5-

W9-ANO-055

The National Hockey League

Official Guide & Record Book

2014

HOCKEY FIGHTS CANCER™

THE NATIONAL HOCKEY LEAGUE
Official Guide & Record Book/2014

TERMS & CONDITIONS FOR USING THE DATA CONTAINED IN THIS BOOK

ATTENTION: PLEASE READ THIS DOCUMENT CAREFULLY BEFORE USING THIS BOOK (THE "BOOK") AND/OR THE DATA IT CONTAINS (THE "DATA"). INDIVIDUALS OR ENTITIES USING THE DATA ("END USERS") AGREE TO BE BOUND BY THE TERMS OF THIS LICENSE. IF YOU DO NOT AGREE TO THE TERMS OF THIS LICENSE, DO NOT USE THE DATA AND PROMPTLY RETURN THE UNUSED BOOK AND PROOF OF PAYMENT TO THE FOLLOWING ADDRESS FOR A REFUND:

Diamond Sports Data, Inc.
194 Dovercourt Road, Toronto, Ontario, M6J 3C8
dda.nhl@sympatico.ca.

Dan Diamond & Associates, Inc. (the "Publisher") owns, and retains ownership of, the Data. The Publisher reserves any right not expressly granted to End Users.

1. License. End-Users are granted a limited, non-exclusive license to do only the following, subject to the restrictions set out in Section 2 below:
   (a) End-Users may use the Data for personal, non-commercial purposes.
   (b) End-Users may reproduce individual player records, tables and data panels in connection with bona fide private study and research.
   (c) End-Users who are journalists may reproduce individual player records, tables and data panels for use by the broadcast and print media.
2. Restrictions. End-Users may NOT reproduce the Data, in whole or in part, in any form or by any means, electronic or mechanical, including photocopying, recording, or by any information storage and retrieval system now known or hereafter invented, without written permission from the Publisher. End-Users may NOT sublicense, assign, or distribute (via the World Wide Web or otherwise) copies of the Data, in whole or in part, to others. END-USERS MAY NOT MODIFY, ADAPT, TRANSLATE, RENT, LEASE, LOAN, RESELL FOR PROFIT, DISTRIBUTE, OR OTHERWISE ASSIGN OR TRANSFER THE DATA, OR CREATE DERIVATIVE WORKS BASED UPON THE DATA OR ANY PART THEREOF, EXCEPT AS PROVIDED ABOVE.
3. Commercial Users. Commercial users (such as sports reference and sports gaming websites) may obtain a license to use customized Data upon payment of a reasonable fee. Please contact the Publisher at the address provided above.
4. Termination. This License is effective until terminated. This License will terminate immediately without notice from the Publisher if the End User fails to comply with any of its provisions. Upon termination End Users must destroy the Data and all copies thereof.
5. General. This License will be governed by and construed in accordance with the laws of the province of Ontario and the laws of Canada applicable therein, and shall inure to the benefit of the Publisher and End-Users and their successors, assigns and legal representatives. If any provision of this License is held by a court of competent jurisdiction to be invalid or unenforceable to any extent under applicable law, that provision will be enforced to the maximum extent permissible and the remaining provisions of this License will remain in full force and effect. Any notices or other communications to be sent to the Publishers must be mailed first class, postage prepaid, to the address provided above. This Agreement constitutes the entire agreement between the parties with respect to the subject matter hereof, and all prior proposals, agreements, representations, statements and undertakings are hereby expressly cancelled and superseded. This Agreement may not be changed or amended except by a written instrument executed by a duly authorized officer of the Publisher.
6. Acknowledgment. BY USING THE DATA, THE END-USER ACKNOWLEDGES THAT IT HAS READ THIS LICENSE, UNDERSTANDS IT, AND AGREES TO BE BOUND BY ITS TERMS AND CONDITIONS. Should you have any questions concerning this License, contact the Publisher at the address provided above.

Copyright © 2013 by the National Hockey League.
Compiled by the NHL Public Relations Department and the 30 NHL Club Public Relations Directors.
Printed in Canada. All rights reserved under the Pan-American and International Copyright Conventions.
Published in Canada by: Diamond Sports Data, Inc., 194 Dovercourt Road, Toronto, Ontario M6J 3C8 Canada
ISBN in Canada 978-1-894801-26-3

Published in the United States by: Triumph Books, 814 N. Franklin Street, Chicago, Illinois 60610
ISBN in USA 978-1-60078-916-8

Staff

For the NHL: Dave McCarthy; Supervising Editor: Greg Inglis; Statistician: Benny Ercolani;
Editorial Staff: Dave Baker, John Dellapina, David Keon, Jennifer Moad, Kelley Rosset, Susan Snow, Julie Young.

Senior Managing Editor: Ralph Dinger
Associate Managing Editor: Paul Bontje
Production Editors: John Pasternak, Alex Dubiel, Becky Gowing
Photo Editor: Eric Zweig
Publisher: Dan Diamond

Data Management and Typesetting: Caledon Data Management, Eden, Ontario
Printing Consultant: Sunrise Consulting Inc., Toronto, Ontario
Printed in the United States of America by Ripon Printers, Ripon, Wisconsin
Production Management: Diamond Sports Data, Inc., Toronto, Ontario
Contributors and Photo Credits: see page 671

Distribution

Trade sales and distribution in Canada by:
North 49 Books, 35 Prince Andrew Drive, Toronto, Ontario M3C 2H2 416/449-4000; Fax 416/449-9924
Dan Diamond and Associates, Inc., Toronto 416/531-6535 dda.nhl@sympatico.ca www.nhlofficialguide.com

Trade sales and distribution in the United States by:
Triumph Books, 814 North Franklin Street, Chicago, Illinois 60610 800/335-5323; Fax 312/663-3557

International distribution:
For information on international distrtibution opportunities, contact the publisher at dda.nhl@sympatico.ca

Licensed by the National Hockey League®
NHL and the NHL Shield are registered trademarks of the National Hockey League.
All NHL logos and marks and team logos and marks depicted herein are the property of the NHL and the respective teams and may not be reproduced without the prior written consent of Enterprises, L.P. © NHL 2012. All Rights Reserved.

The National Hockey League
1185 Avenue of the Americas, 14th Floor, New York, New York 10036
1800 McGill College Ave., Suite 2600, Montreal, Quebec H3A 3J6
50 Bay Street, 11th Floor, Toronto, Ontario M5J 2X8

Table of Contents

Table of Contents *continued*

Introduction

WELCOME TO THE 82ND EDITION OF *THE NATIONAL HOCKEY LEAGUE OFFICIAL GUIDE & RECORD BOOK*, the definitive statistical record of the NHL. A labor dispute, a lockout and protracted negotiations resulted in the cancellation of 510 games in 2012-13. Teams played a condensed 48-game schedule that ran from January 19 to April 27, 2013. There were no inter-conference games and an Eastern Conference team did not face off against a team from the Western Conference until game one of the Stanley Cup Final, a 4-3 triple overtime win by Chicago at home vs. Boston. This would prove to be the first of three overtime games in a well-played Final and the longest of the 27 overtime games played in pursuit of the Stanley Cup in 2013. The Blackhawks clinched the Cup in regulation time in game six on June 24, getting goals from Bryan Bickell and Dave Bolland in the last two minutes of the third period to win their second Cup since 2010. Each clubs's 2012-13 results can be found on the last of its four pages of detailed statistics beginning with Anaheim on page 21. An in-depth stat pack for the 2013 Stanley Cup Playoffs begins on page 245. A list of every playoff overtime game since 1918 begins on page 274 with 2013's games on page 276.

After the disappointments and tensions of the September lockout, NHL clubs and players were quick to return the focus of the sport from the negotiating table to the ice, displaying skill and intense competition night after night. The Blackhawks, eventual Stanley Cup champions, didn't lose in regulation time until the 25th game of the season. And later in the season, the Pittsburgh Penguins won 15 consecutive games. Given the shortened 48-game schedule it is no surprise that these two clubs finished atop their respective Conferences with 77 and 72 points. (New records for Longest Team Points Streak can be found on page 165 as can the record for Longest Winning Streak. NHL final standings for 2012-13 are found on page 141.)

For the fifth time since 1998, the NHL's regular-season schedule has been structured to provide a break so that top players can travel to Sochi, Russia and play for their nations' Olympic teams from February 12 to 23, 2014. The previous four Olympic hockey competitions have seen three pairs of teams meet in the gold medal final. In Nagano (1998), the Czech Republic defeated Russia; in Salt Lake City (2002) and Vancouver (2010), Canada defeated the USA; while in Torino (2006), Sweden defeated Finland. Since NHLers have taken part in the tournament, North American teams have not reached the gold medal game when the games are played on the wider European-sized ice. Conversely, European teams have never played for gold on an NHL-sized rink. Will this trend hold? A galaxy of the NHL's big-game star players, including 2010's golden goal scorer Sidney Crosby (CAN), Patrick Kane (USA), Evgeni Malkin (RUS), Alex Ovechkin (RUS), Zach Parise (USA), Daniel and Henrik Sedin (SWE) and Jonathan Toews (CAN), expect to have their say in Sochi in February. Olympic hockey schedules for both men's and women's competition are found on page 15. Olympic scoring statistics for active NHL players begin on page 19. Goaltenders' Olympic results are found on page 20.

Future Olympians will undoubtedly be found amongst the 211 players selected in the 2013 Entry Draft (Entry Draft coverage begins on page 218.) This year's first selection, Nathan MacKinnon, is the youngest player chosen first overall since the modern universal draft began in 1969. He is the third 17-year old selected first overall, joining Pierre Turgeon (1987) and Sidney Crosby (2005). Also noteworthy is the fact that players born in 22 American states were selected in the 2013 Entry Draft. The traditional hockey incubators of Minnesota, Massachusetts, Michigan and New York topped the table, but players from California, Arizona, Texas and Florida were selected as well. A quarter century after Wayne Gretzky joined the Los Angeles Kings, high-quality youth hockey programs flourish in various parts of the USA. (2013 Entry Draft Analysis by birthplace, position and birth year is found on page 222.) And for fans of statistics that are interesting but don't mean much, left wing Adam Erne from the Quebec Remparts of the QMJHL was taken by Tampa Bay 10,000th overall since the modern draft began in 1969!

Anchoring this and every edition of the *NHL Official Guide & Record Book* is data on every one of the more than 7,000 players who have appeared in an NHL game, plus more than 1,000 prospects who have yet to do so. See the Prospect Register (page 281), Active Player Register (348), Goaltender Register (591), Retired Player Index (616), Retired Goaltender Index (659), regular-season and playoff Record Books (164 and 248), Award Winners (210), All-Star Teams (234) or Hockey Hall of Fame sections (241). A register of 2013's free agent signings is found on page 666, a trade register on page 668 and late additions on page 615.

A key to the abbreviations and symbols used in individual player and goaltender data panels, along with useful information on how to use the Registers, is found on page 280. Each NHL club's minor-pro affiliates are found on page 14. A list of league abbreviations used in the Prospect, Player and Goaltender Registers is found on page 670. The league's revised Conferences and Divisions are listed on the inside front cover. The new Division-based playoff format is detailed on page 257. Two photos of the NHL goal of the year for 2013 are found on page 671. This play by Eric Fehr of the Capitals was ranked number one on the NHL Network's Top 10 Countdown.

Thanks to readers, correspondents, members of the media and hockey communications professionals throughout the game who make good use of what we produce. This is the 30th and largest edition of the combined *NHL Official Guide & Record Book*. Our mandate is simple and has not changed; if it has happened in the NHL, or if it's about to happen, it's in the *Guide*.

Best wishes,

Dan Diamond
Publisher

ACCURACY REMAINS THE *GUIDE & RECORD BOOK*'S TOP PRIORITY.

We appreciate comments and clarification from our readers. Please direct these to:

- Ralph Dinger — Senior Managing Editor, 194 Dovercourt Road, Toronto, Ontario M6J 3C8. e-mail: ralph.dda@sympatico.ca.
- Greg Inglis — 1185 Avenue of the Americas, New York, New York 10036 . . . or . . .
- David Keon — 50 Bay Street, 11th Floor, Toronto, Ontario, M5J 2X8

Your involvement makes a better book.

NATIONAL HOCKEY LEAGUE

New York
1185 Avenue of the Americas,
New York, NY 10036,
212/789-2000, Fax: 212/789-2020, PR Fax: 212/789-2070

Montréal
1800 McGill College Avenue,
Suite 2600,
Montréal, Québec, H3A 3J6
514/841-9220, Fax: 514/841-1040

Toronto
50 Bay Street,
11th Floor,
Toronto, Ontario, M5J 2X8
416/359-7900, Fax: 416/981-2779

League and Club websites: www.nhl.com

Executive
Commissioner .... Gary B. Bettman
Deputy Commissioner .... William Daly
Chief Operating Officer .... John Collins
Senior Executive Vice President of Hockey Operations .... Colin Campbell

Commissioner and League Presidents

Gary B. Bettman

Gary B. Bettman took office as the NHL's first Commissioner on February 1, 1993. Since the League was formed in 1917, there have been five League Presidents.

NHL President	Years in Office
Frank Calder	1917-1943
Mervyn "Red" Dutton	1943-1946
Clarence Campbell	1946-1977
John A. Ziegler, Jr.	1977-1992
Gil Stein	1992-1993

Hockey Hall of Fame

Hockey Hall of Fame
Brookfield Place
30 Yonge Street, Toronto, Ontario M5E 1X8
Phone: 416/360-7735 • Executive Fax: 416/360-1501

Pat Quinn – Chairman of the Board
Jeff Denomme – President and CEO
Craig Baines – Vice-President, Development & Building Operations
Peter Jagla – Vice-President, Marketing & Attraction Services
Ron Ellis - Program Director, HHOF Development Association
Kelly Masse – Director, Corporate & Media Relations
Craig Beckim – Manager, Merchandising & Retail Operations
Darren Boyko – Manager, Special Projects & International Business
Sarah Lee – Manager, Special Events & Hospitality
Jackie Schwartz – Manager, Marketing & Promotions

D.K. (Doc) Seaman Resource Centre and Archives
400 Kipling Avenue, Toronto, Ontario M8V 3L1
Phone: 416/360-7735 • Fax: 416/251-5770
www.hhof.com, www.imagesonice.net

Phil Pritchard – Vice President, Resource Centre and Curator
Craig Campbell – Manager, Resource Centre and Archives
Izak Westgate – Manager, Outreach and Asst. Curator
Steve Poirier – Coordinator, HHOF Images and Archival Services
Miragh Bitove – Archivist & Collections Registrar

National Hockey League Players' Association

20 Bay Street, Suite 1700, Toronto, Ontario M5J 2N8
Phone: 416/313-2300 • Fax: 416/313-2301
www.nhlpa.com

Donald Fehr – Executive Director
Don Zaveklo – General Counsel
Mathieu Schneider – Special Assistant to the Executive Director
Mike Ouellet – Chief of Business Affairs
Roman Stoykewych – Associate Counsel, Labour
Robert DeGregory – Associate Counsel, Labour
Maria Dennis – Associate Counsel, Labour
Roland Lee – Director, Salary Cap and Marketplace and Associate Counsel
Alex Dagg – Director, Operations
Adam Larry – Director, Licensing and Associate Counsel
Kim Murdoch – Director, Player Insurance & Pensions
Richard Smit – Director, Finance and HRR
Devin Smith – Director, Marketing & Community Relations
Jonathan Weatherdon – Director, Communications
Tyler Currie – Director, International Affairs
Stephen Frank – Director, Information Technology
Casey Rovinelli – Director, Digital Marketing
Colin Campbell – Director, Corporate Sponsorship

BOARD OF GOVERNORS

Chairman of the Board – Jeremy M. Jacobs

Anaheim Ducks

Henry Samueli .... Governor
Susan Samueli .... Alternate Governor
Michael Schulman .... Alternate Governor
Tim Ryan .... Alternate Governor
Bob Murray .... Alternate Governor

Boston Bruins

Jeremy M. Jacobs .... Governor
Charles Jacobs .... Alternate Governor
Jeremy Jacobs, Jr. .... Alternate Governor
Louis Jacobs .... Alternate Governor
Harry J. Sinden .... Alternate Governor
Cam Neely .... Alternate Governor
Peter Chiarelli .... Alternate Governor

Buffalo Sabres

Terry Pegula .... Governor
Ted Black .... Alternate Governor
Darcy Regier .... Alternate Governor
Ken Sawyer .... Alternate Governor
Cliff Benson .... Alternate Governor

Calgary Flames

N. Murray Edwards .... Governor
Ken King .... Alternate Governor
Alvin Libin .... Alternate Governor

Carolina Hurricanes

Peter Karmanos, Jr. .... Governor
Jim Rutherford .... Alternate Governor
Michael Amendola .... Alternate Governor
Jason Karmanos .... Alternate Governor
Ron Francis .... Alternate Governor

Chicago Blackhawks

W. Rockwell Wirtz .... Governor
Robert J. Pulford .... Alternate Governor
John A. Ziegler, Jr. .... Alternate Governor
John McDonough .... Alternate Governor

Colorado Avalanche

Josh Kroenke .... Governor
Mark Waggoner .... Alternate Governor
Greg Sherman .... Alternate Governor
Joe Sakic .... Alternate Governor

Columbus Blue Jackets

John P. McConnell .... Governor
Mike Priest .... Alternate Governor
John Davidson .... Alternate Governor

Dallas Stars

Tom Gaglardi .... Governor
Jim Lites .... Alternate Governor
Jim Nill .... Alternate Governor
Mike Modano .... Alternate Governor

Detroit Red Wings

Michael Ilitch .... Governor
Jim Devellano .... Alternate Governor
Ken Holland .... Alternate Governor
Christopher Ilitch .... Alternate Governor
Rob Carr .... Alternate Governor
Tom Wilson .... Alternate Governor

Edmonton Oilers

Daryl Katz .... Governor
Patrick LaForge .... Alternate Governor
Kevin Lowe .... Alternate Governor

Florida Panthers

Cliff Viner .... Governor
Bill Torrey .... Alternate Governor
Michael Yormark .... Alternate Governor

Los Angeles Kings

Philip F. Anschutz .... Governor
Dean Lombardi .... Alternate Governor
Dan Beckerman .... Alternate Governor

Minnesota Wild

Craig Leopold .... Governor
Philip Falcone .... Alternate Governor
Jac Sperling .... Alternate Governor
Chuck Fletcher .... Alternate Governor

Montréal Canadiens

Geoff Molson .... Governor
Kevin Gilmore .... Alternate Governor
Fred Steer .... Alternate Governor
Michael Andlauer .... Alternate Governor
Andrew T. Molson .... Alternate Governor
Marc Bergevin .... Alternate Governor

Nashville Predators

Tom Cigarran .... Governor
Herbert Fritch .... Alternate Governor
David Poile .... Alternate Governor
Jeff Cogen .... Alternate Governor
Sean Henry .... Alternate Governor
Joel Dobberpuhl .... Alternate Governor

New Jersey Devils

Joshua Harris .... Governor
David Blitzer .... Alternate Governor
Lou Lamoriello .... Alternate Governor
Scott O'Neil .... Alternate Governor

New York Islanders

Charles Wang .... Governor
Roy Reichbach .... Alternate Governor
Arthur J. McCarthy .... Alternate Governor
Michael J. Picker .... Alternate Governor
Garth Snow .... Alternate Governor

New York Rangers

James L. Dolan .... Governor
Glen Sather .... Alternate Governor
Hank Ratner .... Alternate Governor
Dave Howard .... Alternate Governor

Ottawa Senators

Eugene Melnyk .... Governor
Sheldon Plener .... Alternate Governor
Cyril Leeder .... Alternate Governor
Erin Crowe .... Alternate Governor
Bryan Murray .... Alternate Governor

Philadelphia Flyers

Edward M. Snider .... Governor
Philip I. Weinberg .... Alternate Governor
Peter Luukko .... Alternate Governor
Paul Holmgren .... Alternate Governor

Phoenix Coyotes

George Gosbee .... Governor
Don Maloney .... Alternate Governor
Anthony LeBlanc .... Alternate Governor
Craig Stewart .... Alternate Governor

Pittsburgh Penguins

David Morehouse .... Governor
Ronald Burkle .... Alternate Governor
Anthony Liberati .... Alternate Governor
Ray Shero .... Alternate Governor
Travis WIlliams .... Alternate Governor
Mario Lemieux .... Alternate Governor

St. Louis Blues

Thomas Stillman .... Governor
Doug Armstrong .... Alternate Governor

San Jose Sharks

Hasso Plattner .... Governor
Doug Wilson .... Alternate Governor
John Tortora .... Alternate Governor

Tampa Bay Lightning

Jeff Vinik .... Governor
Steve Yzerman .... Alternate Governor
Tod Leiweke .... Alternate Governor

Toronto Maple Leafs

Larry Tanenbaum .... Governor
Dale Lastman .... Alternate Governor
Dave Nonis .... Alternate Governor
Tim Leiweke .... Alternate Governor

Vancouver Canucks

Francesco Aquilini .... Governor
Paolo Aquilini .... Alternate Governor
Roberto Aquilini .... Alternate Governor
Michael Gillis .... Alternate Governor
Victor de Boris .... Alternate Governor

Washington Capitals

Ted Leonsis .... Governor
Richard M. Patrick .... Alternate Governor
George McPhee .... Alternate Governor

Winnipeg Jets

Mark Chipman .... Governor
Kevin Cheveldayoff .... Alternate Governor
Patrick Phillips .... Alternate Governor

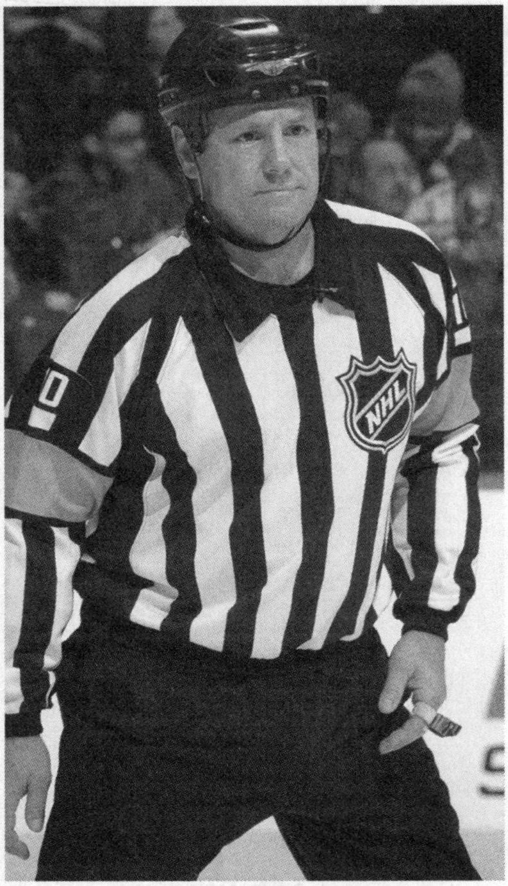

Paul Devorski (above) has worked 1,450 regular-season games, the most for any active referee. Brad Lazarowich (below) leads all linesmen, having worked 1,786 regular-season games.

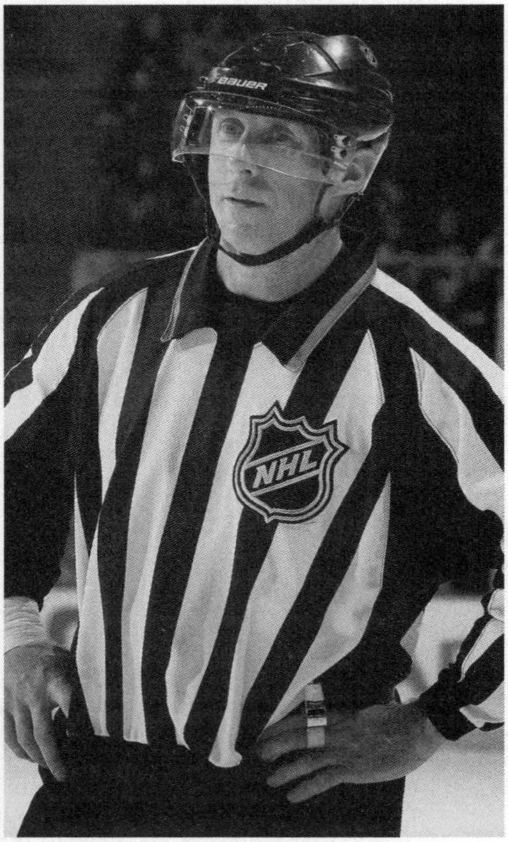

NHL On-Ice Officials

Total NHL Games and 2012-13 Games columns count regular-season games only.

Referees

#	Name	Birthplace	*Age	First NHL Game	Total NHL Games	2012-13 Games
42	Darcy Burchell	St. Catharines, Ont.	35	Jan 29, 2013	5	5
6	Francis Charron	Ottawa, Ont.	30	Apr 5, 2010	69	41
10	Paul Devorski	Guelph, Ont.	55	Oct 14, 1989	1450	42
19	Gord Dwyer	Halifax, N.S.	36	Nov 19, 2005	497	43
27	Eric Furlatt	Trois-Rivieres, Que.	42	Oct 8, 2001	728	43
47	Trevor Hanson	Richmond, BC	29			
2	Mike Hasenfratz	Regina, Sask.	47	Oct 21, 2000	645	42
22	Ghislain Hebert	Bathurst, NB	32	Mar 2, 2009	145	40
43	Jean Hebert	Moncton, NB	33	Mar 30, 2011	25	10
8	Dave Jackson	Montreal, Que.	48	Dec 22, 1990	1258	43
25	Marc Joannette	Verdun, Que.	44	Oct 1, 1999	853	44
18	Greg Kimmerly	Toronto, Ont.	49	Nov 30, 1996	935	42
44	Trent Knorr	Powell River, BC	27			
32	Tom Kowal	Vernon, B.C.	45	Oct 29, 1999	736	44
40	Steve Kozari	Penticton, B.C.	40	Oct 15, 2005	464	44
14	Dennis LaRue	Savannah, GA	54	Mar 26, 1991	1126	42
17	Frederick L'Ecuyer	Trois-Rivieres, Que.	36	Oct 11, 2007	255	42
28	Chris Lee	Saint John, N.B.	43	Apr 2, 2000	713	43
3	Mike Leggo	North Bay, Ont.	48	Mar 3, 1998	925	43
41	Mark Lemelin	Albuquerque, NM	32	Jan 21, 2013	6	6
46	Dave Lewis	Pickering, Ont.	30			
49	Thomas John Luxmore	Timmins, Ont.	28			
26	Rob Martell	Winnipeg, Man.	49	Mar 14, 1984	[1] 813	42
4	Wes McCauley	Georgetown, Ont.	41	Jan 20, 2003	587	44
45	Jon McIsaac	Truro, NS	29			
34	Brad Meier	Dayton, OH	46	Oct 23, 1999	853	43
36	Dean Morton	Peterborough, Ont.	45	Nov 11, 2000	407	40
13	Dan O'Halloran	Essex, Ont.	49	Oct 1, 1995	1006	43
9	Dan O'Rourke	Calgary, Alta.	41	Oct 2, 1999	[2] 584	44
20	Tim Peel	Toronto, Ont.	47	Oct 21, 1999	860	44
16	Brian Pochmara	Detroit, MI	36	Dec 23, 2005	394	44
33	Kevin Pollock	Kincardine, Ont.	43	Mar 28, 2000	858	42
37	Kyle Rehman	Stettler, Alta.	35	Jan 22, 2008	234	42
5	Chris Rooney	Boston, MA	38	Nov 22, 2000	753	43
48	Graham Skilliter	La Ronge, Sask.	29	Jan 28, 2013	6	6
38	Francois St. Laurent	Greenfield Park, Que.	36	Nov 10, 2005	334	44
12	Justin St. Pierre	Dolbeau, Que.	41	Nov 9, 2005	493	42
11	Kelly Sutherland	Richmond, BC	42	Dec 19, 2000	790	44
21	Don Van Massenhoven	Parkhill, Ont.	53	Nov 11, 1993	1209	43
29	Ian Walsh	Philadelphia, PA	41	Oct 14, 2000	697	43
23	Brad Watson	Regina, Sask.	52	Mar 7, 1996	956	43

[1] plus 3 games as a linesman. [2] plus 120 games as a linesman.

Linesmen

#	Name	Birthplace	*Age	First NHL Game	Total NHL Games	2012-13 Games
75	Derek Amell	Port Colborne, Ont.	45	Oct 11, 1997	993	44
59	Steve Barton	Vankleek Hill, Ont.	41	Nov 1, 2000	768	43
96	David Brisebois	Sudbury, Ont.	37	Oct 11, 1999	730	44
74	Lonnie Cameron	Victoria, B.C.	49	Oct 5, 1996	1106	44
67	Pierre Champoux	Ville St-Pierre, Que.	50	Oct 8, 1988	1516	0
50	Scott Cherrey	Drayton, Ont.	37	Oct 6, 2007	389	44
76	Michel Cormier	Trois-Rivieres, Que.	39	Oct 10, 2003	631	43
88	Mike Cvik	Calgary, Alta.	51	Oct 8, 1987	1678	43
54	Greg Devorski	Guelph, Ont.	44	Oct 9, 1993	1272	43
68	Scott Driscoll	Seaforth, Ont.	45	Oct 10, 1992	1344	44
82	Ryan Galloway	Winnipeg, Man.	41	Oct 17, 2002	656	43
66	Darren Gibbs	Edmonton, Alta.	47	Oct 1, 1997	958	44
98	John Grandt	Denver, CO	28	Jan 22, 2013	24	24
91	Don Henderson	Calgary, Alta.	45	Mar 11, 1995	1094	43
55	Shane Heyer	Summerland, B.C.	49	Oct 6, 1988	[3] 1256	43
71	Brad Kovachik	Woodstock, Ont.	42	Oct 10, 1996	1068	43
86	Brad Lazarowich	Vancouver, B.C.	51	Oct 9, 1986	1786	44
78	Brian Mach	Little Falls, MN	39	Oct 7, 2000	835	44
83	Matt MacPherson	Antigonish, NS	30	Oct 11, 2011	94	43
90	Andy McElman	Chicago Heights, IL	52	Oct 3, 1993	1255	44
89	Steve Miller	Stratford, Ont.	41	Oct 11, 2000	824	44
97	Jean Morin	Sorel, Que.	50	Oct 5, 1991	1357	44
79	Kiel Murchison	Cloverdale, BC	28	Jan 21, 2013	24	24
93	Brian Murphy	Dover, NH	48	Oct 7, 1988	[4] 1472	43
95	Jonny Murray	Beauport, Que.	39	Oct 7, 2000	836	43
70	Derek Nansen	Ottawa, Ont.	41	Oct 11, 2002	684	44
80	Thor Nelson	Westminister, CA	45	Feb 16, 1995	974	43
77	Tim Nowak	Buffalo, NY	46	Oct 8, 1993	1278	43
94	Bryan Pancich	Great Falls, MT	31	Oct 3, 2009	241	44
65	Pierre Racicot	Verdun, Que.	46	Oct 12, 1993	1307	44
73	Vaughan Rody	Winnipeg, Man.	44	Oct 8, 2000	806	43
84	Anthony Sericolo	Troy, NY	45	Oct 21, 1998	929	44
57	Jay Sharrers	New Westminster, B.C.	46	Oct 6, 1990	[5] 1190	43
92	Mark Shewchyk	Waterdown, Ont.	38	Oct 9, 2003	635	44
56	Mark Wheler	North Battleford, Sask.	48	Oct 10, 1992	1370	43

[3] plus 386 games as a referee. [4] plus 88 games as a referee. [5] plus 136 games as a referee.

– Age at start of 2013-14 season

NHL History

1917 — National Hockey League organized November 26 in Montreal following suspension of operations by the National Hockey Association of Canada Limited (NHA). Montreal Canadiens, Montreal Wanderers, Ottawa Senators and Quebec Bulldogs attended founding meeting. Delegates decided to use NHA rules.

Toronto Arenas were later admitted as fifth team; Quebec decided not to operate during the first season. Quebec players allocated to remaining four teams.

Frank Calder elected president and secretary-treasurer.

First NHL games played December 19, with Toronto only arena with artificial ice. Clubs played 22-game split schedule.

1918 — Emergency meeting held January 3 due to destruction by fire of Montreal Arena which was home ice for both Canadiens and Wanderers.

Wanderers withdrew, reducing the NHL to three teams; Canadiens played remaining home games at 3,250-seat Jubilee rink.

Quebec franchise sold to P.J. Quinn of Toronto on October 18 on the condition that the team operate in Quebec City for 1918-19 season. Quinn did not attend the November League meeting and Quebec did not play in 1918-19.

1919-20 — NHL reactivated Quebec Bulldogs franchise. Former Quebec players returned to the club. New Mount Royal Arena became home of Canadiens. Toronto Arenas changed name to St. Patricks. Clubs played 24-game split schedule.

1920-21 — H.P. Thompson of Hamilton, Ontario made application for the purchase of an NHL franchise. Quebec franchise shifted to Hamilton with other NHL teams providing players to strengthen the club.

1921-22 — Split schedule abandoned. First and second place teams at the end of full schedule to play for championship.

1922-23 — Clubs agreed that players could not be sold or traded to clubs in any other league without first being offered to all other clubs in the NHL. Norman Albert made the first broadcast of a hockey game on February 8, 1923. The first NHL game was broadcast on February 14, 1923. Foster Hewitt called his first game on February 16, 1923. All games were broadcast on Toronto radio station CFCA.

1923-24 — Ottawa's new 10,000-seat arena opened. First U.S. franchise granted to Boston for following season.

Dr. Cecil Hart Trophy donated to NHL to be awarded to the player judged most useful to his team.

1924-25 — New franchises granted to Boston and Montreal (later named Maroons). NHL now six team league with two clubs in Montreal. Inaugural game in new Montreal Forum played November 29, 1924 as Canadiens defeated Toronto 7-1. Hamilton finished first in the standings, receiving a bye into the finals. But Hamilton players, demanding $200 each for additional games in the playoffs, went on strike. The NHL suspended all players, fining them $200 each. Stanley Cup finalist to be the winner of NHL semi-final between Toronto and Canadiens.

Lady Byng Trophy donated to NHL.

Clubs played 30-game schedule.

1925-26 — Hamilton club dropped from NHL. Players signed by new New York Americans franchise. Pittsburgh Pirates granted franchise. Prince of Wales Trophy donated to NHL.

Clubs played 36-game schedule.

1926-27 — New York Rangers granted franchise May 15, 1926. Chicago Black Hawks and Detroit Cougars granted franchises September 25, 1926. NHL now ten-team league with an American and a Canadian Division.

Stanley Cup came under the control of NHL. In previous seasons, winners of the now-defunct Western or Pacific Coast leagues would play NHL champion in Cup finals.

Toronto franchise sold to a new company controlled by Hugh Aird and Conn Smythe. Name changed from St. Patricks to Maple Leafs.

Clubs played 44-game schedule.

The Montreal Canadiens donated the Vezina Trophy to be awarded to the team allowing the fewest goals-against in regular season play. The winning team would, in turn, present the trophy to the goaltender playing in the greatest number of games during the season.

1930-31 — Detroit franchise changed name from Cougars to Falcons. Pittsburgh transferred to Philadelphia for one season. Pirates changed name to Philadelphia Quakers. Trading deadline for teams set at February 15 of each year. NHL approved operation of farm teams by Rangers, Americans, Falcons and Bruins. Four-sided electric arena clock first demonstrated.

1931-32 — Philadelphia dropped out. Ottawa withdrew for one season. New Maple Leaf Gardens completed.

Clubs played 48-game schedule.

1932-33 — Detroit franchise changed name from Falcons to Red Wings. Franchise application received from St. Louis but refused because of additional travel costs. Ottawa team resumed play.

1933-34 — First All-Star Game played as a benefit for injured player Ace Bailey. Leafs defeated All-Stars 7-3 in Toronto.

1934-35 — Ottawa franchise transferred to St. Louis. Team called St. Louis Eagles and consisted largely of Ottawa's players.

1935-36 — Ottawa-St. Louis franchise terminated. Montreal Canadiens finished season with very poor record. To strengthen the club, NHL gave Canadiens first call on the services of all French-Canadian players for three seasons.

1937-38 — Second benefit All-Star game staged November 2 in Montreal in aid of the family of the late Canadiens star Howie Morenz.

Montreal Maroons withdrew from the NHL on June 22, 1938, leaving seven clubs in the League.

1938-39 — Expenses for each club regulated at $5 per man per day for meals and $2.50 per man per day for accommodation.

1939-40 — Benefit All-Star Game played October 29, 1939 in Montreal for the children of the late Albert (Babe) Siebert.

1940-41 — Ross-Tyer puck adopted as the official puck of the NHL. Early in the season it was apparent that this puck was too soft. The Spalding puck was adopted in its place.

On May 16, 1941, Arthur Ross, NHL governor from Boston, donated a perpetual trophy to be awarded annually to the player voted outstanding in the league. Due to wartime restrictions, the trophy was never awarded.

1941-42 — New York Americans changed name to Brooklyn Americans.

1942-43 — Brooklyn Americans withdrew from NHL, leaving six teams: Boston, Chicago, Detroit, Montreal, New York and Toronto. Playoff format saw first-place team play third-place team and second play fourth.

Clubs played 50-game schedule.

Frank Calder, president of the NHL since its inception, died in Montreal. Meryn "Red" Dutton, former manager of the New York Americans, became president. The NHL commissioned the Calder Memorial Trophy to be awarded to the League's outstanding rookie each year.

1945-46 — Philadelphia, Los Angeles and San Francisco applied for NHL franchises.

The Philadelphia Arena Company of the American Hockey League applied for an injunction to prevent the possible operation of an NHL franchise in that city.

1946-47 — Mervyn Dutton retired as president of the NHL prior to the start of the season. He was succeeded by Clarence S. Campbell.

Individual trophy winners and all-star team members to receive $1,000 awards.

Playoff guarantees for players introduced.

Clubs played 60-game schedule.

1947-48 — The first annual All-Star Game for the benefit of the players' pension fund was played when the All-Stars defeated the Stanley Cup Champion Toronto Maple Leafs 4-3 in Toronto on October 13, 1947.

Criteria for awarding Art Ross Trophy changed. Now awarded to top scorer. Elmer Lach was its first winner.

Philadelphia and Los Angeles franchise applications refused.

National Hockey League Pension Society formed.

1949-50 — Clubs played 70-game schedule.

First intra-league draft held April 30, 1950. Clubs allowed to protect 30 players. Remaining players available for $25,000 each.

1951-52 — Referees included in the League's pension plan.

1952-53 — In May of 1952, City of Cleveland applied for NHL franchise. Application denied. In March of 1953, the Cleveland Barons of the AHL challenged the NHL champions for the Stanley Cup. The NHL governors did not accept this challenge.

1953-54 — The James Norris Memorial Trophy presented to the NHL for annual presentation to the League's best defenseman.

Intra-league draft rules amended to allow teams to protect 18 skaters and two goaltenders, claiming price reduced to $15,000.

1954-55 — Each arena to operate an "out-of-town" scoreboard.

1956-57 — Referees and linesmen to wear shirts of black and white vertical stripes. Standardized signals for referees and linesmen introduced.

1960-61 — Canadian National Exhibition, City of Toronto and NHL reach agreement for the construction of a Hockey Hall of Fame on the CNE grounds. Hall opens on August 26, 1961.

1963-64 — Player development league established with clubs operated by NHL franchises located in Minneapolis, St. Paul, Indianapolis, Omaha and, beginning in 1964-65, Tulsa. First universal amateur draft took place. All players of qualifying age (17) unaffected by sponsorship of junior teams available to be drafted.

1964-65 — Conn Smythe Trophy presented to the NHL to be awarded annually to the outstanding player in the Stanley Cup playoffs.

Minimum age of players subject to amateur draft changed to 18.

1965-66 — NHL announced expansion plans for a second six-team division to begin play in 1967-68.

1966-67 — Fourteen applications for NHL franchises received.

Lester Patrick Trophy presented to the NHL to be awarded annually for outstanding service to hockey in the United States.

NHL sponsorship of junior teams ceased, making all players of qualifying age not already on NHL-sponsored lists eligible for the amateur draft.

1967-68 — Six new teams added: California Seals, Los Angeles Kings, Minnesota North Stars, Philadelphia Flyers, Pittsburgh Penguins, St. Louis Blues. New teams to play in West Division. Remaining six teams to play in East Division.

Minimum age of players subject to amateur draft changed to 20.

Clubs played 74-game schedule.

Clarence S. Campbell Trophy awarded to team finishing the regular season in first place in West Division.

California Seals change name to Oakland Seals on December 8, 1967.

1968-69 — Clubs played 76-game schedule.

Amateur draft expanded to cover any amateur player of qualifying age throughout the world.

1970-71 — Two new teams added: Buffalo Sabres and Vancouver Canucks. These teams joined East Division: Chicago switched to West Division. Oakland Seals change name to California Golden Seals prior to season.

Clubs played 78-game schedule.

1971-72 — Playoff format amended. In each division, first to play fourth; second to play third.

1972-73 — Soviet Nationals and Canadian NHL stars play eight pre-season games. Canadians win 4-3-1.

Two new teams added. Atlanta Flames join West Division; New York Islanders join East Division.

1974-75 — Two new teams added: Kansas City Scouts and Washington Capitals. Teams realigned into two nine-team conferences, the Prince of Wales made up of the Norris and Adams Divisions, and the Clarence Campbell made up of the Smythe and Patrick Divisions.

Clubs played 80-game schedule.

1976-77 — California franchise transferred to Cleveland. Team named Cleveland Barons. Kansas City franchise transferred to Denver. Team named Colorado Rockies.

1977-78 — Clarence S. Campbell retires as NHL president. Succeeded by John A. Ziegler, Jr.

1978-79 — Cleveland and Minnesota franchises merge, leaving NHL with 17 teams. Merged team placed in Adams Division, playing home games in Minnesota.

Minimum age of players subject to amateur draft changed to 19.

1979-80 — Four new teams added: Edmonton Oilers, Hartford Whalers, Quebec Nordiques and Winnipeg Jets.

Minimum age of players subject to entry draft changed to 18.

1980-81 — Atlanta franchise shifted to Calgary, retaining "Flames" name.

1981-82 — Teams realigned within existing divisions. New groupings based on geographical areas. Unbalanced schedule adopted.

1982-83 — Colorado Rockies franchise shifted to East Rutherford, New Jersey. Team named New Jersey Devils. Franchise moved to Patrick Division from Smythe; Winnipeg moved to Smythe from Norris.

1991-92 — San Jose Sharks added, making the NHL a 22-team league. NHL celebrates 75th Anniversary Season. The 1991-92 regular season suspended due to a players' strike on April 1, 1992. Play resumed April 12, 1992.

1992-93 — Gil Stein named NHL president (October, 1992). Gary Bettman named first NHL Commissioner (February, 1993). Ottawa Senators and Tampa Bay Lightning added, making the NHL a 24-team league. NHL celebrates Stanley Cup Centennial. Clubs played 84-game schedule.

NHL History — *continued*

1993-94 — Mighty Ducks of Anaheim and Florida Panthers added, making the NHL a 26-team league. Minnesota franchise shifted to Dallas, team named Dallas Stars. Prince of Wales and Clarence Campbell Conferences renamed Eastern and Western. Adams, Patrick, Norris and Smythe Divisions renamed Northeast, Atlantic, Central and Pacific. Winnipeg moved to Central Division from Pacific; Tampa Bay moved to Atlantic Division from Central; Pittsburgh moved to Northeast Division from Atlantic.

1994-95 — A lockout resulted in the cancellation of 468 games from October 1, 1994 to January 19, 1995. Clubs played a 48-game schedule that began January 20, 1995 and ended May 3, 1995. No inter-conference games were played.

1995-96 — Quebec franchise transferred to Denver. Team named Colorado Avalanche and placed in Pacific Division of Western Conference. Clubs to play 82-game schedule.

1996-97 — Winnipeg franchise transferred to Phoenix. Team named Phoenix Coyotes and placed in Central Division of Western Conference.

1997-98 — Hartford franchise transferred to Raleigh. Team named Carolina Hurricanes and remains in Northeast Division of Eastern Conference.

1998-99 — The addition of the Nashville Predators made the NHL a 27-team league and brought about the creation of two new divisions and a League-wide realignment in preparation for further expansion to 30 teams by 2000-2001. Nashville was added to the Central Division of the Western Conference, while Toronto moved into the Northeast Division of the Eastern Conference. Pittsburgh was shifted from the Northeast to the Atlantic, while Carolina left the Northeast for the newly created Southeast Division of the Eastern Conference. Florida, Tampa Bay and Washington also joined the Southeast. In the Western Conference, Calgary, Colorado, Edmonton and Vancouver make up the new Northwest Division. Dallas and Phoenix moved from the Central to the Pacific Division.

The NHL retired uniform number 99 in honor of all-time scoring leader Wayne Gretzky who retired at the end of the season.

1999-2000 — Atlanta Thrashers added, making the NHL a 28-team league.

2000-01 — Columbus Blue Jackets and Minnesota Wild added, making the NHL a 30-team league.

2003-04 — First outdoor NHL game. 57,167 attend Heritage Classic at Edmonton's Commonwealth Stadium. Montreal defeated Edmonton 4-3, November 22, 2003.

2004-05 — A lockout resulted in the cancellation of the season.

2007-08 — NHL-record crowd of 71,217 fills Buffalo's Ralph Wilson Stadium on New Year's Day for the 2008 Winter Classic, the first NHL outdoor game in the United States. Sidney Crosby's shootout goal gives the Pittsburgh Penguins a 2-1 win over the Buffalo Sabres.

2011-12 — Atlanta franchise transferred to Winnipeg. Team named Winnipeg Jets.

2012-13 — A lockout resulted in the cancellation of 510 games from October 11, 2012 to January 18, 2013. Clubs played a 48-game schedule that began January 19, 2013 and ended April 27, 2013. No inter-conference games were played.

2013-14 — The NHL's clubs are re-aligned into two conferences each consisting of two divisions. The new alignment places several clubs in more geographically appropriate groupings. The Eastern Conference is made up of the Atlantic and Metropolitan divisions, each with eight teams. The Western Conference is made up of the Central and Pacific divisions, each with seven teams. All 30 teams play in all 30 arenas at least once a season.

NHL Attendance

Season	Regular Season Games	Regular Season Attendance	Playoffs Games	Playoffs Attendance	Total Attendance
1967-68	444	4,938,043	40	495,089	5,433,132
1968-69	456	5,550,613	33	431,739	5,982,352
1969-70	456	5,992,065	34	461,694	6,453,759
1970-71	546	7,257,677	43	707,633	7,965,310
1971-72	546	7,609,368	36	582,666	8,192,034
1972-73	624	8,575,651	38	624,637	9,200,288
1973-74	624	8,640,978	38	600,442	9,241,420
1974-75	720	9,521,536	51	784,181	10,305,717
1975-76	720	9,103,761	48	726,279	9,830,040
1976-77	720	8,563,890	44	646,279	9,210,169
1977-78	720	8,526,564	45	686,634	9,213,198
1978-79	680	7,758,053	45	694,521	8,452,574
1979-80	840	10,533,623	67	976,699	11,510,322
1980-81	840	10,726,198	68	966,390	11,692,588
1981-82	840	10,710,894	71	1,058,948	11,769,842
1982-83	840	11,020,610	66	1,088,222	12,028,832
1983-84	840	11,359,386	70	1,107,400	12,466,786
1984-85	840	11,633,730	70	1,107,500	12,741,230
1985-86	840	11,621,000	72	1,152,503	12,773,503
1986-87	840	11,855,880	87	1,383,967	13,239,847
1987-88	840	12,117,512	83	1,336,901	13,454,413
1988-89	840	12,417,969	82	1,327,214	13,745,183
1989-90	840	12,579,651	85	1,355,593	13,935,244
1990-91	840	12,343,897	92	1,442,203	13,786,100
1991-92	880	12,769,676	86	1,327,920	14,097,596
1992-93	1,008	14,158,177 [1]	83	1,346,034	15,504,211
1993-94	1,092	16,105,604 [2]	90	1,440,095	17,545,699
1994-95	624 [3]	9,233,884	81	1,329,130	10,563,014
1995-96	1,066	17,041,614	86	1,540,140	18,581,754
1996-97	1,066	17,640,529	82	1,494,878	19,135,407
1997-98	1,066	17,264,678	82	1,507,416	18,772,094
1998-99	1,107	18,001,741	86	1,509,411	19,511,152
1999-2000	1,148	18,800,139	83	1,524,629	20,324,768
2000-01	1,230	20,373,379	86	1,584,011	21,957,390
2001-02	1,230	20,614,613	90	1,691,174	22,305,787
2002-03	1,230	20,408,704	89	1,636,120	22,044,824
2003-04	1,230	20,356,199	89	1,708,691	22,064,890
2004-05	....	....	....	....	....
2005-06	1,230	20,854,169	83	1,530,405	22,384,574
2006-07	1,230	20,861,787	81	1,496,501	22,358,288
2007-08	1,230	21,236,255	85	1,587,054	22,823,309
2008-09	1,230	21,475,223	87	1,639,602	23,114,825
2009-10	1,230	20,996,455	90	1,702,371	22,698,826
2010-11	1,230	21,112,139	89	1,667,624	22,779,763
2011-12	1,230	21,468,121	86	1,591,856	23,059,977
2012-13	720 [4]	12,792,707	86	1,631,683	14,424,390

NHL Expansion: the NHL operated as a six-team league from 1942-43 to 1966-67. Six teams were added in 1967-68: California (later to move to Cleveland), Los Angeles, Minnesota (later to move to Dallas), Philadelphia, Pittsburgh and St. Louis. In 1970-71: Buffalo and Vancouver. In 1972-73: Atlanta (later to move to Calgary) and NYIslanders. In 1974-75: Kansas City (later to move to Colorado and then to New Jersey) and Washington. In 1979-80, Hartford (later to move to Carolina), Edmonton, Quebec (later to move to Colorado) and Winnipeg (later to move to Phoenix). In 1991-92, San Jose. In 1992-93, Ottawa and Tampa Bay. In 1993-94, Anaheim and Florida. In 1998-99, Nashville. In 1999-2000, Atlanta (later to move to Winnipeg). In 2000-01, Columbus and Minnesota.

[1] Includes 24 neutral site games • [2] Includes 26 neutral site games
[3] Lockout resulted in the cancellation of 468 games. • [4] Lockout resulted in the cancellation of 510 games.

Major Rule Changes

1910-11 — Game changed from two 30-minute periods to three 20-minute periods.

1911-12 — National Hockey Association (forerunner of the NHL) originated six-man hockey, replacing seven-man game.

1917-18 — Goalies permitted to fall to the ice to make saves. Previously a goaltender was penalized for dropping to the ice.

1918-19 — Penalty rules amended. For minor fouls, substitutes not allowed until penalized player had served three minutes. For major fouls, no substitutes for five minutes. For match fouls, no substitutes allowed for the remainder of the game.

With the addition of two lines painted on the ice twenty feet from center, three playing zones were created, producing a forty-foot neutral center ice area in which forward passing was permitted. Kicking the puck was permitted in this neutral zone.

Tabulation of assists began.

1921-22 — Goaltenders allowed to pass the puck forward up to their own blue line.

Overtime limited to twenty minutes.

Minor penalties changed from three minutes to two minutes.

1923-24 — Match foul defined as actions deliberately injuring or disabling an opponent. For such actions, a player was fined not less than $50 and ruled off the ice for the balance of the game. A player assessed a match penalty may be replaced by a substitute at the end of 20 minutes. Match penalty recipients must meet with the League president who can assess additional punishment.

1925-26 — Delayed penalty rules introduced. Each team must have a minimum of four players on the ice at all times.

Two rules were amended to encourage offense: No more than two defensemen permitted to remain inside a team's own blue line when the puck has left the defensive zone. A faceoff to be called for ragging the puck unless shorthanded.

Team captains only players allowed to talk to referees.

Goaltender's leg pads limited to 12-inch width.

Timekeeper's gong to mark end of periods rather than referee's whistle. Teams to dress a maximum of 12 players for each game from a roster of no more than 14 players.

1926-27 — Blue lines repositioned to sixty feet from each goal-line, thereby enlarging the neutral zone and standardizing distance from blue line to goal.

Uniform goal nets adopted throughout NHL with goal posts securely fastened to the ice.

1927-28 — To further encourage offense, forward passes allowed in defending and neutral zones and goaltender's pads reduced in width from 12 to 10 inches.

Game standardized at three twenty-minute periods of stop-time separated by ten-minute intermissions.

Teams to change ends after each period.

Ten minutes of sudden-death overtime to be played if the score is tied after regulation time.

Minor penalty to be assessed to any player other than a goaltender for deliberately picking up the puck while it is in play. Minor penalty to be assessed for deliberately shooting the puck out of play.

The Art Ross goal net adopted as the official net of the NHL.

Maximum length of hockey sticks limited to 53 inches measured from heel of blade to end of handle. No minimum length stipulated.

Home teams given choice of end to defend at start of game.

1928-29 — Forward passing permitted in defensive and neutral zones and into attacking zone if pass receiver is in neutral zone when pass is made. No forward passing allowed inside attacking zone.

Minor penalty to be assessed to any player who delays the game by passing the puck back into his defensive zone.

Ten-minute overtime without sudden-death provision to be played in games tied after regulation time. Games tied after this overtime period declared a draw.

Exclusive of goaltenders, team to dress at least 8 and no more than 12 skaters.

Major Rule Changes — *continued*

1929-30 — Forward passing permitted inside all three zones but not permitted across either blue line.

Kicking the puck allowed, but a goal cannot be scored by kicking the puck in.

No more than three players including the goaltender may remain in their defensive zone when the puck has gone up ice. Minor penalties to be assessed for the first two violations of this rule in a game; major penalties thereafter.

Goaltenders forbidden to hold the puck. Pucks caught must be cleared immediately. For infringement of this rule, a faceoff to be taken ten feet in front of the goal with no player except the goaltender standing between the faceoff spot and the goal-line.

Highsticking penalties introduced.

Maximum number of players in uniform increased from 12 to 15.

December 21, 1929 — Forward passing rules instituted at the beginning of the 1929-30 season more than doubled number of goals scored. Partway through the season, these rules were further amended to read, ''No attacking player allowed to precede the play when entering the opposing defensive zone.'' This is similar to modern offside rule.

1930-31 — A player without a complete stick ruled out of play and forbidden from taking part in further action until a new stick is obtained. A player who has broken his stick must obtain a replacement at his bench.

A further refinement of the offside rule stated that the puck must first be propelled into the attacking zone before any player of the attacking side can enter that zone; for infringement of this rule a faceoff to take place at the spot where the infraction took place.

1931-32 — Though there is no record of a team attempting to play with two goaltenders on the ice, a rule was instituted which stated that each team was allowed only one goaltender on the ice at one time.

Attacking players forbidden to impede the movement or obstruct the vision of opposing goaltenders.

Defending players with the exception of the goaltender forbidden from falling on the puck within 10 feet of the net.

1932-33 — Each team to have captain on the ice at all times. Maximum number of players in uniform reduced to 14 from 15.

If the goaltender is removed from the ice to serve a penalty, the manager of the club to appoint a substitute.

Match penalty with substitution after five minutes instituted for kicking another player.

1933-34 — Number of players permitted to stand in defensive zone restricted to three including goaltender.

Visible time clocks required in each rink.

Two referees replace one referee and one linesman.

1934-35 — Penalty shot awarded when a player is tripped and thus prevented from having a clear shot on goal, having no player to pass to other than the offending player. Shot taken from inside a 10-foot circle located 38 feet from the goal. The goaltender must not advance more than one foot from his goal-line when the shot is taken.

1937-38 — Rules introduced governing icing the puck.

Penalty shot awarded when a player other than a goaltender falls on the puck within 10 feet of the goal.

1938-39 — Penalty shot modified to allow puck carrier to skate in before shooting.

One referee and one linesman replace two referee system.

Blue line widened to 12 inches.

Maximum number of players in uniform increased from 14 to 15.

1939-40 — A substitute replacing a goaltender removed from ice to serve a penalty may use a goaltender's stick and gloves but no other goaltending equipment.

1940-41 — Flooding ice surface between periods made obligatory.

1941-42 — Penalty shots classified as minor and major. Minor shot to be taken from a line 28 feet from the goal. Major shot, awarded when a player is tripped with only the goaltender to beat, permits the player taking the penalty shot to skate right into the goalkeeper and shoot from point-blank range.

One referee and two linesmen employed to officiate games.

For playoffs, standby minor league goaltenders employed by NHL as emergency substitutes.

1942-43 — Because of wartime restrictions on train scheduling, regular-season overtime was discontinued on November 21, 1942.

Player limit reduced from 15 to 14. Minimum of 12 men in uniform abolished.

1943-44 — Red line at center ice introduced to speed up the game and reduce offside calls. This rule is considered to mark the beginning of the modern era in the NHL.

1945-46 — Goal indicator lights synchronized with official time clock required at all rinks.

1946-47 — System of signals by officials to indicate infractions introduced.

Linesmen from neutral cities employed for all games.

1947-48 — Goal awarded when a player with the puck has an open net to shoot at and a thrown stick prevents the shot on goal. Major penalty to any player who throws his stick in any zone other than defending zone. If a stick is thrown by a player in his defending zone but the thrown stick is not considered to have prevented a goal, a penalty shot is awarded.

All playoff games played until a winner determined, with 20-minute sudden-death overtime periods separated by 10-minute intermissions.

1949-50 — Ice surface painted white.

Clubs allowed to dress 17 players exclusive of goaltenders.

Major penalties incurred by goaltenders served by a member of the goaltender's team instead of resulting in a penalty shot.

1950-51 — Each team required to provide an emergency goaltender in attendance with full equipment at each game for use by either team in the event of illness or injury to a regular goaltender.

1951-52 — Home teams to wear basic white uniforms; visiting teams basic colored uniforms.

Goal crease enlarged from 3 × 7 feet to 4 × 8 feet.

Number of players in uniform reduced to 15 plus goaltenders.

Faceoff circles enlarged from 10-foot to 15-foot radius.

1952-53 — Teams permitted to dress 15 skaters on the road and 16 at home.

1953-54 — Number of players in uniform set at 16 plus goaltenders.

1954-55 — Number of players in uniform set at 18 plus goaltenders up to December 1 and 16 plus goaltenders thereafter. Teams agree to wear colored uniforms at home and white uniforms on the road.

1956-57 — Player serving a minor penalty allowed to return to ice when a goal is scored by opposing team.

1959-60 — Players prevented from leaving their benches to enter into an altercation. Substitutions permitted providing substitutes do not enter into altercation.

1960-61 — Number of players in uniform set at 16 plus goaltenders.

1961-62 — Penalty shots to be taken by the player against whom the foul was committed. In the event of a penalty shot called in a situation where a particular player hasn't been fouled, the penalty shot to be taken by any player on the ice when the foul was committed.

1964-65 — No body contact on faceoffs.

In playoff games, each team to have its substitute goaltender dressed in his regular uniform except for leg pads and body protector. All previous rules governing standby goaltenders terminated.

1965-66 — Teams required to dress two goaltenders for each regular-season game. Maximum stick length increased to 55 inches.

1966-67 — Substitution allowed on coincidental major penalties.

Between-periods intermissions fixed at 15 minutes.

1967-68 — If a penalty incurred by a goaltender is a co-incident major, the penalty to be served by a player of the goaltender's team on the ice at the time the penalty was called. Limit of curvature of hockey stick blade set at 1½ inches.

1969-70 — Limit of curvature of hockey stick blade set at 1 inch.

1970-71 — Home teams to wear basic white uniforms; visiting teams to wear basic colored uniforms.

Limit of curvature of hockey stick blade set at ½ inch.

Minor penalty for deliberately shooting the puck out of the playing area.

1971-72 — Number of players in uniform set at 17 plus 2 goaltenders.

Third man to enter an altercation assessed an automatic game misconduct penalty.

1972-73 — Minimum width of stick blade reduced to 2 inches from 2½ inches.

1974-75 — Bench minor penalty imposed if a penalized player does not proceed directly and immediately to the penalty box.

1976-77 — Rule dealing with fighting amended to provide a major and game misconduct penalty for any player who is clearly the instigator of a fight.

1977-78 — Teams requesting a stick measurement to be assessed a minor penalty in the event that the measured stick does not violate the rules.

1979-80 — Wearing of helmets made mandatory for players entering the NHL.

1980-81 — Maximum stick length increased to 58 inches.

1981-82 — If both of a team's listed goaltenders are incapacitated, the team can dress and play any eligible goaltender who is available.

1982-83 — Number of players in uniform set at 18 plus 2 goaltenders.

1983-84 — Five-minute sudden-death overtime to be played in regular-season games that are tied at the end of regulation time.

1985-86 — Substitutions allowed in the event of co-incidental minor penalties. Maximum stick length increased to 60 inches.

1986-87 — Delayed off-side is no longer in effect once the players of the offending team have cleared the opponents' defensive zone.

1990-91 — The goal lines, blue lines, defensive zone face-off circles and markings all moved one foot out from the end boards, creating 11 feet of room behind the nets and shrinking the neutral zone from 60 to 58 feet.

1991-92 — Video replays employed to assist referees in goal/no goal situations. Size of goal crease increased. Crease changed to semi-circular configuration. Time clock to record tenths of a second in last minute of each period and overtime. Major and game misconduct penalty for checking from behind into boards. Penalties added for crease infringement and unnecessary contact with goaltender. Goal disallowed if puck enters net while a player of the attacking team is standing on the goal crease line, is in the goal crease or places his stick in the goal crease.

1992-93 — No substitutions allowed in the event of coincidental minor penalties called when both teams are at full strength. Minor penalty for attempting to draw a penalty ("diving"). Major and game misconduct penalty for checking from behind into goal frame. Game misconduct penalty for instigating a fight. High sticking redefined to include any use of the stick above waist-height. Previous rule stipulated shoulder-height.

1993-94 — High sticking redefined to allow goals scored with a high stick below the height of the crossbar of the goal frame.

1996-97 — Maximum stick length increased to 63 inches. All players must be clear of the attacking zone prior to the puck being shot into that zone. The opportunity to "tag-up" and return into the zone has been removed.

1998-99 — The league instituted a two-referee system with each team to play 20 regular-season games with two referees and a pair of linesmen. Goal line moved to 13 feet from end boards. Goal crease altered to extend one foot beyond each goal post (eight feet across in total. Sides of crease squared off, extending 4'6". Only the top of the crease remains rounded. Only the top of the crease remains rounded.

1999-2000 — Each team to play 25 home and 25 road games using the two-referee system. Crease rule revised to implement a ''no harm, no foul, no video review'' standard. Teams to play with four skaters and a goaltender in regular-season overtime. If a goal is scored in regular-season overtime, the winner is awarded two points and the loser one point. In no goal is scored in overtime, both teams are awarded one point.

2000-01 — All games to be played using the two-referee system.

2002-03 — "Hurry-up" faceoff and line-change rules implemented.

2003-04 — Home teams to wear basic colored uniforms; visiting teams to wear basic white uniforms. Maximum length of goaltender's pads set at 38 inches.

2005-06 — The NHL adopted a comprehensive package of rule changes that included the following:

Goal line moved to 11 feet from end boards; blue lines moved to 75 feet from end boards, reducing neutral zone from 54 feet to 50 feet. Center red line eliminated for two-line passes. "Tag-up" off-side rule reinstituted. Goaltender not permitted to play the puck outside a designated trapezoid-shaped area behind the net. A team that ices the puck is not permitted to make any player substitutions prior to the ensuing faceoff. A player who instigates a fight in the final five minutes of regulation time or at any time of overtime to receive a minor, a major, a misconduct and an automatic one-game suspension. The size of goaltender equipment reduced. If a game remains tied after five minutes of overtime, winner determined by shootout.

2011-12 — Rules and penalties modified to address contact with the head.

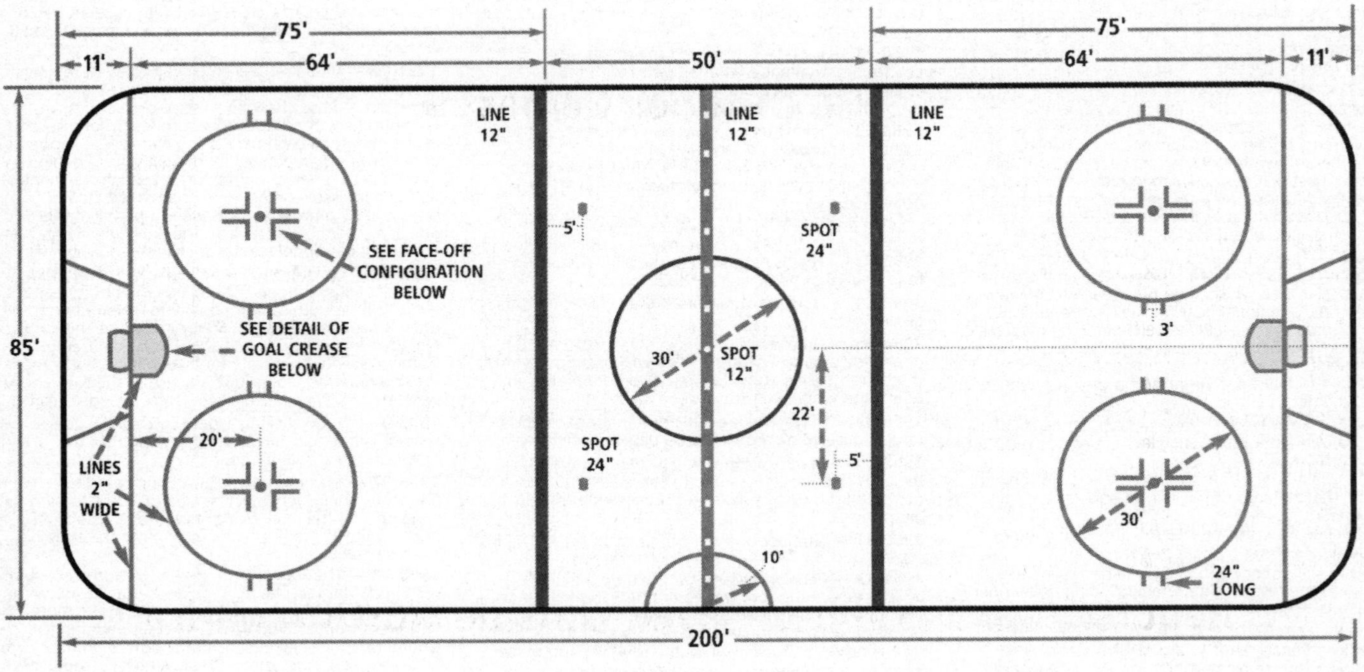

NHL RINK DIMENSIONS

FACEOFF CONFIGURATION

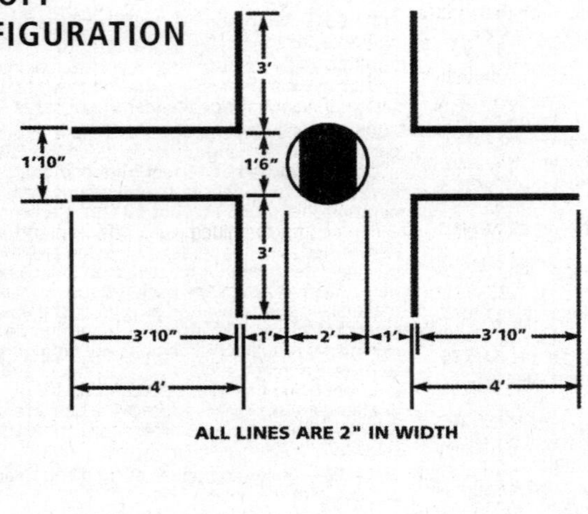

ALL LINES ARE 2" IN WIDTH

CREASE DIMENSIONS

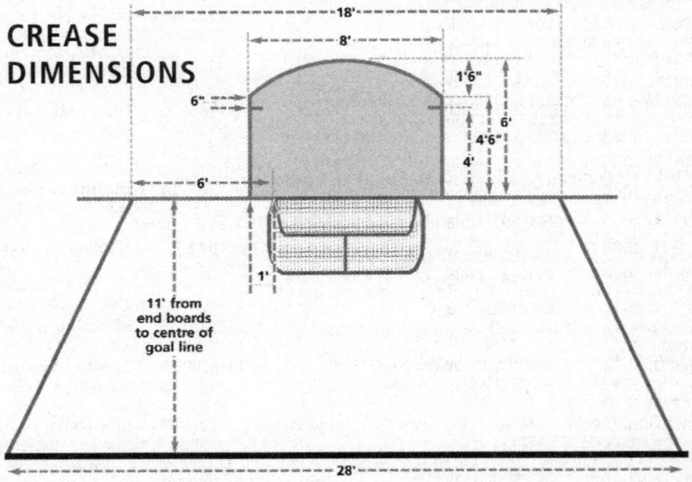

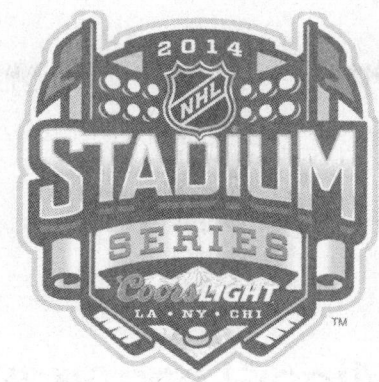

NHL Outdoor Games

Date	Location	Venue	Attendance	Final Score				Game-Winning Goal	Time of GWG	Temperature
Nov. 22, 2003**	Edmonton, Alberta	Commonwealth Stadium	57,167	Montreal	4	Edmonton	3	Richard Zednik	14:18 (3rd)	0°F/-18°C
Jan. 1, 2008*	Buffalo, New York	Ralph Wilson Stadium	71,217	Pittsburgh	2	Buffalo	1	Sidney Crosby	Shootout	33°F/+1°C
Jan. 1, 2009*	Chicago, Illinois	Wrigley Field	40,818	Detroit	6	Chicago	4	Brian Rafalski	3:07 (3rd)	32°F/0°C
Jan. 1, 2010*	Boston, Massachusetts	Fenway Park	38,112	Boston	2	Philadelphia	1	Marco Sturm	1:57 (OT)	35°F/+2°C
Jan. 1, 2011*	Pittsburgh, Pennsylvania	Heinz Field	68,111	Washington	3	Pittsburgh	1	Eric Fehr	11:59 (3rd)	50°F/+10°C
Feb. 20, 2011**	Calgary, Alberta	McMahon Stadium	41,022	Calgary	4	Montreal	0	Rene Bourque	8:09 (1st)	18°F/-8°C
Jan. 2, 2012*	Philadelphia, Pennsylvania	Citizens Bank Park	46,967	NY Rangers	3	Philadelphia	2	Brad Richards	5:21 (3rd)	41°F/+5°C
Jan. 1, 2014*	Ann Arbor, Michigan	Michigan Stadium	*est.*115,000	Toronto		Detroit				
Jan. 25, 2014***	Los Angeles, California	Dodger Stadium	*est.*56,000	Anaheim		Los Angeles				
Jan. 26, 2014***	New York, New York	Yankee Stadium	*est.*50,000	NY Rangers		New Jersey				
Jan. 29, 2014***	New York, New York	Yankee Stadium	*est.*50,000	NY Rangers		NY Islanders				
Mar. 1, 2014***	Chicago, Illinois	Soldier Field	*est.*61,500	Pittsburgh		Chicago				
Mar. 2, 2014**	Vancouver, B.C.	BC Place	*est.*54,000	Ottawa		Vancouver				

** - Winter Classic; ** - Heritage Classic; *** - Coors Light NHL Stadium Series*

Regular-Season Games Played Outside North America

Date	Location	Venue	Attendance	Final Score				Game-Winning Goal	Time of GWG
Oct. 3, 1997	Tokyo, Japan	Yoyogi Arena	10,500	Vancouver	3	Anaheim	2	Pavel Bure	14:41 (2nd)
Oct. 4, 1997	Tokyo, Japan	Yoyogi Arena	10,500	Anaheim	3	Vancouver	2	J.J. Daigneault	13:38 (3rd)
Oct. 9, 1998	Tokyo, Japan	Yoyogi Arena	10,000	San Jose	3	Calgary	3	...	...
Oct. 10, 1998	Tokyo, Japan	Yoyogi Arena	10,000	Calgary	5	San Jose	3	Dave Roche	11:41 (2nd)
Oct. 7, 2000	Saitama, Japan	Saitama Super Arena	13,849	Nashville	3	Pittsburgh	1	Vitali Yachmanev	8:01 (2nd)
Oct. 8, 2000	Saitama, Japan	Saitama Super Arena	13,426	Pittsburgh	3	Nashville	1	Martin Straka	16:16 (3rd)
Sept. 29, 2007	London, England	O2 Arena	17,551	Los Angeles	4	Anaheim	1	Rob Blake	10:15 (2nd)
Sept. 30, 2007	London, England	O2 Arena	17,300	Anaheim	4	Los Angeles	1	Chris Kunitz	15:19 (1st)
Oct. 4, 2008	Prague, Czech Republic	O2 Arena	17,085	NY Rangers	2	Tampa Bay	1	Brandon Dubinsky	14:16 (3rd)
Oct. 4, 2008	Stockholm, Sweden	Ericsson Globe Arena	13,699	Pittsburgh	4	Ottawa	3	Tyler Kennedy	4:35 (OT)
Oct. 5, 2008	Prague, Czech Republic	O2 Arena	17,085	NY Rangers	2	Tampa Bay	1	Scott Gomez	12:12 (2nd)
Oct. 5, 2008	Stockholm, Sweden	Ericsson Globe Arena	13,699	Ottawa	3	Pittsburgh	1	Dany Heatley	12:17 (3rd)
Oct. 2, 2009	Helsinki, Finland	Hartwell Arena	12,056	Florida	4	Chicago	3	Ville Koistinen	Shootout
Oct. 2, 2009	Stockholm, Sweden	Ericsson Globe Arena	13,850	St. Louis	4	Detroit	3	Paul Kariya	17:36 (2nd)
Oct. 3, 2009	Helsinki, Finland	Hartwell Arena	11,526	Chicago	4	Florida	0	Brian Campbell	3:05 (1st)
Oct. 3, 2009	Stockholm, Sweden	Ericsson Globe Arena	13,850	St. Louis	5	Detroit	3	Patrick Berglund	13:37 (2nd)
Oct. 7, 2010	Helsinki, Finland	Hartwell Arena	12,355	Carolina	4	Minnesota	3	Brandon Sutter	18:03 (2nd)
Oct. 8, 2010	Helsinki, Finland	Hartwell Arena	13,465	Carolina	2	Minnesota	1	Jeff Skinner	Shootout
Oct. 8, 2010	Stockholm, Sweden	Ericsson Globe Arena	11,324	San Jose	3	Columbus	2	Logan Couture	10:15 (3rd)
Oct. 9, 2010	Stockholm, Sweden	Ericsson Globe Arena	11,324	Columbus	3	San Jose	2	Ethan Moreau	1:56 (OT)
Oct. 9, 2010	Prague, Czech Republic	O2 Arena	15,299	Phoenix	5	Boston	2	Scottie Upshall	15:02 (2nd)
Oct. 10, 2010	Prague, Czech Republic	O2 Arena	12,990	Boston	3	Phoenix	0	Milan Lucic	12:11 (2nd)
Oct. 7, 2011	Helsinki, Finland	Hartwell Arena	13,349	Buffalo	4	Anaheim	2	Ville Leino	8:30 (1st)
Oct. 7, 2011	Stockholm, Sweden	Ericsson Globe Arena	13,800	Los Angeles	3	NY Rangers	2	Jack Johnson	4:08 (OT)
Oct. 8, 2011	Stockholm, Sweden	Ericsson Globe Arena	13,800	Anaheim	2	NY Rangers	1	Bobby Ryan	Shootout
Oct. 8, 2011	Berlin, Germany	O2 World	14,300	Buffalo	4	Los Angeles	2	Paul Gaustad	13:19 (2nd)

NHL Clubs' Minor-League Affiliations, 2013-14

NHL Club	Minor-League Affiliates
Anaheim	Norfolk Admirals (AHL) Utah Grizzlies (ECHL)
Boston	Providence Bruins (AHL) South Carolina Stingrays (ECHL)
Buffalo	Rochester Americans (AHL)
Calgary	Abbotsford Heat (AHL) Utah Grizzlies (ECHL)
Carolina	Charlotte Checkers (AHL) Florida Everblades (ECHL)
Chicago	Rockford IceHogs (AHL) Toledo Walleye (ECHL)
Colorado	Lake Erie Monsters (AHL) Denver Cutthroats (CHL)
Columbus	Springfield Falcons (AHL) Evansville IceMen (ECHL)
Dallas	Texas Stars (AHL) Idaho Steelheads (ECHL)
Detroit	Grand Rapids Griffins (AHL) Toledo Walleye (ECHL)
Edmonton	Oklahoma City Barons (AHL) Bakersfield Condors (ECHL)
Florida	San Antonio Rampage (AHL) Cincinnati Cyclones (ECHL)
Los Angeles	Manchester Monarchs (AHL) Ontario (CA) Reign (ECHL)
Minnesota	Iowa Wild (AHL) Orlando Solar Bears (ECHL) Quad City Mallards (CHL)
Montreal	Hamilton Bulldogs (AHL) Wheeling Nailers (ECHL)

NHL Club	Minor-League Affiliates
Nashville	Milwaukee Admirals (AHL) Cincinnati Cyclones (ECHL)
New Jersey	Albany Devils (AHL)
NY Islanders	Bridgeport Sound Tigers (AHL) Stockton Thunder (ECHL)
NY Rangers	Hartford Wolf Pack (AHL) Greenville Road Warriors (ECHL)
Ottawa	Binghamton Senators (AHL) Elmira Jackals (ECHL)
Philadelphia	Adirondack Phantoms (AHL) Greenville Road Warriors (ECHL)
Phoenix	Portland Pirates (AHL) Gwinnett Gladiators (ECHL) Arizona Sundogs (CHL)
Pittsburgh	Wilkes-Barre/Scranton Penguins (AHL) Wheeling Nailers (ECHL)
St. Louis	Chicago Wolves (AHL) Evansville IceMen (ECHL)
San Jose	Worcester Sharks (AHL) San Francisco Bulls (ECHL)
Tampa Bay	Syracuse Crunch (AHL) Florida Everblades (ECHL)
Toronto	Toronto Marlies (AHL) Orlando Solar Bears (ECHL)
Vancouver	Utica Comets (AHL) Kalamazoo Wings (ECHL)
Washington	Hershey Bears (AHL) Reading Royals (ECHL)
Winnipeg	St. John's IceCaps (AHL) Ontario (CA) Reign (ECHL)

NHL Players at the 2014 Olympic Winter Games

FOR THE FIFTH TIME SINCE 1997-98, the NHL's 2013-14 regular season will be interrupted in order to allow the League's players to represent their countries at the Olympic Winter Games in Sochi, Russia.

Twelve teams, divided into three groups of four, will play for Olympic gold. Each team will play the three opponents in its group from Feb. 12 to Feb. 16. Russia, Slovakia, the USA and Slovenia will compete in Group A; Finland, Canada, Norway and Austria in Group B; and the Czech Republic, Sweden, Switzerland and Latvia in Group C.

At the conclusion of the Preliminary Round, all 12 teams will be ranked in one group. The top four teams will advance to the quarterfinals. The remaining teams play a single Qualification Playoff on Feb. 18: 5 vs.12, 6 vs.11, 7 vs.10 and 8 vs.9. The four winners qualify for the quarterfinals. Single-game playoffs will then determine the winner of the quarterfinals (Feb. 19), the semifinals (Feb. 21), the bronze medal game (Feb. 22) and the gold medal game (Feb. 23).

2014 Men's Olympic Hockey Schedule

Start times listed in Sochi local time (GMT + 4).
EST is 9 hours earlier than local time in Sochi.
PST is 12 hours earlier than local time in Sochi.

Preliminary Round (round robin)

Feb. 12	Czech Republic	vs.	Sweden	9:00 pm
	Latvia	vs.	Switzerland	9:00 pm
Feb.13	Finland	vs.	Austria	noon
	Russia	vs.	Slovenia	4:30 pm
	Slovakia	vs.	USA	4:30 pm
	Canada	vs.	Norway	9:00 pm
Feb. 14	Czech Republic	vs.	Latvia	noon
	Sweden	vs.	Switzerland	4:30 pm
	Canada	vs.	Austria	9:00 pm
	Norway	vs.	Finland	9:00 pm
Feb. 15	Slovakia	vs.	Slovenia	noon
	USA	vs.	Russia	4:30 pm
	Switzerland	vs.	Czech Republic	9:00 pm
	Sweden	vs.	Latvia	9:00 pm
Feb. 16	Austria	vs.	Norway	noon
	Russia	vs.	Slovakia	4:30 pm
	Slovenia	vs.	USA	4:30 pm
	Finland	vs.	Canada	9:00 pm

Qualification Playoff Round (single elimination)

Feb. 18	Qualification Playoff Game 1	noon
	Qualification Playoff Game 2	4:30 pm
	Qualification Playoff Game 3	9:00 pm
	Qualification Playoff Game 4	9:00 pm

Playoff Round (single elimination)

Feb. 19	Quarterfinal 1	noon
	Quarterfinal 2	4:30 pm
	Quarterfinal 3	9:00 pm
	Quarterfinal 4	9:00 pm

Note: If qualified, USA to play at noon or 9:00 pm; If qualified, Canada to play at 4:30 pm.

Feb. 21	Semifinal	4:00 pm
	Semifinal	9:00 pm
Feb. 22	Bronze Medal Game	7:00 pm
Feb. 23	Gold Medal Game	4:00 pm

2014 Women's Olympic Hockey Schedule

Start times listed in Sochi local time (GMT + 4).
EST is 9 hours earlier than local time in Sochi.
PST is 12 hours earlier than local time in Sochi.

Preliminary Round (round robin)

Feb. 8	USA	vs.	Finland	noon
	Canada	vs.	Switzerland	5:00 pm
Feb. 9	Sweden	vs.	Japan	noon
	Russia	vs.	Germany	5:00 pm
Feb. 10	USA	vs.	Switzerland	2:00 pm
	Finalnd	vs.	Canada	7:00 pm
Feb. 11	Germany	vs.	Sweden	2:00 pm
	Russia	vs.	Japan	7:00 pm
Feb.12	Switzerland	vs.	Finland	noon
	Canada	vs.	USA	4:30 pm
Feb. 13	Japan	vs.	Germany	noon
	Sweden	vs.	Russia	9:00 pm

Playoff Round (single elimination)

Feb. 15	Quarterfinal 1	noon
	Quarterfinal 2	4:30 pm
Feb. 16	Placement Game 1	noon
	Placement Game 2	9:00 pm
Feb. 17	Semifinal	4:30 pm
	Semifinal	9:00 pm
Feb. 18	Placement Game 7th/8th	noon
	Placement Game 5th/6th	4:30 pm

Finals

Feb. 20	Bronze Medal Game	4:00 pm
	Gold Medal Game	9:00 pm

Cumulative Medal Standings, Women's Olympic Hockey, 1998-2010

	G	S	B	Total	Last Medal
1. Canada	3	1	0	4	Gold 10
2. USA	1	2	1	4	Silver 10
3. Sweden	0	1	1	2	Silver 06
4. Finland	0	0	2	2	Bronze 10

Cumulative Medal Standings, Men's Olympic Hockey, 1920-2010

	G	S	B	Total	Last Medal
1. Canada	8	4	2	14	Gold 10
2. USSR/Russia*	8	2	2	12	Bronze 02
3. USA	2	8	1	11	Silver 10
4. Sweden	2	2	4	8	Gold 06
5. Czechoslovakia/Czech Rep.	1	4	5	10	Bronze 06
6. Great Britain	1	0	1	2	Gold 36
7. Finland	0	2	3	5	Bronze 10
8. W. Germany	0	0	2	2	Bronze 76
9. Switzerland	0	0	2	2	Bronze 48

** Soviet Union/Russia played as the Unified Team in 1992.*

Vancouver, B.C., Canada • 2010

Preliminary Round

(Note: W = 3 pts; OTW = 2 pts; OTL = 1 pt.)

Group A

Team	GP	W	OTW	OTL	L	GF	GA	Pts
USA	3	3	0	0	0	14	5	9
CAN	3	1	1	0	1	14	7	5
SUI	3	0	1	1	1	8	10	3
NOR	3	0	0	1	2	5	19	1

Group B

Team	GP	W	OTW	OTL	L	GF	GA	Pts
RUS	3	2	0	1	0	13	6	7
CZE	3	2	0	0	1	10	7	6
SVK	3	1	1	0	1	9	4	5
LAT	3	0	0	0	3	4	19	0

Group C

Team	GP	W	OTW	OTL	L	GF	GA	Pts
SWE	3	3	0	0	0	9	2	9
FIN	3	2	0	0	1	10	4	6
BLR	3	1	0	0	2	8	12	3
GER	3	0	0	0	3	3	12	0

Qualification Playoff

Switzerland	3	Belarus	2	(SO)
Czech Republic	3	Latvia	3	(OT)
Canada	8	Germany	2	
Slovakia	4	Norway	3	

Quarterfinals

USA	2	Switzerland	0
Finland	2	Czech Republic	0
Canada	7	Russia	3
Slovakia	4	Sweden	3

Semifinals

USA	6	Finland	1
Canada	3	Slovakia	2

Bronze Medal game

Finland	5	Slovakia	3

Gold Medal game

Canada	3	USA	2	(OT)

2010 Final Rankings, Men

1. Canada
2. USA
3. Finland
4. Slovakia
5. Sweden
6. Russia
7. Czech Republic
8. Switzerland
9. Belarus
10. Norway
11. Germany
12. Latvia

2010 Scoring Leaders

Player	Team	GP	G	A	PTS	PIM
Pavol Demitra	Slovakia	7	3	7	10	2
Marian Hossa	Slovakia	7	3	6	9	6
Zach Parise	USA	6	4	4	8	0
Brian Rafalski	USA	6	4	4	8	2
Jonathan Toews	Canada	7	1	7	8	2
Jarome Iginla	Canada	7	5	2	7	0
Sidney Crosby	Canada	7	4	3	7	4
Dany Heatley	Canada	7	4	3	7	4
Ryan Getzlaf	Canada	7	3	4	7	2
Niklas Hagman	Finland	6	4	2	6	2
Evgeni Malkin	Russia	4	3	3	6	0
Michal Handzus	Slovakia	7	3	3	6	0
Shea Weber	Canada	7	2	4	6	2
Richard Zednik	Slovakia	7	2	4	6	6
Nicklas Backstrom	Sweden	4	1	5	6	0
Dan Boyle	Canada	7	1	5	6	2
Eric Staal	Canada	7	1	5	6	6
Duncan Keith	Canada	7	0	6	6	2

2010 Goaltending Leaders

(Minimum 150 Mins)

Player	Team	GP	Min	GA	SO	GAA
Henrik Lundqvist	Sweden	3	179	4	2	1.34
Ryan Miller	USA	6	355	8	1	1.35
Roberto Luongo	Canada	5	308	9	1	1.76
Tomas Vokoun	Czech Rep.	5	304	9	0	1.78
Jaroslav Halak	Slovakia	7	423	17	1	2.41

Torino, Italy • 2006

Preliminary Round

Group A

Team	GP	W	L	T	GF	GA	Pts
Finland	5	5	0	0	19	2	10
Switzerland	5	2	1	2	10	12	6
Canada	5	3	2	0	15	9	6
Czech Republic	5	2	3	0	14	12	4
Germany	5	0	3	2	7	16	2
Italy	5	0	3	2	9	23	2

Group B

Team	GP	W	L	T	GF	GA	Pts
Slovakia	5	5	0	0	18	8	10
Russia	5	4	1	0	23	11	8
Sweden	5	3	2	0	15	12	6
United States	5	1	3	1	13	13	3
Kazakhstan	5	1	4	0	9	16	2
Latvia	5	0	4	1	11	29	1

Quarterfinals

Sweden	6	Switzerland	2
Finland	4	USA	3
Russia	2	Canada	0
Czech Republic	3	Slovakia	1

Semifinals

Sweden	7	Czech Republic	3
Finland	4	Russia	0

Bronze Medal game

Czech Republic	3	Russia	0

Gold Medal game

Sweden	3	Finland	2

2006 Final Rankings, Men

1. Sweden
2. Finland
3. Czech Republic
4. Russia
5. Slovakia
6. Switzerland
7. Canada
8. USA
9. Kazakhstan
10. Germany
11. Italy
12. Latvia

2006 Scoring Leaders

Player	Team	GP	G	A	PTS	PIM
Teemu Selanne	Finland	8	6	5	11	4
Saku Koivu	Finland	8	3	8	11	12
Daniel Alfredsson	Sweden	8	5	5	10	4
Marián Hossa	Slovakia	6	5	5	10	4
Ville Peltonen	Finland	8	4	5	9	6
Olli Jokinen	Finland	8	6	2	8	2
Jere Lehtinen	Finland	8	3	5	8	0
Mats Sundin	Sweden	8	3	5	8	4
Martin Straka	Czech Rep.	8	2	6	8	6
Pavel Datsyuk	Russia	8	1	7	8	10

2006 Goaltending Leaders

(Minimum 150 Mins)

Player	Team	GP	Min	GA	SO	GAA
Antero Niittymaki	Finland	6	359	8	3	1.34
Evgeni Nabokov	Russia	7	359	8	3	1.34
David Aebischer	Switz.	4	200	7	0	2.10
Peter Budaj	Slovakia	3	179	6	0	2.01
Martin Brodeur	Canada	4	239	8	0	2.01

Salt Lake City, Utah, USA • 2002

Preliminary Round

Group A

Team	GP	W	L	T	GF	GA	Pts
Germany	3	3	0	0	10	3	6
Latvia	3	1	1	1	11	12	3
Austria	3	1	2	0	7	9	2
Slovakia	3	0	2	1	8	12	1

Group B

Team	GP	W	L	T	GF	GA	Pts
Belarus	3	2	1	0	5	3	4
Ukraine	3	2	1	0	9	5	4
Switzerland	3	1	1	1	7	9	3
France	3	0	2	1	6	10	1

Final Round

Group C

Team	GP	W	L	T	GF	GA	Pts
Sweden	3	3	0	0	14	4	6
Czech Rep.	3	1	1	1	12	7	3
Canada	3	1	1	1	8	10	3
Germany	3	0	3	0	5	18	0

Group D

Team	GP	W	L	T	GF	GA	Pts
USA	3	2	0	1	16	3	5
Finland	3	2	1	0	11	8	4
Russia	3	1	1	1	9	9	3
Belarus	3	0	3	0	6	22	0

Quarterfinals

Belarus	4	Sweden	3
Russia	2	Czech Republic	1
USA	5	Germany	0
Canada	2	Finland	1

Semifinals

Canada	7	Belarus	1
USA	3	Russia	2

Bronze Medal game

Russia	7	Belarus	2

Gold Medal game

Canada	5	USA	2

2002 Final Rankings, Men

1. Canada
2. USA
3. Russia
4. Belarus
5-8. Czech Republic
5-8. Finland
5-8. Germany
5-8. Sweden
9. Latvia
10. Ukraine
11. Switzerland
12. Austria
13. Slovakia
14. France

2002 Scoring Leaders

Player	Team	GP	G	A	PTS	PIM
Mats Sundin	Sweden	4	5	4	9	10
Brett Hull	USA	6	3	5	8	6
John LeClair	USA	6	6	1	7	2
Joe Sakic	Canada	6	4	3	7	0
Marian Hossa	Slovakia	2	4	2	6	0
J-J Aeschlimann	Switzerland	4	3	3	6	2
Philippe Bozon	France	4	3	3	6	2
Len Soccio	Germany	7	3	3	6	8
Mario Lemieux	Canada	5	2	4	6	0
Steve Yzerman	Canada	6	2	4	6	2
Nicklas Lidstrom	Sweden	4	1	5	6	0
Mike Modano	USA	6	0	6	6	0

2002 Goaltending Leaders

(Minimum 150 Mins)

Player	Team	GP	Min	GA	SO	GAA
Martin Gerber	Switzerland	3	157	4	0	1.52
Martin Brodeur	Canada	5	300	9	0	1.80
Dominik Hasek	Czech Rep.	4	239	8	0	2.01
Mike Richter	USA	4	240	9	1	2.34
N. Khabibulin	Russia	6	359	14	1	2.34
Tommy Salo	Sweden	3	179	7	0	2.35

Nagano, Japan • 1998

Preliminary Round

Group A

Team	GP	W	L	T	GF	GA	Pts
Kazakhstan	3	2	0	1	14	11	5
Slovakia	3	1	1	1	9	9	3
Italy	3	1	2	0	11	11	2
Austria	3	0	1	2	9	12	2

Group B

Team	GP	W	L	T	GF	GA	Pts
Belarus	3	2	0	1	14	4	5
Germany	3	2	1	0	7	9	4
France	3	1	2	0	5	8	2
Japan	3	0	2	1	5	10	1

Final Round

Group A

Team	GP	W	L	T	GF	GA	Pts
Canada	3	3	0	0	12	3	6
Sweden	3	2	1	0	11	7	4
USA	3	1	2	0	8	10	2
Belarus	3	0	3	0	4	15	0

Group B

Team	GP	W	L	T	GF	GA	Pts
Russia	3	3	0	0	15	6	6
Czech Rep.	3	2	1	0	12	4	4
Finland	3	1	2	0	11	9	2
Kazakhstan	3	0	3	0	6	25	0

Quarterfinals

Canada	4	Kazakhstan	1
Czech Republic	4	USA	1
Finland	2	Sweden	1
Russia	4	Belarus	1

Semifinals

Note: SO = Shootout

Czech Republic	2	Canada	1 (SO)
Russia	7	Finland	4

Bronze Medal game

Finland	3	Canada	2

Gold Medal game

Czech Republic	1	Russia	0

1998 Final Rankings, Men

1. Czech Republic
2. Russia
3. Finland
4. Canada
5–8. USA
5–8. Sweden
5–8. Belarus
5–8. Kazakhstan
9. Germany
10. Slovakia
11. France
12. Italy
13. Japan
14. Austria

1998 Scoring Leaders

Player	Team	GP	G	A	PTS	PIM
Teemu Selanne	Finland	5	4	6	10	8
Saku Koivu	Finland	6	2	8	10	4
Pavel Bure	Russia	6	9	0	9	2
Alex. Koreshkov	Kazakhstan	7	3	6	9	2
Phillipe Bozon	France	4	5	2	7	4
K. Shafranov	Kazakhstan	7	4	3	7	6
Dominik Lavoie	Austria	4	5	1	6	8
Jere Lehtinen	Finland	6	4	2	6	2
Alexei Yashin	Russia	6	3	3	6	0
Serge Poudrier	France	6	2	4	6	4
Sergei Fedorov	Russia	6	1	5	6	8

1998 Goaltending Leaders

(Minimum 150 Mins)

Player	Team	GP	Min	GA	SO	GAA
Dominik Hasek	Czech Rep.	6	369	6	2	0.97
Patrick Roy	Canada	6	369	9	1	1.46
M. Shtalenkov	Russia	5	290	8	0	1.65
Tommy Salo	Sweden	4	238	9	0	2.27
Dusty Imoo	Japan	3	189	8	0	2.54
Mike Rosati	Italy	4	215	12	0	3.35

Lillehammer, Norway • 1994

Group A

Team	GP	W	L	T	GF	GA	PTS
Finland	5	5	0	0	25	4	10
Germany	5	3	2	0	11	14	6
Czech Rep.	5	3	2	0	16	11	6
Russia	5	3	2	0	20	14	6
Austria	5	1	4	0	13	28	2
Norway	5	0	5	0	5	19	0

Group B

Team	GP	W	L	T	GF	GA	PTS
Slovakia	5	3	0	2	26	14	8
Canada	5	3	1	1	17	11	7
Sweden	5	3	1	1	23	13	7
USA	5	1	1	3	21	17	5
Italy	5	1	4	0	15	31	2
France	5	0	4	1	11	27	1

Quarterfinals

Canada	3	Czech Rep.	2
Finland	6	USA	1
Sweden	3	Germany	0
Russia	3	Slovakia	2

Semifinals

Canada	5	Finland	3
Sweden	4	Russia	3

Bronze Medal Game

Finland	4	Russia	0

Gold Medal Game

Note: SO = Shootout

Sweden	3	Canada	2 (SO)

1994 Final Rankings

1. Sweden
2. Canada
3. Finland
4. Russia
5. Czech Republic
6. Slovakia
7. Germany
8. USA
9. Italy
10. France
11. Norway
12. Austria

1994 Scoring Leaders

Player	Team	GP	G	A	PTS	PIM
Ziggy Palffy	Slovakia	8	3	7	10	8
Miroslav Satan	Slovakia	8	9	0	9	0
Peter Stastny	Slovakia	8	5	4	9	9
Hakan Loob	Sweden	8	4	5	9	2
Gates Orlando	Italy	7	3	6	9	41
Patrik Juhlin	Sweden	8	7	1	8	16
Jiri Kucera	Czech Rep.	8	6	2	8	4
Marty Dallman	Austria	7	4	4	8	8
Mika Nieminen	Finland	8	3	5	8	0
David Sacco	USA	8	3	5	8	12
Peter Forsberg	Sweden	8	2	6	8	6

Albertville, France • 1992

Group A

Team	GP	W	L	T	GF	GA	PTS
USA	5	4	0	1	18	7	9
Sweden	5	3	0	2	22	11	8
Finland	5	3	0	1	22	11	7
Germany	5	2	3	0	11	12	4
Italy	5	1	4	0	18	24	2
Poland	5	0	5	0	4	30	0

Group B

Team	GP	W	L	T	GF	GA	PTS
Canada	5	4	1	0	28	9	8
Unified Team*	5	4	1	0	32	10	8
Czech.	5	4	1	0	25	15	8
France	5	2	3	0	14	22	4
Switzerland	5	1	4	0	13	25	2
Norway	5	0	5	0	7	38	0

* Soviet Union/Russia played as Unified Team in 1992.

Medal Round

Note: SO = Shootout

Canada	4	Germany	3 (SO)
Czechoslovakia	3	Sweden	1
USA	4	France	1
Unified Team	6	Finland	1

Semifinals

Canada	4	Czechoslovakia	2
Unified Team	5	USA	2

Bronze Medal Game

Czechoslovakia	6	USA	1

Gold Medal Game

Unified Team	3	Canada	1

1992 Final Rankings

1. Unified Team
2. Canada
3. Czechoslovakia
4. USA
5. Sweden
6. Germany
7. Finland
8. France
9. Norway
10. Switzerland
11. Poland
12. Italy

1992 Scoring Leaders

Player	Team	GP	G	A	PTS	PIM
Joe Juneau	Canada	8	6	9	15	5
Andrei Khomutov	Unified	8	7	7	14	2
Robert Lang	Czech.	8	5	8	13	8
Teemu Selanne	Finland	8	7	4	11	6
Eric Lindros	Canada	8	5	6	11	5
H. Jarvenpaa	Finland	8	5	6	11	14
V. Bykov	Unified	8	4	7	11	2
Yuri Khmylev	Unified	8	4	6	10	4
Mika Nieminen	Finland	8	4	6	10	6
N. Borschevsky	Unified	8	7	2	9	0

Calgary, Alberta, Canada • 1988

Group A

Team	GP	W	L	T	GF	GA	PTS
Finland	5	3	1	1	22	8	7
Sweden	5	2	0	3	23	10	7
Canada	5	3	1	1	17	12	7
Switzerland	5	3	2	0	19	10	6
Poland	5	0	4	1	3	13	1
France	5	1	4	0	10	41	0

Group B

Team	GP	W	L	T	GF	GA	PTS
Soviet Union	5	5	0	0	32	10	10
W. Germany	5	4	1	0	19	12	8
Czech.	5	3	2	0	23	14	6
USA	5	2	3	0	27	27	4
Austria	5	0	4	1	12	29	1
Norway	5	0	4	1	11	32	1

Final Round

Team	GP	W	L	T	GF	GA	PTS
Soviet Union	5	4	1	0	25	7	8
Finland	5	3	1	1	18	10	7
Sweden	5	2	1	2	15	16	6
Canada	5	2	2	1	17	14	5
W. Germany	5	1	4	0	8	26	2
Czech.	5	1	4	0	12	22	2

1988 Final Rankings

1. Soviet Union
2. Finland
3. Sweden
4. Canada
5. W. Germany
6. Czechoslovakia
7. USA
8. Switzerland
9. Austria
10. Poland
11. France
12. Norway

1988 Scoring Leaders

Player	Team	GP	G	A	PTS	PIM
Vladimir Krutov	Soviet Union	8	6	9	15	0
Igor Larionov	Soviet Union	8	4	9	13	4
V. Fetisov	Soviet Union	8	4	9	13	6
Corey Millen	USA	6	6	5	11	4
Dusan Pasek	Czech.	8	6	5	11	8
Sergei Makarov	Soviet Union	8	3	8	11	10
Erkki Lehtonen	Finland	8	4	6	10	2
Anders Eldebrink	Sweden	8	4	6	10	4
Igor Liba	Czech.	8	4	6	10	8
Gerd Truntschka	W. Germany	8	3	7	10	10
Raimo Helminen	Finland	7	2	8	10	4

Sarajevo, Yugoslavia • 1984

Group A

Team	GP	W	L	T	GF	GA	PTS
Soviet Union	5	5	0	0	42	5	10
Sweden	5	3	1	1	34	15	7
W. Germany	5	3	1	1	27	17	7
Poland	5	1	4	0	16	37	2
Italy	5	1	4	0	15	31	2
Yugoslavia	5	1	4	0	8	37	2

Group B

Czech.	5	5	0	0	38	7	10
Canada	5	4	1	0	24	10	8
Finland	5	2	2	1	27	19	5
USA	5	1	2	2	16	17	4
Austria	5	1	4	0	13	37	2
Norway	5	0	4	1	15	43	1

Final Round

Team	GP	W	L	T	GF	GA	PTS
Soviet Union	3	3	0	0	16	1	6
Czech.	3	2	1	0	6	2	4
Sweden	3	1	2	0	3	12	2
Canada	3	0	3	0	0	10	0

Consolation Round

W. Germany	1	1	0	0	7	4	2
USA	1	1	0	0	7	4	2
Finland	1	0	1	0	4	7	0
Poland	1	0	1	0	4	7	0

1984 Final Rankings

1. Soviet Union
2. Czechoslovakia
3. Sweden
4. Canada
5. W. Germany
6. Finland
7. USA
8. Poland

1984 Scoring Leaders

Player	Team	GP	G	A	PTS	PIM
Erich Kuhnhackl	W. Germany	6	8	6	14	12
Peter Gradin	Sweden	7	9	4	13	6
N. Drozdetski	Soviet Union	7	10	2	12	2
V. Fetisov	Soviet Union	7	3	8	11	8
Petri Skriko	Finland	6	6	4	10	8
Vladimir Ruzicka	Czech.	7	4	6	10	0
R. Summanen	Finland	6	4	6	10	4
Darius Rusnak	Czech.	7	4	6	10	6
Jiri Hrdina	Czech.	7	4	6	10	10
Vincent Lukac	Czech.	7	4	5	9	2
Viktor Tjumenev	Soviet Union	6	0	9	9	2

Lake Placid, NY, USA • 1980

Red Division

Team	GP	W	L	T	GF	GA	PTS
Soviet Union	5	5	0	0	51	11	10
Finland	5	3	2	0	26	18	6
Canada	5	3	2	0	28	12	6
Poland	5	2	3	0	15	23	4
Holland	5	1	3	1	16	43	3
Japan	5	0	4	1	7	36	1

Blue Division

Sweden	5	4	0	1	26	7	9
USA	5	4	0	1	25	10	9
Czech.	5	3	2	0	34	16	6
Romania	5	1	3	1	13	29	3
W. Germany	5	1	4	0	21	30	2
Norway	5	0	4	1	9	36	1

Final Round

Team	GP	W	L	T	GF	GA	PTS
USA	3	2	0	1	10	7	5
Soviet Union	3	2	1	0	16	8	4
Sweden	3	0	1	2	7	14	2
Finland	3	0	2	1	7	11	1

1980 Final Rankings

1. USA
2. Soviet Union
3. Sweden
4. Finland
5. Czechoslovakia
6. Canada
7. Poland
8. Holland
9. Romania
10. W. Germany
11. Norway
12. Japan

1980 Scoring Leaders

Player	Team	GP	G	A	PTS	PIM
Milan Novy	Czech.	6	7	8	15	0
Peter Stastny	Czech.	6	7	7	14	6
Jaroslav Pouzar	Czech.	6	8	5	13	8
Alexander Golikov	Soviet Union	7	7	6	13	6
Jukka Porvari	Finland	7	7	4	11	4
Boris Mikhailov	Soviet Union	7	6	5	11	2
Vladimir Krutov	Soviet Union	7	6	5	11	4
Sergei Makarov	Soviet Union	7	5	6	11	2
Marian Stastny	Czech.	6	5	6	11	4
Mark Johnson	USA	7	5	6	11	6

Innsbruck, Austria • 1976

Group A

Team	GP	W	L	T	GF	GA	PTS
Soviet Union	5	5	0	0	40	11	10
Czech.	5	3	2	0	17	10	6
W. Germany	5	2	3	0	21	24	4
Finland	5	2	3	0	19	18	4
USA	5	2	3	0	15	21	4
Poland	5	0	5	0	9	37	0

Group B

Romania	5	4	1	0	23	15	8
Austria	5	3	2	0	18	14	6
Japan	5	3	2	0	20	18	6
Yugoslavia	5	3	2	0	22	19	6
Switzerland	5	2	3	0	24	22	4
Bulgaria	5	0	5	0	19	38	0

1976 Final Rankings

1. Soviet Union
2. Czechoslovakia
3. W. Germany
4. Finland
5. USA
6. Poland
7. Romania
8. Austria
9. Japan
10. Yugoslavia
11. Switzerland
12. Bulgaria

1976 Scoring Leaders

Player	Team	GP	G	A	PTS	PIM
Vladimir Shadrin	Soviet Union	5	6	4	10	0
Alexander Maltsev	Soviet Union	5	5	5	10	0
Victor Shalimov	Soviet Union	5	5	5	10	2
Erich Kuhnhackl	W. Germany	5	5	5	10	10
Valeri Kharlamov	Soviet Union	5	3	6	9	6
Ernst Kopf	W. Germany	5	3	5	8	2
Vladimir Petrov	Soviet Union	5	4	3	7	8
A. Yakushev	Soviet Union	5	3	4	7	2
Bob Dobek	USA	5	3	4	7	4
Lorenz Funk	W. Germany	5	2	5	7	4
Victor Zhluktov	Soviet Union	5	1	6	7	2

Sapporo, Japan • 1972

Group A

Team	GP	W	L	T	GF	GA	PTS
Soviet Union	5	4	0	1	33	13	9
USA	5	3	2	0	18	15	6
Czech.	5	3	2	0	26	13	6
Sweden	5	2	2	1	17	13	5
Finland	5	2	3	0	14	24	4
Poland	5	0	5	0	9	39	0

Group B

W. Germany	4	3	1	0	22	10	6
Norway	4	3	1	0	16	14	6
Japan	4	2	1	1	17	16	5
Switzerland	4	0	2	2	9	16	2
Yugoslavia	4	0	3	1	9	17	1

1972 Final Rankings

1. Soviet Union
2. USA
3. Czechoslovakia
4. Sweden
5. Finland
6. Poland
7. W. Germany
8. Norway
9. Japan
10. Switzerland
11. Yugoslavia

1972 Scoring Leaders

Player	Team	GP	G	A	PTS	PIM
Valeri Kharlamov	Soviet Union	5	9	6	15	2
V. Nedomansky	Czech.	5	6	3	9	0
Vladimir Vikulov	Soviet Union	5	5	4	9	0
Craig Sarner	USA	5	4	5	9	0
Kevin Ahearn	USA	5	4	3	7	0
Alexander Maltsev	Soviet Union	5	4	3	7	0
Anatoli Firsov	Soviet Union	5	2	5	7	0
Yuri Blinov	Soviet Union	5	3	3	6	0
Jiri Kochta	Czech.	5	3	3	6	0
Richard Farda	Czech.	5	1	5	6	0

Grenoble, France • 1968

Group A

Team	GP	W	L	T	GF	GA	PTS
Soviet Union	7	6	1	0	48	10	12
Czech.	7	5	1	1	33	17	11
Canada	7	5	2	0	28	15	10
Sweden	7	4	2	1	23	18	9
Finland	7	3	3	1	17	23	7
USA	7	2	4	1	23	28	5
W. Germany	7	1	6	0	13	39	2
E. Germany	7	0	7	0	13	48	0

Group B

Yugoslavia	5	5	0	0	33	9	10
Japan	5	4	1	0	27	12	8
Norway	5	3	2	0	15	15	6
Romania	5	2	3	0	22	23	4
Austria	5	1	4	0	12	27	2
France	5	0	5	0	9	32	0

1968 Final Rankings

1. Soviet Union
2. Czechoslovakia
3. Canada
4. Sweden
5. Finland
6. USA
7. W. Germany
8. E. Germany
9. Yugoslavia
10. Japan
11. Norway
12. Romania
13. Austria
14. France

1968 Scoring Leaders

Player	Team	GP	G	A	PTS	PIM
Anatoli Firsov	Soviet Union	7	12	4	16	4
Vladimir Vikulov	Soviet Union	7	2	10	12	2
Vyatch. Starshinov	Soviet Union	7	6	6	12	2
Victor Populanov	Soviet Union	7	6	6	12	10
Josef Golonka	Czech.	7	4	6	10	8
Jan Hrbaty	Czech.	7	2	7	9	2
Fran Huck	Canada	7	4	5	9	10
Marshall Johnston	Canada	7	2	6	8	4
Jack Morrison	USA	7	2	6	8	10
V. Nedomansky	Czech.	7	5	2	7	4

Innsbruck, Austria • 1964

Group A

Team	GP	W	L	T	GF	GA	PTS
Soviet Union	7	7	0	0	54	10	14
Sweden	7	5	2	0	47	16	10
Czech.	7	5	2	0	38	19	10
Canada	7	5	2	0	32	17	10
USA	7	2	5	0	29	33	4
Finland	7	2	5	0	10	31	4
W. Germany	7	2	5	0	13	49	4
Switzerland	7	0	7	0	9	57	0

Group B

Poland	7	6	1	0	40	13	12
Norway	7	5	2	0	40	19	10
Japan	7	4	2	1	35	31	9
Romania	7	3	3	1	31	28	7
Austria	7	3	3	1	24	28	7
Yugoslavia	7	3	3	1	29	37	7
Italy	7	2	5	0	24	42	4
Hungary	7	0	7	0	14	39	0

1964 Final Rankings

1. Soviet Union
2. Sweden
3. Czechoslovakia
4. Canada
5. USA
6. Finland
7. W. Germany
8. Switzerland
9. Poland
10. Norway
11. Japan
12. Romania
13. Austria
14. Yugoslavia
15. Italy
16. Hungary

1964 Scoring Leaders

Player	Team	GP	G	A	PTS	PIM
Sven Tumba	Sweden	7	8	3	11	0
Ulf Sterner	Sweden	7	6	5	11	0
Victor Yakushev	Soviet Union	7	7	3	10	0
Boris Mayorov	Soviet Union	7	7	3	10	0
Jiri Dolana	Czech.	7	7	3	10	0
Vy. Starshinov	Soviet Union	7	7	3	10	6
Josef Cerny	Czech.	7	5	5	10	2
A. Andersson	Sweden	7	7	2	9	8
K. Loktev	Soviet Union	7	4	5	9	8
Gary Dineen	Canada	7	3	6	9	10

Squaw Valley, CA, USA • 1960

Group A

Team	GP	W	L	T	GF	GA	PTS
Canada	2	2	0	0	24	3	4
Sweden	2	1	1	0	21	5	2
Japan	2	0	2	0	1	38	0

Group B

Soviet Union	2	2	0	0	16	4	4
W. Germany	2	1	1	0	4	9	2
Finland	2	0	2	0	5	12	0

Group C

USA	2	2	0	0	19	6	4
Czech.	2	1	1	0	23	6	2
Australia	2	0	2	0	2	30	0

Final Round

Team	GP	W	L	T	GF	GA	PTS
USA	5	5	0	0	29	11	10
Canada	5	4	1	0	31	12	8
Soviet Union	5	2	2	1	24	19	5
Czech.	5	2	3	0	21	23	4
Sweden	5	1	3	1	19	19	3
W. Germany	5	0	5	0	5	45	0

Consolation Round

Finland	4	3	0	1	50	11	7
Japan	4	2	1	1	32	22	5
Australia	4	0	4	0	8	57	0

1960 Final Rankings

1. USA
2. Canada
3. Soviet Union
4. Czechoslovakia
5. Sweden
6. W. Germany
7. Finland
8. Japan
9. Australia

1960 Scoring Leaders

Player	Team	GP	G	A	PTS	PIM
Fred Etcher	Canada	7	9	12	21	0
Bobby Attersley	Canada	7	6	12	18	4
Bill Cleary	USA	7	7	7	14	2
Bill Christian	USA	7	2	11	13	2
G. Samolenko	Canada	7	8	4	12	0
Lars E. Lundvall	Sweden	7	8	4	12	2
Vaclav Panucek	Czech.	7	7	5	12	0
John Mayasich	USA	7	7	5	12	2
Nisse Nilsson	Sweden	7	7	5	12	4
V. Alexandrov	Soviet Union	7	7	5	12	8
Butch Martin	Canada	7	6	6	12	14
Ronald Petersson	Sweden	7	4	8	12	2

Cortina d'Ampezzo, Italy • 1956

Group A

Team	GP	W	L	T	GF	GA	PTS
Canada	3	3	0	0	30	1	6
W. Germany	3	1	1	1	9	6	3
Italy	3	0	1	2	5	7	2
Austria	3	0	2	1	2	32	1

Group B

Czech.	2	2	0	0	12	6	4
USA	2	1	1	0	7	4	2
Poland	2	0	2	0	3	12	0

Group C

Soviet Union	2	2	0	0	15	4	4
Sweden	2	1	1	0	7	10	2
Switzerland	2	0	2	0	8	16	0

Final Round

Team	GP	W	L	T	GF	GA	PTS
Soviet Union	5	5	0	0	25	5	10
USA	5	4	1	0	26	12	8
Canada	5	3	2	0	23	11	6
Sweden	5	1	3	1	10	17	3
Czech.	5	1	4	0	20	30	2
W. Germany	5	0	4	1	6	35	1

Consolation Round

Italy	3	3	0	0	21	7	6
Poland	3	2	1	0	12	10	4
Switzerland	3	1	2	0	12	8	2
Austria	3	0	3	0	9	19	0

1956 Final Rankings

1. Soviet Union
2. USA
3. Canada
4. Sweden
5. Czechoslovakia
6. W. Germany
7. Italy
8. Poland
9. Switzerland
10. Austria

1956 Scoring Leaders

Player	Team	GP	G	A	PTS	PIM
Jim Logan	Canada	8	7	5	12	2
Paul Knox	Canada	8	7	5	12	2
Vsevolod Bobrov	Soviet Union	7	9	2	11	4
Gerry Theberge	Canada	8	9	2	11	8
Jack McKenzie	Canada	8	7	4	11	4
John Mayasich	USA	7	7	3	10	2
Alexei Guryshev	Soviet Union	7	7	2	9	0
Vlastimil Bubnik	Czech.	7	5	4	9	14
George Scholes	Canada	8	5	3	8	2

Oslo, Norway • 1952

Team	GP	W	L	T	GF	GA	PTS
Canada	8	7	0	1	71	1	15
USA	8	6	1	1	43	21	13
Sweden	8	6	2	0	48	19	12
Czech.	8	6	2	0	47	18	12
Switzerland	8	4	4	0	40	40	8
Poland	8	2	5	1	21	56	5
Finland	8	2	6	0	21	60	4
W. Germany	8	1	6	1	21	53	3
Norway	8	0	8	0	15	46	0

1952 Final Rankings

1. Canada
2. USA
3. Sweden
4. Czechoslovakia
5. Switzerland
6. Poland
7. Finland
8. W. Germany
9. Norway

St. Moritz, Switzerland • 1948

Team	GP	W	L	T	GF	GA	PTS
Canada	7	6	0	1	57	2	13
Czech.	7	6	0	1	76	15	13
Switzerland	7	5	2	0	62	17	10
Sweden	7	4	3	0	53	23	8
Great Britain	7	3	4	0	36	43	6
Poland	7	2	5	0	25	74	4
Austria	7	1	6	0	31	64	2
Italy	7	0	7	0	23	125	0

* USA also competed as an unofficial entry.

1948 Final Rankings

1. Canada
2. Czechoslovakia
3. Switzerland
4. Sweden
5. Great Britain
6. Poland
7. Austria
8. Italy

Garmisch-Partenkirchen, Germany • 1936

Group A

Team	GP	W	L	T	GF	GA	PTS
Canada	3	3	0	0	24	3	6
Austria	3	2	1	0	11	7	4
Poland	3	1	2	0	11	12	2
Latvia	3	0	0	3	3	27	0

Group B

Germany	3	2	1	0	5	1	4
USA	3	2	1	0	5	2	4
Italy	3	1	2	0	2	5	2
Switzerland	3	1	2	0	1	5	2

Group C

Czech.	3	3	0	0	10	0	6
Hungary	3	2	1	0	14	5	4
France	3	1	2	0	4	7	2
Belgium	3	0	3	0	4	20	6

Group D

Great Britain	2	2	0	0	4	0	4
Sweden	2	1	1	0	2	1	2
Japan	2	0	2	0	0	5	0

Group A Semifinal Round

Team	GP	W	L	T	GF	GA	PTS
Great Britain	3	2	0	1	8	3	5
Canada	3	2	1	0	22	4	4
Germany	3	1	1	1	5	8	3
Hungary	3	0	0	3	2	22	0

Group B Semifinal Round

USA	3	3	0	0	5	1	6
Czech.	3	2	1	0	6	4	4
Sweden	3	1	2	0	3	6	2
Austria	3	0	3	0	1	4	0

Final Round

Team	GP	W	L	T	GF	GA	PTS
Great Britain	3	2	0	1	7	1	5
Canada	3	2	1	0	9	2	4
USA	3	1	1	1	2	1	3
Czech.	3	0	3	0	0	14	0

1936 Final Rankings

1. Great Britain
2. Canada
3. USA
4. Czechoslovakia
5. Germany
5. Sweden
7. Hungary
7. Austria

Lake Placid, NY, USA • 1932

Team	GP	W	L	T	GF	GA	PTS
Canada	6	5	0	1	32	4	11
USA	6	4	1	1	27	5	9
Germany	6	2	4	0	7	26	4
Poland	6	0	6	0	3	34	0

1932 Final Rankings

1. Canada
2. USA
3. Germany
4. Poland

St. Moritz, Switzerland • 1928

Group A

Team	GP	W	L	T	GF	GA	PTS
Great Britain	3	2	1	0	10	6	4
France	3	2	1	0	6	5	4
Belgium	3	2	1	0	9	10	4
Hungary	3	0	3	0	2	6	0

Group B

Sweden	2	1	0	1	5	2	3
Czech.	2	1	1	0	3	5	2
Poland	2	0	0	1	4	5	1

Group C

Switzerland	2	1	0	1	5	4	3
Austria	2	0	0	2	4	4	2
Germany	2	0	0	1	0	1	1

Final Round

Team	GP	W	L	T	GF	GA	PTS
Canada	3	3	0	0	38	0	6
Sweden	3	2	1	0	7	12	4
Switzerland	3	1	2	0	4	17	2
Great Britain	3	0	3	0	1	21	0

1928 Final Rankings

1. Canada
2. Sweden
3. Switzerland
4. Great Britain
5. France
5. Czechoslovakia
5. Austria
8. Belgium
8. Poland
8. Germany
11. Hungary

Chamonix, France • 1924

Group A

Team	GP	W	L	T	GF	GA	PTS
Canada	3	3	0	0	85	0	6
Sweden	3	2	1	0	18	25	4
Czech.	3	1	2	0	14	41	2
Switzerland	3	0	3	0	2	53	0

Group B

USA	3	3	0	0	52	0	6
Great Britain	3	2	1	0	34	16	4
France	3	1	2	0	9	42	2
Belgium	3	0	3	0	8	35	0

Final Round

Canada	3	3	0	0	47	3	6
USA	3	2	1	0	32	6	4
Great Britain	3	1	2	0	6	33	2
Sweden	3	0	3	0	3	46	0

1924 Final Rankings

1. Canada
2. USA
3. Great Britain
4. Sweden
5. Czechoslovakia
5. France
7. Switzerland
7. Belgium

Antwerp, Belgium • 1920

Hockey was played at the 1920 Summer Olympics in Antwerp, Belgium. The IIHF has declared this the first World Championship.

1920 Final Rankings

1. Canada
2. USA
3. Czechoslovakia
4. Sweden
5. Switzerland
6–7. Belgium
6–7. France

Women's Olympic Results and Rankings, 2010 to 1998

Vancouver, B.C., Canada • 2010

Sweden	3	Switzerland	0
Canada	18	Slovakia	0
USA	12	China	1
Finland	5	Russia	1
Switzerland	1	Canada	10
Sweden	6	Slovakia	2
Russia	0	USA	13
Finland	2	China	1
Canada	13	Sweden	1
Slovakia	2	Switzerland	5
USA	6	Finland	0
China	1	Russia	2

Classification Round

Switzerland	6	China	0
Russia	4	Slovakia	2

Semi-final Games

USA	9	Sweden	1
Canada	5	Finland	0

Seventh-Place Game

China	3	Slovakia	1

Fifth-Place Game

Switzerland	2	Russia	1

Bronze Medal Game

Finland	3	Sweden	2 (OT)

Gold Medal Game

Canada	2	USA	0

2010 Final Rankings, Women

1 Canada
2 USA
3 Finland
4 Sweden
5 Switzerland
6 Russia
7 China
8 Slovakia

Torino, Italy • 2006

Finland	3	Germany	0
Sweden	3	Russia	1
USA	6	Switzerland	0
Canada	16	Italy	0
Canada	12	Russia	0
USA	5	Germany	0
Sweden	11	Italy	0
Finland	4	Switzerland	0
Russia	5	Italy	1
Canada	8	Sweden	1
Germany	2	Switzerland	1
USA	7	Finland	3

Classification Round

Russia	6	Suwitzerland	2
Germany	5	Italy	2

Semi-final Games

Sweden	3	USA	2 (SO)
Canada	6	Finland	0

Seventh-Place Game

Switzerland	11	Italy	0

Fifth-Place Game

Germany	1	Russia	0

Bronze Medal Game

USA	4	Finland	0

Gold Medal Game

Canada	4	Sweden	1

2006 Final Rankings, Women

1 Canada
2 Sweden
3 USA
4 Finland
5 Germany
6 Russia
7 Switzerland
8 Italy

Salt Lake City, Utah, USA • 2002

Canada	7	Kazakhstan	0
Sweden	3	Russia	2
USA	10	Germany	0
Finland	4	China	0
Russia	0	Canada	7
Sweden	7	Kazakhstan	0
Finland	3	Germany	1
China	1	USA	12
Kazakhstan	1	Russia	4
USA	5	Finland	0
Germany	5	China	5
Canada	11	Sweden	0

Classification Round

Russia	5	China	0
Germany	4	Kazakhstan	0

Semi-final Games

Canada	7	Finland	3
USA	4	Sweden	0

Seventh-Place Game

China	2	Kazakhstan	1 (OT)

Fifth-Place Game

Russia	5	Germany	0

Bronze Medal Game

Sweden	2	Finland	0

Gold Medal Game

Canada	3	USA	2

2002 Final Rankings, Women

1 Canada
2 USA
3 Sweden
4 Finland
5 Russia
6 Germany
7 China
8 Kazakhstan

Nagano, Japan • 1998

Sweden	0	Finland	6
Canada	13	Japan	0
China	0	USA	5
Finland	11	Japan	1
USA	7	Sweden	1
Canada	2	China	0
Sweden	3	Canada	5
Japan	1	China	6
USA	4	Finland	2
China	3	Sweden	1
USA	10	Japan	0
Finland	2	Canada	4
Japan	0	Sweden	5
Finland	6	China	1
Canada	4	USA	7

Bronze Medal Game

Finland	4	China	1

Gold Medal Game

USA	3	Canada	1

1998 Final Rankings, Women

1 USA
2 Canada
3 Finland
4 China
5 Sweden
6 Japan

Olympic Results, Active NHL Players

Medal	Player	Year	Team	GP	G	A	Pts	PIM
	Alfredsson, Daniel	1998	SWE	4	2	3	5	2
	Alfredsson, Daniel	2002	SWE	4	1	4	5	2
G	Alfredsson, Daniel	2006	SWE	8	5	5	10	4
	Alfredsson, Daniel	2010	SWE	4	3	0	3	0
	Antropov, Nik	2006	KAZ	5	1	0	1	4
S	Aucoin, Adrian	1994	CAN	4	0	0	0	2
S	Backes, David	2010	USA	6	1	2	3	2
	Backstrom, Nicklas	2010	SWE	4	1	5	6	0
	Bartulis, Oskars	2010	LAT	4	0	0	0	2
G	Bergeron, Patrice	2010	CAN	7	0	1	1	2
	Bertuzzi, Todd	2006	CAN	6	0	3	3	6
	Bouwmeester, Jay	2006	CAN	6	0	0	0	0
G	Boyle, Dan	2010	CAN	7	1	5	6	2
G	Brewer, Eric	2002	CAN	6	2	0	2	0
S	Brown, Dustin	2010	USA	6	0	0	0	0
S	Callahan, Ryan	2010	USA	6	0	1	1	2
	Chara, Zdeno	2006	SVK	6	1	1	2	2
	Chara, Zdeno	2010	SVK	7	0	3	3	6
	Cole, Erik	2006	USA	6	1	2	3	0
G	Crosby, Sidney	2010	CAN	7	4	3	7	4
B	Datsyuk, Pavel	2002	RUS	6	1	2	3	0
	Datsyuk, Pavel	2006	RUS	8	1	7	8	10
	Datsyuk, Pavel	2010	RUS	4	1	2	3	2
	Daugavins, Kaspars	2010	LAT	4	0	0	0	2
	Diaz, Raphael	2010	SUI	5	0	0	0	4
	Doan, Shane	2006	CAN	6	2	1	3	2
G	Doughty, Drew	2010	CAN	7	0	2	2	2
	Dvorak, Radek	2002	CZE	4	0	0	0	0
	Ehrhoff, Christian	2002	GER	7	0	0	0	8
	Ehrhoff, Christian	2006	GER	5	1	1	2	4
	Ehrhoff, Christian	2010	GER	4	0	0	0	4
	Elias, Patrik	2002	CZE	4	1	1	2	0
B	Elias, Patrik	2006	CZE	1	0	0	0	2
	Elias, Patrik	2010	CZE	5	2	2	4	2
	Enstrom, Toby	2010	SWE	4	0	2	2	4
B	Erat, Martin	2006	CZE	8	1	1	2	4
	Erat, Martin	2010	CZE	5	0	1	1	2
	Eriksson, Loui	2010	SWE	4	3	1	4	0
	Fedotenko, Ruslan	2002	UKR	1	1	0	1	4
B	Filppula, Valtteri	2010	FIN	6	3	0	3	0
	Fleischmann, Tomas	2010	CZE	5	1	2	3	2
	Franzen, Johan	2010	SWE	4	1	1	2	2
	Gaborik, Marian	2006	SVK	6	3	4	7	4
	Gaborik, Marian	2010	SVK	7	4	1	5	6
G	Gagne, Simon	2002	CAN	6	1	3	4	0
	Gagne, Simon	2006	CAN	6	1	2	3	6
G	Getzlaf, Ryan	2010	CAN	7	3	4	7	2
	Gionta, Brian	2006	USA	6	4	0	4	2
S	Gleason, Tim	2010	USA	6	0	0	0	0
	Goc, Marcel	2006	GER	5	1	0	1	0
	Goc, Marcel	2010	GER	4	2	1	3	0
	Gomez, Scott	2006	USA	6	1	4	5	10
B	Gonchar, Sergei	1998	RUS	6	0	2	2	0
B	Gonchar, Sergei	2002	RUS	6	0	0	0	2
	Gonchar, Sergei	2006	RUS	8	0	2	2	8
	Gonchar, Sergei	2010	RUS	4	1	0	1	2
	Hagman, Niklas	2002	FIN	4	1	2	3	0
S	Hagman, Niklas	2006	FIN	8	0	1	1	2
B	Hagman, Niklas	2010	FIN	6	4	2	6	2
G	Hamrlik, Roman	1998	CZE	6	1	0	1	2
	Hamrlik, Roman	2002	CZE	4	0	1	1	2
	Handzus, Michal	2002	SVK	2	1	0	1	6
	Handzus, Michal	2010	SVK	7	3	3	6	0
	Havlat, Martin	2002	CZE	4	3	1	4	27
	Havlat, Martin	2010	CZE	5	0	2	2	0
	Heatley, Dany	2006	CAN	6	2	1	3	8
G	Heatley, Dany	2010	CAN	7	4	3	7	4
	Hecht, Jochen	1998	GER	4	1	0	1	6
	Hecht, Jochen	2002	GER	4	1	1	2	2
	Hecht, Jochen	2010	GER	4	0	1	1	2
	Hejda, Jan	2010	CZE	5	0	0	0	4
G	Hejduk, Milan	1998	CZE	4	0	0	0	2
	Hejduk, Milan	2002	CZE	4	1	0	1	0
B	Hejduk, Milan	2006	CZE	8	2	1	3	2
B	Hemsky, Ales	2006	CZE	8	1	2	3	2
	Holos, Jonas	2010	NOR	4	0	1	1	2
	Holzer, Korbinian	2010	GER	4	0	0	0	2
	Hornqvist, Patric	2010	SWE	4	1	0	1	4
	Hossa, Marian	2002	SVK	2	4	2	6	0
	Hossa, Marian	2006	SVK	6	5	5	10	4
	Hossa, Marian	2010	SVK	7	3	6	9	6
G	Iginla, Jarome	2002	CAN	6	3	1	4	0
	Iginla, Jarome	2006	CAN	6	2	1	3	4
G	Iginla, Jarome	2010	CAN	7	5	2	7	0
G	Jagr, Jaromir	1998	CZE	6	1	4	5	2
	Jagr, Jaromir	2002	CZE	4	2	3	5	4
B	Jagr, Jaromir	2006	CZE	8	2	5	7	6
	Jagr, Jaromir	2010	CZE	5	2	1	3	6
S	Johnson, Erik	2010	USA	6	1	0	1	4
S	Johnson, Jack	2010	USA	6	0	1	1	2
S	Jokinen, Jussi	2006	FIN	8	1	3	4	2
	Jokinen, Olli	2002	FIN	4	2	1	3	0
S	Jokinen, Olli	2006	FIN	8	6	2	8	2
B	Jokinen, Olli	2010	FIN	6	3	1	4	2
G	Jovanovski, Ed	2002	CAN	6	0	3	3	4
	Jurcina, Milan	2006	SVK	6	0	1	1	8
	Jurcina, Milan	2010	SVK	7	0	0	0	2
	Kaberle, Tomas	2002	CZE	4	0	1	1	2
B	Kaberle, Tomas	2006	CZE	8	2	2	4	2
	Kaberle, Tomas	2010	CZE	5	1	2	3	0
S	Kane, Patrick	2010	USA	6	3	2	5	2
	Karsums, Martins	2010	LAT	4	0	2	2	2
G	Keith, Duncan	2010	CAN	7	0	6	6	2
S	Kesler, Ryan	2010	USA	6	2	0	2	2
S	Kessel, Phil	2010	USA	6	1	1	2	0
	Knuble, Mike	2006	USA	6	1	1	2	4
S	Koivu, Mikko	2006	FIN	8	0	0	0	6
B	Koivu, Mikko	2010	FIN	6	0	4	4	2
B	Koivu, Saku	1994	FIN	8	4	3	7	12
B	Koivu, Saku	1998	FIN	6	2	8	10	4
S	Koivu, Saku	2006	FIN	8	3	8	11	12

Olympic Results, Active NHL Players *continued*

Medal	Player	Year	Team	GP	G	A	Pts	PIM
B	Koivu, Saku	2010	FIN	6	0	2	2	6
	Kopecky, Tomas	2010	SVK	7	1	0	1	2
	Kostitsyn, Sergei	2010	BLR	4	2	3	5	0
B	Kotalik, Ales	2006	CZE	4	0	0	0	0
B	Kovalchuk, Ilya	2002	RUS	6	1	2	3	14
	Kovalchuk, Ilya	2006	RUS	8	4	1	5	31
	Kovalchuk, Ilya	2010	RUS	4	1	2	3	0
	Krejci, David	2010	CZE	5	2	1	3	6
G	Kronwall, Niklas	2006	SWE	2	1	1	2	8
	Kronwall, Niklas	2010	SWE	4	0	0	0	2
B	Kuba, Filip	2006	CZE	8	1	0	1	0
	Kuba, Filip	2010	CZE	5	0	1	1	0
	Langenbrunner, Jamie	1998	USA	3	0	0	0	4
S	Langenbrunner, Jamie	2010	USA	6	1	3	4	0
	Lecavalier, Vincent	2006	CAN	6	0	3	3	16
	Leopold, Jordan	2006	USA	6	1	0	1	4
B	Lepisto, Sami	2010	FIN	6	0	1	1	6
	Liles, John-Michael	2006	USA	6	0	2	2	2
S	Lydman, Toni	2006	FIN	8	1	0	1	10
B	Lydman, Toni	2010	FIN	6	0	0	0	2
	Malkin, Evgeni	2006	RUS	7	2	4	6	31
	Malkin, Evgeni	2010	RUS	4	3	3	6	0
S	Malone, Ryan	2010	USA	6	3	2	5	6
	Markov, Andrei	2006	RUS	8	1	2	3	6
	Markov, Andrei	2010	RUS	4	0	2	2	0
G	Marleau, Patrick	2010	CAN	7	2	3	5	0
	Meszaros, Andrej	2006	SVK	6	0	2	2	4
	Meszaros, Andrej	2010	SVK	7	0	0	0	4
	Michalek, Milan	2010	CZE	5	2	0	2	0
	Michalek, Zbynek	2010	CZE	5	0	0	0	2
B	Miettinen, Antti	2010	FIN	6	1	0	1	0
G	Morrow, Brenden	2010	CAN	7	2	1	3	2
	Murray, Douglas	2010	SWE	4	0	0	0	0
	Nash, Rick	2006	CAN	6	0	1	1	10
G	Nash, Rick	2010	CAN	7	2	3	5	0
	Oduya, Johnny	2010	SWE	4	0	0	0	12
	Ohlund, Mattias	1998	SWE	4	0	1	1	4
	Ohlund, Mattias	2002	SWE	4	0	2	2	2
G	Ohlund, Mattias	2006	SWE	6	0	2	2	2
	Ohlund, Mattias	2010	SWE	4	1	0	1	2
B	Olesz, Rostislav	2006	CZE	8	0	0	0	2
S	Orpik, Brooks	2010	USA	6	0	0	0	0
	Ovechkin, Alex	2006	RUS	8	5	0	5	8
	Ovechkin, Alex	2010	RUS	4	2	2	4	2
G	Pahlsson, Samuel	2006	SWE	8	2	2	4	8
	Pahlsson, Samuel	2010	SWE	3	0	1	1	2
S	Parise, Zach	2010	USA	6	4	4	8	0
S	Pavelski, Joe	2010	USA	6	0	3	3	4
G	Perry, Corey	2010	CAN	7	4	1	5	2
B	Pitkanen, Joni	2010	FIN	5	1	2	3	29
	Plekanec, Tomas	2010	CZE	5	2	1	3	2
	Pock, Thomas	2002	AUT	4	0	0	0	2
	Polak, Roman	2010	CZE	5	0	0	0	4
	Ponikarovsky, Alexei	2002	UKR	4	1	1	2	6
S	Poti, Tom	2002	USA	6	0	1	1	4
B	Prospal, Vinny	2006	CZE	8	4	2	6	2
	Radulov, Alexander	2010	RUS	4	1	1	2	4
	Redden, Wade	2006	CAN	6	1	0	1	0
	Regehr, Robyn	2006	CAN	6	0	1	1	2
	Richards, Brad	2006	CAN	6	2	2	4	6
G	Richards, Mike	2010	CAN	7	2	3	5	0
	Ruutu, Jarkko	2002	FIN	4	0	0	0	4
S	Ruutu, Jarkko	2006	FIN	8	0	0	0	31
B	Ruutu, Jarkko	2010	FIN	6	2	1	3	14
B	Ruutu, Tuomo	2010	FIN	6	1	0	1	2
S	Ryan, Bobby	2010	USA	6	1	1	2	2
	Salo, Sami	2002	FIN	4	0	0	0	0
S	Salo, Sami	2006	FIN	6	1	3	4	0
B	Salo, Sami	2010	FIN	6	1	1	2	4
G	Samuelsson, Mikael	2006	SWE	8	1	3	4	2
	Sbisa, Luca	2010	SUI	5	0	0	0	0
G	Seabrook, Brent	2010	CAN	7	0	1	1	2
G	Sedin, Daniel	2006	SWE	8	1	3	4	2
	Sedin, Daniel	2010	SWE	4	1	2	3	0
G	Sedin, Henrik	2006	SWE	8	3	1	4	2
	Sedin, Henrik	2010	SWE	4	0	2	2	2
	Seidenberg, Dennis	2002	GER	7	1	1	2	8
	Seidenberg, Dennis	2006	GER	5	0	0	0	6
	Seidenberg, Dennis	2010	GER	4	1	0	1	2
	Sekera, Andrej	2010	SVK	7	1	0	1	0
	Selanne, Teemu	1992	FIN	8	7	4	11	6
	Selanne, Teemu	1998	FIN	5	4	6	10	8
	Selanne, Teemu	2002	FIN	4	3	0	3	2
S	Selanne, Teemu	2006	FIN	8	6	5	11	4
B	Selanne, Teemu	2010	FIN	6	0	2	2	0
	Semin, Alexander	2010	RUS	4	0	2	2	4
G	Smyth, Ryan	2002	CAN	6	0	1	1	0
	Smyth, Ryan	2006	CAN	6	0	1	1	4
G	Spacek, Jaroslav	1998	CZE	6	0	0	0	4
	Spacek, Jaroslav	2002	CZE	4	0	0	0	0
B	Spacek, Jaroslav	2006	CZE	8	0	1	1	2
	St. Louis, Martin	2006	CAN	6	2	1	3	0
G	Staal, Eric	2010	CAN	7	1	5	6	6
S	Stastny, Paul	2010	USA	6	1	2	3	0
	Streit, Mark	2002	SUI	4	1	1	2	0
	Streit, Mark	2006	SUI	6	2	1	3	6
	Streit, Mark	2010	SUI	5	0	3	3	0
	Sturm, Marco	1998	GER	2	0	0	0	0
	Sturm, Marco	2002	GER	5	0	1	1	0
	Sturm, Marco	2010	GER	4	0	1	1	0
	Sulzer, Alexander	2006	GER	5	0	1	1	2
	Sulzer, Alexander	2010	GER	4	0	0	0	4
S	Suter, Ryan	2010	USA	6	0	4	4	2
	Svatos, Marek	2006	SVK	6	0	0	0	0
	Tallinder, Henrik	2010	SWE	4	0	0	0	4
	Thornton, Joe	2006	CAN	6	1	2	3	0
G	Thornton, Joe	2010	CAN	7	1	1	2	0
B	Timonen, Kimmo	1998	FIN	6	0	1	1	2
	Timonen, Kimmo	2002	FIN	4	0	1	1	2
S	Timonen, Kimmo	2006	FIN	8	1	4	5	2
B	Timonen, Kimmo	2010	FIN	6	2	2	4	2
G	Toews, Jonathan	2010	CAN	7	1	7	8	2
	Tyutin, Fedor	2006	RUS	8	0	1	1	4
	Tyutin, Fedor	2010	RUS	4	0	2	2	2
	Visnovsky, Lubomir	1998	SVK	3	0	0	0	2
	Visnovsky, Lubomir	2002	SVK	3	1	2	3	0
	Visnovsky, Lubomir	2006	SVK	6	1	1	2	0
	Visnovsky, Lubomir	2010	SVK	7	2	1	3	0
	Volchenkov, Anton	2006	RUS	8	0	0	0	2
	Volchenkov, Anton	2010	RUS	4	0	1	1	2
G	Weber, Shea	2010	CAN	7	2	4	6	2
	Weber, Yannick	2010	SUI	5	0	0	0	6
S	Whitney, Ryan	2010	USA	6	0	0	0	0
	Zetterberg, Henrik	2002	SWE	4	0	1	1	0
G	Zetterberg, Henrik	2006	SWE	8	3	3	6	0
	Zetterberg, Henrik	2010	SWE	4	1	0	1	2
B	Zidlicky, Marek	2006	CZE	7	4	1	5	16
	Zidlicky, Marek	2010	CZE	5	0	5	5	2
	Zuccarello, Mats	2010	NOR	4	1	2	3	2

Olympic Results, Active NHL Goaltenders

Medal	Goaltender	Year	Team	GPI	W	L	T	Mins	GA	SO	Avg
S	Backstrom, Niklas	2006	FIN	Did not play – spare goaltender							
B	Backstrom, Niklas	2010	FIN	2	1	0	0	110	2	1	1.09
	Brodeur, Martin	1998	CAN	Did not play – spare goaltender							
G	Brodeur, Martin	2002	CAN	5	4	0	1	300	9	0	1.80
	Brodeur, Martin	2006	CAN	4	2	2	0	239	8	0	2.01
G	Brodeur, Martin	2010	CAN	2	1	1	0	124	6	0	2.90
B	Bryzgalov, Ilya	2002	RUS	Did not play – spare goaltender							
	Bryzgalov, Ilya	2006	RUS	1	0	1	0	60	5	0	5.00
	Bryzgalov, Ilya	2010	RUS	2	0	1	0	101	3	0	1.78
	Budaj, Peter	2006	SVK	3	2	1	0	179	6	0	2.01
	Budaj, Peter	2010	SVK	Did not play – spare goaltender							
	DiPietro, Rick	2006	USA	4	1	3	0	237	9	0	2.28
G	Fleury, Marc-Andre	2010	CAN	Did not play – spare goaltender							
	Greiss, Thomas	2006	GER	1	0	1	0	60	5	0	5.00
	Greiss, Thomas	2010	GER	3	0	3	0	179	15	0	5.03
	Gustavsson, Jonas	2010	SWE	1	1	0	0	60	2	0	2.00
	Halak, Jaroslav	2010	SVK	7	3	4	0	423	17	1	2.41
	Hedberg, Johan	1998	SWE	Did not play – spare goaltender							
	Hedberg, Johan	2002	SWE	1	1	0	0	60	1	0	1.00
	Hiller, Jonas	2010	SUI	5	2	3	0	316	13	0	2.47
G	Khabibulin, Nikolai	1992	RUS	Did not play – spare goaltender							
B	Khabibulin, Nikolai	2002	RUS	6	3	2	1	359	14	1	2.34
	Khabibulin, Nikolai	2006	RUS	Did not play – injured							
S	Kiprusoff, Miikka	2006	FIN	Did not play – injured							
B	Kiprusoff, Miikka	2010	FIN	5	3	2	0	250	11	1	2.64
S	Lehtonen, Kari	2006	FIN	Did not play – injured							
	Lundqvist, Henrik	2006	SWE	6	5	1	0	360	14	0	2.33
	Lundqvist, Henrik	2010	SWE	3	2	1	0	179	4	2	1.34
	Luongo, Roberto	2006	CAN	2	1	1	0	119	3	0	1.51
G	Luongo, Roberto	2010	CAN	5	5	0	0	308	9	1	1.76
S	Miller, Ryan	2010	USA	6	5	1	0	355	8	1	1.35
	Nabokov, Evgeni	2006	RUS	7	4	2	0	359	8	3	1.34
	Nabokov, Evgeni	2010	RUS	3	2	1	0	144	10	0	4.16
	Pavelec, Ondrej	2010	CZE	Did not play – spare goaltender							
S	Quick, Jonathan	2010	USA	Did not play – spare goaltender							
S	Thomas, Tim	2010	USA	1	0	0	0	12	1	0	5.21
	Varlamov, Semyon	2010	RUS	Did not play – spare goaltender							
B	Vokoun, Tomas	2006	CZE	7	3	4	0	342	14	1	2.46
	Vokoun, Tomas	2010	CZE	5	3	2	0	304	9	0	1.78

Anaheim Ducks

Key Off-Season Signings/Acquisitions

2013

June 27 • Re-signed D **Ben Lovejoy**.
July 5 • Acquired RW **Jakob Silfverberg**, LW **Stefan Noesen** and a 1st-round pick in the 2014 NHL Draft from Ottawa for LW **Bobby Ryan**.
5 • Re-signed C **Saku Koivu**.
7 • Re-signed LW **Matt Beleskey**.
16 • Signed LW **Dustin Penner**.
26 • Re-signed RW **Kyle Palmieri**.

2012-13 Results: 30W-12L-3OTL-3SOL 66PTS
1ST, Pacific Division • 2ND, Western Conference

Year-by-Year Record

		Home				Road				Overall									
Season	**GP**	**W**	**L**	**T**	**OL**	**W**	**L**	**T**	**OL**	**W**	**L**	**T**	**OL**	**GF**	**GA**	**Pts.**	**Div. Fin.**	**Conf. Fin.**	**Playoff Result**
2012-13	48	16	7	....	1	14	5	....	5	30	12	....	6	140	118	66	1st, Pac.	2nd, West	Lost Conf. Quarter-Final
2011-12	82	21	18	....	2	13	18	....	10	34	36	....	12	204	231	80	5th, Pac.	13th, West	Out of Playoffs
2010-11	82	26	13	....	2	21	17	....	3	47	30	....	5	239	235	99	2nd, Pac.	4th, West	Lost Conf. Quarter-Final
2009-10	82	25	11	....	5	14	21	....	6	39	32	....	11	238	251	89	4th, Pac.	11th, West	Out of Playoffs
2008-09	82	20	18	....	3	22	15	....	4	42	33	....	7	245	238	91	2nd, Pac.	8th, West	Lost Conf. Semi-Final
2007-08	82	28	9	....	4	19	18	....	4	47	27	....	8	205	191	102	2nd, Pac.	4th, West	Lost Conf. Quarter-Final
2006-07	**82**	**26**	**6**	....	**9**	**22**	**14**	....	**5**	**48**	**20**	....	**14**	**258**	**208**	**110**	**1st, Pac.**	**2nd, West**	**Won Stanley Cup**
2005-06*	82	26	10	....	5	17	17	....	7	43	27	....	12	254	229	98	3rd, Pac.	6th, West	Lost Conf. Final
2004-05*	....	....	....	....	....	....	....	....	....	....	....	....	....	....	....	....			
2003-04*	82	19	11	7	4	10	24	3	4	29	35	10	8	184	213	76	4th, Pac.	12th, West	Out of Playoffs
2002-03*	82	22	10	7	2	18	17	2	4	40	27	9	6	203	193	95	2nd, Pac.	7th, West	Lost Final
2001-02*	82	15	19	5	2	14	23	3	1	29	42	8	3	175	198	69	5th, Pac.	13th, West	Out of Playoffs
2000-01*	82	15	20	4	2	10	21	7	3	25	41	11	5	188	245	66	5th, Pac.	15th, West	Out of Playoffs
1999-2000*	82	19	13	7	2	15	20	5	1	34	33	12	3	217	227	83	5th, Pac.	9th, West	Out of Playoffs
1998-99*	82	21	14	6	....	14	20	7	....	35	34	13	....	215	206	83	3rd, Pac.	6th, West	Lost Conf. Quarter-Final
1997-98*	82	12	23	6	....	14	20	7	....	26	43	13	....	205	261	65	6th, Pac.	12th, West	Out of Playoffs
1996-97*	82	23	12	6	....	13	21	7	....	36	33	13	....	245	233	85	2nd, Pac.	4th, West	Lost Conf. Semi-Final
1995-96*	82	22	15	4	....	13	24	4	....	35	39	8	....	234	247	78	4th, Pac.	9th, West	Out of Playoffs
1994-95*	48	11	9	4	....	5	18	1	....	16	27	5	....	125	164	37	6th, Pac.	12th, West	Out of Playoffs
1993-94*	84	14	26	2	....	19	20	3	....	33	46	5	....	229	251	71	4th, Pac.	9th, West	Out of Playoffs

* Mighty Ducks of Anaheim

2013-14 Schedule

Oct.	Wed.	2	at Colorado
	Sat.	5	at Minnesota
	Sun.	6	at Winnipeg
	Thu.	10	NY Rangers
	Sun.	13	Ottawa*
	Wed.	16	Calgary
	Fri.	18	Phoenix
	Sun.	20	Dallas*
	Tue.	22	at Toronto
	Thu.	24	at Montreal
	Fri.	25	at Ottawa
	Sun.	27	at Columbus
	Tue.	29	at Philadelphia
	Thu.	31	at Boston
Nov.	Sat.	2	at Buffalo
	Mon.	4	at NY Rangers
	Wed.	6	Phoenix
	Fri.	8	Buffalo
	Sun.	10	Vancouver*
	Tue.	12	at Florida
	Thu.	14	at Tampa Bay
	Fri.	15	at Carolina
	Mon.	18	at Pittsburgh
	Wed.	20	New Jersey
	Fri.	22	Tampa Bay
	Sat.	23	at Phoenix
	Tue.	26	at Dallas
	Fri.	29	Calgary*
	Sat.	30	at San Jose
Dec.	Tue.	3	Los Angeles
	Fri.	6	at Chicago
	Sat.	7	at St. Louis
	Mon.	9	NY Islanders
	Wed.	11	Minnesota
	Sun.	15	Edmonton*
	Tue.	17	at Detroit
	Fri.	20	at New Jersey
	Sat.	21	at NY Islanders
	Mon.	23	at Washington
	Sat.	28	Phoenix*
	Sun.	29	at San Jose
	Tue.	31	San Jose*
Jan.	Fri.	3	Edmonton
	Sun.	5	Vancouver*
	Tue.	7	Boston
	Thu.	9	at Nashville
	Sat.	11	at Phoenix
	Sun.	12	Detroit*
	Wed.	15	Vancouver
	Fri.	17	at Chicago
	Sat.	18	at St. Louis
	Tue.	21	Winnipeg
	Thu.	23	Los Angeles
	Sat.	25	at Los Angeles
	Tue.	28	Minnesota
	Thu.	30	Philadelphia
Feb.	Sat.	1	Dallas
	Mon.	3	Columbus
	Wed.	5	Chicago
	Sat.	8	at Nashville
	Fri.	28	St. Louis
Mar.	Sun.	2	Carolina*
	Wed.	5	Montreal
	Fri.	7	Pittsburgh
	Mon.	10	Toronto
	Wed.	12	at Calgary
	Fri.	14	at Colorado
	Sat.	15	at Los Angeles
	Tue.	18	Washington
	Thu.	20	at San Jose
	Sun.	23	Florida*
	Wed.	26	at Calgary
	Fri.	28	at Edmonton
	Sat.	29	at Vancouver
	Mon.	31	Winnipeg
Apr.	Wed.	2	Edmonton
	Fri.	4	Nashville
	Sun.	6	at Edmonton
	Mon.	7	at Vancouver
	Wed.	9	San Jose
	Sat.	12	at Los Angeles
	Sun.	13	Colorado*

* Denotes afternoon game.

The Ducks signed both Corey Perry and Ryan Getzlaf to long-term contracts during the 2012-13 season. Getzlaf ranked among the NHL's top scorers with 49 points during the 48-game season and Perry tied him for the team lead with 15 goals.

PACIFIC DIVISION
21st NHL Season

Franchise date: June 15, 1993

2013-14 Player Personnel

FORWARDS	HT	WT	*Age	Place of Birth	S	2012-13 Club
BELESKEY, Matt	6-0	198	25	Windsor, Ont.	L	Coventry-Anaheim
BONINO, Nick	6-1	194	25	Hartford, CT	L	Neumarkt/Egna-Anaheim
COGLIANO, Andrew	5-10	180	26	Toronto, Ont.	L	Klagenfurt-Anaheim
CRAMAROSSA, Joseph	6-1	200	20	Toronto, Ont.	L	Belleville
ETEM, Emerson	6-1	210	21	Long Beach, CA	L	Norfolk-Anaheim
FRIBERG, Max	5-11	203	20	Skovde, Sweden	R	Timra-Norfolk
GETZLAF, Ryan	6-4	221	28	Regina, Sask.	R	Anaheim
HOLLAND, Peter	6-2	195	22	Toronto, Ont.	L	Norfolk-Anaheim
KOIVU, Saku	5-10	182	38	Turku, Finland	L	Anaheim
KURTZ, John	6-2	204	24	Oakville, Ont.	L	Norfolk
LAGANIERE, Antoine	6-5	207	23	L'Ile-Cadieux, Que.	L	Yale
MAROON, Patrick	6-3	229	25	St Louis, MO	L	Norfolk-Anaheim
MITCHELL, John	6-5	216	27	Neenah, WI	L	Norfolk
NOESEN, Stefan	6-1	200	20	Plano, TX	R	Plymouth
PALMIERI, Kyle	5-11	196	22	Smithtown, NY	R	Norfolk-Anaheim
PENNER, Dustin	6-4	242	31	Winkler, Man.	L	Los Angeles
PERRY, Corey	6-3	212	28	Peterborough, Ont.	R	Anaheim
RAKELL, Rickard	6-1	197	20	Sundbyberg, Sweden	R	Plymouth-Anaheim
SARAULT, Charles	5-11	188	21	Ottawa, Ont.	L	Sarnia-Norfolk
SELANNE, Teemu	6-0	200	43	Helsinki, Finland	R	Anaheim
SILFVERBERG, Jakob	6-2	195	22	Gavle, Sweden	R	Binghamton-Ottawa
SMITH-PELLY, Devante	6-0	225	21	Scarborough, Ont.	R	Norfolk-Anaheim
STAUBITZ, Brad	6-1	215	29	Bright's Grove, Ont.	R	Anaheim
STORTINI, Zack	6-4	215	28	Elliot Lake, Ont.	R	Hamilton
WAGNER, Chris	5-11	201	22	Wellesley, MA	R	Norfolk
WHITNEY, Steven	5-7	164	22	Reading, MA	R	Boston College-Norfolk
WINNIK, Daniel	6-2	213	28	Toronto, Ont.	L	Anaheim
DEFENSEMEN						
ALLEN, Bryan	6-5	229	33	Kingston, Ont.	L	Anaheim
BEAUCHEMIN, Francois	6-1	207	33	Sorel, Que.	L	Anaheim
CLARK, Mat	6-3	225	22	Wheat Ridge, CO	R	Norfolk
CUMISKEY, Kyle	5-10	185	26	Abbotsford, B.C.	L	MODO
FOWLER, Cam	6-1	196	21	Windsor, Ont.	L	Sodertalje-Anaheim
GAGNE, Kevin	5-8	176	21	Edmundston, N.B.	L	Saint John-Rimouski-Norfolk
GRANT, Alex	6-2	185	24	Antigonish, N.S.	R	Wilkes-Barre
LINDHOLM, Hampus	6-3	200	19	Helsingborg, Sweden	L	Norfolk
LOVEJOY, Ben	6-2	215	29	Concord, NH	R	Pittsburgh-Anaheim
SBISA, Luca	6-2	204	23	Ozieri, Italy	L	Lugano-Anaheim
SOURAY, Sheldon	6-4	237	37	Elk Point, Alta.	L	Anaheim
VATANEN, Sami	5-10	180	22	Jyvaskyla, Finland	R	Norfolk-Anaheim
WARG, Stefan	6-2	187	23	Stockholm, Sweden	R	Vasteras
YONKMAN, Nolan	6-6	253	32	Punnichy, Sask.	R	San Antonio-Florida

GOALTENDERS	HT	WT	*Age	Place of Birth	C	2012-13 Club
ANDERSEN, Frederik	6-4	245	23	Herning, Denmark	L	Norfolk
BOBKOV, Igor	6-6	228	22	Surgut, USSR	L	Norfolk
FASTH, Viktor	6-0	186	31	Kalix, Sweden	L	Tingsryd-Norfolk-Anaheim
GIBSON, John	6-3	212	20	Pittsburgh, PA	L	Kitchener-Norfolk
HILLER, Jonas	6-2	194	31	Felben Wellhausen, Switz.	R	Anaheim

* – Age at start of 2013-14 season

Bruce Boudreau

Head Coach

Born: Toronto, Ont., January 9, 1955.

Bruce Boudreau was named head coach in Anaheim on November 30, 2011. In his first full season with the team in 2012-13, he led the Ducks to a division title.

As head coach of the Washington Capitals between 2007 and 2011, Boudreau won the 2007-08 Jack Adams Award (NHL Coach of the Year) and led his club to the 2009-10 Presidents' Trophy as the NHL's top club in the regular season with a franchise record 54 wins and 121 points. He compiled a record of 201-88-40 (.672 winning percentage) with the Capitals and won the Southeast Division four times. He became the fastest coach in modern day NHL history to win 200 games (Nov. 21, 2011 vs. Phoenix) and recorded more wins (184) in his first 300 NHL games than any NHL coach all-time.

Boudreau was named interim head coach of the Capitals on November 22, 2007. On that date, Washington was 30th in the NHL standings. Boudreau led the club to a 37-17-7 finish, as the Capitals won the Southeast Division. Boudreau, whose interim tag was removed on December 26, 2007, became the first coach since Bill Barber (2001) to win the Jack Adams Award after taking over a team midseason. In 2008-09, he led the Capitals to their first playoff series win since 1988.

Before joining the Capitals, Boudreau spent nine seasons as an AHL head coach, including a Calder Cup championship with the Hershey Bears in 2006. Boudreau began his coaching career in the Colonial Hockey League with Muskegon in 1992-93 and was named the International Hockey League Coach of the Year in 1993-94 with Fort Wayne. He also served as head coach and director of hockey operations for Mississippi (ECHL), where he won the 1999 Kelly Cup championship.

Boudreau played parts of eight NHL seasons with the Toronto Maple Leafs and Chicago Blackhawks between 1976 and 1986, recording 28 goals and 42 assists for 70 points in 141 career games. He was selected by the Maple Leafs in the third round of the 1975 NHL Entry Draft. As a Canadian junior playing for the Toronto Marlboros in 1974-75, he scored 68 goals and added 97 assists for 165 points, a Canadian Hockey League record until Bobby Smith and Wayne Gretzky surpassed the mark during the 1977-78 season. Boudreau also ranks 11th all-time in scoring in AHL history with 316 goals and 799 points and led all AHL players in scoring during the 1980s. He won the AHL scoring title in 1987-88 and was a member of the 1992 Calder Cup champion Adirondack Red Wings

2012-13 Scoring

* – rookie

Regular Season

Pos	#	Player	Team	GP	G	A	Pts	TOI	+/–	PIM	PP	SH	GW	S	%
C	15	Ryan Getzlaf	ANA	44	15	34	49	20:11	14	41	4	3	3	99	15.2
R	10	Corey Perry	ANA	44	15	21	36	19:04	10	72	5	0	5	128	11.7
R	9	Bobby Ryan	ANA	46	11	19	30	16:35	3	17	2	0	1	101	10.9
C	11	Saku Koivu	ANA	47	8	19	27	17:36	4	18	4	0	0	55	14.5
R	8	Teemu Selanne	ANA	46	12	12	24	15:41	–10	28	3	0	1	96	12.5
D	23	Francois Beauchemin	ANA	48	6	18	24	23:27	19	22	1	0	0	74	8.1
C	7	Andrew Cogliano	ANA	48	13	10	23	15:22	14	6	0	2	1	79	16.5
C	51	Kyle Palmieri	ANA	42	10	11	21	12:19	2	9	2	0	5	92	10.9
C	34	Daniel Winnik	ANA	48	6	13	19	16:49	13	16	0	0	1	95	6.3
D	44	Sheldon Souray	ANA	44	7	10	17	20:55	19	52	2	0	3	80	8.8
L	39	Matt Beleskey	ANA	42	8	5	13	12:00	2	56	2	0	1	61	13.1
C	13	Nick Bonino	ANA	27	5	8	13	15:53	–3	8	1	0	0	37	13.5
D	4	Cam Fowler	ANA	37	1	10	11	20:26	–4	4	1	0	0	50	2.0
R	65 *	Emerson Etem	ANA	38	3	7	10	11:27	7	9	0	0	0	48	6.3
D	6	Ben Lovejoy	PIT	3	0	0	0	13:36	–2	0	0	0	0	7	0.0
			ANA	32	0	10	10	18:13	6	29	0	0	0	51	0.0
			Total	35	0	10	10	17:49	4	29	0	0	0	58	0.0
C	19	Matthew Lombardi	PHX	21	4	4	8	14:08	0	4	1	0	1	39	10.3
			ANA	7	0	0	0	13:25	–2	4	0	0	0	5	0.0
			Total	28	4	4	8	13:57	–2	8	1	0	1	44	9.1
D	5	Luca Sbisa	ANA	41	1	7	8	19:50	0	23	0	0	1	39	2.6
C	20	David Steckel	TOR	13	0	1	1	7:04	–2	0	0	0	0	4	0.0
			ANA	21	1	5	6	10:37	2	4	0	0	0	19	5.3
			Total	34	1	6	7	9:15	0	4	0	0	0	23	4.3
D	32	Toni Lydman	ANA	35	0	6	6	19:23	–1	12	0	0	0	28	0.0
D	55	Bryan Allen	ANA	41	0	6	6	18:44	1	34	0	0	0	25	0.0
C	74 *	Peter Holland	ANA	21	3	2	5	11:35	4	4	1	0	0	26	11.5
R	18	Radek Dvorak	ANA	9	4	0	4	13:08	2	2	0	0	1	17	23.5
L	62 *	Patrick Maroon	ANA	13	2	1	3	9:47	–1	10	0	0	0	21	9.5
D	45 *	Sami Vatanen	ANA	8	2	0	2	15:49	3	0	1	0	0	6	33.3
R	25	Brad Staubitz	ANA	15	1	1	2	6:12	0	41	0	0	1	5	20.0
C	64	Brandon McMillan	ANA	6	0	1	1	8:44	–1	2	0	0	0	2	0.0
D	40	Jordan Hendry	ANA	2	0	0	0	17:34	0	0	0	0	0	0	0.0
R	67 *	Rickard Rakell	ANA	4	0	0	0	8:57	–2	0	0	0	0	3	0.0
R	77	Devante Smith-Pelly	ANA	7	0	0	0	8:59	–4	0	0	0	0	5	0.0

Goaltending

No.	Goaltender	GPI	Mins	Avg	W	L	OT	EN	SO	GA	SA	S%	G	A	PIM
30	Viktor Fasth	25	1428	2.18	15	6	2	3	4	52	661	.921	0	0	0
1	Jonas Hiller	26	1498	2.36	15	6	4	1	1	59	675	.913	0	1	2
	Totals	**48**	**2936**	**2.35**	**30**	**12**	**6**	**4**	**5**	**115**	**1340**	**.914**			

Playoffs

Pos	#	Player	Team	GP	G	A	Pts	TOI	+/–	PIM	PP	SH	GW	OT	S	%
C	15	Ryan Getzlaf	ANA	7	3	3	6	21:27	2	6	1	1	0	0	15	20.0
D	23	Francois Beauchemin	ANA	7	2	4	6	25:22	–2	4	1	0	0	0	13	15.4
C	51	Kyle Palmieri	ANA	7	3	2	5	10:34	5	4	0	0	0	0	11	27.3
R	65 *	Emerson Etem	ANA	7	3	2	5	12:50	4	2	0	0	0	0	12	25.0
C	13	Nick Bonino	ANA	7	3	1	4	16:37	2	4	2	0	2	1	16	18.8
R	9	Bobby Ryan	ANA	7	2	2	4	16:17	1	0	0	0	0	0	15	13.3
L	39	Matt Beleskey	ANA	7	2	1	3	11:01	1	2	1	0	0	0	13	15.4
R	8	Teemu Selanne	ANA	7	1	2	3	13:59	1	6	1	0	1	0	16	6.3
C	11	Saku Koivu	ANA	7	1	2	3	17:52	–4	6	1	0	0	0	6	16.7
D	4	Cam Fowler	ANA	7	0	3	3	22:44	3	0	0	0	0	0	9	0.0
C	20	David Steckel	ANA	7	1	1	2	9:46	1	0	0	0	0	0	7	14.3
R	10	Corey Perry	ANA	7	0	2	2	20:20	0	4	0	0	0	0	24	0.0
D	6	Ben Lovejoy	ANA	7	0	2	2	21:05	4	0	0	0	0	0	13	0.0
D	44	Sheldon Souray	ANA	6	0	1	1	19:31	–2	4	0	0	0	0	13	0.0
D	55	Bryan Allen	ANA	7	0	1	1	17:22	1	2	0	0	0	0	5	0.0
C	34	Daniel Winnik	ANA	7	0	1	1	15:04	–4	7	0	0	0	0	22	0.0
C	7	Andrew Cogliano	ANA	7	0	1	1	15:46	–3	4	0	0	0	0	11	0.0
D	32	Toni Lydman	ANA	3	0	0	0	15:08	1	0	0	0	0	0	1	0.0
D	5	Luca Sbisa	ANA	5	0	0	0	21:25	–2	4	0	0	0	0	3	0.0

Goaltending

No.	Goaltender	GPI	Mins	Avg	W	L	EN	SO	GA	SA	S%	G	A	PIM
1	Jonas Hiller	7	439	2.46	3	4	0	1	18	218	.917	0	1	0
	Totals	**7**	**439**	**2.46**	**3**	**4**	**0**	**1**	**18**	**218**	**.917**			

Coaching Record

			Regular Season				Playoffs			
Season	Team	League	GC	W	L	O/T	GC	W	L	T
1992-93	Muskegon	CoHL	60	28	27	5	7	3	4	....
1993-94	Fort Wayne	IHL	81	41	29	11	18	10	8	....
1994-95	Fort Wayne	IHL	39	15	21	3	....	....	....	....
1996-97	Mississippi	ECHL	70	34	26	10	3	0	3	....
1997-98	Mississippi	ECHL	70	34	27	9	....	....	....	....
1998-99	Mississippi	ECHL	70	41	22	7	18	14	4	....
99-2000	Lowell	AHL	80	33	36	11	7	3	4	....
2000-01	Lowell	AHL	80	35	35	10	4	1	3	....
2001-02	Manchester	AHL	80	38	28	14	5	2	3	....
2002-03	Manchester	AHL	80	40	23	17	3	0	3	....
2003-04	Manchester	AHL	80	40	28	12	6	2	4	....
2004-05	Manchester	AHL	80	51	21	8	6	2	4	....
2005-06	Hershey	AHL	80	44	21	15	21	16	5	....
2006-07	Hershey	AHL	80	51	17	12	19	13	6	....
2007-08	Hershey	AHL	15	8	7	0	....	....	....	....
2007-08	**Washington**	**NHL**	**61**	**37**	**17**	**7**	**7**	**3**	**4**	....
2008-09	**Washington**	**NHL**	**82**	**50**	**24**	**8**	**14**	**7**	**7**	....
2009-10	**Washington**	**NHL**	**82**	**54**	**15**	**13**	**7**	**3**	**4**	....
2010-11	**Washington**	**NHL**	**82**	**48**	**23**	**11**	**9**	**4**	**5**	....
2011-12	**Washington**	**NHL**	**22**	**12**	**9**	**1**	....	....	....	....
2011-12	**Anaheim**	**NHL**	**58**	**27**	**23**	**8**	....	....	....	....
2012-13	**Anaheim**	**NHL**	**48**	**30**	**12**	**6**	**7**	**3**	**4**	....
	NHL Totals		**435**	**258**	**123**	**54**	**44**	**20**	**24**	....

Jack Adams Award (2008)

Club Records

Team

(Figures in brackets for season records are games played; records for fewest points, wins, ties, losses, goals, goals against are for 70 or more games)

Most Points **110** 2006-07 (82)
Most Wins **48** 2006-07 (82)
Most Ties **13** 1996-97 (82), 1997-98 (82), 1998-99 (82)
Most Losses **46** 1993-94 (84)
Most Goals **258** 2006-07 (82)
Most Goals Against **261** 1997-98 (82)
Fewest Points **65** 1997-98 (82)
Fewest Wins **25** 2000-01 (82)
Fewest Ties **5** 1993-94 (84)
Fewest Losses **20** 2006-07 (82)
Fewest Goals **175** 2001-02 (82)
Fewest Goals Against **191** 2007-08 (82)
Longest Winning Streak
Overall .... **7** Feb. 20-Mar. 7/99
Home .... **13** Jan. 26-Mar. 20/13
Away .... **7** Nov. 28-Dec. 13/06
Longest Undefeated Streak
Overall .... **12** Feb. 22-Mar. 19/97 (7W, 5T)
Home .... **14** Feb. 12-Apr. 9/97 (10W, 4T)
Away .... **7** Nov. 28-Dec. 13/06 (7W)
Longest Losing Streak
Overall .... **8** Oct. 12-30/96, Nov. 3-20/05
Home .... **8** Jan. 10-Feb. 9/01
Away .... **13** Oct. 29-Dec. 22/11
Longest Winless Streak
Overall .... **9** Three times
Home .... **11** Jan. 5-Feb. 14/01 (8L, 3T/OL)
Away .... **13** Nov. 1-Dec. 27/03 (11L, 2T/OL)
Most Shutouts, Season **9** 2002-03 (82)
Most PIM, Season **1,843** 1997-98 (82)
Most Goals, Game .... **8** Jan. 21/98 (Fla. 3 at Ana. 8), Mar. 21/04 (Det. 6 at Ana. 8)

Individual

Most Seasons .... **14** Teemu Selanne
Most Games .... **902** Teemu Selanne
Most Goals, Career .... **448** Teemu Selanne
Most Assists, Career .... **513** Teemu Selanne
Most Points, Career .... **961** Teemu Selanne (448G, 513A)
Most PIM, Career .... **812** George Parros
Most Shutouts, Career .... **32** Jean-Sebastien Giguere
Longest Consecutive Games Streak .... **276** Andy McDonald (Oct. 17/03-Dec. 12/07)
Most Goals, Season .... **52** Teemu Selanne (1997-98)
Most Assists, Season .... **66** Ryan Getzlaf (2008-09)
Most Points, Season .... **109** Teemu Selanne (1996-97; 51G, 58A)
Most PIM, Season .... **285** Todd Ewen (1995-96)
Most Points, Defenseman, Season .... **69** Scott Niedermayer (2006-07; 15G, 54A)
Most Points, Center, Season .... **91** Ryan Getzlaf (2008-09; 25G, 66A)
Most Points, Right Wing, Season .... **109** Teemu Selanne (1996-97; 51G, 58A)
Most Points, Left Wing, Season .... **108** Paul Kariya (1995-96; 50G, 58A)
Most Points, Rookie, Season .... **57** Bobby Ryan (2008-09; 31G, 26A)
Most Shutouts, Season .... **8** Jean-Sebastien Giguere (2002-03)
Most Goals, Game .... **3** Thirty-four times
Most Assists, Game .... **5** Dmitri Mironov (Dec. 12/97), Teemu Selanne (Nov. 19/06), Ryan Getzlaf (Oct. 29/08)
Most Points, Game .... **5** Fifteen times

General Managers' History

Jack Ferreira, 1993-94 to 1997-98; Pierre Gauthier, 1998-99 to 2001-02; Bryan Murray, 2002-03, 2003-04; Al Coates, 2004-05; Brian Burke, 2005-06 to 2007-08; Brian Burke and Bob Murray, 2008-09; Bob Murray, 2009-10 to date.

Coaching History

Ron Wilson, 1993-94 to 1996-97; Pierre Page, 1997-98; Craig Hartsburg, 1998-99, 1999-2000; Craig Hartsburg and Guy Charron, 2000-01; Bryan Murray, 2001-02; Mike Babcock, 2002-03 to 2004-05; Randy Carlyle, 2005-06 to 2010-11; Randy Carlyle and Bruce Boudreau, 2011-12; Bruce Boudreau, 2012-13 to date.

Captains' History

Troy Loney, 1993-94; Randy Ladouceur, 1994-95, 1995-96; Paul Kariya, 1996-97; Paul Kariya and Teemu Selanne, 1997-98; Paul Kariya, 1998-99 to 2002-03; Steve Rucchin, 2003-04; Scott Niedermayer, 2005-06, 2006-07; Chris Pronger, 2007-08; Scott Niedermayer, 2008-09, 2009-10; Ryan Getzlaf, 2010-11 to date.

All-time Record vs. Other Clubs

Regular Season

	Total								At Home								On Road							
	GP	W	L	T	OL	GF	GA	PTS	GP	W	L	T	OL	GF	GA	PTS	GP	W	L	T	OL	GF	GA	PTS
Boston	24	10	9	2	3	62	65	25	12	4	4	2	2	26	31	12	12	6	5	0	1	36	34	13
Buffalo	26	8	14	3	1	55	78	20	13	5	8	0	0	27	39	10	13	3	6	3	1	28	39	10
Calgary	82	41	33	7	1	231	220	90	41	27	8	6	0	136	100	60	41	14	25	1	1	95	120	30
Carolina	26	12	12	2	0	68	73	26	13	7	5	1	0	38	39	15	13	5	7	1	0	30	34	11
Chicago	77	42	26	5	4	203	183	93	37	23	10	3	1	106	78	50	40	19	16	2	3	97	105	43
Colorado	73	32	29	7	5	199	194	76	37	18	14	3	2	101	96	41	36	14	15	4	3	98	98	35
Columbus	47	23	17	1	6	131	125	53	24	12	7	1	4	75	65	29	23	11	10	0	2	56	60	24
Dallas	107	38	58	5	6	244	315	87	53	24	25	3	1	137	147	52	54	14	33	2	5	107	168	35
Detroit	75	20	43	7	5	172	234	52	38	16	18	4	0	95	102	36	37	4	25	3	5	77	132	16
Edmonton	82	42	34	2	4	218	199	90	41	22	16	2	1	116	107	47	41	20	18	0	3	102	92	43
Florida	23	10	9	3	1	61	63	24	12	5	6	1	0	34	36	11	11	5	3	2	1	27	27	13
Los Angeles	112	49	41	11	11	325	317	120	56	29	13	7	7	188	151	72	56	20	28	4	4	137	166	48
Minnesota	47	22	16	2	7	110	116	53	24	14	7	0	3	65	58	31	23	8	9	2	4	45	58	22
Montreal	22	10	9	2	1	69	67	23	11	5	5	0	1	35	33	11	11	5	4	2	0	34	34	12
Nashville	55	30	18	2	5	146	124	67	28	20	5	0	3	86	55	43	27	10	13	2	2	60	69	24
New Jersey	24	8	13	1	2	54	71	19	13	6	6	1	0	35	33	13	11	2	7	0	2	19	38	6
NY Islanders	24	9	10	4	1	61	64	23	13	5	4	3	1	32	35	14	11	4	6	1	0	29	29	9
NY Rangers	25	14	6	1	4	76	68	33	12	8	2	0	2	43	35	18	13	6	4	1	2	33	33	15
Ottawa	23	12	7	3	1	58	55	28	12	6	3	2	1	29	24	15	11	6	4	1	0	29	31	13
Philadelphia	24	9	8	5	2	69	75	25	13	5	4	2	2	46	46	14	11	4	4	3	0	23	29	11
Phoenix	105	57	32	5	11	314	285	130	53	32	15	3	3	164	133	70	52	25	17	2	8	150	152	60
Pittsburgh	24	10	12	2	0	74	75	22	11	7	4	0	0	38	32	14	13	3	8	2	0	36	43	8
St. Louis	75	33	32	5	5	212	233	76	37	20	15	2	0	111	104	42	38	13	17	3	5	101	129	34
San Jose	113	52	52	4	5	297	320	113	57	25	27	2	3	151	163	55	56	27	25	2	2	146	157	58
Tampa Bay	24	14	9	1	0	69	55	29	12	7	4	1	0	38	31	15	12	7	5	0	0	31	24	14
Toronto	32	9	18	5	0	81	99	23	14	6	7	1	0	44	39	13	18	3	11	4	0	37	60	10
Vancouver	82	32	35	9	6	224	259	79	40	14	15	7	4	110	124	39	42	18	20	2	2	114	135	40
Washington	25	13	9	1	2	76	66	29	12	6	4	1	1	41	38	14	13	7	5	0	1	35	28	15
Winnipeg	14	7	6	0	1	44	41	15	7	3	3	0	1	22	23	7	7	4	3	0	0	22	18	8
Totals	**1492**	**668**	**617**	**107**	**100**	**4003**	**4139**	**1543**	**746**	**381**	**264**	**58**	**43**	**2169**	**1997**	**863**	**746**	**287**	**353**	**49**	**57**	**1834**	**2142**	**680**

Playoffs

	Series	W	L	GP	W	L	T	GF	GA	Last Mtg.	Rnd.	Result
Calgary	1	1	0	7	4	3	0	17	16	2006	CQF	W 4-3
Colorado	1	1	0	4	4	0	0	16	4	2006	CSF	W 4-0
Dallas	2	1	1	12	6	6	0	27	34	2008	CQF	L 2-4
Detroit	6	2	4	32	14	18	0	78	93	2013	CQF	L 3-4
Edmonton	1	0	1	5	1	4	0	13	16	2006	CF	L 1-4
Minnesota	2	2	0	9	8	1	0	21	10	2007	CQF	W 4-1
Nashville	1	0	1	6	2	4	0	20	22	2011	CQF	L 2-4
New Jersey	1	0	1	7	3	4	0	12	19	2003	F	L 3-4
Ottawa	1	1	0	5	4	1	0	16	11	2007	F	W 4-1
Phoenix	1	1	0	7	4	3	0	17	17	1997	CQF	W 4-3
San Jose	1	1	0	6	4	2	0	18	10	2009	CQF	W 4-2
Vancouver	1	1	0	5	4	1	0	14	8	2007	CSF	W 4-1
Totals	**19**	**11**	**8**	**105**	**58**	**47**	**0**	**269**	**260**			

Playoff Results 2013-2009

Year	Round	Opponent	Result	GF	GA
2013	CQF	Detroit	L 3-4	21	18
2011	CQF	Nashville	L 2-4	20	22
2009	CSF	Detroit	L 3-4	17	22
	CQF	San Jose	W 4-2	18	10

Abbreviations: Round: F – Final; **CF** – conference final; **CSF** – conference semi-final; **CQF** – conference quarter-final.

2012-13 Results

Jan.	19	at Vancouver	7-3		12	at Minnesota	2-1
	21	at Calgary	5-4		14	at Dallas	2-1†
	25	Vancouver	0-5		16	at St. Louis	1-2*
	26	Nashville	3-2†		18	San Jose	5-3
	29	at San Jose	2-3†		20	Chicago	4-2
Feb.	1	Minnesota	3-1		22	Detroit	1-5
	2	Los Angeles	7-4		24	Detroit	1-2
	4	San Jose	2-1		25	San Jose	3-5
	6	at Colorado	3-0		27	at San Jose	0-4
	8	at Dallas	1-3		29	at Chicago	2-1
	9	at St. Louis	6-5†		31	at Columbus	1-2*
	12	at Chicago	3-2†	**Apr.**	1	at Dallas	4-0
	15	at Detroit	5-2		3	Dallas	5-2
	16	at Nashville	3-2†		5	Dallas	1-3
	18	Columbus	3-2		7	Los Angeles	4-3†
	24	Colorado	4-3*		8	Edmonton	2-1
	25	at Los Angeles	2-5		10	Colorado	1-4
	27	Nashville	5-1		13	at Los Angeles	1-2
Mar.	1	Minnesota	3-2		17	Columbus	2-3*
	2	at Phoenix	4-5†		19	at Calgary	1-3
	4	at Phoenix	4-5†		21	at Edmonton	3-1
	6	Phoenix	2-0		22	at Edmonton	3-0
	8	Calgary	4-0		25	at Vancouver	3-1
	10	St. Louis	4-2		27	Phoenix	3-5

* – Overtime † – Shootout

Carolina totals include Hartford, 1993-94 to 1996-97.
Phoenix totals include Winnipeg, 1993-94 to 1995-96.
Colorado totals include Quebec, 1993-94 to 1994-95.
Winnipeg totals include Atlanta Thrashers, 1999-2000 to 2010-11.

Entry Draft Selections 2013-1999

Name in bold denotes played in NHL.

2013
Pick
26 Shea Theodore
45 Nick Sorensen
87 Keaton Thompson
147 Grant Besse
177 Miro Aaltonen

2012
Pick
6 Hampus Lindholm
36 Nicolas Kerdiles
87 Frederik Andersen
97 Kevin Roy
108 Andrew O'Brien
127 Brian Cooper
187 Kenton Helgesen
210 Jaycob Megna

2011
Pick
30 **Rickard Rakell**
39 John Gibson
53 William Karlsson
65 Joseph Cramarossa
83 Andy Welinski
143 Max Friberg
160 Josh Manson

2010
Pick
12 **Cam Fowler**
29 **Emerson Etem**
42 **Devante Smith-Pelly**
122 Chris Wagner
132 Tim Heed
161 Andreas Dahlstrom
177 Kevin Lind
192 Brett Perlini

2009
Pick
15 **Peter Holland**
26 **Kyle Palmieri**
37 **Mat Clark**
76 Igor Bobkov
106 **Sami Vatanen**
136 Radoslav Illo
166 Scott Valentine

2008
Pick
17 **Jake Gardiner**
35 Nicolas Deschamps
39 Eric O'Dell
43 **Justin Schultz**
71 Josh Brittain
83 Marco Cousineau
85 **Brandon McMillan**
113 Ryan Hegarty
143 Stefan Warg
208 Nick Pryor

2007
Pick
19 Logan MacMillan
42 **Eric Tangradi**
63 **Maxime Macenauer**
92 Justin Vaive
93 **Steven Kampfer**
98 Sebastian Stefaniszin
121 Mattias Modig
151 Brett Morrison

2006
Pick
19 Mark Mitera
38 Bryce Swan
83 John de Gray
112 **Matt Beleskey**
172 **Petteri Wirtanen**

2005
Pick
2 **Bobby Ryan**
31 **Brendan Mikkelson**
63 Jason Bailey
127 Bobby Bolt
141 **Brian Salcido**
197 Jean-Philippe Levasseur

2004
Pick
9 **Ladislav Smid**
39 Jordan Smith
74 Kyle Klubertanz
75 **Tim Brent**
172 Matt Auffrey
203 Gabriel Bouthillette
236 Matt Christie
269 **Janne Pesonen**

2003
Pick
19 **Ryan Getzlaf**
28 **Corey Perry**
86 Shane Hynes
90 Juha Alen
119 Nathan Saunders
186 **Drew Miller**
218 Dirk Southern
250 **Shane O'Brien**
280 Ville Mantymaa

2002
Pick
7 **Joffrey Lupul**
37 **Tim Brent**
71 Brian Lee
103 Joonas Vihko
140 George Davis
173 Luke Fritshaw
261 Francois Caron
267 Chris Petrow

2001
Pick
5 **Stanislav Chistov**
35 **Mark Popovic**
69 Joel Stepp
102 **Timo Parssinen**
105 Vladimir Korsunov
118 Brandon Rogers
137 **Joel Perrault**
170 Jan Tabacek
224 **Tony Martensson**
232 **Martin Gerber**
264 **P.A. Parenteau**

2000
Pick
12 **Alexei Smirnov**
44 **Ilya Bryzgalov**
98 **Jonas Ronnqvist**
134 Peter Podhradsky
153 Bill Cass

1999
Pick
44 **Jordan Leopold**
83 **Niclas Havelid**
105 Alexandr Chagodayev
141 Maxim Rybin
173 Jan Sandstrom
230 **Petr Tenkrat**
258 Brian Gornick

Bob Murray

Executive Vice President and General Manager

Born: Kingston, Ont., November 26, 1954.

Bob Murray was named executive vice president and general manager of the Anaheim Ducks on November 12, 2008 after 3 1/2 years as senior vice president of hockey operations. He was named to that original position on July 14, 2005. Murray's astute judgment of hockey talent and player evaluation were instrumental in several trades and acquisitions the Ducks made over his tenure, highlighted by a Stanley Cup championship in 2007.

Murray's responsibilities include overseeing all aspects of player development, playing a key role in the club's professional scouting efforts, contract negotiations and all matters relating to the National Hockey League. He has been instrumental in the organization's success at both the NHL and AHL level. Both the Ducks and American Hockey League's Portland Pirates made Conference Final appearances in 2006, making Anaheim the only organization to have both their NHL and AHL teams advance to their league's respective Conference Finals.

Prior to joining the Ducks, Murray worked as a professional scout with the Vancouver Canucks from 1999 to 2005 under then-general manager Brian Burke (1998 to 2004). Murray's scouting expertise helped to build teams that recorded 100+ point season two years in a row (2002-03 and 2003-04) and advanced to the Stanley Cup playoffs four seasons in a row (2001 to 2004). Before his stint in Vancouver, he served as a scouting consultant for Anaheim during the 1998-99 season.

Murray was a member of the Chicago Blackhawks organization for 25 years, serving as general manager from 1997 to 1999. He was promoted to the post after serving as assistant general manager under Bob Pulford for two seasons. Before joining upper management, Murray was named the director of player personnel in 1991 and was largely responsible for the club's entry draft selections over eight seasons.

Drafted by the Blackhawks in 1974, Murray spent his entire 1,008-game, 15-year career in a Chicago uniform. He became just the fourth player in Blackhawks history to reach the 1,000-game plateau. In addition, he became the first defenseman in club history to appear in 100 postseason contests, reaching the mark during the 1990 Stanley Cup playoffs. In all, Murray had 132 goals and 382 assists for 514 points, and currently ranks second in all-time points among Blackhawk defensemen. He was named to both the 1981 and 1983 NHL All-Star Games. Murray retired at the conclusion of the 1989-90 season. Known for his work ethic, intelligence and determination as a player, Murray remained with the organization as a professional scout following his retirement in 1990.

Club Directory

Honda Center

Anaheim Ducks
Honda Center
2695 E. Katella Ave.
Anaheim, CA 92806
Phone **714/940-2900**
FAX 714/940-2953
Ticket Information 877/WILDWING
www.anaheimducks.com
Capacity: 17,174

Executive Management
Owners. . . . . Henry and Susan Samueli
Chief Executive Officer . . . . Michael Schulman
Executive Vice President/General Manager . . . . Bob Murray
Executive Vice President/Chief Operating Officer . . . Tim Ryan
Senior Vice President, Hockey Operations . . . . David McNab
Chief Financial Officer/Vice President of Finance . . . Doug Heller
Vice President, Human Resources . . . . Jay Scott
Vice President/COO, Anaheim Arena. . . . . Kevin Starkey
Vice President, Chief Marketing Officer. . . . . Aaron Teats
Vice President Sales/Chief Revenue Officer . . . . John Viola
Vice President of Finance, Anaheim Arena. . . . . Angela Wergechik
Executive Assistants . . . . Cheryl Gorman, Janet Conley

Coaching Staff
Head Coach . . . . Bruce Boudreau
Assistant Coaches. . . . . Bob Woods, Brad Lauer, Scott Niedermayer
Goaltending Consultant / Video Coordinator . . . . . Dwayne Roloson / Joe Piscotty

Hockey Operations
Director of Player Personnel . . . . Rick Paterson
Scouting Directors, Amateur / Pro . . . . Martin Madden / Dave Baseggio
Director of Player Development. . . . . Todd Marchant
Scouting Staff . . . . Glen Cochrane, Jeff Crisp, Jan-Åke Danielson, Casey Hankinson, Konstantin Krylov, Matt Laatsch, Martin Madden, Sr., Kevin Murray, Steve Lyons, Jim Pappin, Jim Sandlak, Stephane Pilotte
Hockey Ops, Senior Manager / Manager . . . . Maureen Norvall / Ryan Lichtenfels
Strength and Conditioning Coach. . . . . Sean Skahan
Athletic Trainers, Head / Assistant . . . . Joe Huff / Mike Hannegan
Massage Therapist . . . . James Partida
Equipment Manager / Asst. Mgr. / Assistant . . . . . . Doug Shearer / Chris Aldrich / Chris Kincaid
Team Physicians / Oral Surgeon. . . . . Drs. Craig Milhouse, Orr Limpisvasti / Bao-Thy Grant

Legal
General Counsel / Asst. General Counsel . . . . Bernard Schneider / Katie Rodin

Broadcasting
TV: FSN Prime Ticket (Cable), KDOC-TV. . . . . John Ahlers, Brian Hayward
Radio: KLAA AM 830 & Ducks Radio Network . . . . Steve Carroll, Dan Wood
Host-Producer / Postgame Radio Host . . . . Kent French / Josh Brewster
Broadcasting Associate . . . . Tiffany Spiritosanto

Communications
Director of Media & Communications . . . . Alex Gilchrist
Managers, Media & Communications . . . . Steve Hoem, Lauren O'Gorman
Game Night Communications Staff . . . Chelsea Gonye, Sam Kieckhefer, Lisa Parris, Larry Woodard

Community Relations
Director of Community Relations . . . . Wendy Arciero
Community Relations Managers / Coordinator . . . . Jesse Bryson, Colleen MacKinnon / Ashley Forbes

Entertainment
Director of Production & Entertainment. . . . . Rich Cooley
Entertainment Manager . . . . Chris Brown
Arena Vision Editor-Producer . . . . Davin Maske
Producer / Associate Producer / Coordinator . . . . . . Peter Uvalle / Gabe Suarez / Sarah Moews

Fan Development
Director of Fan Development . . . . Matt Savant
Sr. Manager, Fan Development & Education . . . . . . Joseph Hwang
Fan Development Manager / Coordinators . . . . Champ Baginski / Jason Cooper, Mike Hermosa

Finance
Controller / Financial Analyst / Payroll . . . . Melody Martin / Rosanna Sitzman / Regina Terrana
Accounting Asst./Accounts Payable. . . . . Rob Dumlao/Lou Rae Campbell

Human Resources
Human Resources Managers / Coordinator . . . . Wendy Mulhall, Donna Vass / Lisa Monson

Corporate Partnerships
Corporate Partnerships Director / Managers . . . . . . Greg Rieber / Brian Fling, Graham Siderius

Corporate Partnership Activation
Senior Manager, Corporate Partnership Activation . Sarah Morales
Manager, Corporate Partnership Activation. . . . . . . Keith Shattenkirk
Media Services Associate/ Activation Coordinators . Randy Bernabe / Natalie Bobuk, Katie Bailey

Marketing
Director of Marketing . . . . Tracie Jones
Signature Programs & Events, Sr. Mgr. / Mgr. . . . . . Kris Loomis / Jamie Minkler
Senior Media and Marketing Manager . . . . Adam Mendelsohn
Marketing Manager . . . . Ryan Spillers
The Rinks Corp. Partnerships & Marketing Mgr. . . . Jesse Chatfield
Marketing Coordinators . . . . G.M. Ciallella, Cindy Iwami, Ryan Johnson
Graphic Designers, Senior / Juniors . . . . Mariana Koontz / Jeff Ipjian Ruben Segura

Publications and New Media
Director of Publications and New Media . . . . Adam Brady
Social Media Producer. . . . . Anthony Manderichio
Publications & New Media Associate. . . . . Kyle Shohara

Premium Sales and Service
Director of Premium Sales & Service . . . . Jim Panetta
Premium Account Executives . . . . . . Casey Haakinson, Geoff Matthews, Timothy Thompson
Premium Services Manager / Coordinator . . . . Jana Cannavo / Ariana Zamora

Ticketing
Senior Manager of Ticket Operations . . . . James Bakken
Assistant Mgrs., Ticketing / Premium Ticketing . . . . Jonas Calicdan / Gina Bulgheroni
Group & Inside Sales Ticketing Rep. . . . . Robert Slaby
Ticketing Reps., Premium / Season . . . . Christie Nevin, John Watson / Kameron Kwok

Ticket Sales and Customer Service
Director of Ticket Sales and Service . . . . Lisa Johnson
Manager, Business Development & Retention . . . . . Chris Kenyon
Business Development Acct. Execs. . . . . Angelo Anello, Anthony Bennett, Melissa Garza, Debora Lee, Brett Miller, Phillip Widell
Business Retention Acct. Execs. . . . . Daniel Alvarez, Michelle Carter, Nick Moller
Group Sales Acct. Execs.. . . . . Jennifer D'Anna, Jamie Friedrich, Matt Payne, Sean Sterner
Season and Group Sales Coordinator . . . . Natasha Arena

Boston Bruins

Key Off-Season Signings/Acquisitions

2013

July 4 • Acquired LW **Loui Eriksson**, RW **Matt Fraser**, RW **Reilly Smith** and D **Joe Morrow** from Dallas for C **Rich Peverley**, C **Tyler Seguin** and D **Ryan Button**.

5 • Signed RW **Jarome Iginla**.

10 • Re-signed G **Tuukka Rask**.

12 • Re-signed C **Patrice Bergeron**.

2012-13 Results: 28W-14L-3OTL-3SOL 62PTS
2ND, Northeast Division • 4TH, Eastern Conference

Year-by-Year Record

		Home				Road				Overall									
Season	GP	W	L	T	OL	W	L	T	OL	W	L	T	OL	GF	GA	Pts.	Div. Fin.	Conf. Fin.	Playoff Result
2012-13	48	16	5	....	3	12	9	....	3	28	14	....	6	131	109	62	2nd, NE	4th, East	Lost Final
2011-12	82	24	14	....	3	25	15	....	1	49	29	....	4	269	202	102	1st, NE	2nd, East	Lost Conf. Quarter-Final
2010-11	**82**	**22**	**13**	....	**6**	**24**	**12**	....	**5**	**46**	**25**	....	**11**	**246**	**195**	**103**	**1st, NE**	**3rd, East**	**Won Stanley Cup**
2009-10	82	18	17	....	6	21	13	....	7	39	30	....	13	206	200	91	3rd, NE	6th, East	Lost Conf. Semi-Final
2008-09	82	29	6	....	6	24	13	....	4	53	19	....	10	274	196	116	1st, NE	1st, East	Lost Conf. Semi-Final
2007-08	82	21	16	....	4	20	13	....	8	41	29	....	12	212	222	94	3rd, NE	8th, East	Lost Conf. Quarter-Final
2006-07	82	18	19	....	4	17	22	....	2	35	41	....	6	219	289	76	5th, NE	13th, East	Out of Playoffs
2005-06	82	16	15	....	10	13	22	....	6	29	37	....	16	230	266	74	5th, NE	13th, East	Out of Playoffs
2004-05	....	....	....	....	....	....	....	....	....	....	....	....	....	....	....	....			
2003-04	82	18	12	9	2	23	7	6	5	41	19	15	7	209	188	104	1st, NE	2nd, East	Lost Conf. Quarter-Final
2002-03	82	23	11	5	2	13	20	6	2	36	31	11	4	245	237	87	3rd, NE	7th, East	Lost Conf. Quarter-Final
2001-02	82	23	11	2	5	20	13	4	4	43	24	6	9	236	201	101	1st, NE	1st, East	Lost Conf. Quarter-Final
2000-01	82	21	12	5	3	15	18	3	5	36	30	8	8	227	249	88	4th, NE	9th, East	Out of Playoffs
1999-2000	82	12	17	11	1	12	16	8	5	24	33	19	6	210	248	73	5th, NE	12th, East	Out of Playoffs
1998-99	82	22	10	9	....	17	20	4	....	39	30	13	....	214	181	91	3rd, NE	6th, East	Lost Conf. Semi-Final
1997-98	82	19	16	6	....	20	14	7	....	39	30	13	....	221	194	91	2nd, NE	5th, East	Lost Conf. Quarter-Final
1996-97	82	14	20	7	....	12	27	2	....	26	47	9	....	234	300	61	6th, NE	13th, East	Out of Playoffs
1995-96	82	22	14	5	....	18	17	6	....	40	31	11	....	282	269	91	2nd, NE	5th, East	Lost Conf. Quarter-Final
1994-95	48	15	7	2	....	12	11	1	....	27	18	3	....	150	127	57	3rd, NE	4th, East	Lost Conf. Quarter-Final
1993-94	84	20	14	8	....	22	15	5	....	42	29	13	....	289	252	97	2nd, NE	4th, East	Lost Conf. Semi-Final
1992-93	84	29	10	3	....	22	16	4	....	51	26	7	....	332	268	109	1st, Adams		Lost Div. Semi-Final
1991-92	80	23	11	6	....	13	21	6	....	36	32	12	....	270	275	84	2nd, Adams		Lost Conf. Final
1990-91	80	26	9	5	....	18	15	7	....	44	24	12	....	299	264	100	1st, Adams		Lost Conf. Final
1989-90	80	23	13	4	....	23	12	5	....	46	25	9	....	289	232	101	1st, Adams		Lost Final
1988-89	80	17	15	8	....	20	14	6	....	37	29	14	....	289	256	88	2nd, Adams		Lost Div. Final
1987-88	80	24	13	3	....	20	17	3	....	44	30	6	....	300	251	94	2nd, Adams		Lost Final
1986-87	80	25	11	4	....	14	23	3	....	39	34	7	....	301	276	85	3rd, Adams		Lost Div. Semi-Final
1985-86	80	24	9	7	....	13	22	5	....	37	31	12	....	311	288	86	3rd, Adams		Lost Div. Semi-Final
1984-85	80	21	15	4	....	15	19	6	....	36	34	10	....	303	287	82	4th, Adams		Lost Div. Semi-Final
1983-84	80	25	12	3	....	24	13	3	....	49	25	6	....	336	261	104	1st, Adams		Lost Div. Semi-Final
1982-83	80	28	6	6	....	22	14	4	....	50	20	10	....	327	228	110	1st, Adams		Lost Conf. Final
1981-82	80	24	12	4	....	19	15	6	....	43	27	10	....	323	285	96	2nd, Adams		Lost Div. Final
1980-81	80	26	10	4	....	11	20	9	....	37	30	13	....	316	272	87	2nd, Adams		Lost Prelim. Round
1979-80	80	27	9	4	....	19	12	9	....	46	21	13	....	310	234	105	2nd, Adams		Lost Quarter-Final
1978-79	80	25	10	5	....	18	13	9	....	43	23	14	....	316	270	100	1st, Adams		Lost Semi-Final
1977-78	80	29	6	5	....	22	12	6	....	51	18	11	....	333	218	113	1st, Adams		Lost Final
1976-77	80	27	7	6	....	22	16	2	....	49	23	8	....	312	240	106	1st, Adams		Lost Final
1975-76	80	27	5	8	....	21	10	9	....	48	15	17	....	313	237	113	1st, Adams		Lost Semi-Final
1974-75	80	29	5	6	....	11	21	8	....	40	26	14	....	345	245	94	2nd, Adams		Lost Prelim. Round
1973-74	78	33	4	2	....	19	13	7	....	52	17	9	....	349	221	113	1st, East		Lost Final
1972-73	78	27	10	2	....	24	12	3	....	51	22	5	....	330	235	107	2nd, East		Lost Quarter-Final
1971-72	**78**	**28**	**4**	**7**	....	**26**	**9**	**4**	....	**54**	**13**	**11**	....	**330**	**204**	**119**	**1st, East**		**Won Stanley Cup**
1970-71	78	33	4	2	....	24	10	5	....	57	14	7	....	399	207	121	1st, East		Lost Quarter-Final
1969-70	**76**	**27**	**3**	**8**	....	**13**	**14**	**11**	....	**40**	**17**	**19**	....	**277**	**216**	**99**	**2nd, East**		**Won Stanley Cup**
1968-69	76	29	3	6	....	13	15	10	....	42	18	16	....	303	221	100	2nd, East		Lost Semi-Final
1967-68	74	22	9	6	....	15	18	4	....	37	27	10	....	259	216	84	3rd, East		Lost Quarter-Final
1966-67	70	10	21	4	....	7	22	6	....	17	43	10	....	182	253	44	6th,		Out of Playoffs
1965-66	70	15	17	3	....	6	26	3	....	21	43	6	....	174	275	48	5th,		Out of Playoffs
1964-65	70	12	17	6	....	9	26	0	....	21	43	6	....	166	253	48	6th,		Out of Playoffs
1963-64	70	13	15	7	....	5	25	5	....	18	40	12	....	170	212	48	6th,		Out of Playoffs
1962-63	70	7	18	10	....	7	21	7	....	14	39	17	....	198	281	45	6th,		Out of Playoffs
1961-62	70	9	22	4	....	6	25	4	....	15	47	8	....	177	306	38	6th,		Out of Playoffs
1960-61	70	13	17	5	....	2	25	8	....	15	42	13	....	176	254	43	6th,		Out of Playoffs
1959-60	70	21	11	3	....	7	23	5	....	28	34	8	....	220	241	64	5th,		Out of Playoffs
1958-59	70	21	11	3	....	11	18	6	....	32	29	9	....	205	215	73	2nd,		Lost Semi-Final
1957-58	70	15	14	6	....	12	14	9	....	27	28	15	....	199	194	69	4th,		Lost Final
1956-57	70	20	9	6	....	14	15	6	....	34	24	12	....	195	174	80	3rd,		Lost Final
1955-56	70	14	14	7	....	9	20	6	....	23	34	13	....	147	185	59	5th,		Out of Playoffs
1954-55	70	16	10	9	....	7	16	12	....	23	26	21	....	169	188	67	4th,		Lost Semi-Final
1953-54	70	22	8	5	....	10	20	5	....	32	28	10	....	177	181	74	4th,		Lost Semi-Final
1952-53	70	19	10	6	....	9	19	7	....	28	29	13	....	152	172	69	3rd,		Lost Final
1951-52	70	15	12	8	....	10	17	8	....	25	29	16	....	162	176	66	4th,		Lost Semi-Final
1950-51	70	13	12	10	....	9	18	8	....	22	30	18	....	178	197	62	4th,		Lost Semi-Final
1949-50	70	15	12	8	....	7	20	8	....	22	32	16	....	198	228	60	5th,		Out of Playoffs
1948-49	60	18	10	2	....	11	13	6	....	29	23	8	....	178	163	66	2nd,		Lost Semi-Final
1947-48	60	12	8	10	....	11	16	3	....	23	24	13	....	167	168	59	3rd,		Lost Semi-Final
1946-47	60	18	7	5	....	8	16	6	....	26	23	11	....	190	175	63	3rd,		Lost Semi-Final
1945-46	50	11	5	4	....	13	13	4	....	24	18	8	....	167	156	56	2nd,		Lost Final
1944-45	50	11	12	2	....	5	18	2	....	16	30	4	....	179	219	36	4th,		Lost Semi-Final
1943-44	50	15	8	2	....	4	18	3	....	19	26	5	....	223	268	43	5th,		Out of Playoffs
1942-43	50	17	3	5	....	7	14	4	....	24	17	9	....	195	176	57	2nd,		Lost Final
1941-42	48	17	4	3	....	8	13	3	....	25	17	6	....	160	118	56	3rd,		Lost Semi-Final
1940-41	**48**	**15**	**4**	**5**	....	**12**	**4**	**8**	....	**27**	**8**	**13**	....	**168**	**102**	**67**	**1st,**		**Won Stanley Cup**
1939-40	48	20	3	1	....	11	9	4	....	31	12	5	....	170	98	67	1st,		Lost Semi-Final
1938-39	**48**	**20**	**2**	**2**	....	**16**	**8**	**0**	....	**36**	**10**	**2**	....	**156**	**76**	**74**	**1st,**		**Won Stanley Cup**
1937-38	48	18	3	3	....	12	8	4	....	30	11	7	....	142	89	67	1st, Amn.		Lost Semi-Final
1936-37	48	9	11	4	....	14	7	3	....	23	18	7	....	120	110	53	2nd, Amn.		Lost Quarter-Final
1935-36	48	15	8	1	....	7	12	5	....	22	20	6	....	92	83	50	2nd, Amn.		Lost Quarter-Final
1934-35	48	17	7	0	....	9	9	6	....	26	16	6	....	129	112	58	1st, Amn.		Lost Semi-Final
1933-34	48	11	11	2	....	7	14	3	....	18	25	5	....	111	130	41	4th, Amn.		Out of Playoffs
1932-33	48	19	2	3	....	6	13	5	....	25	15	8	....	124	88	58	1st, Amn.		Lost Semi-Final
1931-32	48	11	10	3	....	4	11	9	....	15	21	12	....	122	117	42	4th, Amn.		Out of Playoffs
1930-31	44	16	1	5	....	12	9	1	....	28	10	6	....	143	90	62	1st, Amn.		Lost Semi-Final
1929-30	44	21	1	0	....	17	4	1	....	38	5	1	....	179	98	77	1st, Amn.		Lost Final
1928-29	**44**	**15**	**6**	**1**	....	**11**	**7**	**4**	....	**26**	**13**	**5**	....	**89**	**52**	**57**	**1st, Amn.**		**Won Stanley Cup**
1927-28	44	13	4	5	....	7	9	6	....	20	13	11	....	77	70	51	1st, Amn.		Lost Semi-Final
1926-27	44	15	7	0	....	6	13	3	....	21	20	3	....	97	89	45	2nd, Amn.		Lost Final
1925-26	36	10	7	1	....	7	8	3	....	17	15	4	....	92	85	38	4th,		Out of Playoffs
1924-25	30	3	12	0	....	3	12	0	....	6	24	0	....	49	119	12	6th,		Out of Playoffs

2013-14 Schedule

Oct.	Thu.	3	Tampa Bay		Sat.	4	Winnipeg*
	Sat.	5	Detroit		Tue.	7	at Anaheim
	Thu.	10	Colorado		Thu.	9	at Los Angeles
	Sat.	12	at Columbus		Sat.	11	at San Jose
	Mon.	14	Detroit*		Tue.	14	Toronto
	Thu.	17	at Florida		Thu.	16	at Dallas
	Sat.	19	at Tampa Bay		Sun.	19	at Chicago*
	Wed.	23	at Buffalo		Mon.	20	Los Angeles*
	Thu.	24	San Jose		Sat.	25	at Philadelphia*
	Sat.	26	New Jersey		Mon.	27	at NY Islanders
	Wed.	30	at Pittsburgh		Tue.	28	Florida
	Thu.	31	Anaheim		Thu.	30	Montreal
Nov.	Sat.	2	at NY Islanders	**Feb.**	Sat.	1	Edmonton*
	Tue.	5	Dallas		Tue.	4	Vancouver
	Thu.	7	Florida		Thu.	6	at St. Louis
	Sat.	9	Toronto		Sat.	8	Ottawa*
	Mon.	11	Tampa Bay*		Wed.	26	at Buffalo
	Thu.	14	Columbus	**Mar.**	Sat.	1	Washington*
	Fri.	15	at Ottawa		Sun.	2	at NY Rangers
	Mon.	18	at Carolina		Tue.	4	Florida
	Tue.	19	at NY Rangers		Thu.	6	Washington
	Thu.	21	St. Louis		Sat.	8	at Tampa Bay
	Sat.	23	Carolina*		Sun.	9	at Florida*
	Mon.	25	Pittsburgh		Wed.	12	at Montreal
	Wed.	27	at Detroit		Thu.	13	Phoenix
	Fri.	29	NY Rangers*		Sat.	15	Carolina*
	Sat.	30	Columbus		Mon.	17	Minnesota
Dec.	Thu.	5	at Montreal		Tue.	18	at New Jersey
	Sat.	7	Pittsburgh		Fri.	21	at Colorado
	Sun.	8	at Toronto		Sat.	22	at Phoenix
	Tue.	10	at Calgary		Mon.	24	Montreal
	Thu.	12	at Edmonton		Thu.	27	Chicago
	Sat.	14	at Vancouver		Sat.	29	at Washington*
	Tue.	17	Calgary		Sun.	30	at Philadelphia
	Thu.	19	at Buffalo	**Apr.**	Wed.	2	at Detroit
	Sat.	21	Buffalo		Thu.	3	at Toronto
	Mon.	23	at Nashville		Sat.	5	Philadelphia*
	Fri.	27	Ottawa		Tue.	8	at Minnesota
	Sat.	28	at Ottawa		Thu.	10	at Winnipeg
	Tue.	31	NY Islanders		Sat.	12	Buffalo*
Jan.	Thu.	2	Nashville		Sun.	13	at New Jersey*

* Denotes afternoon game.

ATLANTIC DIVISION
90th NHL Season

Franchise date: November 1, 1924

2013-14 Player Personnel

FORWARDS	HT	WT	*Age	Place of Birth	S	2012-13 Club
BERGERON, Patrice	6-2	194	28	Ancienne-Lorette, Que.	R	Lugano-Boston
CAMARA, Anthony	6-0	192	20	Toronto, Ont.	L	Barrie
CAMPBELL, Gregory	6-0	197	29	London, Ont.	L	Boston
CAMPER, Carter	5-9	176	25	Rocky River, OH	R	Providence (AHL)
CARON, Jordan	6-2	202	22	Sayabec, Que.	L	Providence (AHL)-Boston
ERIKSSON, Loui	6-2	196	28	Goteborg, Sweden	L	Davos-Dallas
FRASER, Matt	6-1	204	23	Red Deer, Alta.	L	Texas-Dallas
IGINLA, Jarome	6-1	210	36	Edmonton, Alta.	R	Calgary-Pittsburgh
JOHNSON, Nick	6-2	200	27	Calgary, Alta.	R	Idaho-Port (AHL)-Phx
KELLY, Chris	6-0	198	32	Toronto, Ont.	L	Martigny-Boston
KNIGHT, Jared	5-11	203	21	Battle Creek, MI	R	Prov (AHL)-South Carolina
KREJCI, David	6-0	188	27	Sternberk, Czech.	R	Pardubice-Boston
LINDBLAD, Matt	5-11	193	23	Winnetka, IL	L	Dartmouth-Providence (AHL)
LUCIC, Milan	6-4	220	25	Vancouver, B.C.	L	Boston
MARCHAND, Brad	5-9	183	25	Halifax, N.S.	L	Boston
PAILLE, Daniel	6-0	200	29	Welland, Ont.	L	Ilves-Boston
SAVARD, Marc	5-10	191	36	Ottawa, Ont.	L	Boston
SMITH, Reilly	6-0	185	22	Toronto, Ont.	L	Texas-Dallas
SODERBERG, Carl	6-3	198	27	Malmo, Sweden	L	Linkoping-Boston
SPOONER, Ryan	5-10	180	21	Ottawa, Ont.	L	Providence (AHL)-Boston
THORNTON, Shawn	6-2	217	36	Oshawa, Ont.	R	Boston
DEFENSEMEN						
BARTKOWSKI, Matt	6-1	196	25	Pittsburgh, PA	L	Providence (AHL)-Boston
BOYCHUK, Johnny	6-2	225	29	Edmonton, Alta.	R	Salzburg-Boston
CHARA, Zdeno	6-9	255	36	Trencin, Czechoslovakia	L	Lev Praha-Boston
HAMILTON, Dougie	6-5	199	20	Toronto, Ont.	R	Boston
KRUG, Torey	5-9	180	22	Livonia, MI	L	Providence (AHL)-Boston
McQUAID, Adam	6-5	209	26	Charlottetown, P.E.I.	R	Boston
MILLER, Kevan	6-2	200	25	Los Angeles, CA	R	Providence (AHL)
MOORE, Mike	6-1	210	28	Calgary, Alta.	L	Milwaukee
MORROW, Joe	6-1	204	20	Edmonton, Alta.	L	Wilkes-Barre-Texas
SEIDENBERG, Dennis	6-1	210	32	Schwenningen, W. Germany	L	Mannheim-Boston
WARSOFSKY, David	5-8	160	23	Marshfield, MA	L	Providence (AHL)

GOALTENDERS	HT	WT	*Age	Place of Birth	C	2012-13 Club
JOHNSON, Chad	6-3	205	27	Calgary, Alta.	L	Portland (AHL)-Phoenix
RASK, Tuukka	6-3	185	26	Savonlinna, Finland	L	Plzen-Boston
SVEDBERG, Niklas	6-0	176	24	Sollentuna, Sweden	L	Providence (AHL)

* – Age at start of 2013-14 season

Coaching History

Art Ross, 1924-25 to 1933-34; Frank Patrick, 1934-35, 1935-36; Art Ross, 1936-37 to 1938-39; Cooney Weiland, 1939-40, 1940-41; Art Ross, 1941-42 to 1944-45; Dit Clapper, 1945-46 to 1948-49; George Boucher, 1949-50; Lynn Patrick, 1950-51 to 1953-54; Lynn Patrick and Milt Schmidt, 1954-55; Milt Schmidt, 1955-56 to 1960-61; Phil Watson, 1961-62; Phil Watson and Milt Schmidt, 1962-63; Milt Schmidt, 1963-64 to 1965-66; Harry Sinden, 1966-67 to 1969-70; Tom Johnson, 1970-71, 1971-72; Tom Johnson and Bep Guidolin, 1972-73; Bep Guidolin, 1973-74; Don Cherry, 1974-75 to 1978-79; Fred Creighton and Harry Sinden, 1979-80; Gerry Cheevers, 1980-81 to 1983-84; Gerry Cheevers and Harry Sinden, 1984-85; Butch Goring, 1985-86; Butch Goring and Terry O'Reilly, 1986-87; Terry O'Reilly, 1987-88, 1988-89; Mike Milbury, 1989-90, 1990-91; Rick Bowness, 1991-92; Brian Sutter, 1992-93 to 1994-95; Steve Kasper, 1995-96, 1996-97; Pat Burns, 1997-98 to 1999-2000; Pat Burns and Mike Keenan, 2000-01; Robbie Ftorek, 2001-02; Robbie Ftorek and Mike O'Connell, 2002-03; Mike Sullivan, 2003-04 to 2005-06; Dave Lewis, 2006-07; Claude Julien, 2007-08 to date.

Claude Julien

Head Coach

Born: Orleans, Ont., April 23, 1960.

The Boston Bruins named Claude Julien the 28th head coach in club history on June 21, 2007. In his first season behind the bench in 2007-08, he guided the Bruins back to the playoffs for the first time since 2003-04. In 2008-09, the Bruins posted the best record in the Eastern Conference and were second overall in the NHL, earning Julien the Jack Adams Award for coach of the year. In 2010-11, he guided the team to a Stanley Cup victory for the first time since 1972. Boston reached the Stanley Cup final again in 2013.

Julien joined the Bruins with four years of NHL head coaching experience. In his lone season with New Jersey, he held a record of 47-24-8 before being replaced on April 2, 2007 with three games remaining in the 2006-07 regular season. At the time he was replaced by the Devils, Julien's club was in first place in the Atlantic Division. Prior to being named head coach of the Devils, Julien spent three seasons as the head coach of the Montreal Canadiens, serving from January 2003 until January of 2006. During his tenure with Montreal, Julien led the Canadiens to a record of 72-71-16 in 159 games.

Before joining the NHL coaching ranks, Julien spent four seasons with Hull of the Quebec Major Junior Hockey League and three campaigns with Hamilton of the American Hockey League. While with Hamilton, Julien was co-awarded the Louis A. R. Pieri Award as the league's outstanding coach during the 2002-03 season. Julien has also coached at the international level, having served as an assistant coach to Team Canada at the 2006 World Championship after he led Team Canada to a bronze medal as a head coach at the 2000 World Junior Championship. He will be an associate coach for Canada at the 2014 Sochi Winter Olympics.

A defenseman, Julien's professional playing career spanned 12 seasons from 1981 to 1992, highlighted by stints with the Quebec Nordiques between 1984 and 1986.

2012-13 Scoring

* – rookie

Regular Season

Pos	#	Player	Team	GP	G	A	Pts	TOI	+/–	PIM	PP	SH	GW	S	%
C	63	Brad Marchand	BOS	45	18	18	36	16:57	23	27	4	2	5	91	19.8
R	68	Jaromir Jagr	DAL	34	14	12	26	18:17	–5	20	6	0	2	87	16.1
			BOS	11	2	7	9	18:26	3	2	0	0	2	28	7.1
			Total	45	16	19	35	18:19	–2	22	6	0	4	115	13.9
C	46	David Krejci	BOS	47	10	23	33	18:30	1	20	0	0	5	93	10.8
C	19	Tyler Seguin	BOS	48	16	16	32	17:00	23	16	4	0	2	161	9.9
C	37	Patrice Bergeron	BOS	42	10	22	32	19:17	24	18	2	0	3	125	8.0
L	17	Milan Lucic	BOS	46	7	20	27	16:54	8	75	0	0	0	79	8.9
R	18	Nathan Horton	BOS	43	13	9	22	16:51	1	22	0	0	1	114	11.4
D	33	Zdeno Chara	BOS	48	7	12	19	24:56	14	70	3	0	2	119	5.9
C	49	Rich Peverley	BOS	47	6	12	18	15:15	–9	16	2	0	0	95	6.3
L	20	Daniel Paille	BOS	46	10	7	17	12:40	3	8	0	2	1	70	14.3
D	44	Dennis Seidenberg	BOS	46	4	13	17	23:47	18	10	0	0	2	83	4.8
D	27 *	Dougie Hamilton	BOS	42	5	11	16	17:07	4	14	2	0	0	83	6.0
D	21	Andrew Ference	BOS	48	4	9	13	19:29	9	35	0	0	0	66	6.1
C	11	Gregory Campbell	BOS	48	4	9	13	13:42	2	41	0	1	0	52	7.7
C	23	Chris Kelly	BOS	34	3	6	9	14:58	–8	16	1	0	0	40	7.5
D	6	Wade Redden	STL	23	2	3	5	14:59	–2	11	0	0	0	23	8.7
			BOS	6	1	1	2	15:23	0	0	0	0	0	5	20.0
			Total	29	3	4	7	15:04	–2	11	0	0	0	28	10.7
L	22	Shawn Thornton	BOS	45	3	4	7	8:06	1	60	0	0	0	55	5.5
D	55	Johnny Boychuk	BOS	44	1	5	6	20:24	5	12	0	0	0	75	1.3
L	48	Chris Bourque	BOS	18	1	3	4	12:04	–6	6	0	0	1	24	4.2
L	16	Kaspars Daugavins	OTT	19	1	2	3	11:25	–7	9	0	0	0	23	4.3
			BOS	6	0	1	1	9:42	–1	0	0	0	0	13	0.0
			Total	25	1	3	4	11:00	–8	9	0	0	0	36	2.8
D	54	Adam McQuaid	BOS	32	1	3	4	14:17	0	60	0	0	0	26	3.8
R	38	Jordan Caron	BOS	17	1	2	3	9:24	1	4	0	0	0	20	5.0
C	34	Carl Soderberg	BOS	6	0	2	2	14:43	–2	6	0	0	0	6	0.0
D	43 *	Matt Bartkowski	BOS	11	0	2	2	13:29	0	6	0	0	0	9	0.0
D	47 *	Torey Krug	BOS	1	0	1	1	15:47	–1	0	0	0	0	0	0.0
R	68	Jamie Tardif	BOS	2	0	0	0	4:55	0	0	0	0	0	1	0.0
C	51 *	Ryan Spooner	BOS	4	0	0	0	9:07	0	0	0	0	0	4	0.0
D	45	Aaron Johnson	BOS	10	0	0	0	14:52	0	10	0	0	0	8	0.0
L	29	Jay Pandolfo	BOS	18	0	0	0	9:04	–2	2	0	0	0	11	0.0

Goaltending

No.	Goaltender	GPI	Mins	Avg	W	L	OT	EN	SO	GA	SA	S%	G	A	PIM
40	Tuukka Rask	36	2104	2.00	19	10	5	5	5	70	980	.929	0	1	0
35	Anton Khudobin	14	803	2.32	9	4	1	0	1	31	388	.920	0	0	4
	Totals	**48**	**2923**	**2.18**	**28**	**14**	**6**	**5**	**6**	**106**	**1373**	**.923**			

Playoffs

Pos	#	Player	Team	GP	G	A	Pts	TOI	+/–	PIM	PP	SH	GW	OT	S	%
C	46	David Krejci	BOS	22	9	17	26	22:15	13	14	1	0	2	1	56	16.1
R	18	Nathan Horton	BOS	22	7	12	19	18:29	20	14	2	0	3	0	38	18.4
L	17	Milan Lucic	BOS	22	7	12	19	20:56	12	14	0	0	0	0	42	16.7
C	37	Patrice Bergeron	BOS	22	9	6	15	20:43	2	13	4	0	2	2	71	12.7
D	33	Zdeno Chara	BOS	22	3	12	15	29:31	7	20	0	0	0	0	55	5.5
C	63	Brad Marchand	BOS	22	4	9	13	19:34	4	21	0	0	1	1	57	7.0
R	68	Jaromir Jagr	BOS	22	0	10	10	17:55	–1	8	0	0	0	0	58	0.0
L	20	Daniel Paille	BOS	22	4	5	9	12:31	4	0	0	1	3	1	27	14.8
C	19	Tyler Seguin	BOS	22	1	7	8	16:03	–2	4	0	0	0	0	70	1.4
D	55	Johnny Boychuk	BOS	22	6	1	7	23:55	4	10	0	0	1	0	63	9.5
C	11	Gregory Campbell	BOS	15	3	4	7	11:35	7	11	0	0	1	0	20	15.0
D	47 *	Torey Krug	BOS	15	4	2	6	15:49	5	0	3	0	0	0	34	11.8
D	54	Adam McQuaid	BOS	22	2	2	4	14:46	9	10	0	0	1	0	11	18.2
L	22	Shawn Thornton	BOS	22	0	4	4	7:20	3	18	0	0	0	0	26	0.0
C	23	Chris Kelly	BOS	22	2	1	3	15:40	–7	19	0	0	0	0	26	7.7
D	27 *	Dougie Hamilton	BOS	7	0	3	3	15:47	0	0	0	0	0	0	11	0.0
C	49	Rich Peverley	BOS	21	2	0	2	14:42	–8	12	1	0	0	0	35	5.7
D	6	Wade Redden	BOS	5	1	1	2	15:48	2	0	0	0	0	0	9	11.1
D	43 *	Matt Bartkowski	BOS	7	1	1	2	19:46	–1	4	0	0	0	0	12	8.3
D	21	Andrew Ference	BOS	14	0	2	2	24:31	2	4	0	0	0	0	19	0.0
D	44	Dennis Seidenberg	BOS	18	0	1	1	25:59	1	4	0	0	0	0	30	0.0
C	34	Carl Soderberg	BOS	2	0	0	0	12:15	0	0	0	0	0	0	3	0.0
L	16	Kaspars Daugavins	BOS	6	0	0	0	8:47	–1	2	0	0	0	0	9	0.0

Goaltending

No.	Goaltender	GPI	Mins	Avg	W	L	EN	SO	GA	SA	S%	G	A	PIM
40	Tuukka Rask	22	1466	1.88	14	8	1	3	46	761	.940	0	0	0
	Totals	**22**	**1473**	**1.91**	**14**	**8**	**1**	**3**	**47**	**762**	**.938**			

Coaching Record

			Regular Season				Playoffs			
Season	Team	League	GC	W	L	O/T	GC	W	L	T
1996-97	Hull	QMJHL	70	48	19	3	14	12	2	....
1996-97	Hull	M-Cup	....	....	....	....	5	3	2	....
1997-98	Hull	QMJHL	70	32	37	1	11	6	5	....
1998-99	Hull	QMJHL	70	23	38	9	23	15	8	....
99-2000	Hull	QMJHL	72	42	24	6	15	9	6	....
2000-01	Hamilton	AHL	80	28	41	11	....	....	....	....
2001-02	Hamilton	AHL	80	37	30	13	15	10	5	....
2002-03	Hamilton	AHL	45	33	9	3	....	....	....	....
2002-03	**Montreal**	**NHL**	**36**	**12**	**16**	**8**	....	....	....	....
2003-04	**Montreal**	**NHL**	**82**	**41**	**30**	**11**	**11**	**4**	**7**	....
2004-05	**Montreal**				SEASON CANCELLED					
2005-06	**Montreal**	**NHL**	**41**	**19**	**16**	**6**	....	....	....	....
2006-07	**New Jersey**	**NHL**	**79**	**47**	**24**	**8**	....	....	....	....
2007-08	**Boston**	**NHL**	**82**	**41**	**29**	**12**	**7**	**3**	**4**	....
2008-09	**Boston**	**NHL**	**82**	**53**	**19**	**19**	**11**	**7**	**4**	....
2009-10	**Boston**	**NHL**	**82**	**39**	**30**	**13**	**13**	**7**	**6**	....
2010-11♦	**Boston**	**NHL**	**82**	**46**	**25**	**11**	**25**	**16**	**9**	....
2011-12	**Boston**	**NHL**	**82**	**49**	**29**	**4**	**7**	**3**	**4**	....
2012-13	**Boston**	**NHL**	**48**	**28**	**14**	**6**	**22**	**14**	**8**	....
	NHL Totals		**696**	**375**	**232**	**98**	**96**	**54**	**42**	....

♦ Stanley Cup win.
Jack Adams Award (2009)

Club Records

Team

(Figures in brackets for season records are games played; records for fewest points, wins, ties, losses, goals, goals against are for 70 or more games)

Most Points	**121**	1970-71 (78)
Most Wins	**57**	1970-71 (78)
Most Ties	**21**	1954-55 (70)
Most Losses	**47**	1961-62 (70), 1996-97 (82)
Most Goals	**399**	1970-71 (78)
Most Goals Against	**306**	1961-62 (70)
Fewest Points	**38**	1961-62 (70)
Fewest Wins	**14**	1962-63 (70)
Fewest Ties	**5**	1972-73 (78)
Fewest Losses	**13**	1971-72 (78)
Fewest Goals	**147**	1955-56 (70)
Fewest Goals Against	**172**	1952-53 (70)
Longest Winning Streak		
Overall	**14**	Dec. 3/29-Jan. 9/30
Home	**20**	Dec. 3/29-Mar. 18/30
Away	**8**	Feb. 17-Mar. 8/72, Mar. 15-Apr. 14/93
Longest Undefeated Streak		
Overall	**23**	Dec. 22/40-Feb. 23/41 (15W, 8T)
Home	**27**	Nov. 22/70-Mar. 20/71 (26W, 1T)
Away	**15**	Dec. 22/40-Mar. 16/41 (9W, 6T)
Longest Losing Streak		
Overall	**11**	Dec. 3/24-Jan. 5/25
Home	**11**	Dec. 8/24-Feb. 17/25
Away	**14**	Dec. 27/64-Feb. 21/65
Longest Winless Streak		
Overall	**20**	Jan. 28-Mar. 11/62 (16L, 4T)
Home	**11**	Dec. 8/24-Feb. 17/25 (11L)
Away	**14**	Three times
Most Shutouts, Season	**15**	1927-28 (44)
Most PIM, Season	**2,443**	1987-88 (80)
Most Goals, Game	**14**	Jan. 21/45 (NYR 3 at Bos. 14)

Individual

Most Seasons	**21**	John Bucyk, Raymond Bourque
Most Games	**1,518**	Raymond Bourque
Most Goals, Career	**545**	John Bucyk
Most Assists, Career	**1,111**	Raymond Bourque
Most Points, Career	**1,506**	Raymond Bourque (395G, 1,111A)
Most PIM, Career	**2,095**	Terry O'Reilly
Most Shutouts, Career	**74**	Tiny Thompson
Longest Consecutive Games Streak	**418**	John Bucyk (Jan. 23/69-Mar. 2/75)
Most Goals, Season	**76**	Phil Esposito (1970-71)
Most Assists, Season	**102**	Bobby Orr (1970-71)
Most Points, Season	**152**	Phil Esposito (1970-71; 76G, 76A)
Most PIM, Season	**302**	Jay Miller (1987-88)
Most Points, Defenseman, Season	***139**	Bobby Orr (1970-71; 37G, 102A)
Most Points, Center, Season	**152**	Phil Esposito (1970-71; 76G, 76A)
Most Points, Right Wing, Season	**105**	Ken Hodge (1970-71; 43G, 62A), (1973-74; 50G, 55A) Rick Middleton (1983-84; 47G, 58A)
Most Points, Left Wing, Season	**116**	John Bucyk (1970-71; 51G, 65A)
Most Points, Rookie, Season	**102**	Joe Juneau (1992-93; 32G, 70A)
Most Shutouts, Season	**15**	Hal Winkler (1927-28)
Most Goals, Game	**4**	Twenty one times
Most Assists, Game	**6**	Ken Hodge (Feb. 9/71) Bobby Orr (Jan. 1/73)
Most Points, Game	**7**	Bobby Orr (Nov. 15/73; 3G, 4A) Phil Esposito (Dec. 19/74; 3G, 4A) Barry Pederson (Apr. 4/82; 3G, 4A) Cam Neely (Oct. 16/88; 3G, 4A)

* NHL Record.

Retired Numbers

2	Eddie Shore	1926-1940
3	Lionel Hitchman	1925-1934
4	Bobby Orr	1966-1976
5	Dit Clapper	1927-1947
7	Phil Esposito	1967-1975
8	Cam Neely	1986-1996
9	John Bucyk	1957-1978
15	Milt Schmidt	1936-1955
24	Terry O'Reilly	1971-1985
77	Raymond Bourque	1979-2000

All-time Record vs. Other Clubs

Regular Season

	Total								At Home								On Road							
	GP	W	L	T	OL	GF	GA	PTS	GP	W	L	T	OL	GF	GA	PTS	GP	W	L	T	OL	GF	GA	PTS
Anaheim	24	12	10	2	0	65	62	26	12	6	6	0	0	34	36	12	12	6	4	2	0	31	26	14
Buffalo	268	122	108	29	9	863	868	282	133	73	43	14	3	478	393	163	135	49	65	15	6	385	475	119
Calgary	97	54	32	10	1	341	299	119	50	31	12	6	1	182	132	69	47	23	20	4	0	159	167	50
Carolina	185	97	70	16	2	633	548	212	93	53	32	7	1	320	246	114	92	44	38	9	1	313	302	98
Chicago	578	261	235	79	3	1817	1754	604	288	164	90	34	0	1036	817	362	290	97	145	45	3	781	937	242
Colorado	134	69	49	15	1	526	443	154	65	31	24	9	1	243	199	72	69	38	25	6	0	283	244	82
Columbus	12	7	3	0	2	40	26	16	5	3	2	0	0	14	11	6	7	4	1	0	2	26	15	10
Dallas	127	74	28	23	2	496	335	173	63	43	9	10	1	270	152	97	64	31	19	13	1	226	183	76
Detroit	579	235	246	95	3	1743	1735	568	291	155	91	43	2	1015	774	355	288	80	155	52	1	728	961	213
Edmonton	65	42	17	6	0	243	187	90	33	24	6	3	0	137	83	51	32	18	11	3	0	106	104	39
Florida	74	36	28	6	4	207	191	82	38	16	15	4	3	102	87	39	36	20	13	2	1	105	104	43
Los Angeles	131	80	34	13	4	536	409	177	66	45	12	6	3	297	185	99	65	35	22	7	1	239	224	78
Minnesota	12	2	10	0	0	16	35	4	6	0	6	0	0	6	19	0	6	2	4	0	0	10	16	4
Montreal	721	270	340	103	8	1909	2185	651	361	165	135	56	5	1064	980	391	360	105	205	47	3	845	1205	260
Nashville	17	9	4	1	3	45	40	22	8	5	2	1	0	24	15	11	9	4	2	0	3	21	25	11
New Jersey	140	74	37	19	10	474	381	177	72	40	18	8	6	262	210	94	68	34	19	11	4	212	171	83
NY Islanders	151	77	49	21	4	520	445	179	75	42	20	11	2	273	204	97	76	35	29	10	2	247	241	82
NY Rangers	631	285	240	97	9	1985	1839	676	314	166	100	42	6	1103	871	380	317	119	140	55	3	882	968	296
Ottawa	117	69	33	8	7	372	289	153	60	36	18	5	1	199	154	78	57	33	15	3	6	173	135	75
Philadelphia	180	94	59	21	6	591	534	215	91	52	24	11	4	320	251	119	89	42	35	10	2	271	283	96
Phoenix	67	39	20	7	1	251	208	86	33	22	6	4	1	140	101	49	34	17	14	3	0	111	107	37
Pittsburgh	189	103	60	21	5	727	587	232	93	62	22	6	3	389	261	133	96	41	38	15	2	338	326	99
St. Louis	125	61	39	18	7	467	370	147	62	35	15	9	3	253	172	82	63	26	24	9	4	214	198	65
San Jose	28	14	9	5	0	88	77	33	14	7	4	3	0	45	43	17	14	7	5	2	0	43	34	16
Tampa Bay	77	48	20	9	0	261	201	105	39	29	4	6	0	149	87	64	38	19	16	3	0	112	114	41
Toronto	649	287	256	98	8	1919	1929	680	324	179	95	47	3	1064	859	408	325	108	161	51	5	855	1070	272
Vancouver	109	68	25	15	1	439	303	152	55	39	8	7	1	224	131	86	54	29	17	8	0	215	172	66
Washington	142	74	39	21	8	481	392	177	71	41	18	9	3	248	186	94	71	33	21	12	5	233	206	83
Winnipeg	51	30	15	2	4	164	150	66	25	17	4	2	2	92	74	38	26	13	11	0	2	72	76	28
Defunct Clubs	328	191	106	31	0	1021	746	413	164	112	39	13	0	525	306	237	164	79	67	18	0	496	440	176
Totals	**6008**	**2884**	**2221**	**791**	**112**	**19240**	**17568**	**6671**	**3004**	**1693**	**880**	**376**	**55**	**10508**	**8039**	**3817**	**3004**	**1191**	**1341**	**415**	**57**	**8732**	**9529**	**2854**

Playoffs

	Series	W	L	GP	W	L	T	GF	GA	Last Mtg.	Rnd.	Result
Buffalo	8	6	2	45	25	20	0	155	145	2010	CQF	W 4-2
Carolina	4	3	1	26	15	11	0	80	64	2009	CSF	L 3-4
Chicago	7	5	2	28	18	9	1	112	80	2013	F	L 2-4
Colorado	2	1	1	11	6	5	0	37	36	1983	DSF	W 3-1
Dallas	1	0	1	3	0	3	0	13	20	1981	PRE	L 0-3
Detroit	7	4	3	33	19	14	0	96	98	1957	SF	W 4-1
Edmonton	2	0	2	9	1	8	0	20	41	1990	F	L 1-4
Florida	1	0	1	5	1	4	0	16	22	1996	CQF	L 1-4
Los Angeles	2	2	0	13	8	5	0	56	38	1977	QF	W 4-2
Montreal	33	9	24	170	68	102	0	420	511	2011	CQF	W 4-3
New Jersey	4	1	3	23	8	15	0	60	68	2003	CQF	L 1-4
NY Islanders	2	0	2	11	3	8	0	35	49	1983	CF	L 2-4
NY Rangers	10	7	3	47	26	19	2	130	114	2013	CSF	W 4-1
Philadelphia	6	3	3	31	18	13	0	100	86	2011	CSF	W 4-0
Pittsburgh	5	3	2	23	13	10	0	74	69	2013	CF	W 4-0
St. Louis	2	2	0	8	8	0	0	48	15	1972	SF	W 4-0
Tampa Bay	1	1	0	7	4	3	0	21	21	2011	CF	W 4-3
Toronto	14	6	8	69	34	34	1	175	168	2013	CQF	W 4-3
Vancouver	1	1	0	7	4	3	0	23	8	2011	F	W 4-3
Washington	3	1	2	17	9	8	0	43	37	2012	CQF	L 3-4
Defunct Clubs	3	1	2	11	4	5	2	20	20			
Totals	**118**	**56**	**62**	**597**	**292**	**299**	**6**	**1734**	**1710**			

Calgary totals include Atlanta Flames, 1972-73 to 1979-80.
Carolina totals include Hartford, 1979-80 to 1996-97.
Colorado totals include Quebec, 1979-80 to 1994-95.
Dallas totals include Minnesota North Stars, 1967-68 to 1992-93.
New Jersey totals include Kansas City, 1974-75, 1975-76, and Colorado Rockies, 1976-77 to 1981-82.
Phoenix totals include Winnipeg, 1979-80 to 1995-96.
Winnipeg totals include Atlanta Thrashers, 1999-2000 to 2010-11.

Playoff Results 2013-2009

Year	Round	Opponent	Result	GF	GA
2013	F	Chicago	L 2-4	15	17
	CF	Pittsburgh	W 4-0	12	2
	CSF	NY Rangers	W 4-1	16	10
	CQF	Toronto	W 4-3	22	18
2012	CQF	Washington	L 3-4	15	16
2011	**F**	**Vancouver**	**W 4-3**	**23**	**8**
	CF	Tampa Bay	W 4-3	21	21
	CSF	Philadelphia	W 4-0	20	7
	CQF	Montreal	W 4-3	17	17
2010	CSF	Philadelphia	L 3-4	20	22
	CQF	Buffalo	W 4-2	16	15
2009	CSF	Carolina	L 3-4	17	16
	CQF	Montreal	W 4-0	17	6

Abbreviations: Round: F – Final; **CF** – conference final; **CSF** – conference semi-final; **CQF** – conference quarter-final; **DSF** – division semi-final; **SF** – semi-final; **QF** – quarter-final; **PRE** – preliminary round.

2012-13 Results

Jan.	19	NY Rangers	3-1
	21	Winnipeg	2-1†
	23	at NY Rangers	3-4*
	25	NY Islanders	4-2
	28	at Carolina	5-3
	29	New Jersey	2-1†
	31	Buffalo	4-7
Feb.	2	at Toronto	1-0
	6	at Montreal	2-1
	10	at Buffalo	3-1
	12	NY Rangers	3-4†
	15	at Buffalo	2-4
	17	at Winnipeg	3-2
	21	at Tampa Bay	4-2
	24	at Florida	4-1
	26	at NY Islanders	4-1
	28	Ottawa	2-1*
Mar.	2	Tampa Bay	3-2
	3	Montreal	3-4
	5	at Washington	3-4*
	7	Toronto	4-2
	9	Philadelphia	3-0
	11	at Ottawa	3-2†
	12	at Pittsburgh	2-3
	14	Florida	4-1
	16	Washington	4-1
	17	at Pittsburgh	1-2
	19	at Winnipeg	1-3
	21	at Ottawa	2-1
	23	at Toronto	2-3
	25	Toronto	3-2†
	27	Montreal	5-6†
	30	at Philadelphia	1-3
	31	at Buffalo	2-0
Apr.	2	Ottawa	3-2
	4	New Jersey	1-0
	6	at Montreal	1-2
	8	Carolina	6-2
	10	at New Jersey	5-4
	11	NY Islanders	1-2
	13	at Carolina	2-4
	17	Buffalo	2-3†
	20	Pittsburgh	2-3
	21	Florida	3-0
	23	at Philadelphia	2-5
	25	Tampa Bay	2-0
	27	at Washington	2-3*
	28	Ottawa	2-4

* – Overtime † – Shootout

Entry Draft Selections 2013-1999

Name in bold denotes played in NHL.

2013
Pick
60 Linus Arnesson
90 Peter Cehlarik
120 Ryan Fitzgerald
150 Wiley Sherman
180 Anton Blidh
210 Mitchell Dempsey

2012
Pick
24 Malcolm Subban
85 Matthew Grzelcyk
131 Seth Griffith
145 Cody Payne
175 Matthew Benning
205 Colton Hargrove

2011
Pick
9 **Dougie Hamilton**
40 Alexander Khokhlachev
81 Anthony Camara
121 Brian Ferlin
151 Rob O'Gara
181 Lars Volden

2010
Pick
2 **Tyler Seguin**
32 Jared Knight
45 **Ryan Spooner**
97 Craig Cunningham
135 Justin Florek
165 Zane Gothberg
195 Maxim Chudinov
210 Zach Trotman

2009
Pick
25 **Jordan Caron**
86 Ryan Button
112 **Lane MacDermid**
176 Tyler Randell
206 Ben Sexton

2008
Pick
16 **Joe Colborne**
47 **Max Sauve**
77 Michael Hutchinson
97 **Jamie Arniel**
173 Nick Tremblay
197 Mark Goggin

2007
Pick
8 **Zach Hamill**
35 Tommy Cross
130 Denis Reul
159 Alain Goulet
169 Radim Ostrcil
189 Jordan Knackstedt

2006
Pick
5 **Phil Kessel**
37 Yury Alexandrov
50 **Milan Lucic**
71 **Brad Marchand**
128 **Andrew Bodnarchuk**
158 Levi Nelson

2005
Pick
22 **Matt Lashoff**
39 **Petr Kalus**
83 **Mikko Lehtonen**
100 **Jonathan Sigalet**
106 **Vladimir Sobotka**
154 Wacey Rabbit
172 Lukas Vantuch
217 Brock Bradford

2004
Pick
63 **David Krejci**
64 **Martins Karsums**
108 Ashton Rome
134 **Kris Versteeg**
160 **Ben Walter**
224 **Matt Hunwick**
255 Anton Hedman

2003
Pick
21 **Mark Stuart**
45 **Patrice Bergeron**
66 **Masi Marjamaki**
107 **Byron Bitz**
118 Frank Rediker
129 Patrik Valcak
153 Mike Brown
183 **Nate Thompson**
247 Benoit Mondou
277 Kevin Regan

2002
Pick
29 **Hannu Toivonen**
56 Vladislav Yevseyev
130 Jan Kubista
153 Peter Hamerlik
228 Dmitri Utkin
259 **Yan Stastny**
290 Pavel Frolov

2001
Pick
19 **Shaone Morrisonn**
77 Darren McLachlan
111 Matti Kaltiainen
147 Jiri Jakes
179 **Andrew Alberts**
209 **Jordan Sigalet**
241 **Milan Jurcina**
282 Marcel Rodman

2000
Pick
7 **Lars Jonsson**
27 **Martin Samuelsson**
37 **Andy Hilbert**
59 **Ivan Huml**
66 Tuukka Makela
73 **Sergei Zinovjev**
103 Brett Nowak
174 **Jarno Kultanen**
204 Chris Berti
237 **Zdenek Kutlak**
268 **Pavel Kolarik**
279 Andreas Lindstrom

1999
Pick
21 **Nick Boynton**
56 Matt Zultek
89 **Kyle Wanvig**
118 Jaakko Harikkala
147 Seamus Kotyk
179 Donald Choukalos
207 Greg Barber
236 John Cronin
247 **Mikko Eloranta**
264 Georgy Pujacs

Captains' History

No captain, 1924-25 to 1926-27; Lionel Hitchman, 1927-28 to 1930-31; George Owen, 1931-32; Dit Clapper, 1932-33 to 1937-38; Cooney Weiland, 1938-39; Dit Clapper, 1939-40 to 1945-46; Dit Clapper and John Crawford, 1946-47; John Crawford 1947-48 to 1949-50; Milt Schmidt, 1950-51 to 1953-54; Milt Schmidt, Ed Sanford, 1954-55; Fern Flaman, 1955-56 to 1960-61; Don McKenney, 1961-62, 1962-63; Leo Boivin, 1963-64 to 1965-66; John Bucyk, 1966-67; no captain, 1967-68 to 1972-73; John Bucyk, 1973-74 to 1976-77; Wayne Cashman, 1977-78 to 1982-83; Terry O'Reilly, 1983-84, 1984-85; Raymond Bourque, Rick Middleton (co-captains) 1985-86 to 1987-88; Raymond Bourque, 1988-89 to 1999-2000; Jason Allison, 2000-01; no captain, 2001-02; Joe Thornton, 2002-03 to 2004-05; Joe Thornton and no captain, 2005-06; Zdeno Chara, 2006-07 to date.

General Managers' History

Art Ross, 1924-25 to 1953-54; Lynn Patrick, 1954-55 to 1964-65; Hap Emms, 1965-66, 1966-67; Milt Schmidt, 1967-68 to 1971-72; Harry Sinden, 1972-73 to 1999-2000; Harry Sinden and Mike O'Connell, 2000-01; Mike O'Connell, 2001-02 to 2004-05; Mike O'Connell and Jeff Gorton, 2005-06; Peter Chiarelli, 2006-07 to date.

Peter Chiarelli

General Manager

Born: Nepean, Ont., August 5, 1964.

Peter Chiarelli became just the seventh man in club history to hold the position of general manager when he was named to the post on May 26, 2006. He officially began his position in Boston on July 10, 2006 as a result of a league-arbitrated compensation agreement that saw the Bruins surrender a third-round draft pick in the 2006 NHL Entry Draft (Eric Gryba, 68th overall) to the Ottawa Senators. By his third season in Boston in 2008-09, the Bruins posted the best record in the Eastern Conference and were second overall in the NHL. In 2010-11, Boston won the Stanley Cup for the first time since 1972. The Bruins reached the Stanley Cup final again in 2013.

Chiarelli came to the Bruins after seven seasons with the Ottawa Senators, five as the director of legal relations and the last two as assistant general manager. He was involved in all aspects of that team's hockey operations, including contract research and negotiations, salary arbitration and all player personnel matters. He was also involved in overseeing Ottawa's top developmental affiliate, the Binghamton Senators of the American Hockey League. The Senators had four 100+ point seasons during his tenure and never finished below 94 points, finished with the NHL's top record in 2002-03 (113 points) and the best record in the Eastern Conference in 2005-06 (113 points).

A native of the Ottawa area, Chiarelli played four seasons of college hockey at Harvard University where he served the team as captain and was a teammate of former Bruin Don Sweeney. He had 21 goals and 28 assists for 49 points with 70 penalty minutes in 109 career college games and earned his degree in Economics in 1987. He played professionally in Europe for one year before returning to school and obtaining his law degree from the University of Ottawa. He was admitted to the Ontario bar in 1993 and spent six years as a lawyer and player agent prior to joining the Senators front office in 1999.

Club Directory

TD Garden

Boston Bruins
TD Garden
100 Legends Way
Boston, MA 02114
Phone **617/624-BEAR (2327)**
FAX 617/523-7184
www.bostonbruins.com
Capacity: 17,565

Ownership

Owner & Governor, Boston Bruins; Chairman, NHL Board of Governors	Jeremy M. Jacobs
Principal, Boston Bruins	Charlie Jacobs
Alternate Governors	Charlie Jacobs, Jeremy Jacobs, Jr., Louis Jacobs, Harry Sinden, Peter Chiarelli, Cam Neely
Senior Advisor to the Owner	Harry Sinden

Executive

President	Cam Neely
Sr. Vice President, Sales	Glen Thornborough
Vice President, Finance	Jim Bednarek
Vice President, Marketing	Jen Compton
Vice President, Communications & Content	Matthew Chmura
Vice President, Corporate Partnerships	Chris Johnson
Vice President, Premium Sales & Service	Leah Leahy
Director of Administration	Dale Hamilton-Powers
Executive Assistants	Rita Brandano, Maria Poirier
Administrative Assistant	Karen Ondo

Hockey Operations

General Manager	Peter Chiarelli
Assistant General Managers	Jim Benning, Don Sweeney
Director of Player Personnel	Scott Bradley
Director of Amateur Scouting	TBA
Assistant Director of Amateur Scouting	Scott Fitzgerald
Scouting Staff	Mike Chiarelli, Adam Creighton, Keith Gretzky, Jukka Holtari, Denis LeBlanc, Dean Malkoc, Mike McGraw, Tom McVie, Svenake Svensson
Director of Hockey Administration & Scout	Ryan Nadeau
Assistant to Hockey Administration	Cole Burkhalter
Team Road Services Coordinator	John Bucyk

Coaching

Head Coach	Claude Julien
Assistant Coaches	Doug Houda, Geoff Ward, Doug Jarvis
Goaltending Coach	Bob Essensa
Video Analyst	Jeremy Rogalski

Medical, Training and Equipment

Strength & Conditioning Coach	John Whitesides
Athletic Trainer	Don DelNegro
Physical Therapist	Scott Waugh
Assistant Athletic Trainer & Massage Therapist	Derek Repucci
Equipment Manager	Keith Robinson
Assistant Equipment Managers	Jim 'Beets' Johnson, Matt Falconer
Head Team Physician/Orthopedist	Dr. Peter Asnis
Team Internist	Dr. David Judge

Communications

Assistant Director of Media Relations	Eric Tosi
Director of Publications & Information	Heidi Holland
Digital Content Specialist	Caryn Switaj
Web Video Producer	Jonathan Gotlib
Communications Specialist	Erika Wentzell
Content Specialist	Brandon McNelis

Marketing and Community Relations

Director of Marketing	Chris DiPierro
Director of Community Relations	Kerry Collins
Director of Interactive	Darrell Wood
Digital Marketing Manager	Liz d'Entremont
Digital Content Producer	Michael Berger
Strategic Marketing Manager	Rachel Markovitz
Creative Marketing Manager	Brandon Anthony
Youth Hockey Development Manager	Mike Dargin
Coordinators, Marketing / Promotions	Renee Riva / Andrea Mazzarelli
Community Relations Coordinator	Ashley Hansen
Graphic Designer	Jason Petrie
Digital Marketing Designer	Matt Hunter

Boston Bruins Foundation and Alumni Office

Executive Director, Bruins Foundation	Bob Sweeney
Foundation Manager / Coordinator	Erin McEvoy / Zack Fitzgerald
Boston Bruins Alumni Coordinator	Mal Viola

Sales, Fan Relations and Retail

Client Services Manager, The Premium Club	Tamala Levin
Director of Ticket Sales	Mark Rodrigues
Retail Director	Lauma Cerlins
Business Analyst	Mark Steffan
Ticket Sales Manager	Chad Cardinal
Fan Relations Manager	John Cadigan
Season Sales Account Executives	Matt Gulley, Kevin Stone, Tina Zettel
Group Sales Account Executives	Rachel Hansen, Briana Lynch, Caillin Miller
Fan Relations Representatives	Chris Gutierrez,Ben Papapietro, Keith Ricci, Kaitlin Rowe, Erin Silva, Richard Yutkins

Finance, Legal, Human Resources and Box Office

Controller	Rick McGlinchey
Staff Accountant	Linda Bartlett
Accounting Manager / Coordinator	Wesley Dauer / Rick McGlinchey, Jr.
Payroll & Benefits Manager	Botin Bou-James
Assistant General Counsel	Matt Reece
Legal Assistant	Binnie Hundley
Human Resources Director / Manager	Shauna K. Gilhooly / Kate Green
Director of Box Office	Matthew Whelan
Assistant Director of Ticket Operations	Jim Foley
Assistant Box Office Manager	Courtney McNeice
Ticket Office Receptionist	Jo-Ann Connolly-White

Broadcasting

TV Rightsholder	New England Sports Network (NESN)
Radio play-by-play / analyst	Jack Edwards / Andy Brickley

Buffalo Sabres

Key Off-Season Signings/Acquisitions

2013

May 20 • Re-signed LW **John Scott**.
June 20 • Re-signed G **Jhonas Enroth**.
27 • Re-signed D **Mike Weber**.
30 • Acquired D **Jamie McBain** and a 2nd-round pick (J.T. Compher) in the 2013 NHL Draft from Carolina for D **Andrej Sekera**.
July 2 • Named **Joe Sacco** assistant coach.
3 • Re-signed LW **Matt Ellis**.
6 • Re-signed D **Alexander Sulzer**.
23 • Re-signed C **Luke Adam** and G **Matt Hackett**.

2012-13 Results: 21W-21L-2OTL-4SOL 48PTS
5TH, Northeast Division • 12TH, Eastern Conference

Christian Ehrhoff suited up in 47 of 48 games for Buffalo in 2012-13 and was among the NHL's busiest defensemen with a career-high average of 25:11 minutes of ice time per game.

2013-14 Schedule

Month	Day	Date	Opponent
Oct.	Wed.	2	at Detroit
	Fri.	4	Ottawa
	Sat.	5	at Pittsburgh
	Tue.	8	Tampa Bay
	Thu.	10	Columbus
	Sat.	12	at Chicago
	Mon.	14	Minnesota
	Tue.	15	at NY Islanders
	Thu.	17	Vancouver
	Sat.	19	Colorado
	Wed.	23	Boston
	Fri.	25	at Florida
	Sat.	26	at Tampa Bay
	Mon.	28	Dallas
	Thu.	31	at NY Rangers
Nov.	Sat.	2	Anaheim
	Tue.	5	at San Jose
	Thu.	7	at Los Angeles
	Fri.	8	at Anaheim
	Tue.	12	Los Angeles
	Fri.	15	Toronto
	Sat.	16	at Toronto
	Tue.	19	St. Louis
	Thu.	21	at Philadelphia
	Sun.	24	Detroit*
	Wed.	27	Montreal
	Fri.	29	Toronto
	Sat.	30	at New Jersey
Dec.	Thu.	5	NY Rangers
	Sat.	7	at Montreal
	Tue.	10	Ottawa
	Thu.	12	at Ottawa
	Sat.	14	Calgary*
	Tue.	17	Winnipeg
	Thu.	19	Boston
	Sat.	21	at Boston
	Mon.	23	Phoenix
	Fri.	27	at Toronto
	Sun.	29	Washington*
	Tue.	31	at Winnipeg
Jan.	Thu.	2	at Minnesota
	Sat.	4	New Jersey
	Tue.	7	Carolina
	Thu.	9	Florida
	Sun.	12	at Washington*
	Tue.	14	Philadelphia
	Wed.	15	at Toronto
	Sat.	18	Columbus
	Tue.	21	Florida
	Thu.	23	Carolina
	Sat.	25	at Columbus
	Mon.	27	at Pittsburgh
	Tue.	28	Washington
	Thu.	30	at Phoenix
Feb.	Sat.	1	at Colorado*
	Mon.	3	Edmonton
	Wed.	5	Pittsburgh
	Thu.	6	at Ottawa
	Wed.	26	Boston
	Fri.	28	San Jose
Mar.	Mon.	3	at Dallas
	Thu.	6	at Tampa Bay
	Fri.	7	at Florida
	Sun.	9	Chicago
	Tue.	11	Nashville
	Thu.	13	at Carolina
	Sat.	15	at NY Islanders
	Sun.	16	Montreal
	Tue.	18	at Calgary
	Thu.	20	at Edmonton
	Sun.	23	at Vancouver*
	Tue.	25	at Montreal
	Thu.	27	at Nashville
	Sat.	29	Tampa Bay
Apr.	Tue.	1	New Jersey
	Thu.	3	at St. Louis
	Fri.	4	at Detroit
	Sun.	6	at Philadelphia
	Tue.	8	Detroit
	Thu.	10	at NY Rangers
	Sat.	12	at Boston*
	Sun.	13	NY Islanders*

* Denotes afternoon game.

Year-by-Year Record

		Home				Road				Overall									
Season	**GP**	**W**	**L**	**T**	**OL**	**W**	**L**	**T**	**OL**	**W**	**L**	**T**	**OL**	**GF**	**GA**	**Pts.**	**Div. Fin.**	**Conf. Fin.**	**Playoff Result**
2012-13	48	11	10	....	3	10	11	....	3	21	21	....	6	125	143	48	5th, NE	12th, East	Out of Playoffs
2011-12	82	21	12	....	8	18	20	....	3	39	32	....	11	218	230	89	3rd, NE	9th, East	Out of Playoffs
2010-11	82	21	16	....	4	22	13	....	6	43	29	....	10	245	229	96	3rd, NE	7th, East	Lost Conf. Quarter-Final
2009-10	82	25	10	....	6	20	17	....	4	45	27	....	10	235	207	100	1st, NE	3rd, East	Lost Conf. Quarter-Final
2008-09	82	23	15	....	3	18	17	....	6	41	32	....	9	250	234	91	3rd, NE	10th, East	Out of Playoffs
2007-08	82	20	15	....	6	19	16	....	6	39	31	....	12	255	242	90	4th, NE	10th, East	Out of Playoffs
2006-07	82	28	10	....	3	25	12	....	4	53	22	....	7	308	242	113	1st, NE	1st, East	Lost Conf. Final
2005-06	82	27	11	....	3	25	13	....	3	52	24	....	6	281	239	110	2nd, NE	4th, East	Lost Conf. Final
2004-05	....	....	....	....	....	....	....	....	....	....	....	....	....	....	....	....			
2003-04	82	21	13	4	3	16	21	3	1	37	34	7	4	220	221	85	5th, NE	9th, East	Out of Playoffs
2002-03	82	18	16	5	2	9	21	5	6	27	37	10	8	190	219	72	5th, NE	12th, East	Out of Playoffs
2001-02	82	20	16	5	0	15	19	6	1	35	35	11	1	213	200	82	5th, NE	10th, East	Out of Playoffs
2000-01	82	26	12	3	0	20	18	2	1	46	30	5	1	218	184	98	2nd, NE	5th, East	Lost Conf. Semi-Final
1999-2000	82	21	14	5	1	14	18	6	3	35	32	11	4	213	204	85	3rd, NE	8th, East	Lost Conf. Quarter-Final
1998-99	82	23	12	6	....	14	16	11	....	37	28	17	....	207	175	91	4th, NE	7th, East	Lost Final
1997-98	82	20	13	8	....	16	16	9	....	36	29	17	....	211	187	89	3rd, NE	6th, East	Lost Conf. Final
1996-97	82	24	11	6	....	16	19	6	....	40	30	12	....	237	208	92	1st, NE	3rd, East	Lost Conf. Semi-Final
1995-96	82	19	17	5	....	14	25	2	....	33	42	7	....	247	262	73	5th, NE	11th, East	Out of Playoffs
1994-95	48	15	8	1	....	7	11	6	....	22	19	7	....	130	119	51	4th, NE	7th, East	Lost Conf. Quarter-Final
1993-94	84	22	17	3	....	21	15	6	....	43	32	9	....	282	218	95	4th, NE	6th, East	Lost Conf. Quarter-Final
1992-93	84	25	15	2	....	13	21	8	....	38	36	10	....	335	297	86	4th, Adams		Lost Div. Final
1991-92	80	22	13	5	....	9	24	7	....	31	37	12	....	289	299	74	3rd, Adams		Lost Div. Semi-Final
1990-91	80	15	13	12	....	16	17	7	....	31	30	19	....	292	278	81	3rd, Adams		Lost Div. Semi-Final
1989-90	80	27	11	2	....	18	16	6	....	45	27	8	....	286	248	98	2nd, Adams		Lost Div. Semi-Final
1988-89	80	25	12	3	....	13	23	4	....	38	35	7	....	291	299	83	3rd, Adams		Lost Div. Semi-Final
1987-88	80	19	14	7	....	18	18	4	....	37	32	11	....	283	305	85	3rd, Adams		Lost Div. Semi-Final
1986-87	80	18	18	4	....	10	26	4	....	28	44	8	....	280	308	64	5th, Adams		Out of Playoffs
1985-86	80	23	16	1	....	14	21	5	....	37	37	6	....	296	291	80	5th, Adams		Out of Playoffs
1984-85	80	23	10	7	....	15	18	7	....	38	28	14	....	290	237	90	3rd, Adams		Lost Div. Semi-Final
1983-84	80	25	9	6	....	23	16	1	....	48	25	7	....	315	257	103	2nd, Adams		Lost Div. Semi-Final
1982-83	80	25	7	8	....	13	22	5	....	38	29	13	....	318	285	89	3rd, Adams		Lost Div. Final
1981-82	80	23	8	9	....	16	18	6	....	39	26	15	....	307	273	93	3rd, Adams		Lost Div. Semi-Final
1980-81	80	21	7	12	....	18	13	9	....	39	20	21	....	327	250	99	1st, Adams		Lost Quarter-Final
1979-80	80	27	5	8	....	20	12	8	....	47	17	16	....	318	201	110	1st, Adams		Lost Semi-Final
1978-79	80	19	13	8	....	17	15	8	....	36	28	16	....	280	263	88	2nd, Adams		Lost Prelim. Round
1977-78	80	25	7	8	....	19	12	9	....	44	19	17	....	288	215	105	2nd, Adams		Lost Quarter-Final
1976-77	80	27	8	5	....	21	16	3	....	48	24	8	....	301	220	104	2nd, Adams		Lost Quarter-Final
1975-76	80	28	7	5	....	18	14	8	....	46	21	13	....	339	240	105	2nd, Adams		Lost Quarter-Final
1974-75	80	28	6	6	....	21	10	9	....	49	16	15	....	354	240	113	1st, Adams		Lost Final
1973-74	78	23	10	6	....	9	24	6	....	32	34	12	....	242	250	76	5th, East		Out of Playoffs
1972-73	78	30	6	3	....	7	21	11	....	37	27	14	....	257	219	88	4th, East		Lost Quarter-Final
1971-72	78	11	19	9	....	5	24	10	....	16	43	19	....	203	289	51	6th, East		Out of Playoffs
1970-71	78	16	13	10	....	8	26	5	....	24	39	15	....	217	291	63	5th, East		Out of Playoffs

ATLANTIC DIVISION
44th NHL Season

Franchise date: May 22, 1970

2013-14 Player Personnel

FORWARDS	HT	WT	*Age	Place of Birth	S	2012-13 Club
ENNIS, Tyler	5-9	157	23	Edmonton, Alta.	L	Langnau-Buffalo
FLYNN, Brian	6-1	185	25	Lynnfield, MA	R	Rochester-Buffalo
FOLIGNO, Marcus	6-2	215	22	Buffalo, NY	L	Rochester-Buffalo
GRIGORENKO, Mikhail	6-3	215	19	Khabarovsk, Russia	L	Quebec-Buf-Roch
HODGSON, Cody	6-0	185	23	Toronto, Ont.	R	Rochester-Buffalo
KALETA, Patrick	6-1	206	27	Buffalo, NY	R	Buffalo
LEINO, Ville	6-1	190	29	Savonlinna, Finland	L	Buffalo
McCORMICK, Cody	6-3	221	30	London, Ont.	R	Buffalo-Rochester
OTT, Steve	6-0	190	31	Summerside, P.E.I.	L	Buffalo
PORTER, Kevin	6-0	190	27	Detroit, MI	L	Rochester-Buffalo
SCOTT, John	6-8	270	31	St. Catharines, Ont.	L	Buffalo
STAFFORD, Drew	6-2	214	27	Milwaukee, WI	R	Buffalo
TROPP, Corey	6-0	183	24	Grosse Pointe, MI	R	Rochester
VANEK, Thomas	6-2	205	29	Vienna, Austria	R	Graz-Buffalo
DEFENSEMEN						
EHRHOFF, Christian	6-2	203	31	Moers, West Germany	L	Krefeld-Buffalo
McBAIN, Jamie	6-2	200	25	Edina, MN	R	Pelicans-Carolina
MYERS, Tyler	6-8	227	23	Houston, TX	R	Klagenfurt-Buffalo
PYSYK, Mark	6-1	195	21	Edmonton, Alta.	R	Rochester-Buffalo
SULZER, Alexander	6-1	204	29	Kaufbeuren, West Germany	L	Ingolstadt-Buffalo
TALLINDER, Henrik	6-4	215	34	Stockholm, Sweden	L	New Jersey
WEBER, Mike	6-2	211	25	Pittsburgh, PA	L	Lorenskog-Buffalo
GOALTENDERS	**HT**	**WT**	***Age**	**Place of Birth**	**C**	**2012-13 Club**
ENROTH, Jhonas	5-10	166	25	Stockholm, Sweden	L	Huddinge-Almtuna-Buffalo
MILLER, Ryan	6-2	175	33	East Lansing, MI	L	Buffalo

* – Age at start of 2013-14 season

2012-13 Scoring

* – rookie

Regular Season

Pos	#	Player	Team	GP	G	A	Pts	TOI	+/–	PIM	PP	SH	GW	S	%
L	26	Thomas Vanek	BUF	38	20	21	41	18:24	–1	20	9	1	2	119	16.8
C	19	Cody Hodgson	BUF	48	15	19	34	18:23	–4	20	3	1	1	114	13.2
C	63	Tyler Ennis	BUF	47	10	21	31	17:52	–14	16	2	0	0	108	9.3
C	9	Steve Ott	BUF	48	9	15	24	18:33	3	93	2	0	3	73	12.3
D	10	Christian Ehrhoff	BUF	47	5	17	22	25:11	6	34	1	0	2	102	4.9
R	21	Drew Stafford	BUF	46	6	12	18	17:01	–16	21	0	0	0	121	5.0
L	82 *	Marcus Foligno	BUF	47	5	13	18	13:37	–4	41	1	0	0	55	9.1
C	55	Jochen Hecht	BUF	47	5	9	14	13:41	6	18	0	1	1	69	7.2
D	44	Andrej Sekera	BUF	37	2	10	12	21:12	–2	4	0	0	0	33	6.1
C	65 *	Brian Flynn	BUF	26	6	5	11	14:40	6	0	0	1	1	49	12.2
C	42	Nathan Gerbe	BUF	42	5	5	10	12:30	–3	14	0	1	0	64	7.8
C	12	Kevin Porter	BUF	31	4	5	9	15:13	–1	10	0	1	0	37	10.8
D	57	Tyler Myers	BUF	39	3	5	8	21:18	–8	32	1	0	2	48	6.3
D	6	Mike Weber	BUF	42	1	6	7	18:21	3	70	0	0	0	25	4.0
L	23	Ville Leino	BUF	8	2	4	6	15:48	0	6	1	0	0	11	18.2
D	53 *	Mark Pysyk	BUF	19	1	4	5	16:16	–7	0	1	0	0	21	4.8
C	25 *	Mikhail Grigorenko	BUF	25	1	4	5	10:14	–1	0	0	0	0	31	3.2
D	52	Alexander Sulzer	BUF	17	3	1	4	16:31	3	10	0	0	1	15	20.0
D	27	Adam Pardy	BUF	17	0	4	4	16:30	4	14	0	0	0	6	0.0
C	72	Luke Adam	BUF	4	1	0	1	9:47	1	2	0	0	0	2	50.0
R	36	Patrick Kaleta	BUF	34	1	0	1	10:47	–4	67	0	0	0	34	2.9
L	37	Matt Ellis	BUF	6	0	0	0	6:11	0	0	0	0	0	8	0.0
D	5 *	Chad Ruhwedel	BUF	7	0	0	0	14:11	0	0	0	0	0	8	0.0
C	8	Cody McCormick	BUF	8	0	0	0	6:27	–2	10	0	0	0	6	0.0
L	32	John Scott	BUF	34	0	0	0	5:26	–1	69	0	0	0	15	0.0

Goaltending

No.	Goaltender	GPI	Mins	Avg	W	L	OT	EN	SO	GA	SA	S%	G	A	PIM
1	Jhonas Enroth	12	623	2.60	4	4	1	1	1	27	332	.919	0	0	0
30	Ryan Miller	40	2302	2.81	17	17	5	3	0	108	1270	.915	0	0	2
	Totals	**48**	**2946**	**2.83**	**21**	**21**	**6**	**4**	**1**	**139**	**1606**	**.913**			

Second-generation Sabre Marcus Foligno played 14 games for Buffalo in 2011-12 and 47 in 2012-13. His father Nick Foligno spent almost 10 seasons with the Sabres from 1981 to 1990.

Captains' History

Floyd Smith, 1970-71; Gerry Meehan, 1971-72 to 1973-74; Gerry Meehan and Jim Schoenfeld, 1974-75; Jim Schoenfeld, 1975-76, 1976-77; Danny Gare, 1977-78 to 1980-81; Danny Gare and Gilbert Perreault, 1981-82; Gilbert Perreault, 1982-83 to 1985-86; Gilbert Perreault and Lindy Ruff, 1986-87; Lindy Ruff, 1987-88; Lindy Ruff and Mike Foligno, 1988-89; Mike Foligno, 1989-90; Mike Foligno and Mike Ramsey, 1990-91; Mike Ramsey, 1991-92; Mike Ramsey and Pat LaFontaine, 1992-93; Pat LaFontaine and Alexander Mogilny, 1993-94; Pat LaFontaine, 1994-95 to 1996-97; Donald Audette and Michael Peca, 1997-98; Michael Peca, 1998-99, 1999-2000; no captain, 2000-01; Stu Barnes. 2001-02, 2002-03; Miroslav Satan, Chris Drury, James Patrick, J.P. Dumont, Daniel Briere, 2003-04; Daniel Briere and Chris Drury, 2005-06, 2006-07; Jochen Hecht, Toni Lydman, Brian Campbell, Jaroslav Spacek, Jason Pominville, 2007-08; Craig Rivet, 2008-09 to 2010-11; Jason Pominville, 2011-12, 2012-13.

Ron Rolston

Head Coach

Born: Fenton, MI, October 14, 1966.

Ron Rolston was named head coach of the Buffalo Sabres on May 7, 2013. He had been serving as the club's interim head coach since February 20. Rolston is the 16th head coach in franchise history.

Prior to joining the Sabres, Rolston was the head coach of the Rochester Americans, Buffalo's farm club in the American Hockey League. In his two seasons with the Americans, Rolston compiled a 63-44-17 regular-season record.

Before joining the Americans as head coach in 2011, Rolston spent seven seasons as head coach with USA Hockey's National Team Development Program, where he became the first coach in U.S. history to lead the United States under-18 team to three gold medals (2005, 2009, 2011) at the World Under-18 Championship, adding a silver medal (2007) in his other appearance as head coach. In addition to coaching at the under-18 and under-17 levels, Rolston also served as head coach for the U.S. national junior team at the World Junior Championship in 2007 and 2009. In 2007, he led Team USA to the bronze medal.

Rolston joined USA Hockey after serving as an assistant coach at four different NCAA Division I hockey programs between 1990 and 2004 (Lake Superior State University, 1990 to 1995; Clarkson University, 1996 to 1999; Harvard University, 1999 to 2002; Boston College, 2002 to 2004). He won national championships in 1992 and 1994 with Lake Superior State.

Coaching Record

			Regular Season				Playoffs			
Season	Team	League	GC	W	L	O/T	GC	W	L	T
2004-05	USNTDP	U18	54	37	12	5	....	....	....	....
2005-06	USNTDP	U17	65	38	19	8	....	....	....	....
2006-07	USNTDP	U18	56	37	15	4	....	....	....	....
2007-08	USNTDP	U17	68	30	34	4	....	....	....	....
2008-09	USNTDP	U18	61	41	18	2	....	....	....	....
2009-10	USNTDP	U17	52	18	30	4	....	....	....	....
2010-11	USNTDP	U18	70	39	25	6	....	....	....	....
2011-12	Rochester	AHL	76	36	26	14	3	0	3	0
2012-13	Rochester	AHL	48	27	18	3	....	....	....	....
2012-13	**Buffalo**	**NHL**	**31**	**15**	**11**	**5**	....	....	....	....
	NHL Totals		**31**	**15**	**11**	**5**	....	....	....	....

Coaching History

Punch Imlach, 1970-71; Punch Imlach, Floyd Smith and Joe Crozier, 1971-72; Joe Crozier, 1972-73, 1973-74; Floyd Smith, 1974-75 to 1976-77; Marcel Pronovost, 1977-78; Marcel Pronovost and Billy Inglis, 1978-79; Scotty Bowman, 1979-80; Roger Neilson, 1980-81; Jim Roberts and Scotty Bowman, 1981-82; Scotty Bowman 1982-83 to 1984-85; Jim Schoenfeld and Scotty Bowman, 1985-86; Scotty Bowman, Craig Ramsay and Ted Sator, 1986-87; Ted Sator, 1987-88, 1988-89; Rick Dudley, 1989-90, 1990-91; Rick Dudley and John Muckler, 1991-92; John Muckler, 1992-93 to 1994-95; Ted Nolan, 1995-96, 1996-97; Lindy Ruff, 1997-98 to 2011-12; Lindy Ruff and Ron Rolston, 2012-13; Ron Rolston, 2013-14.

Club Records

Team

(Figures in brackets for season records are games played; records for fewest points, wins, ties, losses, goals, goals against are for 70 or more games)

Most Points **113** 1974-75 (80), 2006-07 (82)
Most Wins **53** 2006-07 (82)
Most Ties **21** 1980-81 (80)
Most Losses **44** 1986-87 (80)
Most Goals **354** 1974-75 (80)
Most Goals Against **308** 1986-87 (80)
Fewest Points **51** 1971-72 (78)
Fewest Wins **16** 1971-72 (78)
Fewest Ties **5** 2000-01 (82)
Fewest Losses **16** 1974-75 (80)
Fewest Goals **190** 2002-03 (82)
Fewest Goals Against **175** 1998-99 (82)
Longest Winning Streak
Overall .... **10** Jan. 4-23/84, Oct. 4-26/06
Home .... **12** Nov. 12/72-Jan. 7/73, Oct. 13-Dec. 10/89
Away .... **10** Dec. 10/83-Jan. 23/84, Oct. 4-Nov. 13/06
Longest Undefeated Streak
Overall .... **14** Mar. 6-Apr. 6/80 (8W, 6T)
Home .... **21** Oct. 8/72-Jan. 7/73 (18W, 3T)
Away .... **10** Dec. 10/83-Jan. 23/84 (10W), Oct. 4-Nov. 13/06 (10W)
Longest Losing Streak
Overall .... **8** Jan. 25-Feb. 13/03
Home .... **7** Oct. 9-Nov. 5/10
Away .... **12** Dec. 17/11-Jan. 21/12
Longest Winless Streak
Overall .... **12** Nov. 23-Dec. 20/91 (8L, 4T), Oct. 25-Nov. 19/02 (10L, 2T/OL)
Home .... **12** Jan. 27-Mar. 10/91 (7L, 5T)
Away .... **23** Oct. 30/71-Feb. 19/72 (15L, 8T)
Most Shutouts, Season **13** 1997-98 (82)
Most PIM, Season ***2,713** 1991-92 (80)
Most Goals, Game .... **14** Jan. 21/75 (Wsh. 2 at Buf. 14), Mar. 19/81 (Tor. 4 at Buf. 14)

Individual

Most Seasons .... **17** Gilbert Perreault
Most Games .... **1,191** Gilbert Perreault
Most Goals, Career .... **512** Gilbert Perreault
Most Assists, Career .... **814** Gilbert Perreault
Most Points, Career .... **1,326** Gilbert Perreault (512G, 814A)
Most PIM, Career .... **3,189** Rob Ray
Most Shutouts, Career .... **55** Dominik Hasek
Longest Consecutive Games Streak .... **776** Craig Ramsay (Mar. 27/73-Feb. 10/83)
Most Goals, Season .... **76** Alexander Mogilny (1992-93)
Most Assists, Season .... **95** Pat LaFontaine (1992-93)
Most Points, Season .... **148** Pat LaFontaine (1992-93; 53G, 95A)
Most PIM, Season .... **354** Rob Ray (1991-92)
Most Points, Defenseman, Season .... **81** Phil Housley (1989-90; 21G, 60A)
Most Points, Center, Season .... **148** Pat LaFontaine (1992-93; 53G, 95A)
Most Points, Right Wing, Season .... **127** Alexander Mogilny (1992-93; 76G, 51A)
Most Points, Left Wing, Season .... **95** Rick Martin (1974-75; 52G, 43A)
Most Points, Rookie, Season .... **74** Rick Martin (1971-72; 44G, 30A)
Most Shutouts, Season .... **13** Dominik Hasek (1997-98)
Most Goals, Game .... **5** Dave Andreychuk (Feb. 6/86)
Most Assists, Game .... **5** Gilbert Perreault (Feb. 1/76), (Mar. 9/80), (Jan. 4/84); Dale Hawerchuk (Jan. 15/92); Pat LaFontaine (Mar. 19/92), (Dec. 31/92), (Feb. 10/93)
Most Points, Game .... **7** Gilbert Perreault (Feb. 1/76; 2G, 5A)

* NHL Record.

Retired Numbers

2	Tim Horton	1972-1974
7	Rick Martin	1971-1981
11	Gilbert Perreault	1970-1987
14	Rene Robert	1971-1979
16	Pat Lafontaine	1991-1996
18	Danny Gare	1974-1981

All-time Record vs. Other Clubs

Regular Season

	Total								At Home								On Road							
	GP	W	L	T	OL	GF	GA	PTS	GP	W	L	T	OL	GF	GA	PTS	GP	W	L	T	OL	GF	GA	PTS
Anaheim	26	15	8	3	0	78	55	33	13	7	3	3	0	39	28	17	13	8	5	0	0	39	27	16
Boston	268	117	111	29	11	868	863	274	135	71	43	15	6	475	385	163	133	46	68	14	5	393	478	111
Calgary	97	48	33	16	0	347	301	112	48	30	13	5	0	196	135	65	49	18	20	11	0	151	166	47
Carolina	186	96	66	18	6	639	538	216	92	54	30	7	1	360	263	116	94	42	36	11	5	279	275	100
Chicago	111	53	45	13	0	354	323	119	56	34	15	7	0	207	144	75	55	19	30	6	0	147	179	44
Colorado	133	59	50	20	4	463	453	142	66	36	19	9	2	256	216	83	67	23	31	11	2	207	237	59
Columbus	14	5	8	1	0	35	41	11	8	4	4	0	0	23	20	8	6	1	4	1	0	12	21	3
Dallas	112	54	41	17	0	363	329	125	55	31	13	11	0	200	147	73	57	23	28	6	0	163	182	52
Detroit	116	53	47	13	3	403	386	122	57	34	14	8	1	238	170	77	59	19	33	5	2	165	216	45
Edmonton	65	21	34	10	0	209	242	52	33	13	13	7	0	118	117	33	32	8	21	3	0	91	125	19
Florida	75	43	26	4	2	221	180	92	38	24	11	3	0	114	80	51	37	19	15	1	2	107	100	41
Los Angeles	113	55	39	18	1	432	359	129	56	31	16	9	0	236	160	71	57	24	23	9	1	196	199	58
Minnesota	12	7	5	0	0	30	28	14	6	2	4	0	0	13	17	4	6	5	1	0	0	17	11	10
Montreal	258	119	102	31	6	768	791	275	128	69	35	19	5	396	336	162	130	50	67	12	1	372	455	113
Nashville	15	7	6	1	1	40	40	16	7	1	4	1	1	20	26	4	8	6	2	0	0	20	14	12
New Jersey	139	71	45	17	6	464	401	165	70	38	22	8	2	250	207	86	69	33	23	9	4	214	194	79
NY Islanders	153	75	56	18	4	467	431	172	77	42	24	9	2	255	215	95	76	33	32	9	2	212	216	77
NY Rangers	165	78	54	25	8	543	510	189	84	47	24	10	3	324	257	107	81	31	30	15	5	219	253	82
Ottawa	116	57	42	10	7	330	304	131	57	31	19	3	4	177	142	69	59	26	23	7	3	153	162	62
Philadelphia	161	63	75	20	3	477	511	149	79	40	29	8	2	263	226	90	82	23	46	12	1	214	285	59
Phoenix	68	39	21	7	1	242	184	86	35	22	7	5	1	137	88	50	33	17	14	2	0	105	96	36
Pittsburgh	173	64	68	35	6	579	557	169	86	40	24	17	5	315	236	102	87	24	44	18	1	264	321	67
St. Louis	108	45	48	13	2	341	364	105	55	30	19	6	0	207	174	66	53	15	29	7	2	134	190	39
San Jose	29	18	6	4	1	113	83	41	15	14	1	0	0	67	41	28	14	4	5	4	1	46	42	13
Tampa Bay	77	49	23	5	0	251	192	103	38	23	13	2	0	124	103	48	39	26	10	3	0	127	89	55
Toronto	188	104	61	18	5	684	522	231	95	62	25	6	2	375	251	132	93	42	36	12	3	309	271	99
Vancouver	110	46	45	19	0	369	363	111	55	29	18	8	0	199	160	66	55	17	27	11	0	170	203	45
Washington	143	83	43	15	2	517	375	183	71	44	20	6	1	272	183	95	72	39	23	9	1	245	192	88
Winnipeg	51	21	19	1	10	175	153	53	26	14	8	0	4	107	71	32	25	7	11	1	6	68	82	21
Defunct Clubs	46	25	13	8	0	191	139	58	23	13	5	5	0	94	63	31	23	12	8	3	0	97	76	27
Totals	**3328**	**1590**	**1240**	**409**	**89**	**10993**	**10018**	**3678**	**1664**	**930**	**495**	**197**	**42**	**6057**	**4661**	**2099**	**1664**	**660**	**745**	**212**	**47**	**4936**	**5357**	**1579**

Playoffs

	Series	W	L	GP	W	L	T	GF	GA	Last Mtg.	Rnd.	Result
Boston	8	2	6	45	20	25	0	145	155	2010	CQF	L 2-4
Carolina	1	0	1	7	3	4	0	17	22	2006	CF	L 3-4
Chicago	2	2	0	9	8	1	0	36	17	1980	QF	W 4-0
Colorado	2	0	2	8	2	6	0	27	35	1985	DSF	L 2-3
Dallas	3	1	2	13	5	8	0	37	39	1999	F	L 2-4
Montreal	7	3	4	35	17	18	0	111	124	1998	CSF	W 4-0
New Jersey	1	0	1	7	3	4	0	14	14	1994	CQF	L 3-4
NY Islanders	4	1	3	21	8	13	0	62	70	2007	CQF	W 4-1
NY Rangers	2	2	0	9	6	3	0	28	19	2007	CSF	W 4-2
Ottawa	4	3	1	21	13	8	0	52	47	2007	CF	L 1-4
Philadelphia	9	3	6	50	21	29	0	141	146	2011	CQF	L 3-4
Pittsburgh	2	0	2	10	4	6	0	26	26	2001	CSF	L 3-4
St. Louis	1	1	0	3	2	1	0	7	8	1976	PRE	W 2-1
Toronto	1	1	0	5	4	1	0	21	16	1999	CF	W 4-1
Vancouver	2	2	0	7	6	1	0	28	14	1981	PRE	W 3-0
Washington	1	0	1	6	2	4	0	11	13	1998	CF	L 2-4
Totals	**50**	**21**	**29**	**256**	**124**	**132**	**0**	**763**	**765**			

Playoff Results 2013-2009

Year	Round	Opponent	Result	GF	GA
2011	CQF	Philadelphia	L 3-4	18	22
2010	CQF	Boston	L 2-4	15	16

Abbreviations: Round: F – Final; **CF** – conference final; **CSF** – conference semi-final; **CQF** – conference quarter-final; **DSF** – division semi-final; **QF** – quarter-final; **PRE** – preliminary round.

Calgary totals include Atlanta Flames, 1972-73 to 1979-80.
Carolina totals include Hartford, 1979-80 to 1996-97.
Colorado totals include Quebec, 1979-80 to 1994-95.
Dallas totals include Minnesota North Stars, 1970-71 to 1992-93.
New Jersey totals include Kansas City, 1974-75, 1975-76, and Colorado Rockies, 1976-77 to 1981-82.
Phoenix totals include Winnipeg, 1979-80 to 1995-96.
Winnipeg totals include Atlanta Thrashers, 1999-2000 to 2010-11.

2012-13 Results

Jan.	20	Philadelphia	5-2
	21	at Toronto	2-1
	24	at Carolina	3-6
	25	Carolina	1-3
	27	at Washington	2-3
	29	Toronto	3-4*
	31	at Boston	7-4
Feb.	2	at Montreal	1-6
	3	Florida	3-4
	5	at Ottawa	3-4
	7	Montreal	5-4†
	9	at NY Islanders	3-2
	10	Boston	1-3
	12	at Ottawa	0-2
	15	Boston	4-2
	17	Pittsburgh	3-4
	19	Winnipeg	1-2
	21	at Toronto	1-3
	23	NY Islanders	0-4
	26	at Tampa Bay	2-1
	28	at Florida	4-3†
Mar.	2	New Jersey	4-3†
	3	at NY Rangers	2-3†
	5	at Carolina	3-4
	7	at New Jersey	2-3†
	10	at Philadelphia	2-3
	12	NY Rangers	3-1
	16	Ottawa	3-4*
	17	at Washington	3-5
	19	at Montreal	3-2*
	21	Toronto	5-4†
	23	at Montreal	2-1
	26	at Tampa Bay	1-2
	28	at Florida	4-5†
	30	Washington	3-4†
	31	Boston	0-2
Apr.	2	at Pittsburgh	4-1
	5	Ottawa	4-2
	7	New Jersey	3-2†
	9	at Winnipeg	1-4
	11	Montreal	1-5
	13	Philadelphia	1-0
	14	Tampa Bay	3-1
	17	at Boston	3-2†
	19	NY Rangers	4-8
	22	Winnipeg	1-2
	23	at Pittsburgh	4-2
	26	NY Islanders	2-1†

* – Overtime † – Shootout

Entry Draft Selections 2013-1999

Name in bold denotes played in NHL.

2013
Pick
8 Rasmus Ristolainen
16 Nikita Zadorov
35 J.T. Compher
38 Connor Hurley
52 Justin Bailey
69 Nicholas Baptiste
129 Calvin Petersen
130 Gustav Possler
143 Anthony Florentino
159 Sean Malone
189 Eric Locke

2012
Pick
12 **Mikhail Grigorenko**
14 Zemgus Girgensons
44 Jake McCabe
73 Justin Kea
133 Logan Nelson
163 Linus Ullmark
193 Brady Austin
204 Judd Peterson

2011
Pick
16 Joel Armia
77 Daniel Catenacci
107 Colin Jacobs
137 Alex Lepkowski
167 Nathan Lieuwen
197 Brad Navin

2010
Pick
23 **Mark Pysyk**
68 Jerome Gauthier-Leduc
75 Kevin Sundher
83 Matt MacKenzie
98 Steven Shipley
143 Gregg Sutch
173 Cedrick Henley
203 Christian Isackson
208 Riley Boychuk

2009
Pick
13 **Zack Kassian**
66 **Brayden McNabb**
104 **Marcus Foligno**
134 Mark Adams
164 Connor Knapp
194 Maxime Legault

2008
Pick
12 **Tyler Myers**
26 **Tyler Ennis**
44 **Luke Adam**
81 Corey Fienhage
101 Justin Jokinen
104 Jordon Southorn
134 Jacob Lagace
164 Nick Crawford

2007
Pick
31 **T.J. Brennan**
59 Drew Schiestel
89 **Corey Tropp**
139 Brad Eidsness
147 Jean-Simon Allard
179 **Paul Byron**
187 Nick Eno
209 Drew Mackenzie

2006
Pick
24 Dennis Persson
46 **Jhonas Enroth**
57 **Mike Weber**
117 Felix Schutz
147 Alex Biega
207 Benjamin Breault

2005
Pick
13 Marek Zagrapan
48 Philip Gogulla
87 **Marc-Andre Gragnani**
96 **Chris Butler**
142 **Nathan Gerbe**
182 Adam Dennis
191 Vyacheslav Buravchikov
208 Matt Generous
227 Andrew Orpik

2004
Pick
13 **Drew Stafford**
43 **Michael Funk**
71 **Andrej Sekera**
145 Michal Valent
176 **Patrick Kaleta**
207 **Mark Mancari**
241 **Mike Card**
273 Dylan Hunter

2003
Pick
5 **Thomas Vanek**
65 Branislav Fabry
74 **Clarke MacArthur**
106 **Jan Hejda**
114 Denis Ezhov
150 Thomas Morrow
172 Pavel Voroshnin
202 **Nathan Paetsch**
235 Jeff Weber
266 Louis-Philippe Martin

2002
Pick
11 **Keith Ballard**
20 **Daniel Paille**
76 Michael Tessier
82 John Adams
108 Jakub Hulva
121 Marty Magers
178 Maxim Scheviev
208 **Radoslav Hecl**
241 **Dennis Wideman**
271 Martin Cizek

2001
Pick
22 **Jiri Novotny**
32 **Derek Roy**
50 **Chris Thorburn**
55 **Jason Pominville**
155 Michal Vondrka
234 Calle Aslund
247 Marek Dubec
279 Ryan Jorde

2000
Pick
15 Artem Kryukov
48 Gerard Dicaire
111 Ghyslain Rousseau
149 Denis Denisov
213 Vasily Bizyayev
220 **Paul Gaustad**
258 **Sean McMorrow**
277 Ryan Courtney

1999
Pick
20 **Barrett Heisten**
35 **Milan Bartovic**
55 **Doug Janik**
64 **Mike Zigomanis**
73 Tim Preston
117 Karel Mosovsky
138 **Ryan Miller**
146 Matt Kinch
178 Seneque Hyacinthe
206 Bret DeCecco
235 Brad Self
263 Craig Brunel

General Managers' History

Punch Imlach, 1970-71 to 1977-78; Punch Imlach and John Anderson, 1978-79; Scotty Bowman, 1979-80 to 1985-86; Scotty Bowman and Gerry Meehan, 1986-87; Gerry Meehan, 1987-88 to 1992-93; John Muckler, 1993-94 to 1996-97; Darcy Regier, 1997-98 to date.

Darcy Regier

General Manager

Born: Swift Current, Sask., November 27, 1957.

Darcy Regier was named general manager of the Buffalo Sabres on June 11, 1997 after a lengthy management apprenticeship in the New York Islanders organization. As a player, Regier played eight pro seasons, including part of the 1977-78 season with the Cleveland Barons and parts of the 1982-83 and 1983-84 campaigns with the New York Islanders.

He began his career as an administrator with the Islanders in 1984-85 and went on to serve in a variety of capacities including director of administration, assistant director of hockey operations, assistant coach and assistant general manager. He also served as an assistant coach with Hartford in 1991-92.

While with the Islanders, Regier benefited from working with talented managers and coaches including Bill Torrey and Al Arbour. As a minor pro player with Indianapolis of the CHL he became associated with another important influence on his hockey career, current Detroit Red Wing executive Jim Devellano.

Club Directory

First Niagara Center

Buffalo Sabres
First Niagara Center
One Seymour H. Knox III Plaza
Buffalo, NY 14203
Phone **716/855-4100**
Fax 716/855-4110
Tickets, U.S.: 888/GO-SABRES
Canada: 888/669-GOAL
www.sabres.com
Capacity: 19,070

Executive

Owner	Terrence M. Pegula
President	Theodore N. Black
Senior Advisors	Ken Sawyer, Clifford Benson

Hockey Department

General Manager	Darcy Regier
Assistant General Manager	Kevin Devine
Assistant to the General Manager	Mark Jakubowski
Director, Hockey Technologies/Innovation	Scott Schranz
Coordinator, Hockey Operations	Michael Bermingham
Scouting Directors, Pro / Amateur	Jon Christiano / Al MacAdam
Pro Scouts	Eric Weinrich, John Van Boxmeer, Fredrik Andersson, Graham Beamish, Teemu Numminen
Head Amateur Scout	Dave Torrie
Amateur Scouts	Al McAdam, Iouri Khmylev, Craig Benning, Kim Gellert, Eric Weissman, Toby O'Brien, Monty Trottier, Fredrik Andersson, Austin Dunne, Paul Merritt, Bo Berglund, Norm Poisson, Jussi Kari-Koskinen, Keith Hendrickson, Teemu Numminen, Brandon Jay, Victor Nybladh, Jim Kovachik, Chris Moulton
Hockey Technologies Manager	Kyle Kiebzak
Hockey Ops Asst. / Hockey Relations Coord.	Brett Ruff / Jessica Kindron

Coaching Staff

Head Coach	Ron Rolston
Assistant Coaches	Joe Sacco, Teppo Numminen
Goaltender Coach / Admin. Asst. Coach	Jim Corsi / Corey Smith
Strength & Conditioning Coach / Assistant Coach	Doug McKenney / J.T. Allaire
Hockey Data Analyst / Video Assistant	Jason Nightingale / Neil McKenney
Athletic Trainer / Assitant Trainer	Tim Macre / Bob Mowry
Massage Therapist / Physical Therapist	Chuck Garlow / Michael Adesso
Equipment Managers	Dave Williams, Rip Simonick
Assistant Equipment Manager / Assistant	George Babcock / Keith Hayes

Medical

Medical Director	Les Bisson, M.D.
Team Physicians	Nicholas Aquino, M.D., William Hartrich, M.D., Mark Feinberg, M.D.
Oral Surgeon / Team Dentist	Steven Jenson, DDS, David Croglio, DDS
Team Doctor Emeritus	John L. Butsch, M.D.

Legal

V.P., Legal Affairs & Human Resources	Dave Zygaj

Finance and Administration

V.P., Finance & Business Operations	Chuck LaMattina
Corporate Controller / Accounting Manager	Kristin Zirnheld / Christine Ivansitz
Payroll & Human Resource Manager / Assistant	Birgid Haensel / Ann Pastwick
Accounts Payable Clerk / Executive Assistants	Kim Binkley / Fay McNamara, Nadine Leone
IT Systems Consultant	Christian Tabone

Broadcast and Game Presentation

V.P., Broadcasting	Chrisanne Bellas
Game Presentation Director / Coordinator	Jenifer Rehac / Kelsey Schneider
TV Producer / TV Director	Joe Pinter / Matt Gould
Lead Feature Editor / Videographer/Editor	Drew Boeing / Mark Blaszak
Lead Editor / Production Coordinator	Jason Holler / Jason Wiese
Videoboard Director/Editor	Jeff Hill
Broadcast Team	Rick Jeanneret (Play-by-Play), Rob Ray (Color), Dan Dunleavy (Play-by-Play/Reporter), Brian Duff (Studio Host), Mike Robitaille, Danny Gare (Analysts)
Host, Sabres Hockey Hotline	Kevin Sylvester

Merchandise

Director, Merchandise	Mike Kaminska
Merchandise Mgrs., Inventory / Event Sales	Glenn Barker, Jeff Smith
Store Manager / Asst. Store Manager	Theresa Cerabone / Katie Mumbach-Kay

Marketing

VP, Marketing & Brand Strategy	Brent Rossi
Database Marketing Manager	Tom Matheny
Media Managers, Digital / Social	Scott Miner / Craig Kannalley
Digital Content Manager / Coordinator	Kevin Snow / Chris Ryndak
Marketing Coordinator	Cara Foligno
V.P., Creative Services / Sr. Graphic Designer	Frank Cravotta / Vicki Sitek
Graphic Designers	Melissa Gebhardt, Lindsey Caber

Public and Community Relations

V.P., Public & Community Relations	Michael Gilbert
Director, Media Relations	Chris Bandura
P.R. Assistants	Ian Ott, Marc Heintzman
Community Relations Director	Rich Jureller
Community Relations Manager/Assistant	Teresa Belbas / Lauren Yurko
Youth Hockey Coord. / Team Photographer	Ed Grudzinski / Bill Wippert
President, Alumni Relations	Rob Ray
Corporate & Community Relations Liaison	Gilbert Perreault

Sales and Business Development

V.P. Sales & Business Development	John Livsey
Director, Corporate Sales / Account Executive	Joe Foy / Rob Nugent
Director, Business Development	Pete Petrella
Partnership Services Sr. Manager / Manager	Jon Latke / Katy Ryan
Fulfillment Coordinator	Joe Hartman

Ticket Sales and Operations

V.P., Tickets & Service	John Sinclair
Box Office Manager / Asst. Mgr. / Coord.	Marty Maloney / Paul Barker / Gretchen Knott
Ticket Administrator	Melissa Rugg
Account Services Reps.	Roxanne Anderson, Melissa Eagen, Kevin Kennedy, Kristin Debellis
Special Consultant	Joe Crozier
Coordinator, Suite Services	Michelle Mitchell

First Niagara Center Staff

V.P.s, Arena Operations / Arena Events	Stan Makowski, Jr. / Jennifer Van Rysdam
V.P., Arena Services / Director, Arena Ops.	Thomas Ahern / Beth Giuliani Gatto
Managers, Marketing / Events	Tracy Mancini / Charlie Cannan, Robert Neumann
Managers, Technical Communications	Mike Queeno, Ray Riel
Chief Engineer / Dir., Bldg. Services / Security Mgr.	Bruce Johnson / Dennis Hooper / Marc Brenner

Calgary Flames

2012-13 Results: 19W-25L-1OTL-3SOL 42PTS
4TH, Northwest Division • 13TH, Western Conference

Key Off-Season Signings/Acquisitions

2013

June 27 • Acquired RW **David Jones** and D **Shane O'Brien** from Colorado for LW **Alex Tanguay** and D **Cory Sarich**.

July 2 • Acquired LW **T.J. Galiardi** from San Jose for a 4th-round pick in the 2015 NHL Draft.

4 • Re-signed RW **Brian McGrattan**.

5 • Acquired D **Kris Russell** from St. Louis for a 5th-round pick in the 2014 NHL Draft.

5 • Signed G **Karri Ramo**.

5 • Re-signed D **Chris Butler**.

10 • Re-signed C **Mikael Backlund**.

20 • Re-signed C **Paul Byron**.

31 • Re-signed D **T.J. Brodie**.

Curtis Glencross (#20) celebrates a goal with teammates Mark Giordano (#5) Dennis Wideman (#26) and Lee Stempniak (#22). Glencross was the Flames' top goal scorer with 15 during the 2012-13 season.

2013-14 Schedule

Oct.	Thu.	3	at Washington
	Fri.	4	at Columbus
	Sun.	6	Vancouver
	Wed.	9	Montreal
	Fri.	11	New Jersey
	Wed.	16	at Anaheim
	Sat.	19	at San Jose
	Mon.	21	at Los Angeles
	Tue.	22	at Phoenix
	Thu.	24	at Dallas
	Sat.	26	Washington
	Wed.	30	Toronto
Nov.	Fri.	1	Detroit
	Sun.	3	at Chicago
	Tue.	5	at Minnesota
	Thu.	7	at St. Louis
	Fri.	8	at Colorado
	Tue.	12	San Jose
	Thu.	14	Dallas
	Sat.	16	Edmonton
	Mon.	18	at Winnipeg
	Wed.	20	Columbus
	Fri.	22	Florida
	Wed.	27	Chicago
	Fri.	29	at Anaheim*
	Sat.	30	at Los Angeles
Dec.	Wed.	4	Phoenix
	Fri.	6	Colorado
	Sat.	7	at Edmonton
	Tue.	10	Boston
	Thu.	12	Carolina
	Sat.	14	at Buffalo*
	Sun.	15	at NY Rangers
	Tue.	17	at Boston
	Thu.	19	at Detroit
	Sat.	21	at Pittsburgh*
	Mon.	23	St. Louis
	Fri.	27	Edmonton
	Sun.	29	Vancouver*
	Tue.	31	Philadelphia
Jan.	Fri.	3	Tampa Bay
	Mon.	6	at Colorado
	Tue.	7	at Phoenix
	Thu.	9	St. Louis
	Sat.	11	Pittsburgh
	Mon.	13	at Carolina
	Tue.	14	at Nashville
	Thu.	16	Winnipeg
	Sat.	18	at Vancouver
	Mon.	20	at San Jose
	Wed.	22	Phoenix
	Fri.	24	Nashville
	Tue.	28	Chicago
	Thu.	30	San Jose
Feb.	Sat.	1	Minnesota
	Tue.	4	at Montreal
	Thu.	6	at NY Islanders
	Sat.	8	at Philadelphia*
	Thu.	27	Los Angeles
Mar.	Sat.	1	at Edmonton
	Mon.	3	at Minnesota
	Wed.	5	Ottawa
	Fri.	7	NY Islanders
	Sat.	8	at Vancouver
	Mon.	10	Los Angeles
	Wed.	12	Anaheim
	Fri.	14	at Dallas
	Sat.	15	at Phoenix
	Tue.	18	Buffalo
	Fri.	21	Nashville
	Sat.	22	at Edmonton
	Mon.	24	San Jose
	Wed.	26	Anaheim
	Fri.	28	NY Rangers
	Sun.	30	at Ottawa*
Apr.	Tue.	1	at Toronto
	Thu.	3	at Tampa Bay
	Fri.	4	at Florida
	Mon.	7	at New Jersey
	Wed.	9	Los Angeles
	Fri.	11	Winnipeg
	Sun.	13	at Vancouver*

* Denotes afternoon game.

Year-by-Year Record

		Home				Road				Overall									
Season	GP	W	L	T	OL	W	L	T	OL	W	L	T	OL	GF	GA	Pts.	Div. Fin.	Conf. Fin.	Playoff Result
2012-13	48	13	9	....	2	6	16	....	2	19	25	....	4	128	160	42	4th, NW	13th, West	Out of Playoffs
2011-12	82	23	12	....	6	14	17	....	10	37	29	....	16	202	226	90	2nd, NW	9th, West	Out of Playoffs
2010-11	82	23	13	....	5	18	16	....	7	41	29	....	12	250	237	94	2nd, NW	10th, West	Out of Playoffs
2009-10	82	20	17	....	4	20	15	....	6	40	32	....	10	204	210	90	3rd, NW	10th, West	Out of Playoffs
2008-09	82	27	10	....	4	19	20	....	2	46	30	....	6	254	248	98	2nd, NW	5th, West	Lost Conf. Quarter-Final
2007-08	82	21	11	....	9	21	19	....	1	42	30	....	10	229	227	94	3rd, NW	7th, West	Lost Conf. Quarter-Final
2006-07	82	30	9	....	2	13	20	....	8	43	29	....	10	258	226	96	3rd, NW	8th, West	Lost Conf. Quarter-Final
2005-06	82	30	7	....	4	16	18	....	7	46	25	....	11	218	200	103	1st, NW	3rd, West	Lost Conf. Quarter-Final
2004-05	....	....	....	....	....	....	....	....	....	....	....	....	....	....	....	....			
2003-04	82	21	14	5	1	21	16	2	2	42	30	7	3	200	176	94	3rd, NW	6th, West	Lost Final
2002-03	82	14	16	10	1	15	20	3	3	29	36	13	4	186	228	75	5th, NW	12th, West	Out of Playoffs
2001-02	82	20	14	5	2	12	21	7	1	32	35	12	3	201	220	79	4th, NW	11th, West	Out of Playoffs
2000-01	82	12	18	9	2	15	18	6	2	27	36	15	4	197	236	73	4th, NW	11th, West	Out of Playoffs
1999-2000	82	20	14	6	1	11	22	4	4	31	36	10	5	211	256	77	4th, NW	12th, West	Out of Playoffs
1998-99	82	15	20	6	....	15	20	6	....	30	40	12	....	211	234	72	3rd, NW	9th, West	Out of Playoffs
1997-98	82	18	17	6	....	8	24	9	....	26	41	15	....	217	252	67	5th, Pac.	11th, West	Out of Playoffs
1996-97	82	21	18	2	....	11	23	7	....	32	41	9	....	214	239	73	5th, Pac.	10th, West	Out of Playoffs
1995-96	82	18	18	5	....	16	19	6	....	34	37	11	....	241	240	79	2nd, Pac.	6th, West	Lost Conf. Quarter-Final
1994-95	48	15	7	2	....	9	10	5	....	24	17	7	....	163	135	55	1st, Pac.	3rd, West	Lost Conf. Quarter-Final
1993-94	84	25	12	5	....	17	17	8	....	42	29	13	....	302	256	97	1st, Pac.	3rd, West	Lost Conf. Quarter-Final
1992-93	84	23	14	5	....	20	16	6	....	43	30	11	....	322	282	97	2nd, Smythe		Lost Div. Semi-Final
1991-92	80	19	14	7	....	12	23	5	....	31	37	12	....	296	305	74	5th, Smythe		Out of Playoffs
1990-91	80	29	8	3	....	17	18	5	....	46	26	8	....	344	263	100	2nd, Smythe		Lost Div. Semi-Final
1989-90	80	28	7	5	....	14	16	10	....	42	23	15	....	348	265	99	1st, Smythe		Lost Div. Semi-Final
1988-89	**80**	**32**	**4**	**4**	....	**22**	**13**	**5**	....	**54**	**17**	**9**	....	**354**	**226**	**117**	**1st, Smythe**		**Won Stanley Cup**
1987-88	80	26	11	3	....	22	12	6	....	48	23	9	....	397	305	105	1st, Smythe		Lost Div. Final
1986-87	80	25	13	2	....	21	18	1	....	46	31	3	....	318	289	95	2nd, Smythe		Lost Div. Semi-Final
1985-86	80	23	11	6	....	17	20	3	....	40	31	9	....	354	315	89	2nd, Smythe		Lost Final
1984-85	80	23	11	6	....	18	16	6	....	41	27	12	....	363	302	94	3rd, Smythe		Lost Div. Semi-Final
1983-84	80	22	11	7	....	12	21	7	....	34	32	14	....	311	314	82	2nd, Smythe		Lost Div. Final
1982-83	80	21	12	7	....	11	22	7	....	32	34	14	....	321	317	78	2nd, Smythe		Lost Div. Final
1981-82	80	20	11	9	....	9	23	8	....	29	34	17	....	334	345	75	3rd, Smythe		Lost Div. Semi-Final
1980-81	80	25	5	10	....	14	22	4	....	39	27	14	....	329	298	92	3rd, Patrick		Lost Semi-Final
1979-80*	80	18	15	7	....	17	17	6	....	35	32	13	....	282	269	83	4th, Patrick		Lost Prelim. Round
1978-79*	80	25	11	4	....	16	20	4	....	41	31	8	....	327	280	90	4th, Patrick		Lost Prelim. Round
1977-78*	80	20	13	7	....	14	14	12	....	34	27	19	....	274	252	87	3rd, Patrick		Lost Prelim. Round
1976-77*	80	22	11	7	....	12	23	5	....	34	34	12	....	264	265	80	3rd, Patrick		Lost Prelim. Round
1975-76*	80	19	14	7	....	16	19	5	....	35	33	12	....	262	237	82	3rd, Patrick		Lost Prelim. Round
1974-75*	80	24	9	7	....	10	22	8	....	34	31	15	....	243	233	83	4th, Patrick		Out of Playoffs
1973-74*	78	17	15	7	....	13	19	7	....	30	34	14	....	214	238	74	4th, West		Lost Quarter-Final
1972-73*	78	16	16	7	....	9	22	8	....	25	38	15	....	191	239	65	7th, West		Out of Playoffs

* Atlanta Flames

PACIFIC DIVISION
42nd NHL Season

Franchise date: June 6, 1972

Transferred from Atlanta to Calgary, June 24, 1980.

2013-14 Player Personnel

FORWARDS	HT	WT	*Age	Place of Birth	S	2012-13 Club
BACKLUND, Mikael	6-0	198	24	Vasteras, Sweden	L	Vasteras-Calgary
BAERTSCHI, Sven	5-11	187	20	Langenthal, Switzerland	L	Abbotsford-Calgary
BEGIN, Steve	6-0	192	35	Trois-Rivieres, Que.	L	Calgary
BOUMA, Lance	6-1	210	23	Provost, Alta.	L	Abbotsford
BYRON, Paul	5-9	144	24	Ottawa, Ont.	L	Abbotsford-Calgary
CAMMALLERI, Mike	5-9	190	31	Richmond Hill, Ont.	L	Calgary
GALIARDI, T.J.	6-2	195	25	Calgary, Alta.	L	Bietigheim-San Jose
GLENCROSS, Curtis	6-1	197	30	Kindersley, Sask.	L	Calgary
HORAK, Roman	6-0	170	22	Ceske Budejovice, Czech.	L	Abbotsford-Calgary
HUDLER, Jiri	5-10	186	29	Olomouc, Czech.	L	Lev Praha-Trinec-Calgary
JACKMAN, Tim	6-2	225	31	Minot, ND	R	Calgary
JONES, Blair	6-2	216	27	Central Butte, Sask.	R	Abbotsford-Calgary
JONES, David	6-2	210	29	Guelph, Ont.	R	Colorado
McGRATTAN, Brian	6-4	235	32	Hamilton, Ont.	R	Abbotsford-Nsh-Cgy-Milwaukee
MONAHAN, Sean	6-2	187	18	Brampton, Ont.	L	Ottawa (OHL)
STAJAN, Matt	6-1	192	29	Mississauga, Ont.	L	Calgary
STEMPNIAK, Lee	5-11	196	30	Buffalo, NY	R	Calgary
DEFENSEMEN						
BRODIE, T.J.	6-1	182	23	Chatham, Ont.	L	Calgary
BUTLER, Chris	6-1	196	26	St. Louis, MO	L	Karlskrona-Calgary
GIORDANO, Mark	6-0	200	29	Toronto, Ont.	L	Calgary
O'BRIEN, Shane	6-3	230	30	Port Hope, Ont.	L	Colorado
RUSSELL, Kris	5-10	173	26	Caroline, Alta.	L	TPS-St. Louis
SMITH, Derek	6-1	197	28	Belleville, Ont.	L	Calgary
WIDEMAN, Dennis	6-0	200	30	Kitchener, Ont.	R	Calgary

GOALTENDERS	HT	WT	*Age	Place of Birth	C	2012-13 Club
MacDONALD, Joey	6-0	197	33	Pictou, N.S.	L	Calgary
RAMO, Karri	6-0	215	27	Asikkala, Finland	L	Omsk

* – Age at start of 2013-14 season

Captains' History

Keith McCreary, 1972-73 to 1974-75; Pat Quinn, 1975-76, 1976-77; Tom Lysiak, 1977-78, 1978-79; Jean Pronovost, 1979-80; Brad Marsh, 1980-81; Phil Russell, 1981-82, 1982-83; Lanny McDonald, Doug Risebrough, 1983-84; Lanny McDonald, Doug Risebrough, Jim Peplinski, 1984-85 to 1986-87; Lanny McDonald, Jim Peplinski, 1987-88; Lanny McDonald, Jim Peplinski, Tim Hunter, 1988-89; Brad McCrimmon, 1989-90; alternating captains, 1990-91; Joe Nieuwendyk, 1991-92 to 1994-95; Theoren Fleury, 1995-96, 1996-97; Todd Simpson, 1997-98, 1998-99; Steve Smith, 1999-2000; Steve Smith and Dave Lowry, 2000-01; Dave Lowry; Bob Boughner and Craig Conroy, 2001-02; Bob Boughner and Craig Conroy, 2002-03; Jarome Iginla, 2003-04 to 2012-13.

Coaching History

Bernie Geoffrion, 1972-73, 1973-74; Bernie Geoffrion and Fred Creighton, 1974-75; Fred Creighton, 1975-76 to 1978-79; Al MacNeil, 1979-80 to 1981-82; Bob Johnson, 1982-83 to 1986-87; Terry Crisp, 1987-88 to 1989-90; Doug Risebrough, 1990-91; Doug Risebrough and Guy Charron, 1991-92; Dave King, 1992-93 to 1994-95; Pierre Page, 1995-96, 1996-97; Brian Sutter, 1997-98 to 1999-2000; Don Hay and Greg Gilbert, 2000-01; Greg Gilbert, 2001-02; Greg Gilbert, Al MacNeil and Darryl Sutter, 2002-03; Darryl Sutter, 2003-04 to 2005-06; Jim Playfair, 2006-07; Mike Keenan, 2007-08, 2008-09; Brent Sutter, 2009-10 to 2011-12; Bob Hartley, 2012-13 to date.

Bob Hartley

Head Coach

Born: Hawkesbury, Ont., September 9, 1960.

The Calgary Flames announced the hiring of Bob Hartley as head coach on May 31, 2012. Hartley joined the Flames following a championship season with the ZSC Lions of Switzerland's National League A in 2011-12. Hartley brings a wealth of experience and winning to the Flames, having coached the Colorado Avalanche for five seasons, during which they won the 2001 Stanley Cup, and coaching the Atlanta Thrashers for parts of five seasons. He also led the Hershey Bears to the 1997 Calder Cup and has Junior A and Major Junior championship rings among his accomplishments.

Hartley began his coaching career with the Junior A team in his hometown of Hawkesbury, Ontario. After guiding the club to two championships, he was named head coach of the Laval Titan of the Quebec Major Junior Hockey League in 1991. After an appearance in the 1993 Memorial Cup, Hartley's was hired by the Quebec Nordiques as an assistant coach with their American Hockey League affiliate, the Cornwall Aces. He took over as head coach in 1994, guiding the Aces to two division titles during the team's three-year history.

When the Nordiques relocated to Colorado, Hartley became the head coach of their AHL affiliate, the Hershey Bears. He guided the team to four consecutive playoff appearances and a Calder Cup title in 1997. A season later, Hartley was hired as the Colorado Avalanche bench boss. During his five seasons, the Avalanche won four division titles and made four appearances in the Conference Finals. In his third season of 2000-01, Colorado won the Presidents' Trophy and the Stanley Cup. He became the only coach in team history to record 40 or more wins during his first four seasons as head coach. When his tenure with the Avalanche franchise ended in December of 2002 he had a franchise record 193 wins.

One month later, Hartley was appointed head coach of the Atlanta Thrashers. He guided the young Thrashers through four seasons of steady improvements including the 2006-07 campaign in which they won their first Southeast Division title, setting new franchise records for wins (43-28-11) and points (97) and gaining its first playoff berth. A slow start for the Thrashers in 2007-08 season resulted in Hartley and the club parting ways.

Hartley was enjoying a successful media career as a hockey analyst with RDS, but in the summer of 2011, he signed as head coach for the ZSC Lions in Zurich, Switzerland.

2012-13 Scoring

* – rookie

Regular Season

Pos	#	Player	Team	GP	G	A	Pts	TOI	+/–	PIM	PP	SH	GW	S	%
L	13	Mike Cammalleri	CGY	44	13	19	32	18:03	–15	25	5	0	3	102	12.7
R	22	Lee Stempniak	CGY	47	9	23	32	17:54	2	12	4	0	2	113	8.0
L	40	Alex Tanguay	CGY	40	11	16	27	19:21	–13	22	2	1	1	44	25.0
C	24	Jiri Hudler	CGY	42	10	17	27	17:09	–13	22	5	0	0	56	17.9
L	20	Curtis Glencross	CGY	40	15	11	26	18:14	–8	18	3	1	3	92	16.3
C	18	Matt Stajan	CGY	43	5	18	23	17:09	7	26	0	0	1	44	11.4
D	26	Dennis Wideman	CGY	46	6	16	22	25:01	–9	12	4	0	1	94	6.4
C	10	Roman Cervenka	CGY	39	9	8	17	13:08	–13	14	1	0	0	51	17.6
C	11	Mikael Backlund	CGY	32	8	8	16	15:07	–6	29	2	0	1	88	9.1
D	5	Mark Giordano	CGY	47	4	11	15	23:09	–7	40	1	1	1	58	6.9
D	7	T.J. Brodie	CGY	47	2	12	14	20:13	–9	8	0	0	0	44	4.5
L	47 *	Sven Baertschi	CGY	20	3	7	10	13:24	0	6	0	0	0	28	10.7
L	25	Steve Begin	CGY	36	4	4	8	7:59	–2	22	0	1	2	31	12.9
D	44	Chris Butler	CGY	44	1	7	8	17:02	–10	19	0	1	0	40	2.5
L	51	Roman Horak	CGY	20	2	5	7	14:31	–5	2	0	0	0	28	7.1
R	15	Tim Jackman	CGY	42	1	4	5	7:35	–9	76	0	0	0	42	2.4
R	16	Brian McGrattan	NSH	2	0	0	0	6:17	0	0	0	0	0	0	0.0
			CGY	19	3	0	3	7:11	–4	49	0	0	1	18	16.7
			Total	21	3	0	3	7:06	–4	49	0	0	1	18	16.7
D	42 *	Mark Cundari	CGY	4	1	2	3	19:46	–2	2	1	0	0	8	12.5
C	59 *	Max Reinhart	CGY	11	1	2	3	14:25	–3	4	0	0	0	26	3.8
D	6	Cory Sarich	CGY	28	0	2	2	14:51	–8	16	0	0	0	14	0.0
L	58 *	Ben Hanowski	CGY	5	1	0	1	13:17	0	0	0	0	0	4	25.0
C	32	Paul Byron	CGY	4	0	1	1	10:27	–2	2	0	0	0	1	0.0
C	38 *	Ben Street	CGY	6	0	1	1	13:36	–1	0	0	0	0	13	0.0
D	33	Anton Babchuk	CGY	7	0	1	1	11:51	–1	0	0	0	0	5	0.0
D	3	Brett Carson	CGY	10	0	1	1	10:55	–1	0	0	0	0	8	0.0
C	19	Blair Jones	CGY	15	0	1	1	10:44	–6	10	0	0	0	22	0.0
D	27	Derek Smith	CGY	22	0	1	1	12:14	–5	10	0	0	0	18	0.0
C	46 *	Carter Bancks	CGY	2	0	0	0	14:41	0	0	0	0	0	0	0.0
R	29 *	Akim Aliu	CGY	5	0	0	0	10:51	–2	14	0	0	0	2	0.0

Goaltending

No.	Goaltender	GPI	Mins	Avg	W	L	OT	EN	SO	GA	SA	S%	G	A	PIM
35	Joey MacDonald	21	1148	2.87	8	9	1	2	0	55	562	.902	0	0	0
41	Daniel Taylor	2	120	3.00	1	1	0	0	0	6	68	.912	0	0	0
37	* Leland Irving	6	270	3.33	2	1	1	0	0	15	128	.883	0	1	0
34	Miikka Kiprusoff	24	1344	3.44	8	14	2	2	0	77	650	.882	0	1	0
	Totals	**48**	**2901**	**3.25**	**19**	**25**	**4**	**4**	**0**	**157**	**1412**	**.889**			

Coaching Record

Season	Team	League	Regular Season GC	W	L	O/T	Playoffs GC	W	L	T
1987-88	Hawkesbury	CJHL	56	9	47	0	....	....	....	....
1988-89	Hawkesbury	CJHL	56	35	19	2	....	....	....	....
1989-90	Hawkesbury	CJHL	56	40	14	2	....	....	....	....
1990-91	Hawkesbury	CJHL	56	42	7	7	....	....	....	....
1991-92	Laval	QMJHL	67	37	25	5	10	4	6	....
1992-93	Laval	QMJHL	70	43	25	2	13	12	1	....
1992-93	Laval	M-Cup	....	....	....	....	5	2	3	....
1994-95	Cornwall	AHL	80	38	33	9	15	8	7	....
1995-96	Cornwall	AHL	80	34	39	7	8	3	5	....
1996-97	Hershey	AHL	80	43	27	10	23	15	8	....
1997-98	Hershey	AHL	80	36	37	7	7	3	4	....
1998-99	**Colorado**	**NHL**	**82**	**44**	**28**	**10**	**19**	**11**	**8**	....
99-2000	**Colorado**	**NHL**	**82**	**42**	**28**	**12**	**17**	**11**	**6**	....
2000-01 ♦	**Colorado**	**NHL**	**82**	**52**	**16**	**14**	**23**	**16**	**7**	....
2001-02	**Colorado**	**NHL**	**82**	**45**	**28**	**9**	**21**	**11**	**10**	....
2002-03	**Colorado**	**NHL**	**31**	**10**	**8**	**13**	....	....	....	....
2002-03	**Atlanta**	**NHL**	**39**	**19**	**14**	**6**	....	....	....	....
2003-04	**Atlanta**	**NHL**	**82**	**33**	**37**	**12**	....	....	....	....
2004-05	**Atlanta**				SEASON CANCELLED					
2005-06	**Atlanta**	**NHL**	**82**	**41**	**33**	**8**	....	....	....	....
2006-07	**Atlanta**	**NHL**	**82**	**43**	**28**	**11**	**4**	**0**	**4**	....
2007-08	**Atlanta**	**NHL**	**6**	**0**	**6**	**0**	....	....	....	....
2011-12	ZSC Lions Zurich	Swiss	50	27	33	....	15	12	3	....
2012-13	**Calgary**	**NHL**	**48**	**19**	**25**	**4**	....	....	....	....
	NHL Totals		**698**	**348**	**251**	**99**	**84**	**49**	**35**	....

♦ Stanley Cup win.

Club Records

Team

(Figures in brackets for season records are games played; records for fewest points, wins, ties, losses, goals, goals against are for 70 or more games)

Most Points	**117**	1988-89 (80)
Most Wins	**54**	1988-89 (80)
Most Ties	**19**	1977-78 (80)
Most Losses	**41**	1996-97 (82), 1997-98 (82), 1999-2000 (82)
Most Goals	**397**	1987-88 (80)
Most Goals Against	**345**	1981-82 (80)
Fewest Points	**65**	1972-73 (78)
Fewest Wins	**25**	1972-73 (78)
Fewest Ties	**3**	1986-87 (80)
Fewest Losses	**17**	1988-89 (80)
Fewest Goals	**186**	2002-03 (82)
Fewest Goals Against	**176**	2003-04 (82)
Longest Winning Streak		
Overall	**10**	Oct. 14-Nov. 3/78
Home	**10**	Nov. 7-Dec. 12/06
Away	**7**	Nov. 10-Dec. 4/88
Longest Undefeated Streak		
Overall	**13**	Nov. 10-Dec. 8/88 (12W, 1T)
Home	**18**	Dec. 29/90-Mar. 14/91 (17W, 1T)
Away	**9**	Feb. 20-Mar. 21/88 (6W, 3T), Nov. 11-Dec. 16/90 (6W, 3T)
Longest Losing Streak		
Overall	**11**	Dec. 14/85-Jan. 7/86
Home	**6**	Dec. 5-31/98, Jan. 8-25/10
Away	**11**	Feb. 28-Apr. 6/13
Longest Winless Streak		
Overall	**11**	Dec. 14/85-Jan. 7/86 (11L), Jan. 5-26/93 (9L, 2T)
Home	**10**	Oct. 21-Dec. 4/00 (6L, 4T/OL)
Away	**13**	Feb. 3-Mar. 29/73 (10L, 3T), Feb. 18-Apr. 6/13 (12L, 1OL/SOL)
Most Shutouts, Season	**11**	2003-04 (82)
Most PIM, Season	**2,643**	1991-92 (80)
Most Goals, Game	**13**	Feb. 10/93 (S.J. 1 at Cgy. 13)

Individual

Most Seasons	**16**	Jarome Iginla
Most Games	**1,219**	Jarome Iginla
Most Goals, Career	**525**	Jarome Iginla
Most Assists, Career	**609**	Al MacInnis
Most Points, Career	**1,095**	Jarome Iginla (525G, 570A)
Most PIM, Career	**2,405**	Tim Hunter
Most Shutouts, Career	**41**	Miikka Kiprusoff
Longest Consecutive Games Streak	**441**	Jarome Iginla (Oct. 4/07-Mar. 26/13)
Most Goals, Season	**66**	Lanny McDonald (1982-83)
Most Assists, Season	**82**	Kent Nilsson (1980-81)
Most Points, Season	**131**	Kent Nilsson (1980-81; 49G, 82A)
Most PIM, Season	**375**	Tim Hunter (1988-89)
Most Points, Defenseman, Season	**103**	Al MacInnis (1990-91; 28G, 75A)
Most Points, Center, Season	**131**	Kent Nilsson (1980-81; 49G, 82A)
Most Points, Right Wing, Season	**110**	Joe Mullen (1988-89; 51G, 59A)
Most Points, Left Wing, Season	**90**	Gary Roberts (1991-92; 53G, 37A)
Most Points, Rookie, Season	**92**	Joe Nieuwendyk (1987-88; 51G, 41A)
Most Shutouts, Season	**10**	Miikka Kiprusoff (2005-06)
Most Goals, Game	**5**	Joe Nieuwendyk (Jan. 11/89)
Most Assists, Game	**6**	Guy Chouinard (Feb. 25/81) Gary Suter (Apr. 4/86)
Most Points, Game	**7**	Sergei Makarov (Feb. 25/90; 2G, 5A)

Records include Atlanta Flames, 1972-73 through 1979-80.

Retired Numbers

9	Lanny McDonald	1981-1989
30	Mike Vernon	1982-1994; 2000-2002

Honored Numbers

2	Al MacInnis	1981-1994

All-time Record vs. Other Clubs

Regular Season

	Total								At Home								On Road							
	GP	W	L	T	OL	GF	GA	PTS	GP	W	L	T	OL	GF	GA	PTS	GP	W	L	T	OL	GF	GA	PTS
Anaheim	82	34	33	7	8	220	231	83	41	26	13	1	1	120	95	54	41	8	20	6	7	100	136	29
Boston	97	33	54	10	0	299	341	76	47	20	23	4	0	167	159	44	50	13	31	6	0	132	182	32
Buffalo	97	33	45	16	3	301	347	85	49	20	18	11	0	166	151	51	48	13	27	5	3	135	196	34
Carolina	63	38	17	7	1	267	205	84	32	24	6	2	0	154	99	50	31	14	11	5	1	113	106	34
Chicago	155	61	63	26	5	456	486	153	78	35	27	13	3	240	231	86	77	26	36	13	2	216	255	67
Colorado	146	66	53	20	7	482	459	159	73	36	24	9	4	251	214	85	73	30	29	11	3	231	245	74
Columbus	47	22	20	0	5	121	128	49	23	14	5	0	4	71	56	32	24	8	15	0	1	50	72	17
Dallas	155	69	55	25	6	487	469	169	77	41	19	14	3	252	195	99	78	28	36	11	3	235	274	70
Detroit	150	66	64	16	4	490	486	152	76	42	26	6	2	266	217	92	74	24	38	10	2	224	269	60
Edmonton	214	106	86	19	3	750	709	234	107	62	35	9	1	413	337	134	107	44	51	10	2	337	372	100
Florida	23	11	7	3	2	56	56	27	11	5	4	1	1	28	30	12	12	6	3	2	1	28	26	15
Los Angeles	216	109	82	21	4	813	723	243	109	65	31	12	1	459	345	143	107	44	51	9	3	354	378	100
Minnesota	74	41	20	4	9	171	166	95	37	23	7	3	4	89	76	53	37	18	13	1	5	82	90	42
Montreal	105	35	54	15	1	294	353	86	54	21	26	7	0	168	175	49	51	14	28	8	1	126	178	37
Nashville	56	25	25	4	2	149	154	56	27	14	8	3	2	77	62	33	29	11	17	1	0	72	92	23
New Jersey	93	58	22	11	2	364	252	129	45	30	6	8	1	195	118	69	48	28	16	3	1	169	134	60
NY Islanders	106	42	43	20	1	331	357	105	52	25	15	11	1	183	157	62	54	17	28	9	0	148	200	43
NY Rangers	107	53	35	15	4	415	339	125	52	29	11	10	2	225	155	70	55	24	24	5	2	190	184	55
Ottawa	31	15	11	4	1	93	73	35	16	10	5	1	0	54	34	21	15	5	6	3	1	39	39	14
Philadelphia	109	42	53	12	2	359	386	98	55	25	20	9	1	214	183	60	54	17	33	3	1	145	203	38
Phoenix	172	80	66	20	6	626	573	186	87	48	28	9	2	344	268	107	85	32	38	11	4	282	305	79
Pittsburgh	96	38	39	18	1	347	326	95	49	27	13	8	1	210	151	63	47	11	26	10	0	137	175	32
St. Louis	157	73	66	14	4	488	479	164	78	40	30	5	3	245	211	88	79	33	36	9	1	243	268	76
San Jose	97	50	36	8	3	299	280	111	48	27	16	4	1	161	126	59	49	23	20	4	2	138	154	52
Tampa Bay	26	12	10	1	3	90	81	28	13	7	5	0	1	44	37	15	13	5	5	1	2	46	44	13
Toronto	124	59	52	12	1	465	423	131	66	39	22	5	0	257	202	83	58	20	30	7	1	208	221	48
Vancouver	250	123	84	33	10	856	797	289	124	69	36	15	4	461	363	157	126	54	48	18	6	395	434	132
Washington	85	40	32	13	0	310	267	93	41	25	9	7	0	163	105	57	44	15	23	6	0	147	162	36
Winnipeg	13	7	5	1	0	41	32	15	6	6	0	0	0	26	11	12	7	1	5	1	0	15	21	3
Defunct Clubs	26	15	7	4	0	94	67	34	13	8	4	1	0	51	34	17	13	7	3	3	0	43	33	17
Totals	**3172**	**1456**	**1239**	**379**	**98**	**10534**	**10045**	**3389**	**1586**	**863**	**492**	**188**	**43**	**5754**	**4597**	**1957**	**1586**	**593**	**747**	**191**	**55**	**4780**	**5448**	**1432**

Playoffs

	Series	W	L	GP	W	L	T	GF	GA	Last Mtg.	Rnd.	Result
Anaheim	1	0	1	7	3	4	0	16	17	2006	CQF	L 3-4
Chicago	4	2	2	18	9	9	0	53	54	2009	CQF	L 2-4
Dallas	1	0	1	6	2	4	0	18	25	1981	SF	L 2-4
Detroit	3	1	2	14	6	8	0	26	38	2007	CQF	L 2-4
Edmonton	5	1	4	30	11	19	0	96	132	1991	DSF	L 3-4
Los Angeles	6	2	4	26	13	13	0	112	105	1993	DSF	L 2-4
Montreal	2	1	1	11	5	6	0	32	31	1989	F	W 4-2
NY Rangers	1	0	1	4	1	3	0	8	14	1980	PRE	L 1-3
Philadelphia	2	1	1	11	4	7	0	28	43	1981	QF	W 4-3
Phoenix	3	1	2	13	6	7	0	43	45	1987	DSF	L 2-4
St. Louis	1	1	0	7	4	3	0	28	22	1986	CF	W 4-3
San Jose	3	1	2	20	10	10	0	68	57	2008	CQF	L 3-4
Tampa Bay	1	0	1	7	3	4	0	14	13	2004	F	L 3-4
Toronto	1	0	1	2	0	2	0	5	9	1979	PRE	L 0-2
Vancouver	6	4	2	32	17	15	0	101	96	2004	CQF	W 4-3
Totals	**40**	**15**	**25**	**208**	**94**	**114**	**0**	**648**	**701**			

Playoff Results 2013-2009

Year	Round	Opponent	Result	GF	GA
2009	CQF	Chicago	L 2-4	16	21

Abbreviations: Round: F – Final; **CF** – conference final; **CSF** – conference semi-final; **CQF** – conference quarter-final; **DSF** – division semi-final; **SF** – semi-final; **QF** – quarter-final; **PRE** – preliminary round.

Carolina totals include Hartford, 1979-80 to 1996-97.
Colorado totals include Quebec, 1979-80 to 1994-95.
Dallas totals include Minnesota North Stars, 1972-73 to 1992-93.
New Jersey totals include Kansas City, 1974-75, 1975-76, and Colorado Rockies, 1976-77 to 1981-82.
Phoenix totals include Winnipeg, 1979-80 to 1995-96.
Winnipeg totals include Atlanta Thrashers, 1999-2000 to 2010-11.

2012-13 Results

Jan.	20	San Jose	1-4		13	Detroit	5-2
	21	Anaheim	4-5		15	Nashville	6-3
	23	at Vancouver	2-3†		18	at Dallas	3-4
	26	Edmonton	4-3		21	at Nashville	3-5
	31	Colorado	3-6		22	at Columbus	1-5
Feb.	2	Chicago	2-3†		24	St. Louis	3-2
	5	at Detroit	4-1		26	at Chicago	0-2
	7	at Columbus	4-3*		27	Colorado	4-3
	9	at Vancouver	1-5		29	Columbus	4-6
	11	Minnesota	1-2†	**Apr.**	1	at Edmonton	1-4
	13	Dallas	7-4		3	Edmonton	2-8
	15	St. Louis	2-5		5	at San Jose	1-2
	17	at Dallas	4-3		6	at Vancouver	2-5
	18	at Phoenix	0-4		8	at Colorado	3-1
	20	Los Angeles	1-3		10	Vancouver	1-4
	23	Minnesota	3-1		12	Phoenix	3-2*
	24	Phoenix	5-4		13	at Edmonton	4-1
	26	at Minnesota	1-2*		15	Minnesota	3-4
	28	at Colorado	4-5		17	Detroit	3-2
Mar.	3	Vancouver	4-2		19	Anaheim	3-1
	6	San Jose	4-1		21	at Minnesota	4-1
	8	at Anaheim	0-4		23	at Nashville	3-4
	9	at Los Angeles	2-6		25	at St. Louis	1-4
	11	at Los Angeles	1-3		26	at Chicago	1-3

* – Overtime † – Shootout

Entry Draft Selections 2013-1999

Name in bold denotes played in NHL.

2013

Pick	
6	Sean Monahan
22	Emile Poirier
28	Morgan Klimchuk
67	Keegan Kanzig
135	Eric Roy
157	Tim Harrison
187	Rushan Rafikov
198	John Gilmour

2012

Pick	
21	Mark Jankowski
42	Patrick Sieloff
75	Jon Gillies
105	Brett Kulak
124	Ryan Culkin
165	Coda Gordon
186	Matthew Deblouw

2011

Pick	
13	**Sven Baertschi**
45	Markus Granlund
57	Tyler Wotherspoon
104	John Gaudreau
164	Laurent Brossoit

2010

Pick	
64	**Max Reinhart**
73	Joey Leach
103	John Ramage
108	Bill Arnold
133	Michael Ferland
193	Patrick Holland

2009

Pick	
23	**Tim Erixon**
74	Ryan Howse
111	Henrik Bjorklund
141	Spencer Bennett
171	Joni Ortio
201	Gaelan Patterson

2008

Pick	
25	**Greg Nemisz**
48	Mitch Wahl
78	**Lance Bouma**
108	Nicholas Larson
114	**T.J. Brodie**
168	Ryley Grantham
198	Alexander Deilert

2007

Pick	
24	**Mikael Backlund**
70	**John Negrin**
116	**Keith Aulie**
143	Mickey Renaud
186	C.J. Severyn

2006

Pick	
26	**Leland Irving**
87	John Armstrong
89	Aaron Marvin
118	Hugo Carpentier
149	Juuso Puustinen
179	Jordan Fulton
187	Devin Didiomete
209	Per Jonsson

2005

Pick	
26	**Matt Pelech**
69	Gord Baldwin
74	Dan Ryder
111	J.D. Watt
128	Kevin Lalande
158	**Matt Keetley**
179	**Brett Sutter**
221	Myles Rumsey

2004

Pick	
24	**Kris Chucko**
70	**Brandon Prust**
98	**Dustin Boyd**
118	Aki Seitsonen
121	Kris Hogg
173	**Adam Pardy**
182	Fred Wikner
200	Matt Schneider
213	James Spratt
279	**Adam Cracknell**

2003

Pick	
9	**Dion Phaneuf**
39	**Tim Ramholt**
97	Ryan Donally
112	**Jamie Tardif**
143	**Greg Moore**
173	**Tyler Johnson**
206	Thomas Bellemare
240	Cam Cunning
270	Kevin Harvey

2002

Pick	
10	**Eric Nystrom**
39	Brian McConnell
90	**Matthew Lombardi**
112	Yuri Artemenkov
141	Jiri Cetkovsky
142	Emanuel Peter
146	Viktor Bobrov
159	Kristofer Persson
176	**Curtis McElhinney**
206	**David Van Der Gulik**
207	Pierre Johnsson
238	Jyri Marttinen

2001

Pick	
14	**Chuck Kobasew**
41	Andrei Taratukhin
56	Andrei Medvedev
108	**Tomi Maki**
124	Yegor Shastin
145	James Hakewill
164	Yuri Trubachev
207	Garrett Bembridge
220	**Dave Moss**
233	Joe Campbell
251	Ville Hamalainen

2000

Pick	
9	**Brent Krahn**
40	**Kurtis Foster**
46	**Jarret Stoll**
116	Levente Szuper
141	Wade Davis
155	**Travis Moen**
176	**Jukka Hentunen**
239	David Hajek
270	**Micki DuPont**

1999

Pick	
11	**Oleg Saprykin**
38	Dan Cavanaugh
77	**Craig Anderson**
106	Roman Rozakov
135	Matt Doman
153	Jesse Cook
166	Cory Pecker
170	**Matt Underhill**
190	Blair Stayzer
252	Dmitri Kirilenko

General Managers' History

Cliff Fletcher, 1972-73 to 1990-91; Doug Risebrough, 1991-92 to 1994-95; Doug Risebrough and Al Coates, 1995-96; Al Coates, 1996-97 to 1999-2000; Craig Button, 2000-01 to 2002-03; Darryl Sutter, 2003-04 to 2009-10; Darryl Sutter and Jay Feaster, 2010-11; Jay Feaster, 2011-12 to date.

Jay Feaster

General Manager

Born: Williamstown, PA, July 30, 1962.

Jay Feaster joined the Calgary Flames in July 2010 as assistant general manager. He was named acting general manager on December 28, 2010 and, on May 16, 2011 was named general manager of the team. Feaster and senior vice president & assistant general manager Michael Holditch are central figures with the Flames hockey management group.

Feaster joined the Flames organization to build on his decorated managerial career that includes a Stanley Cup championship as general manager of the Tampa Bay Lightning in 2004 and a Calder Cup championship as the president of the Hershey Bears (American Hockey League) in 1997. The native of Williamstown, Pennsylvania was originally named general manager of the Lightning on February 10, 2002. In addition to a Stanley Cup championship, the Lightning won back to back Southeast Division titles in 2002-03 and 2003-04.

Feaster was named the 2004 Sporting News NHL Executive of the Year based on a vote of other NHL GMs and hockey executives. Prior to being named general manager, he spent three seasons with the club in the assistant general manager's position. In that capacity, Feaster was responsible for all contractual, collective bargaining and NHL legal issues, as well as the organization's scouting department and its developmental league affiliates.

To join the Lightning, Feaster resigned his post as president of the Hershey Bears and vice president of Hershey Entertainment. In that capacity, Feaster oversaw the operations of the Bears, the Hershey Wildcats professional soccer team and Hersheypark Arena/Stadium, including the star Pavilion. Feaster, who spent nine years with the Bears, led the team to a division title (1993-94) and a Calder Cup Championship (1997), while establishing three consecutive single-season attendance records (1991-92 to 1993-94) and entering into a five-year affiliation agreement with the NHL's Colorado Avalanche. For his work, he was named the AHL's Executive of the Year in 1997. He originally joined Hershey Entertainment as assistant to the president in 1989 and was named general manager of the Bears and Hersheypark Arena/Stadium in 1990.

Prior to joining Hershey Entertainment, Feaster practiced law with the firm of McNees, Wallace & Nurick in Harrisburg, Pennsylvania. Feaster is a Summa Cum Laude graduate of Susquehanna University and a Cum Laude graduate of the Georgetown Law Center in Washington, DC.

Club Directory

Scotiabank Saddledome

Calgary Flames
Scotiabank Saddledome
P.O. Box 1540 Station M
Calgary, Alberta T2P 3B9
Phone **403/777-2177**
FAX 403/777-2195
www.calgaryflames.com
Capacity: 19,289

Owners . . . . . N. Murray Edwards (Chairman), Alvin G. Libin, Allan P. Markin, Jeff McCaig, Clayton H. Riddell

Executive

President & Chief Executive Officer	Ken King
Senior V.P., Finance and Administration & CFO	John Bean
General Manager	Jay Feaster
Assistant G.M./Sr. VP of Hockey Admin.	Michael Holditch
V.P., Building Operations	Libby Raines
V.P., Advertising, Sponsorship & Marketing	Jim Bagshaw
V.P., Sales, Customer Service & Ticketing	Rollie Cyr
V.P., Communications	Peter Hanlon
V.P., Business Development	Jim Peplinski
V.P., Food and Beverage	Mark Vaillant

Hockey Club Personnel

General Manager	Jay Feaster
Assistant G.M./Player Personnel	John Weisbrod
Assistant G.M./Sr. VP of Hockey Admin.	Michael Holditch
Special Assistant to the G.M.	Craig Conroy
Director, Hockey Administration	Mike Burke
Director, Player Development	Ron Sutter
Director of Amateur Scouting	Tod Button
Director, Video and Statistical Analysis	Chris Snow
Head Coach	Bob Hartley
Associate Coach	Jacques Cloutier
Assistant Coach	Martin Gelinas
Goaltending Coach	Clint Malarchuk
Senior Video Analyst	Jamie Pringle
Team Services Manager	Sean O'Brien
Exec. Asst. to GM and Hockey Operations	Brenda Koyich
Exec. Asst. to Sr. V.P. Hockey Ops and AGM	Anita Cranston
Pro Scouts	Michael Goulet, Steve Leach, Steve Pleau, David Volek

Scouts . . . . . Frank Anzalone, Jim Cummins, Ari Haanpaa, Bobbie Hagelin, Bob MacMillan, Fred Parker, Blair Reid, Rob Sumner, Tom Webster PT: Mike Adessa, Ritchie Thibeau

Medical/Training Staff

Strength & Conditioning Coach	Rich Hesketh
Athletic Therapist	Morris Boyer
Assistant Athletic Therapist	Schad Richea
Physiotherapist	Kent Kobelka
Equipment Manager	Mark DePasquale
Assistant Equipment Manager	Corey Osmak
Massage Therapist	Bryan Lentz
Dressing Room Attendant	Ben Dumaine
Head Physician	Dr. Kelly Brett
Team Physician/Sports Medicine	Dr. Jim Thorne
Team Orthopedic Surgeons	Dr. Nicholas Mohtadi, Dr. Richard Boorman
Team Dentist	Dr. Bill Blair, Dr. Kristin Yont
Team Optometrist	Dr. Derek Gaume

Abbotsford Heat

Head Coach	Troy Ward
Assistant Coach	TBD
Goaltending Coach	Jordan Sigalet
Vice-President, Communications	Peter Hanlon
Director, Communications & Media Relations	Sean Kelso
Administrative Assistant, Communications	Bernie Hargrave

Administration

Senior V.P., Finance and Administration & CFO	John Bean
Exec. Asst. to President/CEO	Judy O'Brien
Director, Business Analytics	Deniece Kennedy
Director, Human Resources	Betty Mah

Marketing/Ticketing

V.P. Advertising, Sponsorship & Marketing	Jim Bagshaw
V.P. Sales, Customer Service & Ticketing	Rollie Cyr
V.P. Business Development	Jim Peplinski
Senior Director, Sponsorship & Sales	Pat Halls
Director, Corporate Sponsorship	Kevin Gross
Director, Sponsorship & Sales	Mark Stiles
Executive Assistant Marketing	Suzanna Chapman
Executive Assistant to V.P. of Sales, Customer Service & Ticketing	Tracy Wood
Director, Executive Suites	Mike Mungiello
Director of Sales	Mike Franco
Director, Customer Service	Marc Leost
Director, Broadcast & Production	Carlo Petrini
Assistant Manager, In Game Entertainment	Steve Edgar
Director, Retail	Brent Gibbs
Manager, Publications	Laurie Wheeler
Director, Marketing	Jillian Frechette
Digital Content Manager	Jason Johnson

Scotiabank Saddledome

V.P. Building Operations	Libby Raines
V.P. Food and Beverage	Mark Vaillant
Director, Building Operations	Rob Blanchard
Manager, Building Operations	Andrew Higgins
Senior Food Services Manager	Sheila Parisien
Manager, Security and Loss Prevention	Bob Godun

Miscellaneous

Radio Affiliate	The FAN 960 (960 AM)
TV Affiliate	Rogers Sportsnet, CBC-TV, TSN

Carolina Hurricanes

Key Off-Season Signings/Acquisitions

2013

June 30 • Acquired D **Andrej Sekera** from Buffalo for D **Jamie McBain** and a 2nd-round pick (J.T. Compher) in the 2013 NHL Draft.

July 5 • Signed D **Mike Komisarek** and G **Anton Khudobin**.

9 • Re-signed C **Riley Nash**.

11 • Signed RW **Aaron Palushaj**.

19 • Re-signed RW **Zac Dalpe**.

26 • Signed LW **Nathan Gerbe**.

2012-13 Results: 19W-25L-3OTL-1SOL 42PTS
3RD, Southeast Division • 13TH, Eastern Conference

Staal in the family! The Carolina Hurricanes called up youngest brother Jared Staal (#13) and played him on a line with Jordan and Eric when he made his NHL debut against the New York Rangers on April 25, 2013. Marc Staal of the Rangers was out with an injury at the time.

2013-14 Schedule

Oct.	Fri.	4	Detroit
	Sun.	6	Philadelphia*
	Tue.	8	at Pittsburgh
	Thu.	10	at Washington
	Fri.	11	Los Angeles
	Sun.	13	Phoenix*
	Tue.	15	Chicago
	Thu.	17	at Toronto
	Sat.	19	at NY Islanders
	Thu.	24	at Minnesota
	Fri.	25	at Colorado
	Mon.	28	Pittsburgh
Nov.	Fri.	1	Tampa Bay
	Sat.	2	at NY Rangers
	Tue.	5	Philadelphia
	Thu.	7	NY Islanders
	Sat.	9	Minnesota
	Tue.	12	Colorado
	Fri.	15	Anaheim
	Sat.	16	at St. Louis
	Mon.	18	Boston
	Thu.	21	at Detroit
	Sat.	23	at Boston*
	Sun.	24	Ottawa*
	Wed.	27	at New Jersey
	Fri.	29	New Jersey
Dec.	Sun.	1	Vancouver*
	Tue.	3	at Washington
	Thu.	5	at Nashville
	Fri.	6	San Jose
	Mon.	9	at Vancouver
	Tue.	10	at Edmonton
	Thu.	12	at Calgary
	Sat.	14	at Phoenix
	Fri.	20	Washington
	Sat.	21	at Tampa Bay
	Mon.	23	Columbus
	Fri.	27	Pittsburgh
	Sun.	29	at Toronto
	Tue.	31	Montreal
Jan.	Thu.	2	at Washington
	Sat.	4	at NY Islanders
	Sun.	5	Nashville
	Tue.	7	at Buffalo
	Thu.	9	Toronto
	Fri.	10	at Columbus
	Mon.	13	Calgary
	Sat.	18	Florida
	Sun.	19	Tampa Bay*
	Tue.	21	at Philadelphia
	Thu.	23	at Buffalo
	Fri.	24	Ottawa
	Mon.	27	Columbus
	Tue.	28	at Montreal
	Fri.	31	St. Louis
Feb.	Tue.	4	Winnipeg
	Fri.	7	Florida
	Sat.	8	Montreal
	Thu.	27	at Dallas
Mar.	Sat.	1	at Los Angeles*
	Sun.	2	at Anaheim*
	Tue.	4	at San Jose
	Fri.	7	NY Rangers
	Sat.	8	at New Jersey
	Tue.	11	NY Rangers
	Thu.	13	Buffalo
	Sat.	15	at Boston*
	Sun.	16	Edmonton*
	Tue.	18	at Columbus
	Fri.	21	at Chicago
	Sat.	22	at Winnipeg
	Tue.	25	NY Islanders
	Thu.	27	at Florida
	Sat.	29	Columbus
	Mon.	31	at Ottawa
Apr.	Tue.	1	at Pittsburgh
	Thu.	3	Dallas
	Sat.	5	New Jersey
	Tue.	8	at NY Rangers
	Thu.	10	Washington
	Fri.	11	at Detroit
	Sun.	13	at Philadelphia*

* Denotes afternoon game.

METROPOLITAN DIVISION

35th NHL Season

Franchise date: June 22, 1979

Transferred from Hartford to Carolina, June 25, 1997.

Year-by-Year Record

		Home				Road				Overall									
Season	GP	W	L	T	OL	W	L	T	OL	W	L	T	OL	GF	GA	Pts.	Div. Fin.	Conf. Fin.	Playoff Result
2012-13	48	9	14	....	1	10	11	....	3	19	25	....	4	128	160	42	3rd, SE	13th, East	Out of Playoffs
2011-12	82	20	14	....	7	13	19	....	9	33	33	....	16	213	243	82	5th, SE	12th, East	Out of Playoffs
2010-11	82	22	14	....	5	18	17	....	6	40	31	....	11	236	239	91	3rd, SE	9th, East	Out of Playoffs
2009-10	82	21	17	....	3	14	20	....	7	35	37	....	10	230	256	80	3rd, SE	11th, East	Out of Playoffs
2008-09	82	26	14	....	1	19	16	....	6	45	30	....	7	239	226	97	2nd, SE	6th, East	Lost Conf. Final
2007-08	82	24	13	....	4	19	20	....	2	43	33	....	6	252	249	92	2nd, SE	9th, East	Out of Playoffs
2006-07	82	21	16	....	4	19	18	....	4	40	34	....	8	241	253	88	3rd, SE	11th, East	Out of Playoffs
2005-06	**82**	**31**	**8**	....	**2**	**21**	**14**	....	**6**	**52**	**22**	....	**8**	**294**	**260**	**112**	**1st, SE**	**2nd, East**	**Won Stanley Cup**
2004-05	....	....	....	....	....	....	....	....	....	....	....	....	....	....	....	....			
2003-04	82	13	18	8	2	15	16	6	4	28	34	14	6	172	209	76	3rd, SE	11th, East	Out of Playoffs
2002-03	82	12	17	9	3	10	26	2	3	22	43	11	6	171	240	61	5th, SE	15th, East	Out of Playoffs
2001-02	82	15	13	11	2	20	13	5	3	35	26	16	5	217	217	91	1st, SE	3rd, East	Lost Final
2000-01	82	23	15	3	0	15	17	6	3	38	32	9	3	212	225	88	2nd, SE	8th, East	Lost Conf. Quarter-Final
1999-2000	82	20	16	5	0	17	19	5	0	37	35	10	0	217	216	84	3rd, SE	9th, East	Out of Playoffs
1998-99	82	20	12	9	....	14	18	9	....	34	30	18	....	210	202	86	1st, SE	3rd, East	Lost Conf. Quarter-Final
1997-98	82	16	18	7	....	17	23	1	....	33	41	8	....	200	219	74	6th, NE	9th, East	Out of Playoffs
1996-97*	82	23	15	3	....	9	24	8	....	32	39	11	....	226	256	75	5th, NE	10th, East	Out of Playoffs
1995-96*	82	22	15	4	....	12	24	5	....	34	39	9	....	237	259	77	4th, NE	10th, East	Out of Playoffs
1994-95*	48	12	10	2	....	7	14	3	....	19	24	5	....	127	141	43	5th, NE	10th, East	Out of Playoffs
1993-94*	84	14	22	6	....	13	26	3	....	27	48	9	....	227	288	63	6th, NE	13th, East	Out of Playoffs
1992-93*	84	12	25	5	....	14	27	1	....	26	52	6	....	284	369	58	5th, Adams		Out of Playoffs
1991-92*	80	13	17	10	....	13	24	3	....	26	41	13	....	247	283	65	4th, Adams		Lost Div. Semi-Final
1990-91*	80	18	16	6	....	13	22	5	....	31	38	11	....	238	276	73	4th, Adams		Lost Div. Semi-Final
1989-90*	80	17	18	5	....	21	15	4	....	38	33	9	....	275	268	85	4th, Adams		Lost Div. Semi-Final
1988-89*	80	21	17	2	....	16	21	3	....	37	38	5	....	299	290	79	4th, Adams		Lost Div. Semi-Final
1987-88*	80	21	14	5	....	14	24	2	....	35	38	7	....	249	267	77	4th, Adams		Lost Div. Semi-Final
1986-87*	80	26	9	5	....	17	21	2	....	43	30	7	....	287	270	93	1st, Adams		Lost Div. Semi-Final
1985-86*	80	21	17	2	....	19	19	2	....	40	36	4	....	332	302	84	4th, Adams		Lost Div. Final
1984-85*	80	17	18	5	....	13	23	4	....	30	41	9	....	268	318	69	5th, Adams		Out of Playoffs
1983-84*	80	19	16	5	....	9	26	5	....	28	42	10	....	288	320	66	5th, Adams		Out of Playoffs
1982-83*	80	13	22	5	....	6	32	2	....	19	54	7	....	261	403	45	5th, Adams		Out of Playoffs
1981-82*	80	13	17	10	....	8	24	8	....	21	41	18	....	264	351	60	5th, Adams		Out of Playoffs
1980-81*	80	14	17	9	....	7	24	9	....	21	41	18	....	292	372	60	4th, Norris		Out of Playoffs
1979-80*	80	22	12	6	....	5	22	13	....	27	34	19	....	303	312	73	4th, Norris		Lost Prelim. Round

* Hartford Whalers

2013-14 Player Personnel

FORWARDS	HT	WT	*Age	Place of Birth	S	2012-13 Club
BLANCHARD, Nicolas	6-3	205	26	Granby, Que.	L	Charlotte-Carolina
BOWMAN, Drayson	6-1	195	24	Grand Rapids, MI	L	Charlotte-Carolina
DALPE, Zac	6-1	195	23	Paris, Ont.	R	Charlotte-Carolina
DWYER, Patrick	5-11	175	30	Spokane, WA	R	Carolina
GERBE, Nathan	5-5	178	26	Oxford, MI	L	Buffalo
LINDHOLM, Elias	6-1	192	18	Boden , Sweden	R	Brynas
NASH, Riley	6-1	200	24	Consort, Alta.	R	Charlotte-Carolina
PALUSHAJ, Aaron	6-0	200	24	Livonia, MI	R	Hamilton-Colorado
RASK, Victor	6-2	200	20	Leksand, Sweden	L	Calgary (WHL)-Charlotte
RUUTU, Tuomo	6-0	205	30	Vantaa, Finland	L	Carolina
SEMIN, Alexander	6-2	209	29	Krasnoyarsk, USSR	R	Krasnoyarsk-Nizhny Novgorod-Car
SKINNER, Jeff	5-11	200	21	Markham, Ont.	L	Carolina
STAAL, Eric	6-4	205	28	Thunder Bay, Ont.	L	Carolina
STAAL, Jared	6-4	210	23	Thunder Bay, Ont.	R	Charlotte-Carolina
STAAL, Jordan	6-4	220	25	Thunder Bay, Ont.	L	Carolina
SUTTER, Brett	6-0	200	26	Viking, Alta.	L	Charlotte-Carolina
TERRY, Chris	5-10	195	24	Brampton, Ont.	L	Charlotte-Carolina
TLUSTY, Jiri	6-0	209	25	Slany, Czech.	L	Kladno-Carolina
WELSH, Jeremy	6-3	210	25	Bayfield, Ont.	L	Charlotte-Carolina
WESTGARTH, Kevin	6-4	234	29	Amherstburg, Ont.	R	Carolina
DEFENSEMEN						
BELLEMORE, Brett	6-4	225	25	Windsor, Ont.	R	Charlotte-Carolina
FAULK, Justin	6-0	215	21	South St. Paul, MN	R	Charlotte-Carolina
GLEASON, Tim	6-0	217	30	Clawson, MI	L	Carolina
HARRISON, Jay	6-4	220	30	Oshawa, Ont.	L	Carolina
JORDAN, Michal	6-1	195	23	Zlin, Czech.	L	Charlotte-Carolina
KOMISAREK, Mike	6-4	235	31	West Islip, NY	R	Toronto-Toronto (AHL)
MURPHY, Ryan	5-11	185	20	Aurora, Ont.	R	Kitch-Car-Charlotte
PITKANEN, Joni	6-3	220	30	Oulu, Finland	L	Carolina
SEKERA, Andrej	6-0	201	27	Bojnice, Czech.	L	Bratislava-Buffalo
GOALTENDERS	**HT**	**WT**	***Age**	**Place of Birth**	**C**	**2012-13 Club**
KHUDOBIN, Anton	5-11	203	27	Ust-Kamenogorsk, USSR	L	Mytischi-Boston
PETERS, Justin	6-1	210	27	Blyth, Ont.	L	Charlotte-Carolina
WARD, Cam	6-1	185	29	Saskatoon, Sask.	L	Carolina

* – Age at start of 2013-14 season

2012-13 Scoring

* – rookie

Regular Season

Pos	#	Player	Team	GP	G	A	Pts	TOI	+/–	PIM	PP	SH	GW	S	%
C	12	Eric Staal	CAR	48	18	35	53	20:59	5	54	3	1	4	152	11.8
R	28	Alexander Semin	CAR	44	13	31	44	20:56	14	46	4	0	1	150	8.7
C	19	Jiri Tlusty	CAR	48	23	15	38	18:14	15	18	4	0	3	117	19.7
C	11	Jordan Staal	CAR	48	10	21	31	20:06	–18	32	1	0	1	114	8.8
C	53	Jeff Skinner	CAR	42	13	11	24	18:27	–21	26	5	0	0	159	8.2
D	77	Joe Corvo	CAR	40	6	11	17	18:45	–3	14	3	0	2	71	8.5
R	39	Patrick Dwyer	CAR	46	8	8	16	15:25	–7	12	1	1	0	93	8.6
D	27	Justin Faulk	CAR	38	5	10	15	24:00	1	15	1	1	0	76	6.6
D	44	Jay Harrison	CAR	47	3	7	10	19:54	–10	51	0	0	2	54	5.6
R	15	Tuomo Ruutu	CAR	17	4	5	9	15:14	–6	8	0	0	0	30	13.3
C	20 *	Riley Nash	CAR	32	4	5	9	12:48	–4	8	0	0	0	36	11.1
D	25	Joni Pitkanen	CAR	22	1	8	9	22:49	2	12	0	0	0	34	2.9
D	47	Marc-Andre Bergeron	T.B.	12	1	4	5	12:21	3	4	0	0	0	22	4.5
			CAR	13	0	4	4	15:03	–7	5	0	0	0	21	0.0
			Total	25	1	8	9	13:45	–4	9	0	0	0	43	2.3
D	6	Tim Gleason	CAR	42	0	9	9	19:34	–3	40	0	0	0	36	0.0
D	4	Jamie McBain	CAR	40	1	7	8	18:25	0	12	0	0	0	46	2.2
D	24 *	Bobby Sanguinetti	CAR	37	2	4	6	14:45	–6	4	0	0	1	48	4.2
L	21	Drayson Bowman	CAR	37	3	2	5	11:42	–7	17	0	0	0	68	4.4
R	8	Kevin Westgarth	CAR	31	2	2	4	5:43	1	45	0	0	0	16	12.5
R	59	Chad LaRose	CAR	35	2	2	4	12:50	–8	29	0	0	0	65	3.1
C	22	Zac Dalpe	CAR	10	1	2	3	12:18	–7	0	0	0	0	18	5.6
C	37	Tim Brent	CAR	30	0	3	3	9:47	–3	8	0	0	0	23	0.0
R	29	Tim Wallace	CAR	28	1	1	2	10:01	–9	17	0	0	0	20	5.0
D	73 *	Brett Bellemore	CAR	8	0	2	2	13:45	–2	7	0	0	0	3	0.0
L	58 *	Chris Terry	CAR	3	1	0	1	9:36	0	0	0	0	1	1	100.0
C	23 *	Jeremy Welsh	CAR	5	0	1	1	5:50	1	0	0	0	0	4	0.0
R	14	Andreas Nodl	CAR	8	0	1	1	8:28	–1	2	0	0	0	6	0.0
D	5	Marc-Andre Gragnani	CAR	1	0	0	0	7:53	0	0	0	0	0	0	0.0
R	13 *	Jared Staal	CAR	2	0	0	0	13:23	–2	2	0	0	0	3	0.0
L	42	Brett Sutter	CAR	3	0	0	0	8:20	–1	4	0	0	0	2	0.0
D	7 *	Ryan Murphy	CAR	4	0	0	0	21:03	–4	2	0	0	0	7	0.0
D	47 *	Michal Jordan	CAR	5	0	0	0	10:41	–2	2	0	0	0	2	0.0
C	72 *	Nicolas Blanchard	CAR	9	0	0	0	8:40	–2	20	0	0	0	6	0.0

Goaltending

No.	Goaltender	GPI	Mins	Avg	W	L	OT	EN	SO	GA	SA	S%	G	A	PIM
30	Cam Ward	17	929	2.84	9	6	1	1	0	44	477	.908	0	0	0
31	Dan Ellis	19	997	3.13	6	8	2	1	1	52	555	.906	0	2	0
35	Justin Peters	19	954	3.46	4	11	1	6	1	55	506	.891	0	0	0
	Totals	**48**	**2898**	**3.29**	**19**	**25**	**4**	**8**	**2**	**159**	**1546**	**.897**			

Captains' History

Rick Ley, 1979-80; Rick Ley and Mike Rogers, 1980-81; Dave Keon, 1981-82; Russ Anderson, 1982-83; Mark Johnson, 1983-84; Mark Johnson and Ron Francis, 1984-85; Ron Francis, 1985-86 to 1990-91; Randy Ladouceur, 1991-92; Pat Verbeek, 1992-93 to 1994-95; Brendan Shanahan, 1995-96; Kevin Dineen, 1996-97, 1997-98; Keith Primeau, 1998-99; Keith Primeau and Ron Francis, 1999-2000; Ron Francis, 2000-01 to 2003-04; Rod Brind'Amour, 2005-06 to 2008-09; Rod Brind'Amour and Eric Staal, 2009-10; Eric Staal, 2010-11 to date.

Kirk Muller

Head Coach

Born: Kingston, Ont., February 8, 1966.

Kirk Muller was named head coach of the Carolina Hurricanes on November 28, 2011 and spent his first full season behind the bench in 2012-13. He is the 12th person to serve as head coach in franchise history, and the third since the team relocated to North Carolina in 1997.

Muller began the 2011-12 season in his first professional head coaching job with the Nashville Predators' American Hockey League affiliate Milwaukee Admirals. Prior to joining the Admirals, Muller spent five seasons as an assistant coach with the Montreal Canadiens, helping the Habs reach the playoffs four consecutive seasons, including a trip to the Eastern Conference Final in 2010. Muller worked extensively with the Habs' penalty killing unit throughout his tenure in Montreal, helping it finish in the top half of the NHL in each season under his watch, including a seventh-place ranking in 2010-11 and a perfect 21-for-21 performance during the 2011 Stanley Cup playoffs. Prior to joining the Canadiens on June 20, 2006, Muller spent one season as head coach with the Queen's University Golden Gaels in his hometown of Kingston. He also served as an assistant coach for Canada at the 2005 Lotto Cup and the 2006 Under-18 World Championship.

As a player, Muller totaled 357 goals and 602 assists (959 points) in 1,349 career NHL games over 19 seasons with the New Jersey Devils, Montreal Canadiens, New York Islanders, Toronto Maple Leafs, Florida Panthers and Dallas Stars from 1984 to 2003. He skated in 127 career Stanley Cup playoff games, totaling 69 points (33 goals, 36 assists), including the Stanley Cup-clinching goal for the Canadiens in the 1993 Stanley Cup Final. A six-time NHL All-Star, Muller posted 30-or-more goals five times in his career, 20-or-more goals nine times, and had seven 70-point seasons. He established career highs with New Jersey in 1987-88 and Montreal in 1992-93, totaling 37 goals, 57 assists and 94 points in each of those seasons. Muller served as captain for both the Devils (1989 to 1991) and the Canadiens (1994-95).

Prior to turning professional, Muller played junior hockey in the Ontario Hockey League for Kingston and Guelph, and represented Canada at the 1984 Olympic Games. He made his NHL debut for New Jersey straight out of junior hockey in 1984, after the Devils selected him second overall in the 1984 NHL Entry Draft, behind only Mario Lemieux.

Coaching Record

			Regular Season				Playoffs			
Season	Team	League	GC	W	L	O/T	GC	W	L	T
2011-12	Milwaukee	AHL	17	10	6	1	....	....	....	....
2011-12	**Carolina**	**NHL**	**57**	**25**	**20**	**12**	....	....	....	....
2012-13	**Carolina**	**NHL**	**48**	**19**	**25**	**4**	....	....	....	....
	NHL Totals		**105**	**44**	**45**	**16**	....	....	....	....

Jiri Tlusty led the Hurricanes with 23 goals in 2012-13, giving him six more goals than the previous career-high 17 he had scored in 79 games in 2011-12.

Club Records

Team

(Figures in brackets for season records are games played; records for fewest points, wins, ties, losses, goals, goals against are for 70 or more games)

Most Points 112 2005-06 (82)
Most Wins 52 2005-06 (82)
Most Ties 19 1979-80 (80)
Most Losses 54 1982-83 (80)
Most Goals 332 1985-86 (80)
Most Goals Against 403 1982-83 (80)
Fewest Points 45 1982-83 (80)
Fewest Wins 19 1982-83 (80)
Fewest Ties 4 1985-86 (80)
Fewest Losses 22 2005-06 (82)
Fewest Goals 171 2002-03 (82)
Fewest Goals Against 202 1998-99 (82)

Longest Winning Streak
Overall .... 9 Oct. 22-Nov. 11/05, Dec. 31/05-Jan. 19/06, Mar. 18-Apr. 07/09
Home .... 12 Feb. 20-Apr. 7/09
Away .... 6 Nov. 10-Dec. 7/90

Longest Undefeated Streak
Overall .... 10 Jan. 20-Feb. 10/82 (6W, 4T)
Home .... 12 Feb. 20-Apr. 7/09 (12W)
Away .... 8 Nov. 11-Dec. 5/96 (4W, 4T)

Longest Losing Streak
Overall .... 14 Oct. 10-Nov. 13/09
Home .... 8 Mar. 14-Apr. 9/13
Away .... 13 Dec. 18/82-Feb. 5/83, Oct. 3-Nov. 28/09

Longest Winless Streak
Overall .... 14 Jan. 4-Feb. 9/92 (8L, 6T), Oct. 10-Nov. 13/09 (10L, 4OL/SOL)
Home .... 13 Jan. 15-Mar. 10/85 (11L, 2T)
Away .... 15 Nov. 11/79-Jan. 9/80 (11L, 4T), Jan. 7-Mar. 2/03 (13L, 2T/OL)

Most Shutouts, Season 8 1998-99 (82)
Most PIM, Season 2,354 1992-93 (84)
Most Goals, Game .... 11 Feb. 12/84 (Edm. 0 at Hfd. 11), Oct. 19/85 (Mtl. 6 at Hfd. 11), Jan. 17/86 (Que. 6 at Hfd. 11), Mar. 15/86 (Chi. 4 at Hfd. 11)

Individual

Most Seasons .... 16 Ron Francis
Most Games .... 1,186 Ron Francis
Most Goals, Career .... 382 Ron Francis
Most Assists, Career .... 793 Ron Francis
Most Points, Career .... 1,175 Ron Francis (382G, 793A)
Most PIM, Career .... 1,439 Kevin Dineen
Most Shutouts, Career .... 21 Cam Ward
Longest Consecutive Games Streak .... 419 Dave Tippett (Mar. 3/84-Oct. 7/89)
Most Goals, Season .... 56 Blaine Stoughton (1979-80)
Most Assists, Season .... 69 Ron Francis (1989-90)
Most Points, Season .... 105 Mike Rogers (1979-80; 44G, 61A), (1980-81; 40G, 65A)
Most PIM, Season .... 358 Torrie Robertson (1985-86)
Most Points, Defenseman, Season .... 69 Dave Babych (1985-86; 14G, 55A)
Most Points, Center, Season .... 105 Mike Rogers (1979-80; 44G, 61A), (1980-81; 40G, 65A)
Most Points, Right Wing, Season .... 100 Blaine Stoughton (1979-80; 56G, 44A)
Most Points, Left Wing, Season .... 89 Geoff Sanderson (1992-93; 46G, 43A)
Most Points, Rookie, Season .... 72 Sylvain Turgeon (1983-84; 40G, 32A)
Most Shutouts, Season .... 6 Arturs Irbe (1998-99), (2000-01); Kevin Weekes (2003-04); Cam Ward (2008-09)
Most Goals, Game .... 4 Jordy Douglas (Feb. 3/80); Ron Francis (Feb. 12/84); Eric Staal (Mar. 7/09)
Most Assists, Game .... 6 Ron Francis (Mar. 5/87)
Most Points, Game .... 6 Paul Lawless (Jan. 4/87; 2G, 4A); Ron Francis (Mar. 5/87; 6A), (Oct. 8/89; 3G, 3A); Eric Staal (Mar. 7/09; 4G, 2A)

Records include Hartford Whalers, 1979-80 through 1996-97.

Retired Numbers

2	Glen Wesley	1994-2008
10	Ron Francis	1981-1991; 1998-2004
17	Rod Brind'Amour	2000-2010

All-time Record vs. Other Clubs

Regular Season

	Total								At Home								On Road							
	GP	W	L	T	OL	GF	GA	PTS	GP	W	L	T	OL	GF	GA	PTS	GP	W	L	T	OL	GF	GA	PTS
Anaheim	26	12	10	2	2	73	68	28	13	7	4	1	1	34	30	16	13	5	6	1	1	39	38	12
Boston	185	72	95	16	2	548	633	162	92	39	42	9	2	302	313	89	93	33	53	7	0	246	320	73
Buffalo	186	72	92	18	4	538	639	166	94	41	40	11	2	275	279	95	92	31	52	7	2	263	360	71
Calgary	63	18	38	7	0	205	267	43	31	12	14	5	0	106	113	29	32	6	24	2	0	99	154	14
Chicago	65	28	29	7	1	199	223	64	33	17	12	4	0	109	98	38	32	11	17	3	1	90	125	26
Colorado	134	44	67	21	2	416	511	111	66	27	26	12	1	216	223	67	68	17	41	9	1	200	288	44
Columbus	13	6	7	0	0	31	38	12	7	4	3	0	0	18	20	8	6	2	4	0	0	13	18	4
Dallas	69	25	35	6	3	207	253	59	36	15	17	4	0	114	126	34	33	10	18	2	3	93	127	25
Detroit	67	26	32	8	1	204	223	61	33	19	13	1	0	111	91	39	34	7	19	7	1	93	132	22
Edmonton	66	21	33	12	0	227	235	54	32	13	12	7	0	127	104	33	34	8	21	5	0	100	131	21
Florida	103	51	36	11	5	284	290	118	51	33	13	3	2	162	127	71	52	18	23	8	3	122	163	47
Los Angeles	67	28	30	8	1	242	261	65	34	17	12	5	0	120	122	39	33	11	18	3	1	122	139	26
Minnesota	14	8	3	2	1	42	33	19	5	5	0	0	0	13	7	10	9	3	3	2	1	29	26	9
Montreal	184	64	95	20	5	533	666	153	93	37	41	13	2	272	314	89	91	27	54	7	3	261	352	64
Nashville	17	5	9	1	2	39	51	13	9	4	2	1	2	26	27	11	8	1	7	0	0	13	24	2
New Jersey	120	46	58	12	4	354	383	108	60	26	25	8	1	179	180	61	60	20	33	4	3	175	203	47
NY Islanders	120	61	43	9	7	393	364	138	60	31	21	5	3	213	190	70	60	30	22	4	4	180	174	68
NY Rangers	119	50	56	7	6	335	390	113	59	31	23	3	2	188	179	67	60	19	33	4	4	147	211	46
Ottawa	87	45	32	8	2	238	229	100	42	26	11	4	1	123	99	57	45	19	21	4	1	115	130	43
Philadelphia	118	30	64	14	10	325	438	84	59	16	30	9	4	176	217	45	59	14	34	5	6	149	221	39
Phoenix	68	32	28	8	0	238	224	72	34	15	13	6	0	111	101	36	34	17	15	2	0	127	123	36
Pittsburgh	125	55	54	11	5	442	455	126	64	32	26	5	1	230	219	70	61	23	28	6	4	212	236	56
St. Louis	70	26	37	5	2	201	229	59	35	15	18	2	0	102	105	32	35	11	19	3	2	99	124	27
San Jose	28	14	14	0	0	87	93	28	14	8	6	0	0	44	34	16	14	6	8	0	0	43	59	12
Tampa Bay	106	49	40	10	7	310	318	115	54	29	15	7	3	163	157	68	52	20	25	3	4	147	161	47
Toronto	104	55	35	11	3	376	331	124	52	28	17	6	1	197	168	63	52	27	18	5	2	179	163	61
Vancouver	65	25	27	11	2	194	225	63	32	15	12	5	0	106	107	35	33	10	15	6	2	88	118	28
Washington	149	54	74	14	7	403	465	129	75	29	34	10	2	212	223	70	74	25	40	4	5	191	242	59
Winnipeg	78	46	22	4	6	252	224	102	39	20	14	1	4	117	122	45	39	26	8	3	2	135	102	57
Totals	**2616**	**1068**	**1195**	**263**	**90**	**7936**	**8759**	**2489**	**1308**	**611**	**516**	**147**	**34**	**4166**	**4095**	**1403**	**1308**	**457**	**679**	**116**	**56**	**3770**	**4664**	**1086**

Playoffs

	Series	W	L	GP	W	L	T	GF	GA	Last Mtg.	Rnd.	Result
Boston	4	1	3	26	11	15	0	64	80	2009	CSF	W 4-3
Buffalo	1	1	0	7	4	3	0	22	17	2006	CF	W 4-3
Colorado	2	1	1	9	5	4	0	35	34	1987	DSF	L 2-4
Detroit	1	0	1	5	1	4	0	7	14	2002	F	L 1-4
Edmonton	1	1	0	7	4	3	0	19	16	2006	F	W 4-3
Montreal	7	2	5	39	16	23	0	106	125	2006	CQF	W 4-2
New Jersey	4	3	1	24	14	10	0	51	56	2009	CQF	W 4-3
Pittsburgh	1	0	1	4	0	4	0	9	20	2009	CF	L 0-4
Toronto	1	1	0	6	4	2	0	10	6	2002	CF	W 4-2
Totals	**22**	**10**	**12**	**127**	**59**	**68**	**0**	**323**	**368**			

Playoff Results 2013-2009

Year	Round	Opponent	Result	GF	GA
2009	CF	Pittsburgh	L 0-4	9	20
	CSF	Boston	W 4-3	16	17
	CQF	New Jersey	W 4-3	17	15

Abbreviations: Round: F – Final; **CF** – conference final; **CSF** – conference semi-final; **CQF** – conference quarter-final; **DSF** – division semi-final.

Calgary totals include Atlanta Flames, 1979-80.
Dallas totals include Minnesota North Stars, 1979-80 to 1992-93.
Phoenix totals include Winnipeg, 1979-80 to 1995-96.
Colorado totals include Quebec, 1979-80 to 1994-95.
New Jersey totals include Colorado Rockies, 1979-80 to 1981-82.
Winnipeg totals include Atlanta Thrashers, 1999-2000 to 2010-11.

2012-13 Results

Jan.	19	at Florida	1-5
	22	Tampa Bay	1-4
	24	Buffalo	6-3
	25	at Buffalo	3-1
	28	Boston	3-5
Feb.	1	Ottawa	1-0
	2	at Philadelphia	3-5
	4	at Toronto	4-1
	7	at Ottawa	3-2*
	9	at Philadelphia	3-4*
	11	at NY Islanders	6-4
	12	at New Jersey	4-2
	14	Toronto	3-1
	18	at Montreal	0-3
	21	Winnipeg	3-4
	23	Tampa Bay	2-5
	24	at NY Islanders	4-2
	26	at Washington	0-3
	28	Pittsburgh	4-1
Mar.	2	Florida	6-2
	3	at Florida	3-2
	5	Buffalo	4-3
	7	Montreal	2-4
	9	New Jersey	6-3
	12	at Washington	4-0
	14	Washington	2-3
	16	at Tampa Bay	1-4
	18	at NY Rangers	1-2†
	19	Florida	1-4
	21	New Jersey	1-4
	26	Winnipeg	1-4
	28	at Toronto	3-6
	30	at Winnipeg	3-1
Apr.	1	at Montreal	1-4
	2	Washington	3-5
	4	Tampa Bay	0-5
	6	NY Rangers	1-4
	8	at Boston	2-6
	9	Pittsburgh	3-5
	11	at Washington	1-3
	13	Boston	4-2
	16	at Ottawa	2-3
	18	at Winnipeg	3-4*
	20	Philadelphia	3-5
	21	at Tampa Bay	3-2
	23	NY Islanders	4-3†
	25	NY Rangers	3-4*
	27	at Pittsburgh	3-8

* – Overtime † – Shootout

Entry Draft Selections 2013-1999

Name in bold denotes played in NHL.

2013

Pick	
5	Elias Lindholm
66	Brett Pesce
126	Brent Pedersen
156	Tyler Ganly

2012

Pick	
38	Phillip Di Giuseppe
47	Brock McGinn
69	Daniel Altshuller
99	Erik Karlsson
115	Trevor Carrick
120	Jaccob Slavin
129	Brendan Woods
159	Collin Olson
189	Brendan Collier

2011

Pick	
12	**Ryan Murphy**
42	Victor Rask
73	Keegan Lowe
103	Gregory Hofmann
163	Matt Mahalak
193	Brody Sutter

2010

Pick	
7	**Jeff Skinner**
37	**Justin Faulk**
53	Mark Alt
67	Danny Biega
85	Austin Levi
105	Justin Shugg
167	Tyler Stahl
187	Frederik Andersen

2009

Pick	
27	Philippe Paradis
51	Brian Dumoulin
88	Mattias Lindstrom
131	Matt Kennedy
178	Rasmus Rissanen
208	Tommi Kivisto

2008

Pick	
14	**Zach Boychuk**
45	**Zac Dalpe**
105	**Michal Jordan**
165	**Mike Murphy**
195	Samuel Morneau

2007

Pick	
11	**Brandon Sutter**
72	**Drayson Bowman**
102	Justin McCrae
132	**Chris Terry**
162	**Brett Bellemore**

2006

Pick	
63	**Jamie McBain**
93	Harrison Reed
123	Bobby Hughes
153	Stefan Chaput
183	Nick Dodge
213	Justin Krueger

2005

Pick	
3	**Jack Johnson**
58	Nate Hagemo
64	Joe Barnes
94	Jakub Vojta
123	Ondrej Otcenas
145	Tim Kunes
159	Risto Korhonen
192	**Nicolas Blanchard**
198	Kyle Lawson

2004

Pick	
4	**Andrew Ladd**
38	**Justin Peters**
69	**Casey Borer**
109	**Brett Carson**
137	Magnus Akerlund
202	Ryan Pottruff
235	Jonas Fiedler
268	Martin Vagner

2003

Pick	
2	**Eric Staal**
31	**Danny Richmond**
102	Aaron Dawson
126	Kevin Nastiuk
130	Matej Trojovsky
137	**Tyson Strachan**
198	**Shay Stephenson**
230	Jamie Hoffmann
262	Ryan Rorabeck

2002

Pick	
25	**Cam Ward**
91	Jesse Lane
160	Daniel Manzato
224	Adam Taylor

2001

Pick	
15	Igor Knyazev
46	**Mike Zigomanis**
91	Kevin Estrada
110	Rob Zepp
181	Daniel Boisclair
211	Sean Curry
244	Carter Trevisani
274	Peter Reynolds

2000

Pick	
32	**Tomas Kurka**
80	**Ryan Bayda**
97	**Niclas Wallin**
110	Jared Newman
181	J.D. Forrest
212	Magnus Kahnberg
235	Craig Kowalski
276	Troy Ferguson

1999

Pick	
16	**David Tanabe**
49	**Brett Lysak**
84	**Brad Fast**
113	Ryan Murphy
174	**Damian Surma**
202	Jim Baxter
231	David Evans
237	Antti Jokela
259	Yevgeny Kurilin

Coaching History

Don Blackburn, 1979-80; Don Blackburn and Larry Pleau, 1980-81; Larry Pleau, 1981-82; Larry Kish, Larry Pleau and John Cuniff, 1982- 83; Jack Evans, 1983-84 to 1986-87; Jack Evans and Larry Pleau, 1987-88; Larry Pleau, 1988-89; Rick Ley, 1989-90, 1990-91; Jim Roberts, 1991-92; Paul Holmgren, 1992-93; Paul Holmgren and Pierre Maguire, 1993-94; Paul Holmgren, 1994-95; Paul Holmgren and Paul Maurice, 1995-96; Paul Maurice, 1996-97 to 2002-03; Paul Maurice and Peter Laviolette, 2003-04; Peter Laviolette, 2004-05 to 2007-08; Peter Laviolette and Paul Maurice, 2008-09; Paul Maurice, 2009-10, 2010-11; Paul Maurice and Kirk Muller, 2011-12; Kirk Muller, 2012-13 to date.

General Managers' History

Jack Kelley, 1979-80; Jack Kelley and Larry Pleau, 1980-81; Larry Pleau, 1981-82, 1982-83; Emile Francis, 1983-84 to 1988-89; Eddie Johnston, 1989-90 to 1991-92; Brian Burke, 1992-93; Paul Holmgren, 1993-94; Jim Rutherford, 1994-95 to date.

Jim Rutherford

President and General Manager

Born: Beeton, Ont., February 17, 1949.

Jim Rutherford, a former NHL goaltender, is the franchise's seventh general manager and the only general manager of the Carolina Hurricanes. Named to his position on June 28, 1994, Rutherford has always taken an aggressive approach towards improving the fortunes of the franchise through trades and the NHL Entry Draft. In 2002, the team reached the Stanley Cup Finals for the first time in history. The Hurricanes won the Stanley Cup in 2006.

A veteran of 13 NHL seasons, Rutherford began his professional goaltending career in 1969 as a first-round selection of the Detroit Red Wings. While playing for Detroit, Pittsburgh, Toronto and Los Angeles, Rutherford collected 14 career shutouts. For five seasons he also served as the Red Wings' player representative. Rutherford also played for Team Canada at the World Championships in Vienna in 1977 and Moscow in 1979.

After his playing days with the Red Wings, Rutherford joined Compuware to serve as the director of hockey operations for Compuware Sports Corporation. Rutherford gained a wealth of experience in youth hockey and junior programs. As a former player, coach, and general manager, his ability to develop players and produce winning programs is widely respected throughout the hockey community.

He started his management career by guiding Compuware Sports Corporation's purchase of the Windsor Spitfires of the Ontario Hockey League in April of 1984. During the next four years, Rutherford acted as general manager of the Spitfires. After the Spitfires advanced to the 1988 Memorial Cup finals, Rutherford led Compuware's efforts to bring the first American-based OHL franchise to Detroit on December 11, 1989. Rutherford was voted the 1987 executive of the year in both the OHL and the Canadian Hockey League and won the OHL executive of the year award again in 1988.

Club Directory

PNC Arena

Carolina Hurricanes
1400 Edwards Mill Rd.
Raleigh, NC 27607
Phone **919/467-7825**
FAX 919/462-0123
Tickets 1.866.NHL.CANES
www.carolinahurricanes.com
Capacity: 18,680

Executive Management

Chief Executive Officer/Owner/Governor	Peter Karmanos, Jr.
President/General Manager	Jim Rutherford
Executive Vice President/Assistant General Manager	Jason Karmanos
Executive Vice President/Chief Financial Officer	Mike Amendola
Executive Vice President/General Manager, PNC Arena	Davin Olsen

Hockey Operations

Vice President of Hockey Operations	Ron Francis
Head Coach	Kirk Muller
Assistant Coaches	Rod Brind'Amour, Dave Lewis, John MacLean
Goaltending Coach	Greg Stefan
Director of Defensemen Development	Glen Wesley
Director of Forwards Development	Cory Stillman
Video Coach	Chris Huffine
Head Ath. Trainer/Strength Conditioning Coach	Peter Friesen
Assistant Athletic Trainer	Doug Bennett
Equipment Managers	Skip Cunningham, Bob Gorman, Jorge Alves
Vice President of Team Operations	Brian Tatum
Executive Assistant to the President/G.M.	Mari Jeter
Video Scout/Hockey Operations Assistant	Darren Yorke
Scouting Directors, Amateur / Pro	Tony MacDonald / Marshall Johnston
Amateur Scouts	Sheldon Ferguson, Robert Kron, Bob Luccini, Bert Marshall
Pro Scouts	Dave Hunter, Gene Reilly
Charlotte Checkers Head Coach/G.M.	Jeff Daniels
Charlotte Checkers Assistant Coach	Geordie Kinnear
Charlotte Checkers Head Athletic Trainer	Brian Maddox
Charlotte Checkers Equipment Managers	Steve Latin, Donny White

Administration

Receptionists	Mary Lou Ruetz, Janet Davis

Arena Operations

Vice President of Guest Relations, PNC Arena	Larry Perkins
Director of Arena Marketing	Crystal Pace
Guest Services Coordinator/Executive Assistant	April Keeley
Director of Safety and Security	Clinton Peterson
Director of Parking and Traffic	Jared Wright
Director of Event and Guest Services	Steve Congress
Director of Premium Services	Suzanne Golden
Director of Production	Rob Douglas
Senior Director of Operations and Facilities	Dan McGowan
Director of Facilities / Operations Manager	Alan Wobbleton / Melvin Terrell
Vice President of Ticket Operations	Bill Nowicki
Director of Arena Box Office	Joe Sousa
Arena Box Office Manager	Erin Latore

Broadcasters

Television Play-by-Play / Analyst	John Forslund / Tripp Tracy
Radio Play-by-Play	Chuck Kaiton
Sideline Reporter/Host	Chantel McCabe

Communications

Senior Director of Communications	Mike Sundheim
Director of Media Relations and Broadcasting	Kyle Hanlin
Team Photographer	Gregg Forwerck

Finance/Information Technology

Senior Vice President/General Counsel	William Traurig
Accountant	Shaun Nicholson
Accounts Payable / Receivable	Michael Arrington / Patty Hilliard, Temika Smith-Harris
Payroll/Human Resources	Crystal DeDitius, Keitha Stanley
Assistant to the CFO	Stacey Ustin
Vice President of Information Technology	Glenn Johnson
Director IT Services	Myatt Williams
Client/Server Technologist / Developer	Larry Kelly / Alex Byrd

Food and Beverage

Senior Director of VAB Catering	Chris Diamond
Director of Concessions / Director of Catering	Rick Rhodes / Katrina Ryan
Director of Suites Food and Beverage	Lori Holtz
Commissary Manager	Gary Berry
Chefs	Michael Flood, Dennis Atkinson, Kevin Heintz, Lecan Huynh, Pete Aiello
Concessions Manager / Catering Manager	Jim O'Brien / Frankie McGee
Assistant Managers, Concessions / Catering	Barbara Couch / Skip Roach

Marketing

Vice President of Marketing/ Exec. Dir., Kids 'n Community Foundation	Doug Warf
Senior Director of Marketing and Brand Development	Ben Aycock
Dir. of Canesvision and In-Game Marketing	Stephen Rutherford
Dir. of Community Relations and Promotions	Jon Chase
Web Producer / Social Media Specialist	Michael Smith / Coop Elias
Manager of Creative Services	Lauren Baxter
Senior Graphic Designer	Andrew Roman
Youth and Amateur Hockey Coordinator	Shane Willis
Mascot Coordinator	George Brown
Promotions/Fan Development Coordinator	Ryan O'Quinn
Sr. Coordinator, Community Relations/ Asst. Dir., Kids 'n Community Foundation	Kristina Boyce
Community Relations Coordinator	Gabby Pinto

Gale Force Media, CanesVision and Wolfpack TV

Senior Producer	Don Sill
Producers	Chris Burns, Logan McDonald
Graphics Producer	Rachel Cannon

Merchandise

Director of Merchandise	James Blitch

Sales

Vice President of Corporate Sponsorships	Jim Ballweg
Senior Corporate Sales Executives	Rick Francis, Johnny Gill, Todd Yunker
Corporate Sales Executive	Justin Buck
Client Services Coordinator	Marie Bobalik
Vice President of Ticket Sales / Assistant	Kyle Prairie / Karen Prince
Director of Ticket Sales	Peterson Avetta
Account Executives/Business Development	Michael Miller, Greg Perna, Jonathan Kramer
Client Relations Representative	Brian Friedhaber
Hurricanes Group Sales Manager	Brian Kapusta
PNC Arena Group Sales Manager	Brian Slais
Senior Group Sales Representative	Rich Davis

Chicago Blackhawks

Key Off-Season Signings/Acquisitions

2013

- **June 30** • Re-signed LW **Bryan Bickell**.
- **July 3** • Re-signed D **Nick Leddy**.
- **5** • Signed G **Nikolai Khabibulin**.
- **5** • Re-signed C **Michal Handzus** and D **Michal Rozsival**.
- **12** • Re-signed C **Marcus Kruger**.
- **19** • Signed D **Theo Peckham** and D **Mike Kostka**.
- **24** • Signed LW **Brad Winchester**.

2012-13 Results: 36W-7L-0OTL-5SOL 77PTS
1ST, Central Division • 1ST, Western Conference

2013-14 Schedule

Oct.	Tue.	1	Washington		Mon.	30	Los Angeles
	Sat.	5	Tampa Bay	**Jan.**	Thu.	2	at NY Islanders
	Wed.	9	at St. Louis		Fri.	3	at New Jersey
	Fri.	11	NY Islanders		Sun.	5	San Jose
	Sat.	12	Buffalo		Wed.	8	NY Rangers
	Tue.	15	at Carolina		Sat.	11	at Montreal
	Thu.	17	St. Louis		Sun.	12	Edmonton
	Sat.	19	Toronto		Tue.	14	Colorado
	Tue.	22	at Florida		Fri.	17	Anaheim
	Thu.	24	at Tampa Bay		Sun.	19	Boston*
	Sat.	26	Minnesota		Wed.	22	at Detroit
	Mon.	28	at Minnesota		Thu.	23	at Minnesota
	Tue.	29	Ottawa		Sun.	26	Winnipeg
Nov.	Sat.	2	at Winnipeg*		Tue.	28	at Calgary
	Sun.	3	Calgary		Wed.	29	at Vancouver
	Wed.	6	Winnipeg	**Feb.**	Sat.	1	at San Jose
	Sat.	9	at Dallas		Mon.	3	at Los Angeles
	Sun.	10	Edmonton		Wed.	5	at Anaheim
	Thu.	14	Phoenix		Fri.	7	at Phoenix
	Sat.	16	at Nashville		Thu.	27	at NY Rangers
	Sun.	17	San Jose	**Mar.**	Sat.	1	Pittsburgh
	Tue.	19	at Colorado		Tue.	4	Colorado
	Thu.	21	at Winnipeg		Thu.	6	Columbus
	Sat.	23	at Vancouver		Sun.	9	at Buffalo
	Mon.	25	at Edmonton		Wed.	12	at Colorado
	Wed.	27	at Calgary		Fri.	14	Nashville
	Fri.	29	at Dallas		Sun.	16	Detroit
	Sat.	30	at Phoenix		Tue.	18	at Philadelphia
Dec.	Tue.	3	Dallas		Wed.	19	St. Louis
	Thu.	5	at Minnesota		Fri.	21	Carolina
	Fri.	6	Anaheim		Sun.	23	Nashville
	Sun.	8	Florida		Tue.	25	Dallas
	Tue.	10	at Dallas		Thu.	27	at Boston
	Wed.	11	Philadelphia		Fri.	28	at Ottawa
	Sat.	14	at Toronto		Sun.	30	at Pittsburgh
	Sun.	15	Los Angeles	**Apr.**	Thu.	3	Minnesota
	Tue.	17	at Nashville		Fri.	4	at Columbus
	Fri.	20	Vancouver		Sun.	6	St. Louis
	Mon.	23	New Jersey		Wed.	9	Montreal
	Fri.	27	Colorado		Fri.	11	at Washington
	Sat.	28	at St. Louis		Sat.	12	at Nashville

* Denotes afternoon game.

CENTRAL DIVISION
88th NHL Season

Franchise date: September 25, 1926

Year-by-Year Record

		Home				Road				Overall									
Season	**GP**	**W**	**L**	**T**	**OL**	**W**	**L**	**T**	**OL**	**W**	**L**	**T**	**OL**	**GF**	**GA**	**Pts.**	**Div. Fin.**	**Conf. Fin.**	**Playoff Result**
2012-13	**48**	**18**	**3**	....	**3**	**18**	**4**	....	**2**	**36**	**7**	....	**5**	**155**	**102**	**77**	**1st, Cen.**	**1st, West**	**Won Stanley Cup**
2011-12	82	27	8	....	6	18	18	....	5	45	26	....	11	248	238	101	4th, Cen.	6th, West	Lost Conf. Quarter-Final
2010-11	82	24	17	....	0	20	12	....	9	44	29	....	9	258	225	97	3rd, Cen.	8th, West	Lost Conf. Quarter-Final
2009-10	**82**	**29**	**8**	....	**4**	**23**	**14**	....	**4**	**52**	**22**	....	**8**	**271**	**209**	**112**	**1st, Cen.**	**2nd, West**	**Won Stanley Cup**
2008-09	82	24	9	....	8	22	15	....	4	46	24	....	12	264	216	104	2nd, Cen.	4th, West	Lost Conf. Final
2007-08	82	23	16	....	2	17	18	....	6	40	34	....	8	239	235	88	3rd, Cen.	10th, West	Out of Playoffs
2006-07	82	17	20	....	4	14	22	....	5	31	42	....	9	201	258	71	5th, Cen.	13th, West	Out of Playoffs
2005-06	82	16	19	....	6	10	24	....	7	26	43	....	13	211	285	65	4th, Cen.	14th, West	Out of Playoffs
2004-05	....	....	....	....	....	....	....	....	....	....	....	....	....	....	....	....			
2003-04	82	13	17	6	5	7	26	5	3	20	43	11	8	188	259	59	5th, Cen.	15th, West	Out of Playoffs
2002-03	82	17	15	7	2	13	18	6	4	30	33	13	6	207	226	79	3rd, Cen.	9th, West	Out of Playoffs
2001-02	82	28	7	5	1	13	20	8	0	41	27	13	1	216	207	96	3rd, Cen.	5th, West	Lost Conf. Quarter-Final
2000-01	82	14	21	4	2	15	19	4	3	29	40	8	5	210	246	71	4th, Cen.	12th, West	Out of Playoffs
1999-2000	82	16	19	5	1	17	18	5	1	33	37	10	2	242	245	78	3rd, Cen.	11th, West	Out of Playoffs
1998-99	82	20	17	4	....	9	24	8	....	29	41	12	....	202	248	70	3rd, Cen.	10th, West	Out of Playoffs
1997-98	82	14	19	8	....	16	20	5	....	30	39	13	....	192	199	73	5th, Cen.	9th, West	Out of Playoffs
1996-97	82	16	21	4	....	18	14	9	....	34	35	13	....	223	210	81	5th, Cen.	8th, West	Lost Conf. Quarter-Final
1995-96	82	22	13	6	....	18	15	8	....	40	28	14	....	273	220	94	2nd, Cen.	3rd, West	Lost Conf. Semi-Final
1994-95	48	11	10	3	....	13	9	2	....	24	19	5	....	156	115	53	3rd, Cen.	4th, West	Lost Conf. Final
1993-94	84	21	16	5	....	18	20	4	....	39	36	9	....	254	240	87	5th, Cen.	6th, West	Lost Conf. Quarter-Final
1992-93	84	25	11	6	....	22	14	6	....	47	25	12	....	279	230	106	1st, Norris		Lost Div. Semi-Final
1991-92	80	23	9	8	....	13	20	7	....	36	29	15	....	257	236	87	2nd, Norris		Lost Final
1990-91	80	28	8	4	....	21	15	4	....	49	23	8	....	284	211	106	1st, Norris		Lost Div. Semi-Final
1989-90	80	25	13	2	....	16	20	4	....	41	33	6	....	316	294	88	1st, Norris		Lost Conf. Final
1988-89	80	16	14	10	....	11	27	2	....	27	41	12	....	297	335	66	4th, Norris		Lost Conf. Final
1987-88	80	21	17	2	....	9	24	7	....	30	41	9	....	284	328	69	3rd, Norris		Lost Div. Semi-Final
1986-87	80	18	13	9	....	11	24	5	....	29	37	14	....	290	310	72	3rd, Norris		Lost Div. Semi-Final
1985-86	80	23	12	5	....	16	21	3	....	39	33	8	....	351	349	86	1st, Norris		Lost Div. Semi-Final
1984-85	80	22	16	2	....	16	19	5	....	38	35	7	....	309	299	83	2nd, Norris		Lost Conf. Final
1983-84	80	25	13	2	....	5	29	6	....	30	42	8	....	277	311	68	4th, Norris		Lost Div. Semi-Final
1982-83	80	29	8	3	....	18	15	7	....	47	23	10	....	338	268	104	1st, Norris		Lost Conf. Final
1981-82	80	20	13	7	....	10	25	5	....	30	38	12	....	332	363	72	4th, Norris		Lost Conf. Final
1980-81	80	21	11	8	....	10	22	8	....	31	33	16	....	304	315	78	2nd, Smythe		Lost Prelim. Round
1979-80	80	21	12	7	....	13	15	12	....	34	27	19	....	241	250	87	1st, Smythe		Lost Quarter-Final
1978-79	80	18	12	10	....	11	24	5	....	29	36	15	....	244	277	73	1st, Smythe		Lost Quarter-Final
1977-78	80	20	9	11	....	12	20	8	....	32	29	19	....	230	220	83	1st, Smythe		Lost Quarter-Final
1976-77	80	19	16	5	....	7	27	6	....	26	43	11	....	240	298	63	3rd, Smythe		Lost Prelim. Round
1975-76	80	17	15	8	....	15	15	10	....	32	30	18	....	254	261	82	1st, Smythe		Lost Quarter-Final
1974-75	80	24	12	4	....	13	23	4	....	37	35	8	....	268	241	82	3rd, Smythe		Lost Quarter-Final
1973-74	78	20	6	13	....	21	8	10	....	41	14	23	....	272	164	105	2nd, West		Lost Semi-Final
1972-73	78	26	9	4	....	16	18	5	....	42	27	9	....	284	225	93	1st, West		Lost Final
1971-72	78	28	3	8	....	18	14	7	....	46	17	15	....	256	166	107	1st, West		Lost Semi-Final
1970-71	78	30	6	3	....	19	14	6	....	49	20	9	....	277	184	107	1st, West		Lost Final
1969-70	76	26	7	5	....	19	15	4	....	45	22	9	....	250	170	99	1st, East		Lost Semi-Final
1968-69	76	20	14	4	....	14	19	5	....	34	33	9	....	280	246	77	6th, East		Out of Playoffs
1967-68	74	20	13	4	....	12	13	12	....	32	26	16	....	212	222	80	4th, East		Lost Semi-Final
1966-67	70	24	5	6	....	17	12	6	....	41	17	12	....	264	170	94	1st,		Lost Semi-Final
1965-66	70	21	8	6	....	16	17	2	....	37	25	8	....	240	187	82	2nd,		Lost Semi-Final
1964-65	70	20	13	2	....	14	15	6	....	34	28	8	....	224	176	76	3rd,		Lost Final
1963-64	70	26	4	5	....	10	18	7	....	36	22	12	....	218	169	84	2nd,		Lost Semi-Final
1962-63	70	17	9	9	....	15	12	8	....	32	21	17	....	194	178	81	2nd,		Lost Semi-Final
1961-62	70	20	10	5	....	11	16	8	....	31	26	13	....	217	186	75	3rd,		Lost Final
1960-61	**70**	**20**	**6**	**9**	....	**9**	**18**	**8**	....	**29**	**24**	**17**	....	**198**	**180**	**75**	**3rd,**		**Won Stanley Cup**
1959-60	70	18	11	6	....	10	18	7	....	28	29	13	....	191	180	69	3rd,		Lost Semi-Final
1958-59	70	14	12	9	....	14	17	4	....	28	29	13	....	197	208	69	3rd,		Lost Semi-Final
1957-58	70	15	17	3	....	9	22	4	....	24	39	7	....	163	202	55	5th,		Out of Playoffs
1956-57	70	12	15	8	....	4	24	7	....	16	39	15	....	169	225	47	6th,		Out of Playoffs
1955-56	70	9	19	7	....	10	20	5	....	19	39	12	....	155	216	50	6th,		Out of Playoffs
1954-55	70	6	21	8	....	7	19	9	....	13	40	17	....	161	235	43	6th,		Out of Playoffs
1953-54	70	8	21	6	....	4	30	1	....	12	51	7	....	133	242	31	6th,		Out of Playoffs
1952-53	70	14	11	10	....	13	17	5	....	27	28	15	....	169	175	69	4th,		Lost Semi-Final
1951-52	70	9	19	7	....	8	25	2	....	17	44	9	....	158	241	43	6th,		Out of Playoffs
1950-51	70	8	22	5	....	5	25	5	....	13	47	10	....	171	280	36	6th,		Out of Playoffs
1949-50	70	13	18	4	....	9	20	6	....	22	38	10	....	203	244	54	6th,		Out of Playoffs
1948-49	60	13	12	5	....	8	19	3	....	21	31	8	....	173	211	50	5th,		Out of Playoffs
1947-48	60	10	17	3	....	10	17	3	....	20	34	6	....	195	225	46	6th,		Out of Playoffs
1946-47	60	10	17	3	....	9	20	1	....	19	37	4	....	193	274	42	6th,		Out of Playoffs
1945-46	50	15	5	5	....	8	15	2	....	23	20	7	....	200	178	53	3rd,		Lost Semi-Final
1944-45	50	9	14	2	....	4	16	5	....	13	30	7	....	141	194	33	5th,		Out of Playoffs
1943-44	50	15	6	4	....	7	17	1	....	22	23	5	....	178	187	49	4th,		Lost Final
1942-43	50	14	3	8	....	3	15	7	....	17	18	15	....	179	180	49	5th,		Out of Playoffs
1941-42	48	15	8	1	....	7	15	2	....	22	23	3	....	145	155	47	4th,		Lost Quarter-Final
1940-41	48	11	10	3	....	5	15	4	....	16	25	7	....	112	139	39	5th,		Lost Semi-Final
1939-40	48	15	7	2	....	8	12	4	....	23	19	6	....	112	120	52	4th,		Lost Quarter-Final
1938-39	48	5	13	6	....	7	15	2	....	12	28	8	....	91	132	32	7th,		Out of Playoffs
1937-38	**48**	**10**	**10**	**4**	....	**4**	**15**	**5**	....	**14**	**25**	**9**	....	**97**	**139**	**37**	**3rd, Amn.**		**Won Stanley Cup**
1936-37	48	8	13	3	....	6	14	4	....	14	27	7	....	99	131	35	4th, Amn.		Out of Playoffs
1935-36	48	15	7	2	....	6	12	6	....	21	19	8	....	93	92	50	3rd, Amn.		Lost Quarter-Final
1934-35	48	12	9	3	....	14	8	2	....	26	17	5	....	118	88	57	2nd, Amn.		Lost Quarter-Final
1933-34	**48**	**13**	**4**	**7**	....	**7**	**13**	**4**	....	**20**	**17**	**11**	....	**88**	**83**	**51**	**2nd, Amn.**		**Won Stanley Cup**
1932-33	48	12	7	5	....	4	13	7	....	16	20	12	....	88	101	44	4th, Amn.		Out of Playoffs
1931-32	48	13	5	6	....	5	14	5	....	18	19	11	....	86	101	47	2nd, Amn.		Lost Quarter-Final
1930-31	44	13	8	1	....	11	9	2	....	24	17	3	....	108	78	51	2nd, Amn.		Lost Final
1929-30	44	12	9	1	....	9	9	4	....	21	18	5	....	117	111	47	2nd, Amn.		Lost Quarter-Final
1928-29	44	3	13	6	....	4	16	2	....	7	29	8	....	33	85	22	5th, Amn.		Out of Playoffs
1927-28	44	2	18	2	....	5	16	1	....	7	34	3	....	68	134	17	5th, Amn.		Out of Playoffs
1926-27	44	12	8	2	....	7	14	1	....	19	22	3	....	115	116	41	3rd, Amn.		Lost Quarter-Final

2013-14 Player Personnel

FORWARDS	HT	WT	*Age	Place of Birth	S	2012-13 Club
BEACH, Kyle	6-3	208	23	Vancouver, B.C.	R	Rockford
BICKELL, Bryan	6-4	233	27	Bowmanville, Ont.	L	Znojmo-Chicago
BOLLIG, Brandon	6-2	223	26	St. Charles, MO	L	Rockford-Chicago
DANAULT, Phillip	6-0	184	20	Victoriaville, Que.	L	Victoriaville-Moncton-Rockford
HANDZUS, Michal	6-5	215	36	Banska Bystrica, Czech.	L	B. Bystrica-S.J.-Chi
HAYES, Jimmy	6-6	221	23	Boston, MA	R	Rockford-Chicago
HOSSA, Marian	6-1	210	34	Stara Lubovna, Czech.	L	Chicago
KANE, Patrick	5-11	181	24	Buffalo, NY	L	Biel-Chicago
KRUGER, Marcus	6-0	181	23	Stockholm, Sweden	L	Rockford-Chicago
LeBLANC, Drew	6-0	195	24	Hermantown, MN	R	St. Cloud State-Chicago
McNEILL, Mark	6-1	211	20	Langley, B.C.	R	Prince Albert-Rockford
MORIN, Jeremy	6-1	192	22	Auburn, NY	R	Rockford-Chicago
PIRRI, Brandon	6-0	183	22	Toronto, Ont.	L	Rockford-Chicago
SAAD, Brandon	6-1	202	20	Pittsburgh, PA	L	Rockford-Chicago
SHARP, Patrick	6-1	199	31	Winnipeg, Man.	R	Chicago
SHAW, Andrew	5-10	180	22	Belleville, Ont.	R	Rockford-Chicago
SMITH, Ben	5-11	207	25	Winston-Salem, NC	R	Rockford-Chicago
TOEWS, Jonathan	6-2	208	25	Winnipeg, Man.	L	Chicago
WINCHESTER, Brad	6-5	230	32	Madison, WI	L	Milwaukee
DEFENSEMEN						
BROOKBANK, Sheldon	6-1	202	32	Lanigan, Sask.	R	Chicago
CLENDENING, Adam	5-11	187	20	Niagara Falls, NY	R	Rockford
HJALMARSSON, Niklas	6-3	207	26	Eksjo, Sweden	L	Bolzano-Chicago
KEITH, Duncan	6-1	200	30	Winnipeg, Man.	L	Chicago
KOSTKA, Mike	6-1	200	27	Etobicoke, Ont.	R	Toronto (AHL)-Toronto
LEDDY, Nick	6-0	191	22	Eden Prairie, MN	L	Rockford-Chicago
ODUYA, Johnny	6-0	190	32	Stockholm, Sweden	L	Flying Farangs-Chicago
OLSEN, Dylan	6-2	214	22	Salt Lake City, UT	L	Rockford
PECKHAM, Theo	6-2	236	25	Richmond Hill, Ont.	L	San Francisco-Edm-Oklahoma City
ROZSIVAL, Michal	6-1	212	35	Vlasim, Czech.	R	Chicago
SEABROOK, Brent	6-3	221	28	Richmond, B.C.	R	Chicago
STANTON, Ryan	6-2	196	24	St. Albert, Alta.	L	Rockford-Chicago

GOALTENDERS	HT	WT	*Age	Place of Birth	C	2012-13 Club
CRAWFORD, Corey	6-2	208	28	Montreal, Que.	L	Chicago
KHABIBULIN, Nikolai	6-1	208	40	Sverdlovsk, USSR	L	Edmonton
RAANTA, Antti	6-0	182	24	Rauma, Finland	L	Assat

* – Age at start of 2013-14 season

Joel Quenneville

Head Coach

Born: Windsor, Ont., September 15, 1958.

Joel Quenneville was named the 37th head coach in Chicago Blackhawks history on October 16, 2008 and in 2009-10 he guided the team to its first Stanley Cup championship since 1961. Quenneville led Chicago to another Stanley Cup title in 2013. He originally joined the Blackhawks as a pro scout in September 2008. Quenneville has been a proven winner throughout his career as a head coach in the NHL, including seven seasons with the St. Louis Blues (1996 to 2004) and three with the Colorado Avalanche (2005 to 2008). In his first season behind the bench in Chicago, he led the Blackhawks to the Western Conference Final in just their second playoff appearance since the 1996-97 season.

One of only three men in the history of the NHL to have played in and coached 800 or more games, Quenneville is the winningest coach in Blues history, having compiled a 307-191-95 record. He won the 2000 Jack Adams Award as the league's top coach. Quenneville was drafted by the Toronto Maple Leafs in the first round (21st overall) of the 1978 NHL Entry Draft. He spent 13 seasons as an NHL defenseman, netting 54 goals, 136 assists, 190 points and 705 penalty minutes in 803 career games with the Toronto Maple Leafs, Colorado Rockies, New Jersey Devils, Hartford Whalers and Washington Capitals.

Quenneville retired as an active player after the 1991-92 season, when he served as a player-coach for the American Hockey League's St. John's Maple Leafs. Quenneville broke into coaching with the AHL's Springfield Indians before serving as an assistant coach for the Quebec Nordiques/Colorado Avalanche organization for two and a half seasons. He helped Colorado capture the 1996 Stanley Cup in that position before accepting his first NHL head coaching job with St. Louis for the 1996-97 campaign.

Coaching Record

			Regular Season				Playoffs			
Season	Team	League	GC	W	L	O/T	GC	W	L	T
1993-94	Springfield	AHL	80	29	38	13	6	2	4	....
1996-97	**St. Louis**	**NHL**	**40**	**18**	**15**	**7**	**6**	**2**	**4**	....
1997-98	**St. Louis**	**NHL**	**82**	**45**	**29**	**8**	**10**	**6**	**4**	....
1998-99	**St. Louis**	**NHL**	**82**	**37**	**32**	**13**	**13**	**6**	**7**	....
99-2000	**St. Louis**	**NHL**	**82**	**51**	**19**	**12**	**7**	**3**	**4**	....
2000-01	**St. Louis**	**NHL**	**82**	**43**	**22**	**17**	**15**	**9**	**6**	....
2001-02	**St. Louis**	**NHL**	**82**	**43**	**27**	**12**	**10**	**5**	**5**	....
2002-03	**St. Louis**	**NHL**	**82**	**41**	**24**	**17**	**7**	**3**	**4**	....
2003-04	**St. Louis**	**NHL**	**61**	**29**	**23**	**9**	....	....	....	....
2004-05	**Colorado**				SEASON CANCELLED					
2005-06	**Colorado**	**NHL**	**82**	**43**	**30**	**9**	**9**	**4**	**5**	....
2006-07	**Colorado**	**NHL**	**82**	**44**	**31**	**7**	....	....	....	....
2007-08	**Colorado**	**NHL**	**82**	**44**	**31**	**7**	**10**	**4**	**6**	....
2008-09	**Chicago**	**NHL**	**78**	**45**	**22**	**11**	**17**	**9**	**8**	....
2009-10♦	**Chicago**	**NHL**	**82**	**52**	**22**	**8**	**22**	**16**	**6**	....
2010-11	**Chicago**	**NHL**	**82**	**44**	**29**	**9**	**7**	**3**	**4**	....
2011-12	**Chicago**	**NHL**	**82**	**45**	**26**	**11**	**6**	**2**	**4**	....
2012-13♦	**Chicago**	**NHL**	**48**	**36**	**7**	**5**	**23**	**16**	**7**	....
	NHL Totals		**1211**	**660**	**389**	**162**	**162**	**88**	**74**	....

♦ Stanley Cup win.
Jack Adams Award (2000)
Assistant coach Mike Haviland posted a 3-1-0 record as replacement coach when Joel Quenneville was sidelined with an ulcer, February 16 to 23, 2011. All games are credited to Quenneville's coaching record.

2012-13 Scoring

* – rookie

Regular Season

Pos	#	Player	Team	GP	G	A	Pts	TOI	+/–	PIM	PP	SH	GW	S	%
R	88	Patrick Kane	CHI	47	23	32	55	20:03	11	8	8	0	3	138	16.7
C	19	Jonathan Toews	CHI	47	23	25	48	19:20	28	27	2	2	5	143	16.1
R	81	Marian Hossa	CHI	40	17	14	31	18:02	20	16	4	1	6	116	14.7
L	20 *	Brandon Saad	CHI	46	10	17	27	16:27	17	12	0	1	2	98	10.2
D	2	Duncan Keith	CHI	47	3	24	27	24:06	16	31	2	0	0	91	3.3
L	25	Viktor Stalberg	CHI	47	9	14	23	14:07	16	25	0	0	1	113	8.0
L	29	Bryan Bickell	CHI	48	9	14	23	12:48	12	25	0	0	2	82	11.0
D	7	Brent Seabrook	CHI	47	8	12	20	21:59	12	23	3	0	1	65	12.3
R	10	Patrick Sharp	CHI	28	6	14	20	18:49	8	14	1	0	1	88	6.8
D	8	Nick Leddy	CHI	48	6	12	18	17:25	15	10	2	0	2	65	9.2
C	65	Andrew Shaw	CHI	48	9	6	15	15:03	6	38	2	0	2	64	14.1
C	36	Dave Bolland	CHI	35	7	7	14	16:20	–7	22	1	0	1	46	15.2
C	16	Marcus Kruger	CHI	47	4	9	13	14:09	3	24	0	0	2	50	8.0
D	27	Johnny Oduya	CHI	48	3	9	12	20:31	12	10	0	0	0	52	5.8
D	32	Michal Rozsival	CHI	27	0	12	12	18:06	18	14	0	0	0	13	0.0
R	67	Michael Frolik	CHI	45	3	7	10	12:31	5	8	0	0	1	98	3.1
D	4	Niklas Hjalmarsson	CHI	46	2	8	10	20:54	15	22	0	0	0	43	4.7
C	26	Michal Handzus	S.J.	28	1	1	2	13:32	–9	12	0	0	0	31	3.2
			CHI	11	1	5	6	12:06	7	4	0	0	0	10	10.0
			Total	39	2	6	8	13:08	–2	16	0	0	0	41	4.9
R	39	Jimmy Hayes	CHI	10	1	3	4	14:19	0	0	0	0	0	13	7.7
L	13	Daniel Carcillo	CHI	23	2	1	3	8:59	1	11	0	0	1	23	8.7
L	11 *	Jeremy Morin	CHI	3	1	1	2	13:01	1	0	0	0	0	7	14.3
R	22	Jamal Mayers	CHI	19	0	2	2	6:58	2	16	0	0	0	10	0.0
R	28	Ben Smith	CHI	1	1	0	1	18:21	1	0	0	0	0	1	100.0
D	17	Sheldon Brookbank	CHI	26	1	0	1	12:45	–2	21	0	1	0	25	4.0
D	42 *	Shawn Lalonde	CHI	1	0	0	0	14:47	1	0	0	0	0	0	0.0
C	37 *	Brandon Pirri	CHI	1	0	0	0	17:55	0	0	0	0	0	2	0.0
D	55 *	Ryan Stanton	CHI	1	0	0	0	17:05	1	2	0	0	0	1	0.0
C	14 *	Drew Leblanc	CHI	2	0	0	0	13:20	–3	0	0	0	0	3	0.0
L	52 *	Brandon Bollig	CHI	25	0	0	0	8:00	–1	51	0	0	0	34	0.0

Goaltending

No.	Goaltender	GPI	Mins	Avg	W	L	OT	EN	SO	GA	SA	S%	G	A	PIM
30	Ray Emery	21	1116	1.94	17	1	0	0	3	36	460	.922	0	0	0
50	Corey Crawford	30	1761	1.94	19	5	5	1	3	57	769	.926	0	0	4
33	Carter Hutton	1	59	3.05	0	1	0	0	0	3	28	.893	0	0	0
	Totals	**48**	**2945**	**1.98**	**36**	**7**	**5**	**1**	**7**	**97**	**1258**	**.923**			

Ray Emery and Corey Crawford shared a shutout vs. St. Louis on Feb. 28, 2013

Playoffs

Pos	#	Player	Team	GP	G	A	Pts	TOI	+/–	PIM	PP	SH	GW	OT	S	%
R	88	Patrick Kane	CHI	23	9	10	19	20:55	7	8	0	0	2	1	88	10.2
L	29	Bryan Bickell	CHI	23	9	8	17	15:22	11	14	1	0	2	1	49	18.4
R	10	Patrick Sharp	CHI	23	10	6	16	18:15	1	8	2	0	2	0	91	11.0
R	81	Marian Hossa	CHI	22	7	9	16	19:56	8	2	3	0	2	0	70	10.0
C	19	Jonathan Toews	CHI	23	3	11	14	21:33	9	18	1	0	0	0	70	4.3
D	2	Duncan Keith	CHI	22	2	11	13	27:37	10	18	0	0	0	0	51	3.9
C	26	Michal Handzus	CHI	23	3	8	11	16:03	7	6	0	1	0	0	17	17.6
R	67	Michael Frolik	CHI	23	3	7	10	13:09	1	6	0	1	1	0	46	6.5
C	65	Andrew Shaw	CHI	23	5	4	9	14:49	2	35	1	0	2	1	36	13.9
D	27	Johnny Oduya	CHI	23	3	5	8	22:44	12	16	0	0	1	0	30	10.0
C	36	Dave Bolland	CHI	18	3	3	6	13:30	–2	24	0	0	1	0	29	10.3
L	20 *	Brandon Saad	CHI	23	1	5	6	16:23	–1	4	0	0	0	0	50	2.0
C	16	Marcus Kruger	CHI	23	3	2	5	13:48	–2	2	0	0	1	0	27	11.1
D	4	Niklas Hjalmarsson	CHI	23	0	5	5	23:14	10	4	0	0	0	0	12	0.0
D	7	Brent Seabrook	CHI	23	3	1	4	23:04	–1	4	0	0	2	2	39	7.7
D	32	Michal Rozsival	CHI	23	0	4	4	19:15	9	16	0	0	0	0	14	0.0
L	25	Viktor Stalberg	CHI	19	0	3	3	10:35	–1	6	0	0	0	0	27	0.0
D	8	Nick Leddy	CHI	23	0	2	2	14:20	–8	4	0	0	0	0	31	0.0
L	13	Daniel Carcillo	CHI	4	0	1	1	6:41	2	6	0	0	0	0	3	0.0
D	17	Sheldon Brookbank	CHI	1	0	0	0	6:50	–2	0	0	0	0	0	0	0.0
R	28	Ben Smith	CHI	1	0	0	0	10:23	–1	0	0	0	0	0	1	0.0
L	52 *	Brandon Bollig	CHI	5	0	0	0	8:51	–1	2	0	0	0	0	6	0.0

Goaltending

No.	Goaltender	GPI	Mins	Avg	W	L	EN	SO	GA	SA	S%	G	A	PIM
50	Corey Crawford	23	1504	1.84	16	7	2	1	46	674	.932	0	0	0
	Totals	**23**	**1510**	**1.91**	**16**	**7**	**2**	**1**	**48**	**676**	**.929**			

Coaching History

Pete Muldoon, 1926-27; Barney Stanley and Hugh Lehman, 1927-28; Herb Gardiner and Dick Irvin, 1928-29; Tom Shaughnessy and Bill Tobin, 1929-30; Dick Irvin, 1930-31; Bill Tobin, 1931-32; Emil Iverson, Godfrey Matheson and Tommy Gorman, 1932-33; Tommy Gorman, 1933-34; Clem Loughlin, 1934-35 to 1936-37; Bill Stewart, 1937-38; Bill Stewart and Paul Thompson, 1938-39; Paul Thompson, 1939-40 to 1943-44; Paul Thompson and Johnny Gottselig, 1944-45; Johnny Gottselig, 1945-46, 1946-47; Johnny Gottselig and Charlie Conacher, 1947-48; Charlie Conacher, 1948-49, 1949-50; Ebbie Goodfellow, 1950-51, 1951-52; Sid Abel, 1952-53, 1953-54; Frank Eddolls, 1954-55; Dick Irvin, 1955-56; Tommy Ivan, 1956-57; Tommy Ivan and Rudy Pilous, 1957-58; Rudy Pilous, 1958-59 to 1962-63; Billy Reay, 1963-64 to 1975-76; Billy Reay and Bill White, 1976-77; Bob Pulford, 1977-78, 1978-79; Eddie Johnston, 1979-80; Keith Magnuson, 1980-81; Keith Magnuson and Bob Pulford, 1981-82; Orval Tessier, 1982-83, 1983-84; Orval Tessier and Bob Pulford, 1984-85; Bob Pulford, 1985-86, 1986-87; Bob Murdoch, 1987-88; Mike Keenan, 1988-89 to 1991-92; Darryl Sutter, 1992-93 to 1994-95; Craig Hartsburg, 1995-96 to 1997-98; Dirk Graham and Lorne Molleken, 1998-99; Lorne Molleken and Bob Pulford, 1999-2000; Alpo Suhonen, 2000-01; Brian Sutter, 2001-02 to 2004-05; Trent Yawney, 2005-06; Trent Yawney and Denis Savard, 2006-07; Denis Savard, 2007-08; Denis Savard and Joel Quenneville, 2008-09; Joel Quenneville, 2009-10 to date.

Club Records

Team

(Figures in brackets for season records are games played; records for fewest points, wins, ties, losses, goals, goals against are for 70 or more games)

Most Points **112** 2009-10 (82)
Most Wins **52** 2009-10 (82)
Most Ties **23** 1973-74 (78)
Most Losses **56** 2005-06 (82)
Most Goals **351** 1985-86 (80)
Most Goals Against **363** 1981-82 (80)
Fewest Points **31** 1953-54 (70)
Fewest Wins **12** 1953-54 (70)
Fewest Ties **6** 1989-90 (80)
Fewest Losses **14** 1973-74 (78)
Fewest Goals ***133** 1953-54 (70)
Fewest Goals Against **164** 1973-74 (78)
Longest Winning Streak
Overall .... **11** Feb. 15-Mar. 6/13
Home .... **13** Nov. 11-Dec. 20/70
Away .... **7** Dec. 9-29/64
Longest Undefeated Streak
Overall .... **15** Jan. 14-Feb. 16/67 (12W, 3T), Oct. 29-Dec. 3/75 (6W, 9T)
Home .... **18** Oct. 11-Dec. 20/70 (16W, 2T)
Away .... **12** Nov. 2-Dec. 16/67 (6W, 6T)
Longest Losing Streak
Overall .... **12** Feb. 25-Mar. 25/51
Home .... **10** Jan. 29-Mar. 21/28
Away .... **19** Nov. 10/03-Jan. 29/04
Longest Winless Streak
Overall .... **21** Dec. 17/50-Jan. 28/51 (18L, 3T)
Home .... **15** Dec. 16/28-Feb. 28/29 (11L, 4T)
Away .... **22** Dec. 19/50-Mar. 25/51 (20L, 2T)
Most Shutouts, Season **15** 1969-70 (76)
Most PIM, Season **2,663** 1991-92 (80)
Most Goals, Game .... **12** Jan. 30/69 (Chi. 12 at Phi. 0)

Individual

Most Seasons .... **22** Stan Mikita
Most Games .... **1,394** Stan Mikita
Most Goals, Career .... **604** Bobby Hull
Most Assists, Career .... **926** Stan Mikita
Most Points, Career .... **1,467** Stan Mikita (541G, 926A)
Most PIM, Career .... **1,495** Chris Chelios
Most Shutouts, Career .... **74** Tony Esposito
Longest Consecutive Games Streak .... **884** Steve Larmer (Oct. 6/82-Apr. 15/93)
Most Goals, Season .... **58** Bobby Hull (1968-69)
Most Assists, Season .... **87** Denis Savard (1981-82, 1987-88)
Most Points, Season .... **131** Denis Savard (1987-88; 44G, 87A)
Most PIM, Season .... **408** Mike Peluso (1991-92)
Most Points, Defenseman, Season .... **85** Doug Wilson (1981-82; 39G, 46A)
Most Points, Center, Season .... **131** Denis Savard (1987-88; 44G, 87A)
Most Points, Right Wing, Season .... **101** Steve Larmer (1990-91; 44G, 57A)
Most Points, Left Wing, Season .... **107** Bobby Hull (1968-69; 58G, 49A)
Most Points, Rookie, Season .... **90** Steve Larmer (1982-83; 43G, 47A)
Most Shutouts, Season .... **15** Tony Esposito (1969-70)
Most Goals, Game .... **5** Grant Mulvey (Feb. 3/82)
Most Assists, Game .... **6** Pat Stapleton (Mar. 30/69)
Most Points, Game .... **7** Max Bentley (Jan. 28/43; 4G, 3A), Grant Mulvey (Feb. 3/82; 5G, 2A)

* NHL Record.

General Managers' History

Major Frederic McLaughlin, 1926-27 to 1931-32; Major Frederic McLaughlin and Tommy Gorman, 1932-33; Tommy Gorman, 1933-34; Clem Loughlin, 1934-35 to 1935-36; Bill Tobin, 1936-37 to 1953-54; Tommy Ivan, 1954-55 to 1976-77; Bob Pulford, 1977-78 to 1989-90; Mike Keenan, 1990-91, 1991-92; Mike Keenan and Bob Pulford, 1992-93; Bob Pulford, 1993-94 to 1996-97; Bob Murray, 1997-98, 1998-99; Bob Murray and Bob Pulford, 1999-2000; Mike Smith, 2000-01 to 2002-03; Mike Smith and Bob Pulford, 2003-04; Bob Pulford, 2004-05; Dale Tallon, 2005-06 to 2008-09; Stan Bowman, 2009-10 to date.

Retired Numbers

1	Glenn Hall	1957-1967
3	Pierre Pilote	1955-1968
	Keith Magnuson	1969-1980
9	Bobby Hull	1957-1972
18	Denis Savard	1980-1990, 1995-1997
21	Stan Mikita	1958-1980
35	Tony Esposito	1969-1984

All-time Record vs. Other Clubs

Regular Season

	Total								At Home								On Road							
	GP	W	L	T	OL	GF	GA	PTS	GP	W	L	T	OL	GF	GA	PTS	GP	W	L	T	OL	GF	GA	PTS
Anaheim	77	30	41	5	1	183	203	66	40	19	18	2	1	105	97	41	37	11	23	3	0	78	106	25
Boston	578	238	259	79	2	1754	1817	557	290	148	95	45	2	937	781	343	288	90	164	34	0	817	1036	214
Buffalo	111	45	52	13	1	323	354	104	55	30	18	6	1	179	147	67	56	15	34	7	0	144	207	37
Calgary	155	68	60	26	1	486	456	163	77	38	26	13	0	255	216	89	78	30	34	13	1	231	240	74
Carolina	65	30	27	7	1	223	199	68	32	18	10	3	1	125	90	40	33	12	17	4	0	98	109	28
Colorado	111	49	47	9	6	362	385	113	56	30	19	3	4	187	172	67	55	19	28	6	2	175	213	46
Columbus	73	43	23	2	5	246	201	93	36	22	11	1	2	113	84	47	37	21	12	1	3	133	117	46
Dallas	253	124	95	31	3	855	766	282	125	73	37	15	0	460	332	161	128	51	58	16	3	395	434	121
Detroit	725	278	354	84	9	1994	2254	649	364	166	141	51	6	1088	1028	389	361	112	213	33	3	906	1226	260
Edmonton	120	56	47	12	5	421	414	129	60	30	19	7	4	225	201	71	60	26	28	5	1	196	213	58
Florida	27	15	7	3	2	91	65	35	14	7	4	2	1	45	38	17	13	8	3	1	1	46	27	18
Los Angeles	180	86	73	17	4	596	551	193	91	45	35	9	2	308	256	101	89	41	38	8	2	288	295	92
Minnesota	47	19	19	1	8	120	131	47	23	10	10	1	2	59	65	23	24	9	9	0	6	61	66	24
Montreal	555	150	299	103	3	1399	1842	406	276	96	125	55	0	741	765	247	279	54	174	48	3	658	1077	159
Nashville	86	44	30	4	8	247	246	100	44	26	15	1	2	129	119	55	42	18	15	3	6	118	127	45
New Jersey	101	43	34	21	3	337	293	110	50	26	13	10	1	189	138	63	51	17	21	11	2	148	155	47
NY Islanders	102	43	38	20	1	324	347	107	52	28	18	5	1	175	172	62	50	15	20	15	0	149	175	45
NY Rangers	579	245	235	98	1	1696	1652	589	290	131	115	43	1	880	800	306	289	114	120	55	0	816	852	283
Ottawa	24	15	7	2	0	64	62	32	11	7	2	2	0	27	23	16	13	8	5	0	0	37	39	16
Philadelphia	128	43	55	30	0	381	395	116	63	27	17	19	0	213	180	73	65	16	38	11	0	168	215	43
Phoenix	129	60	46	15	8	431	366	143	63	33	16	10	4	223	159	80	66	27	30	5	4	208	207	63
Pittsburgh	125	65	41	17	2	445	384	149	63	41	11	10	1	247	165	93	62	24	30	7	1	198	219	56
St. Louis	286	138	108	35	5	950	874	316	144	84	40	18	2	524	410	188	142	54	68	17	3	426	464	128
San Jose	82	35	36	5	6	238	249	81	41	21	16	2	2	129	128	46	41	14	20	3	4	109	121	35
Tampa Bay	32	15	9	5	3	96	79	38	17	10	5	2	0	54	38	22	15	5	4	3	3	42	41	16
Toronto	639	259	284	96	0	1816	1920	614	321	159	120	42	0	979	838	360	318	100	164	54	0	837	1082	254
Vancouver	174	80	65	22	7	548	470	189	86	53	23	7	3	302	209	116	88	27	42	15	4	246	261	73
Washington	87	40	34	11	2	300	282	93	43	24	12	6	1	164	126	55	44	16	22	5	1	136	156	38
Winnipeg	12	9	3	0	0	40	33	18	5	4	1	0	0	17	10	8	7	5	2	0	0	23	23	10
Defunct Clubs	279	131	107	41	0	724	614	303	139	79	40	20	0	408	268	178	140	52	67	21	0	316	346	125
Totals	**5942**	**2496**	**2535**	**814**	**97**	**17690**	**17904**	**5903**	**2971**	**1485**	**1032**	**410**	**44**	**9487**	**8055**	**3424**	**2971**	**1011**	**1503**	**404**	**53**	**8203**	**9849**	**2479**

Playoffs

	Series	W	L	GP	W	L	T	GF	GA	Last Mtg.	Rnd.	Result
Boston	7	2	5	28	9	18	1	80	112	2013	F	W 4-2
Buffalo	2	0	2	9	1	8	0	17	36	1980	QF	L 0-4
Calgary	4	2	2	18	9	9	0	54	53	2009	CQF	W 4-2
Colorado	2	0	2	12	4	8	0	28	49	1997	CQF	L 2-4
Dallas	6	4	2	33	19	14	0	120	118	1991	DSF	L 2-4
Detroit	16	9	7	81	43	38	0	236	224	2013	CSF	W 4-3
Edmonton	4	1	3	20	8	12	0	77	102	1992	CF	W 4-0
Los Angeles	2	2	0	10	8	2	0	24	18	2013	CF	W 4-1
Minnesota	1	1	0	5	4	1	0	17	7	2013	CQF	W 4-1
Montreal	17	5	12	81	29	50	2	185	261	1976	QF	L 0-4
Nashville	1	1	0	6	4	2	0	17	15	2010	CQF	W 4-2
NY Islanders	2	0	2	6	0	6	0	6	21	1979	QF	L 0-4
NY Rangers	5	4	1	24	14	10	0	66	54	1973	SF	W 4-1
Philadelphia	2	2	0	10	8	2	0	45	30	2010	F	W 4-2
Phoenix	1	0	1	6	2	4	0	12	17	2012	CQF	L 2-4
Pittsburgh	2	1	1	8	4	4	0	24	23	1992	F	L 0-4
St. Louis	10	7	3	50	28	22	0	171	142	2002	CQF	L 1-4
San Jose	1	1	0	4	4	0	0	13	7	2010	CF	W 4-0
Toronto	9	3	6	38	15	22	1	89	111	1995	CQF	W 4-3
Vancouver	5	3	2	28	16	12	0	92	77	2011	CQF	L 3-4
Defunct Clubs	4	2	2	9	5	3	1	16	15			
Totals	**103**	**50**	**53**	**486**	**234**	**247**	**5**	**1389**	**1492**			

Playoff Results 2013-2009

Year	Round	Opponent	Result	GF	GA
2013	**F**	**Boston**	**W 4-2**	**17**	**15**
	CF	Los Angeles	W 4-1	14	11
	CSF	Detroit	W 4-3	16	15
	CQF	Minnesota	W 4-1	17	7
2012	CQF	Phoenix	L 2-4	12	17
2011	CQF	Vancouver	L 3-4	22	16
2010	**F**	**Philadelphia**	**W 4-2**	**25**	**22**
	CF	San Jose	W 4-0	13	7
	CSF	Vancouver	W 4-2	23	18
	CQF	Nashville	W 4-2	17	15
2009	CF	Detroit	L 1-4	10	19
	CSF	Vancouver	W 4-2	23	19
	CQF	Calgary	W 4-2	21	16

Abbreviations: Round: F – Final; **CF** – conference final; **CSF** – conference semi-final; **CQF** – conference quarter-final; **DSF** – division semi-final; **SF** – semi-final; **QF** – quarter-final.

Calgary totals include Atlanta Flames, 1972-73 to 1979-80.
Carolina totals include Hartford, 1979-80 to 1996-97.
Colorado totals include Quebec, 1979-80 to 1994-95.
Dallas totals include Minnesota North Stars, 1967-68 to 1992-93.
New Jersey totals include Kansas City, 1974-75, 1975-76, and Colorado Rockies, 1976-77 to 1981-82.
Phoenix totals include Winnipeg, 1979-80 to 1995-96.
Winnipeg totals include Atlanta Thrashers, 1999-2000 to 2010-11.

2012-13 Results

Jan.	19	at Los Angeles	5-2		8	at Colorado	2-6
	20	at Phoenix	6-4		10	Edmonton	5-6
	22	St. Louis	3-2		14	at Columbus	2-1†
	24	at Dallas	3-2*		16	at Dallas	8-1
	26	at Columbus	3-2		18	at Colorado	5-2
	27	Detroit	2-1*		20	at Anaheim	2-4
	30	at Minnesota	2-3†		25	Los Angeles	4-5
Feb.	1	at Vancouver	1-2†		26	Calgary	2-0
	2	at Calgary	3-2†		29	Anaheim	1-2
	5	at San Jose	5-3		31	at Detroit	7-1
	7	at Phoenix	6-2	**Apr.**	1	Nashville	3-2†
	10	at Nashville	3-0		4	St. Louis	3-4†
	12	Anaheim	2-3†		6	at Nashville	1-0
	15	San Jose	4-1		7	Nashville	5-3
	17	Los Angeles	3-2		9	at Minnesota	1-0
	19	Vancouver	4-3†		12	Detroit	3-2†
	22	San Jose	2-1		14	at St. Louis	2-0
	24	Columbus	1-0		15	Dallas	5-2
	25	Edmonton	3-2*		19	Nashville	5-4*
	28	at St. Louis	3-0		20	Phoenix	2-3†
Mar.	1	Columbus	4-3*		22	at Vancouver	1-3
	3	at Detroit	2-1†		24	at Edmonton	4-1
	5	Minnesota	5-3		26	Calgary	3-1
	6	Colorado	3-2		27	at St. Louis	1-3

* – Overtime † – Shootout

Entry Draft Selections 2013-1999

Name in bold denotes played in NHL.

2013
Pick
30 Ryan Hartman
51 Carl Dahlstrom
74 John Hayden
111 Robin Norell
121 Tyler Motte
134 Luke Johnson
181 Anthony Louis
211 Robin Press

2012
Pick
18 Teuvo Teravainen
48 Dillon Fournier
79 Chris Calnan
139 Garret Ross
149 Travis Brown
169 Vincent Hinostroza
191 Brandon Whitney
199 Matt Tomkins

2011
Pick
18 Mark McNeill
26 Phillip Danault
36 Adam Clendening
43 **Brandon Saad**
70 Michael Paliotta
79 Klas Dahlbeck
109 Maxim Shalunov
139 **Andrew Shaw**
169 Sam Jardine
199 Alex Broadhurst
211 Johan Mattsson

2010
Pick
24 Kevin Hayes
35 Ludvig Rensfeldt
54 Justin Holl
58 Kent Simpson
60 Stephen Johns
90 Joakim Nordstrom
120 Rob Flick
151 Mirko Hoefflin
180 Nick Mattson
191 Mac Carruth

2009
Pick
28 **Dylan Olsen**
59 **Brandon Pirri**
89 Dan Delisle
119 Byron Froese
149 **Marcus Kruger**
177 David Pacan
195 Paul Phillips
209 David Gilbert

2008
Pick
11 Kyle Beach
68 **Shawn Lalonde**
132 Teigan Zahn
162 Jonathan Carlsson
169 **Ben Smith**
179 Braden Birch
192 Joe Gleason

2007
Pick
1 **Patrick Kane**
38 **Bill Sweatt**
56 **Akim Aliu**
69 Maxime Tanguay
86 Josh Unice
126 Joe Lavin
156 Richard Greenop

2006
Pick
3 **Jonathan Toews**
33 Igor Makarov
61 Simon Danis-Pepin
76 Tony Lagerstrom
95 Ben Shutron
96 Joe Palmer
156 Jan-Mikael Juutilainen
169 Chris Auger
186 Peter Leblanc

2005
Pick
7 **Jack Skille**
43 **Mike Blunden**
54 Dan Bertram
68 **Evan Brophey**
108 **Niklas Hjalmarsson**
113 Nathan Davis
117 Denis Istomin
134 Brennan Turner
167 Joe Fallon
188 Joe Charlebois
202 David Kuchejda
203 Adam Hobson

2004
Pick
3 **Cam Barker**
32 **Dave Bolland**
41 **Bryan Bickell**
45 Ryan Garlock
54 Jakub Sindel
68 **Adam Berti**
120 Mitch Maunu
123 Karel Hromas
131 Trevor Kell
140 **Jake Dowell**
165 Scott McCulloch
196 **Petri Kontiola**
214 **Troy Brouwer**
223 Jared Walker
229 Eric Hunter
256 Matthew Ford
260 Marko Anttila

2003
Pick
14 **Brent Seabrook**
52 **Corey Crawford**
59 **Michal Barinka**
151 **Lasse Kukkonen**
156 Alexei Ivanov
181 Johan Andersson
211 **Mike Brodeur**
245 **Dustin Byfuglien**
275 Michael Grenzy
282 **Chris Porter**

2002
Pick
21 **Anton Babchuk**
54 **Duncan Keith**
93 Alexander Kojevnikov
128 **Matt Ellison**
156 **James Wisniewski**
188 Kevin Kantee
219 Tyson Kellerman
251 Jason Kostadine
282 **Adam Burish**

2001
Pick
9 **Tuomo Ruutu**
29 **Adam Munro**
59 **Matt Keith**
73 **Craig Anderson**
104 Brent MacLellan
115 Vladimir Gusev
119 Alexei Zotkin
142 Tommi Jaminki
174 Alexander Golovin
186 Petr Puncochar
205 Teemu Jaaskelainen
216 Oleg Minakov
268 Jeff Miles

2000
Pick
10 **Mikhail Yakubov**
11 **Pavel Vorobiev**
49 **Jonas Nordqvist**
74 **Igor Radulov**
106 Scott Balan
117 **Olli Malmivaara**
151 Alexander Barkunov
177 Michael Ayers
193 Joey Martin
207 Cliff Loya
225 Vladislav Luchkin
240 **Adam Berkhoel**
262 Peter Flache
271 **Reto Von Arx**
291 Arne Ramholt

1999
Pick
23 **Steve McCarthy**
46 Dimitri Levinski
63 Stepan Mokhov
134 Michael Jacobsen
165 **Michael Leighton**
194 Mattias Wennerberg
195 Yorick Treille
223 Andrew Carver

Captains' History

Dick Irvin, 1926-27 to 1928-29; Duke Dukowski, 1929-30; Ty Arbour, 1930-31; Cy Wentworth, 1931-32; Helge Bostrom, 1932-33; Charlie Gardiner, 1933-34; no captain, 1934-35; Johnny Gottselig, 1935-36 to 1939-40; Earl Seibert, 1940-41, 1941-42; Doug Bentley, 1942-43, 1943-44; Clint Smith 1944-45; John Mariucci, 1945-46; Red Hamill, 1946-47; John Mariucci, 1947-48; Gaye Stewart, 1948-49; Doug Bentley, 1949-50; Jack Stewart, 1950-51, 1951-52; Bill Gadsby, 1952-53, 1953-54; Gus Mortson, 1954-55 to 1956-57; no captain, 1957-58; Ed Litzenberger, 1958-59 to 1960-61; Pierre Pilote, 1961-62 to 1967-68, no captain, 1968-69; Pat Stapleton, 1969-70; no captain, 1970-71 to 1974-75; Stan Mikita and Pit Martin, 1975-76; Stan Mikita, Pit Martin and Keith Magnuson, 1976-77; Keith Magnuson, 1977-78, 1978-79; Keith Magnuson and Terry Ruskowski, 1979-80; Terry Ruskowski, 1980-81, 1981-82; Darryl Sutter, 1982-83 to 1984-85; Darryl Sutter and Bob Murray, 1985-86; Darryl Sutter, 1986-87; no captain, 1987-88; Denis Savard and Dirk Graham, 1988-89; Dirk Graham, 1989-90 to 1994-95; Chris Chelios, 1995-96 to 1998-99; Doug Gilmour, 1999-2000; Tony Amonte, 2000-01, 2001-02; Alex Zhamnov, 2002-03, 2003-04; Adrian Aucoin and Martin Lapointe, 2005-06, 2006-07; no captain, 2007-08; Jonathan Toews, 2008-09 to date.

Stan Bowman

General Manager

Born: Montreal, Que., June 28, 1973.

Stan Bowman was named general manager of the Chicago Blackhawks on July 14, 2009. In his first season on the job in 2009-10, the Blackhawks won the Stanley Cup for the first time since 1961. They won it again in 2013. Prior to being named to the position, Bowman had served for eight years in the Blackhawks operations department.

Bowman originally joined the Blackhawks in 2001, serving for four seasons as special assistant to the G.M. before being promoted to director of hockey operations from 2005 to 2007. As assistant G.M. from 2007 to 2009, Bowman attended to the day-to-day administration of the hockey operations department including contract negotiations, free agency, salary arbitration, player movement and player assignment. He also tracked the progress of the Blackhawks prospects at the club's minor league affiliate in Rockford and assisted with player evaluation, prospect development and scouting.

Bowman graduated from the University of Notre Dame in 1995 with degrees in Finance and Computer Applications. He was born in Montreal where his father, current Blackhawks senior advisor and Hall of Fame member Scotty Bowman, was coaching at the time.

Club Directory

United Center

Chicago Blackhawks
United Center
1901 W. Madison Street
Chicago, IL 60612
Phone **312/455-7000**
FAX 312/455-7042
www.chicagoblackhawks.com
Capacity: 19,717

Management

Chairman	W. Rockwell "Rocky" Wirtz
President/CEO	John F. McDonough
Executive Vice President	Jay Blunk
Vice President/General Manager	Stan Bowman
Vice President/Asst. to the President	Al MacIsaac
Vice President, Ticket Ops and Customer Relations	Chris Werner
Assistant General Manager	Norm Maciver
Sr. Exec Asst./Marketing Coordinator	Kayla Kindred
Coordinator, Special Projects/Sr. Exec. Mgmt.	Jillian Smith
Exec. Asst. to VP/GM and Hockey Operations	Lauren Peterson

Coaching Staff

Head Coach	Joel Quenneville
Assistant Coaches	Mike Kitchen, Jamie Kompon
Goaltending Coach	Steve Weeks
Strength and Conditioning Coach	Paul Goodman
Video Coach	Tim Campbell
Skating and Skills Development	Kevin Delaney
Developmental Goaltending Coach	Andrew Allen

Training/Equipment Staff

Athletic Trainers, Head / Assistant	Mike Gapski / Jeff Thomas
Massage Therapist	Pawel Prylinski
Equipment Manager / Asst. Manager / Assistant	Troy Parchman / Clint Reif / Jim Heintzelman

Medical

Head Team Physician, Orthopaedics	Dr. Michael Terry
Lead Team Internal Medicine Physician	William Harper
Team Physicians	Drs. George Chiampas, Angelo Costas, Ari Levy, Bradley Merk
Team Dentists	DDS Russ Baer, Martin Marcus, Michael Marcus
Mental Skills Coach	James Gary

Hockey Operations and Scouting

Senior Advisor, Hockey Operations	Scotty Bowman
Director, Player Personnel	Pierre Gauthier
Scouting Directors, Amateur / Pro	Mark Kelley / Ryan Stewart
Director, Player Development	Barry Smith
General Manager, Minor League Affiliations	Mark Bernard
Director, Player Recruitment	Ron Anderson
Chief Amateur Scout	Bruce Franklin
Senior Director, Team Services	Tony Ommen
Manager, Hockey Ops / Administration	Ian Gentile
Coordinator, Hockey Ops / Administration	Kyle Davidson
Player Development Coach	Keith Carney
Player Recruitment	Rick Comley
Amateur Scouts	Mike Doneghy, Gord Donnelly, Michel Dumas, Darrell May, Jim McKellar, Peter Nevin, Jad Ramsay
European Scouts, Head / Amateur / Pro	Niklas Blomgren / Karel Pavlik / Mats Hallin
Pro Scouts	Dennis Bonvie, Alex Brooks, Don Lever
Hockey Analytics/Video Analyst	Adam Gill
Team Security	Brian Higgins

Communications, Public Relations and Community Relations

Senior Director, Comm. and Community Relations	Brandon Faber
Director, Public Relations	Adam Rogowin
Manager, Community Relations	Ashley Hinton
Manger, Media Relations	Rob Tillotson
Coordinator, Team Photography	Chase Agnello-Dean
Assistant, Public Relations	Meghan Bower

Broadcasters

Television Play-By-Play / Analyst / Studio Host	Pat Foley / Eddie Olczyk / Steve Konroyd
Radio Play-By-Play / Analyst / Studio Host	John Wiedeman / Troy Murray / Judd Sirott

Marketing and Youth Hockey

Sr. Exec. Director, Marketing	Pete Hassen
Director, Youth Hockey	Annie Camins
Manager, In-Game Presentation and Entertainment	A.J. Dolan
Manager, Charitable Partnerships	Elizabeth Queen
Coords, Event Marketing / Mascot	Brian Howe / Joe Doyle
Assistant, Youth Hockey	Nick Rocca

Finance

Sr. Director, Finance	T.J. Skattum
Accounting Manager	Michael Dorsch
Payroll Administrator	Patricia Walsh

Human Resources

Sr. Exec. Director, Human Resources	Marie Sutera
Coordinator, Human Resources	Kyleen King
Office Coordinator	Leanne Mayville

Corporate Sponsorships

Sr. Exec. Director, Corporate Sponsorships	Steve Waight
Manager, Corporate Sponsorships	Sara Bailey
Manager, Client Services	Kelly Smith
Coordinator, Market Research and Sponsor Events	Brian Dahm
Account Execs., Corporate Sponsorships	Ryan Gallante, Sean Keefer, Greg Zinsmeister

New Media and Creative Services

Sr. Director, New Media and Creative Services	Adam Kempenaar
Manager, Creative Services	John Sandberg
Coordinator, New Media	Brad Boron
Graphic Designer, Creative Services	Chris Weibring
Team Historian	Bob Verdi

Tickets Operations and Customer Relations

Exec. Director, Ticket Operations	Jim Bare
Sr. Director, Ticket Sales and Service	Dan Rozenblat
Sr. Manager, Customer Service	Julie Lovins
Sr. Manager, Group Sales and Special Projects	Steve DiLenardi
Manager, Youth Hockey Sales	Eric Dumais
Assistant, Ticket Operations	Allison Westfall
Sr. Account Exec., Group Sales	Nick Zombolas
Account Execs., Ticket Sales	Andrew Roan, Jake Tuton
Sr. Customer Service Execs.	T.R. Johnson, Kathie Raimondi
Customer Service Execs.	Matt Brooks, Neil Desmond, Lindsay Dresser, Kevin LeClair, Shannon Pyrz, Shilpa Rupani

Colorado Avalanche

2012-13 Results: 16W-25L-5OTL-2SOL 39PTS
5TH, Northwest Division • 15TH, Western Conference

Key Off-Season Signings/Acquisitions

2013

May 10 • Named **Joe Sakic** Executive VP/Hockey Operations.

23 • Named **Patrick Roy** Head Coach and VP/Hockey Operations.

June 27 • Acquired LW **Alex Tanguay** and D **Cory Sarich** from Calgary for RW **David Jones** and D **Shane O'Brien**.

July 5 • Signed D **Andre Benoit**.

18 • Re-signed C **Matt Duchene**.

Matt Duchene celebrates a goal with P.A. Parenteau. The two players tied for the team lead with 43 points in 2012-13, with Parenteau collecting 18 goals and 25 assists to Duchene's 17 and 26.

2013-14 Schedule

Month	Day	Date	Opponent	Month	Day	Date	Opponent
Oct.	Wed.	2	Anaheim		Mon.	6	Calgary
	Fri.	4	Nashville		Wed.	8	Ottawa
	Tue.	8	at Toronto		Fri.	10	NY Islanders
	Thu.	10	at Boston		Sat.	11	at Minnesota
	Sat.	12	at Washington		Tue.	14	at Chicago
	Tue.	15	Dallas		Thu.	16	New Jersey
	Thu.	17	Detroit		Sat.	18	at Nashville
	Sat.	19	at Buffalo		Tue.	21	Toronto
	Mon.	21	at Pittsburgh		Fri.	24	at Florida
	Fri.	25	Carolina		Sat.	25	at Tampa Bay
	Sun.	27	Winnipeg		Mon.	27	at Dallas
Nov.	Fri.	1	at Dallas		Thu.	30	Minnesota
	Sat.	2	Montreal	**Feb.**	Sat.	1	Buffalo*
	Wed.	6	Nashville		Mon.	3	at New Jersey
	Fri.	8	Calgary		Tue.	4	at NY Rangers
	Sun.	10	Washington		Thu.	6	at Philadelphia
	Tue.	12	at Carolina		Sat.	8	at NY Islanders
	Thu.	14	at St. Louis		Wed.	26	Los Angeles
	Sat.	16	Florida		Fri.	28	Phoenix
	Tue.	19	Chicago	**Mar.**	Sun.	2	Tampa Bay
	Thu.	21	at Phoenix		Tue.	4	at Chicago
	Sat.	23	at Los Angeles		Thu.	6	at Detroit
	Wed.	27	St. Louis		Sat.	8	St. Louis*
	Fri.	29	at Minnesota*		Mon.	10	Winnipeg
	Sat.	30	Minnesota		Wed.	12	Chicago
Dec.	Thu.	5	at Edmonton		Fri.	14	Anaheim
	Fri.	6	at Calgary		Sun.	16	at Ottawa*
	Sun.	8	at Vancouver*		Tue.	18	at Montreal
	Tue.	10	Phoenix		Wed.	19	at Winnipeg
	Thu.	12	at Winnipeg		Fri.	21	Boston
	Sat.	14	Minnesota		Tue.	25	at Nashville
	Mon.	16	Dallas		Thu.	27	Vancouver
	Tue.	17	at Dallas		Sat.	29	San Jose*
	Thu.	19	Edmonton	**Apr.**	Tue.	1	at Columbus
	Sat.	21	at Los Angeles*		Thu.	3	NY Rangers
	Mon.	23	at San Jose		Sat.	5	at St. Louis*
	Fri.	27	at Chicago		Sun.	6	Pittsburgh
	Sun.	29	Winnipeg		Tue.	8	at Edmonton
	Tue.	31	Columbus		Thu.	10	at Vancouver
Jan.	Thu.	2	Philadelphia		Fri.	11	at San Jose
	Sat.	4	San Jose*		Sun.	13	at Anaheim*

* Denotes afternoon game.

Year-by-Year Record

		Home				Road				Overall									
Season	GP	W	L	T	OL	W	L	T	OL	W	L	T	OL	GF	GA	Pts.	Div. Fin.	Conf. Fin.	Playoff Result
2012-13	48	12	9	....	3	4	16	....	4	16	25	....	7	116	152	39	5th, NW	15th, West	Out of Playoffs
2011-12	82	22	17	....	2	19	18	....	4	41	35	....	6	208	220	88	3rd, NW	11th, West	Out of Playoffs
2010-11	82	16	21	....	4	14	23	....	4	30	44	....	8	227	288	68	4th, NW	14th, West	Out of Playoffs
2009-10	82	24	14	....	3	19	16	....	6	43	30	....	9	244	233	95	2nd, NW	8th, West	Lost Conf. Quarter-Final
2008-09	82	18	21	....	2	14	24	....	3	32	45	....	5	199	257	69	5th, NW	15th, West	Out of Playoffs
2007-08	82	27	12	....	2	17	19	....	5	44	31	....	7	231	219	95	2nd, NW	6th, West	Lost Conf. Semi-Final
2006-07	82	22	16	....	3	22	15	....	4	44	31	....	7	272	251	95	4th, NW	9th, West	Out of Playoffs
2005-06	82	25	10	....	6	18	20	....	3	43	30	....	9	283	257	95	2nd, NW	7th, West	Lost Conf. Semi-Final
2004-05	....	....	....	....	....	....	....	....	....	....	....	....	....	....	....	....			
2003-04	82	19	14	6	2	21	8	7	5	40	22	13	7	236	198	100	2nd, NW	4th, West	Lost Conf. Semi-Final
2002-03	82	21	9	8	3	21	10	5	5	42	19	13	8	251	194	105	1st, NW	3rd, West	Lost Conf. Quarter-Final
2001-02	82	24	12	4	1	21	16	4	0	45	28	8	1	212	169	99	1st, NW	2nd, West	Lost Conf. Final
2000-01	**82**	**28**	**6**	**5**	**2**	**24**	**10**	**5**	**2**	**52**	**16**	**10**	**4**	**270**	**192**	**118**	**1st, NW**	**1st, West**	**Won Stanley Cup**
1999-2000	82	25	12	4	0	17	16	7	1	42	28	11	1	233	201	96	1st, NW	3rd, West	Lost Conf. Final
1998-99	82	21	14	6	....	23	14	4	....	44	28	10	....	239	205	98	1st, NW	2nd, West	Lost Conf. Final
1997-98	82	21	10	10	....	18	16	7	....	39	26	17	....	231	205	95	1st, Pac.	4th, West	Lost Conf. Quarter-Final
1996-97	82	26	10	5	....	23	14	4	....	49	24	9	....	277	205	107	1st, Pac.	1st, West	Lost Conf. Final
1995-96	**82**	**24**	**10**	**7**	....	**23**	**15**	**3**	....	**47**	**25**	**10**	....	**326**	**240**	**104**	**1st, Pac.**	**2nd, West**	**Won Stanley Cup**
1994-95*	48	19	1	4	....	11	12	1	....	30	13	5	....	185	134	65	1st, NE	1st, East	Lost Conf. Quarter-Final
1993-94*	84	19	17	6	....	15	25	2	....	34	42	8	....	277	292	76	5th, NE	11th, East	Out of Playoffs
1992-93*	84	23	17	2	....	24	10	8	....	47	27	10	....	351	300	104	2nd, Adams		Lost Div. Semi-Final
1991-92*	80	18	19	3	....	2	29	9	....	20	48	12	....	255	318	52	5th, Adams		Out of Playoffs
1990-91*	80	9	23	8	....	7	27	6	....	16	50	14	....	236	354	46	5th, Adams		Out of Playoffs
1989-90*	80	8	26	6	....	4	35	1	....	12	61	7	....	240	407	31	5th, Adams		Out of Playoffs
1988-89*	80	16	20	4	....	11	26	3	....	27	46	7	....	269	342	61	5th, Adams		Out of Playoffs
1987-88*	80	15	23	2	....	17	20	3	....	32	43	5	....	271	306	69	5th, Adams		Out of Playoffs
1986-87*	80	20	13	7	....	11	26	3	....	31	39	10	....	267	276	72	4th, Adams		Lost Div. Final
1985-86*	80	23	13	4	....	20	18	2	....	43	31	6	....	330	289	92	1st, Adams		Lost Div. Semi-Final
1984-85*	80	24	12	4	....	17	18	5	....	41	30	9	....	323	275	91	2nd, Adams		Lost Conf. Final
1983-84*	80	24	11	5	....	18	17	5	....	42	28	10	....	360	278	94	3th, Adams		Lost Div. Final
1982-83*	80	23	10	7	....	11	24	5	....	34	34	12	....	343	336	80	4th, Adams		Lost Div. Semi-Final
1981-82*	80	24	13	3	....	9	18	13	....	33	31	16	....	356	345	82	4th, Adams		Lost Conf. Final
1980-81*	80	18	11	11	....	12	21	7	....	30	32	18	....	314	318	78	4th, Adams		Lost Prelim. Round
1979-80*	80	17	16	7	....	8	28	4	....	25	44	11	....	248	313	61	5th, Adams		Out of Playoffs

* Quebec Nordiques

CENTRAL DIVISION
35th NHL Season

Franchise date: June 22, 1979

Transferred from Quebec to Denver, June 21, 1995.

2013-14 Player Personnel

FORWARDS	HT	WT	*Age	Place of Birth	S	2012-13 Club
AGOZZINO, Andrew	5-9	185	22	Kleinburg, Ont.	L	Lake Erie
BORDELEAU, Patrick	6-6	225	27	Montreal, Que.	L	Lake Erie-Colorado
CAREY, Paul	6-1	196	25	Boston, MA	L	Lake Erie
CHEEK, Trevor	6-2	198	20	Vancouver, WA	L	Cgy (WHL)-Van (WHL)-Edmonton
DESBIENS, Guillaume	6-3	216	28	Alma, Que.	R	Chicago (AHL)
DOWNIE, Steve	5-11	191	26	Newmarket, Ont.	R	Colorado
DUCHENE, Matt	5-11	200	22	Haliburton, Ont.	L	Frolunda-Ambri-Colorado
HEARD, Mitchell	6-1	188	21	Bowmanville, Ont.	L	Plymouth-Lake Erie
HISHON, Joey	5-10	175	21	Stratford, Ont.	L	Lake Erie
LANDESKOG, Gabriel	6-1	204	20	Stockholm, Sweden	L	Djurgarden-Colorado
LERG, Bryan	5-10	175	27	Livonia, MI	L	Lake Erie
MacKINNON, Nathan	6-0	182	18	Halifax, N.S.	R	Halifax
MALONE, Brad	6-2	207	24	Miramichi, N.B.	L	Lake Erie-Colorado
McGINN, Jamie	6-1	210	25	Fergus, Ont.	L	Colorado
McLEOD, Cody	6-2	210	29	Binscarth, Man.	L	Colorado
MEURS, Garrett	5-11	175	20	Wingham, Ont.	R	Plymouth
MITCHELL, John	6-1	204	28	Oakville, Ont.	L	Colorado
OLVER, Mark	5-10	170	25	Burnaby, B.C.	L	Lake Erie-Colorado
O'REILLY, Ryan	6-0	200	22	Clinton, Ont.	L	Magnitogorsk-Colorado
PARENTEAU, P.A.	6-0	193	30	Hull, Que.	R	Colorado
SGARBOSSA, Michael	5-11	175	21	Campbellville, Ont.	L	Lake Erie-Colorado
SMITH, Colin	5-10	162	20	Edmonton, Alta.	R	Kamloops
STASTNY, Paul	6-0	208	27	Quebec City, Que.	L	EHC Munchen-Colorado
TANGUAY, Alex	6-1	194	33	Ste-Justine, Que.	L	Calgary
VAN DER GULIK, David	5-10	173	30	Abbotsford, B.C.	L	Lake Erie-Colorado
WYMAN, J.T.	6-2	199	27	Edina, MN	R	Syracuse-Tampa Bay
DEFENSEMEN						
BARRIE, Tyson	5-10	191	22	Victoria, B.C.	R	Lake Erie-Colorado
BEAUPRE, Gabriel	6-2	180	20	Levis, Que.	L	Val-d'Or-Denver-Lake Erie
BENOIT, Andre	5-11	186	29	St. Albert, Ont.	L	Binghamton-Ottawa
ELLIOTT, Stefan	6-1	192	22	Vancouver, B.C.	R	Colorado-Lake Erie
GUENIN, Nate	6-3	207	30	Sewickley, PA	R	Norfolk
HEJDA, Jan	6-4	237	35	Prague, Czech.	L	Colorado
HOLDEN, Nick	6-4	207	26	St. Albert, Alta.	L	Springfield-Columbus
HUNWICK, Matt	5-11	190	28	Warren, MI	L	Colorado
JOHNSON, Erik	6-4	232	25	Bloomington, MN	R	Colorado
LAURIDSEN, Markus	6-1	205	22	Gentofte, Denmark	L	Lake Erie-Denver
SARICH, Cory	6-4	207	35	Saskatoon, Sask.	R	Calgary
SIEMENS, Duncan	6-4	209	20	Edmonton, Alta.	L	Saskatoon
STOLLERY, Karl	5-11	165	25	Camrose, Alta.	L	Lake Erie
WILSON, Ryan	6-1	207	26	Windsor, Ont.	L	Colorado

GOALTENDERS	HT	WT	*Age	Place of Birth	C	2012-13 Club
AITTOKALLIO, Sami	6-1	174	21	Tampere, Finland	L	Lake Erie-Colorado
GIGUERE, Jean-Sebastien	6-1	202	36	Montreal, Que.	L	Colorado
MILLAN, Kieran	6-0	190	24	Edmonton, Alta.	L	Denver-Lake Erie
PATTERSON, Kent	6-0	184	24	St. Louis Park, MN	L	Denver-Lake Erie
PICKARD, Calvin	6-0	196	21	Moncton, N.B.	L	Lake Erie
VARLAMOV, Semyon	6-2	209	25	Kuybyshev, USSR	L	Yaroslavl-Colorado

* – Age at start of 2013-14 season

Coaching History

Jacques Demers, 1979-80; Maurice Filion and Michel Bergeron, 1980-81; Michel Bergeron, 1981-82 to 1986-87; Andre Savard and Ron Lapointe, 1987-88; Ron Lapointe and Jean Perron, 1988-89; Michel Bergeron, 1989-90; Dave Chambers, 1990-91; Dave Chambers and Pierre Page, 1991-92; Pierre Page, 1992-93, 1993-94; Marc Crawford, 1994-95 to 1997-98; Bob Hartley, 1998-99 to 2001-02; Bob Hartley and Tony Granato, 2002-03; Tony Granato, 2003-04; Joel Quenneville, 2004-05 to 2007-08; Tony Granato, 2008-09; Joe Sacco, 2009-10 to 2012-13; Patrick Roy, 2013-14.

Captains' History

Marc Tardif, 1979-80, 1980-81; Robbie Ftorek and Andre Dupont, 1981-82; Mario Marois, 1982-83 to 1984-85; Mario Marois and Peter Stastny, 1985-86; Peter Stastny, 1986-87 to 1989-90; Joe Sakic and Steven Finn, 1990-91; Mike Hough, 1991-92; Joe Sakic, 1992-93 to 2008-09; Adam Foote, 2009-10, 2010-11; Milan Hejduk, 2011-12; Gabriel Landeskog, 2012-13 to date.

2012-13 Scoring

* – rookie

Regular Season

Pos	#	Player	Team	GP	G	A	Pts	TOI	+/–	PIM	PP	SH	GW	S	%
R	15	P.A. Parenteau	COL	48	18	25	43	19:08	–11	38	6	0	1	105	17.1
C	9	Matt Duchene	COL	47	17	26	43	20:55	–12	12	2	0	3	132	12.9
C	26	Paul Stastny	COL	40	9	15	24	19:21	–7	14	2	0	1	87	10.3
L	11	Jamie McGinn	COL	47	11	11	22	17:17	–13	26	3	0	2	128	8.6
C	7	John Mitchell	COL	47	10	10	20	16:44	5	18	1	0	1	72	13.9
C	90	Ryan O'Reilly	COL	29	6	14	20	18:30	–3	4	3	0	0	66	9.1
L	92	Gabriel Landeskog	COL	36	9	8	17	19:19	–4	22	0	3	1	109	8.3
D	41	* Tyson Barrie	COL	32	2	11	13	21:34	–11	10	1	0	1	58	3.4
L	55	Cody McLeod	COL	48	8	4	12	13:05	4	83	0	0	0	79	10.1
R	23	Milan Hejduk	COL	29	4	7	11	13:08	–7	0	2	0	0	41	9.8
D	8	Jan Hejda	COL	46	1	9	10	19:41	–3	28	0	0	1	50	2.0
R	12	Chuck Kobasew	COL	37	5	4	9	11:16	6	21	0	0	1	43	11.6
R	54	David Jones	COL	33	3	6	9	16:49	–11	6	1	0	2	62	4.8
R	17	Aaron Palushaj	COL	25	2	7	9	11:18	–2	8	0	0	0	29	6.9
C	40	Mark Olver	COL	32	4	2	6	9:02	–5	6	0	0	0	33	12.1
D	22	Matt Hunwick	COL	43	0	6	6	21:31	4	16	0	0	0	57	0.0
D	4	Greg Zanon	COL	44	0	6	6	19:19	–16	28	0	0	0	40	0.0
L	58	Patrick Bordeleau	COL	46	2	3	5	6:13	–7	70	0	0	0	24	8.3
C	24	Tomas Vincour	DAL	15	2	1	3	8:50	0	2	0	0	0	11	18.2
			COL	2	0	1	1	9:03	–1	2	0	0	0	1	0.0
			Total	17	2	2	4	8:51	–1	4	0	0	0	12	16.7
D	46	Stefan Elliott	COL	18	1	3	4	17:30	–3	2	0	0	0	35	2.9
D	5	Shane O'Brien	COL	28	0	4	4	15:30	0	60	0	0	0	28	0.0
D	6	Erik Johnson	COL	31	0	4	4	20:45	–3	18	0	0	0	64	0.0
D	44	Ryan Wilson	COL	12	0	3	3	18:30	4	8	0	0	0	23	0.0
C	42	* Brad Malone	COL	13	1	1	2	8:47	–7	16	0	0	0	10	10.0
L	14	David Van Der Gulik	COL	9	0	2	2	9:26	2	6	0	0	0	10	0.0
R	27	Steve Downie	COL	2	0	1	1	8:53	1	6	0	0	0	2	0.0
C	43	* Michael Sgarbossa	COL	6	0	0	0	10:21	–3	4	0	0	0	6	0.0

Goaltending

No.	Goaltender	GPI	Mins	Avg	W	L	OT	EN	SO	GA	SA	S%	G	A	PIM
30	* Sami Aittokallio	1	49	2.45	0	0	0	0	0	2	25	.920	0	0	0
35	Jean-Sebastien Giguere	18	908	2.84	5	4	4	1	0	43	469	.908	0	0	4
1	Semyon Varlamov	35	1950	3.02	11	21	3	6	3	98	1007	.903	0	1	0
	Totals	**48**	**2930**	**3.07**	**16**	**25**	**7**	**7**	**3**	**150**	**1508**	**.901**			

Patrick Roy

Head Coach and Vice President of Hockey Operations

Born: Quebec City, Que., October 5, 1965.

The Colorado Avalanche announced on May 23, 2013 that the organization had reached an agreement in principle with Patrick Roy to become the franchise's head coach and vice president of hockey operations. He was formally introduced at a press conference on May 28. Roy is the sixth head coach in Avalanche history and the 14th in franchise history. In addition to his head coaching duties, Roy will work with executive vice president of hockey operations Joe Sakic in all player personnel decisions.

Roy spent the previous eight seasons as head coach and general manager of the Quebec Remparts of the Quebec Major Junior Hockey League. He guided the Remparts to a 348-159-37 record (.674) in 544 regular-season games behind the bench, which included leading Quebec to the 2006 Memorial Cup title as the Canadian Hockey League champions. He is also a part owner of the QMJHL franchise.

Roy, who was inducted into the Hockey Hall of Fame in 2006, retired with the most regular season wins in NHL history (551), a number that currently ranks second all-time. The four-time Stanley Cup champion is still the winningest goaltender in Stanley Cup playoff history with 151 postseason wins. Roy is the only player in league history to win the Conn Smythe Trophy as playoff MVP three times (1986, 1993, 2001). The Quebec City native backstopped the Montreal Canadiens to two Stanley Cup championships (1986, 1993), the first of which was his rookie campaign. Traded to Colorado on December 6, 1995, Roy led the Avalanche to the Stanley Cup during the club's first season in Denver (1996) and again in 2001. He is the only goaltender in NHL history to win 200 or more games with two different teams. Roy won the Vezina Trophy three times (1989, 1990, 1992) and the William Jennings Trophy five times (1987, 1988, 1989, 1992, 2002). He was selected to the NHL All-Star Team on six occasions, the First Team in 1988-89, 1989-90, 1991-92 and 2001-02 and the Second Team in 1987-88 and 1990-91. He participated in 11 NHL All-Star Games and was named to the NHL All-Rookie Team in 1985-86.

Roy, who is the Avalanche's all-time goaltending leader in nearly every statistical category, had his number 33 retired by the organization on October 28, 2003.

Coaching Record

			Regular Season				Playoffs			
Season	Team	League	GC	W	L	O/T	GC	W	L	T
2005-06	Quebec	QMJHL	65	51	12	2	23	14	9	....
2005-06	Quebec	M-Cup	....	....	....	....	4	3	1	....
2006-07	Quebec	QMJHL	69	36	28	5	5	1	4	....
2007-08	Quebec	QMJHL	70	38	28	4	6	2	4	....
2008-09	Quebec	QMJHL	68	49	16	3	17	9	8	....
2009-10	Quebec	QMJHL	68	41	20	7	9	4	5	....
2010-11	Quebec	QMJHL	68	48	16	4	18	11	7	....
2011-12	Quebec	QMJHL	68	43	18	7	11	7	4	....
2012-13	Quebec	QMJHL	68	42	21	5	11	5	6	....

Club Records

Team

(Figures in brackets for season records are games played; records for fewest points, wins, ties, losses, goals, goals against are for 70 or more games)

Most Points **118** 2000-01 (82)
Most Wins **52** 2000-01 (82)
Most Ties **18** 1980-81 (80)
Most Losses **61** 1989-90 (80)
Most Goals **360** 1983-84 (80)
Most Goals Against **407** 1989-90 (80)
Fewest Points **31** 1989-90 (80)
Fewest Wins **12** 1989-90 (80)
Fewest Ties **5** 1987-88 (80)
Fewest Losses **16** 2000-01 (82)
Fewest Goals **199** 2008-09 (82)
Fewest Goals Against **169** 2001-02 (82)
Longest Winning Streak
  Overall . . . . **12** Jan. 10-Feb. 7/99
  Home . . . . **10** Nov. 26/83-Jan. 10/84, Mar. 6-Apr. 16/95
  Away . . . . **7** Jan. 10-Feb. 7/99
Longest Undefeated Streak
  Overall . . . . **12** Dec. 23/96-Jan. 20/97 (9W, 3T), Jan. 10-Feb. 7/99 (12W)
  Home . . . . **14** Nov. 19/83-Jan. 21/84 (11W, 3T)
  Away . . . . **10** Jan. 10-Mar. 3/99 (8W, 2T)
Longest Losing Streak
  Overall . . . . **14** Oct. 21-Nov. 19/90
  Home . . . . **8** Oct. 21-Nov. 24/90
  Away . . . . **18** Jan. 18-Apr. 1/90
Longest Winless Streak
  Overall . . . . **17** Oct. 21-Nov. 25/90 (15L, 2T)
  Home . . . . **11** Nov. 14-Dec. 26/89 (7L, 4T)
  Away . . . . **33** Oct. 8/91-Feb. 27/92 (25L, 8T)
Most Shutouts, Season **11** 2001-02 (82)
Most PIM, Season **2,104** 1989-90 (80)
Most Goals, Game . . . . **12** Feb. 1/83 (Hfd. 3 at Que. 12), Oct. 20/84 (Que. 12 at Tor. 3), Dec. 5/95 (S.J. 2 at Col. 12)

Individual

Most Seasons . . . . **20** Joe Sakic
Most Games . . . . **1,378** Joe Sakic
Most Goals, Career . . . . **625** Joe Sakic
Most Assists, Career . . . . **1,016** Joe Sakic
Most Points, Career . . . . **1,641** Joe Sakic (625G, 1,016A)
Most PIM, Career . . . . **1,562** Dale Hunter
Most Shutouts, Career . . . . **37** Patrick Roy
Longest Consecutive Games Streak . . . . **312** Dale Hunter (Oct. 9/80-Mar. 13/84)
Most Goals, Season . . . . **57** Michel Goulet (1982-83)
Most Assists, Season . . . . **93** Peter Stastny (1981-82)
Most Points, Season . . . . **139** Peter Stastny (1981-82; 46G, 93A)
Most PIM, Season . . . . **301** Gord Donnelly (1987-88)
Most Points, Defenseman, Season . . . . **82** Steve Duchesne (1992-93; 20G, 62A)
Most Points, Center, Season . . . . **139** Peter Stastny (1981-82; 46G, 93A)
Most Points, Right Wing, Season . . . . **103** Jacques Richard (1980-81; 52G, 51A)
Most Points, Left Wing, Season . . . . **121** Michel Goulet (1983-84; 56G, 65A)
Most Points, Rookie, Season . . . . **109** Peter Stastny (1980-81; 39G, 70A)
Most Shutouts, Season . . . . **9** Patrick Roy (2001-02)
Most Goals, Game . . . . **5** Mats Sundin (Mar. 5/92), Mike Ricci (Feb. 17/94)
Most Assists, Game . . . . **5** Eight times
Most Points, Game . . . . **8** Peter Stastny (Feb. 22/81; 4G, 4A), Anton Stastny (Feb. 22/81; 3G, 5A)

Records include Quebec Nordiques, 1979-80 through 1994-95.

Retired Numbers

3	J.C. Tremblay*	1972-1979
8	Marc Tardif*	1979-1983
16	Michel Goulet*	1979-1990
19	Joe Sakic	1988-2009
21	Peter Forsberg	1994-04, 07-08, 2010-11
26	Peter Stastny*	1980-1990
33	Patrick Roy	1995-2003
52**	Adam Foote	1991-04, 08-11
77	Raymond Bourque	2000-2001

* Quebec Nordiques
** Ceremony to take place November 2, 2013

All-time Record vs. Other Clubs

Regular Season

	Total								At Home								On Road							
	GP	W	L	T	OL	GF	GA	PTS	GP	W	L	T	OL	GF	GA	PTS	GP	W	L	T	OL	GF	GA	PTS
Anaheim	73	34	25	7	7	194	199	82	36	18	13	4	1	98	98	41	37	16	12	3	6	96	101	41
Boston	134	50	69	15	0	443	526	115	69	25	38	6	0	244	283	56	65	25	31	9	0	199	243	59
Buffalo	133	54	57	20	2	453	463	130	67	33	22	11	1	237	207	78	66	21	35	9	1	216	256	52
Calgary	146	60	65	20	1	459	482	141	73	32	29	11	1	245	231	76	73	28	36	9	0	214	251	65
Carolina	134	69	43	21	1	511	416	160	68	42	17	9	0	288	200	93	66	27	26	12	1	223	216	67
Chicago	111	53	45	9	4	385	362	119	55	30	17	6	2	213	175	68	56	23	28	3	2	172	187	51
Columbus	47	33	10	1	3	162	93	70	24	18	5	0	1	85	48	37	23	15	5	1	2	77	45	33
Dallas	113	51	43	12	7	357	330	121	57	31	15	7	4	197	139	73	56	20	28	5	3	160	191	48
Detroit	113	46	57	5	5	345	386	102	57	25	24	4	4	184	188	58	56	21	33	1	1	161	198	44
Edmonton	146	68	66	8	4	487	518	148	74	38	31	4	1	260	249	81	72	30	35	4	3	227	269	67
Florida	29	18	6	3	2	102	80	41	14	7	4	3	0	42	34	17	15	11	2	0	2	60	46	24
Los Angeles	116	50	54	8	4	409	414	112	57	30	23	3	1	223	189	64	59	20	31	5	3	186	225	48
Minnesota	74	35	28	3	8	208	191	81	37	19	15	2	1	104	90	41	37	16	13	1	7	104	101	40
Montreal	133	52	66	15	0	435	505	119	66	34	27	5	0	223	229	73	67	18	39	10	0	212	276	46
Nashville	55	23	22	5	5	147	153	56	28	14	10	2	2	71	70	32	27	9	12	3	3	76	83	24
New Jersey	78	35	34	8	1	263	261	79	38	20	14	4	0	135	104	44	40	15	20	4	1	128	157	35
NY Islanders	73	35	33	4	1	251	251	75	38	22	12	3	1	134	108	48	35	13	21	1	0	117	143	27
NY Rangers	76	35	34	7	0	261	280	77	38	21	14	3	0	153	137	45	38	14	20	4	0	108	143	32
Ottawa	39	24	11	4	0	158	112	52	18	14	3	1	0	81	54	29	21	10	8	3	0	77	58	23
Philadelphia	76	27	33	14	2	238	265	70	39	16	10	12	1	139	131	45	37	11	23	2	1	99	134	25
Phoenix	112	52	43	12	5	370	379	121	56	28	20	5	3	187	183	64	56	24	23	7	2	183	196	57
Pittsburgh	76	36	32	7	1	312	294	80	36	19	14	2	1	153	135	41	40	17	18	5	0	159	159	39
St. Louis	112	53	46	11	2	358	341	119	57	33	16	7	1	201	148	74	55	20	30	4	1	157	193	45
San Jose	78	40	29	5	4	250	207	89	38	22	11	4	1	130	88	49	40	18	18	1	3	120	119	40
Tampa Bay	33	18	12	3	0	107	81	39	17	12	3	2	0	62	35	26	16	6	9	1	0	45	46	13
Toronto	70	36	25	9	0	267	223	81	32	18	9	5	0	123	101	41	38	18	16	4	0	144	122	40
Vancouver	146	67	56	15	8	476	444	157	73	35	26	8	4	231	207	82	73	32	30	7	4	245	237	75
Washington	73	29	35	9	0	224	264	67	37	16	16	5	0	111	128	37	36	13	19	4	0	113	136	30
Winnipeg	17	7	7	1	2	48	49	17	9	3	4	0	2	27	29	8	8	4	3	1	0	21	20	9
Totals	**2616**	**1190**	**1086**	**261**	**79**	**8680**	**8569**	**2720**	**1308**	**675**	**462**	**138**	**33**	**4581**	**4018**	**1521**	**1308**	**515**	**624**	**123**	**46**	**4099**	**4551**	**1199**

Playoffs

	Series	W	L	GP	W	L	T	GF	GA	Last Mtg.	Rnd.	Result
Anaheim	1	0	1	4	0	4	0	4	16	2006	CSF	L 0-4
Boston	2	1	1	11	5	6	0	36	37	1983	DSF	L 1-3
Buffalo	2	2	0	8	6	2	0	35	27	1985	DSF	W 3-2
Carolina	2	1	1	9	4	5	0	34	35	1987	DSF	W 4-2
Chicago	2	2	0	12	8	4	0	49	28	1997	CQF	W 4-2
Dallas	4	2	2	24	14	10	0	66	62	2006	CQF	W 4-1
Detroit	6	3	3	34	17	17	0	88	97	2008	CSF	L 0-4
Edmonton	2	1	1	12	7	5	0	35	30	1998	CQF	L 3-4
Florida	1	1	0	4	4	0	0	15	4	1996	F	W 4-0
Los Angeles	2	2	0	14	8	6	0	33	23	2002	CQF	W 4-3
Minnesota	2	1	1	13	7	6	0	34	28	2008	CQF	W 4-2
Montreal	5	2	3	31	14	17	0	85	105	1993	DSF	L 2-4
New Jersey	1	1	0	7	4	3	0	19	11	2001	F	W 4-3
NY Islanders	1	0	1	4	0	4	0	9	18	1982	CF	L 0-4
NY Rangers	1	0	1	6	2	4	0	19	25	1995	CQF	L 2-4
Philadelphia	2	0	2	11	4	7	0	29	39	1985	CF	L 2-4
Phoenix	1	1	0	5	4	1	0	17	10	2000	CQF	W 4-1
St. Louis	1	1	0	5	4	1	0	17	11	2001	CF	W 4-1
San Jose	4	2	2	25	12	13	0	62	71	2010	CQF	L 2-4
Vancouver	2	2	0	10	8	2	0	40	26	2001	CQF	W 4-0
Totals	**44**	**25**	**19**	**249**	**132**	**117**	**0**	**726**	**703**			

Calgary totals include Atlanta Flames, 1979-80.
Dallas totals include Minnesota North Stars, 1979-80 to 1992-93.
Phoenix totals include Winnipeg, 1979-80 to 1995-96.
Carolina totals include Hartford, 1979-80 to 1996-97.
New Jersey totals include Colorado Rockies, 1979-80 to 1981-82.
Winnipeg totals include Atlanta Thrashers, 1999-2000 to 2010-11.

Playoff Results 2013-2009

Year	Round	Opponent	Result	GF	GA
2010	CQF	San Jose	L 2-4	11	19

Abbreviations: Round: F – Final; **CF** – conference final; **CSF** – conference semi-final; **CQF** – conference quarter-final; **DSF** – division semi-final.

2012-13 Results

Jan.	19	at Minnesota	2-4		12	Edmonton	0-4
	22	Los Angeles	3-1		14	at Minnesota	3-5
	24	Columbus	4-0		16	Minnesota	4-6
	26	at San Jose	0-4		18	Chicago	2-5
	28	at Edmonton	1-4		20	Dallas	4-3
	30	at Vancouver	0-3		23	at Dallas	2-5
	31	at Calgary	6-3		24	Vancouver	2-3
Feb.	2	Edmonton	3-1		27	at Calgary	3-4
	4	Dallas	2-3		28	at Vancouver	1-4
	6	Anaheim	0-3		30	Nashville	1-0*
	11	Phoenix	2-3*	**Apr.**	1	at Detroit	2-3
	14	at Minnesota	4-3†		2	at Nashville	1-3
	16	at Edmonton	4-6		5	Detroit	2-3*
	18	Nashville	6-5		6	at Phoenix	0-4
	20	St. Louis	1-0*		8	Calgary	1-3
	23	at Los Angeles	1-4		10	at Anaheim	4-1
	24	at Anaheim	3-4*		11	at Los Angeles	2-3†
	26	at San Jose	2-3†		13	Vancouver	4-3
	28	Calgary	5-4		15	Columbus	3-4*
Mar.	3	at Columbus	1-2*		19	Edmonton	1-4
	5	at Detroit	1-2		21	St. Louis	5-3
	6	at Chicago	2-3		23	at St. Louis	1-3
	8	Chicago	6-2		26	at Phoenix	5-4†
	10	San Jose	3-2*		27	Minnesota	1-3

* – Overtime † – Shootout

Entry Draft Selections 2013-1999

Name in bold denotes played in NHL.

2013

Pick	
1	Nathan MacKinnon
32	Chris Bigras
63	Spencer Martin
93	Mason Geertsen
123	Will Butcher
153	Ben Storm
183	Wilhelm Westlund

2012

Pick	
41	Mitchell Heard
72	Troy Bourke
132	Michael Clarke
162	Joseph Blandisi
192	Colin Smith

2011

Pick	
2	**Gabriel Landeskog**
11	Duncan Siemens
93	Joachim Nermark
123	Garrett Meurs
153	Gabriel Beaupre
183	Dillon Donnelly

2010

Pick	
17	Joey Hishon
49	Calvin Pickard
71	Michael Bournival
95	Stephen Silas
107	**Sami Aittokallio**
137	Troy Rutkowski
139	Luke Walker
197	Luke Moffatt

2009

Pick	
3	**Matt Duchene**
33	**Ryan O'Reilly**
49	**Stefan Elliott**
64	**Tyson Barrie**
124	Kieran Millan
154	Brandon Maxwell
184	Gus Young

2008

Pick	
50	**Cameron Gaunce**
61	Peter Delmas
110	Kelsey Tessier
140	**Mark Olver**
167	Joel Chouinard
170	**Jonas Holos**
200	Nathan Condon

2007

Pick	
14	**Kevin Shattenkirk**
45	**Colby Cohen**
49	Trevor Cann
55	**T.J. Galiardi**
105	**Brad Malone**
113	Kent Patterson
135	Paul Carey
155	Jens Hellgren
195	Johan Alcen

2006

Pick	
18	**Chris Stewart**
51	Nigel Williams
59	Codey Burki
81	Mike Carman
110	Kevin Montgomery
201	Billy Sauer

2005

Pick	
34	**Ryan Stoa**
44	**Paul Stastny**
47	Tom Fritsche
52	Chris Durand
88	**T.J. Hensick**
124	**Ray Macias**
166	Jason Lynch
168	**Justin Mercier**
222	**Kyle Cumiskey**

2004

Pick	
21	**Wojtek Wolski**
55	**Victor Oreskovich**
72	Denis Parshin
154	Richard Demen-Willaume
184	**Derek Peltier**
215	Ian Keserich
239	**Brandon Yip**
249	J.D. Corbin
281	Steve McClellan

2003

Pick	
63	**David Liffiton**
131	David Svagrovsky
146	Mark McCutcheon
163	**Brad Richardson**
204	Linus Videll
225	Brett Hemingway
257	Darryl Yacboski
288	**David Jones**

2002

Pick	
28	**Jonas Johansson**
61	**Johnny Boychuk**
94	Eric Lundberg
107	Mikko Kalteva
129	**Tom Gilbert**
164	**Tyler Weiman**
195	Taylor Christie
227	Ryan Steeves
258	Sergei Shemetov
289	Sean Collins

2001

Pick	
63	**Peter Budaj**
97	**Danny Bois**
130	Colt King
143	Frantisek Skladany
144	**Cody McCormick**
149	Mikko Viitanen
165	Pierre-Luc Emond
184	Scott Horvath
196	**Charlie Stephens**
227	**Marek Svatos**

2000

Pick	
14	**Vaclav Nedorost**
47	**Jared Aulin**
50	Sergei Soin
63	Agris Saviels
88	**Kurt Sauer**
92	Sergei Klyazmin
119	**Brian Fahey**
159	**John-Michael Liles**
189	Chris Bahen
221	Aaron Molnar
252	**Darryl Bootland**
266	Sean Kotary
285	Blake Ward

1999

Pick	
25	**Mikhail Kuleshov**
45	**Martin Grenier**
93	**Branko Radivojevic**
112	Sanny Lindstrom
122	Kristian Kovac
142	Will Magnuson
152	**Jordan Krestanovich**
158	Anders Lovdahl
183	**Riku Hahl**
212	**Radim Vrbata**
240	**Jeff Finger**

General Managers' History

Maurice Filion, 1979-80 to 1987-88; Martin Madden, 1988-89; Martin Madden and Maurice Filion, 1989-90; Pierre Page, 1990-91 to 1993-94; Pierre Lacroix, 1994-95 to 2005-06; Francois Giguere, 2006-07 to 2008-09; Greg Sherman, 2009-10 to date.

Greg Sherman

General Manager/Executive V.P. and Alt. Governor

Born: Scranton, PA, March 30, 1970.

Greg Sherman was named general manager of the Colorado Avalanche on June 3, 2009. At the time of his appointment, he had spent the last seven years as the team's assistant general manager and had been associated with the franchise for 13 years. In his first few weeks on the job, Sherman oversaw the selection of Matt Duchene with the third pick in the 2009 NHL Entry Draft. The team showed a 26-point improvement in 2009-10 and returned to the playoffs. In the 2011 Entry Draft, Sherman made Gabriel Landeskog the second overall selection and he went on to win the Calder Trophy as rookie of the year in 2011-12.

In his previous role in Colorado, Sherman worked on contract negotiations, arbitration cases, salary cap management and matters concerning personnel at all levels of the organization. In addition, Sherman also served as a liaison between the Avalanche and its American Hockey League affiliate, the Lake Erie Monsters. He oversaw and coordinated all financial obligations of both clubs.

Born in Scranton, Pennsylvania and raised in Denver, Sherman has spent most of his life in Colorado. He attended the University of San Diego and received his Bachelor in Accountancy in May 1992.

Club Directory

Pepsi Center

Colorado Avalanche
Pepsi Center
1000 Chopper Circle
Denver, CO 80204
Phone **303/405-1100**
FAX 303/893-0614
Press Box 303/575-1926
www.coloradoavalanche.com
Capacity: 18,007

Executive	
Owner	E. Stanley Kroenke
President & Governor	Josh Kroenke
Exec. VP of Hockey Operations/Alt. Governor	Joe Sakic
General Manager/Alt. Governor	Greg Sherman
Assistant General Manager	Craig Billington
Vice President of Hockey Administration	Charlotte Grahame
Advisor	Pierre Lacroix
Coaching Staff	
Head Coach/VP of Hockey Operations	Patrick Roy
Assistant Coaches	Tim Army, Andre Tourigny
Video Coach	Mario Duhamel
Goaltending Coach	Francois Allaire
Defense Development Consultant	Adam Foote
Training Staff	
Head Athletic Trainer	Matthew Sokolowski
Assistant Athletic Trainer/Physical Therapist	Scott Woodward
Head Equipment Manager	Mark Miller
Assistant Equipment Managers	Cliff Halstead, Brad Lewkow
Inventory Manager	Wayne Flemming
Strength & Conditioning Coach	Casey Bond
Massage Therapist	Gregorio Pradera
Scouting	
Director of Player Personnel	Brad Smith
Assistant Director of Player Personnel	Garth Joy
Pro Scouts	Dan Laperriere, Terry Martin
Director of Amateur Scouting	Richard Pracey
Assistant Director of Amateur Scouting	Alan Hepple
Scouts	Anders Carlsson, Adam Deadmarsh, John Harrington, Rick Lanz, Joni Lehto, Don Paarup, Guy Perron, Neil Shea
Communications/Team Services	
Sr. V.P., Communications & Business Operations	Jean Martineau
Exec. Director of Media Services	Brendan McNicholas
Team Services Coordinator	Erin DeGraff
Website/Media Relations Coordinator	Ron Knabenbauer
Lake Erie Monsters (AHL affiliate)	
Director of AHL Operations	David Oliver
Head Coach	Dean Chynoweth
Assistant Coach	Randy Ladouceur
Goaltending Coach	Jean-Ian Filiatrault
Head Athletic Trainer	Brent Woodside
Head Equipment Manager	Dusty Halstead
Team Information	
Practice Facility	South Suburban Family Sports Center
Television Outlet	Altitude Sports & Entertainment Network
Radio	Altitude Radio Network

One of four 2009 draft picks to have reach the NHL with the Avalanche, Tyson Barrie led the team with an average time on ice of 21:34 per game during the 32 games he played in 2012-13.

Columbus Blue Jackets

Key Off-Season Signings/Acquisitions

2013

June 26 • Re-signed C **Artem Anisimov**.
July 1 • Re-signed G **Sergei Bobrovsky**.
2 • Re-signed LW **Blake Comeau**.
5 • Signed RW **Nathan Horton**.
7 • Signed RW **Jack Skille**.
15 • Re-signed D **David Savard**.
25 • Re-signed D **Cody Goloubef**.

2012-13 Results: 24W-17L-3OTL-4SOL 55PTS
4TH, Central Division • 9TH, Western Conference

Year-by-Year Record

		Home				Road				Overall									
Season	GP	W	L	T	OL	W	L	T	OL	W	L	T	OL	GF	GA	Pts.	Div. Fin.	Conf. Fin.	Playoff Result
2012-13	48	14	5	....	5	10	12	....	2	24	17	....	7	120	119	55	4th, Cen.	9th, West	Out of Playoffs
2011-12	82	17	21	....	3	12	25	....	4	29	46	....	7	202	262	65	5th, Cen.	15th, West	Out of Playoffs
2010-11	82	17	19	....	5	17	16	....	8	34	35	....	13	215	258	81	5th, Cen.	13th, West	Out of Playoffs
2009-10	82	20	12	....	9	12	23	....	6	32	35	....	15	216	259	79	5th, Cen.	14th, West	Out of Playoffs
2008-09	82	25	13	....	3	16	18	....	7	41	31	....	10	226	230	92	4th, Cen.	7th, West	Lost Conf. Quarter-Final
2007-08	82	20	14	....	7	14	22	....	5	34	36	....	12	193	218	80	4th, Cen.	13th, West	Out of Playoffs
2006-07	82	18	19	....	4	15	23	....	3	33	42	....	7	201	249	73	4th, Cen.	11th, West	Out of Playoffs
2005-06	82	23	18	....	0	12	25	....	4	35	43	....	4	223	279	74	3rd, Cen.	13th, West	Out of Playoffs
2004-05	....	....	....	....	....	....	....	....	....	....	....	....	....	....	....	....			
2003-04	82	17	18	4	2	8	27	4	2	25	45	8	4	177	238	62	4th, Cen.	14th, West	Out of Playoffs
2002-03	82	20	14	5	2	9	28	3	1	29	42	8	3	213	263	69	5th, Cen.	15th, West	Out of Playoffs
2001-02	82	14	18	5	4	8	29	3	1	22	47	8	5	164	255	57	5th, Cen.	15th, West	Out of Playoffs
2000-01	82	19	15	4	3	9	24	5	3	28	39	9	6	190	233	71	5th, Cen.	13th, West	Out of Playoffs

2013-14 Schedule

Oct.	Fri.	4	Calgary
	Sat.	5	at NY Islanders
	Thu.	10	at Buffalo
	Sat.	12	Boston
	Tue.	15	at Detroit
	Thu.	17	at Montreal
	Sat.	19	at Washington
	Sun.	20	Vancouver
	Tue.	22	New Jersey
	Fri.	25	Toronto
	Sun.	27	Anaheim
Nov.	Fri.	1	at Pittsburgh
	Sat.	2	Pittsburgh
	Tue.	5	Ottawa
	Thu.	7	NY Rangers
	Sat.	9	NY Islanders
	Tue.	12	at Washington
	Thu.	14	at Boston
	Fri.	15	Montreal
	Sun.	17	at Ottawa*
	Tue.	19	at Edmonton
	Wed.	20	at Calgary
	Fri.	22	at Vancouver
	Mon.	25	at Toronto
	Wed.	27	Nashville
	Fri.	29	Edmonton
	Sat.	30	at Boston
Dec.	Tue.	3	Tampa Bay
	Fri.	6	Minnesota
	Mon.	9	at Pittsburgh
	Tue.	10	New Jersey
	Thu.	12	at NY Rangers
	Sat.	14	St. Louis
	Mon.	16	Winnipeg
	Thu.	19	at Philadelphia
	Sat.	21	Philadelphia
	Mon.	23	at Carolina
	Fri.	27	at New Jersey
	Sun.	29	Pittsburgh
	Tue.	31	at Colorado
Jan.	Thu.	2	at Phoenix
	Sat.	4	at St. Louis
	Mon.	6	at NY Rangers
	Fri.	10	Carolina
	Sat.	11	at Winnipeg
	Mon.	13	Tampa Bay
	Fri.	17	Washington
	Sat.	18	at Buffalo
	Tue.	21	Los Angeles
	Thu.	23	Philadelphia
	Sat.	25	Buffalo
	Mon.	27	at Carolina
	Tue.	28	Ottawa
	Thu.	30	Washington
Feb.	Sat.	1	Florida
	Mon.	3	at Anaheim
	Thu.	6	at Los Angeles
	Fri.	7	at San Jose
	Thu.	27	at New Jersey
Mar.	Sat.	1	Florida*
	Mon.	3	at Toronto
	Tue.	4	Dallas
	Thu.	6	at Chicago
	Sat.	8	at Nashville
	Mon.	10	at Dallas
	Tue.	11	Detroit
	Thu.	13	San Jose
	Sat.	15	at Minnesota
	Tue.	18	Carolina
	Thu.	20	at Montreal
	Fri.	21	NY Rangers
	Sun.	23	at NY Islanders*
	Tue.	25	Detroit
	Fri.	28	Pittsburgh
	Sat.	29	at Carolina
Apr.	Tue.	1	Colorado
	Thu.	3	at Philadelphia
	Fri.	4	Chicago
	Sun.	6	NY Islanders
	Tue.	8	Phoenix
	Fri.	11	at Tampa Bay
	Sat.	12	at Florida

* Denotes afternoon game.

In his first season with Columbus in 2012-13, Sergei Bobrovsky won the Vezina Trophy as the NHL's best goalie. Bobrovsky ranked second in the league with a .932 save percentage and sixth with a 2.00 goals-against average.

METROPOLITAN DIVISION
14th NHL Season

Franchise date: June 25, 1997

2013-14 Player Personnel

FORWARDS	HT	WT	*Age	Place of Birth	S	2012-13 Club
ANISIMOV, Artem	6-4	200	25	Yaroslavl, USSR	L	Yaroslavl-Columbus
ATKINSON, Cam	5-7	173	24	Riverside, CT	R	Springfield-Columbus
AUDY-MARCHESSAULT, Jon	5-9	175	22	Cap-Rouge, Que.	R	Springfield-Columbus
BASS, Cody	6-0	205	26	Owen Sound, Ont.	R	Springfield
BOLL, Jared	6-2	219	27	Charlotte, NC	R	TuTo Hockey-Columbus
CALVERT, Matt	5-10	187	23	Brandon, Man.	L	Springfield-Columbus
CHAPUT, Michael	6-2	194	21	Ile Bizard, Que.	L	Springfield
COLLINS, Sean	6-3	205	24	Saskatoon, Sask.	L	Springfield-Columbus
COMEAU, Blake	6-0	195	27	Meadow Lake, Sask.	R	Calgary-Columbus
CRAIG, Ryan	6-2	221	31	Abbotsford, B.C.	L	Springfield
DUBINSKY, Brandon	6-1	210	27	Anchorage, AK	L	Alaska-Columbus
FOLIGNO, Nick	6-0	210	25	Buffalo, NY	L	Columbus
GABORIK, Marian	6-1	204	31	Trencin, Czech.	L	NY Rangers-Columbus
HORTON, Nathan	6-2	229	28	Welland, Ont.	R	Boston
JENNER, Boone	6-2	202	20	Dorchester, Ont.	L	Oshawa-Springfield
JOHANSEN, Ryan	6-3	205	21	Port Moody, B.C.	R	Springfield-Columbus
LETESTU, Mark	5-11	195	28	Elk Point, Alta.	R	Almtuna-Columbus
MACHACEK, Spencer	6-1	200	24	Lethbridge, Alta.	R	St. John's-Springfield
MacKENZIE, Derek	5-11	180	32	Sudbury, Ont.	L	Columbus
SKILLE, Jack	6-1	219	26	Madison, WI	R	Rosenborg-Florida
UMBERGER, R.J.	6-2	220	31	Pittsburgh, PA	L	Columbus
DEFENSEMEN						
ERIXON, Tim	6-2	190	22	Port Chester, NY	L	Springfield-Columbus
GOLOUBEF, Cody	6-1	190	23	Mississauga, Ont.	R	Springfield-Columbus
JOHNSON, Jack	6-1	231	26	Indianapolis, IN	L	Columbus
McNEILL, Patrick	6-0	198	26	Strathroy, Ont.	L	Hershey
MELART, Ilari	6-4	227	24	Helsinki, Finland	L	HIFK
MURRAY, Ryan	6-1	201	20	Regina, Sask.	L	Everett
NIKITIN, Nikita	6-3	217	27	Omsk, USSR	L	Omsk-Columbus
PARLETT, Blake	6-1	205	24	Bracebridge, Ont.	R	Connecticut-Springfield
PROUT, Dalton	6-3	219	23	LaSalle, Ont.	R	Springfield-Columbus
ST. DENIS, Frederic	5-11	193	27	Greenfield Park, Que.	L	Hamilton
SAVARD, David	6-2	219	22	St. Hyacinthe, Que.	R	Springfield-Columbus
TYUTIN, Fedor	6-2	216	30	Izhevsk, USSR	L	Mytischi-Columbus
WEBER, Will	6-4	219	24	Gaylord, MI	L	Springfield-Evansville
WISNIEWSKI, James	6-0	208	29	Canton, MI	R	Columbus

GOALTENDERS	HT	WT	*Age	Place of Birth	C	2012-13 Club
BOBROVSKY, Sergei	6-2	190	25	Novokuznetsk, USSR	L	St. Petersburg-Columbus
McELHINNEY, Curtis	6-2	207	30	London, Ont.	L	Springfield
McKENNA, Mike	6-3	195	30	St. Louis, MO	R	Peoria
SMITH, Jeremy	6-0	173	24	Dearborn, MI	L	Milwaukee

* – Age at start of 2013-14 season

Fedor Tyutin was the only Columbus defenseman to see action in every game during the 2012-13 season. He also established a career high in plus-minus at +9.

2012-13 Scoring

* – rookie

Regular Season

Pos	#	Player	Team	GP	G	A	Pts	TOI	+/–	PIM	PP	SH	GW	S	%
L	22	Vinny Prospal	CBJ	48	12	18	30	16:31	3	32	4	0	2	85	14.1
C	55	Mark Letestu	CBJ	46	13	14	27	16:30	7	10	3	2	2	92	14.1
R	10	Marian Gaborik	NYR	35	9	10	19	18:40	–8	8	1	0	4	113	8.0
			CBJ	12	3	5	8	18:04	5	6	0	0	1	38	7.9
			Total	47	12	15	27	18:31	–3	14	1	0	5	151	7.9
D	51	Fedor Tyutin	CBJ	48	4	18	22	24:05	9	28	0	0	1	56	7.1
C	17	Brandon Dubinsky	CBJ	29	2	18	20	18:24	2	76	1	0	0	50	4.0
L	71	Nick Foligno	CBJ	45	6	13	19	16:31	6	28	1	0	2	69	8.7
D	7	Jack Johnson	CBJ	44	5	14	19	25:58	–5	12	3	0	1	96	5.2
C	42	Artem Anisimov	CBJ	35	11	7	18	16:24	–6	12	1	0	3	68	16.2
R	13	Cam Atkinson	CBJ	35	9	9	18	15:35	9	4	1	0	1	91	9.9
C	18	R.J. Umberger	CBJ	48	8	10	18	18:29	3	16	2	0	0	96	8.3
L	11	Matt Calvert	CBJ	42	9	7	16	14:10	–9	32	0	1	2	63	14.3
D	21	James Wisniewski	CBJ	30	5	9	14	22:49	–1	15	4	0	0	62	8.1
L	14	Blake Comeau	CGY	33	4	3	7	12:17	–9	14	0	1	1	44	9.1
			CBJ	9	2	3	5	11:41	5	6	0	0	0	4	50.0
			Total	42	6	6	12	12:09	–4	20	0	1	1	48	12.5
C	19	Ryan Johansen	CBJ	40	5	7	12	16:05	–7	12	0	0	2	84	6.0
R	15	Derek Dorsett	CBJ	24	3	6	9	15:59	–11	53	0	0	0	38	7.9
D	6	Nikita Nikitin	CBJ	38	3	6	9	21:11	2	17	1	0	0	60	5.0
C	24	Derek MacKenzie	CBJ	43	3	5	8	10:20	1	36	0	0	0	33	9.1
D	47 *	Dalton Prout	CBJ	28	1	6	7	18:31	15	25	0	0	0	16	6.3
R	40	Jared Boll	CBJ	43	2	4	6	8:04	1	100	0	0	0	19	10.5
D	20 *	Tim Erixon	CBJ	31	0	5	5	15:41	4	14	0	0	0	21	0.0
D	33	Adrian Aucoin	CBJ	36	0	4	4	16:20	–8	16	0	0	0	26	0.0
C	9	Colton Gillies	CBJ	27	1	1	2	8:17	1	17	0	0	0	17	5.9
D	48 *	Cody Goloubef	CBJ	11	1	0	1	14:48	–3	0	0	0	1	14	7.1
D	29 *	Nick Holden	CBJ	2	0	0	0	8:34	1	0	0	0	0	2	0.0
C	36 *	Jon Audy-Marchessault	CBJ	2	0	0	0	10:56	–1	0	0	0	0	0	0.0
D	58	David Savard	CBJ	4	0	0	0	13:12	–3	0	0	0	0	1	0.0
C	43 *	Sean Collins	CBJ	5	0	0	0	12:29	–2	6	0	0	0	0	0.0
C	34 *	Nick Drazenovic	CBJ	8	0	0	0	9:55	–2	4	0	0	0	5	0.0

Goaltending

No.	Goaltender	GPI	Mins	Avg	W	L	OT	EN	SO	GA	SA	S%	G	A	PIM
72	Sergei Bobrovsky	38	2219	2.00	21	11	6	3	4	74	1084	.932	0	0	0
35	Steve Mason	13	712	2.95	3	6	1	3	0	35	346	.899	0	0	0
	Totals	**48**	**2950**	**2.34**	**24**	**17**	**7**	**6**	**4**	**115**	**1436**	**.920**			

Coaching History

Dave King, 2000-01, 2001-02; Dave King and Doug MacLean, 2002-03; Doug MacLean and Gerard Gallant, 2003-04; Gerard Gallant, 2004-05, 2005-06; Gerard Gallant, Gary Agnew and Ken Hitchcock, 2006-07; Ken Hitchcock, 2007-08, 2008-09; Ken Hitchcock and Claude Noel, 2009-10; Scott Arniel, 2010-11; Scott Arniel and Todd Richards, 2011-12; Todd Richards, 2012-13 to date.

Todd Richards

Head Coach

Born: Robbinsdale, MN, October 20, 1966.

Todd Richards was named head coach of the Columbus Blue Jackets on May 14, 2012. He joined the Blue Jackets as an assistant coach on June 20, 2011 and took over as interim head coach on January 9, 2012. He spent his first full season as Blue Jackets bench boss in 2012-13.

Before joining the Blue Jackets, Richards was the head coach of the Minnesota Wild from 2009 to 2011 after being named the second head coach in Wild history on June 16, 2009. In 2008-09, he served as an assistant coach with the San Jose Sharks and helped the club capture the Presidents' Trophy with an NHL-best 53-18-11 record. He was responsible for the power play in San Jose and that unit ranked third in the NHL at 24.2 percent in 2008-09. During his stint with the Wild, the club's power play unit converted nearly 19 percent of its man advantage opportunities.

Prior to his stint with the Sharks, Richards spent two seasons as the head coach of the Wilkes-Barre/Scranton Penguins in the American Hockey League from 2006 to 2008, leading the club to the 2008 Calder Cup Final. He also coached the PlanetUSA squad at the 2007 AHL All-Star Classic in Toronto. He began his coaching career as an assistant with the American Hockey League's Milwaukee Admirals from 2002 to 2006, helping the club to a pair of West Division titles, two appearances in the Calder Cup Final and the 2004 Calder Cup championship.

Richards played four seasons at the University of Minnesota from 1985 to 1989. He was a three-time WCHA Second All-Star Team pick, helping the Golden Gophers win Western Collegiate Hockey Association titles in 1988 and 1989 and reach the NCAA title game in 1989. He served as the team's captain and earned Second Team All-America honors as a senior. He is the University of Minnesota's all-time leading scorer among defensemen with 30 goals, 128 assists and 158 points.

Montreal's third pick, 33rd overall, in the 1985 Entry Draft, Richards made his professional debut in 1990 and appeared in eight career NHL games with the Hartford Whalers between 1990 and 1992, collecting four assists and four penalty minutes. His playing career would span 13 seasons, mostly in the AHL and International Hockey League. He helped Springfield win the 1991 Calder Cup championship, was a three-time IHL All-Star and won the 2001 Turner Cup title with the Orlando Solar Bears. He wrapped up his career in 2001-02 with Servette Geneve in Switzerland.

Coaching Record

			Regular Season				Playoffs			
Season	Team	League	GC	W	L	O/T	GC	W	L	T
2006-07	Wilkes-Barre	AHL	80	51	23	6	11	5	6	....
2007-08	Wilkes-Barre	AHL	80	47	26	6	23	14	9	....
2009-10	**Minnesota**	**NHL**	**82**	**38**	**36**	**8**	....	....	....	....
2010-11	**Minnesota**	**NHL**	**82**	**39**	**35**	**8**	....	....	....	....
2011-12	**Columbus**	**NHL**	**41**	**18**	**21**	**2**	....	....	....	....
2012-13	**Columbus**	**NHL**	**48**	**24**	**17**	**7**	....	....	....	....
	NHL Totals		**253**	**119**	**109**	**25**	....	....	....	....

Club Records

Team

(Figures in brackets for season records are games played.)

Most Points .... 92 — 2008-09 (82)
Most Wins .... 41 — 2008-09 (82)
Most Ties .... 9 — 2000-01 (82)
Most Losses .... 47 — 2001-02 (82)
Most Goals .... 226 — 2008-09 (82)
Most Goals Against .... 279 — 2005-06 (82)
Fewest Points .... 57 — 2001-02 (82)
Fewest Wins .... 22 — 2001-02 (82)
Fewest Ties .... 8 — 2001-02 (82), 2002-03 (82), 2003-04 (82)
Fewest Losses .... 31 — 2008-09 (82)
Fewest Goals .... 164 — 2001-02 (82)
Fewest Goals Against .... 218 — 2007-08 (82)

Longest Winning Streak
- **Overall** .... 6 — Mar. 24-Apr. 3/06
- **Home** .... 6 — Dec. 26/07-Jan. 15/08
- **Away** .... 6 — Jan. 19-Feb. 18/11

Longest Undefeated Streak
- **Overall** .... 6 — Mar. 24-Apr. 3/06 (6W)
- **Home** .... 6 — Dec. 26/07-Jan. 15/08 (6W)
- **Away** .... 4 — Jan. 3-11/03 (3W, 1T/OL), Dec. 2-12/06 (4W)

Longest Losing Streak
- **Overall** .... 9 — Dec. 10-26/09
- **Home** .... 6 — Oct. 12-Nov. 9/01, Mar. 9-27/11
- **Away** .... 13 — Nov. 21/09-Jan. 5/10

Longest Winless Streak
- **Overall** .... 9 — Dec. 4-23/03 (8L, 1T/OL), Dec. 10-26/09 (7L, 2OL/SOL)
- **Home** .... 8 — Oct. 4-Nov. 9/01 (6L, 2T/OL), Dec. 4-31/03 (7L, 1T/OL)
- **Away** .... 14 — Oct. 9-Dec. 23/03 (13L, 1T/OL)

Most Shutouts, Season .... 11 — 2007-08 (82), 2008-09 (82)
Most PIM, Season .... 1,505 — 2002-03 (82)
Most Goals, Game .... 8 — Mar. 7/09 (CBJ 8 at Det. 2), Mar. 25/10 (CBJ 8 at Chi. 3), Nov. 10/10 (CBJ 8 at St.L. 1)

Individual

Most Seasons .... 10 — Rostislav Klesla
Most Games .... 674 — Rick Nash
Most Goals, Career .... 289 — Rick Nash
Most Assists, Career .... 258 — Rick Nash
Most Points, Career .... 547 — Rick Nash (289G, 258A)
Most PIM, Career .... 1,025 — Jody Shelley
Most Shutouts, Career .... 19 — Steve Mason
Longest Consecutive Games Streak .... 288 — R.J. Umberger (Oct. 10/08-Jan. 10/12)
Most Goals, Season .... 41 — Rick Nash (2003-04)
Most Assists, Season .... 52 — Ray Whitney (2002-03)
Most Points, Season .... 79 — Rick Nash (2008-09; 40G, 39A)
Most PIM, Season .... 249 — Jody Shelley (2002-03)
Most Points, Defenseman, Season .... 45 — Jaroslav Spacek (2002-03; 9G, 36A)
Most Points, Center, Season .... 68 — Andrew Cassels (2002-03; 20G, 48A)
Most Points, Right Wing, Season .... 65 — David Vyborny (2005-06; 22G, 43A)
Most Points, Left Wing, Season .... 79 — Rick Nash (2008-09; 40G, 39A)
Most Points, Rookie, Season .... 39 — Rick Nash (2002-03; 17G, 22A)
Most Shutouts, Season .... 10 — Steve Mason (2008-09)
Most Goals, Game .... 4 — Geoff Sanderson (Mar. 29/03)
Most Assists, Game .... 5 — Espen Knutsen (Mar. 24/01)
Most Points, Game .... 5 — Espen Knutsen (Mar. 24/01; 5A), Geoff Sanderson (Mar. 29/03; 4G, 1A), Andrew Cassels (Mar. 29/03; 1G, 4A), David Vyborny (Feb. 28/04; 1G, 4A)

Captains' History

Lyle Odelein, 2000-01, 2001-02; Ray Whitney, 2002-03; Luke Richardson, 2003-04; Luke Richardson and Adam Foote, 2005-06; Adam Foote, 2006-07; Adam Foote and Rick Nash, 2007-08; Rick Nash, 2008-09 to 2011-12; no captain, 2012-13.

All-time Record vs. Other Clubs

Regular Season

	Total								At Home								On Road							
	GP	W	L	T	OL	GF	GA	PTS	GP	W	L	T	OL	GF	GA	PTS	GP	W	L	T	OL	GF	GA	PTS
Anaheim	47	23	20	1	3	125	131	50	23	12	10	0	1	60	56	25	24	11	10	1	2	65	75	25
Boston	12	5	5	0	2	26	40	12	7	3	3	0	1	15	26	7	5	2	2	0	1	11	14	5
Buffalo	14	8	5	1	0	41	35	17	6	4	1	1	0	21	12	9	8	4	4	0	0	20	23	8
Calgary	47	25	16	0	6	128	121	56	24	16	4	0	4	72	50	36	23	9	12	0	2	56	71	20
Carolina	13	7	6	0	0	38	31	14	6	4	2	0	0	18	13	8	7	3	4	0	0	20	18	6
Chicago	73	28	35	2	8	201	246	66	37	15	16	1	5	117	133	36	36	13	19	1	3	84	113	30
Colorado	47	13	30	1	3	93	162	30	23	7	14	1	1	45	77	16	24	6	16	0	2	48	85	14
Dallas	47	16	25	0	6	106	139	38	24	8	12	0	4	55	72	20	23	8	13	0	2	51	67	18
Detroit	74	23	39	1	11	169	243	58	38	14	16	1	7	81	113	36	36	9	23	0	4	88	130	22
Edmonton	47	15	26	3	3	119	166	36	24	10	10	3	1	65	80	24	23	5	16	0	2	54	86	12
Florida	12	8	4	0	0	34	28	16	6	4	2	0	0	16	12	8	6	4	2	0	0	18	16	8
Los Angeles	47	20	24	1	2	108	138	43	23	12	9	0	2	60	71	26	24	8	15	1	0	48	67	17
Minnesota	46	22	20	1	3	112	116	48	22	14	7	1	0	59	47	29	24	8	13	0	3	53	69	19
Montreal	11	6	4	1	0	25	22	13	4	2	2	0	0	10	9	4	7	4	2	1	0	15	13	9
Nashville	74	23	40	1	10	168	231	57	36	16	15	0	5	86	99	37	38	7	25	1	5	82	132	20
New Jersey	12	3	7	1	1	25	34	8	7	3	4	0	0	17	20	6	5	0	3	1	1	8	14	2
NY Islanders	14	9	1	1	3	49	38	22	8	6	0	1	1	30	18	14	6	3	1	0	2	19	20	8
NY Rangers	12	6	4	1	1	38	33	14	7	5	2	0	0	24	14	10	5	1	2	1	1	14	19	4
Ottawa	11	4	5	2	0	31	34	10	5	3	1	1	0	18	14	7	6	1	4	1	0	13	20	3
Philadelphia	11	2	6	3	0	22	35	7	6	2	2	2	0	12	11	6	5	0	4	1	0	10	24	1
Phoenix	47	17	24	4	2	109	131	40	23	11	10	1	1	58	57	24	24	6	14	3	1	51	74	16
Pittsburgh	14	5	6	0	3	44	50	13	7	3	1	0	3	25	24	9	7	2	5	0	0	19	26	4
St. Louis	73	26	34	3	10	185	227	65	36	17	13	2	4	97	96	40	37	9	21	1	6	88	131	25
San Jose	47	17	26	0	4	107	133	38	24	13	9	0	2	67	49	28	23	4	17	0	2	40	84	10
Tampa Bay	13	4	6	1	2	25	30	11	6	3	2	1	0	15	12	7	7	1	4	0	2	10	18	4
Toronto	10	3	6	1	0	22	35	7	4	1	3	0	0	10	17	2	6	2	3	1	0	12	18	5
Vancouver	47	15	23	2	7	116	163	39	24	9	10	2	3	58	78	23	23	6	13	0	4	58	85	16
Washington	14	4	6	1	3	39	45	12	8	2	4	0	2	21	26	6	6	2	2	1	1	18	19	6
Winnipeg	14	9	5	0	0	35	26	18	7	5	2	0	0	18	13	10	7	4	3	0	0	17	13	8
Totals	**950**	**366**	**458**	**33**	**93**	**2340**	**2863**	**858**	**475**	**224**	**186**	**18**	**47**	**1250**	**1319**	**513**	**475**	**142**	**272**	**15**	**46**	**1090**	**1544**	**345**

Playoffs

	Series	W	L	GP	W	L	T	GF	GA	Last Mtg.	Rnd.	Result
Detroit	1	0	1	4	0	4	0	7	18	2009	CQF	L 0-4
Totals	**1**	**0**	**1**	**4**	**0**	**4**	**0**	**7**	**18**			

Winnipeg totals include Atlanta Thrashers, 1999-2000 to 2010-11.

Playoff Results 2013-2009

Year	Round	Opponent	Result	GF	GA
2009	CQF	Detroit	L 0-4	7	18

Abbreviations: Round: CQF – conference quarter-final.

2012-13 Results

Jan.	19	at Nashville	3-2†		9	Detroit	3-0
	21	Detroit	3-4†		10	at Detroit	3-2†
	23	at Phoenix	1-5		12	Vancouver	1-2†
	24	at Colorado	0-4		14	Chicago	1-2†
	26	Chicago	2-3		16	Phoenix	1-0†
	28	Dallas	2-1		19	Nashville	4-3
	29	at Minnesota	2-3		22	Calgary	5-1
	31	St. Louis	1-4		23	at Nashville	2-5
Feb.	2	Detroit	4-2		26	at Vancouver	0-1†
	5	Los Angeles	2-4		28	at Edmonton	4-6
	7	Calgary	3-4*		29	at Calgary	6-4
	10	Edmonton	1-3		31	Anaheim	2-1*
	11	San Jose	6-2	**Apr.**	4	at Nashville	3-1
	15	at Los Angeles	1-2		5	at St. Louis	1-3
	16	at Phoenix	3-5		7	Minnesota	0-3
	18	at Anaheim	2-3		9	San Jose	4-0
	21	at Detroit	3-2		12	St. Louis	4-1
	23	at St. Louis	1-2		13	at Minnesota	3-2†
	24	at Chicago	0-1		15	at Colorado	4-3*
	26	Dallas	4-5*		17	at Anaheim	3-2*
Mar.	1	at Chicago	3-4*		18	at Los Angeles	1-2
	3	Colorado	2-1*		21	at San Jose	4-3
	5	Edmonton	4-3†		25	at Dallas	3-1
	7	Vancouver	2-1*		27	Nashville	3-1

* – Overtime † – Shootout

Entry Draft Selections 2013-2000

Name in bold denotes played in NHL.

2013

Pick	
14	Alexander Wennberg
19	Kerby Rychel
27	Marko Dano
50	Dillon Heatherington
89	Oliver Bjorkstrand
105	Nick Moutrey
165	Markus Soberg
195	Peter Quenneville

2012

Pick	
2	Ryan Murray
31	Oscar Dansk
62	Joonas Korpisalo
95	Josh Anderson
152	Daniel Zaar
182	Gianluca Curcuruto

2011

Pick	
37	Boone Jenner
66	T.J. Tynan
98	Mike Reilly
128	Seth Ambroz
158	Lukas Sedlak
188	Anton Forsberg

2010

Pick	
4	**Ryan Johansen**
34	Dalton Smith
55	Petr Straka
94	Brandon Archibald
102	Mathieu Corbeil
124	Austin Madaisky
154	**Dalton Prout**
184	Martin Ouellette

2009

Pick	
21	**John Moore**
56	Kevin Lynch
94	**David Savard**
137	Thomas Larkin
167	Anton Blomqvist
197	Kyle Neuber

2008

Pick	
6	**Nikita Filatov**
37	**Cody Goloubef**
107	Steven Delisle
118	Drew Olson
127	**Matt Calvert**
135	**Tomas Kubalik**
137	Brent Regner
157	**Cam Atkinson**
187	**Sean Collins**

2007

Pick	
7	**Jakub Voracek**
37	Stefan Legein
53	Will Weber
68	Jake Hansen
94	**Maksim Mayorov**
158	**Allen York**
211	Trent Vogelhuber

2006

Pick	
6	**Derick Brassard**
69	**Steve Mason**
85	**Tom Sestito**
113	Ben Wright
129	Robert Nyholm
136	Nick Sucharski
142	Maxime Frechette
159	Jesse Dudas
189	**Derek Dorsett**
194	Matt Marquardt

2005

Pick	
6	**Gilbert Brule**
55	**Adam McQuaid**
67	**Kris Russell**
101	**Jared Boll**
131	**Tomas Popperle**
177	Derek Reinhart
189	Kirill Starkov
201	Trevor Hendrikx

2004

Pick	
8	**Alexandre Picard**
46	**Adam Pineault**
59	Kyle Wharton
93	**Dan LaCosta**
96	Andrey Plekhanov
133	Petr Pohl
167	Rob Page
190	**Lennart Petrell**
198	Justin Vienneau
231	Brian McGuirk
233	Matt Greer
271	**Grant Clitsome**

2003

Pick	
4	**Nikolai Zherdev**
46	**Dan Fritsche**
71	Dmitry Kosmachev
103	Kevin Jarman
104	**Philippe Dupuis**
138	Arsi Piispanen
168	**Marc Methot**
200	Alexander Guskov
233	Mathieu Gravel
283	Trevor Hendrikx

2002

Pick	
1	**Rick Nash**
41	**Joakim Lindstrom**
65	**Ole-Kristian Tollefsen**
96	Jeff Genovy
98	Ivan Tkachenko
119	Jekabs Redlihs
133	**Lasse Pirjeta**
168	Tim Konsorada
184	**Jaroslav Balastik**
199	**Greg Mauldin**
225	**Steven Goertzen**
231	Jaroslav Kracik
263	Sergei Mozyakin

2001

Pick	
8	**Pascal Leclaire**
38	**Tim Jackman**
53	Kiel McLeod
85	**Aaron Johnson**
87	Per Mars
141	**Cole Jarrett**
173	Justin Aikins
187	Artem Vostrikov
204	Raffaele Sannitz
236	Ryan Bowness
242	**Andrew Murray**

2000

Pick	
4	**Rostislav Klesla**
69	Ben Knopp
133	**Petteri Nummelin**
138	Scott Heffernan
150	Tyler Kolarik
169	Shane Bendera
200	Janne Jokila
231	Peter Zingoni
278	Martin Paroulek
286	**Andrej Nedorost**
292	Louis Mandeville

General Managers' History

Doug MacLean, 2000-01 to 2006-07; Scott Howson, 2007-08 to 2011-12; Scott Howson and Jarmo Kekalainen, 2012-13; Jarmo Kekalainen, 2013-14.

Jarmo Kekalainen

General Manager

Born: Tampere, Finland, July 3, 1966.

Jarmo Kekalainen was named the third general manager in Columbus Blue Jackets history on February 13, 2013. He joined the club after serving as the president and general manager of Jokerit in the Finnish Elite League since 2010. He works closely with Blue Jackets president of hockey operations John Davidson on all hockey-related matters involving the club. Kekalainen owns a bachelor's degree in management from Clarkson University and earned a master's in business marketing from the University of Tampere.

Prior to his stint with Jokerit, Kekalainen spent eight seasons with the St. Louis Blues from 2002 to 2010. He joined the Blues as director of amateur scouting and was named assistant general manager as well in 2005. Kekalainen was involved in all facets of hockey operations, including professional scouting efforts and overseeing the club's amateur scouting and draft preparations. During his eight years in St. Louis, the Blues drafted players such as David Backes, Roman Polak, David Perron, T.J. Oshie, Patrik Berglund and Alex Pietrangelo.

Kekalainen was a member of the Ottawa Senators hockey operations department from 1995 to 2002 and served in a variety of roles with the club. He served as Ottawa's director of player personnel for three years and also oversaw the amateur draft and the club's scouting efforts in Europe. Among the players selected by Ottawa during this time were Jason Spezza, Marian Hossa, Martin Havlat, Antoine Vermette and Ray Emery. While working with the Senators, he also served as general manager of HIFK Helsinki in the Finnish Elite League from 1995 to 1999 and led the club to the league championship in 1998.

As a player, Kekalainen appeared in 55 career NHL games with the Senators and Boston Bruins during his career. He also played in the American Hockey League and his native Finland before wrapping up his playing career with Vasteras IK in the Swedish Elite League in 1994-95. Before signing with the Bruins, Kekalainen played two seasons at Clarkson University from 1987 to 1989. He was named to the Eastern Collegiate Athletic Conference First All-Star Team after tallying 19 goals and 25 assists for 44 points in 31 games during the 1988-89 season. He also represented Finland at the 1986 World Junior Championship and the 1991 Canada Cup Tournament.

Club Directory

Nationwide Arena

Columbus Blue Jackets
Nationwide Arena
200 W. Nationwide Blvd.
Columbus, Ohio 43215
Phone **614/246-4625**
FAX 614/246-4007
www.BlueJackets.com
Capacity: 18,144

Ownership/Senior Management

Majority Owner/Governor	John P. McConnell
President/Alternate Governor	Mike Priest
President, Hockey Operations/Alternate Governor	John Davidson

Executive Staff – Business Operations

Executive Vice President, Business Operations	Larry Hoepfner
Senior Vice President/General Counsel	Greg Kirstein
Senior Vice President/Chief Marketing Officer	John Browne
Chief Financial Officer	T.J. LaMendola
Vice President, Digital Marketing & Media	Marc Gregory
Vice President, Communications & Team Services	Todd Sharrock
Vice President, Marketing	J.D. Kershaw
Vice President, Corporate Development	A.J. Poole
Vice President, Community Relations and Executive Director of CBJ Foundation	Jen Bowden
Vice President, Ticket Sales & Service	Joe Andrade

Hockey Operations

General Manager	Jarmo Kekalainen
Assistant General Managers	Chris MacFarland, Bill Zito
Senior Advisor, Hockey Operations	Craig Patrick
Director of Amateur Scouting	Paul Castron
Head Amateur Scout / Amateur Scouts	Ville Siren / Marshall Davidson, Greg Drechsel, John Hill, Rob Riley, Andy Schneider
Regional Scouts	Niklas Evertsson, Basil McRae, Chris Morehouse, Milan Tichy
European Scout	Josef Boumedienne
Pro Scouts	Peter Dineen, Blake Geoffrion, Bob Halkidis, Sam McMaster
Video Scouts, Pro / Amateur	Mike Battaglia / Scott Harris
Hockey Operations	John McConnell II
Athletic Trainers, Head / Assistants	Mike Vogt / Nates Goto, Chris Strickland
Equipment Manager / Assistant Mgr. / Assistant	Tim LeRoy / Jamie Healy / Jason Stypinski
Executive Administrative Assistant	Christina Gest

Coaching Staff

Head Coach	Todd Richards
Associate Coach	Craig Hartsburg
Assistant Coaches	Dan Hinote, TBA
Goaltending Coach	Ian Clark
Coaches, Strength & Conditioning / Development	Kevin Collins / Chris Clark
Video Assistant Coach	Dan Singleton

Corporate Development and Premium Seating

Director of Premium Sales and Service	Marcus Lyons
Director of Corporate Development Services	Craig Smith
Director of Corporate Development	Ryan Shirk
Partnership Account Specialists	Amber Ribarchak, Amy Ranallo, Janny Lavery, Molly Taylor
Corporate Development Account Executives	Evan Ashton, Sean Siebenkittel, Ashley Smith
Corporate Development Sales Coordinator	Doug Vinci
Premium Seating Account Execs. / Specialist	Carson Barnes, Mike Minnix / Christina Leonard

Communications and Team Services

Director of Communications	Karen Davis
Managers, Communications / Team Services	Richard Bowness / Julie Gamble

Community Relations

Managers, Mascot Services / CBJ Foundation	Jason Zumpano / Alison Pegg
Community Relations Manager / Coordinator	Colleen Cheek / Katie Massey

Game Operations and Event Presentation

Director of Game Operations/Event Presentation	Derek Dawley
Managers, Event Presentation / Sr. Production	Lynn Truitt / Jeff Coltoniak
Senior Editor-Producer / Broadcast Engineer	David Traube / Rick Shepherd

Marketing and Fan Development

Directors, CRM & Analytics / Marketing	Jeff Eldersveld / Jim Riley
Director of Digital Media	Marcus Stephenson
Mgrs., Partnership Activation / Fan Development	Becky Magaw / Joel Siegman
Fan Development/Marketing Coordinator	Mason Fisher
CRM Coordinator / Digital Producer	Alexander Karp / Will Maetzold
Digital Content and Community Manager	Rob Mixer
Graphics, Senior Designer / Designer	Jason Duignan / Anthony Zych

Human Resources and Legal

Human Resources Director / Assistant	Cheryl Sparks / Ryan Leitenberger
Payroll Manager / Staff Counsel / Paralegal	Christine Parthemore / Pete Olsen / Ken Erney

Finance and Information Technology

Controller / Staff Accountants	Wendy Rohaly / Michael Fullen, Nora Ludwig
Director of IT / Systems Analyst	Jim Connolly / Matthew DeStephen
Accounts Payable Coordinator	Zachary Kramer
Office Coordinator/Receptionist	Beth Carlisle

Ticket Sales and Operations

Directors, Ticket Ops / Service & Retention	Mark Metz / Kelly Jones
Directors, New Business / Group Sales	Drew Ribarchak / Nick Myerr
Ticket Operations Managers	Brandon Haas, Abby Miller
Group Event Specialists	Erica Ganyard, James Garland, Josh Hafer, Grant Jamieson, Brian Thompson, Marc Witt
Season Ticket Sales Account Execs.	Ian Bernadas, Sean Tobin, Cody Johnson, Tim McDonough
Season Ticket Service Coordinators	Megan Cooper, Justin Dunn, Michelle Furr, Caitlin Reagan
Ticket Sales Coordinator	Shivani Banker
Inside Sales Representatives	Victoria Centers, Emily Clingan, Andrew Exler, Zayna Ibrahim, Zachary Joy, Joe Lombardi, Carmelo Marzullo, Donovan Powell, Joe Powell, Courtney Spiegel, Tara Smeak, Zach Wilson

Broadcasting

Director of Broadcasting	Russ Mollohan
FOX Sports Ohio Play-By-Play / Color	Jeff Rimer / Bill Davidge
Radio Play-By-Play Announcer	Bob McElligott
Broadcast Associate and Team Ambassador	Jody Shelley

Dallas Stars

2012-13 Results: 22W-22L-3OTL-1SOL 48PTS
5TH, Pacific Division • 11TH, Western Conference

Key Off-Season Signings/Acquisitions

2013

April 29 • Named **Jim Nill** general manager.

June 7 • Acquired D **Sergei Gonchar** from Ottawa for a 6th-round pick (Chris LeBlanc) in the 2013 NHL Draft.

21 • Named **Lindy Ruff** head coach.

July 3 • Re-signed D **Jordie Benn**.

4 • Acquired C **Rich Peverley**, C **Tyler Seguin** and D **Ryan Button** from Boston for LW **Loui Eriksson**, RW **Matt Fraser**, RW **Reilly Smith** and D **Joe Morrow**.

5 • Acquired C **Shawn Horcoff** from Edmonton for D **Philip Larsen** and a 7th-round pick in the 2016 NHL Draft.

5 • Signed G **Dan Ellis**.

8 • Signed C **Chris Mueller**.

24 • Named **James Patrick** assistant coach.

Jamie Benn celebrates a goal with Ryan Whitney during the Stars 20th year in Dallas in 2012-13. Benn was the team's top point-getter with 33 in 41 games played during the season.

2013-14 Schedule

Oct.	Thu.	3	Florida
	Sat.	5	Washington
	Fri.	11	at Winnipeg
	Sat.	12	at Minnesota
	Tue.	15	at Colorado
	Thu.	17	San Jose
	Sat.	19	at Los Angeles
	Sun.	20	at Anaheim*
	Thu.	24	Calgary
	Sat.	26	Winnipeg
	Mon.	28	at Buffalo
	Tue.	29	at Montreal
Nov.	Fri.	1	Colorado
	Sun.	3	at Ottawa*
	Tue.	5	at Boston
	Thu.	7	at Detroit
	Sat.	9	Chicago
	Wed.	13	at Edmonton
	Thu.	14	at Calgary
	Sun.	17	at Vancouver*
	Thu.	21	NY Rangers
	Sat.	23	at St. Louis
	Tue.	26	Anaheim
	Fri.	29	Chicago
Dec.	Sun.	1	Edmonton*
	Tue.	3	at Chicago
	Thu.	5	at Toronto
	Sat.	7	Philadelphia*
	Tue.	10	Chicago
	Thu.	12	at Nashville
	Sat.	14	at Winnipeg*
	Mon.	16	at Colorado
	Tue.	17	Colorado
	Thu.	19	Vancouver
	Sat.	21	at San Jose
	Mon.	23	at Los Angeles
	Fri.	27	Nashville
	Sun.	29	St. Louis*
	Tue.	31	Los Angeles
Jan.	Thu.	2	Montreal
	Sat.	4	Detroit
	Mon.	6	at NY Islanders
	Thu.	9	at New Jersey
	Fri.	10	at NY Rangers
	Sun.	12	NY Islanders*
	Tue.	14	Edmonton
	Thu.	16	Boston
	Sat.	18	at Minnesota
	Mon.	20	at Nashville
	Tue.	21	Minnesota
	Thu.	23	Toronto
	Sat.	25	Pittsburgh
	Mon.	27	Colorado
	Thu.	30	New Jersey
Feb.	Sat.	1	at Anaheim
	Tue.	4	at Phoenix
	Wed.	5	at San Jose
	Sat.	8	Phoenix
	Thu.	27	Carolina
Mar.	Sat.	1	Tampa Bay*
	Mon.	3	Buffalo
	Tue.	4	at Columbus
	Thu.	6	Vancouver
	Sat.	8	Minnesota
	Mon.	10	Columbus
	Tue.	11	at St. Louis
	Fri.	14	Calgary
	Sun.	16	at Winnipeg
	Tue.	18	at Pittsburgh
	Thu.	20	at Philadelphia
	Sat.	22	Ottawa*
	Mon.	24	Winnipeg
	Tue.	25	at Chicago
	Fri.	28	Nashville
	Sat.	29	at St. Louis
Apr.	Tue.	1	at Washington
	Thu.	3	at Carolina
	Sat.	5	at Tampa Bay
	Sun.	6	at Florida*
	Tue.	8	Nashville
	Fri.	11	St. Louis
	Sun.	13	at Phoenix

* Denotes afternoon game.

CENTRAL DIVISION
47th NHL Season

Franchise date: June 5, 1967

Transferred from Minnesota to Dallas, June 9, 1993.

Year-by-Year Record

		Home				Road				Overall									
Season	GP	W	L	T	OL	W	L	T	OL	W	L	T	OL	GF	GA	Pts.	Div. Fin.	Conf. Fin.	Playoff Result
2012-13	48	11	11	....	2	11	11	....	2	22	22	....	4	130	142	48	5th, Pac.	11th, West	Out of Playoffs
2011-12	82	22	16	....	3	20	19	....	2	42	35	....	5	211	222	89	4th, Pac.	10th, West	Out of Playoffs
2010-11	82	22	11	....	8	20	18	....	3	42	29	....	11	227	233	95	5th, Pac.	9th, West	Out of Playoffs
2009-10	82	23	11	....	7	14	20	....	7	37	31	....	14	237	254	88	5th, Pac.	12th, West	Out of Playoffs
2008-09	82	20	16	....	5	16	19	....	6	36	35	....	11	230	257	83	3rd, Pac.	12th, West	Out of Playoffs
2007-08	82	23	16	....	2	22	14	....	5	45	30	....	7	242	207	97	3rd, Pac.	5th, West	Lost Conf. Final
2006-07	82	28	11	....	2	22	14	....	5	50	25	....	7	226	197	107	3rd, Pac.	6th, West	Lost Conf. Quarter-Final
2005-06	82	28	11	....	2	25	12	....	4	53	23	....	6	265	218	112	1st, Pac.	2nd, West	Lost Conf. Quarter-Final
2004-05	....	....	....	....	....	....	....	....	....	....	....	....	....	....	....	....			
2003-04	82	26	7	8	0	15	19	5	2	41	26	13	2	194	175	97	2nd, Pac.	5th, West	Lost Conf. Quarter-Final
2002-03	82	28	5	6	2	18	12	9	2	46	17	15	4	245	169	111	1st, Pac.	1st, West	Lost Conf. Semi-Final
2001-02	82	18	13	6	4	18	15	7	1	36	28	13	5	215	213	90	4th, Pac.	10th, West	Out of Playoffs
2000-01	82	26	10	5	0	22	14	3	2	48	24	8	2	241	187	106	1st, Pac.	3rd, West	Lost Conf. Semi-Final
1999-2000	82	21	11	5	4	22	12	5	2	43	23	10	6	211	184	102	1st, Pac.	2nd, West	Lost Final
1998-99	**82**	**29**	**8**	**4**	....	**22**	**11**	**8**	....	**51**	**19**	**12**	....	**236**	**168**	**114**	**1st, Pac.**	**1st, West**	**Won Stanley Cup**
1997-98	82	26	8	7	....	23	14	4	....	49	22	11	....	242	167	109	1st, Cen.	1st, West	Lost Conf. Final
1996-97	82	25	13	3	....	23	13	5	....	48	26	8	....	252	198	104	1st, Cen.	2nd, West	Lost Conf. Quarter-Final
1995-96	82	14	18	9	....	12	24	5	....	26	42	14	....	227	280	66	6th, Cen.	11th, West	Out of Playoffs
1994-95	48	9	10	5	....	8	13	3	....	17	23	8	....	136	135	42	5th, Cen.	8th, West	Lost Conf. Quarter-Final
1993-94	84	23	12	7	....	19	17	6	....	42	29	13	....	286	265	97	3rd, Cen.	4th, West	Lost Conf. Semi-Final
1992-93*	84	18	17	7	....	18	21	3	....	36	38	10	....	272	293	82	5th, Norris		Out of Playoffs
1991-92*	80	20	16	4	....	12	26	2	....	32	42	6	....	246	278	70	4th, Norris		Lost Div. Semi-Final
1990-91*	80	19	15	6	....	8	24	8	....	27	39	14	....	256	266	68	4th, Norris		Lost Final
1989-90*	80	26	12	2	....	10	28	2	....	36	40	4	....	284	291	76	4th, Norris		Lost Div. Semi-Final
1988-89*	80	17	15	8	....	10	22	8	....	27	37	16	....	258	278	70	3rd, Norris		Lost Div. Semi-Final
1987-88*	80	10	24	6	....	9	24	7	....	19	48	13	....	242	349	51	5th, Norris		Out of Playoffs
1986-87*	80	17	20	3	....	13	20	7	....	30	40	10	....	296	314	70	5th, Norris		Out of Playoffs
1985-86*	80	21	15	4	....	17	18	5	....	38	33	9	....	327	305	85	2nd, Norris		Lost Div. Semi-Final
1984-85*	80	14	19	7	....	11	24	5	....	25	43	12	....	268	321	62	4th, Norris		Lost Div. Final
1983-84*	80	22	14	4	....	17	17	6	....	39	31	10	....	345	344	88	1st, Norris		Lost Conf. Final
1982-83*	80	23	6	11	....	17	18	5	....	40	24	16	....	321	290	96	2nd, Norris		Lost Div. Final
1981-82*	80	21	7	12	....	16	16	8	....	37	23	20	....	346	288	94	1st, Norris		Lost Div. Semi-Final
1980-81*	80	23	10	7	....	12	18	10	....	35	28	17	....	291	263	87	3rd, Adams		Lost Final
1979-80*	80	25	8	7	....	11	20	9	....	36	28	16	....	311	253	88	3rd, Adams		Lost Semi-Final
1978-79*	80	19	15	6	....	9	25	6	....	28	40	12	....	257	289	68	4th, Adams		Out Of Playoffs
1977-78*	80	12	24	4	....	6	29	5	....	18	53	9	....	218	325	45	5th, Smythe		Out of Playoffs
1976-77*	80	17	14	9	....	6	25	9	....	23	39	18	....	240	310	64	2nd, Smythe		Lost Prelim. Round
1975-76*	80	15	22	3	....	5	31	4	....	20	53	7	....	195	303	47	4th, Smythe		Out of Playoffs
1974-75*	80	17	20	3	....	6	30	4	....	23	50	7	....	221	341	53	4th, Smythe		Out of Playoffs
1973-74*	78	18	15	6	....	5	23	11	....	23	38	17	....	235	275	63	7th, West		Out of Playoffs
1972-73*	78	26	8	5	....	11	22	6	....	37	30	11	....	254	230	85	3rd, West		Lost Quarter-Final
1971-72*	78	22	11	6	....	15	18	6	....	37	29	12	....	212	191	86	2nd, West		Lost Quarter-Final
1970-71*	78	16	15	8	....	12	19	8	....	28	34	16	....	191	223	72	4th, West		Lost Semi-Final
1969-70*	76	11	16	11	....	8	19	11	....	19	35	22	....	224	257	60	3rd, West		Lost Quarter-Final
1968-69*	76	11	21	6	....	7	22	9	....	18	43	15	....	189	270	51	6th, West		Out of Playoffs
1967-68*	74	17	12	8	....	10	20	7	....	27	32	15	....	191	226	69	4th, West		Lost Semi-Final

* Minnesota North Stars

2013-14 Player Personnel

FORWARDS	HT	WT	*Age	Place of Birth	S	2012-13 Club
BENN, Jamie	6-2	205	24	Victoria, B.C.	L	Hamburg Freez.-Dallas
CHIASSON, Alex	6-3	202	23	Montreal, Que.	R	Texas-Dallas
COLE, Erik	6-2	212	34	Oswego, NY	L	Montreal-Dallas
EAKIN, Cody	6-0	190	22	Winnipeg, Man.	L	Texas-Dallas
FIDDLER, Vernon	5-11	197	33	Edmonton, Alta.	L	Dallas
GARBUTT, Ryan	6-0	190	28	Winnipeg, Man.	L	Dallas
HORCOFF, Shawn	6-1	208	35	Trail, B.C.	L	Edmonton
MacDERMID, Lane	6-3	205	24	Hartford, CT	L	Prov (AHL)-Bos-Dal
MUELLER, Chris	5-11	203	27	West Seneca, NY	R	Milwaukee-Nashville
NICHUSHKIN, Valeri	6-4	202	18	Chelyabinsk, Russia	L	Chelyabinsk Jr.-Chelmet-Chelyabinsk
PEVERLEY, Rich	6-0	195	31	Guelph, Ont.	R	JYP-Boston
ROUSSEL, Antoine	5-11	192	23	Roubaix, France	L	Texas-Dallas
SCEVIOUR, Colton	6-0	201	24	Red Deer, Alta.	R	Texas-Dallas
SEGUIN, Tyler	6-1	182	21	Brampton, Ont.	R	Biel-Boston
WHITNEY, Ray	5-10	180	41	Fort Saskatchewan, Alta.	R	Dallas
DEFENSEMEN						
BENN, Jordie	6-1	200	26	Victoria, B.C.	L	Texas-Dallas
CONNAUTON, Kevin	6-1	196	23	Edmonton, Alta.	L	Chicago (AHL)-Texas
DALEY, Trevor	5-11	198	29	Toronto, Ont.	L	Dallas
DILLON, Brenden	6-3	209	22	Surrey, B.C.	L	Texas-Dallas
GOLIGOSKI, Alex	5-11	181	28	Grand Rapids, MN	L	Dallas
GONCHAR, Sergei	6-2	212	39	Chelyabinsk, USSR	L	Ottawa-Magnitogorsk
OLEKSIAK, Jamie	6-7	252	20	Toronto, Ont.	L	Texas-Dallas
ROBIDAS, Stephane	5-11	196	36	Sherbrooke, Que.	R	HIFK-Dallas
ROME, Aaron	6-1	218	30	Nesbitt, Man.	L	Dallas
GOALTENDERS	**HT**	**WT**	***Age**	**Place of Birth**	**C**	**2012-13 Club**
ELLIS, Dan	6-1	191	33	Saskatoon, Sask.	L	Charlotte-Carolina
LEHTONEN, Kari	6-4	217	29	Helsinki, Finland	L	Dallas
NILSTORP, Cristopher	6-3	192	29	Burlov, Sweden	R	Texas-Dallas

* – Age at start of 2013-14 season

2012-13 Scoring

* – rookie

Regular Season

Pos	#	Player	Team	GP	G	A	Pts	TOI	+/–	PIM	PP	SH	GW	S	%
L	14	Jamie Benn	DAL	41	12	21	33	19:54	–12	40	3	0	3	110	10.9
L	21	Loui Eriksson	DAL	48	12	17	29	20:07	–9	8	2	1	3	104	11.5
L	13	Ray Whitney	DAL	32	11	18	29	19:23	1	4	4	0	1	62	17.7
D	33	Alex Goligoski	DAL	47	3	24	27	22:23	4	18	0	0	0	80	3.8
C	20	Cody Eakin	DAL	48	7	17	24	15:05	1	31	3	0	1	67	10.4
L	38	Vernon Fiddler	DAL	46	4	13	17	12:51	3	48	1	0	0	56	7.1
L	60 *	Antoine Roussel	DAL	39	7	7	14	9:23	3	85	0	0	0	46	15.2
L	72	Erik Cole	MTL	19	3	3	6	15:39	1	10	0	0	2	41	7.3
			DAL	28	6	1	7	16:53	–7	10	1	0	0	45	13.3
			Total	47	9	4	13	16:23	–6	20	1	0	2	86	10.5
D	6	Trevor Daley	DAL	44	4	9	13	21:24	1	14	2	0	0	58	6.9
D	3	Stephane Robidas	DAL	48	1	12	13	22:14	2	56	0	0	0	46	2.2
L	24	Eric Nystrom	DAL	48	7	4	11	14:21	–3	61	0	1	3	49	14.3
C	40	Ryan Garbutt	DAL	36	3	7	10	9:55	1	32	0	0	0	59	5.1
R	18 *	Reilly Smith	DAL	37	3	6	9	10:55	0	8	0	0	0	34	8.8
D	4 *	Brenden Dillon	DAL	48	3	5	8	21:22	1	65	0	0	1	75	4.0
R	12 *	Alex Chiasson	DAL	7	6	1	7	14:04	3	0	1	0	1	13	46.2
D	58 *	Jordie Benn	DAL	26	1	5	6	17:18	–4	10	1	0	0	31	3.2
D	36	Philip Larsen	DAL	32	2	3	5	14:52	–10	18	1	0	0	30	6.7
D	27	Aaron Rome	DAL	27	0	5	5	15:20	–2	18	0	0	0	15	0.0
R	25 *	Matt Fraser	DAL	12	1	2	3	11:47	0	0	0	0	0	17	5.9
L	28 *	Lane MacDermid	BOS	3	0	0	0	3:34	0	10	0	0	0	1	0.0
			DAL	6	2	0	2	5:05	1	9	0	0	0	3	66.7
			Total	9	2	0	2	4:35	1	19	0	0	0	4	50.0
D	43 *	Jamie Oleksiak	DAL	16	0	2	2	14:50	–5	14	0	0	0	11	0.0
C	23	Tom Wandell	DAL	18	1	0	1	8:26	0	4	0	0	1	14	7.1
C	22 *	Colton Sceviour	DAL	1	0	1	1	4:51	–1	0	0	0	0	0	0.0
C	17	Toby Petersen	DAL	1	0	0	0	6:40	0	0	0	0	0	0	0.0
L	48	Francis Wathier	DAL	1	0	0	0	5:40	0	0	0	0	0	0	0.0

Goaltending

No.	Goaltender	GPI	Mins	Avg	W	L	OT	EN	SO	GA	SA	S%	G	A	PIM
32	Kari Lehtonen	36	1986	2.66	15	14	3	3	1	88	1050	.916	0	2	0
41	Cristopher Nilstorp	5	291	3.09	1	3	1	0	0	15	146	.897	0	0	0
31	* Richard Bachman	13	609	3.25	6	5	0	2	0	33	288	.885	0	0	0
	Totals	**48**	**2906**	**2.91**	**22**	**22**	**4**	**5**	**1**	**141**	**1489**	**.905**			

Lindy Ruff

Head Coach

Born: Warburg, Alta., February 17, 1960.

Dallas Stars general manager Jim Nill announced on Friday, June 21, 2013, that Lindy Ruff had been hired as the 22nd head coach in franchise history. He is the seventh head coach in Dallas Stars history.

Ruff is the 12th-winningest head coach in NHL history, one of only 17 to reach the 500-victory plateau, and has the third-most wins of any active NHL coach. Dallas marks his second stint as an NHL head coach after departing the Buffalo Sabres as their all-time franchise leader in wins with a 571-432-162 record. During Ruff's tenure in Buffalo, the team made eight postseason appearances, including four trips to the Eastern Conference Final as well as an appearance in the 1999 Stanley Cup Final. In 2006, he was awarded the Jack Adams Award as the league's top coach for guiding his team to the Conference Final. Ruff was nominated again for the accolade in 2007 for posting consecutive 50-win campaigns and for leading his club to the Presidents' Trophy, which is earned annually by the top team in the regular season.

In Ruff's eight postseason appearances in Buffalo he earned a 57-44 record, which is tied for the 15th-most playoff victories in NHL history. He is also one of only 21 NHL head coaches to guide his team through at least 100 postseason contests.

No stranger to international competition, Ruff coached Canada's national team to a silver medal at the World Championships in 2009, served as an associate coach for the gold medal-winning team at the 2010 Winter Olympic Games in Vancouver, and served as head coach once more at the 2013 World Championships. He will be an associate coach again at the 2014 Olympics.

Prior to his coaching career, the native of Warburg, Alberta, played 691 games in the NHL from 1979 to 1991, posting 300 points (105 goals, 195 assists). He was Buffalo's second-round selection (32nd overall) in 1979.

Coaching Record

			Regular Season				Playoffs			
Season	**Team**	**League**	**GC**	**W**	**L**	**O/T**	**GC**	**W**	**L**	**T**
1997-98	Buffalo	NHL	82	36	29	17	15	10	5	....
1998-99	Buffalo	NHL	82	37	28	17	21	14	7	....
99-2000	Buffalo	NHL	82	35	32	15	5	1	4	....
2000-01	Buffalo	NHL	82	46	30	6	13	7	6	....
2001-02	Buffalo	NHL	82	35	35	12	....	....	....	....
2002-03	Buffalo	NHL	82	27	37	18	....	....	....	....
2003-04	Buffalo	NHL	82	37	34	11	....	....	....	....
2004-05	Buffalo				SEASON CANCELLED					
2005-06	Buffalo	NHL	82	52	24	6	18	11	7	....
2006-07	Buffalo	NHL	82	53	22	7	16	9	7	....
2007-08	Buffalo	NHL	82	39	31	12	....	....	....	....
2008-09	Buffalo	NHL	82	41	32	9	....	....	....	....
2009-10	Buffalo	NHL	82	45	27	10	6	2	4	....
2010-11	Buffalo	NHL	82	43	29	10	7	3	4	....
2011-12	Buffalo	NHL	82	39	32	11	....	....	....	....
2012-13	Buffalo	NHL	17	6	10	1	....	....	....	....
	NHL Totals		**1165**	**571**	**432**	**162**	**101**	**57**	**44**	....

Jack Adams Award (2006)

Assistant coaches Brian McCutheon and Scott Arniel posted an 0-1-0 record as replacement coach when Lindy Ruff was sidelined due to a family medical emergency, March 20, 2006. Game is credited to Ruff's coaching record.

Assistant coach James Patrick posted a 2-1-0 record as replacement coach after Lindy Ruff suffered broken ribs on February 6, 2012 and was sidelined from February 8 to 11. Games are credited to Ruff's coaching record.

After making a one-game debut with Dallas in 2011-12, Brenden Dillon was one of only six NHL rookies to suit up for all of his team's games in 2012-13. Dillon ranked third among rookies in total time on ice.

Coaching History

Wren Blair, 1967-68; Wren Blair and John Muckler, 1968-69; Wren Blair and Charlie Burns, 1969-70; Jack Gordon, 1970-71 to 1972-73; Jack Gordon and Parker MacDonald, 1973-74; Jack Gordon and Charlie Burns, 1974-75; Ted Harris, 1975-76, 1976-77; Ted Harris, André Beaulieu and Lou Nanne, 1977-78; Harry Howell and Glen Sonmor, 1978-79; Glen Sonmor, 1979-80 to 1981-82; Glen Sonmor and Murray Oliver, 1982-83; Bill Mahoney, 1983-84, 1984-85; Lorne Henning, 1985-86; Lorne Henning and Glen Sonmor, 1986-87; Herb Brooks, 1987-88; Pierre Page, 1988-89, 1989-90; Bob Gainey, 1990-91 to 1994-95; Bob Gainey and Ken Hitchcock, 1995-96; Ken Hitchcock, 1996-97 to 2000-01; Ken Hitchcock and Rick Wilson, 2001-02; Dave Tippett, 2002-03 to 2008-09; Marc Crawford, 2009-10, 2010-11; Glen Gulutzan, 2011-12, 2012-13; Lindy Ruff, 2013-14.

Club Records

Team

(Figures in brackets for season records are games played; records for fewest points, wins, ties, losses, goals, goals against are for 70 or more games)

Most Points **114** 1998-99 (82)
Most Wins **53** 2005-06 (82)
Most Ties **22** 1969-70 (76)
Most Losses **53** 1975-76 (80), 1977-78 (80)
Most Goals **346** 1981-82 (80)
Most Goals Against **349** 1987-88 (80)
Fewest Points **45** 1977-78 (80)
Fewest Wins **18** 1968-69 (76), 1977-78 (80)
Fewest Ties **4** 1989-90 (80)
Fewest Losses **19** 1998-99 (82)
Fewest Goals **189** 1968-69 (76)
Fewest Goals Against **167** 1997-98 (82)
Longest Winning Streak
Overall .... **7** Mar. 16-28/80, Mar. 16-Apr. 2/97, Nov. 22-Dec. 5/97, Jan. 29-Feb. 11/08
Home .... **11** Nov. 4-Dec. 27/72
Away .... **8** Dec. 13/10-Jan. 20/11
Longest Undefeated Streak
Overall .... **15** Dec. 6/98-Jan. 6/99 (12W, 3T)
Home .... **17** Jan. 23-Mar. 20/04 (13W, 4T/OL)
Away .... **10** Jan. 12-Mar. 4/99 (8W, 2T), Dec. 27/02-Feb. 25/03 (7W, 3T/OL)
Longest Losing Streak
Overall .... **10** Feb. 1-20/76
Home .... **6** Jan. 17-Feb. 4/70, Feb. 21-Mar. 8/09
Away .... **10** Dec. 12/09-Jan. 21/10
Longest Winless Streak
Overall .... **20** Jan. 15-Feb. 28/70 (15L, 5T)
Home .... **12** Jan. 17-Feb. 25/70 (8L, 4T)
Away .... **23** Oct. 25/74-Jan. 28/75 (19L, 4T)
Most Shutouts, Season **11** 2000-01 (82), 2002-03 (82)
Most PIM, Season **2,313** 1987-88 (80)
Most Goals, Game .... **15** Nov. 11/81 (Wpg. 2 at Min. 15)

Individual

Most Seasons .... **21** Mike Modano
Most Games .... **1,459** Mike Modano
Most Goals, Career .... **557** Mike Modano
Most Assists, Career .... **802** Mike Modano
Most Points, Career .... **1,359** Mike Modano (557G, 802A)
Most PIM, Career .... **1,883** Shane Churla
Most Shutouts, Career .... **40** Marty Turco
Longest Consecutive Games Streak .... **442** Danny Grant (Dec. 4/68-Apr. 7/74)
Most Goals, Season .... **55** Dino Ciccarelli (1981-82), Brian Bellows (1989-90)
Most Assists, Season .... **76** Neal Broten (1985-86)
Most Points, Season .... **114** Bobby Smith (1981-82; 43G, 71A)
Most PIM, Season .... **382** Basil McRae (1987-88)
Most Points, Defenseman, Season .... **77** Craig Hartsburg (1981-82; 17G, 60A)
Most Points, Center, Season .... **114** Bobby Smith (1981-82; 43G, 71A)
Most Points, Right Wing, Season .... **106** Dino Ciccarelli (1981-82; 55G, 51A)
Most Points, Left Wing, Season .... **99** Brian Bellows (1989-90; 55G, 44A)
Most Points, Rookie, Season .... **98** Neal Broten (1981-82; 38G, 60A)
Most Shutouts, Season .... **9** Ed Belfour (1997-98), Marty Turco (2003-04)
Most Goals, Game .... **5** Tim Young (Jan. 15/79)
Most Assists, Game .... **5** Murray Oliver (Oct. 24/71), Larry Murphy (Oct. 17/89), Brad Richards (Feb. 28/08)
Most Points, Game .... **7** Bobby Smith (Nov. 11/81; 4G, 3A)

Records include Minnesota North Stars, 1967-68 through 1992-93.

Retired Numbers

7	Neal Broten	1980-1995, 1996-1997
8	Bill Goldsworthy*	1967-1976
19	Bill Masterton*	1967-1968

* Minnesota North Stars

All-time Record vs. Other Clubs

Regular Season

	Total								At Home								On Road							
	GP	W	L	T	OL	GF	GA	PTS	GP	W	L	T	OL	GF	GA	PTS	GP	W	L	T	OL	GF	GA	PTS
Anaheim	107	64	29	5	9	315	244	142	54	38	11	2	3	168	107	81	53	26	18	3	6	147	137	61
Boston	127	30	74	23	0	335	496	83	64	20	31	13	0	183	226	53	63	10	43	10	0	152	270	30
Buffalo	112	41	52	17	2	329	363	101	57	28	22	6	1	182	163	63	55	13	30	11	1	147	200	38
Calgary	155	61	62	25	7	469	487	154	78	39	23	11	5	274	235	94	77	22	39	14	2	195	252	60
Carolina	69	38	25	6	0	253	207	82	33	21	10	2	0	127	93	44	36	17	15	4	0	126	114	38
Chicago	253	98	120	31	4	766	855	231	128	61	49	16	2	434	395	140	125	37	71	15	2	332	460	91
Colorado	113	50	47	12	4	330	357	116	56	31	17	5	3	191	160	70	57	19	30	7	1	139	197	46
Columbus	47	31	11	0	5	139	106	67	23	15	6	0	2	67	51	32	24	16	5	0	3	72	55	35
Detroit	243	102	105	34	2	782	819	240	121	58	43	18	2	406	363	136	122	44	62	16	0	376	456	104
Edmonton	120	62	40	15	3	410	380	142	60	35	17	7	1	214	162	78	60	27	23	8	2	196	218	64
Florida	25	11	8	3	3	74	69	28	12	4	4	2	2	37	43	12	13	7	4	1	1	37	26	16
Los Angeles	219	105	72	32	10	712	643	252	110	64	31	13	2	393	294	143	109	41	41	19	8	319	349	109
Minnesota	47	30	14	1	2	142	114	63	24	19	3	1	1	92	56	40	23	11	11	0	1	50	58	23
Montreal	123	32	70	21	0	315	468	85	62	19	31	12	0	163	209	50	61	13	39	9	0	152	259	35
Nashville	55	31	21	1	2	144	117	65	27	19	7	0	1	77	43	39	28	12	14	1	1	67	74	26
New Jersey	98	50	39	9	0	320	293	109	50	30	14	6	0	179	125	66	48	20	25	3	0	141	168	43
NY Islanders	102	37	47	16	2	297	368	92	50	19	22	8	1	147	181	47	52	18	25	8	1	150	187	45
NY Rangers	130	39	68	22	1	374	452	101	64	21	31	11	1	201	231	54	66	18	37	11	0	173	221	47
Ottawa	26	16	8	0	2	86	66	34	14	9	5	0	0	54	38	18	12	7	3	0	2	32	28	16
Philadelphia	141	38	70	32	1	385	493	109	70	28	25	16	1	224	224	73	71	10	45	16	0	161	269	36
Phoenix	161	80	62	13	6	515	472	179	81	40	30	9	2	266	232	91	80	40	32	4	4	249	240	88
Pittsburgh	134	57	63	12	2	441	476	128	68	38	22	6	2	258	227	84	66	19	41	6	0	183	249	44
St. Louis	263	100	116	43	4	800	845	247	131	63	44	22	2	435	379	150	132	37	72	21	2	365	466	97
San Jose	111	58	42	5	6	303	285	127	55	26	21	4	4	154	143	60	56	32	21	1	2	149	142	67
Tampa Bay	30	19	8	3	0	92	68	41	14	8	5	1	0	47	38	17	16	11	3	2	0	45	30	24
Toronto	204	89	86	28	1	705	677	207	100	52	36	11	1	375	314	116	104	37	50	17	0	330	363	91
Vancouver	173	81	67	22	3	552	553	187	87	46	29	12	0	297	249	104	86	35	38	10	3	255	304	83
Washington	87	42	27	16	2	304	247	102	44	23	11	8	2	163	118	56	43	19	16	8	0	141	129	46
Winnipeg	14	11	2	0	1	47	33	23	7	6	1	0	0	19	10	12	7	5	1	0	1	28	23	11
Defunct Clubs	65	29	24	12	0	207	191	70	33	19	8	6	0	123	86	44	32	10	16	6	0	84	105	26
Totals	**3554**	**1532**	**1479**	**459**	**84**	**10943**	**11244**	**3607**	**1777**	**899**	**609**	**228**	**41**	**5950**	**5195**	**2067**	**1777**	**633**	**870**	**231**	**43**	**4993**	**6049**	**1540**

Playoffs

	Series	W	L	GP	W	L	T	GF	GA	Last Mtg.	Rnd.	Result
Anaheim	2	1	1	12	6	6	0	34	27	2008	CQF	W 4-2
Boston	1	1	0	3	3	0	0	20	13	1981	PRE	W 3-0
Buffalo	3	2	1	13	8	5	0	39	37	1999	F	W 4-2
Calgary	1	1	0	6	4	2	0	25	18	1981	SF	W 4-2
Chicago	6	2	4	33	14	19	0	118	120	1991	DSF	W 4-2
Colorado	4	2	2	24	10	14	0	62	66	2006	CQF	L 1-4
Detroit	4	0	4	24	8	16	0	50	72	2008	CF	L 2-4
Edmonton	8	6	2	42	27	15	0	118	104	2003	CQF	W 4-2
Los Angeles	1	1	0	7	4	3	0	26	21	1968	QF	W 4-3
Montreal	2	1	1	13	6	7	0	37	48	1980	QF	W 4-3
New Jersey	1	0	1	6	2	4	0	9	15	2000	F	L 2-4
NY Islanders	1	0	1	5	1	4	0	16	26	1981	F	L 1-4
Philadelphia	2	0	2	11	3	8	0	26	41	1980	SF	L 1-4
Pittsburgh	1	0	1	6	2	4	0	16	28	1991	F	L 2-4
St. Louis	12	6	6	66	34	32	0	197	187	2001	CSF	L 0-4
San Jose	3	3	0	17	12	5	0	46	30	2008	CSF	W 4-2
Toronto	2	2	0	7	6	1	0	35	26	1983	DSF	W 3-1
Vancouver	2	0	2	12	4	8	0	23	31	2007	CQF	L 3-4
Totals	**56**	**28**	**28**	**307**	**154**	**153**	**0**	**897**	**910**			

Calgary totals include Atlanta Flames, 1972-73 to 1979-80. Carolina totals include Hartford, 1979-80 to 1996-97.
Colorado totals include Quebec, 1979-80 to 1994-95.
New Jersey totals include Kansas City, 1974-75, 1975-76, and Colorado Rockies, 1976-77 to 1981-82.
Phoenix totals include Winnipeg, 1979-80 to 1995-96. Winnipeg totals include Atlanta Thrashers, 1999-2000 to 2010-11.

Playoff Results 2013-2009

(Last playoff appearance: 2008)

Abbreviations: Round: F – Final; **CF** – conference final; **CSF** – conference semi-final; **CQF** – conference quarter-final; **DSF** – division semi-final; **SF** – semi-final; **QF** – quarter-final; **PRE** – preliminary round.

2012-13 Results

Jan.	19	Phoenix	4-3		12	Nashville	0-4
	20	at Minnesota	0-1		14	Anaheim	1-2†
	22	at Detroit	2-1		16	Chicago	1-8
	24	Chicago	2-3*		18	Calgary	4-3
	26	St. Louis	3-4		20	at Colorado	3-4
	28	at Columbus	1-2		21	at Los Angeles	2-0
	29	at Detroit	1-4		23	Colorado	5-2
Feb.	1	Phoenix	4-3†		25	Minnesota	4-7
	2	at Phoenix	0-2		29	Minnesota	5-3
	4	at Colorado	3-2		31	Los Angeles	2-3
	6	at Edmonton	3-2*	**Apr.**	1	Anaheim	0-4
	8	Anaheim	3-1		3	at Anaheim	2-5
	12	at Edmonton	4-1		5	at Anaheim	3-1
	13	at Calgary	4-7		7	at San Jose	5-4†
	15	at Vancouver	4-3		9	Los Angeles	5-1
	17	Calgary	3-4		12	at Nashville	5-2
	21	Vancouver	3-4		13	San Jose	2-1
	23	San Jose	3-1		15	at Chicago	2-5
	25	at Nashville	4-5*		18	Vancouver	5-1
	26	at Columbus	5-4*		19	at St. Louis	1-2
	28	Edmonton	1-5		21	at Los Angeles	3-4*
Mar.	3	St. Louis	4-1		23	at San Jose	2-3
	7	at Los Angeles	5-2		25	Columbus	1-3
	9	at Phoenix	1-2		27	Detroit	0-3

* – Overtime † – Shootout

Entry Draft Selections 2013-1999

Name in bold denotes played in NHL.

2013
Pick
10 Valeri Nichushkin
29 Jason Dickinson
40 Remi Elie
54 Philippe Desrosiers
68 Niklas Hansson
101 Nicholas Paul
131 Cole Ully
149 Matej Paulovic
182 Aleksi Makela

2012
Pick
13 Radek Faksa
43 Ludwig Bystrom
54 Mike Winther
61 Devin Shore
74 Esa Lindell
104 Gemel Smith
134 Branden Troock
144 Henri Kiviaho
183 Dmitry Sinitsyn

2011
Pick
14 **Jamie Oleksiak**
44 Brett Ritchie
105 Emil Molin
135 Troy Vance
165 Matej Stransky
195 Jyrki Jokipakka

2010
Pick
11 Jack Campbell
41 Patrik Nemeth
77 Alexander Guptill
109 Alex Theriau
131 John Klingberg

2009
Pick
8 **Scott Glennie**
38 **Alex Chiasson**
69 **Reilly Smith**
129 **Tomas Vincour**
159 Curtis McKenzie

2008
Pick
59 Tyler Beskorowany
89 Scott Winkler
149 **Philip Larsen**
176 Matthew Tassone
209 Mike Bergin

2007
Pick
50 Nico Sacchetti
64 Sergei Korostin
112 **Colton Sceviour**
128 Austin Smith
129 **Jamie Benn**
136 Ondrej Roman
149 Michael Neal
172 Luke Gazdic

2006
Pick
27 **Ivan Vishnevskiy**
90 Aaron Snow
120 **Richard Bachman**
138 **David McIntyre**
150 Max Warn

2005
Pick
28 **Matt Niskanen**
33 **James Neal**
71 **Rich Clune**
75 **Perttu Lindgren**
146 **Tom Wandell**
160 **Matt Watkins**
223 Pat McGann

2004
Pick
28 **Mark Fistric**
34 Johan Fransson
52 **Raymond Sawada**
56 **Nicklas Grossmann**
86 John Lammers
104 Fredrik Naslund
183 Trevor Ludwig
218 Sergei Kukushkin
248 Lukas Vomela
280 Matt McKnight

2003
Pick
33 **Loui Eriksson**
36 **Vojtech Polak**
54 **B.J. Crombeen**
99 Matt Nickerson
134 Alexander Naurov
144 Eero Kilpelainen
165 Gino Guyer
185 **Francis Wathier**
195 **Drew Bagnall**
196 Elias Granath
259 Niko Vainio

2002
Pick
26 Martin Vagner
32 Janos Vas
34 **Tobias Stephan**
42 Marius Holtet
43 **Trevor Daley**
78 Geoff Waugh
110 Jarkko A. Immonen
147 David Bararuk
180 Kirill Sidorenko
210 Bryan Hamm
243 Tuomas Mikkonen
273 Ned Havern

2001
Pick
26 **Jason Bacashihua**
70 Yared Hagos
92 Anthony Aquino
126 Daniel Volrab
161 **Mike Smith**
167 Michal Blazek
192 **Jussi Jokinen**
255 Marco Rosa
265 Dale Sullivan
285 Marek Tomica

2000
Pick
25 **Steve Ott**
60 **Dan Ellis**
68 **Joel Lundqvist**
91 Alexei Tereschenko
123 Vadim Khomitski
139 Ruslan Bernikov
162 Artem Chernov
192 Ladislav Vlcek
219 Marco Tuokko
224 **Antti Miettinen**

1999
Pick
32 **Michael Ryan**
66 **Dan Jancevski**
96 **Mathias Tjarnqvist**
126 Jeff Bateman
156 Gregor Baumgartner
184 Justin Cox
186 Brett Draney
215 **Jeff MacMillan**
243 Brian Sullivan
265 Jamie Chamberlain
272 Mikhail Donika

General Managers' History

Wren Blair, 1967-68 to 1973-74; Jack Gordon, 1974-75 to 1976-77; Jack Gordon and Lou Nanne, 1977-78; Lou Nanne, 1978-79 to 1986-87; Lou Nanne and Jack Ferreira, 1987-88; Jack Ferreira, 1988-89, 1989-90; Bob Clarke, 1990-91, 1991-92; Bob Gainey, 1992-93 to 2000-01; Bob Gainey and Doug Armstrong, 2001-02; Doug Armstrong, 2002-03 to 2006-07; Doug Armstrong and Brett Hull/Les Jackson, 2007-08; Brett Hull/Les Jackson, 2008-09; Joe Nieuwendyk, 2009-10 to 2012-13; Jim Nill, 2013-14.

Captains' History

Bob Woytowich, 1967-68; Moose Vasko, 1968-69; Claude Larose, 1969-70; Ted Harris, 1970-71 to 1973-74; Bill Goldsworthy, 1974-75, 1975-76; Bill Hogaboam, 1976-77; Nick Beverley, 1977-78; J.P. Parise, 1978-79; Paul Shmyr, 1979-80, 1980-81; Tim Young, 1981-82; Craig Hartsburg, 1982-83; Craig Hartsburg and Brian Bellows, 1983-84; Craig Hartsburg, 1984-85 to 1987-88; Curt Fraser, Bob Rouse and Curt Giles, 1988-89; Curt Giles, 1989-90, 1990-91; Mark Tinordi, 1991-92 to 1993-94; Neal Broten and Derian Hatcher, 1994-95; Derian Hatcher, 1995-96 to 2002-03; Mike Modano, 2003-04 to 2005-06; Brenden Morrow, 2006-07 to 2012-13.

Jim Nill

General Manager

Born: Hanna, Alta., April 11, 1958.

Jim Nill was appointed general manager of the Dallas Stars on April 29, 2013. He becomes the 11th General Manager in franchise history and the sixth since the team moved to Dallas.

Nill concluded his 15th season as assistant general manager of the Detroit Red Wings, and his 19th season overall as a member of the management team, in 2012-13. His responsibilities with Detroit included directing the amateur scouting department and overseeing all selections at the annual NHL Draft, as well as managing the development of the organization's prospects at both the professional and amateur levels. During Nill's tenure in Detroit, the Red Wings had more wins than any other franchise in the NHL, won the Stanley Cup four times (1997, 1998, 2002 and 2008), the Presidents' Trophy six times (1995, 1996, 2002, 2004, 2006 and 2008), the Central Division title 12 times, and won seven regular season Western Conference titles while never missing the playoffs. He was an integral part of Detroit's drafting of Pavel Datsyuk, Henrik Zetterberg, Niklas Kronwall, Valtteri Filppula, Jimmy Howard and Johan Franzen. Nill was also general manager of Team Canada for the 2004 World Championship, winning a gold medal.

Nill joined the Red Wings' front office in the summer of 1994 following three seasons with the Ottawa Senators. Previously, Nill enjoyed a nine-season NHL career as a right winger with the Boston Bruins, Vancouver Canucks, St. Louis Blues, Winnipeg Jets and Red Wings. He collected 58 goals, 87 assists and 854 penalty minutes in 524 regular season games. Nill later went to Adirondack of the American Hockey League as a player/coach, retiring as a player after the 1990-91 season. A member of the 1979-80 Canadian national and Olympic team, he was a fifth-round pick of the St. Louis Blues (89th overall) in the 1978 draft.

Club Directory

American Airlines Center

Dallas Stars
Office Address:
2601 Ave. of the Stars
Frisco, TX 75034
Phone **214/387-5500**
FAX 214/387-5564
Ticket Information 214/GO STARS
www.dallasstars.com
Capacity: 18,532

Executives	
Owner and Governor	Tom Gaglardi
President, CEO and Alternate Governor	James R. Lites
Executive Vice President, Chief Operating Officer	Jason Farris
Executive Vice President, Chief Revenue Officer	Brad Alberts
Executive Advisor and Alternate Governor	Mike Modano
Executive Assistant to the President	Aanya Reiten
Hockey Operations	
General Manager	Jim Nill
Assistant G.M.	Les Jackson
Director of Hockey Operations/Texas Stars G.M.	Scott White
Director of Hockey Administration	Mark Janko
Advisor to Hockey Operations	Mark Recchi
Head Coach	Lindy Ruff
Assistant Coaches	Curt Fraser, James Patrick
Goaltending Coach	Mike Valley
Coordinators, Video / Player Development	Kelly Forbes / J.J. McQueen
Director, Team Services	Jason Rademan
Scouting Directors, Amateur / European	Joe McDonnell / Kari Takko
Pro Scouts	Paul McIntosh, Danny O'Brien, Doug Overton
Amateur Scouts	Bob Gernander, Dennis Holland, Jiri Hrdina, Jimmy Johnston, Mark Leach, Alex LePore, Rickard Oquist, Borys Protsenko, Shane Turner, Bobby Vermette
Athletic Trainers, Head / Associate	Dave Zeis / Craig Lowry
Equipment Head / Assistant Mgr. / Assistant	Steve Sumner / Dennis Soetaert / Josh Richards
Strength and Conditioning Coach	Brad Jellis
Massage Therapist	Cleo Bates
Executive Assistant, Hockey Operations	Katie Purcell
Production and Entertainment	
Vice President, Production and Entertainment	Jason Walsh
Play-By-Play / Analyst	Ralph Strangis / Daryl Reaugh
Reporter / Director-Producer	Ali Lucia / Mark Vittorio
Associate Producer / Associate Director	John Sponsler / Doug Foster
Radio Analyst	Bruce LeVine
Director, Game Entertainment	Jason Danby
Editors	Hunter Lee Harrington, Jeff Lewis, Jerry Miranda
Animator / Web Producer	Jeffrey Neal / Cody Eastwood
Ice Girls Director	Christina Swanson
Business Operations	
Assistant Vice President, Business Operations	Bill Herman
Communications	
Senior Director, Communications	Tom Holy
Corporate Communications Coordinator	Joe Calvillo
Media Relations Coordinators	Ben Fromstein, Greg Ramirez
Dallas Stars Foundation	
Executive Director, Dallas Stars Foundation	Jessica Dunn
Coordinators, Dallas Stars Foundation	Christa Melia, Dana Swann
Corporate Partnerships	
Vice President, Corporate Partnerships	Grady Raskin
Vice President, Business Development	Dan Stuchal
Manager, Youth Hockey Development	Frances Gulick
Director, Corporate Sponsorships	Mallory Martin
Senior Account Executives	Christine MacDonald, Jessica Reveruzzi
Activation Directors	Whitney Allen, Lisa Solomon
Activation Coordinators	Shae Bryan, Molly Lee
Finance and Administration	
Vice President, Finance and Administration	Toni May
Director, Finance	Martha Riddell
Payroll Manager / Accounts Payable	Marie Brumfield / Tina Forbes
Staff Accountant / Human Resources Generalist	Candace Kent / Megan Lippe
Corporate Operations	
Vice President and Chief Information Officer	Daniel Doggendorf
Vice President, Corporate Support & Development	Ed Reusch
Senior Technology Engineer	David Leija
Technology Engineers	Alex Cheng, Rudy Duarte, Jchon Paradise
Data Manager	Leslie Horn
Front Desk Receptionist	Robbyn Good
Marketing	
Marketing, Vice President / Director	Kelly Calvert / Todd McVeigh
Community Development Director / Manager	Chrissy Matthews / Joan Holdburg
Managers, Social Media / Advertising / Promo	Alex Cerda / Kelly Briggs / Steve Phillips
Director, Alumni Association	Bob Bassen
Graphic Designers	Chase Hargrove, Anna Kremer
Sales and Marketing Administrator	Kalie Hagood
Ticket Operations	
Ticket Operations, Director / Managers	Mac Amin / Jeff Gogerty, John Schloffman
Ticket Sales	
Vice President, Ticket Sales and Service	Matt Bowman
Director, New Business and Premium Sales	Ryan Hoopes
Directors, Customer Service / Group Sales	Daniel Venegas / Scott Bolton
Dr Pepper StarCenter	
Assistant Vice President	Keith Andresen

Key Off-Season Signings/Acquisitions

2013

June 18 • Re-signed C **Pavel Datsyuk**.
29 • Re-signed LW **Drew Miller** and D **Jakub Kindl**.
July 5 • Signed RW **Daniel Alfredsson** and C **Stephen Weiss**.
16 • Re-signed D **Brendan Smith**.
Aug. 6 • Re-signed C **Joakim Andersson**.

Detroit Red Wings

2012-13 Results: 24W-16L-3OTL-5SOL 56PTS
3RD, Central Division • 7TH, Western Conference

2013-14 Schedule

Oct.	Wed.	2	Buffalo	**Jan.**	Wed.	1	Toronto*
	Fri.	4	at Carolina		Sat.	4	at Dallas
	Sat.	5	at Boston		Thu.	9	at San Jose
	Thu.	10	Phoenix		Sat.	11	at Los Angeles
	Sat.	12	Philadelphia		Sun.	12	at Anaheim*
	Mon.	14	at Boston*		Thu.	16	at NY Rangers
	Tue.	15	Columbus		Sat.	18	Los Angeles
	Thu.	17	at Colorado		Mon.	20	St. Louis
	Sat.	19	at Phoenix		Wed.	22	Chicago
	Mon.	21	San Jose		Fri.	24	Montreal
	Wed.	23	Ottawa		Sun.	26	Florida*
	Sat.	26	NY Rangers		Tue.	28	at Philadelphia
	Wed.	30	at Vancouver		Fri.	31	Washington
Nov.	Fri.	1	at Calgary	**Feb.**	Sun.	2	at Washington*
	Sat.	2	at Edmonton		Mon.	3	Vancouver
	Mon.	4	at Winnipeg		Thu.	6	at Florida
	Thu.	7	Dallas		Sat.	8	at Tampa Bay
	Sat.	9	Tampa Bay		Wed.	26	at Montreal
	Tue.	12	Winnipeg		Thu.	27	at Ottawa
	Fri.	15	Washington	**Mar.**	Tue.	4	at New Jersey
	Sat.	16	at NY Islanders		Thu.	6	Colorado
	Tue.	19	Nashville		Fri.	7	New Jersey
	Thu.	21	Carolina		Sun.	9	at NY Rangers
	Sat.	23	Ottawa		Tue.	11	at Columbus
	Sun.	24	at Buffalo*		Fri.	14	Edmonton
	Wed.	27	Boston		Sun.	16	at Chicago
	Fri.	29	at NY Islanders*		Tue.	18	Toronto
Dec.	Sun.	1	at Ottawa*		Thu.	20	Pittsburgh
	Wed.	4	Philadelphia		Sat.	22	at Minnesota*
	Fri.	6	at New Jersey		Sun.	23	Minnesota
	Sat.	7	Florida		Tue.	25	at Columbus
	Tue.	10	at Florida		Thu.	27	Montreal
	Thu.	12	at Tampa Bay		Sat.	29	at Toronto
	Sat.	14	Pittsburgh		Sun.	30	Tampa Bay*
	Sun.	15	Tampa Bay*	**Apr.**	Wed.	2	Boston
	Tue.	17	Anaheim		Fri.	4	Buffalo
	Thu.	19	Calgary		Sat.	5	at Montreal
	Sat.	21	at Toronto		Tue.	8	at Buffalo
	Mon.	23	NY Islanders		Wed.	9	at Pittsburgh
	Sat.	28	at Florida		Fri.	11	Carolina
	Mon.	30	at Nashville		Sun.	13	at St. Louis*

* Denotes afternoon game.

Year-by-Year Record

		Home				Road				Overall									
Season	**GP**	**W**	**L**	**T**	**OL**	**W**	**L**	**T**	**OL**	**W**	**L**	**T**	**OL**	**GF**	**GA**	**Pts.**	**Div. Fin.**	**Conf. Fin.**	**Playoff Result**
2012-13	48	13	7	....	4	11	9	....	4	24	16	....	8	124	115	56	3rd, Cen.	7th, West	Lost Conf. Semi-Final
2011-12	82	31	7	....	3	17	21	....	3	48	28	....	6	248	203	102	3rd, Cen.	5th, West	Lost Conf. Quarter-Final
2010-11	82	21	14	....	6	26	11	....	4	47	25	....	10	261	241	104	1st, Cen.	3rd, West	Lost Conf. Semi-Final
2009-10	82	25	10	....	6	19	14	....	8	44	24	....	14	229	216	102	2nd, Cen.	5th, West	Lost Conf. Semi-Final
2008-09	82	27	9	....	5	24	12	....	5	51	21	....	10	295	244	112	1st, Cen.	2nd, West	Lost Final
2007-08	**82**	**29**	**9**	....	**3**	**25**	**12**	....	**4**	**54**	**21**	....	**7**	**257**	**184**	**115**	**1st, Cen.**	**1st, West**	**Won Stanley Cup**
2006-07	82	29	4	....	8	21	15	....	5	50	19	....	13	254	199	113	1st, Cen.	1st, West	Lost Conf. Final
2005-06	82	27	9	....	5	31	7	....	3	58	16	....	8	305	209	124	1st, Cen.	1st, West	Lost Conf. Quarter-Final
2004-05	....	....	....	....	....	....	....	....	....	....	....	....	....	....	....	....			
2003-04	82	30	7	4	0	18	14	7	2	48	21	11	2	255	189	109	1st, Cen.	1st, West	Lost Conf. Semi-Final
2002-03	82	28	6	5	2	20	14	5	2	48	20	10	4	269	203	110	1st, Cen.	2nd, West	Lost Conf. Quarter-Final
2001-02	**82**	**28**	**7**	**5**	**1**	**23**	**10**	**5**	**3**	**51**	**17**	**10**	**4**	**251**	**187**	**116**	**1st, Cen.**	**1st, West**	**Won Stanley Cup**
2000-01	82	27	9	3	2	22	11	6	2	49	20	9	4	253	202	111	1st, Cen.	2nd, West	Lost Conf. Quarter-Final
1999-2000	82	28	9	3	1	20	13	7	1	48	22	10	2	278	210	108	2nd, Cen.	4th, West	Lost Conf. Semi-Final
1998-99	82	27	12	2	....	16	20	5	....	43	32	7	....	245	202	93	1st, Cen.	3rd, West	Lost Conf. Semi-Final
1997-98	**82**	**25**	**8**	**8**	....	**19**	**15**	**7**	....	**44**	**23**	**15**	....	**250**	**196**	**103**	**2nd, Cen.**	**2nd, West**	**Won Stanley Cup**
1996-97	**82**	**20**	**12**	**9**	....	**18**	**14**	**9**	....	**38**	**26**	**18**	....	**253**	**197**	**94**	**2nd, Cen.**	**3rd, West**	**Won Stanley Cup**
1995-96	82	36	3	2	....	26	10	5	....	62	13	7	....	325	181	131	1st, Cen.	1st, West	Lost Conf. Final
1994-95	48	17	4	3	....	16	7	1	....	33	11	4	....	180	117	70	1st, Cen.	1st, West	Lost Final
1993-94	84	23	13	6	....	23	17	2	....	46	30	8	....	356	275	100	1st, Cen.	1st, West	Lost Conf. Quarter-Final
1992-93	84	25	14	3	....	22	14	6	....	47	28	9	....	369	280	103	2nd, Norris		Lost Div. Semi-Final
1991-92	80	24	12	4	....	19	13	8	....	43	25	12	....	320	256	98	1st, Norris		Lost Div. Final
1990-91	80	26	14	0	....	8	24	8	....	34	38	8	....	273	298	76	3rd, Norris		Lost Div. Semi-Final
1989-90	80	20	14	6	....	8	24	8	....	28	38	14	....	288	323	70	5th, Norris		Out of Playoffs
1988-89	80	20	14	6	....	14	20	6	....	34	34	12	....	313	316	80	1st, Norris		Lost Div. Semi-Final
1987-88	80	24	10	6	....	17	18	5	....	41	28	11	....	322	269	93	1st, Norris		Lost Conf. Final
1986-87	80	20	14	6	....	14	22	4	....	34	36	10	....	260	274	78	2nd, Norris		Lost Conf. Final
1985-86	80	10	26	4	....	7	31	2	....	17	57	6	....	266	415	40	5th, Norris		Out of Playoffs
1984-85	80	19	14	7	....	8	27	5	....	27	41	12	....	313	357	66	3rd, Norris		Lost Div. Semi-Final
1983-84	80	18	20	2	....	13	22	5	....	31	42	7	....	298	323	69	3rd, Norris		Lost Div. Semi-Final
1982-83	80	14	19	7	....	7	25	8	....	21	44	15	....	263	344	57	5th, Norris		Out of Playoffs
1981-82	80	15	19	6	....	6	28	6	....	21	47	12	....	270	351	54	6th, Norris		Out of Playoffs
1980-81	80	16	15	9	....	3	28	9	....	19	43	18	....	252	339	56	5th, Norris		Out of Playoffs
1979-80	80	14	21	5	....	12	22	6	....	26	43	11	....	268	306	63	5th, Norris		Out of Playoffs
1978-79	80	15	17	8	....	8	24	8	....	23	41	16	....	252	295	62	5th, Norris		Out of Playoffs
1977-78	80	22	11	7	....	10	23	7	....	32	34	14	....	252	266	78	2nd, Norris		Lost Quarter-Final
1976-77	80	12	22	6	....	4	33	3	....	16	55	9	....	183	309	41	5th, Norris		Out of Playoffs
1975-76	80	17	15	8	....	9	29	2	....	26	44	10	....	226	300	62	4th, Norris		Out of Playoffs
1974-75	80	17	17	6	....	6	28	6	....	23	45	12	....	259	335	58	4th, Norris		Out of Playoffs
1973-74	78	21	12	6	....	8	27	4	....	29	39	10	....	255	319	68	6th, East		Out of Playoffs
1972-73	78	22	12	5	....	15	17	7	....	37	29	12	....	265	243	86	5th, East		Out of Playoffs
1971-72	78	25	11	3	....	8	24	7	....	33	35	10	....	261	262	76	5th, East		Out of Playoffs
1970-71	78	17	15	7	....	5	30	4	....	22	45	11	....	209	308	55	7th, East		Out of Playoffs
1969-70	76	20	11	7	....	20	10	8	....	40	21	15	....	246	199	95	3rd, East		Lost Quarter-Final
1968-69	76	23	8	7	....	10	23	5	....	33	31	12	....	239	221	78	5th, East		Out of Playoffs
1967-68	74	18	15	4	....	9	20	8	....	27	35	12	....	245	257	66	6th, East		Out of Playoffs
1966-67	70	21	11	3	....	6	28	1	....	27	39	4	....	212	241	58	5th,		Out of Playoffs
1965-66	70	20	8	7	....	11	19	5	....	31	27	12	....	221	194	74	4th,		Lost Final
1964-65	70	25	7	3	....	15	16	4	....	40	23	7	....	224	175	87	1st,		Lost Semi-Final
1963-64	70	23	9	3	....	7	20	8	....	30	29	11	....	191	204	71	4th,		Lost Final
1962-63	70	19	10	6	....	13	15	7	....	32	25	13	....	200	194	77	4th,		Lost Final
1961-62	70	17	11	7	....	6	22	7	....	23	33	14	....	184	219	60	5th,		Out of Playoffs
1960-61	70	15	13	7	....	10	16	9	....	25	29	16	....	195	215	66	4th,		Lost Final
1959-60	70	18	14	3	....	8	15	12	....	26	29	15	....	186	197	67	4th,		Lost Semi-Final
1958-59	70	13	17	5	....	12	20	3	....	25	37	8	....	167	218	58	6th,		Out of Playoffs
1957-58	70	16	11	8	....	13	18	4	....	29	29	12	....	176	207	70	3rd,		Lost Semi-Final
1956-57	70	23	7	5	....	15	13	7	....	38	20	12	....	198	157	88	1st,		Lost Semi-Final
1955-56	70	21	6	8	....	9	18	8	....	30	24	16	....	183	148	76	2nd,		Lost Final
1954-55	**70**	**25**	**5**	**5**	....	**17**	**12**	**6**	....	**42**	**17**	**11**	....	**204**	**134**	**95**	**1st,**		**Won Stanley Cup**
1953-54	**70**	**24**	**4**	**7**	....	**13**	**15**	**7**	....	**37**	**19**	**14**	....	**191**	**132**	**88**	**1st,**		**Won Stanley Cup**
1952-53	70	20	5	10	....	16	11	8	....	36	16	18	....	222	133	90	1st,		Lost Semi-Final
1951-52	**70**	**24**	**7**	**4**	....	**20**	**7**	**8**	....	**44**	**14**	**12**	....	**215**	**133**	**100**	**1st,**		**Won Stanley Cup**
1950-51	70	25	3	7	....	19	10	6	....	44	13	13	....	236	139	101	1st,		Lost Semi-Final
1949-50	**70**	**19**	**9**	**7**	....	**18**	**10**	**7**	....	**37**	**19**	**14**	....	**229**	**164**	**88**	**1st,**		**Won Stanley Cup**
1948-49	60	21	6	3	....	13	13	4	....	34	19	7	....	195	145	75	1st,		Lost Final
1947-48	60	16	9	5	....	14	9	7	....	30	18	12	....	187	148	72	2nd,		Lost Final
1946-47	60	14	10	6	....	8	17	5	....	22	27	11	....	190	193	55	4th,		Lost Semi-Final
1945-46	50	16	5	4	....	4	15	6	....	20	20	10	....	146	159	50	4th,		Lost Semi-Final
1944-45	50	19	5	1	....	12	9	4	....	31	14	5	....	218	161	67	2nd,		Lost Final
1943-44	50	18	5	2	....	8	13	4	....	26	18	6	....	214	177	58	2nd,		Lost Semi-Final
1942-43	**50**	**16**	**4**	**5**	....	**9**	**10**	**6**	....	**25**	**14**	**11**	....	**169**	**124**	**61**	**1st,**		**Won Stanley Cup**
1941-42	48	14	7	3	....	5	18	1	....	19	25	4	....	140	147	42	5th,		Lost Final
1940-41	48	14	5	5	....	7	11	6	....	21	16	11	....	112	102	53	3rd,		Lost Final
1939-40	48	11	10	3	....	5	16	3	....	16	26	6	....	91	126	38	5th,		Lost Semi-Final
1938-39	48	14	8	2	....	4	16	4	....	18	24	6	....	107	128	42	5th,		Lost Semi-Final
1937-38	48	8	10	6	....	4	15	5	....	12	25	11	....	99	133	35	4th, Amn.		Out of Playoffs
1936-37	**48**	**14**	**5**	**5**	....	**11**	**9**	**4**	....	**25**	**14**	**9**	....	**128**	**102**	**59**	**1st, Amn.**		**Won Stanley Cup**
1935-36	**48**	**14**	**5**	**5**	....	**10**	**11**	**3**	....	**24**	**16**	**8**	....	**124**	**103**	**56**	**1st, Amn.**		**Won Stanley Cup**
1934-35	48	11	8	5	....	8	14	2	....	19	22	7	....	127	114	45	4th, Amn.		Out of Playoffs
1933-34	48	15	5	4	....	9	9	6	....	24	14	10	....	113	98	58	1st, Amn.		Lost Final
1932-33*	48	17	3	4	....	8	12	4	....	25	15	8	....	111	93	58	2nd, Amn.		Lost Semi-Final
1931-32	48	15	3	6	....	3	17	4	....	18	20	10	....	95	108	46	3rd, Amn.		Lost Quarter-Final
1930-31**	44	10	7	5	....	6	14	2	....	16	21	7	....	102	105	39	4th, Amn.		Out of Playoffs
1929-30	44	9	10	3	....	5	14	3	....	14	24	6	....	117	133	34	4th, Amn.		Out of Playoffs
1928-29	44	11	6	5	....	8	10	4	....	19	16	9	....	72	63	47	3rd, Amn.		Lost Quarter-Final
1927-28	44	9	10	3	....	10	9	3	....	19	19	6	....	88	79	44	4th, Amn.		Out of Playoffs
1926-27***	44	5	16	0	....	7	12	4	....	12	28	4	....	76	105	28	5th, Amn.		Out of Playoffs

* Team name changed to Red Wings. ** Team name changed to Falcons. *** Team named Cougars.

ATLANTIC DIVISION
88th NHL Season

Franchise date: September 25, 1926

2013-14 Player Personnel

FORWARDS	HT	WT	*Age	Place of Birth	S	2012-13 Club
ABDELKADER, Justin	6-1	219	26	Muskegon, MI	L	Detroit
ALFREDSSON, Daniel	5-11	196	40	Gothenburg, Sweden	R	Ottawa
ANDERSSON, Joakim	6-2	206	24	Munkedal, Sweden	L	Grand Rapids-Detroit
BERTUZZI, Todd	6-3	229	38	Sudbury, Ont.	L	Detroit
CLEARY, Dan	6-0	208	34	Carbonear, Nfld.	L	Detroit
DATSYUK, Pavel	5-11	198	35	Sverdlovsk, USSR	L	CSKA-Detroit
EAVES, Patrick	6-0	187	29	Calgary, Alta.	R	Detroit
EMMERTON, Cory	6-0	191	25	St. Thomas, Ont.	L	SaiPa-Detroit
FRANZEN, Johan	6-3	223	33	Landsbro, Sweden	L	Detroit
HELM, Darren	5-11	192	26	Winnipeg, Man.	L	Detroit
MILLER, Drew	6-2	178	29	Dover, NJ	L	Braehead-Detroit
NYQUIST, Gustav	5-10	185	24	Halmstad, Sweden	L	Grand Rapids-Detroit
SAMUELSSON, Mikael	6-2	218	36	Mariefred, Sweden	R	Detroit
TATAR, Tomas	5-10	186	22	Ilava, Czech.	L	Piestany-Grand Rapids-Det
TOOTOO, Jordin	5-9	199	30	Churchill, Man.	R	Detroit
WEISS, Stephen	5-11	190	30	Toronto, Ont.	L	Florida
ZETTERBERG, Henrik	5-11	197	32	Njurunda, Sweden	L	Zug-Detroit
DEFENSEMEN						
DeKEYSER, Danny	6-3	190	23	Detroit, MI	L	Detroit-Grand Rapids
ERICSSON, Jonathan	6-4	221	29	Karlskrona, Sweden	L	Vita Hasten-Sodertalje-Det
KINDL, Jakub	6-3	216	26	Sumperk, Czech.	L	Pardubice-Detroit
KRONWALL, Niklas	6-0	190	32	Stockholm, Sweden	L	Detroit
LASHOFF, Brian	6-3	212	23	Albany, NY	L	Grand Rapids-Detroit
QUINCEY, Kyle	6-2	207	28	Kitchener, Ont.	L	Denver-Detroit
SMITH, Brendan	6-1	198	24	Toronto, Ont.	L	Grand Rapids-Detroit
GOALTENDERS	**HT**	**WT**	***Age**	**Place of Birth**	**C**	**2012-13 Club**
GUSTAVSSON, Jonas	6-3	192	28	Danderyd, Sweden	L	Detroit-Grand Rapids
HOWARD, Jimmy	6-0	218	29	Syracuse, NY	L	Detroit

* – Age at start of 2013-14 season

Mike Babcock

Head Coach

Born: Manitouwadge, Ont., April 29, 1963.

Mike Babcock became the 26th coach in Detroit Red Wings history on July 14, 2005. In 2008, he led the Red Wings to the Stanley Cup. The Red Wings reached the Finals again in 2009 and topped 50 wins during the regular season in each of Babcock's first four years with the team. He coached Canada to an Olympic gold medal in 2010 and will serve as head coach again at the 2014 Sochi Olympics.

Babcock brought a winning track record to Detroit from all levels of play, including college and junior hockey, the American Hockey League, the NHL and international hockey. He is the only man to coach Team Canada to victories at both the World Junior Championship (1997) and the senior World Championship (2004.) Prior to joining the Red Wings, he had spent two seasons with Anaheim, leading the team to the Stanley Cup Finals in his first season behind the bench in 2002-03. He became the first rookie coach to reach the Finals since Florida's Doug MacLean in 1996. With a four-game sweep over Detroit in the first round of the playoffs, the Ducks became the first team since the 1952 Red Wings (over Toronto) to sweep a defending Stanley Cup champion.

Before joining Anaheim, Babcock spent two seasons as head coach of the Cincinnati Mighty Ducks (2000 to 2002), the primary development affiliate for both Detroit and Anaheim in the American Hockey League. He led the club to a franchise-best 41 wins and 95 points in 2000-01. Babcock moved to Cincinnati after a successful six-year run as the head coach of the Spokane Chiefs of the Western Hockey League (1994 through 2000). He was twice named WHL coach of the year (1996 and 2000) after taking the Chiefs to the league finals in both seasons. He began his WHL coaching career with the Moose Jaw Warriors in 1991-92. In Canadian university play, Babcock won a national championship and was named the coach of the year with the Lethbridge Pronghorns in 1993-94. In 1988, he was named head coach at Red Deer College in Red Deer, Alberta. He spent three seasons at the school, winning the Alberta college championship and coach of the year award in 1989.

Babcock played in the WHL for Saskatoon (1980-81) and Kelowna (1982-83), where he was team captain. In between, he spent a year at the University of Saskatoon. Babcock also played four years at McGill University (1983 to 1987), twice being named an All-Star defenseman. He earned his bachelor's degree in physical education and attended graduate school in sports psychology at McGill.

2012-13 Scoring

* – rookie

Regular Season

Pos	#	Player	Team	GP	G	A	Pts	TOI	+/–	PIM	PP	SH	GW	S	%
C	13	Pavel Datsyuk	DET	47	15	34	49	20:10	21	14	8	0	6	107	14.0
L	40	Henrik Zetterberg	DET	46	11	37	48	20:31	2	18	4	2	5	173	6.4
C	93	Johan Franzen	DET	41	14	17	31	18:05	13	41	6	0	1	116	12.1
D	55	Niklas Kronwall	DET	48	5	24	29	24:21	–5	44	2	0	2	67	7.5
C	24	Damien Brunner	DET	44	12	14	26	15:35	–6	12	3	0	1	123	9.8
C	51	Valtteri Filppula	DET	41	9	8	17	17:46	–4	6	3	0	0	78	11.5
R	11	Daniel Cleary	DET	48	9	6	15	16:26	–6	40	5	1	0	93	9.7
L	8	Justin Abdelkader	DET	48	10	3	13	14:48	6	34	0	0	0	96	10.4
D	4	Jakub Kindl	DET	41	4	9	13	18:33	15	28	1	0	2	76	5.3
D	52	Jonathan Ericsson	DET	45	3	10	13	21:19	6	29	0	0	1	34	8.8
C	25	Cory Emmerton	DET	48	5	3	8	10:48	–1	4	0	0	0	55	9.1
L	20	Drew Miller	DET	44	4	4	8	13:49	–8	2	1	0	2	54	7.4
C	63	* Joakim Andersson	DET	38	3	5	8	12:05	2	8	0	0	0	43	7.0
R	22	Jordin Tootoo	DET	42	3	5	8	9:04	0	78	0	0	1	45	6.7
R	17	Patrick Eaves	DET	34	2	6	8	10:34	–1	4	0	0	1	42	4.8
D	2	* Brendan Smith	DET	34	0	8	8	18:24	1	36	0	0	0	33	0.0
C	21	* Tomas Tatar	DET	18	4	3	7	11:22	2	4	1	0	0	32	12.5
C	14	* Gustav Nyquist	DET	22	3	3	6	13:02	0	6	0	0	0	46	6.5
D	23	* Brian Lashoff	DET	31	1	4	5	17:47	–10	15	0	0	0	26	3.8
D	18	Ian White	DET	25	2	2	4	19:35	5	4	0	0	0	27	7.4
R	44	Todd Bertuzzi	DET	7	2	1	3	15:31	3	2	0	0	0	10	20.0
D	27	Kyle Quincey	DET	36	1	2	3	19:13	7	18	0	0	0	36	2.8
R	37	Mikael Samuelsson	DET	4	0	1	1	12:51	–3	0	0	0	0	4	0.0
D	28	Carlo Colaiacovo	DET	6	0	1	1	18:54	–4	2	0	0	0	12	0.0
D	65	* Danny DeKeyser	DET	11	0	1	1	18:02	4	2	0	0	0	15	0.0
C	43	Darren Helm	DET	1	0	0	0	12:27	0	2	0	0	0	1	0.0
C	15	* Riley Sheahan	DET	1	0	0	0	6:47	0	0	0	0	0	1	0.0
L	39	Jan Mursak	DET	2	0	0	0	5:38	0	4	0	0	0	0	0.0

Goaltending

No.	Goaltender	GPI	Mins	Avg	W	L	OT	EN	SO	GA	SA	S%	G	A	PIM
34	* Petr Mrazek	2	119	2.02	1	1	0	0	0	4	51	.922	0	0	0
35	Jimmy Howard	42	2446	2.13	21	13	7	2	5	87	1129	.923	0	1	0
50	Jonas Gustavsson	7	349	2.92	2	2	1	0	0	17	140	.879	0	1	2
	Totals	**48**	**2928**	**2.25**	**24**	**16**	**8**	**2**	**5**	**110**	**1322**	**.917**			

Playoffs

Pos	#	Player	Team	GP	G	A	Pts	TOI	+/–	PIM	PP	SH	GW	OT	S	%
L	40	Henrik Zetterberg	DET	14	4	8	12	19:58	3	8	1	0	1	1	58	6.9
R	11	Daniel Cleary	DET	14	4	6	10	16:47	–1	2	1	0	0	0	20	20.0
C	24	Damien Brunner	DET	14	5	4	9	13:06	2	4	0	0	1	1	31	16.1
C	13	Pavel Datsyuk	DET	14	3	6	9	20:58	2	4	0	0	0	0	39	7.7
C	93	Johan Franzen	DET	14	4	2	6	19:30	–7	8	3	0	0	0	40	10.0
C	51	Valtteri Filppula	DET	14	2	4	6	16:36	–4	4	0	0	1	0	24	8.3
D	2	* Brendan Smith	DET	14	2	3	5	19:07	–3	10	0	0	1	0	17	11.8
C	14	* Gustav Nyquist	DET	14	2	3	5	12:35	3	2	1	0	1	1	26	7.7
D	4	Jakub Kindl	DET	14	1	4	5	17:43	4	10	1	0	1	0	24	4.2
C	63	* Joakim Andersson	DET	14	1	4	5	13:19	2	10	0	0	0	0	19	5.3
L	8	Justin Abdelkader	DET	12	2	1	3	16:57	4	33	0	1	0	0	33	6.1
R	17	Patrick Eaves	DET	13	1	2	3	10:00	–1	4	0	0	0	0	16	6.3
D	52	Jonathan Ericsson	DET	14	0	3	3	22:32	2	2	0	0	0	0	7	0.0
R	37	Mikael Samuelsson	DET	5	1	1	2	13:04	–1	2	0	0	0	0	8	12.5
L	20	Drew Miller	DET	6	1	1	2	13:12	1	2	0	0	1	0	4	25.0
D	55	Niklas Kronwall	DET	14	0	2	2	25:20	–1	4	0	0	0	0	13	0.0
D	27	Kyle Quincey	DET	14	0	2	2	19:02	–3	12	0	0	0	0	15	0.0
D	28	Carlo Colaiacovo	DET	9	0	1	1	15:14	3	2	0	0	0	0	4	0.0
C	25	Cory Emmerton	DET	13	0	1	1	10:25	–2	4	0	0	0	0	11	0.0
R	22	Jordin Tootoo	DET	1	0	0	0	6:24	0	2	0	0	0	0	0	0.0
D	65	* Danny DeKeyser	DET	2	0	0	0	17:53	0	0	0	0	0	0	0	0.0
R	44	Todd Bertuzzi	DET	6	0	0	0	9:39	–2	2	0	0	0	0	6	0.0

Goaltending

No.	Goaltender	GPI	Mins	Avg	W	L	EN	SO	GA	SA	S%	G	A	PIM
35	Jimmy Howard	14	859	2.44	7	7	2	1	35	461	.924	0	0	2
	Totals	**14**	**863**	**2.57**	**7**	**7**	**2**	**1**	**37**	**463**	**.920**			

Coaching Record

			Regular Season				Playoffs			
Season	Team	League	GC	W	L	O/T	GC	W	L	T
1991-92	Moose Jaw	WHL	72	33	36	3	4	0	4	....
1992-93	Moose Jaw	WHL	72	27	42	3	....	....	....	....
1993-94	U of Lethbridge	CIAU	28	19	7	2	....	....	....	....
1994-95	Spokane	WHL	72	32	36	4	11	6	5	....
1995-96	Spokane	WHL	72	50	18	4	9	3	6	....
1996-97	Spokane	WHL	72	35	33	4	9	4	5	....
1997-98	Spokane	WHL	72	45	23	4	18	10	8	....
1998-99	Spokane	WHL	72	19	44	9	....	....	....	....
99-2000	Spokane	WHL	72	47	19	6	20	15	5	....
2000-01	Cincinnati	AHL	80	41	26	13	4	1	3	....
2001-02	Cincinnati	AHL	80	33	33	14	3	1	2	....
2002-03	**Anaheim**	**NHL**	**82**	**40**	**27**	**15**	**21**	**15**	**6**	....
2003-04	**Anaheim**	**NHL**	**82**	**29**	**35**	**18**	....	....	....	....
2004-05	**Anaheim**				SEASON CANCELLED					
2005-06	**Detroit**	**NHL**	**82**	**58**	**16**	**8**	**6**	**2**	**4**	....
2006-07	**Detroit**	**NHL**	**82**	**50**	**19**	**13**	**18**	**10**	**8**	....
2007-08♦	**Detroit**	**NHL**	**82**	**54**	**21**	**7**	**22**	**16**	**6**	....
2008-09	**Detroit**	**NHL**	**82**	**51**	**21**	**10**	**23**	**15**	**8**	....
2009-10	**Detroit**	**NHL**	**82**	**44**	**24**	**14**	**12**	**5**	**7**	....
2010-11	**Detroit**	**NHL**	**82**	**47**	**25**	**10**	**11**	**7**	**4**	....
2011-12	**Detroit**	**NHL**	**82**	**48**	**28**	**6**	**5**	**1**	**4**	....
2012-13	**Detroit**	**NHL**	**48**	**24**	**16**	**8**	**14**	**7**	**7**	....
	NHL Totals		**786**	**445**	**232**	**109**	**132**	**78**	**54**	....

♦ Stanley Cup win.

Club Records

Team

(Figures in brackets for season records are games played; records for fewest points, wins, ties, losses, goals, goals against are for 70 or more games)

Most Points 131 1995-96 (82)
Most Wins *62 1995-96 (82)
Most Ties 18 1952-53 (70), 1980-81 (80), 1996-97 (82)
Most Losses 57 1985-86 (80)
Most Goals 369 1992-93 (84)
Most Goals Against 415 1985-86 (80)
Fewest Points 40 1985-86 (80)
Fewest Wins 16 1976-77 (80)
Fewest Ties 4 1966-67 (70)
Fewest Losses 13 1950-51 (70), 1995-96 (82)
Fewest Goals 167 1958-59 (70)
Fewest Goals Against 132 1953-54 (70)

Longest Winning Streak
Overall .... 9 Seven times
Home .... *23 Nov. 5/11-Feb. 19/12
Away .... *12 Mar. 1-Apr. 15/06

Longest Undefeated Streak
Overall .... 15 Nov. 27-Dec. 28/52 (8W, 7T)
Home .... 19 Dec. 31/00-Apr.7/01 (17W, 2T/OL)
Away .... 15 Oct. 18-Dec. 20/51 (10W, 5T)

Longest Losing Streak
Overall .... 14 Feb. 24-Mar. 25/82
Home .... 7 Feb. 20-Mar. 25/82
Away .... 14 Oct. 19-Dec. 21/66

Longest Winless Streak
Overall .... 19 Feb. 26-Apr. 3/77 (18L, 1T)
Home .... 10 Dec. 11/85-Jan. 18/86 (9L, 1T)
Away .... 26 Dec. 15/76-Apr. 3/77 (23L, 3T)

Most Shutouts, Season 13 1953-54 (70)
Most. PIM, Season 2,393 1985-86 (80)
Most Goals, Game .... 15 Jan. 23/44 (NYR 0 at Det. 15)

Individual

Most Seasons .... 25 Gordie Howe
Most Games .... 1,687 Gordie Howe
Most Goals, Career .... 786 Gordie Howe
Most Assists, Career ...... 1,063 Steve Yzerman
Most Points, Career .... 1,809 Gordie Howe (786G, 1,023A)
Most PIM, Career .... 2,090 Bob Probert
Most Shutouts, Career .... 85 Terry Sawchuk
Longest Consecutive Games Streak .... 548 Alex Delvecchio (Dec. 13/56-Nov. 11/64)
Most Goals, Season .... 65 Steve Yzerman (1988-89)
Most Assists, Season .... 90 Steve Yzerman (1988-89)
Most Points, Season .... 155 Steve Yzerman (1988-89; 65G, 90A)
Most PIM, Season .... 398 Bob Probert (1987-88)
Most Points, Defenseman, Season .... 80 Nicklas Lidstrom (2005-06; 16G, 64A)
Most Points, Center, Season .... 155 Steve Yzerman (1988-89; 65G, 90A)
Most Points, Right Wing, Season .... 103 Gordie Howe (1968-69; 44G, 59A)
Most Points, Left Wing, Season .... 105 John Ogrodnick (1984-85; 55G, 50A)
Most Points, Rookie, Season .... 87 Steve Yzerman (1983-84; 39G, 48A)
Most Shutouts, Season .... 12 Terry Sawchuk (1951-52), (1953-54), (1954-55); Glenn Hall (1955-56)
Most Goals, Game .... 6 Syd Howe (Feb. 3/44)
Most Assists, Game .... *7 Billy Taylor (Mar. 16/47)
Most Points, Game .... 7 Carl Liscombe (Nov. 5/42; 3G, 4A), Don Grosso (Feb. 3/44; 1G, 6A), Billy Taylor (Mar. 16/47; 7A)

* NHL Record.

Retired Numbers

1	Terry Sawchuk	1949-55, 57-64, 1968-69
5*	Nicklas Lidstrom	1991-2012
7	Ted Lindsay	1944-57, 64-65
9	Gordie Howe	1946-1971
10	Alex Delvecchio	1951-1973
12	Sid Abel	1938-43, 45-52
19	Steve Yzerman	1983-2006

* Ceremony to take place March 6, 2014.

All-time Record vs. Other Clubs

Regular Season

	Total								At Home								On Road							
	GP	W	L	T	OL	GF	GA	PTS	GP	W	L	T	OL	GF	GA	PTS	GP	W	L	T	OL	GF	GA	PTS
Anaheim	75	48	18	7	2	234	172	105	37	30	4	3	0	132	77	63	38	18	14	4	2	102	95	42
Boston	579	249	234	95	1	1735	1743	594	288	156	80	52	0	961	728	364	291	93	154	43	1	774	1015	230
Buffalo	116	50	52	13	1	386	403	114	59	35	18	5	1	216	165	76	57	15	34	8	0	170	238	38
Calgary	150	68	65	16	1	486	490	153	74	40	23	10	1	269	224	91	76	28	42	6	0	217	266	62
Carolina	67	33	26	8	0	223	204	74	34	20	7	7	0	132	93	47	33	13	19	1	0	91	111	27
Chicago	725	363	265	84	13	2254	1994	823	361	216	106	33	6	1226	906	471	364	147	159	51	7	1028	1088	352
Colorado	113	62	41	5	5	386	345	134	56	34	17	1	4	198	161	73	57	28	24	4	1	188	184	61
Columbus	74	50	16	1	7	243	169	108	36	27	6	0	3	130	88	57	38	23	10	1	4	113	81	51
Dallas	243	107	97	34	5	819	782	253	122	62	42	16	2	456	376	142	121	45	55	18	3	363	406	111
Edmonton	119	59	36	13	11	433	393	142	60	37	16	3	4	228	177	81	59	22	20	10	7	205	216	61
Florida	23	14	2	5	2	74	51	35	11	6	1	3	1	38	26	16	12	8	1	2	1	36	25	19
Los Angeles	190	82	79	27	2	661	668	193	95	48	34	13	0	364	314	109	95	34	45	14	2	297	354	84
Minnesota	47	30	9	3	5	155	108	68	24	16	4	1	3	92	55	36	23	14	5	2	2	63	53	32
Montreal	568	201	271	96	0	1457	1726	498	283	132	98	53	0	812	722	317	285	69	173	43	0	645	1004	181
Nashville	85	49	24	4	8	267	212	110	43	29	7	2	5	153	97	65	42	20	17	2	3	114	115	45
New Jersey	87	40	35	11	1	288	279	92	44	28	14	2	0	176	135	58	43	12	21	9	1	112	144	34
NY Islanders	97	46	44	6	1	311	321	99	48	26	19	2	1	169	143	55	49	20	25	4	0	142	178	44
NY Rangers	575	261	210	103	1	1762	1582	626	288	167	76	45	0	1016	708	379	287	94	134	58	1	746	874	247
Ottawa	25	16	8	1	0	85	64	33	12	8	4	0	0	44	26	16	13	8	4	1	0	41	38	17
Philadelphia	124	47	56	21	0	399	436	115	63	34	19	10	0	225	193	78	61	13	37	11	0	174	243	37
Phoenix	131	65	41	22	3	463	399	155	66	36	21	8	1	254	210	81	65	29	20	14	2	209	189	74
Pittsburgh	139	62	58	16	3	475	480	143	69	42	13	12	2	269	192	98	70	20	45	4	1	206	288	45
St. Louis	273	118	110	37	8	882	840	281	137	68	48	17	4	491	403	157	136	50	62	20	4	391	437	124
San Jose	82	51	24	4	3	298	221	109	40	30	7	1	2	148	78	63	42	21	17	3	1	150	143	46
Tampa Bay	32	25	5	2	0	135	76	52	15	13	1	1	0	58	25	27	17	12	4	1	0	77	51	25
Toronto	644	275	273	93	3	1831	1855	646	325	170	107	46	2	979	798	388	319	105	166	47	1	852	1057	258
Vancouver	162	84	54	18	6	581	517	192	81	49	20	8	4	323	233	110	81	35	34	10	2	258	284	82
Washington	101	45	40	16	0	330	332	106	51	24	16	11	0	174	147	59	50	21	24	5	0	156	185	47
Winnipeg	14	10	4	0	0	62	41	20	8	6	2	0	0	30	19	12	6	4	2	0	0	32	22	8
Defunct Clubs	282	125	103	54	0	794	682	304	141	76	40	25	0	430	307	177	141	49	63	29	0	364	375	127
Totals	**5942**	**2735**	**2300**	**815**	**92**	**18509**	**17585**	**6377**	**2971**	**1665**	**870**	**390**	**46**	**10193**	**7826**	**3766**	**2971**	**1070**	**1430**	**425**	**46**	**8316**	**9759**	**2611**

Playoffs

	Series	W	L	GP	W	L	T	GF	GA	Last Mtg.	Rnd.	Result
Anaheim	6	4	2	32	18	14	0	93	78	2013	CQF	W 4-3
Boston	7	3	4	33	14	19	0	98	96	1957	SF	L 1-4
Calgary	3	2	1	14	8	6	0	38	26	2007	CQF	W 4-2
Carolina	1	1	0	5	4	1	0	14	7	2002	F	W 4-1
Chicago	16	7	9	81	38	43	0	224	236	2013	CSF	L 3-4
Colorado	6	3	3	34	17	17	0	97	88	2008	CSF	W 4-0
Columbus	1	1	0	4	4	0	0	18	7	2009	CQF	W 4-0
Dallas	4	4	0	24	16	8	0	72	50	2008	CF	W 4-2
Edmonton	3	0	3	16	4	12	0	43	58	2006	CQF	L 2-4
Los Angeles	2	1	1	10	6	4	0	32	21	2001	CQF	L 2-4
Montreal	12	7	5	62	29	33	0	149	161	1978	QF	L 1-4
Nashville	3	2	1	17	9	8	0	38	34	2012	CQF	L 1-4
New Jersey	1	0	1	4	0	4	0	7	16	1995	F	L 0-4
NY Rangers	5	4	1	23	13	10	0	57	49	1950	F	W 4-3
Philadelphia	1	1	0	4	4	0	0	16	6	1997	F	W 4-0
Phoenix	4	4	0	23	16	7	0	88	56	2011	CQF	W 4-0
Pittsburgh	2	1	1	13	7	6	0	34	24	2009	F	L 3-4
St. Louis	7	5	2	40	24	16	0	125	103	2002	CSF	W 4-1
San Jose	5	2	3	29	15	14	0	99	69	2011	CSF	L 3-4
Toronto	23	11	12	117	59	58	0	321	311	1993	DSF	L 3-4
Vancouver	1	1	0	6	4	2	0	22	16	2002	CQF	W 4-2
Washington	1	1	0	4	4	0	0	13	7	1998	F	W 4-0
Defunct Clubs	4	3	1	10	7	2	1	21	13			
Totals	**118**	**68**	**50**	**605**	**320**	**284**	**1**	**1719**	**1532**			

Playoff Results 2013-2009

Year	Round	Opponent	Result	GF	GA
2013	CSF	Chicago	L 3-4	15	16
	CQF	Anaheim	W 4-3	18	21
2012	CQF	Nashville	L 1-4	9	13
2011	CSF	San Jose	L 3-4	18	18
	CQF	Phoenix	W 4-0	18	10
2010	CSF	San Jose	L 1-4	17	15
	CQF	Phoenix	W 4-3	26	18
2009	F	Pittsburgh	L 3-4	17	14
	CF	Chicago	W 4-1	19	10
	CSF	Anaheim	W 4-3	22	17
	CQF	Columbus	W 4-0	18	7

Abbreviations: Round: F – Final; **CF** – conference final; **CSF** – conference semi-final; **CQF** – conference quarter-final; **DSF** – division semi-final; **SF** – semi-final; **QF** – quarter-final.

Calgary totals include Atlanta Flames, 1972-73 to 1979-80.
Carolina totals include Hartford, 1979-80 to 1996-97.
Colorado totals include Quebec, 1979-80 to 1994-95.
Dallas totals include Minnesota North Stars, 1967-68 to 1992-93.
New Jersey totals include Kansas City, 1974-75, 1975-76, and Colorado Rockies, 1976-77 to 1981-82.
Phoenix totals include Winnipeg, 1979-80 to 1995-96.
Winnipeg totals include Atlanta Thrashers, 1999-2000 to 2010-11.

2012-13 Results

Jan.	19	at St. Louis	0-6		9	at Columbus	0-3
	21	at Columbus	4-3†		10	Columbus	2-3†
	22	Dallas	1-2		13	at Calgary	2-5
	25	Minnesota	5-3		15	at Edmonton	3-2*
	27	at Chicago	1-2*		16	at Vancouver	5-2
	29	Dallas	4-1		20	Minnesota	2-4
Feb.	1	St. Louis	5-3		22	at Anaheim	5-1
	2	at Columbus	2-4		24	at Anaheim	2-1
	5	Calgary	1-4		25	at Phoenix	3-2
	7	at St. Louis	5-1		28	at San Jose	0-2
	9	Edmonton	2-1		31	Chicago	1-7
	10	Los Angeles	3-2	Apr.	1	Colorado	3-2
	13	St. Louis	3-4*		4	at Phoenix	2-4
	15	Anaheim	2-5		5	at Colorado	3-2*
	17	at Minnesota	2-3		7	St. Louis	0-1
	19	at Nashville	3-4*		11	San Jose	2-3†
	21	Columbus	2-3		12	at Chicago	2-3†
	23	Nashville	4-0		14	at Nashville	3-0
	24	Vancouver	8-3		17	at Calgary	2-3
	27	at Los Angeles	1-2		20	at Vancouver	1-2†
	28	at San Jose	2-1†		22	Phoenix	4-0
Mar.	3	Chicago	1-2†		24	Los Angeles	3-1
	5	Colorado	2-1		25	Nashville	5-2
	7	Edmonton	3-0		27	at Dallas	3-0

* – Overtime † – Shootout

Entry Draft Selections 2013-1999

Name in bold denotes played in NHL.

2013
Pick
20 Anthony Mantha
48 Zach Nastasiuk
58 Tyler Bertuzzi
79 Mattias Janmark-Nylen
109 David Pope
139 Mitchell Wheaton
169 Marc McNulty
199 Hampus Melen

2012
Pick
49 Martin Frk
80 Jake Paterson
110 Andreas Athanasiou
140 Michael McKee
170 James De Haas
200 Rasmus Bodin

2011
Pick
35 Tomas Jurco
48 Xavier Ouellet
55 Ryan Sproul
85 Alan Quine
115 Marek Tvrdon
145 Philippe Hudon
146 Mattias Backman
175 Richard Nedomlel
205 Alexei Marchenko

2010
Pick
21 **Riley Sheahan**
51 Calle Jarnkrok
81 Louis-Marc Aubry
111 Teemu Pulkkinen
141 **Petr Mrazek**
171 Brooks Macek
201 Ben Marshall

2009
Pick
32 Landon Ferraro
60 **Tomas Tatar**
75 Andrej Nestrasil
90 Gleason Fournier
150 Nick Jensen
180 Mitch Callahan
210 Adam Almqvist

2008
Pick
30 **Thomas McCollum**
91 Max Nicastro
121 **Gustav Nyquist**
151 Julien Cayer
181 Stephen Johnston
211 Jesper Samuelsson

2007
Pick
27 **Brendan Smith**
88 **Joakim Andersson**
148 Randy Cameron
178 Zack Torquato
208 Bryan Rufenach

2006
Pick
41 **Cory Emmerton**
47 **Shawn Matthias**
62 Dick Axelsson
92 Daniel Larsson
182 **Jan Mursak**
191 Nick Oslund
212 Logan Pyett

2005
Pick
19 **Jakub Kindl**
42 **Justin Abdelkader**
80 Christofer Lofberg
103 **Mattias Ritola**
132 **Darren Helm**
137 Johan Ryno
151 Jeff May
175 Juho Mielonen
214 Bretton Stamler

2004
Pick
97 **Johan Franzen**
128 Evan McGrath
151 Sergei Kolosov
162 Tyler Haskins
192 Anton Axelsson
226 Steven Covington
257 Gennady Stolyarov
290 Nils Backstrom

2003
Pick
64 **Jimmy Howard**
132 **Kyle Quincey**
164 Ryan Oulahen
170 Andreas Sundin
194 Stefan Blom
226 Tomas Kollar
258 Vladimir Kutny
289 Mikael Johansson

2002
Pick
58 **Jiri Hudler**
63 **Tomas Fleischmann**
95 **Valtteri Filppula**
131 Johan Berggren
166 Logan Koopmans
197 Jimmy Cuddihy
229 **Derek Meech**
260 Pierre-Olivier Beaulieu
262 Christian Soderstrom
291 **Jonathan Ericsson**

2001
Pick
62 Igor Grigorenko
121 **Drew MacIntyre**
129 Miroslav Blatak
157 Andreas Jamtin
195 Nick Pannoni
258 **Dmitri Bykov**
288 Francois Senez

2000
Pick
29 **Niklas Kronwall**
38 **Tomas Kopecky**
102 Stefan Liv
127 Dmitri Semenov
128 Alexander Seluyanov
130 Aaron Van Leusen
187 Per Backer
196 Paul Ballantyne
228 Jimmie Svensson
251 Todd Jackson
260 Yevgeny Bumagin

1999
Pick
120 Jari Tolsa
149 Andrei Maximenko
181 **Kent McDonell**
210 **Henrik Zetterberg**
238 Anton Borodkin
266 Ken Davis

Club Directory

Joe Louis Arena

Detroit Red Wings
Joe Louis Arena
19 Steve Yzerman Drive
Detroit, MI 48226
Phone **313/394-7000**
FAX PR: 313/567-0296
Media Hotline: 313/396-7599
www.detroitredwings.com
Capacity: 20,066

Owner/Governor	Mike Ilitch
Owner/Secretary-Treasurer	Marian Ilitch
President and CEO, Ilitch Holdings/ Alternate Governor Red Wings	Christopher Ilitch
Senior Vice President/Alternate Governor	Jim Devellano
Executive Vice President/General Manager	Ken Holland
Assistant General Manager/Hockey Admin.	Ryan Martin
Advisor to Hockey Operations	Chris Chelios
Special Assistant to the General Manager	Kris Draper
Director of Player Development	Jiri Fischer
President and CEO, Olympia Entertainment/ Alternate Governor Red Wings	Tom Wilson
Vice President Olympia Entertainment/ General Counsel Red Wings	Robert E. Carr
Head Coach	Mike Babcock
Associate Coach	Tom Renney
Assistant Coach	Bill Peters
Assistant Coach/Video	Keith McKittrick
Goaltending Coach	Jim Bedard
Goaltending Development Coach	Chris Osgood
Director of Pro Scouting	Mark Howe
Pro Scouts	Glenn Merkosky, Bruce Haralson, Kirk Maltby
Director of Amateur Scouting	Tyler Wright
Chief Amateur Scout	Jeff Finley
Amateur Scouts	Dave Kolb, Mario Marois, Andrew Dickson, Kelly Harper, Len Quesnelle, Sam Lites, Marty Stein
Director of European Scouting	Hakan Andersson
European Scouts	Vladimir Havluj, Ari Vouri, Nikolai Vakourov
Vice President of Finance	Paul MacDonald
Executive Assistant	Kim Brodie
General Accountant	Bridget Merritt
Administrative Assistant	Julie Dailey
Head Athletic Therapist	Piet Van Zant
Head Equipment Manager	Paul Boyer
Assistant Athletic Therapist	Russ Baumann
Assistant Equipment Managers	John Remejes, Dan Kerstetter
Team Masseurs	Sergei Tchekmarev, Ainars Treiguts
Senior Director of Communications	John Hahn
Director, Detroit Red Wings Foundation	Lynsie DeLoss Estes
Media Relations Manager	Todd Beam
Community Relations Manager	Christy Hammond
Public Relations Coordinator	Kyle Kujawa
Medical Director	Dr. Donald Weaver
Team Physicians	Dr. Anthony Colucci, Dr. Doug Plagens
Team Dentists	Dr. Jeffrey Boogren, Dr. Randy Freij
Team Photographer	Dave Reginek
Radio Announcers, 97.1 The Ticket	Ken Kal, Paul Woods
Television Announcers, Fox Sports Detroit	Ken Daniels, Mickey Redmond

General Managers' History

Art Duncan, 1926-27; Jack Adams, 1927-28 to 1961-62; Sid Abel, 1962-63 to 1969-70; Sid Abel and Ned Harkness, 1970-71; Ned Harkness, 1971-72, 1972-73; Ned Harkness and Jimmy Skinner, 1973-74; Alex Delvecchio, 1974-75, 1975-76; Alex Delvecchio and Ted Lindsay, 1976-77; Ted Lindsay, 1977-78 to 1979-80; Jimmy Skinner, 1980-81, 1981-82; Jim Devellano, 1982-83 to 1989-90; Bryan Murray, 1990-91 to 1993-94; Jim Devellano (Senior Vice President/Hockey), 1994-95 to 1996-97; Ken Holland, 1997-98 to date.

Ken Holland

Executive Vice President and General Manager

Born: Vernon, B.C., November 10, 1955.

Ken Holland has served in the Red Wings front office since 1985, and has been the club's general manager since July 18, 1997. He has established himself as one of the most innovative and aggressive GMs in the National Hockey League. Detroit's Stanley Cup victory in 2008 marked the team's third championship under his leadership. Holland began his tenure as the club's general manager after serving as assistant general manager for the previous three seasons. He will be part of the management group for Team Canada at the 2014 Sochi Winter Olympics.

Holland oversees all aspects of hockey operations including all matters relating to player personnel, development, contract negotiations and player movements, though he now takes a less prominent role in the NHL draft than he did during his seven years as the club's director of amateur scouting.

At the conclusion of his playing days as a goaltender, spending most of his pro career at the American Hockey League level, Holland began his off-ice career in 1985 as a western Canada scout followed by five years as an amateur scouting director before promotions led to his current position as general manager.

A native of Vernon, British Columbia, Holland played in the junior ranks for Medicine Hat (WHL) in 1974-75. He was Toronto's 13th pick (188th overall) in the 1975 draft but never saw action with the Maple Leafs. Holland twice signed with NHL teams as a free agent — in 1980 with Hartford and 1983 with Detroit. He spent most of his pro career with AHL clubs in Binghamton and Springfield, along with Adirondack, but did appear in four NHL games, making his debut with Hartford in 1980-81 and playing three contests for Detroit in 1983-84.

Coaching History

Art Duncan and Duke Keats, 1926-27; Jack Adams, 1927-28 to 1946-47; Tommy Ivan, 1947-48 to 1953-54; Jimmy Skinner, 1954-55 to 1956-57; Jimmy Skinner and Sid Abel, 1957-58; Sid Abel, 1958-59 to 1967-68; Bill Gadsby, 1968-69; Bill Gadsby and Sid Abel, 1969-70; Ned Harkness and Doug Barkley, 1970-71; Doug Barkley and Johnny Wilson, 1971-72; Johnny Wilson, 1972-73; Ted Garvin and Alex Delvecchio, 1973-74; Alex Delvecchio, 1974-75; Doug Barkley and Alex Delvecchio, 1975-76; Alex Delvecchio and Larry Wilson, 1976-77; Bobby Kromm, 1977-78, 1978-79; Bobby Kromm and Ted Lindsay, 1979-80; Ted Lindsay and Wayne Maxner, 1980-81; Wayne Maxner and Billy Dea, 1981-82; Nick Polano, 1982-83 to 1984-85; Harry Neale and Brad Park, 1985-86; Jacques Demers, 1986-87 to 1989-90; Bryan Murray, 1990-91 to 1992-93; Scotty Bowman, 1993-94 to 1997-98; Dave Lewis, Barry Smith (co-coaches) and Scotty Bowman, 1998-99; Scotty Bowman, 1999-2000 to 2001-02; Dave Lewis, 2002-03 to 2004-05; Mike Babcock, 2005-06 to date.

Captains' History

Art Duncan, 1926-27; Reg Noble, 1927-28 to 1929-30; George Hay, 1930-31; Carson Cooper, 1931-32; Larry Aurie, 1932-33; Herbie Lewis, 1933-34; Ebbie Goodfellow, 1934-35; Doug Young, 1935-36 to 1937-38; Ebbie Goodfellow, 1938-39 to 1940-41; Ebbie Goodfellow and Syd Howe, 1941-42; Sid Abel, 1942-43; Mud Bruneteau, Flash Hollett, 1943-44; Flash Hollett, 1944-45; Flash Hollett and Sid Abel, 1945-46; Sid Abel, 1946-47 to 1951-52; Ted Lindsay, 1952-53 to 1955-56; Red Kelly, 1956-57, 1957-58; Gordie Howe, 1958-59 to 1961-62; Alex Delvecchio, 1962-63 to 1972-73; Alex Delvecchio, Nick Libett, Red Berenson, Gary Bergman, Ted Harris, Mickey Redmond and Larry Johnston, 1973-74; Marcel Dionne, 1974-75; Danny Grant and Terry Harper, 1975-76; Danny Grant and Dennis Polonich, 1976-77; Dan Maloney and Dennis Hextall, 1977-78; Dennis Hextall, Nick Libett and Paul Woods, 1978-79; Dale McCourt, 1979-80; Errol Thompson and Reed Larson, 1980-81; Reed Larson, 1981-82; Danny Gare, 1982-83 to 1985-86; Steve Yzerman, 1986-87 to 2005-06; Nicklas Lidstrom, 2006-07 to 2011-12; Henrik Zetterberg, 2012-13 to date.

Edmonton Oilers

2012-13 Results: 19W-22L-4OTL-3SOL 45PTS
3RD, Northwest Division • 12TH, Western Conference

Key Off-Season Signings/Acquisitions

2013

June 10 • Named **Dallas Eakins** head coach.
28 • Named **Keith Acton** associate coach.
July 5 • Signed D **Andrew Ference**, G **Jason LaBarbera** and RW **Boyd Gordon**.
5 • Acquired D **Philip Larsen** and a 7th-round pick in the 2016 NHL Draft from Dallas for C **Shawn Horcoff**.
6 • Signed G **Richard Bachman**.
6 • Re-signed LW **Ryan Jones**.
10 • Acquired LW **David Perron** from St. Louis for LW **Magnus Paajarvi** and a 2nd-round pick in the 2014 NHL Draft.
18 • Signed D **Denis Grebeshkov**.
22 • Re-signed C **Sam Gagner**.

Year-by-Year Record

Season	GP	Home W	Home L	Home T	Home OL	Road W	Road L	Road T	Road OL	Overall W	Overall L	Overall T	Overall OL	GF	GA	Pts.	Div. Fin.	Conf. Fin.	Playoff Result
2012-13	48	9	11	....	4	10	11	....	3	19	22	....	7	125	134	45	3rd, NW	12th, West	Out of Playoffs
2011-12	82	18	17	....	6	14	23	....	4	32	40	....	10	212	239	74	5th, NW	14th, West	Out of Playoffs
2010-11	82	13	22	....	6	12	23	....	6	25	45	....	12	193	269	62	5th, NW	15th, West	Out of Playoffs
2009-10	82	18	19	....	4	9	28	....	4	27	47	....	8	214	284	62	5th, NW	15th, West	Out of Playoffs
2008-09	82	18	17	....	6	20	18	....	3	38	35	....	9	234	248	85	4th, NW	11th, West	Out of Playoffs
2007-08	82	23	17	....	1	18	18	....	5	41	35	....	6	235	251	88	4th, NW	9th, West	Out of Playoffs
2006-07	82	19	19	....	3	13	24	....	4	32	43	....	7	195	248	71	5th, NW	12th, West	Out of Playoffs
2005-06	82	20	15	....	6	21	13	....	7	41	28	....	13	256	251	95	3rd, NW	8th, West	Lost Final
2004-05	....	....	....	....	....	....	....	....	....	....	....	....	....	....	....	....			
2003-04	82	22	12	4	3	14	17	8	2	36	29	12	5	221	208	89	4th, NW	9th, West	Out of Playoffs
2002-03	82	20	12	5	4	16	14	6	5	36	26	11	9	231	230	92	4th, NW	8th, West	Lost Conf. Quarter-Final
2001-02	82	23	14	4	0	15	14	8	4	38	28	12	4	205	182	92	3rd, NW	9th, West	Out of Playoffs
2000-01	82	23	9	7	2	16	19	5	1	39	28	12	3	243	222	93	2nd, NW	6th, West	Lost Conf. Quarter-Final
1999-2000	82	18	11	9	3	14	15	7	5	32	26	16	8	226	212	88	2nd, NW	7th, West	Lost Conf. Quarter-Final
1998-99	82	17	19	5	....	16	18	7	....	33	37	12	....	230	226	78	2nd, NW	8th, West	Lost Conf. Quarter-Final
1997-98	82	20	16	5	....	15	21	5	....	35	37	10	....	215	224	80	3rd, Pac.	7th, West	Lost Conf. Semi-Final
1996-97	82	21	16	4	....	15	21	5	....	36	37	9	....	252	247	81	3rd, Pac.	7th, West	Lost Conf. Semi-Final
1995-96	82	15	21	5	....	15	23	3	....	30	44	8	....	240	304	68	5th, Pac.	10th, West	Out of Playoffs
1994-95	48	11	12	1	....	6	15	3	....	17	27	4	....	136	183	38	5th, Pac.	11th, West	Out of Playoffs
1993-94	84	17	22	3	....	8	23	11	....	25	45	14	....	261	305	64	6th, Pac.	11th, West	Out of Playoffs
1992-93	84	16	21	5	....	10	29	3	....	26	50	8	....	242	337	60	5th, Smythe		Out of Playoffs
1991-92	80	22	13	5	....	14	21	5	....	36	34	10	....	295	297	82	3rd, Smythe		Lost Conf. Final
1990-91	80	22	15	3	....	15	22	3	....	37	37	6	....	272	272	80	3rd, Smythe		Lost Conf. Final
1989-90	**80**	**23**	**11**	**6**	....	**15**	**17**	**8**	....	**38**	**28**	**14**	....	**315**	**283**	**90**	**2nd, Smythe**		**Won Stanley Cup**
1988-89	80	21	16	3	....	17	18	5	....	38	34	8	....	325	306	84	3rd, Smythe		Lost Div. Semi-Final
1987-88	**80**	**28**	**8**	**4**	....	**16**	**17**	**7**	....	**44**	**25**	**11**	....	**363**	**288**	**99**	**2nd, Smythe**		**Won Stanley Cup**
1986-87	**80**	**29**	**6**	**5**	....	**21**	**18**	**1**	....	**50**	**24**	**6**	....	**372**	**284**	**106**	**1st, Smythe**		**Won Stanley Cup**
1985-86	80	32	6	2	....	24	11	5	....	56	17	7	....	426	310	119	1st, Smythe		Lost Div. Final
1984-85	**80**	**26**	**7**	**7**	....	**23**	**13**	**4**	....	**49**	**20**	**11**	....	**401**	**298**	**109**	**1st, Smythe**		**Won Stanley Cup**
1983-84	**80**	**31**	**5**	**4**	....	**26**	**13**	**1**	....	**57**	**18**	**5**	....	**446**	**314**	**119**	**1st, Smythe**		**Won Stanley Cup**
1982-83	80	25	9	6	....	22	12	6	....	47	21	12	....	424	315	106	1st, Smythe		Lost Final
1981-82	80	31	5	4	....	17	12	11	....	48	17	15	....	417	295	111	1st, Smythe		Lost Div. Semi-Final
1980-81	80	17	13	10	....	12	22	6	....	29	35	16	....	328	327	74	4th, Smythe		Lost Quarter-Final
1979-80	80	17	14	9	....	11	25	4	....	28	39	13	....	301	322	69	4th, Smythe		Lost Prelim. Round

2013-14 Schedule

Oct.	Tue.	1	Winnipeg
	Sat.	5	at Vancouver
	Mon.	7	New Jersey
	Thu.	10	Montreal
	Sat.	12	at Toronto
	Mon.	14	at Washington
	Tue.	15	at Pittsburgh
	Thu.	17	at NY Islanders
	Sat.	19	at Ottawa*
	Tue.	22	at Montreal
	Thu.	24	Washington
	Sat.	26	at Phoenix*
	Sun.	27	at Los Angeles
	Tue.	29	Toronto
Nov.	Sat.	2	Detroit
	Tue.	5	at Florida
	Thu.	7	at Tampa Bay
	Sat.	9	at Philadelphia*
	Sun.	10	at Chicago
	Wed.	13	Dallas
	Fri.	15	San Jose
	Sat.	16	at Calgary
	Tue.	19	Columbus
	Thu.	21	Florida
	Mon.	25	Chicago
	Thu.	28	at Nashville
	Fri.	29	at Columbus
Dec.	Sun.	1	at Dallas*
	Tue.	3	Phoenix
	Thu.	5	Colorado
	Sat.	7	Calgary
	Tue.	10	Carolina
	Thu.	12	Boston
	Fri.	13	at Vancouver
	Sun.	15	at Anaheim*
	Tue.	17	at Los Angeles
	Thu.	19	at Colorado
	Sat.	21	St. Louis
	Mon.	23	Winnipeg
	Fri.	27	at Calgary
	Sat.	28	Philadelphia
	Tue.	31	at Phoenix
Jan.	Thu.	2	at San Jose
	Fri.	3	at Anaheim
	Sun.	5	Tampa Bay
	Tue.	7	St. Louis
	Fri.	10	Pittsburgh
	Sun.	12	at Chicago
	Tue.	14	at Dallas
	Thu.	16	at Minnesota
	Sat.	18	at Winnipeg*
	Tue.	21	Vancouver
	Fri.	24	Phoenix
	Sun.	26	Nashville
	Mon.	27	at Vancouver
	Wed.	29	San Jose
Feb.	Sat.	1	at Boston*
	Mon.	3	at Buffalo
	Thu.	6	at NY Rangers
	Fri.	7	at New Jersey
	Thu.	27	Minnesota
Mar.	Sat.	1	Calgary
	Tue.	4	Ottawa
	Thu.	6	NY Islanders
	Sun.	9	Los Angeles
	Tue.	11	at Minnesota
	Thu.	13	at St. Louis
	Fri.	14	at Detroit
	Sun.	16	at Carolina*
	Tue.	18	Nashville
	Thu.	20	Buffalo
	Sat.	22	Calgary
	Tue.	25	San Jose
	Fri.	28	Anaheim
	Sun.	30	NY Rangers
Apr.	Tue.	1	at San Jose
	Wed.	2	at Anaheim
	Fri.	4	at Phoenix
	Sun.	6	Anaheim
	Tue.	8	Colorado
	Thu.	10	Los Angeles
	Sat.	12	Vancouver

* Denotes afternoon game.

Selected first overall in the 2012 NHL Entry Draft, Nail Yakupov led all NHL rookies, and topped the Oilers, with 17 goals and a 21.0 shooting percentage during the 2012-13 season.

PACIFIC DIVISION
35th NHL Season

Franchise date: June 22, 1979

2013-14 Player Personnel

FORWARDS	HT	WT	*Age	Place of Birth	S	2012-13 Club
ACTON, Will	6-2	190	26	Stouffville, Ont.	L	Toronto (AHL)
BROWN, Mike	5-11	205	28	Chicago, IL	R	Toronto-Edmonton
EAGER, Ben	6-2	240	29	Ottawa, Ont.	L	Oklahoma City-Edmonton
EBERLE, Jordan	5-11	184	23	Regina, Sask.	R	Oklahoma City-Edmonton
GAGNER, Sam	5-11	195	24	London, Ont.	R	Klagenfurt-Edmonton
GORDON, Boyd	6-0	200	29	Unity, Sask.	R	Phoenix
HALL, Taylor	6-1	194	21	Calgary, Alta.	L	Oklahoma City-Edmonton
HAMILTON, Ryan	6-2	230	28	Oshawa, Ont.	L	Toronto (AHL)-Toronto
HARTIKAINEN, Teemu	6-1	215	23	Kuopio, Finland	L	Oklahoma City-Edmonton
HEMSKY, Ales	6-0	185	30	Pardubice, Czech.	R	Pardubice-Edmonton
JOENSUU, Jesse	6-4	209	25	Pori, Finland	L	NY Islanders-Assat
JONES, Ryan	6-1	205	29	Chatham, Ont.	L	Edmonton
NUGENT-HOPKINS, Ryan	6-1	175	20	Burnaby, B.C.	L	Oklahoma City-Edmonton
PERRON, David	5-11	196	25	Sherbrooke, Que.	R	St. Louis
SMYTH, Ryan	6-1	192	37	Banff, Alta.	L	Edmonton
YAKUPOV, Nail	5-11	185	19	Nizhnekamsk, Russia	L	Nizhnekamsk-Edmonton
DEFENSEMEN						
FERENCE, Andrew	5-11	189	34	Edmonton, Alta.	L	C. Budejovice-Boston
GREBESHKOV, Denis	6-0	209	29	Yaroslavl, USSR	L	St. Petersburg-Khanty-Mansiisk
LARSEN, Philip	6-0	190	23	Esbjerg, Denmark	R	Lukko-Dallas
NURSE, Darnell	6-4	185	18	Hamilton, Ont.	L	Sault Ste. Marie
PETRY, Jeff	6-3	196	25	Ann Arbor, MI	R	Edmonton
POTTER, Corey	6-3	206	29	Lansing, MI	R	Vienna Capitals-Edmonton
SCHULTZ, Justin	6-2	185	23	Kelowna, B.C.	R	Oklahoma City-Edmonton
SCHULTZ, Nick	6-1	200	31	Strasbourg, Sask.	L	Edmonton
SMID, Ladislav	6-3	210	27	Frydlant V Cechach, Czech.	L	Liberec-Edmonton

GOALTENDERS	HT	WT	*Age	Place of Birth	C	2012-13 Club
BACHMAN, Richard	5-10	175	26	Salt Lake City, UT	L	Texas-Dallas
DUBNYK, Devan	6-5	210	27	Regina, Sask.	L	Edmonton
LaBARBERA, Jason	6-3	234	33	Burnaby, B.C.	L	Phoenix

* – Age at start of 2013-14 season

Captains' History

Ron Chipperfield, 1979-80; Blair MacDonald and Lee Fogolin, Jr., 1980-81; Lee Fogolin, Jr., 1981-82, 1982-83; Wayne Gretzky, 1983-84 to 1987-88; Mark Messier, 1988-89 to 1990-91; Kevin Lowe, 1991-92; Craig MacTavish, 1992-93, 1993-94; Shayne Corson, 1994-95; Kelly Buchberger, 1995-96 to 1998-99; Doug Weight, 1999-2000, 2000-01; Jason Smith, 2001-02 to 2006-07; Ethan Moreau, 2007-08 to 2009-10; Shawn Horcoff, 2010-11 to 2012-13.

Coaching History

Glen Sather, 1979-80; Bryan Watson and Glen Sather, 1980-81; Glen Sather, 1981-82 to 1988-89; John Muckler, 1989-90, 1990-91; Ted Green, 1991-92, 1992-93; Ted Green and Glen Sather, 1993-94; George Burnett and Ron Low, 1994-95; Ron Low, 1995-96 to 1998-99; Kevin Lowe, 1999-2000; Craig MacTavish, 2000-01 to 2008-09; Pat Quinn, 2009-10; Tom Renney, 2010-11, 2011-12; Ralph Krueger, 2012-13; Dallas Eakins, 2013-14.

Dallas Eakins

Head Coach

Born: Dade City, FL, February 27, 1967.

General manager Craig MacTavish appointed Dallas Eakins the new head coach of the Edmonton Oilers on June 10, 2013. Eakins is the 12th head coach in Oilers franchise history.

Eakins spent the previous eight seasons in the Toronto Maple Leafs organization, where he served as an assistant coach with the Maple Leafs for two seasons (2006 to 2008), before becoming the head coach of the Leafs' American Hockey League affiliate, the Toronto Marlies, in 2009. He was also an assistant coach with the Marlies in 2005-06 and served as the Maple Leafs' director of player development for one season in 2008-09.

In four seasons as head coach of the Marlies, Eakins accumulated a record of 157-114-41. He was one of two head coaches who represented the Western Conference at the AHL All-Star Game in 2011-12 and 2012-13. After knocking off the Oilers' AHL affiliate, the Oklahoma City Barons, in the 2012 playoffs Eakins' Marlies went on to the Calder Cup Final, losing out to the Norfolk Admirals.

Drafted in the 10th round, 208th overall by the Washington Capitals in 1985, Eakins recorded nine assists in 120 career NHL games and patrolled the blueline for the Winnipeg Jets, Florida Panthers, St. Louis Blues, Phoenix Coyotes, Toronto Maple Leafs, Calgary Flames, New York Rangers and the New York Islanders.

The Dade City, Florida native finished his playing career with minor league stops in the International Hockey League and the AHL, where he played in 882 games, registering 222 points (43 goals, 179 assists). His minor league stops included Baltimore, Moncton, Cincinnati, Worchester, Springfield, Binghamton, New Haven, St. John's, and the Chicago Wolves, where he won a Calder Cup. Eakins concluded his playing career in 2003-04, captaining the Manitoba Moose.

Coaching Record

			Regular Season				Playoffs			
Season	Team	League	GC	W	L	O/T	GC	W	L	T
2009-10	Toronto	AHL	80	33	35	12	....	....	....	....
2010-11	Toronto	AHL	80	37	32	11	....	....	....	....
2011-12	Toronto	AHL	76	44	24	8	17	11	6	....
2012-13	Toronto	AHL	76	43	23	10	9	5	4	....

2012-13 Scoring

* – rookie

Regular Season

Pos	#	Player	Team	GP	G	A	Pts	TOI	+/–	PIM	PP	SH	GW	S	%
L	4	Taylor Hall	EDM	45	16	34	50	18:37	5	33	4	0	4	154	10.4
C	89	Sam Gagner	EDM	48	14	24	38	19:24	–6	23	4	0	1	113	12.4
C	14	Jordan Eberle	EDM	48	16	21	37	18:59	–4	16	3	0	3	133	12.0
R	64 *	Nail Yakupov	EDM	48	17	14	31	14:33	–4	24	6	0	2	81	21.0
D	19 *	Justin Schultz	EDM	48	8	19	27	21:26	–17	8	4	0	3	85	9.4
C	93	Ryan Nugent-Hopkins	EDM	40	4	20	24	18:51	3	8	2	0	0	78	5.1
R	83	Ales Hemsky	EDM	38	9	11	20	15:42	–6	16	5	0	1	82	11.0
L	91	Magnus Paajarvi	EDM	42	9	7	16	14:07	–1	14	2	1	2	75	12.0
D	6	Ryan Whitney	EDM	34	4	9	13	18:28	–7	23	0	0	0	30	13.3
L	94	Ryan Smyth	EDM	47	2	11	13	15:22	–5	40	0	1	0	69	2.9
C	10	Shawn Horcoff	EDM	31	7	5	12	16:51	8	24	3	0	1	41	17.1
D	2	Jeff Petry	EDM	48	3	9	12	21:54	1	29	0	1	0	66	4.5
C	37	Lennart Petrell	EDM	35	3	6	9	11:31	–4	4	0	1	0	23	13.0
D	15	Nick Schultz	EDM	48	1	8	9	18:37	–13	24	0	0	0	33	3.0
L	28	Ryan Jones	EDM	27	2	5	7	12:58	0	17	0	0	0	38	5.3
R	52	Jerred Smithson	FLA	35	2	3	5	10:21	–4	10	0	0	0	22	9.1
			EDM	10	1	0	1	11:43	0	2	0	0	0	7	14.3
			Total	45	3	3	6	10:39	–4	12	0	0	0	29	10.3
D	45	Mark Fistric	EDM	25	0	6	6	15:20	6	32	0	0	0	9	0.0
D	44	Corey Potter	EDM	33	3	1	4	17:27	8	6	0	0	0	36	8.3
D	5	Ladislav Smid	EDM	48	1	3	4	20:19	–1	55	0	0	0	30	3.3
C	56	Teemu Hartikainen	EDM	23	1	2	3	10:34	–8	6	1	0	0	21	4.8
C	20	Eric Belanger	EDM	26	0	3	3	14:07	–1	10	0	0	0	31	0.0
L	55	Ben Eager	EDM	14	1	1	2	9:39	–4	25	0	0	0	14	7.1
R	13	Mike Brown	TOR	12	0	1	1	4:39	1	70	0	0	0	2	0.0
			EDM	27	1	0	1	8:47	–8	53	0	0	0	16	6.3
			Total	39	1	1	2	7:31	–7	123	0	0	0	18	5.6
C	57	Anton Lander	EDM	11	0	1	1	11:01	–4	2	0	0	0	11	0.0
R	62 *	Mark Arcobello	EDM	1	0	0	0	18:15	0	0	0	0	0	0	0.0
L	16	Darcy Hordichuk	EDM	4	0	0	0	2:02	–1	2	0	0	0	0	0.0
D	24	Theo Peckham	EDM	4	0	0	0	17:38	–1	6	0	0	0	2	0.0
C	54 *	Chris VandeVelde	EDM	11	0	0	0	7:02	–3	4	0	0	0	7	0.0

Goaltending

No.	Goaltender	GPI	Mins	Avg	W	L	OT	EN	SO	GA	SA	S%	G	A	PIM
35	Nikolai Khabibulin	12	684	2.54	4	6	1	1	1	29	376	.923	0	0	0
40	Devan Dubnyk	38	2101	2.57	14	16	6	4	2	90	1132	.920	0	0	0
34	Yann Danis	3	110	3.82	1	0	0	0	0	7	59	.881	0	0	0
	Totals	**48**	**2924**	**2.69**	**19**	**22**	**7**	**5**	**3**	**131**	**1572**	**.917**			

The Oilers' first pick (14th overall) back in 2004, Devan Dubnyk has established himself as the number-one goaltender in Edmonton.

Club Records

Team

(Figures in brackets for season records are games played; records for fewest points, wins, ties, losses, goals, goals against are for 70 or more games)

Most Points .... 119 — 1983-84 (80), 1985-86 (80)
Most Wins .... 57 — 1983-84 (80)
Most Ties .... 16 — 1980-81 (80), 1999-2000 (82)
Most Losses .... 50 — 1992-93 (84)
Most Goals .... *446 — 1983-84 (80)
Most Goals Against .... 337 — 1992-93 (84)
Fewest Points .... 60 — 1992-93 (84)
Fewest Wins .... 25 — 1993-94 (84)
Fewest Ties .... 5 — 1983-84 (80)
Fewest Losses .... 17 — 1981-82 (80), 1985-86 (80)
Fewest Goals .... 195 — 2006-07 (82)
Fewest Goals Against .... 182 — 2001-02 (82)
Longest Winning Streak
Overall .... 9 — Feb. 20-Mar. 13/01
Home .... 8 — Jan. 19-Feb. 22/85, Feb. 24-Apr. 2/86
Away .... 8 — Dec. 9/86-Jan. 17/87
Longest Undefeated Streak
Overall .... 15 — Oct. 11-Nov. 9/84 (12W, 3T)
Home .... 14 — Nov. 15/89-Jan. 6/90 (11W, 3T)
Away .... 9 — Jan. 17-Mar. 2/82 (6W, 3T), Nov. 23/82-Jan. 18/83 (7W, 2T)
Longest Losing Streak
Overall .... 13 — Dec. 31/09-Jan. 30/10
Home .... 9 — Oct. 16-Nov. 24/93
Away .... 11 — Dec. 23/09-Feb. 10/10
Longest Winless Streak
Overall .... 14 — Oct. 11-Nov. 7/93 (13L, 1T)
Home .... 9 — Oct. 16-Nov. 24/93 (9L)
Away .... 11 — Dec. 18/01-Feb. 8/02 (7L, 4T/OL), Dec. 23/09-Feb. 10/10 (11 losses)
Most Shutouts, Season .... 8 — 1997-98 (82); 2000-01 (82); 2001-02 (82)
Most PIM, Season .... 2,173 — 1987-88 (80)
Most Goals, Game .... 13 — Nov. 19/83 (N.J. 4 at Edm. 13), Nov. 8/85 (Van. 0 at Edm. 13)

Individual

Most Seasons .... 15 — Kevin Lowe
Most Games .... 1,037 — Kevin Lowe
Most Goals, Career .... 583 — Wayne Gretzky
Most Assists, Career ...... 1,086 — Wayne Gretzky
Most Points, Career .... 1,669 — Wayne Gretzky (583G, 1,086A)
Most PIM, Career .... 1,747 — Kelly Buchberger
Most Shutouts, Career .... 23 — Tommy Salo
Longest Consecutive Games Streak .... 518 — Craig MacTavish (Oct. 12/86-Jan. 2/93)
Most Goals, Season .... *92 — Wayne Gretzky (1981-82)
Most Assists, Season .... *163 — Wayne Gretzky (1985-86)
Most Points, Season .... *215 — Wayne Gretzky (1985-86; 52G, 163A)
Most PIM, Season .... 286 — Steve Smith (1987-88)
Most Points, Defenseman, Season .... 138 — Paul Coffey (1985-86; 48G, 90A)
Most Points, Center, Season .... *215 — Wayne Gretzky (1985-86; 52G, 163A)
Most Points, Right Wing, Season .... 135 — Jari Kurri (1984-85; 71G, 64A)
Most Points, Left Wing, Season .... 106 — Mark Messier (1982-83; 48G, 58A)
Most Points, Rookie, Season .... 75 — Jari Kurri (1980-81; 32G, 43A)
Most Shutouts, Season .... 8 — Curtis Joseph (1997-98), Tommy Salo (2000-01)
Most Goals, Game .... 5 — Wayne Gretzky (Feb. 18/81), (Dec. 30/81), (Dec. 15/84), (Dec. 6/87); Jari Kurri (Nov. 19/83); Pat Hughes (Feb. 3/84)
Most Assists, Game .... *7 — Wayne Gretzky (Feb. 15/80), (Dec. 11/85), (Feb. 14/86)
Most Points, Game .... 8 — Wayne Gretzky (Nov. 19/83; 3G, 5A), (Jan. 4/84; 4G, 4A); Paul Coffey (Mar. 14/86; 2G, 6A); Sam Gagner (Feb. 2/12; 4G, 4A)

* NHL Record.

Retired Numbers

3	Al Hamilton	1972-1980
7	Paul Coffey	1980-1987
9	Glenn Anderson	1980-91, 1996
11	Mark Messier	1980-1991
17	Jari Kurri	1980-1990
31	Grant Fuhr	1981-1991
99	Wayne Gretzky	1979-1988

All-time Record vs. Other Clubs

Regular Season

	Total								At Home								On Road							
	GP	W	L	T	OL	GF	GA	PTS	GP	W	L	T	OL	GF	GA	PTS	GP	W	L	T	OL	GF	GA	PTS
Anaheim	82	38	38	2	4	199	218	82	41	21	16	0	4	92	102	46	41	17	22	2	0	107	116	36
Boston	65	17	39	6	3	187	243	43	32	11	16	3	2	104	106	27	33	6	23	3	1	83	137	16
Buffalo	65	34	20	10	1	242	209	79	32	21	8	3	0	125	91	45	33	13	12	7	1	117	118	34
Calgary	214	89	101	19	5	709	750	202	107	53	40	10	4	372	337	120	107	36	61	9	1	337	413	82
Carolina	66	33	21	12	0	235	227	78	34	21	8	5	0	131	100	47	32	12	13	7	0	104	127	31
Chicago	120	52	55	12	1	414	421	117	60	29	26	5	0	213	196	63	60	23	29	7	1	201	225	54
Colorado	146	70	59	8	9	518	487	157	72	38	25	4	5	269	227	85	74	32	34	4	4	249	260	72
Columbus	47	29	10	3	5	166	119	66	23	18	4	0	1	86	54	37	24	11	6	3	4	80	65	29
Dallas	120	43	54	15	8	380	410	109	60	25	21	8	6	218	196	64	60	18	33	7	2	162	214	45
Detroit	119	47	54	13	5	393	433	112	59	27	20	10	2	216	205	66	60	20	34	3	3	177	228	46
Florida	22	11	8	3	0	64	51	25	10	6	3	1	0	31	21	13	12	5	5	2	0	33	30	12
Los Angeles	185	87	66	30	2	737	661	206	93	45	33	15	0	382	319	105	92	42	33	15	2	355	342	101
Minnesota	73	28	33	4	8	167	196	68	37	16	15	3	3	88	91	38	36	12	18	1	5	79	105	30
Montreal	75	34	34	4	3	250	247	75	40	22	18	0	0	139	126	44	35	12	16	4	3	111	121	31
Nashville	56	23	26	3	4	160	164	53	27	12	12	0	3	71	80	27	29	11	14	3	1	89	84	26
New Jersey	70	32	24	9	5	258	237	78	34	15	11	6	2	140	119	38	36	17	13	3	3	118	118	40
NY Islanders	66	26	25	14	1	230	228	67	32	19	8	5	0	116	90	43	34	7	17	9	1	114	138	24
NY Rangers	64	29	24	9	2	230	227	69	31	14	14	3	0	108	100	31	33	15	10	6	2	122	127	38
Ottawa	31	14	11	4	2	92	82	34	16	7	7	2	0	50	47	16	15	7	4	2	2	42	35	18
Philadelphia	65	28	29	8	0	200	224	64	31	17	8	6	0	106	86	40	34	11	21	2	0	94	138	24
Phoenix	174	98	56	11	9	723	611	216	88	54	24	6	4	370	278	118	86	44	32	5	5	353	333	98
Pittsburgh	66	36	25	4	1	289	234	77	33	23	9	1	0	154	106	47	33	13	16	3	1	135	128	30
St. Louis	119	52	53	11	3	394	395	118	59	29	24	4	2	197	192	64	60	23	29	7	1	197	203	54
San Jose	96	43	36	12	5	286	277	103	49	25	15	7	2	152	124	59	47	18	21	5	3	134	153	44
Tampa Bay	27	16	8	2	1	79	70	35	13	9	4	0	0	36	30	18	14	7	4	2	1	43	40	17
Toronto	90	41	39	8	2	362	326	92	48	24	16	6	2	189	155	56	42	17	23	2	0	173	171	36
Vancouver	216	110	77	19	10	811	712	249	108	63	33	7	5	430	330	138	108	47	44	12	5	381	382	111
Washington	64	27	30	6	1	230	226	61	32	17	11	4	0	128	96	38	32	10	19	2	1	102	130	23
Winnipeg	13	8	3	1	1	46	30	18	7	4	1	1	1	27	19	10	6	4	2	0	0	19	11	8
Totals	**2616**	**1195**	**1058**	**262**	**101**	**9051**	**8715**	**2753**	**1308**	**685**	**450**	**125**	**48**	**4740**	**4023**	**1543**	**1308**	**510**	**608**	**137**	**53**	**4311**	**4692**	**1210**

Playoffs

	Series	W	L	GP	W	L	T	GF	GA	Last Mtg.	Rnd.	Result
Anaheim	1	1	0	5	4	1	0	16	13	2006	CF	W 4-1
Boston	2	2	0	9	8	1	0	41	20	1990	F	W 4-1
Calgary	5	4	1	30	19	11	0	132	96	1991	DSF	W 4-3
Carolina	1	0	1	7	3	4	0	16	19	2006	F	L 3-4
Chicago	4	3	1	20	12	8	0	102	77	1992	CF	L 0-4
Colorado	2	1	1	12	5	7	0	30	35	1998	CQF	W 4-3
Dallas	8	2	6	42	15	27	0	104	118	2003	CQF	L 2-4
Detroit	3	3	0	16	12	4	0	58	43	2006	CQF	W 4-2
Los Angeles	7	5	2	36	24	12	0	154	127	1992	DSF	W 4-2
Montreal	1	1	0	3	3	0	0	15	6	1981	PRE	W 3-0
NY Islanders	3	1	2	15	6	9	0	47	58	1984	F	W 4-1
Philadelphia	3	2	1	15	8	7	0	49	44	1987	F	W 4-3
Phoenix	6	6	0	26	22	4	0	120	75	1990	DSF	W 4-3
San Jose	1	1	0	6	4	2	0	19	12	2006	CSF	W 4-2
Vancouver	2	2	0	9	7	2	0	35	20	1992	DF	W 4-2
Totals	**49**	**34**	**15**	**251**	**152**	**99**	**0**	**938**	**763**			

Playoff Results 2013-2009

(Last playoff appearance: 2006)

Abbreviations: Round: F – Final; **CF** – conference final; **CSF** – conference semi-final; **CQF** – conference quarter-final; **DF** – division final; **DSF** – division semi-final; **PRE** – preliminary round.

Calgary totals include Atlanta Flames, 1979-80.
Colorado totals include Quebec, 1979-80 to 1994-95.
New Jersey totals include Colorado Rockies, 1979-80 to 1981-82.
Winnipeg totals include Atlanta Thrashers, 1999-2000 to 2010-11.
Carolina totals include Hartford, 1979-80 to 1996-97.
Dallas totals include Minnesota North Stars, 1979-80 to 1992-93.
Phoenix totals include Winnipeg, 1979-80 to 1995-96.

2012-13 Results

Jan.	20	at Vancouver	3-2†		10	at Chicago	6-5
	22	San Jose	3-6		12	at Colorado	4-0
	24	Los Angeles	2-1*		15	Detroit	2-3*
	26	at Calgary	3-4		17	Nashville	3-2
	28	Colorado	4-1		20	San Jose	3-4†
	30	at Phoenix	2-1*		23	St. Louis	0-3
	31	at San Jose	2-3†		25	at Nashville	2-3
Feb.	2	at Colorado	1-3		26	at St. Louis	3-0
	4	Vancouver	2-3*		28	Columbus	6-4
	6	Dallas	2-3*		30	Vancouver	4-0
	9	at Detroit	1-2	**Apr.**	1	Calgary	4-1
	10	at Columbus	3-1		3	at Calgary	8-2
	12	Dallas	1-4		4	at Vancouver	0-4
	16	Colorado	6-4		6	at Los Angeles	1-4
	19	Los Angeles	1-3		8	at Anaheim	1-2
	21	Minnesota	1-3		10	Phoenix	1-3
	23	Phoenix	3-2†		13	Calgary	1-4
	25	at Chicago	2-3*		16	Minnesota	3-5
	28	at Dallas	5-1		19	at Colorado	4-1
Mar.	1	at St. Louis	2-4		21	Anaheim	1-3
	3	at Minnesota	2-4		22	Anaheim	0-3
	5	at Columbus	3-4†		24	Chicago	1-4
	7	at Detroit	0-3		26	at Minnesota	6-1
	8	at Nashville	0-6		27	Vancouver	7-2

* – Overtime † – Shootout

Entry Draft Selections 2013-1999

Name in bold denotes played in NHL.

2013
Pick
7 Darnell Nurse
56 Marc-Olivier Roy
83 Bogdan Yakimov
88 Anton Slepyshev
94 Jackson Houck
96 Kyle Platzer
113 Aidan Muir
128 Evan Campbell
158 Ben Betker
188 Gregory Chase

2012
Pick
1 **Nail Yakupov**
32 Mitchell Moroz
63 Jujhar Khaira
91 Daniil Zharkov
93 Erik Gustafsson
123 Joey Laleggia
153 John McCarron

2011
Pick
1 **Ryan Nugent-Hopkins**
19 Oscar Klefbom
31 David Musil
62 Samu Perhonen
74 Travis Ewanyk
92 Dillon Simpson
114 Tobias Rieder
122 Martin Gernat
182 Frans Tuohimaa

2010
Pick
1 **Taylor Hall**
31 Tyler Pitlick
46 Martin Marincin
48 Curtis Hamilton
61 Ryan Martindale
91 Jeremie Blain
121 Tyler Bunz
162 Brandon Davidson
166 Drew Czerwonka
181 Kristians Pelss
202 Kellen Jones

2009
Pick
10 **Magnus Paajarvi**
40 **Anton Lander**
71 Troy Hesketh
82 Cameron Abney
99 Kyle Bigos
101 Toni Rajala
133 Olivier Roy

2008
Pick
22 **Jordan Eberle**
103 **Johan Motin**
133 **Philippe Cornet**
163 **Teemu Hartikainen**
193 Jordan Bendfeld

2007
Pick
6 **Sam Gagner**
15 **Alex Plante**
21 **Riley Nash**
97 **Linus Omark**
127 **Milan Kytnar**
157 William Quist

2006
Pick
45 **Jeff Petry**
75 **Theo Peckham**
133 Bryan Pitton
140 Cody Wild
170 Alexander Bumagin

2005
Pick
25 **Andrew Cogliano**
36 **Taylor Chorney**
81 **Danny Syvret**
86 Robby Dee
97 **Chris Vande Velde**
120 Viacheslav Trukhno
157 Fredrik Pettersson
220 Matthew Glasser

2004
Pick
14 **Devan Dubnyk**
25 **Rob Schremp**
44 Roman Tesliuk
57 Geoff Paukovich
112 **Liam Reddox**
146 **Bryan Young**
177 Max Gordichuk
208 Stephane Goulet
242 Tyler Spurgeon
274 Bjorn Bjurling

2003
Pick
22 **Marc Pouliot**
51 **Colin McDonald**
68 **Jean-Francois Jacques**
72 Mikhail Zhukov
94 **Zack Stortini**
147 Kalle Olsson
154 David Rohlfs
184 Dragan Umicevic
214 **Kyle Brodziak**
215 **Mathieu Roy**
248 Josef Hrabal
278 **Troy Bodie**

2002
Pick
15 Jesse Niinimaki
31 **Jeff Deslauriers**
36 **Jarret Stoll**
44 **Matt Greene**
79 Brock Radunske
106 Ivan Koltsov
111 Jonas Almtorp
123 invalid pick
148 Glenn Fisher
181 **Mikko Luoma**
205 J.F. Dufort
211 Patrick Murphy
244 **Dwight Helminen**
245 Tomas Micka
274 Fredrik Johansson

2001
Pick
13 **Ales Hemsky**
43 **Doug Lynch**
52 Ed Caron
84 Kenny Smith
133 **Jussi Markkanen**
154 Jake Brenk
185 Mikael Svensk
215 Dan Baum
248 **Kari Haakana**
272 **Ales Pisa**
278 **Shay Stephenson**

2000
Pick
17 **Alexei Mikhnov**
35 **Brad Winchester**
83 Alexander Liubimov
113 Lou Dickenson
152 Paul Flache
184 Shaun Norrie
211 Joe Cullen
215 **Matthew Lombardi**
247 Jason Platt
274 Yevgeny Muratov

1999
Pick
13 **Jani Rita**
36 **Alexei Semenov**
41 **Tony Salmelainen**
81 **Adam Hauser**
91 **Mike Comrie**
139 Jonathan Fauteux
171 Chris Legg
199 Christian Chartier
256 Tamas Groschl

General Managers' History

Larry Gordon, 1979-80; Glen Sather, 1980-81 to 1999-2000; Kevin Lowe, 2000-01 to 2007-08; Steve Tambellini, 2008-09 to 2011-12; Steve Tambellini and Craig MacTavish, 2012-13; Craig MacTavish, 2013-14.

Craig MacTavish

General Manager

Born: London, Ont., August 15, 1958.

Craig MacTavish was named the fifth general manager of the Edmonton Oilers on April 15, 2013 after starting the 2012-13 season as the Oilers' senior vice president of hockey operations. MacTavish had been head coach of the Chicago Wolves of the American Hockey League in 2011-12, where he led the Vancouver Canucks' American Hockey League affiliate to a 42-27-7 record.

Named the eighth head coach in Oilers history on June 22, 2000, MacTavish compiled a career record of 301-252-103 (.537) in 656 regular-season games over the course of eight seasons (2000-01 to 2008-09). He became the 36th coach in NHL history to win 300-or-more games with a 5-3 win versus the Vancouver Canucks on April 4, 2009. He completed his coaching tenure behind the Oilers bench after the 2008-09 season, ranking second among Edmonton coaches in games coached, wins, losses, ties/overtime losses and winning percentage, and ranked 36th all-time in NHL history in wins and 41st in games coached.

The former Edmonton captain has a 19-17 record (.528) in the Stanley Cup playoffs and became the third coach to lead the Oilers to the Stanley Cup Final in 2006. MacTavish guided the Oilers to their first trip to the Stanley Cup Final since 1990 as Edmonton fell in seven games to the Carolina Hurricanes. After finishing the regular season in eighth place in the NHL's Western Conference standings with a 41-28-13 record, MacTavish led the Oilers to within a game of their sixth Stanley Cup.

After departing the Oilers organization following the 2008-09 season, MacTavish earned a master's degree in business from Queen's University and spent two years as an analyst for the NHL on TSN.

Coaching Record

			Regular Season				Playoffs			
Season	**Team**	**League**	**GC**	**W**	**L**	**O/T**	**GC**	**W**	**L**	**T**
2000-01	Edmonton	NHL	82	39	28	15	6	2	4	....
2001-02	Edmonton	NHL	82	38	28	16	....	....	....	....
2002-03	Edmonton	NHL	82	36	26	20	6	2	4	....
2003-04	Edmonton	NHL	82	36	29	17	....	....	....	....
2004-05	Edmonton				SEASON CANCELLED					
2005-06	Edmonton	NHL	82	41	28	13	24	15	9	....
2006-07	Edmonton	NHL	82	32	43	7	....	....	....	....
2007-08	Edmonton	NHL	82	41	35	6	....	....	....	....
2008-09	Edmonton	NHL	82	38	35	9	....	....	....	....
	NHL Totals		**656**	**301**	**252**	**103**	**36**	**19**	**17**	....

Club Directory

Rexall Place

Edmonton Oilers
11230 – 110 Street
Edmonton, Alberta T5G 3H7
Phone **780/414-GOAL(4625)**
Press Box 780/409-3780
Media Lounge 780/409-3778
FAX 780/409-5890
www.edmontonoilers.com
Capacity: 16,839

Owner & Governor	Daryl A. Katz (Rexall Sports Corp)
President, COO & Alternate Governor	Patrick LaForge
President of Hockey Ops & Alternate Governor	Kevin Lowe
Manager of Hockey Administration	Connie Hadden
Chief Revenue Officer	Stew MacDonald
Chief Financial Officer	Darryl Boessenkool
Executive Assistants to the President / CFO	Lisa Nicolson / Bobbie-Jo Dawe
Security	Michael Fluker

Hockey Operations

General Manager	Craig MacTavish
Senior VP, Hockey Operations	Scott Howson
Asst. G.M & Dir. of Hockey Ops/Legal Affairs	Ricky Olczyk
Head Coach	Dallas Eakins
Assistant Coaches	Kelly Buchberger, Steve Smith
Goaltending Coach / Consultant	Frederic Chabot / Sylvain Rodrigue
Video Coordinator	Myles Fee
Player Development, Sr. Director / Director	Rick Carriere / Mike Sillinger
Consultant, Player Development	Billy Moores
Skating & Skills Coach	Steve Serdachny
Performance / Fitness Consultants	Dr. Kimberley Amirault / Simon Bennett
Dir. of Research, Analysis & Software Development	Sean Draper
Director of Amateur and Free Agent Scouting	Bob Green
Manager of Scouting Information	James McGregor
Head Scouts, Amateur / Pro	Stu MacGregor / Morey Gare
Amateur Scouts	Bob Brown, Bill Dandy, Brad Davis, Kent Hawley, Scott Harlow, Frank Musil, Pelle Eklund, Robert Nordmark, James Crosson, Joseph Cucci, Matti Virmanen, Dave Heinz
Pro Scouts	Michael Abbamont, Dave Semenko, Chris Cichocki, Duane Sutter
Family Liaison	Jill Metz

Medical and Training Staff

Athletic Therapists, Head / Assistant	T.D. Forss / Chris Davie
Equipment Manager / Assistant Managers	Jeff Lang / Brad Harrison, Chris Hamelin
Massage Therapist / Physical Therapy Consultant	Steve Lines / Ryan Williams
Team Medical Chief of Staff	Dr. Dhiren Naidu
Medical Staff	Drs. John Clarke, Jeff Robinson, Ben Eastwood, Tony Sneazwell, David Magee, Brent Saik

Communications and Broadcast

Director, Communications & Media Relations	J.J. Hebert
Manager, Communications & Team Services	Patrick Garland
Coordinator, Communications & Media Relations	Shawn May
Director of Broadcast	Don Metz

Finance and Administration

Vice President, Business Operations & Development	Jason Quilley
Director, Human Resources	Tandy Kustiak
General Counsel	Keely Brown
Vice President, Facility Operations	Tom Cornwall
Manager, Administration & Operations	Sherry Smith
Corporate Controller	Roger Dang
Controller / Assistant Controller	Zeshan Qureshi / Corinne Carey
Accounting	Christine Marceau, Jamie Schenknecht
Coordinator, Accts Rec.	Sheri Carver
Managers, Payroll	Shawna Quigley, Lanette Vermeersch
Director, IT / Analyst	Kevin Flemming / Raphael Caluttung,
Infrastructure Analyst	David Kagan
Director, Operations & Analysis / Business Analyst	Sharon Lyseng / Angela Frecon
Sharepoint Architect	Kelvin Sun
Manager, Ticket Operations	Gavin Morton
Accounting Team Lead	Travis Nielsen, Eric Motuzas
Coordinator, Facility Operations	Gilbert da Silva
Operations Assistant	Macy Beley
Receptionists / Operations Assistant	Sandy Langley, Lynn Berglund

Corporate Partnerships

Sr. Directors, Corp. Partnerships	Lisa Munro, Craig Purcell
Directors, Partnerships / Suites / Sales	Andrew Hore and J.F.Amyot / Bob Haromy / Abe Hajar
Coordinator, Exec Suites / Sponsorship	Michelle Schwendeman
Partner Activation Specialists	Stephen Rausch, Sara Ripko, Brent Frew, Shandy Lo

Ticket Sales and Customer Relations

Sr. Director, Ticket Sales and Customer Relationships	Bill Makris
Manager, Customer Relationships	Jody Young
Ticket Accounts, Sr. Exec. / Execs.	Erik Hapke / Daniel Troiani, Derek Perchaluk, Jennifer Tessier
Customer Experience Reps	Raelene Dufva, Pierre Farage, Keenyn Bijou, Kyla Ostafichuk
Supervisors, Ticket Services	Tony Bao and Dianne Kalita

Marketing

Director, Brand Marketing & CRM	Christine McAnally
Vice President, Communications & Media Content	Steve Hogle
Director, Website & New Media	Marc Ciampa
Digital Media Producer / Reporter-Host	TBA / Tom Gazzola
Coordinator, New Media Content	TBA
Video Producer	Devin Lacombe
Coordinator, Web Apps	Heather Weigum
Director, Brand	Debbie George
Manager. Brand Mktg & Database	Avery Hardy
Sr. Manager, Community & Fan Relations/Marketing	Kevin Radomski
Coordinator, Community & Fan Relations	Darcy Steen
Director / Manager, Social Media	Ryan Frankson / TBA
Coordinator, Social Media & Comm.	Andrea Goss
Lead Designer	Joey Angeles
Event Coordinators	Brad Ellard, Kyle Ferguson
Game Night Director / Team Photographer	Ben Broder / Andy Devlin

Community

Exec. Dir., Oilers Community Foundation	Natalie Minckler
Coordinators	Dwain Tomkow, Diane Gurnham, Lauren Gilley, Erin Barrett
Community Coordinator	Cheryl Thomas

Radio/TV Broadcasters

Television Outlets	Sportsnet, CBXT TV and TSN
Radio Flagship Station	630 CHED (AM); Jack Michaels (play-by-play) & Bob Stauffer (color)

Florida Panthers

Key Off-Season Signings/Acquisitions

2013

June 14 • Acquired RW **Bobby Butler** from Nashville for D **T.J. Brennan**.
July 5 • Signed RW **Joey Crabb**, D **Mike Mottau** and C **Jesse Winchester**.
5 • Re-signed C **Shawn Matthias**.
8 • Signed D **Matt Gilroy**.
15 • Re-signed G **Jacob Markstrom**.
16 • Re-signed C **Greg Rallo** and D **Michael Caruso**.
22 • Re-signed D **Colby Robak**.
24 • Re-signed C **Scott Timmins**.
31 • Signed C **Scott Gomez**.
Aug. 5 • Signed C **Steve Pinizzotto**.

2012-13 Results: 15W-27L-5OTL-1SOL 36PTS
5TH, Southeast Division • 15TH, Eastern Conference

Year-by-Year Record

		Home				Road				Overall									
Season	**GP**	**W**	**L**	**T**	**OL**	**W**	**L**	**T**	**OL**	**W**	**L**	**T**	**OL**	**GF**	**GA**	**Pts.**	**Div. Fin.**	**Conf. Fin.**	**Playoff Result**
2012-13	48	8	11	....	5	7	16	....	1	15	27	....	6	112	171	36	5th, SE	15th, East	Out of Playoffs
2011-12	82	21	9	....	11	17	17	....	7	38	26	....	18	203	227	94	1st, SE	3rd, East	Lost Conf. Quarter-Final
2010-11	82	16	17	....	8	14	23	....	4	30	40	....	12	195	229	72	5th, SE	15th, East	Out of Playoffs
2009-10	82	16	16	....	9	16	21	....	4	32	37	....	13	208	244	77	5th, SE	14th, East	Out of Playoffs
2008-09	82	22	12	....	7	19	18	....	4	41	30	....	11	234	231	93	3rd, SE	9th, East	Out of Playoffs
2007-08	82	18	15	....	8	20	20	....	1	38	35	....	9	216	226	85	3rd, SE	11th, East	Out of Playoffs
2006-07	82	23	12	....	6	12	19	....	10	35	31	....	16	247	257	86	4th, SE	12th, East	Out of Playoffs
2005-06	82	25	11	....	5	12	23	....	6	37	34	....	11	240	257	85	4th, SE	11th, East	Out of Playoffs
2004-05	....	....	....	....	....	....	....	....	....	....	....	....	....	....	....	....			
2003-04	82	16	15	7	3	12	20	8	1	28	35	15	4	188	221	75	4th, SE	12th, East	Out of Playoffs
2002-03	82	8	21	7	5	16	15	6	4	24	36	13	9	176	237	70	4th, SE	13th, East	Out of Playoffs
2001-02	82	11	23	3	4	11	21	7	2	22	44	10	6	180	250	60	4th, SE	14th, East	Out of Playoffs
2000-01	82	12	18	7	4	10	20	6	5	22	38	13	9	200	246	66	3rd, SE	12th, East	Out of Playoffs
1999-2000	82	26	9	4	2	17	18	2	4	43	27	6	6	244	209	98	2nd, SE	5th, East	Lost Conf. Quarter-Final
1998-99	82	17	17	7	....	13	17	11	....	30	34	18	....	210	228	78	2nd, SE	9th, East	Out of Playoffs
1997-98	82	11	24	6	....	13	19	9	....	24	43	15	....	203	256	63	6th, Atl.	12th, East	Out of Playoffs
1996-97	82	21	12	8	....	14	16	11	....	35	28	19	....	221	201	89	3rd, Atl.	4th, East	Lost Conf. Quarter-Final
1995-96	82	25	12	4	....	16	19	6	....	41	31	10	....	254	234	92	3rd, Atl.	4th, East	Lost Final
1994-95	48	9	12	3	....	11	10	3	....	20	22	6	....	115	127	46	5th, Atl.	9th, East	Out of Playoffs
1993-94	84	15	18	9	....	18	16	8	....	33	34	17	....	233	233	83	5th, Atl.	9th, East	Out of Playoffs

2013-14 Schedule

Oct.	Thu.	3	at Dallas	**Jan.**	Sat.	4	Nashville
	Sat.	5	at St. Louis		Mon.	6	at Montreal
	Tue.	8	at Philadelphia		Thu.	9	at Buffalo
	Thu.	10	at Tampa Bay		Sat.	11	at New Jersey
	Fri.	11	Pittsburgh		Tue.	14	NY Islanders
	Sun.	13	Los Angeles*		Thu.	16	San Jose
	Tue.	15	at Nashville		Sat.	18	at Carolina
	Thu.	17	Boston		Mon.	20	at Pittsburgh
	Sat.	19	Minnesota		Tue.	21	at Buffalo
	Tue.	22	Chicago		Fri.	24	Colorado
	Fri.	25	Buffalo		Sun.	26	at Detroit*
	Sun.	27	Tampa Bay*		Tue.	28	at Boston
Nov.	Fri.	1	St. Louis		Thu.	30	at Toronto
	Sat.	2	at Washington	**Feb.**	Sat.	1	at Columbus
	Tue.	5	Edmonton		Tue.	4	Toronto
	Thu.	7	at Boston		Thu.	6	Detroit
	Sat.	9	at Ottawa*		Fri.	7	at Carolina
	Sun.	10	at NY Rangers		Thu.	27	Washington
	Tue.	12	Anaheim	**Mar.**	Sat.	1	at Columbus*
	Fri.	15	at Minnesota		Sun.	2	at NY Islanders*
	Sat.	16	at Colorado		Tue.	4	at Boston
	Tue.	19	at Vancouver		Fri.	7	Buffalo
	Thu.	21	at Edmonton		Sun.	9	Boston*
	Fri.	22	at Calgary		Tue.	11	Phoenix
	Mon.	25	Philadelphia		Thu.	13	at Tampa Bay
	Wed.	27	NY Rangers		Fri.	14	New Jersey
	Sat.	30	Pittsburgh		Sun.	16	Vancouver*
Dec.	Tue.	3	Ottawa		Tue.	18	at San Jose
	Thu.	5	Winnipeg		Thu.	20	at Phoenix
	Sat.	7	at Detroit		Sat.	22	at Los Angeles*
	Sun.	8	at Chicago		Sun.	23	at Anaheim*
	Tue.	10	Detroit		Tue.	25	Ottawa
	Fri.	13	Washington		Thu.	27	Carolina
	Sun.	15	at Montreal		Sat.	29	Montreal
	Tue.	17	at Toronto		Mon.	31	at New Jersey
	Thu.	19	at Ottawa	**Apr.**	Tue.	1	at NY Islanders
	Fri.	20	at Winnipeg		Fri.	4	Calgary
	Mon.	23	Tampa Bay		Sun.	6	Dallas*
	Sat.	28	Detroit		Tue.	8	Philadelphia
	Sun.	29	Montreal*		Thu.	10	Toronto
	Tue.	31	NY Rangers*		Sat.	12	Columbus

* Denotes afternoon game.

Selected third overall behind Ryan Nugent-Hopkins and Gabriel Landeskog in the 2011 Entry Draft, Jonathan Huberdeau made his NHL debut in 2012-13 and won the Calder Trophy as rookie of the year. His 31 points tied him with Nail Yakupov for the lead among rookies, though he had 14 goals to Yakupov's 17.

ATLANTIC DIVISION
21st NHL Season

Franchise date: June 14, 1993

2013-14 Player Personnel

FORWARDS	HT	WT	*Age	Place of Birth	S	2012-13 Club
BARKOV, Aleksander	6-3	209	18	Tampere, Finland	L	Tappara
BERGENHEIM, Sean	5-10	205	29	Helsinki, Finland	L	HIFK
BJUGSTAD, Nick	6-5	211	21	Minneapolis, MN	R	U. of Minnesota-Florida
BUTLER, Bobby	6-0	189	26	Marlborough, MA	R	Albany-N.J.-Nsh
CRABB, Joey	6-1	190	30	Anchorage, AK	R	Alaska-Hershey-Wsh
FLEISCHMANN, Tomas	6-1	192	29	Koprivnice, Czech.	L	Florida
GOC, Marcel	6-1	197	30	Calw, West Germany	L	Mannheim-Florida
GOMEZ, Scott	5-11	198	33	Anchorage, AK	L	Alaska-San Jose
HOWDEN, Quinton	6-3	183	21	Winnipeg, Man.	L	San Antonio-Florida
HUBERDEAU, Jonathan	6-1	171	20	Saint-Jerome, Que.	L	Saint John-Florida
KOPECKY, Tomas	6-3	203	31	Ilava, Czech.	L	Trencin-Florida
MATSUMOTO, Jon	6-0	184	26	Ottawa, Ont.	L	Worcester-Chicago (AHL)
MATTHIAS, Shawn	6-4	220	25	Mississauga, Ont.	L	Florida
PINIZZOTTO, Steve	6-1	200	29	Mississauga, Ont.	R	Chicago (AHL)-Vancouver
RALLO, Greg	6-0	195	32	Gurnee, IL	R	San Antonio-Florida
SELLECK, Eric	6-2	208	25	Spencerville, Ont.	L	San Antonio-Florida
SHORE, Drew	6-2	195	22	Denver, CO	R	San Antonio-Florida
TIMMINS, Scott	5-11	191	24	Hamilton, Ont.	L	San Antonio-Florida
TROCHECK, Vincent	5-11	190	20	Pittsburgh, PA	R	Saginaw-Plymouth
UPSHALL, Scottie	6-0	200	29	Fort McMurray, Alta.	L	Florida
VERSTEEG, Kris	5-11	183	27	Lethbridge, Alta.	R	Florida
WINCHESTER, Jesse	6-1	206	29	Long Sault, Ont.	R	TuTo Hockey-Jokerit
DEFENSEMEN						
CAMPBELL, Brian	5-10	190	34	Strathroy, Ont.	L	Florida
CARUSO, Michael	6-2	191	25	Mississauga, Ont.	L	San Antonio-Florida
GILROY, Matt	6-1	199	29	North Bellmore, NY	R	Connecticut-NY Rangers
GUDBRANSON, Erik	6-5	210	21	Ottawa, Ont.	R	San Antonio-Florida
JOVANOVSKI, Ed	6-3	220	37	Windsor, Ont.	L	Florida
KULIKOV, Dmitry	6-1	205	22	Lipetsk, USSR	L	Yaroslavl-Florida
MOTTAU, Mike	6-0	190	35	Quincy, MA	L	San Antonio-Toronto (AHL)
PETROVIC, Alex	6-4	205	21	Edmonton, Alta.	R	San Antonio-Florida
ROBAK, Colby	6-3	194	23	Dauphin, Man.	L	San Antonio-Florida
WEAVER, Mike	5-10	180	35	Bramalea, Ont.	R	Florida

GOALTENDERS	HT	WT	*Age	Place of Birth	C	2012-13 Club
CLEMMENSEN, Scott	6-2	201	36	Des Moines, IA	L	Florida
GRUMET-MORRIS, Dov	6-2	205	31	Evanston, IL	L	San Antonio
HOUSER, Michael	6-2	190	21	Wexford, PA	L	Cincinnati
MARKSTROM, Jacob	6-3	178	23	Gavle, Sweden	L	San Antonio-Florida

* – Age at start of 2013-14 season

2012-13 Scoring

* – rookie

Regular Season

Pos	#	Player	Team	GP	G	A	Pts	TOI	+/-	PIM	PP	SH	GW	S	%
L	14	Tomas Fleischmann	FLA	48	12	23	35	18:44	–10	16	2	1	2	121	9.9
C	11	* Jonathan Huberdeau	FLA	48	14	17	31	16:55	–15	18	2	0	1	112	12.5
R	82	Tomas Kopecky	FLA	47	15	12	27	17:41	–8	28	4	1	0	92	16.3
D	51	Brian Campbell	FLA	48	8	19	27	26:25	–22	12	6	0	2	70	11.4
C	18	Shawn Matthias	FLA	48	14	7	21	15:11	–8	16	2	1	1	106	13.2
C	57	Marcel Goc	FLA	42	9	10	19	18:16	–6	8	4	0	1	92	9.8
C	88	Peter Mueller	FLA	43	8	9	17	16:15	–11	18	2	0	0	131	6.1
C	15	* Drew Shore	FLA	43	3	10	13	15:48	–10	14	1	1	1	96	3.1
R	12	Jack Skille	FLA	40	3	9	12	13:19	–9	11	0	0	0	69	4.3
D	3	* T.J. Brennan	BUF	10	1	0	1	14:48	–1	6	1	0	0	18	5.6
			FLA	19	2	7	9	17:40	–8	2	0	0	0	24	8.3
			Total	29	3	7	10	16:41	–9	8	1	0	0	42	7.1
D	7	Dmitry Kulikov	FLA	34	3	7	10	20:58	–5	22	2	0	2	52	5.8
D	17	Filip Kuba	FLA	44	1	9	10	21:13	–18	24	0	0	0	50	2.0
D	43	Mike Weaver	FLA	27	1	8	9	20:08	–3	8	0	0	0	21	4.8
R	19	Scottie Upshall	FLA	27	4	1	5	13:29	–8	25	1	0	1	54	7.4
R	27	Alex Kovalev	FLA	14	2	3	5	15:36	–1	6	1	0	1	21	9.5
R	32	Kris Versteeg	FLA	10	2	2	4	16:53	–8	8	0	0	0	20	10.0
C	9	Stephen Weiss	FLA	17	1	3	4	18:27	–13	25	1	0	0	19	5.3
D	44	Erik Gudbranson	FLA	32	0	4	4	18:44	–22	47	0	0	0	49	0.0
D	23	Tyson Strachan	FLA	38	0	4	4	18:57	–13	40	0	0	0	42	0.0
R	22	George Parros	FLA	39	1	1	2	6:36	–15	57	0	0	0	16	6.3
C	37	Greg Rallo	FLA	10	1	0	1	9:33	–5	2	1	0	0	10	10.0
C	27	* Nick Bjugstad	FLA	11	1	0	1	15:12	–8	2	0	0	0	17	5.9
L	76	* Eric Selleck	FLA	2	0	1	1	7:55	2	17	0	0	0	2	0.0
D	55	Ed Jovanovski	FLA	6	0	1	1	15:39	–4	0	0	0	0	6	0.0
D	47	* Colby Robak	FLA	16	0	1	1	15:10	–1	17	0	0	0	15	0.0
D	62	* Michael Caruso	FLA	2	0	0	0	7:55	–1	0	0	0	0	0	0.0
R	52	Jonathan Rheault	FLA	5	0	0	0	10:34	0	0	0	0	0	5	0.0
C	75	* Scott Timmins	FLA	5	0	0	0	10:35	–2	4	0	0	0	6	0.0
D	72	* Alex Petrovic	FLA	6	0	0	0	18:46	–8	25	0	0	0	5	0.0
D	34	Nolan Yonkman	FLA	7	0	0	0	9:46	–1	11	0	0	0	4	0.0
C	42	* Quinton Howden	FLA	18	0	0	0	10:27	–11	2	0	0	0	22	0.0

Goaltending

No.	Goaltender	GPI	Mins	Avg	W	L	OT	EN	SO	GA	SA	S%	G	A	PIM
35	* Jacob Markstrom	23	1266	3.22	8	14	1	5	0	68	685	.901	0	0	0
60	Jose Theodore	15	766	3.29	4	6	3	1	0	42	391	.893	0	0	2
30	Scott Clemmensen	19	866	3.67	3	7	2	1	0	53	421	.874	0	0	0
	Totals	**48**	**2915**	**3.50**	**15**	**27**	**6**	**7**	**0**	**170**	**1504**	**.887**			

Kevin Dineen

Head Coach

Born: Quebec City, Que., October 28, 1963.

Kevin Dineen was named to the position as the head coach of the Florida Panthers on June 1, 2011. In his first year behind the bench in 2011-12, he led the Panthers to the first division title in franchise history and the first playoff berth since the 1999-2000 season.

Prior to being hired in Florida, Dineen had spent the previous six seasons as the head coach of the Portland Pirates (AHL), where he compiled a record of 266-155-59 with a .616 winning percentage, the best in the franchise's history. During this tenure with Portland, his teams won at least 40 games in four of out six seasons, won a pair of division titles (2005-06 and 2010-11) and advanced to the AHL's Eastern Conference Finals twice (2005-06 and 2007-08).

A third-round draft pick of the Hartford Whalers in the 1982 NHL Entry Draft, Dineen played in 1,188 career National Hockey League games with Hartford (1984 to 1991 and 1995 to 1997), Philadelphia (1991 to 1995), Carolina (1997 to 1999), Ottawa (1999-2000) and Columbus (2000 to 2003). Throughout his 19-year NHL playing career, he scored 355 goals with 405 assists and 2,229 penalty minutes. He also served as team captain while playing for Philadelphia, Hartford and Carolina. Dineen appeared in two NHL All-Star Games while playing for Hartford (1988 and 1989). He was named the 1990-91 NHL Man of the Year and was a three-time finalist for the Bill Masterton Memorial Trophy (1995, 2001 and 2002). After retiring as a player on November 5, 2002, Dineen spent two seasons working in the Columbus Blue Jackets hockey operations department.

As a coach for Portland in the AHL for six seasons, Dineen demonstrated the ability to develop young talent. He guided young stars like Corey Perry, Bobby Ryan, Ryan Getzlaf and Dustin Penner before they moved to the NHL with the Anaheim Ducks, then coached three straight winners of the AHL Rookie of the Year award – Buffalo farmhands Nathan Gerbe, Tyler Ennis and Luke Adam.

Dineen comes from one of the most prominent hockey families. His father, Bill, was a two-time NHL All-Star with the Detroit Red Wings who later was head coach of the Flyers for a season and a half at the time Kevin played for Philadelphia. His brothers Gord and Peter also played in the NHL. Gord is currently an assistant with the Toronto Marlies of the AHL, while Peter is a scout for the Columbus Blue Jackets. Brothers Shawn and Jerry played minor league hockey – Shawn is now a professional scout with the Nashville Predators, where he worked with Panthers assistant general manager Mike Santos; Jerry is the video coach of the New York Rangers.

Coaching Record

			Regular Season				Playoffs			
Season	Team	League	GC	W	L	O/T	GC	W	L	T
2005-06	Portland	AHL	80	53	19	8	19	11	8	....
2006-07	Portland	AHL	80	37	31	12	....	....	....	....
2007-08	Portland	AHL	80	45	26	9	18	11	7	....
2008-09	Portland	AHL	80	39	31	10	5	1	4	....
2009-10	Portland	AHL	80	45	24	11	4	0	4	....
2010-11	Portland	AHL	80	47	24	9	12	6	6	....
2011-12	**Florida**	**NHL**	**82**	**38**	**26**	**18**	**7**	**3**	**4**	....
2012-13	**Florida**	**NHL**	**48**	**15**	**27**	**6**	....	....	....	....
	NHL Totals		**130**	**53**	**53**	**24**	**7**	**3**	**4**	....

Brian Campbell had a busy season for Florida in 2012-13, trailing only Ryan Suter of Minnesota for total time on ice and ranking third behind Suter and Ottawa's Erik Karlsson in time-on-ice per game.

Coaching History

Roger Neilson, 1993-94, 1994-95; Doug MacLean, 1995-96, 1996-97; Doug MacLean and Bryan Murray, 1997-98; Terry Murray, 1998-99, 1999-2000; Terry Murray and Duane Sutter, 2000-01; Duane Sutter and Mike Keenan, 2001-02; Mike Keenan, 2002-03; Mike Keenan, Rick Dudley and John Torchetti, 2003-04; Jacques Martin, 2004-05 to 2007-08; Peter DeBoer, 2008-09 to 2010-11; Kevin Dineen, 2011-12 to date.

Club Records

Team

(Figures in brackets for season records are games played; records for fewest points, wins, ties, losses, goals, goals against are for 70 or more games)

Most Points	**98**	1999-2000 (82)
Most Wins	**43**	1999-2000 (82)
Most Ties	**19**	1996-97 (82)
Most Losses	**44**	2001-02 (82)
Most Goals	**254**	1995-96 (82)
Most Goals Against	**257**	2005-06 (82), 2006-07 (82)
Fewest Points	**60**	2001-02 (82)
Fewest Wins	**22**	2000-01 (82), 2001-02 (82)
Fewest Ties	**6**	1999-2000 (82)
Fewest Losses	**26**	2011-12 (82)
Fewest Goals	**176**	2002-03 (82)
Fewest Goals Against	**201**	1996-97 (82)
Longest Winning Streak		
Overall	**7**	Nov. 2-14/95, Mar. 17-29/06, Mar. 2-16/08
Home	**5**	Nov. 5-14/95, Mar. 17-Apr. 1/06, Mar. 6-16/08, Jan. 27-Feb. 13/09, Jan. 16-31/10, Mar. 4-17/12
Away	**5**	Nov. 30-Dec. 12/08
Longest Undefeated Streak		
Overall	**12**	Oct. 5-30/96 (8W, 4T)
Home	**8**	Nov. 5-26/95 (7W, 1T)
Away	**7**	Dec. 7-29/93 (5W, 2T), Oct. 5-29/96 (4W, 3T)
Longest Losing Streak		
Overall	**13**	Feb. 7-Mar. 23/98
Home	**6**	Feb. 25-Mar. 23/98
Away	**13**	Oct. 27-Dec. 17/05
Longest Winless Streak		
Overall	**15**	Feb. 1-Mar. 23/98 (14L, 1T)
Home	**13**	Feb. 5-Mar. 24/03 (11L, 2T/OL)
Away	**16**	Jan. 2-Mar. 21/98 (12L, 4T)
Most Shutouts, Season	**9**	2008-09 (82)
Most PIM, Season	**1,994**	2001-02 (82)
Most Goals, Game	**10**	Nov. 26/97 (Bos. 5 at Fla. 10)

Individual

Most Seasons	**11**	Stephen Weiss
Most Games	**654**	Stephen Weiss
Most Goals, Career	**188**	Olli Jokinen
Most Assists, Career	**249**	Stephen Weiss
Most Points, Career	**419**	Olli Jokinen (188G, 231A)
Most PIM, Career	**1,702**	Paul Laus
Most Shutouts, Career	**26**	Roberto Luongo
Longest Consecutive Games Streak	**376**	Olli Jokinen (Dec. 27/02-Apr. 5/08)
Most Goals, Season	**59**	Pavel Bure (2000-01)
Most Assists, Season	**53**	Viktor Kozlov (1999-2000)
Most Points, Season	**94**	Pavel Bure (1999-2000; 58G, 36A)
Most PIM, Season	**354**	Peter Worrell (2001-02)
Most Points, Defenseman, Season	**57**	Robert Svehla (1995-96; 8G, 49A)
Most Points, Center, Season	**91**	Olli Jokinen (2006-07; 39G, 52A)
Most Points, Right Wing, Season	**94**	Pavel Bure (1999-2000; 58G, 36A)
Most Points, Left Wing, Season	**71**	Ray Whitney (1999-2000; 29G, 42A)
Most Points, Rookie, Season	**50**	Jesse Belanger (1993-94; 17G, 33A)
Most Shutouts, Season	**7**	Roberto Luongo (2003-04), Tomas Vokoun (2009-10)
Most Goals, Game	**4**	Mark Parrish (Oct. 30/98), Pavel Bure (Jan. 1/00), (Feb. 10/01)
Most Assists, Game	**4**	Eight times
Most Points, Game	**6**	Olli Jokinen (Mar. 17/07; 2G, 4A)

Captains' History

Brian Skrudland, 1993-94 to 1996-97; Scott Mellanby, 1997-98 to 2000-01; Pavel Bure, 2001-02; no captain, 2002-03; Olli Jokinen, 2003-04 to 2007-08; no captain, 2008-09; Bryan McCabe, 2009-10, 2010-11; no captain, 2011-12; Ed Jovanovski, 2012-13 to date.

All-time Record vs. Other Clubs

Regular Season

	Total								At Home								On Road							
	GP	W	L	T	OL	GF	GA	PTS	GP	W	L	T	OL	GF	GA	PTS	GP	W	L	T	OL	GF	GA	PTS
Anaheim	23	10	9	3	1	63	61	24	11	4	5	2	0	27	27	10	12	6	4	1	1	36	34	14
Boston	74	32	31	6	5	191	207	75	36	14	15	2	5	104	105	35	38	18	16	4	0	87	102	40
Buffalo	75	28	37	4	6	180	221	66	37	17	16	1	3	100	107	38	38	11	21	3	3	80	114	28
Calgary	23	9	8	3	3	56	56	24	12	4	4	2	2	26	28	12	11	5	4	1	1	30	28	12
Carolina	103	41	40	11	11	290	284	104	52	26	10	8	8	163	122	68	51	15	30	3	3	127	162	36
Chicago	27	9	14	3	1	65	91	22	13	4	7	1	1	27	46	10	14	5	7	2	0	38	45	12
Colorado	29	8	15	3	3	80	102	22	15	4	10	0	1	46	60	9	14	4	5	3	2	34	42	13
Columbus	12	4	4	0	4	28	34	12	6	2	1	0	3	16	18	7	6	2	3	0	1	12	16	5
Dallas	25	11	11	3	0	69	74	25	13	5	7	1	0	26	37	11	12	6	4	2	0	43	37	14
Detroit	23	4	11	5	3	51	74	16	12	2	6	2	2	25	36	8	11	2	5	3	1	26	38	8
Edmonton	22	8	8	3	3	51	64	22	12	5	2	2	3	30	33	15	10	3	6	1	0	21	31	7
Los Angeles	24	9	11	3	1	64	64	22	11	5	2	3	1	29	26	14	13	4	9	0	0	35	38	8
Minnesota	13	3	7	1	2	22	40	9	7	2	4	0	1	14	21	5	6	1	3	1	1	8	19	4
Montreal	74	34	26	6	8	184	194	82	38	18	14	3	3	104	101	42	36	16	12	3	5	80	93	40
Nashville	18	7	5	3	3	43	41	20	9	5	1	1	2	27	19	13	9	2	4	2	1	16	22	7
New Jersey	80	26	41	7	6	172	226	65	40	15	17	4	4	93	101	38	40	11	24	3	2	79	125	27
NY Islanders	81	39	27	8	7	234	220	93	40	21	11	6	2	127	114	50	41	18	16	2	5	107	106	43
NY Rangers	80	32	36	6	6	185	229	76	40	18	15	2	5	98	106	43	40	14	21	4	1	87	123	33
Ottawa	75	28	40	3	4	203	241	63	38	14	22	1	1	110	124	30	37	14	18	2	3	93	117	33
Philadelphia	80	29	39	7	5	200	241	70	39	11	23	1	4	94	133	27	41	18	16	6	1	106	108	43
Phoenix	24	9	10	3	2	69	65	23	11	4	6	0	1	32	29	9	13	5	4	3	1	37	36	14
Pittsburgh	76	32	31	4	9	213	214	77	38	20	15	1	2	111	98	43	38	12	16	3	7	102	116	34
St. Louis	25	7	14	3	1	44	59	18	12	4	5	2	1	26	26	11	13	3	9	1	0	18	33	7
San Jose	24	8	9	7	0	60	71	23	12	4	3	5	0	33	34	13	12	4	6	2	0	27	37	10
Tampa Bay	109	57	32	10	10	341	283	134	54	32	10	4	8	180	137	76	55	25	22	6	2	161	146	58
Toronto	63	24	27	7	5	181	184	60	33	13	13	5	2	93	92	33	30	11	14	2	3	88	92	27
Vancouver	23	6	9	6	2	53	70	20	11	5	4	1	1	27	34	12	12	1	5	5	1	26	36	8
Washington	108	43	49	9	7	274	324	102	54	24	21	4	5	146	150	57	54	19	28	5	2	128	174	45
Winnipeg	79	31	31	5	12	213	250	79	40	18	15	1	6	107	116	43	39	13	16	4	6	106	134	36
Totals	**1492**	**588**	**632**	**142**	**130**	**3879**	**4284**	**1448**	**746**	**320**	**284**	**65**	**77**	**2041**	**2080**	**782**	**746**	**268**	**348**	**77**	**53**	**1838**	**2204**	**666**

Playoffs

	Series	W	L	GP	W	L	T	GF	GA	Last Mtg.	Rnd.	Result
Boston	1	1	0	5	4	1	0	22	16	1996	CQF	W 4-1
Colorado	1	0	1	4	0	4	0	4	15	1996	F	L 0-4
New Jersey	2	0	2	11	3	8	0	23	30	2012	CQF	L 3-4
NY Rangers	1	0	1	5	1	4	0	10	13	1997	CQF	L 1-4
Philadelphia	1	1	0	6	4	2	0	15	11	1996	CSF	W 4-2
Pittsburgh	1	1	0	7	4	3	0	20	15	1996	CF	W 4-3
Totals	**7**	**3**	**4**	**38**	**16**	**22**	**0**	**94**	**100**			

Playoff Results 2013-2009

Year	Round	Opponent	Result	GF	GA
2012	CQF	New Jersey	L 3-4	17	18

Abbreviations: Round: F – Final; **CF** – conference final; **CSF** – conference semi-final; **CQF** – conference quarter-final.

Colorado totals include Quebec, 1993-94 to 1994-95.
Phoenix totals include Winnipeg, 1993-94 to 1995-96.

Carolina totals include Hartford, 1993-94 to 1996-97.
Winnipeg totals include Atlanta Thrashers, 1999-2000 to 2010-11.

2012-13 Results

Jan.	19	Carolina	5-1		8	Winnipeg	2-3*
	21	at Ottawa	0-4		10	Montreal	2-5
	22	at Montreal	1-4		12	Tampa Bay	2-3
	24	Ottawa	1-3		14	at Boston	1-4
	26	Philadelphia	1-7		16	NY Islanders	3-4
	29	at Tampa Bay	2-5		19	at Carolina	4-1
	31	Winnipeg	6-3		21	at NY Rangers	3-1
Feb.	3	at Buffalo	4-3		23	at New Jersey	1-2
	5	at Winnipeg	2-3*		24	at NY Islanders	0-3
	7	at Philadelphia	3-2†		26	at Toronto	2-3
	9	at Washington	0-5		28	Buffalo	5-4†
	12	Washington	5-6*		30	New Jersey	3-2*
	14	Montreal	0-1*	**Apr.**	2	at Tampa Bay	3-2†
	16	Tampa Bay	5-6*		6	Washington	3-4
	18	Toronto	0-3		7	Ottawa	2-1
	21	at Philadelphia	5-2		11	at Winnipeg	2-7
	22	at Pittsburgh	1-3		13	Pittsburgh	1-3
	24	Boston	1-4		16	at NY Islanders	2-5
	26	Pittsburgh	6-4		18	at NY Rangers	1-6
	28	Buffalo	3-4†		20	at New Jersey	2-6
Mar.	2	at Carolina	2-6		21	at Boston	0-3
	3	Carolina	2-3		23	NY Rangers	3-2
	5	Winnipeg	4-1		25	Toronto	0-4
	7	at Washington	1-7		27	at Tampa Bay	5-3

* – Overtime † – Shootout

Entry Draft Selections 2013-1999

Name in bold denotes played in NHL.

2013
Pick
2 Aleksander Barkov
31 Ian McCoshen
92 Evan Cowley
97 Michael Downing
98 Matt Buckles
122 Christopher Clapperton
152 Joshua Brown
206 MacKenzie Weegar

2012
Pick
23 Michael Matheson
84 Steven Hodges
114 Alexander Delnov
174 Francis Beauvillier
194 Jonatan Nielsen

2011
Pick
3 **Jonathan Huberdeau**
33 Rocco Grimaldi
59 Rasmus Bengtsson
64 Vincent Trocheck
76 Logan Shaw
87 Jonathan Racine
91 Kyle Rau
124 Yaroslav Kosov
154 Eddie Wittchow
184 Iiro Pakarinen

2010
Pick
3 **Erik Gudbranson**
19 **Nick Bjugstad**
25 **Quinton Howden**
33 John McFarland
36 **Alex Petrovic**
50 Connor Brickley
69 Joe Basaraba
92 Sam Brittain
93 Ben Gallacher
99 Joonas Donskoi
123 Zach Hyman
153 Corey Durocher
183 R.J. Boyd

2009
Pick
14 **Dmitry Kulikov**
44 **Drew Shore**
67 Josh Birkholz
107 Garrett Wilson
135 Corban Knight
138 Wade Megan
165 **Scott Timmins**

2008
Pick
31 **Jacob Markstrom**
46 **Colby Robak**
80 Adam Comrie
100 AJ Jenks
190 **Matt Bartkowski**

2007
Pick
10 **Keaton Ellerby**
40 **Michal Repik**
71 **Evgeni Dadonov**
101 Matt Rust
131 John Lee
181 Corey Syvret
191 Ryan Watson
202 Sergei Gayduchenko

2006
Pick
10 **Michael Frolik**
73 Brady Calla
103 **Michael Caruso**
116 Derrick Lapoint
155 Peter Aston
193 Marc Cheverie

2005
Pick
20 **Kenndal McArdle**
32 Tyler Plante
90 Dan Collins
93 Olivier Legault
104 Matt Duffy
161 **Brian Foster**
164 Roman Derlyuk
224 Zach Bearson

2004
Pick
7 **Rostislav Olesz**
37 David Shantz
53 **David Booth**
105 Evan Schafer
152 Bret Nasby
267 Spencer Dillon
283 Luke Beaverson

2003
Pick
3 **Nathan Horton**
25 **Anthony Stewart**
38 **Kamil Kreps**
55 **Stefan Meyer**
105 **Martin Lojek**
124 James Pemberton
141 Dan Travis
162 Martin Tuma
171 Denis Stasyuk
223 Dany Roussin
234 Petr Kadlec
264 John Hecimovic
265 **Tanner Glass**

2002
Pick
3 **Jay Bouwmeester**
9 **Petr Taticek**
40 **Rob Globke**
67 **Gregory Campbell**
134 Topi Jaakola
158 Vince Bellissimo
169 Jeremy Swanson
196 Mikael Vuorio
200 Denis Yachmenev
232 Peter Hafner

2001
Pick
4 **Stephen Weiss**
24 **Lukas Krajicek**
34 Greg Watson
64 **Tomas Malec**
68 **Grant McNeill**
117 Mike Woodford
136 Billy Thompson
169 Dustin Johner
200 Toni Koivisto
231 Kyle Bruce
263 Jan Blanar
267 **Ivan Majesky**

2000
Pick
58 Vladimir Sapozhnikov
77 Robert Fried
82 Sean O'Connor
115 Chris Eade
120 Davis Parley
190 **Josh Olson**
234 **Janis Sprukts**
253 Mathew Sommerfeld

1999
Pick
12 **Denis Shvidki**
40 **Alex Auld**
70 **Niklas Hagman**
80 Jean-Francois Laniel
103 Morgan McCormick
109 Rod Sarich
169 Brad Woods
198 Travis Eagles
227 Jonathon Charron

General Managers' History

Bob Clarke, 1993-94; Bryan Murray, 1994-95 to 1999-2000; Bryan Murray and Bill Torrey, 2000-01; Bill Torrey and Chuck Fletcher, 2001-02; Rick Dudley, 2002-03, 2003-04; Mike Keenan, 2004-05, 2005-06; Jacques Martin, 2006-07 to 2008-09; Randy Sexton, 2009-10; Dale Tallon, 2010-11 to date.

Dale Tallon

Executive Vice President and General Manager

Born: Noranda, Que., October 19, 1950.

Dale Tallon was named general manager of the Florida Panthers on May 17, 2010. After joining Florida, Tallon conducted a successful 2010 NHL Entry Draft that saw the club stockpile 13 picks, including three first-round selections (No. 3 - D Erik Gudbranson, No. 19 - C Nick Bjugstad and No. 25 - C Quinton Howden). The hiring of head coach Kevin Dineen, and acquisitions such as Brian Campbell before the 2011-12 season helped Florida win the first division title in franchise history and return to the playoffs for the first time since 1999-2000. Jonathan Huberdeau, whom the Panthers selected third overall in 2011, won the Calder Trophy as rookie of the year in 2012-13.

Prior to joining the Panthers, Tallon spent 33 years with the Blackhawks organization as a front office executive, player and broadcast personality. He served as Chicago's general manager from June 2005 to July 2009 after having served as assistant general manager from November 2003 to June 2005. Tallon was responsible for drafting or acquiring many of the players who led the Blackhawks to the Stanley Cup in 2010, including Jonathan Toews, Patrick Kane, Marian Hossa, Patrick Sharp, Kris Versteeg, John Madden and Brian Campbell.

As a player, Tallon was the Vancouver Canucks' first-round selection (second overall) in the 1970 NHL Draft. The Noranda, Quebec native played in 642 NHL contests with Vancouver (1970 to 1973), Chicago (1973 to 1978) and Pittsburgh (1978 to 1980) registering 336 points (98 goals, 238 assists) and 568 penalty minutes.Tallon recorded a career-high 17 goals in 69 games with Vancouver during the 1971-72 season and appeared in the 1971 and 1972 NHL All-Star Games. In 1972, Tallon was picked as an alternate for Team Canada for the Summit Series against the Soviet Union. After retiring following the 1979-80 season, Tallon served as a color analyst for Chicago radio and television broadcasts for 16 seasons.

Prior to joining the Panthers, Tallon spent the 2009-10 season serving as a senior advisor of hockey operations for the Blackhawks. He also served four years (1998 to 2002) as director of player personnel before returning to the radio and television booth prior to the 2002-03 season.

Club Directory

BB&T Center

Florida Panthers
BB&T Center
One Panther Parkway
Sunrise, FL 33323
Phone **954/835-7000**
FAX 954/835-7700
www.floridapanthers.com
Capacity: 17,040

Ownership	
General Partner/Chairman of the Board/ Chief Executive Officer/Governor	Cliff Viner
Partners	Alan Cohen, Steve Cohen, David Epstein, Dr. Elliott Hahn, H. Wayne Huizenga, Bernie Kosar, Richard C. Lehman, M.D., Albert E. Maroone, Michael E. Maroone, James L Nederlander, Robert Printz, Michael Rashes, Jordan Zimmerman
Executive	
President	Michael R. Yormark
Exec. Vice President & G.M., Hockey Ops	Dale Tallon
Sr. Vice President, Sales & Service	Ryan McCoy
Sr. Vice President, Communications and Public Affairs	Matthew F. Sacco
Sr. Vice President / G.M., BB&T Center	Brett Stefansson
Sr. Vice President, Marketing & Brand Strategy	Steve Ziff
Vice President/G.M., Saveology.com Iceplex	Jeff Campol
Vice President, Human Resources & Payroll	Elisa Hernandez
Vice President, Managing Dir. 360 Premium	Rick Lassiter
Vice President, Sales & Fan Experience	Shawn Kuzmin
Vice President, Finance & Controller	Luciana Midili
Vice President, Broadcasting & Panthers Alumni	Randy Moller
Vice President, Chief Financial Officer	Louis Partenza
Vice President, Partnership Marketing	Matthew Rickoff
Vice President, General Counsel	Ed Wildermuth
Assistant to the President	Israel Mantilla
Hockey Operations	
Exec. Vice President/General Manager	Dale Tallon
Assistant General Manager	Mike Santos
Alternate Governor	William Torrey
Team Services Manager	Mike Dixon
Director, Scouting	Scott Luce
Director, Player Development	Brian Skrudland
Manager, Player Development	Bryan McCabe
Pro Scout	Peter Mahovlich, Al Tuer
Head Amateur Scout	Erin Ginnell
Assistant Head Amateur Scout	Jason Bukala
Amateur Scouts	Fred Bandel, Craig Demetrick, Paul Gallagher, Jari Kekalainen, Kent Nilsson, Vadim Podrezov, Mike Yandle
Coaching Staff	
Head Coach	Kevin Dineen
Assistant Coaches	Gord Murphy, Craig Ramsay
Goaltending Coach	Robb Tallas
Strength & Conditioning Coach	Craig Slaunwhite
Skating & Skills Coach	Paul Vincent
Video Coach	Jason Cipolla
Training Staff	
Athletic Trainer	David Zenobi
Assistant Athletic Trainer	Tommy Alva
Physical Therapist	Steve Dischiavi
Equipment Manager	Chris Scoppetto
Assistant Equipment Manager	Chris Moody
Equipment Assistant	Jason MacDonald
Communications and Media Content	
Director, Communications	Justin Copertino
Sr. Manager, Communications & Digital Media	Glenn Odebralski
Broadcasting	
Television	FOX Sports Florida
Play-By-Play	Steve Goldstein
Television Analyst	Bill Lindsay
Panthers Preview/Review Host	Allison Williams/Frank Forte
Radio	560 WQAM
Radio Play-By-Play	Randy Moller

Los Angeles Kings

2012-13 Results: 27W-16L-1OTL-4SOL 59PTS
2ND, Pacific Division • 5TH, Western Conference

Key Off-Season Signings/Acquisitions

2013

June 18 • Re-signed D **Slava Voynov**.

23 • Acquired RW **Matt Frattin**, G **Ben Scrivens** and a 2nd-round pick in the 2014 or 2015 NHL Draft from Toronto for G **Jonathan Bernier**.

July 4 • Re-signed D **Keaton Ellerby**.

5 • Signed D **Jeff Schultz**.

12 • Re-signed D **Jake Muzzin**.

15 • Re-signed D **Alec Martinez**.

16 • Acquired LW **Daniel Carcillo** from Chicago for a conditional pick in the 2015 NHL Draft.

18 • Re-signed RW **Dustin Brown**.

21 • Re-signed C **Jordan Nolan**.

23 • Re-signed C **Trevor Lewis**.

Aug. 2 • Re-signed LW **Kyle Clifford**.

Kings forwards Jeff Carter (left) and Anze Kopitar look for a scoring chance in front of Sharks goalie Antti Niemi and defenseman Douglas Murray. Carter ranked among the NHL leaders with 26 goals in 2012-13 while Kopitar led the Kings with 32 assists and 42 points.

2013-14 Schedule

Oct.	Thu.	3	at Minnesota
	Fri.	4	at Winnipeg
	Mon.	7	NY Rangers
	Wed.	9	Ottawa
	Fri.	11	at Carolina
	Sun.	13	at Florida*
	Tue.	15	at Tampa Bay
	Thu.	17	at Nashville
	Sat.	19	Dallas
	Mon.	21	Calgary
	Thu.	24	Phoenix
	Sun.	27	Edmonton
	Tue.	29	at Phoenix
	Wed.	30	San Jose
Nov.	Sat.	2	Nashville
	Thu.	7	Buffalo
	Sat.	9	Vancouver
	Tue.	12	at Buffalo
	Thu.	14	at NY Islanders
	Fri.	15	at New Jersey
	Sun.	17	at NY Rangers
	Tue.	19	Tampa Bay
	Thu.	21	New Jersey
	Sat.	23	Colorado
	Mon.	25	at Vancouver
	Wed.	27	at San Jose
	Sat.	30	Calgary
Dec.	Mon.	2	St. Louis
	Tue.	3	at Anaheim
	Sat.	7	NY Islanders
	Tue.	10	at Montreal
	Wed.	11	at Toronto
	Sat.	14	at Ottawa*
	Sun.	15	at Chicago
	Tue.	17	Edmonton
	Thu.	19	San Jose
	Sat.	21	Colorado*
	Mon.	23	Dallas
	Sat.	28	at Nashville
	Mon.	30	at Chicago
	Tue.	31	at Dallas
Jan.	Thu.	2	at St. Louis
	Sat.	4	Vancouver
	Tue.	7	Minnesota
	Thu.	9	Boston
	Sat.	11	Detroit
	Mon.	13	Vancouver
	Thu.	16	at St. Louis
	Sat.	18	at Detroit
	Mon.	20	at Boston*
	Tue.	21	at Columbus
	Thu.	23	at Anaheim
	Sat.	25	Anaheim
	Mon.	27	at San Jose
	Tue.	28	at Phoenix
	Thu.	30	Pittsburgh
Feb.	Sat.	1	Philadelphia*
	Mon.	3	Chicago
	Thu.	6	Columbus
	Wed.	26	at Colorado
	Thu.	27	at Calgary
Mar.	Sat.	1	Carolina*
	Mon.	3	Montreal
	Thu.	6	at Winnipeg
	Sun.	9	at Edmonton
	Mon.	10	at Calgary
	Thu.	13	Toronto
	Sat.	15	Anaheim
	Mon.	17	Phoenix
	Thu.	20	Washington
	Sat.	22	Florida*
	Mon.	24	at Philadelphia
	Tue.	25	at Washington
	Thu.	27	at Pittsburgh
	Sat.	29	Winnipeg
	Mon.	31	Minnesota
Apr.	Wed.	2	Phoenix
	Thu.	3	at San Jose
	Sat.	5	at Vancouver
	Wed.	9	at Calgary
	Thu.	10	at Edmonton
	Sat.	12	Anaheim

* Denotes afternoon game.

Year-by-Year Record

Season	GP	Home W	Home L	Home T	Home OL	Road W	Road L	Road T	Road OL	Overall W	Overall L	Overall T	Overall OL	GF	GA	Pts.	Div. Fin.	Conf. Fin.	Playoff Result
2012-13	48	19	4	....	1	8	12	....	4	27	16	....	5	133	118	59	2nd, Pac.	5th, West	Lost Conf. Final
2011-12	**82**	**22**	**14**	....	**5**	**18**	**13**	....	**10**	**40**	**27**	....	**15**	**194**	**179**	**95**	**3rd, Pac.**	**8th, West**	**Won Stanley Cup**
2010-11	82	25	13	....	3	21	17	....	3	46	30	....	6	219	198	98	4th, Pac.	7th, West	Lost Conf. Quarter-Final
2009-10	82	22	13	....	6	24	14	....	3	46	27	....	9	241	219	101	3rd, Pac.	6th, West	Lost Conf. Quarter-Final
2008-09	82	18	15	....	8	16	22	....	3	34	37	....	11	207	234	79	5th, Pac.	14th, West	Out of Playoffs
2007-08	82	17	21	....	3	15	22	....	4	32	43	....	7	231	266	71	5th, Pac.	15th, West	Out of Playoffs
2006-07	82	16	16	....	9	11	25	....	5	27	41	....	14	227	283	68	4th, Pac.	14th, West	Out of Playoffs
2005-06	82	26	14	....	1	16	21	....	4	42	35	....	5	249	270	89	4th, Pac.	10th, West	Out of Playoffs
2004-05	....	....	....	....	....	....	....	....	....	....	....	....	....	....	....	....			
2003-04	82	15	16	9	1	13	13	7	8	28	29	16	9	205	217	81	3rd, Pac.	11th, West	Out of Playoffs
2002-03	82	19	19	2	1	14	18	4	5	33	37	6	6	203	221	78	3rd, Pac.	10th, West	Out of Playoffs
2001-02	82	22	12	6	1	18	15	5	3	40	27	11	4	214	190	95	3rd, Pac.	7th, West	Lost Conf. Quarter-Final
2000-01	82	20	12	8	1	18	16	5	2	38	28	13	3	252	228	92	3rd, Pac.	7th, West	Lost Conf. Semi-Final
1999-2000	82	21	13	5	2	18	14	7	2	39	27	12	4	245	228	94	2nd, Pac.	5th, West	Lost Conf. Quater-Final
1998-99	82	18	20	3	....	14	25	2	....	32	45	5	....	189	222	69	5th, Pac.	11th, West	Out of Playoffs
1997-98	82	22	16	3	....	16	17	8	....	38	33	11	....	227	225	87	2nd, Pac.	5th, West	Lost Conf. Quater-Final
1996-97	82	18	16	7	....	10	27	4	....	28	43	11	....	214	268	67	6th, Pac.	12th, West	Out of Playoffs
1995-96	82	16	16	9	....	8	24	9	....	24	40	18	....	256	302	66	6th, Pac.	12th, West	Out of Playoffs
1994-95	48	7	11	6	....	9	12	3	....	16	23	9	....	142	174	41	4th, Pac.	9th, West	Out of Playoffs
1993-94	84	18	19	5	....	9	26	7	....	27	45	12	....	294	322	66	5th, Pac.	10th, West	Out of Playoffs
1992-93	84	22	15	5	....	17	20	5	....	39	35	10	....	338	340	88	3rd, Smythe		Lost Final
1991-92	80	20	11	9	....	15	20	5	....	35	31	14	....	287	296	84	2nd, Smythe		Lost Div. Semi-Final
1990-91	80	26	9	5	....	20	15	5	....	46	24	10	....	340	254	102	1st, Smythe		Lost Div. Final
1989-90	80	21	16	3	....	13	23	4	....	34	39	7	....	338	337	75	4th, Smythe		Lost Div. Final
1988-89	80	25	12	3	....	17	19	4	....	42	31	7	....	376	335	91	2nd, Smythe		Lost Div. Final
1987-88	80	19	18	3	....	11	24	5	....	30	42	8	....	318	359	68	4th, Smythe		Lost Div. Semi-Final
1986-87	80	20	17	3	....	11	24	5	....	31	41	8	....	318	341	70	4th, Smythe		Lost Div. Semi-Final
1985-86	80	9	27	4	....	14	22	4	....	23	49	8	....	284	389	54	5th, Smythe		Out of Playoffs
1984-85	80	20	14	6	....	14	18	8	....	34	32	14	....	339	326	82	4th, Smythe		Lost Div. Semi-Final
1983-84	80	13	19	8	....	10	25	5	....	23	44	13	....	309	376	59	5th, Smythe		Out of Playoffs
1982-83	80	20	13	7	....	7	28	5	....	27	41	12	....	308	365	66	5th, Smythe		Out of Playoffs
1981-82	80	19	15	6	....	5	26	9	....	24	41	15	....	314	369	63	4th, Smythe		Lost Div. Final
1980-81	80	22	11	7	....	21	13	6	....	43	24	13	....	337	290	99	2nd, Norris		Lost Prelim. Round
1979-80	80	18	13	9	....	12	23	5	....	30	36	14	....	290	313	74	2nd, Norris		Lost Prelim. Round
1978-79	80	20	13	7	....	14	21	5	....	34	34	12	....	292	286	80	3rd, Norris		Lost Prelim. Round
1977-78	80	18	16	6	....	13	18	9	....	31	34	15	....	243	245	77	3rd, Norris		Lost Prelim. Round
1976-77	80	20	13	7	....	14	18	8	....	34	31	15	....	271	241	83	2nd, Norris		Lost Quarter-Final
1975-76	80	22	13	5	....	16	20	4	....	38	33	9	....	263	265	85	2nd, Norris		Lost Quarter-Final
1974-75	80	22	7	11	....	20	10	10	....	42	17	21	....	269	185	105	2nd, Norris		Lost Prelim. Round
1973-74	78	22	13	4	....	11	20	8	....	33	33	12	....	233	231	78	3rd, West		Lost Quarter-Final
1972-73	78	21	11	7	....	10	25	4	....	31	36	11	....	232	245	73	6th, West		Out of Playoffs
1971-72	78	14	23	2	....	6	26	7	....	20	49	9	....	206	305	49	7th, West		Out of Playoffs
1970-71	78	17	14	8	....	8	26	5	....	25	40	13	....	239	303	63	5th, West		Out of Playoffs
1969-70	76	12	22	4	....	2	30	6	....	14	52	10	....	168	290	38	6th, West		Out of Playoffs
1968-69	76	19	14	5	....	5	28	5	....	24	42	10	....	185	260	58	4th, West		Lost Semi-Final
1967-68	74	20	13	4	....	11	20	6	....	31	33	10	....	200	224	72	2nd, West		Lost Quarter-Final

PACIFIC DIVISION
47th NHL Season

Franchise date: June 5, 1967

2013-14 Player Personnel

FORWARDS	HT	WT	*Age	Place of Birth	S	2012-13 Club
BROWN, Dustin	6-0	212	28	Ithaca, NY	R	Zurich-Los Angeles
CARCILLO, Daniel	6-0	203	28	King City, Ont.	L	Chicago
CARTER, Jeff	6-4	210	28	London, Ont.	R	Los Angeles
CLIFFORD, Kyle	6-2	209	22	Ayr, Ont.	L	Ontario-Los Angeles
FRASER, Colin	6-1	189	28	Sicamous, B.C.	L	Los Angeles
FRATTIN, Matt	6-0	200	25	Edmonton, Alta.	R	Toronto (AHL)-Toronto
KING, Dwight	6-4	232	24	Meadow Lake, Sask.	L	Los Angeles-Manchester
KOPITAR, Anze	6-3	225	26	Jesenice, Yugoslavia	L	Mora-Los Angeles
LEWIS, Trevor	6-1	199	26	Salt Lake City, UT	R	Utah-Los Angeles
NOLAN, Jordan	6-3	225	24	St. Catharines, Ont.	L	Manchester-Los Angeles
RICHARDS, Mike	5-11	200	28	Kenora, Ont.	L	Los Angeles
STOLL, Jarret	6-1	212	31	Melville, Sask.	R	Los Angeles
WILLIAMS, Justin	6-1	188	31	Cobourg, Ont.	R	Los Angeles
DEFENSEMEN						
DOUGHTY, Drew	6-1	208	23	London, Ont.	R	Los Angeles
ELLERBY, Keaton	6-5	221	24	Strathmore, Alta.	L	Florida-Los Angeles
GREENE, Matt	6-3	232	30	Grand Ledge, MI	R	Los Angeles
MARTINEZ, Alec	6-1	206	26	Rochester Hills, MI	L	TPS-Allen-Los Angeles
MITCHELL, Willie	6-3	212	36	Port McNeill, B.C.	L	Los Angeles
REGEHR, Robyn	6-3	225	33	Recife, Brazil	L	Buffalo-Los Angeles
SCHULTZ, Jeff	6-6	230	27	Calgary, Alta.	L	Washington
VOYNOV, Slava	6-0	190	23	Chelyabinsk, USSR	R	Manchester-Los Angeles

GOALTENDERS	HT	WT	*Age	Place of Birth	C	2012-13 Club
QUICK, Jonathan	6-1	218	27	Milford, CT	L	Los Angeles
SCRIVENS, Ben	6-2	192	27	Spruce Grove, Alta.	L	Toronto (AHL)-Toronto

* – Age at start of 2013-14 season

Darryl Sutter

Head Coach

Born: Viking, Alta., August 19, 1958.

Darryl Sutter was named the 24th head coach in Kings history on December 20, 2011. The team had a record of 15-14-4 when Sutter took over and posted a mark of 25-13-11 under him. A strong finish saw them claim the eighth and final playoff spot in the Western Conference and an impressive 16-4 playoff run saw the Kings win the Stanley Cup for the first time in franchise history. It was also Sutter's first Stanley Cup win. The Kings reached the Western Conference final in 2013.

Sutter had a career head coaching record of 409-320-131 in 860 regular season games over 12 seasons when hired by the Kings. His team's had eclipsed the 40-win mark four times, 100 points twice and finished in first place three times. He is also only one of nine head coaches in NHL history to lead three different teams to 100 wins. Only Scotty Bowman and Ron Wilson have coached four different teams to 100 wins. Sutter led the Calgary Flames to Game 7 of the 2004 Stanley Cup Final and Chicago to the 1995 Western Conference Final.

Before coming to Los Angeles, Sutter was the general manager of the Flames from the 2003-04 season until he resigned on December 28, 2010. Sutter also served as Calgary's head coach from 2002-03 through 2005-06. He was the head coach of the San Jose Sharks for parts of six seasons (1997-98 through the start of the 2002-03 season), where he worked under current Kings president/general manager Dean Lombardi, then the GM of the Sharks. As in Calgary, the Sharks increased their point total every season Sutter was the head coach. He led San Jose to a first-place finish in the Pacific Division in 2001-02 with a 44-27-11 record (99 points). Sutter was relieved of his duties with the Sharks on December 1, 2002.

Sutter was the head coach of the Chicago Blackhawks for three seasons (1992-93 through 1994-95) and served as Chicago's assistant coach in 1987-88 and as associate coach in 1990-91 and 1991-92. He led Chicago to a first-place finish in the Norris Division (and the best record in the Campbell Conference) in 1992-93 with a 47-25-12 record and 106 points. Sutter's head coaching experience also includes two seasons in the International Hockey League, where he coached the Saginaw Hawks in 1988-89 and he led the Indianapolis Ice to the Turner Cup Championship in 1989-90.

As a player, Sutter played in 406 career NHL regular season games (all with the Blackhawks), recording 279 points (161 goals, 118 assists) and 288 penalty minutes. He scored 20-plus goals in five of his eight NHL seasons, including a career-high 40 goals in 1980-81. He served as Chicago's captain from 1982 to 1985 and again in 1986-87. Darryl is one of seven Sutter brothers, six of whom played in the NHL. His son Brett currently plays in the Carolina Hurricanes organization.

Coaching Record

			Regular Season				Playoffs			
Season	Team	League	GC	W	L	O/T	GC	W	L	T
1992-93	Chicago	NHL	84	47	25	12	4	0	4	....
1993-94	Chicago	NHL	84	39	36	9	6	2	4	....
1994-95	Chicago	NHL	48	24	19	5	16	9	7	....
1997-98	San Jose	NHL	82	34	38	10	6	2	4	....
1998-99	San Jose	NHL	82	31	33	18	6	2	4	....
99-2000	San Jose	NHL	82	35	30	17	12	5	7	....
2000-01	San Jose	NHL	82	40	27	15	6	2	4	....
2001-02	San Jose	NHL	82	44	27	11	12	7	5	....
2002-03	San Jose	NHL	24	8	12	4	....	....	....	....
2002-03	Calgary	NHL	46	19	18	9	....	....	....	....
2003-04	Calgary	NHL	82	42	30	10	26	15	11	....
2004-05	Calgary				SEASON CANCELLED					
2005-06	Calgary	NHL	82	46	25	11	7	3	4	....
2011-12♦	Los Angeles	NHL	49	25	13	11	20	16	4	....
2012-13	Los Angeles	NHL	48	27	16	5	18	9	9	....
	NHL Totals		957	461	349	147	139	72	67	....

♦ Stanley Cup win.

2012-13 Scoring

* – rookie

Regular Season

Pos	#	Player	Team	GP	G	A	Pts	TOI	+/–	PIM	PP	SH	GW	S	%
C	11	Anze Kopitar	L.A.	47	10	32	42	20:28	14	16	0	0	1	98	10.2
C	77	Jeff Carter	L.A.	48	26	7	33	17:34	0	16	8	0	8	133	19.5
R	14	Justin Williams	L.A.	48	11	22	33	16:59	15	22	1	0	3	142	7.7
C	10	Mike Richards	L.A.	48	12	20	32	16:21	–8	42	6	0	3	82	14.6
L	23	Dustin Brown	L.A.	46	18	11	29	19:30	6	22	8	0	1	142	12.7
D	26	Slava Voynov	L.A.	48	6	19	25	22:18	5	14	1	0	2	79	7.6
D	8	Drew Doughty	L.A.	48	6	16	22	26:23	4	36	3	0	0	114	5.3
C	28	Jarret Stoll	L.A.	48	7	11	18	16:31	1	28	1	1	3	73	9.6
D	6*	Jake Muzzin	L.A.	45	7	9	16	17:53	16	35	3	0	1	77	9.1
L	13	Kyle Clifford	L.A.	48	7	7	14	10:36	1	51	0	0	1	56	12.5
C	22	Trevor Lewis	L.A.	48	5	9	14	15:12	5	19	0	1	2	92	5.4
R	25	Dustin Penner	L.A.	33	2	12	14	12:41	–2	18	0	0	0	61	3.3
D	7	Rob Scuderi	L.A.	48	1	11	12	21:47	–6	4	0	0	0	33	3.0
L	74	Dwight King	L.A.	47	4	6	10	12:45	–3	11	0	0	0	60	6.7
C	24	Colin Fraser	L.A.	34	2	5	7	9:22	–4	25	0	0	0	19	10.5
C	71	Jordan Nolan	L.A.	44	2	4	6	8:28	–5	46	0	0	0	23	8.7
R	15	Brad Richardson	L.A.	16	1	5	6	10:53	2	10	0	0	0	27	3.7
C	73*	Tyler Toffoli	L.A.	10	2	3	5	11:58	3	2	1	0	0	20	10.0
D	27	Alec Martinez	L.A.	27	1	4	5	16:01	–2	10	0	0	0	30	3.3
D	44	Robyn Regehr	BUF	29	0	2	2	18:39	–4	21	0	0	0	15	0.0
			L.A.	12	0	2	2	21:16	0	2	0	0	0	12	0.0
			Total	41	0	4	4	19:25	–4	23	0	0	0	27	0.0
D	5	Keaton Ellerby	FLA	9	0	0	0	15:11	–2	36	0	0	0	8	0.0
			L.A.	35	0	3	3	14:17	5	16	0	0	0	15	0.0
			Total	44	0	3	3	14:28	3	52	0	0	0	23	0.0
D	2	Matt Greene	L.A.	5	0	1	1	15:17	–1	8	0	0	0	3	0.0

Goaltending

No.	Goaltender	GPI	Mins	Avg	W	L	OT	EN	SO	GA	SA	S%	G	A	PIM
45	Jonathan Bernier	14	768	1.88	9	3	1	1	1	24	306	.922	0	1	0
32	Jonathan Quick	37	2134	2.45	18	13	4	2	1	87	889	.902	0	0	2
	Totals	**48**	**2917**	**2.34**	**27**	**16**	**5**	**3**	**2**	**114**	**1198**	**.905**			

Playoffs

Pos	#	Player	Team	GP	G	A	Pts	TOI	+/–	PIM	PP	SH	GW	OT	S	%
C	77	Jeff Carter	L.A.	18	6	7	13	19:37	6	14	1	0	0	0	56	10.7
D	26	Slava Voynov	L.A.	18	6	7	13	21:54	9	0	0	0	4	1	34	17.6
C	10	Mike Richards	L.A.	15	3	9	12	19:08	5	8	1	0	0	0	23	13.0
R	14	Justin Williams	L.A.	18	6	3	9	18:35	0	8	1	0	2	0	57	10.5
C	11	Anze Kopitar	L.A.	18	3	6	9	21:14	–2	12	1	0	1	0	32	9.4
C	73*	Tyler Toffoli	L.A.	12	2	4	6	10:46	5	0	1	0	0	0	19	10.5
R	25	Dustin Penner	L.A.	18	3	2	5	14:32	4	8	0	0	1	0	35	8.6
L	74	Dwight King	L.A.	18	2	3	5	14:46	–4	2	0	1	0	0	19	10.5
D	8	Drew Doughty	L.A.	18	2	3	5	27:57	–7	8	1	0	0	0	32	6.3
L	23	Dustin Brown	L.A.	18	3	1	4	18:46	2	8	2	0	0	0	31	9.7
C	22	Trevor Lewis	L.A.	18	1	2	3	16:24	–3	2	1	0	1	0	25	4.0
D	6*	Jake Muzzin	L.A.	17	0	3	3	15:50	–2	6	0	0	0	0	14	0.0
D	7	Rob Scuderi	L.A.	18	0	3	3	23:18	9	0	0	0	0	0	12	0.0
D	27	Alec Martinez	L.A.	7	0	2	2	13:14	–4	8	0	0	0	0	4	0.0
D	2	Matt Greene	L.A.	9	0	2	2	15:28	3	6	0	0	0	0	4	0.0
L	13	Kyle Clifford	L.A.	14	0	2	2	10:21	–1	8	0	0	0	0	16	0.0
C	24	Colin Fraser	L.A.	16	0	2	2	8:27	–2	10	0	0	0	0	6	0.0
R	15	Brad Richardson	L.A.	11	0	1	1	10:46	–3	0	0	0	0	0	10	0.0
C	28	Jarret Stoll	L.A.	12	0	1	1	16:01	–2	4	0	0	0	0	11	0.0
D	44	Robyn Regehr	L.A.	18	0	1	1	21:13	–8	6	0	0	0	0	16	0.0
L	70*	Tanner Pearson	L.A.	1	0	0	0	5:44	0	0	0	0	0	0	0	0.0
D	5	Keaton Ellerby	L.A.	5	0	0	0	10:43	0	0	0	0	0	0	3	0.0
C	71	Jordan Nolan	L.A.	7	0	0	0	8:52	0	4	0	0	0	0	1	0.0

Goaltending

No.	Goaltender	GPI	Mins	Avg	W	L	EN	SO	GA	SA	S%	G	A	PIM
45	Jonathan Bernier	1	30	0.00	0	0	0	0	0	9	1.000	0	0	0
32	Jonathan Quick	18	1099	1.86	9	9	0	3	34	518	.934	0	1	14
	Totals	**18**	**1135**	**1.80**	**9**	**9**	**0**	**3**	**34**	**527**	**.935**			

Captains' History

Bob Wall, 1967-68, 1968-69; Larry Cahan, 1969-70, 1970-71; Bob Pulford, 1971-72, 1972-73; Terry Harper, 1973-74, 1974-75; Mike Murphy, 1975-76 to 1980-81; Dave Lewis, 1981-82, 1982-83; Terry Ruskowski, 1983-84, 1984-85; Dave Taylor, 1985-86 to 1988-89; Wayne Gretzky, 1989-90 to 1991-92; Wayne Gretzky and Luc Robitaille, 1992-93; Wayne Gretzky, 1993-94, 1994-95; Wayne Gretzky and Rob Blake, 1995-96; Rob Blake, 1996-97 to 2000-01; Mattias Norstrom, 2001-02 to 2006-07; Rob Blake, 2007-08; Dustin Brown, 2008-09 to date.

Coaching History

Red Kelly, 1967-68, 1968-69; Hal Laycoe and Johnny Wilson, 1969-70; Larry Regan, 1970-71; Larry Regan and Fred Glover, 1971-72; Bob Pulford, 1972-73 to 1976-77; Ron Stewart, 1977-78; Bob Berry, 1978-79 to 1980-81; Parker MacDonald and Don Perry, 1981-82; Don Perry, 1982-83; Don Perry, Rogie Vachon and Roger Neilson, 1983-84; Pat Quinn, 1984-85, 1985-86; Pat Quinn and Mike Murphy 1986-87; Mike Murphy, Rogie Vachon and Robbie Ftorek, 1987-88; Robbie Ftorek, 1988-89; Tom Webster, 1989-90 to 1991-92; Barry Melrose, 1992-93, 1993-94; Barry Melrose and Rogie Vachon, 1994-95; Larry Robinson, 1995-96 to 1998-99; Andy Murray, 1999-2000 to 2004-05; Andy Murray and John Torchetti, 2005-06; Marc Crawford, 2006-07, 2007-08; Terry Murray, 2008-09 to 2010-11; Terry Murray and Darryl Sutter, 2011-12; Darryl Sutter, 2012-13 to date.

Club Records

Team

(Figures in brackets for season records are games played; records for fewest points, wins, ties, losses, goals, goals against are for 70 or more games)

Most Points	**105**	1974-75 (80)
Most Wins	**46**	1990-91 (80), 2009-10 (82), 2010-11 (82)
Most Ties	**21**	1974-75 (80)
Most Losses	**52**	1969-70 (76)
Most Goals	**376**	1988-89 (80)
Most Goals Against	**389**	1985-86 (80)
Fewest Points	**38**	1969-70 (76)
Fewest Wins	**14**	1969-70 (76)
Fewest Ties	**5**	1998-99 (82)
Fewest Losses	**17**	1974-75 (80)
Fewest Goals	**168**	1969-70 (76)
Fewest Goals Against	**179**	2011-12 (82)
Longest Winning Streak		
Overall	**9**	Jan. 21-Feb. 6/10
Home	**12**	Oct. 10-Dec. 5/92
Away	**8**	Dec. 18/74-Jan. 16/75
Longest Undefeated Streak		
Overall	**11**	Feb. 28-Mar. 24/74 (9W, 2T)
Home	**13**	Oct. 10-Dec. 8/92 (12W, 1T)
Away	**11**	Oct. 10-Dec. 11/74 (6W, 5T)
Longest Losing Streak		
Overall	**11**	Mar. 16-Apr. 4/04
Home	**9**	Feb. 8-Mar. 12/86
Away	**11**	Jan. 11-Feb. 15/70
Longest Winless Streak		
Overall	**17**	Jan. 29-Mar. 5/70 (13L, 4T)
Home	**9**	Jan. 29-Mar. 5/70 (8L, 1T), Feb. 8-Mar. 12/86 (9L)
Away	**20**	Jan. 11-Apr. 3/70 (16L, 4T)
Most Shutouts, Season	**11**	2011-12 (82)
Most PIM, Season	**2,247**	1992-93 (84)
Most Goals, Game	**12**	Nov. 29/84 (Van. 1 at L.A. 12)

Individual

Most Seasons	**17**	Dave Taylor
Most Games	**1,111**	Dave Taylor
Most Goals, Career	**557**	Luc Robitaille
Most Assists, Career	**757**	Marcel Dionne
Most Points Career	**1,307**	Marcel Dionne (550G, 757A)
Most PIM, Career	**1,846**	Marty McSorley
Most Shutouts, Career	**32**	Rogie Vachon
Longest Consecutive Games Streak	**330**	Anze Kopitar (Mar. 21/07-Mar. 26/11)
Most Goals, Season	**70**	Bernie Nicholls (1988-89)
Most Assists, Season	**122**	Wayne Gretzky (1990-91)
Most Points, Season	**168**	Wayne Gretzky (1988-89; 54G, 114A)
Most PIM, Season	**399**	Marty McSorley (1992-93)
Most Points, Defenseman, Season	**76**	Larry Murphy (1980-81; 16G, 60A)
Most Points, Center, Season	**168**	Wayne Gretzky (1988-89; 54G, 114A)
Most Points, Right Wing, Season	**112**	Dave Taylor (1980-81; 47G, 65A)
Most Points, Left Wing, Season	***125**	Luc Robitaille (1992-93; 63G, 62A)
Most Points, Rookie, Season	**84**	Luc Robitaille (1986-87; 45G, 39A)
Most Shutouts, Season	**10**	Jonathan Quick (2011-12)
Most Goals, Game	**4**	Seventeen times
Most Assists, Game	**6**	Bernie Nicholls (Dec. 1/88), Tomas Sandstrom (Oct. 9/93)
Most Points, Game	**8**	Bernie Nicholls (Dec. 1/88; 2G, 6A)

* NHL Record.

Retired Numbers

16	Marcel Dionne	1975-1987
18	Dave Taylor	1977-1994
20	Luc Robitaille	1986-94, 97-01, 2003-2006
30	Rogie Vachon	1971-1978
99	Wayne Gretzky	1988-1996

All-time Record vs. Other Clubs

Regular Season

	Total								At Home								On Road							
	GP	W	L	T	OL	GF	GA	PTS	GP	W	L	T	OL	GF	GA	PTS	GP	W	L	T	OL	GF	GA	PTS
Anaheim	112	52	40	11	9	317	325	124	56	32	15	4	5	166	137	73	56	20	25	7	4	151	188	51
Boston	131	38	79	13	1	409	536	90	65	23	34	7	1	224	239	54	66	15	45	6	0	185	297	36
Buffalo	113	40	55	18	0	359	432	98	57	24	24	9	0	199	196	57	56	16	31	9	0	160	236	41
Calgary	216	86	105	21	4	723	813	197	107	54	43	9	1	378	354	118	109	32	62	12	3	345	459	79
Carolina	67	31	26	8	2	261	242	72	33	19	11	3	0	139	122	41	34	12	15	5	2	122	120	31
Chicago	180	77	81	17	5	551	596	176	89	40	38	8	3	295	288	91	91	37	43	9	2	256	308	85
Colorado	116	58	47	8	3	414	409	127	59	34	18	5	2	225	186	75	57	24	29	3	1	189	223	52
Columbus	47	26	17	1	3	138	108	56	24	15	8	1	0	67	48	31	23	11	9	0	3	71	60	25
Dallas	219	82	97	32	8	643	712	204	109	49	38	19	3	349	319	120	110	33	59	13	5	294	393	84
Detroit	190	81	78	27	4	668	661	193	95	47	33	14	1	354	297	109	95	34	45	13	3	314	364	84
Edmonton	185	68	79	30	8	661	737	174	92	35	36	15	6	342	355	91	93	33	43	15	2	319	382	83
Florida	24	12	9	3	0	64	64	27	13	9	4	0	0	38	35	18	11	3	5	3	0	26	29	9
Minnesota	47	21	14	5	7	118	108	54	23	11	7	2	3	62	56	27	24	10	7	3	4	56	52	27
Montreal	135	27	88	20	0	370	567	74	68	19	40	9	0	204	267	47	67	8	48	11	0	166	300	27
Nashville	55	28	21	3	3	156	139	62	28	14	12	0	2	82	78	30	27	14	9	3	1	74	61	32
New Jersey	93	51	29	11	2	366	294	115	46	30	10	6	0	208	141	66	47	21	19	5	2	158	153	49
NY Islanders	97	42	42	12	1	306	312	97	48	24	17	7	0	173	146	55	49	18	25	5	1	133	166	42
NY Rangers	125	44	62	16	3	391	466	107	64	26	26	10	2	210	223	64	61	18	36	6	1	181	243	43
Ottawa	25	16	7	2	0	90	63	34	13	11	1	1	0	58	25	23	12	5	6	1	0	32	38	11
Philadelphia	137	40	81	15	1	366	489	96	70	22	40	8	0	204	238	52	67	18	41	7	1	162	251	44
Phoenix	203	78	93	25	7	685	742	188	100	43	41	14	2	361	347	102	103	35	52	11	5	324	395	86
Pittsburgh	148	70	57	18	3	512	467	161	72	45	17	8	2	275	192	100	76	25	40	10	1	237	275	61
St. Louis	187	69	94	22	2	550	599	162	93	44	36	12	1	313	264	101	94	25	58	10	1	237	335	61
San Jose	126	54	54	7	11	354	379	126	63	34	22	4	3	186	168	75	63	20	32	3	8	168	211	51
Tampa Bay	27	9	15	2	1	56	71	21	14	2	10	2	0	27	43	6	13	7	5	0	1	29	28	15
Toronto	139	60	57	21	1	475	471	142	68	35	23	10	0	242	199	80	71	25	34	11	1	233	272	62
Vancouver	227	96	96	32	3	767	757	227	115	59	38	16	2	434	347	136	112	37	58	16	1	333	410	91
Washington	100	53	32	13	2	384	346	121	51	30	14	6	1	201	152	67	49	23	18	7	1	183	194	54
Winnipeg	14	8	2	0	4	53	44	20	7	5	0	0	2	35	23	12	7	3	2	0	2	18	21	8
Defunct Clubs	69	38	20	11	0	232	185	87	35	27	6	2	0	141	76	56	34	11	14	9	0	91	109	31
Totals	**3554**	**1455**	**1577**	**424**	**98**	**11439**	**12134**	**3432**	**1777**	**862**	**662**	**211**	**42**	**6192**	**5561**	**1977**	**1777**	**593**	**915**	**213**	**56**	**5247**	**6573**	**1455**

Playoffs

	Series	W	L	GP	W	L	T	GF	GA	Last Mtg.	Rnd.	Result
Boston	2	0	2	13	5	8	0	38	56	1977	QF	L 2-4
Calgary	6	4	2	26	13	13	0	105	112	1993	DSF	W 4-2
Chicago	2	0	2	10	2	8	0	18	24	2013	CF	L 1-4
Colorado	2	0	2	14	6	8	0	23	33	2002	CQF	L 3-4
Dallas	1	0	1	7	3	4	0	21	26	1968	QF	L 3-4
Detroit	2	1	1	10	4	6	0	21	32	2001	CQF	W 4-2
Edmonton	7	2	5	36	12	24	0	127	154	1992	DSF	L 2-4
Montreal	1	0	1	5	1	4	0	12	15	1993	F	L 1-4
New Jersey	1	1	0	6	4	2	0	16	8	2012	F	W 4-2
NY Islanders	1	0	1	4	1	3	0	10	21	1980	PRE	L 1-3
NY Rangers	2	0	2	6	1	5	0	14	32	1981	PRE	L 1-3
Phoenix	1	1	0	5	4	1	0	14	8	2012	CF	W 4-1
St. Louis	4	2	2	18	8	10	0	40	48	2013	CQF	W 4-2
San Jose	2	1	1	13	6	7	0	34	30	2013	CSF	W 4-3
Toronto	3	1	2	12	5	7	0	31	41	1993	CF	W 4-3
Vancouver	5	3	2	28	15	13	0	96	93	2012	CQF	W 4-1
Defunct Clubs	1	0	1	7	4	3	0	23	25			
Totals	**43**	**17**	**26**	**220**	**94**	**126**	**0**	**643**	**758**			

Playoff Results 2013-2009

Year	Round	Opponent	Result	GF	GA
2013	CF	Chicago	L 1-4	11	14
	CSF	San Jose	W 4-3	14	10
	CQF	St. Louis	W 4-2	12	10
2012	**F**	**New Jersey**	**W 4-2**	**16**	**8**
	CF	Phoenix	W 4-1	14	8
	CSF	St. Louis	W 4-0	15	6
	CQF	Vancouver	W 4-1	12	8
2011	CQF	San Jose	L 2-4	20	20
2010	CQF	Vancouver	L 2-4	18	25

Abbreviations: Round: F – Final; **CF** – conference final; **CSF** – conference semi-final; **CQF** – conference quarter-final; **DSF** – division semi-final; **QF** – quarter-final; **PRE** – preliminary round.

Calgary totals include Atlanta Flames, 1972-73 to 1979-80.
Carolina totals include Hartford, 1979-80 to 1996-97.
Colorado totals include Quebec, 1979-80 to 1994-95.
Dallas totals include Minnesota North Stars, 1967-68 to 1992-93.
New Jersey totals include Kansas City, 1974-75, 1975-76, and Colorado Rockies, 1976-77 to 1981-82.
Phoenix totals include Winnipeg, 1979-80 to 1995-96.
Winnipeg totals include Atlanta Thrashers, 1999-2000 to 2010-11.

2012-13 Results

Jan.	19	Chicago	2-5		12	at Phoenix	2-5
	22	at Colorado	1-3		14	at San Jose	3-4
	24	at Edmonton	1-2*		16	San Jose	5-2
	26	at Phoenix	4-2		18	Phoenix	4-0
	28	Vancouver	3-2†		19	Phoenix	3-2
	31	Nashville	1-2†		21	Dallas	0-2
Feb.	2	at Anaheim	4-7		23	Vancouver	0-1
	5	at Columbus	4-2		25	at Chicago	5-4
	7	at Nashville	0-3		28	at St. Louis	4-2
	10	at Detroit	2-3		30	at Minnesota	3-4†
	11	at St. Louis	4-1		31	at Dallas	3-2
	15	Columbus	2-1	**Apr.**	2	at Phoenix	1-3
	17	at Chicago	2-3		4	Minnesota	3-0
	19	at Edmonton	3-1		6	Edmonton	4-1
	20	at Calgary	3-1		7	at Anaheim	3-4†
	23	Colorado	4-1		9	at Dallas	1-5
	25	Anaheim	5-2		11	Colorado	3-2†
	27	Detroit	2-1		13	Anaheim	2-1
Mar.	2	at Vancouver	2-5		16	at San Jose	2-3†
	4	Nashville	5-1		18	Columbus	2-1
	5	St. Louis	6-4		21	Dallas	4-3*
	7	Dallas	2-5		23	at Minnesota	1-2
	9	Calgary	6-2		24	at Detroit	1-3
	11	Calgary	3-1		27	San Jose	3-2

* – Overtime † – Shootout

Entry Draft Selections 2013-1999

Name in bold denotes played in NHL.

2013
Pick
37 Valentin Zykov
103 Justin Auger
118 Hudson Fasching
146 Patrik Bartosak
148 Jonny Brodzinski
178 Zachary Leslie
191 Dominik Kubalik

2012
Pick
30 **Tanner Pearson**
121 Nikolay Prokhorkin
151 Colin Miller
171 Tomas Hyka
181 Paul Ladue
211 Nick Ebert

2011
Pick
49 Christopher Gibson
80 Andy Andreoff
82 Nick Shore
110 Michael Mersch
140 Joel Lowry
200 Michael Schumacher

2010
Pick
15 Derek Forbort
47 **Tyler Toffoli**
70 Jordan Weal
148 Kevin Gravel
158 Maxim Kitsyn

2009
Pick
5 **Brayden Schenn**
35 **Kyle Clifford**
84 Nicolas Deslauriers
95 Jean-Francois Berube
96 Linden Vey
126 David Kolomatis
156 Michael Pelech
179 Brandon Kozun
186 **Jordan Nolan**
198 Nic Dowd

2008
Pick
2 **Drew Doughty**
13 **Colten Teubert**
32 **Slava Voynov**
63 Robert Czarnik
74 Andrew Campbell
88 Geordie Wudrick
123 **Andrei Loktionov**
153 Justin Azevedo
183 Garrett Roe

2007
Pick
4 **Thomas Hickey**
52 **Oscar Moller**
61 **Wayne Simmonds**
82 Bryan Cameron
95 **Alec Martinez**
109 **Dwight King**
124 Linden Rowat
137 Joshua Turnbull
184 Josh Kidd
188 Matt Fillier

2006
Pick
11 **Jonathan Bernier**
17 **Trevor Lewis**
48 Joe Ryan
74 Jeff Zatkoff
86 Bud Holloway
114 Niclas Andersen
134 David Meckler
144 Martin Nolet
164 Constantin Braun

2005
Pick
11 **Anze Kopitar**
50 Dany Roussin
60 T.J. Fast
72 **Jonathan Quick**
139 Patrik Hersley
184 Ryan McGinnis
206 Josh Meyers
226 John Seymour

2004
Pick
11 **Lauri Tukonen**
95 Paul Baier
110 Ned Lukacevic
143 Eric Neilson
174 **Scott Parse**
205 Mike Curry
221 **Daniel Taylor**
238 **Yutaka Fukufuji**
264 Valtteri Tenkanen

2003
Pick
13 **Dustin Brown**
26 **Brian Boyle**
27 **Jeff Tambellini**
44 **Konstantin Pushkarev**
82 Ryan Munce
152 **Brady Murray**
174 **Esa Pirnes**
231 **Matt Zaba**
244 Mike Sullivan
274 Marty Guerin

2002
Pick
18 **Denis Grebeshkov**
50 Sergei Anshakov
66 **Petr Kanko**
104 **Aaron Rome**
115 Mark Rooneem
152 Greg Hogeboom
157 Joel Andresen
185 Ryan Murphy
215 Mikhail Lyubushin
248 Tuukka Pulliainen
279 **Connor James**

2001
Pick
18 Jens Karlsson
30 **David Steckel**
49 **Mike Cammalleri**
51 **Jaroslav Bednar**
83 Henrik Juntunen
116 **Richard Petiot**
152 Terry Denike
153 Tuukka Mantyla
214 **Cristobal Huet**
237 Mike Gabinet
277 Sebastien Laplante

2000
Pick
20 **Alex Frolov**
54 **Andreas Lilja**
86 **Yanick Lehoux**
118 **Lubomir Visnovsky**
165 Nathan Marsters
201 Yevgeny Fedorov
206 Tim Eriksson
218 Craig Olynick
245 Dan Welch
250 Flavien Conne
282 Carl Grahn

1999
Pick
43 Andrei Shefer
74 Jason Crain
76 **Frantisek Kaberle**
92 Cory Campbell
104 **Brian McGrattan**
125 Daniel Johansson
133 Jean-Francois Nogues
193 Kevin Baker
222 **George Parros**
250 **Noah Clarke**

General Managers' History

Larry Regan, 1967-68 to 1972-73; Larry Regan and Jake Milford, 1973-74; Jake Milford, 1974-75 to 1976-77; George Maguire, 1977-78 to 1982-83; George Maguire and Rogie Vachon, 1983-84; Rogie Vachon, 1984-85 to 1991-92; Nick Beverley, 1992-93, 1993-94; Sam McMaster, 1994-95 to 1996-97; Dave Taylor, 1997-98 to 2005-06; Dean Lombardi, 2006-07 to date.

Dean Lombardi

President and General Manager

Born: Holyoke, MA, March 5, 1958.

The Kings entered into a new executive era when the club hired Dean Lombardi as president and general manager on April 21, 2006. Coming to Los Angeles as a veteran of 20 NHL seasons in the front office as an executive and a pro scout, Lombardi brought a well-earned reputation for being one of hockey's true visionaries while possessing a solid track record of success, building from within, and of development on the ice and infrastructure off the ice. In 2010, the Kings returned to the playoffs for the first time since 2002 and in 2012 they became Stanley Cup champions for the first time in franchise history. Los Angeles reached the Western Conference final in 2013.

Lombardi was formerly a member of the San Jose Sharks front office for 13 years, including seven seasons as general manager, followed by three years as a pro scout for the Philadelphia Flyers from 2003 to 2006, As an executive in the San Jose front office beginning in 1990, Lombardi first served as assistant general manager (a post he held the previous two seasons with the Minnesota North Stars) for the expansion Sharks before being elevated to vice president, director of hockey operations in 1992. Four years later, he was promoted to executive vice president and general manager. During his tenure as general manager in San Jose from 1996 to 2003, Lombardi helped build the Sharks into one of the premier teams in the NHL.

Prior to joining the North Stars, Lombardi spent three seasons as a player representative, including the representation of five members of the 1988 United States Olympic team, and at the time he joined Minnesota's front office Lombardi was only the second former player agent to be employed in an NHL front office (Brian Burke/Vancouver Canucks was the other).

Born in Holyoke, Massachusetts, and raised in nearby Ludlow, Lombardi received his undergraduate degree from the University of New Haven where he finished third in his class. On the ice he was the hockey team's captain his final two seasons, and he received a full athletic scholarship and the school's student-athlete of the year award. In 1985, Lombardi earned his Law degree (with honors) from Tulane Law School where he specialized in Labor Law.

Club Directory

STAPLES Center

Los Angeles Kings
STAPLES Center
1111 South Figueroa Street
Los Angeles, CA 90015
Phone **213/742-7100**
GM FAX 310/535-4525
www.lakings.com
Capacity: 18,118

Ownership
Owner . . . . . Philip F. Anschutz
Owner . . . . . Edward P. Roski, Jr.
Alternate Governor . . . . . Dan Beckerman
Executive Assistant to the Alternate Governor . . . . . Tanya Brice

Kings Executive
President/General Manager, Alternate Governor . . . . . Dean Lombardi
President, Business Operations, Alt. Governor . . . . . Luc Robitaille
Chief Operating Officer . . . . . Kelly Cheeseman
Executive Assistant, President/General Manager . . . . . Tiffany Frost
Executive Assistant, President, Business Ops . . . . . Kehly Sloane
Executive Assistant, Chief Operating Officer . . . . . Alicia Briones
Office Coordinator . . . . . Kiki Oldani

Hockey Operations
Assistant General Manager . . . . . Rob Blake
Special Assistant to the General Manager . . . . . Jack Ferreira
Vice President/Hockey Ops and Legal Affairs . . . . . Jeff Solomon
Director of Team Operations . . . . . Marshall Dickerson

Coaches
Head Coach . . . . . Darryl Sutter
Assistant Coaches . . . . . John Stevens, Davis Payne
Goaltending Coach . . . . . Bill Ranford
Video Coordinator . . . . . Zach Ziegler

Player Development
Player Development . . . . . Nelson Emerson
Senior Advisor/Development Coach . . . . . Mike O'Connell
Goaltender Development . . . . . Kim Dillabaugh

Training Staff – Medical
Head Athletic Trainer . . . . . Chris Kingsley
Assistant Athletic Trainer . . . . . Myles Hirayama
Massage Therapist . . . . . Chris Pikosky
Strength and Conditioning Coach . . . . . Ryan van Asten

Training Staff – Equipment
Head Equipment Manager . . . . . Darren Granger
Assistant Equipment Managers . . . . . Dana Bryson / Denver Wilson

Medical
Team Physician / Internist . . . . . Dr. Ronald Kvitne / Dr. Michael Mellman
Team Dentist / Opthalmologist . . . . . Dr. Ken Ochi / Dr. Howard Lazerson

Scouts/Hockey Operations
Scouting Operations Coordinator/Asst. to the G.M. . . . . . Lee Callans
Senior Pro Scout / Pro Scout . . . . . Rob Laird / Alyn McCauley
Directors of Amateur Scouting . . . . . Mark Yannetti, Michael Futa
Amateur Scouts . . . . . Bob Crocker, Denis Fugere, Tony Gasparini, Brent McEwen, Christian Ruuttu
Collegiate Scouts . . . . . Mike Donnelly, Mark Mullen
Video Technicians . . . . . Bob Friedlander, Bill Gurney

Broadcasters
TV Station / Play-by-Play / Color . . . . . FOX Sports West / Bob Miller / Jim Fox
Radio Flagship / Play-by-Play / Color . . . . . KTLK AM 1150 / Nick Nickson / Daryl Evans

Communications and Content
Vice President, Communications and Broadcasting . . . . . Michael Altieri
Senior Director, Communications and Content . . . . . Jeff Moeller
Director of Production . . . . . Aaron Brenner
Senior Manager, Communications . . . . . Mike Kalinowski
Manager, Communications and Broadcasting . . . . . Jeremy Zager
Associate Producer . . . . . Rob McPherson
Beat Reporter . . . . . Jon Rosen

Fan Development and Community Relations
Director, Fan Development/Community Relations . . . . . James Cefaly

Finance
Staff Accountant / Finance Manager . . . . . Charles Borjon / Yvonne Luong

Game Presentation and Events
Sr. Director, Game Presentation and Events . . . . . Danny Zollars
Sr. Manager, Game Presentation and Events . . . . . Brooklyn Boyars
Supervisor, Game Presentation and Events . . . . . Tim Smith
Coordinator, Game Presentation and Events . . . . . Janelle Morgan
Assistant, Game Presentation and Events . . . . . Vanessa Manning
Public Address Announcer / Music Director . . . . . Dave Joseph / Dieter Ruehle

Group Sales
Vice President, Group Sales . . . . . Matt Rosenfeld
Group Sales Director / Manager . . . . . Mason Donley / Aaron Kulik
Group Sales Account Exec. / Sales Reps. . . . . . Stephen Fiamengo / Melina Kent, Charlie Brooks

Humans Resources
Senior Manager, Human Resources . . . . . Cassy Niehaus

Marketing
Vice President, Marketing . . . . . Jonathan Lowe
Director, Marketing . . . . . Heather Bardocz
Manager, Digital Media . . . . . Pat Donahue
Coordinators, Marketing & Promo . . . . . Kevin Polizzotto
Senior Producer, Digital Media . . . . . Edward Valencia

Sponsorship Sales and Service
Sr. Vice President, Corporate Partnerships . . . . . Bill Pedigo
Sr. Director, Corporate Partnerships . . . . . Josh Veilleux
Director, Partnership Activation . . . . . Nam McGrail
Sr. Manager, Admin. / Manager, Partnerships . . . . . Katie Ranne / Kim Cantor

Ticket Sales and Service
Senior Director, Ticket Sales and Service . . . . . Josh Bender
Senior Manager, Digital Strategy and Analytics . . . . . Aaron LeValley
Director, Ticket Operations . . . . . Elizabeth Hauck
Senior Manager of Ticket Sales and Service . . . . . Adam Cheever
Senior Manager, CRM and Analytics . . . . . Lisa Rollins

Minnesota Wild

2012-13 Results: 26W-19L-1OTL-2SOL 55PTS
2ND, Northwest Division • 8TH, Western Conference

Key Off-Season Signings/Acquisitions

2013

June 12 • Re-signed LW **Stephane Veilleux**.
17 • Re-signed D **Marco Scandella**.
24 • Re-signed G **Niklas Backstrom**.
30 • Acquired RW **Nino Niederreiter** from NY Islanders for RW **Cal Clutterbuck** and a 3rd-round pick (Eamon McAdam) in the 2013 NHL Draft.
July 5 • Signed D **Keith Ballard** and LW **Matt Cooke**.
5 • Re-signed D **Jared Spurgeon**.
12 • Signed D **Jonathon Blum**.

Year-by-Year Record

Season	GP	Home W	Home L	Home T	Home OL	Road W	Road L	Road T	Road OL	Overall W	Overall L	Overall T	Overall OL	GF	GA	Pts.	Div. Fin.	Conf. Fin.	Playoff Result
2012-13	48	14	8	....	2	12	11	....	1	26	19	....	3	122	127	55	2nd, NW	8th, West	Lost Conf. Quarter-Final
2011-12	82	20	17	....	4	15	19	....	7	35	36	....	11	177	226	81	4th, NW	12th, West	Out of Playoffs
2010-11	82	19	17	....	5	20	18	....	3	39	35	....	8	206	233	86	3rd, NW	12th, West	Out of Playoffs
2009-10	82	25	12	....	4	13	24	....	4	38	36	....	8	219	246	84	4th, NW	13th, West	Out of Playoffs
2008-09	82	23	11	....	7	17	22	....	2	40	33	....	9	219	200	89	3rd, NW	9th, West	Out of Playoffs
2007-08	82	25	11	....	5	19	17	....	5	44	28	....	10	223	218	98	1st, NW	3rd, West	Lost Conf. Quarter-Final
2006-07	82	29	7	....	5	19	19	....	3	48	26	....	8	235	191	104	2nd, NW	7th, West	Lost Conf. Quarter-Final
2005-06	82	23	16	....	2	15	20	....	6	38	36	....	8	231	215	84	5th, NW	11th, West	Out of Playoffs
2004-05	....	....	....	....	....	....	....	....	....	....	....	....	....	....	....	....			
2003-04	82	19	13	7	2	11	16	13	1	30	29	20	3	188	183	83	5th, NW	10th, West	Out of Playoffs
2002-03	82	25	13	3	0	17	16	7	1	42	29	10	1	198	178	95	3rd, NW	6th, West	Lost Conf. Final
2001-02	82	14	14	8	5	12	21	4	4	26	35	12	9	195	238	73	5th, NW	12th, West	Out of Playoffs
2000-01	82	14	13	10	4	11	26	3	1	25	39	13	5	168	210	68	5th, NW	14th, West	Out of Playoffs

2013-14 Schedule

Month	Day	Date	Opponent
Oct.	Thu.	3	Los Angeles
	Sat.	5	Anaheim
	Tue.	8	at Nashville
	Thu.	10	Winnipeg
	Sat.	12	Dallas
	Mon.	14	at Buffalo
	Tue.	15	at Toronto
	Thu.	17	at Tampa Bay
	Sat.	19	at Florida
	Tue.	22	Nashville
	Thu.	24	Carolina
	Sat.	26	at Chicago
	Mon.	28	Chicago
Nov.	Fri.	1	Montreal
	Sun.	3	New Jersey
	Tue.	5	Calgary
	Thu.	7	at Washington
	Sat.	9	at Carolina
	Wed.	13	Toronto
	Fri.	15	Florida
	Sun.	17	Winnipeg
	Tue.	19	at Montreal
	Wed.	20	at Ottawa
	Sat.	23	at Winnipeg*
	Mon.	25	at St. Louis
	Wed.	27	Phoenix
	Fri.	29	Colorado*
	Sat.	30	at Colorado
Dec.	Mon.	2	Philadelphia
	Thu.	5	Chicago
	Fri.	6	at Columbus
	Sun.	8	San Jose*
	Wed.	11	at Anaheim
	Thu.	12	at San Jose
	Sat.	14	at Colorado
	Tue.	17	Vancouver
	Thu.	19	at Pittsburgh
	Sun.	22	at NY Rangers
	Mon.	23	at Philadelphia
	Fri.	27	at Winnipeg
	Sun.	29	NY Islanders
	Tue.	31	St. Louis*
Jan.	Thu.	2	Buffalo
	Sat.	4	Washington
	Tue.	7	at Los Angeles
	Thu.	9	at Phoenix
	Sat.	11	Colorado
	Sun.	12	at Nashville
	Tue.	14	Ottawa
	Thu.	16	Edmonton
	Sat.	18	Dallas
	Tue.	21	at Dallas
	Thu.	23	Chicago
	Sat.	25	at San Jose
	Tue.	28	at Anaheim
	Thu.	30	at Colorado
Feb.	Sat.	1	at Calgary
	Tue.	4	Tampa Bay
	Thu.	6	Nashville
	Thu.	27	at Edmonton
	Fri.	28	at Vancouver
Mar.	Mon.	3	Calgary
	Sat.	8	at Dallas
	Sun.	9	St. Louis
	Tue.	11	Edmonton
	Thu.	13	NY Rangers
	Sat.	15	Columbus
	Mon.	17	at Boston
	Tue.	18	at NY Islanders
	Thu.	20	at New Jersey
	Sat.	22	Detroit*
	Sun.	23	at Detroit
	Wed.	26	Vancouver
	Thu.	27	at St. Louis
	Sat.	29	at Phoenix
	Mon.	31	at Los Angeles
Apr.	Thu.	3	at Chicago
	Sat.	5	Pittsburgh
	Mon.	7	at Winnipeg
	Tue.	8	Boston
	Thu.	10	St. Louis
	Sun.	13	Nashville

* Denotes afternoon game.

Zach Parise battles for position in front of Ducks goalie Jonas Hiller and defenseman Sheldon Souray. In his first season with the Wild in 2012-13, Parise led the team with 18 goals and 38 points in 48 games played.

CENTRAL DIVISION
14th NHL Season

Franchise date: June 25, 1997

2013-14 Player Personnel

FORWARDS	HT	WT	*Age	Place of Birth	S	2012-13 Club
BRODZIAK, Kyle	6-2	209	29	St. Paul, Alta.	R	Minnesota
BULMER, Brett	6-4	214	21	Prince George, B.C.	R	Houston
COOKE, Matt	5-11	205	35	Belleville, Ont.	L	Pittsburgh
COYLE, Charlie	6-3	222	21	E. Weymouth, MA	R	Houston-Minnesota
DOWELL, Jake	6-0	202	28	Eau Claire, WI	L	Houston-Minnesota
GRANLUND, Mikael	5-10	186	21	Oulu, Finland	L	Houston-Minnesota
HEATLEY, Dany	6-4	220	32	Freiburg, West Germany	L	Minnesota
KOIVU, Mikko	6-3	217	30	Turku, Finland	L	TPS-Minnesota
KONOPKA, Zenon	6-0	209	32	Niagara on the Lake, Ont.	L	Minnesota
McMILLAN, Carson	6-1	197	25	Brandon, Man.	R	Houston
MITCHELL, Torrey	5-11	190	28	Montreal, Que.	R	San Francisco-Minnesota
NIEDERREITER, Nino	6-2	208	21	Chur, Switzerland	L	Bridgeport
PARISE, Zach	5-11	195	29	Minneapolis, MN	L	Minnesota
POMINVILLE, Jason	6-0	185	30	Repentigny, Que.	R	Mannheim-Buf-Min
RUPP, Mike	6-5	243	33	Cleveland, OH	L	NY Rangers-Minnesota
VEILLEUX, Stephane	6-1	200	31	Beauceville, Que.	L	Houston-Minnesota
ZUCKER, Jason	5-11	186	21	Las Vegas, NV	L	Houston-Minnesota

DEFENSEMEN	HT	WT	*Age	Place of Birth	S	2012-13 Club
BALLARD, Keith	5-11	208	30	Baudette, MN	L	Vancouver
BLUM, Jonathon	6-1	186	24	Long Beach, CA	R	Milwaukee-Nashville
BRODIN, Jonas	6-1	180	20	Karlstad, Sweden	L	Houston-Minnesota
KAMPFER, Steven	5-11	197	25	Ann Arbor, MI	R	Houston
PROSSER, Nate	6-2	207	27	Elk River, MN	R	Minnesota
SCANDELLA, Marco	6-3	210	23	Montreal, Que.	L	Houston-Minnesota
SPURGEON, Jared	5-9	185	23	Edmonton, Alta.	R	Langnau-Minnesota
STONER, Clayton	6-4	213	28	Port McNeill, B.C.	L	B. Bystrica-Minnesota
SUTER, Ryan	6-1	198	28	Madison, WI	L	Minnesota

GOALTENDERS	HT	WT	*Age	Place of Birth	C	2012-13 Club
BACKSTROM, Niklas	6-2	194	35	Helsinki, Finland	L	Minnesota
HARDING, Josh	6-2	202	29	Regina, Sask.	R	Minnesota-Houston
KUEMPER, Darcy	6-5	205	23	Saskatoon, Sask.	L	Houston-Orlando-Minnesota

* – Age at start of 2013-14 season

Mike Yeo

Head Coach

Born: North Bay, Ont., July 31, 1973.

Mike Yeo was named head coach of the Minnesota Wild on June 17, 2011. The hiring came 366 days after Yeo had been tabbed to lead the Houston Aeros, the Wild's primary developmental affiliate in the American Hockey League. In his one year as a head coach, he led the Aeros to an appearance in the Calder Cup Finals. Yeo joined the Wild franchise with the Aeros after spending the previous five seasons as assistant coach of the NHL's Pittsburgh Penguins. During Yeo's tenure in Pittsburgh he helped lead the Penguins to the 2008-09 Stanley Cup championship. Yeo led the Wild to their first playoff appearance since 2008 in 2013.

Yeo played five seasons with the Aeros (1994 to 1999) and was the captain of Houston's 1999 Turner Cup Championship team. He joined the Aeros in 1994 after playing the previous four seasons with the Sudbury Wolves (Ontario Hockey Leaue). As a left winger, he accumulated 127 points (55 goals, 72 assists) and 511 penalty minutes over 317 games during his Aeros playing career. Yeo enjoyed career-highs of 20 goals, 21 assists, 41 points and 128 penalty minutes during the 1997-98 season while serving as team captain. The native of North Bay, Ontario posted 18 points (six goals, 12 assists) and 65 penalty minutes in 57 games during the 1998-99 season. He also added four assists and 11 penalty minutes in nine games during the Aeros' run to the Turner Cup. Yeo joined the Wilkes-Barre/Scranton Penguins for the 1999-2000 season and played in 19 games before suffering a career-ending knee injury.

After his injury, Yeo joined the Wilkes-Barre/Scranton coaching staff where he spent six seasons as the assistant coach of Pittsburgh's AHL affiliate. During his tenure in Wilkes-Barre/Scranton, Yeo helped the Penguins to a Western Conference championship in 2001, an Eastern Conference championship in 2005, and two trips to the Calder Cup Finals. He made the jump to the NHL's Pittsburgh Penguins under head coach Michel Therrien in December 2005. During his first full season in 2006-07, Yeo helped the Penguins to a 47-point improvement from the previous season, the fourth-largest turnaround from one season to the next in NHL history. In Yeo's second season, he helped lead the Penguins to the Stanley Cup Final for the first time since the 1992 season. Yeo remained on staff in Pittsburgh during the 2008-09 season after Dan Byslma replaced Therrien on February 15, 2009, and the Penguins went on to win their third Stanley Cup championship in franchise history.

Coaching Record

			Regular Season				Playoffs			
Season	Team	League	GC	W	L	O/T	GC	W	L	T
2010-11	Houston	AHL	80	46	28	6	24	14	10	....
2011-12	**Minnesota**	**NHL**	**82**	**35**	**36**	**11**	....	....	....	....
2012-13	**Minnesota**	**NHL**	**48**	**26**	**19**	**3**	**5**	**1**	**4**	....
	NHL Totals		**130**	**61**	**55**	**14**	**5**	**1**	**4**	....

2012-13 Scoring

* – rookie

Regular Season

Pos	#	Player	Team	GP	G	A	Pts	TOI	+/–	PIM	PP	SH	GW	S	%
L	11	Zach Parise	MIN	48	18	20	38	20:40	2	16	7	0	4	182	9.9
C	9	Mikko Koivu	MIN	48	11	26	37	21:05	2	26	0	0	3	127	8.7
R	29	Jason Pominville	BUF	37	10	15	25	20:53	1	8	1	1	1	94	10.6
			MIN	10	4	5	9	17:31	0	0	1	0	1	24	16.7
			Total	47	14	20	34	20:10	1	8	2	1	2	118	11.9
D	20	Ryan Suter	MIN	48	4	28	32	27:16	2	24	3	0	1	91	4.4
R	10	Devin Setoguchi	MIN	48	13	14	27	14:26	5	20	5	0	3	97	13.4
C	7	Matt Cullen	MIN	42	7	20	27	15:53	9	10	0	0	0	79	8.9
L	15	Dany Heatley	MIN	36	11	10	21	18:32	–12	8	3	0	1	83	13.3
C	96	Pierre-Marc Bouchard	MIN	43	8	12	20	13:56	3	8	0	0	2	71	11.3
D	46	Jared Spurgeon	MIN	39	5	10	15	21:32	1	4	4	0	2	67	7.5
C	63 *	Charlie Coyle	MIN	37	8	6	14	15:03	3	28	1	0	2	50	16.0
D	77	Tom Gilbert	MIN	43	3	10	13	19:19	–11	18	1	0	0	36	8.3
C	21	Kyle Brodziak	MIN	48	8	4	12	17:21	–18	20	1	1	1	88	9.1
D	25 *	Jonas Brodin	MIN	45	2	9	11	23:12	3	10	1	0	0	51	3.9
R	22	Cal Clutterbuck	MIN	42	4	6	10	13:44	–5	27	0	0	1	87	4.6
D	4	Clayton Stoner	MIN	48	0	10	10	18:12	0	42	0	0	0	40	0.0
C	17	Torrey Mitchell	MIN	45	4	4	8	10:29	–8	21	0	0	1	39	10.3
C	64 *	Mikael Granlund	MIN	27	2	6	8	13:10	–4	6	0	0	0	36	5.6
L	16 *	Jason Zucker	MIN	20	4	1	5	11:15	4	8	0	0	0	34	11.8
C	27	Mike Rupp	NYR	8	0	0	0	6:14	–3	12	0	0	0	2	0.0
			MIN	32	1	3	4	8:53	1	67	0	0	0	27	3.7
			Total	40	1	3	4	8:21	–2	79	0	0	0	29	3.4
D	44	Justin Falk	MIN	36	0	3	3	13:12	–9	40	0	0	0	27	0.0
D	6	Marco Scandella	MIN	6	1	0	1	14:25	–1	4	0	0	0	7	14.3
D	5	Brett Clark	MIN	8	0	1	1	14:04	–9	0	0	0	0	6	0.0
L	47 *	Johan Larsson	MIN	1	0	0	0	14:02	0	0	0	0	0	2	0.0
C	18	Jake Dowell	MIN	2	0	0	0	8:32	0	0	0	0	0	3	0.0
D	39	Nate Prosser	MIN	17	0	0	0	11:15	4	4	0	0	0	5	0.0
C	28	Zenon Konopka	MIN	37	0	0	0	8:26	–4	117	0	0	0	18	0.0

Goaltending

No.		Goaltender	GPI	Mins	Avg	W	L	OT	EN	SO	GA	SA	S%	G	A	PIM
35	*	Darcy Kuemper	6	288	2.08	1	2	0	0	0	10	119	.916	0	0	0
32		Niklas Backstrom	42	2368	2.48	24	15	3	2	2	98	1072	.909	0	0	2
37		Josh Harding	5	185	3.24	1	1	0	0	1	10	73	.863	0	0	0
31	*	Matt Hackett	1	59	5.08	0	1	0	0	0	5	33	.848	0	0	0
		Totals	**48**	**2920**	**2.57**	**26**	**19**	**3**	**2**	**3**	**125**	**1299**	**.904**			

Playoffs

Pos	#	Player	Team	GP	G	A	Pts	TOI	+/–	PIM	PP	SH	GW	OT	S	%
C	7	Matt Cullen	MIN	5	0	3	3	19:07	1	2	0	0	0	0	8	0.0
C	96	Pierre-Marc Bouchard	MIN	5	1	1	2	14:36	2	0	0	0	0	0	10	10.0
R	22	Cal Clutterbuck	MIN	5	1	1	2	15:51	0	4	0	0	0	0	11	9.1
D	6	Marco Scandella	MIN	5	1	1	2	18:01	–1	0	0	0	0	0	6	16.7
L	16 *	Jason Zucker	MIN	5	1	1	2	13:29	1	0	0	0	1	1	11	9.1
C	21	Kyle Brodziak	MIN	5	0	2	2	20:40	0	4	0	0	0	0	9	0.0
C	63 *	Charlie Coyle	MIN	5	0	2	2	18:09	–4	2	0	0	0	0	11	0.0
L	11	Zach Parise	MIN	5	1	0	1	21:23	–7	2	0	0	0	0	17	5.9
C	17	Torrey Mitchell	MIN	5	1	0	1	11:24	–4	0	0	0	0	0	8	12.5
R	10	Devin Setoguchi	MIN	5	1	0	1	16:04	–2	0	0	0	0	0	12	8.3
D	4	Clayton Stoner	MIN	1	0	1	1	8:18	1	0	0	0	0	0	0	0.0
R	29	Jason Pominville	MIN	2	0	0	0	13:32	–1	0	0	0	0	0	4	0.0
L	19	Stephane Veilleux	MIN	2	0	0	0	7:31	0	0	0	0	0	0	1	0.0
C	28	Zenon Konopka	MIN	2	0	0	0	9:52	–2	0	0	0	0	0	2	0.0
C	27	Mike Rupp	MIN	4	0	0	0	6:38	–3	12	0	0	0	0	2	0.0
D	44	Justin Falk	MIN	4	0	0	0	11:33	–3	2	0	0	0	0	0	0.0
C	9	Mikko Koivu	MIN	5	0	0	0	20:30	–6	8	0	0	0	0	11	0.0
D	77	Tom Gilbert	MIN	5	0	0	0	16:16	–2	2	0	0	0	0	0	0.0
D	20	Ryan Suter	MIN	5	0	0	0	31:37	–5	0	0	0	0	0	5	0.0
D	46	Jared Spurgeon	MIN	5	0	0	0	21:15	–3	2	0	0	0	0	8	0.0
D	25 *	Jonas Brodin	MIN	5	0	0	0	26:23	–3	0	0	0	0	0	3	0.0

Goaltending

No.		Goaltender	GPI	Mins	Avg	W	L	EN	SO	GA	SA	S%	G	A	PIM
37		Josh Harding	5	245	2.94	1	4	1	0	12	135	.911	0	0	0
35	*	Darcy Kuemper	2	73	3.29	0	0	0	0	4	33	.879	0	0	0
		Totals	**5**	**319**	**3.20**	**1**	**4**	**1**	**0**	**17**	**169**	**.899**			

Club Records

Team

(Figures in brackets for season records are games played.)

Most Points **104** 2006-07 (82)
Most Wins **48** 2006-07 (82)
Most Ties **20** 2003-04 (82)
Most Losses **39** 2000-01 (82)
Most Goals **235** 2006-07 (82)
Most Goals Against **246** 2009-10 (82)
Fewest Points **68** 2000-01 (82)
Fewest Wins **25** 2000-01 (82)
Fewest Ties **10** 2002-03 (82)
Fewest Losses **26** 2006-07 (82)
Fewest Goals **168** 2000-01 (82)
Fewest Goals Against **178** 2002-03 (82)

Longest Winning Streak
Overall .... **9** Mar. 8-24/07
Home .... **8** Oct. 5-Nov. 2/06, Dec. 5/06-Jan. 2/07
Away .... **7** Nov. 13-Dec. 10/11

Longest Undefeated Streak
Overall .... **9** Dec. 13-30/03 (4W, 5T/OL) Mar. 8-24/07 (9W)
Home .... **9** Dec. 13/00-Jan. 10/01 (5W, 4T/OL)
Away .... **7** Dec. 6-30/03 (2W, 5T/OL)

Longest Losing Streak
Overall .... **8** Mar. 10-26/11
Home .... **5** Feb. 28-Mar. 13/12, Apr. 1-21/13
Away .... **11** Nov. 20/06-Jan. 9/07 Dec. 13/11-Jan. 19/12

Longest Winless Streak
Overall .... **12** Mar. 11-Apr. 4/01 (9L, 3T/OL)
Home .... **8** Feb. 26-Mar. 28/01 (5L, 3T/OL)
Away .... **12** Dec. 18/03-Jan. 31/04 (5L, 7T/OL)

Most Shutouts, Season **8** 2006-07 (82), 2008-09 (82)
Most PIM, Season **1,209** 2001-02 (82), 2005-06 (82)
Most Goals, Game .... **8** Mar. 25/04 (Min. 8 at Chi. 2) Apr. 10/09 (Nsh. 2 at Min. 8)

Individual

Most Seasons .... **10** Nick Schultz, Pierre-Marc Bouchard
Most Games .... **743** Nick Schultz
Most Goals, Career .... **219** Marian Gaborik
Most Assists, Career .... **279** Mikko Koivu
Most Points, Career .... **437** Marian Gaborik (219G, 218A)
Most PIM, Career .... **698** Matt Johnson
Most Shutouts, Career .... **28** Niklas Backstrom
Longest Consecutive Games Streak .... **288** Antti Laaksonen (Oct. 6/00-Dec. 29/03)
Most Goals, Season .... **42** Marian Gaborik (2007-08)
Most Assists, Season .... **50** Pierre-Marc Bouchard (2007-08)
Most Points, Season .... **83** Marian Gaborik (2007-08; 42G, 41A)
Most PIM, Season .... **201** Matt Johnson (2002-03)
Most Points, Defenseman, Season .... **46** Brent Burns (2010-11; 17G, 29A)
Most Points, Center, Season .... **71** Mikko Koivu (2009-10; 22G, 49A)
Most Points, Right Wing, Season .... **83** Marian Gaborik (2007-08; 42G, 41A)
Most Points, Left Wing, Season .... **79** Brian Rolston (2005-06; 34G, 45A)
Most Points, Rookie, Season .... **36** Marian Gaborik (2000-01; 18G, 18A)
Most Shutouts, Season .... **8** Niklas Backstrom (2008-09)
Most Goals, Game .... **5** Marian Gaborik (Dec. 20/07)
Most Assists, Game .... **4** Andrew Brunette (Mar. 10/02) Marian Gaborik (Oct. 26/02) Pascal Dupuis (Mar. 25/04) Eric Belanger (Nov. 15/07) Mikko Koivu (Oct. 16/08, Jan. 2/11)
Most Points, Game .... **6** Marian Gaborik (Oct. 26/02; 2G, 4A), (Dec. 20/07; 5G, 1A)

Captains' History

Sean O'Donnell, Scott Pellerin, Wes Walz, Brad Bombardir, Darby Hendrickson, 2000-01; Jim Dowd, Filip Kuba, Brad Brown, Andrew Brunette, 2001-02; Brad Bombardir, Matt Johnson, Sergei Zholtok, 2002-03; Brad Brown, Andrew Brunette, Richard Park, Brad Bombardir, Jim Dowd, 2003-04; Alex Henry, Filip Kuba, Willie Mitchell, Brian Rolston, Wes Walz, 2005-06; Brian Rolston, Keith Carney, Mark Parrish, 2006-07; Pavol Demitra, Brian Rolston, Mark Parrish, Nick Schultz, Marian Gaborik, 2007-08; Mikko Koivu, Kim Johnsson, Andrew Brunette, 2008-09; Mikko Koivu, 2009-10 to date.

General Managers' History

Doug Risebrough, 2000-01 to 2008-09; Chuck Fletcher, 2009-10 to date.

Coaching History

Jacques Lemaire, 2000-01 to 2008-09; Todd Richards, 2009-10, 2010-11; Mike Yeo, 2011-12 to date.

All-time Record vs. Other Clubs

Regular Season

	Total								At Home								On Road							
	GP	W	L	T	OL	GF	GA	PTS	GP	W	L	T	OL	GF	GA	PTS	GP	W	L	T	OL	GF	GA	PTS
Anaheim	47	23	20	2	2	116	110	50	23	13	7	2	1	58	45	29	24	10	13	0	1	58	65	21
Boston	12	10	1	0	1	35	16	21	6	4	1	0	1	16	10	9	6	6	0	0	0	19	6	12
Buffalo	12	5	5	0	2	28	30	12	6	1	3	0	2	11	17	4	6	4	2	0	0	17	13	8
Calgary	74	29	34	4	7	166	171	69	37	18	12	1	6	90	82	43	37	11	22	3	1	76	89	26
Carolina	14	4	6	2	2	33	42	12	9	4	3	2	0	26	29	10	5	0	3	0	2	7	13	2
Chicago	47	27	18	1	1	131	120	56	24	15	8	0	1	66	61	31	23	12	10	1	0	65	59	25
Colorado	74	36	29	3	6	191	208	81	37	20	12	1	4	101	104	45	37	16	17	2	2	90	104	36
Columbus	46	23	16	1	6	116	112	53	24	16	5	0	3	69	53	35	22	7	11	1	3	47	59	18
Dallas	47	16	23	1	7	114	142	40	23	12	9	0	2	58	50	26	24	4	14	1	5	56	92	14
Detroit	47	14	24	3	6	108	155	37	23	7	8	2	6	53	63	22	24	7	16	1	0	55	92	15
Edmonton	73	41	23	4	5	196	167	91	36	23	11	1	1	105	79	48	37	18	12	3	4	91	88	43
Florida	13	9	2	1	1	40	22	20	6	4	0	1	1	19	8	10	7	5	2	0	0	21	14	10
Los Angeles	47	21	16	5	5	108	118	52	24	11	7	3	3	52	56	28	23	10	9	2	2	56	62	24
Montreal	11	4	4	1	2	29	37	11	5	2	2	0	1	12	18	5	6	2	2	1	1	17	19	6
Nashville	47	20	20	5	2	124	133	47	24	13	8	3	0	78	67	29	23	7	12	2	2	46	66	18
New Jersey	12	3	5	2	2	29	40	10	6	2	2	1	1	17	19	6	6	1	3	1	1	12	21	4
NY Islanders	14	8	5	0	1	39	34	17	7	5	1	0	1	21	17	11	7	3	4	0	0	18	17	6
NY Rangers	14	5	8	0	1	36	42	11	8	3	4	0	1	24	26	7	6	2	4	0	0	12	16	4
Ottawa	11	2	6	1	2	26	39	7	6	1	3	1	1	15	22	4	5	1	3	0	1	11	17	3
Philadelphia	13	4	8	1	0	20	38	9	5	2	2	1	0	9	13	5	8	2	6	0	0	11	25	4
Phoenix	47	22	20	3	2	119	117	49	23	11	9	2	1	63	56	25	24	11	11	1	1	56	61	24
Pittsburgh	13	9	3	1	0	42	24	19	6	3	2	1	0	17	16	7	7	6	1	0	0	25	8	12
St. Louis	47	22	15	5	5	117	109	54	24	14	6	2	2	69	50	32	23	8	9	3	3	48	59	22
San Jose	47	19	23	2	3	107	130	43	23	11	9	1	2	58	58	25	24	8	14	1	1	49	72	18
Tampa Bay	14	9	3	1	1	43	32	20	7	5	2	0	0	23	17	10	7	4	1	1	1	20	15	10
Toronto	10	3	7	0	0	23	29	6	4	2	2	0	0	11	8	4	6	1	5	0	0	12	21	2
Vancouver	73	30	29	5	9	186	193	74	37	19	13	2	3	107	88	43	36	11	16	3	6	79	105	31
Washington	12	7	5	0	0	23	24	14	6	6	0	0	0	15	7	12	6	1	5	0	0	8	17	2
Winnipeg	12	6	3	1	2	36	31	15	6	3	1	1	1	18	13	8	6	3	2	0	1	18	18	7
Totals	**950**	**431**	**381**	**55**	**83**	**2381**	**2465**	**1000**	**475**	**250**	**152**	**28**	**45**	**1281**	**1152**	**573**	**475**	**181**	**229**	**27**	**38**	**1100**	**1313**	**427**

Playoffs

	Series	W	L	GP	W	L	T	GF	GA	Last Mtg.	Rnd.	Result
Anaheim	2	0	2	9	1	8	0	10	21	2007	CQF	L 1-4
Chicago	1	0	1	5	1	4	0	7	17	2013	CQF	L 1-4
Colorado	2	1	1	13	6	7	0	28	34	2008	CQF	L 2-4
Vancouver	1	1	0	7	4	3	0	26	17	2003	CSF	W 4-3
Totals	**6**	**2**	**4**	**34**	**12**	**22**	**0**	**71**	**89**			

Winnipeg totals include Atlanta Thrashers, 1999-2000 to 2010-11.

Playoff Results 2013-2009

Year	Round	Opponent	Result	GF	GA
2013	CQF	Chicago	L 1-4	7	17

Abbreviations: Round: CSF – conference semi-final; **CQF** – conference quarter-final.

2012-13 Results

Month	Date	Opponent	Score	Month	Date	Opponent	Score
Jan.	19	Colorado	4-2		12	Anaheim	1-2
	20	Dallas	1-0		14	Colorado	5-3
	22	Nashville	1-3		16	at Colorado	6-4
	25	at Detroit	3-5		18	at Vancouver	3-1
	27	at St. Louis	4-5*		20	at Detroit	4-2
	29	Columbus	3-2		23	San Jose	2-0
	30	Chicago	3-2†		25	at Dallas	7-4
Feb.	1	at Anaheim	1-3		27	Phoenix	4-3*
	4	at Phoenix	1-2		29	at Dallas	3-5
	7	Vancouver	1-4		30	Los Angeles	4-3†
	9	Nashville	2-1*	**Apr.**	1	St. Louis	1-4
	11	at Calgary	2-1†		3	at San Jose	2-4
	12	at Vancouver	1-2		4	at Los Angeles	0-3
	14	Colorado	3-4†		7	at Columbus	3-0
	17	Detroit	3-2		9	Chicago	0-1
	21	at Edmonton	3-1		11	St. Louis	0-2
	23	at Calgary	1-3		13	Columbus	2-3†
	26	Calgary	2-1*		15	at Calgary	4-3
	28	at Phoenix	4-3		16	at Edmonton	5-3
Mar.	1	at Anaheim	2-3		18	at San Jose	1-6
	3	Edmonton	4-2		21	Calgary	1-4
	5	at Chicago	3-5		23	Los Angeles	2-1
	9	at Nashville	2-1†		26	Edmonton	1-6
	10	Vancouver	4-2		27	at Colorado	3-1

* – Overtime † – Shootout

Entry Draft Selections 2013-2000

Name in bold denotes played in NHL.

2013

Pick	
46	Gustav Olofsson
81	Kurtis Gabriel
107	Dylan Labbe
137	Carson Soucy
167	Avery Peterson
197	Nolan De Jong
200	Alexandre Belanger

2012

Pick	
7	Mathew Dumba
46	Raphael Bussieres
68	John Draeger
98	Adam Gilmour
128	Daniel Gunnarsson
158	Christoph Bertschy
188	Louis Nanne

2011

Pick	
10	**Jonas Brodin**
28	Zack Phillips
60	Mario Lucia
131	Nick Seeler
161	Steve Michalek
191	Tyler Graovac

2010

Pick	
9	**Mikael Granlund**
39	**Brett Bulmer**
56	**Johan Larsson**
59	**Jason Zucker**
159	Johan Gustafsson
189	Dylen McKinlay

2009

Pick	
16	**Nick Leddy**
77	**Matt Hackett**
103	**Kris Foucault**
116	Alex Fallstrom
161	**Darcy Kuemper**
163	Jere Sallinen
182	Erik Haula
193	Anthony Hamburg

2008

Pick	
23	**Tyler Cuma**
55	**Marco Scandella**
115	Sean Lorenz
145	Eero Elo

2007

Pick	
16	**Colton Gillies**
110	**Justin Falk**
140	**Cody Almond**
170	Harri Ilvonen
200	**Carson McMillan**

2006

Pick	
9	**James Sheppard**
40	Ondrej Fiala
72	**Cal Clutterbuck**
102	Kyle Medvec
132	Niko Hovinen
162	Julian Walker
192	Chris Hickey

2005

Pick	
4	**Benoit Pouliot**
57	**Matt Kassian**
65	Kristofer Westblom
110	Kyle Bailey
122	Morten Madsen
129	Anthony Aiello
199	Riley Emmerson

2004

Pick	
12	A.J. Thelen
42	Roman Voloshenko
78	**Peter Olvecky**
79	**Clayton Stoner**
111	**Ryan Jones**
114	**Patrick Bordeleau**
117	Julien Sprunger
161	Jean-Claude Sawyer
175	Aaron Boogaard
195	Jean-Michel Rizk
206	**Anton Khudobin**
272	**Kyle Wilson**

2003

Pick	
20	**Brent Burns**
56	**Patrick O'Sullivan**
78	**Danny Irmen**
157	Marcin Kolusz
187	Miroslav Kopriva
207	Georgy Misharin
219	Adam Courchaine
251	Mathieu Melanson
281	Jean-Michel Bolduc

2002

Pick	
8	**Pierre-Marc Bouchard**
38	**Josh Harding**
72	Mike Erickson
73	**Barry Brust**
155	Armands Berzins
175	**Matt Foy**
204	Niklas Eckerblom
237	**Christoph Brandner**
268	Mikhail Tyulyapkin
269	Mika Hannula

2001

Pick	
6	**Mikko Koivu**
36	**Kyle Wanvig**
74	Chris Heid
93	**Stephane Veilleux**
103	**Tony Virta**
202	**Derek Boogaard**
239	Jake Riddle

2000

Pick	
3	**Marian Gaborik**
33	**Nick Schultz**
99	Marc Cavosie
132	**Maxim Sushinsky**
170	**Erik Reitz**
199	Brian Passmore
214	**Peter Bartos**
232	**Lubomir Sekeras**
255	Eric Johansson

Chuck Fletcher

General Manager

Born: Montreal, Que., April 29, 1967.

The Minnesota Wild announced the hiring of Chuck Fletcher as the second general manager in club history on May 22, 2009. During the summer of 2012, Fletcher made his mark with the acquisition of Zach Parise and Ryan Suter, two of the biggest names available on the free-agent market, and the Wild made their first playoff appearance since 2008 in the spring of 2013.

Fletcher has been to the Stanley Cup Finals in management with three different teams (Florida, Anaheim and Pittsburgh). With the Penguins from 2006 to 2009, he worked closely with general manager Ray Shero on all hockey-related matters, including scouting, overseeing the development of young prospects and contract negotiations. Fletcher also managed hockey operations for the club's American Hockey League affiliate, the Wilkes-Barre/Scranton Penguins. Under his leadership, Wilkes-Barre/Scranton reached the AHL's Calder Cup finals in 2007-08, and the division finals in 2008-09.

Fletcher, the son of Hockey Hall of Famer Cliff Fletcher, had extensive NHL management experience before he joined the Penguins in July 2006 – including a four-year stint with the Anaheim Ducks from 2003 to 2006 as director of hockey operations, assistant general manager, and vice president of amateur scouting and player development.

The Montreal native also spent nine years in the front office of the Florida Panthers from 1993 to 2002, working seven seasons as assistant general manager and part of one season (2001-02) as interim general manager. In 1996, the Panthers advanced to the Stanley Cup Finals.

Fletcher graduated from Harvard in 1990 and spent one year as the sales and merchandising coordinator for Hockey Canada and two years as a player representative for Newport Sports Management before making the transition to the front office.

Club Directory

Xcel Energy Center

Minnesota Wild
317 Washington Street
St. Paul, MN 55102
Phone **651/602-6000**
FAX 651/222-1055
Tickets 651/222-9453
www.wild.com
Capacity: 17,954

Board Members . . . . Craig Leipold (Owner/Governor), Philip Falcone (Minority Owner), Mark Falcone, Quinn Martin, Mark Pacchini and Jac Sperling

Investors in MSE . . . Craig Leipold (Owner/Governor), Philip Falcone (Minority Owner); Limited Partners: Robert Hubbard, Stanley E. Hubbard, Stanley S. Hubbard, Horace H. Irvine III, Robert Marvin, Robert O. Naegele, Jr., Ford Nicholson, Todd Nicholson, Vance Opperman and Michael Reilly

Owner/Governor	Craig Leipold
Minority Owner	Philip Falcone
General Manager	Chuck Fletcher
Chief Operating Officer	Matt Majka
Executive Vice President, Chief Financial Officer	Jeff Pellegrom
Vice President and General Counsel	Steve Weinreich
Vice President, Facility Admin. / G.M., RiverCentre	Jim Ibister
Vice President/G.M., Xcel Energy Center	Jack Larson
Vice President Corp. Partnerships and Retail Mgmt.	Carin Anderson
Vice President, Brand Content & Communications	John Maher
Executive Assistant	Deb Hanson
Executive Assistant	Stephanie Huseby
Admin. Assistant, Ticket Sales and Service	Tawnya Vidnovic
Hockey Operations	
Assistant General Manager	Brent Flahr
Assistant to the G.M. and G.M. Iowa Wild	Jim Mill
Head Coach	Mike Yeo
Assistant Coaches	Rick Wilson, Darryl Sydor, Darby Hendrickson
Goalie Coach	Bob Mason
Strength and Conditioning Coach	Kirk Olson
Coordinators, Video / Amateur Scouting	Jonas Plumb / Guy Lapointe
Director, Player Personnel/Development	Blair Mackasey/Brad Bombardir
Sr. Director, Team Ops. and Business Integration	Frank Buonomo
Director, Hockey Administration	Shep Harder
Hockey Operations Advisor	Andrew Brunette
Coordinator, Hockey Operations	Ben Resnick
Director, Media Relations	Aaron Sickman
Manager, Digital Content	Ryan Stanzel
Coordinator, Media Relations	Carly Peters
Scouts	Marc Chamard, Craig Channell, Paul Charles, Brian Fortin, Christopher Hamel, Jamie Hislop, Brian Hunter, Chris Kelleher, Martin Nanne, Frank Neal, Ricard Perrson, Pavel Routa, Ernie Vargas, Darren Yopyk
Head Athletic Trainer / Assistant	Don Fuller / John Worley
Head Equipment Manager / Assistants	Tony DaCosta / Matt Benz, Rick Bronwell
Message Therapist	Travis Green
Hockey Ops Administrator / Travel Coordinator	Cindy Sweiger / Mary Kenna
Medical Staff	Drs. Sheldon Burns, Joel Boyd, Brad Nelson, Dan Peterson
Oral Surgeon / Team Dentists	David Hamlar / Kyle Edlund, Mike Nanne, Mike Pelke
Ticket Sales and Service	
Senior Director, Fan Relations	Maria Troje
Director, Ticket Sales	Matt Cords
Director, Ticket Operations	Chris Turns
Managers, Group Sales / Inside Sales	Jason Stern / Emily Iverson
Marketing Intelligence	
Vice President, Marketing Intelligence	Mitch Helgerson
Director, Marketing Partnerships	Wayne Petersen
Marketing Manager	Bridget Johnson
Retail Operation	
Retail Operations Manager	Scott Sarkis
Managers, Arena Store / Warehouse	Bill Berg / Joe Ferens
Managers, Maplewood / Burnsville stores	Ryan Geris / Jerry Hudson
Corporate Partnerships and Suite Sales	
Senior Account Executive	Bryan Bellows
Account Executives	Jeff Hunsaker, Brandon Latack
Sr. Mgr. Partnership Activation	Ed Souter
Suite Sales Manager	Mark Fasching
Brand Content and Communications/Broadcasting	
Manager, Game Presentation	Paul Loomis
Manager, Production Facilities Operations	Hank Dolan
Manager, Broadcasting and Production	Maggie Kukar
Coordinators, Radio Ops / Production Services	Kevin Falness / Dustin Peterson
Radio Play-By-Play / Analyst	Bob Kurtz / Tom Reid
Television Play-By-Play / Analyst	Anthony LaPanta / Mike Greenlay
Manager, Web and Creative Services	Matt Minnichsoffer
Managing Editor, Wild.com	Mike Doyle
Lead Graphic Designer / Graphic Designer	Rebecca Finlay / Allison Thompson
Team Curator / Mascot Coordinator	Roger Godin / Robert Hathaway
Community Relations	
Sr. Director, Community Partnerships and Director, Player Development	Brad Bombardir
Executive Director, Wild Foundation	Rachel Schuldt
Finance and Accounting	
Controller	Trevor Shannon
Risk Manager / Sr. Accounting Manager	Maggie Hobbs / Kara Hanson
Human Resources	
Human Resources Director / Generalist	Monica Laurent / Rachel Link
Information Technology	
Helpdesk Manager / IT Generalist	Mike Vevea / Adam Lucht
Miscellaneous	
Radio Network Flagship	KFAN 100.3 FM
Television Network	FOX Sports Net North
Team Photographer / Public Address Announcer	Bruce Kluckhohn / Adam Abrams

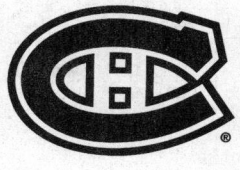

Montreal Canadiens

Key Off-Season Signings/Acquisitions

2013

June 13 • Re-signed D **Davis Drewiske**.
28 • Re-signed RW **Michael Blunden**.
July 5 • Signed C **Daniel Briere**.
5 • Acquired RW **George Parros** from Florida for LW **Philippe Lefebvre** and a 7th-round pick in the 2014 NHL Draft.
10 • Re-signed C **Gabriel Dumont**.
13 • Re-signed C **Ryan White**.

2012-13 Results: 29W-14L-3OTL-2SOL 63PTS
1ST, Northeast Division • 2ND, Eastern Conference

Year-by-Year Record

Season	GP	Home W	Home L	Home T	Home OL	Road W	Road L	Road T	Road OL	Overall W	Overall L	Overall T	Overall OL	GF	GA	Pts.	Div. Fin.	Conf. Fin.	Playoff Result
2012-13	48	14	7	....	3	15	7	....	2	29	14	....	5	149	126	63	1st, NE	2nd, East	Lost Conf. Quarter-Final
2011-12	82	16	15	....	10	15	20	....	6	31	35	....	16	212	226	78	5th, NE	15th, East	Out of Playoffs
2010-11	82	24	11	....	6	20	19	....	2	44	30	....	8	216	209	96	2nd, NE	6th, East	Lost Conf. Quarter-Final
2009-10	82	20	16	....	5	19	17	....	5	39	33	....	10	217	223	88	4th, NE	8th, East	Lost Conf. Final
2008-09	82	24	10	....	7	17	20	....	4	41	30	....	11	249	247	93	2nd, NE	8th, East	Lost Conf. Quarter-Final
2007-08	82	22	13	....	6	25	12	....	4	47	25	....	10	262	222	104	1st, NE	1st, East	Lost Conf. Semi-Final
2006-07	82	26	12	....	3	16	22	....	3	42	34	....	6	245	256	90	4th, NE	10th, East	Out of Playoffs
2005-06	82	24	13	....	4	18	18	....	5	42	31	....	9	243	247	93	3rd, NE	7th, East	Lost Conf. Quarter-Final
2004-05	....	....	....	....	....	....	....	....	....	....	....	....	....	....	....	....			
2003-04	82	23	13	4	1	18	17	3	3	41	30	7	4	208	192	93	4th, NE	7th, East	Lost Conf. Semi-Final
2002-03	82	16	16	5	4	14	19	3	5	30	35	8	9	206	234	77	4th, NE	10th, East	Out of Playoffs
2001-02	82	21	13	6	1	15	18	6	2	36	31	12	3	207	209	87	4th, NE	8th, East	Lost Conf. Semi-Final
2000-01	82	15	20	4	2	13	20	4	4	28	40	8	6	206	232	70	5th, NE	11th, East	Out of Playoffs
1999-2000	82	18	17	5	1	17	17	4	3	35	34	9	4	196	194	83	4th, NE	10th, East	Out of Playoffs
1998-99	82	21	15	5	....	11	24	6	....	32	39	11	....	184	209	75	5th, NE	11th, East	Out of Playoffs
1997-98	82	15	17	9	....	22	15	4	....	37	32	13	....	235	208	87	4th, NE	7th, East	Lost Conf. Semi-Final
1996-97	82	17	17	7	....	14	19	8	....	31	36	15	....	249	276	77	4th, NE	8th, East	Lost Conf. Quarter-Final
1995-96	82	23	12	6	....	17	20	4	....	40	32	10	....	265	248	90	3rd, NE	6th, East	Lost Conf. Quarter-Final
1994-95	48	15	5	4	....	3	18	3	....	18	23	7	....	125	148	43	6th, NE	11th, East	Out of Playoffs
1993-94	84	26	12	4	....	15	17	10	....	41	29	14	....	283	248	96	3rd, NE	5th, East	Lost Conf. Quarter-Final
1992-93	**84**	**27**	**13**	**2**	....	**21**	**17**	**4**	....	**48**	**30**	**6**	....	**326**	**280**	**102**	**3rd, Adams**		**Won Stanley Cup**
1991-92	80	27	8	5	....	14	20	6	....	41	28	11	....	267	207	93	1st, Adams		Lost Div. Final
1990-91	80	23	12	5	....	16	18	6	....	39	30	11	....	273	249	89	2nd, Adams		Lost Div. Final
1989-90	80	26	8	6	....	15	20	5	....	41	28	11	....	288	234	93	3rd, Adams		Lost Div. Final
1988-89	80	30	6	4	....	23	12	5	....	53	18	9	....	315	218	115	1st, Adams		Lost Final
1987-88	80	26	8	6	....	19	14	7	....	45	22	13	....	298	238	103	1st, Adams		Lost Div. Final
1986-87	80	27	9	4	....	14	20	6	....	41	29	10	....	277	241	92	2nd, Adams		Lost Conf. Final
1985-86	**80**	**25**	**11**	**4**	....	**15**	**22**	**3**	....	**40**	**33**	**7**	....	**330**	**280**	**87**	**2nd, Adams**		**Won Stanley Cup**
1984-85	80	24	10	6	....	17	17	6	....	41	27	12	....	309	262	94	1st, Adams		Lost Div. Final
1983-84	80	19	19	2	....	16	21	3	....	35	40	5	....	286	295	75	4th, Adams		Lost Conf. Final
1982-83	80	25	6	9	....	17	18	5	....	42	24	14	....	350	286	98	2nd, Adams		Lost Div. Semi-Final
1981-82	80	25	6	9	....	21	11	8	....	46	17	17	....	360	223	109	1st, Adams		Lost Div. Semi-Final
1980-81	80	31	7	2	....	14	15	11	....	45	22	13	....	332	232	103	1st, Norris		Lost Prelim. Round
1979-80	80	30	7	3	....	17	13	10	....	47	20	13	....	328	240	107	1st, Norris		Lost Quarter-Final
1978-79	**80**	**29**	**6**	**5**	....	**23**	**11**	**6**	....	**52**	**17**	**11**	....	**337**	**204**	**115**	**1st, Norris**		**Won Stanley Cup**
1977-78	**80**	**32**	**4**	**4**	....	**27**	**6**	**7**	....	**59**	**10**	**11**	....	**359**	**183**	**129**	**1st, Norris**		**Won Stanley Cup**
1976-77	**80**	**33**	**1**	**6**	....	**27**	**7**	**6**	....	**60**	**8**	**12**	....	**387**	**171**	**132**	**1st, Norris**		**Won Stanley Cup**
1975-76	**80**	**32**	**3**	**5**	....	**26**	**8**	**6**	....	**58**	**11**	**11**	....	**337**	**174**	**127**	**1st, Norris**		**Won Stanley Cup**
1974-75	80	27	8	5	....	20	6	14	....	47	14	19	....	374	225	113	1st, Norris		Lost Semi-Final
1973-74	78	24	12	3	....	21	12	6	....	45	24	9	....	293	240	99	2nd, East		Lost Quarter-Final
1972-73	**78**	**29**	**4**	**6**	....	**23**	**6**	**10**	....	**52**	**10**	**16**	....	**329**	**184**	**120**	**1st, East**		**Won Stanley Cup**
1971-72	78	29	3	7	....	17	13	9	....	46	16	16	....	307	205	108	3rd, East		Lost Quarter-Final
1970-71	**78**	**29**	**7**	**3**	....	**13**	**16**	**10**	....	**42**	**23**	**13**	....	**291**	**216**	**97**	**3rd, East**		**Won Stanley Cup**
1969-70	76	21	9	8	....	17	13	8	....	38	22	16	....	244	201	92	5th, East		Out of Playoffs
1968-69	**76**	**26**	**7**	**5**	....	**20**	**12**	**6**	....	**46**	**19**	**11**	....	**271**	**202**	**103**	**1st, East**		**Won Stanley Cup**
1967-68	**74**	**26**	**5**	**6**	....	**16**	**17**	**4**	....	**42**	**22**	**10**	....	**236**	**167**	**94**	**1st, East**		**Won Stanley Cup**
1966-67	70	19	9	7	....	13	16	6	....	32	25	13	....	202	188	77	2nd,		Lost Final
1965-66	**70**	**23**	**11**	**1**	....	**18**	**10**	**7**	....	**41**	**21**	**8**	....	**239**	**173**	**90**	**1st,**		**Won Stanley Cup**
1964-65	**70**	**20**	**8**	**7**	....	**16**	**15**	**4**	....	**36**	**23**	**11**	....	**211**	**185**	**83**	**2nd,**		**Won Stanley Cup**
1963-64	70	22	7	6	....	14	14	7	....	36	21	13	....	209	167	85	1st,		Lost Semi-Final
1962-63	70	15	10	10	....	13	9	13	....	28	19	23	....	225	183	79	3rd,		Lost Semi-Final
1961-62	70	26	2	7	....	16	12	7	....	42	14	14	....	259	166	98	1st,		Lost Semi-Final
1960-61	70	24	6	5	....	17	13	5	....	41	19	10	....	254	188	92	1st,		Lost Semi-Final
1959-60	**70**	**23**	**4**	**8**	....	**17**	**14**	**4**	....	**40**	**18**	**12**	....	**255**	**178**	**92**	**1st,**		**Won Stanley Cup**
1958-59	**70**	**21**	**8**	**6**	....	**18**	**10**	**7**	....	**39**	**18**	**13**	....	**258**	**158**	**91**	**1st,**		**Won Stanley Cup**
1957-58	**70**	**23**	**8**	**4**	....	**20**	**9**	**6**	....	**43**	**17**	**10**	....	**250**	**158**	**96**	**1st,**		**Won Stanley Cup**
1956-57	**70**	**23**	**6**	**6**	....	**12**	**17**	**6**	....	**35**	**23**	**12**	....	**210**	**155**	**82**	**2nd,**		**Won Stanley Cup**
1955-56	**70**	**29**	**5**	**1**	....	**16**	**10**	**9**	....	**45**	**15**	**10**	....	**222**	**131**	**100**	**1st,**		**Won Stanley Cup**
1954-55	70	26	5	4	....	15	13	7	....	41	18	11	....	228	157	93	2nd,		Lost Final
1953-54	70	27	5	3	....	8	19	8	....	35	24	11	....	195	141	81	2nd,		Lost Final
1952-53	**70**	**18**	**12**	**5**	....	**10**	**11**	**14**	....	**28**	**23**	**19**	....	**155**	**148**	**75**	**2nd,**		**Won Stanley Cup**
1951-52	70	22	8	5	....	12	18	5	....	34	26	10	....	195	164	78	2nd,		Lost Final
1950-51	70	17	10	8	....	8	20	7	....	25	30	15	....	173	184	65	3rd,		Lost Final
1949-50	70	17	8	10	....	12	14	9	....	29	22	19	....	172	150	77	2nd,		Lost Semi-Final
1948-49	60	19	8	3	....	9	15	6	....	28	23	9	....	152	126	65	3rd,		Lost Semi-Final
1947-48	60	13	13	4	....	7	16	7	....	20	29	11	....	147	169	51	5th,		Out of Playoffs
1946-47	60	19	6	5	....	15	10	5	....	34	16	10	....	189	138	78	1st,		Lost Final
1945-46	**50**	**16**	**6**	**3**	....	**12**	**11**	**2**	....	**28**	**17**	**5**	....	**172**	**134**	**61**	**1st,**		**Won Stanley Cup**
1944-45	50	21	2	2	....	17	6	2	....	38	8	4	....	228	121	80	1st,		Lost Semi-Final
1943-44	**50**	**22**	**0**	**3**	....	**16**	**5**	**4**	....	**38**	**5**	**7**	....	**234**	**109**	**83**	**1st,**		**Won Stanley Cup**
1942-43	50	14	4	7	....	5	15	5	....	19	19	12	....	181	191	50	4th,		Lost Semi-Final
1941-42	48	12	10	2	....	6	17	1	....	18	27	3	....	134	173	39	6th,		Lost Quarter-Final
1940-41	48	11	9	4	....	5	17	2	....	16	26	6	....	121	147	38	6th,		Lost Quarter-Final
1939-40	48	5	14	5	....	5	19	0	....	10	33	5	....	90	168	25	7th,		Out of Playoffs
1938-39	48	8	11	5	....	7	13	4	....	15	24	9	....	115	146	39	6th,		Lost Quarter-Final
1937-38	48	13	4	7	....	5	13	6	....	18	17	13	....	123	128	49	3rd, Cdn.		Lost Quarter-Final
1936-37	48	16	8	0	....	8	10	6	....	24	18	6	....	115	111	54	1st, Cdn.		Lost Semi-Final
1935-36	48	5	11	8	....	6	15	3	....	11	26	11	....	82	123	33	4th, Cdn.		Out of Playoffs
1934-35	48	11	11	2	....	8	12	4	....	19	23	6	....	110	145	44	3rd, Cdn.		Lost Quarter-Final
1933-34	48	16	6	2	....	6	14	4	....	22	20	6	....	99	101	50	2nd, Cdn.		Lost Quarter-Final
1932-33	48	15	5	4	....	3	20	1	....	18	25	5	....	92	115	41	3rd, Cdn.		Lost Quarter-Final
1931-32	48	18	3	3	....	7	13	4	....	25	16	7	....	128	111	57	1st, Cdn.		Lost Semi-Final
1930-31	**44**	**15**	**3**	**4**	....	**11**	**7**	**4**	....	**26**	**10**	**8**	....	**129**	**89**	**60**	**1st, Cdn.**		**Won Stanley Cup**
1929-30	**44**	**13**	**5**	**4**	....	**8**	**9**	**5**	....	**21**	**14**	**9**	....	**142**	**114**	**51**	**2nd, Cdn.**		**Won Stanley Cup**
1928-29	44	12	4	6	....	10	3	9	....	22	7	15	....	71	43	59	1st, Cdn.		Lost Semi-Final
1927-28	44	12	7	3	....	14	4	4	....	26	11	7	....	116	48	59	1st, Cdn.		Lost Semi-Final
1926-27	44	15	5	2	....	13	9	0	....	28	14	2	....	99	67	58	2nd, Cdn.		Lost Semi-Final
1925-26	36	5	12	1	....	6	12	0	....	11	24	1	....	79	108	23	7th,		Out of Playoffs
1924-25	30	10	5	0	....	7	6	2	....	17	11	2	....	93	56	36	3rd,		Lost Final
1923-24	**24**	**10**	**2**	**0**	....	**3**	**9**	**0**	....	**13**	**11**	**0**	....	**59**	**48**	**26**	**2nd,**		**Won Stanley Cup**
1922-23	24	10	2	0	....	3	7	2	....	13	9	2	....	73	61	28	2nd,		Lost NHL Final
1921-22	24	8	3	1	....	4	8	0	....	12	11	1	....	88	94	25	3rd,		Out of Playoffs
1920-21	24	9	3	0	....	4	8	0	....	13	11	0	....	112	99	26	3rd and 2nd*		Out of Playoffs
1919-20	24	8	4	0	....	5	7	0	....	13	11	0	....	129	113	26	2nd and 3rd*		Out of Playoffs
1918-19	18	7	2	0	....	3	6	0	....	10	8	0	....	88	78	20	1st and 2nd*		Cup Final but no Decision
1917-18	22	8	3	0	....	5	6	0	....	13	9	0	....	115	84	26	1st and 3rd*		Lost NHL Final

* Season played in two halves with no combined standing at end.
From 1917-18 through 1925-26, NHL champions played against PCHA/WCHL champions for Stanley Cup.

2013-14 Schedule

Month	Day	Date	Opponent
Oct.	Tue.	1	Toronto
	Sat.	5	Philadelphia
	Wed.	9	at Calgary
	Thu.	10	at Edmonton
	Sat.	12	at Vancouver
	Tue.	15	at Winnipeg
	Thu.	17	Columbus
	Sat.	19	Nashville
	Tue.	22	Edmonton
	Thu.	24	Anaheim
	Sat.	26	San Jose
	Mon.	28	at NY Rangers
	Tue.	29	Dallas
Nov.	Fri.	1	at Minnesota
	Sat.	2	at Colorado
	Tue.	5	St. Louis
	Thu.	7	at Ottawa
	Sun.	10	NY Islanders
	Tue.	12	Tampa Bay
	Fri.	15	at Columbus
	Sat.	16	NY Rangers
	Tue.	19	Minnesota
	Fri.	22	at Washington
	Sat.	23	Pittsburgh
	Wed.	27	at Buffalo
	Fri.	29	at Washington*
	Sat.	30	Toronto
Dec.	Mon.	2	New Jersey
	Wed.	4	at New Jersey
	Thu.	5	Boston
	Sat.	7	Buffalo
	Tue.	10	Los Angeles
	Thu.	12	at Philadelphia
	Sat.	14	at NY Islanders
	Sun.	15	Florida
	Tue.	17	Phoenix
	Thu.	19	at St. Louis
	Sat.	21	at Nashville
	Sat.	28	at Tampa Bay
	Sun.	29	at Florida*
	Tue.	31	at Carolina
Jan.	Thu.	2	at Dallas
	Sat.	4	Ottawa
	Mon.	6	Florida
	Wed.	8	at Philadelphia
	Sat.	11	Chicago
	Tue.	14	New Jersey
	Thu.	16	at Ottawa
	Sat.	18	at Toronto
	Wed.	22	at Pittsburgh
	Fri.	24	at Detroit
	Sat.	25	Washington
	Tue.	28	Carolina
	Thu.	30	at Boston
Feb.	Sat.	1	Tampa Bay*
	Sun.	2	Winnipeg*
	Tue.	4	Calgary
	Thu.	6	Vancouver
	Sat.	8	at Carolina
	Wed.	26	Detroit
	Thu.	27	at Pittsburgh
Mar.	Sat.	1	Toronto
	Mon.	3	at Los Angeles
	Wed.	5	at Anaheim
	Thu.	6	at Phoenix
	Sat.	8	at San Jose
	Wed.	12	Boston
	Sat.	15	Ottawa
	Sun.	16	at Buffalo
	Tue.	18	Colorado
	Thu.	20	Columbus
	Sat.	22	at Toronto
	Mon.	24	at Boston
	Tue.	25	Buffalo
	Thu.	27	at Detroit
	Sat.	29	at Florida
Apr.	Tue.	1	at Tampa Bay
	Fri.	4	at Ottawa
	Sat.	5	Detroit
	Wed.	9	at Chicago
	Thu.	10	NY Islanders
	Sat.	12	NY Rangers

* Denotes afternoon game.

ATLANTIC DIVISION
97th NHL Season

Franchise date: November 26, 1917

2013-14 Player Personnel

FORWARDS	HT	WT	*Age	Place of Birth	S	2012-13 Club
BLUNDEN, Mike	6-4	211	26	Toronto, Ont.	R	Hamilton-Montreal
BOURQUE, Rene	6-2	211	31	Lac La Biche, Alta.	L	Montreal
BRIERE, Daniel	5-10	179	35	Gatineau, Que.	R	Eisbaren Berlin-Phi
DESHARNAIS, David	5-7	177	27	Laurier-Station, Que.	L	Fribourg-Montreal
ELLER, Lars	6-2	201	24	Rodovre, Denmark	L	JYP-Montreal
GALCHENYUK, Alex	6-1	194	19	Milwaukee, WI	L	Sarnia-Montreal
GALLAGHER, Brendan	5-8	175	21	Edmonton, Alta.	R	Hamilton-Montreal
GIONTA, Brian	5-7	175	34	Rochester, NY	R	Montreal
MOEN, Travis	6-2	215	31	Stewart Valley, Sask.	L	Montreal
PACIORETTY, Max	6-2	210	24	New Canaan, CT	L	Ambri-Montreal
PARROS, George	6-5	228	33	Washington, PA	R	Florida
PLEKANEC, Tomas	5-11	198	30	Kladno, Czech.	L	Kladno-Montreal
PRUST, Brandon	6-2	192	29	London, Ont.	L	Montreal
WHITE, Ryan	6-0	199	25	Brandon, Man.	R	Montreal
DEFENSEMEN						
BOUILLON, Francis	5-8	198	37	New York, NY	L	Montreal
DIAZ, Raphael	5-11	194	27	Baar, Switz.	R	Zug-Montreal
DREWISKE, Davis	6-1	220	28	Hudson, WI	L	Los Angeles-Montreal
EMELIN, Alexei	6-2	219	27	Togliatti, USSR	L	Kazan-Montreal
GORGES, Josh	6-1	201	29	Kelowna, B.C.	L	Montreal
MARKOV, Andrei	6-0	207	34	Voskresensk, USSR	L	Chekhov-Montreal
SUBBAN, P.K.	6-0	206	24	Toronto, Ont.	R	Montreal

GOALTENDERS	HT	WT	*Age	Place of Birth	C	2012-13 Club
BUDAJ, Peter	6-1	195	31	Banska Bystrica, Czech.	L	Montreal
PRICE, Carey	6-3	221	26	Anahim Lake, B.C.	L	Montreal

* – Age at start of 2013-14 season

Michel Therrien

Head Coach

Born: Montreal, Que., November 4, 1963.

The Montreal Canadiens announced the appointment of Michel Therrien as the club's head coach on June 5, 2012. After finishing 15th in the Eastern Conference in 2011-12, Therrien led the Canadiens to a division title in 2012-13.

This is Therrien's second stint with the Canadiens, having previously served as a head coach in the organization from 1997 to 2003. The Montreal native joined the franchise in June 1997 taking over behind the bench of the Canadiens' American Hockey League affiliate in Fredericton. In 1999-2000, he became the first head coach of the Quebec Citadelles leading the team to the Atlantic Division Championship in its inaugural season. On November 20, 2000, Therrien became the 25th head coach in Canadiens history. He led the Canadiens to their first playoff appearance in four years in 2001-02.

After Montreal, Therrien spent six years with the Pittsburgh Penguins organization, coaching the club's AHL affiliate in Wilkes-Barre/Scranton from 2003 to 2005, before being promoted to Pittsburgh and leading the Penguins to new heights from 2005 to 2009. Therrien's team was off to a 21-1-3 start in the AHL when he was summoned to Pittsburgh to take over as head coach on December 15, 2005. In 2006-07, his second season behind the Pens' bench, he was a finalist for the Jack Adams Award as NHL coach of the year after leading the Penguins to 105 points and a 47-point improvement over the previous season. It was the fourth-biggest turnaround from one season to the next in NHL history. In 2007-08 under Therrien's guidance, the Penguins kept the same pace and earned 102 regular season points making their way to the Stanley Cup Final, dropping a six-game decision to the Detroit Red Wings. It was the Penguins first division title since 1997-98 and their first berth to the Cup finals since 1991-92.

Before joining the Canadiens, Therrien coached the Laval Titan and the Granby Predateurs in the Quebec Major Junior Hockey League, winning the Memorial Cup with Granby in 1996. In his playing days, he was a solid defenseman who captured the Calder Cup in 1985 as a member of the Sherbrooke Canadiens.

Coaching Record

			Regular Season				Playoffs			
Season	Team	League	GC	W	L	O/T	GC	W	L	T
1990-91	Laval	QMJHL	3	2	1	0	....	....	....	....
1991-92	Laval	QMJHL	3	1	2	....	....	....	....	....
1993-94	Laval	QMJHL	58	41	16	1	21	14	7	....
1993-94	Laval	M-Cup	....	....	....	....	5	2	3	....
1994-95	Laval	QMJHL	63	41	21	1	20	14	6	....
1995-96	Granby	QMJHL	62	49	11	2	20	16	4	....
1995-96	Granby	M-Cup	....	....	....	....	4	3	1	....
1996-97	Granby	QMJHL	67	42	19	6	5	1	4	....
1997-98	Fredericton	AHL	80	33	32	15	4	1	3	....
1998-99	Fredericton	AHL	80	33	36	11	15	9	6	....
99-2000	Quebec	AHL	80	37	34	9	3	0	3	....
2000-01	**Montreal**	**NHL**	**62**	**23**	**27**	**12**	....	....	....	....
2000-01	Quebec	AHL	19	12	6	1	....	....	....	....
2001-02	**Montreal**	**NHL**	**82**	**36**	**31**	**15**	**12**	**6**	**6**	....
2002-03	**Montreal**	**NHL**	**46**	**18**	**19**	**9**	....	....	....	....
2003-04	Wilkes-Barre	AHL	80	34	28	18	24	12	12	....
2004-05	Wilkes-Barre	AHL	80	39	27	14	11	5	6	....
2005-06	**Pittsburgh**	**NHL**	**51**	**14**	**29**	**8**	....	....	....	....
2005-06	Wilkes-Barre	AHL	25	21	1	3	....	....	....	....
2006-07	**Pittsburgh**	**NHL**	**82**	**47**	**24**	**11**	**5**	**1**	**4**	....
2007-08	**Pittsburgh**	**NHL**	**82**	**47**	**27**	**8**	**20**	**14**	**6**	....
2008-09	**Pittsburgh**	**NHL**	**57**	**27**	**25**	**5**	....	....	....	....
2012-13	**Montreal**	**NHL**	**48**	**29**	**14**	**5**	**5**	**1**	**4**	....
	NHL Totals		**510**	**241**	**196**	**73**	**42**	**22**	**20**	....

2012-13 Scoring

* – rookie

Regular Season

Pos	#	Player	Team	GP	G	A	Pts	TOI	+/–	PIM	PP	SH	GW	S	%
L	67	Max Pacioretty	MTL	44	15	24	39	16:30	8	28	4	0	0	163	9.2
D	76	P.K. Subban	MTL	42	11	27	38	23:14	12	57	7	0	0	126	8.7
R	73	Michael Ryder	DAL	19	6	8	14	16:22	4	8	2	0	2	42	14.3
			MTL	27	10	11	21	15:49	–2	8	6	0	3	59	16.9
			Total	46	16	19	35	16:02	2	16	8	0	5	101	15.8
C	14	Tomas Plekanec	MTL	47	14	19	33	19:12	3	24	4	0	2	133	10.5
D	79	Andrei Markov	MTL	48	10	20	30	24:07	–9	14	8	0	4	79	12.7
C	81	Lars Eller	MTL	46	8	22	30	14:49	8	45	1	0	1	84	9.5
R	11 *	Brendan Gallagher	MTL	44	15	13	28	13:51	10	33	3	0	3	117	12.8
C	51	David Desharnais	MTL	48	10	18	28	16:27	–2	26	2	0	3	66	15.2
C	27 *	Alex Galchenyuk	MTL	48	9	18	27	12:19	14	20	0	0	2	79	11.4
R	21	Brian Gionta	MTL	48	14	12	26	18:07	3	8	5	0	3	112	12.5
L	8	Brandon Prust	MTL	38	5	9	14	13:38	11	110	0	0	1	39	12.8
D	61	Raphael Diaz	MTL	23	1	13	14	20:33	4	6	0	0	0	34	2.9
R	17	Rene Bourque	MTL	27	7	6	13	16:19	–1	32	2	0	1	63	11.1
D	74	Alexei Emelin	MTL	38	3	9	12	19:40	2	33	0	0	0	33	9.1
D	26	Josh Gorges	MTL	48	2	7	9	21:23	4	15	0	0	0	40	5.0
D	55	Francis Bouillon	MTL	48	1	8	9	18:04	4	21	0	0	0	46	2.2
D	44	Davis Drewiske	L.A.	20	1	3	4	14:27	3	14	1	0	0	20	5.0
			MTL	9	1	2	3	16:49	0	0	0	0	0	8	12.5
			Total	29	2	5	7	15:11	3	14	1	0	0	28	7.1
L	32	Travis Moen	MTL	45	2	4	6	11:39	–4	32	0	0	0	32	6.3
R	20	Colby Armstrong	MTL	37	2	3	5	11:12	1	12	0	0	0	33	6.1
C	37 *	Gabriel Dumont	MTL	10	1	2	3	9:40	1	13	0	0	0	20	5.0
C	24	Jeff Halpern	NYR	30	0	1	1	9:09	–5	8	0	0	0	13	0.0
			MTL	16	1	1	2	12:06	–3	2	0	0	1	13	7.7
			Total	46	1	2	3	10:11	–8	10	0	0	1	26	3.8
D	22	Tomas Kaberle	MTL	10	0	3	3	13:32	4	0	0	0	0	11	0.0
D	68	Yannick Weber	MTL	6	0	2	2	13:45	–1	2	0	0	0	3	0.0
D	40 *	Nathan Beaulieu	MTL	6	0	2	2	15:22	5	0	0	0	0	8	0.0
D	42 *	Jarred Tinordi	MTL	8	0	2	2	11:42	5	2	0	0	0	5	0.0
C	53	Ryan White	MTL	26	1	0	1	9:24	1	67	0	0	0	16	6.3
D	64 *	Greg Pateryn	MTL	3	0	0	0	9:36	0	0	0	0	0	0	0.0
R	45	Mike Blunden	MTL	5	0	0	0	8:20	–1	4	0	0	0	5	0.0

Goaltending

No.	Goaltender	GPI	Mins	Avg	W	L	OT	EN	SO	GA	SA	S%	G	A	PIM
30	Peter Budaj	13	656	2.29	8	1	1	0	1	25	273	.908	0	0	0
31	Carey Price	39	2249	2.59	21	13	4	2	3	97	1018	.905	0	0	0
	Totals	**48**	**2918**	**2.55**	**29**	**14**	**5**	**2**	**4**	**124**	**1293**	**.904**			

Playoffs

Pos	#	Player	Team	GP	G	A	Pts	TOI	+/–	PIM	PP	SH	GW	OT	S	%
D	76	P.K. Subban	MTL	5	2	2	4	23:56	–1	31	1	0	0	0	21	9.5
C	14	Tomas Plekanec	MTL	5	0	4	4	20:53	–5	2	0	0	0	0	15	0.0
R	17	Rene Bourque	MTL	5	2	1	3	16:08	–1	10	1	0	0	0	17	11.8
C	27 *	Alex Galchenyuk	MTL	5	1	2	3	13:00	–4	0	0	0	0	0	15	6.7
R	11 *	Brendan Gallagher	MTL	5	2	0	2	14:26	–7	5	1	0	1	0	22	9.1
R	73	Michael Ryder	MTL	5	1	1	2	14:50	0	2	0	0	0	0	8	12.5
C	53	Ryan White	MTL	3	1	0	1	9:05	–1	23	0	0	0	0	4	25.0
R	21	Brian Gionta	MTL	2	0	1	1	17:09	–2	0	0	0	0	0	5	0.0
C	24	Jeff Halpern	MTL	3	0	1	1	14:24	1	0	0	0	0	0	8	0.0
L	8	Brandon Prust	MTL	4	0	1	1	15:26	–3	14	0	0	0	0	7	0.0
D	79	Andrei Markov	MTL	5	0	1	1	23:53	–1	0	0	0	0	0	7	0.0
C	51	David Desharnais	MTL	5	0	1	1	17:13	1	2	0	0	0	0	3	0.0
D	42 *	Jarred Tinordi	MTL	5	0	1	1	13:05	–3	15	0	0	0	0	4	0.0
R	45	Mike Blunden	MTL	1	0	0	0	8:12	0	10	0	0	0	0	1	0.0
C	81	Lars Eller	MTL	1	0	0	0	8:43	0	0	0	0	0	0	0	0.0
C	37 *	Gabriel Dumont	MTL	3	0	0	0	6:20	0	12	0	0	0	0	3	0.0
R	20	Colby Armstrong	MTL	4	0	0	0	11:31	–1	15	0	0	0	0	2	0.0
L	67	Max Pacioretty	MTL	4	0	0	0	17:16	0	4	0	0	0	0	13	0.0
D	55	Francis Bouillon	MTL	5	0	0	0	16:02	–3	17	0	0	0	0	5	0.0
L	32	Travis Moen	MTL	5	0	0	0	12:53	–2	17	0	0	0	0	5	0.0
D	26	Josh Gorges	MTL	5	0	0	0	21:18	–4	4	0	0	0	0	5	0.0
D	61	Raphael Diaz	MTL	5	0	0	0	22:22	–4	0	0	0	0	0	10	0.0

Goaltending

No.	Goaltender	GPI	Mins	Avg	W	L	EN	SO	GA	SA	S%	G	A	PIM
31	Carey Price	4	239	3.26	1	2	0	0	13	123	.894	0	0	0
30	Peter Budaj	2	63	6.67	0	2	0	0	7	31	.774	0	0	0
	Totals	**5**	**303**	**3.96**	**1**	**4**	**0**	**0**	**20**	**154**	**.870**			

Coaching History

Jack Laviolette, 1909-10; Adolphe Lecours, 1910-11; Napoleon Dorval, 1911-12, 1912-13; Jimmy Gardner, 1913-14, 1914-15; Newsy Lalonde, 1915-16 to 1920-21; Newsy Lalonde and Léo Dandurand, 1921-22; Léo Dandurand, 1922-23 to 1925-26; Cecil Hart, 1926-27 to 1931-32; Newsy Lalonde, 1932-33, 1933-34; Newsy Lalonde and Léo Dandurand, 1934-35; Sylvio Mantha, 1935-36; Cecil Hart, 1936-37, 1937-38; Cecil Hart and Jules Dugal, 1938-39; Babe Siebert, 1939*; Pit Lepine, 1939-40; Dick Irvin 1940-41 to 1954-55; Toe Blake, 1955-56 to 1967-68; Claude Ruel, 1968-69, 1969-70; Claude Ruel and Al MacNeil, 1970-71; Scotty Bowman, 1971-72 to 1978-79; Bernie Geoffrion and Claude Ruel, 1979-80; Claude Ruel, 1980-81; Bob Berry, 1981-82, 1982-83; Bob Berry and Jacques Lemaire, 1983-84; Jacques Lemaire, 1984-85; Jean Perron, 1985-86 to 1987-88; Pat Burns, 1988-89 to 1991-92; Jacques Demers, 1992-93 to 1994-95; Jacques Demers, Jacques Laperriere, Mario Tremblay, 1995-96; Mario Tremblay, 1996-97; Alain Vigneault, 1997-98 to 1999-2000; Alain Vigneault and Michel Therrien, 2000-01; Michel Therrien, 2001-02; Michel Therrien and Claude Julien, 2002-03; Claude Julien, 2003-04, 2004-05; Claude Julien and Bob Gainey, 2005-06; Guy Carbonneau, 2006-07, 2007-08; Guy Carbonneau and Bob Gainey, 2008-09; Jacques Martin, 2009-10, 2010-11; Jacques Martin and Randy Cunneyworth, 2011-12; Michel Therrien, 2012-13 to date.

* Named coach in summer but died before 1939-40 season began.

Club Records

Team

(Figures in brackets for season records are games played; records for fewest points, wins, ties, losses, goals, goals against are for 70 or more games)

Most Points	*132	1976-77 (80)
Most Wins	60	1976-77 (80)
Most Ties	23	1962-63 (70)
Most Losses	40	1983-84 (80), 2000-01 (82)
Most Goals	387	1976-77 (80)
Most Goals Against	295	1983-84 (80)
Fewest Points	65	1950-51 (70)
Fewest Wins	25	1950-51 (70)
Fewest Ties	5	1983-84 (80)
Fewest Losses	*8	1976-77 (80)
Fewest Goals	155	1952-53 (70)
Fewest Goals Against	*131	1955-56 (70)
Longest Winning Streak		
Overall	12	Jan. 6-Feb. 3/68
Home	13	Nov. 2/43-Jan. 8/44, Jan. 30-Mar. 26/77
Away	8	Dec. 18/77-Jan. 18/78, Jan. 21-Feb. 21/82
Longest Undefeated Streak		
Overall	28	Dec. 18/77-Feb. 23/78 (23W, 5T)
Home	*34	Nov. 1/76-Apr. 2/77 (28W, 6T)
Away	*23	Nov. 27/74-Mar. 12/75 (14W, 9T)
Longest Losing Streak		
Overall	12	Feb. 13-Mar. 13/26
Home	7	Dec. 16/39-Jan. 18/40, Oct. 28-Nov. 25/00
Away	10	Jan. 16-Mar. 13/26
Longest Winless Streak		
Overall	12	Feb. 13-Mar. 13/26 (12L), Nov. 28-Dec. 29/35 (8L, 4T)
Home	15	Dec. 16/39-Mar. 7/40 (12L, 3T)
Away	12	Nov. 26/33-Jan. 28/34 (8L, 4T), Oct. 20-Dec. 13/51 (8L, 4T)
Most Shutouts, Season	*22	1928-29 (44)
Most PIM, Season	1,847	1995-96 (82)
Most Goals, Game	*16	Mar. 3/20 (Mtl. 16 at Que. 3)

Individual

Most Seasons	20	Henri Richard, Jean Béliveau
Most Games	1,256	Henri Richard
Most Goals, Career	544	Maurice Richard
Most Assists, Career	728	Guy Lafleur
Most Points, Career	1,246	Guy Lafleur (518G, 728A)
Most PIM, Career	2,248	Chris Nilan
Most Shutouts, Career	75	George Hainsworth
Longest Consecutive Games Streak	560	Doug Jarvis (Oct. 8/75-Apr. 4/82)
Most Goals, Season	60	Steve Shutt (1976-77), Guy Lafleur (1977-78)
Most Assists, Season	82	Pete Mahovlich (1974-75)
Most Points, Season	136	Guy Lafleur (1976-77; 56G, 80A)
Most PIM, Season	358	Chris Nilan (1984-85)
Most Points, Defenseman, Season	85	Larry Robinson (1976-77; 19G, 66A)
Most Points, Center, Season	117	Pete Mahovlich (1974-75; 35G, 82A)
Most Points, Right Wing, Season	136	Guy Lafleur (1976-77; 56G, 80A)
Most Points, Left Wing, Season	110	Mats Naslund (1985-86; 43G, 67A)
Most Points, Rookie, Season	71	Mats Naslund (1982-83; 26G, 45A), Kjell Dahlin (1985-86; 32G, 39A)
Most Shutouts, Season	*22	George Hainsworth (1928-29)
Most Goals, Game	6	Newsy Lalonde (Jan. 10/20)
Most Assists, Game	6	Elmer Lach (Feb. 6/43)
Most Points, Game	8	Maurice Richard (Dec. 28/44; 5G, 3A), Bert Olmstead (Jan. 9/54; 4G, 4A)

* NHL Record.

Retired Numbers

1	Jacques Plante	1952-1963
2	Doug Harvey	1947-1961
3	Butch Bouchard	1941-1956
4	Jean Béliveau	1950-1971
5	Bernard Geoffrion	1950-1964
7	Howie Morenz	1923-1937
9	Maurice Richard	1942-1960
10	Guy Lafleur	1971-1984
12	Dickie Moore	1951-1963
	Yvan Cournoyer	1963-1979
16	Henri Richard	1955-1975
	Elmer Lach	1940-1954
18	Serge Savard	1966-1981
19	Larry Robinson	1972-1989
23	Bob Gainey	1973-1989
29	Ken Dryden	1970-1979
33	Patrick Roy	1984-1996

Captains' History

Jack Laviolette, 1909-10; Newsy Lalonde, 1910-11; Jack Laviolette, 1911-12; Newsy Lalonde, 1912-13; Jimmy Gardner, 1913-14, 1914-15; Howard McNamara, 1915-16; Newsy Lalonde, 1916-17 to 1921-22; Sprague Cleghorn, 1922-23 to 1924-25; Bill Coutu, 1925-26; Sylvio Mantha, 1926-27 to 1931-32; George Hainsworth, 1932-33; Sylvio Mantha, 1933-34 to 1935-36; Babe Siebert, 1936-37 to 1938-39; Walt Buswell, 1939-40; Toe Blake, 1940-41 to 1946-47; Toe Blake and Bill Durnan, 1947-48; Butch Bouchard, 1948-49 to 1955-56; Maurice Richard, 1956-57 to 1959-60; Doug Harvey, 1960-61; Jean Béliveau, 1961-62 to 1970-71; Henri Richard, 1971-72 to 1974-75; Yvan Cournoyer, 1975-76 to 1977-78; Yvan Cournoyer and Serge Savard (interim), 1978-79; Serge Savard, 1979-80, 1980-81; Bob Gainey, 1981-82 to 1988-89; Guy Carbonneau and Chris Chelios, 1989-90; Guy Carbonneau, 1990-91 to 1993-94; Kirk Muller and Mike Keane, 1994-95; Mike Keane and Pierre Turgeon, 1995-96; Pierre Turgeon and Vincent Damphousse, 1996-97; Vincent Damphousse, 1997-98, 1998-99; Saku Koivu, 1999-2000 to 2008-09; no captain, 2009-10; Brian Gionta, 2010-11 to date.

All-time Record vs. Other Clubs

Regular Season

	Total								At Home								On Road							
	GP	W	L	T	OL	GF	GA	PTS	GP	W	L	T	OL	GF	GA	PTS	GP	W	L	T	OL	GF	GA	PTS
Anaheim	22	10	9	2	1	67	69	23	11	4	4	2	1	34	34	11	11	6	5	0	0	33	35	12
Boston	721	348	263	103	7	2185	1909	806	360	208	102	47	3	1205	845	466	361	140	161	56	4	980	1064	340
Buffalo	258	108	105	31	14	791	768	261	130	68	43	12	7	455	372	155	128	40	62	19	7	336	396	106
Calgary	105	55	34	15	1	353	294	126	51	29	14	8	0	178	126	66	54	26	20	7	1	175	168	60
Carolina	184	100	59	20	5	666	533	225	91	57	25	7	2	352	261	123	93	43	34	13	3	314	272	102
Chicago	555	302	150	103	0	1842	1399	707	279	177	54	48	0	1077	658	402	276	125	96	55	0	765	741	305
Colorado	133	66	49	15	3	505	435	150	67	39	16	10	2	276	212	90	66	27	33	5	1	229	223	60
Columbus	11	4	3	1	3	22	25	12	7	2	2	1	2	13	15	7	4	2	1	0	1	9	10	5
Dallas	123	70	32	21	0	468	315	161	61	39	13	9	0	259	152	87	62	31	19	12	0	209	163	74
Detroit	568	271	199	96	2	1726	1457	640	285	173	68	43	1	1004	645	390	283	98	131	53	1	722	812	250
Edmonton	75	37	30	4	4	247	250	82	35	19	10	4	2	121	111	44	40	18	20	0	2	126	139	38
Florida	74	34	31	6	3	194	184	77	36	17	13	3	3	93	80	40	38	17	18	3	0	101	104	37
Los Angeles	135	88	27	20	0	567	370	196	67	48	8	11	0	300	166	107	68	40	19	9	0	267	204	89
Minnesota	11	6	3	1	1	37	29	14	6	3	2	1	0	19	17	7	5	3	1	0	1	18	12	7
Nashville	14	8	4	1	1	37	41	18	7	5	1	0	1	22	19	11	7	3	3	1	0	15	22	7
New Jersey	139	67	59	10	3	436	384	147	69	36	25	6	2	208	176	80	70	31	34	4	1	228	208	67
NY Islanders	151	79	49	15	8	489	434	181	75	45	16	9	5	268	206	104	76	34	33	6	3	221	228	77
NY Rangers	611	326	188	94	3	2066	1589	749	306	202	63	40	1	1185	705	445	305	124	125	54	2	881	884	304
Ottawa	116	57	46	5	8	333	335	127	59	32	21	4	2	175	163	70	57	25	25	1	6	158	172	57
Philadelphia	178	80	66	30	2	567	535	192	90	44	31	14	1	306	268	103	88	36	35	16	1	261	267	89
Phoenix	64	43	12	9	0	277	171	95	32	27	3	2	0	154	71	56	32	16	9	7	0	123	100	39
Pittsburgh	195	115	52	23	5	769	552	258	97	68	17	10	2	433	257	148	98	47	35	13	3	336	295	110
St. Louis	122	71	27	22	2	464	328	166	62	41	12	7	2	261	172	91	60	30	15	15	0	203	156	75
San Jose	28	14	8	4	2	85	71	34	14	10	2	2	0	48	25	22	14	4	6	2	2	37	46	12
Tampa Bay	76	39	29	6	2	213	186	86	37	21	13	1	2	107	89	45	39	18	16	5	0	106	97	41
Toronto	719	340	283	88	8	2195	1995	776	359	210	101	43	5	1243	906	468	360	130	182	45	3	952	1089	308
Vancouver	118	76	27	13	2	469	311	167	58	41	11	5	1	255	145	88	60	35	16	8	1	214	166	79
Washington	150	71	56	17	6	485	386	165	76	41	24	8	3	270	178	93	74	30	32	9	3	215	208	72
Winnipeg	51	33	11	2	5	158	112	73	26	19	4	0	3	93	60	41	25	14	7	2	2	65	52	32
Defunct Clubs	461	246	155	60	0	1365	1075	552	231	148	58	25	0	779	469	321	230	98	97	35	0	586	606	231
Totals	**6168**	**3164**	**2066**	**837**	**101**	**20078**	**16542**	**7266**	**3084**	**1873**	**776**	**382**	**53**	**11193**	**7603**	**4181**	**3084**	**1291**	**1290**	**455**	**48**	**8885**	**8939**	**3085**

Playoffs

	Series	W	L	GP	W	L	T	GF	GA	Last Mtg.	Rnd.	Result
Boston	33	24	9	170	102	68	0	511	420	2011	CQF	L 3-4
Buffalo	7	4	3	35	18	17	0	124	111	1998	CSF	L 0-4
Calgary	2	1	1	11	6	5	0	31	32	1989	F	L 2-4
Carolina	7	5	2	39	23	16	0	125	106	2006	CQF	L 2-4
Chicago	17	12	5	81	50	29	2	261	185	1976	QF	W 4-0
Colorado	5	3	2	31	17	14	0	105	85	1993	DSF	W 4-2
Dallas	2	1	1	13	7	6	0	48	37	1980	QF	L 3-4
Detroit	12	5	7	62	33	29	0	161	149	1978	QF	W 4-1
Edmonton	1	0	1	3	0	3	0	6	15	1981	PRE	L 0-3
Los Angeles	1	1	0	5	4	1	0	15	12	1993	F	W 4-1
New Jersey	1	0	1	5	1	4	0	11	22	1997	CQF	L 1-4
NY Islanders	4	3	1	22	14	8	0	64	55	1993	CF	W 4-1
NY Rangers	14	7	7	61	34	25	2	188	158	1996	CQF	L 2-4
Ottawa	1	0	1	5	1	4	0	9	20	2013	CQF	L 1-4
Philadelphia	6	3	3	31	16	15	0	93	89	2010	CF	L 1-4
Pittsburgh	2	2	0	13	8	5	0	37	33	2010	CSF	W 4-3
St. Louis	3	3	0	12	12	0	0	42	14	1977	QF	W 4-0
Tampa Bay	1	0	1	4	0	4	0	5	14	2004	CSF	L 0-4
Toronto	15	8	7	71	42	29	0	215	160	1979	QF	W 4-0
Vancouver	1	1	0	5	4	1	0	20	9	1975	QF	W 4-1
Washington	1	1	0	7	4	3	0	20	22	2010	CQF	W 4-3
Defunct Clubs	10*	5	4	28	15	9	4	70	71			
Totals	**146***	**89**	**56**	**714**	**411**	**295**	**8**	**2161**	**1819**			

Calgary totals include Atlanta Flames, 1972-73 to 1979-80.
Colorado totals include Quebec, 1979-80 to 1994-95.
New Jersey totals include Kansas City, 1974-75, 1975-76, and Colorado Rockies, 1976-77 to 1981-82.
Phoenix totals include Winnipeg, 1979-80 to 1995-96.
Carolina totals include Hartford, 1979-80 to 1996-97.
Dallas totals include Minnesota North Stars, 1967-68 to 1992-93.
Winnipeg totals include Atlanta Thrashers, 1999-2000 to 2010-11.

Playoff Results 2013-2009

Year	Round	Opponent	Result	GF	GA
2013	CQF	Ottawa	L 1-4	9	20
2011	CQF	Boston	L 3-4	17	17
2010	CF	Philadelphia	L 1-4	7	17
	CSF	Pittsburgh	W 4-3	19	18
	CQF	Washington	W 4-3	20	22
2009	CQF	Boston	L 0-4	6	17

Abbreviations: Round: F – Final; **CF** – conference final; **CSF** – conference semi-final; **CQF** – conference quarter-final; **DSF** – division semi-final; **QF** – quarter-final; **PRE** – preliminary round.

2012-13 Results

Jan.	19	Toronto	1-2		9	at Tampa Bay	4-3
	22	Florida	4-1		10	at Florida	5-2
	24	at Washington	4-1		13	Ottawa	4-3†
	27	New Jersey	4-3*		16	at New Jersey	2-1
	29	Winnipeg	4-3		19	Buffalo	2-3*
	30	at Ottawa	1-5		21	at NY Islanders	5-2
Feb.	2	Buffalo	6-1		23	Buffalo	1-2
	3	Ottawa	2-1		26	at Pittsburgh	0-1
	6	Boston	1-2		27	at Boston	6-5†
	7	at Buffalo	4-5†		30	NY Rangers	3-0
	9	Toronto	0-6	**Apr.**	1	Carolina	4-1
	12	at Tampa Bay	4-3†		3	at Philadelphia	3-5
	14	at Florida	1-0*		4	Winnipeg	4-1
	16	Philadelphia	4-1		6	Boston	2-1
	18	Carolina	3-0		9	Washington	2-3
	19	at NY Rangers	3-1		11	at Buffalo	5-1
	21	NY Islanders	3-4*		13	at Toronto	1-5
	23	NY Rangers	3-0		15	Philadelphia	3-7
	25	at Ottawa	1-2†		17	at Pittsburgh	4-6
	27	at Toronto	5-2		18	Tampa Bay	3-2
Mar.	2	Pittsburgh	6-7*		20	Washington	1-5
	3	at Boston	4-3		23	at New Jersey	2-3
	5	at NY Islanders	3-6		25	at Winnipeg	4-2
	7	at Carolina	4-2		27	at Toronto	4-1

* – Overtime † – Shootout

Entry Draft Selections 2013-1999

Name in bold denotes played in NHL.

2013
Pick
25 Michael McCarron
34 Jacob De La Rose
36 Zachary Fucale
55 Artturi Lehkonen
71 Connor Crisp
86 Sven Andrighetto
116 Martin Reway
176 Jeremy Gregoire

2012
Pick
3 **Alex Galchenyuk**
33 Sebastian Collberg
51 Dalton Thrower
64 Tim Bozon
94 Brady Vail
122 Charles Hudon
154 Erik Nystrom

2011
Pick
17 **Nathan Beaulieu**
97 Josiah Didier
108 Olivier Archambault
113 Magnus Nygren
138 Darren Dietz
168 Daniel Pribyl
198 Colin Sullivan

2010
Pick
22 **Jarred Tinordi**
113 Mark MacMillan
117 Morgan Ellis
147 **Brendan Gallagher**
207 John Westin

2009
Pick
18 **Louis Leblanc**
65 Joonas Nattinen
79 Mac Bennett
109 Alexander Avtsin
139 **Gabriel Dumont**
169 Dustin Walsh
199 Michael Cichy
211 Petteri Simila

2008
Pick
56 Danny Kristo
86 Steve Quailer
116 Jason Missiaen
138 Maxim Trunev
206 Patrick Johnson

2007
Pick
12 **Ryan McDonagh**
22 **Max Pacioretty**
43 **P.K. Subban**
65 Olivier Fortier
73 **Yannick Weber**
133 Joe Stejskal
142 Andrew Conboy
163 Nichlas Torp
192 Scott Kishel

2006
Pick
20 David Fischer
49 **Ben Maxwell**
53 **Mathieu Carle**
66 **Ryan White**
139 Pavel Valentenko
199 Cameron Cepek

2005
Pick
5 **Carey Price**
45 **Guillaume Latendresse**
121 Juraj Mikus
130 Mathieu Aubin
190 **Matt D'Agostini**
200 **Sergei Kostitsyn**
229 Philippe Paquet

2004
Pick
18 **Kyle Chipchura**
84 **Alexei Emelin**
100 **J.T. Wyman**
150 **Mikhail Grabovski**
181 Loic Lacasse
212 Jon Gleed
246 **Greg Stewart**
262 **Mark Streit**
278 Alex Dulac-Lemelin

2003
Pick
10 **Andrei Kostitsyn**
40 Cory Urquhart
61 **Maxim Lapierre**
79 **Ryan O'Byrne**
113 **Corey Locke**
123 Danny Stewart
177 Chris Heino-Lindberg
188 **Mark Flood**
217 Oskari Korpikari
241 Jimmy Bonneau
271 **Jaroslav Halak**

2002
Pick
14 **Chris Higgins**
45 Tomas Linhart
99 Michael Lambert
182 **Andre Deveaux**
212 **Jonathan Ferland**
275 Konstantin Korneev

2001
Pick
7 **Mike Komisarek**
25 **Alexander Perezhogin**
37 **Duncan Milroy**
71 **Tomas Plekanec**
109 **Martti Jarventie**
171 Eric Himelfarb
203 Andrew Archer
266 Viktor Ujcik

2000
Pick
13 **Ron Hainsey**
16 **Marcel Hossa**
78 **Jozef Balej**
79 Tyler Hanchuck
109 Johan Eneqvist
114 Christian Larrivee
145 Ryan Glenn
172 Scott Selig
182 Petr Chvojka
243 Joni Puurula
275 Jonathan Gauthier

1999
Pick
39 Alexander Buturlin
58 **Matt Carkner**
97 Chris Dyment
107 Evan Lindsay
136 Dusty Jamieson
145 Marc-Andre Thinel
150 Matt Shasby
167 Sean Dixon
196 Vadim Tarasov
225 Mikko Hyytia
253 Jerome Marois

General Managers' History

Jack Laviolette and Joseph Cattarinich, 1909-1910; George Kennedy, 1910-11 to 1920-21; Leo Dandurand, 1921-22 to 1934-35; Ernest Savard, 1935-36; Cecil Hart, 1936-37, 1937-38; Cecil Hart and Jules Dugal, 1938-39; Jules Dugal, 1939-40; Tom P. Gorman, 1940-41 to 1945-46; Frank J. Selke, 1946-47 to 1963-64; Sam Pollock, 1964-65 to 1977-78; Irving Grundman, 1978-79 to 1982-83; Serge Savard, 1983-84 to 1994-95; Serge Savard and Réjean Houle, 1995-96; Réjean Houle, 1996-97 to 1999-2000; Réjean Houle and Andre Savard, 2000-01; Andre Savard, 2001-02, 2002-03; Bob Gainey, 2003-04 to 2008-09; Bob Gainey and Pierre Gauthier, 2009-10; Pierre Gauthier, 2010-11, 2011-12; Marc Bergevin, 2012-13 to date.

Marc Bergevin

Executive Vice President and General Manager

Born: Montreal, Que., August 11, 1965.

The Montreal Canadiens announced the appointment of Marc Bergevin as executive vice president and general manager on May 2, 2012. Bergevin became the 17th general manager in Canadiens history after having spent the previous seven seasons with the Chicago Blackhawks where he was the assistant general manager under Stan Bowman in 2011-12. After finishing 15th in the Eastern Conference in 2011-12, the Canadiens won a division title in 2012-13 and Bergevin finished third in voting as NHL General Manager of the Year.

Bergevin held various positions within the Blackhawks organization, including director of player personnel for two seasons (2009 to 2011), and won the Stanley Cup in 2009-10. He served as an assistant coach on Joel Quenneville's staff during the 2008-09 campaign and also spent three years on the Blackhawks scouting staff (2005 to 2008), including one season as director of professional scouting (2007-08).

Originally selected by the Blackhawks in the third round (60th overall) in the 1983 NHL Entry Draft, Bergevin enjoyed a 20-season career as a defenseman in the National Hockey League, collecting 181 points (36 goals, 145 assists) in 1,191 regular season games with Chicago, the New York Islanders, Hartford Whalers, Tampa Bay Lightning, Detroit Red Wings, St. Louis Blues, Pittsburgh Penguins and Vancouver Canucks. Bergevin also skated in 80 playoff contests, reaching the Conference Finals in 1996 (Detroit) and in 2001 (Pittsburgh). He played his junior hockey in the Quebec Major Junior Hockey League with the Chicoutimi Sagueneens, from 1982 to 1984.

Club Directory

Bell Centre

Club de hockey Canadien
1909, avenue des
Canadiens-de-Montréal
Montréal, QC H4B 5G0
Phone: **514/932-2582**
Media Hotline: 514/989-2835
www.canadiens.com
Capacity: 21,273

Executive Management
Owner, President and CEO, Club de hockey Canadien, Bell Centre & evenko . . . . . Geoff Molson
Executive VP and Chief Operating Officer . . . . . Kevin Gilmore
Executive VP Hockey and General Manager . . . . . Marc Bergevin
Executive VP and Chief Financial Officer . . . . . Fred Steer
Executive VP and General Manager, Facilities Ops. . . . . . Alain Gauthier
Senior Vice President, Communications . . . . . Donald Beauchamp
Senior Vice President, Chief Legal Officer . . . . . France Margaret Bélanger
President, Effix – Advertising and Sponsorship Sales . . . . François Seigneur
President, Canadiens Alumni . . . . . Réjean Houle
Executive VP & General Manager, evenko . . . . . Jacques Aubé
Executive Assistant to the Owner, President and CEO . . . Rolande Bernier
Executive Assistant to COO . . . . . Carina Houle

Hockey Operations
Executive Assistant to the General Manager . . . . . Susan Cryans
Assistant General Managers . . . . . Larry Carrière, Rick Dudley
Director of Player Personnel . . . . . Scott Mellanby
Director of Amateur Scouting . . . . . Trevor Timmins
Director of Legal Affairs . . . . . John Sedgwick
Director of Player Development . . . . . Martin Lapointe
Player Development Coach . . . . . Patrice Brisebois
Head Coach . . . . . Michel Therrien
Assistant Coaches . . . . . Clément Jodoin, Gerard Gallant, Jean-Jacques Daigneault
Goaltending Coach . . . . . Stéphane Waite
Video Coach . . . . . Mario Leblanc
Strength & Conditioning Coach . . . . . Pierre Allard
Professional Scouts . . . . . Doug Gibson, Vaughn Karpan, Ethan Moreau, Mark Mowers
Assistant Director of Amateur Scouting . . . . . Frank Jay
Chief Amateur Scout . . . . . Shane Churla
Amateur Scouting Staff . . . . . Donald Audette, Alvin Backus, Elmer Benning, Bill Berglund, Serge Boisvert, Bobby Kinsella, Michal Krupa, Hannu Laine, Scott Masters, Christer Rockstrom, Artem Telepin, Pat Westrum
Team Services & Hockey Admin. Manager . . . . . Claudine Crépin
Scouting Coordinator . . . . . Ken Morin
Team Services Coordinator . . . . . Alain Gagnon

Medical and Training Staff
Chief Surgeon . . . . . Dr. David S. Mulder
Head Team Physician . . . . . Dr. Vincent J. Lacroix
Head Orthopedic Surgeon . . . . . Dr. Paul A. Martineau
Assistants to the Chief Surgeon . . . . . Dr. Tarek Razek, Dr. Kosar Khwaja, Dr. Dan Beckelbaum
Dentist . . . . . Dr. Jean-François Desjardins
Consultant, Ophthalmology . . . . . Dr. John Little
Consultant, Sports Psychology . . . . . Dr. Sylvain Guimond
Head Athletic Therapist / Athletic Therapist . . . . . Graham Rynbend / Nick Addey-Jibb
Consultants, Ostheopathy / Physiotherapy . . . . . Dave Campbell / Donald Balmforth
Equipment Manager . . . . . Pierre Gervais
Assistants to the Equipment Manager . . . . . Patrick Langlois, Pierre Ouellette, Richard Généreux

Communications
Director of Media Relations . . . . . Dominick Saillant
Executive Assistant to the VP Communications . . . . . Sylvie Lambert
Manager, Research and Translation . . . . . Carl Lavigne
Communications Coordinator . . . . . François Marchand

Community Relations
Director of Community Relations / Exec. Dir., Children's Foundation . . . . . Geneviève Paquette
Project Manager, Children's Foundation . . . . . Patrick Mahoney
Community Relations Coordinator . . . . . Anne-Marie Bégin
Coordinator, Donations and Administration, Children's Foundation . . . . . Sylvie Nadeau
Coordinator, Fundraising, Children's Foundation . . . . . Ryan Frank

Marketing and Sales
Vice President, Sales . . . . . Vincent Lucier
Executive Director, Luxury Suites and Services . . . . . Richard Primeau
Executive Director, Marketing . . . . . Jon Trzcienski
Director, Group Sales . . . . . Pierre Constant
Director, Publications and Creative Services . . . . . Jean Simard
Director, Digital Media . . . . . Alexandre Harvey
Group Manager, HabsTV and Editorial . . . . . Shauna Denis
Group Manager, Game Production . . . . . Paul Gallant
Group Manager, Consumer Products . . . . . Mathieu Lapointe
Manager, Creative Services . . . . . David Bayreuther
Managers, Digital Media / Graphic Design . . . . . Vincent Cauchy / Éric Pelletier
Manager, Luxury Suites Services . . . . . Sabina D'Ascoli
Manager, Advertising and Fan Development . . . . . Kim Marois
Manager, Business Development and Events . . . . . David McGinnis
Manager, Sponsor Integration and Branding . . . . . Véronique Poulin
Manager, Youth Hockey Development . . . . . Stéphane Verret

Building Operations
Executive Assistant to the VP Operations . . . . . Maryse Cartwright
Director of Ticket Office . . . . . Cathy D'Ascoli
Assistants to the Director of Ticket Office . . . . . Lucie Masse, Isabelle Naud-Rodrigue
Director of Building Operations . . . . . Xavier Luydlin
Director of Retail and Concession Operations . . . . . Alec Beaudry
Director of Customer Satisfaction . . . . . Caroline Hamel

Information Technology
Vice President, Info and Communication Tech. . . . . . Pierre-Éric Belzile
Senior IT Analyst Development / Technician . . . . . Louis Pennimpede / Roger Miron

Finance
Executive Assistantto the Chief Financial Officer . . . . . Christine Ouellette
Controller . . . . . Raymond Lamarche
Administrator, Payroll Services . . . . . Teresa Nola

Broadcasting
Play-by-play – Radio/TV: Pierre Houde (RDS), Martin McGuire (COGECO 98.5 FM), John Bartlett (TSN Radio 990)
Colormen – Radio/TV: Marc Denis (RDS), Dany Dubé (COGECO 98.5 FM), Sergio Momesso (TSN Radio 990)
Radio/television flagships: RDS (Cable 33), COGECO (985 FM), TSN Radio (990 AM)

Nashville Predators

Key Off-Season Signings/Acquisitions

2013

April 30 • Re-signed RW **Patric Hornqvist**.
May 22 • Named **Phil Housley** assistant coach.
June 10 • Re-signed D **Roman Josi**.
July 5 • Signed RW **Viktor Stalberg**, C **Matt Cullen**, LW **Eric Nystrom** and C **Matt Hendricks**.
17 • Re-signed LW **Rich Clune**.
25 • Re-signed LW **Nick Spaling**.

2012-13 Results: 16W-23L-3OTL-6SOL 41PTS
5TH, Central Division • 14TH, Western Conference

Year-by-Year Record

		Home				Road				Overall									
Season	GP	W	L	T	OL	W	L	T	OL	W	L	T	OL	GF	GA	Pts.	Div. Fin.	Conf. Fin.	Playoff Result
2012-13	48	11	9	....	4	5	14	....	5	16	23	....	9	111	139	41	5th, Cen.	14th, West	Out of Playoffs
2011-12	82	26	10	....	5	22	16	....	3	48	26	....	8	237	210	104	2nd, Cen.	4th, West	Lost Conf. Semi-Final
2010-11	82	24	9	....	8	20	18	....	3	44	27	....	11	219	194	99	2nd, Cen.	5th, West	Lost Conf. Semi-Final
2009-10	82	24	14	....	3	23	15	....	3	47	29	....	6	225	225	100	3rd, Cen.	7th, West	Lost Conf. Quarter-Final
2008-09	82	24	13	....	4	16	21	....	4	40	34	....	8	213	233	88	5th, Cen.	10th, West	Out of Playoffs
2007-08	82	23	14	....	4	18	18	....	5	41	32	....	9	230	229	91	2nd, Cen.	8th, West	Lost Conf. Quarter-Final
2006-07	82	28	8	....	5	23	15	....	3	51	23	....	8	272	212	110	2nd, Cen.	4th, West	Lost Conf. Quarter-Final
2005-06	82	32	8	....	1	17	17	....	7	49	25	....	8	259	227	106	2nd, Cen.	4th, West	Lost Conf. Quarter-Final
2004-05	....	....	....	....	....	....	....	....	....	....	....	....	....	....	....	....			
2003-04	82	22	10	7	2	16	19	4	2	38	29	11	4	216	217	91	3rd, Cen.	8th, West	Lost Conf. Quarter-Final
2002-03	82	18	17	5	1	9	18	8	6	27	35	13	7	183	206	74	4th, Cen.	13th, West	Out of Playoffs
2001-02	82	17	16	8	0	11	25	5	0	28	41	13	0	196	230	69	4th, Cen.	14th, West	Out of Playoffs
2000-01	82	16	18	7	0	18	18	2	3	34	36	9	3	186	200	80	3rd, Cen.	10th, West	Out of Playoffs
1999-2000	82	15	21	3	2	13	19	4	5	28	40	7	7	199	240	70	4th, Cen.	13th, West	Out of Playoffs
1998-99	82	15	22	4	....	13	25	3	....	28	47	7	....	190	261	63	4th, Cen.	12th, West	Out of Playoffs

2013-14 Schedule

Oct.	Thu.	3	at St. Louis
	Fri.	4	at Colorado
	Tue.	8	Minnesota
	Thu.	10	Toronto
	Sat.	12	NY Islanders
	Tue.	15	Florida
	Thu.	17	Los Angeles
	Sat.	19	at Montreal
	Sun.	20	at Winnipeg
	Tue.	22	at Minnesota
	Thu.	24	Winnipeg
	Sat.	26	St. Louis
	Thu.	31	at Phoenix
Nov.	Sat.	2	at Los Angeles
	Wed.	6	at Colorado
	Fri.	8	at Winnipeg
	Sun.	10	at New Jersey
	Tue.	12	at NY Islanders
	Fri.	15	at Pittsburgh
	Sat.	16	Chicago
	Tue.	19	at Detroit
	Thu.	21	at Toronto
	Sat.	23	NY Rangers
	Mon.	25	Phoenix
	Wed.	27	at Columbus
	Thu.	28	Edmonton
	Sat.	30	Philadelphia
Dec.	Tue.	3	Vancouver
	Thu.	5	Carolina
	Sat.	7	at Washington
	Tue.	10	at NY Rangers
	Thu.	12	Dallas
	Sat.	14	San Jose
	Tue.	17	Chicago
	Thu.	19	at Tampa Bay
	Sat.	21	Montreal
	Mon.	23	Boston
	Fri.	27	at Dallas
	Sat.	28	Los Angeles
	Mon.	30	Detroit
Jan.	Thu.	2	at Boston
	Sat.	4	at Florida
	Sun.	5	at Carolina
	Tue.	7	San Jose
	Thu.	9	Anaheim
	Sat.	11	Ottawa
	Sun.	12	Minnesota
	Tue.	14	Calgary
	Thu.	16	at Philadelphia
	Sat.	18	Colorado
	Mon.	20	Dallas
	Thu.	23	at Vancouver
	Fri.	24	at Calgary
	Sun.	26	at Edmonton
	Tue.	28	at Winnipeg
	Fri.	31	New Jersey
Feb.	Sat.	1	at St. Louis
	Thu.	6	at Minnesota
	Sat.	8	Anaheim
	Thu.	27	Tampa Bay
Mar.	Sat.	1	Winnipeg*
	Tue.	4	Pittsburgh
	Thu.	6	St. Louis
	Sat.	8	Columbus
	Mon.	10	at Ottawa
	Tue.	11	at Buffalo
	Fri.	14	at Chicago
	Sat.	15	St. Louis
	Tue.	18	at Edmonton
	Wed.	19	at Vancouver
	Fri.	21	at Calgary
	Sun.	23	at Chicago
	Tue.	25	Colorado
	Thu.	27	Buffalo
	Fri.	28	at Dallas
	Sun.	30	Washington
Apr.	Fri.	4	at Anaheim
	Sat.	5	at San Jose
	Tue.	8	at Dallas
	Thu.	10	Phoenix
	Sat.	12	Chicago
	Sun.	13	at Minnesota

* Denotes afternoon game.

It was another busy season for Shea Weber in 2012-13 as he played all 48 games on the schedule and ranked fourth in the NHL in total time on ice. Weber's average of 25:55 minutes of ice time per game ranked sixth in the league.

CENTRAL DIVISION
16th NHL Season

Franchise date: June 25, 1997

2013-14 Player Personnel

FORWARDS	HT	WT	*Age	Place of Birth	S	2012-13 Club
BECK, Taylor	6-2	208	22	St. Catharines, Ont.	R	Milwaukee-Nashville
BOURQUE, Gabriel	5-10	192	23	Rimouski, Que.	L	Milwaukee-Nashville
BUDISH, Zach	6-3	218	22	Edina, MN	R	U. of Minnesota-Milwaukee
CEHLIN, Patrick	5-11	177	22	Huddinge, Sweden	R	Milwaukee-Cincinnati
CLUNE, Rich	5-10	207	26	Toronto, Ont.	L	Manchester-Nashville
CULLEN, Matt	6-0	200	36	Virginia, MN	L	Minnesota
FISHER, Mike	6-1	208	33	Peterborough, Ont.	R	Nashville
FORSBERG, Filip	6-1	194	19	Ostervala, Sweden	R	Leksand-Nashville
GAUSTAD, Paul	6-5	220	31	Fargo, ND	L	Nashville
HENDERSON, Kevin	6-3	210	26	Toronto, Ont.	L	Milwaukee-Nashville
HENDRICKS, Matt	6-0	211	32	Blaine, MN	L	Washington
HORNQVIST, Patric	6-0	190	26	Sollentuna, Sweden	R	Martigny-Djurgarden-Nsh
LEGWAND, David	6-2	204	33	Detroit, MI	L	Nashville
NYSTROM, Eric	6-1	193	30	Syosset, NY	L	Stavanger-Dallas
RASK, Joonas	5-10	176	23	Savonlinna, Finland	R	Jokerit-Nsh-Milwaukee
SALOMAKI, Miikka	5-11	203	20	Raahe, Finland	L	Karpat
SHALLA, Josh	6-2	208	22	Whitby, Ont.	L	Cincinnati-Milwaukee
SISSONS, Colton	6-1	189	19	North Vancouver, B.C.	R	Kelowna
SMITH, Craig	6-1	199	24	Madison, WI	R	KalPa-Nsh-Milwaukee
SPALING, Nick	6-1	198	25	Palmerston, Ont.	L	Nashville
STALBERG, Viktor	6-3	209	27	Stockholm, Sweden	L	Frolunda-Mytischi-Chi
VAN GUILDER, Mark	6-2	205	29	Roseville, MN	R	Milwaukee
WATSON, Austin	6-3	201	21	Ann Arbor, MI	R	Milwaukee-Nashville
WILSON, Colin	6-1	212	23	Greenwich, CT	L	Nashville
DEFENSEMEN						
BARTLEY, Victor	6-0	212	25	Maple Ridge, B.C.	L	Milwaukee-Nashville
BITETTO, Anthony	6-0	215	23	Island Park, NY	L	Cincinnati-Milwaukee
EKHOLM, Mattias	6-4	202	23	Borlange, Sweden	L	Milwaukee-Nashville
ELLIS, Ryan	5-10	179	22	Hamilton, Ont.	R	Milwaukee-Nashville
JARVINEN, Joonas	6-3	234	24	Turku, Finland	L	Milwaukee
JONES, Seth	6-5	210	18	Arlington, TX	R	Portland (WHL)
JOSI, Roman	6-1	198	23	Bern, Switzerland	L	Bern-Nashville
KLEIN, Kevin	6-1	204	28	Kitchener, Ont.	R	Herlev-Nashville
ROUSSEL, Charles-Olivier	6-1	205	22	St. Eustache, Que.	R	Milwaukee-Cincinnati
VALENTINE, Scott	6-1	213	22	Ottawa, Ont.	L	Milwaukee
WEBER, Shea	6-4	234	28	Sicamous, B.C.	R	Nashville

GOALTENDERS	HT	WT	*Age	Place of Birth	C	2012-13 Club
HELLBERG, Magnus	6-6	195	22	Uppsala, Sweden	L	Milwaukee-Cincinnati
HUTTON, Carter	6-1	195	27	Thunder Bay, Ont.	L	Rockford-Chicago
MAZANEC, Marek	6-4	197	22	Pisek, Czech.	R	Plzen Jr.-Pisek-Plzen
RINNE, Pekka	6-5	206	30	Kempele, Finland	L	Dynamo Minsk-Nashville

* – Age at start of 2013-14 season

2012-13 Scoring

* – rookie

Regular Season

Pos	#	Player	Team	GP	G	A	Pts	TOI	+/–	PIM	PP	SH	GW	S	%
D	6	Shea Weber	NSH	48	9	19	28	25:55	–2	48	3	0	1	124	7.3
C	11	David Legwand	NSH	48	12	13	25	18:25	–6	20	2	0	2	78	15.4
C	12	Mike Fisher	NSH	38	10	11	21	19:27	6	27	1	0	0	68	14.7
C	33	Colin Wilson	NSH	25	7	12	19	16:34	1	4	2	0	1	26	26.9
D	59	Roman Josi	NSH	48	5	13	18	23:31	–7	8	1	0	1	96	5.2
L	57	Gabriel Bourque	NSH	34	11	5	16	15:49	6	4	3	1	2	50	22.0
L	74	Sergei Kostitsyn	NSH	46	3	12	15	16:43	–5	11	1	0	0	42	7.1
R	27	Patric Hornqvist	NSH	24	4	10	14	16:13	–1	14	4	0	1	87	4.6
D	8	Kevin Klein	NSH	47	3	11	14	20:25	–1	9	0	0	0	54	5.6
C	13	Nick Spaling	NSH	47	9	4	13	15:51	–10	18	1	0	2	57	15.8
C	15	Craig Smith	NSH	44	4	8	12	13:51	–11	20	2	0	0	83	4.8
R	24	Matt Halischuk	NSH	36	5	6	11	11:57	1	10	0	0	1	51	9.8
R	19	Bobby Butler	N.J.	14	1	1	2	9:58	–6	0	1	0	0	13	7.7
			NSH	20	3	6	9	11:22	–2	4	0	0	0	28	10.7
			Total	34	4	7	11	10:48	–8	4	1	0	0	41	9.8
L	16 *	Rich Clune	NSH	47	4	5	9	9:24	3	113	0	0	1	46	8.7
R	18	Brandon Yip	NSH	34	3	5	8	12:02	–3	26	0	0	0	35	8.6
L	56 *	Taylor Beck	NSH	16	3	4	7	16:05	0	2	1	0	0	39	7.7
D	7	Jonathon Blum	NSH	35	1	6	7	14:17	–1	6	0	0	0	26	3.8
D	64 *	Victor Bartley	NSH	24	0	7	7	19:32	2	6	0	0	0	19	0.0
D	4	Ryan Ellis	NSH	32	2	4	6	16:22	–2	15	2	0	0	48	4.2
C	17	Chris Mueller	NSH	18	2	3	5	10:42	–4	6	0	0	1	22	9.1
C	28	Paul Gaustad	NSH	23	2	3	5	15:13	–1	20	0	0	0	35	5.7
L	23	Zach Boychuk	CAR	1	0	0	0	10:13	0	0	0	0	0	0	0.0
			PIT	7	0	0	0	11:37	–2	2	0	0	0	6	0.0
			NSH	5	1	1	2	13:42	1	4	0	0	0	8	12.5
			Total	13	1	1	2	12:18	–1	6	0	0	0	14	7.1
L	50 *	Daniel Bang	NSH	8	0	2	2	12:54	–2	0	0	0	0	13	0.0
L	46	Kevin Henderson	NSH	4	1	0	1	14:41	–1	0	0	0	0	3	33.3
L	52 *	Austin Watson	NSH	6	1	0	1	12:42	–2	0	0	0	0	4	25.0
C	72 *	Joonas Rask	NSH	2	0	1	1	8:00	–1	0	0	0	0	0	0.0
C	9 *	Filip Forsberg	NSH	5	0	1	1	15:28	–5	0	0	0	0	14	0.0
D	42 *	Mattias Ekholm	NSH	1	0	0	0	16:05	–1	0	0	0	0	0	0.0
D	75	Hal Gill	NSH	32	0	0	0	13:23	–3	12	0	0	0	8	0.0

Goaltending

No.	Goaltender	GPI	Mins	Avg	W	L	OT	EN	SO	GA	SA	S%	G	A	PIM
35	Pekka Rinne	43	2444	2.43	15	16	8	2	5	99	1101	.910	0	1	8
30	Chris Mason	11	467	3.73	1	7	1	3	0	29	229	.873	0	0	0
	Totals	**48**	**2929**	**2.72**	**16**	**23**	**9**	**5**	**5**	**133**	**1335**	**.900**			

Captains' History

Tom Fitzgerald, 1998-99 to 2001-02; Greg Johnson, 2002-03 to 2005-06; Kimmo Timonen, 2006-07; Jason Arnott, 2007-08 to 2009-10; Shea Weber, 2010-11 to date.

Coaching History

Barry Trotz, 1998-99 to date.

Barry Trotz

Head Coach

Born: Winnipeg, Man., July 15, 1962.

The only head coach in the history of the Nashville Predators, Barry Trotz was hired on August 6, 1997 and is currently the longest-tenured coach in the NHL. During the 2011-12 season, Trotz joined Lindy Ruff and Hall of Famer Toe Blake as the only coaches in history to win 500 games while coaching just one NHL team (though Ruff is now coaching his second team in Dallas).

Trotz was hired after serving four seasons as head coach and director of hockey operations for the American Hockey League's Portland Pirates. He and assistant Paul Gardner spent the 1997-98 season scouting in preparation for the inaugural season of the Predators. In his sixth season behind the bench in 2003-04, Trotz led Nashville into the playoffs for the first time. During the 2006-07 season, Nashville was in contention for first overall in the NHL, setting club records with 51 wins and 110 points.Trotz was nominated for the Jack Adams Award as coach of the year for the first time in 2009-10 and received a second nomination in 2010-11.

Trotz began his coaching career in 1984 as assistant coach with the University of Manitoba for one season, before serving two seasons as the head coach and general manager of the Dauphin Kings Junior Hockey Club from 1985 to 1987. He became head coach of the University of Manitoba during the 1987 season and also served as a scout for the Spokane Chiefs of the Western Hockey League that season. Trotz joined the Washington Capitals organization as their chief western scout during the 1988 season. The Winnipeg, Manitoba native was appointed an assistant coach of the Capitals' American Hockey League affiliate in Baltimore prior to the 1991 season before being named head coach prior to the 1992 season. When the franchise relocated to Portland, he guided the Pirates to two AHL Calder Cup Final appearances in the club's first four seasons. He led the Pirates to a league-best 43-27-10 record, captured the Calder Cup championship and was named the American Hockey League coach of the year following the 1994-95 season.

In 1995, Trotz guided Portland to a new North American professional hockey league record 17-game unbeaten streak (14-0-3) to start the season. He was named head coach for the U.S. team at the American Hockey League All-Star Game in 1996.

Prior to his coaching career, Trotz played junior hockey for the Western Hockey League's Regina Pats from 1979 to 1983. During that time, he recorded 39 goals, 121 assists for 160 points, along with 490 penalty minutes in 204 games.

Coaching Record

			Regular Season				Playoffs			
Season	Team	League	GC	W	L	O/T	GC	W	L	T
1992-93	Baltimore	AHL	80	28	40	12	7	3	4	....
1993-94	Portland	AHL	80	43	27	10	8	6	2	....
1994-95	Portland	AHL	80	46	22	12	7	3	4	....
1995-96	Portland	AHL	80	32	34	14	24	14	10	....
1996-97	Portland	AHL	80	37	26	17	5	2	3	....
1998-99	**Nashville**	**NHL**	**82**	**28**	**47**	**7**	....	....	....	....
99-2000	**Nashville**	**NHL**	**82**	**28**	**40**	**14**	....	....	....	....
2000-01	**Nashville**	**NHL**	**82**	**34**	**36**	**12**	....	....	....	....
2001-02	**Nashville**	**NHL**	**82**	**28**	**41**	**13**	....	....	....	....
2002-03	**Nashville**	**NHL**	**82**	**27**	**35**	**20**	....	....	....	....
2003-04	**Nashville**	**NHL**	**82**	**38**	**29**	**15**	**6**	**2**	**4**	....
2004-05	**Nashville**				SEASON CANCELLED					
2005-06	**Nashville**	**NHL**	**82**	**49**	**25**	**8**	**5**	**1**	**4**	....
2006-07	**Nashville**	**NHL**	**82**	**51**	**23**	**8**	**5**	**1**	**4**	....
2007-08	**Nashville**	**NHL**	**82**	**41**	**32**	**9**	**6**	**2**	**4**	....
2008-09	**Nashville**	**NHL**	**82**	**40**	**34**	**8**	....	....	....	....
2009-10	**Nashville**	**NHL**	**82**	**47**	**29**	**6**	**6**	**2**	**4**	....
2010-11	**Nashville**	**NHL**	**82**	**44**	**27**	**11**	**12**	**6**	**6**	....
2011-12	**Nashville**	**NHL**	**82**	**48**	**26**	**8**	**10**	**5**	**5**	....
2012-13	**Nashville**	**NHL**	**48**	**16**	**23**	**9**	....	....	....	....
	NHL Totals		**1114**	**519**	**447**	**148**	**50**	**19**	**31**	....

Club Records

Team

(Figures in brackets for season records are games played; records for fewest points, wins, ties, losses, goals, goals against are for 70 or more games)

Most Points	**110**	2006-07 (82)
Most Wins	**51**	2006-07 (82)
Most Ties	**13**	2001-02 (82), 2002-03 (82)
Most Losses	**47**	1998-99 (82)
Most Goals	**272**	2006-07 (82)
Most Goals Against	**261**	1998-99 (82)
Fewest Points	**63**	1998-99 (82)
Fewest Wins	**27**	2002-03 (82)
Fewest Ties	**7**	1998-99 (82) 1999-2000 (82)
Fewest Losses	**23**	2006-07 (82)
Fewest Goals	**183**	2002-03 (82)
Fewest Goals Against	**194**	2010-11 (82)
Longest Winning Streak		
Overall	**8**	Oct. 5-25/05
Home	**8**	Jan. 6-Feb. 8/07
Away	**7**	Oct. 16-Nov. 4/06
Longest Undefeated Streak		
Overall	**8**	Dec. 18/99-Jan. 1/00 (5W, 3T/OL), Oct. 5-25/05 (8W)
Home	**11**	Dec. 20/03-Jan. 31/04 (9W, 2T/OL), Nov. 3-Dec. 23/01 (8W, 3T/OL)
Away	**7**	Oct. 16-Nov. 4/06 (7W)
Longest Losing Streak		
Overall	**8**	Apr. 4-19/13
Home	**6**	Jan. 21-Feb. 15/99, Feb. 26-Mar. 21/02, Feb. 21-Mar. 20/08, Apr. 4-15/13
Away	**10**	Mar. 14-Apr. 27/13
Longest Winless Streak		
Overall	**15**	Mar. 10-Apr. 6/03 (10L, 5T/OL)
Home	**9**	Jan. 21-Mar. 2/99 (8L, 1T)
Away	**10**	Mar. 14-Apr. 27/13 (7L, 3OL/SOL)
Most Shutouts, Season	**11**	2006-07 (82)
Most PIM, Season	**1,533**	2005-06 (82)
Most Goals, Game	**9**	Mar. 4/04 (Nsh. 9 at Pit. 4), Mar. 18/06 (Cgy. 4 at Nsh. 9)

Individual

Most Seasons	**14**	David Legwand
Most Games	**894**	David Legwand
Most Goals, Career	**200**	David Legwand
Most Assists, Career	**326**	David Legwand
Most Points, Career	**526**	David Legwand (200G, 326A)
Most PIM, Career	**725**	Jordin Tootoo
Most Shutouts, Career	**30**	Pekka Rinne
Longest Consecutive Games Streak	**269**	Karlis Skrastins (Feb. 21/00-Apr. 6/03)
Most Goals, Season	**33**	Jason Arnott (2008-09)
Most Assists, Season	**54**	Paul Kariya (2005-06)
Most Points, Season	**85**	Paul Kariya (2005-06; 31G, 54A)
Most PIM, Season	**242**	Patrick Cote (1998-99)
Most Points, Defenseman, Season	**55**	Kimmo Timonen (2006-07; 13G, 42A)
Most Points, Center, Season	**72**	Jason Arnott (2007-08; 28G, 44A)
Most Points, Right Wing, Season	**72**	J.P. Dumont (2007-08; 29G, 43A)
Most Points, Left Wing, Season	**85**	Paul Kariya (2005-06; 31G, 54A)
Most Points, Rookie, Season	**37**	Alexander Radulov (2006-07; 18G, 19A)
Most Shutouts, Season	**7**	Pekka Rinne (2008-09) (2009-10)
Most Goals, Game	**3**	Twenty one times
Most Assists, Game	**5**	Marek Zidlicky (Feb. 18/04)
Most Points, Game	**5**	Marek Zidlicky (Feb. 18/04; 5A), Dan Hamhuis (Mar. 4/04; 1G, 4A), J.P. Dumont (Oct. 22/09; 1G, 4A)

All-time Record vs. Other Clubs

Regular Season

	Total								At Home								On Road							
	GP	W	L	T	OL	GF	GA	PTS	GP	W	L	T	OL	GF	GA	PTS	GP	W	L	T	OL	GF	GA	PTS
Anaheim	55	23	23	2	7	124	146	55	27	15	7	2	3	69	60	35	28	8	16	0	4	55	86	20
Boston	17	7	8	1	1	40	45	16	9	5	4	0	0	25	21	10	8	2	4	1	1	15	24	6
Buffalo	15	7	6	1	1	40	40	16	8	2	5	0	1	14	20	5	7	5	1	1	0	26	20	11
Calgary	56	27	20	4	5	154	149	63	29	17	9	1	2	92	72	37	27	10	11	3	3	62	77	26
Carolina	17	11	4	1	1	51	39	24	8	7	1	0	0	24	13	14	9	4	3	1	1	27	26	10
Chicago	86	38	38	4	6	246	247	86	42	21	15	3	3	127	118	48	44	17	23	1	3	119	129	38
Colorado	55	27	21	5	2	153	147	61	27	15	9	3	0	83	76	33	28	12	12	2	2	70	71	28
Columbus	74	50	17	1	6	231	168	107	38	30	4	1	3	132	82	64	36	20	13	0	3	99	86	43
Dallas	55	23	30	1	1	117	144	48	28	15	12	1	0	74	67	31	27	8	18	0	1	43	77	17
Detroit	85	32	41	4	8	212	267	76	42	20	17	2	3	115	114	45	43	12	24	2	5	97	153	31
Edmonton	56	30	20	3	3	164	160	66	29	15	11	3	0	84	89	33	27	15	9	0	3	80	71	33
Florida	18	8	7	3	0	41	43	19	9	5	2	2	0	22	16	12	9	3	5	1	0	19	27	7
Los Angeles	55	24	25	3	3	139	156	54	27	10	14	3	0	61	74	23	28	14	11	0	3	78	82	31
Minnesota	47	22	15	5	5	133	124	54	23	14	5	2	2	66	46	32	24	8	10	3	3	67	78	22
Montreal	14	5	5	1	3	41	37	14	7	3	1	1	2	22	15	9	7	2	4	0	1	19	22	5
New Jersey	17	7	7	0	3	41	50	17	9	2	5	0	2	18	26	6	8	5	2	0	1	23	24	11
NY Islanders	15	10	3	0	2	42	34	22	8	6	2	0	0	22	17	12	7	4	1	0	2	20	17	10
NY Rangers	16	7	7	1	1	37	47	16	7	2	4	0	1	17	25	5	9	5	3	1	0	20	22	11
Ottawa	15	6	9	0	0	37	44	12	7	3	4	0	0	15	15	6	8	3	5	0	0	22	29	6
Philadelphia	16	6	7	3	0	32	45	15	7	3	2	2	0	16	15	8	9	3	5	1	0	16	30	7
Phoenix	55	26	24	2	3	158	149	57	28	15	10	2	1	79	69	33	27	11	14	0	2	79	80	24
Pittsburgh	17	9	5	2	1	57	47	21	9	6	2	0	1	34	21	13	8	3	3	2	0	23	26	8
St. Louis	85	42	31	4	8	190	208	96	43	22	12	3	6	99	98	53	42	20	19	1	2	91	110	43
San Jose	55	24	23	2	6	138	148	56	27	14	11	1	1	69	69	30	28	10	12	1	5	69	79	26
Tampa Bay	16	6	7	2	1	43	47	15	9	4	4	0	1	25	25	9	7	2	3	2	0	18	22	6
Toronto	13	7	5	1	0	39	30	15	4	3	1	0	0	14	9	6	9	4	4	1	0	25	21	9
Vancouver	56	20	29	2	5	142	175	47	29	11	12	1	5	76	79	28	27	9	17	1	0	66	96	19
Washington	17	6	6	1	4	43	44	17	9	4	2	1	2	24	21	11	8	2	4	0	2	19	23	6
Winnipeg	16	9	4	1	2	51	43	21	8	6	2	0	0	30	20	12	8	3	2	1	2	21	23	9
Totals	**1114**	**519**	**447**	**60**	**88**	**2936**	**3023**	**1186**	**557**	**295**	**189**	**34**	**39**	**1548**	**1392**	**663**	**557**	**224**	**258**	**26**	**49**	**1388**	**1631**	**523**

Playoffs

	Series	W	L	GP	W	L	T	GF	GA	Last Mtg.	Rnd.	Result
Anaheim	1	1	0	6	4	2	0	22	20	2011	CQF	W 4-2
Chicago	1	0	1	6	2	4	0	15	17	2010	CQF	L 2-4
Detroit	3	1	2	17	8	9	0	34	38	2012	CQF	W 4-1
Phoenix	1	0	1	5	1	4	0	9	12	2012	CSF	L 1-4
San Jose	2	0	2	10	2	8	0	24	33	2007	CQF	L 1-4
Vancouver	1	0	1	6	2	4	0	11	14	2011	CSF	L 2-4
Totals	**9**	**2**	**7**	**50**	**19**	**31**	**0**	**115**	**134**			

Playoff Results 2013-2009

Year	Round	Opponent	Result	GF	GA
2012	CSF	Phoenix	L 1-4	9	12
	CQF	Detroit	W 4-1	13	9
2011	CSF	Vancouver	L 2-4	11	14
	CQF	Anaheim	W 4-2	22	20
2010	CQF	Chicago	L 2-4	15	17

Abbreviations: Round: CSF – conference semi-final; **CQF** – conference quarter-final.

Winnipeg totals include Atlanta Thrashers, 1999-2000 to 2010-11.

2012-13 Results

Jan.	19	Columbus	2-3†		9	Minnesota	1-2†
	21	St. Louis	3-4†		12	at Dallas	4-0
	22	at Minnesota	3-1		14	at Vancouver	4-7
	24	at St. Louis	0-3		15	at Calgary	3-6
	26	at Anaheim	2-3†		17	at Edmonton	2-3
	28	at Phoenix	0-4		19	at Columbus	3-4
	31	at Los Angeles	2-1†		21	Calgary	5-3
Feb.	2	at San Jose	2-1†		23	Columbus	5-2
	5	at St. Louis	6-1		25	Edmonton	3-2
	7	Los Angeles	3-0		28	Phoenix	4-7
	9	at Minnesota	1-2*		30	at Colorado	0-1*
	10	Chicago	0-3	**Apr.**	1	at Chicago	2-3†
	12	San Jose	1-0*		2	Colorado	3-1
	14	Phoenix	3-0		4	Columbus	1-3
	16	Anaheim	2-3†		6	Chicago	0-1
	18	at Colorado	5-6		7	at Chicago	3-5
	19	Detroit	4-3*		9	St. Louis	0-1
	22	Vancouver	0-1		12	Dallas	2-5
	23	at Detroit	0-4		14	Detroit	0-3
	25	Dallas	5-4*		15	Vancouver	2-5
	27	at Anaheim	1-5		19	at Chicago	4-5*
Mar.	2	at San Jose	1-2		23	Calgary	4-3
	4	at Los Angeles	1-5		25	at Detroit	2-5
	8	Edmonton	6-0		27	at Columbus	1-3

* – Overtime † – Shootout

Entry Draft Selections 2013-1999

Name in bold denotes played in NHL.

2013

Pick	
4	Seth Jones
64	Jonathan Diaby
95	Felix Girard
99	Juuse Saros
125	Saku Maenalanen
140	Teemu Kivihalme
155	Emil Pettersson
171	Tommy Veilleux
185	Wade Murphy
203	Janne Juvonen

2012

Pick	
37	Pontus Aberg
50	Colton Sissons
66	Jimmy Vesey
89	Brendan Leipsic
112	Zachary Stepan
118	Mikko Vainonen
164	Simon Fernholm
172	Max Gortz
179	Marek Mazanec

2011

Pick	
38	Magnus Hellberg
52	Miikka Salomaki
94	Josh Shalla
112	Garrett Noonan
142	Simon Karlsson
170	Chase Balisy
202	Brent Andrews

2010

Pick	
18	**Austin Watson**
78	Taylor Aronson
126	Patrick Cehlin
168	Anthony Bitetto
194	David Elsner
198	**Joonas Rask**

2009

Pick	
11	**Ryan Ellis**
41	Zach Budish
42	Charles-Olivier Roussel
70	**Taylor Beck**
72	Michael Latta
98	**Craig Smith**
102	**Mattias Ekholm**
110	Nick Oliver
132	**Gabriel Bourque**
192	Cam Reid

2008

Pick	
7	**Colin Wilson**
18	Chet Pickard
38	**Roman Josi**
136	Taylor Stefishen
166	Jeff Foss
201	Jani Lajunen
207	**Anders Lindback**

2007

Pick	
23	**Jonathon Blum**
54	Jeremy Smith
58	**Nick Spaling**
81	**Ryan Thang**
114	Ben Ryan
119	Mark Santorelli
144	**Andreas Thuresson**
174	Robert Dietrich
204	Atte Engren

2006

Pick	
56	**Blake Geoffrion**
105	Niko Snellman
146	**Mark Dekanich**
176	Ryan Flynn
206	Viktor Sjodin

2005

Pick	
18	**Ryan Parent**
78	**Teemu Laakso**
79	**Cody Franson**
150	**Cal O'Reilly**
176	Ryan Maki
213	Scott Todd
230	**Patric Hornqvist**

2004

Pick	
15	**Alexander Radulov**
81	Vaclav Meidl
107	Nick Fugere
139	Kyle Moir
147	**Janne Niskala**
178	**Mike Santorelli**
193	Kevin Schaeffer
209	Stanislav Balan
243	Denis Kulyash
258	**Pekka Rinne**
275	Craig Switzer

2003

Pick	
7	**Ryan Suter**
35	Konstantin Glazachev
37	**Kevin Klein**
49	**Shea Weber**
76	Richard Stehlik
89	Paul Brown
92	**Alexander Sulzer**
98	Grigory Shafigulin
117	Teemu Lassila
133	Rustam Sidikov
210	Andrei Mukhachev
213	Miroslav Hanuljak
268	Lauris Darzins

2002

Pick	
6	**Scottie Upshall**
102	**Brandon Segal**
138	Patrick Jarrett
172	**Mike McKenna**
203	Josh Morrow
235	Kaleb Betts
264	Matt Davis
266	Steven Spencer

2001

Pick	
12	**Dan Hamhuis**
33	**Timofei Shishkanov**
42	Tomas Slovak
75	Denis Platonov
76	Oliver Setzinger
98	**Jordin Tootoo**
178	Anton Lavrentiev
240	Gustav Grasberg
271	**Mikko Lehtonen**

2000

Pick	
6	**Scott Hartnell**
36	Daniel Widing
72	Mattias Nilsson
89	**Libor Pivko**
131	**Matt Hendricks**
137	**Mike Stuart**
154	**Matt Koalska**
173	Tomas Harant
197	Zbynek Irgl
203	Jure Penko
236	Mats Christeen
284	Martin Hohener

1999

Pick	
6	**Brian Finley**
33	**Jonas Andersson**
52	**Adam Hall**
54	**Andrew Hutchinson**
61	Ed Hill
65	**Jan Lasak**
72	Brett Angel
121	Yevgeny Pavlov
124	Alexandre Krevsun
131	Konstantin Panov
162	**Timo Helbling**
191	**Martin Erat**
205	Kyle Kettles
220	Miroslav Durak
248	**Darren Haydar**

General Managers' History

David Poile, 1998-99 to date.

David Poile

President of Hockey Operations and General Manager

Born: Toronto, Ont., February 14, 1949.

Hired as the first general manager in franchise history on July 9, 1997, David Poile has been committed to building the team through the NHL Draft. In 2003-04, Nashville reached the playoffs for the first time in franchise history. During the 2006-07 season, the team was in contention for first overall in the NHL, setting club records with 51 wins and 110 points. Though forced to rebuild the roster for 2007-08, the Predators reached the playoffs for the fourth year in a row. Poile has an impressive reputation as an NHL leader and in 2001 he received the Lester Patrick Trophy for his contributions to hockey in the United States. His father, Norman "Bud" Poile, had won the honor in 1989. He served as Associate G.M. for the 2010 U.S. Olympic Team and U.S. squads for the 2009 and 2010 IIHF World Championships and will be general manager of the 2014 U.S. Olympic team at Sochi. He was a finalist for the NHL's inaugural G.M. of the Year Award in 2010 and was a finalist for the award again in 2011 and 2012.

Prior to joining Nashville, Poile spent 15 seasons as vice president/general manager of the Washington Capitals. During his tenure in Washington, the Capitals made 14 postseason appearances, winning their only Patrick Division title in 1989 and advancing to the Conference Finals in 1990. During Poile's 15 years in Washington, the Capitals compiled a record of 594-454-132, finished second in the Patrick Division seven times and recorded 90-or-more points seven different seasons.

Poile started his professional hockey career as an administrative assistant for the Atlanta Flames in 1972, shortly after graduating from Northeastern University in Boston. At Northeastern, he was hockey team captain, leading scorer and most valuable player for two years. In 1977, he was named assistant general manager of the Atlanta Flames (who moved to Calgary in 1980), serving as the manager and coordinator of the Flames farm club.

Poile was instrumental in the NHL's adoption of the instant replay rule in 1991. He was awarded *Inside Hockey*'s man of the year for his leadership on the issue. He has also been honored three times as *The Sporting News* NHL executive of the year in 1982-83, 1983-84 and 2006-07. Poile served as general manager of the 1998 and 1999 U.S. national teams for the World Championships.

Club Directory

Bridgestone Arena

Nashville Predators
Bridgestone Arena
501 Broadway
Nashville, TN 37203
Phone **615/770-2300**
FAX 615/770-2309
Ticket Information 615/770-PUCK
www.nashvillepredators.com
Capacity: 17,113

Owner	Predators Holdings LLC
Investor Group	Christopher Cigarran, Thomas Cigarran, Joel and Holly Dobberpuhl, David Freeman, Herbert Fritch, DeWitt Thompson V, John Thompson, W. Brett Wilson & Warren Woo
Chairman and Alternate Governor	Thomas Cigarran
Governor	Joel Dobberpuhl
Pres. of Hockey Ops/G.M./Alt. Gov.	David Poile
Chief Executive Officer/Alt. Gov.	Jeff Cogen
President/COO	Sean Henry
Exec. V.P./Chief Sales & Marketing Officer	Chris Parker
Exec. V.P., General Counsel and Chief Financial Officer	Michelle Kennedy
Sr. V.P., Hockey Communications and P.R.	Gerry Helper
Sr. V.P., Corporate Development	Chris Junghans
Hockey Operations	
Assistant General Manager	Paul Fenton
Director of Hockey Operations	Brian Poile
Hockey Operations Manager / Assistant	Brandon Walker / Paul Cook
Hockey Operations Advisor	Brent Peterson
Head Coach	Barry Trotz
Associate Coach	Peter Horachek
Assistant Coaches	Phil Housley, Lane Lambert
Goaltending Coach	Mitch Korn
Strength and Conditioning Coach	David Good
Video Coordinator/Assistant	Lawrence Feloney / Zach Ziegler
Chief Amateur Scout	Jeff Kealty
Professional Scouts	Nick Beverley, Shawn Dineen, Vaclav Nedomansky
North American Amateur Scouts	Tom Nolan, Ryan Rezmierski, Glen Sanders, David Westby
European Scouts	Martin Bakula, Lucas Bergman, Janne Kekalainen
Head Athletic Trainer / Assistant Trainer	Andy Hosler/D.J. Amadio
Equipment Manager / Asst. Manager	Pete Rogers / Jeff Camelio
Equipment Assistant / Locker Room Attendant	Brad Peterson / Craig 'Partner' Baugh
Medical Staff	
Team Doctors	Drs. John E. Kuhn, Paul J. Rummo, Charles L. Cox, Alex Diamond, Daniel S. Weikert, Mark Melson, Gary Solomon, Joseph L. Fredi, Stephane Braun, Kevin Hagan, Blair Summitt, Wesley Thayer, Jason Wendel, Jody Jones, Cliff Brown
Communications/Development	
Manager of Hockey Communications	Kevin Wilson
Corp. Communications Coordinator	Jessica Jones
Digital Media Coordinator	Jimi Russell
Community Relations Director / Coordinator	Rebecca King / Kristen Finch
Team Photographer	John Russell
Corporate Partnerships	
Senior Directors, Corporate Partnerships	Delmar Smith, Charlie Severn
Senior Director, New Business Development	Bob Flynn
Senior Director, Service and Retention	Britt Kincheloe
Account Executives, Corporate Partnerships	Jack Burk, Will Myers
Sr. Account Service Mgr., Corporate Partnerships	Jennifer Maxwell
Account Service Mgrs., Corporate Partnerships	Jordan Bridges, Paige Ciuffo
Sales Coordinator	Lindsay Rutledge
Marketing	
Marketing Director	Danny Shaklan
Mgr., Marketing Entertainment / Interactive	Adam DeVault / Sarah Ryan
Youth Hockey & Fan Development Director	Andee Boiman
Youth Hockey & Fan Development Coordinator	Elizabeth Wardlow
Marketing Coordinator	Sandy Weaver
Marketing Associates	Katie Hamilton, Kelsey Morris, Hannah Foster
Manager, Creative Services	Chuck Stevens
Graphic Designers	Jackie Fisher, Brennan Scott
Premium Seats	
Director, Premium Seat Sales	Chris Burton
Senior Manager, Premium Seat Sales	Tim Wilson
Account Manager, Premium Seats	Rebecca Swan
Finance/Administration/Human Resources	
Sr. Vice President, Finance	Beth Snider
Vice President, Human Resources	Allison Simms
Director, Payroll / Accounting. Coordinator	Susan Charnley / Brandy Tatum
Controller / Project Specialist	Jane Avinger / Rick Bailey
Exec. Assistant / Office Assistant	Elaine Lewis / Maggie France
Human Resources Generalist	Courtni Hinton
Associate General Council	Sean Marshall
Administrative Assistant	Pier Vaughn
Event Technology	
Event Presentation Manager	Patrick Abell
Game Presentation Coordinator	Chris Smith
Information Systems Director / Coordinator	Casey Millar / Michael Paul
Broadcast	
Broadcasting, Sr. Director / Producer	Bob Kohl / David White
Television Play-by-Play Announcer / Color	Pete Weber / Terry Crisp
Radio Play-by-Play Announcer / Color	Tom Callahan / Stu Grimson
Video Production Manager	Mitch Jordan
Videographer/Editor / Assistant	Brett Newkirk / Vickie Chien
Ticket Operations	
Vice President of Ticket Sales	Nat Harden
Ticket Sales Director / Manager	Marty Mulford / Brad Gillispie
Director of Business Strategy	Jordan Kolosey
Database Research Coordinator	Mike Connolly
Manager, Business Director	Paul Tarrants
Vice President of Event Operations	David Chadwell
Ticket Operations Manager / Coordinator	Sara Shear / Taylor Cain
Manager, Fan Relations	Emily Burley

New Jersey Devils

2012-13 Results: 19W-19L-3OTL-7SOL 48PTS
5TH, Atlantic Division • 11TH, Eastern Conference

Key Off-Season Signings/Acquisitions

2013

- **June 20** • Re-signed RW **Mattias Tedenby** and C **Andrei Loktionov**.
- **30** • Acquired G **Cory Schneider** from Vancouver for a 1st-round pick (Bo Horvat) in the 2013 NHL Draft.
- **July 1** • Re-signed D **Peter Harrold**.
- **4** • Re-signed LW **Patrik Elias** and RW **Dainius Zubrus**.
- **5** • Signed LW **Ryane Clowe**, RW **Michael Ryder** and LW **Rostislav Olesz**.
- **10** • Re-signed D **Marek Zidlicky**.
- **18** • Re-signed C **Jacob Josefson**.
- **19** • Named **Mike Foligno** assistant coach.
- **23** • Signed RW **Jaromir Jagr**.

With 20 NHL seasons in the books, Martin Brodeur is the NHL's all-time goaltending leader in games (1,220), minutes played (71,786), wins (669), shutouts (121) and 40-or-more win season (8). He also holds the single-season records for wins (48) and minutes played (4,697), both in 2006-07.

2013-14 Schedule

Oct.	Thu.	3	at Pittsburgh	**Jan.**	Fri.	3	Chicago
	Fri.	4	NY Islanders		Sat.	4	at Buffalo
	Mon.	7	at Edmonton		Tue.	7	Philadelphia
	Tue.	8	at Vancouver		Thu.	9	Dallas
	Fri.	11	at Calgary		Sat.	11	Florida
	Sun.	13	at Winnipeg		Sun.	12	at Toronto
	Thu.	17	at Ottawa		Tue.	14	at Montreal
	Sat.	19	NY Rangers		Thu.	16	at Colorado
	Tue.	22	at Columbus		Sat.	18	at Phoenix
	Thu.	24	Vancouver		Tue.	21	St. Louis
	Sat.	26	at Boston		Fri.	24	Washington
	Tue.	29	Tampa Bay		Sun.	26	NY Rangers*
Nov.	Sat.	2	Philadelphia		Tue.	28	at St. Louis
	Sun.	3	at Minnesota		Thu.	30	at Dallas
	Thu.	7	at Philadelphia		Fri.	31	at Nashville
	Fri.	8	at Toronto	**Feb.**	Mon.	3	Colorado
	Sun.	10	Nashville		Fri.	7	Edmonton
	Tue.	12	at NY Rangers		Sat.	8	at Washington
	Fri.	15	Los Angeles		Thu.	27	Columbus
	Sat.	16	Pittsburgh	**Mar.**	Sat.	1	at NY Islanders*
	Wed.	20	at Anaheim		Sun.	2	San Jose*
	Thu.	21	at Los Angeles		Tue.	4	Detroit
	Sat.	23	at San Jose		Fri.	7	at Detroit
	Mon.	25	Winnipeg		Sat.	8	Carolina
	Wed.	27	Carolina		Tue.	11	at Philadelphia
	Fri.	29	at Carolina		Fri.	14	at Florida
	Sat.	30	Buffalo		Sat.	15	at Tampa Bay
Dec.	Mon.	2	at Montreal		Tue.	18	Boston
	Wed.	4	Montreal		Thu.	20	Minnesota
	Fri.	6	Detroit		Sat.	22	NY Rangers
	Sat.	7	at NY Rangers		Sun.	23	Toronto
	Tue.	10	at Columbus		Thu.	27	Phoenix
	Fri.	13	at Pittsburgh		Sat.	29	at NY Islanders
	Sat.	14	Tampa Bay		Mon.	31	Florida
	Wed.	18	Ottawa	**Apr.**	Tue.	1	at Buffalo
	Fri.	20	Anaheim		Fri.	4	Washington
	Sat.	21	at Washington		Sat.	5	at Carolina
	Mon.	23	at Chicago		Mon.	7	Calgary
	Fri.	27	Columbus		Thu.	10	at Ottawa
	Sat.	28	at NY Islanders		Fri.	11	NY Islanders
	Tue.	31	Pittsburgh*		Sun.	13	Boston*

* Denotes afternoon game.

METROPOLITAN DIVISION
40th NHL Season

Franchise date: June 11, 1974

Transferred from Denver to New Jersey, June 30, 1982.
Transferred from Kansas City to Denver, August 25, 1976.

Year-by-Year Record

		Home				Road				Overall									
Season	**GP**	**W**	**L**	**T**	**OL**	**W**	**L**	**T**	**OL**	**W**	**L**	**T**	**OL**	**GF**	**GA**	**Pts.**	**Div. Fin.**	**Conf. Fin.**	**Playoff Result**
2012-13	48	13	9	....	2	6	10	....	8	19	19	....	10	112	129	48	5th, Atl.	11th, East	Out of Playoffs
2011-12	82	24	13	....	4	24	15	....	2	48	28	....	6	228	209	102	4th, Atl.	6th, East	Lost Final
2010-11	82	22	16	....	3	16	23	....	2	38	39	....	5	174	209	81	4th, Atl.	11th, East	Out of Playoffs
2009-10	82	27	10	....	4	21	17	....	3	48	27	....	7	222	191	103	1st, Atl.	2nd, East	Lost Conf. Quarter-Final
2008-09	82	28	12	....	1	23	15	....	3	51	27	....	4	244	209	106	1st, Atl.	3rd, East	Lost Conf. Quarter-Final
2007-08	82	25	14	....	2	21	15	....	5	46	29	....	7	206	197	99	2nd, Atl.	4th, East	Lost Conf. Quarter-Final
2006-07	82	25	10	....	6	24	14	....	3	49	24	....	9	216	201	107	1st, Atl.	2nd, East	Lost Conf. Semi-Final
2005-06	82	27	11	....	3	19	16	....	6	46	27	....	9	242	229	101	1st, Atl.	3rd, East	Lost Conf. Semi-Final
2004-05	....	....	....	....	....	....	....	....	....	....	....	....	....	....	....	....			
2003-04	82	22	13	5	1	21	12	7	1	43	25	12	2	213	164	100	2nd, Atl.	6th, East	Lost Conf. Quarter-Final
2002-03	**82**	**25**	**11**	**3**	**2**	**21**	**9**	**7**	**4**	**46**	**20**	**10**	**6**	**216**	**166**	**108**	**1st, Atl.**	**2nd, East**	**Won Stanley Cup**
2001-02	82	22	13	4	2	19	15	5	2	41	28	9	4	205	187	95	3rd, Atl.	6th, East	Lost Conf. Quarter-Final
2000-01	82	24	11	6	0	24	8	6	3	48	19	12	3	295	195	111	1st, Atl.	1st, East	Lost Final
1999-2000	**82**	**28**	**9**	**3**	**1**	**17**	**15**	**5**	**4**	**45**	**24**	**8**	**5**	**251**	**203**	**103**	**2nd, Atl.**	**4th, East**	**Won Stanley Cup**
1998-99	82	19	14	8	....	28	10	3	....	47	24	11	....	248	196	105	1st, Atl.	1st, East	Lost Conf. Quarter-Final
1997-98	82	29	10	2	....	19	13	9	....	48	23	11	....	225	166	107	1st, Atl.	1st, East	Lost Conf. Quarter-Final
1996-97	82	23	9	9	....	22	14	5	....	45	23	14	....	231	182	104	1st, Atl.	1st, East	Lost Conf. Semi-Final
1995-96	82	22	17	2	....	15	16	10	....	37	33	12	....	215	202	86	6th, Atl.	9th, East	Out of Playoffs
1994-95	**48**	**14**	**4**	**6**	....	**8**	**14**	**2**	....	**22**	**18**	**8**	....	**136**	**121**	**52**	**2nd, Atl.**	**5th, East**	**Won Stanley Cup**
1993-94	84	29	11	2	....	18	14	10	....	47	25	12	....	306	220	106	2nd, Atl.	2nd, East	Lost Conf. Final
1992-93	84	24	14	4	....	16	23	3	....	40	37	7	....	308	299	87	4th, Patrick		Lost Div. Semi-Final
1991-92	80	24	12	4	....	14	19	3	....	38	31	11	....	289	259	87	4th, Patrick		Lost Div. Semi-Final
1990-91	80	23	10	7	....	9	23	8	....	32	33	15	....	272	264	79	4th, Patrick		Lost Div. Semi-Final
1989-90	80	22	15	3	....	15	19	6	....	37	34	9	....	295	288	83	2nd, Patrick		Lost Div. Semi-Final
1988-89	80	17	18	5	....	10	23	7	....	27	41	12	....	281	325	66	5th, Patrick		Out of Playoffs
1987-88	80	23	16	1	....	15	20	5	....	38	36	6	....	295	296	82	4th, Patrick		Lost Conf. Final
1986-87	80	20	17	3	....	9	28	3	....	29	45	6	....	293	368	64	6th, Patrick		Out of Playoffs
1985-86	80	17	21	2	....	11	28	1	....	28	49	3	....	300	374	59	6th, Patrick		Out of Playoffs
1984-85	80	13	21	6	....	9	27	4	....	22	48	10	....	264	346	54	5th, Patrick		Out of Playoffs
1983-84	80	10	28	2	....	7	28	5	....	17	56	7	....	231	350	41	5th, Patrick		Out of Playoffs
1982-83	80	11	20	9	....	6	29	5	....	17	49	14	....	230	338	48	5th, Patrick		Out of Playoffs
1981-82**	80	14	21	5	....	4	28	8	....	18	49	13	....	241	362	49	5th, Smythe		Out of Playoffs
1980-81**	80	15	16	9	....	7	29	4	....	22	45	13	....	258	344	57	5th, Smythe		Out of Playoffs
1979-80**	80	12	20	8	....	7	28	5	....	19	48	13	....	234	308	51	6th, Smythe		Out of Playoffs
1978-79**	80	8	24	8	....	7	29	4	....	15	53	12	....	210	331	42	4th, Smythe		Out of Playoffs
1977-78**	80	17	14	9	....	2	26	12	....	19	40	21	....	257	305	59	2nd, Smythe		Lost Prelim. Round
1976-77**	80	12	20	8	....	8	26	6	....	20	46	14	....	226	307	54	5th, Smythe		Out of Playoffs
1975-76*	80	8	24	8	....	4	32	4	....	12	56	12	....	190	351	36	5th, Smythe		Out of Playoffs
1974-75*	80	12	20	8	....	3	34	3	....	15	54	11	....	184	328	41	5th, Smythe		Out of Playoffs

* Kansas City Scouts. ** Colorado Rockies.

2013-14 Player Personnel

FORWARDS	HT	WT	*Age	Place of Birth	S	2012-13 Club
BARCH, Krys	6-1	220	33	Hamilton, Ont.	L	New Jersey
BELL, Myles	6-0	210	20	Calgary, Alta.	L	Kelowna
BERNIER, Steve	6-3	220	28	Quebec City, Que.	R	New Jersey
BLACK, Graham	5-11	175	20	Regina, Sask.	L	Swift Current
BOUCHER, Reid	5-11	195	20	Lansing, MI	L	Sarnia-Albany
BOYCHUK, Riley	6-5	220	22	Vancouver, B.C.	L	Fort Worth
CARTER, Ryan	6-1	205	30	White Bear Lake, MN	L	New Jersey
CLOWE, Ryane	6-2	225	31	St. John's, Nfld.	L	San Jose-NY Rangers
ELIAS, Patrik	6-1	195	37	Trebic, Czech.	L	New Jersey
GIONTA, Stephen	5-7	185	29	Rochester, NY	R	Albany-New Jersey
HENRIQUE, Adam	6-0	195	23	Brantford, Ont.	L	Albany-New Jersey
HOEFFEL, Mike	6-4	205	24	North Oaks, MN	L	Albany
JAGR, Jaromir	6-3	240	41	Kladno, Czech.	L	Kladno-Dallas-Boston
JANSSEN, Cam	6-0	215	29	St. Louis, MO	R	Albany-New Jersey
JOHNSON, Ben	5-11	190	19	Hancock, MI	L	Windsor
JOSEFSON, Jacob	6-1	190	22	Stockholm, Sweden	L	Albany-New Jersey
KUJAWINSKI, Ryan	6-2	205	18	Kirkland Lake, Ont.	L	Kingston
LOKTIONOV, Andrei	5-10	180	23	Voskresensk, USSR	L	Manchester-Alb-N.J.
MATTEAU, Stefan	6-3	215	19	Chicago, IL	L	Blainville-Bois.-New Jersey
OLESZ, Rostislav	6-2	215	27	Bilovec, Czech.	L	Rockford
PELLEY, Rod	5-11	200	29	Kitimat, B.C.	L	Norfolk
PESONEN, Harri	6-0	200	25	Muurame, Finland	L	Albany-New Jersey
RYDER, Michael	6-1	200	33	Bonavista, Nfld.	R	Dallas-Montreal
SESTITO, Tim	5-11	200	29	Rome, NY	L	Albany-New Jersey
SISLO, Mike	6-0	195	25	Superior, WI	R	Albany
TEDENBY, Mattias	5-9	175	23	Vetlanda, Sweden	L	Albany-New Jersey
THOMSON, Ben	6-3	205	20	Brampton, Ont.	L	Kitchener
WHITNEY, Joe	5-6	170	25	Reading, MA	L	Albany
WOHLBERG, David	6-1	200	23	Southfield, MI	L	Albany
ZAJAC, Darcy	6-1	205	27	Winnipeg, Man.	R	Albany
ZAJAC, Travis	6-3	205	28	Winnipeg, Man.	R	New Jersey
ZUBRUS, Dainius	6-5	225	35	Elektrenai, USSR	L	New Jersey
DEFENSEMEN						
BURLON, Brandon	6-0	195	23	Nobleton, Ont.	L	Albany
FAYNE, Mark	6-3	215	26	Nashua, NH	R	New Jersey
GELINAS, Eric	6-4	210	22	Vanier, Ont.	L	Albany-New Jersey
GREENE, Andy	5-11	190	30	Trenton, MI	L	New Jersey
HARROLD, Peter	6-0	185	30	Kirtland Hills, OH	R	New Jersey
HELGESON, Seth	6-5	215	22	Faribault, MN	L	U. of Minnesota-Albany
HRABARENKA, Raman	6-4	235	21	Mogilev, Belarus	R	Albany
LARSSON, Adam	6-3	205	20	Skelleftea, Sweden	R	Albany-New Jersey
McPHERSON, Corbin	6-5	220	25	Folsom, CA	R	Albany
MERRILL, Jon	6-4	205	21	Oklahoma City, OK	L	U. of Michigan-Albany
SALVADOR, Bryce	6-3	215	37	Brandon, Man.	L	New Jersey
SCARLETT, Reece	6-1	175	20	Edmonton, Alta.	R	Swift Current
SEVERSON, Damon	6-2	195	19	Brandon, Man.	R	Kelowna-Albany
URBOM, Alexander	6-5	215	22	Stockholm, Sweden	L	Albany-New Jersey
VOLCHENKOV, Anton	6-1	225	31	Moscow, USSR	L	Nizhny Novgorod-New Jersey
YOUNG, Harry	6-5	230	23	Windsor, Ont.	L	Trenton-Kalamazoo-Albany
ZIDLICKY, Marek	5-11	190	36	Most, Czech.	R	Kladno-New Jersey

GOALTENDERS	HT	WT	*Age	Place of Birth	C	2012-13 Club
BRODEUR, Anthony	5-11	180	18	Paterson, NJ	L	Shattuck
BRODEUR, Martin	6-2	220	41	Montreal, Que.	L	New Jersey
CLERMONT, Maxime	6-1	200	21	Montreal, Que.	L	Elmira-Albany
KINKAID, Keith	6-2	190	24	Farmingville, NY	L	Albany-New Jersey
SCHNEIDER, Cory	6-2	195	27	Marblehead, MA	L	Ambri-Vancouver
WEDGEWOOD, Scott	6-1	195	21	Etobicoke, Ont.	L	Trenton-Albany

* – Age at start of 2013-14 season

2012-13 Scoring

* – rookie

Regular Season

Pos	#	Player	Team	GP	G	A	Pts	TOI	+/–	PIM	PP	SH	GW	S	%
L	26	Patrik Elias	N.J.	48	14	22	36	18:43	5	22	5	1	0	118	11.9
L	17	Ilya Kovalchuk	N.J.	37	11	20	31	24:44	–6	18	2	4	5	123	8.9
R	23	David Clarkson	N.J.	48	15	9	24	17:35	–6	78	6	0	5	180	8.3
C	19	Travis Zajac	N.J.	48	7	13	20	19:31	–5	22	1	1	1	82	8.5
D	2	Marek Zidlicky	N.J.	48	4	15	19	20:59	–12	38	1	0	0	101	4.0
L	15	Steve Sullivan	PHX	33	5	7	12	14:21	–8	20	2	0	0	48	10.4
			N.J.	9	2	3	5	15:15	–4	4	2	0	1	13	15.4
			Total	42	7	10	17	14:33	–12	24	4	0	1	61	11.5
C	14	Adam Henrique	N.J.	42	11	5	16	18:19	–3	16	3	2	2	78	14.1
D	6	Andy Greene	N.J.	48	4	12	16	23:02	12	20	2	1	1	63	6.3
R	18	Steve Bernier	N.J.	47	8	7	15	13:45	–7	17	2	0	1	88	9.1
C	20	Ryan Carter	N.J.	44	6	9	15	13:03	–2	31	0	1	1	63	9.5
R	11	Stephen Gionta	N.J.	48	4	10	14	13:01	2	14	0	0	0	58	6.9
C	21	Andrei Loktionov	N.J.	28	8	4	12	14:15	–2	4	1	0	0	47	17.0
L	12	Alexei Ponikarovsky	WPG	12	2	0	2	11:52	–2	6	0	0	1	10	20.0
			N.J.	30	2	5	7	13:40	1	8	0	0	0	41	4.9
			Total	42	4	5	9	13:09	–1	14	0	0	1	51	7.8
C	8	Dainius Zubrus	N.J.	22	2	7	9	16:47	–3	12	0	0	0	22	9.1
R	16	Matt D'Agostini	STL	16	1	1	2	11:52	–4	2	0	0	0	19	5.3
			N.J.	13	2	2	4	12:51	–1	6	0	0	0	14	14.3
			Total	29	3	3	6	12:18	–5	8	0	0	0	33	9.1
D	29	Mark Fayne	N.J.	31	1	5	6	18:05	6	16	0	1	0	34	2.9
D	5	Adam Larsson	N.J.	37	0	6	6	18:06	4	12	0	0	0	30	0.0
D	10	Peter Harrold	N.J.	23	2	3	5	17:37	–8	6	1	0	0	36	5.6
D	28	Anton Volchenkov	N.J.	37	1	4	5	16:03	–1	37	0	0	0	38	2.6
D	7	Henrik Tallinder	N.J.	25	1	3	4	17:34	0	10	0	0	0	22	4.5
C	15	* Stefan Matteau	N.J.	17	1	2	3	9:11	–1	6	0	0	0	22	4.5
C	9	Jacob Josefson	N.J.	22	1	2	3	12:58	–10	2	0	0	0	20	5.0
D	24	Bryce Salvador	N.J.	39	0	2	2	21:19	–12	22	0	0	0	29	0.0
R	25	Tom Kostopoulos	N.J.	15	1	0	1	9:05	0	18	0	0	0	13	7.7
C	12	Matt Anderson	N.J.	2	0	1	1	5:46	1	0	0	0	0	0	0.0
L	21	Mattias Tedenby	N.J.	4	0	1	1	8:59	0	2	0	0	0	2	0.0
D	32	* Eric Gelinas	N.J.	1	0	0	0	15:59	–1	0	0	0	0	1	0.0
D	33	* Alexander Urbom	N.J.	1	0	0	0	14:11	–1	0	0	0	0	0	0.0
R	25	Cam Janssen	N.J.	4	0	0	0	3:58	–1	2	0	0	0	0	0.0
C	9	* Harri Pesonen	N.J.	4	0	0	0	9:11	–1	2	0	0	0	3	0.0
C	15	Tim Sestito	N.J.	6	0	0	0	7:52	1	2	0	0	0	4	0.0
R	22	Kry Barch	N.J.	22	0	0	0	5:51	1	44	0	0	0	4	0.0

Goaltending

No.	Goaltender	GPI	Mins	Avg	W	L	OT	EN	SO	GA	SA	S%	G	A	PIM
31	* Jeff Frazee	1	19	0.00	0	0	0	1	0	0	3	1.000	0	0	0
30	Martin Brodeur	29	1757	2.22	13	9	7	2	2	65	654	.901	1	2	0
35	* Keith Kinkaid	1	26	2.31	0	0	0	1	0	1	13	.923	0	0	0
1	Johan Hedberg	19	1108	2.76	6	10	3	1	1	51	435	.883	0	1	4
	Totals	**48**	**2938**	**2.49**	**19**	**19**	**10**	**5**	**3**	**122**	**1110**	**.890**			

Captains' History

Simon Nolet, 1974-75 to 1976-77; Wilf Paiement, 1977-78; Gary Croteau, 1978-79; Mike Christie, Rene Robert and Lanny McDonald, 1979-80; Lanny McDonald, 1980-81; Lanny McDonald and Rob Ramage, 1981-82; Don Lever, 1982-83; Don Lever and Mel Bridgman, 1983-84; Mel Bridgman, 1984-85 to 1986-87; Kirk Muller, 1987-88 to 1990-91; Bruce Driver, 1991-92; Scott Stevens, 1992-93 to 2002-03; Scott Stevens and Scott Neidermayer, 2003-04; no captain, 2005-06; Patrik Elias, 2006-07; Patrik Elias and Jamie Langenbrunner, 2007-08; Jamie Langenbrunner, 2008-09 to 2010-11; Zach Parise, 2011-12; Bryce Salvador, 2012-13 to date.

Lou Lamoriello

President, CEO and General Manager

Born: Providence, RI, October 21, 1942.

Lou Lamoriello has been president and general manager of the Devils since 1987-88 following more than 20 years with Providence College as a player, coach and administrator. He was inducted into the Hockey Hall of Fame's Builder category in November, 2009 and elected to the U.S. Hockey Hall of Fame in 2012. His trades, signings and draft choices helped lead the Devils to their first Stanley Cup Championship in 1995 and were followed by victories again in 2000 and 2003. During his tenure, the Devils have had 13 100-point seasons, five Eastern Conference playoff titles and nine Atlantic Division regular-season championships. In 2005-06, Lamoriello took over behind the bench and coached the Devils to first place in the Atlantic Division.

While at Providence, Lamoriello served as hockey coach for 15 seasons, compiling an impressive .578 winning percentage (248-179-13), while guiding the Friars to 12 post-season tournaments in a row. During his last five seasons (1978-83) of coaching, the school compiled a record of 107-58-4 and had more players drafted by the National Hockey League after entering college than any other college team during those years. Lamoriello helped propel numerous players and administrators toward NHL careers during his tenure at Providence. He was hired as president of the Devils on April 30, 1987, and assumed the responsibility of general manager on September 10, 1987. Lamoriello was G.M. of Team USA for the first World Cup of Hockey in 1996 as the U.S. captured the championship. He was also the G.M. for the 1998 U.S. Olympic Team.

Coaching Record

			Regular Season				Playoffs			
Season	Team	League	GC	W	L	O/T	GC	W	L	T
2005-06	New Jersey	NHL	50	32	14	4	9	5	4	....
2006-07	New Jersey	NHL	3	2	0	1	11	5	6	....
	NHL Totals		**53**	**34**	**14**	**5**	**20**	**10**	**10**	

Posted an 0-1 playoff record as replacement coach when Jim Schoenfeld was suspended, May 10, 1988. Loss is credited to Schoenfeld's coaching record.

Drafted by the Devils in the second round of the 1994 Entry Draft, Patrik Elias has played 1,090 regular-season games for the Devils and is the club's all-time leading scorer.

Club Records

Team

(Figures in brackets for season records are games played; records for fewest points, wins, ties, losses, goals, goals against are for 70 or more games)

Most Points **111** 2000-01 (82)
Most Wins **51** 2008-09 (82)
Most Ties ***21** 1977-78 (80)
.... **15** 1990-91 (80)
Most Losses **56** 1975-76 (80), 1983-84 (80)
Most Goals **308** 1992-93 (84)
Most Goals Against **374** 1985-86 (80)
Fewest Points ***36** 1975-76 (80)
41 1983-84 (80)
Fewest Wins ***12** 1975-76 (80)
17 1982-83 (80), 1983-84 (80)
Fewest Ties **3** 1985-86 (80)
Fewest Losses **19** 2000-01 (82)
Fewest Goals **174** 2010-11 (82)
Fewest Goals Against **164** 2003-04 (82)
Longest Winning Streak
Overall .... **13** Feb. 26-Mar. 23/01
Home .... **11** Feb. 9-Mar. 20/09
Away .... **10** Feb. 27-Apr. 7/01
Longest Undefeated Streak
Overall .... **13** Four times
Home .... **15** Jan. 8-Mar. 15/97 (9W, 6T)
Away .... **10** Feb. 27-Apr. 7/01 (10W)
Longest Losing Streak
Overall .... ***14** Dec. 30/75-Jan. 29/76
10 Oct. 14-Nov. 4/83
Home .... **9** Dec. 22/85-Feb. 6/86
Away .... **12** Oct. 19-Dec. 1/83
Longest Winless Streak
Overall .... ***27** Feb. 12-Apr. 4/76 (21L, 6T)
18 Oct. 20-Nov. 26/82 (14L 4T)
Home .... ***14** Feb. 12-Mar. 30/76 (10L, 4T), Feb. 4-Mar. 31/79 (12L, 2T)
9 Dec. 22/85-Feb. 6/86 (9L)
Away .... ***32** Nov. 12/77-Mar. 15/78 (22L, 10T)
14 Dec. 26/82-Mar. 5/83 (13L, 1T)
Most Shutouts, Season **14** 2003-04 (82)
Most PIM, Season **2,494** 1988-89 (80)
Most Goals, Game .... **9** Nine times

Individual

Most Seasons .... **20** Ken Daneyko
Most Games .... **1,283** Ken Daneyko
Most Goals, Career .... **375** Patrik Elias
Most Assists, Career .... **555** Patrik Elias
Most Points, Career .... **930** Patrik Elias (375G, 555A)
Most PIM, Career .... **2,519** Ken Daneyko
Most Shutouts, Career ..... ****121** Martin Brodeur
Longest Consecutive Games Streak .... **401** Travis Zajac (Oct. 26/06-Apr. 10/11)
Most Goals, Season .... **48** Brian Gionta (2005-06)
Most Assists, Season .... **60** Scott Stevens (1993-94)
Most Points, Season .... **96** Patrik Elias (2000-01; 40G, 56A)
Most PIM, Season .... **295** Krzysztof Oliwa (1997-98)
Most Points, Defenseman, Season .... **78** Scott Stevens (1993-94; 18G, 60A)
Most Points, Center, Season .... **94** Kirk Muller (1987-88; 37G, 57A)
Most Points, Right Wing, Season .... **89** Brian Gionta (2005-06; 48G, 41A)
Most Points, Left Wing, Season .... **96** Patrik Elias (2000-01; 40G, 56A)
Most Points, Rookie, Season .... **70** Scott Gomez (1999-2000; 19G, 51A)
Most Shutouts, Season .... **12** Martin Brodeur (2006-07)
Most Goals, Game .... **4** Six times
Most Assists, Game .... **5** Greg Adams (Oct. 10/85), Kirk Muller (Mar. 25/87), Tom Kurvers (Feb. 13/89), Scott Gomez (Mar. 30/03)
Most Points, Game .... **6** Kirk Muller (Oct. 29/86; 3G, 3A)

* Records include Kansas City Scouts and Colorado Rockies, 1974-75 through 1981-82.
** NHL Record.

General Managers' History

Sid Abel, 1974-75; Sid Abel and Baz Bastien, 1975-76; Ray Miron, 1976-77 to 1980-81; Bill MacMillan, 1981-82, 1982-83; Bill MacMillan and Max McNab, 1983-84; Max McNab 1984-85 to 1986-87; Lou Lamoriello, 1987-88 to date.

Retired Numbers

3	Ken Daneyko	1982-2003
4	Scott Stevens	1991-2005
27	Scott Niedermayer	1991-2004

All-time Record vs. Other Clubs

Regular Season

	Total								At Home								On Road							
	GP	W	L	T	OL	GF	GA	PTS	GP	W	L	T	OL	GF	GA	PTS	GP	W	L	T	OL	GF	GA	PTS
Anaheim	24	15	8	1	0	71	54	31	11	9	2	0	0	38	19	18	13	6	6	1	0	33	35	13
Boston	140	47	69	19	5	381	474	118	68	23	33	11	1	171	212	58	72	24	36	8	4	210	262	60
Buffalo	139	51	65	17	6	401	464	125	69	27	31	9	2	194	214	65	70	24	34	8	4	207	250	60
Calgary	93	24	57	11	1	252	364	60	48	17	28	3	0	134	169	37	45	7	29	8	1	118	195	23
Carolina	120	62	44	12	2	383	354	138	60	36	20	4	0	203	175	76	60	26	24	8	2	180	179	62
Chicago	101	37	41	21	2	293	337	97	51	23	16	11	1	155	148	58	50	14	25	10	1	138	189	39
Colorado	78	35	34	8	1	261	263	79	40	21	14	4	1	157	128	47	38	14	20	4	0	104	135	32
Columbus	12	8	2	1	1	34	25	18	5	4	0	1	0	14	8	9	7	4	2	0	1	20	17	9
Dallas	98	39	48	9	2	293	320	89	48	25	19	3	1	168	141	54	50	14	29	6	1	125	179	35
Detroit	87	36	39	11	1	279	288	84	43	22	12	9	0	144	112	53	44	14	27	2	1	135	176	31
Edmonton	70	29	32	9	0	237	258	67	36	16	17	3	0	118	118	35	34	13	15	6	0	119	140	32
Florida	80	47	23	7	3	226	172	104	40	26	10	3	1	125	79	56	40	21	13	4	2	101	93	48
Los Angeles	93	31	49	11	2	294	366	75	47	21	21	5	0	153	158	47	46	10	28	6	2	141	208	28
Minnesota	12	7	3	2	0	40	29	16	6	4	1	1	0	21	12	9	6	3	2	1	0	19	17	7
Montreal	139	62	65	10	2	384	436	136	70	35	31	4	0	208	228	74	69	27	34	6	2	176	208	62
Nashville	17	10	5	0	2	50	41	22	8	3	4	0	1	24	23	7	9	7	1	0	1	26	18	15
NY Islanders	222	83	111	22	6	653	768	194	110	50	46	11	3	351	353	114	112	33	65	11	3	302	415	80
NY Rangers	222	91	97	27	7	665	734	216	112	59	43	7	3	366	344	128	110	32	54	20	4	299	390	88
Ottawa	78	46	23	5	4	203	180	101	39	24	12	2	1	109	90	51	39	22	11	3	3	94	90	50
Philadelphia	221	98	101	18	4	653	737	218	110	63	38	8	1	368	338	135	111	35	63	10	3	285	399	83
Phoenix	66	21	36	9	0	192	219	51	32	14	12	6	0	104	93	34	34	7	24	3	0	88	126	17
Pittsburgh	212	105	87	17	3	700	690	230	107	56	37	13	1	368	326	126	105	49	50	4	2	332	364	104
St. Louis	98	36	46	14	2	305	337	88	49	22	19	7	1	151	136	52	49	14	27	7	1	154	201	36
San Jose	29	17	8	2	2	96	70	38	16	10	4	1	1	58	36	22	13	7	4	1	1	38	34	16
Tampa Bay	82	50	20	7	5	276	189	112	42	28	10	2	2	151	95	60	40	22	10	5	3	125	94	52
Toronto	125	42	57	20	6	372	412	110	61	23	19	15	4	204	194	65	64	19	38	5	2	168	218	45
Vancouver	102	31	52	17	2	292	352	81	52	21	23	6	2	157	166	50	50	10	29	11	0	135	186	31
Washington	189	83	92	13	1	554	622	180	94	49	37	7	1	288	268	106	95	34	55	6	0	266	354	74
Winnipeg	51	30	13	3	5	159	118	68	26	15	7	1	3	77	58	34	25	15	6	2	2	82	60	34
Defunct Clubs	16	6	5	5	0	44	46	17	8	4	2	2	0	25	19	10	8	2	3	3	0	19	27	7
Totals	**3016**	**1279**	**1332**	**328**	**77**	**9043**	**9719**	**2963**	**1508**	**750**	**568**	**159**	**31**	**4804**	**4460**	**1690**	**1508**	**529**	**764**	**169**	**46**	**4239**	**5259**	**1273**

Playoffs

	Series	W	L	GP	W	L	T	GF	GA	Last Mtg.	Rnd.	Result
Anaheim	1	1	0	7	4	3	0	19	12	2003	F	W 4-3
Boston	4	3	1	23	15	8	0	68	60	2003	CQF	W 4-1
Buffalo	1	1	0	7	4	3	0	14	14	1994	CQF	W 4-3
Carolina	4	1	3	24	10	14	0	56	51	2009	CQF	L 3-4
Colorado	1	0	1	7	3	4	0	11	19	2001	F	L 3-4
Dallas	1	1	0	6	4	2	0	15	9	2000	F	W 4-2
Detroit	1	1	0	4	4	0	0	16	7	1995	F	W 4-0
Florida	2	2	0	11	8	3	0	30	23	2012	CQF	W 4-3
Los Angeles	1	0	1	6	2	4	0	8	16	2012	F	L 2-4
Montreal	1	1	0	5	4	1	0	22	11	1997	CQF	W 4-1
NY Islanders	1	1	0	6	4	2	0	23	18	1988	DSF	W 4-2
NY Rangers	6	2	4	34	16	18	0	90	93	2012	CF	W 4-2
Ottawa	3	1	2	18	7	11	0	40	41	2007	CSF	L 1-4
Philadelphia	6	3	3	30	14	16	0	77	75	2012	CSF	W 4-1
Pittsburgh	5	2	3	29	15	14	0	86	80	2001	CF	W 4-1
Tampa Bay	2	2	0	11	8	3	0	33	22	2007	CQF	W 4-2
Toronto	2	2	0	13	8	5	0	37	27	2001	CSF	W 4-3
Washington	2	1	1	13	6	7	0	43	44	1990	DSF	L 2-4
Totals	**44**	**25**	**19**	**254**	**136**	**118**	**0**	**688**	**622**			

Playoff Results 2013-2009

Year	Round	Opponent	Result	GF	GA
2012	F	Los Angeles	L 2-4	8	16
	CF	NY Rangers	W 4-2	15	14
	CSF	Philadelphia	W 4-1	18	11
	CQF	Florida	W 4-3	18	17
2010	CQF	Philadelphia	L 1-4	9	15
2009	CQF	Carolina	L 3-4	15	17

Abbreviations: Round: F – Final; **CF** – conference final; **CSF** – conference semi-final; **CQF** – conference quarter-final; **DSF** – division semi-final.

Calgary totals include Atlanta Flames, 1974-75 to 1979-80.
Colorado totals include Quebec, 1979-80 to 1994-95.
Phoenix totals include Winnipeg, 1979-80 to 1995-96.
Carolina totals include Hartford, 1979-80 to 1996-97.
Dallas totals include Minnesota North Stars, 1974-75 to 1992-93.
Winnipeg totals include Atlanta Thrashers, 1999-2000 to 2010-11.

2012-13 Results

Jan.	19	at NY Islanders	2-1		9	at Carolina	3-6
	22	Philadelphia	3-0		10	Winnipeg	3-2†
	25	Washington	3-2*		13	Philadelphia	5-2
	27	at Montreal	3-4*		15	at Philadelphia	1-2†
	29	at Boston	1-2†		16	Montreal	1-2
	31	NY Islanders	4-5*		19	NY Rangers	2-3
Feb.	2	at Pittsburgh	1-5		21	at Carolina	4-1
	3	at NY Islanders	3-0		23	Florida	2-1
	5	NY Rangers	3-1		25	at Ottawa	2-3†
	7	Tampa Bay	4-2		29	at Tampa Bay	4-5†
	9	Pittsburgh	3-1		30	at Florida	2-3*
	10	at Pittsburgh	3-1	**Apr.**	1	NY Islanders	1-3
	12	Carolina	2-4		4	at Boston	0-1
	15	Philadelphia	5-3		6	Toronto	1-2
	16	at NY Islanders	1-5		7	at Buffalo	2-3†
	18	Ottawa	1-2†		10	Boston	4-5
	21	at Washington	3-2		12	Ottawa	0-2
	23	at Washington	1-5		15	at Toronto	0-2
	24	Winnipeg	2-4		18	at Philadelphia	3-0
	28	at Winnipeg	1-3		20	Florida	6-2
Mar.	2	at Buffalo	3-4†		21	at NY Rangers	1-4
	4	at Toronto	2-4		23	Montreal	3-2
	5	Tampa Bay	2-5		25	Pittsburgh	3-2
	7	Buffalo	3-2†		27	at NY Rangers	0-4

* – Overtime † – Shootout

Entry Draft Selections 2013-1999

Name in bold denotes played in NHL.

2013
Pick
42 Steven Santini
73 Ryan Kujawinski
100 Miles Wood
160 Myles Bell
208 Anthony Brodeur

2012
Pick
29 **Stefan Matteau**
60 Damon Severson
90 Ben Johnson
96 Ben Thomson
135 Graham Black
150 Alexander Kerfoot
180 Artur Gavrus

2011
Pick
4 **Adam Larsson**
69 forfeited pick
75 Blake Coleman
99 Reid Boucher
129 Blake Pietila
159 Reece Scarlett
189 Patrick Daly

2010
Pick
38 Jon Merrill
84 Scott Wedgewood
114 Joe Faust
174 Maxime Clermont
204 Mauro Jorg

2009
Pick
20 **Jacob Josefson**
54 **Eric Gelinas**
73 **Alexander Urbom**
114 Seth Helgeson
144 Derek Rodwell
174 Ashton Bernard
204 Curtis Gedig

2008
Pick
24 **Mattias Tedenby**
52 Brandon Burlon
54 **Patrice Cormier**
82 **Adam Henrique**
112 Matt Delahey
142 Kory Nagy
172 David Wohlberg
202 Harry Young
205 Jean-Sebastien Berube

2007
Pick
57 Mike Hoeffel
79 **Nick Palmieri**
87 Corbin McPherson
117 **Matt Halischuk**
177 Vili Sopanen
207 Ryan Molle

2006
Pick
30 **Matthew Corrente**
58 **Alexander Vasyunov**
67 Kirill Tulupov
77 **Vladimir Zharkov**
107 Tyler Miller
148 **Olivier Magnan**
178 Tony Romano
208 Kyell Henegan

2005
Pick
23 **Niclas Bergfors**
38 **Jeff Frazee**
84 **Mark Fraser**
99 **Patrick Davis**
155 **Mark Fayne**
170 Sean Zimmerman
218 Alexander Sundstrom

2004
Pick
20 **Travis Zajac**
155 Alexander Mikhailishin
185 Josh Disher
216 **Pierre-Luc Letourneau-Leblond**
217 **Tyler Eckford**
250 Nathan Perkovich
282 Valeri Klimov

2003
Pick
17 **Zach Parise**
42 **Petr Vrana**
93 Ivan Khomutov
167 Zach Tarkir
197 Jason Smith
261 **Joey Tenute**
292 Arseny Bondarev

2002
Pick
51 Anton Kadeykin
53 **Barry Tallackson**
64 **Jason Ryznar**
84 Marek Chvatal
85 Ahren Nittel
117 **Cam Janssen**
154 Krisjanis Redlihs
187 Eric Johansson
218 **Ilkka Pikkarainen**
250 Dan Glover
281 Bill Kinkel

2001
Pick
28 Adrian Foster
44 Igor Pohanka
48 **Tuomas Pihlman**
60 Victor Uchevatov
67 Robin Leblanc
72 **Brandon Nolan**
128 Andrei Posnov
163 **Andreas Salomonsson**
194 James Massen
229 **Aaron Voros**
257 Yevgeny Gamalei

2000
Pick
22 **David Hale**
39 Teemu Laine
56 **Alexander Suglobov**
57 Matt DeMarchi
62 **Paul Martin**
67 Max Birbraer
76 **Mike Rupp**
125 Phil Cole
135 **Mike Danton**
164 Matus Kostur
194 **Deryk Engelland**
198 Ken Magowan
257 Warren McCutcheon

1999
Pick
27 Ari Ahonen
42 **Mike Commodore**
50 Brett Clouthier
95 Andre Lakos
100 Teemu Kesa
185 Scott Cameron
214 Chris Hartsburg
242 Justin Dziama

Coaching History

Bep Guidolin, 1974-75; Bep Guidolin, Sid Abel and Eddie Bush, 1975-76; Johnny Wilson, 1976-77; Pat Kelly, 1977-78; Pat Kelly and Aldo Guidolin, 1978-79; Don Cherry, 1979-80; Bill MacMillan, 1980-81; Bert Marshall and Marshall Johnston, 1981-82; Bill MacMillan, 1982-83; Bill MacMillan and Tom McVie, 1983-84; Doug Carpenter, 1984-85 to 1986-87; Doug Carpenter and Jim Schoenfeld, 1987-88; Jim Schoenfeld, 1988-89; Jim Schoenfeld and John Cunniff, 1989-90; John Cunniff and Tom McVie, 1990-91; Tom McVie, 1991-92; Herb Brooks, 1992-93; Jacques Lemaire, 1993-94 to 1997-98; Robbie Ftorek, 1998-99; Robbie Ftorek and Larry Robinson, 1999-2000; Larry Robinson, 2000-01; Larry Robinson and Kevin Constantine, 2001-02; Pat Burns, 2002-03 to 2004-05; Larry Robinson and Lou Lamoriello, 2005-06; Claude Julien and Lou Lamoriello, 2006-07; Brent Sutter, 2007-08, 2008-09; Jacques Lemaire, 2009-10; John MacLean and Jacques Lemaire, 2010-11; Peter DeBoer, 2011-12 to date.

Club Directory

Prudential Center

New Jersey Devils
Prudential Center
25 Lafayette Street
Newark, NJ 07102
Phone **973/757-6100**
FAX 973/757-6399
www.newjerseydevils.com
Capacity: 17,625

Owner/Chairman/Governor	Joshua Harris
Owner/Vice Chairman/Alternate Governor	David Blitzer
President/General Manager/Alternate Governor	Lou Lamoriello
CEO, NJ Devils & Prudential Center/Alt. Governor	Scott O'Neil
Senior Advisor to the Chairman	Jeff Vanderbeek
Exec. Vice President, Hockey Ops/Director, Scouting	David Conte
Exec. Vice President, Operations	Peter McMullen
Sr. Vice President, Hockey Ops/ General Manager, Albany/Scout	Chris Lamoriello
Senior Vice President, Communications	Mike Levine
Vice President, Hockey Operations	Stephen Pellegrini
Hockey Club Personnel	
Head Coach	Peter DeBoer
Assistant Coaches	Dave Barr, Scott Stevens, Mike Foligno
Goaltending Coach	Chris Terreri
Special Assignment Coaches	Jacques Laperriere, Jacques Lemaire
Assistant Director, Scouting	Claude Carrier
Scouting Staff	Timo Blomqvist, Jeremy Conte, Glen Dirk, Milt Fisher, Dan Labraaten, Scott Lachance, Pierre Mondou, Gates Orlando, Larry Perris, Marcel Pronovost, Lou Reycroft, Vaclav Slansky, Jr., Steve Smith, Geoff Stevens, Ed Thomlinson
Pro Scouting Staff	Bob Hoffmeyer, Jan Ludvig
Hockey Operations Video Coordinator	Taran Singleton
Video Assistant	Matthew DeMado
Scouting Staff Assistant	Callie A. Smith
Head Trainer	Richard Stinziano
Assistant Trainer	Kevin Morley
Equipment Manager	Rich Matthews
Assistant Equipment Managers	Jason McGrath, Mike Thibault
Strength/Conditioning Coordinator	Michael Vasalani
Massage Therapist	Brian Smith
Team Orthopedist	Dr. Barry Fisher
Team Cardiologist	Dr. Joseph Niznik
Team Dentists	Dr. H. Hugh Gardy, Dr. Jason Schepis
Team Optometrist	Dr. Paul Berman
Exercise Physiologist	Dr. Garret Caffrey
Video Consultant	Mitch Kaufman
Head Coach, Albany	Rick Kowalsky
Assistant Coach, Albany	Tommy Albelin
Goaltending Coach, Albany	Dave Caruso
Video Coordinators, Albany	Mike Regan, Sean Andrake
Athletic Trainer, Albany	TBA
Equipment Manager, Albany	Andrew Schmidt
Assistant Equipment Manager, Albany	Elliot Newton
President's Office	
Hockey Operations Executive Assistant to the President/General Manager	Marie Carnevale
Administrative Assistant	Christine Garcia
Communications	
Director, Communications	Pete Albietz
Director, Website Content	Eric Marin
Assistant Director, Communications	Daniel Beam
Staff Assistant	Valentino Sisti
Computer Operations	
Sr. Director, Programming/Computer Operations	Jack Skelley
Alumni	
Alumni Representatives	Ken Daneyko, Bruce Driver, Grant Marshall, Jim Dowd
Television/Radio	
Television Outlet	MSG Plus
Television Play-by-Play / Color	Steve Cangialosi / Glenn Resch
Radio Outlet	SportsRadio 66 WFAN & 101.9 FM
Radio Play-by-Play/ Color	Matt Loughlin / Sherry Ross

Peter DeBoer

Head Coach

Born: Dunnville, Ont., June 13, 1968.

New Jersey Devils general manager Lou Lamoriello introduced Peter DeBoer as the 21st coach in franchise history on July 19, 2011. He had spent the previous three seasons as head coach of the Florida Panthers. In his first season behind the bench with the Devils in 2011-12, DeBoer led New Jersey to the Stanley Cup Final.

DeBoer joined the NHL coaching ranks with Florida in 2008 after 13 seasons of leading teams in the Ontario Hockey League. The current part-owner of the OHL's Oshawa Generals is a two-time winner of the OHL coach of the year – both coming with the Plymouth Whalers, in 1998-99 and 1999-2000. He coached the Kitchener Rangers to the Memorial Cup twice, winning it in 2003. DeBoer also served as an assistant coach for Team Canada at the 2010 World Championship and was a member of the gold medal-winning Canadian staff at the 2005 World Junior Championship.

As a player, DeBoer won the 1988 Memorial Cup as a member of the Windsor Spitfires. He was a 12th-round selection of the Toronto Maple Leafs in the 1988 NHL Entry Draft and played two full seasons professionally with the Milwaukee Admirals of the International Hockey League. He holds a law degree from the University of Windsor/University of Detroit.

Coaching Record

			Regular Season				Playoffs			
Season	Team	League	GC	W	L	O/T	GC	W	L	T
1995-96	Detroit	OHL	66	40	22	4	17	9	8	....
1996-97	Detroit	OHL	66	26	34	6	5	1	4	....
1997-98	Plymouth	OHL	66	37	22	7	15	8	7	....
1998-99	Plymouth	OHL	66	51	13	4	11	7	4	....
99-2000	Plymouth	OHL	68	45	18	5	23	15	8	....
2000-01	Plymouth	OHL	68	43	15	10	19	14	5	....
2001-02	Kitchener	OHL	68	35	22	11	4	0	4	....
2002-03	Kitchener	OHL	68	46	14	8	21	16	5	....
2002-03	Kitchener	M-Cup	....	....	....	....	4	4	0	....
2003-04	Kitchener	OHL	68	34	26	8	5	1	4	....
2004-05	Kitchener	OHL	68	35	20	13	15	9	6	....
2005-06	Kitchener	OHL	68	47	19	2	5	1	4	....
2006-07	Kitchener	OHL	68	47	17	4	9	5	4	....
2007-08	Kitchener	OHL	68	53	11	4	20	16	4	....
2007-08	Kitchener	M-Cup	....	....	....	....	5	2	3	....
2008-09	**Florida**	**NHL**	**82**	**41**	**30**	**11**	....	....	....	....
2009-10	**Florida**	**NHL**	**82**	**32**	**37**	**13**	....	....	....	....
2010-11	**Florida**	**NHL**	**82**	**30**	**40**	**12**	....	....	....	....
2011-12	**New Jersey**	**NHL**	**82**	**48**	**28**	**6**	**24**	**14**	**10**	....
2012-13	**New Jersey**	**NHL**	**48**	**19**	**19**	**10**	....	....	....	....
	NHL Totals		**376**	**170**	**154**	**52**	**24**	**14**	**10**	....

Key Off-Season Signings/Acquisitions

2013

May 17 • Re-signed LW **Eric Boulton**.

June 30 • Acquired RW **Cal Clutterbuck** and a 3rd-round pick (Eamon McAdam) in the 2013 NHL Draft from Minnesota for RW **Nino Niederreiter**.

July 5 • Signed C **Peter Regin** and C **Pierre-Marc Bouchard**.

5 • Re-signed G **Evgeni Nabokov** and D **Travis Hamonic**.

8 • Re-signed G **Kevin Poulin**.

15 • Re-signed C **Josh Bailey**.

18 • Re-signed D **Thomas Hickey**.

New York Islanders

2012-13 Results: 24W-17L-4OTL-3SOL 55PTS
3RD, Atlantic Division • 8TH, Eastern Conference

Battling to keep possession of the puck in front of Sidney Crosby, John Tavares officially entered the debate for best player in the game in 2012-13 with a third-place finish behind Alex Ovechkin and Crosby in voting for the Hart Trophy as NHL MVP. Tavares was also third in the league with 28 goals.

2013-14 Schedule

Oct.	Fri.	4	at New Jersey	**Jan.**	Thu.	2	Chicago
	Sat.	5	Columbus		Sat.	4	Carolina
	Tue.	8	Phoenix		Mon.	6	Dallas
	Fri.	11	at Chicago		Tue.	7	at Toronto
	Sat.	12	at Nashville		Fri.	10	at Colorado
	Tue.	15	Buffalo		Sun.	12	at Dallas*
	Thu.	17	Edmonton		Tue.	14	at Florida
	Sat.	19	Carolina		Thu.	16	at Tampa Bay
	Tue.	22	Vancouver		Sat.	18	at Philadelphia
	Fri.	25	at Pittsburgh		Mon.	20	Philadelphia*
	Sat.	26	Philadelphia		Tue.	21	at NY Rangers
	Tue.	29	NY Rangers		Thu.	23	Pittsburgh
Nov.	Fri.	1	at Ottawa		Sat.	25	St. Louis*
	Sat.	2	Boston		Mon.	27	Boston
	Tue.	5	at Washington		Wed.	29	NY Rangers
	Thu.	7	at Carolina		Fri.	31	at NY Rangers
	Sat.	9	at Columbus	**Feb.**	Tue.	4	at Washington
	Sun.	10	at Montreal		Thu.	6	Calgary
	Tue.	12	Nashville		Sat.	8	Colorado
	Thu.	14	Los Angeles		Thu.	27	Toronto
	Sat.	16	Detroit	**Mar.**	Sat.	1	New Jersey*
	Tue.	19	at Toronto		Sun.	2	Florida*
	Fri.	22	at Pittsburgh		Tue.	4	at Winnipeg
	Sat.	23	at Philadelphia		Thu.	6	at Edmonton
	Wed.	27	Winnipeg		Fri.	7	at Calgary
	Fri.	29	Detroit*		Mon.	10	at Vancouver
	Sat.	30	Washington		Fri.	14	San Jose
Dec.	Tue.	3	Pittsburgh		Sat.	15	Buffalo
	Thu.	5	at St. Louis		Tue.	18	Minnesota
	Sat.	7	at Los Angeles		Sun.	23	Columbus*
	Mon.	9	at Anaheim		Tue.	25	at Carolina
	Tue.	10	at San Jose		Thu.	27	at Tampa Bay
	Thu.	12	at Phoenix		Sat.	29	New Jersey
	Sat.	14	Montreal	**Apr.**	Tue.	1	Florida
	Tue.	17	Tampa Bay		Wed.	2	at Ottawa
	Fri.	20	at NY Rangers		Sat.	5	Washington*
	Sat.	21	Anaheim		Sun.	6	at Columbus
	Mon.	23	at Detroit		Tue.	8	Ottawa
	Sat.	28	New Jersey		Thu.	10	at Montreal
	Sun.	29	at Minnesota		Fri.	11	at New Jersey
	Tue.	31	at Boston		Sun.	13	at Buffalo*

* Denotes afternoon game.

Year-by-Year Record

		Home				Road				Overall									
Season	**GP**	**W**	**L**	**T**	**OL**	**W**	**L**	**T**	**OL**	**W**	**L**	**T**	**OL**	**GF**	**GA**	**Pts.**	**Div. Fin.**	**Conf. Fin.**	**Playoff Result**
2012-13	48	10	11	....	3	14	6	....	4	24	17	....	7	139	139	55	3rd, Atl.	8th, East	Lost Conf. Quarter-Final
2011-12	82	17	18	....	6	17	19	....	5	34	37	....	11	203	255	79	5th, Atl.	14th, East	Out of Playoffs
2010-11	82	17	18	....	6	13	21	....	7	30	39	....	13	229	264	73	5th, Atl.	14th, East	Out of Playoffs
2009-10	82	23	14	....	4	11	23	....	7	34	37	....	11	222	264	79	5th, Atl.	13th, East	Out of Playoffs
2008-09	82	17	18	....	6	9	29	....	3	26	47	....	9	201	279	61	5th, Atl.	15th, East	Out of Playoffs
2007-08	82	18	18	....	5	17	20	....	4	35	38	....	9	194	243	79	5th, Atl.	13th, East	Out of Playoffs
2006-07	82	22	13	....	6	18	17	....	6	40	30	....	12	248	240	92	4th, Atl.	8th, East	Lost Conf. Quarter-Final
2005-06	82	20	18	....	3	16	22	....	3	36	40	....	6	230	278	78	4th, Atl.	12th, East	Out of Playoffs
2004-05	....	....	....	....	....	....	....	....	....	....	....	....	....	....	....	....			
2003-04	82	25	11	4	1	13	18	7	3	38	29	11	4	237	210	91	3rd, Atl.	8th, East	Lost Conf. Quarter-Final
2002-03	82	18	18	5	0	17	16	6	2	35	34	11	2	224	231	83	3rd, Atl.	8th, East	Lost Conf. Quarter-Final
2001-02	82	21	13	5	2	21	15	3	2	42	28	8	4	239	220	96	2nd, Atl.	5th, East	Lost Conf. Quarter-Final
2000-01	82	12	27	1	1	9	24	6	2	21	51	7	3	185	268	52	5th, Atl.	15th, East	Out of Playoffs
1999-2000	82	10	25	5	1	14	23	4	0	24	48	9	1	194	275	58	5th, Atl.	13th, East	Out of Playoffs
1998-99	82	11	23	7	....	13	25	3	....	24	48	10	....	194	244	58	5th, Atl.	13th, East	Out of Playoffs
1997-98	82	17	20	4	....	13	21	7	....	30	41	11	....	212	225	71	4th, Atl.	10th, East	Out of Playoffs
1996-97	82	19	18	4	....	10	23	8	....	29	41	12	....	240	250	70	7th, Atl.	12th, East	Out of Playoffs
1995-96	82	14	21	6	....	8	29	4	....	22	50	10	....	229	315	54	7th, Atl.	12th, East	Out of Playoffs
1994-95	48	10	11	3	....	5	17	2	....	15	28	5	....	126	158	35	7th, Atl.	13th, East	Out of Playoffs
1993-94	84	23	15	4	....	13	21	8	....	36	36	12	....	282	264	84	4th, Atl.	8th, East	Lost Conf. Quarter-Final
1992-93	84	20	19	3	....	20	18	4	....	40	37	7	....	335	297	87	3rd, Patrick		Lost Conf. Final
1991-92	80	20	15	5	....	14	20	6	....	34	35	11	....	291	299	79	5th, Patrick		Out of Playoffs
1990-91	80	15	19	6	....	10	26	4	....	25	45	10	....	223	290	60	6th, Patrick		Out of Playoffs
1989-90	80	15	17	8	....	16	21	3	....	31	38	11	....	281	288	73	4th, Patrick		Lost Div. Semi-Final
1988-89	80	19	18	3	....	9	29	2	....	28	47	5	....	265	325	61	6th, Patrick		Out of Playoffs
1987-88	80	24	10	6	....	15	21	4	....	39	31	10	....	308	267	88	1st, Patrick		Lost Div. Semi-Final
1986-87	80	20	15	5	....	15	18	7	....	35	33	12	....	279	281	82	3rd, Patrick		Lost Div. Final
1985-86	80	22	11	7	....	17	18	5	....	39	29	12	....	327	284	90	3rd, Patrick		Lost Div. Semi-Final
1984-85	80	26	11	3	....	14	23	3	....	40	34	6	....	345	312	86	3rd, Patrick		Lost Div. Final
1983-84	80	28	11	1	....	22	15	3	....	50	26	4	....	357	269	104	1st, Patrick		Lost Final
1982-83	**80**	**26**	**11**	**3**	....	**16**	**15**	**9**	....	**42**	**26**	**12**	....	**302**	**226**	**96**	**2nd, Patrick**		**Won Stanley Cup**
1981-82	**80**	**33**	**3**	**4**	....	**21**	**13**	**6**	....	**54**	**16**	**10**	....	**385**	**250**	**118**	**1st, Patrick**		**Won Stanley Cup**
1980-81	**80**	**23**	**6**	**11**	....	**25**	**12**	**3**	....	**48**	**18**	**14**	....	**355**	**260**	**110**	**1st, Patrick**		**Won Stanley Cup**
1979-80	**80**	**26**	**9**	**5**	....	**13**	**19**	**8**	....	**39**	**28**	**13**	....	**281**	**247**	**91**	**2nd, Patrick**		**Won Stanley Cup**
1978-79	80	31	3	6	....	20	12	8	....	51	15	14	....	358	214	116	1st, Patrick		Lost Semi-Final
1977-78	80	29	3	8	....	19	14	7	....	48	17	15	....	334	210	111	1st, Patrick		Lost Quarter-Final
1976-77	80	24	11	5	....	23	10	7	....	47	21	12	....	288	193	106	2nd, Patrick		Lost Semi-Final
1975-76	80	24	8	8	....	18	13	9	....	42	21	17	....	297	190	101	2nd, Patrick		Lost Semi-Final
1974-75	80	22	6	12	....	11	19	10	....	33	25	22	....	264	221	88	3rd, Patrick		Lost Semi-Final
1973-74	78	13	17	9	....	6	24	9	....	19	41	18	....	182	247	56	8th, East		Out of Playoffs
1972-73	78	10	25	4	....	2	35	2	....	12	60	6	....	170	347	30	8th, East		Out of Playoffs

METROPOLITAN DIVISION
42nd NHL Season

Franchise date: June 6, 1972

2013-14 Player Personnel

FORWARDS	HT	WT	*Age	Place of Birth	S	2012-13 Club
BAILEY, Josh	6-1	190	23	Bowmanville, Ont.	L	Bietigheim-NY Islanders
BOUCHARD, Pierre-Marc	5-11	171	29	Sherbrooke, Que.	L	Minnesota
BOULTON, Eric	6-0	224	37	Halifax, N.S.	L	NY Islanders
CIZIKAS, Casey	5-11	187	22	Toronto, Ont.	L	Bridgeport-NY Islanders
CLUTTERBUCK, Cal	5-11	213	25	Welland, Ont.	R	Minnesota
GRABNER, Michael	6-1	186	25	Villach, Austria	L	Villach-NY Islanders
LEE, Anders	6-2	225	23	Edina, MN	L	U. of Notre Dame-NYI
MARTIN, Matt	6-3	206	24	Windsor, Ont.	L	NY Islanders
McDONALD, Colin	6-1	210	29	New Haven, CT	R	Bridgeport-NY Islanders
MOULSON, Matt	6-0	205	29	North York, Ont.	L	NY Islanders
NELSON, Brock	6-3	196	21	Warroad, MN	L	Bridgeport-NY Islanders
NIELSEN, Frans	6-1	180	29	Herning, Denmark	L	Lukko-NY Islanders
OKPOSO, Kyle	6-0	212	25	St. Paul, MN	R	NY Islanders
PERSSON, John	6-2	209	21	Ostersund, Sweden	L	Bridgeport
REGIN, Peter	6-2	195	27	Herning, Denmark	L	Langenthal-Ottawa
STROME, Ryan	6-1	188	20	Mississauga, Ont.	R	Niagara-Bridgeport
SUNDSTROM, Johan	6-3	201	21	Gothenburg, Sweden	R	Bridgeport
TAVARES, John	6-0	199	23	Mississauga, Ont.	L	Bern-NY Islanders
DEFENSEMEN						
CARKNER, Matt	6-4	227	32	Winchester, Ont.	R	NY Islanders
de HAAN, Calvin	6-1	187	22	Carp, Ont.	L	Bridgeport
DONOVAN, Matt	6-0	195	23	Edmond, OK	L	Bridgeport
FINLEY, Joe	6-8	249	26	Edina, MN	L	Rochester-NY Islanders
HAMONIC, Travis	6-1	206	23	St. Malo, Man.	R	Bridgeport-NY Islanders
HICKEY, Thomas	5-11	190	24	Calgary, Alta.	L	Manchester-NY Islanders
MacDONALD, Andrew	6-0	185	27	Judique, N.S.	L	Karlovy Vary-Sokolov-NYI
MAYFIELD, Scott	6-4	209	20	St. Louis, MO	R	U. of Denver-Bridgeport
NESS, Aaron	5-10	182	23	Roseau, MN	L	Bridgeport
PEDAN, Andrey	6-4	207	20	Kaunas, Lithuania	L	Guelph-Bridgeport
STRAIT, Brian	6-1	200	25	Boston, MA	L	Wilkes-Barre-NY Islanders
VISNOVSKY, Lubomir	5-10	197	37	Topolcany, Czech.	L	Bratislava-NY Islanders

GOALTENDERS	HT	WT	*Age	Place of Birth	C	2012-13 Club
NABOKOV, Evgeni	6-0	202	38	Ust-Kamenogorsk, USSR	L	NY Islanders
NILSSON, Anders	6-5	227	23	Lulea, Sweden	L	Bridgeport
POULIN, Kevin	6-2	192	23	Montreal, Que.	L	Bridgeport-NY Islanders

* – Age at start of 2013-14 season

2012-13 Scoring

* – rookie

Regular Season

Pos	#	Player	Team	GP	G	A	Pts	TOI	+/-	PIM	PP	SH	GW	S	%
C	91	John Tavares	NYI	48	28	19	47	20:46	–2	18	9	0	5	162	17.3
L	26	Matt Moulson	NYI	47	15	29	44	19:09	–3	4	8	0	0	154	9.7
R	24	Brad Boyes	NYI	48	10	25	35	18:12	–6	16	1	0	1	97	10.3
C	51	Frans Nielsen	NYI	48	6	23	29	18:01	–3	12	2	1	1	93	6.5
D	2	Mark Streit	NYI	48	6	21	27	23:20	–14	22	3	0	1	83	7.2
R	21	Kyle Okposo	NYI	48	4	20	24	16:57	–2	38	0	0	0	101	4.0
R	40	Michael Grabner	NYI	45	16	5	21	14:47	4	12	2	1	3	108	14.8
C	12	Josh Bailey	NYI	38	11	8	19	16:22	7	6	0	0	1	76	14.5
R	13	Colin McDonald	NYI	45	7	10	17	11:22	–1	32	1	0	0	82	8.5
C	53 *	Casey Cizikas	NYI	45	6	9	15	10:47	0	14	0	0	1	45	13.3
D	11	Lubomir Visnovsky	NYI	35	3	11	14	22:48	12	20	1	0	0	69	4.3
C	10	Keith Aucoin	NYI	41	6	6	12	12:29	–1	4	1	0	1	50	12.0
D	47	Andrew MacDonald	NYI	48	3	9	12	23:31	–2	20	1	0	1	45	6.7
L	17	Matt Martin	NYI	48	4	7	11	11:54	–2	63	1	0	1	67	6.0
D	3	Travis Hamonic	NYI	48	3	7	10	22:48	–8	28	1	0	1	83	3.6
L	41	David Ullstrom	NYI	20	2	3	5	9:29	–2	6	0	0	1	28	7.1
C	16	Marty Reasoner	NYI	31	0	5	5	11:13	–3	4	0	0	0	34	0.0
D	14 *	Thomas Hickey	NYI	39	1	3	4	16:51	9	8	0	0	1	40	2.5
D	37 *	Brian Strait	NYI	19	0	4	4	17:09	4	10	0	0	0	13	0.0
D	4	Radek Martinek	NYI	13	3	0	3	16:08	–2	4	0	0	1	12	25.0
C	27 *	Anders Lee	NYI	2	1	1	2	8:12	–3	0	0	0	0	2	50.0
L	6	Jesse Joensuu	NYI	7	0	2	2	10:08	2	6	0	0	0	15	0.0
D	7	Matt Carkner	NYI	22	0	2	2	12:35	–2	46	0	0	0	19	0.0
D	52 *	Joe Finley	NYI	16	0	1	1	11:57	–5	20	0	0	0	2	0.0
L	36	Eric Boulton	NYI	15	0	0	0	5:40	–4	36	0	0	0	5	0.0

Goaltending

No.	Goaltender	GPI	Mins	Avg	W	L	OT	EN	SO	GA	SA	S%	G	A	PIM
20	Evgeni Nabokov	41	2475	2.50	23	11	7	6	3	103	1139	.910	0	4	6
60	Kevin Poulin	5	258	3.02	1	3	0	1	0	13	122	.893	0	0	0
39	Rick DiPietro	3	176	4.09	0	3	0	1	0	12	83	.855	0	0	0
	Totals	**48**	**2927**	**2.79**	**24**	**17**	**7**	**8**	**3**	**136**	**1352**	**.899**			

Playoffs

Pos	#	Player	Team	GP	G	A	Pts	TOI	+/-	PIM	PP	SH	GW	OT	S	%
C	91	John Tavares	NYI	6	3	2	5	20:34	–4	4	0	0	1	0	21	14.3
D	2	Mark Streit	NYI	6	2	3	5	20:17	–1	4	1	0	0	0	8	25.0
R	21	Kyle Okposo	NYI	6	3	1	4	19:12	–1	5	0	1	1	0	14	21.4
C	53 *	Casey Cizikas	NYI	6	2	2	4	10:46	1	12	0	0	0	0	8	25.0
R	40	Michael Grabner	NYI	6	1	3	4	12:30	2	0	0	0	0	0	13	7.7
R	13	Colin McDonald	NYI	6	2	1	3	11:57	2	2	0	0	0	0	14	14.3
L	26	Matt Moulson	NYI	6	2	1	3	17:23	–4	10	1	0	0	0	15	13.3
R	24	Brad Boyes	NYI	6	0	3	3	19:05	–3	2	0	0	0	0	13	0.0
C	10	Keith Aucoin	NYI	6	0	3	3	12:18	1	10	0	0	0	0	9	0.0
C	12	Josh Bailey	NYI	6	0	3	3	20:14	–1	0	0	0	0	0	16	0.0
D	11	Lubomir Visnovsky	NYI	6	0	2	2	22:50	2	2	0	0	0	0	11	0.0
C	51	Frans Nielsen	NYI	6	0	2	2	17:59	–2	0	0	0	0	0	16	0.0
D	37 *	Brian Strait	NYI	6	1	0	1	20:34	1	12	0	0	0	0	5	20.0
L	17	Matt Martin	NYI	6	1	0	1	12:09	0	14	0	0	0	0	8	12.5
L	41	David Ullstrom	NYI	3	0	1	1	7:03	1	0	0	0	0	0	2	0.0
D	7	Matt Carkner	NYI	4	0	1	1	12:40	0	2	0	0	0	0	2	0.0
D	3	Travis Hamonic	NYI	6	0	1	1	24:59	–4	23	0	0	0	0	6	0.0
C	16	Marty Reasoner	NYI	1	0	0	0	12:51	–1	17	0	0	0	0	3	0.0
L	6	Jesse Joensuu	NYI	1	0	0	0	8:26	0	0	0	0	0	0	1	0.0
C	29 *	Brock Nelson	NYI	1	0	0	0	7:44	–1	0	0	0	0	0	0	0.0
D	4	Radek Martinek	NYI	2	0	0	0	18:06	–2	2	0	0	0	0	3	0.0
D	14 *	Thomas Hickey	NYI	2	0	0	0	18:17	–2	2	0	0	0	0	1	0.0
D	47	Andrew MacDonald	NYI	4	0	0	0	23:26	0	4	0	0	0	0	8	0.0

Goaltending

No.	Goaltender	GPI	Mins	Avg	W	L	EN	SO	GA	SA	S%	G	A	PIM
60	Kevin Poulin	2	52	1.15	0	0	0	0	1	15	.933	0	0	0
20	Evgeni Nabokov	6	324	4.44	2	4	0	0	24	152	.842	0	0	0
	Totals	**6**	**377**	**3.98**	**2**	**4**	**0**	**0**	**25**	**167**	**.850**			

Jack Capuano

Head Coach

Born: Cranston, RI, July 7, 1966.

Jack Capuano was named the interim head coach of the New York Islanders on November 15, 2010. Islanders general manager Garth Snow announced his decision to remove the "interim" title and officially name Capuano the club's head coach on April 12, 2011. In 2012-13, he guided the Islanders into the playoffs for the first time since 2007.

Capuano made his debut in the midst of one of the worst winless streaks in team history and was tasked with turning the season around. Right after Capuano took the reigns, the team posted a 1-8-2 record, but that wouldn't last. After their rough start, Capuano led the Islanders to a 25-21-8 record in their last 54 games of the season, making the Islanders one of the best teams in the Eastern Conference after December 15. The coach had a 15-12-6 record after the All-Star Break.

Capuano joined the Islanders organization in the 2005-06 season as an assistant coach with the Islanders. The native of Cranston, Rhode Island, was named head coach of the Bridgeport Sound Tigers on April 30, 2007. In four seasons he had a 133-100-22 mark as head coach of the Sound Tigers. From 1997 to 2005 he served as the general manager of the Pee Dee Pride of the East Coast Hockey League. Capuano also served as the head coach of the 2005 U.S. Under-18 Select Team at the Five Nations Cup in Slovakia.

Capuano began his coaching career in 1995 as an assistant coach with the Tallahassee Tiger Sharks of the ECHL after ending a pro playing career that included stints with Boston, Vancouver and Toronto of the NHL and Springfield and Maine of the American Hockey League. The former First Team All-American captained the University of Maine to a Hockey East championship and NCAA Frozen Four appearance in 1998.

Coaching Record

			Regular Season				Playoffs			
Season	Team	League	GC	W	L	O/T	GC	W	L	T
....	NY Islanders	NHL	48	24	17	7	6	2	4	....
1996-97	Knoxville	ECHL	16	7	8	1	....	....	....	....
1997-98	Pee Dee	ECHL	70	34	25	11	8	3	5	....
1998-99	Pee Dee	ECHL	70	51	15	4	13	7	6	....
2000-01	Pee Dee	ECHL	15	9	5	1	....	....	....	....
2007-08	Bridgeport	AHL	80	40	36	4	....	....	....	....
2008-09	Bridgeport	AHL	80	49	23	8	5	1	4	....
2009-10	Bridgeport	AHL	80	38	32	10	5	1	4	....
2010-11	Bridgeport	AHL	15	6	9	0	....	....	....	....
2010-11	**NY Islanders**	**NHL**	**65**	**26**	**29**	**10**	....	....	....	....
2011-12	**NY Islanders**	**NHL**	**82**	**34**	**37**	**11**	....	....	....	....
2012-13	**NY Islanders**	**NHL**	**48**	**24**	**17**	**7**	**6**	**2**	**4**	....
	NHL Totals		**195**	**84**	**83**	**28**	**6**	**2**	**4**	....

Coaching History

Phil Goyette and Earl Ingarfield, 1972-73; Al Arbour, 1973-74 to 1985-86; Terry Simpson, 1986-87, 1987-88; Terry Simpson and Al Arbour, 1988-89; Al Arbour, 1989-90 to 1993-94; Lorne Henning, 1994-95; Mike Milbury, 1995-96; Mike Milbury and Rick Bowness, 1996-97; Rick Bowness and Mike Milbury, 1997-98; Mike Milbury and Bill Stewart, 1998-99; Butch Goring, 1999-2000; Butch Goring and Lorne Henning, 2000-01; Peter Laviolette, 2001-02, 2002-03; Steve Stirling, 2003-04, 2004-05; Steve Stirling and Brad Shaw, 2005-06; Ted Nolan, 2006-07, 2007-08; Scott Gordon, 2008-09, 2009-10; Scott Gordon and Jack Capuano, 2010-11; Jack Capuano, 2011-12 to date.

Club Records

Team

(Figures in brackets for season records are games played; records for fewest points, wins, ties, losses, goals, goals against are for 70 or more games)

Most Points	**118**	1981-82 (80)
Most Wins	**54**	1981-82 (80)
Most Ties	**22**	1974-75 (80)
Most Losses	**60**	1972-73 (78)
Most Goals	**385**	1981-82 (80)
Most Goals Against	**347**	1972-73 (78)
Fewest Points	**30**	1972-73 (78)
Fewest Wins	**12**	1972-73 (78)
Fewest Ties	**4**	1983-84 (80)
Fewest Losses	**15**	1978-79 (80)
Fewest Goals	**170**	1972-73 (78)
Fewest Goals Against	**190**	1975-76 (80)
Longest Winning Streak		
Overall	**15**	Jan. 21-Feb. 20/82
Home	**14**	Jan. 2-Feb. 25/82
Away	**8**	Feb. 27-Mar. 29/81
Longest Undefeated Streak		
Overall	**15**	Three times
Home	**23**	Oct. 17/78-Jan. 20/79 (19W, 4T), Jan. 2-Apr. 3/82 (21W, 2T)
Away	**8**	Three times
Longest Losing Streak		
Overall	**14**	Oct. 23-Nov. 24/10
Home	**7**	Nov. 13-Dec. 14/99
Away	**15**	Jan. 20-Mar. 31/73
Longest Winless Streak		
Overall	**15**	Nov. 22-Dec. 21/72 (12L, 3T)
Home	**9**	Mar. 2-Apr. 6/99 (7L, 2T)
Away	**20**	Nov. 3/72-Jan. 13/73 (19L, 1T)
Most Shutouts, Season	**10**	1975-76 (80)
Most PIM, Season	**1,857**	1986-87 (80)
Most Goals, Game	**11**	Dec. 20/83 (Pit. 3 at NYI 11), Mar. 3/84 (NYI 11 at Tor. 6)

Individual

Most Seasons	**17**	Billy Smith
Most Games	**1,123**	Bryan Trottier
Most Goals, Career	**573**	Mike Bossy
Most Assists, Career	**853**	Bryan Trottier
Most Points, Career	**1,353**	Bryan Trottier (500G, 853A)
Most PIM, Career	**1,879**	Mick Vukota
Most Shutouts, Career	**25**	Glenn Resch
Longest Consecutive Games Streak	**576**	Billy Harris (Oct. 7/72-Nov. 30/79)
Most Goals, Season	**69**	Mike Bossy (1978-79)
Most Assists, Season	**87**	Bryan Trottier (1978-79)
Most Points, Season	**147**	Mike Bossy (1981-82; 64G, 83A)
Most PIM, Season	**356**	Brian Curran (1986-87)
Most Points, Defenseman, Season	**101**	Denis Potvin (1978-79; 31G, 70A)
Most Points, Center, Season	**134**	Bryan Trottier (1978-79; 47G, 87A)
Most Points, Right Wing, Season	**147**	Mike Bossy (1981-82; 64G, 83A)
Most Points, Left Wing, Season	**100**	John Tonelli (1984-85; 42G, 58A)
Most Points, Rookie, Season	**95**	Bryan Trottier (1975-76; 32G, 63A)
Most Shutouts, Season	**7**	Glenn Resch (1975-76)
Most Goals, Game	**5**	Bryan Trottier (Dec. 23/78), (Feb. 13/82) John Tonelli (Jan. 6/81)
Most Assists, Game	**6**	Mike Bossy (Jan. 6/81)
Most Points, Game	**8**	Bryan Trottier (Dec. 23/78; 5G, 3A)

Captains' History

Ed Westfall, 1972-73 to 1975-76; Ed Westfall and Clark Gillies, 1976-77; Clark Gillies, 1977-78, 1978-79; Denis Potvin, 1979-80 to 1986-87; Brent Sutter, 1987-88 to 1990-91; Brent Sutter and Pat Flatley, 1991-92; Pat Flatley, 1992-93 to 1995-96; no captain, 1996-97; Bryan McCabe and Trevor Linden, 1997-98; Trevor Linden, 1998-99; Kenny Jonsson, 1999-2000, 2000-01; Michael Peca, 2001-02 to 2003-04; Alexei Yashin, 2005-06, 2006-07; Bill Guerin, 2007-08; Bill Guerin and no captain, 2008-09; Doug Weight, 2009-10, 2010-11; Mark Streit, 2011-12, 2012-13.

Retired Numbers

5	Denis Potvin	1973-1988
9	Clark Gillies	1974-1986
19	Bryan Trottier	1975-1990
22	Mike Bossy	1977-1987
23	Bob Nystrom	1972-1986
31	Billy Smith	1972-1989

All-time Record vs. Other Clubs

Regular Season

	Total								At Home								On Road							
	GP	W	L	T	OL	GF	GA	PTS	GP	W	L	T	OL	GF	GA	PTS	GP	W	L	T	OL	GF	GA	PTS
Anaheim	24	11	8	4	1	64	61	27	11	6	4	1	0	29	29	13	13	5	4	3	1	35	32	14
Boston	151	53	74	21	3	445	520	130	76	31	35	10	0	241	247	72	75	22	39	11	3	204	273	58
Buffalo	153	60	70	18	5	431	467	143	76	34	31	9	2	216	212	79	77	26	39	9	3	215	255	64
Calgary	106	44	42	20	0	357	331	108	54	28	17	9	0	200	148	65	52	16	25	11	0	157	183	43
Carolina	120	50	58	9	3	364	393	112	60	26	29	4	1	174	180	57	60	24	29	5	2	190	213	55
Chicago	102	39	41	20	2	347	324	100	50	20	14	15	1	175	149	56	52	19	27	5	1	172	175	44
Colorado	73	34	33	4	2	251	251	74	35	21	13	1	0	143	117	43	38	13	20	3	2	108	134	31
Columbus	14	4	7	1	2	38	49	11	6	3	2	0	1	20	19	7	8	1	5	1	1	18	30	4
Dallas	102	49	35	16	2	368	297	116	52	26	16	8	2	187	150	62	50	23	19	8	0	181	147	54
Detroit	97	45	44	6	2	321	311	98	49	25	18	4	2	178	142	56	48	20	26	2	0	143	169	42
Edmonton	66	26	26	14	0	228	230	66	34	18	7	9	0	138	114	45	32	8	19	5	0	90	116	21
Florida	81	34	37	8	2	220	234	78	41	21	17	2	1	106	107	45	40	13	20	6	1	114	127	33
Los Angeles	97	43	41	12	1	312	306	99	49	26	17	5	1	166	133	58	48	17	24	7	0	146	173	41
Minnesota	14	6	7	0	1	34	39	13	7	4	3	0	0	17	18	8	7	2	4	0	1	17	21	5
Montreal	151	57	78	15	1	434	489	130	76	36	34	6	0	228	221	78	75	21	44	9	1	206	268	52
Nashville	15	5	9	0	1	34	42	11	7	3	3	0	1	17	20	7	8	2	6	0	0	17	22	4
New Jersey	222	117	76	22	7	768	653	263	112	68	30	11	3	415	302	150	110	49	46	11	4	353	351	113
NY Rangers	244	106	113	19	6	783	827	237	122	64	46	8	4	435	386	140	122	42	67	11	2	348	441	97
Ottawa	78	20	44	11	3	212	280	54	40	11	22	6	1	121	151	29	38	9	22	5	2	91	129	25
Philadelphia	245	93	121	26	5	746	804	217	124	56	50	15	3	417	375	130	121	37	71	11	2	329	429	87
Phoenix	67	31	23	12	1	240	215	75	33	15	9	8	1	122	99	39	34	16	14	4	0	118	116	36
Pittsburgh	227	98	96	22	11	800	807	229	112	58	39	8	7	430	373	131	115	40	57	14	4	370	434	98
St. Louis	103	48	32	20	3	357	318	119	53	27	13	11	2	196	140	67	50	21	19	9	1	161	178	52
San Jose	29	12	12	3	2	90	83	29	14	6	5	2	1	46	44	15	15	6	7	1	1	44	39	14
Tampa Bay	82	40	35	3	4	241	222	87	41	23	16	1	1	125	105	48	41	17	19	2	3	116	117	39
Toronto	139	68	58	7	6	491	447	149	68	38	23	3	4	258	200	83	71	30	35	4	2	233	247	66
Vancouver	100	49	36	13	2	341	306	113	50	27	12	10	1	180	142	65	50	22	24	3	1	161	164	48
Washington	193	86	84	13	10	644	609	195	96	49	41	2	4	347	297	104	97	37	43	11	6	297	312	91
Winnipeg	51	28	17	2	4	184	150	62	25	13	12	0	0	86	71	26	26	15	5	2	4	98	79	36
Defunct Clubs	26	15	5	6	0	110	74	36	13	11	0	2	0	75	33	24	13	4	5	4	0	35	41	12
Totals	**3172**	**1371**	**1362**	**347**	**92**	**10255**	**10139**	**3181**	**1586**	**794**	**578**	**170**	**44**	**5488**	**4724**	**1802**	**1586**	**577**	**784**	**177**	**48**	**4767**	**5415**	**1379**

Playoffs

	Series	W	L	GP	W	L	T	GF	GA	Last Mtg.	Rnd.	Result
Boston	2	2	0	11	8	3	0	49	35	1983	CF	W 4-2
Buffalo	4	3	1	21	13	8	0	70	62	2007	CQF	L 1-4
Chicago	2	2	0	6	6	0	0	21	6	1979	QF	W 4-0
Colorado	1	1	0	4	4	0	0	18	9	1982	CF	W 4-0
Dallas	1	1	0	5	4	1	0	26	16	1981	F	W 4-1
Edmonton	3	2	1	15	9	6	0	58	47	1984	F	L 1-4
Los Angeles	1	1	0	4	3	1	0	21	10	1980	PRE	W 3-1
Montreal	4	1	3	22	8	14	0	55	64	1993	CF	L 1-4
New Jersey	1	0	1	6	2	4	0	18	23	1988	DSF	L 2-4
NY Rangers	8	5	3	39	20	19	0	129	132	1994	CQF	L 0-4
Ottawa	1	0	1	5	1	4	0	7	13	2003	CQF	L 1-4
Philadelphia	4	1	3	25	11	14	0	69	83	1987	DF	L 3-4
Pittsburgh	4	3	1	25	13	12	0	84	83	2013	CQF	L 2-4
Tampa Bay	1	0	1	5	1	4	0	5	12	2004	CQF	L 1-4
Toronto	3	1	2	17	9	8	0	54	42	2002	CQF	L 3-4
Vancouver	2	2	0	6	6	0	0	26	14	1982	F	W 4-0
Washington	6	5	1	30	18	12	0	99	88	1993	DSF	W 4-2
Totals	**48**	**30**	**18**	**246**	**136**	**110**	**0**	**809**	**739**			

Playoff Results 2013-2009

Year	Round	Opponent	Result	GF	GA
2013	CQF	Pittsburgh	L 2-4	17	25

Abbreviations: Round: F – Final; **CF** – conference final; **CQF** – conference quarter-final; **DF** – division final; **DSF** – division semi-final; **QF** – quarter-final; **PRE** – preliminary round.

Calgary totals include Atlanta Flames, 1972-73 to 1979-80. Carolina totals include Hartford, 1979-80 to 1996-97.
Colorado totals include Quebec, 1979-80 to 1994-95. Dallas totals include Minnesota North Stars, 1972-73 to 1992-93.
New Jersey totals include Kansas City, 1974-75, 1975-76, and Colorado Rockies, 1976-77 to 1981-82.
Phoenix totals include Winnipeg, 1979-80 to 1995-96. Winnipeg totals include Atlanta Thrashers, 1999-2000 to 2010-11.

2012-13 Results

Jan.	19	New Jersey	1-2		9	Washington	5-2
	21	Tampa Bay	4-3		10	at Pittsburgh	1-6
	24	at Toronto	7-4		14	at Tampa Bay	2-0
	25	at Boston	2-4		16	at Florida	4-3
	27	at Winnipeg	4-5*		19	Ottawa	3-5
	29	at Pittsburgh	4-1		21	Montreal	2-5
	31	at New Jersey	5-4*		22	Pittsburgh	2-4
Feb.	3	New Jersey	0-3		24	Florida	3-0
	5	Pittsburgh	2-4		26	at Washington	3-2
	7	at NY Rangers	1-4		28	at Philadelphia	4-3†
	9	Buffalo	2-3		30	at Pittsburgh	0-2
	11	Carolina	4-6	**Apr.**	1	at New Jersey	3-1
	14	at NY Rangers	4-3†		2	Winnipeg	5-2
	16	New Jersey	5-1		4	at Washington	1-2†
	18	Philadelphia	0-7		6	Tampa Bay	4-2
	19	at Ottawa	1-3		9	Philadelphia	4-1
	21	at Montreal	4-3*		11	at Boston	2-1
	23	at Buffalo	4-0		13	NY Rangers	0-1*
	24	Carolina	2-4		16	Florida	5-2
	26	Boston	1-4		18	at Toronto	5-3
	28	Toronto	4-5*		20	at Winnipeg	5-4†
Mar.	3	Ottawa	3-2†		23	at Carolina	3-4†
	5	Montreal	6-3		25	at Philadelphia	1-2
	7	NY Rangers	1-2*		26	at Buffalo	1-2†

* – Overtime † – Shootout

Entry Draft Selections 2013-1999

Name in bold denotes played in NHL.

2013

Pick	
15	Ryan Pulock
70	Eamon McAdam
76	Taylor Cammarata
106	Stephon Williams
136	Viktor Crus Rydberg
166	Alan Quine
196	Kyle Burroughs

2012

Pick	
4	Griffin Reinhart
34	Ville Pokka
65	Adam Pelech
103	Loic Leduc
125	Doyle Somerby
155	Jesse Graham
185	Jake Bischoff

2011

Pick	
5	Ryan Strome
34	Scott Mayfield
50	Johan Sundstrom
63	Andrey Pedan
95	Robbie Russo
125	John Persson
127	Brenden Kichton
185	Mitchell Theoret

2010

Pick	
5	**Nino Niederreiter**
30	**Brock Nelson**
65	Kirill Kabanov
82	Jason Clark
125	Tony Dehart
185	Cody Rosen

2009

Pick	
1	**John Tavares**
12	**Calvin De Haan**
31	**Mikko Koskinen**
62	**Anders Nilsson**
92	**Casey Cizikas**
122	**Anton Klementyev**
152	**Anders Lee**

2008

Pick	
9	**Josh Bailey**
36	Corey Trivino
40	**Aaron Ness**
53	**Travis Hamonic**
66	David Toews
72	Jyri Niemi
73	Kirill Petrov
96	**Matt Donovan**
102	**David Ullstrom**
126	**Kevin Poulin**
148	**Matt Martin**
156	**Jared Spurgeon**
175	**Justin Dibenedetto**

2007

Pick	
62	**Mark Katic**
76	Jason Gregoire
106	Maxim Gratchev
166	Blake Kessel
196	Simon Lacroix

2006

Pick	
7	**Kyle Okposo**
60	**Jesse Joensuu**
70	Robin Figren
100	**Rhett Rakhshani**
108	Jase Weslosky
115	Tomas Marcinko
119	Doug Rogers
126	**Shane Sims**
141	Kim Johansson
160	**Andrew MacDonald**
171	Brian Day
173	Stefan Ridderwall
190	Troy Mattila

2005

Pick	
15	**Ryan O'Marra**
46	**Dustin Kohn**
76	Shea Guthrie
144	**Masi Marjamaki**
180	Tyrell Mason
196	Nick Tuzzolino
210	Luciano Aquino

2004

Pick	
16	**Petteri Nokelainen**
47	**Blake Comeau**
82	Sergei Ogorodnikov
115	**Wes O'Neill**
148	**Steve Regier**
179	Jaroslav Mrazek
210	Emil Axelsson
227	**Chris Campoli**
244	Jason Pitton
276	Sylvain Michaud

2003

Pick	
15	**Robert Nilsson**
48	Dmitri Chernykh
53	Evgeny Tunik
58	**Jeremy Colliton**
120	Stefan Blaho
182	**Bruno Gervais**
212	Denis Rehak
238	Cody Blanshan
246	Igor Volkov

2002

Pick	
22	**Sean Bergenheim**
87	**Frans Nielsen**
149	Marcus Paulsson
189	Alexei Stonkus
220	Brad Topping
252	Martin Chabada
283	Per Braxenholm

2001

Pick	
101	Cory Stillman
132	Dusan Salficky
166	**Andy Chiodo**
197	Jan Holub
228	Mike Bray
260	Bryan Perez
280	Roman Kuhtinov
287	Juha-Pekka Ketola

2000

Pick	
1	**Rick DiPietro**
5	**Raffi Torres**
101	Arto Tukio
105	Vladimir Gorbunov
136	Dmitri Upper
148	Kristofer Ottosson
202	**Ryan Caldwell**
264	Dmitri Altarev
267	**Tomi Pettinen**

1999

Pick	
5	**Tim Connolly**
8	**Taylor Pyatt**
10	**Branislav Mezei**
28	**Kristian Kudroc**
78	**Mattias Weinhandl**
87	Brian Collins
101	**Juraj Kolnik**
102	Johan Halvardsson
130	**Justin Mapletoft**
140	Adam Johnson
163	**Bjorn Melin**
228	**Radek Martinek**
255	Brett Henning
268	Tyler Scott

General Managers' History

Bill Torrey, 1972-73 to 1991-92; Don Maloney, 1992-93 to 1994-95; Don Maloney, Darcy Regier and Mike Milbury, 1995-96; Mike Milbury, 1996-97 to 2005-06; Neil Smith and Garth Snow, 2006-07; Garth Snow, 2007-08 to date.

Garth Snow

General Manager

Born: Wrentham, MA, June 28, 1969.

Former Islanders' goaltender Garth Snow retired as a player on July 18, 2006 to become the fifth general manager of the New York Islanders. In his first season as general manager, Snow successfully bolstered the lineup with several key additions that helped to propel the Islanders into the postseason for the first time since the 2003–04 season and earned Snow the title of NHL Executive of the Year from *Sports Illustrated*.

Snow spent four seasons with the Islanders and 12 in the NHL. The goaltender was 135-147-44 with a 2.80 goals-against average and .901 save percentage over 368 games with Quebec, Philadelphia, Vancouver, Pittsburgh and the Islanders. Originally selected in the sixth round by Quebec in the 1987 NHL Entry Draft, the native of Wrentham, Massachusetts signed with the Islanders as a free agent on July 1, 2001.

Club Directory

Nassau Veterans Memorial Coliseum

New York Islanders
Executive Office
1255 Hempstead Turnpike
Uniondale, NY 11553
Phone **516/501-6700**
FAX 516/501-6850
www.newyorkislanders.com
Arena
Nassau Veterans
Memorial Coliseum
Uniondale, NY 11553
Capacity: 16,170

Owner and Governor	Charles B. Wang
General Manager and Alternate Governor	Garth Snow
Alternate Governors	Art McCarthy, Roy Reichbach
Sr. Vice President & Alternate Governor	Michael Picker
Sr. Vice President of Marketing and Sales	Paul Lancey
President of Bridgeport Sound Tigers (AHL)	Howard Saffan
Hockey Operations	
Manager, Hockey Administration	Joanne Holewa
Director of Pro Scouting	Ken Morrow
Sr. Advisor to the G.M. & Assistant Coach	Doug Weight
Assistant to the General Manager	Kerry Gwydir
Head Coach	Jack Capuano
Assistant Coach	Brent Thompson
Director of Sports Performance	Sean Donellan
Goaltending Coach	Mike Dunham
Skill Development Coach	Bernie Cassell
Video Coach	Matt Bertani
Head Amateur Scout / Player Development	Trent Klatt
Player Development	Eric Cairns, Geoff Sanderson
Equipment Manager / Asst. Manager / Assistant	Scott Boggs / Richard Krouse / Tom Kitz
Head Athletic Trainer / Assistant Trainer	Matt Bain / Philip E. Watson
Massage Therapist	Jim Miccio
Strength and Conditioning Coach	Derrek Douglas
Chief European Scout	Velli-Pekka Kautonen
Scouts	Mario Saraceno, Chris O'Sullivan, Tim Maclean, Anders Kallur, David Hymovitz, Jay Saraceno, Jeff Napierala, Don McDuff
Administration	
Deputy General Counsel	Stacey Sabo
Human Resources Manager / Coordinator	Michele Finkelstein / Jillian Haskel
IT Manager	Pawel Tauter
Receptionist / Office Attendant	Bonnie Dreher / Todd Aronovich
Corporate Partnerships and Islanders Networking Club	
V.P., Sponsorship & Partnerships Marketing	Mike Bossy
Director, Corporate Partnerships	Amy Fleischer
Managers, Coporate Partnerships	Ingrid Dodd
Manager, Partnership Marketing	Stephen Smyth
Coordinators, Partnership Marketing	Caroline Seiter, Kathryn Lazarski
Coordinator, Executive Suites	Tina Brennan
Ticket Sales and Operations	
Vice President of Ticket Sales	Ralph Sellitti
Ticket Manager	Adam Ortiz
Ticket Operations Coordinator / Assistant	Steve Aprill / Alfred Jahn
Customer Service Director	Kerry Cornils
Customer Service Coordinator / Rep	Stephanie Mascone / John Cloghessy
Group Sales Director / Coordinator	Eric Nadeau / Grant Comarato
Senior Sales Executive, Group Tickets	Cliff Gault
Sales Execs, Group Tickets	Sean Cassin, Scott Hill, Matt Hansen, Chris Stellato, Bryan Hess
Senior Sales Executives	Steven Beisel, Marc Gerstein, Jeffrey Guida
Sales Execs, Tickets	Marty Asalone, Vito Cataldo, David Vangrov, Michael Winkler, Tom Giulietti
Marketing and Client Services	
Director of Marketing	Thomas Rakoczy
Marketing Coordinator	Kristina Hjertkvist
Graphic Designers	Cristina Weigel, Douglas Bouchelle
Media Relations / Communications	
Director of Communications	Kimber Auerbach
Islanders TV Director	Susie Schopp
Communications Manager	Jesse Eisenberg
Website Coordinator	Travis Betts
Communication Coordinator	Greg Picker
Radio Producer and Broadcaster	Chris King
Islanders TV Producer	Ryan Mason
Game Operations	
Vice President, Operations	Tim Beach
Community Relations Manager	Ann Rina
Event Operations Coordinator	Joe Giarroputo
Game Operations	Erin Willey
Manager, Video Production & Game Ops Coord.	Brian Jones
Manager, Amateur Hockey Development	Jocelyne Cummings
Game Operations and Events Assistant	Alexa Conforti
Retail and Merchandise Operations	
Director of Retail Operations	Terry Goldstein
Pro Shop Manager / Asst. Manager	Tim Murray / Dale Ianuzzi
Finance	
Controller / Accounting Manager	Frank Romano / Chris Vardaro
Payroll Manager / A/P Coordinator	Christine Bowler / Janet Nelson
Staff Accountants	Erica Zervas, Jennifer Penning

New York Rangers

Key Off-Season Signings/Acquisitions

2013

June 21 • Named **Alain Vigneault** head coach.
30 • Acquired D **Justin Falk** from Minnesota for C **Benn Ferriero** and a 6th-round pick in the 2014 NHL Draft.
July 5 • Signed C **Dominic Moore**, D **Aaron Johnson** and LW **Benoit Pouliot**.
8 • Re-signed D **Ryan McDonagh**.
10 • Re-signed LW **Carl Hagelin**.
30 • Re-signed LW **Mats Zuccarello**.

2013-14 Schedule

Oct.	Thu.	3	at Phoenix
	Mon.	7	at Los Angeles
	Tue.	8	at San Jose
	Thu.	10	at Anaheim
	Sat.	12	at St. Louis
	Wed.	16	at Washington
	Sat.	19	at New Jersey
	Thu.	24	at Philadelphia
	Sat.	26	at Detroit
	Mon.	28	Montreal
	Tue.	29	at NY Islanders
	Thu.	31	Buffalo
Nov.	Sat.	2	Carolina
	Mon.	4	Anaheim
	Wed.	6	Pittsburgh
	Thu.	7	at Columbus
	Sun.	10	Florida
	Tue.	12	New Jersey
	Sat.	16	at Montreal
	Sun.	17	Los Angeles
	Tue.	19	Boston
	Thu.	21	at Dallas
	Sat.	23	at Nashville
	Mon.	25	at Tampa Bay
	Wed.	27	at Florida
	Fri.	29	at Boston*
	Sat.	30	Vancouver*
Dec.	Mon.	2	Winnipeg
	Thu.	5	at Buffalo
	Sat.	7	New Jersey
	Sun.	8	Washington
	Tue.	10	Nashville
	Thu.	12	Columbus
	Sun.	15	Calgary
	Wed.	18	Pittsburgh
	Fri.	20	NY Islanders
	Sun.	22	Minnesota
	Mon.	23	Toronto
	Fri.	27	at Washington
	Sun.	29	at Tampa Bay
	Tue.	31	at Florida*
Jan.	Fri.	3	at Pittsburgh
	Sat.	4	at Toronto
	Mon.	6	Columbus
	Wed.	8	at Chicago
	Fri.	10	Dallas
	Sun.	12	Philadelphia
	Tue.	14	Tampa Bay
	Thu.	16	Detroit
	Sat.	18	at Ottawa*
	Sun.	19	Washington
	Tue.	21	NY Islanders
	Thu.	23	St. Louis
	Sun.	26	at New Jersey*
	Wed.	29	at NY Islanders
	Fri.	31	NY Islanders
Feb.	Tue.	4	Colorado
	Thu.	6	Edmonton
	Fri.	7	at Pittsburgh
	Thu.	27	Chicago
Mar.	Sat.	1	at Philadelphia*
	Sun.	2	Boston
	Wed.	5	Toronto
	Fri.	7	at Carolina
	Sun.	9	Detroit
	Tue.	11	at Carolina
	Thu.	13	at Minnesota
	Fri.	14	at Winnipeg
	Sun.	16	San Jose*
	Tue.	18	at Ottawa
	Fri.	21	at Columbus
	Sat.	22	at New Jersey
	Mon.	24	Phoenix
	Wed.	26	Philadelphia
	Fri.	28	at Calgary
	Sun.	30	at Edmonton
Apr.	Tue.	1	at Vancouver
	Thu.	3	at Colorado
	Sat.	5	Ottawa
	Tue.	8	Carolina
	Thu.	10	Buffalo
	Sat.	12	at Montreal

* Denotes afternoon game.

METROPOLITAN DIVISION
88th NHL Season

Franchise date: May 15, 1926

2012-13 Results: 26W-18L-0OTL-4SOL 56PTS
2ND, Atlantic Division • 6TH, Eastern Conference

Year-by-Year Record

		Home				Road				Overall									
Season	GP	W	L	T	OL	W	L	T	OL	W	L	T	OL	GF	GA	Pts.	Div. Fin.	Conf. Fin.	Playoff Result
2012-13	48	16	6	....	2	10	12	....	2	26	18	....	4	130	112	56	2nd, Atl.	6th, East	Lost Conf. Semi-Final
2011-12	82	27	12	....	2	24	12	....	5	51	24	....	7	226	187	109	1st, Atl.	1st, East	Lost Conf. Final
2010-11	82	20	17	....	4	24	16	....	1	44	33	....	5	233	198	93	3rd, Atl.	8th, East	Lost Conf. Quarter-Final
2009-10	82	18	17	....	6	20	16	....	5	38	33	....	11	222	218	87	4th, Atl.	9th, East	Out of Playoffs
2008-09	82	26	11	....	4	17	19	....	5	43	30	....	9	210	218	95	4th, Atl.	7th, East	Lost Conf. Quarter-Final
2007-08	82	25	13	....	3	17	14	....	10	42	27	....	13	213	199	97	3rd, Atl.	5th, East	Lost Conf. Semi-Final
2006-07	82	21	15	....	5	21	15	....	5	42	30	....	10	242	216	94	3rd, Atl.	6th, East	Lost Conf. Semi-Final
2005-06	82	25	10	....	6	19	16	....	6	44	26	....	12	257	215	100	3rd, Atl.	6th, East	Lost Conf. Quarter-Final
2004-05	....	....	....	....	....	....	....	....	....	....	....	....	....	....	....	....			
2003-04	82	13	21	3	4	14	19	4	4	27	40	7	8	206	250	69	4th, Atl.	13th, East	Out of Playoffs
2002-03	82	17	18	4	2	15	18	6	2	32	36	10	4	210	231	78	4th, Atl.	9th, East	Out of Playoffs
2001-02	82	19	19	2	1	17	19	2	3	36	38	4	4	227	258	80	4th, Atl.	11th, East	Out of Playoffs
2000-01	82	17	20	3	1	16	23	2	0	33	43	5	1	250	290	72	4th, Atl.	10th, East	Out of Playoffs
1999-2000	82	15	20	5	1	14	18	7	2	29	38	12	3	218	246	73	4th, Atl.	11th, East	Out of Playoffs
1998-99	82	17	19	5	....	16	19	6	....	33	38	11	....	217	227	77	4th, Atl.	10th, East	Out of Playoffs
1997-98	82	14	18	9	....	11	21	9	....	25	39	18	....	197	231	68	5th, Atl.	11th, East	Out of Playoffs
1996-97	82	21	14	6	....	17	20	4	....	38	34	10	....	258	231	86	4th, Atl.	5th, East	Lost Conf. Final
1995-96	82	22	10	9	....	19	17	5	....	41	27	14	....	272	237	96	2nd, Atl.	3rd, East	Lost Conf. Semi-Final
1994-95	48	11	10	3	....	11	13	0	....	22	23	3	....	139	134	47	4th, Atl.	8th, East	Lost Conf. Semi-Final
1993-94	**84**	**28**	**8**	**6**	....	**24**	**16**	**2**	....	**52**	**24**	**8**	....	**299**	**231**	**112**	**1st, Atl.**	**1st, East**	**Won Stanley Cup**
1992-93	84	20	17	5	....	14	22	6	....	34	39	11	....	304	308	79	6th, Patrick		Out of Playoffs
1991-92	80	28	8	4	....	22	17	1	....	50	25	5	....	321	246	105	1st, Patrick		Lost Div. Final
1990-91	80	22	11	7	....	14	20	6	....	36	31	13	....	297	265	85	2nd, Patrick		Lost Div. Semi-Final
1989-90	80	20	11	9	....	16	20	4	....	36	31	13	....	279	267	85	1st, Patrick		Lost Div. Final
1988-89	80	21	17	2	....	16	18	6	....	37	35	8	....	310	307	82	3rd, Patrick		Lost Div. Semi-Final
1987-88	80	22	13	5	....	14	21	5	....	36	34	10	....	300	283	82	5th, Patrick		Out of Playoffs
1986-87	80	18	18	4	....	16	20	4	....	34	38	8	....	307	323	76	4th, Patrick		Lost Div. Semi-Final
1985-86	80	20	18	2	....	16	20	4	....	36	38	6	....	280	276	78	4th, Patrick		Lost Conf. Final
1984-85	80	16	18	6	....	10	26	4	....	26	44	10	....	295	345	62	4th, Patrick		Lost Div. Semi-Final
1983-84	80	27	12	1	....	15	17	8	....	42	29	9	....	314	304	93	4th, Patrick		Lost Div. Semi-Final
1982-83	80	24	13	3	....	11	22	7	....	35	35	10	....	306	287	80	4th, Patrick		Lost Div. Final
1981-82	80	19	15	6	....	20	12	8	....	39	27	14	....	316	306	92	2nd, Patrick		Lost Div. Final
1980-81	80	17	13	10	....	13	23	4	....	30	36	14	....	312	317	74	4th, Patrick		Lost Semi-Final
1979-80	80	22	10	8	....	16	22	2	....	38	32	10	....	308	284	86	3rd, Patrick		Lost Quarter-Final
1978-79	80	19	13	8	....	21	16	3	....	40	29	11	....	316	292	91	3rd, Patrick		Lost Final
1977-78	80	18	15	7	....	12	22	6	....	30	37	13	....	279	280	73	4th, Patrick		Lost Prelim. Round
1976-77	80	17	18	5	....	12	19	9	....	29	37	14	....	272	310	72	4th, Patrick		Out of Playoffs
1975-76	80	16	16	8	....	13	26	1	....	29	42	9	....	262	333	67	4th, Patrick		Out of Playoffs
1974-75	80	21	11	8	....	16	18	6	....	37	29	14	....	319	276	88	2nd, Patrick		Lost Prelim. Round
1973-74	78	26	7	6	....	14	17	8	....	40	24	14	....	300	251	94	3rd, East		Lost Semi-Final
1972-73	78	26	8	5	....	21	15	3	....	47	23	8	....	297	208	102	3rd, East		Lost Semi-Final
1971-72	78	26	6	7	....	22	11	6	....	48	17	13	....	317	192	109	2nd, East		Lost Final
1970-71	78	30	2	7	....	19	16	4	....	49	18	11	....	259	177	109	2nd, East		Lost Semi-Final
1969-70	76	22	8	8	....	16	14	8	....	38	22	16	....	246	189	92	4th, East		Lost Quarter-Final
1968-69	76	27	7	4	....	14	19	5	....	41	26	9	....	231	196	91	3rd, East		Lost Quarter-Final
1967-68	74	22	8	7	....	17	15	5	....	39	23	12	....	226	183	90	2nd, East		Lost Quarter-Final
1966-67	70	18	12	5	....	12	16	7	....	30	28	12	....	188	189	72	4th,		Lost Semi-Final
1965-66	70	12	16	7	....	6	25	4	....	18	41	11	....	195	261	47	6th,		Out of Playoffs
1964-65	70	8	19	8	....	12	19	4	....	20	38	12	....	179	246	52	5th,		Out of Playoffs
1963-64	70	14	13	8	....	8	25	2	....	22	38	10	....	186	242	54	5th,		Out of Playoffs
1962-63	70	12	17	6	....	10	19	6	....	22	36	12	....	211	233	56	5th,		Out of Playoffs
1961-62	70	16	11	8	....	10	21	4	....	26	32	12	....	195	207	64	4th,		Lost Semi-Final
1960-61	70	15	15	5	....	7	23	5	....	22	38	10	....	204	248	54	5th,		Out of Playoffs
1959-60	70	10	15	10	....	7	23	5	....	17	38	15	....	187	247	49	6th,		Out of Playoffs
1958-59	70	14	16	5	....	12	16	7	....	26	32	12	....	201	217	64	5th,		Out of Playoffs
1957-58	70	14	15	6	....	18	10	7	....	32	25	13	....	195	188	77	2nd,		Lost Semi-Final
1956-57	70	15	12	8	....	11	18	6	....	26	30	14	....	184	227	66	4th,		Lost Semi-Final
1955-56	70	20	7	8	....	12	21	2	....	32	28	10	....	204	203	74	3rd,		Lost Semi-Final
1954-55	70	10	12	13	....	7	23	5	....	17	35	18	....	150	210	52	5th,		Out of Playoffs
1953-54	70	18	12	5	....	11	19	5	....	29	31	10	....	161	182	68	5th,		Out of Playoffs
1952-53	70	11	14	10	....	6	23	6	....	17	37	16	....	152	211	50	6th,		Out of Playoffs
1951-52	70	16	13	6	....	7	21	7	....	23	34	13	....	192	219	59	5th,		Out of Playoffs
1950-51	70	14	11	10	....	6	18	11	....	20	29	21	....	169	201	61	5th,		Out of Playoffs
1949-50	70	19	12	4	....	9	19	7	....	28	31	11	....	170	189	67	4th,		Lost Final
1948-49	60	13	12	5	....	5	19	6	....	18	31	11	....	133	172	47	6th,		Out of Playoffs
1947-48	60	11	12	7	....	10	14	6	....	21	26	13	....	176	201	55	4th,		Lost Semi-Final
1946-47	60	11	14	5	....	11	18	1	....	22	32	6	....	167	186	50	5th,		Out of Playoffs
1945-46	50	8	12	5	....	5	16	4	....	13	28	9	....	144	191	35	6th,		Out of Playoffs
1944-45	50	7	11	7	....	4	18	3	....	11	29	10	....	154	247	32	6th,		Out of Playoffs
1943-44	50	4	17	4	....	2	22	1	....	6	39	5	....	162	310	17	6th,		Out of Playoffs
1942-43	50	7	13	5	....	4	18	3	....	11	31	8	....	161	253	30	6th,		Out of Playoffs
1941-42	48	15	8	1	....	14	9	1	....	29	17	2	....	177	143	60	1st,		Lost Semi-Final
1940-41	48	13	7	4	....	8	12	4	....	21	19	8	....	143	125	50	4th,		Lost Quarter-Final
1939-40	**48**	**17**	**4**	**3**	....	**10**	**7**	**7**	....	**27**	**11**	**10**	....	**136**	**77**	**64**	**2nd,**		**Won Stanley Cup**
1938-39	48	13	8	3	....	13	8	3	....	26	16	6	....	149	105	58	2nd,		Lost Semi-Final
1937-38	48	15	5	4	....	12	10	2	....	27	15	6	....	149	96	60	2nd, Amn.		Lost Quarter-Final
1936-37	48	9	7	8	....	10	13	1	....	19	20	9	....	117	106	47	3rd, Amn.		Lost Final
1935-36	48	11	6	7	....	8	11	5	....	19	17	12	....	91	96	50	4th, Amn.		Out of Playoffs
1934-35	48	11	8	5	....	11	12	1	....	22	20	6	....	137	139	50	3rd, Amn.		Lost Semi-Final
1933-34	48	11	7	6	....	10	12	2	....	21	19	8	....	120	113	50	3rd, Amn.		Lost Quarter-Final
1932-33	**48**	**12**	**7**	**5**	....	**11**	**10**	**3**	....	**23**	**17**	**8**	....	**135**	**107**	**54**	**3rd, Amn.**		**Won Stanley Cup**
1931-32	48	13	7	4	....	10	10	4	....	23	17	8	....	134	112	54	1st, Amn.		Lost Final
1930-31	44	10	9	3	....	9	7	6	....	19	16	9	....	106	87	47	3rd, Amn.		Lost Semi-Final
1929-30	44	11	5	6	....	6	12	4	....	17	17	10	....	136	143	44	3rd, Amn.		Lost Semi-Final
1928-29	44	12	6	4	....	9	7	6	....	21	13	10	....	72	65	52	2nd, Amn.		Lost Final
1927-28	**44**	**10**	**8**	**4**	....	**9**	**8**	**5**	....	**19**	**16**	**9**	....	**94**	**79**	**47**	**2nd, Amn.**		**Won Stanley Cup**
1926-27	44	13	5	4	....	12	8	2	....	25	13	6	....	95	72	56	1st, Amn.		Lost Quarter-Final

2013-14 Player Personnel

FORWARDS	HT	WT	*Age	Place of Birth	S	2012-13 Club
ASHAM, Arron	5-11	205	35	Portage La Prairie, Man.	R	NY Rangers
BOYLE, Brian	6-7	244	28	Hingham, MA	L	NY Rangers
BRASSARD, Derick	6-1	202	26	Hull, Que.	L	Salzburg-CBJ-NYR
CALLAHAN, Ryan	5-11	190	28	Rochester, NY	R	NY Rangers
DORSETT, Derek	6-0	192	26	Kindersley, Sask.	R	Salzburg-CBJ-NYR
HAGELIN, Carl	5-11	186	25	Sodertalje, Sweden	L	Sodertalje-NY Rangers
HALEY, Micheal	5-10	204	27	Guelph, Ont.	L	Connecticut-NY Rangers
KREIDER, Chris	6-3	226	22	Boxford, MA	L	Connecticut-NY Rangers
MASHINTER, Brandon	6-4	220	25	Bradford, Ont.	L	Wor-NYR-Connecticut
MILLER, J.T.	6-1	200	20	East Palestine, OH	L	Connecticut-NY Rangers
MOORE, Dominic	6-0	192	33	Sarnia, Ont.	L	(none)
NASH, Rick	6-4	212	29	Brampton, Ont.	L	Davos-NY Rangers
POULIOT, Benoit	6-3	199	27	Alfred, Ont.	L	Tampa Bay
POWE, Darroll	5-11	212	28	Saskatoon, Sask.	L	Minnesota-NY Rangers
PYATT, Taylor	6-4	230	32	Thunder Bay, Ont.	L	NY Rangers
RICHARDS, Brad	6-0	196	33	Murray Harbour, P.E.I.	L	NY Rangers
STEPAN, Derek	6-0	196	23	Hastings, MN	R	KalPa-NY Rangers
ZUCCARELLO, Mats	5-7	179	26	Oslo, Norway	L	Magnitogorsk-NY Rangers

DEFENSEMEN	HT	WT	*Age	Place of Birth	S	2012-13 Club
BICKEL, Stu	6-4	207	26	Chanhassen, MN	R	Connecticut-NY Rangers
DEL ZOTTO, Michael	6-0	195	23	Stouffville, Ont.	L	Rapperswil-NY Rangers
FALK, Justin	6-5	215	24	Snowflake, Man.	L	Minnesota
GIRARDI, Dan	6-1	203	29	Welland, Ont.	R	NY Rangers
JOHNSON, Aaron	6-2	211	30	Port Hawkesbury, N.S.	L	Providence (AHL)-Boston
McDONAGH, Ryan	6-1	213	24	St.Paul, MN	L	Astana-NY Rangers
MOORE, John	6-3	202	22	Winnetka, IL	L	Sprfld-CBJ-NYR
STAAL, Marc	6-4	207	26	Thunder Bay, Ont.	L	NY Rangers
STRALMAN, Anton	5-11	190	27	Tibro, Sweden	R	NY Rangers
SYVRET, Danny	5-11	203	28	Millgrove, Ont.	L	Adirondack

GOALTENDERS	HT	WT	*Age	Place of Birth	C	2012-13 Club
BIRON, Martin	6-2	186	36	Lac-St-Charles, Que.	L	NY Rangers
LUNDQVIST, Henrik	6-1	188	31	Are, Sweden	L	NY Rangers

* – Age at start of 2013-14 season

Captains' History

Bill Cook, 1926-27 to 1936-37; Art Coulter, 1937-38 to 1941-42; Ott Heller, 1942-43 to 1944-45; Neil Colville 1945-46 to 1948-49; Buddy O'Connor, 1949-50; Frank Eddolls, 1950-51; Frank Eddolls and Allan Stanley, 1951-52; Allan Stanley, 1952-53; Allan Stanley and Don Raleigh, 1953-54; Don Raleigh, 1954-55; Harry Howell, 1955-56, 1956-57; Red Sullivan, 1957-58 to 1960-61; Andy Bathgate, 1961-62, 1962-63; Andy Bathgate and Camille Henry, 1963-64; Camille Henry and Bob Nevin, 1964-65; Bob Nevin 1965-66 to 1970-71; Vic Hadfield, 1971-72 to 1973-74; Brad Park, 1974-75; Brad Park and Phil Esposito, 1975-76; Phil Esposito, 1976-77, 1977-78; Dave Maloney, 1978-79, 1979-80; Dave Maloney, Walt Tkaczuk and Barry Beck, 1980-81; Barry Beck, 1981-82 to 1985-86; Ron Greschner, 1986-87; Ron Greschner and Kelly Kisio, 1987-88; Kelly Kisio, 1988-89 to 1990-91; Mark Messier, 1991-92 to 1996-97; Brian Leetch, 1997-98 to 1999-2000; Mark Messier, 2000-01 to 2003-04; no captain, 2005-06; Jaromir Jagr, 2006-07, 2007-08; Chris Drury, 2008-09 to 2010-11; Ryan Callahan, 2011-12 to date.

Alain Vigneault

Head Coach

Born: Quebec City, Que., May 14, 1961.

The New York Rangers officially named Alain Vigneault as the club's head coach on June 21, 2013. He is the 35th head coach in franchise history. A three-time Jack Adams Award finalist, and the 2007 winner of the award presented to the NHL's top coach, Vigneault joined the Rangers after spending seven season with the Vancouver Canucks where he recorded five seasons with 100 or more points.

After being a successful head coach in the Quebec Major Junior Hockey League and as an assistant with the Ottawa Senators, Vigneault earned his first NHL head coaching job with the Canadiens in 1997-98, leading the club to the second round of the playoffs that season. He became the Canucks head coach prior to the 2006-07 season. His most successful season behind the bench in Vancouver was 2010-11 when the Canucks won 54 games, totaled 117 points, captured the Presidents' Trophy as the top team in the league over the regular season, and then fell just one victory shy of winning the Stanley Cup. A year later Vigneault's Canucks edged the Rangers by just two points, 111 to 109, to win the Presidents' Trophy again.

Coaching Record

			Regular Season				Playoffs			
Season	Team	League	GC	W	L	O/T	GC	W	L	T
1986-87	Trois-Rivieres	QMJHL	70	28	40	2	....	....	....	....
1987-88	Hull	QMJHL	70	43	23	4	19	12	7	....
1987-88	Hull	M-Cup	....	....	....	....	4	1	3	....
1988-89	Hull	QMJHL	70	40	25	5	9	5	4	....
1989-90	Hull	QMJHL	70	36	29	5	11	4	7	....
1990-91	Hull	QMJHL	70	36	27	7	6	2	4	....
1991-92	Hull	QMJHL	70	41	24	5	6	2	4	....
1995-96	Beauport	QMJHL	31	19	7	5	20	13	7	....
1996-97	Beauport	QMJHL	70	24	44	2	4	1	3	....
1997-98	**Montreal**	**NHL**	**82**	**37**	**32**	**13**	**10**	**4**	**6**	....
1998-99	**Montreal**	**NHL**	**82**	**32**	**39**	**11**	....	....	....	....
99-2000	**Montreal**	**NHL**	**82**	**35**	**34**	**13**	....	....	....	....
2000-01	**Montreal**	**NHL**	**20**	**5**	**13**	**2**	....	....	....	....
2003-04	PEI	QMJHL	70	40	19	11	11	6	5	....
2004-05	PEI	QMJHL	70	24	39	7	....	....	....	....
2005-06	Manitoba	AHL	80	44	24	12	13	7	6	....
2006-07	**Vancouver**	**NHL**	**82**	**49**	**26**	**7**	**12**	**5**	**7**	....
2007-08	**Vancouver**	**NHL**	**82**	**39**	**33**	**10**	....	....	....	....
2008-09	**Vancouver**	**NHL**	**82**	**45**	**27**	**10**	**10**	**6**	**4**	....
2009-10	**Vancouver**	**NHL**	**82**	**49**	**28**	**5**	**12**	**6**	**6**	....
2010-11	**Vancouver**	**NHL**	**82**	**54**	**19**	**9**	**25**	**15**	**10**	....
2011-12	**Vancouver**	**NHL**	**82**	**51**	**22**	**9**	**5**	**1**	**4**	....
2012-13	**Vancouver**	**NHL**	**48**	**26**	**15**	**7**	**4**	**0**	**4**	....
	NHL Totals		**806**	**422**	**288**	**96**	**78**	**37**	**41**	....

Jack Adams Award (2007)

2012-13 Scoring

* – rookie

Regular Season

Pos	#	Player	Team	GP	G	A	Pts	TOI	+/-	PIM	PP	SH	GW	S	%
C	21	Derek Stepan	NYR	48	18	26	44	20:55	25	12	4	1	6	108	16.7
L	61	Rick Nash	NYR	44	21	21	42	19:58	16	26	3	1	3	176	11.9
C	19	Brad Richards	NYR	46	11	23	34	18:48	8	14	3	0	1	110	10.0
R	24	Ryan Callahan	NYR	45	16	15	31	21:30	9	12	6	2	4	144	11.1
C	16	Derick Brassard	CBJ	34	7	11	18	16:31	–2	16	1	0	1	63	11.1
			NYR	13	5	6	11	16:38	3	0	2	0	0	25	20.0
			Total	47	12	17	29	16:33	1	16	3	0	1	88	13.6
L	62	Carl Hagelin	NYR	48	10	14	24	17:18	10	18	1	0	1	132	7.6
D	4	Michael Del Zotto	NYR	46	3	18	21	23:10	6	18	0	1	0	81	3.7
D	27	Ryan McDonagh	NYR	47	4	15	19	24:21	13	22	0	0	1	83	4.8
L	29	Ryane Clowe	S.J.	28	0	11	11	16:27	–4	79	0	0	0	65	0.0
			NYR	12	3	5	8	17:01	5	14	1	0	0	22	13.6
			Total	40	3	16	19	16:37	1	93	1	0	0	87	3.4
D	5	Dan Girardi	NYR	46	2	12	14	25:24	–1	16	0	0	1	81	2.5
L	14	Taylor Pyatt	NYR	48	6	5	11	13:06	5	6	1	0	0	56	10.7
D	18	Marc Staal	NYR	21	2	9	11	24:27	4	14	1	0	0	20	10.0
C	36	Mats Zuccarello	NYR	15	3	5	8	16:25	10	8	0	0	0	27	11.1
D	6	Anton Stralman	NYR	48	4	3	7	18:02	14	16	0	0	0	66	6.1
D	17	John Moore	CBJ	17	0	1	1	14:30	–5	2	0	0	0	14	0.0
			NYR	13	1	5	6	11:46	9	5	0	0	0	15	6.7
			Total	30	1	6	7	13:19	4	7	0	0	0	29	3.4
C	22	Brian Boyle	NYR	38	2	3	5	14:12	–13	29	0	0	1	56	3.6
C	47 *	J.T. Miller	NYR	26	2	2	4	13:31	–7	8	1	0	0	43	4.7
C	20 *	Chris Kreider	NYR	23	2	1	3	10:06	–1	6	0	0	0	19	10.5
D	44	Steve Eminger	NYR	35	0	3	3	13:02	9	8	0	0	0	22	0.0
R	45	Arron Asham	NYR	27	2	0	2	6:37	2	50	0	0	0	14	14.3
R	36	Benn Ferriero	NYR	4	0	1	1	9:36	0	0	0	0	0	4	0.0
C	28	Kris Newbury	NYR	6	0	1	1	7:53	1	9	0	0	0	4	0.0
D	40	Roman Hamrlik	WSH	4	0	1	1	15:35	–1	2	0	0	0	2	0.0
			NYR	12	0	0	0	10:06	–3	6	0	0	0	5	0.0
			Total	16	0	1	1	11:28	–4	8	0	0	0	7	0.0
R	42	Brandon Segal	NYR	1	0	0	0	5:21	0	2	0	0	0	0	0.0
L	58 *	Christian Thomas	NYR	1	0	0	0	12:46	0	0	0	0	0	2	0.0
L	40 *	Brandon Mashinter	NYR	4	0	0	0	5:55	–2	0	0	0	0	2	0.0
C	32	Micheal Haley	NYR	9	0	0	0	6:37	–1	12	0	0	0	4	0.0
D	97	Matt Gilroy	NYR	15	0	0	0	9:33	–3	6	0	0	0	14	0.0
D	41	Stu Bickel	NYR	16	0	0	0	5:31	–2	49	0	0	0	2	0.0
C	8	Darroll Powe	MIN	8	0	0	0	10:13	1	9	0	0	0	5	0.0
			NYR	34	0	0	0	8:42	–2	18	0	0	0	18	0.0
			Total	42	0	0	0	8:59	–1	27	0	0	0	23	0.0

Goaltending

No.	Goaltender	GPI	Mins	Avg	W	L	OT	EN	SO	GA	SA	S%	G	A	PIM
30	Henrik Lundqvist	43	2575	2.05	24	16	3	6	2	88	1190	.926	0	1	0
43	Martin Biron	6	336	2.32	2	2	1	1	0	13	156	.917	0	0	0
	Totals	**48**	**2927**	**2.21**	**26**	**18**	**4**	**7**	**2**	**108**	**1353**	**.920**			

Playoffs

Pos	#	Player	Team	GP	G	A	Pts	TOI	+/-	PIM	PP	SH	GW	OT	S	%
C	16	Derick Brassard	NYR	12	2	10	12	18:54	1	2	1	0	1	0	22	9.1
C	36	Mats Zuccarello	NYR	12	1	6	7	16:21	–2	4	0	0	0	0	22	4.5
L	62	Carl Hagelin	NYR	12	3	3	6	18:05	6	0	0	0	0	0	35	8.6
C	21	Derek Stepan	NYR	12	4	1	5	22:30	4	2	0	0	2	0	32	12.5
C	22	Brian Boyle	NYR	11	3	2	5	18:49	–1	2	1	0	0	0	16	18.8
R	24	Ryan Callahan	NYR	12	2	3	5	23:22	2	6	0	0	0	0	40	5.0
L	61	Rick Nash	NYR	12	1	4	5	20:27	3	0	0	0	0	0	42	2.4
L	14	Taylor Pyatt	NYR	12	2	2	4	13:32	2	4	0	0	0	0	19	10.5
D	5	Dan Girardi	NYR	12	2	2	4	25:58	2	2	2	0	0	0	17	11.8
D	27	Ryan McDonagh	NYR	12	1	3	4	25:52	1	6	0	0	0	0	21	4.8
R	45	Arron Asham	NYR	10	2	0	2	6:40	0	6	0	0	1	0	7	28.6
C	20 *	Chris Kreider	NYR	8	1	1	2	9:42	0	0	0	0	1	1	8	12.5
D	4	Michael Del Zotto	NYR	12	1	1	2	21:10	–3	8	0	0	0	0	17	5.9
D	44	Steve Eminger	NYR	11	0	2	2	12:44	1	4	0	0	0	0	3	0.0
C	19	Brad Richards	NYR	10	1	0	1	14:43	–3	2	0	0	0	0	18	5.6
D	40	Roman Hamrlik	NYR	2	0	1	1	7:16	0	2	0	0	0	0	0	0.0
L	29	Ryane Clowe	NYR	2	0	1	1	7:07	–1	0	0	0	0	0	0	0.0
R	15	Derek Dorsett	NYR	11	0	1	1	10:45	–5	28	0	0	0	0	13	0.0
D	17	John Moore	NYR	12	0	1	1	17:07	0	2	0	0	0	0	16	0.0
D	18	Marc Staal	NYR	1	0	0	0	17:17	–1	0	0	0	0	0	0	0.0
C	32	Micheal Haley	NYR	2	0	0	0	6:01	–1	0	0	0	0	0	0	0.0
C	28	Kris Newbury	NYR	3	0	0	0	6:09	–1	2	0	0	0	0	2	0.0
C	8	Darroll Powe	NYR	3	0	0	0	6:25	0	2	0	0	0	0	2	0.0
D	6	Anton Stralman	NYR	10	0	0	0	21:06	1	0	0	0	0	0	10	0.0

Goaltending

No.	Goaltender	GPI	Mins	Avg	W	L	EN	SO	GA	SA	S%	G	A	PIM
30	Henrik Lundqvist	12	756	2.14	5	7	1	2	27	411	.934	0	0	0
	Totals	**12**	**760**	**2.21**	**5**	**7**	**1**	**2**	**28**	**412**	**.932**			

Coaching History

Lester Patrick, 1926-27 to 1938-39; Frank Boucher, 1939-40 to 1947-48; Frank Boucher and Lynn Patrick, 1948-49; Lynn Patrick, 1949-50; Neil Colville, 1950-51; Neil Colville and Bill Cook, 1951-52; Bill Cook, 1952-53; Frank Boucher and Muzz Patrick, 1953-54; Muzz Patrick, 1954-55; Phil Watson, 1955-56 to 1958-59; Phil Watson, Muzz Patrick and Alf Pike, 1959-60; Alf Pike, 1960-61; Doug Harvey, 1961-62; Muzz Patrick and Red Sullivan, 1962-63; Red Sullivan, 1963-64, 1964-65; Red Sullivan and Emile Francis, 1965-66; Emile Francis, 1966-67, 1967-68; Bernie Geoffrion and Emile Francis, 1968-69; Emile Francis, 1969-70 to 1972-73; Larry Popein and Emile Francis, 1973-74; Emile Francis, 1974-75; Ron Stewart and John Ferguson, 1975-76; John Ferguson, 1976-77; Jean-Guy Talbot, 1977-78; Fred Shero, 1978-79, 1979-80; Fred Shero and Craig Patrick, 1980-81; Herb Brooks, 1981-82 to 1983-84; Herb Brooks and Craig Patrick, 1984-85; Ted Sator, 1985-86; Ted Sator, Tom Webster and Phil Esposito, 1986-87; Michel Bergeron, 1987-88; Michel Bergeron and Phil Esposito, 1988-89; Roger Neilson, 1989-90 to 1991-92; Roger Neilson and Ron Smith, 1992-93; Mike Keenan, 1993-94; Colin Campbell, 1994-95 to 1996-97; Colin Campbell and John Muckler, 1997-98; John Muckler, 1998-99; John Muckler and John Tortorella, 1999-2000; Ron Low, 2000-01, 2001-02; Bryan Trottier and Glen Sather, 2002-03; Glen Sather and Tom Renney, 2003-04; Tom Renney, 2004-05 to 2007-08; Tom Renney and John Tortorella, 2008-09; John Tortorella, 2009-10 to 2012-13; Alain Vigneault, 2013-14.

Club Records

Team

(Figures in brackets for season records are games played; records for fewest points, wins, ties, losses, goals, goals against are for 70 or more games)

Most Points **112** 1993-94 (84)
Most Wins **52** 1993-94 (84)
Most Ties **21** 1950-51 (70)
Most Losses **44** 1984-85 (80)
Most Goals **321** 1991-92 (80)
Most Goals Against **345** 1984-85 (80)
Fewest Points **47** 1965-66 (70)
Fewest Wins **17** 1952-53 (70), 1954-55 (70), 1959-60 (70)
Fewest Ties **4** 2001-02 (82)
Fewest Losses **17** 1971-72 (78)
Fewest Goals **150** 1954-55 (70)
Fewest Goals Against **177** 1970-71 (78)

Longest Winning Streak
Overall .... **10** Dec. 19/39-Jan. 13/40, Jan. 19-Feb. 10/73
Home .... **14** Dec. 19/39-Feb. 25/40
Away .... **7** Jan. 12-Feb. 12/35, Oct. 28-Nov. 29/78

Longest Undefeated Streak
Overall .... **19** Nov. 23/39-Jan. 13/40 (14W, 5T)
Home .... **24** Oct. 14/70-Jan. 31/71 (18W, 6T), Oct. 24/95-Feb.15/96 (18W, 6T)
Away .... **11** Nov. 5/39-Jan. 13/40 (6W, 5T)

Longest Losing Streak
Overall .... **11** Oct. 30-Nov. 27/43
Home .... **7** Oct. 20-Nov. 14/76, Mar. 24-Apr. 14/93
Away .... **10** Oct. 30-Dec. 23/43, Feb. 8-Mar. 15/61

Longest Winless Streak
Overall .... **21** Jan. 23-Mar. 19/44 (17L, 4T)
Home .... **10** Jan. 30-Mar. 19/44 (7L, 3T)
Away .... **16** Oct. 9-Dec. 20/52 (12L, 4T)

Most Shutouts, Season **13** 1928-29 (44)
Most PIM, Season **2,018** 1989-90 (80)
Most Goals, Game .... **12** Nov. 21/71 (Cal. 1 at NYR 12)

Individual

Most Seasons .... **18** Rod Gilbert
Most Games .... **1,160** Harry Howell
Most Goals, Career .... **406** Rod Gilbert
Most Assists, Career .... **741** Brian Leetch
Most Points, Career .... **1,021** Rod Gilbert (406G, 615A)
Most PIM, Career .... **1,226** Ron Greschner
Most Shutouts, Career .... **49** Ed Giacomin
Longest Consecutive Games Streak .... **560** Andy Hebenton (Oct. 7/55-Mar. 24/63)
Most Goals, Season .... **54** Jaromir Jagr (2005-06)
Most Assists, Season .... **80** Brian Leetch (1991-92)
Most Points, Season .... **123** Jaromir Jagr (2005-06; 54G, 69A)
Most PIM, Season .... **305** Troy Mallette (1989-90)
Most Points, Defenseman, Season .... **102** Brian Leetch (1991-92; 22G, 80A)
Most Points, Center, Season .... **109** Jean Ratelle (1971-72; 46G, 63A)
Most Points, Right Wing, Season .... **123** Jaromir Jagr (2005-06; 54G, 69A)
Most Points, Left Wing, Season .... **106** Vic Hadfield (1971-72; 50G, 56A)
Most Points, Rookie, Season .... **76** Mark Pavelich (1981-82; 33G, 43A)
Most Shutouts, Season .... **13** John Ross Roach (1928-29)
Most Goals, Game .... **5** Don Murdoch (Oct. 12/76), Mark Pavelich (Feb. 23/83)
Most Assists, Game .... **5** Walt Tkaczuk (Feb. 12/72), Rod Gilbert (Mar. 2/75), (Mar. 30/75), (Oct. 8/76), Don Maloney (Jan. 3/87), Brian Leetch (Apr. 18/95), Wayne Gretzky (Feb. 15/99)
Most Points, Game .... **7** Steve Vickers (Feb. 18/76; 3G, 4A)

Retired Numbers

1	Ed Giacomin	1965-1975
2	Brian Leetch	1987-2004
3	Harry Howell	1952-1969
7	Rod Gilbert	1960-1977
9	Andy Bathgate	1952-1964
	Adam Graves	1991-2001
11	Mark Messier	1991-97; 2000-04
35	Mike Richter	1989-2003

All-time Record vs. Other Clubs

Regular Season

	Total								At Home								On Road							
	GP	W	L	T	OL	GF	GA	PTS	GP	W	L	T	OL	GF	GA	PTS	GP	W	L	T	OL	GF	GA	PTS
Anaheim	25	10	13	1	1	68	76	22	13	6	6	1	0	33	33	13	12	4	7	0	1	35	43	9
Boston	631	249	283	97	2	1839	1985	597	317	143	119	55	0	968	882	341	314	106	164	42	2	871	1103	256
Buffalo	165	62	73	25	5	510	543	154	81	35	28	15	3	253	219	88	84	27	45	10	2	257	324	66
Calgary	107	39	53	15	0	339	415	93	55	26	24	5	0	184	190	57	52	13	29	10	0	155	225	36
Carolina	119	62	48	7	2	390	335	133	60	37	17	4	2	211	147	80	59	25	31	3	0	179	188	53
Chicago	579	236	243	98	2	1652	1696	572	289	120	114	55	0	852	816	295	290	116	129	43	2	800	880	277
Colorado	76	34	31	7	4	280	261	79	38	20	12	4	2	143	108	46	38	14	19	3	2	137	153	33
Columbus	12	5	6	1	0	33	38	11	5	3	1	1	0	19	14	7	7	2	5	0	0	14	24	4
Dallas	130	69	38	22	1	452	374	161	66	37	18	11	0	221	173	85	64	32	20	11	1	231	201	76
Detroit	575	211	260	103	1	1582	1762	526	287	135	94	58	0	874	746	328	288	76	166	45	1	708	1016	198
Edmonton	64	26	27	9	2	227	230	63	33	12	14	6	1	127	122	31	31	14	13	3	1	100	108	32
Florida	80	42	28	6	4	229	185	94	40	22	14	4	0	123	87	48	40	20	14	2	4	106	98	46
Los Angeles	125	65	43	16	1	466	391	147	61	37	18	6	0	243	181	80	64	28	25	10	1	223	210	67
Minnesota	14	9	5	0	0	42	36	18	6	4	2	0	0	16	12	8	8	5	3	0	0	26	24	10
Montreal	611	191	323	94	3	1589	2066	479	305	127	123	54	1	884	881	309	306	64	200	40	2	705	1185	170
Nashville	16	8	5	1	2	47	37	19	9	3	4	1	1	22	20	8	7	5	1	0	1	25	17	11
New Jersey	222	104	85	27	6	734	665	241	110	58	30	20	2	390	299	138	112	46	55	7	4	344	366	103
NY Islanders	244	119	99	19	7	827	783	264	122	69	37	11	5	441	348	154	122	50	62	8	2	386	435	110
Ottawa	77	33	37	3	4	204	221	73	38	14	22	0	2	104	114	30	39	19	15	3	2	100	107	43
Philadelphia	272	119	109	37	7	811	813	282	136	62	47	23	4	430	390	151	136	57	62	14	3	381	423	131
Phoenix	68	38	24	6	0	257	229	82	34	22	10	2	0	144	114	46	34	16	14	4	0	113	115	36
Pittsburgh	254	118	104	23	9	902	855	268	128	66	50	9	3	478	420	144	126	52	54	14	6	424	435	124
St. Louis	131	75	40	16	0	463	354	166	63	45	12	6	0	251	151	96	68	30	28	10	0	212	203	70
San Jose	29	20	6	3	0	108	76	43	13	9	3	1	0	51	39	19	16	11	3	2	0	57	37	24
Tampa Bay	83	42	29	5	7	268	242	96	43	24	13	2	4	145	116	54	40	18	16	3	3	123	126	42
Toronto	596	222	273	95	6	1715	1889	545	299	129	111	56	3	930	876	317	297	93	162	39	3	785	1013	228
Vancouver	111	73	30	8	0	452	318	154	57	39	13	5	0	243	148	83	54	34	17	3	0	209	170	71
Washington	197	87	86	18	6	673	680	198	98	48	38	9	3	360	325	108	99	39	48	9	3	313	355	90
Winnipeg	51	24	17	1	9	150	143	58	26	10	10	1	5	72	74	26	25	14	7	0	4	78	69	32
Defunct Clubs	278	169	64	45	0	901	581	383	139	87	30	22	0	460	290	196	139	82	34	23	0	441	291	187
Totals	**5942**	**2561**	**2482**	**808**	**91**	**18210**	**18279**	**6021**	**2971**	**1449**	**1034**	**447**	**41**	**9672**	**8335**	**3386**	**2971**	**1112**	**1448**	**361**	**50**	**8538**	**9944**	**2635**

Playoffs

	Series	W	L	GP	W	L	T	GF	GA	Last Mtg.	Rnd.	Result
Boston	10	3	7	47	19	26	2	114	130	2013	CSF	L 1-4
Buffalo	2	0	2	9	3	6	0	19	28	2007	CSF	L 2-4
Calgary	1	1	0	4	3	1	0	14	8	1980	PRE	W 3-1
Chicago	5	1	4	24	10	14	0	54	66	1973	SF	L 1-4
Colorado	1	1	0	6	4	2	0	25	19	1995	CQF	W 4-2
Detroit	5	1	4	23	10	13	0	49	57	1950	F	L 3-4
Florida	1	1	0	5	4	1	0	13	10	1997	CQF	W 4-1
Los Angeles	2	2	0	6	5	1	0	32	14	1981	PRE	W 3-1
Montreal	14	7	7	61	25	34	2	158	188	1996	CQF	W 4-2
New Jersey	6	4	2	34	18	16	0	93	90	2012	CF	L 2-4
NY Islanders	8	3	5	39	19	20	0	132	129	1994	CQF	W 4-0
Ottawa	1	1	0	7	4	3	0	14	13	2012	CQF	W 4-3
Philadelphia	10	4	6	47	20	27	0	153	157	1997	CF	L 1-4
Pittsburgh	4	0	4	20	4	16	0	57	79	2008	CSF	L 1-4
St. Louis	1	1	0	6	4	2	0	29	22	1981	QF	W 4-2
Toronto	8	5	3	35	19	16	0	86	86	1971	QF	W 4-2
Vancouver	1	1	0	7	4	3	0	21	19	1994	F	W 4-3
Washington	8	4	4	48	23	25	0	121	132	2013	CQF	W 4-3
Winnipeg	1	1	0	4	4	0	0	17	6	2007	CQF	W 4-0
Defunct Clubs	9	6	3	22	11	7	4	43	29			
Totals	**98**	**47**	**51**	**454**	**213**	**233**	**8**	**1244**	**1282**			

Calgary totals include Atlanta Flames, 1972-73 to 1979-80.
Colorado totals include Quebec, 1979-80 to 1994-95.
New Jersey totals include Kansas City, 1974-75, 1975-76, and Colorado Rockies, 1976-77 to 1981-82.
Phoenix totals include Winnipeg, 1979-80 to 1995-96.
Carolina totals include Hartford, 1979-80 to 1996-97.
Dallas totals include Minnesota North Stars, 1967-68 to 1992-93.
Winnipeg totals include Atlanta Thrashers, 1999-2000 to 2010-11.

Playoff Results 2013-2009

Year	Round	Opponent	Result	GF	GA
2013	CSF	Boston	L 1-4	10	16
	CQF	Washington	W 4-3	16	12
2012	CF	New Jersey	L 2-4	14	15
	CSF	Washington	W 4-3	15	13
	CQF	Ottawa	W 4-3	14	13
2011	CQF	Washington	L 1-4	8	13
2009	CQF	Washington	L 3-4	11	19

Abbreviations: Round: F – Final; **CF** – conference final; **CSF** – conference semi-final; **CQF** – conference quarter-final; **SF** – semi-final; **QF** – quarter-final; **PRE** – preliminary round.

2012-13 Results

Jan.	19	at Boston	1-3		12	at Buffalo	1-3
	20	Pittsburgh	3-6		14	at Winnipeg	1-3
	23	Boston	4-3*		16	at Pittsburgh	0-3
	24	at Philadelphia	1-2		18	Carolina	2-1†
	26	Toronto	5-2		19	at New Jersey	3-2
	29	Philadelphia	2-1		21	Florida	1-3
	31	Pittsburgh	0-3		24	Washington	2-3†
Feb.	2	at Tampa Bay	3-2		26	at Philadelphia	5-2
	5	at New Jersey	1-3		28	at Ottawa	0-3
	7	NY Islanders	4-1		30	at Montreal	0-3
	10	Tampa Bay	5-1	**Apr.**	1	Winnipeg	4-2
	12	at Boston	4-3†		3	Pittsburgh	6-1
	14	NY Islanders	3-4†		5	at Pittsburgh	1-2†
	17	Washington	2-1		6	at Carolina	4-1
	19	Montreal	1-3		8	at Toronto	3-4
	21	at Ottawa	2-3†		10	Toronto	3-2†
	23	at Montreal	0-3		13	at NY Islanders	1-0*
	26	Winnipeg	3-4		16	at Philadelphia	2-4
	28	Tampa Bay	4-1		18	Florida	6-1
Mar.	3	Buffalo	3-2†		19	at Buffalo	8-4
	5	Philadelphia	4-2		21	New Jersey	4-1
	7	at NY Islanders	2-1*		23	at Florida	2-3
	8	Ottawa	2-3		25	at Carolina	4-3*
	10	at Washington	4-1		27	New Jersey	4-0

* – Overtime † – Shootout

Entry Draft Selections 2013-1999

Name in bold denotes played in NHL.

2013
Pick
65 Adam Tambellini
75 Pavel Buchnevich
80 Anthony Duclair
110 Ryan Graves
170 Mackenzie Skapski

2012
Pick
28 Brady Skjei
59 Cristoval Nieves
119 Calle Andersson
142 Thomas Spelling

2011
Pick
15 **J.T. Miller**
72 Steven Fogarty
106 Michael St. Croix
134 Shane McColgan
136 Samuel Noreau
172 Peter Ceresnak

2010
Pick
10 Dylan McIlrath
40 **Christian Thomas**
100 Andrew Yogan
130 Jason Wilson
157 Jesper Fast
190 Randy McNaught

2009
Pick
19 **Chris Kreider**
47 Ethan Werek
80 Ryan Bourque
127 **Roman Horak**
140 Scott Stajcer
170 Dan Maggio
200 Mikhail Pashnin

2008
Pick
20 **Michael Del Zotto**
51 **Derek Stepan**
75 **Evgeny Grachev**
90 **Tomas Kundratek**
111 **Dale Weise**
141 Chris Doyle
171 Mitch Gaulton

2007
Pick
17 Alexei Cherepanov
48 Antoine Lafleur
138 Max Campbell
168 **Carl Hagelin**
193 David Skokan
198 Danny Hobbs

2006
Pick
21 **Bobby Sanguinetti**
54 **Artem Anisimov**
84 Ryan Hillier
104 David Kveton
137 Tomas Zaborsky
174 Eric Hunter
204 Lukas Zeliska

2005
Pick
12 **Marc Staal**
40 **Michael Sauer**
56 **Marc-Andre Cliche**
66 **Brodie Dupont**
77 Dalyn Flatt
107 **Tom Pyatt**
147 Trevor Koverko
178 Greg Beller
211 **Ryan Russell**

2004
Pick
6 **Al Montoya**
19 **Lauri Korpikoski**
36 Darin Olver
48 **Dane Byers**
51 Bruce Graham
60 **Brandon Dubinsky**
73 Zdenek Bahensky
80 Billy Ryan
127 **Ryan Callahan**
135 Roman Psurny
169 Jordan Foote
247 Jonathan Paiement
266 **Jakub Petruzalek**

2003
Pick
12 **Hugh Jessiman**
50 **Ivan Baranka**
75 Ken Roche
122 **Corey Potter**
149 **Nigel Dawes**
176 Ivan Dornic
179 Philippe Furrer
180 **Chris Holt**
209 **Dylan Reese**
243 Jan Marek

2002
Pick
33 Lee Falardeau
81 Marcus Jonasen
127 **Nate Guenin**
143 Mike Walsh
177 Jake Taylor
194 Kim Hirschovits
226 **Joey Crabb**
240 **Petr Prucha**
270 Rob Flynn

2001
Pick
10 **Dan Blackburn**
40 **Fedor Tyutin**
79 **Garth Murray**
113 **Bryce Lampman**
139 Shawn Collymore
176 **Marek Zidlicky**
206 Petr Preucil
226 Pontus Petterstrom
230 Leonid Zhvachkin
238 **Ryan Hollweg**
269 Juris Stals

2000
Pick
64 **Filip Novak**
95 **Dominic Moore**
112 Premysl Duben
140 Nathan Martz
143 Brandon Snee
175 Sven Helfenstein
205 **Henrik Lundqvist**
238 Danny Eberly
269 Martin Richter

1999
Pick
4 **Pavel Brendl**
9 **Jamie Lundmark**
59 David Inman
79 Johan Asplund
90 Patrick Aufiero
137 Garrett Bembridge
177 Jay Dardis
197 Arto Laatikainen
226 Yevgeny Gusakov
251 Petter Henning
254 Alexei Bulatov

General Managers' History

Lester Patrick, 1926-27 to 1944-45; Lester Patrick and Frank Boucher, 1945-46; Frank Boucher, 1946-47 to 1954-55; Muzz Patrick, 1955-56 to 1963-64; Muzz Patrick and Emile Francis, 1964-65; Emile Francis, 1965-66 to 1974-75; Emile Francis and John Ferguson, 1975-76; John Ferguson, 1976-77, 1977-78; Fred Shero, 1978-79, 1979-80; Fred Shero and Craig Patrick, 1980-81; Craig Patrick, 1981-82 to 1985-86; Phil Esposito, 1986-87 to 1988-89; Neil Smith, 1989-90 to 1999-2000; Glen Sather, 2000-01 to date.

Glen Sather

President and General Manager

Born: High River, Alta., September 2, 1943.

Glen Sather, who spent parts of four seasons with the New York Rangers as a player from 1970 to 1974, became the franchise's 12th president and tenth general manager on June 2, 2000. He also served as coach of the team from January 30, 2003, to February 25, 2004.

Sather joined the Rangers following a 24-year career with the Edmonton Oilers, where he was the architect of five Stanley Cup championships between 1984 and 1990. One of the most respected executives in the National Hockey League, Sather was honored for his tremendous achievements in 1997 by becoming the first member of the Oilers organization to be selected to the Hockey Hall of Fame.

Named coach and vice president of hockey operations for the Oilers when the franchise joined the NHL in June of 1979, Sather became general manager and club president in May of 1980. He coached through the 1988-89 season and also returned for 60 games behind the bench in 1993-94. Sather-coached teams won the Stanley Cup four times in the 1980s. As general manager, Sather was instrumental in the Oilers' fifth Cup triumph in 1990.

He played for six different teams during a 10-year NHL career. He scored 80 goals in 658 games.

Coaching Record

			Regular Season				Playoffs			
Season	Team	League	GC	W	L	O/T	GC	W	L	T
1979-80	Edmonton	NHL	80	28	39	13	3	0	3	....
1980-81	Edmonton	NHL	62	25	26	11	9	5	4	....
1981-82	Edmonton	NHL	80	48	17	15	5	2	3	....
1982-83	Edmonton	NHL	80	47	21	12	16	11	5	....
1983-84♦	Edmonton	NHL	80	57	18	5	19	15	4	....
1984-85♦	Edmonton	NHL	80	49	20	11	18	15	3	....
1985-86	Edmonton	NHL	80	56	17	7	10	6	4	....
1986-87♦	Edmonton	NHL	80	50	24	6	21	16	5	....
1987-88♦*	Edmonton	NHL	80	44	25	11	19	16	2	1
1988-89	Edmonton	NHL	80	38	34	8	7	3	4	....
1993-94	Edmonton	NHL	60	22	27	11	....	....	....	....
2002-03	NY Rangers	NHL	28	11	10	7	....	....	....	....
2003-04	NY Rangers	NHL	62	22	29	11	....	....	....	....
	NHL Totals		**932**	**497**	**307**	**128**	**127**	**89**	**37**	**1**

♦ Stanley Cup win.
Jack Adams Award (1986)
* Playoff game May 24, 1988 suspended due to power failure. Score tied.

Club Directory

Madison Square Garden

New York Rangers
14th Floor
2 Pennsylvania Plaza
New York, New York 10121
Phone **212/465-6486**
PR FAX 212/465-6494
www.newyorkrangers.com
Capacity: 18,200

Team Executive Management
Exec. Chairman, The Madison Square Garden Company. James L. Dolan
President & CEO, The Madison Square Garden Company Hank J. Ratner
President, MSG Sports . . . . Scott O'Neil
President and G.M. . . . . Glen Sather
Executive V.P., Marketing & Sales . . . . Howard Jacobs
Sr. V.P., Finance & Controller . . . . John Cudmore
Deputy General Counsel & Sr. V.P.,
Legal & Business Affairs – Team Ops. . . . . Marc Schoenfeld
Sr. V.P., Marketing . . . . Janet Duch
Sr. V.P., Sports Team Operations . . . . Mark Piazza
Sr. V.P., Legal & Business Affairs – Sports Ops . . . . John Master
V.P., Public Relations and Player Recruitment . . . . John Rosasco

Hockey Club Personnel
Asst. G.M., Player Personnel, Assistant Coach and
G.M. – Hartford Wolf Pack. . . . . Jim Schoenfeld
Asst. G.M. . . . . Jeff Gorton
Head Coach . . . . Alain Vigneault
Associate Coach . . . . Scott Arniel
Assistant Coaches . . . . Ulf Samuelsson, Daniel Lacroix
Assistant Coach and Goaltending Coach . . . . Benoit Allaire
Video Coach . . . . Jerry Dineen
Director, Player Personnel . . . . Gordie Clark
Director, Professional Scouting. . . . . Kevin Maxwell
Hockey Consultant . . . . Doug Risebrough
Hockey and Business Operations . . . . Adam Graves
Head Professional Scout, Europe . . . . Anders Hedberg
European Scouts . . . . Jan Gajdosik, Otto Hascak, Vladimir Lutchenko
Amateur Scouts. . . . . Mike Barnett, Larry Bernard, Rich Brown, Brendon Clark, Daniel Dore, Ernie Gare, Tom Thompson
Professional Scouts . . . . Rick Kehoe, Gilles Leger, Justin Sather, Peter Stephan
Head Athletic Trainer. . . . . Jim Ramsay
Equipment Manager / Assistant Manager. . . . . Acacio Marques / Jason Levy
Massage Therapist/Assistant Trainer. . . . . Bruce Lifrieri
Strength and Conditioning Coach . . . . Reg Grant
Strength and Conditioning Consultant – Europe. . . . . . . Daniel Hedin
Video Analyst . . . . Jim Sullivan
Manager, MSG Training Center Operations . . . . Alex Case

Sports Team Operations
V.P., Sports Team Operations. . . . . Jason Vogel
Administrator, Sports Team Operations . . . . Brian Wendth
Coordinator, Sports Team Ops and Integrated Marketing. . Caroline Giglio

Hockey Operations
Managers, Scouting / Hockey Administration . . . . Victor Saljanin / Katie Condon
Executive Administrative Assistant . . . . Barbara Steppe
Director, Operations, MSG Training Center . . . . Miguel Vazquez
Manager, Building Operations, MSG Training Center . . . Kristine DeRosa

Medical Staff
Team Physician and Orthopedic Surgeon . . . . Dr. Andrew Feldman
Assistant Team Physician . . . . Dr. Anthony Maddalo
Medical Consultants . . . . Drs. Ronald Weissman, Ron Preston, Martin Posner
Team Dentists . . . . Drs. Don Salomon, Joe Esposito

Public Relations
V.P., Business Public Relations . . . . Stacey Escudero
Public Relations, Director / Coordinator . . . . Brendan McIntyre / Dino Ticinelli

Marketing
V.P., Marketing and Programming . . . . Jeanie Baumgartner
Director, Marketing Programs/Brands. . . . . Mark Gallego
Coordinator, Marketing Programs . . . . Jane Stanton
Coordinator, Marketing. . . . . Jessica Quinlan
Design Director / Art Directors . . . . Joanecy Kagalingan / Tarek Awad

Event Presentation
V.P., Event Presentation. . . . . Greg Kwizak
Music Director, MSG Sports. . . . . Ray Castoldi
Coordinating Producer, MSG Sports. . . . . Faith Astrada
Production Assistant . . . . Danielle Nardi

Community Relations and Fan Development
V.P., Community Relations. . . . . Kerryann Tomlinson
Director, Fan Development . . . . Rick Nadeau
Coordinator, Field Marketing and Fan Development. . . . Mike Fasulo
Manager, Community Relations. . . . . David Martella
Manager, Alumni and Community Relations . . . . Anthony Zucconi
Director, Special Projects and Comm. Relations Rep. . . . . Rod Gilbert

MSG Interactive
Manager, MSG Interactive Websites – Teams . . . . Ryan Braithwaite

MSG Photo Services
Official Photographer of Madison Square Garden. . . . . . George Kalinsky
MSG Photo Services, V.P. / Coordinator . . . . Rebecca Taylor / Gina Licata

Finance
V.P., Finance . . . . Jeanine McGrory
Director, Accounting . . . . Paul Kohler
Director, Accounting Suites and Teams . . . . Dean Cannizzo
Director, Finance Marketing Partnerships . . . . Brandy Champion
Sr. Staff Accountant . . . . Lissette Bayon
Staff Accountants . . . . Ahmed Abady, Mark Herrero
Coordinator, Accounts Payable . . . . Dularie Harris
Sr. Administrative Assistant . . . . Mabel Martinez

Legal and Business Affairs
V.P.s, Legal & Business Affairs . . . . Jamaal Lesane, Christina Song

Additional Information
Television / Radio Network. . . . . MSG Network / MSG Radio

Ottawa Senators

Key Off-Season Signings/Acquisitions

2013

July 5 • Acquired LW **Bobby Ryan** from Anaheim for RW **Jakob Silfverberg**, LW **Stefan Noesen** and a 1st-round pick in the 2014 NHL Draft.
5 • Signed LW **Clarke MacArthur**.
8 • Signed D **Joe Corvo**.
10 • Re-signed D **Mark Borowiecki** and LW **David Dziurzynski**.
12 • Re-signed RW **Erik Condra**.
18 • Re-signed C **Mike Hoffman**.
22 • Re-signed D **Patrick Wiercioch**.

2012-13 Results: 25W-17L-2OTL-4SOL 56PTS
4TH, Northeast Division • 7TH, Eastern Conference

Year-by-Year Record

		Home				Road				Overall									
Season	**GP**	**W**	**L**	**T**	**OL**	**W**	**L**	**T**	**OL**	**W**	**L**	**T**	**OL**	**GF**	**GA**	**Pts.**	**Div. Fin.**	**Conf. Fin.**	**Playoff Result**
2012-13	48	15	6	....	3	10	11	....	3	25	17	....	6	116	104	56	4th, NE	7th, East	Lost Conf. Semi-Final
2011-12	82	20	17	....	4	21	14	....	6	41	31	....	10	249	240	92	2nd, NE	8th, East	Lost Conf. Quarter-Final
2010-11	82	16	20	....	5	16	20	....	5	32	40	....	10	192	250	74	5th, NE	13th, East	Out of Playoffs
2009-10	82	26	11	....	4	18	21	....	2	44	32	....	6	225	238	94	2nd, NE	5th, East	Lost Conf. Quarter-Final
2008-09	82	22	12	....	7	14	23	....	4	36	35	....	11	217	237	83	4th, NE	11th, East	Out of Playoffs
2007-08	82	22	15	....	4	21	16	....	4	43	31	....	8	261	247	94	2nd, NE	7th, East	Lost Conf. Quarter-Final
2006-07	82	25	13	....	3	23	12	....	6	48	25	....	9	288	222	105	2nd, NE	4th, East	Lost Final
2005-06	82	29	9	....	3	23	12	....	6	52	21	....	9	314	211	113	1st, NE	1st, East	Lost Conf. Semi-Final
2004-05	....	....	....	....	....	....	....	....	....	....	....	....	....	....	....	....			
2003-04	82	23	8	5	5	20	15	5	1	43	23	10	6	262	189	102	3rd, NE	5th, East	Lost Conf. Quarter-Final
2002-03	82	28	9	3	1	24	12	5	0	52	21	8	1	263	182	113	1st, NE	1st, East	Lost Conf. Final
2001-02	82	21	13	3	4	18	14	6	3	39	27	9	7	243	208	94	3rd, NE	7th, East	Lost Conf. Semi-Final
2000-01	82	26	7	5	3	22	14	4	1	48	21	9	4	274	205	109	1st, NE	2nd, East	Lost Conf. Quarter-Final
1999-2000	82	24	10	5	2	17	18	6	0	41	28	11	2	244	210	95	2nd, NE	6th, East	Lost Conf. Quarter-Final
1998-99	82	22	11	8	....	22	12	7	....	44	23	15	....	239	179	103	1st, NE	2nd, East	Lost Conf. Quarter-Final
1997-98	82	18	16	7	....	16	17	8	....	34	33	15	....	193	200	83	5th, NE	8th, East	Lost Conf. Semi-Final
1996-97	82	16	17	8	....	15	19	7	....	31	36	15	....	226	234	77	3rd, NE	7th, East	Lost Conf. Quarter-Final
1995-96	82	8	28	5	....	10	31	0	....	18	59	5	....	191	291	41	6th, NE	13th, East	Out of Playoffs
1994-95	48	5	16	3	....	4	18	2	....	9	34	5	....	117	174	23	7th, NE	14th, East	Out of Playoffs
1993-94	84	8	30	4	....	6	31	5	....	14	61	9	....	201	397	37	7th, NE	14th, East	Out of Playoffs
1992-93	84	9	29	4	....	1	41	0	....	10	70	4	....	202	395	24	6th, Adams		Out of Playoffs

2013-14 Schedule

Oct.	Fri.	4	at Buffalo
	Sat.	5	at Toronto
	Wed.	9	at Los Angeles
	Sat.	12	at San Jose
	Sun.	13	at Anaheim*
	Tue.	15	at Phoenix
	Thu.	17	New Jersey
	Sat.	19	Edmonton*
	Wed.	23	at Detroit
	Fri.	25	Anaheim
	Sun.	27	San Jose*
	Tue.	29	at Chicago
Nov.	Fri.	1	NY Islanders
	Sun.	3	Dallas*
	Tue.	5	at Columbus
	Thu.	7	Montreal
	Sat.	9	Florida*
	Tue.	12	Philadelphia
	Fri.	15	Boston
	Sun.	17	Columbus*
	Tue.	19	at Philadelphia
	Wed.	20	Minnesota
	Sat.	23	at Detroit
	Sun.	24	at Carolina*
	Wed.	27	at Washington
	Thu.	28	Vancouver
Dec.	Sun.	1	Detroit*
	Tue.	3	at Florida
	Thu.	5	at Tampa Bay
	Sat.	7	Toronto
	Mon.	9	Philadelphia
	Tue.	10	at Buffalo
	Thu.	12	Buffalo
	Sat.	14	Los Angeles*
	Mon.	16	St. Louis
	Wed.	18	at New Jersey
	Thu.	19	Florida
	Sat.	21	Phoenix*
	Mon.	23	Pittsburgh
	Fri.	27	at Boston
	Sat.	28	Boston
	Mon.	30	Washington
Jan.	Thu.	2	Winnipeg
	Sat.	4	at Montreal
	Wed.	8	at Colorado
	Sat.	11	at Nashville
	Tue.	14	at Minnesota
	Thu.	16	Montreal
	Sat.	18	NY Rangers*
	Tue.	21	at Washington
	Thu.	23	at Tampa Bay
	Fri.	24	at Carolina
	Tue.	28	at Columbus
	Thu.	30	Tampa Bay
Feb.	Sat.	1	at Toronto
	Mon.	3	at Pittsburgh
	Tue.	4	at St. Louis
	Thu.	6	Buffalo
	Sat.	8	at Boston*
	Thu.	27	Detroit
Mar.	Sun.	2	at Vancouver*
	Tue.	4	at Edmonton
	Wed.	5	at Calgary
	Sat.	8	at Winnipeg*
	Mon.	10	Nashville
	Sat.	15	at Montreal
	Sun.	16	Colorado*
	Tue.	18	NY Rangers
	Thu.	20	Tampa Bay
	Sat.	22	at Dallas*
	Mon.	24	at Tampa Bay
	Tue.	25	at Florida
	Fri.	28	Chicago
	Sun.	30	Calgary*
	Mon.	31	Carolina
Apr.	Wed.	2	NY Islanders
	Fri.	4	Montreal
	Sat.	5	at NY Rangers
	Tue.	8	at NY Islanders
	Thu.	10	New Jersey
	Sat.	12	Toronto
	Sun.	13	at Pittsburgh

* Denotes afternoon game.

A rash of injuries saw Ottawa's offense tumble from fourth best in the NHL in 2011-12 to fourth worst in 2012-13. Goalie Craig Anderson also battled injuries, but his brilliant play in just 24 games helped Ottawa return to the playoffs and saw Anderson rank fourth in voting for the Vezina Trophy and 12th for the Hart as MVP.

ATLANTIC DIVISION
22nd NHL Season

Franchise date: December 16, 1991

2013-14 Player Personnel

FORWARDS	HT	WT	*Age	Place of Birth	S	2012-13 Club
CONACHER, Cory	5-8	179	23	Burlington, Ont.	L	Syracuse-T.B.-Ott
CONDRA, Erik	6-0	190	27	Trenton, MI	R	Fussen-Riessersee-Ottawa
DA COSTA, Stephane	5-11	183	24	Paris, France	R	Binghamton-Ottawa
DZIURZYNSKI, David	6-3	214	23	Lloydminster, Alta.	L	Binghamton-Ottawa
GRANT, Derek	6-3	203	23	Abbotsford, B.C.	L	Binghamton-Ottawa
GREENING, Colin	6-3	212	27	St. John's, Nfld.	L	Aalborg-Ottawa
HOFFMAN, Mike	6-0	185	23	Kitchener, Ont.	L	Binghamton-Ottawa
KASSIAN, Matt	6-5	247	26	Edmonton, Alta.	L	Houston-Ottawa
MacARTHUR, Clarke	6-0	191	28	Lloydminster, Alta.	L	Crimmitschau-Toronto
MICHALEK, Milan	6-2	225	28	Jindrichuv Hradec, Czech.	L	C. Budejovice-Ottawa
NEIL, Chris	6-1	215	34	Markdale, Ont.	R	Ottawa
O'BRIEN, Jim	6-2	200	24	Maplewood, MN	R	Ottawa
PAGEAU, Jean-Gabriel	5-9	172	20	Ottawa, Ont.	R	Binghamton-Ottawa
RYAN, Bobby	6-2	200	26	Cherry Hill, NJ	R	Mora-Anaheim
SMITH, Zack	6-2	212	25	Medicine Hat, Alta.	L	Frederikshavn-Ottawa
SPEZZA, Jason	6-3	216	30	Mississauga, Ont.	R	Rapperswil-Ottawa
STONE, Mark	6-2	211	21	Winnipeg, Man.	R	Binghamton-Ottawa
TURRIS, Kyle	6-1	195	24	New Westminster, B.C.	R	Karpat-Ottawa
ZIBANEJAD, Mika	6-2	212	20	Huddinge, Sweden	R	Binghamton-Ottawa
DEFENSEMEN						
BOROWIECKI, Mark	6-2	205	24	Ottawa, Ont.	L	Binghamton-Ottawa
CORVO, Joe	6-0	204	36	Oak Park, IL	R	Carolina
COWEN, Jared	6-5	230	22	Saskatoon, Sask.	L	Binghamton-Ottawa
GRYBA, Eric	6-3	214	25	Saskatoon, Sask.	R	Binghamton-Ottawa
KARLSSON, Erik	6-0	180	23	Landsbro, Sweden	R	Jokerit-Ott-Frolunda Jr.
METHOT, Marc	6-3	227	28	Ottawa, Ont.	L	Ottawa
PHILLIPS, Chris	6-3	221	35	Calgary, Alta.	L	Ottawa
WIERCIOCH, Patrick	6-4	200	23	Burnaby, B.C.	L	Binghamton-Ottawa

GOALTENDERS	HT	WT	*Age	Place of Birth	C	2012-13 Club
ANDERSON, Craig	6-2	180	32	Park Ridge, IL	L	Ottawa
LEHNER, Robin	6-4	210	22	Goteborg, Sweden	L	Binghamton-Ottawa

* – Age at start of 2013-14 season

Paul MacLean

Head Coach

Born: Grostenquin, France, March 9, 1958.

Ottawa Senators general manager Bryan Murray announced the hiring of Paul MacLean as the club's head coach on June 14, 2011. In hs first season behind the bench in Ottawa in 2011-12, MacLean led the Senators back to the postseason after finishing 26th in the NHL's overall standings the year before. He won the Jack Adams Award as coach of the year in 2012-13 for guiding an injury-ravaged Ottawa team to the playoffs again.

MacLean joined the Senators after spending the previous six seasons as assistant coach to Mike Babcock with the Detroit Red Wings. During his tenure with Detroit, the Red Wings finished first in the Central Division five times and made two appearances in the Stanley Cup Final, winning in six games over the Pittsburgh Penguins in 2008 and losing in seven games to Pittsburgh in 2009. During his six seasons with Detroit, the team posted a 304-126-62 record in 492 regular-season games (.681 winning percentage).

Prior to joining Detroit, MacLean was hired in 2002 by Bryan Murray, who was then the general manager of the Mighty Ducks of Anaheim. MacLean spent two seasons as an assistant to Babcock, the Mighty Ducks' head coach at that time. In his first season in Anaheim, the club made its first Stanley Cup Final appearance and posted a 69-62-33 record (.521) during MacLean's two seasons as an assistant with the Ducks. In his last eight seasons as an assistant coach, MacLean was part of a team that has reached the Stanley Cup Final on three occasions.

Before joining the Anaheim coaching staff in 2002, MacLean, who was born in Grostenquin, France, but grew up in Antigonish, Nova Scotia, was head coach of the Quad City Mallards of the United Hockey League (UHL) from 2000 to 2002. MacLean led the Mallards to a two-season record of 112-27-9 (.787) and the 2001 Colonial Cup championship. MacLean was the head coach of the International Hockey League's Kansas City Blades from 1997 to 2000. He spent one season as an assistant coach with the Phoenix Coyotes in 1996-97 and was head coach at Peoria (IHL) from 1993 to 1996. While with Peoria, MacLean was named The Hockey News Minor League Coach of the Year in 1994 after leading the Rivermen to a 51-24-6 mark and a division title. He was also a scout with the St. Louis Blues for two seasons from 1991 to 1993.

MacLean spent 11 seasons in the National Hockey League as a forward with St. Louis, Winnipeg and Detroit from 1980-81 to 1990-91. He played in 719 NHL regular-season games, scoring 324 goals and adding 349 assists for 673 points. He recorded eight seasons of 30 or more goals. He also appeared in 53 playoff games, scoring 21 goals and 35 points. MacLean set career highs in goals (41) and points (101) during the 1984-85 season with Winnipeg and was named to the Campbell Conference All-Star Team. MacLean also represented Canada internationally at the 1980 Winter Olympics, held in Lake Placid, New York.

Coaching Record

			Regular Season				Playoffs			
Season	Team	League	GC	W	L	O/T	GC	W	L	T
1993-94	Peoria	IHL	81	51	24	6	6	2	4	....
1994-95	Peoria	IHL	81	51	19	11	9	4	5	....
1995-96	Peoria	IHL	82	39	38	5	12	6	6	....
1997-98	Kansas City	IHL	82	41	29	12	11	6	5	....
1998-99	Kansas City	IHL	82	44	31	7	3	1	2	....
99-2000	Kansas City	IHL	82	36	37	9	....	....	....	....
2000-01	Quad City	UHL	74	55	12	7	12	10	2	....
2001-02	Quad City	UHL	74	57	15	2	12	6	6	....
2011-12	**Ottawa**	**NHL**	**82**	**41**	**31**	**10**	**7**	**3**	**4**	....
2012-13	**Ottawa**	**NHL**	**48**	**25**	**17**	**6**	**10**	**5**	**5**	....
	NHL Totals		**130**	**66**	**48**	**16**	**17**	**8**	**9**	....

Jack Adams Award (2013)

2012-13 Scoring

* – rookie

Regular Season

Pos	#	Player	Team	GP	G	A	Pts	TOI	+/-	PIM	PP	SH	GW	S	%
C	7	Kyle Turris	OTT	48	12	17	29	19:38	6	24	3	0	2	118	10.2
C	89	* Cory Conacher	T.B.	35	9	15	24	14:21	-3	16	1	0	2	53	17.0
			OTT	12	2	3	5	12:50	6	4	0	0	1	14	14.3
			Total	47	11	18	29	13:58	3	20	1	0	3	67	16.4
D	55	Sergei Gonchar	OTT	45	3	24	27	23:59	4	26	2	0	3	85	3.5
R	11	Daniel Alfredsson	OTT	47	10	16	26	19:20	1	33	3	0	2	101	9.9
C	93	* Mika Zibanejad	OTT	42	7	13	20	13:33	9	6	3	0	0	90	7.8
R	33	* Jakob Silfverberg	OTT	48	10	9	19	16:13	9	12	2	1	2	134	7.5
C	14	Colin Greening	OTT	47	8	11	19	14:43	5	11	2	0	2	80	10.0
D	46	* Patrick Wiercioch	OTT	42	5	14	19	15:41	9	39	3	0	0	81	6.2
C	15	Zack Smith	OTT	48	4	11	15	15:08	-9	56	0	0	0	94	4.3
D	65	Erik Karlsson	OTT	17	6	8	14	27:09	8	8	2	1	2	79	7.6
D	4	Chris Phillips	OTT	48	5	9	14	21:02	-5	43	1	0	0	89	5.6
L	9	Milan Michalek	OTT	23	4	10	14	18:11	8	17	0	0	0	58	6.9
R	25	Chris Neil	OTT	48	4	8	12	13:51	0	144	0	0	3	87	4.6
R	22	Erik Condra	OTT	48	4	8	12	13:10	3	34	0	0	0	73	5.5
D	3	Marc Methot	OTT	47	2	9	11	22:13	2	31	0	0	0	53	3.8
L	73	Guillaume Latendresse	OTT	27	6	4	10	14:48	-2	8	1	0	0	53	11.3
D	61	Andre Benoit	OTT	33	3	7	10	16:25	-3	8	1	0	2	50	6.0
C	18	Jim O'Brien	OTT	29	5	1	6	11:25	-2	8	1	0	0	38	13.2
D	62	* Eric Gryba	OTT	33	2	4	6	20:16	-3	26	0	0	0	51	3.9
C	19	Jason Spezza	OTT	5	2	3	5	19:10	3	2	1	0	0	12	16.7
C	44	* Jean-Gabriel Pageau	OTT	9	2	2	4	11:29	3	0	0	0	2	14	14.3
C	13	Peter Regin	OTT	27	0	3	3	11:31	-4	8	0	0	0	37	0.0
L	59	* Dave Dziurzynski	OTT	12	2	0	2	12:32	-1	13	0	0	0	20	10.0
C	24	* Stephane Da Costa	OTT	9	1	1	2	11:51	-3	0	0	0	0	15	6.7
D	2	Jared Cowen	OTT	7	1	0	1	20:17	1	10	0	0	0	8	12.5
L	28	* Matt Kassian	OTT	15	1	0	1	6:22	0	47	0	0	0	6	16.7
D	10	Mike Lundin	OTT	11	0	1	1	15:30	-2	0	0	0	0	13	0.0
C	68	* Mike Hoffman	OTT	3	0	0	0	12:19	-1	2	0	0	0	6	0.0
R	16	* Mark Stone	OTT	4	0	0	0	10:00	-1	2	0	0	0	3	0.0
C	57	* Derek Grant	OTT	5	0	0	0	8:39	-1	0	0	0	0	5	0.0
D	74	* Mark Borowiecki	OTT	6	0	0	0	12:59	1	18	0	0	0	1	0.0

Goaltending

No.	Goaltender	GPI	Mins	Avg	W	L	OT	EN	SO	GA	SA	S%	G	A	PIM
41	Craig Anderson	24	1421	1.69	12	9	2	1	3	40	677	.941	0	0	0
40	* Robin Lehner	12	735	2.20	5	3	4	0	0	27	424	.936	0	0	0
30	Ben Bishop	13	758	2.45	8	5	0	1	1	31	399	.922	0	0	0
	Totals	**48**	**2931**	**2.05**	**25**	**17**	**6**	**2**	**4**	**100**	**1502**	**.933**			

Playoffs

Pos	#	Player	Team	GP	G	A	Pts	TOI	+/-	PIM	PP	SH	GW	OT	S	%
R	11	Daniel Alfredsson	OTT	10	4	6	10	19:09	5	6	3	1	0	0	27	14.8
C	7	Kyle Turris	OTT	10	6	3	9	19:57	2	13	1	1	1	1	29	20.7
D	65	Erik Karlsson	OTT	10	1	7	8	26:44	0	6	0	0	0	0	28	3.6
R	22	Erik Condra	OTT	10	1	6	7	13:36	-1	2	1	0	0	0	14	7.1
C	44	* Jean-Gabriel Pageau	OTT	10	4	2	6	12:52	4	8	1	0	1	0	21	19.0
D	55	Sergei Gonchar	OTT	10	0	6	6	23:55	-3	14	0	0	0	0	16	0.0
L	9	Milan Michalek	OTT	10	3	2	5	17:50	3	2	0	1	0	0	29	10.3
D	3	Marc Methot	OTT	10	1	4	5	22:44	1	6	0	0	1	0	18	5.6
C	14	Colin Greening	OTT	10	3	1	4	15:56	-1	2	0	0	1	1	21	14.3
R	33	* Jakob Silfverberg	OTT	10	2	2	4	16:39	-1	2	1	0	0	0	22	9.1
C	93	* Mika Zibanejad	OTT	10	1	3	4	13:35	-3	0	0	0	0	0	21	4.8
R	25	Chris Neil	OTT	10	0	4	4	12:41	0	39	0	0	0	0	10	0.0
C	89	* Cory Conacher	OTT	8	3	0	3	11:57	-2	31	1	0	1	0	9	33.3
D	61	Andre Benoit	OTT	5	0	3	3	15:27	4	0	0	0	0	0	9	0.0
D	2	Jared Cowen	OTT	10	0	3	3	18:33	-6	21	0	0	0	0	8	0.0
L	73	Guillaume Latendresse	OTT	3	1	1	2	13:55	1	6	0	0	0	0	5	20.0
C	15	Zack Smith	OTT	10	1	1	2	13:17	-2	31	0	0	0	0	9	11.1
L	28	* Matt Kassian	OTT	5	0	2	2	8:50	1	17	0	0	0	0	5	0.0
C	19	Jason Spezza	OTT	3	0	1	1	18:26	-1	0	0	0	0	0	6	0.0
D	4	Chris Phillips	OTT	10	0	1	1	21:08	6	21	0	0	0	0	12	0.0
D	46	* Patrick Wiercioch	OTT	1	0	0	0	1:47	0	0	0	0	0	0	1	0.0
R	16	* Mark Stone	OTT	1	0	0	0	11:23	0	0	0	0	0	0	2	0.0
D	62	* Eric Gryba	OTT	4	0	0	0	12:11	0	17	0	0	0	0	2	0.0

Goaltending

No.	Goaltender	GPI	Mins	Avg	W	L	EN	SO	GA	SA	S%	G	A	PIM
40	* Robin Lehner	2	49	2.45	0	1	0	0	2	25	.920	0	0	0
41	Craig Anderson	10	578	3.01	5	4	0	0	29	352	.918	0	0	0
	Totals	**10**	**630**	**2.95**	**5**	**5**	**0**	**0**	**31**	**377**	**.918**			

Coaching History

Rick Bowness, 1992-93 to 1994-95; Rick Bowness, Dave Allison and Jacques Martin, 1995-96; Jacques Martin, 1996-97 to 2000-01; Jacques Martin and Roger Neilson, 2001-02; Jacques Martin, 2002-03, 2003-04; Bryan Murray, 2004-05 to 2006-07; John Paddock and Bryan Murray, 2007-08; Craig Hartsburg and Cory Clouston, 2008-09; Cory Clouston, 2009-10, 2010-11; Paul MacLean, 2011-12 to date.

Club Records

Team

(Figures in brackets for season records are games played; records for fewest points, wins, ties, losses, goals, goals against are for 70 or more games)

Most Points	113	2002-03 (82), 2005-06 (82)
Most Wins	52	2002-03 (82), 2005-06 (82)
Most Ties	15	1996-97 (82), 1997-98 (82), 1998-99 (82)
Most Losses	70	1992-93 (84)
Most Goals	312	2005-06 (82)
Most Goals Against	397	1993-94 (84)
Fewest Points	24	1992-93 (84)
Fewest Wins	10	1992-93 (84)
Fewest Ties	4	1992-93 (84)
Fewest Losses	21	2000-01 (82), 2002-03 (82), 2005-06 (82)
Fewest Goals	191	1995-96 (82)
Fewest Goals Against	179	1998-99 (82)
Longest Winning Streak		
Overall	11	Jan. 14-Feb. 4/10
Home	9	Mar. 5-Apr. 7/09
Away	6	Mar. 18-Apr. 5/03, Jan. 14-Feb. 3/10
Longest Undefeated Streak		
Overall	11	Four times
Home	12	Dec. 18/03-Jan. 24/04 (10W, 2T/OL)
Away	7	Three times
Longest Losing Streak		
Overall	14	Mar. 2-Apr. 7/93
Home	11	Oct. 27-Dec. 8/93
Away	*38	Oct. 10/92-Apr. 3/93**
Longest Winless Streak		
Overall	21	Oct. 10-Nov. 23/92 (20L, 1T)
Home	*17	Oct. 28/95-Jan. 27/96 (15L, 2T)
Away	*38	Oct. 10/92-Apr. 3/93 (38L)
Most Shutouts, Season	10	2001-02 (82)
Most PIM, Season	1,716	1992-93 (84)
Most Goals, Game	11	Nov. 13/01 (Ott. 11 at Wsh. 5)

** NHL records do not include neutral site games

Individual

Most Seasons	17	Daniel Alfredsson
Most Games, Career	1,178	Daniel Alfredsson
Most Goals, Career	426	Daniel Alfredsson
Most Assists, Career	682	Daniel Alfredsson
Most Points, Career	1,108	Daniel Alfredsson (426G, 682A)
Most PIM, Career	2,005	Chris Neil
Most Shutouts, Career	30	Patrick Lalime
Longest Consecutive Games Streak	292	Alexei Yashin (Dec. 31/95-Apr. 17/99)
Most Goals, Season	50	Dany Heatley (2005-06), (2006-07)
Most Assists, Season	71	Jason Spezza (2005-06)
Most Points, Season	105	Dany Heatley (2006-07; 50G, 55A)
Most PIM, Season	318	Mike Peluso (1992-93)
Most Points, Defenseman, Season	78	Erik Karlsson (2011-12; 19G, 59A)
Most Points, Center, Season	94	Alexei Yashin (1998-99; 44G, 50A)
Most Points, Right Wing, Season	103	Daniel Alfredsson (2005-06; 43G, 60A)
Most Points, Left Wing, Season	105	Dany Heatley (2006-07; 50G, 55A)
Most Points, Rookie, Season	79	Alexei Yashin (1993-94; 30G, 49A)
Most Shutouts, Season	8	Patrick Lalime (2002-03)
Most Goals, Game	4	Marian Hossa (Jan. 2/03), Dany Heatley (Oct. 29/05), Daniel Alfredsson (Nov. 2/05), Martin Havlat (Nov. 2/05), Alex Kovalev (Jan. 3/10)
Most Assists, Game	5	Marian Hossa (Jan. 4/01)
Most Points, Game	7	Daniel Alfredsson (Jan. 24/08; 3G, 4A)

* NHL Record.

General Managers' History

Mel Bridgman, 1992-93; Randy Sexton, 1993-94, 1994-95; Randy Sexton and Pierre Gauthier, 1995-96; Pierre Gauthier, 1996-97, 1997-98; Rick Dudley, 1998-99; Marshall Johnston, 1999-2000 to 2001-02; John Muckler, 2002-03 to 2006-07; Bryan Murray, 2007-08 to date.

Captains' History

Laurie Boschman, 1992-93; Brad Shaw, Mark Lamb and Gord Dineen, 1993-94; Randy Cunneyworth, 1994-95 to 1997-98; Alexei Yashin, 1998-99; Daniel Alfredsson, 1999-2000 to 2012-13.

Retired Numbers

8	Frank Finnigan	1924-1934

All-time Record vs. Other Clubs

Regular Season

	Total								At Home								On Road							
	GP	W	L	T	OL	GF	GA	PTS	GP	W	L	T	OL	GF	GA	PTS	GP	W	L	T	OL	GF	GA	PTS
Anaheim	23	8	10	3	2	55	58	21	11	4	4	1	2	31	29	11	12	4	6	2	0	24	29	10
Boston	117	40	63	8	6	289	372	94	57	21	30	3	3	135	173	48	60	19	33	5	3	154	199	46
Buffalo	116	49	45	10	12	304	330	120	59	26	18	7	8	162	153	67	57	23	27	3	4	142	177	53
Calgary	31	12	13	4	2	73	93	30	15	7	4	3	1	39	39	18	16	5	9	1	1	34	54	12
Carolina	87	34	41	8	4	229	238	80	45	22	16	4	3	130	115	51	42	12	25	4	1	99	123	29
Chicago	24	7	11	2	4	62	64	20	13	5	6	0	2	39	37	12	11	2	5	2	2	23	27	8
Colorado	39	11	22	4	2	112	158	28	21	8	10	3	0	58	77	19	18	3	12	1	2	54	81	9
Columbus	11	5	2	2	2	34	31	14	6	4	0	1	1	20	13	10	5	1	2	1	1	14	18	4
Dallas	26	10	16	0	0	66	86	20	12	5	7	0	0	28	32	10	14	5	9	0	0	38	54	10
Detroit	25	8	14	1	2	64	85	19	13	4	7	1	1	38	41	10	12	4	7	0	1	26	44	9
Edmonton	31	13	13	4	1	82	92	31	15	6	6	2	1	35	42	15	16	7	7	2	0	47	50	16
Florida	75	44	26	3	2	241	203	93	37	21	12	2	2	117	93	46	38	23	14	1	0	124	110	47
Los Angeles	25	7	15	2	1	63	90	17	12	6	4	1	1	38	32	14	13	1	11	1	0	25	58	3
Minnesota	11	8	2	1	0	39	26	17	5	4	1	0	0	17	11	8	6	4	1	1	0	22	15	9
Montreal	116	54	52	5	5	335	333	118	57	31	23	1	2	172	158	65	59	23	29	4	3	163	175	53
Nashville	15	9	5	0	1	44	37	19	8	5	2	0	1	29	22	11	7	4	3	0	0	15	15	8
New Jersey	78	27	38	5	8	180	203	67	39	14	19	3	3	90	94	34	39	13	19	2	5	90	109	33
NY Islanders	78	47	16	11	4	280	212	109	38	24	7	5	2	129	91	55	40	23	9	6	2	151	121	54
NY Rangers	77	41	31	3	2	221	204	87	39	17	18	3	1	107	100	38	38	24	13	0	1	114	104	49
Philadelphia	78	33	36	8	1	226	242	75	39	19	14	6	0	121	112	44	39	14	22	2	1	105	130	31
Phoenix	27	13	12	2	0	93	83	28	14	7	6	1	0	47	41	15	13	6	6	1	0	46	42	13
Pittsburgh	85	31	39	9	6	247	284	77	43	16	18	5	4	129	140	41	42	15	21	4	2	118	144	36
St. Louis	25	11	12	2	0	64	78	24	13	6	7	0	0	30	43	12	12	5	5	2	0	34	35	12
San Jose	24	9	10	4	1	61	61	23	12	4	4	4	0	37	34	12	12	5	6	0	1	24	27	11
Tampa Bay	77	48	24	2	3	277	195	101	38	27	11	0	0	139	81	54	39	21	13	2	3	138	114	47
Toronto	95	49	38	3	5	270	265	106	47	26	16	1	4	133	131	57	48	23	22	2	1	137	134	49
Vancouver	31	11	15	2	3	65	92	27	15	6	7	1	1	33	42	14	16	5	8	1	2	32	50	13
Washington	78	36	33	5	4	245	244	81	39	23	14	1	1	139	112	48	39	13	19	4	3	106	132	33
Winnipeg	51	29	14	2	6	196	154	66	26	15	6	1	4	101	66	35	25	14	8	1	2	95	88	31
Totals	**1576**	**704**	**668**	**115**	**89**	**4517**	**4613**	**1612**	**788**	**383**	**297**	**60**	**48**	**2323**	**2154**	**874**	**788**	**321**	**371**	**55**	**41**	**2194**	**2459**	**738**

Playoffs

	Series	W	L	GP	W	L	T	GF	GA	Last Mtg.	Rnd.	Result
Anaheim	1	0	1	5	1	4	0	11	16	2007	F	L 1-4
Buffalo	4	1	3	21	8	13	0	47	52	2007	CF	W 4-1
Montreal	1	1	0	5	4	1	0	20	9	2013	CQF	W 4-1
New Jersey	3	2	1	18	11	7	0	41	40	2007	CSF	W 4-1
NY Islanders	1	1	0	5	4	1	0	13	7	2003	CQF	W 4-1
NY Rangers	1	0	1	7	3	4	0	13	14	2012	CQF	L 3-4
Philadelphia	2	2	0	11	8	3	0	28	12	2003	CSF	W 4-2
Pittsburgh	4	1	3	20	7	13	0	53	72	2013	CSF	L 1-4
Tampa Bay	1	1	0	5	4	1	0	23	13	2006	CQF	W 4-1
Toronto	4	0	4	24	8	16	0	42	57	2004	CQF	L 3-4
Washington	1	0	1	5	1	4	0	7	18	1998	CSF	L 1-4
Totals	**23**	**9**	**14**	**126**	**59**	**67**	**0**	**298**	**310**			

Playoff Results 2013-2009

Year	Round	Opponent	Result	GF	GA
2013	CSF	Pittsburgh	L 1-4	11	22
	CQF	Montreal	W 4-1	20	9
2012	CQF	NY Rangers	L 3-4	13	14
2010	CQF	Pittsburgh	L 2-4	19	24

Abbreviations: Round: F – Final; **CF** – conference final; **CSF** – conference semi-final; **CQF** – conference quarter-final.

Colorado totals include Quebec, 1992-93 to 1994-95.
Dallas totals include Minnesota North Stars, 1992-93.
Winnipeg totals include Atlanta Thrashers, 1999-2000 to 2010-11.
Carolina totals include Hartford, 1992-93 to 1996-97.
Phoenix totals include Winnipeg, 1992-93 to 1995-96.

2012-13 Results

Jan.	19	at Winnipeg	4-1
	21	Florida	4-0
	24	at Florida	3-1
	25	at Tampa Bay	4-6
	27	Pittsburgh	1-2†
	29	Washington	3-2
	30	Montreal	5-1
Feb.	1	at Carolina	0-1
	3	at Montreal	1-2
	5	Buffalo	4-3
	7	Carolina	2-3*
	9	Winnipeg	0-1
	12	Buffalo	2-0
	13	at Pittsburgh	2-4
	16	at Toronto	0-3
	18	at New Jersey	2-1†
	19	NY Islanders	3-1
	21	NY Rangers	3-2†
	23	Toronto	3-2
	25	Montreal	2-1†
	28	at Boston	1-2*
Mar.	2	at Philadelphia	1-2
	3	at NY Islanders	2-3†
	6	at Toronto	4-5
	8	at NY Rangers	3-2
	11	Boston	2-3†
	13	at Montreal	3-4†
	16	at Buffalo	4-3*
	17	Winnipeg	4-1
	19	at NY Islanders	5-3
	21	Boston	1-2
	23	Tampa Bay	5-3
	25	New Jersey	3-2†
	28	NY Rangers	3-0
	30	Toronto	0-4
Apr.	2	at Boston	2-3
	5	at Buffalo	2-4
	7	at Florida	1-2
	9	at Tampa Bay	2-3
	11	at Philadelphia	3-1
	12	at New Jersey	2-0
	16	Carolina	3-2
	18	Washington	3-1
	20	Toronto	1-4
	22	Pittsburgh	1-3
	25	at Washington	2-1*
	27	Philadelphia	1-2
	28	at Boston	4-2

* – Overtime † – Shootout

Entry Draft Selections 2013-1999

Name in bold denotes played in NHL.

2013
Pick
- 17 Curtis Lazar
- 78 Marcus Hogberg
- 102 Tobias Lindberg
- 108 Ben Harpur
- 138 Vincent Dunn
- 161 Chris Leblanc
- 168 Quentin Shore

2012
Pick
- 15 Cody Ceci
- 76 Chris Driedger
- 82 Jarrod Maidens
- 106 Timothy Boyle
- 136 Robert Baillargeon
- 166 Francois Brassard
- 196 Mikael Wikstrand

2011
Pick
- 6 **Mika Zibanejad**
- 21 Stefan Noesen
- 24 Matt Puempel
- 61 Shane Prince
- 96 **Jean-Gabriel Pageau**
- 126 Fredrik Claesson
- 156 Darren Kramer
- 171 Max McCormick
- 186 Jordan Fransoo
- 204 Ryan Dzingel

2010
Pick
- 76 Jakub Culek
- 106 Marcus Sorensen
- 178 **Mark Stone**
- 196 Bryce Aneloski

2009
Pick
- 9 **Jared Cowen**
- 39 **Jakob Silfverberg**
- 46 **Robin Lehner**
- 100 Chris Wideman
- 130 **Mike Hoffman**
- 146 Jeff Costello
- 160 Corey Cowick
- 190 Brad Peltz
- 191 Michael Sdao

2008
Pick
- 15 **Erik Karlsson**
- 42 **Patrick Wiercioch**
- 79 **Zack Smith**
- 109 **Andre Petersson**
- 119 **Derek Grant**
- 139 **Mark Borowiecki**
- 199 Emil Sandin

2007
Pick
- 29 **Jim O'Brien**
- 60 Ruslan Bashkirov
- 90 Louie Caporusso
- 120 Ben Blood

2006
Pick
- 28 **Nick Foligno**
- 68 **Eric Gryba**
- 91 **Kaspars Daugavins**
- 121 Pierre-Luc Lessard
- 151 Ryan Daniels
- 181 Kevin Koopman
- 211 **Erik Condra**

2005
Pick
- 9 **Brian Lee**
- 70 Vitali Anikeyenko
- 95 **Cody Bass**
- 98 **Ilya Zubov**
- 115 Janne Kolehmainen
- 136 Tomas Kudelka
- 186 Dmitri Megalinsky
- 204 **Colin Greening**

2004
Pick
- 23 **Andrej Meszaros**
- 58 Kirill Lyamin
- 77 Shawn Weller
- 87 **Peter Regin**
- 89 Jeff Glass
- 122 **Alexander Nikulin**
- 141 Jim McKenzie
- 156 **Roman Wick**
- 219 Joe Cooper
- 251 Matthew McIlvane
- 284 John Wikner

2003
Pick
- 29 **Patrick Eaves**
- 67 Igor Mirnov
- 100 Philippe Seydoux
- 135 Mattias Karlsson
- 142 Tim Cook
- 166 Sergei Gimayev
- 228 Will Colbert
- 260 Ossi Louhivaara
- 291 **Brian Elliott**

2002
Pick
- 16 **Jakub Klepis**
- 47 **Alexei Kaigorodov**
- 75 Arttu Luttinen
- 113 Scott Dobben
- 125 Johan Bjork
- 150 Brock Hooton
- 246 Josef Vavra
- 276 Vitali Atyushov

2001
Pick
- 2 **Jason Spezza**
- 23 **Tim Gleason**
- 81 Neil Komadoski
- 99 **Ray Emery**
- 127 **Christoph Schubert**
- 162 Stefan Schauer
- 193 **Brooks Laich**
- 218 Jan Platil
- 223 **Brandon Bochenski**
- 235 Neil Petruic
- 256 Gregg Johnson
- 286 **Toni Dahlman**

2000
Pick
- 21 **Anton Volchenkov**
- 45 **Mathieu Chouinard**
- 55 **Antoine Vermette**
- 87 Jan Bohac
- 122 Derrick Byfuglien
- 156 **Greg Zanon**
- 157 Grant Potulny
- 158 Sean Connolly
- 188 Jason Maleyko
- 283 James Demone

1999
Pick
- 26 **Martin Havlat**
- 48 **Simon Lajeunesse**
- 62 Teemu Sainomaa
- 94 **Chris Kelly**
- 154 Andrew Ianiero
- 164 **Martin Prusek**
- 201 Mikko Ruutu
- 209 **Layne Ulmer**
- 213 **Alexandre Giroux**
- 269 Konstantin Gorovikov

Bryan Murray

Executive Vice President and General Manager

Born: Shawville, Que., December 5, 1942.

On June 18, 2007, Bryan Murray was appointed as the seventh general manager of the Ottawa Senators. Murray had joined the organization on June 8, 2004, when he was named the club's head coach. Murray resigned as senior vice president and general manager of Anaheim to take the coaching position in Ottawa. As coach in Ottawa in 2006–07, Murray led the Senators to the Stanley Cup Final for the first time in franchise history, only to lose to his former Anaheim team. He also has previous front office experience as vice president and general manager of the Florida Panthers from 1994 to 2001, assembling a team that reached the Stanley Cup Final in just its third year of existence in 1996.

Murray, who was back behind the bench in Ottawa briefly in 2007-08, began his NHL career as head coach of the Washington Capials in 1981. He has served 16+ years behind the bench, coaching more than 1,300 regular-season and playoff games, including 672 wins. He earned the Jack Adams Award as coach of the year in 1983-84. Murray's regular-season coaching record in Ottawa is 107-55-20 and includes winning the 2007 Prince of Wales Trophy as the NHL's Eastern Conference champions.

Coaching Record

			Regular Season				Playoffs			
Season	Team	League	GC	W	L	O/T	GC	W	L	T
1981-82	Washington	NHL	66	25	28	13	....	....	....	....
1982-83	Washington	NHL	80	39	25	16	4	1	3	....
1983-84	Washington	NHL	80	48	27	5	8	4	4	....
1984-85	Washington	NHL	80	46	25	9	5	2	3	....
1985-86	Washington	NHL	80	50	23	7	9	5	4	....
1986-87	Washington	NHL	80	38	32	10	7	3	4	....
1987-88	Washington	NHL	80	38	33	9	14	7	7	....
1988-89	Washington	NHL	80	41	29	10	6	2	4	....
1989-90	Washington	NHL	46	18	24	4	....	....	....	....
1990-91	Detroit	NHL	80	34	38	8	7	3	4	....
1991-92	Detroit	NHL	80	43	25	12	11	4	7	....
1992-93	Detroit	NHL	84	47	28	9	7	3	4	....
1997-98	Florida	NHL	59	17	31	11	....	....	....	....
2001-02	Anaheim	NHL	82	29	42	11	....	....	....	....
2004-05	Ottawa				SEASON CANCELLED					
2005-06	Ottawa	NHL	82	52	21	9	10	5	5	....
2006-07	Ottawa	NHL	82	48	25	9	20	13	7	....
2007-08	Ottawa	NHL	18	7	9	2	4	0	4	....
	NHL Totals		**1239**	**620**	**465**	**154**	**112**	**52**	**60**	....

Jack Adams Award (1984)

Club Directory

Canadian Tire Centre

Ottawa Senators
Canadian Tire Centre
1000 Palladium Drive
Ottawa, Ontario
K2V 1A5
Phone **613/599-0250**
FAX 613/599-5562
www.ottawasenators.com
Capacity: 19,153

Executive

Owner, Governor and Chairman	Eugene Melnyk
President and Alternate Governor	Cyril Leeder
Exec. V.P., CFO and Alternate Governor	Erin Crowe
Exec. V.P., G.M. and Alternate Governor	Bryan Murray
V.P. and Executive Director, Canadian Tire Centre	Tom Conroy
Exec. Assistant to the President	Kathy Downs
Exec. Assistant to the Exec. V.P. and CFO	Colette Hiscott

Hockey Operations

Assistant General Manager	Tim Murray
Director of Player Personnel	Pierre Dorion
Director of Hockey Operations and Player Development	Randy Lee
Manager of Hockey Administration	Allison Vaughan
Head Coach	Paul MacLean
Assistant Coaches	Dave Cameron, Mark Reeds, Rick Wamsley
Video Coach	Tim Pattyson
Scouting and Development Consultant	Jason Smith
Conditioning Coach	Chris Schwarz
Manager, Team Services	Jordan Silmser
Head Athletic Therapist	Gerry Townend
Assistant Athletic Therapist	Domenic Nicoletta
Equipment Manager	Scott Allegrino
Assistant Equipment Manager	John Gervais
Massage Therapist	Shawn Markwick

Scouts

Scouts	Vaclav Burda, George Fargher, Bob Janecyk, Bob Lowes, Bill McCarthy, Trent Mann, Lew Mongelluzzo, Greg Royce, Mikko Ruutu
Pro Scouts	Jim Clark, Rob Murphy, Nick Polano

Communications

Director, Communications	Brian Morris
Manager, Communications	Chris Moore
Coordinator, Communications	Amanda Nigh
Content Producer/Editor	Chris Lund
Translator	Eric Tremblay

Broadcasting

Vice-President, Broadcast	Jim Steel
Video Producer	Christopher Skinner

Legal

Senior Legal Council	Richard Stacey

Corporate & Ticket Sales and Service

Sr. V.P., Corporate & Ticketing Sales	Mark Bonneau
Exec. Ass't. to Sr. V.P., Corp. & Ticketing	Brooke Brown
Director, Corporate Partnerships	Bill Courchaine
Senior Exec. Assistant, Corporate Partnerships	Cheryl Blake
Sr. Corporate Account Managers	Steve Chestnut, Jimi Duff, Michael Lummack
Director, Business Development	Gina Gianetto
Director, Sales	Jim Orban
Manager, Sales	Chris Atack
Manager, Group Sales	Devon Hogan
Director, Premium Services	Christine Clancy
Manager, Premium Client Services	Tracey Bonner
Manager, Corporate Services	Kristin Wood

Finance

Controller	Derek Winch

Information Technology

Director, IT	Darren Just
IT Architect	Don Morin

Marketing

Vice-President, Marketing	Jeff Kyle
Exec. Assistant to the VP, Marketing	Deborah Wilson
Director, Merchandise Operations	Kevin Lawton
Director, Game Entertainment	Glen Gower
Director, Fan and Community Development	Aaron Robinson
Art Director	Edtmun Jasvins
Director, Promotions & Marketing Services	Lisa Strangway
Director, Marketing	Isabelle Perreault-Lachapelle
Director, Advertising & Promotions	Michael Wallace

Operations and Events

Assistant to the V.P. & Executive Director	Linda Julian
Director, Engineering & Operations	Ed Healy
Manager, Canadian Tire Centre Marketing	Krista Galbraith
Manager, engineering	Konstantinos Capordelis
Manager, Guest Services & Fan Loyalty	Erin Moretto
Manager, Operations & Production	Tim Swords
Manager, event planning	Karen Speers

People Department

Director, People Department	Sandi Horner

Sens Foundation

President	Danielle Robinson

Miscellaneous

Radio	Team 1200 (English), 94,5 FM (French)
Television	Rogers Sportsnet, TVA and RDS
Team Photographer	Freestyle Photography (Andre Ringuette)
Anthem singer	Lyndon Slewidge
Mascot	Spartacat

Philadelphia Flyers

Key Off-Season Signings/Acquisitions

2013

- **June 12** • Acquired D **Mark Streit** from NY Islanders for a 4th-round pick in the 2014 NHL Draft and RW **Shane Harper**.
- **July 4** • Re-signed C **Adam Hall**.
- **5** • Signed G **Ray Emery** and G **Yann Danis**.
- **5** • Re-signed C **Claude Giroux**.
- **6** • Signed C **Vincent Lecavalier**.
- **9** • Re-signed D **Erik Gustafsson**.
- **10** • Re-signed D **Oliver Lauridsen**.
- **20** • Re-signed C **Sean Couturier**.

2012-13 Results: 23W-22L-1OTL-2SOL 49PTS
4TH, Atlantic Division • 10TH, Eastern Conference

Year-by-Year Record

		Home				Road				Overall									
Season	GP	W	L	T	OL	W	L	T	OL	W	L	T	OL	GF	GA	Pts.	Div. Fin.	Conf. Fin.	Playoff Result
2012-13	48	15	7	....	2	8	15	....	1	23	22	....	3	133	141	49	4th, Atl.	10th, East	Out of Playoffs
2011-12	82	22	13	....	6	25	13	....	3	47	26	....	9	264	232	103	3rd, Atl.	5th, East	Lost Conf. Semi-Final
2010-11	82	22	12	....	7	25	11	....	5	47	23	....	12	259	223	106	1st, Atl.	2nd, East	Lost Conf. Semi-Final
2009-10	82	24	14	....	3	17	21	....	3	41	35	....	6	236	225	88	3rd, Atl.	7th, East	Lost Final
2008-09	82	24	13	....	4	20	14	....	7	44	27	....	11	264	238	99	3rd, Atl.	5th, East	Lost Conf. Quarter-Final
2007-08	82	21	14	....	6	21	15	....	5	42	29	....	11	248	233	95	4th, Atl.	6th, East	Lost Conf. Final
2006-07	82	10	24	....	7	12	24	....	5	22	48	....	12	214	303	56	5th, Atl.	15th, East	Out of Playoffs
2005-06	82	22	13	....	6	23	13	....	5	45	26	....	11	267	259	101	2nd, Atl.	5th, East	Lost Conf. Quarter-Final
2004-05	....	....	....	....	....	....	....	....	....	....	....	....	....	....	....	....			
2003-04	82	24	11	3	3	16	10	12	3	40	21	15	6	229	186	101	1st, Atl.	3rd, East	Lost Conf. Final
2002-03	82	21	10	8	2	24	10	5	2	45	20	13	4	211	166	107	2nd, Atl.	4th, East	Lost Conf. Semi-Final
2001-02	82	20	13	5	3	22	14	5	0	42	27	10	3	234	192	97	1st, Atl.	2nd, East	Lost Conf. Quarter-Final
2000-01	82	26	11	4	0	17	14	7	3	43	25	11	3	240	207	100	2nd, Atl.	4th, East	Lost Conf. Quarter-Final
1999-2000	82	25	6	7	3	20	16	5	0	45	22	12	3	237	179	105	1st, Atl.	1st, East	Lost Conf. Final
1998-99	82	21	9	11	....	16	17	8	....	37	26	19	....	231	196	93	2nd, Atl.	5th, East	Lost Conf. Quarter-Final
1997-98	82	24	11	6	....	18	18	5	....	42	29	11	....	242	193	95	2nd, Atl.	3rd, East	Lost Conf. Quarter-Final
1996-97	82	23	12	6	....	22	12	7	....	45	24	13	....	274	217	103	2nd, Atl.	2nd, East	Lost Final
1995-96	82	27	9	5	....	18	15	8	....	45	24	13	....	282	208	103	1st, Atl.	1st, East	Lost Conf. Semi-Final
1994-95	48	16	7	1	....	12	9	3	....	28	16	4	....	150	132	60	1st, Atl.	3rd, East	Lost Conf. Final
1993-94	84	19	20	3	....	16	19	7	....	35	39	10	....	294	314	80	6th, Atl.	10th, East	Out of Playoffs
1992-93	84	23	14	5	....	13	23	6	....	36	37	11	....	319	319	83	5th, Patrick		Out of Playoffs
1991-92	80	22	11	7	....	10	26	4	....	32	37	11	....	252	273	75	6th, Patrick		Out of Playoffs
1990-91	80	18	16	6	....	15	21	4	....	33	37	10	....	252	267	76	5th, Patrick		Out of Playoffs
1989-90	80	17	19	4	....	13	20	7	....	30	39	11	....	290	297	71	6th, Patrick		Out of Playoffs
1988-89	80	22	15	3	....	14	21	5	....	36	36	8	....	307	285	80	4th, Patrick		Lost Conf. Final
1987-88	80	20	14	6	....	18	19	3	....	38	33	9	....	292	292	85	3rd, Patrick		Lost Div. Semi-Final
1986-87	80	29	9	2	....	17	17	6	....	46	26	8	....	310	245	100	1st, Patrick		Lost Final
1985-86	80	33	6	1	....	20	17	3	....	53	23	4	....	335	241	110	1st, Patrick		Lost Div. Semi-Final
1984-85	80	32	4	4	....	21	16	3	....	53	20	7	....	348	241	113	1st, Patrick		Lost Final
1983-84	80	25	10	5	....	19	16	5	....	44	26	10	....	350	290	98	3rd, Patrick		Lost Div. Semi-Final
1982-83	80	29	8	3	....	20	15	5	....	49	23	8	....	326	240	106	1st, Patrick		Lost Div. Semi-Final
1981-82	80	25	10	5	....	13	21	6	....	38	31	11	....	325	313	87	3rd. Patrick		Lost Div. Semi-Final
1980-81	80	23	9	8	....	18	15	7	....	41	24	15	....	313	249	97	2nd, Patrick		Lost Quarter-Final
1979-80	80	27	5	8	....	21	7	12	....	48	12	20	....	327	254	116	1st, Patrick		Lost Final
1978-79	80	26	10	4	....	14	15	11	....	40	25	15	....	281	248	95	2nd, Patrick		Lost Quarter-Final
1977-78	80	29	6	5	....	16	14	10	....	45	20	15	....	296	200	105	2nd, Patrick		Lost Semi-Final
1976-77	80	33	6	1	....	15	10	15	....	48	16	16	....	323	213	112	1st, Patrick		Lost Semi-Final
1975-76	80	36	2	2	....	15	11	14	....	51	13	16	....	348	209	118	1st, Patrick		Lost Final
1974-75	**80**	**32**	**6**	**2**	....	**19**	**12**	**9**	....	**51**	**18**	**11**	....	**293**	**181**	**113**	**1st, Patrick**		**Won Stanley Cup**
1973-74	**78**	**28**	**6**	**5**	....	**22**	**10**	**7**	....	**50**	**16**	**12**	....	**273**	**164**	**112**	**1st, West**		**Won Stanley Cup**
1972-73	78	27	8	4	....	10	22	7	....	37	30	11	....	296	256	85	2nd, West		Lost Semi-Final
1971-72	78	19	13	7	....	7	25	7	....	26	38	14	....	200	236	66	5th, West		Out of Playoffs
1970-71	78	20	10	9	....	8	23	8	....	28	33	17	....	207	225	73	3rd, West		Lost Quarter-Final
1969-70	76	11	14	13	....	6	21	11	....	17	35	24	....	197	225	58	5th, West		Out of Playoffs
1968-69	76	14	16	8	....	6	19	13	....	20	35	21	....	174	225	61	3rd, West		Lost Quarter-Final
1967-68	74	17	13	7	....	14	19	4	....	31	32	11	....	173	179	73	1st, West		Lost Quarter-Final

2013-14 Schedule

Oct.	Wed.	2	Toronto		Sat.	4	at Phoenix
	Sat.	5	at Montreal		Tue.	7	at New Jersey
	Sun.	6	at Carolina*		Wed.	8	Montreal
	Tue.	8	Florida		Sat.	11	Tampa Bay*
	Fri.	11	Phoenix		Sun.	12	at NY Rangers
	Sat.	12	at Detroit		Tue.	14	at Buffalo
	Tue.	15	Vancouver		Thu.	16	Nashville
	Thu.	17	Pittsburgh		Sat.	18	NY Islanders
	Thu.	24	NY Rangers		Mon.	20	at NY Islanders*
	Sat.	26	at NY Islanders		Tue.	21	Carolina
	Tue.	29	Anaheim		Thu.	23	at Columbus
Nov.	Fri.	1	Washington		Sat.	25	Boston*
	Sat.	2	at New Jersey		Tue.	28	Detroit
	Tue.	5	at Carolina		Thu.	30	at Anaheim
	Thu.	7	New Jersey	**Feb.**	Sat.	1	at Los Angeles*
	Sat.	9	Edmonton*		Mon.	3	at San Jose
	Tue.	12	at Ottawa		Thu.	6	Colorado
	Wed.	13	at Pittsburgh		Sat.	8	Calgary*
	Fri.	15	at Winnipeg		Thu.	27	San Jose
	Tue.	19	Ottawa	**Mar.**	Sat.	1	NY Rangers*
	Thu.	21	Buffalo		Sun.	2	at Washington*
	Sat.	23	NY Islanders		Wed.	5	Washington
	Mon.	25	at Florida		Sat.	8	at Toronto
	Wed.	27	at Tampa Bay		Tue.	11	New Jersey
	Fri.	29	Winnipeg*		Sat.	15	Pittsburgh*
	Sat.	30	at Nashville		Sun.	16	at Pittsburgh
Dec.	Mon.	2	at Minnesota		Tue.	18	Chicago
	Wed.	4	at Detroit		Thu.	20	Dallas
	Sat.	7	at Dallas*		Sat.	22	St. Louis*
	Mon.	9	at Ottawa		Mon.	24	Los Angeles
	Wed.	11	at Chicago		Wed.	26	at NY Rangers
	Thu.	12	Montreal		Fri.	28	Toronto
	Sun.	15	at Washington*		Sun.	30	Boston
	Tue.	17	Washington	**Apr.**	Tue.	1	at St. Louis
	Thu.	19	Columbus		Thu.	3	Columbus
	Sat.	21	at Columbus		Sat.	5	at Boston*
	Mon.	23	Minnesota		Sun.	6	Buffalo
	Sat.	28	at Edmonton		Tue.	8	at Florida
	Mon.	30	at Vancouver		Thu.	10	at Tampa Bay
	Tue.	31	at Calgary		Sat.	12	at Pittsburgh*
Jan.	Thu.	2	at Colorado		Sun.	13	Carolina*

* Denotes afternoon game.

Though the 2012-13 season was just 48 games long, Jakub Voracek still set a career high — and led the Flyers — with 22 goals. His 46 points trailed only Claude Giroux, who led the club for the third straight season with 48 points.

METROPOLITAN DIVISION
47th NHL Season

Franchise date: June 5, 1967

2013-14 Player Personnel

FORWARDS	HT	WT	*Age	Place of Birth	S	2012-13 Club
COUTURIER, Sean	6-3	197	20	Phoenix, AZ	L	Adirondack-Philadelphia
GIROUX, Claude	5-11	172	25	Hearst, Ont.	R	Eisbaren Berlin-Phi
HALL, Adam	6-2	212	33	Kalamazoo, MI	R	Ravensburg-T.B.-Car-Phi
HARTNELL, Scott	6-2	210	31	Regina, Sask.	L	Philadelphia
HOLMSTROM, Ben	6-1	197	26	Colorado Springs, CO	R	Adirondack
LECAVALIER, Vincent	6-4	208	33	Ile Bizard, Que.	L	Tampa Bay
NEWBURY, Kris	5-11	205	31	Brampton, Ont.	L	Connecticut-NY Rangers
READ, Matt	5-10	185	27	Ilderton, Ont.	R	Sodertalje-Philadelphia
RINALDO, Zac	5-11	185	23	Mississauga, Ont.	L	Adirondack-Philadelphia
SCHENN, Brayden	6-1	190	22	Saskatoon, Sask.	L	Adirondack-Philadelphia
SIMMONDS, Wayne	6-2	183	25	Scarborough, Ont.	R	Crimmitschau-Liberec-Phi
TALBOT, Maxime	5-11	190	29	Lemoyne, Que.	L	Ilves-Philadelphia
VORACEK, Jakub	6-2	214	24	Kladno, Czech.	L	Lev Praha-Philadelphia
WELLWOOD, Eric	5-11	180	23	Windsor, Ont.	L	Adirondack-Philadelphia
DEFENSEMEN						
BOURDON, Marc-Andre	6-0	206	24	St-Hyacinthe, Que.	L	Adirondack
COBURN, Braydon	6-5	220	28	Calgary, Alta.	L	Philadelphia
GERVAIS, Bruno	6-1	200	28	Longueuil, Que.	R	Heilbronn-Philadelphia
GROSSMANN, Nicklas	6-4	230	28	Stockholm, Sweden	L	Sodertalje-Philadelphia
GUSTAFSSON, Erik	5-10	180	24	Kvissleby, Sweden	L	Adirondack-Philadelphia
MESZAROS, Andrej	6-2	223	27	Povazska Bystrica, Czech.	L	Philadelphia
PRONGER, Chris	6-6	220	38	Dryden, Ont.	L	Philadelphia
SCHENN, Luke	6-2	229	23	Saskatoon, Sask.	R	Philadelphia
STREIT, Mark	5-11	191	35	Bern, Switz.	L	NY Islanders-Bern
TIMONEN, Kimmo	5-10	194	38	Kuopio, Finland	L	Philadelphia

GOALTENDERS	HT	WT	*Age	Place of Birth	C	2012-13 Club
DANIS, Yann	6-0	185	32	Lafontaine, Que.	L	Oklahoma City-Edmonton
EMERY, Ray	6-2	196	31	Cayuga, Ont.	L	Chicago
MASON, Steve	6-4	217	25	Oakville, Ont.	R	Columbus-Philadelphia

* – Age at start of 2013-14 season

Peter Laviolette

Head Coach

Born: Norwood, MA, December 7, 1964.

Peter Laviolette was named the 17th coach in Flyers history on December 4, 2009. Taking over the team two months into the season, Laviolette's Flyers would clinch a playoff berth in the final game on the schedule and go on to reach the Stanley Cup Final before losing to the Chicago Blackhawks. Along the way, they became just the third team in NHL history to rally from a three-games-to-nothing deficit when they beat the Boston Bruins in the second round of the playoffs.

Previously, Laviolette had coached the Carolina Hurricanes from 2003-04 until partway through the 2008-09 season. In 2005-06 he led the Hurricanes to a club-record 52 wins and 112 points in the regular-season and a Stanley Cup championship. Laviolette's career as an NHL head coach began with the New York Islanders in 2001-02. He led the team to the playoffs two years in a row after the club had failed to reach the postseason for seven straight seasons. Prior to joining the Islanders, Laviolette served as an assistant coach with the Boston Bruins after two years of guiding Boston's AHL affiliate, Providence. In 1998-99, Laviolette led the Providence Bruins to a 56-16-8 regular-season record, and a 15-4 playoff record that culminated with Providence hoisting the Calder Cup and Laviolette being named AHL coach of the year.

Laviolette played 11 seasons of professional hockey, mostly in the AHL and IHL, but did play 12 games with the New York Rangers during the 1988-89 season. He was a member of the 1988 and 1994 U.S. Olympic hockey teams, and captained the 1994 Olympic squad.

In the spring of 2004, Laviolette helped assure the United States a spot in the 2006 Olympic Games in Torino, Italy, when he guided Team USA to a bronze medal at the 2004 World Championship in the Czech Republic. He also served as an assistant to San Jose Sharks head coach Ron Wilson behind the bench for Team USA in the 2004 World Cup of Hockey and was head coach again at the 2005 World Championship and 2006 Olympics.

Coaching Record

			Regular Season				Playoffs			
Season	Team	League	GC	W	L	O/T	GC	W	L	T
1997-98	Wheeling	ECHL	70	37	24	9	15	8	7	....
1998-99	Providence	AHL	80	56	16	8	19	15	4	....
99-2000	Providence	AHL	80	33	38	9	14	10	4	....
2001-02	**NY Islanders**	**NHL**	**82**	**42**	**28**	**12**	**7**	**3**	**4**	....
2002-03	**NY Islanders**	**NHL**	**82**	**35**	**34**	**13**	**5**	**1**	**4**	....
2003-04	**Carolina**	**NHL**	**52**	**20**	**22**	**10**	....	....	....	....
2004-05	**Carolina**		SEASON CANCELLED							
2005-06♦	**Carolina**	**NHL**	**82**	**52**	**22**	**8**	**25**	**16**	**9**	....
2006-07	**Carolina**	**NHL**	**82**	**40**	**34**	**8**	....	....	....	....
2007-08	**Carolina**	**NHL**	**82**	**43**	**33**	**6**	....	....	....	....
2008-09	**Carolina**	**NHL**	**25**	**12**	**11**	**2**	....	....	....	....
2009-10	**Philadelphia**	**NHL**	**57**	**28**	**24**	**5**	**23**	**14**	**9**	....
2010-11	**Philadelphia**	**NHL**	**82**	**47**	**23**	**12**	**11**	**4**	**7**	....
2011-12	**Philadelphia**	**NHL**	**82**	**47**	**26**	**9**	**11**	**5**	**6**	....
2012-13	**Philadelphia**	**NHL**	**48**	**23**	**22**	**3**	....	....	....	....
	NHL Totals		**756**	**389**	**279**	**88**	**82**	**43**	**39**	....

♦ Stanley Cup win.

2012-13 Scoring

* – rookie

Regular Season

Pos	#	Player	Team	GP	G	A	Pts	TOI	+/-	PIM	PP	SH	GW	S	%
R	28	Claude Giroux	PHI	48	13	35	48	21:10	–7	22	6	1	2	137	9.5
R	93	Jakub Voracek	PHI	48	22	24	46	17:14	–7	35	8	0	3	129	17.1
R	17	Wayne Simmonds	PHI	45	15	17	32	15:38	–7	82	6	0	4	110	13.6
D	44	Kimmo Timonen	PHI	45	5	24	29	21:45	3	36	3	0	1	78	6.4
C	10	Brayden Schenn	PHI	47	8	18	26	15:31	–8	24	2	0	0	79	10.1
R	24	Matt Read	PHI	42	11	13	24	18:01	1	2	1	0	2	72	15.3
C	48	Daniel Briere	PHI	34	6	10	16	16:03	–13	10	3	0	1	87	6.9
L	12	Simon Gagne	L.A.	11	0	5	5	13:45	2	2	0	0	0	20	0.0
			PHI	27	5	6	11	14:17	–3	6	2	0	0	56	8.9
			Total	38	5	11	16	14:08	–1	8	2	0	0	76	6.6
C	14	Sean Couturier	PHI	46	4	11	15	15:53	–8	10	0	0	0	75	5.3
L	26	Ruslan Fedotenko	PHI	47	4	9	13	12:34	8	12	0	0	1	43	9.3
L	19	Scott Hartnell	PHI	32	8	3	11	15:52	–5	70	4	0	1	74	10.8
D	22	Luke Schenn	PHI	47	3	8	11	21:51	3	34	0	0	0	81	3.7
C	25	Maxime Talbot	PHI	35	5	5	10	15:25	2	23	0	1	0	41	12.2
R	9	Mike Knuble	PHI	28	4	4	8	12:55	–4	20	1	0	1	31	12.9
D	29	Erik Gustafsson	PHI	27	3	5	8	20:08	–1	2	0	0	1	36	8.3
D	27	Bruno Gervais	PHI	37	1	5	6	17:07	–17	10	0	0	0	49	2.0
L	15 *	Tye McGinn	PHI	18	3	2	5	12:43	0	19	0	0	1	33	9.1
C	36	Zac Rinaldo	PHI	32	3	2	5	8:22	–7	85	0	0	0	15	20.0
D	3	Kurtis Foster	PHI	23	1	4	5	13:05	0	25	1	0	0	21	4.8
D	5	Braydon Coburn	PHI	33	1	4	5	22:36	–10	41	0	0	0	38	2.6
D	8	Nicklas Grossmann	PHI	30	1	3	4	18:19	–1	21	0	0	0	21	4.8
R	18	Adam Hall	T.B.	20	0	4	4	10:17	3	23	0	0	0	16	0.0
			CAR	6	0	0	0	10:30	–2	0	0	0	0	3	0.0
			PHI	11	0	0	0	10:58	–1	0	0	0	0	15	0.0
			Total	37	0	4	4	10:31	0	23	0	0	0	34	0.0
D	38 *	Oliver Lauridsen	PHI	15	2	1	3	15:08	0	34	0	0	2	14	14.3
D	32 *	Brandon Manning	PHI	6	0	2	2	14:48	4	0	0	0	0	5	0.0
D	41	Andrej Meszaros	PHI	11	0	2	2	18:27	–9	2	0	0	0	18	0.0
R	42 *	Jason Akeson	PHI	1	1	0	1	12:23	2	0	0	0	0	2	50.0
L	37	Jay Rosehill	PHI	11	1	0	1	6:47	–4	64	0	0	1	7	14.3
L	37	Harry Zolnierczyk	PHI	7	0	1	1	7:22	0	36	0	0	0	4	0.0
D	23	Kent Huskins	DET	11	0	0	0	15:20	–3	4	0	0	0	2	0.0
			PHI	8	0	1	1	16:06	0	0	0	0	0	2	0.0
			Total	19	0	1	1	15:39	–3	4	0	0	0	4	0.0
L	45	Jody Shelley	PHI	1	0	0	0	7:58	0	0	0	0	0	0	0.0
D	34 *	Matthew Konan	PHI	2	0	0	0	15:55	0	0	0	0	0	4	0.0
D	6	Andreas Lilja	PHI	4	0	0	0	16:46	–1	0	0	0	0	2	0.0
L	11 *	Eric Wellwood	PHI	4	0	0	0	9:25	0	0	0	0	0	2	0.0
L	21 *	Scott Laughton	PHI	5	0	0	0	11:31	0	0	0	0	0	10	0.0

Goaltending

No.	Goaltender	GPI	Mins	Avg	W	L	OT	EN	SO	GA	SA	S%	G	A	PIM
35	Steve Mason	7	378	1.90	4	2	0	1	0	12	215	.944	0	1	0
33	Brian Boucher	4	144	2.50	0	2	0	1	0	6	55	.891	0	0	0
30	Ilya Bryzgalov	40	2298	2.79	19	17	3	7	1	107	1066	.900	0	3	0
49	Michael Leighton	1	59	5.08	0	1	0	0	0	5	26	.808	0	0	0
	Totals	**48**	**2901**	**2.87**	**23**	**22**	**3**	**9**	**1**	**139**	**1371**	**.899**			

Coaching History

Keith Allen, 1967-68, 1968-69; Vic Stasiuk, 1969-70, 1970-71; Fred Shero, 1971-72 to 1977-78; Bob McCammon and Pat Quinn, 1978-79; Pat Quinn, 1979-80, 1980-81; Pat Quinn and Bob McCammon, 1981-82; Bob McCammon, 1982-83, 1983-84; Mike Keenan, 1984-85 to 1987-88; Paul Holmgren, 1988-89 to 1990-91; Paul Holmgren and Bill Dineen, 1991-92; Bill Dineen, 1992-93; Terry Simpson, 1993-94; Terry Murray, 1994-95 to 1996-97; Wayne Cashman and Roger Neilson, 1997-98; Roger Neilson, 1998-99, 1999-2000; Craig Ramsay and Bill Barber, 2000-01; Bill Barber, 2001-02; Ken Hitchcock, 2002-03 to 2005-06; Ken Hitchcock and John Stevens, 2006-07; John Stevens, 2007-08, 2008-09; John Stevens and Peter Laviolette, 2009-10; Peter Laviolette, 2010-11 to date.

Captains' History

Lou Angotti, 1967-68; Ed Van Impe, 1968-69 to 1971-72; Ed Van Impe and Bobby Clarke, 1972-73; Bobby Clarke, 1973-74 to 1978-79; Mel Bridgman, 1979-80, 1980-81; Bill Barber, 1981-82; Bill Barber and Bobby Clarke, 1982-83; Bobby Clarke, 1983-84; Dave Poulin, 1984-85 to 1988-89; Dave Poulin and Ron Sutter, 1989-90; Ron Sutter, 1990-91; Rick Tocchet, 1991-92; no captain, 1992-93; Kevin Dineen, 1993-94; Eric Lindros, 1994-95 to 1998-99; Eric Lindros and Eric Desjardins, 1999-2000; Eric Desjardins, 2000-01; Eric Desjardins and Keith Primeau, 2001-02; Keith Primeau, 2002-03, 2003-04; Keith Primeau and Derian Hatcher, 2005-06; Peter Forsberg, 2006-07; Jason Smith, 2007-08; Mike Richards, 2008-09 to 2010-11; Chris Pronger, 2011-12; Claude Giroux, 2012-13 to date.

Club Records

Team

(Figures in brackets for season records are games played; records for fewest points, wins, ties, losses, goals, goals against are for 70 or more games)

Most Points	118	1975-76 (80)
Most Wins	53	1984-85 (80), 1985-86 (80)
Most Ties	*24	1969-70 (76)
Most Losses	48	2006-07 (82)
Most Goals	350	1983-84 (80)
Most Goals Against	319	1992-93 (84)
Fewest Points	56	2006-07 (82)
Fewest Wins	17	1969-70 (76)
Fewest Ties	4	1985-86 (80)
Fewest Losses	12	1979-80 (80)
Fewest Goals	173	1967-68 (74)
Fewest Goals Against	164	1973-74 (78)
Longest Winning Streak		
Overall	13	Oct. 19-Nov. 17/85
Home	20	Jan. 4-Apr. 3/76
Away	8	Dec. 22/82-Jan. 16/83
Longest Undefeated Streak		
Overall	*35	Oct. 14/79-Jan. 6/80 (25W, 10T)
Home	26	Oct. 11/79-Feb. 3/80 (19W, 7T)
Away	16	Oct. 20/79-Jan. 6/80 (11W, 5T)
Longest Losing Streak		
Overall	9	Dec. 8-27/06
Home	13	Nov. 29/06-Feb. 8/07
Away	8	Oct. 25-Nov. 26/72, Mar. 3-29/88
Longest Winless Streak		
Overall	12	Feb. 24-Mar. 16/99 (8L, 4T)
Home	13	Nov. 29/06-Feb. 8/07 (13L)
Away	19	Oct. 23/71-Jan. 27/72 (15L, 4T)
Most Shutouts, Season	13	1974-75 (80)
Most PIM, Season	2,621	1980-81 (80)
Most Goals, Game	13	Mar. 22/84 (Pit. 4 at Phi. 13), Oct. 18/84 (Van. 2 at Phi. 13)

Individual

Most Seasons	15	Bobby Clarke
Most Games	1,144	Bobby Clarke
Most Goals, Career	420	Bill Barber
Most Assists, Career	852	Bobby Clarke
Most Points, Career	1,210	Bobby Clarke (358G, 852A)
Most PIM, Career	1,817	Rick Tocchet
Most Shutouts, Career	50	Bernie Parent
Longest Consecutive Game Streak	484	Rod Brind'Amour (Feb. 24/93-Apr. 18/99)
Most Goals, Season	61	Reggie Leach (1975-76)
Most Assists, Season	89	Bobby Clarke (1974-75), (1975-76)
Most Points, Season	123	Mark Recchi (1992-93; 53G, 70A)
Most PIM, Season	*472	Dave Schultz (1974-75)
Most Points, Defenseman, Season	82	Mark Howe (1985-86; 24G, 58A)
Most Points, Center, Season	119	Bobby Clarke (1975-76; 30G, 89A)
Most Points, Right Wing, Season	123	Mark Recchi (1992-93; 53G, 70A)
Most Points, Left Wing, Season	112	Bill Barber (1975-76; 50G, 62A)
Most Points, Rookie, Season	82	Mikael Renberg (1993-94; 38G, 44A)
Most Shutouts, Season	12	Bernie Parent (1973-74), (1974-75)
Most Goals, Game	4	Sixteen times
Most Assists, Game	6	Eric Lindros (Feb. 26/97)
Most Points, Game	8	Tom Bladon (Dec. 11/77; 4G, 4A)

* NHL Record.

Retired Numbers

1	Bernie Parent	1967-1971, 1973-1979
4	Barry Ashbee	1970-1974
7	Bill Barber	1972-1985
16	Bobby Clarke	1969-1984

All-time Record vs. Other Clubs

Regular Season

	Total								At Home								On Road							
	GP	W	L	T	OL	GF	GA	PTS	GP	W	L	T	OL	GF	GA	PTS	GP	W	L	T	OL	GF	GA	PTS
Anaheim	24	10	7	5	2	75	69	27	11	4	3	3	1	29	23	12	13	6	4	2	1	46	46	15
Boston	180	65	86	21	8	534	591	159	89	37	39	10	3	283	271	87	91	28	47	11	5	251	320	72
Buffalo	161	78	58	20	5	511	477	181	82	47	20	12	3	285	214	109	79	31	38	8	2	226	263	72
Calgary	109	55	40	12	2	386	359	124	54	34	15	3	2	203	145	73	55	21	25	9	0	183	214	51
Carolina	118	74	26	14	4	438	325	166	59	40	11	5	3	221	149	88	59	34	15	9	1	217	176	78
Chicago	128	55	43	30	0	395	381	140	65	38	16	11	0	215	168	87	63	17	27	19	0	180	213	53
Colorado	76	35	23	14	4	265	238	88	37	24	9	2	2	134	99	52	39	11	14	12	2	131	139	36
Columbus	11	6	2	3	0	35	22	15	5	4	0	1	0	24	10	9	6	2	2	2	0	11	12	6
Dallas	141	71	38	32	0	493	385	174	71	45	10	16	0	269	161	106	70	26	28	16	0	224	224	68
Detroit	124	56	47	21	0	436	399	133	61	37	13	11	0	243	174	85	63	19	34	10	0	193	225	48
Edmonton	65	29	28	8	0	224	200	66	34	21	11	2	0	138	94	44	31	8	17	6	0	86	106	22
Florida	80	44	26	7	3	241	200	98	41	17	15	6	3	108	106	43	39	27	11	1	0	133	94	55
Los Angeles	137	82	37	15	3	489	366	182	67	42	16	7	2	251	162	93	70	40	21	8	1	238	204	89
Minnesota	13	8	3	1	1	38	20	18	8	6	1	0	1	25	11	13	5	2	2	1	0	13	9	5
Montreal	178	68	76	30	4	535	567	170	88	36	34	16	2	267	261	90	90	32	42	14	2	268	306	80
Nashville	16	7	3	3	3	45	32	20	9	5	2	1	1	30	16	12	7	2	1	2	2	15	16	8
New Jersey	221	105	88	18	10	737	653	238	111	66	30	10	5	399	285	147	110	39	58	8	5	338	368	91
NY Islanders	245	126	87	26	6	804	746	284	121	73	33	11	4	429	329	161	124	53	54	15	2	375	417	123
NY Rangers	272	116	112	37	7	813	811	276	136	65	53	14	4	423	381	148	136	51	59	23	3	390	430	128
Ottawa	78	37	29	8	4	242	226	86	39	23	12	2	2	130	105	50	39	14	17	6	2	112	121	36
Phoenix	69	42	24	2	1	255	201	87	35	25	9	0	1	144	93	51	34	17	15	2	0	111	108	36
Pittsburgh	264	142	84	30	8	957	813	322	132	92	28	8	4	532	349	196	132	50	56	22	4	425	464	126
St. Louis	141	83	40	17	1	497	363	184	70	47	13	10	0	272	161	104	71	36	27	7	1	225	202	80
San Jose	31	13	11	4	3	87	86	33	15	6	5	2	2	48	46	16	16	7	6	2	1	39	40	17
Tampa Bay	82	42	29	8	3	248	227	95	40	20	11	7	2	126	99	49	42	22	18	1	1	122	128	46
Toronto	165	89	52	22	2	575	450	202	82	51	23	8	0	306	198	110	83	38	29	14	2	269	252	92
Vancouver	111	69	29	13	0	459	325	151	57	38	18	1	0	243	171	77	54	31	11	12	0	216	154	74
Washington	194	102	67	19	6	675	582	229	99	61	30	6	2	373	276	130	95	41	37	13	4	302	306	99
Winnipeg	51	33	11	3	4	188	141	73	25	15	5	2	3	99	76	35	26	18	6	1	1	89	65	38
Defunct Clubs	69	37	18	14	0	239	156	88	34	24	4	6	0	137	67	54	35	13	14	8	0	102	89	34
Totals	**3554**	**1779**	**1224**	**457**	**94**	**11916**	**10411**	**4109**	**1777**	**1043**	**489**	**193**	**52**	**6386**	**4700**	**2331**	**1777**	**736**	**735**	**264**	**42**	**5530**	**5711**	**1778**

Playoffs

	Series	W	L	GP	W	L	T	GF	GA	Last Mtg.	Rnd.	Result
Boston	6	3	3	31	13	18	0	86	100	2011	CSF	L 0-4
Buffalo	9	6	3	50	29	21	0	146	141	2011	CQF	W 4-3
Calgary	2	1	1	11	7	4	0	43	28	1981	QF	L 3-4
Chicago	2	0	2	10	2	8	0	30	45	2010	F	L 2-4
Colorado	2	2	0	11	7	4	0	39	29	1985	CF	W 4-2
Dallas	2	2	0	11	8	3	0	41	26	1980	SF	W 4-1
Detroit	1	0	1	4	0	4	0	6	16	1997	F	L 0-4
Edmonton	3	1	2	15	7	8	0	44	49	1987	F	L 3-4
Florida	1	0	1	6	2	4	0	11	15	1996	CSF	L 2-4
Montreal	6	3	3	31	15	16	0	89	93	2010	CF	W 4-1
New Jersey	6	3	3	30	16	14	0	75	77	2012	CSF	L 1-4
NY Islanders	4	3	1	25	14	11	0	83	69	1987	DF	W 4-3
NY Rangers	10	6	4	47	27	20	0	157	153	1997	CF	W 4-1
Ottawa	2	0	2	11	3	8	0	12	28	2003	CSF	L 2-4
Pittsburgh	6	4	2	35	19	16	0	121	115	2012	CQF	W 4-2
St. Louis	2	0	2	11	3	8	0	20	34	1969	QF	L 0-4
Tampa Bay	2	1	1	13	7	6	0	45	34	2004	CF	L 3-4
Toronto	6	5	1	36	22	14	0	119	85	2004	CSF	W 4-2
Vancouver	1	1	0	3	2	1	0	15	9	1979	PRE	W 2-1
Washington	4	2	2	23	11	12	0	78	85	2008	CQF	W 4-3
Totals	**77**	**43**	**34**	**414**	**214**	**200**	**0**	**1260**	**1231**			

Playoff Results 2013-2009

Year	Round	Opponent	Result	GF	GA
2012	CSF	New Jersey	L 1-4	11	18
	CQF	Pittsburgh	W 4-2	30	26
2011	CSF	Boston	L 0-4	7	20
	CQF	Buffalo	W 4-3	22	18
2010	F	Chicago	L 2-4	22	25
	CF	Montreal	W 4-1	17	7
	CSF	Boston	W 4-3	22	20
	CQF	New Jersey	W 4-1	15	9
2009	CQF	Pittsburgh	L 2-4	16	18

Abbreviations: Round: F – Final; **CF** – conference final; **CSF** – conference semi-final; **CQF** – conference quarter-final; **DF** – division final; **SF** – semi-final; **QF** – quarter-final; **PRE** – preliminary round.

Calgary totals include Atlanta Flames, 1972-73 to 1979-80.
Colorado totals include Quebec, 1979-80 to 1994-95.
New Jersey totals include Kansas City, 1974-75, 1975-76, and Colorado Rockies, 1976-77 to 1981-82.
Phoenix totals include Winnipeg, 1979-80 to 1995-96.
Carolina totals include Hartford, 1979-80 to 1996-97.
Dallas totals include Minnesota North Stars, 1967-68 to 1992-93.
Winnipeg totals include Atlanta Thrashers, 1999-2000 to 2010-11.

2012-13 Results

Jan.	19	Pittsburgh	1-3		7	Pittsburgh	4-5
	20	at Buffalo	2-5		9	at Boston	0-3
	22	at New Jersey	0-3		10	Buffalo	3-2
	24	NY Rangers	2-1		13	at New Jersey	2-5
	26	at Florida	7-1		15	New Jersey	2-1†
	27	at Tampa Bay	1-5		18	at Tampa Bay	2-4
	29	at NY Rangers	1-2		24	at Pittsburgh	1-2*
Feb.	1	at Washington	2-3		26	NY Rangers	2-5
	2	Carolina	5-3		28	NY Islanders	3-4†
	5	Tampa Bay	2-1		30	Boston	3-1
	7	Florida	2-3†		31	Washington	5-4*
	9	Carolina	4-3*	**Apr.**	3	Montreal	5-3
	11	at Toronto	2-5		4	at Toronto	5-3
	12	at Winnipeg	3-2		6	at Winnipeg	1-4
	15	at New Jersey	3-5		9	at NY Islanders	1-4
	16	at Montreal	1-4		11	Ottawa	1-3
	18	at NY Islanders	7-0		13	at Buffalo	0-1
	20	at Pittsburgh	6-5		15	at Montreal	7-3
	21	Florida	2-5		16	NY Rangers	4-2
	23	Winnipeg	5-3		18	New Jersey	0-3
	25	Toronto	2-4		20	at Carolina	5-3
	27	Washington	4-1		23	Boston	5-2
Mar.	2	Ottawa	2-1		25	NY Islanders	2-1
	5	at NY Rangers	2-4		27	at Ottawa	2-1

* – Overtime † – Shootout

Entry Draft Selections 2013-1999

Name in bold denotes played in NHL.

2013

Pick	
11	Samuel Morin
41	Robert Hagg
72	Tyrell Goulbourne
132	Terrance Amorosa
162	Merrick Madsen
192	David Drake

2012

Pick	
20	**Scott Laughton**
45	Anthony Stolarz
78	Shayne Gostisbehere
111	Fredric Larsson
117	Taylor Leier
141	Reece Willcox
201	Valeri Vasiliev

2011

Pick	
8	**Sean Couturier**
68	Nick Cousins
116	Colin Suellentrop
118	Marcel Noebels
176	Petr Placek
206	Derek Mathers

2010

Pick	
89	Michael Chaput
119	**Tye McGinn**
149	Michael Parks
179	Nick Luukko
206	Ricard Blidstrand
209	Brendan Ranford

2009

Pick	
81	Adam Morrison
87	Simon Bertilsson
142	Nic Riopel
153	Dave Labrecque
172	**Eric Wellwood**
196	**Oliver Lauridsen**

2008

Pick	
19	**Luca Sbisa**
67	**Marc-Andre Bourdon**
84	Jacob Deserres
178	**Zac Rinaldo**
196	Joacim Eriksson

2007

Pick	
2	**James van Riemsdyk**
41	**Kevin Marshall**
66	Garrett Klotz
122	Mario Kempe
152	**Jon Kalinski**
161	**Patrick Maroon**
182	Brad Phillips

2006

Pick	
22	**Claude Giroux**
39	**Andreas Nodl**
42	Mike Ratchuk
55	Denis Bodrov
79	**Jon Matsumoto**
101	Joonas Lehtivuori
109	Jakub Kovar
145	**Jon Rheault**
175	Michael Dupont
205	Andrei Popov

2005

Pick	
29	**Steve Downie**
91	**Oskars Bartulis**
119	**Jeremy Duchesne**
152	Josh Beaulieu
174	John Flatters
215	Matt Clackson

2004

Pick	
92	Rob Bellamy
101	R.J. Anderson
124	**David Laliberte**
144	Chris Zarb
149	Gino Pisellini
170	Ladislav Scurko
171	Frederik Cabana
232	**Martin Houle**
253	Travis Gawryletz
286	**Triston Grant**
291	John Carter

2003

Pick	
11	**Jeff Carter**
24	**Mike Richards**
69	**Colin Fraser**
81	**Stefan Ruzicka**
85	**Alexandre Picard**
87	**Ryan Potulny**
95	Rick Kozak
108	Kevin Romy
140	David Tremblay
191	Rejean Beauchemin
193	Ville Hostikka

2002

Pick	
4	**Joni Pitkanen**
105	Rosario Ruggeri
126	Konstantin Baranov
161	Dov Grumet-Morris
192	Nikita Korovkin
193	**Joey Mormina**
201	Mathieu Brunelle

2001

Pick	
27	**Jeff Woywitka**
95	**Patrick Sharp**
146	**Jussi Timonen**
150	Bernd Bruckler
158	Roman Malek
172	**Dennis Seidenberg**
177	Andrei Razin
208	Thierry Douville
225	**David Printz**

2000

Pick	
28	**Justin Williams**
94	Alexander Drozdetsky
171	**Roman Cechmanek**
195	Colin Shields
210	John Eichelberger
227	**Guillaume Lefebvre**
259	Regan Kelly
287	Milan Kopecky

1999

Pick	
22	**Maxime Ouellet**
119	Jeff Feniak
160	Konstantin Rudenko
200	Pavel Kasparik
208	**Vaclav Pletka**
224	David Nystrom

General Managers' History

Bud Poile, 1967-68, 1968-69; Bud Poile and Keith Allen, 1969-70; Keith Allen, 1970-71 to 1982-83; Bob McCammon, 1983-84; Bob Clarke, 1984-85 to 1989-90; Russ Farwell, 1990-91 to 1993-94; Bob Clarke, 1994-95 to 2005-06; Bob Clarke and Paul Holmgren, 2006-07; Paul Holmgren, 2007-08 to date.

Paul Holmgren

General Manager

Born: St. Paul, MN, December 2, 1955.

Paul Holmgren was named interim general manager of the Philadelphia Flyers on November 11, 2006, replacing Bob Clarke who resigned on October 22. On March 14, 2007, Holmgren was officially announced as the club's new g.m. In his first full season on the job in 2007-08, the Flyers returned to the playoffs after finishing last overall in the NHL the year before. They reached the Stanley Cup Final in 2010. Prior to his promotion, Holmgren had served the previous seven seasons as the team's assistant general manager. He rejoined the Flyers organization as a scout after being replaced as the Hartford Whalers' head coach on November 6, 1995. He had served as a head coach with both the Whalers and the Flyers and also served as general manager in Hartford during the 1993–94 season.

Holmgren retired from playing after the 1984-85 season, having recorded 144 goals and 179 assists for 323 points and 1,684 penalty minutes in 527 career regular season NHL games with the Flyers and the Minnesota North Stars. He recorded 138 goals and 171 assists for 309 points and 1,600 penalty minutes in 500 games over parts of nine seasons with the Flyers (1975-76 to 1983-84). His 1,600 penalty minutes with the Flyers are second all-time in club history. Holmgren was drafted from the University of Minnesota by the Flyers in the sixth round (108th overall) of the 1975 NHL Entry Draft.

Coaching Record

			Regular Season				Playoffs			
Season	Team	League	GC	W	L	O/T	GC	W	L	T
1988-89	Philadelphia	NHL	80	36	36	8	19	10	9	....
1989-90	Philadelphia	NHL	80	30	39	11	....	....	....	....
1990-91	Philadelphia	NHL	80	33	37	10	....	....	....	....
1991-92	Philadelphia	NHL	24	8	14	2	....	....	....	....
1992-93	Hartford	NHL	84	26	52	6	....	....	....	....
1993-94	Hartford	NHL	17	4	11	2	....	....	....	....
1994-95	Hartford	NHL	48	19	24	5	....	....	....	....
1995-96	Hartford	NHL	12	5	6	1	....	....	....	....
	NHL Totals		**425**	**161**	**219**	**45**	**19**	**10**	**9**	....

Club Directory

Wells Fargo Center

Philadelphia Flyers
Wells Fargo Center
3601 South Broad Street
Philadelphia, PA 19148-5290
Phone **215/465-4500**
PR FAX 215/218-7837
www.philadelphiaflyers.com
Capacity: 19,541

Executive Management

Chairman . . . . Ed Snider
President and COO of Comcast-Spectacor. . . . . Peter A. Luukko
General Manager . . . . Paul Holmgren
Senior Vice President. . . . . Bob Clarke
Executive Vice President . . . . Keith Allen
Governor . . . . Ed Snider
Alternate Governors . . . . Paul Holmgren, Peter A. Luukko, Phil Weinberg
Senior Vice President, Business Operations . . . . Shawn Tilger
Executive Assistants . . . . Sharon Allison, Cheri Arnao, Ann Marie Nasuti

Hockey Club Personnel

Assistant General Managers . . . . Barry Hanrahan, John Paddock
Director of Hockey Operations . . . . Chris Pryor
Director of Player Development. . . . . Ian Laperriere
Director of Player Personnel . . . . Dave Brown
Head Coach . . . . Peter Laviolette
Assistant Coaches. . . . . Craig Berube, Kevin McCarthy, Joe Mullen
Goaltending Coach. . . . . Jeff Reese
Player Development Coach . . . . Derian Hatcher
Video Coach. . . . . Adam Patterson
Pro Scouts . . . . John Chapman, Al Hill, Don Luce
Scouting Staff. . . . . . . Andre Beaulieu, Wade Clarke, Ross Fitzpatrick, Mark Greig, Joakim Grundberg ,Todd Hearty, Ken Hoodikoff, , Neil Little, Jack McIlhargey, Antero Niittymaki, Simon Nolet, Dennis Patterson, Nick Pryor, John Riley, Ilkka Sinisalo, Vaclav Slansky
Scouting Consultant . . . . Bill Barber
Director, Team Services. . . . . Bryan Hardenbergh
Executive Assistant . . . . Dianna Taylor
Administrative Assistant . . . . Jody Clarke

Medical / Training Staff

Team Physicians . . . . Peter DeLuca, M.D.; Gary Dorshimer, M.D.; Guy Lanzi, D.M.D.; Frank Brady, D.C.
Athletic Trainer/Strength & Conditioning Coach . . . Jim McCrossin
Assistant Athletic Trainer. . . . . Sal Raffa
Assistant Strength & Conditioning Coach . . . . Ryan Podell
Massage Therapist . . . . Brad Smith
Head Equipment Manager . . . . Derek Settlemyre
Equipment Managers . . . . Harry Bricker, Anthony Oratorio, Luke Clarke
Assistant Equipment Trainer . . . . Mike Craytor

Communications

Senior Director, Communications . . . . Zack Hill
Manager, Public Relations. . . . . Joe Siville
Manager, Broadcasting & Media Services . . . . Brian Smith

Community Relations

Senior Director,
Project Development. . . . . Linda Mantai
Ambassadors of Hockey. . . . . Bob Kelly, Todd Fedoruk, Gary Dornhoefer, Bernie Parent
Fan Relations Assistant . . . . Jerry Callahan

Customer Service

Vice President, Customer Solutions . . . . Cindy Stutman
Director, Customer Service . . . . Lauren Pawlowski
Senior Customer Service Account Manager. . . . . . Courtney Sams
Customer Service Account Managers . . . . Steve Coskey, Vincent Galasso, Tom Griendling, Niles McFate, Sean Naylor
Client Communications Coordinator. . . . . Shannon Bowes

Game Presentation

Senior Director, Game Presentation. . . . . Anthony Gioia
Game Presentation Coordinator . . . . Corinne Yamada
Producer/Director . . . . Artie Halstead
Graphics Designer / Video Editor . . . . Mike Cahill / Chris Shay
Public Address Announcer / Anthem Singer . . . . . . Lou Nolan / Lauren Hart

Marketing

Senior Director, Marketing . . . . Joe Heller
Manager, Youth & Amateur Hockey . . . . Rob Baer
Publicist . . . . Alicia DeFillipo
Community Relations Coordinator . . . . Jason Tempesta
Marketing Manager . . . . Hung Tran
Marketing Coordinator, Flyers Skate Zone. . . . . Brett Bruneteau

Business Development

Vice President, Business Development. . . . . Rob Johnson
Director, Digital Media . . . . Lauren Cochran
Inside Reporter . . . . Anthony SanFilippo
Digital Media Coordinator. . . . . Samantha Wood

Ticket Sales

Vice President, Sales. . . . . Bryan Anton
Director, Ticket Sales. . . . . Tim Gobs
Direct Marketing Coordinator . . . . Justine Pletnick
Account Executives . . . . Steve Greenblatt, Dan Ryan, Ben Schlegel, Josh Wentz
Client Development Executives. . . . . James Darlington, Travis Kraus, Tony Sukanick, Fran Walmsley, Nick Marchesiello,Owen Mullin, Bret Sokirka
Sales Associates . . . . Brian Gatti, Brian Hawkins, , Kyle Hofstaedter, Kevin Leis, Jenna Matta, Ryan Pirrone

Ticketing

Vice President, Ticket Operations . . . . Cecilia Baker
Senior Director, Ticket Operations & Processing. . . . Dan McGinnis
Ticket Office Manager / Asst. Manager . . . . Linda Fleischer / Michael Snyder
Ticket Office Administration . . . . Joan Kadlec

Finance

Chief Financial Officer. . . . . Angelo Cardone
Controller. . . . . Judy Zdunkiewicz
Manager of Reporting . . . . Tom Griendling
Staff Accountants . . . . Tyler Deane, Sara Bonner
Payroll Accountant / Accounting Clerk . . . . Renee Eiler / Michele Dominic
Team Consultant . . . . Ron Ryan

Phoenix Coyotes

Key Off-Season Signings/Acquisitions

2013

- **May 16** • Re-signed LW **Rob Klinkhammer**.
- **July 1** • Re-signed G **Mike Smith**.
- **5** • Signed C **Mike Ribeiro** and G **Thomas Greiss**.
- **5** • Re-signed C **Kyle Chipchura**, D **Michael Stone** and D **Chris Summers**.
- **9** • Re-signed C **Andy Miele**.
- **10** • Named **Newell Brown** assistant coach.
- **11** • Signed C **Tim Kennedy**.
- **11** • Re-signed LW **Lauri Korpikoski**.
- **19** • Signed RW **Brandon Yip**.
- **22** • Re-signed D **David Rundblad**.

2012-13 Results: 21W-18L-3OTL-6SOL 51PTS
4TH, Pacific Division • 10TH, Western Conference

Year-by-Year Record

		Home				Road				Overall									
Season	**GP**	**W**	**L**	**T**	**OL**	**W**	**L**	**T**	**OL**	**W**	**L**	**T**	**OL**	**GF**	**GA**	**Pts.**	**Div. Fin.**	**Conf. Fin.**	**Playoff Result**
2012-13	48	14	8	....	2	7	10	....	7	21	18	....	9	125	131	51	4th, Pac.	10th, West	Out of Playoffs
2011-12	82	22	13	....	6	20	14	....	7	42	27	....	13	216	204	97	1st, Pac.	3rd, West	Lost Conf. Final
2010-11	82	21	13	....	7	22	13	....	6	43	26	....	13	231	226	99	3rd, Pac.	6th, West	Lost Conf. Quarter-Final
2009-10	82	29	10	....	2	21	15	....	5	50	25	....	7	225	202	107	2nd, Pac.	4th, West	Lost Conf. Quarter-Final
2008-09	82	23	15	....	3	13	24	....	4	36	39	....	7	208	252	79	4th, Pac.	13th, West	Out of Playoffs
2007-08	82	17	20	....	4	21	17	....	3	38	37	....	7	214	231	83	4th, Pac.	12th, West	Out of Playoffs
2006-07	82	18	20	....	3	13	26	....	2	31	46	....	5	216	284	67	5th, Pac.	15th, West	Out of Playoffs
2005-06	82	19	18	....	4	19	21	....	1	38	39	....	5	246	271	81	5th, Pac.	12th, West	Out of Playoffs
2004-05	....	....	....	....	....	....	....	....	....	....	....	....	....	....	....	....			
2003-04	82	11	19	7	4	11	17	11	2	22	36	18	6	188	245	68	5th, Pac.	13th, West	Out of Playoffs
2002-03	82	17	16	6	2	14	19	5	3	31	35	11	5	204	230	78	4th, Pac.	11th, West	Out of Playoffs
2001-02	82	27	8	3	3	13	19	6	3	40	27	9	6	228	210	95	2nd, Pac.	6th, West	Lost Conf. Quarter-Final
2000-01	82	21	11	7	2	14	16	10	1	35	27	17	3	214	212	90	4th, Pac.	9th, West	Out of Playoffs
1999-2000	82	22	16	2	1	17	15	6	3	39	31	8	4	232	228	90	3rd, Pac.	6th, West	Lost Conf. Quarter-Final
1998-99	82	23	13	5	....	16	18	7	....	39	31	12	....	205	197	90	2nd, Pac.	4th, West	Lost Conf. Quarter-Final
1997-98	82	19	16	6	....	16	19	6	....	35	35	12	....	224	227	82	4th, Cen.	6th, West	Lost Conf. Quarter-Final
1996-97	82	15	19	7	....	23	18	0	....	38	37	7	....	240	243	83	3rd, Cen.	5th, West	Lost Conf. Quarter-Final
1995-96*	82	22	16	3	....	14	24	3	....	36	40	6	....	275	291	78	5th, Cen.	8th, West	Lost Conf. Quarter-Final
1994-95*	48	10	10	4	....	6	15	3	....	16	25	7	....	157	177	39	6th, Cen.	10th, West	Out of Playoffs
1993-94*	84	15	23	4	....	9	28	5	....	24	51	9	....	245	344	57	6th, Cen.	12th, West	Out of Playoffs
1992-93*	84	23	16	3	....	17	21	4	....	40	37	7	....	322	320	87	4th, Smythe		Lost Div. Semi-Final
1991-92*	80	20	14	6	....	13	18	9	....	33	32	15	....	251	244	81	4th, Smythe		Lost Div. Semi-Final
1990-91*	80	17	18	5	....	9	25	6	....	26	43	11	....	260	288	63	5th, Smythe		Out of Playoffs
1989-90*	80	22	13	5	....	15	19	6	....	37	32	11	....	298	290	85	3rd, Smythe		Lost Div. Semi-Final
1988-89*	80	17	18	5	....	9	24	7	....	26	42	12	....	300	355	64	5th, Smythe		Out of Playoffs
1987-88*	80	20	14	6	....	13	22	5	....	33	36	11	....	292	310	77	3rd, Smythe		Lost Div. Semi-Final
1986-87*	80	25	12	3	....	15	20	5	....	40	32	8	....	279	271	88	3rd, Smythe		Lost Div. Final
1985-86*	80	18	19	3	....	8	28	4	....	26	47	7	....	295	372	59	3rd, Smythe		Lost Div. Semi-Final
1984-85*	80	21	13	6	....	22	14	4	....	43	27	10	....	358	332	96	2nd, Smythe		Lost Div. Final
1983-84*	80	17	15	8	....	14	23	3	....	31	38	11	....	340	374	73	4th, Smythe		Lost Div. Semi-Final
1982-83*	80	22	16	2	....	11	23	6	....	33	39	8	....	311	333	74	4th, Smythe		Lost Div. Semi-Final
1981-82*	80	18	13	9	....	15	20	5	....	33	33	14	....	319	332	80	2nd, Norris		Lost Div. Semi-Final
1980-81*	80	7	25	8	....	2	32	6	....	9	57	14	....	246	400	32	6th, Smythe		Out of Playoffs
1979-80*	80	13	19	8	....	7	30	3	....	20	49	11	....	214	314	51	5th, Smythe		Out of Playoffs

* Winnipeg Jets

2013-14 Schedule

Oct.	Thu.	3	NY Rangers
	Sat.	5	at San Jose
	Tue.	8	at NY Islanders
	Thu.	10	at Detroit
	Fri.	11	at Philadelphia
	Sun.	13	at Carolina*
	Tue.	15	Ottawa
	Fri.	18	at Anaheim
	Sat.	19	Detroit
	Tue.	22	Calgary
	Thu.	24	at Los Angeles
	Sat.	26	Edmonton*
	Tue.	29	Los Angeles
	Thu.	31	Nashville
Nov.	Sat.	2	at San Jose
	Tue.	5	Vancouver
	Wed.	6	at Anaheim
	Sat.	9	Washington
	Tue.	12	at St. Louis
	Thu.	14	at Chicago
	Sat.	16	Tampa Bay
	Thu.	21	Colorado
	Sat.	23	Anaheim
	Mon.	25	at Nashville
	Wed.	27	at Minnesota
	Sat.	30	Chicago
Dec.	Tue.	3	at Edmonton
	Wed.	4	at Calgary
	Fri.	6	at Vancouver
	Tue.	10	at Colorado
	Thu.	12	NY Islanders
	Sat.	14	Carolina
	Tue.	17	at Montreal
	Thu.	19	at Toronto
	Sat.	21	at Ottawa*
	Mon.	23	at Buffalo
	Fri.	27	San Jose
	Sat.	28	at Anaheim*
	Tue.	31	Edmonton
Jan.	Thu.	2	Columbus
	Sat.	4	Philadelphia
	Tue.	7	Calgary
	Thu.	9	Minnesota
	Sat.	11	Anaheim
	Mon.	13	at Winnipeg
	Tue.	14	at St. Louis
	Thu.	16	Vancouver
	Sat.	18	New Jersey
	Mon.	20	Toronto
	Wed.	22	at Calgary
	Fri.	24	at Edmonton
	Sun.	26	at Vancouver*
	Tue.	28	Los Angeles
	Thu.	30	Buffalo
Feb.	Sat.	1	Pittsburgh
	Tue.	4	Dallas
	Fri.	7	Chicago
	Sat.	8	at Dallas
	Thu.	27	at Winnipeg
	Fri.	28	at Colorado
Mar.	Sun.	2	St. Louis
	Tue.	4	Vancouver
	Thu.	6	Montreal
	Sat.	8	at Washington
	Mon.	10	at Tampa Bay
	Tue.	11	at Florida
	Thu.	13	at Boston
	Sat.	15	Calgary
	Mon.	17	at Los Angeles
	Thu.	20	Florida
	Sat.	22	Boston
	Mon.	24	at NY Rangers
	Tue.	25	at Pittsburgh
	Thu.	27	at New Jersey
	Sat.	29	Minnesota
Apr.	Tue.	1	Winnipeg
	Wed.	2	at Los Angeles
	Fri.	4	Edmonton
	Tue.	8	at Columbus
	Thu.	10	at Nashville
	Sat.	12	San Jose
	Sun.	13	Dallas

* Denotes afternoon game.

Battling Anaheim's Ryan Getzlaf behind the Phoenix net, defenseman Oliver Ekman-Larsson led the Coyotes with 25:05 of ice time per game and was sixth overall in the NHL in terms of total time on ice. He also led the team with 21 assists.

PACIFIC DIVISION
35th NHL Season

Franchise date: June 22, 1979

Transferred from Winnipeg to Phoenix, July 1, 1996.

2013-14 Player Personnel

FORWARDS	HT	WT	*Age	Place of Birth	S	2012-13 Club
BISSONNETTE, Paul	6-2	216	28	Welland, Ont.	L	Cardiff-Phoenix
BOEDKER, Mikkel	6-0	211	23	Brondby, Denmark	L	Lukko-Phoenix
CHIPCHURA, Kyle	6-2	203	27	Westlock, Alta.	L	Arizona-Phoenix
DOAN, Shane	6-1	223	36	Halkirk, Alta.	R	Phoenix
HANZAL, Martin	6-6	236	26	Pisek, Czech.	L	C. Budejovice-Phoenix
KENNEDY, Tim	5-11	180	27	Buffalo, NY	L	Worcester-San Jose
KLINKHAMMER, Rob	6-3	214	27	Lethbridge, Alta.	L	Portland (AHL)-Phoenix
KORPIKOSKI, Lauri	6-1	205	27	Turku, Finland	L	TPS-Phoenix
McMILLAN, Brandon	5-11	190	23	Richmond, B.C.	L	Norfolk-Ana-Port (AHL)
MOSS, Dave	6-4	210	31	Livonia, MI	R	Phoenix
RIBEIRO, Mike	6-0	180	33	Montreal, Que.	L	Washington
VERMETTE, Antoine	6-1	198	31	St-Agapit, Que.	L	Phoenix
VRBATA, Radim	6-1	194	32	Mlada Boleslav, Czech.	R	Ml. Boleslav-Phoenix
YIP, Brandon	6-1	200	28	Vancouver, B.C.	R	Nashville
DEFENSEMEN						
EKMAN-LARSSON, Oliver	6-2	190	22	Karlskrona, Sweden	L	Portland (AHL)-Phoenix
KLESLA, Rostislav	6-3	223	31	Novy Jicin, Czech.	L	Trinec-Phoenix
MICHALEK, Zbynek	6-2	210	30	Jindrichuv Hradec, Czech.	R	Phoenix
MORRIS, Derek	6-0	200	35	Edmonton, Alta.	R	Phoenix
RUNDBLAD, David	6-2	195	22	Lycksele, Sweden	R	Portland (AHL)-Phoenix
SCHLEMKO, David	6-1	190	26	Edmonton, Alta.	L	Arizona-Phoenix
STONE, Michael	6-3	210	23	Winnipeg, Man.	R	Portland (AHL)-Phoenix
SUMMERS, Chris	6-2	209	25	Ann Arbor, MI	L	Portland (AHL)-Phoenix
YANDLE, Keith	6-1	190	27	Boston, MA	L	Phoenix

GOALTENDERS	HT	WT	*Age	Place of Birth	C	2012-13 Club
GREISS, Thomas	6-1	215	27	Straubing, West Germany	L	Hannover Scorp.-S.J.-Wor
SMITH, Mike	6-4	215	31	Kingston, Ont.	L	Phoenix

* – Age at start of 2013-14 season

2012-13 Scoring

* – rookie

Regular Season

Pos	#	Player	Team	GP	G	A	Pts	TOI	+/–	PIM	PP	SH	GW	S	%
D	3	Keith Yandle	PHX	48	10	20	30	22:14	4	54	5	0	3	130	7.7
R	17	Radim Vrbata	PHX	34	12	16	28	18:18	6	14	2	1	1	106	11.3
R	19	Shane Doan	PHX	48	13	14	27	18:03	6	37	0	0	2	129	10.1
L	89	Mikkel Boedker	PHX	48	7	19	26	18:28	0	12	3	0	2	83	8.4
D	23	Oliver Ekman-Larsson	PHX	48	3	21	24	25:05	5	26	0	0	1	101	3.0
C	11	Martin Hanzal	PHX	39	11	12	23	18:32	2	24	4	0	2	93	11.8
C	50	Antoine Vermette	PHX	48	13	8	21	18:14	–3	36	3	0	3	91	14.3
R	18	David Moss	PHX	45	5	15	20	15:33	3	21	1	1	0	82	6.1
C	24	Kyle Chipchura	PHX	46	5	9	14	9:41	1	50	0	0	0	37	13.5
C	15	Boyd Gordon	PHX	48	4	10	14	15:00	0	8	0	0	0	59	6.8
L	28	Lauri Korpikoski	PHX	36	6	5	11	17:07	–3	12	1	0	0	83	7.2
C	36	Rob Klinkhammer	PHX	22	5	6	11	12:13	7	10	1	0	1	34	14.7
D	53	Derek Morris	PHX	39	0	11	11	21:23	–6	36	0	0	0	68	0.0
D	29 *	Michael Stone	PHX	40	5	4	9	16:41	2	16	1	0	0	50	10.0
D	16	Rostislav Klesla	PHX	38	2	6	8	17:37	0	22	0	0	0	44	4.5
R	32	Nick Johnson	PHX	17	4	2	6	9:57	3	0	1	0	1	23	17.4
D	6	David Schlemko	PHX	30	1	5	6	17:13	8	12	0	0	0	35	2.9
L	12	Paul Bissonnette	PHX	28	0	6	6	5:25	2	36	0	0	0	13	0.0
R	14	Chris Conner	PHX	12	1	1	2	11:22	3	2	0	0	0	15	6.7
D	4	Zbynek Michalek	PHX	34	0	2	2	21:18	4	14	0	0	0	42	0.0
D	2	David Rundblad	PHX	8	0	1	1	13:44	–5	0	0	0	0	9	0.0
C	21 *	Andy Miele	PHX	1	0	0	0	9:02	1	0	0	0	0	0	0.0
C	44 *	Chris Brown	PHX	5	0	0	0	7:38	0	2	0	0	0	6	0.0
D	20 *	Chris Summers	PHX	6	0	0	0	12:39	–3	9	0	0	0	5	0.0
C	49	Alexandre Bolduc	PHX	14	0	0	0	7:37	–4	2	0	0	0	17	0.0

Goaltending

No.	Goaltender	GPI	Mins	Avg	W	L	OT	EN	SO	GA	SA	S%	G	A	PIM
31	Chad Johnson	4	247	1.21	2	0	2	0	1	5	108	.954	0	0	0
41	Mike Smith	34	1956	2.58	15	12	5	2	5	84	938	.910	0	0	0
1	Jason LaBarbera	15	726	2.64	4	6	2	2	0	32	418	.923	0	0	0
	Totals	**48**	**2945**	**2.55**	**21**	**18**	**9**	**4**	**6**	**125**	**1467**	**.915**			

Mike Smith's five shutouts for Phoenix in 2012-13 earned him a share of the NHL lead along with Jimmy Howard, Tuukka Rask, Cory Schneider and Pekka Rinne.

Don Maloney

General Manager

Born: Lindsay, Ont., September 5, 1958.

Don Maloney was signed as general manager of the Phoenix Coyotes on May 30, 2007. Maloney has steered the team through turbulent times and guided the Coyotes to the most successful season in franchise history in 2009-10, setting club records with 50 wins and 107 points. He was rewarded for his efforts by being named the inauguarl winner of the NHL General Manager of the Year Award in 2010. In 2011-12, the Coyotes won the first division title in franchise history and advanced to the second round of the playoffs for the first time since 1987.

Maloney joined the Coyotes from the New York Rangers for whom he served as vice president of player personnel and assistant general manager. He assisted Rangers' president and g.m. Glen Sather in all player transactions and contract negotiations and was involved with the team's professional and amateur scouting operations. Maloney spent 10 seasons in the Rangers' front office. He played a key role in the Rangers' development of several prospects into productive NHL players, including Henrik Lundqvist. Maloney also served as assistant general manager for Team Canada squads that won gold medals at the 2003 and 2004 World Championships.

Maloney's first front office position in the NHL was as assistant general manager of the New York Islanders following his retirement as a player with the club on January 17, 1991. Maloney later served as Islanders' general manager from August 17, 1992 to December 2, 1995. Among the players drafted by the Islanders during Maloney's tenure with the club were Todd Bertuzzi, Bryan McCabe, Ziggy Palffy, Tommy Salo and Darius Kasparaitis. Maloney then served as Eastern professional scout for the San Jose Sharks during the 1996-97 season prior to joining the Rangers' front office.

As a player, Maloney registered 214 goals, 350 assists, and 564 points as well as 815 penalty minutes in 765 regular-season games over 13 NHL campaigns with the Rangers, Hartford Whalers and Islanders. He also collected 22 goals, 35 assists, and 57 points in 94 career playoff games. Maloney spent 11 seasons with the Rangers after being selected by the club in the second round (26th overall) of the 1978 NHL Entry Draft. He helped lead the Rangers to the 1980 Stanley Cup Final by posting 20 points (7 goals, 13 assists) that postseason, a playoff record for rookies at the time. Maloney played in the NHL All-Star Game in 1983 and 1984. He was named MVP of the 1984 game.

General Managers' History

John Ferguson, 1979-80 to 1987-88; John Ferguson and Mike Smith, 1988-89; Mike Smith, 1989-90 to 1992-93; Mike Smith and John Paddock, 1993-94; John Paddock, 1994-95, 1995-96; John Paddock and Bobby Smith, 1996-97; Bobby Smith, 1997-98 to 1999-2000; Bobby Smith and Cliff Fletcher, 2000-01; Michael Barnett, 2001-02 to 2006-07; Don Maloney, 2007-08 to date.

Coaching History

Tom McVie and Bill Sutherland, 1979-80; Tom McVie, Bill Sutherland and Mike Smith, 1980-81; Tom Watt, 1981-82, 1982-83; Tom Watt and Barry Long, 1983-84; Barry Long, 1984-85; Barry Long and John Ferguson, 1985-86; Dan Maloney, 1986-87, 1987-88; Dan Maloney and Rick Bowness, 1988-89; Bob Murdoch, 1989-90, 1990-91; John Paddock, 1991-92 to 1993-94; John Paddock and Terry Simpson, 1994-95; Terry Simpson, 1995-96; Don Hay, 1996-97; Jim Schoenfeld, 1997-98, 1998-99; Bob Francis, 1999-2000 to 2002-03; Bob Francis and Rick Bowness, 2003-04; Rick Bowness, 2004-05; Wayne Gretzky, 2005-06 to 2008-09; Dave Tippett, 2009-10 to date.

Club Records

Team

(Figures in brackets for season records are games played; records for fewest points, wins, ties, losses, goals, goals against are for 70 or more games)

Most Points **107** 2009-10 (82)
Most Wins **50** 2009-10 (82)
Most Ties **18** 2003-04 (82)
Most Losses **57** 1980-81 (80)
Most Goals **358** 1984-85 (80)
Most Goals Against **400** 1980-81 (80)
Fewest Points **32** 1980-81 (80)
Fewest Wins **9** 1980-81 (80)
Fewest Ties **6** 1995-96 (82)
Fewest Losses **25** 2009-10 (82)
Fewest Goals **188** 2003-04 (82)
Fewest Goals Against **197** 1998-99 (82)
Longest Winning Streak
Overall .... **9** Mar. 8-27/85, Mar. 4-21/10
Home .... **10** Nov. 21-Dec. 29/09
Away .... **8** Feb. 25-Apr. 6/85
Longest Undefeated Streak
Overall .... **14** Oct. 25-Nov. 28/98 (12W, 2T)
Home .... **11** Dec. 23/83-Feb. 5/84 (6W, 5T), Oct. 15-Dec. 20/98 (10W, 1T)
Away .... **9** Feb. 25-Apr. 7/85 (8W, 1T), Dec. 7/03-Jan. 9/04 (5W, 4T/OL)
Longest Losing Streak
Overall .... **10** Nov. 30-Dec. 20/80, Feb. 6-25/94
Home .... **6** Oct. 6-Nov. 3/07, Jan. 27-Feb. 16/09
Away .... **13** Jan. 26-Apr. 14/94
Longest Winless Streak
Overall .... ***30** Oct. 19-Dec. 20/80 (23L, 7T)
Home .... **14** Oct. 19-Dec. 14/80 (9L, 5T)
Away .... **18** Oct. 10-Dec. 20/80 (16L, 2T)
Most Shutouts, Season **9** 1998-99 (82), 2010-11 (82)
Most PIM, Season **2,278** 1987-88 (80)
Most Goals, Game .... **12** Feb. 25/85 (Wpg. 12 at NYR 5)

Individual

Most Seasons .... **17** Shane Doan
Most Games .... **1,246** Shane Doan
Most Goals, Career .... **379** Dale Hawerchuk
Most Assists, Career .... **553** Thomas Steen
Most Points, Career .... **929** Dale Hawerchuk (379G, 550A)
Most PIM, Career .... **1,508** Keith Tkachuk
Most Shutouts, Career .... **21** Nikolai Khabibulin, Ilya Bryzgalov
Longest Consecutive Games Streak .... **475** Dale Hawerchuk (Dec. 19/82-Dec. 10/88)
Most Goals, Season .... **76** Teemu Selanne (1992-93)
Most Assists, Season .... **79** Phil Housley (1992-93)
Most Points, Season .... **132** Teemu Selanne (1992-93; 76G, 56A)
Most PIM, Season .... **347** Tie Domi (1993-94)
Most Points, Defenseman, Season .... **97** Phil Housley (1992-93; 18G, 79A)
Most Points, Center, Season .... **130** Dale Hawerchuk (1984-85; 53G, 77A)
Most Points, Right Wing, Season .... **132** Teemu Selanne (1992-93; 76G, 56A)
Most Points, Left Wing, Season .... **98** Keith Tkachuk (1995-96; 50G, 48A)
Most Points, Rookie, Season .... ***132** Teemu Selanne (1992-93; 76G, 56A)
Most Shutouts, Season .... **8** Nikolai Khabibulin (1998-99), Ilya Bryzgalov (2009-10), Mike Smith (2011-12)
Most Goals, Game .... **5** Willy Lindstrom (Mar. 2/82), Alexei Zhamnov (Apr. 1/95)
Most Assists, Game .... **5** Dale Hawerchuk (Mar. 6/84), (Mar. 18/89), (Mar. 4/90), Phil Housley (Jan. 18/93), Keith Tkachuk (Feb. 23/01)
Most Points, Game .... **6** Willy Lindstrom (Mar. 2/82; 5G, 1A), Dale Hawerchuk (Dec. 14/83; 3G, 3A), (Mar. 5/88; 2G, 4A), (Mar. 18/89; 1G, 5A), Thomas Steen (Oct. 24/84; 2G, 4A), Ed Olczyk (Dec. 21/91; 2G, 4A)

* NHL Record.
Records include Winnipeg Jets, 1979-80 through 1995-96.

Captains' History

Lars-Erik Sjoberg, 1979-80; Morris Lukowich and Scott Campbell, 1980-81; Dave Christian and Barry Long, 1981-82; Dave Christian and Lucien DeBlois, 1982-83; Lucien DeBlois, 1983-84; Dale Hawerchuk, 1984-85 to 1988-89; Randy Carlyle, Dale Hawerchuk and Thomas Steen (tri-captains), 1989-90; Randy Carlyle and Thomas Steen (co-captains), 1990-91; Troy Murray, 1991-92; Troy Murray and Dean Kennedy, 1992-93; Dean Kennedy and Keith Tkachuk, 1993-94; Keith Tkachuk, 1994-95; Kris King, 1995-96; Keith Tkachuk, 1996-97 to 2000-01; Teppo Numminen, 2001-02, 2002-03; Shane Doan, 2003-04 to date.

Retired Numbers

7	Keith Tkachuk	1991-2001
9	Bobby Hull*	1972-1980
10	Dale Hawerchuk*	1981-1990
25	Thomas Steen*	1981-1995
27	Teppo Numminen*	1988-2003
97	Jeremy Roenick	1996-2001

* Winnipeg Jets

All-time Record vs. Other Clubs

Regular Season

	Total								At Home								On Road							
	GP	W	L	T	OL	GF	GA	PTS	GP	W	L	T	OL	GF	GA	PTS	GP	W	L	T	OL	GF	GA	PTS
Anaheim	105	43	49	5	8	285	314	99	52	25	20	2	5	152	150	57	53	18	29	3	3	133	164	42
Boston	67	21	38	7	1	208	251	50	34	14	16	3	1	107	111	32	33	7	22	4	0	101	140	18
Buffalo	68	22	38	7	1	184	242	52	33	14	16	2	1	96	105	31	35	8	22	5	0	88	137	21
Calgary	172	72	78	20	2	573	626	166	85	42	32	11	0	305	282	95	87	30	46	9	2	268	344	71
Carolina	68	28	29	8	3	224	238	67	34	15	15	2	2	123	127	34	34	13	14	6	1	101	111	33
Chicago	129	54	56	15	4	366	431	127	66	34	25	5	2	207	208	75	63	20	31	10	2	159	223	52
Colorado	112	48	46	12	6	379	370	114	56	25	21	7	3	196	183	60	56	23	25	5	3	183	187	54
Columbus	47	26	16	4	1	131	109	57	24	15	6	3	0	74	51	33	23	11	10	1	1	57	58	24
Dallas	161	68	71	13	9	472	515	158	80	36	36	4	4	240	249	80	81	32	35	9	5	232	266	78
Detroit	131	44	59	22	6	399	463	116	65	22	26	14	3	189	209	61	66	22	33	8	3	210	254	55
Edmonton	174	65	92	11	6	611	723	147	86	37	41	5	3	333	353	82	88	28	51	6	3	278	370	65
Florida	24	12	7	3	2	65	69	29	13	5	3	3	2	36	37	15	11	7	4	0	0	29	32	14
Los Angeles	203	100	71	25	7	742	685	232	103	57	33	11	2	395	324	127	100	43	38	14	5	347	361	105
Minnesota	47	22	19	3	3	117	119	50	24	12	10	1	1	61	56	26	23	10	9	2	2	56	63	24
Montreal	64	12	41	9	2	171	277	35	32	9	15	7	1	100	123	26	32	3	26	2	1	71	154	9
Nashville	55	27	19	2	7	149	158	63	27	16	8	0	3	80	79	35	28	11	11	2	4	69	79	28
New Jersey	66	36	21	9	0	219	192	81	34	24	7	3	0	126	88	51	32	12	14	6	0	93	104	30
NY Islanders	67	24	30	12	1	215	240	61	34	14	15	4	1	116	118	33	33	10	15	8	0	99	122	28
NY Rangers	68	24	34	6	4	229	257	58	34	14	15	4	1	115	113	33	34	10	19	2	3	114	144	25
Ottawa	27	12	13	2	0	83	93	26	13	6	6	1	0	42	46	13	14	6	7	1	0	41	47	13
Philadelphia	69	25	41	2	1	201	255	53	34	15	17	2	0	108	111	32	35	10	24	0	1	93	144	21
Pittsburgh	68	26	37	3	2	217	250	57	34	15	14	3	2	125	119	35	34	11	23	0	0	92	131	22
St. Louis	132	55	57	18	2	382	424	130	66	33	26	7	0	206	208	73	66	22	31	11	2	176	216	57
San Jose	120	54	51	7	8	337	362	123	61	31	23	3	4	177	169	69	59	23	28	4	4	160	193	54
Tampa Bay	29	13	16	0	0	77	89	26	16	7	9	0	0	36	42	14	13	6	7	0	0	41	47	12
Toronto	88	47	33	8	0	351	312	102	42	23	13	6	0	177	147	52	46	24	20	2	0	174	165	50
Vancouver	172	65	84	20	3	527	604	153	84	40	32	10	2	291	288	92	88	25	52	10	1	236	316	61
Washington	67	26	28	12	1	211	243	65	33	17	9	7	0	118	114	41	34	9	19	5	1	93	129	24
Winnipeg	16	13	2	1	0	53	29	27	9	8	0	1	0	33	16	17	7	5	2	0	0	20	13	10
Totals	**2616**	**1084**	**1176**	**266**	**90**	**8178**	**8940**	**2524**	**1308**	**625**	**509**	**131**	**43**	**4364**	**4226**	**1424**	**1308**	**459**	**667**	**135**	**47**	**3814**	**4714**	**1100**

Playoffs

	Series	W	L	GP	W	L	T	GF	GA	Last Mtg.	Rnd.	Result
Anaheim	1	0	1	7	3	4	0	17	17	1997	CQF	L 3-4
Calgary	3	2	1	13	7	6	0	45	43	1987	DSF	W 4-2
Chicago	1	1	0	6	4	2	0	17	12	2012	CQF	W 4-2
Colorado	1	0	1	5	1	4	0	10	17	2000	CQF	L 1-4
Detroit	4	0	4	23	7	16	0	56	88	2011	CQF	L 0-4
Edmonton	6	0	6	26	4	22	0	75	120	1990	DSF	L 3-4
Los Angeles	1	0	1	5	1	4	0	8	14	2012	CF	L 1-4
Nashville	1	1	0	5	4	1	0	12	9	2012	CSF	W 4-1
St. Louis	2	0	2	11	4	7	0	29	39	1999	CQF	L 3-4
San Jose	1	0	1	5	1	4	0	7	13	2002	CQF	L 1-4
Vancouver	2	0	2	13	5	8	0	34	50	1993	DSF	L 2-4
Totals	**23**	**4**	**19**	**119**	**41**	**78**	**0**	**310**	**422**			

Playoff Results 2013-2009

Year	Round	Opponent	Result	GF	GA
2012	CF	Los Angeles	L 1-4	8	14
	CSF	Nashville	W 4-1	12	9
	CQF	Chicago	W 4-2	17	12
2011	CQF	Detroit	L 0-4	10	18
2010	CQF	Detroit	L 3-4	18	26

Abbreviations: Round: CF – conference final; **CSF** – conference semi-final; **CQF** – conference quarter-final; **DSF** – division semi-final.

Calgary totals include Atlanta Flames, 1979-80.
Colorado totals include Quebec, 1979-80 to 1994-95.
New Jersey totals include Colorado Rockies, 1979-80 to 1981-82.
Carolina totals include Hartford, 1979-80 to 1996-97.
Dallas totals include Minnesota North Stars, 1979-80 to 1992-93.
Winnipeg totals include Atlanta Thrashers, 1999-2000 to 2010-11.

2012-13 Results

Jan.	19	at Dallas	3-4		9	Dallas	2-1
	20	Chicago	4-6		12	Los Angeles	5-2
	23	Columbus	5-1		14	at St. Louis	0-3
	24	at San Jose	3-5		16	at Columbus	0-1†
	26	Los Angeles	2-4		18	at Los Angeles	0-4
	28	Nashville	4-0		19	at Los Angeles	2-3
	30	Edmonton	1-2*		21	Vancouver	1-2
Feb.	1	at Dallas	3-4†		25	Detroit	2-3
	2	Dallas	2-0		27	at Minnesota	3-4*
	4	Minnesota	2-1		28	at Nashville	7-4
	7	Chicago	2-6		30	at San Jose	2-3†
	9	at San Jose	1-0†	**Apr.**	2	Los Angeles	3-1
	11	at Colorado	3-2*		4	Detroit	4-2
	14	at Nashville	0-3		6	Colorado	4-0
	16	Columbus	5-3		8	at Vancouver	0-2
	18	Calgary	4-0		10	at Edmonton	3-1
	23	at Edmonton	2-3†		12	at Calgary	2-3*
	24	at Calgary	4-5		15	San Jose	0-4
	26	at Vancouver	4-2		18	at St. Louis	1-2†
	28	Minnesota	3-4		20	at Chicago	3-2†
Mar.	2	Anaheim	5-4†		22	at Detroit	0-4
	4	Anaheim	5-4†		24	San Jose	2-1
	6	at Anaheim	0-2		26	Colorado	4-5†
	7	St. Louis	3-6		27	at Anaheim	5-3

* – Overtime † – Shootout

Entry Draft Selections 2013-1999

Name in bold denotes played in NHL.

2013
Pick
- 12 Max Domi
- 39 Laurent Dauphin
- 62 Pavel Laplante
- 133 Connor Clifton
- 163 Brendan Burke
- 193 Jedd Soleway

2012
Pick
- 27 Henrik Samuelsson
- 58 Jordan Martinook
- 88 James Melindy
- 102 Rhett Holland
- 148 Niklas Tikkinen
- 178 Hunter Fejes
- 184 Marek Langhamer
- 208 Justin Hache

2011
Pick
- 20 Connor Murphy
- 51 Alexander Ruuttu
- 56 Lucas Lessio
- 84 Harrison Ruopp
- 111 Kale Kessy
- 141 Darian Dziurzynski
- 155 Andrew Fritsch
- 196 Zac Larraza

2010
Pick
- 13 Brandon Gormley
- 27 Mark Visentin
- 52 Phil Lane
- 57 Oscar Lindberg
- 138 Louis Domingue

2009
Pick
- 6 **Oliver Ekman-Larsson**
- 36 **Chris Brown**
- 91 Mike Lee
- 97 Jordan Szwarz
- 105 Justin Weller
- 157 Evan Bloodoff

2008
Pick
- 8 **Mikkel Boedker**
- 28 **Viktor Tikhonov**
- 49 **Jared Staal**
- 69 **Michael Stone**
- 76 Mathieu Brodeur
- 99 Colin Long
- 159 Brett Hextall
- 189 Tim Billingsley

2007
Pick
- 3 **Kyle Turris**
- 30 Nick Ross
- 32 **Brett Maclean**
- 36 Joel Gistedt
- 103 Vladimir Ruzicka
- 123 Maxim Goncharov
- 153 Scott Darling

2006
Pick
- 8 **Peter Mueller**
- 29 **Chris Summers**
- 88 Jonas Ahnelov
- 130 Brett Bennett
- 131 Martin Latal
- 152 Jordan Bendfeld
- 188 Chris Frank
- 196 **Benn Ferriero**

2005
Pick
- 17 **Martin Hanzal**
- 59 Pier-Olivier Pelletier
- 105 **Keith Yandle**
- 148 Anton Krysanov
- 212 Pat Brosnihan

2004
Pick
- 5 **Blake Wheeler**
- 35 Logan Stephenson
- 50 **Enver Lisin**
- 103 Roman Tomanek
- 119 **Kevin Porter**
- 168 Kevin Cormier
- 199 **Chad Kolarik**
- 240 **Aaron Gagnon**
- 261 Will Engasser
- 265 **Daniel Winnik**

2003
Pick
- 77 Tyler Redenbach
- 80 Dmitri Pestunov
- 115 Liam Lindstrom
- 178 Ryan Gibbons
- 208 Randall Gelech
- 242 Eduard Lewandowski
- 272 Sean Sullivan
- 290 Loic Burkhalter

2002
Pick
- 19 Jakub Koreis
- 23 **Ben Eager**
- 46 **David LeNeveu**
- 70 **Joe Callahan**
- 80 **Matt Jones**
- 97 Lance Monych
- 132 **John Zeiler**
- 186 Jeff Pietrasiak
- 216 Ladislav Kouba
- 249 Marcus Smith
- 280 Russell Spence

2001
Pick
- 11 **Fredrik Sjostrom**
- 31 **Matthew Spiller**
- 45 Martin Podlesak
- 78 Beat Forster
- 148 David Klema
- 180 Scott Polaski
- 210 Steve Belanger
- 243 Frantisek Lukes
- 273 Severin Blindenbacher

2000
Pick
- 19 **Krys Kolanos**
- 53 Alexander Tatarinov
- 85 **Ramzi Abid**
- 160 Nate Kiser
- 186 Brent Gauvreau
- 217 Igor Samoilov
- 249 Sami Venalainen
- 281 Peter Fabus

1999
Pick
- 15 Scott Kelman
- 19 **Kirill Safronov**
- 53 **Brad Ralph**
- 71 **Jason Jaspers**
- 116 Ryan Lauzon
- 123 Preston Mizzi
- 168 Erik Lewerstrom
- 234 **Goran Bezina**
- 262 Alexei Litvinenko

Dave Tippett

Head Coach

Born: Moosomin, Sask., August 25, 1961.

Dave Tippett was named the 17th head coach in Coyotes/Jets history on September 24, 2009. In his first season with the team in 2009-10, he led the Coyotes to a club-record 50 wins and 107 points and the team's first playoff appearance since 2001-02. Tippett was rewarded with the Jack Adams Award as coach of the year. In 2011-12, the Coyotes won the first division title in franchise history and advanced to the second round of the playoffs for the first time since 1987.

Prior to Phoenix, Tippett spent seven seasons as the head coach of the Dallas Stars from 2002-03 to 2008-09. Under Tippett's leadership, the Stars won two Pacific Division titles (2002-03 and 2005-06), made the playoffs in five out of six years and reached the Western Conference Final in 2008. His 271 career regular-season coaching victories rank him second all-time in Stars history.

Tippett joined the Stars organization on May 16, 2002 after serving as an assistant coach with the Los Angeles Kings for three seasons. Prior to becoming a coach, Tippett played 11 years as a forward in the National Hockey League with the Hartford Whalers, Washington Capitals, Pittsburgh Penguins and Philadelphia Flyers. He ended his playing career in 1995 as a player-assistant coach with the Houston Aeros (IHL). Internationally, he captained the 1984 Canadian Olympic team in Sarajevo, Yugoslavia, and he earned a silver medal as a member of the Canadian Olympic team in Albertville, France, in 1992. He was a member of the 1982 NCAA Division I championship squad at the University of North Dakota with former Stars defenseman Craig Ludwig. Tippett became head coach of the Houston Aeros in 1995-96. In 1999, he led the team to the Turner Cup championship and was named the IHL coach of the year.

Coaching Record

			Regular Season				Playoffs			
Season	Team	League	GC	W	L	O/T	GC	W	L	T
1995-96	Houston	IHL	42	17	18	7	....	....	....	....
1996-97	Houston	IHL	82	44	30	8	13	8	5	....
1997-98	Houston	IHL	82	50	22	10	4	1	3	....
1998-99	Houston	IHL	82	54	15	13	19	11	8	....
2002-03	**Dallas**	**NHL**	**82**	**46**	**17**	**19**	**12**	**6**	**6**	....
2003-04	**Dallas**	**NHL**	**82**	**41**	**26**	**15**	**5**	**1**	**4**	....
2004-05	**Dallas**				SEASON CANCELLED					
2005-06	**Dallas**	**NHL**	**82**	**53**	**23**	**6**	**5**	**1**	**4**	....
2006-07	**Dallas**	**NHL**	**82**	**50**	**25**	**7**	**7**	**3**	**4**	....
2007-08	**Dallas**	**NHL**	**82**	**45**	**30**	**7**	**18**	**10**	**8**	....
2008-09	**Dallas**	**NHL**	**82**	**36**	**35**	**11**	....	....	....	....
2009-10	**Phoenix**	**NHL**	**82**	**50**	**25**	**7**	**7**	**3**	**4**	....
2010-11	**Phoenix**	**NHL**	**82**	**43**	**26**	**13**	**4**	**0**	**4**	....
2011-12	**Phoenix**	**NHL**	**82**	**42**	**27**	**13**	**16**	**9**	**7**	....
2012-13	**Phoenix**	**NHL**	**48**	**21**	**18**	**9**	....	....	....	....
	NHL Totals		**786**	**427**	**252**	**107**	**74**	**33**	**41**	....

Jack Adams Award (2010)

Posted a 2-1-2 record as replacement coach when Andy Murray was sidelined following a car accident, February 26 to March 6, 2002, All games are credited to Murray's coaching record.

Club Directory

Jobing.com Arena

Phoenix Coyotes
6751 N. Sunset Blvd. #200
Glendale, AZ 85305
Phone **623/772-3200**
FAX 623/872-2000
Tickets 480/563-PUCK

Jobing.com Arena
9400 W. Maryland Avenue
Glendale, AZ 85305
Phone 623/772-3200
FAX 623/772-3201
www.PhoenixCoyotes.com
Capacity: 17,125

Club Officers and Executives

Executive Chairman and Governor	George Gosbee
President, CEO & Alternate Governor	Anthony LeBlanc
Strategic Advisor to the CEO & Chairman	Mike Nealy
Executive Vice President, G.M. & Alt. Governor	Don Maloney
Vice President of Hockey Operations & Asst. G.M.	Brad Treliving
Exec. Support/Legal & Risk Mgmt. Coord.	Gail Avisar

Hockey Operations

Head Coach	Dave Tippett
Associate Coach	Jim Playfair
Assistant Coach	Newell Brown
Asst. to the G.M./Goaltending Coach	Sean Burke
Development Coach	Dave King
Video Coach / Power Skating Coach	Steve Peters / Mark Ciaccio
Sr. Director of Hockey Operations	Chris O'Hearn
Hockey Operations Coordinator	Bob Teofilo
Executive Assistant/Hockey Ops.	Ashley James
Head Athletic Trainer / Assistant Trainer	Jason Serbus / Mike Ermatinger
Strength & Conditioning Coordinator	Tommy Powers
Manual Therapist	Mike Griebel
Equipment: Head Mgr. / Mgr. / Asst. Mgr.	Stan Wilson / Tony Silva / Jason Rudee
Manager of Team Services	Rick Braunstein
Team Services Coordinator/Security	Jim O'Neal
Scouting Directors, Amateur / Pro	Rick Knickle / Frank Effinger
Professional / European Scouts	Derek MacKinnon, David MacLean / Robert Neuhauser
Amateur Scouts	Norm Gosselin, Trevor Hanson, Mike MacFarlane, Tim Keon, Gary Knickle, Tim Bernhardt, Rob Pulford, Glen Zacharias
Team Internist	Robert Luberto, D.O.
Team Orthopedic Surgeons	Dr. Doug Freeberg, Dr. Gary Waslewski
Team Dentists	Dr. Lawrence Emmott, Dr. Rick Landgrin, Byron J. Larsen, DDS
Team Opthamologists	Dr. George Reiss, Dr. Jeffery Edelstein
Portland (AHL) Coaches, Head / Assistant	Ray Edwards / John Slaney
Portland (AHL) Goaltending/Video Coach	Mike Minard
Portland (AHL) Trainer / Equipment Mgr.	Mike Booi / John Krouse

Broadcasting

Director of Broadcasting	Doug Cannon
TV Play-by-Play Announcer	Matt McConnell
TV/Radio Color Analyst / Host	Tyson Nash / Todd Walsh
Radio Play-by-Play Announcer / Host	Bob Heethuis / Luke Lapinski

Communications

Vice President of Communications	Rich Nairn
Media Relations Director / Coordinator	Chris Wojcik / Greg Dillard

Community Relations

Director of Community Relations	Kimberly Trichel
Community Relations Manager / Coordinator	Matt Shott / Ann Pickrell

Corporate Partnerships & Service

Director of Corporate Partnerships	Brittany Grant
Corporate Partnerships Managers	Pam Craven / Lindsay Foletta
Corporate Partner Service Coordinator	Taylor Popish

Finance & Accounting

Sr. Vice President of Finance	Joe Leibfried
Assistant Controller	Stephanie Johnson
Administrators, A/P / Payroll	Kathy Kelly / Lollie Gonzales

Game Operations

Lead Editor/Production Manager	Rachel Regnier
Field Producer / Producer/Editor	Rachel Korchin / Robert Clark

Human Resources

Vice President of Human Resources	Julie Atherton
Receptionist	Jessica Glass

Marketing

Vice President of Marketing	Ted Santiago
Manager of Creative Services	Scott Jenner
Marketing Manager / Database Mktg. Coord.	Trent Nielsen / Stephanie Richter

News Content

Sr. Director of News Content	Dave Vest

Ticket Operations

Sr. Director of Ticket Operations	Doug Vanderheyden
Box Office Manager	Julia Kincade
Ticket Operations Supervisor	Jakub Jaroszewicz

Ticket Sales & Service

Sr. Director of Premium & Suite Sales	Grant Buckborough
Ticket Sales Sr. Director / Director	Ken Troupe / Justin Brickner
Premium Seating Sr. Mgr. / Mgrs.	Mike Briody / Mike Ostrowski, James Whitener
Premium Seating Execs. / Service Rep.	Matt McClelland, Dave Paris / Leah Adler
Manager of Service & Retention	Lindsay Kray
Service & Retention Account Execs.	Karalyn Katchmark, Sean Sanford, Matt Herold
Business Development Account Execs.	Zach Fish, Drew Bennett, Josh Pitts, Phil Martin, Sean Phelan, Marshall Spalding
Group Sales Mgr. / Sr. Exec. / Execs	TBA / Steve Gonzales / Jack Mertes, Katarina Hinsberg, Pete Musser, Will Rimer, Scott Schwartz
Inside Sales Mgr. / Reps	Jesse Whalen / Daniel Zamora, Mike Kann, Michelle Sondheim, Matt Hergenrader, Ryan Jacobsen, Celina Encinas, James Kim, Tyler Kern, Ian Kalanges, John Baker, Craig Campbell, Whitney Macleod

Technology

Director of IT / Analyst System Administrator	Monty Low / Justin Ferguson

Arena Management Group

Sr. Vice President & General Manager	Jim Foss

Team Information

Regional Sports Network / Radio Station	FOX Sports Arizona / FOX Sports 910
Team Photographer	Norm Hall

Pittsburgh Penguins

2012-13 Results: 36W-12L-0OTL-0SOL 72PTS
1ST, Atlantic Division • 1ST, Eastern Conference

Key Off-Season Signings/Acquisitions

2013

- **June 13** • Re-signed C **Evgeni Malkin**.
- **24** • Acquired LW **Harry Zolnierczyk** from Anaheim for D **Alex Grant**.
- **27** • Re-signed LW **Chris Kunitz**.
- **July 2** • Re-signed D **Kris Letang** and RW **Pascal Dupuis**.
- **5** • Signed D **Rob Scuderi**, C **Andrew Ebbett** and RW **Chris Conner**.
- **5** • Re-signed RW **Craig Adams**.
- **10** • Signed RW **Matt D'Agostini**.
- **18** • Re-signed LW **Dustin Jeffrey**.
- **19** • Signed D **Brendan Mikkelson**.
- **24** • Re-signed D **Robert Bortuzzo**.

Likely en route to a scoring title during a brilliant comeback in 2012-13, Sidney Crosby was sidelined for the final 12 games of the regular season when a fluky deflection saw a puck hit him in the face and break his jaw. He returned in time for the playoffs wearing a special plastic protector.

2013-14 Schedule

Oct.	Thu.	3	New Jersey		Tue.	31	at New Jersey*
	Sat.	5	Buffalo	**Jan.**	Fri.	3	NY Rangers
	Tue.	8	Carolina		Sun.	5	Winnipeg*
	Fri.	11	at Florida		Tue.	7	at Vancouver
	Sat.	12	at Tampa Bay		Fri.	10	at Edmonton
	Tue.	15	Edmonton		Sat.	11	at Calgary
	Thu.	17	at Philadelphia		Wed.	15	Washington
	Sat.	19	Vancouver*		Mon.	20	Florida
	Mon.	21	Colorado		Wed.	22	Montreal
	Fri.	25	NY Islanders		Thu.	23	at NY Islanders
	Sat.	26	at Toronto		Sat.	25	at Dallas
	Mon.	28	at Carolina		Mon.	27	Buffalo
	Wed.	30	Boston		Thu.	30	at Los Angeles
Nov.	Fri.	1	Columbus	**Feb.**	Sat.	1	at Phoenix
	Sat.	2	at Columbus		Mon.	3	Ottawa
	Wed.	6	at NY Rangers		Wed.	5	at Buffalo
	Sat.	9	at St. Louis		Fri.	7	NY Rangers
	Wed.	13	Philadelphia		Thu.	27	Montreal
	Fri.	15	Nashville	**Mar.**	Sat.	1	at Chicago
	Sat.	16	at New Jersey		Tue.	4	at Nashville
	Mon.	18	Anaheim		Thu.	6	at San Jose
	Wed.	20	at Washington		Fri.	7	at Anaheim
	Fri.	22	NY Islanders		Mon.	10	at Washington
	Sat.	23	at Montreal		Tue.	11	Washington
	Mon.	25	at Boston		Sat.	15	at Philadelphia*
	Wed.	27	Toronto		Sun.	16	Philadelphia
	Fri.	29	at Tampa Bay*		Tue.	18	Dallas
	Sat.	30	at Florida		Thu.	20	at Detroit
Dec.	Tue.	3	at NY Islanders		Sat.	22	Tampa Bay*
	Thu.	5	San Jose		Sun.	23	St. Louis*
	Sat.	7	at Boston		Tue.	25	Phoenix
	Mon.	9	Columbus		Thu.	27	Los Angeles
	Fri.	13	New Jersey		Fri.	28	at Columbus
	Sat.	14	at Detroit		Sun.	30	Chicago
	Mon.	16	Toronto	**Apr.**	Tue.	1	Carolina
	Wed.	18	at NY Rangers		Thu.	3	at Winnipeg
	Thu.	19	Minnesota		Sat.	5	at Minnesota
	Sat.	21	Calgary*		Sun.	6	at Colorado
	Mon.	23	at Ottawa		Wed.	9	Detroit
	Fri.	27	at Carolina		Sat.	12	Philadelphia*
	Sun.	29	at Columbus		Sun.	13	Ottawa

* Denotes afternoon game.

Year-by-Year Record

		Home				Road				Overall									
Season	**GP**	**W**	**L**	**T**	**OL**	**W**	**L**	**T**	**OL**	**W**	**L**	**T**	**OL**	**GF**	**GA**	**Pts.**	**Div. Fin.**	**Conf. Fin.**	**Playoff Result**
2012-13	48	18	6	....	0	18	6	....	0	36	12	....	0	165	119	72	1st, Atl.	1st, East	Lost Conf. Final
2011-12	82	29	10	....	2	22	15	....	4	51	25	....	6	282	221	108	2nd, Atl.	4th, East	Lost Conf. Quarter-Final
2010-11	82	25	14	....	2	24	11	....	6	49	25	....	8	238	199	106	2nd, Atl.	4th, East	Lost Conf. Quarter-Final
2009-10	82	25	12	....	4	22	16	....	3	47	28	....	7	257	237	101	2nd, Atl.	4th, East	Lost Conf. Semi-Final
2008-09	**82**	**25**	**13**	....	**3**	**20**	**15**	....	**6**	**45**	**28**	....	**9**	**264**	**239**	**99**	**2nd, Atl.**	**4th, East**	**Won Stanley Cup**
2007-08	82	26	10	....	5	21	17	....	3	47	27	....	8	247	216	102	1st, Atl.	2nd, East	Lost Final
2006-07	82	26	10	....	5	21	14	....	6	47	24	....	11	277	246	105	2nd, Atl.	5th, East	Lost Conf. Quarter-Final
2005-06	82	12	21	....	8	10	25	....	6	22	46	....	14	244	316	58	5th, Atl.	15th, East	Out of Playoffs
2004-05	....	....	....	....	....	....	....	....	....	....	....	....	....	....	....	....			
2003-04	82	13	22	6	0	10	25	2	4	23	47	8	4	190	303	58	5th, Atl.	15th, East	Out of Playoffs
2002-03	82	15	22	2	2	12	22	4	3	27	44	6	5	189	255	65	5th, Atl.	14th, East	Out of Playoffs
2001-02	82	16	20	4	1	12	21	4	4	28	41	8	5	198	249	69	5th, Atl.	12th, East	Out of Playoffs
2000-01	82	24	15	2	0	18	13	7	3	42	28	9	3	281	256	96	3rd, Atl.	6th, East	Lost Conf. Final
1999-2000	82	23	11	7	0	14	20	1	6	37	31	8	6	241	236	88	3rd, Atl.	7th, East	Lost Conf. Semi-Final
1998-99	82	21	10	10	....	17	20	4	....	38	30	14	....	242	225	90	3rd, Atl.	8th, East	Lost Conf. Semi-Final
1997-98	82	21	10	10	....	19	14	8	....	40	24	18	....	228	188	98	1st, NE	2nd, East	Lost Conf. Quarter-Final
1996-97	82	25	11	5	....	13	25	3	....	38	36	8	....	285	280	84	2nd, NE	6th, East	Lost Conf. Quarter-Final
1995-96	82	32	9	0	....	17	20	4	....	49	29	4	....	362	284	102	1st, NE	2nd, East	Lost Conf. Final
1994-95	48	18	5	1	....	11	11	2	....	29	16	3	....	181	158	61	2nd, NE	2nd, East	Lost Conf. Semi-Final
1993-94	84	25	9	8	....	19	18	5	....	44	27	13	....	299	285	101	1st, NE	3rd, East	Lost Conf. Quarter-Final
1992-93	84	32	6	4	....	24	15	3	....	56	21	7	....	367	268	119	1st, Patrick		Lost Div. Final
1991-92	**80**	**21**	**13**	**6**	....	**18**	**19**	**3**	....	**39**	**32**	**9**	....	**343**	**308**	**87**	**3rd, Patrick**		**Won Stanley Cup**
1990-91	**80**	**25**	**12**	**3**	....	**16**	**21**	**3**	....	**41**	**33**	**6**	....	**342**	**305**	**88**	**1st, Patrick**		**Won Stanley Cup**
1989-90	80	22	15	3	....	10	25	5	....	32	40	8	....	318	359	72	5th, Patrick		Out of Playoffs
1988-89	80	24	13	3	....	16	20	4	....	40	33	7	....	347	349	87	2nd, Patrick		Lost Div. Final
1987-88	80	22	12	6	....	14	23	3	....	36	35	9	....	319	316	81	6th, Patrick		Out of Playoffs
1986-87	80	19	15	6	....	11	23	6	....	30	38	12	....	297	290	72	5th, Patrick		Out of Playoffs
1985-86	80	20	15	5	....	14	23	3	....	34	38	8	....	313	305	76	5th, Patrick		Out of Playoffs
1984-85	80	17	20	3	....	7	31	2	....	24	51	5	....	276	385	53	6th, Patrick		Out of Playoffs
1983-84	80	7	29	4	....	9	29	2	....	16	58	6	....	254	390	38	6th, Patrick		Out of Playoffs
1982-83	80	14	22	4	....	4	31	5	....	18	53	9	....	257	394	45	6th, Patrick		Out of Playoffs
1981-82	80	21	11	8	....	10	25	5	....	31	36	13	....	310	337	75	4th, Patrick		Lost Div. Semi-Final
1980-81	80	21	16	3	....	9	21	10	....	30	37	13	....	302	345	73	3rd, Norris		Lost Prelim. Round
1979-80	80	20	13	7	....	10	24	6	....	30	37	13	....	251	303	73	3rd, Norris		Lost Prelim. Round
1978-79	80	23	12	5	....	13	19	8	....	36	31	13	....	281	279	85	2nd, Norris		Lost Quarter-Final
1977-78	80	16	15	9	....	9	22	9	....	25	37	18	....	254	321	68	4th, Norris		Out of Playoffs
1976-77	80	22	12	6	....	12	21	7	....	34	33	13	....	240	252	81	3rd, Norris		Lost Prelim. Round
1975-76	80	23	11	6	....	12	22	6	....	35	33	12	....	339	303	82	3rd, Norris		Lost Prelim. Round
1974-75	80	25	5	10	....	12	23	5	....	37	28	15	....	326	289	89	3rd, Norris		Lost Quarter-Final
1973-74	78	15	18	6	....	13	23	3	....	28	41	9	....	242	273	65	5th, West		Out of Playoffs
1972-73	78	24	11	4	....	8	26	5	....	32	37	9	....	257	265	73	5th, West		Out of Playoffs
1971-72	78	18	15	6	....	8	23	8	....	26	38	14	....	220	258	66	4th, West		Lost Quarter-Final
1970-71	78	18	12	9	....	3	25	11	....	21	37	20	....	221	240	62	6th, West		Out of Playoffs
1969-70	76	17	13	8	....	9	25	4	....	26	38	12	....	182	238	64	2nd, West		Lost Semi-Final
1968-69	76	12	20	6	....	8	25	5	....	20	45	11	....	189	252	51	5th, West		Out of Playoffs
1967-68	74	15	12	10	....	12	22	3	....	27	34	13	....	195	216	67	5th, West		Out of Playoffs

METROPOLITAN DIVISION
47th NHL Season

Franchise date: June 5, 1967

2013-14 Player Personnel

FORWARDS	HT	WT	*Age	Place of Birth	S	2012-13 Club
ADAMS, Craig	6-0	197	36	Seria, Brunei	R	Pittsburgh
BENNETT, Beau	6-2	207	21	Gardena, CA	R	Wilkes-Barre-Pittsburgh
CONNER, Chris	5-8	180	29	Westland, MI	L	Portland (AHL)-Phoenix
CROSBY, Sidney	5-11	200	26	Cole Harbour, N.S.	L	Pittsburgh
D'AGOSTINI, Matt	6-0	198	26	Sault Ste. Marie, Ont.	R	Riessersee-StL-N.J.
DRAZENOVIC, Nick	6-0	192	26	Prince George, B.C.	L	Columbus-Springfield
DUPUIS, Pascal	6-1	205	34	Laval, Que.	L	Pittsburgh
EBBETT, Andrew	5-9	174	30	Calgary, Alta.	L	Chicago (AHL)-Vancouver
FARNHAM, Bobby	5-10	180	24	North Andover, MA	L	Wheeling-Wilkes-Barre
GIBBONS, Brian	5-8	170	25	Braintree, MA	L	Wilkes-Barre
GLASS, Tanner	6-1	210	29	Regina, Sask.	L	B. Bystrica-Pittsburgh
JEFFREY, Dustin	6-1	205	25	Sarnia, Ont.	L	Zagreb-Pittsburgh
JOKINEN, Jussi	5-11	198	30	Kalajoki, Finland	L	Karpat-Car-Pit
KUHNHACKL, Tom	6-2	172	21	Landshut, Germany	L	Wheeling-Wilkes-Barre
KUNITZ, Chris	6-0	193	34	Regina, Sask.	L	Pittsburgh
MacINTYRE, Steve	6-5	250	33	Brock, Sask.	L	Wilkes-Barre-Pittsburgh
MALKIN, Evgeni	6-3	195	27	Magnitogorsk, USSR	L	Magnitogorsk-Pittsburgh
MEGNA, Jayson	6-1	195	23	Northbrook, IL	R	Wilkes-Barre
NEAL, James	6-2	208	26	Whitby, Ont.	L	Pittsburgh
PAYERL, Adam	6-3	218	22	Kitchener, Ont.	R	Wilkes-Barre-Wheeling
SILL, Zach	6-0	202	25	Truro, N.S.	L	Wilkes-Barre
SUTTER, Brandon	6-3	183	24	Huntington, NY	R	Pittsburgh
THOMPSON, Paul	6-1	198	24	Melrose, MA	R	Wilkes-Barre
UHER, Dominik	6-1	199	20	Frydek-Mistek, Czech.	L	Wilkes-Barre-Wheeling
VITALE, Joe	5-11	205	28	St. Louis, MO	R	Pittsburgh
ZLOBIN, Anton	5-11	189	20	Moscow, Russia	R	Val-d'Or
ZOLNIERCZYK, Harry	5-11	175	26	Toronto, Ont.	L	Adi-Phi-Norfolk
DEFENSEMEN						
BORTUZZO, Robert	6-4	215	24	Thunder Bay, Ont.	R	Wilkes-Barre-Pittsburgh
D'AGOSTINO, Nick	6-2	197	23	Mississauga, Ont.	L	Cornell
DESPRES, Simon	6-4	214	22	Laval, Que.	L	Wilkes-Barre-Pittsburgh
DUMOULIN, Brian	6-4	219	22	Biddeford, ME	L	Wilkes-Barre
ENGELLAND, Deryk	6-2	202	31	Edmonton, Alta.	R	Rosenborg-Pittsburgh
HARRINGTON, Scott	6-2	205	20	Kingston, Ont.	L	London-Wilkes-Barre
LETANG, Kris	6-0	201	26	Montreal, Que.	R	Pittsburgh
MARTIN, Paul	6-1	200	32	Minneapolis, MN	L	Pittsburgh
McNEILL, Reid	6-4	204	21	London, Ont.	L	Wheeling-Wilkes-Barre
MIKKELSON, Brendan	6-3	210	26	Regina, Sask.	L	Vasteras-T.B.-Syr
NISKANEN, Matt	6-0	209	26	Virginia, MN	R	Pittsburgh
ORPIK, Brooks	6-2	219	33	San Francisco, CA	L	Pittsburgh
RUOPP, Harrison	6-3	205	20	Zehner, Sask.	R	Prince Albert
SAMUELSSON, Philip	6-2	194	22	Leksand, Sweden	L	Wilkes-Barre
SCUDERI, Rob	6-1	219	34	Syosset, NY	L	Los Angeles
GOALTENDERS	**HT**	**WT**	***Age**	**Place of Birth**	**C**	**2012-13 Club**
FLEURY, Marc-Andre	6-2	180	28	Sorel, Que.	L	Pittsburgh
HARTZELL, Eric	6-4	205	24	White Bear Lake, MN	L	Quinnipiac
VOKOUN, Tomas	6-1	210	37	Karlovy Vary, Czech.	R	Pittsburgh
ZATKOFF, Jeff	6-2	179	26	Detroit, MI	L	Wilkes-Barre

* – Age at start of 2013-14 season

Ray Shero

Executive Vice President and General Manager

Born: St. Paul, MN, July 28, 1962.

The Pittsburgh Penguins signed Ray Shero to a five-year contract as their new general manager on May 25, 2006. His fresh ideas and calm but firm management style helped transform the Penguins organization in his first year on the job as the team made the playoffs in 2006-07 for the first time since 2000-01. In 2007-08 the team posted the second-best record in the Eastern Conference and advanced to the Stanley Cup Final. They won the Stanley Cup in 2009. Shero was named NHL General Manager of the Year in 2012-13. He will be an assistant general manager with Team USA at the 2014 Sochi Winter Olympics.

Shero is the son of the late Fred Shero, who coached the Philadelphia Flyers for seven years and led them to back-to-back Stanley Cup championships in 1973-74 and 1974-75. Fred Shero also was g.m. and coach of the New York Rangers from 1978 to 1980. He was elected to the Hockey Hall of Fame in 2013. Ray Shero played college hockey at St. Lawrence University, serving twice as team captain, and was drafted by the Los Angeles Kings in 1982. He worked as a player agent for seven years before entering NHL management.

Before joining the Penguins, Shero had been assistant general manager of the Nashville Predators for eight seasons, working closely with Predators g.m. David Poile on all aspects of the club's hockey operations. His specific responsibilities included scouting at the amateur and professional levels, contract negotiations, and personnel matters such as arbitration, in addition to overseeing operations of the Predators top minor-league affiliate, the Milwaukee Admirals of the American Hockey League. Before joining the Predators organization, Shero spent six seasons as assistant general manager of the Ottawa Senators – joining the club in its second year of existence as an expansion team.

Both Ottawa and Nashville made significant improvement during Shero's tenure as assistant g.m., building with youth while adhering to a budget and business plan. The Predators went 49-25-8 and established a club record with 106 points in 2005-06, qualifying for the Stanley Cup playoffs for the second straight season. They had the third-best record in the Western Conference and fifth-best in the NHL.

Shero also played an important role in the success of the Milwaukee Admirals, Nashville's top affiliate in the American Hockey League. In 2003-04, the Admirals led the AHL in wins (43) and points (102) and won the Calder Cup by defeating the

2012-13 Scoring

* – rookie

Regular Season

Pos	#	Player	Team	GP	G	A	Pts	TOI	+/–	PIM	PP	SH	GW	S	%
C	87	Sidney Crosby	PIT	36	15	41	56	21:06	26	16	3	0	1	124	12.1
L	14	Chris Kunitz	PIT	48	22	30	52	18:01	30	39	9	0	5	113	19.5
L	9	Pascal Dupuis	PIT	48	20	18	38	17:30	31	26	2	1	2	140	14.3
D	58	Kris Letang	PIT	35	5	33	38	25:38	16	8	1	0	1	95	5.3
L	18	James Neal	PIT	40	21	15	36	17:28	5	26	9	0	6	136	15.4
R	12	Jarome Iginla	CGY	31	9	13	22	19:17	–7	22	2	0	2	100	9.0
			PIT	13	5	6	11	17:40	2	9	4	0	1	34	14.7
			Total	44	14	19	33	18:48	–5	31	6	0	3	134	10.4
C	71	Evgeni Malkin	PIT	31	9	24	33	19:42	5	36	4	0	3	99	9.1
L	10	Brenden Morrow	DAL	29	6	5	11	14:55	–8	18	1	0	1	31	19.4
			PIT	15	6	8	14	14:44	5	19	1	0	1	24	25.0
			Total	44	12	13	25	14:51	–3	37	2	0	2	55	21.8
D	7	Paul Martin	PIT	34	6	17	23	25:19	14	16	2	0	1	38	15.8
L	36	Jussi Jokinen	CAR	33	6	5	11	15:35	–8	18	2	0	3	61	9.8
			PIT	10	7	4	11	14:55	3	6	1	0	0	13	53.8
			Total	43	13	9	22	15:25	–5	24	3	0	3	74	17.6
L	24	Matt Cooke	PIT	48	8	13	21	14:42	–2	36	0	0	1	61	13.1
C	16	Brandon Sutter	PIT	48	11	8	19	16:24	3	4	3	0	5	82	13.4
D	2	Matt Niskanen	PIT	40	4	10	14	20:21	4	12	0	0	2	67	6.0
R	19 *	Beau Bennett	PIT	26	3	11	14	12:18	7	6	1	0	2	30	10.0
C	48	Tyler Kennedy	PIT	46	6	5	11	12:27	–6	19	1	0	1	100	6.0
R	27	Craig Adams	PIT	48	3	6	9	11:09	–1	28	0	1	0	46	6.5
D	44	Brooks Orpik	PIT	46	0	8	8	22:17	17	32	0	0	0	32	0.0
D	47 *	Simon Despres	PIT	33	2	5	7	15:06	9	20	0	0	0	33	6.1
C	17	Dustin Jeffrey	PIT	24	3	3	6	11:30	1	2	0	0	0	26	11.5
D	3	Douglas Murray	S.J.	29	0	3	3	17:08	–8	26	0	0	0	13	0.0
			PIT	14	1	2	3	18:29	–1	9	0	0	0	14	7.1
			Total	43	1	5	6	17:35	–9	35	0	0	0	27	3.7
D	5	Deryk Engelland	PIT	42	0	6	6	13:55	5	54	0	0	0	31	0.0
C	46	Joe Vitale	PIT	33	2	3	5	9:31	–7	17	0	0	1	26	7.7
D	41 *	Robert Bortuzzo	PIT	15	2	2	4	13:17	3	27	0	0	0	10	20.0
L	15	Tanner Glass	PIT	48	1	1	2	10:04	–11	62	1	0	0	38	2.6
L	33	Steve MacIntyre	PIT	1	0	0	0	4:31	0	12	0	0	0	0	0.0
C	23	Trevor Smith	PIT	1	0	0	0	10:24	0	0	0	0	0	0	0.0
D	42	Dylan Reese	PIT	3	0	0	0	15:15	0	0	0	0	0	1	0.0
D	4	Mark Eaton	PIT	23	0	0	0	17:58	9	4	0	0	0	8	0.0

Goaltending

No.	Goaltender	GPI	Mins	Avg	W	L	OT	EN	SO	GA	SA	S%	G	A	PIM
29	Marc-Andre Fleury	33	1858	2.39	23	8	0	2	1	74	881	.916	0	2	2
92	Tomas Vokoun	20	1029	2.45	13	4	0	1	3	42	519	.919	0	2	2
	Totals	**48**	**2898**	**2.46**	**36**	**12**	**0**	**3**	**5**	**119**	**1403**	**.915**			

Tomas Vokoun and Marc-Andre Fleury shared a shutout vs. Montreal on Mar. 26, 2013

Playoffs

Pos	#	Player	Team	GP	G	A	Pts	TOI	+/–	PIM	PP	SH	GW	OT	S	%
C	71	Evgeni Malkin	PIT	15	4	12	16	20:29	–2	26	0	0	1	0	67	6.0
D	58	Kris Letang	PIT	15	3	13	16	27:37	2	8	2	0	1	0	49	6.1
C	87	Sidney Crosby	PIT	14	7	8	15	23:05	–3	8	2	0	0	0	59	11.9
R	12	Jarome Iginla	PIT	15	4	8	12	15:45	–4	16	2	0	0	0	34	11.8
L	9	Pascal Dupuis	PIT	15	7	4	11	18:52	2	12	0	2	0	0	37	18.9
D	7	Paul Martin	PIT	15	2	9	11	26:38	5	4	1	0	0	0	23	8.7
L	18	James Neal	PIT	13	6	4	10	17:42	–3	8	2	0	1	0	51	11.8
L	14	Chris Kunitz	PIT	15	5	5	10	18:18	–1	6	3	0	1	1	32	15.6
C	48	Tyler Kennedy	PIT	9	2	3	5	12:33	6	2	0	0	1	0	12	16.7
L	10	Brenden Morrow	PIT	14	2	2	4	13:47	–2	8	0	0	1	0	9	22.2
L	24	Matt Cooke	PIT	15	0	4	4	15:08	1	35	0	0	0	0	17	0.0
D	3	Douglas Murray	PIT	15	2	1	3	15:19	–3	32	0	0	0	0	12	16.7
C	16	Brandon Sutter	PIT	15	2	1	3	16:17	–1	0	0	0	0	0	25	8.0
D	4	Mark Eaton	PIT	8	0	3	3	17:16	2	0	0	0	0	0	6	0.0
L	36	Jussi Jokinen	PIT	8	0	3	3	11:00	3	4	0	0	0	0	8	0.0
D	44	Brooks Orpik	PIT	12	1	1	2	25:08	2	10	0	0	1	1	7	14.3
D	2	Matt Niskanen	PIT	15	0	2	2	18:54	–4	11	0	0	0	0	17	0.0
L	15	Tanner Glass	PIT	5	1	0	1	8:13	0	4	0	0	0	0	3	33.3
R	19 *	Beau Bennett	PIT	6	1	0	1	11:05	2	0	1	0	1	0	11	9.1
C	46	Joe Vitale	PIT	6	0	1	1	9:53	–1	6	0	0	0	0	5	0.0
R	27	Craig Adams	PIT	15	0	1	1	12:01	1	10	0	0	0	0	13	0.0
D	47 *	Simon Despres	PIT	3	0	0	0	11:07	0	0	0	0	0	0	0	0.0
D	5	Deryk Engelland	PIT	7	0	0	0	15:27	–6	8	0	0	0	0	3	0.0

Goaltending

No.	Goaltender	GPI	Mins	Avg	W	L	EN	SO	GA	SA	S%	G	A	PIM
92	Tomas Vokoun	11	685	2.01	6	5	0	1	23	345	.933	0	0	0
29	Marc-Andre Fleury	5	290	3.52	2	2	0	1	17	145	.883	0	1	0
	Totals	**15**	**980**	**2.45**	**8**	**7**	**0**	**2**	**40**	**490**	**.918**			

Captains' History

Ab McDonald, 1967-68; Earl Ingarfield, 1968-69; no captain, 1968-69 to 1972-73; Ron Schock, 1973-74 to 1976-77; Jean Pronovost, 1977-78; Orest Kindrachuk, 1978-79 to 1980-81; Randy Carlyle, 1981-82 to 1983-84; Mike Bullard, 1984-85, 1985-86; Mike Bullard and Terry Ruskowski, 1986-87; Dan Frawley and Mario Lemieux, 1987-88; Mario Lemieux, 1988-89 to 1993-94; Ron Francis, 1994-95; Mario Lemieux, 1995-96, 1996-97; Ron Francis, 1997-98; Jaromir Jagr, 1998-99 to 2000-01; Mario Lemieux, 2001-02 to 2004-05; Mario Lemieux and no captain, 2005-06; no captain, 2006-07; Sidney Crosby, 2007-08 to date.

Coaching History

Red Sullivan, 1967-68, 1968-69; Red Kelly, 1969-70 to 1971-72; Red Kelly and Ken Schinkel, 1972-73; Ken Schinkel and Marc Boileau, 1973-74; Marc Boileau, 1974-75; Marc Boileau and Ken Schinkel, 1975-76; Ken Schinkel, 1976-77; Johnny Wilson, 1977-78 to 1979-80; Eddie Johnston, 1980-81 to 1982-83; Lou Angotti, 1983-84; Bob Berry, 1984-85 to 1986-87; Pierre Creamer, 1987-88; Gene Ubriaco, 1988-89; Gene Ubriaco and Craig Patrick, 1989-90; Bob Johnson, 1990-91; Scotty Bowman, 1991-92, 1992-93; Eddie Johnston, 1993-94 to 1995-96; Eddie Johnston and Craig Patrick, 1996-97; Kevin Constantine, 1997-98, 1998-99; Kevin Constantine and Herb Brooks, 1999-2000; Ivan Hlinka, 2000-01; Ivan Hlinka and Rick Kehoe, 2001-02; Rick Kehoe, 2002-03; Ed Olczyk, 2003-04, 2004-05; Ed Olczyk and Michel Therrien, 2005-06; Michel Therrien, 2006-07, 2007-08; Michel Therrien and Dan Bylsma, 2008-09; Dan Bylsma, 2009-10 to date.

Club Records

Team

(Figures in brackets for season records are games played; records for fewest points, wins, ties, losses, goals, goals against are for 70 or more games)

Most Points **119** 1992-93 (84)
Most Wins **56** 1992-93 (84)
Most Ties **20** 1970-71 (78)
Most Losses **58** 1983-84 (80)
Most Goals **367** 1992-93 (84)
Most Goals Against **394** 1982-83 (80)
Fewest Points **38** 1983-84 (80)
Fewest Wins **16** 1983-84 (80)
Fewest Ties **4** 1995-96 (82)
Fewest Losses **21** 1992-93 (84)
Fewest Goals **182** 1969-70 (76)
Fewest Goals Against **188** 1997-98 (82)

Longest Winning Streak
Overall .... ***17** Mar. 9-Apr. 10/93
Home .... **12** Feb. 22-Mar. 30/13
Away .... **7** Mar. 14-Apr. 9/93, Oct. 3-Nov. 3/09, Nov. 6-Dec. 11/10

Longest Undefeated Streak
Overall .... **18** Mar. 9-Apr. 14/93 (17W, 1T)
Home .... **20** Nov. 30/74-Feb. 22/75 (12W, 8T)
Away .... **8** Mar. 14-Apr. 14/93 (7W, 1T)

Longest Losing Streak
Overall .... **18** Jan. 13-Feb. 22/04
Home .... ***14** Dec. 31/03-Feb. 22/04
Away .... **18** Dec. 23/82-Mar. 4/83

Longest Winless Streak
Overall .... **18** Jan. 2-Feb. 10/83 (17L, 1T), Jan. 13-Feb. 22/04 (18L)
Home .... **16** Dec. 31/03-Mar. 4/04 (15L, 1T/OL)
Away .... **18** Oct. 25/70-Jan. 14/71 (11L, 7T), Dec. 23/82-Mar. 4/83 (18L)

Most Shutouts, Season **9** 1998-99 (82)
Most PIM, Season **2,670** 1988-89 (80)
Most Goals, Game .... **12** Mar. 15/75 (Wsh. 1 at Pit. 12), Dec. 26/91 (Tor. 1 at Pit. 12)

Individual

Most Seasons .... **17** Mario Lemieux
Most Games .... **915** Mario Lemieux
Most Goals, Career .... **690** Mario Lemieux
Most Assists, Career ..... **1,033** Mario Lemieux
Most Points, Career ...... **1,723** Mario Lemieux (690G, 1,033A)
Most PIM, Career .... **1,048** Kevin Stevens
Most Shutouts, Career .... **23** Marc-Andre Fleury
Longest Consecutive Games Streak .... **313** Ron Schock (Oct. 24/73-Apr. 3/77)
Most Goals, Season .... **85** Mario Lemieux (1988-89)
Most Assists, Season .... **114** Mario Lemieux (1988-89)
Most Points, Season .... **199** Mario Lemieux (1988-89; 85G, 114A)
Most PIM, Season .... **409** Paul Baxter (1981-82)
Most Points, Defenseman, Season .... **113** Paul Coffey (1988-89; 30G, 83A)
Most Points, Center, Season .... **199** Mario Lemieux (1988-89; 85G, 114A)
Most Points, Right Wing, Season .... ***149** Jaromir Jagr (1995-96; 62G, 87A)
Most Points, Left Wing, Season .... **123** Kevin Stevens (1991-92; 54G, 69A)
Most Points, Rookie, Season .... **102** Sidney Crosby (2005-06; 39G, 63A)
Most Shutouts, Season .... **7** Tom Barrasso (1997-98)
Most Goals, Game .... **5** Mario Lemieux (Dec. 31/88), (Apr. 9/93), (Mar. 26/96)
Most Assists, Game .... **6** Ron Stackhouse (Mar. 8/75); Greg Malone (Nov. 28/79); Mario Lemieux (Oct. 15/88), (Dec. 5/92), (Nov. 1/95)
Most Points, Game .... **8** Mario Lemieux (Oct. 15/88; 2G, 6A), (Dec. 31/88; 5G, 3A)

* NHL Record.

General Managers' History

Jack Riley, 1967-68 to 1969-70; Red Kelly, 1970-71; Red Kelly and Jack Riley, 1971-72; Jack Riley, 1972-73; Jack Riley and Jack Button, 1973-74; Jack Button, 1974-75; Wren Blair, 1975-76; Wren Blair and Baz Bastien, 1976-77; Baz Bastien, 1977-78 to 1982-83; Eddie Johnston, 1983-84 to 1987-88; Tony Esposito, 1988-89; Tony Esposito and Craig Patrick, 1989-90; Craig Patrick, 1990-91 to 2005-06; Ray Shero, 2006-07 to date.

Retired Numbers

21	Michel Brière	1969-1970
66	Mario Lemieux	1984-2006

All-time Record vs. Other Clubs

Regular Season

	Total								At Home								On Road							
	GP	W	L	T	OL	GF	GA	PTS	GP	W	L	T	OL	GF	GA	PTS	GP	W	L	T	OL	GF	GA	PTS
Anaheim	24	12	8	2	2	75	74	28	13	8	3	2	0	43	36	18	11	4	5	0	2	32	38	10
Boston	189	65	100	21	3	587	727	154	96	40	39	15	2	326	338	97	93	25	61	6	1	261	389	57
Buffalo	173	74	62	35	2	557	579	185	87	45	23	18	1	321	264	109	86	29	39	17	1	236	315	76
Calgary	96	40	38	18	0	326	347	98	47	26	11	10	0	175	137	62	49	14	27	8	0	151	210	36
Carolina	125	59	50	11	5	455	442	134	61	32	22	6	1	236	212	71	64	27	28	5	4	219	230	63
Chicago	125	43	63	17	2	384	445	105	62	31	23	7	1	219	198	70	63	12	40	10	1	165	247	35
Colorado	76	33	35	7	1	294	312	74	40	18	17	5	0	159	159	41	36	15	18	2	1	135	153	33
Columbus	14	9	4	0	1	50	44	19	7	5	2	0	0	26	19	10	7	4	2	0	1	24	25	9
Dallas	134	65	56	12	1	476	441	143	66	41	19	6	0	249	183	88	68	24	37	6	1	227	258	55
Detroit	139	61	61	16	1	480	475	139	70	46	20	4	0	288	206	96	69	15	41	12	1	192	269	43
Edmonton	66	26	35	4	1	234	289	57	33	17	13	3	0	128	135	37	33	9	22	1	1	106	154	20
Florida	76	40	29	4	3	214	213	87	38	23	11	3	1	116	102	50	38	17	18	1	2	98	111	37
Los Angeles	148	60	69	18	1	467	512	139	76	41	25	10	0	275	237	92	72	19	44	8	1	192	275	47
Minnesota	13	3	8	1	1	24	42	8	7	1	5	0	1	8	25	3	6	2	3	1	0	16	17	5
Montreal	195	57	108	23	7	552	769	144	98	38	45	13	2	295	336	91	97	19	63	10	5	257	433	53
Nashville	17	6	8	2	1	47	57	15	8	3	2	2	1	26	23	9	9	3	6	0	0	21	34	6
New Jersey	212	90	97	17	8	690	700	205	105	52	45	4	4	364	332	112	107	38	52	13	4	326	368	93
NY Islanders	227	107	92	22	6	807	800	242	115	61	38	14	2	434	370	138	112	46	54	8	4	373	430	104
NY Rangers	254	113	110	23	8	855	902	257	126	60	48	14	4	435	424	138	128	53	62	9	4	420	478	119
Ottawa	85	45	29	9	2	284	247	101	42	23	13	4	2	144	118	52	43	22	16	5	0	140	129	49
Philadelphia	264	92	137	30	5	813	957	219	132	60	50	22	0	464	425	142	132	32	87	8	5	349	532	77
Phoenix	68	39	26	3	0	250	217	81	34	23	11	0	0	131	92	46	34	16	15	3	0	119	125	35
St. Louis	135	50	63	18	4	426	454	122	67	33	21	12	1	246	198	79	68	17	42	6	3	180	256	43
San Jose	29	11	12	3	3	106	86	28	12	5	4	1	2	46	38	13	17	6	8	2	1	60	48	15
Tampa Bay	77	40	28	5	4	245	213	89	39	24	9	3	3	146	98	54	38	16	19	2	1	99	115	35
Toronto	167	75	70	17	5	603	597	172	84	44	33	6	1	333	275	95	83	31	37	11	4	270	322	77
Vancouver	106	59	35	11	1	428	369	130	53	34	12	7	0	233	179	75	53	25	23	4	1	195	190	55
Washington	200	96	83	16	5	735	716	213	99	55	35	7	2	375	312	119	101	41	48	9	3	360	404	94
Winnipeg	51	38	10	0	3	192	132	79	25	21	3	0	1	108	63	43	26	17	7	0	2	84	69	36
Defunct Clubs	69	35	16	18	0	256	194	88	35	22	6	7	0	148	93	51	34	13	10	11	0	108	101	37
Totals	**3554**	**1543**	**1542**	**383**	**86**	**11912**	**12352**	**3555**	**1777**	**932**	**608**	**205**	**32**	**6497**	**5627**	**2101**	**1777**	**611**	**934**	**178**	**54**	**5415**	**6725**	**1454**

Playoffs

	Series	W	L	GP	W	L	T	GF	GA	Last Mtg.	Rnd.	Result
Boston	5	2	3	23	10	13	0	69	74	2013	CF	L 0-4
Buffalo	2	2	0	10	6	4	0	26	26	2001	CSF	W 4-3
Carolina	1	1	0	4	4	0	0	20	9	2009	CF	W 4-0
Chicago	2	1	1	8	4	4	0	23	24	1992	F	W 4-0
Dallas	1	1	0	6	4	2	0	28	16	1991	F	W 4-2
Detroit	2	1	1	13	6	7	0	24	34	2009	F	W 4-3
Florida	1	0	1	7	3	4	0	15	20	1996	CF	L 3-4
Montreal	2	0	2	13	5	8	0	33	37	2010	CSF	L 3-4
New Jersey	5	3	2	29	14	15	0	80	86	2001	CF	L 1-4
NY Islanders	4	1	3	25	12	13	0	83	84	2013	CQF	W 4-2
NY Rangers	4	4	0	20	16	4	0	79	57	2008	CSF	W 4-1
Ottawa	4	3	1	20	13	7	0	72	53	2013	CSF	W 4-1
Philadelphia	6	2	4	35	16	19	0	115	121	2012	CQF	L 2-4
St. Louis	3	1	2	13	6	7	0	40	45	1981	PRE	L 2-3
Tampa Bay	1	0	1	7	3	4	0	14	22	2011	CQF	L 3-4
Toronto	3	0	3	12	4	8	0	27	39	1999	CSF	L 2-4
Washington	8	7	1	49	30	19	0	164	143	2009	CSF	W 4-3
Defunct Clubs	1	1	0	4	4	0	0	13	6			
Totals	**55**	**30**	**25**	**298**	**160**	**138**	**0**	**925**	**896**			

Playoff Results 2013-2009

Year	Round	Opponent	Result	GF	GA
2013	CF	Boston	L 0-4	2	12
	CSF	Ottawa	W 4-1	22	11
	CQF	NY Islanders	W 4-2	25	17
2012	CQF	Philadelphia	L 2-4	26	30
2011	CQF	Tampa Bay	L 3-4	14	22
2010	CSF	Montreal	L 3-4	18	19
	CQF	Ottawa	W 4-2	24	19
2009	**F**	**Detroit**	**W 4-3**	**14**	**17**
	CF	Carolina	W 4-0	20	9
	CSF	Washington	W 4-3	27	22
	CQF	Philadelphia	W 4-2	18	16

Abbreviations: Round: F – Final; **CF** – conference final; **CSF** – conference semi-final; **CQF** – conference quarter-final; **DF** – division final; **PRE** – preliminary round.

Calgary totals include Atlanta Flames, 1972-73 to 1979-80.
Colorado totals include Quebec, 1979-80 to 1994-95.
New Jersey totals include Kansas City, 1974-75, 1975-76, and Colorado Rockies, 1976-77 to 1981-82.
Phoenix totals include Winnipeg, 1979-80 to 1995-96.
Carolina totals include Hartford, 1979-80 to 1996-97.
Dallas totals include Minnesota North Stars, 1967-68 to 1992-93.
Winnipeg totals include Atlanta Thrashers, 1999-2000 to 2010-11.

2012-13 Results

Jan.	19	at Philadelphia	3-1		9	at Toronto	5-4†
	20	at NY Rangers	6-3		10	NY Islanders	6-1
	23	Toronto	2-5		12	Boston	3-2
	25	at Winnipeg	2-4		14	at Toronto	3-1
	27	at Ottawa	2-1†		16	NY Rangers	3-0
	29	NY Islanders	1-4		17	Boston	2-1
	31	at NY Rangers	3-0		19	Washington	2-1
Feb.	2	New Jersey	5-1		22	at NY Islanders	4-2
	3	at Washington	6-3		24	Philadelphia	2-1*
	5	at NY Islanders	4-2		26	Montreal	1-0
	7	Washington	5-2		28	Winnipeg	4-0
	9	at New Jersey	1-3		30	NY Islanders	2-0
	10	New Jersey	1-3	**Apr.**	2	Buffalo	1-4
	13	Ottawa	4-2		3	at NY Rangers	1-6
	15	at Winnipeg	3-1		5	NY Rangers	2-1†
	17	at Buffalo	4-3		9	at Carolina	5-3
	20	Philadelphia	5-6		11	at Tampa Bay	6-3
	22	Florida	3-1		13	at Florida	3-1
	24	Tampa Bay	5-3		17	Montreal	6-4
	26	at Florida	4-6		20	at Boston	3-2
	28	at Carolina	1-4		22	at Ottawa	3-1
Mar.	2	at Montreal	7-6*		23	Buffalo	2-4
	4	Tampa Bay	4-3		25	at New Jersey	2-3
	7	at Philadelphia	5-4		27	Carolina	8-3

* – Overtime † – Shootout

Entry Draft Selections 2013-1999

Name in bold denotes played in NHL.

2013
Pick
44 Tristan Jarry
77 Jake Guentzel
119 Ryan Segalla
164 Dane Birks
179 Blaine Byron
209 Troy Josephs

2012
Pick
8 Derrick Pouliot
22 Olli Maatta
52 Teddy Blueger
81 Oskar Sundqvist
83 Matt Murray
92 Matia Marcantuoni
113 Sean Maguire
143 Clark Seymour
173 Anton Zlobin

2011
Pick
23 Joe Morrow
54 Scott Harrington
144 Dominik Uher
174 Josh Archibald
209 Scott Wilson

2010
Pick
20 **Beau Bennett**
80 Bryan Rust
110 Tom Kuhnhackl
140 Kenny Agostino
152 Joe Rogalski
170 Reid McNeill

2009
Pick
30 **Simon Despres**
61 Philip Samuelsson
63 **Ben Hanowski**
121 Nick Petersen
123 Alex Velischek
151 Andy Bathgate
181 Viktor Ekbom

2008
Pick
120 Nathan Moon
150 **Alexander Pechurski**
180 Patrick Killeen
210 Nick D'Agostino

2007
Pick
20 Angelo Esposito
51 Keven Veilleux
78 **Robert Bortuzzo**
80 Casey Pierro-Zabotel
111 **Luca Caputi**
118 Alex Grant
141 **Jake Muzzin**
171 **Dustin Jeffrey**

2006
Pick
2 **Jordan Staal**
32 **Carl Sneep**
65 **Brian Strait**
125 **Chad Johnson**
185 Timo Seppanen

2005
Pick
1 **Sidney Crosby**
61 Michael Gergen
62 **Kris Letang**
125 Tommi Leinonen
126 Tim Crowder
194 Jean-Philippe Paquet
195 **Joe Vitale**

2004
Pick
2 **Evgeni Malkin**
31 Johannes Salmonsson
61 **Alex Goligoski**
67 **Nick Johnson**
85 Brian Gifford
99 **Tyler Kennedy**
130 Michal Sersen
164 Moises Gutierrez
194 Chris Peluso
222 Jordan Morrison
228 David Brown
259 Brian Ihnacak

2003
Pick
1 **Marc-Andre Fleury**
32 **Ryan Stone**
70 **Jonathan Filewich**
73 **Daniel Carcillo**
121 **Paul Bissonnette**
161 Evgeni Isakov
169 Lukas Bolf
199 **Andy Chiodo**
229 Stephen Dixon
232 **Joe Jensen**
263 **Matt Moulson**

2002
Pick
5 **Ryan Whitney**
35 Ondrej Nemec
69 **Erik Christensen**
101 Daniel Fernholm
136 Andrew Sertich
137 **Cam Paddock**
171 Robert Goepfert
202 Patrik Baertschi
234 **Maxime Talbot**
239 Ryan Lannon
265 Dwight Labrosse

2001
Pick
21 **Colby Armstrong**
54 **Noah Welch**
86 **Drew Fata**
96 Alexandre Rouleau
120 **Tomas Surovy**
131 Ben Eaves
156 Andy Schneider
217 Tomas Duba
250 Brandon Crawford-West

2000
Pick
18 **Brooks Orpik**
52 **Shane Endicott**
84 Peter Hamerlik
124 **Michel Ouellet**
146 **David Koci**
185 Patrick Foley
216 Jim Abbott
248 Steve Crampton
273 **Roman Simicek**
280 Nick Boucher

1999
Pick
18 **Konstantin Koltsov**
51 **Matt Murley**
57 Jeremy Van Hoof
86 **Sebastien Caron**
115 **Ryan Malone**
144 Tomas Skvaridlo
157 Vladimir Malenkykh
176 Doug Meyer
204 **Tom Kostopoulos**
233 Darcy Robinson
261 Andrew McPherson

Dan Bylsma

Head Coach

Born: Grand Haven, MI, September 19, 1970.

Dan Bylsma was named interim head coach of the Pittsburgh Penguins on February 15, 2009 and had the interim tag removed on April 28. He took over a Penguins team that was six points out of a playoff spot with 25 games to go and guided them to the Stanley Cup. Bylsma was the 14th rookie head coach, and just the fourth in 50 years, to win the Stanley Cup. Of these, only Montreal's Al MacNeil (1970-71) took over in midseason. In 2010-11 he won the Jack Adams Award as coach of the year for guiding an injury-riddled Penguins club to a 49 wins and 106 points. In 2014, Bylsma will serve as head coach for Team USA at the Sochi Winter Olympics.

Bylsma played nine NHL seasons as a right winger with Los Angeles and Anaheim from 1995 to 2004. A role player who excelled at killing penalties and blocking shots, he played 429 NHL regular-season games and also played in the 2003 Stanley Cup Final with Anaheim. He retired as a player following the 2003-04 season. The native of Grand Haven, Michigan began his coaching career as an assistant with the Cincinnati Mighty Ducks of the AHL in 2004-05. He made his NHL coaching debut as an assistant with the New York Islanders in 2005-06.

Bylsma joined the Penguins organization as an assistant to Todd Richards in Wilkes-Barre/Scranton in 2006-07. The Baby Penguins won the AHL East Division and Eastern Conference championships in 2007-08 and advanced to the Calder Cup Final. When Richards accepted the job as an assistant coach with the NHL's San Jose Sharks in the offseason, Bylsma was elevated to head coach at Wilkes-Barre/Scranton.

Bylsma was an outstanding athlete at West Michigan Christian High School, winning a state individual golf championship and starting in left field on a state championship baseball team. He played Junior B hockey for St. Mary's of the Ontario Hockey Association before playing four years of college hockey at Bowling Green. He was twice selected to the Central Collegiate Hockey Association (CCHA) All-Academic Team. Dan and his father, Jay, also have written four books about sports for kids and families, including "So Your Son Wants to Play in the NHL" and "So You Want to Play in the NHL." He operates Dan Bylsma's Western Michigan Hockey Camp and has established the Dan Bylsma Charitable Trust Fund, which provides a means to assist children with the high cost of participating in youth sports, especially hockey.

Coaching Record

			Regular Season				Playoffs			
Season	Team	League	GC	W	L	O/T	GC	W	L	T
2008-09	Wilkes-Barre	AHL	55	36	16	3	....	....	....	....
2008-09♦	**Pittsburgh**	**NHL**	**25**	**18**	**3**	**4**	**24**	**16**	**8**	....
2009-10	**Pittsburgh**	**NHL**	**82**	**47**	**28**	**7**	**13**	**7**	**6**	....
2010-11	**Pittsburgh**	**NHL**	**82**	**49**	**25**	**8**	**7**	**3**	**4**	....
2011-12	**Pittsburgh**	**NHL**	**82**	**51**	**25**	**6**	**6**	**2**	**4**	....
2012-13	**Pittsburgh**	**NHL**	**48**	**36**	**12**	**0**	**15**	**8**	**7**	....
	NHL Totals		**319**	**201**	**93**	**25**	**65**	**36**	**29**	....

♦ Stanley Cup win.
Jack Adams Award (2011)

Club Directory

CONSOL Energy Center

Pittsburgh Penguins
CONSOL Energy Center
1001 Fifth Avenue
Pittsburgh, PA 15219
Phone **412/642-1300**
PR FAX 412/255-1988
www.pittsburghpenguins.com
Capacity: 18,387

Executive Management	
Co-Owner/Chairman	Mario Lemieux
Co-Owner	Ron Burkle
CEO/President	David Morehouse
COO/General Counsel	Travis Williams
Hockey Operations	
Executive V.P./General Manager	Ray Shero
Assistant General Manager	Jason Botterill
Assistant to the General Manager	Tom Fitzgerald
Director of Player Personnel	Dan Mackinnon
Head Coach	Dan Bylsma
Assistant Coaches	Tony Granato, Jacques Martin, Todd Reirden
Goaltending Coach	TBA
AHL Head Coach / Assistant Coach	John Hynes / Alain Nasreddine
Strength & Conditioning Coach	Mike Kadar
Player Development Coach	Bill Guerin
Goaltender Development Coach	Mike Bales
Manager of Team Services	Jim Britt
Hockey Operations Assistant	Erik Heasley
Video Coordinator	Andy Saucier
Head Athletic Trainer / Asst. Trainer	Chris Stewart / Curtis Bell, Patrick Steidle
Head Team Physician	Dr. Christopher Harner
Associate Team Physician/ Assistant Team Phys.	Dr. Tanya Hagen / Dr. Dharmesh Vyas
Head Equipment Mgr. / Asst. Mgrs.	Dana Heinze / Paul Defazio, Daniel Kroll
Equipment Assistant	Jon Taglianetti
Physical Therapist	Rick Joreitz
Massage Therapist	Dave Sanctis
Skating Consultant	Marianne Watkins
Mental Training Consultant	Aimee Kimball
Scouting	
Director of Professional Scouting	Derek Clancey
Professional Scouts	Andre Savard, Don Waddell
Director of Amateur Scouting	Jay Heinbuck
Assistant Director of Amateur Scouting	Randy Sexton
Head European Scout	Patrik Allvin
Amateur Scouts	Scott Bell, Chris DiPiero, Brian Fitzgerald, Luc Gauthier, Wayne Meier, Ron Pyette, Al Santilli, Tommy Westlund, Warren Young
Administration	
Director, Government Affairs	TBA
Director, Outreach	Kimberly Wood
Executive Assistants	Amber Auchey, Mary Beth Bertoni
Shipping/Receiving Coordinator / Receptionist	Brett Hart / Kelly Hart
Partnership Sales	
Sr. Vice President, Sales & Service	David Peart
Sr. Director, Corporate Sales	Kimberly Bogesdorfer
Sr. Director, Media	Mark Turley
Senior Managers, Client Services	Lori Wineland, Julie Klausner
Managers, Corporate Sales	Robbie Hofmann, Lindsay Mulvihill
Coordinator, Corporate Sales & Service	Amanda Susko
Corporate Sales Liaison	Pierre Larouche
Communications	
Vice President, Communications	Tom McMillan
Communications Director	Jennifer Bullano
Content Director / Manager	Sam Kasan / Michelle Crechiolo
New Media Video Producer	Mark Cottington
Communications Manager	Jason Seidling
Marketing	
Vice President, Marketing	James Santilli
Executive Director, Strategic Planning	Rich Hixon
Sr. Director, Marketing	Ross Miller
Director, Fan Development & Special Events	Jill Shipley
New Media Sr. Director / Coordinator	Jeremy Zimmer / Melissa Marchionna
Director, Community/Alumni Relations	Cindy Himes
Director, Amateur Hockey	Mark Shuttleworth
Sr. Creative Director / Graphic Designers	Barbara Pilarski / Erin Halley, Lori Haramia
Manager, Amateur Hockey Development	Max Malone
Manager, Youth Hockey Programs	Michael Chaisson
Community Relations Coordinator	Kathleen Unger
Community Relations/Alumni Liaison	Ed Johnston
Fan Development Coordinator	Laura Spencer
Game Entertainment	
Sr. Director, Production and Game Presentation	Rod Murray
Director, Game Presentation	Billy Wareham
Director, Production Operations	Stephen Finerty
Pens TV Host	Katie O'Malley
Game Entertainment Producers	Michael Davenport, Leo McCafferty, John Otte
Motion Graphics Designers	Nick Schultz, Aaron Spiegel
Finance	
Vice President & Controller	Kevin Hart
Director, Finance / Sr. Accountant	Mark Kuczinski / Troy Ussack
Payroll Manager / Accounts Payable	Andrea Winschel / Tawni Love
CONSOL Energy Center Operations	
Sr. Directors, Arena Ops / Technology	Brian Magness / Erik Watts
Director, Video Production & Technical Ops	Andrew Warren
Building Audio Engineer	Brian Duffy
Systems Administrator	Walt Greene, Jason Henry
Jr. Systems Administrator	Jay Girlardo
Building Audio/Video Specialist	Aaron Miller
Ticketing	
Vice President, Ticket Sales	Chad Slencak
Directors, Customer Service / Ticket Sales	Kathy Davis / George Murphy
Database Marketing Director / Manager	Erin Exley / Dana DiCello
Manager, Box Office Operations	Jason Onufer
Box Office Manager / Coordinator	Caroline Coulson / Kelly Gabany
Ticket Sales Account Execs.	George Birman, Jeff Blizman, Bonnie Golinski, Nicole Kyslinger, Chuck Pukansky
Managers, Group Sales / Premium Seating	Michael Zatchey / Kyle Lux
Premium Service Representative	Jonathan Seelnacht
Customer Service Representatives	Holly Homistek, Daniel Gardner
Penguins Foundation	
President, Penguins Foundation	David Soltesz
Manager, Foundation Programs / Program Coord.	Jaime Greenwald / Lindsay Thomes
Broadcasting	
Executive Producer, Penguins Radio Network	Ray Walker
Radio Broadcasters / HD Radio Host	Phil Bourque, Mike Lange / TBA

St. Louis Blues

2012-13 Results: 29W-17L-1OTL-1SOL 60PTS
2ND, Central Division • 4TH, Western Conference

Key Off-Season Signings/Acquisitions

2013

May 24 • Re-signed RW **Adam Cracknell**.
28 • Re-signed D **Ian Cole**.
June 25 • Re-signed C **Patrik Berglund**.
26 • Re-signed D **Kevin Shattenkirk**.
July 3 • Re-signed D **Jordan Leopold**.
5 • Signed C **Maxim Lapierre**, C **Keith Aucoin** and C **Alexandre Bolduc**.
10 • Acquired LW **Magnus Paajarvi** and a 2nd-round pick in the 2014 NHL Draft from Edmonton for LW **David Perron**.
11 • Signed C **Derek Roy**.
19 • Re-signed RW **Chris Stewart**.
25 • Re-signed G **Jake Allen**.
Aug. 1 • Re-signed D **Jay Bouwmeester**.

David Backes and Alex Pietrangelo discuss strategy in a game against Anaheim on March 10, 2013. Backes scored only six goals during 2012-13 season, but led the Blues with 22 assists. Pietrangelo was among the NHL leaders in time on ice per game at 25:06.

2013-14 Schedule

Oct.	Thu.	3	Nashville		Tue.	7	at Edmonton
	Sat.	5	Florida		Thu.	9	at Calgary
	Wed.	9	Chicago		Fri.	10	at Vancouver
	Sat.	12	NY Rangers		Tue.	14	Phoenix
	Tue.	15	San Jose		Thu.	16	Los Angeles
	Thu.	17	at Chicago		Sat.	18	Anaheim
	Fri.	18	at Winnipeg		Mon.	20	at Detroit
	Fri.	25	Vancouver		Tue.	21	at New Jersey
	Sat.	26	at Nashville		Thu.	23	at NY Rangers
	Tue.	29	Winnipeg		Sat.	25	at NY Islanders*
Nov.	Fri.	1	at Florida		Tue.	28	New Jersey
	Sat.	2	at Tampa Bay		Fri.	31	at Carolina
	Tue.	5	at Montreal	**Feb.**	Sat.	1	Nashville
	Thu.	7	Calgary		Tue.	4	Ottawa
	Sat.	9	Pittsburgh		Thu.	6	Boston
	Tue.	12	Phoenix		Sat.	8	Winnipeg*
	Thu.	14	Colorado		Wed.	26	at Vancouver
	Sat.	16	Carolina		Fri.	28	at Anaheim
	Sun.	17	at Washington	**Mar.**	Sun.	2	at Phoenix
	Tue.	19	at Buffalo		Tue.	4	Tampa Bay
	Thu.	21	at Boston		Thu.	6	at Nashville
	Sat.	23	Dallas		Sat.	8	at Colorado*
	Mon.	25	Minnesota		Sun.	9	at Minnesota
	Wed.	27	at Colorado		Tue.	11	Dallas
	Fri.	29	at San Jose*		Thu.	13	Edmonton
Dec.	Mon.	2	at Los Angeles		Sat.	15	at Nashville
	Thu.	5	NY Islanders		Mon.	17	Winnipeg
	Sat.	7	Anaheim		Wed.	19	at Chicago
	Tue.	10	at Winnipeg		Sat.	22	at Philadelphia*
	Thu.	12	Toronto		Sun.	23	at Pittsburgh*
	Sat.	14	at Columbus		Tue.	25	at Toronto
	Mon.	16	at Ottawa		Thu.	27	Minnesota
	Tue.	17	San Jose		Sat.	29	Dallas
	Thu.	19	Montreal	**Apr.**	Tue.	1	Philadelphia
	Sat.	21	at Edmonton		Thu.	3	Buffalo
	Mon.	23	at Calgary		Sat.	5	Colorado*
	Sat.	28	Chicago		Sun.	6	at Chicago
	Sun.	29	at Dallas*		Tue.	8	Washington
	Tue.	31	at Minnesota*		Thu.	10	at Minnesota
Jan.	Thu.	2	Los Angeles		Fri.	11	at Dallas
	Sat.	4	Columbus		Sun.	13	Detroit*

* Denotes afternoon game.

Year-by-Year Record

Season	GP	Home W	Home L	Home T	Home OL	Road W	Road L	Road T	Road OL	Overall W	Overall L	Overall T	Overall OL	GF	GA	Pts.	Div. Fin.	Conf. Fin.	Playoff Result
2012-13	48	15	8	....	1	14	9	....	1	29	17	....	2	129	115	60	2nd, Cen.	4th, West	Lost Conf. Quarter-Final
2011-12	82	30	6	....	5	19	16	....	6	49	22	....	11	210	165	109	1st, Cen.	2nd, West	Lost Conf. Semi-Final
2010-11	82	23	13	....	5	15	20	....	6	38	33	....	11	240	234	87	4th, Cen.	11th, West	Out of Playoffs
2009-10	82	18	18	....	5	22	14	....	5	40	32	....	10	225	223	90	4th, Cen.	9th, West	Out of Playoffs
2008-09	82	23	13	....	5	18	18	....	5	41	31	....	10	233	233	92	3rd, Cen.	6th, West	Lost Conf. Quarter-Final
2007-08	82	20	15	....	6	13	21	....	7	33	36	....	13	205	237	79	5th, Cen.	14th, West	Out of Playoffs
2006-07	82	18	19	....	4	16	16	....	9	34	35	....	13	214	254	81	3rd, Cen.	10th, West	Out of Playoffs
2005-06	82	12	23	....	6	9	23	....	9	21	46	....	15	197	292	57	5th, Cen.	15th, West	Out of Playoffs
2004-05	....	....	....	....	....	....	....	....	....	....	....	....	....	....	....	....			
2003-04	82	23	11	7	0	16	19	4	2	39	30	11	2	191	198	91	2nd, Cen.	7th, West	Lost Conf. Quarter-Final
2002-03	82	23	11	4	3	18	13	7	3	41	24	11	6	253	222	99	2nd, Cen.	5th, West	Lost Conf. Quarter-Final
2001-02	82	27	12	1	1	16	15	7	3	43	27	8	4	227	188	98	2nd, Cen.	4th, West	Lost Conf. Semi-Final
2000-01	82	28	5	5	3	15	17	7	2	43	22	12	5	249	195	103	2nd, Cen.	4th, West	Lost Conf. Final
1999-2000	82	24	9	7	1	27	10	4	0	51	19	11	1	248	165	114	1st, Cen.	1st, West	Lost Conf. Quarter-Final
1998-99	82	18	17	6	....	19	15	7	....	37	32	13	....	237	209	87	2nd, Cen.	5th, West	Lost Conf. Semi-Final
1997-98	82	26	10	5	....	19	19	3	....	45	29	8	....	256	204	98	3rd, Cen.	3rd, West	Lost Conf. Semi-Final
1996-97	82	17	20	4	....	19	15	7	....	36	35	11	....	236	239	83	4th, Cen.	6th, West	Lost Conf. Quarter-Final
1995-96	82	15	17	9	....	17	17	7	....	32	34	16	....	219	248	80	4th, Cen.	5th, West	Lost Conf. Semi-Final
1994-95	48	16	6	2	....	12	9	3	....	28	15	5	....	178	135	61	2nd, Cen.	2nd, West	Lost Conf. Quarter-Final
1993-94	84	23	11	8	....	17	22	3	....	40	33	11	....	270	283	91	4th, Cen.	5th, West	Lost Conf. Quarter-Final
1992-93	84	22	13	7	....	15	23	4	....	37	36	11	....	282	278	85	4th, Norris		Lost Div. Final
1991-92	80	25	12	3	....	11	21	8	....	36	33	11	....	279	266	83	3rd, Norris		Lost Div. Semi-Final
1990-91	80	24	9	7	....	23	13	4	....	47	22	11	....	310	250	105	2nd, Norris		Lost Div. Final
1989-90	80	20	15	5	....	17	19	4	....	37	34	9	....	295	279	83	2nd, Norris		Lost Div. Final
1988-89	80	22	11	7	....	11	24	5	....	33	35	12	....	275	285	78	2nd, Norris		Lost Div. Final
1987-88	80	18	17	5	....	16	21	3	....	34	38	8	....	278	294	76	2nd, Norris		Lost Div. Final
1986-87	80	21	12	7	....	11	21	8	....	32	33	15	....	281	293	79	1st, Norris		Lost Div. Semi-Final
1985-86	80	23	11	6	....	14	23	3	....	37	34	9	....	302	291	83	3rd, Norris		Lost Conf. Final
1984-85	80	21	12	7	....	16	19	5	....	37	31	12	....	299	288	86	1st, Norris		Lost Div. Semi-Final
1983-84	80	23	14	3	....	9	27	4	....	32	41	7	....	293	316	71	2nd, Norris		Lost Div. Final
1982-83	80	16	16	8	....	9	24	7	....	25	40	15	....	285	316	65	4th, Norris		Lost Div. Semi-Final
1981-82	80	22	14	4	....	10	26	4	....	32	40	8	....	315	349	72	3rd Norris		Lost Div. Final
1980-81	80	29	7	4	....	16	11	13	....	45	18	17	....	352	281	107	1st, Smythe		Lost Quarter-Final
1979-80	80	20	13	7	....	14	21	5	....	34	34	12	....	266	278	80	2nd, Smythe		Lost Prelim. Round
1978-79	80	14	20	6	....	4	30	6	....	18	50	12	....	249	348	48	3rd, Smythe		Out of Playoffs
1977-78	80	12	20	8	....	8	27	5	....	20	47	13	....	195	304	53	4th, Smythe		Out of Playoffs
1976-77	80	22	13	5	....	10	26	4	....	32	39	9	....	239	276	73	1st, Smythe		Lost Quarter-Final
1975-76	80	20	12	8	....	9	25	6	....	29	37	14	....	249	290	72	3rd, Smythe		Lost Prelim. Round
1974-75	80	23	13	4	....	12	18	10	....	35	31	14	....	269	267	84	2nd, Smythe		Lost Prelim. Round
1973-74	78	16	16	7	....	10	24	5	....	26	40	12	....	206	248	64	6th, West		Out of Playoffs
1972-73	78	21	11	7	....	11	23	5	....	32	34	12	....	233	251	76	4th, West		Lost Quarter-Final
1971-72	78	17	17	5	....	11	22	6	....	28	39	11	....	208	247	67	3rd, West		Lost Semi-Final
1970-71	78	23	7	9	....	11	18	10	....	34	25	19	....	223	208	87	2nd, West		Lost Quarter-Final
1969-70	76	24	9	5	....	13	18	7	....	37	27	12	....	224	179	86	1st, West		Lost Final
1968-69	76	21	8	9	....	16	17	5	....	37	25	14	....	204	157	88	1st, West		Lost Final
1967-68	74	18	12	7	....	9	19	9	....	27	31	16	....	177	191	70	3rd, West		Lost Final

CENTRAL DIVISION
47th NHL Season

Franchise date: June 5, 1967

2013-14 Player Personnel

FORWARDS	HT	WT	*Age	Place of Birth	S	2012-13 Club
ANDRONOV, Sergei	6-2	190	24	Penza, USSR	L	Peoria
AUCOIN, Keith	5-8	171	34	Waltham, MA	R	Toronto (AHL)-NY Islanders
BACKES, David	6-3	221	29	Blaine, MN	R	St. Louis
BEACH, Cody	6-5	190	21	Nanaimo, B.C.	R	Peoria-Evansville
BERGLUND, Patrik	6-3	217	25	Vasteras, Sweden	L	Vasteras-St. Louis
BOLDUC, Alexandre	6-3	208	28	Montreal, Que.	L	Portland (AHL)-Phoenix
CANNONE, Pat	5-11	204	27	Bayport, NY	R	Binghamton
CRACKNELL, Adam	6-2	210	28	Prince Albert, Sask.	R	Peoria-St. Louis
GRACHEV, Evgeny	6-4	225	23	Khabarovsk, USSR	L	Peoria
JASKIN, Dmitrij	6-2	196	20	Omsk, Russia	L	Moncton-St. Louis
LAPIERRE, Maxim	6-2	207	28	St. Leonard, Que.	R	Vancouver
MANCARI, Mark	6-3	225	28	London, Ont.	R	Rochester
McRAE, Philip	6-2	200	23	Minneapolis, MN	L	Peoria
OSHIE, T.J.	5-11	189	26	Mt. Vernon, WA	R	St. Louis
PAAJARVI, Magnus	6-3	200	22	Norrkoping, Sweden	L	Oklahoma City-Edmonton
PORTER, Chris	6-1	206	29	Toronto, Ont.	L	Peoria-St. Louis
RATTIE, Ty	6-0	176	20	Calgary, Alta.	R	Portland (WHL)
REAVES, Ryan	6-1	224	26	Winnipeg, Man.	R	Orlando-St. Louis
ROY, Derek	5-9	184	30	Ottawa, Ont.	L	Dallas-Vancouver
SCHWARTZ, Jaden	5-10	190	21	Melfort, Sask.	L	Peoria-St. Louis
SHATTOCK, Tyler	6-2	205	23	Vernon, B.C.	R	Peoria-Evansville
SOBOTKA, Vladimir	5-10	197	26	Trebic, Czech.	L	Slavia-St. Louis
STEEN, Alex	5-11	212	29	Winnipeg, Man.	L	MODO-St. Louis
STEWART, Chris	6-2	231	25	Toronto, Ont.	R	Crimmitschau-Liberec-StL
TARASENKO, Vladimir	6-0	219	21	Yaroslavl, USSR	L	St. Petersburg-St. Louis
VEILLEUX, Yannick	6-2	195	20	Saint-Hippolyte, Que.	L	Moncton-Peoria
WANNSTROM, Sebastian	6-1	180	22	Gavle, Sweden	R	Peoria-Evansville-Brynas
DEFENSEMEN						
BOUWMEESTER, Jay	6-4	212	30	Edmonton, Alta.	L	Calgary-St. Louis
CHORNEY, Taylor	6-1	189	26	Thunder Bay, Ont.	L	Peoria
COLE, Ian	6-1	219	24	Ann Arbour, MI	L	Peoria-St. Louis
EDMUNDSON, Joel	6-5	190	20	Brandon, MB	L	Moose Jaw-Kamloops
FAIRCHILD, Cade	5-11	175	24	Duluth, MN	L	Peoria
HAKANPAA, Jani	6-5	218	21	Kirkkonummi, Finland	R	Blues-Peoria
JACKMAN, Barret	6-0	203	32	Trail, B.C.	L	St. Louis
LEOPOLD, Jordan	6-1	206	33	Golden Valley, MN	L	Buffalo-St. Louis
PIETRANGELO, Alex	6-3	201	23	King City, Ont.	R	St. Louis
POLAK, Roman	6-0	236	27	Ostrava, Czech.	R	Vitkovice-St. Louis
PONICH, Brett	6-7	220	22	Edmonton, Alta.	L	Evansville-Peoria-Alaska
SHATTENKIRK, Kevin	5-11	207	24	New Rochelle, NY	R	TPS-St. Louis
SHIELDS, David	6-3	204	22	Buffalo, NY	R	Peoria

GOALTENDERS	HT	WT	*Age	Place of Birth	C	2012-13 Club
ALLEN, Jake	6-2	195	23	Fredericton, N.B.	L	Peoria-St. Louis
BINNINGTON, Jordan	6-2	162	20	Richmond Hill, Ont.	L	Owen Sound
ELLIOTT, Brian	6-2	209	28	Newmarket, Ont.	L	St. Louis-Peoria
HALAK, Jaroslav	5-10	186	28	Bratislava, Czech.	L	Weiswasser-St. Louis
LUNDSTROM, Niklas	6-2	187	20	Varmdo, Sweden	L	AIK-AIK Jr.

* – Age at start of 2013-14 season

Coaching History

Lynn Patrick and Scotty Bowman, 1967-68; Scotty Bowman, 1968-69, 1969-70; Al Arbour and Scotty Bowman, 1970-71; Sid Abel, Bill McCreary and Al Arbour, 1971-72; Al Arbour and Jean-Guy Talbot, 1972-73; Jean-Guy Talbot and Lou Angotti, 1973-74; Lou Angotti, Lynn Patrick and Garry Young, 1974-75; Garry Young, Lynn Patrick and Leo Boivin, 1975-76; Emile Francis, 1976-77; Leo Boivin and Barclay Plager, 1977-78; Barclay Plager, 1978-79; Barclay Plager and Red Berenson, 1979-80; Red Berenson, 1980-81; Red Berenson and Emile Francis, 1981-82; Emile Francis and Barclay Plager, 1982-83; Jacques Demers, 1983-84 to 1985-86; Jacques Martin, 1986-87, 1987-88; Brian Sutter, 1988-89 to 1991-92; Bob Plager and Bob Berry, 1992-93; Bob Berry, 1993-94; Mike Keenan, 1994-95, 1995-96; Mike Keenan, Jim Roberts and Joel Quenneville, 1996-97; Joel Quenneville, 1997-98 to 2002-03; Joel Quenneville and Mike Kitchen, 2003-04; Mike Kitchen, 2004-05, 2005-06; Mike Kitchen and Andy Murray, 2006-07; Andy Murray, 2007-08, 2008-09; Andy Murray and Davis Payne, 2009-10; Davis Payne, 2010-11; Davis Payne and Ken Hitchcock, 2011-12; Ken Hitchcock, 2012-13 to date.

Ken Hitchcock

Head Coach

Born: Edmonton, Alta., December 17, 1951.

Ken Hitchcock was named the 24th head coach in St. Louis Blues history on November 6, 2011. The team was 6-7-0 at the time. Hitchcock led the Blues to a record of 43-15-11 the rest of the way and third place in the overall standings. He was rewarded with the Jack Adams Award as coach of the year.

In 14 full seasons behind the bench prior to his arrival in St. Louis, Hitchcock led his teams to nine Stanley Cup playoffs appearances and six division titles while recording at least 40 wins nine times and 100 points on eight occasions. He won the Stanley Cup with Dallas in 1999 when the team set club records with 51 wins and 114 points. He also won the Presidents' Trophy twice and was nominated for the Jack Adams Award three times. In Philadelphia from 2002 to 2006, he posted three straight 100-point seasons. While coaching Columbus, Hitchcock became the 13th coach in NHL history to record 500 wins on February 19, 2009.

Hitchcock began his professional coaching career as an assistant coach with the Philadelphia Flyers from 1990 to 1993 before spending two-plus seasons as the head coach of the Kalamazoo Wings/Michigan K-Wings, Dallas' International Hockey League affiliate. Prior to joining the professional ranks, Hitchcock was one of the winningest coaches in the history of the Western Hockey League with the Kamloops Blazers from 1984 to 1990. He was the league's coach of the year in 1986-87 and 1989-90 and was also named the Canadian Major Junior coach of the year in 1989-90 after leading Kamloops to the WHL championship.

Hitchcock has also represented Canada at numerous international competitions, including serving as an associate coach at the Winter Olympics in 2002 (gold), 2006, 2010 (gold), and will again in 2014. He also helped Team Canada win the World Cup of Hockey Tournament in 2004 as an associate coach and was an assistant on gold medal-winning squads at the 2002 World Championship and the 1987 World Junior Championships.

2012-13 Scoring

* – rookie

Regular Season

Pos	#	Player	Team	GP	G	A	Pts	TOI	+/-	PIM	PP	SH	GW	S	%
R	25	Chris Stewart	STL	48	18	18	36	15:49	0	40	6	0	3	97	18.6
R	42	David Backes	STL	48	6	22	28	19:36	5	62	1	0	1	100	6.0
C	20	Alexander Steen	STL	40	8	19	27	18:59	5	14	3	0	3	129	6.2
C	21	Patrik Berglund	STL	48	17	8	25	16:49	–2	12	5	2	3	74	23.0
L	57	David Perron	STL	48	10	15	25	18:00	0	44	2	0	2	84	11.9
D	27	Alex Pietrangelo	STL	47	5	19	24	25:06	0	10	2	0	0	93	5.4
D	22	Kevin Shattenkirk	STL	48	5	18	23	21:18	2	20	2	0	0	84	6.0
D	19	Jay Bouwmeester	CGY	33	6	9	15	25:09	–11	16	1	0	0	55	10.9
			STL	14	1	6	7	23:23	5	6	0	0	0	24	4.2
			Total	47	7	15	22	24:38	–6	22	1	0	0	79	8.9
C	10	Andy McDonald	STL	37	7	14	21	17:15	–2	16	1	0	2	86	8.1
C	74	T.J. Oshie	STL	30	7	13	20	19:05	–5	15	2	1	1	65	10.8
R	91	* Vladimir Tarasenko	STL	38	8	11	19	13:24	1	10	3	0	1	75	10.7
C	17	Vladimir Sobotka	STL	48	8	11	19	15:27	–4	35	1	0	2	69	11.6
C	9	* Jaden Schwartz	STL	45	7	6	13	12:28	–4	4	0	0	1	50	14.0
D	5	Barret Jackman	STL	46	3	9	12	19:19	6	39	0	0	0	39	7.7
D	33	Jordan Leopold	BUF	24	2	6	8	21:08	–6	14	0	0	0	38	5.3
			STL	15	0	2	2	18:22	–2	0	0	0	0	22	0.0
			Total	39	2	8	10	20:04	–8	14	0	0	0	60	3.3
L	32	Chris Porter	STL	29	2	6	8	11:38	5	0	0	0	2	46	4.3
D	4	Kris Russell	STL	33	1	6	7	16:02	6	9	1	0	0	41	2.4
R	75	Ryan Reaves	STL	43	4	2	6	7:26	3	79	0	0	1	24	16.7
R	79	Adam Cracknell	STL	20	2	4	6	8:36	3	4	0	0	0	21	9.5
D	46	Roman Polak	STL	48	1	5	6	18:25	–2	48	0	0	1	39	2.6
C	12	Scott Nichol	STL	30	1	0	1	9:46	–2	25	0	0	1	13	7.7
R	15	Jamie Langenbrunner	STL	4	0	1	1	9:46	1	0	0	0	0	5	0.0
D	28	Ian Cole	STL	15	0	1	1	17:44	–4	10	0	0	0	10	0.0
C	23	Andrew Murray	STL	1	0	0	0	7:49	0	0	0	0	0	2	0.0
R	26	* Dmitrij Jaskin	STL	2	0	0	0	7:29	–1	0	0	0	0	2	0.0

Goaltending

No.	Goaltender	GPI	Mins	Avg	W	L	OT	EN	SO	GA	SA	S%	G	A	PIM
41	Jaroslav Halak	16	813	2.14	6	5	1	2	3	29	286	.899	0	1	0
1	Brian Elliott	24	1292	2.28	14	8	1	1	3	49	526	.907	0	0	0
34	* Jake Allen	15	804	2.46	9	4	0	0	1	33	346	.905	0	0	0
	Totals	**48**	**2920**	**2.34**	**29**	**17**	**2**	**3**	**7**	**114**	**1161**	**.902**			

Playoffs

Pos	#	Player	Team	GP	G	A	Pts	TOI	+/-	PIM	PP	SH	GW	OT	S	%
C	20	Alexander Steen	STL	6	3	0	3	20:56	2	6	1	1	1	1	17	17.6
R	42	David Backes	STL	6	1	2	3	20:32	0	0	0	0	0	0	19	5.3
C	17	Vladimir Sobotka	STL	6	0	3	3	16:36	0	0	0	0	0	0	6	0.0
C	74	T.J. Oshie	STL	6	2	0	2	18:31	–4	2	1	0	0	0	6	33.3
D	5	Barret Jackman	STL	6	1	1	2	20:12	–1	10	0	0	1	0	7	14.3
C	21	Patrik Berglund	STL	6	1	1	2	17:46	–3	2	0	0	0	0	11	9.1
D	27	Alex Pietrangelo	STL	6	1	1	2	26:33	2	2	0	0	0	0	14	7.1
D	22	Kevin Shattenkirk	STL	6	0	2	2	18:38	–1	6	0	0	0	0	12	0.0
L	57	David Perron	STL	6	0	2	2	17:11	–3	6	0	0	0	0	12	0.0
L	32	Chris Porter	STL	6	1	0	1	9:14	0	0	0	0	0	0	7	14.3
D	19	Jay Bouwmeester	STL	6	0	1	1	25:07	0	0	0	0	0	0	7	0.0
D	46	Roman Polak	STL	6	0	1	1	20:09	–2	2	0	0	0	0	8	0.0
R	25	Chris Stewart	STL	6	0	1	1	16:32	0	0	0	0	0	0	17	0.0
C	9	* Jaden Schwartz	STL	6	0	1	1	16:06	1	2	0	0	0	0	13	0.0
R	91	* Vladimir Tarasenko	STL	1	0	0	0	5:51	0	0	0	0	0	0	0	0.0
R	79	Adam Cracknell	STL	5	0	0	0	7:59	–1	0	0	0	0	0	5	0.0
D	33	Jordan Leopold	STL	6	0	0	0	16:32	–2	0	0	0	0	0	0	0.0
C	10	Andy McDonald	STL	6	0	0	0	17:31	0	0	0	0	0	0	10	0.0
R	75	Ryan Reaves	STL	6	0	0	0	7:30	–1	2	0	0	0	0	6	0.0

Goaltending

No.	Goaltender	GPI	Mins	Avg	W	L	EN	SO	GA	SA	S%	G	A	PIM
1	Brian Elliott	6	378	1.90	2	4	0	0	12	149	.919	0	0	0
	Totals	**6**	**381**	**1.89**	**2**	**4**	**0**	**0**	**12**	**149**	**.919**			

Coaching Record

			Regular Season				Playoffs			
Season	Team	League	GC	W	L	O/T	GC	W	L	T
1984-85	Kamloops	WHL	71	52	17	2	15	10	5	....
1985-86	Kamloops	WHL	72	49	19	4	16	14	2	....
1985-86	Kamloops	M-Cup	....	....	....	....	4	1	3	....
1986-87	Kamloops	WHL	72	55	14	3	13	8	5	....
1987-88	Kamloops	WHL	72	45	26	1	18	12	6	....
1988-89	Kamloops	WHL	72	34	33	5	16	8	8	....
1989-90	Kamloops	WHL	72	56	16	0	17	14	3	....
1989-90	Kamloops	M-Cup	....	....	....	....	3	0	3	....
1993-94	Kalamazoo	IHL	81	48	26	7	5	1	4	....
1994-95	Kalamazoo	IHL	81	43	24	14	16	10	6	....
1995-96	Michigan	IHL	40	19	10	11	....	....	....	....
1995-96	**Dallas**	**NHL**	**43**	**15**	**23**	**5**	....	....	....	....
1996-97	**Dallas**	**NHL**	**82**	**48**	**26**	**8**	**7**	**3**	**4**	....
1997-98	**Dallas**	**NHL**	**82**	**49**	**22**	**11**	**17**	**10**	**7**	....
1998-99 ♦	**Dallas**	**NHL**	**82**	**51**	**19**	**12**	**23**	**16**	**7**	....
99-2000	**Dallas**	**NHL**	**82**	**43**	**23**	**16**	**23**	**14**	**9**	....
2000-01	**Dallas**	**NHL**	**82**	**48**	**24**	**10**	**10**	**4**	**6**	....
2001-02	**Dallas**	**NHL**	**50**	**23**	**17**	**10**	....	....	....	....
2002-03	**Philadelphia**	**NHL**	**82**	**45**	**20**	**17**	**13**	**6**	**7**	....
2003-04	**Philadelphia**	**NHL**	**82**	**40**	**21**	**21**	**18**	**11**	**7**	....
2004-05	**Philadelphia**				SEASON CANCELLED					
2005-06	**Philadelphia**	**NHL**	**82**	**45**	**26**	**11**	**6**	**2**	**4**	....
2006-07	**Philadelphia**	**NHL**	**8**	**1**	**6**	**1**	....	....	....	....
2006-07	**Columbus**	**NHL**	**62**	**28**	**29**	**5**	....	....	....	....
2007-08	**Columbus**	**NHL**	**82**	**34**	**36**	**12**	....	....	....	....
2008-09	**Columbus**	**NHL**	**82**	**41**	**31**	**10**	**4**	**0**	**4**	....
2009-10	**Columbus**	**NHL**	**58**	**22**	**27**	**9**	....	....	....	....
2011-12	**St. Louis**	**NHL**	**69**	**43**	**15**	**11**	**9**	**4**	**5**	....
2012-13	**St. Louis**	**NHL**	**48**	**29**	**17**	**2**	**6**	**2**	**4**	....
	NHL Totals		**1158**	**605**	**382**	**171**	**136**	**72**	**64**	....

♦ Stanley Cup win.
Jack Adams Award (2012)

Club Records

Team

(Figures in brackets for season records are games played; records for fewest points, wins, ties, losses, goals, goals against are for 70 or more games)

Most Points	**114**	1999-2000 (82)
Most Wins	**51**	1999-2000 (82)
Most Ties	**19**	1970-71 (78)
Most Losses	**50**	1978-79 (80)
Most Goals	**352**	1980-81 (80)
Most Goals Against	**349**	1981-82 (80)
Fewest Points	**48**	1978-79 (80)
Fewest Wins	**18**	1978-79 (80)
Fewest Ties	**7**	1983-84 (80)
Fewest Losses	**18**	1980-81 (80)
Fewest Goals	**177**	1967-68 (74)
Fewest Goals Against	**157**	1968-69 (76)
Longest Winning Streak		
Overall	**10**	Jan. 3-23/02
Home	**9**	Jan. 26-Feb. 26/91
Away	**10**	Jan. 21-Mar. 2/00
Longest Undefeated Streak		
Overall	**12**	Nov. 10-Dec. 8/68 (5W, 7T), Nov. 24-Dec. 26/00 (11W, 1T/OL)
Home	**11**	Four times
Away	**11**	Jan. 21-Mar. 4/00 (10W, 1T/OL)
Longest Losing Streak		
Overall	**13**	Mar. 16-Apr. 8/06
Home	**7**	Oct. 22-Nov. 26/05, Nov. 25-Dec. 17/06
Away	**10**	Jan. 20-Mar. 8/82, Dec. 29/05-Feb. 1/06, Feb. 16-Mar. 15/08
Longest Winless Streak		
Overall	**13**	Mar. 16-Apr. 8/06 (13L)
Home	**7**	Dec. 28/82-Jan. 25/83 (5L, 2T), Oct. 22-Nov. 26/05 (7L)
Away	**17**	Jan. 23-Apr. 7/74 (14L, 3T)
Most Shutouts, Season	**15**	2011-12 (82)
Most PIM, Season	**2,041**	1990-91 (80)
Most Goals, Game	**11**	Feb. 26/94 (St.L. 11 at Ott. 1)

Individual

Most Seasons	**13**	Bernie Federko
Most Games	**927**	Bernie Federko
Most Goals, Career	**527**	Brett Hull
Most Assists, Career	**721**	Bernie Federko
Most Points, Career	**1,073**	Bernie Federko (352G, 721A)
Most PIM, Career	**1,786**	Brian Sutter
Most Shutouts, Career	**16**	Glenn Hall, Jaroslav Halak
Longest Consecutive Games Streak	**662**	Garry Unger (Feb. 7/71-Apr. 8/79)
Most Goals, Season	**86**	Brett Hull (1990-91)
Most Assists, Season	**90**	Adam Oates (1990-91)
Most Points, Season	**131**	Brett Hull (1990-91; 86G, 45A)
Most PIM, Season	**306**	Bob Gassoff (1975-76)
Most Points, Defenseman, Season	**78**	Jeff Brown (1992-93; 25G, 53A)
Most Points, Center, Season	**115**	Adam Oates (1990-91; 25G, 90A)
Most Points, Right Wing, Season	**131**	Brett Hull (1990-91; 86G, 45A)
Most Points, Left Wing, Season	**102**	Brendan Shanahan (1993-94; 52G, 50A)
Most Points, Rookie, Season	**73**	Jorgen Pettersson (1980-81; 37G, 36A)
Most Shutouts, Season	**9**	Brian Elliott (2011-12)
Most Goals, Game	**6**	Red Berenson (Nov. 7/68)
Most Assists, Game	**5**	Brian Sutter (Nov. 22/83), Bernie Federko (Feb. 27/88), Adam Oates (Jan. 26/91), Dallas Drake (Oct. 29/03)
Most Points, Game	**7**	Red Berenson (Nov. 7/68; 6G, 1A), Garry Unger (Mar. 13/71; 3G, 4A)

All-time Record vs. Other Clubs

Regular Season

	Total								At Home								On Road							
	GP	W	L	T	OL	GF	GA	PTS	GP	W	L	T	OL	GF	GA	PTS	GP	W	L	T	OL	GF	GA	PTS
Anaheim	75	37	27	5	6	233	212	85	38	22	8	3	5	129	101	52	37	15	19	2	1	104	111	33
Boston	125	46	61	18	0	370	467	110	63	28	26	9	0	198	214	65	62	18	35	9	0	172	253	45
Buffalo	108	50	45	13	0	364	341	113	53	31	15	7	0	190	134	69	55	19	30	6	0	174	207	44
Calgary	157	70	68	14	5	479	488	159	79	37	31	9	2	268	243	85	78	33	37	5	3	211	245	74
Carolina	70	39	25	5	1	229	201	84	35	21	10	3	1	124	99	46	35	18	15	2	0	105	102	38
Chicago	286	113	126	35	12	874	950	273	142	71	51	17	3	464	426	162	144	42	75	18	9	410	524	111
Colorado	112	48	49	11	4	341	358	111	55	31	18	4	2	193	157	68	57	17	31	7	2	148	201	43
Columbus	73	44	23	3	3	227	185	94	37	27	8	1	1	131	88	56	36	17	15	2	2	96	97	38
Dallas	263	120	96	43	4	845	800	287	132	74	37	21	0	466	365	169	131	46	59	22	4	379	435	118
Detroit	273	118	112	37	6	840	882	279	136	66	47	20	3	437	391	155	137	52	65	17	3	403	491	124
Edmonton	119	56	46	11	6	395	394	129	60	30	20	7	3	203	197	70	59	26	26	4	3	192	197	59
Florida	25	15	7	3	0	59	44	33	13	9	3	1	0	33	18	19	12	6	4	2	0	26	26	14
Los Angeles	187	96	67	22	2	599	550	216	94	59	24	10	1	335	237	129	93	37	43	12	1	264	313	87
Minnesota	47	20	16	5	6	109	117	51	23	12	5	3	3	59	48	30	24	8	11	2	3	50	69	21
Montreal	122	29	70	22	1	328	464	81	60	15	29	15	1	156	203	46	62	14	41	7	0	172	261	35
Nashville	85	39	29	4	13	208	190	95	42	21	15	1	5	110	91	48	43	18	14	3	8	98	99	47
New Jersey	98	48	35	14	1	337	305	111	49	28	13	7	1	201	154	64	49	20	22	7	0	136	151	47
NY Islanders	103	35	46	20	2	318	357	92	50	20	19	9	2	178	161	51	53	15	27	11	0	140	196	41
NY Rangers	131	40	73	16	2	354	463	98	68	28	29	10	1	203	212	67	63	12	44	6	1	151	251	31
Ottawa	25	12	11	2	0	78	64	26	12	5	5	2	0	35	34	12	13	7	6	0	0	43	30	14
Philadelphia	141	41	79	17	4	363	497	103	71	28	34	7	2	202	225	65	70	13	45	10	2	161	272	38
Phoenix	132	59	51	18	4	424	382	140	66	33	22	11	0	216	176	77	66	26	29	7	4	208	206	63
Pittsburgh	135	67	48	18	2	454	426	154	68	45	16	6	1	256	180	97	67	22	32	12	1	198	246	57
San Jose	83	49	28	2	4	249	206	104	44	24	18	1	1	125	107	50	39	25	10	1	3	124	99	54
Tampa Bay	31	18	8	3	2	110	86	41	14	11	3	0	0	54	35	22	17	7	5	3	2	56	51	19
Toronto	207	91	88	25	3	660	669	210	105	59	30	14	2	355	288	134	102	32	58	11	1	305	381	76
Vancouver	174	90	59	18	7	583	494	205	86	50	23	9	4	312	239	113	88	40	36	9	3	271	255	92
Washington	87	38	36	12	1	301	286	89	44	22	14	8	0	174	137	52	43	16	22	4	1	127	149	37
Winnipeg	15	9	3	1	2	48	36	21	6	4	1	0	1	19	11	9	9	5	2	1	1	29	25	12
Defunct Clubs	65	36	14	15	0	226	155	87	32	25	4	3	0	131	55	53	33	11	10	12	0	95	100	34
Totals	**3554**	**1573**	**1446**	**432**	**103**	**11005**	**11069**	**3681**	**1777**	**936**	**578**	**218**	**45**	**5957**	**5026**	**2135**	**1777**	**637**	**868**	**214**	**58**	**5048**	**6043**	**1546**

Playoffs

	Series	W	L	GP	W	L	T	GF	GA	Last Mtg.	Rnd.	Result
Boston	2	0	2	8	0	8	0	15	48	1972	SF	L 0-4
Buffalo	1	0	1	3	1	2	0	8	7	1976	PRE	L 1-2
Calgary	1	0	1	7	3	4	0	22	28	1986	CF	L 3-4
Chicago	10	3	7	50	22	28	0	142	171	2002	CQF	W 4-1
Colorado	1	0	1	5	1	4	0	11	17	2001	CF	L 1-4
Dallas	12	6	6	66	32	34	0	187	197	2001	CSF	W 4-0
Detroit	7	2	5	40	16	24	0	103	125	2002	CSF	L 1-4
Los Angeles	4	2	2	18	10	8	0	48	40	2013	CQF	L 2-4
Montreal	3	0	3	12	0	12	0	14	42	1977	QF	L 0-4
NY Rangers	1	0	1	6	2	4	0	22	29	1981	QF	L 2-4
Philadelphia	2	2	0	11	8	3	0	34	20	1969	QF	W 4-0
Phoenix	2	2	0	11	7	4	0	39	29	1999	CQF	W 4-3
Pittsburgh	3	2	1	13	7	6	0	45	40	1981	PRE	W 3-2
San Jose	4	2	2	23	12	11	0	61	51	2012	CQF	W 4-1
Toronto	5	3	2	31	17	14	0	88	90	1996	CQF	W 4-2
Vancouver	3	0	3	18	6	12	0	53	55	2009	CQF	L 0-4
Totals	**61**	**24**	**37**	**322**	**144**	**178**	**0**	**892**	**989**			

Calgary totals include Atlanta Flames, 1972-73 to 1979-80.
Carolina totals include Hartford, 1979-80 to 1996-97.
Colorado totals include Quebec, 1979-80 to 1994-95.
Dallas totals include Minnesota North Stars, 1967-68 to 1992-93.
New Jersey totals include Kansas City, 1974-75, 1975-76, and Colorado Rockies, 1976-77 to 1981-82.
Phoenix totals include Winnipeg, 1979-80 to 1995-96.
Winnipeg totals include Atlanta Thrashers, 1999-2000 to 2010-11.

Playoff Results 2013-2009

Year	Round	Opponent	Result	GF	GA
2013	CQF	Los Angeles	L 2-4	10	12
2012	CSF	Los Angeles	L 0-4	6	15
	CQF	San Jose	W 4-1	14	8
2009	CQF	Vancouver	L 0-4	5	11

Abbreviations: Round: CF – conference final; **CSF** – conference semi-final; **CQF** – conference quarter-final; **SF** – semi-final; **QF** – quarter-final; **PRE** – preliminary round.

Retired Numbers

2	Al MacInnis	1994-2004
3	Bob Gassoff	1973-1977
8	Barclay Plager	1967-1977
11	Brian Sutter	1976-1988
16	Brett Hull	1987-1998
24	Bernie Federko	1976-1989

General Managers' History

Lynn Patrick, 1967-68; Scotty Bowman, 1968-69 to 1970-71; Lynn Patrick and Sid Abel, 1971-72; Sid Abel, 1972-73; Charles Catto, 1973-74; Gerry Ehman and Dennis Ball, 1974-75; Dennis Ball, 1975-76; Emile Francis, 1976-77 to 1982-83; Ron Caron, 1983-84 to 1993-94; Mike Keenan, 1994-95, 1995-96; Mike Keenan and Ron Caron, 1996-97; Larry Pleau, 1997-98 to 2009-10; Doug Armstrong, 2010-11 to date.

2012-13 Results

Jan.	19	Detroit	6-0		10	at Anaheim	2-4
	21	at Nashville	4-3†		12	San Jose	4-2
	22	at Chicago	2-3		14	Phoenix	3-0
	24	Nashville	3-0		16	Anaheim	2-1*
	26	at Dallas	4-3		19	at Vancouver	2-3
	27	Minnesota	5-4*		23	at Edmonton	3-0
	31	at Columbus	4-1		24	at Calgary	2-3
Feb.	1	at Detroit	3-5		26	Edmonton	0-3
	5	Nashville	1-6		28	Los Angeles	2-4
	7	Detroit	1-5	**Apr.**	1	at Minnesota	4-1
	9	Anaheim	5-6†		4	at Chicago	4-3†
	11	Los Angeles	1-4		5	Columbus	3-1
	13	at Detroit	4-3*		7	at Detroit	1-0
	15	at Calgary	5-2		9	at Nashville	1-0
	17	at Vancouver	4-3†		11	at Minnesota	2-0
	19	San Jose	1-2		12	at Columbus	1-4
	20	at Colorado	0-1*		14	Chicago	0-2
	23	Columbus	2-1		16	Vancouver	2-1†
	28	Chicago	0-3		18	Phoenix	2-1†
Mar.	1	Edmonton	4-2		19	Dallas	2-1
	3	at Dallas	1-4		21	at Colorado	3-5
	5	at Los Angeles	4-6		23	Colorado	3-1
	7	at Phoenix	6-3		25	Calgary	4-1
	9	at San Jose	4-3*		27	Chicago	3-1

* – Overtime † – Shootout

Entry Draft Selections 2013-1999

Name in bold denotes played in NHL.

2013

Pick	
47	Thomas Vannelli
57	William Carrier
112	Zachary Pochiro
173	Santeri Saari

2012

Pick	
25	Jordan Schmaltz
56	Sam Kurker
67	Mackenzie MacEachern
86	Colton Parayko
116	Nicholas Walters
146	Francois Tremblay
176	Petteri Lindbohm
206	Tyrel Seaman

2011

Pick	
32	Ty Rattie
41	**Dmitrij Jaskin**
46	Joel Edmundson
88	Jordan Binnington
102	Yannick Veilleux
132	Niklas Lundstrom
162	Ryan Tesink
192	Teemu Eronen

2010

Pick	
14	**Jaden Schwartz**
16	**Vladimir Tarasenko**
44	Sebastian Wannstrom
74	Max Gardiner
104	Jani Hakanpaa
134	Cody Beach
164	Stephen Macaulay

2009

Pick	
17	**David Rundblad**
48	Brett Ponich
78	Sergei Andronov
108	Tyler Shattock
168	David Shields
202	Max Tardy

2008

Pick	
4	**Alex Pietrangelo**
33	**Philip McRae**
34	**Jake Allen**
65	Jori Lehtera
70	James Livingston
87	Ian Schultz
95	David Warsofsky
125	Kristofer Berglund
155	Anthony Nigro
185	Paul Karpowich

2007

Pick	
13	**Lars Eller**
18	**Ian Cole**
26	**David Perron**
39	Simon Hjalmarsson
44	**Aaron Palushaj**
85	Brett Sonne
96	**Cade Fairchild**
100	Travis Erstad
160	**Anthony Peluso**
190	Trevor Nill

2006

Pick	
1	**Erik Johnson**
25	**Patrik Berglund**
31	**Tomas Kana**
64	**Jonas Junland**
94	Ryan Turek
106	Reto Berra
124	Andy Sackrison
154	Matthew McCollem
184	Alexander Hellstrom

2005

Pick	
24	**T.J. Oshie**
37	**Scott Jackson**
85	**Ben Bishop**
156	**Ryan Reaves**
169	Mike Gauthier
171	**Nick Drazenovic**
219	Nikolai Lemtyugov

2004

Pick	
17	**Marek Schwarz**
49	**Carl Soderberg**
83	Viktor Alexandrov
116	Michal Birner
136	**Nikita Nikitin**
180	**Roman Polak**
211	David Fredriksson
277	Jonathan Michel Boutin

2003

Pick	
30	**Shawn Belle**
62	**David Backes**
84	Konstantin Barulin
88	**Zack Fitzgerald**
101	Konstantin Zakharov
127	**Alexandre Bolduc**
148	**Lee Stempniak**
159	**Chris Beckford-Tseu**
189	Jonathan Lehun
221	Evgeny Skachkov
253	Andrei Pervyshin
284	Juhamatti Aaltonen

2002

Pick	
48	Alexei Shkotov
62	Andrei Mikhnov
89	Tomas Troliga
120	Robin Jonsson
165	Justin Maiser
190	**DJ King**
221	Jonas Johnson
253	**Tom Koivisto**
284	Ryan MacMurchy

2001

Pick	
57	**Jay McClement**
89	Tuomas Nissinen
122	Igor Valeev
159	Dmitri Semin
190	Brett Scheffelmaier
253	**Petr Cajanek**
270	Grant Jacobsen
283	Simon Skoog

2000

Pick	
30	**Jeff Taffe**
65	**Dave Morisset**
75	**Justin Papineau**
96	Antoine Bergeron
129	Troy Riddle
167	**Craig Weller**
229	Brett Lutes
261	**Reinhard Divis**
293	Lauri Kinos

1999

Pick	
17	**Barret Jackman**
85	**Peter Smrek**
114	Chad Starling
143	Trevor Byrne
180	Tore Vikingstad
203	Phil Osaer
221	**Colin Hemingway**
232	**Alexander Khavanov**
260	Brian McMeekin
270	James Desmarais

Captains' History

Al Arbour, 1967-68 to 1969-70; Red Berenson and Barclay Plager, 1970-71; Barclay Plager, 1971-72 to 1975-76; no captain, 1976-77; Red Berenson, 1977-78; Barry Gibbs, 1978-79; Brian Sutter, 1979-80 to 1987-88; Bernie Federko, 1988-89; Rick Meagher, 1989-90; Scott Stevens, 1990-91; Garth Butcher, 1991-92; Brett Hull, 1992-93 to 1994-95; Brett Hull, Shayne Corson and Wayne Gretzky, 1995-96; no captain, 1996-97; Chris Pronger, 1997-98 to 2001-02; Al MacInnis, 2002-03, 2003-04; Dallas Drake, 2005-06, 2006-07; Eric Brewer, 2007-08 to 2010-11; David Backes, 2011-12 to date.

Doug Armstrong

Executive Vice President and General Manager

Born: Sarnia, Ont., September 24, 1964.

Doug Armstrong was named the Blues' executive vice president and general manager on July 1, 2010 after serving two seasons with the club as vice president of player personnel. In his second season on the job in 2011-12, Armstrong acquired goalie Brian Elliott to share the net with Jaroslav Halak and hired Ken Hitchcock as coach after a slow start. The result was the best defensive record in the NHL and 49 wins and 109 points for the second-best performance in franchise history. Armstrong was rewarded with a selection as the NHL G.M. of the Year.

Prior to being hired in St. Louis, Armstrong spent 17 years with the Dallas Stars organization and the last six seasons (from January 25, 2002, to 2008) as the club's general manager. He was a part of the Stars' organization since the club moved to Dallas in 1993 and helped lead the franchise to two Presidents' Trophies, two Western Conference titles and the 1999 Stanley Cup championship. Prior to being named the team's seventh general manager, Armstrong served nine years as the assistant general manager under Bob Gainey. As Gainey's assistant, Armstrong worked on contract negotiations and season scheduling, and handled the day-to-day operations of the hockey department.

On the international level, Armstrong was the associate director of player personnel for Team Canada at the 2010 Winter Olympics in Vancouver and will be involved with the management team again at Sochi in 2014. He also served as general manager for Team Canada and won the silver medal at the 2009 World Championship in Switzerland. He was the assistant general manager for Team Canada at the 2007 World Championship and 2008 World Championship (silver medal) and served as a special advisor to Steve Yzerman for the Canadian team that won gold at the 2007 World Championship. Armstrong is the son of former NHL linesman Neil Armstrong who was inducted into the Hockey Hall of Fame in 1991.

Club Directory

Scottrade Center

St. Louis Blues
Scottrade Center
1401 Clark Avenue at Brett Hull Way
St. Louis, MO 63103
Phone **314/622-2500**
FAX 314/622-2582
www.stlouisblues.com
Capacity: 19,150

Executive

Chairman and Governor	Tom Stillman
Exec. V.P., General Manager, St. Louis Blues	Doug Armstrong
Chief Operating Officer	Bruce Affleck
Sr. V.P., Marketing and Public Relations	Mike Caruso
Sr. V.P., Sales	Todd Lambert
Sr. V.P., Chief Financial Officer	Phil Siddle
Sr. V.P., Sponsorship	Eric Stisser
Sr. V.P., Events and New Business, Scottrade Center	John Urban
Vice President, Corporate and Sponsorship Sales	Bryan Lucas
Vice President, Hockey Operations	Dave Taylor
Vice President, Marketing	Karrie Yager
Exec. Asst., Hockey Operations	Donna Lembke
Exec. Asst. to the Chairman/COO	Lisa Cwiklowski

Hockey Operations

Assistant G.M.	Kevin McDonald
Senior Advisor to the General Manager	Al MacInnis
Director, Pro Scouting	Rob DiMaio
Director, Amateur Scouting	Bill Armstrong
Director, Player Development	Tim Taylor
Consultant to Hockey Operations	Sergei Zubov
Head Coach	Ken Hitchcock
Associate Coach	Brad Shaw
Assistant Coaches	Ray Bennett, Gary Agnew
Goaltending Coach	Corey Hirsch
Strength and Conditioning Coach	Nelson Ayotte
Video Coach	Dan Brooks
Sr. Director, Media Relations/Team Services	Rich Jankowski
Assistant Director, Media Relations	Dan O'Neill
Director, Hockey Administration	Ryan Miller

Scouting

Professional Scout	Tony Feltrin
Part-Time Professional Scout	Wayne Mundey
Senior Advisor for Amateur Scouting	Larry Pleau
Amateur Scouts	Mike Antonovich, Marshall Davidson, Dan Ginnell, J Niemiec, Michel Picard, Anders Ostberg, Ville Siren, Jan Vopat
Part-Time Amateur Scouts	Corey Banika, Blair Nicholson, Vincent Montalbano

Training

Athletic Trainer / Asst. Athletic Trainer	Ray Barile / Chris Palmer
Equipment Manager / Asst. Manager / Assistant	Bert Godin / Joel Farnsworth / Chad O'Neil
Massage Therapist	Jeff Wright

Medical

Orthopedic Surgeons	Drs. Matt Matava, Rick Wright
Internists	Drs. Aaron Birenbaum, Dr. William Birenbaum
Neurosurgeon	Dr. Ralph Dacey
General / Plastic Surgeons	Dr. Michael Brunt / Dr. Tom Francel
Oral Surgeon	Dr. Ken Kram
Ophthalmologist / Optometrist	Dr. Gill Grand / Dr. David Seibel

Broadcasting

Radio / Television Stations	KMOX, 1120 AM / FS Midwest
Dir., Broadcasting and Radio Play-by-Play / Color	Chris Kerber / Kelly Chase
Community Relations and KMOX Radio	Bob Plager
Television Play-by-Play / Color	John Kelly / Darren Pang, Bernie Federko
FS Midwest Analyst / Host	Jim Hayes / Pat Parris

Marketing

Director, Alumni Relations	Terry Yake
Director, Marketing Communications	Matt Gardner
Director, Event Presentation	Chris Frome
Director, Community Relations	Randy Girsch
Director, Event Presentation and Amateur Hockey	Lamont Buford
Director, Website	Chris Pinkert

Sponsorship

Director, Sponsorship Sales	Deni Allen
Corporate Sales Executive	Matt Poling
Marketing/Sponsorship Assistant	Donna Ferguson

Ticket Sales

Director, Client Services and Fan Development	Matt Brown
Director, Suite Sales	Nick Wierciak
Coordinator, Suite Sales	Melissa Weissman

Group Ticket Sales

Group Sales Senior Director / Manager	Jennifer Nevins / Kari Takmajian

Finance

Finance Controller	Keith Hegger
Managers, Accounting	Craig Bryant, Mike Tonjes, Kristy Atwater
Manager, IT	Larry Womack

Retail

Retail Director / Manager	George Pavlik / Barry Smith

Box Office

Senior Director, Ticket Operations	Tere Hubert

San Jose Sharks

2012-13 Results: 25W-16L-3OTL-4SOL 57PTS
3RD, Pacific Division • 6TH, Western Conference

Key Off-Season Signings/Acquisitions

2013

June 20 • Re-signed LW **Raffi Torres**.
26 • Re-signed C **James Sheppard** and C **Andrew Desjardins**.
27 • Re-signed D **Jason Demers**.
30 • Acquired C **Tyler Kennedy** from Pittsburgh for a 2nd-round pick (later traded) in the 2013 NHL Draft.
July 5 • Re-signed C **Logan Couture** and D **Scott Hannan**.
30 • Re-signed C **Joe Pavelski**.
Aug. 2 • Re-signed C **Bracken Kearns**.

Year-by-Year Record

		Home				Road				Overall									
Season	**GP**	**W**	**L**	**T**	**OL**	**W**	**L**	**T**	**OL**	**W**	**L**	**T**	**OL**	**GF**	**GA**	**Pts.**	**Div. Fin.**	**Conf. Fin.**	**Playoff Result**
2012-13	48	17	2	....	5	8	14	....	2	25	16	....	7	124	116	57	3rd, Pac.	6th, West	Lost Conf. Semi-Final
2011-12	82	26	12	....	3	17	17	....	7	43	29	....	10	228	210	96	2nd, Pac.	7th, West	Lost Conf. Quarter-Final
2010-11	82	25	11	....	5	23	14	....	4	48	25	....	9	248	213	105	1st, Pac.	2nd, West	Lost Conf. Final
2009-10	82	27	6	....	8	24	14	....	3	51	20	....	11	264	215	113	1st, Pac.	1st, West	Lost Conf. Final
2008-09	82	32	5	....	4	21	13	....	7	53	18	....	11	257	204	117	1st, Pac.	1st, West	Lost Conf. Quarter-Final
2007-08	82	22	13	....	6	27	10	....	4	49	23	....	10	222	193	108	1st, Pac.	2nd, West	Lost Conf. Semi-Final
2006-07	82	25	12	....	4	26	14	....	1	51	26	....	5	258	199	107	2nd, Pac.	5th, West	Lost Conf. Semi-Final
2005-06	82	25	9	....	7	19	18	....	4	44	27	....	11	266	242	99	2nd, Pac.	5th, West	Lost Conf. Semi-Final
2004-05	....	....	....	....	....	....	....	....	....	....	....	....	....	....	....	....			
2003-04	82	24	8	7	2	19	13	5	4	43	21	12	6	219	183	104	1st, Pac.	2nd, West	Lost Conf. Final
2002-03	82	17	16	5	3	11	21	4	5	28	37	9	8	214	239	73	5th, Pac.	14th, West	Out of Playoffs
2001-02	82	25	11	3	2	19	16	5	1	44	27	8	3	248	199	99	1st, Pac.	3rd, West	Lost Conf. Semi-Final
2000-01	82	22	14	4	1	18	13	8	2	40	27	12	3	217	192	95	2nd, Pac.	5th, West	Lost Conf. Quarter-Final
1999-2000	82	21	14	3	3	14	16	7	4	35	30	10	7	225	214	87	4th, Pac.	8th, West	Lost Conf. Semi-Final
1998-99	82	17	15	9	....	14	18	9	....	31	33	18	....	196	191	80	4th, Pac.	7th, West	Lost Conf. Quarter-Final
1997-98	82	17	19	5	....	17	19	5	....	34	38	10	....	210	216	78	4th, Pac.	8th, West	Lost Conf. Quarter-Final
1996-97	82	14	23	4	....	13	24	4	....	27	47	8	....	211	278	62	7th, Pac.	13th, West	Out of Playoffs
1995-96	82	12	26	3	....	8	29	4	....	20	55	7	....	252	357	47	7th, Pac.	13th, West	Out of Playoffs
1994-95	48	10	13	1	....	9	12	3	....	19	25	4	....	129	161	42	3rd, Pac.	7th, West	Lost Conf. Semi-Final
1993-94	84	19	13	10	....	14	22	6	....	33	35	16	....	252	265	82	3rd, Pac.	8th, West	Lost Conf. Semi-Final
1992-93	84	8	33	1	....	3	38	1	....	11	71	2	....	218	414	24	6th, Smythe		Out of Playoffs
1991-92	80	14	23	3	....	3	35	2	....	17	58	5	....	219	359	39	6th, Smythe		Out of Playoffs

2013-14 Schedule

Oct.	Thu.	3	Vancouver
	Sat.	5	Phoenix
	Tue.	8	NY Rangers
	Thu.	10	at Vancouver
	Sat.	12	Ottawa
	Tue.	15	at St. Louis
	Thu.	17	at Dallas
	Sat.	19	Calgary
	Mon.	21	at Detroit
	Thu.	24	at Boston
	Sat.	26	at Montreal
	Sun.	27	at Ottawa*
	Wed.	30	at Los Angeles
Nov.	Sat.	2	Phoenix
	Tue.	5	Buffalo
	Thu.	7	Vancouver
	Sun.	10	at Winnipeg
	Tue.	12	at Calgary
	Thu.	14	at Vancouver
	Fri.	15	at Edmonton
	Sun.	17	at Chicago
	Thu.	21	Tampa Bay
	Sat.	23	New Jersey
	Wed.	27	Los Angeles
	Fri.	29	St. Louis*
	Sat.	30	Anaheim
Dec.	Tue.	3	at Toronto
	Thu.	5	at Pittsburgh
	Fri.	6	at Carolina
	Sun.	8	at Minnesota*
	Tue.	10	NY Islanders
	Thu.	12	Minnesota
	Sat.	14	at Nashville
	Tue.	17	at St. Louis
	Thu.	19	at Los Angeles
	Sat.	21	Dallas
	Mon.	23	Colorado
	Fri.	27	at Phoenix
	Sun.	29	Anaheim
	Tue.	31	at Anaheim*
Jan.	Thu.	2	Edmonton
	Sat.	4	at Colorado*
	Sun.	5	at Chicago
	Tue.	7	at Nashville
	Thu.	9	Detroit
	Sat.	11	Boston
	Tue.	14	at Washington
	Thu.	16	at Florida
	Sat.	18	at Tampa Bay*
	Mon.	20	Calgary
	Thu.	23	Winnipeg
	Sat.	25	Minnesota
	Mon.	27	Los Angeles
	Wed.	29	at Edmonton
	Thu.	30	at Calgary
Feb.	Sat.	1	Chicago
	Mon.	3	Philadelphia
	Wed.	5	Dallas
	Fri.	7	Columbus
	Thu.	27	at Philadelphia
	Fri.	28	at Buffalo
Mar.	Sun.	2	at New Jersey*
	Tue.	4	Carolina
	Thu.	6	Pittsburgh
	Sat.	8	Montreal
	Tue.	11	Toronto
	Thu.	13	at Columbus
	Fri.	14	at NY Islanders
	Sun.	16	at NY Rangers*
	Tue.	18	Florida
	Thu.	20	Anaheim
	Sat.	22	Washington
	Mon.	24	at Calgary
	Tue.	25	at Edmonton
	Thu.	27	Winnipeg
	Sat.	29	at Colorado*
Apr.	Tue.	1	Edmonton
	Thu.	3	Los Angeles
	Sat.	5	Nashville
	Wed.	9	at Anaheim
	Fri.	11	Colorado
	Sat.	12	at Phoenix

* Denotes afternoon game.

Logan Couture led the Sharks with 21 goals in 2012-13, making him one of just 12 NHL players to score more than 20 goals during the 48-game campaign.

PACIFIC DIVISION
23rd NHL Season

Franchise date: May 9, 1990

2013-14 Player Personnel

FORWARDS	HT	WT	*Age	Place of Birth	S	2012-13 Club
BURISH, Adam	6-1	195	30	Madison, WI	R	San Jose
BURNS, Brent	6-5	230	28	Ajax, Ont.	R	San Jose
COUTURE, Logan	6-1	200	24	Guelph, Ont.	L	Geneve-San Jose
CRANE, Chris	6-1	190	21	Virginia Beach, VA	R	Ohio State-Worcester
DESJARDINS, Andrew	6-1	195	27	Lively, Ont.	R	San Jose
EMANUELSSON, Petter	6-0	200	22	Kiruna, Sweden	R	Skelleftea
GOGOL, Curt	6-1	190	22	Calgary, Alta.	L	Worcester
HAMILTON, Freddie	6-1	195	21	Toronto, Ont.	R	Worcester
HAVLAT, Martin	6-2	210	32	Mlada Boleslav, Czech.	L	San Jose
HAYES, Eriah	6-4	210	25	La Crescent, MN	R	Minnesota State-Worcester
HERTL, Tomas	6-2	210	19	Prague, Czech Rep.	L	Slavia
KEARNS, Bracken	6-0	195	32	Vancouver, B.C.	R	Worcester-San Jose
KENNEDY, Tyler	5-11	185	27	Sault Ste. Marie, Ont.	R	Pittsburgh
LIVINGSTON, James	6-1	210	23	Halifax, N.S.	R	Worcester
MARLEAU, Patrick	6-2	220	34	Aneroid, Sask.	L	San Jose
McCARTHY, John	6-1	190	27	Boston, MA	L	Worcester
NIETO, Matthew	5-11	190	20	Long Beach, CA	L	Boston University
OLEKSUK, Travis	6-0	200	24	Thunder Bay, Ont.	L	Worcester
PAVELSKI, Joe	5-11	190	29	Plover, WI	R	Dynamo Minsk-San Jose
PELECH, Matt	6-4	230	26	Toronto, Ont.	R	Worcester-San Jose
REID, Brodie	6-1	190	24	Delta, B.C.	R	Worcester
SCHWARTZ, Rylan	5-10	200	23	Wilcox, Sask.	L	Colorado College-Worcester
SHEPPARD, James	6-1	215	25	Halifax, N.S.	L	Worcester-San Jose
STALBERG, Sebastian	6-1	185	23	Gothenburg, Sweden	R	Worcester
TARASOV, Daniil	6-1	195	22	Moscow, Russia	L	Worcester-San Francisco
THORNTON, Joe	6-4	220	34	London, Ont.	L	Davos-San Jose
TIERNEY, Chris	6-0	195	19	Keswick, Ont.	L	London
TORRES, Raffi	6-0	215	31	Toronto, Ont.	L	Phoenix-San Jose
VIEDENSKY, Marek	6-3	210	23	Handlova, Czech.	R	Worcester-San Francisco
WINGELS, Tommy	6-0	200	25	Evanston, IL	R	KooKoo-San Jose
DEFENSEMEN						
ABELTSHAUSER, Konrad	6-5	225	21	Bad Tolz, Germany	L	Halifax
ACOLATSE, Sena	6-0	210	22	Hayward, CA	R	Worcester
BIGOS, Kyle	6-4	235	24	Upland, CA	R	Merrimack
BOYLE, Dan	5-11	190	37	Ottawa, Ont.	R	San Jose
BRAUN, Justin	6-2	205	26	St. Paul, MN	R	Tappara-San Jose
COMRIE, Adam	6-4	215	23	Kanata, Ont.	L	Reading-Worcester
DAVISON, Rob	6-2	215	33	St. Catharines, Ont.	L	Salzburg
DEMELO, Dylan	6-1	195	20	London, Ont.	R	Mississauga-Worcester
DEMERS, Jason	6-1	195	25	Dorval, Que.	R	Karpat-San Jose
DOHERTY, Taylor	6-7	235	22	Cambridge, Ont.	R	Worcester
HANNAN, Scott	6-1	215	34	Richmond, B.C.	L	Nashville-San Jose
IRWIN, Matt	6-2	210	25	Brentwood Bay, B.C.	L	Worcester-San Jose
PETRECKI, Nicholas	6-3	230	24	Schenectady, NY	L	Binghamton-San Jose
STUART, Brad	6-2	215	33	Rocky Mountain House, Alta.	L	San Jose
TENNYSON, Matt	6-2	205	23	Pleasanton, CA	R	Worcester-San Jose
VLASIC, Marc-Edouard	6-1	205	26	Montreal, Que.	L	San Jose
GOALTENDERS	**HT**	**WT**	***Age**	**Place of Birth**	**C**	**2012-13 Club**
ANDERSON, J.P.	5-11	185	21	Toronto, Ont.	R	Sarnia
GROSENICK, Troy	6-1	190	24	Brookfield, WI	L	Union College
NIEMI, Antti	6-2	210	30	Vantaa, Finland	L	Pelicans-San Jose
SATERI, Harri	6-1	205	23	Toijala, Finland	L	Worcester
STALOCK, Alex	6-0	190	26	St. Paul, MN	L	Worcester-San Jose

* – Age at start of 2013-14 season

Todd McLellan

Head Coach

Born: Melville, Sask., October 3, 1967.

The San Jose Sharks introduced Todd McLellan as their new head coach on June 12, 2008. In his first three seasons as an NHL head coach, McLellan posted a 152-63-31 record behind the San Jose Sharks bench, tying him with Mike Keenan for the most wins by any NHL head coach in their first three years. In his five years with the Sharks, the team has posted four 40-plus win seasons, three 100-point seasons, captured a Presidents' Trophy (2009), three Pacific Division titles and made back-to-back appearances in the Western Conference Final (2010, 2011). They have never failed to reach the playoffs.

During the 2010-11 campaign, McLellan's Sharks tied for the third-most wins in the NHL (48), were second in power play percentage (23.5%), led the NHL in shots per game (34.5) and were second in faceoff percentage (53.7%). In 2009-10, McLellan's team finished in the top-five among all NHL teams in goals per game (3.13), power play (21.0 percent), penalty killing (85.0), faceoff percentage (55.6) and even-strength goal differential (plus-32). He became just the third coach in NHL history to record 50-plus wins in his first two seasons. In his first season as an NHL head coach, he was named as a finalist for the Jack Adams Award and became just the sixth NHL coach (and first since 1990) to lead his team to the Presidents' Trophy for the best overall regular season record (53-18-11) in his first season.

Before joining San Jose, McLellan spent three seasons as an assistant coach under Mike Babcock with the Detroit Red Wings. During that span, no NHL team won more games (162) or earned more points (352) than Detroit. One of McLellan's key responsibilities was working with the Red Wings power play, which finished third in the NHL in 2007-08 (20.7) and first in 2005-06 (22.1). Prior to being hired in Detroit, McLellan spent four seasons as head coach of the Houston Aeros in the American Hockey League, capturing the Calder Cup championship and being named Minor League coach of the year by The Hockey News in 2003. In 2000-01, he was the head coach of the Cleveland Lumberjacks of the International Hockey League. From 1994-95 through 1999-00, McLellan coached the Swift Current Broncos of the Western Hockey League, where he also served as general manager in his final four seasons. He was named 2000 WHL coach of the year and 1997 WHL executive of the year. The team captured division titles in 1996 and 2000. In 18 years as a head and assistant coach, McLellan's teams have never missed the playoffs.

McLellan played his junior hockey with Saskatoon (WHL) and was drafted by the New York Islanders in the fifth round (106th overall) in the 1986 NHL Entry Draft. He played parts of two seasons with Springfield in the AHL and played in five games with the Islanders in 1987-88, posting two points (one goal, one assist) before a shoulder injury ended his career.

2012-13 Scoring

* – rookie

Regular Season

Pos	#	Player	Team	GP	G	A	Pts	TOI	+/–	PIM	PP	SH	GW	S	%
C	19	Joe Thornton	S.J.	48	7	33	40	18:22	6	26	2	0	1	85	8.2
C	39	Logan Couture	S.J.	48	21	16	37	18:05	7	4	7	0	5	151	13.9
C	12	Patrick Marleau	S.J.	48	17	14	31	19:06	–2	24	6	1	3	150	11.3
C	8	Joe Pavelski	S.J.	48	16	15	31	18:54	2	10	5	0	5	130	12.3
D	88	Brent Burns	S.J.	30	9	11	20	16:16	0	20	2	0	0	81	11.1
D	22	Dan Boyle	S.J.	46	7	13	20	22:47	3	27	5	0	0	97	7.2
R	9	Martin Havlat	S.J.	40	8	10	18	15:50	7	30	1	0	1	89	9.0
L	13	Raffi Torres	PHX	28	5	7	12	12:59	–1	13	0	0	0	40	12.5
			S.J.	11	2	4	6	13:57	1	4	1	0	0	20	10.0
			Total	39	7	11	18	13:16	0	17	1	0	0	60	11.7
C	23	Scott Gomez	S.J.	39	2	13	15	13:32	–10	22	0	0	0	58	3.4
L	21	T.J. Galiardi	S.J.	36	5	9	14	13:52	1	14	1	0	0	68	7.4
C	57	Tommy Wingels	S.J.	42	5	8	13	14:14	–9	26	0	1	0	69	7.2
D	52	* Matt Irwin	S.J.	38	6	6	12	19:06	–1	10	4	0	0	79	7.6
D	44	Marc-Edouard Vlasic	S.J.	48	3	4	7	20:49	5	29	0	0	0	59	5.1
D	61	Justin Braun	S.J.	41	0	7	7	18:48	–5	6	0	0	0	48	0.0
D	7	Brad Stuart	S.J.	48	0	6	6	20:27	4	25	0	0	0	39	0.0
C	15	James Sheppard	S.J.	32	1	3	4	11:44	–9	12	0	0	1	40	2.5
C	10	Andrew Desjardins	S.J.	42	2	1	3	10:07	–6	61	0	0	0	51	3.9
D	5	Jason Demers	S.J.	22	1	2	3	18:37	–4	10	0	0	0	27	3.7
R	37	Adam Burish	S.J.	46	1	2	3	10:34	–7	25	0	1	0	39	2.6
L	46	Tim Kennedy	S.J.	13	2	0	2	13:35	–3	2	0	0	1	24	8.3
D	80	* Matt Tennyson	S.J.	4	0	2	2	15:42	2	2	0	0	0	8	0.0
D	27	Scott Hannan	NSH	29	0	1	1	19:29	–11	20	0	0	0	20	0.0
			S.J.	4	0	0	0	18:16	–3	2	0	0	0	5	0.0
			Total	33	0	1	1	19:20	–14	22	0	0	0	25	0.0
C	38	Bracken Kearns	S.J.	1	0	0	0	12:04	0	0	0	0	0	0	0.0
D	54	* Nick Petrecki	S.J.	1	0	0	0	11:58	0	0	0	0	0	0	0.0
R	42	* Matt Pelech	S.J.	2	0	0	0	9:03	0	7	0	0	0	0	0.0

Goaltending

No.	Goaltender	GPI	Mins	Avg	W	L	OT	EN	SO	GA	SA	S%	G	A	PIM
31	Antti Niemi	43	2581	2.16	24	12	6	3	4	93	1220	.924	0	1	2
1	Thomas Greiss	6	308	2.53	1	4	0	1	1	13	153	.915	0	0	0
32	* Alex Stalock	2	42	2.86	0	0	1	0	0	2	13	.846	0	0	0
	Totals	**48**	**2948**	**2.28**	**25**	**16**	**7**	**4**	**5**	**112**	**1390**	**.919**			

Playoffs

Pos	#	Player	Team	GP	G	A	Pts	TOI	+/–	PIM	PP	SH	GW	OT	S	%
C	8	Joe Pavelski	S.J.	11	4	8	12	21:12	0	0	3	0	0	0	36	11.1
C	39	Logan Couture	S.J.	11	5	6	11	20:31	–6	0	5	0	3	1	33	15.2
C	19	Joe Thornton	S.J.	11	2	8	10	20:16	5	2	1	0	0	0	25	8.0
C	12	Patrick Marleau	S.J.	11	5	3	8	21:17	0	2	1	0	1	1	41	12.2
D	22	Dan Boyle	S.J.	11	3	5	8	22:11	–3	2	1	0	1	0	26	11.5
D	88	Brent Burns	S.J.	11	2	2	4	17:49	–1	8	0	0	0	0	31	6.5
D	27	Scott Hannan	S.J.	11	0	4	4	17:18	1	4	0	0	0	0	9	0.0
D	7	Brad Stuart	S.J.	11	1	2	3	19:09	3	2	0	0	0	0	10	10.0
D	44	Marc-Edouard Vlasic	S.J.	11	1	1	2	20:39	2	6	0	0	0	0	11	9.1
L	21	T.J. Galiardi	S.J.	11	1	1	2	16:49	1	6	0	0	1	0	19	5.3
C	23	Scott Gomez	S.J.	9	0	2	2	15:01	0	6	0	0	0	0	12	0.0
C	57	Tommy Wingels	S.J.	11	0	2	2	13:53	1	6	0	0	0	0	20	0.0
L	13	Raffi Torres	S.J.	5	1	0	1	17:41	–1	2	0	0	1	1	12	8.3
D	61	Justin Braun	S.J.	11	0	1	1	19:37	–1	0	0	0	0	0	14	0.0
D	52	* Matt Irwin	S.J.	11	0	1	1	17:47	–4	4	0	0	0	0	18	0.0
D	5	Jason Demers	S.J.	1	0	0	0	3:47	0	2	0	0	0	0	0	0.0
R	9	Martin Havlat	S.J.	2	0	0	0	4:04	0	0	0	0	0	0	1	0.0
L	46	Tim Kennedy	S.J.	3	0	0	0	8:44	0	2	0	0	0	0	0	0.0
R	37	Adam Burish	S.J.	6	0	0	0	10:14	0	4	0	0	0	0	9	0.0
C	38	Bracken Kearns	S.J.	7	0	0	0	7:36	–1	2	0	0	0	0	4	0.0
C	10	Andrew Desjardins	S.J.	11	0	0	0	10:57	1	6	0	0	0	0	9	0.0
C	15	James Sheppard	S.J.	11	0	0	0	10:28	–1	4	0	0	0	0	11	0.0

Goaltending

No.	Goaltender	GPI	Mins	Avg	W	L	EN	SO	GA	SA	S%	G	A	PIM
31	Antti Niemi	11	673	1.87	7	4	1	0	21	298	.930	0	1	0
	Totals	**11**	**680**	**1.94**	**7**	**4**	**1**	**0**	**22**	**299**	**.926**			

Coaching Record

			Regular Season				Playoffs			
Season	Team	League	GC	W	L	O/T	GC	W	L	T
1994-95	Swift Current	WHL	72	31	34	7	6	2	4	....
1995-96	Swift Current	WHL	72	36	31	5	6	2	4	....
1996-97	Swift Current	WHL	72	44	23	5	10	4	4	....
1997-98	Swift Current	WHL	72	44	19	9	12	7	5	....
1998-99	Swift Current	WHL	72	34	32	6	6	2	4	....
99-2000	Swift Current	WHL	72	47	18	7	12	6	6	....
2000-01	Cleveland	IHL	82	43	32	7	4	0	4	....
2001-02	Houston	AHL	80	39	26	15	14	8	6	....
2002-03	Houston	AHL	80	47	23	10	23	15	8	....
2003-04	Houston	AHL	80	28	34	18	2	0	2	....
2004-05	Houston	AHL	80	40	28	12	5	1	4	....
2008-09	**San Jose**	**NHL**	**82**	**53**	**18**	**11**	**6**	**2**	**4**	....
2009-10	**San Jose**	**NHL**	**82**	**51**	**20**	**11**	**15**	**8**	**7**	....
2010-11	**San Jose**	**NHL**	**82**	**48**	**25**	**9**	**18**	**9**	**9**	....
2011-12	**San Jose**	**NHL**	**82**	**43**	**29**	**10**	**5**	**1**	**4**	....
2012-13	**San Jose**	**NHL**	**48**	**25**	**16**	**7**	**11**	**7**	**4**	....
	NHL Totals		**376**	**220**	**108**	**48**	**55**	**27**	**28**	....

Assistant coaches Matt Shaw and Jay Woodcrofl posted an 1-2-0 record as replacement coach when Todd McLellan was sidelined due to a concussion suffered February 26, 2012. McLellan returned March 5. Games are credited to McLellan's coaching record.

Club Records

Team

(Figures in brackets for season records are games played; records for fewest points, wins, ties, losses, goals, goals against are for 70 or more games)

Most Points	117	2008-09 (82)
Most Wins	53	2008-09 (82)
Most Ties	18	1998-99 (82)
Most Losses	*71	1992-93 (84)
Most Goals	266	2005-06 (82)
Most Goals Against	414	1992-93 (84)
Fewest Points	24	1992-93 (84)
Fewest Wins	11	1992-93 (84)
Fewest Ties	*2	1992-93 (84)
Fewest Losses	18	2008-09 (82)
Fewest Goals	196	1998-99 (82)
Fewest Goals Against	183	2003-04 (82)
Longest Winning Streak		
Overall	11	Feb. 21-Mar. 14/08
Home	9	Oct. 9-Nov. 8/08
Away	10	Nov. 14-Dec. 31/07
Longest Undefeated Streak		
Overall	10	Nov. 27-Dec. 19/01 (9W, 1T/OL)
Home	11	Nov. 15-Dec. 29/03 (8W, 3T/OL)
Away	10	Dec. 26/00-Feb. 16/01 (6W, 4T/OL)
Longest Losing Streak		
Overall	*17	Jan. 4-Feb. 12/93
Home	9	Nov. 19-Dec. 19/92
Away	19	Nov. 27/92-Feb. 12/93
Longest Winless Streak		
Overall	20	Dec. 29/92-Feb. 12/93 (19L, 1T)
Home	9	Nov. 19-Dec. 19/92 (9L), Oct. 16-Nov. 18/03 (4L, 5T/OL)
Away	19	Nov. 27/92-Feb. 12/93 (19L)
Most Shutouts, Season	11	2003-04 (82), 2006-07 (82)
Most PIM, Season	2,134	1992-93 (84)
Most Goals, Game	10	Jan. 13/96 (S.J. 10 at Pit. 8), Mar. 30/02 (CBJ 2 at S.J. 10)

Individual

Most Seasons	15	Patrick Marleau
Most Games, Career	1,165	Patrick Marleau
Most Goals, Career	404	Patrick Marleau
Most Assists, Career	502	Joe Thornton
Most Points, Career	861	Patrick Marleau (404G, 457A)
Most PIM, Career	1,001	Jeff Odgers
Most Shutouts, Career	50	Evgeni Nabokov
Longest Consecutive Games Streak	379	Joe Thornton (Dec. 1/05-Mar. 27/10)
Most Goals, Season	56	Jonathan Cheechoo (2005-06)
Most Assists, Season	92	Joe Thornton (2006-07)
Most Points, Season	114	Joe Thornton (2006-07; 22G, 92A)
Most PIM, Season	326	Link Gaetz (1991-92)
Most Points, Defenseman, Season	64	Sandis Ozolinsh (1993-94; 26G, 38A)
Most Points, Center, Season	114	Joe Thornton (2006-07; 22G, 92A)
Most Points, Right Wing, Season	93	Jonathan Cheechoo (2005-06; 56G, 37A)
Most Points, Left Wing, Season	83	Patrick Marleau (2009-10; 44G, 39A)
Most Points, Rookie, Season	59	Pat Falloon (1991-92; 25G, 34A)
Most Shutouts, Season	9	Evgeni Nabokov (2003-04)
Most Goals, Game	4	Owen Nolan (Dec. 19/95)
Most Assists, Game	4	Nineteen times
Most Points, Game	6	Owen Nolan (Oct. 4/99; 3G, 3A)

* NHL Record.

Captains' History

Doug Wilson, 1991-92, 1992-93; Bob Errey, 1993-94; Bob Errey and Jeff Odgers, 1994-95; Jeff Odgers, 1995-96; Todd Gill, 1996-97, 1997-98; Owen Nolan, 1998-99 to 2002-03; Mike Ricci, Vincent Damphousse, Alyn McCauley, Patrick Marleau, 2003-04; Patrick Marleau, 2005-06 to 2008-09; Rob Blake, 2009-10; Joe Thornton, 2010-11 to date.

Coaching History

George Kingston, 1991-92, 1992-93; Kevin Constantine, 1993-94, 1994-95; Kevin Constantine and Jim Wiley, 1995-96; Al Sims, 1996-97; Darryl Sutter, 1997-98 to 2001-02; Darryl Sutter, Cap Raeder and Ron Wilson, 2002-03; Ron Wilson, 2003-04 to 2007-08; Todd McLellan, 2008-09 to date.

General Managers' History

Jack Ferreira, 1991-92; Chuck Grillo (V.P. Director of Player Personnel), 1992-93 to 1995-96; Chuck Grillo and Dean Lombardi, 1996-97; Dean Lombardi, 1997-98 to 2002-03; Doug Wilson, 2003-04 to date.

All-time Record vs. Other Clubs

Regular Season

	Total								At Home								On Road							
	GP	W	L	T	OL	GF	GA	PTS	GP	W	L	T	OL	GF	GA	PTS	GP	W	L	T	OL	GF	GA	PTS
Anaheim	113	57	45	4	7	320	297	125	56	27	24	2	3	157	146	59	57	30	21	2	4	163	151	66
Boston	28	9	13	5	1	77	88	24	14	5	6	2	1	34	43	13	14	4	7	3	0	43	45	11
Buffalo	29	7	17	4	1	83	113	19	14	6	4	4	0	42	46	16	15	1	13	0	1	41	67	3
Calgary	97	39	46	8	4	280	299	90	49	22	21	4	2	154	138	50	48	17	25	4	2	126	161	40
Carolina	28	14	13	0	1	93	87	29	14	8	5	0	1	59	43	17	14	6	8	0	0	34	44	12
Chicago	82	42	28	5	7	249	238	96	41	24	12	3	2	121	109	53	41	18	16	2	5	128	129	43
Colorado	78	33	35	5	5	207	250	76	40	21	18	1	0	119	120	43	38	12	17	4	5	88	130	33
Columbus	47	30	13	0	4	133	107	64	23	19	2	0	2	84	40	40	24	11	11	0	2	49	67	24
Dallas	111	48	46	5	12	285	303	113	56	23	23	1	9	142	149	56	55	25	23	4	3	143	154	57
Detroit	82	27	46	4	5	221	298	63	42	18	19	3	2	143	150	41	40	9	27	1	3	78	148	22
Edmonton	96	41	36	12	7	277	286	101	47	24	14	5	4	153	134	57	49	17	22	7	3	124	152	44
Florida	24	9	7	7	1	71	60	26	12	6	3	2	1	37	27	15	12	3	4	5	0	34	33	11
Los Angeles	126	65	48	7	6	379	354	143	63	40	18	3	2	211	168	85	63	25	30	4	4	168	186	58
Minnesota	47	26	14	2	5	130	107	59	24	15	6	1	2	72	49	33	23	11	8	1	3	58	58	26
Montreal	28	10	13	4	1	71	85	25	14	8	3	2	1	46	37	19	14	2	10	2	0	25	48	6
Nashville	55	29	18	2	6	148	138	66	28	17	6	1	4	79	69	39	27	12	12	1	2	69	69	27
New Jersey	29	10	15	2	2	70	96	24	13	5	6	1	1	34	38	12	16	5	9	1	1	36	58	12
NY Islanders	29	14	11	3	1	83	90	32	15	8	5	1	1	39	44	18	14	6	6	2	0	44	46	14
NY Rangers	29	6	18	3	2	76	108	17	16	3	10	2	1	37	57	9	13	3	8	1	1	39	51	8
Ottawa	24	11	9	4	0	61	61	26	12	7	5	0	0	27	24	14	12	4	4	4	0	34	37	12
Philadelphia	31	14	13	4	0	86	87	32	16	7	7	2	0	40	39	16	15	7	6	2	0	46	48	16
Phoenix	120	59	46	7	8	362	337	133	59	32	17	4	6	193	160	74	61	27	29	3	2	169	177	59
Pittsburgh	29	15	10	3	1	86	106	34	17	9	6	2	0	48	60	20	12	6	4	1	1	38	46	14
St. Louis	83	32	43	2	6	206	249	72	39	13	21	1	4	99	124	31	44	19	22	1	2	107	125	41
Tampa Bay	30	13	13	2	2	99	87	30	14	7	6	1	0	54	42	15	16	6	7	1	2	45	45	15
Toronto	39	14	20	5	0	99	124	33	18	7	8	3	0	42	48	17	21	7	12	2	0	57	76	16
Vancouver	97	41	42	9	5	277	301	96	50	22	19	5	4	149	144	53	47	19	23	4	1	128	157	43
Washington	31	21	9	1	0	100	78	43	15	11	3	1	0	53	35	23	16	10	6	0	0	47	43	20
Winnipeg	14	10	1	2	1	48	26	23	7	5	1	1	0	26	15	11	7	5	0	1	1	22	11	12
Totals	**1656**	**746**	**688**	**121**	**101**	**4677**	**4860**	**1714**	**828**	**419**	**298**	**58**	**53**	**2494**	**2298**	**949**	**828**	**327**	**390**	**63**	**48**	**2183**	**2562**	**765**

Playoffs

	Series	W	L	GP	W	L	T	GF	GA	Last Mtg.	Rnd.	Result
Anaheim	1	0	1	6	2	4	0	10	18	2009	CQF	L 2-4
Calgary	3	2	1	20	10	10	0	57	68	2008	CQF	W 4-3
Chicago	1	0	1	4	0	4	0	7	13	2010	CF	L 0-4
Colorado	4	2	2	25	13	12	0	71	62	2010	CQF	W 4-2
Dallas	3	0	3	17	5	12	0	30	46	2008	CSF	L 2-4
Detroit	5	3	2	29	14	15	0	69	99	2011	CSF	W 4-3
Edmonton	1	0	1	6	2	4	0	12	19	2006	CSF	L 2-4
Los Angeles	2	1	1	13	7	6	0	30	34	2013	CSF	L 3-4
Nashville	2	2	0	10	8	2	0	33	24	2007	CQF	W 4-1
Phoenix	1	1	0	5	4	1	0	13	7	2002	CQF	W 4-1
St. Louis	4	2	2	23	11	12	0	51	61	2012	CQF	L 1-4
Toronto	1	0	1	7	3	4	0	21	26	1994	CSF	L 3-4
Vancouver	2	1	1	9	5	4	0	28	28	2013	CQF	W 4-0
Totals	**30**	**14**	**16**	**174**	**84**	**90**	**0**	**432**	**505**			

Carolina totals include Hartford, 1991-92 to 1996-97.
Dallas totals include Minnesota North Stars, 1991-92 to 1992-93.
Winnipeg totals include Atlanta Thrashers, 1999-2000 to 2010-11.

Playoff Results 2013-2009

Year	Round	Opponent	Result	GF	GA
2013	CSF	Los Angeles	L 3-4	10	14
	CQF	Vancouver	W 4-0	15	8
2012	CQF	St. Louis	L 1-4	8	14
2011	CF	Vancouver	L 1-4	13	20
	CSF	Detroit	W 4-3	18	18
	CQF	Los Angeles	W 4-2	20	20
2010	CF	Chicago	L 0-4	7	13
	CSF	Detroit	W 4-1	15	17
	CQF	Colorado	W 4-2	19	11
2009	CQF	Anaheim	L 2-4	10	18

Abbreviations: Round: CF – conference final; **CSF** – conference semi-final; **CQF** – conference quarter-final.

Colorado totals include Quebec, 1991-92 to 1994-95.
Phoenix totals include Winnipeg, 1991-92 to 1995-96.

2012-13 Results

Jan.	20	at Calgary	4-1		12	at St. Louis	2-4
	22	at Edmonton	6-3		14	Los Angeles	4-3
	24	Phoenix	5-3		16	at Los Angeles	2-5
	26	Colorado	4-0		18	at Anaheim	3-5
	27	Vancouver	4-1		20	at Edmonton	4-3†
	29	Anaheim	3-2†		23	at Minnesota	0-2
	31	Edmonton	3-2†		25	at Anaheim	5-3
Feb.	2	Nashville	1-2†		27	Anaheim	4-0
	4	at Anaheim	1-2		28	Detroit	2-0
	5	Chicago	3-5		30	Phoenix	3-2†
	9	Phoenix	0-1†	**Apr.**	1	Vancouver	3-2
	11	at Columbus	2-6		3	Minnesota	4-2
	12	at Nashville	0-1*		5	Calgary	2-1
	15	at Chicago	1-4		7	Dallas	4-5†
	19	at St. Louis	2-1		9	at Columbus	0-4
	22	at Chicago	1-2		11	at Detroit	3-2†
	23	at Dallas	1-3		13	at Dallas	1-2
	26	Colorado	3-2†		15	at Phoenix	4-0
	28	Detroit	1-2†		16	Los Angeles	3-2†
Mar.	2	Nashville	2-1		18	Minnesota	6-1
	5	at Vancouver	3-2†		21	Columbus	3-4
	6	at Calgary	1-4		23	Dallas	3-2
	9	St. Louis	3-4*		24	at Phoenix	1-2
	10	at Colorado	2-3*		27	at Los Angeles	2-3

* – Overtime † – Shootout

Entry Draft Selections 2013-1999

Name in bold denotes played in NHL.

2013
Pick
18 Mirco Mueller
49 Gabryel Boudreau
117 Fredrik Bergvik
141 Michael Brodzinski
151 Gage Ausmus
201 Jacob Jackson
207 Emil Galimov

2012
Pick
17 Tomas Hertl
55 Chris Tierney
109 Christophe Lalancette
138 Daniel O'Regan
168 Clifford Watson
198 Joakim Ryan

2011
Pick
47 Matthew Nieto
89 Justin Sefton
133 Sean Kuraly
166 Daniil Sobchenko
179 Dylan Demelo
194 Colin Blackwell

2010
Pick
28 **Charlie Coyle**
88 Max Gaede
127 Cody Ferriero
129 Freddie Hamilton
136 Isaac MacLeod
163 Konrad Abeltshauser
188 Lee Moffie
200 Chris Crane

2009
Pick
43 William Wrenn
57 Taylor Doherty
147 Phil Varone
189 Marek Viedensky
207 Dominik Bielke

2008
Pick
62 Justin Daniels
92 Samuel Groulx
106 Harri Sateri
146 Julien Demers
177 **Tommy Wingels**
186 **Jason Demers**
194 Drew Daniels

2007
Pick
9 **Logan Couture**
28 **Nicholas Petrecki**
83 **Timo Pielmeier**
91 Tyson Sexsmith
165 Patrik Zackrisson
173 **Nick Bonino**
201 **Justin Braun**
203 **Frazer McLaren**

2006
Pick
16 **Ty Wishart**
36 **Jamie McGinn**
98 James Delory
143 Ashton Rome
202 **John McCarthy**
203 Jay Barriball

2005
Pick
8 **Devin Setoguchi**
35 **Marc-Edouard Vlasic**
112 **Alex Stalock**
140 Taylor Dakers
149 **Derek Joslin**
162 P.J. Fenton
183 Will Colbert
193 Tony Lucia

2004
Pick
22 **Lukas Kaspar**
94 **Thomas Greiss**
126 **Torrey Mitchell**
129 Jason Churchill
153 **Steven Zalewski**
201 **Mike Vernace**
225 David MacDonald
234 Derek MacIntyre
288 Brian Mahoney-Wilson
289 Christian Jensen

2003
Pick
6 **Milan Michalek**
16 **Steve Bernier**
43 **Josh Hennessy**
47 **Matt Carle**
139 Patrick Ehelechner
201 Jonathan Tremblay
205 **Joe Pavelski**
216 Kai Hospelt
236 Alexander Hult
267 Brian O'Hanley
276 Carter Lee

2002
Pick
27 Mike Morris
52 Dan Spang
86 Jonas Fiedler
139 **Kris Newbury**
163 Tom Walsh
217 **Tim Conboy**
288 Michael Hutchins

2001
Pick
20 **Marcel Goc**
106 **Christian Ehrhoff**
107 **Dimitri Patzold**
140 **Tomas Plihal**
175 **Ryane Clowe**
182 **Tom Cavanagh**

2000
Pick
41 Tero Maatta
104 **Jon DiSalvatore**
142 Michal Pinc
166 **Nolan Schaefer**
183 Michal Macho
246 **Chad Wiseman**
256 Pasi Saarinen

1999
Pick
14 **Jeff Jillson**
82 Mark Concannon
111 Willie Levesque
155 **Niko Dimitrakos**
229 Eric Betournay
241 **Douglas Murray**
257 **Hannes Hyvonen**

Doug Wilson

Executive Vice President and General Manager

Born: Ottawa, Ont., July 5, 1957.

In his nine seasons in charge of the Sharks hockey department, Doug Wilson has guided the team to its most successful era since the franchise's inception, capturing the Presidents' Trophy (2009) and five Pacific Division titles (2004, 2008, 2009, 2010, 2011). Under Wilson, the Sharks advanced to the Western Conference Final in 2004, 2010 and 2011.

Wilson has overall authority regarding all hockey-related operations. He oversees player personnel decisions, contract negotiation, scouting, player evaluation and draft day preparation. In his previous role as the team's director of pro development (1997 to 2003), the 16-year NHL veteran's responsibilities included evaluating talent at all professional and minor league levels and continuous assessment of the Sharks roster and reserve list. Working closely with the entire hockey department, Wilson has played a major role in creating a positive atmosphere in the Sharks dressing room.

Wilson draws on a vast amount of hockey knowledge. He was an integral member of the NHL Players' Association for four years (1993 to 1997) and is a past president of the NHLPA and served a consultant to Team Canada, winners of four consecutive World Junior gold medals in the 1990s. His brother Murray was a member of four Stanley Cup championship teams with Montreal in the 1970s. With the Ottawa 67s in junior, Wilson played for Hall of Famer Hec Kilrea, junior hockey's winningest coach.

In 2004, Wilson was named to the NHL's Game Committee, a panel of players, coaches, executives and media responsible for examining all aspects of the game. This committee included Hall of Fame Coach Scotty Bowman, Pittsburgh's Mario Lemieux and St. Louis Blues President of Hockey Operations John Davidson, among others.

A first-round draft choice (sixth overall) by the Blackhawks in 1977 after a stellar junior career, Wilson played 14 seasons in Chicago and still ranks as that club's highest scoring defenseman with 225 goals and 554 assists for 779 points. He led all Blackhawks defensemen in scoring for 10 consecutive seasons (1980-81 through 1990-91) and captured the 1982 James Norris Memorial Trophy, as the League's top defenseman, when he tallied 39 goals and 85 points — still Blackhawks single-season records for goals and points for a defenseman.

Acquired by San Jose from Chicago just before the Sharks inaugural season (1991-92), Wilson brought instant credibility and respect to the young franchise. He played two seasons for the Sharks, serving as the franchise's first team captain (1991 to 1993). He played his 1,000th NHL game on Nov. 21, 1992 and was named San Jose's nominee (1992 and 1993) for the King Clancy Award for leadership and humanitarian contributions both on-and off-the-ice.

Wilson announced his retirement as a member of the Sharks during training camp in 1993-94 after playing 1,024 regular-season and 95 playoff games. He was selected to play in a total of seven NHL All-Star Games (six with Chicago and one with San Jose) and earned one First and two Second Team All-Star selections.

Club Directory

SAP Center at San Jose

San Jose Sharks
SAP Center at San Jose
525 West Santa Clara Street
San Jose, CA 95113
Phone **408/287-7070**
FAX 408/999-5797
www.sjsharks.com
Capacity: 17,562

San Jose Sports and Entertainment Enterprises Ownership Group
Hasso Plattner, Gary Valenzuela, Gordon Russell, Rudy Staedler

San Jose Sports and Entertainment Board of Directors
Hasso Plattner, Gary Valenzuela, Scott McNealy, Rouven Westphal

Hockey Operations
Executive Vice President & General Manager . . . . . Doug Wilson
Vice President & Assistant General Manager . . . . . Wayne Thomas
Assistant General Manager . . . . . Joe Will
Head Coach . . . . . Todd McLellan
Associate Coach . . . . . Larry Robinson
Assistant Coaches . . . . . Jim Johnson, Jay Woodcroft
Goaltending Development Coach . . . . . Corey Schwab
Development Coach . . . . . Mike Ricci
Video Coordinator . . . . . Brett Heimlich
Directors, Scouting / Pro Scouting . . . . . Tim Burke / John Ferguson
Scouts . . . . . Gilles Cote, Pat Funk, Jack Gardiner, Dirk Graham, Rob Grillo, Brian Gross, Shin Larsson, Bryan Marchment, Jason Rowe
Director of Hockey Administration . . . . . Rosemary Tebaldi
Team Services Manager . . . . . Ryan Stenn
Athletic Trainers, Head / Assistant . . . . . Ray Tufts, ATC / Wes Howard, ATC
Strength & Conditioning Coordinator . . . . . Mike Potenza
Massage Therapist . . . . . Arnulfo Aguirre, CMT, ART
Equipment Manager / Assistant Manager . . . . . Mike Aldrich / Vinny Ferraiuolo
Equipment Assistant & Equipment Transportation . . Roy Sneesby
Cleaning Specialist . . . . . Norma Hernandez
Team Physician / Internists . . . . . Arthur J. Ting, M.D. / Greg Whitley, M.D., John Chiu, M.D.
Team Dentists . . . . . Don Goudy, D.D.S., Robert Bonahoom, D.D.S.
Team Vision Specialist . . . . . Allen Boghossian M.D.
Medical Staff . . . . . Steve Franzino, M.D., Robert Millard, M.D., Mark Sontag, M.D.
Chiropractic Consultant . . . . . Mike McMurray, D.C.
Manual Therapy Consultant . . . . . Tobe Hanson

Business and Building Operations
Chief Operating Officer . . . . . John Tortora
Executive V.P., Business and Building Ops . . . . . Jim Goddard
Vice President, Sales & Service . . . . . John Castro
Vice President, Finance . . . . . Ken Caveney
Vice President, People . . . . . Fiona Ow Giuffre
Vice President, Sharks Ice & Worcester Sharks . . . . . Jon Gustafson
Vice President, Building Operations . . . . . Rich Sotelo
Executive Assistants . . . . . Rebeca Gomez, Mary Grace Miller, Michelle Simmons

Ticket Sales
Senior Ticket Operations Manager . . . . . Scott Fitzsimmons
Account Sales Managers . . . . . Ted Chuba, Mike Hollywood, Adam King, Mike Nieves
Account Service Managers . . . . . Kayla Chickos, Sharon Holman, Julie Kennedy

Corporate Partnerships
Senior Sales Managers, Corporate Partnerships . . . . Jennifer Birmingham, Michael Farrell
Senior Service Manager, Corporate Partnerships . . . Reza Wiriaatmadja
Sales Managers, Corporate Partnerships . . . . . Kevin Hilton, Matt Mendes
Service Managers, Corporate Partnerships . . . . . Jennifer De Carlo, Patrick Luck

Suite Sales and Service
Suite Sales & Service Director / Manager . . . . . Bruce Ross / Kathy Payne-Tovar

Event Presentation
Director of Event Presentation . . . . . Steve Maroni

Marketing and Digital Media
Director of Marketing & Digital Media . . . . . Doug Bentz
Manager, Marketing . . . . . Courtney Jankovich
Graphic Designer . . . . . Brittney Thorp
Digital Content Developers . . . . . Patrick Hooper, Sarah Peters

Media Relations
Director of Media Relations . . . . . Scott Emmert
Media Relations Manager . . . . . Ben Guerrero

Public Relations and Fan Development / Sharks Foundation
Director of Public Relations & Fan Development . . . Jim Sparaco
Mascot Ops Manager / Fan Development Coord. . . Tim Patnode / Tim Howell
Sharks Foundation Manager / Coordinator . . . . . Jeff Cafuir / Kelly Esrey

Broadcasting
Director of Broadcasting . . . . . Frank Albin
Television Play-By-Play / Color Analyst . . . . . Randy Hahn / Drew Remenda
Radio Play-By-Play / Color Analyst . . . . . Dan Rusanowsky / Jamie Baker
Production Associate . . . . . Elisabeth Farkas

Building Operations
Directors, Booking & Events / Guest Services . . . . . Steve Kirsner, James Hamnett / David Cahill
Directors, Building Services / Ticket Operations . . . . Monte Chavez / Patrick Doherty
Facilities Technical Director / Chief Engineer . . . . . Greg Carrolan / Mike Vitolo
Building Services Managers . . . . . Bruce Tharaldson, Ray Romero
Managers, Technical Services / Ticket Operations . . . Mike O'Brien / Judy Jones
Ushering & Emergency Medical Manager . . . . . Mike McCarroll
Receptionist/Administrative Assistant . . . . . Jeannine Turner
Receptionist . . . . . Nancy Perez

Finance
Controller . . . . . Stephanie Reitz

Information Technology
Director of Information Technology . . . . . Uy Ut

Human Resources
HR Operations Manager . . . . . Bethany Lopusnak

Legal
Associate Counsel . . . . . Maggie Carlyle

Miscellaneous
Television Rightsholder . . . . . Comcast SportsNet California
Radio Network Flagship . . . . . 98.5/102.1 KFOX (KUFX FM)
Team Photographers . . . . . Don Smith, Rocky Widner
P.A. Announcer / Mascot . . . . . Danny Miller / S.J. Sharkie

Tampa Bay Lightning

Key Off-Season Signings/Acquisitions

2013

May 6 • Re-signed D **Radko Gudas**.
June 3 • Named **Rick Bowness** associate coach.
26 • Re-signed D **Keith Aulie**.
July 1 • Re-signed LW **Pierre-Cedric Labrie**.
3 • Re-signed G **Cedrick Desjardins** and D **Matt Taormina**.
5 • Signed C **Valtteri Filppula**.

2012-13 Results: 18W-26L-1OTL-3SOL 40PTS
4TH, Southeast Division • 14TH, Eastern Conference

Year-by-Year Record

		Home				Road				Overall									
Season	**GP**	**W**	**L**	**T**	**OL**	**W**	**L**	**T**	**OL**	**W**	**L**	**T**	**OL**	**GF**	**GA**	**Pts.**	**Div. Fin.**	**Conf. Fin.**	**Playoff Result**
2012-13	48	12	10	....	2	6	16	....	2	18	26	....	4	148	150	40	4th, SE	14th, East	Out of Playoffs
2011-12	82	25	14	....	2	13	22	....	6	38	36	....	8	235	281	84	3rd, SE	10th, East	Out of Playoffs
2010-11	82	25	11	....	5	21	14	....	6	46	25	....	11	247	240	103	2nd, SE	5th, East	Lost Conf. Final
2009-10	82	21	14	....	6	13	22	....	6	34	36	....	12	217	260	80	4th, SE	12th, East	Out of Playoffs
2008-09	82	12	18	....	11	12	22	....	7	24	40	....	18	210	279	66	5th, SE	14th, East	Out of Playoffs
2007-08	82	20	18	....	3	11	24	....	6	31	42	....	9	223	267	71	5th, SE	15th, East	Out of Playoffs
2006-07	82	22	18	....	1	22	15	....	4	44	33	....	5	253	261	93	2nd, SE	7th, East	Lost Conf. Quarter-Final
2005-06	82	25	14	....	2	18	19	....	4	43	33	....	6	252	260	92	2nd, SE	8th, East	Lost Conf. Quarter-Final
2004-05	....	....	....	....	....	....	....	....	....	....	....	....	....	....	....	....			
2003-04	**82**	**24**	**10**	**4**	**3**	**22**	**12**	**4**	**3**	**46**	**22**	**8**	**6**	**245**	**192**	**106**	**1st, SE**	**1st, East**	**Won Stanley Cup**
2002-03	82	22	9	7	3	14	16	9	2	36	25	16	5	219	210	93	1st, SE	3rd, East	Lost Conf. Semi-Final
2001-02	82	16	17	5	3	11	23	6	1	27	40	11	4	178	219	69	3rd, SE	13th, East	Out of Playoffs
2000-01	82	17	19	3	2	7	28	3	3	24	47	6	5	201	280	59	5th, SE	14th, East	Out of Playoffs
1999-2000	82	13	20	4	4	6	27	5	3	19	47	9	7	204	310	54	4th, SE	14th, East	Out of Playoffs
1998-99	82	12	25	4	....	7	29	5	....	19	54	9	....	179	292	47	4th, SE	14th, East	Out of Playoffs
1997-98	82	11	23	7	....	6	32	3	....	17	55	10	....	151	269	44	7th, Atl.	13th, East	Out of Playoffs
1996-97	82	15	18	8	....	17	22	2	....	32	40	10	....	217	247	74	6th, Atl.	11th, East	Out of Playoffs
1995-96	82	22	14	5	....	16	18	7	....	38	32	12	....	238	248	88	5th, Atl.	8th, East	Lost Conf. Quarter-Final
1994-95	48	10	14	0	....	7	14	3	....	17	28	3	....	120	144	37	6th, Atl.	12th, East	Out of Playoffs
1993-94	84	14	22	6	....	16	21	5	....	30	43	11	....	224	251	71	7th, Atl.	12th, East	Out of Playoffs
1992-93	84	12	27	3	....	11	27	4	....	23	54	7	....	245	332	53	6th, Norris		Out of Playoffs

2013-14 Schedule

Oct.	Thu.	3	at Boston		Sun.	5	at Edmonton
	Sat.	5	at Chicago		Tue.	7	at Winnipeg
	Tue.	8	at Buffalo		Thu.	9	Washington
	Thu.	10	Florida		Sat.	11	at Philadelphia*
	Sat.	12	Pittsburgh		Mon.	13	at Columbus
	Tue.	15	Los Angeles		Tue.	14	at NY Rangers
	Thu.	17	Minnesota		Thu.	16	NY Islanders
	Sat.	19	Boston		Sat.	18	San Jose*
	Thu.	24	Chicago		Sun.	19	at Carolina*
	Sat.	26	Buffalo		Thu.	23	Ottawa
	Sun.	27	at Florida*		Sat.	25	Colorado
	Tue.	29	at New Jersey		Tue.	28	at Toronto
Nov.	Fri.	1	at Carolina		Thu.	30	at Ottawa
	Sat.	2	St. Louis	**Feb.**	Sat.	1	at Montreal*
	Thu.	7	Edmonton		Tue.	4	at Minnesota
	Sat.	9	at Detroit		Thu.	6	Toronto
	Mon.	11	at Boston*		Sat.	8	Detroit
	Tue.	12	at Montreal		Thu.	27	at Nashville
	Thu.	14	Anaheim	**Mar.**	Sat.	1	at Dallas*
	Sat.	16	at Phoenix		Sun.	2	at Colorado
	Tue.	19	at Los Angeles		Tue.	4	at St. Louis
	Thu.	21	at San Jose		Thu.	6	Buffalo
	Fri.	22	at Anaheim		Sat.	8	Boston
	Mon.	25	NY Rangers		Mon.	10	Phoenix
	Wed.	27	Philadelphia		Thu.	13	Florida
	Fri.	29	Pittsburgh*		Sat.	15	New Jersey
Dec.	Tue.	3	at Columbus		Mon.	17	Vancouver
	Thu.	5	Ottawa		Wed.	19	at Toronto
	Sat.	7	Winnipeg		Thu.	20	at Ottawa
	Tue.	10	at Washington		Sat.	22	at Pittsburgh*
	Thu.	12	Detroit		Mon.	24	Ottawa
	Sat.	14	at New Jersey		Thu.	27	NY Islanders
	Sun.	15	at Detroit*		Sat.	29	at Buffalo
	Tue.	17	at NY Islanders		Sun.	30	at Detroit*
	Thu.	19	Nashville	**Apr.**	Tue.	1	Montreal
	Sat.	21	Carolina		Thu.	3	Calgary
	Mon.	23	at Florida		Sat.	5	Dallas
	Sat.	28	Montreal		Tue.	8	Toronto
	Sun.	29	NY Rangers		Thu.	10	Philadelphia
Jan.	Wed.	1	at Vancouver		Fri.	11	Columbus
	Fri.	3	at Calgary		Sun.	13	at Washington*

* Denotes afternoon game.

Steven Stamkos (left) and Martin St. Louis were the NHL's top two scorers in 2012-13. St. Louis led the league with 43 assists and 60 points while Stamkos finished second in both goals (29, behind Alex Ovechkin's 32) and points (57).

ATLANTIC DIVISION
22nd NHL Season

Franchise date: December 16, 1991

2013-14 Player Personnel

FORWARDS	HT	WT	*Age	Place of Birth	S	2012-13 Club
ANGELIDIS, Mike	6-1	212	28	Woodbridge, Ont.	L	Syracuse-Tampa Bay
BROWN, J.T.	5-11	177	23	High Point, NC	R	Syracuse
CONNOLLY, Brett	6-2	200	21	Prince George, B.C.	R	Syracuse-Tampa Bay
CROMBEEN, B.J.	6-2	209	28	Denver, CO	R	Orlando-Tampa Bay
DROUIN, Jonathan	5-11	186	18	Ste-Agathe, Que.	L	Halifax
FILPPULA, Valtteri	6-0	195	29	Vantaa, Finland	L	Jokerit-Detroit
JOHNSON, Tyler	5-9	182	23	Spokane, WA	R	Syracuse-Tampa Bay
KILLORN, Alex	6-1	202	24	Halifax, N.S.	L	Syracuse-Tampa Bay
LABRIE, Pierre-Cedric	6-3	234	26	Baie Comeau, Que.	R	Syracuse-Tampa Bay
MALONE, Ryan	6-4	224	33	Pittsburgh, PA	L	Tampa Bay
PURCELL, Teddy	6-3	203	28	St. Johns, Nfld.	R	Tampa Bay
PYATT, Tom	5-11	188	26	Thunder Bay, Ont.	L	Tampa Bay
ST. LOUIS, Martin	5-8	180	38	Laval, Que.	L	Tampa Bay
STAMKOS, Steven	6-1	191	23	Markham, Ont.	R	Tampa Bay
THOMPSON, Nate	6-0	212	28	Anchorage, AK	L	Alaska-Tampa Bay
TYRELL, Dana	5-11	192	24	Airdrie, Alta.	L	B. Bystrica-T.B.-Syr
WALKER, Geoff	6-3	225	25	Charlottetown, P.E.I.	R	Lake Erie
DEFENSEMEN						
AULIE, Keith	6-6	228	24	Rouleau, Sask.	L	Syracuse-Tampa Bay
BARBERIO, Mark	6-1	185	23	Montreal, Que.	L	Syracuse-Tampa Bay
BREWER, Eric	6-4	216	34	Vernon, B.C.	L	Tampa Bay
CARLE, Matt	6-0	205	29	Anchorage, AK	L	Tampa Bay
GUDAS, Radko	6-0	204	23	Prague, Czech.	R	Syracuse-Tampa Bay
HEDMAN, Victor	6-6	233	22	Ornskoldsvik, Sweden	L	Astana-Tampa Bay
LEE, Brian	6-3	200	26	Moorhead, MN	R	Tampa Bay-Syracuse
OHLUND, Mattias	6-4	233	37	Pitea, Sweden	L	Tampa Bay
SALO, Sami	6-3	215	39	Turku, Finland	R	Tampa Bay
SUSTR, Andrej	6-8	225	22	Plzen, Czech.	R	Nebraska-Omaha-T.B.-Syr
TAORMINA, Matt	5-10	182	26	Warren, MI	L	Syracuse-Tampa Bay

GOALTENDERS	HT	WT	*Age	Place of Birth	C	2012-13 Club
BISHOP, Ben	6-7	214	26	Denver, CO	L	Binghamton-Ottawa-T.B.
LINDBACK, Anders	6-6	210	25	Gavle, Sweden	L	Ilves-Tampa Bay

* – Age at start of 2013-14 season

2012-13 Scoring

* – rookie

Regular Season

Pos	#	Player	Team	GP	G	A	Pts	TOI	+/-	PIM	PP	SH	GW	S	%
R	26	Martin St. Louis	T.B.	48	17	43	60	21:59	0	14	3	0	2	112	15.2
C	91	Steven Stamkos	T.B.	48	29	28	57	22:01	–4	32	10	0	2	157	18.5
R	16	Teddy Purcell	T.B.	48	11	25	36	16:44	–1	12	3	0	2	94	11.7
C	4	Vincent Lecavalier	T.B.	39	10	22	32	17:52	–5	29	5	0	0	86	11.6
D	25	Matthew Carle	T.B.	48	5	17	22	23:44	1	4	2	0	0	66	7.6
L	67	Benoit Pouliot	T.B.	34	8	12	20	13:14	8	15	0	0	1	60	13.3
D	77	Victor Hedman	T.B.	44	4	16	20	22:39	1	31	0	0	0	76	5.3
C	17 *	Alexander Killorn	T.B.	38	7	12	19	16:49	–6	14	1	0	2	82	8.5
D	6	Sami Salo	T.B.	46	2	15	17	20:59	5	16	1	0	0	48	4.2
C	11	Tom Pyatt	T.B.	43	8	8	16	13:34	5	12	0	0	1	60	13.3
C	44	Nate Thompson	T.B.	45	7	8	15	14:20	–2	17	0	0	0	58	12.1
D	2	Eric Brewer	T.B.	48	4	8	12	20:30	3	30	1	0	1	56	7.1
R	71 *	Richard Panik	T.B.	25	5	4	9	11:19	–2	4	1	0	1	34	14.7
L	12	Ryan Malone	T.B.	24	6	2	8	15:44	–3	22	2	0	1	37	16.2
R	19	B.J. Crombeen	T.B.	44	1	7	8	11:04	4	112	0	0	0	50	2.0
D	3	Keith Aulie	T.B.	45	2	5	7	12:49	1	60	0	0	0	37	5.4
C	63 *	Tyler Johnson	T.B.	14	3	3	6	13:04	3	4	0	0	0	11	27.3
D	75 *	Radko Gudas	T.B.	22	2	3	5	16:59	3	38	0	0	1	31	6.5
L	74 *	Ondrej Palat	T.B.	14	2	2	4	11:44	5	0	0	0	1	16	12.5
C	42	Dana Tyrell	T.B.	21	1	3	4	10:21	–3	4	0	0	0	19	5.3
L	76 *	Pierre-Cedric Labrie	T.B.	19	2	1	3	8:33	2	30	0	0	0	16	12.5
R	14	Brett Connolly	T.B.	5	1	0	1	10:16	–3	0	1	0	0	10	10.0
D	29	Brendan Mikkelson	T.B.	4	0	1	1	9:45	1	6	0	0	0	0	0.0
D	28	Mathieu Roy	T.B.	1	0	0	0	14:07	–1	0	0	0	0	0	0.0
R	34	J.T. Wyman	T.B.	1	0	0	0	13:31	–1	0	0	0	0	0	0.0
L	10	Mike Angelidis	T.B.	1	0	0	0	7:22	0	0	0	0	0	0	0.0
D	8 *	Mark Barberio	T.B.	2	0	0	0	15:29	–2	0	0	0	0	1	0.0
D	55	Matt Taormina	T.B.	2	0	0	0	16:38	–1	0	0	0	0	0	0.0
D	62 *	Andrej Sustr	T.B.	2	0	0	0	10:43	1	0	0	0	0	2	0.0
D	15	Brian Lee	T.B.	22	0	0	0	13:55	–13	16	0	0	0	13	0.0

Goaltending

No.	Goaltender	GPI	Mins	Avg	W	L	OT	EN	SO	GA	SA	S%	G	A	PIM
32	Mathieu Garon	18	910	2.90	5	9	2	1	0	44	427	.897	0	0	0
39	Anders Lindback	24	1304	2.90	10	10	1	3	0	63	642	.902	0	1	0
30	Ben Bishop	9	502	2.99	3	4	1	2	1	25	302	.917	0	0	2
30	Cedrick Desjardins	3	160	3.00	0	3	0	1	0	8	73	.890	0	0	0
	Totals	**48**	**2904**	**3.04**	**18**	**26**	**4**	**7**	**1**	**147**	**1451**	**.899**			

Selected 208th overall among the 211 players drafted in 2011, Ondrej Palat reached the NHL in 2012-13 when he made his debut for Tampa Bay on March 4, 2013.

Jon Cooper

Head Coach

Born: Prince George, B.C., August 23, 1967.

The Tampa Bay Lightning named Jon Cooper as the eighth head coach in franchise history on March 25, 2013. Cooper joined the Lightning after having spent the previous three seasons behind the bench of Tampa Bay's top minor league affiliate, the Norfolk Admirals, from 2010 to 2012 and the Syracuse Crunch in 2012-13. He compiled a 133-62-26 regular-season record (.661) in 221 games in the American Hockey League.

Cooper was awarded the Louis A.R. Pieri Memorial Award as the AHL's top coach in 2011-12 after guiding the Admirals to a franchise-record 55 wins and 113 points en route to the team's first Calder Cup Championship. Along the way, Cooper and his team set a North American professional hockey record, winning a remarkable 28 consecutive games. Norfolk also earned the Macgregor Kilpatrick Trophy as the AHL's regular-season points champion, while capturing the league's East Division title. Cooper led Norfolk to a 94-44-18 record in the regular season and a 17-7 mark in the playoffs during two seasons behind the bench. In 2012-13, he led the Syracuse Crunch to a 39-18-8 record, the best in the AHL at the time, despite a number of key players being recalled to the Lightning before he himself was summoned to Tampa Bay.

Before joining the AHL ranks, Cooper also found success in the United States Hockey League with the Green Bay Gamblers, posting an 84-27-9 record in two seasons. Under Cooper's guidance the Gamblers posted back-to-back seasons with the best record in the USHL and won the 2010 Clark Cup. In his first season in 2008-09, Green Bay saw a 50-point improvement from the previous year, setting a USHL record for largest single-season improvement. He was rewarded with the 2009 and 2010 USHL General Manager of the Year Awards, as well as being named the 2010 USHL Coach of the Year.

Cooper played high school hockey at Notre Dame in Wilcox, Saskatchewan. He then moved on to Hofstra University in the NCAA, where he played four seasons of Division I lacrosse and spent one season on Hofstra's hockey team. He then went on to earn a law degree from Thomas M. Cooley Law School in Lansing, Michigan, eventually closing his practice in 2003 to pursue a career in coaching.

Coaching Record

			Regular Season				Playoffs			
Season	Team	League	GC	W	L	O/T	GC	W	L	T
2003-04	Texarkana	NAHL	56	30	24	2	4	0	4	0
2004-05	Texarkana	NAHL	56	36	15	5	9	4	5	0
2005-06	Texarkana	NAHL	58	42	12	4	8	3	5	0
2006-07	St. Louis	NAHL	62	43	14	5	12	9	3	0
2007-08	St. Louis	NAHL	58	47	9	2	11	9	1	1
2008-09	Green Bay	USHL	60	39	17	4	7	4	3	....
2009-10	Green Bay	USHL	60	45	10	5	12	9	3	....
2010-11	Norfolk	AHL	80	39	26	15	6	2	4	....
2011-12	Norfolk	AHL	76	55	18	3	18	15	3	....
2012-13	Syracuse	AHL	65	39	18	8	....	....	....	....
2012-13*	**Tampa Bay**	**NHL**	**15**	**4**	**8**	**3**	....	....	....	....
	NHL Totals		**15**	**4**	**8**	**3**	....	....	....	....

* Hired by Tampa Bay on March 25, 2013 but did not appear behind the bench until March 29. Assistant coaches Dan Lacroix, Martin Raymond, and Steve Thomas worked a 3-2 loss at Winnipeg on March 24. Lacroix and Thomas worked a 2-1 win vs. Buffalo on March 26.

Coaching History

Terry Crisp, 1992-93 to 1996-97; Terry Crisp, Rick Paterson and Jacques Demers, 1997-98; Jacques Demers, 1998-99; Steve Ludzik, 1999-2000; Steve Ludzik and John Tortorella, 2000-01; John Tortorella, 2001-02 to 2007-08; Barry Melrose and Rick Tocchet, 2008-09; Rick Tocchet, 2009-10; Guy Boucher, 2010-11, 2011-12; Guy Boucher and Jon Cooper, 2012-13; Jon Cooper, 2013-14.

Club Records

Team

(Figures in brackets for season records are games played; records for fewest points, wins, ties, losses, goals, goals against are for 70 or more games)

Most Points	**106**	2003-04 (82)
Most Wins	**46**	2003-04 (82), 2010-11 (82)
Most Ties	**16**	2002-03 (82)
Most Losses	**55**	1997-98 (82)
Most Goals	**247**	2010-11 (82)
Most Goals Against	**332**	1992-93 (84)
Fewest Points	**44**	1997-98 (82)
Fewest Wins	**17**	1997-98 (82)
Fewest Ties	**6**	2000-01 (82)
Fewest Losses	**22**	2003-04 (82)
Fewest Goals	**151**	1997-98 (82)
Fewest Goals Against	**192**	2003-04 (82)
Longest Winning Streak		
Overall	**8**	Feb. 23-Mar. 6/04
Home	**8**	Mar. 17-Apr. 8/06
Away	**7**	Jan. 7-Feb. 1/07
Longest Undefeated Streak		
Overall	**13**	Mar. 7-Apr. 2/03 (7W, 6T/OL)
Home	**10**	Jan. 29-Mar. 12/04 (9W, 1T/OL)
Away	**7**	Feb. 23-Mar. 10/04 (6W, 1T/OL), Jan. 7-Feb. 1/07 (7W)
Longest Losing Streak		
Overall	**13**	Jan. 3-Feb. 2/98
Home	**10**	Jan. 3-Feb. 26/98
Away	**11**	Oct. 24-Dec. 10/97
Longest Winless Streak		
Overall	**16**	Oct. 10-Nov. 17/97 (15L, 1T), Jan. 2-Feb. 5/98 (14L, 2T)
Home	**11**	Jan. 2-Feb. 26/98 (10L, 1T)
Away	**17**	Dec. 2/99-Feb. 19/00 (14L, 3T/OL)
Most Shutouts, Season	**9**	2001-02 (82)
Most PIM, Season	**1,823**	1997-98 (82)
Most Goals, Game	**9**	Nov. 8/03 (Pit. 0 at T.B. 9)

Individual

Most Seasons	**14**	Vincent Lecavalier
Most Games, Career	**1,037**	Vincent Lecavalier
Most Goals, Career	**383**	Vincent Lecavalier
Most Assists, Career	**556**	Martin St. Louis
Most Points, Career	**892**	Martin St. Louis (336G, 556A)
Most PIM, Career	**828**	Chris Gratton
Most Shutouts, Career	**14**	Nikolai Khabibulin
Longest Consecutive Games Streak	**499**	Martin St. Louis (Nov. 17/05-Dec. 6/11)
Most Goals, Season	**60**	Steven Stamkos (2011-12)
Most Assists, Season	**68**	Brad Richards (2005-06), Martin St. Louis (2010-11)
Most Points, Season	**108**	Vincent Lecavalier (2006-07; 52G, 56A)
Most PIM, Season	**265**	Zenon Konopka (2009-10)
Most Points, Defenseman, Season	**65**	Roman Hamrlik (1995-96; 16G, 49A)
Most Points, Center, Season	**108**	Vincent Lecavalier (2006-07; 52G, 56A)
Most Points, Right Wing, Season	**102**	Martin St. Louis (2006-07; 43G, 59A)
Most Points, Left Wing, Season	**80**	Cory Stillman (2003-04; 25G, 55A), Vinny Prospal (2005-06; 25G, 55A)
Most Points, Rookie, Season	**62**	Brad Richards (2000-01; 21G, 41A)
Most Shutouts, Season	**7**	Nikolai Khabibulin (2001-02)
Most Goals, Game	**4**	Chris Kontos (Oct. 7/92)
Most Assists, Game	**5**	Mark Recchi (Mar. 1/09), Martin St. Louis (Nov. 18/10)
Most Points, Game	**6**	Doug Crossman (Nov. 7/92; 3G, 3A)

Captains' History

No captain, 1992-93 to 1994-95; Paul Ysebaert, 1995-96, 1996-97; Paul Ysebaert and Mikael Renberg, 1997-98; Rob Zamuner, 1998-99; Bill Houlder, Chris Gratton and Vincent Lecavalier, 1999-2000; Vincent Lecavalier, 2000-01; no captain, 2001-02; Dave Andreychuk, 2002-03 to 2004-05; Dave Andreychuk and no captain, 2005-06; Tim Taylor, 2006-07, 2007-08; Vincent Lecavalier, 2008-09 to 2012-13.

All-time Record vs. Other Clubs

Regular Season

	Total								At Home								On Road							
	GP	W	L	T	OL	GF	GA	PTS	GP	W	L	T	OL	GF	GA	PTS	GP	W	L	T	OL	GF	GA	PTS
Anaheim	24	9	11	1	3	55	69	22	12	5	6	0	1	24	31	11	12	4	5	1	2	31	38	11
Boston	77	20	43	9	5	201	261	54	38	16	17	3	2	114	112	37	39	4	26	6	3	87	149	17
Buffalo	77	23	43	5	6	192	251	57	39	10	22	3	4	89	127	27	38	13	21	2	2	103	124	30
Calgary	26	13	11	1	1	81	90	28	13	7	5	1	0	44	46	15	13	6	6	0	1	37	44	13
Carolina	106	47	44	10	5	318	310	109	52	29	19	3	1	161	147	62	54	18	25	7	4	157	163	47
Chicago	32	12	14	5	1	79	96	30	15	7	4	3	1	41	42	18	17	5	10	2	0	38	54	12
Colorado	33	12	14	3	4	81	107	31	16	9	4	1	2	46	45	21	17	3	10	2	2	35	62	10
Columbus	13	8	4	1	0	30	25	17	7	6	1	0	0	18	10	12	6	2	3	1	0	12	15	5
Dallas	30	8	17	3	2	68	92	21	16	3	10	2	1	30	45	9	14	5	7	1	1	38	47	12
Detroit	32	5	24	2	1	76	135	13	17	4	11	1	1	51	77	10	15	1	13	1	0	25	58	3
Edmonton	27	9	14	2	2	70	79	22	14	5	6	2	1	40	43	13	13	4	8	0	1	30	36	9
Florida	109	42	46	10	11	283	341	105	55	24	20	6	5	146	161	59	54	18	26	4	6	137	180	46
Los Angeles	27	16	7	2	2	71	56	36	13	6	5	0	2	28	29	14	14	10	2	2	0	43	27	22
Minnesota	14	4	8	1	1	32	43	10	7	2	3	1	1	15	20	6	7	2	5	0	0	17	23	4
Montreal	76	31	33	6	6	186	213	74	39	16	14	5	4	97	106	41	37	15	19	1	2	89	107	33
Nashville	16	8	6	2	0	47	43	18	7	3	2	2	0	22	18	8	9	5	4	0	0	25	25	10
New Jersey	82	25	44	7	6	189	276	63	40	13	19	5	3	94	125	34	42	12	25	2	3	95	151	29
NY Islanders	82	39	35	3	5	222	241	86	41	22	14	2	3	117	116	49	41	17	21	1	2	105	125	37
NY Rangers	83	36	38	5	4	242	268	81	40	19	16	3	2	126	123	43	43	17	22	2	2	116	145	38
Ottawa	77	27	43	2	5	195	277	61	39	16	20	2	1	114	138	35	38	11	23	0	4	81	139	26
Philadelphia	82	32	39	8	3	227	248	75	42	19	20	1	2	128	122	41	40	13	19	7	1	99	126	34
Phoenix	29	16	13	0	0	89	77	32	13	7	6	0	0	47	41	14	16	9	7	0	0	42	36	18
Pittsburgh	77	32	38	5	2	213	245	71	38	20	16	2	0	115	99	42	39	12	22	3	2	98	146	29
St. Louis	31	10	16	3	2	86	110	25	17	7	6	3	1	51	56	18	14	3	10	0	1	35	54	7
San Jose	30	15	13	2	0	87	99	32	16	9	6	1	0	45	45	19	14	6	7	1	0	42	54	13
Toronto	72	25	39	2	6	186	244	58	36	13	20	1	2	88	113	29	36	12	19	1	4	98	131	29
Vancouver	24	6	13	2	3	66	97	17	12	5	5	0	2	42	46	12	12	1	8	2	1	24	51	5
Washington	110	36	61	6	7	286	378	85	55	22	29	2	2	144	171	48	55	14	32	4	5	142	207	37
Winnipeg	78	40	27	4	7	248	221	91	39	26	9	1	3	140	93	56	39	14	18	3	4	108	128	35
Totals	**1576**	**606**	**758**	**112**	**100**	**4206**	**4992**	**1424**	**788**	**350**	**335**	**56**	**47**	**2217**	**2347**	**803**	**788**	**256**	**423**	**56**	**53**	**1989**	**2645**	**621**

Playoffs

	Series	W	L	GP	W	L	T	GF	GA	Last Mtg.	Rnd.	Result
Boston	1	0	1	7	3	4	0	21	21	2011	CF	L 3-4
Calgary	1	1	0	7	4	3	0	13	14	2004	F	W 4-3
Montreal	1	1	0	4	4	0	0	14	5	2004	CSF	W 4-0
New Jersey	2	0	2	11	3	8	0	22	33	2007	CQF	L 2-4
NY Islanders	1	1	0	5	4	1	0	12	5	2004	CQF	W 4-1
Ottawa	1	0	1	5	1	4	0	13	23	2006	CQF	L 1-4
Philadelphia	2	1	1	13	6	7	0	34	45	2004	CF	W 4-3
Pittsburgh	1	1	0	7	4	3	0	22	14	2011	CQF	W 4-3
Washington	2	2	0	10	8	2	0	30	25	2011	CSF	W 4-0
Totals	**12**	**7**	**5**	**69**	**37**	**32**	**0**	**181**	**185**			

Carolina totals include Hartford, 1992-93 to 1996-97.
Dallas totals include Minnesota North Stars, 1992-93.
Winnipeg totals include Atlanta Thrashers, 1999-2000 to 2010-11.
Colorado totals include Quebec, 1992-93 to 1994-95.
Phoenix totals include Winnipeg, 1992-93 to 1995-96.

Playoff Results 2013-2009

Year	Round	Opponent	Result	GF	GA
2011	CF	Boston	L 3-4	21	21
	CSF	Washington	W 4-0	16	10
	CQF	Pittsburgh	W 4-3	22	14

Abbreviations: Round: F – Final; **CF** – conference final; **CSF** – conference semi-final; **CQF** – conference quarter-final.

2012-13 Results

Jan.	19	Washington	6-3		9	Montreal	3-4
	21	at NY Islanders	3-4		12	at Florida	3-2
	22	at Carolina	4-1		14	NY Islanders	0-2
	25	Ottawa	6-4		16	Carolina	4-1
	27	Philadelphia	5-1		18	Philadelphia	4-2
	29	Florida	5-2		20	at Toronto	2-4
Feb.	1	Winnipeg	8-3		23	at Ottawa	3-5
	2	NY Rangers	2-3		24	at Winnipeg	2-3
	5	at Philadelphia	1-2		26	Buffalo	2-1
	7	at New Jersey	2-4		29	New Jersey	5-4†
	10	at NY Rangers	1-5	**Apr.**	2	Florida	2-3†
	12	Montreal	3-4†		4	at Carolina	5-0
	14	Washington	3-4		6	at NY Islanders	2-4
	16	at Florida	6-5*		7	at Washington	2-4
	19	Toronto	4-2		9	Ottawa	3-2
	21	Boston	2-4		11	Pittsburgh	3-6
	23	at Carolina	5-2		13	at Washington	5-6*
	24	at Pittsburgh	3-5		14	at Buffalo	1-3
	26	Buffalo	1-2		16	at Winnipeg	3-4†
	28	at NY Rangers	1-4		18	at Montreal	2-3
Mar.	2	at Boston	2-3		21	Carolina	2-3
	4	at Pittsburgh	3-4		24	Toronto	5-2
	5	at New Jersey	5-2		25	at Boston	0-2
	7	Winnipeg	1-2		27	Florida	3-5

* – Overtime † – Shootout

Entry Draft Selections 2013-1999

Name in bold denotes played in NHL.

2013

Pick	
3	Jonathan Drouin
33	Adam Erne
124	Kristers Gudlevskis
154	Henri Ikonen
184	Saku Salminen
186	Joel Vermin

2012

Pick	
10	Slater Koekkoek
19	Andrei Vasilevsky
40	Dylan Blujus
53	Brian Hart
71	Tanner Richard
101	Cedric Paquette
161	Jake Dotchin
202	Nikita Gusev

2011

Pick	
27	Vladislav Namestnikov
58	Nikita Kucherov
148	Nikita Nesterov
178	Adam Wilcox
201	Matthew Peca
208	**Ondrej Palat**

2010

Pick	
6	**Brett Connolly**
63	Brock Beukeboom
66	**Radko Gudas**
72	Adam Janosik
96	Geoffrey Schemitsch
118	Jimmy Mullin
156	Brendan O'Donnell
186	Teigan Zahn

2009

Pick	
2	**Victor Hedman**
29	**Carter Ashton**
52	**Richard Panik**
93	Alex Hutchings
148	Michael Zador
162	Jaroslav Janus
183	Kirill Gotovets

2008

Pick	
1	**Steven Stamkos**
117	**James Wright**
122	**Dustin Tokarski**
147	Kyle DeCoste
152	**Mark Barberio**
160	Luke Witkowski
182	Matias Sointu
203	David Carle

2007

Pick	
47	**Dana Tyrell**
75	Luca Cunti
77	**Alex Killorn**
107	Mitch Fadden
150	Matt Marshall
167	**Johan Harju**
183	Torrie Jung
197	Michael Ward
210	Justin Courtnall

2006

Pick	
15	**Riku Helenius**
78	**Kevin Quick**
168	Dane Crowley
198	Denis Kazionov

2005

Pick	
30	**Vladimir Mihalik**
73	**Radek Smolenak**
89	Chris Lawrence
92	Marek Bartanus
102	**Blair Jones**
133	Stanislav Lascek
163	Marek Kvapil
165	Kevin Beech
225	John Wessbecker

2004

Pick	
30	Andy Rogers
65	Mark Tobin
102	**Mike Lundin**
158	Brandon Elliott
163	Dusty Collins
188	Jan Zapletal
191	**Karri Ramo**
245	Justin Keller

2003

Pick	
34	Mike Egener
41	**Matt Smaby**
96	Jonathan Boutin
192	**Doug O'Brien**
224	**Gerald Coleman**
227	**Jay Rosehill**
255	Raimonds Danilics
256	Brady Greco
273	Albert Vishnyakov
286	Zbynek Hrdel
287	**Nick Tarnasky**

2002

Pick	
60	Adam Henrich
100	Dmitri Kazionov
135	Joe Pearce
162	Gerard Dicaire
170	P.J. Atherton
174	Karri Akkanen
183	**Paul Ranger**
213	**Fredrik Norrena**
233	Vasily Koshechkin
255	**Ryan Craig**
256	**Darren Reid**
286	Alexei Glukhov
287	John Toffey

2001

Pick	
3	**Alexander Svitov**
47	Alexander Polushin
61	Andreas Holmqvist
94	**Evgeny Artyukhin**
123	Aaron Lobb
138	Paul Lynch
188	Art Femenella
219	Dennis Packard
222	Jeremy Van Hoof
252	J.F. Soucy
259	Dmitri Bezrukov
261	Vitali Smolyaninov
281	Ilja Solarev
289	Henrik Bergfors

2000

Pick	
8	**Nikita Alexeev**
34	Ruslan Zainullin
81	**Alexander Kharitonov**
126	Johan Hagglund
161	Pavel Sedov
191	Aaron Gionet
222	Marek Priechodsky
226	**Brian Eklund**
233	Alexander Polukeyev
263	**Thomas Ziegler**

1999

Pick	
47	**Sheldon Keefe**
67	**Evgeny Konstantinov**
75	Brett Scheffelmaier
88	**Jimmie Olvestad**
127	**Kaspars Astashenko**
148	Michal Lanicek
182	**Fedor Fedorov**
187	Ivan Rachunek
216	Erkki Rajamaki
244	Mikko Kuparinen

General Managers' History

Phil Esposito, 1992-93 to 1997-98; Phil Esposito and Jacques Demers, 1998-99; Rick Dudley, 1999-2000, 2000-01; Rick Dudley and Jay Feaster, 2001-02; Jay Feaster, 2002-03 to 2007-08; Brian Lawton, 2008-09, 2009-10; Steve Yzerman, 2010-11 to date.

Steve Yzerman

Vice President and General Manager

Born: Cranbrook, B.C., May 9, 1965.

Steve Yzerman – the iconic Detroit Red Wing player and executive – was named the sixth general manager in Lightning history on May 25, 2010. In his first season wih the club in 2010-11 Yzerman was a finalist for the G.M of the Year award as Tampa Bay returned to the playoffs for the first time since 2006-07 and reached the Eastern Conference Final after tying a club record with 46 wins during the regular season.

Before joining the Lightning Yzerman spent four seasons as vice president with the Red Wings, working closely with general manager Ken Holland, senior vice president Jim Devellano and assistant general manager Jim Nill on evaluating talent at both the professional and amateur levels. He also contributed valuable input on trades, free agent signings and at the Entry Draft each summer. Yzerman served as general manager for Canada at the 2007 and 2008 World Championships, bringing home gold and silver respectively. He then led Canada to an Olympic gold medal victory on home ice in Vancouver at the 2010 Winter Olympics as executive director, and will serve in that role again for the 2014 Sochi Olympics. Yzerman also won an Olympic gold medal as a player with Canada in 2002.

Yzerman is a four-time Stanley Cup champion, winning three as a player (1997, 1998 and 2002) and another as a member of Detroit's management team (2008). Overall he spent 27 seasons with the franchise. He was inducted into the Hockey Hall of Fame in 2009, his first year of eligibility. Recognized as one of the best centers in NHL history, Yzerman retired on July 3, 2006 after a remarkable 22-year NHL career with the Red Wings. He ranks among the NHL's all-time leaders with 1,514 career games, 692 goals, 1,063 assists and 1,755 career points. Even more impressive than his career statistics may be his 20-year run as captain in Detroit, the longest tenure in NHL and major sports history. Yzerman was named captain of the Red Wings prior to the 1986-87 season, making him the youngest captain in franchise history at 21-years-old.

During his illustrious career Yzerman was selected to the NHL All-Star Game on 9 occasions. He also won the Bill Masterton Trophy (perseverance, sportsmanship and dedication to hockey) in 2003, the Frank J. Selke Trophy (best defensive forward) in 2000, the Conn Smythe Trophy (playoff MVP) in 1998, the Lester B. Pearson Trophy (the NHLPA's top player) in 1989 and was also selected to the NHL All-Rookie Team in 1984.

Club Directory

Tampa Bay Times Forum

Tampa Bay Lightning
Tampa Bay Times Forum
401 Channelside Drive
Tampa, FL 33602
Phone **813/301-6500**
FAX 813/301-1480
Ticket Info. 813/301-6600
www.tampabaylightning.com
Capacity: 19,758

Executive Staff

Owner, Governor & Chairman	Jeff Vinik
Chief Executive Officer and Alternate Governor	Tod Leiweke
Chief Operating Officer	Steve Griggs
VP and General Manager	Steve Yzerman
Exec. VPs, Finance / Communications / Sales	Robert Canton / Bill Wickett / Jamie Spencer
EVP and General Counsel	Jim Shimberg
Sr. VP, Corporate Sponsorships & Activation	Bill Abercrombie
VPs, Corporate Relations / Partnerships	Phil Esposito / Kyle Draper
VPs, H.R. / Corporate & Community Affairs	Keith Harris / Dave Andreychuk
VPs, Guest Experience / Ticket Ops.	Mary Milne / Jim Mannino
VPs, Event Booking / Event Presentation	Elmer Straub / John Franzone
VP, Philanthropy & Community Initiatives	Elizabeth Frazier
Sr. VP, Marketing	Lynn Wittenburg
Exec. Asst. to Owner and CEO / EVP Finance	Sharon Love Lewis
Exec. Asst. to COO/General Counsel	Sabrina Odria

Coaching Staff

Head Coach	Jon Cooper
Assistant Coaches	Rick Bowness, George Gwozdecky
Goaltending Coach / Video Coach	Frantz Jean / Nigel Kirwan
Player Development Coach	Steve Thomas
Strength & Conditioning Coach / Manual Therapist	Mark Lambert / Christian Rivas

Hockey Operations

Asst. G.M., G.M., Syracuse Crunch	Julien BriseBois
Asst. G.M., Director of Player Personnel	Pat Verbeek
Senior Advisor to the General Manager	Tom Kurvers
Director of Amateur Scouting	Al Murray
Head Scouts, Pro / Amateur	Greg Malone / Darryl Plandowski
Director of Team Services	Ryan Belec
Manager of Hockey Administration	Elizabeth Sylvia
Head Athletic Trainer / Assistant Trainer	Tom Mulligan / Mike Poirier
Equipment Manager / Assistant Managers	Ray Thill / Rob Kennedy, Clay Roffer
Statistical Analyst	Michael Peterson

Media

Media Relations Manager	Brian Breseman
P.R. Coordinator	Trevor van Knotsenburg
Beat Reporter and Media Relations Assistant	Missy Zielinski

Community Relations and Lightning Foundation

Senior Director of Community Relations	Kasey Smith
Director, Youth Hockey	Brian Bradley
Coordinators	Heidi Hamlin, Kelley Cureton, Tom Garavaglia

Finance

Director of Business Strategy	Chris Kamke
Business Analyst / Finance Manager	Matthew Samost / Michelle Davidson
Senior Accountant	Tim Ennis
Managers, Accounts Payable / Receivable	Donna Clark / Angela Edwards

Human Resources

Associate General Counsel	Danna Haydar
Human Resources Manager	Nicole Parente
Front Desk Administrator	Audrey Flowers

Information Technology

Director of IT Services / IT Help Desk	Ian Steele / Bryan Ririe

Ticket Office

Ticket Supervisors, Sports / Event	Helen Junker / Bobby Loman
Premium / Staffing Supervisor	Missy Davis
Box Office Coordinators	Alayn Hornick, Justin Andrews, Chris Sprunger

Client Sales and Services

Executive Suite Director / Specialists	Amanda Graul, Toni Angeli, Danielle Lail
Account Membership Executives	Alyson Bradley, Shannon Dixie, Vince Massi, Dan Schlindwein, Joe Russano, Justin Versaggi
Season Ticket Membership Manager / Asst. Mgr.	Lakisha Sharpe / Thomas Gregory
Coordinators, Member Services / Ticket Services	Erin Bailey / Charlene Beverly

Corporate Partnership & Activation

Sr. Dir. of Partnership Development & Activation	Mike Harrison
Director of Partnership Activation	Julia Wyman
Manager of Partnership Development	Suzy O'Malley
Corporate Partnership Sales Mgrs.	Tim Post, Bob Rossi
Sr. Corporate Partnership Activation Manager	Erik Langner
Corporate Partnership Activation	Amy Bigelow, Nicole Pincus, Bree Maddocks

Ticket Sales

Sr. Director of New Business Development	Ryan Bringger
Directors, Inside Sales / Group Sales	Ryan Cook / Ryan Niemeyer
Director, Season Ticket Membership	Travis Pelleymounter
Corporate Sales Managers	Madeline Anthony, Ryan Wellman, Rich Sadowsky, Trent Gerhart, Adam Lawson, Michael Lopez, Gary Napert, Rich Sadowsky, Mike Sarage, Brian Specia, Jim Van Dam
Suite Sales Director / Managers	Matt Hill / Adam Laws, Katie Valone
Group Sales	Alison Goodman, Brian Boksen, Chris Duffy, Oisin Crean, Kate Kasunic, Stephen Gerhard, Tyler Thompson
Account Representatives	T.J. Abone, Emily Williams, Tony Econ, Grant Smith, Tommy Curtis, Daniel Lozada, Caroline Wright
Database Coordinator	T.J. Aufiero

Marketing

Director of Marketing	Kelsey Carlson
Digital Media Director / Manager	James Royer / Julie Dolak
Marketing Managers, Event / Sports	Jennifer Renspie / Erin Allison
Creative Services Mgr. / Graphic Designers	Brittany Austin / Tucker Brooks, Carolina Bermudez
Coordinators	Erin Allison, Justin Savoie, Brian Babcock, Patrick Gardenier

Arena Management

G.M.s, Tampa Bay Times Forum / SportService	Darryl Benge / Bruce Ground
Directors, Arena Departments	Rhett Blewett, Maurizio Manetti
Managers, Arena Departments	Steven Butler, Kevin Alexander, Amy Ford, Tom Miracle, Stevan Simms, Tripp Turbiville, Susan Danielik
Coordinator / Operations Analyst	Samantha Nemeroff / Sam Carr

Broadcast

Managers, Radio / A/V / Production Systems	Matt Sammon / J.C. Kent / Jorge Rosell
Flagship Station, Television	SunSports Network
Radio Stations	WDAE 970, WWJB 1450, WSRQ 1530/107.5, WWCN 770, WYCG 104.9, WBSR 1450, WDGF 1350
TV Play-by-Play / Color / Reporter	Rick Peckham / Bobby "The Chief" Taylor / Paul Kennedy
Radio Play-by-Play / Analyst	David Mishkin / Phil Esposito

Toronto Maple Leafs

2012-13 Results: 26W-17L-0OTL-5SOL 57PTS
3RD, Northeast Division • 5TH, Eastern Conference

Key Off-Season Signings/Acquisitions

2013

- **June 13** • Re-signed RW **Colton Orr**.
- **23** • Acquired G **Jonathan Bernier** from Los Angeles for RW **Matt Frattin**, G **Ben Scrivens** and a 2nd-round pick in the 2014 or 2015 NHL Draft.
- **30** • Acquired C **Dave Bolland** from Chicago for a 2nd- (Carl Dahlstrom) and 4th-round pick (later traded) in the 2013 NHL Draft and a 4th-round pick in 2014.
- **July 5** • Signed RW **David Clarkson**.
- **5** • Re-signed C **Tyler Bozak** and LW **Frazer McLaren**.
- **22** • Re-signed D **Carl Gunnarsson**.
- **30** • Re-signed D **Mark Fraser**.

2013-14 Schedule

Oct.	Tue.	1	at Montreal
	Wed.	2	at Philadelphia
	Sat.	5	Ottawa
	Tue.	8	Colorado
	Thu.	10	at Nashville
	Sat.	12	Edmonton
	Tue.	15	Minnesota
	Thu.	17	Carolina
	Sat.	19	at Chicago
	Tue.	22	Anaheim
	Fri.	25	at Columbus
	Sat.	26	Pittsburgh
	Tue.	29	at Edmonton
	Wed.	30	at Calgary
Nov.	Sat.	2	at Vancouver*
	Fri.	8	New Jersey
	Sat.	9	at Boston
	Wed.	13	at Minnesota
	Fri.	15	at Buffalo
	Sat.	16	Buffalo
	Tue.	19	NY Islanders
	Thu.	21	Nashville
	Sat.	23	Washington
	Mon.	25	Columbus
	Wed.	27	at Pittsburgh
	Fri.	29	at Buffalo
	Sat.	30	at Montreal
Dec.	Tue.	3	San Jose
	Thu.	5	Dallas
	Sat.	7	at Ottawa
	Sun.	8	Boston
	Wed.	11	Los Angeles
	Thu.	12	at St. Louis
	Sat.	14	Chicago
	Mon.	16	at Pittsburgh
	Tue.	17	Florida
	Thu.	19	Phoenix
	Sat.	21	Detroit
	Mon.	23	at NY Rangers
	Fri.	27	Buffalo
	Sun.	29	Carolina
Jan.	Wed.	1	at Detroit*
	Sat.	4	NY Rangers
	Tue.	7	NY Islanders
	Thu.	9	at Carolina
	Fri.	10	at Washington
	Sun.	12	New Jersey
	Tue.	14	at Boston
	Wed.	15	Buffalo
	Sat.	18	Montreal
	Mon.	20	at Phoenix
	Tue.	21	at Colorado
	Thu.	23	at Dallas
	Sat.	25	at Winnipeg
	Tue.	28	Tampa Bay
	Thu.	30	Florida
Feb.	Sat.	1	Ottawa
	Tue.	4	at Florida
	Thu.	6	at Tampa Bay
	Sat.	8	Vancouver
	Thu.	27	at NY Islanders
Mar.	Sat.	1	at Montreal
	Mon.	3	Columbus
	Wed.	5	at NY Rangers
	Sat.	8	Philadelphia
	Mon.	10	at Anaheim
	Tue.	11	at San Jose
	Thu.	13	at Los Angeles
	Sun.	16	at Washington*
	Tue.	18	at Detroit
	Wed.	19	Tampa Bay
	Sat.	22	Montreal
	Sun.	23	at New Jersey
	Tue.	25	St. Louis
	Fri.	28	at Philadelphia
	Sat.	29	Detroit
Apr.	Tue.	1	Calgary
	Thu.	3	Boston
	Sat.	5	Winnipeg
	Tue.	8	at Tampa Bay
	Thu.	10	at Florida
	Sat.	12	at Ottawa

* Denotes afternoon game.

ATLANTIC DIVISION
97th NHL Season

Franchise date: November 26, 1917

Year-by-Year Record

		Home				Road				Overall									
Season	GP	W	L	T	OL	W	L	T	OL	W	L	T	OL	GF	GA	Pts.	Div. Fin.	Conf. Fin.	Playoff Result
2012-13	48	13	9	....	2	13	8	....	3	26	17	....	5	145	133	57	3rd, NE	5th, East	Lost Conf. Quarter-Final
2011-12	82	18	16	....	7	17	21	....	3	35	37	....	10	231	264	80	4th, NE	13th, East	Out of Playoffs
2010-11	82	18	15	....	8	19	19	....	3	37	34	....	11	218	251	85	4th, NE	10th, East	Out of Playoffs
2009-10	82	18	17	....	6	12	21	....	8	30	38	....	14	214	267	74	5th, NE	15th, East	Out of Playoffs
2008-09	82	16	16	....	9	18	19	....	4	34	35	....	13	250	293	81	5th, NE	12th, East	Out of Playoffs
2007-08	82	18	17	....	6	18	18	....	5	36	35	....	11	231	260	83	5th, NE	12th, East	Out of Playoffs
2006-07	82	21	15	....	5	19	16	....	6	40	31	....	11	258	269	91	3rd, NE	9th, East	Out of Playoffs
2005-06	82	26	12	....	3	15	21	....	5	41	33	....	8	257	270	90	4th, NE	9th, East	Out of Playoffs
2004-05	....	....	....	....	....	....	....	....	....	....	....	....	....	....	....	....			
2003-04	82	22	14	3	2	23	10	7	1	45	24	10	3	242	204	103	2nd, NE	4th, East	Lost Conf. Semi-Final
2002-03	82	24	13	4	0	20	15	3	3	44	28	7	3	236	208	98	2nd, NE	5th, East	Lost Conf. Quarter-Final
2001-02	82	24	11	6	0	19	14	4	4	43	25	10	4	249	207	100	2nd, NE	4th, East	Lost Conf. Final
2000-01	82	19	11	7	4	18	18	4	1	37	29	11	5	232	207	90	3rd, NE	7th, East	Lost Conf. Semi-Final
1999-2000	82	24	12	5	0	21	15	2	3	45	27	7	3	246	222	100	1st, NE	3rd, East	Lost Conf. Semi-Final
1998-99	82	23	13	5	....	22	17	2	....	45	30	7	....	268	231	97	2nd, NE	4th, East	Lost Conf. Final
1997-98	82	16	20	5	....	14	23	4	....	30	43	9	....	194	237	69	6th, Cen.	10th, West	Out of Playoffs
1996-97	82	18	20	3	....	12	24	5	....	30	44	8	....	230	273	68	6th, Cen.	11th, West	Out of Playoffs
1995-96	82	19	15	7	....	15	21	5	....	34	36	12	....	247	252	80	3rd, Cen.	4th, West	Lost Conf. Quarter-Final
1994-95	48	15	7	2	....	6	12	6	....	21	19	8	....	135	146	50	4th, Cen.	5th, West	Lost Conf. Quarter-Final
1993-94	84	23	15	4	....	20	14	8	....	43	29	12	....	280	243	98	2nd, Cen.	2nd, West	Lost Conf. Final
1992-93	84	25	11	6	....	19	18	5	....	44	29	11	....	288	241	99	3rd, Norris		Lost Conf. Final
1991-92	80	21	16	3	....	9	27	4	....	30	43	7	....	234	294	67	5th, Norris		Out of Playoffs
1990-91	80	15	21	4	....	8	25	7	....	23	46	11	....	241	318	57	5th, Norris		Out of Playoffs
1989-90	80	24	14	2	....	14	24	2	....	38	38	4	....	337	358	80	3rd, Norris		Lost Div. Semi-Final
1988-89	80	15	20	5	....	13	26	1	....	28	46	6	....	259	342	62	5th, Norris		Out of Playoffs
1987-88	80	14	20	6	....	7	29	4	....	21	49	10	....	273	345	52	4th, Norris		Lost Div. Semi-Final
1986-87	80	22	14	4	....	10	28	2	....	32	42	6	....	286	319	70	4th, Norris		Lost Div. Final
1985-86	80	16	21	3	....	9	27	4	....	25	48	7	....	311	386	57	4th, Norris		Lost Div. Final
1984-85	80	10	28	2	....	10	24	6	....	20	52	8	....	253	358	48	5th, Norris		Out of Playoffs
1983-84	80	17	16	7	....	9	29	2	....	26	45	9	....	303	387	61	5th, Norris		Out of Playoffs
1982-83	80	20	15	5	....	8	25	7	....	28	40	12	....	293	330	68	3rd, Norris		Lost Div. Semi-Final
1981-82	80	12	20	8	....	8	24	8	....	20	44	16	....	298	380	56	5th, Norris		Out of Playoffs
1980-81	80	14	21	5	....	14	16	10	....	28	37	15	....	322	367	71	5th, Adams		Lost Prelim. Round
1979-80	80	17	19	4	....	18	21	1	....	35	40	5	....	304	327	75	4th, Adams		Lost Prelim. Round
1978-79	80	20	12	8	....	14	21	5	....	34	33	13	....	267	252	81	3rd, Adams		Lost Quarter-Final
1977-78	80	21	13	6	....	20	16	4	....	41	29	10	....	271	237	92	3rd, Adams		Lost Semi-Final
1976-77	80	18	13	9	....	15	19	6	....	33	32	15	....	301	285	81	3rd, Adams		Lost Quarter-Final
1975-76	80	23	12	5	....	11	19	10	....	34	31	15	....	294	276	83	3rd, Adams		Lost Quarter-Final
1974-75	80	19	12	9	....	12	21	7	....	31	33	16	....	280	309	78	3rd, Adams		Lost Quarter-Final
1973-74	78	21	11	7	....	14	16	9	....	35	27	16	....	274	230	86	4th, East		Lost Quarter-Final
1972-73	78	20	12	7	....	7	29	3	....	27	41	10	....	247	279	64	6th, East		Out of Playoffs
1971-72	78	21	11	7	....	12	20	7	....	33	31	14	....	209	208	80	4th, East		Lost Quarter-Final
1970-71	78	24	9	6	....	13	24	2	....	37	33	8	....	248	211	82	4th, East		Lost Quarter-Final
1969-70	76	18	13	7	....	11	21	6	....	29	34	13	....	222	242	71	6th, East		Out of Playoffs
1968-69	76	20	8	10	....	15	18	5	....	35	26	15	....	234	217	85	4th, East		Lost Quarter-Final
1967-68	74	24	9	4	....	9	22	6	....	33	31	10	....	209	176	76	5th, East		Out of Playoffs
1966-67	**70**	**21**	**8**	**6**	....	**11**	**19**	**5**	....	**32**	**27**	**11**	....	**204**	**211**	**75**	**3rd,**		**Won Stanley Cup**
1965-66	70	22	9	4	....	12	16	7	....	34	25	11	....	208	187	79	3rd,		Lost Semi-Final
1964-65	70	17	15	3	....	13	11	11	....	30	26	14	....	204	173	74	4th,		Lost Semi-Final
1963-64	**70**	**22**	**7**	**6**	....	**11**	**18**	**6**	....	**33**	**25**	**12**	....	**192**	**172**	**78**	**3rd,**		**Won Stanley Cup**
1962-63	**70**	**21**	**8**	**6**	....	**14**	**15**	**6**	....	**35**	**23**	**12**	....	**221**	**180**	**82**	**1st,**		**Won Stanley Cup**
1961-62	**70**	**25**	**5**	**5**	....	**12**	**17**	**6**	....	**37**	**22**	**11**	....	**232**	**180**	**85**	**2nd,**		**Won Stanley Cup**
1960-61	70	21	6	8	....	18	13	4	....	39	19	12	....	234	176	90	2nd,		Lost Semi-Final
1959-60	70	20	9	6	....	15	17	3	....	35	26	9	....	199	195	79	2nd,		Lost Final
1958-59	70	17	13	5	....	10	19	6	....	27	32	11	....	189	201	65	4th,		Lost Final
1957-58	70	12	16	7	....	9	22	4	....	21	38	11	....	192	226	53	6th,		Out of Playoffs
1956-57	70	12	16	7	....	9	18	8	....	21	34	15	....	174	192	57	5th,		Out of Playoffs
1955-56	70	19	10	6	....	5	23	7	....	24	33	13	....	153	181	61	4th,		Lost Semi-Final
1954-55	70	14	10	11	....	10	14	11	....	24	24	22	....	147	135	70	3rd,		Lost Semi-Final
1953-54	70	22	6	7	....	10	18	7	....	32	24	14	....	152	131	78	3rd,		Lost Semi-Final
1952-53	70	17	12	6	....	10	18	7	....	27	30	13	....	156	167	67	5th,		Out of Playoffs
1951-52	70	17	10	8	....	12	15	8	....	29	25	16	....	168	157	74	3rd,		Lost Semi-Final
1950-51	**70**	**22**	**8**	**5**	....	**19**	**8**	**8**	....	**41**	**16**	**13**	....	**212**	**138**	**95**	**2nd,**		**Won Stanley Cup**
1949-50	70	18	9	8	....	13	18	4	....	31	27	12	....	176	173	74	3rd,		Lost Semi-Final
1948-49	**60**	**12**	**8**	**10**	....	**10**	**17**	**3**	....	**22**	**25**	**13**	....	**147**	**161**	**57**	**4th,**		**Won Stanley Cup**
1947-48	**60**	**22**	**3**	**5**	....	**10**	**12**	**8**	....	**32**	**15**	**13**	....	**182**	**143**	**77**	**1st,**		**Won Stanley Cup**
1946-47	**60**	**20**	**8**	**2**	....	**11**	**11**	**8**	....	**31**	**19**	**10**	....	**209**	**172**	**72**	**2nd,**		**Won Stanley Cup**
1945-46	50	10	13	2	....	9	11	5	....	19	24	7	....	174	185	45	5th,		Out of Playoffs
1944-45	**50**	**13**	**9**	**3**	....	**11**	**13**	**1**	....	**24**	**22**	**4**	....	**183**	**161**	**52**	**3rd,**		**Won Stanley Cup**
1943-44	50	13	11	1	....	10	12	3	....	23	23	4	....	214	174	50	3rd,		Lost Semi-Final
1942-43	50	17	6	2	....	5	13	7	....	22	19	9	....	198	159	53	3rd,		Lost Semi-Final
1941-42	**48**	**18**	**6**	**0**	....	**9**	**12**	**3**	....	**27**	**18**	**3**	....	**158**	**136**	**57**	**2nd,**		**Won Stanley Cup**
1940-41	48	16	5	3	....	12	9	3	....	28	14	6	....	145	99	62	2nd,		Lost Semi-Final
1939-40	48	15	3	6	....	10	14	0	....	25	17	6	....	134	110	56	3rd,		Lost Final
1938-39	48	13	8	3	....	6	12	6	....	19	20	9	....	114	107	47	3rd,		Lost Final
1937-38	48	13	6	5	....	11	9	4	....	24	15	9	....	151	127	57	1st, Cdn.		Lost Final
1936-37	48	14	9	1	....	8	12	4	....	22	21	5	....	119	115	49	3rd, Cdn.		Lost Quarter-Final
1935-36	48	15	4	5	....	8	15	1	....	23	19	6	....	126	106	52	2nd, Cdn.		Lost Final
1934-35	48	16	6	2	....	14	8	2	....	30	14	4	....	157	111	64	1st, Cdn.		Lost Final
1933-34	48	19	2	3	....	7	11	6	....	26	13	9	....	174	119	61	1st, Cdn.		Lost Semi-Final
1932-33	48	16	4	4	....	8	14	2	....	24	18	6	....	119	111	54	1st, Cdn.		Lost Final
1931-32	**48**	**17**	**4**	**3**	....	**6**	**14**	**4**	....	**23**	**18**	**7**	....	**155**	**127**	**53**	**2nd, Cdn.**		**Won Stanley Cup**
1930-31	44	15	4	3	....	7	9	6	....	22	13	9	....	118	99	53	2nd, Cdn.		Lost Quarter-Final
1929-30	44	10	8	4	....	7	13	2	....	17	21	6	....	116	124	40	4th, Cdn.		Out of Playoffs
1928-29	44	15	5	2	....	6	13	3	....	21	18	5	....	85	69	47	3rd, Cdn.		Lost Semi-Final
1927-28	44	9	8	5	....	9	10	3	....	18	18	8	....	89	88	44	4th, Cdn.		Out of Playoffs
1926-27*	44	10	10	2	....	5	14	3	....	15	24	5	....	79	94	35	5th, Cdn.		Out of Playoffs
1925-26	36	11	5	2	....	1	16	1	....	12	21	3	....	92	114	27	6th,		Out of Playoffs
1924-25	30	10	5	0	....	9	6	0	....	19	11	0	....	90	84	38	2nd,		Lost NHL S-Final
1923-24	24	7	5	0	....	3	9	0	....	10	14	0	....	59	85	20	3rd,		Out of Playoffs
1922-23	24	10	1	1	....	3	9	0	....	13	10	1	....	82	88	27	3rd,		Out of Playoffs
1921-22	**24**	**8**	**4**	**0**	....	**5**	**6**	**1**	....	**13**	**10**	**1**	....	**98**	**97**	**27**	**2nd,**		**Won Stanley Cup**
1920-21	24	9	3	0	....	6	6	0	....	15	9	0	....	105	100	30	2nd and 1st***		Lost NHL Final
1919-20**	24	8	4	0	....	4	8	0	....	12	12	0	....	119	106	24	3rd and 2nd***		Out of Playoffs
1918-19	18	5	4	0	....	0	9	0	....	5	13	0	....	64	92	10	3rd and 3rd***		Out of Playoffs
1917-18	**22**	**10**	**1**	**0**	....	**3**	**8**	**0**	....	**13**	**9**	**0**	....	**108**	**109**	**26**	**2nd and 1st*** **		**Won Stanley Cup**

* Name changed from St. Patricks to Maple Leafs (February, 1927). ** Name changed from Arenas to St. Patricks.
*** Season played in two halves with no combined standing at end.
From 1917-18 through 1925-26, NHL champions played against PCHA/WCHL champions for Stanley Cup.

2013-14 Player Personnel

FORWARDS	HT	WT	*Age	Place of Birth	S	2012-13 Club
ASHTON, Carter	6-3	215	22	Winnipeg, Man.	L	Toronto (AHL)
BODIE, Troy	6-4	220	28	Portage La Prairie, Man.	R	Norfolk-Portland (AHL)
BOLLAND, Dave	6-0	184	27	Mimico, Ont.	R	Chicago
BOZAK, Tyler	6-1	195	27	Regina, Sask.	R	Toronto
CLARKSON, David	6-1	200	29	Toronto, Ont.	R	Salzburg-New Jersey
COLBORNE, Joe	6-5	213	23	Calgary, Alta.	L	Toronto (AHL)-Toronto
D'AMIGO, Jerry	5-11	213	22	Binghamton, NY	L	Toronto (AHL)
KADRI, Nazem	6-0	188	22	London, Ont.	L	Toronto (AHL)-Toronto
KESSEL, Phil	6-0	202	25	Madison, WI	R	Toronto
KULEMIN, Nikolai	6-1	225	27	Magnitogorsk, USSR	L	Magnitogorsk-Toronto
LUPUL, Joffrey	6-1	206	30	Fort Saskatchewan, Alta.	R	Avtomobilist-Toronto
McCLEMENT, Jay	6-1	205	30	Kingston, Ont.	L	Toronto
McLAREN, Frazer	6-5	230	25	Winnipeg, Man.	L	Worcester-S.J.-Tor
ORR, Colton	6-3	222	31	Winnipeg, Man.	R	Toronto
SMITH, Trevor	6-1	195	28	Ottawa, Ont.	L	Wilkes-Barre-Pittsburgh
van RIEMSDYK, James	6-3	200	24	Middletown, NJ	L	Toronto
DEFENSEMEN						
BLACKER, Jesse	6-2	190	22	Toronto, Ont.	R	Toronto (AHL)
BRENNAN, T.J.	6-1	213	24	Willingboro, NJ	L	Rochester-Buf.-Fla.
FRANSON, Cody	6-5	213	26	Sicamous, B.C.	R	Brynas-Toronto
FRASER, Mark	6-4	220	27	Ottawa, Ont.	L	Toronto (AHL)-Toronto
GARDINER, Jake	6-2	184	23	Minnetonka, MN	L	Toronto (AHL)-Toronto
GRANBERG, Petter	6-3	205	21	Gallivare, Sweden	R	Skelleftea
GUNNARSSON, Carl	6-2	196	26	Orebro, Sweden	L	Orebro-Toronto
HOLZER, Korbinian	6-3	205	25	Munich, West Germany	R	Toronto (AHL)-Toronto
LILES, John-Michael	5-10	185	32	Indianapolis, IN	L	Toronto
MARSHALL, Kevin	6-1	201	24	Boucherville, Que.	L	Hershey-Toronto (AHL)
PHANEUF, Dion	6-3	214	28	Edmonton, Alta.	L	Toronto
RANGER, Paul	6-3	210	29	Whitby, Ont.	L	Toronto (AHL)

GOALTENDERS	HT	WT	*Age	Place of Birth	C	2012-13 Club
BERNIER, Jonathan	6-0	185	25	Laval, Que.	L	Heilbronn-Los Angeles
MacINTYRE, Drew	6-1	190	30	Charlottetown, P.E.I.	L	Lev Praha-Reading-Tor (AHL)
REIMER, James	6-2	208	25	Morweena, Man.	L	Toronto

* – Age at start of 2013-14 season

Coaching History

Dick Carroll, 1917-18, 1918-19; Frank Heffernan and Harry Sproule, 1919-20; Frank Carroll, 1920-21; George O'Donohue, 1921-22; George O'Donohue and Charles Querrie, 1922-23; Charles Querrie, 1923-24; Eddie Powers, 1924-25, 1925-26; Charles Querrie, Mike Rodden and Alex Romeril, 1926-27; Conn Smythe, 1927-28 to 1929-30; Conn Smythe and Art Duncan, 1930-31; Art Duncan, Conn Smythe and Dick Irvin, 1931-32; Dick Irvin, 1932-33 to 1939-40; Hap Day, 1940-41 to 1949-50; Joe Primeau, 1950-51 to 1952-53; King Clancy, 1953-54 to 1955-56; Howie Meeker, 1956-57; Billy Reay, 1957-58; Billy Reay and Punch Imlach, 1958-59; Punch Imlach, 1959-60 to 1968-69; John McLellan, 1969-70 to 1972-73; Red Kelly, 1973-74 to 1976-77; Roger Neilson, 1977-78, 1978-79; Floyd Smith, Dick Duff and Punch Imlach, 1979-80; Joe Crozier and Mike Nykoluk, 1980-81; Mike Nykoluk, 1981-82 to 1983-84; Dan Maloney, 1984-85, 1985-86; John Brophy, 1986-87, 1987-88; John Brophy and George Armstrong, 1988-89; Doug Carpenter, 1989-90; Doug Carpenter and Tom Watt, 1990-91; Tom Watt, 1991-92; Pat Burns, 1992-93 to 1994-95; Pat Burns and Nick Beverley, 1995-96; Mike Murphy, 1996-97, 1997-98; Pat Quinn, 1998-99 to 2005-06; Paul Maurice, 2006-07, 2007-08; Ron Wilson, 2008-09 to 2010-11; Ron Wilson and Randy Carlyle, 2011-12; Randy Carlyle, 2012-13 to date.

Randy Carlyle

Head Coach

Born: Sudbury, Ont., April 19, 1956.

Randy Carlyle was hired as the head coach of the Toronto Maple Leafs on March 2, 2012. The move brought Carlyle back to where he had begun his NHL career as a player in 1976-77. In his first full season behind the bench in Toronto in 2012-13, Carlyle led the Maple Leafs into the playoffs for the first time since 2004.

Carlyle's first NHL coaching job was in Anaheim, where he was hired on August 1, 2005. In his first season behind the bench in 2005-06, he led the Ducks to the Western Conference Final. He led Anaheim to its first Stanley Cup championship in 2007. Prior to joining the Ducks, Carlyle had served as the head coach of the Manitoba Moose, the Vancouver Canucks' primary development team. In all, Carlyle spent six seasons between 1996 and 2005 as head coach in Manitoba (both in the International and American Hockey Leagues) with his team posting an overall record of 222-159-52-7. He had the additional duties of general manager of the Moose from 1996 to 2000, and served as club president for the 2001-02 season. Carlyle helped the Moose to a 47-21-14 record for 108 points in 1998-99, for which he was named the IHL's general manager of the year.

Following the 2001-02 season, Carlyle joined the coaching staff of the Washington Capitals. He served as an assistant coach with Washington for two seasons (2002 to 2004), before rejoining Manitoba in 2004–05.

Carlyle played 17 seasons in the NHL with Toronto, Pittsburgh and Winnipeg. He appeared in 1,055 games and had 148 goals and 499 assists for 647 points. Known as a fiery, tough-nosed defenseman, he was selected to play in four NHL All-Star Games, winning the Norris Trophy as the league's top defenseman in 1981. At the conclusion of his playing career in 1993, Carlyle remained with the Winnipeg organization's hockey operations staff, eventually becoming an assistant coach for the 1995-96 season.

2012-13 Scoring

* – rookie

Regular Season

Pos	#	Player	Team	GP	G	A	Pts	TOI	+/-	PIM	PP	SH	GW	S	%
C	81	Phil Kessel	TOR	48	20	32	52	19:48	-3	18	6	0	4	161	12.4
C	43	Nazem Kadri	TOR	48	18	26	44	16:03	15	23	5	0	1	107	16.8
L	21	James van Riemsdyk	TOR	48	18	14	32	19:12	-7	26	5	0	3	140	12.9
D	4	Cody Franson	TOR	45	4	25	29	18:47	4	8	3	0	0	70	5.7
C	42	Tyler Bozak	TOR	46	12	16	28	20:18	-1	6	4	1	3	61	19.7
D	3	Dion Phaneuf	TOR	48	9	19	28	25:10	-4	65	3	0	1	88	10.2
L	41	Nikolai Kulemin	TOR	48	7	16	23	16:44	-5	22	0	0	0	72	9.7
L	16	Clarke MacArthur	TOR	40	8	12	20	14:54	3	26	2	0	1	62	12.9
R	19	Joffrey Lupul	TOR	16	11	7	18	16:07	8	12	3	0	3	42	26.2
C	11	Jay McClement	TOR	48	8	9	17	15:14	0	11	0	0	0	48	16.7
C	84	Mikhail Grabovski	TOR	48	9	7	16	15:34	-10	24	0	0	1	80	11.3
D	36	Carl Gunnarsson	TOR	37	1	14	15	21:16	5	14	0	0	0	28	3.6
R	39	Matt Frattin	TOR	25	7	6	13	13:13	6	4	0	0	3	42	16.7
D	24	John-Michael Liles	TOR	32	2	9	11	18:46	-1	4	0	0	0	47	4.3
C	47	* Leo Komarov	TOR	42	4	5	9	13:56	-1	18	0	0	3	51	7.8
D	53	Mike Kostka	TOR	35	0	8	8	22:04	-7	27	0	0	0	49	0.0
D	45	Mark Fraser	TOR	45	0	8	8	16:57	18	85	0	0	0	33	0.0
D	23	Ryan O'Byrne	COL	34	1	3	4	18:51	-8	54	0	0	0	21	4.8
			TOR	8	1	1	2	17:10	4	6	0	0	0	5	20.0
			Total	42	2	4	6	18:31	-4	60	0	0	0	26	7.7
L	38	Frazer McLaren	S.J.	1	0	0	0	6:54	0	0	0	0	0	0	0.0
			TOR	35	3	2	5	5:09	0	102	0	0	2	20	15.0
			Total	36	3	2	5	5:12	0	102	0	0	2	20	15.0
R	28	Colton Orr	TOR	44	1	3	4	6:23	4	155	0	0	0	13	7.7
D	51	Jake Gardiner	TOR	12	0	4	4	20:28	0	0	0	0	0	12	0.0
D	55	* Korbinian Holzer	TOR	22	2	1	3	18:30	-12	28	0	0	1	16	12.5
L	48	Ryan Hamilton	TOR	10	0	2	2	10:51	1	0	0	0	0	6	0.0
D	8	Mike Komisarek	TOR	4	0	0	0	15:20	2	2	0	0	0	1	0.0
C	32	* Joe Colborne	TOR	5	0	0	0	9:07	-1	2	0	0	0	4	0.0

Goaltending

No.	Goaltender	GPI	Mins	Avg	W	L	OT	EN	SO	GA	SA	S%	G	A	PIM
40	* Jussi Rynnas	1	10	0.00	0	0	0	0	0	0	6	1.000	0	0	0
34	James Reimer	33	1856	2.46	19	8	5	4	4	76	995	.924	0	1	0
30	Ben Scrivens	20	1025	2.69	7	9	0	2	2	46	542	.915	0	0	6
	Totals	**48**	**2911**	**2.64**	**26**	**17**	**5**	**6**	**6**	**128**	**1549**	**.917**			

Playoffs

Pos	#	Player	Team	GP	G	A	Pts	TOI	+/-	PIM	PP	SH	GW	OT	S	%
L	21	James van Riemsdyk	TOR	7	2	5	7	19:41	-1	4	1	0	0	0	33	6.1
C	81	Phil Kessel	TOR	7	4	2	6	18:28	3	2	1	0	2	0	29	13.8
D	4	Cody Franson	TOR	7	3	3	6	22:49	0	0	1	0	0	0	15	20.0
D	51	Jake Gardiner	TOR	6	1	4	5	23:01	-3	0	1	0	0	0	9	11.1
R	19	Joffrey Lupul	TOR	7	3	1	4	18:59	-1	4	1	0	0	0	27	11.1
C	43	Nazem Kadri	TOR	7	1	3	4	13:34	5	10	0	0	0	0	14	7.1
L	16	Clarke MacArthur	TOR	5	2	1	3	12:21	-1	2	0	0	1	0	7	28.6
D	3	Dion Phaneuf	TOR	7	1	2	3	25:22	-6	6	0	0	0	0	16	6.3
C	42	Tyler Bozak	TOR	5	1	1	2	21:43	0	4	0	1	0	0	13	7.7
R	39	Matt Frattin	TOR	6	0	2	2	13:46	-1	0	0	0	0	0	12	0.0
C	84	Mikhail Grabovski	TOR	7	0	2	2	19:06	-10	2	0	0	0	0	16	0.0
L	48	Ryan Hamilton	TOR	2	0	1	1	8:08	0	0	0	0	0	0	3	0.0
D	45	Mark Fraser	TOR	4	0	1	1	18:26	1	7	0	0	0	0	4	0.0
L	41	Nikolai Kulemin	TOR	7	0	1	1	18:10	-9	0	0	0	0	0	9	0.0
D	36	Carl Gunnarsson	TOR	7	0	1	1	22:05	-7	0	0	0	0	0	7	0.0
L	38	Frazer McLaren	TOR	1	0	0	0	7:46	0	2	0	0	0	0	1	0.0
D	53	Mike Kostka	TOR	1	0	0	0	22:22	-3	0	0	0	0	0	0	0.0
C	32	* Joe Colborne	TOR	2	0	0	0	13:28	0	0	0	0	0	0	3	0.0
D	24	John-Michael Liles	TOR	4	0	0	0	15:25	4	2	0	0	0	0	3	0.0
D	23	Ryan O'Byrne	TOR	6	0	0	0	15:13	2	4	0	0	0	0	0	0.0
R	28	Colton Orr	TOR	7	0	0	0	6:30	-1	18	0	0	0	0	4	0.0
C	11	Jay McClement	TOR	7	0	0	0	14:43	-4	0	0	0	0	0	4	0.0
C	47	* Leo Komarov	TOR	7	0	0	0	9:12	0	17	0	0	0	0	5	0.0

Goaltending

No.	Goaltender	GPI	Mins	Avg	W	L	EN	SO	GA	SA	S%	G	A	PIM
34	James Reimer	7	438	2.88	3	4	1	0	21	272	.923	0	0	0
	Totals	**7**	**439**	**3.01**	**3**	**4**	**1**	**0**	**22**	**273**	**.919**			

Coaching Record

			Regular Season				Playoffs			
Season	Team	League	GC	W	L	O/T	GC	W	L	T
1996-97	Manitoba	IHL	32	16	14	2	....	....	....	....
1997-98	Manitoba	IHL	82	39	36	7	3	0	3	....
1998-99	Manitoba	IHL	82	47	21	14	5	2	3	....
99-2000	Manitoba	IHL	82	37	31	14	2	0	2	....
2000-01	Manitoba	IHL	82	39	31	12	13	6	7	....
2004-05	Manitoba	AHL	80	44	26	10	14	6	8	....
2005-06	**Anaheim**	**NHL**	**82**	**43**	**27**	**12**	**16**	**9**	**7**	....
2006-07♦	**Anaheim**	**NHL**	**82**	**48**	**20**	**14**	**21**	**16**	**5**	....
2007-08	**Anaheim**	**NHL**	**82**	**47**	**27**	**8**	**6**	**2**	**4**	....
2008-09	**Anaheim**	**NHL**	**82**	**42**	**33**	**7**	**13**	**7**	**6**	....
2009-10	**Anaheim**	**NHL**	**82**	**39**	**32**	**11**	....	....	....	....
2010-11	**Anaheim**	**NHL**	**82**	**47**	**30**	**5**	**6**	**2**	**4**	....
2011-12	**Anaheim**	**NHL**	**24**	**7**	**13**	**4**	....	....	....	....
2011-12	**Toronto**	**NHL**	**18**	**6**	**9**	**3**	....	....	....	....
2012-13	**Toronto**	**NHL**	**48**	**26**	**17**	**5**	**7**	**3**	**4**	....
	NHL Totals		**582**	**305**	**208**	**69**	**69**	**39**	**30**	....

♦ Stanley Cup win.

Club Records

Team

(Figures in brackets for season records are games played; records for fewest points, wins, ties, losses, goals, goals against are for 70 or more games)

Most Points	**103**	2003-04 (82)
Most Wins	**45**	1998-99 (82), 1999-2000 (82), 2003-04 (82)
Most Ties	**22**	1954-55 (70)
Most Losses	**52**	1984-85 (80)
Most Goals	**337**	1989-90 (80)
Most Goals Against	**387**	1983-84 (80)
Fewest Points	**48**	1984-85 (80)
Fewest Wins	**20**	1981-82 (80), 1984-85 (80)
Fewest Ties	**4**	1989-90 (80)
Fewest Losses	**16**	1950-51 (70)
Fewest Goals	**147**	1954-55 (70)
Fewest Goals Against	***131**	1953-54 (70)
Longest Winning Streak		
Overall	**10**	Oct. 7-28/93
Home	**9**	Nov. 11-Dec. 26/53, Mar. 6-Apr. 7/07
Away	**7**	Three times
Longest Undefeated Streak		
Overall	**11**	Oct. 15-Nov. 8/50 (8W, 3T), Jan. 6-Feb. 1/94 (7W, 4T)
Home	**18**	Nov. 28/33-Mar. 10/34 (15W, 3T), Oct. 31/53-Jan. 23/54 (16W, 2T)
Away	**9**	Nov. 30/47-Jan. 11/48 (4W, 5T)
Longest Losing Streak		
Overall	**10**	Jan. 15-Feb. 8/67
Home	**7**	Nov. 11-Dec. 5/84
Away	**11**	Feb. 20-Apr. 1/88
Longest Winless Streak		
Overall	**15**	Dec. 26/87-Jan. 25/88 (11L, 4T)
Home	**11**	Dec. 19/87-Jan. 25/88 (7L, 4T), Feb. 11-Mar. 29/12 (9L, 2OL/SOL)
Away	**18**	Oct. 6/82-Jan. 5/83 (13L, 5T)
Most Shutouts, Season	**13**	1953-54 (70)
Most PIM, Season	**2,419**	1989-90 (80)
Most Goals, Game	**14**	Mar. 16/57 (NYR 1 at Tor. 14)

Individual

Most Seasons	**21**	George Armstrong
Most Games	**1,187**	George Armstrong
Most Goals, Career	**420**	Mats Sundin
Most Assists, Career	**620**	Borje Salming
Most Points, Career	**987**	Mats Sundin (420G, 567A)
Most PIM, Career	**2,265**	Tie Domi
Most Shutouts, Career	**62**	Turk Broda
Longest Consecutive Games Streak	**486**	Tim Horton (Feb. 11/61-Feb. 4/68)
Most Goals, Season	**54**	Rick Vaive (1981-82)
Most Assists, Season	**95**	Doug Gilmour (1992-93)
Most Points, Season	**127**	Doug Gilmour (1992-93; 32G, 95A)
Most PIM, Season	**365**	Tie Domi (1997-98)
Most Points, Defenseman, Season	**79**	Ian Turnbull (1976-77; 22G, 57A)
Most Points, Center, Season	**127**	Doug Gilmour (1992-93; 32G, 95A)
Most Points, Right Wing, Season	**97**	Wilf Paiement (1980-81; 40G, 57A)
Most Points, Left Wing, Season	**99**	Dave Andreychuk (1993-94; 53G, 46A)
Most Points, Rookie, Season	**66**	Peter Ihnacak (1982-83; 28G, 38A)
Most Shutouts, Season	**13**	Harry Lumley (1953-54)
Most Goals, Game	**6**	Corb Denneny (Jan. 26/21), Darryl Sittler (Feb. 7/76)
Most Assists, Game	**6**	Babe Pratt (Jan. 8/44), Doug Gilmour (Feb. 13/93)
Most Points, Game	***10**	Darryl Sittler (Feb. 7/76; 6G, 4A)

* NHL Record.

Retired Numbers

5	Bill Barilko	1946-1951
6	Ace Bailey	1926-1934

Honored Numbers

1	Turk Broda	1936-43, 1945-52
	Johnny Bower	1958-1970
4	Hap Day	1926-1937
	Red Kelly	1959-1967
7	King Clancy	1930-1937
	Tim Horton	1949-50, 1951-70
9	Charlie Conacher	1929-1938
	Ted Kennedy	1942-55, 1956-57
10	Syl Apps	1936-43, 1945-48
	George Armstrong	1949-50, 1951-71
13	Mats Sundin	1994-2008
17	Wendel Clark	1985-94, 96-98, 2000
21	Borje Salming	1973-1989
27	Frank Mahovlich	1956-1968
	Darryl Sittler	1970-1982
93	Doug Gilmour	1992-97, 2003

All-time Record vs. Other Clubs

Regular Season

	Total								At Home								On Road							
	GP	W	L	T	OL	GF	GA	PTS	GP	W	L	T	OL	GF	GA	PTS	GP	W	L	T	OL	GF	GA	PTS
Anaheim	32	18	8	5	1	99	81	42	18	11	2	4	1	60	37	27	14	7	6	1	0	39	44	15
Boston	649	264	279	98	8	1929	1919	634	325	166	106	51	2	1070	855	385	324	98	173	47	6	859	1064	249
Buffalo	188	66	96	18	8	522	684	158	93	39	38	12	4	271	309	94	95	27	58	6	4	251	375	64
Calgary	124	53	55	12	4	423	465	122	58	31	18	7	2	221	208	71	66	22	37	5	2	202	257	51
Carolina	104	38	49	11	6	331	376	93	52	20	26	5	1	163	179	46	52	18	23	6	5	168	197	47
Chicago	639	284	258	96	1	1920	1816	665	318	164	99	54	1	1082	837	383	321	120	159	42	0	838	979	282
Colorado	70	25	35	9	1	223	267	60	38	16	17	4	1	122	144	37	32	9	18	5	0	101	123	23
Columbus	10	6	1	1	2	35	22	15	6	3	1	1	1	18	12	8	4	3	0	0	1	17	10	7
Dallas	204	87	88	28	1	677	705	203	104	50	37	17	0	363	330	117	100	37	51	11	1	314	375	86
Detroit	644	276	275	93	0	1855	1831	645	319	167	105	47	0	1057	852	381	325	109	170	46	0	798	979	264
Edmonton	90	41	40	8	1	326	362	91	42	23	17	2	0	171	173	48	48	18	23	6	1	155	189	43
Florida	63	32	22	7	2	184	181	73	30	17	10	2	1	92	88	37	33	15	12	5	1	92	93	36
Los Angeles	139	58	59	21	1	471	475	138	71	35	24	11	1	272	233	82	68	23	35	10	0	199	242	56
Minnesota	10	7	3	0	0	29	23	14	6	5	1	0	0	21	12	10	4	2	2	0	0	8	11	4
Montreal	719	291	331	88	9	1995	2195	679	360	185	124	45	6	1089	952	421	359	106	207	43	3	906	1243	258
Nashville	13	5	6	1	1	30	39	12	9	4	4	1	0	21	25	9	4	1	2	0	1	9	14	3
New Jersey	125	63	35	20	7	412	372	153	64	40	15	5	4	218	168	89	61	23	20	15	3	194	204	64
NY Islanders	139	64	61	7	7	447	491	142	71	37	27	4	3	247	233	81	68	27	34	3	4	200	258	61
NY Rangers	596	279	215	95	7	1889	1715	660	297	165	90	39	3	1013	785	372	299	114	125	56	4	876	930	288
Ottawa	95	43	41	3	8	265	270	97	48	23	18	2	5	134	137	53	47	20	23	1	3	131	133	44
Philadelphia	165	54	86	22	3	450	575	133	83	31	36	14	2	252	269	78	82	23	50	8	1	198	306	55
Phoenix	88	33	46	8	1	312	351	75	46	20	23	2	1	165	174	43	42	13	23	6	0	147	177	32
Pittsburgh	167	75	70	17	5	597	603	172	83	41	28	11	3	322	270	96	84	34	42	6	2	275	333	76
St. Louis	207	91	88	25	3	669	660	210	102	59	29	11	3	381	305	132	105	32	59	14	0	288	355	78
San Jose	39	20	14	5	0	124	99	45	21	12	7	2	0	76	57	26	18	8	7	3	0	48	42	19
Tampa Bay	72	45	20	2	5	244	186	97	36	23	10	1	2	131	98	49	36	22	10	1	3	113	88	48
Vancouver	134	52	59	22	1	456	465	127	65	28	25	11	1	231	219	68	69	24	34	11	0	225	246	59
Washington	129	57	60	10	2	440	446	126	63	34	22	6	1	256	206	75	66	23	38	4	1	184	240	51
Winnipeg	49	28	14	1	6	176	124	63	24	14	6	1	3	89	68	32	25	14	8	0	3	87	56	31
Defunct Clubs	465	242	173	50	0	1468	1260	534	232	158	53	21	0	861	515	337	233	84	120	29	0	607	745	197
Totals	**6168**	**2697**	**2587**	**783**	**101**	**18998**	**19058**	**6278**	**3084**	**1621**	**1018**	**393**	**52**	**10469**	**8750**	**3687**	**3084**	**1076**	**1569**	**390**	**49**	**8529**	**10308**	**2591**

Playoffs

	Series	W	L	GP	W	L	T	GF	GA	Last Mtg.	Rnd.	Result
Boston	14	8	6	69	34	34	1	168	175	2013	CQF	L 3-4
Buffalo	1	0	1	5	1	4	0	16	21	1999	CF	L 1-4
Calgary	1	1	0	2	2	0	0	9	5	1979	PRE	W 2-0
Carolina	1	0	1	6	2	4	0	6	10	2002	CF	L 2-4
Chicago	9	6	3	38	22	15	1	111	89	1995	CQF	L 3-4
Dallas	2	0	2	7	1	6	0	26	35	1983	DSF	L 1-3
Detroit	23	12	11	117	58	59	0	311	321	1993	DSF	W 4-3
Los Angeles	3	2	1	12	7	5	0	41	31	1993	CF	L 3-4
Montreal	15	7	8	71	29	42	0	160	215	1979	QF	L 0-4
New Jersey	2	0	2	13	5	8	0	27	37	2001	CSF	L 3-4
NY Islanders	3	2	1	17	8	9	0	42	54	2002	CQF	W 4-3
NY Rangers	8	3	5	35	16	19	0	86	86	1971	QF	L 2-4
Ottawa	4	4	0	24	16	8	0	57	42	2004	CQF	W 4-3
Philadelphia	6	1	5	36	14	22	0	85	119	2004	CSF	L 2-4
Pittsburgh	3	3	0	12	8	4	0	39	27	1999	CSF	W 4-2
St. Louis	5	2	3	31	14	17	0	90	88	1996	CQF	L 2-4
San Jose	1	1	0	7	4	3	0	26	21	1994	CSF	W 4-3
Vancouver	1	0	1	5	1	4	0	9	16	1994	CF	L 1-4
Defunct Clubs	8	6	2	24	12	10	2	59	57			
Totals	**110**	**58**	**52**	**531**	**254**	**273**	**4**	**1368**	**1449**			

Calgary totals include Atlanta Flames, 1972-73 to 1979-80.
Colorado totals include Quebec, 1979-80 to 1994-95.
New Jersey totals include Kansas City, 1974-75, 1975-76, and Colorado Rockies, 1976-77 to 1981-82.
Phoenix totals include Winnipeg, 1979-80 to 1995-96.
Carolina totals include Hartford, 1979-80 to 1996-97.
Dallas totals include Minnesota North Stars, 1967-68 to 1992-93.
Winnipeg totals include Atlanta Thrashers, 1999-2000 to 2010-11.

Playoff Results 2013-2009

Year	Round	Opponent	Result	GF	GA
2013	CQF	Boston	L 3-4	18	22

Abbreviations: Round: CF – conference final; **CSF** – conference semi-final; **CQF** – conference quarter-final; **DSF** – division semi-final; **QF** – quarter-final; **PRE** – preliminary round.

2012-13 Results

Jan.	19	at Montreal	2-1
	21	Buffalo	1-2
	23	at Pittsburgh	5-2
	24	NY Islanders	4-7
	26	at NY Rangers	2-5
	29	at Buffalo	4-3*
	31	Washington	3-2
Feb.	2	Boston	0-1
	4	Carolina	1-4
	5	at Washington	3-2
	7	at Winnipeg	3-2
	9	at Montreal	6-0
	11	Philadelphia	5-2
	14	at Carolina	1-3
	16	Ottawa	3-0
	18	at Florida	3-0
	19	at Tampa Bay	2-4
	21	Buffalo	3-1
	23	at Ottawa	2-3
	25	at Philadelphia	4-2
	27	Montreal	2-5
	28	at NY Islanders	5-4*
Mar.	4	New Jersey	4-2
	6	Ottawa	5-4
	7	at Boston	2-4
	9	Pittsburgh	4-5†
	12	at Winnipeg	2-5
	14	Pittsburgh	1-3
	16	Winnipeg	4-5†
	20	Tampa Bay	4-2
	21	at Buffalo	4-5†
	23	Boston	3-2
	25	at Boston	2-3†
	26	Florida	3-2
	28	Carolina	6-3
	30	at Ottawa	4-0
Apr.	4	Philadelphia	3-5
	6	at New Jersey	2-1
	8	NY Rangers	4-3
	10	at NY Rangers	2-3†
	13	Montreal	5-1
	15	New Jersey	2-0
	16	at Washington	1-5
	18	NY Islanders	3-5
	20	at Ottawa	4-1
	24	at Tampa Bay	2-5
	25	at Florida	4-0
	27	Montreal	1-4

* – Overtime † – Shootout

Entry Draft Selections 2013-1999

Name in bold denotes played in NHL.

2013

Pick	
21	Frederik Gauthier
82	Carter Verhaeghe
142	Fabrice Herzog
172	Antoine Bibeau
202	Andreas Johnson

2012

Pick	
5	Morgan Rielly
35	Matthew Finn
126	Dominic Toninato
156	Connor Brown
157	Ryan Rupert
209	Viktor Loov

2011

Pick	
22	Tyler Biggs
25	Stuart Percy
86	Josh Leivo
100	Tom Nilsson
130	Tony Cameranesi
152	David Broll
173	Dennis Robertson
190	Garret Sparks
203	Max Everson

2010

Pick	
43	Brad Ross
62	Greg McKegg
79	Sondre Olden
116	Petter Granberg
144	Sam Carrick
146	Daniel Brodin
182	Josh Nicholls

2009

Pick	
7	**Nazem Kadri**
50	Kenny Ryan
58	Jesse Blacker
68	Jamie Devane
128	Eric Knodel
158	Jerry D'Amigo
188	Barron Smith

2008

Pick	
5	**Luke Schenn**
60	**Jimmy Hayes**
98	Mikhail Stefanovich
128	**Greg Pateryn**
129	Joel Champagne
130	Jerome Flaake
158	Grant Rollheiser
188	Andrew MacWilliam

2007

Pick	
74	Dale Mitchell
99	**Matt Frattin**
104	Ben Winnett
134	Juraj Mikus
164	Chris Didomenico
194	**Carl Gunnarsson**

2006

Pick	
13	**Jiri Tlusty**
44	**Nikolai Kulemin**
99	**James Reimer**
111	**Korbinian Holzer**
161	**Viktor Stalberg**
166	Tyler Ruegsegger
180	**Leo Komarov**

2005

Pick	
21	**Tuukka Rask**
82	**Phil Oreskovic**
153	Alex Berry
173	Johan Dahlberg
216	**Anton Stralman**
228	**Chad Rau**

2004

Pick	
90	**Justin Pogge**
113	Roman Kukumberg
157	Dmitri Vorobiev
187	**Robbie Earl**
220	Maxim Semenov
252	Jan Steber
285	Pierce Norton

2003

Pick	
57	John Doherty
91	Martin Sagat
125	Konstantin Volkov
158	**John Mitchell**
220	**Jeremy Williams**
237	Shaun Landolt

2002

Pick	
24	**Alex Steen**
57	**Matt Stajan**
74	Todd Ford
88	Dominic D'Amour
122	David Turon
191	**Ian White**
222	Scott May
254	**Jarkko Immonen**
285	**Staffan Kronwall**

2001

Pick	
17	**Carlo Colaiacovo**
39	**Karel Pilar**
65	**Brendan Bell**
82	**Jay Harrison**
88	Nicolas Corbeil
134	**Kyle Wellwood**
168	**Maxim Kondratiev**
183	Jaroslav Sklenar
198	Ivan Kolozvary
213	Jan Chovan
246	**Tomas Mojzis**
276	Mike Knoepfli

2000

Pick	
24	**Brad Boyes**
51	**Kris Vernarsky**
70	**Mikael Tellqvist**
90	Jean-Francois Racine
100	Miguel Delisle
179	Vadim Sozinov
209	Markus Seikola
223	Lubos Velebny
254	Alexander Shinkar
265	**Jean-Philippe Cote**

1999

Pick	
24	Luca Cereda
60	Peter Reynolds
108	Mirko Murovic
110	Jon Zion
151	Vaclav Zavoral
161	Jan Sochor
211	Vladimir Kulikov
239	**Pierre Hedin**
267	Peter Metcalf

Captains' History

Bert Corbeau, 1926-27; Hap Day, 1927-28 to 1936-37; Charlie Conacher, 1937-38; Red Horner, 1938-39, 1939-40; Syl Apps, 1940-41 to 1942-43; Bob Davidson, 1943-44, 1944-45; Syl Apps, 1945-46 to 1947-48; Ted Kennedy, 1948-49 to 1954-55; Sid Smith, 1955-56; Jimmy Thomson, Ted Kennedy, 1956-57; George Armstrong, 1957-58 to 1968-69; Dave Keon, 1969-70 to 1974-75; Darryl Sittler, 1975-76 to 1980-81; Rick Vaive, 1981-82 to 1985-86; no captain, 1986-87 to 1988-89; Rob Ramage, 1989-90, 1990-91; Wendel Clark, 1991-92 to 1993-94; Doug Gilmour, 1994-95 to 1996-97; Mats Sundin, 1997-98 to 2007-08; no captain, 2008-09, 2009-10; Dion Phaneuf, 2010-11 to date.

General Managers' History

Charles Querrie, 1917-18 to 1926-27; Conn Smythe, 1927-28 to 1953-54; Hap Day, 1954-55 to 1956-57; Howie Meeker, summer 1957; Stafford Smythe 1957-58; Stafford Smythe and Punch Imlach, 1958-59; Punch Imlach, 1959-60 to 1968-69; Jim Gregory, 1969-70 to 1978-79; Punch Imlach, 1979-80, 1980-81; Punch Imlach and Gerry McNamara, 1981-82; Gerry McNamara, 1982-83 to 1986-87; Gerry McNamara and Gord Stellick, 1987-88; Gord Stellick, 1988-89; Floyd Smith, 1989-90, 1990-91; Cliff Fletcher, 1991-92 to 1996-97; Ken Dryden, 1997-98, 1998-99; Pat Quinn, 1999-2000 to 2002-03; John Ferguson Jr., 2003-04 to 2006-07; John Ferguson Jr. and Cliff Fletcher, 2007-08; Cliff Fletcher and Brian Burke, 2008-09; Brian Burke, 2009-10 to 2011-12; Brian Burke and Dave Nonis, 2012-13; Dave Nonis, 2013-14.

Dave Nonis

Senior Vice President and General Manager

Born: Burnaby, B.C., May 25, 1966.

David Nonis was named senior vice president and general manager of the Toronto Maple Leafs on January 9, 2013. He originally joined the Maple Leafs organization as the senior vice president of hockey operations on December 6, 2008. Nonis also serves as the general manager of the Toronto Marlies, the American Hockey League affiliate of the Maple Leafs.

Prior to joining the Maple Leafs, Nonis had been named the Anaheim Ducks' senior advisor of hockey operations on June 20, 2008. Previously, he was the senior vice president and general manager of the Vancouver Canucks from 2004 to 2008, during which time his team compiled a record of 130-91-25. Nonis originally joined the Canucks in 1990 and spent four years with the team before moving on to a four-year term as the NHL's manager of hockey operations. He returned to Vancouver in 1998 as senior vice president, director of hockey operations. Since coming to Toronto, Nonis has also worked in a management capacity for Canada in international hockey, serving as general manager of Team Canada for the World Championship in 2011 and assistant general manager in 2012.

A native of Burnaby, British Columbia, Nonis played hockey for the University of Maine where he served as captain for two seasons, leading his team to back-to-back NCAA championship tournaments and graduating with a B.A. in 1988. He played one season professionally in Denmark before returning to Maine in 1989 to serve on the coaching staff of his alma mater. He earned his M.B.A. from Maine in 1990.

Club Directory

Air Canada Centre

Toronto Maple Leafs
Air Canada Centre
40 Bay St.
Toronto, Ontario M5J 2X2
Phone **416/815-5700**
FAX 416/359-9331
mapleleafs.nhl.com
Capacity: 18,819

Board of Directors
Lawrence M. Tanenbaum, George Cope, Dale Lastman, Nadir Mohamed, Edward Rogers, Mary Ann Turcke

Maple Leaf Sports & Entertainment	
Chairman, NHL Governor	Lawrence M. Tanenbaum
Alternate NHL Governor	Dale Lastman
President and CEO	Tim Leiweke
Chief Operating Officer	Tom Anselmi
Chief Financial Officer	Ian Clarke
Chief Facilities & Live Entertainment Officer	Bob Hunter
Chief Commercial Officer	Dave Hopkinson
Chief Legal & Development Officer	Peter Miller
Hockey Operations	
Senior Vice President and General Manager	David Nonis
Vice President of Hockey Operations	Dave Poulin
Vice President and Assistant General Manager	Claude Loiselle
Senior Advisor	Cliff Fletcher
Head Coach	Randy Carlyle
Assistant Coaches	Greg Cronin, Dave Farrish, Scott Gordon, Chris Dennis
Goaltending Coach	Rick St. Croix
Director of Player Development	Jim Hughes
Player Development Coordinator	Bobby Carpenter
Player Development Advisor	Steve Staios
Sports Psychologist	Dana Sinclair
Director, Hockey and Scouting Administration	Reid Mitchell
Strength and Conditioning Coordinator	Anthony Belza
Manager, Team Services	Dave Griffiths
Video Coordinator	Adam Jancelewicz
Director of Amateur Scouting	Dave Morrison
Director of Pro Scouting	Steve Kasper
Pro Scouts	Rob Cowie, Mike Penny, Tom Watt
Amateur Scouts	Scott Carter, Gary Harker, John Lilley, Garth Malarchuk, Mike Palmateer, Allan Power, George Armstrong, Pierre Rioux, Roy Stasiuk, Pat Dapuzzo, John McMorrow, Darryl Stanley, Bud Stefanski
European Scouts	Thommie Bergman, Joe Gibbs, Peter Ihnacak, Nikolai Ladygin, Jari Gronstrand
Community Representatives	Wendel Clark, Darryl Sittler
Executive Assistants, Hockey Operations	Sandi Dunn, Catherine Grey
Medical and Training Staff	
Head Athletic Therapist	Paul Ayotte
Athletic Therapist	Marty Dudgeon
Massage Therapist	Todd Bean
Equipment Manager	Brian Papineau
Assistant Equipment Managers	Tom Blatchford, Bobby Hastings
Medical Director, Maple Leafs and Marlies	Dr. Noah Forman
Orthopedic Consultant	Dr. John Theodoropoulos
Team Dentists	Dr. Marvin Lean, Dr. Charles Goldberg
Communications	
Director, Media Relations	Pat Park
Manager, Media Relations	Craig Downey
Coordinator, Media Relations	Aaron Gogishvili
Broadcasting	
Senior Director, Broadcast and Content	Frank Hayward
Senior Producer, Broadcast and Networks	Mark Askin
Talent, Leafs TV	Joe Bowen, Dan Dunleavy, Paul Hendrick, Tessa Bonhomme, Bob McGill, Greg Millen
Toronto Radio, Play-By-Play	Joe Bowen, Dan Dunleavy (mid-week)
Television Play-By-Play	Joe Bowen (mid-week)
Television Analysts	Bob McGill, Greg Millen

Selected seventh overall in the 2009 NHL Entry Draft and brought along slowly, Nazem Kadri finished second in Leafs scoring with 44 points in 2012-13 and was tied for second on the club with 18 goals.

Vancouver Canucks

Key Off-Season Signings/Acquisitions

2013

May 29 • Re-signed **Tom Sestito**.
June 25 • Named **John Tortorella** head coach.
July 5 • Signed C **Brad Richardson** and D **Yannick Weber**.
6 • Signed C **Mike Santorelli**.
12 • Signed C **Benn Ferriero**.
23 • Named **Mike Sullivan** and **Glen Gulutzan** assistant coaches.
24 • Re-signed C **Jordan Schroeder**.
25 • Re-signed RW **Dale Weise**.

2012-13 Results: 26W-15L-1OTL-6SOL 59PTS
1ST, Northwest Division • 3RD, Western Conference

Dan Hamhuis wears a uniform honoring the Vancouver Millionaires of the old Pacific Coast Hockey Association in a game against Detroit on March 16, 2013. Hamhuis led Canucks defensemen with 20 assists and 24 points during the 2012-13 season.

2013-14 Schedule

Oct.	Thu.	3	at San Jose	**Jan.**	Wed.	1	Tampa Bay
	Sat.	5	Edmonton		Sat.	4	at Los Angeles
	Sun.	6	at Calgary		Sun.	5	at Anaheim*
	Tue.	8	New Jersey		Tue.	7	Pittsburgh
	Thu.	10	San Jose		Fri.	10	St. Louis
	Sat.	12	Montreal		Mon.	13	at Los Angeles
	Tue.	15	at Philadelphia		Wed.	15	at Anaheim
	Thu.	17	at Buffalo		Thu.	16	at Phoenix
	Sat.	19	at Pittsburgh*		Sat.	18	Calgary
	Sun.	20	at Columbus		Tue.	21	at Edmonton
	Tue.	22	at NY Islanders		Thu.	23	Nashville
	Thu.	24	at New Jersey		Sun.	26	Phoenix*
	Fri.	25	at St. Louis		Mon.	27	Edmonton
	Mon.	28	Washington		Wed.	29	Chicago
	Wed.	30	Detroit		Fri.	31	at Winnipeg
Nov.	Sat.	2	Toronto*	**Feb.**	Mon.	3	at Detroit
	Tue.	5	at Phoenix		Tue.	4	at Boston
	Thu.	7	at San Jose		Thu.	6	at Montreal
	Sat.	9	at Los Angeles		Sat.	8	at Toronto
	Sun.	10	at Anaheim*		Wed.	26	St. Louis
	Thu.	14	San Jose		Fri.	28	Minnesota
	Sun.	17	Dallas*	**Mar.**	Sun.	2	Ottawa*
	Tue.	19	Florida		Tue.	4	at Phoenix
	Fri.	22	Columbus		Thu.	6	at Dallas
	Sat.	23	Chicago		Sat.	8	Calgary
	Mon.	25	Los Angeles		Mon.	10	NY Islanders
	Thu.	28	at Ottawa		Wed.	12	at Winnipeg
	Sat.	30	at NY Rangers*		Fri.	14	at Washington
Dec.	Sun.	1	at Carolina*		Sun.	16	at Florida*
	Tue.	3	at Nashville		Mon.	17	at Tampa Bay
	Fri.	6	Phoenix		Wed.	19	Nashville
	Sun.	8	Colorado*		Sun.	23	Buffalo*
	Mon.	9	Carolina		Wed.	26	at Minnesota
	Fri.	13	Edmonton		Thu.	27	at Colorado
	Sat.	14	Boston		Sat.	29	Anaheim
	Tue.	17	at Minnesota	**Apr.**	Tue.	1	NY Rangers
	Thu.	19	at Dallas		Sat.	5	Los Angeles
	Fri.	20	at Chicago		Mon.	7	Anaheim
	Sun.	22	Winnipeg*		Thu.	10	Colorado
	Sun.	29	at Calgary*		Sat.	12	at Edmonton
	Mon.	30	Philadelphia		Sun.	13	Calgary*

* Denotes afternoon game.

Year-by-Year Record

		Home				Road				Overall									
Season	**GP**	**W**	**L**	**T**	**OL**	**W**	**L**	**T**	**OL**	**W**	**L**	**T**	**OL**	**GF**	**GA**	**Pts.**	**Div. Fin.**	**Conf. Fin.**	**Playoff Result**
2012-13	48	15	6	....	3	11	9	....	4	26	15	....	7	127	121	59	1st, NW	3rd, West	Lost Conf. Quarter-Final
2011-12	82	27	10	....	4	24	12	....	5	51	22	....	9	249	198	111	1st, NW	1st, West	Lost Conf. Quarter-Final
2010-11	82	27	9	....	5	27	10	....	4	54	19	....	9	262	185	117	1st, NW	1st, West	Lost Final
2009-10	82	30	8	....	3	19	20	....	2	49	28	....	5	272	222	103	1st, NW	3rd, West	Lost Conf. Semi-Final
2008-09	82	24	12	....	5	21	15	....	5	45	27	....	10	246	220	100	1st, NW	3rd, West	Lost Conf. Semi-Final
2007-08	82	21	15	....	5	18	18	....	5	39	33	....	10	213	215	88	5th, NW	11th, West	Out of Playoffs
2006-07	82	26	11	....	4	23	15	....	3	49	26	....	7	222	201	105	1st, NW	3rd, West	Lost Conf. Semi-Final
2005-06	82	25	10	....	6	17	22	....	2	42	32	....	8	256	255	92	4th, NW	9th, West	Out of Playoffs
2004-05	....	....	....	....	....	....	....	....	....	....	....	....	....	....	....	....			
2003-04	82	21	13	7	0	22	11	3	5	43	24	10	5	235	194	101	1st, NW	3rd, West	Lost Conf. Quarter-Final
2002-03	82	22	13	6	0	23	10	7	1	45	23	13	1	264	208	104	2nd, NW	4th, West	Lost Conf. Semi-Final
2001-02	82	23	11	5	2	19	19	2	1	42	30	7	3	254	211	94	2nd, NW	8th, West	Lost Conf. Quarter-Final
2000-01	82	21	12	5	3	15	16	6	4	36	28	11	7	239	238	90	3rd, NW	8th, West	Lost Conf. Quarter-Final
1999-2000	82	16	14	5	6	14	15	10	2	30	29	15	8	227	237	83	3rd, NW	10th, West	Out of Playoffs
1998-99	82	14	21	6	....	9	26	6	....	23	47	12	....	192	258	58	4th, NW	13th, West	Out of Playoffs
1997-98	82	15	22	4	....	10	21	10	....	25	43	14	....	224	273	64	7th, Pac.	13th, West	Out of Playoffs
1996-97	82	20	17	4	....	15	23	3	....	35	40	7	....	257	273	77	4th, Pac.	9th, West	Out of Playoffs
1995-96	82	15	19	7	....	17	16	8	....	32	35	15	....	278	278	79	3rd, Pac.	7th, West	Lost Conf. Quarter-Final
1994-95	48	10	8	6	....	8	10	6	....	18	18	12	....	153	148	48	2nd, Pac.	6th, West	Lost Conf. Semi-Final
1993-94	84	20	19	3	....	21	21	0	....	41	40	3	....	279	276	85	2nd, Pac.	7th, West	Lost Final
1992-93	84	27	11	4	....	19	18	5	....	46	29	9	....	346	278	101	1st, Smythe		Lost Div. Final
1991-92	80	23	10	7	....	19	16	5	....	42	26	12	....	285	250	96	1st, Smythe		Lost Div. Final
1990-91	80	18	17	5	....	10	26	4	....	28	43	9	....	243	315	65	4th, Smythe		Lost Div. Semi-Final
1989-90	80	13	16	11	....	12	25	3	....	25	41	14	....	245	306	64	5th, Smythe		Out of Playoffs
1988-89	80	19	15	6	....	14	24	2	....	33	39	8	....	251	253	74	4th, Smythe		Lost Div. Semi-Final
1987-88	80	15	20	5	....	10	26	4	....	25	46	9	....	272	320	59	5th, Smythe		Out of Playoffs
1986-87	80	17	19	4	....	12	24	4	....	29	43	8	....	282	314	66	5th, Smythe		Out of Playoffs
1985-86	80	17	18	5	....	6	26	8	....	23	44	13	....	282	333	59	4th, Smythe		Lost Div. Semi-Final
1984-85	80	15	21	4	....	10	25	5	....	25	46	9	....	284	401	59	5th, Smythe		Out of Playoffs
1983-84	80	20	16	4	....	12	23	5	....	32	39	9	....	306	328	73	3rd, Smythe		Lost Div. Semi-Final
1982-83	80	20	12	8	....	10	23	7	....	30	35	15	....	303	309	75	3rd, Smythe		Lost Div. Semi-Final
1981-82	80	20	8	12	....	10	25	5	....	30	33	17	....	290	286	77	2nd, Smythe		Lost Final
1980-81	80	17	12	11	....	11	20	9	....	28	32	20	....	289	301	76	3rd, Smythe		Lost Prelim. Round
1979-80	80	14	17	9	....	13	20	7	....	27	37	16	....	256	281	70	3rd, Smythe		Lost Prelim. Round
1978-79	80	15	18	7	....	10	24	6	....	25	42	13	....	217	291	63	2nd, Smythe		Lost Prelim. Round
1977-78	80	13	15	12	....	7	28	5	....	20	43	17	....	239	320	57	3rd, Smythe		Out of Playoffs
1976-77	80	13	21	6	....	12	21	7	....	25	42	13	....	235	294	63	4th, Smythe		Out of Playoffs
1975-76	80	22	11	7	....	11	21	8	....	33	32	15	....	271	272	81	2nd, Smythe		Lost Prelim. Round
1974-75	80	23	12	5	....	15	20	5	....	38	32	10	....	271	254	86	1st, Smythe		Lost Quarter-Final
1973-74	78	14	18	7	....	10	25	4	....	24	43	11	....	224	296	59	7th, East		Out of Playoffs
1972-73	78	17	18	4	....	5	29	5	....	22	47	9	....	233	339	53	7th, East		Out of Playoffs
1971-72	78	14	20	5	....	6	30	3	....	20	50	8	....	203	297	48	7th, East		Out of Playoffs
1970-71	78	17	18	4	....	7	28	4	....	24	46	8	....	229	296	56	6th, East		Out of Playoffs

PACIFIC DIVISION
44th NHL Season

Franchise date: May 22, 1970

2013-14 Player Personnel

FORWARDS	HT	WT	*Age	Place of Birth	S	2012-13 Club
BOOTH, David	6-0	212	28	Detroit, MI	L	Vancouver
BURROWS, Alexandre	6-1	195	32	Pincourt, Que.	L	Vancouver
HANSEN, Jannik	6-1	195	27	Herlev, Denmark	R	Tappara-Vancouver
HIGGINS, Chris	6-0	193	30	Smithtown, NY	L	Vancouver
KASSIAN, Zack	6-3	214	22	Windsor, Ont.	R	Chicago (AHL)-Vancouver
KESLER, Ryan	6-2	202	29	Livonia, MI	R	Vancouver
RICHARDSON, Brad	5-11	191	28	Belleville, Ont.	L	Los Angeles
SCHROEDER, Jordan	5-8	175	23	Prior Lake, MN	R	Chicago (AHL)-Vancouver
SEDIN, Daniel	6-1	187	33	Ornskoldsvik, Sweden	L	Vancouver
SEDIN, Henrik	6-2	188	33	Ornskoldsvik, Sweden	L	Vancouver
SESTITO, Tom	6-5	228	26	Rome, NY	L	Sheffield-Phi-Adi-Van
WEISE, Dale	6-2	210	25	Winnipeg, Man.	R	Tilburg-Vancouver
DEFENSEMEN						
ALBERTS, Andrew	6-5	206	32	Minneapolis, MN	L	Vancouver
BIEKSA, Kevin	6-1	206	32	Grimsby, Ont.	R	Vancouver
EDLER, Alexander	6-4	220	27	Ostersund, Sweden	L	Vancouver
GARRISON, Jason	6-2	218	28	White Rock, B.C.	L	Vancouver
HAMHUIS, Dan	6-1	202	30	Smithers, B.C.	L	Vancouver
TANEV, Chris	6-2	185	23	Toronto, Ont.	R	Chicago (AHL)-Vancouver
WEBER, Yannick	5-11	199	25	Morges, Switz.	R	Geneve-Montreal

GOALTENDERS	HT	WT	*Age	Place of Birth	C	2012-13 Club
LACK, Eddie	6-4	187	25	Norrtalje, Sweden	L	Chicago (AHL)
LUONGO, Roberto	6-3	217	34	Montreal, Que.	L	Vancouver

* – Age at start of 2013-14 season

John Tortorella
Head Coach
Born: Boston, MA, June 24, 1958.

Vancouver Canucks president and general manager Mike Gillis announced on June 25, 2013 that John Tortorella had been named head coach of the Vancouver Canucks. He is the 17th head coach in club history.

Tortorella is a Boston, Massachusetts native who arrived in Vancouver with 13 years of NHL head coaching experience between the New York Rangers and Tampa Bay Lightning. He led the Lightning to the Stanley Cup in 2003-04 and was recognized with the Jack Adams Award as NHL coach of the year that season. Tortorella is currently the NHL's all-time win leader among American-born coaches and ranks fifth among active coaches for most games coached entering the 2013-14 season. In addition to his NHL head coaching experience, Tortorella has also acted as an assistant coach with the New York Rangers (1999-00), Phoenix Coyotes (1997 to 1999) and the Buffalo Sabres (1989 to 1995). He had success at the AHL and ACHL level, winning the league championships with the Rochester Americans (AHL) in the 1995-96 season and the Virginia Lancers (ACHL) in the 1986-87 campaign.

On the international stage, Tortorella served as an assistant coach for the silver medal-winning Team USA at the 2010 Winter Olympic Games in Vancouver. He also served as Team USA's head coach at the 2008 World Championship and assistant coach at the 2005 World Championship.

Prior to taking the helm behind the bench, Tortorella played right wing as a member of Salem State College and the University of Maine. He continued his playing career in Sweden before returning to North America where he joined the Hampton Road Gulls, Erie Golden Blades and Virginia Lancers of the ACHL.

Coaching Record

			Regular Season				Playoffs			
Season	Team	League	GC	W	L	O/T	GC	W	L	T
1995-96	Rochester	AHL	80	37	34	9	19	15	4	....
1996-97	Rochester	AHL	80	40	30	10	10	6	4	....
99-2000	**NY Rangers**	**NHL**	**4**	**0**	**3**	**1**	....	....	....	....
2000-01	**Tampa Bay**	**NHL**	**43**	**12**	**27**	**4**	....	....	....	....
2001-02	**Tampa Bay**	**NHL**	**82**	**27**	**40**	**15**	....	....	....	....
2002-03	**Tampa Bay**	**NHL**	**82**	**36**	**25**	**21**	**11**	**5**	**6**	....
2003-04♦	**Tampa Bay**	**NHL**	**82**	**46**	**22**	**14**	**23**	**16**	**7**	....
2004-05	**Tampa Bay**				SEASON CANCELLED					
2005-06	**Tampa Bay**	**NHL**	**82**	**43**	**33**	**6**	**5**	**1**	**4**	....
2006-07	**Tampa Bay**	**NHL**	**82**	**44**	**33**	**5**	**6**	**2**	**4**	....
2007-08	**Tampa Bay**	**NHL**	**82**	**31**	**42**	**9**	....	....	....	....
2008-09	**NY Rangers**	**NHL**	**21**	**12**	**7**	**2**	**7**	**3**	**4**	....
2009-10	**NY Rangers**	**NHL**	**82**	**38**	**33**	**11**	....	....	....	....
2010-11	**NY Rangers**	**NHL**	**82**	**44**	**33**	**5**	**5**	**1**	**4**	....
2011-12	**NY Rangers**	**NHL**	**82**	**51**	**24**	**7**	**20**	**10**	**10**	....
2012-13	**NY Rangers**	**NHL**	**48**	**26**	**18**	**4**	**12**	**5**	**7**	....
	NHL Totals		**854**	**410**	**340**	**104**	**89**	**43**	**46**	....

♦ Stanley Cup win.
Jack Adams Award (2004)
Jim Schoenfeld posted an 0-1 playoff record as replacement coach when John Tortorella was suspended, April 26, 2009. Loss is credited to Tortorella's coaching record.

2012-13 Scoring

* – rookie

Regular Season

Pos	#	Player	Team	GP	G	A	Pts	TOI	+/–	PIM	PP	SH	GW	S	%
C	33	Henrik Sedin	VAN	48	11	34	45	19:20	19	24	1	1	1	70	15.7
L	22	Daniel Sedin	VAN	47	12	28	40	19:01	12	18	3	0	3	138	8.7
C	15	Derek Roy	DAL	30	4	18	22	18:58	3	4	1	0	1	65	6.2
			VAN	12	3	3	6	17:39	1	2	1	0	0	20	15.0
			Total	42	7	21	28	18:35	4	6	2	0	1	85	8.2
R	36	Jannik Hansen	VAN	47	10	17	27	17:33	12	8	1	0	2	99	10.1
L	14	Alexandre Burrows	VAN	47	13	11	24	18:54	15	54	1	0	2	140	9.3
D	2	Dan Hamhuis	VAN	47	4	20	24	23:23	9	12	0	1	0	61	6.6
L	21	Mason Raymond	VAN	46	10	12	22	15:49	2	16	4	0	1	79	12.7
D	23	Alexander Edler	VAN	45	8	14	22	23:50	–5	37	5	0	0	113	7.1
D	5	Jason Garrison	VAN	47	8	8	16	21:41	18	28	3	0	2	94	8.5
L	20	Chris Higgins	VAN	41	10	5	15	16:24	–4	10	0	0	1	77	13.0
C	17	Ryan Kesler	VAN	17	4	9	13	18:57	–5	12	2	0	1	36	11.1
D	3	Kevin Bieksa	VAN	36	6	6	12	21:56	6	48	2	0	1	77	7.8
R	9	Zack Kassian	VAN	39	7	4	11	13:28	–7	51	2	0	1	49	14.3
C	40	Maxim Lapierre	VAN	48	4	6	10	12:35	–6	45	0	0	1	54	7.4
C	45 *	Jordan Schroeder	VAN	31	3	6	9	13:42	0	4	1	0	2	28	10.7
D	8	Christopher Tanev	VAN	38	2	5	7	17:17	4	10	0	0	1	20	10.0
R	32	Dale Weise	VAN	40	3	3	6	9:33	–7	43	0	0	2	35	8.6
C	25	Andrew Ebbett	VAN	28	1	5	6	12:19	–1	4	0	0	0	23	4.3
L	29	Tom Sestito	PHI	7	2	0	2	5:46	1	12	0	0	1	3	66.7
			VAN	23	1	0	1	6:37	–3	53	0	0	0	11	9.1
			Total	30	3	0	3	6:25	–2	65	0	0	1	14	21.4
L	7	David Booth	VAN	12	1	2	3	12:45	–3	4	0	0	0	27	3.7
D	18	Cam Barker	VAN	14	0	2	2	14:11	–3	4	0	0	0	19	0.0
D	4	Keith Ballard	VAN	36	0	2	2	15:28	–2	29	0	0	0	35	0.0
D	41	Andrew Alberts	VAN	24	0	1	1	15:10	–7	32	0	0	0	15	0.0
L	42 *	Bill Sweatt	VAN	1	0	0	0	12:24	–1	0	0	0	0	0	0.0
D	38	Derek Joslin	VAN	2	0	0	0	16:59	–2	0	0	0	0	2	0.0
L	46 *	Nicklas Jensen	VAN	2	0	0	0	13:51	–1	0	0	0	0	0	0.0
D	26 *	Frank Corrado	VAN	3	0	0	0	19:24	–1	0	0	0	0	4	0.0
R	44	Andrew Gordon	VAN	6	0	0	0	8:25	–1	0	0	0	0	2	0.0
C	27	Manny Malhotra	VAN	9	0	0	0	11:07	–3	0	0	0	0	2	0.0
R	13	Steve Pinizzotto	VAN	12	0	0	0	9:59	–6	29	0	0	0	9	0.0

Goaltending

No.	Goaltender	GPI	Mins	Avg	W	L	OT	EN	SO	GA	SA	S%	G	A	PIM
35	Cory Schneider	30	1733	2.11	17	9	4	1	5	61	835	.927	0	1	0
1	Roberto Luongo	20	1197	2.56	9	6	3	2	2	51	551	.907	0	0	0
	Totals	**48**	**2944**	**2.34**	**26**	**15**	**7**	**3**	**7**	**115**	**1389**	**.917**			

Playoffs

Pos	#	Player	Team	GP	G	A	Pts	TOI	+/–	PIM	PP	SH	GW	OT	S	%
L	14	Alexandre Burrows	VAN	4	2	1	3	20:35	1	6	1	0	0	0	11	18.2
L	22	Daniel Sedin	VAN	4	0	3	3	20:42	–2	14	0	0	0	0	11	0.0
C	33	Henrik Sedin	VAN	4	0	3	3	20:44	0	4	0	0	0	0	5	0.0
C	17	Ryan Kesler	VAN	4	2	0	2	23:06	–2	0	1	0	0	0	13	15.4
D	2	Dan Hamhuis	VAN	4	1	1	2	25:13	0	8	0	0	0	0	7	14.3
L	21	Mason Raymond	VAN	4	1	1	2	16:49	2	0	0	0	0	0	9	11.1
D	3	Kevin Bieksa	VAN	4	1	0	1	25:50	–1	8	0	0	0	0	6	16.7
D	23	Alexander Edler	VAN	4	1	0	1	26:57	–1	2	0	0	0	0	12	8.3
C	15	Derek Roy	VAN	4	0	1	1	17:15	–1	2	0	0	0	0	7	0.0
L	29	Tom Sestito	VAN	1	0	0	0	5:51	0	2	0	0	0	0	0	0.0
R	13	Steve Pinizzotto	VAN	1	0	0	0	3:57	0	0	0	0	0	0	1	0.0
C	25	Andrew Ebbett	VAN	2	0	0	0	4:29	0	0	0	0	0	0	2	0.0
D	41	Andrew Alberts	VAN	4	0	0	0	13:04	–2	2	0	0	0	0	1	0.0
L	20	Chris Higgins	VAN	4	0	0	0	16:40	–2	0	0	0	0	0	5	0.0
C	40	Maxim Lapierre	VAN	4	0	0	0	9:30	1	6	0	0	0	0	4	0.0
R	36	Jannik Hansen	VAN	4	0	0	0	18:11	0	2	0	0	0	0	9	0.0
D	5	Jason Garrison	VAN	4	0	0	0	23:43	1	2	0	0	0	0	15	0.0
R	32	Dale Weise	VAN	4	0	0	0	5:37	–2	4	0	0	0	0	2	0.0
R	9	Zack Kassian	VAN	4	0	0	0	12:04	–1	4	0	0	0	0	4	0.0
D	26 *	Frank Corrado	VAN	4	0	0	0	12:18	–1	0	0	0	0	0	2	0.0

Goaltending

No.	Goaltender	GPI	Mins	Avg	W	L	EN	SO	GA	SA	S%	G	A	PIM
1	Roberto Luongo	3	140	2.57	0	2	0	0	6	71	.915	0	0	0
35	Cory Schneider	2	117	4.62	0	2	0	0	9	75	.880	0	0	0
	Totals	**4**	**259**	**3.47**	**0**	**4**	**0**	**0**	**15**	**146**	**.897**			

Coaching History

Hal Laycoe, 1970-71, 1971-72; Vic Stasiuk, 1972-73; Bill McCreary and Phil Maloney, 1973-74; Phil Maloney, 1974-75, 1975-76; Phil Maloney and Orland Kurtenbach, 1976-77; Orland Kurtenbach, 1977-78; Harry Neale, 1978-79 to 1980-81; Harry Neale and Roger Neilson, 1981-82; Roger Neilson, 1982-83; Roger Neilson and Harry Neale, 1983-84; Bill Laforge and Harry Neale, 1984-85; Tom Watt, 1985-86, 1986-87; Bob McCammon, 1987-88 to 1989-90; Bob McCammon and Pat Quinn, 1990-91; Pat Quinn, 1991-92 to 1993-94; Rick Ley, 1994-95; Rick Ley and Pat Quinn, 1995-96; Tom Renney, 1996-97; Tom Renney and Mike Keenan, 1997-98; Mike Keenan and Marc Crawford, 1998-99; Marc Crawford, 1999-2000 to 2005-06; Alain Vigneault, 2006-07 to 2012-13; John Tortorella, 2013-14.

Club Records

Team

(Figures in brackets for season records are games played; records for fewest points, wins, ties, losses, goals, goals against are for 70 or more games)

Most Points **117** 2010-11 (82)
Most Wins **54** 2010-11 (82)
Most Ties **20** 1980-81 (80)
Most Losses **50** 1971-72 (78)
Most Goals **346** 1992-93 (84)
Most Goals Against **401** 1984-85 (80)
Fewest Points **48** 1971-72 (78)
Fewest Wins **20** 1971-72 (78), 1977-78 (80)
Fewest Ties **3** 1993-94 (84)
Fewest Losses **19** 2010-11 (82)
Fewest Goals **192** 1998-99 (82)
Fewest Goals Against **185** 2010-11 (82)

Longest Winning Streak
Overall .... **10** Nov. 9-30/02
Home .... **11** Feb. 3-Mar. 19/09
Away .... **9** Mar. 5-29/11

Longest Undefeated Streak
Overall **14** Jan.26-Feb. 25/03 (10W, 4T/OL)
Home .... **18** Nov. 4/92-Jan. 16/93 (16W, 2T)
Away .... **9** Feb. 4-Mar. 3/03 (6W, 3T/OL), Mar. 5-29/11 (9W)

Longest Losing Streak
Overall .... **10** Oct. 23-Nov. 11/97
Home .... **6** Dec. 18/70-Jan. 20/71
Away .... **12** Nov. 28/81-Feb. 6/82

Longest Winless Streak
Overall .... **13** Nov. 9-Dec. 7/73 (10L, 3T)
Home .... **11** Dec. 18/70-Feb. 6/71 (10L, 1T)
Away .... **20** Jan. 2-Apr. 2/86 (14L, 6T)

Most Shutouts, Season **10** 2008-09 (82)
Most PIM, Season **2,326** 1992-93 (84)
Most Goals, Game .... **11** Mar. 28/71 (Cal. 5 at Van. 11), Nov. 25/86 (L.A. 5 at Van. 11), Mar. 1/92 (Cgy. 0 at Van. 11)

Individual

Most Seasons .... **16** Trevor Linden
Most Games .... **1,140** Trevor Linden
Most Goals, Career .... **346** Markus Naslund
Most Assists, Career .... **610** Henrik Sedin
Most Points, Career .... **792** Henrik Sedin (182G, 610A)
Most PIM, Career .... **2,127** Gino Odjick
Most Shutouts, Career .... **35** Roberto Luongo
Longest Consecutive Games Streak .... **534** Brendan Morrison (Mar. 16/00-Dec. 10/07)
Most Goals, Season .... **60** Pavel Bure (1992-93), (1993-94)
Most Assists, Season .... **83** Henrik Sedin (2009-10)
Most Points, Season .... **112** Henrik Sedin (2009-10; 29G, 83A)
Most PIM, Season .... **372** Donald Brashear (1997-98)
Most Points, Defenseman, Season .... **63** Doug Lidster (1986-87; 12G, 51A)
Most Points, Center, Season .... **112** Henrik Sedin (2009-10; 29G, 83A)
Most Points, Right Wing, Season .... **110** Pavel Bure (1992-93; 60G, 50A)
Most Points, Left Wing, Season .... **104** Markus Naslund (2002-03; 48G, 56A), Daniel Sedin (2010-11; 41G, 63A)
Most Points, Rookie, Season .... **60** Ivan Hlinka (1981-82; 23G, 37A), Pavel Bure (1991-92; 34G, 26A)
Most Shutouts, Season .... **9** Roberto Luongo (2008-09)
Most Goals, Game .... **4** Twelve times
Most Assists, Game .... **6** Patrik Sundstrom (Feb. 29/84)
Most Points, Game .... **7** Patrik Sundstrom (Feb. 29/84; 1G, 6A)

Retired Numbers

12	Stan Smyl	1978-1991
16	Trevor Linden	1988-1998; 2001-2008
19	Markus Naslund	1996-2008

All-time Record vs. Other Clubs

Regular Season

	Total								At Home								On Road							
	GP	W	L	T	OL	GF	GA	PTS	GP	W	L	T	OL	GF	GA	PTS	GP	W	L	T	OL	GF	GA	PTS
Anaheim	82	41	30	9	2	259	224	93	42	22	17	2	1	135	114	47	40	19	13	7	1	124	110	46
Boston	109	26	66	15	2	303	439	69	54	17	28	8	1	172	215	43	55	9	38	7	1	131	224	26
Buffalo	110	45	44	19	2	363	369	111	55	27	17	11	0	203	170	65	55	18	27	8	2	160	199	46
Calgary	250	94	118	33	5	797	856	226	126	54	50	18	4	434	395	130	124	40	68	15	1	363	461	96
Carolina	65	29	25	11	0	225	194	69	33	17	10	6	0	118	88	40	32	12	15	5	0	107	106	29
Chicago	174	72	75	22	5	470	548	171	88	46	27	15	0	261	246	107	86	26	48	7	5	209	302	64
Colorado	146	64	58	15	9	444	476	152	73	34	27	7	5	237	245	80	73	30	31	8	4	207	231	72
Columbus	47	30	9	2	6	163	116	68	23	17	3	0	3	85	58	37	24	13	6	2	3	78	58	31
Dallas	173	70	76	22	5	553	552	167	86	41	33	10	2	304	255	94	87	29	43	12	3	249	297	73
Detroit	162	60	78	18	6	517	581	144	81	36	32	10	3	284	258	85	81	24	46	8	3	233	323	59
Edmonton	216	87	101	19	9	712	811	202	108	49	43	12	4	382	381	114	108	38	58	7	5	330	430	88
Florida	23	11	5	6	1	70	53	29	12	6	1	5	0	36	26	17	11	5	4	1	1	34	27	12
Los Angeles	227	99	90	32	6	757	767	236	112	59	33	16	4	410	333	138	115	40	57	16	2	347	434	98
Minnesota	73	38	24	5	6	193	186	87	36	22	6	3	5	105	79	52	37	16	18	2	1	88	107	35
Montreal	118	29	76	13	0	311	469	71	60	17	35	8	0	166	214	42	58	12	41	5	0	145	255	29
Nashville	56	34	19	2	1	175	142	71	27	17	8	1	1	96	66	36	29	17	11	1	0	79	76	35
New Jersey	102	54	31	17	0	352	292	125	50	29	10	11	0	186	135	69	52	25	21	6	0	166	157	56
NY Islanders	100	38	47	13	2	306	341	91	50	25	22	3	0	164	161	53	50	13	25	10	2	142	180	38
NY Rangers	111	30	73	8	0	318	452	68	54	17	34	3	0	170	209	37	57	13	39	5	0	148	243	31
Ottawa	31	18	11	2	0	92	65	38	16	10	5	1	0	50	32	21	15	8	6	1	0	42	33	17
Philadelphia	111	29	67	13	2	325	459	73	54	11	30	12	1	154	216	35	57	18	37	1	1	171	243	38
Phoenix	172	87	60	20	5	604	527	199	88	53	24	10	1	316	236	117	84	34	36	10	4	288	291	82
Pittsburgh	106	36	57	11	2	369	428	85	53	24	23	4	2	190	195	54	53	12	34	7	0	179	233	31
St. Louis	174	66	88	18	2	494	583	152	88	39	39	9	1	255	271	88	86	27	49	9	1	239	312	64
San Jose	97	47	36	9	5	301	277	108	47	24	15	4	4	157	128	56	50	23	21	5	1	144	149	52
Tampa Bay	24	16	5	2	1	97	66	35	12	9	0	2	1	51	24	21	12	7	5	0	0	46	42	14
Toronto	134	60	50	22	2	465	456	144	69	34	22	11	2	246	225	81	65	26	28	11	0	219	231	63
Washington	85	37	37	9	2	277	272	85	42	21	15	5	1	149	131	48	43	16	22	4	1	128	141	37
Winnipeg	12	8	2	1	1	40	28	18	6	4	1	1	0	20	11	9	6	4	1	0	1	20	17	9
Defunct Clubs	38	24	11	3	0	153	116	51	19	14	3	2	0	82	48	30	19	10	8	1	0	71	68	21
Totals	**3328**	**1379**	**1469**	**391**	**89**	**10505**	**11145**	**3238**	**1664**	**795**	**613**	**210**	**46**	**5618**	**5165**	**1846**	**1664**	**584**	**856**	**181**	**43**	**4887**	**5980**	**1392**

Playoffs

	Series	W	L	GP	W	L	T	GF	GA	Last Mtg.	Rnd.	Result
Anaheim	1	0	1	5	1	4	0	8	14	2007	CSF	L 1-4
Boston	1	0	1	7	3	4	0	8	23	2011	F	L 3-4
Buffalo	2	0	2	7	1	6	0	14	28	1981	PRE	L 0-3
Calgary	6	2	4	32	15	17	0	96	101	2004	CQF	L 3-4
Chicago	5	2	3	28	12	16	0	77	92	2011	CQF	W 4-3
Colorado	2	0	2	10	2	8	0	26	40	2001	CQF	L 0-4
Dallas	2	2	0	12	8	4	0	31	23	2007	CQF	W 4-3
Detroit	1	0	1	6	2	4	0	16	22	2002	CQF	L 2-4
Edmonton	2	0	2	9	2	7	0	20	35	1992	DF	L 2-4
Los Angeles	5	2	3	28	13	15	0	93	96	2012	CQF	L 1-4
Minnesota	1	0	1	7	3	4	0	17	26	2003	CSF	L 3-4
Montreal	1	0	1	5	1	4	0	9	20	1975	QF	L 1-4
Nashville	1	1	0	6	4	2	0	14	11	2011	CSF	W 4-2
NY Islanders	2	0	2	6	0	6	0	14	26	1982	F	L 0-4
NY Rangers	1	0	1	7	3	4	0	19	21	1994	F	L 3-4
Philadelphia	1	0	1	3	1	2	0	9	15	1979	PRE	L 1-2
Phoenix	2	2	0	13	8	5	0	50	34	1993	DSF	W 4-2
St. Louis	3	3	0	18	12	6	0	55	53	2009	CQF	W 4-0
San Jose	2	1	1	9	4	5	0	28	28	2013	CQF	L 0-4
Toronto	1	1	0	5	4	1	0	16	9	1994	CF	W 4-1
Totals	**42**	**16**	**26**	**223**	**99**	**124**	**0**	**620**	**717**			

Playoff Results 2013-2009

Year	Round	Opponent	Result	GF	GA
2013	CQF	San Jose	L 0-4	8	15
2012	CQF	Los Angeles	L 1-4	8	12
2011	F	Boston	L 3-4	8	23
	CF	San Jose	W 4-1	20	13
	CSF	Nashville	W 4-2	14	11
	CQF	Chicago	W 4-3	16	22
2010	CSF	Chicago	L 2-4	18	23
	CQF	Los Angeles	W 4-2	25	18
2009	CSF	Chicago	L 2-4	19	23
	CQF	St. Louis	W 4-0	11	5

Abbreviations: Round: F – Final; **CF** – conference final; **CSF** – conference semi-final; **CQF** – conference quarter-final; **DF** – division final; **DSF** – division semi-final; **QF** – quarter-final; **PRE** – preliminary round.

2012-13 Results

Jan.	19	Anaheim	3-7		12	at Columbus	2-1†
	20	Edmonton	2-3†		14	Nashville	7-4
	23	Calgary	3-2†		16	Detroit	2-5
	25	at Anaheim	5-0		18	Minnesota	1-3
	27	at San Jose	1-4		19	St. Louis	3-2
	28	at Los Angeles	2-3†		21	at Phoenix	2-1
	30	Colorado	3-0		23	at Los Angeles	1-0
Feb.	1	Chicago	2-1†		24	at Colorado	3-2
	4	at Edmonton	3-2*		26	Columbus	1-0†
	7	at Minnesota	4-1		28	Colorado	4-1
	9	Calgary	5-1		30	at Edmonton	0-4
	12	Minnesota	2-1	**Apr.**	1	at San Jose	2-3
	15	Dallas	3-4		4	Edmonton	4-0
	17	St. Louis	3-4†		6	Calgary	5-2
	19	at Chicago	3-4†		8	Phoenix	2-0
	21	at Dallas	4-3		10	at Calgary	4-1
	22	at Nashville	1-0		13	at Colorado	3-4
	24	at Detroit	3-8		15	at Nashville	5-2
	26	Phoenix	2-4		16	at St. Louis	1-2†
Mar.	2	Los Angeles	5-2		18	at Dallas	1-5
	3	at Calgary	2-4		20	Detroit	2-1†
	5	San Jose	2-3†		22	Chicago	3-1
	7	at Columbus	1-2*		25	Anaheim	1-3
	10	at Minnesota	2-4		27	at Edmonton	2-7

* – Overtime † – Shootout

Calgary totals include Atlanta Flames, 1972-73 to 1979-80.
Colorado totals include Quebec, 1979-80 to 1994-95.
New Jersey totals include Kansas City, 1974-75, 1975-76, and Colorado Rockies, 1976-77 to 1981-82.
Phoenix totals include Winnipeg, 1979-80 to 1995-96.
Carolina totals include Hartford, 1979-80 to 1996-97.
Dallas totals include Minnesota North Stars, 1970-71 to 1992-93.
Winnipeg totals include Atlanta Thrashers, 1999-2000 to 2010-11.

Entry Draft Selections 2013-1999

Name in bold denotes played in NHL.

2013

Pick	
9	Bo Horvat
24	Hunter Shinkaruk
85	Cole Cassels
115	Jordan Subban
145	Anton Cederholm
175	Mike Williamson
205	Miles Liberati

2012

Pick	
26	Brendan Gaunce
57	Alexandre Mallet
147	Ben Hutton
177	Wesley Myron
207	Matthew Beattie

2011

Pick	
29	**Nicklas Jensen**
71	David Honzik
90	Alexandre Grenier
101	Joseph Labate
120	Ludwig Blomstrand
150	**Frank Corrado**
180	Pathrik Westerholm
210	Henrik Tommernes

2010

Pick	
115	Patrick McNally
145	Adam Polasek
172	Alex Friesen
175	Jonathan Iilahti
205	Sawyer Hannay

2009

Pick	
22	**Jordan Schroeder**
53	Anton Rodin
83	Kevin Connauton
113	Jeremy Price
143	Peter Andersson
173	Joe Cannata
187	Steven Anthony

2008

Pick	
10	**Cody Hodgson**
41	**Yann Sauve**
131	Prab Rai
161	Mats Froshaug
191	Morgan Clark

2007

Pick	
25	Patrick White
33	Taylor Ellington
145	Charles-Antoine Messier
146	Ilja Kablukov
176	Taylor Matson
206	Dan Gendur

2006

Pick	
14	**Michael Grabner**
82	Daniel Rahimi
163	**Sergei Shirokov**
167	Juraj Simek
197	Evan Fuller

2005

Pick	
10	**Luc Bourdon**
51	**Mason Raymond**
114	Alexandre Vincent
138	Matt Butcher
185	**Kris Fredheim**
205	**Mario Bliznak**

2004

Pick	
26	**Cory Schneider**
91	**Alexander Edler**
125	Andrew Sarauer
159	**Mike Brown**
189	Julien Ellis
254	David Schulz
287	**Jannik Hansen**

2003

Pick	
23	**Ryan Kesler**
60	Marc-Andre Bernier
111	**Brandon Nolan**
128	Ty Morris
160	Nicklas Danielsson
190	Chad Brownlee
222	Francois-Pierre Guenette
252	Sergei Topol
254	**Nathan McIver**
285	Matthew Hansen

2002

Pick	
49	Kirill Koltsov
55	Denis Grot
68	**Brett Skinner**
83	Lukas Mensator
114	John Laliberte
151	**Rob McVicar**
214	Marc-Andre Roy
223	Ilja Krikunov
247	Matt Violin
277	Thomas Nussli
278	Matt Gens

2001

Pick	
16	**R.J. Umberger**
66	**Fedor Fedorov**
114	Evgeny Gladskikh
151	**Kevin Bieksa**
212	**Jason King**
245	Konstantin Mikhailov

2000

Pick	
23	**Nathan Smith**
71	Thatcher Bell
93	Tim Branham
144	Pavel Duma
208	**Brandon Reid**
241	Nathan Barrett
272	Tim Smith

1999

Pick	
2	**Daniel Sedin**
3	**Henrik Sedin**
69	Rene Vydareny
129	Ryan Thorpe
172	Josh Reed
189	Kevin Swanson
218	Markus Kankaanpera
271	Darrell Hay

General Managers' History

Bud Poile, 1970-71, 1971-72; Bud Poile and Hal Laycoe, 1972-73; Hal Laycoe and Phil Maloney, 1973-74; Phil Maloney, 1974-75 to 1976-77; Jake Milford, 1977-78 to 1981-82; Harry Neale, 1982-83 to 1984-85; Jack Gordon, 1985-86, 1986-87; Pat Quinn, 1987-88 to 1996-97; Pat Quinn and Mike Keenan, 1997-98; Brian Burke, 1998-99 to 2003-04; David Nonis, 2004-05 to 2007-08; Mike Gillis, 2008-09 to date.

Mike Gillis

President and General Manager

Born: Sudbury, Ont., December 1, 1958.

The Vancouver Canucks announced on April 23, 2008, that Mike Gillis had been named the tenth general manager in club history. Gillis joined the Canucks organization after spending the previous 16 years as a player representative. In his first two seasons with the club, the Canucks won the Northwest Division title. In his third season of 2010-11, Gillis won the NHL's G.M of the Year Award after Vancouver set new club records with 54 wins and 117 points. The team won the Presidents' Trophy for the first time and reached the seventh game of the Stanley Cup Final. The Canucks won the Presidents' Trophy again in 2011-12.

Gillis began his NHL career in 1978 as a member of the Colorado Rockies. In 246 NHL regular season games, Gillis recorded 76 points (33 goals, 43 assists) and 186 penalty minutes with Colorado and Boston before a leg injury forced him to retire in 1985. He then returned to Kingston, Ontario, where he had grown up, to obtain his law degree from Queen's University in 1990. Gillis began his career as a NHL player representative in 1992 and became one of the most successful in his industry. His ability to evaluate players, negotiate contracts and his extensive knowledge of the Collective Bargaining Agreement, provided him the opportunity to work with a number of the NHL's most elite players.

Club Directory

Rogers Arena

Vancouver Canucks
Rogers Arena
800 Griffiths Way
Vancouver, B.C. V6B 6G1
Phone **604/899-4600**
FAX 604/899-4640
www.canucks.com
Capacity: 18,910

Executive Directory – Vancouver Canucks Limited Partnership	
Chairman, Canucks L.P. and Governor, NHL	Francesco Aquilini
Alternate Governors, NHL	Roberto Aquilini, Paolo Aquilini
Executive Office Manager	Cheryl Loveseth
President, G.M. and Alt. Governor, NHL	Michael D. Gillis
Executive Assistants	Joan Stobbs, Andrea Lobo
Chief Operating Officer and Alt. Governor, NHL	Victor de Bonis
Executive Vice President, Sales and Marketing	Trent Carroll
Vice President, Hockey Ops and Assistant G.M.	Laurence Gilman
Vice President, Player Personnel and Assistant G.M.	Lorne Henning
Vice President and G.M., Arena Operations	Michael Doyle
Vice President, Business and General Counsel	Chris Gear
Vice President, Finance and CFO	Todd Kobus
Vice President, Communications and Community Partnerships	TC Carling
Vice President, Marketing and Game Presentation	Ali Gardiner
Vice President, Construction	Harvey Jones
Hockey Operations	
President, G.M. and Alt. Governor, NHL	Michael D. Gillis
Executive Assistant	Joan Stobbs
Vice President, Player Personnel and Asst. G.M.	Lorne Henning
Vice President, Hockey Operations and Asst. G.M.	Laurence Gilman
Senior Advisor to the General Manager	Stan Smyl
Head Coach	John Tortorella
Assistant Coach	TBA
Assistant Coach	TBA
Assistant Coach, Video	Darryl Williams
Goaltending Coach	Roland Melanson
Strength & Conditioning Coach	Roger Takahashi
Skill Coach	Glenn Carnegie
Director, Human Performance	Dr. Mike Wilkinson
Director, Player Development	Dave Gagner
Director, Player Personnel	Eric Crawford
Director, Hockey Administration	Jonathan Wall
Head Coach, Utica Comets	Travis Green
Assistant Coaches, Utica Comets	Nolan Baumgartner, Mike Foligno
Vice President, Communications and Community Partnerships	TC Carling
Director, Media Relations and Team Operations	Ben Brown
Manager, Media Relations and Publications	Stephanie Maniago
Coordinator, Media Relations and Publications	Jen Rollins
Director, Community Partnerships	Alex Mitchell
Director of Charitable, Corporate and On-Ice Events	Karen Christiansen
Program Manager, Community Partnerships	Jessica Hoffman
Program Manager, Community Partnerships	Tara Clarke
Manager, Hockey Development and Alumni Liaison	Rod Brathwaite
Coordinator, Community Partnerships and Mascot Liaison	Paul Buckley
Scouting Staff	
Chief Amateur Scout	Ron Delorme
Associate Chief Scout	Thomas Gradin
Amateur Scouts	Brian Chapman, Sergei Chibisov, Tim Lenardon, Harold Snepsts, Darrell Young, Judd Brackett, Inge Hammarstrom, Richard Rose, Ken Cook, Edward Hampson, Dan Palango, Wyatt Smith
Director, Player Personnel	Eric Crawford
Professional Scouts	Lucien DeBlois, Lars Lindgren, Brett Henning, Neil Komadoski, Jonathan Bates
Director of Hockey Administration	Jonathan Wall
Scouting Coordinator	Mike Brown
Medical and Training Staff	
Head Athletic Trainer	Mike Burnstein
Assistant Athletic Trainers	Jon Sanderson, Dave Zarn
Equipment Manager	Pat O'Neill
Assistant Equipment Manager	Jamie Hendricks
Equipment Assistant	Brian Hamilton
Game Dressing Room Attendants	John Jukich, Ron Shute, Brian Brumwell, Ferdie De Guzman
Team Physician	Dr. Bill Regan
Team Dentist	Dr. Jeffrey Norden
Team Chiropractor	Dr. Glenn Cashman
Team Optometrist	Dr. Alan R. Boyco
Broadcast	
Director, Facilities & In-House Broadcast	Paul Brettell
Director, Game Presentation & Broadcast Operations	Mike Hall
Associate Producer	Josh Grunberg
Senior Broadcast Technician	Greg Story
Multimedia Senior Producer/Producer	Jason Steensma/Gayla Anderson
Production Assistant & Editor	Rory McGarry
Reporter	Joey Kenward

Captains' History

Orland Kurtenbach, 1970-71 to 1973-74; no captain, 1974-75; Andre Boudrias, 1975-76; Chris Oddleifson, 1976-77; Don Lever, 1977-78; Don Lever and Kevin McCarthy, 1978-79; Kevin McCarthy, 1979-80 to 1981-82; Stan Smyl, 1982-83 to 1989-90; Dan Quinn, Doug Lidster and Trevor Linden, 1990-91; Trevor Linden, 1991-92 to 1996-97; Mark Messier, 1997-98 to 1999-2000; Markus Naslund, 2000-01 to 2007-08; Roberto Luongo, 2008-09, 2009-10; Henrik Sedin, 2010-11 to date.

Key Off-Season Signings/Acquisitions

2013

July 2 • Re-signed D **Tomas Kundratek**.
8 • Signed D **Tyson Strachan**.
10 • Re-signed D **Karl Alzner**.

Washington Capitals

2012-13 Results: 27W-18L-3OTL-0SOL 57PTS
1ST, Southeast Division • 3RD, Eastern Conference

After a slow start to the 2012-13 season, coach Adam Oates moved Alex Ovechkin from left wing to right wing. Ovechkin responded with 23 goals over his final 23 games to lead the Capitals to a division title, lead the NHL with 32 goals, and win the Hart Trophy as most valuable player.

2013-14 Schedule

Oct.	Tue.	1	at Chicago
	Thu.	3	Calgary
	Sat.	5	at Dallas
	Thu.	10	Carolina
	Sat.	12	Colorado
	Mon.	14	Edmonton
	Wed.	16	NY Rangers
	Sat.	19	Columbus
	Tue.	22	at Winnipeg
	Thu.	24	at Edmonton
	Sat.	26	at Calgary
	Mon.	28	at Vancouver
Nov.	Fri.	1	at Philadelphia
	Sat.	2	Florida
	Tue.	5	NY Islanders
	Thu.	7	Minnesota
	Sat.	9	at Phoenix
	Sun.	10	at Colorado
	Tue.	12	Columbus
	Fri.	15	at Detroit
	Sun.	17	St. Louis
	Wed.	20	Pittsburgh
	Fri.	22	Montreal
	Sat.	23	at Toronto
	Wed.	27	Ottawa
	Fri.	29	Montreal*
	Sat.	30	at NY Islanders
Dec.	Tue.	3	Carolina
	Sat.	7	Nashville
	Sun.	8	at NY Rangers
	Tue.	10	Tampa Bay
	Fri.	13	at Florida
	Sun.	15	Philadelphia*
	Tue.	17	at Philadelphia
	Fri.	20	at Carolina
	Sat.	21	New Jersey
	Mon.	23	Anaheim
	Fri.	27	NY Rangers
	Sun.	29	at Buffalo*
	Mon.	30	at Ottawa
Jan.	Thu.	2	Carolina
	Sat.	4	at Minnesota
	Thu.	9	at Tampa Bay
	Fri.	10	Toronto
	Sun.	12	Buffalo*
	Tue.	14	San Jose
	Wed.	15	at Pittsburgh
	Fri.	17	at Columbus
	Sun.	19	at NY Rangers
	Tue.	21	Ottawa
	Fri.	24	at New Jersey
	Sat.	25	at Montreal
	Tue.	28	at Buffalo
	Thu.	30	at Columbus
	Fri.	31	at Detroit
Feb.	Sun.	2	Detroit*
	Tue.	4	NY Islanders
	Thu.	6	Winnipeg
	Sat.	8	New Jersey
	Thu.	27	at Florida
Mar.	Sat.	1	at Boston*
	Sun.	2	Philadelphia*
	Wed.	5	at Philadelphia
	Thu.	6	at Boston
	Sat.	8	Phoenix
	Mon.	10	Pittsburgh
	Tue.	11	at Pittsburgh
	Fri.	14	Vancouver
	Sun.	16	Toronto*
	Tue.	18	at Anaheim
	Thu.	20	at Los Angeles
	Sat.	22	at San Jose
	Tue.	25	Los Angeles
	Sat.	29	Boston*
	Sun.	30	at Nashville
Apr.	Tue.	1	Dallas
	Fri.	4	at New Jersey
	Sat.	5	at NY Islanders*
	Tue.	8	at St. Louis
	Thu.	10	at Carolina
	Fri.	11	Chicago
	Sun.	13	Tampa Bay*

* Denotes afternoon game.

Year-by-Year Record

		Home				Road				Overall									
Season	**GP**	**W**	**L**	**T**	**OL**	**W**	**L**	**T**	**OL**	**W**	**L**	**T**	**OL**	**GF**	**GA**	**Pts.**	**Div. Fin.**	**Conf. Fin.**	**Playoff Result**
2012-13	48	15	8	....	1	12	10	....	2	27	18	....	3	149	130	57	1st, SE	3rd, East	Lost Conf. Quarter-Final
2011-12	82	26	11	....	4	16	21	....	4	42	32	....	8	222	230	92	2nd, SE	7th, East	Lost Conf. Semi-Final
2010-11	82	25	8	....	8	23	15	....	3	48	23	....	11	224	197	107	1st, SE	1st, East	Lost Conf. Semi-Final
2009-10	82	30	5	....	6	24	10	....	7	54	15	....	13	318	233	121	1st, SE	1st, East	Lost Conf. Quarter-Final
2008-09	82	29	9	....	3	21	15	....	5	50	24	....	8	272	245	108	1st, SE	2nd, East	Lost Conf. Semi-Final
2007-08	82	23	15	....	3	20	16	....	5	43	31	....	8	242	231	94	1st, SE	3rd, East	Lost Conf. Quarter-Final
2006-07	82	17	17	....	7	11	23	....	7	28	40	....	14	235	286	70	5th, SE	14th, East	Out of Playoffs
2005-06	82	16	18	....	7	13	23	....	5	29	41	....	12	237	306	70	5th, SE	14th, East	Out of Playoffs
2004-05	....	....	....	....	....	....	....	....	....	....	....	....	....	....	....	....			
2003-04	82	13	20	6	2	10	26	4	1	23	46	10	3	186	253	59	5th, SE	14th, East	Out of Playoffs
2002-03	82	24	13	2	2	15	16	6	4	39	29	8	6	224	220	92	2nd, SE	6th, East	Lost Conf. Quarter-Final
2001-02	82	21	12	6	2	15	21	5	0	36	33	11	2	228	240	85	2nd, SE	9th, East	Out of Playoffs
2000-01	82	24	9	6	2	17	18	4	2	41	27	10	4	233	211	96	1st, SE	3rd, East	Lost Conf. Quarter-Final
1999-2000	82	26	5	8	2	18	19	4	0	44	24	12	2	227	194	102	1st, SE	2nd, East	Lost Conf. Quarter-Final
1998-99	82	16	23	2	....	15	22	4	....	31	45	6	....	200	218	68	3rd, SE	12th, East	Out of Playoffs
1997-98	82	23	12	6	....	17	18	6	....	40	30	12	....	219	202	92	3rd, Atl.	4th, East	Lost Final
1996-97	82	19	17	5	....	14	23	4	....	33	40	9	....	214	231	75	5th, Atl.	9th, East	Out of Playoffs
1995-96	82	21	15	5	....	18	17	6	....	39	32	11	....	234	204	89	4th, Atl.	7th, East	Lost Conf. Quarter-Final
1994-95	48	15	6	3	....	7	12	5	....	22	18	8	....	136	120	52	3rd, Atl.	6th, East	Lost Conf. Quarter-Final
1993-94	84	17	16	9	....	22	19	1	....	39	35	10	....	277	263	88	3rd, Atl.	7th, East	Lost Conf. Semi-Final
1992-93	84	21	15	6	....	22	19	1	....	43	34	7	....	325	286	93	2nd, Patrick		Lost Div. Semi-Final
1991-92	80	25	12	3	....	20	15	5	....	45	27	8	....	330	275	98	2nd, Patrick		Lost Div. Semi-Final
1990-91	80	21	14	5	....	16	22	2	....	37	36	7	....	258	258	81	3rd, Patrick		Lost Div. Final
1989-90	80	19	18	3	....	17	20	3	....	36	38	6	....	284	275	78	3rd, Patrick		Lost Conf. Final
1988-89	80	25	12	3	....	16	17	7	....	41	29	10	....	305	259	92	1st, Patrick		Lost Div. Semi-Final
1987-88	80	22	14	4	....	16	19	5	....	38	33	9	....	281	249	85	2nd, Patrick		Lost Div. Final
1986-87	80	22	15	3	....	16	17	7	....	38	32	10	....	285	278	86	2nd, Patrick		Lost Div. Semi-Final
1985-86	80	30	8	2	....	20	15	5	....	50	23	7	....	315	272	107	2nd, Patrick		Lost Div. Final
1984-85	80	27	11	2	....	19	14	7	....	46	25	9	....	322	240	101	2nd, Patrick		Lost Div. Semi-Final
1983-84	80	26	11	3	....	22	16	2	....	48	27	5	....	308	226	101	2nd, Patrick		Lost Div. Final
1982-83	80	22	12	6	....	17	13	10	....	39	25	16	....	306	283	94	3rd, Patrick		Lost Div. Semi-Final
1981-82	80	16	16	8	....	10	25	5	....	26	41	13	....	319	338	65	5th, Patrick		Out of Playoffs
1980-81	80	16	17	7	....	10	19	11	....	26	36	18	....	286	317	70	5th, Patrick		Out of Playoffs
1979-80	80	20	14	6	....	7	26	7	....	27	40	13	....	261	293	67	5th, Patrick		Out of Playoffs
1978-79	80	15	19	6	....	9	22	9	....	24	41	15	....	273	338	63	4th, Norris		Out of Playoffs
1977-78	80	10	23	7	....	7	26	7	....	17	49	14	....	195	321	48	5th, Norris		Out of Playoffs
1976-77	80	17	15	8	....	7	27	6	....	24	42	14	....	221	307	62	4th, Norris		Out of Playoffs
1975-76	80	6	26	8	....	5	33	2	....	11	59	10	....	224	394	32	5th, Norris		Out of Playoffs
1974-75	80	7	28	5	....	1	39	0	....	8	67	5	....	181	446	21	5th, Norris		Out of Playoffs

METROPOLITAN DIVISION
40th NHL Season

Franchise date: June 11, 1974

2013-14 Player Personnel

FORWARDS	HT	WT	*Age	Place of Birth	S	2012-13 Club
BACKSTROM, Nicklas	6-1	213	25	Gavle, Sweden	L	Dynamo Moscow-Washington
BEAGLE, Jay	6-3	215	27	Calgary, Alta.	R	Washington
BROUWER, Troy	6-3	213	28	Vancouver, B.C.	R	Washington
CHIMERA, Jason	6-3	213	34	Edmonton, Alta.	L	Chomutov-Washington
ERAT, Martin	6-0	200	32	Trebic, Czech.	L	Nashville-Washington
FEHR, Eric	6-4	212	28	Winkler, Man.	R	HPK-Washington
JOHANSSON, Marcus	6-1	205	22	Landskrona, Sweden	L	Bofors-Washington
LAICH, Brooks	6-2	210	30	Wawota, Sask.	L	Kloten-Washington
LATTA, Michael	6-0	209	22	Kitchener, Ont.	R	Milwaukee-Hershey
MITCHELL, Garrett	5-10	180	22	Regina, Sask.	R	Hershey
OVECHKIN, Alex	6-3	230	28	Moscow, USSR	R	Washington
PERREAULT, Mathieu	5-10	185	25	Drummondville, Que.	L	HIFK-Washington
STOA, Ryan	6-3	200	26	Bloomington, MN	L	Hershey
VOLPATTI, Aaron	6-0	225	28	Revelstoke, B.C.	L	Vancouver-Washington
WARD, Joel	6-1	226	32	Toronto, Ont.	R	Washington
WELLMAN, Casey	6-0	173	25	Brentwood, CA	R	San Antonio-Hershey
WILSON, Tom	6-4	205	19	Toronto, Ont.	R	Plymouth-Her-Wsh
DEFENSEMEN						
ALZNER, Karl	6-3	213	25	Burnaby, B.C.	L	Washington
CARLSON, John	6-3	212	23	Natick, MA	R	Washington
ERSKINE, John	6-4	220	33	Kingston, Ont.	L	Washington
GREEN, Mike	6-1	207	27	Calgary, Alta.	R	Washington
HILLEN, Jack	5-10	190	27	Minnetonka, MN	L	Washington
KUNDRATEK, Tomas	6-2	195	23	Prerov, Czech.	R	Hershey-Washington
OLEKSY, Steven	6-0	190	27	Chesterfield, MI	R	Hershey-Washington
ORLOV, Dmitry	6-0	210	22	Novokuznetsk, USSR	L	Hershey-Washington
SCHILLING, Cameron	6-2	197	24	Carmel, IN	L	Hershey-Washington
SCHMIDT, Nate	6-0	194	22	St. Cloud, MN	L	U. of Minnesota-Hershey
STRACHAN, Tyson	6-3	215	28	Melfort, Sask.	R	San Antonio-Florida

GOALTENDERS	HT	WT	*Age	Place of Birth	C	2012-13 Club
GRUBAUER, Philipp	6-1	186	21	Rosenheim, Germany	L	Reading-Hershey-Washington
HOLTBY, Braden	6-2	203	24	Lloydminster, Sask.	L	Hershey-Washington
LEGGIO, David	6-0	180	29	Buffalo, NY	L	Rochester
NEUVIRTH, Michal	6-1	209	25	Usti nad Labem, Czech.	L	Sparta-Washington

* – Age at start of 2013-14 season

Adam Oates

Head Coach

Born: Weston, Ont., August 27, 1962.

The Washington Capitals named Adam Oates the team's head coach on June 26, 2012 and he guided the team to a division title in 2012-13. Oates became the 16th head coach in Washington Capitals history with his first head coaching job after three seasons as an assistant coach. Oates was an assistant coach for the Tampa Bay Lightning during the 2009-10 season before moving to New Jersey in 2010-11. He was behind the bench as an assistant for the Devils during the team's 2012 run to the Stanley Cup final.

Elected to the Hockey Hall of Fame in 2012, Oates played 19 seasons in the NHL from 1985 to 2004. He appeared in 1,337 games and collected 1,420 points (341 goals, 1,079 assists) with Detroit, St. Louis, Boston, Washington, Philadelphia, Anaheim and Edmonton. Only Wayne Gretzky, Bobby Orr and Mario Lemieux averaged more assists per game than Oates in NHL history. During the 1990s only Gretzky (662) recorded more assists than Oates (636). The Weston, Ontario, native ranks sixth all-time in assists and 16th all-time in points in NHL history. The former center led or was tied for the league lead in assists three times in his career (1992-93, 2000-01 and 2001-02) and ranked in the top-10 in assists in 12 of his 19 seasons. Oates was named an NHL All-Star five times (1991 to 1994 and 1997) and was a six-time Lady Bing finalist during his career (runner-up in four straight seasons).

Oates was originally signed as an undrafted free agent by the Detroit Red Wings on June 28, 1985, after spending four seasons with RPI of the NCAA. He played in 387 games for the Capitals from 1996 to 2002, compiling 363 points (73 goals, 290 assists) to rank 18th in scoring and 10th in assists among all players in the Capitals history. Wearing number 77 for the Capitals, Oates was an alternate captain during the 1997-98 season when the team advanced to the Stanley Cup final. He served as the team's captain from 1999 to 2001.

Coaching Record

			Regular Season				Playoffs			
Season	Team	League	GC	W	L	O/T	GC	W	L	T
2012-13	Washington	NHL	48	27	18	3	7	3	4	....
	NHL Totals		48	27	18	3	7	3	4	....

2012-13 Scoring

* – rookie

Regular Season

Pos	#	Player	Team	GP	G	A	Pts	TOI	+/–	PIM	PP	SH	GW	S	%
R	8	Alex Ovechkin	WSH	48	32	24	56	20:53	2	36	16	0	4	220	14.5
C	9	Mike Ribeiro	WSH	48	13	36	49	17:50	–4	53	6	0	1	63	20.6
C	19	Nicklas Backstrom	WSH	48	8	40	48	19:54	8	20	3	0	1	82	9.8
R	20	Troy Brouwer	WSH	47	19	14	33	18:32	–5	28	7	1	5	111	17.1
D	52	Mike Green	WSH	35	12	14	26	24:51	–3	20	4	0	2	96	12.5
R	10	Martin Erat	NSH	36	4	17	21	18:55	–7	26	1	0	1	60	6.7
			WSH	9	1	2	3	13:54	0	4	0	0	1	9	11.1
			Total	45	5	19	24	17:55	–7	30	1	0	2	69	7.2
C	90	Marcus Johansson	WSH	34	6	16	22	16:35	3	4	3	0	1	40	15.0
D	74	John Carlson	WSH	48	6	16	22	23:01	11	18	0	0	0	97	6.2
R	42	Joel Ward	WSH	39	8	12	20	15:07	7	12	1	1	1	52	15.4
R	16	Eric Fehr	WSH	41	9	8	17	13:22	14	10	2	1	2	72	12.5
C	85	Mathieu Perreault	WSH	39	6	11	17	11:40	7	20	2	0	1	47	12.8
L	25	Jason Chimera	WSH	47	3	11	14	12:40	–5	48	0	0	0	92	3.3
L	17	Wojtek Wolski	WSH	27	4	5	9	13:21	1	6	0	0	2	49	8.2
D	38	Jack Hillen	WSH	23	3	6	9	17:36	9	14	0	0	1	28	10.7
D	61	Steve Oleksy	WSH	28	1	8	9	17:16	9	33	0	0	0	25	4.0
C	26	Matt Hendricks	WSH	48	5	3	8	11:43	–6	73	0	0	1	54	9.3
C	83	Jay Beagle	WSH	48	2	6	8	12:06	–1	14	0	0	1	56	3.6
D	36	* Tomas Kundratek	WSH	25	1	6	7	16:08	–5	8	0	0	0	23	4.3
D	4	John Erskine	WSH	30	3	3	6	18:27	10	34	0	0	0	32	9.4
D	27	Karl Alzner	WSH	48	1	4	5	20:57	–6	14	0	0	0	39	2.6
C	21	Brooks Laich	WSH	9	1	3	4	16:32	2	6	0	0	0	10	10.0
D	55	Jeff Schultz	WSH	26	0	3	3	14:15	–6	12	0	0	0	12	0.0
R	15	Joey Crabb	WSH	26	2	0	2	9:25	–1	8	0	0	0	20	10.0
L	24	Aaron Volpatti	VAN	16	1	0	1	7:18	0	28	0	0	0	11	9.1
			WSH	17	0	1	1	9:18	–2	7	0	0	0	10	0.0
			Total	33	1	1	2	8:20	–2	35	0	0	0	21	4.8
D	3	Tom Poti	WSH	16	0	2	2	15:13	–2	2	0	0	0	8	0.0
D	81	Dmitry Orlov	WSH	5	0	1	1	14:56	5	0	0	0	0	1	0.0
D	45	* Cameron Schilling	WSH	1	0	0	0	11:58	–1	0	0	0	0	0	0.0

Goaltending

No.	Goaltender	GPI	Mins	Avg	W	L	OT	EN	SO	GA	SA	S%	G	A	PIM
70	Braden Holtby	36	2089	2.58	23	12	1	2	4	90	1123	.920	0	2	2
30	Michal Neuvirth	13	723	2.74	4	5	2	0	0	33	367	.910	0	0	0
31	* Philipp Grubauer	2	84	3.57	0	1	0	0	0	5	59	.915	0	0	0
	Totals	**48**	**2910**	**2.68**	**27**	**18**	**3**	**2**	**4**	**130**	**1551**	**.916**			

Playoffs

Pos	#	Player	Team	GP	G	A	Pts	TOI	+/–	PIM	PP	SH	GW	OT	S	%
D	52	Mike Green	WSH	7	2	2	4	25:31	0	4	1	0	1	1	19	10.5
R	42	Joel Ward	WSH	7	1	3	4	13:11	–1	6	1	0	0	0	8	12.5
C	85	Mathieu Perreault	WSH	7	1	3	4	13:37	3	0	0	0	0	0	10	10.0
L	25	Jason Chimera	WSH	7	1	2	3	13:39	1	4	0	0	0	0	15	6.7
C	19	Nicklas Backstrom	WSH	7	1	2	3	19:46	–2	0	0	0	0	0	14	7.1
C	9	Mike Ribeiro	WSH	7	1	1	2	18:32	–2	10	0	0	1	1	13	7.7
R	8	Alex Ovechkin	WSH	7	1	1	2	20:44	–2	4	1	0	0	0	30	3.3
R	20	Troy Brouwer	WSH	7	1	1	2	19:33	0	10	0	0	0	0	13	7.7
D	27	Karl Alzner	WSH	7	1	1	2	22:18	3	2	0	0	0	0	19	5.3
C	90	Marcus Johansson	WSH	7	1	1	2	16:59	–3	0	0	0	1	0	13	7.7
C	83	Jay Beagle	WSH	7	1	0	1	9:38	–5	4	0	0	0	0	8	12.5
D	4	John Erskine	WSH	7	0	1	1	19:27	–4	4	0	0	0	0	6	0.0
D	38	Jack Hillen	WSH	7	0	1	1	16:37	–4	6	0	0	0	0	7	0.0
D	74	John Carlson	WSH	7	0	1	1	22:28	–4	4	0	0	0	0	21	0.0
D	61	Steve Oleksy	WSH	7	0	1	1	15:09	–1	4	0	0	0	0	7	0.0
R	43	* Tom Wilson	WSH	3	0	0	0	6:52	–1	0	0	0	0	0	4	0.0
R	10	Martin Erat	WSH	4	0	0	0	14:31	1	4	0	0	0	0	3	0.0
C	26	Matt Hendricks	WSH	7	0	0	0	10:31	–2	0	0	0	0	0	3	0.0
R	16	Eric Fehr	WSH	7	0	0	0	15:52	–2	6	0	0	0	0	13	0.0

Goaltending

No.	Goaltender	GPI	Mins	Avg	W	L	EN	SO	GA	SA	S%	G	A	PIM
70	Braden Holtby	7	433	2.22	3	4	0	1	16	205	.922	0	0	2
	Totals	**7**	**437**	**2.20**	**3**	**4**	**0**	**1**	**16**	**205**	**.922**			

Captains' History

Doug Mohns, 1974-75; Bill Clement and Yvon Labre, 1975-76; Yvon Labre, 1976-77, 1977-78; Guy Charron, 1978-79; Ryan Walter, 1979-80 to 1981-82; Rod Langway, 1982-83 to 1991-92; Rod Langway and Kevin Hatcher, 1992-93; Kevin Hatcher, 1993-94; Dale Hunter, 1994-95 to 1998-99; Adam Oates, 1999-2000, 2000-01; Brendan Witt and Steve Konowalchuk, 2001-02; Steve Konowalchuk, 2002-03; Steve Konowalchuk and no captain, 2003-04; Jeff Halpern, 2005-06; Chris Clark, 2006-07 to 2008-09; Chris Clark and Alex Ovechkin, 2009-10; Alex Ovechkin, 2010-11 to date.

Coaching History

Jim Anderson, Red Sullivan and Milt Schmidt, 1974-75; Milt Schmidt and Tom McVie, 1975-76; Tom McVie, 1976-77, 1977-78; Danny Belisle, 1978-79; Danny Belisle and Gary Green, 1979-80; Gary Green, 1980-81; Gary Green, Roger Crozier and Bryan Murray, 1981-82; Bryan Murray, 1982-83 to 1988-89; Bryan Murray and Terry Murray, 1989-90; Terry Murray, 1990-91 to 1992-93; Terry Murray and Jim Schoenfeld, 1993-94; Jim Schoenfeld, 1994-95 to 1996-97; Ron Wilson, 1997-98 to 2001-02; Bruce Cassidy, 2002-03; Bruce Cassidy and Glen Hanlon, 2003-04; Glen Hanlon, 2004-05 to 2006-07; Glen Hanlon and Bruce Boudreau, 2007-08; Bruce Boudreau, 2008-09 to 2010-11; Bruce Boudreau and Dale Hunter, 2011-12; Adam Oates, 2012-13 to date.

Club Records

Team

(Figures in brackets for season records are games played; records for fewest points, wins, ties, losses, goals, goals against are for 70 or more games)

Most Points	**121**	2009-10 (82)
Most Wins	**54**	2009-10 (82)
Most Ties	**18**	1980-81 (80)
Most Losses	**67**	1974-75 (80)
Most Goals	**330**	1991-92 (80)
Most Goals Against	***446**	1974-75 (80)
Fewest Points	***21**	1974-75 (80)
Fewest Wins	***8**	1974-75 (80)
Fewest Ties	**5**	1974-75 (80), 1983-84 (80)
Fewest Losses	**15**	2009-10 (82)
Fewest Goals	**181**	1974-75 (80)
Fewest Goals Against	**194**	1999-00 (82)
Longest Winning Streak		
Overall	**14**	Jan. 13-Feb. 7/10
Home	**13**	Jan. 5-Mar. 6/10
Away	**6**	Feb. 26-Apr. 1/84, Feb. 20-Mar. 15/11
Longest Undefeated Streak		
Overall	**14**	Nov. 24-Dec. 23/82 (9W, 5T), Jan. 17-Feb. 18/84 (13W, 1T), Jan. 13-Feb. 7/10 (14W)
Home	**13**	Nov. 25/92-Jan. 31/93 (9W, 4T), Dec. 27/99-Feb. 23/00 (11W, 2T/OL), Jan. 5-Mar. 6/10 (13W)
Away	**10**	Nov. 24/82-Jan. 8/83 (6W, 4T)
Longest Losing Streak		
Overall	***17**	Feb. 18-Mar. 26/75
Home	**11**	Feb. 18-Mar. 30/75
Away	**37**	Oct. 9/74-Mar. 26/75
Longest Winless Streak		
Overall	**25**	Nov. 29/75-Jan. 21/76 (22L, 3T)
Home	**14**	Dec. 3/75-Jan. 21/76 (11L, 3T)
Away	**37**	Oct. 9/74-Mar. 26/75 (37L)
Most Shutouts, Season	**9**	1995-96 (82)
Most PIM, Season	**2,204**	1989-90 (80)
Most Goals, Game	**12**	Feb. 6/90 (Que. 2 at Wsh. 12), Jan. 11/03 (Fla. 2 at Wsh. 12)

Individual

Most Seasons	**16**	Olie Kolzig
Most Games	**983**	Calle Johansson
Most Goals, Career	**472**	Peter Bondra
Most Assists, Career	**418**	Michal Pivonka
Most Points, Career	**825**	Peter Bondra (472G, 353A)
Most PIM, Career	**2,003**	Dale Hunter
Most Shutouts, Career	**35**	Olie Kolzig
Longest Consecutive Games Streak	**422**	Bob Carpenter (Oct. 7/81-Nov. 22/86)
Most Goals, Season	**65**	Alex Ovechkin (2007-08)
Most Assists, Season	**76**	Dennis Maruk (1981-82)
Most Points, Season	**136**	Dennis Maruk (1981-82; 60G, 76A)
Most PIM, Season	**339**	Alan May (1989-90)
Most Points, Defenseman, Season	**81**	Larry Murphy (1986-87; 23G, 58A)
Most Points, Center, Season	**136**	Dennis Maruk (1981-82; 60G, 76A)
Most Points, Right Wing, Season	**102**	Mike Gartner (1984-85; 50G, 52A)
Most Points, Left Wing, Season	**112**	Alex Ovechkin (2007-08; 65G, 47A)
Most Points, Rookie, Season	**106**	Alex Ovechkin (2005-06; 52G, 54A)
Most Shutouts, Season	**9**	Jim Carey (1995-96)
Most Goals, Game	**5**	Bengt Gustafsson (Jan. 8/84), Peter Bondra (Feb. 5/94)
Most Assists, Game	**6**	Mike Ridley (Jan. 7/89)
Most Points, Game	**7**	Dino Ciccarelli (Mar. 18/89; 4G, 3A), Jaromir Jagr (Jan. 11/03; 3G, 4A)

* NHL Record.

Retired Numbers

5	Rod Langway	1982-1993
7	Yvon Labre	1974-1981
11	Mike Gartner	1979-1989
32	Dale Hunter	1987-1999

All-time Record vs. Other Clubs

Regular Season

	Total								At Home								On Road							
	GP	W	L	T	OL	GF	GA	PTS	GP	W	L	T	OL	GF	GA	PTS	GP	W	L	T	OL	GF	GA	PTS
Anaheim	25	11	12	1	1	66	76	24	13	6	6	0	1	28	35	13	12	5	6	1	0	38	41	11
Boston	142	47	66	21	8	392	481	123	71	26	29	12	4	206	233	68	71	21	37	9	4	186	248	55
Buffalo	143	45	80	15	3	375	517	108	72	24	37	9	2	192	245	59	71	21	43	6	1	183	272	49
Calgary	85	32	40	13	0	267	310	77	44	23	15	6	0	162	147	52	41	9	25	7	0	105	163	25
Carolina	149	81	47	14	7	465	403	183	74	45	22	4	3	242	191	97	75	36	25	10	4	223	212	86
Chicago	87	36	39	11	1	282	300	84	44	23	15	5	1	156	136	52	43	13	24	6	0	126	164	32
Colorado	73	35	28	9	1	264	224	80	36	19	12	4	1	136	113	43	37	16	16	5	0	128	111	37
Columbus	14	9	3	1	1	45	39	20	6	3	1	1	1	19	18	8	8	6	2	0	0	26	21	12
Dallas	87	29	41	16	1	247	304	75	43	16	18	8	1	129	141	41	44	13	23	8	0	118	163	34
Detroit	101	40	43	16	2	332	330	98	50	24	21	5	0	185	156	53	51	16	22	11	2	147	174	45
Edmonton	64	31	27	6	0	226	230	68	32	20	10	2	0	130	102	42	32	11	17	4	0	96	128	26
Florida	108	56	36	9	7	324	274	128	54	30	14	5	5	174	128	70	54	26	22	4	2	150	146	58
Los Angeles	100	34	53	13	0	346	384	81	49	19	23	7	0	194	183	45	51	15	30	6	0	152	201	36
Minnesota	12	5	6	0	1	24	23	11	6	5	1	0	0	17	8	10	6	0	5	0	1	7	15	1
Montreal	150	62	68	17	3	386	485	144	74	35	29	9	1	208	215	80	76	27	39	8	2	178	270	64
Nashville	17	10	6	1	0	44	43	21	8	6	2	0	0	23	19	12	9	4	4	1	0	21	24	9
New Jersey	189	93	71	13	12	622	554	211	95	55	28	6	6	354	266	122	94	38	43	7	6	268	288	89
NY Islanders	193	94	83	13	3	609	644	204	97	49	35	11	2	312	297	111	96	45	48	2	1	297	347	93
NY Rangers	197	92	81	18	6	680	673	208	99	51	35	9	4	355	313	115	98	41	46	9	2	325	360	93
Ottawa	78	37	32	5	4	244	245	83	39	22	11	4	2	132	106	50	39	15	21	1	2	112	139	33
Philadelphia	194	73	97	19	5	582	675	170	95	41	40	13	1	306	302	96	99	32	57	6	4	276	373	74
Phoenix	67	29	25	12	1	243	211	71	34	20	8	5	1	129	93	46	33	9	17	7	0	114	118	25
Pittsburgh	200	88	90	16	6	716	735	198	101	51	37	9	4	404	360	115	99	37	53	7	2	312	375	83
St. Louis	87	37	37	12	1	286	301	87	43	23	16	4	0	149	127	50	44	14	21	8	1	137	174	37
San Jose	31	9	20	1	1	78	100	20	16	6	9	0	1	43	47	13	15	3	11	1	0	35	53	7
Tampa Bay	110	68	30	6	6	378	286	148	55	37	11	4	3	207	142	81	55	31	19	2	3	171	144	67
Toronto	129	62	52	10	5	446	440	139	66	39	21	4	2	240	184	84	63	23	31	6	3	206	256	55
Vancouver	85	39	36	9	1	272	277	88	43	23	16	4	0	141	128	50	42	16	20	5	1	131	149	38
Winnipeg	79	42	25	5	7	257	224	96	39	24	9	3	3	140	114	54	40	18	16	2	4	117	110	42
Defunct Clubs	20	6	13	1	0	58	81	13	10	2	8	0	0	28	42	4	10	4	5	1	0	30	39	9
Totals	**3016**	**1332**	**1287**	**303**	**94**	**9556**	**9869**	**3061**	**1508**	**767**	**539**	**153**	**49**	**5141**	**4591**	**1736**	**1508**	**565**	**748**	**150**	**45**	**4415**	**5278**	**1325**

Playoffs

	Series	W	L	GP	W	L	T	GF	GA	Last Mtg.	Rnd.	Result
Boston	3	2	1	17	8	9	0	37	43	2012	CQF	W 4-3
Buffalo	1	1	0	6	4	2	0	13	11	1998	CF	W 4-2
Detroit	1	0	1	4	0	4	0	7	13	1998	F	L 0-4
Montreal	1	0	1	7	3	4	0	22	20	2010	CQF	L 3-4
New Jersey	2	1	1	13	7	6	0	44	43	1990	DSF	W 4-2
NY Islanders	6	1	5	30	12	18	0	88	99	1993	DSF	L 2-4
NY Rangers	8	4	4	48	25	23	0	132	121	2013	CQF	L 3-4
Ottawa	1	1	0	5	4	1	0	18	7	1998	CSF	W 4-1
Philadelphia	4	2	2	23	12	11	0	85	78	2008	CQF	L 3-4
Pittsburgh	8	1	7	49	19	30	0	143	164	2009	CSF	L 3-4
Tampa Bay	2	0	2	10	2	8	0	25	30	2011	CSF	L 0-4
Totals	**37**	**13**	**24**	**212**	**96**	**116**	**0**	**614**	**629**			

Playoff Results 2013-2009

Year	Round	Opponent	Result	GF	GA
2013	CQF	NY Rangers	L 3-4	12	16
2012	CSF	NY Rangers	L 3-4	13	15
	CQF	Boston	W 4-3	16	15
2011	CSF	Tampa Bay	L 0-4	10	16
	CQF	NY Rangers	W 4-1	13	8
2010	CQF	Montreal	L 3-4	22	20
2009	CSF	Pittsburgh	L 3-4	22	27
	CQF	NY Rangers	W 4-3	19	11

Abbreviations: Round: F – Final; **CF** – conference final; **CSF** – conference semi-final; **CQF** – conference quarter-final; **DSF** – division semi-final.

Calgary totals include Atlanta Flames, 1974-75 to 1979-80.
Carolina totals include Hartford, 1979-80 to 1996-97.
Colorado totals include Quebec, 1979-80 to 1994-95.
Dallas totals include Minnesota North Stars, 1974-75 to 1992-93.
New Jersey totals include Kansas City, 1974-75, 1975-76, and Colorado Rockies, 1976-77 to 1981-82.
Phoenix totals include Winnipeg, 1979-80 to 1995-96.
Winnipeg totals include Atlanta Thrashers, 1999-2000 to 2010-11.

2012-13 Results

Jan.	19	at Tampa Bay	3-6		12	Carolina	0-4
	22	Winnipeg	2-4		14	at Carolina	3-2
	24	Montreal	1-4		16	at Boston	1-4
	25	at New Jersey	2-3*		17	Buffalo	5-3
	27	Buffalo	3-2		19	at Pittsburgh	1-2
	29	at Ottawa	2-3		21	at Winnipeg	4-0
	31	at Toronto	2-3		22	at Winnipeg	6-1
Feb.	1	Philadelphia	3-2		24	at NY Rangers	3-2†
	3	Pittsburgh	3-6		26	NY Islanders	2-3
	5	Toronto	2-3		30	at Buffalo	4-3†
	7	at Pittsburgh	2-5		31	at Philadelphia	4-5*
	9	Florida	5-0	**Apr.**	2	at Carolina	5-3
	12	at Florida	6-5*		4	NY Islanders	2-1†
	14	at Tampa Bay	4-3		6	at Florida	4-3
	17	at NY Rangers	1-2		7	Tampa Bay	4-2
	21	New Jersey	2-3		9	at Montreal	3-2
	23	New Jersey	5-1		11	Carolina	3-1
	26	Carolina	3-0		13	Tampa Bay	6-5*
	27	at Philadelphia	1-4		16	Toronto	5-1
Mar.	2	at Winnipeg	3-0		18	at Ottawa	1-3
	5	Boston	4-3*		20	at Montreal	5-1
	7	Florida	7-1		23	Winnipeg	5-3
	9	at NY Islanders	2-5		25	Ottawa	1-2*
	10	NY Rangers	1-4		27	Boston	3-2*

* – Overtime † – Shootout

Entry Draft Selections 2013-1999

Name in bold denotes played in NHL.

2013

Pick	
23	Andre Burakovsky
53	Madison Bowey
61	Zachary Sanford
144	Blake Heinrich
174	Brian Pinho
204	Tyler Lewington

2012

Pick	
11	**Filip Forsberg**
16	**Thomas Wilson**
77	Chandler Stephenson
100	Thomas Di Pauli
107	Austin Wuthrich
137	Connor Carrick
167	Riley Barber
195	Christian Djoos
197	Jaynen Rissling
203	Sergey Kostenko

2011

Pick	
117	Steffen Soberg
147	Patrick Koudys
177	Travis Boyd
207	Garrett Haar

2010

Pick	
26	Evgeny Kuznetsov
86	Stanislav Galiev
112	**Philipp Grubauer**
142	Caleb Herbert
176	Samuel Carrier

2009

Pick	
24	**Marcus Johansson**
55	**Dmitry Orlov**
85	**Cody Eakin**
115	Patrick Wey
145	Brett Flemming
175	Garrett Mitchell
205	Benjamin Casavant

2008

Pick	
21	Anton Gustafsson
27	**John Carlson**
57	Eric Mestery
58	Dmitry Kugryshev
93	**Braden Holtby**
144	Joel Broda
174	Greg Burke
204	**Stefan Della Rovere**

2007

Pick	
5	**Karl Alzner**
34	Josh Godfrey
46	Theo Ruth
84	Phil Desimone
108	Brett Bruneteau
125	Brett Leffler
154	Dan Dunn
180	Justin Taylor
185	Nick Larson
199	Andrew Glass

2006

Pick	
4	**Nicklas Backstrom**
23	**Semyon Varlamov**
34	**Michal Neuvirth**
35	Francois Bouchard
52	Keith Seabrook
97	**Oskar Osala**
122	Luke Lynes
127	Maxime Lacroix
157	Brent Gwidt
177	**Mathieu Perreault**

2005

Pick	
14	Sasha Pokulok
27	**Joe Finley**
109	Andrew Thomas
118	Patrick McNeill
143	Daren Machesney
181	**Tim Kennedy**
209	Viktor Dovgan

2004

Pick	
1	**Alex Ovechkin**
27	**Jeff Schultz**
29	**Mike Green**
33	**Chris Bourque**
62	Mikhail Yunkov
66	**Sami Lepisto**
88	Clayton Barthel
132	Oscar Hedman
138	Pasi Salonen
166	Peter Guggisberg
197	**Andrew Gordon**
230	Justin Mrazek
263	**Travis Morin**

2003

Pick	
18	**Eric Fehr**
83	Steve Werner
109	Andreas Valdix
155	Josh Robertson
249	**Andrew Joudrey**
279	Mark Olafson

2002

Pick	
12	**Steve Eminger**
13	**Alexander Semin**
17	**Boyd Gordon**
59	Maxime Daigneault
77	Patrick Wellar
92	Derek Krestanovich
109	Jevon Desautels
118	Petr Dvorak
145	Rob Gherson
179	Marian Havel
209	Joni Lindlof
242	Igor Ignatushkin
272	Patric Blomdahl

2001

Pick	
58	**Nathan Paetsch**
90	**Owen Fussey**
125	Jeff Lucky
160	Artem Ternavsky
191	Zbynek Novak
221	**Johnny Oduya**
249	Matt Maglione
254	Peter Polcik
275	Robert Muller
284	Viktor Hubl

2000

Pick	
26	**Brian Sutherby**
43	**Matt Pettinger**
61	**Jakub Cutta**
121	Ryan Vanbuskirk
163	Ivan Nepryayev
289	Bjorn Nord

1999

Pick	
7	**Kris Beech**
29	**Michal Sivek**
31	**Charlie Stephens**
34	**Ross Lupaschuk**
37	**Nolan Yonkman**
132	**Roman Tvrdon**
175	Kyle Clark
192	David Bornhammar
219	Maxim Orlov
249	Igor Shadilov

General Managers' History

Milt Schmidt, 1974-75; Milt Schmidt and Max McNab, 1975-76; Max McNab, 1976-77 to 1980-81; Max McNab and Roger Crozier, 1981-82; David Poile, 1982-83 to 1996-97; George McPhee, 1997-98 to date.

George McPhee

Vice President and General Manager

Born: Wallaceburg, Ont., July 2, 1958.

On June 9, 1997, George McPhee became the fifth general manager of the Washington Capitals. In his first year on the job, McPhee led the Caps to the Stanley Cup Final for the first time in franchise history. He has since rebuilt the Capitals with younger players and used the first overall choice at the 2004 NHL Entry Draft to select Alex Ovechkin. The Capitals finished first in the Southeast Division from 2007-08 to 2010-11 and also in 2012-13. They shattered club records with 54 wins and 121 points in 2009-10 and won the Presidents' Trophy for the first time in franchise history.

Prior to joining the Capitals, McPhee spent five years in the front office of the Vancouver Canucks where he served as vice president of hockey operations and alternate governor. He has earned degrees in both law and business and, while attending law school at Rutgers University, interned at the United States Court of International Trade in 1991.

A back injury forced McPhee to retire as an active player at the conclusion of the 1988-89 season, after a seven year playing career with the New York Rangers and New Jersey Devils. McPhee originally signed as a free agent with the Rangers in July, 1982, after graduating from Bowling Green State University with a business degree. McPhee did not waste any time in college, tallying 40 goals and 48 assists in his freshman season and easily winning CCHA rookie of the year honors. His outstanding collegiate hockey career was capped off when he was named the recipient of the Hobey Baker Award as the top U.S. collegiate player in his senior season. McPhee also earned All-America honors as a senior and finished his career at Bowling Green as the CCHA's all-time leading scorer with 114-153-267. He was the first player in CCHA history to make the Conference's all-academic team three straight seasons.

Club Directory

Verizon Center

Washington Capitals
627 N. Glebe Road, Suite 850
Arlington, VA 22203
Phone **202/266-2200**
PR FAX 202/266-2360
www.washingtoncaps.com
Capacity: 18,506

Ownership	Monumental Sports & Entertainment
Chairman and Majority Owner	Ted Leonsis
Vice Chairman and President, C.O.O.	Dick Patrick
Vice Chairmen	Raul Fernandez, Sheila Johnson
MSE Partners	Scott Brickman, Neil D. Cohen, Jack Davies, Richard Fairbank, Michelle D. Freeman, Richard Kay, Jeong Kim, Mark D. Lerner, Roger Mody, Anthony Nader, Fred Schaufeld, George Stamas, Earl Stafford, Cliff White
Hockey Operations	
Vice President and General Manager	George McPhee
Assistant General Manager, Dir. of Legal Affairs	Don Fishman
Head Coach	Adam Oates
Assistant Coaches	Calle Johansson, Blaine Forsythe
Video Coach	Brett Leonhardt
Director of Goaltending & Goaltending Coach	Dave Prior
Associate Goaltending Coach	Olie Kolzig
Strength and Conditioning Coach	Mark Nemish
Physiologist	Jack Blatherwick
Director, Team Operations	Katy Headman
Hockey Operations Assistants	Eric Garvey, Evan Gold
Manager, Team Services	Ian Anderson
Hershey Bears, Head Coach / Assistant Coach	Mike Haviland, Ryan Mougenel
Scouting Staff	
Assistant General Manager, Dir. Player Personnel	Brian MacLellan
Director, Player Development	Steve Richmond
Director, Amateur Scouting	Ross Mahoney
Pro Scouts	Jason Fitzsimmons, Chris Patrick, Martin Pouliot
Amateur Scouts	Darrell Baumgartner, Steve Bowman, Alan Haworth, Phil Horner, Ed McColgan, Wil Nichol, Terry Richardson, A.J. Toews
European Scouts	Vojtech Kucera, Petri Skriko, Mats Weiderstal
Director, Scouting Operations	Kris Wagner
Medical Staff	
Head Athletic Trainer / Assistant Trainer	Greg Smith / Ben Reisz
Massage Therapist	Curtis Millar
Team Physician / Team Internist	Ben Shaffer, MD / Chris Walsh, MD
Team Ophthalmologist / Team Dentist	Thomas Clinch, MD / Thomas Lenz, DDS, PC
Training Staff	
Head Equipment Manager	Brock Myles
Assistant Equipment Manager	Craig Leydig
Equipment Assistant	Dave Marin
Business Operations	
Vice President, Administration	Michelle Trostle
Senior Director, Information Technology	Brian McPartland
Office Assistant / Receptionist	Valerie Garrett / Chuquita Pettus
Chief Building Engineer	Larry Hollen
Building Engineer	Pedro Pena
Communications	
Senior Vice President, Communications and CCO, Monumental Sports & Entertainment	Kurt Kehl
Senior Director, Communications	Sergey Kocharov
Director, Community Relations	Nadia Wajid
Senior Writer	Mike Vogel
Media Relations Manager	Pace Sagester
Digital Content Producer	James Heuser
Communications Coordinator	Megan Eichenberg
Broadcasting	
Radio Rightsholder	WJFK
Radio Play-by-Play / Analyst	John Walton / Ken Sabourin
Television Rightsholder	Comcast SportsNet
Television Play-by-Play / Analyst	Joe Beninati / Craig Laughlin
Television Reporters / Studio Analyst	Al Koken, Jill Sorenson / Alan May

The fourth pick overall in the 2006 Entry Draft, Nicklas Backstrom had a bounce-back season in 2012-13. Though he scored just eight goals, his 40 assists trailed only NHL scoring leader Martin St. Louis and Sidney Crosby.

Winnipeg Jets

Key Off-Season Signings/Acquisitions

2013

June 30 • Acquired RW **Michael Frolik** from Chicago for a 3rd- (John Hayden) and 5th-round pick (Luke Johnson) in the 2013 NHL Draft.
2 • Re-signed D **Grant Clitsome**.
4 • Re-signed G **Al Montoya**.
5 • Acquired RW **Devin Setoguchi** from Minnesota for a 2nd-round pick in the 2014 NHL Draft.
6 • Signed RW **Andrew Gordon** and D **Adam Pardy**.
11 • Signed RW **Matt Halischuk**.
16 • Re-signed C **Eric Tangradi**.
19 • Re-signed D **Paul Postma**.
20 • Re-signed D **Zach Redmond**.
22 • Re-signed C **Bryan Little**.
23 • Re-signed RW **Anthony Peluso**.
26 • Re-signed RW **Blake Wheeler**.
29 • Re-signed D **Zach Bogosian**.

2012-13 Results: 24W-21L-0OTL-3SOL 51PTS
2ND, Southeast Division • 9TH, Eastern Conference

Year-by-Year Record

		Home				Road				Overall									
Season	**GP**	**W**	**L**	**T**	**OL**	**W**	**L**	**T**	**OL**	**W**	**L**	**T**	**OL**	**GF**	**GA**	**Pts.**	**Div. Fin.**	**Conf. Fin.**	**Playoff Result**
2012-13	48	13	10	....	1	11	11	....	2	24	21	....	3	128	144	51	2nd, SE	9th, East	Out of Playoffs
2011-12	82	23	13	....	5	14	22	....	5	37	35	....	10	225	246	84	4th, SE	11th, East	Out of Playoffs
2010-11*	82	17	17	....	7	17	19	....	5	34	36	....	12	223	269	80	4th, SE	12th, East	Out of Playoffs
2009-10*	82	19	16	....	6	16	18	....	7	35	34	....	13	234	256	83	2nd, SE	10th, East	Out of Playoffs
2008-09*	82	18	21	....	2	17	20	....	4	35	41	....	6	257	280	76	4th, SE	13th, East	Out of Playoffs
2007-08*	82	19	19	....	3	15	21	....	5	34	40	....	8	216	272	76	4th, SE	14th, East	Out of Playoffs
2006-07*	82	23	12	....	6	20	16	....	5	43	28	....	11	246	245	97	1st, SE	3rd, East	Lost Conf. Quarter-Final
2005-06*	82	24	13	....	4	17	20	....	4	41	33	....	8	281	275	90	3rd, SE	10th, East	Out of Playoffs
2004-05*	....	....	....	....	....	....	....	....	....	....	....	....	....	....	....	....			
2003-04*	82	18	17	4	2	15	20	4	2	33	37	8	4	214	243	78	2nd, SE	10th, East	Out of Playoffs
2002-03*	82	15	19	4	3	16	20	3	2	31	39	7	5	226	284	74	3rd, SE	11th, East	Out of Playoffs
2001-02*	82	11	21	9	0	8	26	2	5	19	47	11	5	187	288	54	5th, SE	15th, East	Out of Playoffs
2000-01*	82	10	23	6	2	13	22	6	0	23	45	12	2	211	289	60	4th, SE	13th, East	Out of Playoffs
1999-2000*	82	9	26	3	3	5	31	4	1	14	57	7	4	170	313	39	5th, SE	15th, East	Out of Playoffs

* Atlanta Thrashers

2013-14 Schedule

Oct.	Tue.	1	at Edmonton
	Fri.	4	Los Angeles
	Sun.	6	Anaheim
	Thu.	10	at Minnesota
	Fri.	11	Dallas
	Sun.	13	New Jersey
	Tue.	15	Montreal
	Fri.	18	St. Louis
	Sun.	20	Nashville
	Tue.	22	Washington
	Thu.	24	at Nashville
	Sat.	26	at Dallas
	Sun.	27	at Colorado
	Tue.	29	at St. Louis
Nov.	Sat.	2	Chicago*
	Mon.	4	Detroit
	Wed.	6	at Chicago
	Fri.	8	Nashville
	Sun.	10	San Jose
	Tue.	12	at Detroit
	Fri.	15	Philadelphia
	Sun.	17	at Minnesota
	Mon.	18	Calgary
	Thu.	21	Chicago
	Sat.	23	Minnesota*
	Mon.	25	at New Jersey
	Wed.	27	at NY Islanders
	Fri.	29	at Philadelphia*
Dec.	Mon.	2	at NY Rangers
	Thu.	5	at Florida
	Sat.	7	at Tampa Bay
	Tue.	10	St. Louis
	Thu.	12	Colorado
	Sat.	14	Dallas*
	Mon.	16	at Columbus
	Tue.	17	at Buffalo
	Fri.	20	Florida
	Sun.	22	at Vancouver*
	Mon.	23	at Edmonton
	Fri.	27	Minnesota
	Sun.	29	at Colorado
	Tue.	31	Buffalo
Jan.	Thu.	2	at Ottawa
	Sat.	4	at Boston*
	Sun.	5	at Pittsburgh*
	Tue.	7	Tampa Bay
	Sat.	11	Columbus
	Mon.	13	Phoenix
	Thu.	16	at Calgary
	Sat.	18	Edmonton*
	Tue.	21	at Anaheim
	Thu.	23	at San Jose
	Sat.	25	Toronto
	Sun.	26	at Chicago
	Tue.	28	Nashville
	Fri.	31	Vancouver
Feb.	Sun.	2	at Montreal*
	Tue.	4	at Carolina
	Thu.	6	at Washington
	Sat.	8	at St. Louis*
	Thu.	27	Phoenix
Mar.	Sat.	1	at Nashville*
	Tue.	4	NY Islanders
	Thu.	6	Los Angeles
	Sat.	8	Ottawa*
	Mon.	10	at Colorado
	Wed.	12	Vancouver
	Fri.	14	NY Rangers
	Sun.	16	Dallas
	Mon.	17	at St. Louis
	Wed.	19	Colorado
	Sat.	22	Carolina
	Mon.	24	at Dallas
	Thu.	27	at San Jose
	Sat.	29	at Los Angeles
	Mon.	31	at Anaheim
Apr.	Tue.	1	at Phoenix
	Thu.	3	Pittsburgh
	Sat.	5	at Toronto
	Mon.	7	Minnesota
	Thu.	10	Boston
	Fri.	11	at Calgary

* Denotes afternoon game.

Captain Andrew Ladd was Winnipeg's best offensive performer in 2012-13, leading the team in assists (28) and points (46), tying defenseman Grant Clistome for the lead in plus-minus (+10) and finishing just one goal behind Blake Wheeler for the team lead in goals with 18.

CENTRAL DIVISION
15th NHL Season

Franchise date: June 25, 1997

Transferred from Atlanta to Winnipeg, June 21, 2011.

2013-14 Player Personnel

FORWARDS	HT	WT	*Age	Place of Birth	S	2012-13 Club
FROLIK, Michael	6-1	198	25	Kladno, Czech.	L	Chomutov-Chicago
HALISCHUK, Matt	5-11	187	25	Toronto, Ont.	R	Nashville-Milwaukee
JOKINEN, Olli	6-2	210	34	Kuopio, Finland	L	Winnipeg
KANE, Evander	6-2	195	22	Vancouver, B.C.	L	Dynamo Minsk-Winnipeg
LADD, Andrew	6-3	205	27	Maple Ridge, B.C.	L	Winnipeg
LITTLE, Bryan	5-11	185	25	Edmonton, Alta.	R	Winnipeg
PELUSO, Anthony	6-3	235	24	North York, Ont.	R	Peoria-Winnipeg
SCHEIFELE, Mark	6-2	192	20	Kitchener, Ont.	R	Barrie-Winnipeg
SETOGUCHI, Devin	6-2	205	26	Taber, Alta.	R	Ontario-Minnesota
SLATER, Jim	6-0	200	30	Lapeer, MI	L	Winnipeg
TANGRADI, Eric	6-4	221	24	Philadelphia, PA	L	Wilkes-Barre-Pit-Wpg
THORBURN, Chris	6-3	230	30	Sault Ste. Marie, Ont.	R	Winnipeg
WHEELER, Blake	6-5	205	27	Robbinsdale, MN	R	EHC Munchen-Winnipeg
WRIGHT, James	6-4	200	23	Saskatoon, Sask.	L	San Antonio-Winnipeg
DEFENSEMEN						
BOGOSIAN, Zach	6-3	215	23	Massena, NY	R	Winnipeg
BYFUGLIEN, Dustin	6-5	265	28	Minneapolis, MN	R	Winnipeg
CLITSOME, Grant	5-11	215	28	Gloucester, Ont.	L	Winnipeg
ENSTROM, Toby	5-10	180	28	Nordingra, Sweden	L	Salzburg-Winnipeg
PARDY, Adam	6-4	220	29	Bonavista, Nfld.	L	Rochester-Buffalo
POSTMA, Paul	6-3	195	24	Red Deer, Alta.	R	St. John's-Winnipeg
REDMOND, Zach	6-2	197	25	Traverse City, MI	R	St. John's-Winnipeg
STUART, Mark	6-2	213	29	Rochester, MN	L	Florida (ECHL)-Winnipeg
TROUBA, Jacob	6-2	196	19	Rochester, MI	R	U. of Michigan

GOALTENDERS	HT	WT	*Age	Place of Birth	C	2012-13 Club
MONTOYA, Al	6-2	203	28	Chicago, IL	L	Winnipeg
PASQUALE, Eddie	6-3	215	22	Toronto, Ont.	L	St. John's
PAVELEC, Ondrej	6-3	220	26	Kladno, Czech.	L	Liberec-Pelicans-Winnipeg

* – Age at start of 2013-14 season

2012-13 Scoring

* – rookie

Regular Season

Pos	#	Player	Team	GP	G	A	Pts	TOI	+/–	PIM	PP	SH	GW	S	%
L	16	Andrew Ladd	WPG	48	18	28	46	19:40	10	22	3	0	4	121	14.9
R	26	Blake Wheeler	WPG	48	19	22	41	18:48	–3	28	2	0	2	129	14.7
L	9	Evander Kane	WPG	48	17	16	33	20:27	–3	80	2	0	4	190	8.9
R	18	Bryan Little	WPG	48	7	25	32	19:47	8	4	2	0	2	84	8.3
D	33	Dustin Byfuglien	WPG	43	8	20	28	24:24	–1	34	4	0	2	142	5.6
C	80	Nik Antropov	WPG	40	6	12	18	15:57	6	16	2	0	0	56	10.7
D	24	Grant Clitsome	WPG	44	4	12	16	18:50	10	18	2	0	0	56	7.1
C	13	Kyle Wellwood	WPG	39	6	9	15	12:58	0	2	0	0	2	37	16.2
D	39	Tobias Enstrom	WPG	22	4	11	15	22:31	–8	8	1	0	2	21	19.0
C	12	Olli Jokinen	WPG	45	7	7	14	17:07	–19	14	0	0	0	85	8.2
D	44	Zach Bogosian	WPG	33	5	9	14	23:07	–5	29	0	0	0	85	5.9
D	6	Ron Hainsey	WPG	47	0	13	13	22:51	–8	10	0	0	0	52	0.0
C	8	Alexander Burmistrov	WPG	44	4	6	10	15:38	0	14	0	0	0	55	7.3
D	4 *	Paul Postma	WPG	34	4	5	9	15:01	–5	6	2	0	0	32	12.5
R	20	Antti Miettinen	WPG	22	3	2	5	12:38	–3	2	0	0	2	26	11.5
C	17	James Wright	WPG	38	2	3	5	11:35	–5	31	0	0	0	32	6.3
C	15	Mike Santorelli	FLA	24	2	1	3	11:05	–7	2	0	0	0	21	9.5
			WPG	10	0	1	1	13:43	–5	0	0	0	0	14	0.0
			Total	34	2	2	4	11:51	–12	2	0	0	0	35	5.7
R	22	Chris Thorburn	WPG	42	2	2	4	6:19	–5	70	0	0	0	13	15.4
D	5	Mark Stuart	WPG	42	2	2	4	16:42	5	53	0	0	0	40	5.0
D	25 *	Zach Redmond	WPG	8	1	3	4	19:34	0	12	0	1	0	13	7.7
C	27	Eric Tangradi	PIT	5	0	0	0	8:32	2	0	0	0	0	4	0.0
			WPG	36	1	3	4	10:17	–4	22	0	0	0	44	2.3
			Total	41	1	3	4	10:05	–2	22	0	0	0	48	2.1
C	21	Aaron Gagnon	WPG	10	3	0	3	8:09	2	2	0	0	1	11	27.3
C	19	Jim Slater	WPG	26	1	1	2	10:27	–3	19	0	0	0	22	4.5
R	14 *	Anthony Peluso	WPG	5	0	2	2	4:59	1	14	0	0	0	4	0.0
D	7	Derek Meech	WPG	16	0	1	1	14:41	0	2	0	0	0	5	0.0
C	55 *	Mark Scheifele	WPG	4	0	0	0	11:31	0	0	0	0	0	6	0.0
C	28	Patrice Cormier	WPG	10	0	0	0	3:53	–3	7	0	0	0	4	0.0

Goaltending

No.	Goaltender	GPI	Mins	Avg	W	L	OT	EN	SO	GA	SA	S%	G	A	PIM
31	Ondrej Pavelec	44	2553	2.80	21	20	3	5	0	119	1251	.905	0	0	2
35	Al Montoya	7	351	2.91	3	1	0	0	1	17	168	.899	0	0	0
	Totals	**48**	**2917**	**2.90**	**24**	**21**	**3**	**5**	**1**	**141**	**1424**	**.901**			

Claude Noel

Head Coach

Born: Kirkland Lake, Ont., October 31, 1955.

Claude Noel was hired on June 24, 2011, as the first head coach of the Winnipeg Jets and the sixth head coach in the history of the franchise dating back to the inception of the Atlanta Thrashers in 1999. Noel was the former coach of the American Hockey League's Manitoba Moose, where he spent the 2010-11 season. Previously, Noel had spent three seasons with the Columbus Blue Jackets from 2007 to 2010. He began the 2009-10 season as an assistant coach before taking over from Ken Hitchcock as interim head coach on February 3, 2010.

Before his time with the Blue Jackets, Noel spent four seasons as head coach of the Milwaukee Admirals, the AHL affiliate of the Nashville Predators. During that time he recorded three 100-point seasons, won two West Division titles and made two appearances in the Calder Cup Finals. During the 2003-04 season, the club compiled a 46-24-10 record and went 16-6 in the Calder Cup playoffs en route to capturing the organization's first Calder Cup championship. Noel was subsequently named the coach of the year when he was honored with the Louis A.R. Pieri Memorial Award.

Noel made his coaching debut in the ECHL with the Roanoke Valley Rebels in 1990-91 and served as head coach and director of hockey operations for the ECHL's Dayton Bombers from 1991 to 1993. In 1993 he joined the Kalamazoo Wings (later the Michigan K-Wings), the International Hockey League affiliate of the Dallas Stars, as an assistant coach. He succeeded then coach Ken Hitchcock behind the bench during the 1995-96 season and served in that capacity through the 1997-98 campaign. From 1998 to 2002 he was an assistant coach with the Milwaukee Admirals and in 2002-03 was named ECHL coach of the year with the Toledo Storm before returning to Milwaukee as head coach prior to the 2003-04 season.

As a player, Noel appeared in seven games with the Washington Capitals during the 1979-80 season. He spent most of his playing career in the AHL and IHL and was named the IHL's Most Valuable Player in 1982-83 after leading the Toledo Goaldiggers to the Turner Cup championship. He also won a Calder Cup as a member of the Hershey Bears in 1979-80. Noel wrapped up his playing career with Milwaukee in 1987-88. Noel was born in Kirkland Lake, Ontario and was raised in Virginiatown and North Bay, Ontario. He moved away from home at age 20 to play junior hockey for the Kitchener Rangers.

Coaching Record

			Regular Season				Playoffs			
Season	Team	League	GC	W	L	O/T	GC	W	L	T
1990-91	Roanoke	ECHL	64	26	31	7	....	....	....	....
1991-92	Dayton	ECHL	64	32	26	6	3	0	3	....
1992-93	Dayton	ECHL	64	35	23	6	3	0	3	....
1995-96	Kalamazoo	IHL	42	21	14	7	10	6	4	....
1996-97	Michigan	IHL	82	31	44	7	4	1	3	....
1997-98	Michigan	IHL	82	36	39	7	4	1	3	....
2002-03	Toledo	ECHL	72	47	15	10	7	4	3	....
2003-04	Milwaukee	AHL	80	46	24	10	22	16	6	....
2004-05	Milwaukee	AHL	80	47	24	9	7	3	4	....
2005-06	Milwaukee	AHL	80	49	21	10	21	14	7	....
2006-07	Milwaukee	AHL	80	41	25	14	4	0	4	....
2009-10	**Columbus**	**NHL**	**24**	**10**	**8**	**6**	....	....	....	....
2010-11	Manitoba	AHL	80	43	30	7	14	7	7	....
2011-12	**Winnipeg**	**NHL**	**82**	**37**	**35**	**10**	....	....	....	....
2012-13	**Winnipeg**	**NHL**	**48**	**24**	**21**	**3**	....	....	....	....
	NHL Totals		**154**	**71**	**64**	**19**	....	....	....	....

Blake Wheeler's team-leading 19 goals in 2012-13 were only two short of his career high set during his rookie season of 2008-09 when he had 21 goals in 81 games.

Club Records

Team

(Figures in brackets for season records are games played.)

Most Points	**97**	2006-07 (82)
Most Wins	**43**	2006-07 (82)
Most Ties	**12**	2000-01 (82)
Most Losses	**57**	1999-2000 (82)
Most Goals	**281**	2005-06 (82)
Most Goals Against	**313**	1999-2000 (82)
Fewest Points	**39**	1999-2000 (82)
Fewest Wins	**14**	1999-2000 (82)
Fewest Ties	**7**	1999-2000 (82), 2002-03 (82)
Fewest Losses	**28**	2006-07 (82)
Fewest Goals	**170**	1999-2000 (82)
Fewest Goals Against	**243**	2003-04 (82)
Longest Winning Streak		
Overall	**6**	Mar. 6-16/09, Nov. 19-30/10
Home	**7**	Mar. 2-18/07
Away	**4**	Jan. 13-Feb. 7/03, Nov. 3-21/07, Feb. 3-16/09, Nov. 12-Dec. 5/09
Longest Undefeated Streak		
Overall	**6**	Mar. 6-16/09 (6W), Nov. 19-30/10 (6W)
Home	**7**	Mar. 2-18/07 (7W)
Away	**7**	Oct. 21-Nov. 13/00 (3W, 4T/OL)
Longest Losing Streak		
Overall	**12**	Jan. 24-Feb. 20/00
Home	**11**	Jan. 24-Mar. 16/00
Away	**10**	Oct. 6-Nov. 18/01, Feb. 16-Mar. 18/08
Longest Winless Streak		
Overall	**16**	Jan. 16-Feb. 20/00 (14L, 2T/OL)
Home	***17**	Jan. 19-Mar. 29/00 (15L, 2T/OL)
Away	**10**	Oct. 6-Nov. 18/01 (10L)
Most Shutouts, Season	**5**	2005-06 (82), 2007-08 (82), 2010-11 (82)
Most PIM, Season	**1,505**	2003-04 (82)
Most Goals, Game	**9**	Nov. 12/05 (Atl. 9 at Car. 0)

Individual

Most Seasons	**8**	Ilya Kovalchuk
Most Games	**594**	Ilya Kovalchuk
Most Goals, Career	**328**	Ilya Kovalchuk
Most Assists, Career	**287**	Ilya Kovalchuk
Most Points, Career	**615**	Ilya Kovalchuk (328G, 287A)
Most PIM, Career	**639**	Eric Boulton
Most Shutouts, Career	**14**	Kari Lehtonen
Longest Consecutive Games Streak	**252**	Vyacheslav Kozlov (Jan. 9/07-Jan. 21/10)
Most Goals, Season	**52**	Ilya Kovalchuk (2005-06), (2007-08)
Most Assists, Season	**69**	Marc Savard (2005-06)
Most Points, Season	**100**	Marian Hossa (2006-07; 43G, 57A)
Most PIM, Season	**226**	Jeff Odgers (2000-01)
Most Points, Defenseman, Season	**53**	Dustin Byfuglien (2010-11; 20G, 33A), (2011-12; 12G, 41A)
Most Points, Center, Season	**97**	Marc Savard (2005-06; 28G, 69A)
Most Points, Right Wing, Season	**100**	Marian Hossa (2006-07; 43G, 57A)
Most Points, Left Wing, Season	**98**	Ilya Kovalchuk (2005-06; 52G, 46A)
Most Points, Rookie, Season	**67**	Dany Heatley (2001-02; 26G, 41A)
Most Shutouts, Season	**4**	Kari Lehtonen (2006-07), (2007-08), Ondrej Pavelec (2010-11), (2011-12)
Most Goals, Game	**4**	Pascal Rheaume (Jan. 19/02), Ilya Kovalchuk (Nov. 11/05)
Most Assists, Game	**4**	Seven times
Most Points, Game	**5**	Seven times

* NHL Record.

Records include Atlanta Thrashers, 1999-2000 through 2010-11.

Captains' History

Kelly Buchberger, 1999-2000; Steve Staios, 2000-01; Ray Ferraro, 2001-02; Shawn McEachern, 2002-03, 2003-04; Scott Mellanby, 2005-06, 2006-07; Bobby Holik, 2007-08; no captain and Ilya Kovalchuk, 2008-09; Ilya Kovalchuk, 2009-10; Andrew Ladd, 2010-11 to date.

Coaching History

Curt Fraser, 1999-2000 to 2001-02; Curt Fraser, Don Waddell and Bob Hartley, 2002-03; Bob Hartley, 2003-04 to 2006-07; Bob Hartley and Don Waddell, 2007-08; John Anderson, 2008-09, 2009-10; Craig Ramsay, 2010-11; Claude Noel, 2011-12 to date.

General Managers' History

Don Waddell, 1999-2000 to 2009-10; Rick Dudley, 2010-11; Kevin Cheveldayoff, 2011-12 to date.

All-time Record vs. Other Clubs

Regular Season

	Total								At Home								On Road							
	GP	W	L	T	OL	GF	GA	PTS	GP	W	L	T	OL	GF	GA	PTS	GP	W	L	T	OL	GF	GA	PTS
Anaheim	14	7	7	0	0	41	44	14	7	3	4	0	0	18	22	6	7	4	3	0	0	23	22	8
Boston	51	19	25	2	5	150	164	45	26	13	12	0	1	76	72	27	25	6	13	2	4	74	92	18
Buffalo	51	29	16	1	5	153	175	64	25	17	4	1	3	82	68	38	26	12	12	0	2	71	107	26
Calgary	13	5	7	1	0	32	41	11	7	5	1	1	0	21	15	11	6	0	6	0	0	11	26	0
Carolina	78	28	37	4	9	224	252	69	39	10	22	3	4	102	135	27	39	18	15	1	5	122	117	42
Chicago	12	3	6	0	3	33	40	9	7	2	3	0	2	23	23	6	5	1	3	0	1	10	17	3
Colorado	17	9	5	1	2	49	48	21	8	3	3	1	1	20	21	8	9	6	2	0	1	29	27	13
Columbus	14	5	8	0	1	26	35	11	7	3	4	0	0	13	17	6	7	2	4	0	1	13	18	5
Dallas	14	3	10	0	1	33	47	7	7	2	4	0	1	23	28	5	7	1	6	0	0	10	19	2
Detroit	14	4	8	0	2	41	62	10	6	2	4	0	0	22	32	4	8	2	4	0	2	19	30	6
Edmonton	13	4	8	1	0	30	46	9	6	2	4	0	0	11	19	4	7	2	4	1	0	19	27	5
Florida	79	43	23	5	8	250	213	99	39	22	9	4	4	134	106	52	40	21	14	1	4	116	107	47
Los Angeles	14	6	8	0	0	44	53	12	7	4	3	0	0	21	18	8	7	2	5	0	0	23	35	4
Minnesota	12	5	6	1	0	31	36	11	6	3	3	0	0	18	18	6	6	2	3	1	0	13	18	5
Montreal	51	16	29	2	4	112	158	38	25	9	12	2	2	52	65	22	26	7	17	0	2	60	93	16
Nashville	16	6	7	1	2	43	51	15	8	4	1	1	2	23	21	11	8	2	6	0	0	20	30	4
New Jersey	51	18	26	3	4	118	159	43	25	8	14	2	1	60	82	19	26	10	12	1	3	58	77	24
NY Islanders	51	21	24	2	4	150	184	48	26	9	12	2	3	79	98	23	25	12	12	0	1	71	86	25
NY Rangers	51	26	21	1	3	143	150	56	25	11	12	0	2	69	78	24	26	15	9	1	1	74	72	32
Ottawa	51	20	29	2	0	154	196	42	25	10	14	1	0	88	95	21	26	10	15	1	0	66	101	21
Philadelphia	51	15	29	3	4	141	188	37	26	7	15	1	3	65	89	18	25	8	14	2	1	76	99	19
Phoenix	16	2	10	1	3	29	53	8	7	2	3	0	2	13	20	6	9	0	7	1	1	16	33	2
Pittsburgh	51	13	33	0	5	132	192	31	26	9	15	0	2	69	84	20	25	4	18	0	3	63	108	11
St. Louis	15	5	7	1	2	36	48	13	9	3	4	1	1	25	29	8	6	2	3	0	1	11	19	5
San Jose	14	2	10	2	0	26	48	6	7	1	5	1	0	11	22	3	7	1	5	1	0	15	26	3
Tampa Bay	78	34	27	4	13	221	248	85	39	22	8	3	6	128	108	53	39	12	19	1	7	93	140	32
Toronto	49	20	24	1	4	124	176	45	25	11	12	0	2	56	87	24	24	9	12	1	2	68	89	21
Vancouver	12	3	8	1	0	28	40	7	6	2	4	0	0	17	20	4	6	1	4	1	0	11	20	3
Washington	79	32	35	5	7	224	257	76	40	20	16	2	2	110	117	44	39	12	19	3	5	114	140	32
Totals	**1032**	**403**	**493**	**45**	**91**	**2818**	**3404**	**942**	**516**	**219**	**227**	**26**	**44**	**1449**	**1609**	**508**	**516**	**184**	**266**	**19**	**47**	**1369**	**1795**	**434**

Playoffs

	Series	W	L	GP	W	L	T	GF	GA	Last Mtg.	Rnd.	Result
NY Rangers	1	0	1	4	0	4	0	6	17	2007	CQF	L 0-4
Totals	**1**	**0**	**1**	**4**	**0**	**4**	**0**	**6**	**17**			

Playoff Results 2013-2009

(Last playoff appearance: 2007)

Abbreviations: Round: CQF – conference quarter-final.

2012-13 Results

Jan.	19	Ottawa	1-4		10	at New Jersey	2-3†
	21	at Boston	1-2†		12	Toronto	5-2
	22	at Washington	4-2		14	NY Rangers	3-1
	25	Pittsburgh	4-2		16	at Toronto	5-4†
	27	NY Islanders	5-4*		17	at Ottawa	1-4
	29	at Montreal	3-4		19	Boston	3-1
	31	at Florida	3-6		21	Washington	0-4
Feb.	1	at Tampa Bay	3-8		22	Washington	1-6
	5	Florida	3-2*		24	Tampa Bay	3-2
	7	Toronto	2-3		26	at Carolina	4-1
	9	at Ottawa	1-0		28	at Pittsburgh	0-4
	12	Philadelphia	2-3		30	Carolina	1-3
	15	Pittsburgh	1-3	**Apr.**	1	at NY Rangers	2-4
	17	Boston	2-3		2	at NY Islanders	2-5
	19	at Buffalo	2-1		4	at Montreal	1-4
	21	at Carolina	4-3		6	Philadelphia	4-1
	23	at Philadelphia	3-5		9	Buffalo	4-1
	24	at New Jersey	4-2		11	Florida	7-2
	26	at NY Rangers	4-3		16	Tampa Bay	4-3†
	28	New Jersey	3-1		18	Carolina	4-3*
Mar.	2	Washington	0-3		20	NY Islanders	4-5†
	5	at Florida	1-4		22	at Buffalo	2-1
	7	at Tampa Bay	2-1		23	at Washington	3-5
	8	at Florida	3-2*		25	Montreal	2-4

* – Overtime † – Shootout

Entry Draft Selections 2013-1999

Name in bold denotes played in NHL.

2013

Pick	
13	Joshua Morrissey
43	Nicolas Petan
59	Eric Comrie
84	Jimmy Lodge
91	J.C. Lipon
104	Andrew Copp
114	Jan Kostalek
127	Tucker Poolman
190	Brenden Kichton
194	Marcus Karlstrom

2012

Pick	
9	Jacob Trouba
39	Lukas Sutter
70	Scott Kosmachuk
130	Connor Hellebuyck
160	Ryan Olsen
190	Jamie Phillips

2011

Pick	
7	**Mark Scheifele**
67	Adam Lowry
78	Brennan Serville
119	Zachary Yuen
149	Austen Brassard
157	Jason Kasdorf
187	Aaron Harstad

2010

Pick	
8	**Alexander Burmistrov**
87	Julian Melchiori
101	Ivan Telegin
128	Fredrik Pettersson-Wentzel
150	Yasin Cisse
155	Kendall McFaull
160	Tanner Lane
169	Sebastian Owuya
199	Peter Stoykewych

2009

Pick	
4	**Evander Kane**
34	**Carl Klingberg**
45	**Jeremy Morin**
117	Eddie Pasquale
120	Ben Chiarot
125	Cody Sol
155	Jimmy Bubnick
185	Levko Koper
203	Jordan Samuels-Thomas

2008

Pick	
3	**Zach Bogosian**
29	Daultan Leveille
64	Danick Paquette
94	Vinny Saponari
124	Nicklas Lasu
154	Chris Carrozzi
184	**Zach Redmond**

2007

Pick	
67	**Spencer Machacek**
115	Niclas Lucenius
175	John Albert
205	**Paul Postma**

2006

Pick	
12	**Bryan Little**
43	Riley Holzapfel
80	Michael Forney
135	Alex Kangas
165	Jonas Enlund
195	Jesse Martin
200	**Arturs Kulda**
210	Will O'Neill

2005

Pick	
16	Alex Bourret
41	**Ondrej Pavelec**
49	Chad Denny
53	Andrew Kozek
116	**Jordan Smotherman**
135	Tomas Pospisil
187	**Andrei Zubarev**
207	Myles Stoesz

2004

Pick	
10	**Boris Valabik**
40	**Grant Lewis**
76	**Scott Lehman**
106	Chad Painchaud
142	Juraj Gracik
186	Dan Turple
204	Miikka Tuomainen
237	Mitch Carefoot
270	Matt Siddall

2003

Pick	
8	**Braydon Coburn**
110	Jim Sharrow
116	**Guillaume Desbiens**
136	Michael Vannelli
145	**Brett Sterling**
175	Mike Hamilton
203	Denis Loginov
239	**Tobias Enstrom**
269	Rylan Kaip

2002

Pick	
2	**Kari Lehtonen**
30	**Jim Slater**
116	**Patrick Dwyer**
124	Lane Manson
144	Paul Flache
167	Brad Schell
198	**Nathan Oystrick**
230	Colton Fretter
236	Tyler Boldt
257	Pauli Levokari

2001

Pick	
1	**Ilya Kovalchuk**
80	**Michael Garnett**
100	Brian Sipotz
112	Milan Gajic
135	**Colin Stuart**
189	**Pasi Nurminen**
199	Matt Suderman
201	Colin FitzRandolph
262	Mario Cartelli

2000

Pick	
2	**Dany Heatley**
31	Ilja Nikulin
42	Libor Ustrnul
107	Carl Mallette
108	Blake Robson
147	Matt McRae
168	Zdenek Smid
178	Jeff Dwyer
180	**Darcy Hordichuk**
230	Samu Isosalo
242	Evan Nielsen
244	Eric Bowen
288	Mark McRae
290	**Simon Gamache**

1999

Pick	
1	**Patrik Stefan**
30	**Luke Sellars**
68	**Zdenek Blatny**
98	David Kaczowka
99	Rob Zepp
128	**Derek MacKenzie**
159	Yuri Dobryshkin
188	Stephen Baby
217	**Garnet Exelby**
245	**Tommi Santala**
246	Raymond DiLauro

Kevin Cheveldayoff

Executive Vice President and General Manager

Born: Blaine Lake, Sask., February 4, 1970.

Kevin Cheveldayoff was given his first assignment as general manager of an NHL hockey club when he was named to the position by the Winnipeg Jets on June 8, 2011. Prior to joining the Jets, he had spent two seasons with the Chicago Blackhawks and served as the club's assistant general manager/senior director, hockey operations in 2010-11. During Cheveldayoff's tenure, the Blackhawks won the 2010 Stanley Cup championship, the team's first since 1961.

Before joining the Blackhawks on August 3, 2009, Cheveldayoff spent the previous 12 seasons as the general manager of the Chicago Wolves, guiding the franchise to four league championships, which included the 2002 and 2008 Calder Cup titles in the American Hockey League and the 1998 and 2000 International Hockey League's Turner Cup. Overall, Cheveldayoff was a part of seven league championships during his 15-year management career before being hired in Winnipeg, including two Turner Cup titles in three seasons as the assistant vice president of hockey operations and assistant coach for the Denver and Utah Grizzlies (1994 to 1997).

Cheveldayoff was the architect of 12 Wolves teams that compiled a .615 regular-season winning percentage (544-320-114) and 10 postseason berths from 1997 to 2009. Eight of those clubs reached the 100-point mark during the regular season while earning four division titles and six postseason conference championships.

Cheveldayoff was originally drafted by the New York Islanders with their first pick (16th overall) in the 1988 NHL Entry Draft. He began his career in the AHL with the Capital District Islanders, serving as the alternate captain from 1991 to 1993. He held the same role with the Salt Lake Golden Eagles in 1993-94, earning the team's "Unsung Hero Award" after racking up a career-high 216 penalty minutes in 73 games. Known as a defensive defenseman during his playing days, a knee injury cut his professional career short after five seasons.

Club Directory

MTS Centre

Winnipeg Jets
MTS Centre
345 Graham Avenue
Winnipeg, Manitoba, R3C 5S6
Phone **204/987-7825**
FAX 204/926-5555
www.winnipegjets.com
Twitter @NHLJets
Capacity: 15,004

Senior Management

Chairman and Governor	Mark Chipman
President and Chief Executive Officer	Jim Ludlow
Exec. V.P. and Chief Financial Officer	John Olfert
Exec. V.P. and General Manager, Winnipeg Jets	Kevin Cheveldayoff
Sr. V.P. and Director Hockey Ops/Asst. G.M.	Craig Heisinger
Sr. V.P. and General Manager – MTS Centre	Kevin Donnelly
Sr. V.P., Sales & Marketing	Norva Riddell
VP, People & Patron Services	Robert Thorsten
General Manager – MTS Iceplex	Gavin Johnstone

Hockey Operations

Exec. V.P. and General Manager, Winnipeg Jets	Kevin Cheveldayoff
Sr. V.P. and Director Hockey Ops/Asst. G.M.	Craig Heisinger
Assistant General Manager	Larry Simmons
Manager, Hockey Ops & Team Services	TBA
Executive Assistant, Hockey Ops	Sandra Smith
Head Coach	Claude Noel
Assistant Coaches	Charlie Huddy, Perry Pearn, Pascal Vincent
Goaltending Coach	Wade Flaherty
Video Coach	Tony Borgford
Head Equipment Manager	Jason McMaster
Assistant Equipment Managers	Mark Grehan, Mike Flaman
Head Athletic Therapist	Rob Milette
Assistant Athletic Therapist	Brad Shaw
Asst. Athletic Therapist/Strength & Conditioning	Lee Stubbs
Massage Therapist	Al Pritchard
Coordinator, Team Travel	Silvana Gosgnach
Director Security, Winnipeg Jets	Ken Shipley
Coordinator, Team Services	Chris Kreviazuk
Scouting & Video Coordinator	Barrett Leganchuk

Scouting Staff

Director, Pro Scouting	Mark Dobson
Director, Amateur Scouting	Marcel Comeau
Head Scout	Mark Hillier
Pro Scouts	Jack Birch, John Perpich, Bruce Southern, Peter Ratchuk, Carter Sears, Ryan Bowness
Amateur Scouts	Tavis MacMillan, Evgeny Bogdanovich, Fredrik Jax, Pat Carmichael, Chris Snell, Scott Scoville, Bob Owen, Yanick Lemay, Ed Friesen, Brian Renfrew, Vladimir Havluj, Scott Robson, Max Giese
Coordinator, Player Development	Jimmy Roy

Medical Staff

Head Physician	Dr. Peter MacDonald
Assistant Physicians	Dr. Greg Stranges, Dr. Jamie Dubberley
Primary Care	Dr. Mike MacKay, Dr. Swee Teo
Team Dentist	Dr. Gene Solmundson

Marketing & Communications

Senior Director Marketing & Brand Management	Dorian Morphy
Director Corporate Communications	Scott Brown
Director, Game Production & Broadcast Services	Kyle Balharry
Communications Coordinators	Christina Caligiuri, Kalen Qually
Manager, Marketing	Andrew Wilkinson
Senior Producer, Visual Media	Steve Godkin
Producer, Visual Media	Curtis Robson
Coordinator, Event Production	Nate Rollo
Coordinators, Web Content	Kristi Hennesy, Rhéanne Marcoux
Coordinator, Digital Media	Fabio Bellisario
Senior Graphic Designer	Josh Dudych
Graphic Designer	Jessie Greenwood

Sales

Director Ticket Administration & CRM	Mitch Brennan
Director Ticket Sales & Account Service	Linzy Jones
Director Corporate Partnerships	Jeff Mager

Retail Operations

Director Retail Operations	Dave Blackmore
Director Retail Development	Dan Suga
Assistant Manager Retail Operations	Shane Tucker

Community Relations

Manager, Community Relations	Barrett Paulsen
Community Relations Coordinator	Katie Dicks

Finance

Senior Director Finance	Lorna Daniels
Senior Director Business Operations	Audrey Gan
Controller	Lindsay Yurick

Event Management

Director, Event Management & Security	Kim Boulet
Director, Event Marketing	Alayne Nott
Sr. Manager Broadcast Services & Event Production	Lloyd Fox
Manager, Professional Audio & Video Services	Brian Johnson

Information Systems

Director Information Technology	Dan Gill
Systems Administrator	Darryl Elyk
Network Administrator	Ryan Cullen

Winnipeg Jets True North Foundation

Executive Director, WJTN Foundation	Dwayne Green

Building Operations

Senior Director, Facility Operations	Ed Meichsner
Chief Engineer	Derek King

2012-13 Final Standings

Standings

Abbreviations: GP - games played; **W** - wins; **L** - losses; **OT** - overtime and shootout losses; **GF** - goals for; **GA** - goals against; **PTS** - points.

Note: teams receive two points for a Win (W), one point for an Overtime or Shootout Loss (OT)

EASTERN CONFERENCE

Northeast Division

		GP	W	L	OT	GF	GA	PTS
Montreal	(2)	48	29	14	5	149	126	63
Boston	(4)	48	28	14	6	131	109	62
Toronto	(5)	48	26	17	5	145	133	57
Ottawa	(7)	48	25	17	6	116	104	56
Buffalo		48	21	21	6	125	143	48

Atlantic Division

		GP	W	L	OT	GF	GA	PTS
Pittsburgh	(1)	48	36	12	0	165	119	72
NY Rangers	(6)	48	26	18	4	130	112	56
NY Islanders	(8)	48	24	17	7	139	139	55
Philadelphia		48	23	22	3	133	141	49
New Jersey		48	19	19	10	112	129	48

Southeast Division

		GP	W	L	OT	GF	GA	PTS
Washington	(3)	48	27	18	3	149	130	57
Winnipeg		48	24	21	3	128	144	51
Carolina		48	19	25	4	128	160	42
Tampa Bay		48	18	26	4	148	150	40
Florida		48	15	27	6	112	171	36

WESTERN CONFERENCE

Central Division

		GP	W	L	OT	GF	GA	PTS
Chicago	(1)	48	36	7	5	155	102	77
St. Louis	(4)	48	29	17	2	129	115	60
Detroit	(7)	48	24	16	8	124	115	56
Columbus		48	24	17	7	120	119	55
Nashville		48	16	23	9	111	139	41

Pacific Division

		GP	W	L	OT	GF	GA	PTS
Anaheim	(2)	48	30	12	6	140	118	66
Los Angeles	(5)	48	27	16	5	133	118	59
San Jose	(6)	48	25	16	7	124	116	57
Phoenix		48	21	18	9	125	131	51
Dallas		48	22	22	4	130	142	48

Northwest Division

		GP	W	L	OT	GF	GA	PTS
Vancouver	(3)	48	26	15	7	127	121	59
Minnesota	(8)	48	26	19	3	122	127	55
Edmonton		48	19	22	7	125	134	45
Calgary		48	19	25	4	128	160	42
Colorado		48	16	25	7	116	152	39

Alex Ovechkin follows through on a shot that would net his 28th goal of the 2012-13 season during a 5-1 victory over Toronto on April 16, 2013. Two games later, Ovechkin notched his 30th en route to leading the NHL in goals for the third time in his eight-year career. He finished with 32 goals in 48 games.

INDIVIDUAL LEADERS

Goal Scoring

Player	Team	GP	G
Alex Ovechkin	Washington	48	32
Steven Stamkos	Tampa Bay	48	29
John Tavares	NY Islanders	48	28
Jeff Carter	Los Angeles	48	26
Jonathan Toews	Chicago	47	23
Patrick Kane	Chicago	47	23
Jiri Tlusty	Carolina	48	23
Chris Kunitz	Pittsburgh	48	22
Jakub Voracek	Philadelphia	48	22
James Neal	Pittsburgh	40	21
Rick Nash	NY Rangers	44	21
Logan Couture	San Jose	48	21
Thomas Vanek	Buffalo	38	20
Pascal Dupuis	Pittsburgh	48	20
Phil Kessel	Toronto	48	20

Assists

Player	Team	GP	A
Martin St. Louis	Tampa Bay	48	43
Sidney Crosby	Pittsburgh	36	41
Nicklas Backstrom	Washington	48	40
Henrik Zetterberg	Detroit	46	37
Mike Ribeiro	Washington	48	36
Eric Staal	Carolina	48	35
Claude Giroux	Philadelphia	48	35
Ryan Getzlaf	Anaheim	44	34
Taylor Hall	Edmonton	45	34
Pavel Datsyuk	Detroit	47	34
Henrik Sedin	Vancouver	48	34
Kris Letang	Pittsburgh	35	33
Joe Thornton	San Jose	48	33
Anze Kopitar	Los Angeles	47	32
Patrick Kane	Chicago	47	32
Phil Kessel	Toronto	48	32

Power-play Goals

Player	Team	GP	PP
Alex Ovechkin	Washington	48	16
Steven Stamkos	Tampa Bay	48	10
Thomas Vanek	Buffalo	38	9
James Neal	Pittsburgh	40	9
Chris Kunitz	Pittsburgh	48	9
John Tavares	NY Islanders	48	9

Shorthand Goals

Player	Team	GP	SH
Ilya Kovalchuk	New Jersey	37	4
Gabriel Landeskog	Colorado	36	3
Ryan Getzlaf	Anaheim	44	3
9 Players With			2

Game-winning Goals

Player	Team	GP	GW
Jeff Carter	Los Angeles	48	8
Marian Hossa	Chicago	40	6
James Neal	Pittsburgh	40	6
Pavel Datsyuk	Detroit	47	6
Derek Stepan	NY Rangers	48	6
16 Players With			5

Shots

Player	Team	GP	S
Alex Ovechkin	Washington	48	220
Evander Kane	Winnipeg	48	190
Zach Parise	Minnesota	48	182
David Clarkson	New Jersey	48	180
Rick Nash	NY Rangers	44	176
Henrik Zetterberg	Detroit	46	173

Shooting Percentage

(minimum 48 shots)

Player	Team	GP	G	S	%
Patrik Berglund	St. Louis	48	17	74	23.0
Gabriel Bourque	Nashville	34	11	50	22.0
Brenden Morrow	Dal., Pit.	44	12	55	21.8
Nail Yakupov*	Edmonton	48	17	81	21.0
Mike Ribeiro	Washington	48	13	63	20.6
Brad Marchand	Boston	45	18	91	19.8

Plus/Minus

Player	Team	GP	+/–
Pascal Dupuis	Pittsburgh	48	31
Chris Kunitz	Pittsburgh	48	30
Jonathan Toews	Chicago	47	28
Sidney Crosby	Pittsburgh	36	26
Derek Stepan	NY Rangers	48	25

** – rookie eligible for Calder Trophy*

Individual Leaders

Abbreviations: GP – games played; **G** – goals; **A** – assists; **Pts** – points; **+/–** – difference between Goals For (**GF**) scored when a player is on the ice with his team at even strength or shorthanded and Goals Against (**GA**) scored when the same player is on the ice with his team at even strength or on a power play; **PIM** – penalties in minutes; **PP** – power play goals; **SH** – shorthanded goals; **GW** – game-winning goals; **S** – shots on goal; **%** – percentage of shots on goal resulting in goals.

Individual Scoring Leaders for Art Ross Trophy

Player	Team	GP	G	A	Pts	+/-	PIM	PP	SH	GW	S	%
Martin St. Louis	Tampa Bay	48	17	43	60	0	14	3	0	2	112	15.2
Steven Stamkos	Tampa Bay	48	29	28	57	-4	32	10	0	2	157	18.5
Alex Ovechkin	Washington	48	32	24	56	2	36	16	0	4	220	14.5
Sidney Crosby	Pittsburgh	36	15	41	56	26	16	3	0	1	124	12.1
Patrick Kane	Chicago	47	23	32	55	11	8	8	0	3	138	16.7
Eric Staal	Carolina	48	18	35	53	5	54	3	1	4	152	11.8
Chris Kunitz	Pittsburgh	48	22	30	52	30	39	9	0	5	113	19.5
Phil Kessel	Toronto	48	20	32	52	-3	18	6	0	4	161	12.4
Taylor Hall	Edmonton	45	16	34	50	5	33	4	0	4	154	10.4
Ryan Getzlaf	Anaheim	44	15	34	49	14	41	4	3	3	99	15.2
Pavel Datsyuk	Detroit	47	15	34	49	21	14	8	0	6	107	14.0
Mike Ribeiro	Washington	48	13	36	49	-4	53	6	0	1	63	20.6
Jonathan Toews	Chicago	47	23	25	48	28	27	2	2	5	143	16.1
Claude Giroux	Philadelphia	48	13	35	48	-7	22	6	1	2	137	9.5
Henrik Zetterberg	Detroit	46	11	37	48	2	18	4	2	5	173	6.4
Nicklas Backstrom	Washington	48	8	40	48	8	20	3	0	1	82	9.8
John Tavares	NY Islanders	48	28	19	47	-2	18	9	0	5	162	17.3
Jakub Voracek	Philadelphia	48	22	24	46	-7	35	8	0	3	129	17.1
Andrew Ladd	Winnipeg	48	18	28	46	10	22	3	0	4	121	14.9
Henrik Sedin	Vancouver	48	11	34	45	19	24	1	1	1	70	15.7
Derek Stepan	NY Rangers	48	18	26	44	25	12	4	1	6	108	16.7
Nazem Kadri	Toronto	48	18	26	44	15	23	5	0	1	107	16.8
Matt Moulson	NY Islanders	47	15	29	44	-3	4	8	0	0	154	9.7
Alexander Semin	Carolina	44	13	31	44	14	46	4	0	1	150	8.7
P.A. Parenteau	Colorado	48	18	25	43	-11	38	6	0	1	105	17.1
Matt Duchene	Colorado	47	17	26	43	-12	12	2	0	3	132	12.9

Defencemen Scoring Leaders

Player	Team	GP	G	A	Pts	+/-	PIM	PP	SH	GW	S	%
P.K. Subban	Montreal	42	11	27	38	12	57	7	0	0	126	8.7
Kris Letang	Pittsburgh	35	5	33	38	16	8	1	0	1	95	5.3
Ryan Suter	Minnesota	48	4	28	32	2	24	3	0	1	91	4.4
Andrei Markov	Montreal	48	10	20	30	-9	14	8	0	4	79	12.7
Keith Yandle	Phoenix	48	10	20	30	4	54	5	0	3	130	7.7
Kimmo Timonen	Philadelphia	45	5	24	29	3	36	3	0	1	78	6.4
Niklas Kronwall	Detroit	48	5	24	29	-5	44	2	0	2	67	7.5
Cody Franson	Toronto	45	4	25	29	4	8	3	0	0	70	5.7
Dion Phaneuf	Toronto	48	9	19	28	-4	65	3	0	1	88	10.2
Shea Weber	Nashville	48	9	19	28	-2	48	3	0	1	124	7.3
Dustin Byfuglien	Winnipeg	43	8	20	28	-1	34	4	0	2	142	5.6
Brian Campbell	Florida	48	8	19	27	-22	12	6	0	2	70	11.4
Justin Schultz*	Edmonton	48	8	19	27	-17	8	4	0	3	85	9.4
Mark Streit	NY Islanders	48	6	21	27	-14	22	3	0	1	83	7.2
Sergei Gonchar	Ottawa	45	3	24	27	4	26	2	0	3	85	3.5
Duncan Keith	Chicago	47	3	24	27	16	31	2	0	0	91	3.3
Alex Goligoski	Dallas	47	3	24	27	4	18	0	0	0	80	3.8
Mike Green	Washington	35	12	14	26	-3	20	4	0	2	96	12.5
Slava Voynov	Los Angeles	48	6	19	25	5	14	1	0	2	79	7.6
Francois Beauchemin	Anaheim	48	6	18	24	19	22	1	0	0	74	8.1
Alex Pietrangelo	St. Louis	47	5	19	24	0	10	2	0	0	93	5.4
Dan Hamhuis	Vancouver	47	4	20	24	9	12	0	1	0	61	6.6
Oliver Ekman-Larsson	Phoenix	48	3	21	24	5	26	0	0	1	101	3.0
Paul Martin	Pittsburgh	34	6	17	23	14	16	2	0	1	38	15.8
Kevin Shattenkirk	St. Louis	48	5	18	23	2	20	2	0	0	84	6.0
Alexander Edler	Vancouver	45	8	14	22	-5	37	5	0	0	113	7.1

* — rookie eligible for Calder Trophy

Tampa Bay's Martin St. Louis puts in a rebound off Florida goalie Jacob Markstrom for his 17th and final goal of the 2012-13 season. With an NHL-best 43 assists, St. Louis led the league in scoring for the second time

CONSECUTIVE SCORING STREAKS

Goals

Games	Player	Team	G
6	Steven Stamkos	Tampa Bay	7
5	Patrick Marleau	San Jose	9
5	Chris Kunitz	Pittsburgh	7
5	Patrick Kane	Chicago	7
5	John Tavares	NY Islanders	7
5	Justin Williams	Los Angeles	6
5	Rick Nash	NY Rangers	6
5	Alex Ovechkin	Washington	6
5	Steven Stamkos	Tampa Bay	6
5	Jeff Carter	Los Angeles	5

Assists

Games	Player	Team	A
10	Sergei Gonchar	Ottawa	14
7	Nicklas Backstrom	Washington	13
7	Andrew Ladd	Winnipeg	10
6	Kris Letang	Pittsburgh	12
6	Joe Thornton	San Jose	11
6	Sidney Crosby	Pittsburgh	10
6	Sidney Crosby	Pittsburgh	10
6	Martin St. Louis	Tampa Bay	9
6	Vernon Fiddler	Dallas	8
6	Claude Giroux	Philadelphia	8
6	Henrik Zetterberg	Detroit	7
6	Matt Moulson	NY Islanders	7

Points

Games	Player	Team	G	A	PTS
11	Eric Staal	Carolina	8	9	17
10	Steven Stamkos	Tampa Bay	10	7	17
10	Sergei Gonchar	Ottawa	1	14	15
10	Sam Gagner	Edmonton	3	8	11
9	Alex Ovechkin	Washington	10	5	15
9	Nicklas Backstrom	Washington	1	14	15
8	Sidney Crosby	Pittsburgh	5	15	20
8	Steven Stamkos	Tampa Bay	7	9	16
8	Patrick Kane	Chicago	6	9	15
8	Tobias Enstrom	Winnipeg	2	10	12
8	Patrick Kane	Chicago	7	5	12
8	Jiri Tlusty	Carolina	6	5	11
8	Evander Kane	Winnipeg	6	4	10
8	Mike Fisher	Nashville	5	4	9

Individual Rookie Scoring Leaders

Player	Team	GP	G	A	Pts	+/–	PIM	PP	SH	GW	S	%
Nail Yakupov	Edmonton	48	17	14	31	-4	24	6	0	2	81	21.0
Jonathan Huberdeau	Florida	48	14	17	31	-15	18	2	0	1	112	12.5
Cory Conacher	T.B., Ott.	47	11	18	29	3	20	1	0	3	67	16.4
Brendan Gallagher	Montreal	44	15	13	28	10	33	3	0	3	117	12.8
Brandon Saad	Chicago	46	10	17	27	17	12	0	1	2	98	10.2
Alex Galchenyuk	Montreal	48	9	18	27	14	20	0	0	2	79	11.4
Justin Schultz	Edmonton	48	8	19	27	-17	8	4	0	3	85	9.4
Mika Zibanejad	Ottawa	42	7	13	20	9	6	3	0	0	90	7.8
Jakob Silfverberg	Ottawa	48	10	9	19	9	12	2	1	2	134	7.5
Vladimir Tarasenko	St. Louis	38	8	11	19	1	10	3	0	1	75	10.7
Alexander Killorn	Tampa Bay	38	7	12	19	-6	14	1	0	2	82	8.5
Patrick Wiercioch	Ottawa	42	5	14	19	9	39	3	0	0	81	6.2
Marcus Foligno	Buffalo	47	5	13	18	-4	41	1	0	0	55	9.1
Jake Muzzin	Los Angeles	45	7	9	16	16	35	3	0	1	77	9.1
Dougie Hamilton	Boston	42	5	11	16	4	14	2	0	0	83	6.0
Casey Cizikas	NY Islanders	45	6	9	15	0	14	0	0	1	45	13.3
Charlie Coyle	Minnesota	37	8	6	14	3	28	1	0	2	50	16.0
Antoine Roussel	Dallas	39	7	7	14	3	85	0	0	0	46	15.2
Beau Bennett	Pittsburgh	26	3	11	14	7	6	1	0	2	30	10.0

Goal Scoring

Player	Team	GP	G
Nail Yakupov	Edmonton	48	17
Brendan Gallagher	Montreal	44	15
Jonathan Huberdeau	Florida	48	14
Cory Conacher	T.B., Ott.	47	11
Brandon Saad	Chicago	46	10
Jakob Silfverberg	Ottawa	48	10
Alex Galchenyuk	Montreal	48	9
Charlie Coyle	Minnesota	37	8
Vladimir Tarasenko	St. Louis	38	8
Justin Schultz	Edmonton	48	8

Assists

Player	Team	GP	A
Justin Schultz	Edmonton	48	19
Cory Conacher	T.B., Ott.	47	18
Alex Galchenyuk	Montreal	48	18
Brandon Saad	Chicago	46	17
Jonathan Huberdeau	Florida	48	17
Patrick Wiercioch	Ottawa	42	14
Nail Yakupov	Edmonton	48	14
Mika Zibanejad	Ottawa	42	13
Brendan Gallagher	Montreal	44	13
Marcus Foligno	Buffalo	47	13

Power-play Goals

Player	Team	GP	PP
Nail Yakupov	Edmonton	48	6
Matt Irwin	San Jose	38	4
Justin Schultz	Edmonton	48	4
5 Players With			3

Shorthand Goals

Player	Team	GP	SH
Zach Redmond	Winnipeg	8	1
Brian Flynn	Buffalo	26	1
Drew Shore	Florida	43	1
Brandon Saad	Chicago	46	1
Jakob Silfverberg	Ottawa	48	1

Game-winning Goals

Player	Team	GP	GW
Leo Komarov	Toronto	42	3
Brendan Gallagher	Montreal	44	3
Cory Conacher	T.B., Ott.	47	3
Justin Schultz	Edmonton	48	3
10 Players With			2

Shots

Player	Team	GP	S
Jakob Silfverberg	Ottawa	48	134
Brendan Gallagher	Montreal	44	117
Jonathan Huberdeau	Florida	48	112
Brandon Saad	Chicago	46	98
Drew Shore	Florida	43	96

Shooting Percentage

(minimum 48 shots)

Player	Team	GP	G	S	%
Nail Yakupov	Edmonton	48	17	81	21.0
Cory Conacher	T.B., Ott.	47	11	67	16.4
Charlie Coyle	Minnesota	37	8	50	16.0
Jaden Schwartz	St. Louis	45	7	50	14.0
Brendan Gallagher	Montreal	44	15	117	12.8
Jon. Huberdeau	Florida	48	14	112	12.5
Brian Flynn	Buffalo	26	6	49	12.2

Plus/Minus

Player	Team	GP	+/–
Brandon Saad	Chicago	46	17
Jake Muzzin	Los Angeles	45	16
Dalton Prout	Columbus	28	15
Alex Galchenyuk	Montreal	48	14
Brendan Gallagher	Montreal	44	10
Simon Despres	Pittsburgh	33	9
Thomas Hickey	NY Islanders	39	9
Patrick Wiercioch	Ottawa	42	9
Mika Zibanejad	Ottawa	42	9
Jakob Silfverberg	Ottawa	48	9

Three-or-More-Goal Games

Player	Team	Date		Final Score				G
Justin Abdelkader	Detroit	Mar.	22	Det.	5	Ana.	1	3
Nick Bonino	Anaheim	Feb	2	L.A.	4	Ana.	7	3
Mike Cammalleri	Calgary	Feb.	13	Dal.	4	Cgy.	7	3
Jeff Carter	Los Angeles	Mar.	4	Nsh.	1	L.A.	5	3
Andrew Cogliano	Anaheim	Mar.	2	Ana.	4	Phx.	5	3
Marian Gaborik	NY Rangers	Jan.	23	Bos.	3	NYR	4	3
Curtis Glencross	Calgary	Mar.	15	Nsh.	3	Cgy.	6	3
Taylor Hall	Edmonton	Mar.	30	Van.	0	Edm.	4	3
Scott Hartnell	Philadelphia	Apr.	15	Phi.	7	Mtl.	3	3
Nazem Kadri	Toronto	Feb.	28	Tor.	5	NYI	4	3
Nazem Kadri	Toronto	Mar.	30	Tor.	4	Ott.	0	3
Tomas Kopecky	Florida	Feb.	26	Pit.	4	Fla.	6	3
Chris Kunitz	Pittsburgh	Feb	3	Pit.	6	Wsh.	3	4
Chris Kunitz	Pittsburgh	Mar.	10	NYI	1	Pit.	6	3
James Neal	Pittsburgh	Apr.	27	Car.	3	Pit.	8	3
Alex Ovechkin	Washington	Feb.	23	N.J.	1	Wsh.	5	3
Alex Ovechkin	Washington	Apr	06	Wsh.	4	Fla.	3	3
Kyle Palmieri	Anaheim	Feb.	27	Nsh.	1	Ana.	5	3
Matt Read	Philadelphia	Jan.	26	Phi.	7	Fla.	1	3
Brad Richards	NY Rangers	Apr.	19	NYR	8	Buf.	4	3
Wayne Simmonds	Philadelphia	Apr.	20	Phi.	5	Car.	3	3
Vladimir Sobotka	St. Louis	Mar.	9	St.L.	4	S.J.	3	3
Martin St. Louis	Tampa Bay	Apr.	24	Tor.	2	T.B.	5	3
Eric Staal	Carolina	Jan.	24	Buf.	3	Car.	6	3
Steve Sullivan	Phoenix	Jan.	23	CBJ	1	Phx.	5	3
John Tavares	NY Islanders	Feb.	16	N.J.	1	NYI	5	3
Jiri Tlusty	Carolina	Apr	02	Wsh.	5	Car.	3	3
Thomas Vanek	Buffalo	Jan	31	Buf.	7	Bos.	4	3
Jakub Voracek	Philadelphia	Feb.	20	Phi.	6	Pit.	5	3
Radim Vrbata	Phoenix	Apr.	27	Phx.	5	Ana.	3	3
Nail Yakupov*	Edmonton	Apr.	27	Van.	2	Edm.	7	3
Henrik Zetterberg	Detroit	Feb	1	St.L.	3	Det.	5	3

* — rookie eligible for Calder Trophy

2012-13 Penalty Shots

(For shootout statistics, see page 143.)

Scored

Ilya Kovalchuk (N.J.) scored against Ilya Bryzgalov (Phi.) Jan. 22. Final score: Phi. 0 at N.J. 3

Patrik Berglund (St.L.) scored against Pekka Rinne (Nsh.) Jan. 24. Final score: Nsh. 0 at St.L. 3

Jonathan Huberdeau (Fla.) scored against Ilya Bryzgalov (Phi.) Feb. 21. Final score: Fla. 5 at Phi. 2

Brad Marchand (Bos.) scored against Braden Holtby (Wsh.) Mar. 5. Final score: Bos. 3 at Wsh. 4

Jonathan Huberdeau (Fla.) scored against Ondrej Pavelec (Wpg.) Mar. 5. Final score: Wpg. 1 at Fla. 4

Rich Clune (Nsh.) scored against Kari Lehtonen (Dal.) Mar. 12. Final score: Nsh. 4 at Dal. 0

Henrik Sedin (Van.) scored against Chris Mason (Nsh.) Mar. 14. Final score: Nsh. 4 at Van. 7

Tom Kostopoulos (N.J.) scored against Mathieu Garon (T.B.) Mar. 29. Final score: N.J. 4 at T.B. 5

Stopped

Guillaume Latendresse (Ott.) stopped by **Jose Theodore** (Fla.) Jan. 24. Final score: Ott. 3 at Fla. 1

Ryan Garbutt (Dal.) stopped by **Corey Crawford** (Chi.) Jan. 24. Final score: Chi. 3 at Dal. 2

Alexandre Burrows (Van.) stopped by **Jonas Hiller** (Ana.) Jan. 25. Final score: Van. 5 at Ana. 0

Pierre-Marc Bouchard (Min.) stopped by **Steve Mason** (CBJ) Jan. 29. Final score: CBJ 2 at Min. 3

Taylor Hall (Edm.) stopped by **Roberto Luongo** (Van.) Feb. 4. Final score: Van. 3 at Edm. 2

Jarome Iginla (Cgy.) stopped by **Jimmy Howard** (Det.) Feb. 5. Final score: Cgy. 4 at Det. 1

John Tavares (NYI) stopped by **Ryan Miller** (Buf.) Feb. 9. Final score: Buf. 3 at NYI 2

David Ullstrom (NYI) stopped by **Johan Hedberg** (N.J.) Feb. 16. Final score: N.J. 1 at NYI 5

Steve Bernier (N.J.) stopped by **Braden Holtby** (Wsh.) Feb. 23. Final score: N.J. 1 at Wsh. 5

Dustin Brown (L.A.) stopped by **Viktor Fasth** (Ana.) Feb. 25. Final score: Ana. 2 at L.A. 5

Mikhail Grabovski (Tor.) stopped by **Carey Price** (Mtl.) Feb. 27. Final score: Mtl. 5 at Tor. 2

Michael Grabner (NYI) stopped by **James Reimer** (Tor.) Feb. 28. Final score: Tor. 5 at NYI 4

Andrew Cogliano (Ana.) stopped by **Jason LaBarbera** (Phx.) Mar. 6. Final score: Phx. 0 at Ana. 2

Eric Staal (Car.) stopped by **Carey Price** (Mtl.) Mar. 7. Final score: Mtl. 4 at Car. 2

Mikael Backlund (Cgy.) stopped by **Jonas Gustavsson** (Det.) Mar. 13. Final score: Det. 2 at Cgy. 5

Marian Gaborik (NYR) stopped by **Ondrej Pavelec** (Wpg.) Mar. 14. Final score: NYR 1 at Wpg. 3

Jannik Hansen (Van.) stopped by **Jimmy Howard** (Det.) Mar. 16. Final score: Det. 5 at Van. 2

Tommy Wingels (S.J.) stopped by **Jonathan Bernier** (L.A.) Mar. 16. Final score: S.J. 2 at L.A. 5

Antoine Roussel (Dal.) stopped by **Joey MacDonald** (Cgy.) Mar. 18. Final score: Cgy. 3 at Dal. 4

Andrew Desjardins (S.J.) stopped by **Niklas Backstrom** (Min.) Mar. 23. Final score: S.J. 0 at Min. 2

Lauri Korpikoski (Phx.) stopped by **Jonas Gustavsson** (Det.) Mar. 25. Final score: Det. 3 at Phx. 2

Johnny Boychuk (Bos.) stopped by **Martin Brodeur** (N.J.) Apr. 10. Final score: Bos. 5 at N.J. 4

Bobby Butler (Nsh.) stopped by **Jimmy Howard** (Det.) Apr. 14. Final score: Det. 3 at Nsh. 0

Quinton Howden (Fla.) stopped by **Martin Brodeur** (N.J.) Apr. 20. Final score: Fla. 2 at N.J. 6

Evander Kane (Wpg.) stopped by **Jhonas Enroth** (Buf.) Apr. 22. Final score: Wpg. 2 at Buf. 1

Benoit Pouliot (T.B.) stopped by **Jacob Markstrom** (Fla.) Apr. 27. Final score: Fla. 5 at T.B. 3

Total Shots: 34
Total Goals: 8
Total Saves: 26

Florida's Jonathan Huberdeau was awarded a penalty shot on this play after being interfered with by Philadelphia defenseman Kimmo Timonen. Huberdeau beat Ilya Bryzgalov for his first of two penalty shot goals during the 2012-13 season.

Goaltending Leaders

Minimum 13 games

Goals Against Average

Goaltender	Team	GPI	MINS	GA	Avg
Craig Anderson	Ottawa	24	1421	40	1.69
Jonathan Bernier	Los Angeles	14	768	24	1.88
Ray Emery	Chicago	21	1116	36	1.94
Corey Crawford	Chicago	30	1761	57	1.94
Tuukka Rask	Boston	36	2104	70	2.00
Sergei Bobrovsky	Columbus	38	2219	74	2.00

Wins

Goaltender	Team	GPI	MINS	W	L	OT
Niklas Backstrom	Minnesota	42	2368	24	15	3
Henrik Lundqvist	NY Rangers	43	2575	24	16	3
Antti Niemi	San Jose	43	2581	24	12	6
Marc-Andre Fleury	Pittsburgh	33	1858	23	8	0
Braden Holtby	Washington	36	2089	23	12	1
Evgeni Nabokov	NY Islanders	41	2475	23	11	7

Save Percentage

Goaltender	Team	GPI	MINS	GA	SA	S%	W	L	OT
Craig Anderson	Ottawa	24	1421	40	677	.941	12	9	2
Sergei Bobrovsky	Columbus	38	2219	74	1084	.932	21	11	6
Tuukka Rask	Boston	36	2104	70	980	.929	19	10	5
Cory Schneider	Vancouver	30	1733	61	835	.927	17	9	4
Henrik Lundqvist	NY Rangers	43	2575	88	1190	.926	24	16	3
Corey Crawford	Chicago	30	1761	57	769	.926	19	5	5

Shutouts

Goaltender	Team	GPI	MINS	SO	W	L	OT
Cory Schneider	Vancouver	30	1733	5	17	9	4
Mike Smith	Phoenix	34	1956	5	15	12	5
Tuukka Rask	Boston	36	2104	5	19	10	5
Pekka Rinne	Nashville	43	2444	5	15	16	8
Jimmy Howard	Detroit	42	2446	5	21	13	7
5 goaltenders with				4			

Team-by-Team Point Totals

2008-09 to 2012-13

(Ranked by five-year point %)

Team	12-13	11-12	10-11	09-10	08-09	Pts%
Chicago	77	101	97	112	104	.653
Vancouver	59	111	117	103	100	.652
San Jose	57	96	105	113	117	.649
Pittsburgh	72	108	106	101	99	.646
Washington	57	92	107	121	108	.645
Detroit	56	102	104	102	112	.633
Boston	62	102	103	91	116	.630
Philadelphia	49	103	106	88	99	.592
NY Rangers	56	109	93	87	95	.585
New Jersey	48	102	81	103	106	.585
St. Louis	60	109	87	90	92	.582
Phoenix	51	97	99	107	79	.576
Los Angeles	59	95	98	101	79	.574
Nashville	41	104	99	100	88	.574
Anaheim	66	80	99	89	91	.565
Buffalo	48	89	96	100	91	.564
Montreal	63	78	96	88	93	.556
Calgary	42	90	94	90	98	.551
Dallas	48	89	95	88	83	.536
Ottawa	56	92	74	94	83	.531
Minnesota	55	81	86	84	89	.525
Carolina	42	82	91	80	97	.521
Toronto	57	80	85	74	81	.501
Winnipeg	51	84	80	83	76	.497
Tampa Bay	40	84	103	80	66	.496
Columbus	55	65	81	79	92	.495
Florida	36	94	72	77	93	.495
Colorado	39	88	68	95	69	.477
NY Islanders	55	79	73	79	61	.461
Edmonton	45	74	62	62	85	.436

Team Record When Scoring First Goal of a Game

Team	FG	W	L	OT
Anaheim	24	18	2	4
Boston	26	19	4	3
Buffalo	24	16	4	4
Calgary	25	15	9	1
Carolina	19	11	6	2
Chicago	29	26	2	1
Colorado	16	9	4	3
Columbus	20	12	6	2
Dallas	23	16	5	2
Detroit	25	16	7	2
Edmonton	24	12	6	6
Florida	17	11	4	2
Los Angeles	26	21	3	2
Minnesota	23	18	4	1
Montreal	29	21	5	3
Nashville	18	11	2	5
New Jersey	19	14	1	4
NY Islanders	23	17	3	3
NY Rangers	21	18	2	1
Ottawa	25	18	5	2
Philadelphia	26	18	6	2
Phoenix	19	14	1	4
Pittsburgh	31	25	6	0
San Jose	25	20	3	2
St. Louis	29	23	5	1
Tampa Bay	19	13	6	0
Toronto	32	19	9	4
Vancouver	31	20	6	5
Washington	26	17	8	1
Winnipeg	23	16	6	1

Team Plus/Minus Differential

Team	GF	PPGF	Net GF	GA	PPGA	Net GA	Goal Differential
Chicago	155	25	130	102	18	84	+46
Pittsburgh	165	42	123	119	34	85	+38
Boston	131	18	113	109	21	88	+25
Anaheim	140	29	111	118	30	88	+23
NY Rangers	130	24	106	112	28	84	+22
Montreal	149	42	107	126	35	91	+16
Washington	149	44	105	130	36	94	+11
Los Angeles	133	33	100	118	27	91	+9
St. Louis	129	29	100	115	23	92	+8
Vancouver	127	26	101	121	27	94	+7
Ottawa	116	25	91	104	20	84	+7
Detroit	124	34	90	115	30	85	+5
Columbus	120	22	98	119	25	94	+4
Phoenix	125	25	100	131	34	97	+3
Toronto	145	31	114	133	19	114	0
Tampa Bay	148	31	117	150	30	120	-3
NY Islanders	139	31	108	139	28	111	-3
Buffalo	125	23	102	143	37	106	-4
San Jose	124	34	90	116	22	94	-4
Minnesota	122	27	95	127	26	101	-6
Dallas	130	29	101	142	34	108	-7
Winnipeg	128	20	108	144	28	116	-8
New Jersey	112	28	84	129	32	97	-13
Edmonton	125	34	91	134	29	105	-14
Nashville	111	24	87	139	34	105	-18
Philadelphia	133	37	96	141	26	115	-19
Carolina	128	24	104	160	36	124	-20
Colorado	116	21	95	152	36	116	-21
Calgary	128	31	97	160	28	132	-35
Florida	112	29	83	171	39	132	-49

Team Record When Leading, Trailing, Tied

Team	Leading after 1 period			Leading after 2 periods			Trailing after 1 period			Trailing after 2 periods			Tied after 1 period			Tied after 2 periods		
	W	L	OT	W	L	OT	W	L	OT	W	L	OT	W	L	OT	W	L	OT
Anaheim	12	0	3	17	0	2	8	10	1	5	11	1	10	2	2	8	1	3
Boston	13	2	2	15	4	4	2	7	3	3	7	2	13	5	1	10	3	0
Buffalo	6	2	2	9	0	4	1	10	1	3	15	2	14	9	3	9	6	0
Calgary	11	4	1	12	2	1	1	15	0	1	19	1	7	6	3	6	4	2
Carolina	9	3	1	14	1	0	4	13	2	2	16	2	6	9	1	3	8	2
Chicago	17	1	1	26	1	2	3	3	3	4	5	1	16	3	1	6	1	2
Colorado	7	2	1	9	2	3	4	16	3	4	22	3	5	7	3	3	1	1
Columbus	8	2	1	13	0	0	4	9	1	3	14	3	12	6	5	8	3	4
Dallas	14	3	2	12	3	2	2	13	2	2	15	0	6	6	0	8	4	2
Detroit	9	4	1	18	2	1	4	9	3	2	11	3	11	3	4	4	3	4
Edmonton	11	3	2	12	0	4	5	9	0	4	16	2	3	10	5	3	6	1
Florida	7	2	2	6	0	1	3	22	3	3	24	2	5	3	1	6	3	3
Los Angeles	15	1	0	19	1	2	5	10	1	3	11	0	7	5	4	5	4	3
Minnesota	9	2	1	18	1	1	6	12	1	2	14	2	11	5	1	6	4	0
Montreal	15	3	1	17	2	2	1	7	1	4	12	1	13	4	3	8	0	2
Nashville	7	1	3	8	1	1	0	12	1	1	18	2	9	10	5	7	4	6
New Jersey	8	2	1	12	1	3	4	10	4	3	14	3	7	7	5	4	4	4
NY Islanders	13	2	1	16	2	1	5	5	2	2	7	5	6	10	4	6	8	1
NY Rangers	13	0	1	16	0	0	5	10	1	3	16	1	8	8	2	7	2	3
Ottawa	8	2	2	19	1	1	3	10	2	3	10	1	14	5	2	3	6	4
Philadelphia	13	3	1	17	0	3	1	12	0	2	14	0	9	7	2	4	8	0
Phoenix	13	1	2	15	0	1	2	11	5	2	14	4	6	6	2	4	4	4
Pittsburgh	21	4	0	19	1	0	5	5	0	4	8	0	10	3	0	13	3	0
San Jose	14	2	1	15	1	2	4	9	1	4	13	1	7	5	5	6	2	4
St. Louis	15	3	1	19	2	0	5	9	0	5	13	1	9	5	1	5	2	1
Tampa Bay	13	3	0	11	3	0	2	13	3	2	20	4	3	10	1	5	3	0
Toronto	16	4	2	20	2	1	3	6	1	2	12	3	7	7	2	4	3	1
Vancouver	15	2	4	18	2	3	2	6	2	1	9	2	9	7	1	7	4	2
Washington	12	3	0	19	3	0	9	9	2	5	11	2	6	6	1	3	4	1
Winnipeg	10	2	0	18	2	0	5	11	2	1	14	0	9	8	1	5	5	3

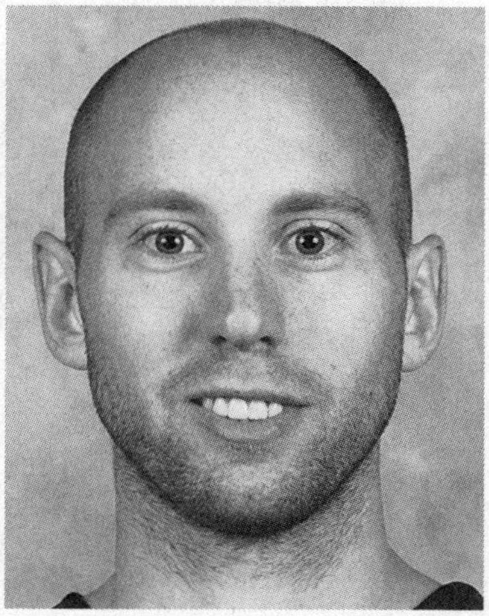

Although limited to 24 games due to an injury in 2012-13, Ottawa's Craig Anderson had a save percentage of .941 for the best mark since the statistic was officially introduced in 1976-77. He also led the NHL with a 1.69 goals against average.

Team Statistics

TEAMS' HOME AND ROAD RECORD

Eastern Conference

	Home							Road						
Team	GP	W	L	OT	GF	GA	PTS	GP	W	L	OT	GF	GA	PTS
PIT	24	18	6	0	79	52	36	24	18	6	0	86	67	36
MTL	24	14	7	3	70	59	31	24	15	7	2	79	67	32
BOS	24	16	5	3	71	51	35	24	12	9	3	60	58	27
TOR	24	13	9	2	74	70	28	24	13	8	3	71	63	29
WSH	24	15	8	1	77	60	31	24	12	10	2	72	70	26
NYR	24	16	6	2	77	51	34	24	10	12	2	53	61	22
OTT	24	15	6	3	59	45	33	24	10	11	3	57	59	23
NYI	24	10	11	3	68	73	23	24	14	6	4	71	66	32
WPG	24	13	10	1	68	66	27	24	11	11	2	60	78	24
PHI	24	15	7	2	70	64	32	24	8	15	1	63	77	17
N.J.	24	13	9	2	66	59	28	24	6	10	8	46	70	20
BUF	24	11	10	3	63	71	25	24	10	11	3	62	72	23
CAR	24	9	14	1	67	83	19	24	10	11	3	61	77	23
T.B.	24	12	10	2	82	69	26	24	6	16	2	66	81	14
FLA	24	8	11	5	65	81	21	24	7	16	1	47	90	15
Totals	**360**	**198**	**129**	**33**	**1056**	**954**	**429**	**360**	**162**	**159**	**39**	**954**	**1056**	**363**

Western Conference

CHI	24	18	3	3	77	57	39	24	18	4	2	78	45	38
ANA	24	16	7	1	72	61	33	24	14	5	5	68	57	33
ST.L.	24	15	8	1	59	52	31	24	14	9	1	70	63	29
L.A.	24	19	4	1	74	44	39	24	8	12	4	59	74	20
VAN	24	15	6	3	70	54	33	24	11	9	4	57	67	26
S.J.	24	17	2	5	73	49	39	24	8	14	2	51	67	18
DET	24	13	7	4	68	57	30	24	11	9	4	56	58	26
MIN	24	14	8	2	54	57	30	24	12	11	1	68	70	25
CBJ	24	14	5	5	64	51	33	24	10	12	2	56	68	22
PHX	24	14	8	2	74	62	30	24	7	10	7	51	69	21
DAL	24	11	11	2	65	74	24	24	11	11	2	65	68	24
EDM	24	9	11	4	61	71	22	24	10	11	3	64	63	23
CGY	24	13	9	2	78	80	28	24	6	16	2	50	80	14
NSH	24	11	9	4	59	59	26	24	5	14	5	52	80	15
COL	24	12	9	3	65	68	27	24	4	16	4	51	84	12
Totals	**360**	**211**	**107**	**42**	**1013**	**896**	**464**	**360**	**149**	**163**	**48**	**896**	**1013**	**346**
	720	**409**	**236**	**75**	**2069**	**1850**	**893**	**720**	**311**	**322**	**87**	**1850**	**2069**	**709**

Though his stay in Pittsburgh proved brief, Jarome Iginla arrived in a trade from Calgary in time to help the Penguins notch their 15th consecutive win on March 30, 2013. The streak is tied for the second longest in NHL history behind Pittsburgh's 17-gamer in 1992-93.

TEAMS' DIVISIONAL RECORD

Northeast Division

	Against Own Division							Against Other Divisions						
Team	GP	W	L	OT	GF	GA	PTS	GP	W	L	OT	GF	GA	PTS
MTL	18	9	6	3	50	50	21	30	20	8	2	99	76	42
BOS	18	10	6	2	46	45	22	30	18	8	4	85	64	40
TOR	18	10	6	2	53	40	22	30	16	11	3	92	93	35
OTT	18	7	8	3	41	48	17	30	18	9	3	75	56	39
BUF	18	9	7	2	48	55	20	30	12	14	4	77	88	28
Totals	**90**	**45**	**33**	**12**	**238**	**238**	**102**	**150**	**84**	**50**	**16**	**428**	**377**	**184**

Atlantic Division

PIT	18	12	6	0	56	41	24	30	24	6	0	109	78	48
NYR	18	10	6	2	46	38	22	30	16	12	2	84	74	34
NYI	18	7	9	2	38	51	16	30	17	8	5	101	88	39
PHI	18	6	10	2	43	55	14	30	17	12	1	90	86	35
N.J.	18	10	6	2	44	42	22	30	9	13	8	68	87	26
Totals	**90**	**45**	**37**	**8**	**227**	**227**	**98**	**150**	**83**	**51**	**16**	**452**	**413**	**182**

Southeast Division

WSH	18	15	3	0	73	43	30	30	12	15	3	76	87	27
WPG	18	10	8	0	50	60	20	30	14	13	3	78	84	31
CAR	18	5	12	1	38	60	11	30	14	13	3	90	100	31
T.B.	18	9	6	3	69	53	21	30	9	20	1	79	97	19
FLA	18	6	8	4	55	69	16	30	9	19	2	57	102	20
Totals	**90**	**45**	**37**	**8**	**285**	**285**	**98**	**150**	**58**	**80**	**12**	**380**	**470**	**128**

Central Division

CHI	18	16	1	1	53	29	33	30	20	6	4	102	73	44
ST.L.	18	11	7	0	43	41	22	30	18	10	2	86	74	38
DET	18	6	6	6	43	51	18	30	18	10	2	81	64	38
CBJ	18	9	6	3	44	42	21	30	15	11	4	76	77	34
NSH	18	3	11	4	36	56	10	30	13	12	5	75	83	31
Totals	**90**	**45**	**34**	**11**	**244**	**244**	**101**	**150**	**84**	**49**	**17**	**420**	**371**	**185**

Pacific Division

ANA	18	8	7	3	52	54	19	30	22	5	3	88	64	47
L.A.	18	9	7	2	51	54	20	30	18	9	3	82	64	39
S.J.	18	9	7	2	49	45	20	30	16	9	5	75	71	37
PHX	18	9	7	2	45	49	20	30	12	11	7	80	82	31
DAL	18	10	6	2	47	42	22	30	12	16	2	83	100	26
Totals	**90**	**45**	**34**	**11**	**244**	**244**	**101**	**150**	**80**	**50**	**20**	**408**	**381**	**180**

Northwest Division

VAN	18	11	6	1	52	42	23	30	15	9	6	75	79	36
MIN	18	12	5	1	53	47	25	30	14	14	2	69	80	30
EDM	18	10	7	1	63	44	21	30	9	15	6	62	90	24
CGY	18	7	8	3	47	60	17	30	12	17	1	81	100	25
COL	18	5	13	0	45	67	10	30	11	12	7	71	85	29
Totals	**90**	**45**	**39**	**6**	**260**	**260**	**96**	**150**	**61**	**67**	**22**	**358**	**434**	**144**

TEAM STREAKS

Consecutive Wins

Games	Team	From	To
15	Pittsburgh	Mar. 2	Mar. 30
11	Chicago	Feb. 15	Mar. 6
8	Washington	Apr. 2	Apr. 16
7	San Jose	Jan. 20	Jan. 31
7	Minnesota	Mar. 14	Mar. 27
7	San Jose	Mar. 25	Apr. 5
7	Pittsburgh	Apr. 5	Apr. 22
7	Chicago	Apr. 6	Apr. 19
6	Chicago	Jan. 19	Jan. 27
6	Vancouver	Jan. 30	Feb. 12
6	Anaheim	Feb. 9	Feb. 24
6	Boston	Feb. 17	Mar. 2
6	Vancouver	Mar. 19	Mar. 28
6	St. Louis	Apr. 1	Apr. 11

Consecutive Home Wins

Games	Team	From	To
13	Anaheim	Jan. 26	Mar. 20
12	Pittsburgh	Feb. 22	Mar. 30
9	Chicago	Feb. 15	Mar. 6
8	Calgary	Feb. 23	Mar. 27
8	Vancouver	Mar. 19	Apr. 22
7	San Jose	Mar. 14	Apr. 5
7	Los Angeles	Apr. 4	Apr. 27

Consecutive Road Wins

Games	Team	From	To
6	Chicago	Feb. 2	Mar. 3
5	Pittsburgh	Mar. 2	Mar. 22
5	Montreal	Mar. 7	Mar. 21
5	Minnesota	Mar. 9	Mar. 25
5	Detroit	Mar. 15	Mar. 25
5	St. Louis	Apr. 1	Apr. 11
5	Pittsburgh	Apr. 9	Apr. 22

TEAM PENALTIES

Abbreviations: GP – games played; **PEN** – total penalty minutes including bench minutes; **BMI** – total bench minor minutes; **AVG** – average penalty minutes/game calculated by dividing total penalty minutes by games played

Team	GP	PEN	BMI	AVG
CHI	48	444	6	9.3
NYR	48	444	12	9.3
NYI	48	461	6	9.6
DET	48	469	6	9.8
NSH	48	471	10	9.8
L.A.	48	481	10	10.0
PHX	48	504	12	10.5
N.J.	48	509	14	10.6
CGY	48	518	6	10.8
WSH	48	516	8	10.8
EDM	48	522	16	10.9
S.J.	48	521	4	10.9
ANA	48	535	10	11.1
ST.L.	48	531	16	11.1
WPG	48	535	8	11.1
CAR	48	538	8	11.2
FLA	48	541	6	11.3
MIN	48	545	6	11.4
PIT	48	563	12	11.7
T.B.	48	577	10	12.0
BOS	48	584	14	12.2
COL	48	598	8	12.5
CBJ	48	605	10	12.6
VAN	48	609	4	12.7
DAL	48	623	18	13.0
BUF	48	630	8	13.1
MTL	48	636	12	13.3
OTT	48	655	6	13.6
PHI	48	755	18	15.7
TOR	48	776	12	16.2
Totals	**720**	**16696**	**296**	**23.2**

The New York Rangers were the NHL's least penalized team in 2012-13. Derek Stepan led the Rangers with 44 points in 48 games while serving only 12 minutes in the penalty box.

TEAMS' POWER-PLAY RECORD

Abbreviations: ADV – total advantages; **PPGF** – power-play goals for; **%** – calculated by dividing number of power-play goals by total advantages.

	Home					Road					Overall				
	Team	GP	ADV	PPGF	%	Team	GP	ADV	PPGF	%	Team	GP	ADV	PPGF	%
1	Phi.	24	79	22	27.8	Wsh.	24	83	22	26.5	Wsh.	48	164	44	26.8
2	Wsh.	24	81	22	27.2	Min.	24	68	16	23.5	Pit.	48	170	42	24.7
3	Pit.	24	80	21	26.3	Pit.	24	90	21	23.3	Phi.	48	171	37	21.6
4	S.J.	24	82	21	25.6	Tor.	24	78	15	19.2	Ana.	48	135	29	21.5
5	T.B.	24	91	22	24.2	NYI	24	68	13	19.1	Mtl.	48	203	42	20.7
6	Det.	24	97	23	23.7	Ana.	24	63	12	19.0	Fla.	48	142	29	20.4
7	Ana.	24	72	17	23.6	Edm.	24	84	16	19.0	S.J.	48	169	34	20.1
8	Nsh.	24	68	16	23.5	Cgy.	24	84	16	19.0	Edm.	48	169	34	20.1
9	Mtl.	24	98	22	22.4	Mtl.	24	105	20	19.0	Cgy.	48	155	31	20.0
10	Fla.	24	82	18	22.0	L.A.	24	81	15	18.5	L.A.	48	166	33	19.9
11	St.L.	24	84	18	21.4	Fla.	24	60	11	18.3	NYI	48	156	31	19.9
12	L.A.	24	85	18	21.2	Col.	24	68	12	17.6	St.L.	48	149	29	19.5
13	Edm.	24	85	18	21.2	Bos.	24	58	10	17.2	T.B.	48	163	31	19.0
14	Cgy.	24	71	15	21.1	St.L.	24	65	11	16.9	Tor.	48	166	31	18.7
15	NYI	24	88	18	20.5	Phi.	24	92	15	16.3	Det.	48	185	34	18.4
16	Dal.	24	92	18	19.6	Ott.	24	81	13	16.0	Min.	48	151	27	17.9
17	NYR	24	83	16	19.3	Chi.	24	72	11	15.3	Nsh.	48	140	24	17.1
18	Phx.	24	86	16	18.6	S.J.	24	87	13	14.9	Dal.	48	171	29	17.0
19	Tor.	24	88	16	18.2	Van.	24	81	12	14.8	Chi.	48	150	25	16.7
20	N.J.	24	94	17	18.1	Car.	24	83	12	14.5	Ott.	48	157	25	15.9
21	Chi.	24	78	14	17.9	Dal.	24	79	11	13.9	N.J.	48	176	28	15.9
22	Van.	24	84	14	16.7	N.J.	24	82	11	13.4	Van.	48	165	26	15.8
23	CBJ	24	86	14	16.3	Det.	24	88	11	12.5	NYR	48	153	24	15.7
24	Buf.	24	82	13	15.9	T.B.	24	72	9	12.5	Col.	48	140	21	15.0
25	Ott.	24	76	12	15.8	Buf.	24	81	10	12.3	Bos.	48	122	18	14.8
26	Wpg.	24	78	12	15.4	Wpg.	24	67	8	11.9	Phx.	48	169	25	14.8
27	Car.	24	82	12	14.6	CBJ	24	69	8	11.6	Car.	48	165	24	14.5
28	Min.	24	83	11	13.3	NYR	24	70	8	11.4	CBJ	48	155	22	14.2
29	Bos.	24	64	8	12.5	Nsh.	24	72	8	11.1	Buf.	48	163	23	14.1
30	Col.	24	72	9	12.5	Phx.	24	83	9	10.8	Wpg.	48	145	20	13.8
	Totals	**720**	**2471**	**493**	**20.0**		**720**	**2314**	**379**	**16.4**		**720**	**4785**	**872**	**18.2**

TEAMS' PENALTY KILLING RECORD

Abbreviations: TSH – total times shorthanded; **PPGA** – power-play goals against; **%** – calculated by dividing times short minus power-play goals against by times short.

	Home					Road					Overall				
	Team	GP	TSH	PPGA	%	Team	GP	TSH	PPGA	%	Team	GP	TSH	PPGA	%
1	Col.	24	92	8	91.3	Chi.	24	70	7	90.0	Ott.	48	167	20	88.0
2	Tor.	24	73	7	90.4	Bos.	24	76	9	88.2	Tor.	48	157	19	87.9
3	Ott.	24	80	8	90.0	Ott.	24	87	12	86.2	Chi.	48	141	18	87.2
4	St.L.	24	66	7	89.4	Dal.	24	85	12	85.9	Bos.	48	163	21	87.1
5	L.A.	24	70	8	88.6	Tor.	24	84	12	85.7	Phi.	48	184	26	85.9
6	CBJ	24	67	8	88.1	Cgy.	24	76	11	85.5	S.J.	48	147	22	85.0
7	Phi.	24	91	11	87.9	Edm.	24	89	14	84.3	St.L.	48	150	23	84.7
8	S.J.	24	64	8	87.5	Phi.	24	93	15	83.9	Van.	48	169	27	84.0
9	Van.	24	78	10	87.2	S.J.	24	83	14	83.1	Edm.	48	175	29	83.4
10	NYR	24	80	11	86.3	Mtl.	24	84	15	82.1	L.A.	48	161	27	83.2
11	Bos.	24	87	12	86.2	N.J.	24	88	16	81.8	CBJ	48	144	25	82.6
12	Wpg.	24	70	10	85.7	Van.	24	91	17	81.3	Det.	48	164	30	81.7
13	Pit.	24	69	10	85.5	St.L.	24	84	16	81.0	Ana.	48	162	30	81.5
14	Ana.	24	79	12	84.8	NYI	24	72	14	80.6	Cgy.	48	151	28	81.5
15	Chi.	24	71	11	84.5	Det.	24	81	16	80.2	NYR	48	148	28	81.1
16	Min.	24	70	11	84.3	T.B.	24	78	16	79.5	N.J.	48	169	32	81.1
17	Det.	24	83	14	83.1	Phx.	24	82	17	79.3	Dal.	48	179	34	81.0
18	Edm.	24	86	15	82.6	L.A.	24	91	19	79.1	Min.	48	135	26	80.7
19	T.B.	24	77	14	81.8	Buf.	24	99	21	78.8	T.B.	48	155	30	80.6
20	Phx.	24	87	17	80.5	Ana.	24	83	18	78.3	NYI	48	142	28	80.3
21	Wsh.	24	71	14	80.3	CBJ	24	77	17	77.9	Col.	48	183	36	80.3
22	N.J.	24	81	16	80.2	Min.	24	65	15	76.9	Phx.	48	169	34	79.9
23	NYI	24	70	14	80.0	Wsh.	24	92	22	76.1	Mtl.	48	173	35	79.8
24	Buf.	24	79	16	79.7	Car.	24	82	20	75.6	Wpg.	48	138	28	79.7
25	Car.	24	79	16	79.7	Pit.	24	98	24	75.5	Pit.	48	167	34	79.6
26	Nsh.	24	62	13	79.0	NYR	24	68	17	75.0	Buf.	48	178	37	79.2
27	Mtl.	24	89	20	77.5	Fla.	24	77	20	74.0	Wsh.	48	163	36	77.9
28	Cgy.	24	75	17	77.3	Wpg.	24	68	18	73.5	Car.	48	161	36	77.6
29	Dal.	24	94	22	76.6	Nsh.	24	77	21	72.7	Nsh.	48	139	34	75.5
30	Fla.	24	74	19	74.3	Col.	24	91	28	69.2	Fla.	48	151	39	74.2
	Totals	**720**	**2314**	**379**	**83.6**		**720**	**2471**	**493**	**80.0**		**720**	**4785**	**872**	**81.8**

SHORTHAND GOALS FOR

	Home			Road			Overall		
	Team	GP	SHGF	Team	GP	SHGF	Team	GP	SHGF
1	N.J.	24	5	N.J.	24	6	N.J.	48	11
2	NYR	24	3	Buf.	24	5	Buf.	48	7
3	Chi.	24	3	Bos.	24	5	Cgy.	48	6
4	Phi.	24	2	Cgy.	24	4	Chi.	48	5
5	St.L.	24	2	Ana.	24	3	Bos.	48	5
6	Van.	24	2	Fla.	24	3	NYR	48	5
7	Buf.	24	2	Chi.	24	2	Ana.	48	5
8	Cgy.	24	2	NYR	24	2	Fla.	48	4
9	Ott.	24	2	Wsh.	24	2	Edm.	48	4
10	Col.	24	2	Car.	24	2	Wsh.	48	3
11	Edm.	24	2	Det.	24	2	Car.	48	3
12	Ana.	24	2	CBJ	24	2	St.L.	48	3
13	Wpg.	24	1	S.J.	24	2	Det.	48	3
14	L.A.	24	1	Edm.	24	2	CBJ	48	3
15	NYI	24	1	Pit.	24	1	Col.	48	3
16	Fla.	24	1	Tor.	24	1	S.J.	48	3
17	Dal.	24	1	Phx.	24	1	Phi.	48	2
18	Phx.	24	1	Col.	24	1	Pit.	48	2
19	CBJ	24	1	Dal.	24	1	Ott.	48	2
20	Wsh.	24	1	St.L.	24	1	L.A.	48	2
21	Car.	24	1	Nsh.	24	1	NYI	48	2
22	Det.	24	1	L.A.	24	1	Dal.	48	2
23	Pit.	24	1	NYI	24	1	Phx.	48	2
24	S.J.	24	1	Min.	24	1	Van.	48	2
25	Bos.	24	0	Ott.	24	0	Wpg.	48	1
26	Mtl.	24	0	Phi.	24	0	Tor.	48	1
27	T.B.	24	0	Wpg.	24	0	Nsh.	48	1
28	Nsh.	24	0	T.B.	24	0	Min.	48	1
29	Min.	24	0	Mtl.	24	0	Mtl.	48	0
30	Tor.	24	0	Van.	24	0	T.B.	48	0
	Totals	**720**	**41**		**720**	**52**		**720**	**93**

SHORTHAND GOALS AGAINST

	Home			Road			Overall		
	Team	GP	SHGA	Team	GP	SHGA	Team	GP	SHGA
1	NYI	24	0	Car.	24	0	NYI	48	0
2	Min.	24	0	Fla.	24	0	Min.	48	0
3	Ott.	24	0	L.A.	24	0	Ott.	48	1
4	Edm.	24	0	NYI	24	0	L.A.	48	1
5	Phi.	24	1	Min.	24	0	Fla.	48	1
6	Wpg.	24	1	Pit.	24	1	Edm.	48	1
7	L.A.	24	1	Ott.	24	1	Bos.	48	2
8	Bos.	24	1	Tor.	24	1	Mtl.	48	2
9	Mtl.	24	1	Wsh.	24	1	CBJ	48	2
10	Fla.	24	1	CBJ	24	1	Phx.	48	2
11	Cgy.	24	1	Phx.	24	1	Cgy.	48	2
12	Phx.	24	1	Ana.	24	1	Phi.	48	3
13	CBJ	24	1	Dal.	24	1	Pit.	48	3
14	Col.	24	1	Edm.	24	1	Wpg.	48	3
15	S.J.	24	1	Nsh.	24	1	Dal.	48	3
16	T.B.	24	2	Bos.	24	1	Col.	48	3
17	St.L.	24	2	Cgy.	24	1	Van.	48	3
18	Dal.	24	2	Mtl.	24	1	NYR	48	4
19	Van.	24	2	Van.	24	1	Tor.	48	4
20	NYR	24	2	Chi.	24	2	T.B.	48	4
21	Det.	24	2	NYR	24	2	Wsh.	48	4
22	Pit.	24	2	Col.	24	2	Car.	48	4
23	Nsh.	24	3	Phi.	24	2	Nsh.	48	4
24	Tor.	24	3	Wpg.	24	2	S.J.	48	4
25	Wsh.	24	3	T.B.	24	2	Chi.	48	5
26	N.J.	24	3	N.J.	24	3	St.L.	48	5
27	Chi.	24	3	Det.	24	3	Det.	48	5
28	Buf.	24	4	S.J.	24	3	Ana.	48	5
29	Car.	24	4	St.L.	24	3	N.J.	48	6
30	Ana.	24	4	Buf.	24	3	Buf.	48	7
	Totals	**720**	**52**		**720**	**41**		**720**	**93**

Regular-Season Overtime Results

2012-13 to 1992-93

Team	2012-13				2011-12				2010-11				2009-10				2008-09				2007-08				2006-07				2005-06				2003-04				2002-03			
	GP	W	L	SO	GP	W	L	SO	GP	W	L	SO	GP	W	L	SO	GP	W	L	SO	GP	W	L	SO	GP	W	L	SO	GP	W	L	SO	GP	W	L	T	GP	W	L	T
ANA	13	7	3	3	17	2	5	10	18	9	3	6	19	3	3	13	19	5	4	10	20	4	1	15	23	5	4	14	18	3	5	10	22	4	8	10	21	6	6	9
BOS	11	5	3	3	15	2	1	12	14	1	5	8	27	4	4	19	17	3	4	10	21	3	5	13	19	4	2	13	22	4	8	10	30	8	7	15	21	6	4	11
BUF	14	8	2	4	23	5	4	14	25	10	9	6	20	6	4	10	19	2	4	13	21	5	3	13	22	5	3	14	17	6	1	10	13	2	4	7	21	3	8	10
CGY	6	2	1	3	20	1	10	9	23	2	5	16	15	2	3	10	12	3	4	5	16	3	7	6	15	2	5	8	15	2	4	9	13	3	3	7	19	2	6	11
CAR/HFD	6	2	3	1	21	4	7	10	22	6	6	10	19	5	5	9	17	7	2	8	13	5	3	5	14	6	3	5	20	4	6	10	25	5	6	14	15	4	3	8
CHI	16	11	0	5	22	4	4	14	19	4	4	11	23	6	2	15	22	6	5	11	17	4	4	9	18	3	2	13	22	7	7	8	23	4	8	11	23	6	4	13
COL/QUE	12	5	5	2	22	7	4	11	20	6	7	7	18	2	4	12	17	3	1	13	18	4	4	10	15	3	3	9	15	3	3	9	28	8	7	13	23	4	6	13
CBJ	17	10	3	4	13	2	2	9	23	5	5	13	20	3	5	12	21	5	3	13	17	2	4	11	16	4	2	10	18	6	1	11	18	6	4	8	28	7	8	13
DAL/MIN	8	4	3	1	16	4	1	11	21	5	4	12	23	2	4	17	22	5	5	12	15	3	4	8	22	6	3	13	21	3	5	13	18	3	2	13	24	5	4	15
DET	12	4	3	5	18	3	3	12	23	9	6	8	25	5	5	15	19	3	6	10	14	2	2	10	18	3	5	10	15	3	5	7	20	7	2	11	21	7	4	10
EDM	11	4	4	3	17	2	3	12	16	2	3	11	17	1	2	14	16	1	5	10	25	4	2	19	11	1	4	6	26	6	4	16	23	6	5	12	27	7	9	11
FLA	10	4	5	1	25	1	7	17	22	6	5	11	21	2	3	16	18	4	3	11	18	4	3	11	21	3	8	10	23	8	6	9	24	5	4	15	26	4	9	13
L.A.	8	3	1	4	24	3	6	15	17	1	4	12	23	4	1	18	19	3	3	13	14	2	4	8	20	2	8	10	15	4	4	7	27	2	9	16	19	6	7	6
MIN	10	7	1	2	24	2	2	20	16	5	3	8	18	5	1	12	17	3	6	8	19	6	2	11	25	7	1	17	14	1	5	8	24	1	3	20	19	8	1	10
MTL	10	5	3	2	23	2	4	17	16	5	5	6	25	8	5	12	22	4	4	14	20	5	4	11	14	2	1	11	18	7	6	5	16	5	4	7	19	2	9	8
NSH	14	5	3	6	16	3	3	10	19	2	7	10	20	6	2	12	20	6	3	11	17	5	4	8	17	3	3	11	17	3	5	9	22	7	4	11	24	8	6	10
N.J.	13	3	3	7	22	4	2	16	15	7	3	5	15	2	2	11	19	9	2	8	22	7	3	12	22	3	1	18	22	4	5	13	21	7	2	12	25	5	7	13
NYI	13	6	4	3	21	3	7	11	24	7	7	10	25	6	5	14	15	3	4	8	19	5	6	8	22	2	7	13	18	3	3	12	17	2	4	11	18	5	2	11
NYR	12	8	0	4	19	8	2	9	17	3	2	12	15	1	7	7	22	3	3	16	25	4	4	17	22	3	5	14	23	4	8	11	18	3	8	7	20	6	4	10
OTT	12	6	2	4	21	5	6	10	14	2	5	7	16	5	1	10	18	3	5	10	14	3	3	8	13	2	3	8	13	2	3	8	19	3	6	10	16	7	1	8
PHI	6	3	1	2	19	6	2	11	18	3	5	10	12	2	3	7	21	6	5	10	17	3	5	9	16	3	6	7	22	7	5	10	23	2	6	15	23	6	4	13
PHX/WPG	14	5	3	6	22	3	3	16	20	2	7	11	26	5	1	20	11	1	4	6	16	4	1	11	12	2	3	7	15	6	2	7	29	5	6	18	20	4	5	11
PIT	5	5	0	0	17	2	3	12	23	5	5	13	21	6	5	10	21	6	3	12	16	1	4	11	27	6	5	16	19	4	8	7	19	7	4	8	14	3	5	6
ST.L.	11	9	1	1	18	3	1	14	18	3	5	10	20	3	5	12	20	4	4	12	17	1	8	8	23	4	7	12	22	3	7	12	24	11	2	11	19	2	8	9
S.J.	15	8	3	4	22	3	5	14	19	5	4	10	19	1	5	13	21	4	6	11	19	3	4	12	8	1	3	4	21	9	4	8	21	3	6	12	23	6	6	11
T.B.	6	2	1	3	21	10	5	6	25	8	5	12	21	5	5	11	23	2	8	13	13	2	8	3	20	5	3	12	18	6	2	10	18	4	6	8	23	2	5	16
TOR	7	2	0	5	19	5	5	9	18	2	5	11	23	5	10	8	23	4	6	13	19	5	7	7	19	4	4	11	18	7	1	10	17	4	3	10	17	7	3	7
VAN	13	6	1	6	24	7	2	15	17	4	4	9	13	4	1	8	18	5	3	10	20	4	1	15	24	12	3	9	16	4	4	8	26	11	5	10	19	5	1	13
WSH	10	7	3	0	19	7	4	8	25	9	5	11	24	6	7	11	18	6	3	9	19	7	4	8	19	4	3	12	21	2	6	13	14	1	3	10	20	6	6	8
WPG/ATL	9	6	0	3	20	6	6	8	27	10	5	12	19	2	7	10	17	4	5	8	23	6	2	15	25	7	7	11	18	5	3	10	18	6	4	8	19	7	5	7
Totals	**162**	**162**	**65**	**97**	**300**	**119**		**181**	**297**	**148**		**149**	**301**	**117**		**184**	**282**	**123**		**159**	**272**	**116**		**156**	**281**	**117**		**164**	**281**	**136**		**145**	**315**	**145**		**170**	**313**	**156**		**157**

Team	2001-02				2000-01				1999-2000				1998-99				1997-98				1996-97				1995-96				1994-95				1993-94				1992-93			
	GP	W	L	T	GP	W	L	T	GP	W	L	T	GP	W	L	T	GP	W	L	T	GP	W	L	T	GP	W	L	T	GP	W	L	T	GP	W	L	T	GP	W	L	T
ANA	14	3	3	8	20	4	5	11	18	3	3	12	17	1	3	13	20	3	4	13	16	3	0	13	16	6	2	8	7	2	0	5	12	2	5	5	...	...	...	...
BOS	24	9	9	6	20	4	8	8	26	1	6	19	17	2	2	13	17	3	1	13	15	3	3	9	19	2	6	11	8	2	3	3	17	2	2	13	15	5	3	7
BUF	16	4	1	11	10	4	1	5	20	5	4	11	23	3	3	17	21	3	1	17	21	5	4	12	15	2	6	7	9	1	1	7	13	0	4	9	18	4	4	10
CGY	17	2	3	12	22	3	4	15	26	11	5	10	16	3	1	12	22	4	3	15	16	3	4	9	16	2	3	11	9	1	1	7	18	3	2	13	19	4	4	11
CAR/HFD	27	6	5	16	18	6	3	9	14	4	0	10	24	1	5	18	12	2	2	8	18	3	4	11	14	2	3	9	9	1	1	7	14	4	1	9	18	3	9	6
CHI	17	3	1	13	15	2	5	8	17	5	2	10	15	1	2	12	18	1	4	13	19	1	5	13	19	1	4	14	7	2	0	5	16	2	5	9	16	1	3	12
COL/QUE	13	4	1	8	20	6	4	10	17	5	1	11	12	2	0	10	22	2	3	17	15	2	3	10	6	1	0	5	8	0	0	8	15	3	3	9	15	4	1	10
CBJ	15	2	5	8	18	3	6	9	...	...	...	...	...	...	...	...	...	...	...	...	...	...	...	...	...	...	...	...	...	...	...	...	...	...	...	...	...	...	...	...
DAL/MIN	21	3	5	13	16	6	2	8	19	3	6	10	16	3	1	12	17	5	1	11	15	4	3	8	15	1	0	14	9	0	1	8	22	6	3	13	10	0	0	10
DET	24	10	4	10	23	10	4	9	16	4	2	10	10	2	1	7	15	0	0	15	27	7	2	18	11	3	1	7	4	0	0	4	15	5	2	8	11	2	0	9
EDM	19	3	4	12	20	5	3	12	27	3	8	16	20	3	5	12	15	3	2	10	16	1	6	9	14	4	2	8	7	1	2	4	21	1	6	14	17	5	4	8
FLA	16	0	6	10	24	2	9	13	15	3	6	6	21	1	2	18	20	3	2	15	26	3	4	19	13	0	3	10	9	0	3	6	24	2	5	17	...	...	...	...
L.A.	18	3	4	11	19	3	3	13	21	5	4	12	12	5	2	5	16	3	2	11	14	0	3	11	23	3	2	18	9	0	0	9	18	3	3	12	13	2	1	10
MIN	21	0	9	12	22	4	5	13	...	...	...	...	...	...	...	...	...	...	...	...	...	...	...	...	...	...	...	...	...	...	...	...	...	...	...	...	...	...	...	...
MTL	17	2	3	12	16	2	6	8	17	4	4	9	15	0	4	11	20	3	4	13	21	2	4	15	15	2	3	10	10	1	2	7	19	3	2	14	14	5	3	6
NSH	18	5	0	13	17	5	3	9	18	4	7	7	10	1	2	7	...	...	...	...	...	...	...	...	...	...	...	...	...	...	...	...	...	...	...	...	...	...	...	...
N.J.	19	6	4	9	20	5	3	12	16	3	5	8	15	3	1	11	16	2	3	11	17	1	2	14	19	7	0	12	11	1	2	8	14	1	1	12	11	4	0	7
NYI	18	6	4	8	12	2	3	7	15	5	1	9	17	1	6	10	13	0	2	11	17	3	2	12	17	2	5	10	7	1	1	5	19	5	2	12	13	3	3	7
NYR	13	5	4	4	11	5	1	5	21	6	3	12	19	5	3	11	24	2	4	18	13	3	0	10	17	2	1	14	3	0	0	3	12	3	1	8	17	2	4	11
OTT	19	3	7	9	16	3	4	9	15	2	2	11	18	1	2	15	17	2	0	15	17	0	2	15	8	0	3	5	7	1	1	5	17	4	4	9	10	0	6	4
PHI	16	3	3	10	19	5	3	11	21	6	3	12	24	2	3	19	15	3	1	11	18	3	2	13	20	4	3	13	8	3	1	4	18	3	5	10	17	4	2	11
PHX/WPG	19	4	6	9	23	3	3	17	16	4	4	8	15	2	1	12	14	0	2	12	16	5	4	7	8	2	0	6	9	0	2	7	15	1	5	9	11	2	2	7
PIT	20	7	5	8	15	3	3	9	17	3	6	8	22	7	1	14	23	3	2	18	13	1	4	8	9	3	2	4	5	1	1	3	19	4	2	13	10	3	0	7
ST.L.	18	6	4	8	23	6	5	12	17	5	1	11	15	1	1	13	12	2	2	8	13	1	1	11	18	1	1	16	7	1	1	5	17	4	2	11	17	2	4	11
S.J.	13	2	3	8	22	7	3	12	21	4	7	10	21	1	2	18	12	0	2	10	12	3	1	8	9	1	1	7	5	1	0	4	19	2	1	16	10	3	5	2
T.B.	19	4	4	11	13	2	5	6	16	0	7	9	12	1	2	9	13	0	3	10	16	4	2	10	18	3	3	12	7	2	2	3	18	3	4	11	14	3	4	7
TOR	17	3	4	10	19	3	5	11	17	7	3	7	14	6	1	7	10	1	0	9	10	1	1	8	18	4	2	12	8	0	0	8	17	4	1	12	13	1	1	11
VAN	14	4	3	7	23	5	7	11	27	4	8	15	13	0	1	12	17	0	3	14	14	5	2	7	20	1	4	15	13	0	1	12	12	5	4	3	10	1	0	9
WSH	19	6	2	11	16	2	4	10	19	5	2	12	11	2	3	6	17	4	1	12	13	2	2	9	16	4	1	11	9	0	1	8	14	2	2	10	11	2	2	7
WPG/ATL	19	3	5	11	16	2	2	12	11	0	4	7	...	...	...	...	...	...	...	...	...	...	...	...	...	...	...	...	...	...	...	...	...	...	...	...	...	...	...	...
Totals	**270**	**121**		**149**	**274**	**122**		**152**	**260**	**114**		**146**	**222**	**60**		**162**	**219**	**54**		**165**	**214**	**70**		**144**	**201**	**64**		**137**	**101**	**26**		**75**	**214**	**74**		**140**	**165**	**65**		**100**

Abbreviations: GP – games played; **W** – overtime win; **L** – overtime loss;
SO – game tied after overtime. Game decided in shootout. (2005-06 to date); See page 143.
T – game tied after overtime. (Up to and including 2003-04.)

2012-13 Shootout Summary

Team Shootout Statistics

	GP	W	L	W%	G	S	S%	SA	GA	Sv%
Anaheim	9	6	3	.667	15	30	.500	30	10	.667
Boston	7	4	3	.571	9	29	.310	29	8	.724
Buffalo	11	7	4	.636	12	32	.375	33	10	.697
Calgary	3	0	3	.000	2	11	.182	9	5	.444
Carolina	2	1	1	.500	2	4	.500	5	2	.600
Chicago	11	6	5	.545	16	38	.421	40	15	.625
Colorado	4	2	2	.500	6	10	.600	11	5	.545
Columbus	9	5	4	.556	11	28	.393	26	7	.731
Dallas	3	2	1	.667	3	8	.375	10	3	.700
Detroit	7	2	5	.286	5	23	.217	22	8	.636
Edmonton	5	2	3	.400	5	11	.454	13	6	.538
Florida	4	3	1	.750	5	10	.500	11	3	.727
Los Angeles	6	2	4	.333	9	21	.429	22	12	.455
Minnesota	6	4	2	.667	9	15	.600	15	8	.467
Montreal	5	3	2	.600	6	19	.316	20	5	.750
Nashville	8	2	6	.250	9	32	.281	32	14	.563
New Jersey	9	2	7	.222	6	29	.207	27	12	.556
NY Islanders	7	4	3	.571	8	20	.400	19	6	.684
NY Rangers	8	4	4	.500	9	28	.321	27	8	.704
Ottawa	8	4	4	.500	11	30	.367	32	12	.625
Philadelphia	3	1	2	.333	3	9	.333	9	5	.444
Phoenix	10	4	6	.400	8	29	.276	29	12	.586
Pittsburgh	3	3	0	1.000	6	8	.750	8	2	.750
St. Louis	6	5	1	.833	14	22	.636	21	7	.667
San Jose	12	8	4	.667	13	37	.351	33	9	.727
Tampa Bay	4	1	3	.250	2	10	.200	9	4	.556
Toronto	5	0	5	.000	3	24	.125	24	9	.625
Vancouver	11	5	6	.455	8	33	.242	35	12	.657
Washington	3	3	0	1.000	5	9	.556	9	1	.889
Winnipeg	5	2	3	.400	6	22	.273	21	6	.714
Totals	**97**				**226**	**631**	**.358**			

Team Shootout Leaders

Wins

	W	L	W%
San Jose	**8**	4	.667
Buffalo	**7**	4	.636
Anaheim	**6**	3	.667
Chicago	**6**	5	.625
St. Louis	**5**	1	.833
Columbus	**5**	4	.556
Vancouver	**5**	6	.454
6 teams tied with	**4**		

Goals Scored

	G	S	S%
Chicago	**16**	38	.421
Anaheim	**15**	30	.500
St. Louis	**14**	22	.636
San Jose	**13**	37	.351
Buffalo	**12**	32	.375
Columbus	**11**	28	.393
Ottawa	**11**	30	.367
Minnesota	**9**	15	.600
Los Angeles	**9**	21	.429
NY Rangers	**9**	28	.321
Boston	**9**	29	.310
Nashville	**9**	32	.281

Fewest Goals Against

	GA	SA	Sv%
Washington	**1**	9	.889
Carolina	**2**	5	.600
Pittsburgh	**2**	8	.750
Dallas	**3**	10	.700
Florida	**3**	11	.727
Tampa Bay	**4**	9	.556
Calgary	**5**	9	.444
Philadelphia	**5**	9	.444
Montreal	**5**	20	.750
Colorado	**5**	11	.545

Winning Percentage

	W	L	Win%
Washington	3	0	**1.000**
Pittsburgh	3	0	**1.000**
St. Louis	5	1	**.833**
Florida	3	1	**.750**
Dallas	2	1	**.667**
Minnesota	4	2	**.667**
San Jose	8	4	**.667**
Anaheim	6	3	**.667**
Buffalo	7	4	**.636**
Montreal	3	2	**.600**

Shootout Abbreviations

G ....Goals Scored
GA......Goals Against
GDG ...Game Deciding Goal
S.........Shots Taken
SA ......Shots Against
S% ....Goal Scoring %
Sv%....Save %

Individual Shootout Leaders – Goaltenders

Goaltender Shootout Wins

	Team	W	L
Antti Niemi	S.J.	**8**	4
Ryan Miller	Buf.	**7**	3
Viktor Fasth	Ana.	**5**	1
Sergei Bobrovsky	CBJ	**5**	4
Ben Bishop	Ott.	**4**	0
Brian Elliott	St.L.	**4**	1
Niklas Backstrom	Min.	**4**	2
Tuukka Rask	Bos.	**4**	2
Henrik Lundqvist	NYR	**4**	3
Evgeni Nabokov	NYI	**4**	3
Mike Smith	Phx.	**4**	4
Corey Crawford	Chi.	**4**	5

Goaltender Shootout Shots Against

	Team	SA	GA	Sv%
Corey Crawford	Chi.	**34**	14	.588
Antti Niemi	S.J.	**33**	9	.727
Pekka Rinne	Nsh.	**32**	14	.563
Ryan Miller	Buf.	**31**	8	.742
Sergei Bobrovsky	CBJ	**26**	7	.731
Tuukka Rask	Bos.	**26**	7	.731
Henrik Lundqvist	NYR	**25**	6	.760
James Reimer	Tor.	**24**	9	.625
Mike Smith	Phx.	**23**	10	.565
Cory Schneider	Van.	**21**	7	.667
Ondrej Pavelec	Wpg.	**21**	6	.714

Goaltender Shootout Save Percentage

(min. 15 shots faced)	Team	Sv%	SA	GA
Ben Bishop	Ott.	**.842**	19	3
Henrik Lundqvist	NYR	**.760**	25	6
Ryan Miller	Buf.	**.742**	31	8
Sergei Bobrovsky	CBJ	**.731**	26	7
Tuukka Rask	Bos.	**.731**	26	7
Antti Niemi	S.J.	**.727**	33	9
Ondrej Pavelec	Wpg.	**.714**	21	6
Evgeni Nabokov	NYI	**.684**	19	6
Cory Schneider	Van.	**.667**	21	7
Viktor Fasth	Ana.	**.650**	20	7

Chicago's Patrick Kane beats Sergei Bobrovsky of Columbus for one of his NHL-best six shootout goals during the 2012-13 season.

Individual Shootout Leaders – Skaters

Shootout Goals Scored

	Team	G	S	S%
Patrick Kane	Chi.	**6**	11	.546
Craig Smith	Nsh.	**5**	7	.714
Corey Perry	Ana.	**5**	8	.625
Jonathan Toews	Chi.	**5**	11	.454
Andy McDonald	St.L.	**4**	4	1.000
Alexander Steen	St.L.	**4**	5	.800
Artem Anisimov	CBJ	**4**	6	.667
Logan Couture	S.J.	**4**	6	.667
Jakob Silfverberg	Ott.	**4**	7	.571
Jason Pominville	Buf.	**4**	8	.500
17 players tied with		**3**		

Shootout Shots Taken

	Team	G	S	S%
Patrick Kane	Chi.	6	**11**	.546
Jonathan Toews	Chi.	5	**11**	.454
Mikkel Boedker	Phx.	2	**9**	.222
Corey Perry	Ana.	5	**8**	.625
Jason Pominville	Buf.	4	**8**	.500
Patrik Elias	N.J.	2	**8**	.250
Joe Pavelski	S.J.	1	**8**	.125
15 players tied with			**7**	

Shootout Scoring Percentage

(min. 4 shots taken)	Team	S%	G	S
Andy McDonald	St.L.	**1.000**	4	4
Alex Steen	St.L.	**.800**	4	5
Ryan Getzlaf	Ana.	**.750**	3	4
Mark Letestu	CBJ	**.750**	3	4
Craig Smith	Nsh.	**.714**	5	7
Artem Anisimov	CBJ	**.667**	4	6
Logan Couture	S.J.	**.667**	4	6
Corey Perry	Ana.	**.625**	5	8
Nick Bonino	Ana.	**.600**	3	5
Tyler Bozak	Tor.	**.600**	3	5
Jeff Carter	L.A.	**.600**	3	5
Thomas Vanek	Buf.	**.600**	3	5

Shootout Game-Deciding Goals

	Team	GDG	G	S
Corey Perry	Ana.	**3**	5	8
Patrick Kane	Chi.	**3**	6	11
Matt Cullen	Min.	**2**	3	3
Maxim Lapierre	Van.	**2**	2	3
Patrick Marleau	S.J.	**2**	2	3
T.J. Oshie	St.L.	**2**	2	3
Andy McDonald	St.L.	**2**	4	4
Sam Gagner	Edm.	**2**	2	5
Thomas Vanek	Buf.	**2**	3	5
Artem Anisimov	CBJ	**2**	4	6
Mikko Koivu	Min.	**2**	3	6
6 players tied with		**2**		

Shootout Register, 2012-13

Skaters

Player	Team	S	G	S%	GDG
Daniel Alfredsson	Ott.	7	1	.143	0
Artem Anisimov	CBJ	6	4	.667	2
Nik Antropov	Wpg.	1	0	.000	0
Cam Atkinson	CBJ	4	1	.250	0
Nicklas Backstrom	Wsh.	1	1	1.000	1
Josh Bailey	NYI	1	1	1.000	1
Taylor Beck	Nsh.	1	0	.000	0
Jamie Benn	Dal.	2	2	1.000	1
Patrice Bergeron	Bos.	7	3	.429	2
Patrik Berglund	St.L.	1	0	.000	0
Mikkel Boedker	Phx.	9	2	.222	1
Zach Bogosian	Wpg.	1	1	1.000	1
Nick Bonino	Ana.	5	3	.600	1
Chris Bourque	Bos.	2	0	.000	0
Gabriel Bourque	Nsh.	3	1	.333	0
Rene Bourque	Mtl.	1	0	.000	0
Brad Boyes	NYI	6	2	.333	0
Dan Boyle	S.J.	7	2	.286	1
Tyler Bozak	Tor.	5	3	.600	0
Derick Brassard	CBJ	2	1	.500	1
Daniel Brière	Phi.	1	0	.000	0
Dustin Brown	L.A.	4	2	.500	1
Damien Brunner	Det.	7	2	.286	2
Brent Burns	S.J.	1	0	.000	0
Alexandre Burrows	Van.	7	1	.143	0
Bobby Butler	N.J.	1	0	.000	0
Dustin Byfuglien	Wpg.	1	0	.000	0
Ryan Callahan	NYR	7	3	.429	1
Matt Calvert	CBJ	4	1	.250	1
Mike Cammalleri	Cgy.	1	0	.000	0
Jeff Carter	L.A.	5	3	.600	1
Roman Cervenka	Cgy.	1	0	.000	0
David Clarkson	N.J.	4	1	.250	1
Ryane Clowe	S.J.	3	0	.000	0
Andrew Cogliano	Ana.	1	0	.000	0
Logan Couture	S.J.	6	4	.667	1
Sidney Crosby	Pit.	2	2	1.000	0
Matt Cullen	Min.	3	3	1.000	2
Pavel Datsyuk	Det.	7	2	.286	0
Kaspars Daugavins	Ott.	3	1	.333	1
David Desharnais	Mtl.	4	2	.500	1
Shane Doan	Phx.	1	0	.000	0
Drew Doughty	L.A.	1	0	.000	0
Matt Duchene	Col.	3	2	.667	1
Pascal Dupuis	Pit.	1	0	.000	0
Jordan Eberle	Edm.	2	2	1.000	0
Alexander Edler	Van.	4	0	.000	0
Oliver Ekman-Larsson	Phx.	3	1	.333	1
Patrik Elias	N.J.	8	2	.250	1
Lars Eller	Mtl.	2	1	.500	1
Ryan Ellis	Nsh.	1	0	.000	0
Tyler Ennis	Buf.	7	1	.143	0
Martin Erat	Nsh.	4	0	.000	0
Loui Eriksson	Dal.	2	0	.000	0
Valtteri Filppula	Det.	1	0	.000	0
Mike Fisher	Nsh.	2	0	.000	0
Cody Franson	Tor.	1	0	.000	0
Johan Franzen	Det.	1	0	.000	0
Matt Fraser	Dal.	1	0	.000	0
Matt Frattin	Tor.	1	0	.000	0
Marian Gaborik	NYR	3	0	.000	0
Simon Gagne	L.A.	1	0	.000	0
Sam Gagner	Edm.	5	2	.400	2
Alex Galchenyuk	Mtl.	5	2	.400	0
Brendan Gallagher	Mtl.	2	1	.500	1
Nathan Gerbe	Buf.	2	1	.500	1
Ryan Getzlaf	Ana.	4	3	.750	0
Brian Gionta	Mtl.	2	0	.000	0
Claude Giroux	Phi.	3	2	.667	1
Curtis Glencross	Cgy.	1	0	.000	0
Mikhail Grabovski	Tor.	2	0	.000	0
Carl Hagelin	NYR	1	0	.000	0
Michal Handzus	S.J.- Chi.	8	3	.375	2
Jannik Hansen	Van.	1	0	.000	0
Jochen Hecht	Buf.	1	0	.000	0
Victor Hedman	T.B.	3	1	.333	0
Milan Hejduk	Col.	2	1	.500	1
Ales Hemsky	Edm.	3	1	.333	0
Matt Hendricks	Wsh.	3	1	.333	1
Adam Henrique	N.J.	2	0	.000	0
Chris Higgins	Van.	3	2	.667	0
Cody Hodgson	Buf.	1	0	.000	0
Patric Hornqvist	Nsh.	1	0	.000	0
Nathan Horton	Bos.	2	0	.000	0
Marian Hossa	Chi.	3	2	.667	0
Jonathan Huberdeau	Fla.	4	2	.500	1
Jiri Hudler	Cgy.	2	1	.500	0
Jarome Iginla	Cgy.	1	0	.000	0
Jaromir Jagr	Dal.	1	1	1.000	1
Ryan Johansen	CBJ	6	1	.167	0
Jack Johnson	CBJ	1	0	.000	0
Jussi Jokinen	Pit.	1	1	1.000	1
Olli Jokinen	Wpg.	2	0	.000	0
Blair Jones	Cgy.	1	0	.000	0
Jacob Josefson	N.J.	1	0	.000	0
Roman Josi	Nsh.	1	0	.000	0
Nazem Kadri	Tor.	5	0	.000	0
Evander Kane	Wpg.	2	0	.000	0
Patrick Kane	Chi.	11	6	.546	3
Zack Kassian	Van.	3	1	.333	1
Ryan Kesler	Van.	3	0	.000	0
Phil Kessel	Tor.	2	0	.000	0
Mikko Koivu	Min.	6	3	.500	2
Saku Koivu	Ana.	3	2	.667	1
Anze Kopitar	L.A.	4	2	.500	0
Lauri Korpikoski	Phx.	1	0	.000	0
Sergei Kostitsyn	Nsh.	2	1	.500	1
Ilya Kovalchuk	N.J.	6	2	.333	0
Chris Kreider	NYR	1	0	.000	0
David Krejci	Bos.	4	1	.250	1
Nikolai Kulemin	Tor.	2	0	.000	0
Andrew Ladd	Wpg.	4	2	.500	0
Gabriel Landeskog	Col.	1	0	.000	0
Maxim Lapierre	Van.	3	2	.667	2
Nick Leddy	Chi.	1	0	.000	0
David Legwand	Nsh.	7	2	.286	0
Ville Leino	Buf.	1	0	.000	0
Mark Letestu	CBJ	4	3	.750	1
Bryan Little	Wpg.	2	0	.000	0
Andrei Loktionov	N.J.	1	0	.000	0
Joffrey Lupul	Tor.	1	0	.000	0
Clarke MacArthur	Tor.	2	0	.000	0
Evgeni Malkin	Pit.	2	1	.500	1
Brad Marchand	Bos.	6	2	.333	1
Patrick Marleau	S.J.	3	2	.667	2
Shawn Matthias	Fla.	1	0	.000	0
Andy McDonald	St.L.	4	4	1.000	2
Milan Michalek	Ott.	1	0	.000	0
Antti Miettinen	Wpg.	1	0	.000	0
J.T. Miller	NYR	2	1	.500	0
John Mitchell	Col.	1	0	.000	0
Peter Mueller	Fla.	4	2	.500	1
Rick Nash	NYR	7	3	.429	2
Riley Nash	Car.	1	1	1.000	1
James Neal	Pit.	2	2	1.000	1
Frans Nielsen	NYI	7	2	.286	2
Ryan Nugent-Hopkins	Edm.	1	0	.000	0
Gustav Nyquist	Det.	2	0	.000	0
T.J. Oshie	St.L.	3	2	.667	2
Steve Ott	Buf.	3	1	.333	1
Alex Ovechkin	Wsh.	3	3	1.000	1
Richard Panik	T.B.	1	0	.000	0
P.A. Parenteau	Col.	3	3	1.000	0
Zach Parise	Min.	6	3	.500	0
Joe Pavelski	S.J.	8	1	.125	1
David Perron	St.L.	2	1	.500	0
Corey Perry	Ana.	8	5	.625	3
Rich Peverley	Bos.	1	0	.000	0
Dion Phaneuf	Tor.	1	0	.000	0
Tomas Plekanec	Mtl.	2	0	.000	0
Jason Pominville	Buf.	8	4	.500	2
Teddy Purcell	T.B.	3	1	.333	1
Mason Raymond	Van.	3	1	.333	1
Matt Read	Phi.	3	1	.333	0
Peter Regin	Ott.	1	1	1.000	1
Mike Ribeiro	Wsh.	2	0	.000	0
Brad Richards	NYR	3	0	.000	0
Mike Richards	L.A.	4	2	.500	0
Derek Roy	Van.	2	0	.000	0
Michal Rozsival	Chi.	2	1	.500	1
David Rundblad	Phx.	1	0	.000	0
Bobby Ryan	Ana.	5	2	.400	1
Michael Ryder	Mtl.	1	0	.000	0
Brandon Saad	Chi.	4	1	.250	1
Martin St Louis	T.B.	1	0	.000	0
Mike Santorelli	Fla.- Wpg.	3	2	.667	2
Brayden Schenn	Phi.	1	0	.000	0
David Schlemko	Phx.	1	1	1.000	1
Jordan Schroeder	Van.	3	1	.333	1
Daniel Sedin	Van.	1	0	.000	0
Tyler Seguin	Bos.	7	3	.429	0
Teemu Selanne	Ana.	4	0	.000	0
Alexander Semin	Car.	1	0	.000	0
Patrick Sharp	Chi.	2	0	.000	0
Kevin Shattenkirk	St.L.	2	1	.500	1
Andrew Shaw	Chi.	3	1	.333	1
James Sheppard	S.J.	1	0	.000	0
Jakob Silfverberg	Ott.	7	4	.571	1
Wayne Simmonds	Phi.	1	0	.000	0
Jeff Skinner	Car.	1	1	1.000	0
Craig Smith	Nsh.	7	5	.714	1
Zack Smith	Ott.	1	0	.000	0
Jason Spezza	Ott.	1	1	1.000	0
Drew Stafford	Buf.	4	2	.500	1
Steven Stamkos	T.B.	2	0	.000	0
Alex Steen	St.L.	5	4	.800	0
Lee Stempniak	Cgy.	1	0	.000	0
Derek Stepan	NYR	2	1	.500	0
Chris Stewart	St.L.	3	2	.667	0
Jarret Stoll	L.A.	1	0	.000	0
Steve Sullivan	Phx.-N.J.	5	2	.400	1
Alex Tanguay	Cgy.	3	1	.333	0
Vladimir Tarasenko	St.L.	2	0	.000	0
John Tavares	NYI	6	3	.500	1
Jiri Tlusty	Car.	1	0	.000	0
Jonathan Toews	Chi.	11	5	.454	0
Raffi Torres	S.J.	1	1	1.000	1
Kyle Turris	Ott.	6	2	.333	0
James van Riemsdyk	Tor.	2	0	.000	0
Thomas Vanek	Buf.	5	3	.600	2
Antoine Vermette	Phx.	3	0	.000	0
Radim Vrbata	Phx.	6	2	.333	0
Kyle Wellwood	Wpg.	1	0	.000	0
Blake Wheeler	Wpg.	5	2	.400	0
Ray Whitney	Dal.	2	0	.000	0
Patrick Wiercioch	Ott.	1	0	.000	0
Justin Williams	L.A.	1	0	.000	0
Colin Wilson	Nsh.	2	0	.000	0
James Wisniewski	CBJ	1	0	.000	0
Brandon Yip	Nsh.	1	0	.000	0
Travis Zajac	N.J.	4	1	.250	0
Henrik Zetterberg	Det.	5	1	.200	0
Mika Zibanejad	Ott.	2	1	.500	1
Marek Zidlicky	N.J.	1	0	.000	0
Mats Zuccarello	NYR	2	1	.500	1

Goaltenders

Goaltender	Team	W	L	SA	GA	Sv %
Jake Allen	St.L.	1	0	2	0	1.000
Craig Anderson	Ott.	0	1	3	3	.000
Niklas Backstrom	Min.	4	2	15	8	.467
Jonathan Bernier	L.A.	0	1	3	3	.000
Martin Biron	NYR	0	1	2	2	.000
Ben Bishop	Ott.-T.B.	4	1	22	5	.773
Sergei Bobrovsky	CBJ	5	4	26	7	.731
Martin Brodeur	N.J.	0	4	11	6	.455
Ilya Bryzgalov	Phi.	1	2	9	5	.444
Peter Budaj	Mtl.	1	1	9	2	.778
Corey Crawford	Chi.	4	5	34	14	.588
Devan Dubnyk	Edm.	1	3	11	6	.455
Brian Elliott	St.L.	4	1	19	7	.632
Dan Ellis	Car.	1	1	5	2	.600
Ray Emery	Chi.	2	0	6	1	.833
Jhonas Enroth	Buf.	0	1	2	2	.000
Viktor Fasth	Ana.	5	1	20	7	.650
Marc-Andre Fleury	Pit.	3	0	8	2	.750
Mathieu Garon	T.B.	1	1	4	1	.750
J-S Giguere	Col.	1	1	5	3	.400
Jonas Gustavsson	Det.	1	0	3	0	1.000
Johan Hedberg	N.J.	2	3	16	6	.625
Jonas Hiller	Ana.	1	2	10	3	.700
Braden Holtby	Wsh.	3	0	9	1	.889
Jimmy Howard	Det.	1	5	19	8	.579
Leland Irving	Cgy.	0	1	2	2	.000
Chad Johnson	Phx.	0	1	3	1	.667
Nikolai Khabibulin	Edm.	1	0	2	0	1.000
Anton Khudobin	Bos.	0	1	3	1	.667
Miikka Kiprusoff	Cgy.	0	2	7	3	.571
Jason LaBarbera	Phx.	0	1	3	1	.667
Robin Lehner	Ott.	0	3	10	6	.400
Kari Lehtonen	Dal.	2	1	10	3	.700
Anders Lindback	T.B.	0	1	2	1	.500
Henrik Lundqvist	NYR	4	3	25	6	.760
Roberto Luongo	Van.	2	3	14	5	.643
Jacob Markstrom	Fla.	2	0	7	1	.857
Ryan Miller	Buf.	7	3	31	8	.742
Evgeni Nabokov	NYI	4	3	19	6	.684
Antti Niemi	S.J.	8	4	33	9	.727
Ondrej Pavelec	Wpg.	2	3	21	6	.714
Carey Price	Mtl.	2	1	11	3	.727
Jonathan Quick	L.A.	2	3	19	9	.526
Tuukka Rask	Bos.	4	2	26	7	.731
James Reimer	Tor.	0	5	24	9	.625
Pekka Rinne	Nsh.	2	6	32	14	.563
Cory Schneider	Van.	3	3	21	7	.667
Mike Smith	Phx.	4	4	23	10	.565
Jose Theodore	Fla.	1	1	4	2	.500
Semyon Varlamov	Col.	1	1	6	2	.667

NHL Record Book

All-Time Standings of NHL Teams

(ranked by percentage)

Active Teams

Team	Games	Wins	Losses	Ties	OT Losses	SO Losses	Goals For	Goals Against	Points	Pts %	First Season
Montreal	6168	3164	2066	837	58	43	20078	16542	7266	.589	1917-18
Philadelphia	3554	1779	1224	457	51	43	11916	10411	4109	.578	1967-68
Boston	6008	2884	2221	791	66	46	19240	17568	6671	.555	1924-25
Buffalo	3328	1590	1240	409	48	41	10993	10018	3678	.553	1970-71
Detroit	5942	2735	2300	815	51	41	18509	17585	6377	.537	1926-27
Calgary	3172	1456	1239	379	55	43	10534	10045	3389	.534	1972-73
Nashville	1114	519	447	60	51	37	2936	3023	1186	.532	1998-99
Minnesota	950	431	381	55	39	44	2381	2465	1000	.526	2000-01
Edmonton	2616	1195	1058	262	56	45	9051	8715	2753	.526	1979-80
Colorado	2616	1190	1086	261	52	27	8680	8569	2720	.520	1979-80
St. Louis	3554	1573	1446	432	56	47	11005	11069	3681	.518	1967-68
San Jose	1656	746	688	121	61	40	4677	4860	1714	.518	1991-92
Anaheim	1492	668	617	107	53	47	4003	4139	1543	.517	1993-94
Ottawa	1576	704	668	115	48	41	4517	4613	1612	.511	1992-93
Toronto	6168	2697	2587	783	56	45	18997	19058	6278	.509	1917-18
Washington	3016	1332	1287	303	52	42	9556	9869	3061	.507	1974-75
Dallas	3554	1532	1479	459	48	36	10943	11244	3607	.507	1967-68
NY Rangers	5942	2561	2482	808	51	40	18210	18279	6021	.507	1926-27
NY Islanders	3172	1371	1362	347	57	35	10255	10139	3181	.501	1972-73
Pittsburgh	3554	1543	1542	383	56	30	11912	12352	3555	.500	1967-68
Chicago	5942	2496	2535	814	50	47	17690	17904	5903	.497	1926-27
New Jersey	3016	1279	1332	328	41	36	9043	9719	2963	.491	1974-75
Vancouver	3328	1379	1469	391	43	46	10505	11145	3238	.486	1970-71
Florida	1492	588	632	142	74	56	3879	4284	1448	.485	1993-94
Los Angeles	3554	1455	1577	424	57	41	11439	12134	3432	.483	1967-68
Phoenix	2616	1084	1176	266	48	42	8178	8940	2524	.482	1979-80
Carolina	2616	1068	1195	263	58	32	7936	8759	2489	.476	1979-80
Winnipeg	1032	403	493	45	55	36	2818	3404	942	.456	1999-2000
Tampa Bay	1576	606	758	112	64	36	4206	4992	1424	.452	1992-93
Columbus	950	366	458	33	43	50	2340	2863	858	.452	2000-01

Defunct Teams

Team	Games	Wins	Losses	Ties	Goals For	Goals Against	Points	Pts %	First Season	Last Season
Ottawa Senators	542	258	221	63	1458	1333	579	.534	1917-18	1933-34
Montreal Maroons	622	271	260	91	1474	1405	633	.509	1924-25	1937-38
NY/Brooklyn Americans	784	255	402	127	1643	2182	637	.406	1925-26	1941-42
Hamilton Tigers	126	47	78	1	414	475	95	.377	1920-21	1924-25
Cleveland Barons	160	47	87	26	470	617	120	.375	1976-77	1977-78
Pittsburgh Pirates	212	67	122	23	376	519	157	.370	1925-26	1929-30
Calif./Oakland Seals	698	182	401	115	1826	2580	479	.343	1967-68	1975-76
St. Louis Eagles	48	11	31	6	86	144	28	.292	1934-35	1934-35
Quebec Bulldogs	24	4	20	0	91	177	8	.167	1919-20	1919-20
Montreal Wanderers	6	1	5	0	17	35	2	.167	1917-18	1917-18
Philadelphia Quakers	44	4	36	4	76	184	12	.136	1930-31	1930-31

Calgary totals include Atlanta Flames, 1972-73 to 1979-80.
Carolina totals include Hartford Whalers, 1979-80 to 1996-97.
Colorado totals include Quebec Nordiques, 1979-80 to 1994-95.
Dallas totals include Minnesota North Stars, 1967-68 to 1992-93.
Detroit totals include Cougars, 1926-27 to 1929-30, and Falcons, 1930-31 to 1931-32.
New Jersey totals include Kansas City Scouts, 1974-75 to 1975-76, and Colorado Rockies, 1976-77 to 1981-82.
Phoenix totals include Winnipeg Jets, 1979-80 to 1995-96.
Toronto totals include Arenas, 1917-18 to 1918-19, and St. Patricks, 1919-20 to 1925-26.
Winnipeg totals include Atlanta Thrashers, 1999-2000 to 2010-11.

Year-By-Year Final Standings & Leading Scorers

*Stanley Cup winner

1917-18

First Half

Team	GP	W	L	T	GF	GA	PTS
Montreal	14	10	4	0	81	47	20
Toronto	14	8	6	0	71	75	16
Ottawa	14	5	9	0	67	79	10
**Mtl. Wanderers	6	1	5	0	17	35	2

**Montreal Arena burned down and Wanderers forced to withdraw from League. Montreal Canadiens and Toronto each counted a win for defaulted games with Wanderers.

Second Half

Team	GP	W	L	T	GF	GA	PTS
*Toronto	8	5	3	0	37	34	10
Ottawa	8	4	4	0	35	35	8
Montreal	8	3	5	0	34	37	6

Leading Scorers

Player	Team	GP	G	A	PTS	PIM
Joe Malone	Montreal	20	44	4	48	30
Cy Denneny	Ottawa	20	36	10	46	80
Reg Noble	Toronto	20	30	10	40	35
Newsy Lalonde	Montreal	14	23	7	30	51
Corb Denneny	Toronto	21	20	9	29	14
Harry Cameron	Toronto	21	17	10	27	28
Didier Pitre	Montreal	20	17	6	23	29
Eddie Gerard	Ottawa	20	13	7	20	26
Jack Darragh	Ottawa	18	14	5	19	26
Frank Nighbor	Ottawa	10	11	8	19	6
Harry Meeking	Toronto	21	10	9	19	28

1918-19

First Half

Team	GP	W	L	T	GF	GA	PTS
• Montreal	10	7	3	0	57	50	14
Ottawa	10	5	5	0	39	39	10
Toronto	10	3	7	0	42	49	6

Second Half

Team	GP	W	L	T	GF	GA	PTS
Ottawa	8	7	1	0	32	14	14
Montreal	8	3	5	0	31	28	6
Toronto	8	2	6	0	22	43	4

• NHL Champion. Stanley Cup not awarded due to influenza epidemic.

Leading Scorers

Player	Team	GP	G	A	PTS	PIM
Newsy Lalonde	Montreal	17	22	10	32	40
Odie Cleghorn	Montreal	17	22	6	28	22
Frank Nighbor	Ottawa	18	19	9	28	27
Cy Denneny	Ottawa	18	18	4	22	58
Didier Pitre	Montreal	17	14	5	19	12
Alf Skinner	Toronto	17	12	4	16	26
Harry Cameron	Tor., Ott.	14	11	3	14	35
Jack Darragh	Ottawa	14	11	3	14	33
Ken Randall	Toronto	15	8	6	14	27
Sprague Cleghorn	Ottawa	18	7	6	13	27

1919-20

First Half

Team	GP	W	L	T	GF	GA	PTS
Ottawa	12	9	3	0	59	23	18
Montreal	12	8	4	0	62	51	16
Toronto	12	5	7	0	52	62	10
Quebec	12	2	10	0	44	81	4

Second Half

Team	GP	W	L	T	GF	GA	PTS
*Ottawa	12	10	2	0	62	41	20
Toronto	12	7	5	0	67	44	14
Montreal	12	5	7	0	67	62	10
Quebec	12	2	10	0	47	96	4

Leading Scorers

Player	Team	GP	G	A	PTS	PIM
Joe Malone	Quebec	24	39	10	49	12
Newsy Lalonde	Montreal	23	37	9	46	34
Frank Nighbor	Ottawa	23	26	15	41	18
Corb Denneny	Toronto	24	24	12	36	20
Jack Darragh	Ottawa	23	22	14	36	22
Reg Noble	Toronto	24	24	9	33	52
Amos Arbour	Montreal	22	21	5	26	13
Cully Wilson	Toronto	23	20	6	26	86
Didier Pitre	Montreal	22	14	12	26	6
Punch Broadbent	Ottawa	21	19	6	25	40

1920-21

First Half

Team	GP	W	L	T	GF	GA	PTS
*Ottawa	10	8	2	0	49	23	16
Toronto	10	5	5	0	39	47	10
Montreal	10	4	6	0	37	51	8
Hamilton	10	3	7	0	34	38	6

Second Half

Team	GP	W	L	T	GF	GA	PTS
Toronto	14	10	4	0	66	53	20
Montreal	14	9	5	0	75	48	18
Ottawa	14	6	8	0	48	52	12
Hamilton	14	3	11	0	58	94	6

Leading Scorers

Player	Team	GP	G	A	PTS	PIM
Newsy Lalonde	Montreal	24	33	10	43	36
Babe Dye	Ham., Tor.	24	35	5	40	32
Cy Denneny	Ottawa	24	34	5	39	10
Joe Malone	Hamilton	20	28	9	37	6
Frank Nighbor	Ottawa	24	19	10	29	10
Reg Noble	Toronto	24	19	8	27	54
Harry Cameron	Toronto	24	18	9	27	35
Goldie Prodgers	Hamilton	24	18	9	27	8
Corb Denneny	Toronto	20	19	7	26	29
Jack Darragh	Ottawa	24	11	15	26	20

1921-22

Team	GP	W	L	T	GF	GA	PTS
Ottawa	24	14	8	2	106	84	30
*Toronto	24	13	10	1	98	97	27
Montreal	24	12	11	1	88	94	25
Hamilton	24	7	17	0	88	105	14

Leading Scorers

Player	Team	GP	G	A	PTS	PIM
Punch Broadbent	Ottawa	24	32	14	46	28
Cy Denneny	Ottawa	22	27	12	39	20
Babe Dye	Toronto	24	31	7	38	39
Harry Cameron	Toronto	24	18	17	35	22
Joe Malone	Hamilton	24	24	7	31	4
Corb Denneny	Toronto	24	19	9	28	28
Reg Noble	Toronto	24	17	11	28	19
Sprague Cleghorn	Montreal	24	17	9	26	80
Georges Boucher	Ottawa	23	13	12	25	12
Odie Cleghorn	Montreal	23	21	3	24	26

1922-23

Team	GP	W	L	T	GF	GA	PTS
*Ottawa	24	14	9	1	77	54	29
Montreal	24	13	9	2	73	61	28
Toronto	24	13	10	1	82	88	27
Hamilton	24	6	18	0	81	110	12

Leading Scorers

Player	Team	GP	G	A	PTS	PIM
Babe Dye	Toronto	22	26	11	37	19
Cy Denneny	Ottawa	24	23	11	34	28
Billy Boucher	Montreal	24	24	7	31	55
Jack Adams	Toronto	23	19	9	28	42
Mickey Roach	Hamilton	24	17	10	27	8
Odie Cleghorn	Montreal	24	19	6	25	18
Georges Boucher	Ottawa	24	14	9	23	58
Reg Noble	Toronto	24	12	11	23	47
Cully Wilson	Hamilton	23	16	5	21	46
Aurel Joliat	Montreal	24	12	9	21	37

1923-24

Team	GP	W	L	T	GF	GA	PTS
Ottawa	24	16	8	0	74	54	32
*Montreal	24	13	11	0	59	48	26
Toronto	24	10	14	0	59	85	20
Hamilton	24	9	15	0	63	68	18

Leading Scorers

Player	Team	GP	G	A	PTS	PIM
Cy Denneny	Ottawa	22	22	2	24	10
Georges Boucher	Ottawa	21	13	10	23	38
Billy Boucher	Montreal	23	16	6	22	48
Billy Burch	Hamilton	24	16	6	22	6
Aurel Joliat	Montreal	24	15	5	20	27
Babe Dye	Toronto	19	16	3	19	23
Jack Adams	Toronto	22	14	4	18	51
Reg Noble	Toronto	24	12	5	17	79
Frank Nighbor	Ottawa	20	11	6	17	16
Howie Morenz	Montreal	24	13	3	16	20
King Clancy	Ottawa	24	8	8	16	26

1924-25

Team	GP	W	L	T	GF	GA	PTS
Hamilton	30	19	10	1	90	60	39
Toronto	30	19	11	0	90	84	38
• Montreal	30	17	11	2	93	56	36
Ottawa	30	17	12	1	83	66	35
Mtl. Maroons	30	9	19	2	45	65	20
Boston	30	6	24	0	49	119	12

• NHL Champion (Stanley Cup won by Victoria Cougars, WCHL)

Leading Scorers

Player	Team	GP	G	A	PTS	PIM
Babe Dye	Toronto	29	38	8	46	41
Cy Denneny	Ottawa	29	27	15	42	16
Aurel Joliat	Montreal	25	30	11	41	85
Howie Morenz	Montreal	30	28	11	39	46
Red Green	Hamilton	30	19	15	34	81
Jack Adams	Toronto	27	21	10	31	67
Billy Boucher	Montreal	30	17	13	30	92
Billy Burch	Hamilton	27	20	7	27	10
Jimmy Herberts	Boston	30	17	7	24	55
Hooley Smith	Ottawa	30	10	13	23	81

1925-26

Team	GP	W	L	T	GF	GA	PTS
Ottawa	36	24	8	4	77	42	52
*Mtl. Maroons	36	20	11	5	91	73	45
Pittsburgh	36	19	16	1	82	70	39
Boston	36	17	15	4	92	85	38
NY Americans	36	12	20	4	68	89	28
Toronto	36	12	21	3	92	114	27
Montreal	36	11	24	1	79	108	23

Leading Scorers

Player	Team	GP	G	A	PTS	PIM
Nels Stewart	Mtl. Maroons	36	34	8	42	119
Cy Denneny	Ottawa	36	24	12	36	18
Carson Cooper	Boston	36	28	3	31	10
Jimmy Herberts	Boston	36	26	5	31	47
Howie Morenz	Montreal	31	23	3	26	39
Jack Adams	Toronto	36	21	5	26	52
Aurel Joliat	Montreal	35	17	9	26	52
Billy Burch	NY Americans	36	22	3	25	33
Hooley Smith	Ottawa	28	16	9	25	53
Frank Nighbor	Ottawa	35	12	13	25	40

1926-27

Canadian Division

Team	GP	W	L	T	GF	GA	PTS
*Ottawa	44	30	10	4	86	69	64
Montreal	44	28	14	2	99	67	58
Mtl. Maroons	44	20	20	4	71	68	44
NY Americans	44	17	25	2	82	91	36
Toronto	44	15	24	5	79	94	35

American Division

Team	GP	W	L	T	GF	GA	PTS
NY Rangers	44	25	13	6	95	72	56
Boston	44	21	20	3	97	89	45
Chicago	44	19	22	3	115	116	41
Pittsburgh	44	15	26	3	79	108	33
Detroit	44	12	28	4	76	105	28

Leading Scorers

Player	Team	GP	G	A	PTS	PIM
Bill Cook	NY Rangers	44	33	4	37	58
Dick Irvin	Chicago	43	18	18	36	34
Howie Morenz	Montreal	44	25	7	32	49
Frank Fredrickson	Det., Bos.	41	18	13	31	46
Babe Dye	Chicago	41	25	5	30	14
Ace Bailey	Toronto	42	15	13	28	82
Frank Boucher	NY Rangers	44	13	15	28	17
Billy Burch	NY Americans	43	19	8	27	40
Harry Oliver	Boston	42	18	6	24	17
Duke Keats	Bos., Det.	42	16	8	24	52

1927-28

Canadian Division

Team	GP	W	L	T	GF	GA	PTS
Montreal	44	26	11	7	116	48	59
Mtl. Maroons	44	24	14	6	96	77	54
Ottawa	44	20	14	10	78	57	50
Toronto	44	18	18	8	89	88	44
NY Americans	44	11	27	6	63	128	28

American Division

Team	GP	W	L	T	GF	GA	PTS
Boston	44	20	13	11	77	70	51
*NY Rangers	44	19	16	9	94	79	47
Pittsburgh	44	19	17	8	67	76	46
Detroit	44	19	19	6	88	79	44
Chicago	44	7	34	3	68	134	17

Leading Scorers

Player	Team	GP	G	A	PTS	PIM
Howie Morenz	Montreal	43	33	18	51	66
Aurel Joliat	Montreal	44	28	11	39	105
Frank Boucher	NY Rangers	44	23	12	35	15
George Hay	Detroit	42	22	13	35	20
Nels Stewart	Mtl. Maroons	41	27	7	34	104
Art Gagne	Montreal	44	20	10	30	75
Bun Cook	NY Rangers	44	14	14	28	45
Bill Carson	Toronto	32	20	6	26	36
Frank Finnigan	Ottawa	38	20	5	25	34
Bill Cook	NY Rangers	43	18	6	24	42
Duke Keats	Det., Chi.	38	14	10	24	60

1928-29

Canadian Division

Team	GP	W	L	T	GF	GA	PTS
Montreal	44	22	7	15	71	43	59
NY Americans	44	19	13	12	53	53	50
Toronto	44	21	18	5	85	69	47
Ottawa	44	14	17	13	54	67	41
Mtl. Maroons	44	15	20	9	67	65	39

American Division

Team	GP	W	L	T	GF	GA	PTS
*Boston	44	26	13	5	89	52	57
NY Rangers	44	21	13	10	72	65	52
Detroit	44	19	16	9	72	63	47
Pittsburgh	44	9	27	8	46	80	26
Chicago	44	7	29	8	33	85	22

Leading Scorers

Player	Team	GP	G	A	PTS	PIM
Ace Bailey	Toronto	44	22	10	32	78
Nels Stewart	Mtl. Maroons	44	21	8	29	74
Carson Cooper	Detroit	43	18	9	27	14
Howie Morenz	Montreal	42	17	10	27	47
Andy Blair	Toronto	44	12	15	27	41
Frank Boucher	NY Rangers	44	10	16	26	8
Harry Oliver	Boston	43	17	6	23	24
Bill Cook	NY Rangers	43	15	8	23	41
Jimmy Ward	Mtl. Maroons	43	14	8	22	46

Seven players tied with 19 points

1929-30

Canadian Division

Team	GP	W	L	T	GF	GA	PTS
Mtl. Maroons	44	23	16	5	141	114	51
*Montreal	44	21	14	9	142	114	51
Ottawa	44	21	15	8	138	118	50
Toronto	44	17	21	6	116	124	40
NY Americans	44	14	25	5	113	161	33

American Division

Team	GP	W	L	T	GF	GA	PTS
Boston	44	38	5	1	179	98	77
Chicago	44	21	18	5	117	111	47
NY Rangers	44	17	17	10	136	143	44
Detroit	44	14	24	6	117	133	34
Pittsburgh	44	5	36	3	102	185	13

Leading Scorers

Player	Team	GP	G	A	PTS	PIM
Cooney Weiland	Boston	44	43	30	73	27
Frank Boucher	NY Rangers	42	26	36	62	16
Dit Clapper	Boston	44	41	20	61	48
Bill Cook	NY Rangers	44	29	30	59	56
Hec Kilrea	Ottawa	44	36	22	58	72
Nels Stewart	Mtl. Maroons	44	39	16	55	81
Howie Morenz	Montreal	44	40	10	50	72
Normie Himes	NY Americans	44	28	22	50	15
Joe Lamb	Ottawa	44	29	20	49	119
Dutch Gainor	Boston	42	18	31	49	39

1930-31

Canadian Division

Team	GP	W	L	T	GF	GA	PTS
*Montreal	44	26	10	8	129	89	60
Toronto	44	22	13	9	118	99	53
Mtl. Maroons	44	20	18	6	105	106	46
NY Americans	44	18	16	10	76	74	46
Ottawa	44	10	30	4	91	142	24

American Division

Team	GP	W	L	T	GF	GA	PTS
Boston	44	28	10	6	143	90	62
Chicago	44	24	17	3	108	78	51
NY Rangers	44	19	16	9	106	87	47
Detroit	44	16	21	7	102	105	39
Philadelphia	44	4	36	4	76	184	12

Leading Scorers

Player	Team	GP	G	A	PTS	PIM
Howie Morenz	Montreal	39	28	23	51	49
Ebbie Goodfellow	Detroit	44	25	23	48	32
Charlie Conacher	Toronto	37	31	12	43	78
Bill Cook	NY Rangers	43	30	12	42	39
Ace Bailey	Toronto	40	23	19	42	46
Joe Primeau	Toronto	38	9	32	41	18
Nels Stewart	Mtl. Maroons	42	25	14	39	75
Frank Boucher	NY Rangers	44	12	27	39	20
Cooney Weiland	Boston	44	25	13	38	14
Bun Cook	NY Rangers	44	18	17	35	72
Aurel Joliat	Montreal	43	13	22	35	73

1931-32

Canadian Division

Team	GP	W	L	T	GF	GA	PTS
Montreal	48	25	16	7	128	111	57
*Toronto	48	23	18	7	155	127	53
Mtl. Maroons	48	19	22	7	142	139	45
NY Americans	48	16	24	8	95	142	40

American Division

Team	GP	W	L	T	GF	GA	PTS
NY Rangers	48	23	17	8	134	112	54
Chicago	48	18	19	11	86	101	47
Detroit	48	18	20	10	95	108	46
Boston	48	15	21	12	122	117	42

Leading Scorers

Player	Team	GP	G	A	PTS	PIM
Busher Jackson	Toronto	48	28	25	53	63
Joe Primeau	Toronto	46	13	37	50	25
Howie Morenz	Montreal	48	24	25	49	46
Charlie Conacher	Toronto	44	34	14	48	66
Bill Cook	NY Rangers	48	34	14	48	33
Dave Trottier	Mtl. Maroons	48	26	18	44	94
Hooley Smith	Mtl. Maroons	43	11	33	44	49
Babe Siebert	Mtl. Maroons	48	21	18	39	64
Dit Clapper	Boston	48	17	22	39	21
Aurel Joliat	Montreal	48	15	24	39	46

1932-33

Canadian Division

Team	GP	W	L	T	GF	GA	PTS
Toronto	48	24	18	6	119	111	54
Mtl. Maroons	48	22	20	6	135	119	50
Montreal	48	18	25	5	92	115	41
NY Americans	48	15	22	11	91	118	41
Ottawa	48	11	27	10	88	131	32

American Division

Team	GP	W	L	T	GF	GA	PTS
Boston	48	25	15	8	124	88	58
Detroit	48	25	15	8	111	93	58
*NY Rangers	48	23	17	8	135	107	54
Chicago	48	16	20	12	88	101	44

Leading Scorers

Player	Team	GP	G	A	PTS	PIM
Bill Cook	NY Rangers	48	28	22	50	51
Busher Jackson	Toronto	48	27	17	44	43
Baldy Northcott	Mtl. Maroons	48	22	21	43	30
Hooley Smith	Mtl. Maroons	48	20	21	41	66
Paul Haynes	Mtl. Maroons	48	16	25	41	18
Aurel Joliat	Montreal	48	18	21	39	53
Marty Barry	Boston	48	24	13	37	40
Bun Cook	NY Rangers	48	22	15	37	35
Nels Stewart	Boston	47	18	18	36	62
Howie Morenz	Montreal	46	14	21	35	32
Johnny Gagnon	Montreal	48	12	23	35	64
Eddie Shore	Boston	48	8	27	35	102
Frank Boucher	NY Rangers	46	7	28	35	4

1933-34

Canadian Division

Team	GP	W	L	T	GF	GA	PTS
Toronto	48	26	13	9	174	119	61
Montreal	48	22	20	6	99	101	50
Mtl. Maroons	48	19	18	11	117	122	49
NY Americans	48	15	23	10	104	132	40
Ottawa	48	13	29	6	115	143	32

American Division

Team	GP	W	L	T	GF	GA	PTS
Detroit	48	24	14	10	113	98	58
*Chicago	48	20	17	11	88	83	51
NY Rangers	48	21	19	8	120	113	50
Boston	48	18	25	5	111	130	41

Leading Scorers

Player	Team	GP	G	A	PTS	PIM
Charlie Conacher	Toronto	42	32	20	52	38
Joe Primeau	Toronto	45	14	32	46	8
Frank Boucher	NY Rangers	48	14	30	44	4
Marty Barry	Boston	48	27	12	39	12
Cecil Dillon	NY Rangers	48	13	26	39	10
Nels Stewart	Boston	48	21	17	38	68
Busher Jackson	Toronto	38	20	18	38	38
Aurel Joliat	Montreal	48	22	15	37	27
Hooley Smith	Mtl. Maroons	47	18	19	37	58
Paul Thompson	Chicago	48	20	16	36	17

1934-35

Canadian Division

Team	GP	W	L	T	GF	GA	PTS
Toronto	48	30	14	4	157	111	64
*Mtl. Maroons	48	24	19	5	123	92	53
Montreal	48	19	23	6	110	145	44
NY Americans	48	12	27	9	100	142	33
St. Louis	48	11	31	6	86	144	28

American Division

Team	GP	W	L	T	GF	GA	PTS
Boston	48	26	16	6	129	112	58
Chicago	48	26	17	5	118	88	57
NY Rangers	48	22	20	6	137	139	50
Detroit	48	19	22	7	127	114	45

Leading Scorers

Player	Team	GP	G	A	PTS	PIM
Charlie Conacher	Toronto	47	36	21	57	24
Syd Howe	St.L., Det.	50	22	25	47	34
Larry Aurie	Detroit	48	17	29	46	24
Frank Boucher	NY Rangers	48	13	32	45	2
Busher Jackson	Toronto	42	22	22	44	27
Herbie Lewis	Detroit	47	16	27	43	26
Art Chapman	NY Americans	47	9	34	43	4
Marty Barry	Boston	48	20	20	40	33
Sweeney Schriner	NY Americans	48	18	22	40	6
Nels Stewart	Boston	47	21	18	39	45
Paul Thompson	Chicago	48	16	23	39	20

1935-36

Canadian Division

Team	GP	W	L	T	GF	GA	PTS
Mtl. Maroons	48	22	16	10	114	106	54
Toronto	48	23	19	6	126	106	52
NY Americans	48	16	25	7	109	122	39
Montreal	48	11	26	11	82	123	33

American Division

Team	GP	W	L	T	GF	GA	PTS
*Detroit	48	24	16	8	124	103	56
Boston	48	22	20	6	92	83	50
Chicago	48	21	19	8	93	92	50
NY Rangers	48	19	17	12	91	96	50

Leading Scorers

Player	Team	GP	G	A	PTS	PIM
Sweeney Schriner	NY Americans	48	19	26	45	8
Marty Barry	Detroit	48	21	19	40	16
Paul Thompson	Chicago	45	17	23	40	19
Bill Thoms	Toronto	48	23	15	38	29
Charlie Conacher	Toronto	44	23	15	38	74
Hooley Smith	Mtl. Maroons	47	19	19	38	75
Doc Romnes	Chicago	48	13	25	38	6
Art Chapman	NY Americans	47	10	28	38	14
Herbie Lewis	Detroit	45	14	23	37	25
Baldy Northcott	Mtl. Maroons	48	15	21	36	41

1936-37

Canadian Division

Team	GP	W	L	T	GF	GA	PTS
Montreal	48	24	18	6	115	111	54
Mtl. Maroons	48	22	17	9	126	110	53
Toronto	48	22	21	5	119	115	49
NY Americans	48	15	29	4	122	161	34

American Division

Team	GP	W	L	T	GF	GA	PTS
*Detroit	48	25	14	9	128	102	59
Boston	48	23	18	7	120	110	53
NY Rangers	48	19	20	9	117	106	47
Chicago	48	14	27	7	99	131	35

Leading Scorers

Player	Team	GP	G	A	PTS	PIM
Sweeney Schriner	NY Americans	48	21	25	46	17
Syl Apps	Toronto	48	16	29	45	10
Marty Barry	Detroit	48	17	27	44	6
Larry Aurie	Detroit	45	23	20	43	20
Busher Jackson	Toronto	46	21	19	40	12
Johnny Gagnon	Montreal	48	20	16	36	38
Bob Gracie	Mtl. Maroons	47	11	25	36	18
Nels Stewart	Bos., NYA	43	23	12	35	37
Paul Thompson	Chicago	47	17	18	35	28
Bill Cowley	Boston	46	13	22	35	4

1937-38

Canadian Division

Team	GP	W	L	T	GF	GA	PTS
Toronto	48	24	15	9	151	127	57
NY Americans	48	19	18	11	110	111	49
Montreal	48	18	17	13	123	128	49
Mtl. Maroons	48	12	30	6	101	149	30

American Division

Team	GP	W	L	T	GF	GA	PTS
Boston	48	30	11	7	142	89	67
NY Rangers	48	27	15	6	149	96	60
*Chicago	48	14	25	9	97	139	37
Detroit	48	12	25	11	99	133	35

Leading Scorers

Player	Team	GP	G	A	PTS	PIM
Gordie Drillon	Toronto	48	26	26	52	4
Syl Apps	Toronto	47	21	29	50	9
Paul Thompson	Chicago	48	22	22	44	14
Georges Mantha	Montreal	47	23	19	42	12
Cecil Dillon	NY Rangers	48	21	18	39	6
Bill Cowley	Boston	48	17	22	39	8
Sweeney Schriner	NY Americans	49	21	17	38	22
Bill Thoms	Toronto	48	14	24	38	14
Clint Smith	NY Rangers	48	14	23	37	0
Nels Stewart	NY Americans	48	19	17	36	29
Neil Colville	NY Rangers	45	17	19	36	11

1938-39

Team	GP	W	L	T	GF	GA	PTS
*Boston	48	36	10	2	156	76	74
NY Rangers	48	26	16	6	149	105	58
Toronto	48	19	20	9	114	107	47
NY Americans	48	17	21	10	119	157	44
Detroit	48	18	24	6	107	128	42
Montreal	48	15	24	9	115	146	39
Chicago	48	12	28	8	91	132	32

Leading Scorers

Player	Team	GP	G	A	PTS	PIM
Toe Blake	Montreal	48	24	23	47	10
Sweeney Schriner	NY Americans	48	13	31	44	20
Bill Cowley	Boston	34	8	34	42	2
Clint Smith	NY Rangers	48	21	20	41	2
Marty Barry	Detroit	48	13	28	41	4
Syl Apps	Toronto	44	15	25	40	4
Tom Anderson	NY Americans	48	13	27	40	14
Johnny Gottselig	Chicago	48	16	23	39	15
Paul Haynes	Montreal	47	5	33	38	27
Roy Conacher	Boston	47	26	11	37	12
Lorne Carr	NY Americans	46	19	18	37	16
Neil Colville	NY Rangers	48	18	19	37	12
Phil Watson	NY Rangers	48	15	22	37	42

1939-40

Team	GP	W	L	T	GF	GA	PTS
Boston	48	31	12	5	170	98	67
*NY Rangers	48	27	11	10	136	77	64
Toronto	48	25	17	6	134	110	56
Chicago	48	23	19	6	112	120	52
Detroit	48	16	26	6	91	126	38
NY Americans	48	15	29	4	106	140	34
Montreal	48	10	33	5	90	168	25

Leading Scorers

Player	Team	GP	G	A	PTS	PIM
Milt Schmidt	Boston	48	22	30	52	37
Woody Dumart	Boston	48	22	21	43	16
Bobby Bauer	Boston	48	17	26	43	2
Gordie Drillon	Toronto	43	21	19	40	13
Bill Cowley	Boston	48	13	27	40	24
Bryan Hextall	NY Rangers	48	24	15	39	52
Neil Colville	NY Rangers	48	19	19	38	22
Syd Howe	Detroit	46	14	23	37	17
Toe Blake	Montreal	48	17	19	36	48
Murray Armstrong	NY Americans	48	16	20	36	12

1940-41

Team	GP	W	L	T	GF	GA	PTS
*Boston	48	27	8	13	168	102	67
Toronto	48	28	14	6	145	99	62
Detroit	48	21	16	11	112	102	53
NY Rangers	48	21	19	8	143	125	50
Chicago	48	16	25	7	112	139	39
Montreal	48	16	26	6	121	147	38
NY Americans	48	8	29	11	99	186	27

Leading Scorers

Player	Team	GP	G	A	PTS	PIM
Bill Cowley	Boston	46	17	45	62	16
Bryan Hextall	NY Rangers	48	26	18	44	16
Gordie Drillon	Toronto	42	23	21	44	2
Syl Apps	Toronto	41	20	24	44	6
Lynn Patrick	NY Rangers	48	20	24	44	12
Syd Howe	Detroit	48	20	24	44	8
Neil Colville	NY Rangers	48	14	28	42	28
Eddie Wiseman	Boston	48	16	24	40	10
Bobby Bauer	Boston	48	17	22	39	2
Sweeney Schriner	Toronto	48	24	14	38	6
Roy Conacher	Boston	40	24	14	38	7
Milt Schmidt	Boston	44	13	25	38	23

1941-42

Team	GP	W	L	T	GF	GA	PTS
NY Rangers	48	29	17	2	177	143	60
*Toronto	48	27	18	3	158	136	57
Boston	48	25	17	6	160	118	56
Chicago	48	22	23	3	145	155	47
Detroit	48	19	25	4	140	147	42
Montreal	48	18	27	3	134	173	39
Brooklyn	48	16	29	3	133	175	35

Leading Scorers

Player	Team	GP	G	A	PTS	PIM
Bryan Hextall	NY Rangers	48	24	32	56	30
Lynn Patrick	NY Rangers	47	32	22	54	18
Don Grosso	Detroit	48	23	30	53	13
Phil Watson	NY Rangers	48	15	37	52	48
Sid Abel	Detroit	48	18	31	49	45
Toe Blake	Montreal	47	17	28	45	19
Bill Thoms	Chicago	47	15	30	45	8
Gordie Drillon	Toronto	48	23	18	41	6
Syl Apps	Toronto	38	18	23	41	0
Tom Anderson	Brooklyn	48	12	29	41	54

1942-43

Team	GP	W	L	T	GF	GA	PTS
*Detroit	50	25	14	11	169	124	61
Boston	50	24	17	9	195	176	57
Toronto	50	22	19	9	198	159	53
Montreal	50	19	19	12	181	191	50
Chicago	50	17	18	15	179	180	49
NY Rangers	50	11	31	8	161	253	30

Leading Scorers

Player	Team	GP	G	A	PTS	PIM
Doug Bentley	Chicago	50	33	40	73	18
Bill Cowley	Boston	48	27	45	72	10
Max Bentley	Chicago	47	26	44	70	2
Lynn Patrick	NY Rangers	50	22	39	61	28
Lorne Carr	Toronto	50	27	33	60	15
Billy Taylor	Toronto	50	18	42	60	2
Bryan Hextall	NY Rangers	50	27	32	59	28
Toe Blake	Montreal	48	23	36	59	28
Elmer Lach	Montreal	45	18	40	58	14
Buddy O'Connor	Montreal	50	15	43	58	2

1943-44

Team	GP	W	L	T	GF	GA	PTS
*Montreal	50	38	5	7	234	109	83
Detroit	50	26	18	6	214	177	58
Toronto	50	23	23	4	214	174	50
Chicago	50	22	23	5	178	187	49
Boston	50	19	26	5	223	268	43
NY Rangers	50	6	39	5	162	310	17

Leading Scorers

Player	Team	GP	G	A	PTS	PIM
Herb Cain	Boston	48	36	46	82	4
Doug Bentley	Chicago	50	38	39	77	22
Lorne Carr	Toronto	50	36	38	74	9
Carl Liscombe	Detroit	50	36	37	73	17
Elmer Lach	Montreal	48	24	48	72	23
Clint Smith	Chicago	50	23	49	72	4
Bill Cowley	Boston	36	30	41	71	12
Bill Mosienko	Chicago	50	32	38	70	10
Art Jackson	Boston	49	28	41	69	8
Gus Bodnar	Toronto	50	22	40	62	18

1944-45

Team	GP	W	L	T	GF	GA	PTS
Montreal	50	38	8	4	228	121	80
Detroit	50	31	14	5	218	161	67
*Toronto	50	24	22	4	183	161	52
Boston	50	16	30	4	179	219	36
Chicago	50	13	30	7	141	194	33
NY Rangers	50	11	29	10	154	247	32

Leading Scorers

Player	Team	GP	G	A	PTS	PIM
Elmer Lach	Montreal	50	26	54	80	37
Maurice Richard	Montreal	50	50	23	73	36
Toe Blake	Montreal	49	29	38	67	15
Bill Cowley	Boston	49	25	40	65	2
Ted Kennedy	Toronto	49	29	25	54	14
Bill Mosienko	Chicago	50	28	26	54	0
Joe Carveth	Detroit	50	26	28	54	6
Ab DeMarco	NY Rangers	50	24	30	54	10
Clint Smith	Chicago	50	23	31	54	0
Syd Howe	Detroit	46	17	36	53	6

1945-46

Team	GP	W	L	T	GF	GA	PTS
*Montreal	50	28	17	5	172	134	61
Boston	50	24	18	8	167	156	56
Chicago	50	23	20	7	200	178	53
Detroit	50	20	20	10	146	159	50
Toronto	50	19	24	7	174	185	45
NY Rangers	50	13	28	9	144	191	35

Leading Scorers

Player	Team	GP	G	A	PTS	PIM
Max Bentley	Chicago	47	31	30	61	6
Gaye Stewart	Toronto	50	37	15	52	8
Toe Blake	Montreal	50	29	21	50	2
Clint Smith	Chicago	50	26	24	50	2
Maurice Richard	Montreal	50	27	21	48	50
Bill Mosienko	Chicago	40	18	30	48	12
Ab DeMarco	NY Rangers	50	20	27	47	20
Elmer Lach	Montreal	50	13	34	47	34
Alex Kaleta	Chicago	49	19	27	46	17
Billy Taylor	Toronto	48	23	18	41	14
Pete Horeck	Chicago	50	20	21	41	34

1946-47

Team	GP	W	L	T	GF	GA	PTS
Montreal	60	34	16	10	189	138	78
*Toronto	60	31	19	10	209	172	72
Boston	60	26	23	11	190	175	63
Detroit	60	22	27	11	190	193	55
NY Rangers	60	22	32	6	167	186	50
Chicago	60	19	37	4	193	274	42

Leading Scorers

Player	Team	GP	G	A	PTS	PIM
Max Bentley	Chicago	60	29	43	72	12
Maurice Richard	Montreal	60	45	26	71	69
Billy Taylor	Detroit	60	17	46	63	35
Milt Schmidt	Boston	59	27	35	62	40
Ted Kennedy	Toronto	60	28	32	60	27
Doug Bentley	Chicago	52	21	34	55	18
Bobby Bauer	Boston	58	30	24	54	4
Roy Conacher	Detroit	60	30	24	54	6
Bill Mosienko	Chicago	59	25	27	52	2
Woody Dumart	Boston	60	24	28	52	12

1947-48

Team	GP	W	L	T	GF	GA	PTS
*Toronto	60	32	15	13	182	143	77
Detroit	60	30	18	12	187	148	72
Boston	60	23	24	13	167	168	59
NY Rangers	60	21	26	13	176	201	55
Montreal	60	20	29	11	147	169	51
Chicago	60	20	34	6	195	225	46

Leading Scorers

Player	Team	GP	G	A	PTS	PIM
Elmer Lach	Montreal	60	30	31	61	72
Buddy O'Connor	NY Rangers	60	24	36	60	8
Doug Bentley	Chicago	60	20	37	57	16
Gaye Stewart	Tor., Chi.	61	27	29	56	83
Max Bentley	Chi., Tor.	59	26	28	54	14
Bud Poile	Tor., Chi.	58	25	29	54	17
Maurice Richard	Montreal	53	28	25	53	89
Syl Apps	Toronto	55	26	27	53	12
Ted Lindsay	Detroit	60	33	19	52	95
Roy Conacher	Chicago	52	22	27	49	4

1948-49

Team	GP	W	L	T	GF	GA	PTS
Detroit	60	34	19	7	195	145	75
Boston	60	29	23	8	178	163	66
Montreal	60	28	23	9	152	126	65
*Toronto	60	22	25	13	147	161	57
Chicago	60	21	31	8	173	211	50
NY Rangers	60	18	31	11	133	172	47

Leading Scorers

Player	Team	GP	G	A	PTS	PIM
Roy Conacher	Chicago	60	26	42	68	8
Doug Bentley	Chicago	58	23	43	66	38
Sid Abel	Detroit	60	28	26	54	49
Ted Lindsay	Detroit	50	26	28	54	97
Jim Conacher	Det., Chi.	59	26	23	49	43
Paul Ronty	Boston	60	20	29	49	11
Harry Watson	Toronto	60	26	19	45	0
Billy Reay	Montreal	60	22	23	45	33
Gus Bodnar	Chicago	59	19	26	45	14
Johnny Peirson	Boston	59	22	21	43	45

1949-50

Team	GP	W	L	T	GF	GA	PTS
*Detroit	70	37	19	14	229	164	88
Montreal	70	29	22	19	172	150	77
Toronto	70	31	27	12	176	173	74
NY Rangers	70	28	31	11	170	189	67
Boston	70	22	32	16	198	228	60
Chicago	70	22	38	10	203	244	54

Leading Scorers

Player	Team	GP	G	A	PTS	PIM
Ted Lindsay	Detroit	69	23	55	78	141
Sid Abel	Detroit	69	34	35	69	46
Gordie Howe	Detroit	70	35	33	68	69
Maurice Richard	Montreal	70	43	22	65	114
Paul Ronty	Boston	70	23	36	59	8
Roy Conacher	Chicago	70	25	31	56	16
Doug Bentley	Chicago	64	20	33	53	28
Johnny Peirson	Boston	57	27	25	52	49
Metro Prystai	Chicago	65	29	22	51	31
Bep Guidolin	Chicago	70	17	34	51	42

1950-51

Team	GP	W	L	T	GF	GA	PTS
Detroit	70	44	13	13	236	139	101
*Toronto	70	41	16	13	212	138	95
Montreal	70	25	30	15	173	184	65
Boston	70	22	30	18	178	197	62
NY Rangers	70	20	29	21	169	201	61
Chicago	70	13	47	10	171	280	36

Leading Scorers

Player	Team	GP	G	A	PTS	PIM
Gordie Howe	Detroit	70	43	43	86	74
Maurice Richard	Montreal	65	42	24	66	97
Max Bentley	Toronto	67	21	41	62	34
Sid Abel	Detroit	69	23	38	61	30
Milt Schmidt	Boston	62	22	39	61	33
Ted Kennedy	Toronto	63	18	43	61	32
Ted Lindsay	Detroit	67	24	35	59	110
Tod Sloan	Toronto	70	31	25	56	105
Red Kelly	Detroit	70	17	37	54	24
Sid Smith	Toronto	70	30	21	51	10
Cal Gardner	Toronto	66	23	28	51	42

1951-52

Team	GP	W	L	T	GF	GA	PTS
*Detroit	70	44	14	12	215	133	100
Montreal	70	34	26	10	195	164	78
Toronto	70	29	25	16	168	157	74
Boston	70	25	29	16	162	176	66
NY Rangers	70	23	34	13	192	219	59
Chicago	70	17	44	9	158	241	43

Leading Scorers

Player	Team	GP	G	A	PTS	PIM
Gordie Howe	Detroit	70	47	39	86	78
Ted Lindsay	Detroit	70	30	39	69	123
Elmer Lach	Montreal	70	15	50	65	36
Don Raleigh	NY Rangers	70	19	42	61	14
Sid Smith	Toronto	70	27	30	57	6
Bernie Geoffrion	Montreal	67	30	24	54	66
Bill Mosienko	Chicago	70	31	22	53	10
Sid Abel	Detroit	62	17	36	53	32
Ted Kennedy	Toronto	70	19	33	52	33
Milt Schmidt	Boston	69	21	29	50	57
Johnny Peirson	Boston	68	20	30	50	30

1952-53

Team	GP	W	L	T	GF	GA	PTS
Detroit	70	36	16	18	222	133	90
*Montreal	70	28	23	19	155	148	75
Boston	70	28	29	13	152	172	69
Chicago	70	27	28	15	169	175	69
Toronto	70	27	30	13	156	167	67
NY Rangers	70	17	37	16	152	211	50

Leading Scorers

Player	Team	GP	G	A	PTS	PIM
Gordie Howe	Detroit	70	49	46	95	57
Ted Lindsay	Detroit	70	32	39	71	111
Maurice Richard	Montreal	70	28	33	61	112
Wally Hergesheimer	NY Rangers	70	30	29	59	10
Alex Delvecchio	Detroit	70	16	43	59	28
Paul Ronty	NY Rangers	70	16	38	54	20
Metro Prystai	Detroit	70	16	34	50	12
Red Kelly	Detroit	70	19	27	46	8
Bert Olmstead	Montreal	69	17	28	45	83
Fleming Mackell	Boston	65	27	17	44	63
Jim McFadden	Chicago	70	23	21	44	29

1953-54

Team	GP	W	L	T	GF	GA	PTS
*Detroit	70	37	19	14	191	132	88
Montreal	70	35	24	11	195	141	81
Toronto	70	32	24	14	152	131	78
Boston	70	32	28	10	177	181	74
NY Rangers	70	29	31	10	161	182	68
Chicago	70	12	51	7	133	242	31

Leading Scorers

Player	Team	GP	G	A	PTS	PIM
Gordie Howe	Detroit	70	33	48	81	109
Maurice Richard	Montreal	70	37	30	67	112
Ted Lindsay	Detroit	70	26	36	62	110
Bernie Geoffrion	Montreal	54	29	25	54	87
Bert Olmstead	Montreal	70	15	37	52	85
Red Kelly	Detroit	62	16	33	49	18
Dutch Reibel	Detroit	69	15	33	48	18
Ed Sandford	Boston	70	16	31	47	42
Fleming Mackell	Boston	67	15	32	47	60
Ken Mosdell	Montreal	67	22	24	46	64
Paul Ronty	NY Rangers	70	13	33	46	18

1954-55

Team	GP	W	L	T	GF	GA	PTS
*Detroit	70	42	17	11	204	134	95
Montreal	70	41	18	11	228	157	93
Toronto	70	24	24	22	147	135	70
Boston	70	23	26	21	169	188	67
NY Rangers	70	17	35	18	150	210	52
Chicago	70	13	40	17	161	235	43

Leading Scorers

Player	Team	GP	G	A	PTS	PIM
Bernie Geoffrion	Montreal	70	38	37	75	57
Maurice Richard	Montreal	67	38	36	74	125
Jean Béliveau	Montreal	70	37	36	73	58
Dutch Reibel	Detroit	70	25	41	66	15
Gordie Howe	Detroit	64	29	33	62	68
Red Sullivan	Chicago	69	19	42	61	51
Bert Olmstead	Montreal	70	10	48	58	103
Sid Smith	Toronto	70	33	21	54	14
Ken Mosdell	Montreal	70	22	32	54	82
Danny Lewicki	NY Rangers	70	29	24	53	8

1955-56

Team	GP	W	L	T	GF	GA	PTS
*Montreal	70	45	15	10	222	131	100
Detroit	70	30	24	16	183	148	76
NY Rangers	70	32	28	10	204	203	74
Toronto	70	24	33	13	153	181	61
Boston	70	23	34	13	147	185	59
Chicago	70	19	39	12	155	216	50

Leading Scorers

Player	Team	GP	G	A	PTS	PIM
Jean Béliveau	Montreal	70	47	41	88	143
Gordie Howe	Detroit	70	38	41	79	100
Maurice Richard	Montreal	70	38	33	71	89
Bert Olmstead	Montreal	70	14	56	70	94
Tod Sloan	Toronto	70	37	29	66	100
Andy Bathgate	NY Rangers	70	19	47	66	59
Bernie Geoffrion	Montreal	59	29	33	62	66
Dutch Reibel	Detroit	68	17	39	56	10
Alex Delvecchio	Detroit	70	25	26	51	24
Dave Creighton	NY Rangers	70	20	31	51	43
Bill Gadsby	NY Rangers	70	9	42	51	84

1956-57

Team	GP	W	L	T	GF	GA	PTS
Detroit	70	38	20	12	198	157	88
*Montreal	70	35	23	12	210	155	82
Boston	70	34	24	12	195	174	80
NY Rangers	70	26	30	14	184	227	66
Toronto	70	21	34	15	174	192	57
Chicago	70	16	39	15	169	225	47

Leading Scorers

Player	Team	GP	G	A	PTS	PIM
Gordie Howe	Detroit	70	44	45	89	72
Ted Lindsay	Detroit	70	30	55	85	103
Jean Béliveau	Montreal	69	33	51	84	105
Andy Bathgate	NY Rangers	70	27	50	77	60
Ed Litzenberger	Chicago	70	32	32	64	48
Maurice Richard	Montreal	63	33	29	62	74
Don McKenney	Boston	69	21	39	60	31
Dickie Moore	Montreal	70	29	29	58	56
Henri Richard	Montreal	63	18	36	54	71
Norm Ullman	Detroit	64	16	36	52	47

1957-58

Team	GP	W	L	T	GF	GA	PTS
*Montreal	70	43	17	10	250	158	96
NY Rangers	70	32	25	13	195	188	77
Detroit	70	29	29	12	176	207	70
Boston	70	27	28	15	199	194	69
Chicago	70	24	39	7	163	202	55
Toronto	70	21	38	11	192	226	53

Leading Scorers

Player	Team	GP	G	A	PTS	PIM
Dickie Moore	Montreal	70	36	48	84	65
Henri Richard	Montreal	67	28	52	80	56
Andy Bathgate	NY Rangers	65	30	48	78	42
Gordie Howe	Detroit	64	33	44	77	40
Bronco Horvath	Boston	67	30	36	66	71
Ed Litzenberger	Chicago	70	32	30	62	63
Fleming Mackell	Boston	70	20	40	60	72
Jean Béliveau	Montreal	55	27	32	59	93
Alex Delvecchio	Detroit	70	21	38	59	22
Don McKenney	Boston	70	28	30	58	22

1958-59

Team	GP	W	L	T	GF	GA	PTS
*Montreal	70	39	18	13	258	158	91
Boston	70	32	29	9	205	215	73
Chicago	70	28	29	13	197	208	69
Toronto	70	27	32	11	189	201	65
NY Rangers	70	26	32	12	201	217	64
Detroit	70	25	37	8	167	218	58

Leading Scorers

Player	Team	GP	G	A	PTS	PIM
Dickie Moore	Montreal	70	41	55	96	61
Jean Béliveau	Montreal	64	45	46	91	67
Andy Bathgate	NY Rangers	70	40	48	88	48
Gordie Howe	Detroit	70	32	46	78	57
Ed Litzenberger	Chicago	70	33	44	77	37
Bernie Geoffrion	Montreal	59	22	44	66	30
Red Sullivan	NY Rangers	70	21	42	63	56
Andy Hebenton	NY Rangers	70	33	29	62	8
Don McKenney	Boston	70	32	30	62	20
Tod Sloan	Chicago	59	27	35	62	79

1959-60

Team	GP	W	L	T	GF	GA	PTS
*Montreal	70	40	18	12	255	178	92
Toronto	70	35	26	9	199	195	79
Chicago	70	28	29	13	191	180	69
Detroit	70	26	29	15	186	197	67
Boston	70	28	34	8	220	241	64
NY Rangers	70	17	38	15	187	247	49

Leading Scorers

Player	Team	GP	G	A	PTS	PIM
Bobby Hull	Chicago	70	39	42	81	68
Bronco Horvath	Boston	68	39	41	80	60
Jean Béliveau	Montreal	60	34	40	74	57
Andy Bathgate	NY Rangers	70	26	48	74	28
Henri Richard	Montreal	70	30	43	73	66
Gordie Howe	Detroit	70	28	45	73	46
Bernie Geoffrion	Montreal	59	30	41	71	36
Don McKenney	Boston	70	20	49	69	28
Vic Stasiuk	Boston	69	29	39	68	121
Dean Prentice	NY Rangers	70	32	34	66	43

1960-61

Team	GP	W	L	T	GF	GA	PTS
Montreal	70	41	19	10	254	188	92
Toronto	70	39	19	12	234	176	90
*Chicago	70	29	24	17	198	180	75
Detroit	70	25	29	16	195	215	66
NY Rangers	70	22	38	10	204	248	54
Boston	70	15	42	13	176	254	43

Leading Scorers

Player	Team	GP	G	A	PTS	PIM
Bernie Geoffrion	Montreal	64	50	45	95	29
Jean Béliveau	Montreal	69	32	58	90	57
Frank Mahovlich	Toronto	70	48	36	84	131
Andy Bathgate	NY Rangers	70	29	48	77	22
Gordie Howe	Detroit	64	23	49	72	30
Norm Ullman	Detroit	70	28	42	70	34
Red Kelly	Toronto	64	20	50	70	12
Dickie Moore	Montreal	57	35	34	69	62
Henri Richard	Montreal	70	24	44	68	91
Alex Delvecchio	Detroit	70	27	35	62	26

1961-62

Team	GP	W	L	T	GF	GA	PTS
Montreal	70	42	14	14	259	166	98
*Toronto	70	37	22	11	232	180	85
Chicago	70	31	26	13	217	186	75
NY Rangers	70	26	32	12	195	207	64
Detroit	70	23	33	14	184	219	60
Boston	70	15	47	8	177	306	38

Leading Scorers

Player	Team	GP	G	A	PTS	PIM
Bobby Hull	Chicago	70	50	34	84	35
Andy Bathgate	NY Rangers	70	28	56	84	44
Gordie Howe	Detroit	70	33	44	77	54
Stan Mikita	Chicago	70	25	52	77	97
Frank Mahovlich	Toronto	70	33	38	71	87
Alex Delvecchio	Detroit	70	26	43	69	18
Ralph Backstrom	Montreal	66	27	38	65	29
Norm Ullman	Detroit	70	26	38	64	54
Bill Hay	Chicago	60	11	52	63	34
Claude Provost	Montreal	70	33	29	62	22

1962-63

Team	GP	W	L	T	GF	GA	PTS
*Toronto	70	35	23	12	221	180	82
Chicago	70	32	21	17	194	178	81
Montreal	70	28	19	23	225	183	79
Detroit	70	32	25	13	200	194	77
NY Rangers	70	22	36	12	211	233	56
Boston	70	14	39	17	198	281	45

Leading Scorers

Player	Team	GP	G	A	PTS	PIM
Gordie Howe	Detroit	70	38	48	86	100
Andy Bathgate	NY Rangers	70	35	46	81	54
Stan Mikita	Chicago	65	31	45	76	69
Frank Mahovlich	Toronto	67	36	37	73	56
Henri Richard	Montreal	67	23	50	73	57
Jean Béliveau	Montreal	69	18	49	67	68
John Bucyk	Boston	69	27	39	66	36
Alex Delvecchio	Detroit	70	20	44	64	8
Bobby Hull	Chicago	65	31	31	62	27
Murray Oliver	Boston	65	22	40	62	38

1963-64

Team	GP	W	L	T	GF	GA	PTS
Montreal	70	36	21	13	209	167	85
Chicago	70	36	22	12	218	169	84
*Toronto	70	33	25	12	192	172	78
Detroit	70	30	29	11	191	204	71
NY Rangers	70	22	38	10	186	242	54
Boston	70	18	40	12	170	212	48

Leading Scorers

Player	Team	GP	G	A	PTS	PIM
Stan Mikita	Chicago	70	39	50	89	146
Bobby Hull	Chicago	70	43	44	87	50
Jean Béliveau	Montreal	68	28	50	78	42
Andy Bathgate	NYR, Tor.	71	19	58	77	34
Gordie Howe	Detroit	69	26	47	73	70
Kenny Wharram	Chicago	70	39	32	71	18
Murray Oliver	Boston	70	24	44	68	41
Phil Goyette	NY Rangers	67	24	41	65	15
Rod Gilbert	NY Rangers	70	24	40	64	62
Dave Keon	Toronto	70	23	37	60	6

1964-65

Team	GP	W	L	T	GF	GA	PTS
Detroit	70	40	23	7	224	175	87
*Montreal	70	36	23	11	211	185	83
Chicago	70	34	28	8	224	176	76
Toronto	70	30	26	14	204	173	74
NY Rangers	70	20	38	12	179	246	52
Boston	70	21	43	6	166	253	48

Leading Scorers

Player	Team	GP	G	A	PTS	PIM
Stan Mikita	Chicago	70	28	59	87	154
Norm Ullman	Detroit	70	42	41	83	70
Gordie Howe	Detroit	70	29	47	76	104
Bobby Hull	Chicago	61	39	32	71	32
Alex Delvecchio	Detroit	68	25	42	67	16
Claude Provost	Montreal	70	27	37	64	28
Rod Gilbert	NY Rangers	70	25	36	61	52
Pierre Pilote	Chicago	68	14	45	59	162
John Bucyk	Boston	68	26	29	55	24
Ralph Backstrom	Montreal	70	25	30	55	41
Phil Esposito	Chicago	70	23	32	55	44

1965-66

Team	GP	W	L	T	GF	GA	PTS
*Montreal	70	41	21	8	239	173	90
Chicago	70	37	25	8	240	187	82
Toronto	70	34	25	11	208	187	79
Detroit	70	31	27	12	221	194	74
Boston	70	21	43	6	174	275	48
NY Rangers	70	18	41	11	195	261	47

Leading Scorers

Player	Team	GP	G	A	PTS	PIM
Bobby Hull	Chicago	65	54	43	97	70
Stan Mikita	Chicago	68	30	48	78	58
Bobby Rousseau	Montreal	70	30	48	78	20
Jean Béliveau	Montreal	67	29	48	77	50
Gordie Howe	Detroit	70	29	46	75	83
Norm Ullman	Detroit	70	31	41	72	35
Alex Delvecchio	Detroit	70	31	38	69	16
Bob Nevin	NY Rangers	69	29	33	62	10
Henri Richard	Montreal	62	22	39	61	47
Murray Oliver	Boston	70	18	42	60	30

1966-67

Team	GP	W	L	T	GF	GA	PTS
Chicago	70	41	17	12	264	170	94
Montreal	70	32	25	13	202	188	77
*Toronto	70	32	27	11	204	211	75
NY Rangers	70	30	28	12	188	189	72
Detroit	70	27	39	4	212	241	58
Boston	70	17	43	10	182	253	44

Leading Scorers

Player	Team	GP	G	A	PTS	PIM
Stan Mikita	Chicago	70	35	62	97	12
Bobby Hull	Chicago	66	52	28	80	52
Norm Ullman	Detroit	68	26	44	70	26
Kenny Wharram	Chicago	70	31	34	65	21
Gordie Howe	Detroit	69	25	40	65	53
Bobby Rousseau	Montreal	68	19	44	63	58
Phil Esposito	Chicago	69	21	40	61	40
Phil Goyette	NY Rangers	70	12	49	61	6
Doug Mohns	Chicago	61	25	35	60	58
Henri Richard	Montreal	65	21	34	55	28
Alex Delvecchio	Detroit	70	17	38	55	10

1967-68

East Division

Team	GP	W	L	T	GF	GA	PTS
*Montreal	74	42	22	10	236	167	94
NY Rangers	74	39	23	12	226	183	90
Boston	74	37	27	10	259	216	84
Chicago	74	32	26	16	212	222	80
Toronto	74	33	31	10	209	176	76
Detroit	74	27	35	12	245	257	66

West Division

Team	GP	W	L	T	GF	GA	PTS
Philadelphia	74	31	32	11	173	179	73
Los Angeles	74	31	33	10	200	224	72
St. Louis	74	27	31	16	177	191	70
Minnesota	74	27	32	15	191	226	69
Pittsburgh	74	27	34	13	195	216	67
Oakland	74	15	42	17	153	219	47

Leading Scorers

Player	Team	GP	G	A	PTS	PIM
Stan Mikita	Chicago	72	40	47	87	14
Phil Esposito	Boston	74	35	49	84	21
Gordie Howe	Detroit	74	39	43	82	53
Jean Ratelle	NY Rangers	74	32	46	78	18
Rod Gilbert	NY Rangers	73	29	48	77	12
Bobby Hull	Chicago	71	44	31	75	39
Norm Ullman	Det., Tor.	71	35	37	72	28
Alex Delvecchio	Detroit	74	22	48	70	14
John Bucyk	Boston	72	30	39	69	8
Kenny Wharram	Chicago	74	27	42	69	18

1968-69

East Division

Team	GP	W	L	T	GF	GA	PTS
*Montreal	76	46	19	11	271	202	103
Boston	76	42	18	16	303	221	100
NY Rangers	76	41	26	9	231	196	91
Toronto	76	35	26	15	234	217	85
Detroit	76	33	31	12	239	221	78
Chicago	76	34	33	9	280	246	77

West Division

Team	GP	W	L	T	GF	GA	PTS
St. Louis	76	37	25	14	204	157	88
Oakland	76	29	36	11	219	251	69
Philadelphia	76	20	35	21	174	225	61
Los Angeles	76	24	42	10	185	260	58
Pittsburgh	76	20	45	11	189	252	51
Minnesota	76	18	43	15	189	270	51

Leading Scorers

Player	Team	GP	G	A	PTS	PIM
Phil Esposito	Boston	74	49	77	126	79
Bobby Hull	Chicago	74	58	49	107	48
Gordie Howe	Detroit	76	44	59	103	58
Stan Mikita	Chicago	74	30	67	97	52
Ken Hodge	Boston	75	45	45	90	75
Yvan Cournoyer	Montreal	76	43	44	87	31
Alex Delvecchio	Detroit	72	25	58	83	8
Red Berenson	St. Louis	76	35	47	82	43
Jean Béliveau	Montreal	69	33	49	82	55
Frank Mahovlich	Detroit	76	49	29	78	38
Jean Ratelle	NY Rangers	75	32	46	78	26

1969-70

East Division

Team	GP	W	L	T	GF	GA	PTS
Chicago	76	45	22	9	250	170	99
*Boston	76	40	17	19	277	216	99
Detroit	76	40	21	15	246	199	95
NY Rangers	76	38	22	16	246	189	92
Montreal	76	38	22	16	244	201	92
Toronto	76	29	34	13	222	242	71

West Division

Team	GP	W	L	T	GF	GA	PTS
St. Louis	76	37	27	12	224	179	86
Pittsburgh	76	26	38	12	182	238	64
Minnesota	76	19	35	22	224	257	60
Oakland	76	22	40	14	169	243	58
Philadelphia	76	17	35	24	197	225	58
Los Angeles	76	14	52	10	168	290	38

Leading Scorers

Player	Team	GP	G	A	PTS	PIM
Bobby Orr	Boston	76	33	87	120	125
Phil Esposito	Boston	76	43	56	99	50
Stan Mikita	Chicago	76	39	47	86	50
Phil Goyette	St. Louis	72	29	49	78	16
Walt Tkaczuk	NY Rangers	76	27	50	77	38
Jean Ratelle	NY Rangers	75	32	42	74	28
Red Berenson	St. Louis	67	33	39	72	38
Jean-Paul Parise	Minnesota	74	24	48	72	72
Gordie Howe	Detroit	76	31	40	71	58
Frank Mahovlich	Detroit	74	38	32	70	59
Dave Balon	NY Rangers	76	33	37	70	100
John McKenzie	Boston	72	29	41	70	114

1970-71

East Division

Team	GP	W	L	T	GF	GA	PTS
Boston	78	57	14	7	399	207	121
NY Rangers	78	49	18	11	259	177	109
*Montreal	78	42	23	13	291	216	97
Toronto	78	37	33	8	248	211	82
Buffalo	78	24	39	15	217	291	63
Vancouver	78	24	46	8	229	296	56
Detroit	78	22	45	11	209	308	55

West Division

Team	GP	W	L	T	GF	GA	PTS
Chicago	78	49	20	9	277	184	107
St. Louis	78	34	25	19	223	208	87
Philadelphia	78	28	33	17	207	225	73
Minnesota	78	28	34	16	191	223	72
Los Angeles	78	25	40	13	239	303	63
Pittsburgh	78	21	37	20	221	240	62
California	78	20	53	5	199	320	45

Leading Scorers

Player	Team	GP	G	A	PTS	PIM
Phil Esposito	Boston	78	76	76	152	71
Bobby Orr	Boston	78	37	102	139	91
John Bucyk	Boston	78	51	65	116	8
Ken Hodge	Boston	78	43	62	105	113
Bobby Hull	Chicago	78	44	52	96	32
Norm Ullman	Toronto	73	34	51	85	24
Wayne Cashman	Boston	77	21	58	79	100
John McKenzie	Boston	65	31	46	77	120
Dave Keon	Toronto	76	38	38	76	4
Jean Béliveau	Montreal	70	25	51	76	40
Fred Stanfield	Boston	75	24	52	76	12

1971-72

East Division

Team	GP	W	L	T	GF	GA	PTS
*Boston	78	54	13	11	330	204	119
NY Rangers	78	48	17	13	317	192	109
Montreal	78	46	16	16	307	205	108
Toronto	78	33	31	14	209	208	80
Detroit	78	33	35	10	261	262	76
Buffalo	78	16	43	19	203	289	51
Vancouver	78	20	50	8	203	297	48

West Division

Team	GP	W	L	T	GF	GA	PTS
Chicago	78	46	17	15	256	166	107
Minnesota	78	37	29	12	212	191	86
St. Louis	78	28	39	11	208	247	67
Pittsburgh	78	26	38	14	220	258	66
Philadelphia	78	26	38	14	200	236	66
California	78	21	39	18	216	288	60
Los Angeles	78	20	49	9	206	305	49

Leading Scorers

Player	Team	GP	G	A	PTS	PIM
Phil Esposito	Boston	76	66	67	133	76
Bobby Orr	Boston	76	37	80	117	106
Jean Ratelle	NY Rangers	63	46	63	109	4
Vic Hadfield	NY Rangers	78	50	56	106	142
Rod Gilbert	NY Rangers	73	43	54	97	64
Frank Mahovlich	Montreal	76	43	53	96	36
Bobby Hull	Chicago	78	50	43	93	24
Yvan Cournoyer	Montreal	73	47	36	83	15
John Bucyk	Boston	78	32	51	83	4
Bobby Clarke	Philadelphia	78	35	46	81	87
Jacques Lemaire	Montreal	77	32	49	81	26

1972-73

East Division

Team	GP	W	L	T	GF	GA	PTS
*Montreal	78	52	10	16	329	184	120
Boston	78	51	22	5	330	235	107
NY Rangers	78	47	23	8	297	208	102
Buffalo	78	37	27	14	257	219	88
Detroit	78	37	29	12	265	243	86
Toronto	78	27	41	10	247	279	64
Vancouver	78	22	47	9	233	339	53
NY Islanders	78	12	60	6	170	347	30

West Division

Team	GP	W	L	T	GF	GA	PTS
Chicago	78	42	27	9	284	225	93
Philadelphia	78	37	30	11	296	256	85
Minnesota	78	37	30	11	254	230	85
St. Louis	78	32	34	12	233	251	76
Pittsburgh	78	32	37	9	257	265	73
Los Angeles	78	31	36	11	232	245	73
Atlanta	78	25	38	15	191	239	65
California	78	16	46	16	213	323	48

Leading Scorers

Player	Team	GP	G	A	PTS	PIM
Phil Esposito	Boston	78	55	75	130	87
Bobby Clarke	Philadelphia	78	37	67	104	80
Bobby Orr	Boston	63	29	72	101	99
Rick MacLeish	Philadelphia	78	50	50	100	69
Jacques Lemaire	Montreal	77	44	51	95	16
Jean Ratelle	NY Rangers	78	41	53	94	12
Mickey Redmond	Detroit	76	52	41	93	24
John Bucyk	Boston	78	40	53	93	12
Frank Mahovlich	Montreal	78	38	55	93	51
Jim Pappin	Chicago	76	41	51	92	82

1973-74

East Division

Team	GP	W	L	T	GF	GA	PTS
Boston	78	52	17	9	349	221	113
Montreal	78	45	24	9	293	240	99
NY Rangers	78	40	24	14	300	251	94
Toronto	78	35	27	16	274	230	86
Buffalo	78	32	34	12	242	250	76
Detroit	78	29	39	10	255	319	68
Vancouver	78	24	43	11	224	296	59
NY Islanders	78	19	41	18	182	247	56

West Division

Team	GP	W	L	T	GF	GA	PTS
*Philadelphia	78	50	16	12	273	164	112
Chicago	78	41	14	23	272	164	105
Los Angeles	78	33	33	12	233	231	78
Atlanta	78	30	34	14	214	238	74
Pittsburgh	78	28	41	9	242	273	65
St. Louis	78	26	40	12	206	248	64
Minnesota	78	23	38	17	235	275	63
California	78	13	55	10	195	342	36

Leading Scorers

Player	Team	GP	G	A	PTS	PIM
Phil Esposito	Boston	78	68	77	145	58
Bobby Orr	Boston	74	32	90	122	82
Ken Hodge	Boston	76	50	55	105	43
Wayne Cashman	Boston	78	30	59	89	111
Bobby Clarke	Philadelphia	77	35	52	87	113
Rick Martin	Buffalo	78	52	34	86	38
Syl Apps Jr.	Pittsburgh	75	24	61	85	37
Darryl Sittler	Toronto	78	38	46	84	55
Lowell MacDonald	Pittsburgh	78	43	39	82	14
Brad Park	NY Rangers	78	25	57	82	148
Dennis Hextall	Minnesota	78	20	62	82	138

1974-75

PRINCE OF WALES CONFERENCE

Norris Division

Team	GP	W	L	T	GF	GA	PTS
Montreal	80	47	14	19	374	225	113
Los Angeles	80	42	17	21	269	185	105
Pittsburgh	80	37	28	15	326	289	89
Detroit	80	23	45	12	259	335	58
Washington	80	8	67	5	181	446	21

Adams Division

Team	GP	W	L	T	GF	GA	PTS
Buffalo	80	49	16	15	354	240	113
Boston	80	40	26	14	345	245	94
Toronto	80	31	33	16	280	309	78
California	80	19	48	13	212	316	51

CLARENCE CAMPBELL CONFERENCE

Patrick Division

Team	GP	W	L	T	GF	GA	PTS
*Philadelphia	80	51	18	11	293	181	113
NY Rangers	80	37	29	14	319	276	88
NY Islanders	80	33	25	22	264	221	88
Atlanta	80	34	31	15	243	233	83

Smythe Division

Team	GP	W	L	T	GF	GA	PTS
Vancouver	80	38	32	10	271	254	86
St. Louis	80	35	31	14	269	267	84
Chicago	80	37	35	8	268	241	82
Minnesota	80	23	50	7	221	341	53
Kansas City	80	15	54	11	184	328	41

Leading Scorers

Player	Team	GP	G	A	PTS	PIM
Bobby Orr	Boston	80	46	89	135	101
Phil Esposito	Boston	79	61	66	127	62
Marcel Dionne	Detroit	80	47	74	121	14
Guy Lafleur	Montreal	70	53	66	119	37
Pete Mahovlich	Montreal	80	35	82	117	64
Bobby Clarke	Philadelphia	80	27	89	116	125
Rene Robert	Buffalo	74	40	60	100	75
Rod Gilbert	NY Rangers	76	36	61	97	22
Gilbert Perreault	Buffalo	68	39	57	96	36
Rick Martin	Buffalo	68	52	43	95	72

1975-76

PRINCE OF WALES CONFERENCE

Norris Division

Team	GP	W	L	T	GF	GA	PTS
*Montreal	80	58	11	11	337	174	127
Los Angeles	80	38	33	9	263	265	85
Pittsburgh	80	35	33	12	339	303	82
Detroit	80	26	44	10	226	300	62
Washington	80	11	59	10	224	394	32

Adams Division

Team	GP	W	L	T	GF	GA	PTS
Boston	80	48	15	17	313	237	113
Buffalo	80	46	21	13	339	240	105
Toronto	80	34	31	15	294	276	83
California	80	27	42	11	250	278	65

CLARENCE CAMPBELL CONFERENCE

Patrick Division

Team	GP	W	L	T	GF	GA	PTS
Philadelphia	80	51	13	16	348	209	118
NY Islanders	80	42	21	17	297	190	101
Atlanta	80	35	33	12	262	237	82
NY Rangers	80	29	42	9	262	333	67

Smythe Division

Team	GP	W	L	T	GF	GA	PTS
Chicago	80	32	30	18	254	261	82
Vancouver	80	33	32	15	271	272	81
St. Louis	80	29	37	14	249	290	72
Minnesota	80	20	53	7	195	303	47
Kansas City	80	12	56	12	190	351	36

Leading Scorers

Player	Team	GP	G	A	PTS	PIM
Guy Lafleur	Montreal	80	56	69	125	36
Bobby Clarke	Philadelphia	76	30	89	119	136
Gilbert Perreault	Buffalo	80	44	69	113	36
Bill Barber	Philadelphia	80	50	62	112	104
Pierre Larouche	Pittsburgh	76	53	58	111	33
Jean Ratelle	Bos., NYR	80	36	69	105	18
Pete Mahovlich	Montreal	80	34	71	105	76
Jean Pronovost	Pittsburgh	80	52	52	104	24
Darryl Sittler	Toronto	79	41	59	100	90
Syl Apps Jr.	Pittsburgh	80	32	67	99	24

1976-77

PRINCE OF WALES CONFERENCE

Norris Division

Team	GP	W	L	T	GF	GA	PTS
*Montreal	80	60	8	12	387	171	132
Los Angeles	80	34	31	15	271	241	83
Pittsburgh	80	34	33	13	240	252	81
Washington	80	24	42	14	221	307	62
Detroit	80	16	55	9	183	309	41

Adams Division

Team	GP	W	L	T	GF	GA	PTS
Boston	80	49	23	8	312	240	106
Buffalo	80	48	24	8	301	220	104
Toronto	80	33	32	15	301	285	81
Cleveland	80	25	42	13	240	292	63

CLARENCE CAMPBELL CONFERENCE

Patrick Division

Team	GP	W	L	T	GF	GA	PTS
Philadelphia	80	48	16	16	323	213	112
NY Islanders	80	47	21	12	288	193	106
Atlanta	80	34	34	12	264	265	80
NY Rangers	80	29	37	14	272	310	72

Smythe Division

Team	GP	W	L	T	GF	GA	PTS
St. Louis	80	32	39	9	239	276	73
Minnesota	80	23	39	18	240	310	64
Chicago	80	26	43	11	240	298	63
Vancouver	80	25	42	13	235	294	63
Colorado	80	20	46	14	226	307	54

Leading Scorers

Player	Team	GP	G	A	PTS	PIM
Guy Lafleur	Montreal	80	56	80	136	20
Marcel Dionne	Los Angeles	80	53	69	122	12
Steve Shutt	Montreal	80	60	45	105	28
Rick MacLeish	Philadelphia	79	49	48	97	42
Gilbert Perreault	Buffalo	80	39	56	95	30
Tim Young	Minnesota	80	29	66	95	58
Jean Ratelle	Boston	78	33	61	94	22
Lanny McDonald	Toronto	80	46	44	90	77
Darryl Sittler	Toronto	73	38	52	90	89
Bobby Clarke	Philadelphia	80	27	63	90	71

1977-78

PRINCE OF WALES CONFERENCE

Norris Division

Team	GP	W	L	T	GF	GA	PTS
*Montreal	80	59	10	11	359	183	129
Detroit	80	32	34	14	252	266	78
Los Angeles	80	31	34	15	243	245	77
Pittsburgh	80	25	37	18	254	321	68
Washington	80	17	49	14	195	321	48

Adams Division

Team	GP	W	L	T	GF	GA	PTS
Boston	80	51	18	11	333	218	113
Buffalo	80	44	19	17	288	215	105
Toronto	80	41	29	10	271	237	92
Cleveland	80	22	45	13	230	325	57

CLARENCE CAMPBELL CONFERENCE

Patrick Division

Team	GP	W	L	T	GF	GA	PTS
NY Islanders	80	48	17	15	334	210	111
Philadelphia	80	45	20	15	296	200	105
Atlanta	80	34	27	19	274	252	87
NY Rangers	80	30	37	13	279	280	73

Smythe Division

Team	GP	W	L	T	GF	GA	PTS
Chicago	80	32	29	19	230	220	83
Colorado	80	19	40	21	257	305	59
Vancouver	80	20	43	17	239	320	57
St. Louis	80	20	47	13	195	304	53
Minnesota	80	18	53	9	218	325	45

Leading Scorers

Player	Team	GP	G	A	PTS	PIM
Guy Lafleur	Montreal	78	60	72	132	26
Bryan Trottier	NY Islanders	77	46	77	123	46
Darryl Sittler	Toronto	80	45	72	117	100
Jacques Lemaire	Montreal	76	36	61	97	14
Denis Potvin	NY Islanders	80	30	64	94	81
Mike Bossy	NY Islanders	73	53	38	91	6
Terry O'Reilly	Boston	77	29	61	90	211
Gilbert Perreault	Buffalo	79	41	48	89	20
Bobby Clarke	Philadelphia	71	21	68	89	83
Lanny McDonald	Toronto	74	47	40	87	54
Wilf Paiement	Colorado	80	31	56	87	114

1978-79

PRINCE OF WALES CONFERENCE

Norris Division

Team	GP	W	L	T	GF	GA	PTS
*Montreal	80	52	17	11	337	204	115
Pittsburgh	80	36	31	13	281	279	85
Los Angeles	80	34	34	12	292	286	80
Washington	80	24	41	15	273	338	63
Detroit	80	23	41	16	252	295	62

Adams Division

Team	GP	W	L	T	GF	GA	PTS
Boston	80	43	23	14	316	270	100
Buffalo	80	36	28	16	280	263	88
Toronto	80	34	33	13	267	252	81
Minnesota	80	28	40	12	257	289	68

CLARENCE CAMPBELL CONFERENCE

Patrick Division

Team	GP	W	L	T	GF	GA	PTS
NY Islanders	80	51	15	14	358	214	116
Philadelphia	80	40	25	15	281	248	95
NY Rangers	80	40	29	11	316	292	91
Atlanta	80	41	31	8	327	280	90

Smythe Division

Team	GP	W	L	T	GF	GA	PTS
Chicago	80	29	36	15	244	277	73
Vancouver	80	25	42	13	217	291	63
St. Louis	80	18	50	12	249	348	48
Colorado	80	15	53	12	210	331	42

Leading Scorers

Player	Team	GP	G	A	PTS	PIM
Bryan Trottier	NY Islanders	76	47	87	134	50
Marcel Dionne	Los Angeles	80	59	71	130	30
Guy Lafleur	Montreal	80	52	77	129	28
Mike Bossy	NY Islanders	80	69	57	126	25
Bob MacMillan	Atlanta	79	37	71	108	14
Guy Chouinard	Atlanta	80	50	57	107	14
Denis Potvin	NY Islanders	73	31	70	101	58
Bernie Federko	St. Louis	74	31	64	95	14
Dave Taylor	Los Angeles	78	43	48	91	124
Clark Gillies	NY Islanders	75	35	56	91	68

1979-80

PRINCE OF WALES CONFERENCE

Norris Division

Team	GP	W	L	T	GF	GA	PTS
Montreal	80	47	20	13	328	240	107
Los Angeles	80	30	36	14	290	313	74
Pittsburgh	80	30	37	13	251	303	73
Hartford	80	27	34	19	303	312	73
Detroit	80	26	43	11	268	306	63

Adams Division

Team	GP	W	L	T	GF	GA	PTS
Buffalo	80	47	17	16	318	201	110
Boston	80	46	21	13	310	234	105
Minnesota	80	36	28	16	311	253	88
Toronto	80	35	40	5	304	327	75
Quebec	80	25	44	11	248	313	61

CLARENCE CAMPBELL CONFERENCE

Patrick Division

Team	GP	W	L	T	GF	GA	PTS
Philadelphia	80	48	12	20	327	254	116
*NY Islanders	80	39	28	13	281	247	91
NY Rangers	80	38	32	10	308	284	86
Atlanta	80	35	32	13	282	269	83
Washington	80	27	40	13	261	293	67

Smythe Division

Team	GP	W	L	T	GF	GA	PTS
Chicago	80	34	27	19	241	250	87
St. Louis	80	34	34	12	266	278	80
Vancouver	80	27	37	16	256	281	70
Edmonton	80	28	39	13	301	322	69
Winnipeg	80	20	49	11	214	314	51
Colorado	80	19	48	13	234	308	51

Leading Scorers

Player	Team	GP	G	A	PTS	PIM
Marcel Dionne	Los Angeles	80	53	84	137	32
Wayne Gretzky	Edmonton	79	51	86	137	21
Guy Lafleur	Montreal	74	50	75	125	12
Gilbert Perreault	Buffalo	80	40	66	106	57
Mike Rogers	Hartford	80	44	61	105	10
Bryan Trottier	NY Islanders	78	42	62	104	68
Charlie Simmer	Los Angeles	64	56	45	101	65
Blaine Stoughton	Hartford	80	56	44	100	16
Darryl Sittler	Toronto	73	40	57	97	62
Blair MacDonald	Edmonton	80	46	48	94	6
Bernie Federko	St. Louis	79	38	56	94	24

1980-81

PRINCE OF WALES CONFERENCE

Norris Division

Team	GP	W	L	T	GF	GA	PTS
Montreal	80	45	22	13	332	232	103
Los Angeles	80	43	24	13	337	290	99
Pittsburgh	80	30	37	13	302	345	73
Hartford	80	21	41	18	292	372	60
Detroit	80	19	43	18	252	339	56

Adams Division

Team	GP	W	L	T	GF	GA	PTS
Buffalo	80	39	20	21	327	250	99
Boston	80	37	30	13	316	272	87
Minnesota	80	35	28	17	291	263	87
Quebec	80	30	32	18	314	318	78
Toronto	80	28	37	15	322	367	71

CLARENCE CAMPBELL CONFERENCE

Patrick Division

Team	GP	W	L	T	GF	GA	PTS
*NY Islanders	80	48	18	14	355	260	110
Philadelphia	80	41	24	15	313	249	97
Calgary	80	39	27	14	329	298	92
NY Rangers	80	30	36	14	312	317	74
Washington	80	26	36	18	286	317	70

Smythe Division

Team	GP	W	L	T	GF	GA	PTS
St. Louis	80	45	18	17	352	281	107
Chicago	80	31	33	16	304	315	78
Vancouver	80	28	32	20	289	301	76
Edmonton	80	29	35	16	328	327	74
Colorado	80	22	45	13	258	344	57
Winnipeg	80	9	57	14	246	400	32

Leading Scorers

Player	Team	GP	G	A	PTS	PIM
Wayne Gretzky	Edmonton	80	55	109	164	28
Marcel Dionne	Los Angeles	80	58	77	135	70
Kent Nilsson	Calgary	80	49	82	131	26
Mike Bossy	NY Islanders	79	68	51	119	32
Dave Taylor	Los Angeles	72	47	65	112	130
Peter Stastny	Quebec	77	39	70	109	37
Charlie Simmer	Los Angeles	65	56	49	105	62
Mike Rogers	Hartford	80	40	65	105	32
Bernie Federko	St. Louis	78	31	73	104	47
Jacques Richard	Quebec	78	52	51	103	39
Rick Middleton	Boston	80	44	59	103	16
Bryan Trottier	NY Islanders	73	31	72	103	74

1981-82

CLARENCE CAMPBELL CONFERENCE

Norris Division

Team	GP	W	L	T	GF	GA	PTS
Minnesota	80	37	23	20	346	288	94
Winnipeg	80	33	33	14	319	332	80
St. Louis	80	32	40	8	315	349	72
Chicago	80	30	38	12	332	363	72
Toronto	80	20	44	16	298	380	56
Detroit	80	21	47	12	270	351	54

Smythe Division

Team	GP	W	L	T	GF	GA	PTS
Edmonton	80	48	17	15	417	295	111
Vancouver	80	30	33	17	290	286	77
Calgary	80	29	34	17	334	345	75
Los Angeles	80	24	41	15	314	369	63
Colorado	80	18	49	13	241	362	49

PRINCE OF WALES CONFERENCE

Adams Division

Team	GP	W	L	T	GF	GA	PTS
Montreal	80	46	17	17	360	223	109
Boston	80	43	27	10	323	285	96
Buffalo	80	39	26	15	307	273	93
Quebec	80	33	31	16	356	345	82
Hartford	80	21	41	18	264	351	60

Patrick Division

Team	GP	W	L	T	GF	GA	PTS
*NY Islanders	80	54	16	10	385	250	118
NY Rangers	80	39	27	14	316	306	92
Philadelphia	80	38	31	11	325	313	87
Pittsburgh	80	31	36	13	310	337	75
Washington	80	26	41	13	319	338	65

Leading Scorers

Player	Team	GP	G	A	PTS	PIM
Wayne Gretzky	Edmonton	80	92	120	212	26
Mike Bossy	NY Islanders	80	64	83	147	22
Peter Stastny	Quebec	80	46	93	139	91
Dennis Maruk	Washington	80	60	76	136	128
Bryan Trottier	NY Islanders	80	50	79	129	88
Denis Savard	Chicago	80	32	87	119	82
Marcel Dionne	Los Angeles	78	50	67	117	50
Bobby Smith	Minnesota	80	43	71	114	82
Dino Ciccarelli	Minnesota	76	55	51	106	138
Dave Taylor	Los Angeles	78	39	67	106	130

1982-83

CLARENCE CAMPBELL CONFERENCE

Norris Division

Team	GP	W	L	T	GF	GA	PTS
Chicago	80	47	23	10	338	268	104
Minnesota	80	40	24	16	321	290	96
Toronto	80	28	40	12	293	330	68
St. Louis	80	25	40	15	285	316	65
Detroit	80	21	44	15	263	344	57

Smythe Division

Team	GP	W	L	T	GF	GA	PTS
Edmonton	80	47	21	12	424	315	106
Calgary	80	32	34	14	321	317	78
Vancouver	80	30	35	15	303	309	75
Winnipeg	80	33	39	8	311	333	74
Los Angeles	80	27	41	12	308	365	66

PRINCE OF WALES CONFERENCE

Adams Division

Team	GP	W	L	T	GF	GA	PTS
Boston	80	50	20	10	327	228	110
Montreal	80	42	24	14	350	286	98
Buffalo	80	38	29	13	318	285	89
Quebec	80	34	34	12	343	336	80
Hartford	80	19	54	7	261	403	45

Patrick Division

Team	GP	W	L	T	GF	GA	PTS
Philadelphia	80	49	23	8	326	240	106
*NY Islanders	80	42	26	12	302	226	96
Washington	80	39	25	16	306	283	94
NY Rangers	80	35	35	10	306	287	80
New Jersey	80	17	49	14	230	338	48
Pittsburgh	80	18	53	9	257	394	45

Leading Scorers

Player	Team	GP	G	A	PTS	PIM
Wayne Gretzky	Edmonton	80	71	125	196	59
Peter Stastny	Quebec	75	47	77	124	78
Denis Savard	Chicago	78	35	86	121	99
Mike Bossy	NY Islanders	79	60	58	118	20
Marcel Dionne	Los Angeles	80	56	51	107	22
Barry Pederson	Boston	77	46	61	107	47
Mark Messier	Edmonton	77	48	58	106	72
Michel Goulet	Quebec	80	57	48	105	51
Glenn Anderson	Edmonton	72	48	56	104	70
Kent Nilsson	Calgary	80	46	58	104	10
Jari Kurri	Edmonton	80	45	59	104	22

1983-84

CLARENCE CAMPBELL CONFERENCE

Norris Division

Team	GP	W	L	T	GF	GA	PTS
Minnesota	80	39	31	10	345	344	88
St. Louis	80	32	41	7	293	316	71
Detroit	80	31	42	7	298	323	69
Chicago	80	30	42	8	277	311	68
Toronto	80	26	45	9	303	387	61

Smythe Division

Team	GP	W	L	T	GF	GA	PTS
*Edmonton	80	57	18	5	446	314	119
Calgary	80	34	32	14	311	314	82
Vancouver	80	32	39	9	306	328	73
Winnipeg	80	31	38	11	340	374	73
Los Angeles	80	23	44	13	309	376	59

PRINCE OF WALES CONFERENCE

Adams Division

Team	GP	W	L	T	GF	GA	PTS
Boston	80	49	25	6	336	261	104
Buffalo	80	48	25	7	315	257	103
Quebec	80	42	28	10	360	278	94
Montreal	80	35	40	5	286	295	75
Hartford	80	28	42	10	288	320	66

Patrick Division

Team	GP	W	L	T	GF	GA	PTS
NY Islanders	80	50	26	4	357	269	104
Washington	80	48	27	5	308	226	101
Philadelphia	80	44	26	10	350	290	98
NY Rangers	80	42	29	9	314	304	93
New Jersey	80	17	56	7	231	350	41
Pittsburgh	80	16	58	6	254	390	38

Leading Scorers

Player	Team	GP	G	A	PTS	PIM
Wayne Gretzky	Edmonton	74	87	118	205	39
Paul Coffey	Edmonton	80	40	86	126	104
Michel Goulet	Quebec	75	56	65	121	76
Peter Stastny	Quebec	80	46	73	119	73
Mike Bossy	NY Islanders	67	51	67	118	8
Barry Pederson	Boston	80	39	77	116	64
Jari Kurri	Edmonton	64	52	61	113	14
Bryan Trottier	NY Islanders	68	40	71	111	59
Bernie Federko	St. Louis	79	41	66	107	43
Rick Middleton	Boston	80	47	58	105	14

1984-85

CLARENCE CAMPBELL CONFERENCE

Norris Division

Team	GP	W	L	T	GF	GA	PTS
St. Louis	80	37	31	12	299	288	86
Chicago	80	38	35	7	309	299	83
Detroit	80	27	41	12	313	357	66
Minnesota	80	25	43	12	268	321	62
Toronto	80	20	52	8	253	358	48

Smythe Division

Team	GP	W	L	T	GF	GA	PTS
*Edmonton	80	49	20	11	401	298	109
Winnipeg	80	43	27	10	358	332	96
Calgary	80	41	27	12	363	302	94
Los Angeles	80	34	32	14	339	326	82
Vancouver	80	25	46	9	284	401	59

PRINCE OF WALES CONFERENCE

Adams Division

Team	GP	W	L	T	GF	GA	PTS
Montreal	80	41	27	12	309	262	94
Quebec	80	41	30	9	323	275	91
Buffalo	80	38	28	14	290	237	90
Boston	80	36	34	10	303	287	82
Hartford	80	30	41	9	268	318	69

Patrick Division

Team	GP	W	L	T	GF	GA	PTS
Philadelphia	80	53	20	7	348	241	113
Washington	80	46	25	9	322	240	101
NY Islanders	80	40	34	6	345	312	86
NY Rangers	80	26	44	10	295	345	62
New Jersey	80	22	48	10	264	346	54
Pittsburgh	80	24	51	5	276	385	53

Leading Scorers

Player	Team	GP	G	A	PTS	PIM
Wayne Gretzky	Edmonton	80	73	135	208	52
Jari Kurri	Edmonton	73	71	64	135	30
Dale Hawerchuk	Winnipeg	80	53	77	130	74
Marcel Dionne	Los Angeles	80	46	80	126	46
Paul Coffey	Edmonton	80	37	84	121	97
Mike Bossy	NY Islanders	76	58	59	117	38
John Ogrodnick	Detroit	79	55	50	105	30
Denis Savard	Chicago	79	38	67	105	56
Bernie Federko	St. Louis	76	30	73	103	27
Mike Gartner	Washington	80	50	52	102	71

1985-86

CLARENCE CAMPBELL CONFERENCE

Norris Division

Team	GP	W	L	T	GF	GA	PTS
Chicago	80	39	33	8	351	349	86
Minnesota	80	38	33	9	327	305	85
St. Louis	80	37	34	9	302	291	83
Toronto	80	25	48	7	311	386	57
Detroit	80	17	57	6	266	415	40

Smythe Division

Team	GP	W	L	T	GF	GA	PTS
Edmonton	80	56	17	7	426	310	119
Calgary	80	40	31	9	354	315	89
Winnipeg	80	26	47	7	295	372	59
Vancouver	80	23	44	13	282	333	59
Los Angeles	80	23	49	8	284	389	54

PRINCE OF WALES CONFERENCE

Adams Division

Team	GP	W	L	T	GF	GA	PTS
Quebec	80	43	31	6	330	289	92
*Montreal	80	40	33	7	330	280	87
Boston	80	37	31	12	311	288	86
Hartford	80	40	36	4	332	302	84
Buffalo	80	37	37	6	296	291	80

Patrick Division

Team	GP	W	L	T	GF	GA	PTS
Philadelphia	80	53	23	4	335	241	110
Washington	80	50	23	7	315	272	107
NY Islanders	80	39	29	12	327	284	90
NY Rangers	80	36	38	6	280	276	78
Pittsburgh	80	34	38	8	313	305	76
New Jersey	80	28	49	3	300	374	59

Leading Scorers

Player	Team	GP	G	A	PTS	PIM
Wayne Gretzky	Edmonton	80	52	163	215	52
Mario Lemieux	Pittsburgh	79	48	93	141	43
Paul Coffey	Edmonton	79	48	90	138	120
Jari Kurri	Edmonton	78	68	63	131	22
Mike Bossy	NY Islanders	80	61	62	123	14
Peter Stastny	Quebec	76	41	81	122	60
Denis Savard	Chicago	80	47	69	116	111
Mats Naslund	Montreal	80	43	67	110	16
Dale Hawerchuk	Winnipeg	80	46	59	105	44
Neal Broten	Minnesota	80	29	76	105	47

1986-87

CLARENCE CAMPBELL CONFERENCE

Norris Division

Team	GP	W	L	T	GF	GA	PTS
St. Louis	80	32	33	15	281	293	79
Detroit	80	34	36	10	260	274	78
Chicago	80	29	37	14	290	310	72
Toronto	80	32	42	6	286	319	70
Minnesota	80	30	40	10	296	314	70

Smythe Division

Team	GP	W	L	T	GF	GA	PTS
*Edmonton	80	50	24	6	372	284	106
Calgary	80	46	31	3	318	289	95
Winnipeg	80	40	32	8	279	271	88
Los Angeles	80	31	41	8	318	341	70
Vancouver	80	29	43	8	282	314	66

PRINCE OF WALES CONFERENCE

Adams Division

Team	GP	W	L	T	GF	GA	PTS
Hartford	80	43	30	7	287	270	93
Montreal	80	41	29	10	277	241	92
Boston	80	39	34	7	301	276	85
Quebec	80	31	39	10	267	276	72
Buffalo	80	28	44	8	280	308	64

Patrick Division

Team	GP	W	L	T	GF	GA	PTS
Philadelphia	80	46	26	8	310	245	100
Washington	80	38	32	10	285	278	86
NY Islanders	80	35	33	12	279	281	82
NY Rangers	80	34	38	8	307	323	76
Pittsburgh	80	30	38	12	297	290	72
New Jersey	80	29	45	6	293	368	64

Leading Scorers

Player	Team	GP	G	A	PTS	PIM
Wayne Gretzky	Edmonton	79	62	121	183	28
Jari Kurri	Edmonton	79	54	54	108	41
Mario Lemieux	Pittsburgh	63	54	53	107	57
Mark Messier	Edmonton	77	37	70	107	73
Doug Gilmour	St. Louis	80	42	63	105	58
Dino Ciccarelli	Minnesota	80	52	51	103	92
Dale Hawerchuk	Winnipeg	80	47	53	100	54
Michel Goulet	Quebec	75	49	47	96	61
Tim Kerr	Philadelphia	75	58	37	95	57
Raymond Bourque	Boston	78	23	72	95	36

1987-88

CLARENCE CAMPBELL CONFERENCE

Norris Division

Team	GP	W	L	T	GF	GA	PTS
Detroit	80	41	28	11	322	269	93
St. Louis	80	34	38	8	278	294	76
Chicago	80	30	41	9	284	328	69
Toronto	80	21	49	10	273	345	52
Minnesota	80	19	48	13	242	349	51

Smythe Division

Team	GP	W	L	T	GF	GA	PTS
Calgary	80	48	23	9	397	305	105
*Edmonton	80	44	25	11	363	288	99
Winnipeg	80	33	36	11	292	310	77
Los Angeles	80	30	42	8	318	359	68
Vancouver	80	25	46	9	272	320	59

PRINCE OF WALES CONFERENCE

Adams Division

Team	GP	W	L	T	GF	GA	PTS
Montreal	80	45	22	13	298	238	103
Boston	80	44	30	6	300	251	94
Buffalo	80	37	32	11	283	305	85
Hartford	80	35	38	7	249	267	77
Quebec	80	32	43	5	271	306	69

Patrick Division

Team	GP	W	L	T	GF	GA	PTS
NY Islanders	80	39	31	10	308	267	88
Washington	80	38	33	9	281	249	85
Philadelphia	80	38	33	9	292	292	85
New Jersey	80	38	36	6	295	296	82
NY Rangers	80	36	34	10	300	283	82
Pittsburgh	80	36	35	9	319	316	81

Leading Scorers

Player	Team	GP	G	A	PTS	PIM
Mario Lemieux	Pittsburgh	77	70	98	168	92
Wayne Gretzky	Edmonton	64	40	109	149	24
Denis Savard	Chicago	80	44	87	131	95
Dale Hawerchuk	Winnipeg	80	44	77	121	59
Luc Robitaille	Los Angeles	80	53	58	111	82
Peter Stastny	Quebec	76	46	65	111	69
Mark Messier	Edmonton	77	37	74	111	103
Jimmy Carson	Los Angeles	80	55	52	107	45
Hakan Loob	Calgary	80	50	56	106	47
Michel Goulet	Quebec	80	48	58	106	56

1988-89

CLARENCE CAMPBELL CONFERENCE

Norris Division

Team	GP	W	L	T	GF	GA	PTS
Detroit	80	34	34	12	313	316	80
St. Louis	80	33	35	12	275	285	78
Minnesota	80	27	37	16	258	278	70
Chicago	80	27	41	12	297	335	66
Toronto	80	28	46	6	259	342	62

Smythe Division

Team	GP	W	L	T	GF	GA	PTS
*Calgary	80	54	17	9	354	226	117
Los Angeles	80	42	31	7	376	335	91
Edmonton	80	38	34	8	325	306	84
Vancouver	80	33	39	8	251	253	74
Winnipeg	80	26	42	12	300	355	64

PRINCE OF WALES CONFERENCE

Adams Division

Team	GP	W	L	T	GF	GA	PTS
Montreal	80	53	18	9	315	218	115
Boston	80	37	29	14	289	256	88
Buffalo	80	38	35	7	291	299	83
Hartford	80	37	38	5	299	290	79
Quebec	80	27	46	7	269	342	61

Patrick Division

Team	GP	W	L	T	GF	GA	PTS
Washington	80	41	29	10	305	259	92
Pittsburgh	80	40	33	7	347	349	87
NY Rangers	80	37	35	8	310	307	82
Philadelphia	80	36	36	8	307	285	80
New Jersey	80	27	41	12	281	325	66
NY Islanders	80	28	47	5	265	325	61

Leading Scorers

Player	Team	GP	G	A	PTS	PIM
Mario Lemieux	Pittsburgh	76	85	114	199	100
Wayne Gretzky	Los Angeles	78	54	114	168	26
Steve Yzerman	Detroit	80	65	90	155	61
Bernie Nicholls	Los Angeles	79	70	80	150	96
Rob Brown	Pittsburgh	68	49	66	115	118
Paul Coffey	Pittsburgh	75	30	83	113	193
Joe Mullen	Calgary	79	51	59	110	16
Jari Kurri	Edmonton	76	44	58	102	69
Jimmy Carson	Edmonton	80	49	51	100	36
Luc Robitaille	Los Angeles	78	46	52	98	65

1989-90

CLARENCE CAMPBELL CONFERENCE

Norris Division

Team	GP	W	L	T	GF	GA	PTS
Chicago	80	41	33	6	316	294	88
St. Louis	80	37	34	9	295	279	83
Toronto	80	38	38	4	337	358	80
Minnesota	80	36	40	4	284	291	76
Detroit	80	28	38	14	288	323	70

Smythe Division

Team	GP	W	L	T	GF	GA	PTS
Calgary	80	42	23	15	348	265	99
*Edmonton	80	38	28	14	315	283	90
Winnipeg	80	37	32	11	298	290	85
Los Angeles	80	34	39	7	338	337	75
Vancouver	80	25	41	14	245	306	64

PRINCE OF WALES CONFERENCE

Adams Division

Team	GP	W	L	T	GF	GA	PTS
Boston	80	46	25	9	289	232	101
Buffalo	80	45	27	8	286	248	98
Montreal	80	41	28	11	288	234	93
Hartford	80	38	33	9	275	268	85
Quebec	80	12	61	7	240	407	31

Patrick Division

Team	GP	W	L	T	GF	GA	PTS
NY Rangers	80	36	31	13	279	267	85
New Jersey	80	37	34	9	295	288	83
Washington	80	36	38	6	284	275	78
NY Islanders	80	31	38	11	281	288	73
Pittsburgh	80	32	40	8	318	359	72
Philadelphia	80	30	39	11	290	297	71

Leading Scorers

Player	Team	GP	G	A	PTS	PIM
Wayne Gretzky	Los Angeles	73	40	102	142	42
Mark Messier	Edmonton	79	45	84	129	79
Steve Yzerman	Detroit	79	62	65	127	79
Mario Lemieux	Pittsburgh	59	45	78	123	78
Brett Hull	St. Louis	80	72	41	113	24
Bernie Nicholls	L.A., NYR	79	39	73	112	86
Pierre Turgeon	Buffalo	80	40	66	106	29
Pat LaFontaine	NY Islanders	74	54	51	105	38
Paul Coffey	Pittsburgh	80	29	74	103	95
Joe Sakic	Quebec	80	39	63	102	27
Adam Oates	St. Louis	80	23	79	102	30

1990-91

CLARENCE CAMPBELL CONFERENCE

Norris Division

Team	GP	W	L	T	GF	GA	PTS
Chicago	80	49	23	8	284	211	106
St. Louis	80	47	22	11	310	250	105
Detroit	80	34	38	8	273	298	76
Minnesota	80	27	39	14	256	266	68
Toronto	80	23	46	11	241	318	57

Smythe Division

Team	GP	W	L	T	GF	GA	PTS
Los Angeles	80	46	24	10	340	254	102
Calgary	80	46	26	8	344	263	100
Edmonton	80	37	37	6	272	272	80
Vancouver	80	28	43	9	243	315	65
Winnipeg	80	26	43	11	260	288	63

PRINCE OF WALES CONFERENCE

Adams Division

Team	GP	W	L	T	GF	GA	PTS
Boston	80	44	24	12	299	264	100
Montreal	80	39	30	11	273	249	89
Buffalo	80	31	30	19	292	278	81
Hartford	80	31	38	11	238	276	73
Quebec	80	16	50	14	236	354	46

Patrick Division

Team	GP	W	L	T	GF	GA	PTS
*Pittsburgh	80	41	33	6	342	305	88
NY Rangers	80	36	31	13	297	265	85
Washington	80	37	36	7	258	258	81
New Jersey	80	32	33	15	272	264	79
Philadelphia	80	33	37	10	252	267	76
NY Islanders	80	25	45	10	223	290	60

Leading Scorers

Player	Team	GP	G	A	PTS	PIM
Wayne Gretzky	Los Angeles	78	41	122	163	16
Brett Hull	St. Louis	78	86	45	131	22
Adam Oates	St. Louis	61	25	90	115	29
Mark Recchi	Pittsburgh	78	40	73	113	48
John Cullen	Pit., Hfd.	78	39	71	110	101
Joe Sakic	Quebec	80	48	61	109	24
Steve Yzerman	Detroit	80	51	57	108	34
Theoren Fleury	Calgary	79	51	53	104	136
Al MacInnis	Calgary	78	28	75	103	90
Steve Larmer	Chicago	80	44	57	101	79

1991-92

CLARENCE CAMPBELL CONFERENCE

Norris Division

Team	GP	W	L	T	GF	GA	PTS
Detroit	80	43	25	12	320	256	98
Chicago	80	36	29	15	257	236	87
St. Louis	80	36	33	11	279	266	83
Minnesota	80	32	42	6	246	278	70
Toronto	80	30	43	7	234	294	67

Smythe Division

Team	GP	W	L	T	GF	GA	PTS
Vancouver	80	42	26	12	285	250	96
Los Angeles	80	35	31	14	287	296	84
Edmonton	80	36	34	10	295	297	82
Winnipeg	80	33	32	15	251	244	81
Calgary	80	31	37	12	296	305	74
San Jose	80	17	58	5	219	359	39

PRINCE OF WALES CONFERENCE

Adams Division

Team	GP	W	L	T	GF	GA	PTS
Montreal	80	41	28	11	267	207	93
Boston	80	36	32	12	270	275	84
Buffalo	80	31	37	12	289	299	74
Hartford	80	26	41	13	247	283	65
Quebec	80	20	48	12	255	318	52

Patrick Division

Team	GP	W	L	T	GF	GA	PTS
NY Rangers	80	50	25	5	321	246	105
Washington	80	45	27	8	330	275	98
*Pittsburgh	80	39	32	9	343	308	87
New Jersey	80	38	31	11	289	259	87
NY Islanders	80	34	35	11	291	299	79
Philadelphia	80	32	37	11	252	273	75

Leading Scorers

Player	Team	GP	G	A	PTS	PIM
Mario Lemieux	Pittsburgh	64	44	87	131	94
Kevin Stevens	Pittsburgh	80	54	69	123	254
Wayne Gretzky	Los Angeles	74	31	90	121	34
Brett Hull	St. Louis	73	70	39	109	48
Luc Robitaille	Los Angeles	80	44	63	107	95
Mark Messier	NY Rangers	79	35	72	107	76
Jeremy Roenick	Chicago	80	53	50	103	23
Steve Yzerman	Detroit	79	45	58	103	64
Brian Leetch	NY Rangers	80	22	80	102	26
Adam Oates	St.L., Bos.	80	20	79	99	22

1992-93

CLARENCE CAMPBELL CONFERENCE

Norris Division

Team	GP	W	L	T	GF	GA	PTS
Chicago	84	47	25	12	279	230	106
Detroit	84	47	28	9	369	280	103
Toronto	84	44	29	11	288	241	99
St. Louis	84	37	36	11	282	278	85
Minnesota	84	36	38	10	272	293	82
Tampa Bay	84	23	54	7	245	332	53

Smythe Division

Team	GP	W	L	T	GF	GA	PTS
Vancouver	84	46	29	9	346	278	101
Calgary	84	43	30	11	322	282	97
Los Angeles	84	39	35	10	338	340	88
Winnipeg	84	40	37	7	322	320	87
Edmonton	84	26	50	8	242	337	60
San Jose	84	11	71	2	218	414	24

PRINCE OF WALES CONFERENCE

Adams Division

Team	GP	W	L	T	GF	GA	PTS
Boston	84	51	26	7	332	268	109
Quebec	84	47	27	10	351	300	104
*Montreal	84	48	30	6	326	280	102
Buffalo	84	38	36	10	335	297	86
Hartford	84	26	52	6	284	369	58
Ottawa	84	10	70	4	202	395	24

Patrick Division

Team	GP	W	L	T	GF	GA	PTS
Pittsburgh	84	56	21	7	367	268	119
Washington	84	43	34	7	325	286	93
NY Islanders	84	40	37	7	335	297	87
New Jersey	84	40	37	7	308	299	87
Philadelphia	84	36	37	11	319	319	83
NY Rangers	84	34	39	11	304	308	79

Leading Scorers

Player	Team	GP	G	A	PTS	PIM
Mario Lemieux	Pittsburgh	60	69	91	160	38
Pat LaFontaine	Buffalo	84	53	95	148	63
Adam Oates	Boston	84	45	97	142	32
Steve Yzerman	Detroit	84	58	79	137	44
Teemu Selanne	Winnipeg	84	76	56	132	45
Pierre Turgeon	NY Islanders	83	58	74	132	26
Alexander Mogilny	Buffalo	77	76	51	127	40
Doug Gilmour	Toronto	83	32	95	127	100
Luc Robitaille	Los Angeles	84	63	62	125	100
Mark Recchi	Philadelphia	84	53	70	123	95

1993-94

EASTERN CONFERENCE

Northeast Division

Team		GP	W	L	T	GF	GA	PTS
Pittsburgh	(2)	84	44	27	13	299	285	101
Boston	(4)	84	42	29	13	289	252	97
Montreal	(5)	84	41	29	14	283	248	96
Buffalo	(6)	84	43	32	9	282	218	95
Quebec		84	34	42	8	277	292	76
Hartford		84	27	48	9	227	288	63
Ottawa		84	14	61	9	201	397	37

Atlantic Division

Team		GP	W	L	T	GF	GA	PTS
*NY Rangers	(1)	84	52	24	8	299	231	112
New Jersey	(3)	84	47	25	12	306	220	106
Washington	(7)	84	39	35	10	277	263	88
NY Islanders	(8)	84	36	36	12	282	264	84
Florida		84	33	34	17	233	233	83
Philadelphia		84	35	39	10	294	314	80
Tampa Bay		84	30	43	11	224	251	71

WESTERN CONFERENCE

Central Division

Team		GP	W	L	T	GF	GA	PTS
Detroit	(1)	84	46	30	8	356	275	100
Toronto	(3)	84	43	29	12	280	243	98
Dallas	(4)	84	42	29	13	286	265	97
St. Louis	(5)	84	40	33	11	270	283	91
Chicago	(6)	84	39	36	9	254	240	87
Winnipeg		84	24	51	9	245	344	57

Pacific Division

Team		GP	W	L	T	GF	GA	PTS
Calgary	(2)	84	42	29	13	302	256	97
Vancouver	(7)	84	41	40	3	279	276	85
San Jose	(8)	84	33	35	16	252	265	82
Anaheim		84	33	46	5	229	251	71
Los Angeles		84	27	45	12	294	322	66
Edmonton		84	25	45	14	261	305	64

Leading Scorers

Player	Team	GP	G	A	PTS	PIM
Wayne Gretzky	Los Angeles	81	38	92	130	20
Sergei Fedorov	Detroit	82	56	64	120	34
Adam Oates	Boston	77	32	80	112	45
Doug Gilmour	Toronto	83	27	84	111	105
Pavel Bure	Vancouver	76	60	47	107	86
Jeremy Roenick	Chicago	84	46	61	107	125
Mark Recchi	Philadelphia	84	40	67	107	46
Brendan Shanahan	St. Louis	81	52	50	102	211
Dave Andreychuk	Toronto	83	53	46	99	98
Jaromir Jagr	Pittsburgh	80	32	67	99	61

1994-95

EASTERN CONFERENCE

Northeast Division

Team		GP	W	L	T	GF	GA	PTS
Quebec	(1)	48	30	13	5	185	134	65
Pittsburgh	(3)	48	29	16	3	181	158	61
Boston	(4)	48	27	18	3	150	127	57
Buffalo	(7)	48	22	19	7	130	119	51
Hartford		48	19	24	5	127	141	43
Montreal		48	18	23	7	125	148	43
Ottawa		48	9	34	5	117	174	23

Atlantic Division

Philadelphia	(2)	48	28	16	4	150	132	60
*New Jersey	(5)	48	22	18	8	136	121	52
Washington	(6)	48	22	18	8	136	120	52
NY Rangers	(8)	48	22	23	3	139	134	47
Florida		48	20	22	6	115	127	46
Tampa Bay		48	17	28	3	120	144	37
NY Islanders		48	15	28	5	126	158	35

WESTERN CONFERENCE

Central Division

Detroit	(1)	48	33	11	4	180	117	70
St. Louis	(3)	48	28	15	5	178	135	61
Chicago	(4)	48	24	19	5	156	115	53
Toronto	(5)	48	21	19	8	135	146	50
Dallas	(8)	48	17	23	8	136	135	42
Winnipeg		48	16	25	7	157	177	39

Pacific Division

Calgary	(2)	48	24	17	7	163	135	55
Vancouver	(6)	48	18	18	12	153	148	48
San Jose	(7)	48	19	25	4	129	161	42
Los Angeles		48	16	23	9	142	174	41
Edmonton		48	17	27	4	136	183	38
Anaheim		48	16	27	5	125	164	37

Leading Scorers

Player	Team	GP	G	A	PTS	PIM
Jaromir Jagr	Pittsburgh	48	32	38	70	37
Eric Lindros	Philadelphia	46	29	41	70	60
Alex Zhamnov	Winnipeg	48	30	35	65	20
Joe Sakic	Quebec	47	19	43	62	30
Ron Francis	Pittsburgh	44	11	48	59	18
Theoren Fleury	Calgary	47	29	29	58	112
Paul Coffey	Detroit	45	14	44	58	72
Mikael Renberg	Philadelphia	47	26	31	57	20
John LeClair	Mtl., Phi.	46	26	28	54	30
Mark Messier	NY Rangers	46	14	39	53	40
Adam Oates	Boston	48	12	41	53	8

1995-96

EASTERN CONFERENCE

Northeast Division

Team		GP	W	L	T	GF	GA	PTS
Pittsburgh	(2)	82	49	29	4	362	284	102
Boston	(5)	82	40	31	11	282	269	91
Montreal	(6)	82	40	32	10	265	248	90
Hartford		82	34	39	9	237	259	77
Buffalo		82	33	42	7	247	262	73
Ottawa		82	18	59	5	191	291	41

Atlantic Division

Philadelphia	(1)	82	45	24	13	282	208	103
NY Rangers	(3)	82	41	27	14	272	237	96
Florida	(4)	82	41	31	10	254	234	92
Washington	(7)	82	39	32	11	234	204	89
Tampa Bay	(8)	82	38	32	12	238	248	88
New Jersey		82	37	33	12	215	202	86
NY Islanders		82	22	50	10	229	315	54

WESTERN CONFERENCE

Central Division

Detroit	(1)	82	62	13	7	325	181	131
Chicago	(3)	82	40	28	14	273	220	94
Toronto	(4)	82	34	36	12	247	252	80
St. Louis	(5)	82	32	34	16	219	248	80
Winnipeg	(8)	82	36	40	6	275	291	78
Dallas		82	26	42	14	227	280	66

Pacific Division

*Colorado	(2)	82	47	25	10	326	240	104
Calgary	(6)	82	34	37	11	241	240	79
Vancouver	(7)	82	32	35	15	278	278	79
Anaheim		82	35	39	8	234	247	78
Edmonton		82	30	44	8	240	304	68
Los Angeles		82	24	40	18	256	302	66
San Jose		82	20	55	7	252	357	47

Leading Scorers

Player	Team	GP	G	A	PTS	PIM
Mario Lemieux	Pittsburgh	70	69	92	161	54
Jaromir Jagr	Pittsburgh	82	62	87	149	96
Joe Sakic	Colorado	82	51	69	120	44
Ron Francis	Pittsburgh	77	27	92	119	56
Peter Forsberg	Colorado	82	30	86	116	47
Eric Lindros	Philadelphia	73	47	68	115	163
Paul Kariya	Anaheim	82	50	58	108	20
Teemu Selanne	Wpg., Ana.	79	40	68	108	22
Alexander Mogilny	Vancouver	79	55	52	107	16
Sergei Fedorov	Detroit	78	39	68	107	48

1996-97

EASTERN CONFERENCE

Northeast Division

Team		GP	W	L	T	GF	GA	PTS
Buffalo	(2)	82	40	30	12	237	208	92
Pittsburgh	(6)	82	38	36	8	285	280	84
Ottawa	(7)	82	31	36	15	226	234	77
Montreal	(8)	82	31	36	15	249	276	77
Hartford		82	32	39	11	226	256	75
Boston		82	26	47	9	234	300	61

Atlantic Division

New Jersey	(1)	82	45	23	14	231	182	104
Philadelphia	(3)	82	45	24	13	274	217	103
Florida	(4)	82	35	28	19	221	201	89
NY Rangers	(5)	82	38	34	10	258	231	86
Washington		82	33	40	9	214	231	75
Tampa Bay		82	32	40	10	217	247	74
NY Islanders		82	29	41	12	240	250	70

WESTERN CONFERENCE

Central Division

Dallas	(2)	82	48	26	8	252	198	104
*Detroit	(3)	82	38	26	18	253	197	94
Phoenix	(5)	82	38	37	7	240	243	83
St. Louis	(6)	82	36	35	11	236	239	83
Chicago	(8)	82	34	35	13	223	210	81
Toronto		82	30	44	8	230	273	68

Pacific Division

Colorado	(1)	82	49	24	9	277	205	107
Anaheim	(4)	82	36	33	13	245	233	85
Edmonton	(7)	82	36	37	9	252	247	81
Vancouver		82	35	40	7	257	273	77
Calgary		82	32	41	9	214	239	73
Los Angeles		82	28	43	11	214	268	67
San Jose		82	27	47	8	211	278	62

Leading Scorers

Player	Team	GP	G	A	PTS	PIM
Mario Lemieux	Pittsburgh	76	50	72	122	65
Teemu Selanne	Anaheim	78	51	58	109	34
Paul Kariya	Anaheim	69	44	55	99	6
John LeClair	Philadelphia	82	50	47	97	58
Wayne Gretzky	NY Rangers	82	25	72	97	28
Jaromir Jagr	Pittsburgh	63	47	48	95	40
Mats Sundin	Toronto	82	41	53	94	59
Ziggy Palffy	NY Islanders	80	48	42	90	43
Ron Francis	Pittsburgh	81	27	63	90	20
Brendan Shanahan	Hfd., Det.	81	47	41	88	131

1997-98

EASTERN CONFERENCE

Northeast Division

Team		GP	W	L	T	GF	GA	PTS
Pittsburgh	(2)	82	40	24	18	228	188	98
Boston	(5)	82	39	30	13	221	194	91
Buffalo	(6)	82	36	29	17	211	187	89
Montreal	(7)	82	37	32	13	235	208	87
Ottawa	(8)	82	34	33	15	193	200	83
Carolina		82	33	41	8	200	219	74

Atlantic Division

New Jersey	(1)	82	48	23	11	225	166	107
Philadelphia	(3)	82	42	29	11	242	193	95
Washington	(4)	82	40	30	12	219	202	92
NY Islanders		82	30	41	11	212	225	71
NY Rangers		82	25	39	18	197	231	68
Florida		82	24	43	15	203	256	63
Tampa Bay		82	17	55	10	151	269	44

WESTERN CONFERENCE

Central Division

Dallas	(1)	82	49	22	11	242	167	109
*Detroit	(3)	82	44	23	15	250	196	103
St. Louis	(4)	82	45	29	8	256	204	98
Phoenix	(6)	82	35	35	12	224	227	82
Chicago		82	30	39	13	192	199	73
Toronto		82	30	43	9	194	237	69

Pacific Division

Colorado	(2)	82	39	26	17	231	205	95
Los Angeles	(5)	82	38	33	11	227	225	87
Edmonton	(7)	82	35	37	10	215	224	80
San Jose	(8)	82	34	38	10	210	216	78
Calgary		82	26	41	15	217	252	67
Anaheim		82	26	43	13	205	261	65
Vancouver		82	25	43	14	224	273	64

Leading Scorers

Player	Team	GP	G	A	PTS	PIM
Jaromir Jagr	Pittsburgh	77	35	67	102	64
Peter Forsberg	Colorado	72	25	66	91	94
Pavel Bure	Vancouver	82	51	39	90	48
Wayne Gretzky	NY Rangers	82	23	67	90	28
John LeClair	Philadelphia	82	51	36	87	32
Ziggy Palffy	NY Islanders	82	45	42	87	34
Ron Francis	Pittsburgh	81	25	62	87	20
Teemu Selanne	Anaheim	73	52	34	86	30
Jason Allison	Boston	81	33	50	83	60
Jozef Stumpel	Los Angeles	77	21	58	79	53

1998-99

EASTERN CONFERENCE

Northeast Division

Team		GP	W	L	T	GF	GA	PTS
Ottawa	(2)	82	44	23	15	239	179	103
Toronto	(4)	82	45	30	7	268	231	97
Boston	(6)	82	39	30	13	214	181	91
Buffalo	(7)	82	37	28	17	207	175	91
Montreal		82	32	39	11	184	209	75

Atlantic Division

New Jersey	(1)	82	47	24	11	248	196	105
Philadelphia	(5)	82	37	26	19	231	196	93
Pittsburgh	(8)	82	38	30	14	242	225	90
NY Rangers		82	33	38	11	217	227	77
NY Islanders		82	24	48	10	194	244	58

Southeast Division

Carolina	(3)	82	34	30	18	210	202	86
Florida		82	30	34	18	210	228	78
Washington		82	31	45	6	200	218	68
Tampa Bay		82	19	54	9	179	292	47

WESTERN CONFERENCE

Central Division

Detroit	(3)	82	43	32	7	245	202	93
St Louis	(5)	82	37	32	13	237	209	87
Chicago		82	29	41	12	202	248	70
Nashville		82	28	47	7	190	261	63

Pacific Division

*Dallas	(1)	82	51	19	12	236	168	114
Phoenix	(4)	82	39	31	12	205	197	90
Anaheim	(6)	82	35	34	13	215	206	83
San Jose	(7)	82	31	33	18	196	191	80
Los Angeles		82	32	45	5	189	222	69

Northwest Division

Colorado	(2)	82	44	28	10	239	205	98
Edmonton	(8)	82	33	37	12	230	226	78
Calgary		82	30	40	12	211	234	72
Vancouver		82	23	47	12	192	258	58

Leading Scorers

Player	Team	GP	G	A	PTS	PIM
Jaromir Jagr	Pittsburgh	81	44	83	127	66
Teemu Selanne	Anaheim	75	47	60	107	30
Paul Kariya	Anaheim	82	39	62	101	40
Peter Forsberg	Colorado	78	30	67	97	108
Joe Sakic	Colorado	73	41	55	96	29
Alexei Yashin	Ottawa	82	44	50	94	54
Eric Lindros	Philadelphia	71	40	53	93	120
Theoren Fleury	Cgy., Col.	75	40	53	93	86
John LeClair	Philadelphia	76	43	47	90	30
Pavol Demitra	St Louis	82	37	52	89	16

1999-2000

EASTERN CONFERENCE

Northeast Division

Team		GP	W	L	T	OTL	GF	GA	PTS
Toronto	(3)	82	45	27	7	3	246	222	100
Ottawa	(6)	82	41	28	11	2	244	210	95
Buffalo	(8)	82	35	32	11	4	213	204	85
Montreal		82	35	34	9	4	196	194	83
Boston		82	24	33	19	6	210	248	73

Atlantic Division

Philadelphia	(1)	82	45	22	12	3	237	179	105
*New Jersey	(4)	82	45	24	8	5	251	203	103
Pittsburgh	(7)	82	37	31	8	6	241	236	88
NY Rangers		82	29	38	12	3	218	246	73
NY Islanders		82	24	48	9	1	194	275	58

Southeast Division

Washington	(2)	82	44	24	12	2	227	194	102
Florida	(5)	82	43	27	6	6	244	209	98
Carolina		82	37	35	10	0	217	216	84
Tampa Bay		82	19	47	9	7	204	310	54
Atlanta		82	14	57	7	4	170	313	39

WESTERN CONFERENCE

Central Division

St. Louis	(1)	82	51	19	11	1	248	165	114
Detroit	(4)	82	48	22	10	2	278	210	108
Chicago		82	33	37	10	2	242	245	78
Nashville		82	28	40	7	7	199	240	70

Pacific Division

Team		GP	W	L	T	OTL	GF	GA	PTS
Dallas	(2)	82	43	23	10	6	211	184	102
Los Angeles	(5)	82	39	27	12	4	245	228	94
Phoenix	(6)	82	39	31	8	4	232	228	90
San Jose	(8)	82	35	30	10	7	225	214	87
Anaheim		82	34	33	12	3	217	227	83

Northwest Division

Team		GP	W	L	T	OTL	GF	GA	PTS
Colorado	(3)	82	42	28	11	1	233	201	96
Edmonton	(7)	82	32	26	16	8	226	212	88
Vancouver		82	30	29	15	8	227	237	83
Calgary		82	31	36	10	5	211	256	77

Leading Scorers

Player	Team	GP	G	A	PTS	PIM
Jaromir Jagr	Pittsburgh	63	42	54	96	50
Pavel Bure	Florida	74	58	36	94	16
Mark Recchi	Philadelphia	82	28	63	91	50
Paul Kariya	Anaheim	74	42	44	86	24
Teemu Selanne	Anaheim	79	33	52	85	12
Owen Nolan	San Jose	78	44	40	84	110
Tony Amonte	Chicago	82	43	41	84	48
Mike Modano	Dallas	77	38	43	81	48
Joe Sakic	Colorado	60	28	53	81	28
Steve Yzerman	Detroit	78	35	44	79	34

2000-01

EASTERN CONFERENCE

Northeast Division

Team		GP	W	L	T	OTL	GF	GA	PTS
Ottawa	(2)	82	48	21	9	4	274	205	109
Buffalo	(5)	82	46	30	5	1	218	184	98
Toronto	(7)	82	37	29	11	5	232	207	90
Boston		82	36	30	8	8	227	249	88
Montreal		82	28	40	8	6	206	232	70

Atlantic Division

Team		GP	W	L	T	OTL	GF	GA	PTS
New Jersey	(1)	82	48	19	12	3	295	195	111
Philadelphia	(4)	82	43	25	11	3	240	207	100
Pittsburgh	(6)	82	42	28	9	3	281	256	96
NY Rangers		82	33	43	5	1	250	290	72
NY Islanders		82	21	51	7	3	185	268	52

Southeast Division

Team		GP	W	L	T	OTL	GF	GA	PTS
Washington	(3)	82	41	27	10	4	233	211	96
Carolina	(8)	82	38	32	9	3	212	225	88
Florida		82	22	38	13	9	200	246	66
Atlanta		82	23	45	12	2	211	289	60
Tampa Bay		82	24	47	6	5	201	280	59

WESTERN CONFERENCE

Central Division

Team		GP	W	L	T	OTL	GF	GA	PTS
Detroit	(2)	82	49	20	9	4	253	202	111
St. Louis	(4)	82	43	22	12	5	249	195	103
Nashville		82	34	36	9	3	186	200	80
Chicago		82	29	40	8	5	210	246	71
Columbus		82	28	39	9	6	190	233	71

Pacific Division

Team		GP	W	L	T	OTL	GF	GA	PTS
Dallas	(3)	82	48	24	8	2	241	187	106
San Jose	(5)	82	40	27	12	3	217	192	95
Los Angeles	(7)	82	38	28	13	3	252	228	92
Phoenix		82	35	27	17	3	214	212	90
Anaheim		82	25	41	11	5	188	245	66

Northwest Division

Team		GP	W	L	T	OTL	GF	GA	PTS
*Colorado	(1)	82	52	16	10	4	270	192	118
Edmonton	(6)	82	39	28	12	3	243	222	93
Vancouver	(8)	82	36	28	11	7	239	238	90
Calgary		82	27	36	15	4	197	236	73
Minnesota		82	25	39	13	5	168	210	68

Leading Scorers

Player	Team	GP	G	A	PTS	PIM
Jaromir Jagr	Pittsburgh	81	52	69	121	42
Joe Sakic	Colorado	82	54	64	118	30
Patrik Elias	New Jersey	82	40	56	96	51
Alex Kovalev	Pittsburgh	79	44	51	95	96
Jason Allison	Boston	82	36	59	95	85
Martin Straka	Pittsburgh	82	27	68	95	38
Pavel Bure	Florida	82	59	33	92	58
Doug Weight	Edmonton	82	25	65	90	91
Ziggy Palffy	Los Angeles	73	38	51	89	20
Peter Forsberg	Colorado	73	27	62	89	54

2001-02

EASTERN CONFERENCE

Northeast Division

Team		GP	W	L	T	OTL	GF	GA	PTS
Boston	(1)	82	43	24	6	9	236	201	101
Toronto	(4)	82	43	25	10	4	249	207	100
Ottawa	(7)	82	39	27	9	7	243	208	94
Montreal	(8)	82	36	31	12	3	207	209	87
Buffalo		82	35	35	11	1	213	200	82

Atlantic Division

Team		GP	W	L	T	OTL	GF	GA	PTS
Philadelphia	(2)	82	42	27	10	3	234	192	97
NY Islanders	(5)	82	42	28	8	4	239	220	96
New Jersey	(6)	82	41	28	9	4	205	187	95
NY Rangers		82	36	38	4	4	227	258	80
Pittsburgh		82	28	41	8	5	198	249	69

Southeast Division

Team		GP	W	L	T	OTL	GF	GA	PTS
Carolina	(3)	82	35	26	16	5	217	217	91
Washington		82	36	33	11	2	228	240	85
Tampa Bay		82	27	40	11	4	178	219	69
Florida		82	22	44	10	6	180	250	60
Atlanta		82	19	47	11	5	187	288	54

WESTERN CONFERENCE

Central Division

Team		GP	W	L	T	OTL	GF	GA	PTS
*Detroit	(1)	82	51	17	10	4	251	187	116
St. Louis	(4)	82	43	27	8	4	227	188	98
Chicago	(5)	82	41	27	13	1	216	207	96
Nashville		82	28	41	13	0	196	230	69
Columbus		82	22	47	8	5	164	255	57

Pacific Division

Team		GP	W	L	T	OTL	GF	GA	PTS
San Jose	(3)	82	44	27	8	3	248	199	99
Phoenix	(6)	82	40	27	9	6	228	210	95
Los Angeles	(7)	82	40	27	11	4	214	190	95
Dallas		82	36	28	13	5	215	213	90
Anaheim		82	29	42	8	3	175	198	69

Northwest Division

Team		GP	W	L	T	OTL	GF	GA	PTS
Colorado	(2)	82	45	28	8	1	212	169	99
Vancouver	(8)	82	42	30	7	3	254	211	94
Edmonton		82	38	28	12	4	205	182	92
Calgary		82	32	35	12	3	201	220	79
Minnesota		82	26	35	12	9	195	238	73

Leading Scorers

Player	Team	GP	G	A	PTS	PIM
Jarome Iginla	Calgary	82	52	44	96	77
Markus Naslund	Vancouver	81	40	50	90	50
Todd Bertuzzi	Vancouver	72	36	49	85	110
Mats Sundin	Toronto	82	41	39	80	94
Jaromir Jagr	Washington	69	31	48	79	30
Joe Sakic	Colorado	82	26	53	79	18
Pavol Demitra	St. Louis	82	35	43	78	46
Adam Oates	Wsh., Phi.	80	14	64	78	28
Mike Modano	Dallas	78	34	43	77	38
Ron Francis	Carolina	80	27	50	77	18

2002-03

EASTERN CONFERENCE

Northeast Division

Team		GP	W	L	T	OTL	GF	GA	PTS
Ottawa	(1)	82	52	21	8	1	263	182	113
Toronto	(5)	82	44	28	7	3	236	208	98
Boston	(7)	82	36	31	11	4	245	237	87
Montreal		82	30	35	8	9	206	234	77
Buffalo		82	27	37	10	8	190	219	72

Atlantic Division

Team		GP	W	L	T	OTL	GF	GA	PTS
*New Jersey	(2)	82	46	20	10	6	216	166	108
Philadelphia	(4)	82	45	20	13	4	211	166	107
NY Islanders	(8)	82	35	34	11	2	224	231	83
NY Rangers		82	32	36	10	4	210	231	78
Pittsburgh		82	27	44	6	5	189	255	65

Southeast Division

Team		GP	W	L	T	OTL	GF	GA	PTS
Tampa Bay	(3)	82	36	25	16	5	219	210	93
Washington	(6)	82	39	29	8	6	224	220	92
Atlanta		82	31	39	7	5	226	284	74
Florida		82	24	36	13	9	176	237	70
Carolina		82	22	43	11	6	171	240	61

WESTERN CONFERENCE

Central Division

Team		GP	W	L	T	OTL	GF	GA	PTS
Detroit	(2)	82	48	20	10	4	269	203	110
St. Louis	(5)	82	41	24	11	6	253	222	99
Chicago		82	30	33	13	6	207	226	79
Nashville		82	27	35	13	7	183	206	74
Columbus		82	29	42	8	3	213	263	69

Pacific Division

Team		GP	W	L	T	OTL	GF	GA	PTS
Dallas	(1)	82	46	17	15	4	245	169	111
Anaheim	(7)	82	40	27	9	6	203	193	95
Los Angeles		82	33	37	6	6	203	221	78
Phoenix		82	31	35	11	5	204	230	78
San Jose		82	28	37	9	8	214	239	73

Northwest Division

Team		GP	W	L	T	OTL	GF	GA	PTS
Colorado	(3)	82	42	19	13	8	251	194	105
Vancouver	(4)	82	45	23	13	1	264	208	104
Minnesota	(6)	82	42	29	10	1	198	178	95
Edmonton	(8)	82	36	26	11	9	231	230	92
Calgary		82	29	36	13	4	186	228	75

Leading Scorers

Player	Team	GP	G	A	PTS	PIM
Peter Forsberg	Colorado	75	29	77	106	70
Markus Naslund	Vancouver	82	48	56	104	52
Joe Thornton	Boston	77	36	65	101	109
Milan Hejduk	Colorado	82	50	48	98	52
Todd Bertuzzi	Vancouver	82	46	51	97	144
Pavol Demitra	St. Louis	78	36	57	93	32
Glen Murray	Boston	82	44	48	92	64
Mario Lemieux	Pittsburgh	67	28	63	91	43
Dany Heatley	Atlanta	77	41	48	89	58
Ziggy Palffy	Los Angeles	76	37	48	85	47
Mike Modano	Dallas	79	28	57	85	30

2003-04

EASTERN CONFERENCE

Northeast Division

Team		GP	W	L	T	OTL	GF	GA	PTS
Boston	(2)	82	41	19	15	7	209	188	104
Toronto	(4)	82	45	24	10	3	242	204	103
Ottawa	(5)	82	43	23	10	6	262	189	102
Montreal	(7)	82	41	30	7	4	208	192	93
Buffalo		82	37	34	7	4	220	221	85

Atlantic Division

Team		GP	W	L	T	OTL	GF	GA	PTS
Philadelphia	(3)	82	40	21	15	6	229	186	101
New Jersey	(6)	82	43	25	12	2	213	164	100
NY Islanders	(8)	82	38	29	11	4	237	210	91
NY Rangers		82	27	40	7	8	206	250	69
Pittsburgh		82	23	47	8	4	190	303	58

Southeast Division

Team		GP	W	L	T	OTL	GF	GA	PTS
*Tampa Bay	(1)	82	46	22	8	6	245	192	106
Atlanta		82	33	37	8	4	214	243	78
Carolina		82	28	34	14	6	172	209	76
Florida		82	28	35	15	4	188	221	75
Washington		82	23	46	10	3	186	253	59

WESTERN CONFERENCE

Central Division

Team		GP	W	L	T	OTL	GF	GA	PTS
Detroit	(1)	82	48	21	11	2	255	189	109
St. Louis	(7)	82	39	30	11	2	191	198	91
Nashville	(8)	82	38	29	11	4	216	217	91
Columbus		82	25	45	8	4	177	238	62
Chicago		82	20	43	11	8	188	259	59

Pacific Division

Team		GP	W	L	T	OTL	GF	GA	PTS
San Jose	(2)	82	43	21	12	6	219	183	104
Dallas	(5)	82	41	26	13	2	194	175	97
Los Angeles		82	28	29	16	9	205	217	81
Anaheim		82	29	35	10	8	184	213	76
Phoenix		82	22	36	18	6	188	245	68

Northwest Division

Team		GP	W	L	T	OTL	GF	GA	PTS
Vancouver	(3)	82	43	24	10	5	235	194	101
Colorado	(4)	82	40	22	13	7	236	198	100
Calgary	(6)	82	42	30	7	3	200	176	94
Edmonton		82	36	29	12	5	221	208	89
Minnesota		82	30	29	20	3	188	183	83

Leading Scorers

Player	Team	GP	G	A	PTS	PIM
Martin St. Louis	Tampa Bay	82	38	56	94	24
Ilya Kovalchuk	Atlanta	81	41	46	87	63
Joe Sakic	Colorado	81	33	54	87	42
Markus Naslund	Vancouver	78	35	49	84	58
Marian Hossa	Ottawa	81	36	46	82	46
Patrik Elias	New Jersey	82	38	43	81	44
Daniel Alfredsson	Ottawa	77	32	48	80	24
Cory Stillman	Tampa Bay	81	25	55	80	36
Robert Lang	Wsh., Det.	69	30	49	79	24
Brad Richards	Tampa Bay	82	26	53	79	12
Alex Tanguay	Colorado	69	25	54	79	42

2004-05

SEASON CANCELLED

2005-06

EASTERN CONFERENCE

Northeast Division

Team		GP	W	L	OL	GF	GA	PTS
Ottawa	(1)	82	52	21	9	314	211	113
Buffalo	(4)	82	52	24	6	281	239	110
Montreal	(7)	82	42	31	9	243	247	93
Toronto		82	41	33	8	257	270	90
Boston		82	29	37	16	230	266	74

Atlantic Division

Team		GP	W	L	OL	GF	GA	PTS
New Jersey	(3)	82	46	27	9	242	229	101
Philadelphia	(5)	82	45	26	11	267	259	101
NY Rangers	(6)	82	44	26	12	257	215	100
NY Islanders		82	36	40	6	230	278	78
Pittsburgh		82	22	46	14	244	316	58

Southeast Division

Team		GP	W	L	OL	GF	GA	PTS
*Carolina	(2)	82	52	22	8	294	260	112
Tampa Bay	(8)	82	43	33	6	252	260	92
Atlanta		82	41	33	8	281	275	90
Florida		82	37	34	11	240	257	85
Washington		82	29	41	12	237	306	70

WESTERN CONFERENCE

Central Division

Team		GP	W	L	OL	GF	GA	PTS
Detroit	(1)	82	58	16	8	305	209	124
Nashville	(4)	82	49	25	8	259	227	106
Columbus		82	35	43	4	223	279	74
Chicago		82	26	43	13	211	285	65
St. Louis		82	21	46	15	197	292	57

Pacific Division

Team		GP	W	L	OL	GF	GA	PTS
Dallas	(2)	82	53	23	6	265	218	112
San Jose	(5)	82	44	27	11	266	242	99
Anaheim	(6)	82	43	27	12	254	229	98
Los Angeles		82	42	35	5	249	270	89
Phoenix		82	38	39	5	246	271	81

Northwest Division

Team		GP	W	L	OL	GF	GA	PTS
Calgary	(3)	82	46	25	11	218	200	103
Colorado	(7)	82	43	30	9	283	257	95
Edmonton	(8)	82	41	28	13	256	251	95
Vancouver		82	42	32	8	256	255	92
Minnesota		82	38	36	8	231	215	84

Leading Scorers

Player	Team	GP	G	A	PTS	PIM
Joe Thornton	Bos., S.J.	81	29	96	125	61
Jaromir Jagr	NY Rangers	82	54	69	123	72
Alex Ovechkin	Washington	81	52	54	106	52
Dany Heatley	Ottawa	82	50	53	103	86
Daniel Alfredsson	Ottawa	77	43	60	103	50
Sidney Crosby	Pittsburgh	81	39	63	102	110
Eric Staal	Carolina	82	45	55	100	81
Ilya Kovalchuk	Atlanta	78	52	46	98	68
Marc Savard	Atlanta	82	28	69	97	100
Jonathan Cheechoo	San Jose	82	56	37	93	58

2006-07

EASTERN CONFERENCE

Northeast Division

Team		GP	W	L	OL	GF	GA	PTS
Buffalo	(1)	82	53	22	7	308	242	113
Ottawa	(4)	82	48	25	9	288	222	105
Toronto		82	40	31	11	258	269	91
Montreal		82	42	34	6	245	256	90
Boston		82	35	41	6	219	289	76

Atlantic Division

Team		GP	W	L	OL	GF	GA	PTS
New Jersey	(2)	82	49	24	9	216	201	107
Pittsburgh	(5)	82	47	24	11	277	246	105
NY Rangers	(6)	82	42	30	10	242	216	94
NY Islanders	(8)	82	40	30	12	248	240	92
Philadelphia		82	22	48	12	214	303	56

Southeast Division

Team		GP	W	L	OL	GF	GA	PTS
Atlanta	(3)	82	43	28	11	246	245	97
Tampa Bay	(7)	82	44	33	5	253	261	93
Carolina		82	40	34	8	241	253	88
Florida		82	35	31	16	247	257	86
Washington		82	28	40	14	235	286	70

WESTERN CONFERENCE

Central Division

Team		GP	W	L	OL	GF	GA	PTS
Detroit	(1)	82	50	19	13	254	199	113
Nashville	(4)	82	51	23	8	272	212	110
St. Louis		82	34	35	13	214	254	81
Columbus		82	33	42	7	201	249	73
Chicago		82	31	42	9	201	258	71

Pacific Division

Team		GP	W	L	OL	GF	GA	PTS
*Anaheim	(2)	82	48	20	14	258	208	110
San Jose	(5)	82	51	26	5	258	199	107
Dallas	(6)	82	50	25	7	226	197	107
Los Angeles		82	27	41	14	227	283	68
Phoenix		82	31	46	5	216	284	67

Northwest Division

Team		GP	W	L	OL	GF	GA	PTS
Vancouver	(3)	82	49	26	7	222	201	105
Minnesota	(7)	82	48	26	8	235	191	104
Calgary	(8)	82	43	29	10	258	226	96
Colorado		82	44	31	7	272	251	95
Edmonton		82	32	43	7	195	248	71

Leading Scorers

Player	Team	GP	G	A	PTS	PIM
Sidney Crosby	Pittsburgh	79	36	84	120	60
Joe Thornton	San Jose	82	22	92	114	44
Vincent Lecavalier	Tampa Bay	82	52	56	108	44
Dany Heatley	Ottawa	82	50	55	105	74
Martin St. Louis	Tampa Bay	82	43	59	102	28
Marian Hossa	Atlanta	82	43	57	100	49
Joe Sakic	Colorado	82	36	64	100	46
Jaromir Jagr	NY Rangers	82	30	66	96	78
Marc Savard	Boston	82	22	74	96	96
Daniel Briere	Buffalo	81	32	63	95	89

2007-08

EASTERN CONFERENCE

Northeast Division

Team		GP	W	L	OL	GF	GA	PTS
Montreal	(1)	82	47	25	10	262	222	104
Ottawa	(7)	82	43	31	8	261	247	94
Boston	(8)	82	41	29	12	212	222	94
Buffalo		82	39	31	12	255	242	90
Toronto		82	36	35	11	231	260	83

Atlantic Division

Team		GP	W	L	OL	GF	GA	PTS
Pittsburgh	(2)	82	47	27	8	247	216	102
New Jersey	(4)	82	46	29	7	206	197	99
NY Rangers	(5)	82	42	27	13	213	199	97
Philadelphia	(6)	82	42	29	11	248	233	95
NY Islanders		82	35	38	9	194	243	79

Southeast Division

Team		GP	W	L	OL	GF	GA	PTS
Washington	(3)	82	43	31	8	242	231	94
Carolina		82	43	33	6	252	249	92
Florida		82	38	35	9	216	226	85
Atlanta		82	34	40	8	216	272	76
Tampa Bay		82	31	42	9	223	267	71

WESTERN CONFERENCE

Central Division

Team		GP	W	L	OL	GF	GA	PTS
*Detroit	(1)	82	54	21	7	257	184	115
Nashville	(8)	82	41	32	9	230	229	91
Chicago		82	40	34	8	239	235	88
Columbus		82	34	36	12	193	218	80
St. Louis		82	33	36	13	205	237	79

Pacific Division

Team		GP	W	L	OL	GF	GA	PTS
San Jose	(2)	82	49	23	10	222	193	108
Anaheim	(4)	82	47	27	8	205	191	102
Dallas	(5)	82	45	30	7	242	207	97
Phoenix		82	38	37	7	214	231	83
Los Angeles		82	32	43	7	231	266	71

Northwest Division

Team		GP	W	L	OL	GF	GA	PTS
Minnesota	(3)	82	44	28	10	223	218	98
Colorado	(6)	82	44	31	7	231	219	95
Calgary	(7)	82	42	30	10	229	227	94
Edmonton		82	41	35	6	235	251	88
Vancouver		82	39	33	10	213	215	88

Leading Scorers

Player	Team	GP	G	A	PTS	PIM
Alex Ovechkin	Washington	82	65	47	112	40
Evgeni Malkin	Pittsburgh	82	47	59	106	78
Jarome Iginla	Calgary	82	50	48	98	83
Pavel Datsyuk	Detroit	82	31	66	97	20
Joe Thornton	San Jose	82	29	67	96	59
Henrik Zetterberg	Detroit	75	43	49	92	34
Vincent Lecavalier	Tampa Bay	81	40	52	92	89
Jason Spezza	Ottawa	76	34	58	92	66
Daniel Alfredsson	Ottawa	70	40	49	89	34
Ilya Kovalchuk	Atlanta	79	52	35	87	52

2008-09

EASTERN CONFERENCE

Northeast Division

Team		GP	W	L	OL	GF	GA	PTS
Boston	(1)	82	53	19	10	274	196	116
Montreal	(8)	82	41	30	11	249	247	93
Buffalo		82	41	32	9	250	234	91
Ottawa		82	36	35	11	217	237	83
Toronto		82	34	35	13	250	293	81

Atlantic Division

Team		GP	W	L	OL	GF	GA	PTS
New Jersey	(3)	82	51	27	4	244	209	106
*Pittsburgh	(4)	82	45	28	9	264	239	99
Philadelphia	(5)	82	44	27	11	264	238	99
NY Rangers	(7)	82	43	30	9	210	218	95
NY Islanders		82	26	47	9	201	279	61

Southeast Division

Team		GP	W	L	OL	GF	GA	PTS
Washington	(2)	82	50	24	8	272	245	108
Carolina	(6)	82	45	30	7	239	226	97
Florida		82	41	30	11	234	231	93
Atlanta		82	35	41	6	257	280	76
Tampa Bay		82	24	40	18	210	279	66

WESTERN CONFERENCE

Central Division

Team		GP	W	L	OL	GF	GA	PTS
Detroit	(2)	82	51	21	10	295	244	112
Chicago	(4)	82	46	24	12	264	216	104
St. Louis	(6)	82	41	31	10	233	233	92
Columbus	(7)	82	41	31	10	226	230	92
Nashville		82	40	34	8	213	233	88

Pacific Division

Team		GP	W	L	OL	GF	GA	PTS
San Jose	(1)	82	53	18	11	257	204	117
Anaheim	(8)	82	42	33	7	245	238	91
Dallas		82	36	35	11	230	257	83
Phoenix		82	36	39	7	208	252	79
Los Angeles		82	34	37	11	207	234	79

Northwest Division

Team		GP	W	L	OL	GF	GA	PTS
Vancouver	(3)	82	45	27	10	246	220	100
Calgary	(5)	82	46	30	6	254	248	98
Minnesota		82	40	33	9	219	200	89
Edmonton		82	38	35	9	234	248	85
Colorado		82	32	45	5	199	257	69

Leading Scorers

Player	Team	GP	G	A	PTS	PIM
Evgeni Malkin	Pittsburgh	82	35	78	113	80
Alex Ovechkin	Washington	79	56	54	110	72
Sidney Crosby	Pittsburgh	77	33	70	103	76
Pavel Datsyuk	Detroit	81	32	65	97	34
Zach Parise	New Jersey	82	45	49	94	24
Ilya Kovalchuk	Atlanta	79	43	48	91	50
Ryan Getzlaf	Anaheim	81	25	66	91	121
Jarome Iginla	Calgary	82	35	54	89	37
Marc Savard	Boston	82	25	63	88	70
Nicklas Backstrom	Washington	82	22	66	88	46

2009-10

EASTERN CONFERENCE

Northeast Division

Team		GP	W	L	OL	GF	GA	PTS
Buffalo	(3)	82	45	27	10	235	207	100
Ottawa	(5)	82	44	32	6	225	238	94
Boston	(6)	82	39	30	13	206	200	91
Montreal	(8)	82	39	33	10	217	223	88
Toronto		82	30	38	14	214	267	74

Atlantic Division

Team		GP	W	L	OL	GF	GA	PTS
New Jersey	(2)	82	48	27	7	222	191	103
Pittsburgh	(4)	82	47	28	7	257	237	101
Philadelphia	(7)	82	41	35	6	236	225	88
NY Rangers		82	38	33	11	222	218	87
NY Islanders		82	34	37	11	222	264	79

Southeast Division

Team		GP	W	L	OL	GF	GA	PTS
Washington	(1)	82	54	15	13	318	233	121
Atlanta		82	35	34	13	234	256	83
Carolina		82	35	37	10	230	256	80
Tampa Bay		82	34	36	12	217	260	80
Florida		82	32	37	13	208	244	77

WESTERN CONFERENCE

Central Division

Team		GP	W	L	OL	GF	GA	PTS
*Chicago	(2)	82	52	22	8	271	209	112
Detroit	(5)	82	44	24	14	229	216	102
Nashville	(7)	82	47	29	6	225	225	100
St. Louis		82	40	32	10	225	223	90
Columbus		82	32	35	15	216	259	79

Pacific Division

Team		GP	W	L	OL	GF	GA	PTS
San Jose	(1)	82	51	20	11	264	215	113
Phoenix	(4)	82	50	25	7	225	202	107
Los Angeles	(6)	82	46	27	9	241	219	101
Anaheim		82	39	32	11	238	251	89
Dallas		82	37	31	14	237	254	88

Northwest Division

Team		GP	W	L	OL	GF	GA	PTS
Vancouver	(3)	82	49	28	5	272	222	103
Colorado	(8)	82	43	30	9	244	233	95
Calgary		82	40	32	10	204	210	90
Minnesota		82	38	36	8	219	246	84
Edmonton		82	27	47	8	214	284	62

Leading Scorers

Player	Team	GP	G	A	PTS	PIM
Henrik Sedin	Vancouver	82	29	83	112	48
Sidney Crosby	Pittsburgh	81	51	58	109	71
Alex Ovechkin	Washington	72	50	59	109	89
Nicklas Backstrom	Washington	82	33	68	101	50
Steven Stamkos	Tampa Bay	82	51	44	95	38
Martin St. Louis	Tampa Bay	82	29	65	94	12
Brad Richards	Dallas	80	24	67	91	14
Joe Thornton	San Jose	79	20	69	89	54
Patrick Kane	Chicago	82	30	58	88	20
Marian Gaborik	NY Rangers	76	42	44	86	37

2010-11

EASTERN CONFERENCE

Northeast Division

Team		GP	W	L	OT	GF	GA	PTS
*Boston	(3)	82	46	25	11	246	195	103
Montreal	(6)	82	44	30	8	216	209	96
Buffalo	(7)	82	43	29	10	245	229	96
Toronto		82	37	34	11	218	251	85
Ottawa		82	32	40	10	192	250	74

Atlantic Division

Team		GP	W	L	OT	GF	GA	PTS
Philadelphia	(2)	82	47	23	12	259	223	106
Pittsburgh	(4)	82	49	25	8	238	199	106
NY Rangers	(8)	82	44	33	5	233	198	93
New Jersey		82	38	39	5	174	209	81
NY Islanders		82	30	39	13	229	264	73

Southeast Division

Team		GP	W	L	OT	GF	GA	PTS
Washington	(1)	82	48	23	11	224	197	107
Tampa Bay	(5)	82	46	25	11	247	240	103
Carolina		82	40	31	11	236	239	91
Atlanta		82	34	36	12	223	269	80
Florida		82	30	40	12	195	229	72

WESTERN CONFERENCE

Central Division

Team		GP	W	L	OT	GF	GA	PTS
Detroit	(3)	82	47	25	10	261	241	104
Nashville	(5)	82	44	27	11	219	194	99
Chicago	(8)	82	44	29	9	258	225	97
St. Louis		82	38	33	11	240	234	87
Columbus		82	34	35	13	215	258	81

Pacific Division

Team		GP	W	L	OT	GF	GA	PTS
San Jose	(2)	82	48	25	9	248	213	105
Anaheim	(4)	82	47	30	5	239	235	99
Phoenix	(6)	82	43	26	13	231	226	99
Los Angeles	(7)	82	46	30	6	219	198	98
Dallas		82	42	29	11	227	233	95

Northwest Division

Team		GP	W	L	OT	GF	GA	PTS
Vancouver	(1)	82	54	19	9	262	185	117
Calgary		82	41	29	12	250	237	94
Minnesota		82	39	35	8	206	233	86
Colorado		82	30	44	8	227	288	68
Edmonton		82	25	45	12	193	269	62

Leading Scorers

Player	Team	GP	G	A	PTS	PIM
Daniel Sedin	Vancouver	82	41	63	104	32
Martin St. Louis	Tampa Bay	82	31	68	99	12
Corey Perry	Anaheim	82	50	48	98	104
Henrik Sedin	Vancouver	82	19	75	94	40
Steven Stamkos	Tampa Bay	82	45	46	91	74
Jarome Iginla	Calgary	82	43	43	86	40
Alex Ovechkin	Washington	79	32	53	85	41
Teemu Selanne	Anaheim	73	31	49	80	49
Henrik Zetterberg	Detroit	80	24	56	80	40
Brad Richards	Dallas	72	28	49	77	24

2011-12

EASTERN CONFERENCE

Northeast Division

Team		GP	W	L	OT	GF	GA	PTS
Boston	(2)	82	49	29	4	269	202	102
Ottawa	(8)	82	41	31	10	249	240	92
Buffalo		82	39	32	11	218	230	89
Toronto		82	35	37	10	231	264	80
Montreal		82	31	35	16	212	226	78

Atlantic Division

Team		GP	W	L	OT	GF	GA	PTS
NY Rangers	(1)	82	51	24	7	226	187	109
Pittsburgh	(4)	82	51	25	6	282	221	108
Philadelphia	(5)	82	47	26	9	264	232	103
New Jersey	(6)	82	48	28	6	228	209	102
NY Islanders		82	34	37	11	203	255	79

Southeast Division

Team		GP	W	L	OT	GF	GA	PTS
Florida	(3)	82	38	26	18	203	227	94
Washington	(7)	82	42	32	8	222	230	92
Tampa Bay		82	38	36	8	235	281	84
Winnipeg		82	37	35	10	225	246	84
Carolina		82	33	33	16	213	243	82

WESTERN CONFERENCE

Central Division

Team		GP	W	L	OT	GF	GA	PTS
St. Louis	(2)	82	49	22	11	210	165	109
Nashville	(4)	82	48	26	8	237	210	104
Detroit	(5)	82	48	28	6	248	203	102
Chicago	(6)	82	45	26	11	248	238	101
Columbus		82	29	46	7	202	262	65

Pacific Division

Team		GP	W	L	OT	GF	GA	PTS
Phoenix	(3)	82	42	27	13	216	204	97
San Jose	(7)	82	43	29	10	228	210	96
*Los Angeles	(8)	82	40	27	15	194	179	95
Dallas		82	42	35	5	211	222	89
Anaheim		82	34	36	12	204	231	80

Northwest Division

Team		GP	W	L	OT	GF	GA	PTS
Vancouver	(1)	82	51	22	9	249	198	111
Calgary		82	37	29	16	202	226	90
Colorado		82	41	35	6	208	220	88
Minnesota		82	35	36	11	177	226	81
Edmonton		82	32	40	10	212	239	74

Leading Scorers

Player	Team	GP	G	A	PTS	PIM
Evgeni Malkin	Pittsburgh	75	50	59	109	70
Steven Stamkos	Tampa Bay	82	60	37	97	66
Claude Giroux	Philadelphia	77	28	65	93	29
Jason Spezza	Ottawa	80	34	50	84	36
Ilya Kovalchuk	New Jersey	77	37	46	83	33
Phil Kessel	Toronto	82	37	45	82	20
James Neal	Pittsburgh	80	40	41	81	87
John Tavares	NY Islanders	82	31	50	81	26
Henrik Sedin	Vancouver	82	14	67	81	52
Patrik Elias	New Jersey	81	26	52	78	16

2012-13

EASTERN CONFERENCE

Northeast Division

Team		GP	W	L	OT	GF	GA	PTS
Montreal	(2)	48	29	14	5	149	126	63
Boston	(4)	48	28	14	6	131	109	62
Toronto	(5)	48	26	17	5	145	133	57
Ottawa	(7)	48	25	17	6	116	104	56
Buffalo		48	21	21	6	125	143	48

Atlantic Division

Team		GP	W	L	OT	GF	GA	PTS
Pittsburgh	(1)	48	36	12	0	165	119	72
NY Rangers	(6)	48	26	18	4	130	112	56
NY Islanders	(8)	48	24	17	7	139	139	55
Philadelphia		48	23	22	3	133	141	49
New Jersey		48	19	19	10	112	129	48

Southeast Division

Team		GP	W	L	OT	GF	GA	PTS
Washington	(3)	48	27	18	3	149	130	57
Winnipeg		48	24	21	3	128	144	51
Carolina		48	19	25	4	128	160	42
Tampa Bay		48	18	26	4	148	150	40
Florida		48	15	27	6	112	171	36

WESTERN CONFERENCE

Central Division

Team		GP	W	L	OT	GF	GA	PTS
*Chicago	(1)	48	36	7	5	155	102	77
St. Louis	(4)	48	29	17	2	129	115	60
Detroit	(7)	48	24	16	8	124	115	56
Columbus		48	24	17	7	120	119	55
Nashville		48	16	23	9	111	139	41

Pacific Division

Team		GP	W	L	OT	GF	GA	PTS
Anaheim	(2)	48	30	12	6	140	118	66
Los Angeles	(5)	48	27	16	5	133	118	59
San Jose	(6)	48	25	16	7	124	116	57
Phoenix		48	21	18	9	125	131	51
Dallas		48	22	22	4	130	142	48

Northwest Division

Team		GP	W	L	OT	GF	GA	PTS
Vancouver	(3)	48	26	15	7	127	121	59
Minnesota	(8)	48	26	19	3	122	127	55
Edmonton		48	19	22	7	125	134	45
Calgary		48	19	25	4	128	160	42
Colorado		48	16	25	7	116	152	39

Leading Scorers

Player	Team	GP	G	A	PTS	PIM
Martin St. Louis	Tampa Bay	48	17	43	60	14
Steven Stamkos	Tampa Bay	48	29	28	57	32
Alex Ovechkin	Washington	48	32	24	56	36
Sidney Crosby	Pittsburgh	36	15	41	56	16
Patrick Kane	Chicago	47	23	32	55	8
Eric Staal	Carolina	48	18	35	53	54
Chris Kunitz	Pittsburgh	48	22	30	52	39
Phil Kessel	Toronto	48	20	32	52	18
Taylor Hall	Edmonton	45	16	34	50	33
Ryan Getzlaf	Anaheim	44	15	34	49	41

Note: Detailed statistics for 2012-13 are listed in the Final Statistics, 2012-13 section of the *NHL Guide & Record Book*. **See page 141.**

With a sixth-place finish in the NHL scoring race in 2011-12 and an eighth-place finish in 2012-13, Phil Kessel is the first Maple Leaf to crack the top 10 in scoring since Mats Sundin in 2001-02 and the first to do so in back-to-back seasons since Doug Gilmour in 1992-93 and 1993-94.

Team Records

Regular Season

FINAL STANDINGS

MOST POINTS, ONE SEASON:
132 – Montreal Canadiens, 1976-77. 60W-8L-12T. 80GP
131 – Detroit Red Wings, 1995-96. 62W-13L-7T. 82GP
129 – Montreal Canadiens, 1977-78. 59W-10L-11T. 80GP

BEST POINTS PERCENTAGE, ONE SEASON:
.875 – Boston Bruins, 1929-30. 38W-5L-1T. 77PTS in 44GP
.830 – Montreal Canadiens, 1943-44. 38W-5L-7T. 83PTS in 50GP
.825 – Montreal Canadiens, 1976-77. 60W-8L-12T. 132PTS in 80GP
.806 – Montreal Canadiens, 1977-78. 59W-10L-11T. 129PTS in 80GP
.802 – Chicago Blackhawks, 2012-13. 36W-7L-5OTL. 77PTS in 48GP
.800 – Montreal Canadiens, 1944-45. 38W-8L-4T. 80PTS in 50GP

FEWEST POINTS, ONE SEASON:
8 – Quebec Bulldogs, 1919-20. 4W-20L-0T. 24GP
10 – Toronto Arenas, 1918-19. 5W-13L-0T. 18GP
12 – Hamilton Tigers, 1920-21. 6W-18L-0T. 24GP
– Hamilton Tigers, 1922-23. 6W-18L-0T. 24GP
– Boston Bruins, 1924-25. 6W-24L-0T. 30GP
– Philadelphia Quakers, 1930-31. 4W-36L-4T. 44GP

FEWEST POINTS, ONE SEASON (MINIMUM 70-GAME SCHEDULE):
21 – Washington Capitals, 1974-75. 8W-67L-5T. 80GP
24 – Ottawa Senators, 1992-93. 10W-70L-4T. 84GP
– San Jose Sharks, 1992-93. 11W-71L-2T. 84GP
30 – New York Islanders, 1972-73. 12W-60L-6T. 78GP

WORST POINTS PERCENTAGE, ONE SEASON:
.131 – Washington Capitals, 1974-75. 8W-67L-5T. 21PTS in 80GP
.136 – Philadelphia Quakers, 1930-31. 4W-36L-4T. 12PTS in 44GP
.143 – Ottawa Senators, 1992-93. 10W-70L-4T. 24PTS in 84GP
– San Jose Sharks, 1992-93. 11W-71L-2T. 24PTS in 84GP
.148 – Pittsburgh Pirates, 1929-30. 5W-36L-3T. 13PTS in 44GP

TEAM WINS

Most Wins

MOST WINS, ONE SEASON:
62 – Detroit Red Wings, 1995-96. 82GP
60 – Montreal Canadiens, 1976-77. 80GP
59 – Montreal Canadiens, 1977-78. 80GP

MOST HOME WINS, ONE SEASON:
36 – Philadelphia Flyers, 1975-76. 40GP
– Detroit Red Wings, 1995-96. 41GP
33 – Boston Bruins, 1970-71. 39GP
– Boston Bruins, 1973-74. 39GP
– Montreal Canadiens, 1976-77. 40GP
– Philadelphia Flyers, 1976-77. 40GP
– New York Islanders, 1981-82. 40GP
– Philadelphia Flyers, 1985-86. 40GP

MOST ROAD WINS, ONE SEASON:
31 – Detroit Red Wings, 2005-06. 41GP
28 – New Jersey Devils, 1998-99. 41GP
27 – Montreal Canadiens, 1976-77. 40GP
– Montreal Canadiens, 1977-78. 40GP
– St. Louis Blues, 1999-2000. 41GP
– San Jose Sharks, 2007-08. 41GP
– Vancouver Canucks, 2010-11. 41GP
26 – Boston Bruins, 1971-72. 39GP
– Montreal Canadiens, 1975-76. 40GP
– Edmonton Oilers, 1983-84. 40GP
– Detroit Red Wings, 1995-96. 41GP
– San Jose Sharks, 2006-07. 41GP
– Detroit Red Wings, 2010-11. 41GP

Fewest Wins

FEWEST WINS, ONE SEASON:
4 – Quebec Bulldogs, 1919-20. 24GP
– Philadelphia Quakers, 1930-31. 44GP
5 – Toronto Arenas, 1918-19. 18GP
Pittsburgh Pirates, 1929-30. 44GP

FEWEST WINS, ONE SEASON (MINIMUM 70-GAME SCHEDULE):
8 – Washington Capitals, 1974-75. 80GP
9 – Winnipeg Jets, 1980-81. 80GP
10 – Ottawa Senators, 1992-93. 84GP

FEWEST HOME WINS, ONE SEASON:
2 – Chicago Blackhawks, 1927-28. 22GP
3 – Boston Bruins, 1924-25. 15GP
– Chicago Blackhawks, 1928-29. 22GP
– Philadelphia Quakers, 1930-31. 22GP

FEWEST HOME WINS, ONE SEASON (MINIMUM 70-GAME SCHEDULE):
6 – Chicago Blackhawks, 1954-55. 35GP
– Washington Capitals, 1975-76. 40GP
7 – Boston Bruins, 1962-63. 35GP
– Washington Capitals, 1974-75. 40GP
– Winnipeg Jets, 1980-81. 40GP
– Pittsburgh Penguins, 1983-84. 40GP

FEWEST ROAD WINS, ONE SEASON:
0 – Toronto Arenas, 1918-19. 9GP
– Quebec Bulldogs, 1919-20. 12GP
– Pittsburgh Pirates, 1929-30. 22GP
1 – Hamilton Tigers, 1921-22. 12GP
– Toronto St. Patricks, 1925-26. 18GP
– Philadelphia Quakers, 1930-31. 22GP
– New York Americans, 1940-41. 24GP
– Washington Capitals, 1974-75. 40GP
* – Ottawa Senators, 1992-93. 41GP

FEWEST ROAD WINS, ONE SEASON (MINIMUM 70-GAME SCHEDULE):
1 – Washington Capitals, 1974-75. 40GP
*** – Ottawa Senators**, 1992-93. 41GP
2 – Boston Bruins, 1960-61. 35GP
– Los Angeles Kings, 1969-70. 38GP
– New York Islanders, 1972-73. 39GP
– California Golden Seals, 1973-74. 39GP
– Colorado Rockies, 1977-78. 40GP
– Winnipeg Jets, 1980-81. 40GP
– Quebec Nordiques, 1991-92. 40GP

TEAM LOSSES

Fewest Losses

FEWEST LOSSES, ONE SEASON:
5 – Ottawa Senators, 1919-20. 24GP
– Boston Bruins, 1929-30. 44GP
– Montreal Canadiens, 1943-44. 50GP

FEWEST HOME LOSSES, ONE SEASON:
0 – Ottawa Senators, 1922-23. 12GP
– Montreal Canadiens, 1943-44. 25GP
1 – Toronto Arenas, 1917-18. 11GP
– Ottawa Senators, 1918-19. 9GP
– Ottawa Senators, 1919-20. 12GP
– Toronto St. Patricks, 1922-23. 12GP
– Boston Bruins, 1929-30. 22GP
– Boston Bruins, 1930-31. 22GP
– Montreal Canadiens, 1976-77. 40GP
– Quebec Nordiques, 1994-95. 24GP

FEWEST ROAD LOSSES, ONE SEASON:
3 – Montreal Canadiens, 1928-29. 22GP
4 – Ottawa Senators, 1919-20. 12GP
– Montreal Canadiens, 1927-28. 22GP
– Boston Bruins, 1929-30. 20GP
– Boston Bruins, 1940-41. 24GP
– Chicago Blackhawks, 2012-13. 24GP

FEWEST LOSSES, ONE SEASON (MINIMUM 70-GAME SCHEDULE):
8 – Montreal Canadiens, 1976-77. 80GP
10 – Montreal Canadiens, 1972-73. 78GP
– Montreal Canadiens, 1977-78. 80GP
11 – Montreal Canadiens, 1975-76. 80GP

FEWEST HOME LOSSES, ONE SEASON (MINIMUM 70-GAME SCHEDULE):
1 – Montreal Canadiens, 1976-77. 40GP
2 – Montreal Canadiens, 1961-62. 35GP
– New York Rangers, 1970-71. 39GP
– Philadelphia Flyers, 1975-76. 40GP

FEWEST ROAD LOSSES, ONE SEASON (MINIMUM 70-GAME SCHEDULE):
6 – Montreal Canadiens, 1972-73. 39GP
– Montreal Canadiens, 1974-75. 40GP
– Montreal Canadiens, 1977-78. 40GP
7 – Detroit Red Wings, 1951-52. 35GP
– Montreal Canadiens, 1976-77. 40GP
– Philadelphia Flyers, 1979-80. 40GP
– Boston Bruins, 2003-04. 41GP
– Detroit Red Wings, 2005-06. 41GP

Most Losses

MOST LOSSES, ONE SEASON:
71 – San Jose Sharks, 1992-93. 84GP
70 – Ottawa Senators, 1992-93. 84GP
67 – Washington Capitals, 1974-75. 80GP
61 – Quebec Nordiques, 1989-90. 80GP
– Ottawa Senators, 1993-94. 84GP

MOST HOME LOSSES, ONE SEASON:
***32 – San Jose Sharks**, 1992-93. 41GP
29 – Pittsburgh Penguins, 1983-84. 40GP
* – Ottawa Senators, 1993-94. 41GP

MOST ROAD LOSSES, ONE SEASON:
***40 – Ottawa Senators**, 1992-93. 41GP
39 – Washington Capitals, 1974-75. 40GP
37 – California Golden Seals, 1973-74. 39GP
* – San Jose Sharks, 1992-93. 41GP

* – Does not include neutral site games

TEAM TIES

Most Ties

MOST TIES, ONE SEASON:
24 – Philadelphia Flyers, 1969-70. 76GP
23 – Montreal Canadiens, 1962-63. 70GP
– Chicago Blackhawks, 1973-74. 78GP

MOST HOME TIES, ONE SEASON:
13 – New York Rangers, 1954-55. 35GP
– Philadelphia Flyers, 1969-70. 38GP
– California Golden Seals, 1971-72. 39GP
– California Golden Seals, 1972-73. 39GP
– Chicago Blackhawks, 1973-74. 39GP

MOST ROAD TIES, ONE SEASON:
15 – Philadelphia Flyers, 1976-77. 40GP
14 – Montreal Canadiens, 1952-53. 35GP
– Montreal Canadiens, 1974-75. 40GP
– Philadelphia Flyers, 1975-76. 40GP

Fewest Ties

FEWEST TIES, ONE SEASON (Since 1926-27):
1 – Boston Bruins, 1929-30. 44GP
2 – Montreal Canadiens, 1926-27. 44GP
– New York Americans, 1926-27. 44GP
– Boston Bruins, 1938-39. 48GP
– New York Rangers, 1941-42. 48GP
– San Jose Sharks, 1992-93. 84GP

FEWEST TIES, ONE SEASON (MINIMUM 70-GAME SCHEDULE):
2 – San Jose Sharks, 1992-93. 84GP
3 – New Jersey Devils, 1985-86. 80GP
– Calgary Flames, 1986-87. 80GP
– Vancouver Canucks, 1993-94. 84GP

WINNING STREAKS

LONGEST WINNING STREAK, ONE SEASON:
17 Games – Pittsburgh Penguins, Mar. 9 – Apr. 10, 1993.
15 Games – New York Islanders, Jan. 21 – Feb. 20, 1982.
– Pittsburgh Penguins, Mar. 2 – Mar. 30, 2013.
14 Games – Boston Bruins, Dec. 3, 1929 – Jan. 9, 1930.
– Washington Capitals, Jan.13 – Feb. 7, 2010.

LONGEST HOME WINNING STREAK, ONE SEASON:
23 Games – Detroit Red Wings, Nov. 5, 2011 – Feb. 19, 2012.
20 Games – Boston Bruins, Dec. 3, 1929 – Mar. 18, 1930.
– Philadelphia Flyers, Jan. 4 – Apr. 3, 1976.

LONGEST ROAD WINNING STREAK, ONE SEASON:
12 Games – Detroit Red Wings, Mar. 1 – Apr. 15, 2006.
10 Games – Buffalo Sabres, Dec. 10, 1983 – Jan. 23, 1984.
– St. Louis Blues, Jan. 21 – Mar. 2, 2000.
– New Jersey Devils, Feb. 27 – Apr. 7, 2001.
– Buffalo Sabres, Oct. 4 – Nov. 13, 2006.
– San Jose Sharks, Nov. 14 – Dec. 31, 2007.

LONGEST WINNING STREAK FROM START OF SEASON:
10 Games – Toronto Maple Leafs, 1993-94.
– Buffalo Sabres, 2006-07.
8 Games – Toronto Maple Leafs, 1934-35.
– Buffalo Sabres, 1975-76.
– Nashville Predators, 2005-06.
7 Games – Edmonton Oilers, 1983-84.
– Quebec Nordiques, 1985-86.
– Pittsburgh Penguins, 1986-87.
– Pittsburgh Penguins, 1994-95.
– Washington Capitals, 2011-12
– San Jose Sharks, 2012-13.

LONGEST HOME WINNING STREAK FROM START OF SEASON:
11 Games – Chicago Blackhawks, 1963-64.
10 Games – Ottawa Senators, 1925-26.
9 Games – Montreal Canadiens, 1953-54.
– Chicago Blackhawks, 1971-72.
– San Jose Sharks, 2008-09.

LONGEST ROAD WINNING STREAK FROM START OF SEASON:
10 Games – Buffalo Sabres, Oct.4 – Nov. 13, 2006.
9 Games – New Jersey Devils, Oct. 8 – Nov. 12, 2009.
7 Games – Toronto Maple Leafs, Nov. 14 – Dec. 15, 1940.
– Philadelphia Flyers, Oct. 12 – Nov. 16, 1985.
– Detroit Red Wings, Oct. 6 – Nov. 6, 2005.
– Pittsburgh Penguins, Oct. 3 – Nov. 3, 2009

LONGEST WINNING STREAK, INCLUDING PLAYOFFS:
15 Games – Detroit Red Wings, Feb. 27 – Apr. 5, 1955.
(9 regular-season games, 6 playoff games)
– New Jersey Devils, Mar. 28 – Apr. 29, 2006.
(11 regular-season games, 4 playoff games)

LONGEST HOME WINNING STREAK, INCLUDING PLAYOFFS:
24 Games – Philadelphia Flyers, Jan. 4 – Apr. 25, 1976.
(20 regular-season games, 4 playoff games)

LONGEST ROAD WINNING STREAK, INCLUDING PLAYOFFS:
11 Games – New Jersey Devils, Feb. 27 – Apr. 17, 2001.
(10 regular-season games, 1 playoff game)

UNDEFEATED STREAKS

LONGEST UNDEFEATED STREAK, ONE SEASON:
35 Games – Philadelphia Flyers, Oct. 14, 1979 – Jan. 6, 1980. 25W-10T
28 Games – Montreal Canadiens, Dec. 18, 1977 – Feb. 23, 1978. 23W-5T

LONGEST HOME UNDEFEATED STREAK, ONE SEASON:
34 Games – Montreal Canadiens, Nov. 1, 1976 – Apr. 2, 1977. 28W-6T
27 Games – Boston Bruins, Nov. 22, 1970 – Mar. 20, 1971. 26W-1T

LONGEST ROAD UNDEFEATED STREAK, ONE SEASON:
23 Games – Montreal Canadiens, Nov. 27, 1974 – Mar. 12, 1975. 14W-9T
17 Games – Montreal Canadiens, Dec. 18, 1977 – Mar. 1, 1978. 14W-3T

LONGEST UNDEFEATED STREAK FROM START OF SEASON:
15 Games – Edmonton Oilers, 1984-85. 12W-3T
14 Games – Montreal CanaKdiens, 1943-44. 11W-3T

LONGEST HOME UNDEFEATED STREAK FROM START OF SEASON:
26 Games – Philadelphia Flyers, Oct. 11, 1979 – Feb. 3, 1980. 19W-7T

LONGEST ROAD UNDEFEATED STREAK FROM START OF SEASON:
15 Games – Detroit Red Wings, Oct. 18 – Dec. 20, 1951. 10W-5T

LONGEST UNDEFEATED STREAK, INCLUDING PLAYOFFS:
24 Games – Montreal Canadiens, Feb. 21 – Apr. 11, 1980.
15W-6T in regular season and 3W in playoffs.
21 Games – Philadelphia Flyers, Mar. 9 – May 4, 1975.
13W-1T in regular season and 7W in playoffs.
– Pittsburgh Penguins, Mar. 9 – Apr. 22, 1993.
17W-1T in regular season and 3W in playoffs.

LONGEST HOME UNDEFEATED STREAK, INCLUDING PLAYOFFS:
38 Games – Montreal Canadiens, Nov. 1, 1976 – Apr. 26, 1977.
28W-6T in regular season and 4W in playoffs.

LONGEST ROAD UNDEFEATED STREAK, INCLUDING PLAYOFFS:
13 Games – Philadelphia Flyers, Feb. 26 – Apr. 21, 1977. 6W-4T in regular season and 3W in playoffs.
– Montreal Canadiens, Feb. 26 – Apr. 20, 1980. 6W-4T in regular season and 3W in playoffs.
– New York Islanders, Mar. 16 – May 1, 1980. 3W-3T in regular season and 7W in playoffs.

TEAM POINT STREAKS

LONGEST TEAM POINT STREAK, ONE SEASON:
35 Games – Philadelphia Flyers, Oct. 14, 1979 – Jan. 6, 1980. 25W-10T
28 Games – Montreal Canadiens, Dec. 18, 1977 – Feb. 23, 1978. 23W-5T
24 Games – Chicago Blackhawks, Jan. 19 – Mar. 6, 2013. 21W-3OL

LONGEST TEAM POINT STREAK FROM START OF SEASON:
24 Games – Chicago Blackhawks, Jan. 19 – Mar. 6, 2013. 21W-3OL
16 Games – Anaheim Ducks, Oct. 6 – Nov. 9, 2006. 12W-4OL
15 Games – Edmonton Oilers, Oct. 11 – Nov. 9, 1984. 12W-3T
14 Games – Montreal Canadiens, Oct. 30 – Dec. 4, 1943. 11W-3T

LOSING STREAKS

LONGEST LOSING STREAK, ONE SEASON:
17 Games – Washington Capitals, Feb. 18 – Mar. 26, 1975.
– San Jose Sharks, Jan. 4 – Feb. 12, 1993.
15 Games – Philadelphia Quakers, Nov. 29, 1930 – Jan. 8, 1931.

LONGEST HOME LOSING STREAK, ONE SEASON:
14 Games – Pittsburgh Penguins, Dec. 31, 2003 – Feb. 22, 2004.
11 Games – Boston Bruins, Dec. 8, 1924 – Feb. 17, 1925.
– Washington Capitals, Feb. 18 – Mar. 30, 1975.
– Ottawa Senators, Oct. 27 – Dec. 8, 1993.

LONGEST ROAD LOSING STREAK, ONE SEASON:
***38 Games – Ottawa Senators**, Oct. 10, 1992 – Apr. 3, 1993.
37 Games – Washington Capitals, Oct. 9, 1974 – Mar. 26, 1975.

LONGEST LOSING STREAK FROM START OF SEASON:
11 Games – New York Rangers, 1943-44.
7 Games – Montreal Canadiens, 1938-39.
– Chicago Blackhawks, 1947-48.
– Washington Capitals, 1983-84.
– Chicago Blackhawks, 1997-98.

LONGEST HOME LOSING STREAK FROM START OF SEASON:
8 Games – Los Angeles Kings, Oct. 13 – Nov. 6, 1971.

LONGEST ROAD LOSING STREAK FROM START OF SEASON:
***38 Games – Ottawa Senators**, Oct. 10, 1992 – Apr. 3, 1993.

WINLESS STREAKS

LONGEST WINLESS STREAK, ONE SEASON:
30 Games – Winnipeg Jets, Oct. 19 – Dec. 20, 1980. 23L-7T
27 Games – Kansas City Scouts, Feb. 12 – Apr. 4, 1976. 21L-6T
25 Games – Washington Capitals, Nov. 29, 1975 – Jan. 21, 1976. 22L-3T

LONGEST HOME WINLESS STREAK, ONE SEASON:
17 Games – Ottawa Senators, Oct. 28, 1995 – Jan. 27, 1996. 15L-2T
– Atlanta Thrashers, Jan. 19 – Mar. 29, 2000. 15L-2T
16 Games – Pittsburgh Penguins, Dec. 31, 2003 – Mar. 4, 2004. 15L-1T

LONGEST ROAD WINLESS STREAK, ONE SEASON:
***38 Games – Ottawa Senators**, Oct. 10, 1992 – Apr. 3, 1993. 38L
37 Games – Washington Capitals, Oct. 9, 1974 – Mar. 26, 1975. 37L

LONGEST WINLESS STREAK FROM START OF SEASON:
15 Games – New York Rangers, 1943-44. 14L-1T
11 Games – Pittsburgh Pirates, 1927-28. 8L-3T
– Minnesota North Stars, 1973-74. 5L-6T
– San Jose Sharks, 1995-96. 7L-4T

LONGEST HOME WINLESS STREAK FROM START OF SEASON:
11 Games – Pittsburgh Penguins, Oct. 8 – Nov. 19, 1983. 9L-2T

LONGEST ROAD WINLESS STREAK FROM START OF SEASON:
***38 Games – Ottawa Senators**, Oct. 10, 1992 – Apr. 3, 1993. 38L

NON-SHUTOUT STREAKS

LONGEST NON-SHUTOUT STREAK:
264 Games – Calgary Flames, Nov. 12, 1981 – Jan. 9, 1985.
261 Games – Los Angeles Kings, Mar. 15, 1986 – Oct. 22, 1989.
244 Games – Washington Capitals, Oct. 31, 1989 – Nov. 11, 1993.
236 Games – New York Rangers, Dec. 20, 1989 – Dec. 13, 1992.
230 Games – Quebec Nordiques, Feb. 10, 1980 – Jan. 12, 1983.

LONGEST NON-SHUTOUT STREAK, INCLUDING PLAYOFFS:
264 Games – Los Angeles Kings, Mar. 15, 1986 – Apr. 6, 1989. (5 playoff games in 1987; 5 in 1988; 2 in 1989).
262 Games – Chicago Blackhawks, Mar. 14, 1970 – Feb. 21, 1973. (8 playoff games in 1970; 18 in 1971; 8 in 1972).
251 Games – Quebec Nordiques, Feb. 10, 1980 – Jan. 12, 1983. (5 playoff games in 1981; 16 in 1982).
246 Games – Pittsburgh Penguins, Jan. 7, 1989 – Oct. 26, 1991. (11 playoff games in 1989; 24 in 1991).

TEAM GOALS

Most Goals

MOST GOALS, ONE SEASON:
446 – Edmonton Oilers, 1983-84. 80GP
426 – Edmonton Oilers, 1985-86. 80GP
424 – Edmonton Oilers, 1982-83. 80GP
417 – Edmonton Oilers, 1981-82. 80GP
401 – Edmonton Oilers, 1984-85. 80GP

MOST GOALS, ONE TEAM, ONE GAME:
16 – Montreal Canadiens, Mar. 3, 1920, at Quebec. Montreal won 16-3.

MOST GOALS, BOTH TEAMS, ONE GAME:
21 – Montreal Canadiens (14), Toronto St. Patricks (7), Jan. 10, 1920, at Montreal.
– Edmonton Oilers (12), Chicago Blackhawks (9), Dec. 11, 1985, at Chicago.
20 – Edmonton Oilers (12), Minnesota North Stars (8), Jan. 4, 1984, at Edmonton.
– Toronto Maple Leafs (11), Edmonton Oilers (9), Jan. 8, 1986, at Toronto.
19 – Montreal Wanderers (10), Toronto Arenas (9), Dec. 19, 1917, at Montreal.
– Montreal Canadiens (16), Quebec Bulldogs (3), Mar. 3, 1920, at Quebec.
– Montreal Canadiens (13), Hamilton Tigers (6), Feb. 26, 1921, at Montreal.
– Boston Bruins (10), New York Rangers (9), Mar. 4, 1944, at Boston.
– Detroit Red Wings (10), Boston Bruins (9), Mar. 16, 1944, at Detroit.
– Vancouver Canucks (10), Minnesota North Stars (9), Oct. 7, 1983, at Vancouver.

MOST GOALS, ONE TEAM, ONE PERIOD:
9 – Buffalo Sabres, Mar. 19, 1981, at Buffalo, second period during 14-4 win over Toronto.
8 – Detroit Red Wings, Jan. 23, 1944, at Detroit, third period during 15-0 win over NY Rangers.
– Boston Bruins, Mar. 16, 1969, at Boston, second period during 11-3 win over Toronto.
– New York Rangers, Nov. 21, 1971, at NY Rangers, third period during 12-1 win over California.
– Philadelphia Flyers, Mar. 31, 1973, at Philadelphia, second period during 10-2 win over NY Islanders.
– Buffalo Sabres, Dec. 21, 1975, at Buffalo, third period during 14-2 win over Washington.
– Minnesota North Stars, Nov. 11, 1981, at Minnesota, second period during 15-2 win over Winnipeg.
– Pittsburgh Penguins, Dec. 17, 1991, at Pittsburgh, second period during 10-2 win over San Jose.
– Washington Capitals, Feb. 3, 1999, at Washington, second period during 10-1 win over Tampa Bay.

MOST GOALS, BOTH TEAMS, ONE PERIOD:
12 – Buffalo Sabres (9), Toronto Maple Leafs (3), Mar. 19, 1981, at Buffalo, second period. Buffalo won 14-4.
– Edmonton Oilers (6), Chicago Blackhawks (6), Dec. 11, 1985, at Chicago, second period. Edmonton won 12-9.
10 – New York Rangers (7), New York Americans (3), Mar. 16, 1939, at NY Americans, third period. NY Rangers won 11-5.
– Toronto Maple Leafs (6), Detroit Red Wings (4), Mar. 17, 1946, at Detroit, third period. Toronto won 11-7.
– Buffalo Sabres (6), Vancouver Canucks (4), Jan. 8, 1976, at Buffalo, third period. Buffalo won 8-5.
– Buffalo Sabres (5), Montreal Canadiens (5), Oct. 26, 1982, at Montreal, first period. Teams tied 7-7.
– Quebec Nordiques (6), Boston Bruins (4), Dec. 7, 1982, at Quebec, second period. Quebec won 10-5.
– Vancouver Canucks (6), Calgary Flames (4), Jan. 16, 1987, at Vancouver, first period. Vancouver won 9-5.
– Detroit Red Wings (7), Winnipeg Jets (3), Nov. 25, 1987, at Detroit, third period. Detroit won 10-8.
– Chicago Blackhawks (5), St. Louis Blues (5), Mar. 15, 1988, at St. Louis, third period. Teams tied 7-7.

MOST CONSECUTIVE GOALS, ONE TEAM, ONE GAME:
15 – Detroit Red Wings, Jan. 23, 1944, at Detroit during 15-0 win over NY Rangers.

Fewest Goals

FEWEST GOALS, ONE SEASON:
33 – Chicago Blackhawks, 1928-29. 44GP
45 – Montreal Maroons, 1924-25. 30GP
46 – Pittsburgh Pirates, 1928-29. 44GP

FEWEST GOALS, ONE SEASON (MINIMUM 70-GAME SCHEDULE):
133 – Chicago Blackhawks, 1953-54. 70GP
147 – Toronto Maple Leafs, 1954-55. 70GP
– Boston Bruins, 1955-56. 70GP
150 – New York Rangers, 1954-55. 70GP

TEAM POWER-PLAY GOALS

MOST POWER-PLAY GOALS, ONE SEASON:
119 – Pittsburgh Penguins, 1988-89. 80GP
113 – Detroit Red Wings, 1992-93. 84GP
111 – New York Rangers, 1987-88. 80GP
110 – Pittsburgh Penguins, 1987-88. 80GP
– Winnipeg Jets, 1987-88. 80GP

TEAM SHORTHAND GOALS

MOST SHORTHAND GOALS, ONE SEASON:
36 – Edmonton Oilers, 1983-84. 80GP
28 – Edmonton Oilers, 1986-87. 80GP
27 – Edmonton Oilers, 1985-86. 80GP
– Edmonton Oilers, 1988-89. 80GP

TEAM GOALS-PER-GAME

HIGHEST GOALS-PER-GAME AVERAGE, ONE SEASON:
5.58 – Edmonton Oilers, 1983-84. 446G in 80GP.
5.38 – Montreal Canadiens, 1919-20. 129G in 24GP.
5.33 – Edmonton Oilers, 1985-86. 426G in 80GP.
5.30 – Edmonton Oilers, 1982-83. 424G in 80GP.
5.23 – Montreal Canadiens, 1917-18. 115G in 22GP.

LOWEST GOALS-PER-GAME AVERAGE, ONE SEASON:
0.75 – Chicago Blackhawks, 1928-29. 33G in 44GP.
1.05 – Pittsburgh Pirates, 1928-29. 46G in 44GP.
1.20 – New York Americans, 1928-29. 53G in 44GP.

TEAM ASSISTS

MOST ASSISTS, ONE SEASON:
737 – Edmonton Oilers, 1985-86. 80GP
736 – Edmonton Oilers, 1983-84. 80GP
706 – Edmonton Oilers, 1981-82. 80GP

FEWEST ASSISTS, ONE SEASON (Since 1926-27):
45 – New York Rangers, 1926-27. 44GP

FEWEST ASSISTS, ONE SEASON (MINIMUM 70-GAME SCHEDULE):
206 – Chicago Blackhawks, 1953-54. 70GP

TEAM TOTAL POINTS

MOST SCORING POINTS, ONE SEASON:
1,182 – Edmonton Oilers, 1983-84. (446G-736A) 80GP
1,163 – Edmonton Oilers, 1985-86. (426G-737A) 80GP
1,123 – Edmonton Oilers, 1981-82. (417G-706A) 80GP

MOST SCORING POINTS, ONE TEAM, ONE GAME:
40 – Buffalo Sabres, Dec. 21, 1975, at Buffalo. Buffalo defeated Washington 14-2, and had 26A.
39 – Minnesota North Stars, Nov. 11, 1981, at Minnesota. Minnesota defeated Winnipeg 15-2, and had 24A.
37 – Detroit Red Wings, Jan. 23, 1944, at Detroit. Detroit defeated NY Rangers 15-0, and had 22A.
– Toronto Maple Leafs, Mar. 16, 1957, at Toronto. Toronto defeated NY Rangers 14-1, and had 23A.
– Buffalo Sabres, Feb. 25, 1978, at Cleveland. Buffalo defeated Cleveland 13-3, and had 24A.
– Calgary Flames, Feb. 10, 1993, at Calgary. Calgary defeated San Jose 13-1, and had 24A.

MOST SCORING POINTS, BOTH TEAMS, ONE GAME:
62 – Edmonton Oilers, Chicago Blackhawks, Dec. 11, 1985, at Chicago. Edmonton won 12-9. Edmonton had 24A, Chicago, 17A.
53 – Quebec Nordiques, Washington Capitals, Feb. 22, 1981, at Washington. Quebec won 11-7. Quebec had 22A, Washington, 13A.
– Edmonton Oilers, Minnesota North Stars, Jan. 4, 1984, at Edmonton. Edmonton won 12-8. Edmonton had 20A, Minnesota, 13A.
– Minnesota North Stars, St. Louis Blues, Jan. 27, 1984, at St. Louis. Minnesota won 10-8. Minnesota had 19A, St. Louis, 16A.
– Toronto Maple Leafs, Edmonton Oilers, Jan. 8, 1986, at Toronto. Toronto won 11-9. Toronto had 17A, Edmonton, 16A.
52 – Montreal Maroons, New York Americans, Feb. 18, 1936, at NY Americans. Teams tied 8-8. NY Americans had 20A, Montreal, 16A. (3A allowed for each goal.)
– Vancouver Canucks, Minnesota North Stars, Oct. 7, 1983, at Vancouver. Vancouver won 10-9. Vancouver had 16A, Minnesota, 17A.

MOST SCORING POINTS, ONE TEAM, ONE PERIOD:
23 – New York Rangers, Nov. 21, 1971, at NY Rangers, third period during 12-1 win over California. NY Rangers had 8G, 15A.
– Buffalo Sabres, Dec. 21, 1975, at Buffalo, third period during 14-2 win over Washington. Buffalo had 8G, 15A.
– Buffalo Sabres, Mar. 19, 1981, at Buffalo, second period during 14-4 win over Toronto. Buffalo had 9G, 14A.

22 – Detroit Red Wings, Jan. 23, 1944, at Detroit, third period during 15-0 win over NY Rangers. Detroit had 8G, 14A.
– Boston Bruins, Mar. 16, 1969, at Boston, second period during 11-3 win over Toronto. Boston had 8G, 14A.
– Minnesota North Stars, Nov. 11, 1981, at Minnesota, second period during 15-2 win over Winnipeg. Minnesota had 8G, 14A.
– Pittsburgh Penguins, Dec. 17, 1991, at Pittsburgh, second period during 10-2 win over San Jose. Pittsburgh had 8G, 14A.
– Washington Capitals, Feb. 3, 1999, at Washington, second period during 10-1 win over Tampa Bay. Washington had 8G, 14A.

MOST SCORING POINTS, BOTH TEAMS, ONE PERIOD:
35 – Edmonton, Oilers, Chicago Blackhawks, Dec. 11, 1985, at Chicago, second period. Edmonton won 12-9. Edmonton had 6G, 12A; Chicago, 6G, 11A.
31 – Buffalo Sabres, Toronto Maple Leafs, Mar. 19, 1981, at Buffalo, second period. Buffalo won 14-4. Buffalo had 9G, 14A; Toronto, 3G, 5A.
29 – Winnipeg Jets, Detroit Red Wings, Nov. 25, 1987, at Detroit, third period. Detroit won 10-8. Detroit had 7G, 13A; Winnipeg, 3G, 6A.
– Chicago Blackhawks, St. Louis Blues, Mar. 15, 1988, at St. Louis, third period. Teams tied 7-7. St. Louis had 5G, 10A; Chicago, 5G, 9A.

FASTEST GOALS

FASTEST SIX GOALS, BOTH TEAMS:
3:00 – Quebec Nordiques, Washington Capitals, Feb. 22, 1981, at Washington. Scorers: Peter Stastny, Quebec, 18:51; Pierre Lacroix, Quebec, 19:57 (first period); Anton Stastny, Quebec, 0:34; Jacques Richard, Quebec, 1:07 and 1:37; Rick Green, Washington, 1:51 (second period). Quebec won 11-7.
3:15 – Montreal Canadiens, Toronto Maple Leafs, Jan. 4, 1944, at Montreal, first period. Scorers: Maurice Richard, Montreal, 14:10; Don Webster, Toronto, 15:13; Fern Majeau, Montreal, 15:41; Phil Watson, Montreal, 15:52; Lorne Carr, Toronto, 16:55; Butch Bouchard, Montreal, 17:25. Montreal won 6-3.

FASTEST FIVE GOALS, BOTH TEAMS:
1:24 – Chicago Blackhawks, Toronto Maple Leafs, Oct. 15, 1983, at Toronto, second period. Scorers: Gaston Gingras, Toronto, 16:49; Denis Savard, Chicago, 17:12; Steve Larmer, Chicago, 17:27; Denis Savard, Chicago, 17:42; John Anderson, Toronto, 18:13. Toronto won 10-8.
1:39 – Detroit Red Wings, Toronto Maple Leafs, Nov. 15, 1944, at Toronto, third period. Scorers: Ted Kennedy, Toronto, 10:36 and 10:55; Harold Jackson, Detroit, 11:48; Steve Wojciechowski, Detroit, 12:02; Don Grosso, Detroit, 12:15. Detroit won 8-4.

FASTEST FIVE GOALS, ONE TEAM:
2:07 – Pittsburgh Penguins, Nov. 22, 1972, at Pittsburgh, third period. Scorers: Bryan Hextall, Jr., 12:00; Jean Pronovost, 12:18; Al McDonough, 13:40; Ken Schinkel, 13:49; Ron Schock, 14:07. Pittsburgh defeated St. Louis 10-4.
2:37 – New York Islanders, Jan. 26, 1982, at NY Islanders, first period. Scorers: Duane Sutter, 1:31; John Tonelli, 2:30; Bryan Trottier, 2:46 and 3:31; Duane Sutter, 4:08. NY Islanders defeated Pittsburgh 9-2.
2:55 – Boston Bruins, Dec. 19, 1974, at Boston. Scorers: Bobby Schmautz, 19:13 (first period); Ken Hodge, 0:18; Phil Esposito, 0:43; Don Marcotte, 0:58; John Bucyk, 2:08 (second period). Boston defeated NY Rangers 11-3.

FASTEST FOUR GOALS, BOTH TEAMS:
0:53 – Chicago Blackhawks, Toronto Maple Leafs, Oct. 15, 1983, at Toronto, second period. Scorers: Gaston Gingras, Toronto, 16:49; Denis Savard, Chicago, 17:12; Steve Larmer, Chicago, 17:27; Denis Savard, Chicago, 17:42. Toronto won 10-8.
0:57 – Quebec Nordiques, Detroit Red Wings, Jan. 27, 1990, at Quebec, first period. Scorers: Paul Gillis, Quebec, 18:01; Claude Loiselle, Quebec, 18:12; Joe Sakic, Quebec, 18:27; Jimmy Carson, Detroit, 18:58. Detroit won 8-6.
1:01 – Colorado Rockies, New York Rangers, Jan. 15, 1980, at NY Rangers, first period. Scorers: Doug Sulliman, NY Rangers, 7:52; Eddie Johnstone, NY Rangers, 7:57; Warren Miller, NY Rangers, 8:20; Rob Ramage, Colorado, 8:53. Teams tied 6-6.
– Chicago Blackhawks, Toronto Maple Leafs, Oct. 15, 1983, at Toronto, second period. Scorers: Denis Savard, Chicago, 17:12; Steve Larmer, Chicago, 17:27; Denis Savard, Chicago, 17:42; John Anderson, Toronto, 18:13. Toronto won 10-8.

FASTEST FOUR GOALS, ONE TEAM:
1:20 – Boston Bruins, Jan. 21, 1945, at Boston, second period. Scorers: Bill Thoms, 6:34; Frank Mario, 7:08 and 7:27; Ken Smith, 7:54. Boston defeated NY Rangers 14-3.

FASTEST THREE GOALS, BOTH TEAMS:
0:15 – Minnesota North Stars, New York Rangers, Feb. 10, 1983, at Minnesota, second period. Scorers: Mark Pavelich, NY Rangers, 19:18; Ron Greschner, NY Rangers, 19:27; Willi Plett, Minnesota, 19:33. Minnesota won 7-5.
0:18 – Montreal Canadiens, New York Rangers, Dec. 12, 1963, at Montreal, first period. Scorers: Dave Balon, Montreal, 0:58; Gilles Tremblay, Montreal, 1:04; Camille Henry, NY Rangers, 1:16. Montreal won 6-4.
– California Golden Seals, Buffalo Sabres, Feb. 1, 1976, at California, third period. Scorers: Jim Moxey, California, 19:38; Wayne Merrick, California, 19:45; Danny Gare, Buffalo, 19:56. Buffalo won 9-5.

FASTEST THREE GOALS, ONE TEAM:
0:20 – Boston Bruins, Feb. 25, 1971, at Boston, third period. Scorers: John Bucyk, 4:50; Ed Westfall, 5:02; Ted Green, 5:10. Boston defeated Vancouver 8-3.
0:21 – Chicago Blackhawks, Mar. 23, 1952, at NY Rangers, third period. Bill Mosienko scored all three goals, at 6:09, 6:20 and 6:30. Chicago defeated NY Rangers 7-6.
– Washington Capitals, Nov. 23, 1990, at Washington, first period. Scorers: Michal Pivonka, 16:18; Stephen Leach, 16:29 and 16:39. Washington defeated Pittsburgh 7-3.

FASTEST THREE GOALS FROM START OF PERIOD, BOTH TEAMS:
1:05 – Hartford Whalers, Montreal Canadiens, Mar. 11, 1989, at Montreal, second period. Scorers: Kevin Dineen, Hartford, 0:11; Guy Carbonneau, Montreal, 0:36; Petr Svoboda, Montreal, 1:05. Montreal won 5-3.

FASTEST THREE GOALS FROM START OF PERIOD, ONE TEAM:
0:53 – Calgary Flames, Feb. 10, 1993, at Calgary, third period. Scorers: Gary Suter, 0:17; Chris Lindberg, 0:40; Ron Stern, 0:53. Calgary defeated San Jose 13-1.

FASTEST TWO GOALS, BOTH TEAMS:
0:02 – St. Louis Blues, Boston Bruins, Dec. 19, 1987, at Boston, third period. Scorers: Ken Linseman, Boston, 19:50; Doug Gilmour, St. Louis, 19:52. St. Louis won 7-5.
* 0:03 – Chicago Blackhawks, Minnesota North Stars, Nov. 5, 1988, at Minnesota, third period. Scorers: Steve Thomas, Chicago, 6:03; Dave Gagner, Minnesota, 6:06. Teams tied 5-5.

** – Newspaper accounts of this game note that the clock was slow to start after the first goal was scored.*

FASTEST TWO GOALS, ONE TEAM:
0:03 – Minnesota Wild, Jan. 21, 2004, at Minnesota, third period. Scorers: Jim Dowd, 19:44; Richard Park, 19:47. Minnesota defeated Chicago 4-2.
0:04 – Montreal Maroons, Jan. 3, 1931, at Montreal, third period. Nels Stewart scored both goals, at 8:24 and 8:28. Mtl. Maroons defeated Boston 5-3.
– Buffalo Sabres, Oct. 17, 1974, at Buffalo, third period. Scorers: Lee Fogolin, Jr., 14:55; Don Luce, 14:59. Buffalo defeated California 6-1.
– Toronto Maple Leafs, Dec. 29, 1988, at Quebec, third period. Scorers: Ed Olczyk, 5:24; Gary Leeman, 5:28. Toronto defeated Quebec 6-5.
– Calgary Flames, Oct. 17, 1989, at Quebec, third period. Scorers: Doug Gilmour, 19:45; Paul Ranheim, 19:49. Teams tied 8-8.
– NY Rangers, Oct. 9, 1991, at NY Rangers, third period. Scorers: Kris King, 19:45; James Patrick, 19:49. NY Rangers defeated NY Islanders 5-3.
– Winnipeg Jets, Dec. 15, 1995, at Winnipeg, second period. Deron Quint scored both goals, at 7:51 and 7:55. Winnipeg defeated Edmonton 9-4.

FASTEST TWO GOALS FROM START OF GAME, ONE TEAM:
0:24 – Edmonton Oilers, Mar. 28, 1982, at Los Angeles. Scorers: Mark Messier, 0:14; Dave Lumley, 0:24. Edmonton defeated Los Angeles 6-2.
0:27 – Boston Bruins, Feb. 14, 2003, at Florida. Mike Knuble scored both goals, at 0:10 and 0:27. Boston defeated Florida 6-5.
0:29 – Pittsburgh Penguins, Dec. 6, 1980, at Pittsburgh. Scorers: George Ferguson, 0:17; Greg Malone, 0:29. Pittsburgh defeated Chicago 6-4.

FASTEST TWO GOALS FROM START OF PERIOD, BOTH TEAMS:
0:14 – New York Rangers, Quebec Nordiques, Nov. 5, 1983, at Quebec, third period. Scorers: Andre Savard, Quebec, 0:08; Pierre Larouche, NY Rangers, 0:14. Teams tied 4-4.
0:25 – St. Louis Blues, Chicago Blackhawks, Feb. 2, 2006, at St. Louis, second period. Scorers: Peter Cajanek, St. Louis, 0:10; Tyler Arnason, Chicago, 0:25. St. Louis won 6-5.
0:28 – Boston Bruins, Montreal Canadiens, Oct. 11, 1989, at Montreal, third period. Scorers: Jim Wiemer, Boston 0:10; Tom Chorske, Montreal 0:28. Montreal won 4-2.

FASTEST TWO GOALS FROM START OF PERIOD, ONE TEAM:
0:21 – Chicago Blackhawks, Nov. 5, 1983, at Minnesota, second period. Scorers: Ken Yaremchuk, 0:12; Darryl Sutter, 0:21. Minnesota defeated Chicago 10-5.
0:24 – Edmonton Oilers, Mar. 28, 1982, at Los Angeles, first period. Scorers: Mark Messier, 0:14; Dave Lumley, 0:24. Edmonton defeated Los Angeles 6-2.
0:27 – Boston Bruins, Feb. 14, 2003, at Florida. Mike Knuble scored both goals, at 0:10 and 0:27. Boston defeated Florida 6-5.

50, 40, 30, 20-GOAL SCORERS

MOST 50-OR-MORE GOAL SCORERS, ONE SEASON:
3 – Edmonton Oilers, 1983-84. 80GP. Wayne Gretzky, 87; Glenn Anderson, 54; Jari Kurri, 52.
– Edmonton Oilers, 1985-86. 80GP. Jari Kurri, 68; Glenn Anderson, 54; Wayne Gretzky, 52.
2 – Boston Bruins, 1970-71. 78GP. Phil Esposito, 76; John Bucyk, 51.
– Boston Bruins, 1973-74. 78GP. Phil Esposito, 68; Ken Hodge, 50.
– Philadelphia Flyers, 1975-76. 80GP. Reggie Leach, 61; Bill Barber, 50.
– Pittsburgh Penguins, 1975-76. 80GP. Pierre Larouche, 53; Jean Pronovost, 52.
– Montreal Canadiens, 1976-77. 80GP. Steve Shutt, 60; Guy Lafleur, 56.
– Los Angeles Kings, 1979-80. 80GP. Charlie Simmer, 56; Marcel Dionne, 53.
– Montreal Canadiens, 1979-80. 80GP. Pierre Larouche, 50; Guy Lafleur, 50.
– Los Angeles Kings, 1980-81. 80GP. Marcel Dionne, 58; Charlie Simmer, 56.
– Edmonton Oilers, 1981-82. 80GP. Wayne Gretzky, 92; Mark Messier, 50.
– New York Islanders, 1981-82. 80GP. Mike Bossy, 64; Bryan Trottier, 50.
– Edmonton Oilers, 1984-85. 80GP. Wayne Gretzky, 73; Jari Kurri, 71.
– Washington Capitals, 1984-85. 80GP. Bob Carpenter, 53; Mike Gartner, 50.
– Edmonton Oilers, 1986-87. 80GP. Wayne Gretzky, 62; Jari Kurri, 54.
– Calgary Flames, 1987-88. 80GP. Joe Nieuwendyk, 51; Hakan Loob, 50.
– Los Angeles Kings, 1987-88. 80GP. Jimmy Carson, 55; Luc Robitaille, 53.
– Calgary Flames, 1988-89. 80GP. Joe Nieuwendyk, 51; Joe Mullen, 51.
– Los Angeles Kings, 1988-89. 80GP. Bernie Nicholls, 70; Wayne Gretzky, 54.
– Buffalo Sabres, 1992-93. 84GP. Alexander Mogilny, 76; Pat LaFontaine, 53.
– Pittsburgh Penguins, 1992-93. 84GP. Mario Lemieux, 69; Kevin Stevens, 55.
– St. Louis Blues, 1992-93. 84GP. Brett Hull, 54; Brendan Shanahan, 51.
– Detroit Red Wings, 1993-94. 84GP. Sergei Fedorov, 56; Ray Sheppard, 52.
– St. Louis Blues, 1993-94. 84GP. Brett Hull, 57; Brendan Shanahan, 52.
– Pittsburgh Penguins, 1995-96. 82GP. Mario Lemieux, 69; Jaromir Jagr, 62.

MOST 40-OR-MORE GOAL SCORERS, ONE SEASON:

4 – Edmonton Oilers, 1982-83. 80GP. Wayne Gretzky, 71; Glenn Anderson, 48; Mark Messier, 48; Jari Kurri, 45.
– Edmonton Oilers, 1983-84. 80GP. Wayne Gretzky, 87; Glenn Anderson, 54; Jari Kurri, 52; Paul Coffey, 40.
– Edmonton Oilers, 1984-85. 80GP. Wayne Gretzky, 73; Jari Kurri, 71; Mike Krushelnyski, 43; Glenn Anderson, 42.
– Edmonton Oilers, 1985-86. 80GP. Jari Kurri, 68; Glenn Anderson, 54; Wayne Gretzky, 52; Paul Coffey, 48.
– Calgary Flames, 1987-88. 80GP. Joe Nieuwendyk, 51; Hakan Loob, 50; Mike Bullard, 48; Joe Mullen, 40.
3 – Boston Bruins, 1970-71. 78GP. Phil Esposito, 76; John Bucyk, 51; Ken Hodge, 43.
– New York Rangers, 1971-72. 78GP. Vic Hadfield, 50; Jean Ratelle, 46; Rod Gilbert, 43.
– Buffalo Sabres, 1975-76. 80GP. Danny Gare, 50; Rick Martin, 49; Gilbert Perreault, 44.
– Montreal Canadiens, 1979-80. 80GP. Guy Lafleur, 50; Pierre Larouche, 50; Steve Shutt, 47.
– Buffalo Sabres, 1979-80. 80GP. Danny Gare, 56; Rick Martin, 45; Gilbert Perreault, 40.
– Los Angeles Kings, 1980-81. 80GP. Marcel Dionne, 58; Charlie Simmer, 56; Dave Taylor, 47.
– Los Angeles Kings, 1984-85. 80GP. Marcel Dionne, 46; Bernie Nicholls, 46; Dave Taylor, 41.
– New York Islanders, 1984-85. 80GP. Mike Bossy, 58; Brent Sutter, 42; John Tonelli, 42.
– Chicago Blackhawks, 1985-86. 80GP. Denis Savard, 47; Troy Murray, 45; Al Secord, 40.
– Chicago Blackhawks, 1987-88. 80GP. Denis Savard, 44; Rick Vaive, 43; Steve Larmer, 41.
– Edmonton Oilers, 1987-88. 80GP. Craig Simpson, 43; Jari Kurri, 43; Wayne Gretzky, 40.
– Los Angeles Kings, 1988-89. 80GP. Bernie Nicholls, 70; Wayne Gretzky, 54; Luc Robitaille, 46.
– Los Angeles Kings, 1990-91. 80GP. Luc Robitaille, 45; Tomas Sandstrom, 45; Wayne Gretzky, 41.
– Pittsburgh Penguins, 1991-92. 80GP. Kevin Stevens, 54; Mario Lemieux, 44; Joe Mullen, 42.
– Pittsburgh Penguins, 1992-93. 84GP. Mario Lemieux, 69; Kevin Stevens, 55; Rick Tocchet, 48.
– Calgary Flames, 1993-94. 84GP. Gary Roberts, 41; Robert Reichel, 40; Theoren Fleury, 40.
– Pittsburgh Penguins, 1995-96. 82GP. Mario Lemieux, 69; Jaromir Jagr, 62; Petr Nedved, 45.

MOST 30-OR-MORE GOAL SCORERS, ONE SEASON:

6 – Buffalo Sabres, 1974-75. 80GP. Rick Martin, 52; Rene Robert, 40; Gilbert Perreault, 39; Don Luce, 33; Rick Dudley, 31; Danny Gare, 31.
– New York Islanders, 1977-78. 80GP. Mike Bossy, 53; Bryan Trottier, 46; Clark Gillies, 35; Denis Potvin, 30; Bob Nystrom, 30; Bob Bourne, 30.
– Winnipeg Jets, 1984-85. 80GP. Dale Hawerchuk, 53; Paul MacLean, 41; Laurie Boschman, 32; Brian Mullen, 32; Doug Smail, 31; Thomas Steen, 30.
5 – Chicago Blackhawks, 1968-69. 76GP
– Boston Bruins, 1970-71. 78GP
– Montreal Canadiens, 1971-72. 78GP
– Philadelphia Flyers, 1972-73. 78GP
– Boston Bruins, 1973-74. 78GP
– Montreal Canadiens, 1974-75. 80GP
– Montreal Canadiens, 1975-76. 80GP
– Pittsburgh Penguins, 1975-76. 80GP
– New York Islanders, 1978-79. 80GP
– Detroit Red Wings, 1979-80. 80GP
– Philadelphia Flyers, 1979-80. 80GP
– New York Islanders, 1980-81. 80GP
– St. Louis Blues, 1980-81. 80GP
– Chicago Blackhawks, 1981-82. 80GP
– Edmonton Oilers, 1981-82. 80GP
– Montreal Canadiens, 1981-82. 80GP
– Quebec Nordiques, 1981-82. 80GP
– Washington Capitals, 1981-82. 80GP
– Edmonton Oilers, 1982-83. 80GP
– Edmonton Oilers, 1983-84. 80GP
– Edmonton Oilers, 1984-85. 80GP
– Los Angeles Kings, 1984-85. 80GP
– Edmonton Oilers, 1985-86. 80GP
– Edmonton Oilers, 1986-87. 80GP
– Edmonton Oilers, 1987-88. 80GP
– Edmonton Oilers, 1988-89. 80GP
– Detroit Red Wings, 1991-92. 80GP
– New York Rangers, 1991-92. 80GP
– Pittsburgh Penguins, 1991-92. 80GP
– Detroit Red Wings, 1992-93. 84GP
– Pittsburgh Penguins, 1992-93. 84GP

MOST 20-OR-MORE GOAL SCORERS, ONE SEASON:

11 – Boston Bruins, 1977-78. 80GP. Peter McNab, 41; Terry O'Reilly, 29; Bobby Schmautz, 27; Stan Jonathan, 27; Jean Ratelle, 25; Rick Middleton, 25; Wayne Cashman, 24; Gregg Sheppard, 23; Brad Park, 22; Don Marcotte, 20; Bob Miller, 20.
10 – Boston Bruins, 1970-71. 78GP
– Montreal Canadiens, 1974-75. 80GP
– St. Louis Blues, 1980-81. 80GP

100-POINT SCORERS

MOST 100-OR-MORE-POINT SCORERS, ONE SEASON:

4 – Boston Bruins, 1970-71. 78GP. Phil Esposito, 76G-76A-152PTS; Bobby Orr, 37G-102A-139PTS; John Bucyk, 51G-65A-116PTS; Ken Hodge, 43G-62A-105PTS.
– Edmonton Oilers, 1982-83. 80GP. Wayne Gretzky, 71G-125A-196PTS; Mark Messier, 48G-58A-106PTS; Glenn Anderson, 48G-56A-104PTS; Jari Kurri, 45G-59A-104PTS.
– Edmonton Oilers, 1983-84. 80GP. Wayne Gretzky, 87G-118A-205PTS; Paul Coffey, 40G-86A-126PTS; Jari Kurri, 52G-61A-113PTS; Mark Messier, 37G-64A-101PTS.
– Edmonton Oilers,1985-86. 80GP. Wayne Gretzky, 52G-163A-215PTS; Paul Coffey, 48G-90A-138PTS; Jari Kurri, 68G-63A-131PTS; Glenn Anderson, 54G-48A-102PTS.
– Pittsburgh Penguins,1992-93. 84GP. Mario Lemieux, 69G-91A-160PTS; Kevin Stevens, 55G-56A-111PTS; Rick Tocchet, 48G-61A-109PTS; Ron Francis, 24G-76A-100PTS.
3 – Boston Bruins, 1973-74. 78GP. Phil Esposito, 68G-77A-145PTS; Bobby Orr, 32G-90A-122PTS; Ken Hodge, 50G-55A-105PTS.
– New York Islanders, 1978-79. 80GP. Bryan Trottier, 47G-87A-134PTS; Mike Bossy, 69G-57A-126PTS; Denis Potvin, 31G-70A-101PTS.
– Los Angeles Kings, 1980-81. 80GP. Marcel Dionne, 58G-77A-135PTS; Dave Taylor, 47G-65A-112PTS; Charlie Simmer, 56G-49A-105PTS.
– Edmonton Oilers, 1984-85. 80GP. Wayne Gretzky, 73G-135A-208PTS; Jari Kurri, 71G-64A-135PTS; Paul Coffey, 37G-84A-121PTS.
– New York Islanders, 1984-85. 80GP. Mike Bossy, 58G-59A-117PTS; Brent Sutter, 42G-60A-102PTS; John Tonelli, 42G-58A-100PTS.
– Edmonton Oilers, 1986-87. 80GP. Wayne Gretzky, 62G-121A-183PTS; Jari Kurri, 54G-54A-108PTS; Mark Messier, 37G-70A-107PTS.
– Pittsburgh Penguins, 1988-89. 80GP. Mario Lemieux, 85G-114A-199PTS; Rob Brown, 49G-66A-115PTS; Paul Coffey, 30G-83A-113PTS.
– Pittsburgh Penguins, 1995-96. 82GP. Mario Lemieux, 69G-92A-161PTS; Jaromir Jagr, 62G-87A-149PTS; Ron Francis, 27G-92A-119PTS.

SHOTS ON GOAL

MOST SHOTS, BOTH TEAMS, ONE GAME:

141 – New York Americans, Pittsburgh Pirates, Dec. 26, 1925, at NY Americans. NY Americans won 3-1 with 73 shots; Pittsburgh had 68 shots.

MOST SHOTS, ONE TEAM, ONE GAME:

83 – Boston Bruins, Mar. 4, 1941, at Boston. Boston defeated Chicago 3-2.
73 – New York Americans, Dec. 26, 1925, at NY Americans. NY Americans defeated Pittsburgh 3-1.
– Boston Bruins, Mar. 21, 1991, at Boston. Boston tied Quebec 3-3.
72 – Boston Bruins, Dec. 10, 1970, at Boston. Boston defeated Buffalo 8-2.

MOST SHOTS, ONE TEAM, ONE PERIOD:

33 – Boston Bruins, Mar. 4, 1941, at Boston, second period. Boston defeated Chicago 3-2.

TEAM GOALS AGAINST

Fewest Goals Against

FEWEST GOALS AGAINST, ONE SEASON:

42 – Ottawa Senators, 1925-26. 36GP
43 – Montreal Canadiens, 1928-29. 44GP
48 – Montreal Canadiens, 1923-24. 24GP
– Montreal Canadiens, 1927-28. 44GP

FEWEST GOALS AGAINST, ONE SEASON (MINIMUM 70-GAME SCHEDULE):

131 – Toronto Maple Leafs, 1953-54. 70GP
– Montreal Canadiens, 1955-56. 70GP
132 – Detroit Red Wings, 1953-54. 70GP
133 – Detroit Red Wings, 1951-52. 70GP
– Detroit Red Wings, 1952-53. 70GP

LOWEST GOALS-AGAINST-PER-GAME AVERAGE, ONE SEASON:

0.98 – Montreal Canadiens, 1928-29. 43GA in 44GP.
1.09 – Montreal Canadiens, 1927-28. 48GA in 44GP.
1.17 – Ottawa Senators, 1925-26. 42GA in 36GP.

Most Goals Against

MOST GOALS AGAINST, ONE SEASON:

446 – Washington Capitals, 1974-75. 80GP
415 – Detroit Red Wings, 1985-86. 80GP
414 – San Jose Sharks, 1992-93. 84GP
407 – Quebec Nordiques, 1989-90. 80GP
403 – Hartford Whalers, 1982-83. 80GP

HIGHEST GOALS-AGAINST-PER-GAME AVERAGE, ONE SEASON:

7.38 – Quebec Bulldogs, 1919-20. 177GA in 24GP.
6.20 – New York Rangers, 1943-44. 310GA in 50GP.
5.58 – Washington Capitals, 1974-75. 446GA in 80GP.

MOST POWER-PLAY GOALS AGAINST, ONE SEASON:

122 – Chicago Blackhawks, 1988-89. 80GP
120 – Pittsburgh Penguins, 1987-88. 80GP
116 – Washington Capitals, 2005-06. 82GP
115 – New Jersey Devils, 1988-89. 80GP
– Ottawa Senators, 1992-93. 84GP
114 – Los Angeles Kings, 1992-93. 84GP

MOST SHORTHAND GOALS AGAINST, ONE SEASON:

22 – Pittsburgh Penguins, 1984-85. 80GP
– Minnesota North Stars, 1991-92. 80GP
– Colorado Avalanche, 1995-96. 82GP
21 – Calgary Flames, 1984-85. 80GP
– Pittsburgh Penguins, 1989-90. 80GP

TEAM SHOOTOUT RECORDS

MOST SHOOTOUT GAMES, ONE SEASON:
20 – Phoenix, 2009-10 (14W, 6L)
– Minnesota, 2011-12 (11W, 9L)
19 – Edmonton, 2007-08 (15W, 4L)
– Boston, 2009-10 (10W, 9L)

MOST SHOOTOUT GAMES, ALL-TIME:
94 – NY Rangers (54W, 40L)
93 – Edmonton (48W, 45L)
92 – New Jersey (56W, 36L)
– Boston (46W, 46L)
– Chicago (45W, 47L)

MOST SHOOTOUT WINS, ONE SEASON:
15 – Edmonton, 2007-08, 19GP
14 – Phoenix, 2009-10, 20GP
12 – Dallas, 2005-06, 13GP
– New Jersey, 2011-12, 16GP

MOST SHOOTOUT WINS, ALL-TIME:
56 – New Jersey, 92GP
54 – Pittsburgh, 84GP
– NY Rangers, 94GP

MOST SHOOTOUT HOME WINS, ONE SEASON:
8 – Edmonton, 2007-08, 9GP
– New Jersey, 2011-12, 12GP
7 – NY Rangers, 2008-09, 9GP
– NY Islanders, 2009-10, 9GP
– Anaheim, 2007-08, 10GP
– Minnesota, 2006-07, 11GP

MOST SHOOTOUT HOME WINS, ALL-TIME:
32 – New Jersey, 50GP
26 – NY Rangers, 42GP
25 – Los Angeles, 49GP

MOST SHOOTOUT ROAD WINS, ONE SEASON:
8 – Phoenix, 2009-10, 12GP
– Calgary, 2010-11, 12GP
7 – NY Rangers, 2011-12, 7GP
– Dallas, 2005-06, 8GP
– Dallas, 2006-07, 9GP
– Edmonton, 2007-08, 10GP
– Boston, 2009-10, 10GP
– Pittsburgh, 2010-11, 10GP

MOST SHOOTOUT ROAD WINS, ALL-TIME:
31 – Pittsburgh, 49GP
30 – Colorado, 45GP
– Dallas, 45GP

MOST SHOOTOUT SHOTS TAKEN, ONE SEASON:
90 – Phoenix, 2009-10, 20GP
75 – Dallas, 2009-10, 17GP
74 – Los Angeles, 2009-10, 18GP

MOST SHOOTOUT SHOTS TAKEN, ALL-TIME:
352 – NY Rangers, 94GP
336 – Los Angeles, 89GP
335 – Edmonton, 93GP

MOST SHOOTOUT GOALS SCORED, ONE SEASON:
34 – Phoenix, 2009-10, 20GP
28 – New Jersey, 2011-12, 16GP
27 – Minnesota, 2006-07, 17GP
– Los Angeles, 2009-10, 18GP

MOST SHOOTOUT GOALS SCORED, ALL-TIME:
122 – Los Angeles, 89GP (336S)
– New Jersey, 92GP (303S)
118 – Buffalo, 91GP (333S)

BEST SHOOTOUT SCORING PERCENTAGE, ONE SEASON:
.750 – Pittsburgh, 2006-07, 3GP (6G, 8S)
.636 – St. Louis, 2005-06, 6GP (14G, 22S)
.600 – Colorado, 2011-12, 4GP (6G, 10S)
– Minnesota, 2012-13, 6GP (9G, 15S)

BEST SHOOTOUT SCORING PERCENTAGE, ALL-TIME:
.403 – New Jersey, 92GP (122G, 303S)
.386 – Colorado, 75GP (102G, 264S)
.373 – NY Islanders, 83GP (110G, 295S)
– Pittsburgh, 84GP (107G, 287S)

FEWEST SHOOTOUT GOALS AGAINST, ONE SEASON:
1 – Washington, 2012-13, 3GP (9SA)
2 – Colorado, 2010-11, 7GP (27SA)
– Pittsburgh, 2012-13, 3GP (8SA)
– Carolina, 2012-13, 2GP (5SA)

FEWEST SHOOTOUT GOALS AGAINST, ALL-TIME:
66 – Carolina, 56GP (175SA)
70 – Tampa Bay, 71GP (248SA)
75 – Pittsburgh, 84GP (284SA)

BEST SHOOTOUT WINNING PERCENTAGE, ONE SEASON:
1.000 – Pittsburgh, 2012-13, 3GP (3W)
– Washington, 2012-13, 3GP (3W)
.923 – Dallas, 2005-06, 13GP (12W)

BEST SHOOTOUT WINNING PERCENTAGE, ALL-TIME:
.643 – Pittsburgh, 84GP (54W)
.640 – Colorado, 75GP (48W)
.609 – New Jersey, 92GP (56W)

SHUTOUTS

MOST SHUTOUTS, ONE SEASON:
22 – Montreal Canadiens, 1928-29. All by George Hainsworth. 44GP
16 – New York Americans, 1928-29. Roy Worters 13, Flat Walsh 3. 44GP
15 – Ottawa Senators, 1925-26. All by Alex Connell. 36GP
– Ottawa Senators, 1927-28. All by Alex Connell. 44GP
– Boston Bruins, 1927-28. All by Hal Winkler. 44GP
– Chicago Blackhawks, 1969-70. All by Tony Esposito. 76GP
– St. Louis Blues, 2011-12. Brian Elliott 9, Jaroslav Halak 6. 82GP

MOST CONSECUTIVE SHUTOUTS, ONE SEASON:
6 – Ottawa Senators, Jan. 31 – Feb. 18, 1928. All by Alex Connell.

MOST CONSECUTIVE SHUTOUTS TO START SEASON:
5 – Toronto Maple Leafs, Nov. 13 – 22, 1930. Lorne Chabot 3, Benny Grant 2.

MOST GAMES SHUTOUT, ONE SEASON:
20 – Chicago Blackhawks, 1928-29. 44GP

MOST CONSECUTIVE GAMES SHUTOUT:
8 – Chicago Blackhawks, Feb. 7 – 28, 1929.

MOST CONSECUTIVE GAMES SHUTOUT TO START SEASON:
3 – Montreal Maroons, Nov. 11 – 18, 1930.

TEAM PENALTIES

MOST PENALTY MINUTES, ONE SEASON:
2,713 – Buffalo Sabres, 1991-92. 80GP
2,670 – Pittsburgh Penguins, 1988-89. 80GP
2,663 – Chicago Blackhawks, 1991-92. 80GP
2,643 – Calgary Flames, 1991-92. 80GP
2,621 – Philadelphia Flyers, 1980-81. 80GP

MOST PENALTIES, BOTH TEAMS, ONE GAME:
85 – Edmonton Oilers (44), Los Angeles Kings (41), Feb. 28, 1990, at Los Angeles. Edmonton received 26 minors, 7 majors, 6 10-minute misconducts, 4 game misconducts and 1 match penalty; Los Angeles received 26 minors, 9 majors, 3 10-minute misconducts and 3 game misconducts.

MOST PENALTY MINUTES, BOTH TEAMS, ONE GAME:
419 – Ottawa Senators (206), Philadelphia Flyers (213), Mar. 5, 2004, at Philadelphia. Ottawa received 8 minors, 10 majors, 4 10-minute misconducts and 10 game misconducts. Philadelphia received 9 minors, 11 majors, 4 10-minute misconducts and 10 game misconducts.

MOST PENALTIES, ONE TEAM, ONE GAME:
44 – Edmonton Oilers, Feb. 28, 1990, at Los Angeles. Edmonton received 26 minors, 7 majors, 6 10-minute misconducts, 4 game misconducts and 1 match penalty.
42 – Minnesota North Stars, Feb. 26, 1981, at Boston. Minnesota received 18 minors, 13 majors, 4 10-minute misconducts and 7 game misconducts.
– Boston Bruins, Feb. 26, 1981, at Boston vs. Minnesota. Boston received 20 minors, 13 majors, 3 10-minute misconducts and 6 game misconducts.

MOST PENALTY MINUTES, ONE TEAM, ONE GAME:
213 – Philadelphia Flyers, Mar. 5, 2004, at Philadelphia. Philadelphia received 9 minors, 11 majors, 4 10-minute misconducts and 10 game misconducts.

MOST PENALTIES, BOTH TEAMS, ONE PERIOD:
67 – Minnesota North Stars (34), Boston Bruins (33), Feb. 26, 1981, at Boston, first period. Minnesota received 15 minors, 8 majors, 4 10-minute misconducts and 7 game misconducts. Boston had 16 minors, 8 majors, 3 10-minute misconducts and 6 game misconducts.

MOST PENALTY MINUTES, BOTH TEAMS, ONE PERIOD:
409 – Ottawa Senators (200), Philadelphia Flyers (209), Mar. 5, 2004, at Philadelphia, third period. Ottawa received 5 minors, 10 majors, 4 10-minute misconducts and 10 game misconducts. Philadelphia received 7 minors, 11 majors, 4 10-minute misconducts and 10 game misconducts.

MOST PENALTIES, ONE TEAM, ONE PERIOD:
34 – Minnesota North Stars, Feb. 26, 1981, at Boston, first period. Minnesota received 15 minors, 8 majors, 4 10-minute misconducts and 7 game misconducts.

MOST PENALTY MINUTES, ONE TEAM, ONE PERIOD:
209 – Philadelphia Flyers, Mar. 5, 2004, at Philadelphia vs. Ottawa, third period. Philadelphia received 7 minors, 11 majors, 4 10-minute misconducts and 10 game misconducts.
200 – Ottawa Senators, Mar. 5, 2004, at Philadelphia, third period. Ottawa received 5 minors, 10 majors, 4 10-minute misconducts and 10 game misconducts.

NHL Individual Scoring Records – History

Six individual scoring records stand as benchmarks in the history of the game: most goals, single-season and career; most assists, single-season and career; and most points, single-season and career. The evolution of these six records is traced here, beginning with 1917-18, the NHL's first season. New research has resulted in changes to scoring records in the NHL's first nine seasons.

MOST GOALS, ONE SEASON

44 —Joe Malone, Montreal, 1917-18.
Scored goal #44 against Toronto's Harry Holmes on March 2, 1918 and finished the season with 44 goals.
50 —Maurice Richard, Montreal, 1944-45.
Scored goal #45 against Toronto's Frank McCool on February 25, 1945 and finished the season with 50 goals.
50 —Bernie Geoffrion, Montreal, 1960-61.
Scored goal #50 against Toronto's Cesare Maniago on March 16, 1961 and finished the season with 50 goals.
50 —Bobby Hull, Chicago, 1961-62.
Scored goal #50 against NY Rangers' Gump Worsley on March 25, 1962 and finished the season with 50 goals.
54 —Bobby Hull, Chicago, 1965-66.
Scored goal #51 against NY Rangers' Cesare Maniago on March 12, 1966 and finished the season with 54 goals.
58 —Bobby Hull, Chicago, 1968-69.
Scored goal #55 against Boston's Gerry Cheevers on March 20, 1969 and finished the season with 58 goals.
76 —Phil Esposito, Boston, 1970-71.
Scored goal #59 against Los Angeles' Denis DeJordy on March 11, 1971 and finished the season with 76 goals.
92 —Wayne Gretzky, Edmonton, 1981-82.
Scored goal #77 against Buffalo's Don Edwards on February 24, 1982 and finished the season with 92 goals.

MOST ASSISTS, ONE SEASON

10 —Cy Denneny, Ottawa, 1917-18.
—Reg Noble, Toronto, 1917-18.
—Harry Cameron, Toronto, 1917-18.
—Newsy Lalonde, Montreal, 1918-19.
15 —Frank Nighbor, Ottawa, 1919-20.
—Jack Darragh, Ottawa, 1920-21.
17 —Harry Cameron, Toronto, 1921-22.
18 —Dick Irvin, Chicago, 1926-27.
—Howie Morenz, Montreal, 1927-28.
36 —Frank Boucher, NY Rangers, 1929-30.
37 —Joe Primeau, Toronto, 1931-32.
45 —Bill Cowley, Boston, 1940-41.
—Bill Cowley, Boston, 1942-43.
49 —Clint Smith, Chicago, 1943-44.
54 —Elmer Lach, Montreal, 1944-45.
55 —Ted Lindsay, Detroit, 1949-50.
56 —Bert Olmstead, Montreal, 1955-56.
58 —Jean Beliveau, Montreal, 1960-61.
—Andy Bathgate, NY Rangers/Toronto, 1963-64.
59 —Stan Mikita, Chicago, 1964-65.
62 —Stan Mikita, Chicago, 1966-67.
77 —Phil Esposito, Boston, 1968-69.
87 —Bobby Orr, Boston, 1969-70.
102 —Bobby Orr, Boston, 1970-71.
109 —Wayne Gretzky, Edmonton, 1980-81.
120 —Wayne Gretzky, Edmonton, 1981-82.
125 —Wayne Gretzky, Edmonton, 1982-83.
135 —Wayne Gretzky, Edmonton, 1984-85.
163 —Wayne Gretzky, Edmonton, 1985-86.

MOST POINTS, ONE SEASON

48 —Joe Malone, Montreal, 1917-18.
49 —Joe Malone, Montreal, 1919-20.
51 —Howie Morenz, Montreal, 1927-28.
73 —Cooney Weiland, Boston, 1929-30.
—Doug Bentley, Chicago, 1942-43.
82 —Herb Cain, Boston, 1943-44.
86 —Gordie Howe, Detroit, 1950-51.
95 —Gordie Howe, Detroit, 1952-53.
96 —Dickie Moore, Montreal, 1958-59.
97 —Bobby Hull, Chicago, 1965-66.
—Stan Mikita, Chicago, 1966-67.
126 —Phil Esposito, Boston, 1968-69.
152 —Phil Esposito, Boston, 1970-71.
164 —Wayne Gretzky, Edmonton, 1980-81.
212 —Wayne Gretzky, Edmonton, 1981-82.
215 —Wayne Gretzky, Edmonton, 1985-86.

MOST REGULAR-SEASON GOALS, CAREER

44 —Joe Malone, Montreal.
Malone led the NHL in goals in the league's first season with 44 goals in 20 games in 1917-18.
54 —Cy Denneny, Ottawa.
Denneny passed Malone during the 1918-19 season, and led the NHL in goals with 54 after two seasons.
143 —Joe Malone, Montreal, Quebec Bulldogs, Hamilton.
Malone passed Denneny during the 1919-20 season and finished his career with 143 goals.
248 —Cy Denneny, Ottawa, Boston.
Denneny passed Malone with goal #144 during the 1922-23 season and finished his career with 248 goals.
271 —Howie Morenz, Montreal, Chicago, NY Rangers.
Morenz passed Denneny with goal #249 during the 1933-34 season and finished his career with 271 goals.
324 —Nels Stewart, Montreal Maroons, Boston, NY Americans.
Stewart passed Morenz with goal #272 during the 1936-37 season and finished his career with 324 goals.
544 —Maurice Richard, Montreal.
Richard passed Stewart with goal #325 on Nov. 8, 1952 and finished his career with 544 goals.
801 —Gordie Howe, Detroit, Hartford.
Howe passed Richard with goal #545 on Nov. 10, 1963 and finished his career with 801 goals.
894 —Wayne Gretzky, Edmonton, Los Angeles, St. Louis, NY Rangers.
Gretzky passed Howe with goal #802 on March 23, 1994 and finished his career with 894 goals.

Gordie Howe of the Detroit Red Wings checks out the curved blades on the sticks of Chicago superstars Bobby Hull and Stan Mikita before a practice at the Detroit Olympia on December 7, 1966. Hull and Mikita pushed the single-season records for goals, assists and points to new heights in the late 1960s, while Howe continued to add to his then-unprecedented career totals in those categories.

Nels Stewart led the NHL in both goals and points as a rookie with the Montreal Maroons in 1925-26 and continued to put up impressive numbers for that era throughout the course of his 15-year career. He was the first player in NHL history to reach the 300-goal plateau and his total of 324 remained a record for 12 years until being surpassed by Maurice Richard.

MOST REGULAR-SEASON ASSISTS, CAREER

(minimum 100 assists)

100 —Frank Boucher, Ottawa, NY Rangers.
In 1930-31, Boucher became the first NHL player to reach the 100-assist milestone.

263 —Frank Boucher, Ottawa, NY Rangers.
Boucher retired as the NHL's career assist leader in 1938 with 253. He returned to the NHL in 1943-44 and remained the NHL's career assist leader until he was overtaken by Bill Cowley in 1943-44. He finished his career with 263 assists.

353 —Bill Cowley, St. Louis Eagles, Boston.
Cowley passed Boucher with assist #264 in 1943-44. He retired as the NHL's career assist leader in 1947 with 353.

408 —Elmer Lach, Montreal.
Lach passed Cowley with assist #354 in 1951-52. He retired as the NHL's career assist leader in 1954 with 408.

1,049 —Gordie Howe, Detroit, Hartford.
Howe passed Lach with assist #409 in 1957-58. He retired as the NHL's career assist leader in 1980 with 1,049.

1,963 —Wayne Gretzky, Edmonton, Los Angeles, St. Louis, NY Rangers.
Gretzky passed Howe with assist #1,050 in 1987-88. He retired as the NHL's current career assist leader with 1,963.

MOST REGULAR-SEASON POINTS, CAREER

(minimum 100 points)

100 —Joe Malone, Montreal, Quebec Bulldogs, Hamilton.
In 1919-20, Malone became the first player in NHL history to record 100 points.

200 —Cy Denneny, Ottawa.
In 1923-24, Denneny became the first player in NHL history to record 200 points.

300 —Cy Denneny, Ottawa.
In 1926-27, Denneny became the first player in NHL history to record 300 points.

333 —Cy Denneny, Ottawa, Boston.
Denneny retired as the NHL's career point-scoring leader in 1929 with 333 points.

472 —Howie Morenz, Montreal, Chicago, NY Rangers.
Morenz passed Cy Denneny with point #334 in 1931-32. At the time his career ended in 1937, he was the NHL's career point- scoring leader with 472 points.

515 —Nels Stewart, Montreal Maroons, Boston, NY Americans.
Stewart passed Morenz with point #473 in 1938-39. He retired as the NHL's career point-scoring leader in 1940 with 515 points.

528 —Syd Howe, Ottawa, Philadelphia Quakers, Toronto, St. Louis Eagles, Detroit.
Howe passed Nels Stewart with point #516 on March 8, 1945.
He retired as the NHL's career point-scoring leader in 1946 with 528 points.

548 —Bill Cowley, St. Louis Eagles, Boston.
Cowley passed Syd Howe with point #529 on Feb. 12, 1947.
He retired as the NHL's career point-scoring leader in 1947 with 548 points.

610 —Elmer Lach, Montreal.
Lach passed Bill Cowley with point #549 on Feb. 23, 1952. He remained the NHL's career point-scoring leader until he was overtaken by Maurice Richard in 1953-54. He finished his career with 623 points.

946 —Maurice Richard, Montreal.
Richard passed teammate Elmer Lach with point #611 on Dec. 12, 1953. He remained the NHL's career point-scoring leader until he was overtaken by Gordie Howe in 1959-60. He finished his career with 965 points.

1,850 —Gordie Howe, Detroit, Hartford.
Howe passed Richard with point #947 on Jan. 16, 1960. He retired as the NHL's career point-scoring leader in 1980 with 1,850 points.

2,857 —Wayne Gretzky, Edmonton, Los Angeles, St. Louis, NY Rangers.
Gretzky passed Howe with point #1,851 on Oct. 15, 1989. He retired as the NHL's current career points leader with 2,857.

Individual Records

Regular Season

SEASONS

MOST SEASONS:
26 – Gordie Howe, Detroit, 1946-47 – 1970-71; Hartford, 1979-80.
– Chris Chelios, Montreal, Chicago, Detroit, Atlanta 1983-84 – 2003-04, 2005-06 – 2009-10.
25 – Mark Messier, Edmonton, NY Rangers, Vancouver, 1979-80 – 2003-04.
24 – Alex Delvecchio, Detroit, 1950-51 – 1973-74.
– Tim Horton, Toronto, NY Rangers, Pittsburgh, Buffalo, 1949-50, 1951-52 – 1973-74.
23 – John Bucyk, Detroit, Boston, 1955-56 – 1977-78.
– Ron Francis, Hartford, Pittsburgh, Carolina, Toronto, 1981-82 – 2003-04.
– Al MacInnis, Calgary, St. Louis, 1981-82 – 2003-04.
– Dave Andreychuk, Buffalo, Toronto, New Jersey, Boston, Colorado, Tampa Bay, 1982-83 – 2003-04, 2005-06.

GAMES

MOST GAMES:
1,767 – Gordie Howe, Detroit, 1946-47 – 1970-71; Hartford, 1979-80.
1,756 – Mark Messier, Edmonton, NY Rangers, Vancouver, 1979-80 – 2003-04.
1,731 – Ron Francis, Hartford, Pittsburgh, Carolina, Toronto, 1981-82 – 2003-04.
1,652 – Mark Recchi, Pittsburgh, Philadelphia, Montreal, Carolina, Tampa Bay, Boston, 1988-89 – 2003-04, 2005-06 – 2010-11.
1,651 – Chris Chelios, Montreal, Chicago, Detroit, Atlanta, 1983-84 – 2003-04, 2005-06 – 2009-10.
1,639 – Dave Andreychuk, Buffalo, Toronto, New Jersey, Boston, Colorado, Tampa Bay, 1982-83 – 2003-04, 2005-06.
1,635 – Scott Stevens, Washington, St. Louis, New Jersey, 1982-83 – 2003-04.

MOST GAMES, INCLUDING PLAYOFFS:
1,992 – Mark Messier, Edmonton, NY Rangers, Vancouver, 1,756 regular-season games, 236 playoff games.
1,924 – Gordie Howe, Detroit, Hartford, 1,767 regular-season games, 157 playoff games.
1,917 – Chris Chelios, Montreal, Chicago, Detroit, Atlanta, 1,651 regular-season games, 266 playoff games.
1,902 – Ron Francis, Hartford, Pittsburgh, Carolina, Toronto, 1,731 regular-season games, 171 playoff games.
1,868 – Scott Stevens, Washington, St. Louis, New Jersey, 1,635 regular-season games, 233 playoff games.

MOST CONSECUTIVE GAMES:
964 – Doug Jarvis, Montreal, Washington, Hartford, Oct. 8, 1975 – Oct. 10, 1987.
914 – Garry Unger, Toronto, Detroit, St. Louis, Atlanta, Feb. 24, 1968 – Dec. 21, 1979.
884 – Steve Larmer, Chicago, Oct. 6, 1982 – Apr. 15, 1993.
776 – Craig Ramsay, Buffalo, Mar. 27, 1973 – Feb. 10, 1983.
635 – Jay Bouwmeester, Florida, Calgary, St. Louis, Mar. 6, 2004 – Apr. 27, 2013.
630 – Andy Hebenton, NY Rangers, Boston, Oct. 7, 1955 – Mar. 22, 1964.

GOALS

MOST GOALS:
894 – Wayne Gretzky, Edmonton, Los Angeles, St. Louis, NY Rangers, in 20 seasons. 1,487GP
801 – Gordie Howe, Detroit, Hartford, in 26 seasons. 1,767GP
741 – Brett Hull, Calgary, St. Louis, Dallas, Detroit, Phoenix, in 19 seasons. 1,269GP
731 – Marcel Dionne, Detroit, Los Angeles, NY Rangers, in 18 seasons. 1,348GP
717 – Phil Esposito, Chicago, Boston, NY Rangers, in 18 seasons. 1,282GP

MOST GOALS, INCLUDING PLAYOFFS:
1,016 – Wayne Gretzky, Edmonton, Los Angeles, St. Louis, NY Rangers, 894G in 1,487 regular-season games, 122G in 208 playoff games.
869 – Gordie Howe, Detroit, Hartford, 801G in 1,767 regular-season games, 68G in 157 playoff games.
844 – Brett Hull, Calgary, St. Louis, Dallas, Detroit, Phoenix, 741G in 1,269 regular-season games, 103G in 202 playoff games.
803 – Mark Messier, Edmonton, NY Rangers, Vancouver, 694G in 1,756 regular-season games, 109G in 236 playoff games.
778 – Phil Esposito, Chicago, Boston, NY Rangers, 717G in 1,282 regular-season games, 61G in 130 playoff games.

MOST GOALS, ONE SEASON:
92 – Wayne Gretzky, Edmonton, 1981-82. 80GP – 80 game schedule.
87 – Wayne Gretzky, Edmonton, 1983-84. 74GP – 80 game schedule.
86 – Brett Hull, St. Louis, 1990-91. 78GP – 80 game schedule.
85 – Mario Lemieux, Pittsburgh, 1988-89. 76GP – 80 game schedule.
76 – Phil Esposito, Boston, 1970-71. 78GP – 78 game schedule.
– Alexander Mogilny, Buffalo, 1992-93. 77GP – 84 game schedule.
– Teemu Selanne, Winnipeg, 1992-93. 84GP – 84 game schedule.
73 – Wayne Gretzky, Edmonton, 1984-85. 80GP – 80 game schedule.
72 – Brett Hull, St. Louis, 1989-90. 80GP – 80 game schedule.
71 – Wayne Gretzky, Edmonton, 1982-83. 80GP – 80 game schedule.
– Jari Kurri, Edmonton, 1984-85. 73GP – 80 game schedule.
70 – Mario Lemieux, Pittsburgh, 1987-88. 77GP – 80 game schedule.
– Bernie Nicholls, Los Angeles, 1988-89. 79GP – 80 game schedule.
– Brett Hull, St. Louis, 1991-92. 73GP – 80 game schedule.

MOST GOALS, ONE SEASON, INCLUDING PLAYOFFS:
100 – Wayne Gretzky, Edmonton, 1983-84, 87G in 74 regular-season games, 13G in 19 playoff games.
97 – Wayne Gretzky, Edmonton, 1981-82, 92G in 80 regular-season games, 5G in 5 playoff games.
– Mario Lemieux, Pittsburgh, 1988-89, 85G in 76 regular-season games, 12G in 11 playoff games.
– Brett Hull, St. Louis, 1990-91, 86G in 78 regular-season games, 11G in 13 playoff games.
90 – Wayne Gretzky, Edmonton, 1984-85, 73G in 80 regular-season games, 17G in 18 playoff games.
– Jari Kurri, Edmonton, 1984-85, 71G in 80 regular-season games, 19G in 18 playoff games.
85 – Mike Bossy, NY Islanders, 1980-81, 68G in 79 regular-season games, 17G in 18 playoff games.
– Brett Hull, St. Louis, 1989-90, 72G in 80 regular-season games, 13G in 12 playoff games.
83 – Wayne Gretzky, Edmonton, 1982-83, 71G in 73 regular-season games, 12G in 16 playoff games.
– Alexander Mogilny, Buffalo, 1992-93, 76G in 77 regular-season games, 7G in 7 playoff games.

MOST GOALS, 50 GAMES FROM START OF SEASON:
61 – Wayne Gretzky, Edmonton, 1981-82. Oct. 7, 1981 – Jan. 22, 1982. (80-game schedule)
– Wayne Gretzky, Edmonton, 1983-84. Oct. 5, 1983 – Jan. 25, 1984. (80-game schedule)
54 – Mario Lemieux, Pittsburgh, 1988-89. Oct. 7, 1988 – Jan. 31, 1989. (80-game schedule)
53 – Wayne Gretzky, Edmonton, 1984-85. Oct. 11, 1984 – Jan. 28, 1985. (80-game schedule)
52 – Brett Hull, St. Louis, 1990-91. Oct. 4, 1990 – Jan. 26, 1991. (80-game schedule)
50 – Maurice Richard, Montreal, 1944-45. Oct. 28, 1944 – Mar. 18, 1945. (50-game schedule)
– Mike Bossy, NY Islanders, 1980-81. Oct. 11, 1980 – Jan. 24, 1981. (80-game schedule)
– Brett Hull, St. Louis, 1991-92. Oct. 5, 1991 – Jan. 28, 1992. (80-game schedule)

MOST GOALS, ONE GAME:
7 – Joe Malone, Quebec, Jan. 31, 1920, at Quebec. Quebec 10, Toronto 6.
6 – Newsy Lalonde, Montreal, Jan. 10, 1920, at Montreal. Montreal 14, Toronto 7.
– Joe Malone, Quebec, Mar. 10, 1920, at Quebec. Quebec 10, Ottawa 4.
– Corb Denneny, Toronto, Jan. 26, 1921, at Toronto. Toronto 10, Hamilton 3.
– Cy Denneny, Ottawa, Mar. 7, 1921, at Ottawa. Ottawa 12, Hamilton 5.
– Syd Howe, Detroit, Feb. 3, 1944, at Detroit. Detroit 12, NY Rangers 2.
– Red Berenson, St. Louis, Nov. 7, 1968, at Philadelphia. St. Louis 8, Philadelphia 0.
– Darryl Sittler, Toronto, Feb. 7, 1976, at Toronto. Toronto 11, Boston 4.

Though pictured in the uniform of the Montreal Canadiens, Joe Malone was with the Quebec Bulldogs when he scored seven goals in a single game on January 31, 1920. Malone's mark is the oldest in the NHL record book.

Wayne Gretzky slips the puck past Buffalo's Don Edwards with just under seven minutes remaining in the third period on February 24, 1982. It was Gretzky's record-breaking 77th goal of the season, scored in his 64th game. Gretzky added two more later in the match and pushed his total to 92 by season's end. This single-season goal-scoring record still stands.

MOST GOALS, ONE ROAD GAME:

6 – Red Berenson, St. Louis, Nov. 7, 1968, at Philadelphia. St. Louis 8, Philadelphia 0.
5 – Joe Malone, Montreal, Dec. 19, 1917, at Ottawa. Montreal 7, Ottawa 4.
– Red Green, Hamilton, Dec. 5, 1924, at Toronto. Hamilton 10, Toronto 3.
– Babe Dye, Toronto, Dec. 22, 1924, at Boston. Toronto 10, Boston 1.
– Punch Broadbent, Mtl. Maroons, Jan. 7, 1925, at Hamilton. Mtl. Maroons 6, Hamilton 2.
– Don Murdoch, NY Rangers, Oct. 12, 1976, at Minnesota. NY Rangers 10, Minnesota 4.
– Tim Young, Minnesota, Jan. 15, 1979, at NY Rangers. Minnesota 8, NY Rangers 1.
– Willy Lindstrom, Winnipeg, Mar. 2, 1982, at Philadelphia. Winnipeg 7, Philadelphia 6.
– Bengt Gustafsson, Washington, Jan. 8, 1984, at Philadelphia. Washington 7, Philadelphia 1.
– Wayne Gretzky, Edmonton, Dec. 15, 1984, at St. Louis. Edmonton 8, St. Louis 2.
– Dave Andreychuk, Buffalo, Feb. 6, 1986, at Boston. Buffalo 8, Boston 6.
– Mats Sundin, Quebec, Mar. 5, 1992, at Hartford. Quebec 10, Hartford 4.
– Mario Lemieux, Pittsburgh, Apr. 9, 1993, at NY Rangers. Pittsburgh 10, NY Rangers 4.
– Mike Ricci, Quebec, Feb. 17, 1994, at San Jose. Quebec 8, San Jose 2.
– Alex Zhamnov, Winnipeg, Apr. 1, 1995, at Los Angeles. Winnipeg 7, Los Angeles 7.
– Johan Franzem, Detroit, Feb 2, 2011, at Ottawa. Detroit 7, Ottawa 5.

MOST GOALS, ONE PERIOD:

4 – Busher Jackson, Toronto, Nov. 20, 1934, at St. Louis, third period. Toronto 5, St. Louis 2.
– Max Bentley, Chicago, Jan. 28, 1943, at Chicago, third period. Chicago 10, NY Rangers 1.
– Clint Smith, Chicago, Mar. 4, 1945, at Chicago, third period. Chicago 6, Montreal 4.
– Red Berenson, St. Louis, Nov. 7, 1968, at Philadelphia, second period. St. Louis 8, Philadelphia 0.
– Wayne Gretzky, Edmonton, Feb. 18, 1981, at Edmonton, third period. Edmonton 9, St. Louis 2.
– Grant Mulvey, Chicago, Feb. 3, 1982, at Chicago, first period. Chicago 9, St. Louis 5.
– Bryan Trottier, NY Islanders, Feb. 13, 1982, at NY Islanders, second period. NY Islanders 8, Philadelphia 2.
– Al Secord, Chicago, Jan. 7, 1987, at Chicago, second period. Chicago 6, Toronto 4.
– Joe Nieuwendyk, Calgary, Jan. 11, 1989, at Calgary, second period. Calgary 8, Winnipeg 3.
– Peter Bondra, Washington, Feb. 5, 1994, at Washington, first period. Washington 6, Tampa Bay 3.
– Mario Lemieux, Pittsburgh, Jan. 26, 1997, at Montreal, third period. Pittsburgh 5, Montreal 2.

ASSISTS

MOST ASSISTS:

1,963 – Wayne Gretzky, Edmonton, Los Angeles, St. Louis, NY Rangers, in 20 seasons. 1,487GP
1,249 – Ron Francis, Hartford, Pittsburgh, Carolina, Toronto, in 23 seasons. 1,731GP
1,193 – Mark Messier, Edmonton, NY Rangers, Vancouver, in 25 seasons. 1,756GP
1,169 – Raymond Bourque, Boston, Colorado, in 22 seasons. 1,612GP
1,135 – Paul Coffey, Edmonton, Pittsburgh, Los Angeles, Detroit, Hartford, Philadelphia, Chicago, Carolina, Boston, in 21 seasons. 1,409GP

MOST ASSISTS, INCLUDING PLAYOFFS:

2,223 – Wayne Gretzky, Edmonton, Los Angeles, St. Louis, NY Rangers, 1,963A in 1,487 regular-season games, 260A in 208 playoff games.
1,379 – Mark Messier, Edmonton, NY Rangers, Vancouver, 1,193A in 1,756 regular-season games, 186A in 236 playoff games.
1,346 – Ron Francis, Hartford, Pittsburgh, Carolina, Toronto, 1,249A in 1,731 regular-season games, 97A in 171 playoff games.
1,308 – Raymond Bourque, Boston, Colorado, 1,169A in 1,612 regular-season games, 139A in 214 playoff games.
1,272 – Paul Coffey, Edmonton, Pittsburgh, Los Angeles, Detroit, Hartford, Philadelphia, Chicago, Carolina, Boston, 1,135A in 1,409 regular-season games, 137A in 194 playoff games.

MOST ASSISTS, ONE SEASON:

163 – Wayne Gretzky, Edmonton, 1985-86. 80GP – 80 game schedule.
135 – Wayne Gretzky, Edmonton, 1984-85. 80GP – 80 game schedule.
125 – Wayne Gretzky, Edmonton, 1982-83. 80GP – 80 game schedule.
122 – Wayne Gretzky, Los Angeles, 1990-91. 78GP – 80 game schedule.
121 – Wayne Gretzky, Edmonton, 1986-87. 79GP – 80 game schedule.
120 – Wayne Gretzky, Edmonton, 1981-82. 80GP – 80 game schedule.
118 – Wayne Gretzky, Edmonton, 1983-84. 74GP – 80 game schedule.
114 – Mario Lemieux, Pittsburgh, 1988-89. 76GP – 80 game schedule.
– Wayne Gretzky, Los Angeles, 1988-89. 78GP – 80 game schedule.
109 – Wayne Gretzky, Edmonton, 1980-81. 80GP – 80 game schedule.
– Wayne Gretzky, Edmonton, 1987-88. 64GP – 80 game schedule.
102 – Bobby Orr, Boston, 1970-71. 78GP – 78 game schedule.
– Wayne Gretzky, Los Angeles, 1989-90. 73GP – 80 game schedule.

MOST ASSISTS, ONE SEASON, INCLUDING PLAYOFFS:

174 – Wayne Gretzky, Edmonton, 1985-86,
163A in 80 regular-season games, 11A in 10 playoff games.
165 – Wayne Gretzky, Edmonton, 1984-85,
135A in 80 regular-season games, 30A in 18 playoff games.
151 – Wayne Gretzky, Edmonton, 1982-83,
125A in 80 regular-season games, 26A in 16 playoff games.
150 – Wayne Gretzky, Edmonton, 1986-87,
121A in 79 regular-season games, 29A in 21 playoff games.
140 – Wayne Gretzky, Edmonton, 1983-84,
118A in 74 regular-season games, 22A in 19 playoff games.
– Wayne Gretzky, Edmonton, 1987-88,
109A in 64 regular-season games, 31A in 19 playoff games.
133 – Wayne Gretzky, Los Angeles, 1990-91,
122A in 78 regular-season games, 11A in 12 playoff games.
131 – Wayne Gretzky, Los Angeles, 1988-89,
114A in 78 regular-season games, 17A in 11 playoff games.
127 – Wayne Gretzky, Edmonton, 1981-82,
120A in 80 regular-season games, 7A in 5 playoff games.
123 – Wayne Gretzky, Edmonton, 1980-81,
109A in 80 regular-season games, 14A in 9 playoff games.
121 – Mario Lemieux, Pittsburgh, 1988-89,
114A in 76 regular-season games, 7A in 11 playoff games.

MOST ASSISTS, ONE GAME:

7 – Billy Taylor, Detroit, Mar. 16, 1947, at Chicago. Detroit 10, Chicago 6.
– Wayne Gretzky, Edmonton, Feb. 15, 1980, at Edmonton. Edmonton 8, Washington 2.
– Wayne Gretzky, Edmonton, Dec. 11, 1985, at Chicago. Edmonton 12, Chicago 9.
– Wayne Gretzky, Edmonton, Feb. 14, 1986, at Edmonton. Edmonton 8, Quebec 2.
6 – Six assists have been recorded in one game on 24 occasions since Elmer Lach of Montreal first accomplished the feat vs. Boston on Feb. 6, 1943. The most recent player is Eric Lindros of Philadelphia on Feb. 26, 1997 at Ottawa.

MOST ASSISTS, ONE ROAD GAME:

7 – Billy Taylor, Detroit, Mar. 16, 1947, at Chicago. Detroit 10, Chicago 6.
– Wayne Gretzky, Edmonton, Dec. 11, 1985, at Chicago. Edmonton 12, Chicago 9.
6 – Bobby Orr, Boston, Jan. 1, 1973, at Vancouver. Boston 8, Vancouver 2.
– Patrik Sundstrom, Vancouver, Feb. 29, 1984, at Pittsburgh. Vancouver 9, Pittsburgh 5.
– Mario Lemieux, Pittsburgh, Dec. 5, 1992, at San Jose. Pittsburgh 9, San Jose 4.
– Eric Lindros, Philadelphia, Feb. 26, 1997, at Ottawa. Philadelphia 8, Ottawa 5.

MOST ASSISTS, ONE PERIOD:

5 – Dale Hawerchuk, Winnipeg, Mar. 6, 1984, at Los Angeles, second period. Winnipeg 7, Los Angeles 3.
4 – Four assists have been recorded in one period on 70 occasions since Mickey Roach of Hamilton first accomplished the feat vs. Toronto on Feb. 23, 1921. The most recent player is Rostislav Klesla of Phoenix on Mar. 28, 2013 vs. Nashville.

POINTS

MOST POINTS:

2,857 – Wayne Gretzky, Edmonton, Los Angeles, St. Louis, NY Rangers, in 20 seasons. 1,487GP (894G-1,963A)
1,887 – Mark Messier, Edmonton, NY Rangers, Vancouver, in 25 seasons. 1,756GP (694G-1,193A)
1,850 – Gordie Howe, Detroit, Hartford, in 26 seasons. 1,767GP (801G-1,049A)
1,798 – Ron Francis, Hartford, Pittsburgh, Carolina, Toronto, in 23 seasons. 1,731GP (549G-1,249A)
1,771 – Marcel Dionne, Detroit, Los Angeles, NY Rangers, in 18 seasons. 1,348GP (731G-1,040A)

MOST POINTS, INCLUDING PLAYOFFS:

3,239 – Wayne Gretzky, Edmonton, Los Angeles, St. Louis, NY Rangers,
2,857PTS in 1,487 regular-season games, 382PTS in 208 playoff games.
2,182 – Mark Messier, Edmonton, NY Rangers, Vancouver,
1,887PTS in 1,756 regular-season games, 295PTS in 236 playoff games.
2,010 – Gordie Howe, Detroit, Hartford,
1,850PTS in 1,767 regular-season games, 160PTS in 157 playoff games.
1,941 – Ron Francis, Hartford, Pittsburgh, Carolina, Toronto,
1,798PTS in 1,731 regular-season games, 143PTS in 171 playoff games
1,940 – Steve Yzerman, Detroit,
1,755PTS in 1,514 regular-season games, 185PTS in 196 playoff games.

MOST POINTS, ONE SEASON:

215 – Wayne Gretzky, Edmonton, 1985-86. 80GP – 80 game schedule.
212 – Wayne Gretzky, Edmonton, 1981-82. 80GP – 80 game schedule.
208 – Wayne Gretzky, Edmonton, 1984-85. 80GP – 80 game schedule.
205 – Wayne Gretzky, Edmonton, 1983-84. 74GP – 80 game schedule.
199 – Mario Lemieux, Pittsburgh, 1988-89. 76GP – 80 game schedule.
196 – Wayne Gretzky, Edmonton, 1982-83. 80GP – 80 game schedule.
183 – Wayne Gretzky, Edmonton, 1986-87. 79GP – 80 game schedule.
168 – Mario Lemieux, Pittsburgh, 1987-88, 77GP – 80 game schedule.
– Wayne Gretzky, Los Angeles, 1988-89. 78GP – 80 game schedule.
164 – Wayne Gretzky, Edmonton, 1980-81. 80GP – 80 game schedule.
163 – Wayne Gretzky, Los Angeles, 1990-91. 78GP – 80 game schedule.
161 – Mario Lemieux, Pittsburgh, 1995-96. 70GP – 82 game schedule.
160 – Mario Lemieux, Pittsburgh, 1992-93. 60GP – 84 game schedule.

MOST POINTS, ONE SEASON, INCLUDING PLAYOFFS:

255 – Wayne Gretzky, Edmonton, 1984-85,
208PTS in 80 regular-season games, 47PTS in 18 playoff games.
240 – Wayne Gretzky, Edmonton, 1983-84,
205PTS in 74 regular-season games, 35PTS in 19 playoff games.
234 – Wayne Gretzky, Edmonton, 1982-83,
196PTS in 80 regular-season games, 38PTS in 16 playoff games.
– Wayne Gretzky, Edmonton, 1985-86,
215PTS in 80 regular-season games, 19PTS in 10 playoff games.
224 – Wayne Gretzky, Edmonton, 1981-82,
212PTS in 80 regular-season games, 12PTS in 5 playoff games.
218 – Mario Lemieux, Pittsburgh, 1988-89,
199PTS in 76 regular-season games, 19PTS in 11 playoff games.
217 – Wayne Gretzky, Edmonton, 1986-87,
183PTS in 79 regular-season games, 34PTS in 21 playoff games.
192 – Wayne Gretzky, Edmonton, 1987-88,
149PTS in 64 regular-season games, 43PTS in 19 playoff games.
190 – Wayne Gretzky, Los Angeles, 1988-89,
168PTS in 78 regular-season games, 22PTS in 11 playoff games.
188 – Mario Lemieux, Pittsburgh, 1995-96,
161PTS in 70 regular-season games, 27PTS in 18 playoff games.
185 – Wayne Gretzky, Edmonton, 1980-81,
164PTS in 80 regular-season games, 21PTS in 9 playoff games.

MOST POINTS, ONE GAME:

10 – Darryl Sittler, Toronto, Feb. 7, 1976, at Toronto, 6G-4A. Toronto 11, Boston 4.
8 – Maurice Richard, Montreal, Dec. 28, 1944, at Montreal, 5G-3A. Montreal 9, Detroit 1.
– Bert Olmstead, Montreal, Jan. 9, 1954, at Montreal, 4G-4A. Montreal 12, Chicago 1.
– Tom Bladon, Philadelphia, Dec. 11, 1977, at Philadelphia, 4G-4A. Philadelphia 11, Cleveland 1.
– Bryan Trottier, NY Islanders, Dec. 23, 1978, at NY Islanders, 5G-3A. NY Islanders 9, NY Rangers 4.
– Peter Stastny, Quebec, Feb. 22, 1981, at Washington, 4G-4A. Quebec 11, Washington 7.
– Anton Stastny, Quebec, Feb. 22, 1981, at Washington, 3G-5A. Quebec 11, Washington 7.
– Wayne Gretzky, Edmonton, Nov. 19, 1983, at Edmonton, 3G-5A. Edmonton 13, New Jersey 4.
– Wayne Gretzky, Edmonton, Jan. 4, 1984, at Edmonton, 4G-4A. Edmonton 12, Minnesota 8.
– Paul Coffey, Edmonton, Mar. 14, 1986, at Edmonton, 2G-6A. Edmonton 12, Detroit 3.
– Mario Lemieux, Pittsburgh, Oct. 15, 1988, at Pittsburgh, 2G-6A. Pittsburgh 9, St. Louis 2.
– Bernie Nicholls, Los Angeles, Dec. 1, 1988, at Los Angeles, 2G-6A. Los Angeles 9, Toronto 3.
– Mario Lemieux, Pittsburgh, Dec. 31, 1988, at Pittsburgh, 5G-3A. Pittsburgh 8, New Jersey 6.
– Sam Gagner, Edmonton, Feb. 2, 2012, at Edmonton. 4G-4A.

MOST POINTS, ONE ROAD GAME:

8 – Peter Stastny, Quebec, Feb. 22, 1981, at Washington. 4G-4A. Quebec 11, Washington 7.
– Anton Stastny, Quebec, Feb. 22, 1981, at Washington. 3G-5A. Quebec 11, Washington 7.
7 – Red Green, Hamilton, Dec. 5, 1924, at Toronto. 5G-2A. Hamilton 10, Toronto 3.
– Billy Taylor, Detroit, Mar. 16, 1947, at Chicago. 7A. Detroit 10, Chicago 6.
– Red Berenson, St. Louis, Nov. 7, 1968, at Philadelphia. 6G-1A. St. Louis 8, Philadelphia 0.
– Gilbert Perreault, Buffalo, Feb. 1, 1976, at California. 2G-5A. Buffalo 9, California 5.
– Peter Stastny, Quebec, Apr. 1, 1982, at Boston. 3G-4A. Quebec 8, Boston 5.
– Wayne Gretzky, Edmonton, Nov. 6, 1983, at Winnipeg. 4G-3A. Edmonton 8, Winnipeg 5.
– Patrik Sundstrom, Vancouver, Feb. 29, 1984, at Pittsburgh. 1G-6A. Vancouver 9, Pittsburgh 5.
– Wayne Gretzky, Edmonton, Dec. 11, 1985, at Chicago. 7A. Edmonton 12, Chicago 9.
– Cam Neely, Boston, Oct. 16, 1988, at Chicago. 3G-4A. Boston 10, Chicago 3.
– Mario Lemieux, Pittsburgh, Jan. 21, 1989, at Edmonton. 2G-5A. Pittsburgh 7, Edmonton 4.
– Dino Ciccarelli, Washington, Mar. 18, 1989, at Hartford. 4G-3A. Washington 8, Hartford 2.
– Mats Sundin, Quebec, Mar. 5, 1992, at Hartford. 5G-2A. Quebec 10, Hartford 4.
– Mario Lemieux, Pittsburgh, Dec. 5, 1992, at San Jose. 1G-6A. Pittsburgh 9, San Jose 4.
– Eric Lindros, Philadelphia, Feb. 26, 1997, at Ottawa. 1G-6A. Philadelphia 8, Ottawa 5.
– Daniel Alfredsson, Ottawa, Jan. 24, 2008, at Tampa Bay. 3G-4A. Ottawa 8, Tampa Bay 4.

MOST POINTS, ONE PERIOD:
6 – Bryan Trottier, NY Islanders, Dec. 23, 1978, at NY Islanders, second period. 3G-3A. NY Islanders 9, NY Rangers 4.
5 – Bill Cook, NY Rangers, Mar. 12, 1933, at NY Americans, third period. 3G-2A. NY Rangers 8, NY Americans 2.
– Les Cunningham, Chicago, Jan. 28, 1940, at Chicago, third period. 2G-3A. Chicago 8, Montreal 1.
– Max Bentley, Chicago, Jan. 28, 1943, at Chicago, third period. 4G-1A. Chicago 10, NY Rangers 1.
– Leo Labine, Boston, Nov. 28, 1954, at Boston, second period. 3G-2A. Boston 6, Detroit 2.
– Darryl Sittler, Toronto, Feb. 7, 1976, at Toronto, second period. 3G-2A. Toronto 11, Boston 4.
– Grant Mulvey, Chicago, Feb. 3, 1982, at Chicago, first period. 4G-1A. Chicago 9, St. Louis 5.
– Dale Hawerchuk, Winnipeg, Mar. 6, 1984, at Los Angeles, second period. 5A. Winnipeg 7, Los Angeles 3.
– Jari Kurri, Edmonton, Oct. 26, 1984, at Edmonton, second period. 2G-3A. Edmonton 8, Los Angeles 2.
– Pat Elynuik, Winnipeg, Jan. 20, 1989, at Winnipeg, second period. 2G-3A. Winnipeg 7, Pittsburgh 3.
– Ray Ferraro, Hartford, Dec. 9, 1989, at Hartford, first period. 3G-2A. Hartford 7, New Jersey 3.
– Stephane Richer, Montreal, Feb. 14, 1990, at Montreal, first period. 2G-3A. Montreal 10, Vancouver 1.
– Cliff Ronning, Vancouver, Apr. 15, 1993, at Los Angeles, third period. 3G-2A. Vancouver 8, Los Angeles 6.
– Peter Forsberg, Colorado, Mar. 3, 1999, at Florida, third period. 2G-3A. Colorado 7, Florida 5.
– Sam Gagner, Edmonton, Feb. 2, 2012, at Edmonton, third period 3G-2A.

POWER-PLAY AND SHORTHAND GOALS

MOST POWER-PLAY GOALS, CAREER:
274 – Dave Andreychuk, Buffalo, Toronto, New Jersey, Boston, Colorado, Tampa Bay, in 23 seasons. 1,639GP
265 – Brett Hull, Calgary, St. Louis, Dallas, Detroit, Phoenix, in 19 seasons. 1,269GP
251 – Teemu Selanne, Winnipeg, Anaheim, San Jose, Colorado, in 21 seasons. 1,387GP
249 – Phil Esposito, Chicago, Boston, NY Rangers, in 18 seasons. 1,282GP

MOST POWER-PLAY GOALS, ONE SEASON:
34 – Tim Kerr, Philadelphia, 1985-86. 76GP – 80 game schedule.
32 – Dave Andreychuk, Buffalo, Toronto, 1992-93. 83GP – 84 game schedule.
31 – Joe Nieuwendyk, Calgary, 1987-88. 75GP – 80 game schedule.
– Mario Lemieux, Pittsburgh, 1988-89. 76GP – 80 game schedule.
– Mario Lemieux, Pittsburgh, 1995-96. 70GP – 82 game schedule.
29 – Michel Goulet, Quebec, 1987-88. 80GP – 80 game schedule.
– Brett Hull, St. Louis, 1990-91. 78GP – 80 game schedule.
– Brett Hull, St. Louis, 1992-93. 80GP – 84 game schedule.

MOST POWER-PLAY GOALS, ONE GAME
4 – Camille Henry, NY Rangers, Mar. 13, 1954, at Detroit. NY Rangers 5, Detroit 2.
– Bernie Geoffrion, Montreal, Feb. 19, 1955, at Montreal. Montreal 10, NY Rangers 2.
– Bryan Trottier, NY Islanders, Feb. 13, 1982, at NY Islanders. NY Islanders 8, Philadephia 2.
– Chris Valentine, Washington, Feb. 27, 1982, at Washington. Washington 7, Hartford 1.
– Dave Andreychuk, Buffalo, Mar. 19, 1992, at Los Angeles. Buffalo 8, Los Angeles 2.
– Mario Lemieux, Pittsburgh, Mar. 20, 1993, at Pittsburgh. Pittsburgh 9, Philadelphia 3.
– Luc Robitaille, Los Angeles, Nov. 25, 1993, at Quebec. Quebec 8, Los Angeles 6.
– Scott Mellanby, St. Louis, Mar. 6, 2003, at St. Louis. St. Louis 6, Phoenix 3.

MOST SHORTHAND GOALS, ONE SEASON:
13 – Mario Lemieux, Pittsburgh, 1988-89. 76GP – 80 game schedule.
12 – Wayne Gretzky, Edmonton, 1983-84. 74GP – 80 game schedule.
11 – Wayne Gretzky, Edmonton, 1984-85. 80GP – 80 game schedule.
10 – Marcel Dionne, Detroit, 1974-75. 80GP – 80 game schedule.
– Mario Lemieux, Pittsburgh, 1987-88. 77GP – 80 game schedule.
– Dirk Graham, Chicago, 1988-89. 80GP – 80 game schedule.

MOST SHORTHAND GOALS, ONE GAME:
3 – Theoren Fleury, Calgary, Mar. 9, 1991, at St. Louis. Calgary 8, St. Louis 4.

OVERTIME SCORING

MOST OVERTIME GOALS, CAREER:
17 – Jaromir Jagr, Pittsburgh, Washington, NY Rangers, Philadelphia, Dallas.
15 – Mats Sundin, Quebec, Toronto.
– Sergei Fedorov, Detroit, Anaheim, Columbus, Washington.
– Patrik Elias, New Jersey.
14 – Ilya Kovalchuk, Atlanta, New Jersey.
13 – Steve Thomas, Toronto, Chicago, NY Islanders, New Jersey, Anaheim.
– Olli Jokinen, Los Angeles, NY Islanders, Florida, NY Rangers.
– Scott Niedermayer, New Jersey, Anaheim.
12 – Nels Stewart, Mtl. Maroons, Boston, NY Americans.
– Brett Hull, Calgary, St. Louis, Dallas, Detroit, Phoenix.
– Brendan Shanahan, New Jersey, St. Louis, Hartford, Detroit, NY Rangers.
– Alex Ovechkin, Washington.

MOST OVERTIME ASSISTS, CAREER:
21 – Nicklas Lidstrom, Detroit.
18 – Mark Messier, Edmonton, NY Rangers, Vancouver.
– Pavol Demitra, Ottawa, St. Louis, Los Angeles, Minnesota, Vancouver.
– Tomas Kaberle, Toronto.
– Patrik Elias, New Jersey.
17 – Adam Oates, Detroit, St. Louis, Boston, Washington, Philadelphia, Anaheim.
– Cory Stillman, Calgary, St. Louis, Tampa Bay, Carolina, Ottawa, Florida.
– Ray Whitney, San Jose, Edmonton, Florida, Columbus, Detroit, Carolina, Phoenix.

MOST OVERTIME POINTS, CAREER:
33 – Patrik Elias, New Jersey. 15G-18A
31 – Sergei Fedorov, Detroit, Anaheim, Columbus, Washington. 15G-16A
29 – Jaromir Jagr, Pittsburgh, Washington, NY Rangers, Philadelphia, Dallas. 17G-12A
– Ilya Kovalchuk, Atlanta, New Jersey. 14G-15A
28 – Mats Sundin, Quebec, Toronto. 15G-13A
27 – Pavol Demitra, Ottawa, St. Louis, Los Angeles, Minnesota, Vancouver. 9G-18A
26 – Mark Messier, Edmonton, NY Rangers, Vancouver. 8G-18A
25 – Tomas Kaberle, Toronto, Boston. 7G-18A
– Nicklas Lidstrom, Detroit. 4G-21A

MOST OVERTIME GOALS, ONE SEASON:
5 – Steven Stamkos, Tampa Bay, 2011-12.
4 – Howie Morenz, Montreal, 1929-30.
– Frank Finnigan, Ottawa, 1929-30.
– Johnny Gagnon, Montreal 1936-37.
– Mats Sundin, Toronto, 1999-2000.
– Scott Niedermayer, New Jersey, 2001-02.
– Patrik Elias, New Jersey, 2003-04.
– Markus Naslund, Vancouver, 2003-04.
– Olli Jokinen, Florida, 2005-06.
– Daniel Sedin, Vancouver, 2006-07.
– Ilya Kovalchuk, New Jersey, 2010-11.

SHOOTOUT GOALS

MOST SHOOTOUT GOALS, ONE SEASON:
11 – Ilya Kovalchuk, New Jersey, 2011-12. 14S
10 – Wojtek Wolski, Colorado, 2008-09. 12S
– Jussi Jokinen, Dallas, 2005-06. 13S
– Alex Tanguay, Calgary, 2010-11. 16S

MOST SHOOTOUT GOALS, ALL-TIME:
33 – Pavel Datsyuk, Detroit. 72S
32 – Zach Parise, New Jersey. 69S
31 – Jussi Jokinen, Dallas, Tampa Bay, Carolina, Pittsburgh. 67S
– Brad Boyes, Boston, St. Louis, Buffalo, NY Islanders. 70S

MOST SHOOTOUT SHOTS TAKEN, ONE SEASON:
18 – Radim Vrbata, Phoenix, 2009-10. 8G
17 – Lauri Korpikoski, Phoenix, 2009-10. 7G
– Jack Johnson, Los Angeles, 2009-10. 6G
– Sam Gagner, Edmonton, 2007-08. 5G

MOST SHOOTOUT SHOTS TAKEN, ALL-TIME:
74 – Rick Nash, Columbus, NY Rangers. 29G
72 – Pavel Datsyuk, Detroit. 33G
– Brad Richards, Tampa Bay, Dallas, NY Rangers. 26G
70 – Brad Boyes, Boston, St. Louis, Buffalo, NY Islanders. 31G
– Mikko Koivu, Minnesota. 30G
– Radim Vrbata, Carolina, Chicago, Phoenix, Tampa Bay. 30G

BEST SHOOTOUT SCORING PERCENTAGE, ONE SEASON: *minimum 5 shots*
.900 – Jarret Stoll, Los Angeles, 2010-11. 9G-10S
.857 – Petteri Nummelin, Minnesota, 2006-07. 6G-7S
.833 – Wojtek Wolski, Colorado, 2008-09. 10G-12S
– Daniel Alfredsson, Ottawa, 2011-12. 5G-6S
– Patrik Elias, New Jersey, 2007-08. 5G-6S
– Matt Hendricks, Washington, 2011-12. 5G-6S
– Thomas Vanek, Buffalo, 2010-11. 5G-6S

BEST SHOOTOUT SCORING PERCENTAGE, CAREER: *minimum 10 shots*
.800 – Petteri Nummelin, Minnesota. 8G-10S
.600 – Matt Hendricks, Colorado, Washington. 9G-12S
.587 – Vyacheslav Kozlov, Atlanta. 27G-46S
.583 – Trevor Linden, Vancouver. 7G-12S

MOST GAME DECIDING SHOOTOUT GOALS, ONE SEASON:
7 – Ilya Kovalchuk, New Jersey, 2011-12. 14S
6 – Adrian Aucoin, Phoenix, 2009-10. 9S
5 – Miroslav Satan, NY Islanders, 2005-06. 10S
– Vyacheslav Kozlov, Atlanta, 2006-07. 11S
– Viktor Kozlov, New Jersey, 2005-06. 12S
– Phil Kessel, Boston, 2007-08. 13S
– Ales Kotalik, Buffalo, Edmonton, 2008-09. 13S

MOST GAME DECIDING SHOOTOUT GOALS, CAREER:
13 – Phil Kessel, Boston, Toronto. 52S
– Sidney Crosby, Pittsburgh. 54S
– Erik Christensen, Pittsburgh, Atlanta, Anaheim, NY Rangers, Minnesota. 55S
– Patrick Kane, Chicago. 66S

SCORING BY A CENTER

MOST GOALS BY A CENTER, CAREER:
894 – Wayne Gretzky, Edmonton, Los Angeles, St. Louis, NY Rangers, in 20 seasons. 1,487GP
731 – Marcel Dionne, Detroit, Los Angeles, NY Rangers, in 18 seasons. 1,348GP
717 – Phil Esposito, Chicago, Boston, NY Rangers, in 18 seasons. 1,282GP
694 – Mark Messier, Edmonton, NY Rangers, Vancouver, in 25 seasons. 1,756GP
692 – Steve Yzerman, Detroit, in 22 seasons. 1,514GP

MOST GOALS BY A CENTER, ONE SEASON:
92 – Wayne Gretzky, Edmonton, 1981-82. 80GP – 80 game schedule.
87 – Wayne Gretzky, Edmonton, 1983-84. 74GP – 80 game schedule.
85 – Mario Lemieux, Pittsburgh, 1988-89. 76GP – 80 game schedule.
76 – Phil Esposito, Boston, 1970-71. 78GP – 78 game schedule.
73 – Wayne Gretzky, Edmonton, 1984-85. 80GP – 80 game schedule.

MOST ASSISTS BY A CENTER, CAREER:
1,963 – Wayne Gretzky, Edmonton, Los Angeles, St. Louis, NY Rangers, in 20 seasons. 1,487GP
1,249 – Ron Francis, Hartford, Pittsburgh, Carolina, Toronto, in 23 seasons. 1,731GP
1,193 – Mark Messier, Edmonton, NY Rangers, Vancouver, in 25 seasons. 1,756GP
1,079 – Adam Oates, Detroit, St. Louis, Boston, Washington, Philadelphia, Anaheim, Edmonton, in 19 seasons. 1,337GP
1,063 – Steve Yzerman, Detroit, in 22 seasons. 1,514GP

MOST ASSISTS BY A CENTER, ONE SEASON:
163 – Wayne Gretzky, Edmonton, 1985-86. 80GP – 80 game schedule.
135 – Wayne Gretzky, Edmonton, 1984-85. 80GP – 80 game schedule.
125 – Wayne Gretzky, Edmonton, 1982-83. 80GP – 80 game schedule.
122 – Wayne Gretzky, Los Angeles, 1990-91. 78GP – 80 game schedule.
121 – Wayne Gretzky, Edmonton, 1986-87. 79GP – 80 game schedule.

MOST POINTS BY A CENTER, CAREER:
2,857 – Wayne Gretzky, Edmonton, Los Angeles, St. Louis, NY Rangers, in 20 seasons. 1,487GP (894G-1,963A)
1,887 – Mark Messier, Edmonton, NY Rangers, Vancouver, in 25 seasons. 1,756GP (694G-1,193A)
1,798 – Ron Francis, Hartford, Pittsburgh, Carolina, Toronto, in 23 seasons. 1,731GP (549G-1,249A)
1,771 – Marcel Dionne, Detroit, Los Angeles, NY Rangers, in 18 seasons. 1,348GP (731G-1,040A)
1,755 – Steve Yzerman, Detroit, in 22 seasons. 1,514GP (692G-1,063A)

MOST POINTS BY A CENTER, ONE SEASON:
215 – Wayne Gretzky, Edmonton, 1985-86. 80GP – 80 game schedule.
212 – Wayne Gretzky, Edmonton, 1981-82. 80GP – 80 game schedule.
208 – Wayne Gretzky, Edmonton, 1984-85. 80GP – 80 game schedule.
205 – Wayne Gretzky, Edmonton, 1983-84. 74GP – 80 game schedule.
199 – Mario Lemieux, Pittsburgh, 1988-89. 76GP – 80 game schedule.

SCORING BY A LEFT WING

MOST GOALS BY A LEFT WING, CAREER:
668 – Luc Robitaille, Los Angeles, Pittsburgh, NY Rangers, Detroit, in 19 seasons. 1,431GP
656 – Brendan Shanahan, New Jersey, St. Louis, Hartford, Detroit, NY Rangers, in 21 seasons. 1,524GP
640 – Dave Andreychuk, Buffalo, Toronto, New Jersey, Boston, Colorado, Tampa Bay, in 23 seasons. 1,639GP
610 – Bobby Hull, Chicago, Winnipeg, Hartford, in 16 seasons. 1,063GP
556 – John Bucyk, Detroit, Boston, in 23 seasons. 1,540GP

Bobby Hull became just the second player in NHL history (after Gordie Howe) to reach the 600-goal plateau during the 1971-72 season. Sixteen others have topped 600 since, but Hull still ranks fourth among left wingers.

MOST GOALS BY A LEFT WING, ONE SEASON:
65 – Alex Ovechkin, Washington, 2007-08. 82GP – 82 game schedule.
63 – Luc Robitaille, Los Angeles, 1992-93. 84GP – 84 game schedule.
60 – Steve Shutt, Montreal, 1976-77. 80GP – 80 game schedule.
58 – Bobby Hull, Chicago, 1968-69. 74GP – 76 game schedule.
57 – Michel Goulet, Quebec, 1982-83. 80GP – 80 game schedule.

MOST ASSISTS BY A LEFT WING, CAREER:
813 – John Bucyk, Detroit, Boston, in 23 seasons. 1,540GP
726 – Luc Robitaille, Los Angeles, Pittsburgh, NY Rangers, Detroit, in 19 seasons. 1,431GP
698 – Dave Andreychuk, Buffalo, Toronto, New Jersey, Boston, Colorado, Tampa Bay, in 23 seasons. 1,639GP
– Brendan Shanahan, New Jersey, St. Louis, Hartford, Detroit, NY Rangers, in 21 seasons. 1,524GP
656 – Ray Whitney, San Jose, Edmonton, Florida, Columbus, Detroit, Carolina, Phoenix, Dallas, in 21 seasons. 1,261GP
604 – Michel Goulet, Quebec, Chicago, in 15 seasons. 1,089GP

MOST ASSISTS BY A LEFT WING, ONE SEASON:
70 – Joe Juneau, Boston, 1992-93. 84GP – 84 game schedule.
69 – Kevin Stevens, Pittsburgh, 1991-92. 80GP – 80 game schedule.
67 – Mats Naslund, Montreal, 1985-86. 80GP – 80 game schedule.
65 – John Bucyk, Boston, 1970-71. 78GP – 78 game schedule.
– Michel Goulet, Quebec, 1983-84. 75GP – 80 game schedule.
64 – Mark Messier, Edmonton, 1983-84. 73GP – 80 game schedule.

MOST POINTS BY A LEFT WING, CAREER:
1,394 – Luc Robitaille, Los Angeles, Pittsburgh, NY Rangers, Detroit, in 19 seasons. 1,431GP (668G-726A)
1,369 – John Bucyk, Detroit, Boston, in 23 seasons. 1,540GP (556G-813A)
1,354 – Brendan Shanahan, New Jersey, St. Louis, Hartford, Detroit, NY Rangers, in 21 seasons. 1,524GP (656G-698A)
1,338 – Dave Andreychuk, Buffalo, Toronto, New Jersey, Boston, Colorado, Tampa Bay, in 23 seasons. 1,639GP (640G-698A)
1,170 – Bobby Hull, Chicago, Winnipeg, Hartford, in 16 seasons. 1,063GP (610G-560A)

MOST POINTS BY A LEFT WING, ONE SEASON:
125 – Luc Robitaille, Los Angeles, 1992-93. 84GP – 84 game schedule.
123 – Kevin Stevens, Pittsburgh, 1991-92. 80GP – 80 game schedule.
121 – Michel Goulet, Quebec, 1983-84. 75GP – 80 game schedule.
116 – John Bucyk, Boston, 1970-71. 78GP – 78 game schedule.
112 – Bill Barber, Philadelphia, 1975-76. 80GP – 80 game schedule.
– Alex Ovechkin, Washington, 2007-08. 82GP – 82 game schedule.

SCORING BY A RIGHT WING

MOST GOALS BY A RIGHT WING, CAREER:
801 – Gordie Howe, Detroit, Hartford, in 26 seasons. 1,767GP
741 – Brett Hull, Calgary, St. Louis, Dallas, Detroit, Phoenix, in 19 seasons. 1,269GP
708 – Mike Gartner, Washington, Minnesota, NY Rangers, Toronto, Phoenix, in 19 seasons. 1,432GP
681 – Jaromir Jagr, Pittsburgh, Washington, NY Rangers, Philadelphia, Dallas, Boston, in 19 seasons. 1,391GP
675 – Teemu Selanne, Winnipeg, Anaheim, San Jose, Colorado, in 20 seasons. 1,387GP
608 – Dino Ciccarelli, Minnesota, Washington, Detroit, Tampa Bay, Florida, in 19 seasons. 1,232GP

MOST GOALS BY A RIGHT WING, ONE SEASON:
86 – Brett Hull, St. Louis, 1990-91. 78GP – 80 game schedule.
76 – Alexander Mogilny, Buffalo, 1992-93. 77GP – 84 game schedule.
– Teemu Selanne, Winnipeg, 1992-93. 84GP – 84 game schedule.
72 – Brett Hull, St. Louis, 1989-90. 80GP – 80 game schedule.
71 – Jari Kurri, Edmonton, 1984-85. 73GP – 80 game schedule.
70 – Brett Hull, St. Louis, 1991-92. 73GP – 80 game schedule.

MOST ASSISTS BY A RIGHT WING, CAREER:
1,049 – Gordie Howe, Detroit, Hartford, in 26 seasons. 1,767GP
1,007 – Jaromir Jagr, Pittsburgh, Washington, NY Rangers, Philadelphia, Dallas, Boston, in 19 seasons. 1,391GP
956 – Mark Recchi, Pittsburgh, Philadelphia, Montreal, Carolina, Atlanta, Boston, in 22 seasons. 1,652GP
797 – Jari Kurri, Edmonton, Los Angeles, NY Rangers, Anaheim, Colorado, in 17 seasons. 1,251GP
793 – Guy Lafleur, Montreal, NY Rangers, Quebec, in 17 seasons. 1,126GP

MOST ASSISTS BY A RIGHT WING, ONE SEASON:
87 – Jaromir Jagr, Pittsburgh, 1995-96. 82GP – 82 game schedule.
83 – Mike Bossy, NY Islanders, 1981-82. 80GP – 80 game schedule.
– Jaromir Jagr, Pittsburgh, 1998-99. 81GP – 82 game schedule.
80 – Guy Lafleur, Montreal, 1976-77. 80GP – 80 game schedule.
77 – Guy Lafleur, Montreal, 1978-79. 80GP – 80 game schedule.

MOST POINTS BY A RIGHT WING, CAREER:
1,850 – Gordie Howe, Detroit, Hartford, in 26 seasons. 1,767GP (801G-1,049A)
1,688 – Jaromir Jagr, Pittsburgh, Washington, NY Rangers, Philadelphia, Dallas, Boston, in 19 seasons. 1,391GP (681G-1,007A)
1,533 – Mark Recchi, Pittsburgh, Philadelphia, Montreal, Carolina, Atlanta, Boston, in 22 seasons. 1,652GP (577G-956A)
1,430 – Teemu Selanne, Winnipeg, Anaheim, San Jose, Colorado, in 20 seasons. 1,387GP (675G-755A)
1,398 – Jari Kurri, Edmonton, Los Angeles, NY Rangers, Anaheim, Colorado, in 17 seasons. 1,251GP (601G-797A)
1,391 – Brett Hull, Calgary, St. Louis, Dallas, Detroit, Phoenix, in 19 seasons. 1,269GP (741G-650A)

MOST POINTS BY A RIGHT WING, ONE SEASON:
149 – Jaromir Jagr, Pittsburgh, 1995-96. 82GP – 82 game schedule.
147 – Mike Bossy, NY Islanders, 1981-82. 80GP – 80 game schedule.
136 – Guy Lafleur, Montreal, 1976-77. 80GP – 80 game schedule.
135 – Jari Kurri, Edmonton, 1984-85. 73GP – 80 game schedule.
132 – Guy Lafleur, Montreal, 1977-78. 78GP – 80 game schedule.
– Teemu Selanne, Winnipeg, 1992-93. 84GP – 84 game schedule.

SCORING BY A DEFENSEMAN

MOST GOALS BY A DEFENSEMAN, CAREER:
410 – Raymond Bourque, Boston, Colorado, in 22 seasons. 1,612GP
396 – Paul Coffey, Edmonton, Pittsburgh, Los Angeles, Detroit, Hartford, Philadelphia, Chicago, Carolina, Boston, in 21 seasons. 1,409GP
340 – Al MacInnis, Calgary, St. Louis, in 23 seasons. 1,416GP
338 – Phil Housley, Buffalo, Winnipeg, St. Louis, Calgary, New Jersey, Washington, Chicago, Toronto, in 21 seasons. 1,495GP
310 – Denis Potvin, NY Islanders, in 15 seasons. 1,060GP

MOST GOALS BY A DEFENSEMAN, ONE SEASON:
48 – Paul Coffey, Edmonton, 1985-86. 79GP – 80 game schedule.
46 – Bobby Orr, Boston, 1974-75. 80GP – 80 game schedule.
40 – Paul Coffey, Edmonton, 1983-84. 80GP – 80 game schedule.
39 – Doug Wilson, Chicago, 1981-82. 76GP – 80 game schedule.
37 – Bobby Orr, Boston, 1970-71. 78GP – 78 game schedule.
– Bobby Orr, Boston, 1971-72. 76GP – 78 game schedule.
– Paul Coffey, Edmonton, 1984-85. 80GP – 80 game schedule.

MOST GOALS BY A DEFENSEMAN, ONE GAME:
5 – Ian Turnbull, Toronto, Feb. 2, 1977, at Toronto. Toronto 9, Detroit 1.
4 – Harry Cameron, Toronto, Dec. 26, 1917, at Toronto. Toronto 7, Montreal 5.
– Harry Cameron, Montreal, Mar. 3, 1920, at Quebec. Montreal 16, Quebec 3.
– Sprague Cleghorn, Montreal, Jan. 14, 1922, at Montreal. Montreal 10, Hamilton 6.
– John McKinnon, Pittsburgh, Nov. 19, 1929, at Pittsburgh. Pittsburgh 10, Toronto 5.
– Hap Day, Toronto, Nov. 19, 1929, at Pittsburgh. Pittsburgh 10, Toronto 5.
– Tom Bladon, Philadelphia, Dec. 11, 1977, at Philadelphia. Philadelphia 11, Cleveland 1.
– Ian Turnbull, Los Angeles, Dec. 12, 1981, at Los Angeles. Los Angeles 7, Vancouver 5.
– Paul Coffey, Edmonton, Oct. 26, 1984, at Calgary. Edmonton 6, Calgary 5.

MOST ASSISTS BY A DEFENSEMAN, CAREER:
1,169 – Raymond Bourque, Boston, Colorado, in 22 seasons. 1,612GP
1,135 – Paul Coffey, Edmonton, Pittsburgh, Los Angeles, Detroit, Hartford, Philadelphia, Chicago, Carolina, Boston, in 21 seasons. 1,409GP
934 – Al MacInnis, Calgary, St. Louis, in 23 seasons. 1,416GP
929 – Larry Murphy, Los Angeles, Washington, Minnesota, Pittsburgh, Toronto, Detroit, in 21 seasons. 1,615GP
894 – Phil Housley, Buffalo, Winnipeg, St. Louis, Calgary, New Jersey, Washington, Chicago, Toronto, in 21 seasons. 1,495GP

MOST ASSISTS BY A DEFENSEMAN, ONE SEASON:
102 – Bobby Orr, Boston, 1970-71. 78GP – 78 game schedule.
90 – Bobby Orr, Boston, 1973-74. 74GP – 78 game schedule.
– Paul Coffey, Edmonton, 1985-86. 79GP – 80 game schedule.
89 – Bobby Orr, Boston, 1974-75. 80GP – 80 game schedule.
87 – Bobby Orr, Boston, 1969-70. 76GP – 78 game schedule.

MOST ASSISTS BY A DEFENSEMAN, ONE GAME:
6 – Babe Pratt, Toronto, Jan. 8, 1944, at Toronto. Toronto 12, Boston 3.
– Pat Stapleton, Chicago, Mar. 30, 1969, at Chicago. Chicago 9, Detroit 5.
– Bobby Orr, Boston, Jan. 1, 1973, at Vancouver. Boston 8, Vancouver 2.
– Ron Stackhouse, Pittsburgh, Mar. 8, 1975, at Pittsburgh. Pittsburgh 8, Philadelphia 2.
– Paul Coffey, Edmonton, Mar. 14, 1986, at Edmonton. Edmonton 12, Detroit 3.
– Gary Suter, Calgary, Apr. 4, 1986, at Calgary. Calgary 9, Edmonton 3.

MOST POINTS BY A DEFENSEMAN, CAREER:
1,579 – Raymond Bourque, Boston, Colorado, in 22 seasons. 1,612GP (410G-1,169A)
1,531 – Paul Coffey, Edmonton, Pittsburgh, Los Angeles, Detroit, Hartford, Philadelphia, Chicago, Carolina, Boston, in 21 seasons. 1,409GP (396G-1,135A)
1,274 – Al MacInnis, Calgary, St. Louis, in 23 seasons. 1,416GP (340G-934A)
1,232 – Phil Housley, Buffalo, Winnipeg, St. Louis, Calgary, New Jersey, Washington, Chicago, Toronto, in 21 seasons. 1,495GP (338G-894A)
1,216 – Larry Murphy, Los Angeles, Washington, Minnesota, Pittsburgh, Toronto, Detroit, in 21 seasons. 1,615GP (287G-929A)

MOST POINTS BY A DEFENSEMAN, ONE SEASON:
139 – Bobby Orr, Boston, 1970-71. 78GP – 78 game schedule.
138 – Paul Coffey, Edmonton, 1985-86. 79GP – 80 game schedule.
135 – Bobby Orr, Boston, 1974-75. 80GP – 80 game schedule.
126 – Paul Coffey, Edmonton, 1983-84. 80GP – 80 game schedule.
122 – Bobby Orr, Boston, 1973-74. 74GP – 78 game schedule.

MOST POINTS BY A DEFENSEMAN, ONE GAME:
8 – Tom Bladon, Philadelphia, Dec. 11, 1977, at Philadelphia. 4G-4A. Philadelphia 11, Cleveland 1.
– Paul Coffey, Edmonton, Mar. 14, 1986, at Edmonton. 2G-6A. Edmonton 12, Detroit 3.
7 – Bobby Orr, Boston, Nov. 15, 1973, at Boston. 3G-4A. Boston 10, NY Rangers 2.

SCORING BY A GOALTENDER

MOST POINTS BY A GOALTENDER, CAREER:
48 – Tom Barrasso, Buffalo, Pittsburgh, Ottawa, Carolina, Toronto, St. Louis, in 19 seasons. 777GP
46 – Grant Fuhr, Edmonton, Toronto, Buffalo, Los Angeles, St. Louis, Calgary, in 19 seasons. 868GP

MOST POINTS BY A GOALTENDER, ONE SEASON:
14 – Grant Fuhr, Edmonton, 1983-84. 45GP – 80 game schedule.
9 – Curtis Joseph, St. Louis, 1991-92. 60GP – 80 game schedule.
8 – Mike Palmateer, Washington, 1980-81. 49GP – 80 game schedule.
– Grant Fuhr, Edmonton, 1987-88. 75GP – 80 game schedule.
– Ron Hextall, Philadelphia, 1988-89. 64GP – 80 game schedule.
– Tom Barrasso, Pittsburgh, 1992-93. 63GP – 84 game schedule.

MOST POINTS BY A GOALTENDER, ONE GAME:
3 – Jeff Reese, Calgary, Feb. 10, 1993, at Calgary. Calgary 13, San Jose 1.

From Eddie Shore to Bobby Orr to Zdeno Chara, Boston has boasted some of the best blueliners in NHL history. Raymond Bourque spent 20+ of his 22 NHL seasons with the Bruins and collected more goals, more assists and more points than any defenseman in league history.

SCORING BY A ROOKIE

MOST GOALS BY A ROOKIE, ONE SEASON:
76 – Teemu Selanne, Winnipeg, 1992-93. 84GP – 84 game schedule.
53 – Mike Bossy, NY Islanders, 1977-78. 73GP – 80 game schedule.
52 – Alex Ovechkin, Washington, 2005-06. 81GP – 82 game schedule.
51 – Joe Nieuwendyk, Calgary, 1987-88. 75GP – 80 game schedule.
45 – Dale Hawerchuk, Winnipeg, 1981-82. 80GP – 80 game schedule.
– Luc Robitaille, Los Angeles, 1986-87. 79GP – 80 game schedule.

MOST GOALS BY A PLAYER IN HIS FIRST NHL SEASON, ONE GAME:
5 – Joe Malone, Montreal, three occasions, 1917-18.
– Harry Hyland, Mtl. Wanderers, Dec. 19, 1917, at Montreal. Mtl Wanderers 10, Toronto 9.
– Mickey Roach, Toronto, Mar. 6, 1920, at Toronto. Toronto 11, Quebec 2.
– Howie Meeker, Toronto, Jan. 8, 1947, at Toronto. Toronto 10, Chicago 4.
– Don Murdoch, NY Rangers, Oct. 12, 1976, at Minnesota. NY Rangers 10, Minnesota 4.

MOST GOALS BY A PLAYER IN HIS FIRST NHL GAME:
5 – Joe Malone, Montreal, Dec. 19, 1917, at Ottawa. Montreal 7, Ottawa 4.
– Harry Hyland, Mtl. Wanderers, Dec. 19, 1917, at Montreal. Mtl Wanderers 10, Toronto 9.
3 – Alex Smart, Montreal, Jan. 14, 1943, at Montreal. Montreal 5, Chicago 1.
– Real Cloutier, Quebec, Oct. 10, 1979, at Quebec. Atlanta 5, Quebec 3.
– Fabian Brunnstrom, Dallas, Oct. 15, 2008, at Dallas. Dallas 6, Nashville 4.
– Derek Stepan, NY Rangers, Oct. 9, 2010, at Buffalo. NY Rangers 6, Buffalo 3.

MOST ASSISTS BY A ROOKIE, ONE SEASON:
70 – Peter Stastny, Quebec, 1980-81. 77GP – 80 game schedule.
– Joe Juneau, Boston, 1992-93. 84GP – 84 game schedule.
63 – Bryan Trottier, NY Islanders, 1975-76. 80GP – 80 game schedule.
– Sidney Crosby, Pittsburgh, 2005–06. 81GP – 82 game schedule.
62 – Sergei Makarov, Calgary, 1989-90. 80GP – 80 game schedule.
60 – Larry Murphy, Los Angeles, 1980-81. 80GP – 80 game schedule.

MOST ASSISTS BY A PLAYER IN HIS FIRST NHL SEASON, ONE GAME:
7 – Wayne Gretzky, Edmonton, Feb. 15, 1980, at Edmonton. Edmonton 8, Washington 2.
6 – Gary Suter, Calgary, Apr. 4, 1986, at Calgary. Calgary 9, Edmonton 3.

MOST ASSISTS BY A PLAYER IN HIS FIRST NHL GAME:
4 – Dutch Reibel, Detroit, Oct. 8, 1953, at Detroit. Detroit 4, NY Rangers 1.
– Roland Eriksson, Minnesota, Oct. 6, 1976, at NY Rangers. NY Rangers 6, Minnesota 5.
3 – Al Hill, Philadelphia, Feb. 14, 1977, at Philadelphia. Philadelphia 6, St. Louis 4.
– Jarno Kultanen, Boston, Oct. 5, 2000, at Boston. Boston 4, Ottawa 4.
– Stanislav Chistov, Anaheim, Oct. 10, 2002, at St. Louis. Anaheim 4, St. Louis 3.
– Dominic Moore, NY Rangers, Nov. 1, 2003, at Montreal. NY Rangers 5, Montreal 1.

MOST POINTS BY A ROOKIE, ONE SEASON:
132 – Teemu Selanne, Winnipeg, 1992-93. 84GP – 84 game schedule.
109 – Peter Stastny, Quebec, 1980-81. 77GP – 80 game schedule.
106 – Alex Ovechkin, Washington, 2005-06. 81GP – 82 game schedule.
103 – Dale Hawerchuk, Winnipeg, 1981-82. 80GP – 80 game schedule.
102 – Joe Juneau, Boston, 1992-93. 84GP – 84 game schedule.
– Sidney Crosby, Pittsburgh, 2005–06. 81GP – 82 game schedule.
100 – Mario Lemieux, Pittsburgh, 1984-85. 73GP – 80 game schedule.

MOST POINTS BY A PLAYER IN HIS FIRST NHL SEASON, ONE GAME:
8 – Peter Stastny, Quebec, Feb. 22, 1981, at Washington. 4G-4A. Quebec 11, Washington 7.
– Anton Stastny, Quebec, Feb. 22, 1981, at Washington. 3G-5A. Quebec 11, Washington 7.
7 – Wayne Gretzky, Edmonton, Feb. 15, 1980, at Edmonton. 7A. Edmonton 8, Washington 2.
– Sergei Makarov, Calgary, Feb. 25, 1990, at Calgary. 2G-5A. Calgary 10, Edmonton 4.
6 – Wayne Gretzky, Edmonton, Mar. 29, 1980, at Toronto. 2G-4A. Edmonton 8, Toronto 5.
– Gary Suter, Calgary, Apr. 4, 1986, at Calgary. 6A. Calgary 9, Edmonton 3.

MOST POINTS BY A PLAYER IN HIS FIRST NHL GAME:
5 – Joe Malone, Montreal, Dec. 19, 1917, at Ottawa. 5G*. Montreal 7, Ottawa 4.
– Harry Hyland, Mtl. Wanderers, Dec. 19, 1917, at Montreal. 5G*. Mtl Wanderers 10, Toronto 9.
– Al Hill, Philadelphia, Feb. 14, 1977, at Philadelphia. 2G-3A. Philadelphia 6, St. Louis 4.
4 – Alex Smart, Montreal, Jan. 14, 1943, at Montreal. 3G-1A. Montreal 5, Chicago 1.
– Dutch Reibel, Detroit, Oct. 8, 1953, at Detroit. 4A. Detroit 4, NY Rangers 1.
– Roland Eriksson, Minnesota, Oct. 6, 1976, at NY Rangers. 4A. NY Rangers 6, Minnesota 5.
– Stanislav Chistov, Anaheim, Oct. 10, 2002, at St. Louis. 1G-3A. Anaheim 4, St. Louis 3.

** – Official assists not awarded in 1917-18.*

SCORING BY A ROOKIE DEFENSEMAN

MOST GOALS BY A ROOKIE DEFENSEMAN, ONE SEASON:
23 – Brian Leetch, NY Rangers, 1988-89. 68GP – 80 game schedule.
22 – Barry Beck, Colorado, 1977-78. 75GP – 80 game schedule.
20 – Dion Phaneuf, Calgary, 2005-06. 82GP – 82 game schedule.

MOST ASSISTS BY A ROOKIE DEFENSEMAN, ONE SEASON:
60 – Larry Murphy, Los Angeles, 1980-81. 80GP – 80 game schedule.
55 – Chris Chelios, Montreal, 1984-85. 74GP – 80 game schedule.
50 – Stefan Persson, NY Islanders, 1977-78. 66GP – 80 game schedule.
– Gary Suter, Calgary, 1985-86. 80GP – 80 game schedule.
49 – Nicklas Lidstrom, Detroit, 1991-92. 80GP – 80 game schedule.

MOST POINTS BY A ROOKIE DEFENSEMAN, ONE SEASON:
76 – Larry Murphy, Los Angeles, 1980-81. 80GP – 80 game schedule.
71 – Brian Leetch, NY Rangers, 1988-89. 68GP – 80 game schedule.
68 – Gary Suter, Calgary, 1985-86. 80GP – 80 game schedule.
66 – Phil Housley, Buffalo, 1982-83. 77GP – 80 game schedule.
65 – Raymond Bourque, Boston, 1979-80. 80GP – 80 game schedule.

Mike Bossy (left) of the New York Islanders became the first rookie in NHL history to score 50 goals when he netted 53 back in 1977-78. Teemu Selanne (right) celebrates his record-breaking 54th with the Winnipeg Jets in 1992-93 en route to setting new rookie records with 76 goals and 132 points. Selanne's marks seem destined to stand the test of time, as does Bossy's record of nine-straight 50-goal seasons.

PER-GAME SCORING AVERAGES

HIGHEST GOALS-PER-GAME AVERAGE, CAREER
(AMONG PLAYERS WITH 200-OR-MORE GOALS):
.762 – Mike Bossy, NY Islanders, 1977-78 – 1986-87, with 573G in 752GP.
.756 – Cy Denneny, Ottawa, Boston, 1917-18 – 1928-29, with 248G in 328GP.
.754 – Mario Lemieux, Pittsburgh, 1984-85 – 1996-97, 2000-01 – 2003-04, 2005-06, with 690G in 915GP.
.742 – Babe Dye, Toronto, Hamilton, Chicago, NY Americans, 1919-20 – 1930-31, with 201G in 271GP.
.623 – Pavel Bure, Vancouver, Florida, NY Rangers, 1991-92 – 2002-03, with 437G in 702GP.

HIGHEST GOALS-PER-GAME AVERAGE, ONE SEASON
(AMONG PLAYERS WITH 20-OR-MORE GOALS):
2.20 – Joe Malone, Montreal, 1917-18, with 44G in 20GP.
1.80 – Cy Denneny, Ottawa, 1917-18, with 36G in 20GP.
1.64 – Newsy Lalonde, Montreal, 1917-18, with 23G in 14GP.
1.63 – Joe Malone, Quebec, 1919-20, with 39G in 24GP.
1.61 – Newsy Lalonde, Montreal, 1919-20, with 37G in 23GP.

HIGHEST GOALS-PER-GAME AVERAGE, ONE SEASON
(AMONG PLAYERS WITH 50-OR-MORE GOALS):
1.18 – Wayne Gretzky, Edmonton, 1983-84, with 87G in 74GP.
1.15 – Wayne Gretzky, Edmonton, 1981-82, with 92G in 80GP.
– Mario Lemieux, Pittsburgh, 1992-93, with 69G in 60GP.
1.12 – Mario Lemieux, Pittsburgh, 1988-89, with 85G in 76GP.
1.10 – Brett Hull, St. Louis, 1990-91, with 86G in 78GP.
1.02 – Cam Neely, Boston, 1993-94, with 50G in 49GP.
1.00 – Maurice Richard, Montreal, 1944-45, with 50G in 50GP.

HIGHEST ASSISTS-PER-GAME AVERAGE, CAREER
(AMONG PLAYERS WITH 300-OR-MORE ASSISTS):
1.320 – Wayne Gretzky, Edmonton, Los Angeles, St. Louis, NY Rangers, 1979-80 – 1998-99, with 1,963A in 1,487GP.
1.129 – Mario Lemieux, Pittsburgh, 1984-85 – 1996-97, 2000-01 – 2003-04, 2005-06, with 1,033A in 915GP.
.982 – Bobby Orr, Boston, Chicago, 1966-67 – 1978-79, with 645A in 657GP.
.909 – Sidney Crosby, Pittsburgh, 2005-06 – 2012-13, with 427A in 470GP.
.898 – Peter Forsberg, Quebec, Colorado, Philadelphia, Nashville, 1994-95 – 2000-01, 2002-03, 2003-04, 2005-06 – 2007-08, 2010-11 with 636A in 708GP.

HIGHEST ASSISTS-PER-GAME AVERAGE, ONE SEASON
(AMONG PLAYERS WITH 35-OR-MORE ASSISTS):
2.04 – Wayne Gretzky, Edmonton, 1985-86, with 163A in 80GP.
1.70 – Wayne Gretzky, Edmonton, 1987-88, with 109A in 64GP.
1.69 – Wayne Gretzky, Edmonton, 1984-85, with 135A in 80GP.
1.59 – Wayne Gretzky, Edmonton, 1983-84, with 118A in 74GP.
1.56 – Wayne Gretzky, Edmonton, 1982-83, with 125A in 80GP.
– Wayne Gretzky, Los Angeles, 1990-91, with 122A in 78GP.
1.53 – Wayne Gretzky, Edmonton, 1986-87, with 121A in 79GP.
1.52 – Mario Lemieux, Pittsburgh, 1992-93, with 91A in 60GP.
1.50 – Wayne Gretzky, Edmonton, 1981-82, with 120A in 80GP.
– Mario Lemieux, Pittsburgh, 1988-89, with 114A in 76GP.

HIGHEST POINTS-PER-GAME AVERAGE, CAREER
(AMONG PLAYERS WITH 500-OR-MORE POINTS):
1.921 – Wayne Gretzky, Edmonton, Los Angeles, St. Louis, NY Rangers, 1979-80 – 1998-99, with 2,857PTS (894G-1,963A) in 1,487GP.
1.883 – Mario Lemieux, Pittsburgh, 1984-85 – 1996-97, 2000-01 – 2003-04, 2005-06, with 1,723PTS (690G-1,033A) in 915GP.
1.497 – Mike Bossy, NY Islanders, 1977-78 – 1986-87, with 1,126PTS (573G-553A) in 752GP.
1.415 – Sidney Crosby, Pittsburgh, 2005-06 – 2012-13, with 665PTS (238G-427A) in 470GP.
1.393 – Bobby Orr, Boston, Chicago, 1966-67 – 1978-79, with 915PTS (270G-645A) in 657GP.

HIGHEST POINTS-PER-GAME AVERAGE, ONE SEASON
(AMONG PLAYERS WITH 50-OR-MORE POINTS):
2.77 – Wayne Gretzky, Edmonton, 1983-84, with 205PTS in 74GP.
2.69 – Wayne Gretzky, Edmonton, 1985-86, with 215PTS in 80GP.
2.67 – Mario Lemieux, Pittsburgh, 1992-93, with 160PTS in 60GP.
2.65 – Wayne Gretzky, Edmonton, 1981-82, with 212PTS in 80GP.
2.62 – Mario Lemieux, Pittsburgh, 1988-89, with 199PTS in 76GP.
2.60 – Wayne Gretzky, Edmonton, 1984-85, with 208PTS in 80GP.
2.45 – Wayne Gretzky, Edmonton, 1982-83, with 196PTS in 80GP.
2.33 – Wayne Gretzky, Edmonton, 1987-88, with 149PTS in 64GP.
2.32 – Wayne Gretzky, Edmonton, 1986-87, with 183PTS in 79GP.
2.30 – Mario Lemieux, Pittsburgh, 1995-96, with 161PTS in 70GP.
2.18 – Mario Lemieux, Pittsburgh, 1987-88, with 168PTS in 77GP.
2.15 – Wayne Gretzky, Los Angeles, 1988-89, with 168PTS in 78GP.
2.09 – Wayne Gretzky, Los Angeles, 1990-91, with 163PTS in 78GP.
2.08 – Mario Lemieux, Pittsburgh, 1989-90, with 123PTS in 59GP.

SCORING PLATEAUS

MOST 20-OR-MORE GOAL SEASONS:
22 – Gordie Howe, Detroit, Hartford, in 26 seasons.
20 – Ron Francis, Hartford, Pittsburgh, Carolina, Toronto, in 23 seasons.
19 – Dave Andreychuk, Buffalo, Toronto, New Jersey, Boston, Colorado, Tampa Bay, in 23 seasons.
– Brendan Shanahan, New Jersey, St. Louis, Hartford, Detroit, NY Rangers, in 21 seasons.
17 – Marcel Dionne, Detroit, Los Angeles, NY Rangers, in 18 seasons.
– Mike Gartner, Washington, Minnesota, NY Rangers, Toronto, Phoenix, in 19 seasons.
– Wayne Gretzky, Edmonton, Los Angeles, St. Louis, NY Rangers, in 20 seasons.
– Mark Messier, Edmonton, NY Rangers, Vancouver, in 25 seasons.
– Brett Hull, Calgary, St. Louis, Dallas, Detroit, Phoenix, in 19 seasons.
– Joe Sakic, Quebec, Colorado, in 20 seasons.
– Mats Sundin, Quebec, Toronto, Vancouver, in 18 seasons.
– Jaromir Jagr, Pittsburgh, Washington, NY Rangers, Philadelphia, Dallas, Boston in 19 seasons.
– Teemu Selanne, Winnipeg, Anaheim, San Jose, Colorado, in 20 seasons.

MOST CONSECUTIVE 20-OR-MORE GOAL SEASONS:
22 – Gordie Howe, Detroit, 1949-50 – 1970-71.
19 – Brendan Shanahan, New Jersey, St. Louis, Hartford, Detroit, NY Rangers, 1988-89 – 2007-08.
17 – Marcel Dionne, Detroit, Los Angeles, NY Rangers, 1971-72 – 1987-88.
– Brett Hull, Calgary, St. Louis, Dallas, Detroit, 1987-88 – 2003-04.
– Jaromir Jagr, Pittsburgh, Washington, NY Rangers, 1990-91 – 2007-08.
– Mats Sundin, Quebec, Toronto, 1990-91 – 2007-08.

Though knee injuries cut short his career, Bobby Orr at his best was an extraordinary player. A two-time NHL scoring champion as a defenseman, Orr averaged nearly one assist per game during his playing days. He ranks third in highest career assists-per-game and fifth in highest career points-per-game average.

MOST 30-OR-MORE GOAL SEASONS:
17 – Mike Gartner, Washington, Minnesota, NY Rangers, Toronto, Phoenix, in 19 seasons.
15 – Jaromir Jagr, Pittsburgh, Washington, NY Rangers, Philadelphia, Dallas, Boston in 19 seasons.
14 – Gordie Howe, Detroit, Hartford, in 26 seasons.
– Marcel Dionne, Detroit, Los Angeles, NY Rangers, in 18 seasons.
– Wayne Gretzky, Edmonton, Los Angeles, St. Louis, NY Rangers, in 20 seasons.
13 – Bobby Hull, Chicago, Winnipeg, Hartford, in 16 seasons.
– Phil Esposito, Chicago, Boston, NY Rangers, in 18 seasons.
– Brett Hull, Calgary, St. Louis, Dallas, Detroit, Phoenix, in 19 seasons.
– Mats Sundin, Quebec, Toronto, Vancouver, in 18 seasons.

MOST CONSECUTIVE 30-OR-MORE GOAL SEASONS:
15 – Mike Gartner, Washington, Minnesota, NY Rangers, Toronto, 1979-80 – 1993-94.
– Jaromir Jagr, Pittsburgh, Washington, NY Rangers, 1991-92 – 2006-07.
13 – Bobby Hull, Chicago, 1959-60 – 1971-72.
– Phil Esposito, Boston, NY Rangers, 1967-68 – 1979-80.
– Wayne Gretzky, Edmonton, Los Angeles, 1979-80 – 1991-92.

MOST 40-OR-MORE GOAL SEASONS:
12 – Wayne Gretzky, Edmonton, Los Angeles, St. Louis, NY Rangers, in 20 seasons.
10 – Marcel Dionne, Detroit, Los Angeles, NY Rangers, in 18 seasons.
– Mario Lemieux, Pittsburgh, in 17 seasons.
9 – Mike Bossy, NY Islanders, in 10 seasons.
– Mike Gartner, Washington, Minnesota, NY Rangers, Toronto, Phoenix, in 19 seasons.

MOST CONSECUTIVE 40-OR-MORE GOAL SEASONS:
12 – Wayne Gretzky, Edmonton, Los Angeles, 1979-80 – 1990-91.
9 – Mike Bossy, NY Islanders, 1977-78 – 1985-86.
8 – Luc Robitaille, Los Angeles, 1986-87 – 1993-94.
7 – Phil Esposito, Boston, 1968-69 – 1974-75.
– Michel Goulet, Quebec, 1981-82 – 1987-88.
– Jari Kurri, Edmonton, 1982-83 – 1988-89.

MOST 50-OR-MORE GOAL SEASONS:
9 – Mike Bossy, NY Islanders, in 10 seasons.
– Wayne Gretzky, Edmonton, Los Angeles, St. Louis, NY Rangers, in 20 seasons.
6 – Guy Lafleur, Montreal, NY Rangers, Quebec, in 17 seasons.
– Marcel Dionne, Detroit, Los Angeles, NY Rangers, in 18 seasons.
– Mario Lemieux, Pittsburgh, in 17 seasons.
5 – Bobby Hull, Chicago, Winnipeg, Hartford, in 16 seasons.
– Phil Esposito, Chicago, Boston, NY Rangers, in 18 seasons.
– Brett Hull, Calgary, St. Louis, Dallas, Detroit, Phoenix, in 19 seasons.
– Steve Yzerman, Detroit, in 22 seasons.
– Pavel Bure, Vancouver, Florida, NY Rangers, in 12 seasons.

MOST CONSECUTIVE 50-OR-MORE GOAL SEASONS:
9 – Mike Bossy, NY Islanders, 1977-78 – 1985-86.
8 – Wayne Gretzky, Edmonton, 1979-80 – 1986-87.
6 – Guy Lafleur, Montreal, 1974-75 – 1979-80.
5 – Phil Esposito, Boston, 1970-71 – 1974-75.
– Marcel Dionne, Los Angeles, 1978-79 – 1982-83.
– Brett Hull, St. Louis, 1989-90 – 1993-94.

MOST 60-OR-MORE GOAL SEASONS:
5 – Mike Bossy, NY Islanders, in 10 seasons.
– Wayne Gretzky, Edmonton, Los Angeles, St. Louis, NY Rangers, in 20 seasons.
4 – Phil Esposito, Chicago, Boston, NY Rangers, in 18 seasons.
– Mario Lemieux, Pittsburgh, in 17 seasons.

MOST CONSECUTIVE 60-OR-MORE GOAL SEASONS:
4 – Wayne Gretzky, Edmonton, 1981-82 – 1984-85.
3 – Mike Bossy, NY Islanders, 1980-81 – 1982-83.
– Brett Hull, St. Louis, 1989-90 – 1991-92.
2 – Phil Esposito, Boston, 1970-71 – 1971-72, 1973-74 – 1974-75.
– Jari Kurri, Edmonton, 1984-85 – 1985-86.
– Mario Lemieux, Pittsburgh, 1987-88 – 1988-89.
– Steve Yzerman, Detroit, 1988-89 – 1989-90.
– Pavel Bure, Vancouver, 1992-93 – 1993-94.

MOST 100-OR-MORE POINT SEASONS:
15 – Wayne Gretzky, Edmonton, Los Angeles, St. Louis, NY Rangers, in 20 seasons.
10 – Mario Lemieux, Pittsburgh, in 17 seasons.
8 – Marcel Dionne, Detroit, Los Angeles, NY Rangers, in 18 seasons.
7 – Mike Bossy, NY Islanders, in 10 seasons.
– Peter Stastny, Quebec, New Jersey, St. Louis, in 15 seasons.

MOST CONSECUTIVE 100-OR-MORE POINT SEASONS:
13 – Wayne Gretzky, Edmonton, Los Angeles, 1979-80 – 1991-92.
6 – Bobby Orr, Boston, 1969-70 – 1974-75.
– Guy Lafleur, Montreal, 1974-75 – 1979-80.
– Mike Bossy, NY Islanders,1980-81 – 1985-86.
– Peter Stastny, Quebec, 1980-81 – 1985-86.
– Mario Lemieux, Pittsburgh, 1984-85 – 1989-90.
– Steve Yzerman, Detroit, 1987-88 – 1992-93.

THREE-OR-MORE-GOAL GAMES

MOST THREE-OR-MORE GOAL GAMES, CAREER:
50 – Wayne Gretzky, Edmonton, Los Angeles, St. Louis, NY Rangers, in 20 seasons, 37 three-goal games, 9 four-goal games, 4 five-goal games.
40 – Mario Lemieux, Pittsburgh, in 17 seasons, 27 three-goal games, 10 four-goal games, 3 five-goal games.
39 – Mike Bossy, NY Islanders, in 10 seasons, 30 three-goal games, 9 four-goal games.
33 – Brett Hull, Calgary, St. Louis, Dallas, Detroit, Phoenix, in 19 seasons, 30 three-goal games, 3 four-goal games.
32 – Phil Esposito, Chicago, Boston, NY Rangers, in 18 seasons, 27 three-goal games, 5 four-goal games.

MOST THREE-OR-MORE GOAL GAMES, ONE SEASON:
10 – Wayne Gretzky, Edmonton, 1981-82. 6 three-goal games, 3 four-goal games, 1 five-goal game.
– Wayne Gretzky, Edmonton, 1983-84. 6 three-goal games, 4 four-goal games.
9 – Mike Bossy, NY Islanders, 1980-81. 6 three-goal games, 3 four-goal games.
– Mario Lemieux, Pittsburgh, 1988-89. 7 three-goal games, 1 four-goal game, 1 five-goal game.
8 – Brett Hull, St. Louis, 1991-92. 8 three-goal games.
7 – Joe Malone, Montreal, 1917-18. 2 three-goal games, 2 four-goal games, 3 five-goal games.
– Phil Esposito, Boston, 1970-71. 7 three-goal games.
– Rick Martin, Buffalo, 1975-76. 6 three-goal games, 1 four-goal game.
– Alexander Mogilny, Buffalo, 1992-93. 5 three-goal games, 2 four-goal games.

SCORING STREAKS

LONGEST CONSECUTIVE GOAL-SCORING STREAK:
16 Games – Punch Broadbent, Ottawa, 1921-22. 27G
14 Games – Joe Malone, Montreal, 1917-18. 35G
13 Games – Newsy Lalonde, Montreal, 1920-21. 24G
– Charlie Simmer, Los Angeles, 1979-80. 17G
12 Games – Cy Denneny, Ottawa, 1917-18. 23G
– Dave Lumley, Edmonton, 1981-82. 15G
– Mario Lemieux, Pittsburgh, 1992-93. 18G

LONGEST CONSECUTIVE ASSIST-SCORING STREAK:
23 Games – Wayne Gretzky, Los Angeles, 1990-91. 48A
18 Games – Adam Oates, Boston, 1992-93. 28A
17 Games – Wayne Gretzky, Edmonton, 1983-84. 38A
– Paul Coffey, Edmonton, 1985-86. 27A
– Wayne Gretzky, Los Angeles, 1989-90. 35A
16 Games – Jaromir Jagr, Pittsburgh, 2000-01. 24A

LONGEST CONSECUTIVE POINT-SCORING STREAK:
51 Games – Wayne Gretzky, Edmonton, 1983-84. 61G-92A-153PTS
46 Games – Mario Lemieux, Pittsburgh, 1989-90. 39G-64A-103PTS
39 Games – Wayne Gretzky, Edmonton, 1985-86. 33G-75A-108PTS
30 Games – Wayne Gretzky, Edmonton, 1982-83. 24G-52A-76PTS
– Mats Sundin, Quebec, 1992-93. 21G-25A-46PTS

LONGEST CONSECUTIVE POINT-SCORING STREAK FROM START OF SEASON:
51 Games – Wayne Gretzky, Edmonton, 1983-84. 61G-92A-153PTS. Streak ended by Los Angeles and goaltender Markus Mattsson on Jan. 28, 1984.

LONGEST CONSECUTIVE POINT-SCORING STREAK BY A DEFENSEMAN:
28 Games – Paul Coffey, Edmonton, 1985-86. 16G-39A-55PTS
19 Games – Raymond Bourque, Boston, 1987-88. 6G-21A-27PTS
17 Games – Raymond Bourque, Boston, 1984-85. 4G-24A-28PTS
– Brian Leetch, NY Rangers, 1991-92. 5G-24A-29PTS
16 Games – Gary Suter, Calgary, 1987-88. 8G-17A-25PTS
15 Games – Bobby Orr, Boston, 1970-71. 10G-23A-33PTS
– Bobby Orr, Boston, 1973-74. 8G-15A-23PTS
– Steve Duchesne, Quebec, 1992-93. 4G-17A-21PTS
– Chris Chelios, Chicago, 1995-96. 4G-16A-20PTS

LONGEST CONSECUTIVE POINT-SCORING STREAK BY A ROOKIE:
20 Games – Paul Stastny, Colorado, 2006-07. 11G-18A-29PTS
17 Games – Teemu Selanne, Winnipeg, 1992-93. 20G-14A-34PTS
16 Games – Peter Stastny, Quebec, 1980-81
15 Games – Jude Drouin, Minnesota North Stars, 1970-71

FASTEST GOALS AND ASSISTS

FASTEST GOAL FROM START OF A GAME:
0:05 – Doug Smail, Winnipeg, Dec. 20, 1981, at Winnipeg. Winnipeg 5, St. Louis 4.
– Bryan Trottier, NY Islanders, Mar. 22, 1984, at Boston. NY Islanders 3, Boston 3.
– Alexander Mogilny, Buffalo, Dec. 21, 1991, at Toronto. Buffalo 4, Toronto 1.
0:06 – Henry Boucha, Detroit, Jan. 28, 1973, at Montreal. Detroit 4, Montreal 2.
– Jean Pronovost, Pittsburgh, Mar. 25, 1976, at St. Louis. St. Louis 5, Pittsburgh 2.
– Alex Burrows, Vancouver, Mar. 16, 2013, at Vancouver. Detroit 5, Vancouver 2
0:07 – Charlie Conacher, Toronto, Feb. 6, 1932, at Toronto. Toronto 6, Boston 0.
– Danny Gare, Buffalo, Dec. 17, 1978, at Buffalo. Buffalo 6, Vancouver 3.
– Tiger Williams, Los Angeles, Feb. 14, 1987, at Los Angeles. Los Angeles 5, Harford 2.
– Evgeni Malkin, Pittsburgh, Jan. 5, 2011, at Pittsburgh. Pittsburgh 8, Tampa Bay 1.

FASTEST GOAL FROM START OF A PERIOD:
0:04 – Claude Provost, Montreal, Nov. 9, 1957, at Montreal, second period. Montreal 4, Boston 2.
– **Denis Savard**, Chicago, Jan. 12, 1986, at Chicago, third period. Chicago 4, Hartford 2.

FASTEST GOAL BY A PLAYER IN HIS FIRST NHL GAME:
0:15 – Gus Bodnar, Toronto, Oct. 30, 1943, at Toronto. Toronto 5, NY Rangers 2.
0:18 – Danny Gare, Buffalo, Oct. 10, 1974, at Buffalo. Buffalo 9, Boston 5.
0:20 – Alexander Mogilny, Buffalo, Oct. 5, 1989, at Buffalo. Buffalo 4, Quebec 3.

FASTEST TWO GOALS FROM START OF A GAME:
0:27 – Mike Knuble, Boston, Feb. 14, 2003, at Florida. 0:10 and 0:27. Boston 6, Florida 5.

FASTEST TWO GOALS:
0:04 – Nels Stewart, Mtl. Maroons, Jan. 3, 1931, at Mtl. Maroons. 8:24 and 8:28, third period. Mtl. Maroons 5, Boston 3.
– **Deron Quint**, Winnipeg, Dec. 15, 1995, at Winnipeg. 7:51 and 7:55, second period. Winnipeg 9, Edmonton 4.
0:05 – Pete Mahovlich, Montreal, Feb. 20, 1971, at Montreal. 12:16 and 12:21, third period. Montreal 7, Chicago 1.
– Nathan Gerbe, Buffalo, January 21, 2011at Buffalo. 16:38 and 16:43, third period. NY Islanders 5, Buffalo 2.
0:06 – Jim Pappin, Chicago, Feb. 16, 1972, at Chicago. 2:57 and 3:03, third period. Chicago 3, Philadelphia 3.
– Ralph Backstrom, Los Angeles, Nov. 2, 1972, at Los Angeles. 8:30 and 8:36, third period. Los Angeles 5, Boston 2.
– Lanny McDonald, Calgary, Mar. 22, 1984, at Calgary. 16:23 and 16:29, first period. Detroit 6, Calgary 4.
– Sylvain Turgeon, Hartford, Mar. 28, 1987, at Hartford. 13:59 and 14:05, second period. Hartford 5, Pittsburgh 4.

FASTEST THREE GOALS:
0:21 – Bill Mosienko, Chicago, Mar. 23, 1952, at NY Rangers, against goaltender Lorne Anderson. Mosienko scored at 6:09, 6:20 and 6:30 of third period, all with both teams at full strength. Chicago 7, NY Rangers 6.
0:44 – Jean Béliveau, Montreal, Nov. 5, 1955, at Montreal, against goaltender Terry Sawchuk. Béliveau scored at 0:42, 1:08 and 1:26 of second period, all with Montreal holding a 6-4 man advantage. Montreal 4, Boston 2.

FASTEST THREE ASSISTS:
0:21 – Gus Bodnar, Chicago, Mar. 23, 1952, at NY Rangers, Bodnar assisted on Bill Mosienko's three goals at 6:09, 6:20 and 6:30 of third period. Chicago 7, NY Rangers 6.
0:44 – Bert Olmstead, Montreal, Nov. 5, 1955, at Montreal, Olmstead assisted on Jean Béliveau's three goals at 0:42, 1:08 and 1:26 of second period. Montreal 4, Boston 2.

SHOTS ON GOAL

MOST SHOTS ON GOAL, ONE SEASON:
550 – Phil Esposito, Boston, 1970-71. 78GP – 78 game schedule.
528 – Alex Ovechkin, Washington, 2008-09. 79GP – 82 game schedule.
446 – Alex Ovechkin, Washington, 2007-08. 82GP – 82 game schedule.
429 – Paul Kariya, Anaheim, 1998-99. 82GP – 82 game schedule.
426 – Phil Esposito, Boston, 1971-72. 76GP – 78 game schedule.

After making a brief debut with the Devils during the NHL's 75th anniversary season of 1991-92, Martin Brodeur won the Calder Trophy as rookie of the year in 1993-94. He has gone on to set every major regular-season record for goaltenders in his brilliant career.

PENALTIES

MOST PENALTY MINUTES, CAREER:
3,966 – Tiger Williams, Toronto, Vancouver, Detroit, Los Angeles, Hartford, in 14 seasons. 962GP
3,565 – Dale Hunter, Quebec, Washington, Colorado, in 19 seasons. 1,407GP
3,515 – Tie Domi, Toronto, NY Rangers, Winnipeg, in 16 seasons. 1,020GP
3,381 – Marty McSorley, Pittsburgh, Edmonton, Los Angeles, NY Rangers, San Jose, Boston, in 17 seasons. 961GP
3,300 – Bob Probert, Detroit, Chicago, in 17 seasons. 935GP

MOST PENALTY MINUTES, CAREER, INCLUDING PLAYOFFS:
4,421 – Tiger Williams, Toronto, Vancouver, Detroit, Los Angeles, Hartford, 3,966 in 962 regular-season games; 455 in 83 playoff games.
4,294 – Dale Hunter, Quebec, Washington, Colorado, 3,565 in 1,407 regular-season games; 729 in 186 playoff games.
3,755 – Marty McSorley, Pittsburgh, Edmonton, Los Angeles, NY Rangers, San Jose, Boston, 3,381 in 961 regular-season games; 374 in 115 playoff games.
3,753 – Tie Domi, Toronto, NY Rangers, Winnipeg, 3,515 in 1,020 regular-season games; 238 in 98 playoff games.
3,584 – Chris Nilan, Montreal, NY Rangers, Boston, 3,043 in 688 regular-season games; 541 in 111 playoff games.

MOST PENALTY MINUTES, ONE SEASON:
472 – Dave Schultz, Philadelphia, 1974-75.
409 – Paul Baxter, Pittsburgh, 1981-82.
408 – Mike Peluso, Chicago, 1991-92.
405 – Dave Schultz, Los Angeles, Pittsburgh, 1977-78.

MOST PENALTIES, ONE GAME:
10 – Chris Nilan, Boston, Mar. 31, 1991, at Boston vs. Hartford. 6 minors, 2 majors, 1 10-minute misconduct, 1 game misconduct.
9 – Jim Dorey, Toronto, Oct. 16, 1968, at Toronto vs. Pittsburgh. 4 minors, 2 majors, 2 10-minute misconducts, 1 game misconduct.
– Dave Schultz, Pittsburgh, Apr. 6, 1978, at Detroit. 5 minors, 2 majors, 2 10-minute misconducts.
– Randy Holt, Los Angeles, Mar. 11, 1979, at Philadelphia. 1 minor, 3 majors, 2 10-minute misconducts, 3 game misconducts.
– Russ Anderson, Pittsburgh, Jan. 19, 1980, at Pittsburgh vs. Edmonton. 3 minors, 3 majors, 3 game misconducts.
– Kim Clackson, Quebec, Mar. 8, 1981, at Quebec vs. Chicago. 4 minors, 3 majors, 2 game misconducts.
– Terry O'Reilly, Boston, Dec. 19, 1984, at Hartford. 5 minors, 3 majors, 1 game misconduct.
– Larry Playfair, Los Angeles, Dec. 9, 1986, at NY Islanders. 6 minors, 2 majors, 1 10-minute misconduct.
– Marty McSorley, Los Angeles, Apr. 14, 1992, at Vancouver. 5 minors, 2 majors, 1 10-minute misconduct, 1 game misconduct.
– Reed Low, St. Louis, Dec. 31, 2002, at Detroit. 4 minors, 1 major, 1 10-minute misconduct, 3 game misconducts.

MOST PENALTY MINUTES, ONE GAME:
67 – Randy Holt, Los Angeles, Mar. 11, 1979, at Philadelphia. 1 minor, 3 majors, 2 10-minute misconducts, 3 game misconducts.
57 – Brad Smith, Toronto, Nov. 15, 1986, at Toronto vs. Detroit. 1 minor, 3 majors, 2 10-minute misconducts, 2 game misconducts.
– Reed Low, St. Louis, Feb. 28, 2002, at St. Louis vs. Calgary. 1 minor, 3 majors, 1 10-minute misconduct, 3 game misconducts.

MOST PENALTIES, ONE PERIOD:
9 – Randy Holt, Los Angeles, Mar. 11, 1979, at Philadelphia, first period. 1 minor, 3 majors, 2 10-minute misconducts, 3 game misconducts.

MOST PENALTY MINUTES, ONE PERIOD:
67 – Randy Holt, Los Angeles, Mar. 11, 1979, at Philadelphia, first period. 1 minor, 3 majors, 2 10-minute misconducts, 3 game misconducts.

GOALTENDING

MOST GAMES APPEARED IN BY A GOALTENDER, CAREER:
1,220 – Martin Brodeur, New Jersey, 1991-92 – 2003-04, 2005-06 – 2012-13.
1,029 – Patrick Roy, Montreal, Colorado,1984-85 – 2002-03.
971 – Terry Sawchuk, Detroit, Boston, Toronto, Los Angeles, NY Rangers, 1949-50 – 1969-70.
963 – Ed Belfour, Chicago, San Jose, Dallas, Toronto, Florida, 1988-89 – 2003-04, 2005-06, 2006-07.
943 – Curtis Joseph, St. Louis, Edmonton, Toronto, Detroit, Phoenix, Calgary, 1989-90 – 2003-04, 2005-06 – 2008-09.

MOST CONSECUTIVE COMPLETE GAMES BY A GOALTENDER:
502 – Glenn Hall, Detroit, Chicago. Played 502 games from beginning of 1955-56 season through first 12 games of 1962-63 season. In his 503rd straight game, Nov. 7, 1962, at Chicago, Hall was removed from the game against Boston with a back injury in the first period.

MOST GAMES APPEARED IN BY A GOALTENDER, ONE SEASON:
79 – Grant Fuhr, St. Louis, 1995-96.
78 – Martin Brodeur, New Jersey, 2006-07.
77 – Martin Brodeur, New Jersey, 1995-96.
– Bill Ranford, Edmonton, Boston, 1995-96.
– Arturs Irbe, Carolina, 2000-01.
– Marc Denis, Columbus, 2002-03.
– Evgeni Nabokov, San Jose, 2007-08.
– Martin Brodeur, New Jersey, 2007-08.
– Martin Brodeur, New Jersey, 2009-10.

MOST MINUTES PLAYED BY A GOALTENDER, CAREER:
71,786 – Martin Brodeur, New Jersey, 1991-92 – 2003-04, 2005-06 – 2012-13.
60,235 – Patrick Roy, Montreal, Colorado, 1984-85 – 2002-03.
57,194 – Terry Sawchuk, Detroit, Boston, Toronto, Los Angeles, NY Rangers, 1949-50 – 1969-70.

MOST MINUTES PLAYED BY A GOALTENDER, ONE SEASON:
4,697 – Martin Brodeur, New Jersey, 2006-07.
4,635 – Martin Brodeur, New Jersey, 2007-08.
4,561 – Evgeni Nabokov, San Jose, 2007-08.
4,555 – Martin Brodeur, New Jersey, 2003-04.
4,511 – Marc Denis, Columbus, 2002-03.

MOST SHUTOUTS, CAREER:
121 – Martin Brodeur, New Jersey, in 20 seasons. (1991-92, 1993-94 – 2003-04, 2005-06 – 2012-13)
103 – Terry Sawchuk, Detroit, Boston, Toronto, Los Angeles, NY Rangers, in 21 seasons. (1949-50 – 1969-70)
94 – George Hainsworth, Montreal, Toronto, in 11 seasons. (1926-27 – 1936-37)

MOST SHUTOUTS, ONE SEASON:
22 – George Hainsworth, Montreal, 1928-29. 44GP
15 – Alec Connell, Ottawa, 1925-26. 36GP
– Alec Connell, Ottawa, 1927-28. 44GP
– Hal Winkler, Boston, 1927-28. 44GP
– Tony Esposito, Chicago, 1969-70. 63GP
14 – George Hainsworth, Montreal, 1926-27. 44GP

LONGEST SHUTOUT SEQUENCE BY A GOALTENDER:
461:29 – Alec Connell, Ottawa, 1927-28, six consecutive shutouts.
(Forward passing not permitted in attacking zones in 1927-28.)
343:05 – George Hainsworth, Montreal, 1928-29, four consecutive shutouts.
(Forward passing not permitted in attacking zones in 1928-29.)
332:01 – Brian Boucher, Phoenix, 2003-04, five consecutive shutouts.
324:40 – Roy Worters, NY Americans, 1930-31, four consecutive shutouts.
309:21 – Bill Durnan, Montreal, 1948-49, four consecutive shutouts.

MOST WINS BY A GOALTENDER, CAREER:
669 – Martin Brodeur, New Jersey, in 20 seasons. 1,220 GP
551 – Patrick Roy, Montreal, Colorado, in 19 seasons. 1,029GP
484 – Ed Belfour, Chicago, San Jose, Dallas, Toronto, Florida, in 17 seasons. 963GP
454 – Curtis Joseph, St. Louis, Edmonton, Toronto, Detroit, Phoenix, Calgary, in 19 seasons. 943GP
447 – Terry Sawchuk, Detroit, Boston, Toronto, Los Angeles, NY Rangers, in 21 seasons. 971GP

MOST WINS BY A GOALTENDER, ONE SEASON:
48 – Martin Brodeur, New Jersey, 2006-07. 78GP
47 – Bernie Parent, Philadelphia, 1973-74. 73GP
– Roberto Luongo, Vancouver, 2006-07. 76GP
46 – Evgeni Nabokov, San Jose, 2007-08. 77GP
45 – Miikka Kiprusoff, Calgary, 2008-09. 76GP
– Martin Brodeur, New Jersey, 2009-10. 77GP

LONGEST WINNING STREAK BY A GOALTENDER, ONE SEASON:
17 – Gilles Gilbert, Boston, 1975-76.
14 – Tiny Thompson, Boston, 1929-30.
– Ross Brooks, Boston, 1973-74.
– Don Beaupre, Minnesota, 1985-86.
– Tom Barrasso, Pittsburgh, 1992-93.

LONGEST UNDEFEATED STREAK BY A GOALTENDER, ONE SEASON:
32 Games – Gerry Cheevers, Boston, 1971-72. 24W-8T
31 Games – Pete Peeters, Boston, 1982-83. 26W-5T
27 Games – Pete Peeters, Philadelphia, 1979-80. 22W-5T

LONGEST UNDEFEATED STREAK BY A GOALTENDER IN HIS FIRST NHL SEASON:
23 Games – Grant Fuhr, Edmonton, 1981-82. 15W-8T

LONGEST UNDEFEATED STREAK BY A GOALTENDER FROM START OF CAREER:
16 Games – Patrick Lalime, Pittsburgh, 1996-97. 14W-2T

MOST 30-OR-MORE WIN SEASONS BY A GOALTENDER:
14 – Martin Brodeur, New Jersey, in 20 seasons.
13 – Patrick Roy, Montreal, Colorado, in 19 seasons.
9 – Ed Belfour, Chicago, San Jose, Dallas, Toronto, Florida, in 17 seasons.
8 – Tony Esposito, Montreal, Chicago, in 16 seasons.
7 – Jacques Plante, Montreal, NY Rangers, St. Louis, Toronto, Boston, in 18 seasons.
– Ken Dryden, Montreal, in 8 seasons.
– Curtis Joseph, St. Louis, Edmonton, Toronto, Detroit, Phoenix, Calgary, in 19 seasons.
– Dominik Hasek, Chicago, Buffalo, Detroit, Ottawa, in 16 seasons.
– Henrik Lundqvist, NY Rangers, in 8 seasons.
– Miikka Kiprusoff, San Jose, Calgary, in 12 seasons.
– Ryan Miller, Buffalo, in 10 seasons.
– Roberto Luongo, NY Islanders, Florida, Vancouver, in 13 seasons.

MOST CONSECUTIVE 30-OR-MORE WIN SEASONS BY A GOALTENDER:
12 – Martin Brodeur, New Jersey, 1995-96 – 2003-04, 2005-06 – 2007-08.
8 – Patrick Roy, Montreal, Colorado, 1995-96 – 2002-03.
7 – Tony Esposito, Chicago, 1969-70 – 1975-76.
– Miikka Kiprusoff, Calgary, 2005-06 – 2011-12.
– Henrik Lundqvist, NY Rangers, 2005-06 – 2011-12.
– Roberto Luongo, Florida, Vancouver, 2005-06 – 2011-12.
– Ryan Miller, Buffalo, 2005-06 – 2011-12.
6 – Jacques Plante, Montreal, 1954-55 – 1959-60.
– Marty Turco, Dallas, 2002-03, 2003-04, 2005-06 – 2008-09.

MOST 40-OR-MORE WIN SEASONS BY A GOALTENDER:
8 – Martin Brodeur, New Jersey, in 20 seasons.
3 – Terry Sawchuk, Detroit, Boston, Toronto, Los Angeles, NY Rangers, in 21 seasons.
– Jacques Plante, Montreal, NY Rangers, St. Louis, Toronto, Boston, in 18 seasons.
– Miikka Kiprusoff, San Jose, Calgary, in 12 seasons.
– Evgeni Nabokov, San Jose, NY Islanders, in 12 seasons.
2 – Bernie Parent, Boston, Philadelphia, Toronto, in 13 seasons.
– Ken Dryden, Montreal, in 8 seasons.
– Ed Belfour, Chicago, San Jose, Dallas, Toronto, Florida, in 17 seasons.
– Ryan Miller, Buffalo, in 10 seasons.
– Roberto Luongo, NY islanders, Florida, Vancouver, in 13 seasons.
– Marc-Andre Fleury, Pittsburgh, in 9 seasons.

MOST CONSECUTIVE 40-OR-MORE WIN SEASONS BY A GOALTENDER:
3 – Martin Brodeur, New Jersey, 2005-06 – 2007-08.
– Evgeni Nabokov, San Jose, 2007-08 – 2009-10.
2 – Terry Sawchuk, Detroit, 1950-51 – 1951-52.
– Bernie Parent, Philadelphia, 1973-74 – 1974-75.
– Ken Dryden, Montreal, 1975-76 – 1976-77.
– Martin Brodeur, New Jersey, 1999-2000 – 2000-01.
– Miikka Kiprusoff, Calgary, 2005-06 – 2006-07.

MOST LOSSES BY A GOALTENDER, CAREER:
380 – Martin Brodeur, New Jersey in 20 seasons. 1,220GP
352 – Gump Worsley, NY Rangers, Montreal, Minnesota, in 21 seasons. 861GP
– Curtis Joseph, St. Louis, Edmonton, Toronto, Detroit, Phoenix, Calgary, in 19 seasons. 943GP
351 – Gilles Meloche, Chicago, California, Cleveland, Minnesota, Pittsburgh, in 18 seasons. 788GP
346 – John Vanbiesbrouck, NY Rangers, Florida, Philadelphia, NY Islanders, New Jersey, in 20 seasons. 882GP
341 – Sean Burke, New Jersey, Hartford, Carolina, Vancouver, Philadelphia, Florida, Phoenix, Tampa Bay, Los Angeles, in 18 seasons. 820GP

MOST LOSSES BY A GOALTENDER, ONE SEASON:
48 – Gary Smith, California, 1970-71. 71GP
47 – Al Rollins, Chicago, 1953-54. 66GP
46 – Peter Sidorkiewicz, Ottawa, 1992-93. 64GP

GOALTENDER SHOOTOUT RECORDS

MOST SHOOTOUT WINS, ONE SEASON:
10 – Mathieu Garon, Edmonton, 2007-08. 10GP
– Jonathan Quick, Los Angelesm 2010-11. 10GP
– Ryan Miller, Buffalo, 2006-07. 14GP
– Martin Brodeur, New Jersey, 2006-07. 16GP

MOST SHOOTOUT WINS, CAREER:
45 – Henrik Lundqvist, NY Rangers. 75GP
43 – Ryan Miller, Buffalo. 70GP
42 – Martin Brodeur, New Jersey. 67GP
39 – Marc-Andre Fleury, Pittsburgh. 56GP

MOST SHOOTOUT SHOTS AGAINST, ONE SEASON:
62 – Ilya Bryzgalov, Phoenix, 2009-10. 17GA
60 – Martin Brodeur, New Jersey, 2006-07. 20GA
54 – Roberto Luongo, Vancouver, 2007-08. 15GA
– Jimmy Howard, Detroit, 2009-10. 17GA

MOST SHOOTOUT SHOTS AGAINST, CAREER:
287 – Henrik Lundqvist, NY Rangers. 68GA
240 – Ryan Miller, Buffalo. 71GA
237 – Roberto Luongo, Florida, Vancouver. 79GA
228 – Martin Brodeur, New Jersey. 67GA

BEST SHOOTOUT SAVE PERCENTAGE, ONE SEASON: *(minimum 20 shots)*
.938 – Mathieu Garon, Edmonton, 2007-08. 32S-2GA
.917 – Semyon Varlamov, Colorado, 2011-12. 24S-2GA
.900 – Marc Denis, Tampa Bay, 2006-07. 20S-2GA
.879 – Johan Holmqvist, Tampa Bay, 2006-07. 33S-4GA

BEST SHOOTOUT SAVE PERCENTAGE, CAREER: *(minimum 40 shots)*
.854 – Marc Denis, Columbus, Tampa Bay, Montreal. 41S-6GA
.775 – Semyon Varlamov, Washington, Colorado. 71S-16GA
.764 – Brent Johnson, Washington, Pittsburgh. 55S-13GA
.763 – Henrik Lundqvist, NY Rangers. 287S-68GA

Active NHL Players' Three-or-More-Goal Games

Regular Season

Teams named are the ones the players were with at the time of their multiple-scoring games. Players listed alphabetically.

Pittsburgh's Chris Kunitz is congratulated after his third goal of the game in a 6-3 victory over Washington on February 3, 2013. Kunitz later scored another for the only four-goal game in the NHL during the 2012-13 season.

Player	Team(s)	3-Goals	4-Goals	5-Goals
Abdelkader, Justin	Detroit	1	—	—
Alfredsson, Daniel	Ottawa	7	1	—
Antropov, Nik	Toronto	2	—	—
Atkinson, Cam	Columbus	1	—	—
Backes, David	St. Louis	1	—	—
Belanger, Eric	Los Angeles	1	—	—
Bergenheim, Sean	NY Islanders	1	—	—
Bergeron, Marc-Andre	Edmonton	1	—	—
Bergeron, Patrice	Boston	1	—	—
Bertuzzi, Todd	Vancouver	5	—	—
Bonino, Nick	Anaheim	1	—	—
Booth, David	Florida	2	—	—
Boulton, Eric	Atlanta	1	—	—
Bourque, Rene	Calgary	3	—	—
Boyes, Brad	Boston	1	—	—
Boyle, Dan	Tampa Bay	1	—	—
Briere, Daniel	Buf., Phi.	5	—	—
Brouwer, Troy	Washington	1	—	—
Brown, Dustin	Los Angeles	3	—	—
Brunnstrom, Fabian	Dallas	1	—	—
Burrows, Alexandre	Vancouver	3	—	—
Byfuglien, Dustin	Chicago	1	—	—
Callahan, Ryan	NY Rangers	2	—	—
Calvert, Matt	Columbus	1	—	—
Cammalleri, Mike	Cgy., Mtl.	5	—	—
Carcillo, Daniel	Phoenix	1	—	—
Carter, Jeff	Phi., CBJ, L.A.	5	—	—
Chara, Zdeno	Boston	1	—	—
Cleary, Daniel	Detroit	1	—	—
Clowe, Ryane	San Jose	1	—	—
Cogliano, Andrew	Anaheim	2	—	—
Cole, Erik	Car., Edm., Mtl.	7	—	—
Comeau, Blake	NY Islanders	1	—	—
Corvo, Joe	Carolina	1	—	—
Crombeen, B.J.	St. Louis	1	—	—
Crosby, Sidney	Pittsburgh	7	—	—
Cullen, Matt	Carolina	1	—	—
Doan, Shane	Phoenix	1	—	—
Duchene, Matt	Colorado	1	—	—
Dupuis, Pascal	Pittsburgh	1	—	—
Dvorak, Radek	NYR, Fla.	2	1	—
Eaves, Patrick	Detroit	1	—	—
Elias, Patrik	New Jersey	7	1	—
Eller, Lars	Montreal	—	1	—
Erat, Martin	Nashville	2	—	—
Eriksson, Loui	Dallas	2	—	—
Fiddler, Vernon	Phoenix	1	—	—
Filatov, Nikita	Columbus	1	—	—
Fisher, Mike	Ottawa	1	—	—
Fleischmann, Tomas	Colorado	1	—	—
Franzen, Johan	Detroit	1	—	1
Gaborik, Marian	Min., NYR	12	1	1
Gagne, Simon	Philadelphia	3	—	—
Gagner, Sam	Edmonton	1	1	—
Gionta, Brian	New Jersey	1	—	—
Glencross, Curtis	Calgary	2	—	—
Gomez, Scott	New Jersey	2	—	—
Gonchar, Sergei	Washington	1	—	—
Grabner, Michael	Van., NYI	2	—	—
Hall, Taylor	Edmonton	3	—	—
Handzus, Michal	St.L., L.A.	2	—	—
Hanzal, Martin	Phoenix	1	—	—
Hartnell, Scott	Nsh., Phi.	7	—	—
Havlat, Martin	Ottawa	3	1	—
Heatley, Dany	Atl., Ott., S.J.	8	1	—
Hecht, Jochen	Buffalo	1	—	—
Hejduk, Milan	Colorado	4	—	—
Hemsky, Alex	Edmonton	1	—	—
Higgins, Chris	Montreal	1	—	—
Horcoff, Shawn	Edmonton	1	—	—
Horton, Nathan	Florida	2	—	—
Hossa, Marian	Ott., Atl.	6	1	—
Iginla, Jarome	Calgary	11	1	—
Jagr, Jaromir	Pit., NYR	13	1	—
Jokinen, Jussi	Dallas	—	1	—
Jokinen, Olli	Fla., Phx., Cgy.,	7	—	—
Jovanovski, Ed	Phoenix	1	—	—
Kaberle, Tomas	Toronto	1	—	—
Kadri, Nazim	Toronto	2	—	—
Kelly, Chris	Ottawa	1	—	—
Kesler, Ryan	Vancouver	3	—	—
Kessel, Phil	Bos., Tor.	3	—	—
Knuble, Mike	Philadelphia	1	—	—
Kobasew, Chuck	Cgy., Min.	2	—	—
Koivu, Saku	Mtl., Ana.	2	—	—
Kopecky, Tomas	Florida	1	—	—
Kopitar, Anze	Los Angeles	2	—	—
Kostitsyn, Andrei	Montreal	1	—	—
Kostitsyn, Sergei	Nashville	1	—	—
Krejci, David	Boston	2	—	—
Kunitz, Chris	Ana., Pit.	3	1	—
Ladd, Andrew	Chicago	1	—	—
Laich, Brooks	Washington	1	—	—
Langenbrunner, Jamie	New Jersey	1	—	—
Langkow, Daymond	Phx., Cgy.	3	—	—
Lapierre, Maxim	Montreal	1	—	—
Larose, Chad	Carolina	1	—	—
Latendresse, Guillaume	Minnesota	1	—	—
Lecavalier, Vincent	Tampa Bay	6	—	—
Legwand, David	Nashville	2	—	—
Leino, Ville	Philadelphia	1	—	—
Little, Bryan	Atlanta	1	—	—
Lombardi, Matthew	Calgary	1	—	—
Lucic, Milan	Boston	2	—	—
Lupul, Joffrey	Phi., Tor.	3	—	—
Malkin, Evgeni	Pittsburgh	9	—	—
Malone, Ryan	Pit., T.B.	4	—	—
Marchand, Brad	Boston	1	—	—
Marleau, Patrick	San Jose	4	—	—
McClement, Jay	St. Louis	1	—	—
Michalek, Milan	Ottawa	2	—	—
Morrow, Brenden	Dallas	1	—	—
Moss, Dave	Calgary	1	—	—
Moulson, Matt	NY Islanders	2	1	—
Mueller, Peter	Phoenix	2	—	—
Nash, Rick	Columbus	5	—	—
Neal, James	Dal., Pit.	3	—	—
Nugent-Hopkins, Ryan	Edmonton	1	—	—
Ott, Steve	Dallas	1	—	—
Ovechkin, Alex	Washington	10	2	—
Pacioretty, Max	Montreal	1	—	—
Palmieiri, Kyle	Anaheim	1	—	—
Parise, Zach	New Jersey	2	—	—
Perreault, Mathieu	Washington	1	—	—
Perron, David	St. Louis	1	—	—
Perry, Corey	Anaheim	5	—	—
Petersen, Toby	Pittsburgh	1	—	—
Plekanec, Thomas	Montreal	1	—	—
Pominville, Jason	Buffalo	2	—	—
Prospal, Vinny	Ana., T.B.	2	—	—
Purcell, Teddy	Tampa Bay	2	—	—
Pyatt, Taylor	Buffalo	2	—	—
Raymond, Mason	Vancouver	2	—	—
Read, Matt	Philadelphia	1	—	—
Reinprecht, Steve	Col., Phx., Fla.	4	—	—
Ribeiro, Mike	Dallas	1	—	—
Richards, Brad	NY Rangers	1	—	—
Richards, Mike	Philadelphia	2	—	—
Richardson, Brad	Los Angeles	1	—	—
Roy, Derek	Buffalo	4	—	—
Rupp, Mike	Pittsburgh	1	—	—
Ruutu, Tuomo	Carolina	1	—	—
Ryan, Bobby	Anaheim	3	—	—
Ryder, Michael	Montreal	2	—	—
St. Louis, Martin	Tampa Bay	7	—	—
Salo, Sami	Ottawa	1	—	—
Samuelsson, Mikael	Vancouver	1	—	—
Sedin, Daniel	Vancouver	4	1	—
Sedin, Henrik	Vancouver	1	—	—
Seguin, Tyler	Boston	1	—	—
Selanne, Teemu	Wpg., Ana., S.J.	20	2	—
Semin, Alexander	Washington	7	—	—
Setoguchi, Devin	San Jose	1	—	—
Sharp, Patrick	Chicago	2	—	—
Sim, Jon	Florida	1	—	—
Simmonds, Wayne	Philadelphia	1	—	—
Smyth, Ryan	Edmonton	5	—	—
Sobotka, Vladimir	St. Louis	1	—	—
Souray, Sheldon	Montreal	1	—	—
Spezza, Jason	Ottawa	4	—	—
Staal, Eric	Carolina	12	1	—
Staal, Jordan	Pittsburgh	2	—	—
Stafford, Drew	Buffalo	6	—	—
Stalberg, Viktor	Chicago	1	—	—
Stamkos, Steven	Tampa Bay	5	—	—
Stastny, Paul	Colorado	1	—	—
Steen, Alex	Toronto	1	—	—
Stempniak, Lee	Phx., Cgy.	1	—	—
Stepan, Derek	NY Rangers	1	—	—
Stewart, Anthony	Atlanta	1	—	—
Stewart, Chris	Colorado	2	—	—
Sturm, Marco	S.J., Bos.	2	—	—
Subban, P.K.	Montreal	1	—	—
Sullivan, Steve	Tor., Chi., Nsh., Phx.	7	1	—
Tanguay, Alex	Colorado	2	—	—
Tavares, John	NY Islanders	4	—	—
Thornton, Joe	Bos., S.J.	4	—	—
Tlusty, Jiri	Carolina	1	—	—
Toews, Jonathan	Chicago	2	—	—
Torres, Raffi	Vancouver	1	—	—
Umberger, R.J.	Phi., CBJ	3	—	—
Upshall, Scottie	Phoenix	1	—	—
Vanek, Thomas	Buffalo	7	1	—
van Riemsdyk, James	Philadelphia	1	—	—
Vermette, Antoine	Ottawa	1	—	—
Versteeg, Kris	Florida	1	—	—
Visnovsky, Lubomir	L.A., Ana.	2	—	—
Voracek, Jakub	Philadelphia	1	—	—
Vrbata, Radim	Col., Car., Phx.	4	—	—
Weiss, Stephen	Florida	2	—	—
Wellwood, Kyle	Toronto	1	—	—
Wheeler, Blake	Boston	1	—	—
Whitney, Ray	CBJ, Car., Phx.	4	—	—
Williams, Jason	Detroit	1	—	—
Williams, Justin	Carolina	1	—	—
Yakupov, Nail	Edmonton	1	—	—
Zetterberg, Henrik	Detroit	5	—	—
Zubrus, Dainius	Mtl., N.J.	1	1	—

Top 100 All-Time Goal-Scoring Leaders

* active player

	Player	Goals	Games	Goals per game	Seasons
1.	**Wayne Gretzky**, Edm., L.A., St.L., NYR	**894**	1487	.601	20
2.	**Gordie Howe**, Det., Hfd.	**801**	1767	.453	26
3.	**Brett Hull**, Cgy., St.L., Dal., Det., Phx.	**741**	1269	.584	20
4.	**Marcel Dionne**, Det., L.A., NYR	**731**	1348	.542	18
5.	**Phil Esposito**, Chi., Bos., NYR	**717**	1282	.559	18
6.	**Mike Gartner**, Wsh., Min., NYR, Tor., Phx.	**708**	1432	.494	19
7.	**Mark Messier**, Edm., NYR, Van.	**694**	1756	.395	25
8.	**Steve Yzerman**, Det.	**692**	1514	.457	22
9.	**Mario Lemieux**, Pit.	**690**	915	.754	18
* 10.	**Jaromir Jagr**, Pit., Wsh., NYR, Phi., Dal., Bos.	**681**	1391	.490	19
* 11.	**Teemu Selanne**, Wpg., Ana., S.J., Col.	**675**	1387	.487	20
12.	**Luc Robitaille**, L.A., Pit., NYR, Det.	**668**	1431	.467	19
13.	**Brendan Shanahan**, N.J., St.L., Hfd., Det., NYR	**656**	1524	.430	21
14.	**Dave Andreychuk**, Buf., Tor., N.J., Bos., Col., T.B.	**640**	1639	.390	23
15.	**Joe Sakic**, Que., Col.	**625**	1378	.454	20
16.	**Bobby Hull**, Chi., Wpg., Hfd.	**610**	1063	.574	16
17.	**Dino Ciccarelli**, Min., Wsh., Det., T.B., Fla.	**608**	1232	.494	19
18.	**Jari Kurri**, Edm., L.A., NYR, Ana., Col.	**601**	1251	.480	17
19.	**Mark Recchi**, Pit., Phi., Mtl., Car., Atl., T.B., Bos.	**577**	1652	.349	22
20.	**Mike Bossy**, NYI	**573**	752	.762	10
21.	**Joe Nieuwendyk**, Cgy., Dal., N.J., Tor., Fla.	**564**	1257	.449	20
22.	**Mats Sundin**, Que., Tor., Van.	**564**	1346	.419	18
23.	**Mike Modano**, Min., Dal., Det.	**561**	1499	.374	22
24.	**Guy Lafleur**, Mtl., NYR, Que.	**560**	1126	.497	17
25.	**John Bucyk**, Det., Bos.	**556**	1540	.361	23
26.	**Ron Francis**, Hfd., Pit., Car., Tor.	**549**	1731	.317	23
27.	**Michel Goulet**, Que., Chi.	**548**	1089	.503	15
28.	**Maurice Richard**, Mtl.	**544**	978	.556	18
29.	**Stan Mikita**, Chi.	**541**	1394	.388	22
30.	**Keith Tkachuk**, Wpg., Phx., St.L., Atl.	**538**	1201	.448	18
31.	**Frank Mahovlich**, Tor., Det., Mtl.	**533**	1181	.451	18
* 32.	**Jarome Iginla**, Cgy., Pit.	**530**	1232	.430	17
33.	**Bryan Trottier**, NYI, Pit.	**524**	1279	.410	18
34.	**Pat Verbeek**, N.J., Hfd., NYR, Dal., Det.	**522**	1424	.367	20
35.	**Dale Hawerchuk**, Wpg., Buf., St.L., Phi.	**518**	1188	.436	16
36.	**Pierre Turgeon**, Buf., NYI, Mtl., St.L., Dal., Col.	**515**	1294	.398	19
37.	**Jeremy Roenick**, Chi., Phx., Phi., L.A., S.J.	**513**	1363	.376	20
38.	**Gilbert Perreault**, Buf.	**512**	1191	.430	17
39.	**Jean Beliveau**, Mtl.	**507**	1125	.451	20
40.	**Peter Bondra**, Wsh., Ott., Atl., Chi.	**503**	1081	.465	16
41.	**Joe Mullen**, St.L., Cgy., Pit., Bos.	**502**	1062	.473	17
42.	**Lanny McDonald**, Tor., Col., Cgy.	**500**	1111	.450	16
43.	**Glenn Anderson**, Edm., Tor., NYR, St.L.	**498**	1129	.441	16
44.	**Jean Ratelle**, NYR, Bos.	**491**	1281	.383	21
45.	**Norm Ullman**, Det., Tor.	**490**	1410	.348	20
46.	**Brian Bellows**, Min., Mtl., T.B., Ana., Wsh.	**485**	1188	.408	17
47.	**Darryl Sittler**, Tor., Phi., Det.	**484**	1096	.442	15
48.	**Sergei Fedorov**, Det., Ana., CBJ, Wsh.	**483**	1248	.387	18
49.	**Bernie Nicholls**, L.A., NYR, Edm., N.J., Chi., S.J.	**475**	1127	.421	18
50.	**Alexander Mogilny**, Buf., Van., N.J., Tor.	**473**	990	.478	16
51.	**Denis Savard**, Chi., Mtl., T.B.	**473**	1196	.395	17
52.	**Pat LaFontaine**, NYI, Buf., NYR	**468**	865	.541	15
53.	**Alex Delvecchio**, Det.	**456**	1549	.294	24
54.	**Theoren Fleury**, Cgy., Col., NYR, Chi.	**455**	1084	.420	15
55.	**Rod Brind'Amour**, St.L., Phi., Car.	**452**	1484	.305	21
56.	**Peter Stastny**, Que., N.J., St.L.	**450**	977	.461	15
57.	**Doug Gilmour**, St.L., Cgy., Tor., N.J., Chi., Buf., Mtl.	**450**	1474	.305	20
58.	**Rick Middleton**, NYR, Bos.	**448**	1005	.446	14
59.	**Rick Vaive**, Van., Tor., Chi., Buf.	**441**	876	.503	13
60.	**Steve Larmer**, Chi., NYR	**441**	1006	.438	15
61.	**Rick Tocchet**, Phi., Pit., L.A., Bos., Wsh., Phx.	**440**	1144	.385	18
62.	**Gary Roberts**, Cgy., Car., Tor., Fla., Pit., T.B.	**438**	1224	.358	22
63.	**Pavel Bure**, Van., Fla., NYR	**437**	702	.623	12
* 64.	**Marian Hossa**, Ott., Atl., Pit., Det., Chi	**434**	1018	.426	15
65.	**Vincent Damphousse**, Tor., Edm., Mtl., S.J.	**432**	1378	.313	18
66.	**Dave Taylor**, L.A.	**431**	1111	.388	17
67.	**Alex Kovalev**, NYR, Pit., Mtl., Ott., Fla.	**430**	1316	.327	19
68.	**Bill Guerin**, N.J., Edm., Bos., Dal., St.L., S.J., NYI, Pit.	**429**	1263	.340	18
69.	**Yvan Cournoyer**, Mtl.	**428**	968	.442	16
* 70.	**Daniel Alfredsson**, Ott.	**426**	1178	.362	17
71.	**Brian Propp**, Phi., Bos., Min., Hfd.	**425**	1016	.418	15
72.	**Steve Shutt**, Mtl., L.A.	**424**	930	.456	13
73.	**Owen Nolan**, Que., Col., S.J., Tor., Phx., Cgy., Min.	**422**	1200	.352	18
74.	**Stephane Richer**, Mtl., N.J., T.B., St.L., Pit.	**421**	1054	.399	17
75.	**Steve Thomas**, Tor., Chi., NYI, N.J., Ana., Det.	**421**	1235	.341	20
76.	**Bill Barber**, Phi.	**420**	903	.465	12
77.	**Ilya Kovalchuk**, Atl., N.J.	**417**	816	.511	11
78.	**Jason Arnott**, Edm., N.J., Dal., Nsh., Wsh., St.L.	**417**	1244	.335	18
79.	**Tony Amonte**, NYR, Chi., Phx., Phi., Cgy.	**416**	1174	.354	16
80.	**Garry Unger**, Tor., Det., St.L., Atl., L.A., Edm.	**413**	1105	.374	16
81.	**John MacLean**, N.J., S.J., NYR, Dal.	**413**	1194	.346	18
82.	**Raymond Bourque**, Bos., Col.	**410**	1612	.254	22
83.	**Ray Ferraro**, Hfd., NYI, NYR, L.A., Atl., St.L.	**408**	1258	.324	18
84.	**John LeClair**, Mtl., Phi., Pit.	**406**	967	.420	16
85.	**Rod Gilbert**, NYR	**406**	1065	.381	18
* 86.	**Patrick Marleau**, S.J.	**404**	1165	.347	15
87.	**John Ogrodnick**, Det., Que., NYR	**402**	928	.433	14
88.	**Paul Kariya**, Ana., Col., Nsh., St.L.	**402**	989	.406	15
89.	**Dave Keon**, Tor., Hfd.	**396**	1296	.306	18
90.	**Paul Coffey**, Edm., Pit., L.A., Det., Hfd., Phi., Chi., Car., Bos.	**396**	1409	.281	21
91.	**Cam Neely**, Van., Bos.	**395**	726	.544	13
92.	**Pierre Larouche**, Pit., Mtl., Hfd., NYR	**395**	812	.486	14
93.	**Markus Naslund**, Pit., Van., NYR	**395**	1117	.354	15
94.	**Tomas Sandstrom**, NYR, L.A., Pit., Det., Ana.	**394**	983	.401	15
95.	**Bernie Geoffrion**, Mtl., NYR	**393**	883	.445	16
96.	**Jean Pronovost**, Pit., Atl., Wsh.	**391**	998	.392	14
97.	**Dean Prentice**, NYR, Bos., Det., Pit., Min.	**391**	1378	.284	22
98.	**Rick Martin**, Buf., L.A.	**384**	685	.561	11
* 99.	**Vincent Lecavalier**, T.B.	**383**	1037	.369	14
100.	**Reggie Leach**, Bos., Cal., Phi., Det.	**381**	934	.408	13

Lanny McDonald is the only player in NHL history to finish his career with exactly 500 goals scored in regular-season play. He added another 44 in 117 playoff games.

Top 100 Active Goal-Scoring Leaders

	Player	Goals	Games	Goals per game	Seasons
1.	**Jaromir Jagr**, Pit., Wsh., NYR, Phi., Dal., Bos.	**681**	1391	.490	19
2.	**Teemu Selanne**, Wpg., Ana., S.J., Col.	**675**	1387	.487	20
3.	**Jarome Iginla**, Cgy., Pit.	**530**	1232	.430	17
4.	**Marian Hossa**, Ott., Atl., Pit., Det., Chi.	**434**	1018	.426	15
5.	**Daniel Alfredsson**, Ott.	**426**	1178	.362	17
6.	**Patrick Marleau**, S.J.	**404**	1165	.347	15
7.	**Vincent Lecavalier**, T.B.	**383**	1037	.369	14
8.	**Ryan Smyth**, Edm., NYI, Col., L.A.	**376**	1198	.314	18
9.	**Ray Whitney**, S.J., Edm., Fla., CBJ, Det., Car., Phx., Dal.	**376**	1261	.298	21
10.	**Milan Hejduk**, Col.	**375**	1020	.368	14
11.	**Patrik Elias**, N.J.	**375**	1090	.344	17
12.	**Alex Ovechkin**, Wsh.	**371**	601	.617	8
13.	**Dany Heatley**, Atl., Ott., S.J., Min.	**360**	787	.457	11
14.	**Martin St. Louis**, Cgy., T.B.	**340**	979	.347	14
15.	**Marian Gaborik**, Min., NYR, CBJ	**336**	769	.437	12
16.	**Joe Thornton**, Bos., S.J.	**331**	1125	.294	15
17.	**Shane Doan**, Wpg., Phx.	**331**	1246	.266	17
18.	**Rick Nash**, CBJ, NYR	**310**	718	.432	10
19.	**Todd Bertuzzi**, NYI, Van., Fla., Det., Ana., Cgy.	**305**	1100	.277	17
20.	**Olli Jokinen**, L.A., NYI, Fla., Phx., Cgy., NYR, Wpg.	**299**	1087	.275	15
21.	**Daniel Sedin**, Van.	**291**	906	.321	12
22.	**Steve Sullivan**, N.J., Tor., Chi., Nsh., Pit., Phx.	**290**	1011	.287	17
23.	**Simon Gagne**, Phi., T.B., L.A.	**288**	799	.360	13
24.	**Daniel Briere**, Phx., Buf., Phi.	**286**	847	.338	15
25.	**Mike Knuble**, Det., NYR, Bos., Phi., Wsh.	**278**	1068	.260	16
26.	**Daymond Langkow**, T.B., Phi., Phx., Cgy.	**270**	1090	.248	16
27.	**Eric Staal**, Car.	**268**	690	.388	9
28.	**Henrik Zetterberg**, Det.	**263**	714	.368	10
29.	**Brad Richards**, T.B., Dal., NYR	**256**	900	.284	12
30.	**Pavel Datsyuk**, Det.	**255**	779	.327	11
31.	**Vinny Prospal**, Phi., Ott., Fla., T.B., Ana., NYR, CBJ	**255**	1108	.230	16
32.	**Thomas Vanek**, Buf.	**250**	585	.427	8
33.	**Brenden Morrow**, Dal., Pit.	**249**	850	.293	13
34.	**Alex Tanguay**, Col., Cgy., Mtl., T.B.	**249**	922	.270	13
35.	**Saku Koivu**, Mtl., Ana.	**244**	1059	.230	17
36.	**Jamie Langenbrunner**, Dal., N.J., St.L.	**243**	1109	.219	18
37.	**Marco Sturm**, S.J., Bos., L.A., Wsh., Van., Fla.	**242**	938	.258	14
38.	**Sidney Crosby**, Pit.	**238**	470	.506	8
39.	**Brian Gionta**, N.J., Mtl.	**231**	695	.332	11
40.	**Scott Hartnell**, Nsh., Phi.	**230**	875	.263	12
41.	**Jeff Carter**, Phi., CBJ, L.A.	**228**	564	.404	8
42.	**Jason Spezza**, Ott.	**228**	611	.373	10
43.	**Erik Cole**, Car., Edm., Mtl., Dal.	**228**	749	.304	11
44.	**Martin Havlat**, Ott., Chi., Min., S.J.	**224**	700	.320	12
45.	**Radek Dvorak**, Fla., NYR, Edm., St.L., Atl., Dal., Ana.	**223**	1200	.186	17
46.	**Corey Perry**, Ana.	**220**	574	.383	8
47.	**Evgeni Malkin**, Pit.	**217**	458	.474	7
48.	**Sergei Gonchar**, Wsh., Bos., Pit., Ott.	**217**	1177	.184	18
49.	**Michael Ryder**, Mtl., Bos., Dal.	**213**	677	.315	9
50.	**Zach Parise**, N.J., Min.	**212**	550	.385	8
51.	**Alexander Semin**, Wsh., Car.	**210**	513	.409	8
52.	**Mike Cammalleri**, L.A., Cgy., Mtl.	**210**	606	.347	10
53.	**Steven Stamkos**, T.B.	**208**	373	.558	5
54.	**Dainius Zubrus**, Phi., Mtl., Wsh., Buf., N.J.	**208**	1087	.191	16
55.	**Mike Fisher**, Ott., Nsh.	**206**	812	.254	13
56.	**Matt Cullen**, Ana., Fla., Car., NYR, Ott., Min.	**202**	1073	.188	15
57.	**David Legwand**, Nsh.	**200**	894	.224	14
58.	**Patrick Sharp**, Phi., Chi.	**199**	595	.334	10
59.	**Nathan Horton**, Fla., Bos.	**198**	591	.335	9
60.	**Radim Vrbata**, Col., Car., Chi., Phx., T.B.	**195**	712	.274	11
61.	**Nik Antropov**, Tor., NYR, Atl., Wpg.	**193**	788	.245	13
62.	**Justin Williams**, Phi., Car., L.A.	**190**	755	.252	12
63.	**Jason Pominville**, Buf., Min.	**189**	588	.321	9
64.	**Mike Ribeiro**, Mtl., Dal., Wsh.	**186**	785	.237	13
65.	**Jochen Hecht**, St.L., Edm., Buf.	**186**	833	.223	14
66.	**Phil Kessel**, Bos., Tor.	**185**	504	.367	7
67.	**Henrik Sedin**, Van.	**182**	940	.194	12
68.	**Dustin Brown**, L.A.	**181**	641	.282	9
69.	**Michal Handzus**, St.L., Phx., Phi., Chi., L.A., S.J.	**181**	950	.191	14
70.	**Pascal Dupuis**, Min., NYR, Atl., Pit.	**175**	798	.219	12
71.	**Ryan Malone**, Pit., T.B.	**174**	584	.298	9
72.	**Anze Kopitar**, L.A.	**173**	522	.331	7
73.	**Ruslan Fedotenko**, Phi., T.B., NYI, Pit., NYR	**173**	863	.200	12
74.	**Chris Kunitz**, Ana., Atl., Pit.	**172**	581	.296	9
75.	**Scott Gomez**, N.J., NYR, Mtl., S.J.	**171**	941	.182	13
76.	**Milan Michalek**, S.J., Ott.	**170**	549	.310	9
77.	**Derek Roy**, Buf., Dal., Van.	**168**	591	.284	9
78.	**Brad Boyes**, S.J., Bos., St.L., Buf., NYI	**168**	606	.277	9
79.	**Jonathan Toews**, Chi.	**167**	408	.409	6
80.	**Johan Franzen**, Det.	**164**	513	.320	8
81.	**Martin Erat**, Nsh., Wsh.	**164**	732	.224	11
82.	**Mike Richards**, Phi., L.A.	**163**	575	.283	8
83.	**Joffrey Lupul**, Ana., Edm., Phi., Tor.	**162**	531	.305	9
84.	**Shawn Horcoff**, Edm.	**162**	796	.204	12
85.	**Dan Cleary**, Chi., Edm., Phx., Det.	**160**	869	.184	15
86.	**Ryan Kesler**, Van.	**157**	578	.272	9
87.	**Antoine Vermette**, Ott., CBJ, Phx.	**157**	670	.234	9
88.	**Tomas Plekanec**, Mtl.	**156**	598	.261	9
89.	**Roman Hamrlik**, T.B., Edm., NYI, Cgy., Mtl., Wsh., NYR	**155**	1395	.111	20
90.	**Patrice Bergeron**, Bos.	**153**	579	.264	9
91.	**Matt Cooke**, Van., Wsh., Pit.	**153**	935	.164	14
92.	**Ryan Getzlaf**, Ana.	**152**	556	.273	8
93.	**Alexandre Burrows**, Van.	**152**	569	.267	8
94.	**R.J. Umberger**, Phi., CBJ	**151**	599	.252	8
95.	**Joe Pavelski**, S.J.	**150**	479	.313	7
96.	**Loui Eriksson**, Dal.	**150**	501	.299	7
97.	**Patrick Kane**, Chi.	**149**	446	.334	6
98.	**Mikael Samuelsson**, S.J., NYR, Pit., Fla., Det., Van.	**148**	673	.220	12
99.	**Bobby Ryan**, Ana.	**147**	378	.389	6
100.	**Jeff Halpern**, Wsh., Dal., T.B., L.A., Mtl., NYR	**147**	907	.162	13

Patrick Marleau scored the 400th goal of his career versus Colorado on March 10, 2013. Marleau had a fast start to the 2012-13 season with two goals in each of his first four games. He became the first player to begin a season with four consecutive multi-goal games since Cy Denneny in the NHL's first season of 1917-18.

Top 100 All-Time Assist Leaders

* active player

Among players in the top 100 all-time assist leaders, Peter Forsberg's assists-per-game rate of .898 trails only Wayne Gretzky, Mario Lemieux and Bobby Orr. Forsberg had 636 assists in 708 games played.

	Player	Assists	Games	Assists per game	Seasons
1.	**Wayne Gretzky**, Edm., L.A., St.L., NYR	**1963**	1487	1.320	20
2.	**Ron Francis**, Hfd., Pit., Car., Tor.	**1249**	1731	.722	23
3.	**Mark Messier**, Edm., NYR, Van.	**1193**	1756	.679	25
4.	**Raymond Bourque**, Bos., Col.	**1169**	1612	.725	22
5.	**Paul Coffey**, Edm., Pit., L.A., Det., Hfd., Phi., Chi., Car., Bos.	**1135**	1409	.806	21
6.	**Adam Oates**, Det., St.L., Bos., Wsh., Phi., Ana., Edm.	**1079**	1337	.807	19
7.	**Steve Yzerman**, Det.	**1063**	1514	.702	22
8.	**Gordie Howe**, Det., Hfd.	**1049**	1767	.594	26
9.	**Marcel Dionne**, Det., L.A., NYR	**1040**	1348	.772	18
10.	**Mario Lemieux**, Pit.	**1033**	915	1.129	18
11.	**Joe Sakic**, Que., Col.	**1016**	1378	.737	20
* 12.	**Jaromir Jagr**, Pit., Wsh., NYR, Phi., Dal., Bos.	**1007**	1391	.724	19
13.	**Doug Gilmour**, St.L., Cgy., Tor., N.J., Chi., Buf., Mtl.	**964**	1474	.654	20
14.	**Mark Recchi**, Pit., Phi., Mtl., Car., Atl., T.B., Bos.	**956**	1652	.579	22
15.	**Al MacInnis**, Cgy., St.L.	**934**	1416	.660	23
16.	**Larry Murphy**, L.A., Wsh., Min., Pit., Tor., Det.	**929**	1615	.575	21
17.	**Stan Mikita**, Chi.	**926**	1394	.664	22
18.	**Bryan Trottier**, NYI, Pit.	**901**	1279	.704	18
19.	**Phil Housley**, Buf., Wpg., St.L., Cgy., N.J., Wsh., Chi., Tor.	**894**	1495	.598	21
20.	**Dale Hawerchuk**, Wpg., Buf., St.L., Phi.	**891**	1188	.750	16
21.	**Nicklas Lidstrom**, Det.	**878**	1564	.561	20
22.	**Phil Esposito**, Chi., Bos., NYR	**873**	1282	.681	18
23.	**Denis Savard**, Chi., Mtl., T.B.	**865**	1196	.723	17
24.	**Bobby Clarke**, Phi.	**852**	1144	.745	15
25.	**Alex Delvecchio**, Det.	**825**	1549	.533	24
26.	**Gilbert Perreault**, Buf.	**814**	1191	.683	17
27.	**Mike Modano**, Min., Dal., Det.	**813**	1499	.542	22
28.	**John Bucyk**, Det., Bos.	**813**	1540	.528	23
29.	**Pierre Turgeon**, Buf., NYI, Mtl., St.L., Dal., Col.	**812**	1294	.628	19
30.	**Jari Kurri**, Edm., L.A., NYR, Ana., Col.	**797**	1251	.637	17
31.	**Guy Lafleur**, Mtl., NYR, Que.	**793**	1126	.704	17
32.	**Peter Stastny**, Que., N.J., St.L.	**789**	977	.808	15
* 33.	**Joe Thornton**, Bos., S.J.	**787**	1125	.700	15
34.	**Mats Sundin**, Que., Tor., Van.	**785**	1346	.583	18
35.	**Brian Leetch**, NYR, Tor., Bos.	**781**	1205	.648	18
36.	**Jean Ratelle**, NYR, Bos.	**776**	1281	.606	21
37.	**Vincent Damphousse**, Tor., Edm., Mtl., S.J.	**773**	1378	.561	18
38.	**Chris Chelios**, Mtl., Chi., Det., Atl.	**763**	1651	.462	26
39.	**Bernie Federko**, St.L., Det.	**761**	1000	.761	14
40.	**Doug Weight**, NYR, Edm., St.L., Car., Ana., NYI	**755**	1238	.610	20
* 41.	**Teemu Selanne**, Wpg., Ana., S.J., Col.	**755**	1387	.544	20
42.	**Larry Robinson**, Mtl., L.A.	**750**	1384	.542	20
43.	**Denis Potvin**, NYI	**742**	1060	.700	15
44.	**Norm Ullman**, Det., Tor.	**739**	1410	.524	20
45.	**Bernie Nicholls**, L.A., NYR, Edm., N.J., Chi., S.J.	**734**	1127	.651	18
46.	**Rod Brind'Amour**, St.L., Phi., Car.	**732**	1484	.493	21
47.	**Luc Robitaille**, L.A., Pit., NYR, Det.	**726**	1431	.507	19
48.	**Jean Beliveau**, Mtl.	**712**	1125	.633	20
49.	**Scott Stevens**, Wsh., St.L., N.J.	**712**	1635	.435	22
50.	**Jeremy Roenick**, Chi., Phx., Phi., L.A., S.J.	**703**	1363	.516	20
51.	**Brendan Shanahan**, N.J., St.L., Hfd., Det., NYR	**698**	1524	.458	21
52.	**Dave Andreychuk**, Buf., Tor., N.J., Bos., Col., T.B.	**698**	1639	.426	23
53.	**Dale Hunter**, Que., Wsh., Col.	**697**	1407	.495	19
54.	**Sergei Fedorov**, Det., Ana., CBJ, Wsh.	**696**	1248	.558	18
55.	**Henri Richard**, Mtl.	**688**	1256	.548	20
56.	**Brad Park**, NYR, Bos., Det.	**683**	1113	.614	17
* 57.	**Daniel Alfredsson**, Ott.	**682**	1178	.579	17
58.	**Bobby Smith**, Min., Mtl.	**679**	1077	.630	15
* 59.	**Ray Whitney**, S.J., Edm., Fla., CBJ, Det., Car., Phx., Dal.	**656**	1261	.520	21
60.	**Brett Hull**, Cgy., St.L., Dal., Det., Phx.	**650**	1269	.512	20
61.	**Bobby Orr**, Bos., Chi.	**645**	657	.982	12
62.	**Gary Suter**, Cgy., Chi., S.J.	**641**	1145	.560	17
63.	**Dave Taylor**, L.A.	**638**	1111	.574	17
64.	**Darryl Sittler**, Tor., Phi., Det.	**637**	1096	.581	15
65.	**Borje Salming**, Tor., Det.	**637**	1148	.555	17
66.	**Peter Forsberg**, Que., Col., Phi., Nsh.	**636**	708	.898	14
67.	**Neal Broten**, Min., Dal., N.J., L.A.	**634**	1099	.577	17
68.	**Theoren Fleury**, Cgy., Col., NYR, Chi.	**633**	1084	.584	15
69.	**Mike Gartner**, Wsh., Min., NYR, Tor., Phx.	**627**	1432	.438	19
70.	**Andy Bathgate**, NYR, Tor., Det., Pit.	**624**	1069	.584	17
71.	**Sergei Zubov**, NYR, Pit., Dal.	**619**	1068	.580	16
72.	**Rod Gilbert**, NYR	**615**	1065	.577	18
* 73.	**Henrik Sedin**, Van.	**610**	940	.649	12
74.	**Michel Goulet**, Que., Chi.	**604**	1089	.555	15
75.	**Kirk Muller**, N.J., Mtl., NYI, Tor., Fla., Dal.	**602**	1349	.446	19
76.	**Glenn Anderson**, Edm., Tor., NYR, St.L.	**601**	1129	.532	16
77.	**Alex Kovalev**, NYR, Pit., Mtl., Ott., Fla.	**599**	1316	.455	19
78.	**Dino Ciccarelli**, Min., Wsh., Det., T.B., Fla.	**592**	1232	.481	19
79.	**Doug Wilson**, Chi., S.J.	**590**	1024	.576	16
80.	**Dave Keon**, Tor., Hfd.	**590**	1296	.455	18
81.	**Paul Kariya**, Ana., Col., Nsh., St.L.	**587**	989	.594	15
82.	**Dave Babych**, Wpg., Hfd., Van., Phi., L.A.	**581**	1195	.486	19
83.	**Brian Propp**, Phi., Bos., Min., Hfd.	**579**	1016	.570	15
* 84.	**Jarome Iginla**, Cgy., Pit.	**576**	1232	.468	17
* 85.	**Martin St. Louis**, Cgy., T.B.	**572**	979	.584	14
86.	**Steve Larmer**, Chi., NYR	**571**	1006	.568	15
87.	**Frank Mahovlich**, Tor., Det., Mtl.	**570**	1181	.483	18
88.	**Scott Niedermayer**, N.J., Ana.	**568**	1263	.450	18
89.	**Craig Janney**, Bos., St.L., S.J., Wpg., Phx., T.B., NYI	**563**	760	.741	12
90.	**Cliff Ronning**, St.L., Van., Phx., Nsh., L.A., Min., NYI	**563**	1137	.495	18
91.	**Joe Nieuwendyk**, Cgy., Dal., N.J., Tor., Fla.	**562**	1257	.447	20
92.	**Joe Mullen**, St.L., Cgy., Pit., Bos.	**561**	1062	.528	17
* 93.	**Brad Richards**, T.B., Dal., NYR	**560**	900	.622	12
94.	**Bobby Hull**, Chi., Wpg., Hfd.	**560**	1063	.527	16
95.	**Alexander Mogilny**, Buf., Van., N.J., Tor.	**559**	990	.565	16
* 96.	**Saku Koivu**, Mtl., Ana.	**559**	1059	.528	17
* 97.	**Sergei Gonchar**, Wsh., Bos., Pit., Ott.	**558**	1177	.474	18
* 98.	**Patrik Elias**, N.J.	**555**	1090	.509	17
99.	**Mike Bossy**, NYI	**553**	752	.735	10
100.	**Thomas Steen**, Wpg.	**553**	950	.582	14

Top 100 Active Assist Leaders

	Player	Assists	Games	Assists per game	Seasons
1.	**Jaromir Jagr**, Pit., Wsh., NYR, Phi., Dal., Bos.	**1007**	1391	.724	19
2.	**Joe Thornton**, Bos., S.J.	**787**	1125	.700	15
3.	**Teemu Selanne**, Wpg., Ana., S.J., Col.	**755**	1387	.544	20
4.	**Daniel Alfredsson**, Ott.	**682**	1178	.579	17
5.	**Ray Whitney**, S.J., Edm., Fla., CBJ, Det., Car., Phx., Dal.	**656**	1261	.520	21
6.	**Henrik Sedin**, Van.	**610**	940	.649	12
7.	**Jarome Iginla**, Cgy., Pit.	**576**	1232	.468	17
8.	**Martin St. Louis**, Cgy., T.B.	**572**	979	.584	14
9.	**Brad Richards**, T.B., Dal., NYR	**560**	900	.622	12
10.	**Saku Koivu**, Mtl., Ana.	**559**	1059	.528	17
11.	**Sergei Gonchar**, Wsh., Bos., Pit., Ott.	**558**	1177	.474	18
12.	**Patrik Elias**, N.J.	**555**	1090	.509	17
13.	**Scott Gomez**, N.J., NYR, Mtl., S.J.	**530**	941	.563	13
14.	**Alex Tanguay**, Col., Cgy., Mtl., T.B.	**513**	922	.556	13
15.	**Pavel Datsyuk**, Det.	**512**	779	.657	11
16.	**Vinny Prospal**, Phi., Ott., Fla., T.B., Ana., NYR, CBJ	**510**	1108	.460	16
17.	**Marian Hossa**, Ott., Atl., Pit., Det., Chi.	**501**	1018	.492	15
18.	**Vincent Lecavalier**, T.B.	**491**	1037	.473	14
19.	**Shane Doan**, Wpg., Phx.	**484**	1246	.388	17
20.	**Roman Hamrlik**, T.B., Edm., NYI, Cgy., Mtl., Wsh., NYR	**483**	1395	.346	20
21.	**Tomas Kaberle**, Tor., Bos., Car., Mtl.	**476**	984	.484	14
22.	**Daniel Sedin**, Van.	**467**	906	.515	12
23.	**Steve Sullivan**, N.J., Tor., Chi., Nsh., Pit., Phx.	**457**	1011	.452	17
24.	**Patrick Marleau**, S.J.	**457**	1165	.392	15
25.	**Todd Bertuzzi**, NYI, Van., Fla., Det., Ana., Cgy.	**449**	1100	.408	17
26.	**Ryan Smyth**, Edm., NYI, Col., L.A.	**443**	1198	.370	18
27.	**Milan Hejduk**, Col.	**430**	1020	.422	14
28.	**Sidney Crosby**, Pit.	**427**	470	.909	8
29.	**Kimmo Timonen**, Nsh., Phi.	**425**	1015	.419	14
30.	**Mike Ribeiro**, Mtl., Dal., Wsh.	**423**	785	.539	13
31.	**Jamie Langenbrunner**, Dal., N.J., St.L.	**420**	1109	.379	18
32.	**Henrik Zetterberg**, Det.	**409**	714	.573	10
33.	**Dany Heatley**, Atl., Ott., S.J., Min.	**403**	787	.512	11
34.	**Daymond Langkow**, T.B., Phi., Phx., Cgy.	**402**	1090	.369	16
35.	**Olli Jokinen**, L.A., NYI, Fla., Phx., Cgy., NYR, Wpg.	**398**	1087	.366	15
36.	**Jason Spezza**, Ott.	**393**	611	.643	10
37.	**Dan Boyle**, Fla., T.B., S.J.	**393**	879	.447	14
38.	**Daniel Briere**, Phx., Buf., Phi.	**373**	847	.440	15
39.	**Ryan Getzlaf**, Ana.	**369**	556	.664	8
40.	**Alex Ovechkin**, Wsh.	**364**	601	.606	8
41.	**Matt Cullen**, Ana., Fla., Car., NYR, Ott., Min.	**360**	1073	.336	15
42.	**Eric Staal**, Car.	**359**	690	.520	9
43.	**Ed Jovanovski**, Fla., Van., Phx.	**359**	1091	.329	17
44.	**Radek Dvorak**, Fla., NYR, Edm., St.L., Atl., Dal., Ana.	**358**	1200	.298	17
45.	**Wade Redden**, Ott., NYR, St.L., Bos.	**348**	1023	.340	14
46.	**Lubomir Visnovsky**, L.A., Edm., Ana., NYI	**344**	806	.427	12
47.	**Evgeni Malkin**, Pit.	**343**	458	.749	7
48.	**Dainius Zubrus**, Phi., Mtl., Wsh., Buf., N.J.	**340**	1087	.313	16
49.	**Marian Gaborik**, Min., NYR, CBJ	**338**	769	.440	12
50.	**Zdeno Chara**, NYI, Ott., Bos.	**334**	1055	.317	15
51.	**Martin Havlat**, Ott., Chi., Min., S.J.	**333**	700	.476	12
52.	**Brian Campbell**, Buf., S.J., Chi., Fla.	**326**	756	.431	13
53.	**David Legwand**, Nsh.	**326**	894	.365	14
54.	**Martin Erat**, Nsh., Wsh.	**320**	732	.437	11
55.	**Derek Morris**, Cgy., Col., Phx., NYR, Bos.	**320**	1044	.307	15
56.	**Ales Hemsky**, Edm.	**318**	597	.533	10
57.	**Simon Gagne**, Phi., T.B., L.A.	**309**	799	.387	13
58.	**Andrei Markov**, Mtl.	**308**	684	.450	12
59.	**Justin Williams**, Phi., Car., L.A.	**308**	755	.408	12
60.	**Nicklas Backstrom**, Wsh.	**306**	413	.741	6
61.	**Anze Kopitar**, L.A.	**303**	522	.580	7
62.	**Tim Connolly**, NYI, Buf., Tor.	**300**	697	.430	12
63.	**Brenden Morrow**, Dal., Pit.	**293**	850	.345	13
64.	**Derek Roy**, Buf., Dal., Van.	**287**	591	.486	9
65.	**Michal Handzus**, St.L., Phx., Phi., Chi., L.A., S.J.	**286**	950	.301	14
66.	**Shawn Horcoff**, Edm.	**285**	796	.358	12
67.	**Patrice Bergeron**, Bos.	**280**	579	.484	9
68.	**Mikko Koivu**, Min.	**279**	536	.521	8
69.	**Rick Nash**, CBJ, NYR	**279**	718	.389	10
70.	**Adrian Aucoin**, Van., T.B., NYI, Chi., Cgy., Phx., CBJ	**278**	1108	.251	18
71.	**Jochen Hecht**, St.L., Edm., Buf.	**277**	833	.333	14
72.	**Jason Pominville**, Buf., Min.	**276**	588	.469	9
73.	**Pavel Kubina**, T.B., Tor., Atl., Phi.	**276**	970	.285	14
74.	**Patrick Kane**, Chi.	**275**	446	.617	6
75.	**Nik Antropov**, Tor., NYR, Atl., Wpg.	**272**	788	.345	13
76.	**Mike Knuble**, Det., NYR, Bos., Phi., Wsh.	**270**	1068	.253	16
77.	**Paul Stastny**, Col.	**263**	467	.563	7
78.	**Filip Kuba**, Fla., Min., T.B., Ott.	**263**	836	.315	14
79.	**Mike Richards**, Phi., L.A.	**262**	575	.456	8
80.	**Marek Zidlicky**, Nsh., Min., N.J.	**259**	618	.419	9
81.	**Tom Poti**, Edm., NYR, NYI, Wsh.	**258**	824	.313	13
82.	**Scott Hartnell**, Nsh., Phi.	**255**	875	.291	12
83.	**Duncan Keith**, Chi.	**250**	607	.412	8
84.	**Mattias Ohlund**, Van., T.B.	**250**	909	.275	13
85.	**Stephen Weiss**, Fla.	**249**	654	.381	11
86.	**Mike Cammalleri**, L.A., Cgy., Mtl.	**247**	606	.408	10
87.	**Corey Perry**, Ana.	**245**	574	.427	8
88.	**Marco Sturm**, S.J., Bos., L.A., Wsh., Van., Fla.	**245**	938	.261	14
89.	**Alexander Semin**, Wsh., Car.	**242**	513	.472	8
90.	**Steve Reinprecht**, L.A., Col., Cgy., Phx., Fla.	**242**	663	.365	11
91.	**Pierre-Marc Bouchard**, Min.	**241**	565	.427	10
92.	**Tomas Plekanec**, Mtl.	**240**	598	.401	9
93.	**Brad Boyes**, S.J., Bos., St.L., Buf., NYI	**239**	606	.394	9
94.	**Thomas Vanek**, Buf.	**238**	585	.407	8
95.	**Brad Stuart**, S.J., Bos., Cgy., L.A., Det.	**237**	924	.256	13
96.	**Zach Parise**, N.J., Min.	**236**	550	.429	8
97.	**John-Michael Liles**, Col., Tor.	**236**	621	.380	9
98.	**Erik Cole**, Car., Edm., Mtl., Dal.	**236**	749	.315	11
99.	**Jay Bouwmeester**, Fla., Cgy., St.L.	**235**	764	.308	10
100.	**Dion Phaneuf**, Cgy., Tor.	**234**	600	.390	8

Henrik Sedin became the 76th player in NHL history to record 600 career assists when he set up Alex Burrows for a goal in the second period of Vancouver's 5-2 win over Calgary on April 6, 2013. Sedin has led the NHL in assists three times in his career.

Top 100 All-Time Point Leaders

* active player

Player	Points	Games	Points per game	Goals	Assists	Seasons
1. **Wayne Gretzky**, Edm., L.A., St.L., NYR	**2857**	1487	1.921	894	1963	20
2. **Mark Messier**, Edm., NYR, Van.	**1887**	1756	1.075	694	1193	25
3. **Gordie Howe**, Det., Hfd.	**1850**	1767	1.047	801	1049	26
4. **Ron Francis**, Hfd., Pit., Car., Tor.	**1798**	1731	1.039	549	1249	23
5. **Marcel Dionne**, Det., L.A., NYR	**1771**	1348	1.314	731	1040	18
6. **Steve Yzerman**, Det.	**1755**	1514	1.159	692	1063	22
7. **Mario Lemieux**, Pit.	**1723**	915	1.883	690	1033	18
* 8. **Jaromir Jagr**, Pit., Wsh., NYR, Phi., Dal., Bos.	**1688**	1391	1.214	681	1007	19
9. **Joe Sakic**, Que., Col.	**1641**	1378	1.191	625	1016	20
10. **Phil Esposito**, Chi., Bos., NYR	**1590**	1282	1.240	717	873	18
11. **Raymond Bourque**, Bos., Col.	**1579**	1612	.980	410	1169	22
12. **Mark Recchi**, Pit., Phi., Mtl., Car., Atl., T.B., Bos.	**1533**	1652	.928	577	956	22
13. **Paul Coffey**, Edm., Pit., L.A., Det., Hfd., Phi., Chi., Car., Bos.	**1531**	1409	1.087	396	1135	21
14. **Stan Mikita**, Chi.	**1467**	1394	1.052	541	926	22
* 15. **Teemu Selanne**, Wpg., Ana., S.J., Col.	**1430**	1387	1.031	675	755	20
16. **Bryan Trottier**, NYI, Pit.	**1425**	1279	1.114	524	901	18
17. **Adam Oates**, Det., St.L., Bos., Wsh., Phi., Ana., Edm.	**1420**	1337	1.062	341	1079	19
18. **Doug Gilmour**, St.L., Cgy., Tor., N.J., Chi., Buf., Mtl.	**1414**	1474	.959	450	964	20
19. **Dale Hawerchuk**, Wpg., Buf., St.L., Phi.	**1409**	1188	1.186	518	891	16
20. **Jari Kurri**, Edm., L.A., NYR, Ana., Col.	**1398**	1251	1.118	601	797	17
21. **Luc Robitaille**, L.A., Pit., NYR, Det.	**1394**	1431	.974	668	726	19
22. **Brett Hull**, Cgy., St.L., Dal., Det., Phx.	**1391**	1269	1.096	741	650	20
23. **Mike Modano**, Min., Dal., Det.	**1374**	1499	.917	561	813	22
24. **John Bucyk**, Det., Bos.	**1369**	1540	.889	556	813	23
25. **Brendan Shanahan**, N.J., St.L., Hfd., Det., NYR	**1354**	1524	.888	656	698	21
26. **Guy Lafleur**, Mtl., NYR, Que.	**1353**	1126	1.202	560	793	17
27. **Mats Sundin**, Que., Tor., Van.	**1349**	1346	1.002	564	785	18
28. **Denis Savard**, Chi., Mtl., T.B.	**1338**	1196	1.119	473	865	17
29. **Dave Andreychuk**, Buf., Tor., N.J., Bos., Col., T.B.	**1338**	1639	.816	640	698	23
30. **Mike Gartner**, Wsh., Min., NYR, Tor., Phx.	**1335**	1432	.932	708	627	19
31. **Pierre Turgeon**, Buf., NYI, Mtl., St.L., Dal., Col.	**1327**	1294	1.026	515	812	19
32. **Gilbert Perreault**, Buf.	**1326**	1191	1.113	512	814	17
33. **Alex Delvecchio**, Det.	**1281**	1549	.827	456	825	24
34. **Al MacInnis**, Cgy., St.L.	**1274**	1416	.900	340	934	23
35. **Jean Ratelle**, NYR, Bos.	**1267**	1281	.989	491	776	21
36. **Peter Stastny**, Que., N.J., St.L.	**1239**	977	1.268	450	789	15
37. **Phil Housley**, Buf., Wpg., St.L., Cgy., N.J., Wsh., Chi., Tor.	**1232**	1495	.824	338	894	21
38. **Norm Ullman**, Det., Tor.	**1229**	1410	.872	490	739	20
39. **Jean Beliveau**, Mtl.	**1219**	1125	1.084	507	712	20
40. **Jeremy Roenick**, Chi., Phx., Phi., L.A., S.J.	**1216**	1363	.892	513	703	20
41. **Larry Murphy**, L.A., Wsh., Min., Pit., Tor., Det.	**1216**	1615	.753	287	929	21
42. **Bobby Clarke**, Phi.	**1210**	1144	1.058	358	852	15
43. **Bernie Nicholls**, L.A., NYR, Edm., N.J., Chi., S.J.	**1209**	1127	1.073	475	734	18
44. **Vincent Damphousse**, Tor., Edm., Mtl., S.J.	**1205**	1378	.874	432	773	18
45. **Dino Ciccarelli**, Min., Wsh., Det., T.B., Fla.	**1200**	1232	.974	608	592	19
46. **Rod Brind'Amour**, St.L., Phi., Car.	**1184**	1484	.798	452	732	21
47. **Sergei Fedorov**, Det., Ana., CBJ, Wsh.	**1179**	1248	.945	483	696	18
48. **Bobby Hull**, Chi., Wpg., Hfd.	**1170**	1063	1.101	610	560	16
49. **Michel Goulet**, Que., Chi.	**1152**	1089	1.058	548	604	15
50. **Nicklas Lidstrom**, Det.	**1142**	1564	.730	264	878	20
51. **Bernie Federko**, St.L., Det.	**1130**	1000	1.130	369	761	14
52. **Mike Bossy**, NYI	**1126**	752	1.497	573	553	10
53. **Joe Nieuwendyk**, Cgy., Dal., N.J., Tor., Fla.	**1126**	1257	.896	564	562	20
54. **Darryl Sittler**, Tor., Phi., Det.	**1121**	1096	1.023	484	637	15
* 55. **Joe Thornton**, Bos., S.J.	**1118**	1125	.994	331	787	15
* 56. **Daniel Alfredsson**, Ott.	**1108**	1178	.941	426	682	17
* 57. **Jarome Iginla**, Cgy., Pit.	**1106**	1232	.898	530	576	17
58. **Frank Mahovlich**, Tor., Det., Mtl.	**1103**	1181	.934	533	570	18
59. **Glenn Anderson**, Edm., Tor., NYR, St.L.	**1099**	1129	.973	498	601	16
60. **Theoren Fleury**, Cgy., Col., NYR, Chi.	**1088**	1084	1.004	455	633	15
61. **Dave Taylor**, L.A.	**1069**	1111	.962	431	638	17
62. **Keith Tkachuk**, Wpg., Phx., St.L., Atl.	**1065**	1201	.887	538	527	18
63. **Joe Mullen**, St.L., Cgy., Pit., Bos.	**1063**	1062	1.001	502	561	17
64. **Pat Verbeek**, N.J., Hfd., NYR, Dal., Det.	**1063**	1424	.746	522	541	20
65. **Denis Potvin**, NYI	**1052**	1060	.992	310	742	15
66. **Henri Richard**, Mtl.	**1046**	1256	.833	358	688	20
67. **Bobby Smith**, Min., Mtl.	**1036**	1077	.962	357	679	15
68. **Doug Weight**, NYR, Edm., St.L., Car., Ana., NYI	**1033**	1238	.834	278	755	20
69. **Alexander Mogilny**, Buf., Van., N.J., Tor.	**1032**	990	1.042	473	559	16
* 70. **Ray Whitney**, S.J., Edm., Fla., CBJ, Det., Car., Phx., Dal.	**1032**	1261	.818	376	656	21
71. **Alex Kovalev**, NYR, Pit., Mtl., Ott., Fla.	**1029**	1316	.782	430	599	19
72. **Brian Leetch**, NYR, Tor., Bos.	**1028**	1205	.853	247	781	18
73. **Brian Bellows**, Min., Mtl., T.B., Ana., Wsh.	**1022**	1188	.860	485	537	17
74. **Rod Gilbert**, NYR	**1021**	1065	.959	406	615	18
75. **Dale Hunter**, Que., Wsh., Col.	**1020**	1407	.725	323	697	19
76. **Pat LaFontaine**, NYI, Buf., NYR	**1013**	865	1.171	468	545	15
77. **Steve Larmer**, Chi., NYR	**1012**	1006	1.006	441	571	15
78. **Lanny McDonald**, Tor., Col., Cgy.	**1006**	1111	.905	500	506	16
79. **Brian Propp**, Phi., Bos., Min., Hfd.	**1004**	1016	.988	425	579	15
80. **Paul Kariya**, Ana., Col., Nsh., St.L.	**989**	989	1.000	402	587	15
81. **Rick Middleton**, NYR, Bos.	**988**	1005	.983	448	540	14
82. **Dave Keon**, Tor., Hfd.	**986**	1296	.761	396	590	18
83. **Andy Bathgate**, NYR, Tor., Det., Pit.	**973**	1069	.910	349	624	17
84. **Maurice Richard**, Mtl.	**965**	978	.987	544	421	18
85. **Kirk Muller**, N.J., Mtl., NYI, Tor., Fla., Dal.	**959**	1349	.711	357	602	19
86. **Larry Robinson**, Mtl., L.A.	**958**	1384	.692	208	750	20
87. **Rick Tocchet**, Phi., Pit., L.A., Bos., Wsh., Phx.	**952**	1144	.832	440	512	18
88. **Chris Chelios**, Mtl., Chi., Det., Atl.	**948**	1651	.574	185	763	26
89. **Jason Arnott**, Edm., N.J., Dal., Nsh., Wsh., St.L.	**938**	1244	.754	417	521	18
* 90. **Marian Hossa**, Ott., Atl., Pit., Det., Chi.	**935**	1018	.918	434	501	15
91. **Steve Thomas**, Tor., Chi., NYI, N.J., Ana., Det.	**933**	1235	.755	421	512	20
* 92. **Patrik Elias**, N.J.	**930**	1090	.853	375	555	17
93. **Neal Broten**, Min., Dal., N.J., L.A.	**923**	1099	.840	289	634	17
94. **Bobby Orr**, Bos., Chi.	**915**	657	1.393	270	645	12
* 95. **Martin St. Louis**, Cgy., T.B.	**912**	979	.932	340	572	14
96. **Gary Roberts**, Cgy., Car., Tor., Fla., Pit., T.B.	**910**	1224	.743	438	472	22
97. **Scott Stevens**, Wsh., St.L., N.J.	**908**	1635	.555	196	712	22
98. **Tony Amonte**, NYR, Chi., Phx., Phi., Cgy.	**900**	1174	.767	416	484	16
99. **Ray Ferraro**, Hfd., NYI, NYR, L.A., Atl., St.L.	**898**	1258	.714	408	490	18
100. **Brad Park**, NYR, Bos., Det.	**896**	1113	.805	213	683	17

Jaromir Jagr poses with the puck from his 1,000th career assist, which he picked up on March 29, 2013. Jagr is the 12th NHL player to reach that milestone.

Top 100 Active Points Leaders

	Player	Points	Games	Points per game	Goals	Assists	Seasons
1.	**Jaromir Jagr**, Pit., Wsh., NYR, Phi., Dal., Bos.	**1688**	1391	1.214	681	1007	19
2.	**Teemu Selanne**, Wpg., Ana., S.J., Col.	**1430**	1387	1.031	675	755	20
3.	**Joe Thornton**, Bos., S.J.	**1118**	1125	.994	331	787	15
4.	**Daniel Alfredsson**, Ott.	**1108**	1178	.941	426	682	17
5.	**Jarome Iginla**, Cgy., Pit.	**1106**	1232	.898	530	576	17
6.	**Ray Whitney**, S.J., Edm., Fla., CBJ, Det., Car., Phx., Dal.	**1032**	1261	.818	376	656	21
7.	**Marian Hossa**, Ott., Atl., Pit., Det., Chi.	**935**	1018	.918	434	501	15
8.	**Patrik Elias**, N.J.	**930**	1090	.853	375	555	17
9.	**Martin St. Louis**, Cgy., T.B.	**912**	979	.932	340	572	14
10.	**Vincent Lecavalier**, T.B.	**874**	1037	.843	383	491	14
11.	**Patrick Marleau**, S.J.	**861**	1165	.739	404	457	15
12.	**Ryan Smyth**, Edm., NYI, Col., L.A.	**819**	1198	.684	376	443	18
13.	**Ilya Kovalchuk**, Atl., N.J.	**816**	816	1.000	417	399	11
14.	**Brad Richards**, T.B., Dal., NYR	**816**	900	.907	256	560	12
15.	**Shane Doan**, Wpg., Phx.	**815**	1246	.654	331	484	17
16.	**Milan Hejduk**, Col.	**805**	1020	.789	375	430	14
17.	**Saku Koivu**, Mtl., Ana.	**803**	1059	.758	244	559	17
18.	**Henrik Sedin**, Van.	**792**	940	.843	182	610	12
19.	**Sergei Gonchar**, Wsh., Bos., Pit., Ott.	**775**	1177	.658	217	558	18
20.	**Pavel Datsyuk**, Det.	**767**	779	.985	255	512	11
21.	**Vinny Prospal**, Phi., Ott., Fla., T.B., Ana., NYR, CBJ	**765**	1108	.690	255	510	16
22.	**Dany Heatley**, Atl., Ott., S.J., Min.	**763**	787	.970	360	403	11
23.	**Alex Tanguay**, Col., Cgy., Mtl., T.B.	**762**	922	.826	249	513	13
24.	**Daniel Sedin**, Van.	**758**	906	.837	291	467	12
25.	**Todd Bertuzzi**, NYI, Van., Fla., Det., Ana., Cgy.	**754**	1100	.685	305	449	17
26.	**Steve Sullivan**, N.J., Tor., Chi., Nsh., Pit., Phx.	**747**	1011	.739	290	457	17
27.	**Alex Ovechkin**, Wsh.	**735**	601	1.223	371	364	8
28.	**Scott Gomez**, N.J., NYR, Mtl., S.J.	**701**	941	.745	171	530	13
29.	**Olli Jokinen**, L.A., NYI, Fla., Phx., Cgy., NYR, Wpg.	**697**	1087	.641	299	398	15
30.	**Marian Gaborik**, Min., NYR, CBJ	**674**	769	.876	336	338	12
31.	**Henrik Zetterberg**, Det.	**672**	714	.941	263	409	10
32.	**Daymond Langkow**, T.B., Phi., Phx., Cgy.	**672**	1090	.617	270	402	16
33.	**Sidney Crosby**, Pit.	**665**	470	1.415	238	427	8
34.	**Jamie Langenbrunner**, Dal., N.J., St.L.	**663**	1109	.598	243	420	18
35.	**Daniel Briere**, Phx., Buf., Phi.	**659**	847	.778	286	373	15
36.	**Roman Hamrlik**, T.B., Edm., NYI, Cgy., Mtl., Wsh., NYR	**638**	1395	.457	155	483	20
37.	**Eric Staal**, Car.	**627**	690	.909	268	359	9
38.	**Jason Spezza**, Ott.	**621**	611	1.016	228	393	10
39.	**Mike Ribeiro**, Mtl., Dal., Wsh.	**609**	785	.776	186	423	13
40.	**Simon Gagne**, Phi., T.B., L.A.	**597**	799	.747	288	309	13
41.	**Rick Nash**, CBJ, NYR	**589**	718	.820	310	279	10
42.	**Radek Dvorak**, Fla., NYR, Edm., St.L., Atl., Dal., Ana.	**581**	1200	.484	223	358	17
43.	**Tomas Kaberle**, Tor., Bos., Car., Mtl.	**563**	984	.572	87	476	14
44.	**Matt Cullen**, Ana., Fla., Car., NYR, Ott., Min.	**562**	1073	.524	202	360	15
45.	**Evgeni Malkin**, Pit.	**560**	458	1.223	217	343	7
46.	**Martin Havlat**, Ott., Chi., Min., S.J.	**557**	700	.796	224	333	12
47.	**Mike Knuble**, Det., NYR, Bos., Phi., Wsh.	**548**	1068	.513	278	270	16
48.	**Dainius Zubrus**, Phi., Mtl., Wsh., Buf., N.J.	**548**	1087	.504	208	340	16
49.	**Brenden Morrow**, Dal., Pit.	**542**	850	.638	249	293	13
50.	**Kimmo Timonen**, Nsh., Phi.	**536**	1015	.528	111	425	14
51.	**David Legwand**, Nsh.	**526**	894	.588	200	326	14
52.	**Dan Boyle**, Fla., T.B., S.J.	**525**	879	.597	132	393	14
53.	**Ryan Getzlaf**, Ana.	**521**	556	.937	152	369	8
54.	**Justin Williams**, Phi., Car., L.A.	**498**	755	.660	190	308	12
55.	**Ed Jovanovski**, Fla., Van., Phx.	**495**	1091	.454	136	359	17
56.	**Thomas Vanek**, Buf.	**488**	585	.834	250	238	8
57.	**Marco Sturm**, S.J., Bos., L.A., Wsh., Van., Fla.	**487**	938	.519	242	245	14
58.	**Scott Hartnell**, Nsh., Phi.	**485**	875	.554	230	255	12
59.	**Martin Erat**, Nsh., Wsh.	**484**	732	.661	164	320	11
60.	**Zdeno Chara**, NYI, Ott., Bos.	**478**	1055	.453	144	334	15
61.	**Anze Kopitar**, L.A.	**476**	522	.912	173	303	7

Patrik Elias picked up a goal and two assists to reach the 900-point plateau in New Jersey's 4-3 loss to Montreal on January 27, 2013. Elias is the Devils' all-time scoring leader.

	Player	Points	Games	Points per game	Goals	Assists	Seasons
62.	**Michal Handzus**, St.L., Phx., Phi., Chi., L.A., S.J.	**467**	950	.492	181	286	14
63.	**Corey Perry**, Ana.	**465**	574	.810	220	245	8
64.	**Jason Pominville**, Buf., Min.	**465**	588	.791	189	276	9
65.	**Nik Antropov**, Tor., NYR, Atl., Wpg.	**465**	788	.590	193	272	13
66.	**Erik Cole**, Car., Edm., Mtl., Dal.	**464**	749	.619	228	236	11
67.	**Lubomir Visnovsky**, L.A., Edm., Ana., NYI	**464**	806	.576	120	344	12
68.	**Jochen Hecht**, St.L., Edm., Buf.	**463**	833	.556	186	277	14
69.	**Mike Cammalleri**, L.A., Cgy., Mtl.	**457**	606	.754	210	247	10
70.	**Wade Redden**, Ott., NYR, St.L., Bos.	**457**	1023	.447	109	348	14
71.	**Derek Roy**, Buf., Dal., Van.	**455**	591	.770	168	287	9
72.	**Alexander Semin**, Wsh., Car.	**452**	513	.881	210	242	8
73.	**Ales Hemsky**, Edm.	**451**	597	.755	133	318	10
74.	**Zach Parise**, N.J., Min.	**448**	550	.815	212	236	8
75.	**Shawn Horcoff**, Edm.	**447**	796	.562	162	285	12
76.	**Brian Gionta**, N.J., Mtl.	**445**	695	.640	231	214	11
77.	**Patrice Bergeron**, Bos.	**433**	579	.748	153	280	9
78.	**Mike Fisher**, Ott., Nsh.	**432**	812	.532	206	226	13
79.	**Michael Ryder**, Mtl., Bos., Dal.	**431**	677	.637	213	218	9
80.	**Tim Connolly**, NYI, Buf., Tor.	**431**	697	.618	131	300	12
81.	**Mike Richards**, Phi., L.A.	**425**	575	.739	163	262	8
82.	**Patrick Kane**, Chi.	**424**	446	.951	149	275	6
83.	**Nicklas Backstrom**, Wsh.	**415**	413	1.005	109	306	6
84.	**Radim Vrbata**, Col., Car., Chi., Phx., T.B.	**413**	712	.580	195	218	11
85.	**Jeff Carter**, Phi., CBJ, L.A.	**410**	564	.727	228	182	8
86.	**Brad Boyes**, S.J., Bos., St.L., Buf., NYI	**407**	606	.672	168	239	9
87.	**Derek Morris**, Cgy., Col., Phx., NYR, Bos.	**407**	1044	.390	87	320	15
88.	**Patrick Sharp**, Phi., Chi.	**405**	595	.681	199	206	10
89.	**Chris Kunitz**, Ana., Atl., Pit.	**403**	581	.694	172	231	9
90.	**Nathan Horton**, Fla., Bos.	**402**	591	.680	198	204	9
91.	**Andrei Markov**, Mtl.	**399**	684	.583	91	308	12
92.	**Adrian Aucoin**, Van., T.B., NYI, Chi., Cgy., Phx., CBJ	**399**	1108	.360	121	278	18
93.	**Paul Stastny**, Col.	**398**	467	.852	135	263	7
94.	**Mikko Koivu**, Min.	**398**	536	.743	119	279	8
95.	**Tomas Plekanec**, Mtl.	**396**	598	.662	156	240	9
96.	**Stephen Weiss**, Fla.	**394**	654	.602	145	249	11
97.	**Brian Campbell**, Buf., S.J., Chi., Fla.	**392**	756	.519	66	326	13
98.	**Dustin Brown**, L.A.	**388**	641	.605	181	207	9
99.	**Steven Stamkos**, T.B.	**386**	373	1.035	208	178	5
100.	**Steve Reinprecht**, L.A., Col., Cgy., Phx., Fla.	**382**	663	.576	140	242	11

Top 100 All-Time Games Played Leaders

* active player

	Player	Games Played	Seasons
1.	**Gordie Howe**, Det., Hfd.	**1767**	26
2.	**Mark Messier**, Edm., NYR, Van.	**1756**	25
3.	**Ron Francis**, Hfd., Pit., Car., Tor.	**1731**	23
4.	**Mark Recchi**, Pit., Phi., Mtl., Car., Atl., T.B., Bos.	**1652**	22
5.	**Chris Chelios**, Mtl., Chi., Det., Atl.	**1651**	26
6.	**Dave Andreychuk**, Buf., Tor., N.J., Bos., Col., T.B.	**1639**	23
7.	**Scott Stevens**, Wsh., St.L., N.J.	**1635**	22
8.	**Larry Murphy**, L.A., Wsh., Min., Pit., Tor., Det.	**1615**	21
9.	**Raymond Bourque**, Bos., Col.	**1612**	22
10.	**Nicklas Lidstrom**, Det.	**1564**	20
11.	**Alex Delvecchio**, Det.	**1549**	24
12.	**John Bucyk**, Det., Bos.	**1540**	23
13.	**Brendan Shanahan**, N.J., St.L., Hfd., Det., NYR	**1524**	21
14.	**Steve Yzerman**, Det.	**1514**	22
15.	**Mike Modano**, Min., Dal., Det.	**1499**	22
16.	**Phil Housley**, Buf., Wpg., St.L., Cgy., N.J., Wsh., Chi., Tor.	**1495**	21
17.	**Wayne Gretzky**, Edm., L.A., St.L., NYR	**1487**	20
18.	**Rod Brind'Amour**, St.L., Phi., Car.	**1484**	21
19.	**Doug Gilmour**, St.L., Cgy., Tor., N.J., Chi., Buf., Mtl.	**1474**	20
20.	**Glen Wesley**, Bos., Hfd., Car., Tor.	**1457**	20
21.	**Tim Horton**, Tor., NYR, Pit., Buf.	**1446**	24
22.	**Mike Gartner**, Wsh., Min., NYR, Tor., Phx.	**1432**	19
23.	**Luc Robitaille**, L.A., Pit., NYR, Det.	**1431**	19
24.	**Scott Mellanby**, Phi., Edm., Fla., St.L., Atl.	**1431**	21
25.	**Pat Verbeek**, N.J., Hfd., NYR, Dal., Det.	**1424**	20
26.	**Luke Richardson**, Tor., Edm., Phi., CBJ, T.B., Ott.	**1417**	21
27.	**Al MacInnis**, Cgy., St.L.	**1416**	23
28.	**Harry Howell**, NYR, Oak., Cal., L.A.	**1411**	21
29.	**Norm Ullman**, Det., Tor.	**1410**	20
30.	**Paul Coffey**, Edm., Pit., L.A., Det., Hfd., Phi., Chi., Car., Bos.	**1409**	21
31.	**Dale Hunter**, Que., Wsh., Col.	**1407**	19
* 32.	**Roman Hamrlik**, T.B., Edm., NYI, Cgy., Mtl., Wsh., NYR	**1395**	20
33.	**Stan Mikita**, Chi.	**1394**	22
* 34.	**Jaromir Jagr**, Pit., Wsh., NYR, Phi., Dal., Bos.	**1391**	19
35.	**Doug Mohns**, Bos., Chi., Min., Atl., Wsh.	**1390**	22
* 36.	**Teemu Selanne**, Wpg., Ana., S.J., Col.	**1387**	20
37.	**Larry Robinson**, Mtl., L.A.	**1384**	20
38.	**Trevor Linden**, Van., NYI, Mtl., Wsh.	**1382**	19
39.	**Vincent Damphousse**, Tor., Edm., Mtl., S.J.	**1378**	18
40.	**Joe Sakic**, Que., Col.	**1378**	20
41.	**Dean Prentice**, NYR, Bos., Det., Pit., Min.	**1378**	22
42.	**Teppo Numminen**, Wpg., Phx., Dal., Buf.	**1372**	20
43.	**Jeremy Roenick**, Chi., Phx., Phi., L.A., S.J.	**1363**	20
44.	**Ron Stewart**, Tor., Bos., St.L., NYR, Van., NYI	**1353**	21
45.	**Kirk Muller**, N.J., Mtl., NYI, Tor., Fla., Dal.	**1349**	19
46.	**Marcel Dionne**, Det., L.A., NYR	**1348**	18
47.	**Mats Sundin**, Que., Tor., Van.	**1346**	18
48.	**Adam Oates**, Det., St.L., Bos., Wsh., Phi., Ana., Edm.	**1337**	19
49.	**Guy Carbonneau**, Mtl., St.L., Dal.	**1318**	19
50.	**Alex Kovalev**, NYR, Pit., Mtl., Ott., Fla.	**1316**	19
51.	**Red Kelly**, Det., Tor.	**1316**	20
52.	**Bobby Holik**, Hfd., N.J., NYR, Atl.	**1314**	18
53.	**Dave Keon**, Tor., Hfd.	**1296**	18
54.	**Pierre Turgeon**, Buf., NYI, Mtl., St.L., Dal., Col.	**1294**	19
55.	**Darryl Sydor**, L.A., Dal., CBJ, T.B., Pit., St.L.	**1291**	18
56.	**Mathieu Schneider**, Mtl., NYI, Tor., NYR, L.A., Det., Ana., Atl., Van., Phx.	**1289**	21
57.	**Ken Daneyko**, N.J.	**1283**	20
58.	**Phil Esposito**, Chi., Bos., NYR	**1282**	18
59.	**Jean Ratelle**, NYR, Bos.	**1281**	21
60.	**James Patrick**, NYR, Hfd., Cgy., Buf.	**1280**	21
61.	**Bryan Trottier**, NYI, Pit.	**1279**	18
62.	**Martin Gelinas**, Edm., Que., Van., Car., Cgy., Fla., Nsh.	**1273**	19
63.	**Rob Blake**, L.A., Col., S.J.	**1270**	20
64.	**Brett Hull**, Cgy., St.L., Dal., Det., Phx.	**1269**	20
65.	**Bill Guerin**, N.J., Edm., Bos., Dal., St.L., S.J., NYI, Pit.	**1263**	18
66.	**Scott Niedermayer**, N.J., Ana.	**1263**	18
* 67.	**Ray Whitney**, S.J., Edm., Fla., CBJ, Det., Car., Phx., Dal.	**1261**	21
68.	**Ray Ferraro**, Hfd., NYI, NYR, L.A., Atl., St.L.	**1258**	18
69.	**Joe Nieuwendyk**, Cgy., Dal., N.J., Tor., Fla.	**1257**	20
70.	**Brian Rolston**, N.J., Col., Bos., Min., NYI	**1256**	17
71.	**Craig Ludwig**, Mtl., NYI, Min., Dal.	**1256**	17
72.	**Henri Richard**, Mtl.	**1256**	20
73.	**Kevin Lowe**, Edm., NYR	**1254**	19
74.	**Jari Kurri**, Edm., L.A., NYR, Ana., Col.	**1251**	17
75.	**Sergei Fedorov**, Det., Ana., CBJ, Wsh.	**1248**	18
76.	**Bill Gadsby**, Chi., NYR, Det.	**1248**	20
* 77.	**Shane Doan**, Wpg., Phx.	**1246**	17
78.	**Jason Arnott**, Edm., N.J., Dal., Nsh., Wsh., St.L.	**1244**	18
79.	**Allan Stanley**, NYR, Chi., Bos., Tor., Phi.	**1244**	21
80.	**Doug Weight**, NYR, Edm., St.L., Car., Ana., NYI	**1238**	20

Dave Keon played 1,062 games with the Toronto Maple Leafs between 1960 and 1975. He later played 234 games in three seasons with the Hartford Whalers from 1979 to 1982 for a total of 1,296. Keon also played 301 games during four seasons in the World Hockey Association.

	Player	Games Played	Seasons
81.	**Steve Thomas**, Tor., Chi., NYI, N.J., Ana., Det.	**1235**	20
* 82.	**Jarome Iginla**, Cgy., Pit.	**1232**	17
83.	**Dino Ciccarelli**, Min., Wsh., Det., T.B., Fla.	**1232**	19
84.	**Ed Westfall**, Bos., NYI	**1226**	18
85.	**Sean O'Donnell**, L.A., Min., N.J., Bos., Phx., Ana., Phi., Chi.	**1224**	17
86.	**Gary Roberts**, Cgy., Car., Tor., Fla., Pit., T.B.	**1224**	22
87.	**Brad McCrimmon**, Bos., Phi., Cgy., Det., Hfd., Phx.	**1222**	18
* 88.	**Martin Brodeur**, N.J.	**1220**	20
89.	**Eric Nesterenko**, Tor., Chi.	**1219**	21
90.	**Claude Lemieux**, Mtl., N.J., Col., Phx., Dal., S.J.	**1215**	21
91.	**Marcel Pronovost**, Det., Tor.	**1206**	21
92.	**Brian Leetch**, NYR, Tor., Bos.	**1205**	18
93.	**Keith Tkachuk**, Wpg., Phx., St.L., Atl.	**1201**	18
* 94.	**Radek Dvorak**, Fla., NYR, Edm., St.L., Atl., Dal., Ana.	**1200**	17
95.	**Owen Nolan**, Que., Col., S.J., Tor., Phx., Cgy., Min.	**1200**	18
* 96.	**Ryan Smyth**, Edm., NYI, Col., L.A.	**1198**	18
97.	**Denis Savard**, Chi., Mtl., T.B.	**1196**	17
98.	**Todd Marchant**, NYR, Edm., CBJ, Ana.	**1195**	17
99.	**Dave Babych**, Wpg., Hfd., Van., Phi., L.A.	**1195**	19
100.	**John MacLean**, N.J., S.J., NYR, Dal.	**1194**	18

Top 100 Active Games Played Leaders

	Player	Games Played	Seasons
1.	**Roman Hamrlik**, T.B., Edm., NYI, Cgy., Mtl., Wsh., NYR	**1395**	20
2.	**Jaromir Jagr**, Pit., Wsh., NYR, Phi., Dal., Bos.	**1391**	19
3.	**Teemu Selanne**, Wpg., Ana., S.J., Col.	**1387**	20
4.	**Ray Whitney**, S.J., Edm., Fla., CBJ, Det., Car., Phx., Dal.	**1261**	21
5.	**Shane Doan**, Wpg., Phx.	**1246**	17
6.	**Jarome Iginla**, Cgy., Pit.	**1232**	17
7.	**Martin Brodeur**, N.J.	**1220**	20
8.	**Radek Dvorak**, Fla., NYR, Edm., St.L., Atl., Dal., Ana.	**1200**	17
9.	**Ryan Smyth**, Edm., NYI, Col., L.A.	**1198**	18
10.	**Daniel Alfredsson**, Ott.	**1178**	17
11.	**Sergei Gonchar**, Wsh., Bos., Pit., Ott.	**1177**	18
12.	**Patrick Marleau**, S.J.	**1165**	15
13.	**Joe Thornton**, Bos., S.J.	**1125**	15
14.	**Jamie Langenbrunner**, Dal., N.J., St.L.	**1109**	18
15.	**Vinny Prospal**, Phi., Ott., Fla., T.B., Ana., NYR, CBJ	**1108**	16
16.	**Adrian Aucoin**, Van., T.B., NYI, Chi., Cgy., Phx., CBJ	**1108**	18
17.	**Hal Gill**, Bos., Tor., Pit., Mtl., Nsh.	**1102**	15
18.	**Todd Bertuzzi**, NYI, Van., Fla., Det., Ana., Cgy.	**1100**	17
19.	**Ed Jovanovski**, Fla., Van., Phx.	**1091**	17
20.	**Daymond Langkow**, T.B., Phi., Phx., Cgy.	**1090**	16
21.	**Patrik Elias**, N.J.	**1090**	17
22.	**Olli Jokinen**, L.A., NYI, Fla., Phx., Cgy., NYR, Wpg.	**1087**	15
23.	**Dainius Zubrus**, Phi., Mtl., Wsh., Buf., N.J.	**1087**	16
24.	**Matt Cullen**, Ana., Fla., Car., NYR, Ott., Min.	**1073**	15
25.	**Chris Phillips**, Ott.	**1073**	15
26.	**Mike Knuble**, Det., NYR, Bos., Phi., Wsh.	**1068**	16
27.	**Saku Koivu**, Mtl., Ana.	**1059**	17
28.	**Zdeno Chara**, NYI, Ott., Bos.	**1055**	15
29.	**Derek Morris**, Cgy., Col., Phx., NYR, Bos.	**1044**	15
30.	**Vincent Lecavalier**, T.B.	**1037**	14
31.	**Wade Redden**, Ott., NYR, St.L., Bos.	**1023**	14
32.	**Milan Hejduk**, Col.	**1020**	14
33.	**Marian Hossa**, Ott., Atl., Pit., Det., Chi.	**1018**	15
34.	**Kimmo Timonen**, Nsh., Phi.	**1015**	14
35.	**Steve Sullivan**, N.J., Tor., Chi., Nsh., Pit., Phx.	**1011**	17
36.	**Tomas Kaberle**, Tor., Bos., Car., Mtl.	**984**	14
37.	**Martin St. Louis**, Cgy., T.B.	**979**	14
38.	**Michal Handzus**, St.L., Phx., Phi., Chi., L.A., S.J.	**950**	14
39.	**Robyn Regehr**, Cgy., Buf., L.A.	**943**	13
40.	**Scott Gomez**, N.J., NYR, Mtl., S.J.	**941**	13
41.	**Scott Hannan**, S.J., Col., Wsh., Cgy., Nsh.	**941**	14
42.	**Henrik Sedin**, Van.	**940**	12
43.	**Marco Sturm**, S.J., Bos., L.A., Wsh., Van., Fla.	**938**	14
44.	**Matt Cooke**, Van., Wsh., Pit.	**935**	14
45.	**Brad Stuart**, S.J., Bos., Cgy., L.A., Det.	**924**	13
46.	**Alex Tanguay**, Col., Cgy., Mtl., T.B.	**922**	13
47.	**Cory Sarich**, Buf., T.B., Cgy.	**915**	14
48.	**Jamal Mayers**, St.L., Tor., Cgy., S.J., Chi.	**915**	15
49.	**Mattias Ohlund**, Van., T.B.	**909**	13
50.	**Jeff Halpern**, Wsh., Dal., T.B., L.A., Mtl., NYR	**907**	13
51.	**Daniel Sedin**, Van.	**906**	12
52.	**Brad Richards**, T.B., Dal., NYR	**900**	12
53.	**David Legwand**, Nsh.	**894**	14
54.	**Eric Brewer**, NYI, Edm., St.L., T.B.	**888**	14
55.	**Dan Boyle**, Fla., T.B., S.J.	**879**	14
56.	**Scott Hartnell**, Nsh., Phi.	**875**	12
57.	**Dan Cleary**, Chi., Edm., Phx., Det.	**869**	15
58.	**Manny Malhotra**, NYR, Dal., CBJ, S.J., Van.	**864**	14
59.	**Ruslan Fedotenko**, Phi., T.B., NYI, Pit., NYR	**863**	12
60.	**Brenden Morrow**, Dal., Pit.	**850**	13
61.	**Toni Lydman**, Cgy., Buf., Ana.	**847**	12
62.	**Stephane Robidas**, Mtl., Dal., Chi.	**847**	13
63.	**Daniel Briere**, Phx., Buf., Phi.	**847**	15
64.	**Filip Kuba**, Fla., Min., T.B., Ott.	**836**	14
65.	**Jochen Hecht**, St.L., Edm., Buf.	**833**	14
66.	**Tom Poti**, Edm., NYR, NYI, Wsh.	**824**	13
67.	**Eric Belanger**, L.A., Car., Atl., Min., Wsh., Phx., Edm.	**820**	12
68.	**Mike Fisher**, Ott., Nsh.	**812**	13
69.	**Nick Schultz**, Min., Edm.	**811**	11
70.	**Sami Salo**, Ott., Van., T.B.	**807**	14
71.	**Lubomir Visnovsky**, L.A., Edm., Ana., NYI	**806**	12
72.	**Taylor Pyatt**, NYI, Buf., Van., Phx., NYR	**803**	12
73.	**Craig Adams**, Car., Chi., Pit.	**799**	12
74.	**Simon Gagne**, Phi., T.B., L.A.	**799**	13
75.	**Samuel Pahlsson**, Bos., Ana., Chi., CBJ, Van.	**798**	11
76.	**Pascal Dupuis**, Min., NYR, Atl., Pit.	**798**	12
77.	**Shawn Horcoff**, Edm.	**796**	12
78.	**Nikolai Khabibulin**, Phx., T.B., Chi., Edm.	**795**	17
79.	**Nik Antropov**, Tor., NYR, Atl., Wpg.	**788**	13
80.	**Dany Heatley**, Atl., Ott., S.J., Min.	**787**	11
81.	**Mike Ribeiro**, Mtl., Dal., Wsh.	**785**	13
82.	**Michal Rozsival**, Pit., NYR, Phx., Chi.	**783**	12

Steve Sullivan missed a full season and parts of two others between February of 2007 and the early stages of 2008-09 recovering from a serious back injury. He had played 723 games at that time and set a goal of making it to 1,000 when he came back. He reached that plateau on March 28, 2013.

	Player	Games Played	Seasons
83.	**Arron Asham**, Mtl., NYI, N.J., Phi., Pit., NYR	**783**	14
84.	**Chris Neil**, Ott.	**779**	11
85.	**Pavel Datsyuk**, Det.	**779**	11
86.	**Marian Gaborik**, Min., NYR, CBJ	**769**	12
87.	**Jay Bouwmeester**, Fla., Cgy., St.L.	**764**	10
88.	**Andrew Ference**, Pit., Cgy., Bos.	**760**	13
89.	**Sheldon Souray**, N.J., Mtl., Edm., Dal., Ana.	**758**	14
90.	**Brian Campbell**, Buf., S.J., Chi., Fla.	**756**	13
91.	**Justin Williams**, Phi., Car., L.A.	**755**	12
92.	**Erik Cole**, Car., Edm., Mtl., Dal.	**749**	11
93.	**Roberto Luongo**, NYI, Fla., Van.	**747**	13
94.	**Richard Park**, Pit., Ana., Phi., Min., Van., NYI	**738**	14
95.	**Martin Erat**, Nsh., Wsh.	**732**	11
96.	**Bryce Salvador**, St.L., N.J.	**731**	11
97.	**Francis Bouillon**, Mtl., Nsh.	**724**	13
98.	**Willie Mitchell**, N.J., Min., Dal., Van., L.A.	**719**	12
99.	**Rick Nash**, CBJ, NYR	**718**	10
100.	**Henrik Zetterberg**, Det.	**714**	10

Goaltending Records

All-Time Shutout Leaders (Minimum 54 Shutouts)

Goaltender	Team	Shutouts	Games	Seasons
1. ***Martin Brodeur**	New Jersey	**121**	1,220	20
(1991-2013)				
2. **Terry Sawchuk**	Detroit	85	734	14
(1949-1970)	Boston	11	102	2
	Toronto	4	91	3
	Los Angeles	2	36	1
	NY Rangers	1	8	1
	Total	**103**	971	21
3. **George Hainsworth**	Montreal	75	318	7½
(1926-1937)	Toronto	19	147	3½
	Total	**94**	465	11
4. **Glenn Hall**	Detroit	17	148	4
(1952-1971)	Chicago	51	618	10
	St. Louis	16	140	4
	Total	**84**	906	18
5. **Jacques Plante**	Montreal	58	556	11
(1952-1973)	NY Rangers	5	98	2
	St. Louis	10	69	2
	Toronto	7	106	2¾
	Boston	2	8	¼
	Total	**82**	837	18
6. **Alec Connell**	Ottawa	64	293	8
(1924-1937)	Detroit	6	48	1
	NY Americans	0	1	1
	Mtl. Maroons	11	75	2
	Total	**81**	417	12
7. **Tiny Thompson**	Boston	74	468	10¼
(1928-1940)	Detroit	7	85	1¾
	Total	**81**	553	12
8. **Dominik Hasek**	Chicago	1	25	2
(1990-2008)	Buffalo	55	491	9
	Detroit	20	176	4
	Ottawa	5	43	1
	Total	**81**	735	16
9. **Tony Esposito**	Montreal	2	13	1
(1968-1984)	Chicago	74	873	15
	Total	**76**	886	16
10. **Ed Belfour**	Chicago	30	415	7⅔
(1988-2007)	San Jose	1	13	⅓
	Dallas	27	307	5
	Toronto	17	170	3
	Florida	1	58	1
	Total	**76**	963	17
11. **Lorne Chabot**	NY Rangers	21	80	2
(1926-1937)	Toronto	32	214	5
	Montreal	8	47	1
	Chicago	8	48	1
	Mtl. Maroons	2	16	1
	NY Americans	1	6	1
	Total	**72**	411	11
12. **Harry Lumley**	Detroit	26	324	6½
(1943-1960)	NY Rangers	0	1	½
	Chicago	5	134	2
	Toronto	34	267	4
	Boston	6	78	3
	Total	**71**	804	16
13. **Roy Worters**	Pittsburgh Pirates	22	123	3
(1925-1937)	NY Americans	45	360	9
	**Montreal	0	1	
	Total	**67**	484	12
14. **Patrick Roy**	Montreal	29	551	11½
(1984-2003)	Colorado	37	478	7½
	Total	**66**	1,029	19
15. **Turk Broda**	Toronto	**62**	629	14
(1936-1952)				
16. ***Roberto Luongo**	NY Islanders	1	24	1
(1999-2013)	Florida	26	317	5
	Vancouver	35	406	7
	Total	**62**	747	13
17. **Clint Benedict**	Ottawa	19	158	7
(1917-1930)	Mtl. Maroons	39	204	6
	Total	**58**	362	13
18. **John Ross Roach**	Toronto	13	222	7
(1921-1935)	NY Rangers	30	89	4
	Detroit	15	180	3
	Total	**58**	491	14
19. ***Evgeni Nabokov**	San Jose	50	563	10
(1999-2013)	NY Islanders	5	83	2
	Total	**55**	646	12
20. **Bernie Parent**	Boston	1	57	2
(1965-1979)	Philadelphia	50	486	9½
	Toronto	3	65	1½
	Total	**54**	608	13
21. **Ed Giacomin**	NY Rangers	49	539	10¼
(1965-1978)	Detroit	5	71	2¾
	Total	**54**	610	13

* Active goalie
** Played 1 game for Montreal in 1929-30.

Ten or More Shutouts, One Season

Number of Shutouts	Goaltender	Team	Season	Length of Schedule
22	George Hainsworth	Montreal	1928-29	44
15	Alec Connell	Ottawa	1925-26	36
	Alec Connell	Ottawa	1927-28	44
	Hal Winkler	Boston	1927-28	44
	Tony Esposito	Chicago	1969-70	76
14	George Hainsworth	Montreal	1926-27	44
13	Clint Benedict	Mtl. Maroons	1926-27	44
	Alec Connell	Ottawa	1926-27	44
	George Hainsworth	Montreal	1927-28	44
	John Ross Roach	NY Rangers	1928-29	44
	Roy Worters	NY Americans	1928-29	44
	Harry Lumley	Toronto	1953-54	70
	Dominik Hasek	Buffalo	1997-98	82
12	Tiny Thompson	Boston	1928-29	44
	Charlie Gardiner	Chicago	1930-31	44
	Terry Sawchuk	Detroit	1951-52	70
	Terry Sawchuk	Detroit	1953-54	70
	Terry Sawchuk	Detroit	1954-55	70
	Glenn Hall	Detroit	1955-56	70
	Bernie Parent	Philadelphia	1973-74	78
	Bernie Parent	Philadelphia	1974-75	80
	Martin Brodeur	New Jersey	2006-07	82
11	Lorne Chabot	NY Rangers	1927-28	44
	Hap Holmes	Detroit	1927-28	44
	Roy Worters	Pittsburgh Pirates	1927-28	44
	Clint Benedict	Mtl. Maroons	1928-29	44
	Joe Miller	Pittsburgh Pirates	1928-29	44
	Tiny Thompson	Boston	1932-33	48
	Terry Sawchuk	Detroit	1950-51	70
	Dominik Hasek	Buffalo	2000-01	82
	Martin Brodeur	New Jersey	2003-04	82
	Henrik Lundqvist	NY Rangers	2010-11	82
10	Lorne Chabot	NY Rangers	1926-27	44
	Lorne Chabot	Toronto	1928-29	44
	Dolly Dolson	Detroit	1928-29	44
	John Ross Roach	Detroit	1932-33	48
	Charlie Gardiner	Chicago	1933-34	48
	Tiny Thompson	Boston	1935-36	48
	Frank Brimsek	Boston	1938-39	48
	Bill Durnan	Montreal	1948-49	60
	Harry Lumley	Toronto	1952-53	70
	Gerry McNeil	Montreal	1952-53	70
	Tony Esposito	Chicago	1973-74	78
	Ken Dryden	Montreal	1976-77	80
	Martin Brodeur	New Jersey	1996-97	82
	Martin Brodeur	New Jersey	1997-98	82
	Byron Dafoe	Boston	1998-99	82
	Roman Cechmanek	Philadelphia	2000-01	82
	Ed Belfour	Toronto	2003-04	82
	Miikka Kiprusoff	Calgary	2005-06	82
	Henrik Lundqvist	NY Rangers	2007-08	82
	Steve Mason	Columbus	2008-09	82
	Jonathan Quick	Los Angeles	2011-12	82

All-Time Win Leaders

(Minimum 270 Wins)

	Goaltender	Wins	GP	Dec.	Losses	OT/Ties
1.	* Martin Brodeur	**669**	1,220	1,197	380	148
2.	Patrick Roy	**551**	1,029	997	315	131
3.	Ed Belfour	**484**	963	929	320	125
4.	Curtis Joseph	**454**	943	902	352	96
5.	Terry Sawchuk	**447**	971	949	330	172
6.	Jacques Plante	**437**	837	828	246	145
7.	Tony Esposito	**423**	886	880	306	151
8.	Glenn Hall	**407**	906	896	326	163
9.	Grant Fuhr	**403**	868	812	295	114
10.	Chris Osgood	**401**	744	712	216	95
11.	Dominik Hasek	**389**	735	707	223	95
12.	Mike Vernon	**385**	781	750	273	92
13.	John Vanbiesbrouck	**374**	882	839	346	119
14.	Andy Moog	**372**	713	669	209	88
15.	Tom Barrasso	**369**	777	732	277	86
16.	Rogie Vachon	**355**	795	773	291	127
17.	* Roberto Luongo	**348**	747	723	289	86
18.	* Evgeni Nabokov	**335**	646	618	207	76
19.	Gump Worsley	**335**	861	837	352	150
20.	* Nikolai Khabibulin	**332**	795	762	334	96
21.	Harry Lumley	**330**	803	801	329	142
22.	Sean Burke	**324**	820	775	341	110
23.	Miikka Kiprusoff	**319**	623	603	213	71
24.	Billy Smith	**305**	680	643	233	105
25.	Olaf Kolzig	**303**	719	687	297	87
26.	Turk Broda	**302**	629	627	224	101
27.	Mike Richter	**301**	666	632	258	73
28.	* Tomas Vokoun	**300**	700	666	288	78
29.	Ron Hextall	**296**	608	579	214	69
30.	Mike Liut	**294**	664	639	271	74
31.	Ed Giacomin	**289**	609	594	209	96
32.	* Jose Theodore	**286**	648	609	254	69
33.	Dan Bouchard	**286**	655	631	232	113
34.	Tiny Thompson	**284**	553	553	194	75
35.	* Henrik Lundqvist	**276**	511	504	171	57
36.	Marty Turco	**275**	543	508	167	66
37.	Bernie Parent	**271**	608	590	198	121
38.	Kelly Hrudey	**271**	677	624	265	88
39.	Gilles Meloche	**270**	788	752	351	131

* active player

Active Shutout Leaders

(Minimum 30 Shutouts)

	Goaltender	Teams	Shutouts	Games	Seasons
1.	Martin Brodeur	New Jersey	**121**	1,220	20
2.	Roberto Luongo	NYI, Fla., Van.	**62**	747	13
3.	Evgeni Nabokov	San Jose, NY Islanders	**55**	646	12
4.	Tomas Vokoun	Mtl., Nsh., Fla., Wsh., Pit.	**51**	700	15
5.	Nikolai Khabibulin	Wpg., Phx., T.B., Chi., Edm.	**46**	795	17
6.	Henrik Lundqvist	NY Rangers	**45**	511	8
7.	Jean-Sebastien Giguere	Hfd., Cgy., Ana., Tor., Col.	**36**	575	15
8.	Jose Theodore	Mtl., Col., Wsh., Min., Fla.	**33**	648	16
9.	Tim Thomas	Boston	**31**	378	8
10.	Pekka Rinne	Nashville	**30**	293	7
11.	Ilya Bryzgalov	Ana., Phx., Phi.	**30**	425	10

All-Time Penalty-Minute Leaders

(Regular season. Minimum 3,000 minutes)

	Player	Penalty Mins.	Games	Mins. per game	Seasons
1.	**Tiger Williams**, Tor., Van., Det., L.A., Hfd.	**3966**	962	4.12	14
2.	**Dale Hunter**, Que., Wsh., Col.	**3565**	1407	2.53	19
3.	**Tie Domi**, Tor., NYR, Wpg.	**3515**	1020	3.45	16
4.	**Marty McSorley**, Pit., Edm., L.A., NYR, S.J., Bos.	**3381**	961	3.52	17
5.	**Bob Probert**, Det., Chi.	**3300**	935	3.53	16
6.	**Rob Ray**, Buf., Ott.	**3207**	900	3.56	15
7.	**Craig Berube**, Phi., Tor., Cgy., Wsh., NYI	**3149**	1054	2.99	17
8.	**Tim Hunter**, Cgy., Que., Van., S.J.	**3146**	815	3.86	16
9.	**Chris Nilan**, Mtl., NYR, Bos.	**3043**	688	4.42	13

Goals-Against Average Leaders (Minimum 25 games played)

(Exceptions: Minimum 13 games played, 1994-95, 2012-13; minimum 26 games played, 1992-93 to 1993-94; minimum 15 games played, 1917-18 to 1925-26)

Season	Goaltender, Team	GP	Mins.	GA	SO	AVG.
2012-13	Craig Anderson, Ottawa	24	1,421	40	3	1.69
2011-12	Brian Elliott, St. Louis	38	2,235	58	9	1.56
2010-11	Tim Thomas, Boston	57	3,634	112	9	2.00
2009-10	Tuukka Rask, Boston	45	2,562	84	5	1.97
2008-09	Tim Thomas, Boston	54	3,259	114	5	2.10
2007-08	Chris Osgood, Detroit	43	2,409	84	4	2.09
2006-07	Niklas Backstrom, Minnesota	41	2,227	73	5	1.97
2005-06	Miikka Kiprusoff, Calgary	74	4,380	151	10	2.07
2003-04	Miikka Kiprusoff, Calgary	38	2,301	65	4	1.69
2002-03	Marty Turco, Dallas	55	3,203	92	7	1.72
2001-02	Patrick Roy, Colorado	63	3,773	122	9	1.94
2000-01	Marty Turco, Dallas	26	1,266	40	3	1.90
99-2000	Brian Boucher, Philadelphia	35	2,038	65	4	1.91
1998-99	Ron Tugnutt, Ottawa	43	2,508	75	3	1.79
1997-98	Ed Belfour, Dallas	61	3,581	112	9	1.88
1996-97	Martin Brodeur, New Jersey	67	3,838	120	10	1.88
1995-96	Ron Hextall, Philadelphia	53	3,102	112	4	2.17
1994-95	Dominik Hasek, Buffalo	41	2,416	85	5	2.11
1993-94	Dominik Hasek, Buffalo	58	3,358	109	7	1.95
1992-93	Felix Potvin, Toronto	48	2,781	116	2	2.50
1991-92	Patrick Roy, Montreal	67	3,935	155	5	2.36
1990-91	Ed Belfour, Chicago	74	4,127	170	4	2.47
1989-90	Mike Liut, Hartford, Washington	37	2,161	91	4	2.53
1988-89	Patrick Roy, Montreal	48	2,744	113	4	2.47
1987-88	Pete Peeters, Washington	35	1,896	88	2	2.78
1986-87	Brian Hayward, Montreal	37	2,178	102	1	2.81
1985-86	Bob Froese, Philadelphia	51	2,728	116	5	2.55
1984-85	Tom Barrasso, Buffalo	54	3,248	144	5	2.66
1983-84	Pat Riggin, Washington	41	2,299	102	4	2.66
1982-83	Pete Peeters, Boston	62	3,611	142	8	2.36
1981-82	Denis Herron, Montreal	27	1,547	68	3	2.64
1980-81	Richard Sevigny, Montreal	33	1,777	71	2	2.40
1979-80	Bob Sauve, Buffalo	32	1,880	74	4	2.36
1978-79	Ken Dryden, Montreal	47	2,814	108	5	2.30
1977-78	Ken Dryden, Montreal	52	3,071	105	5	2.05
1976-77	Michel Larocque, Montreal	26	1,525	53	4	2.09
1975-76	Ken Dryden, Montreal	62	3,580	121	8	2.03
1974-75	Bernie Parent, Philadelphia	68	4,041	137	12	2.03
1973-74	Bernie Parent, Philadelphia	73	4,314	136	12	1.89
1972-73	Ken Dryden, Montreal	54	3,165	119	6	2.26
1971-72	Tony Esposito, Chicago	48	2,780	82	9	1.77
1970-71	Jacques Plante, Toronto	40	2,329	73	4	1.88
1969-70	Ernie Wakely, St. Louis	30	1,651	58	4	2.11
1968-69	Jacques Plante, St. Louis	37	2,139	70	5	1.96
1967-68	Gump Worsley, Montreal	40	2,213	73	6	1.98
1966-67	Glenn Hall, Chicago	32	1,664	66	2	2.38
1965-66	Johnny Bower, Toronto	35	1,998	75	3	2.25
1964-65	Johnny Bower, Toronto	34	2,040	81	3	2.38
1963-64	Johnny Bower, Toronto	51	3,009	106	5	2.11
1962-63	Don Simmons, Toronto	28	1,680	69	1	2.46
1961-62	Jacques Plante, Montreal	70	4,200	166	4	2.37
1960-61	Charlie Hodge, Montreal	30	1,800	74	4	2.47
1959-60	Jacques Plante, Montreal	69	4,140	175	3	2.54
1958-59	Jacques Plante, Montreal	67	4,000	144	9	2.16
1957-58	Jacques Plante, Montreal	57	3,386	119	9	2.11
1956-57	Jacques Plante, Montreal	61	3,660	122	9	2.00
1955-56	Jacques Plante, Montreal	64	3,840	119	7	1.86
1954-55	Harry Lumley, Toronto	69	4,140	134	8	1.94
1953-54	Harry Lumley, Toronto	69	4,140	128	13	1.86
1952-53	Terry Sawchuk, Detroit	63	3,780	120	9	1.90
1951-52	Terry Sawchuk, Detroit	70	4,200	133	12	1.90
1950-51	Al Rollins, Toronto	40	2,367	70	5	1.77
1949-50	Bill Durnan, Montreal	64	3,840	141	8	2.20
1948-49	Bill Durnan, Montreal	60	3,600	126	10	2.10
1947-48	Turk Broda, Toronto	60	3,600	143	5	2.38
1946-47	Bill Durnan, Montreal	60	3,600	138	4	2.30
1945-46	Bill Durnan, Montreal	40	2,400	104	4	2.60
1944-45	Bill Durnan, Montreal	50	3,000	121	1	2.42
1943-44	Bill Durnan, Montreal	50	3,000	109	2	2.18
1942-43	Johnny Mowers, Detroit	50	3,010	124	6	2.47
1941-42	Frank Brimsek, Boston	47	2,930	115	3	2.35
1940-41	Turk Broda, Toronto	48	2,970	99	5	2.00
1939-40	Dave Kerr, NY Rangers	48	3,000	77	8	1.54
1938-39	Frank Brimsek, Boston	43	2,610	68	10	1.56
1937-38	Tiny Thompson, Boston	48	2,970	89	7	1.80
1936-37	Normie Smith, Detroit	48	2,980	102	6	2.05
1935-36	Tiny Thompson, Boston	48	2,930	82	10	1.68
1934-35	Lorne Chabot, Chicago	48	2,940	88	8	1.80
1933-34	Wilf Cude, Detroit, Montreal	30	1,920	47	5	1.47
1932-33	Tiny Thompson, Boston	48	3,000	88	11	1.76
1931-32	Charlie Gardiner, Chicago	48	2,989	92	4	1.85
1930-31	Roy Worters, NY Americans	44	2,760	74	8	1.61
1929-30	Tiny Thompson, Boston	44	2,680	98	3	2.19
1928-29	George Hainsworth, Montreal	44	2,800	43	22	0.92
1927-28	George Hainsworth, Montreal	44	2,730	48	13	1.05
1926-27	Clint Benedict, Mtl. Maroons	43	2,748	65	13	1.42
1925-26	Alec Connell, Ottawa	36	2,251	42	15	1.12
1924-25	Georges Vezina, Montreal	30	1,860	56	5	1.81
1923-24	Georges Vezina, Montreal	24	1,459	48	3	1.97
1922-23	Clint Benedict, Ottawa	24	1,478	54	4	2.18
1921-22	Clint Benedict, Ottawa	24	1,508	84	2	3.34
1920-21	Clint Benedict, Ottawa	24	1,457	75	2	3.09
1919-20	Clint Benedict, Ottawa	24	1,444	64	5	2.66
1918-19	Clint Benedict, Ottawa	18	1,113	53	2	2.86
1917-18	Georges Vezina, Montreal	21	1,282	84	1	3.93

All-Time Regular-Season NHL Coaching Register

Regular Season, 1917-2013

Coach	Team	Games Coached	Wins	Losses	O/T	Years	Cup Wins	Career
Abel, Sid	Chicago	140	39	79	22	2		
	Detroit	811	340	339	132	12		
	St. Louis	10	3	6	1	1		
	Kansas City	3	0	3	0	1		
	Totals	**964**	**382**	**427**	**155**	**16**		**1952-76**
Adams, Jack	**Detroit**	**964**	**413**	**390**	**161**	**20**	**3**	**1927-47**
Agnew, Gary	**Columbus**	**5**	**0**	**4**	**1**	**1**		**2006-07**
Allen, Keith	**Philadelphia**	**150**	**51**	**67**	**32**	**2**		**1967-69**
Allison, Dave	**Ottawa**	**25**	**2**	**22**	**1**	**1**		**1995-96**
Anderson, Jim	**Washington**	**54**	**4**	**45**	**5**	**1**		**1974-75**
Anderson, John	**Atlanta**	**164**	**70**	**75**	**19**	**2**		**2008-10**
Angotti, Lou	St. Louis	32	6	20	6	2		
	Pittsburgh	80	16	58	6	1		
	Totals	**112**	**22**	**78**	**12**	**3**		**1973-84**
Arbour, Al	St. Louis	107	42	40	25	3		
	NY Islanders	1500	740	537	223	20	4	
	Totals	**1607**	**782**	**577**	**248**	**23**	**4**	**1970-08**
Armstrong, George	**Toronto**	**47**	**17**	**26**	**4**	**1**		**1988-89**
Arniel, Scott	**Columbus**	**123**	**45**	**60**	**18**	**2**		**2010-12**
Babcock, Mike	Anaheim	164	69	62	33	3		
	Detroit	622	376	170	76	8	1	
	Totals	**786**	**445**	**232**	**109**	**11**	**1**	**2002-13**
Barber, Bill	**Philadelphia**	**136**	**73**	**40**	**23**	**2**		**2000-02**
Barkley, Doug	**Detroit**	**77**	**20**	**46**	**11**	**3**		**1970-76**
Beaulieu, Andre	**Minnesota**	**32**	**6**	**23**	**3**	**1**		**1977-78**
Belisle, Danny	**Washington**	**96**	**28**	**51**	**17**	**2**		**1978-80**
Berenson, Red	**St. Louis**	**204**	**100**	**72**	**32**	**3**		**1979-82**
Bergeron, Michel	Quebec	634	265	283	86	8		
	NY Rangers	158	73	67	18	2		
	Totals	**792**	**338**	**350**	**104**	**10**		**1980-90**
Berry, Bob	Los Angeles	240	107	94	39	3		
	Montreal	223	116	71	36	3		
	Pittsburgh	240	88	127	25	3		
	St. Louis	157	73	63	21	2		
	Totals	**860**	**384**	**355**	**121**	**11**		**1978-94**
Beverley, Nick	**Toronto**	**17**	**9**	**6**	**2**	**1**		**1995-96**
Blackburn, Don	**Hartford**	**140**	**42**	**63**	**35**	**2**		**1979-81**
Blair, Wren	**Minnesota**	**147**	**48**	**65**	**34**	**3**		**1967-70**
Blake, Toe	**Montreal**	**914**	**500**	**255**	**159**	**13**	**8**	**1955-68**
Boileau, Marc	**Pittsburgh**	**151**	**66**	**61**	**24**	**3**		**1973-76**
Boivin, Leo	**St. Louis**	**97**	**28**	**53**	**16**	**2**		**1975-78**
Boucher, Frank	**NY Rangers**	**527**	**181**	**263**	**83**	**11**	**1**	**1939-54**
Boucher, George	Mtl. Maroons	12	6	5	1	1		
	Ottawa	48	13	29	6	1		
	St. Louis	35	9	20	6	1		
	Boston	70	22	32	16	1		
	Totals	**165**	**50**	**86**	**29**	**4**		**1930-50**
Boucher, Guy	**Tampa Bay**	**195**	**97**	**78**	**20**	**3**		**2010-13**
Boudreau, Bruce	Washington	329	201	88	40	5		
	Anaheim	106	57	35	14	2		
	Totals	**435**	**258**	**123**	**54**	**6**		**2007-13**
Bowman, Scotty	St. Louis	238	110	83	45	4		
	Montreal	634	419	110	105	8	5	
	Buffalo	404	210	134	60	7		
	Pittsburgh	164	95	53	16	2	1	
	Detroit	701	410	193	98	9	3	
	Totals	**2141**	**1244**	**573**	**324**	**30**	**9**	**1967-02**
Bowness, Rick	Winnipeg	28	8	17	3	1		
	Boston	80	36	32	12	1		
	Ottawa	235	39	178	18	4		
	NY Islanders	100	38	50	12	2		
	Phoenix	20	2	12	6	2		
	Totals	**463**	**123**	**289**	**51**	**10**		**1988-05**
Brooks, Herb	NY Rangers	285	131	113	41	4		
	Minnesota	80	19	48	13	1		
	New Jersey	84	40	37	7	1		
	Pittsburgh	57	29	21	7	1		
	Totals	**506**	**219**	**219**	**68**	**7**		**1981-00**
Brophy, John	**Toronto**	**193**	**64**	**111**	**18**	**3**		**1986-89**
Burnett, George	**Edmonton**	**35**	**12**	**20**	**3**	**1**		**1994-95**
Burns, Charlie	**Minnesota**	**86**	**22**	**50**	**14**	**2**		**1969-75**
Burns, Pat	Montreal	320	174	104	42	4		
	Toronto	281	133	107	41	4		
	Boston	254	105	97	52	4		
	New Jersey	164	89	45	30	3	1	
	Totals	**1019**	**501**	**353**	**165**	**15**	**1**	**1988-05**
Bush, Eddie	**Kansas City**	**32**	**1**	**23**	**8**	**1**		**1975-76**
Bylsma, Dan	**Pittsburgh**	**319**	**201**	**93**	**25**	**5**	**1**	**2008-13**
Campbell, Colin	**NY Rangers**	**269**	**118**	**108**	**43**	**4**		**1994-98**
Capuano, Jack	**NY Islanders**	**195**	**84**	**83**	**28**	**3**		**2010-13**
Carbonneau, Guy	**Montreal**	**230**	**124**	**83**	**23**	**3**		**2006-09**
Carlyle, Randy	Anaheim	516	273	182	61	7	1	
	Toronto	66	32	26	8	2		
	Totals	**582**	**305**	**208**	**69**	**8**	**1**	**2005-13**
Carpenter, Doug	New Jersey	290	100	166	24	4		
	Toronto	91	39	47	5	2		
	Totals	**381**	**139**	**213**	**29**	**6**		**1984-91**
Carroll, Dick	**Toronto**	**40**	**18**	**22**	**0**	**2**	**1**	**1917-19**
Carroll, Frank	**Toronto**	**24**	**15**	**9**	**0**	**1**		**1920-21**
Cashman, Wayne	**Philadelphia**	**61**	**32**	**20**	**9**	**1**		**1997-98**

Coach	Team	Games Coached	Wins	Losses	O/T	Years	Cup Wins	Career
Cassidy, Bruce	**Washington**	**110**	**47**	**47**	**16**	**2**		**2002-04**
Chambers, Dave	**Quebec**	**98**	**19**	**64**	**15**	**2**		**1990-92**
Chapman, Art	NY Americans	48	8	29	11	1		
	Brooklyn	48	16	29	3	1		
	Totals	**96**	**24**	**58**	**14**	**2**		**1940-42**
Charron, Guy	Calgary	16	6	7	3	1		
	Anaheim	49	14	26	9	1		
	Totals	**65**	**20**	**33**	**12**	**2**		**1991-01**
Cheevers, Gerry	**Boston**	**376**	**204**	**126**	**46**	**5**		**1980-85**
Cherry, Don	Boston	400	231	105	64	5		
	Colorado	80	19	48	13	1		
	Totals	**480**	**250**	**153**	**77**	**6**		**1974-80**
Clancy, King	Mtl. Maroons	18	6	11	1	1		
	Toronto	210	80	81	49	3		
	Totals	**228**	**86**	**92**	**50**	**4**		**1937-56**
Clapper, Dit	**Boston**	**230**	**102**	**88**	**40**	**4**		**1945-49**
Cleghorn, Odie	**Pittsburgh**	**168**	**62**	**86**	**20**	**4**		**1925-29**
Cleghorn, Sprague	**Mtl. Maroons**	**48**	**19**	**22**	**7**	**1**		**1931-32**
Clouston, Cory	**Ottawa**	**198**	**95**	**83**	**20**	**3**		**2008-11**
Colville, Neil	**NY Rangers**	**93**	**26**	**41**	**26**	**2**		**1950-52**
Conacher, Charlie	**Chicago**	**162**	**56**	**84**	**22**	**3**		**1947-50**
Conacher, Lionel	**NY Americans**	**44**	**14**	**25**	**5**	**1**		**1929-30**
Constantine, Kevin	San Jose	157	55	78	24	3		
	Pittsburgh	189	86	64	39	3		
	New Jersey	31	20	8	3	1		
	Totals	**377**	**161**	**150**	**66**	**7**		**1993-02**
Cook, Bill	**NY Rangers**	**117**	**34**	**59**	**24**	**2**		**1951-53**
Cooper, Jon	**Tampa Bay ***	**15**	**4**	**8**	**3**	**1**		**2012-13**

* Hired by Tampa Bay on March 25, 2013 but did not appear behind the bench until March 29. Assistant coaches Dan Lacroix, Martin Raymond, and Steve Thomas worked a 3-2 loss at Winnipeg on March 24. Lacroix and Thomas worked a 2-1 win vs. Buffalo on March 26.

Coach	Team	Games Coached	Wins	Losses	O/T	Years	Cup Wins	Career
Crawford, Marc	Quebec	48	30	13	5	1		
	Colorado	246	135	75	36	3	1	
	Vancouver	529	246	189	94	8		
	Los Angeles	164	59	84	21	2		
	Dallas	164	79	60	25	2		
	Totals	**1151**	**549**	**421**	**181**	**16**	**1**	**1994-11**
Creamer, Pierre	**Pittsburgh**	**80**	**36**	**35**	**9**	**1**		**1987-88**
Creighton, Fred	Atlanta	348	156	136	56	5		
	Boston	73	40	20	13	1		
	Totals	**421**	**196**	**156**	**69**	**6**		**1974-80**
Crisp, Terry	Calgary	240	144	63	33	3	1	
	Tampa Bay	391	142	204	45	6		
	Totals	**631**	**286**	**267**	**78**	**9**	**1**	**1987-98**
Crozier, Joe	Buffalo	192	77	80	35	3		
	Toronto	40	13	22	5	1		
	Totals	**232**	**90**	**102**	**40**	**4**		**1971-81**
Crozier, Roger	**Washington**	**1**	**0**	**1**	**0**	**1**		**1981-82**
Cunneyworth, Randy	**Montreal**	**50**	**18**	**23**	**9**	**1**		**2011-12**
Cunniff, John	Hartford	13	3	9	1	1		
	New Jersey	133	59	56	18	2		
	Totals	**146**	**62**	**65**	**19**	**3**		**1982-91**
Curry, Alex	**Ottawa**	**36**	**24**	**8**	**4**	**1**		**1925-26**
Dandurand, Leo	**Montreal**	**163**	**78**	**76**	**9**	**6**	**1**	**1921-35**
Day, Hap	**Toronto**	**546**	**259**	**206**	**81**	**10**	**5**	**1940-50**
Dea, Billy	**Detroit**	**11**	**3**	**8**	**0**	**1**		**1981-82**
DeBoer, Peter	Florida	246	103	107	36	3		
	New Jersey	130	67	47	16	2		
	Totals	**376**	**170**	**154**	**52**	**5**		**2008-13**
Delvecchio, Alex	**Detroit**	**245**	**82**	**131**	**32**	**4**		**1973-77**
Demers, Jacques	Quebec	80	25	44	11	1		
	St. Louis	240	106	106	28	3		
	Detroit	320	137	136	47	4		
	Montreal	220	107	86	27	4	1	
	Tampa Bay	147	34	96	17	2		
	Totals	**1007**	**409**	**468**	**130**	**14**	**1**	**1979-99**
Denneny, Cy	**Ottawa**	**48**	**11**	**27**	**10**	**1**		**1932-33**
Dineen, Bill	**Philadelphia**	**140**	**60**	**60**	**20**	**2**		**1991-93**
Dineen, Kevin	**Florida**	**130**	**53**	**53**	**24**	**2**		**2011-13**
Dudley, Rick	Buffalo	188	85	72	31	3		
	Florida	40	13	15	12	1		
	Totals	**228**	**98**	**87**	**43**	**4**		**1989-04**
Duff, Dick	**Toronto**	**2**	**0**	**2**	**0**	**1**		**1979-80**
Dugal, Jules	**Montreal**	**18**	**9**	**6**	**3**	**1**		**1938-39**
Duncan, Art	Detroit	33	10	21	2	1		
	Toronto	47	21	16	10	2		
	Totals	**80**	**31**	**37**	**12**	**3**		**1926-32**
Dutton, Red	**NY Americans**	**192**	**66**	**97**	**29**	**4**		**1936-40**
Eddolls, Frank	**Chicago**	**70**	**13**	**40**	**17**	**1**		**1954-55**
Esposito, Phil	**NY Rangers**	**45**	**24**	**21**	**0**	**2**		**1986-89**
Evans, Jack	California	80	27	42	11	1		
	Cleveland	160	47	87	26	2		
	Hartford	374	163	174	37	5		
	Totals	**614**	**237**	**303**	**74**	**8**		**1975-88**
Ferguson, John	NY Rangers	121	43	59	19	2		
	Winnipeg	14	7	6	1	1		
	Totals	**135**	**50**	**65**	**20**	**3**		**1975-86**
Filion, Maurice	**Quebec**	**6**	**1**	**3**	**2**	**1**		**1980-81**
Francis, Bob	**Phoenix**	**390**	**165**	**144**	**81**	**5**		**1999-04**
Francis, Emile	NY Rangers	654	342	209	103	10		
	St. Louis	124	46	64	14	3		
	Totals	**778**	**388**	**273**	**117**	**13**		**1965-83**
Fraser, Curt	**Atlanta**	**279**	**64**	**169**	**46**	**4**		**1999-03**
Fredrickson, Frank	**Pittsburgh**	**44**	**5**	**36**	**3**	**1**		**1929-30**

Coach	Team	Games Coached	Wins	Losses	O/T	Years	Cup Wins	Career
Ftorek, Robbie	Los Angeles	132	65	56	11	2		
	New Jersey	156	88	44	24	2		
	Boston	155	76	52	27	2		
	Totals	443	229	152	62	6		1987-03
Gadsby, Bill	Detroit	78	35	31	12	2		1968-70
Gainey, Bob	Minnesota	244	95	119	30	3		
	Dallas	171	70	71	30	3		
	Montreal	57	29	21	7	2		
	Totals	472	194	211	67	8		1990-09
Gallant, Gerard	Columbus	142	56	76	10	4		2003-07
Gardiner, Herb	Chicago	32	5	23	4	1		1928-29
Gardner, Jimmy	Hamilton	30	19	10	1	1		1924-25
Garvin, Ted	Detroit	11	2	8	1	1		1973-74
Geoffrion, Bernie	NY Rangers	43	22	18	3	1		
	Atlanta	208	77	92	39	3		
	Montreal	30	15	9	6	1		
	Totals	281	114	119	48	5		1968-80
Gerard, Eddie	Ottawa	22	9	13	0	1		
	Mtl. Maroons	294	129	122	43	7	1	
	NY Americans	92	34	40	18	2		
	St. Louis	13	2	11	0	1		
	Totals	421	174	186	61	11	1	1917-35
Gilbert, Greg	Calgary	121	42	56	23	3		2000-03
Gill, David	Ottawa	132	64	41	27	3	1	1926-29
Glover, Fred	Oakland	152	51	76	25	2		
	California	204	45	131	28	4		
	Los Angeles	68	18	42	8	1		
	Totals	424	114	249	61	6		1968-74
Goodfellow, Ebbie	Chicago	140	30	91	19	2		1950-52
Gordon, Jackie	Minnesota	289	116	123	50	5		1970-75
Gordon, Scott	NY Islanders	181	64	94	23	3		2008-11
Goring, Butch	Boston	93	42	38	13	2		
	NY Islanders	147	41	88	18	2		
	Totals	240	83	126	31	4		1985-01
Gorman, Tommy	NY Americans	80	31	33	16	2		
	Chicago	73	28	28	17	2	1	
	Mtl. Maroons	174	74	71	29	4	1	
	Totals	327	133	132	62	8	2	1925-38
Gottselig, Johnny	Chicago	187	62	105	20	4		1944-48
Goyette, Phil	NY Islanders	48	6	38	4	1		1972-73
Graham, Dirk	Chicago	59	16	35	8	1		1998-99
Granato, Tony	Colorado	215	104	78	33	3		2002-09
Green, Gary	Washington	157	50	78	29	3		1979-82
Green, Pete	Ottawa	150	94	52	4	6	3	1919-25
Green, Shorty	NY Americans	44	11	27	6	1		1927-28
Green, Ted	Edmonton	188	65	102	21	3		1991-94
Gretzky, Wayne	Phoenix	328	143	161	24	4		2005-09
Guidolin, Aldo	Colorado	59	12	39	8	1		1978-79
Guidolin, Bep	Boston	104	72	23	9	2		
	Kansas City	125	26	84	15	2		
	Totals	229	98	107	24	4		1972-76
Gulutzan, Glen	Dallas	130	64	57	9	2		2011-13
Hanlon, Glen	Washington	239	78	122	39	5		2003-08
Harkness, Ned	Detroit	38	12	22	4	1		1970-71
Harris, Ted	Minnesota	179	48	104	27	3		1975-78
Hart, Cecil	Montreal	394	196	125	73	9	2	1926-39
Hartley, Bob	Colorado	359	193	108	58	5	1	
	Atlanta	291	136	118	37	6		
	Calgary	48	19	25	4	1		
	Totals	698	348	251	99	11	1	1998-13
Hartsburg, Craig	Chicago	246	104	102	40	3		
	Anaheim	197	80	82	35	3		
	Ottawa	48	17	24	7	1		
	Totals	491	201	208	82	7		1995-09
Harvey, Doug	NY Rangers	70	26	32	12	1		1961-62
Hay, Don	Phoenix	82	38	37	7	1		
	Calgary	68	23	28	17	1		
	Totals	150	61	65	24	2		1996-01
Heffernan, Frank	Toronto	12	5	7	0	1		1919-20
Helmer, Rosie	NY Americans	48	16	25	7	1		1935-36
Henning, Lorne	Minnesota	158	68	72	18	2		
	NY Islanders	65	19	39	7	2		
	Totals	223	87	111	25	4		1985-01
Hitchcock, Ken	Dallas	503	277	154	72	7	1	
	Philadelphia	254	131	73	50	5		
	Columbus	284	125	123	36	4		
	St. Louis	117	72	32	13	2		
	Totals	1158	605	382	171	17	1	1995-13
Hlinka, Ivan	Pittsburgh	86	42	32	12	2		2000-02
Holmgren, Paul	Philadelphia	264	107	126	31	4		
	Hartford	161	54	93	14	4		
	Totals	425	161	219	45	8		1988-96
Howell, Harry	Minnesota	11	3	6	2	1		1978-79
Hunter, Dale	Washington	60	30	23	7	1		2011-12
Imlach, Punch	Toronto	770	370	275	125	12	4	
	Buffalo	119	32	62	25	2		
	Totals	889	402	337	150	14	4	1958-80
Ingarfield, Earl	NY Islanders	30	6	22	2	1		1972-73
Inglis, Bill	Buffalo	56	28	18	10	1		1978-79
Irvin, Dick	Chicago	126	45	62	19	3		
	Toronto	426	215	152	59	9	1	
	Montreal	896	431	313	152	15	3	
	Totals	1448	691	527	230	27	4	1928-56
Ivan, Tommy	Detroit	470	262	118	90	7	3	
	Chicago	103	26	56	21	2		
	Totals	573	288	174	111	9	3	1947-58
Iverson, Emil	Chicago	21	8	7	6	1		1932-33

Coach	Team	Games Coached	Wins	Losses	O/T	Years	Cup Wins	Career
Johnson, Bob	Calgary	400	193	155	52	5		
	Pittsburgh	80	41	33	6	1	1	
	Totals	480	234	188	58	6	1	1982-91
Johnson, Tom	Boston	208	142	43	23	3	1	1970-73
Johnston, Eddie	Chicago	80	34	27	19	1		
	Pittsburgh	516	232	224	60	7		
	Totals	596	266	251	79	8		1979-97
Johnston, Marshall	California	69	13	45	11	2		
	Colorado	56	15	32	9	1		
	Totals	125	28	77	20	3		1973-82
Julien, Claude	Montreal	159	72	62	25	4		
	New Jersey	79	47	24	8	1		
	Boston	458	256	146	65	6	1	
	Totals	696	375	232	98	11	1	2002-13
Kasper, Steve	Boston	164	66	78	20	2		1995-97
Keats, Duke	Detroit	11	2	7	2	1		1926-27
Keenan, Mike	Philadelphia	320	190	102	28	4		
	Chicago	320	153	126	41	4		
	NY Rangers	84	52	24	8	1	1	
	St. Louis	163	75	66	22	3		
	Vancouver	108	36	54	18	2		
	Boston	74	33	26	15	1		
	Florida	153	45	73	35	3		
	Calgary	164	88	60	16	2		
	Totals	1386	672	531	183	20	1	1984-09
Kehoe, Rick	Pittsburgh	160	55	81	22	2		2001-03
Kelly, Pat	Colorado	101	22	54	25	2		1977-79
Kelly, Red	Los Angeles	150	55	75	20	2		
	Pittsburgh	274	90	132	52	4		
	Toronto	318	133	123	62	4		
	Totals	742	278	330	134	10		1967-77
King, Dave	Calgary	216	109	76	31	3		
	Columbus	204	64	106	34	3		
	Totals	420	173	182	65	6		1992-03
Kingston, George	San Jose	164	28	129	7	2		1991-93
Kish, Larry	Hartford	49	12	32	5	1		1982-83
Kitchen, Mike	St. Louis	131	38	70	23	4		2003-07
Kromm, Bobby	Detroit	231	79	111	41	3		1977-80
Krueger, Ralph	Edmonton	48	19	22	7	1		2012-13
Kurtenbach, Orland	Vancouver	125	36	62	27	2		1976-78
LaForge, Bill	Vancouver	20	4	14	2	1		1984-85
Lalonde, Newsy	Montreal	207	96	97	14	8		
	NY Americans	44	17	25	2	1		
	Ottawa	88	31	45	12	2		
	Totals	339	144	167	28	11		1917-35
Lamoriello, Lou	New Jersey	53	34	14	5	2		2005-07
Laperriere, Jacques	Montreal	1	0	1	0	1		1995-96
Lapointe, Ron	Quebec	89	33	50	6	2		1987-89
Laviolette, Peter	NY Islanders	164	77	62	25	2		
	Carolina	323	167	122	34	6	1	
	Philadelphia	269	145	95	29	4		
	Totals	756	389	279	88	12	1	2001-13
Laycoe, Hal	Los Angeles	24	5	18	1	1		
	Vancouver	156	44	96	16	2		
	Totals	180	49	114	17	3		1969-72
Lehman, Hugh	Chicago	21	3	17	1	1		1927-28
Lemaire, Jacques	Montreal	97	48	37	12	2		
	New Jersey	509	276	166	67	7	1	
	Minnesota	656	293	255	108	9		
	Totals	1262	617	458	187	18	1	1983-11
Lepine, Pit	Montreal	48	10	33	5	1		1939-40
LeSueur, Percy	Hamilton	10	3	7	0	1		1923-24
Lewis, Dave	Detroit *	169	100	42	27	4		
	Boston	82	35	41	6	1		
	Totals	251	135	83	33	5		1998-07

* Shared a record of 4-1-0 with co-coach Barry Smith in 1998-99

Coach	Team	Games Coached	Wins	Losses	O/T	Years	Cup Wins	Career
Ley, Rick	Hartford	160	69	71	20	2		
	Vancouver	124	47	50	27	2		
	Totals	284	116	121	47	4		1989-96
Lindsay, Ted	Detroit	29	5	21	3	2		1979-81
Long, Barry	Winnipeg	205	87	93	25	3		1983-86
Loughlin, Clem	Chicago	144	61	63	20	3		1934-37
Low, Ron	Edmonton	341	139	162	40	5		
	NY Rangers	164	69	81	14	2		
	Totals	505	208	243	54	7		1994-02
Lowe, Kevin	Edmonton	82	32	26	24	1		1999-00
Ludzik, Steve	Tampa Bay	121	31	67	23	2		1999-01
MacDonald, Parker	Minnesota	61	20	30	11	1		
	Los Angeles	42	13	24	5	1		
	Totals	103	33	54	16	2		1973-82
MacLean, Doug	Florida	187	83	71	33	3		
	Columbus	79	24	43	12	2		
	Totals	266	107	114	45	5		1995-04
MacLean, John	New Jersey	33	9	22	2	1		2010-11
MacLean, Paul	Ottawa	130	66	48	16	2		2011-13
MacMillan, Bill	Colorado	80	22	45	13	1		
	New Jersey	100	19	67	14	2		
	Totals	180	41	112	27	3		1980-84
MacNeil, Al	Montreal	55	31	15	9	1	1	
	Atlanta	80	35	32	13	1		
	Calgary	171	72	66	33	3		
	Totals	306	138	113	55	5	1	1970-03
MacTavish, Craig	Edmonton	656	301	252	103	9		2000-09
Magnuson, Keith	Chicago	132	49	57	26	2		1980-82
Mahoney, Bill	Minnesota	93	42	39	12	2		1983-85
Maloney, Dan	Toronto	160	45	100	15	2		
	Winnipeg	212	91	93	28	3		
	Totals	372	136	193	43	5		1984-89

Coach	Team	Games Coached	Wins	Losses	O/T	Years	Cup Wins	Career
Maloney, Phil	**Vancouver**	**232**	**95**	**105**	**32**	**4**		**1973-77**
Mantha, Sylvio	**Montreal**	**48**	**11**	**26**	**11**	**1**		**1935-36**
Marshall, Bert	**Colorado**	**24**	**3**	**17**	**4**	**1**		**1981-82**
Martin, Jacques	St. Louis	160	66	71	23	2		
	Ottawa	692	341	235	116	9		
	Florida	246	110	100	36	4		
	Montreal	196	96	75	25	3		
	Totals	**1294**	**613**	**481**	**200**	**18**		**1986-12**
Matheson, Godfrey	**Chicago**	**2**	**0**	**2**	**0**	**1**		**1932-33**
Maurice, Paul	Hartford	152	61	72	19	2		
	Carolina	768	323	319	126	11		
	Toronto	164	76	66	22	2		
	Totals	**1084**	**460**	**457**	**167**	**15**		**1995-12**
Maxner, Wayne	**Detroit**	**129**	**34**	**68**	**27**	**2**		**1980-82**
McCammon, Bob	Philadelphia	218	119	68	31	4		
	Vancouver	294	102	156	36	4		
	Totals	**512**	**221**	**224**	**67**	**8**		**1978-91**
McCreary, Bill	St. Louis	24	6	14	4	1		
	Vancouver	41	9	25	7	1		
	California	32	8	20	4	1		
	Totals	**97**	**23**	**59**	**15**	**3**		**1971-75**
McGuire, Pierre	**Hartford**	**67**	**23**	**37**	**7**	**1**		**1993-94**
McLellan, John	**Toronto**	**310**	**126**	**139**	**45**	**4**		**1969-73**
McLellan, Todd	**San Jose**	**376**	**220**	**108**	**48**	**5**		**2008-13**
McVie, Tom	Washington	204	49	122	33	3		
	Winnipeg	105	20	67	18	2		
	New Jersey	153	57	74	22	3		
	Totals	**462**	**126**	**263**	**73**	**8**		**1975-92**
Meeker, Howie	**Toronto**	**70**	**21**	**34**	**15**	**1**		**1956-57**
Melrose, Barry	Los Angeles	209	79	101	29	3		
	Tampa Bay	16	5	7	4	1		
	Totals	**225**	**84**	**108**	**33**	**4**		**1992-09**
Milbury, Mike	Boston	160	90	49	21	2		
	NY Islanders	191	56	111	24	4		
	Totals	**351**	**146**	**160**	**45**	**6**		**1989-99**
Molleken, Lorne	**Chicago**	**47**	**18**	**19**	**10**	**2**		**1998-00**
Muckler, John	Minnesota	35	6	23	6	1		
	Edmonton	160	75	65	20	2	1	
	Buffalo	268	125	109	34	4		
	NY Rangers	185	70	88	27	3		
	Totals	**648**	**276**	**285**	**87**	**10**	**1**	**1968-00**
Muldoon, Pete	**Chicago**	**44**	**19**	**22**	**3**	**1**		**1926-27**
Muller, Kirk	**Carolina**	**105**	**44**	**45**	**16**	**2**		**2011-13**
Munro, Dunc	**Mtl. Maroons**	**76**	**37**	**29**	**10**	**2**		**1929-31**
Murdoch, Bob	Chicago	80	30	41	9	1		
	Winnipeg	160	63	75	22	2		
	Totals	**240**	**93**	**116**	**31**	**3**		**1987-91**
Murphy, Mike	Los Angeles	65	20	37	8	2		
	Toronto	164	60	87	17	2		
	Totals	**229**	**80**	**124**	**25**	**4**		**1986-98**
Murray, Andy	Los Angeles	480	215	176	89	7		
	St. Louis	258	118	102	38	4		
	Totals	**738**	**333**	**278**	**127**	**11**		**1999-10**
Murray, Bryan	Washington	672	343	246	83	9		
	Detroit	244	124	91	29	3		
	Florida	59	17	31	11	1		
	Anaheim	82	29	42	11	1		
	Ottawa	182	107	55	20	4		
	Totals	**1239**	**620**	**465**	**154**	**18**		**1981-08**
Murray, Terry	Washington	325	163	134	28	5		
	Philadelphia	212	118	64	30	3		
	Florida	200	79	79	42	3		
	Los Angeles	275	139	106	30	4		
	Totals	**1012**	**499**	**383**	**130**	**15**		**1989-12**
Nanne, Lou	**Minnesota**	**29**	**7**	**18**	**4**	**1**		**1977-78**
Neale, Harry	Vancouver	407	142	189	76	6		
	Detroit	35	8	23	4	1		
	Totals	**442**	**150**	**212**	**80**	**7**		**1978-86**
Neilson, Roger	Toronto	160	75	62	23	2		
	Buffalo	80	39	20	21	1		
	Vancouver	133	51	61	21	3		
	Los Angeles	28	8	17	3	1		
	NY Rangers	280	141	104	35	4		
	Florida	132	53	56	23	2		
	Philadelphia	185	92	57	36	3		
	Ottawa	2	1	1	0	1		
	Totals	**1000**	**460**	**378**	**162**	**16**		**1977-02**
Noel, Claude	Columbus	24	10	8	6	1		
	Winnipeg	130	61	56	13	2		
	Totals	**154**	**71**	**64**	**19**	**3**		**2009-13**
Nolan, Ted	Buffalo	164	73	72	19	2		
	NY Islanders	163	74	68	21	2		
	Totals	**327**	**147**	**140**	**40**	**4**		**1995-08**
Nykoluk, Mike	**Toronto**	**280**	**89**	**144**	**47**	**4**		**1980-84**
Oates, Adam	**Washington**	**48**	**27**	**18**	**3**	**1**		**2012-13**
O'Connell, Mike	**Boston**	**9**	**3**	**3**	**3**	**1**		**2002-03**
O'Donoghue, George	**Toronto**	**29**	**15**	**13**	**1**	**2**	**1**	**1921-23**
Olczyk, Ed	**Pittsburgh**	**113**	**31**	**64**	**18**	**3**		**2003-06**
Oliver, Murray	**Minnesota**	**37**	**18**	**12**	**7**	**1**		**1982-83**
Olmstead, Bert	**Oakland** *	**74**	**15**	**42**	**17**	**1**		**1967-68**

* Olmstead, who was also GM, turned over bench duties to assistant coach Gord Fashoway for the last 22 games of the season. Fashoway posted a 5-11-6 record. All games are credited to Olmstead's coaching record.

Coach	Team	Games Coached	Wins	Losses	O/T	Years	Cup Wins	Career
O'Reilly, Terry	**Boston**	**227**	**115**	**86**	**26**	**3**		**1986-89**
Paddock, John	Winnipeg	281	106	138	37	4		
	Ottawa	64	36	22	6	1		
	Totals	**345**	**142**	**160**	**43**	**5**		**1991-08**
Page, Pierre	Minnesota	160	63	77	20	2		
	Quebec	230	98	103	29	3		
	Calgary	164	66	78	20	2		
	Anaheim	82	26	43	13	1		
	Totals	**636**	**253**	**301**	**82**	**8**		**1988-98**
Park, Brad	**Detroit**	**45**	**9**	**34**	**2**	**1**		**1985-86**
Paterson, Rick	**Tampa Bay**	**6**	**0**	**6**	**0**	**1**		**1997-98**
Patrick, Craig	NY Rangers	95	37	45	13	2		
	Pittsburgh	74	29	36	9	2		
	Totals	**169**	**66**	**81**	**22**	**4**		**1980-97**
Patrick, Frank	**Boston**	**96**	**48**	**36**	**12**	**2**		**1934-36**
Patrick, Lester	**NY Rangers**	**604**	**281**	**216**	**107**	**13**	**2**	**1926-39**
Patrick, Lynn	NY Rangers	107	40	51	16	2		
	Boston	310	117	130	63	5		
	St. Louis	26	8	15	3	3		
	Totals	**443**	**165**	**196**	**82**	**10**		**1948-76**
Patrick, Muzz	**NY Rangers**	**136**	**43**	**66**	**27**	**4**		**1953-63**
Payne, Davis	**St. Louis**	**137**	**67**	**55**	**15**	**3**		**2009-12**
Perron, Jean	Montreal	240	126	84	30	3	1	
	Quebec	47	16	26	5	1		
	Totals	**287**	**142**	**110**	**35**	**4**	**1**	**1985-89**
Perry, Don	**Los Angeles**	**168**	**52**	**85**	**31**	**3**		**1981-84**
Pike, Alf	**NY Rangers**	**123**	**36**	**66**	**21**	**2**		**1959-61**
Pilous, Rudy	**Chicago**	**387**	**162**	**151**	**74**	**6**	**1**	**1957-63**
Plager, Barclay	**St. Louis**	**178**	**49**	**96**	**33**	**4**		**1977-83**
Plager, Bob	**St. Louis**	**11**	**4**	**6**	**1**	**1**		**1992-93**
Playfair, Jim	**Calgary**	**82**	**43**	**29**	**10**	**1**		**2006-07**
Pleau, Larry	**Hartford**	**224**	**81**	**117**	**26**	**5**		**1980-89**
Polano, Nick	**Detroit**	**240**	**79**	**127**	**34**	**3**		**1982-85**
Popein, Larry	**NY Rangers**	**41**	**18**	**14**	**9**	**1**		**1973-74**
Powers, Eddie	**Toronto**	**66**	**31**	**32**	**3**	**2**		**1924-26**
Primeau, Joe	**Toronto**	**210**	**97**	**71**	**42**	**3**	**1**	**1950-53**
Pronovost, Marcel	**Buffalo**	**104**	**52**	**29**	**23**	**2**		**1977-79**
Pulford, Bob	Los Angeles	396	178	150	68	5		
	Chicago	433	185	180	68	7		
	Totals	**829**	**363**	**330**	**136**	**12**		**1972-00**
Quenneville, Joel	St. Louis	593	307	191	95	8		
	Colorado	246	131	92	23	4		
	Chicago	372	222	106	44	5	2	
	Totals	**1211**	**660**	**389**	**162**	**17**	**2**	**1996-13**
Querrie, Charles	**Toronto**	**72**	**29**	**38**	**5**	**3**		**1922-27**
Quinn, Mike	**Quebec**	**24**	**4**	**20**	**0**	**1**		**1919-20**
Quinn, Pat	Philadelphia	262	141	73	48	4		
	Los Angeles	202	75	101	26	3		
	Vancouver	280	141	111	28	5		
	Toronto	574	300	196	78	8		
	Edmonton	82	27	47	8	1		
	Totals	**1400**	**684**	**528**	**188**	**21**		**1978-10**
Raeder, Cap	**San Jose**	**1**	**1**	**0**	**0**	**1**		**2002-03**
Ramsay, Craig	Buffalo	21	4	15	2	1		
	Philadelphia	28	12	12	4	1		
	Atlanta	82	34	36	12	1		
	Totals	**131**	**50**	**63**	**18**	**3**		**1986-11**
Randall, Ken	**Hamilton**	**14**	**6**	**8**	**0**	**1**		**1923-24**
Reay, Billy	Toronto	90	26	50	14	2		
	Chicago	1012	516	335	161	14		
	Totals	**1102**	**542**	**385**	**175**	**16**		**1957-77**
Regan, Larry	**Los Angeles**	**88**	**27**	**47**	**14**	**2**		**1970-72**
Renney, Tom	Vancouver	101	39	53	9	2		
	NY Rangers	327	164	117	46	6		
	Edmonton	164	57	85	22	2		
	Totals	**592**	**260**	**255**	**77**	**10**		**1996-12**
Richards, Todd	Minnesota	164	77	71	16	2		
	Columbus	89	42	38	9	2		
	Totals	**253**	**119**	**109**	**25**	**4**		**2009-13**
Risebrough, Doug	**Calgary**	**144**	**71**	**56**	**17**	**2**		**1990-92**
Roberts, Jim	Buffalo	45	21	16	8	1		
	Hartford	80	26	41	13	1		
	St. Louis	9	3	3	3	1		
	Totals	**134**	**50**	**60**	**24**	**3**		**1981-97**
Robinson, Larry	Los Angeles	328	122	161	45	4		
	New Jersey	173	87	56	30	4	1	
	Totals	**501**	**209**	**217**	**75**	**8**	**1**	**1995-06**
Rodden, Mike	**Toronto**	**2**	**0**	**2**	**0**	**1**		**1926-27**
Rolston, Ron	**Buffalo**	**31**	**15**	**11**	**5**	**1**		**2012-13**
Romeril, Alex	**Toronto**	**13**	**7**	**5**	**1**	**1**		**1926-27**
Ross, Art	Mtl. Wanderers	6	1	5	0	1		
	Hamilton	24	6	18	0	1		
	Boston	772	387	290	95	17	2	
	Totals	**802**	**394**	**313**	**95**	**19**	**2**	**1917-45**
Ruel, Claude	**Montreal**	**305**	**172**	**82**	**51**	**5**	**1**	**1968-81**
Ruff, Lindy	**Buffalo**	**1165**	**571**	**432**	**162**	**16**		**1997-13**
Sacco, Joe	**Colorado**	**294**	**130**	**134**	**30**	**4**		**2009-13**
Sather, Glen	Edmonton	842	464	268	110	11	4	
	NY Rangers	90	33	39	18	2		
	Totals	**932**	**497**	**307**	**128**	**13**	**4**	**1979-04**
Sator, Ted	NY Rangers	99	41	48	10	2		
	Buffalo	207	96	89	22	3		
	Totals	**306**	**137**	**137**	**32**	**4**		**1985-89**
Savard, Andre	**Quebec**	**24**	**10**	**13**	**1**	**1**		**1987-88**
Savard, Denis	**Chicago**	**147**	**65**	**66**	**16**	**3**		**2006-09**
Schinkel, Ken	**Pittsburgh**	**203**	**83**	**92**	**28**	**4**		**1972-77**
Schmidt, Milt	Boston	726	245	360	121	11		
	Washington	44	5	34	5	2		
	Totals	**770**	**250**	**394**	**126**	**13**		**1954-76**

Coach	Team	Games Coached	Wins	Losses	O/T	Years	Cup Wins	Career
Schoenfeld, Jim	Buffalo	43	19	19	5	1		
	New Jersey	124	50	59	15	3		
	Washington	249	113	102	34	4		
	Phoenix	164	74	66	24	2		
	Totals	**580**	**256**	**246**	**78**	**10**		**1985-99**
Shaughnessy, Tom	**Chicago**	**21**	**10**	**8**	**3**	**1**		**1929-30**
Shaw, Brad	**NY Islanders**	**40**	**18**	**18**	**4**	**1**		**2005-06**
Shero, Fred	Philadelphia	554	308	151	95	7	2	
	NY Rangers	180	82	74	24	3		
	Totals	**734**	**390**	**225**	**119**	**10**	**2**	**1971-81**
Simpson, Joe	**NY Americans**	**144**	**42**	**72**	**30**	**3**		**1932-35**
Simpson, Terry	NY Islanders	187	81	82	24	3		
	Philadelphia	84	35	39	10	1		
	Winnipeg	97	43	47	7	2		
	Totals	**368**	**159**	**168**	**41**	**6**		**1986-96**
Sims, Al	**San Jose**	**82**	**27**	**47**	**8**	**1**		**1996-97**
Sinden, Harry	**Boston**	**327**	**153**	**116**	**58**	**6**	**1**	**1966-85**
Skinner, Jimmy	**Detroit**	**247**	**123**	**78**	**46**	**4**	**1**	**1954-58**
Smeaton, Cooper	**Philadelphia**	**44**	**4**	**36**	**4**	**1**		**1930-31**
Smith, Alf	**Ottawa**	**18**	**12**	**6**	**0**	**1**		**1918-19**
Smith, Barry	**Detroit ***	**5**	**4**	**1**	**0**	**1**		**1998-99**
	* Results Shared with co-coach Dave Lewis							
Smith, Floyd	Buffalo	241	143	62	36	4		
	Toronto	68	30	33	5	1		
	Totals	**309**	**173**	**95**	**41**	**5**		**1971-80**
Smith, Mike	**Winnipeg**	**23**	**2**	**17**	**4**	**1**		**1980-81**
Smith, Ron	**NY Rangers**	**44**	**15**	**22**	**7**	**1**		**1992-93**
Smythe, Conn	**Toronto**	**135**	**58**	**57**	**20**	**5**		**1927-32**
Sonmor, Glen	**Minnesota**	**421**	**177**	**161**	**83**	**7**		**1978-87**
Sproule, Harvey	**Toronto**	**12**	**7**	**5**	**0**	**1**		**1919-20**
Stanley, Barney	**Chicago**	**23**	**4**	**17**	**2**	**1**		**1927-28**
Stasiuk, Vic	Philadelphia	154	45	68	41	2		
	California	75	21	38	16	1		
	Vancouver	78	22	47	9	1		
	Totals	**307**	**88**	**153**	**66**	**4**		**1969-73**
Stevens, John	Philadelphia	263	120	109	34	4		
	Los Angeles	4	2	2	0	1		
	Totals	**267**	**122**	**111**	**34**	**5**		**2006-12**
Stewart, Bill J.	**Chicago**	**69**	**22**	**35**	**12**	**2**	**1**	**1937-39**
Stewart, Bill D.	**NY Islanders**	**37**	**11**	**19**	**7**	**1**		**1998-99**
Stewart, Ron	NY Rangers	39	15	20	4	1		
	Los Angeles	80	31	34	15	1		
	Totals	**119**	**46**	**54**	**19**	**2**		**1975-78**
Stirling, Steve	**NY Islanders**	**124**	**56**	**51**	**17**	**3**		**2003-06**
Suhonen, Alpo	**Chicago**	**82**	**29**	**41**	**12**	**1**		**2000-01**
Sullivan, Mike	**Boston**	**164**	**70**	**56**	**38**	**3**		**2003-06**
Sullivan, Red	NY Rangers	196	58	103	35	4		
	Pittsburgh	150	47	79	24	2		
	Washington	18	2	16	0	1		
	Totals	**364**	**107**	**198**	**59**	**7**		**1962-75**
Sutherland, Bill	**Winnipeg**	**32**	**7**	**22**	**3**	**2**		**1979-81**
Sutter, Brent	New Jersey	164	97	56	11	2		
	Calgary	246	118	90	38	3		
	Totals	**410**	**215**	**146**	**49**	**5**		**2007-12**
Sutter, Brian	St. Louis	320	153	124	43	4		
	Boston	216	120	73	23	3		
	Calgary	246	87	117	42	3		
	Chicago	246	91	103	52	4		
	Totals	**1028**	**451**	**417**	**160**	**14**		**1988-05**
Sutter, Darryl	Chicago	216	110	80	26	3		
	San Jose	434	192	167	75	6		
	Calgary	210	107	73	30	4		
	Los Angeles	97	52	29	16	2	1	
	Totals	**957**	**461**	**349**	**147**	**14**	**1**	**1992-13**
Sutter, Duane	**Florida**	**72**	**22**	**35**	**15**	**2**		**2000-02**
Talbot, Jean-Guy	St. Louis	120	52	53	15	2		
	NY Rangers	80	30	37	13	1		
	Totals	**200**	**82**	**90**	**28**	**3**		**1972-78**
Tessier, Orval	**Chicago**	**213**	**99**	**93**	**21**	**3**		**1982-85**
Therrien, Michel	Montreal	238	106	91	41	4		
	Pittsburgh	272	135	105	32	4		
	Totals	**510**	**241**	**196**	**73**	**8**		**2000-13**
Thompson, Paul	**Chicago**	**272**	**104**	**127**	**41**	**7**		**1938-45**
Thompson, Percy	**Hamilton**	**48**	**13**	**35**	**0**	**2**		**1920-22**
Tippett, Dave	Dallas	492	271	156	65	7		
	Phoenix	294	156	96	42	4		
	Totals	**786**	**427**	**252**	**107**	**11**		**2002-13**
Tobin, Bill	**Chicago**	**71**	**29**	**29**	**13**	**2**		**1929-32**
Tocchet, Rick	**Tampa Bay**	**148**	**53**	**69**	**26**	**2**		**2008-10**
Torchetti, John	Florida	27	10	12	5	1		
	Los Angeles	12	5	7	0	1		
	Totals	**39**	**15**	**19**	**5**	**2**		**2003-06**
Tortorella, John	NY Rangers	319	171	118	30	6		
	Tampa Bay	535	239	222	74	8	1	
	Totals	**854**	**410**	**340**	**104**	**14**	**1**	**1999-13**
Tremblay, Mario	**Montreal**	**159**	**71**	**63**	**25**	**2**		**1995-97**
Trottier, Bryan	**NY Rangers**	**54**	**21**	**26**	**7**	**1**		**2002-03**
Trotz, Barry	**Nashville**	**1114**	**519**	**447**	**148**	**15**		**1998-13**
Ubriaco, Gene	**Pittsburgh**	**106**	**50**	**47**	**9**	**2**		**1988-90**
Vachon, Rogie	**Los Angeles**	**10**	**4**	**3**	**3**	**3**		**1983-95**
Vigneault, Alain	Montreal	266	109	118	39	4		
	Vancouver	540	313	170	57	7		
	Totals	**806**	**422**	**288**	**96**	**11**		**1997-13**
Waddell, Don	**Atlanta**	**86**	**38**	**39**	**9**	**2**		**2002-08**
Watson, Bryan	**Edmonton**	**18**	**4**	**9**	**5**	**1**		**1980-81**
Watson, Phil	NY Rangers	295	119	124	52	5		
	Boston	84	16	55	13	2		
	Totals	**379**	**135**	**179**	**65**	**7**		**1955-63**
Watt, Tom	Winnipeg	181	72	85	24	3		
	Vancouver	160	52	87	21	2		
	Toronto	149	52	80	17	2		
	Totals	**490**	**176**	**252**	**62**	**7**		**1981-92**
Webster, Tom	NY Rangers	18	5	9	4	1		
	Los Angeles	240	115	94	31	3		
	Totals	**258**	**120**	**103**	**35**	**4**		**1986-92**
Weiland, Cooney	**Boston**	**96**	**58**	**20**	**18**	**2**	**1**	**1939-41**
White, Bill	**Chicago**	**46**	**16**	**24**	**6**	**1**		**1976-77**
Wiley, Jim	**San Jose**	**57**	**17**	**37**	**3**	**1**		**1995-96**
Wilson, Johnny	Los Angeles	52	9	34	9	1		
	Detroit	145	67	56	22	2		
	Colorado	80	20	46	14	1		
	Pittsburgh	240	91	105	44	3		
	Totals	**517**	**187**	**241**	**89**	**7**		**1969-80**
Wilson, Larry	**Detroit**	**36**	**3**	**29**	**4**	**1**		**1976-77**
Wilson, Rick	**Dallas**	**32**	**13**	**11**	**8**	**1**		**2001-02**
Wilson, Ron	Anaheim	296	120	145	31	4		
	Washington	410	192	159	59	5		
	San Jose	385	206	122	57	6		
	Toronto	310	130	135	45	4		
	Totals	**1401**	**648**	**561**	**192**	**19**		**1993-12**
Yawney, Trent	**Chicago**	**103**	**33**	**55**	**15**	**2**		**2005-07**
Yeo, Mike	**Minnesota**	**130**	**61**	**55**	**14**	**2**		**2011-13**
Young, Garry	California	12	2	7	3	1		
	St. Louis	98	41	41	16	2		
	Totals	**110**	**43**	**48**	**19**	**3**		**1972-76**

Paul MacLean (left) won the Jack Adams Award as coach of the year in 2012-13. A finalist the year before, MacLean guided Ottawa to a playoff berth despite numerous injuries. Joel Quenneville (center) led Chicago to the best regular-season record in the NHL and a Stanley Cup championship. Bruce Boudreau (right) led Anaheim back into the playoffs in his first full season with the club.

Year-by-Year Individual Regular-Season Leaders

Season	Goals	G	Assists	A	Points	Pts.	Penalty Minutes	PIM
1917-18	Joe Malone	44	Cy Denneny, Reg Noble, Harry Cameron	10	Joe Malone	48	Joe Hall	100
1918-19	Newsy Lalonde	22	Newsy Lalonde	10	Newsy Lalonde	32	Joe Hall	135
1919-20	Joe Malone	39	Frank Nighbor	15	Joe Malone	49	Cully Wilson	86
1920-21	Babe Dye	35	Jack Darragh	15	Newsy Lalonde	43	Bert Corbeau	86
1921-22	Punch Broadbent	32	Harry Cameron	17	Punch Broadbent	46	Sprague Cleghorn	63
1922-23	Babe Dye	26	Eddie Gerard	13	Babe Dye	37	Georges Boucher	58
1923-24	Cy Denneny	22	Georges Boucher	10	Cy Denneny	24	Reg Noble	79
1924-25	Babe Dye	38	Cy Denneny, Red Green	15	Babe Dye	46	Georges Boucher	95
1925-26	Nels Stewart	34	Frank Nighbor	13	Nels Stewart	42	Bert Corbeau	121
1926-27	Bill Cook	33	Dick Irvin	18	Bill Cook	37	Nels Stewart	133
1927-28	Howie Morenz	33	Howie Morenz	18	Howie Morenz	51	Eddie Shore	165
1928-29	Ace Bailey	22	Frank Boucher	16	Ace Bailey	32	Red Dutton	139
1929-30	Cooney Weiland	43	Frank Boucher	36	Cooney Weiland	73	Joe Lamb	119
1930-31	Charlie Conacher	31	Joe Primeau	32	Howie Morenz	51	Harvey Rockburn	118
1931-32	Charlie Conacher, Bill Cook	34	Joe Primeau	37	Busher Jackson	53	Red Dutton	107
1932-33	Bill Cook	28	Frank Boucher	28	Bill Cook	50	Red Horner	144
1933-34	Charlie Conacher	32	Joe Primeau	32	Charlie Conacher	52	Red Horner	126 *
1934-35	Charlie Conacher	36	Art Chapman	34	Charlie Conacher	57	Red Horner	125
1935-36	Charlie Conacher, Bill Thoms	23	Art Chapman	28	Sweeney Schriner	45	Red Horner	167
1936-37	Larry Aurie, Nels Stewart	23	Syl Apps	29	Sweeney Schriner	46	Red Horner	124
1937-38	Gordie Drillon	26	Syl Apps	29	Gordie Drillon	52	Art Coulter	90
1938-39	Roy Conacher	26	Bill Cowley	34	Toe Blake	47	Red Horner	85
1939-40	Bryan Hextall	24	Milt Schmidt	30	Milt Schmidt	52	Red Horner	87
1940-41	Bryan Hextall	26	Bill Cowley	45	Bill Cowley	62	Jimmy Orlando	99
1941-42	Lynn Patrick	32	Phil Watson	37	Bryan Hextall	56	Pat Egan	124
1942-43	Doug Bentley	33	Bill Cowley	45	Doug Bentley	73	Jimmy Orlando	89 *
1943-44	Doug Bentley	38	Clint Smith	49	Herb Cain	82	Mike McMahon	98
1944-45	Maurice Richard	50	Elmer Lach	54	Elmer Lach	80	Pat Egan	86
1945-46	Gaye Stewart	37	Elmer Lach	34	Max Bentley	61	Jack Stewart	73
1946-47	Maurice Richard	45	Billy Taylor	46	Max Bentley	72	Gus Mortson	133
1947-48	Ted Lindsay	33	Doug Bentley	37	Elmer Lach	61	Bill Barilko	147
1948-49	Sid Abel	28	Doug Bentley	43	Roy Conacher	68	Bill Ezinicki	145
1949-50	Maurice Richard	43	Ted Lindsay	55	Ted Lindsay	78	Bill Ezinicki	144
1950-51	Gordie Howe	43	Gordie Howe, Ted Kennedy	43	Gordie Howe	86	Gus Mortson	142
1951-52	Gordie Howe	47	Elmer Lach	50	Gordie Howe	86	Gus Kyle	127
1952-53	Gordie Howe	49	Gordie Howe	46	Gordie Howe	95	Maurice Richard	112
1953-54	Maurice Richard	37	Gordie Howe	48	Gordie Howe	81	Gus Mortson	132
1954-55	Maurice Richard, Bernie Geoffrion	38	Bert Olmstead	48	Bernie Geoffrion	75	Fern Flaman	150
1955-56	Jean Beliveau	47	Bert Olmstead	56	Jean Beliveau	88	Lou Fontinato	202
1956-57	Gordie Howe	44	Ted Lindsay	55	Gordie Howe	89	Gus Mortson	147
1957-58	Dickie Moore	36	Henri Richard	52	Dickie Moore	84	Lou Fontinato	152
1958-59	Jean Beliveau	45	Dickie Moore	55	Dickie Moore	96	Ted Lindsay	184
1959-60	Bobby Hull, Bronco Horvath	39	Don McKenney	49	Bobby Hull	81	Carl Brewer	150
1960-61	Bernie Geoffrion	50	Jean Beliveau	58	Bernie Geoffrion	95	Pierre Pilote	165
1961-62	Bobby Hull	50	Andy Bathgate	56	Bobby Hull, Andy Bathgate	84	Lou Fontinato	167
1962-63	Gordie Howe	38	Henri Richard	50	Gordie Howe	86	Howie Young	273
1963-64	Bobby Hull	43	Andy Bathgate	58	Stan Mikita	89	Vic Hadfield	151
1964-65	Norm Ullman	42	Stan Mikita	59	Stan Mikita	87	Carl Brewer	177
1965-66	Bobby Hull	54	Stan Mikita, Bobby Rousseau, Jean Beliveau	48	Bobby Hull	97	Reggie Fleming	166
1966-67	Bobby Hull	52	Stan Mikita	62	Stan Mikita	97	John Ferguson	177
1967-68	Bobby Hull	44	Phil Esposito	49	Stan Mikita	87	Barclay Plager	153
1968-69	Bobby Hull	58	Phil Esposito	77	Phil Esposito	126	Forbes Kennedy	219
1969-70	Phil Esposito	43	Bobby Orr	87	Bobby Orr	120	Keith Magnuson	213
1970-71	Phil Esposito	76	Bobby Orr	102	Phil Esposito	152	Keith Magnuson	291
1971-72	Phil Esposito	66	Bobby Orr	80	Phil Esposito	133	Bryan Watson	212
1972-73	Phil Esposito	55	Phil Esposito	75	Phil Esposito	130	Dave Schultz	259
1973-74	Phil Esposito	68	Bobby Orr	90	Phil Esposito	145	Dave Schultz	348
1974-75	Phil Esposito	61	Bobby Orr, Bobby Clarke	89	Bobby Orr	135	Dave Schultz	472
1975-76	Reggie Leach	61	Bobby Clarke	89	Guy Lafleur	125	Steve Durbano	370
1976-77	Steve Shutt	60	Guy Lafleur	80	Guy Lafleur	136	Tiger Williams	338
1977-78	Guy Lafleur	60	Bryan Trottier	77	Guy Lafleur	132	Dave Schultz	405
1978-79	Mike Bossy	69	Bryan Trottier	87	Bryan Trottier	134	Tiger Williams	298
1979-80	Charlie Simmer, Danny Gare, Blaine Stoughton	56	Wayne Gretzky	86	Marcel Dionne, Wayne Gretzky	137	Jimmy Mann	287
1980-81	Mike Bossy	68	Wayne Gretzky	109	Wayne Gretzky	164	Tiger Williams	343
1981-82	Wayne Gretzky	92	Wayne Gretzky	120	Wayne Gretzky	212	Paul Baxter	409
1982-83	Wayne Gretzky	71	Wayne Gretzky	125	Wayne Gretzky	196	Randy Holt	275
1983-84	Wayne Gretzky	87	Wayne Gretzky	118	Wayne Gretzky	205	Chris Nilan	338
1984-85	Wayne Gretzky	73	Wayne Gretzky	135	Wayne Gretzky	208	Chris Nilan	358
1985-86	Jari Kurri	68	Wayne Gretzky	163	Wayne Gretzky	215	Joe Kocur	377
1986-87	Wayne Gretzky	62	Wayne Gretzky	121	Wayne Gretzky	183	Tim Hunter	361
1987-88	Mario Lemieux	70	Wayne Gretzky	109	Mario Lemieux	168	Bob Probert	398
1988-89	Mario Lemieux	85	Mario Lemieux, Wayne Gretzky	114	Mario Lemieux	199	Tim Hunter	375
1989-90	Brett Hull	72	Wayne Gretzky	102	Wayne Gretzky	142	Basil McRae	351
1990-91	Brett Hull	86	Wayne Gretzky	122	Wayne Gretzky	163	Rob Ray	350
1991-92	Brett Hull	70	Wayne Gretzky	90	Mario Lemieux	131	Mike Peluso	408
1992-93	Teemu Selanne, Alexander Mogilny	76	Adam Oates	97	Mario Lemieux	160	Marty McSorley	399
1993-94	Pavel Bure	60	Wayne Gretzky	92	Wayne Gretzky	130	Tie Domi	347
1994-95	Peter Bondra	34	Ron Francis	48	Jaromir Jagr, Eric Lindros	70	Enrico Ciccone	225
1995-96	Mario Lemieux	69	Mario Lemieux, Ron Francis	92	Mario Lemieux	161	Matthew Barnaby	335
1996-97	Keith Tkachuk	52	Mario Lemieux, Wayne Gretzky	72	Mario Lemieux	122	Gino Odjick	371
1997-98	Teemu Selanne, Peter Bondra	52	Jaromir Jagr, Wayne Gretzky	67	Jaromir Jagr	102	Donald Brashear	372
1998-99	Teemu Selanne	47	Jaromir Jagr	83	Jaromir Jagr	127	Rob Ray	261
99-2000	Pavel Bure	58	Mark Recchi	63	Jaromir Jagr	96	Denny Lambert	219
2000-01	Pavel Bure	59	Jaromir Jagr, Adam Oates	69	Jaromir Jagr	121	Matthew Barnaby	265
2001-02	Jarome Iginla	52	Adam Oates	64	Jarome Iginla	96	Peter Worell	354
2002-03	Milan Hejduk	50	Peter Forsberg	77	Peter Forsberg	106	Jody Shelley	249
2003-04	Rick Nash, Jarome Iginla, Ilya Kovalchuk	41	Scott Gomez, Martin St. Louis	56	Martin St. Louis	94	Sean Avery	261
2004-05	....	....	....	....	....	....	....	....
2005-06	Jonathan Cheechoo	56	Joe Thornton	96	Joe Thornton	125	Sean Avery	257
2006-07	Vincent Lecavalier	52	Joe Thornton	92	Sidney Crosby	120	Ben Eager	233
2007-08	Alex Ovechkin	65	Joe Thornton	67	Alex Ovechkin	112	Daniel Carcillo	324
2008-09	Alex Ovechkin	56	Evgeni Malkin	78	Evgeni Malkin	113	Daniel Carcillo	254
2009-10	Sidney Crosby, Steven Stamkos	51	Henrik Sedin	83	Henrik Sedin	112	Zenon Konopka	265
2010-11	Corey Perry	50	Henrik Sedin	75	Daniel Sedin	104	Zenon Konopka	307
2011-12	Steven Stamkos	60	Henrik Sedin	67	Evgeni Malkin	109	Derek Dorsett	235
2012-13	Alex Ovechkin	32	Martin St. Louis	43	Martin St. Louis	60	Colton Orr	155

* Match Misconduct penalty not included in total penalty minutes.
1946-47 was the first season that a Match penalty was automaticaly written into the player's total penalty minutes as 20 minutes.
Beginning in 1947-48 all penalties, Match, Game Misconduct, and Misconduct, are written as 10 minutes.

One Season Scoring Records

Goals-Per-Game Leaders, One Season

(Among players with 20 goals or more in one season)

Player	Team	Season	Games	Goals	Goals per game average
Joe Malone	Montreal	1917-18	20	44	2.20
Cy Denneny	Ottawa	1917-18	20	36	1.80
Newsy Lalonde	Montreal	1917-18	14	23	1.64
Joe Malone	Quebec	1919-20	24	39	1.63
Newsy Lalonde	Montreal	1919-20	23	37	1.61
Reg Noble	Toronto	1917-18	20	30	1.50
Babe Dye	Ham., Tor.	1920-21	24	35	1.46
Cy Denneny	Ottawa	1920-21	24	34	1.42
Joe Malone	Hamilton	1920-21	20	28	1.40
Newsy Lalonde	Montreal	1920-21	24	33	1.38
Punch Broadbent	Ottawa	1921-22	24	32	1.33
Babe Dye	Toronto	1924-25	29	38	1.31
Babe Dye	Toronto	1921-22	24	31	1.29
Newsy Lalonde	Montreal	1918-19	17	22	1.29
Odie Cleghorn	Montreal	1918-19	17	22	1.29
Cy Denneny	Ottawa	1921-22	22	27	1.23
Aurel Joliat	Montreal	1924-25	25	30	1.20
Wayne Gretzky	Edmonton	1983-84	74	87	1.18
Babe Dye	Toronto	1922-23	22	26	1.18
Wayne Gretzky	Edmonton	1981-82	80	92	1.15
Mario Lemieux	Pittsburgh	1992-93	60	69	1.15
Frank Nighbor	Ottawa	1919-20	23	26	1.13
Mario Lemieux	Pittsburgh	1988-89	76	85	1.12
Brett Hull	St. Louis	1990-91	78	86	1.10
Cam Neely	Boston	1993-94	49	50	1.02
Maurice Richard	Montreal	1944-45	50	50	1.00
Reg Noble	Toronto	1919-20	24	24	1.00
Corb Denneny	Toronto	1919-20	24	24	1.00
Joe Malone	Hamilton	1921-22	24	24	1.00
Billy Boucher	Montreal	1922-23	24	24	1.00
Cy Denneny	Ottawa	1923-24	22	22	1.00
Alexander Mogilny	Buffalo	1992-93	77	76	0.99
Mario Lemieux	Pittsburgh	1995-96	70	69	0.99
Cooney Weiland	Boston	1929-30	44	43	0.98
Phil Esposito	Boston	1970-71	78	76	0.97
Jari Kurri	Edmonton	1984-85	73	71	0.97

Adam Oates, who made a successful debut as an NHL head coach with Washington in 2012-13, established the highest number of assists per game for any player other than Wayne Gretzky or Mario Lemieux when he was a member of the St. Louis Blues in 1990-91.

Assists-Per-Game Leaders, One Season

(Among players with 35 assists or more in one season)

Player	Team	Season	Games	Assists	Assists per game average
Wayne Gretzky	Edmonton	1985-86	80	163	2.04
Wayne Gretzky	Edmonton	1987-88	64	109	1.70
Wayne Gretzky	Edmonton	1984-85	80	135	1.69
Wayne Gretzky	Edmonton	1983-84	74	118	1.59
Wayne Gretzky	Edmonton	1982-83	80	125	1.56
Wayne Gretzky	Los Angeles	1990-91	78	122	1.56
Wayne Gretzky	Edmonton	1986-87	79	121	1.53
Mario Lemieux	Pittsburgh	1992-93	60	91	1.52
Wayne Gretzky	Edmonton	1981-82	80	120	1.50
Mario Lemieux	Pittsburgh	1988-89	76	114	1.50
Adam Oates	St. Louis	1990-91	61	90	1.48
Wayne Gretzky	Los Angeles	1988-89	78	114	1.46
Wayne Gretzky	Los Angeles	1989-90	73	102	1.40
Wayne Gretzky	Edmonton	1980-81	80	109	1.36
Mario Lemieux	Pittsburgh	1991-92	64	87	1.36
Mario Lemieux	Pittsburgh	1989-90	59	78	1.32
Bobby Orr	Boston	1970-71	78	102	1.31
Mario Lemieux	Pittsburgh	1995-96	70	92	1.31
Mario Lemieux	Pittsburgh	1987-88	77	98	1.27
Bobby Orr	Boston	1973-74	74	90	1.22
Wayne Gretzky	Los Angeles	1991-92	74	90	1.22
Joe Thornton	Bos., S.J.	2005-06	81	96	1.19
Ron Francis	Pittsburgh	1995-96	77	92	1.19
Mario Lemieux	Pittsburgh	1985-86	79	93	1.18
Bobby Clarke	Philadelphia	1975-76	76	89	1.17
Peter Stastny	Quebec	1981-82	80	93	1.16
Adam Oates	Boston	1992-93	84	97	1.15
Doug Gilmour	Toronto	1992-93	83	95	1.14
Wayne Gretzky	Los Angeles	1993-94	81	92	1.14
Paul Coffey	Edmonton	1985-86	79	90	1.14
Bobby Orr	Boston	1969-70	76	87	1.14
Bryan Trottier	NY Islanders	1978-79	76	87	1.14
Bobby Orr	Boston	1972-73	63	72	1.14
Bill Cowley	Boston	1943-44	36	41	1.14
Sidney Crosby	**Pittsburgh**	**2012-13**	**36**	**41**	**1.14**
Pat LaFontaine	Buffalo	1992-93	84	95	1.13
Steve Yzerman	Detroit	1988-89	80	90	1.13
Paul Coffey	Pittsburgh	1987-88	46	52	1.13
Joe Thornton	San Jose	2006-07	82	92	1.12
Bobby Orr	Boston	1974-75	80	89	1.11
Bobby Clarke	Philadelphia	1974-75	80	89	1.11
Paul Coffey	Pittsburgh	1988-89	75	83	1.11
Wayne Gretzky	Los Angeles	1992-93	45	49	1.11
Denis Savard	Chicago	1982-83	78	86	1.10
Denis Savard	Chicago	1981-82	80	87	1.09
Denis Savard	Chicago	1987-88	80	87	1.09
Wayne Gretzky	Edmonton	1979-80	79	86	1.09
Ron Francis	Pittsburgh	1994-95	44	48	1.09
Paul Coffey	Edmonton	1983-84	80	86	1.08
Elmer Lach	Montreal	1944-45	50	54	1.08
Peter Stastny	Quebec	1985-86	76	81	1.07
Jaromir Jagr	Pittsburgh	1995-96	82	87	1.06
Mark Messier	Edmonton	1989-90	79	84	1.06
Sidney Crosby	Pittsburgh	2006-07	79	84	1.06
Peter Forsberg	Colorado	1995-96	82	86	1.05
Paul Coffey	Edmonton	1984-85	80	84	1.05
Marcel Dionne	Los Angeles	1979-80	80	84	1.05
Bobby Orr	Boston	1971-72	76	80	1.05
Mike Bossy	NY Islanders	1981-82	80	83	1.04
Adam Oates	Boston	1993-94	77	80	1.04
Phil Esposito	Boston	1968-69	74	77	1.04
Bryan Trottier	NY Islanders	1983-84	68	71	1.04
Jason Spezza	Ottawa	2005-06	68	71	1.04
Pete Mahovlich	Montreal	1974-75	80	82	1.03
Kent Nilsson	Calgary	1980-81	80	82	1.03
Peter Stastny	Quebec	1982-83	75	77	1.03
Peter Forsberg	Colorado	2002-03	75	77	1.03
Denis Savard	Chicago	1988-89	58	59	1.02
Jaromir Jagr	Pittsburgh	1998-99	81	83	1.02
Doug Gilmour	Toronto	1993-94	83	84	1.01
Henrik Sedin	Vancouver	2009-10	82	83	1.01
Bernie Nicholls	Los Angeles	1988-89	79	80	1.01
Guy Lafleur	Montreal	1979-80	74	75	1.01
Guy Lafleur	Montreal	1976-77	80	80	1.00
Marcel Dionne	Los Angeles	1984-85	80	80	1.00
Brian Leetch	NY Rangers	1991-92	80	80	1.00
Bryan Trottier	NY Islanders	1977-78	77	77	1.00
Mike Bossy	NY Islanders	1983-84	67	67	1.00
Jean Ratelle	NY Rangers	1971-72	63	63	1.00
Steve Yzerman	Detroit	1993-94	58	58	1.00
Ron Francis	Hartford	1985-86	53	53	1.00
Guy Chouinard	Calgary	1980-81	52	52	1.00

Points-Per-Game Leaders, One Season

(Among players with 50 points or more in one season)

Player	Team	Season	Games	Points	Points per game average
Wayne Gretzky	Edmonton	1983-84	74	205	2.77
Wayne Gretzky	Edmonton	1985-86	80	215	2.69
Mario Lemieux	Pittsburgh	1992-93	60	160	2.67
Wayne Gretzky	Edmonton	1981-82	80	212	2.65
Mario Lemieux	Pittsburgh	1988-89	76	199	2.62
Wayne Gretzky	Edmonton	1984-85	80	208	2.60
Wayne Gretzky	Edmonton	1982-83	80	196	2.45
Wayne Gretzky	Edmonton	1987-88	64	149	2.33
Wayne Gretzky	Edmonton	1986-87	79	183	2.32
Mario Lemieux	Pittsburgh	1995-96	70	161	2.30
Mario Lemieux	Pittsburgh	1987-88	77	168	2.18
Wayne Gretzky	Los Angeles	1988-89	78	168	2.15
Wayne Gretzky	Los Angeles	1990-91	78	163	2.09
Mario Lemieux	Pittsburgh	1989-90	59	123	2.08
Wayne Gretzky	Edmonton	1980-81	80	164	2.05
Mario Lemieux	Pittsburgh	1991-92	64	131	2.05
Bill Cowley	Boston	1943-44	36	71	1.97
Phil Esposito	Boston	1970-71	78	152	1.95
Wayne Gretzky	Los Angeles	1989-90	73	142	1.95
Steve Yzerman	Detroit	1988-89	80	155	1.94
Bernie Nicholls	Los Angeles	1988-89	79	150	1.90
Adam Oates	St. Louis	1990-91	61	115	1.89
Phil Esposito	Boston	1973-74	78	145	1.86
Jari Kurri	Edmonton	1984-85	73	135	1.85
Mike Bossy	NY Islanders	1981-82	80	147	1.84
Jaromir Jagr	Pittsburgh	1995-96	82	149	1.82
Mario Lemieux	Pittsburgh	1985-86	79	141	1.78
Bobby Orr	Boston	1970-71	78	139	1.78
Jari Kurri	Edmonton	1983-84	64	113	1.77
Mario Lemieux	Pittsburgh	2000-01	43	76	1.77
Pat LaFontaine	Buffalo	1992-93	84	148	1.76
Bryan Trottier	NY Islanders	1978-79	76	134	1.76
Mike Bossy	NY Islanders	1983-84	67	118	1.76
Paul Coffey	Edmonton	1985-86	79	138	1.75
Phil Esposito	Boston	1971-72	76	133	1.75
Peter Stastny	Quebec	1981-82	80	139	1.74
Wayne Gretzky	Edmonton	1979-80	79	137	1.73
Jean Ratelle	NY Rangers	1971-72	63	109	1.73
Marcel Dionne	Los Angeles	1979-80	80	137	1.71
Herb Cain	Boston	1943-44	48	82	1.71
Guy Lafleur	Montreal	1976-77	80	136	1.70
Dennis Maruk	Washington	1981-82	80	136	1.70
Phil Esposito	Boston	1968-69	74	126	1.70
Guy Lafleur	Montreal	1974-75	70	119	1.70
Mario Lemieux	Pittsburgh	1986-87	63	107	1.70
Adam Oates	Boston	1992-93	84	142	1.69
Bobby Orr	Boston	1974-75	80	135	1.69
Marcel Dionne	Los Angeles	1980-81	80	135	1.69
Guy Lafleur	Montreal	1977-78	78	132	1.69
Guy Lafleur	Montreal	1979-80	74	125	1.69
Rob Brown	Pittsburgh	1988-89	68	115	1.69
Jari Kurri	Edmonton	1985-86	78	131	1.68
Brett Hull	St. Louis	1990-91	78	131	1.68
Phil Esposito	Boston	1972-73	78	130	1.67
Cooney Weiland	Boston	1929-30	44	73	1.66
Alexander Mogilny	Buffalo	1992-93	77	127	1.65
Peter Stastny	Quebec	1982-83	75	124	1.65
Bobby Orr	Boston	1973-74	74	122	1.65
Kent Nilsson	Calgary	1980-81	80	131	1.64
Denis Savard	Chicago	1987-88	80	131	1.64
Wayne Gretzky	Los Angeles	1991-92	74	121	1.64
Steve Yzerman	Detroit	1992-93	84	137	1.63
Marcel Dionne	Los Angeles	1978-79	80	130	1.63
Dale Hawerchuk	Winnipeg	1984-85	80	130	1.63
Mark Messier	Edmonton	1989-90	79	129	1.63
Bryan Trottier	NY Islanders	1983-84	68	111	1.63
Pat LaFontaine	Buffalo	1991-92	57	93	1.63
Charlie Simmer	Los Angeles	1980-81	65	105	1.62
Guy Lafleur	Montreal	1978-79	80	129	1.61
Bryan Trottier	NY Islanders	1981-82	80	129	1.61
Phil Esposito	Boston	1974-75	79	127	1.61
Steve Yzerman	Detroit	1989-90	79	127	1.61
Peter Stastny	Quebec	1985-86	76	122	1.61
Mario Lemieux	Pittsburgh	1996-97	76	122	1.61
Michel Goulet	Quebec	1983-84	75	121	1.61
Sidney Crosby	Pittsburgh	2010-11	41	66	1.61
Wayne Gretzky	Los Angeles	1993-94	81	130	1.60
Bryan Trottier	NY Islanders	1977-78	77	123	1.60
Bobby Orr	Boston	1972-73	63	101	1.60
Guy Chouinard	Calgary	1980-81	52	83	1.60
Elmer Lach	Montreal	1944-45	50	80	1.60
Pierre Turgeon	NY Islanders	1992-93	83	132	1.59
Steve Yzerman	Detroit	1987-88	64	102	1.59
Mike Bossy	NY Islanders	1978-79	80	126	1.58
Paul Coffey	Edmonton	1983-84	80	126	1.58
Marcel Dionne	Los Angeles	1984-85	80	126	1.58
Bobby Orr	Boston	1969-70	76	120	1.58
Eric Lindros	Philadelphia	1995-96	73	115	1.58
Charlie Simmer	Los Angeles	1979-80	64	101	1.58
Teemu Selanne	Winnipeg	1992-93	84	132	1.57
Jaromir Jagr	Pittsburgh	1998-99	81	127	1.57
Bobby Clarke	Philadelphia	1975-76	76	119	1.57
Guy Lafleur	Montreal	1975-76	80	125	1.56
Dave Taylor	Los Angeles	1980-81	72	112	1.56
Sidney Crosby	**Pittsburgh**	**2012-13**	**36**	**56**	**1.56**
Denis Savard	Chicago	1982-83	78	121	1.55
Ron Francis	Pittsburgh	1995-96	77	119	1.55
Joe Thornton	Bos., S.J.	2005-06	81	125	1.54
Mike Bossy	NY Islanders	1985-86	80	123	1.54
Kevin Stevens	Pittsburgh	1991-92	80	123	1.54
Bobby Orr	Boston	1971-72	76	117	1.54
Mike Bossy	NY Islanders	1984-85	76	117	1.54
Kevin Stevens	Pittsburgh	1992-93	72	111	1.54
Doug Bentley	Chicago	1943-44	50	77	1.54
Doug Gilmour	Toronto	1992-93	83	127	1.53
Marcel Dionne	Los Angeles	1976-77	80	122	1.53
Sidney Crosby	Pittsburgh	2006-07	79	120	1.52
Jaromir Jagr	Pittsburgh	99-2000	63	96	1.52
Eric Lindros	Philadelphia	1996-97	52	79	1.52
Eric Lindros	Philadelphia	1994-95	46	70	1.52
Marcel Dionne	Detroit	1974-75	80	121	1.51
Mike Bossy	NY Islanders	1980-81	79	119	1.51
Paul Coffey	Edmonton	1984-85	80	121	1.51
Dale Hawerchuk	Winnipeg	1987-88	80	121	1.51
Paul Coffey	Pittsburgh	1988-89	75	113	1.51
Alex Ovechkin	Washington	2009-10	72	109	1.51
Jaromir Jagr	Pittsburgh	1996-97	63	95	1.51
Cam Neely	Boston	1993-94	49	74	1.51

Bernie Nicholls had the greatest scoring season of any player not in the Hockey Hall of Fame when he collected 70 goals and 80 assists for 150 points in 79 games with the Los Angeles Kings in 1988-89. His points-per-game average for the season was 1.90.

The dueling debut of rookies Alex Ovechkin and Sidney Crosby was one of the big stories of the 2005-06 season. Crosby became the youngest player in NHL history to reach 100 points that year while Ovechkin became just the third player to top 50 goals and 100 points in his rookie campaign.

Rookie Scoring Records

All-Time Top 50 Goal-Scoring Rookies

	Rookie	Team	Position	Season	GP	G	A	PTS
1.	* Teemu Selanne	Winnipeg	Right wing	1992-93	84	**76**	56	132
2.	* Mike Bossy	NY Islanders	Right wing	1977-78	73	**53**	38	91
3.	* Alex Ovechkin	Washington	Left wing	2005-06	81	**52**	54	106
4.	* Joe Nieuwendyk	Calgary	Center	1987-88	75	**51**	41	92
5.	* Dale Hawerchuk	Winnipeg	Center	1981-82	80	**45**	58	103
	* Luc Robitaille	Los Angeles	Left wing	1986-87	79	**45**	39	84
7.	Rick Martin	Buffalo	Left wing	1971-72	73	**44**	30	74
	Barry Pederson	Boston	Center	1981-82	80	**44**	48	92
9.	* Steve Larmer	Chicago	Right wing	1982-83	80	**43**	47	90
	* Mario Lemieux	Pittsburgh	Center	1984-85	73	**43**	57	100
11.	Eric Lindros	Philadelphia	Center	1992-93	61	**41**	34	75
12.	Darryl Sutter	Chicago	Left wing	1980-81	76	**40**	22	62
	Sylvain Turgeon	Hartford	Left wing	1983-84	76	**40**	32	72
	Warren Young	Pittsburgh	Left wing	1984-85	80	**40**	32	72
15.	* Eric Vail	Atlanta	Left wing	1974-75	72	**39**	21	60
	* Peter Stastny	Quebec	Center	1980-81	77	**39**	70	109
	Anton Stastny	Quebec	Left wing	1980-81	80	**39**	46	85
	Steve Yzerman	Detroit	Center	1983-84	80	**39**	48	87
	Sidney Crosby	Pittsburgh	Center	2005-06	81	**39**	63	102
20.	* Gilbert Perreault	Buffalo	Center	1970-71	78	**38**	34	72
	Neal Broten	Minnesota	Center	1981-82	73	**38**	60	98
	Ray Sheppard	Buffalo	Right wing	1987-88	74	**38**	27	65
	Mikael Renberg	Philadelphia	Left wing	1993-94	83	**38**	44	82
24.	Jorgen Pettersson	St. Louis	Left wing	1980-81	62	**37**	36	73
	Jimmy Carson	Los Angeles	Center	1986-87	80	**37**	42	79
26.	Mike Foligno	Detroit	Right wing	1979-80	80	**36**	35	71
	Paul MacLean	Winnipeg	Right wing	1981-82	74	**36**	25	61
	Mike Bullard	Pittsburgh	Center	1981-82	75	**36**	27	63
	Tony Granato	NY Rangers	Right wing	1988-89	78	**36**	27	63
30.	Marian Stastny	Quebec	Right wing	1981-82	74	**35**	54	89
	Brian Bellows	Minnesota	Right wing	1982-83	78	**35**	30	65
	Tony Amonte	NY Rangers	Right wing	1991-92	79	**35**	34	69
33.	Nels Stewart	Mtl. Maroons	Center	1925-26	36	**34**	8	42
	* Danny Grant	Minnesota	Left wing	1968-69	75	**34**	31	65
	Norm Ferguson	Oakland	Right wing	1968-69	76	**34**	20	54
	Brian Propp	Philadelphia	Left wing	1979-80	80	**34**	41	75
	Wendel Clark	Toronto	Left wing	1985-86	66	**34**	11	45
	* Pavel Bure	Vancouver	Right wing	1991-92	65	**34**	26	60
	Michael Grabner	NY Islanders	Right wing	2010-11	76	**34**	18	52
40.	* Willi Plett	Atlanta	Right wing	1976-77	64	**33**	23	56
	Dale McCourt	Detroit	Center	1977-78	76	**33**	39	72
	Steve Bozek	Los Angeles	Center	1981-82	71	**33**	23	56
	Ron Flockhart	Philadelphia	Center	1981-82	72	**33**	39	72
	Mark Pavelich	NY Rangers	Center	1981-82	79	**33**	43	76
	Jason Arnott	Edmonton	Center	1993-94	78	**33**	35	68
	* Evgeni Malkin	Pittsburgh	Center	2006-07	78	**33**	52	85
47.	Bill Mosienko	Chicago	Right wing	1943-44	50	**32**	38	70
	Michel Bergeron	Detroit	Right wing	1975-76	72	**32**	27	59
	* Bryan Trottier	NY Islanders	Center	1975-76	80	**32**	63	95
	Don Murdoch	NY Rangers	Right wing	1976-77	59	**32**	24	56
	Jari Kurri	Edmonton	Left wing	1980-81	75	**32**	43	75
	Bobby Carpenter	Washington	Center	1981-82	80	**32**	35	67
	Petr Klima	Detroit	Left wing	1985-86	74	**32**	24	56
	Kjell Dahlin	Montreal	Right wing	1985-86	77	**32**	39	71
	Darren Turcotte	NY Rangers	Right wing	1989-90	76	**32**	34	66
	Joe Juneau	Boston	Center	1992-93	84	**32**	70	102
	Marek Svatos	Colorado	Right wing	2005-06	61	**32**	18	50
	Logan Couture	San Jose	Center	2010-11	79	**32**	24	56

* Calder Trophy Winner

All-Time Top 50 Point-Scoring Rookies

	Rookie	Team	Position	Season	GP	G	A	PTS
1.	* Teemu Selanne	Winnipeg	Right wing	1992-93	84	76	56	**132**
2.	* Peter Stastny	Quebec	Center	1980-81	77	39	70	**109**
3.	* Alex Ovechkin	Washington	Left wing	2005-06	81	52	54	**106**
4.	* Dale Hawerchuk	Winnipeg	Center	1981-82	80	45	58	**103**
5.	Joe Juneau	Boston	Center	1992-93	84	32	70	**102**
	Sidney Crosby	Pittsburgh	Center	2005-06	81	39	63	**102**
7.	* Mario Lemieux	Pittsburgh	Center	1984-85	73	43	57	**100**
8.	Neal Broten	Minnesota	Center	1981-82	73	38	60	**98**
9.	* Bryan Trottier	NY Islanders	Center	1975-76	80	32	63	**95**
10.	Barry Pederson	Boston	Center	1981-82	80	44	48	**92**
	* Joe Nieuwendyk	Calgary	Center	1987-88	75	51	41	**92**
12.	* Mike Bossy	NY Islanders	Right wing	1977-78	73	53	38	**91**
13.	* Steve Larmer	Chicago	Right wing	1982-83	80	43	47	**90**
14.	Marian Stastny	Quebec	Right wing	1981-82	74	35	54	**89**
15.	Steve Yzerman	Detroit	Center	1983-84	80	39	48	**87**
16.	* Sergei Makarov	Calgary	Right wing	1989-90	80	24	62	**86**
17.	Anton Stastny	Quebec	Left wing	1980-81	80	39	46	**85**
18.	* Evgeni Malkin	Pittsburgh	Center	2006-07	78	33	52	**85**
19.	* Luc Robitaille	Los Angeles	Left wing	1986-87	79	45	39	**84**
20.	Mikael Renberg	Philadelphia	Left wing	1993-94	83	38	44	**82**
21.	Jimmy Carson	Los Angeles	Center	1986-87	80	37	42	**79**
	Sergei Fedorov	Detroit	Center	1990-91	77	31	48	**79**
	Alexei Yashin	Ottawa	Center	1993-94	83	30	49	**79**
24.	Paul Stastny	Colorado	Center	2006-07	82	28	50	**78**
25.	Marcel Dionne	Detroit	Center	1971-72	78	28	49	**77**
26.	Larry Murphy	Los Angeles	Defense	1980-81	80	16	60	**76**
	Mark Pavelich	NY Rangers	Center	1981-82	79	33	43	**76**
	Dave Poulin	Philadelphia	Center	1983-84	73	31	45	**76**
29.	Brian Propp	Philadelphia	Left wing	1979-80	80	34	41	**75**
	Jari Kurri	Edmonton	Left wing	1980-81	75	32	43	**75**
	Denis Savard	Chicago	Center	1980-81	76	28	47	**75**
	Mike Modano	Minnesota	Center	1989-90	80	29	46	**75**
	Eric Lindros	Philadelphia	Center	1992-93	61	41	34	**75**
34.	Rick Martin	Buffalo	Left wing	1971-72	73	44	30	**74**
	* Bobby Smith	Minnesota	Center	1978-79	80	30	44	**74**
36.	Jorgen Pettersson	St. Louis	Left wing	1980-81	62	37	36	**73**
37.	* Gilbert Perreault	Buffalo	Center	1970-71	78	38	34	**72**
	Dale McCourt	Detroit	Center	1977-78	76	33	39	**72**
	Ron Flockhart	Philadelphia	Center	1981-82	72	33	39	**72**
	Sylvain Turgeon	Hartford	Left wing	1983-84	76	40	32	**72**
	Carey Wilson	Calgary	Center	1984-85	74	24	48	**72**
	Warren Young	Pittsburgh	Left wing	1984-85	80	40	32	**72**
	Alex Zhamnov	Winnipeg	Center	1992-93	68	25	47	**72**
	* Patrick Kane	Chicago	Right wing	2007-08	82	21	51	**72**
45.	Mike Foligno	Detroit	Right wing	1979-80	80	36	35	**71**
	Dave Christian	Winnipeg	Center	1980-81	80	28	43	**71**
	Mats Naslund	Montreal	Left wing	1982-83	74	26	45	**71**
	Kjell Dahlin	Montreal	Right wing	1985-86	77	32	39	**71**
	* Brian Leetch	NY Rangers	Defense	1988-89	68	23	48	**71**
50.	Bill Mosienko	Chicago	Right wing	1943-44	50	32	38	**70**
	* Scott Gomez	New Jersey	Center	99-2000	82	19	51	**70**

* Calder Trophy Winner

50-Goal Seasons

Rick Martin

Bill Barber

Mike Bullard

Player	Team	Date of 50th Goal	Score	Goaltender	Player's Game No.	Team Game No.	Total Goals	Total Games	Age When First 50th Scored (Yrs. & Mos.)
Maurice Richard	Mtl.	Mar. 18/45	Mtl. 4 at Bos. 2	Harvey Bennett	50	50	50	50	23.7
Bernie Geoffrion	Mtl.	Mar. 16/61	Tor. 2 at Mtl. 5	Cesare Maniago	62	68	50	64	30.1
Bobby Hull	Chi.	Mar. 25/62	Chi. 1 at NYR 4	Gump Worsley	70	70	50	70	23.2
Bobby Hull	Chi.	Mar. 2/66	Det. 4 at Chi. 5	Hank Bassen	52	57	54	65	
Bobby Hull	Chi.	Mar. 18/67	Chi. 5 at Tor. 9	Bruce Gamble	63	66	52	66	
Bobby Hull	Chi.	Mar. 5/69	NYR 4 at Chi. 4	Ed Giacomin	64	66	58	74	
Phil Esposito	Bos.	Feb. 20/71	Bos. 4 at L.A. 5	Denis DeJordy	58	58	76	78	29.0
John Bucyk	Bos.	Mar. 16/71	Bos. 11 at Det. 4	Roy Edwards	69	69	51	78	35.10
Phil Esposito	Bos.	Feb. 20/72	Bos. 3 at Chi. 1	Tony Esposito	60	60	66	76	
Bobby Hull	Chi.	Apr. 2/72	Det. 1 at Chi. 6	Andy Brown	78	78	50	78	
Vic Hadfield	NYR	Apr. 2/72	Mtl. 6 at NYR 5	Denis DeJordy	78	78	50	78	31.6
Phil Esposito	Bos.	Mar. 25/73	Buf. 1 at Bos. 6	Roger Crozier	75	75	55	78	
Mickey Redmond	Det.	Mar. 27/73	Det. 8 at Tor. 1	Ron Low	73	75	52	76	25.3
Rick MacLeish	Phi.	Apr. 1/73	Phi. 4 at Pit. 5	Cam Newton	78	78	50	78	23.2
Phil Esposito	Bos.	Feb. 20/74	Bos. 5 at Min. 5	Cesare Maniago	56	56	68	78	
Mickey Redmond	Det.	Mar. 23/74	NYR 3 at Det. 5	Ed Giacomin	69	71	51	76	
Ken Hodge	Bos.	Apr. 6/74	Bos. 2 at Mtl. 6	Michel Larocque	75	77	50	76	29.10
Rick Martin	Buf.	Apr. 7/74	St.L. 2 at Buf. 5	Wayne Stephenson	78	78	52	78	22.9
Phil Esposito	Bos.	Feb. 8/75	Bos. 8 at Det. 5	Jim Rutherford	54	54	61	79	
Guy Lafleur	Mtl.	Mar. 29/75	K.C. 1 at Mtl. 4	Denis Herron	66	76	53	70	23.6
Danny Grant	Det.	Apr. 2/75	Wsh. 3 at Det. 8	John Adams	78	78	50	80	29.2
Rick Martin	Buf.	Apr. 3/75	Bos. 2 at Buf. 4	Ken Broderick	67	79	52	68	
Reggie Leach	Phi.	Mar. 14/76	Atl. 1 at Phi. 6	Dan Bouchard	69	69	61	80	25.11
Jean Pronovost	Pit.	Mar. 24/76	Bos. 5 at Pit. 5	Gilles Gilbert	74	74	52	80	30.3
Guy Lafleur	Mtl.	Mar. 27/76	K.C. 2 at Mtl. 8	Denis Herron	76	76	56	80	
Bill Barber	Phi.	Apr. 3/76	Buf. 2 at Phi. 5	Al Smith	79	79	50	80	23.9
Pierre Larouche	Pit.	Apr. 3/76	Wsh. 5 at Pit. 4	Ron Low	75	79	53	76	20.5
Danny Gare	Buf.	Apr. 4/76	Tor. 2 at Buf. 5	Gord McRae	79	80	50	79	21.11
Steve Shutt	Mtl.	Mar. 1/77	Mtl. 5 at NYI 4	Glenn Resch	65	65	60	80	24.8
Guy Lafleur	Mtl.	Mar. 6/77	Mtl. 1 at Buf. 4	Don Edwards	68	68	56	80	
Marcel Dionne	L.A.	Apr. 2/77	Min. 2 at L.A. 7	Pete LoPresti	79	79	53	80	25.8
Guy Lafleur	Mtl.	Mar. 8/78	Wsh. 3 at Mtl. 4	Jim Bedard	63	65	60	78	
Mike Bossy	NYI	Apr. 1/78	Wsh. 2 at NYI 3	Bernie Wolfe	69	76	53	73	21.2
Mike Bossy	NYI	Feb. 24/79	Det. 1 at NYI 3	Rogie Vachon	58	58	69	80	
Marcel Dionne	L.A.	Mar. 11/79	L.A. 3 at Phi. 6	Wayne Stephenson	68	68	59	80	
Guy Lafleur	Mtl.	Mar. 31/79	Pit. 3 at Mtl. 5	Denis Herron	76	76	52	80	
Guy Chouinard	Atl.	Apr. 6/79	NYR 2 at Atl. 9	John Davidson	79	79	50	80	22.5
Marcel Dionne	L.A.	Mar. 12/80	L.A. 2 at Pit. 4	Nick Ricci	70	70	53	80	
Mike Bossy	NYI	Mar. 16/80	NYI 6 at Chi. 1	Tony Esposito	68	71	51	75	
Charlie Simmer	L.A.	Mar. 19/80	Det. 3 at L.A. 4	Jim Rutherford	57	73	56	64	26.0
Pierre Larouche	Mtl.	Mar. 25/80	Chi. 4 at Mtl. 8	Tony Esposito	72	75	50	73	
Danny Gare	Buf.	Mar. 27/80	Det. 1 at Buf. 10	Jim Rutherford	71	75	56	76	
Blaine Stoughton	Hfd.	Mar. 28/80	Hfd. 4 at Van. 4	Glen Hanlon	75	75	56	80	27.0
Guy Lafleur	Mtl.	Apr. 2/80	Mtl. 7 at Det. 2	Rogie Vachon	72	78	50	74	
Wayne Gretzky	Edm.	Apr. 2/80	Min. 1 at Edm. 1	Gary Edwards	78	79	51	79	19.2
Reggie Leach	Phi.	Apr. 3/80	Wsh. 2 at Phi. 4	empty net	75	79	50	76	
Mike Bossy	NYI	Jan. 24/81	Que. 3 at NYI 7	Ron Grahame	50	50	68	79	
Charlie Simmer	L.A.	Jan. 26/81	L.A. 7 at Que. 5	Michel Dion	51	51	56	65	
Marcel Dionne	L.A.	Mar. 8/81	L.A. 4 at Wpg. 1	Markus Mattsson	68	68	58	80	
Wayne Babych	St.L.	Mar. 12/81	St.L. 3 at Mtl. 4	Richard Sevigny	70	68	54	78	22.9
Wayne Gretzky	Edm.	Mar. 15/81	Edm. 3 at Cgy. 3	Pat Riggin	69	69	55	80	
Rick Kehoe	Pit.	Mar. 16/81	Pit. 7 at Edm. 6	Eddie Mio	70	70	55	80	29.7
Jacques Richard	Que.	Mar. 29/81	Mtl. 0 at Que. 4	Richard Sevigny	76	75	52	78	28.6
Dennis Maruk	Wsh.	Apr. 5/81	Det. 2 at Wsh. 7	Larry Lozinski	80	80	50	80	25.3
Wayne Gretzky	Edm.	Dec. 30/81	Phi. 5 at Edm. 7	empty net	39	39	92	80	
Dennis Maruk	Wsh.	Feb. 21/82	Wpg. 3 at Wsh. 6	Doug Soetaert	61	61	60	80	
Mike Bossy	NYI	Mar. 4/82	Tor. 1 at NYI 10	Michel Larocque	66	66	64	80	
Dino Ciccarelli	Min.	Mar. 8/82	St.L. 1 at Min. 8	Mike Liut	67	68	55	76	22.1
Rick Vaive	Tor.	Mar. 24/82	St.L. 3 at Tor. 4	Mike Liut	72	75	54	77	22.10
Blaine Stoughton	Hfd.	Mar. 28/82	Min. 5 at Hfd. 2	Gilles Meloche	76	76	52	80	
Rick Middleton	Bos.	Mar. 28/82	Bos. 5 at Buf. 9	Paul Harrison	72	77	51	75	28.11
Marcel Dionne	L.A.	Mar. 30/82	Cgy. 7 at L.A. 5	Pat Riggin	75	77	50	78	
Mark Messier	Edm.	Mar. 31/82	L.A. 3 at Edm. 7	Mario Lessard	78	79	50	78	21.3
Bryan Trottier	NYI	Apr. 3/82	Phi. 3 at NYI 6	Pete Peeters	79	79	50	80	25.9
Lanny McDonald	Cgy.	Feb. 18/83	Cgy. 1 at Buf. 5	Bob Sauve	60	60	66	80	30.0
Wayne Gretzky	Edm.	Feb. 19/83	Edm. 10 at Pit. 7	Nick Ricci	60	60	71	80	
Michel Goulet	Que.	Mar. 5/83	Hfd. 3 at Que. 10	Mike Veisor	67	67	57	80	22.11
Mike Bossy	NYI	Mar. 12/83	Wsh. 2 at NYI 6	Al Jensen	70	71	60	79	
Marcel Dionne	L.A.	Mar. 17/83	Que. 3 at L.A. 4	Dan Bouchard	71	71	56	80	
Al Secord	Chi.	Mar. 20/83	Tor. 3 at Chi. 7	Mike Palmateer	73	73	54	80	25.0
Rick Vaive	Tor.	Mar. 30/83	Tor. 4 at Det. 2	Gilles Gilbert	76	78	51	78	
Wayne Gretzky	Edm.	Jan. 7/84	Hfd. 3 at Edm. 5	Greg Millen	42	42	87	74	
Michel Goulet	Que.	Mar. 8/84	Que. 8 at Pit. 6	Denis Herron	63	69	56	75	
Rick Vaive	Tor.	Mar. 14/84	Min. 3 at Tor. 3	Gilles Meloche	69	72	52	76	
Mike Bullard	Pit.	Mar. 14/84	Pit. 6 at L.A. 7	Markus Mattsson	71	72	51	76	23.0
Jari Kurri	Edm.	Mar. 15/84	Edm. 2 at Mtl. 3	Rick Wamsley	57	73	52	64	23.10
Glenn Anderson	Edm.	Mar. 21/84	Hfd. 3 at Edm. 5	Greg Millen	76	76	54	80	23.6
Tim Kerr	Phi.	Mar. 22/84	Pit. 4 at Phi. 13	Denis Herron	74	75	54	79	24.3

Player	Team	Date of 50th Goal	Score		Goaltender	Player's Game No.	Team Game No.	Total Goals	Total Games	Age When First 50th Scored (Yrs. & Mos.)
Mike Bossy	NYI	Mar. 31/84	NYI 3	at Wsh. 1	Pat Riggin	67	79	51	67	
Wayne Gretzky	Edm.	Jan. 26/85	Pit. 3	at Edm. 6	Denis Herron	49	49	73	80	
Jari Kurri	Edm.	Feb. 3/85	Hfd. 3	at Edm. 6	Greg Millen	50	53	71	73	
Mike Bossy	NYI	Mar. 5/85	Phi. 5	at NYI 4	Bob Froese	61	65	58	76	
Michel Goulet	Que.	Mar. 6/85	Buf. 3	at Que. 4	Tom Barrasso	62	73	55	69	
Tim Kerr	Phi.	Mar. 7/85	Wsh. 6	at Phi. 9	Pat Riggin	63	65	54	74	
John Ogrodnick	Det.	Mar. 13/85	Det. 6	at Edm. 7	Grant Fuhr	69	69	55	79	25.9
Bob Carpenter	Wsh.	Mar. 21/85	Wsh. 2	at Mtl. 3	Steve Penney	72	72	53	80	21.9
Dale Hawerchuk	Wpg.	Mar. 29/85	Chi. 5	at Wpg. 5	W. Skorodenski	77	77	53	80	21.11
Mike Gartner	Wsh.	Apr. 7/85	Pit. 3	at Wsh. 7	Brian Ford	80	80	50	80	25.5
Jari Kurri	Edm.	Mar. 4/86	Edm. 6	at Van. 2	Richard Brodeur	63	65	68	78	
Mike Bossy	NYI	Mar. 11/86	Cgy. 4	at NYI 8	Reggie Lemelin	67	67	61	80	
Glenn Anderson	Edm.	Mar. 14/86	Det. 3	at Edm. 12	Greg Stefan	63	71	54	72	
Michel Goulet	Que.	Mar. 17/86	Que. 8	at Mtl. 6	Patrick Roy	67	72	53	75	
Wayne Gretzky	Edm.	Mar. 18/86	Wpg. 2	at Edm. 6	Brian Hayward	72	72	52	80	
Tim Kerr	Phi.	Mar. 20/86	Pit. 1	at Phi. 5	Roberto Romano	68	72	58	76	
Wayne Gretzky	Edm.	Feb. 4/87	Edm. 6	at Min. 5	Don Beaupre	55	55	62	79	
Dino Ciccarelli	Min.	Mar. 7/87	Pit. 7	at Min. 3	Gilles Meloche	66	66	52	80	
Mario Lemieux	Pit.	Mar. 12/87	Que. 3	at Pit. 6	Mario Gosselin	53	70	54	63	21.5
Tim Kerr	Phi.	Mar. 17/87	NYR 1	at Phi. 4	J. Vanbiesbrouck	67	71	58	75	
Jari Kurri	Edm.	Mar. 17/87	N.J. 4	at Edm. 7	Craig Billington	69	70	54	79	
Mario Lemieux	Pit.	Feb. 2/88	Wsh. 2	at Pit. 3	Pete Peeters	51	54	70	77	
Steve Yzerman	Det.	Mar. 1/88	Buf. 0	at Det. 4	Tom Barrasso	64	64	50	64	22.10
Joe Nieuwendyk	Cgy.	Mar. 12/88	Buf. 4	at Cgy. 10	Tom Barrasso	66	70	51	75	21.5
Craig Simpson	Edm.	Mar. 15/88	Buf. 4	at Edm. 6	Jacques Cloutier	71	71	56	80	21.1
Jimmy Carson	L.A.	Mar. 26/88	Chi. 5	at L.A. 9	Darren Pang	77	77	55	88	19.8
Luc Robitaille	L.A.	Apr. 1/88	L.A. 6	at Cgy. 3	Mike Vernon	79	79	53	80	21.10
Hakan Loob	Cgy.	Apr. 3/88	Min. 1	at Cgy. 4	Don Beaupre	80	80	50	80	27.9
Stephane Richer	Mtl.	Apr. 3/88	Mtl. 4	at Buf. 4	Tom Barrasso	72	80	50	72	21.10
Mario Lemieux	Pit.	Jan. 20/89	Pit. 3	at Wpg. 7	Pokey Reddick	44	46	85	76	
Bernie Nicholls	L.A.	Jan. 28/89	Edm. 7	at L.A. 6	Grant Fuhr	51	51	70	79	27.7
Steve Yzerman	Det.	Feb. 5/89	Det. 6	at Wpg. 2	Pokey Reddick	55	55	65	80	
Wayne Gretzky	L.A.	Mar. 4/89	Phi. 2	at L.A. 6	Ron Hextall	66	67	54	78	
Joe Nieuwendyk	Cgy.	Mar. 21/89	NYI 1	at Cgy. 4	Mark Fitzpatrick	72	74	51	77	
Joe Mullen	Cgy.	Mar. 31/89	Wpg. 1	at Cgy. 4	Bob Essensa	78	79	51	79	32.1
Brett Hull	St.L.	Feb. 6/90	Tor. 4	at St.L. 6	Jeff Reese	54	54	72	80	25.6
Steve Yzerman	Det.	Feb. 24/90	Det. 3	at NYI 3	Glenn Healy	63	63	62	79	
Cam Neely	Bos.	Mar. 10/90	Bos. 3	at NYI 3	Mark Fitzpatrick	69	71	55	76	24.9
Brian Bellows	Min.	Mar. 22/90	Min. 5	at Det. 1	Tim Cheveldae	75	75	55	80	25.6
Pat LaFontaine	NYI	Mar. 24/90	NYI 5	at Edm. 5	Bill Ranford	71	77	54	74	25.1
Stephane Richer	Mtl.	Mar. 24/90	Mtl. 4	at Hfd. 7	Peter Sidorkiewicz	75	77	51	75	
Gary Leeman	Tor.	Mar. 28/90	NYI 6	at Tor. 3	Mark Fitzpatrick	78	78	51	80	26.1
Luc Robitaille	L.A.	Mar. 31/90	L.A. 3	at Van. 6	Kirk McLean	79	79	52	80	
Brett Hull	St.L.	Jan. 25/91	St.L. 9	at Det. 4	David Gagnon	49	49	86	78	
Cam Neely	Bos.	Mar. 26/91	Bos. 7	at Que. 4	empty net	67	78	51	69	
Theoren Fleury	Cgy.	Mar. 26/91	Van. 2	at Cgy. 7	Bob Mason	77	77	51	79	22.9
Steve Yzerman	Det.	Mar. 30/91	NYR 5	at Det. 6	Mike Richter	79	79	51	80	
Brett Hull	St.L.	Jan. 28/92	St.L. 3	at L.A. 3	Kelly Hrudey	50	50	70	73	
Jeremy Roenick	Chi.	Mar. 7/92	Chi. 2	at Bos. 1	Daniel Berthiaume	67	67	53	80	22.2
Kevin Stevens	Pit.	Mar. 24/92	Pit. 3	at Det. 4	Tim Cheveldae	74	74	54	80	26.11
Gary Roberts	Cgy.	Mar. 31/92	Edm. 2	at Cgy. 5	Bill Ranford	73	77	53	76	25.10
Alexander Mogilny	Buf.	Feb. 3/93	Hfd. 2	at Buf. 3	Sean Burke	46	53	76	77	23.11
Teemu Selanne	Wpg.	Feb. 28/93	Min. 6	at Wpg. 7	Darcy Wakaluk	63	63	76	84	22.6
Pavel Bure	Van.	Mar. 1/93	Van. 5	at Buf. 2*	Grant Fuhr	63	63	60	83	21.11
Steve Yzerman	Det.	Mar. 10/93	Det. 6	at Edm. 3	Bill Ranford	70	70	58	84	
Luc Robitaille	L.A.	Mar. 15/93	L.A. 4	at Buf. 2	Grant Fuhr	69	69	63	84	
Brett Hull	St.L.	Mar. 20/93	St.L. 2	at L.A. 3	Robb Stauber	73	73	54	80	
Mario Lemieux	Pit.	Mar. 21/93	Pit. 6	at Edm. 4**	Ron Tugnutt	48	72	69	60	
Kevin Stevens	Pit.	Mar. 21/93	Pit. 6	at Edm. 4**	Ron Tugnutt	62	72	55	72	
Dave Andreychuk	Tor.	Mar. 23/93	Tor. 5	at Wpg. 4	Bob Essensa	72	73	54	83	29.6
Pat LaFontaine	Buf.	Mar. 28/93	Ott. 1	at Buf. 3	Peter Sidorkiewicz	75	75	53	84	
Pierre Turgeon	NYI	Apr. 2/93	NYI 3	at NYR 2	Mike Richter	75	76	58	83	23.8
Mark Recchi	Phi.	Apr. 3/93	T.B. 2	at Phi. 6	J-C Bergeron	77	77	53	84	25.2
Brendan Shanahan	St.L.	Apr. 15/93	T.B. 5	at St.L. 6	Pat Jablonski	71	84	51	71	24.3
Jeremy Roenick	Chi.	Apr. 15/93	Tor. 2	at Chi. 3	Felix Potvin	84	84	50	84	
Cam Neely	Bos.	Mar. 7/94	Wsh. 3	at Bos. 6	Don Beaupre	44	66	50	49	
Sergei Fedorov	Det.	Mar. 15/94	Van. 2	at Det. 5	Kirk McLean	67	69	56	82	24.3
Pavel Bure	Van.	Mar. 23/94	Van. 6	at L.A. 3	empty net	65	73	60	76	
Adam Graves	NYR	Mar. 23/94	NYR 5	at Edm. 3	Bill Ranford	74	74	52	84	25.11
Dave Andreychuk	Tor.	Mar. 24/94	S.J. 2	at Tor. 1	Arturs Irbe	73	74	53	83	
Brett Hull	St.L.	Mar. 25/94	Dal. 3	at St.L. 5	Andy Moog	71	74	52	81	
Ray Sheppard	Det.	Mar. 29/94	Hfd. 2	at Det. 6	Sean Burke	74	76	52	82	27.10
Brendan Shanahan	St.L.	Apr. 12/94	St.L. 5	at Dal. 9	Andy Moog	80	83	52	81	
Mike Modano	Dal.	Apr. 12/94	St.L. 5	at Dal. 9	Curtis Joseph	75	83	50	76	23.11
Mario Lemieux	Pit.	Feb. 23/96	Hfd. 4	at Pit. 5	Sean Burke	50	59	69	70	
Jaromir Jagr	Pit.	Feb. 23/96	Hfd. 4	at Pit. 5	Sean Burke	59	59	62	82	24.0
Alexander Mogilny	Van.	Feb. 29/96	St.L. 2	at Van. 2	Grant Fuhr	60	63	55	79	
Peter Bondra	Wsh.	Apr. 3/96	Wsh. 5	at Buf. 1	Andrei Trefilov	62	77	52	67	28.1
Joe Sakic	Col.	Apr. 7/96	Col. 4	at Dal. 1	empty net	79	79	51	82	26.7
John LeClair	Phi.	Apr. 10/96	Phi. 5	at N.J. 1	Corey Schwab	80	80	51	82	26.7
Keith Tkachuk	Wpg.	Apr. 12/96	L.A. 3	at Wpg. 5	empty net	75	81	50	76	24.0
Paul Kariya	Ana.	Apr. 14/96	Wpg. 2	at Ana. 5	N. Khabibulin	82	82	50	82	21.5
Keith Tkachuk	Phx.	Apr. 6/97	Phx. 1	at Col. 2	Patrick Roy	78	79	52	81	
Teemu Selanne	Ana.	Apr. 9/97	L.A. 1	at Ana. 4	empty net	77	81	51	78	
Mario Lemieux	Pit.	Apr. 11/97	Pit. 2	at Fla. 4	J. Vanbiesbrouck	75	81	50	76	

John Ogrodnick

Gary Roberts

Dave Andreychuk

Alex Ovechkin

Player	Team	Date of 50th Goal	Score	Goaltender	Player's Game No.	Team Game No.	Total Goals	Total Games	Age When First 50th Scored (Yrs. & Mos.)
John LeClair	Phi.	Apr. 13/97	N.J. 4 at Phi. 5	Mike Dunham	82	82	50	82	
Teemu Selanne	Ana.	Mar. 25/98	Ana. 3 at Chi. 2	Jeff Hackett	66	71	52	73	
John LeClair	Phi.	Apr. 13/98	Phi. 1 at Buf. 2	Dominik Hasek	79	79	51	82	
Pavel Bure	Van.	Apr. 17/98	Cgy. 4 at Van. 2	Dwayne Roloson	81	81	51	82	
Peter Bondra	Wsh.	Apr. 18/98	Wsh. 4 at Car. 3	Mike Fountain	75	80	52	76	
Pavel Bure	Fla.	Mar. 18/00	Fla. 4 at NYI 2	empty net	63	71	58	74	
Pavel Bure	Fla.	Mar. 16/01	Pit. 6 at Fla. 3	Johan Hedberg	72	72	59	82	
Joe Sakic	Col.	Apr. 4/01	Ana. 1 at Col. 1	J-S Giguere	80	80	54	82	
Jaromir Jagr	Pit.	Apr. 4/01	T.B. 2 at Pit. 4	Kevin Weekes	80	80	52	81	
Jarome Iginla	Cgy.	Apr. 7/02	Cgy. 2 at Chi. 3	Jocelyn Thibault	79	79	52	82	24.9
Milan Hejduk	Col.	Apr. 6/03	St. L. 2 at Col. 5	Brent Johnson	82	82	50	82	27.1
Jaromir Jagr	NYR	Mar. 24/06	NYR 2 at Fla. 3	Roberto Luongo	70	70	54	82	
Ilya Kovalchuk	Atl.	Apr. 6/06	Atl. 2 at T.B. 3	Sean Burke	72	76	52	78	22.11
Jonathan Cheechoo	S.J.	Apr. 10/06	S.J. 3 at Phx. 2	David LeNeveu	78	78	56	82	25.8
Alex Ovechkin	Wsh.	Apr. 13/06	Wsh. 3 at Atl. 5	Mike Dunham	78	79	52	81	20.6
Dany Heatley	Ott.	Apr. 18/06	Ott. 5 at NYR 1	Henrik Lundqvist	82	82	50	82	25.2
Vincent Lecavalier	T.B.	Mar. 30/07	T.B. 4 at Car. 2	Cam Ward	78	78	52	82	26.11
Dany Heatley	Ott.	Apr. 7/07	Ott. 6 at Bos. 3	Tim Thomas	82	82	50	82	
Alex Ovechkin	Wsh.	Mar. 3/08	Bos. 2 at Wsh. 10	Tim Thomas	67	67	65	82	
Ilya Kovalchuk	Atl.	Mar. 18/08	Atl. 2 at Phi. 3	Antero Niittymaki	72	75	52	79	
Jarome Iginla	Cgy.	Apr. 5/08	Cgy. 7 at Van. 1	Curtis Sanford	82	82	50	82	
Alex Ovechkin	Wsh.	Mar. 19/09	Wsh. 5 at T.B. 2	Mike McKenna	70	73	56	79	
Alex Ovechkin	Wsh.	Apr. 9/10	Atl. 2 at Wsh. 5	Ondrej Pavelec	71	81	50	72	
Steven Stamkos	T.B.	Apr. 10/10	Fla. 3 at T.B. 4	S. Clemmensen	81	81	51	82	20.2
Sidney Crosby	Pit.	Apr. 11/10	Pit. 6 at NYI 5	Dwayne Roloson	81	82	51	81	22.8
Corey Perry	Ana.	Apr. 6/11	S.J. 2 at Ana. 6	Antero Niittymaki	80	80	50	82	25.11
Steven Stamkos	T.B.	Mar. 13/12	Bos. 1 at T.B. 6	Marty Turco	69	69	60	82	
Evgeni Malkin	Pit.	Apr. 7/12	Phi. 2 at Pit. 4	Sergei Bobrovsky	75	82	50	82	25.8

* neutral site game played at Hamilton; ** neutral site game played at Cleveland

Gordie Howe

100-Point Seasons

Player	Team	Date of 100th Point	G or A	Score	Player's Game No.	Team Game No.	G - A PTS	Total Games	Age when first 100th point scored (Yrs. & Mos.)
Phil Esposito	Bos.	Mar. 2/69	(G)	Pit. 0 at Bos. 4	60	62	49-77 — 126	74	27.1
Bobby Hull	Chi.	Mar. 20/69	(G)	Chi. 5 at Bos. 5	71	71	58-49 — 107	76	30.2
Gordie Howe	Det.	Mar. 30/69	(G)	Det. 5 at Chi. 9	76	76	44-59 — 103	76	41.0
Bobby Orr	Bos.	Mar. 15/70	(G)	Det. 5 at Bos. 5	67	67	33-87 — 120	76	22.11
Phil Esposito	Bos.	Feb. 6/71	(A)	Buf. 3 at Bos. 4	51	51	76-76 — 152	78	
Bobby Orr	Bos.	Feb. 20/71	(A)	Bos. 4 at L.A. 5	58	58	37-102 — 139	78	
John Bucyk	Bos.	Mar. 13/71	(G)	Bos. 6 at Van. 3	68	68	51-65 — 116	78	35.10
Ken Hodge	Bos.	Mar. 21/71	(A)	Buf. 7 at Bos. 5	72	72	43-62 — 105	78	26.9
Jean Ratelle	NYR	Feb. 18/72	(A)	NYR 2 at Cal. 2	58	58	46-63 — 109	63	31.4
Phil Esposito	Bos.	Feb. 19/72	(A)	Bos. 6 at Min. 4	59	59	66-67 — 133	76	
Bobby Orr	Bos.	Mar. 2/72	(A)	Van. 3 at Bos. 7	64	64	37-80 — 117	76	
Vic Hadfield	NYR	Mar. 25/72	(A)	NYR 3 at Mtl. 3	74	74	50-56 — 106	78	31.5
Phil Esposito	Bos.	Mar. 3/73	(A)	Bos. 1 at Mtl. 5	64	64	55-75 — 130	78	
Bobby Clarke	Phi.	Mar. 29/73	(G)	Atl. 2 at Phi. 4	76	76	37-67 — 104	78	23.7
Bobby Orr	Bos.	Mar. 31/73	(G)	Bos. 3 at Tor. 7	62	77	29-72 — 101	63	
Rick MacLeish	Phi.	Apr. 1/73	(G)	Phi. 4 at Pit. 5	78	78	50-50 — 100	78	23.3
Phil Esposito	Bos.	Feb. 13/74	(A)	Bos. 9 at Cal. 6	53	53	68-77 — 145	78	
Bobby Orr	Bos.	Mar. 12/74	(A)	Buf. 0 at Bos. 4	62	66	32-90 — 122	74	
Ken Hodge	Bos.	Mar. 24/74	(A)	Mtl. 3 at Bos. 6	72	72	50-55 — 105	76	
Phil Esposito	Bos.	Feb. 8/75	(A)	Bos. 8 at Det. 5	54	54	61-66 — 127	79	
Bobby Orr	Bos.	Feb. 13/75	(A)	Bos. 1 at Buf. 3	57	57	46-89 — 135	80	
Guy Lafleur	Mtl.	Mar. 7/75	(G)	Wsh. 4 at Mtl. 8	56	66	53-66 — 119	70	24.6
Marcel Dionne	Det.	Mar. 9/75	(A)	Det. 5 at Phi. 8	67	67	47-74 — 121	80	23.7
Pete Mahovlich	Mtl.	Mar. 9/75	(G)	Mtl. 5 at NYR 3	67	67	35-82 — 117	80	29.5
Bobby Clarke	Phi.	Mar. 22/75	(A)	Min. 0 at Phi. 4	72	72	27-89 — 116	80	
Rene Robert	Buf.	Apr. 5/75	(A)	Buf. 4 at Tor. 2	74	80	40-60 — 100	74	26.4
Guy Lafleur	Mtl.	Mar. 10/76	(G)	Mtl. 5 at Chi. 1	69	69	56-69 — 125	80	
Bobby Clarke	Phi.	Mar. 11/76	(A)	Buf. 1 at Phi. 6	64	68	30-89 — 119	76	
Bill Barber	Phi.	Mar. 18/76	(A)	Van. 2 at Phi. 3	71	71	50-62 — 112	80	23.8
Gilbert Perreault	Buf.	Mar. 21/76	(A)	K.C. 1 at Buf. 3	73	73	44-69 — 113	80	25.4
Pierre Larouche	Pit.	Mar. 24/76	(G)	Bos. 5 at Pit. 5	70	74	53-58 — 111	76	20.4
Pete Mahovlich	Mtl.	Mar. 28/76	(A)	Mtl. 2 at Bos. 2	77	77	34-71 — 105	80	
Jean Ratelle	Bos.	Mar. 30/76	(G)	Buf. 4 at Bos. 4	77	77	36-69 — 105	80	
Jean Pronovost	Pit.	Apr. 3/76	(A)	Wsh. 5 at Pit. 4	79	79	52-52 — 104	80	30.4
Darryl Sittler	Tor.	Apr. 3/76	(A)	Bos. 4 at Tor. 2	78	79	41-59 — 100	79	25.7
Guy Lafleur	Mtl.	Feb. 26/77	(A)	Cle. 3 at Mtl. 5	63	63	56-80 — 136	80	
Marcel Dionne	L.A.	Mar. 5/77	(G)	Pit. 3 at L.A. 3	67	67	53-69 — 122	80	
Steve Shutt	Mtl.	Mar. 27/77	(A)	Mtl. 6 at Det. 0	77	77	60-45 — 105	80	24.9

Pierre Larouche

Player	Team	Date of 100th Point	G or A	Score	Player's Game No.	Team Game No.	G - A PTS	Total Games	Age when first 100th point scored (Yrs. & Mos.)
Bryan Trottier	NYI	Feb. 25/78	(A)	Chi. 1 at NYI 7	59	60	46-77 — 123	77	21.7
Guy Lafleur	Mtl.	Feb. 28/78	(G)	Det. 3 at Mtl. 9	69	61	60-72 — 132	78	
Darryl Sittler	Tor.	Mar. 12/78	(A)	Tor. 7 at Pit. 1	67	67	45-72 — 117	80	
Guy Lafleur	Mtl.	Feb. 27/79	(A)	Mtl. 3 at NYI 7	61	61	52-77 — 129	80	
Bryan Trottier	NYI	Mar. 6/79	(A)	Buf. 3 at NYI 2	59	63	47-87 — 134	76	
Marcel Dionne	L.A.	Mar. 8/79	(G)	L.A. 4 at Buf. 6	66	66	59-71 — 130	80	
Mike Bossy	NYI	Mar. 11/79	(G)	NYI 4 at Bos. 4	66	66	69-57 — 126	80	22.2
Bob MacMillan	Atl.	Mar. 15/79	(A)	Atl. 4 at Phi. 5	68	69	37-71 — 108	79	26.6
Guy Chouinard	Atl.	Mar. 30/79	(G)	L.A. 3 at Atl. 5	75	75	50-57 — 107	80	22.5
Denis Potvin	NYI	Apr. 8/79	(A)	NYI 5 at NYR 2	73	80	31-70 — 101	73	25.5
Marcel Dionne	L.A.	Feb. 6/80	(A)	L.A. 3 at Hfd. 7	53	53	53-84 — 137	80	
Guy Lafleur	Mtl.	Feb. 10/80	(A)	Mtl. 3 at Bos. 2	55	55	50-75 — 125	74	
Wayne Gretzky	Edm.	Feb. 24/80	(A)	Bos. 4 at Edm. 2	61	62	51-86 — 137	79	19.2
Bryan Trottier	NYI	Mar. 30/80	(A)	NYI 9 at Que. 6	75	77	42-62 — 104	78	
Gilbert Perreault	Buf.	Apr. 1/80	(A)	Buf. 5 at Atl. 2	77	77	40-66 — 106	80	
Mike Rogers	Hfd.	Apr. 4/80	(A)	Que. 2 at Hfd. 9	79	79	44-61 — 105	80	25.5
Charlie Simmer	L.A.	Apr. 5/80	(G)	Van. 5 at L.A. 3	64	80	56-45 — 101	64	26.0
Blaine Stoughton	Hfd.	Apr. 6/80	(A)	Det. 3 at Hfd. 5	80	80	56-44 — 100	80	27.0
Wayne Gretzky	Edm.	Feb. 6/81	(G)	Wpg. 4 at Edm. 10	53	53	55-109 — 164	80	
Marcel Dionne	L.A.	Feb. 12/81	(A)	L.A. 5 at Chi. 5	58	58	58-77 — 135	80	
Charlie Simmer	L.A.	Feb. 14/81	(A)	Bos. 5 at L.A. 4	59	59	56-49 — 105	65	
Kent Nilsson	Cgy.	Feb. 27/81	(G)	Hfd. 1 at Cgy. 5	64	64	49-82 — 131	80	24.6
Mike Bossy	NYI	Mar. 3/81	(G)	Edm. 8 at NYI 8	65	66	68-51 — 119	79	
Dave Taylor	L.A.	Mar. 14/81	(G)	Min. 4 at L.A. 10	63	70	47-65 — 112	72	25.3
Mike Rogers	Hfd.	Mar. 22/81	(G)	Tor. 3 at Hfd. 3	74	74	40-65 — 105	80	
Bernie Federko	St.L.	Mar. 28/81	(A)	Buf. 4 at St.L. 7	74	76	31-73 — 104	78	24.10
Rick Middleton	Bos.	Mar. 28/81	(A)	Chi. 2 at Bos. 5	76	76	44-59 — 103	80	27.4
Bryan Trottier	NYI	Mar. 29/81	(G)	NYI 5 at Wsh. 4	69	76	31-72 — 103	73	
Jacques Richard	Que.	Mar. 29/81	(G)	Mtl. 0 at Que. 4	75	76	52-51 — 103	78	28.6
Peter Stastny	Que.	Mar. 29/81	(A)	Mtl. 0 at Que. 4	73	76	39-70 — 109	77	24.6
Wayne Gretzky	Edm.	Dec. 27/81	(G)	L.A. 3 at Edm. 10	38	38	92-120 — 212	80	
Mike Bossy	NYI	Feb. 13/82	(A)	Phi. 2 at NYI 8	55	55	64-83 — 147	80	
Peter Stastny	Que.	Feb. 16/82	(A)	Wpg. 3 at Que. 7	60	60	46-93 — 139	80	
Dennis Maruk	Wsh.	Feb. 20/82	(G)	Wsh. 3 at Min. 7	60	60	60-76 — 136	80	26.3
Bryan Trottier	NYI	Feb. 23/82	(G)	Chi. 1 at NYI 5	61	61	50-79 — 129	80	
Denis Savard	Chi.	Feb. 27/82	(A)	Chi. 5 at L.A. 3	64	64	32-87 — 119	80	21.1
Bobby Smith	Min.	Mar. 3/82	(A)	Det. 4 at Min. 6	66	66	43-71 — 114	80	24.1
Marcel Dionne	L.A.	Mar. 6/82	(G)	L.A. 6 at Hfd. 7	64	66	50-67 — 117	78	
Dave Taylor	L.A.	Mar. 20/82	(A)	Pit. 5 at L.A. 7	71	72	39-67 — 106	78	
Dale Hawerchuk	Wpg.	Mar. 24/82	(G)	L.A. 3 at Wpg. 5	74	74	45-58 — 103	80	18.11
Dino Ciccarelli	Min.	Mar. 27/82	(A)	Min. 6 at Bos. 5	72	76	55-52 — 107	76	21.8
Glenn Anderson	Edm.	Mar. 28/82	(G)	Edm. 6 at L.A. 2	78	78	38-67 — 105	80	21.7
Mike Rogers	NYR	Apr. 2/82	(G)	Pit. 7 at NYR 5	79	79	38-65 — 103	80	
Wayne Gretzky	Edm.	Jan. 5/83	(A)	Edm. 8 at Wpg. 3	42	42	71-125 — 196	80	
Mike Bossy	NYI	Mar. 3/83	(A)	Tor. 1 at NYI 5	66	67	60-58 — 118	79	
Peter Stastny	Que.	Mar. 5/83	(A)	Hfd. 3 at Que. 10	62	67	47-77 — 124	75	
Denis Savard	Chi.	Mar. 6/83	(G)	Mtl. 4 at Chi. 5	65	67	35-86 — 121	78	
Mark Messier	Edm.	Mar. 23/83	(G)	Edm. 4 at Wpg. 7	73	76	48-58 — 106	77	22.2
Barry Pederson	Bos.	Mar. 26/83	(A)	Hfd. 4 at Bos. 7	73	76	46-61 — 107	77	22.0
Marcel Dionne	L.A.	Mar. 26/83	(A)	Edm. 9 at L.A. 3	75	75	56-51 — 107	80	
Michel Goulet	Que.	Mar. 27/83	(A)	Que. 6 at Buf. 6	77	77	57-48 — 105	80	22.11
Glenn Anderson	Edm.	Mar. 29/83	(A)	Edm. 7 at Van. 4	70	78	48-56 — 104	72	
Jari Kurri	Edm.	Mar. 29/83	(A)	Edm. 7 at Van. 4	78	78	45-59 — 104	80	22.10
Kent Nilsson	Cgy.	Mar. 29/83	(G)	L.A. 3 at Cgy. 5	78	78	46-58 — 104	80	
Wayne Gretzky	Edm.	Dec. 18/83	(G)	Edm. 7 at Wpg. 5	34	34	87-118 — 205	74	
Paul Coffey	Edm.	Mar. 4/84	(A)	Mtl. 1 at Edm. 6	68	68	40-86 — 126	80	22.9
Michel Goulet	Que.	Mar. 4/84	(A)	Que. 1 at Buf. 1	62	67	56-65 — 121	75	
Jari Kurri	Edm.	Mar. 7/84	(G)	Chi. 4 at Edm. 7	53	69	52-61 — 113	64	
Peter Stastny	Que.	Mar. 8/84	(A)	Que. 8 at Pit. 6	69	69	46-73 — 119	80	
Mike Bossy	NYI	Mar. 8/84	(G)	Tor. 5 at NYI 9	56	68	51-67 — 118	67	
Barry Pederson	Bos.	Mar. 14/84	(A)	Bos. 4 at Det. 2	71	71	39-77 — 116	80	
Bryan Trottier	NYI	Mar. 18/84	(G)	NYI 4 at Hfd. 5	62	73	40-71 — 111	68	
Bernie Federko	St.L.	Mar. 20/84	(A)	Wpg. 3 at St.L. 9	75	76	41-66 — 107	79	
Rick Middleton	Bos.	Mar. 27/84	(G)	Bos. 6 at Que. 4	77	77	47-58 — 105	80	
Dale Hawerchuk	Wpg.	Mar. 27/84	(G)	Wpg. 3 at L.A. 3	77	77	37-65 — 102	80	
Mark Messier	Edm.	Mar. 27/84	(G)	Edm. 9 at Cgy. 2	72	79	37-64 — 101	73	
Wayne Gretzky	Edm.	Dec. 29/84	(A)	Det. 3 at Edm. 6	35	35	73-135 — 208	80	
Jari Kurri	Edm.	Jan. 29/85	(G)	Edm. 4 at Cgy. 2	48	51	71-64 — 135	73	
Mike Bossy	NYI	Feb. 23/85	(G)	Bos. 1 at NYI 7	56	60	58-59 — 117	76	
Dale Hawerchuk	Wpg.	Feb. 25/85	(A)	Wpg. 12 at NYR 5	64	64	53-77 — 130	80	
Marcel Dionne	L.A.	Mar. 5/85	(A)	Pit. 0 at L.A. 6	66	66	46-80 — 126	80	
Brent Sutter	NYI	Mar. 12/85	(A)	NYI 6 at St.L. 5	68	68	42-60 — 102	72	22.10
John Ogrodnick	Det.	Mar. 22/85	(A)	NYR 3 at Det. 5	73	73	55-50 — 105	79	25.9
Paul Coffey	Edm.	Mar. 26/85	(G)	Edm. 7 at NYI 5	74	74	37-84 — 121	80	
Denis Savard	Chi.	Mar. 29/85	(A)	Chi. 5 at Wpg. 5	75	76	38-67 — 105	79	
Peter Stastny	Que.	Apr. 2/85	(A)	Bos. 4 at Que. 6	74	77	32-68 — 100	75	
Bernie Federko	St.L.	Apr. 4/85	(A)	NYR 5 at St.L. 4	74	78	30-73 — 103	76	
Paul MacLean	Wpg.	Apr. 6/85	(A)	Wpg. 6 at Edm. 5	78	79	41-60 — 101	79	27.1
Bernie Nicholls	L.A.	Apr. 6/85	(A)	Van. 4 at L.A. 4	80	80	46-54 — 100	80	22.9
John Tonelli	NYI	Apr. 6/85	(G)	N.J. 5 at NYI 5	80	80	42-58 — 100	80	28.1
Mike Gartner	Wsh.	Apr. 7/85	(G)	Pit. 3 at Wsh. 7	80	80	50-52 — 102	80	25.6
Mario Lemieux	Pit.	Apr. 7/85	(G)	Pit. 3 at Wsh. 7	73	80	43-57 — 100	73	19.6

Wayne Gretzky

Bobby Smith

Paul MacLean

Paul Coffey

Brett Hull

Al MacInnis

Player	Team	Date of 100th Point	G or A	Score		Player's Game No.	Team Game No.	G - A PTS	Total Games	Age when first 100th point scored (Yrs. & Mos.)
Wayne Gretzky	Edm.	Jan. 4/86	(A)	Hfd. 3	at Edm. 4	39	39	52-163 — 215	80	
Mario Lemieux	Pit.	Feb. 15/86	(G)	Van. 4	at Pit. 9	55	56	48-93 — 141	79	
Paul Coffey	Edm.	Feb. 19/86	(A)	Tor. 5	at Edm. 9	59	60	48-90 — 138	79	
Peter Stastny	Que.	Mar. 1/86	(A)	Buf. 8	at Que. 4	66	68	41-81 — 122	76	
Jari Kurri	Edm.	Mar. 2/86	(G)	Phi. 1	at Edm. 2	62	64	68-63 — 131	78	
Mike Bossy	NYI	Mar. 8/86	(G)	Wsh. 6	at NYI 2	65	65	61-62 — 123	80	
Denis Savard	Chi.	Mar. 12/86	(A)	Buf. 7	at Chi. 6	69	69	47-69 — 116	80	
Mats Naslund	Mtl.	Mar. 13/86	(A)	Mtl. 2	at Bos. 3	70	70	43-67 — 110	80	26.4
Michel Goulet	Que.	Mar. 24/86	(A)	Que. 1	at Min. 0	70	75	53-50 — 103	75	
Glenn Anderson	Edm.	Mar. 25/86	(G)	Edm. 7	at Det. 2	66	74	54-48 — 102	72	
Neal Broten	Min.	Mar. 26/86	(A)	Min. 6	at Tor. 1	76	76	29-76 — 105	80	26.4
Dale Hawerchuk	Wpg.	Mar. 31/86	(A)	Wpg. 5	at L.A. 2	78	78	46-59 — 105	80	
Bernie Federko	St.L.	Apr. 5/86	(G)	Chi. 5	at St.L. 7	79	79	34-68 — 102	80	
Wayne Gretzky	Edm.	Jan. 11/87	(A)	Cgy. 3	at Edm. 5	42	42	62-121 — 183	79	
Jari Kurri	Edm.	Mar. 14/87	(A)	Buf. 3	at Edm. 5	67	68	54-54 — 108	79	
Mario Lemieux	Pit.	Mar. 18/87	(A)	St.L. 4	at Pit. 5	55	72	54-53 — 107	63	
Mark Messier	Edm.	Mar. 19/87	(A)	Edm. 4	at Cgy. 5	71	71	37-70 — 107	77	
Dino Ciccarelli	Min.	Mar. 30/87	(A)	NYR 6	at Min. 5	78	78	52-51 — 103	80	
Doug Gilmour	St.L.	Apr. 2/87	(A)	Buf. 3	at St.L. 5	78	78	42-63 — 105	80	23.10
Dale Hawerchuk	Wpg.	Apr. 5/87	(A)	Wpg. 3	at Cgy. 1	80	80	47-53 — 100	80	
Mario Lemieux	Pit.	Jan. 20/88	(G)	Pit. 8	at Chi. 3	45	48	70-98 — 168	77	
Wayne Gretzky	Edm.	Feb. 11/88	(A)	Edm. 7	at Van. 2	43	56	40-109 — 149	64	
Denis Savard	Chi.	Feb. 12/88	(A)	St.L. 3	at Chi. 4	57	57	44-87 — 131	80	
Dale Hawerchuk	Wpg.	Feb. 23/88	(G)	Wpg. 4	at Pit. 3	61	61	44-77 — 121	80	
Steve Yzerman	Det.	Feb. 27/88	(A)	Det. 4	at Que. 5	63	63	50-52 — 102	64	22.10
Peter Stastny	Que.	Mar. 8/88	(A)	Hfd. 4	at Que. 6	63	67	46-65 — 111	76	
Mark Messier	Edm.	Mar. 15/88	(A)	Buf. 4	at Edm. 6	68	71	37-74 — 111	77	
Jimmy Carson	L.A.	Mar. 26/88	(A)	Chi. 5	at L.A. 9	77	77	55-52 — 107	80	19.8
Hakan Loob	Cgy.	Mar. 26/88	(A)	Van. 1	at Cgy. 6	76	76	50-56 — 106	80	27.9
Mike Bullard	Cgy.	Mar. 26/88	(A)	Van. 1	at Cgy. 6	76	76	48-55 — 103	79	27.1
Michel Goulet	Que.	Mar. 27/88	(A)	Pit. 6	at Que. 3	76	76	48-58 — 106	80	
Luc Robitaille	L.A.	Mar. 30/88	(G)	Cgy. 7	at L.A. 9	78	78	53-58 — 111	80	22.1
Mario Lemieux	Pit.	Dec. 31/88	(A)	N.J. 6	at Pit. 8	36	38	85-114 — 199	76	
Wayne Gretzky	L.A.	Jan. 21/89	(A)	L.A. 4	at Hfd. 5	47	48	54-114 — 168	78	
Bernie Nicholls	L.A.	Jan. 21/89	(A)	L.A. 4	at Hfd. 5	48	48	70-80 — 150	79	
Steve Yzerman	Det.	Jan. 27/89	(G)	Tor. 1	at Det. 8	50	50	65-90 — 155	80	
Rob Brown	Pit.	Mar. 16/89	(A)	Pit. 2	at N.J. 1	60	72	49-66 — 115	68	20.11
Paul Coffey	Pit.	Mar. 20/89	(A)	Pit. 2	at Min. 7	69	74	30-83 — 113	75	
Joe Mullen	Cgy.	Mar. 23/89	(A)	L.A. 2	at Cgy. 4	74	75	51-59 — 110	79	32.1
Jari Kurri	Edm.	Mar. 29/89	(A)	Edm. 5	at Van. 2	75	79	44-58 — 102	76	
Jimmy Carson	Edm.	Apr. 2/89	(A)	Edm. 2	at Cgy. 4	80	80	49-51 — 100	80	
Mario Lemieux	Pit.	Jan. 28/90	(G)	Pit. 2	at Buf. 7	50	50	45-78 — 123	59	
Wayne Gretzky	L.A.	Jan. 30/90	(A)	N.J. 2	at L.A. 5	51	51	40-102 — 142	73	
Steve Yzerman	Det.	Feb. 19/90	(A)	Mtl. 5	at Det. 5	61	61	62-65 — 127	79	
Mark Messier	Edm.	Feb. 20/90	(A)	Edm. 4	at Van. 2	62	62	45-84 — 129	79	
Brett Hull	St.L.	Mar. 3/90	(A)	NYI 4	at St.L. 5	67	67	72-41 — 113	80	25.7
Bernie Nicholls	NYR	Mar. 12/90	(A)	L.A. 6	at NYR 2	70	71	39-73 — 112	79	
Pierre Turgeon	Buf.	Mar. 25/90	(G)	N.J. 4	at Buf. 3	76	76	40-66 — 106	80	20.7
Paul Coffey	Pit.	Mar. 25/90	(A)	Pit. 2	at Hfd. 4	77	77	29-74 — 103	80	
Pat LaFontaine	NYI	Mar. 27/90	(G)	Cgy. 4	at NYI 2	72	78	54-51 — 105	74	25.1
Adam Oates	St.L.	Mar. 29/90	(G)	Pit. 4	at St.L. 5	79	79	23-79 — 102	80	27.7
Joe Sakic	Que.	Mar. 31/90	(G)	Hfd. 3	at Que. 2	79	79	39-63 — 102	80	20.8
Ron Francis	Hfd.	Mar. 31/90	(G)	Hfd. 3	at Que. 2	79	79	32-69 — 101	80	27.0
Luc Robitaille	L.A.	Apr. 1/90	(A)	L.A. 4	at Cgy. 8	80	80	52-49 — 101	80	
Wayne Gretzky	L.A.	Jan. 30/91	(A)	N.J. 4	at L.A. 2	50	51	41-122 — 163	78	
Brett Hull	St.L.	Feb. 23/91	(G)	Bos. 2	at St.L. 9	60	62	86-45 — 131	78	
Mark Recchi	Pit.	Mar. 5/91	(G)	Van. 1	at Pit. 4	66	67	40-73 — 113	78	23.1
Steve Yzerman	Det.	Mar. 10/91	(G)	Det. 4	at St.L. 1	72	72	51-57 — 108	80	
John Cullen	Hfd.	Mar. 16/91	(G)	N.J. 2	at Hfd. 6	71	71	39-71 — 110	78	26.7
Adam Oates	St.L.	Mar. 17/91	(A)	St.L. 4	at Chi. 6	54	73	25-90 — 115	61	
Joe Sakic	Que.	Mar. 19/91	(G)	Edm. 7	at Que. 6	74	74	48-61 — 109	80	
Steve Larmer	Chi.	Mar. 24/91	(A)	Min. 4	at Chi. 5	76	76	44-57 — 101	80	29.9
Theoren Fleury	Cgy.	Mar. 26/91	(G)	Van. 2	at Cgy. 7	77	77	51-53 — 104	79	22.9
Al MacInnis	Cgy.	Mar. 28/91	(A)	Edm. 4	at Cgy. 4	78	78	28-75 — 103	78	27.8
Brett Hull	St.L.	Mar. 2/92	(G)	St.L. 5	at Van. 3	66	66	70-39 — 109	73	
Wayne Gretzky	L.A.	Mar. 3/92	(A)	Phi. 1	at L.A. 4	60	66	31-90 — 121	74	
Kevin Stevens	Pit.	Mar. 7/92	(A)	Pit. 3	at L.A. 5	66	66	54-69 — 123	80	26.11
Mario Lemieux	Pit.	Mar. 10/92	(A)	Cgy. 2	at Pit. 5	53	67	44-87 — 131	64	
Luc Robitaille	L.A.	Mar. 17/92	(A)	Wpg. 4	at L.A. 5	73	73	44-63 — 107	80	
Mark Messier	NYR	Mar. 22/92	(G)	N.J. 3	at NYR 6	74	75	35-72 — 107	79	
Jeremy Roenick	Chi.	Mar. 29/92	(A)	Tor. 1	at Chi. 5	77	77	53-50 — 103	80	22.2
Steve Yzerman	Det.	Apr. 14/92	(G)	Det. 7	at Min. 4	79	80	45-58 — 103	79	
Brian Leetch	NYR	Apr. 16/92	(G)	Pit. 1	at NYR 7	80	80	22-80 — 102	80	24.1
Mario Lemieux	Pit.	Dec. 31/92	(G)	Tor. 3	at Pit. 3	38	39	69-91 — 160	60	
Pat LaFontaine	Buf.	Feb. 10/93	(A)	Buf. 6	at Wpg. 2	55	55	53-95 — 148	84	
Adam Oates	Bos.	Feb. 14/93	(A)	Bos. 3	at T.B. 3	58	58	45-97 — 142	84	
Steve Yzerman	Det.	Feb. 24/93	(A)	Det. 7	at Buf. 10	64	64	58-79 — 137	84	
Pierre Turgeon	NYI	Feb. 28/93	(G)	NYI 7	at Hfd. 6	62	63	58-74 — 132	83	
Doug Gilmour	Tor.	Mar. 3/93	(A)	Min. 1	at Tor. 3	64	64	32-95 — 127	83	
Alexander Mogilny	Buf.	Mar. 5/93	(A)	Hfd. 4	at Buf. 2	58	65	76-51 — 127	77	24.1
Mark Recchi	Phi.	Mar. 7/93	(G)	Phi. 3	at N.J. 7	66	66	53-70 — 123	84	
Teemu Selanne	Wpg.	Mar. 9/93	(G)	Wpg. 4	at T.B. 2	68	68	76-56 — 132	84	22.7
Luc Robitaille	L.A.	Mar. 15/93	(A)	L.A. 4	at Buf. 2	69	69	63-62 — 125	84	

Player	Team	Date of 100th Point	G or A	Score		Player's Game No.	Team Game No.	G - A PTS	Total Games	Age when first 100th point scored (Yrs. & Mos.)
Kevin Stevens	Pit.	Mar. 23/93	(A)	S.J. 2	at Pit. 7	63	73	55-56 — 111	72	
Mats Sundin	Que.	Mar. 27/93	(G)	Phi. 3	at Que. 8	71	75	47-67 — 114	80	22.1
Pavel Bure	Van.	Apr. 1/93	(G)	Van. 5	at T.B. 3	77	77	60-50 — 110	83	22.0
Jeremy Roenick	Chi.	Apr. 4/93	(G)	St.L. 4	at Chi. 5	79	79	50-57 — 107	84	
Craig Janney	St.L.	Apr. 4/93	(G)	St.L. 4	at Chi. 5	79	79	24-82 — 106	84	25.7
Rick Tocchet	Pit.	Apr. 7/93	(G)	Mtl. 3	at Pit. 4	77	81	48-61 — 109	80	28.11
Joe Sakic	Que.	Apr. 8/93	(A)	Que. 2	at Bos. 6	75	81	48-57 — 105	78	
Ron Francis	Pit.	Apr. 9/93	(A)	Pit. 10	at NYR 4	82	82	24-76 — 100	84	
Brett Hull	St.L.	Apr. 11/93	(G)	Min. 1	at St.L. 5	78	82	54-47 — 101	80	
Theoren Fleury	Cgy.	Apr. 11/93	(G)	Cgy. 3	at Van. 6	82	82	34-66 — 100	83	
Joe Juneau	Bos.	Apr. 14/93	(A)	Bos. 4	at Ott. 2	84	84	32-70 — 102	84	25.3
Wayne Gretzky	L.A.	Feb. 14/94	(A)	Bos. 3	at L.A. 2	56	56	38-92 — 130	81	
Sergei Fedorov	Det.	Mar. 1/94	(A)	Cgy. 2	at Det. 5	63	63	56-64 — 120	82	24.2
Doug Gilmour	Tor.	Mar. 23/94	(G)	Tor. 1	at Fla. 1	74	74	27-84 — 111	83	
Adam Oates	Bos.	Mar. 26/94	(A)	Mtl. 3	at Bos. 6	68	75	32-80 — 112	77	
Mark Recchi	Phi.	Mar. 27/94	(A)	Ana. 3	at Phi. 2	76	76	40-67 — 107	84	
Pavel Bure	Van.	Mar. 28/94	(A)	Tor. 2	at Van. 3	68	76	60-47 — 107	76	
Jeremy Roenick	Chi.	Mar. 31/94	(G)	Chi. 3	at Wsh. 6	78	78	46-61 — 107	84	
Brendan Shanahan	St.L.	Apr. 12/94	(G)	St.L. 5	at Dal. 9	80	83	52-50 — 102	81	25.2
Mario Lemieux	Pit.	Jan. 16/96	(G)	Col. 5	at Pit. 2	38	44	69-92 — 161	70	
Jaromir Jagr	Pit.	Feb. 6/96	(G)	Bos. 5	at Pit. 6	52	52	62-87 — 149	82	23.11
Ron Francis	Pit.	Mar. 9/96	(A)	N.J. 4	at Pit. 3	61	66	27-92 — 119	77	
Peter Forsberg	Col.	Mar. 9/96	(A)	Col. 7	at Van. 5	68	68	30-86 — 116	82	22.7
Joe Sakic	Col.	Mar. 17/96	(A)	Edm. 1	at Col. 8	70	70	51-69 — 120	82	
Eric Lindros	Phi.	Mar. 25/96	(A)	Hfd. 0	at Phi. 3	65	73	47-68 — 115	73	23
Teemu Selanne	Ana.	Mar. 25/96	(A)	Ana. 1	at Det. 5	70	73	40-68 — 108	79	
Alexander Mogilny	Van.	Mar. 25/96	(A)	L.A. 1	at Van. 4	72	75	55-52 — 107	79	
Wayne Gretzky	St.L.	Mar. 28/96	(A)	N.J. 4	at St.L. 4	76	75	23-79 — 102	80	
Doug Weight	Edm.	Mar. 30/96	(G)	Tor. 4	at Edm. 3	76	76	25-79 — 104	82	25.3
Sergei Fedorov	Det.	Apr. 2/96	(A)	Det. 3	at S.J. 6	72	76	39-68 — 107	78	
Paul Kariya	Ana.	Apr. 7/96	(G)	Ana. 5	at S.J. 3	78	78	50-58 — 108	82	21.5
Mario Lemieux	Pit.	Mar. 8/97	(A)	Phi. 2	at Pit. 3	61	65	50-72 — 122	76	
Teemu Selanne	Ana.	Apr. 1/97	(A)	Chi. 3	at Ana. 3	74	78	51-58 — 109	78	
Jaromir Jagr	Pit.	Apr. 15/98	(G)	T.B. 1	at Pit. 5	76	80	35-67 — 102	77	
Jaromir Jagr	Pit.	Mar. 13/99	(G)	Phi. 0	at Pit. 4	65	65	44-83 — 127	81	
Teemu Selanne	Ana.	Apr. 5/99	(A)	Ana. 2	at Det. 3	69	76	47-60 — 107	75	
Paul Kariya	Ana.	Apr. 17/99	(G)	Ana. 3	at S.J. 3	82	82	39-62 — 101	82	
Jaromir Jagr	Pit.	Mar. 10/01	(G)	Cgy. 3	at Pit. 6	68	68	52-69 — 121	81	
Joe Sakic	Col.	Mar. 18/01	(G)	Min. 3	at Col. 4	72	72	54-64 — 118	82	
Markus Naslund	Van.	Mar. 27/03	(A)	Phx. 1	at Van. 5	78	78	48-56 — 104	82	29.8
Peter Forsberg	Col.	Mar. 31/03	(A)	S.J. 1	at Col. 3	72	79	29-77 — 106	79	
Joe Thornton	Bos.	Apr. 4/03	(A)	Buf. 5	at Bos. 8	77	82	36-65 — 101	77	23.9
Jaromir Jagr	NYR	Mar. 18/06	A	Tor. 2	at NYR 5	67	67	54-69 — 123	82	
Joe Thornton	S.J.	Mar. 21/06	A	S.J. 6	at St.L. 0	66	67	29-96 — 125	81	
Alex Ovechkin	Wsh.	Apr. 10/06	G	Wsh. 2	at Bos. 1	77	78	52-54 — 106	81	20.6
Dany Heatley	Ott.	Apr. 13/06	A	Fla. 5	at Ott. 4	80	80	50-53 — 103	82	25.2
Daniel Alfredsson	Ott.	Apr. 15/06	A	Ott. 1	at Tor. 5	76	81	43-60 — 103	77	33.4
Eric Staal	Car.	Apr. 15/06	A	Car. 2	at T.B. 3	81	81	45-55 — 100	82	21.5
Sidney Crosby	Pit.	Apr. 17/06	A	NYI 1	at Pit. 6	80	81	39-63 — 102	81	18.8
Sidney Crosby	Pit.	Mar. 10/07	G	NYR 2	at Pit. 3	65	68	36-84 — 120	79	
Joe Thornton	S.J.	Mar. 22/07	A	S.J. 5	at Atl. 1	75	75	22-92 — 114	82	
Vincent Lecavalier	T.B.	Mar. 24/07	A	Ott. 7	at T.B. 2	76	76	52-56 — 108	82	26.11
Dany Heatley	Ott.	Mar. 31/07	G	Ott. 5	at NYI 2	79	79	50-55 — 105	82	
Martin St. Louis	T.B.	Mar. 31/07	A	Wsh. 2	at T.B. 5	79	79	43-59 — 102	82	31.10
Marian Hossa	Atl.	Apr. 7/07	A	T.B. 2	at Atl. 3	82	82	43-57 — 100	82	28.3
Joe Sakic	Col.	Apr. 8/07	G	Cgy. 3	at Col. 6	82	82	36-64 — 100	82	
Alex Ovechkin	Wsh.	Mar. 18/08	A	Wsh. 4	at Nsh. 2	74	74	65-47 — 112	82	
Evgeni Malkin	Pit.	Mar. 22/08	G	N.J. 1	at Pit. 7	75	75	47-59 — 106	82	21.8
Evgeni Malkin	Pit.	Mar. 17/09	G	Atl. 2	at Pit. 6	72	72	35-78 — 113	82	
Alex Ovechkin	Wsh.	Mar. 27/09	G	T.B. 3	at Wsh. 5	73	76	56-54 — 110	79	
Sidney Crosby	Pit.	Apr. 7/09	G	Pit. 6	at T.B. 4	75	80	33-70 — 103	77	
Henrik Sedin	Van.	Mar. 27/10	A	Van. 2	at S.J. 4	75	75	29-83 — 112	82	29.7
Alex Ovechkin	Wsh.	Mar. 28/10	A	Cgy. 5	at Wsh. 3	65	75	50-59 — 109	72	
Sidney Crosby	Pit.	Apr. 6/10	A	Wsh. 6	at Pit. 3	78	79	51-58 — 109	81	
Nicklas Backstrom	Wsh.	Apr. 9/10	A	Atl. 2	at Wsh. 5	81	81	33-68 — 101	82	22.5
Daniel Sedin	Van.	Mar. 31/11	A	L.A. 1	at Van. 3	78	78	41-63 — 104	82	30.7
Evgeni Malkin	Pit.	Mar. 29/12	G	Pit. 3	at NYI 5	70	77	50-59 — 109	75	

Kevin Stevens

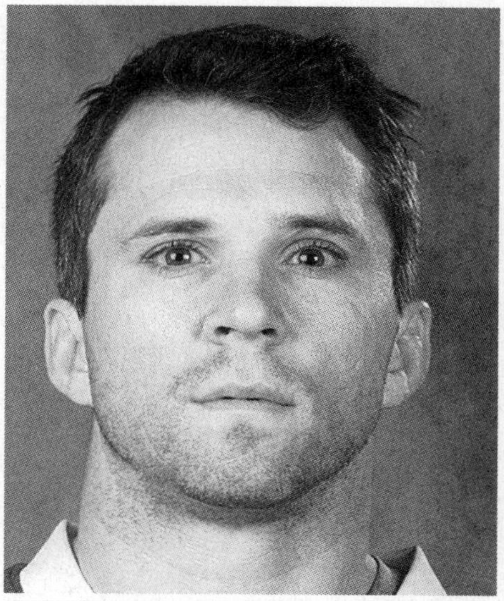

Martin St. Louis

Sidney Crosby

Five-or-more-Goal Games

Player	Team	Date	Score			Opposing Goaltender(s)
SEVEN GOALS						
Joe Malone	Quebec Bulldogs	Jan. 31/20	Tor. 6	at	Que. 10	Ivan Mitchell (4) Howard Lockhart (3)
SIX GOALS						
Newsy Lalonde	Montreal	Jan. 10/20	Tor. 7	at	Mtl. 14	Ivan Mitchell (2) Howard Lockhart (4)
Joe Malone	Quebec Bulldogs	Mar. 10/20	Ott. 4	at	Que. 10	Clint Benedict
Corb Denneny	Toronto St. Pats	Jan. 26/21	Ham. 3	at	Tor. 10	Howard Lockhart
Cy Denneny	Ottawa Senators	Mar. 7/21	Ham. 5	at	Ott. 12	Howard Lockhart
Syd Howe	Detroit	Feb. 3/44	NYR 2	at	Det. 12	Ken McAuley
Red Berenson	St. Louis	Nov. 7/68	St.L. 8	at	Phi. 0	Doug Favell
Darryl Sittler	Toronto	Feb. 7/76	Bos. 4	at	Tor. 11	Dave Reece
FIVE GOALS						
Joe Malone	Montreal	Dec. 19/17	Mtl. 7	at	Ott. 4	Clint Benedict
Harry Hyland	Mtl. Wanderers	Dec. 19/17	Tor. 9	at	Mtl. W. 10	Art Brooks, Sammy Hebert
Joe Malone	Montreal	Jan. 12/18	Ott. 4	at	Mtl. 9	Clint Benedict
Joe Malone	Montreal	Feb. 2/18	Tor. 2	at	Mtl. 11	Hap Holmes
Mickey Roach	Toronto St. Pats	Mar. 6/20	Que. 2	at	Tor. 11	Howard Lockhart
Newsy Lalonde	Montreal	Feb. 16/21	Ham. 5	at	Mtl. 10	Howard Lockhart
Babe Dye	Toronto St. Pats	Dec. 16/22	Mtl. 2	at	Tor. 7	Georges Vezina
Red Green	Hamilton Tigers	Dec. 5/24	Ham. 10	at	Tor. 3	John Ross Roach
Babe Dye	Toronto St. Pats	Dec. 22/24	Tor. 10	at	Bos. 1	Hec Fowler
Punch Broadbent	Mtl. Maroons	Jan. 7/25	Mtl. 6	at	Ham. 2	Jake Forbes
Pit Lepine	Montreal	Dec. 14/29	Ott. 4	at	Mtl. 6	Alex Connell
Howie Morenz	Montreal	Mar. 18/30	NYA 3	at	Mtl. 8	Roy Worters
Charlie Conacher	Toronto	Jan. 19/32	NYA 3	at	Tor. 11	Roy Worters (3) Al Shields (2)
Ray Getliffe	Montreal	Feb. 6/43	Bos. 3	at	Mtl. 8	Frank Brimsek
Maurice Richard	Montreal	Dec. 28/44	Det. 1	at	Mtl. 9	Harry Lumley
Howie Meeker	Toronto	Jan. 8/47	Chi. 4	at	Tor. 10	Paul Bibeault
Bernie Geoffrion	Montreal	Feb. 19/55	NYR 2	at	Mtl. 10	Gump Worsley
Bobby Rousseau	Montreal	Feb. 1/64	Det. 3	at	Mtl. 9	Roger Crozier
Yvan Cournoyer	Montreal	Feb. 15/75	Chi. 3	at	Mtl. 12	Mike Veisor
Don Murdoch	NY Rangers	Oct. 12/76	NYR 10	at	Min. 4	Gary Smith
Ian Turnbull	Toronto	Feb. 2/77	Det. 1	at	Tor. 9	Ed Giacomin (2) Jim Rutherford (3)
Bryan Trottier	NY Islanders	Dec. 23/78	NYR 4	at	NYI 9	Wayne Thomas (4) John Davidson (1)
Tim Young	Minnesota	Jan. 15/79	Min. 8	at	NYR 1	Doug Soetaert (3) Wayne Thomas (2)
John Tonelli	NY Islanders	Jan. 6/81	Tor. 3	at	NYI 6	Jiri Crha (4) empty net (1)
Wayne Gretzky	Edmonton	Feb. 18/81	St.L. 2	at	Edm. 9	Mike Liut (3) Ed Staniowski (2)
Wayne Gretzky	Edmonton	Dec. 30/81	Phi. 5	at	Edm. 7	Pete Peeters (4) empty net (1)
Grant Mulvey	Chicago	Feb. 3/82	St.L. 5	at	Chi. 9	Mike Liut (4) Gary Edwards (1)
Bryan Trottier	NY Islanders	Feb. 13/82	Phi. 2	at	NYI 8	Pete Peeters
Willy Lindstrom	Winnipeg	Mar. 2/82	Wpg. 7	at	Phi. 6	Pete Peeters
Mark Pavelich	NY Rangers	Feb. 23/83	Hfd. 3	at	NYR 11	Greg Millen
Jari Kurri	Edmonton	Nov. 19/83	N.J. 4	at	Edm. 13	Glenn Resch (3) Ron Low (2)
Bengt Gustafsson	Washington	Jan. 8/84	Wsh. 7	at	Phi. 1	Pelle Lindbergh
Pat Hughes	Edmonton	Feb. 3/84	Cgy. 5	at	Edm. 10	Don Edwards (3) Reggie Lemelin (2)
Wayne Gretzky	Edmonton	Dec. 15/84	Edm. 8	at	St.L. 2	Rick Wamsley (4) Mike Liut(1)
Dave Andreychuk	Buffalo	Feb. 6/86	Buf. 8	at	Bos. 6	Pat Riggin (1) Doug Keans (4)
Wayne Gretzky	Edmonton	Dec. 6/87	Min. 4	at	Edm. 10	Don Beaupre (4) Kari Takko (1)
Mario Lemieux	Pittsburgh	Dec. 31/88	N.J. 6	at	Pit. 8	Bob Sauve (3) Chris Terreri (1) empty net (1)
Joe Nieuwendyk	Calgary	Jan. 11/89	Wpg. 3	at	Cgy. 8	Daniel Berthiaume
Mats Sundin	Quebec	Mar. 5/92	Que. 10	at	Hfd. 4	Peter Sidorkiewicz (3) Kay Whitmore (2)
Mario Lemieux	Pittsburgh	Apr. 9/93	Pit. 10	at	NYR 4	Corey Hirsch (3) Mike Richter (2)
Peter Bondra	Washington	Feb. 5/94	T.B. 3	at	Wsh. 6	Daren Puppa (4) Pat Jablonski (1)
Mike Ricci	Quebec	Feb. 17/94	Que. 8	at	S.J. 2	Arturs Irbe (3) Jimmy Waite (2)
Alex Zhamnov	Winnipeg	Apr. 1/95	Wpg. 7	at	L.A. 7	Kelly Hrudey (3) Grant Fuhr (2)
Mario Lemieux	Pittsburgh	Mar. 26/96	St.L. 4	at	Pit. 8	Grant Fuhr (1) Jon Casey (4)
Sergei Fedorov	Detroit	Dec. 26/96	Wsh. 4	at	Det. 5	Jim Carey
Marian Gaborik	Minnesota	Dec. 20/07	NYR 3	at	Min. 6	Henrik Lundqvist
Johan Franzen	Detroit	Feb. 2/11	Det. 7	at	Ott. 5	Robin Lehner (2) Brian Elliott (2) empty net (1)

Players' 500th Goals

Regular Season

Player	Team	Date	Game No.	Score			Opposing Goaltender	Total Goals	Total Games
Maurice Richard	Montreal	Oct. 19/57	863	Chi. 1	at	Mtl. 3	Glenn Hall	544	978
Gordie Howe	Detroit	Mar. 14/62	1,045	Det. 2	at	NYR 3	Gump Worsley	801	1,767
Bobby Hull	Chicago	Feb. 21/70	861	NYR. 2	at	Chi. 4	Ed Giacomin	610	1,063
Jean Béliveau	Montreal	Feb. 11/71	1,101	Min. 2	at	Mtl. 6	Gilles Gilbert	507	1,125
Frank Mahovlich	Montreal	Mar. 21/73	1,105	Van. 2	at	Mtl. 3	Dunc Wilson	533	1,181
Phil Esposito	Boston	Dec. 22/74	803	Det. 4	at	Bos. 5	Jim Rutherford	717	1,282
John Bucyk	Boston	Oct. 30/75	1,370	St.L. 2	at	Bos. 3	Yves Bélanger	556	1,540
Stan Mikita	Chicago	Feb. 27/77	1,221	Van. 4	at	Chi. 3	Cesare Maniago	541	1,394
Marcel Dionne	Los Angeles	Dec. 14/82	887	L.A. 2	at	Wsh. 7	Al Jensen	731	1,348
Guy Lafleur	Montreal	Dec. 20/83	918	Mtl. 6	at	N.J. 0	Glenn Resch	560	1,126
Mike Bossy	NY Islanders	Jan. 2/86	647	Bos. 5	at	NYI 7	empty net	573	752
Gilbert Perreault	Buffalo	Mar. 9/86	1,159	N.J. 3	at	Buf. 4	Alain Chevrier	512	1,191
Wayne Gretzky	Edmonton	Nov. 22/86	575	Van. 2	at	Edm. 5	empty net	894	1,487
Lanny McDonald	Calgary	Mar. 21/89	1,107	NYI 1	at	Cgy. 4	Mark Fitzpatrick	500	1,111
Bryan Trottier	NY Islanders	Feb. 13/90	1,104	Cgy. 4	at	NYI 2	Rick Wamsley	524	1,279
Mike Gartner	NY Rangers	Oct. 14/91	936	Wsh. 5	at	NYR 3	Mike Liut	708	1,432
Michel Goulet	Chicago	Feb. 16/92	951	Cgy. 5	at	Chi. 5	Jeff Reese	548	1,089
Jari Kurri	Los Angeles	Oct. 17/92	833	Bos. 6	at	L.A. 8	empty net	601	1,251
Dino Ciccarelli	Detroit	Jan. 8/94	946	Det. 6	at	L.A. 3	Kelly Hrudey	608	1,232
Mario Lemieux	Pittsburgh	Oct. 26/95	605	Pit. 7	at	NYI 5	Tommy Soderstrom	690	915
Mark Messier	NY Rangers	Nov. 6/95	1,141	Cgy. 2	at	NYR 4	Rick Tabaracci	694	1,756
Steve Yzerman	Detroit	Jan. 17/96	906	Col. 2	at	Det. 3	Patrick Roy	692	1,514
Dale Hawerchuk	St. Louis	Jan. 31/96	1,103	St.L. 4	at	Tor. 0	Felix Potvin	518	1,188
Brett Hull	St. Louis	Dec. 22/96	693	L.A. 4	at	St.L. 7	Stephane Fiset	741	1,269
Joe Mullen	Pittsburgh	Mar. 14/97	1,052	Pit. 3	at	Col. 6	Patrick Roy	502	1,062
Dave Andreychuk	New Jersey	Mar. 15/97	1,070	Wsh. 2	at	N.J. 3	Bill Ranford	640	1,639
Luc Robitaille	Los Angeles	Jan. 7/99	928	Buf. 2	at	L.A. 4	Dwayne Roloson	668	1,431
Pat Verbeek	Detroit	Mar. 22/00	1,285	Cgy. 2	at	Det. 2	Fred Brathwaite	522	1,424
Ron Francis	Carolina	Jan. 2/02	1,533	Bos. 6	at	Car. 3	Byron Dafoe	549	1,731
Brendan Shanahan	Detroit	Mar. 23/02	1,100	Det. 2	at	Col. 0	Patrick Roy	656	1,524
Joe Sakic	Colorado	Dec. 11/02	1,044	Col. 1	at	Van. 3	Dan Cloutier	625	1,378
Joe Nieuwendyk	New Jersey	Jan. 17/03	1,094	N.J. 2	at	Car. 1	Kevin Weekes	564	1,257
*Jaromir Jagr	Washington	Feb. 4/03	928	Wsh. 5	at	T.B. 1	John Grahame	681	1,391
Pierre Turgeon	Colorado	Nov. 8/05	1,229	S.J. 2	at	Col. 5	Vesa Toskala	515	1,294
Mats Sundin	Toronto	Oct. 14/06	1,162	Cgy. 4	at	Tor. 5	Miikka Kiprusoff	564	1,346
*Teemu Selanne	Anaheim	Nov. 22/06	982	Ana. 2	at	Col. 3	Jose Theodore	675	1,387
Peter Bondra	Chicago	Dec. 22/06	1,050	Tor. 1	at	Chi. 3	J.S. Aubin	503	1,081
Mark Recchi	Pittsburgh	Jan. 26/07	1,303	Pit. 4	at	Dal. 3	Marty Turco	577	1,652
Mike Modano	Dallas	Mar. 13/07	1,225	Phi. 2	at	Dal. 3	Antero Niittymaki	561	1,499
Jeremy Roenick	San Jose	Nov. 10/07	1,267	Phx. 1	at	S.J. 4	Alex Auld	513	1,363
Keith Tkachuk	St. Louis	Apr. 6/08	1,055	St.L. 4	at	CBJ 1	empty net	538	1,201
*Jarome Iginla	Calgary	Jan. 7/12	1,149	Min. 1	at	Cgy. 3	Niklas Backstrom	530	1,232

*Active

Guy Lafleur poses with the puck after becoming the 10th player in NHL history to score 500 goals. Lafleur got the final goal in Montreal's 6-0 win over New Jersey on December 20, 1983. Teammate Steve Shutt scored his 400th goal earlier in the game.

Players' 1,000th Points

Regular Season

Player	Team	Date	Game No.	G or A	Score	Total Points G A PTS	Total Games
Gordie Howe	Detroit	Nov. 27/60	938	(A)	Tor. 0 at Det. 2	801-1,049–1,850	1,767
Jean Béliveau	Montreal	Mar. 3/68	911	(G)	Mtl. 2 at Det. 5	507-712–1,219	1,125
Alex Delvecchio	Detroit	Feb. 16/69	1,143	(A)	L.A. 3 at Det. 6	456-825–1,281	1,549
Bobby Hull	Chicago	Dec. 13/70	909	(A)	Min. 2 at Chi. 5	610-560–1,170	1,063
Norm Ullman	Toronto	Oct. 16/71	1,113	(A)	NYR 5 at Tor. 3	490-739–1,229	1,410
Stan Mikita	Chicago	Oct. 15/72	924	(A)	St.L. 3 at Chi. 1	541-926–1,467	1,394
John Bucyk	Boston	Nov. 9/72	1,144	(G)	Det. 3 at Bos. 8	556-813–1,369	1,540
Frank Mahovlich	Montreal	Feb. 17/73	1,090	(A)	Phi. 7 at Mtl. 6	533-570–1,103	1,181
Henri Richard	Montreal	Dec. 20/73	1,194	(A)	Mtl. 2 at Buf. 2	358-688–1,046	1,256
Phil Esposito	Boston	Feb. 15/74	745	(A)	Bos. 4 at Van. 2	717-873–1,590	1,282
Rod Gilbert	NY Rangers	Feb. 19/77	1,027	(G)	NYR 2 at NYI 5	406-615–1,021	1,065
Jean Ratelle	Boston	Apr. 3/77	1,007	(A)	Tor. 4 at Bos. 7	491-776–1,267	1,281
Marcel Dionne	Los Angeles	Jan. 7/81	740	(G)	L.A. 5 at Hfd. 3	731-1,040–1,771	1,348
Guy Lafleur	Montreal	Mar. 4/81	720	(G)	Wpg. 3 at Mtl. 9	560-793–1,353	1,126
Bobby Clarke	Philadelphia	Mar. 19/81	922	(G)	Bos. 3 at Phi. 5	358-852–1,210	1,144
Gilbert Perreault	Buffalo	Apr. 3/82	871	(A)	Buf. 5 at Mtl. 4	512-814–1,326	1,191
Darryl Sittler	Philadelphia	Jan. 20/83	927	(G)	Cgy. 2 at Phi. 5	484-637–1,121	1,096
Wayne Gretzky	Edmonton	Dec. 19/84	424	(A)	L.A. 3 at Edm. 7	894-1,963–2,875	1,487
Bryan Trottier	NY Islanders	Jan. 29/85	726	(G)	Min. 4 at NYI 4	524-901–1,425	1,279
Mike Bossy	NY Islanders	Jan. 24/86	656	(A)	NYI 7 at Wsh. 5	573-553–1,126	752
Denis Potvin	NY Islanders	Apr. 4/87	987	(G)	Buf. 6 at NYI 6	310-742–1,052	1,060
Bernie Federko	St. Louis	Mar. 19/88	855	(A)	Hfd. 5 at St.L. 3	369-761–1,130	1,000
Lanny McDonald	Calgary	Mar. 7/89	1,101	(G)	Wpg. 5 at Cgy. 9	500-506–1,006	1,111
Peter Stastny	Quebec	Oct. 19/89	682	(G)	Que. 5 at Chi. 3	450-789–1,239	977
Jari Kurri	Edmonton	Jan. 2/90	716	(A)	Edm. 6 at St.L. 4	601-797–1,398	1,251
Denis Savard	Chicago	Mar. 11/90	727	(A)	St.L. 6 at Chi. 4	473-865–1,338	1,196
Paul Coffey	Pittsburgh	Dec. 22/90	770	(A)	Pit. 4 at NYI 3	396-1,135–1,531	1,409
Mark Messier	Edmonton	Jan. 13/91	822	(A)	Edm. 5 at Phi. 3	694-1,193–1,887	1,756
Dave Taylor	Los Angeles	Feb. 5/91	930	(A)	L.A. 3 at Phi. 2	431-638–1,069	1,111
Michel Goulet	Chicago	Feb. 23/91	878	(G)	Chi. 3 at Min. 3	548-604–1,152	1,089
Dale Hawerchuk	Buffalo	Mar. 8/91	781	(G)	Chi. 5 at Buf. 3	518-891–1,409	1,188
Bobby Smith	Minnesota	Nov. 30/91	986	(A)	Min. 4 at Tor. 3	357-679–1,036	1,077
Mike Gartner	NY Rangers	Jan. 4/92	971	(G)	NYR 4 at N.J. 6	708-627–1,335	1,432
Raymond Bourque	Boston	Feb. 29/92	933	(A)	Wsh. 5 at Bos. 5	410-1,169–1,579	1,612
Mario Lemieux	Pittsburgh	Mar. 24/92	513	(A)	Pit. 3 at Det. 4	690-1,033–1,723	915
Glenn Anderson	Toronto	Feb. 22/93	954	(G)	Tor. 8 at Van. 1	498-601–1,099	1,129
Steve Yzerman	Detroit	Feb. 24/93	737	(A)	Det. 7 at Buf. 10	692-1,063–1,755	1,514
Ron Francis	Pittsburgh	Oct. 28/93	893	(G)	Que. 7 at Pit. 3	549-1,249–1,798	1,731
Bernie Nicholls	New Jersey	Feb. 13/94	858	(G)	N.J. 3 at T.B. 3	475-734–1,209	1,127
Dino Ciccarelli	Detroit	Mar. 9/94	957	(G)	Det. 5 at Cgy. 1	608-592–1,200	1,232
Brian Propp	Hartford	Mar. 19/94	1,008	(G)	Hfd. 5 at Phi. 3	425-579–1,004	1,016
Joe Mullen	Pittsburgh	Feb. 7/95	935	(A)	Fla. 3 at Pit. 7	502-561–1,063	1,062
Steve Larmer	NY Rangers	Mar. 8/95	983	(A)	N.J. 4 at NYR 6	441-571–1,012	1,006
Doug Gilmour	Toronto	Dec. 23/95	935	(A)	Edm. 1 at Tor. 6	450-964–1,414	1,474
Larry Murphy	Toronto	Mar. 27/96	1,228	(A)	Tor. 6 at Van. 2	287-929–1,216	1,615
Dave Andreychuk	New Jersey	Apr. 7/96	998	(G)	NYR 2 at N.J. 4	640-698–1,338	1,639
Adam Oates	Washington	Oct. 8/97	830	(G)	Wsh. 6 at NYI 3	341-1,079–1,420	1,337
Phil Housley	Washington	Nov. 8/97	1,081	(A)	Edm. 1 at Wsh. 2	338-894–1,232	1,495
Dale Hunter	Washington	Jan. 9/98	1,308	(A)	Phi. 1 at Wsh. 4	323-697–1,020	1,407
Pat LaFontaine	NY Rangers	Jan. 22/98	847	(G)	Phi. 4 at NYR 3	468-545–1,013	865
Luc Robitaille	Los Angeles	Jan. 29/98	882	(A)	Cgy. 3 at L.A. 5	668-726–1,394	1,431
Al MacInnis	St. Louis	Apr. 7/98	1,056	(A)	St.L. 3 at Det. 5	340-934–1,274	1,416
Brett Hull	Dallas	Nov. 14/98	815	(A)	Dal. 3 at Bos. 1	741-650–1,391	1,269
Brian Bellows	Washington	Jan. 2/99	1,147	(A)	Tor. 2 at Wsh. 5	485-537–1,022	1,188
Pierre Turgeon	St. Louis	Oct. 9/99	881	(G)	St.L. 4 at Edm. 3	515-812–1,327	1,294
Joe Sakic	Colorado	Dec. 27/99	810	(A)	St.L. 1 at Col. 5	625-1,016–1,641	1,378
Pat Verbeek	Detroit	Feb. 27/00	1,275	(A)	T.B. 1 at Det. 3	522-541–1,063	1,424
V. Damphousse	San Jose	Oct. 14/00	1,090	(A)	Bos. 2 at S.J. 5	432-773–1,205	1,378
*Jaromir Jagr	Pittsburgh	Dec. 30/00	763	(G)	Ott. 3 at Pit. 5	681-1,007–1,688	1,391
Mark Recchi	Philadelphia	Mar. 13/01	920	(A)	St.L. 2 at Phi. 5	577-956–1,533	1,652
Theoren Fleury	NY Rangers	Oct. 29/01	960	(A)	Dal. 2 at NYR 4	455-633–1,088	1,084
B. Shanahan	Detroit	Jan. 12/02	1,073	(G)	Dal. 2 at Det. 5	656-698–1,354	1,524
Jeremy Roenick	Philadelphia	Jan. 30/02	961	(G)	Phi. 1 at Ott. 3	513-703–1,216	1,363
Mike Modano	Dallas	Nov. 15/02	965	(A)	Col. 2 at Dal. 4	561-813–1,374	1,499
Joe Nieuwendyk	New Jersey	Feb. 23/03	1,094	(G)	N.J. 4 at Pit. 3	564-562–1,126	1,257
Mats Sundin	Toronto	Mar. 10/03	994	(G)	Tor. 3 at Edm. 2	564-785–1,349	1,346
Sergei Fedorov	Anaheim	Feb. 14/04	965	(A)	Ana. 2 at Van. 1	483-696–1,179	1,248
Alexander Mogilny	Toronto	Mar. 15/04	946	(A)	Tor. 6 at Buf. 5	473-559–1,032	990
Brian Leetch	Boston	Oct. 18/05	1,151	(A)	Bos. 3 at Mtl. 4	247-781–1,028	1,205
*Teemu Selanne	Anaheim	Jan. 30/06	928	(G)	L.A. 3 at Ana. 4	675-755–1,430	1,387
Rod Brind'Amour	Carolina	Nov. 4/06	1,202	(A)	Car. 3 at Ott. 2	452-732–1,184	1,484
Keith Tkachuk	St. Louis	Nov. 30/08	1,077	(G)	St.L. 4 at Atl. 2	538-527–1,065	1,201
Doug Weight	NY Islanders	Jan. 2/09	1,167	(A)	NYI 4 at Phx. 5	278-755–1,033	1,238
Nicklas Lidstrom	Detroit	Oct. 15/09	1,336	(A)	L.A. 2 at Det. 5	264-878–1,142	1,564
*Daniel Alfredsson	Ottawa	Oct. 22/10	1,009	(G)	Ott. 4 at Buf. 2	426-682–1,108	1,178
Alex Kovalev	Ottawa	Nov. 22/10	1,249	(G)	L.A. 2 at Ott. 3	430-599–1,029	1,316
*Jarome Iginla	Calgary	Apr. 1/11	1,103	(G)	Cgy. 3 at St.L. 2	530-576–1,106	1,232
*Joe Thornton	San Jose	Apr. 8/11	994	(G)	S.J. 3 at Phx. 4	331-787–1,118	1,125
*Ray Whitney	Phoenix	Mar. 31/12	1,226	(A)	Ana. 0 at Phx. 4	376-656–1,032	1,261

*Active

Islanders legends Bryan Trottier (top), Mike Bossy (middle) and Denis Potvin (bottom) each reached the 1,000-point plateau over three consecutive seasons in the mid 1980s.

Individual Awards

Hart Memorial Trophy

Art Ross Trophy

Calder Memorial Trophy

James Norris Memorial Trophy

HART MEMORIAL TROPHY

An annual award "to the player adjudged to be the most valuable to his team." Winner selected in a poll by the Professional Hockey Writers' Association in the 30 NHL cities at the end of the regular schedule.

History: The Hart Memorial Trophy was presented by the National Hockey League in 1960 after the original Hart Trophy was retired to the Hockey Hall of Fame. The original Hart Trophy was donated to the NHL in 1924 by Dr. David A. Hart, father of Cecil Hart, former manager-coach of the Montreal Canadiens.

2012-13 Winner: **Alex Ovechkin, Washington Capitals**
Runners-up: **Sidney Crosby, Pittsburgh Penguins**
John Tavares, New York Islanders

Right winger Alex Ovechkin of the Washington Capitals is the winner of the Hart Memorial Trophy for the third time in the past six seasons. He previously won the award in 2007-08 and 2008-09. Ovechkin edged Pittsburgh Penguins center Sidney Crosby 1,090 points to 1,058 - just a 32-points spread from a record-setting 179 ballots cast - in the closest Hart Trophy race since Montreal's Jose Theodore and Calgary's Jarome Iginla finished in a virtual tie in 2002. (Theodore took the award that year because he received more first-place votes.) Ovechkin received 50 first-place votes to Crosby's 46, while John Tavares of the New York Islanders received 38 first-place votes and 38 seconds for a total of 919 points to edge out Jonathan Toews of the Chicago Blackhawks who had 39 first-place votes and 886 points. Sergei Bobrovsky of the Columbus Blue Jackets had four first-place votes to finish fifth in balloting with 311 points. Patrick Kane of Chicago received two first-place votes and 157 points. Ryan Getzlaf of Anaheim (96 points), Steven Stamkos (28) and Martin St. Louis (20) of Tampa Bay and Pavel Datsyuk of Detroit (18) rounded out the top 10.

Ovechkin led the NHL with 32 goals in 48 games, including 23 in his final 23 contests. He also finished tied for third in the league in points (56), first in power-play goals (16), first in power-play points (27) and first in shots on goal (220), leading the Capitals to an 11-1-1 record in April and their fifth Southeast Division title in the last six years. Ovechkin became just the ninth player in NHL history to score 30 or more goals in each of his first eight seasons.

ART ROSS TROPHY

An annual award "to the player who leads the league in scoring points at the end of the regular season."

History: Arthur Howey Ross, former manager-coach of the Boston Bruins, presented the trophy to the National Hockey League in 1947. If two players finish the schedule with the same number of points, the trophy is awarded in the following manner: 1. Player with most goals. 2. Player with fewer games played. 3. Player scoring first goal of the season.

2012-13 Winner: **Martin St. Louis, Tampa Bay Lightning**
Runners-up: **Steven Stamkos, Tampa Bay Lightning**
Alex Ovechkin, Washington Capitals

Martin St. Louis of the Tampa Bay Lightning won the Art Ross Trophy for the second time in his career. St. Louis, who won the award previously in 2003-04, finished the 2012-13 season with 17 goals and an NHL-leading 43 assists for 60 points. He edged out teammate Steven Stamkos, who had 29 goals and 28 assists for 57 points. Washington's Alex Ovechkin was third in the scoring race with 56 points (32 goals, 24 assists). Pittsburgh's Sidney Crosby also had 56 points (15 goals, 41 assists) despite playing just 36 games. St. Louis registered points in 36 of the 48 games he played in and never went consecutive games without registering at least one point. He averaged 1.25 points per game, becoming one of only three players in NHL history to achieve that mark at age 37 or older (Mario Lemieux, 2002-03; Gordie Howe, 1968-69). St. Louis (37 years, 10 months) is the oldest scoring champion in NHL history, a distinction that had been held by Bill Cook of the New York Rangers who led the league in 1932-33 when he was 36. St. Louis' nine-year gap between Art Ross titles is the longest between wins by any player since the award was first presented in 1947-48.

CALDER MEMORIAL TROPHY

An annual award "to the player selected as the most proficient in his first year of competition in the National Hockey League." Winner selected in a poll by the Professional Hockey Writers' Association at the end of the regular schedule.

History: From 1936-37 until his death in 1943, Frank Calder, NHL President, bought a trophy each year to be given permanently to the outstanding rookie. After Calder's death, the NHL presented the Calder Memorial Trophy in his memory and the trophy is to be kept in perpetuity. To be eligible for the award, a player cannot have played more than 25 games in any single preceding season nor in six or more games in each of any two preceding seasons in any major professional league. Beginning in 1990-91, to be eligible for this award a player must not have attained his twenty-sixth birthday by September 15th of the season in which he is eligible.

2012-13 Winner: **Jonathan Huberdeau, Florida Panthers**
Runners-up: **Brendan Gallagher, Montreal Canadiens**
Brandon Saad, Chicago Blackhawks

Center Jonathan Huberdeau of the Florida Panthers won the Calder Memorial Trophy. Huberdeau received 54 first-place votes and 55 seconds among the 179 ballots cast and collected 1,141 points. He edged Montreal Canadiens left winger Brendan Gallagher, who also received 54 first-place ballots and polled 1,048 points. Huberdeau, who was selected third overall in the 2011 NHL Entry Draft behind 2012 Calder winner Gabriel Landeskog (second overall) and runner-up Ryan Nugent-Hopkins (first), becomes the first member of the Florida Panthers to be named the NHL's rookie of the year. Chicago's Brandon Saad received 30 first-place votes and was third in the balloting with 730 points. Minnesota's Jonas Brodin had 24 first-place votes and 621 points, followed by Edmonton's Nail Yakupov (11 and 521), Cory Conacher of Ottawa (four and 232) and Justin Schultz of Edmonton (two and 115).

Huberdeau played in all 48 games for Florida and ranked second on the team and tied for first among NHL rookies with 31 points (14 goals, 17 assists). Among first-year players, he finished third in goals, tied for fourth in assists and third in shots on goal (112). His 16:55 average time on ice led all rookie forwards. Huberdeau set two franchise records, becoming the first Panther to score on two penalty shots in one season and recording the most points by a teenager in team history (four more than Radek Dvorak in 1995-96).

JAMES NORRIS MEMORIAL TROPHY

An annual award "to the defense player who demonstrates throughout the season the greatest all-round ability in the position." Winner selected in a poll by the Professional Hockey Writers' Association at the end of the regular schedule.

History: The James Norris Memorial Trophy was presented in 1953 by the four children of the late James Norris in memory of the former owner-president of the Detroit Red Wings.

2012-13 Winner: **P.K. Subban, Montreal Canadiens**
Runners-up: **Ryan Suter, Minnesota Wild**
Kris Letang, Pittsburgh Penguins

P.K. Subban of the Montreal Canadiens won the James Norris Memorial Trophy for the first time in his first year as a finalist. It was the third year in a row that voting was tight for the NHL's best defenseman as Subban captured 66 first-place votes and 1,266 points to edge out Minnesota's Ryan Suter who received 65 first-place votes and 1,230 points. Kris Letang of Pittsburgh was named first on 31 ballots and collected 914 points. Boston's Zdeno Chara received 10 first-place votes but his 289 points ranked him fifth behind Anaheim's Francois Beauchemin who received just one first-place votes but 290 points in total. Chicago's Duncan Keith (one), Phoenix's Oliver Ekman-Larsson (three) and Montreal's Andrei Markov (one) also received first-place votes.

Subban tied for the lead among NHL defensemen in scoring, recording 38 points (11 goals, 27 assists) in 42 games as the Canadiens won the Northeast Division crown and posted the league's fourth-best record. The 24-year-old Toronto native also led defensemen in power-play scoring with 26 points (seven goals, 19 assists), helping Montreal post the league's fifth-best success rate with the man advantage (20.7%). Subban ranked second on the Canadiens in points, plus-minus (+12) and average ice time per game (23:14).

Vezina Trophy

Lady Byng Memorial Trophy

Frank J. Selke Trophy

Conn Smythe Trophy

VEZINA TROPHY

An annual award "to the goalkeeper adjudged to be the best at his position" as voted by the general managers of each of the 30 clubs.

History: Leo Dandurand, Louis Letourneau and Joe Cattarinich, former owners of the Montreal Canadiens, presented the trophy to the National Hockey League in 1926-27 in memory of Georges Vezina, outstanding goalkeeper of the Canadiens who collapsed during an NHL game on November 28, 1925, and died of tuberculosis a few months later. Before the 1981-82 season, the goalkeeper(s) of the team allowing the fewest number of goals during the regular season were awarded the Vezina Trophy.

2012-13 Winner: **Sergei Bobrovsky, Columbus Blue Jackets**
Runners-up: **Henrik Lundqvist, New York Rangers**
Antti Niemi, San Jose Sharks

Sergei Bobrovsky of the Columbus Blue Jackets captured the Vezina Trophy for the first time in his first year as a finalist. Bobrovsky was named on 26 of 30 ballots, capturing 17 first-place votes and 110 points. Henrik Lundqvist of the New York Rangers, who won the award in 2011-12, was named on 19 ballots, including three first-place votes, for 55 points. Antti Niemi of San Jose received six first-place votes and 46 points to finish third. Ottawa's Craig Anderson received three first-place votes and 22 points. Chicago's Ray Emery received the final first-place vote but finished seventh in balloting with six points behind Boston's Tuukka Rask (12 points) and Detroit's Jimmy Howard (nine points.) Jonas Hiller of Anaheim (three points), Minnesota's Nicklas Backstrom (one point) and Montreal's Carey Price (one point) rounded out the balloting.

Bobrovsky (21-11-6) backstopped Columbus' late-season surge that kept the club in contention for a playoff berth until the final moments of the season. He won eight of his last nine decisions from April 9 to 27, posting a 1.64 goals-against average and .945 save percentage in that span. For the entire season, Bobrovsky ranked second among NHL goaltenders in save percentage (.932) and tied for fifth in goals-against average (2.00).

LADY BYNG MEMORIAL TROPHY

An annual award "to the player adjudged to have exhibited the best type of sportsmanship and gentlemanly conduct combined with a high standard of playing ability." Winner selected in a poll by the Professional Hockey Writers' Association at the end of the regular schedule.

History: Lady Byng, wife of Canada's Governor-General at the time, presented the Lady Byng Trophy in the 1924-25 season. After Frank Boucher of the New York Rangers won the award seven times in eight seasons, he was given the trophy to keep and Lady Byng donated another trophy in 1936. After Lady Byng's death in 1949, the National Hockey League presented a new trophy, changing the name to Lady Byng Memorial Trophy.

2012-13 Winner: **Martin St. Louis, Tampa Bay Lightning**
Runners-up: **Patrick Kane, Chicago Blackhawks**
Matt Moulson, New York Islanders

Martin St. Louis of the Tampa Bay Lightning was the winner of the Lady Byng Memorial Trophy. The right winger has captured the award three times in the past four seasons, winning it previously in 2009-10 and 2010-11. He has been a finalist on four other occasions. St. Louis received 47 first-place votes and was named on 119 ballots among the 179 cast for a total of 824 points, winning a close three-way race. Chicago's Patrick Kane was second with 44 first-place votes and 785 points, while the New York Islanders' Matt Moulson finished in third for the second straight season with 35 first-place votes and 750 points. Four-time winner Pavel Datsyuk of Detroit finished fourth with 13 first-place votes and 536 points. San Jose's Logan Couture was fifth in voting (eight and 354).

The 37-year-old St. Louis became the oldest player in NHL history to lead the league in scoring in 2012-13, winning the Art Ross Trophy for the second time. He led the league with 43 assists and 60 points in 48 games and ranked second among all forwards in overall ice time (1,055:12) but was assessed just 14 penalty minutes.

FRANK J. SELKE TROPHY

An annual award "to the forward who best excels in the defensive aspects of the game." Winner selected in a poll by the Professional Hockey Writers' Association at the end of the regular schedule.

History: Presented to the National Hockey League in 1977 by the Board of Governors of the NHL in honor of Frank J. Selke, one of the great architects of Montreal and Toronto championship teams.

2012-13 Winner: **Jonathan Toews, Chicago Blackhawks**
Runners-up: **Patrice Bergeron, Boston Bruins**
Pavel Datsyuk, Detroit Red Wings

Center Jonathan Toews of the Chicago Blackhawks captured the Frank Selke Trophy for the first time, edging out 2011-12 recipient Patrice Bergeron of the Boston Bruins. Toews received 75 first-place votes among the 179 ballots cast and polled 1,260 points to finish just ahead of Bergeron who received 1,250 points, including 78 first-place votes. Detroit's Pavel Datsyuk was third in voting for the third year in a row after winning the trophy for three straight seasons. He finished with eight first-place votes and 737 points. Datsyuk has been a finalist for the award a record six times.

Toews played a leading role in helping the runaway Presidents' Trophy winners rank first overall in team defense (2.02 goals-against per game). He finished third in the NHL in plus-minus with a career-high +28 rating, including a league-leading +21 on the road; shared the overall lead in takeaways with Datsyuk (56); placed second in the NHL in face-off winning percentage (59.9%, 374 of 559); and played an average of 1:25 per game on the NHL's third-ranked penalty-killing unit (87.2%).

WILLIAM M. JENNINGS TROPHY

An annual award "to the goalkeeper(s) having played a minimum of 25 games (13 games in 2012-13) for the team with the fewest goals scored against it." Winners selected on regular-season play.

History: The Jennings Trophy was presented in 1981-82 by the National Hockey League's Board of Governors to honor the late William M. Jennings, longtime governor and president of the New York Rangers and one of the great builders of hockey in the United States.

2012-13 Winners: **Corey Crawford/Ray Emery, Chicago Blackhawks**
Runners-up: **Craig Anderson, Ottawa Senators**
Tuukka Rask/Anton Khudobin, Boston Bruins

Corey Crawford and Ray Emery combined to win the William M. Jennings Trophy. It was the first time either player won the award and the fourth Jennings Trophy win in Blackhawks history (1994-95, 1992-93, 1990-91 - all by Ed Belfour). Crawford and Emery split responsibilities between the pipes on a Chicago team that allowed a league-low 102 goals, two fewer than the Ottawa Senators and seven better than Boston. Crawford posted a 19-5-5 record, tied for third in the NHL with a 1.94 goals-against average and tied for sixth with a .926 save percentage. Emery set an NHL record by winning his first 12 decisions of the season and finished 17-1-0. He tied Crawford with a 1.94 goals-against average and registered a .922 save percentage. Crawford and Emery each recorded three shutouts and shared another, helping the Blackhawks total seven for the season, tied with St. Louis and Vancouver for the most shutouts in the NHL.

William M. Jennings Trophy

Jack Adams Award

Bill Masterton Memorial Trophy

Lester Patrick Trophy

JACK ADAMS AWARD

An annual award presented by the National Hockey League Broadcasters' Association to "the NHL coach adjudged to have contributed the most to his team's success." Winner selected by a poll among members of the NHL Broadcasters' Association at the end of the regular season.

History: The award was presented by the NHL Broadcasters' Association in 1974 to commemorate the late Jack Adams, coach and general manager of the Detroit Red Wings, whose lifetime dedication to hockey serves as an inspiration to all who aspire to further the game.

2012-13 Winner: **Paul MacLean, Ottawa Senators**
Runners-up: **Joel Quenneville, Chicago Blackhawks**
Bruce Boudreau, Anaheim Ducks

Ottawa Senators head coach Paul MacLean was the winner of the Jack Adams Award. MacLean was a top-three selection on 56 of the 83 ballots cast, including 28 first-place votes, for 206 points. Joel Quenneville of the Chicago Blackhawks was second with 22 first-place votes and 160 points. Anaheim's Bruce Boudreau finished third with 88 points, including six first-place votes. Michel Therrien of Montreal received 10 first-place votes, but was fourth overall with 78 points. Jack Capuano of the Islanders (five), Pittsburgh's Dan Bylsma (four), Randy Carlyle of Toronto (three), Todd Richards of Columbus (three) and Adam Oates of Washington (two) also received first-place votes.

MacLean, who finished third in balloting in 2011-12, won the award for the first time for guiding the Senators (25-17-6) to a berth in the Stanley Cup playoffs despite the extended absence of several key players due to injury. Defenseman Erik Karlsson, the reigning Norris Trophy winner, was limited to 17 games; defenseman Jared Cowen, the ninth overall pick in the 2009 NHL Draft, was sidelined for all but seven games; top forwards Jason Spezza and Milan Michalek played in just five and 23 contests, respectively; and starting goaltender Craig Anderson appeared in just 24 games. MacLean led a youthful Senators lineup, which included an NHL-high 14 rookies making at least one appearance, to the top defensive record in the Eastern Conference (2.08 goals-against per game).

LESTER PATRICK TROPHY

An annual award "for outstanding service to hockey in the United States." Eligible recipients are players, officials, coaches, executives and referees. Winners are selected by an award committee consisting of the commissioner of the NHL, an NHL governor, a representative of the New York Rangers, a member of the Hockey Hall of Fame builder's section, a member of the Hockey Hall of Fame player's section, a member of the U.S. Hockey Hall of Fame, a member of the NHL Broadcasters' Association and a member of the Professional Hockey Writers' Association. Each except the League Commissioner is rotated annually. The winner receives a miniature of the trophy.

History: Presented by the New York Rangers in 1966 to honor the late Lester Patrick, longtime general manager and coach of the New York Rangers, whose teams finished out of the playoffs only once in his first 16 years with the club.

2012 Winners: **Dick Patrick** **2013 Winners:** **T.B.A.**
Bob Chase-Wallenstein

Dick Patrick has been president of the Washington Capitals since the 1982-83 season. In the eight seasons prior to his arrival in Washington, the Capitals never reached the Stanley Cup playoffs. In the next 29 seasons, they reached the playoffs 23 times. Patrick has played an integral role in the growth of the Capitals organization and of amateur hockey in the D.C. area. He is a grandson of the trophy's namesake, Lester Patrick.

Bob Chase-Wallenstein marked his 60th season broadcasting Fort Wayne Komets hockey games in 2012-13. A native of Negaunee, Michigan, Chase-Wallenstein arrived in Fort Wayne, Indiana in 1953 and began calling games for the Comets in what was their second season. In addition to his play-by-play work in hockey, he was the broadcaster for the famed 1954 Milan High School run to the Indiana state boys' basketball championship that was immortalized in the film *Hoosiers*.

BILL MASTERTON MEMORIAL TROPHY

An annual award under the trusteeship of the Professional Hockey Writers' Association to "the National Hockey League player who best exemplifies the qualities of perseverance, sportsmanship and dedication to hockey." Winner selected by a poll among the 30 chapters of the PHWA at the end of the regular season. A $2,500 grant from the PHWA is awarded annually to the Bill Masterton Scholarship Fund, based in Bloomington, MN, in the name of the Masterton Trophy winner.

History: The trophy was presented by the NHL Writers' Association in 1968 to commemorate the late Bill Masterton, a player with the Minnesota North Stars, who exhibited to a high degree the qualities of perseverance, sportsmanship and dedication to hockey, and who died January 15, 1968.

2012-13 Winner: **Josh Harding, Minnesota Wild**
Runners-up: **Sidney Crosby, Pittsburgh Penguins**
Adam McQuaid, Boston Bruins

Minnesota Wild goaltender Josh Harding is the recipient of the Bill Masterton Memorial Trophy. Harding went 1-1-0 with a 3.24 goals-against average, a .863 save percentage and one shutout in five regular-season games with Minnesota this year and 1-4 with a 2.94 average and a .911 save percentage in five playoff starts for the Wild. He stopped all 24 shots faced in his first start of the 2012-13 season in a 1-0 victory against the Dallas Stars on January 20, 2013. Harding was placed on Injured Reserve on February 12 and missed 33 games with the Wild while battling multiple sclerosis, which was diagnosed in the fall of 2012. He was assigned to the Houston Aeros of the American Hockey League on a conditioning assignment April 16 and went 1-1-0, stopping 56 of 61 shots for a 3.00 goals-against average and .918 save percentage in two starts and helped Houston clinch a spot in the Calder Cup playoffs before being recalled by Minnesota on April 22.

CONN SMYTHE TROPHY

An annual award "to the most valuable player for his team in the playoffs." Winner selected by the Professional Hockey Writers' Association at the conclusion of the final game in the Stanley Cup Finals.

History: Presented by Maple Leaf Gardens Limited in 1964 to honor Conn Smythe, the former coach, manager, president and owner-governor of the Toronto Maple Leafs.

2012-13 Winner: **Patrick Kane, Chicago Blackhawks**

Chicago Blackhawks right winger Patrick Kane is the winner of the Conn Smythe Trophy. Kane was at his best down the stretch, tallying seven goals, including two game-winners, in his last eight games of the 2013 playoffs. He recorded his second career playoff hat trick in Game 5 of the Western Conference Final against Los Angeles, including the series-clinching goal in double-overtime, and netted a pair of goals, including the game-winner, in Game 5 of the Stanley Cup Final. Kane's nine goals in 23 playoff games tied him for second among all scorers behind teammate Patrick Sharp, while his 19 postseason points tied for second behind Boston's David Krejci (26). Kane tied Dave Bolland for the team lead in scoring in the Stanley Cup Final with three goals and two assists for five points in six games. The 24-year-old Buffalo, New York, native is the third consecutive U.S.-born player and fourth overall to win the Conn Smythe, joining New York Rangers defenseman Brian Leetch in 1994, Boston Bruins goaltender Tim Thomas in 2011 and Los Angeles Kings goaltender Jonathan Quick in 2012.

King Clancy Memorial Trophy

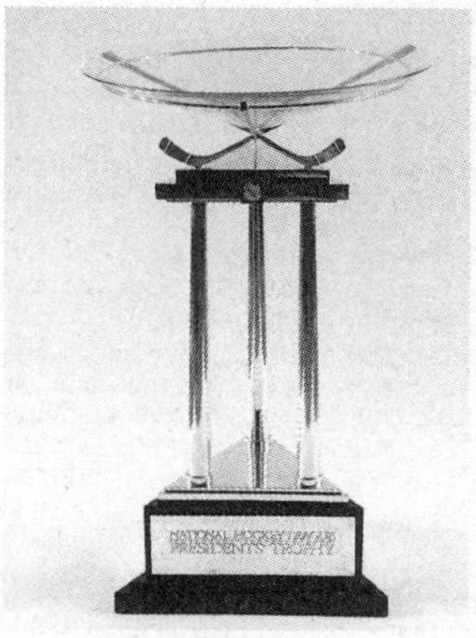

Presidents' Trophy

Maurice "Rocket" Richard Trophy

Ted Lindsay Award

KING CLANCY MEMORIAL TROPHY

An annual award "to the player who best exemplifies leadership qualities on and off the ice and has made a noteworthy humanitarian contribution in his community."

History: The King Clancy Memorial Trophy was presented to the National Hockey League by the Board of Governors in 1988 to honor the late Frank "King" Clancy.

2012-13 Winner: Patrice Bergeron, Boston Bruins

Center Patrice Bergeron of the Boston Bruins is the recipient of the King Clancy Memorial Trophy. Bergeron has demonstrated leadership qualities on and off the ice and made noteworthy humanitarian contributions to his community during his nine seasons with the Bruins by serving as an alternate captain, spending time in the community and working with charitable organizations. Bergeron's Patrice's Pals program brings local hospital patients and children's organizations who may not otherwise have the opportunity to experience a game to TD Garden to watch the Bruins play from the view of a luxury suite and meet and take photographs with Patrice. Among the many organizations he has hosted are: the Make-A-Wish Foundation, Children's Hospital Boston, Franciscan Hospital for Children, Massachusetts General Hospital for Children and numerous special needs hockey teams. One notable guest whom Bergeron has hosted in his Patrice's Pals suite is Matt Brown, a local high school athlete who was paralyzed from the chest down due to a hockey accident in 2010. Bergeron has maintained contact with Brown and his family, hosting them in his suite twice a year since the accident. Bergeron also represents his club at numerous community events throughout the year. He is heavily involved in the Bruins' Annual Holiday Toy Delivery, during which players and other members of the Bruins organization shop for toys to deliver to children in area hospitals who cannot be home for the holidays. Bergeron has spearheaded the shopping and delivery for a number of years, demonstrating his passion for working with children in need.

MAURICE "ROCKET" RICHARD TROPHY

An annual award "presented to the player finishing the regular season as the League's goal-scoring leader."

History: A gift to the NHL from the Montreal Canadiens in 1999, the Maurice "Rocket" Richard Trophy honors one of the game's greatest stars. During his 18-year career with the Canadiens from 1942-43 through 1959-60, Richard was the first player in NHL history to score 50 goals in a season and 500 in his career. He played on eight Stanley Cup champions and led the League in goal scoring five times.

2012-13 Winner: Alex Ovechkin, Washington Capitals
Runners-up Steven Stamkos, Tampa Bay Lightning
John Tavares, New York Islanders

Right winger Alex Ovechkin of the Washington Capitals became the first three-time winner of the Maurice Richard Trophy. After a slow start in which he tallied just twice in his first 10 games, Ovechkin notched 23 goals in his final 23 contests to finish the season with 32 goals and beat Steven Stamkos (29) and John Tavares (28). Ovechkin recorded his 30th goal of the season on April 20, becoming the ninth player in NHL history to score 30 or more goals in each of his first eight seasons. Ovechkin recorded points in nine straight games from March 17 to April 2 (10 goals, five assists), including a five-game goal streak from March 17 to 24.

NHL GENERAL MANAGER OF THE YEAR AWARD

An annual award presented to recognize the work of the league's general managers, voting for this new award is conducted among the 30 club general managers and a panel of NHL executives, print and broadcast media at the conclusion of the regular season.

History: This award was first presented in 2010.

2012-13 Winner: Ray Shero, Pittsburgh Penguins
Runners-up: Bob Murray, Anaheim Ducks
Marc Bergevin, Montreal Canadiens

Ray Shero of the Pittsburgh Penguins is the winner of the NHL General Manager of the Year Award. Shero received 14 first-place votes among the 39 ballots cast, was named on 26 ballots and had a total of 94 points. Anaheim's Bob Murray had 11 first-place votes and 88 points. Marc Bergevin of Montreal was third in voting with seven first-place votes and 75 points. Chicago's Stan Bowman received three first-place votes and had 36 points, while Bryan Murray of Ottawa had two and 23.

Shero made key additions throughout the year to a roster that was already strong, helping to propel the Penguins (36-12-0) to a playoff berth for the seventh consecutive season, their first Atlantic Division title since 2008 and the number-one seed in the Eastern Conference. He obtained center Brandon Sutter and goalie Tomas Vokoun in offseason trades and later brought forwards Jarome Iginla, Brenden Morrow, Jussi Jokinen and defenseman Douglas Murray to Pittsburgh in deals leading up to the trade deadline. Pittsburgh reeled off 15 consecutive victories from March 2 to 30, the second-longest winning streak in NHL history and the league's longest winning streak in 20 years.

TED LINDSAY AWARD

The Ted Lindsay Award is presented annually to the "most outstanding player" in the NHL as voted by fellow members of the National Hockey League Players' Association. The winner receives $20,000, and the two finalists receive $10,000 each to donate to the grassroots hockey program of their choice, through the NHLPA's Goals & Dreams Fund.

History: On April 29, 2010, the Ted Lindsay Award was introduced to recognize Lindsay's pioneering efforts in the establishment of the NHL Players' Association. Carrying on the tradition established by the Lester B. Pearson Award, it remains the only award voted on by the players themselves. The award was originally created in 1971 in honor of the late Lester B. Pearson, former Prime Minister of Canada.

2012-13 Winner: Sidney Crosby, Pittsburgh Penguins
Runners-up: Alex Ovechkin, Washington Capitals
Martin St. Louis, Tampa Bay Lightning

Center Sidney Crosby is the winner of the Ted Lindsay Award for the second time. Crosby previously won the Award in 2006-07 and was also nominated as a finalist in 2009-10. Four Penguins have won the NHL's "Most Outstanding Player" award over the years, including four-time winner Mario Lemieux, three-time winner Jaromir Jagr (twice as a Penguin) and teammate Evgeni Malkin, who won the award in 2011-12.

After missing the majority of the previous two seasons, Crosby returned to star form in 2012-13 and helped lead the Penguins to the best record in the Eastern Conference. Before a broken jaw sidelined him for the final quarter of the regular season, Crosby had amassed a large lead in the race for the NHL scoring title. Despite playing only 36 games during the 48-game season, he still tied for third in the NHL with 56 points, second with 41 assists and fourth in plus-minus at +26 while averaging a league-best 1.56 points per game.

MARK MESSIER NHL LEADERSHIP AWARD
presented by Bridgestone

An annual award presented "to the player who exemplifies great leadership qualitites to his team, on and off the ice during the regular season." Suggestions for nominees are solicited from fans, clubs and NHL personnel, but the selection of the three finalists and the ultimate winner is made by Mark Messier himself.

History: Presented by Bridgestone in honor of one of hockey's great leaders, this award was first handed out in 2007.

2012-13 Winner: **Daniel Alfredsson, Ottawa Senators**
Runners-up: **Dustin Brown, Los Angeles Kings**
Jonathan Toews, Chicago Blackhawks

Ottawa Senators captain Daniel Alfredsson is the recipient of the Mark Messier NHL Leadership Award. When he received the award, Alfredsson was the NHL's longest-serving active captain and led the Senators in numerous categories, including career games played, goals, assists and points. He also took a leadership role off the ice, working with the Boys and Girls Club of Ottawa, the Royal Ottawa Foundation for Mental Health and the Sens Foundation. Alfredsson has supported the Boys and Girls Club of Ottawa for the past 10 seasons, purchasing tickets and suites for club members to attend Senators games and serving as title sponsor of Ringside for Youth, the club's primary fundraising event during the season. Since 2008, he was also the spokesperson and champion for the Royal's "You Know Who I Am" campaign, leading the way to help reduce the stigma surrounding mental health issues. Alfredsson has supported the Royal's "Do It for Daron" campaign to assist in raising the profile of youth mental health issues.

PRESIDENTS' TROPHY

An annual award to the club finishing the regular-season with the best overall record.

History: Presented to the National Hockey League in 1985-86 by the NHL Board of Governors to recognize the team compiling the top regular-season record.

2012-13 Winner: **Chicago Blackhawks**
Runners-up: **Pittsburgh Penguins**
Anaheim Ducks

The Chicago Blackhawks captured the Presidents' Trophy for the second time in franchise history, leading the NHL with 77 points during the 48-game season by posting a record of 36-7-5. Chicago had previously won the Presidents' Trophy in 1990-91 and topped the NHL standings two other times before the presentation of the award (1966-67 and 1969-70). The Blackhawks enjoyed the best start in NHL history in 2012-13, earning points in 24 straight games by posting a record of 21-0-3, and went on to become the first Presidents' Trophy winner to also capture the Stanley Cup since the Detroit Red Wings in 2007-08. The Pittsburgh Penguins won their first Atlantic Division title since 2008 and posted the best record in the Eastern Conference with a mark of 36-12-0 for 72 points. The Anaheim Ducks won their first Pacific Division title since their Stanley Cup season of 2006-07 with a record of 30-12-6 for 66 points.

NHL FOUNDATION PLAYER AWARD

An annual award presented to "an NHL player who applies the core values of hockey – commitment, perseverance and teamwork – to enrich the lives of people in his community." In recognition of this dedication, the NHL Foundation annually awards $25,000 to a current player's charity.

History: NHL players have a long-standing tradition of supporting charities and other important causes in their communities. NHL member clubs are constant in their quest to help local schools, hospitals and charitable organizations. Clubs submit nominations for the NHL Foundation Player Award and the finalists are selected by a judging panel. This award was first presented in 1998.

2012-13 Winner: **Henrik Zetterberg, Detroit Red Wings**

Detroit Red Wings captain Henrik Zetterberg is the recipient of the NHL Foundation Player Award. The NHL Foundation will present $25,000 to the Zetterberg Foundation, to help fund the creation of three water stations in Kemba, Ethiopia, and provide 1,900 people with clean water for a lifetime. This donation will enable more children in the village to attend school as opposed to spending their days walking hours to get water for their families.

Zetterberg and his wife, Emma, give back to the Metro Detroit community through numerous initiatives as well as international causes in Ethiopia, Guatemala and Nepal. Zetterberg hosts children's charities, including Metro Detroit area children's hospitals and mentoring nonprofits, at each Red Wings home game during the regular season in the Zetterberg Foundation Suite. Zetterberg also funds a high school hockey scholarship each year and underwrites the Hockey Weekly High School All-Star Banquet.

As the team spokesman for the Red Wings annual Smoke Detector Collection, Zetterberg personally matches all donations. Working with area fire departments, more than 23,000 smoke detectors have been distributed to low-income and physically disabled residents who could not otherwise afford one or be able to install one in their home. When a local firefighter passed away in the line of duty in May of 2013, Zetterberg contributed to the team fundraiser, helping the Wings raise more than $15,000 for the firefighter's family.

Zetterberg and his wife built the Chige Primary School in Kemba, Ethiopia, in cooperation with Action Aid Ethiopia. The school consists of four classrooms and gives 225 children in Kemba access to a primary school education. The Belta Telo Middle School currently has 780 kids sharing four small classrooms; however, thanks to a donation from the Zetterberg Foundation, construction to add a block of four new classrooms to the school has begun. He also supports microloan programs in Ethiopia and Guatemala to provide women with the opportunity to start their own businesses and work themselves out of poverty. In addition, the Zetterberg Foundation has financed and built six houses for former debt slaves in Nepal.

NATIONAL HOCKEY LEAGUE INDIVIDUAL AWARD WINNERS

CONN SMYTHE TROPHY

	Winner	
2013	Patrick Kane	Chicago
2012	Jonathan Quick	Los Angeles
2011	Tim Thomas	Boston
2010	Jonathan Toews	Chicago
2009	Evgeni Malkin	Pittsburgh
2008	Henrik Zetterberg	Detroit
2007	Scott Niedermayer	Anaheim
2006	Cam Ward	Carolina
2005	....	....
2004	Brad Richards	Tampa Bay
2003	Jean-Sebastien Giguere	Anaheim
2002	Nicklas Lidstrom	Detroit
2001	Patrick Roy	Colorado
2000	Scott Stevens	New Jersey
1999	Joe Nieuwendyk	Dallas
1998	Steve Yzerman	Detroit
1997	Mike Vernon	Detroit
1996	Joe Sakic	Colorado
1995	Claude Lemieux	New Jersey
1994	Brian Leetch	NY Rangers
1993	Patrick Roy	Montreal
1992	Mario Lemieux	Pittsburgh
1991	Mario Lemieux	Pittsburgh
1990	Bill Ranford	Edmonton
1989	Al MacInnis	Calgary
1988	Wayne Gretzky	Edmonton
1987	Ron Hextall	Philadelphia
1986	Patrick Roy	Montreal
1985	Wayne Gretzky	Edmonton
1984	Mark Messier	Edmonton
1983	Billy Smith	NY Islanders
1982	Mike Bossy	NY Islanders
1981	Butch Goring	NY Islanders
1980	Bryan Trottier	NY Islanders
1979	Bob Gainey	Montreal
1978	Larry Robinson	Montreal
1977	Guy Lafleur	Montreal
1976	Reggie Leach	Philadelphia
1975	Bernie Parent	Philadelphia
1974	Bernie Parent	Philadelphia
1973	Yvan Cournoyer	Montreal
1972	Bobby Orr	Boston
1971	Ken Dryden	Montreal
1970	Bobby Orr	Boston
1969	Serge Savard	Montreal
1968	Glenn Hall	St. Louis
1967	Dave Keon	Toronto
1966	Roger Crozier	Detroit
1965	Jean Beliveau	Montreal

FRANK J. SELKE TROPHY

	Winner	Runner-up
2013	Jonathan Toews, Chi.	Patrice Bergeron, Bos.
2012	Patrice Bergeron, Bos.	David Backes, St.L.
2011	Ryan Kesler, Van.	Jonathan Toews, Chi.
2010	Pavel Datsyuk, Det.	Ryan Kesler, Van.
2009	Pavel Datsyuk, Det.	Mike Richards, Phi.
2008	Pavel Datsyuk, Det.	John Madden, N.J.
2007	Rod Brind'Amour, Car.	Samuel Pahlsson, Ana.
2006	Rod Brind'Amour, Car.	Jere Lehtinen, Dal.
2005	....	....
2004	Kris Draper, Det.	John Madden, N.J.
2003	Jere Lehtinen, Dal.	John Madden, N.J.
2002	Michael Peca, NYI	Craig Conroy, Cgy.
2001	John Madden, N.J.	Joe Sakic, Col.
2000	Steve Yzerman, Det.	Michal Handzus, St.L.
1999	Jere Lehtinen, Dal.	Magnus Arvedson, Ott.
1998	Jere Lehtinen, Dal.	Michael Peca, Buf.
1997	Michael Peca, Buf.	Peter Forsberg, Col.
1996	Sergei Fedorov, Det.	Ron Francis, Pit.
1995	Ron Francis, Pit.	Esa Tikkanen, St.L.
1994	Sergei Fedorov, Det.	Doug Gilmour, Tor.
1993	Doug Gilmour, Tor.	Dave Poulin, Bos.
1992	Guy Carbonneau, Mtl.	Sergei Fedorov, Det.
1991	Dirk Graham, Chi.	Esa Tikkanen, Edm.
1990	Rick Meagher, St.L.	Guy Carbonneau, Mtl.
1989	Guy Carbonneau, Mtl.	Esa Tikkanen, Edm.
1988	Guy Carbonneau, Mtl.	Steve Kasper, Bos.
1987	Dave Poulin, Phi.	Guy Carbonneau, Mtl.
1986	Troy Murray, Chi.	Ron Sutter, Phi.
1985	Craig Ramsay, Buf.	Doug Jarvis, Wsh.
1984	Doug Jarvis, Wsh.	Bryan Trottier, NYI
1983	Bobby Clarke, Phi.	Jari Kurri, Edm.
1982	Steve Kasper, Bos.	Bob Gainey, Mtl.
1981	Bob Gainey, Mtl.	Craig Ramsay, Buf.
1980	Bob Gainey, Mtl.	Craig Ramsay, Buf.
1979	Bob Gainey, Mtl.	Don Marcotte, Bos.
1978	Bob Gainey, Mtl.	Craig Ramsay, Buf.

BILL MASTERTON MEMORIAL TROPHY

	Winner	
2013	Josh Harding	Minnesota
2012	Max Pacioretty	Montreal
2011	Ian Laperriere	Philadelphia
2010	Jose Theodore	Washington
2009	Steve Sullivan	Nashville
2008	Jason Blake	Toronto
2007	Phil Kessel	Boston
2006	Teemu Selanne	Anaheim
2005	....	....
2004	Bryan Berard	Chicago
2003	Steve Yzerman	Detroit
2002	Saku Koivu	Montreal
2001	Adam Graves	NY Rangers
2000	Ken Daneyko	New Jersey
1999	John Cullen	Tampa Bay
1998	Jamie McLennan	St. Louis
1997	Tony Granato	San Jose
1996	Gary Roberts	Calgary
1995	Pat LaFontaine	Buffalo
1994	Cam Neely	Boston
1993	Mario Lemieux	Pittsburgh
1992	Mark Fitzpatrick	NY Islanders
1991	Dave Taylor	Los Angeles
1990	Gord Kluzak	Boston
1989	Tim Kerr	Philadelphia
1988	Bob Bourne	Los Angeles
1987	Doug Jarvis	Hartford
1986	Charlie Simmer	Boston
1985	Anders Hedberg	NY Rangers
1984	Brad Park	Detroit
1983	Lanny McDonald	Calgary
1982	Glenn Resch	Colorado
1981	Blake Dunlop	St. Louis
1980	Al MacAdam	Minnesota
1979	Serge Savard	Montreal
1978	Butch Goring	Los Angeles
1977	Ed Westfall	NY Islanders
1976	Rod Gilbert	NY Rangers
1975	Don Luce	Buffalo
1974	Henri Richard	Montreal
1973	Lowell MacDonald	Pittsburgh
1972	Bobby Clarke	Philadelphia
1971	Jean Ratelle	NY Rangers
1970	Pit Martin	Chicago
1969	Ted Hampson	Oakland
1968	Claude Provost	Montreal

ART ROSS TROPHY

	Winner	Runner-up
2013	Martin St. Louis, T.B.	Steven Stamkos, T.B.
2012	Evgeni Malkin, Pit.	Steven Stamkos, T.B.
2011	Daniel Sedin, Van.	Martin St. Louis, T.B.
2010	Henrik Sedin, Van.	Sidney Crosby, Pit.
2009	Evgeni Malkin, Pit.	Alex Ovechkin, Wsh.
2008	Alex Ovechkin, Wsh.	Evgeni Malkin, Pit.
2007	Sidney Crosby, Pit.	Joe Thornton, S.J.
2006	Joe Thornton, Bos., S.J.	Jaromir Jagr, NYR
2005	....	
2004	Martin St. Louis, T.B.	Ilya Kovalchuk, Atl.
2003	Peter Forsberg, Col.	Markus Naslund, Van.
2002	Jarome Iginla, Cgy.	Markus Naslund, Van.
2001	Jaromir Jagr, Pit.	Joe Sakic, Col.
2000	Jaromir Jagr, Pit.	Pavel Bure, Fla.
1999	Jaromir Jagr, Pit.	Teemu Selanne, Ana.
1998	Jaromir Jagr, Pit.	Peter Forsberg, Col.
1997	Mario Lemieux, Pit.	Teemu Selanne, Ana.
1996	Mario Lemieux, Pit.	Jaromir Jagr, Pit.
1995	Jaromir Jagr, Pit.	Eric Lindros, Phi.
1994	Wayne Gretzky, L.A.	Sergei Fedorov, Det.
1993	Mario Lemieux, Pit.	Pat LaFontaine, Buf.
1992	Mario Lemieux, Pit.	Kevin Stevens, Pit.
1991	Wayne Gretzky, L.A.	Brett Hull, St.L.
1990	Wayne Gretzky, L.A.	Mark Messier, Edm.
1989	Mario Lemieux, Pit.	Wayne Gretzky, L.A.
1988	Mario Lemieux, Pit.	Wayne Gretzky, Edm.
1987	Wayne Gretzky, Edm.	Jari Kurri, Edm.
1986	Wayne Gretzky, Edm.	Mario Lemieux, Pit.
1985	Wayne Gretzky, Edm.	Jari Kurri, Edm.
1984	Wayne Gretzky, Edm.	Paul Coffey, Edm.
1983	Wayne Gretzky, Edm.	Peter Stastny, Que.
1982	Wayne Gretzky, Edm.	Mike Bossy, NYI
1981	Wayne Gretzky, Edm.	Marcel Dionne, L.A.
1980	Marcel Dionne, L.A.	Wayne Gretzky, Edm.
1979	Bryan Trottier, NYI	Marcel Dionne, L.A.
1978	Guy Lafleur, Mtl.	Bryan Trottier, NYI
1977	Guy Lafleur, Mtl.	Marcel Dionne, L.A.
1976	Guy Lafleur, Mtl.	Bobby Clarke, Phi.
1975	Bobby Orr, Bos.	Phil Esposito, Bos.
1974	Phil Esposito, Bos.	Bobby Orr, Bos.
1973	Phil Esposito, Bos.	Bobby Clarke, Phi.
1972	Phil Esposito, Bos.	Bobby Orr, Bos.
1971	Phil Esposito, Bos.	Bobby Orr, Bos.
1970	Bobby Orr, Bos.	Phil Esposito, Bos.
1969	Phil Esposito, Bos.	Bobby Hull, Chi.
1968	Stan Mikita, Chi.	Phil Esposito, Bos.
1967	Stan Mikita, Chi.	Bobby Hull, Chi.
1966	Bobby Hull, Chi.	Stan Mikita, Chi.
1965	Stan Mikita, Chi.	Norm Ullman, Det.
1964	Stan Mikita, Chi.	Bobby Hull, Chi.
1963	Gordie Howe, Det.	Andy Bathgate, NYR
1962	Bobby Hull, Chi.	Andy Bathgate, NYR
1961	Bernie Geoffrion, Mtl.	Jean Beliveau, Mtl.
1960	Bobby Hull, Chi.	Bronco Horvath, Bos.
1959	Dickie Moore, Mtl.	Jean Beliveau, Mtl.
1958	Dickie Moore, Mtl.	Henri Richard, Mtl.
1957	Gordie Howe, Det.	Ted Lindsay, Det.
1956	Jean Beliveau, Mtl.	Gordie Howe, Det.
1955	Bernie Geoffrion, Mtl.	Maurice Richard, Mtl.
1954	Gordie Howe, Det.	Maurice Richard, Mtl.
1953	Gordie Howe, Det.	Ted Lindsay, Det.
1952	Gordie Howe, Det.	Ted Lindsay, Det.
1951	Gordie Howe, Det.	Maurice Richard, Mtl.
1950	Ted Lindsay, Det.	Sid Abel, Det.
1949	Roy Conacher, Chi.	Doug Bentley, Chi.
1948*	Elmer Lach, Mtl.	Buddy O'Connor, NYR
1947	Max Bentley, Chi.	Maurice Richard, Mtl.
1946	Max Bentley, Chi.	Gaye Stewart, Tor.
1945	Elmer Lach, Mtl.	Maurice Richard, Mtl.
1944	Herb Cain, Bos.	Doug Bentley, Chi.
1943	Doug Bentley, Chi.	Bill Cowley, Bos.
1942	Bryan Hextall, NYR	Lynn Patrick, NYR
1941	Bill Cowley, Bos.	Bryan Hextall, NYR
1940	Milt Schmidt, Bos.	Woody Dumart, Bos.
1939	Toe Blake, Mtl.	Sweeney Schriner, NYA
1938	Gordie Drillon, Tor.	Syl Apps, Tor.
1937	Sweeney Schriner, NYA	Syl Apps, Tor.
1936	Sweeney Schriner, NYA	Marty Barry, Det.
1935	Charlie Conacher, Tor.	Syd Howe, St.L., Det.
1934	Charlie Conacher, Tor.	Joe Primeau, Tor
1933	Bill Cook, NYR	Busher Jackson, Tor.
1932	Busher Jackson, Tor.	Joe Primeau, Tor.
1931	Howie Morenz, Mtl.	Ebbie Goodfellow, Det.
1930	Cooney Weiland, Bos.	Frank Boucher, NYR
1929	Ace Bailey, Tor.	Nels Stewart, Mtl.M
1928	Howie Morenz, Mtl.	Aurel Joliat, Mtl.
1927	Bill Cook, NYR	Dick Irvin, Chi.
1926	Nels Stewart, Mtl.M.	Cy Denneny, Ott.
1925	Babe Dye, Tor.	Cy Denneny, Ott.
1924	Cy Denneny, Ott.	Billy Boucher, Mtl.
1923	Babe Dye, Tor.	Cy Denneny, Ott.
1922	Punch Broadbent, Ott.	Cy Denneny, Ott.
1921	Newsy Lalonde, Mtl.	Babe Dye, Ham., Tor.
1920	Joe Malone, Que.	Newsy Lalonde, Mtl.
1919	Newsy Lalonde, Mtl.	Odie Cleghorn, Mtl.
1918	Joe Malone, Mtl.	Cy Denneny, Ott.

* Trophy first awarded in 1948.
Scoring leaders listed from 1918 to 1947.

HART MEMORIAL TROPHY

	Winner	Runner-up
2013	Alex Ovechkin, Wsh.	Sidney Crosby, Pit.
2012	Evgeni Malkin, Pit.	Steven Stamkos, T.B.
2011	Corey Perry, Ana.	Daniel Sedin, Van.
2010	Henrik Sedin, Van.	Alex Ovechkin, Wsh.
2009	Alex Ovechkin, Wsh.	Evgeni Malkin, Pit.
2008	Alex Ovechkin, Wsh.	Evgeni Malkin, Pit.
2007	Sidney Crosby, Pit.	Roberto Luongo, Van.
2006	Joe Thornton, Bos., S.J.	Jaromir Jagr, NYR
2005	....	....
2004	Martin St. Louis, T.B.	Jarome Iginla, Cgy.
2003	Peter Forsberg, Col.	Markus Naslund, Van.
2002	Jose Theodore, Mtl.	Jarome Iginla, Cgy.
2001	Joe Sakic, Col.	Mario Lemieux, Pit.
2000	Chris Pronger, St.L.	Jaromir Jagr, Pit.
1999	Jaromir Jagr, Pit.	Alexei Yashin, Ott.
1998	Dominik Hasek, Buf.	Jaromir Jagr, Pit.
1997	Dominik Hasek, Buf.	Paul Kariya, Ana.
1996	Mario Lemieux, Pit.	Mark Messier, NYR
1995	Eric Lindros, Phi.	Jaromir Jagr, Pit.
1994	Sergei Fedorov, Det.	Dominik Hasek, Buf.
1993	Mario Lemieux, Pit.	Doug Gilmour, Tor.
1992	Mark Messier, NYR	Patrick Roy, Mtl.
1991	Brett Hull, St.L.	Wayne Gretzky, L.A.
1990	Mark Messier, Edm.	Raymond Bourque, Bos.
1989	Wayne Gretzky, L.A.	Mario Lemieux, Pit.
1988	Mario Lemieux, Pit.	Grant Fuhr, Edm.
1987	Wayne Gretzky, Edm.	Raymond Bourque, Bos.
1986	Wayne Gretzky, Edm.	Mario Lemieux, Pit.
1985	Wayne Gretzky, Edm.	Dale Hawerchuk, Wpg.
1984	Wayne Gretzky, Edm.	Rod Langway, Wsh.
1983	Wayne Gretzky, Edm.	Pete Peeters, Bos.
1982	Wayne Gretzky, Edm.	Bryan Trottier, NYI
1981	Wayne Gretzky, Edm.	Mike Liut, St.L.
1980	Wayne Gretzky, Edm.	Marcel Dionne, L.A.
1979	Bryan Trottier, NYI	Guy Lafleur, Mtl
1978	Guy Lafleur, Mtl.	Bryan Trottier, NYI
1977	Guy Lafleur, Mtl.	Bobby Clarke, Phi.
1976	Bobby Clarke, Phi.	Denis Potvin, NYI
1975	Bobby Clarke, Phi.	Rogie Vachon, L.A.
1974	Phil Esposito, Bos.	Bernie Parent, Phi.
1973	Bobby Clarke, Phi.	Phil Esposito, Bos.
1972	Bobby Orr, Bos.	Ken Dryden, Mtl.
1971	Bobby Orr, Bos.	Phil Esposito, Bos.
1970	Bobby Orr, Bos.	Tony Esposito, Chi.
1969	Phil Esposito, Bos.	Jean Beliveau, Mtl.
1968	Stan Mikita, Chi.	Jean Beliveau, Mtl.
1967	Stan Mikita, Chi.	Ed Giacomin, NYR
1966	Bobby Hull, Chi.	Jean Beliveau, Mtl.
1965	Bobby Hull, Chi.	Norm Ullman, Det.
1964	Jean Beliveau, Mtl.	Bobby Hull, Chi.
1963	Gordie Howe, Det.	Stan Mikita, Chi.
1962	Jacques Plante, Mtl.	Doug Harvey, NYR
1961	Bernie Geoffrion, Mtl.	Johnny Bower, Tor.
1960	Gordie Howe, Det.	Bobby Hull, Chi.
1959	Andy Bathgate, NYR	Gordie Howe, Det.
1958	Gordie Howe, Det.	Andy Bathgate, NYR
1957	Gordie Howe, Det.	Jean Beliveau, Mtl.
1956	Jean Beliveau, Mtl.	Tod Sloan, Tor.
1955	Ted Kennedy, Tor.	Harry Lumley, Tor.
1954	Al Rollins, Chi.	Red Kelly, Det.
1953	Gordie Howe, Det.	Al Rollins, Chi.
1952	Gordie Howe, Det.	Elmer Lach, Mtl.
1951	Milt Schmidt, Bos.	Maurice Richard, Mtl.
1950	Chuck Rayner, NYR	Ted Kennedy, Tor.
1949	Sid Abel, Det.	Bill Durnan, Mtl.
1948	Buddy O'Connor, NYR	Frank Brimsek, Bos.
1947	Maurice Richard, Mtl.	Milt Schmidt, Bos.
1946	Max Bentley, Chi.	Gaye Stewart, Tor.
1945	Elmer Lach, Mtl.	Maurice Richard, Mtl.
1944	Babe Pratt, Tor.	Bill Cowley, Bos.
1943	Bill Cowley, Bos.	Doug Bentley, Chi.
1942	Tom Anderson, Bro.	Syl Apps, Tor.
1941	Bill Cowley, Bos.	Dit Clapper, Bos.
1940	Ebbie Goodfellow, Det.	Syl Apps, Tor.
1939	Toe Blake, Mtl.	Syl Apps, Tor.
1938	Eddie Shore, Bos.	Paul Thompson, Chi.
1937	Babe Siebert, Mtl.	Lionel Conacher, Mtl.M
1936	Eddie Shore, Bos.	Hooley Smith, Mtl.M
1935	Eddie Shore, Bos.	Charlie Conacher, Tor.
1934	Aurel Joliat, Mtl.	Lionel Conacher, Chi.
1933	Eddie Shore, Bos.	Bill Cook, NYR
1932	Howie Morenz, Mtl.	Ching Johnson, NYR
1931	Howie Morenz, Mtl.	Eddie Shore, Bos.
1930	Nels Stewart, Mtl.M.	Lionel Hitchman, Bos.
1929	Roy Worters, NYA	Ace Bailey, Tor.
1928	Howie Morenz, Mtl.	Roy Worters, Pit.
1927	Herb Gardiner, Mtl.	Bill Cook, NYR
1926	Nels Stewart, Mtl.M.	Sprague Cleghorn, Bos.
1925	Billy Burch, Ham.	Howie Morenz, Mtl.
1924	Frank Nighbor, Ott.	Sprague Cleghorn, Mtl.

WILLIAM M. JENNINGS TROPHY

	Winner	Runner-up
2013	Corey Crawford, Chi.	Craig Anderson, Ott.
	Ray Emery, Chi.	
2012	Brian Elliott, St.L.	Jonathan Quick, L.A.
	Jaroslav Halak, St.L.	
2011	Roberto Luongo, Van.	Pekka Rinne, Nsh.
	Cory Schneider, Van.	
2010	Martin Brodeur, N.J.	Tim Thomas, Bos.
		Tuukka Rask, Bos.
2009	Tim Thomas, Bos.	Niklas Backstrom, Min.
	Manny Fernandez, Bos.	
2008	Chris Osgood, Det.	Jean-Sebastien Giguere, Ana.
	Dominik Hasek, Det.	
2007	Niklas Backstrom, Min.	Dominik Hasek, Det.
	Manny Fernandez, Min.	
2006	Miikka Kiprusoff, Cgy.	Manny Legace, Det.
		Chris Osgood, Det.
2005	....	....
2004	Martin Brodeur, N.J.	Marty Turco, Dal.
2003	Martin Brodeur, N.J.	Marty Turco, Dal.
	Roman Cechmanek, Phi.	Ron Tugnutt, Dal.
	Robert Esche, Phi.	
2002	Patrick Roy, Col.	Tommy Salo, Edm.
2001	Dominik Hasek, Buf.	Ed Belfour, Dal.
		Marty Turco, Dal.
2000	Roman Turek, St.L.	John Vanbiesbrouck, Phi.
		Brian Boucher, Phi.
1999	Ed Belfour, Dal.	Dominik Hasek, Buf.
	Roman Turek, Dal.	
1998	Martin Brodeur, N.J.	Ed Belfour, Dal.
1997	Martin Brodeur, N.J.	Chris Osgood, Det.
	Mike Dunham, N.J.	Mike Vernon, Det.
1996	Chris Osgood, Det.	Martin Brodeur, N.J.
	Mike Vernon, Det.	
1995	Ed Belfour, Chi.	Mike Vernon, Det.
		Chris Osgood, Det.
1994	Dominik Hasek, Buf.	Martin Brodeur, N.J.
	Grant Fuhr, Buf.	Chris Terreri, N.J.
1993	Ed Belfour, Chi.	Felix Potvin, Tor.
		Grant Fuhr, Tor.
1992	Patrick Roy, Mtl.	Ed Belfour, Chi.
1991	Ed Belfour, Chi.	Patrick Roy, Mtl.
1990	Andy Moog, Bos.	Patrick Roy, Mtl.
	Reggie Lemelin, Bos.	Brian Hayward, Mtl.
1989	Patrick Roy, Mtl.	Mike Vernon, Cgy.
	Brian Hayward, Mtl.	Rick Wamsley, Cgy.
1988	Patrick Roy, Mtl.	Clint Malarchuk, Wsh.
	Brian Hayward, Mtl.	Pete Peeters, Wsh.
1987	Patrick Roy, Mtl.	Ron Hextall, Phi.
	Brian Hayward, Mtl.	
1986	Bob Froese, Phi.	Al Jensen, Wsh.
	Darren Jensen, Phi.	Pete Peeters, Wsh.
1985	Tom Barrasso, Buf.	Pat Riggin, Wsh.
	Bob Sauve, Buf.	
1984	Al Jensen, Wsh.	Tom Barrasso, Buf.
	Pat Riggin, Wsh.	Bob Sauve, Buf.
1983	Roland Melanson, NYI	Pete Peeters, Bos.
	Billy Smith, NYI	
1982	Rick Wamsley, Mtl.	Billy Smith, NYI
	Denis Herron, Mtl.	Roland Melanson, NYI

MAURICE "ROCKET" RICHARD TROPHY

	Winner	
2013	Alex Ovechkin	Washington
2012	Steven Stamkos	Tampa Bay
2011	Corey Perry	Anaheim
2010	Sidney Crosby	Pittsburgh
	Steven Stamkos	Tampa Bay
2009	Alex Ovechkin	Washington
2008	Alex Ovechkin	Washington
2007	Vincent Lecavalier	Tampa Bay
2006	Jonathan Cheechoo	San Jose
2005	....	....
2004	Rick Nash	Columbus
	Jarome Iginla	Calgary
	Ilya Kovalchuk	Atlanta
2003	Milan Hejduk	Colorado
2002	Jarome Iginla	Calgary
2001	Pavel Bure	Florida
2000	Pavel Bure	Florida
1999	Teemu Selanne	Anaheim

MARK MESSIER NHL LEADERSHIP AWARD

	Winner	
2013	Daniel Alfredsson	Ottawa
2012	Shane Doan	Phoenix
2011	Zdeno Chara	Boston
2010	Sidney Crosby	Pittsburgh
2009	Jarome Iginla	Calgary
2008	Mats Sundin	Toronto
2007	Chris Chelios	Detroit

NHL GENERAL MANAGER OF THE YEAR AWARD

	Winner	
2013	Ray Shero	Pittsburgh
2012	Doug Armstrong	St. Louis
2011	Mike Gillis	Vancouver
2010	Don Maloney	Phoenix

LADY BYNG MEMORIAL TROPHY

	Winner	Runner-up
2013	Martin St. Louis, T.B.	Patrick Kane, Chi
2012	Brian Campbell, Fla.	Jordan Eberle, Edm.
2011	Martin St. Louis, T.B.	Nicklas Lidstrom, Det.
2010	Martin St. Louis, T.B.	Brad Richards, Dal.
2009	Pavel Datsyuk, Det.	Martin St. Louis, T.B.
2008	Pavel Datsyuk, Det.	Martin St. Louis, T.B.
2007	Pavel Datsyuk, Det.	Martin St. Louis, T.B.
2006	Pavel Datsyuk, Det.	Brad Richards, T.B.
2005	....	....
2004	Brad Richards, T.B.	Daniel Alfredsson, Ott.
2003	Alexander Mogilny, Tor.	Nicklas Lidstrom, Det.
2002	Ron Francis, Car.	Joe Sakic, Col.
2001	Joe Sakic, Col.	Nicklas Lidstrom, Det.
2000	Pavol Demitra, St.L.	Nicklas Lidstrom, Det.
1999	Wayne Gretzky, NYR.	Nicklas Lidstrom, Det.
1998	Ron Francis, Pit.	Teemu Selanne, Ana.
1997	Paul Kariya, Ana.	Teemu Selanne, Ana.
1996	Paul Kariya, Ana.	Adam Oates, Bos.
1995	Ron Francis, Pit.	Adam Oates, Bos.
1994	Wayne Gretzky, L.A.	Adam Oates, Bos.
1993	Pierre Turgeon, NYI	Adam Oates, Bos.
1992	Wayne Gretzky, L.A.	Joe Sakic, Que.
1991	Wayne Gretzky, L.A.	Brett Hull, St.L.
1990	Brett Hull, St.L.	Wayne Gretzky, L.A.
1989	Joe Mullen, Cgy.	Wayne Gretzky, L.A.
1988	Mats Naslund, Mtl.	Wayne Gretzky, Edm.
1987	Joe Mullen, Cgy.	Wayne Gretzky, Edm.
1986	Mike Bossy, NYI	Jari Kurri, Edm.
1985	Jari Kurri, Edm.	Joe Mullen, St.L.
1984	Mike Bossy, NYI	Rick Middleton, Bos.
1983	Mike Bossy, NYI	Rick Middleton, Bos.
1982	Rick Middleton, Bos.	Mike Bossy, NYI
1981	Rick Kehoe, Pit.	Wayne Gretzky, Edm.
1980	Wayne Gretzky, Edm.	Marcel Dionne, L.A.
1979	Bob MacMillan, Atl.	Marcel Dionne, L.A.
1978	Butch Goring, L.A.	Peter McNab, Bos.
1977	Marcel Dionne, L.A.	Jean Ratelle, Bos.
1976	Jean Ratelle, NYR-Bos.	Jean Pronovost, Pit.
1975	Marcel Dionne, Det.	John Bucyk, Bos.
1974	John Bucyk, Bos.	Lowell MacDonald, Pit.
1973	Gilbert Perreault, Buf.	Jean Ratelle, NYR
1972	Jean Ratelle, NYR	John Bucyk, Bos.
1971	John Bucyk, Bos.	Dave Keon, Tor.
1970	Phil Goyette, St.L.	John Bucyk, Bos.
1969	Alex Delvecchio, Det.	Ted Hampson, Oak.
1968	Stan Mikita, Chi.	John Bucyk, Bos.
1967	Stan Mikita, Chi.	Dave Keon, Tor.
1966	Alex Delvecchio, Det.	Bobby Rousseau, Mtl.
1965	Bobby Hull, Chi.	Alex Delvecchio, Det.
1964	Kenny Wharram, Chi.	Dave Keon, Tor.
1963	Dave Keon, Tor.	Camille Henry, NYR
1962	Dave Keon, Tor.	Claude Provost, Mtl.
1961	Red Kelly, Tor.	Norm Ullman, Det.
1960	Don McKenney, Bos.	Andy Hebenton, NYR
1959	Alex Delvecchio, Det.	Andy Hebenton, NYR
1958	Camille Henry, NYR	Don Marshall, Mtl.
1957	Andy Hebenton, NYR	Dutch Reibel, Det.
1956	Dutch Reibel, Det.	Floyd Curry, Mtl.
1955	Sid Smith, Tor.	Danny Lewicki, NYR
1954	Red Kelly, Det.	Don Raleigh, NYR
1953	Red Kelly, Det.	Wally Hergesheimer, NYR
1952	Sid Smith, Tor.	Red Kelly, Det.
1951	Red Kelly, Det.	Woody Dumart, Bos.
1950	Edgar Laprade, NYR	Red Kelly, Det.
1949	Bill Quackenbush, Det.	Harry Watson, Tor.
1948	Buddy O'Connor, NYR	Syl Apps, Tor.
1947	Bobby Bauer, Bos.	Syl Apps, Tor.
1946	Toe Blake, Mtl.	Clint Smith, Chi.
1945	Bill Mosienko, Chi.	Syd Howe, Det.
1944	Clint Smith, Chi.	Herb Cain, Bos.
1943	Max Bentley, Chi.	Buddy O'Connor, Mtl.
1942	Syl Apps, Tor.	Gordie Drillon, Tor.
1941	Bobby Bauer, Bos.	Gordie Drillon, Tor.
1940	Bobby Bauer, Bos.	Clint Smith, NYR
1939	Clint Smith, NYR	Marty Barry, Det.
1938	Gordie Drillon, Tor.	Clint Smith, NYR
1937	Marty Barry, Det.	Gordie Drillon, Tor.
1936	Doc Romnes, Chi.	Sweeney Schriner, NYA
1935	Frank Boucher, NYR	Russ Blinco, Mtl.M
1934	Frank Boucher, NYR	Joe Primeau, Tor.
1933	Frank Boucher, NYR	Joe Primeau, Tor.
1932	Joe Primeau, Tor.	Frank Boucher, NYR
1931	Frank Boucher, NYR	Normie Himes, NYA
1930	Frank Boucher, NYR	Normie Himes, NYA
1929	Frank Boucher, NYR	Harold Darragh, Pit.
1928	Frank Boucher, NYR	George Hay, Det.
1927	Billy Burch, NYA	Dick Irvin, Chi.
1926	Frank Nighbor, Ott.	Billy Burch, NYA
1925	Frank Nighbor, Ott.	none

VEZINA TROPHY

	Winner	Runner-up
2013	Sergei Bobrovsky, CBJ	Henrik Lundqvist, NYR.
2012	Henrik Lundqvist, NYR	Jonathan Quick, L.A.
2011	Tim Thomas, Bos.	Pekka Rinne, Nsh.
2010	Ryan Miller, Buf.	Ilya Bryzgalov, Phx.
2009	Tim Thomas, Bos.	Steve Mason, CBJ
2008	Martin Brodeur, N.J.	Evgeni Nabokov, S.J.
2007	Martin Brodeur, N.J.	Roberto Luongo, Van.
2006	Miikka Kiprusoff, Cgy.	Martin Brodeur, N.J.
2005	....	....
2004	Martin Brodeur, N.J.	Miikka Kiprusoff, Cgy.
2003	Martin Brodeur, N.J.	Marty Turco, Dal.
2002	Jose Theodore, Mtl.	Patrick Roy, Col.
2001	Dominik Hasek, Buf.	Roman Cechmanek, Phi.
2000	Olaf Kolzig, Wsh.	Roman Turek, St.L.
1999	Dominik Hasek, Buf.	Curtis Joseph, Tor.
1998	Dominik Hasek, Buf.	Martin Brodeur, N.J.
1997	Dominik Hasek, Buf.	Martin Brodeur, N.J.
1996	Jim Carey, Wsh.	Chris Osgood, Det.
1995	Dominik Hasek, Buf.	Ed Belfour, Chi.
1994	Dominik Hasek, Buf.	John Vanbiesbrouck, Fla.
1993	Ed Belfour, Chi.	Tom Barrasso, Pit.
1992	Patrick Roy, Mtl.	Kirk McLean, Van.
1991	Ed Belfour, Chi.	Patrick Roy, Mtl.
1990	Patrick Roy, Mtl.	Daren Puppa, Buf.
1989	Patrick Roy, Mtl.	Mike Vernon, Cgy.
1988	Grant Fuhr, Edm.	Tom Barrasso, Buf.
1987	Ron Hextall, Phi.	Mike Liut, Hfd.
1986	John Vanbiesbrouck, NYR	Bob Froese, Phi.
1985	Pelle Lindbergh, Phi.	Tom Barrasso, Buf.
1984	Tom Barrasso, Buf.	Reggie Lemelin, Cgy.
1983	Pete Peeters, Bos.	Roland Melanson, NYI
1982	Billy Smith, NYI	Grant Fuhr, Edm.
1981	Richard Sevigny, Mtl.	Pete Peeters, Phi.
	Denis Herron, Mtl.	Rick St. Croix, Phi.
	Michel Larocque, Mtl.	
1980	Bob Sauve, Buf.	Gerry Cheevers, Bos.
	Don Edwards, Buf.	Gilles Gilbert, Bos.
1979	Ken Dryden, Mtl.	Glenn Resch, NYI
	Michel Larocque, Mtl.	Billy Smith, NYI
1978	Ken Dryden, Mtl.	Bernie Parent, Phi.
	Michel Larocque, Mtl.	Wayne Stephenson, Phi.
1977	Ken Dryden, Mtl.	Glenn Resch, NYI
	Michel Larocque, Mtl.	Billy Smith, NYI
1976	Ken Dryden, Mtl.	Glenn Resch, NYI
		Billy Smith, NYI
1975	Bernie Parent, Phi.	Rogie Vachon, L.A.
		Gary Edwards, L.A.
1974	Bernie Parent, Phi. (tie)	Gilles Gilbert, Bos.
	Tony Esposito, Chi. (tie)	
1973	Ken Dryden, Mtl.	Ed Giacomin, NYR
		Gilles Villemure, NYR
1972	Tony Esposito, Chi.	Cesare Maniago, Min.
	Gary Smith, Chi.	Gump Worsley, Min.
1971	Ed Giacomin, NYR	Tony Esposito, Chi.
	Gilles Villemure, NYR	
1970	Tony Esposito, Chi.	Jacques Plante, St.L.
		Ernie Wakely, St.L.
1969	Jacques Plante, St.L.	Ed Giacomin, NYR
	Glenn Hall, St.L.	
1968	Gump Worsley, Mtl.	Johnny Bower, Tor.
	Rogie Vachon, Mtl.	Bruce Gamble, Tor.
1967	Glenn Hall, Chi.	Charlie Hodge, Mtl.
	Denis DeJordy, Chi.	
1966	Gump Worsley, Mtl.	Glenn Hall, Chi.
	Charlie Hodge, Mtl.	
1965	Terry Sawchuk, Tor.	Roger Crozier, Det.
	Johnny Bower, Tor.	
1964	Charlie Hodge, Mtl.	Glenn Hall, Chi.
1963	Glenn Hall, Chi.	Johnny Bower, Tor.
		Don Simmons, Tor.
1962	Jacques Plante, Mtl.	Johnny Bower, Tor.
1961	Johnny Bower, Tor.	Glenn Hall, Chi.
1960	Jacques Plante, Mtl.	Glenn Hall, Chi.
1959	Jacques Plante, Mtl.	Johnny Bower, Tor.
		Ed Chadwick, Tor.
1958	Jacques Plante, Mtl.	Gump Worsley, NYR
		Marcel Paille, NYR
1957	Jacques Plante, Mtl.	Glenn Hall, Det.
1956	Jacques Plante, Mtl.	Glenn Hall, Det.
1955	Terry Sawchuk, Det.	Harry Lumley, Tor.
1954	Harry Lumley, Tor.	Terry Sawchuk, Det.
1953	Terry Sawchuk, Det.	Gerry McNeil, Mtl.
1952	Terry Sawchuk, Det.	Al Rollins, Tor.
1951	Al Rollins, Tor.	Terry Sawchuk, Det.
1950	Bill Durnan, Mtl.	Harry Lumley, Det.
1949	Bill Durnan, Mtl.	Harry Lumley, Det.
1948	Turk Broda, Tor.	Harry Lumley, Det.
1947	Bill Durnan, Mtl.	Turk Broda, Tor.
1946	Bill Durnan, Mtl.	Frank Brimsek, Bos.
1945	Bill Durnan, Mtl.	Frank McCool, Tor. (tie)
		Harry Lumley, Det. (tie)
1944	Bill Durnan, Mtl.	Paul Bibeault, Tor.
1943	Johnny Mowers, Det.	Turk Broda, Tor.
1942	Frank Brimsek, Bos.	Turk Broda, Tor.
1941	Turk Broda, Tor.	Frank Brimsek, Bos. (tie)
		Johnny Mowers, Det. (tie)
1940	Dave Kerr, NYR	Frank Brimsek, Bos.
1939	Frank Brimsek, Bos.	Dave Kerr, NYR
1938	Tiny Thompson, Bos.	Dave Kerr, NYR
1937	Normie Smith, Det.	Dave Kerr, NYR
1936	Tiny Thompson, Bos.	Mike Karakas, Chi.
1935	Lorne Chabot, Chi.	Alex Connell, Mtl.M
1934	Charlie Gardiner, Chi.	Wilf Cude, Det.
1933	Tiny Thompson, Bos.	John Ross Roach, Det.
1932	Charlie Gardiner, Chi.	Alex Connell, Det.
1931	Roy Worters, NYA	Charlie Gardiner, Chi.
1930	Tiny Thompson, Bos.	Charlie Gardiner, Chi.
1929	George Hainsworth, Mtl.	Tiny Thompson, Bos.
1928	George Hainsworth, Mtl.	Alex Connell, Ott.
1927	George Hainsworth, Mtl.	Clint Benedict, Mtl.M

CALDER MEMORIAL TROPHY

	Winner	Runner-up
2013	Jonathan Huberdeau, Fla.	Brendan Gallagher, Mtl.
2012	Gabriel Landeskog, Col.	Ryan Nugent-Hopkins, Edm.
2011	Jeff Skinner, Car.	Logan Couture, S.J.
2010	Tyler Myers, Buf.	Jimmy Howard, Det.
2009	Steve Mason, CBJ	Bobby Ryan, Ana.
2008	Patrick Kane, Chi.	Nicklas Backstrom, Wsh.
2007	Evgeni Malkin, Pit.	Paul Stastny, Col.
2006	Alex Ovechkin, Wsh.	Sidney Crosby, Pit.
2005	....	....
2004	Andrew Raycroft, Bos.	Michael Ryder, Mtl.
2003	Barret Jackman, St.L.	Henrik Zetterberg, Det.
2002	Dany Heatley, Atl.	Ilya Kovalchuk, Atl.
2001	Evgeni Nabokov, S.J.	Brad Richards, T.B.
2000	Scott Gomez, N.J.	Brad Stuart, S.J.
1999	Chris Drury, Col.	Marian Hossa, Ott.
1998	Sergei Samsonov, Bos.	Mattias Ohlund, Van.
1997	Bryan Berard, NYI	Jarome Iginla, Cgy.
1996	Daniel Alfredsson, Ott.	Eric Daze, Chi.
1995	Peter Forsberg, Que.	Jim Carey, Wsh.
1994	Martin Brodeur, N.J.	Jason Arnott, Edm.
1993	Teemu Selanne, Wpg.	Joe Juneau, Bos.
1992	Pavel Bure, Van.	Nicklas Lidstrom, Det
1991	Ed Belfour, Chi.	Sergei Fedorov, Det.
1990	Sergei Makarov, Cgy.	Mike Modano, Min.
1989	Brian Leetch, NYR	Trevor Linden, Van.
1988	Joe Nieuwendyk, Cgy.	Ray Sheppard, Buf.
1987	Luc Robitaille, L.A.	Ron Hextall, Phi.
1986	Gary Suter, Cgy.	Wendel Clark, Tor.
1985	Mario Lemieux, Pit.	Chris Chelios, Mtl.
1984	Tom Barrasso, Buf.	Steve Yzerman, Det.
1983	Steve Larmer, Chi.	Phil Housley, Buf.
1982	Dale Hawerchuk, Wpg.	Barry Pederson, Bos.
1981	Peter Stastny, Que.	Larry Murphy, L.A.
1980	Raymond Bourque, Bos.	Mike Foligno, Det.
1979	Bobby Smith, Min	Ryan Walter, Wsh.
1978	Mike Bossy, NYI	Barry Beck, Col.
1977	Willi Plett, Atl.	Don Murdoch, NYR
1976	Bryan Trottier, NYI	Glenn Resch, NYI
1975	Eric Vail, Atl.	Pierre Larouche, Pit.
1974	Denis Potvin, NYI	Tom Lysiak, Atl.
1973	Steve Vickers, NYR	Bill Barber, Phi.
1972	Ken Dryden, Mtl.	Rick Martin, Buf.
1971	Gilbert Perreault, Buf.	Jude Drouin, Min.
1970	Tony Esposito, Chi.	Bill Fairbairn, NYR
1969	Danny Grant, Min.	Norm Ferguson, Oak.
1968	Derek Sanderson, Bos.	Jacques Lemaire, Mtl.
1967	Bobby Orr, Bos.	Ed Van Impe, Chi.
1966	Brit Selby, Tor.	Bert Marshall, Det.
1965	Roger Crozier, Det.	Ron Ellis, Tor.
1964	Jacques Laperriere, Mtl.	John Ferguson, Mtl.
1963	Kent Douglas, Tor.	Doug Barkley, Det.
1962	Bobby Rousseau, Mtl.	Cliff Pennington, Bos.
1961	Dave Keon, Tor.	Bob Nevin, Tor.
1960	Bill Hay, Chi.	Murray Oliver, Det.
1959	Ralph Backstrom, Mtl.	Carl Brewer, Tor.
1958	Frank Mahovlich, Tor.	Bobby Hull, Chi.
1957	Larry Regan, Bos.	Ed Chadwick, Tor.
1956	Glenn Hall, Det.	Andy Hebenton, NYR
1955	Ed Litzenberger, Chi.	Don McKenney, Bos.
1954	Camille Henry, NYR	Dutch Reibel, Det.
1953	Gump Worsley, NYR	Gord Hannigan, Tor.
1952	Bernie Geoffrion, Mtl.	Hy Buller, NYR
1951	Terry Sawchuk, Det.	Al Rollins, Tor.
1950	Jack Gelineau, Bos.	Phil Maloney, Bos.
1949	Pentti Lund, NYR	Allan Stanley, NYR
1948	Jim McFadden, Det.	Pete Babando, Bos.
1947	Howie Meeker, Tor.	Jim Conacher, Det.
1946	Edgar Laprade, NYR	George Gee, Chi.
1945	Frank McCool, Tor.	Ken Smith, Bos.
1944	Gus Bodnar, Tor.	Bill Durnan, Mtl.
1943	Gaye Stewart, Tor.	Glen Harmon, Mtl.
1942	Grant Warwick, NYR	Buddy O'Connor, Mtl.
1941	John Quilty, Mtl.	Johnny Mowers, Det.
1940	Kilby MacDonald, NYR	Wally Stanowski, Tor.
1939	Frank Brimsek, Bos.	Roy Conacher, Bos.
1938	Cully Dahlstrom, Chi.	Murph Chamberlain, Tor.
1937	Syl Apps, Tor.	Gordie Drillon, Tor.
1936	Mike Karakas, Chi.	Bucko McDonald, Det.
1935	Sweeney Schriner, NYA	Bert Connelly, NYR
1934	Russ Blinco, Mtl.M.	none
1933	Carl Voss, Det.	none

KING CLANCY MEMORIAL TROPHY

	Winner	
2013	Patrice Bergeron	Boston
2012	Daniel Alfredsson	Ottawa
2011	Doug Weight	NY Islanders
2010	Shane Doan	Phoenix
2009	Ethan Moreau	Edmonton
2008	Vincent Lecavalier	Tampa Bay
2007	Saku Koivu	Montreal
2006	Olaf Kolzig	Washington
2005	....	....
2004	Jarome Iginla	Calgary
2003	Brendan Shanahan	Detroit
2002	Ron Francis	Carolina
2001	Shjon Podein	Colorado
2000	Curtis Joseph	Toronto
1999	Rob Ray	Buffalo
1998	Kelly Chase	St. Louis
1997	Trevor Linden	Vancouver
1996	Kris King	Winnipeg
1995	Joe Nieuwendyk	Calgary
1994	Adam Graves	NY Rangers
1993	Dave Poulin	Boston
1992	Raymond Bourque	Boston
1991	Dave Taylor	Los Angeles
1990	Kevin Lowe	Edmonton
1989	Bryan Trottier	NY Islanders
1988	Lanny McDonald	Calgary

JAMES NORRIS MEMORIAL TROPHY

	Winner	Runner-up
2013	P.K. Subban, Mtl.	Ryan Suter, Min.
2012	Erik Karlsson, Ott.	Shea Weber, Nsh.
2011	Nicklas Lidstrom, Det.	Shea Weber, Nsh.
2010	Duncan Keith, Chi.	Mike Green, Wsh.
2009	Zdeno Chara, Bos.	Mike Green, Wsh.
2008	Nicklas Lidstrom, Det.	Dion Phaneuf, Cgy.
2007	Nicklas Lidstrom, Det.	Scott Niedermayer, Ana.
2006	Nicklas Lidstrom, Det.	Scott Niedermayer, Ana.
2005	....	....
2004	Scott Niedermayer, N.J.	Zdeno Chara, Ott.
2003	Nicklas Lidstrom, Det.	Al MacInnis, St.L.
2002	Nicklas Lidstrom, Det.	Chris Chelios, Det.
2001	Nicklas Lidstrom, Det.	Raymond Bourque, Col.
2000	Chris Pronger, St.L.	Nicklas Lidstrom, Det.
1999	Al MacInnis, St.L.	Nicklas Lidstrom, Det.
1998	Rob Blake, L.A.	Nicklas Lidstrom, Det.
1997	Brian Leetch, NYR	V. Konstantinov, Det.
1996	Chris Chelios, Chi.	Raymond Bourque, Bos.
1995	Paul Coffey, Det.	Chris Chelios, Chi.
1994	Raymond Bourque, Bos.	Scott Stevens, N.J.
1993	Chris Chelios, Chi.	Raymond Bourque, Bos.
1992	Brian Leetch, NYR	Raymond Bourque, Bos.
1991	Raymond Bourque, Bos.	Al MacInnis, Cgy.
1990	Raymond Bourque, Bos.	Al MacInnis, Cgy.
1989	Chris Chelios, Mtl	Paul Coffey, Pit.
1988	Raymond Bourque, Bos.	Scott Stevens, Wsh.
1987	Raymond Bourque, Bos.	Mark Howe, Phi.
1986	Paul Coffey, Edm.	Mark Howe, Phi.
1985	Paul Coffey, Edm.	Raymond Bourque, Bos.
1984	Rod Langway, Wsh.	Paul Coffey, Edm.
1983	Rod Langway, Wsh.	Mark Howe, Phi.
1982	Doug Wilson, Chi.	Raymond Bourque, Bos.
1981	Randy Carlyle, Pit.	Denis Potvin, NYI
1980	Larry Robinson, Mtl.	Borje Salming, Tor.
1979	Denis Potvin, NYI	Larry Robinson, Mtl.
1978	Denis Potvin, NYI	Brad Park, Bos.
1977	Larry Robinson, Mtl.	Borje Salming, Tor.
1976	Denis Potvin, NYI	Brad Park, NYR-Bos.
1975	Bobby Orr, Bos.	Denis Potvin, NYI
1974	Bobby Orr, Bos.	Brad Park, NYR
1973	Bobby Orr, Bos.	Guy Lapointe, Mtl.
1972	Bobby Orr, Bos.	Brad Park, NYR
1971	Bobby Orr, Bos.	Brad Park, NYR
1970	Bobby Orr, Bos.	Brad Park, NYR
1969	Bobby Orr, Bos.	Tim Horton, Tor.
1968	Bobby Orr, Bos.	J.C. Tremblay, Mtl
1967	Harry Howell, NYR	Pierre Pilote, Chi.
1966	Jacques Laperriere, Mtl.	Pierre Pilote, Chi.
1965	Pierre Pilote, Chi.	Jacques Laperriere, Mtl.
1964	Pierre Pilote, Chi.	Tim Horton, Tor.
1963	Pierre Pilote, Chi.	Carl Brewer, Tor.
1962	Doug Harvey, NYR	Pierre Pilote, Chi.
1961	Doug Harvey, Mtl.	Marcel Pronovost, Det.
1960	Doug Harvey, Mtl.	Allan Stanley, Tor.
1959	Tom Johnson, Mtl.	Bill Gadsby, NYR
1958	Doug Harvey, Mtl.	Bill Gadsby, NYR
1957	Doug Harvey, Mtl.	Red Kelly, Det.
1956	Doug Harvey, Mtl.	Bill Gadsby, NYR
1955	Doug Harvey, Mtl.	Red Kelly, Det.
1954	Red Kelly, Det.	Doug Harvey, Mtl.

JACK ADAMS AWARD

	Winner	Runner-up
2013	Paul MacLean, Ott.	Joel Quenneville, Chi.
2012	Ken Hitchcock, St.L.	John Tortorella, NYR
2011	Dan Bylsma, Pit.	Alain Vigneault, Van.
2010	Dave Tippett, Phx.	Barry Trotz, Nsh.
2009	Claude Julien, Bos.	Andy Murray, St.L.
2008	Bruce Boudreau, Wsh.	Guy Carbonneau, Mtl.
2007	Alain Vigneault, Van.	Lindy Ruff, Buf.
2006	Lindy Ruff, Buf.	Peter Laviolette, Car.
2005	....	....
2004	John Tortorella, T.B.	Ron Wilson, S.J.
2003	Jacques Lemaire, Min.	John Tortorella, T.B.
2002	Bob Francis, Phx.	Brian Sutter, Chi.
2001	Bill Barber, Phi.	Scotty Bowman, Det.
2000	Joel Quenneville, St.L.	Alain Vigneault, Mtl.
1999	Jacques Martin, Ott.	Pat Quinn, Tor.
1998	Pat Burns, Bos.	Larry Robinson, L.A.
1997	Ted Nolan, Buf.	Ken Hitchcock, Dal.
1996	Scotty Bowman, Det.	Doug MacLean, Fla.
1995	Marc Crawford, Que.	Scotty Bowman, Det.
1994	Jacques Lemaire, N.J.	Kevin Constantine, S.J.
1993	Pat Burns, Tor.	Brian Sutter, Bos.
1992	Pat Quinn, Van.	Roger Neilson, NYR
1991	Brian Sutter, St.L.	Tom Webster, L.A.
1990	Bob Murdoch, Wpg.	Mike Milbury, Bos.
1989	Pat Burns, Mtl.	Bob McCammon, Van.
1988	Jacques Demers, Det.	Terry Crisp, Cgy.
1987	Jacques Demers, Det.	Jack Evans, Hfd.
1986	Glen Sather, Edm.	Jacques Demers, St.L.
1985	Mike Keenan, Phi.	Barry Long, Wpg.
1984	Bryan Murray, Wsh.	Scotty Bowman, Buf.
1983	Orval Tessier, Chi.	
1982	Tom Watt, Wpg.	
1981	Red Berenson, St.L.	Bob Berry, L.A.
1980	Pat Quinn, Phi.	
1979	Al Arbour, NYI	Fred Shero, NYR
1978	Bobby Kromm, Det.	Don Cherry, Bos.
1977	Scotty Bowman, Mtl.	Tom McVie, Wsh.
1976	Don Cherry, Bos.	
1975	Bob Pulford, L.A.	
1974	Fred Shero, Phi.	

LESTER PATRICK TROPHY

	Winner	
2013	T,B,A,	
2012	Dick Patrick	Bob Chase-Wallestein
2011	Jeff Sauer	Tony Rossi
	Mark Johnson	Bob Pulford
2010	Jerry York	Jack Parker
	Cam Neely	Dave Andrews
2009	Mark Messier	Jim Devellano
	Mike Richter	
2008	Brian Burke	Phil Housley
	Ted Lindsay	Bob Naegele, Jr.
2007	Brian Leetch	Cammi Granato
	Stan Fischler	John Halligan
2006	Red Berenson	Marcel Dionne
	Reed Larson	Glen Sonmor
	Steve Yzerman	
2005	....	
2004	John Davidson	Mike Emrick
	Ray Miron	
2003	Raymond Bourque	Ron DeGregorio
	Willie O'Ree	
2002	Herb Brooks	Larry Pleau
	1960 U.S. Olympic Team	
2001	Gary Bettman	Scotty Bowman
	David Poile	
2000	Mario Lemieux	Craig Patrick
	Lou Vairo	
1999	Harry Sinden	
	1998 U.S. Olympic Women's Team	
1998	Neal Broten	Peter Karmanos
	John Mayasich	Max McNab
1997	Bill Cleary	* Seymour H. Knox III
	Pat LaFontaine	
1996	George Gund	Ken Morrow
	Milt Schmidt	
1995	Bob Fleming	Brian Mullen
	Joe Mullen	
1994	Wayne Gretzky	Robert Ridder
1993	*Frank Boucher	* Mervyn "Red" Dutton
	Bruce McNall	Gil Stein
1992	Al Arbour	Art Berglund
	Lou Lamoriello	
1991	Rod Gilbert	Mike Ilitch
1990	Len Ceglarski	
1989	Dan Kelly	Lou Nanne
	*Lynn Patrick	Bud Poile
1988	Keith Allen	Fred Cusick
	Bob Johnson	
1987	*Hobey Baker	Frank Mathers
1986	John MacInnes	Jack Riley
1985	Jack Butterfield	Arthur M. Wirtz
1984	*Arthur Howey Ross	John A. Ziegler, Jr.
1983	Bill Torrey	
1982	Emile P. Francis	
1981	Charles M. Schulz	
1980	Bobby Clarke	Frederick A. Shero
	Edward M. Snider	1980 U.S. Olympic Team
1979	Bobby Orr	
1978	Phil Esposito	Tom Fitzgerald
	William T. Tutt	William W. Wirtz
1977	Murray A. Armstrong	John P. Bucyk
	John Mariucci	
1976	George A. Leader	Stanley Mikita
	Bruce A. Norris	
1975	William L. Chadwick	Donald M. Clark
	Thomas N. Ivan	
1974	*Weston W. Adams, Sr.	* Charles L. Crovat
	Alex Delvecchio	Murray Murdoch
1973	Walter L. Bush, Jr.	
1972	Clarence S. Campbell	John A. "Snooks" Kelly
	*James D. Norris	Ralph "Cooney" Weiland
1971	William M. Jennings	* Terrance G. Sawchuk
	*John B. Sollenberger	
1970	*James C. V. Hendy	Edward W. Shore
1969	Robert M. Hull	* Edward J. Jeremiah
1968	*Walter A. Brown	* Gen. John R. Kilpatrick
	Thomas F. Lockhart	
1967	*Charles F. Adams	Gordon Howe
	*James Norris, Sr.	
1966	J.J. "Jack" Adams	

* awarded posthumously

PRESIDENTS' TROPHY

	Winner	
2013	Chicago Blackhawks	Pittsburgh Penguins
2012	Vancouver Canucks	New York Rangers
2011	Vancouver Canucks	Washington Capitals
2010	Washington Capitals	San Jose Sharks
2009	San Jose Sharks	Boston Bruins
2008	Detroit Red Wings	San Jose Sharks
2007	Buffalo Sabres	Detroit Red Wings
2006	Detroit Red Wings	Ottawa Senators
2005	....	....
2004	Detroit Red Wings	Tampa Bay Lightning
2003	Ottawa Senators	Dallas Stars
2002	Detroit Red Wings	Boston Bruins
2001	Colorado Avalanche	Detroit Red Wings
2000	St. Louis Blues	Detroit Red Wings
1999	Dallas Stars	New Jersey Devils
1998	Dallas Stars	New Jersey Devils
1997	Colorado Avalanche	Dallas Stars
1996	Detroit Red Wings	Colorado Avalanche
1995	Detroit Red Wings	Quebec Nordiques
1994	New York Rangers	New Jersey Devils
1993	Pittsburgh Penguins	Boston Bruins
1992	New York Rangers	Washington Capitals
1991	Chicago Blackhawks	St. Louis Blues
1990	Boston Bruins	Calgary Flames
1989	Calgary Flames	Montreal Canadiens
1988	Calgary Flames	Montreal Canadiens
1987	Edmonton Oilers	Philadelphia Flyers

TED LINDSAY AWARD

	Winner	
2013	Sidney Crosby	Pittsburgh
2012	Evgeni Malkin	Pittsburgh
2011	Daniel Sedin	Vancouver
2010	Alex Ovechkin	Washington
2009	Alex Ovechkin	Washington
2008	Alex Ovechkin	Washington
2007	Sidney Crosby	Pittsburgh
2006	Jaromir Jagr	NY Rangers
2005	....	....
2004	Martin St. Louis	Tampa Bay
2003	Markus Naslund	Vancouver
2002	Jarome Iginla	Calgary
2001	Joe Sakic	Colorado
2000	Jaromir Jagr	Pittsburgh
1999	Jaromir Jagr	Pittsburgh
1998	Dominik Hasek	Buffalo
1997	Dominik Hasek	Buffalo
1996	Mario Lemieux	Pittsburgh
1995	Eric Lindros	Philadelphia
1994	Sergei Fedorov	Detroit
1993	Mario Lemieux	Pittsburgh
1992	Mark Messier	NY Rangers
1991	Brett Hull	St. Louis
1990	Mark Messier	Edmonton
1989	Steve Yzerman	Detroit
1988	Mario Lemieux	Pittsburgh
1987	Wayne Gretzky	Edmonton
1986	Mario Lemieux	Pittsburgh
1985	Wayne Gretzky	Edmonton
1984	Wayne Gretzky	Edmonton
1983	Wayne Gretzky	Edmonton
1982	Wayne Gretzky	Edmonton
1981	Mike Liut	St. Louis
1980	Marcel Dionne	Los Angeles
1979	Marcel Dionne	Los Angeles
1978	Guy Lafleur	Montreal
1977	Guy Lafleur	Montreal
1976	Guy Lafleur	Montreal
1975	Bobby Orr	Boston
1974	Phil Esposito	Boston
1973	Bobby Clarke	Philadelphia
1972	Jean Ratelle	NY Rangers
1971	Phil Esposito	Boston

NHL LIFETIME ACHIEVEMENT AWARD

	Winner
2013	not awarded
2012	not awarded
2011	not awarded
2010	not awarded
2009	Jean Beliveau
2008	Gordie Howe

NHL FOUNDATION PLAYER AWARD

	Winner	
2013	Henrik Zetterberg	Detroit
2012	Mike Fisher	Nashville
2011	Dustin Brown	Los Angeles
2010	Ryan Miller	Buffalo
2009	Rick Nash	Columbus
2008	Trevor Linden	Vancouver
	Vincent Lecavalier	Tampa Bay
2007	Joe Sakic	Colorado
2006	Marty Turco	Dallas
2004	Jarome Iginla	Calgary
2003	Darren McCarty	Detroit
2002	Ron Francis	Carolina
2001	Olaf Kolzig	Washington
2000	Adam Graves	NY Rangers
1999	Rob Ray	Buffalo
1998	Kelly Chase	St. Louis

NHL Entry Draft

Draft Summary

Following is a summary of the players drafted from the Ontario Hockey League (OHL), Quebec Major Junior Hockey League (QMJHL), Western Hockey League (WHL), United States colleges, United States high schools, European leagues and other North American leagues since 1969. "Other" may include Canadian and U.S. Jr. A and Jr. B, minor professional leagues (AHL, IHL), midget and other teams playing in leagues not listed above.

Year	Total	OHL		QMJHL		WHL		College		Hi School		Int'l		Other	
	Picks	Picks	%	Picks	%	Picks	%	Picks	%	Picks	%	Picks	%	Picks	%
1969	84	36	42.9	11	13.1	20	23.8	7	8.3	-	-	1	1.2	9	10.7
1970	115	51	44.3	13	11.3	22	19.1	16	13.9	-	-	-	-	13	11.3
1971	117	41	35.0	13	11.1	28	23.9	22	18.8	-	-	-	-	13	11.1
1972	152	46	30.3	30	19.7	44	28.9	21	13.8	-	-	-	-	11	7.2
1973	168	56	33.3	24	14.3	49	29.2	25	14.9	-	-	-	-	14	8.3
1974	247	69	27.9	40	16.2	66	26.7	41	16.6	-	-	6	2.4	25	10.1
1975	217	55	25.3	28	12.9	57	26.3	59	27.2	-	-	6	2.8	12	5.5
1976	135	47	34.8	18	13.3	33	24.4	26	19.3	-	-	8	5.9	3	2.2
1977	185	42	22.7	40	21.6	44	23.8	49	26.5	-	-	5	2.7	5	2.7
1978	234	59	25.2	22	9.4	48	20.5	73	31.2	-	-	16	6.8	16	6.8
1979	126	48	38.1	19	15.1	37	29.4	15	11.9	-	-	6	4.8	1	0.8
1980	210	73	34.8	24	11.4	41	19.5	42	20.0	7	3.3	13	6.2	10	4.8
1981	211	59	28.0	28	13.3	37	17.5	21	10.0	17	8.1	32	15.2	17	8.1
1982	252	60	23.8	17	6.7	55	21.8	20	7.9	47	18.7	35	13.9	18	7.1
1983	242	57	23.6	24	9.9	41	16.9	14	5.8	35	14.5	34	14.0	37	15.3
1984	250	55	22.0	16	6.4	37	14.8	22	8.8	44	17.6	40	16.0	36	14.4
1985	252	59	23.4	15	6.0	48	19.0	20	7.9	48	19.0	31	12.3	31	12.3
1986	252	66	26.2	22	8.7	32	12.7	22	8.7	40	15.9	28	11.1	42	16.7
1987	252	32	12.7	17	6.7	36	14.3	40	15.9	69	27.4	38	15.1	20	7.9
1988	252	32	12.7	22	8.7	30	11.9	48	19.0	56	22.2	39	15.5	25	9.9
1989	252	39	15.5	16	6.3	44	17.5	48	19.0	47	18.7	38	15.1	20	7.9
1990	250	39	15.6	14	5.6	33	13.2	38	15.2	57	22.8	53	21.2	16	6.4
1991	264	43	16.3	25	9.5	40	15.2	43	16.3	37	14.0	55	20.8	21	8.0
1992	264	57	21.6	22	8.3	45	17.0	9	3.4	25	9.5	84	31.8	22	8.3
1993	286	60	21.0	23	8.0	44	15.4	17	5.9	33	11.5	78	27.3	31	10.8
1994	286	45	15.7	28	9.8	66	23.1	6	2.1	28	9.8	80	28.0	33	11.5
1995	234	54	23.1	35	15.0	55	23.5	5	2.1	2	0.9	69	29.5	14	6.0
1996	241	51	21.2	31	12.9	54	22.4	25	10.4	6	2.5	58	24.1	16	6.6
1997	246	52	21.1	19	7.7	63	25.6	26	10.6	4	1.6	63	25.6	19	7.7
1998	258	50	19.4	41	15.9	44	17.1	27	10.5	7	2.7	75	29.1	14	5.4
1999	272	52	19.1	20	7.4	40	14.7	36	13.2	9	3.3	94	34.6	21	7.7
2000	293	39	13.3	21	7.2	41	14.0	35	11.9	7	2.4	123	42.0	27	9.2
2001	289	41	14.2	26	9.0	45	15.6	24	8.3	8	2.8	119	41.2	26	9.0
2002	290	35	12.1	23	7.9	43	14.8	41	14.1	6	2.1	110	37.9	32	11.0
2003	292	44	15.1	38	13.0	41	14.0	23	7.9	10	3.4	93	31.8	43	14.7
2004	291	42	14.4	27	9.3	44	15.1	28	9.6	18	6.2	88	30.2	44	15.1
2005	230	43	18.7	23	10.0	43	18.7	13	5.6	18	7.8	50	21.7	40	17.4
2006	213	29	13.6	25	11.7	24	11.2	18	8.4	19	8.9	63	29.5	35	16.4
2007	211	35	16.6	25	11.8	37	17.5	8	3.8	14	6.6	36	17.0	56	56.5
2008	211	46	21.8	27	12.8	37	17.5	9	4.2	15	7.1	39	18.5	38	18.0
2009	210	45	21.4	23	11.0	31	14.8	7	3.3	19	9.0	41	19.5	44	21.0
2010	210	42	20.0	22	10.4	43	20.5	9	4.2	22	10.5	39	18.6	33	15.7
2011	210	46	21.9	22	10.4	33	15.7	11	5.2	18	8.6	48	22.9	32	15.2
2012	211	48	22.7	19	9.0	32	15.2	9	4.3	19	9.0	43	20.4	41	19.4
2013	211	37	17.5	31	14.7	33	15.6	6	2.8	15	7.1	46	21.8	43	20.4
Total		2157	21.2	1069	10.5	1860	18.3	1124	11.0	826	8.1	2023	19.9	1119	11.0

Total Players Drafted (1969-2013): 10,178

Defenseman Seth Jones (left) of the Portland Winterhawks was the top-rated prospect going into the 2013 NHL Entry Draft, but the Colorado Avalanche wanted a forward and selected Nathan MacKinnon (right) of the Halifax Mooseheads with the number-one pick.

History

Year	Location	Date	# Drafted
1963–1970	Montreal	—	321
1971	Queen Elizabeth Hotel, Montreal	June 10	117
1972	Queen Elizabeth Hotel, Montreal	June 8	152
1973	Mount Royal Hotel, Montreal	May 15	168
1974	NHL Montreal Office	May 28	247
1975	NHL Montreal Office	June 3	217
1976	NHL Montreal Office	June 1	135
1977	NHL Montreal Office	June 14	185
1978	Queen Elizabeth Hotel, Montreal	June 15	234
1979	Queen Elizabeth Hotel, Montreal	August 9	126
1980	Montreal Forum	June 11	210
1981	Montreal Forum	June 10	211
1982	Montreal Forum	June 9	252
1983	Montreal Forum	June 8	242
1984	Montreal Forum	June 9	250
1985	Toronto Convention Centre	June 15	252
1986	Montreal Forum	June 21	252
1987	Joe Louis Arena, Detroit	June 13	252
1988	Montreal Forum	June 11	252
1989	Met Sports Center, Minnesota	June 17	252
1990	B.C. Place, Vancouver	June 16	250
1991	Memorial Auditorium, Buffalo	June 22	264
1992	Montreal Forum	June 20	264
1993	Le Colisée, Quebec	June 26	286
1994	Hartford Civic Center	June 28-29	286
1995	Edmonton Coliseum	July 8	234
1996	Kiel Center, St. Louis	June 22	241
1997	Civic Arena, Pittsburgh	June 21	246
1998	Marine Midland Arena, Buffalo	June 27	258
1999	FleetCenter, Boston	June 26	272
2000	Saddledome, Calgary	June 24-25	293
2001	National Car Rental Center, Florida	June 23-24	289
2002	Air Canada Centre, Toronto	June 22-23	290
2003	Gaylord Entertainment Center, Nashville	June 21-22	292
2004	RBC Center, Carolina	June 26-27	291
2005	Sheraton Hotel and Towers, Ottawa	July 30	230
2006	General Motors Place, Vancouver	June 24	213
2007	Nationwide Arena, Columbus	June 22-23	211
2008	Scotiabank Place, Ottawa	June 20-21	211
2009	Bell Centre, Montreal	June 26-27	210
2010	STAPLES Center, Los Angeles	June 25-26	210
2011	Xcel Energy Center, Minnesota	June 24-25	210
2012	CONSOL Energy Center, Pittsburgh	June 22-23	211
2013	Prudential Center, New Jersey	June 30	211

First Selections

Year	Player	Pos	Team	Drafted From	Age
1963	Garry Monahan	LW	Montreal	St. Michael's Juveniles	16.7
1964	Claude Gauthier	RW	Detroit	Comite des jeunes (Rosemont)	16.9
1965	Andre Veilleux	RW	NY Rangers	Montreal Ranger Jr. B	17.5
1966	Barry Gibbs	D	Boston	Estevan Bruins	17.7
1967	Rick Pagnutti	D	Los Angeles	Garson Native Sons	20.6
1968	Michel Plasse	G	Montreal	Drummondville Rangers	20.0
1969	Rejean Houle	LW	Montreal	Montreal Jr. Canadiens	19.8
1970	Gilbert Perreault	C	Buffalo	Montreal Jr. Canadiens	19.7
1971	Guy Lafleur	RW	Montreal	Quebec Remparts	19.9
1972	Billy Harris	RW	NY Islanders	Toronto Marlboros	20.4
1973	Denis Potvin	D	NY Islanders	Ottawa 67's	19.7
1974	Greg Joly	D	Washington	Regina Pats	20.0
1975	Mel Bridgman	C	Philadelphia	Victoria Cougars	20.1
1976	Rick Green	D	Washington	London Knights	20.3
1977	Dale McCourt	C	Detroit	St. Catharines Fincups	20.4
1978	Bobby Smith	C	Minnesota	Ottawa 67's	20.4
1979	Rob Ramage	D	Colorado	London Knights	20.5
1980	Doug Wickenheiser	C	Montreal	Regina Pats	19.2
1981	Dale Hawerchuk	C	Winnipeg	Cornwall Royals	18.2
1982	Gord Kluzak	D	Boston	Nanaimo Islanders	18.3
1983	Brian Lawton	C	Minnesota	Mount St. Charles HS	18.11
1984	Mario Lemieux	C	Pittsburgh	Laval Voisins	18.8
1985	Wendel Clark	LW/D	Toronto	Saskatoon Blades	18.7
1986	Joe Murphy	C	Detroit	Michigan State Spartans	18.8
1987	Pierre Turgeon	C	Buffalo	Granby Bisons	17.10
1988	Mike Modano	C	Minnesota	Prince Albert Raiders	18.0
1989	Mats Sundin	RW	Quebec	Nacka (Sweden)	18.4
1990	Owen Nolan	RW	Quebec	Cornwall Royals	18.4
1991	Eric Lindros	C	Quebec	Oshawa Generals	18.3
1992	Roman Hamrlik	D	Tampa Bay	ZPS Zlin (Czech.)	18.2
1993	Alexandre Daigle	C	Ottawa	Victoriaville Tigres	18.5
1994	Ed Jovanovski	D	Florida	Windsor Spitfires	18.0
1995	Bryan Berard	D	Ottawa	Detroit Jr. Red Wings	18.4
1996	Chris Phillips	D	Ottawa	Prince Albert Raiders	18.3
1997	Joe Thornton	C	Boston	Sault Ste. Marie Greyhounds	17.11
1998	Vincent Lecavalier	C	Tampa Bay	Rimouski Oceanic	18.2
1999	Patrik Stefan	C	Atlanta	Long Beach Ice Dogs (IHL)	18.9
2000	Rick DiPietro	G	NY Islanders	Boston University Terriers	18.9
2001	Ilya Kovalchuk	LW	Atlanta	Spartak (Russia)	18.2
2002	Rick Nash	LW	Columbus	London Knights	18.0
2003	Marc-Andre Fleury	G	Pittsburgh	Cape Breton Screaming Eagles	18.0
2004	Alex Ovechkin	LW	Washington	Dynamo Moscow (Russia)	18.9
2005	Sidney Crosby	C	Pittsburgh	Rimouski Oceanic	17.11
2006	Erik Johnson	D	St. Louis	U.S. National U-18	18.3
2007	Patrick Kane	RW	Chicago	London Knights	18.7
2008	Steven Stamkos	C	Tampa Bay	Sarnia Sting	18.4
2009	John Tavares	C	NY Islanders	London Knights	18.9
2010	Taylor Hall	LW	Edmonton	Windsor Spitfires	18.7
2011	Ryan Nugent-Hopkins	C	Edmonton	Red Deer Rebels	18.2
2012	Nail Yakupov	RW	Edmonton	Sarnia Sting	18.8
2013	Nathan MacKinnon	C	Colorado	Halifax Mooseheads	17.10

Ontario Hockey League Draft Selections by Club

Total	Club	'13	'12	'11	'10	'09	'08	'07	'06	'05	'04	'03	'02	'01	'00	'99	'98	'97	'96	'95	'94	'93	'92	'91	'90	'89	'88	'87	'86	'85	'84	'83	'69 to '82
31	Barrie	–	1	2	2	2	2	–	1	–	–	1	1	1	3	6	3	4	2	–	–	–	–	–	–	–	–	–	–	–	–	–	–
73	Belleville	2	4	1	1	1	3	4	2	2	–	–	2	3	1	5	2	5	–	3	3	–	4	1	2	4	–	2	5	4	4	3	–
37	Brampton	1	1	–	2	2	3	–	4	4	2	4	3	3	6	2	–	–	–	–	–	–	–	–	–	–	–	–	–	–	–	–	–
31	Erie	1	2	–	2	3	1	5	–	2	2	–	2	2	3	2	1	3	–	–	–	–	–	–	–	–	–	–	–	–	–	–	–
87	Guelph	5	4	2	–	5	3	1	1	2	2	1	2	4	1	3	5	1	6	5	7	2	2	–	–	4	–	2	8	3	5	1	–
105	Kingston	2	–	–	2	2	2	–	4	2	–	1	1	2	–	4	1	4	4	3	2	5	3	2	2	–	1	1	4	3	3	1	44
152	Kitchener	2	3	3	1	1	2	4	–	4	2	1	4	1	1	–	5	3	2	4	2	4	1	3	5	7	1	2	3	6	4	8	63
161	London	6	6	2	2	3	1	3	1	3	6	4	2	2	1	4	8	1	4	1	1	4	3	1	3	3	6	2	3	1	7	3	64
32	Mississauga/St. Mike's	1	1	3	3	4	4	–	–	–	4	5	1	5	1	–	–	–	–	–	–	–	–	–	–	–	–	–	–	–	–	–	–
21	Niagara/Mississauga	1	1	3	3	–	1	3	1	1	3	2	–	–	2	–	–	–	–	–	–	–	–	–	–	–	–	–	–	–	–	–	–
164	Oshawa	2	2	5	2	3	2	2	2	–	3	3	3	1	2	3	4	3	1	10	1	4	4	4	2	4	2	3	6	6	6	5	64
144	Ottawa	1	1	2	4	1	2	1	1	2	3	2	–	3	2	6	2	5	2	1	1	4	6	5	5	–	1	2	3	3	2	2	69
47	Owen Sound	3	5	3	4	3	1	1	2	2	1	1	1	–	1	–	1	2	3	2	3	4	2	1	1	–	–	–	–	–	–	–	–
173	Peterborough	–	2	3	2	2	2	1	1	2	5	5	1	2	1	4	1	5	4	5	2	4	4	3	4	2	2	5	2	9	3	7	78
71	Plymouth	1	3	4	3	2	2	3	2	3	3	3	3	3	6	2	2	4	3	6	2	7	2	2	–	–	–	–	–	–	–	–	–
81	Saginaw/North Bay	3	3	4	1	3	3	–	2	3	1	2	2	3	2	2	2	1	1	2	7	2	5	2	4	1	3	3	3	3	4	4	–
38	Sarnia	–	2	1	1	–	4	1	1	3	–	5	2	1	3	1	3	2	7	1	–	–	–	–	–	–	–	–	–	–	–	–	–
122	Sault Ste. Marie	3	3	4	2	1	2	3	–	1	3	1	2	1	1	1	4	1	4	3	4	3	7	2	1	3	2	1	7	5	4	6	37
118	Sudbury	2	–	3	1	2	2	1	2	4	–	1	1	2	–	5	5	3	1	2	2	10	2	8	2	1	–	1	3	5	2	–	45
97	Windsor	1	4	1	4	5	4	2	2	3	2	2	2	2	2	2	1	5	1	4	3	–	3	–	1	2	5	–	7	3	2	2	20

Clubs no longer operating

Total	Club	'13	'12	'11	'10	'09	'08	'07	'06	'05	'04	'03	'02	'01	'00	'99	'98	'97	'96	'95	'94	'93	'92	'91	'90	'89	'88	'87	'86	'85	'84	'83	'69 to '82
27	Brantford	–	–	–	–	–	–	–	–	–	–	–	–	–	–	–	–	–	–	–	–	–	–	–	–	–	–	–	–	–	2	7	18
37	Cornwall	–	–	–	–	–	–	–	–	–	–	–	–	–	–	–	–	–	–	–	–	–	5	3	3	2	3	3	2	2	3	4	7
62	Hamilton	–	–	–	–	–	–	–	–	–	–	–	–	–	–	–	–	–	–	–	–	–	–	2	–	–	4	4	6	3	–	–	43
20	Montreal	–	–	–	–	–	–	–	–	–	–	–	–	–	–	–	–	–	–	–	–	–	–	–	–	–	–	–	–	–	–	–	20
5	Newmarket	–	–	–	–	–	–	–	–	–	–	–	–	–	–	–	–	–	–	–	2	3	–	–	–	–	–	–	–	–	–	–	–
72	Niagara Falls	–	–	–	–	–	–	–	–	–	–	–	–	–	–	–	–	–	6	2	3	4	4	4	4	4	–	–	–	–	–	–	41
52	St. Catharines	–	–	–	–	–	–	–	–	–	–	–	–	–	–	–	–	–	–	–	–	–	–	–	–	–	–	–	–	–	–	–	52
97	Toronto	–	–	–	–	–	–	–	–	–	–	–	–	–	–	–	–	–	–	–	–	–	–	–	–	2	2	1	4	3	4	4	77

Quebec Major Junior Hockey League Draft Selections by Club

Total	Club	'13	'12	'11	'10	'09	'08	'07	'06	'05	'04	'03	'02	'01	'00	'99	'98	'97	'96	'95	'94	'93	'92	'91	'90	'89	'88	'87	'86	'85	'84	'83	'69 to '82
11	Acadie-Bathurst	–	1	–	1	–	–	–	2	–	–	3	2	–	–	2	–	–	–	–	–	–	–	–	–	–	–	–	–	–	–	–	–
27	Baie-Comeau	4	1	1	–	1	2	1	3	–	3	2	1	3	2	–	3	–	–	–	–	–	–	–	–	–	–	–	–	–	–	–	–
12	Blainville-Boisbriand[1]	2	1	1	1	1	2	4	–	–	–	–	–	–	–	–	–	–	–	–	–	–	–	–	–	–	–	–	–	–	–	–	–
19	Cape Breton	1	1	1	1	1	1	–	1	–	3	2	2	1	1	–	3	–	–	–	–	–	–	–	–	–	–	–	–	–	–	–	–
57	Chicoutimi	1	1	1	–	–	3	–	–	4	–	1	3	1	1	–	1	2	–	2	3	1	1	–	1	1	2	2	1	3	–	3	8
59	Drummondville	–	–	2	–	3	–	–	2	2	1	1	–	1	1	–	2	2	3	4	1	2	2	4	–	1	4	2	2	2	1	–	14
81	Gatineau/Hull	2	1	1	3	–	1	1	2	–	4	4	5	2	–	4	3	–	3	3	1	3	3	3	3	2	2	3	4	–	1	3	14
40	Halifax	4	1	2	3	–	–	2	3	1	3	6	–	3	2	–	3	3	1	3	–	–	–	–	–	–	–	–	–	–	–	–	–
80	Lewiston/Sher.	–	–	–	2	1	2	3	2	5	2	1	–	3	–	–	5	1	–	4	2	3	–	–	–	–	–	–	–	–	–	–	44
24	Moncton	–	1	–	2	2	1	1	3	1	2	3	2	–	–	2	2	1	1	–	–	–	–	–	–	–	–	–	–	–	–	–	–
27	PEI/Mtl. Rocket	3	–	–	1	1	2	2	–	2	8	1	3	1	1	2	–	–	–	–	–	–	–	–	–	–	–	–	–	–	–	–	–
32	Quebec	3	3	–	1	1	3	2	2	2	1	3	1	3	–	3	4	–	–	–	–	–	–	–	–	–	–	–	–	–	–	–	–
38	Rimouski	4	2	–	2	2	2	4	–	2	3	4	–	4	2	2	5	–	–	–	–	–	–	–	–	–	–	–	–	–	–	–	–
22	Rouyn-Noranda	2	1	–	1	1	2	1	3	1	–	2	–	–	4	1	3	–	–	–	–	–	–	–	–	–	–	–	–	–	–	–	–
13	Saint John	–	–	5	2	2	1	2	1	–	–	–	–	–	–	–	–	–	–	–	–	–	–	–	–	–	–	–	–	–	–	–	–
88	Shawinigan	1	2	3	1	6	–	1	1	1	3	2	2	1	1	1	3	1	4	2	1	1	3	2	–	2	–	1	2	–	2	5	33
30	Val-d'Or	2	1	3	1	–	2	–	–	2	1	1	1	2	2	3	–	2	4	2	1	–	–	–	–	–	–	–	–	–	–	–	–
41	Victoriaville	2	1	3	–	1	3	1	–	–	–	–	3	1	3	2	1	2	3	1	1	6	2	–	1	–	4	–	–	–	–	–	–

Former club names: [1]–Montreal / St. John's.

Clubs no longer operating

Total	Club	'13	'12	'11	'10	'09	'08	'07	'06	'05	'04	'03	'02	'01	'00	'99	'98	'97	'96	'95	'94	'93	'92	'91	'90	'89	'88	'87	'86	'85	'84	'83	'69 to '82
21	Beauport	–	–	–	–	–	–	–	–	–	–	–	–	–	–	–	–	3	3	7	3	1	3	1	–	–	–	–	–	–	–	–	–
45	Cornwall	–	–	–	–	–	–	–	–	–	–	–	–	–	–	–	–	–	–	–	–	–	–	–	–	–	–	–	–	–	–	–	45
30	Granby	–	–	–	–	–	–	–	–	–	–	–	–	–	–	–	–	1	3	2	5	1	–	2	–	2	–	4	2	2	3	1	–
54	Laval	–	–	–	–	–	–	–	–	–	–	–	–	–	–	–	3	1	2	4	5	2	1	4	3	3	1	3	5	–	2	1	14
12	Longueuil	–	–	–	–	–	–	–	–	–	–	–	–	–	–	–	–	–	–	–	–	–	–	3	2	–	–	1	2	1	2	1	–
32	Montreal Jrs.	–	–	–	–	–	–	–	–	–	–	–	–	–	–	–	–	–	–	–	–	–	–	–	–	–	–	–	–	–	–	–	32
47	Quebec	–	–	–	–	–	–	–	–	–	–	–	–	–	–	–	–	–	–	–	–	–	–	–	–	–	–	–	–	3	2	2	40
15	St. Hyacinthe	–	–	–	–	–	–	–	–	–	–	–	–	–	–	–	–	–	4	–	4	1	2	1	3	–	–	–	–	–	–	–	–
16	St. Jean	–	–	–	–	–	–	–	–	–	–	–	–	–	–	–	–	–	–	1	1	2	1	3	–	1	3	–	1	1	–	2	–
2	St. Jerome	–	–	–	–	–	–	–	–	–	–	–	–	–	–	–	–	–	–	–	–	–	–	–	–	–	–	–	–	–	–	–	2
28	Sorel	–	–	–	–	–	–	–	–	–	–	–	–	–	–	–	–	–	–	–	–	–	–	–	–	–	–	–	–	–	–	–	28
47	Trois Rivieres	–	–	–	–	–	–	–	–	–	–	–	–	–	–	–	–	–	–	–	–	–	1	2	1	3	3	1	–	3	–	3	30
27	Verdun	–	–	–	–	–	–	–	–	–	–	–	–	–	–	–	–	–	–	–	–	–	3	–	–	1	3	–	3	–	3	3	11

Chicago selected Brandon Saad (top) from the Saginaw Spirit of the OHL with the 43rd pick in 2011. The Blackhawks got Corey Crawford from the Moncton Wildcats of the QMJHL 52nd overall in 2003. Both contributed to the Blackhawks' Stanley Cup victory in 2013.

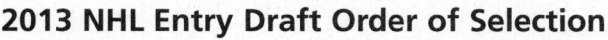

2013 NHL Entry Draft Order of Selection

The first 14 picks of the 2013 Entry Draft were determined by the NHL's annual Draft Drawing, a weighted lottery system used to determine the order of selection.

The 14 teams that did not qualify for the 2013 Stanley Cup Playoffs, or clubs that acquired those clubs' 2013 first-round draft picks, participated in the drawing.

No club can move down more than one position as a result of the Draft Drawing. For 2013, the Colorado Avalanche won the right to the first overall pick, moving up from second overall.

(Note that transferred draft choices are indicated as "N.J. – Van" with the team that selected the player listed at right.)

In the first round of the 2013 Entry Draft, the order of selection was as follows:

a) The winner of the Draft Drawing followed by the remaining non-playoff teams, in inverse order of points. (Note that the original holder of each selection is listed followed by the club that acquired and used that selection in the first round of the 2013 Entry Draft.)

1. Colorado
2. Florida
3. Tampa Bay
4. Nashville
5. Carolina
6. Calgary
7. Edmonton
8. Buffalo
9. N.J. – Van.
10. Dallas
11. Philadelphia
12. Phoenix
13. Winnipeg
14. Columbus

b) Clubs eliminated in the first two rounds of the 2013 Stanley Cup Playoffs, regular-season division winners excluded, in inverse order of points;

15. NY Islanders
16. Min. – Buf.
17. Ottawa
18. Det. – S.J.
19. NYR – CBJ
20. S.J. – Det.
21. Toronto
22. St.L. – Cgy.

c) Regular-season division winning clubs eliminated in the first two rounds of the 2013 Stanley Cup Playoffs, in inverse order of points;

23. Washington
24. Vancouver
25. Montreal
26. Anaheim

d) Clubs eliminated in the 2013 Conference Finals, in inverse order of points;

27. L.A. – CBJ
28. Pit. – Cgy.

e) Loser of Stanley Cup Final

29. Bos. – Dal.

f) Stanley Cup champion

30. Chicago

In the second and subsequent rounds Florida Panthers – the club with the fewest regular-season points – picked first. Colorado Avalanche – the club with the second fewest regular-season points – picked second. Winnipeg Jets received an additional compensatory pick, 59th overall in the second round.

Western Hockey League Draft Selections by Club

Total	Club	'13	'12	'11	'10	'09	'08	'07	'06	'05	'04	'03	'02	'01	'00	'99	'98	'97	'96	'95	'94	'93	'92	'91	'90	'89	'88	'87	'86	'85	'84	'83	'69 to '82
108	Brandon	2	1	1	2	2	2	1	1	2	–	3	4	2	–	–	4	5	2	6	5	2	1	1	1	–	3	3	1	2	3	1	45
44	Calgary	1	3	–	2	2	2	4	1	2	5	3	2	1	4	6	3	–	3	–	–	–	–	–	–	–	–	–	–	–	–	–	–
11	Edmonton	2	3	4	1	1	–	–	–	–	–	–	–	–	–	–	–	–	–	–	–	–	–	–	–	–	–	–	–	–	–	–	–
17	Everett	2	2	–	3	2	1	3	4	–	–	–	–	–	–	–	–	–	–	–	–	–	–	–	–	–	–	–	–	–	–	–	–
114	Kamloops	2	2	–	2	2	–	1	1	2	5	2	5	2	4	4	1	3	4	5	9	2	3	6	4	5	1	3	4	4	4	4	18
45	Kelowna	4	2	1	1	3	4	2	–	2	4	4	1	1	1	2	2	7	4	–	–	–	–	–	–	–	–	–	–	–	–	–	–
22	Kootenay	1	–	1	3	1	–	1	1	3	2	1	3	2	1	2	–	–	–	–	–	–	–	–	–	–	–	–	–	–	–	–	–
92	Lethbridge	–	–	1	–	1	2	2	1	–	2	2	2	1	3	–	1	5	1	3	3	4	3	7	4	3	3	–	1	5	1	2	29
113	Medicine Hat	2	–	1	2	1	2	–	2	4	2	3	3	2	–	1	4	2	7	2	6	1	3	3	1	4	1	5	2	6	1	2	38
68	Moose Jaw	–	2	1	3	–	3	1	1	3	3	3	3	3	5	1	2	4	4	4	3	2	3	2	1	3	–	3	1	4	–	–	–
126	Portland	4	3	4	8	1	–	2	1	3	2	1	2	–	6	1	3	3	1	2	3	4	4	1	1	4	1	3	4	2	5	7	40
85	Prince Albert	1	1	2	–	1	–	–	–	2	4	2	1	4	2	3	3	5	3	4	3	5	2	6	4	3	3	1	6	6	2	2	4
31	Prince George	2	1	–	1	1	–	1	4	1	2	2	–	4	–	2	4	2	2	2	–	–	–	–	–	–	–	–	–	–	–	–	–
52	Red Deer	1	1	2	1	4	1	1	1	1	1	4	4	6	1	1	5	3	4	2	5	3	–	–	–	–	–	–	–	–	–	–	–
117	Regina	2	1	–	2	1	3	3	1	1	–	2	1	2	2	4	2	3	4	2	3	–	4	–	1	5	–	2	3	4	4	8	47
122	Saskatoon	–	3	4	4	3	3	3	–	4	1	–	–	4	1	4	2	2	2	2	4	2	3	2	2	3	4	4	5	1	3	5	42
99	Seattle	1	1	2	1	–	2	1	1	3	2	5	1	5	4	6	2	8	1	5	5	4	2	3	6	2	4	2	1	3	1	–	15
69	Spokane	1	–	3	–	2	3	3	1	4	1	–	3	3	2	1	1	4	5	4	4	4	7	5	1	2	3	1	–	–	–	–	1
71	Swift Current	1	2	3	–	1	4	2	2	1	2	2	4	1	3	1	2	2	1	4	4	5	1	1	2	2	2	5	–	–	–	–	11
57	Tri-City	1	–	1	2	–	2	–	–	2	4	1	3	2	2	1	4	1	6	6	2	2	5	3	3	4	–	–	–	–	–	–	–
24	Vancouver	2	2	2	2	1	3	4	1	3	2	1	1	–	–	–	–	–	–	–	–	–	–	–	–	–	–	–	–	–	–	–	–
9	Victoria/Chilliwack	1	2	–	3	1	–	2	–	–	–	–	–	–	–	–	–	–	–	–	–	–	–	–	–	–	–	–	–	–	–	–	–
	Clubs no longer operating																																
13	Billings	–	–	–	–	–	–	–	–	–	–	–	–	–	–	–	–	–	–	–	–	–	–	–	–	–	–	–	–	–	–	–	13
66	Calgary	–	–	–	–	–	–	–	–	–	–	–	–	–	–	–	–	–	–	–	–	–	–	–	–	–	–	–	2	3	3	3	59
38	Edmonton	–	–	–	–	–	–	–	–	–	–	–	–	–	–	–	–	4	–	–	–	–	–	–	–	–	–	–	–	–	–	–	34
12	Estevan	–	–	–	–	–	–	–	–	–	–	–	–	–	–	–	–	–	–	–	–	–	–	–	–	–	–	–	–	–	–	–	12
39	Flin Flon	–	–	–	–	–	–	–	–	–	–	–	–	–	–	–	–	–	–	–	–	–	–	–	–	–	–	–	–	–	–	–	39
11	Kelowna	–	–	–	–	–	–	–	–	–	–	–	–	–	–	–	–	–	–	–	–	–	–	–	–	–	–	–	–	5	4	2	–
6	Nanaimo	–	–	–	–	–	–	–	–	–	–	–	–	–	–	–	–	–	–	–	–	–	–	–	–	–	–	–	–	–	–	1	5
62	New Westm'r	–	–	–	–	–	–	–	–	–	–	–	–	–	–	–	–	–	–	–	–	–	–	–	–	–	1	2	1	1	2	–	55
12	Tacoma	–	–	–	–	–	–	–	–	–	–	–	–	–	–	–	–	–	–	2	5	2	3	–	–	–	–	–	–	–	–	–	–
2	Vancouver	–	–	–	–	–	–	–	–	–	–	–	–	–	–	–	–	–	–	–	–	–	–	–	–	–	–	–	–	–	–	–	2
79	Victoria	–	–	–	–	–	–	–	–	–	–	–	–	–	–	–	–	–	–	–	2	2	1	–	2	4	4	2	1	2	4	3	52
34	Winnipeg	–	–	–	–	–	–	–	–	–	–	–	–	–	–	–	–	–	–	–	–	–	–	–	–	–	–	–	–	–	–	1	33

U.S. College Hockey Draft Selections by School

Total	Club	'13	'12	'11	'10	'09	'08	'07	'06	'05	'04	'03	'02	'01	'00	'99	'98	'97	'96	'95	'94	'93	'92	'91	'90	'89	'88	'87	'86	'85	'84	'83	'69 to '82
38	Boston College	–	–	–	–	–	1	–	1	1	1	1	3	2	3	–	3	3	2	–	–	–	–	–	–	2	–	2	1	–	–	–	12
56	Boston U.	–	–	3	–	1	1	–	1	–	1	–	3	2	1	3	2	1	1	1	–	1	1	2	2	1	3	2	2	1	1	–	19
28	Bowling Green	–	–	–	–	–	–	–	1	1	–	–	1	1	–	1	1	1	–	–	–	–	1	3	1	2	3	–	–	–	–	1	10
34	Clarkson	–	–	–	1	–	–	–	1	–	–	–	–	–	1	1	3	–	–	–	–	1	1	2	3	1	1	1	–	–	1	1	15
33	Colorado	–	–	–	–	–	–	1	–	1	–	2	1	1	2	1	3	–	–	1	–	–	–	–	2	–	1	–	1	–	3	–	13
36	Cornell	–	2	–	–	–	–	–	–	1	2	2	1	–	2	2	–	1	–	–	–	–	–	–	2	5	2	1	–	2	1	–	10
46	Denver	1	1	1	–	–	–	–	–	2	1	–	1	–	–	1	–	3	–	–	–	–	–	–	–	1	1	4	2	1	–	–	26
35	Harvard	–	–	–	1	–	–	–	–	1	–	–	3	2	2	1	2	1	3	–	1	2	–	–	–	2	1	1	–	2	–	1	9
25	Lake Superior	–	–	–	1	–	–	–	–	–	–	–	1	–	–	1	–	1	1	–	–	1	–	1	3	2	3	–	3	–	1	–	6
22	Maine	–	–	–	–	–	–	–	1	–	1	2	–	–	1	4	1	1	1	–	–	1	–	–	1	2	3	–	1	–	–	1	1
24	Miami U.	–	–	–	–	2	1	1	1	1	2	–	1	1	–	–	1	–	–	–	–	1	1	2	–	2	4	2	–	1	–	–	–
70	Michigan	1	1	–	1	–	–	1	2	1	3	2	3	2	1	2	3	1	3	–	1	1	2	4	5	3	2	1	–	1	1	–	22
49	Michigan State	–	–	–	1	–	–	–	1	–	2	1	4	–	2	2	1	1	1	–	1	1	1	4	5	4	4	1	1	–	2	–	9
46	Michigan Tech	–	–	–	–	–	–	–	–	–	–	–	–	1	–	–	–	–	1	–	2	1	–	2	1	2	1	1	2	2	2	–	29
69	Minnesota	–	–	–	–	1	–	1	1	1	–	2	3	–	3	3	1	2	3	2	–	–	–	–	–	1	1	1	2	–	–	1	40
32	New Hampshire	1	–	–	–	–	–	–	–	–	1	–	1	–	2	1	–	1	–	–	–	–	–	–	–	–	1	–	–	–	2	1	21
40	North Dakota	–	–	1	–	–	–	–	1	–	1	1	1	–	1	1	–	2	–	–	–	–	–	1	1	2	–	–	–	–	1	–	26
30	Northeastern	–	–	1	–	–	–	–	–	–	–	–	–	–	–	1	1	–	–	–	–	–	–	–	1	1	–	–	1	1	–	1	22
24	Northern Mich.	–	–	–	1	–	1	–	–	–	2	2	–	–	1	–	–	–	1	–	–	–	–	1	–	2	1	4	–	–	–	–	8
35	Notre Dame	–	1	1	1	–	–	1	1	–	2	–	2	1	1	2	–	2	1	–	–	–	–	–	–	–	–	–	–	–	–	–	19
21	Ohio State	–	–	–	–	–	–	–	–	1	–	1	2	2	–	1	–	1	1	–	–	1	1	1	1	–	2	2	–	–	1	–	3
37	Providence	1	–	–	–	–	–	–	2	–	–	1	1	–	2	–	2	1	–	–	–	–	–	–	1	–	–	–	1	1	–	2	22
27	RPI	–	–	1	–	–	1	–	–	–	–	–	–	1	2	2	–	1	–	–	–	–	1	3	–	–	2	2	–	1	–	1	9
23	St. Lawrence	–	–	–	–	–	–	–	–	–	–	–	1	–	–	1	–	1	1	–	–	1	–	2	1	1	1	1	1	1	1	–	9
20	Vermont	–	–	–	–	–	–	–	–	1	–	–	–	2	–	–	–	–	1	–	1	–	–	1	–	–	1	–	–	2	1	1	9
26	W. Michigan	–	–	1	–	1	–	–	1	–	–	–	1	–	–	–	1	1	–	–	–	2	–	4	1	1	1	1	2	–	2	2	4
49	Wisconsin	–	2	1	1	–	2	–	–	–	2	–	–	–	3	2	–	–	–	–	–	–	–	1	–	1	–	1	–	1	1	–	31
16	Yale	–	–	–	–	–	–	–	1	–	2	–	3	–	–	–	–	–	–	–	–	1	–	–	–	1	–	2	1	–	–	–	5

Colleges with fewer than 15 players selected: 14 - Brown; 13 - Colgate, Minn.-Duluth; 10 - Dartmouth, Princeton, St.Cloud State; 9 - Ferris State, Merrimack; 7 - Mass.-Lowell; 6 - Illinois-Chicago, St. Louis, Union College; 5 - Nebraska-Omaha, Pennsylvania, Mass.-Amherst, Minnesota State (Mankato); 4 - Alaska-Anchorage; 3 - Babson College, Alaska (Fairbanks); 1 - Air Force, American International College, Army, Bemidji State, Greenway, Hamilton, St. Anselm College, St. Thomas, Salem State, San Diego U., Wisconsin-River Falls.

U.S. High and Prep Schools Draft Selections by School (More than 10 players drafted)

Total	School (State)	'13	'12	'11	'10	'09	'08	'07	'06	'05	'04	'03	'02	'01	'00	'99	'98	'97	'96	'95	'94	'93	'92	'91	'90	'89	'88	'87	'86	'85	'84	'80 to '83
15	Avon Old Farms (CT)	–	–	1	–	1	1	1	–	–	–	–	–	–	–	–	1	1	–	–	–	–	–	–	3	3	–	1	1	1	–	–
16	Belmont Hill (MA)	–	–	–	–	–	–	–	1	–	–	–	–	–	–	–	–	–	–	–	1	–	2	1	2	3	1	1	1	2	–	1
11	Canterbury (CT)	–	–	–	–	–	–	–	–	–	–	1	–	–	–	–	–	–	–	–	–	1	2	–	2	–	3	–	2	–	–	–
16	Catholic Memorial (MA)	–	–	–	–	–	–	–	–	–	2	–	–	–	–	–	1	–	–	–	2	1	2	–	–	3	1	2	–	2	–	–
12	Choate-Rosemary (CT)	–	–	1	–	–	1	–	–	–	–	–	–	–	1	–	–	–	–	–	–	–	1	1	1	–	3	2	–	1	–	–
12	Culver Mil. Acad. (IN)	–	–	–	–	–	–	–	–	–	–	–	–	–	–	–	–	–	–	–	–	2	2	1	2	2	1	2	–	–	–	–
22	Cushing Acad. (MA)	–	–	–	1	–	–	–	1	1	2	–	–	1	–	–	–	1	1	–	2	2	–	1	3	2	3	–	–	–	1	–
14	Deerfield (IL)	–	–	–	–	–	–	1	–	–	1	1	1	–	2	1	–	–	–	–	–	–	–	1	–	2	1	1	–	1	1	–
22	Edina (MN)	1	1	2	–	2	1	–	–	–	–	–	–	–	–	–	–	–	–	–	–	–	1	–	1	2	2	1	–	–	2	6
12	Grand Rapids (MI)	1	1	–	–	–	–	1	–	–	–	–	–	–	–	1	–	–	–	–	–	–	–	1	2	2	1	–	–	–	–	2
15	Hill-Murray (MN)	–	–	–	–	–	–	–	–	–	–	–	–	–	–	–	–	–	–	–	1	–	–	–	3	2	–	3	3	–	3	–
15	Hotchkiss (CT)	1	–	1	–	1	–	–	–	–	1	–	–	1	–	–	–	–	2	1	3	–	–	–	1	–	1	–	1	1	–	–
11	Kent School (CT)	–	1	–	–	–	2	–	–	–	–	–	–	–	–	–	–	–	–	–	2	–	–	–	–	–	–	–	1	2	3	–
14	Minnetonka (MN)	–	–	–	2	1	1	–	–	–	–	–	–	–	–	–	–	–	–	–	–	–	–	1	–	2	–	3	–	2	1	1
13	Mount St. Charles (RI)	–	–	–	–	–	–	–	–	–	–	–	–	–	–	–	–	–	–	–	–	–	–	–	1	1	3	1	2	–	1	4
11	Nobles (MA)	1	3	–	1	1	–	2	–	1	–	–	–	–	–	1	–	–	–	–	–	–	–	–	–	–	–	–	–	1	–	–
19	Northwood (NY)	–	–	–	–	–	1	–	–	–	1	–	–	–	1	–	–	–	–	–	1	1	–	–	3	1	1	2	2	2	–	1
12	Roseau (MN)	–	–	–	–	2	–	–	–	–	–	–	–	–	–	–	–	–	–	–	–	–	–	1	3	1	–	–	1	–	1	3
14	St. Sebastian's (MA)	–	1	–	–	–	–	–	1	–	–	4	1	1	–	–	1	–	–	–	1	2	2	–	–	–	–	–	–	–	–	–
11	St. John's Prep (MA)	1	1	1	–	–	–	–	–	–	–	–	–	–	–	–	–	–	–	–	1	–	–	–	–	–	2	–	–	2	1	2
21	Shattuck-St. Mary's (MN)	1	4	1	3	3	3	1	1	2	–	1	–	–	–	–	–	–	1	–	–	–	–	–	–	–	–	–	–	–	–	–

Schools with 10 players selected: Burnsville (MN), Duluth East (MN), Hibbing (MN), Kent School (CT), Lawrence Academy (MA), Matignon (MA), Thayer Academy (MA).

U.S. College and High School Firsts

Michigan native Mike Modano was playing junior hockey in Saskatchewan when the Minnesota North Stars selected him first overall in 1988.

1967 – First U.S. College Player Drafted • Michigan Tech center Al Karlander was selected 17th overall by the Detroit Red Wings.

1979 – First U.S. College First- Round Selection • Minnesota-born defenseman Mike Ramsey (currently an assistant coach with the Minnesota Wild) was selected 11th overall by the Buffalo Sabres.

1980 – First U.S. High School Player Drafted • Center Jay North of Bloomington-Jefferson H.S. was taken 62nd overall by the Buffalo Sabres in 1980.

1981 – First U.S. High School First- Round Selection • Center Bob Carpenter of St. John's prep school was selected third overall by Washington in 1981.

1983 – First U.S. High School Player Drafted First Overall • Minnesota North Stars selected left winger Brian Lawton from Mount St. Charles H.S. first overall in 1983.

1986 – First U.S. College Player Drafted First Overall • Detroit selected right winger Joe Murphy from Michigan State first overall in 1986.

2003 – Most U.S. College Players Selected in the First Round • The 2003 draft saw seven U.S. college players selected in the first round, the most in Entry Draft history. Six were selected in the first round in 2000 and four in 2001 and 2002. In addition, many players drafted in the first round from the USA U-18 and U-17 teams, high school and prep school programs, U.S. junior and Tier-2 Canadian junior go on to play college hockey.

2013 – Players Born in 22 States Selected • Minnesota, Massachusetts, Michigan and New York led the way, but players born from Alaska to Florida were selected in in 2013.

European Leagues

Ranked by total number of players drafted

Total	Country	'13	'12	'11	'10	'09	'08	'07	'06	'05	'04	'03	'02	'01	'00	'99	'98	'97	'96	'95	'94	'93	'92	'91	'90	'89	'88	'87	'86	'85	'84	'83	'69 to '82
581	Sweden	26	23	25	21	23	19	16	18	15	18	19	24	14	24	24	19	14	16	8	17	18	11	11	7	9	14	15	9	16	14	10	64
550	KHL/Russia/CIS/USSR	8	7	6	4	6	9	7	16	11	24	32	33	36	44	29	22	16	17	27	35	31	45	25	14	18	11	2	1	2	1	5	6
417	CzRep/Slovakia	–	3	5	1	3	2	4	11	15	24	20	21	28	28	20	20	17	14	21	18	15	17	9	21	8	5	11	6	8	13	9	20
355	Finland	10	8	10	7	8	6	4	13	8	14	12	26	29	19	17	12	11	7	12	8	9	8	6	9	3	7	6	10	4	10	9	33
49	Germany	–	–	–	3	1	1	4	2	1	1	4	1	7	1	–	–	1	3	1	1	3	2	1	–	–	2	1	–	1	2	1	4
49	Switzerland	2	1	1	1	–	1	1	3	–	4	5	4	5	7	3	2	3	1	–	1	2	–	1	–	–	–	–	–	–	–	–	1
9	Norway	–	–	1	–	–	1	–	–	–	–	–	1	–	–	–	–	1	–	–	–	–	–	1	2	–	–	2	–	–	–	–	–
6	Denmark	–	1	–	1	–	–	–	–	–	2	–	–	–	–	–	–	–	–	–	–	–	–	–	–	–	–	1	1	–	–	–	–
2	Japan	–	–	–	–	–	–	–	–	–	1	–	–	–	–	–	–	–	–	–	–	–	1	–	–	–	–	–	–	–	–	–	–
2	Poland	–	–	–	–	–	–	–	–	–	–	1	–	–	–	–	–	–	–	–	–	–	–	1	–	–	–	–	–	–	–	–	–
1	Hungary	–	–	–	–	–	–	–	–	–	–	–	–	–	–	1	–	–	–	–	–	–	–	–	–	–	–	–	–	–	–	–	–
1	Latvia	–	–	–	–	–	–	–	–	–	–	–	–	–	–	1	–	–	–	–	–	–	–	–	–	–	–	–	–	–	–	–	–
1	Belarus	–	–	–	1	–	–	–	–	–	–	–	–	–	–	–	–	–	–	–	–	–	–	–	–	–	–	–	–	–	–	–	–
1	Scotland	–	–	–	–	–	–	–	–	–	–	–	–	–	–	–	–	–	–	–	–	–	–	–	–	–	–	–	1	–	–	–	–

Czech Republic and Slovakia

Total	Club	'13	'12	'11	'10	'09	'08	'07	'06	'05	'04	'03	'02	'01	'00	'99	'98	'97	'96	'95	'94	'93	'92	'91	'90	'89	'88	'87	'86	'85	'84	'83	'69 to '82
8	Brno	–	–	–	–	–	–	–	–	–	–	–	–	–	–	–	1	–	–	–	–	–	1	–	2	–	–	3	–	1	–	–	–
33	Ceske Budejovice	–	–	1	–	1	–	–	2	2	1	2	–	2	3	1	1	2	1	3	2	1	–	–	2	1	–	1	–	–	1	1	2
3	Havirov	–	–	–	–	–	–	–	–	–	–	–	2	–	1	–	–	–	–	–	–	–	–	–	–	–	–	–	–	–	–	–	–
28	Jihlava	–	–	–	–	–	–	–	–	–	–	–	–	–	1	–	–	–	2	2	1	1	1	2	3	1	1	3	–	1	3	4	2
4	Karlovy Vary	–	–	–	–	–	–	–	–	–	–	1	1	1	1	–	–	–	–	–	–	–	–	–	–	–	–	–	–	–	–	–	–
23	Kladno	–	–	–	–	–	–	–	3	1	1	1	–	1	1	2	–	–	2	–	2	1	–	2	1	–	–	–	1	–	1	–	3
16	Kosice	–	–	1	–	–	–	–	1	1	–	–	–	1	–	1	1	1	1	–	–	–	–	–	2	–	–	–	1	–	2	–	3
4	Liberec	–	–	–	–	–	–	–	–	1	1	–	–	2	–	–	–	–	–	–	–	–	–	–	–	–	–	–	–	–	–	–	–
34	Litvinov	–	–	–	–	–	–	–	–	–	3	2	–	1	–	1	1	2	2	2	4	2	3	1	2	2	–	–	–	–	2	1	3
6	Martin	–	–	–	–	–	–	–	–	–	1	–	–	1	1	–	–	–	–	2	–	–	–	–	–	–	1	–	–	–	–	–	–
7	Nitra	–	–	–	–	–	–	–	–	–	–	1	–	1	–	–	1	–	1	–	–	1	–	2	–	–	–	–	–	–	–	–	–
7	Olomouc	–	–	–	–	–	–	–	–	–	–	–	–	–	–	–	1	–	–	2	1	–	2	–	–	1	–	–	–	–	–	–	–
14	Pardubice	–	1	–	–	–	–	–	–	–	–	–	3	1	–	–	–	1	–	1	2	–	–	–	–	–	–	1	–	2	–	2	–
15	Plzen	–	1	–	–	–	1	–	–	–	–	–	2	1	1	–	1	–	–	1	1	–	3	–	1	1	–	–	1	–	–	–	–
3	Presov	–	–	–	–	–	–	–	–	1	–	–	–	–	–	–	–	1	–	–	–	1	–	–	–	–	–	–	–	–	–	–	–
30	Slavia Praha	–	1	1	–	–	–	1	–	1	1	2	2	5	3	2	5	4	–	–	–	1	–	–	–	–	–	–	–	–	1	–	–
22	Slovan Bratis.	–	–	–	–	–	–	–	–	–	–	3	1	–	2	2	1	1	1	–	3	–	–	–	1	–	–	1	1	1	–	–	4
29	Sparta Praha	–	–	1	–	–	–	–	1	2	4	1	1	2	1	–	1	1	–	1	–	1	1	–	2	1	2	1	1	1	2	–	1
31	Trencin	–	–	1	–	–	–	1	1	1	4	3	–	2	3	2	–	1	2	1	–	2	2	–	2	1	1	–	–	–	1	–	–
10	Trinec	–	–	–	–	1	1	–	1	1	–	1	1	1	1	2	–	–	–	–	–	–	–	–	–	–	–	–	–	–	–	–	–
19	Vitkovice	–	–	–	–	–	–	–	1	1	2	–	2	–	1	1	1	–	1	1	1	3	1	–	1	–	–	–	–	–	–	–	2
14	Vsetin	–	–	–	–	–	–	1	1	–	1	1	3	2	2	–	1	2	–	–	–	–	–	–	–	–	–	–	–	–	–	–	–
21	Zlin[1]	–	–	–	–	–	–	–	–	1	2	–	–	2	–	2	2	1	–	2	–	1	2	2	–	–	–	1	1	1	–	1	–
8	Zvolen	–	–	–	–	1	–	–	–	–	–	–	–	–	2	2	–	–	1	1	–	–	1	–	–	–	–	–	–	–	–	–	–

Former club names: [1]–Gottwaldov. **Teams with two players selected:** Ingstav Brno, IS Banska Bystrica, Dubnica, Michalovce, Partizan Liptovsky Mikulas, VTJ Pisek, Skalica, Spisska Nova Ves, Topolcany. **Teams with one player selected:** Banik Sokolov, KLH Chomutov, Havlickuv Brod, Ostrava, KC SKP Poprad, Povazska Bystrica, HK Trnava, KHM Zvolen, Slovak U20.

Finland

Total	Club	'13	'12	'11	'10	'09	'08	'07	'06	'05	'04	'03	'02	'01	'00	'99	'98	'97	'96	'95	'94	'93	'92	'91	'90	'89	'88	'87	'86	'85	'84	'83	'69 to '82
17	Assat	–	–	1	–	–	–	–	2	–	–	–	1	–	–	–	1	–	–	1	1	1	–	–	1	–	1	–	–	–	2	2	3
24	Blues Espoo	1	1	1	1	3	1	–	–	1	1	–	1	2	–	2	–	1	–	1	2	–	2	1	1	–	1	–	–	–	–	–	–
42	HIFK Helsinki	–	1	1	1	–	–	–	4	1	2	–	5	2	2	4	2	1	–	1	–	2	–	–	–	1	2	–	–	1	2	2	5
13	HPK	1	–	–	–	–	–	–	1	–	–	–	1	1	3	1	1	1	–	–	–	–	2	–	–	1	–	–	–	–	–	–	–
39	Ilves	1	–	1	2	1	1	–	3	3	–	–	2	4	3	1	2	–	–	2	–	–	–	1	1	–	1	–	1	–	2	2	5
45	Jokerit	1	4	3	1	–	–	–	2	–	1	2	6	4	3	3	1	1	1	–	1	–	3	–	2	–	1	1	–	–	1	–	3
13	JyP Jyvaskyla	–	–	1	–	1	–	–	–	–	1	–	2	1	–	3	–	1	2	–	–	–	–	–	–	–	–	1	–	–	–	–	–
15	KalPa	1	1	1	–	1	1	–	1	–	–	1	–	2	1	–	1	–	–	–	2	1	–	–	–	–	–	1	–	–	–	–	–
29	Karpat	1	1	1	1	1	–	–	–	2	2	3	3	3	–	–	1	1	–	–	–	1	–	1	–	–	–	2	2	–	1	–	2
3	Kiekoo-67	–	–	–	–	–	–	–	–	–	–	–	–	–	–	–	–	–	–	3	–	–	–	–	–	–	–	–	–	–	–	–	–
20	Lukko	–	–	–	–	–	1	1	–	–	1	1	1	3	1	2	–	–	–	–	–	–	1	–	1	–	–	1	–	1	–	2	3
10	Pelicans	1	–	–	–	–	–	1	–	–	1	–	–	–	–	–	–	–	1	–	–	1	–	2	–	–	–	–	–	–	1	1	1
7	SaiPa	–	–	–	–	–	–	–	–	1	1	1	–	1	1	–	–	–	–	–	–	–	–	–	1	–	–	–	–	–	–	–	1
26	Tappara	1	–	–	–	–	2	2	–	–	1	2	2	2	1	–	–	2	1	1	–	–	–	–	1	–	1	–	4	–	–	–	3
37	TPS Turku	1	–	–	–	2	–	–	–	–	1	1	1	3	3	1	3	3	1	3	2	3	–	–	–	–	–	–	1	1	–	–	7

Teams with two players selected: KooKoo Kouvola, K-Vantaa, Sapko Savonlinna, Sport Vaasa, TuTo.
Teams with one player selected: Ahmat Hyvinkaa, Hermes Kokkola, Junkkarit Kalajoki, GrIFK Kauniainen, LeKi, S-Kiekko Seinajoki.

Chosen 147th overall from the WHL's Vancouver Giants in 2010, Montreal's Brendan Gallagher (top) was runner-up to Jonathan Huberdeau for the Calder Trophy in 2012-13. Sweden's Jakob Silfverberg (right) was selected 39th in 2009. He made a strong debut in Ottawa in 2012-13 but was traded to Anaheim in the Bobby Ryan deal after the season.

Note: International draft selections played outside North America in their draft year.

European-born players drafted from the OHL, QMJHL, WHL, U.S. colleges or other North American leagues are not counted as International players.

For analysis by birthplace, see the following page.

2014
NHL Entry Draft
June 27–28, 2014
Wells Fargo Center, Philadelphia

Kontinental Hockey League / Russia / CIS / USSR

Total	Club	'13	'12	'11	'10	'09	'08	'07	'06	'05	'04	'03	'02	'01	'00	'99	'98	'97	'96	'95	'94	'93	'92	'91	'90	'89	'88	'87	'86	'85	'84	'83	'69 to '82
9	Ak Bars Kazan[1]	–	–	–	–	–	1	–	–	–	–	2	–	2	1	1	1	–	–	–	1	–	–	–	–	–	–	–	–	–	–	–	–
17	Atlant Moscow Reg.[2]	–	1	–	–	–	–	–	–	–	–	1	1	1	1	–	3	–	–	–	1	–	2	1	3	1	–	–	–	–	–	1	–
15	Avangard Omsk	–	–	–	–	–	–	1	–	–	1	1	1	6	1	–	–	–	1	–	3	–	–	–	–	–	–	–	–	–	–	–	–
5	CSK VVS Samara	–	–	–	–	–	–	–	–	–	1	1	–	1	–	1	–	–	–	1	–	–	–	–	–	–	–	–	–	–	–	–	–
81	CSKA Moscow	–	2	2	–	–	2	2	3	2	4	5	–	–	–	5	1	2	5	2	5	3	7	4	3	8	5	1	1	1	–	4	2
64	Dynamo Moscow	–	–	–	–	1	–	1	–	–	1	2	–	–	6	2	4	4	1	7	4	3	12	7	4	3	2	–	–	–	–	–	–
4	Dyn-Energ. Yekat.[3]	–	–	–	–	–	–	–	–	–	–	1	–	–	–	1	1	–	1	–	–	–	–	–	–	–	–	–	–	–	–	–	–
16	Elektrostal	–	–	–	–	–	–	–	–	–	–	2	9	1	–	–	1	–	–	–	–	3		–	–	–	–	–	–	–	–	–	–
10	HC CSKA	–	–	–	–	–	–	–	–	–	–	–	5	–	5	–	–	–	–	–	–	–	–	–	–	–	–	–	–	–	–	–	–
4	Kristall Saratov	–	–	–	–	–	–	–	–	–	1	–	–	1	–	–	–	–	–	–	–	1	1	–	–	–	–	–	–	–	–	–	–
37	Krylja Sovetov	–	–	–	–	–	–	–	1	1	2	–	4	1	1	2	1	1	2	3	5	2	3	4	2	1	1	–	–	–	–	–	–
26	Lada Togliatti	–	–	–	–	1	–	–	2	1	2	–	2	2	4	4	1	3	1	–	–	2	1	–	–	–	–	–	–	–	–	–	–
57	Lokomotiv Yaroslavl[4]	2	–	1	–	1	2	1	3	2	–	7	3	1	10	1	6	3	3	6	1	–	–	2	1	–	–	–	–	–	–	–	–
11	Magnitogorsk	–	–	1	–	1	1	–	1	–	2	1	1	3	–	–	–	–	–	–	–	–	–	–	–	–	–	–	–	–	–	–	–
9	Nizhnekamsk	1	–	–	–	–	–	–	1	–	1	–	–	3	2	–	–	1	–	–	–	–	–	–	–	–	–	–	–	–	–	–	–
6	Nizhny Novgorod[5]	–	–	–	–	–	–	–	–	–	–	–	2	–	1	–	–	–	–	–	–	2	–	1	–	–	–	–	–	–	–	–	–
11	Novokuznetsk	–	1	–	1	1	–	–	–	–	1	1	–	1	4	1	–	–	–	–	–	–	–	–	–	–	–	–	–	–	–	–	–
10	Pardaugava Riga[6]	–	–	–	–	–	–	–	–	–	–	–	–	–	–	–	–	–	–	–	–	1	4	1	–	2	1	–	–	–	–	–	1
5	Perm	–	–	–	–	–	–	–	–	–	–	–	1	1	1	–	–	–	–	1	1	–	–	–	–	–	–	–	–	–	–	–	–
20	Severstal Cherepovets[7]	1	–	–	1	–	2	–	1	–	–	2	1	–	2	6	–	–	1	1	–	1	1	–	–	–	–	–	–	–	–	–	–
12	SKA St. Petersburg[8]	–	–	–	–	–	–	–	–	–	–	–	–	2	2	2	–	–	–	–	1	–	1	2	–	–	–	–	–	–	–	–	2
13	Sokol Kiev	–	–	–	–	–	–	–	–	–	–	–	–	–	–	–	1	–	–	2	–	1	3	2	1	1	1	–	–	–	1	–	–
25	Spartak Moscow	–	1	–	–	–	–	–	–	–	2	–	–	6	–	1	–	–	–	1	6	–	4	1	–	–	–	1	–	1	–	–	1
7	THC Tver	–	–	–	–	–	–	–	1	–	3	–	–	1	2	–	–	–	–	–	–	–	–	–	–	–	–	–	–	–	–	–	–
5	Tivali Minsk[9]	–	–	–	–	–	–	–	–	–	1	–	–	–	–	–	–	–	–	–	1	2	–	–	–	–	1	–	–	–	–	–	–
26	Traktor Chelyabinsk	1	–	2	1	–	1	1	1	2	–	–	1	–	–	–	1	1	–	1	2	7	2	–	–	2	–	–	–	–	–	–	–
13	Ufa	1	1	–	–	–	–	–	–	1	–	1	–	–	1	–	–	1	2	1	2	2	–	–	–	–	–	–	–	–	–	–	–
9	Ust-Kamenogorsk	–	–	–	–	–	–	–	–	–	–	1	–	–	–	1	2	–	–	1	2	1	1	–	–	–	–	–	–	–	–	–	–

Former club names: [1]-Ital Kazan, [2]-Khimik Voskresensk, [3]-Avtomobilist Yekaterinburg, [4]-Torpedo Yaroslavl, [5]-Torpedo Gorky, [6]-Dynamo Riga,HC Riga, [7]-Metallurg Cherepovets, [8]-SKA Leningrad, [9]-Dynamo Minsk.

Teams with two players selected: Dizelist Penza, Mechel Chelyabinsk, Neftyanik Almetjevsk, Vityaz Podolsk, Yunost Minsk.

Teams with one player selected: Amur Khabarovsk, Argus Moscow, HC CSKA Moscow 2, Dynamo Khazov, Dynamo-81 Riga, Gazovik Tyumen, HK Gomel, Izohets St. Petersburg, Kapitan Stupino, Khimik Novopolotsk, Metalurgs Liepaja, Mostovik Kurgan, Riga Jr., Spartak St. Petersburg, Sibir Novosibirsk, Sibir Novosibirsk, Slovan Bratislava (SVK), Stalkers-Juniors, HK Zelenograd.

Sweden

Total	Club	'13	'12	'11	'10	'09	'08	'07	'06	'05	'04	'03	'02	'01	'00	'99	'98	'97	'96	'95	'94	'93	'92	'91	'90	'89	'88	'87	'86	'85	'84	'83	'69 to '82
31	AIK Solna	2	–	1	4	–	–	–	–	–	–	–	1	1	–	3	1	1	–	–	1	–	1	1	1	–	–	–	–	4	–	1	8
4	Almtuna	–	–	1	1	1	–	–	–	–	–	–	–	–	–	–	–	–	–	–	–	–	–	–	–	–	–	–	–	–	–	–	2
9	Bjorkloven	–	–	–	–	–	1	–	2	1	–	–	–	–	–	–	–	–	–	–	–	–	–	–	–	–	1	–	–	1	–	–	3
3	Boden	–	–	–	–	–	–	–	–	–	–	–	–	–	–	–	–	–	–	–	1	–	–	–	–	–	–	–	1	–	–	–	1
41	Brynas Gavle	1	3	1	4	3	4	1	1	–	–	2	–	2	1	1	2	1	1	–	–	1	–	–	–	–	–	4	–	–	2	1	5
53	Djurgarden	4	2	3	2	3	1	–	1	1	2	–	2	1	4	1	–	2	2	3	–	1	1	2	1	1	–	2	1	–	1	2	7
3	Falun	–	–	–	–	–	–	–	–	–	–	–	–	–	–	–	–	–	–	–	–	–	–	1	–	–	1	–	–	–	–	–	1
41	Farjestad	2	2	3	–	1	–	–	1	–	–	–	2	1	–	1	6	3	–	2	–	1	2	1	–	1	–	–	–	2	1	1	8
60	Frolunda	4	3	3	1	3	4	5	3	3	4	2	3	3	4	2	1	–	1	1	3	–	1	–	–	1	1	1	–	1	2	–	–
3	Grums	–	–	–	–	–	–	–	–	–	–	–	–	–	1	1	–	–	–	–	1	–	–	–	–	–	–	–	–	–	–	–	–
10	Hammarby	–	–	–	–	–	–	–	1	–	–	–	3	–	1	–	–	1	–	–	–	1	1	–	–	–	–	–	–	–	–	–	2
8	Huddinge	–	1	–	–	–	–	–	1	–	–	–	1	1	–	1	–	–	2	–	–	–	–	1	–	–	–	–	–	–	–	–	–
28	HV 71	–	–	–	1	1	3	1	–	1	2	1	1	–	1	3	4	1	2	–	2	–	–	–	1	–	1	1	–	–	–	–	1
34	Leksand	1	1	1	–	1	–	–	1	1	–	2	–	–	5	–	2	–	1	–	2	2	–	2	–	1	2	1	1	2	2	–	3
13	Linkoping	3	1	3	–	1	1	1	1	1	1	–	–	–	–	–	–	–	–	–	–	–	–	–	–	–	–	–	–	–	–	–	–
17	Lulea	1	1	–	–	1	–	3	–	–	1	–	–	–	2	–	1	1	–	–	–	–	1	–	–	–	1	1	1	–	–	–	2
22	Malmo	1	–	2	–	1	1	1	1	1	1	1	4	–	1	1	–	–	2	–	1	1	1	–	–	–	1	–	–	–	–	–	–
45	MODO	2	3	1	2	1	–	–	–	1	1	–	3	–	3	7	–	3	3	–	–	5	2	2	–	–	–	1	–	–	2	–	3
9	Mora	–	1	1	–	1	–	–	–	–	–	1	–	1	–	–	–	1	1	–	–	–	–	–	–	–	–	–	1	–	–	1	–
3	Morrum	–	–	–	–	–	–	–	–	–	–	–	2	1	–	–	–	–	–	–	–	–	–	–	–	–	–	–	–	–	–	–	–
4	Nacka	–	–	–	–	–	–	–	–	–	–	–	–	–	–	–	–	–	–	–	–	–	2	–	–	1	–	–	1	–	–	–	–
6	Orebro	–	–	–	–	–	–	–	–	–	1	–	–	–	–	–	–	–	–	–	–	–	–	–	–	–	–	1	–	1	–	1	2
3	Ostersund	–	1	–	–	–	–	–	–	–	–	–	–	–	–	–	–	–	–	–	–	–	–	–	–	–	–	1	–	1	–	–	–
3	Pitea	–	–	–	–	–	–	–	–	–	–	–	–	–	–	–	–	–	–	–	1	–	–	–	1	–	–	–	–	–	–	–	1
15	Rogle	2	2	1	–	–	–	1	–	–	–	–	–	–	–	1	–	–	–	1	2	2	–	–	–	–	2	1	–	–	–	–	–
17	Skelleftea	–	1	1	2	3	–	–	–	–	–	–	–	–	–	–	–	1	–	–	–	1	–	–	–	–	1	–	–	–	1	2	4
30	Sodertalje	1	1	1	2	–	–	1	2	3	1	2	–	1	1	–	1	–	–	–	–	1	–	–	–	2	–	–	2	2	2	1	3
3	Stocksund	–	–	–	–	–	–	–	–	–	2	–	–	–	–	–	–	–	–	–	–	–	–	–	–	–	–	–	–	–	–	–	1
3	Team Kiruna	–	–	–	–	–	–	–	–	–	–	–	–	–	–	–	–	–	–	–	–	1	–	–	–	–	–	–	–	–	–	–	2
12	Timra	1	–	–	1	2	–	–	–	–	–	–	1	–	–	1	–	–	–	–	1	–	–	–	–	–	–	–	1	1	–	–	3
3	Tingsryd	1	–	–	–	–	–	–	1	–	–	–	1	–	–	–	–	–	–	–	–	–	–	–	–	–	–	–	–	–	–	–	–
4	Troja/Ljungby	–	–	–	–	–	–	–	–	–	–	1	–	–	–	1	–	–	–	–	–	–	–	–	–	–	1	–	–	1	–	–	–
17	Vasteras	–	–	1	–	–	1	1	3	–	1	–	1	–	1	–	–	–	–	–	1	1	–	1	1	2	2	–	–	–	–	–	–
3	Vita Hasten	–	–	–	–	–	1	–	–	–	–	–	–	1	–	–	–	–	1	–	–	–	–	–	–	–	–	–	–	–	–	–	–

Teams with two players selected: Almtuna, Bofors, Skare, Skovde, Tingsryd. **Teams with one player selected:** Arboga, Arvika, Danderyd Hockey, Fagersta, Jamtland, Karskoga, Kumla, Skovde, Stocksund, S/G Hockey 83 Gavle, Sunne, Talje, Tunabro, Uppsala, Vallentuna, Vasby.

European Draft Firsts

1969 – First European (and Finn) • LW Tommi Salmelainen, 66th overall by St. Louis.

1974 – First Swede • C Per Alexandersson, 49th overall by Toronto. Four other Swedish-born players were selected that year, including defenseman Stefan Persson, 214th overall by the NY Islanders, who became the first European-trained player to be part of a Stanley Cup winner with the Islanders in 1980.

1975 – First Russian • C Viktor Khatulev, 160th overall by Philadelphia.

1976 – First European Taken in the First Round • Swedish D Bjorn Johansson, 5th overall by the California Seals.

1976 – First Swiss • C Jacques Soguel, 121st overall by St. Louis.

1978 – First Czechoslovak • LW Ladislav Svozil, 194th overall by Detroit.

1978 – First Germans • G Bernard Englbrecht, 196th overall by Atlanta and F Gerd Truntschka, 200th overall by St. Louis.

1989 – First European Taken First Overall • Swedish C Mats Sundin, 1st overall by Quebec in 1989.

2013 Entry Draft Analysis

BY BIRTHPLACE

Country of Origin

Country	Players Drafted
Canada	96
USA	57
Sweden	23
Finland	11
Russia	8
Czech Republic	4
Switzerland	4
Denmark	2
Austria	2
Slovakia	2
Norway	1
Latvia	1
Total	**211**

Canadian-Born Players

Province	Players Drafted
Ontario	31
Quebec	24
Alberta	17
British Columbia	15
Saskatchewan	4
Manitoba	3
Nova Scotia	2
Total	**96**

U.S.-Born Players

State	Players Drafted
Minnesota	11
Massachusetts	6
Michigan	5
New York	5
Illinois	4
Connecticut	3
New Jersey	3
Pennsylvania	3
California	2
Iowa	2
Wisconsin	2
Alaska	1
Arizona	1
Colorado	1
Florida	1
Idaho	1
Missouri	1
Montana	1
Nebraska	1
North Dakota	1
South Carolina	1
Texas	1
Total	**57**

BY BIRTH YEAR

Year	Players Drafted
1995	124
1994	66
1993	16
1992	5

BY POSITION

Position	Players Drafted
Defense	69
Center	56
Left wing	39
Right wing	26
Goaltender	21

Notes on 2013 First-Round Selections

1. COLORADO • **NATHAN MacKINNON** *(NAY-thuhn muh-KIHN-uhn)*, C. With a great combination of skill and determination, Nathan MacKinnon led Halifax to the 2013 Memorial Cup championship with a tournament-leading 13 points (seven goals, six assists), including a hat trick in the final game. A great skater with great vision and a great hockey sense, MacKinnon represented Canada at the 2013 World Junior Championship and won a gold medal at the 2012 Ivan Hlinka tournament. MacKinnon is from Cole Harbour, Nova Scotia; the same home town as Sidney Crosby.

2. FLORIDA • **ALEKSANDER BARKOV** *(al-ehx-AN-duhr BAHR-kawv)*, C. Finnish-born but of Russian heritage, Aleksander Barkov is a great all-around player with a high hockey IQ. Barkov is a smart, two-way center who finished among the top 10 in scoring in the Finnish elite league as a 17-year-old in 2012-13. He became the youngest Finnish player to score at the World Junior Championship in 2012 and played at the tournament again in 2013. His father, Alexander, played hockey for Russia and his mother played basketball.

3. TAMPA BAY • **JONATHAN DROUIN** *(JAWN-ah-thuhn DROO-ehn)*, LW. A hard worker with plenty of offensive skill, Jonathan Drouin had 105 points (41 goals, 64 assists) in just 49 games for Halifax in 2012-13 and helped the Mooseheads win the Memorial Cup for the first time. Drouin was named the Canadian Hockey League's Player of the Year, becoming the first player to claim the award in his first year of draft eligibility since Sidney Crosby in 2004-05.

4. NASHVILLE • **SETH JONES** *(SEHTH JOHNZ)*, D. A big, rangy, two-way defenseman, Seth Jones has an excellent hockey sense and strong skating and shooting skills. The youngest member of Team USA's gold medal-winning team at the 2013 World Junior Championship, he also helped Portland reach the Memorial Cup final in 2012-13. Jones previously captained Team USA to gold at the 2012 U-18 World Championship. He is the son of NBA player Popeye Jones.

5. CAROLINA • **ELIAS LINDHOLM** *(eh-LIGH-us LIHND-hohlm)*, C. A gritty, hard-working, two-way player, Elias Lindholm is an excellent skater who finishes his checks very well. Lindholm's father, Mikael, was selected 237th overall by Los Angeles in 1987 and played 18 games for the Kings during the 1989-90 season. His cousin Calle Jarnkrok was drafted 51st by Detroit in 2010. Lindholm won silver medals at the 2013 World Junior Championship and 2012 U-18 Worlds.

6. CALGARY • **SEAN MONAHAN** *(SHAWN MAWN-ah-han)*, C. A good offensive player who sees the ice well, Sean Monahan was voted among the top three in four separate categories – Smartest Player, Best Playmaker, Best Stickhandler and Best on Face-Offs – despite playing with a weak Ottawa team in the OHL in 2012-13. Monahan was the youngest member of Team Canada at the 2012 Canada-Russia Challenge and won gold for Canada at the 2011 Ivan Hlinka Memorial Tournament.

7. EDMONTON • **DARNELL NURSE** *(dahr-NEHL NUHRS)*, D. A strong skater who stands 6'4", Darnell Nurse is a ferocious defender who excels physically. He was also the Ontario Hockey League's Scholastic Player of the Year for 2012-13. Previously, Nurse won gold with Team Canada at the 2012 Ivan Hlinka Tournament and bronze at the 2012 U-18 World Championship. He is the son of former CFL player Richard Nurse and the nephew of former NFL star Donovan McNabb.

8. BUFFALO • **RASMUS RISTOLAINEN** *(RAZ-muhs rihs-toh-LIGH-nehn)*, D. Standing 6'4" and weighing 224 pounds, Rasmus Ristolainen is a mature, reliable, well-rounded defenseman. He has played against men for two seasons in the Finnish elite league and also represented his country at the World Junior Championship in 2012 and 2013. Ristolainen knows how to use his size and strength and also has good puck-handling and passing skills.

9. VANCOUVER • **BO HORVAT** *(BOH HOHR-vat)*, C. A great competitor with a dynamic power game, Bo Horvat is strong on face-offs. He also scored a league-leading 16 goals in 21 games during the 2013 OHL playoffs, including the game-winning goal in Game 7 of the championship series with 0.1 seconds left in regulation. Horvat represented Canada at the 2012 Ivan Hlinka Memorial Tournament alongside London teammate and fellow first-round draft pick Max Domi.

10. DALLAS • **VALERI NICHUSHKIN** *(VAL-uhr-ee nih-KOOSH-kihn)*, RW. At 6'4" and 202 pounds, Valeri Nichushkin is an elite offensive playmaker who can dominate games. He's an excellent skater with excellent vision. Nichushkin scored the winning goal against Canada in overtime of the bronze medal game at the 2013 World Junior Championship and also played for Russia at the U-18 World Championship. In 2012 he won gold at the U-17 World Hockey Challenge.

11. PHILADELPHIA • **SAMUEL MORIN** *(sam-YUHL moh-REHN)*, D. A mobile defenseman with above average offensive skills, Samuel Morin stands 6'6" and brings a physical presence to his game. Named to the QMJHL all-rookie team in 2011-12, Morin missed time due to an injury in 2012-13 but returned in time for the playoffs and had seven points (one goal, six assists) in six games. He then helped Canada win a gold medal at the U-18 World Championship.

12. PHOENIX • **MAX DOMI** *(MAX DOH-mee)*, C/LW. The son of NHL tough guy Tie Domi, Max Domi is a skilled offensive player who stands just 5'9" but weighs 195 pounds and plays with strength and grit. Domi finished second in OHL playoff scoring with 32 points (11 goals, 21 assists) in 21 games for London in 2013 after finishing eighth in the regular season with 87 points (39, 48) in 64 games. Domi was captain of Team Ontario at the 2012 U-17 World Hockey Challenge and won gold for Canada at the 2012 Ivan Hlinka tournament.

13. WINNIPEG • **JOSHUA MORRISSEY** *(JAW-shoo-wuh MOHR-ih-see)*, D. An offensive-minded defenseman who loves to rush the puck, Joshua Morrissey reaches top speed quickly and has a good hockey sense. Playing for Prince Albert in the WHL, he was named the Canadian Hockey League's Scholastic Player of the Year in 2013. Morrissey represented Canada at the U-18 World Championship for the second straight time in 2013 and was the top-scoring defensemen at the tournament as Canada won a gold medal.

14. COLUMBUS • **ALEXANDER WENNBERG** *(al-ehx-AN-duhr WEHN-burgh)*, C. A slick offensive talent who plays the game with speed, Alexander Wennberg is not flashy but plays a skilled, smart game. He goes straight for the net and has a quick release on his shot. Wennberg ranked fourth in scoring as a teenager playing against men for Djurgarden in the Swedish second division in 2012-13. He won silver medals for Sweden at the 2013 World Junior Championship and at the 2012 U-18 World Championship.

15. NY ISLANDERS • **RYAN PULOCK** *(RIGH-uhn POO-lawk)*, D. A well-rounded defenseman with a hard, heavy shot, Ryan Pulock tied for the team lead with 45 points (14 goals, 31 points) in 61 games as captain of the Brandon Wheat Kings in 2012-13 and reached 101 mph on a slap shot at a team skills competition. He had 60 points (19, 41) in 71 games in 2011-12 and broke Wade Redden's franchise record for 16-year-old defensemen with 42 points (8, 34) as a rookie in 2010-11.

16. BUFFALO • **NIKITA ZADOROV** *(nih-KEE-tuh za-DOHR-awv)*, D. A mobile defenseman who uses his size (6'5", 219 lbs,) and stick extremely well, Nikita Zadorov takes the body and battles hard along the boards. With London in the OHL in 2012-13, Zadorov led all rookies in plus-minus at +33. He won gold for Russia at the 2012 U-17 World Hockey Challenge and also played at the 2012 U-18 World Championship, but was a late cut before the 2013 World Junior Championship.

17. OTTAWA • **CURTIS LAZAR** *(KUHR-tihs lah-ZAHR)*, C/RW. A very good two-way player, Curtis Lazar has good puck-handling ability and skates well. As captain of Team British Columbia at the 2011 Canada Winter Games, Lazar had 12 goals and 17 points in six games to break previous tournament records held by Steven Stamkos and Sidney Crosby. He won a gold medal for Canada at the 2012 Ivan Hlinka tournament and helped Edmonton reach the WHL Final in 2013.

18. SAN JOSE • **MIRCO MUELLER** *(MIHR-koh MEW-luhr)*, D. A big (6'3"), explosive puck-moving defenseman, Mirco Mueller plays well in all game situations. He's quick, with a good hockey sense. Mueller played in the Swiss elite league as a 16-year-old in 2011-12 before joining Everett of the WHL in 2012-13 and finishing second among rookie defensemen in scoring. He also represented Switzerland at the World Junior Championship and U-18 World Championship in 2013.

19. COLUMBUS • **KERBY RYCHEL** *(KUHR-bee RIGH-kuhl)*, LW. A solid goal scorer who can also compete hard physically, Kerby Rychel has scored at least 40 goals in two straight OHL seasons for the Windsor Spitfires, where his father – former NHL player Warren Rychel – is general manager and part owner. Rychel scored the winning goal in the gold medal game for Canada at the 2011 U-17 World Hockey Challenge and won bronze at the 2012 U-18 World Championship.

20. DETROIT • **ANTHONY MANTHA** *(AN-thuh-nee MAN-tha)*, RW. A big (6'4", 190 lbs) player who plays a finesse game, Anthony Mantha was the only one of three 50-goal scorers in Major Junior hockey in 2012-13 that was still eligible for the NHL Entry Draft. Mantha's 50 goals in 67 games included five hat tricks and a four-goal game. In 2012, he won bronze with Canada at the U-18 World Championship. Mantha's grandfather, Andre Pronovost, won the Stanley Cup four times with Montreal in the 1950s.

21. TORONTO • **FREDERIK GAUTHIER** *(FREHD-RIHK goh-T'YAY)*, C. A solid two-way player who's always around the puck in his own end, Frederik Gauthier is strong on face-offs. At 6'5" and 214 pounds, he has good size and reach. Though recruited by Harvard, Gauthier joined Rimouski in the QMJHL and led all rookies in face-off winning percentage in 2012-13. He helped Team Canada win gold at the 2013 U-18 World Championship with three assists in seven playoff games. In 2011-12, he was MVP of the Quebec midget AAA league.

22. CALGARY • **EMILE POIRIER** *(eh-MEEL p'wah-REE-ay)*, LW. A quick skater with good two-way instincts, Emile Poirier has a competitive nature and the ability to find open areas on the ice. Poirier led Gatineau with 32 goals in 2012-13 (more than doubling the 15 he scored as a QMJHL rookie in 2011-12), 38 assists and 70 points. His strong play in the playoffs sparked Gatineau's upset of Rimouski in the first round and he finished the playoffs with 10 points (six goals, four assists) in 10 games.

23. WASHINGTON • **ANDRE BURAKOVSKY** *(ahn-DRAY buhr-a-KAWV-skee)*, LW. Though he struggled playing against men in the Swedish elite league, Andre Burakovsky is a dynamic and creative offensive forward. He failed to make Sweden's team for the 2013 World Junior Championship, but starred at the Five Nations tournament. Burakovsky did represent Sweden at the U-18 World Championship in 2012. His father, Robert, was selected 217th overall in 1985 by the Rangers and played 23 games for Ottawa in 1993-94.

24. VANCOUVER • **HUNTER SHINKARUK** *(HUHN-tuhr shihn-KA-ruhk)*, C/LW. A hard worker with passion in his game, Hunter Shinkaruk is an exciting player to watch. He missed his entire midget season with a broken leg, but became rookie of the year in Medicine Hat in 2010-11 and has become a top scorer in the WHL and captain of the Tigers. Shinkaruk had a hat trick, including the overtime winner, in the bronze medal game of the 2012 U-18 World championship.

25. MONTREAL • **MICHAEL McCARRON** *(MIGH-kuhl muh-KAIR-uhn)*, RW. A massive player at 6'5" and 237 pounds, Michael McCarron creates space and causes havoc. He has a strong game down low, soft hands, and a good shot. A product of the U.S. National Team Development Program, McCarron led the team with 182 penalty minutes in 59 games in 2012-13. He played a big role on the U.S. team that won a silver medal at the 2013 U-18 World Championship.

26. ANAHEIM • **SHEA THEODORE** *(SHAY THEE-oh-dohr)*, D. An offensive-minded defenseman with technical skill, Shea Theodore is a smart player with good size (6'1") and good movement. Theodore finished eighth among WHL defensemen in scoring (19 goals, 31 assists, 50 points) with Seattle in 2012-13. He had five assists to help Team Canada win gold at the 2013 U-18 World Championship and was also a gold medalist at the Ivan Hlinka tournament in 2012.

27. COLUMBUS • **MARKO DANO** *(MAHR-koh DA-NOH)*, C. A skilled and opportunistic forward, Marko Dano plays an exciting game. He played as an 18-year-old with Bratislava in the KHL in 2012-13, but his season was shortened due to an injury. Dano had nine points (four goals, five assists) for Slovakia at the 2013 World Junior Championship. He has good instincts around the net and knows how to get open. Dano can also create time and space for his linemates.

28. CALGARY • **MORGAN KLIMCHUK** *(MOHR-guhn KLIHM-chuhk)*, LW. A dangerous offensive player, Morgan Klimchuk is also a smart two-way forward. His 36 goals for Regina in 2012-13 doubled the 18 he'd scored the year before as a WHL rookie. Klimchuk played on the top line with future prospects Connor McDavid and Sam Reinhart on Canada's gold medal team at the 2013 U-18 World Championship and also won gold in 2012 at the Ivan Hlinka tournament.

29. DALLAS • **JASON DICKINSON** *(JAY-suhn DIH-kihn-suhn)*, C. A good offensive player with slick hands, Jason Dickinson can play in all situations. He led Guelph in plus-minus with a +19 in 66 games during the 2012-13 OHL season after being named to the Second All-Rookie team in 2011-12. Dickinson played for Canada's gold medal-winning team at the 2013 Under-18 World Championship, but his tournament was cut short due to an injury.

30. CHICAGO • **RYAN HARTMAN** *(RIGH-uhn HAHRT-man)*, RW. An agitating two-way forward, Ryan Hartman shows no fear in battling for the puck. He sees the ice well and has a good, quick shot. Hartman is a product of the U.S. National Team Development Program who passed on the NCAA to play with Plymouth in the OHL in 2012-13. He won gold with Team USA at the 2012 Under-18 World Championship and the 2013 World Junior Championship.

1: Nathan MacKinnon
C – Colorado

2: Aleksander Barkov
C – Florida

3: Jonathan Drouin
LW – Tampa Bay

4: Seth Jones
D – Nashville

5: Elias Lindholm
C – Carolina

6: Sean Monahan
C – Ottawa

7: Darnell Nurse
D – Edmonton

8: Rasmus Ristolainen
D – Buffalo

9: Bo Horvat
C – London

10: Valeri Nichushkin
RW – Dallas

Players selected first through tenth in the 2013 NHL Entry Draft.

2013 NHL ENTRY DRAFT

FIRST ROUND

Pick	Claimed by		Amateur Club	Position
1	COL	Nathan MacKinnon	Halifax	C
2	FLA	Aleksander Barkov	Tappara	C
3	T.B.	Jonathan Drouin	Halifax	LW
4	NSH	Seth Jones	Portland	D
5	CAR	Elias Lindholm	Brynas	C
6	CGY	Sean Monahan	Ottawa	C
7	EDM	Darnell Nurse	Sault Ste. Marie	D
8	BUF	Rasmus Ristolainen	TPS	D
9	VAN	Bo Horvat	London	C
10	DAL	Valeri Nichushkin	Chelyabinsk	RW
11	PHI	Samuel Morin	Rimouski	D
12	PHX	Max Domi	London	C/LW
13	WPG	Joshua Morrissey	Prince Albert	D
14	CBJ	Alexander Wennberg	Djurgarden	C
15	NYI	Ryan Pulock	Brandon	D
16	BUF	Nikita Zadorov	London	D
17	OTT	Curtis Lazar	Edmonton	C/RW
18	S.J.	Mirco Mueller	Everett	D
19	CBJ	Kerby Rychel	Windsor	LW
20	DET	Anthony Mantha	Val-D'Or	RW
21	TOR	Frederik Gauthier	Rimouski	C
22	CGY	Emile Poirier	Gatineau	LW
23	WSH	Andre Burakovsky	Malmo	LW
24	VAN	Hunter Shinkaruk	Medicine Hat	C/LW
25	MTL	Michael McCarron	USA U-18	RW
26	ANA	Shea Theodore	Seattle	D
27	CBJ	Marko Dano	Bratislava	C
28	CGY	Morgan Klimchuk	Regina	LW
29	DAL	Jason Dickinson	Guelph	C
30	CHI	Ryan Hartman	Plymouth	RW

SECOND ROUND

Pick	Claimed by		Amateur Club	Position
31	FLA	Ian McCoshen	Waterloo	D
32	COL	Chris Bigras	Owen Sound	D
33	T.B.	Adam Erne	Quebec	LW
34	MTL	Jacob de la Rose	Leksand	LW
35	BUF	J.T. Compher	USA U-18	LW
36	MTL	Zachary Fucale	Halifax	G
37	L.A.	Valentin Zykov	Baie-Comeau	LW
38	BUF	Connor Hurley	Edina High	C
39	PHX	Laurent Dauphin	Chicoutimi	C
40	DAL	Remi Elie	London	LW
41	PHI	Robert Hagg	MODO Jr.	D
42	N.J.	Steven Santini	USA U-18	D
43	WPG	Nicolas Petan	Portland	C
44	PIT	Tristan Jarry	Edmonton	G
45	ANA	Nick Sorensen	Quebec	RW
46	MIN	Gustav Olofsson	Green Bay	D
47	STL	Thomas Vannelli	Minnetonka	D
48	DET	Zach Nastasiuk	Owen Sound	RW
49	S.J.	Gabryel Boudreau	Baie-Comeau	LW
50	CBJ	Dillon Heatherington	Swift Current	D
51	CHI	Carl Dahlstrom	Linkoping Jr.	D
52	BUF	Justin Bailey	Kitchener	RW
53	WSH	Madison Bowey	Kelowna	D
54	DAL	Philippe Desrosiers	Rimouski	G
55	MTL	Artturi Lehkonen	Kalpa	LW
56	EDM	Marc-Olivier Roy	Blainville-Boisbriand	C
57	STL	William Carrier	Cape Breton	LW
58	DET	Tyler Bertuzzi	Guelph	LW
59	WPG	Eric Comrie	Tri-City	G
60	BOS	Linus Arnesson	Djurgarden	D
61	WSH	Zachary Sanford	Islanders	LW

THIRD ROUND

Pick	Claimed by		Amateur Club	Position
62	PHX	Yan Pavel Laplante	PEI	C
63	COL	Spencer Martin	Mississauga	G
64	NSH	Jonathan Diaby	Victoriaville	D
65	NYR	Adam Tambellini	Surrey	C
66	CAR	Brett Pesce	New Hampshire	D
67	CGY	Keegan Kanzig	Victoria	D
68	DAL	Niklas Hansson	Rogle Jr.	D
69	BUF	Nicholas Baptiste	Sudbury	RW
70	NYI	Eamon McAdam	Waterloo	G
71	MTL	Connor Crisp	Erie	LW
72	PHI	Tyrell Goulbourne	Kelowna	LW
73	N.J.	Ryan Kujawinski	Kingston	C
74	CHI	John Hayden	USA U-18	C
75	NYR	Pavel Buchnevich	Cherepovets 2	LW
76	NYI	Taylor Cammarata	Waterloo	C/LW
77	PIT	Jake Guentzel	Sioux City	C
78	OTT	Marcus Hogberg	Linkoping Jr.	G
79	DET	Mattias Janmark-Nylen	AIK	C
80	NYR	Anthony Duclair	Quebec	LW
81	MIN	Kurtis Gabriel	Owen Sound	RW
82	TOR	Carter Verhaeghe	Niagara	C
83	EDM	Bogdan Yakimov	Nizhnekamsk 2	C
84	WPG	James Lodge	Saginaw	C
85	VAN	Cole Cassels	Oshawa	C
86	MTL	Sven Andrighetto	Rouyn-Noranda	RW
87	ANA	Keaton Thompson	USA U-18	D
88	EDM	Anton Slepyshev	Ufa	LW
89	CBJ	Oliver Bjorkstrand	Portland	RW
90	BOS	Peter Cehlarik	Lulea Jr.	LW
91	WPG	J.C. Lipon	Kamloops	RW

FOURTH ROUND

Pick	Claimed by		Amateur Club	Position
92	FLA	Evan Cowley	Wichita Falls	G
93	COL	Mason Geertsen	Vancouver	D
94	EDM	Jackson Houck	Vancouver	RW
95	NSH	Felix Girard	Baie-Comeau	C
96	EDM	Kyle Platzer	London	C
97	FLA	Michael Downing	Dubuque	D
98	FLA	Matt Buckles	St. Michael's	C
99	NSH	Juuse Saros	HPK Jr.	G
100	N.J.	Miles Wood	Nobles	LW
101	DAL	Nicholas Paul	Brampton	LW
102	OTT	Tobias Lindberg	Djurgarden Jr.	RW
103	L.A.	Justin Auger	Guelph	RW
104	WPG	Andrew Copp	U of Michigan	C
105	CBJ	Nick Moutrey	Saginaw	C/LW
106	NYI	Stephon Williams	Minnesota State	G
107	MIN	Dylan Labbe	Shawinigan	D
108	OTT	Ben Harpur	Guelph	D
109	DET	David Pope	West Kelowna	LW
110	NYR	Ryan Graves	PEI	D
111	CHI	Robin Norell	Djurgarden Jr.	D
112	STL	Zachary Pochiro	Prince George	LW
113	EDM	Aidan Muir	Victory Honda Midget	W
114	WPG	Jan Kostalek	Rimouski	D
115	VAN	Jordan Subban	Belleville	D
116	MTL	Martin Reway	Gatineau	LW
117	S.J.	Fredrik Bergvik	Frolunda Jr.	G
118	L.A.	Hudson Fasching	USA U-18	RW
119	PIT	Ryan Segalla	Salisbury	D
120	BOS	Ryan Fitzgerald	Valley	C
121	CHI	Tyler Motte	USA U-18	C

FIFTH ROUND

Pick	Claimed by		Amateur Club	Position
122	FLA	Christopher Clapperton	Blainville-Boisbriand	LW
123	COL	Will Butcher	USA U-18	D
124	T.B.	Kristers Gudlevskis	Riga 2	G
125	NSH	Saku Maenalanen	Karpat Jr.	RW
126	CAR	Brent Pedersen	Kitchener	LW
127	WPG	Tucker Poolman	Omaha	D
128	EDM	Evan Campbell	Langley	LW
129	BUF	Calvin Petersen	Waterloo	G
130	BUF	Gustav Possler	MODO Jr.	RW
131	DAL	Cole Ully	Kamloops	LW
132	PHI	Terrance Amorosa	Holderness	D
133	PHX	Connor Clifton	USA U-18	D
134	CHI	Luke Johnson	Lincoln	C
135	CGY	Eric Roy	Brandon	D
136	NYI	Viktor Crus Rydberg	Linkoping Jr.	C
137	MIN	Carson Soucy	Spruce Grove	D
138	OTT	Vincent Dunn	Val-D'Or	C
139	DET	Mitchell Wheaton	Kelowna	D
140	NSH	Teemu Kivihalme	Burnsville	D
141	S.J.	Michael Brodzinski	Muskegon	D
142	TOR	Fabrice Herzog	Zug Jr.	RW
143	BUF	Anthony Florentino	Selects U18 - South Kent	D
144	WSH	Blake Heinrich	Sioux City	D
145	VAN	Anton Cederholm	Rogle Jr.	D
146	L.A.	Patrik Bartosak	Red Deer	G
147	ANA	Grant Besse	Benilde-St. Margaret's	RW
148	L.A.	Jonny Brodzinski	St. Cloud State	C
149	DAL	Matej Paulovic	Farjestad Jr.	LW
150	BOS	Wiley Sherman	Hotchkiss School	D
151	S.J.	Gage Ausmus	USA U-18	D

SIXTH ROUND

Pick	Claimed by		Amateur Club	Position
152	FLA	Joshua Brown	Oshawa	D
153	COL	Ben Storm	Muskegon	D
154	T.B.	Henri Ikonen	Kingston	LW
155	NSH	Emil Pettersson	Timra Jr.	C
156	CAR	Tyler Ganly	Sault Ste. Marie	D
157	CGY	Tim Harrison	Dexter Prep	RW
158	EDM	Ben Betker	Everett	D
159	BUF	Sean Malone	USA U-18	C
160	N.J.	Myles Bell	Kelowna	LW
161	OTT	Chris Leblanc	South Shore	RW
162	PHI	Merrick Madsen	Proctor Academy	G
163	PHX	Brendan Burke	Portland	G
164	PIT	Dane Birks	Merritt	D
165	CBJ	Markus Soberg	Frolunda Jr.	RW
166	NYI	Alan Quine	Belleville	C
167	MIN	Avery Peterson	Grand Rapids	C
168	OTT	Quentin Shore	U of Denver	C
169	DET	Marc McNulty	Prince George	D
170	NYR	Mackenzie Skapski	Kootenay	G
171	NSH	Tommy Veilleux	Victoriaville	LW
172	TOR	Antoine Bibeau	PEI	G
173	STL	Santeri Saari	Jokerit Jr.	D
174	WSH	Brian Pinho	St. John's Prep	C
175	VAN	Mike Williamson	Spruce Grove	D
176	MTL	Jeremy Gregoire	Baie-Comeau	C
177	ANA	Miro Aaltonen	Blues	C
178	L.A.	Zachary Leslie	Guelph	D
179	PIT	Blaine Byron	Smiths Falls	C
180	BOS	Anton Blidh	Frolunda Jr.	LW
181	CHI	Anthony Louis	USA U-18	C

SEVENTH ROUND

Pick	Claimed by		Amateur Club	Position
182	DAL	Aleksi Makela	Ilves Jr.	D
183	COL	Wilhelm Westlund	Farjestad Jr.	D
184	T.B.	Saku Salminen	K-Vantaa	C
185	NSH	Wade Murphy	Penticton	RW
186	T.B.	Joel Vermin	Bern	RW
187	CGY	Rushan Rafikov	Yaroslavl 2	D
188	EDM	Gregory Chase	Calgary	C/RW
189	BUF	Eric Locke	Saginaw	C
190	EDM	Brenden Kichton	Spokane	D
191	L.A.	Dominik Kubalik	Sudbury	LW
192	PHI	David Drake	Des Moines	D
193	PHX	Jedd Soleway	Penticton	C
194	WPG	Marcus Karlstrom	AIK U18	D
195	CBJ	Peter Quenneville	Dubuque	C/RW
196	NYI	Kyle Burroughs	Regina	D
197	MIN	Nolan De Jong	Victoria	D
198	CGY	John Gilmour	Providence	D
199	DET	Hampus Melen	Tingsryd	RW
200	MIN	Alexandre Belanger	Rouyn-Noranda	G
201	S.J.	Jacob Jackson	Tartan	C
202	TOR	Andreas Johnson	Frolunda Jr.	LW
203	NSH	Janne Juvonen	Pelicans Jr.	G
204	WSH	Tyler Lewington	Medicine Hat	D
205	VAN	Miles Liberati	London	D
206	FLA	MacKenzie Weegar	Halifax	D
207	S.J.	Emil Galimov	Yaroslavl	LW
208	N.J.	Anthony Brodeur	Shattuck-St. Mary's	G
209	PIT	Troy Josephs	St. Michael's	C
210	BOS	Mitchell Dempsey	Sault Ste. Marie	LW
211	CHI	Robin Press	Sodertalje	D

First Two Rounds, 2012–2010

2012

FIRST ROUND

Pick	Claimed by		Amateur Club	Position
1	EDM	Nail Yakupov	Sarnia	RW
2	CBJ	Ryan Murray	Everett	D
3	MTL	Alex Galchenyuk	Sarnia	C
4	NYI	Griffin Reinhart	Edmonton	D
5	TOR	Morgan Rielly	Moose Jaw	D
6	ANA	Hampus Lindholm	Rogle Jr.	D
7	MIN	Mathew Dumba	Red Deer	D
8	PIT	Derrick Pouliot	Portland	D
9	WPG	Jacob Trouba	USA U-18	D
10	T.B.	Slater Koekkoek	Peterborough	D
11	WSH	Filip Forsberg	Leksand	RW
12	BUF	Mikhail Grigorenko	Quebec	C
13	DAL	Radek Faksa	Kitchener	C
14	BUF	Zemgus Girgensons	Dubuque	C
15	OTT	Cody Ceci	Ottawa	D
16	WSH	Thomas Wilson	Plymouth	RW
17	S.J.	Tomas Hertl	Slavia	C
18	CHI	Teuvo Teravainen	Jokerit	LW
19	T.B.	Andrey Vasilevskiy	Ufa 2	G
20	PHI	Scott Laughton	Oshawa	C
21	CGY	Mark Jankowski	Stanstead College	C
22	PIT	Olli Maatta	London	D
23	FLA	Michael Matheson	Dubuque	D
24	BOS	Malcolm Subban	Belleville	G
25	STL	Jordan Schmaltz	Green Bay	D
26	VAN	Brendan Gaunce	Belleville	C
27	PHX	Henrik Samuelsson	Edmonton	C
28	NYR	Brady Skjei	USA U-18	D
29	N.J.	Stefan Matteau	USA U-18	C
30	L.A.	Tanner Pearson	Barrie	LW

SECOND ROUND

Pick	Claimed by		Amateur Club	Position
31	CBJ	Oscar Dansk	Brynas Jr.	G
32	EDM	Mitchell Moroz	Edmonton	LW
33	MTL	Sebastian Collberg	Frolunda	RW
34	NYI	Ville Pokka	Karpat	D
35	TOR	Matthew Finn	Guelph	D
36	ANA	Nicolas Kerdiles	USA U-18	LW
37	NSH	Pontus Aberg	Djurgarden	LW
38	CAR	Phillip Di Giuseppe	U.of Michigan	LW
39	WPG	Lukas Sutter	Saskatoon	C
40	T.B.	Dylan Blujus	Brampton	D
41	COL	Mitchell Heard	Plymouth	C
42	CHY	Patrick Sieloff	USA U-18	D
43	DAL	Ludwig Bystrom	MODO Jr.	D
44	BUF	Jake McCabe	U. of Wisconsin	D
45	PHI	Anthony Stolarz	Corpus Christi	G
46	MIN	Raphael Bussieres	Baie-Comeau	LW
47	CAR	Brock McGinn	Guelph	LW
48	CHI	Dillon Fournier	Rouyn-Noranda	D
49	DET	Martin Frk	Halifax	RW
50	NSH	Colton Sissons	Kelowna	C
51	MTL	Dalton Thrower	Saskatoon	D
52	PIT	Teddy Blueger	Shattuck-St. Mary's	C
53	T.B.	Brian Hart	Exeter	RW
54	DAL	Mike Winther	Prince Albert	C
55	S.J.	Chris Tierney	London	C
56	STL	Samuel Kurker	St. John's Prep	RW
57	VAN	Alexandre Mallet	Rimouski	LW
58	PHX	Jordan Martinook	Vancouver	LW
59	NYR	Cristoval "Boo" Nieves	Kent School	C
60	N.J.	Damon Severson	Kelowna	D
61	DAL	Devin Shore	Whitby	C

2011

FIRST ROUND

Pick	Claimed by		Amateur Club	Position
1	EDM	Ryan Nugent-Hopkins	Red Deer	C
2	COL	Gabriel Landeskog	Kitchener	LW
3	FLA	Jonathan Huberdeau	Saint John	C
4	N.J.	Adam Larsson	Skelleftea	D
5	NYI	Ryan Strome	Niagara	C
6	OTT	Mika Zibanejad	Djurgarden	C
7	WPG	Mark Scheifele	Barrie	C
8	PHI	Sean Couturier	Drummondville	C
9	BOS	Dougie Hamilton	Niagara	D
10	MIN	Jonas Brodin	Farjestad	D
11	COL	Duncan Siemens	Saskatoon	D
12	CAR	Ryan Murphy	Kitchener	D
13	CGY	Sven Baertschi	Portland	LW
14	DAL	Jamieson Oleksiak	Northeastern	D
15	NYR	J.T. Miller	USA U-18	C
16	BUF	Joel Armia	Assat	RW
17	MTL	Nathan Beaulieu	Saint John	D
18	CHI	Mark McNeill	Prince Albert	C
19	EDM	Oscar Klefbom	Farjestad	D
20	PHX	Connor Murphy	USA U-18	D
21	OTT	Stefan Noesen	Plymouth	RW
22	TOR	Tyler Biggs	USA U-18	RW
23	PIT	Joe Morrow	Portland	D
24	OTT	Matt Puempel	Peterborough	LW
25	TOR	Stuart Percy	Mississauga St. Michael's	D
26	CHI	Phillip Danault	Victoriaville	LW
27	T.B.	Vladislav Namestnikov	London	C
28	MIN	Zack Phillips	Saint John	C
29	VAN	Nicklas Jensen	Oshawa	LW/RW
30	ANA	Rickard Rakell	Plymouth	RW

SECOND ROUND

Pick	Claimed by		Amateur Club	Position
31	EDM	David Musil	Vancouver	D
32	STL	Ty Rattie	Portland	RW
33	FLA	Rocco Grimaldi	USA U-18	C
34	NYI	Scott Mayfield	Youngstown	D
35	DET	Tomas Jurco	Saint John	RW
36	CHI	Adam Clendening	Boston University	D
37	CBJ	Boone Jenner	Oshawa	C
38	NSH	Magnus Hellberg	Almtuna	G
39	ANA	John Gibson	USA U-18	G
40	BOS	Alexander Khokhlachev	Windsor	C/LW
41	STL	Dmitrij Jaskin	Slavia Praha	RW
42	CAR	Victor Rask	Leksand	C
43	CHI	Brandon Saad	Saginaw	LW
44	DAL	Brett Ritchie	Sarnia	RW
45	CGY	Markus Granlund	HIFK Jr.	C
46	STL	Joel Edmundson	Moose Jaw	D
47	S.J.	Matthew Nieto	Boston University	LW
48	DET	Xavier Ouellet	Montreal	D
49	L.A.	Christopher Gibson	Chicoutimi	G
50	NYI	Johan Sundstrom	Frolunda	C
51	PHX	Alexander Ruuttu	Jokerit Jr.	C
52	NSH	Miikka Salomaki	Karpat	RW
53	ANA	William Karlsson	Vasteras Jr.	C
54	PIT	Scott Harrington	London	D
55	DET	Ryan Sproul	Sault Ste. Marie	D
56	PHX	Lucas Lessio	Oshawa	LW
57	CGY	Tyler Wotherspoon	Portland	D
58	T.B.	Nikita Kucherov	CSKA 2	LW/RW
59	FLA	Rasmus Bengtsson	Rogle Angleholm	D
60	MIN	Mario Lucia	Wayzata	LW
61	OTT	Shane Prince	Ottawa	C

2010

FIRST ROUND

Pick	Claimed by		Amateur Club	Position
1	EDM	Taylor Hall	Windsor	LW
2	BOS	Tyler Seguin	Plymouth	C
3	FLA	Erik Gudbranson	Kingston	D
4	CBJ	Ryan Johansen	Portland	C
5	NYI	Nino Niederreiter	Portland	RW
6	T.B.	Brett Connolly	Prince George	RW
7	CAR	Jeff Skinner	Kitchener	C
8	ATL	Alexander Burmistrov	Barrie	C
9	MIN	Mikael Granlund	HIFK Helsinki	C/W
10	NYR	Dylan McIlrath	Moose Jaw	D
11	DAL	Jack Campbell	USA U-18	G
12	ANA	Cam Fowler	Windsor	D
13	PHX	Brandon Gormley	Moncton	D
14	STL	Jaden Schwartz	Tri-City	C
15	L.A.	Derek Forbort	USA U-18	D
16	STL	Vladimir Tarasenko	Novosibirsk	RW
17	COL	Joey Hishon	Owen Sound	C
18	NSH	Austin Watson	Peterborough	LW
19	FLA	Nick Bjugstad	Blaine	C
20	PIT	Beau Bennett	Penticton	RW
21	DET	Riley Sheahan	U. of Notre Dame	C
22	MTL	Jarred Tinordi	USA U-18	D
23	BUF	Mark Pysyk	Edmonton	D
24	CHI	Kevin Hayes	Nobles	RW
25	FLA	Quinton Howden	Moose Jaw	C
26	WSH	Evgeny Kuznetsov	Chelyabinsk	C
27	PHX	Mark Visentin	Niagara	G
28	S.J.	Charlie Coyle	South Shore	C/RW
29	ANA	Emerson Etem	Medicine Hat	RW
30	NYI	Brock Nelson	Warroad	C

SECOND ROUND

Pick	Claimed by		Amateur Club	Position
31	EDM	Tyler Pitlick	Minnesota State	C
32	BOS	Jared Knight	London	C
33	FLA	John McFarland	Sudbury	LW
34	CBJ	Dalton Smith	Ottawa	LW
35	CHI	Ludvig Rensfeldt	Brynas Jr.	LW
36	FLA	Alexander Petrovic	Red Deer	D
37	CAR	Justin Faulk	USA U-18	D
38	N.J.	Jonathon Merrill	USA U-18	D
39	MIN	Brett Bulmer	Kelowna	RW
40	NYR	Christian Thomas	Oshawa	RW
41	DAL	Patrik Nemeth	AIK-Jr.	D
42	ANA	Devante Smith-Pelly	Mississauga	RW
43	TOR	Brad Ross	Portland	LW
44	STL	Sebastian Wannstrom	Brynas Jr.	RW
45	BOS	Ryan Spooner	Peterborough	C
46	EDM	Martin Marincin	Slovakia U-20	D
47	L.A.	Tyler Toffoli	Ottawa	C
48	EDM	Curtis Hamilton	Saskatoon	LW
49	COL	Calvin Pickard	Seattle	G
50	FLA	Connor Brickley	Des Moines	C
51	DET	Calle Jarnkrok	Brynas	C
52	PHX	Philip Lane	Brampton	RW
53	CAR	Mark Alt	Cretin-Derham	D
54	CHI	Justin Holl	Minnetonka	D
55	CBJ	Petr Straka	Rimouski	RW
56	MIN	Johan Larsson	Brynas Jr.	LW
57	PHX	Oscar Lindberg	Skelleftea Jr.	C
58	CHI	Kent Simpson	Everett	G
59	MIN	Jason Zucker	USA U-18	LW
60	CHI	Stephen Johns	USA U-18	D

Alex Galchenyuk was born in the United States while his Russian father played minor pro hockey in Milwaukee. Chosen third overall in the 2012 NHL Entry Draft despite missing all but two games of the 2011-12 season with a knee injury, Galchenyuk played the full 48 games for Montreal in 2012-13, scoring nine goals and adding 18 assists. He had 61 points in 33 games for Sarnia of the OHL before the NHL season began.

First Round and Other Notable Selections, 2009–1969

2009

FIRST ROUND

Pick		Claimed by	Amateur Club	Position
1	NYI	John Tavares	London	C
2	T.B.	Victor Hedman	MODO Ornskoldsvik	D
3	COL	Matt Duchene	Brampton	C
4	ATL	Evander Kane	Vancouver	C
5	L.A.	Brayden Schenn	Brandon	C
6	PHX	Oliver Ekman-Larsson	Leksand	D
7	TOR	Nazem Kadri	London	C
8	DAL	Scott Glennie	Brandon	RW
9	OTT	Jared Cowen	Spokane	D
10	EDM	Magnus Paajarvi-Svensson	Timra	LW
11	NSH	Ryan Ellis	Windsor	D
12	NYI	Calvin De Haan	Oshawa	D
13	BUF	Zack Kassian	Peterborough	RW
14	FLA	Dmitry Kulikov	Drummondville	D
15	ANA	Peter Holland	Guelph	C
16	MIN	Nick Leddy	Eden Prairie	D
17	STL	David Rundblad	Skelleftea	D
18	MTL	Louis Leblanc	Omaha	C
19	NYR	Chris Kreider	Andover	C
20	N.J.	Jacob Josefson	Djurgarden	C
21	CBJ	John Moore	Chicago Steel	D
22	VAN	Jordan Schroeder	U. of Minnesota	C
23	CGY	Tim Erixon	Skelleftea	D
24	WSH	Marcus Johansson	Farjestad	C
25	BOS	Jordan Caron	Rimouski	RW
26	ANA	Kyle Palmieri	USA U-18	C/RW
27	CAR	Philippe Paradis	Shawinigan	C
28	CHI	Dylan Olsen	Camrose	D
29	T.B.	Carter Ashton	Lethbridge	RW
30	PIT	Simon Despres	Saint John	D

OTHER NOTABLE SELECTIONS

Pick		Claimed by	Amateur Club	Position
33	COL	Ryan O'Reilly	Erie	C
35	L.A.	Kyle Clifford	Barrie	LW
39	OTT	Jakob Silfverberg	Brynas	LW
46	OTT	Robin Lehner	Frolunda Jr.	G
55	WSH	Dmitri Orlov	Novokuznetsk	D
85	WSH	Cody Eakin	Swift Current	C
92	NYI	Casey Cizikas	St. Michael's	C
98	NSH	Craig Smith	Waterloo	C
104	BUF	Marcus Foligno	Sudbury	LW
127	NYR	Roman Horak	Ceske Budejovice	C
129	DAL	Tomas Vincour	Edmonton	C
132	NSH	Gabriel Bourque	Baie-Comeau	LW
149	CHI	Marcus Kruger	Djurgarden	C
186	L.A.	Jordan Nolan	Sault Ste. Marie	C

2008

FIRST ROUND

Pick		Claimed by	Amateur Club	Position
1	T.B.	Steven Stamkos	Sarnia	C
2	L.A.	Drew Doughty	Guelph	D
3	ATL	Zach Bogosian	Peterborough	D
4	STL	Alex Pietrangelo	Niagara	D
5	TOR	Luke Schenn	Kelowna	D
6	CBJ	Nikita Filatov	CSKA 2	LW
7	NSH	Colin Wilson	Boston University	C
8	PHX	Mikkel Boedker	Kitchener	LW
9	NYI	Joshua Bailey	Windsor	C
10	VAN	Cody Hodgson	Brampton	C
11	CHI	Kyle Beach	Everett	C
12	BUF	Tyler Myers	Kelowna	D
13	L.A.	Colten Teubert	Regina	D
14	CAR	Zach Boychuk	Lethbridge	C
15	OTT	Erik Karlsson	Frolunda Jr.	D
16	BOS	Joe Colborne	Camrose	C
17	ANA	Jake Gardiner	Minnetonka	D
18	NSH	Chet Pickard	Tri-City	G
19	PHI	Luca Sbisa	Lethbridge	D
20	NYR	Michael Del Zotto	Oshawa	D
21	WSH	Anton Gustafsson	Frolunda Jr.	C
22	EDM	Jordan Eberle	Regina	C
23	MIN	Tyler Cuma	Ottawa	D
24	N.J.	Mattias Tedenby	HV 71 Jonkoping	LW
25	CGY	Greg Nemisz	Windsor	C
26	BUF	Tyler Ennis	Medicine Hat	C
27	WSH	John Carlson	Indiana	D
28	PHX	Viktor Tikhonov	Cherepovets	W
29	ATL	Daultan Leveille	St. Catharines	C
30	DET	Thomas McCollum	Guelph	G

OTHER NOTABLE SELECTIONS

Pick		Claimed by	Amateur Club	Position
32	L.A.	Slava Voynov	Chelyabinsk	D
51	NYR	Derek Stepan	Shattuck-St. Mary's	C
53	NYI	Travis Hamonic	Moose Jaw	D
79	OTT	Zack Smith	Swift Current	C
82	N.J.	Adam Henrique	Windsor	C
93	WSH	Braden Holtby	Saskatoon	G
148	NYI	Matt Martin	Sarnia	LW
156	NYI	Jared Spurgeon	Spokane	D
186	S.J.	Jason Demers	Victoriaville	D

A Second-Team Canadian Hockey League All-Star while playing with Lewiston in the QMJHL in 2006-07, Jonathan Bernier had already been selected 11th overall by Los Angeles in the 2006 Entry Draft. He was a First-Team AHL All-Star in 2009-10, and then backed up Jonathan Quick in Los Angeles for three seasons before being traded to Toronto on June 23, 2013.

2007

FIRST ROUND

Pick		Claimed by	Amateur Club	Position
1	CHI	Patrick Kane	London	RW
2	PHI	James van Riemsdyk	USA U-18	LW
3	PHX	Kyle Turris	Burnaby	C
4	L.A.	Thomas Hickey	Seattle	D
5	WSH	Karl Alzner	Calgary	D
6	EDM	Sam Gagner	London	C/W
7	CBJ	Jakub Voracek	Halifax	RW
8	BOS	Zach Hamill	Everett	C
9	S.J.	Logan Couture	Ottawa	C
10	FLA	Keaton Ellerby	Kamloops	D
11	CAR	Brandon Sutter	Red Deer	C/RW
12	MTL	Ryan McDonagh	Cretin-Derham	D
13	STL	Lars Eller	Frolunda Jr.	C
14	COL	Kevin Shattenkirk	USA U-18	D
15	EDM	Alex Plante	Calgary	D
16	MIN	Colton Gillies	Saskatoon	C
17	NYR	Alexei Cherepanov	Omsk	RW
18	STL	Ian Cole	USA U-18	D
19	ANA	Logan MacMillan	Halifax	C
20	PIT	Angelo Esposito	Quebec	C
21	EDM	Riley Nash	Salmon Arm	C
22	MTL	Max Pacioretty	Sioux City	LW
23	NSH	Jonathon Blum	Vancouver	D
24	CGY	Mikael Backlund	Vasteras	C
25	VAN	Patrick White	Tri-City	C
26	STL	David Perron	Lewiston	LW
27	DET	Brendan Smith	St. Michael's	D
28	S.J.	Nicholas Petrecki	Omaha	D
29	OTT	Jim O'Brien	U. of Minnesota	C
30	PHX	Nick Ross	Regina	D

OTHER NOTABLE SELECTIONS

Pick		Claimed by	Amateur Club	Position
43	MTL	P.K. Subban	Belleville	D
46	BUF	Jhonas Enroth	Sodertalje	G
55	COL	T.J. Galiardi	Dartmouth	W
58	NSH	Nick Spaling	Kitchener	C
61	L.A.	Wayne Simmonds	Owen Sound	RW
117	N.J.	Matt Halischuk	Kitchener	RW
129	DAL	Jamie Benn	Victoria	LW
168	NYR	Carl Hagelin	Sodertalje Jr	LW
194	TOR	Carl Gunnarson	Linkoping	D

2006

FIRST ROUND

Pick		Claimed by	Amateur Club	Position
1	STL	Erik Johnson	USA U-18	D
2	PIT	Jordan Staal	Peterborough	C
3	CHI	Jonathan Toews	U. of North Dakota	C
4	WSH	Nicklas Backstrom	Brynas Gavle	C
5	BOS	Phil Kessel	U. of Minnesota	C
6	CBJ	Derick Brassard	Drummondville	C
7	NYI	Kyle Okposo	Des Moines	RW
8	PHX	Peter Mueller	Everett	C
9	MIN	James Sheppard	Cape Breton	C
10	FLA	Michael Frolik	Kladno	C
11	L.A.	Jonathan Bernier	Lewiston	G
12	ATL	Bryan Little	Barrie	C
13	TOR	Jiri Tlusty	Kladno	C
14	VAN	Michael Grabner	Spokane	RW
15	T.B.	Riku Helenius	Ilves Tampere	G
16	S.J.	Ty Wishart	Prince George	D
17	L.A.	Trevor Lewis	Des Moines	C
18	COL	Chris Stewart	Kingston	RW
19	ANA	Mark Mitera	U. of Michigan	D
20	MTL	David Fischer	Apple Valley	D
21	NYR	Bobby Sanguinetti	Owen Sound	D
22	PHI	Claude Giroux	Gatineau	RW
23	WSH	Simeon Varlamov	Yaroslavl 2	G
24	BUF	Dennis Persson	Vasteras	D
25	STL	Patrik Berglund	Vasteras	C
26	CGY	Leland Irving	Everett	G
27	DAL	Ivan Vishnevskiy	Rouyn-Noranda	D
28	OTT	Nick Foligno	Sudbury	LW
29	PHX	Chris Summers	USA U-18	D
30	N.J.	Matthew Corrente	Saginaw	D

OTHER NOTABLE SELECTIONS

Pick		Claimed by	Amateur Club	Position
34	Wsh.	Michal Neuvirth	Sparta Jr.	G
39	Phi.	Andreas Nodl	Sioux Falls	RW
44	Tor.	Nikolai Kulemin	Magnitogorsk	W
50	Bos.	Milan Lucic	Vancouver	LW
54	NYR	Artem Anisimov	Yaroslavl	C
69	CBJ	Steve Mason	London	G
71	Bos	Brad Marchand	Moncton	C
72	Min	Cal Clutterbuck	Oshawa	RW
99	Tor	James Reimer	Red Deer	G
161	Tor.	Viktor Stahlberg	Frolunda	LW
177	Wsh	Mathieu Perreault	Acadie-Bathurst	C

2005

FIRST ROUND

Pick	Claimed by		Amateur Club	Position
1	PIT	Sidney Crosby	Rimouski	C
2	ANA	Bobby Ryan	Owen Sound	RW
3	CAR	Jack Johnson	USA U-18	D
4	MIN	Benoit Pouliot	Sudbury	LW
5	MTL	Carey Price	Tri-City	G
6	CBJ	Gilbert Brule	Vancouver	C
7	CHI	Jack Skille	USA U-18	RW
8	S.J.	Devin Setoguchi	Saskatoon	RW
9	OTT	Brian Lee	Moorhead	D
10	VAN	Luc Bourdon	Val d'Or	D
11	L.A.	Anze Kopitar	Sodertalje Jr.	C
12	NYR	Marc Staal	Sudbury	D
13	BUF	Marek Zagrapan	Chicoutimi	C
14	WSH	Sasha Pokulok	Cornell	D
15	NYI	Ryan O'Marra	Erie	C
16	ATL	Alex Bourret	Lewiston	RW
17	PHX	Martin Hanzal	Ceske Budejovice	C
18	NSH	Ryan Parent	Guelph	D
19	DET	Jakub Kindl	Kitchener	D
20	FLA	Kenndal McArdle	Moose Jaw	LW
21	TOR	Tuukka Rask	Ilves Jr.	G
22	BOS	Matt Lashoff	Kitchener	D
23	N.J.	Nicklas Bergfors	Sodertalje	RW
24	STL	T.J. Oshie	Warroad	C
25	EDM	Andrew Cogliano	St. Mike's Buzzers	C
26	CGY	Matt Pelech	Sarnia	D
27	WSH	Joe Finley	Sioux Falls	D
28	DAL	Matt Niskanen	Virginia	D
29	PHI	Steve Downie	Windsor	RW
30	T.B.	Vladimir Mihalik	Presov	D

OTHER NOTABLE SELECTIONS

Pick	Claimed by		Amateur Club	Position
33	DAL	James Neal	Plymouth	LW
35	S.J.	Marc-Edouard Vlasic	Quebec	D
44	COL	Paul Stastny	U. of Denver	C
45	MTL	Guillaume Latendresse	Drummondville	RW
51	VAN	Mason Raymond	Camrose	LW
62	PIT	Kris Letang	Val d'Or	D
71	ATL	Ondrej Pavelec	Poldi Kladno Jr.	G
72	L.A.	Jonathan Quick	Avon Old Farms	G
105	PHX	Keith Yandle	Cushing Academy	D
200	MTL	Sergei Kostitsyn	Gomel	LW
204	OTT	Colin Greening	Upper Canada College	LW
230	NSH	Patric Hornqvist	Vasby	RW

2004

FIRST ROUND

Pick	Claimed by		Amateur Club	Position
1	WSH	Alex Ovechkin	Dynamo Moscow	LW
2	PIT	Evgeni Malkin	Magnitogorsk	C
3	CHI	Cam Barker	Medicine Hat	D
4	CAR	Andrew Ladd	Calgary	LW
5	PHX	Blake Wheeler	Breck	RW
6	NYR	Al Montoya	U. of Michigan	G
7	FLA	Rostislav Olesz	Vitkovice	LW
8	CBJ	Alexandre Picard	Lewiston	LW
9	ANA	Ladislav Smid	Liberec	D
10	ATL	Boris Valabik	Kitchener	D
11	L.A.	Lauri Tukonen	Blues Espoo	RW
12	MIN	A.J. Thelen	Michigan State	D
13	BUF	Drew Stafford	U. of North Dakota	RW
14	EDM	Devan Dubnyk	Kamloops	G
15	NSH	Alexander Radulov	Tver	LW
16	NYI	Petteri Nokelainen	SaiPa	C
17	STL	Marek Schwarz	Sparta Praha	G
18	MTL	Kyle Chipchura	Prince Albert	C
19	NYR	Lauri Korpikoski	TPS Turku Jr.	LW
20	N.J.	Travis Zajac	Salmon Arm	C
21	COL	Wojtek Wolski	Brampton	LW
22	S.J.	Lukas Kaspar	Litvinov	RW
23	OTT	Andrej Meszaros	Trencin	D
24	CGY	Kris Chucko	Salmon Arm	LW
25	EDM	Rob Schremp	London	C
26	VAN	Cory Schneider	Phillips-Andover	G
27	WSH	Jeff Schultz	Calgary	D
28	DAL	Mark Fistric	Vancouver	D
29	WSH	Mike Green	Saskatoon	D
30	T.B.	Andy Rogers	Calgary	D

OTHER NOTABLE SELECTIONS

Pick	Claimed by		Amateur Club	Position
32	CHI	Dave Bolland	London	C
53	FLA	David Booth	Michigan State	LW
60	NYR	Brandon Dubinsky	Portland	C
63	BOS	David Krejci	Kladno Jr.	C
91	VAN	Alexander Edler	Jamtland	D
97	DET	Johan Franzen	Linkoping	C
99	PIT	Tyler Kennedy	Sault Ste. Marie	C
127	NYR	Ryan Callahan	Guelph	RW
134	BOS	Kris Versteeg	Lethbridge	RW
150	MTL	Mikhail Grabovski	Nizhnekamsk	C
214	CHI	Troy Brouwer	Moose Jaw	RW
227	NYI	Chris Campoli	Erie	D
258	NSH	Pekka Rinne	Karpat	G
262	MTL	Mark Streit	Zurich	D
265	PHX	Daniel Winnik	New Hampshire	D
287	VAN	Jannik Hansen	Rodovre	LW

2003

FIRST ROUND

Pick	Claimed by		Amateur Club	Position
1	PIT	Marc-Andre Fleury	Cape Breton	G
2	CAR	Eric Staal	Peterborough	C
3	FLA	Nathan Horton	Oshawa	C
4	CBJ	Nikolai Zherdev	CSKA Moscow	W
5	BUF	Thomas Vanek	U. of Minnesota	LW
6	S.J.	Milan Michalek	Budejovice	RW
7	NSH	Ryan Suter	USA U-18	D
8	ATL	Braydon Coburn	Portland	D
9	CGY	Dion Phaneuf	Red Deer	D
10	MTL	Andrei Kostitsyn	CSKA 2	RW
11	PHI	Jeff Carter	Sault Ste. Marie	C
12	NYR	Hugh Jessiman	Dartmouth	RW
13	L.A.	Dustin Brown	Guelph	RW
14	CHI	Brent Seabrook	Lethbridge	D
15	NYI	Robert Nilsson	Leksand	RW
16	S.J.	Steve Bernier	Moncton	RW
17	N.J.	Zach Parise	North Dakota	C
18	WSH	Eric Fehr	Brandon	RW
19	ANA	Ryan Getzlaf	Calgary	C
20	MIN	Brent Burns	Brampton	RW
21	BOS	Mark Stuart	Colorado College	D
22	EDM	Marc-Antoine Pouliot	Rimouski	C
23	VAN	Ryan Kesler	Ohio State	C
24	PHI	Mike Richards	Kitchener	C
25	FLA	Anthony Stewart	Kingston	C
26	L.A.	Brian Boyle	St. Sebastian's H.S.	C
27	L.A.	Jeff Tambellini	U. of Michigan	LW
28	ANA	Corey Perry	London	RW
29	OTT	Patrick Eaves	Boston College	RW
30	STL	Shawn Belle	Tri-City	D

OTHER NOTABLE SELECTIONS

Pick	Claimed by		Amateur Club	Position
33	DAL	Loui Eriksson	Vastra Frolunda Jr	LW
45	BOS	Patrice Bergeron	Acadie-Bathurst	C
47	S.J.	Matt Carle	River City	D
49	NSH	Shea Weber	Kelowna	D
52	CHI	Corey Crawford	Moncton	G
61	MTL	Maxim Lapierre	Montreal	C
62	STL	David Backes	Lincoln	C
64	DET	Jimmy Howard	U. of Maine	G
148	STL	Lee Stempniak	Dartmouth College	RW
205	S.J.	Joe Pavelski	Waterloo Jr. A	C
214	EDM	Kyle Brodziak	Moose Jaw	C
239	ATL	Tobias Enstrom	MODO Ornskolsvik	D
245	CHI	Dustin Byfuglien	Prince George	RW
263	PIT	Matt Moulson	Cornell	LW
271	MTL	Jaroslav Halak	Bratislava Jr.	G
291	OTT	Brian Elliott	Ajax	G

2002

FIRST ROUND

Pick	Claimed by		Amateur Club	Position
1	CBJ	Rick Nash	London	LW
2	ATL	Kari Lehtonen	Jokerit	G
3	FLA	Jay Bouwmeester	Medicine Hat	D
4	PHI	Joni Pitkanen	Karpat	D
5	PIT	Ryan Whitney	Boston University	D
6	NSH	Scottie Upshall	Kamloops	RW
7	ANA	Joffrey Lupul	Medicine Hat	C
8	MIN	Pierre-Marc Bouchard	Chicoutimi	C
9	FLA	Petr Taticek	Sault Ste. Marie	C
10	CGY	Eric Nystrom	U. of Michigan	LW
11	BUF	Keith Ballard	U. of Minnesota	D
12	WSH	Steve Eminger	Kitchener	D
13	WSH	Alexander Semin	Chelyabinsk	LW
14	MTL	Christopher Higgins	Yale	C
15	EDM	Jesse Niinimaki	Ilves Tampere	C
16	OTT	Jakub Klepis	Portland	C
17	WSH	Boyd Gordon	Red Deer	RW
18	L.A.	Denis Grebeshkov	Yaroslavl	D
19	PHX	Jakub Koreis	Plzen	C
20	BUF	Dan Paille	Guelph	LW
21	CHI	Anton Babchuk	Elektrostal	D
22	NYI	Sean Bergenheim	Jokerit	C
23	PHX	Ben Eager	Oshawa	LW
24	TOR	Alexander Steen	Vastra Frolunda	C
25	CAR	Cam Ward	Red Deer	G
26	DAL	Martin Vagner	Hull	D
27	S.J.	Mike Morris	St. Sebastian's H.S.	RW
28	COL	Jonas Johansson	HV 71 Jonkoping Jr.	RW
29	BOS	Hannu Toivonen	HPK Jr.	G
30	ATL	Jim Slater	Michigan State	C

OTHER NOTABLE SELECTIONS

Pick	Claimed by		Amateur Club	Position
36	EDM	Jarret Stoll	Kootenay	C
54	CHI	Duncan Keith	Michigan State	D
57	TOR	Matt Stajan	Belleville	C
58	DET	Jiri Hudler	Vsetin	C
63	DET	Tomas Fleischmann	Vitkovice Jr.	LW
67	FLA	Gregory Campbell	Plymouth	LW
90	CGY	Matthew Lomardi	Victoriaville	C
95	DET	Valtteri Filppula	Jokerit Jr.	C
234	PIT	Maxime Talbot	Hull	C
240	NYR	Petr Prucha	Pardubice	RW
241	BUF	Dennis Wideman	London	D
291	DET	Jonathan Ericsson	Hasten Jr.	D

2001

FIRST ROUND

Pick	Claimed by		Amateur Club	Position
1	ATL	Ilya Kovalchuk	Spartak	LW
2	OTT	Jason Spezza	Windsor	C
3	T.B.	Alexander Svitov	Avangard Omsk	C
4	FLA	Stephen Weiss	Plymouth	C
5	ANA	Stanislav Chistov	Avangard Omsk	LW
6	MIN	Mikko Koivu	TPS Turku	C
7	MTL	Mike Komisarek	U. of Michigan	D
8	CBJ	Pascal Leclaire	Halifax	G
9	CHI	Tuomo Ruutu	Jokerit	C/LW
10	NYR	Dan Blackburn	Kootenay	G
11	PHX	Fredrik Sjostrom	Vastra Frolunda	RW
12	NSH	Dan Hamhuis	Prince George	D
13	EDM	Ales Hemsky	Hull	RW
14	CGY	Chuck Kobasew	Boston College	C
15	CAR	Igor Knyazev	Spartak	D
16	VAN	R.J. Umberger	Ohio State	C
17	TOR	Carlo Colaiacovo	Erie	D
18	L.A.	Jens Karlsson	Vastra Frolunda	RW
19	BOS	Shaone Morrisonn	Kamloops	D
20	S.J.	Marcel Goc	Schwenningen	C
21	PIT	Colby Armstrong	Red Deer	RW
22	BUF	Jiri Novotny	Budejovice	C
23	OTT	Tim Gleason	Windsor	D
24	FLA	Lukas Krajicek	Peterborough	D
25	MTL	Alexander Perezhogin	Avangard Omsk	C
26	DAL	Jason Bacashihua	Chicago Freeze	G
27	PHI	Jeff Woywitka	Red Deer	D
28	N.J.	Adrian Foster	Saskatoon	C
29	CHI	Adam Munro	Erie	G
30	L.A.	Dave Steckel	Ohio State	C

OTHER NOTABLE SELECTIONS

Pick	Claimed by		Amateur Club	Position
32	BUF	Derek Roy	Kitchener	C
49	L.A.	Michael Cammalleri	U. of Michigan	C
55	BUF	Jason Pominville	Shawinigan	RW
71	MTL	Tomas Plekanec	Kladno	LW
73	CHI	Craig Anderson	Guelph	G
95	PHI	Patrick Sharp	U. of Vermont	C
98	NSH	Jordin Tootoo	Brandon	RW
99	OTT	Ray Emery	SS Marie	G
106	S.J.	Christoph Ehrhoff	Krefeld	D
134	TOR	Kyle Wellwood	Belleville	C
151	VAN	Kevin Bieksa	Bowling Green	D
161	DAL	Mike Smith	Sudbury	G
172	PHI	Dennis Seidenberg	Mannheim	D
175	S.J.	Ryan Clowe	Rimouski	RW
176	NSH	Marek Zidlicky	HIFK Helsinki	D
192	DAL	Jussi Jokinen	Karpat Jr.	F
193	OTT	Brooks Laich	Moose Jaw	C
221	WSH	Johnny Oduya	Victoriaville	D

2000

FIRST ROUND

Pick	Claimed by		Amateur Club	Position
1	NYI	Rick DiPietro	Boston University	G
2	ATL	Dany Heatley	U. of Wisconsin	RW
3	MIN	Marian Gaborik	Dukla Trencin	RW
4	CBJ	Rostislav Klesla	Brampton	D
5	NYI	Raffi Torres	Brampton	LW
6	NSH	Scott Hartnell	Prince Albert	LW
7	BOS	Lars Jonsson	Leksand	D
8	T.B.	Nikita Alexeev	Erie	RW
9	CGY	Brent Krahn	Calgary	G
10	CHI	Mikhail Yakubov	Lada Togliatti	C
11	CHI	Pavel Vorobiev	Yaroslavl	RW
12	ANA	Alexei Smirnov	Tver	LW
13	MTL	Ron Hainsey	U. of Mass-Lowell	D
14	COL	Vaclav Nedorost	Budejovice	C
15	BUF	Artem Kryukov	Yaroslavl	C
16	MTL	Marcel Hossa	Portland	LW
17	EDM	Alexei Mikhnov	Yaroslavl	LW
18	PIT	Brooks Orpik	Boston College	D
19	PHX	Krys Kolanos	Boston College	C
20	L.A.	Alexander Frolov	Yaroslavl 2	LW
21	OTT	Anton Volchenkov	HK Moscow	D
22	N.J.	David Hale	Sioux City	D
23	VAN	Nathan Smith	Swift Current	C
24	TOR	Brad Boyes	Erie	C
25	DAL	Steve Ott	Windsor	C
26	WSH	Brian Sutherby	Moose Jaw	C
27	BOS	Martin Samuelsson	MoDo Ornskoldsvik	RW
28	PHI	Justin Williams	Plymouth	RW
29	DET	Niklas Kronwall	Djurgarden	D
30	STL	Jeff Taffe	U. of Minnesota	C

OTHER NOTABLE SELECTIONS

Pick	Claimed by		Amateur Club	Position
33	MIN	Nick Schultz	Prince Albert	D
44	ANA	Ilya Bryzgalov	Lada Togliatti	G
46	CGY	Jarret Stoll	Kootenay	C
62	COL	Paul Martin	Elk River H.S.	D
95	NYR	Dominic Moore	Harvard	C
118	L.A.	Lubomir Visnovsky	Bratislava	D
155	CGY	Travis Moen	Kelowna	LW
159	COL	John-Michael Liles	Michigan State	D
205	NYR	Henrik Lundqvist	Vastre Frolunda Jr.	G
215	BUF	Matthew Lombardi	Victoriaville	C

1999

FIRST ROUND

Pick	Claimed by		Amateur Club	Position
1	ATL	Patrik Stefan	Long Beach	C
2	VAN	Daniel Sedin	MoDo Ornskoldsvik	LW
3	VAN	Henrik Sedin	MoDo Ornskoldsvik	C
4	NYR	Pavel Brendl	Calgary	RW
5	NYI	Tim Connolly	Erie	C
6	NSH	Brian Finley	Barrie	G
7	WSH	Kris Beech	Calgary	C
8	NYI	Taylor Pyatt	Sudbury	LW
9	NYR	Jamie Lundmark	Moose Jaw	C
10	NYI	Branislav Mezei	Belleville	D
11	CGY	Oleg Saprykin	Seattle	LW
12	FLA	Denis Shvidki	Barrie	RW
13	EDM	Jani Rita	Jokerit	LW
14	S.J.	Jeff Jillson	U. of Michigan	D
15	PHX	Scott Kelman	Seattle	C
16	CAR	David Tanabe	U. of Wisconsin	D
17	STL	Barret Jackman	Regina	D
18	PIT	Konstantin Koltsov	Cherepovets	RW
19	PHX	Kirill Safronov	St. Petersburg	D
20	BUF	Barrett Heisten	U. of Maine	LW
21	BOS	Nick Boynton	Ottawa	D
22	PHI	Maxime Ouellet	Quebec	G
23	CHI	Steve McCarthy	Kootenay	D
24	TOR	Luca Cereda	Ambri	C
25	COL	Mikhail Kuleshov	Cherepovets	LW
26	OTT	Martin Havlat	Trinec	LW
27	N.J.	Ari Ahonen	JyP HT Jr.	G
28	NYI	Kristian Kudroc	Michalovce	D

OTHER NOTABLE SELECTIONS

Pick	Claimed by		Amateur Club	Position
44	ANA	Jordan Leopold	U. of Minnesota	D
91	EDM	Mike Comrie	U. of Michigan	C
115	PIT	Ryan Malone	Omaha	LW
138	BUF	Ryan Miller	Soo	G
165	CHI	Michael Leighton	Windsor	G
191	NSH	Martin Erat	ZPS Zlin Jr.	LW
204	PIT	Tom Kostopolous	London	RW
210	DET	Henrik Zetterberg	Timra	LW
212	COL	Radim Vrbata	Hull	RW
222	L.A.	George Parros	Chicago Freeze	RW

1998

FIRST ROUND

Pick	Claimed by		Amateur Club	Position
1	T.B.	Vincent Lecavalier	Rimouski	C
2	NSH	David Legwand	Plymouth	C
3	S.J.	Brad Stuart	Regina	D
4	VAN	Bryan Allen	Oshawa	D
5	ANA	Vitaly Vishnevski	Yaroslavl 2	D
6	CGY	Rico Fata	London	RW
7	NYR	Manny Malhotra	Guelph	C
8	CHI	Mark Bell	Ottawa	C
9	NYI	Mike Rupp	Erie	RW
10	TOR	Nik Antropov	Ust-Kamenogorsk	C
11	CAR	Jeff Heerema	Sarnia	RW
12	COL	Alex Tanguay	Halifax	LW
13	EDM	Michael Henrich	Barrie	RW
14	PHX	Patrick DesRochers	Sarnia	G
15	OTT	Mathieu Chouinard	Shawinigan	G
16	MTL	Eric Chouinard	Quebec	LW
17	COL	Martin Skoula	Barrie	D
18	BUF	Dmitri Kalinin	Chelyabinsk	D
19	COL	Robyn Regehr	Kamloops	D
20	COL	Scott Parker	Kelowna	RW
21	L.A.	Mathieu Biron	Shawinigan	D
22	PHI	Simon Gagne	Quebec	LW
23	PIT	Milan Kraft	Keramika Plzen Jr.	C
24	STL	Christian Backman	Vastra Frolunda Jr.	D
25	DET	Jiri Fischer	Hull	D
26	N.J.	Mike Van Ryn	U. of Michigan	D
27	N.J.	Scott Gomez	Tri-City	C

OTHER NOTABLE SELECTIONS

Pick	Claimed by		Amateur Club	Position
29	S.J.	Jonathan Cheechoo	Belleville	RW
44	OTT	Mike Fisher	Sudbury	C
45	MTL	Mike Ribeiro	Rouyn-Noranda	C
64	T.B.	Brad Richards	Rimouski	C
68	VAN	Jarkko Ruutu	HIFK Helsinki	RW
71	CAR	Erik Cole	Clarkson	LW
75	MTL	Francois Beauchemin	Laval	D
82	N.J.	Brian Gionta	Boston College	RW
99	EDM	Shawn Horcoff	Michigan State	C
117	FLA	Jaroslav Spacek	Farjestad	D
145	S.J.	Mikael Samuelsson	Sodertalje	LW
161	OTT	Chris Neil	North Bay	RW
162	MTL	Andrei Markov	Khimik Voskresensk	D
164	BUF	Ales Kotalik	Ceske Budejovice Jr.	RW
171	DET	Pavel Datsyuk	Yekateringburg	C
216	MTL	Michael Ryder	Hull	RW
230	NSH	Karlis Skrastins	TPS Turku	D

1997

FIRST ROUND

Pick	Claimed by		Amateur Club	Position
1	BOS	Joe Thornton	Sault Ste. Marie	C
2	S.J.	Patrick Marleau	Seattle	C
3	L.A.	Olli Jokinen	HIFK Helsinki	C
4	NYI	Roberto Luongo	Val-d'Or	G
5	NYI	Eric Brewer	Prince George	D
6	CGY	Daniel Tkaczuk	Barrie	C
7	T.B.	Paul Mara	Sudbury	D
8	BOS	Sergei Samsonov	Detroit	LW
9	WSH	Nick Boynton	Ottawa	D
10	VAN	Brad Ference	Spokane	D
11	MTL	Jason Ward	Erie	RW
12	OTT	Marian Hossa	Dukla Trencin	RW
13	CHI	Daniel Cleary	Belleville	RW
14	EDM	Michel Riesen	Biel-Bienne	RW
15	L.A.	Matt Zultek	Ottawa	LW
16	CHI	Ty Jones	Spokane	RW
17	PIT	Robert Dome	Las Vegas (IHL)	RW
18	ANA	Mikael Holmqvist	Djurgarden	C
19	NYR	Stefan Cherneski	Brandon	RW
20	FLA	Mike Brown	Red Deer	LW
21	BUF	Mika Noronen	Tappara Tampere	G
22	CAR	Nikos Tselios	Belleville	D
23	S.J.	Scott Hannan	Kelowna	D
24	N.J.	J-F Damphousse	Moncton	G
25	DAL	Brenden Morrow	Portland	LW
26	COL	Kevin Grimes	Kingston	D

OTHER NOTABLE SELECTIONS

Pick	Claimed by		Amateur Club	Position
47	FLA	Kristian Huselius	Farjestad	LW
48	BUF	Henrik Tallinder	AIK Solna	D
69	BUF	Maxim Afinogenov	Dynamo Moscow	RW
78	COL	Ville Nieminen	Tappara Tampere	RW
83	L.A.	Joe Corvo	U. of Western Michigan	D
121	EDM	Jason Chimera	Medicine Hat	LW
144	VAN	Matt Cooke	Windsor	C
156	BUF	Brian Campbell	Ottawa	D
177	STL	Ladislav Nagy	Dragon Presov	LW
208	PIT	Andrew Ference	Portland	D

1996

FIRST ROUND

Pick	Claimed by		Amateur Club	Position
1	OTT	Chris Phillips	Prince Albert	D
2	S.J.	Andrei Zyuzin	Salavat Yulayev Ufa	D
3	NYI	J.P. Dumont	Val-d'Or	RW
4	WSH	Alexandre Volchkov	Barrie	C
5	DAL	Ric Jackman	Sault Ste. Marie	D
6	EDM	Boyd Devereaux	Kitchener	C
7	BUF	Erik Rasmussen	U. of Minnesota	LW/C
8	BOS	Johnathan Aitken	Medicine Hat	D
9	ANA	Ruslan Salei	Las Vegas (IHL)	D
10	N.J.	Lance Ward	Red Deer	D
11	PHX	Dan Focht	Tri-City	D
12	VAN	Josh Holden	Regina	C
13	CGY	Derek Morris	Regina	D
14	STL	Marty Reasoner	Boston College	C
15	PHI	Dainius Zubrus	Pembroke Jr. A	RW
16	T.B.	Mario Larocque	Hull	D
17	WSH	Jaroslav Svejkovsky	Tri-City	RW
18	MTL	Matt Higgins	Moose Jaw	C
19	EDM	Matthieu Descoteaux	Shawinigan	D
20	FLA	Marcus Nilson	Djurgarden	LW
21	S.J.	Marco Sturm	Landshut	LW
22	NYR	Jeff Brown	Sarnia	D
23	PIT	Craig Hillier	Ottawa	G
24	PHX	Danny Briere	Drummondville	C
25	COL	Peter Ratchuk	Shattuck-St. Mary's	D
26	DET	Jesse Wallin	Red Deer	D

OTHER NOTABLE SELECTIONS

Pick	Claimed by		Amateur Club	Position
35	ANA	Matt Cullen	St. Cloud State	C
49	N.J.	Colin White	Hull	D
56	NYI	Zdeno Chara	Dukla Trencin	D
59	EDM	Tom Poti	Cushing Academy	D
79	COL	Mark Parrish	St. Cloud State	RW
89	CGY	Toni Lydman	Reipas Lahti	D
96	L.A.	Eric Belanger	Beauport	C
176	COL	Samuel Pahlsson	MoDo Ornskoldsvik	C
179	T.B.	Pavel Kubina	Vitkovice	D
199	N.J.	Willie Mitchell	Melfort Jr. A	D
204	TOR	Tomas Kaberle	Kladno	D
223	HFD	Craig Adams	Harvard	RW
239	OTT	Sami Salo	TPS Turku	D

1995

FIRST ROUND

Pick	Claimed by		Amateur Club	Position
1	OTT	Bryan Berard	Detroit	D
2	NYI	Wade Redden	Brandon	D
3	L.A.	Aki Berg	Kiekko-67 Turku	D
4	ANA	Chad Kilger	Kingston	C
5	T.B.	Daymond Langkow	Tri-City	C
6	EDM	Steve Kelly	Prince Albert	C
7	WPG	Shane Doan	Kamloops	RW
8	MTL	Terry Ryan	Tri-City	LW
9	BOS	Kyle McLaren	Tacoma	D
10	FLA	Radek Dvorak	Ceske Budejovice	RW
11	DAL	Jarome Iginla	Kamloops	RW
12	S.J.	Teemu Riihijarvi	Kiekko-Espoo	LW
13	HFD	Jean-Sebastien Giguere	Halifax	G
14	BUF	Jay McKee	Niagara Falls	D
15	TOR	Jeff Ware	Oshawa	D
16	BUF	Martin Biron	Beauport	G
17	WSH	Brad Church	Prince Albert	LW
18	N.J.	Petr Sykora	Detroit	RW
19	CHI	Dmitri Nabokov	Krylja Sovetov	C/LW
20	CGY	Denis Gauthier	Drummondville	D
21	BOS	Sean Brown	Belleville	D
22	PHI	Brian Boucher	Tri-City	G
23	WSH	Miika Elomo	Kiekko-67 Turku	LW
24	PIT	Aleksey Morozov	Krylja Sovetov	RW
25	COL	Marc Denis	Chicoutimi	G
26	DET	Maxim Kuznetsov	Dynamo Moscow	D

OTHER NOTABLE SELECTIONS

Pick	Claimed by		Amateur Club	Position
31	EDM	Georges Laraque	St-Jean	RW
49	STL	Jochen Hecht	Mannheim	C
67	WPG	Brad Isbister	Portland	LW
79	N.J.	Alyn McCauley	Ottawa	C
87	HFD	Sami Kapanen	HIFK Helsinki	RW
90	S.J.	Vesa Toskala	Ilves Tampere	G
91	NYR	Marc Savard	Oshawa	C
101	STL	Michal Handzus	Banska Bystrica	C
116	S.J.	Miikka Kiprusoff	TPS Turku Jr.	G
122	N.J.	Chris Mason	Prince George	G
144	VAN	Brent Sopel	Swift Current	D
164	MTL	Stephane Robidas	Shawinigan	D
166	FLA	Peter Worrell	Hull	LW
177	BOS	P.J. Axelsson	Vastra Frolunda	LW
192	FLA	Filip Kuba	Vitkovice Jr.	D

1994

FIRST ROUND

Pick	Claimed by		Amateur Club	Position
1	FLA	Ed Jovanovski	Windsor	D
2	ANA	Oleg Tverdovsky	Krylja Sovetov	D
3	OTT	Radek Bonk	Las Vegas (IHL)	C
4	EDM	Jason Bonsignore	Niagara Falls	C
5	HFD	Jeff O'Neill	Guelph	RW
6	EDM	Ryan Smyth	Moose Jaw	LW
7	L.A.	Jamie Storr	Owen Sound	G
8	T.B.	Jason Wiemer	Portland	C
9	NYI	Brett Lindros	Kingston	RW
10	WSH	Nolan Baumgartner	Kamloops	D
11	S.J.	Jeff Friesen	Regina	LW
12	QUE	Wade Belak	Saskatoon	D/RW
13	VAN	Mattias Ohlund	Pitea	D
14	CHI	Ethan Moreau	Niagara Falls	LW
15	WSH	Alexander Kharlamov	CSKA Moscow	C
16	TOR	Eric Fichaud	Chictoutimi	G
17	BUF	Wayne Primeau	Owen Sound	C
18	MTL	Brad Brown	North Bay	D
19	CGY	Chris Dingman	Brandon	LW
20	DAL	Jason Botterill	U. of Michigan	LW
21	BOS	Evgeni Ryabchikov	Molot Perm	G
22	QUE	Jeffrey Kealty	Catholic Memorial H.S.	D
23	DET	Yan Golubovsky	Dynamo 2	D
24	PIT	Chris Wells	Seattle	C
25	N.J.	Vadim Sharifijanov	Salavat Yulayev Ufa	LW
26	NYR	Dan Cloutier	Sault Ste. Marie	G

OTHER NOTABLE SELECTIONS

Pick	Claimed by		Amateur Club	Position
44	MTL	Jose Theodore	St-Jean	G
49	DET	Mathieu Dandenault	Sherbrooke	RW/D
50	PIT	Richard Park	Belleville	D
51	N.J.	Patrik Elias	Kladno	C
64	TOR	Fredrik Modin	Timra	LW
71	N.J.	Sheldon Souray	Tri-City	D
72	QUE	Chris Drury	Fairfield Prep	C
87	QUE	Milan Hejduk	Pardubice	RW
90	NYI	Brad Lukowich	Kamloops	D
124	DAL	Marty Turco	Cambridge Jr. A	G
133	OTT	Daniel Alfredsson	Vastra Frolunda	RW
151	BOS	Andre Roy	Chicoutimi	RW
217	QUE	Tim Thomas	U. of Vermont	G
218	PHI	Johan Hedberg	Leksand	G
219	S.J.	Evgeni Nabokov	Ust-Kamenogorsk	G
226	MTL	Tomas Vokoun	Kladno	G
233	N.J.	Steve Sullivan	Sault Ste. Marie	RW
249	WSH	Richard Zednik	Banska Bystricia	RW
257	DET	Tomas Holmstrom	Bodens IK	LW
286	NYR	Kim Johnsson	Malmo	D

1993

FIRST ROUND

Pick	Claimed by		Amateur Club	Position
1	OTT	Alexandre Daigle	Victoriaville	C
2	HFD	Chris Pronger	Peterborough	D
3	T.B.	Chris Gratton	Kingston	C
4	ANA	Paul Kariya	U. of Maine	LW
5	FLA	Rob Niedermayer	Medicine Hat	C
6	S.J.	Viktor Kozlov	Dynamo Moscow	C
7	EDM	Jason Arnott	Oshawa	C
8	NYR	Niklas Sundstrom	MoDo Ornskoldsvik	RW
9	DAL	Todd Harvey	Detroit	RW/C
10	QUE	Jocelyn Thibault	Sherbrooke	G
11	WSH	Brendan Witt	Seattle	D
12	TOR	Kenny Jonsson	Rogle Angelholm	D
13	N.J.	Denis Pederson	Prince Albert	C/RW
14	QUE	Adam Deadmarsh	Portland	RW
15	WPG	Mats Lindgren	Skelleftea	C/LW
16	EDM	Nick Stajduhar	London	D
17	WSH	Jason Allison	London	C
18	CGY	Jesper Mattsson	Malmo	C
19	TOR	Landon Wilson	Dubuque	RW
20	VAN	Mike Wilson	Sudbury	D
21	MTL	Saku Koivu	TPS Turku	C
22	DET	Anders Eriksson	MoDo Ornskoldsvik	D
23	NYI	Todd Bertuzzi	Guelph	RW
24	CHI	Eric Lecompte	Hull	LW
25	BOS	Kevyn Adams	Miami of Ohio	C
26	PIT	Stefan Bergkvist	Leksand	D

OTHER NOTABLE SELECTIONS

Pick	Claimed by		Amateur Club	Position
28	S.J.	Shean Donovan	Ottawa	RW
32	N.J.	Jay Pandolfo	Boston University	LW
35	DAL	Jamie Langenbrunner	Cloquet	C
39	N.J.	Brendan Morrison	Spokane	D
40	NYI	Bryan McCabe	Spokane	D
41	FLA	Kevin Weekes	Owen Sound	G
71	PHI	Vinny Prospal	Ceske Budejovice	C
72	HFD	Marek Malik	Vitkovice	D
89	STL	Jamal Myers	Western Mich	RW
90	CHI	Eric Daze	Beauport	RW
111	EDM	Miroslav Satan	Dukla Trencin	LW
118	NYI	Tommy Salo	Vasteras	G
124	VAN	Scott Walker	Owen Sound	RW
151	MTL	Darcy Tucker	Kamloops	RW
164	NYR	Todd Marchant	Clarkson	C
174	WSH	Andrew Brunette	Owen Sound	LW
188	HFD	Manny Legace	Niagara Falls	G
207	BOS	Hal Gill	Nashoba H.S.	D
219	STL	Mike Grier	St. Sebastian's H.S.	RW
227	OTT	Pavol Demitra	Dukla Trencin	LW
250	L.A.	Kimmo Timonen	KalPa Kuopio	D

1992

FIRST ROUND

Pick	Claimed by		Amateur Club	Position
1	T.B.	Roman Hamrlik	ZPS Zlin	D
2	OTT	Alexei Yashin	Dynamo Moscow	C
3	S.J.	Mike Rathje	Medicine Hat	D
4	QUE	Todd Warriner	Windsor	LW
5	NYI	Darius Kasparaitis	Dynamo Moscow	D
6	CGY	Cory Stillman	Windsor	LW
7	PHI	Ryan Sittler	Nichols H.S.	LW
8	TOR	Brandon Convery	Sudbury	C
9	HFD	Robert Petrovicky	Dukla Trencin	C
10	S.J.	Andrei Nazarov	Dynamo Moscow	LW
11	BUF	David Cooper	Medicine Hat	D
12	CHI	Sergei Krivokrasov	CSKA Moscow	RW
13	EDM	Joe Hulbig	St. Sebastian's H.S.	LW
14	WSH	Sergei Gonchar	Traktor Chelyabinsk	D
15	PHI	Jason Bowen	Tri-City	D
16	BOS	Dmitri Kvartalnov	San Diego (IHL)	LW
17	WPG	Sergei Bautin	Dynamo Moscow	D
18	N.J.	Jason Smith	Regina	D
19	PIT	Martin Straka	Skoda Plzen	C
20	MTL	David Wilkie	Kamloops	D
21	VAN	Libor Polasek	Vitkovice	C
22	DET	Curtis Bowen	Ottawa	LW
23	TOR	Grant Marshall	Ottawa	RW
24	NYR	Peter Ferraro	Waterloo Jr. A	LW

OTHER NOTABLE SELECTIONS

Pick	Claimed by		Amateur Club	Position
32	WSH	Jim Carey	Catholic Memorial	G
33	MTL	Valeri Bure	Spokane	RW
38	STL	Igor Korolev	Dynamo Moscow	C
40	VAN	Michael Peca	Ottawa	C
42	N.J.	Sergei Brylin	CSKA Moscow	C
46	DET	Darren McCarty	Bellevile	RW
48	NYR	Mattias Norstrom	AIK Solna	D
52	QUE	Manny Fernandez	Laval	G
65	EDM	Kirk Maltby	Owen Sound	RW
68	MTL	Craig Rivet	Kingston	D
88	MIN	Jere Lehtinen	Kiekko-Espoo	RW
117	VAN	Adrian Aucoin	Boston University	D
158	STL	Ian Laperriere	Drummondville	C/RW
186	N.J.	Stephane Yelle	Oshawa	C
204	WPG	Nikolai Khabibulin	CSKA Moscow	G
220	QUE	Anson Carter	Wexford Jr. A	C

1991

FIRST ROUND

Pick	Claimed by		Amateur Club	Position
1	QUE	Eric Lindros	Oshawa	C
2	S.J.	Pat Falloon	Spokane	RW
3	N.J.	Scott Niedermayer	Kamloops	D
4	NYI	Scott Lachance	Boston University	D
5	WPG	Aaron Ward	U. of Michigan	D
6	PHI	Peter Forsberg	MoDo Ornskoldsvik	C
7	VAN	Alek Stojanov	Hamilton	RW
8	MIN	Richard Matvichuk	Saskatoon	D
9	HFD	Patrick Poulin	St-Hyacinthe	C
10	DET	Martin Lapointe	Laval	RW
11	N.J.	Brian Rolston	Detroit Compuware Jr. A	C/RW
12	EDM	Tyler Wright	Swift Current	C
13	BUF	Philippe Boucher	Granby	D
14	WSH	Pat Peake	Detroit	C
15	NYR	Alex Kovalev	Dynamo Moscow	RW
16	PIT	Markus Naslund	MoDo Ornskoldsvik	LW
17	MTL	Brent Bilodeau	Seattle	D
18	BOS	Glen Murray	Sudbury	RW
19	CGY	Niklas Sundblad	AIK Solna	RW
20	EDM	Martin Rucinsky	Litvinov	LW
21	WSH	Trevor Halverson	North Bay	LW
22	CHI	Dean McAmmond	Prince Albert	LW

OTHER NOTABLE SELECTIONS

Pick	Claimed by		Amateur Club	Position
23	S.J.	Ray Whitney	Spokane	LW
26	NYI	Ziggy Palffy	AC Nitra	RW
27	STL	Steve Staios	Niagara Falls	D
30	S.J.	Sandis Ozolinsh	Dynamo Riga	D
40	BOS	Jozef Stumpel	AC Nitra	C
47	TOR	Yanic Perreault	Trois-Rivieres	C
54	DET	Chris Osgood	Medicine Hat	G
58	WSH	Steve Konowalchuk	Portland	LW
59	HFD	Michael Nylander	Huddinge	C
76	DET	Mike Knuble	Kalamazoo Jr. A	RW
81	L.A.	Alexei Zhitnik	Sokol Kiev	D
106	BOS	Mariusz Czerkawski	GKS Tychy	RW
122	PHI	Dmitry Yushkevich	Yaroslavl	D
123	BUF	Sean O'Donnell	Sudbury	D
171	MTL	Brian Savage	Miami of Ohio	LW
203	WPG	Igor Ulanov	Khimik Voskresensk	D

1990

FIRST ROUND

Pick	Claimed by		Amateur Club	Position
1	QUE	Owen Nolan	Cornwall	RW
2	VAN	Petr Nedved	Seattle	C
3	DET	Keith Primeau	Niagara Falls	C
4	PHI	Mike Ricci	Peterborough	C
5	PIT	Jaromir Jagr	Kladno	RW
6	NYI	Scott Scissons	Saskatoon	C
7	L.A.	Darryl Sydor	Kamloops	D
8	MIN	Derian Hatcher	North Bay	D
9	WSH	John Slaney	Cornwall	D
10	TOR	Drake Berehowsky	Kingston	D
11	CGY	Trevor Kidd	Brandon	G
12	MTL	Turner Stevenson	Seattle	RW

Selected 56th overall in the 1996 Entry Draft, Zdeno Chara's skill had not yet caught up to his 6'9" frame during his first four NHL seasons with the New York Islanders. Chara became an All-Star during his next four seasons in Ottawa and has become a superstar, Stanley Cup winner and team captain in Boston.

Pick	Claimed by	Amateur Club	Position
13	NYR Michael Stewart	Michigan State	D
14	BUF Brad May	Niagara Falls	LW
15	HFD Mark Greig	Lethbridge	RW
16	CHI Karl Dykhuis	Hull	D
17	EDM Scott Allison	Prince Albert	C
18	VAN Shawn Antoski	North Bay	LW
19	WPG Keith Tkachuk	Malden Catholic H.S.	LW
20	N.J. Martin Brodeur	St-Hyacinthe	G
21	BOS Bryan Smolinski	Michigan State	C

OTHER NOTABLE SELECTIONS

Pick	Claimed by	Amateur Club	Position
25	PHI Chris Simon	Ottawa	LW
31	TOR Felix Potvin	Chicoutimi	G
34	NYR Doug Weight	Lake Superior State	C
36	HFD Geoff Sanderson	Swift Current	LW
45	DET Vyacheslav Kozlov	Khimik Voskresensk	RW
77	WPG Alexei Zhamnov	Dynamo Moscow	C
85	NYR Sergei Zubov	CSKA Moscow	D
113	MIN Roman Turek	Plzen	G
123	MTL Craig Conroy	Northwood Prep	C
133	L.A. Robert Lang	CHZ Litvinov	C
156	WSH Peter Bondra	Kosice	RW
158	QUE Alexander Karpovtsev	VSZ Dynamo	D
177	WSH Ken Klee	Bowling Green	D
244	NYR Sergei Nemchinov	Krylja Sovetov	LW

1989

FIRST ROUND

Pick	Claimed by	Amateur Club	Position
1	QUE Mats Sundin	Nacka	C
2	NYI Dave Chyzowski	Kamloops	LW
3	TOR Scott Thornton	Belleville	LW
4	WPG Stu Barnes	Tri-City	C
5	N.J. Bill Guerin	Springfield Jr. B.	RW
6	CHI Adam Bennett	Sudbury	D
7	MIN Doug Zmolek	John Marshall H.S.	D
8	VAN Jason Herter	North Dakota	D
9	STL Jason Marshall	Vernon Jr. A	D
10	HFD Bobby Holik	Dukla Jihlava	C
11	DET Mike Sillinger	Regina	C
12	TOR Rob Pearson	Belleville	RW
13	MTL Lindsay Vallis	Seattle	D
14	BUF Kevin Haller	Regina	D
15	EDM Jason Soules	Niagara Falls	D
16	PIT Jamie Heward	Regina	D
17	BOS Shayne Stevenson	Kitchener	RW
18	N.J. Jason Miller	Medicine Hat	LW
19	WSH Olaf Kolzig	Tri-City	G
20	NYR Steven Rice	Kitchener	RW
21	TOR Steve Bancroft	Belleville	D

OTHER NOTABLE SELECTIONS

Pick	Claimed by	Amateur Club	Position
22	QUE Adam Foote	Sault Ste. Marie	D
30	MTL Patrice Brisebois	Laval	D
53	DET Nicklas Lidstrom	Vasteras	D
62	WPG Kris Draper	Canadian National	C
70	CGY Robert Reichel	Litvinov	C
109	WPG Dan Bylsma	Bowling Green	RW
74	DET Sergei Fedorov	CSKA Moscow	C
113	VAN Pavel Bure	CSKA Moscow	RW
116	DET Dallas Drake	Northern Michigan	RW
183	BUF Donald Audette	Laval	RW
191	NYI Vladimir Malakhov	CSKA Moscow	D
196	MIN Arturs Irbe	Dynamo Riga	G
221	DET Vladimir Konstantinov	CSKA Moscow	D

1988

FIRST ROUND

Pick	Claimed by	Amateur Club	Position
1	MIN Mike Modano	Prince Albert	C
2	VAN Trevor Linden	Medicine Hat	RW
3	QUE Curtis Leschyshyn	Saskatoon	D
4	PIT Darrin Shannon	Windsor	LW
5	QUE Daniel Dore	Drummondville	RW
6	TOR Scott Pearson	Kingston	LW
7	L.A. Martin Gelinas	Hull	LW
8	CHI Jeremy Roenick	Thayer Academy	C
9	STL Rod Brind'Amour	Notre Dame Jr. A	C
10	WPG Teemu Selanne	Jokerit	RW
11	HFD Chris Govedaris	Toronto	LW
12	N.J. Corey Foster	Peterborough	D
13	BUF Joel Savage	Victoria	RW
14	PHI Claude Boivin	Drummondville	LW
15	WSH Reggie Savage	Victoriaville	C
16	NYI Kevin Cheveldayoff	Brandon	D
17	DET Kory Kocur	Saskatoon	RW
18	BOS Rob Cimetta	Toronto	W
19	EDM Francois Leroux	St-Jean	D
20	MTL Eric Charron	Trois-Rivieres	D
21	CGY Jason Muzzatti	Michigan State	G

Elected to the U.S. Hockey Hall of Fame in 2013, Bill Guerin was selected fifth overall in the 1989 NHL Entry Draft. He went on to play 18 NHL seasons with eight different teams between 1991 and 2010, collecting 429 goals and 427 assists in 1,263 games.

OTHER NOTABLE SELECTIONS

Pick	Claimed by	Amateur Club	Position
27	TOR Tie Domi	Peterborough	RW
67	PIT Mark Recchi	Kamloops	RW
68	NYR Tony Amonte	Thayer Academy	RW
70	L.A. Rob Blake	Bowling Green	D
76	BUF Keith Carney	Mount St. Charles H.S.	D
81	BOS Joe Juneau	RPI	C
89	BUF Alexander Mogilny	CSKA Moscow	RW
97	BUF Rob Ray	Cornwall	RW
129	QUE Valeri Kamensky	CSKA Moscow	D
198	STL Bret Hedican	North St. Paul H.S.	D
234	QUE Claude Lapointe	Laval	LW/C

1987

FIRST ROUND

Pick	Claimed by	Amateur Club	Position
1	BUF Pierre Turgeon	Granby	C
2	N.J. Brendan Shanahan	London	LW
3	BOS Glen Wesley	Portland	D
4	L.A. Wayne McBean	Medicine Hat	D
5	PIT Chris Joseph	Seattle	D
6	MIN Dave Archibald	Portland	C/LW
7	TOR Luke Richardson	Peterborough	D
8	CHI Jimmy Waite	Chicoutimi	G
9	QUE Bryan Fogarty	Kingston	D
10	NYR Jay More	New Westminster	D
11	DET Yves Racine	Longueuil	D
12	STL Keith Osborne	North Bay	RW
13	NYI Dean Chynoweth	Medicine Hat	D
14	BOS Stephane Quintal	Granby	D
15	QUE Joe Sakic	Swift Current	C
16	WPG Bryan Marchment	Belleville	D
17	MTL Andrew Cassels	Ottawa	C
18	HFD Jody Hull	Peterborough	RW
19	CGY Bryan Deasley	U. of Michigan	LW
20	PHI Darren Rumble	Kitchener	D
21	EDM Peter Soberlak	Swift Current	LW

OTHER NOTABLE SELECTIONS

Pick	Claimed by	Amateur Club	Position
33	MTL John LeClair	Bellows Academy	LW
38	MTL Eric Desjardins	Granby	D
44	MTL Mathieu Schneider	Cornwall	D
71	TOR Joe Sacco	Medford H.S.	RW
110	PIT Shawn McEachern	Matignon H.S.	RW
114	QUE Garth Snow	Mount St. Charles H.S.	G
118	NYI Rob DiMaio	Medicine Hat	RW
149	N.J. Jim Dowd	Brick H.S.	C
166	CGY Theoren Fleury	Moose Jaw	RW

1986

FIRST ROUND

Pick	Claimed by	Amateur Club	Position
1	DET Joe Murphy	Michigan State	RW
2	L.A. Jimmy Carson	Verdun	C
3	N.J. Neil Brady	Medicine Hat	C
4	PIT Zarley Zalapski	Canadian National	D
5	BUF Shawn Anderson	Canadian National	D
6	TOR Vincent Damphousse	Laval	C
7	VAN Dan Woodley	Portland	RW
8	WPG Pat Elynuik	Prince Albert	RW
9	NYR Brian Leetch	Avon Old Farms H.S.	D
10	STL Jocelyn Lemieux	Laval	RW
11	HFD Scott Young	Boston University	RW
12	MIN Warren Babe	Lethbridge	LW
13	BOS Craig Janney	Boston College	C
14	CHI Everett Sanipass	Verdun	LW
15	MTL Mark Pederson	Medicine Hat	LW
16	CGY George Pelawa	Bemidji H.S.	RW
17	NYI Tom Fitzgerald	Austin Prep	RW
18	QUE Ken McRae	Sudbury	C
19	WSH Jeff Greenlaw	Canadian National	LW
20	PHI Kerry Huffman	Guelph	D
21	EDM Kim Issel	Prince Albert	RW

OTHER NOTABLE SELECTIONS

Pick	Claimed by	Amateur Club	Position
22	DET Adam Graves	Windsor	LW
29	WPG Teppo Numminen	Tappara Tampere	D
67	PIT Rob Brown	Kamloops	RW
72	NYR Mark Janssens	Regina	C
81	QUE Ron Tugnutt	Peterborough	G
85	DET Johan Garpenlov	Nacka	LW
114	NYR Darren Turcotte	North Bay	C
141	MTL Lyle Odelein	Moose Jaw	D
143	NYI Rich Pilon	Prince Albert AAA	D
202	BOS Greg Hawgood	Kamloops	D

1985

FIRST ROUND

Pick	Claimed by	Amateur Club	Position
1	TOR Wendel Clark	Saskatoon	LW/D
2	PIT Craig Simpson	Michigan State	LW
3	N.J. Craig Wolanin	Kitchener	D
4	VAN Jim Sandlak	London	RW
5	HFD Dana Murzyn	Calgary	D
6	NYI Brad Dalgarno	Hamilton	RW
7	NYR Ulf Dahlen	Ostersund	LW
8	DET Brent Fedyk	Regina	LW
9	L.A. Craig Duncanson	Sudbury	LW
10	L.A. Dan Gratton	Oshawa	C
11	CHI Dave Manson	Prince Albert	D
12	MTL Jose Charbonneau	Drummondville	RW
13	NYI Derek King	Sault Ste. Marie	LW
14	BUF Calle Johansson	Vastra Frolunda	D

15	QUE	David Latta	Kitchener	LW
16	MTL	Tom Chorske	Minneapolis SW H.S.	LW
17	CGY	Chris Biotti	Belmont Hill H.S.	D
18	WPG	Ryan Stewart	Kamloops	C
19	WSH	Yvon Corriveau	Toronto	LW
20	EDM	Scott Metcalfe	Kingston	LW
21	PHI	Glen Seabrooke	Peterborough	C

OTHER NOTABLE SELECTIONS

24	N.J.	Sean Burke	Toronto	G
27	CGY	Joe Nieuwendyk	Cornell	C
28	NYR	Mike Richter	Northwood Prep	G
32	N.J.	Eric Weinrich	North Yarmouth Academy	D
35	BUF	Benoit Hogue	St-Jean	C
50	DET	Steve Chiasson	Guelph	D
52	BOS	Bill Ranford	New Westminster	G
81	WPG	Fredrik Olausson	Farjestad	D
113	DET	Randy McKay	Michigan Tech	RW
157	BOS	Randy Burridge	Peterborough	LW
188	EDM	Kelly Buchberger	Moose Jaw	RW
189	PHI	Gord Murphy	Oshawa	D
214	VAN	Igor Larionov	CSKA Moscow	C
245	BUF	Ken Baumgartner	Prince Albert	D

1984

FIRST ROUND

1	PIT	Mario Lemieux	Laval	C
2	N.J.	Kirk Muller	Guelph	LW
3	CHI	Eddie Olczyk	Team USA	C
4	TOR	Al Iafrate	Belleville	D
5	MTL	Petr Svoboda	CHZ Litvinov	D
6	L.A.	Craig Redmond	U. of Denver	D
7	DET	Shawn Burr	Kitchener	LW/C
8	MTL	Shayne Corson	Brantford	LW
9	PIT	Doug Bodger	Kamloops	D
10	VAN	J.J. Daigneault	Longueuil	D
11	HFD	Sylvain Cote	Quebec	D
12	CGY	Gary Roberts	Ottawa	LW
13	MIN	David Quinn	Kent H.S.	D
14	NYR	Terry Carkner	Peterborough	D
15	QUE	Trevor Stienburg	Guelph	RW
16	PIT	Roger Belanger	Kingston	C
17	WSH	Kevin Hatcher	North Bay	D
18	BUF	Mikael Andersson	Vastra Frolunda	LW
19	BOS	Dave Pasin	Prince Albert	RW
20	NYI	Duncan MacPherson	Saskatoon	D
21	EDM	Selmar Odelein	Regina	D

OTHER NOTABLE SELECTIONS

25	TOR	Todd Gill	Windsor	D
27	PHI	Scott Mellanby	Henry Carr Jr. B	RW
29	MTL	Stephane Richer	Granby	RW
36	QUE	Jeff Brown	Sudbury	D
51	MTL	Patrick Roy	Granby	G
107	N.J.	Kirk McLean	Oshawa	G
117	CGY	Brett Hull	Penticton Jr. A	RW
119	NYR	Kjell Samuelsson	Leksand	D
166	BOS	Don Sweeney	St. Paul's H.S.	D
171	L.A.	Luc Robitaille	Hull	LW
180	CGY	Gary Suter	U. of Wisconsin	D

1983

FIRST ROUND

1	MIN	Brian Lawton	Mount St. Charles H.S.	LW
2	HFD	Sylvain Turgeon	Hull	LW
3	NYI	Pat LaFontaine	Verdun	C
4	DET	Steve Yzerman	Peterborough	C
5	BUF	Tom Barrasso	Acton-Boxborough	G
6	N.J.	John MacLean	Oshawa	RW
7	TOR	Russ Courtnall	Victoria	RW
8	WPG	Andrew McBain	North Bay	RW
9	VAN	Cam Neely	Portland	RW
10	BUF	Normand Lacombe	New Hampshire	RW
11	BUF	Adam Creighton	Ottawa	C
12	NYR	Dave Gagner	Brantford	C
13	CGY	Dan Quinn	Belleville	C
14	WPG	Bobby Dollas	Laval	D
15	PIT	Bob Errey	Peterborough	LW
16	NYI	Gerald Diduck	Lethbridge	D
17	MTL	Alfie Turcotte	Portland	C
18	CHI	Bruce Cassidy	Ottawa	D
19	EDM	Jeff Beukeboom	Sault Ste. Marie	D
20	HFD	David Jensen	Lawrence Academy	C
21	BOS	Nevin Markwart	Regina	LW

OTHER NOTABLE SELECTIONS

26	MTL	Claude Lemieux	Trois-Rivieres	RW
27	MTL	Sergio Momesso	Shawinigan	LW
41	PHI	Peter Zezel	Toronto	C
82	EDM	Esa Tikkanen	HIFK Helsinki	LW
88	DET	Petr Klima	Dukla Jihlava	W
91	DET	Joe Kocur	Saskatoon	RW
112	L.A.	Kevin Stevens	Silver Lake H.S.	LW
125	PHI	Rick Tocchet	Sault Ste. Marie	RW
139	BUF	Christian Ruuttu	Assat Pori	C
150	N.J.	Viacheslav Fetisov	CSKA Moscow	D
207	CHI	Dominik Hasek	Pardubice	G
223	BUF	Uwe Krupp	Koln	D
241	CGY	Sergei Makarov	CSKA Moscow	RW

1982

FIRST ROUND

1	BOS	Gord Kluzak	Billings	D
2	MIN	Brian Bellows	Kitchener	LW
3	TOR	Gary Nylund	Portland	D
4	PHI	Ron Sutter	Lethbridge	C
5	WSH	Scott Stevens	Kitchener	D
6	BUF	Phil Housley	South St. Paul H.S.	D
7	CHI	Ken Yaremchuk	Portland	C
8	N.J.	Rocky Trottier	Nanaimo	RW
9	BUF	Paul Cyr	Victoria	LW
10	PIT	Rich Sutter	Lethbridge	RW
11	VAN	Michel Petit	Sherbrooke	D
12	WPG	Jim Kyte	Cornwall	D
13	QUE	David Shaw	Kitchener	D
14	HFD	Paul Lawless	Windsor	LW
15	NYR	Chris Kontos	Toronto	LW/C
16	BUF	Dave Andreychuk	Oshawa	LW
17	DET	Murray Craven	Medicine Hat	LW
18	N.J.	Ken Daneyko	Seattle	D
19	MTL	Alain Heroux	Chicoutimi	LW
20	EDM	Jim Playfair	Portland	D
21	NYI	Pat Flatley	U. of Wisconsin	RW

OTHER NOTABLE SELECTIONS

36	NYR	Tomas Sandstrom	Farjestad	RW
43	N.J.	Pat Verbeek	Sudbury	RW
45	TOR	Ken Wregget	Lethbridge	G
56	HFD	Kevin Dineen	U. of Denver	RW
67	HFD	Ulf Samuelsson	Leksand	D
75	WPG	Dave Ellett	Ottawa Jr. A	D
80	MIN	Bob Rouse	Nanaimo	D
88	HFD	Ray Ferraro	Penticton Jr. A	C
119	PHI	Ron Hextall	Brandon	G
120	NYR	Tony Granato	Northwood Prep	RW
134	STL	Doug Gilmour	Cornwall	C
140	PHI	Dave Brown	Saskatoon	RW

1981

FIRST ROUND

1	WPG	Dale Hawerchuk	Cornwall	C
2	L.A.	Doug Smith	Ottawa	C
3	WSH	Bob Carpenter	St. John's Prep	C
4	HFD	Ron Francis	Sault Ste. Marie	C
5	COL	Joe Cirella	Oshawa	D
6	TOR	Jim Benning	Portland	D
7	MTL	Mark Hunter	Brantford	RW
8	EDM	Grant Fuhr	Victoria	G
9	NYR	James Patrick	Prince Albert	D
10	VAN	Garth Butcher	Regina	D
11	QUE	Randy Moller	Lethbridge	D
12	CHI	Tony Tanti	Oshawa	RW
13	MIN	Ron Meighan	Niagara Falls	D
14	BOS	Normand Leveille	Chicoutimi	LW
15	CGY	Al MacInnis	Kitchener	D
16	PHI	Steve Smith	Sault Ste. Marie	D
17	BUF	Jiri Dudacek	Kladno	RW
18	MTL	Gilbert Delorme	Chicoutimi	D
19	MTL	Jan Ingman	Farjestad	LW
20	STL	Marty Ruff	Lethbridge	D
21	NYI	Paul Boutilier	Sherbrooke	D

OTHER NOTABLE SELECTIONS

22	WPG	Scott Arniel	Cornwall	LW
40	MTL	Chris Chelios	Moose Jaw	D
56	CGY	Mike Vernon	Calgary	G
72	NYR	John Vanbiesbrouck	Sault Ste. Marie	G
107	DET	Gerard Gallant	Sherbrooke	LW
108	COL	Bruce Driver	U. of Wisconsin	D
111	EDM	Steve Smith	London	D
145	MTL	Tom Kurvers	Minnesota-Duluth	D
152	WSH	Gaetan Duchesne	Quebec	LW

1980

FIRST ROUND

1	MTL	Doug Wickenheiser	Regina	C
2	WPG	Dave Babych	Portland	D
3	CHI	Denis Savard	Montreal	C
4	L.A.	Larry Murphy	Peterborough	D
5	WSH	Darren Veitch	Regina	D
6	EDM	Paul Coffey	Kitchener	D
7	VAN	Rick Lanz	Oshawa	D
8	HFD	Fred Arthur	Cornwall	D
9	PIT	Mike Bullard	Brantford	C
10	L.A.	Jim Fox	Ottawa	RW
11	DET	Mike Blaisdell	Regina	RW
12	STL	Rik Wilson	Kingston	D
13	CGY	Denis Cyr	Montreal	RW
14	NYR	Jim Malone	Toronto	C
15	CHI	Jerome Dupont	Toronto	D
16	MIN	Brad Palmer	Victoria	LW
17	NYI	Brent Sutter	Red Deer Jr. A	C
18	BOS	Barry Pederson	Victoria	C
19	COL	Paul Gagne	Windsor	LW
20	BUF	Steve Patrick	Brandon	RW
21	PHI	Mike Stothers	Kingston	D

OTHER NOTABLE SELECTIONS

37	MIN	Don Beaupre	Sudbury	G
38	NYI	Kelly Hrudey	Medicine Hat	G
57	CHI	Troy Murray	St. Albert Jr. A	C
61	MTL	Craig Ludwig	North Dakota	D
69	EDM	Jari Kurri	Jokerit	RW
73	L.A.	Bernie Nicholls	Kingston	C
80	NYI	Greg Gilbert	Toronto	LW
81	BOS	Steve Kasper	Verdun	C
106	COL	Aaron Broten	U. of Minnesota	LW/C
120	CHI	Steve Larmer	Niagara Falls	RW
124	MTL	Mike McPhee	RPI	LW
128	WPG	Brian Mullen	U.S. Jr. National	RW
132	EDM	Andy Moog	Billings	G
181	CGY	Hakan Loob	Farjestad	RW

1979

FIRST ROUND

1	COL	Rob Ramage	London	D
2	STL	Perry Turnbull	Portland	C
3	DET	Mike Foligno	Sudbury	RW
4	WSH	Mike Gartner	Niagara Falls	RW
5	VAN	Rick Vaive	Sherbrooke	RW
6	MIN	Craig Hartsburg	Sault Ste. Marie	D
7	CHI	Keith Brown	Portland	D
8	BOS	Raymond Bourque	Verdun	D
9	TOR	Laurie Boschman	Brandon	C
10	MIN	Tom McCarthy	Oshawa	LW
11	BUF	Mike Ramsey	U. of Minnesota	D
12	ATL	Paul Reinhart	Kitchener	D
13	NYR	Doug Sulliman	Kitchener	RW
14	PHI	Brian Propp	Brandon	LW
15	BOS	Brad McCrimmon	Brandon	D
16	L.A.	Jay Wells	Kingston	D
17	NYI	Duane Sutter	Lethbridge	RW
18	HFD	Ray Allison	Brandon	RW
19	WPG	Jimmy Mann	Sherbrooke	RW
20	QUE	Michel Goulet	Quebec	LW
21	EDM	Kevin Lowe	Quebec	D

OTHER NOTABLE SELECTIONS

32	BUF	Lindy Ruff	Lethbridge	D/LW
37	MTL	Mats Naslund	Brynas Gavle	LW
40	WPG	Dave Christian	North Dakota	RW
41	QUE	Dale Hunter	Sudbury	C
42	MIN	Neal Broten	U. of Minnesota	C
44	MTL	Guy Carbonneau	Chicoutimi	C
48	EDM	Mark Messier	St. Albert Jr. A	C
54	ATL	Tim Hunter	Seattle	RW
57	BOS	Keith Crowder	Peterborough	RW
58	MTL	Rick Wamsley	Brantford	G
66	DET	John Ogrodnick	New Westminster	LW
69	EDM	Glenn Anderson	U. of Denver	RW
75	ATL	Jim Peplinski	Toronto	RW
83	QUE	Anton Stastny	Slovan Bratislava	LW
89	VAN	Dirk Graham	Regina	RW/LW
103	WPG	Thomas Steen	Leksand	C
120	BOS	Mike Krushelnyski	Montreal	LW/C

1978

FIRST ROUND

1	MIN	Bobby Smith	Ottawa	C
2	WSH	Ryan Walter	Seattle	C/LW
3	STL	Wayne Babych	Portland	RW
4	VAN	Bill Derlago	Brandon	C
5	COL	Mike Gillis	Kingston	LW
6	PHI	Behn Wilson	Kingston	D
7	PHI	Ken Linseman	Kingston	C
8	MTL	Danny Geoffrion	Cornwall	RW
9	DET	Willie Huber	Hamilton	D
10	CHI	Tim Higgins	Ottawa	RW
11	ATL	Brad Marsh	London	D
12	DET	Brent Peterson	Portland	C
13	BUF	Larry Playfair	Portland	D
14	PHI	Danny Lucas	Sault Ste. Marie	RW
15	NYI	Steve Tambellini	Lethbridge	C
16	BOS	Al Secord	Hamilton	LW
17	MTL	Dave Hunter	Sudbury	LW
18	WSH	Tim Coulis	Hamilton	LW

OTHER NOTABLE SELECTIONS

19	MIN	Steve Payne	Ottawa	LW
21	TOR	Joel Quenneville	Windsor	D
22	VAN	Curt Fraser	Victoria	LW
26	NYR	Don Maloney	Kitchener	LW
32	BUF	Tony McKegney	Kingston	LW
40	VAN	Stan Smyl	New Westminster	RW
54	MIN	Curt Giles	Minnesota-Duluth	D
55	WSH	Bengt Gustafsson	Farjestad	RW
93	NYR	Tom Laidlaw	Northern Michigan	D
103	MTL	Keith Acton	Peterborough	C
109	STL	Paul MacLean	Hull	RW
153	BOS	Craig MacTavish	U. of Mass-Lowell	C
173	STL	Risto Siltanen	Ilves Tampere	D
179	CHI	Darryl Sutter	Lethbridge	LW
231	MTL	Chris Nilan	Northeastern	RW

1977

FIRST ROUND

1	DET	Dale McCourt	St. Catharines	C
2	COL	Barry Beck	New Westminster	D
3	WSH	Robert Picard	Montreal	D
4	VAN	Jere Gillis	Sherbrooke	LW
5	Cle.	Mike Crombeen	Kingston	RW
6	CHI	Doug Wilson	Ottawa	D
7	MIN	Brad Maxwell	New Westminster	D
8	NYR	Lucien DeBlois	Sorel	C
9	STL	Scott Campbell	London	D
10	MTL	Mark Napier	Toronto	RW
11	TOR	John Anderson	Toronto	RW
12	TOR	Trevor Johansen	Toronto	D
13	NYR	Ron Duguay	Sudbury	C/RW
14	BUF	Ric Seiling	St. Catharines	RW/C
15	NYI	Mike Bossy	Laval	RW
16	BOS	Dwight Foster	Kitchener	RW
17	PHI	Kevin McCarthy	Winnipeg	D
18	MTL	Norm Dupont	Montreal	LW

OTHER NOTABLE SELECTIONS

25	MIN	Dave Semenko	Brandon	LW
33	NYI	John Tonelli	Toronto	LW
36	MTL	Rod Langway	New Hampshire	D
40	VAN	Glen Hanlon	Brandon	G
54	MTL	Gordie Roberts	Victoria	D
66	PIT	Mark Johnson	U. of Wisconsin	C
102	PIT	Greg Millen	Peterborough	G
135	PHI	Pete Peeters	Medicine Hat	G
162	MTL	Craig Laughlin	Clarkson	RW

1976

FIRST ROUND

1	WSH	Rick Green	London	D
2	PIT	Blair Chapman	Saskatoon	RW
3	MIN	Glen Sharpley	Hull	C
4	DET	Fred Williams	Saskatoon	C
5	CAL	Bjorn Johansson	Orebro	D
6	NYR	Don Murdoch	Medicine Hat	RW
7	STL	Bernie Federko	Saskatoon	C
8	ATL	Dave Shand	Peterborough	D
9	CHI	Real Cloutier	Quebec	RW
10	ATL	Harold Phillipoff	New Westminster	LW
11	K.C.	Paul Gardner	Oshawa	C
12	MTL	Peter Lee	Ottawa	RW
13	MTL	Rod Schutt	Sudbury	LW
14	NYI	Alex McKendry	Sudbury	W
15	WSH	Greg Carroll	Medicine Hat	C
16	BOS	Clayton Pachal	New Westminster	C/LW
17	PHI	Mark Suzor	Kingston	D
18	MTL	Bruce Baker	Ottawa	RW

OTHER NOTABLE SELECTIONS

19	PIT	Greg Malone	Oshawa	C
20	STL	Brian Sutter	Lethbridge	LW
22	DET	Reed Larson	Minnesota-Duluth	D
30	TOR	Randy Carlyle	Sudbury	D
45	CHI	Thomas Gradin	MoDo Ornskoldsvik	C
47	PIT	Morris Lukowich	Medicine Hat	LW
56	STL	Mike Liut	Bowling Green	G
64	ATL	Kent Nilsson	Djurgarden	C
68	NYI	Ken Morrow	Bowling Green	D
133	MTL	Ron Wilson	St. Catharines	C

1975

FIRST ROUND

1	PHI	Mel Bridgman	Victoria	C
2	K.C.	Barry Dean	Medicine Hat	LW
3	CAL	Ralph Klassen	Saskatoon	C
4	MIN	Bryan Maxwell	Medicine Hat	D
5	DET	Rick Lapointe	Victoria	D
6	TOR	Don Ashby	Calgary	C
7	CHI	Greg Vaydik	Medicine Hat	C
8	ATL	Richard Mulhern	Sherbrooke	D
9	MTL	Robin Sadler	Edmonton	D
10	VAN	Rick Blight	Brandon	RW
11	NYI	Pat Price	Saskatoon	D
12	NYR	Wayne Dillon	Toronto	C
13	PIT	Gord Laxton	New Westminster	G
14	BOS	Doug Halward	Peterborough	D
15	MTL	Pierre Mondou	Montreal	C
16	L.A.	Tim Young	Ottawa	C

OTHER NOTABLE SELECTIONS

17	BUF	Bob Sauve	Laval	G
21	CAL	Dennis Maruk	London	C
22	MTL	Brian Engblom	U. of Wisconsin	D
24	TOR	Doug Jarvis	Peterborough	C
43	CHI	Mike O'Connell	Kingston	D
57	CAL	Greg Smith	Colorado College	D
80	ATL	Willi Plett	St. Catharines	RW
108	PHI	Paul Holmgren	U. of Minnesota	RW
210	L.A.	Dave Taylor	Clarkson	RW

1974

FIRST ROUND

1	WSH	Greg Joly	Regina	D
2	K.C.	Wilf Paiement	St. Catharines	RW
3	CAL	Rick Hampton	St. Catharines	LW/D
4	NYI	Clark Gillies	Regina	LW
5	MTL	Cam Connor	Flin Flon	RW
6	MIN	Doug Hicks	Flin Flon	D
7	MTL	Doug Risebrough	Kitchener	C
8	PIT	Pierre Larouche	Sorel	C
9	DET	Bill Lochead	Oshawa	LW
10	MTL	Rick Chartraw	Kitchener	D/RW
11	BUF	Lee Fogolin Jr.	Oshawa	D
12	MTL	Mario Tremblay	Montreal	RW
13	TOR	Jack Valiquette	Sault Ste. Marie	C
14	NYR	Dave Maloney	Kitchener	D
15	MTL	Gord McTavish	Sudbury	C
16	CHI	Grant Mulvey	Calgary	RW
17	CAL	Ron Chipperfield	Brandon	C
18	BOS	Don Larway	Swift Current	RW

OTHER NOTABLE SELECTIONS

22	NYI	Bryan Trottier	Swift Current	C
25	BOS	Mark Howe	Toronto	D
29	BUF	Danny Gare	Calgary	RW
31	TOR	Tiger Williams	Swift Current	LW
32	NYR	Ron Greschner	New Westminster	D
38	K.C.	Bob Bourne	Saskatoon	C
39	CAL	Charlie Simmer	Sault Ste. Marie	LW
52	CHI	Bob Murray	Cornwall	D
70	CHI	Terry Ruskowski	Swift Current	C
77	VAN	Mike Rogers	Calgary	C
85	TOR	Mike Palmateer	Toronto	G
125	PHI	Reggie Lemelin	Sherbrooke	G
199	MTL	Dave Lumley	New Hampshire	RW
214	NYI	Stefan Persson	Brynas Gavle	D

1973

FIRST ROUND

1	NYI	Denis Potvin	Ottawa	D
2	ATL	Tom Lysiak	Medicine Hat	C
3	VAN	Dennis Ververgaert	London	RW
4	TOR	Lanny McDonald	Medicine Hat	RW
5	STL	John Davidson	Calgary	G
6	BOS	Andre Savard	Quebec	C
7	PIT	Blaine Stoughton	Flin Flon	RW
8	MTL	Bob Gainey	Peterborough	LW
9	VAN	Bob Dailey	Toronto	D
10	TOR	Bob Neely	Peterborough	LW
11	DET	Terry Richardson	New Westminster	G
12	BUF	Morris Titanic	Sudbury	LW
13	CHI	Darcy Rota	Edmonton	LW
14	NYR	Rick Middleton	Oshawa	RW
15	TOR	Ian Turnbull	Ottawa	D
16	ATL	Vic Mercredi	New Westminster	C

OTHER NOTABLE SELECTIONS

21	ATL	Eric Vail	Sudbury	LW
27	PIT	Colin Campbell	Peterborough	D
30	NYR	Pat Hickey	Hamilton	LW
33	NYI	Dave Lewis	Saskatoon	D
49	NYI	Andre St. Laurent	Montreal	C
85	ATL	Ken Houston	Chatham Jr. B.	RW
130	CAL	Larry Patey	Braintree H.S.	C
134	PIT	Gord Lane	New Westminster	D
162	ATL	Greg Fox	U. of Michigan	D

1972

FIRST ROUND

1	NYI	Billy Harris	Toronto	RW
2	ATL	Jacques Richard	Quebec	LW
3	VAN	Don Lever	Niagara Falls	LW
4	MTL	Steve Shutt	Toronto	LW
5	BUF	Jim Schoenfeld	Niagara Falls	D
6	MTL	Michel Larocque	Ottawa	G
7	PHI	Bill Barber	Kitchener	LW
8	MTL	Dave Gardner	Toronto	C
9	STL	Wayne Merrick	Ottawa	C
10	NYR	Al Blanchard	Kitchener	LW
11	TOR	George Ferguson	Toronto	C
12	MIN	Jerry Byers	Kitchener	LW
13	CHI	Phil Russell	Edmonton	D
14	MTL	John Van Boxmeer	Guelph	D
15	NYR	Bob MacMillan	St. Catharines	RW
16	BOS	Mike Bloom	St. Catharines	LW

OTHER NOTABLE SELECTIONS

17	NYI	Lorne Henning	New Westminster	C
23	PHI	Tom Bladon	Edmonton	D
33	NYI	Bob Nystrom	Calgary	RW
39	PHI	Jimmy Watson	Calgary	D
55	PHI	Al MacAdam	U. of PEI	RW
85	BUF	Peter McNab	U. of Denver	C
97	NYI	Richard Brodeur	Cornwall	G
139	TOR	Pat Boutette	Minnesota-Duluth	C/RW
144	NYI	Garry Howatt	Flin Flon	LW

1971

FIRST ROUND

1	MTL	Guy Lafleur	Quebec	RW
2	DET	Marcel Dionne	St. Catharines	C
3	VAN	Jocelyn Guevremont	Montreal	D
4	STL	Gene Carr	Flin Flon	C
5	BUF	Rick Martin	Montreal	LW
6	BOS	Ron Jones	Edmonton	D
7	MTL	Chuck Arnason	Flin Flon	RW
8	PHI	Larry Wright	Regina	C
9	PHI	Pierre Plante	Drummondville	RW
10	NYR	Steve Vickers	Toronto	LW
11	MTL	Murray Wilson	Ottawa	LW
12	CHI	Dan Spring	Edmonton	C
13	NYR	Steve Durbano	Toronto	D
14	BOS	Terry O'Reilly	Oshawa	RW

OTHER NOTABLE SELECTIONS

17	VAN	Bobby Lalonde	Montreal	C
19	BUF	Craig Ramsay	Peterborough	LW
20	MTL	Larry Robinson	Kitchener	D
22	TOR	Rick Kehoe	Hamilton	RW
33	BUF	Bill Hajt	Saskatoon	D
48	L.A.	Neil Komadoski	Winnipeg	D
55	NYR	Jerry Butler	Hamilton	RW

1970

FIRST ROUND

1	BUF	Gilbert Perreault	Montreal	C
2	VAN	Dale Tallon	Toronto	D
3	BOS	Reggie Leach	Flin Flon	RW
4	BOS	Rick MacLeish	Peterborough	C
5	MTL	Ray Martyniuk	Flin Flon	G
6	MTL	Chuck Lefley	Canadian National	LW
7	PIT	Greg Polis	Estevan	LW
8	TOR	Darryl Sittler	London	C
9	BOS	Ron Plumb	Peterborough	D
10	CAL	Chris Oddleifson	Winnipeg	C
11	NYR	Norm Gratton	Montreal	LW
12	DET	Serge Lajeunesse	Montreal	D/RW
13	BOS	Bob Stewart	Oshawa	D
14	CHI	Dan Maloney	London	LW

OTHER NOTABLE SELECTIONS

18	PHI	Bill Clement	Ottawa	C
20	MIN	Fred Barrett	Toronto	D
22	TOR	Errol Thompson	Charlottetown Sr.	LW
25	NYR	Mike Murphy	Toronto	RW
27	BOS	Dan Bouchard	London	G
32	PHI	Bob Kelly	Oshawa	LW
40	DET	Yvon Lambert	Drummondville	LW
59	L.A.	Billy Smith	Cornwall	G
70	CHI	Gilles Meloche	Verdun	G
88	OAK	Terry Murray	Ottawa	D
103	TOR	Ron Low	Dauphin Jr. A	G

1969

FIRST ROUND

1	MTL	Rejean Houle	Montreal	W
2	MTL	Marc Tardif	Montreal	LW
3	BOS	Don Tannahill	Niagara Falls	LW
4	BOS	Frank Spring	Edmonton	RW
5	MIN	Dick Redmond	St. Catharines	D
6	PHI	Bob Currier	Cornwall	C
7	OAK	Tony Featherstone	Peterborough	RW
8	NYR	Andre Dupont	Montreal	D
9	TOR	Ernie Moser	Estevan	RW
10	DET	Jim Rutherford	Hamilton	G
11	BOS	Ivan Boldirev	Oshawa	C
12	NYR	Pierre Jarry	Ottawa	LW

OTHER NOTABLE SELECTIONS

13	CHI	J.P. Bordeleau	Montreal	RW
17	PHI	Bobby Clarke	Flin Flon	C
18	OAK	Ron Stackhouse	Peterborough	D
25	MIN	Gilles Gilbert	London	G
26	PIT	Michel Briere	Shawinigan	C
51	L.A.	Butch Goring	Dauphin Jr. A	C
52	PHI	Dave Schultz	Sorel	LW
55	TOR	Brian Spencer	Swift Current	LW
64	PHI	Don Saleski	Regina	RW

NHL All-Stars

Active Players' All-Star Selection Records

Player	Total	First Team (No.)	First Team Selections	Second Team (No.)	Second Team Selections
GOALTENDER					
Martin Brodeur	**7**	(3)	2002-03; 2003-04; 2006-07.	(4)	1996-97; 1997-98; 2005-06; 2007-08.
Tim Thomas	**2**	(2)	2008-09; 2010-11.	(0)	
Henrik Lundqvist	**2**	(1)	2011-12.	(1)	2012-13.
Roberto Luongo	**2**	(0)		(2)	2003-04; 2006-07.
Miikka Kiprusoff	**1**	(1)	2005-06.	(0)	
Evgeni Nabokov	**1**	(1)	2007-08.	(0)	
Ryan Miller	**1**	(1)	2009-10.	(0)	
Sergei Bobrovsky	**1**	(1)	2012-13.	(0)	
Jose Theodore	**1**	(0)		(1)	2001-02.
Steve Mason	**1**	(0)		(1)	2008-09.
Ilya Bryzgalov	**1**	(0)		(1)	2009-10.
Pekka Rinne	**1**	(0)		(1)	2010-11.
Jonathan Quick	**1**	(0)		(1)	2011-12.
DEFENSE					
Zdeno Chara	**6**	(2)	2003-04; 2008-09.	(4)	2005-06; 2007-08; 2010-11; 2011-12.
Mike Green	**2**	(2)	2008-09; 2009-10.	(0)	
Shea Weber	**2**	(1)	2010-11; 2011-12.	(0)	
Sergei Gonchar	**2**	(0)		(2)	2001-02; 2002-03.
Dan Boyle	**2**	(0)		(2)	2006-07; 2008-09.
Dion Phaneuf	**1**	(1)	2007-08.	(0)	
Duncan Keith	**1**	(1)	2009-10.	(0)	
Erik Karlsson	**1**	(1)	2011-12.	(0)	
P.K. Subban	**1**	(1)	2012-13	(0)	
Ryan Suter	**1**	(1)	2012-13	(0)	
Brian Campbell	**1**	(0)		(1)	2007-08.
Drew Doughty	**1**	(0)		(1)	2009-10.
Lubomir Visnovsky	**1**	(0)		(1)	2010-11.
Alex Pietrangelo	**1**	(0)		(1)	2011-12.
Francois Beachemin	**1**	(0)		(1)	2012-13.
Kris Letang	**1**	(0)		(1)	2012-13.
CENTER					
Evgeni Malkin	**3**	(3)	2007-08; 2008-09; 2011-12.	(0)	
Sidney Crosby	**3**	(2)	2006-07; 2012-13.	(1)	2009-10.
Joe Thornton	**3**	(1)	2005-06.	(2)	2002-03; 2007-08.
Henrik Sedin	**2**	(2)	2009-10; 2010-11.	(0)	
Steven Stamkos	**2**	(0)		(2)	2010-11; 2011-12.
Eric Staal	**1**	(0)		(1)	2005-06.
Vincent Lecavalier	**1**	(0)		(1)	2006-07.
Pavel Datsyuk	**1**	(0)		(1)	2008-09.
Jonathan Toews	**1**	(0)		(1)	2012-13.
RIGHT WING					
Jaromir Jagr	**8**	(7)	1994-95; 1995-96; 1997-98 1998-99; 1999-00; 2000-01; 2005-06.	(1)	1996-97.
Martin St. Louis	**5**	(1)	2003-04.	(4)	2006-07; 2009-10; 2010-11; 2012-13.
Jarome Iginla	**4**	(3)	2001-02; 2007-08; 2008-09.	(1)	2003-04.
Teemu Selanne	**4**	(2)	1992-93; 1996-97.	(2)	1997-98; 1998-99.
Todd Bertuzzi	**1**	(1)	2002-03.	(0)	
Dany Heatley	**1**	(1)	2006-07.	(0)	
Patrick Kane	**1**	(1)	2009-10.	(0)	
Corey Perry	**1**	(1)	2010-11.	(0)	
James Neal	**1**	(1)	2011-12.	(0)	
Alex Ovechkin	**1**	(1)	2012-13.	(0)	
Milan Hejduk	**1**	(0)		(1)	2002-03.
Daniel Alfredsson	**1**	(0)		(1)	2005-06.
Marian Hossa	**1**	(0)		(1)	2008-09.
Marian Gaborik	**1**	(0)		(1)	2011-12.
LEFT WING					
Alex Ovechkin	**7**	(5)	2005-06; 2006-07; 2007-08; 2008-09; 2009-10.	(2)	2010-11; 2012-13.
Daniel Sedin	**2**	(1)	2010-11	(1)	2009-10.
Patrik Elias	**1**	(1)	2000-01.	(0)	
Chris Kunitz	**1**	(1)	2012-13.	(0)	
Dany Heatley	**1**	(0)		(1)	2005-06.
Thomas Vanek	**1**	(0)		(1)	2006-07.
Henrik Zetterberg	**1**	(0)		(1)	2007-08.
Zach Parise	**1**	(0)		(1)	2008-09.
Ray Whitney	**1**	(0)		(1)	2011-12.

Leading NHL All-Stars 1930-31 to 2012-13

Player	Pos.	Team(s)	Total Selections	First Team Selections	Second Team Selections	NHL Seasons
Gordie Howe	RW	Detroit	**21**	12	9	26
Raymond Bourque	D	Bos., Col.	**19**	13	6	22
Wayne Gretzky	C	Edm., L.A., NYR	**15**	8	7	20
Maurice Richard	RW	Montreal	**14**	8	6	18
Bobby Hull	LW	Chicago	**12**	10	2	16
Nicklas Lidstrom	D	Detroit	**12**	10	2	20
Doug Harvey	D	Mtl., NYR	**11**	10	1	19
Glenn Hall	G	Det., Chi., St.L.	**11**	7	4	18
Jean Beliveau	C	Montreal	**10**	6	4	20
Earl Seibert	D	NYR, Chi.	**10**	4	6	15
Bobby Orr	D	Boston	**9**	8	1	12
Ted Lindsay	LW	Detroit	**9**	8	1	17
Mario Lemieux	C	Pittsburgh	**9**	5	4	17
Frank Mahovlich	LW	Tor., Det., Mtl.	**9**	3	6	18
Eddie Shore	D	Boston	**8**	7	1	14
* Jaromir Jagr	RW	Pit., NYR	**8**	7	1	19
* Alex Ovechkin	LW/RW	Washington	**8**	6	2	8
Phil Esposito	C	Boston	**8**	6	2	18
Red Kelly	D	Detroit	**8**	6	2	20
Stan Mikita	C	Chicago	**8**	6	2	22
Mike Bossy	RW	NY Islanders	**8**	5	3	10
Pierre Pilote	D	Chicago	**8**	5	3	14
Luc Robitaille	LW	Los Angeles	**8**	5	3	19
Paul Coffey	D	Edm., Pit., Det.	**8**	4	4	21
Frank Brimsek	G	Boston	**8**	2	6	10
Denis Potvin	D	NY Islanders	**7**	5	2	15
Brad Park	D	NYR, Bos.	**7**	5	2	17
Chris Chelios	D	Mtl., Chi., Det.	**7**	5	2	25
Al MacInnis	D	Cgy., St.L.	**7**	4	3	23
Jacques Plante	G	Mtl., Tor.	**7**	3	4	18
Bill Gadsby	D	Chi., NYR, Det.	**7**	3	4	20
* Martin Brodeur	G	New Jersey	**7**	3	4	20
Terry Sawchuk	G	Detroit	**7**	3	4	21
Bill Durnan	G	Montreal	**6**	6	0	7
Dominik Hasek	G	Buffalo	**6**	6	0	15
Guy Lafleur	RW	Montreal	**6**	6	0	17
Ken Dryden	G	Montreal	**6**	5	1	8
Patrick Roy	G	Mtl., Col.	**6**	4	2	19
Dit Clapper	RW/D	Boston	**6**	3	3	20
Larry Robinson	D	Montreal	**6**	3	3	20
Tim Horton	D	Toronto	**6**	3	3	24
* Zdeno Chara	D	Ott., Bos.	**6**	2	4	15
Borje Salming	D	Toronto	**6**	1	5	17
Bill Cowley	C	Boston	**5**	4	1	13
Busher Jackson	LW	Toronto	**5**	4	1	15
Mark Messier	LW/C	Edm., NYR	**5**	4	1	25
Charlie Conacher	RW	Toronto	**5**	3	2	12
Jack Stewart	D	Detroit	**5**	3	2	12
Toe Blake	LW	Montreal	**5**	3	2	14
Elmer Lach	C	Montreal	**5**	3	2	14
Bill Quackenbush	D	Det., Bos.	**5**	3	2	14
Michel Goulet	LW	Quebec	**5**	3	2	15
Paul Kariya	LW	Anaheim	**5**	3	2	15
Tony Esposito	G	Chicago	**5**	3	2	16
Ken Reardon	D	Montreal	**5**	2	3	7
Syl Apps	C	Toronto	**5**	2	3	10
Ed Giacomin	G	NY Rangers	**5**	2	3	13
John LeClair	LW	Mtl., Phi.	**5**	2	3	16
Brian Leetch	D	NY Rangers	**5**	2	3	17
Jari Kurri	RW	Edmonton	**5**	2	3	17
Scott Stevens	D	Wsh., N.J.	**5**	2	3	21
* Martin St. Louis	RW	Tampa Bay	**5**	1	4	14

* Active

Position Leaders in All-Star Selections

Position	Player	Total	First Team	Second Team	NHL Seasons	Career
GOALTENDER	Glenn Hall	**11**	7	4	18	1952-53 to 1970-71
	Frank Brimsek	**8**	2	6	10	1938-39 to 1949-50
	Jacques Plante	**7**	3	4	18	1952-53 to 1972-73
	* Martin Brodeur	**7**	3	4	20	1991-92 to 2012-13
	Terry Sawchuk	**7**	3	4	21	1949-50 to 1969-70
	Bill Durnan	**6**	6	0	7	1943-44 to 1949-50
	Dominik Hasek	**6**	6	0	15	1990-91 to 2007-08
	Ken Dryden	**6**	5	1	8	1970-71 to 1978-79
	Patrick Roy	**6**	4	2	19	1984-85 to 2002-03
DEFENSE	Raymond Bourque	**19**	13	6	22	1979-80 to 2000-01
	Nicklas Lidstrom	**12**	10	2	20	1991-92 to 2011-12
	Doug Harvey	**11**	10	1	20	1947-48 to 1968-69
	Earl Seibert	**10**	4	6	15	1931-32 to 1945-46
	Bobby Orr	**9**	8	1	12	1966-67 to 1978-79
	Eddie Shore	**8**	7	1	14	1926-27 to 1939-40
	Red Kelly	**8**	6	2	20	1947-48 to 1966-67
	Pierre Pilote	**8**	5	3	14	1955-56 to 1968-69
	Paul Coffey	**8**	4	4	21	1980-81 to 2000-01
CENTER	Wayne Gretzky	**15**	8	7	20	1979-80 to 1998-99
	Jean Beliveau	**10**	6	4	20	1950-51 to 1970-71
	Mario Lemieux	**9**	5	4	18	1984-85 to 2005-06
	Phil Esposito	**8**	6	2	18	1963-64 to 1980-81
	Stan Mikita	**8**	6	2	22	1958-59 to 1979-80
RIGHT WING	Gordie Howe	**21**	12	9	26	1946-47 to 1979-80
	Maurice Richard	**14**	8	6	18	1942-43 to 1959-60
	* Jaromir Jagr	**8**	7	1	19	1990-91 to 2012-13
	Mike Bossy	**8**	5	3	10	1977-78 to 1986-87
	Guy Lafleur	**6**	6	0	17	1971-72 to 1990-91
LEFT WING	Bobby Hull	**12**	10	2	16	1957-58 to 1979-80
	Ted Lindsay	**9**	8	1	17	1944-45 to 1964-65
	Frank Mahovlich	**9**	3	6	18	1956-57 to 1973-74
	Luc Robitaille	**8**	5	3	19	1986-87 to 2005-06
	* Alex Ovechkin	**7**	5	2	8	2005-06 to 2012-13

* active player

All-Star Teams

1930-2013

Voting for the NHL All-Star Team is conducted among the representatives of the Professional Hockey Writers' Association at the end of the season.

Following is a list of the First and Second All-Star Teams since their inception in 1930-31.

2012-13

First Team		Second Team
Sergei Bobrovsky, CBJ	G	Henrik Lundqvist, NYR
P.K. Subban, Mtl.	D	Kris Letang, Pit.
Ryan Suter, Min.	D	Francois Beauchemin, Ana.
Sidney Crosby, Pit.	C	Jonathan Toews, Chi.
Alex Ovechkin, Wsh.	RW	Martin St. Louis, T.B.
Chris Kunitz, Pit.	LW	Alex Ovechkin, Wsh.

2011-12

First Team		Second Team
Henrik Lundqvist, NYR	G	Jonathan Quick, L.A.
Erik Karlsson, Ott.	D	Zdeno Chara, Bos.
Shea Weber, Nsh.	D	Alex Pietrangelo, St. L.
Evgeni Malkin, Pit.	C	Steven Stamkos, T.B.
James Neal, Pit.	RW	Marian Gaborik, NYR
Ilya Kovalchuk, N.J.	LW	Ray Whitney, Phx.

2010-11

First Team		Second Team
Tim Thomas, Bos.	G	Pekka Rinne, Nsh.
Nicklas Lidstrom, Det.	D	Zdeno Chara, Bos.
Shea Weber, Nsh.	D	Lubomir Visnovsky, Ana.
Henrik Sedin, Van.	C	Steven Stamkos, T.B.
Corey Perry, Ana.	RW	Martin St. Louis, T.B.
Daniel Sedin, Van.	LW	Alex Ovechkin, Wsh.

2009-10

First Team		Second Team
Ryan Miller, Buf.	G	Ilya Bryzgalov, Phx.
Duncan Keith, Chi.	D	Drew Doughty, L.A..
Mike Green, Wsh.	D	Nicklas Lidstrom, Det.
Henrik Sedin, Van.	C	Sidney Crosby, Pit.
Patrick Kane, Chi.	RW	Martin St. Louis, T.B.
Alex Ovechkin, Wsh.	LW	Daniel Sedin, Van.

2008-09

First Team		Second Team
Tim Thomas, Bos.	G	Steve Mason, CBJ
Zdeno Chara, Bos	D	Nicklas Lidstrom, Det.
Mike Green, Wsh.	D	Dan Boyle, S.J.
Evgeni Malkin, Pit.	C	Pavel Datsyuk, Det.
Jarome Iginla, Cgy.	RW	Marian Hossa, Det.
Alex Ovechkin, Wsh.	LW	Zach Parise, N.J.

2007-08

First Team		Second Team
Evgeni Nabokov, S.J.	G	Martin Brodeur, N.J.
Nicklas Lidstrom, Det.	D	Brian Campbell, Buf., S.J.
Dion Phaneuf, Cgy.	D	Zdeno Chara, Bos.
Evgeni Malkin, Pit.	C	Joe Thornton, S.J.
Jarome Iginla, Cgy.	RW	Alex Kovalev, Mtl.
Alex Ovechkin, Wsh.	LW	Henrik Zetterberg, Det.

2006-07

First Team		Second Team
Martin Brodeur, N.J.	G	Roberto Luongo, Van.
Nicklas Lidstrom, Det.	D	Chris Pronger, Ana.
Scott Niedermayer, Ana.	D	Dan Boyle, T.B.
Sidney Crosby, Pit.	C	Vincent Lecavalier, T.B.
Dany Heatley, Ott.	RW	Martin St. Louis, T.B.
Alex Ovechkin, Wsh.	LW	Thomas Vanek, Buf.

2005-06

First Team		Second Team
Miikka Kiprusoff, Cgy.	G	Martin Brodeur, N.J.
Nicklas Lidstrom, Det.	D	Zdeno Chara, Ott.
Scott Niedermayer, Ana.	D	Sergei Zubov, Dal.
Joe Thornton, Bos., S.J.	C	Eric Staal, Car.
Jaromir Jagr, NYR	RW	Daniel Alfredsson, Ott.
Alex Ovechkin, Wsh.	LW	Dany Heatley, Ott.

2004-05

Season Cancelled

2003-04

First Team		Second Team
Martin Brodeur, N.J.	G	Roberto Luongo, Fla.
Scott Niedermayer, N.J.	D	Chris Pronger, St.L.
Zdeno Chara, Ott.	D	Bryan McCabe, Tor.
Joe Sakic, Col.	C	Mats Sundin, Tor.
Martin St. Louis, T.B.	RW	Jarome Iginla, Cgy.
Markus Naslund, Van.	LW	Ilya Kovalchuk, Atl.

2002-03

First Team		Second Team
Martin Brodeur, N.J.	G	Marty Turco, Dal.
Al MacInnis, St.L.	D	Sergei Gonchar, Wsh.
Nicklas Lidstrom, Det.	D	Derian Hatcher, Dal.
Peter Forsberg, Col.	C	Joe Thornton, Bos.
Todd Bertuzzi, Van.	RW	Milan Hejduk, Col.
Markus Naslund, Van.	LW	Paul Kariya, Ana.

2001-02

First Team		Second Team
Patrick Roy, Col.	G	Jose Theodore, Mtl.
Nicklas Lidstrom, Det.	D	Rob Blake, Col.
Chris Chelios, Det.	D	Sergei Gonchar, Wsh.
Joe Sakic, Col.	C	Mats Sundin, Tor.
Jarome Iginla, Cgy.	RW	Bill Guerin, Bos.
Markus Naslund, Van.	LW	Brendan Shanahan, Det.

2000-01

First Team		Second Team
Dominik Hasek, Buf.	G	Roman Cechmanek, Phi.
Nicklas Lidstrom, Det.	D	Rob Blake, L.A., Col.
Raymond Bourque, Col.	D	Scott Stevens, N.J.
Joe Sakic, Col.	C	Mario Lemieux, Pit.
Jaromir Jagr, Pit.	RW	Pavel Bure, Fla.
Patrik Elias, N.J.	LW	Luc Robitaille, L.A.

1999-2000

First Team		Second Team
Olaf Kolzig, Wsh.	G	Roman Turek, St.L.
Chris Pronger, St.L.	D	Rob Blake, L.A.
Nicklas Lidstrom, Det.	D	Eric Desjardins, Phi.
Steve Yzerman, Det.	C	Mike Modano, Dal.
Jaromir Jagr, Pit.	RW	Pavel Bure, Fla.
Brendan Shanahan, Det.	LW	Paul Kariya, Ana.

1998-99

First Team		Second Team
Dominik Hasek, Buf.	G	Byron Dafoe, Bos.
Al MacInnis, St.L.	D	Raymond Bourque, Bos.
Nicklas Lidstrom, Det.	D	Eric Desjardins, Phi.
Peter Forsberg, Col.	C	Alexei Yashin, Ott.
Jaromir Jagr, Pit.	RW	Teemu Selanne, Ana.
Paul Kariya, Ana.	LW	John LeClair, Phi.

1997-98

First Team		Second Team
Dominik Hasek, Buf.	G	Martin Brodeur, N.J.
Nicklas Lidstrom, Det.	D	Chris Pronger, St.L.
Rob Blake, L.A.	D	Scott Niedermayer, N.J.
Peter Forsberg, Col.	C	Wayne Gretzky, NYR
Jaromir Jagr, Pit.	RW	Teemu Selanne, Ana.
John LeClair, Phi.	LW	Keith Tkachuk, Phx.

1996-97

First Team		Second Team
Dominik Hasek, Buf.	G	Martin Brodeur, N.J.
Brian Leetch, NYR	D	Chris Chelios, Chi.
Sandis Ozolinsh, Col.	D	Scott Stevens, N.J.
Mario Lemieux, Pit.	C	Wayne Gretzky, NYR
Teemu Selanne, Ana.	RW	Jaromir Jagr, Pit.
Paul Kariya, Ana.	LW	John LeClair, Phi.

1995-96

First Team		Second Team
Jim Carey, Wsh.	G	Chris Osgood, Det.
Chris Chelios, Chi.	D	V. Konstantinov, Det.
Raymond Bourque, Bos.	D	Brian Leetch, NYR
Mario Lemieux, Pit.	C	Eric Lindros, Phi.
Jaromir Jagr, Pit.	RW	Alexander Mogilny, Van.
Paul Kariya, Ana.	LW	John LeClair, Phi.

1994-95

First Team		Second Team
Dominik Hasek, Buf.	G	Ed Belfour, Chi.
Paul Coffey, Det.	D	Raymond Bourque, Bos.
Chris Chelios, Chi.	D	Larry Murphy, Pit.
Eric Lindros, Phi.	C	Alexei Zhamnov, Wpg.
Jaromir Jagr, Pit.	RW	Theoren Fleury, Cgy.
John LeClair, Mtl., Phi.	LW	Keith Tkachuk, Wpg.

1993-94

First Team		Second Team
Dominik Hasek, Buf.	G	John Vanbiesbrouck, Fla.
Raymond Bourque, Bos.	D	Al MacInnis, Cgy.
Scott Stevens, N.J.	D	Brian Leetch, NYR
Sergei Fedorov, Det.	C	Wayne Gretzky, L.A.
Pavel Bure, Van.	RW	Cam Neely, Bos.
Brendan Shanahan, St.L.	LW	Adam Graves, NYR

1992-93

First Team		Second Team
Ed Belfour, Chi.	G	Tom Barrasso, Pit.
Chris Chelios, Chi.	D	Larry Murphy, Pit.
Raymond Bourque, Bos.	D	Al Iafrate, Wsh.
Mario Lemieux, Pit.	C	Pat LaFontaine, Buf.
Teemu Selanne, Wpg.	RW	Alexander Mogilny, Buf.
Luc Robitaille, L.A.	LW	Kevin Stevens, Pit.

1991-92

First Team		Second Team
Patrick Roy, Mtl.	G	Kirk McLean, Van.
Brian Leetch, NYR	D	Phil Housley, Wpg.
Raymond Bourque, Bos.	D	Scott Stevens, N.J.
Mark Messier, NYR	C	Mario Lemieux, Pit.
Brett Hull, St.L.	RW	Mark Recchi, Pit., Phi.
Kevin Stevens, Pit.	LW	Luc Robitaille, L.A.

1990-91

First Team		Second Team
Ed Belfour, Chi.	G	Patrick Roy, Mtl.
Raymond Bourque, Bos.	D	Chris Chelios, Chi.
Al MacInnis, Cgy.	D	Brian Leetch, NYR
Wayne Gretzky, L.A.	C	Adam Oates, St.L.
Brett Hull, St.L.	RW	Cam Neely, Bos.
Luc Robitaille, L.A.	LW	Kevin Stevens, Pit.

1989-90

First Team		Second Team
Patrick Roy, Mtl.	G	Daren Puppa, Buf.
Raymond Bourque, Bos.	D	Paul Coffey, Pit.
Al MacInnis, Cgy.	D	Doug Wilson, Chi.
Mark Messier, Edm.	C	Wayne Gretzky, L.A.
Brett Hull, St.L.	RW	Cam Neely, Bos.
Luc Robitaille, L.A.	LW	Brian Bellows, Min.

1988-89

First Team		Second Team
Patrick Roy, Mtl.	G	Mike Vernon, Cgy.
Chris Chelios, Mtl.	D	Al MacInnis, Cgy.
Paul Coffey, Pit.	D	Raymond Bourque, Bos.
Mario Lemieux, Pit.	C	Wayne Gretzky, L.A.
Joe Mullen, Cgy.	RW	Jari Kurri, Edm.
Luc Robitaille, L.A.	LW	Gerard Gallant, Det.

1987-88

First Team		Second Team
Grant Fuhr, Edm.	G	Patrick Roy, Mtl.
Raymond Bourque, Bos.	D	Gary Suter, Cgy.
Scott Stevens, Wsh.	D	Brad McCrimmon, Cgy.
Mario Lemieux, Pit.	C	Wayne Gretzky, Edm.
Hakan Loob, Cgy.	RW	Cam Neely, Bos.
Luc Robitaille, L.A.	LW	Michel Goulet, Que.

1986-87

First Team		Second Team
Ron Hextall, Phi.	G	Mike Liut, Hfd.
Raymond Bourque, Bos.	D	Larry Murphy, Wsh.
Mark Howe, Phi.	D	Al MacInnis, Cgy.
Wayne Gretzky, Edm.	C	Mario Lemieux, Pit.
Jari Kurri, Edm.	RW	Tim Kerr, Phi.
Michel Goulet, Que.	LW	Luc Robitaille, L.A.

1985-86

First Team		Second Team
John Vanbiesbrouck, NYR	G	Bob Froese, Phi.
Paul Coffey, Edm.	D	Larry Robinson, Mtl.
Mark Howe, Phi.	D	Raymond Bourque, Bos.
Wayne Gretzky, Edm.	C	Mario Lemieux, Pit.
Mike Bossy, NYI	RW	Jari Kurri, Edm.
Michel Goulet, Que.	LW	Mats Naslund, Mtl.

1984-85

First Team		Second Team
Pelle Lindbergh, Phi.	G	Tom Barrasso, Buf.
Paul Coffey, Edm.	D	Rod Langway, Wsh.
Raymond Bourque, Bos.	D	Doug Wilson, Chi.
Wayne Gretzky, Edm.	C	Dale Hawerchuk, Wpg.
Jari Kurri, Edm.	RW	Mike Bossy, NYI
John Ogrodnick, Det.	LW	John Tonelli, NYI

1983-84

First Team		Second Team
Tom Barrasso, Buf.	G	Pat Riggin, Wsh.
Rod Langway, Wsh.	D	Paul Coffey, Edm.
Raymond Bourque, Bos.	D	Denis Potvin, NYI
Wayne Gretzky, Edm.	C	Bryan Trottier, NYI
Mike Bossy, NYI	RW	Jari Kurri, Edm.
Michel Goulet, Que.	LW	Mark Messier, Edm.

1982-83

First Team		Second Team
Pete Peeters, Bos.	G	Roland Melanson, NYI
Mark Howe, Phi.	D	Raymond Bourque, Bos.
Rod Langway, Wsh.	D	Paul Coffey, Edm.
Wayne Gretzky, Edm.	C	Denis Savard, Chi.
Mike Bossy, NYI	RW	Lanny McDonald, Cgy.
Mark Messier, Edm.	LW	Michel Goulet, Que.

1981-82

First Team		Second Team
Billy Smith, NYI	G	Grant Fuhr, Edm.
Doug Wilson, Chi.	D	Paul Coffey, Edm.
Raymond Bourque, Bos.	D	Brian Engblom, Mtl.
Wayne Gretzky, Edm.	C	Bryan Trottier, NYI
Mike Bossy, NYI	RW	Rick Middleton, Bos.
Mark Messier, Edm.	LW	John Tonelli, NYI

1980-81

First Team		Second Team
Mike Liut, St.L.	G	Mario Lessard, L.A.
Denis Potvin, NYI	D	Larry Robinson, Mtl.
Randy Carlyle, Pit.	D	Raymond Bourque, Bos.
Wayne Gretzky, Edm.	C	Marcel Dionne, L.A.
Mike Bossy, NYI	RW	Dave Taylor, L.A.
Charlie Simmer, L.A.	LW	Bill Barber, Phi.

1979-80

First Team		Second Team
Tony Esposito, Chi.	G	Don Edwards, Buf.
Larry Robinson, Mtl.	D	Borje Salming, Tor.
Raymond Bourque, Bos.	D	Jim Schoenfeld, Buf.
Marcel Dionne, L.A.	C	Wayne Gretzky, Edm.
Guy Lafleur, Mtl.	RW	Danny Gare, Buf.
Charlie Simmer, L.A.	LW	Steve Shutt, Mtl.

1978-79

First Team		Second Team
Ken Dryden, Mtl.	G	Glenn Resch, NYI
Denis Potvin, NYI	D	Borje Salming, Tor.
Larry Robinson, Mtl.	D	Serge Savard, Mtl.
Bryan Trottier, NYI	C	Marcel Dionne, L.A.
Guy Lafleur, Mtl.	RW	Mike Bossy, NYI
Clark Gillies, NYI	LW	Bill Barber, Phi.

1977-78

First Team		Second Team
Ken Dryden, Mtl.	G	Don Edwards, Buf.
Denis Potvin, NYI	D	Larry Robinson, Mtl.
Brad Park, Bos.	D	Borje Salming, Tor.
Bryan Trottier, NYI	C	Darryl Sittler, Tor.
Guy Lafleur, Mtl.	RW	Mike Bossy, NYI
Clark Gillies, NYI	LW	Steve Shutt, Mtl.

1976-77

First Team		Second Team
Ken Dryden, Mtl.	G	Rogie Vachon, L.A.
Larry Robinson, Mtl.	D	Denis Potvin, NYI
Borje Salming, Tor.	D	Guy Lapointe, Mtl.
Marcel Dionne, L.A.	C	Gilbert Perreault, Buf.
Guy Lafleur, Mtl.	RW	Lanny McDonald, Tor.
Steve Shutt, Mtl.	LW	Rick Martin, Buf.

1975-76

First Team		Second Team
Ken Dryden, Mtl.	G	Glenn Resch, NYI
Denis Potvin, NYI	D	Borje Salming, Tor.
Brad Park, Bos.	D	Guy Lapointe, Mtl.
Bobby Clarke, Phi.	C	Gilbert Perreault, Buf.
Guy Lafleur, Mtl.	RW	Reggie Leach, Phi.
Bill Barber, Phi.	LW	Rick Martin, Buf.

1974-75

First Team		Second Team
Bernie Parent, Phi.	G	Rogie Vachon, L.A.
Bobby Orr, Bos.	D	Guy Lapointe, Mtl.
Denis Potvin, NYI	D	Borje Salming, Tor.
Bobby Clarke, Phi.	C	Phil Esposito, Bos.
Guy Lafleur, Mtl.	RW	René Robert, Buf.
Rick Martin, Buf.	LW	Steve Vickers, NYR

1973-74

First Team		Second Team
Bernie Parent, Phi.	G	Tony Esposito, Chi.
Bobby Orr, Bos.	D	Bill White, Chi.
Brad Park, NYR	D	Barry Ashbee, Phi.
Phil Esposito, Bos.	C	Bobby Clarke, Phi.
Ken Hodge, Bos.	RW	Mickey Redmond, Det.
Rick Martin, Buf.	LW	Wayne Cashman, Bos.

1972-73

First Team		Second Team
Ken Dryden, Mtl.	G	Tony Esposito, Chi.
Bobby Orr, Bos.	D	Brad Park, NYR
Guy Lapointe, Mtl.	D	Bill White, Chi.
Phil Esposito, Bos.	C	Bobby Clarke, Phi.
Mickey Redmond, Det.	RW	Yvan Cournoyer, Mtl.
Frank Mahovlich, Mtl.	LW	Dennis Hull, Chi.

1971-72

First Team		Second Team
Tony Esposito, Chi.	G	Ken Dryden, Mtl.
Bobby Orr, Bos.	D	Bill White, Chi.
Brad Park, NYR	D	Pat Stapleton, Chi.
Phil Esposito, Bos.	C	Jean Ratelle, NYR
Rod Gilbert, NYR	RW	Yvan Cournoyer, Mtl.
Bobby Hull, Chi.	LW	Vic Hadfield, NYR

1970-71

First Team		Second Team
Ed Giacomin, NYR	G	Jacques Plante, Tor.
Bobby Orr, Bos.	D	Brad Park, NYR
J.C. Tremblay, Mtl.	D	Pat Stapleton, Chi.
Phil Esposito, Bos.	C	Dave Keon, Tor.
Ken Hodge, Bos.	RW	Yvan Cournoyer, Mtl.
John Bucyk, Bos.	LW	Bobby Hull, Chi.

1969-70

First Team		Second Team
Tony Esposito, Chi.	G	Ed Giacomin, NYR
Bobby Orr, Bos.	D	Carl Brewer, Det.
Brad Park, NYR	D	Jacques Laperriere, Mtl.
Phil Esposito, Bos.	C	Stan Mikita, Chi.
Gordie Howe, Det.	RW	John McKenzie, Bos.
Bobby Hull, Chi.	LW	Frank Mahovlich, Det.

1968-69

First Team		Second Team
Glenn Hall, St.L.	G	Ed Giacomin, NYR
Bobby Orr, Bos.	D	Ted Green, Bos.
Tim Horton, Tor.	D	Ted Harris, Mtl.
Phil Esposito, Bos.	C	Jean Béliveau, Mtl.
Gordie Howe, Det.	RW	Yvan Cournoyer, Mtl.
Bobby Hull, Chi.	LW	Frank Mahovlich, Det.

1967-68

First Team		Second Team
Gump Worsley, Mtl.	G	Ed Giacomin, NYR
Bobby Orr, Bos.	D	J.C. Tremblay, Mtl.
Tim Horton, Tor.	D	Jim Neilson, NYR
Stan Mikita, Chi.	C	Phil Esposito, Bos.
Gordie Howe, Det.	RW	Rod Gilbert, NYR
Bobby Hull, Chi.	LW	John Bucyk, Bos.

1966-67

First Team		Second Team
Ed Giacomin, NYR	G	Glenn Hall, Chi.
Pierre Pilote, Chi.	D	Tim Horton, Tor.
Harry Howell, NYR	D	Bobby Orr, Bos.
Stan Mikita, Chi.	C	Norm Ullman, Det.
Kenny Wharram, Chi.	RW	Gordie Howe, Det.
Bobby Hull, Chi.	LW	Don Marshall, NYR

1965-66

First Team		Second Team
Glenn Hall, Chi.	G	Gump Worsley, Mtl.
Jacques Laperriere, Mtl.	D	Allan Stanley, Tor.
Pierre Pilote, Chi.	D	Pat Stapleton, Chi.
Stan Mikita, Chi.	C	Jean Béliveau, Mtl.
Gordie Howe, Det.	RW	Bobby Rousseau, Mtl.
Bobby Hull, Chi.	LW	Frank Mahovlich, Tor.

1964-65

First Team		Second Team
Roger Crozier, Det.	G	Charlie Hodge, Mtl.
Pierre Pilote, Chi.	D	Bill Gadsby, Det.
Jacques Laperriere, Mtl.	D	Carl Brewer, Tor.
Norm Ullman, Det.	C	Stan Mikita, Chi.
Claude Provost, Mtl.	RW	Gordie Howe, Det.
Bobby Hull, Chi.	LW	Frank Mahovlich, Tor.

1963-64

First Team		Second Team
Glenn Hall, Chi.	G	Charlie Hodge, Mtl.
Pierre Pilote, Chi.	D	Moose Vasko, Chi.
Tim Horton, Tor.	D	Jacques Laperriere, Mtl.
Stan Mikita, Chi.	C	Jean Béliveau, Mtl.
Kenny Wharram, Chi.	RW	Gordie Howe, Det.
Bobby Hull, Chi.	LW	Frank Mahovlich, Tor.

1962-63

First Team		Second Team
Glenn Hall, Chi.	G	Terry Sawchuk, Det.
Pierre Pilote, Chi.	D	Tim Horton, Tor.
Carl Brewer, Tor.	D	Moose Vasko, Chi.
Stan Mikita, Chi.	C	Henri Richard, Mtl.
Gordie Howe, Det.	RW	Andy Bathgate, NYR
Frank Mahovlich, Tor.	LW	Bobby Hull, Chi.

1961-62

First Team		Second Team
Jacques Plante, Mtl.	G	Glenn Hall, Chi.
Doug Harvey, NYR	D	Carl Brewer, Tor.
Jean-Guy Talbot, Mtl.	D	Pierre Pilote, Chi.
Stan Mikita, Chi.	C	Dave Keon, Tor.
Andy Bathgate, NYR	RW	Gordie Howe, Det.
Bobby Hull, Chi.	LW	Frank Mahovlich, Tor.

1960-61

First Team		Second Team
Johnny Bower, Tor.	G	Glenn Hall, Chi.
Doug Harvey, Mtl.	D	Allan Stanley, Tor.
Marcel Pronovost, Det.	D	Pierre Pilote, Chi.
Jean Béliveau, Mtl.	C	Henri Richard, Mtl.
Bernie Geoffrion, Mtl.	RW	Gordie Howe, Det.
Frank Mahovlich, Tor.	LW	Dickie Moore, Mtl.

1959-60

First Team		Second Team
Glenn Hall, Chi.	G	Jacques Plante, Mtl.
Doug Harvey, Mtl.	D	Allan Stanley, Tor.
Marcel Pronovost, Det.	D	Pierre Pilote, Chi.
Jean Béliveau, Mtl.	C	Bronco Horvath, Bos.
Gordie Howe, Det.	RW	Bernie Geoffrion, Mtl.
Bobby Hull, Chi.	LW	Dean Prentice, NYR

1958-59

First Team		Second Team
Jacques Plante, Mtl.	*G*	Terry Sawchuk, Det.
Tom Johnson, Mtl.	*D*	Marcel Pronovost, Det.
Bill Gadsby, NYR	*D*	Doug Harvey, Mtl.
Jean Béliveau, Mtl.	*C*	Henri Richard, Mtl.
Andy Bathgate, NYR	*RW*	Gordie Howe, Det.
Dickie Moore, Mtl.	*LW*	Alex Delvecchio, Det.

1957-58

First Team		Second Team
Glenn Hall, Chi.	*G*	Jacques Plante, Mtl.
Doug Harvey, Mtl.	*D*	Fern Flaman, Bos.
Bill Gadsby, NYR	*D*	Marcel Pronovost, Det.
Henri Richard, Mtl.	*C*	Jean Béliveau, Mtl.
Gordie Howe, Det.	*RW*	Andy Bathgate, NYR
Dickie Moore, Mtl.	*LW*	Camille Henry, NYR

1956-57

First Team		Second Team
Glenn Hall, Det.	*G*	Jacques Plante, Mtl.
Doug Harvey, Mtl.	*D*	Fern Flaman, Bos.
Red Kelly, Det.	*D*	Bill Gadsby, NYR
Jean Béliveau, Mtl.	*C*	Ed Litzenberger, Chi.
Gordie Howe, Det.	*RW*	Maurice Richard, Mtl.
Ted Lindsay, Det.	*LW*	Real Chevrefils, Bos.

1955-56

First Team		Second Team
Jacques Plante, Mtl.	*G*	Glenn Hall, Det.
Doug Harvey, Mtl.	*D*	Red Kelly, Det.
Bill Gadsby, NYR	*D*	Tom Johnson, Mtl.
Jean Béliveau, Mtl.	*C*	Tod Sloan, Tor.
Maurice Richard, Mtl.	*RW*	Gordie Howe, Det.
Ted Lindsay, Det.	*LW*	Bert Olmstead, Mtl.

1954-55

First Team		Second Team
Harry Lumley, Tor.	*G*	Terry Sawchuk, Det.
Doug Harvey, Mtl.	*D*	Bob Goldham, Det.
Red Kelly, Det.	*D*	Fern Flaman, Bos.
Jean Béliveau, Mtl.	*C*	Ken Mosdell, Mtl.
Maurice Richard, Mtl.	*RW*	Bernie Geoffrion, Mtl.
Sid Smith, Tor.	*LW*	Danny Lewicki, NYR

1953-54

First Team		Second Team
Harry Lumley, Tor.	*G*	Terry Sawchuk, Det.
Red Kelly, Det.	*D*	Bill Gadsby, Chi.
Doug Harvey, Mtl.	*D*	Tim Horton, Tor.
Ken Mosdell, Mtl.	*C*	Ted Kennedy, Tor.
Gordie Howe, Det.	*RW*	Maurice Richard, Mtl.
Ted Lindsay, Det.	*LW*	Ed Sandford, Bos.

1952-53

First Team		Second Team
Terry Sawchuk, Det.	*G*	Gerry McNeil, Mtl.
Red Kelly, Det.	*D*	Bill Quackenbush, Bos.
Doug Harvey, Mtl.	*D*	Bill Gadsby, Chi.
Fleming MacKell, Bos.	*C*	Alex Delvecchio, Det.
Gordie Howe, Det.	*RW*	Maurice Richard, Mtl.
Ted Lindsay, Det.	*LW*	Bert Olmstead, Mtl.

1951-52

First Team		Second Team
Terry Sawchuk, Det.	*G*	Jim Henry, Bos.
Red Kelly, Det.	*D*	Hy Buller, NYR
Doug Harvey, Mtl.	*D*	Jimmy Thomson, Tor.
Elmer Lach, Mtl.	*C*	Milt Schmidt, Bos.
Gordie Howe, Det.	*RW*	Maurice Richard, Mtl.
Ted Lindsay, Det.	*LW*	Sid Smith, Tor.

1950-51

First Team		Second Team
Terry Sawchuk, Det.	*G*	Chuck Rayner, NYR
Red Kelly, Det.	*D*	Jimmy Thomson, Tor.
Bill Quackenbush, Bos.	*D*	Leo Reise Jr., Det.
Milt Schmidt, Bos.	*C*	Sid Abel, Det.
		Ted Kennedy, Tor. (tied)
Gordie Howe, Det.	*RW*	Maurice Richard, Mtl.
Ted Lindsay, Det.	*LW*	Sid Smith, Tor.

1949-50

First Team		Second Team
Bill Durnan, Mtl.	*G*	Chuck Rayner, NYR
Gus Mortson, Tor.	*D*	Leo Reise Jr., Det.
Ken Reardon, Mtl.	*D*	Red Kelly, Det.
Sid Abel, Det.	*C*	Ted Kennedy, Tor.
Maurice Richard, Mtl.	*RW*	Gordie Howe, Det.
Ted Lindsay, Det.	*LW*	Tony Leswick, NYR

1948-49

First Team		Second Team
Bill Durnan, Mtl.	*G*	Chuck Rayner, NYR
Bill Quackenbush, Det.	*D*	Glen Harmon, Mtl.
Jack Stewart, Det.	*D*	Ken Reardon, Mtl.
Sid Abel, Det.	*C*	Doug Bentley, Chi.
Maurice Richard, Mtl.	*RW*	Gordie Howe, Det.
Roy Conacher, Chi.	*LW*	Ted Lindsay, Det.

1947-48

First Team		Second Team
Turk Broda, Tor.	*G*	Frank Brimsek, Bos.
Bill Quackenbush, Det.	*D*	Ken Reardon, Mtl.
Jack Stewart, Det.	*D*	Neil Colville, NYR
Elmer Lach, Mtl.	*C*	Buddy O'Connor, NYR
Maurice Richard, Mtl.	*RW*	Bud Poile, Chi.
Ted Lindsay, Det.	*LW*	Gaye Stewart, Chi.

1946-47

First Team		Second Team
Bill Durnan, Mtl.	*G*	Frank Brimsek, Bos.
Ken Reardon, Mtl.	*D*	Jack Stewart, Det.
Butch Bouchard, Mtl.	*D*	Bill Quackenbush, Det.
Milt Schmidt, Bos.	*C*	Max Bentley, Chi.
Maurice Richard, Mtl.	*RW*	Bobby Bauer, Bos.
Doug Bentley, Chi.	*LW*	Woody Dumart, Bos.

1945-46

First Team		Second Team
Bill Durnan, Mtl.	*G*	Frank Brimsek, Bos.
Jack Crawford, Bos.	*D*	Ken Reardon, Mtl.
Butch Bouchard, Mtl.	*D*	Jack Stewart, Det.
Max Bentley, Chi.	*C*	Elmer Lach, Mtl.
Maurice Richard, Mtl.	*RW*	Bill Mosienko, Chi.
Gaye Stewart, Tor.	*LW*	Toe Blake, Mtl.
Dick Irvin, Mtl.	*Coach*	Johnny Gottselig, Chi.

1944-45

First Team		Second Team
Bill Durnan, Mtl.	*G*	Mike Karakas, Chi.
Butch Bouchard, Mtl.	*D*	Glen Harmon, Mtl.
Flash Hollett, Det.	*D*	Babe Pratt, Tor.
Elmer Lach, Mtl.	*C*	Bill Cowley, Bos.
Maurice Richard, Mtl.	*RW*	Bill Mosienko, Chi.
Toe Blake, Mtl.	*LW*	Syd Howe, Det.
Dick Irvin, Mtl.	*Coach*	Jack Adams, Det.

1943-44

First Team		Second Team
Bill Durnan, Mtl.	*G*	Paul Bibeault, Tor.
Earl Seibert, Chi.	*D*	Butch Bouchard, Mtl.
Babe Pratt, Tor.	*D*	Dit Clapper, Bos.
Bill Cowley, Bos.	*C*	Elmer Lach, Mtl.
Lorne Carr, Tor.	*RW*	Maurice Richard, Mtl.
Doug Bentley, Chi.	*LW*	Herb Cain, Bos.
Dick Irvin, Mtl.	*Coach*	Hap Day, Tor.

1942-43

First Team		Second Team
Johnny Mowers, Det.	*G*	Frank Brimsek, Bos.
Earl Seibert, Chi.	*D*	Jack Crawford, Bos.
Jack Stewart, Det.	*D*	Flash Hollett, Bos.
Bill Cowley, Bos.	*C*	Syl Apps, Tor.
Lorne Carr, Tor.	*RW*	Bryan Hextall, NYR
Doug Bentley, Chi.	*LW*	Lynn Patrick, NYR
Jack Adams, Det.	*Coach*	Art Ross, Bos.

1941-42

First Team		Second Team
Frank Brimsek, Bos.	*G*	Turk Broda, Tor.
Earl Seibert, Chi.	*D*	Pat Egan, Bro.
Tom Anderson, Bro.	*D*	Bucko McDonald, Tor.
Syl Apps, Tor.	*C*	Phil Watson, NYR
Bryan Hextall, NYR	*RW*	Gordie Drillon, Tor.
Lynn Patrick, NYR	*LW*	Sid Abel, Det.
Frank Boucher, NYR	*Coach*	Paul Thompson, Chi.

1940-41

First Team		Second Team
Turk Broda, Tor.	*G*	Frank Brimsek, Bos.
Dit Clapper, Bos.	*D*	Earl Seibert, Chi.
Wally Stanowski, Tor.	*D*	Ott Heller, NYR
Bill Cowley, Bos.	*C*	Syl Apps, Tor.
Bryan Hextall, NYR	*RW*	Bobby Bauer, Bos.
Sweeney Schriner, Tor.	*LW*	Woody Dumart, Bos.
Cooney Weiland, Bos.	*Coach*	Dick Irvin, Mtl.

1939-40

First Team		Second Team
Dave Kerr, NYR	*G*	Frank Brimsek, Bos.
Dit Clapper, Bos.	*D*	Art Coulter, NYR
Ebbie Goodfellow, Det.	*D*	Earl Seibert, Chi.
Milt Schmidt, Bos.	*C*	Neil Colville, NYR
Bryan Hextall, NYR	*RW*	Bobby Bauer, Bos.
Toe Blake, Mtl.	*LW*	Woody Dumart, Bos.
Paul Thompson, Chi.	*Coach*	Frank Boucher, NYR

1938-39

First Team		Second Team
Frank Brimsek, Bos.	*G*	Earl Robertson, NYA
Eddie Shore, Bos.	*D*	Earl Seibert, Chi.
Dit Clapper, Bos.	*D*	Art Coulter, NYR
Syl Apps, Tor.	*C*	Neil Colville, NYR
Gordie Drillon, Tor.	*RW*	Bobby Bauer, Bos.
Toe Blake, Mtl.	*LW*	Johnny Gottselig, Chi.
Art Ross, Bos.	*Coach*	Red Dutton, NYA

1937-38

First Team		Second Team
Tiny Thompson, Bos.	*G*	Dave Kerr, NYR
Eddie Shore, Bos.	*D*	Art Coulter, NYR
Babe Siebert, Mtl.	*D*	Earl Seibert, Chi.
Bill Cowley, Bos.	*C*	Syl Apps, Tor.
Cecil Dillon, NYR	*RW*	
Gordie Drillon, Tor. *(tied)*		
Paul Thompson, Chi.	*LW*	Toe Blake, Mtl.
Lester Patrick, NYR	*Coach*	Art Ross, Bos.

1936-37

First Team		Second Team
Normie Smith, Det.	*G*	Wilf Cude, Mtl.
Babe Siebert, Mtl.	*D*	Earl Seibert, Chi.
Ebbie Goodfellow, Det.	*D*	Lionel Conacher, Mtl. M.
Marty Barry, Det.	*C*	Art Chapman, NYA
Larry Aurie, Det.	*RW*	Cecil Dillon, NYR
Busher Jackson, Tor.	*LW*	Sweeney Schriner, NYA
Jack Adams, Det.	*Coach*	Cecil Hart, Mtl.

1935-36

First Team		Second Team
Tiny Thompson, Bos.	*G*	Wilf Cude, Mtl.
Eddie Shore, Bos.	*D*	Earl Seibert, Chi.
Babe Siebert, Bos.	*D*	Ebbie Goodfellow, Det.
Hooley Smith, Mtl. M.	*C*	Bill Thoms, Tor.
Charlie Conacher, Tor.	*RW*	Cecil Dillon, NYR
Sweeney Schriner, NYA	*LW*	Paul Thompson, Chi.
Lester Patrick, NYR	*Coach*	Tommy Gorman, Mtl. M.

1934-35

First Team		Second Team
Lorne Chabot, Chi.	*G*	Tiny Thompson, Bos.
Eddie Shore, Bos.	*D*	Cy Wentworth, Mtl. M.
Earl Seibert, NYR	*D*	Art Coulter, Chi.
Frank Boucher, NYR	*C*	Cooney Weiland, Det.
Charlie Conacher, Tor.	*RW*	Dit Clapper, Bos.
Busher Jackson, Tor.	*LW*	Aurel Joliat, Mtl.
Lester Patrick, NYR	*Coach*	Dick Irvin, Tor.

1933-34

First Team		Second Team
Charlie Gardiner, Chi.	*G*	Roy Worters, NYA
King Clancy, Tor.	*D*	Eddie Shore, Bos.
Lionel Conacher, Chi.	*D*	Ching Johnson, NYR
Frank Boucher, NYR	*C*	Joe Primeau, Tor.
Charlie Conacher, Tor.	*RW*	Bill Cook, NYR
Busher Jackson, Tor.	*LW*	Aurel Joliat, Mtl.
Lester Patrick, NYR	*Coach*	Dick Irvin, Tor.

1932-33

First Team		Second Team
John Ross Roach, Det.	*G*	Charlie Gardiner, Chi.
Eddie Shore, Bos.	*D*	King Clancy, Tor.
Ching Johnson, NYR	*D*	Lionel Conacher, Mtl. M.
Frank Boucher, NYR	*C*	Howie Morenz, Mtl.
Bill Cook, NYR	*RW*	Charlie Conacher, Tor.
Baldy Northcott, Mtl. M.	*LW*	Busher Jackson, Tor.
Lester Patrick, NYR	*Coach*	Dick Irvin, Tor.

1931-32

First Team		Second Team
Charlie Gardiner, Chi.	*G*	Roy Worters, NYA
Eddie Shore, Bos.	*D*	Sylvio Mantha, Mtl.
Ching Johnson, NYR	*D*	King Clancy, Tor.
Howie Morenz, Mtl.	*C*	Hooley Smith, Mtl. M.
Bill Cook, NYR	*RW*	Charlie Conacher, Tor.
Busher Jackson, Tor.	*LW*	Aurel Joliat, Mtl.
Lester Patrick, NYR	*Coach*	Dick Irvin, Tor.

1930-31

First Team		Second Team
Charlie Gardiner, Chi.	*G*	Tiny Thompson, Bos.
Eddie Shore, Bos.	*D*	Sylvio Mantha, Mtl.
King Clancy, Tor.	*D*	Ching Johnson, NYR
Howie Morenz, Mtl.	*C*	Frank Boucher, NYR
Bill Cook, NYR	*RW*	Dit Clapper, Bos.
Aurel Joliat, Mtl.	*LW*	Bun Cook, NYR
Lester Patrick, NYR	*Coach*	Dick Irvin, Chi.

NHL ALL-ROOKIE TEAM

Voting for the NHL All-Rookie Team is conducted among the representatives of the Professional Hockey Writers' Association at the end of the season. The rookie all-star team was first selected for the 1982-83 season.

Position	2012-13	2011-12	2010-11	2009-10	2008-09	2007-08	2006-07
Goal	Jake Allen, St. Louis	Jhonas Enroth, Buffalo	Corey Crawford, Chicago	Jimmy Howard, Detroit	Steve Mason, Columbus	Carey Price, Montreal	Mike Smith, Dallas
Defense	Jonas Brodin, Minnesota	Justin Faulk, Carolina	John Carlson, Washington	Tyler Myers, Buffalo	Drew Doughty, Los Angeles	Tobias Enstrom, Atlanta	Matt Carle, San Jose
Defense	Justin Schultz, Edmonton	Jake Gardiner, Toronto	P.K. Subban, Montreal	Michael Del Zotto, NY Rangers	Luke Schenn, Toronto	Tom Gilbert, Edmonton	Marc-Edouard Vlasic, San Jose
Forward	Brendan Gallagher, Montreal	Adam Henrique, New Jersey	Logan Couture, San Jose	John Tavares, NY Islanders	Patrik Berglund, St. Louis	Nicklas Backstrom, Washington	Evgeni Malkin, Pittsburgh
Forward	Jonathan Huberdeau, Florida	Gabriel Landeskog, Colorado	Michael Grabner, NY Islanders	Matt Duchene, Colorado	Bobby Ryan, Anaheim	Patrick Kane, Chicago	Jordan Staal, Pittsburgh
Forward	Brandon Saad, Chicago	Ryan Nugent-Hopkins, Edmonton	Jeff Skinner, Carolina	Niclas Bergfors, N.J., Atl.	Kris Versteeg, Chicago	Jonathan Toews, Chicago	Paul Stastny, Colorado

Position	2005-06	2004-05	2003-04	2002-03	2001-02	2000-01	1999-2000
Goal	Henrik Lundqvist, NY Rangers	*Season Cancelled*	Andrew Raycroft, Boston	Sebastien Caron, Pittsburgh	Dan Blackburn, NY Rangers	Evgeni Nabokov, San Jose	Brian Boucher, Philadelphia
Defense	Andrej Meszaros, Ottawa		John-Michael Liles, Colorado	Jay Bouwmeester, Florida	Nick Boynton, Boston	Lubomir Visnovsky, Los Angeles	Brian Rafalski, New Jersey
Defense	Dion Phaneuf, Calgary		Joni Pitkanen, Philadelphia	Barret Jackman, St. Louis	Rostislav Klesla, Columbus	Colin White, New Jersey	Brad Stuart, San Jose
Forward	Brad Boyes, Boston		Trent Hunter, NY Islanders	Tyler Arnason, Chicago	Dany Heatley, Atlanta	Martin Havlat, Ottawa	Simon Gagne, Philadelphia
Forward	Sidney Crosby, Pittsburgh		Ryan Malone, Pittsburgh	Rick Nash, Columbus	Ilya Kovalchuk, Atlanta	Brad Richards, Tampa Bay	Scott Gomez, New Jersey
Forward	Alex Ovechkin, Washington		Michael Ryder, Montreal	Henrik Zetterberg, Detroit	Kristian Huselius, Florida	Shane Willis, Carolina	Michael York, NY Rangers

Position	1998-99	1997-98	1996-97	1995-96	1994-95	1993-94	1992-93
Goal	Jamie Storr, Los Angeles	Jamie Storr, Los Angeles	Patrick Lalime, Pittsburgh	Corey Hirsch, Vancouver	Jim Carey, Washington	Martin Brodeur, New Jersey	Felix Potvin, Toronto
Defense	Tom Poti, Edmonton	Mattias Ohlund, Vancouver	Bryan Berard, NY Islanders	Ed Jovanovski, Florida	Chris Therien, Philadelphia	Chris Pronger, Hartford	Vladimir Malakhov, NY Islanders
Defense	Sami Salo, Ottawa	Derek Morris, Calgary	Janne Niinimaa, Philadelphia	Kyle McLaren, Boston	Kenny Jonsson, Toronto	Boris Mironov, Wpg./Edm.	Scott Niedermayer, New Jersey
Forward	Chris Drury, Colorado	Sergei Samsonov, Boston	Jarome Iginla, Calgary	Daniel Alfredsson, Ottawa	Peter Forsberg, Quebec	Jason Arnott, Edmonton	Eric Lindros, Philadelphia
Forward	Milan Hejduk, Colorado	Patrick Elias, New Jersey	Jim Campbell, St. Louis	Eric Daze, Chicago	Jeff Friesen, San Jose	Mikael Renberg, Philadelphia	Teemu Selanne, Winnipeg
Forward	Marian Hossa, Ottawa	Mike Johnson, Toronto	Sergei Berezin, Toronto	Petr Sykora, New Jersey	Paul Kariya, Anaheim	Oleg Petrov, Montreal	Joe Juneau, Boston

Position	1991-92	1990-91	1989-90	1988-89	1987-88	1986-87	1985-86
Goal	Dominik Hasek, Chicago	Ed Belfour, Chicago	Bob Essensa, Winnipeg	Peter Sidorkiewicz, Hartford	Darren Pang, Chicago	Ron Hextall, Philadelphia	Patrick Roy, Montreal
Defense	Nicklas Lidstrom, Detroit	Eric Weinrich, New Jersey	Brad Shaw, Hartford	Brian Leetch, NY Rangers	Glen Wesley, Boston	Steve Duchesne, Los Angeles	Gary Suter, Calgary
Defense	Vladimir Konstantinov, Detroit	Rob Blake, Los Angeles	Geoff Smith, Edmonton	Zarley Zalapski, Pittsburgh	Calle Johansson, Buffalo	Brian Benning, St. Louis	Dana Murzyn, Hartford
Forward	Kevin Todd, New Jersey	Sergei Fedorov, Detroit	Mike Modano, Minnesota	Trevor Linden, Vancouver	Joe Nieuwendyk, Calgary	Jimmy Carson, Los Angeles	Mike Ridley, NY Rangers
Forward	Tony Amonte, NY Rangers	Ken Hodge, Boston	Sergei Makarov, Calgary	Tony Granato, NY Rangers	Ray Sheppard, Buffalo	Jim Sandlak, Vancouver	Kjell Dahlin, Montreal
Forward	Gilbert Dionne, Montreal	Jaromir Jagr, Pittsburgh	Rod Brind'Amour, St. Louis	David Volek, NY Islanders	Iain Duncan, Winnipeg	Luc Robitaille, Los Angeles	Wendel Clark, Toronto

Position	1984-85	1983-84	1982-83
Goal	Steve Penney, Montreal	Tom Barrasso, Buffalo	Pelle Lindbergh, Philadelphia
Defense	Chris Chelios, Montreal	Thomas Eriksson, Philadelphia	Scott Stevens, Washington
Defense	Bruce Bell, Quebec	Jamie Macoun, Calgary	Phil Housley, Buffalo
Forward	Mario Lemieux, Pittsburgh	Steve Yzerman, Detroit	Dan Daoust, Mtl./Tor.
Forward	Tomas Sandstrom, NY Rangers	Hakan Loob, Calgary	Steve Larmer, Chicago
Forward	Warren Young, Pittsburgh	Sylvain Turgeon, Hartford	Mats Naslund, Montreal

A member of the NHL All-Rookie team in 2010-11, Montreal's P.K. Subban (left) earned his first selection as a First-Team All-Star in 2012-13 and also won the Norris Trophy as the NHL's best defenseman. Canadiens legend Doug Harvey (right) earned 10 selections to the First-All-Star Team during his Hall of Fame career and won the Norris Trophy seven times.

All-Star Game Results

Year	Venue	Score	Coaches	Attendance
2012	Ottawa	Team Chara 12, Team Alfredsson 9	Claude Julien, Tortorella/MacLellan	20,510
2011	Carolina	Team Lidstrom 11, Team Staal 10	Joel Quenneville, Peter Laviolette	18,680
2009	Montreal	East 12, West 11	Claude Julien, Todd McLellan	21,273
2008	Atlanta	East 8, West 7	John Paddock, Mike Babcock	18,644
2007	Dallas	West 12, East 9	Lindy Ruff, Randy Carlyle	18,532
2004	Minnesota	East 6, West 4	Pat Quinn, Dave Lewis	19,434
2003	Florida	West 6, East 5	Marc Crawford, Jacques Martin	19,250
2002	Los Angeles	World 8, North America 5	Scotty Bowman, Pat Quinn	18,118
2001	Colorado	North America 14, World 12	Joel Quenneville, Jacques Martin	18,646
2000	Toronto	World 9, North America 4	Scotty Bowman, Pat Quinn	19,300
1999	Tampa Bay	North America 8, World 6	Lindy Ruff, Ken Hitchcock	19,758
1998	Vancouver	North America 8, World 7	Jacques Lemaire, Ken Hitchcock	18,422
1997	San Jose	East 11, West 7	Doug MacLean, Ken Hitchcock	17,422
1996	Boston	East 5, West 4	Doug MacLean, Scotty Bowman	17,565
1994	NY Rangers	East 9, West 8	Jacques Demers, Barry Melrose	18,200
1993	Montreal	Wales 16, Campbell 6	Scotty Bowman, Mike Keenan	17,137
1992	Philadelphia	Campbell 10, Wales 6	Bob Gainey, Scotty Bowman	17,380
1991	Chicago	Campbell 11, Wales 5	John Muckler, Mike Milbury	18,472
1990	Pittsburgh	Wales 12, Campbell 7	Pat Burns, Terry Crisp	16,236
1989	Edmonton	Campbell 9, Wales 5	Glen Sather, Terry O'Reilly	17,503
1988	St. Louis	Wales 6, Campbell 5 OT	Mike Keenan, Glen Sather	17,878
1986	Hartford	Wales 4, Campbell 3 OT	Mike Keenan, Glen Sather	15,100
1985	Calgary	Wales 6, Campbell 4	Al Arbour, Glen Sather	16,825
1984	New Jersey	Wales 7, Campbell 6	Al Arbour, Glen Sather	18,939
1983	NY Islanders	Campbell 9, Wales 3	Roger Neilson, Al Arbour	15,230
1982	Washington	Wales 4, Campbell 2	Al Arbour, Glen Sonmor	18,130
1981	Los Angeles	Campbell 4, Wales 1	Pat Quinn, Scotty Bowman	15,761
1980	Detroit	Wales 6, Campbell 3	Scotty Bowman, Al Arbour	21,002
1978	Buffalo	Wales 3, Campbell 2 OT	Scotty Bowman, Fred Shero	16,433
1977	Vancouver	Wales 4, Campbell 3	Scotty Bowman, Fred Shero	15,607
1976	Philadelphia	Wales 7, Campbell 5	Floyd Smith, Fred Shero	16,436
1975	Montreal	Wales 7, Campbell 1	Bep Guidolin, Fred Shero	16,080
1974	Chicago	West 6, East 4	Billy Reay, Scotty Bowman	16,426
1973	NY Rangers	East 5, West 4	Tom Johnson, Billy Reay	16,986
1972	Minnesota	East 3, West 2	Al MacNeil, Billy Reay	15,423
1971	Boston	West 2, East 1	Scotty Bowman, Harry Sinden	14,790
1970	St. Louis	East 4, West 1	Claude Ruel, Scotty Bowman	16,587
1969	Montreal	East 3, West 3	Toe Blake, Scotty Bowman	16,260
1968	Toronto	Toronto 4, All-Stars 3	Punch Imlach, Toe Blake	15,753
1967	Montreal	Montreal 3, All-Stars 0	Toe Blake, Sid Abel	14,284
1965	Montreal	All-Stars 5, Montreal 2	Billy Reay, Toe Blake	13,529
1964	Toronto	All-Stars 3, Toronto 2	Sid Abel, Punch Imlach	14,232
1963	Toronto	All-Stars 3, Toronto 3	Sid Abel, Punch Imlach	14,034
1962	Toronto	Toronto 4, All-Stars 1	Punch Imlach, Rudy Pilous	14,236
1961	Chicago	All-Stars 3, Chicago 1	Sid Abel, Rudy Pilous	14,534
1960	Montreal	All-Stars 2, Montreal 1	Punch Imlach, Toe Blake	13,949
1959	Montreal	Montreal 6, All-Stars 1	Toe Blake, Punch Imlach	13,818
1958	Montreal	Montreal 6, All-Stars 3	Toe Blake, Milt Schmidt	13,989
1957	Montreal	All-Stars 5, Montreal 3	Milt Schmidt, Toe Blake	13,003
1956	Montreal	All-Stars 1, Montreal 1	Jim Skinner, Toe Blake	13,095
1955	Detroit	Detroit 3, All-Stars 1	Jim Skinner, Dick Irvin	10,111
1954	Detroit	All-Stars 2, Detroit 2	King Clancy, Jim Skinner	10,689
1953	Montreal	All-Stars 3, Montreal 1	Lynn Patrick, Dick Irvin	14,153
1952	Detroit	1st Team 1, 2nd Team 1	Tommy Ivan, Dick Irvin	10,680
1951	Toronto	1st Team 2, 2nd Team 2	Joe Primeau, Dick Irvin	11,469
1950	Detroit	Detroit 7, All-Stars 1	Tommy Ivan, Lynn Patrick	9,166
1949	Toronto	All-Stars 3, Toronto 1	Tommy Ivan, Hap Day	13,541
1948	Chicago	All-Stars 3, Toronto 1	Tommy Ivan, Hap Day	12,794
1947	Toronto	All-Stars 4, Toronto 3	Dick Irvin, Hap Day	14,169

There was no All-Star contest during the calendar year of 1966 because the game was moved from the start of season to mid-season. In 1979, the Challenge Cup series between the Soviet Union and Team NHL replaced the All-Star Game. In 1987, Rendez-Vous '87, two games between the Soviet Union and Team NHL replaced the All-Star Game. In 1995, 2005 and 2013 the All-Star Game was not played due to a labour disruption affecting the NHL. In both 2006 and 2010 the All-Star Game was not played because of NHL players' participation in the Olympics.

NHL ALL-STAR GAME MVP

2012	Marian Gaborik, NYR
2011	Patrick Sharp, Chi.
2009	Alex Kovalev, Mtl.
2008	Eric Staal, Car.
2007	Daniel Briere, Buf.
2004	Joe Sakic, Col..
2003	Dany Heatley, Atl.
2002	Eric Daze, Chi.
2001	Bill Guerin, Bos.
2000	Pavel Bure, Fla.
1999	Wayne Gretzky, NYR
1998	Teemu Selanne, Ana.
1997	Mark Recchi, Mtl.
1996	Raymond Bourque, Bos.
1994	Mike Richter, NYR
1993	Mike Gartner, NYR
1992	Brett Hull, St.L.
1991	Vincent Damphousse, Tor.
1990	Mario Lemieux, Pit.
1989	Wayne Gretzky, L.A.
1988	Mario Lemieux, Pit.
1986	Grant Fuhr, Edm.
1985	Mario Lemieux, Pit.
1984	Don Maloney, NYR
1983	Wayne Gretzky, Edm.
1982	Mike Bossy, NYI
1981	Mike Liut, St.L.
1980	Reggie Leach, Phi.
1978	Billy Smith, NYI
1977	Rick Martin, Buf.
1976	Pete Mahovlich, Mtl.
1975	Syl Apps Jr., Pit.
1974	Garry Unger, St.L.
1973	Greg Polis, Pit.
1972	Bobby Orr, Bos.
1971	Bobby Hull, Chi.
1970	Bobby Hull, Chi.
1969	Frank Mahovlich, Det.
1968	Bruce Gamble, Tor.
1967	Henri Richard, Mtl.
1965	Gordie Howe, Det.
1964	Jean Beliveau, Mtl.
1963	Frank Mahovlich, Tor.
1962	Eddie Shack, Tor.

All-Star Game Records 1947 through 2012

TEAM RECORDS

MOST GOALS, BOTH TEAMS, ONE GAME:

26 — North America 14, World 12, 2001 at Colorado
23 — East 12, West 11, 2009 at Montreal
22 — Wales 16, Campbell 6, 1993 at Montreal
21 — West 12, East 9, 2007 at Dallas
— Team Lidstrom 11, Team Staal 10, 2011 at Carolina
— Team Chara 12, Team Alfredsson 9, 2012 at Ottawa
19 — Wales 12, Campbell 7, 1990 at Pittsburgh
18 — East 11, West 7, 1997 at San Jose

FEWEST GOALS, BOTH TEAMS, ONE GAME:

2 — First Team All-Stars 1, Second Team All-Stars 1, 1952 at Detroit
— NHL All-Stars 1, Montreal Canadiens 1, 1956 at Montreal
3 — NHL All-Stars 2, Montreal Canadiens 1, 1960 at Montreal
— Montreal Canadiens 3, NHL All-Stars 0, 1967 at Montreal
— West 2, East 1, 1971 at Boston

MOST GOALS, ONE TEAM, ONE GAME:

16 — Wales 16, Campbell 6, 1993 at Montreal
14 — North America 14, World 12, 2001 at Colorado
12 — Wales 12, Campbell 7, 1990 at Pittsburgh
— World 12, North America 14, 2001 at Colorado
— West 12, East 9, 2007 at Dallas
— East 12, West 11, 2009 at Montreal
— Team Chara 12, Team Alfredsson 9, 2012 at Ottawa

FEWEST GOALS, ONE TEAM, ONE GAME:

0 — NHL All-Stars 0, Montreal Canadiens 3, 1967 at Montreal
1 — 17 times (1981, 1975, 1971, 1970, 1962, 1961, 1960, 1959, both teams 1956, 1955, 1953, both teams 1952, 1950, 1949, 1948)

MOST SHOTS, BOTH TEAMS, ONE GAME (SINCE 1955):

102 — 1994 at NY Rangers — East 9 (56 shots), West 8 (46 shots)
2009 at Montreal — East 12 (48 shots) — West 11 (54 shots)
98 — 2001 at Colorado — North America 14 (53 shots), World 12 (45 shots)
94 — 2012 at Ottawa — Team Chara 12 (44 shots), Team Alfredsson 9 (50 shots)

FEWEST SHOTS, BOTH TEAMS, ONE GAME (SINCE 1955):

52 — 1978 at Buffalo — Campbell 2 (12 shots) Wales 3 (40 shots)
53 — 1960 at Montreal — NHL All-Stars 2 (27 shots) Montreal Canadiens 1 (26 shots)
55 — 1956 at Montreal — NHL All-Stars 1 (28 shots) Montreal Canadiens 1 (27 shots)
— 1971 at Boston — West 2 (28 shots) East 1 (27 shots)

MOST SHOTS, ONE TEAM, ONE GAME (SINCE 1955):

56 — 1994 at NY Rangers — East (9-8 vs. West)
54 — 2009 at Montreal — East (12-11 vs. West)
53 — 2001 at Colorado — North America (14-12 vs. World)
51 — 2008 at Atlanta — West (7-8 vs. East)

FEWEST SHOTS, ONE TEAM, ONE GAME (SINCE 1955):

12 — 1978 at Buffalo — Campbell (2-3 vs. Wales)
17 — 1970 at St. Louis — West (1-4 vs. East)
23 — 1961 at Chicago — Chicago Black Hawks (1-3 vs. NHL All-Stars)
24 — 1976 at Philadelphia — Campbell (5-7 vs. Wales)

MOST POWER-PLAY GOALS, BOTH TEAMS, ONE GAME (SINCE 1950):

3 — 1953 at Montreal — NHL All-Stars 3 (2 power-play goals), Montreal Canadiens 1 (1 power-play goal)
— 1954 at Detroit — NHL All-Stars 2 (1 power-play goal) Detroit Red Wings 2 (2 power-play goals)
— 1958 at Montreal — NHL All-Stars 3 (1 power-play goal) Montreal Canadiens 6 (2 power-play goals)

FEWEST POWER-PLAY GOALS, BOTH TEAMS, ONE GAME (SINCE 1950):

0 — 27 times (1952, 1959, 1960, 1967, 1968, 1969, 1972, 1973, 1976, 1980, 1981, 1984, 1985, 1992, 1994, 1996, 1999, 2000, 2001, 2002, 2003, 2004, 2007, 2008, 2009, 2011, 2012)

FASTEST TWO GOALS, BOTH TEAMS, FROM START OF GAME:

0:37 — 1970 at St. Louis — Jacques Laperriere of East scored at 0:20 and Dean Prentice of West scored at 0:37. Final score: East 4, West 1.

1:20 — 2008 at Atlanta — Rick Nash of West scored at 0:12 and Eric Staal of East scored at 1:20. Final score: East 8, West 7.

2:15 — 1998 at Vancouver — Teemu Selanne scored at 0:53 and Jaromir Jagr scored at 2:15 for World. Final score: North America 8, World 7.

FASTEST TWO GOALS, BOTH TEAMS:

0:08 — 1997 at San Jose — Owen Nolan scored at 18:54 and 19:02 of second period for West. Final Score: East 11, West 7.

0:10 — 1976 at Philadelphia — Dennis Ververgaert scored at 4:33 and at 4:43 of third period for Campbell. Final score: Wales 7, Campbell 5.

0:13 — 1998 at Vancouver — Teemu Selanne scored at 4:00 of first period for World and John LeClair scored at 4:13 for North America. Final score: North America 8, World 7.

FASTEST THREE GOALS, BOTH TEAMS:
0:48 — 2007 at Dallas — Martin Havlat scored at 19:00 of third period for West; Sheldon Souray scored at 19:25 for East; Dion Phaneuf scored at 19:48 for West. Final score: West 12, East 9.

1:08 — 1993 at Montreal — all by Wales — Mike Gartner scored at 3:15 and at 3:37 of first period; Peter Bondra scored at 4:23. Final score: Wales 16, Campbell 6.

1:14 — 1994 at NY Rangers — Bob Kudelski scored at 9:46 of first period for East; Sergei Fedorov scored at 10:20 for West; Eric Lindros scored at 11:00 for East. Final score: East 9, West 8.

FASTEST FOUR GOALS, BOTH TEAMS:
2:16 — 2012 at Ottawa, Marian Hossa scored at 12:04 of third period for Team Chara; Zdeno Chara scored at 12:20 of third period for Team Chara; Corey Perry scored at 13:26 of third period for Team Chara; Daniel Sedin scored at 14:20 of third period for Team Alfredsson. Final score: Team Chara 12, Team Alfredsson 9.
2:24 — 1997 at San Jose — Brendan Shanahan scored at 16:38 of second period for West; Dale Hawerchuk scored at 17:28 for East; Owen Nolan scored at 18:54 and 19:02 for West. Final score: East 11, West 7.

2:49 — 2009 at Montreal — Evgeni Malkin scored at 7:45 of second period for East; Rick Nash scored at 8:27 for West; Milan Hejduk scored at 9:02 for West; Sheldon Souray scored at 10:34 for West.

FASTEST TWO GOALS, ONE TEAM, FROM START OF GAME:
2:15 — 1998 at Vancouver — World — Teemu Selanne scored at 0:53 and Jaromir Jagr scored at 2:15. Final score: North America 8, World 7.

2:48 — 2011 at Carolina — Team Staal — Alex Ovechkin scored at 0:50 and Paul Stastny scored at 2:48. Final score: Team Lidstrom 11, Team Staal 10.

3:37 — 1993 at Montreal — Wales — Mike Gartner scored at 3:15 and at 3:37. Final score: Wales 16, Campbell 6.

FASTEST TWO GOALS, ONE TEAM:
0:08 — 1997 at San Jose — West — Owen Nolan scored at 18:54 and at 19:02 of second period. Final score: East 11, West 7.

0:10 — 1976 at Philadelphia — Campbell — Dennis Ververgaert scored at 4:33 and at 4:43 of third period. Final score: Wales 7, Campbell 5.

0:14 — 1989 at Edmonton — Campbell — Steve Yzerman and Gary Leeman scored at 17:21 and 17:35 of second period. Final score: Campbell 9, Wales 5.

FASTEST THREE GOALS, ONE TEAM:
1:08 — 1993 at Montreal — Wales — Mike Gartner scored at 3:15 and 3:37 of first period; Peter Bondra scored at 4:23. Final score: Wales 16, Campbell 6.

1:22 — 2012 at Ottawa — Team Chara — Marian Hossa scored at 12:04 of third period; Zdeno Chara scored at 12:20; Corey Perry scored at 13:26. Final score: Team Chara 12, Team Alfredsson 9.

1:32 — 1980 at Detroit — Wales — Ron Stackhouse scored at 11:40 of third period; Craig Hartsburg scored at 12:40; Reed Larson scored at 13:12. Final score: Wales 6, Campbell 3.

FASTEST FOUR GOALS, ONE TEAM:
2:57 — 2002 at Los Angeles — World — Sergei Fedorov scored at 16:59 of third period; Markus Naslund scored at 18:17; Alex Zhamnov scored at 19:12; Sami Kapanen scored at 19:56. Final score: World 8, North America 5.

3:29 — 2012 at Ottawa — Team Chara — Marian Hossa scored at 12:04 of third period; Zdeno Chara scored at 12:20; Corey Perry scored at 13:26; Joffrey Lupul scored at 15:33. Final score: Team Chara 12, Team Alfredsson 9.

4:17 — 2007 at Dallas — Brian Rolston scored at 8:30 of second period; Rick Nash scored at 10:40; Martin Havlat scored at 11:34; Yanic Perreault scored at 12:47. Final score: West 12, East 9.

MOST GOALS, BOTH TEAMS, ONE PERIOD:
10 — 1997 at San Jose — Second period — East (6), West (4).
Final score: East 11, West 7.

— 2001 at Colorado — Second period — North America (6), World (4).
Final score: North America 14, World 12.

— 2001 at Colorado — Third period — North America (5), World (5).
Final score: North America 14, World 12.
— 2009 at Montreal — Second period — West (6), East (4).
Final Score: East 12, West 11.

9 — 1990 at Pittsburgh — First period — Wales (7), Campbell (2).
Final score: Wales 12, Campbell 7.

— 2007 at Dallas — Second period — West (6), East (3).
Final score: West 12, East 9.

— 2012 at Ottawa — Third period — Team Chara (6), Team Alfredsson (3).
Final score: Team Chara 12, Team Alfredsson 9.

MOST GOALS, ONE TEAM, ONE PERIOD:
7 — 1990 at Pittsburgh — First period — Wales. Final score: Wales 12, Campbell 7.
6 — 1983 at NY Islanders — Third period — Campbell.
Final score: Campbell 9, Wales 3.

— 1992 at Philadelphia — Second period — Campbell.
Final score: Campbell 10, Wales 6.

— 1993 at Montreal — First period — Wales.
Final score: Wales 16, Campbell 6.

— 1993 at Montreal — Second period — Wales.
Final score: Wales 16, Campbell 6.

— 1997 at San Jose — Second period — East.
Final score: East 11, West 7.

— 2001 at Colorado — Second period — North America.
Final score: North America 14, World 12.

— 2007 at Dallas — Second period — West.
Final score: West 12, East 9.

— 2009 at Montreal — Second period — West.
Final score: East 12, West 11.

— 2012 at Ottawa — Third period — Team Chara.
Final score: Team Chara 12, Team Alfredsson 9.

MOST SHOTS, BOTH TEAMS, ONE PERIOD:
42 — 2009 at Montreal — Second period — West (21), East (21).
Final score: East 12, West 11.

40 — 2012 at Ottawa — Third period — Team Alfredsson (21), Team Chara (19).
Final score: Team Chara 12, Team Alfredsson 9.

39 — 1994 at NY Rangers — Second period — West (21), East (18).
Final score: East 9, West 8.

— 2001 at Colorado — Third period — World (23), North America (16).
Final score: North America 14, World 12.

36 — 1990 at Pittsburgh — Third period — Campbell (22), Wales (14).
Final score: Wales 12, Campbell 7.

— 1994 at NY Rangers — First period — East (19), West (17).
Final score: East 9, West 8.

— 2002 at Los Angeles — Third period — North America (20), World (16).
Final score: World 8, North America 5.

MOST SHOTS, ONE TEAM, ONE PERIOD:
23 — 2001 at Colorado — Third period — World.
Final score: North America 14, World 12.

22 — 1990 at Pittsburgh — Third period — Campbell.
Final score: Wales 12, Campbell 7.

— 1991 at Chicago — Third period — Wales.
Final score: Campbell 11, Wales 5.

— 1993 at Montreal — First period — Wales.
Final score: Wales 16, Campbell 6.

FEWEST SHOTS, BOTH TEAMS, ONE PERIOD:
9 — 1971 at Boston — Third period — East (2), West (7).
Final score: West 2, East 1.

— 1980 at Detroit — Second period — Campbell (4), Wales (5).
Final score: Wales 6, Campbell 3.

13 — 1982 at Washington — Third period — Campbell (6), Wales (7).
Final score: Wales 4, Campbell 2.

14 — 1978 at Buffalo — First period — Campbell (7), Wales (7).
Final score: Wales 3, Campbell 2.

— 1986 at Hartford — First period — Campbell (6), Wales (8).
Final score: Wales 4, Campbell 3.

FEWEST SHOTS, ONE TEAM, ONE PERIOD:
2 — 1971 at Boston — Third period — East.
Final score: West 2, East 1.

— 1978 at Buffalo — Second period — Campbell.
Final score: Wales 3, Campbell 2.

3 — 1978 at Buffalo — Third period — Campbell.
Final score: Wales 3, Campbell 2.

4 — 1955 at Detroit — First period — NHL All-Stars.
Final score: Detroit Red Wings 3, NHL All-Stars 1.

— 1980 at Detroit — Second period — Campbell.
Final score: Wales 6, Campbell 3.

Members of Team Alfredsson celebrate a goal during the 2012 NHL All-Star Game in Ottawa. The 12-9 victory of Team Chara that afternoon marked one of the highest-scoring games in All-Star history.

INDIVIDUAL RECORDS

Games

MOST GAMES PLAYED:
23 — Gordie Howe, 1948 through 1980
19 — Raymond Bourque, 1981 through 2001
18 — Wayne Gretzky, 1980 through 1999
15 — Frank Mahovlich, 1959 through 1974
— Mark Messier, 1982 through 2004

Goals

MOST GOALS, CAREER:
13 — Wayne Gretzky in 18GP
— Mario Lemieux in 10GP
10 — Gordie Howe in 23GP
9 — Teemu Selanne in 10GP
8 — Frank Mahovlich in 15GP
— Luc Robitaille in 8GP

MOST GOALS, ONE GAME:
4 — Wayne Gretzky, Campbell, 1983
— Mario Lemieux, Wales, 1990
— Vince Damphousse, Campbell, 1991
— Mike Gartner, Wales, 1993
— Dany Heatley, East, 2003
3 — Ted Lindsay, Detroit, 1950
— Mario Lemieux, Wales, 1988
— Pierre Turgeon, Wales, 1993
— Mark Recchi, East, 1997
— Owen Nolan, West, 1997
— Teemu Selanne, World, 1998
— Pavel Bure, World, 2000
— Bill Guerin, North America, 2001
— Joe Sakic, West, 2004
— Rick Nash, West, 2008
— Marian Gaborik, Team Chara, 2012

MOST GOALS, ONE PERIOD:
4 — Wayne Gretzky, Campbell, Third period, 1983
3 — Mario Lemieux, Wales, First period, 1990
— Vincent Damphousse, Campbell, Third period, 1991
— Mike Gartner, Wales, First period, 1993

Assists

MOST ASSISTS, CAREER:
16 — Joe Sakic in 12GP
14 — Mark Messier in 15GP
13 — Raymond Bourque in 19GP
12 — Adam Oates in 5GP
— Mats Sundin in 8GP
— Wayne Gretzky in 18GP

MOST ASSISTS, ONE GAME:
5 — Mats Naslund, Wales, 1988
4 — Raymond Bourque, Wales, 1985
— Adam Oates, Campbell, 1991
— Adam Oates, Wales, 1993
— Mark Recchi, Wales, 1993
— Pierre Turgeon, East, 1994
— Fredrik Modin, World, 2001
— Joe Sakic, West, 2007
— Daniel Briere, East, 2007
— Marian Hossa, East, 2007
— Shea Weber, Team Lidstrom, 2011

MOST ASSISTS, ONE PERIOD:
4 — Adam Oates, Wales, First period, 1993
3 — Mark Messier, Campbell, Third period, 1983
3 — Marian Hossa, East, Third period, 2007

Points

MOST POINTS, CAREER:
25 — Wayne Gretzky (13G-12A in 18GP)
23 — Mario Lemieux (13G-10A in 10GP)
22 — Joe Sakic (6G-16A in 12GP)
20 — Mark Messier (6G-14A in 15GP)
19 — Gordie Howe (10G-9A in 23GP)

MOST POINTS, ONE GAME:
6 — Mario Lemieux, Wales, 1988 (3G-3A)
5 — Mats Naslund, Wales, 1988 (5A)
— Adam Oates, Campbell, 1991 (1G-4A)
— Mike Gartner, Wales, 1993 (4G-1A)
— Mark Recchi, Wales, 1993 (1G-4A)
— Pierre Turgeon, Wales, 1993 (3G-2A)
— Bill Guerin, North America, 2001 (3G-2A)
— Dany Heatley, East, 2003 (4G-1A)
— Daniel Briere, East, 2007 (1G-4A)

MOST POINTS, ONE PERIOD:
4 — Wayne Gretzky, Campbell, Third period, 1983 (4G)
— Mike Gartner, Wales, First period, 1993 (3G-1A)
— Adam Oates, Wales, First period, 1993 (4A)
3 — Gordie Howe, NHL All-Stars, Second period, 1965 (1G-2A)
— Pete Mahovlich, Wales, First period, 1976 (1G-2A)
— Mark Messier, Campbell, Third period, 1983 (3A)
— Mario Lemieux, Wales, Second period, 1988 (1G-2A)
— Mario Lemieux, Wales, First period, 1990 (3G)
— Vince Damphousse, Campbell, Third period, 1991 (3G)
— Mark Recchi, Wales, Second period, 1993 (1G-2A)
— Tony Amonte, North America, Second period, 2001 (2G-1A)
— Daniel Alfredsson, East, Second period, 2004 (2G-1A)
— Marian Hossa, East, Third period, 2007 (3A)

Power-Play Goals

MOST POWER-PLAY GOALS, CAREER:
6 — Gordie Howe in 23GP
3 — Bobby Hull in 12GP
— Maurice Richard in 13GP

Fastest Goals

FASTEST GOAL FROM START OF GAME:
0:12 — Rick Nash, West, 2008
0:19 — Ted Lindsay, Detroit, 1950
0:20 — Jacques Laperriere, East, 1970
0:21 — Mario Lemieux, Wales, 1990
0:35 — Vincent Damphousse, North America, 2002

FASTEST GOAL FROM START OF A PERIOD:
0:12 — Rick Nash, West, 2008 (first period)
0:17 — Raymond Bourque, North America, 1999 (second period)
0:19 — Ted Lindsay, Detroit, 1950 (first period)
— Rick Tocchet, Wales, 1993 (second period)
0:20 — Jacques Laperriere, East, 1970 (first period)

FASTEST TWO GOALS, ONE PLAYER, FROM START OF GAME:
3:37 — Mike Gartner, Wales, 1993, at 3:15 and 3:37.
4:00 — Teemu Selanne, World, 1998, at 0:53 and 4:00
5:25 — Wally Hergesheimer, NHL All-Stars, 1953, at 4:06 and 5:25.

FASTEST TWO GOALS, ONE PLAYER, FROM START OF A PERIOD:
3:37 — Mike Gartner, Wales, 1993, at 3:15 and 3:37 of first period.
4:00 — Teemu Selanne, World, 1998, at 0:53 and 4:00 of first period.
4:43 — Dennis Ververgaert, Campbell, 1976, at 4:33 and 4:43 of third period.

FASTEST TWO GOALS, ONE PLAYER:
0:08 — Owen Nolan, West, 1997. Scored at 18:54 and 19:02 of second period.
0:10 — Dennis Ververgaert, Campbell, 1976. Scored at 4:33 and 4:43 of third period.
0:22 — Mike Gartner, Wales, 1993. Scored at 3:15 and 3:37 of first period.

Penalties

MOST PENALTY MINUTES:
25 — Gordie Howe in 23GP
21 — Gus Mortson in 9GP
16 — Harry Howell in 7GP

Goaltenders

MOST GAMES PLAYED:
13 — Glenn Hall from 1955 through 1969
11 — Terry Sawchuk from 1950 through 1968
— Patrick Roy from 1988 through 2003
9 — Martin Brodeur from 1996 through 2007
8 — Jacques Plante from 1956 through 1970

MOST MINUTES PLAYED:
540 — Glenn Hall in 13GP
467 — Terry Sawchuk in 11GP
370 — Jacques Plante in 8GP
250 — Patrick Roy in 11GP
209 — Turk Broda in 4GP

MOST GOALS AGAINST:
31 — Patrick Roy in 11GP
22 — Martin Brodeur in 9GP
— Glenn Hall in 13GP
21 — Mike Vernon in 5GP
19 — Terry Sawchuk in 11GP

BEST GOALS-AGAINST-AVERAGE AMONG THOSE WITH AT LEAST TWO GAMES PLAYED:
0.68 — Gilles Villemure in 3GP
1.49 — Gerry McNeil in 3GP
1.50 — Johnny Bower in 4GP
1.51 — Frank Brimsek in 3GP
1.64 — Gump Worsley in 4GP

Hockey Hall of Fame

(Year of induction is listed after each Honoured Members name)

Location: Brookfield Place, at the corner of Front and Yonge Streets in the heart of downtown Toronto. Easy access from all major highways running into Toronto. Close to TTC subway and Union Station.

Telephone: administration (416) 360-7735; information (416) 360-7765.

Public Hours of Operation: Open every day except Christmas Day, New Year's Day and Induction Day (November 11, 2013). Please call our information number (above) or visit our website (below) for times.

The Hockey Hall of Fame can be booked for private functions after hours.

Website address: www.hhof.com

History: The Hockey Hall of Fame was established in 1943. Members were first honoured in 1945. On August 26, 1961, the Hockey Hall of Fame opened its doors to the public in a building located on the grounds of the Canadian National Exhibition in Toronto. The Hockey Hall of Fame relocated to its current location and welcomed the hockey world on June 18, 1993.

Honour Roll: There are 375 Honoured Members in the Hockey Hall of Fame. 259 have been inducted as players including three women, 101 as builders and 15 as Referees/Linesmen. In addition, there are 90 media honourees.

Founding/Premier Sponsors: Imperial Oil, International Ice Hockey Federation, National Hockey League, National Hockey League Players' Association, Pepsi-Cola Canada, The Toronto Sun, Tim Hortons, The Sports Network (TSN/RDS).

In addition to his three Stanley Cup titles with New Jersey and one with Anaheim, Scott Niedermayer also won the Memorial Cup, a World Junior Championship, a World Championship, the 2004 World Cup and two Olympic gold medals during his career.

PLAYERS

* Abel, Sidney Gerald 1969
* Adams, John James "Jack" 1959
Anderson, Glenn 2008
* Apps, Charles Joseph Sylvanus "Syl" 1961
Armstrong, George Edward 1975
* Bailey, Irvine Wallace "Ace" 1975
* Bain, Donald H. "Dan" 1949
* Baker, Hobart "Hobey" 1945
Barber, William Charles "Bill" 1990
* Barry, Martin J. "Marty" 1965
Bathgate, Andrew James "Andy" 1978
* Bauer, Robert Theodore "Bobby" 1996
Belfour, Ed 2011
Béliveau, Jean Arthur 1972
* Benedict, Clinton S. 1965
* Bentley, Douglas Wagner 1964
* Bentley, Maxwell H. L. 1966
* Blake, Hector "Toe" 1966
Boivin, Leo Joseph 1986
* Boon, Richard R. "Dickie" 1952
Bossy, Michael 1991
* Bouchard, Emile Joseph "Butch" 1966
* Boucher, Frank 1958
* Boucher, Georges "Buck" 1960
Bourque, Raymond 2004
Bower, John William 1976
* Bowie, Russell 1947
* Brimsek, Francis Charles 1966
* Broadbent, Harry L. "Punch" 1962
* Broda, Walter Edward "Turk" 1967
Bucyk, John Paul 1981
* Burch, Billy 1974
Bure, Pavel 2012
* Cameron, Harold Hugh "Harry" 1962
Cheevers, Gerald Michael "Gerry" 1985
Chelios, Chris 2013
Ciccarelli, Dino 2010
* Clancy, Francis Michael "King" 1958
* Clapper, Aubrey "Dit" 1947
Clarke, Robert "Bobby" 1987
* Cleghorn, Sprague 1958
Coffey, Paul 2004
* Colville, Neil MacNeil 1967
* Conacher, Charles W. 1961
* Conacher, Lionel Pretoria 1994
* Conacher, Roy Gordon 1998
* Connell, Alex 1958
* Cook, Fred "Bun" 1995
* Cook, William Osser 1952
* Coulter, Arthur Edmund 1974
Cournoyer, Yvan Serge 1982
* Cowley, William Mailes 1968
* Crawford, Samuel Russell "Rusty" 1962
* Darragh, John Proctor "Jack" 1962
* Davidson, Allan M. "Scotty" 1950
* Day, Clarence Henry "Hap" 1961
Delvecchio, Alex 1977
* Denneny, Cyril "Cy" 1959
Dionne, Marcel 1992
* Drillon, Gordon Arthur 1975
* Drinkwater, Charles Graham 1950
Dryden, Kenneth Wayne 1983
Duff, Dick 2006
* Dumart, Woodrow "Woody" 1992
* Dunderdale, Thomas 1974
* Durnan, William Ronald 1964
* Dutton, Mervyn A. "Red" 1958
* Dye, Cecil Henry "Babe" 1970
Esposito, Anthony James "Tony" 1988
Esposito, Philip Anthony 1984
* Farrell, Arthur F. 1965
Federko, Bernie 2002
Fetisov, Viacheslav 2001
* Flaman, Ferdinand Charles "Fern" 1990
* Foyston, Frank 1958
Francis, Ron 2007
* Fredrickson, Frank 1958
Fuhr, Grant 2003
Gadsby, William Alexander 1970
Gainey, Bob 1992
* Gardiner, Charles Robert "Chuck" 1945
* Gardiner, Herbert Martin "Herb" 1958
* Gardner, James Henry "Jimmy" 1962
Gartner, Michael Alfred 2001
* Geoffrion, Jos. A. Bernard "Boom Boom" 1972
* Gerard, Eddie 1945
Giacomin, Edward "Eddie" 1987
Gilbert, Rodrigue Gabriel "Rod" 1982
Gillies, Clark 2002
Gilmour, Doug 2011
* Gilmour, Hamilton Livingstone "Billy" 1962
* Goheen, Frank Xavier "Moose" 1952
* Goodfellow, Ebenezer R. "Ebbie" 1963
Goulet, Michel 1998
Granato, Cammi 2010
* Grant, Michael "Mike" 1950
* Green, Wilfred "Shorty" 1962
Gretzky, Wayne Douglas 1999
* Griffis, Silas Seth "Si" 1950
* Hainsworth, George 1961
Hall, Glenn Henry 1975
* Hall, Joseph Henry 1961
* Harvey, Douglas Norman 1973
Hawerchuk, Dale Martin 2001
* Hay, George 1958
Heaney, Geraldine 2013
* Hern, William Milton "Riley" 1962
* Hextall, Bryan Aldwyn 1969
* Holmes, Harry "Hap" 1972
* Hooper, Charles Thomas "Tom" 1962
* Horner, George Reginald "Red" 1965
* Horton, Miles Gilbert "Tim" 1977
Howe, Gordon 1972
Howe, Mark 2011
* Howe, Sydney Harris 1965
Howell, Henry Vernon "Harry" 1979
Hull, Brett 2009
Hull, Robert Marvin 1983
* Hutton, John Bower "Bouse" 1962
* Hyland, Harry M. 1962
* Irvin, James Dickenson "Dick" 1958
* Jackson, Harvey "Busher" 1971
James, Angela 2010
* Johnson, Ernest "Moose" 1952
* Johnson, Ivan "Ching" 1958
* Johnson, Thomas Christian 1970
* Joliat, Aurel 1947
* Keats, Gordon "Duke" 1958
Kelly, Leonard Patrick "Red" 1969
* Kennedy, Theodore Samuel "Teeder" 1966
Keon, David Michael 1986
* Kharlamov, Valeri 2005
Kurri, Jari 2001
Lach, Elmer James 1966
Lafleur, Guy Damien 1988
LaFontaine, Pat 2003
* Lalonde, Edouard Charles "Newsy" 1950
Langway, Rod Corry 2002
Laperriere, Jacques 1987
Lapointe, Guy 1993
Laprade, Edgar 1993
Larionov, Igor 2008
* Laviolette, Jean Baptiste "Jack" 1962
* Lehman, Hugh 1958
Lemaire, Jacques Gerard 1984
Lemieux, Mario 1997
* LeSueur, Percy 1961
Leetch, Brian 2009
* Lewis, Herbert A. 1989
Lindsay, Robert Blake Theodore "Ted" 1966
* Lumley, Harry 1980
MacInnis, Al 2007
* MacKay, Duncan "Mickey" 1952
Mahovlich, Frank William 1981
* Malone, Joseph "Joe" 1950
* Mantha, Sylvio 1960
* Marshall, John "Jack" 1965
* Maxwell, Fred G. "Steamer" 1962
McDonald, Lanny 1992
* McGee, Frank 1945
* McGimsie, William George "Billy" 1962
* McNamara, George 1958
Messier, Mark 2007
Mikita, Stanley 1983
Moore, Richard Winston "Dickie" 1974
* Moran, Patrick Joseph "Paddy" 1958
* Morenz, Howie 1945
* Mosienko, William "Billy" 1965
Mullen, Joseph P. 2000
Murphy, Larry 2004
Neely, Cam 2005
Niedermayer, Scott 2013
Nieuwendyk, Joe 2011
* Nighbor, Frank 1947
* Noble, Edward Reginald "Reg" 1962
Oates, Adam 2012
* O'Connor, Herbert William "Buddy" 1988
* Oliver, Harry 1967
Olmstead, Murray Bert "Bert" 1985
Orr, Robert Gordon 1979
Parent, Bernard Marcel 1984
Park, Douglas Bradford "Brad" 1988
* Patrick, Joseph Lynn 1980
* Patrick, Lester 1947
Perreault, Gilbert 1990
* Phillips, Tommy 1945
Pilote, Joseph Albert Pierre Paul 1975
* Pitre, Didier "Pit" 1962
* Plante, Joseph Jacques Omer 1978
Potvin, Denis 1991
* Pratt, Walter "Babe" 1966
* Primeau, A. Joseph 1963
Pronovost, Joseph René Marcel 1978
Pulford, Bob 1991
* Pulford, Harvey 1945
* Quackenbush, Hubert George "Bill" 1976
* Rankin, Frank 1961
Ratelle, Joseph Gilbert Yvan Jean "Jean" 1985
* Rayner, Claude Earl "Chuck" 1973
* Reardon, Kenneth Joseph 1966
Richard, Joseph Henri 1979
* Richard, Joseph Henri Maurice "Rocket" 1961
* Richardson, George Taylor 1950

* Roberts, Gordon 1971
Robinson, Larry 1995
Robitaille, Luc 2009
* Ross, Arthur Howey 1949
Roy, Patrick 2006
* Russell, Blair 1965
* Russell, Ernest 1965
* Ruttan, J.D. "Jack" 1962
Sakic, Joe 2012
Salming, Borje Anders 1996
Savard, Denis Joseph 2000
Savard, Serge 1986
* Sawchuk, Terrance Gordon "Terry" 1971
* Scanlan, Fred 1965
Schmidt, Milton Conrad "Milt" 1961
* Schriner, David "Sweeney" 1962
* Seibert, Earl Walter 1963
* Seibert, Oliver Levi 1961
Shanahan, Brendan 2013
* Shore, Edward W. "Eddie" 1947
Shutt, Stephen 1993
* Siebert, Albert C. "Babe" 1964
* Simpson, Harold Edward "Bullet Joe" 1962
Sittler, Darryl Glen 1989
* Smith, Alfred E. 1962
* Smith, Clint 1991
* Smith, Reginald "Hooley" 1972
* Smith, Thomas James 1973
Smith, William John "Billy" 1993
Stanley, Allan Herbert 1981
* Stanley, Russell "Barney" 1962
Stastny, Peter 1998
Stevens, Scott 2007
* Stewart, John Sherratt "Black Jack" 1964
* Stewart, Nelson "Nels" 1952
* Stuart, Bruce 1961
* Stuart, Hod 1945
Sundin, Mats 2012
* Taylor, Frederick "Cyclone" (O.B.E.) 1947
* Thompson, Cecil R. "Tiny" 1959
Tretiak, Vladislav 1989
* Trihey, Col. Harry J. 1950
Trottier, Bryan 1997
Ullman, Norman V. Alexander "Norm" 1982
* Vezina, Georges 1945
* Walker, John Phillip "Jack" 1960
* Walsh, Martin "Marty" 1962
* Watson, Harry E. 1962
* Watson, Harry 1994
* Weiland, Ralph "Cooney" 1971
* Westwick, Harry 1962
* Whitcroft, Fred 1962
* Wilson, Gordon Allan "Phat" 1962
* Worsley, Lorne John "Gump" 1980
* Worters, Roy 1969
Yzerman, Steve 2009

BUILDERS

* Adams, Charles 1960
* Adams, Weston W. 1972
* Ahearn, Thomas Franklin "Frank" 1962
* Ahearne, John Francis "Bunny" 1977
* Allan, Sir Montagu (C.V.O.) 1945
Allen, Keith 1992
Arbour, Alger Joseph "Al" 1996
* Ballard, Harold Edwin 1977
* Bauer, Father David 1989
* Bickell, John Paris 1978
Bowman, Scotty 1991
* Brooks, Herb 2006
* Brown, George V. 1961
* Brown, Walter A. 1962
* Buckland, Frank 1975
Bush, Walter 2000
* Butterfield, Jack Arlington 1980
* Calder, Frank 1947
* Campbell, Angus D. 1964
* Campbell, Clarence Sutherland 1966
* Cattarinich, Joseph 1977
* Chynoweth, Ed 2008
Costello, Murray 2005
* Dandurand, Joseph Viateur "Leo" 1963
Devellano, Jim 2010
* Dilio, Francis Paul 1964
* Dudley, George S. 1958
* Dunn, James A. 1968
Fletcher, Cliff 2004
Francis, Emile 1982
* Gibson, Dr. John L. "Jack" 1976
* Gorman, Thomas Patrick "Tommy" 1963
Gregory, Jim 2007
* Griffiths, Frank A. 1993
* Hanley, William 1986
* Hay, Charles 1974
* Hendy, James C. 1968
* Hewitt, Foster 1965
* Hewitt, William Abraham 1947
* Hotchkiss, Harley 2006
* Hume, Fred J. 1962
Illitch, Mike 2003
* Imlach, George "Punch" 1984
* Ivan, Thomas N. 1974
* Jennings, William M. 1975
* Johnson, Bob 1992
* Juckes, Gordon W. 1979
* Kilpatrick, Gen. John Reed 1960
Kilrea, Brian Blair 2003
* Knox, Seymour H. III 1993
Lamoriello, Lou 2009
* Leader, George Alfred 1969
* LeBel, Robert 1970
* Lockhart, Thomas F. 1965
* Loicq, Paul 1961
* Mariucci, John 1985
* Mathers, Frank 1992
* McLaughlin, Major Frederic 1963
* Milford, John "Jake" 1984
* Molson, Hon. Hartland de Montarville 1973
Morrison, Ian "Scotty" 1999
* Murray, Monsignor Athol 1998
* Neilson, Roger 2002
* Nelson, Francis 1947
* Norris, Bruce A. 1969
* Norris, Sr., James 1958
* Norris, James Dougan 1962
* Northey, William M. 1947
* O'Brien, John Ambrose 1962
O'Neill, Brian 1994
* Page, Fred 1993
Patrick, Craig 2001
* Patrick, Frank 1950
* Pickard, Allan W. 1958
* Pilous, Rudy 1985
* Poile, Norman "Bud" 1990
* Pollock, Samuel Patterson Smyth 1978
* Raymond, Sen. Donat 1958
* Robertson, John Ross 1947
* Robinson, Claude C. 1947
* Ross, Philip D. 1976
* Sabetzki, Dr. Gunther 1995
Sather, Glen 1997
* Seaman, Daryl "Doc" 2010
* Selke, Frank J. 1960
*** Shero, Fred 2013**
Sinden, Harry James 1983
* Smith, Frank D. 1962
* Smythe, Conn 1958
Snider, Edward M. 1988
* Stanley of Preston, Lord (G.C.B.) 1945
* Sutherland, Cap. James T. 1947
* Tarasov, Anatoli V. 1974
Torrey, Bill 1995
* Turner, Lloyd 1958
* Tutt, William Thayer 1978
* Voss, Carl Potter 1974
* Waghorne, Fred 1961
* Wirtz, Arthur Michael 1971
* Wirtz, William W. "Bill" 1976
Ziegler, John A. Jr. 1987

REFEREES/LINESMEN

Armstrong, Neil 1991
* Ashley, John George 1981
* Chadwick, William L. 1964
* D'Amico, John 1993
* Elliott, Chaucer 1961
* Hayes, George William 1988
* Hewitson, Robert W. 1963
* Ion, Fred J. "Mickey" 1961
Pavelich, Matt 1987
* Rodden, Michael J. "Mike" 1962
Scapinello, Ray 2008
* Smeaton, J. Cooper 1961
* Storey, Roy Alvin "Red" 1967
Udvari, Frank Joseph 1973
Van Hellemond, Andy 1999

Chris Chelios (left) made a brief NHL debut in 1983-84 and went on to play for 26 seasons until he was 48 years old. Chelios only missed the playoffs twice and won the Stanley Cup three times. Geraldine Heaney (center) played 18 seasons of top-level women's hockey, winning seven World Championships and an Olympic gold medal in 2002. Brendan Shanahan (right) is one of the top scoring left wingers in NHL history and a three-time Stanley Cup champion.

Foster Hewitt Memorial Award Winners

In recognition of members of the radio and television industry who made outstanding contributions to their profession and the game during their career in hockey broadcasting. Selected by the NHL Broadcasters' Association.

Cole, Bob, Hockey Night in Canada 1996
* Cusick, Fred, Boston 1984
* Darling, Ted, Buffalo 1994
Davidson, John, MSG Network/HNIC 2009
Emrick, Mike, New Jersey, U.S. networks, 2008
* Gallivan, Danny, Montreal 1984
* Garneau, Richard, Montreal 1999
* Hart, Gene, Philadelphia 1997
* Hewitt, Bill, Hockey Night in Canada 2007
* Hewitt, Foster, Toronto 1984
Irvin, Dick, Montreal 1988
Jeanneret, Rick, Buffalo 2012
Kaiton, Chuck, Hartford/Carolina 2004
* Kelly, Dan, St. Louis 1989
Lange, Mike, Pittsburgh 2001
* Lecavelier, René, Montreal 1984
* Lynch, Budd, Detroit 1985
Maher, Peter, Calgary 2006
Martyn, Bruce, Detroit 1991
McDonald, Jiggs, Los Angeles, Atlanta, NY Islanders 1990
McFarlane, Brian, Hockey Night in Canada 1995
* McKnight, Wes, Toronto 1986
Meeker, Howie, Hockey Night in Canada 1998
Messina, Sal, New York 2005
Miller, Bob, Los Angeles 2000
Neale, Harry, Hockey Night in Canada, Buffalo 2013
* Pettit, Lloyd, Chicago 1986
Phillips, Rod, Edmonton 2003
Redmond, Mickey, Detroit 2011
Robson, Jim, Vancouver 1992
Shaver, Al, Minnesota 1993
* Smith, Doug, Montreal 1985
Tremblay, Gilles, La Soirée du Hockey 2002
Weber, Ron, Washington 2010
Wilson, Bob, Boston 1987

* Deceased

Elmer Ferguson Memorial Award Winners

In recognition of distinguished members of the hockey-writing profession whose words have brought honor to journalism and to hockey. Selected by the Professional Hockey Writers' Association.

* Barton, Charlie, Buffalo-Courier Express 1985
* Beauchamp, Jacques, Montreal Matin/Journal de Montréal 1984
* Brennan, Bill, Detroit News 1987
* Burchard, Jim, New York World Telegram 1984
* Burnett, Red, Toronto Star 1984
* Carroll, Dink, Montreal Gazette 1984
* Coleman, Jim, Southam Newspapers 1984

Conway, Russ, Eagle-Tribune 1999
* Damata, Ted, Chicago Tribune 1984

de Foy, Marc, Le Journal de Montreal/ ruefrontenac.com 2010
Delano, Hugh, New York Post 1991
Desjardins, Marcel, Montréal La Presse 1984
Duhatschek, Eric, Calgary Herald/Globe and Mail 2001
* Dulmage, Jack, Windsor Star 1984
* Dunnell, Milt, Toronto Star 1984

Dupont, Kevin Paul, Boston Globe 2002
Elliott, Helene, Los Angeles Times 2005
Farber, Michael, Montreal Gazette/Sports Illustrated 2003
Fay, Dave, Washington Times 2007
* Ferguson, Elmer, Montreal Herald/Star 1984
* Fitzgerald, Tom, Boston Globe 1984
* Frayne, Trent, Toronto Telegram/Globe and Mail/Sun 1984

Gatecliff, Jack, St. Catharines Standard 1995
Greenberg, Jay, Kansas City Star/Philadelphia Daily News/Sports Illustrated 2013
* Gross, George, Toronto Telegram/Sun 1985

Johnston, Dick, Buffalo News 1986
Jones, Terry, Edmonton Sun 2011
* Kelley, Jim, Buffalo News 2004
* Laney, Al, New York Herald-Tribune 1984
* Larochelle, Claude, Le Soleil 1989

L'Esperance, Zotique, Journal de Montréal/ le Petit Journal 1985
MacGregor, Roy, Globe and Mail 2012
* MacLeod, Rex, Toronto Globe and Mail/Star 1987

Matheson, Jim, Edmonton Journal 2000
* Mayer, Charles, Journal de Montréal/la Patrie 1985
* McKenzie, Ken, The Hockey News 1997

Molinari, Dave, Pittsburgh Post-Gazette 2009
Monahan, Leo, Boston Daily Record/Record-American/ Herald American 1986
Moriarty, Tim, UPI/Newsday 1986
Morrison, Scott, Toronto Sun/Rogers Sportsnet 2006
* Nichols, Joe, New York Times 1984
* O'Brien, Andy, Weekend Magazine 1985

Olan, Ben, New York Associated Press 1987
Orr, Frank, Toronto Star 1989
* O'Meara, Basil, Montreal Star 1984

Pedneault, Yvon, La Presse/Journal de Montréal 1998
* Proudfoot, Jim, Toronto Star 1988

Raymond, Bertrand, Journal de Montréal 1990
Rosa, Fran, Boston Globe 1987
Stevens, Neil, Canadian Press 2008
Strachan, Al, Globe and Mail/Toronto Sun 1993
* Vipond, Jim, Toronto Globe and Mail 1984

Walter, Lewis, Detroit Times 1984
* Young, Scott, Toronto Globe and Mail/Telegram 1988

United States Hockey Hall of Fame

On May 11, 2007, the U.S. Hockey Hall of Fame and USA Hockey came to a historic agreement that transferred rights to the selection process and induction event associated with the Hall, including the Wayne Gretzky International Award, to USA Hockey. As part of the agreement, the U.S. Hockey Hall of Fame Museum, located in Eveleth, Minn., formed a separate Board of Directors to govern the national shrine for American Hockey.

There are 161 enshrined members in the U.S. Hockey Hall of Fame (www.ushockeyhalloffame.com). New members are inducted annually and must have made a significant contribution to hockey in the United States during the course of their career. A special Wayne Gretzky International Award pays tribute to international individuals who have made major contributions to hockey in the USA.

The United States Hockey Hall of Fame Museum was opened on June 21, 1973. It is dedicated to honoring the sport of ice hockey in the United States by preserving those previous memories and legends of the game. It is located in Eveleth, Minn., 60 miles north of Duluth on Highway 53. The facility is open Memorial Day through Labor Day, Monday to Saturday, 9 a.m. to 5 p.m. and Sundays from 10 a.m. to 3 p.m. After Labor Day, it is open Friday through Sunday. Admission is $8.00 for adults, $7.00 for seniors and youths (13-17) and $6.00 for children (6-12). Children under 6 are free. For further information, call 800-443-7825 or 218-744-5167, or visit www.ushockeyhall.com.

INDIVIDUALS

* Abel, Clarence "Taffy" 1973
* Almquist, Oscar 1983

Amonte, Tony 2009
* Baker, Hobart "Hobey" 1973

Barrasso, Tom 2009
* Bartholome, Earl 1977

Berglund, Art 2010
* Bessone, Amo 1992
* Bessone, Peter 1978
* Blake, Robert 1985

Boucha, Henry 1995
* Brimsek, Frank 1973
* Brink, Milton "Curly" 2006
* Brooks, Herb 1990

Broten, Aaron 2007
Broten, Neal 2000
* Brown, George V. 1973
* Brown, Walter A. 1973

Bush, Walter 1980
Carpenter, Bobby 2007
Cavanagh, Joe 1994
Ceglarski, Len 1992
* Chadwick, William 1974
* Chaisson, Ray 1974
* Chase, John P. 1973

Chelios, Chris 2011
Christian, Dave 2001
* Christian, Roger 1989

Christian, William "Bill" 1984
Christiansen, Keith 2005
* Clark, Donald 1978

Claypool, James 1995
Cleary, Robert 1981
Cleary, William 1976
* Conroy, Anthony 1975

Coppo, Paul 2004
* Cunniff, John 2003

Curley, Cindy 2013
Curran, Mike 1998
* Dahlstrom, Carl "Cully" 1973
* Desjardins, Victor 1974
* Desmond, Richard 1988
* Dill, Robert 1979

Dougherty, Richard "Dick" 2003
Emrick, Mike "Doc" 2011
* Everett, Doug 1974

Ftorek, Robbie 1991
* Fullerton, James 1992

Fusco, Mark 2002
Fusco, Scott 2002
Gambucci, Gary 2006
Gambucci, Sergio 1996
* Garrison, John B. 1973

Garrity, Jack 1986
* Gibson, J.C. "Doc" 1973
* Goheen, Frank "Moose" 1973
* Gordon, Malcolm K. 1973

Granato, Cammi 2008
Grant, Wally 1994
Guerin, Bill 2013
* Harding, Francis "Austie" 1975
* Harkness, Nevin D. "Ned" 1994

Hatcher, Derian 2010
Hatcher, Kevin 2010
* Heyliger, Victor 1974
* Holt, Jr. Charles E. 1997

Housley, Phil 2004
Howe, Mark 2003
Hull, Brett 2008
* Iglehart, Stewart 1975

Ikola, Willard 1990
Ilitch, Mike 2004
* Jennings, William M. 1981
* Jeremiah, Edward J. 1973
* Johnson, Bob 1991

Johnson, Mark 2004
Johnson, Paul 2001
* Johnson, Virgil 1974
* Kahler, Nick 1980
* Karakas, Mike 1973

Karmanos, Peter, Jr. 2013
* Kelley, John "Snooks" 1974

Kelley, John H. "Jack" 1993
Kirrane, Jack 1987
LaFontaine, Pat 2003
Lamoriello, Lou 2012
* Lane, Myles J. 1973

Langevin, David R. 1993
Langway, Rod 1999
Larson, Reed 1996
LeClair, John 2009
Leetch, Brian 2008
* Linder, Joseph 1975
* Lockhart, Thomas F. 1973
* LoPresti, Sam L. 1973

MacDonald, Lane 2005
* MacInnes, John 2007
* Mariucci, John 1973
* Marvin, Cal 1982

Mason, Ron 2013
Matchefts, John 1991
* Mather, Bruce 1998

Mayasich, John 1976
McCartan, Jack 1983
Milbury, Mike 2006
Modano, Mike 2012
* Moe, William 1974

Morrow, Ken 1995
* Moseley, Fred 1975

Mullen, Joe 1998
* Murray, Sr. Hugh "Muzz" 1987

Nagobads, Dr. V. George 2010
Nanne, Lou 1998
* Nelson, Hubert "Hub" 1978
* Nyrop, William D. 1997

Olczyk, Ed 2012
* Olson, Eddie 1977
* Owen, Jr. George 1973

Palazzari, Doug 2000
* Palmer, Winthrop 1973

Paradise, Robert 1989
Patrick, Craig 1996
Pleau, Larry 2000
* Pleban, Jon "Connie" 1990
* Purpur, Clifford "Fido" 1974

Ramsey, Mike 2001
Richter, Mike 2008
* Ridder, Robert 1976

Riley, Jack 1979
* Riley, Joe 2002
* Riley, William 1977

Roberts, Gordie 1999
* Roberts, Moe 2005

Roenick, Jeremy 2010
* Romnes, Elwin "Doc" 1973
* Rondeau, Richard 1985
* Ross, Larry 1988
* Schulz, Charles M. 1993

Sheehy, Timothy K. 1997
Snider, Ed 2011
* Stewart, William 1982

Suter, Gary 2011
* Thompson, Clifford R. 1973

Tkachuk, Keith 2011
Trumble, Harold 1985
* Tutt, William Thayer 1973

Vanbiesbrouck, John 2007
* Watson, Sid 1999

Weight, Doug 2013
* Williams, Thomas 1981

Williamson, Murray 2005
Winsor, Alfred "Ralph" 1973
* Winters, Frank "Coddy" 1973
* Wirtz, William W. "Bill" 1984

Woog, Doug 2002
* Wright, Lyle Z. 1973
* Yackel, Ken 1986
* Zamboni, Frank 2009

TEAMS

1960 Olympic Men's Team 2000
1980 Olympic Men's Team 2003
1998 Olympic Women's Team 2009

WAYNE GRETZKY INTERNATIONAL AWARD

Wayne Gretzky 1999
The Howe family 2000
Scotty Morrison 2001
Scotty Bowman 2002
Bobby Hull 2003
* Herb Brooks 2004
* Anatoli Tarasov 2008

Murray Costello 2012

* Deceased

In 1,238 career games over 19 NHL seasons, Doug Weight scored 278 goals and racked up 755 assists. Weight put on the U.S. sweater at nine major international competitions, including the Olympic Winter Games in 1998, 2002 and 2006.

International Ice Hockey Federation Hall of Fame

The IIHF Hall of Fame was founded in 1997. It now boasts 189 greats from 22 countries.

Candidates for election as Honoured Members in the player category shall be chosen on the basis of their playing ability, sportsmanship, character and their contribution to their team or teams and to the game of ice hockey in general.

Candidates for election as Honoured Members in the builder category shall be chosen on the basis of their coaching, managerial or executive ability, where applicable, their sportsmanship and character, and their contribution to their organization or organizations and to the game of ice hockey in general.

Candidates for election as Honoured Members in the referee or linesman category shall be chosen on the basis of their officiating ability, sportsmanship, character and their contribution to the game of ice hockey in general. The Paul Loicq Award, named for the longtime former IIHF president, is presented to honor a person for his service to the international hockey community.

Inductees' names are followed by their country and year of induction.

PLAYERS

Alexandrov, Veniamin, RUS, 2007
Balderis, Helmut, LAT, 1998
Ball, Rudi, GER, 2004
Bergqvist, Sven, SWE, 1999
Bjorn, Lars, SWE, 1998
Bobrov, Vsevolod, RUS, 1997
Bourbonnais, Roger, CAN, 1999
Bouzek, Vladimir, CZE, 2007
Bozon, Phillippe, FRA 2008
Bubnik, Vlastimil, CZE, 1997
Bure, Pavel, RUS 2012
Bye, Karyn, USA, 2011
Cattini, Ferdinand, SUI, 1998
Cattini, Hans, SUI, 1998
Cerny, Josef, CZE, 2007
Christian, Bill, USA, 1998
Cleary, Bill, USA, 1997
Cosby, Gerry, USA, 1997
Craig, Jim, USA, 1999
Curran, Mike, USA, 1999
Davydov, Vitaly, RUS, 2004
Drobny, Jaroslav, CZE, 1997
Dzurilla, Vladimir, SVK, 1998
Erhardt, Carl, G.B., 1998
Fetisov, Viacheslav, RUS, 2005
Firsov, Anatoli, RUS, 1998
Forsberg, Peter, SWE, 2013
Golonka, Josef, SVK, 1998
Goyette, Danielle, CAN, 2013
Granato, Cammi, USA 2008
Gretzky, Wayne, CAN, 2000
Gruth, Henryk, POL, 2006
Gustafsson, Bengt-Ake, SWE, 2003
Gut, Karel, CZE, 1998
Heaney, Geraldine, CAN 2008
Hedberg, Anders, SWE, 1997
Hegen, Dieter, GER 2010
Helminen, Raimo, FIN 2012
Henderson, Paul, CAN, 2013
Hiti, Rudi, SLO, 2009
Hlinka, Ivan, CZE, 2002
Holecek, Jiri, CZE, 1998
Holik, Jiri, CZE, 1999
Holmqvist, Leif, SWE, 1999
Housley, Phil, USA 2012
Huck, Fran, CAN, 1999
Irbe, Arturs, LAT 2010
Jaenecke, Gustav, GER, 1998
James, Angela, CAN 2008
Johnson, Mark, USA, 1999
Johnston, Marshall, CAN, 1998
Jonsson, Tomas, SWE, 2000
Jutila, Timo, FIN, 2003
Kasatonov, Alexei, RUS, 2009
Keinonen, Matti, FIN, 2002
Kharlamov, Valeri, RUS, 1998
Kiessling, Udo, GER, 2000
Kolliker, Jakob, SUI, 2007
Konovalenko, Viktor, RUS, 2007
Krutov, Vladimir, RUS 2010
Kuhnhackl, Erich, GER, 1997
Kurri, Jari, FIN, 2000
Kuzkin, Viktor, RUS, 2005
Lacarriere, Jacques, FRA, 1998
Larionov, Igor RUS 2008
Lemieux, Mario CAN 2008
Loktev, Konstantin, RUS, 2007
Loob, Hakan, SWE, 1998
Lundquist, Vic, CAN, 1997
Lundstrom, Tord, SWE, 2011
Machac, Oldrich, CZE, 1999
MacKenzie, Barry, CAN, 1999
Makarov, Sergei, RUS, 2001
Malecek, Josef, CZE, 2003
Maltsev, Alexander, RUS, 1999
Marjamaki, Pekka, FIN, 1998
Martin, Seth, CAN, 1997
Martinec, Vladimir, CZE, 2001
Mayasich, John, USA, 1997
Mayorov, Boris, RUS, 1999
McCartan, Jack, USA, 1998
McLeod, Jackie, CAN, 1999
Mikhailov, Boris, RUS, 2000
Modry, Bohumil, CZE, 2011
Nanne, Lou, USA, 2004
Naslund, Mats, SWE, 2005
Nedomansky, Vaclav, CZE, 1997
Nieminen-Valila, Riika, FIN, 2010
Nilsson, Kent, SWE, 2006
Nilsson, Nisse, SWE, 2002
Novy, Milan, CZE, 2012
Numminen, Teppo, FIN, 2013
O'Malley, Terry, CAN, 1998
Oksanen, Lasse, FIN, 1999
Pana, Eduard, ROU, 1998
Patton, Peter, G.B., 2002
Peltonen, Esa, FIN, 2007
Petrov, Vladimir, RUS, 2006
Pettersson, Ronald, SWE, 2004
Pospisil, Frantisek, CZE, 1999
Puschnig, Josef, AUT, 1999
Ragulin, Alexander, RUS, 1997
Rampf, Hans, GER, 2001
Rundqvist, Thomas, SWE, 2007
Salming, Borje, SWE, 1998
Schloder, Alois, GER, 2005
Sinden, Harry, CAN, 1997
Sologubov, Nikolai, RUS, 2004
Starshinov, Vyacheslav, RUS, 2007
Stastny, Peter, SVK, 2000
Sterner, Ulf, SWE, 2001
Stoltz, Roland, SWE, 1999
Suchy, Jan, CZE, 2009
Sundin, Mats, SWE, 2013
Tikal, Frantisek, CZE, 2004
Torriani, Bibi, SUI, 1997
Tretiak, Vladislav, RUS, 1997
Trojak, Ladislav, SVK, 2011
Tumba (Johansson), Sven, SWE, 1997
Tureanu, Doru, ROU, 2011
Valtonen, Jorma, FIN, 1999
Vasiliev, Valeri, RUS, 1998
Wahlsten, Vladimir, FIN, 2006
Watson, Harry, CAN, 1998
Yakushev, Alexander, RUS, 2003
Ylonen, Urpo, FIN, 1997
Zabrodsky, Vladimir, CZE, 1997
Ziesche, Joachim, GER, 1999

BUILDERS

Ahearne, Bunny, G.B., 1997
Aljancic Sr., Ernest, SLO, 2002
Bauer, Father David, CAN, 1997
Berglund, Art USA 2008
Berglund, Curt, SWE, 2003
Bokac, Ludek, CZE, 2007
Brooks, Herb, USA, 1999
Brown, Walter, USA, 1997
Buckna, Mike, CAN, 2004
Bush, Walter Jr. USA, 2009
Calcaterra, Enrico, ITA, 1999
Chernyshev, Arkady, RUS, 1999
Dimitriev, Igor, RUS, 2007
Dobida, Hans, AUT, 2007
Edvinsson, Jan-Ake SWE, 2013
Eklow, Rudolf, SWE, 1999
Fagerlund, Rickard SWE 2010
Grunander, Arne, SWE, 1997
Henschel, Heinz, GER, 2003
Hewitt, William, CAN, 1998
Holmes, Derek, CAN, 1999
Horsky, Ladislav, SVK, 2004
Hviid, Jorgen, DEN, 2005
Johannessen, Tore, NOR, 1999
Juckes, Gordon, CAN, 1997
Kawabuchi, Tsutomu, JPN, 2004
Khorozov, Anatoli, UKR, 2006
King, Dave, CAN, 2001
Kostka, Vladimir, CZE, 1997
LeBel, Bob, CAN, 1997
Lindblad, Harry, FIN, 1999
Loicq, Paul, BEL, 1997
Luhti, Cesar W., SUI, 1998
Magnus, Louis, FRA, 1997
Murray, Andy CAN 2012
Numminen, Kalevi, FIN, 2011
Pasztor, Gyorgy, HUN, 2001
Renwick, Gordon, CAN, 2002
Ridder, Bob, USA, 1998
Riley, Jack, USA, 1998
Sabetzki, Dr. Gunther, GER, 1997
Starovoitov, Andrei, RUS, 1997
Starsi, Jan, SVK, 1999
Stromberg, Arne, SWE, 1998
Stubb, Goran, FIN, 2000
Subrt, Miroslav, CZE, 2004
Tarasov, Anatoli, RUS, 1997
Tikhonov, Viktor, RUS, 1998
Tomita, Shoichi, JPN, 2006
Trumble, Hal, USA, 1999
Tsutsumi, Yoshiaki, JPN, 1999
Tutt, Thayer, USA, 2002
Unsinn, Xaver, GER, 1998
Wasservogel, Walter, AUT, 1997
Yurzinov, Vladimir, RUS, 2002

REFEREES

Adamec, Quido, CZE, 2005
Dahlberg, Ove, SWE, 2004
Karandin, Yuri, RUS, 2004
Kompalla, Josef, GER, 2003
Schell, Laszlo, HUN, 2009
Wiitala, Unto, FIN, 2003

PAUL LOICQ AWARD

Montag, Wolf-Dieter, GER, 1998
Neumayer, Roman, GER, 1999
Kukushkin, Vsevolod, RUS, 2000
Kataoka, Isao, JPN, 2001
Marsh, Pat, G.B., 2002
Nagobads, George, USA, 2003
Kukulowicz, Aggie, CAN, 2004
Hrabcek, Rita, AUS, 2005
Tovland, Bo, SWE, 2006
Nadin, Bob, CAN, 2007
Okolicany, Juraj, SVK 2008
Griebel, Harald, GER, 2009
Vairo, Lou, USA 2010
Korolev, Yuri, RUS, 2011
Angus, Kent, CAN, 2012
Miller, Gord, CAN, 2013

CENTENNIAL ALL-STAR TEAM (1908-2008)

Goaltender: Vladislav Tretiak, RUS
Defenseman: Viacheslav Fetisov, RUS
Defenseman: Borje Salming, SWE
Winger: Valeri Kharlamov, RUS
Winger: Sergei Makarov, RUS
Center: Wayne Gretzky, CAN

TRIPLE GOLD CLUB

(Olympics, World Championship, Stanley Cup)

Tomas Jonsson, SWE
Mats Naslund, SWE
Hakan Loob, SWE
Valeri Kamensky, RUS
Alexei Gusarov, RUS
Peter Forsberg, SWE
Vyacheslav Fetisov, RUS
Igor Larionov, RUS
Alexander Mogilny, RUS
Vladimir Malakhov, RUS
Rob Blake, CAN
Joe Sakic, CAN
Brendan Shanahan, CAN
Scott Niedermayer, CAN
Jaromir Jagr, CZE
Jiri Slegr, CZE
Nicklas Lidstrom, SWE
Fredrik Modin, SWE
Chris Pronger, CAN
Niklas Kronwall, SWE
Henrik Zetterberg, SWE
Mikael Samuelsson, SWE
Eric Staal, CAN
Jonathan Toews, CAN
Mike Babcock (coach), CAN
Patrice Bergeron, CAN

MILESTONE TROPHY

1954 Soviet Union World Championship team, 2013

2013

Stanley Cup Playoffs

Results

CONFERENCE QUARTER-FINALS

(Best-of-seven series)

Eastern Conference

Series 'A'

Wed. May 1	(8) NY Islanders 0	at	(1) Pittsburgh 5
Fri. May 3	NY Islanders 4	at	Pittsburgh 3
Sun. May 5	Pittsburgh 5	at	NY Islanders 4*
Tue. May 7	Pittsburgh 4	at	NY Islanders 6
Thu. May 9	NY Islanders 0	at	Pittsburgh 4
Sat. May 11	Pittsburgh 4	at	NY Islanders 3**

* Chris Kunitz scored at 8:44 of overtime
** Brooks Orpik scored at 7:49 of overtime

(Pittsburgh won series 4-2)

Series 'B'

Thu. May 2	(7) Ottawa 4	at	(2) Montreal 2
Fri. May 3	Ottawa 1	at	Montreal 3
Sun. May 5	Montreal 1	at	Ottawa 6
Tue. May 7	Montreal 2	at	Ottawa 3*
Thu. May 9	Ottawa 6	at	Montreal 1

* Kyle Turris scored at 2:32 of overtime

(Ottawa won series 4-1)

Series 'C'

Thu. May 2	(6) NY Rangers 1	at	(3) Washington 3
Sat. May 4	NY Rangers 0	at	Washington 1*
Mon. May 6	Washington 3	at	NY Rangers 4
Wed. May 8	Washington 3	at	NY Rangers 4
Fri. May 10	NY Rangers 1	at	Washington 2**
Sun. May 12	Washington 0	at	NY Rangers 1
Mon. May 13	NY Rangers 5	at	Washington 0

* Mike Green scored at 8:00 of overtime
** Mike Ribeiro scored at 9:24 of overtime

(NY Rangers won series 4-3)

Series 'D'

Wed. May 1	(5) Toronto 1	at	(4) Boston 4
Sat. May 4	Toronto 4	at	Boston 2
Mon. May 6	Boston 5	at	Toronto 2
Wed. May 8	Boston 4	at	Toronto 3*
Fri. May 10	Toronto 2	at	Boston 1
Sun. May 12	Boston 1	at	Toronto 2
Mon. May 13	Toronto 4	at	Boston 5**

* David Krejci scored at 13:06 of overtime
** Patrice Bergeron scored at 6:05 of overtime

(Boston won series 4-3)

Western Conference

Series 'E'

Tue. Apr. 30	(8) Minnesota 1	at	(1) Chicago 2*
Fri. May 3	Minnesota 2	at	Chicago 5
Sun. May 5	Chicago 2	at	Minnesota 3**
Tue. May 7	Chicago 3	at	Minnesota 0
Thu. May 9	Minnesota 1	at	Chicago 5

* Bryan Bickell scored at 16:35 of overtime
** Jason Zucker scored at 2:15 of overtime

(Chicago won series 4-1)

Series 'F'

Tue. Apr. 30	(7) Detroit 1	at	(2) Anaheim 3
Thu. May 2	Detroit 5	at	Anaheim 4*
Sat. May 4	Anaheim 4	at	Detroit 0
Mon. May 6	Anaheim 2	at	Detroit 3**
Wed. May 8	Detroit 2	at	Anaheim 3***
Fri. May 10	Anaheim 3	at	Detroit 4****
Sun. May 12	Detroit 3	at	Anaheim 2

* Gustav Nyquist scored at 1:21 of overtime
** Damien Brunner scored at 15:10 of overtime
*** Nick Bonino scored at 1:54 of overtime
**** Henrik Zetterberg scored at 1:04 of overtime

(Detroit won series 4-3)

Series 'G'

Wed. May 1	(6) San Jose 3	at	(3) Vancouver 1
Fri. May 3	San Jose 3	at	Vancouver 2*
Sun. May 5	Vancouver 2	at	San Jose 5
Tue. May 7	Vancouver 3	at	San Jose 4**

* Raffi Torres scored at 5:31 of overtime
** Patrick Marleau scored at 13:18 of overtime

(San Jose won series 4-0)

Series 'H'

Tue. Apr. 30	(5) Los Angeles 1	at	(4) St. Louis 2*
Thu. May 2	Los Angeles 1	at	St. Louis 2
Sat. May 4	St. Louis 0	at	Los Angeles 1
Mon. May 6	St. Louis 3	at	Los Angeles 4
Wed. May 8	Los Angeles 3	at	St. Louis 2**
Fri. May 10	St. Louis 1	at	Los Angeles 2

* Alex Steen scored at 13:26 of overtime
** Slava Voynov scored at 8:00 of overtime

(Los Angeles won series 4-2)

CONFERENCE SEMI-FINALS

(Best-of-seven series)

Eastern Conference

Series 'I'

Tue. May 14	(7) Ottawa 1	at	(1) Pittsburgh 4
Fri. May 17	Ottawa 3	at	Pittsburgh 4
Sun. May 19	Pittsburgh 1	at	Ottawa 2*
Wed. May 22	Pittsburgh 7	at	Ottawa 3
Fri. May 24	Ottawa 2	at	Pittsburgh 6

* Colin Greening scored at 27:39 of overtime

(Pittsburgh won series 4-1)

Series 'J'

Thu. May 16	(6) NY Rangers 2	at	(4) Boston 3*
Sun. May 19	NY Rangers 2	at	Boston 5
Tue. May 21	Boston 2	at	NY Rangers 1
Thu. May 23	Boston 3	at	NY Rangers 4**
Sat. May 25	NY Rangers 1	at	Boston 3

* Brad Marchand scored at 15:40 of overtime
** Chris Kreider scored at 7:03 of overtime

(Boston won series 4-1)

Western Conference

Series 'K'

Wed. May 15	(7) Detroit 1	at	(1) Chicago 4
Sat. May 18	Detroit 4	at	Chicago 1
Mon. May 20	Chicago 1	at	Detroit 3
Thu. May 23	Chicago 0	at	Detroit 2
Sat. May 25	Detroit 1	at	Chicago 4
Mon. May 27	Chicago 4	at	Detroit 3
Wed. May 29	Detroit 1	at	Chicago 2*

* Brent Seabrook scored at 3:35 of overtime

(Chicago won series 4-3)

Series 'L'

Tue. May 14	(6) San Jose 0	at	(5) Los Angeles 2
Thu. May 16	San Jose 3	at	Los Angeles 4
Sat. May 18	Los Angeles 1	at	San Jose 2*
Tue. May 21	Los Angeles 1	at	San Jose 2
Thu. May 23	San Jose 0	at	Los Angeles 3
Sun. May 26	Los Angeles 1	at	San Jose 2
Tue. May 28	San Jose 1	at	Los Angeles 2

* Logan Couture scored at 1:29 of overtime

(Los Angeles won series 4-3)

CONFERENCE FINALS

(Best-of-seven series)

Eastern Conference

Series 'M'

Sat. June 1	(4) Boston 3	at	(1) Pittsburgh 0
Mon. June 3	Boston 6	at	Pittsburgh 1
Wed. June 5	Pittsburgh 1	at	Boston 2*
Fri. June 7	Pittsburgh 0	at	Boston 1

* Patrice Bergeron scored at 35:19 of overtime

(Boston won series 4-0)

Western Conference

Series 'N'

Sat. June 1	(5) Los Angeles 1	at	(1) Chicago 2
Sun. June 2	Los Angeles 2	at	Chicago 4
Tue. June 4	Chicago 1	at	Los Angeles 3
Thu. June 6	Chicago 3	at	Los Angeles 2
Sat. June 8	Los Angeles 3	at	Chicago 4*

* Patrick Kane scored at 31:40 of overtime

(Chicago won series 4-1)

STANLEY CUP FINAL

(Best-of-seven series)

Series 'O'

Wed. June 12	(4) Boston 3	at	(1) Chicago 4*
Sat. June 15	Boston 2	at	Chicago 1**
Mon. June 17	Chicago 0	at	Boston 2
Wed. June 19	Chicago 6	at	Boston 5***
Sat. June 22	Boston 1	at	Chicago 3
Mon. June 24	Chicago 3	at	Boston 2

* Andrew Shaw scored at 52:08 of overtime
** Daniel Paille scored at 13:48 of overtime
*** Brent Seabrook scored at 9:51 of overtime

(Chicago won series 4-2)

Team Playoff Records

	GP	W	L	GF	GA	%
Chicago	23	16	7	64	48	.696
Boston	22	14	8	65	47	.636
Los Angeles	18	9	9	37	34	.500
Pittsburgh	15	8	7	49	40	.533
San Jose	11	7	4	25	22	.636
Detroit	14	7	7	33	37	.500
Ottawa	10	5	5	31	31	.500
NY Rangers	12	5	7	26	28	.417
Anaheim	7	3	4	21	18	.429
Toronto	7	3	4	18	22	.429
Washington	7	3	4	12	16	.429
St. Louis	6	2	4	10	12	.333
NY Islanders	6	2	4	17	25	.333
Minnesota	5	1	4	7	17	.200
Montreal	5	1	4	9	20	.200
Vancouver	4	0	4	8	15	.000

Individual Leaders

Abbreviations: GP – games played; **G** – goals; **A** – assists; **PTS** – points; **+/–** – difference between Goals For (**GF**) scored when a player is on the ice with his team at even strength or shorthanded and Goals Against (**GA**) scored when the same player is on the ice with his team at even strength or on a power play; **PIM** – penalties in minutes; **PP** – power play goals; **SH** – shorthanded goals; **GW** – game-winning goals; **OT** – overtime goals; **S** – shots on goal; **%** – percentage of shots resulting in goals.

Playoff Scoring Leaders

Player	Team	GP	G	A	PTS	+/–	PIM	PP	SH	GW	OT	S	%
David Krejci	Boston	22	9	17	26	13	14	1	0	2	1	56	16.1
Patrick Kane	Chicago	23	9	10	19	7	8	0	0	2	1	88	10.2
Nathan Horton	Boston	22	7	12	19	20	14	2	0	3	0	38	18.4
Milan Lucic	Boston	22	7	12	19	12	14	0	0	0	0	42	16.7
Bryan Bickell	Chicago	23	9	8	17	11	14	1	0	2	1	49	18.4
Patrick Sharp	Chicago	23	10	6	16	1	8	2	0	2	0	91	11.0
Marian Hossa	Chicago	22	7	9	16	8	2	3	0	2	0	70	10.0
Evgeni Malkin	Pittsburgh	15	4	12	16	-2	26	0	0	1	0	67	6.0
Kris Letang	Pittsburgh	15	3	13	16	2	8	2	0	1	0	49	6.1
Patrice Bergeron	Boston	22	9	6	15	2	13	4	0	2	2	71	12.7
Sidney Crosby	Pittsburgh	14	7	8	15	-3	8	2	0	0	0	59	11.9
Zdeno Chara	Boston	22	3	12	15	7	20	0	0	0	0	55	5.5
Jonathan Toews	Chicago	23	3	11	14	9	18	1	0	0	0	70	4.3
Jeff Carter	Los Angeles	18	6	7	13	6	14	1	0	0	0	56	10.7
Slava Voynov	Los Angeles	18	6	7	13	9	0	0	0	4	1	34	17.6
Brad Marchand	Boston	22	4	9	13	4	21	0	0	1	1	57	7.0
Duncan Keith	Chicago	22	2	11	13	10	18	0	0	0	0	51	3.9
Joe Pavelski	San Jose	11	4	8	12	0	0	3	0	0	0	36	11.1
Henrik Zetterberg	Detroit	14	4	8	12	3	8	1	0	1	1	58	6.9
Jarome Iginla	Pittsburgh	15	4	8	12	-4	16	2	0	0	0	34	11.8
Mike Richards	Los Angeles	15	3	9	12	5	8	1	0	0	0	23	13.0
Derick Brassard	NY Rangers	12	2	10	12	1	2	1	0	1	0	22	9.1
Pascal Dupuis	Pittsburgh	15	7	4	11	2	12	0	2	0	0	37	18.9
Logan Couture	San Jose	11	5	6	11	-6	0	5	0	3	1	33	15.2
Michal Handzus	Chicago	23	3	8	11	7	6	0	1	0	0	17	17.6
Paul Martin	Pittsburgh	15	2	9	11	5	4	1	0	0	0	23	8.7

Playoff Defencemen Scoring Leaders

Player	Team	GP	G	A	PTS	+/–	PIM	PP	SH	GW	OT	S	%
Kris Letang	Pittsburgh	15	3	13	16	2	8	2	0	1	0	49	6.1
Zdeno Chara	Boston	22	3	12	15	7	20	0	0	0	0	55	5.5
Slava Voynov	Los Angeles	18	6	7	13	9	0	0	0	4	1	34	17.6
Duncan Keith	Chicago	22	2	11	13	10	18	0	0	0	0	51	3.9
Paul Martin	Pittsburgh	15	2	9	11	5	4	1	0	0	0	23	8.7
Dan Boyle	San Jose	11	3	5	8	-3	2	1	0	1	0	26	11.5
Johnny Oduya	Chicago	23	3	5	8	12	16	0	0	1	0	30	10.0
Erik Karlsson	Ottawa	10	1	7	8	0	6	0	0	0	0	28	3.6
Johnny Boychuk	Boston	22	6	1	7	4	10	0	0	1	0	63	9.5
Torey Krug*	Boston	15	4	2	6	5	0	3	0	0	0	34	11.8
Cody Franson	Toronto	7	3	3	6	0	0	1	0	0	0	15	20.0
Francois Beauchemin	Anaheim	7	2	4	6	-2	4	1	0	0	0	13	15.4
Sergei Gonchar	Ottawa	10	0	6	6	-3	14	0	0	0	0	16	0.0

GOALTENDING LEADERS

Goals Against Average

Goaltender	Team	GP	Mins	GA	Avg.
Corey Crawford	Chicago	23	1504	46	1.84
Jonathan Quick	Los Angeles	18	1099	34	1.86
Antti Niemi	San Jose	11	673	21	1.87
Tuukka Rask	Boston	22	1466	46	1.88
Tomas Vokoun	Pittsburgh	11	685	23	2.01

Wins

Goaltender	Team	GP	Mins	W	L
Corey Crawford	Chicago	23	1504	16	7
Tuukka Rask	Boston	22	1466	14	8
Jonathan Quick	Los Angeles	18	1099	9	9
Antti Niemi	San Jose	11	673	7	4
Jimmy Howard	Detroit	14	859	7	7

Save Percentage

Goaltender	Team	GP	Mins	GA	SA	S%	W	L
Tuukka Rask	Boston	22	1466	46	761	.940	14	8
Jonathan Quick	Los Angeles	18	1099	34	518	.934	9	9
Henrik Lundqvist	NY Rangers	12	756	27	411	.934	5	7
Tomas Vokoun	Pittsburgh	11	685	23	345	.933	6	5
Corey Crawford	Chicago	23	1504	46	674	.932	16	7

Shutouts

Goaltender	Team	GP	Mins	SO	W	L
Jonathan Quick	Los Angeles	18	1099	3	9	9
Tuukka Rask	Boston	22	1466	3	14	8
Henrik Lundqvist	NY Rangers	12	756	2	5	7
Marc-Andre Fleury	Pittsburgh	5	290	1	2	2
Braden Holtby	Washington	7	433	1	3	4
Jonas Hiller	Anaheim	7	439	1	3	4
Tomas Vokoun	Pittsburgh	11	685	1	6	5
Jimmy Howard	Detroit	14	859	1	7	7
Corey Crawford	Chicago	23	1504	1	16	7

* Rookie

Goals

Player	Team	GP	G
Patrick Sharp	Chicago	23	10
Patrice Bergeron	Boston	22	9
David Krejci	Boston	22	9
Bryan Bickell	Chicago	23	9
Patrick Kane	Chicago	23	9
Sidney Crosby	Pittsburgh	14	7
Pascal Dupuis	Pittsburgh	15	7
Marian Hossa	Chicago	22	7
Nathan Horton	Boston	22	7
Milan Lucic	Boston	22	7

Assists

Player	Team	GP	A
David Krejci	Boston	22	17
Kris Letang	Pittsburgh	15	13
Evgeni Malkin	Pittsburgh	15	12
Zdeno Chara	Boston	22	12
Nathan Horton	Boston	22	12
Milan Lucic	Boston	22	12
Duncan Keith	Chicago	22	11
Jonathan Toews	Chicago	23	11
Derick Brassard	NY Rangers	12	10
Jaromir Jagr	Boston	22	10
Patrick Kane	Chicago	23	10

Power-play Goals

Player	Team	GP	PP
Logan Couture	San Jose	11	5
Patrice Bergeron	Boston	22	4
Daniel Alfredsson	Ottawa	10	3
Joe Pavelski	San Jose	11	3
Johan Franzen	Detroit	14	3
Torey Krug*	Boston	15	3
Chris Kunitz	Pittsburgh	15	3
Marian Hossa	Chicago	22	3
9 players with			2

Game-winning Goals

Player	Team	GP	GW
Slava Voynov	Los Angeles	18	4
Logan Couture	San Jose	11	3
Nathan Horton	Boston	22	3
Daniel Paille	Boston	22	3
12 players with			2

Shorthanded Goals

Player	Team	GP	SH
Pascal Dupuis	Pittsburgh	15	2
Tyler Bozak	Toronto	5	1
Alex Steen	St. Louis	6	1
Kyle Okposo	NY Islanders	6	1
Ryan Getzlaf	Anaheim	7	1
8 more players with			1

Overtime Goals

Player	Team	GP	OT
Patrice Bergeron	Boston	22	2
Brent Seabrook	Chicago	23	2
23 players with			1

Shots

Player	Team	GP	S
Patrick Sharp	Chicago	23	91
Patrick Kane	Chicago	23	88
Patrice Bergeron	Boston	22	71
Marian Hossa	Chicago	22	70
Tyler Seguin	Boston	22	70
Jonathan Toews	Chicago	23	70
Evgeni Malkin	Pittsburgh	15	67
Johnny Boychuk	Boston	22	63

Plus/Minus

Player	Team	GP	+/–
Nathan Horton	Boston	22	20
David Krejci	Boston	22	13
Milan Lucic	Boston	22	12
Johnny Oduya	Chicago	23	12
Bryan Bickell	Chicago	23	11
Duncan Keith	Chicago	22	10
Niklas Hjalmarsson	Chicago	23	10

TEAMS' PLAYOFF HOME/ROAD RECORD

Team	HOME GP	HOME W	HOME L	HOME GF	HOME GA	HOME Win %	ROAD GP	ROAD W	ROAD L	ROAD GF	ROAD GA	ROAD Win %
Chicago	13	11	2	41	23	.846	10	5	5	23	25	.500
Boston	12	8	4	35	26	.667	10	6	4	30	21	.600
Los Angeles	9	8	1	23	12	.889	9	1	8	14	22	.111
Pittsburgh	8	5	3	27	19	.625	7	3	4	22	21	.429
San Jose	5	5	0	15	8	1.000	6	2	4	10	14	.333
Detroit	6	4	2	15	14	.667	8	3	5	18	23	.375
Ottawa	4	3	1	14	11	.750	6	2	4	17	20	.333
NY Rangers	5	4	1	14	11	.800	7	1	6	12	17	.143
Anaheim	4	2	2	12	11	.500	3	1	2	9	7	.333
Toronto	3	1	2	7	10	.333	4	2	2	11	12	.500
Washington	4	3	1	6	7	.750	3	0	3	6	9	.000
St. Louis	3	2	1	6	5	.667	3	0	3	4	7	.000
NY Islanders	3	1	2	13	13	.333	3	1	2	4	12	.333
Minnesota	2	1	1	3	5	.500	3	0	3	4	12	.000
Montreal	3	1	2	6	11	.333	2	0	2	3	9	.000
Vancouver	2	0	2	3	6	.000	2	0	2	5	9	.000
Totals	**86**	**59**	**27**	**240**	**192**	**.686**	**86**	**27**	**59**	**192**	**240**	**.314**

TEAM PENALTIES

Abbreviations: GP – games played; **PEN** – total penalty minutes, including bench penalties; **BMI** – total bench minor minutes; **AVG** – average penalty minutes/game arrived by dividing total penalty minutes by games played

Team	GP	PEN	BMI	AVG
S.J.	11	70	0	6.4
St.L.	6	40	0	6.7
NYR	12	84	2	7.0
L.A.	18	142	6	7.9
Ana.	7	59	0	8.4
Min.	5	44	0	8.8
Chi.	23	209	6	9.1
Det.	14	135	2	9.6
Bos.	22	214	12	9.7
Wsh.	7	76	2	10.9
Tor.	7	84	0	12.0
Pit.	15	222	4	14.8
Van.	4	66	0	16.5
NYI	6	127	0	21.2
Ott.	10	248	4	24.8
Mtl.	5	185	2	37.0
Totals	**86**	**2005**	**40**	**23.3**

TEAMS' POWER-PLAY RECORD

Abbreviations: ADV-total advantages; **PPGF**-power play goals for; **%** arrived by dividing number of power-play goals by total advantages.

	HOME Team	GP	ADV	PPGF	%	ROAD Team	GP	ADV	PPGF	%	OVERALL Team	GP	ADV	PPGF	%
1	S.J.	5	29	10	34.5	Tor.	4	11	3	27.3	Ana.	7	25	7	28.0
2	Ana.	4	16	5	31.3	Ana.	3	9	2	22.2	Tor.	7	21	5	23.8
3	Wsh.	4	11	3	27.3	L.A.	9	24	5	20.8	S.J.	11	50	11	22.0
4	Pit.	8	33	8	24.2	Bos.	10	24	5	20.8	Pit.	15	61	13	21.3
5	Van.	2	5	1	20.0	Van.	2	5	1	20.0	Van.	4	10	2	20.0
6	Tor.	3	10	2	20.0	Pit.	7	28	5	17.9	Wsh.	7	16	3	18.8
7	Ott.	4	21	4	19.0	Det.	8	28	5	17.9	Ott.	10	44	8	18.2
8	Mtl.	3	12	2	16.7	Ott.	6	23	4	17.4	Bos.	22	63	11	17.5
9	Chi.	13	37	6	16.2	Mtl.	2	7	1	14.3	L.A.	18	52	9	17.3
10	Bos.	12	39	6	15.4	St.L.	3	7	1	14.3	Mtl.	5	19	3	15.8
11	NYR	5	21	3	14.3	NYI	3	10	1	10.0	Det.	14	49	7	14.3
12	L.A.	9	28	4	14.3	Chi.	10	33	2	6.1	St.L.	6	17	2	11.8
13	NYI	3	10	1	10.0	S.J.	6	21	1	4.8	Chi.	23	70	8	11.4
14	St.L.	3	10	1	10.0	NYR	7	23	1	4.3	NYI	6	20	2	10.0
15	Det.	6	21	2	9.5	Wsh.	3	5	0	0.0	NYR	12	44	4	9.1
16	Min.	2	9	0	0.0	Min.	3	8	0	0.0	Min.	5	17	0	0.0
	Totals	**86**	**312**	**58**	**18.6**		**86**	**266**	**37**	**13.9**		**86**	**578**	**95**	**16.4**

TEAMS' PENALTY KILLING RECORD

Abbreviations: TSH – Total times shorthanded; **PPGA** – power-play goals against; **%** arrived by dividing times shorthanded minus power-play goals against by times short.

	HOME Team	GP	TSH	PPGA	%	ROAD Team	GP	TSH	PPGA	%	OVERALL Team	GP	TSH	PPGA	%
1	Min.	2	4	0	100.0	St.L.	3	7	0	100.0	Wsh.	7	28	2	92.9
2	Wsh.	4	13	0	100.0	Pit.	7	25	2	92.0	Pit.	15	52	4	92.3
3	L.A.	9	25	1	96.0	Chi.	10	41	4	90.2	Chi.	23	76	7	90.8
4	Pit.	8	27	2	92.6	Ana.	3	10	1	90.0	Bos.	22	71	8	88.7
5	Chi.	13	35	3	91.4	Tor.	4	10	1	90.0	L.A.	18	57	7	87.7
6	Van.	2	9	1	88.9	Bos.	10	30	3	90.0	St.L.	6	15	2	86.7
7	Bos.	12	41	5	87.8	Wsh.	3	15	2	86.7	Tor.	7	20	3	85.0
8	Det.	6	21	3	85.7	L.A.	9	32	6	81.3	Min.	5	13	2	84.6
9	Ott.	4	18	3	83.3	Mtl.	2	14	3	78.6	Ott.	10	44	9	79.5
10	S.J.	5	12	2	83.3	Min.	3	9	2	77.8	Det.	14	49	11	77.6
11	Tor.	3	10	2	80.0	Ott.	6	26	6	76.9	S.J.	11	30	7	76.7
12	NYR	5	9	2	77.8	NYR	7	19	5	73.7	Mtl.	5	25	6	76.0
13	St.L.	3	8	2	75.0	S.J.	6	18	5	72.2	Ana.	7	25	6	76.0
14	Mtl.	3	11	3	72.7	Det.	8	28	8	71.4	NYR	12	28	7	75.0
15	Ana.	4	15	5	66.7	NYI	3	13	4	69.2	Van.	4	24	7	70.8
16	NYI	3	8	3	62.5	Van.	2	15	6	60.0	NYI	6	21	7	66.7
	Totals	**86**	**266**	**37**	**86.1**		**86**	**312**	**58**	**81.4**		**86**	**578**	**95**	**83.6**

SHORTHAND GOALS

GOALS FOR Team	GP	GF	GOALS AGAINST Team	GP	GA
Ott.	10	3	NYR	12	0
Pit.	15	2	S.J.	11	0
Chi.	23	2	Wsh.	7	0
NYI	6	1	NYI	6	0
St.L.	6	1	St.L.	6	0
Tor.	7	1	Van.	4	0
Ana.	7	1	Chi.	23	1
Det.	14	1	L.A.	18	1
L.A.	18	1	Det.	14	1
Bos.	22	1	Tor.	7	1
Van.	4	0	Ana.	7	1
Mtl.	5	0	Mtl.	5	1
Min.	5	0	Min.	5	1
Wsh.	7	0	Bos.	22	2
S.J.	11	0	Ott.	10	2
NYR	12	0	Pit.	15	3
Totals	**86**	**14**		**86**	**14**

STANLEY CUP PLAYOFFS 2013

After scoring nine goals in 48 games during the regular season, Brian Bickell scored nine times in 23 playoff games, including the tying goal in the dying seconds of game six when Chicago staged a late rally to win the Stanley Cup.

Stanley Cup Record Book

History: The Stanley Cup, the oldest trophy competed for by professional athletes in North America, was donated by Frederick Arthur, Lord Stanley of Preston and son of the Earl of Derby, in 1893. Lord Stanley purchased the trophy for 10 guineas ($50 at that time) for presentation to the amateur hockey champions of Canada. Since 1906, when Canadian teams began to pay their players openly, the Stanley Cup has been the symbol of professional hockey supremacy. It has been contested only by NHL teams since 1926-27 and has been under the exclusive control of the NHL since 1947.

Stanley Cup Standings

1918-2013

(ranked by Cup wins)

Teams	Cup Wins	Yrs.	Series	Wins	Losses	Games	Wins	Losses	Ties	Goals For	Goals Against	Winning %
Montreal[1,2]	24	80	146	89	56	714	411	295	8	2161	1819	.581
Toronto[3]	14	65	110	58	52	531	254	273	4	1368	1449	.482
Detroit	11	61	118	68	50	605	320	284	1	1719	1532	.530
Boston	6	68	118	56	62	597	292	299	6	1734	1710	.494
Chicago	5	58	103	50	53	486	234	247	5	1389	1492	.487
Edmonton	5	20	49	34	15	251	152	99	0	938	763	.606
NY Rangers	4	55	98	47	51	454	213	233	8	1244	1282	.478
NY Islanders	4	22	48	30	18	246	136	110	0	809	739	.553
Pittsburgh	3	28	55	30	25	298	160	138	0	925	896	.537
New Jersey[4]	3	22	44	25	19	254	136	118	0	688	622	.535
Philadelphia	2	36	77	43	34	414	214	200	0	1260	1231	.517
Colorado[5]	2	21	44	25	19	249	132	117	0	726	703	.530
Dallas[6]	1	29	56	28	28	307	154	163	0	897	910	.502
Calgary[7]	1	26	40	15	25	208	94	114	0	648	701	.452
Los Angeles	1	27	43	17	26	220	94	126	0	643	758	.427
Carolina[8]	1	13	22	10	12	127	59	68	0	323	358	.465
Anaheim	1	9	19	11	8	105	58	47	0	269	260	.552
Tampa Bay	1	6	12	7	5	69	37	32	0	181	185	.536
St. Louis	0	37	61	24	37	322	144	178	0	892	989	.447
Buffalo	0	29	50	21	29	256	124	132	0	763	765	.484
Vancouver	0	26	42	16	26	223	99	124	0	620	717	.444
Washington	0	24	37	13	24	212	96	116	0	614	629	.453
Phoenix[9]	0	19	23	4	19	119	41	78	0	310	422	.345
San Jose	0	15	30	14	16	174	84	90	0	432	505	.483
Ottawa[10]	0	14	23	9	14	126	59	67	0	298	310	.468
Nashville	0	7	9	2	7	50	19	31	0	115	134	.380
Florida	0	4	7	3	4	38	16	22	0	94	100	.421
Minnesota	0	4	6	2	4	34	12	22	0	71	89	.353
Winnipeg[11]	0	1	1	0	1	4	0	4	0	6	17	.000
Columbus	0	1	1	0	1	4	0	4	0	7	18	.000

1. Includes Stanley Cup championship won in 1916 prior to the formation of the NHL.
2. 1919 final incomplete due to influenza epidemic.
3. Includes Stanley Cup championship won by Toronto Blueshirts in 1914 prior to the formation of the NHL.
4. Includes totals of Colorado Rockies 1976-82.
5. Includes totals of Quebec Nordiques 1979-95.
6. Includes totals of Minnesota North Stars 1967-93.
7. Includes totals of Atlanta Flames 1972-80.
8. Includes totals of Hartford Whalers 1979-97.
9. Includes totals of Winnipeg Jets 1979-96.
10. Modern Ottawa Senators franchise only, 1992 to date.
11. Includes totals of Atlanta Thrashers 1999-2011.

Stanley Cup Winners Prior to Formation of NHL in 1917

Season	Champions	Manager	Coach
1916-17	Seattle Metropolitans	Pete Muldoon	Pete Muldoon
1915-16	Montreal Canadiens	George Kennedy	George Kennedy
1914-15	Vancouver Millionaires	Frank Patrick	Frank Patrick
1913-14	Toronto Blueshirts	Jack Marshall	Scotty Davidson*
1912-13**	Quebec Bulldogs	M.J. Quinn	Joe Malone*
1911-12	Quebec Bulldogs	M.J. Quinn	Charley Nolan
1910-11	Ottawa Senators		Percy LeSueur
1909-10	Montreal Wanderers (Mar. 1910)	Dickie Boon	Pud Glass*
1909-10	Ottawa Senators (Jan. 1910)		Bruce Stuart*
1908-09	Ottawa Senators		Bruce Stuart*
1907-08	Montreal Wanderers	Dickie Boon	Cecil Blachford
1906-07	Montreal Wanderers (Mar. 25, 1907)	Dickie Boon	Cecil Blachford
1906-07	Kenora Thistles (Jan./Mar. 18, 1907)	F.A. Hudson	Tom Phillips*
1905-06	Montreal Wanderers (Mar. 1906)	Cecil Blachford*	
1905-06	Ottawa Silver Seven (Feb. 1906)		Alf Smith
1904-05	Ottawa Silver Seven		Alf Smith
1903-04	Ottawa Silver Seven		Alf Smith
1902-03	Ottawa Silver Seven (Mar. 1903)		Alf Smith
1902-03	Montreal A.A.A. (Feb. 1903)		Clare McKerrow
1901-02	Montreal A.A.A. (Mar. 1902)		Clare McKerrow
1901-02	Winnipeg Victorias (Jan. 1902)		
1900-01	Winnipeg Victorias		Dan Bain*
1899-1900	Montreal Shamrocks		Harry Trihey*
1898-99	Montreal Shamrocks (Mar. 1899)		Harry Trihey*
1898-99	Montreal Victorias (Feb. 1899)		Graham Drinkwater*
1897-98	Montreal Victorias		Frank Richardson*
1896-97	Montreal Victorias		Mike Grant*
1895-96	Montreal Victorias (Dec. 1896)		Mike Grant*
1895-96	Winnipeg Victorias (Feb. 1896)		Jack Armytage*
1894-95	Montreal Victorias		Mike Grant*
1893-94	Montreal A.A.A.		
1892-93	Montreal A.A.A.		

* In the early years the teams were frequently run by the Captain. *Indicates Captain
** Victoria defeated Quebec in challenge series. No official recognition.

Stanley Cup Winners

Year	W-L-T in Finals	Winner	Coach	Finalist	Coach
2013	4-2	Chicago	Joel Quenneville	Boston	Claude Julien
2012	4-2	Los Angeles	Darryl Sutter	New Jersey	Peter DeBoer
2011	4-3	Boston	Claude Julien	Vancouver	Alain Vigneault
2010	4-2	Chicago	Joel Quenneville	Philadelphia	Peter Laviolette
2009	4-3	Pittsburgh	Dan Bylsma	Detroit	Mike Babcock
2008	4-2	Detroit	Mike Babcock	Pittsburgh	Michel Therrien
2007	4-1	Anaheim	Randy Carlyle	Ottawa	Bryan Murray
2006	4-3	Carolina	Peter Laviolette	Edmonton	Craig MacTavish
2005	....	....	....	....	....
2004	4-3	Tampa Bay	John Tortorella	Calgary	Darryl Sutter
2003	4-3	New Jersey	Pat Burns	Anaheim	Mike Babcock
2002	4-1	Detroit	Scotty Bowman	Carolina	Paul Maurice
2001	4-3	Colorado	Bob Hartley	New Jersey	Larry Robinson
2000	4-2	New Jersey	Larry Robinson	Dallas	Ken Hitchcock
1999	4-2	Dallas	Ken Hitchcock	Buffalo	Lindy Ruff
1998	4-0	Detroit	Scotty Bowman	Washington	Ron Wilson
1997	4-0	Detroit	Scotty Bowman	Philadelphia	Terry Murray
1996	4-0	Colorado	Marc Crawford	Florida	Doug MacLean
1995	4-0	New Jersey	Jacques Lemaire	Detroit	Scotty Bowman
1994	4-3	NY Rangers	Mike Keenan	Vancouver	Pat Quinn
1993	4-1	Montreal	Jacques Demers	Los Angeles	Barry Melrose
1992	4-0	Pittsburgh	Scotty Bowman	Chicago	Mike Keenan
1991	4-2	Pittsburgh	Bob Johnson	Minnesota	Bob Gainey
1990	4-1	Edmonton	John Muckler	Boston	Mike Milbury
1989	4-2	Calgary	Terry Crisp	Montreal	Pat Burns
1988	4-0	Edmonton	Glen Sather	Boston	Terry O'Reilly
1987	4-3	Edmonton	Glen Sather	Philadelphia	Mike Keenan
1986	4-1	Montreal	Jean Perron	Calgary	Bob Johnson
1985	4-1	Edmonton	Glen Sather	Philadelphia	Mike Keenan
1984	4-1	Edmonton	Glen Sather	NY Islanders	Al Arbour
1983	4-0	NY Islanders	Al Arbour	Edmonton	Glen Sather
1982	4-0	NY Islanders	Al Arbour	Vancouver	Roger Neilson
1981	4-1	NY Islanders	Al Arbour	Minnesota	Glen Sonmor
1980	4-2	NY Islanders	Al Arbour	Philadelphia	Pat Quinn
1979	4-1	Montreal	Scotty Bowman	NY Rangers	Fred Shero
1978	4-2	Montreal	Scotty Bowman	Boston	Don Cherry
1977	4-0	Montreal	Scotty Bowman	Boston	Don Cherry
1976	4-0	Montreal	Scotty Bowman	Philadelphia	Fred Shero
1975	4-2	Philadelphia	Fred Shero	Buffalo	Floyd Smith
1974	4-2	Philadelphia	Fred Shero	Boston	Bep Guidolin
1973	4-2	Montreal	Scotty Bowman	Chicago	Billy Reay
1972	4-2	Boston	Tom Johnson	NY Rangers	Emile Francis
1971	4-3	Montreal	Al MacNeil	Chicago	Billy Reay
1970	4-0	Boston	Harry Sinden	St. Louis	Scotty Bowman
1969	4-0	Montreal	Claude Ruel	St. Louis	Scotty Bowman
1968	4-0	Montreal	Toe Blake	St. Louis	Scotty Bowman
1967	4-2	Toronto	Punch Imlach	Montreal	Toe Blake
1966	4-2	Montreal	Toe Blake	Detroit	Sid Abel
1965	4-3	Montreal	Toe Blake	Chicago	Billy Reay
1964	4-3	Toronto	Punch Imlach	Detroit	Sid Abel
1963	4-1	Toronto	Punch Imlach	Detroit	Sid Abel
1962	4-2	Toronto	Punch Imlach	Chicago	Rudy Pilous
1961	4-2	Chicago	Rudy Pilous	Detroit	Sid Abel
1960	4-0	Montreal	Toe Blake	Toronto	Punch Imlach
1959	4-1	Montreal	Toe Blake	Toronto	Punch Imlach
1958	4-2	Montreal	Toe Blake	Boston	Milt Schmidt
1957	4-1	Montreal	Toe Blake	Boston	Milt Schmidt
1956	4-1	Montreal	Toe Blake	Detroit	Jimmy Skinner
1955	4-3	Detroit	Jimmy Skinner	Montreal	Dick Irvin
1954	4-3	Detroit	Tommy Ivan	Montreal	Dick Irvin
1953	4-1	Montreal	Dick Irvin	Boston	Lynn Patrick
1952	4-0	Detroit	Tommy Ivan	Montreal	Dick Irvin
1951	4-1	Toronto	Joe Primeau	Montreal	Dick Irvin
1950	4-3	Detroit	Tommy Ivan	NY Rangers	Lynn Patrick
1949	4-0	Toronto	Hap Day	Detroit	Tommy Ivan
1948	4-0	Toronto	Hap Day	Detroit	Tommy Ivan
1947	4-2	Toronto	Hap Day	Montreal	Dick Irvin
1946	4-1	Montreal	Dick Irvin	Boston	Dit Clapper
1945	4-3	Toronto	Hap Day	Detroit	Jack Adams
1944	4-0	Montreal	Dick Irvin	Chicago	Paul Thompson
1943	4-0	Detroit	Jack Adams	Boston	Art Ross
1942	4-3	Toronto	Hap Day	Detroit	Jack Adams
1941	4-0	Boston	Cooney Weiland	Detroit	Ebbie Goodfellow
1940	4-2	NY Rangers	Frank Boucher	Toronto	Dick Irvin
1939	4-1	Boston	Art Ross	Toronto	Dick Irvin
1938	3-1	Chicago	Bill Stewart	Toronto	Dick Irvin
1937	3-2	Detroit	Jack Adams	NY Rangers	Lester Patrick
1936	3-1	Detroit	Jack Adams	Toronto	Dick Irvin
1935	3-0	Mtl. Maroons	Tommy Gorman	Toronto	Dick Irvin
1934	3-1	Chicago	Tommy Gorman	Detroit	Herbie Lewis
1933	3-1	NY Rangers	Lester Patrick	Toronto	Dick Irvin
1932	3-0	Toronto	Dick Irvin	NY Rangers	Lester Patrick
1931	3-2	Montreal	Cecil Hart	Chicago	Dick Irvin
1930	2-0	Montreal	Cecil Hart	Boston	Art Ross
1929	2-0	Boston	Cy Denneny	NY Rangers	Lester Patrick
1928	3-2	NY Rangers	Lester Patrick	Mtl. Maroons	Eddie Gerard
1927	2-0-2	Ottawa	Dave Gill	Boston	Art Ross
		The National Hockey League assumed control of Stanley Cup competition after 1926			
1926	3-1	Mtl. Maroons	Eddie Gerard	Victoria	Lester Patrick
1925	3-1	Victoria	Lester Patrick	Montreal	Leo Dandurand
1924	2-0	Montreal	Leo Dandurand	Cgy. Tigers	Eddie Oatman
1923	2-0	Ottawa	Pete Green	Edm. Eskimos	Ken McKenzie
1922	3-2	Tor. St. Pats	George O'Donoghue	Van. Millionaires	Lloyd Cook/Frank Patrick
1921	3-2	Ottawa	Pete Green	Van. Millionaires	Lloyd Cook/Frank Patrick
1920	3-2	Ottawa	Pete Green	Seattle	Pete Muldoon
1919	2-2-1	No decision - series between Montreal and Seattle cancelled due to influenza epidemic			
1918	3-2	Tor. Arenas	Dick Carroll	Van. Millionaires	Frank Patrick

Championship Trophies

PRINCE OF WALES TROPHY

Beginning with the 1993-94 season, the club which advances to the Stanley Cup Finals as the winner of the Eastern Conference Championship is presented with the Prince of Wales Trophy.

History: His Royal Highness, the Prince of Wales, donated the trophy to the National Hockey League in 1925. It was originally awarded to the winner of the first game played in Madison Square Garden, December 15, 1925 (Montreal Canadiens 3 at NY Americans 1). It was then awarded to the NHL playoff champion in 1925-26 and 1926-27. From 1927-28 through 1937-38, the award was presented to the regular-season champion of the American Division of the NHL. (The team finishing first in the Canadian Division received the O'Brien Trophy during these years.) From 1938-39, when the NHL reverted to one section, to 1966-67, it was presented to the team winning the NHL regular-season championship. With expansion in 1967-68, it again became a divisional trophy, awarded to the regular-season champions of the East Division through to the end of the 1973-74 season. Beginning in 1974-75, it was awarded to the regular-season winner of the conference bearing the name of the trophy. From 1981-82 to 1992-93 the trophy was presented to the playoff champion in the Wales Conference. Since 1993-94, the trophy has been presented to the playoff champion in the Eastern Conference.

2012-13 Winner: Boston Bruins

The Boston Bruins won the Prince of Wales Trophy on June 7, 2013 after defeating the Pittsburgh Penguins 1-0 in game 4 of the Eastern Conference Finals. Before defeating the Penguins, Boston had series wins over the Toronto Maple Leafs and the New York Rangers.

PRINCE OF WALES TROPHY WINNERS

2012-13	Boston	1981-82	NY Islanders	1951-52	Detroit
2011-12	New Jersey	1980-81	Montreal	1950-51	Detroit
2010-11	Boston	1979-80	Buffalo	1949-50	Detroit
2009-10	Philadelphia	1978-79	Montreal	1948-49	Detroit
2008-09	Pittsburgh	1977-78	Montreal	1947-48	Toronto
2007-08	Pittsburgh	1976-77	Montreal	1946-47	Montreal
2006-07	Ottawa	1975-76	Montreal	1945-46	Montreal
2005-06	Carolina	1974-75	Buffalo	1944-45	Montreal
2003-04	Tampa Bay	1973-74	Boston	1943-44	Montreal
2002-03	New Jersey	1972-73	Montreal	1942-43	Detroit
2001-02	Carolina	1971-72	Boston	1941-42	NY Rangers
2000-01	New Jersey	1970-71	Boston	1940-41	Boston
99-2000	New Jersey	1969-70	Chicago	1939-40	Boston
1998-99	Buffalo	1968-69	Montreal	1938-39	Boston
1997-98	Washington	1967-68	Montreal	1937-38	Boston
1996-97	Philadelphia	1966-67	Chicago	1936-37	Detroit
1995-96	Florida	1965-66	Montreal	1935-36	Detroit
1994-95	New Jersey	1964-65	Detroit	1934-35	Boston
1993-94	NY Rangers	1963-64	Montreal	1933-34	Detroit
1992-93	Montreal	1962-63	Toronto	1932-33	Boston
1991-92	Pittsburgh	1961-62	Montreal	1931-32	NY Rangers
1990-91	Pittsburgh	1960-61	Montreal	1930-31	Boston
1989-90	Boston	1959-60	Montreal	1929-30	Boston
1988-89	Montreal	1958-59	Montreal	1928-29	Boston
1987-88	Boston	1957-58	Montreal	1927-28	Boston
1986-87	Philadelphia	1956-57	Detroit	1926-27	Ottawa
1985-86	Montreal	1955-56	Montreal	1925-26	Mtl. Maroons
1984-85	Philadelphia	1954-55	Detroit	Dec. 15/25	Montreal
1983-84	NY Islanders	1953-54	Detroit	1923-24	Montreal*
1982-83	NY Islanders	1952-53	Detroit		

* Engraved by Montreal Canadiens in 1925-26.

CLARENCE S. CAMPBELL BOWL

Beginning with the 1993-94 season, the club which advances to the Stanley Cup Finals as the winner of the Western Conference Championship is presented with the Clarence S. Campbell Bowl.

History: Presented by the member clubs in 1968 for perpetual competition by the National Hockey League in recognition of the services of Clarence S. Campbell, President of the NHL from 1946 to 1977. From 1967-68 through 1973-74, the trophy was awarded to the regular-season champions of the West Division. Beginning in 1974-75, it was awarded to the regular-season winner of the conference bearing the name of the trophy. From 1981-82 to 1992-93 the trophy was presented to the playoff champion in the Campbell Conference. Since 1993-94, the trophy has been presented to the playoff champion in the Western Conference. The trophy itself is a hallmark piece made of sterling silver and was crafted by a British silversmith in 1878.

2012-13 Winner: Chicago Blackhawks

The Chicago Blackhawks won the Clarence S. Campbell Bowl on June 8, 2013 after defeating the Los Angeles Kings 4-3 in game 5 of the Western Conference Finals. Before defeating the Kings, Chicago had series wins over the Minnesota Wild and the Detroit Red Wings.

CLARENCE S. CAMPBELL BOWL WINNERS

2012-13	Chicago	1996-97	Detroit	1981-82	Vancouver
2011-12	Los Angeles	1995-96	Colorado	1980-81	NY Islanders
2010-11	Vancouver	1994-95	Detroit	1979-80	Philadelphia
2009-10	Chicago	1993-94	Vancouver	1978-79	NY Islanders
2008-09	Detroit	1992-93	Los Angeles	1977-78	NY Islanders
2007-08	Detroit	1991-92	Chicago	1976-77	Philadelphia
2006-07	Anaheim	1990-91	Minnesota	1975-76	Philadelphia
2005-06	Edmonton	1989-90	Edmonton	1974-75	Philadelphia
2003-04	Calgary	1988-89	Calgary	1973-74	Philadelphia
2002-03	Anaheim	1987-88	Edmonton	1972-73	Chicago
2001-02	Detroit	1986-87	Edmonton	1971-72	Chicago
2000-01	Colorado	1985-86	Calgary	1970-71	Chicago
99-2000	Dallas	1984-85	Edmonton	1969-70	St. Louis
1998-99	Dallas	1983-84	Edmonton	1968-69	St. Louis
1997-98	Detroit	1982-83	Edmonton	1967-68	Philadelphia

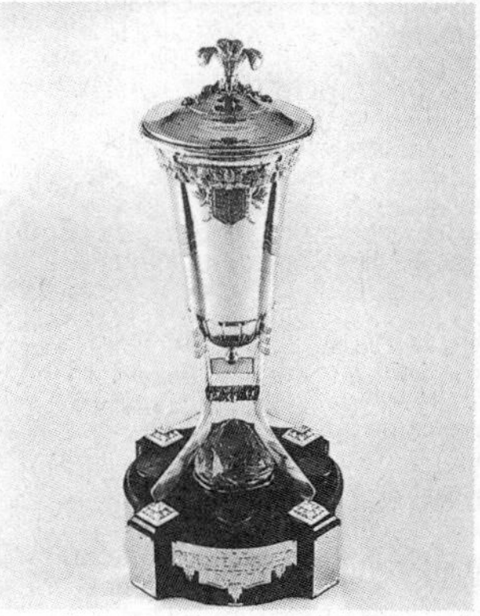

Prince of Wales Trophy

Clarence S. Campbell Bowl

Stanley Cup

Stanley Cup Winners

Rosters and Final Series Scores

2012-13 — Chicago Blackhawks — Jonathan Toews (Captain), Bryan Bickell, Dave Bolland, Brandon Bollig, Sheldon Brookbank, Daniel Carcillo, Corey Crawford, Ray Emery, Michael Frolik, Michal Handzus, Niklas Hjalmarsson, Marian Hossa, Patrick Kane, Duncan Keith, Marcus Kruger, Nick Leddy, Jamal Mayers, Johnny Oduya, Michal Rozsival, Brandon Saad, Brent Seabrook, Patrick Sharp, Andrew Shaw, Ben Smith, Viktor Stalberg, W. Rockwell Wirtz (Chairman), John McDonough (President/CEO), Jay Blunk (Executive Vice President), Stan Bowman (Vice President/General Manager), Al MacIsaac (Vice President/Assistant to the President), Norm Maciver (Assistant General Manager), Scotty Bowman (Senior Advisor), Joel Quenneville (Head Coach), Mike Kitchen, Jamie Kompon (Assistant Coaches), Stephane Waite (Goaltending Coach), Mike Gapski (Head Athletic Trainer), Troy Parchman (Equipment Manager), Jeff Thomas (Assistant Athletic Trainer), Clint Reif (Assistant Equipment Manager), Pawel Prylinski (Massage Therapist), Jim Heintzelman (Equipment Assistant), Paul Goodman (Strength and Conditioning Coach), Tim Campbell (Video Coach), Pierre Gauthier (Director, Player Personnel), Mark Kelley (Director, Amateur Scouting), Barry Smith (Director, Player Development), Ryan Stewart (Director, Pro Scouting), Ron Anderson (Director, Player Recruitment), Tony Ommen (Senior Director, Team Services), Mark Bernard (General Manager, Minor League Affiliates), Dr. Michael Terry (Head Team Physician).

Scores: June 12, at Chicago — Chicago 4, Boston 3; June 15, at Chicago — Boston 2, Chicago 1; June 17, at Boston — Boston 2, Chicago 0; June 19, at Boston — Chicago 6, Boston 5; June 22, at Chicago — Chicago 3, Boston 1; June 24, at Boston — Chicago 3, Boston 2.

2011-12 — Los Angeles Kings — Dustin Brown (Captain), Jonathan Bernier, Jeff Carter, Kyle Clifford, Drew Doughty, Davis Drewiske, Colin Fraser, Simon Gagne, Matt Greene, Dwight King, Anze Kopitar, Trevor Lewis, Alec Martinez, Willie Mitchell, Jordan Nolan, Dustin Penner, Jonathan Quick, Mike Richards, Brad Richardson, Robert Scuderi, Jarret Stoll, Slava Voynov, Kevin Westgarth, Justin Williams, Philip Anschutz (Owner), Nancy Anschutz (Owner), Timothy Leiweke (Governor), Daniel Beckerman (Chief Financial Officer), Ted Fikre (Chief Legal Officer), Dean Lombardi (President/General Manager), Luc Robitaille (President, Business Operations), Ron Hextall (Vice President/Assistant General Manager), Jeffrey Solomon (Vice President/Hockey Operations and Legal Affairs), Darryl Sutter (Head Coach), John Stevens (Assistant Coach), Jamie Kompon (Assistant Coach), Bill Ranford (Goaltending Coach), Chris McGowan (Chief Operating Officer), Michael Altieri (Vice President, Communications and Content), Jack Ferreira (Special Assistant to the General Manager), Mike O'Connell (Player Development), Nelson Emerson (Player Development), Rob Laird (Senior Pro Scout), Michael Futa (Director of Amateur Scouting), Mark Yannetti (Director of Amateur Scouting), Lee Callans (Scouting Operations Coordinator), Marshall Dickerson (Director of Team Operations), Ryan Colville (Video Coordinator), Darren Granger (Head Equipment Manager), Chris Kingsley (Head Athletic Trainer), Dana C. Bryson (Assistant Equipment Manager), Myles Hirayama (Assistant Athletic Trainer).

Scores: May 30, at New Jersey — Los Angeles 2, New Jersey 1; June 2, at New Jersey — Los Angeles 2, New Jersey 1; June 4, at Los Angeles — Los Angeles 4, New Jersey 0; June 5, at Los Angeles — New Jersey 3, Los Angeles 1; June 9, at New Jersey — New Jersey 2, Los Angeles 1; June 11, at Los Angeles — Los Angeles 6, New Jersey 1.

2010-11 — Boston Bruins — Zdeno Chara (Captain), Patrice Bergeron, Johnny Boychuk, Gregory Campbell, Andrew Ference, Nathan Horton, Tomas Kaberle, Chris Kelly, David Krejci, Milan Lucic, Brad Marchand, Adam McQuaid, Daniel Paille, Rich Peverley, Tuukka Rask, Mark Recchi, Michael Ryder, Marc Savard, Tyler Seguin, Dennis Seidenberg, Tim Thomas, Shawn Thornton, Jeremy and Margaret Jacobs, Charlie Jacobs, Louis Jacobs, Jerry Jacobs Jr. (Ownership), Cam Neely (President), Peter Chiarelli (General Manager), Jim Benning, Don Sweeney (Assistant General Managers), Claude Julien (Head Coach), Doug Jarvis, Geoff Ward, Doug Houda (Assistant Coaches), Bob Essensa (Goaltending Coach), Harry Sinden (Senior Advisor), John Bucyk (Team Road Service Coordinator), Scott Bradley (Director of Player Personnel), Wayne Smith (Director of Amateur Scouting), John Weisbrod (Director of Collegiate Scouting), Adam Creighton, Tom McVie (Scouts), Dale Hamilton-Powers (Director of Administration), Matt Chmura (Director of Communications), Ryan Nadeau (Manager of Hockey Administration), Don DelNegro (Athletic Trainer), John Whitesides (Strength and Conditioning Coach), Keith Robinson (Equipment Manager), Derek Repucci (Assistant Trainer and Massage Therapist), Jim "Beets" Johnson (Assistant Equipment Manager), Scott Waugh (Physical Therapist).

Scores: June 1, at Vancouver — Vancouver 1, Boston 0; June 4, at Vancouver — Vancouver 3, Boston 2; June 6, at Boston — Boston 8, Vancouver 1; June 8, at Boston — Boston 4, Vancouver 0; June 10, at Vancouver — Vancouver 1, Boston 0; June 13, at Boston — Boston 5, Vancouver 2; June 15, at Vancouver — Boston 4, Vancouver 0.

2009-10 — Chicago Blackhawks — Jonathan Toews (Captain), Dave Bolland, Nick Boynton, Troy Brouwer, Adam Burish, Dustin Byfuglien, Brian Campbell, Ben Eager, Colin Fraser, Jordan Hendry, Niklas Hjalmarsson, Marian Hossa, Cristobal Huet, Patrick Kane, Duncan Keith, Tomas Kopecky, Andrew Ladd, John Madden, Antti Niemi, Brent Seabrook, Patrick Sharp, Brent Sopel, Kris Versteeg, W. Rockwell Wirtz (Chairman), John McDonough (President), Jay Blunk (Senior VP, Business Operations), Stan Bowman (General Manager), Kevin Cheveldayoff (Assistant General Manager), Al MacIsaac (Senior Director, Hockey Administration/Assistant to the President), Scotty Bowman, Dale Tallon (Senior Advisors, Hockey Operations), Joel Quenneville (Head Coach), John Torchetti, Mike Haviland (Assistant Coaches), Stephane Waite (Goaltending Coach), Paul Goodman (Strength and Conditioning Coach), Brad Aldrich (Video Coach), Paul Vincent (Skating Coach), Marc Bergevin (Director, Player Personnel), Mark Bernard (G.M., Minor League Affiliations), Norm Maciver (Director, Player Development), Mark Kelley (Director, Amateur Scouting), Ron Anderson (Director, Player Recruitment), Michel Dumas (Chief Amateur Scout), Tony Ommen (Director Team Services), Dr. Michael Terry (Head Team Physician), Mike Gapski (Head Athletic Trainer), Troy Parchman (Equipment Manager), Pawel Prylinski (Massage Therapist), Jeff Thomas (Assistant Athletic Trainer), Clint Reif (Assistant Equipment Manager), Jim Heintzelman (Equipment Assistant).

Scores: May 29, at Chicago — Chicago 6, Philadelphia 5; May 31, at Chicago — Chicago 2, Philadelphia 1; June 2 at Philadelphia — Philadelphia 4, Chicago 3; June 4 at Philadelphia — Philadelphia 5, Chicago 3; June 6, at Chicago — Chicago 7, Philadelphia 4; June 9 at Philadelphia — Chicago 4, Philadelphia 3.

2008-09 — Pittsburgh Penguins — Sidney Crosby (Captain), Craig Adams, Philippe Boucher, Matt Cooke, Pascal Dupuis, Mark Eaton, Ruslan Fedotenko, Marc-Andre Fleury, Mathieu Garon, Hal Gill, Eric Godard, Alex Goligoski, Sergei Gonchar, Bill Guerin, Tyler Kennedy, Chris Kunitz, Kris Letang, Evgeni Malkin, Brooks Orpik, Miroslav Satan, Rob Scuderi, Jordan Staal, Petr Sykora, Maxime Talbot, Mike Zigomanis, Mario Lemieux (Co-owner/Chairman), Ron Burkle (Co-owner), Bill Kassling, Tom Grealish, Tony Liberati (Directors), Ken Sawyer (Chief Executive Officer), David Morehouse (President), Ray Shero (Executive Vice President amd General Manager), Chuck Fletcher (Assistant General Manager), Ed Johnston (Senior Advisor, Hockey Operations), Jason Botterill (Director of Hockey Administration), Dan Bylsma (Head Coach), Mike Yeo (Assistant Coach), Tom Fitzgerald (Director of Player Development), GIlles Meloche (Goaltending Coach), Mike Kadar (Strength and Conditioning Coach), Travis Ramsay (Video Coordinator), Chris Stewart (Head Athletic Trainer), Scott Adams (Assistant Athletic Trainer), Mark Mortland (Physical Therapist), Dana Heinze (Equipment Manager), Paul DeFazio, Danny Kroll (Assistant Equipment Managers), Frank Buonomo (Senior Director of Team Services and Communications), Tom McMillan (Vice President, Communications), Dan MacKinnon (Director of Professional Scouting), Jay Heinbuck (Director of Amateur Scouting).

Scores: May 30, at Detroit — Detroit 3, Pittsburgh 1; May 31 at Detroit — Detroit 3, Pittsburgh 1; June 2, at Pittsburgh — Pittsburgh 4, Detroit 2; June 4, at Pittsburgh — Pittsburgh 4, Detroit 2; June 6 at Detroit — Detroit 5, Pittsburgh 0; June 9, at Pittsburgh — Pittsburgh 2, Detroit 1; June 12, at Detroit — Pittsburgh 2, Detroit 1.

2007-08 — Detroit Red Wings — Nicklas Lidstrom (Captain), Chris Chelios, Daniel Cleary, Pavel Datsyuk, Aaron Downey, Dallas Drake, Kris Draper, Valtteri Filppula, Johan Franzen, Dominik Hasek, Darren Helm, Tomas Holmstrom, Jiri Hudler, Tomas Kopecky, Niklas Kronwall, Brett Lebda, Andreas Lilja, Kirk Maltby, Darren McCarty, Derek Meech, Chris Osgood, Brian Rafalski, Mikael Samuelsson, Brad Stuart, Henrik Zetterberg, Michael Ilitch (Owner/Governor), Marian Ilitch (Owner/Secretary-Treasurer), Christopher Ilitch (Vice President/Alternate Governor), Denise Ilitch, Ronald Ilitch, Michael Ilitch Jr., Lisa Ilitch Murray, Atanas Ilitch, Carole Ilitch. Jim Devellano (Senior Vice President/Alternate Governor), Ken Holland (General Manager/Alternate Governor), Steve Yzerman (Vice President/Alternate Governor), Jim Nill (Assistant General Manager), Ryan Martin (Director, Hockey Operations), Scotty Bowman (Consultant), Mike Babcock (Head Coach), Todd McLellan (Associate Coach), Paul MacLean (Assistant Coach), Jim Bedard (Goaltending Consultant), Jay Woodcroft (Video Coordinator), Mark Howe (Director, Pro Scouting), Joe McDonnell (Director, Amateur Scouting), Hakan Andersson (Director, Amateur Scouting Europe), Piet Van Zant (Athletic Trainer), Paul Boyer (Equipment Manager), Russ Baumann, Christopher Scoppetto (Assistant Athletic Trainers).

Scores: May 24, at Detroit — Detroit 4, Pittsburgh 0; May 26, at Detroit — Detroit 3, Pittsburgh 0; May 28, at Pittsburgh — Pittsburgh 3, Detroit 2; May 31, at Pittsburgh — Detroit 2, Pittsburgh 1; June 2, at Detroit — Pittsburgh 4, Detroit 3; June 4, at Pittsburgh — Detroit 3, Pittsburgh 2.

2006-07 — Anaheim Ducks — Scott Niedermayer (Captain), Rob Niedermayer, Chris Pronger, Teemu Selanne, Sean O'Donnell, Brad May, Todd Marchant, Jean-Sebastien Giguere, Andy McDonald, Samuel Pahlsson, Shawn Thornton, Ric Jackman, Joe DiPenta, Kent Huskins, Chris Kunitz, George Parros, Joe Motzko, Ilya Bryzgalov, Francois Beauchemin, Travis Moen, Ryan Carter, Drew Miller, Ryan Shannon, Dustin Penner, Ryan Getzlaf, Corey Perry; Henry Samueli, Susan Samueli (Owners), Michael Schulman (CEO), Brian Burke (Executive Vice President/General Manager), Tim Ryan (Executive Vice President/COO), Bob Wagner (Senior Vice President/Chief Marketing Officer), Bob Murray (Senior Vice President-Hockey Operations), David McNab (Assistant General Manager), Al Coates (Senior Advisor to GM), Randy Carlyle (Head Coach), Dave Farrish, Newell Brown (Assistant Coaches), Francois Allaire (Goaltending Consultant), Sean Skahan (Strength and Conditioning Coach), Joe Trotta (Video Coordinator), Tim Clark (Head Trainer), Mark O'Neill (Equipment Manager), John Allaway (Assistant Equipment Manager), James Partida (Massage Therapist), Rick Paterson (Director of Professional Scouting), Alain Chainey (Director of Amateur Scouting).

Scores: May 28, at Anaheim - Anaheim 3, Ottawa 2; May 30, at Anaheim - Anaheim 1, Ottawa 0; June 2, at Ottawa - Ottawa 5, Anaheim 3; June 4, at Ottawa - Anaheim 3, Ottawa 2; June 6, at Anaheim - Anaheim 6, Ottawa 2.

2005-06 — Carolina Hurricanes — Rod Brind'Amour (Captain), Glen Wesley, Cory Stillman, Kevyn Adams, Craig Adams, Anton Babchuk, Erik Cole, Mike Commodore, Matt Cullen, Martin Gerber, Bret Hedican, Andrew Hutchinson, Frantisek Kaberle, Andrew Ladd, Chad LaRose, Mark Recchi, Eric Staal, Oleg Tverdovsky, Josef Vasicek, Niclas Wallin, Aaron Ward, Cam Ward, Doug Weight, Ray Whitney, Justin Williams; Peter Karmanos Jr., Thomas Thewes (Owners), Jim Rutherford (President/General Manager), Jason Karmanos (Vice President/Assistant General Manager), Mike Amendola (Chief Financial Officer), Peter Laviolette (Head Coach), Kevin McCarthy, Jeff Daniels (Assistant Coaches), Greg Stefan (Goaltending Coach), Chris Huffine (Video Coordinator), Skip Cunningham, Wally Tatomir, Bob Gorman (Equipment Managers), Peter Friesen (Head Athletic Therapist/Strength and Conditioning Coach), Chris Stewart (Associate Athletic Trainer), Brian Tatum (Team Services Manager), Kelly Kirwin (Event Coordinator-Hockey Operations), Mike Sundheim (Director of Media Relations), Kyle Hanlin (Manager of Media Relations), Sheldon Ferguson (Director of Amateur Scouting), Marshall Johnston (Director of Professional Scouting), Claude Larose, Ron Smith (Professional Scouts), Bert Marshall, Tony MacDonald, Martin Madden (Amateur Scouts), Tom Rowe (Lowell (AHL) - Coach).

Scores: June 5, at Carolina - Carolina 5, Edmonton 4; June 7, at Carolina - Carolina 5, Edmonton 0; June 10, at Edmonton - Edmonton 2, Carolina 1; June 12, at Edmonton - Carolina 2, Edmonton 1; June 14, at Carolina - Edmonton 4, Carolina 3; June 17, at Edmonton - Edmonton 4, Carolina 0; June 19, at Carolina - Carolina 3, Edmonton 1.

2003-04 — Tampa Bay Lightning — Dave Andreychuk (Captain), Fredrik Modin, Vincent Lecavalier, Martin St. Louis, Brad Richards, Nikolai Khabibulin, Pavel Kubina, Dan Boyle, Ruslan Fedotenko, Darryl Sydor, Cory Sarich, Tim Taylor, Cory Stillman, Jassen Cullimore, John Grahame, Chris Dingman, Nolan Pratt, Brad Lukowich, Andre Roy, Dmitry Afanasenkov, Martin Cibak, Ben Clymer, Darren Rumble, Stan Neckar, Eric Perrin; William Davidson (Owner), Tom Wilson (Governor), Ron Campbell (President), Jay Feaster (General Manager), John Tortorella (Head Coach), Craig Ramsay (Associate Coach), Jeff Reese (Assistant Coach), Nigel Kirwan (Video Coach), Eric Lawson (Strength and Conditioning Coach), Tom Mulligan (Trainer), Adam Rambo (Assistant Trainer), Ray Thill (Equipment Manager), Dana Heinze, Jim Pickard (Assistant Equipment Managers), Mike Griebel (Massage Therapist), Bill Barber (Director of Player Personnel), Jake Goertzen (Head Scout), Phil Thibodeau (Director of Team Services), Ryan Belec (Assistant to the GM), Rick Paterson (Chief Pro Scout), Kari Kettunen, Glen Zacharias, Steve Baker, Dave Heitz, Yuri Yanchenkov, (Scouts), Bill Wickett (Senior Vice President - Communications), Sean Henry (Executive Vice President/COO).

Scores: May 25, at Tampa Bay - Calgary 4, Tampa Bay 1; May 27, at Tampa Bay - Tampa Bay 4, Calgary 1; May 29, at Calgary - Calgary 3, Tampa Bay 0; May 31, at Calgary - Tampa Bay 1, Calgary 0; June 3, at Tampa Bay - Calgary 3, Tampa Bay 2; June 5, at Calgary - Tampa Bay 3, Calgary 2; June 7, at Tampa Bay - Tampa Bay 2, Calgary 1.

2002-03 — New Jersey Devils — Tommy Albelin, Jiri Bicek, Martin Brodeur, Sergei Brylin, Ken Daneyko, Patrik Elias, Jeff Friesen, Brian Gionta, Scott Gomez, Jamie Langenbrunner, John Madden, Grant Marshall, Jim McKenzie, Scott Niedermayer, Joe Nieuwendyk, Jay Pandolfo, Brian Rafalski, Pascal Rheaume, Mike Rupp, Corey Schwab, Richard Smehlik, Scott Stevens (Captain), Turner Stevenson, Oleg Tverdovsky, Colin White; Raymond Chambers, Lewis Catz (Owners), Peter Simon (Chairman), Lou Lamoriello (CEO/President/General Manager), Pat Burns (Head Coach), Bob Carpenter, John MacLean (Assistant Coaches), Jacques Caron (Goaltending Coach), Larry Robinson (Special Assignment Coach), David Conte (Director - Scouting), Claude Carrier (Assistant Director - Scouting), Chris Lamoriello (Scout/Albany (AHL) - General Manager), Milt Fisher, Dan Labraaten, Marcel Pronovost (Scouts), Bob Hoffmeyer, Jan Ludvig (Pro Scouts), Dr. Barry Fisher (Orthopedist), Chris Modrzynski (Executive Vice President), Terry Farmer (Vice President - Ticket Operations), Vladimir Bure (Fitness Consultant), Taran Singleton (Hockey Operations), Bill Murray (Medical Trainer), Michael Vasalani (Strength and Conditioning Coordinator), Rick Matthews (Equipment Manager), Juergen Merz (Massage Therapist), Alex Abasto (Assistant Equipment Manager).

Scores: May 27, at New Jersey - New Jersey 3, Anaheim 0; May 29, at New Jersey - New Jersey 3, Anaheim 0; May 31, at Anaheim - Anaheim 3, New Jersey 2; June 2, at Anaheim - Anaheim 1, New Jersey 0; June 5, at New Jersey - New Jersey 6, Anaheim 3; June 7, at Anaheim - Anaheim 5, New Jersey 2; June 9, at New Jersey - New Jersey 3, Anaheim 0.

2001-02 — Detroit Red Wings — Steve Yzerman (Captain), Dominik Hasek, Manny Legace, Chris Chelios, Mathieu Dandenault, Steve Duchesne, Jiri Fischer, Nicklas Lidstrom, Fredrik Olausson, Jiri Slegr, Pavel Datsyuk, Boyd Devereaux, Kris Draper, Sergei Fedorov, Tomas Holmstrom, Brett Hull, Igor Larionov, Kirk Maltby, Darren McCarty, Luc Robitaille, Brendan Shanahan, Jason Williams; Michael Ilitch (Owner/Governor), Marian Ilitch (Owner/Secretary Treasurer), Christoper Ilitch (Vice President), Denise Ilitch (Alternate Governor), Ronald Ilitch, Michael Ilitch Jr., Lisa Ilitch Murray, Atanas Ilitch, Carole Ilitch, Jim Devellano (Senior Vice President), Ken Holland (General Manager), Jim Nill (Assistant General Manager), Scotty Bowman (Head Coach), Dave Lewis, Barry Smith (Associate Coaches), Jim Bedard (Goaltending Consultant), Joe Kocur (Video Coordinator), John Wharton (Athletic Trainer), Piet Van Zant (Assistant Athletic Trainer), Paul Boyer (Equipment Manager), Paul MacDonald (Senior Director of Finance), Nancy Beard (Executive Assistant), Dan Belisle, Mark Howe, Bob McCammon (Pro Scouts), Hakan Andersson (Director of European Scouting), Bruce Haralson, Mark Leach, Joe McDonnell, Glenn Merkosky (Scouts).

Scores: June 4, at Detroit - Carolina 3, Detroit 2; June 6, at Detroit - Detroit 3, Carolina 1; June 8, at Carolina - Detroit 3, Carolina 2; June 10, at Carolina - Detroit 3, Carolina 0; June 13, at Detroit - Detroit 3, Carolina 1.

2000-01 — Colorado Avalanche — David Aebischer, Rob Blake, Raymond Bourque, Greg de Vries, Chris Dingman, Chris Drury, Adam Foote, Peter Forsberg, Milan Hejduk, Dan Hinote, Jon Klemm, Eric Messier, Bryan Muir, Ville Nieminen, Scott Parker, Shjon Podein, Nolan Pratt, Dave Reid, Steve Reinprecht, Patrick Roy, Joe Sakic (Captain), Martin Skoula, Alex Tanguay, Stephane Yelle; E. Stanley Kroenke (Owner/Governor), Pierre Lacroix (President/ General Manager), Bob Hartley (Head Coach), Jacques Cloutier, Bryan Trottier (Assistant Coaches), Paul Fixter (Video Coach), Francois Giguere (Vice President - Hockey Operations), Brian MacDonald (Assistant General Manager), Michel Goulet (Vice President - Player Personnel), Jean Martineau (Vice President - Communications and Team Services), Pat Karns (Head Athletic Trainer), Matthew Sokolowski (Assistant Athletic Trainer), Wayne Flemming, Mark Miller (Equipment Managers), Dave Randolph (Assistant Equipment Manager), Paul Goldberg (Strength and Conditioning Coach), Gregorio Pradera (Massage Therapist), Brad Smith (Pro Scout), Jim Hammett (Chief Scout), Garth Joy, Steve Lyons, Joni Lehto, Orval Tessier (Scouts), Charlotte Grahame (Director of Hockey Administration).
Scores: May 26, at Colorado - Colorado 5, New Jersey 0; May 29, at Colorado - New Jersey 2, Colorado 1; May 31, at New Jersey - Colorado 3, New Jersey 1; June 2, at New Jersey - New Jersey 3, Colorado 2; June 4, at Colorado - New Jersey 4, Colorado 1; June 7, at New Jersey - Colorado 4, New Jersey 0; June 9, at Colorado - Colorado 3, New Jersey 1.

1999-2000 — New Jersey Devils — Jason Arnott, Brad Bombardir, Martin Brodeur, Steve Brule, Sergei Brylin, Ken Daneyko, Patrik Elias, Scott Gomez, Bobby Holik, Steve Kelly, Claude Lemieux, John Madden, Vladimir Malakhov, Randy McKay, Alexander Mogilny, Sergei Nemchinov, Scott Niedermayer, Krzysztof Oliwa, Jay Pandolfo, Brian Rafalski, Ken Sutton, Scott Stevens (Captain), Petr Sykora, Chris Terreri, Colin White; Dr. John J. McMullen (Owner/Chairman), Peter S. McMullen (Owner), Lou Lamoriello (President/General Manager), Larry Robinson (Head Coach), Viacheslav Fetisov (Assistant Coach), Jacques Caron (Goaltending Coach), Bob Carpenter (Assistant Coach), John Cuniff (Albany (AHL) - Coach), David Conte (Director of Scouting), Claude Carrier (Assistant Director of Scouting), Milt Fisher, Dan Labraaten, Marcel Pronovost (Scouts), Bob Hoffmeyer (Pro Scout), Dr. Barry Fisher (Orthopedist), Dennis Gendron (Albany (AHL) - Assistant Coach), Robbie Ftorek (Coach), Vladimir Bure (Consultant), Taran Singleton, Marie Carnevale, Callie Smith (Hockey Operations), Bill Murray (Medical Trainer), Michael Vasalani (Strength and Conditioning Coordinator), Dana McGuane (Equipment Manager), Juergen Merz (Massage Therapist), Harry Bricker, Lou Centanni Jr. (Assistant Equipment Managers).
Scores: May 30, at New Jersey - New Jersey 7, Dallas 3; June 1, at New Jersey - Dallas 2, New Jersey 1; June 3, at Dallas - New Jersey 2, Dallas 1; June 5, at Dallas - New Jersey 3, Dallas 1; June 8, at New Jersey - Dallas 1 - New Jersey 0; June 10, at Dallas, New Jersey 2 - Dallas 1.

1998-99 — Dallas Stars — Derian Hatcher (Captain), Mike Modano, Joe Nieuwendyk, Craig Ludwig, Sergei Zubov, Ed Belfour, Guy Carbonneau, Shawn Chambers, Benoit Hogue, Tony Hrkac, Brett Hull, Mike Keane, Jamie Langenbrunner, Jere Lehtinen, Grant Marshall, Richard Matvichuk, Derek Plante, Dave Reid, Brent Severyn, Jon Sim, Brian Skrudland, Blake Sloan, Darryl Sydor, Roman Turek, Pat Verbeek; Thomas Hicks (Chairman/Owner), Jim Lites (President), Bob Gainey (Vice President - Hockey Operations/General Manager), Doug Armstrong (Assistant General Manager), Craig Button (Director of Player Personnel), Ken Hitchcock (Head Coach), Doug Jarvis, Rick Wilson (Assistant Coaches), Rick McLaughlin (Vice President/Chief Financial Officer), Jeff Cogen (Vice President - Marketing and Promotion), Bill Strong (Vice President - Marketing and Broadcasting), Tim Bernhardt (Director of Amateur Scouting), Doug Overton (Director of Pro Scouting), Bob Gernander (Chief Scout), Stu MacGregor (Western Scout), Dave Suprenant (Medical Trainer), Dave Smith, Rich Matthews (Equipment Managers), J.J. McQueen (Strength and Conditioning Coach), Rick St. Croix (Goaltending Consultant), Dan Stuchal (Director of Team Services), Larry Kelly (Director of Public Relations).

Scores: June 8, at Dallas - Buffalo 3, Dallas 2; June 10, at Dallas - Dallas 4, Buffalo 2; June 12, at Buffalo - Dallas 2, Buffalo 1; June 15, at Buffalo - Buffalo 2, Dallas 1; June 17, at Dallas - Dallas 2, Buffalo 0; June 19, at Buffalo - Dallas 2, Buffalo 1.

1997-98 — Detroit Red Wings — Steve Yzerman (Captain), Doug Brown, Mathieu Dandenault, Kris Draper, Anders Eriksson, Sergei Fedorov, Viacheslav Fetisov, Brent Gilchrist, Kevin Hodson, Tomas Holmstrom, Mike Knuble, Joe Kocur, Vladimir Konstantinov, Vyacheslav Kozlov, Martin Lapointe, Igor Larionov, Nicklas Lidstrom, Jamie Macoun, Kirk Maltby, Darren McCarty, Dmitri Mironov, Larry Murphy, Chris Osgood, Bob Rouse, Brendan Shanahan, Aaron Ward; Mike Ilitch, (Owner/Chairman), Marian Ilitch (Owner), Atanas Ilitch, Christopher Ilitch (Vice Presidents), Denise Ilitch, Ronald Ilitch, Michael Ilitch Jr., Lisa Ilitch Murray, Carole Ilitch Trepeck, Jim Devellano (Senior Vice President), Ken Holland (General Manager), Don Waddell (Assistant General Manager), Scotty Bowman (Head Coach), Barry Smith, Dave Lewis (Associate Coaches), Jim Nill (Director of Player Development), Dan Belisle, Mark Howe (Pro Scouts), Jim Bedard (Goaltending Consultant), Hakan Andersson (Director of European Scouting), Mark Leach (USA Scout), Joe McDonnell (Eastern Scout), Bruce Haralson (Western Scout), John Wharton (Athletic Trainer), Paul Boyer (Equipment Manager), Tim Abbott (Assistant Equipment Manager), Bob Huddleston (Masseur), Sergei Mnatsakanov, Wally Crossman (Dressing Room Assistant).
Scores: June 9, at Detroit — Detroit 2, Washington 1; June 11, at Detroit — Detroit 5, Washington 4; June 13, at Washington — Detroit 2, Washington 1; June 16, at Washington — Detroit 4, Washington 1.

1996-97 — Detroit Red Wings — Steve Yzerman (Captain), Doug Brown, Mathieu Dandenault, Kris Draper, Sergei Fedorov, Viacheslav Fetisov, Kevin Hodson, Tomas Holmstrom, Joe Kocur, Vladimir Konstantinov, Vyacheslav Kozlov, Martin Lapointe, Igor Larionov, Nicklas Lidstrom, Kirk Maltby, Darren McCarty, Larry Murphy, Chris Osgood, Jamie Pushor, Bob Rouse, Tomas Sandstrom, Brendan Shanahan, Tim Taylor, Mike Vernon, Aaron Ward; Mike Ilitch (Owner/Chairman), Marian Ilitch (Owner), Atanas Ilitch, Christopher Ilitch (Vice Presidents), Denise Ilitch Lites, Ronald Ilitch, Michael Ilitch Jr., Lisa Ilitch Murray, Carole Ilitch Trepeck, Jim Devellano (Senior Vice President), Scotty Bowman (Head Coach/Director of Player Personnel), Ken Holland (Assistant General Manager), Barry Smith, Dave Lewis (Associate Coaches), Mike Krushelnyski (Assistant Coach), Jim Nill (Director of Player Development), Dan Belisle, Bruce Haralson, Mark Howe (Scouts), Hakan Andersson (Director of European Scouting), John Wharton (Athletic Trainer), Wally Crossman (Dressing Room Assistant), Mark Leach (Scout), Paul Boyer (Equipment Manager), Tim Abbott (Assistant Equipment Manager), Sergei Mnatsakanov (Masseur), Joe McDonnell (Scout).

Scores: May 31, at Philadelphia — Detroit 4, Philadelphia 2; June 3, at Philadelphia — Detroit 4, Philadelphia 2; June 5, at Detroit — Detroit 6, Philadelphia 1; June 7, at Detroit — Detroit 2, Philadelphia 1.

1995-96 — Colorado Avalanche — Rene Corbet, Adam Deadmarsh, Stephane Fiset, Adam Foote, Peter Forsberg, Alexei Gusarov, Dave Hannan, Valeri Kamensky, Mike Keane, Jon Klemm, Uwe Krupp, Sylvain Lefebvre, Claude Lemieux, Curtis Leschyshyn, Troy Murray, Sandis Ozolinsh, Mike Ricci, Patrick Roy, Warren Rychel, Joe Sakic (Captain), Chris Simon, Craig Wolanin, Stephane Yelle, Scott Young; Charlie Lyons (Chairman/CEO), Pierre Lacroix (Executive Vice President/General Manager), Marc Crawford (Head Coach), Joel Quenneville, Jacques Cloutier (Assistant Coaches), Francois Giguere (Assistant General Manager), Michel Goulet (Director of Player Personnel), Dave Draper (Chief Scout), Jean Martineau (Director of Public Relations), Pat Karns (Trainer), Matthew Sokolowski (Assistant Trainer), Rob McLean (Equipment Manager), Mike Kramer, Brock Gibbins (Assistant Equipment Managers), Skip Allen (Strength and Conditioning Coach), Paul Fixter (Video Coordinator), Leo Vyssokov (Massage Therapist).
Scores: June 4, at Colorado — Colorado 3, Florida 1; June 6, at Colorado — Colorado 8, Florida 1; June 8, at Florida — Colorado 3, Florida 2; June 10, at Florida — Colorado 1, Florida 0.

1994-95 — New Jersey Devils — Tommy Albelin, Martin Brodeur, Neal Broten, Sergei Brylin, Bob Carpenter, Shawn Chambers, Tom Chorske, Danton Cole, Ken Daneyko, Kevin Dean, Jim Dowd, Bruce Driver, Bill Guerin, Bobby Holik, Claude Lemieux, John MacLean, Chris McAlpine, Randy McKay, Scott Niedermayer, Mike Peluso, Stephane Richer, Brian Rolston, Scott Stevens (Captain), Chris Terreri, Valeri Zelepukin; Dr. John J. McMullen (Owner/Chairman), Peter S. McMullen (Owner), Lou Lamoriello (President/General Manager), Jacques Lemaire (Head Coach), Jacques Caron (Goaltender Coach), Dennis Gendron, Larry Robinson (Assistant Coaches), Robbie Ftorek (Albany (AHL) - Coach), Alex Abasto (Assistant Equipment Manager), Bob Huddleston (Massage Therapist), David Nichols (Equipment Manager), Ted Schuch (Medical Trainer), Michael Vasalani (Strength and Conditioning Coach), David Conte (Director of Scouting), Milt Fisher, Claude Carrier, Dan Labraaten, Marcel Pronovost (Scouts).
Scores: June 17, at Detroit — New Jersey 2, Detroit 1; June 20, at Detroit — New Jersey 4, Detroit 2; June 22, at New Jersey — New Jersey 5, Detroit 2; June 24, at New Jersey — New Jersey 5, Detroit 2.

1993-94 — New York Rangers — Mark Messier (Captain), Brian Leetch, Kevin Lowe, Adam Graves, Steve Larmer, Glenn Anderson, Jeff Beukeboom, Greg Gilbert, Glenn Healy, Mike Hudson, Alexander Karpovtsev, Joe Kocur, Alex Kovalev, Nick Kypreos, Doug Lidster, Stephane Matteau, Craig MacTavish, Sergei Nemchinov, Brian Noonan, Esa Tikkanen, Mike Richter, Jay Wells, Sergei Zubov, Ed Olczyk, Mike Hartman; Neil Smith (President/General Manager/Governor), Robert Gutkowski, Stanley Jaffe, Kenneth Munoz (Governors), Larry Pleau (Assistant General Manager), Mike Keenan (Head Coach), Colin Campbell (Associate Coach), Dick Todd (Assistant Coach), Matthew Loughren (Manager - Team Operations), Barry Watkins (Director - Communications), Christer Rockstrom, Tony Feltrin, Martin Madden, Herb Hammond, Darwin Bennett (Scouts), Dave Smith, Joe Murphy, Mike Folga, Bruce Lifrieri (Trainers).
Scores: May 31, at New York — Vancouver 3, NY Rangers 2; June 2, at New York — NY Rangers 3, Vancouver 1; June 4, at Vancouver — NY Rangers 5, Vancouver 1; June 7, at Vancouver — NY Rangers 4, Vancouver 2; June 9, at New York — Vancouver 6, at NY Rangers 3; June 11, at Vancouver — Vancouver 4, NY Rangers 1; June 14, at New York — NY Rangers 3, Vancouver 2.

1992-93 — Montreal Canadiens — Guy Carbonneau (Captain), Patrick Roy, Andre Racicot, Rob Ramage, Kirk Muller, Mike Keane, Kevin Haller, Paul DiPietro, John LeClair, Denis Savard, Benoit Brunet, Brian Bellows, Lyle Odelein, Vincent Damphousse, Gary Leeman, Mathieu Schneider, Eric Desjardins, Jesse Belanger, Ed Ronan, Mario Roberge, Donald Dufresne, Todd Ewen, Sean Hill, Patrice Brisebois, Gilbert Dionne, Stephan Lebeau, J.J. Daigneault; Ronald Corey (President), Serge Savard (Managing Director/Vice President - Hockey), Jacques Demers (Head Coach), Jacques Laperriere, Charles Thiffault (Assistant Coaches), Francois Allaire (Goaltending Instructor), Jean Béliveau (Senior Vice President - Corporate Affairs), Jacques Lemaire (Assistant to the Managing Director), André Boudrias (Assistant to the Managing Director/Director of Scouting), Gaeten Lefebvre (Athletic Trainer), John Shipman (Assistant to the Athletic Trainer), Eddy Palchak (Equipment Manager), Pierre Gervais, Robert Boulanger (Assistants to the Equipment Manager).
Scores: June 1, at Montreal — Los Angeles 4, Montreal 1; June 3, at Montreal — Montreal 3, Los Angeles 2; June 5, at Los Angeles — Montreal 4, Los Angeles 3; June 7, at Los Angeles — Montreal 3, Los Angeles 2; June 9, at Montreal — Montreal 4, Los Angeles 1.

1991-92 — Pittsburgh Penguins — Mario Lemieux (Captain), Ron Francis, Bryan Trottier, Kevin Stevens, Bob Errey, Phil Bourque, Troy Loney, Rick Tocchet, Joe Mullen, Jaromir Jagr, Jiri Hrdina, Shawn McEachern, Ulf Samuelsson, Kjell Samuelsson, Larry Murphy, Gordie Roberts, Jim Paek, Paul Stanton, Tom Barrasso, Ken Wregget, Jay Caufield, Jamie Leach, Wendell Young, Grant Jennings, Peter Taglianetti, Jock Callander, Dave Michayluk, Mike Needham, Jeff Chychrun, Ken Priestlay, Jeff Daniels; Morris Belzberg, Howard Baldwin, Thomas Ruta (Owners), Donn Patton (Executive Vice President/Chief Financial Officer), Paul Martha (Executive Vice President/General Counsel), Craig Patrick (Executive Vice President/General Manager), Bob Johnson (Head Coach), Scotty Bowman (Director of Player Development/Coach), Barry Smith, Rick Kehoe, Pierre McGuire, Gilles Meloche, Rick Paterson (Assistant Coaches), Steve Latin (Equipment Manager), Skip Thayer (Trainer), John Welday (Strength and Conditioning Coach), Greg Malone, Les Binkley, Charlie Hodge, John Gill, Ralph Cox (Scouts).
Scores: May 26, at Pittsburgh — Pittsburgh 5, Chicago 4; May 28, at Pittsburgh — Pittsburgh 3, Chicago 1; May 30, at Chicago — Pittsburgh 1, Chicago 0; June 1, at Chicago — Pittsburgh 6, Chicago 5.

1990-91 — Pittsburgh Penguins — Mario Lemieux (Captain), Paul Coffey, Randy Hillier, Bob Errey, Tom Barrasso, Phil Bourque, Jay Caufield, Ron Francis, Randy Gilhen, Jiri Hrdina, Jaromir Jagr, Grant Jennings, Troy Loney, Joe Mullen, Larry Murphy, Jim Paek, Frank Pietrangelo, Barry Pederson, Mark Recchi, Gordie Roberts, Ulf Samuelsson, Paul Stanton, Kevin Stevens, Peter Taglianetti, Bryan Trottier, Scott Young, Wendell Young; Edward J. DeBartolo Sr. (Owner), Marie D. DeBartolo York (President), Paul Martha (Vice President/General Counsel), Craig Patrick (General Manager), Scotty Bowman (Director of Player Development and Recruitment), Bob Johnson (Head Coach), Rick Kehoe, Rick Paterson, Barry Smith (Assistant Coaches), Gilles Meloche (Goaltending Coach/Scout), Steve Latin (Equipment Manager), Skip Thayer (Trainer), John Welday (Strength and Conditioning Coach), Greg Malone (Scout).

Scores: May 15, at Pittsburgh — Minnesota 5, Pittsburgh 4; May 17, at Pittsburgh — Pittsburgh 4, Minnesota 1; May 19, at Minnesota — Minnesota 3, Pittsburgh 1; May 21, at Minnesota — Pittsburgh 5, Minnesota 3; May 23, at Pittsburgh — Pittsburgh 6, Minnesota 4; May 25, at Minnesota — Pittsburgh 8, Minnesota 0.

1989-90 — Edmonton Oilers — Mark Messier (Captain), Jari Kurri, Kevin Lowe, Steve Smith, Jeff Beukeboom, Mark Lamb, Joe Murphy, Glenn Anderson, Adam Graves, Craig MacTavish, Kelly Buchberger, Craig Simpson, Martin Gelinas, Randy Gregg, Charlie Huddy, Geoff Smith, Reijo Ruotsalainen, Craig Muni, Bill Ranford, Dave Brown, Pokey Reddick, Petr Klima, Esa Tikkanen, Grant Fuhr; Peter Pocklington (Owner), Glen Sather (President/General Manager), John Muckler (Head Coach), Ted Green (Co-Coach), Ron Low (Assistant Coach), Bruce MacGregor (Assistant General Manager), Barry Fraser (Director of Player Personnel), Bill Tuele (Director of Public Relations), Werner Baum (Vice President), Dr. Gordon Cameron (Medical Chief of Staff), Dr. David Reid (Team Physician), Ken Lowe (Athletic Therapist), Barrie Stafford (Athletic Trainer), Stuart Poirier (Massage Therapist), Lyle Kulchisky (Assistant Trainer), John Blackwell (Cape Breton (AHL) - Director of Operations), Ace Bailey, Ed Chadwick, Lorne Davis, Harry Howell, Albert Reeves, Matti Vaisanen (Scouts).
Scores: May 15, at Boston — Edmonton 3, Boston 2; May 18, at Boston — Edmonton 7, Boston 2; May 20, at Edmonton — Boston 2, Edmonton 1; May 22, at Edmonton — Edmonton 5, Boston 1; May 24, at Boston — Edmonton 4, Boston 1.

1988-89 — Calgary Flames — Lanny McDonald (Co- Captain), Jim Peplinski (Co-Captain), Tim Hunter, Mike Vernon, Rick Wamsley, Al MacInnis, Brad McCrimmon, Dana Murzyn, Ric Nattress, Joe Mullen, Gary Roberts, Colin Patterson, Hakan Loob, Theoren Fleury, Jiri Hrdina, Gary Suter, Mark Hunter, Joe Nieuwendyk, Brian MacLellan, Joel Otto, Jamie Macoun, Doug Gilmour, Rob Ramage; Norman Green, Harley Hotchkiss, Norman Kwong, Sonia Scurfield, B.J. Seaman, D.K. Seaman (Owners), Cliff Fletcher (President/General Manager), Al MacNeil (Assistant General Manager), Al Coates (Assistant to the President), Terry Crisp (Head Coach), Doug Risebrough, Tom Watt (Assistant Coaches), Glenn Hall (Goaltending Consultant), Jim Murray (Trainer), Al Murray (Assistant Trainer), Bob Stewart (Equipment Manager).
Scores: May 14, at Calgary — Calgary 3, Montreal 2; May 17, at Calgary— Montreal 4, Calgary 2; May 19, at Montreal — Montreal 4, Calgary 3; May 21, at Montreal — Calgary 4, Montreal 2; May 23, at Calgary — Calgary 3, Montreal 2; May 25, at Montreal — Calgary 4, Montreal 2.

1987-88 — Edmonton Oilers — Wayne Gretzky (Captain), Keith Acton, Glenn Anderson, Jeff Beukeboom, Geoff Courtnall, Grant Fuhr, Randy Gregg, Dave Hannan, Charlie Huddy, Mike Krushelnyski, Jari Kurri, Normand Lacombe, Kevin Lowe, Craig MacTavish, Kevin McClelland, Marty McSorley, Mark Messier, Craig Muni, Bill Ranford, Craig Simpson, Steve Smith, Esa Tikkanen; Peter Pocklington (Owner), Glen Sather (General Manager/Coach), John Muckler (Co-Coach), Ted Green (Assistant Coach), Bruce MacGregor (Assistant General Manager), Barry Fraser (Director of Player Personnel), Bill Tuele (Director of Public Relations), Dr. Gordon Cameron (Team Doctor), Peter Millar (Athletic Therapist), Juergen Merz (Massage Therapist), Barrie Stafford (Trainer), Lyle Kulchisky (Assistant Trainer).
Scores: May 18, at Edmonton — Edmonton 2, Boston 1; May 20, at Edmonton — Edmonton 4, Boston 2; May 22, at Boston — Edmonton 6, Boston 3; May 24, at Boston — Boston 3, Edmonton 3 (suspended due to power failure); May 26, at Edmonton — Edmonton 6, Boston 3.

1986-87 — Edmonton Oilers — Wayne Gretzky (Captain), Glenn Anderson, Jeff Beukeboom, Kelly Buchberger, Paul Coffey, Grant Fuhr, Randy Gregg, Charlie Huddy, Dave Hunter, Mike Krushelnyski, Jari Kurri, Moe Lemay, Kevin Lowe, Craig MacTavish, Kevin McClelland, Marty McSorley, Mark Messier, Andy Moog, Craig Muni, Kent Nilsson, Jaroslav Pouzar, Reijo Ruotsalainen, Steve Smith, Esa Tikkanen; Peter Pocklington (Owner), Glen Sather (General Manager/Coach), Bruce MacGregor (Assistant General Manager), John Muckler (Co-Coach), Ted Green, Ron Low (Assistant Coaches), Barry Fraser (Director of Player Personnel), Garnet Bailey, Ed Chadwick, Lorne Davis, Matti Vaisanen (Scouts), Peter Millar (Athletic Therapist), Juergen Merz (Massage Therapist), Dr. Gordon Cameron (Team Doctor), Barrie Stafford (Trainer), Lyle Kulchisky (Assistant Trainer).
Scores: May 17, at Edmonton — Edmonton 4, Philadelphia 2; May 20, at Edmonton — Edmonton 3, Philadelphia 2; May 22, at Philadelphia — Philadelphia 5, Edmonton 3; May 24, at Philadelphia — Edmonton 4, Philadelphia 1; May 26, at Edmonton — Philadelphia 4, Edmonton 3; May 28, at Philadelphia — Philadelphia 3, Edmonton 2; May 31, at Edmonton — Edmonton 3, Philadelphia 1.

1985-86 — Montreal Canadiens — Bob Gainey (Captain), Doug Soetaert, Patrick Roy, Rick Green, David Maley, Ryan Walter, Serge Boisvert, Mario Tremblay, Bobby Smith, Craig Ludwig, Tom Kurvers, Kjell Dahlin, Larry Robinson, Guy Carbonneau, Chris Chelios, Petr Svoboda, Mats Naslund, Lucien DeBlois, Steve Rooney, Gaston Gingras, Mike Lalor, Chris Nilan, John Kordic, Claude Lemieux, Mike McPhee, Brian Skrudland, Stephane Richer; Ronald Corey (President), Serge Savard (General Manager), Jean Perron (Coach), Jacques Laperrière (Assistant Coach), Jean Béliveau, Francois-Xavier Seigneur, Fred Steer (Vice Presidents), Jacques Lemaire, André Boudrias (Assistant General Managers), Claude Ruel (Player Development), Yves Belanger (Athletic Therapist), Gaetan Lefebvre (Assistant Athletic Therapist), Eddy Palchak (Trainer), Sylvain Toupin (Assistant Trainer).
Scores: May 16, at Calgary — Calgary 5, Montreal 2; May 18, at Calgary — Montreal 3, Calgary 2; May 20, at Montreal — Montreal 5, Calgary 3; May 22, at Montreal — Montreal 1, Calgary 0; May 24, at Calgary — Montreal 4, Calgary 3.

1984-85 — Edmonton Oilers — Wayne Gretzky (Captain), Glenn Anderson, Billy Carroll, Paul Coffey, Lee Fogolin Jr., Grant Fuhr, Randy Gregg, Charlie Huddy, Pat Hughes, Dave Hunter, Don Jackson, Mike Krushelnyski, Jari Kurri, Willy Lindstrom, Kevin Lowe, Dave Lumley, Kevin McClelland, Larry Melnyk, Mark Messier, Andy Moog, Mark Napier, Jaroslav Pouzar, Dave Semenko, Esa Tikkanen; Peter Pocklington (Owner), Glen Sather (General Manager/Coach), Bruce MacGregor (Assistant General Manager), John Muckler, Ted Green (Assistant Coaches), Barry Fraser (Director of Player Personnel/Chief Scout), Garnet Bailey, Ed Chadwick, Lorne Davis, Matti Vaisanen (Scouts), Peter Millar (Athletic Therapist), Dr. Gordon Cameron (Team Doctor), Barrie Stafford (Trainer), Lyle Kulchisky (Assistant Trainer).
Scores: May 21, at Philadelphia — Philadelphia 4, Edmonton 1; May 23, at Philadelphia — Edmonton 3, Philadelphia 1; May 25, at Edmonton — Edmonton 4, Philadelphia 3; May 28, at Edmonton — Edmonton 5, Philadelphia 3; May 30, at Edmonton — Edmonton 8, Philadelphia 3.

1983-84 — Edmonton Oilers — Wayne Gretzky (Captain), Glenn Anderson, Paul Coffey, Pat Conacher, Lee Fogolin Jr., Grant Fuhr, Randy Gregg, Charlie Huddy, Pat Hughes, Dave Hunter, Don Jackson, Jari Kurri, Willy Lindstrom, Ken Linseman, Kevin Lowe, Dave Lumley, Kevin McClelland, Mark Messier, Andy Moog, Jaroslav Pouzar, Dave Semenko; Peter Pocklington (Owner), Glen Sather (General Manager/Coach), Bruce MacGregor (Assistant General Manager), John Muckler, Ted Green (Assistant Coaches), Barry Fraser (Director of Player Personnel/Chief Scout), Pete Millar (Athletic Therapist), Barrie Stafford (Trainer), Lyle Kulchisky (Assistant Trainer).
Scores: May 10, at New York — Edmonton 1, NY Islanders 0; May 12, at New York — NY Islanders 6, Edmonton 1; May 15, at Edmonton — Edmonton 7, NY Islanders 2; May 17, at Edmonton — Edmonton 7, NY Islanders 2; May 19, at Edmonton — Edmonton 5, NY Islanders 2.

1982-83 — New York Islanders — Denis Potvin (Captain), Mike Bossy, Bob Bourne, Paul Boutilier, Billy Carroll, Greg Gilbert, Clark Gillies, Butch Goring, Mats Hallin, Tomas Jonsson, Anders Kallur, Gord Lane, Dave Langevin, Mike McEwen, Roland Melanson, Wayne Merrick, Ken Morrow, Bob Nystrom, Stefan Persson, Billy Smith, Brent Sutter, Duane Sutter, John Tonelli, Bryan Trottier; Bill Torrey (President/General Manager), John Pickett Jr. (Chairman), Gerry Ehman (Assistant General Manager/Director of Scouting), Al Arbour (Coach), Lorne Henning (Assistant Coach), Ron Waske (Trainer), Jim Pickard (Assistant Trainer).
Scores: May 10, at Edmonton — NY Islanders 2, Edmonton 0; May 12, at Edmonton — NY Islanders 6, Edmonton 3; May 14, at New York — NY Islanders 5, Edmonton 1; May 17, at New York — NY Islanders 4, Edmonton 2

1981-82 — New York Islanders — Denis Potvin (Captain), Mike Bossy, Bob Bourne, Billy Carroll, Greg Gilbert, Clark Gillies, Butch Goring, Tomas Jonsson, Anders Kallur, Gord Lane, Dave Langevin, Hector Marini, Mike McEwen, Roland Melanson, Wayne Merrick, Ken Morrow, Bob Nystrom, Stefan Persson, Billy Smith, Brent Sutter, Duane Sutter, John Tonelli, Bryan Trottier; Bill Torrey (President/General Manager), John Pickett Jr. (Chairman), Jim Devellano (Assistant General Manager/Director of Scouting), Al Arbour (Coach), Lorne Henning (Assistant Coach), Gerry Ehman (Head Scout), Ron Waske (Trainer), Jim Pickard (Assistant Trainer).
Scores: May 8, at New York — NY Islanders 6, Vancouver 5; May 11, at New York — NY Islanders 6, Vancouver 4; May 13, at Vancouver — NY Islanders 3, Vancouver 0; May 16, at Vancouver — NY Islanders 3, Vancouver 1

1980-81 — New York Islanders — Denis Potvin (Captain), Mike Bossy, Bob Bourne, Billy Carroll, Clark Gillies, Butch Goring, Garry Howatt, Anders Kallur, Gord Lane, Dave Langevin, Bob Lorimer, Hector Marini, Mike McEwen, Roland Melanson, Wayne Merrick, Ken Morrow, Bob Nystrom, Stefan Persson, Jean Potvin, Billy Smith, Duane Sutter, John Tonelli, Bryan Trottier; Bill Torrey (President/General Manager), John Pickett Jr. (Chairman), Al Arbour (Coach), Lorne Henning (Player/Assistant Coach), Jim Devellano (Chief Scout), Gerry Ehman, Mario Saraceno, Harry Boyd (Scouts), Ron Waske (Trainer), Jim Pickard (Assistant Trainer).
Scores: May 12, at New York — NY Islanders 6, Minnesota 3; May 14, at New York — NY Islanders 6, Minnesota 3; May 17, at Minnesota — NY Islanders 7, Minnesota 5; May 19, at Minnesota— Minnesota 4, NY Islanders 2; May 21, at New York — NY Islanders 5, Minnesota 1.

1979-80 — New York Islanders — Denis Potvin (Captain), Mike Bossy, Bob Bourne, Clark Gillies, Butch Goring, Lorne Henning, Garry Howatt, Anders Kallur, Gord Lane, Dave Langevin, Bob Lorimer, Alex McKendry, Wayne Merrick, Ken Morrow, Bob Nystrom, Stefan Persson, Jean Potvin, Glenn Resch, Billy Smith, Duane Sutter, Steve Tambellini, John Tonelli, Bryan Trottier; Bill Torrey (President/General Manager), John Pickett Jr. (Chairman), Al Arbour (Coach), Billy MacMillan (Assistant Coach), Jim Devellano (Chief Scout), Gerry Ehman, Mario Saraceno, Harry Boyd (Scouts), Ron Waske (Trainer), Jim Pickard (Assistant Trainer).
Scores: May 13, at Philadelphia — NY Islanders 4, Philadelphia 3; May 15, at Philadelphia — Philadelphia 8, NY Islanders 3; May 17, at New York — NY Islanders 6, Philadelphia 2; May 19, at New York — NY Islanders 5, Philadelphia 2; May 22, at Philadelphia — Philadelphia 6, NY Islanders 3; May 24, at New York — NY Islanders 5, Philadelphia 4.

1978-79 — Montreal Canadiens — Yvan Cournoyer (Captain), Guy Lafleur, Ken Dryden, Rick Chartraw, Brian Engblom, Bob Gainey, Mario Tremblay, Guy Lapointe, Doug Risebrough, Réjean Houle, Pat Hughes, Michel Larocque, Doug Jarvis, Yvon Lambert, Pierre Larouche, Gilles Lupien, Rod Langway, Jacques Lemaire, Pierre Mondou, Larry Robinson, Mark Napier, Serge Savard, Steve Shutt, Cam Connor, Richard Sévigny; Jacques Courtois (President), Sam Pollock (Director), Irving Grundman (Vice President/Managing Director), Jean Beliveau (Vice President - Corporate Affairs), Scotty Bowman (Coach), Claude Ruel (Director of Player Development), Al MacNeil (Director of Player Personnel), Morgan McCammon (Director), Ron Caron (Director of Recruitment), Eddy Palchak (Trainer), Pierre Meilleur (Assistant Trainer).
Scores: May 13, at Montreal — NY Rangers 4, Montreal 1; May 15, at Montreal — Montreal 6, NY Rangers 2; May 17, at New York — Montreal 4, NY Rangers 1; May 19, at New York — Montreal 4, NY Rangers 3; May 21, at Montreal — Montreal 4, NY Rangers 1.

1977-78 — Montreal Canadiens — Yvan Cournoyer (Captain), Guy Lafleur, Ken Dryden, Michel Larocque, Rick Chartraw, Réjean Houle, Pierre Larouche, Brian Engblom, Yvon Lambert, Jacques Lemaire, Bob Gainey, Guy Lapointe, Doug Jarvis, Gilles Lupien, Pierre Mondou, Larry Robinson, Bill Nyrop, Murray Wilson, Serge Savard, Steve Shutt, Mario Tremblay, Pierre Bouchard, Doug Risebrough; Jacques Courtois (President), Sam Pollock (Vice President/General Manager), Jean Beliveau (Vice President/Director of Corporate Relations), Scotty Bowman (Coach), Peter Bronfman, Edward Bronfman (Directors), Al MacNeil (Director of Player Development), Eddy Palchak (Trainer), Pierre Meilleur (Assistant Trainer), Claude Ruel (Director of Player Development), Floyd Curry, Ron Caron (Assistant General Managers).
Scores: May 13, at Montreal — Montreal 4, Boston 1; May 16, at Montreal — Montreal 3, Boston 2; May 18, at Boston — Boston 4, Montreal 0; May 21, at Boston — Boston 4, Montreal 3; May 23, at Montreal — Montreal 4, Boston 1; May 25, at Boston — Montreal 4, Boston 1.

1976-77 — Montreal Canadiens — Yvan Cournoyer (Captain), Larry Robinson, Guy Lafleur, Pierre Bouchard, Rejean Houle, Yvon Lambert, Bob Gainey, Jacques Lemaire, Guy Lapointe, Ken Dryden, Rick Chartraw, Bill Nyrop, Michel Larocque, Pierre Mondou, Serge Savard, Steve Shutt, Mario Tremblay, Murray Wilson, Doug Jarvis, Mike Polich, Jimmy Roberts, Pete Mahovlich, Doug Risebrough, Jacques Courtois (President), Sam Pollock (Vice President/General Manager), Jean Beliveau (Vice President/Director of Corporate Relations), Scotty Bowman (Coach), Peter Bronfman, Edward Bronfman (Directors), Claude Ruel (Director of Player Development), Floyd Curry, Ron Caron (Assistant General Managers), Pierre Meilleur (Assistant Trainer), Eddy Palchak (Trainer).
Scores: May 7, at Montreal — Montreal 7, Boston 3; May 10, at Montreal — Montreal 3, Boston 0; May 12, at Boston — Montreal 4, Boston 2; May 14, at Boston — Montreal 2, Boston 1.

1975-76 — Montreal Canadiens — Yvan Cournoyer (Captain), Bob Gainey, Larry Robinson, Pierre Bouchard, Rick Chartraw, Ken Dryden, Pete Mahovlich, Guy Lafleur, Yvon Lambert, Michel Larocque, Serge Savard, Doug Jarvis, Jacques Lemaire, Guy Lapointe, Jimmy Roberts, Doug Risebrough, Steve Shutt, Murray Wilson, Mario Tremblay, Bill Nyrop; Jacques Courtois (President), Jean Beliveau (Vice President), Peter Bronfman (Chairman), Edward Bronfman (Director), Sam Pollock (Vice President/General Manager), Scotty Bowman (Coach), Eddy Palchak (Trainer), Pierre Meilleur (Assistant Trainer), Claude Ruel (Director of Player Development).

Scores: May 9, at Montreal — Montreal 4, Philadelphia 3; May 11, at Montreal — Montreal 2, Philadelphia 1; May 13, at Philadelphia — Montreal 3, Philadelphia 2; May 16, at Philadelphia — Montreal 5, Philadelphia 3.

1974-75 — Philadelphia Flyers — Bobby Clarke (Captain), Bernie Parent, Bobby Taylor, Wayne Stephenson, Ed Van Impe, Don Saleski, Tom Bladon, Larry Goodenough, Bill Barber, Gary Dornhoefer, Dave Schultz, Joe Watson, Ross Lonsberry, André Dupont, Terry Crisp, Orest Kindrachuk, Bill Clement, Bob Kelly, Rick MacLeish, Jimmy Watson, Reggie Leach, Ted Harris; Ed Snider (Chairman), Joe Scott (President), Eugene Dixon Jr. (Vice Chairman), Fred Shero (Coach), Keith Allen (Vice President/General Manager), Lou Scheinfeld (Vice President), Mike Nykoluk (Assistant Coach), Marcel Pelletier (Player Personnel Director), Barry Ashbee (Assistant Coach), Frank Lewis (Trainer), Jim McKenzie (Assistant Trainer).
Scores: May 15, at Philadelphia — Philadelphia 4, Buffalo 1; May 18, at Philadelphia — Philadelphia 2, Buffalo 1; May 20, at Buffalo — Buffalo 5, Philadelphia 4; May 22, at Buffalo — Buffalo 4, Philadelphia 2; May 25, at Philadelphia — Philadelphia 5, Buffalo 1; May 27, at Buffalo — Philadelphia 2, Buffalo 0.

1973-74 — Philadelphia Flyers — Bobby Clarke (Captain), Bernie Parent, Bobby Taylor, Bill Clement, Ross Lonsberry, Bill Barber, Orest Kindrachuk, Ed Van Impe, Don Saleski, Gary Dornhoefer, Barry Ashbee, Jimmy Watson, Dave Schultz, André Dupont, Bruce Cowick, Rick MacLeish, Terry Crisp, Bill Flett, Simon Nolet, Joe Watson, Bob Kelly, Tom Bladon; Ed Snider (Chairman), Joe Scott (President), Eugene Dixon Jr. (Vice Chairman), Fred Shero (Coach), Keith Allen (Vice President/General Manager), Mike Nykoluk (Assistant Coach), Marcel Pelletier (Player Personnel Director), Frank Lewis (Trainer), Jim McKenzie (Assistant Trainer).
Scores: May 7, at Boston — Boston 3, Philadelphia 2; May 9, at Boston — Philadelphia 3, Boston 2; May 12, at Philadelphia — Philadelphia 4, Boston 1; May 14, at Philadelphia — Philadelphia 4, Boston 2; May 16, at Boston — Boston 5, Philadelphia 1; May 19, at Philadelphia — Philadelphia 1, Boston 0.

1972-73 — Montreal Canadiens — Henri Richard (Captain), Jacques Laperrière, Ken Dryden, Yvan Cournoyer, Jacques Lemaire, Marc Tardif, Serge Savard, Pete Mahovlich, Guy Lapointe, Réjean Houle, Claude Larose, Pierre Bouchard, Frank Mahovlich, Jimmy Roberts, Chuck Lefley, Guy Lafleur, Bob Murdoch, Michel Plasse, Murray Wilson, Larry Robinson, Steve Shutt; Jacques Courtois (President), Jean Beliveau (Vice President), Peter Bronfman (Chairman), Sam Pollock (Vice President/General Manager), Edward Bronfman (Executive Director), Scotty Bowman (Coach), Bob Williams (Trainer).
Scores: April 29, at Montreal — Montreal 8, Chicago 3; May 1, at Montreal — Montreal 4, Chicago 1; May 3, at Chicago — Chicago 7, Montreal 4; May 6, at Chicago — Montreal 4, Chicago 0; May 8, at Montreal — Chicago 8, Montreal 7; May 10, at Chicago — Montreal 6, Chicago 4.

1971-72 — Boston Bruins — Bobby Orr, Gerry Cheevers, Eddie Johnston, Dallas Smith, Derek Sanderson, Carol Vadnais, Phil Esposito, Fred Stanfield, Don Awrey, Ted Green, Ken Hodge, John Bucyk, Wayne Cashman, John McKenzie, Ed Westfall, Mike Walton, Garnet Bailey, Don Marcotte; Weston Adams (Chairman), Weston Adams Jr. (President), Shelby Davis (Vice President), Charles Mulcahy (Junior Vice President/General Counsel), Eddie Powers (Vice President/Treasurer), Milt Schmidt (General Manager), Tom Johnson (Coach), Dan Canney (Trainer), John Forristall (Assistant Trainer).
Scores: April 30, at Boston — Boston 6, NY Rangers 5; May 2, at Boston — Boston 2, NY Rangers 1; May 4, at New York — NY Rangers 5, Boston 2; May 7, at New York — Boston 3, NY Rangers 2; May 9, at Boston — NY Rangers 3, Boston 2; May 11, at New York — Boston 3, NY Rangers 0.

1970-71 — Montreal Canadiens — Jean Béliveau (Captain), Pierre Bouchard, Yvan Cournoyer, John Ferguson, Jacques Laperrière, Terry Harper, Réjean Houle, Guy Lapointe, Claude Larose, Marc Tardif, Chuck Lefley, Jacques Lemaire, Frank Mahovlich, Henri Richard, Phil Roberto, Pete Mahovlich, Bob Murdoch, Serge Savard (37GP – injured), Bobby Sheehan, Leon Rochefort, J.C. Tremblay, Ken Dryden, Rogie Vachon; David Molson (President), William Molson, Peter Molson (Vice Presidents), Sam Pollock (Vice President/General Manager), Ron Caron (Assistant General Manager), Al MacNeil (Coach), Yves Belanger (Trainer), Phil Langlois, Eddie Palchak (Assistant Trainers).
Scores: May 4, at Chicago — Chicago 2, Montreal 1; May 6, at Chicago — Chicago 5, Montreal 3; May 9, at Montreal — Montreal 4, Chicago 2; May 11, at Montreal — Montreal 5, Chicago 2; May 13, at Chicago — Chicago 2, Montreal 0; May 16, at Montreal — Montreal 4, Chicago 3; May 18, at Chicago — Montreal 3, Chicago 2.

1969-70 — Boston Bruins — Don Awrey, John Bucyk, Garnet Bailey, Wayne Carleton, Wayne Cashman, Gary Doak, Phil Esposito, Ted Green, Ken Hodge, Bobby Orr, Don Marcotte, John McKenzie, Derek Sanderson, Dallas Smith, Rick Smith, Bill Speer, Fred Stanfield, Ed Westfall, Gerry Cheevers, Eddie Johnston, John Adams, Jim Lorentz, Ron Murphy, Bill Lesuk, Ivan Boldirev, Danny Schock; Weston Adams Sr. (Chairman), Weston Adams Jr. (President), Charles Mulcahy, Eddie Powers, Shelby Davis (Vice Presidents), Harry Sinden (Coach), Milt Schmidt (General Manager), Tom Johnson (Assistant General Manager), Dan Canney (Trainer), John Forristall (Assistant Trainer).
Scores: May 3, at St. Louis — Boston 6, St. Louis 1; May 5, at St. Louis — Boston 6, St. Louis 2; May 7, at Boston — Boston 4, St. Louis 1; May 10, at Boston — Boston 4, St. Louis 3.

1968-69 — Montreal Canadiens — Jean Béliveau (Captain), Ralph Backstrom, Jacques Lemaire, Dick Duff, Christian Bordeleau, Mickey Redmond, Yvan Cournoyer, Henri Richard, Bobby Rousseau, John Ferguson, Serge Savard, Terry Harper, Gilles Tremblay, Ted Harris, J.C. Tremblay, Larry Hillman, Jacques Laperrière, Claude Provost, Tony Esposito, Rogie Vachon, Gump Worsley; David Molson (President), William Molson, Peter Molson (Vice Presidents), Sam Pollock (Vice President/General Manager), Claude Ruel (Coach), Larry Aubut (Trainer), Eddie Palchak (Assistant Trainer).
Scores: April 27, at Montreal — Montreal 3, St. Louis 1; April 29, at Montreal — Montreal 3, St. Louis 1; May 1, at St. Louis — Montreal 4, St. Louis 0; May 4, at St. Louis — Montreal 2, St. Louis 1.

1967-68 — Montreal Canadiens — Jean Béliveau (Captain), Ralph Backstrom, Yvan Cournoyer, Dick Duff, John Ferguson, Danny Grant, Terry Harper, Ted Harris, Serge Savard, Jacques Laperrière, Claude Larose, Jacques Lemaire, Claude Provost, Mickey Redmond, Henri Richard, Bobby Rousseau, Gilles Tremblay, J.C. Tremblay, Carol Vadnais, Rogie Vachon, Ernie Wakely, Gump Worsley; Hartland Molson (Chairman), David Molson (President), Sam Pollock (Vice President/General Manager), Toe Blake (Coach), Larry Aubut (Trainer), Eddie Palchak (Assistant Trainer).
Scores: May 5, at St. Louis — Montreal 3, St. Louis 2; May 7, at St. Louis — Montreal 1, St. Louis 0; May 9, at Montreal — Montreal 4, St. Louis 3; May 11, at Montreal — Montreal 3, St. Louis 2.

1966-67 — Toronto Maple Leafs — George Armstrong (Captain), Bob Baun, Johnny Bower, Brian Conacher, Ron Ellis, Aut Erickson, Larry Hillman, Tim Horton, Red Kelly, Larry Jeffrey, Dave Keon, Frank Mahovlich, Milan Marcetta, Jim Pappin, Marcel Pronovost, Bob Pulford, Terry Sawchuk, Eddie Shack, Allan Stanley, Pete Stemkowski, Mike Walton; Stafford Smythe (President), Harold Ballard (Executive Vice President), John Bassett (Chairman), Punch Imlach (General Manager/Coach), King Clancy (Assistant Coach/Assistant General Manager), Bob Davidson (Chief Scout), John Anderson (Business Manager), Bob Haggert (Trainer), Tom Nayler (Assistant Trainer), Karl Elieff (Physiotherapist), Richard Smythe (Mascot).
Scores: April 20, at Montreal — Toronto 2, Montreal 6; April 22, at Montreal — Toronto 3, Montreal 0; April 25, at Toronto — Toronto 3, Montreal 2; April 27, at Toronto — Toronto 2, Montreal 6; April 29, at Montreal — Toronto 4, Montreal 1; May 2, at Toronto — Toronto 3, Montreal 1.

1965-66 — Montreal Canadiens — Jean Béliveau (Captain), Ralph Backstrom, Dave Balon, Yvan Cournoyer, Bobby Rousseau, Dick Duff, John Ferguson, Terry Harper, Ted Harris, Charlie Hodge, Jacques Laperrière, Claude Larose, Noel Price, Claude Provost, Henri Richard, Jimmy Roberts, Leon Rochefort, Jean-Guy Talbot, Gilles Tremblay, J.C. Tremblay, Gump Worsley; Hartland Molson (Chairman), David Molson (President), Sam Pollock (General Manager), Toe Blake (Coach), Andy Galley (Trainer), Larry Aubut (Assistant Trainer).
Scores: April 24, at Montreal — Detroit 3, Montreal 2; April 26, at Montreal — Detroit 5, Montreal 2; April 28, at Detroit — Montreal 4, Detroit 2; May 1, at Detroit — Montreal 2, Detroit 1; May 3, at Montreal — Montreal 5, Detroit 1; May 5, at Detroit — Montreal 3, Detroit 2.

1964-65 — Montreal Canadiens — Jean Béliveau (Captain), Ralph Backstrom, Dave Balon, Red Berenson, Yvan Cournoyer, Dick Duff, John Ferguson, Jean Gauthier, Charlie Hodge, Terry Harper, Ted Harris, Jacques Laperrière, Claude Larose, Garry Peters, Noel Picard, Claude Provost, Henri Richard, Jimmy Roberts, Bobby Rousseau, Jean-Guy Talbot, Gilles Tremblay, J.C. Tremblay, Ernie Wakely, Bryan Watson, Gump Worsley; Hartland Molson (Chairman), David Molson (President), Maurice Richard (Assistant to the President), Sam Pollock (General Manager), Toe Blake (Coach), Andy Galley (Trainer), Larry Aubut (Assistant Trainer).
Scores: April 17, at Montreal — Montreal 3, Chicago 2; April 20, at Montreal — Montreal 2, Chicago 0; April 22, at Chicago — Montreal 1, Chicago 3; April 25, at Chicago — Montreal 1, Chicago 5; April 7, at Montreal — Montreal 6, Chicago 0; April 29, at Chicago — Montreal 1, Chicago 2; May 1, at Montreal — Montreal 4, Chicago 0.

1963-64 — Toronto Maple Leafs — George Armstrong (Captain), Andy Bathgate, Bob Baun, Johnny Bower, Carl Brewer, Gerry Ehman, Billy Harris, Larry Hillman, Dave Keon, Tim Horton, Red Kelly, Frank Mahovlich, Don McKenney, Jim Pappin, Bob Pulford, Eddie Shack, Don Simmons, Allan Stanley, Ron Stewart, Al Arbour, Ed Litzenberger; Stafford Smythe (President), Harold Ballard (Executive Vice President), John Bassett (Chairman), Punch Imlach (Coach/General Manager), King Clancy (Assistant Coach/Assistant General Manager), Bob Haggert (Trainer), Tom Nayler (Assistant Trainer), Hugh Hoult (Stick Boy).
Scores April 11, at Toronto — Toronto 3, Detroit 2; April 14, at Toronto — Toronto 3, Detroit 4; April 16, at Detroit — Toronto 3, Detroit 4; April 18, at Detroit — Toronto 4, Detroit 2; April 21, at Toronto — Toronto 1, Detroit 2; April 23, at Detroit — Toronto 4, Detroit 3; April 25, at Toronto — Toronto 4, Detroit 0.

1962-63 — Toronto Maple Leafs — George Armstrong (Captain), Bob Baun, Johnny Bower, Carl Brewer, Kent Douglas, Dick Duff, Billy Harris, Larry Hillman, Tim Horton, Red Kelly, Dave Keon, Ed Litzenberger, John MacMillan, Frank Mahovlich, Bob Nevin, Bob Pulford, Eddie Shack, Don Simmons, Allan Stanley, Ron Stewart; Stafford Smythe (President), Harold Ballard (Executive Vice President), John Bassett (Chairman), Punch Imlach (Coach/General Manager), King Clancy (Assistant Coach/Assistant General Manager), Bob Haggert (Trainer), Tom Nayler (Assistant Trainer), Hugh Hoult (Stick Boy).
Scores: April 9, at Toronto — Toronto 4, Detroit 2; April 11, at Toronto — Toronto 4, Detroit 2; April 14, at Detroit — Toronto 2, Detroit 3; April 16, at Detroit — Toronto 4, Detroit 2; April 18, at Toronto — Toronto 3, Detroit 1.

1961-62 — Toronto Maple Leafs — George Armstrong (Captain), Al Arbour, Bob Baun, Johnny Bower, Carl Brewer, Dick Duff, Billy Harris, Larry Hillman, Dave Keon, Tim Horton, Red Kelly, Ed Litzenberger, John MacMillan, Frank Mahovlich, Bob Nevin, Bert Olmstead, Bob Pulford, Eddie Shack, Allan Stanley, Don Simmons, Ron Stewart; Stafford Smythe (President), Harold Ballard (Executive Vice President), John Bassett (Vice President), Conn Smythe (Chairman), Punch Imlach (Coach/General Manager), King Clancy (Assistant Coach), Bob Davidson (Chief Scout), Bob Haggert (Trainer), Tom Nayler (Assistant Trainer), Hugh Hoult (Stick Boy).
Scores: April 10, at Toronto — Toronto 4, Chicago 1; April 12, at Toronto — Toronto 3, Chicago 2; April 15, at Chicago — Toronto 0, Chicago 3; April 17, at Chicago — Toronto 1, Chicago 4; April 19, at Toronto —Toronto 8, Chicago 4; April 22, at Chicago — Toronto 2, Chicago 1.

1960-61 — Chicago Black Hawks — Ed Litzenberger (Captain), Al Arbour, Earl Balfour, Murray Balfour, Glenn Hall, Jack Evans, Roy Edwards, Denis DeJordy, Bill Hay, Wayne Hicks, Reggie Fleming, Wayne Hillman, Bobby Hull, Chico Maki, Ab McDonald, Moose Vasko, Stan Mikita, Ron Murphy, Eric Nesterenko, Pierre Pilote, Tod Sloan, Dollard St. Laurent, Kenny Wharram; Arthur Wirtz (President), Arthur Wirtz Jr. (Vice President), James Norris (Chairman), Tommy Ivan (General Manager), Rudy Pilous (Coach), Nick Garen, Walter Humeniuk (Trainers).
Scores: April 6, at Chicago — Chicago 3, Detroit 2; April 8, at Detroit — Detroit 3, Chicago 1; April 10, at Chicago — Chicago 3, Detroit 1; April 12, at Detroit — Detroit 2, Chicago 1; April 14, at Chicago — Chicago 6, Detroit 3; April 16, at Detroit — Chicago 5, Detroit 1.

1959-60 — Montreal Canadiens — Maurice Richard (Captain), Ralph Backstrom, Marcel Bonin, Jean Béliveau, Bernie Geoffrion, Phil Goyette, Doug Harvey, Bill Hicke, Charlie Hodge, Tom Johnson, Albert Langlois, Don Marshall, Dickie Moore, Ab McDonald, Jacques Plante, Henri Richard, André Pronovost, Claude Provost, Bob Turner, Jean-Guy Talbot; Senator Hartland Molson (President), Frank Selke (Managing Director), Ken Reardon (Vice President), Sam Pollock (Personnel Director), Toe Blake (Coach), Hector Dubois, Larry Aubut (Trainers).
Scores: April 7, at Montreal — Montreal 4, Toronto 2; April 9, at Montreal — Montreal 2, Toronto 1; April 12, at Toronto — Montreal 5, Toronto 2; April 14, at Toronto — Montreal 4, Toronto 0.

1958-59 — Montreal Canadiens — Maurice Richard (Captain), Ralph Backstrom, Marcel Bonin, Jean Béliveau, Ian Cushenan, Bernie Geoffrion, Charlie Hodge, Phil Goyette, Doug Harvey, Bill Hicke, Tom Johnson, Albert Langlois, Don Marshall, Ab McDonald, Dickie Moore, Jacques Plante, Ken Mosdell, André Pronovost, Claude Provost, Henri Richard, Jean-Guy Talbot, Bob Turner; Senator Hartland Molson (President), Frank Selke (Managing Director), Ken Reardon (Vice President), Sam Pollock (Personnel Director), Toe Blake (Coach), Hector Dubois, Larry Aubut (Trainers).

Scores: April 9, at Montreal — Montreal 5, Toronto 3; April 11, at Montreal — Montreal 3, Toronto 1; April 14, at Toronto — Toronto 3, Montreal 2; April 16, at Toronto — Montreal 3, Toronto 2; April 18, at Montreal — Montreal 5, Toronto 3.

1957-58 — Montreal Canadiens — Maurice Richard (Captain), Jean Béliveau, Marcel Bonin, Floyd Curry, Connie Broden, Bernie Geoffrion, Phil Goyette, Doug Harvey, Charlie Hodge, Tom Johnson, Albert Langlois, Don Marshall, Ab McDonald, Gerry McNeil, Dickie Moore, Bert Olmstead, Jacques Plante, André Pronovost, Henri Richard, Claude Provost, Dollard St. Laurent, Jean-Guy Talbot, Bob Turner; Senator Hartland Molson (President), Frank Selke (Managing Director), Ken Reardon (Vice President), Toe Blake (Coach), Hector Dubois, Larry Aubut (Trainers).
Scores: April 8, at Montreal —Montreal 2, Boston 1; April 10, at Montreal — Boston 5, Montreal 2; April 13, at Boston — Montreal 3, Boston 0; April 15, at Boston — Boston 3, Montreal 1; April 17, at Montreal — Montreal 3, Boston 2; April 20, at Boston — Montreal 5, Boston 3.

1956-57 — Montreal Canadiens — Maurice Richard (Captain), Jean Béliveau, Connie Broden, Floyd Curry, Bernie Geoffrion, Phil Goyette, Doug Harvey, Tom Johnson, Don Marshall, Gerry McNeil, Dickie Moore, Bert Olmstead, Jacques Plante, André Pronovost, Claude Provost, Henri Richard, Dollard St. Laurent, Jean-Guy Talbot, Bob Turner; William Northey (President), Donat Raymond (Chairman), Ken Reardon (Vice President), Frank Selke (Managing Director), Toe Blake (Coach), Hector Dubois, Larry Aubut (Trainers).
Scores: April 6, at Montreal — Montreal 5, Boston 1; April 9, at Montreal — Montreal 1, Boston 0; April 11, at Boston — Montreal 4, Boston 2; April 14, at Boston — Boston 2, Montreal 0; April 16, at Montreal — Montreal 5, Boston 1.

1955-56 — Montreal Canadiens — Butch Bouchard (Captain), Bob Turner, Jean Béliveau, Bert Olmstead, Floyd Curry, Bernie Geoffrion, Jacques Plante, Doug Harvey, Claude Provost, Charlie Hodge, Henri Richard, Tom Johnson, Maurice Richard, Jackie LeClair, Dollard St. Laurent, Don Marshall, Jean-Guy Talbot, Dickie Moore, Ken Mosdell; Donat Raymond (President), Frank Selke (Managing Director), D'Alton Coleman, William Northey (Vice Presidents), Ken Reardon (Assistant Manager), Toe Blake (Coach), Hector Dubois, Gaston Bettez (Trainers).
Scores: March 31, at Montreal — Montreal 6, Detroit 4; April 3, at Montreal — Montreal 5, Detroit 1; April 5, at Detroit — Detroit 3, Montreal 1; April 8, at Detroit — Montreal 3, Detroit 0; April 10, at Montreal — Montreal 3, Detroit 1.

1954-55 — Detroit Red Wings — Dutch Reibel, Terry Sawchuk, Jim Hay, Vic Stasiuk, Johnny Wilson, Gordie Howe, Red Kelly, Tony Leswick, Ted Lindsay (Captain), Marty Pavelich, Marcel Pronovost, Marcel Bonin, Alex Delvecchio, Bill Dineen, Bob Goldham, Benny Woit, Larry Hillman, Glen Skov; Bruce Norris (President), Marguerite Norris (President), Jack Adams (Manager), Jimmy Skinner (Coach), John Mitchell (Chief Scout), Fred Huber (Publicity Director), Carl Mattson, Lefty Wilson (Trainers).
Scores: April 3, at Detroit — Detroit 4, Montreal 2; April 5, at Detroit — Detroit 7, Montreal 1; April 7, at Montreal — Montreal 4, Detroit 2; April 9, at Montreal — Montreal 5, Detroit 3; April 10, at Detroit — Detroit 5, Montreal 1; April 12, at Montreal — Montreal 6, Detroit 3; April 14, at Detroit — Detroit 3, Montreal 1.

1953-54 — Detroit Red Wings — Marty Pavelich, Jimmy Peters, Marcel Pronovost, Metro Prystai, Dutch Reibel, Terry Sawchuk, Bob Goldham, Gordie Howe, Earl Johnson, Red Kelly, Tony Leswick, Ted Lindsay (Captain), Keith Allen, Al Arbour, Alex Delvecchio, Bill Dineen, Gilles Dube, Dave Gatherum, Glen Skov, Johnny Wilson, Benny Woit; Bruce Norris (Owner), Marguerite Norris (President), Jack Adams (Manager), Tommy Ivan (Coach), John Mitchell (Chief Scout), Fred Huber (Publicity Director), Carl Mattson, Lefty Wilson (Trainers), Wally Crossman (Assistant Trainer).
Scores: April 4, at Detroit — Detroit 3, Montreal 1; April 6, at Detroit — Montreal 3, Detroit 1; April 8, at Montreal — Detroit 5, Montreal 2; April 10, at Montreal — Detroit 2, Montreal 0; April 11, at Detroit — Montreal 1, Detroit 0; April 13, at Montreal — Montreal 4, Detroit 1; April 16, at Detroit — Detroit 2, Montreal 1.

1952-53 — Montreal Canadiens — Floyd Curry, Bernie Geoffrion, Bert Olmstead, Paul Meger, Dick Gamble, Dickie Moore, Tom Johnson, Bud MacPherson, Billy Reay, Ken Mosdell, Paul Masnick, John McCormack, Butch Bouchard (Captain), Maurice Richard, Elmer Lach, Gerry McNeil, Doug Harvey, Dollard St. Laurent, Jacques Plante, Lorne Davis, Calum MacKay, Eddie Mazur, Donat Raymond (President), Dalton Coleman (Director), William Northey (Special Advisor), Frank Selke (Manager), Dick Irvin (Coach), Hector Dubois, Gaston Bettez (Trainers).
Scores: April 9, at Montreal — Montreal 4, Boston 2; April 11, at Montreal — Boston 4, Montreal 1; April 12, at Boston — Montreal 3, Boston 0; April 14, at Boston — Montreal 7, Boston 3; April 16, at Montreal — Montreal 1, Boston 0.

1951-52 — Detroit Red Wings — Metro Prystai, Leo Reise Jr., Terry Sawchuk, Enio Sclisizzi, Glen Skov, Vic Stasiuk, Gordie Howe, Red Kelly, Tony Leswick, Ted Lindsay, Marty Pavelich, Marcel Pronovost, Sid Abel (Captain), Alex Delvecchio, Fred Glover, Bob Goldham, Glenn Hall, Benny Woit, Johnny Wilson, Larry Zeidel; James Norris (President), Bruce Norris (Owner), Jack Adams (Manager), Tommy Ivan (Coach), Fred Huber (Publicity Director), Carson Cooper (Scout), Carl Mattson, Lefty Wilson (Trainers), Wally Crossman (Assistant Trainer).
Scores: April 10, at Montreal — Detroit 3, Montreal 1; April 12, at Montreal — Detroit 2, Montreal 1; April 13, at Detroit — Detroit 3, Montreal 0; April 15, at Detroit — Detroit 3, Montreal 0.

1950-51 — Toronto Maple Leafs — Bill Barilko, Max Bentley, Hugh Bolton, Turk Broda, Fern Flaman, Cal Gardner, Bob Hassard, Bill Juzda, Ted Kennedy (Captain), Joe Klukay, Danny Lewicki, Fleming MacKell, Howie Meeker, Gus Mortson, John McCormack, Al Rollins, Tod Sloan, Sid Smith, Jimmy Thomson, Ray Timgren, Harry Watson; Joe Primeau (Coach), Bill MacBrien (Chairman), Conn Smythe (President/Manager), Hap Day (Assistant Manager), George McCullagh, J.Y. Murdoch (Vice Presidents), J.P. Bickell, Ed Bickle (Directors), Tim Daly (Trainer), Archie Campbell, Tommy Naylor (Assistant Trainers), Dr. Norman Delarue, Dr. James Murray, Dr. Horace MacIntyre (Club Doctors), Ed Fitkin (Publicity Director), Squib Walker (Chief Scout).
Scores: April 11, at Toronto — Toronto 3, Montreal 2; April 14, at Toronto — Montreal 3, Toronto 2; April 17, at Montreal — Toronto 2, Montreal 1; April 19, at Montreal — Toronto 3, Montreal 2; April 21, at Toronto — Toronto 3, Montreal 2.

1949-50 — Detroit Red Wings — Sid Abel (Captain), Pete Babando, Steve Black, Joe Carveth, Gerry Couture, Al Dewsbury, Lee Fogolin, George Gee, Gordie Howe, Red Kelly, Ted Lindsay, Harry Lumley, Clare Martin, Jim McFadden, Max McNab, Marty Pavelich, Jimmy Peters, Marcel Pronovost, Leo Reise Jr., Jack Stewart, Johnny Wilson, Larry Wilson, Doug McKay; James Norris (President), James Norris Jr. (Vice President), Arthur Wirtz (Secretary Treasurer), Jack Adams (Manager), Tommy Ivan (Coach), Fred Huber Jr. (Publicity Director), Carson Cooper (Head Scout), Carl Mattson (Trainer), Walter Humeniuk (Assistant Trainer).
Scores: April 11, at Detroit — Detroit 4, NY Rangers 1; April 13, at Toronto* — NY Rangers 3, Detroit 1; April 15, at Toronto* — Detroit 4, NY Rangers 0; April 18, at Detroit — NY Rangers 4, Detroit 3; April 20, at Detroit — NY Rangers 2, Detroit 1; April 22, at Detroit — Detroit 5, NY Rangers 4; April 23, at Detroit — Detroit 4, NY Rangers 3.
*Ice was unavailable in Madison Square Garden and NY Rangers elected to play second and third games on Toronto ice.

1948-49 — Toronto Maple Leafs — Bill Barilko, Max Bentley, Garth Boesch, Turk Broda, Bob Dawes, Bill Ezinicki, Cal Gardner, Bill Juzda, Ted Kennedy (Captain), Joe Klukay, Vic Lynn, Howie Meeker, Don Metz, Fleming MacKell, Gus Mortson, Sid Smith, Harry Taylor, Ray Timgren, Jimmy Thomson, Harry Watson; Hap Day (Coach), Bill MacBrien (Chairman), Conn Smythe (President/Manager), George McCullagh, J.Y. Murdoch (Vice Presidents), J.P. Bickell, Ed Bickle (Directors), Tim Daly (Trainer), Archie Campbell (Assistant Trainer), Dr. Norman Delarue, Dr. James Murray, Dr. Horace MacIntyre (Club Doctors), Ed Fitkin (Publicity Director), Squib Walker (Chief Scout), Kerry Day (Mascot).
Scores: April 8, at Detroit — Toronto 3, Detroit 2; April 10, at Detroit — Toronto 3, Detroit 1; April 13, at Toronto — Toronto 3, Detroit 1; April 16, at Toronto — Toronto 3, Detroit 1.

1947-48 — Toronto Maple Leafs — Syl Apps (Captain), Bill Barilko, Max Bentley, Garth Boesch, Turk Broda, Les Costello, Bill Ezinicki, Ted Kennedy, Joe Klukay, Vic Lynn, Howie Meeker, Nick Metz, Don Metz, Gus Mortson, Phil Samis, Sid Smith, Wally Stanowski, Jimmy Thomson, Harry Watson; Hap Day (Coach), Conn Smythe (Manager), Tim Daly (Trainer).
Scores: April 7, at Toronto — Toronto 5, Detroit 3; April 10, at Toronto — Toronto 4, Detroit 2; April 11, at Detroit — Toronto 2, Detroit 0; April 14, at Detroit — Toronto 7, Detroit 2.

1946-47 — Toronto Maple Leafs — Turk Broda, Garth Boesch, Gus Mortson, Jimmy Thomson, Wally Stanowski, Bill Barilko, Harry Watson, Bud Poile, Ted Kennedy, Syl Apps (Captain), Don Metz, Nick Metz, Bill Ezinicki, Vic Lynn, Howie Meeker, Gaye Stewart, Joe Klukay, Gus Bodnar, Bob Goldham; Conn Smythe (Manager), Hap Day (Coach), Tim Daly (Trainer).
Scores: April 8, at Montreal — Montreal 6, Toronto 0; April 10, at Montreal — Toronto 4, Montreal 0; April 12, at Toronto — Toronto 4, Montreal 2; April 15, at Toronto — Toronto 2, Montreal 1; April 17, at Montreal — Montreal 3, Toronto 1; April 19, at Toronto — Toronto 2, Montreal 1.

1945-46 — Montreal Canadiens — Elmer Lach, Toe Blake (Captain), Maurice Richard, Bob Fillion, Dutch Hiller, Murph Chamberlain, Ken Mosdell, Buddy O'Connor, Glen Harmon, Jimmy Peters, Butch Bouchard, Billy Reay, Ken Reardon, Leo Lamoureux, Frank Eddolls, Gerry Plamondon, Joe Benoit, Bill Durnan; Tommy Gorman (Manager), Dick Irvin (Coach), Ernie Cook (Trainer).
Scores: March 30, at Montreal — Montreal 4, Boston 3; April 2, at Montreal — Montreal 3, Boston 2; April 4, at Boston — Montreal 4, Boston 2; April 7, at Boston — Boston 3, Montreal 2; April 9, at Montreal — Montreal 6, Boston 3.

1944-45 — Toronto Maple Leafs — Don Metz, Frank McCool, Wally Stanowski, Reg Hamilton, Moe Morris, John McCreedy, Tom O'Neill, Ted Kennedy, Babe Pratt, Gus Bodnar, Art Jackson, Jack McLean, Mel Hill, Nick Metz, Bob Davidson (Captain), Sweeney Schriner, Lorne Carr, Pete Backor, Ross Johnstone; Conn Smythe (Manager), Frank Selke (Business Manager), Hap Day (Coach), Tim Daly (Trainer).
Scores: April 6, at Detroit — Toronto 1, Detroit 0; April 8, at Detroit — Toronto 2, Detroit 0; April 12, at Toronto — Toronto 1, Detroit 0; April 14, at Toronto — Detroit 5, Toronto 3; April 19, at Detroit — Detroit 2, Toronto 0; April 21, at Toronto — Detroit 1, Toronto 0; April 22, at Detroit — Toronto 2, Detroit 1.

1943-44 — Montreal Canadiens — Toe Blake (Captain), Maurice Richard, Elmer Lach, Ray Getliffe, Murph Chamberlain, Phil Watson, Butch Bouchard, Glen Harmon, Buddy O'Connor, Gerry Heffernan, Mike McMahon, Leo Lamoureux, Fern Majeau, Bob Fillion, Bill Durnan; Tommy Gorman (Manager), Dick Irvin (Coach), Ernie Cook (Trainer).
Scores: April 4, at Montreal — Montreal 5, Chicago 1; April 6, at Chicago — Montreal 3, Chicago 1; April 9, at Chicago — Montreal 3, Chicago 2; April 13, at Montreal — Montreal 5, Chicago 4.

1942-43 — Detroit Red Wings — Jack Stewart, Jimmy Orlando, Sid Abel (captain), Alex Motter, Harry Watson, Joe Carveth, Mud Bruneteau, Eddie Wares, Johnny Mowers, Cully Simon, Don Grosso, Carl Liscombe, Connie Brown, Syd Howe, Les Douglas, Harold Jackson, Joe Fisher, Adam Brown; Jack Adams (Manager), Ebbie Goodfellow (Playing Coach), Honey Walker (Trainer).
Scores: April 1, at Detroit — Detroit 6, Boston 2; April 4, at Detroit — Detroit 4, Boston 3; April 7, at Boston — Detroit 4, Boston 0; April 8, at Boston — Detroit 2, Boston 0.

1941-42 — Toronto Maple Leafs — Wally Stanowski, Syl Apps (Captain), Bob Goldham, Gordie Drillon, Hank Goldup, Ernie Dickens, Sweeney Schriner, Bucko McDonald, Bob Davidson, Nick Metz, Bingo Kampman, Don Metz, Gaye Stewart, Turk Broda, John McCreedy, Lorne Carr, Pete Langelle, Billy Taylor, Reg Hamilton; Conn Smythe (Manager), Hap Day (Coach), Frank Selke (Business Manager), Tim Daly (Trainer).
Scores: April 4, at Toronto — Detroit 3, Toronto 2; April 7, at Toronto — Detroit 4, Toronto 2; April 9, at Detroit — Detroit 5, Toronto 2; April 12, at Detroit — Toronto 4, Detroit 3; April 14, at Toronto — Toronto 9, Detroit 3; April 16, at Detroit — Toronto 3, Detroit 0; April 18, at Toronto — Toronto 3, Detroit 1.

1940-41 — Boston Bruins — Bill Cowley, Des Smith, Dit Clapper (Captain), Frank Brimsek, Flash Hollett, Jack Crawford, Bobby Bauer, Pat McReavy, Herb Cain, Mel Hill, Milt Schmidt, Woody Dumart, Roy Conacher, Terry Reardon, Art Jackson, Eddie Wiseman, Jack Shewchuck; Art Ross (Manager), Cooney Weiland (Coach), Win Green (Trainer).
Scores: April 6, at Boston — Detroit 2, Boston 3; April 8, at Boston — Detroit 1, Boston 2; April 10, at Detroit — Boston 4, Detroit 2; April 12, at Detroit — Boston 3, Detroit 1.

1939-40 — New York Rangers — Dave Kerr, Art Coulter (Captain), Ott Heller, Alex Shibicky, Mac Colville, Neil Colville, Phil Watson, Lynn Patrick, Clint Smith, Muzz Patrick, Babe Pratt, Bryan Hextall, Kilby MacDonald, Dutch Hiller, Alf Pike, Stan Smith; Lester Patrick (Manager), Frank Boucher (Coach), Harry Westerby (Trainer).
Scores: April 2, at New York — NY Rangers 2, Toronto 1; April 3, at New York — NY Rangers 6, Toronto 2; April 6, at Toronto — NY Rangers 1, Toronto 2; April 9, at Toronto — NY Rangers 0, Toronto 3; April 11, at Toronto — NY Rangers 2, Toronto 1; April 13, at Toronto — NY Rangers 3, Toronto 2.

1938-39 — Boston Bruins — Bobby Bauer, Mel Hill, Flash Hollett, Roy Conacher, Gord Pettinger, Charlie Sands, Milt Schmidt, Woody Dumart, Jack Crawford, Ray Getliffe, Frank Brimsek, Eddie Shore, Dit Clapper, Bill Cowley, Jack Portland, Red Hamill, Harry Frost, Cooney Weiland (Captain); Art Ross (Manager/Coach), Win Green (Trainer).
Scores: April 6, at Boston — Toronto 1, Boston 2; April 9, at Boston — Toronto 3, Boston 2; April 11, at Toronto — Toronto 1, Boston 3; April 13, at Toronto — Toronto 0, Boston 2; April 16, at Boston — Toronto 1, Boston 3.

1937-38 — Chicago Black Hawks — Art Wiebe, Carl Voss, Harold Jackson, Mike Karakas, Mush March, Jack Shill, Earl Seibert, Cully Dahlstrom, Alex Levinsky, Johnny Gottselig (Captain), Lou Trudel, Pete Palangio, Bill MacKenzie, Doc Romnes, Paul Thompson, Roger Jenkins, Alfie Moore, Bert Connelly, Virgil Johnson, Paul Goodman; Bill Tobin (Vice President), Bill Stewart (Coach), Eddie Froelich (Trainer).
Scores: April 5, at Toronto — Chicago 3, Toronto 1; April 7, at Toronto — Chicago 1, Toronto 5; April 10, at Chicago — Chicago 2, Toronto 1; April 12, at Chicago — Chicago 4, Toronto 1.

1936-37 — Detroit Red Wings — Normie Smith, Pete Kelly, Larry Aurie, Herbie Lewis, Hec Kilrea, Mud Bruneteau, Syd Howe, Wally Kilrea, Jimmy Franks, Bucko McDonald, Gord Pettinger, Ebbie Goodfellow, John Gallagher, Ralph Bowman, John Sorrell, Marty Barry, Earl Robertson, John Sherf, Howie Mackie, Rolly Roulston, Doug Young (Captain); Jack Adams (Manager/Coach), Honey Walker (Trainer).
Scores: April 6, at New York — Detroit 1, NY Rangers 5; April 8, at Detroit — Detroit 4, NY Rangers 2; April 11, at Detroit — Detroit 0, NY Rangers 1; April 13, at Detroit — Detroit 1, NY Rangers 0; April 15, at Detroit — Detroit 3, NY Rangers 0.

1935-36 — Detroit Red Wings — John Sorrell, Syd Howe, Marty Barry, Herbie Lewis, Mud Bruneteau, Wally Kilrea, Hec Kilrea, Gord Pettinger, Bucko McDonald, Ralph Bowman, Pete Kelly, Doug Young (Captain), Ebbie Goodfellow, Normie Smith, Larry Aurie; Jack Adams (Manager/Coach), Honey Walker (Trainer).
Scores: April 5, at Detroit — Detroit 3, Toronto 1; April 7, at Detroit — Detroit 9, Toronto 4; April 9, at Toronto — Detroit 3, Toronto 4; April 11, at Toronto — Detroit 3, Toronto 2.

1934-35 — Montreal Maroons — Lionel Conacher, Cy Wentworth, Alec Connell, Toe Blake, Stewart Evans, Earl Robinson, Bill Miller, Dave Trottier, Jimmy Ward, Baldy Northcott, Hooley Smith (Captain), Russ Blinco, Al Shields, Sammy McManus, Gus Marker, Bob Gracie, Herb Cain, Dutch Gainor; Tommy Gorman (Manager/Coach), Bill O'Brien (Trainer).
Scores: April 4, at Toronto — Mtl. Maroons 3, Toronto 2; April 6, at Toronto — Mtl. Maroons 3, Toronto 1; April 9, at Montreal — Mtl. Maroons 4, Toronto 1.

1933-34 — Chicago Black Hawks — Clarence Abel, Rosie Couture, Lou Trudel, Lionel Conacher, Paul Thompson, Leroy Goldsworthy, Art Coulter, Roger Jenkins, Don McFadyen, Tom Cook, Doc Romnes, Johnny Gottselig, Mush March, Johnny Sheppard, Charlie Gardiner (Captain), Bill Kendall, Jack Leswick; Tommy Gorman (Manager/Coach), Eddie Froelich (Trainer).
Scores: April 3, at Detroit — Chicago 2, Detroit 1; April 5, at Detroit — Chicago 4, Detroit 1; April 8, at Chicago — Detroit 5, Chicago 2; April 10, at Chicago — Chicago 1, Detroit 0.

1932-33 — New York Rangers — Ching Johnson, Butch Keeling, Frank Boucher, Art Somers, Babe Siebert, Bun Cook, Andy Aitkenhead, Ott Heller, Oscar Asmundson, Gord Pettinger, Doug Brennan, Cecil Dillon, Bill Cook (Captain), Murray Murdoch, Earl Seibert; Lester Patrick (Manager/Coach), Harry Westerby (Trainer).
Scores: April 4, at New York — NY Rangers 5, Toronto 1; April 8, at Toronto — NY Rangers 3, Toronto 1; April 11, at Toronto — Toronto 3, NY Rangers 2; April 13, at Toronto — NY Rangers 1, Toronto 0.

1931-32 — Toronto Maple Leafs — Charlie Conacher, Busher Jackson, King Clancy, Andy Blair, Red Horner, Lorne Chabot, Alex Levinsky, Joe Primeau, Harold Darragh, Baldy Cotton, Frank Finnigan, Hap Day (Captain), Ace Bailey, Bob Gracie, Fred Robertson, Earl Miller; Conn Smythe (Manager), Dick Irvin (Coach), Tim Daly (Trainer).
Scores: April 5, at New York — Toronto 6, NY Rangers 4; April 7, at Boston* — Toronto 6, NY Rangers 2; April 9, at Toronto — Toronto 6, NY Rangers 4.

1930-31 — Montreal Canadiens — George Hainsworth, Wildor Larochelle, Marty Burke, Sylvio Mantha (Captain), Howie Morenz, Johnny Gagnon, Aurel Joliat, Armand Mondou, Pit Lepine, Albert Leduc, Georges Mantha, Art Lesieur, Nick Wasnie, Gus Rivers, Jean Pusie; Léo Dandurand (Manager), Cecil Hart (Coach), Ed Dufour (Trainer).
Scores: April 3, at Chicago — Montreal 2, Chicago 1; April 5, at Chicago — Chicago 2, Montreal 1; April 9, at Montreal — Chicago 3, Montreal 2; April 11, at Montreal — Montreal 4, Chicago 2; April 14, at Montreal — Montreal 2, Chicago 0.

1929-30 — Montreal Canadiens — George Hainsworth, Marty Burke, Sylvio Mantha (Captain), Howie Morenz, Bert McCaffrey, Aurel Joliat, Albert Leduc, Pit Lepine, Wildor Larochelle, Nick Wasnie, Gerry Carson, Armand Mondou, Georges Mantha, Gus Rivers; Léo Dandurand (Manager), Cecil Hart (Coach), Ed Dufour (Trainer).
Scores: April 1, at Boston — Montreal 3, Boston 0; April 3, at Montreal — Montreal 4, Boston 3.

1928-29 — Boston Bruins — Tiny Thompson, Eddie Shore, Lionel Hitchman (Captain), Percy Galbraith, Mickey MacKay, Red Green, Dutch Gainor, Harry Oliver, Eddie Rodden, Dit Clapper, Cooney Weiland, Lloyd Klein, Cy Denneny, Bill Carson, George Owen, Myles Lane; Art Ross (Manager/Coach), Win Green (Trainer).
Scores: March 28, at Boston — Boston 2, NY Rangers 0; March 29, at New York — Boston 2, NY Rangers 1.

1927-28 — New York Rangers — Lorne Chabot, Clarence Abel, Leo Bourgeault, Ching Johnson, Bill Cook (Captain), Bun Cook, Frank Boucher, Bill Boyd, Murray Murdoch, Paul Thompson, Alex Gray, Joe Miller, Patsy Callighen; Lester Patrick (Manager/Coach), Harry Westerby (Trainer).
Scores: April 5, at Montreal — Mtl. Maroons 2, NY Rangers 0; April 7, at Montreal — NY Rangers 2, Mtl. Maroons 1; April 10, at Montreal — Mtl. Maroons 2, NY Rangers 0; April 12, at Montreal — NY Rangers 1, Mtl. Maroons 0; April 14, at Montreal — NY Rangers 2, Mtl. Maroons 1.

1926-27 — Ottawa Senators — Alec Connell, King Clancy, Georges Boucher (Captain), Ed Gorman, Frank Finnigan, Alex Smith, Hec Kilrea, Hooley Smith, Cy Denneny, Frank Nighbor, Jack Adams, Milt Halliday; Dave Gill (Manager/Coach).
Scores: April 7, at Boston — Ottawa 0, Boston 0; April 9, at Boston — Ottawa 3, Boston 1; April 11, at Ottawa — Boston 1, Ottawa 1; April 13, at Ottawa — Ottawa 3, Boston 1.

1925-26 — Montreal Maroons — Clint Benedict, Reg Noble, Frank Carson, Dunc Munro (Captain), Nels Stewart, Punch Broadbent, Babe Siebert, Chuck Dinsmore, Merlyn Phillips, Hobie Kitchen, Sam Rothschild, Albert Holway, George Horne, Bernie Brophy; Eddie Gerard (Manager/Coach), Bill O'Brien (Trainer).
Scores: March 30, at Montreal — Mtl. Maroons 3, Victoria 0; April 1, at Montreal — Mtl. Maroons 3, Victoria 0; April 3, at Montreal — Victoria 3, Mtl. Maroons 2; April 6, at Montreal — Mtl. Maroons 2, Victoria 0.

The series in the spring of 1926 ended the annual playoffs between the champions of the East and the champions of the West. Since 1926-27 the annual playoffs in the National Hockey League have decided the Stanley Cup champions.

1924-25 — Victoria Cougars — Hap Holmes, Clem Loughlin (Captain), Gord Fraser, Frank Fredrickson, Jack Walker, Gizzy Hart, Harold Halderson, Frank Foyston, Wally Elmer, Harry Meeking, Jocko Anderson; Lester Patrick (Manager/Coach).
Scores: March 21, at Victoria — Victoria 5, Montreal 2; March 23, at Vancouver — Victoria 3, Montreal 1; March 27, at Victoria — Montreal 4, Victoria 2; March 30, at Victoria — Victoria 6, Montreal 1.

1923-24 — Montreal Canadiens — Georges Vezina, Sprague Cleghorn (Captain), Billy Coutu, Howie Morenz, Aurel Joliat, Billy Boucher, Odie Cleghorn, Sylvio Mantha, Bobby Boucher, Billy Bell, Billy Cameron, Joe Malone, Charles Fortier; Leo Dandurand (Manager/Coach).
Scores: March 22, at Montreal — Montreal 6, Cgy. Tigers 1; March 25, at Ottawa* — Montreal 3, Cgy. Tigers 0.

* Game transferred to Ottawa to benefit from artificial ice surface.

1922-23 — Ottawa Senators — Georges Boucher, Lionel Hitchman, Frank Nighbor, King Clancy, Harry Helman, Clint Benedict, Jack Darragh, Eddie Gerard (Captain), Cy Denneny, Punch Broadbent; Tommy Gorman (Manager), Pete Green (Coach), F. Dolan (Trainer).
Scores: March 29, at Vancouver — Ottawa 2, Edm. Eskimos 1; March 31, at Vancouver — Ottawa 1, Edm. Eskimos 0.

1921-22 — Toronto St. Patricks — Ted Stackhouse, Corb Denneny, Rod Smylie, Lloyd Andrews, John Ross Roach, Harry Cameron, Billy Stuart, Babe Dye, Ken Randall, Reg Noble (Captain), Eddie Gerard (borrowed for one game from Ottawa), Stan Jackson, Ivan Mitchell; Charlie Querrie (Manager), George O'Donoghue (Coach).
Scores: March 17, at Toronto — Van. Millionaires 4, Toronto 3; March 21, at Toronto — Toronto 2, Van. Millionaires 1; March 23, at Toronto — Van. Millionaires 3, Toronto 0; March 25, at Toronto — Toronto 6, Van. Millionaires 0; March 28, at Toronto — Toronto 5, Van. Millionaires 1.

1920-21 — Ottawa Senators — Jack MacKell, Jack Darragh, Morley Bruce, Georges Boucher, Eddie Gerard (Captain), Clint Benedict, Sprague Cleghorn, Frank Nighbor, Punch Broadbent, Cy Denneny, Leth Graham; Tommy Gorman (Manager), Pete Green (Coach), F. Dolan (Trainer).
Scores: March 21, at Vancouver — Van. Millionaires 2, Ottawa 1; March 24, at Vancouver — Ottawa 4, Van. Millionaires 3; March 28, at Vancouver — Ottawa 3, Van. Millionaires 2; March 31, at Vancouver — Van. Millionaires 3, Ottawa 2; April 4, at Vancouver — Ottawa 2, Van. Millionaires 1

1919-20 — Ottawa Senators — Jack MacKell, Jack Darragh, Morley Bruce, Horace Merrill, Georges Boucher, Eddie Gerard (Captain), Clint Benedict, Sprague Cleghorn, Frank Nighbor, Punch Broadbent, Cy Denneny, Tommy Gorman (Manager), Pete Green (Coach).
Scores: March 22, at Ottawa — Ottawa 3, Seattle 2; March 24, at Ottawa — Ottawa 3, Seattle 0; March 27, at Ottawa — Seattle 3, Ottawa 1; March 30, at Toronto* — Seattle 5, Ottawa 2; April 1, at Toronto* — Ottawa 6, Seattle 1.

* Games transferred to Toronto to benefit from artificial ice surface.

1918-19 — No decision, Series halted by Spanish influenza epidemic, illness of several players and death of Joe Hall of Montreal Canadiens from the flu. Five games had been played when the series was halted, each team having won two and tied one. Final scores are listed below.
Scores: March 19, at Seattle — Seattle 7, Montreal 0; March 22, at Seattle — Montreal 4, Seattle 2; March 24, at Seattle — Seattle 7, Montreal 2; March 26, at Seattle — Montreal 0, Seattle 0; March 30, at Seattle — Montreal 4, Seattle 3.

1917-18 — Toronto Arenas — Rusty Crawford, Harry Meeking, Ken Randall (Captain), Corb Denneny, Harry Cameron, Jack Adams, Alf Skinner, Harry Mummery, Hap Holmes, Reg Noble, Sammy Hebert, Jack Marks, Jack Coughlin; Charlie Querrie (Manager), Dick Carroll (Coach), Frank Carroll (Trainer).
Scores: March 20, at Toronto — Toronto 5, Van. Millionaires 3; March 23, at Toronto — Van. Millionaires 6, Toronto 4; March 26, at Toronto — Toronto 6, Van. Millionaires 3; March 28, at Toronto — Van. Millionaires 8, Toronto 1; March 30, at Toronto — Toronto 2, Van. Millionaires 1.

1916-17 — Seattle Metropolitans — Hap Holmes, Ed Carpenter, Cully Wilson, Jack Walker, Bernie Morris, Frank Foyston, Roy Rickey, Jim Riley, Bobby Rowe (Captain); Peter Muldoon (Manager).
Scores: March 17, at Seattle — Montreal 8, Seattle 4; March 20, at Seattle — Seattle 6, Montreal 1; March 23, at Seattle — Seattle 4, Montreal 1; March 26, at Seattle — Seattle 9, Montreal 1.

1915-16 — Montreal Canadiens — Georges Vezina, Bert Corbeau, Jack Laviolette, Newsy Lalonde, Louis Berlinquette, Goldie Prodger, Howard McNamara (Captain), Didier Pitre, Skene Ronan, Amos Arbour, Skinner Poulin, Jack Fournier; George Kennedy (Manager).
Scores: March 20, at Montreal — Portland 2, Montreal 0; March 22, at Montreal — Montreal 2, Portland 1; March 25, at Montreal — Montreal 6, Portland 3; March 28, at Montreal — Portland 6, Montreal 5; March 30, at Montreal — Montreal 2, Portland 1.

1914-15 — Vancouver Millionaires — Ken Mallen, Frank Nighbor, Cyclone Taylor, Hugh Lehman, Lloyd Cook, Mickey MacKay, Barney Stanley, Jim Seaborn, Si Griffis (Captain), Johnny Matz; Frank Patrick (Playing Manager).
Scores: March 22, at Vancouver — Van. Millionaires 6, Ottawa 2; March 24, at Vancouver — Van. Millionaires 8, Ottawa 3; March 26, at Vancouver — Van. Millionaires 12, Ottawa 3.

1913-14 — Toronto Blueshirts — Con Corbeau, Roy McGiffin, Jack Walker, George McNamara, Cully Wilson, Frank Foyston, Harry Cameron, Hap Holmes, Scotty Davidson (Captain), Harriston; Jack Marshall (Playing Manager), Frank Carroll, Dick Carroll (Trainers).

Scores: March 14, at Toronto — Toronto 5, Victoria 2; March 17, at Toronto — Toronto 6, Victoria 5; March 19, at Toronto — Toronto 2, Victoria 1.

Prior to 1914, teams could challenge the Stanley Cup champions for the title, thus there was more than one Championship Series played in most of the seasons between 1894 and 1913.

1912-13 — Quebec Bulldogs — Joe Malone (Captain), Joe Hall, Paddy Moran, Harry Mummery, Tommy Smith, Jack Marks, Rusty Crawford, Billy Creighton, Jeff Malone, Rocket Power; M.J. Quinn (Manager), D. Beland (Trainer).
Scores: March 8, at Quebec — Que. Bulldogs 14, Sydney 3; March 10, at Quebec — Que. Bulldogs 6, Sydney 2.

Victoria challenged Quebec but the Bulldogs refused to put the Stanley Cup in competition so the two teams played an exhibition series with Victoria winning two games to one by scores of 7-5, 3-6, 6-1. It was the first meeting between the Eastern champions and the Western champions. The following year, and until the Western Hockey League disbanded after the 1926 playoffs, the Cup went to the winner of the series between East and West.

1911-12 — Quebec Bulldogs — Goldie Prodger, Joe Hall, Walter Rooney, Paddy Moran, Jack Marks, Jack McDonald, Eddie Oatman, George Leonard, Joe Malone (Captain); Charley Nolan (Coach), M.J. Quinn (Manager), D. Beland (Trainer).
Scores: March 11, at Quebec — Que. Bulldogs 9, Moncton 3; March 13, at Quebec — Que. Bulldogs 8, Moncton 0.

1910-11 — Ottawa Senators — Hamby Shore, Percy LeSueur (Captain), Jack Darragh, Bruce Stuart, Marty Walsh, Bruce Ridpath, Fred Lake, Dubbie Kerr, Alex Currie, Horace Gaul.
Scores: March 13, at Ottawa — Ottawa 7, Galt 4; March 16, at Ottawa — Ottawa 13, Port Arthur 4.

1909-10 — (March) **— Montreal Wanderers —** Cecil Blachford, Moose Johnson, Ernie Russell, Riley Hern, Harry Hyland, Jack Marshall, Pud Glass (Captain), Jimmy Gardner; Dickie Boon (Manager).
Scores: March 12, at Montreal — Mtl. Wanderers 7, Berlin (Kitchener) 3.

By winning the 1910 NHA title, the Montreal Wanderers took possession of the Stanley Cup from Ottawa and accepted a challenge from Berlin, 1910 champions of the OPHL

1909-10 — (January) **— Ottawa Senators —** Dubbie Kerr, Fred Lake, Percy LeSueur, Ken Mallen, Bruce Ridpath, Gord Roberts, Hamby Shore, Bruce Stuart (Captain), Marty Walsh.

The Senators accepted two challenges as defending Cup champions. The first was against Galt in a 2-game, total-goals series, and the second was against Edmonton, also a 2-game, total-goals series.
Scores: January 5, at Ottawa — Ottawa 12, Galt 3; January 7, at Ottawa — Ottawa 3, Galt 1; January 18, at Ottawa — Ottawa 8, Edm. Eskimos 4; January 20, at Ottawa — Ottawa 13, Edm. Eskimos 7.

1908-09 — Ottawa Senators — Fred Lake, Percy LeSueur, Cyclone Taylor, Billy Gilmour, Dubbie Kerr, Edgar Dey, Marty Walsh, Bruce Stuart (Captain).

Ottawa, as champions of the Eastern Canada Hockey Association took over the Stanley Cup in 1909 and, although a challenge was accepted by the Cup trustees from Winnipeg Shamrocks, games could not be arranged because of the lateness of the season. No other challenges were made in 1909.

1907-08 — Montreal Wanderers — Riley Hern, Art Ross, Walter Smaill, Pud Glass, Bruce Stuart, Ernie Russell, Moose Johnson, Cecil Blachford (Captain), Tom Hooper, Larry Gilmour, Ernie Liffiton; Dickie Boon (Manager).
Scores: Wanderers accepted four challenges for the Cup: January 9, at Montreal — Mtl. Wanderers 9, Ott. Victorias 3; January 13, at Montreal — Mtl. Wanderers 13, Ott. Victorias 1; March 10, at Montreal — Mtl. Wanderers 11, Wpg. Maple Leafs 5; March 12, at Montreal — Mtl. Wanderers 9, Wpg. Maple Leafs 3; March 14, at Montreal — Mtl. Wanderers 6, Toronto (OPHL) 4. At start of following season, 1908-09, Wanderers were challenged by Edmonton. Results: December 28, at Montreal — Mtl. Wanderers 7, Edm. Eskimos 3; December 30, at Montreal — Edm. Eskimos 7, Mtl. Wanderers 6. Total goals: Mtl. Wanderers 13, Edm. Eskimos 10.

1906-07 — (March 25) **— Montreal Wanderers —** Billy Strachan, Riley Hern, Lester Patrick (Captain), Hod Stuart, Pud Glass, Ernie Russell, Cecil Blachford, Moose Johnson, Rod Kennedy, Jack Marshall; Dickie Boon (Manager).

1906-07 — (March 18) **— Kenora Thistles —** Eddie Giroux, Si Griffis, Tom Hooper, Fred Whitcroft, Alf Smith, Harry Westwick, Roxy Beaudro, Tommy Phillips (Captain), Russell Phillips.
Scores: March 16, at Winnipeg — Kenora 8, Brandon 6; March 18, at Winnipeg — Kenora 4, Brandon 1; March 23, at Winnipeg — Mtl. Wanderers 7, Kenora 2; March 25, at Winnipeg — Kenora 6, Mtl. Wanderers 5. Total goals: Mtl. Wanderers 12, Kenora 8.

1906-07 — (January) **— Kenora Thistles —** Eddie Giroux, Art Ross, Si Griffis, Tom Hooper, Billy McGimsie, Roxy Beaudro, Tommy Phillips (Captain), Joe Hall, Russell Phillips.
Scores: January 17, at Montreal — Kenora 4, Mtl. Wanderers 2; Jan. 21, at Montreal — Kenora 8, Mtl. Wanderers 6.

1906-07 — (December) **— Montreal Wanderers —** Riley Hern, Billy Strachan, Rod Kennedy, Lester Patrick (Captain), Pud Glass, Ernie Russell, Moose Johnson, Cecil Blachford, Dickie Boon (Manager).

1905-06 — (March) **— Montreal Wanderers —** Henri Menard, Billy Strachan, Rod Kennedy, Lester Patrick, Pud Glass, Ernie Russell, Moose Johnson, Cecil Blachford (Captain), Josh Arnold; Dickie Boon (Manager).
Scores: March 14, at Montreal — Mtl. Wanderers 9, Ottawa 1; March 17, at Ottawa — Ottawa 9, Mtl. Wanderers 3. Total goals: Mtl. Wanderers 12, Ottawa 10. Wanderers accepted a challenge from New Glasgow, N.S., prior to the start of the 1906-07 season. Results: December 27, at Montreal — Mtl. Wanderers 10, New Glasgow 3; December 29, at Montreal — Mtl. Wanderers 7, New Glasgow 2.

1905-06 — (February) **— Ottawa Silver Seven —** Harvey Pulford (Captain), Arthur Moore, Harry Westwick, Frank McGee, Alf Smith (Playing Coach), Billy Gilmour, Billy Hague, Harry Smith, Tommy Smith, Coo Dion, Jack Ebbs.
Scores: February 27, at Ottawa — Ottawa 16, Queen's University 7; February 28, at Ottawa — Ottawa 12, Queen's University 7; March 6, at Ottawa — Ottawa 6, Smiths Falls 5; March 8, at Ottawa — Ottawa 8, Smiths Falls 2.

1904-05 — Ottawa Silver Seven — Dave Finnie, Harvey Pulford (Captain), Arthur Moore, Harry Westwick, Frank McGee, Alf Smith (Playing Coach), Billy Gilmour, Frank White, Horace Gaul, Hamby Shore, Bones Allen.
Scores: January 13, at Ottawa — Ottawa 9, Dawson City 2; January 16, at Ottawa — Ottawa 23, Dawson City 2; March 7, at Ottawa — Rat Portage 9, Ottawa 3; March 9, at Ottawa — Ottawa 4, Rat Portage 2; March 11, at Ottawa — Ottawa 5, Rat Portage 4.

1903-04 — Ottawa Silver Seven — Suddy Gilmour, Arthur Moore, Frank McGee, Bouse Hutton, Billy Gilmour, Jim McGee, Harry Westwick, Harvey Pulford (Captain), Scott, Alf Smith (Playing Coach).
Scores: December 30, at Ottawa — Ottawa 9, Wpg. Rowing Club 1; January 1, at Ottawa — Wpg. Rowing Club 6, Ottawa 2; January 4, at Ottawa — Ottawa 2, Wpg. Rowing Club 0. February 23, at Ottawa — Ottawa 6, Tor. Marlboros 3; February 25, at Ottawa — Ottawa 11, Tor. Marlboros 2; March 2, at Montreal — Ottawa 5, Mtl. Wanderers 5. Following the tie game, a new two-game series was ordered to be played in Ottawa but the Wanderers refused unless the tie game was replayed in Montreal. When no settlement could be reached, the series was abandoned and Ottawa retained the Cup and accepted a two-game challenge from Brandon. Results: (both games at Ottawa), March 9, Ottawa 6, Brandon 3; March 11, Ottawa 9, Brandon 3.

1902-03 — (March) — Ottawa Silver Seven — Suddy Gilmour, Percy Sims, Bouse Hutton, Dave Gilmour, Billy Gilmour, Harry Westwick, Frank McGee, F.H. Wood, A.A. Fraser, Charles Spittal, Harvey Pulford (Captain), Arthur Moore; Alf Smith (Coach).
Scores: March 7, at Montreal — Ottawa 1, Mtl. Victorias 1; March 10, at Ottawa — Ottawa 8, Mtl. Victorias 0. Total goals: Ottawa 9, Mtl. Victorias 1; March 12, at Ottawa — Ottawa 6, Rat Portage 2; March 14, at Ottawa — Ottawa 4, Rat Portage 2.

1902-03 — (February) — Montreal AAA — Tom Hodge, Dickie Boon, Billy Nicholson, Tommy Phillips, Art Hooper, Billy Bellingham, Jack Marshall, Jimmy Gardner, Cecil Blachford, George Smith.
Scores: January 29, at Montreal — Mtl. AAA 8, Wpg. Victorias 1; January 31, at Montreal — Wpg. Victorias 2, Mtl. AAA 2; February 2, at Montreal — Wpg. Victorias 4, Mtl. AAA 2; February 4, at Montreal — Mtl. AAA 5, Wpg. Victorias 1.

1901-02 — (March) — Montreal AAA — Tom Hodge, Dickie Boon, Billy Nicholson, Art Hooper, Billy Bellingham, Jack Marshall, Roland Elliot, Jimmy Gardner.
Scores: March 13, at Winnipeg — Wpg. Victorias 1, Mtl. AAA 0; March 15, at Winnipeg — Mtl. AAA 5, Wpg. Victorias 0; March 17, at Winnipeg — Mtl. AAA 2, Wpg. Victorias 1.

1901-02 — (January) — Winnipeg Victorias — Burke Wood, Tony Gingras, Charles Johnstone, Rod Flett, Magnus Flett, Dan Bain (Captain), Fred Scanlon, F. Cadham, Art Brown.
Scores: January 21, at Winnipeg — Wpg. Victorias 5, Tor Wellingtons 3; January 23, at Winnipeg — Wpg. Victorias 5, Tor. Wellingtons 3.

1900-01 — Winnipeg Victorias — Burke Wood, Jack Marshall, Tony Gingras, Charles Johnstone, Rod Flett, Magnus Flett, Dan Bain (Captain), Art Brown, George Carruthers.
Scores: January 29, at Montreal — Wpg. Victorias 4, Mtl. Shamrocks 3; January 31, at Montreal — Wpg. Victorias 2, Mtl. Shamrocks 1.

1899-1900 — Montreal Shamrocks — oe McKenna, Frank Tansey, Frank Wall, Art Farrell, Fred Scanlon, Harry Trihey (Captain), Jack Brannen.
Scores: February 12, at Montreal — Mtl. Shamrocks 4, Wpg. Victorias 3; February 14, at Montreal — Wpg. Victorias 3, Mtl. Shamrocks 2; February 16, at Montreal — Mtl. Shamrocks 5, Wpg. Victorias 4; March 5, at Montreal — Mtl. Shamrocks 10, Halifax 2; March 7, at Montreal — Mtl. Shamrocks 11, Halifax 0.

1898-99 — (March) — Montreal Shamrocks — Joe McKenna, Frank Tansey, Frank Wall, Harry Trihey (Captain), Art Farrell, Fred Scanlon, Jack Brannen, John Dobby, Charles Hoerner.
Scores: March 14, at Montreal — Mtl. Shamrocks 6, Queen's University 2.

1898-99 — (February) — Montreal Victorias — Gordon Lewis, Mike Grant, Graham Drinkwater (Captain), Cam Davidson, Bob McDougall, Ernie McLea, Frank Richardson, Jack Ewing, Russell Bowie, Douglas Acer, Fred McRobie.
Scores: February 15, at Montreal — Mtl. Victorias 2, Wpg. Victorias 1; February 18, at Montreal — Mtl. Victorias 3, Wpg. Victorias 2.

1897-98 — Montreal Victorias — Gordon Lewis, Hartland McDougall, Mike Grant, Graham Drinkwater, Cam Davidson, Bob McDougall, Ernie McLea, Frank Richardson (Captain), Jack Ewing.

1896-97 — Montreal Victorias — Gordon Lewis, Harold Henderson, Mike Grant (Captain), Cam Davidson, Graham Drinkwater, Bob McDougall, Ernie McLea, Shirley Davidson, Hartland McDougall, Jack Ewing, Percy Molson, David Gillilan, Harry Massey.
Scores: December 27, at Montreal — Mtl. Victorias 15, Ott. Capitals 2.

1895-96 — (December) — Montreal Victorias — Harold Henderson, Mike Grant (Captain), Bob McDougall, Graham Drinkwater, Shirley Davidson, Hartland McDougall, Ernie McLea, Cam Davidson, David Gillilan, Stanley Willett, Gordon Lewis, W. Wallace.
Scores: December 30, at Winnipeg — Mtl. Victorias 6, Wpg. Victorias 5.

1895-96 — (February) — Winnipeg Victorias — Whitey Merritt, Rod Flett, Fred Higginbotham, Jack Armytage (Captain), Tote Campbell, Dan Bain, Charles Johnstone, Attie Howard.
Scores: February 14, at Montreal — Wpg. Victorias 2, Mtl. Victorias 0.

1894-95 — Montreal Victorias — Robert Jones, Harold Henderson, Mike Grant (Captain), Shirley Davidson, Hartland McDougall, Bob McDougall, Norman Rankin, Graham Drinkwater, Roland Elliot, William Pullan, Arthur Fenwick, A. McDougall.

1893-94 — Montreal AAA — Herb Collins, Allan Cameron, George James, Billy Barlow, Clare Mussen, Archie Hodgson, Haviland Routh, Alex Irving, James Stewart, E. O'Brien, Toad Wand, Alex Kingan.
Scores: March 17, at Mtl. Victorias — Mtl. AAA 3, Mtl. Victorias 2; March 22, at Montreal — Mtl. AAA 3, Ott. Capitals 1.

1892-93 — Montreal AAA — Tom Paton, James Stewart, Allan Cameron, Haviland Routh, Archie Hodgson, Billy Barlow, Alex Irving, Alex Kingan, G.S. Low.

All-Time NHL Playoff Formats

1917-18 — The regular-season was split into two halves. The winners of both halves faced each other in a two-game, total-goals series for the NHL championship and the right to meet the PCHA champion in the best-of-five Stanley Cup Finals.

1918-19 — Same as 1917-18, except that the Stanley Cup Finals was extended to a best-of-seven series.

1919-20 — Same as 1917-1918, except that Ottawa won both halves of the split regular-season schedule to earn an automatic berth into the best-of-five Stanley Cup Finals against the PCHA champions.

1921-22 — The top two teams at the conclusion of the regular-season faced each other in a two-game, total-goals series for the NHL championship. The NHL champion then moved on to play the winner of the PCHA-WCHL playoff series in the best-of-five Stanley Cup Finals.

1922-23 — The top two teams at the conclusion of the regular-season faced each other in a two-game, total-goals series for the NHL championship. The NHL champion then moved on to play the PCHA champion in the best-of-three Stanley Cup Semi-Finals, and the winner of the Semi-Finals played the WCHL champion, which had been given a bye, in the best-of-three Stanley Cup Finals.

1923-24 — The top two teams at the conclusion of the regular-season faced each other in a two-game, total-goals series for the NHL championship. The NHL champion then moved on to play the loser of the PCHA-WCHL playoff (the winner of the PCHA-WCHL playoff earned a bye into the Stanley Cup Finals) in the best-of-three Stanley Cup Semi-Finals. The winner of this series met the PCHA-WCHL playoff winner in the best-of-three Stanley Cup Finals.

1924-25 — The first place team (Hamilton) at the conclusion of the regular-season was supposed to play the winner of a two-game, total-goals series between the second (Toronto) and third (Montreal) place clubs. However, Hamilton refused to abide by this new format, demanding greater compensation than offered by the League. Thus, Toronto and Montreal played their two-game, total-goals series, and the winner (Montreal) earned the NHL title and then played the WCHL champion (Victoria) in the best-of-five Stanley Cup Finals.

1925-26 — The format which was intended for 1924-25 went into effect. The winner of the two-game, total-goals series between the second and third place teams squared off against the first place team in the two-game, total-goals NHL championship series. The NHL champion then moved on to play the WHL champion in the best-of-five Stanley Cup Finals.

After the 1925-26 season, the NHL was the only major professional hockey league still in existence and consequently took over sole control of the Stanley Cup competition.

1926-27 — The 10-team league was divided into two divisions — Canadian and American — of five teams apiece. In each division, the winner of the two-game, total-goals series between the second and third place teams faced the first place team in a two-game, total-goals series for the division title. The two division title winners then met in the best-of-five Stanley Cup Finals.

1928-29 — Both first place teams in the two divisions played each other in a best-of-five series. Both second place teams in the two divisions played each other in a two-game, total-goals series as did the two third place teams. The winners of these latter two series then played each other in a best-of-three series for the right to meet the winner of the series between the two first place clubs. This Stanley Cup Final was a best-of-three.

Series A: First in Canadian Division vs. first in American (best-of-five)
Series B: Second in Canadian Division vs. second in American (two-game, total-goals)
Series C: Third in Canadian Division vs. third in American (two-game, total-goals)
Series D: Winner of Series B vs. winner of Series C (best-of-three)
Series E: Winner of Series A vs. winner of Series D (best-of-three) for Stanley Cup

1931-32 — Same as 1928-29, except that Series D was changed to a two-game, total-goals format and Series E was changed to best-of-five.

1936-37 — Same as 1931-32, except that Series B, C, and D were each best-of-three.

1938-39 — With the NHL reduced to seven teams, the two-division system was replaced by one seven-team league. Based on final regular-season standings, the following playoff format was adopted:

Series A: First vs. Second (best-of-seven)
Series B: Third vs. Fourth (best-of-three)
Series C: Fifth vs. Sixth (best-of-three)
Series D: Winner of Series B vs. winner of Series C (best-of-three)
Series E: Winner of Series A vs. winner of Series D (best-of-seven)

1942-43 — With the NHL reduced to six teams (the "original six"), only the top four finishers qualified for playoff action. The best-of-seven Semi-Finals pitted Team #1 vs. Team #3 and Team #2 vs. Team #4. The winners of each Semi-Final series met in the best-of-seven Stanley Cup Finals.

1967-68 — When it doubled in size from 6 to 12 teams, the NHL once again was divided into two divisions — East and West — of six teams apiece. The top four clubs in each division qualified for the playoffs (all series were best-of-seven):

Series A: Team #1 (East) vs. Team #3 (East)
Series B: Team #2 (East) vs. Team #4 (East)
Series C: Team #1 (West) vs. Team #3 (West)
Series D: Team #2 (West) vs. Team #4 (West)
Series E: Winner of Series A vs. winner of Series B
Series F: Winner of Series C vs. winner of Series D
Series G: Winner of Series E vs. Winner of Series F

1970-71 — Same as 1967-68 except that Series E matched the winners of Series A and D, and Series F matched the winners of Series B and C.

1971-72 — Same as 1970-71, except that Series A and C matched Team #1 vs. Team #4, and Series B and D matched Team #2 vs. Team #3.

1974-75 — With the League now expanded to 18 teams in four divisions, a completely new playoff format was introduced. First, the #2 and #3 teams in each of the four divisions were pooled together in the Preliminary round. These eight (#2 and #3) clubs were ranked #1 to #8 based on regular-season record:

Series A: Team #1 vs. Team #8 (best-of-three)
Series B: Team #2 vs. Team #7 (best-of-three)
Series C: Team #3 vs. Team #6 (best-of-three)
Series D: Team #4 vs. Team #5 (best-of-three)
The winners of this Preliminary round then pooled together with the four division winners, which had received byes into this Quarter-Final round. These eight teams were again ranked #1 to #8 based on regular-season record:
Series E: Team #1 vs. Team #8 (best-of-seven)
Series F: Team #2 vs. Team #7 (best-of-seven)
Series G: Team #3 vs. Team #6 (best-of-seven)
Series H: Team #4 vs. Team #5 (best-of-seven)
The four Quarter-Finals winners, which moved on to the Semi-Finals, were then ranked #1 to #4 based on regular season record:
Series I: Team #1 vs. Team #4 (best-of-seven)
Series J: Team #2 vs. Team #3 (best-of-seven)
Series K: Winner of Series I vs. winner of Series J (best-of-seven)

1977-78 — Same as 1974-75, except that the Preliminary round consisted of the #2 teams in the four divisions and the next four teams based on regular-season record (not their standings within their divisions).

1979-80 — With the addition of four WHA franchises, the League expanded its playoff structure to include 16 of its 21 teams. The four first place teams in the four divisions automatically earned playoff berths. Among the 17 other clubs, the top 12, according to regular-season record, also earned berths. All 16 teams were then pooled together and ranked #1 to #16 based on regular-season record:

Series A: Team #1 vs. Team #16 (best-of-five)
Series B: Team #2 vs. Team #15 (best-of-five)
Series C: Team #3 vs. Team #14 (best-of-five)
Series D: Team #4 vs. Team #13 (best-of-five)
Series E: Team #5 vs. Team #12 (best-of-five)
Series F: Team #6 vs. Team #11 (best-of-five)
Series G: Team #7 vs. Team #10 (best-of-five)
Series H: Team #8 vs. Team # 9 (best-of-five)
The eight Preliminary round winners, ranked #1 to #8 based on regular-season record, moved on to the Quarter-Finals:
Series I: Team #1 vs. Team #8 (best-of-seven)
Series J: Team #2 vs. Team #7 (best-of-seven)
Series K: Team #3 vs. Team #6 (best-of-seven)
Series L: Team #4 vs. Team #5 (best-of-seven)
The four Quarter-Finals winners, ranked #1 to #4 based on regular-season record, moved on to the semi-finals:
Series M: Team #1 vs. Team #4 (best-of-seven)
Series N: Team #2 vs. Team #3 (best-of-seven)
Series O: Winner of Series M vs. winner of Series N (best-of-seven)

1981-82 — The first four teams in each division earned playoff berths. In each division, the first-place team opposed the fourth-place team and the second-place team opposed the third-place team in a best-of-five Division Semi-Final series (DSF). In each division, the two winners of the DSF met in a best-of-seven Division Final series (DF). The two DF winners in each conference met in a best-of-seven Conference Final series (CF). In the Prince of Wales Conference, the Adams Division winner opposed the Patrick Division winner; in the Clarence Campbell Conference, the Smythe Division winner opposed the Norris Division winner. The two CF winners met in a best-of-seven Stanley Cup Final (F) series.

1986-87 — Division Semi-Final series changed from best-of-five to best-of-seven.

1993-94 — The NHL's playoff draw is conference-based rather than division-based. At the conclusion of the regular season, the top eight teams in each of the Eastern and Western Conferences qualify for the playoffs. The teams that finish in first place in each of the League's divisions are seeded first and second in each conference's playoff draw and are assured of home ice advantage in the first two playoff rounds. The remaining teams are seeded based on their regular-season point totals. In each conference, the team seeded #1 plays #8; #2 vs. #7; #3 vs. #6; and #4 vs. #5. All series are best-of-seven with home ice rotating on a 2-2-1-1-1 basis, with the exception of matchups between Central and Pacific Division teams. These matchups will be played on a 2-3-2 basis to reduce travel. In a 2-3-2 series, the team with the most points will have its choice to start the series at home or on the road. The Eastern Conference champion will face the Western Conference champion in the Stanley Cup Final.

1994-95 — Same as 1993-94, except that in first, second or third-round playoff series involving Central and Pacific Division teams, the team with the better record has the choice of using either a 2-3-2 or a 2-2-1-1-1 format. When a 2-3-2 format is selected, the higher-ranked team also has the choice of playing games 1, 2, 6 and 7 at home or playing games 3, 4 and 5 at home. The format for the Stanley Cup Final remains 2-2-1-1-1.

1998-99 — The NHL's clubs are re-aligned into two conferences each consisting of three divisions. The number of teams qualifying for the Stanley Cup Playoffs remains unchanged at 16.

First-round playoff berths will be awarded to the first-place team in each division as well as to the next five best teams based on regular-season point totals in each conference. The three division winners in each conference will be seeded first through third, in order of points, for the playoffs and the next five best teams, in order of points, will be seeded fourth through eighth. In each conference, the team seeded #1 will play #8; #2 vs. #7; #3 vs. #6; and #4 vs. #5 in the quarterfinal round. Home-ice in the Conference Quarter-Finals is granted to those teams seeded first through fourth in each conference.

In the Conference Semi-Finals and Conference Finals, teams will be re-seeded according to the same criteria as the Conference Quarter-Finals. Higher seeded teams will have home-ice advantage.

Home-ice advantage for the Stanley Cup Finals will be determined by points.

All series remain best-of-seven.

2013-14 — The NHL's clubs are re-aligned into two conferences each consisting of two divisions. The number of teams qualifying for the Stanley Cup Playoffs remains unchanged at 16.

Twelve first-round playoff berths will be awarded to the top three finishers in each of the four divisions. These clubs will be the first three "seeds" in each division. Two additional "wild card" berths will be awarded to the the next two highest-placed finishers in each conference, ranked on the basis of regular-season points and regardless of division. The first-place finisher with the highest number of regular-season points in the conference will be matched against the wild card team with the lowest number of regular-season points, and the first-place finisher with the second-highest number of regular-season points in the Conference matched against the Wild Card team with the second-lowest number of regular-season points.

In each division, the team seeded #1 plays #4; #2 plays #3.

The two advancing teams in the West and two advancing teams in the East meet in the Conference Finals.

The Eastern and Western Conference champions will meet in the Stanley Cup Final.

Home-ice advantage in the Stanley Cup Final will be determined by points.

All series remain best-of-seven.

Despite recording 11 of their 16 playoff victories at home, the Chicago Blackhawks celebrated with the Stanley Cup on the road in Boston in 2013, as they did in Philadelphia in 2010.

Team Records

1918-2013

GAMES PLAYED

MOST GAMES PLAYED BY ALL TEAMS, ONE PLAYOFF YEAR:
92 — 1991. There were 51 DSF, 24 DF, 11 CF and 6 F games.
90 — 1994. There were 48 CQF, 23 CSF, 12 CF and 7 F games.
— 2002. There were 47 CQF, 25 CSF, 13 CF and 5 F games.

MOST GAMES PLAYED, ONE TEAM, ONE PLAYOFF YEAR:
26 — Philadelphia Flyers, 1987. Won DSF 4-2 vs. NY Rangers, DF 4-3 vs. NY Islanders, CF 4-2 vs. Montreal, and lost F 4-3 vs. Edmonton.
— Calgary Flames, 2004. Won DSF 4-3 vs. Vancouver, DF 4-2 vs. Detroit, CF 4-2 vs. San Jose, and lost F 4-3 vs. Tampa Bay.
25 — New Jersey Devils, 2001. Won CQF 4-2 vs. Carolina, CSF 4-3 vs. Toronto, CF 4-1 vs. Pittsburgh, and lost F 4-3 vs. Colorado.
— Carolina Hurricanes, 2006. Won CQF 4-2 vs. Montreal, CSF 4-1 vs. New Jersey, CF 4-3 vs. Buffalo, and F 4-3 vs. Edmonton
— Boston Bruins, 2011. Won CQF 4-3 vs. Montreal, CSF 4-0 vs. Philadelphia, CF 4-3 vs. Tampa Bay, and F 4-3 vs. Vancouver.
— Vancouver Canucks, 2011. Won CQF 4-3 vs. Chicago, CSF 4-2 vs. Nashville, CF 4-1 vs. San Jose, and lost F 4-3 vs. Boston.

PLAYOFF APPEARANCES

MOST STANLEY CUP CHAMPIONSHIPS (since 1893):
24 — Montreal Canadiens
(1916-24-30-31-44-46-53-56-57-58-59-60-65-66-68-69-71-73-76-77-78-79-86-93)
14 — Toronto Maple Leafs (1914-18-22-32-42-45-47-48-49-51-62-63-64-67)
11 — Detroit Red Wings (1936-37-43-50-52-54-55-97-98-2002-08)

MOST CONSECUTIVE STANLEY CUP CHAMPIONSHIPS:
5 — Montreal Canadiens (1956-57-58-59-60)
4 — Montreal Canadiens (1976-77-78-79)
— NY Islanders (1980-81-82-83)

MOST FINAL SERIES APPEARANCES:
32 — Montreal Canadiens in 96-year history.
24 — Detroit Red Wings in 87-year history.
21 — Toronto Maple Leafs in 96-year history.

MOST CONSECUTIVE FINAL SERIES APPEARANCES:
10 — Montreal Canadiens, (1951-60, inclusive)
5 — Montreal Canadiens, (1965-69, inclusive)
— NY Islanders, (1980-84, inclusive)

MOST YEARS IN PLAYOFFS:
80 — Montreal Canadiens in 96-year history.
68 — Boston Bruins in 89-year history.
65 — Toronto Maple Leafs in 96-year history.

MOST CONSECUTIVE PLAYOFF APPEARANCES:
29 — Boston Bruins (1968-96, inclusive)
28 — Chicago Blackhawks (1970-97, inclusive)
25 — St. Louis Blues (1980-2004, inclusive)
24 — Montreal Canadiens (1971-94, inclusive)
22 — Detroit Red Wings (1991-2013 inclusive)

TEAM WINS

MOST HOME WINS, ONE TEAM, ONE PLAYOFF YEAR:
12 — New Jersey Devils, 2003 in 13 home games.
11 — Edmonton Oilers, 1988 in 11 home games.
— Detroit Red Wings, 2009 in 13 home games.
— Chicago Blackhawks, 2013 in 13 home games.
10 — Edmonton Oilers, 1985 in 10 home games.
— Montreal Canadiens, 1986 in 11 home games.
— Montreal Canadiens, 1993 in 11 home games.
— Carolina Hurricanes, 2006 in 14 home games.
— Anaheim Ducks, 2007 in 12 home games.
— Boston Bruins, 2011 in 13 home games.
— Vancouver Canucks, 2011 in 14 home games.

MOST HOME WINS, ALL TEAMS, ONE PLAYOFF YEAR:
59 — 2013. Of 86 games played, home teams won 59 (30 CQF, 20 CSF, 6 CF and 3 in F).
57 — 1991. Of 92 games played, home teams won 57 (29 DSF, 17 DF, 8 CF and 3 in F).

MOST ROAD WINS, ONE TEAM, ONE PLAYOFF YEAR:
10 — New Jersey Devils, 1995. Won three at Boston in CQF; two at Pittsburgh in CSF; three at Philadelphia in CF; and two at Detroit in F.
— New Jersey Devils, 2000. Won two at Florida in CQF; two at Toronto in CSF; three at Philadelphia in CF; and three at Dallas in F.
— Calgary Flames, 2004. Won three at Vancouver in DSF; two at Detroit in DF; three at San Jose in CF; and two at Tampa Bay in F.
— Los Angeles Kings, 2012. Won three at Vancouver in CQF; two at St. Louis in CSF; three at Phoenix in CF; and two at New Jersey in F.
8 — NY Islanders, 1980. Won two at Los Angeles in PR; three at Boston in QF; two at Buffalo in SF; and one at Philadelphia in F.
— Philadelphia Flyers, 1987. Won two at NY Rangers in DSF; two at NY Islanders in DF; three at Montreal in CF; and one at Edmonton in F.
— Edmonton Oilers, 1990. Won one at Winnipeg in DSF; two at Los Angeles in DF; two at Chicago in CF and three at Boston in F.
— Pittsburgh Penguins, 1992. Won two at Washington in DSF; two at NY Rangers in DF; two at Boston in CF; and two at Chicago in F.
— Vancouver Canucks, 1994. Won three at Calgary in CQF; two at Dallas in CSF; one at Toronto in CF; and two at NY Rangers in F.
— Colorado Avalanche, 1996. Won two at Vancouver in CQF; two at Chicago in CSF; two at Detroit in CF; and two at Florida in F.
— Detroit Red Wings, 1998. Won two at Phoenix in CQF; three at St. Louis in CSF; one at Dallas in CF; and two at Washington in F.
— Colorado Avalanche, 1999. Won three at San Jose in CQF; three at Detroit in CSF; and two at Dallas in CF.
— New Jersey Devils, 2001. Won two at Carolina in CQF; two at Toronto in CSF; two at Pittsburgh in CF; and two at Colorado in F.
— Detroit Red Wings, 2002. Won three at Vancouver in CQF; one at St. Louis in CSF; two at Colorado in CF; and two at Carolina in F.
— Chicago Blackhawks, 2010. Won two at Nashville in CQF; three at Vancouver in CSF; two at San Jose in CF; and one at Philadelphia in F.

MOST ROAD WINS, ALL TEAMS, ONE PLAYOFF YEAR:
47 — 2012. Of 86 games played, road teams won 47 (30 CQF, 7 CSF, 7 CF, 3 F).

MOST OVERTIME WINS, ONE TEAM, ONE PLAYOFF YEAR:
10 — **Montreal Canadiens, 1993.** Won two vs. Quebec in DSF; three vs. Buffalo in DF; two vs. NY Islanders in CF; and three vs. Los Angeles in F.
7 — Carolina Hurricanes, 2002. Won two vs. New Jersey in CQF; one vs. Montreal in CSF; three vs. Toronto in CF; and one vs. Detroit in F.
— Anaheim Mighty Ducks, 2003. Won two vs. Detroit in CQF; two vs. Dallas in CSF; one vs. Minnestoa in CF; and two vs. New Jersey in F.

MOST OVERTIME WINS AT HOME, ONE TEAM, ONE PLAYOFF YEAR:
4 — **St. Louis Blues, 1968.** Won one vs. Philadelphia in QF; three vs. Minnesota in SF.
— **Montreal Canadiens, 1993.** Won one vs. Quebec in DSF; one vs. Buffalo in DF, one vs. NY Islanders in CF; one vs. Los Angeles in F.
— **Chicago Blackhawks, 2013.** Won one vs. Minnesota in CQF; one vs. Detroit in CSF; one vs. Los Angeles in CF; one vs. Boston in F.

MOST OVERTIME WINS ON THE ROAD, ONE TEAM, ONE PLAYOFF YEAR:
6 — **Montreal Canadiens, 1993.** Won one vs. Quebec in DSF; two vs. Buffalo in DF; one vs. NY Islanders in CF; two vs. Los Angeles in F.

TEAM LOSSES

MOST LOSSES, ONE TEAM, ONE PLAYOFF YEAR:
11 — **Philadelphia Flyers, 1987.** Lost two vs. NY Rangers in DSF; three vs. NY Islanders in DF; two vs. Montreal in CF; four vs. Edmonton in F.
— **Calgary Flames, 2004.** Lost three vs. Vancouver in CQF; two vs. Detroit in CSF; two vs. San Jose in CF; four vs. Tampa Bay in F

MOST HOME LOSSES, ONE TEAM, ONE PLAYOFF YEAR:
7 — **Calgary Flames, 2004.** Lost two vs. Vancouver in CQF; one vs. Detroit in CSF; two vs. San Jose in CF; two vs. Tampa Bay in F.
6 — Philadelphia Flyers, 1987. Lost one vs. NY Rangers in DSF; two vs. NY Islanders in DF; two vs. Montreal in CF; one vs. Edmonton in F.
— Washington Capitals, 1998. Lost two vs. Boston in CQF; two vs. Buffalo in CF; two vs. Detroit in F.
— Colorado Avalanche, 1999. Lost two vs. San Jose in CQF; two vs. Detroit in CSF; two vs. Dallas in CF.
— New Jersey Devils, 2001. Lost one vs. Carolina in CQF; two vs. Toronto in CSF; one vs. Pittsburgh in CF; two vs Colorado in F.
— Minnesota Wild, 2003. Lost two vs. Colorado in CQF; two vs. Vancouver in CSF; two vs. Anaheim in CF.

MOST ROAD LOSSES, ONE TEAM, ONE PLAYOFF YEAR:
8 — **Los Angeles Kings, 2013.** Lost two at St. Louis in CQF; three at San Jose in CSF; three at Chicago in CF.
7 — New Jersey Devils, 2003. Lost one at Boston in CQF; one at Tampa Bay in CSF; two at Ottawa in CF; three at Anaheim in F.
— Philadelphia Flyers, 2010. Lost one at New Jersey in CQF; two at Boston in CSF; one at Montreal in CF; three at Chicago in F.

MOST OVERTIME LOSSES, ONE TEAM, ONE PLAYOFF YEAR:
4 — **Montreal Canadiens, 1951.** Lost four vs. Toronto in F.
— **St. Louis Blues, 1968.** Lost one vs. Philadelphia in QF; one vs. Minnesota in SF; two vs. Montreal in F.
— **New York Rangers, 1979.** Lost one vs. Philadelphia in QF; two vs. NY Islanders in SF; one vs. Montreal in F.
— **Los Angeles Kings, 1991.** Lost one vs. Vancouver in DSF; three vs. Edmonton in DF.
— **Los Angeles Kings, 1993.** Lost one vs. Toronto in CF; three vs. Montreal in F.
— **New Jersey Devils, 1994.** Lost one vs. Buffalo in CQF; one vs. Boston in CSF; two vs. NY Rangers in CF.
— **Chicago Blackhawks, 1995.** Lost one vs. Toronto in CQF; three vs. Detroit in CF.
— **Philadelphia Flyers, 1996.** Lost two vs. Tampa Bay in CQF; two vs. Florida in CSF.
— **Dallas Stars, 1999.** Lost two vs. St. Louis in CSF; one vs. Colorado in CF; one vs. Buffalo in F.
— **Detroit Red Wings, 2002.** Lost one vs. Vancouver in CQF; two vs. Colorado in CF; one vs. Carolina in F.
— **New Jersey Devils, 2003.** Lost two vs. Ottawa in CF; two vs. Anaheim in F.
— **Washington Capitals, 2012.** Lost two vs. Boston in CQF; two vs. NY Rangers in CSF.

MOST OVERTIME LOSSES AT HOME, ONE TEAM, ONE PLAYOFF YEAR:
4 — **Detroit Red Wings, 2002.** Lost one vs. Vancouver in CQF; two vs. Colorado in CF; one vs. Carolina in F.

MOST OVERTIME LOSSES ON THE ROAD, ONE TEAM, ONE PLAYOFF YEAR:
3 — **Los Angeles Kings, 1991.** Lost one at Vancouver in DSF; two at Edmonton in DF.
— **Chicago Blackhawks, 1995.** Lost one at Toronto in CQF; two at Detroit in CF.
— **St. Louis Blues, 1996.** Lost two at Toronto in CQF; one at Detroit in CSF.
— **Dallas Stars, 1999.** Lost two at St. Louis in CSF; one at Colorado in CF.
— **New Jersey Devils, 2003.** Lost one at Ottawa in CF; two at Anaheim in F.
— **Los Angeles Kings, 2013.** Lost two at St. Louis in CQF; one at Chicago in CF.
— **New York Rangers, 2013.** Lost two at Washington in CQF; one at Boston in CSF.

PLAYOFF WINNING STREAKS

LONGEST PLAYOFF WINNING STREAK:
14 — **Pittsburgh Penguins.** Streak started May 9, 1992 as Pittsburgh won the first of three straight games in DF vs. NY Rangers. Continued with four wins vs. Boston in 1992 CF and four wins vs. Chicago in 1992 F. Pittsburgh then won the first three games of 1993 DSF vs. New Jersey. New Jersey ended the streak April 25, 1993, at New Jersey with a 4-1 win vs. Pittsburgh in the fourth game of 1993 DSF.
12 — Edmonton Oilers. Streak started May 15, 1984 as Edmonton won the first of three straight games in F vs. NY Islanders. Continued with three wins vs. Los Angeles in 1985 DSF and four wins vs. Winnipeg in 1985 DF. Edmonton then won the first two games of 1985 CF vs. Chicago. Chicago ended the streak May 9, 1985, at Chicago with a 5-2 win vs. Edmonton in the third game of 1985 CF.

MOST CONSECUTIVE WINS, ONE TEAM, ONE PLAYOFF YEAR:
11 — **Chicago Blackhawks** in 1992. Chicago won last three games of DSF vs. St. Louis to win series 4-2, defeated Detroit 4-0 in DF and Edmonton 4-0 in CF.
— **Pittsburgh Penguins** in 1992. Pittsburgh won last three games of DF vs. NY Rangers to win series 4-2, defeated Boston 4-0 in CF and Chicago 4-0 in F.
— **Montreal Canadiens** in 1993. Montreal won last four games of DSF vs. Quebec to win series 4-2, defeated Buffalo 4-0 in DF and won first three games of CF vs. NY Islanders.

PLAYOFF LOSING STREAKS

LONGEST PLAYOFF LOSING STREAK:
16 — **Chicago Black Hawks.** Streak started April 20, 1975 at Chicago with a 6-2 loss in fourth game of QF vs. Buffalo, won by Buffalo 4-1. Continued with four consecutive losses vs. Montreal, in 1976 QF and two straight losses vs. NY Islanders in 1977 best-of-three PRE. Chicago then lost four games vs. Boston in 1978 QF and four games vs. NY Islanders in 1979 QF. Chicago ended the streak April 8, 1980, at Chicago with a 3-2 win vs. St. Louis in the opening game of 1980 PRE.
14 — Los Angeles Kings. Streak started June 3, 1993 at Montreal with a 3-2 loss in second game of F vs. Montreal, won by Montreal 4-1. Los Angeles failed to qualify for the playoffs for the next four years. Then Los Angeles lost four games vs. St. Louis in 1998 CQF; missed the 1999 playoffs and lost four games vs. Detroit in 2000 CQF. Los Angeles then lost the first two games of 2001 CQF vs. Detroit. Los Angeles ended the streak April 15, 2001, at Los Angeles with a 2-1 win vs. Detroit in the third game of 2001 CQF.

Prior to the 2013 Stanley Cup Final, Chicago and Boston had not met in the playoffs since 1978 when Jean Ratelle and the Bruins swept Ivan Boldirev and the Blackhawks during Chicago's record-setting 16-game postseason losing streak.

MOST GOALS IN A SERIES, ONE TEAM

MOST GOALS, ONE TEAM, ONE PLAYOFF SERIES:
44 — Edmonton Oilers in 1985. Edmonton won best-of-seven CF 4-2, outscoring Chicago 44-25.
35 — Edmonton Oilers in 1983. Edmonton won best-of-seven DF 4-1, outscoring Calgary 35-13.
— Calgary Flames in 1995. Calgary lost best-of-seven CQF 4-3, outscoring San Jose 35-26.

MOST GOALS, ONE TEAM, TWO-GAME SERIES:
11 — Buffalo Sabres in 1977. Buffalo won best-of-three PRE 2-0, outscoring Minnesota 11-3.
— Toronto Maple Leafs in 1978. Toronto won best-of-three PRE 2-0, outscoring Los Angeles 11-3.

MOST GOALS, ONE TEAM, THREE-GAME SERIES:
23 — Chicago Blackhawks in 1985. Chicago won best-of-five DSF 3-0, outscoring Detroit 23-8.
20 — Minnesota North Stars in 1981. Minnesota won best-of-five PRE 3-0, outscoring Boston 20-13.
— NY Islanders in 1981. NY Islanders won best-of-five PRE 3-0, outscoring Toronto 20-4.

MOST GOALS, ONE TEAM, FOUR-GAME SERIES:
28 — Boston Bruins in 1972. Boston won best-of-seven SF 4-0, outscoring St. Louis 28-8.

MOST GOALS, ONE TEAM, FIVE-GAME SERIES:
35 — Edmonton Oilers in 1983. Edmonton won best-of-seven DF 4-1, outscoring Calgary 35-13.
32 — Edmonton Oilers in 1987. Edmonton won best-of-seven DSF 4-1, outscoring Los Angeles 32-20.
30 — Calgary Flames in 1988. Calgary won best-of-seven DSF 4-1, outscoring Los Angeles 30-18.

MOST GOALS, ONE TEAM, SIX-GAME SERIES:
44 — Edmonton Oilers in 1985. Edmonton won best-of-seven CF 4-2, outscoring Chicago 44-25.
33 — Montreal Canadiens in 1973. Montreal won best-of-seven F 4-2, outscoring Chicago 33-23.
— Chicago Blackhawks in 1985. Chicago won best-of-seven DF 4-2, outscoring Minnesota 33-29.
— Los Angeles Kings in 1993. Los Angeles won best-of-seven DSF 4-2, outscoring Calgary 33-28.

MOST GOALS, ONE TEAM, SEVEN-GAME SERIES:
35 — Calgary Flames in 1995. Calgary lost best-of-seven CQF 4-3, outscoring San Jose 35-26.
33 — Philadelphia Flyers in 1976. Philadelphia won best-of-seven QF 4-3, outscoring Toronto 33-23.
— Boston Bruins in 1983. Boston won best-of-seven DF 4-3, outscoring Buffalo 33-23.
— Edmonton Oilers in 1984. Edmonton won best-of-seven DF 4-3, outscoring Calgary 33-27.

FEWEST GOALS IN A SERIES, ONE TEAM

FEWEST GOALS, ONE TEAM, TWO-GAME SERIES:
0 — Toronto St. Patricks in 1921. Toronto lost two-game, total-goals NHL F 7-0 vs. Ottawa.
— New York Americans in 1929. NY Americans lost two-game, total-goals QF 1-0 vs. NY Rangers.
— New York Rangers in 1931. NY Rangers lost two-game, total-goals SF 3-0 vs. Chicago.
— Chicago Black Hawks in 1935. Chicago lost two-game, total-goals SF 1-0 vs. Mtl. Maroons.
— Montreal Maroons in 1937. Mtl. Maroons lost best-of-three SF 2-0, outscored by NY Rangers 5-0.
— New York Americans in 1939. NY Americans lost best-of-three QF 2-0, outscored by Toronto 5-0.

FEWEST GOALS, ONE TEAM, THREE-GAME SERIES:
1 — Montreal Maroons in 1936. Mtl. Maroons lost best-of-five SF 3-0, outscored by Detroit 6-1.

FEWEST GOALS, ONE TEAM, FOUR-GAME SERIES:
1 — Minnesota Wild in 2003. Minnesota lost best-of-seven CF 4-0, outscored by Anaheim 9-1.

FEWEST GOALS, ONE TEAM, FIVE-GAME SERIES:
2 — Philadelphia Flyers in 2002. Ottawa won best-of-seven CQF 4-1, while outscoring Philadelphia 11-2.

FEWEST GOALS, ONE TEAM, SIX-GAME SERIES:
5 — Boston Bruins in 1951. Toronto won best-of-seven SF 4-1 with 1 tie, outscoring Boston 17-5.

FEWEST GOALS, ONE TEAM, SEVEN-GAME SERIES:
8 — Vancouver Canucks, in 2011. Boston won best-of-seven F 4-3; while outscoring Vancouver 23-8.
9 — Toronto Maple Leafs, in 1945. Toronto won best-of- seven F 4-3; tied with Detroit in scoring 9-9.
— Detroit Red Wings, in 1945. Toronto won best-of-seven F 4-3; teams tied in scoring 9-9.

Darryl Sutter spent his entire eight-year NHL playing career with the Chicago Blackhawks. He was the team's leading playoff scorer with 12 goals in 1985 when Chicago was involved in some of the highest-scoring series in postseason history.

MOST GOALS IN A SERIES, BOTH TEAMS

MOST GOALS, BOTH TEAMS, ONE PLAYOFF SERIES:
69 — Edmonton Oilers (44), Chicago Black Hawks (25) in 1985. Edmonton won best-of-seven CF 4-2.
62 — Chicago Black Hawks (33), Minnesota North Stars (29) in 1985. Chicago won best-of-seven DF 4-2.
61 — Los Angeles Kings (33), Calgary Flames (28) in 1993. Los Angeles won best-of-seven DSF 4-2.
— Calgary Flames (35), San Jose Sharks (26) in 1995. San Jose won best-of-seven CQF 4-3.

MOST GOALS, BOTH TEAMS, TWO-GAME SERIES:
17 — Toronto St. Patricks (10), Montreal Canadiens (7) in 1918. Toronto won two-game total-goals NHL F.
15 — Boston Bruins (10), Chicago Black Hawks (5) in 1927. Boston won two-game total-goals QF.
— Pittsburgh Penguins (9), St. Louis Blues (6) in 1975. Pittsburgh won best-of-three PRE 2-0.

MOST GOALS, BOTH TEAMS, THREE-GAME SERIES:
33 — Minnesota North Stars (20), Boston Bruins (13) in 1981. Minnesota won best-of-five PRE 3-0.
31 — Chicago Black Hawks (23), Detroit Red Wings (8) in 1985. Chicago won best-of-five DSF 3-0.
28 — Toronto Maple Leafs (18), New York Rangers (10) in 1932. Toronto won best-of-five F 3-0.

MOST GOALS, BOTH TEAMS, FOUR-GAME SERIES:
36 — Boston Bruins (28), St. Louis Blues (8) in 1972. Boston won best-of-seven SF 4-0.
— Minnesota North Stars (18), Toronto Maple Leafs (18) in 1983. Minnesota won best-of-five DSF 3-1.
— Edmonton Oilers (25), Chicago Black Hawks (11) in 1983. Edmonton won best-of-seven CF 4-0.
35 — New York Rangers (23), Los Angeles Kings (12) in 1981. NY Rangers won best-of-five PRE 3-1.

MOST GOALS, BOTH TEAMS, FIVE-GAME SERIES:
52 — Edmonton Oilers (32), Los Angeles Kings (20) in 1987. Edmonton won best-of-seven DSF 4-1.
50 — Los Angeles Kings (27), Edmonton Oilers (23) in 1982. Los Angeles won best-of-five DSF 3-2.
48 — Edmonton Oilers (35), Calgary Flames (13) in 1983. Edmonton won best-of-seven DF 4-1.
— Calgary Flames (30), Los Angeles Kings (18) in 1988. Calgary won best-of-seven DSF 4-1.

MOST GOALS, BOTH TEAMS, SIX-GAME SERIES:
69 — Edmonton Oilers (44), Chicago Black Hawks (25) in 1985. Edmonton won best-of-seven CF 4-2.
62 — Chicago Black Hawks (33), Minnesota North Stars (29) in 1985. Chicago won best-of-seven DF 4-2.
61 — Los Angeles Kings (33), Calgary Flames (28) in 1993. Los Angeles won best-of-seven DSF 4-2.

MOST GOALS, BOTH TEAMS, SEVEN-GAME SERIES:
61 — Calgary Flames (35), San Jose Sharks (26) in 1995. San Jose won best-of-seven CQF 4-3.
60 — Edmonton Oilers (33), Calgary Flames (27) in 1984. Edmonton won best-of-seven DF 4-3.

FEWEST GOALS IN A SERIES, BOTH TEAMS

FEWEST GOALS, BOTH TEAMS, TWO-GAME SERIES:
1 — New York Rangers (1), New York Americans (0) in 1929. NY Rangers won two-game total-goals QF.
— Montreal Maroons (1), Chicago Black Hawks (0) in 1935. Mtl. Maroons won two-game total-goals SF.

FEWEST GOALS, BOTH TEAMS, THREE-GAME SERIES:
7 — Boston Bruins (5), Montreal Canadiens (2) in 1929. Boston won best-of-five SF 3-0.
— Detroit Red Wings (6), Montreal Maroons (1) in 1936. Detroit won best-of-five SF 3-0.

FEWEST GOALS, BOTH TEAMS, FOUR-GAME SERIES:
9 — Toronto Maple Leafs (7), Boston Bruins (2) in 1935. Toronto won best-of-five SF 3-1.

FEWEST GOALS, BOTH TEAMS, FIVE-GAME SERIES:
11 — Montreal Maroons (6), New York Rangers (5) in 1928. NY Rangers won best-of-five F 3-2.

FEWEST GOALS, BOTH TEAMS, SIX-GAME SERIES:
16 — Carolina Hurricanes (10), Toronto Maple Leafs (6) in 2002. Carolina won best-of-seven CF 4-2.

FEWEST GOALS, BOTH TEAMS, SEVEN-GAME SERIES:
18 — Toronto Maple Leafs (9), Detroit Red Wings (9) in 1945. Toronto won best-of-seven F 4-3.

MOST GOALS IN A GAME OR PERIOD

MOST GOALS, ONE TEAM, ONE GAME:
13 — Edmonton Oilers April 9, 1987, vs. Los Angeles at Edmonton. Edmonton won 13-3.
12 — Los Angeles Kings, April 10, 1990, vs. Calgary at Los Angeles. Los Angeles won 12-4.
11 — Montreal Canadiens, March 30, 1944, vs. Toronto at Montreal. Montreal won 11-0.
— Edmonton Oilers, May 4, 1985, vs. Chicago at Edmonton. Edmonton won 11-2.

MOST GOALS, ONE TEAM, ONE PERIOD:
7 — Montreal Canadiens, March 30, 1944, vs. Toronto at Montreal, third period. Montreal won 11-0.

MOST GOALS, BOTH TEAMS, ONE GAME:
18 — Los Angeles Kings (10), Edmonton Oilers (8), April 7, 1982, at Edmonton. Los Angeles won best-of-five DSF 3-2.
17 — Pittsburgh Penguins (10), Philadelphia Flyers (7), April 25, 1989, at Pittsburgh. Pittsburgh won best-of-seven DF 4-3.
16 — Edmonton Oilers (13), Los Angeles Kings (3), April 9, 1987, at Edmonton. Edmonton won best-of-seven DSF 4-1.
— Los Angeles Kings (12), Calgary Flames (4), April 10, 1990, at Los Angeles. Los Angeles won best-of-seven DF 4-2.

MOST GOALS, BOTH TEAMS, ONE PERIOD:
9 — New York Rangers (6), Philadelphia Flyers (3), April 24, 1979, third period, at Philadelphia. NY Rangers won 8-3.
— Los Angeles Kings (5), Calgary Flames (4), April 10, 1990, second period, at Los Angeles. Los Angeles won 12-4.
8 — Chicago Black Hawks (5), Montreal Canadiens (3), May 8, 1973, second period, at Montreal. Chicago won 8-7.
— Chicago Black Hawks (5), Edmonton Oilers (3), May 12, 1985, first period, at Chicago. Chicago won 8-6.
— Edmonton Oilers (6), Winnipeg Jets (2), April 6, 1988, third period, at Edmonton. Edmonton won 7-4.
— Hartford Whalers (5), Montreal Canadiens (3), April 10, 1988, third period, at Montreal. Hartford won 7-5.
— Vancouver Canucks (5), New York Rangers (3), June 9, 1994, third period, at NY Rangers. Vancouver won 6-3.
— Pittsburgh Penguins (5), Ottawa Senators (3), April 20, 2010, second period, at Ottawa. Pittsburgh won 7-4.

TEAM POWER-PLAY GOALS

MOST POWER-PLAY GOALS BY ALL TEAMS, ONE PLAYOFF YEAR:
199 — 1988 in 83 games.

MOST POWER-PLAY GOALS, ONE TEAM, ONE PLAYOFF YEAR:
35 — Minnesota North Stars, 1991 in 23 games.
32 — Edmonton Oilers, 1988 in 18 games.
31 — New York Islanders, 1981 in 18 games.

MOST POWER-PLAY GOALS, ONE TEAM, ONE SERIES:
15 — New York Islanders in 1980 F vs. Philadelphia. NY Islanders won series 4-2.
— Minnesota North Stars in 1991 DSF vs. Chicago. Minnesota won series 4-2.
13 — New York Islanders in 1981 QF vs. Edmonton. NY Islanders won series 4-2.
— Calgary Flames in 1986 CF vs. St. Louis. Calgary won series 4-3.
12 — Toronto Maple Leafs in 1976 QF vs. Philadelphia. Philadelphia won series 4-3.
— Quebec Nordiques in 1987 CQF vs. Hartford. Quebec won series 4-2.
— Colorado Avalanche in 1997 CQF vs. Chicago. Colorado won series 4-2.
— Philadelphia Flyers in 2012 CQF vs. Pittsburgh. Philadelphia won series 4-2.

MOST POWER-PLAY GOALS, BOTH TEAMS, ONE SERIES:
21 — New York Islanders (15), Philadelphia Flyers (6) in 1980 best-of-seven F won by NY Islanders 4-2.
— New York Islanders (13), Edmonton Oilers (8) in 1981 best-of-seven QF won by NY Islanders 4-2.
— Philadelphia Flyers (11), Pittsburgh Penguins (10) in 1989 best-of-seven DF won by Philadelphia 4-3.
— Minnesota North Stars (15), Chicago Black Hawks (6) in 1991 best-of-seven DSF won by Minnesota 4-2.
— Philadelphia Flyers (12), Pittsburgh Penguins (9) in 2012 best-of-seven CQF won by Philadelphia 4-2.
20 — Toronto Maple Leafs (12), Philadelphia Flyers (8) in 1976 best-of-seven QF won by Philadelphia 4-3.

MOST POWER-PLAY GOALS, ONE TEAM, ONE GAME:
6 — Boston Bruins, April 2, 1969, at Boston vs. Toronto. Boston won 10-0.

MOST POWER-PLAY GOALS, BOTH TEAMS, ONE GAME:
8 — Minnesota North Stars (4), St. Louis Blues (4), April 24, 1991, at Minnesota. Minnesota won 8-4.
7 — Minnesota North Stars (4), Edmonton Oilers (3), April 28, 1984, at Minnesota. Edmonton won 8-5.
— Philadelphia Flyers (4), New York Rangers (3), April 13, 1985, at NY Rangers. Philadelphia won 6-5.
— Chicago Black Hawks (5), Edmonton Oilers (2), May 14, 1985, at Edmonton. Edmonton won 10-5.
— Edmonton Oilers (5), Los Angeles Kings (2), April 9, 1987, at Edmonton. Edmonton won 13-3.
— Vancouver Canucks (4), Calgary Flames (3), April 9, 1989, at Vancouver. Vancouver won 5-3.
— Pittsburgh Penguins (4), Philadelphia Flyers (3), April 18, 2012, at Philadelphia. Pittsburgh won 10-5.

MOST POWER-PLAY GOALS, ONE TEAM, ONE PERIOD:
4 — Toronto Maple Leafs, March 26, 1936, second period vs. Boston at Toronto. Toronto won 8-3.
— Minnesota North Stars, April 28, 1984, second period vs. Edmonton at Minnesota. Edmonton won 8-5.
— Boston Bruins, April 11, 1991, third period vs. Hartford at Boston. Boston won 6-1.
— Minnesota North Stars, April 24, 1991, second period vs. St. Louis at Minnesota. Minnesota won 8-4.
— St. Louis Blues, April 27, 1998, third period at Los Angeles. St. Louis won 4-3.

MOST POWER-PLAY GOALS, BOTH TEAMS, ONE PERIOD:
5 — Minnesota North Stars (4), Edmonton Oilers (1), April 28, 1984, at Minnesota. Edmonton won 8-5.
— Vancouver Canucks (3), Calgary Flames (2), April 9, 1989, at Vancouver. Vancouver won 5-3.
— Minnesota North Stars (4), St. Louis Blues (1), April 24, 1991, at Minnesota. Minnesota won 8-4.

TEAM SHORTHAND GOALS

MOST SHORTHAND GOALS BY ALL TEAMS, ONE PLAYOFF YEAR:
33 — 1988, in 83 games.

MOST SHORTHAND GOALS, ONE TEAM, ONE PLAYOFF YEAR:
10 — Edmonton Oilers, 1983, in 16 games.
9 — New York Islanders, 1981, in 19 games.
8 — Philadelphia Flyers, 1989, in 19 games.

MOST SHORTHAND GOALS, ONE TEAM, ONE SERIES:
6 — Calgary Flames in 1995 vs. San Jose in best-of-seven CQF won by San Jose 4-3.
— Vancouver Canucks in 1995 vs. St. Louis in best-of-seven CQF won by Vancouver 4-3.
5 — New York Rangers in 1979 vs. Philadelphia in best-of-seven QF won by NY Rangers 4-1.
— Edmonton Oilers in 1983 vs. Calgary in best-of-seven DF won by Edmonton 4-1.

MOST SHORTHAND GOALS, BOTH TEAMS, ONE SERIES:
7 — Boston Bruins (4), New York Rangers (3), in 1958 SF won by Boston 4-2.
— Edmonton Oilers (5), Calgary Flames (2), in 1983 DF won by Edmonton 4-1.
— Vancouver Canucks (6), St. Louis Blues (1), in 1995 CQF won by Vancouver 4-3.

MOST SHORTHAND GOALS, ONE TEAM, ONE GAME:

3 — Boston Bruins, April 11, 1981, at Minnesota North Stars. Minnesota won 6-3.
— New York Islanders, April 17, 1983, at NY Rangers. NY Rangers won 7-6.
— Edmonton Oilers, April 17, 1983, at Calgary Flames. Edmonton won 10-2.

MOST SHORTHAND GOALS, BOTH TEAMS, ONE GAME:

4 — Boston Bruins (3), Minnesota North Stars (1), April 11, 1981, at Minnesota. Minnesota won 6-3.
— New York Islanders (3), New York Rangers (1), April 17, 1983, at NY Rangers. NY Rangers won 7-6.
3 — Toronto Maple Leafs (2), Detroit Red Wings (1), April 5, 1947, at Toronto. Toronto won 6-1.
— New York Rangers (2), Boston Bruins (1), April 1, 1958, at Boston. NY Rangers won 5-2.
— Minnesota North Stars (2), Philadelphia Flyers (1), May 4, 1980, at Minnesota. Philadelphia won 5-3.
— Winnipeg Jets (2), Edmonton Oilers (1), April 9, 1988, at Winnipeg. Winnipeg won 6-4.
— New York Islanders (2), New Jersey Devils (1), April 14, 1988, at New Jersey. New Jersey won 6-5.
— Toronto Maple Leafs (2), San Jose Sharks (1), May 8, 1994, at San Jose. Toronto won 8-3.
— Montreal Canadiens (2), New Jersey Devils (1), April 17, 1997, at New Jersey. New Jersey won 5-2.
— Dallas Stars (2), San Jose Sharks (1), May 5, 2000, at San Jose. Dallas won 5-4.
— Detroit Red Wings (2), Calgary Flames (1), April 21, 2007, at Detroit. Detroit won 5-1.

MOST SHORTHAND GOALS, ONE TEAM, ONE PERIOD:

2 — Toronto Maple Leafs, April 5, 1947, first period vs. Detroit at Toronto. Toronto won 6-1.
— Toronto Maple Leafs, April 13, 1965, first period vs. Montreal at Toronto. Montreal won 4-3.
— Boston Bruins, April 20, 1969, first period vs. Montreal at Boston. Boston won 3-2.
— Boston Bruins, April 8, 1970, second period vs. NY Rangers at Boston. Boston won 8-2.
— Boston Bruins, April 30, 1972, first period vs. NY Rangers at Boston. Boston won 6-5.
— Chicago Black Hawks, May 3, 1973, first period vs. Montreal at Chicago. Chicago won 7-4.
— Montreal Canadiens, April 23, 1978, first period at Detroit. Montreal won 8-0.
— New York Islanders, April 8, 1980, second period vs. Los Angeles at NY Islanders. NY Islanders won 8-1.
— Los Angeles Kings, April 9, 1980, first period at NY Islanders. Los Angeles won 6-3.
— Boston Bruins, April 13, 1980, second period at Pittsburgh. Boston won 8-3.
— Minnesota North Stars, May 4, 1980, second period vs. Philadelphia at Minnesota. Philadelphia won 5-3.
— Boston Bruins, April 11, 1981, third period at Minnesota North Stars. Minnesota won 6-3.
— New York Islanders, May 12, 1981, first period vs. Minnesota North Stars at NY Islanders. NY Islanders won 6-3.
— Montreal Canadiens, April 7, 1982, third period vs. Quebec at Montreal. Montreal won 5-1.
— Edmonton Oilers, April 24, 1983, third period vs. Chicago at Edmonton. Edmonton won 8-4.
— Winnipeg Jets, April 14, 1985, second period at Calgary. Winnipeg won 5-3.
— Boston Bruins, April 6, 1988, first period vs. Buffalo at Boston. Boston won 7-3.
— New York Islanders, April 14, 1988, third period at New Jersey. New Jersey won 6-5.
— Detroit Red Wings, April 29, 1993, second period at Toronto. Detroit won 7-3.
— Toronto Maple Leafs, May 8, 1994, third period at San Jose. Toronto won 8-3.
— Calgary Flames, May 11, 1995, first period at San Jose. Calgary won 9-2.
— Vancouver Canucks, May 15, 1995, second period at St. Louis. Vancouver won 6-5.
— Montreal Canadiens, April 17, 1997, second period at New Jersey. New Jersey won 5-2.
— Philadelphia Flyers, April 26, 1997, first period vs. Pittsburgh at Philadelphia. Philadelphia won 6-3.
— Phoenix Coyotes, April 24, 1998, second period at Detroit. Phoenix won 7-4.
— Buffalo Sabres, April 27, 1998, second period vs. Philadelphia at Buffalo. Buffalo won 6-1.
— San Jose Sharks, April 30, 1999, third period at Colorado. San Jose won 7-3.
— Detroit Red Wings, April 27, 2002, second period at Vancouver. Detroit won 6-4.
— Detroit Red Wings, April 21, 2007, second period at Detroit. Detroit won 5-1.

MOST SHORTHAND GOALS, BOTH TEAMS, ONE PERIOD:

3 — Toronto Maple Leafs (2), Detroit Red Wings (1), April 5, 1947, first period at Toronto. Toronto won 6-1.
— Toronto Maple Leafs (2), San Jose Sharks (1), May 8, 1994, third period at San Jose. Toronto won 8-3.

FASTEST GOALS

FASTEST FIVE GOALS, BOTH TEAMS:

3:06 — Minnesota North Stars, Chicago Black Hawks, April 21, 1985, at Chicago. Keith Brown scored for Chicago at 1:12 of the second period; Ken Yaremchuk, Chicago, 1:27; Dino Ciccarelli, Minnesota, 2:48; Tony McKegney, Minnesota, 4:07; and Curt Fraser, Chicago, 4:18. Chicago won 6-2 and won best-of-seven DF 4-2.
3:20 — Minnesota North Stars, Philadelphia Flyers, April 29, 1980, at Philadelphia. Paul Shmyr scored for Minnesota at 13:20 of the first period; Steve Christoff, Minnesota, 13:59; Ken Linseman, Philadelphia, 14:54; Tom Gorence, Philadelphia, 15:36; and Ken Linseman, Philadelphia, 16:40. Minnesota won 6-5. Philadelphia won best-of-seven SF 4-1.
3:58 — Detroit Red Wings, Phoenix Coyotes, April 16, 2010, at Phoenix. Henrik Zetterberg scored for Detroit at 6:27 of the second period; Wojtek Wolski, Phoenix, 7:05; Pavel Datsyuk, Detroit, 8:20; Matthew Lombardi, Phoenix, 9:09; Valtteri Filppula, Detroit, 10:25. Detroit won 7-4 and won best-of-seven CQF 4-3.

FASTEST FIVE GOALS, ONE TEAM:

3:36 — Montreal Canadiens, March 30, 1944, at Montreal vs. Toronto. Toe Blake scored at 7:58 and 8:37 of the third period; Maurice Richard, 9:17; Ray Getliffe, 10:33; and Buddy O'Connor, 11:34. Canadiens won 11-0 and won best-of-seven SF 4-1.

FASTEST FOUR GOALS, BOTH TEAMS:

1:33 — Toronto Maple Leafs, Philadelphia Flyers, April 20, 1976, at Philadelphia. Don Saleski scored for Philadelphia at 10:04 of the second period; Bob Neely, Toronto, 10:42; Gary Dornhoefer, Philadelphia, 11:24; and Don Saleski, Philadelphia, 11:37. Philadelphia won 7-1 and won best-of-seven SF 4-3.
1:34 — Calgary Flames, Montreal Canadiens, May 20, 1986, at Montreal. Joel Otto scored for Calgary at 17:59 of the first period; Bobby Smith, Montreal, 18:25; Mats Naslund, Montreal, 19:17; and Bob Gainey, Montreal, 19:33. Montreal won 5-3 and won best-of-seven F 4-1.
1:38 — Boston Bruins, Philadelphia Flyers, April 26, 1977, at Philadelphia. Gregg Sheppard scored for Boston at 14:01 of the second period; Mike Milbury, Boston, 15:01; Gary Dornhoefer, Philadelphia, 15:16; and Jean Ratelle, Boston, 15:39. Boston won 5-4 and won best-of-seven SF 4-0.

FASTEST FOUR GOALS, ONE TEAM:

2:35 — Montreal Canadiens, March 30, 1944, at Montreal. Toe Blake scored at 7:58 and 8:37 of the third period; Maurice Richard, 9:17; and Ray Getliffe, 10:33. Montreal won 11-0 and won best-of-seven SF 4-1.

FASTEST THREE GOALS, BOTH TEAMS:

0:21 — Chicago Black Hawks, Edmonton Oilers, May 7, 1985, at Edmonton. Behn Wilson scored for Chicago at 19:22 of the third period; Jari Kurri, Edmonton, 19:36; and Glenn Anderson, Edmonton, 19:43. Edmonton won 7-3 and won best-of-seven CF 4-2.
0:27 — Phoenix Coyotes, Detroit Red Wings, April 24, 1998, at Detroit. Jeremy Roenick scored for Phoenix at 13:24 of the second period; Mathieu Dandenault, Detroit, 13:32; and Keith Tkachuk, Phoenix, 13:51. Phoenix won 7-4. Detroit won best-of-seven CQF 4-2.
0:30 — Pittsburgh Penguins, Chicago Blackhawks, June 1, 1992, at Chicago. Dirk Graham scored for Chicago at 6:21 of the first period; Kevin Stevens, Pittsburgh, 6:33; and Dirk Graham, Chicago, 6:51. Pittsburgh won 6-5 and won best-of-seven F 4-0.

FASTEST THREE GOALS, ONE TEAM:

0:23 — Toronto Maple Leafs, April 12, 1979, at Toronto vs. Atlanta Flames. Darryl Sittler scored at 4:04 and 4:16 of the first period; and Ron Ellis, 4:27. Toronto won 7-4 and won best-of-three PRE 2-0.
0:38 — New York Rangers, April 12, 1986, at NY Rangers vs. Philadelphia. Jim Weimer scored at 12:29 of the third period; Bob Brooke, 12:43; and Ron Greschner, 13:07. NY Rangers won 5-2 and won best-of-five DSF 3-2.
— Colorado Avalanche, April 18, 2001, at Vancouver. Peter Forsberg scored at 9:11 of the third period; Joe Sakic, 9:28; and Eric Messier, 9:49. Colorado won 5-1 and won best-of-seven CQF 4-0.

FASTEST TWO GOALS, BOTH TEAMS:

0:05 — Pittsburgh Penguins, Buffalo Sabres, April 14, 1979, at Buffalo. Gilbert Perreault scored for Buffalo at 12:59 of the first period; and Jim Hamilton, Pittsburgh, 13:04. Pittsburgh won 4-3 and won best-of-three PRE 2-1.
0:06 — Philadelphia Flyers, Pittsburgh Penguins, April 13, 2012 at Pittsburgh. Claude Giroux scored for Philadelphia at 11:04 of the second period; and Chris Kunitz, Pittsburgh, 11:10. Philadelphia won 8-5. Philadelphia won best-of-seven CQF 4-2.
0:08 — St. Louis Blues, Minnesota North Stars, April 9, 1989, at Minnesota. Bernie Federko scored for St. Louis at 2:28 of the third period; and Perry Berezan, Minnesota, 2:36. Minnesota won 5-4. St. Louis won best-of-seven DSF 4-1.
— Phoenix Coyotes, Detroit Red Wings, April 24, 1998, at Detroit. Jeremy Roenick scored for Phoenix at 13:24 of the second period; and Mathieu Dandenault, Detroit, 13:32. Phoenix won 7-4. Detroit won best-of-seven CQF 4-2.

FASTEST TWO GOALS, ONE TEAM:

0:05 — Detroit Red Wings, April 11, 1965, at Detroit vs. Chicago. Norm Ullman scored at 17:35 and 17:40 of the second period. Detroit won 4-2. Chicago won best-of-seven SF 4-3.

Chicago's Brent Seabrook celebrates his series-winning goal in overtime of game seven against Detroit in the Western Conference semi-final. Seabrook also scored the OT winner in game four of the Stanley Cup Final.

OVERTIME

SHORTEST OVERTIME:
0:09 — Montreal Canadiens, Calgary Flames, May 18, 1986, at Calgary. Montreal won 3-2 on Brian Skrudland's goal at 0:09 of the first overtime period. Montreal won best-of-seven F 4-1.
0:11 — New York Islanders, New York Rangers, April 11, 1975, at NY Rangers. NY Islanders won 4-3 on J.P. Parise's goal at 0:11 of the first overtime period. NY Islanders won best-of-three PRE 2-1.
— Vancouver Canucks, Boston Bruins, June 4, 2011, at Vancouver. Vancouver won 3-2 on Alexandre Burrows' goal at 0:11 of the first overtime period. Boston won best-of-seven F 4-3.

LONGEST OVERTIME:
116:30 — Detroit Red Wings, Montreal Maroons, March 24, 1936, at Montreal. Mtl. Maroons won 1-0 on Mud Bruneteau's goal at 16:30 of the sixth overtime period. Detroit won best-of-five SF 3-0.

MOST OVERTIME GAMES, ONE PLAYOFF YEAR:
28 — 1993. Of 85 games played, 28 went into overtime.
27 — 2013. Of 86 games played, 27 went into overtime.
26 — 2001. Of 86 games played, 26 went into overtime.

FEWEST OVERTIME GAMES, ONE PLAYOFF YEAR:
0 — 1963. None of the 16 games went into overtime, the only year since 1926 that no overtime was required in any playoff series.

MOST OVERTIME GAMES, ONE SERIES:
5 — Toronto Maple Leafs, Montreal Canadiens in 1951. Toronto won best-of-seven F 4-1.
— Phoenix Coyotes, Chicago Blackhawks in 2012. Phoenix won best-of-seven CQF 4-2.
4 — Toronto Maple Leafs, Boston Bruins in 1933. Toronto won best-of-five SF 3-2.
— Boston Bruins, NY Rangers in 1939. Boston won best-of-seven SF 4-3.
— St. Louis Blues, Minnesota North Stars in 1968. St. Louis won best-of-seven SF 4-3.
— Dallas Stars, St. Louis Blues in 1999. Dallas won best-of-seven CSF 4-2.
— Dallas Stars, Edmonton Oilers in 2001. Dallas won best-of-seven CQF 4-2.
— Dallas Stars, San Jose Sharks in 2008. Dallas won best-of-seven CSF 4-2
— Washington Capitals, Boston Bruins in 2012. Washington won best-of-seven CQF 4-3
— Detroit Red Wings, Anaheim Ducks in 2013. Detroit won best-of-seven CQF 4-3

TEAM HAT-TRICKS

MOST HAT-TRICKS, BY ALL TEAMS, ONE PLAYOFF YEAR:
12 — 1983 in 66 games.
— 1988 in 83 games.
11 — 1985 in 70 games.
— 1992 in 86 games.

MOST HAT-TRICKS, ONE TEAM, ONE PLAYOFF YEAR:
6 — Edmonton Oilers in 16 games, 1983.
— Edmonton Oilers in 18 games, 1985.

SHUTOUTS

MOST SHUTOUTS, ONE PLAYOFF YEAR, ALL TEAMS:
25 — 2002. Of 90 games played, Detroit had 6; Ottawa had 4; Carolina, Colorado, St. Louis and Toronto had 3 each; while Los Angeles, New Jersey and Philadelphia had 1 each.
23 — 2004. Of 89 games played, Tampa Bay and Calgary had 5 each; Toronto and San Jose had 3 each; while Boston, Colorado, Detroit, Montreal, Nashville, NY Islanders and Philadelphia had 1 each.
19 — 2001. Of 86 games played, Colorado and New Jersey had 4 each, Toronto had 3, Pittsburgh and Los Angeles had 2 each, while Buffalo, Washington, Detroit and San Jose had 1 each.

FEWEST SHUTOUTS, ONE PLAYOFF YEAR, ALL TEAMS:
0 — 1959. 18 games played.

MOST SHUTOUTS, BOTH TEAMS, ONE SERIES:
5 — Toronto Maple Leafs (3), Detroit Red Wings (2), in 1945. Toronto won best-of-seven F 4-3.
— Toronto Maple Leafs (3), Detroit Red Wings (2), in 1950. Detroit won best-of-seven SF 4-3.

TEAM PENALTIES

FEWEST PENALTIES, BOTH TEAMS, BEST-OF-SEVEN SERIES:
19 — Detroit Red Wings, Toronto Maple Leafs in 1945. Detroit received 10 minors, Toronto received 9 minors. Toronto won best-of-seven F 4-3.

FEWEST PENALTIES, ONE TEAM, BEST-OF-SEVEN SERIES:
9 — Toronto Maple Leafs in 1945 vs. Detroit. Toronto received 9 minors. Toronto won best-of-seven F 4-3.

MOST PENALTIES, BOTH TEAMS, ONE SERIES:
218 — New Jersey Devils, Washington Capitals in 1988. New Jersey received 97 minors, 11 majors, 9 misconducts and 1 match penalty. Washington received 80 minors, 11 majors, 8 misconducts and 1 match penalty. New Jersey won best-of-seven DF 4-3.

MOST PENALTY MINUTES, BOTH TEAMS, ONE SERIES:
654 — New Jersey Devils (349), Washington Capitals (305) in 1988. New Jersey won best-of-seven DF 4-3.

MOST PENALTIES, ONE TEAM, ONE SERIES:
118 — New Jersey Devils in 1988 vs. Washington. New Jersey received 97 minors, 11 majors, 9 misconducts and 1 match penalty. New Jersey won best-of-seven DF 4-3.

MOST PENALTY MINUTES, ONE TEAM, ONE SERIES:
349 — New Jersey Devils in 1988 vs. Washington. New Jersey won best-of-seven DF 4-3.

MOST PENALTIES, BOTH TEAMS, ONE GAME:
66 — Detroit Red Wings (33), St. Louis Blues (33), April 12, 1991, at St. Louis. St. Louis won 6-1.
63 — Minnesota North Stars (34), Chicago Blackhawks (29), April 6, 1990, at Chicago. Chicago won 5-3.
62 — New Jersey Devils (32), Washington Capitals (30), April 22, 1988, at New Jersey. New Jersey won 10-4.

MOST PENALTY MINUTES, BOTH TEAMS, ONE GAME:
298 — Detroit Red Wings (152), St. Louis Blues (146), April 12, 1991, at St. Louis. Detroit received 33 penalties; St. Louis received 33 penalties. St. Louis won 6-1.
267 — New York Rangers (142), Los Angeles Kings (125), April 9, 1981, at Los Angeles. NY Rangers received 31 penalties; Los Angeles received 28 penalties. Los Angeles won 5-4.

MOST PENALTIES, ONE TEAM, ONE GAME:
34 — Minnesota North Stars, April 6, 1990, at Chicago. Chicago won 5-3.
33 — Detroit Red Wings, April 12, 1991, at St. Louis. St. Louis won 6-1.
— St. Louis Blues, April 12, 1991, at St. Louis vs. Detroit. St. Louis won 6-1.

MOST PENALTY MINUTES, ONE TEAM, ONE GAME:
152 — Detroit Red Wings, April 12, 1991, at St. Louis. St. Louis won 6-1.
146 — St. Louis Blues, April 12, 1991, at St. Louis vs. Detroit. St. Louis won 6-1.
142 — New York Rangers, April 9, 1981, at Los Angeles. Los Angeles won 5-4.

MOST PENALTIES, BOTH TEAMS, ONE PERIOD:
43 — New York Rangers (24), Los Angeles Kings (19), April 9, 1981, first period at Los Angeles. Los Angeles won 5-4.

MOST PENALTY MINUTES, BOTH TEAMS, ONE PERIOD:
248 — New York Islanders (124), Boston Bruins (124), April 17, 1980, first period at Boston. NY Islanders won 5-4.

MOST PENALTIES, ONE TEAM, ONE PERIOD:
24 — New York Rangers, April 9, 1981, first period at Los Angeles. Los Angeles won 5-4.
— Montreal Canadiens, May 5, 2013, third period at Ottawa. Ottawa won 6-1.

MOST PENALTY MINUTES, ONE TEAM, ONE PERIOD:
125 — New York Rangers, April 9, 1981, first period at Los Angeles. Los Angeles won 5-4.

Individual Records

GAMES PLAYED

MOST YEARS IN PLAYOFFS:
24 — Chris Chelios, Montreal, Chicago, Detroit (1984-97 inclusive; 1999-2004 inclusive, 2006-2009 inclusive)
21 — Raymond Bourque, Boston, Colorado (1980-96 inclusive; 98-2001 inclusive)
20 — Gordie Howe, Detroit, Hartford
— Larry Robinson, Montreal, Los Angeles
— Larry Murphy, Los Angeles, Washington, Minnesota, Pittsburgh, Toronto, Detroit
— Scott Stevens, Washington, St. Louis, New Jersey
— Steve Yzerman, Detroit
— Nicklas Lidstrom, Detroit

MOST CONSECUTIVE YEARS IN PLAYOFFS:
20 — Larry Robinson, Montreal, Los Angeles (1973-92, inclusive).
— Nicklas Lidstrom, Detroit (1992-2004 inclusive; 2006-2012 inclusive)
19 — Brett Hull, Calgary, St. Louis, Dallas, Detroit (1986-2004, inclusive).
18 — Larry Murphy, Los Angeles, Washington, Minnesota, Pittsburgh, Toronto, Detroit (1984-2001, inclusive).
17 — Brad Park, NY Rangers, Boston, Detroit (1969-85, inclusive).
— Raymond Bourque, Boston (1980-96, inclusive).
— Kris Draper, Detroit (1994-2004 inclusive; 2006-2011 inclusive)

MOST PLAYOFF GAMES:
266 — Chris Chelios, Montreal, Chicago, Detroit
263 — Nicklas Lidstrom, Detroit
247 — Patrick Roy, Montreal, Colorado
236 — Mark Messier, Edmonton, NY Rangers
234 — Claude Lemieux, Montreal, New Jersey, Colorado, Phoenix, Dallas, San Jose

GOALS

MOST GOALS IN PLAYOFFS, CAREER:
122 — Wayne Gretzky, Edmonton, Los Angeles, St. Louis, NY Rangers
109 — Mark Messier, Edmonton, NY Rangers
106 — Jari Kurri, Edmonton, Los Angeles, NY Rangers, Anaheim
103 — Brett Hull, Calgary, St. Louis, Dallas, Detroit
93 — Glenn Anderson, Edmonton, Toronto, NY Rangers, St. Louis

MOST GOALS, ONE PLAYOFF YEAR:
19 — Reggie Leach, Philadelphia, 1976. 16 games.
— Jari Kurri, Edmonton, 1985. 18 games.
18 — Joe Sakic, Colorado, 1996. 22 games.
17 — Newsy Lalonde, Montreal, 1919. 10 games.
— Mike Bossy, NY Islanders, 1981. 18 games.
— Steve Payne, Minnesota, 1981. 19 games.
— Mike Bossy, NY Islanders, 1982. 19 games.
— Mike Bossy, NY Islanders, 1983. 19 games
— Wayne Gretzky, Edmonton, 1985. 18 games.
— Kevin Stevens, Pittsburgh, 1991. 24 games.

MOST GOALS IN ONE SERIES (OTHER THAN FINAL):
12 — Jari Kurri, Edmonton, in 1985 CF, 6 games vs. Chicago.
11 — Newsy Lalonde, Montreal, in 1919 NHL F, 5 games vs. Ottawa.
10 — Tim Kerr, Philadelphia, in 1989 DF, 7 games vs. Pittsburgh.
9 — Reggie Leach, Philadelphia, in 1976 SF, 5 games vs. Boston.
— Bill Barber, Philadelphia, in 1980 SF, 5 games vs. Minnesota.
— Mike Bossy, NY Islanders, in 1983 CF, 6 games vs. Boston.
— Mario Lemieux, Pittsburgh, in 1989 DF, 7 games vs. Philadelphia.
— John Druce, Washington, in 1990 DF, 5 games vs. NY Rangers.
— Johan Franzen, Detroit, in 2008 CSF, 4 games vs. Colorado.

MOST GOALS IN FINAL SERIES (NHL PLAYERS ONLY):
9 — Babe Dye, Toronto, in 1922, 5 games vs. Van. Millionaires.
8 — Alf Skinner, Toronto, in 1918, 5 games vs. Van. Millionaires.
7 — Jean Beliveau, Montreal, in 1956, 5 games vs. Detroit.
— Mike Bossy, NY Islanders, in 1982, 4 games vs. Vancouver.
— Wayne Gretzky, Edmonton, in 1985, 5 games vs. Philadelphia.

MOST GOALS, ONE GAME:
5 — Newsy Lalonde, Montreal, March 1, 1919, at Montreal. Final score: Montreal 6, Ottawa 3.
— Maurice Richard, Montreal, March 23, 1944, at Montreal. Final score: Montreal 5, Toronto 1.
— Darryl Sittler, Toronto, April 22, 1976, at Toronto. Final score: Toronto 8, Philadelphia 5.
— Reggie Leach, Philadelphia, May 6, 1976, at Philadelphia. Final score: Philadelphia 6, Boston 3.
— Mario Lemieux, Pittsburgh, April 25, 1989, at Pittsburgh. Final score: Pittsburgh 10, Philadelphia 7.

MOST GOALS, ONE PERIOD:
4 — Tim Kerr, Philadelphia, April 13, 1985, at NY Rangers, second period. Final score: Philadelphia 6, NY Rangers 5.
— Mario Lemieux, Pittsburgh, April 25, 1989, at Pittsburgh vs. Philadelphia, first period. Final score: Pittsburgh 10, Philadelphia 7.

ASSISTS

MOST ASSISTS IN PLAYOFFS, CAREER:
260 — Wayne Gretzky, Edmonton, Los Angeles, St. Louis, NY Rangers
186 — Mark Messier, Edmonton, NY Rangers
139 — Raymond Bourque, Boston, Colorado
137 — Paul Coffey, Edmonton, Pittsburgh, Los Angeles, Detroit, Philadelphia, Carolina
129 — Nicklas Lidstrom, Detroit

MOST ASSISTS, ONE PLAYOFF YEAR:
31 — Wayne Gretzky, Edmonton, 1988. 19 games.
30 — Wayne Gretzky, Edmonton, 1985. 18 games.
29 — Wayne Gretzky, Edmonton, 1987. 21 games.
28 — Mario Lemieux, Pittsburgh, 1991. 23 games.
26 — Wayne Gretzky, Edmonton, 1983. 16 games.

MOST ASSISTS IN ONE SERIES (OTHER THAN FINAL):
14 — Rick Middleton, Boston, in 1983 DF, 7 games vs. Buffalo.
— Wayne Gretzky, Edmonton, in 1985 CF, 6 games vs. Chicago.
13 — Wayne Gretzky, Edmonton, in 1987 DSF, 5 games vs. Los Angeles.
— Doug Gilmour, Toronto, in 1994 CSF, 7 games vs. San Jose.
11 — Al MacInnis, Calgary, in 1984 DF, 7 games vs. Edmonton.
— Mark Messier, Edmonton, in 1989 DSF, 7 games vs. Los Angeles.
— Mike Ridley, Washington, in 1992 DSF, 7 games vs. Pittsburgh.
— Ron Francis, Pittsburgh, in 1995 CQF, 7 games vs. Washington.
— Henrik Sedin, Vancouver, in 2011 CF, 5 games vs. San Jose.

MOST ASSISTS IN FINAL SERIES:
10 — Wayne Gretzky, Edmonton, in 1988, 4 games plus suspended game vs. Boston.
9 — Jacques Lemaire, Montreal, in 1973, 6 games vs. Chicago.
— Wayne Gretzky, Edmonton, in 1987, 7 games vs. Philadelphia.
— Larry Murphy, Pittsburgh, in 1991, 6 games vs. Minnesota.
— Daniel Briere, Philadelphia, in 2010, 6 games vs. Chicago.

MOST ASSISTS, ONE GAME:
6 — Mikko Leinonen, NY Rangers, April 8, 1982, at NY Rangers. Final score: NY Rangers 7, Philadelphia 3.
— Wayne Gretzky, Edmonton, April 9, 1987, at Edmonton. Final score: Edmonton 13, Los Angeles 3.
5 — Toe Blake, Montreal, March 23, 1944, at Montreal. Final score: Montreal 5, Toronto 1.
— Maurice Richard, Montreal, March 27, 1956, at Montreal. Final score: Montreal 7, NY Rangers 0.
— Bert Olmstead, Montreal, March 30, 1957, at Montreal. Final score: Montreal 8, NY Rangers 3.
— Don McKenney, Boston, April 5, 1958, at Boston. Final score: Boston 8, NY Rangers 2.
— Stan Mikita, Chicago, April 4, 1973, at Chicago. Final score: Chicago 7, St. Louis 1.
— Wayne Gretzky, Edmonton, April 8, 1981, at Montreal. Final score: Edmonton 6, Montreal 3.
— Paul Coffey, Edmonton, May 14, 1985, at Edmonton. Final score: Edmonton 10, Chicago 5.
— Doug Gilmour, St. Louis, April 15, 1986, at Minnesota. Final score: St. Louis 6, Minnesota 3.
— Risto Siltanen, Quebec, April 14, 1987, at Hartford. Final score: Quebec 7, Hartford 5.
— Patrik Sundstrom, New Jersey, April 22, 1988, at New Jersey. Final score: New Jersey 10, Washington 4.
— Geoff Courtnall, St. Louis, April 23, 1998, at St. Louis. Final score: St. Louis 8, Los Angeles 3.

MOST ASSISTS, ONE PERIOD:
3 — Three assists by one player in one period of a playoff game has been recorded on 85 occasions. Zdeno Chara of the Boston Bruins is the most recent to equal this mark with 3 assists in the second period at Toronto, May 8, 2013. Final score: Boston 4, Toronto 3.
— Wayne Gretzky has had 3 assists in one period 5 times; Raymond Bourque, 3 times; Toe Blake, Jean Beliveau, Doug Harvey and Bobby Orr, twice each. Joe Primeau of Toronto was the first player to be credited with 3 assists in one period of a playoff game; third period at Boston vs. NY Rangers, April 7, 1932. Final score: Toronto 6, NY Rangers 2.

POINTS

MOST POINTS IN PLAYOFFS, CAREER:
382 — Wayne Gretzky, Edmonton, Los Angeles, St. Louis, NY Rangers, 122G, 260A
295 — Mark Messier, Edmonton, NY Rangers, 109G, 186A
233 — Jari Kurri, Edmonton, Los Angeles, NY Rangers, Anaheim, 106G, 127A
214 — Glenn Anderson, Edmonton, Toronto, NY Rangers, St. Louis, 93G, 121A
199 — Jaromir Jagr, Pittsburgh, Washington, NY Rangers, Philadelphia, Boston, 78G, 121A

MOST POINTS, ONE PLAYOFF YEAR:
47 — Wayne Gretzky, Edmonton, in 1985. 17 goals, 30 assists in 18 games.
44 — Mario Lemieux, Pittsburgh, in 1991. 16 goals, 28 assists in 23 games.
43 — Wayne Gretzky, Edmonton, in 1988. 12 goals, 31 assists in 19 games.
40 — Wayne Gretzky, Los Angeles, in 1993. 15 goals, 25 assists in 24 games.
38 — Wayne Gretzky, Edmonton, in 1983. 12 goals, 26 assists in 16 games.

MOST POINTS IN ONE SERIES (OTHER THAN FINAL):
19 — Rick Middleton, Boston, in 1983 DF, 7 games vs. Buffalo. 5 goals, 14 assists.
18 — Wayne Gretzky, Edmonton, in 1985 CF, 6 games vs. Chicago. 4 goals, 14 assists.
17 — Mario Lemieux, Pittsburgh, in 1992 DSF, 6 games vs. Washington. 7 goals, 10 assists.
16 — Barry Pederson, Boston, in 1983 DF, 7 games vs. Buffalo. 7 goals, 9 assists.
— Doug Gilmour, Toronto, in 1994 CSF, 7 games vs. San Jose. 3 goals, 13 assists.
15 — Jari Kurri, Edmonton, in 1985 CF, 6 games vs. Chicago. 12 goals, 3 assists.
— Wayne Gretzky, Edmonton, in 1987 DSF, 5 games vs. Los Angeles. 2 goals, 13 assists.
— Tim Kerr, Philadelphia, in 1989 DF, 7 games vs. Pittsburgh. 10 goals, 5 assists.
— Mario Lemieux, Pittsburgh, in 1991 CF, 6 games vs. Boston. 6 goals, 9 assists.

MOST POINTS IN FINAL SERIES:

13 — Wayne Gretzky, Edmonton, in 1988, 4 games plus suspended game vs. Boston. 3 goals, 10 assists.
12 — Gordie Howe, Detroit, in 1955, 7 games vs. Montreal. 5 goals, 7 assists.
— Yvan Cournoyer, Montreal, in 1973, 6 games vs. Chicago. 6 goals, 6 assists.
— Jacques Lemaire, Montreal, in 1973, 6 games vs. Chicago. 3 goals, 9 assists.
— Mario Lemieux, Pittsburgh, in 1991, 5 games vs. Minnesota. 5 goals, 7 assists.
— Daniel Briere, Philadelphia, in 2010, 6 games vs. Chicago. 3 goals, 9 assists.

MOST POINTS, ONE GAME:

8 — Patrik Sundstrom, New Jersey, April 22, 1988, at New Jersey in 10-4 win over Washington. Sundstrom had 3 goals, 5 assists.
— Mario Lemieux, Pittsburgh, April 25, 1989, at Pittsburgh in 10-7 win over Philadelphia. Lemieux had 5 goals, 3 assists.
7 — Wayne Gretzky, Edmonton, April 17, 1983, at Calgary in 10-2 win. Gretzky had 4 goals, 3 assists.
— Wayne Gretzky, Edmonton, April 25,1985, at Winnipeg in 8-3 win. Gretzky had 3 goals, 4 assists.
— Wayne Gretzky, Edmonton, April 9, 1987, at Edmonton in 13-3 win over Los Angeles. Gretzky had 1 goal, 6 assists.
6 — Dickie Moore, Montreal, March 25, 1954, at Montreal in 8-1 win over Boston. Moore had 2 goals, 4 assists.
— Phil Esposito, Boston, April 2, 1969, at Boston in 10-0 win over Toronto. Esposito had 4 goals, 2 assists.
— Darryl Sittler, Toronto, April 22, 1976, at Toronto in 8-5 win over Philadelphia. Sittler had 5 goals, 1 assist.
— Guy Lafleur, Montreal, April 11, 1977, at Montreal in 7-2 win over St. Louis. Lafleur had 3 goals, 3 assists.
— Mikko Leinonen, NY Rangers, April 8, 1982, at NY Rangers in 7-3 win over Philadelphia. Leinonen had 6 assists.
— Paul Coffey, Edmonton, May 14, 1985, at Edmonton in 10-5 win over Chicago. Coffey had 1 goal, 5 assists.
— John Anderson, Hartford, April 12, 1986, at Hartford in 9-4 win over Quebec. Anderson had 2 goals, 4 assists.
— Mario Lemieux, Pittsburgh, April 23, 1992, at Pittsburgh in 6-4 win over Washington. Lemieux had 3 goals, 3 assists.
— Geoff Courtnall, St. Louis, April 23, 1998, at St. Louis in 8-3 win over Los Angeles. Courtnall had 1 goal, 5 assists.
— Patrick Elias, New Jersey, April 22, 2006, at New Jersey in 6-1 win over NY Rangers. Elias had 2 goals, 4 assists.
— Johan Franzen, Detroit, May 6, 2010, at Detroit in 7-1 win over San Jose. Franzen had 4 goals, 2 assists.
— Claude Giroux, Philadelphia, April 13, 2012, at Pittsburgh in 8-5 win. Giroux had 3 goals, 3 assists.

MOST POINTS, ONE PERIOD:

4 — Maurice Richard, Montreal, March 29, 1945, at Montreal, third period, in 10-3 win vs. Toronto. 3 goals, 1 assist.
— Dickie Moore, Montreal, March 25, 1954, at Montreal, first period, in 8-1 win vs. Boston. 2 goals, 2 assists.
— Barry Pederson, Boston, April 8, 1982, at Boston, second period, in 7-3 win vs. Buffalo. 3 goals, 1 assist.
— Peter McNab, Boston, April 11, 1982, at Buffalo, second period, in 5-2 win vs. Buffalo. 1 goal, 3 assists.
— Tim Kerr, Philadelphia, April 13, 1985, at NY Rangers, second period, in 6-5 win vs. NY Rangers. 4 goals.
— Ken Linseman, Boston, April 14, 1985, at Boston, second period, in 7-6 win vs. Montreal. 2 goals, 2 assists.
— Wayne Gretzky, Edmonton, April 12, 1987, at Los Angeles, third period, in 6-3 win vs. Los Angeles. 1 goal, 3 assists.
— Glenn Anderson, Edmonton, April 6, 1988, at Edmonton, third period, in 7-4 win vs. Winnipeg. 3 goals, 1 assist.
— Mario Lemieux, Pittsburgh, April 25, 1989, at Pittsburgh, first period, in 10-7 win vs. Philadelphia. 4 goals.
— Dave Gagner, Minnesota North Stars, April 8, 1991, at Minnesota, first period, in 6-5 loss vs. Chicago. 2 goals, 2 assists.
— Mario Lemieux, Pittsburgh, April 23, 1992, at Pittsburgh, second period, in 6-4 win vs. Washington. 2 goals, 2 assists.
— Alexander Mogilny, New Jersey, April 28, 2001, at New Jersey, second period, in 6-5 win vs. Toronto. 1 goal, 3 assists.
— Brad Richards, Dallas, April 27, 2008, at San Jose, third period, in 5-2 win vs. San Jose. 1 goal, 3 assists.
— Johan Franzen, Detroit, May 6, 2010, at Detroit, first period, in 7-1 win over San Jose. 3 goals, 1 assist.
— Tyler Seguin, Boston, May 17, 2011, at Boston, second period, in 6-5 win over Tampa Bay. 2 goals, 2 assists.

POWER-PLAY GOALS

MOST POWER-PLAY GOALS IN PLAYOFFS, CAREER:

38 — Brett Hull, St. Louis, Dallas, Detroit
35 — Mike Bossy, NY Islanders
34 — Dino Ciccarelli, Minnesota, Washington, Detroit
— Wayne Gretzky, Edmonton, Los Angeles, St. Louis, NY Rangers
30 — Nicklas Lidstrom, Detroit

MOST POWER-PLAY GOALS, ONE PLAYOFF YEAR:

9 — Mike Bossy, NY Islanders, 1981. 18 games vs. Toronto, Edmonton, NY Rangers and Minnesota.
— Cam Neely, Boston, 1991. 19 games vs. Hartford, Montreal and Pittsburgh.
8 — Tim Kerr, Philadelphia, 1989. 19 games.
— John Druce, Washington, 1990. 15 games.
— Brian Propp, Minnesota, 1991. 23 games.
— Mario Lemieux, Pittsburgh, 1992. 15 games.

MOST POWER-PLAY GOALS, ONE PLAYOFF SERIES:

6 — Chris Kontos, Los Angeles, 1989 DSF vs. Edmonton, won by Los Angeles 4-3.
5 — Andy Bathgate, Detroit, 1966 SF vs. Chicago, won by Detroit 4-2.
— Denis Potvin, NY Islanders, 1981 QF vs. Edmonton, won by NY Islanders 4-2.
— Ken Houston, Calgary, 1981 QF vs. Philadelphia, won by Calgary 4-3.
— Rick Vaive, Chicago, 1988 DSF vs. St. Louis, won by St. Louis 4-1.
— Tim Kerr, Philadelphia, 1989 DF vs. Pittsburgh, won by Philadelphia 4-3.
— Mario Lemieux, Pittsburgh, 1989 DF vs. Philadelphia, won by Philadelphia 4-3.
— John Druce, Washington, 1990 DF vs. NY Rangers, won by Washington 4-1.
— Pat LaFontaine, Buffalo, 1992 DSF vs. Boston, won by Boston 4-3.
— Adam Graves, NY Rangers, 1996 CQF vs Montreal, won by NY Rangers 4-2.

MOST POWER-PLAY GOALS, ONE GAME:

3 — Syd Howe, Detroit, March 23, 1939, at Detroit vs. Montreal. Detroit won 7-3.
— Sid Smith, Toronto, April 10, 1949, at Detroit. Toronto won 3-1.
— Phil Esposito, Boston, April 2, 1969, at Boston vs. Toronto. Boston won 10-0.
— John Bucyk, Boston, April 21, 1974, at Boston vs. Chicago. Boston won 8-6.
— Denis Potvin, NY Islanders, April 17, 1981, at NY Islanders vs. Edmonton. NY Islanders won 6-3.
— Tim Kerr, Philadelphia, April 13, 1985, at NY Rangers. Philadelphia won 6-5.
— Jari Kurri, Edmonton, April 9, 1987, at Edmonton vs. Los Angeles. Edmonton won 13-3.
— Mark Johnson, New Jersey, April 22, 1988, at New Jersey vs. Washington. New Jersey won 10-4.
— Dino Ciccarelli, Detroit, April 29, 1993, at Toronto. Detroit won 7-3.
— Dino Ciccarelli, Detroit, May 11, 1995, at Dallas. Detroit won 5-1.
— Valeri Kamensky, Colorado, April 24, 1997, at Colorado vs. Chicago. Colorado won 7-0.
— Jonathan Toews, Chicago May 7, 2010, at Vancouver. Chicago won 7-4.

MOST POWER-PLAY GOALS, ONE PERIOD:

3 — Tim Kerr, Philadelphia, April 13, 1985, at NY Rangers, second period in 6-5 win.
2 — Two power-play goals have been scored by one player in one period on 63 occasions. Charlie Conacher of Toronto was the first to score two power-play goals in one period, setting the mark with two power-play goals in the second period at Toronto vs. Boston, March 26, 1936. Final score: Toronto 8, Boston 3. Logan Couture of the San Jose Sharks is the most recent to equal this mark with two power-play goals in the third period at San Jose, May 5, 2013. Final score: San Jose 5, Vancouver 2.

SHORTHAND GOALS

MOST SHORTHAND GOALS IN PLAYOFFS, CAREER:

12 — Mark Messier, Edmonton, NY Rangers
11 — Wayne Gretzky, Edmonton, Los Angeles, St. Louis
10 — Jari Kurri, Edmonton, Los Angeles, NY Rangers
8 — Ed Westfall, Boston, NY Islanders
— Hakan Loob, Calgary

MOST SHORTHAND GOALS, ONE PLAYOFF YEAR:

3 — Derek Sanderson, Boston, 1969. 1 vs. Toronto in QF, won by Boston 4-0; 2 vs. Montreal in SF, won by Montreal, 4-2.
— Bill Barber, Philadelphia, 1980. All vs. Minnesota in SF, won by Philadelphia 4-1.
— Lorne Henning, NY Islanders, 1980. 1 vs. Boston in QF, won by NY Islanders 4-1; 1 vs. Buffalo in SF, won by NY Islanders 4-2, 1 vs. Philadelphia in F, won by NY Islanders 4-2.
— Wayne Gretzky, Edmonton, 1983. 2 vs. Winnipeg in DSF, won by Edmonton 3-0; 1 vs. Calgary in DF, won by Edmonton 4-1.
— Wayne Presley, Chicago, 1989. All vs. Detroit in DSF, won by Chicago 4-2.
— Todd Marchant, Edmonton, 1997. 1 vs. Dallas in CQF, won by Edmonton 4-3; 2 vs. Colorado in CSF, won by Colorado 4-1.

Jari Kurri's 12 goals against Chicago in the 1985 Western Conference Final set an NHL record that still stands for most goals in one playoff series.

MOST SHORTHAND GOALS, ONE PLAYOFF SERIES:

3 — Bill Barber, Philadelphia, 1980 SF vs. Minnesota, won by Philadelphia 4-1.
— Wayne Presley, Chicago, 1989 DSF vs. Detroit, won by Chicago 4-2.
2 — Mac Colville, NY Rangers, 1940 SF vs. Boston, won by NY Rangers 4-2.
— Jerry Toppazzini, Boston, 1958 SF vs. NY Rangers, won by Boston 4-2.
— Dave Keon, Toronto, 1963 F vs. Detroit, won by Toronto 4-1.
— Bob Pulford, Toronto, 1964 F vs. Detroit, won by Toronto 4-3.
— Serge Savard, Montreal, 1968 F vs. St. Louis, won by Montreal 4-0.
— Derek Sanderson, Boston, 1969 SF vs. Montreal, won by Montreal 4-2.
— Bryan Trottier, NY Islanders, 1980 PR vs. Los Angeles, won by NY Islanders 3-1.
— Bobby Lalonde, Boston, 1981 PR vs. Minnesota, won by Minnesota 3-0.
— Butch Goring, NY Islanders, 1981 SF vs. NY Rangers, won by NY Islanders 4-0.
— Wayne Gretzky, Edmonton, 1983 DSF vs. Winnipeg, won by Edmonton 3-0.
— Mark Messier, Edmonton, 1983 DF vs. Calgary, won by Edmonton 4-1.
— Jari Kurri, Edmonton, 1983 CF vs. Chicago, won by Edmonton 4-0.
— Wayne Gretzky, Edmonton, 1985 DF vs. Winnipeg, won by Edmonton 4-0.
— Kevin Lowe, Edmonton, 1987 F vs. Philadelphia, won by Edmonton 4-3.
— Bob Gould, Washington, 1988 DSF vs. Philadelphia, won by Washington 4-3.
— Dave Poulin, Philadelphia, 1989 DF vs. Pittsburgh, won by Philadelphia 4-3.
— Russ Courtnall, Montreal, 1991 DF vs. Boston, won by Boston 4-3.
— Sergei Fedorov, Detroit, 1992 DSF vs. Minnesota, won by Detroit 4-3.
— Mark Messier, NY Rangers, 1992 DSF vs. New Jersey, won by NY Rangers 4-3.
— Tom Fitzgerald, NY Islanders, 1993 DF vs. Pittsburgh, won by NY Islanders 4-3.
— Mark Osborne, Toronto, 1994 CSF vs. San Jose, won by Toronto 4-3.
— Tony Amonte, Chicago, 1997 CQF vs. Colorado, won by Colorado 4-2.
— Brian Rolston, New Jersey, 1997 CQF vs. Montreal, won by New Jersey 4-1.
— Rod Brind'Amour, Philadelphia, 1997 CQF vs. Pittsburgh, won by Philadelphia 4-1.
— Todd Marchant, Edmonton, 1997 CSF vs. Colorado, won by Colorado 4-1.
— Jeremy Roenick, Phoenix, 1998 CQF vs. Detroit, won by Detroit 4-2.
— Vincent Damphousse, San Jose, 1999 CQF vs. Colorado, won by Colorado 4-2.
— Dixon Ward, Buffalo, 1999 CF vs. Toronto, won by Buffalo 4-1.
— Curtis Brown, Buffalo, 2001 CSF vs. Pittsburgh, won by Pittsburgh 4-3.
— John Madden, New Jersey, 2006 CQF vs. NY Rangers, won by New Jersey 4-0.
— David Legwand, Nashville, 2011 CSF vs. Vancouver, won by Vancouver 4-2.
— Maxime Talbot, Philadelphia, 2012 CQF vs. Pittsburgh, won by Philadelphia 4-2.
— Dustin Brown, Los Angeles, 2012 CQF vs. Vancouver, won by Los Angeles 4-1.
— Pascal Dupuis, Pittsburgh, 2013 CSF vs. Ottawa, won by Pittsburgh 4-1.

MOST SHORTHAND GOALS, ONE GAME:

2 — Dave Keon, Toronto, April 18, 1963, at Toronto, in 3-1 win vs. Detroit.
— Bryan Trottier, NY Islanders, April 8, 1980, at NY Islanders, in 8-1 win vs. Los Angeles.
— Bobby Lalonde, Boston, April 11, 1981, at Minnesota, in 6-3 loss vs. Minnesota.
— Wayne Gretzky, Edmonton, April 6, 1983, at Edmonton, in 6-3 win vs. Winnipeg.
— Jari Kurri, Edmonton, April 24, 1983, at Edmonton, in 8-3 win vs. Chicago.
— Wayne Gretzky, Edmonton, April 25, 1985, at Winnipeg, in 8-3 win by Edmonton.
— Mark Messier, NY Rangers, April 21, 1992, at NY Rangers, in 7-3 loss vs. New Jersey.
— Tom Fitzgerald, NY Islanders, May 8, 1993, at NY Islanders, in 6-5 win vs. Pittsburgh.
— Rod Brind'Amour, Philadelphia, April 26, 1997, at Philadelphia, in 6-3 win vs. Pittsburgh.
— Jeremy Roenick, Phoenix, April 24, 1998, at Detroit, in 7-4 win by Phoenix.
— Vincent Damphousse, San Jose, April 30, 1999, at Colorado, in 7-3 win by San Jose.
— John Madden, New Jersey, April 24, 2006, at New Jersey, in 4-1 win vs. NY Rangers.
— Dustin Brown, Los Angeles, April 13, 2012, at Vancouver, in 4-2 win vs. Vancouver.

MOST SHORTHAND GOALS, ONE PERIOD:

2 — Bryan Trottier, NY Islanders, April 8, 1980, second period, at NY Islanders, in 8-1 win vs. Los Angeles.
— Bobby Lalonde, Boston, April 11, 1981, third period, at Minnesota, in 6-3 loss vs. Minnesota.
— Jari Kurri, Edmonton, April 24, 1983, third period, at Edmonton, in 8-4 win vs. Chicago.
— Rod Brind'Amour, Philadelphia, April 26, 1997, first period, at Philadelphia, in 6-3 win vs. Pittsburgh.
— Jeremy Roenick, Phoenix, April 24, 1998, second period, at Detroit, in 7-4 win by Phoenix.
— Vincent Damphousse, San Jose, April 30, 1999, third period, at Colorado, in 7-3 win vs. Colorado.

GAME-WINNING GOALS

MOST GAME-WINNING GOALS IN PLAYOFFS, CAREER:

24 — Wayne Gretzky, Edmonton, Los Angeles, St. Louis, NY Rangers
— Brett Hull, St. Louis, Dallas, Detroit
19 — Claude Lemieux, Montreal, New Jersey, Colorado
— Joe Sakic, Colorado
18 — Maurice Richard, Montreal

MOST GAME-WINNING GOALS, ONE PLAYOFF YEAR:

7 — Brad Richards, Tampa Bay, 2004. 23 games.
6 — Joe Sakic, Colorado, 1996. 22 games.
— Joe Nieuwendyk, Dallas, 1999. 23 games.
5 — Mike Bossy, NY Islanders, 1983. 19 games.
— Jari Kurri, Edmonton, 1987. 21 games.
— Bobby Smith, Minnesota, 1991. 23 games.
— Mario Lemieux, Pittsburgh, 1992. 15 games.
— Fernando Pisani, Edmonton, 2006. 24 games.
— Johan Franzen, Detroit, 2008. 16 games.
— Dustin Byfuglien, Chicago, 2010. 22 games.

MOST GAME-WINNING GOALS, ONE PLAYOFF SERIES:

4 — Mike Bossy, NY Islanders, 1983 CF vs. Boston, won by NY Islanders 4-2.

OVERTIME GOALS

MOST OVERTIME GOALS IN PLAYOFFS, CAREER:

8 — Joe Sakic, Colorado (2 in 1996; 1 in 1998; 1 in 2001; 2 in 2004; 1 in 2006; 1 in 2008)
6 — Maurice Richard, Montreal
5 — Glenn Anderson, Edmonton, Toronto, St. Louis
4 — Bob Nystrom, NY Islanders
— Dale Hunter, Quebec, Washington
— Wayne Gretzky, Edmonton, Los Angeles
— Stephane Richer, Montreal, New Jersey
— Joe Murphy, Edmonton, Chicago
— Esa Tikkanen, Edmonton, NY Rangers
— Jaromir Jagr, Pittsburgh
— Kirk Muller, Montreal, Dallas
— Jeremy Roenick, Chicago, Philadelphia
— Chris Drury, Colorado, Buffalo
— Jamie Langenbrunner, Dallas, New Jersey

MOST OVERTIME GOALS, ONE PLAYOFF YEAR:

3 — Mel Hill, Boston, 1939. All vs. NY Rangers in best-of-seven SF, won by Boston 4-3.
— Maurice Richard, Montreal, 1951. 2 vs. Detroit in best-of-seven SF, won by Montreal 4-2; 1 vs. Toronto best-of-seven F, won by Toronto 4-1.

MOST OVERTIME GOALS, ONE PLAYOFF SERIES:

3 — Mel Hill, Boston, 1939, SF vs. NY Rangers, won by Boston 4-3. Hill scored at 59:25 of overtime March 21 for a 2-1 win; at 8:24 of overtime, March 23 for a 3-2 win; and at 48:00 of overtime, April 2 for a 2-1 win.

SCORING BY A DEFENSEMAN

MOST GOALS BY A DEFENSEMAN, ONE PLAYOFF YEAR:

12 — Paul Coffey, Edmonton, 1985. 18 games.
11 — Brian Leetch, NY Rangers, 1994. 23 games.
9 — Bobby Orr, Boston, 1970. 14 games.
— Brad Park, Boston, 1978. 15 games.
8 — Denis Potvin, NY Islanders, 1981. 18 games.
— Raymond Bourque, Boston, 1983. 17 games.
— Denis Potvin, NY Islanders, 1983. 20 games.
— Paul Coffey, Edmonton, 1984. 19 games.

MOST GOALS BY A DEFENSEMAN, ONE GAME:

3 — Bobby Orr, Boston, April 11, 1971, at Montreal.
Final score: Boston 5, Montreal 2.
— Dick Redmond, Chicago, April 4, 1973, at Chicago.
Final score: Chicago 7, St. Louis 1.
— Denis Potvin, NY Islanders, April 17, 1981, at NY Islanders.
Final score: NY Islanders 6, Edmonton 3.
— Paul Reinhart, Calgary, April 14, 1983, at Edmonton.
Final score: Edmonton 6, Calgary 3.
— Doug Halward, Vancouver, April 7, 1984, at Vancouver.
Final score: Vancouver 7, Calgary 0.
— Paul Reinhart, Calgary, April 8, 1984, at Vancouver.
Final score: Calgary 5, Vancouver 1.
— Al Iafrate, Washington, April 26, 1993, at Washington.
Final score: Washington 6, NY Islanders 4.
— Eric Desjardins, Montreal, June 3, 1993, at Montreal.
Final score: Montreal 3, Los Angeles 2.
— Gary Suter, Chicago, April 24, 1994, at Chicago.
Final score: Chicago 4, Toronto 3.
— Brian Leetch, NY Rangers, May 22, 1995, at Philadelphia.
Final score: Philadelphia 4, NY Rangers 3.
— Andy Delmore, Philadelphia, May 7, 2000, at Philadelphia.
Final score: Philadelphia 6, Pittsburgh 3.

MOST ASSISTS BY A DEFENSEMAN, ONE PLAYOFF YEAR:

25 — Paul Coffey, Edmonton, 1985. 18 games.
24 — Al MacInnis, Calgary, 1989. 22 games.
23 — Brian Leetch, NY Rangers, 1994. 23 games.
19 — Bobby Orr, Boston, 1972. 15 games.
18 — Raymond Bourque, Boston, 1988. 23 games.
— Raymond Bourque, Boston, 1991. 19 games.
— Larry Murphy, Pittsburgh, 1991. 23 games.
— Chris Pronger, Philadelphia, 2010. 23 games.

MOST ASSISTS BY A DEFENSEMAN, ONE GAME:

5 — Paul Coffey, Edmonton, May 14, 1985, at Edmonton vs. Chicago. Edmonton won 10-5.
— Risto Siltanen, Quebec, April 14, 1987, at Hartford. Quebec won 7-5.

MOST POINTS BY A DEFENSEMAN, ONE PLAYOFF YEAR:

37 — Paul Coffey, Edmonton, 1985. 12 goals, 25 assists in 18 games.
34 — Brian Leetch, NY Rangers, 1994. 11 goals, 23 assists in 23 games.
31 — Al MacInnis, Calgary, 1989. 7 goals, 24 assists in 22 games.
25 — Denis Potvin, NY Islanders, 1981. 8 goals, 17 assists in 18 games.
— Raymond Bourque, Boston, 1991. 7 goals, 18 assists in 19 games.

MOST POINTS BY A DEFENSEMAN, ONE GAME:
6 — Paul Coffey, Edmonton, May 14, 1985, at Edmonton vs. Chicago. 1 goal, 5 assists. Edmonton won 10-5.
5 — Eddie Bush, Detroit, April 9, 1942, at Detroit vs. Toronto. 1 goal, 4 assists. Detroit won 5-2.
— Bob Dailey, Philadelphia, May 1, 1980, at Philadelphia vs. Minnesota. 1 goal, 4 assists. Philadelphia won 7-0.
— Denis Potvin, NY Islanders, April 17, 1981, at NY Islanders vs. Edmonton. 3 goals, 2 assists. NY Islanders won 6-3.
— Risto Siltanen, Quebec, April 14, 1987, at Hartford. 5 assists. Quebec won 7-5.

SCORING BY A ROOKIE

MOST GOALS BY A ROOKIE, ONE PLAYOFF YEAR:
14 — Dino Ciccarelli, Minnesota, 1981. 19 games.
11 — Jeremy Roenick, Chicago, 1990. 20 games.
— Brad Marchand, Boston, 2011. 25 games.
10 — Claude Lemieux, Montreal, 1986. 20 games.
9 — Pat Flatley, NY Islanders, 1984. 21 games

MOST ASSISTS BY A ROOKIE, ONE PLAYOFF YEAR:
14 — Ville Leino, Philadelphia, 2010. 19 games.
13 — Don Maloney, NY Rangers, 1979. 18 games.

MOST POINTS BY A ROOKIE, ONE PLAYOFF YEAR:
21 — Dino Ciccarelli, Minnesota, 1981. 14 goals, 7 assists in 19 games.
— Ville Leino, Philadelphia, 2010. 7 goals, 14 assists in 19 games.
20 — Don Maloney, NY Rangers, 1979. 7 goals, 13 assists in 18 games.

THREE-OR-MORE-GOAL GAMES

MOST THREE-OR-MORE-GOAL GAMES IN PLAYOFFS, CAREER:
10 — Wayne Gretzky, Edmonton, Los Angeles, NY Rangers. Eight three-goal games; two four-goal games.
7 — Maurice Richard, Montreal. Four three-goal games; two four-goal games; one five-goal game.
— Jari Kurri, Edmonton. Six three-goal games; one four-goal game.
6 — Dino Ciccarelli, Minnesota, Washington, Detroit. Five three-goal games; one four-goal game.
5 — Mike Bossy, NY Islanders. Four three-goal games; one four-goal game.

MOST THREE-OR-MORE-GOAL GAMES, ONE PLAYOFF YEAR:
4 — Jari Kurri, Edmonton, 1985. 1 four-goal game, 3 three-goal games.
3 — Mark Messier, Edmonton, 1983. 3 three-goal games.
— Mike Bossy, NY Islanders, 1983. 1 four-goal game, 2 three-goal games
2 — Newsy Lalonde, Montreal, 1919. 1 five-goal game, 1 four-goal game.
— Maurice Richard, Montreal, 1944. 1 five-goal game; 1 three-goal game.
— Doug Bentley, Chicago, 1944. 2 three-goal games.
— Norm Ullman, Detroit, 1964. 2 three-goal games.
— Phil Esposito, Boston, 1970. 2 three-goal games.
— Pit Martin, Chicago, 1973. 2 three-goal games.
— Rick MacLeish, Philadelphia, 1975. 2 three-goal games.
— Lanny McDonald, Toronto, 1977. 1 four-goal game; 1 three-goal game.
— Wayne Gretzky, Edmonton, 1981. 2 three-goal games.
— Wayne Gretzky, Edmonton, 1983. 2 four-goal games.
— Wayne Gretzky, Edmonton, 1985. 2 three-goal games.
— Petr Klima, Detroit, 1988. 2 three-goal games.
— Cam Neely, Boston, 1991. 2 three-goal games.
— Wayne Gretzky, NY Rangers, 1997. 2 three-goal games.
— Daniel Alfredsson, Ottawa, 1998. 2 three-goal games.
— Patrick Marleau, San Jose, 2004. 2 three-goal games.
— Johan Franzen, Detroit, 2008. 2 three-goal games.

MOST THREE-OR-MORE-GOAL GAMES, ONE PLAYOFF SERIES:
3 — Jari Kurri, Edmonton, 1985 CF vs. Chicago, won by Edmonton 4-2. Kurri scored 3 goals May 7 at Edmonton in 7-3 win, 3 goals May 14 at Edmonton in 10-5 win and 4 goals May 16 at Chicago in 8-2 win.
2 — Doug Bentley, Chicago, 1944 SF vs. Detroit, won by Chicago 4-1. Bentley scored 3 goals March 28 at Chicago in 7-1 win and 3 goals March 30 at Detroit in 5-2 win.
— Norm Ullman, Detroit, 1964 SF vs. Chicago, won by Detroit 4-3. Ullman scored 3 goals March 29 at Chicago in 5-4 win and 3 goals April 7 at Detroit in 7-2 win.
— Mark Messier, Edmonton, 1983 DF vs. Calgary, won by Edmonton 4-1. Messier scored 4 goals April 14 at Edmonton in 6-3 win and 3 goals April 17 at Calgary in 10-2 win.
— Mike Bossy, NY Islanders, 1983 CF vs. Boston, won by NY Islanders 4-2. Bossy scored 3 goals May 3 at NY Islanders in 8-3 win and 4 goals May 7 at New York in 8-4 win.
— Johan Franzen, Detroit, 2008 CSF vs. Colorado, won by Detroit 4-0. Franzen scored 3 goals Apr. 26 at Detroit in 5-1 win and 3 goals May 1 at Colorado in 8-2 win.

SCORING STREAKS

LONGEST CONSECUTIVE GOAL-SCORING STREAK, ONE PLAYOFF YEAR:
10 Games — Reggie Leach, Philadelphia, 1976. Streak started April 17 at Toronto and ended May 9 at Montreal. He scored one goal in each of eight games; two in one game; and five in another; a total of 15 goals.

LONGEST CONSECUTIVE POINT-SCORING STREAK, ONE PLAYOFF YEAR:
18 games — Bryan Trottier, NY Islanders, 1981. 11 goals, 18 assists, 29 points.
17 games — Wayne Gretzky, Edmonton, 1988. 12 goals, 29 assists, 41 points.
— Al MacInnis, Calgary, 1989. 7 goals, 19 assists, 26 points.

LONGEST CONSECUTIVE POINT-SCORING STREAK, MORE THAN ONE PLAYOFF YEAR:
27 games — Bryan Trottier, NY Islanders, 1980, 1981 and 1982. 7 games in 1980 (3 goals, 5 assists, 8 points), 18 games in 1981 (11 goals, 18 assists, 29 points), and two games in 1982 (2 goals, 3 assists, 5 points). Total points, 42.
19 games — Wayne Gretzky, Edmonton, Los Angeles, 1988 and 1989. 17 games in 1988 (12 goals, 29 assists, 41 points with Edmonton), 2 games in 1989 (1 goal, 2 assists, 3 points with Los Angeles). Total points, 44.
— Al MacInnis, Calgary, 1989 and 1990. 17 games in 1989 (7 goals, 19 assists, 26 points), and two games in 1990 (2 goals, 1 assist, 3 points). Total points, 29.

FASTEST GOALS

FASTEST GOAL FROM START OF GAME:
0:06 — Don Kozak, Los Angeles, April 17, 1977, at Los Angeles vs. Boston and goaltender Gerry Cheevers. Los Angeles won 7-4.
0:07 — Bob Gainey, Montreal, May 5, 1977, at NY Islanders vs. goaltender Chico Resch. Montreal won 2-1.
— Terry Murray, Philadelphia, April 12, 1981, at Quebec vs. goaltender Dan Bouchard. Quebec won 4-3 in overtime.

FASTEST GOAL FROM START OF PERIOD (OTHER THAN FIRST):
0:06 — Pelle Eklund, Philadelphia, April 25, 1989, at Pittsburgh vs. goaltender Tom Barrasso, second period. Pittsburgh won 10-7.
0:09 — Bill Collins, Minnesota, April 9, 1968, at Minnesota vs. Los Angeles and goaltender Wayne Rutledge, third period. Minnesota won 7-5.
— Dave Balon, Minnesota, April 25, 1968, at St. Louis vs. goaltender Glenn Hall, third period. Minnesota won 5-1.
— Murray Oliver, Minnesota, April 8, 1971, at St. Louis vs. goaltender Ernie Wakely, third period. St. Louis won 4-2.
— Clark Gillies, NY Islanders, April 15, 1977, at Buffalo vs. goaltender Don Edwards, third period. NY Islanders won 4-3.
— Eric Vail, Atlanta, April 11, 1978, at Atlanta vs. Detroit and goaltender Ron Low, third period. Detroit won 5-3.
— Stan Smyl, Vancouver, April 10, 1979, at Philadelphia vs. goaltender Wayne Stephenson, third period. Vancouver won 3-2.
— Wayne Gretzky, Edmonton, April 6, 1983, at Edmonton vs. Winnipeg and goaltender Brian Hayward, second period. Edmonton won 6-3.
— Mark Messier, Edmonton, April 16, 1984, at Calgary vs. goaltender Don Edwards, third period. Edmonton won 5-3.
— Brian Skrudland, Montreal, May 18, 1986, at Calgary vs. goaltender Mike Vernon, first overtime period. Montreal won 3-2.

FASTEST TWO GOALS:
0:05 — Norm Ullman, Detroit, April 11, 1965, at Detroit vs. Chicago and goaltender Glenn Hall. Ullman scored at 17:35 and 17:40 of second period. Detroit won 4-2.

FASTEST TWO GOALS FROM START OF A GAME:
1:08 — Dick Duff, Toronto, April 9, 1963, at Toronto vs. Detroit and goaltender Terry Sawchuk. Duff scored at 0:49 and 1:08. Toronto won 4-2.

FASTEST TWO GOALS FROM START OF A PERIOD:
0:35 — Pat LaFontaine, NY Islanders, May 19, 1984, at Edmonton vs. goaltender Andy Moog. LaFontaine scored at 0:13 and 0:35 of third period. Edmonton won 5-2.

PENALTIES

MOST PENALTY MINUTES IN PLAYOFFS, CAREER:
729 — Dale Hunter, Quebec, Washington, Colorado
541 — Chris Nilan, Montreal, NY Rangers, Boston
529 — Claude Lemieux, Montreal, New Jersey, Colorado, Phoenix, Dallas
471 — Rick Tocchet, Philadelphia, Pittsburgh, Boston, Phoenix
466 — Willi Plett, Atlanta, Calgary, Minnesota, Boston

MOST PENALTIES, ONE GAME:
8 — Forbes Kennedy, Toronto, April 2, 1969, at Boston. Kennedy was assessed 4 minors, 2 majors, 1 10-minute misconduct, 1 game misconduct. Boston won 10-0.
— Kim Clackson, Pittsburgh, April 14, 1980, at Boston. Clackson was assessed 5 minors, 2 majors, 1 10-minute misconduct. Boston won 6-2.

MOST PENALTY MINUTES, ONE GAME:
42 — Dave Schultz, Philadelphia, April 22, 1976, at Toronto. Schultz was assessed 1 minor, 2 majors, 1 10-minute misconduct and 2 game-misconducts. Toronto won 8-5.

MOST PENALTIES, ONE PERIOD AND MOST PENALTY MINUTES, ONE PERIOD:
6 Penalties; 39 Minutes — Ed Hospodar, NY Rangers, April 9, 1981, at Los Angeles, first period. Hospodar was assessed 2 minors, 1 major, 1 10-minute misconduct, 2 game misconducts. Los Angeles won 5-4.

GOALTENDING

MOST PLAYOFF GAMES APPEARED IN BY A GOALTENDER, CAREER:
247 — Patrick Roy, Montreal, Colorado
205 — Martin Brodeur, New Jersey
161 — Ed Belfour, Chicago, Dallas, Toronto
150 — Grant Fuhr, Edmonton, Buffalo, St. Louis
138 — Mike Vernon, Calgary, Detroit, San Jose, Florida

MOST MINUTES PLAYED BY A GOALTENDER, CAREER:
15,209 — Patrick Roy, Montreal, Colorado
12,719 — Martin Brodeur, New Jersey
9,945 — Ed Belfour, Chicago, Dallas, Toronto
8,834 — Grant Fuhr, Edmonton, Buffalo, St. Louis
8,214 — Mike Vernon, Calgary, Detroit, San Jose, Florida

MOST MINUTES PLAYED BY A GOALTENDER, ONE PLAYOFF YEAR:
1,655 — Miikka Kiprusoff, Calgary, 2004. 26 games.
1,544 — Kirk McLean, Vancouver, 1994. 24 games.
— Ed Belfour, Dallas, 1999. 23 games.
1,542 — Tim Thomas, Boston Bruins, 2011. 25 games.
1,540 — Ron Hextall, Philadelphia, 1987. 26 games.

MOST SHUTOUTS IN PLAYOFFS, CAREER:
24 — Martin Brodeur, New Jersey
23 — Patrick Roy, Montreal, Colorado
16 — Curtis Joseph, St. Louis, Edmonton, Toronto, Detroit

MOST SHUTOUTS, ONE PLAYOFF YEAR:
7 — Martin Brodeur, New Jersey, 2003. 24 games.
6 — Dominik Hasek, Detroit, 2002. 23 games.
5 — Jean-Sebastien Giguere, Anaheim, 2003. 21 games.
— Nikolai Khabibulin, Tampa Bay, 2004. 23 games.
— Miikka Kiprusoff, Calgary, 2004. 26 games.

MOST SHUTOUTS, ONE PLAYOFF SERIES:
3 — Clint Benedict, Mtl. Maroons, 1926 F vs. Victoria. 4 games.
— Dave Kerr, NY Rangers, 1940 SF vs. Boston. 6 games.
— Frank McCool, Toronto, 1945 F vs. Detroit. 7 games.
— Turk Broda, Toronto, 1950 SF vs. Detroit. 7 games.
— Felix Potvin, Toronto, 1994 CQF vs. Chicago. 6 games.
— Martin Brodeur, New Jersey, 1995 CQF vs. Boston. 5 games.
— Brent Johnson, St. Louis, 2002 CQF vs. Chicago. 5 games.
— Patrick Lalime, Ottawa, 2002 CQF vs. Philadelphia. 5 games.
— Jean-Sebastien Giguere, Anaheim, 2003 CF vs. Minnesota. 4 games.
— Martin Brodeur, New Jersey, 2003 F vs. Anaheim. 7 games.
— Ed Belfour, Toronto, 2004 CQF vs. Ottawa. 7 games.
— Nikolai Khabibulin, Tampa Bay, 2004 CQF vs. NY Islanders. 5 games.
— Marty Turco, Dallas, 2007 CQF vs. Vancouver. 7 games.
— Michael Leighton, Philadelphia, 2010 CF vs. Montreal. 5 games.

MOST WINS BY A GOALTENDER, CAREER:
151 — Patrick Roy, Montreal, Colorado
113 — Martin Brodeur, New Jersey
92 — Grant Fuhr, Edmonton, Buffalo, St. Louis
88 — Billy Smith, NY Islanders
— Ed Belfour, Chicago, Dallas, Toronto

MOST WINS BY A GOALTENDER, ONE PLAYOFF YEAR:
16 — Sixteen wins by a goaltender in one playoff year has been recorded on 21 occasions. Cory Crawford of the Chicago Blackhawks is the most recent to equal this mark, posting a record of 16 wins and 7 losses in 2013. It was first accomplished by Grant Fuhr of the Edmonton Oilers in 1988.

MOST CONSECUTIVE WINS BY A GOALTENDER, MORE THAN ONE PLAYOFF YEAR:
14 — Tom Barrasso, Pittsburgh, 1992, 1993; 3 wins vs. NY Rangers in 1992 DF, won by Pittsburgh 4-2; 4 wins vs. Boston in 1992 CF, won by Pittsburgh 4-0; 4 wins vs. Chicago in 1992 F, won by Pittsburgh 4-0; 3 wins vs. New Jersey in 1993 DSF, won by Pittsburgh 4-1.

MOST CONSECUTIVE WINS BY A GOALTENDER, ONE PLAYOFF YEAR:
11 — Ed Belfour, Chicago, 1992. 3 wins vs. St. Louis in DSF, won by Chicago 4-2; 4 wins vs. Detroit in DF, won by Chicago 4-0; and 4 wins vs. Edmonton in CF, won by Chicago 4-0.
— Tom Barrasso, Pittsburgh, 1992. 3 wins vs. NY Rangers in DF, won by Pittsburgh 4-2; 4 wins vs. Boston in CF, won by Pittsburgh 4-0; and 4 wins vs. Chicago in F, won by Pittsburgh 4-0.
— Patrick Roy, Montreal, 1993. 4 wins vs. Quebec in DSF, won by Montreal 4-2; 4 wins vs. Buffalo in DF, won by Montreal 4-0; and 3 wins vs. NY Islanders in CF, won by Montreal 4-1.

LONGEST SHUTOUT SEQUENCE:
270:08 — George Hainsworth, Montreal, 1930. Hainsworth's shutout streak began after Murray Murdoch scored a goal for the NY Rangers at 15:34 of the first period in the first game of a SF series on March 28, 1930. Hainsworth did not allow another goal in the final 113:18 of that game, won by Montreal 2-1 at 8:52 of the 4th overtime period. Hainsworth then shutout the NY Rangers in the next and final game of the series on March 30, 1930, won by Montreal 2-0. The streak continued with a 3-0 win over Boston in the opening game of the F series on April 1, 1930. His streak ended on April 3, 1930 when Boston's Eddie Shore scored at 16:50 of the second period in the second game of the F series.

MOST CONSECUTIVE SHUTOUTS:
3 — Clint Benedict, Mtl. Maroons, 1926. Benedict shut out Ottawa 1-0, March 27; he then shut out Victoria twice, 3-0, March 30; 3-0, April 1. Mtl. Maroons won NHL F vs. Ottawa 2 goals to 1 and won the best-of-five F vs. Victoria 3-1.
— John Ross Roach, NY Rangers, 1929. Roach shut out NY Americans twice, 0-0, March 19; 1-0, March 21; he then shut out Toronto 1-0, March 24. NY Rangers won QF vs. NY Americans 1 goal to 0 and won the best-of-three SF vs. Toronto 2-0.
— Frank McCool, Toronto, 1945. McCool shut out Detroit 1-0, April 6; 2-0, April 8; 1-0, April 12. Toronto won the best-of-seven F 4-3.
— Brent Johnson, St. Louis, 2002. Johnson shut out Chicago three times; 2-0, April 20; 4-0, April 21; 1-0, April 23. St. Louis won the best-of-seven CQF 4-1.
— Patrick Lalime, Ottawa, 2002. Lalime shut out Philadelphia three times; 3-0, April 20; 3-0, April 22; 3-0, April 24. Ottawa won the best-of-seven CQF 4-1.
— Jean-Sebastien Giguere, Anaheim, 2003. Giguere shut out Minnesota 1-0, May 10; 2-0, May 12; 4-0, May 14. Anaheim won the best-of-seven CF 4-0.
— Ilya Bryzgalov, Anaheim, 2006. Bryzgalov shut out Calgary, 3-0, May 3; he then shut out Colorado 5-0, May 5; and 3-0, May 7. Anaheim won best-of-seven CQF vs. Calgary 4-3 and won best-of-seven CSF vs. Colorado 4-0.

Early Playoff Records

1893-1918

Team Records

MOST GOALS, BOTH TEAMS, ONE GAME:
25 — Ottawa Silver Seven, Dawson City at Ottawa, Jan. 16, 1905. Ottawa 23, Dawson City 2. Ottawa won best-of-three series 2-0.

MOST GOALS, ONE TEAM, ONE GAME:
23 — Ottawa Silver Seven at Ottawa, Jan. 16, 1905. Ottawa defeated Dawson City 23-2.

MOST GOALS, BOTH TEAMS, BEST-OF-THREE SERIES:
42 — Ottawa Silver Seven, Queen's University at Ottawa, 1906. Ottawa defeated Queen's 16-7, Feb. 27, and 12-7, Feb. 28.

MOST GOALS, ONE TEAM, BEST-OF-THREE SERIES:
32 — Ottawa Silver Seven in 1905 at Ottawa. Defeated Dawson City 9-2, Jan. 13, and 23-2, Jan. 16.

MOST GOALS, BOTH TEAMS, BEST-OF-FIVE SERIES:
39 — Toronto Arenas, Vancouver Millionaires at Toronto, 1918. Toronto won 5-3, Mar. 20; 6-3, Mar. 26; 2-1, Mar. 30. Vancouver won 6-4, Mar. 23, and 8-1, Mar. 28. Toronto scored 18 goals; Vancouver 21.

MOST GOALS, ONE TEAM, BEST-OF-FIVE SERIES:
26 — Vancouver Millionaires in 1915 at Vancouver. Defeated Ottawa Senators 6-2, Mar. 22; 8-3, Mar. 24; and 12-3, Mar. 26.

Individual Records

MOST GOALS IN PLAYOFFS:
63 — Frank McGee, Ottawa Silver Seven, in 22 playoff games. Seven goals in four games, 1903; 21 goals in eight games, 1904; 18 goals in four games, 1905; 17 goals in six games, 1906.

MOST GOALS, ONE PLAYOFF SERIES:
15 — Frank McGee, Ottawa Silver Seven, in two games in 1905 at Ottawa. Scored one goal, Jan. 13, in 9-2 victory over Dawson City and 14 goals, Jan. 16, in 23-2 victory.

MOST GOALS, ONE PLAYOFF GAME:
14 — Frank McGee, Ottawa Silver Seven, at Ottawa, Jan. 16, 1905, in 23-2 victory over Dawson City.

FASTEST THREE GOALS:
40 Seconds — Marty Walsh, Ottawa Senators, at Ottawa, March 16, 1911, at 3:00, 3:10, and 3:40 of third period. Ottawa defeated Port Arthur 13-4.

Now the coach of the Colorado Avalanche, Patrick Roy was a four-time Stanley Cup champion as a player and has the most wins of any goalie in NHL playoff history.

All-Time Playoff Goal Leaders since 1918

(45 or more goals)

Player	Teams	Yrs.	GP	G
Wayne Gretzky	Edm., L.A., St.L., NYR	16	208	122
Mark Messier	Edm., NYR, Van.	17	236	109
Jari Kurri	Edm., L.A., NYR, Ana., Col.	15	200	106
Brett Hull	Cgy., St.L., Dal., Det., Phx.	19	202	103
Glenn Anderson	Edm., Tor., NYR, St.L.	15	225	93
Mike Bossy	NYI	10	129	85
Joe Sakic	Que., Col.	13	172	84
Maurice Richard	Mtl.	15	133	82
Claude Lemieux	Mtl., N.J., Col., Phx., Dal., S.J.	18	234	80
Jean Beliveau	Mtl.	17	162	79
*Jaromir Jagr	Pit., Wsh., NYR, Phi., Dal., Bos.	17	202	78
Mario Lemieux	Pit.	8	107	76
Dino Ciccarelli	Min., Wsh., Det., T.B., Fla.	14	141	73
Esa Tikkanen	Edm., NYR, St.L., N.J., Van., Fla., Wsh.	13	186	72
Bryan Trottier	NYI, Pit.	17	221	71
Steve Yzerman	Det.	20	196	70
Gordie Howe	Det., Hfd.	20	157	68
Joe Nieuwendyk	Cgy., Dal., N.J., Tor., Fla.	16	158	66
Denis Savard	Chi., Mtl., T.B.	16	169	66
Yvan Cournoyer	Mtl.	12	147	64
Peter Forsberg	Que., Col., Phi., Nsh.	13	151	64
Brian Propp	Phi., Bos., Min., Hfd.	13	160	64
Bobby Smith	Min., Mtl.	13	184	64
Bobby Hull	Chi., Wpg., Hfd.	14	119	62
Phil Esposito	Chi., Bos., NYR	15	130	61
Jacques Lemaire	Mtl.	11	145	61
Mark Recchi	Pit., Phi., Mtl., Car., Atl., T.B., Bos.	14	189	61
Joe Mullen	St.L., Cgy., Pit., Bos.	15	143	60
Doug Gilmour	St.L., Cgy., Tor., N.J., Chi., Buf., Mtl.	17	182	60
Brendan Shanahan	N.J., St.L., Hfd., Det., NYR	19	184	60
Stan Mikita	Chi.	18	155	59
Paul Coffey	Edm., Pit., L.A., Det., Hfd., Phi., Chi., Car., Bos.	16	194	59
Guy Lafleur	Mtl., NYR, Que.	14	128	58
Bernie Geoffrion	Mtl., NYR	16	132	58
Luc Robitaille	L.A., Pit., NYR, Det.	15	159	58
Mike Modano	Min., Dal., Det.	16	176	58
Cam Neely	Van., Bos.	9	93	57
*Patrick Marleau	S.J.	13	140	57
Steve Larmer	Chi., NYR	13	140	56
Denis Potvin	NYI	14	185	56
*Henrik Zetterberg	Det.	9	123	55
Rick MacLeish	Phi., Hfd., Pit., Det.	11	114	54
Steve Thomas	Tor., Chi., NYI, N.J., Ana., Det.	16	174	54
Nicklas Lidstrom	Det.	19	263	54
Bill Barber	Phi.	11	129	53
Stephane Richer	Mtl., N.J., T.B., St.L., Pit.	13	134	53
Jeremy Roenick	Chi., Phx., Phi., L.A., S.J.	17	154	53
Rick Tocchet	Phi., Pit., L.A., Bos., Wsh., Phx.	13	145	52
Sergei Fedorov	Det., Ana., CBJ, Wsh.	15	183	52
*Daniel Alfredsson	Ott.	13	121	51
Frank Mahovlich	Tor., Det., Mtl.	14	137	51
Brian Bellows	Min., Mtl., T.B., Ana., Wsh.	13	143	51
Rod Brind'Amour	St.L., Phi., Car.	12	159	51
Steve Shutt	Mtl., L.A.	12	99	50
*Daniel Briere	Phx., Buf., Phi.	8	108	50
Henri Richard	Mtl.	18	180	49
Reggie Leach	Bos., Cal., Phi., Det.	8	94	47
Ted Lindsay	Det., Chi.	16	133	47
Chris Drury	Col., Cgy., Buf., NYR	9	135	47
Clark Gillies	NYI, Buf.	13	164	47
Kevin Stevens	Pit., Bos., L.A., NYR, Phi.	7	103	46
Dickie Moore	Mtl., Tor., St.L.	14	135	46
Ron Francis	Hfd., Pit., Car., Tor.	17	171	46
Tomas Holmstrom	Det.	14	180	46
Rick Middleton	NYR, Bos.	12	114	45
Alex Kovalev	NYR, Pit., Mtl., Ott., Fla.	11	123	45

* Active

All-Time Playoff Assist Leaders since 1918

(65 or more assists)

Player	Teams	Yrs.	GP	A
Wayne Gretzky	Edm., L.A., St.L., NYR	16	208	260
Mark Messier	Edm., NYR, Van.	17	236	186
Raymond Bourque	Bos., Col.	21	214	139
Paul Coffey	Edm., Pit., L.A., Det., Hfd., Phi., Chi., Car., Bos.	16	194	137
Nicklas Lidstrom	Det.	19	263	129
Doug Gilmour	St.L., Cgy., Tor., N.J., Chi., Buf., Mtl.	17	182	128
Jari Kurri	Edm., L.A., NYR, Ana., Col.	15	200	127
Sergei Fedorov	Det., Ana., CBJ, Wsh.	15	183	124
Al MacInnis	Cgy., St.L.	19	177	121
*Jaromir Jagr	Pit., Wsh., NYR, Phi., Dal., Bos.	17	202	121
Glenn Anderson	Edm., Tor., NYR, St.L.	15	225	121
Larry Robinson	Mtl., L.A.	20	227	116
Steve Yzerman	Det.	20	196	115
Larry Murphy	L.A., Wsh., Min., Pit., Tor., Det.	20	215	115
Adam Oates	Det., St.L., Bos., Wsh., Phi., Ana., Edm.	15	163	114
Bryan Trottier	NYI, Pit.	17	221	113
Chris Chelios	Mtl., Chi., Det., Atl.	24	266	113
Denis Savard	Chi., Mtl., T.B.	16	169	109
Denis Potvin	NYI	14	185	108
Peter Forsberg	Que., Col., Phi., Nsh.	13	151	107
Joe Sakic	Que., Col.	13	172	104
Jean Beliveau	Mtl.	17	162	97
Ron Francis	Hfd., Pit., Car., Tor.	17	171	97
Mario Lemieux	Pit.	8	107	96
Bobby Smith	Min., Mtl.	13	184	96
Chris Pronger	Hfd., St.L., Edm., Ana., Phi.	14	173	95
Sergei Zubov	NYR, Pit., Dal.	13	164	93
Gordie Howe	Det., Hfd.	20	157	92
Scott Stevens	Wsh., St.L., N.J.	20	233	92
Stan Mikita	Chi.	18	155	91
Brad Park	NYR, Bos., Det.	17	161	90
Mike Modano	Min., Dal., Det.	16	176	88
Brett Hull	Cgy., St.L., Dal., Det., Phx.	19	202	87
Craig Janney	Bos., St.L., S.J., Wpg., Phx., T.B., NYI	11	120	86
Mark Recchi	Pit., Phi., Mtl., Car., Atl., T.B., Bos.	14	189	86
Brian Propp	Phi., Bos., Min., Hfd.	13	160	84
*Patrik Elias	N.J.	13	162	80
Henri Richard	Mtl.	18	180	80
Jacques Lemaire	Mtl.	11	145	78
Claude Lemieux	Mtl., N.J., Col., Phx., Dal., S.J.	18	234	78
Ken Linseman	Phi., Edm., Bos., Tor.	11	113	77
Bobby Clarke	Phi.	13	136	77
Guy Lafleur	Mtl., NYR, Que.	14	128	76
Phil Esposito	Chi., Bos., NYR	15	130	76
Dale Hunter	Que., Wsh., Col.	18	186	76
*Joe Thornton	Bos., S.J.	12	125	75
Mike Bossy	NYI	10	129	75
Steve Larmer	Chi., NYR	13	140	75
John Tonelli	NYI, Cgy., L.A., Chi., Que.	13	172	75
Brendan Shanahan	N.J., St.L., Hfd., Det., NYR	19	184	74
Scott Niedermayer	N.J., Ana.	15	202	73
Peter Stastny	Que., N.J., St.L.	12	93	72
Bernie Nicholls	L.A., NYR, Edm., N.J., Chi., S.J.	13	118	72
*Scott Gomez	N.J., NYR, Mtl., S.J.	10	149	72
Brian Bellows	Min., Mtl., T.B., Ana., Wsh.	13	143	71
Brian Rafalski	N.J., Det.	10	165	71
Gilbert Perreault	Buf.	11	90	70
*Marian Hossa	Ott., Atl., Pit., Det., Chi.	12	152	70
Geoff Courtnall	Bos., Edm., Wsh., St.L., Van.	15	156	70
Brian Leetch	NYR, Tor., Bos.	8	95	69
Dale Hawerchuk	Wpg., Buf., St.L., Phi.	15	97	69
Alex Delvecchio	Det.	14	121	69
Jeremy Roenick	Chi., Phx., Phi., L.A., S.J.	17	154	69
Luc Robitaille	L.A., Pit., NYR, Det.	15	159	69
*Sergei Gonchar	Wsh., Bos., Pit., Ott.	12	135	68
Bobby Hull	Chi., Wpg., Hfd.	14	119	67
Sandis Ozolinsh	S.J., Col., Car., Fla., Ana., NYR	10	137	67
Frank Mahovlich	Tor., Det., Mtl.	14	137	67
*Pavel Datsyuk	Det.	10	140	67
Igor Larionov	Van., S.J., Det., Fla., N.J.	13	150	67
Bobby Orr	Bos., Chi.	8	74	66
Bernie Federko	St.L., Det.	11	91	66
Jean Ratelle	NYR, Bos.	15	123	66
Charlie Huddy	Edm., L.A., Buf., St.L.	14	183	66
*Sidney Crosby	Pit.	5	82	65
Trevor Linden	Van., NYI, Mtl., Wsh.	12	124	65

All-Time Playoff Point Leaders since 1918

(115 or more points)

Player	Teams	Yrs.	GP	G	A	Pts.
Wayne Gretzky	Edm., L.A., St.L., NYR	16	208	122	260	382
Mark Messier	Edm., NYR, Van.	17	236	109	186	295
Jari Kurri	Edm., L.A., NYR, Ana., Col.	15	200	106	127	233
Glenn Anderson	Edm., Tor., NYR, St.L.	15	225	93	121	214
*Jaromir Jagr	Pit., Wsh., NYR, Phi., Dal., Bos.	17	202	78	121	199
Paul Coffey	Edm., Pit., L.A., Det., Hfd., Phi., Chi., Car., Bos.	16	194	59	137	196
Brett Hull	Cgy., St.L., Dal., Det., Phx.	19	202	103	87	190
Joe Sakic	Que., Col.	13	172	84	104	188
Doug Gilmour	St.L., Cgy., Tor., N.J., Chi., Buf., Mtl.	17	182	60	128	188
Steve Yzerman	Det.	20	196	70	115	185
Bryan Trottier	NYI, Pit.	17	221	71	113	184
Nicklas Lidstrom	Det.	19	263	54	129	183
Raymond Bourque	Bos., Col.	21	214	41	139	180
Jean Beliveau	Mtl.	17	162	79	97	176
Sergei Fedorov	Det., Ana., CBJ, Wsh.	15	183	52	124	176
Denis Savard	Chi., Mtl., T.B.	16	169	66	109	175
Mario Lemieux	Pit.	8	107	76	96	172
Peter Forsberg	Que., Col., Phi., Nsh.	13	151	64	107	171
Denis Potvin	NYI	14	185	56	108	164
Mike Bossy	NYI	10	129	85	75	160
Gordie Howe	Det., Hfd.	20	157	68	92	160
Al MacInnis	Cgy., St.L.	19	177	39	121	160
Bobby Smith	Min., Mtl.	13	184	64	96	160
Claude Lemieux	Mtl., N.J., Col., Phx., Dal., S.J.	18	234	80	78	158
Adam Oates	Det., St.L., Bos., Wsh., Phi., Ana., Edm.	15	163	42	114	156
Larry Murphy	L.A., Wsh., Min., Pit., Tor., Det.	20	215	37	115	152
Stan Mikita	Chi.	18	155	59	91	150
Brian Propp	Phi., Bos., Min., Hfd.	13	160	64	84	148
Mark Recchi	Pit., Phi., Mtl., Car., Atl., T.B., Bos.	14	189	61	86	147
Mike Modano	Min., Dal., Det.	16	176	58	88	146
Larry Robinson	Mtl., L.A.	20	227	28	116	144
Chris Chelios	Mtl., Chi., Det., Atl.	24	266	31	113	144
Ron Francis	Hfd., Pit., Car., Tor.	17	171	46	97	143
Jacques Lemaire	Mtl.	11	145	61	78	139
Phil Esposito	Chi., Bos., NYR	15	130	61	76	137
Guy Lafleur	Mtl., NYR, Que.	14	128	58	76	134
Brendan Shanahan	N.J., St.L., Hfd., Det., NYR	19	184	60	74	134
Esa Tikkanen	Edm., NYR, St.L., N.J., Van., Fla., Wsh.	13	186	72	60	132
Steve Larmer	Chi., NYR	13	140	56	75	131
Bobby Hull	Chi., Wpg., Hfd.	14	119	62	67	129
Henri Richard	Mtl.	18	180	49	80	129
Yvan Cournoyer	Mtl.	12	147	64	63	127
Luc Robitaille	L.A., Pit., NYR, Det.	15	159	58	69	127
Maurice Richard	Mtl.	15	133	82	44	126
Brad Park	NYR, Bos., Det.	17	161	35	90	125
*Patrik Elias	N.J.	13	162	45	80	125
Brian Bellows	Min., Mtl., T.B., Ana., Wsh.	13	143	51	71	122
Jeremy Roenick	Chi., Phx., Phi., L.A., S.J.	17	154	53	69	122
Chris Pronger	Hfd., St.L., Edm., Ana., Phi.	14	173	26	95	121
Ken Linseman	Phi., Edm., Bos., Tor.	11	113	43	77	120
Bobby Clarke	Phi.	13	136	42	77	119
Bernie Geoffrion	Mtl., NYR	16	132	58	60	118
Frank Mahovlich	Tor., Det., Mtl.	14	137	51	67	118
Dino Ciccarelli	Min., Wsh., Det., T.B., Fla.	14	141	73	45	118
Dale Hunter	Que., Wsh., Col.	18	186	42	76	118
Scott Stevens	Wsh., St.L., N.J.	20	233	26	92	118
Sergei Zubov	NYR, Pit., Dal.	13	164	24	93	117
Joe Nieuwendyk	Cgy., Dal., N.J., Tor., Fla.	16	158	66	50	116
John Tonelli	NYI, Cgy., L.A., Chi., Que.	13	172	40	75	115

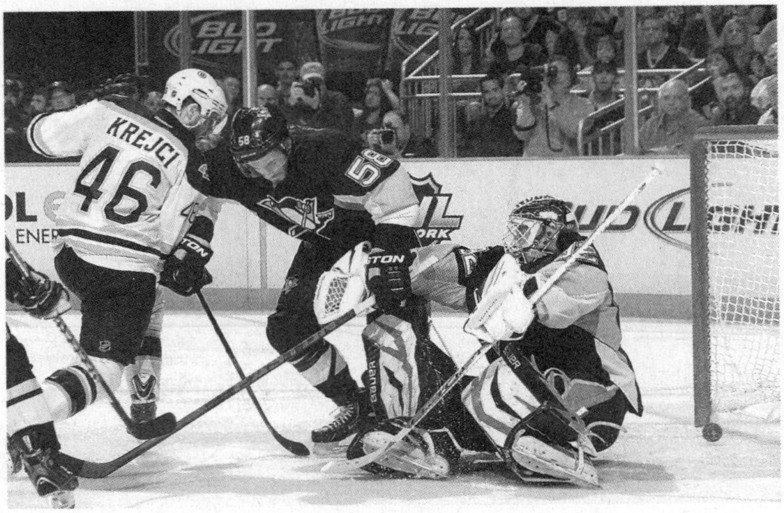

David Krejci pokes the puck past Tomas Vokoun in the third period of game one in the Eastern Conference Final between Boston and Pittsburgh. Krejci was the NHL's playoff scoring leader for the second time in three years in 2013.

Leading Playoff Scorers, 1918–2013

Season	Player, Team	Games Played	Goals	Assists	Points
2012-13	David Krejci, Boston	22	9	17	26
2011-12	Dustin Brown, Los Angeles	20	8	12	20
	Anze Kopitar, Los Angeles	20	8	12	20
2010-11	David Krejci, Boston	25	12	11	23
2009-10	Daniel Briere, Philadelphia	23	12	18	30
2008-09	Evgeni Malkin, Pittsburgh	24	14	22	36
2007-08	Henrik Zetterberg, Detroit	22	13	14	27
	Sidney Crosby, Pittsburgh	20	6	21	27
2006-07	Daniel Alfredsson, Ottawa	20	14	8	22
	Dany Heatley, Ottawa	20	7	15	22
	Jason Spezza, Ottawa	20	7	15	22
2005-06	Eric Staal, Carolina	25	9	19	28
2004-05	*Season Cancelled*				
2003-04	Brad Richards, Tampa Bay	23	12	14	26
2002-03	Jamie Langenbrunner, New Jersey	24	11	7	18
	Scott Niedermayer, New Jersey	24	2	16	18
2001-02	Peter Forsberg, Colorado	20	9	18	27
2000-01	Joe Sakic, Colorado	21	13	13	26
99-2000	Brett Hull, Dallas	23	11	13	24
1998-99	Peter Forsberg, Colorado	19	8	16	24
1997-98	Steve Yzerman, Detroit	22	6	18	24
1996-97	Eric Lindros, Philadelphia	19	12	14	26
1995-96	Joe Sakic, Colorado	22	18	16	34
1994-95	Sergei Fedorov, Detroit	17	7	17	24
1993-94	Brian Leetch, NY Rangers	23	11	23	34
1992-93	Wayne Gretzky, Los Angeles	24	15	25	40
1991-92	Mario Lemieux, Pittsburgh	15	16	18	34
1990-91	Mario Lemieux, Pittsburgh	23	16	28	44
1989-90	Craig Simpson, Edmonton	22	16	15	31
	Mark Messier, Edmonton	22	9	22	31
1988-89	Al MacInnis, Calgary	22	7	24	31
1987-88	Wayne Gretzky, Edmonton	19	12	31	43
1986-87	Wayne Gretzky, Edmonton	21	5	29	34
1985-86	Doug Gilmour, St. Louis	19	9	12	21
	Bernie Federko, St. Louis	19	7	14	21
1984-85	Wayne Gretzky, Edmonton	18	17	30	47
1983-84	Wayne Gretzky, Edmonton	19	13	22	35
1982-83	Wayne Gretzky, Edmonton	16	12	26	38
1981-82	Bryan Trottier, NY Islanders	19	6	23	29
1980-81	Mike Bossy, NY Islanders	18	17	18	35
1979-80	Bryan Trottier, NY Islanders	21	12	17	29
1978-79	Jacques Lemaire, Montreal	16	11	12	23
	Guy Lafleur, Montreal	16	10	13	23
1977-78	Guy Lafleur, Montreal	15	10	11	21
	Larry Robinson, Montreal	15	4	17	21
1976-77	Guy Lafleur, Montreal	14	9	17	26
1975-76	Reggie Leach, Philadelphia	16	19	5	24
1974-75	Rick MacLeish, Philadelphia	17	11	9	20
1973-74	Rick MacLeish, Philadelphia	17	13	9	22
1972-73	Yvan Cournoyer, Montreal	17	15	10	25
1971-72	Phil Esposito, Boston	15	9	15	24
	Bobby Orr, Boston	15	5	19	24
1970-71	Frank Mahovlich, Montreal	20	14	13	27
1969-70	Phil Esposito, Boston	14	13	14	27
1968-69	Phil Esposito, Boston	10	8	10	18
1967-68	Bill Goldsworthy, Minnesota	14	8	7	15
1966-67	Jim Pappin, Toronto	12	7	8	15
1965-66	Norm Ullman, Detroit	12	6	9	15
1964-65	Bobby Hull, Chicago	14	10	7	17
1963-64	Gordie Howe, Detroit	14	9	10	19
1962-63	Gordie Howe, Detroit	11	7	9	16
	Norm Ullman, Detroit	11	4	12	16
1961-62	Stan Mikita, Chicago	12	6	15	21
1960-61	Gordie Howe, Detroit	11	4	11	15
	Pierre Pilote, Chicago	12	3	12	15
1959-60	Henri Richard, Montreal	8	3	9	12
	Bernie Geoffrion, Montreal	8	2	10	12
1958-59	Dickie Moore, Montreal	11	5	12	17
1957-58	Fleming MacKell, Boston	12	5	14	19
1956-57	Bernie Geoffrion, Montreal	10	11	7	18
1955-56	Jean Béliveau, Montreal	10	12	7	19
1954-55	Gordie Howe, Detroit	11	9	11	20
1953-54	Dickie Moore, Montreal	11	5	8	13
1952-53	Ed Sandford, Boston	11	8	3	11
1951-52	Ted Lindsay, Detroit	8	5	2	7
	Floyd Curry, Montreal	11	4	3	7
	Metro Prystai, Detroit	8	2	5	7
	Gordie Howe, Detroit	8	2	5	7
1950-51	Maurice Richard, Montreal	11	9	4	13
	Max Bentley, Toronto	11	2	11	13
1949-50	Pentti Lund, NY Rangers	12	6	5	11
1948-49	Gordie Howe, Detroit	11	8	3	11
1947-48	Ted Kennedy, Toronto	9	8	6	14
1946-47	Maurice Richard, Montreal	10	6	5	11
1945-46	Elmer Lach, Montreal	9	5	12	17
1944-45	Joe Carveth, Detroit	14	5	6	11
1943-44	Toe Blake, Montreal	9	7	11	18
1942-43	Carl Liscombe, Detroit	10	6	8	14
1941-42	Don Grosso, Detroit	12	8	6	14
	Syl Apps, Toronto	13	5	9	14
1940-41	Milt Schmidt, Boston	11	5	6	11
1939-40	Phil Watson, NY Rangers	12	3	6	9
	Neil Colville, NY Rangers	12	2	7	9
1938-39	Bill Cowley, Boston	12	3	11	14
1937-38	Johnny Gottselig, Chicago	10	5	3	8
	Gordie Drillon, Toronto	7	7	1	8
1936-37	Marty Barry, Detroit	10	4	7	11
1935-36	Frank Boll, Toronto	9	7	3	10
1934-35	Baldy Northcott, Mtl. Maroons	7	4	1	5
	Busher Jackson, Toronto	7	3	2	5
	Cy Wentworth, Mtl. Maroons	7	3	2	5
	Charlie Conacher, Toronto	7	1	4	5
1933-34	Larry Aurie, Detroit	9	3	7	10
1932-33	Cecil Dillon, NY Rangers	8	8	2	10
1931-32	Frank Boucher, NY Rangers	7	3	6	9
1930-31	Cooney Weiland, Boston	5	6	3	9
1929-30	Marty Barry, Boston	6	3	3	6
	Cooney Weiland, Boston	6	1	5	6
1928-29	Andy Blair, Toronto	4	3	0	3
	Butch Keeling, NY Rangers	6	3	0	3
	Ace Bailey, Toronto	4	1	2	3
1927-28	Frank Boucher, NY Rangers	9	7	3	10
1926-27	Harry Oliver, Boston	8	4	2	6
	Percy Galbraith, Boston	8	3	3	6
1925-26	Nels Stewart, Mtl. Maroons	8	6	3	9
1924-25	Howie Morenz, Montreal	6	7	1	8
1923-24	Howie Morenz, Montreal	6	7	3	10
1922-23	Punch Broadbent, Ottawa	8	6	1	7
1921-22	Babe Dye, Toronto	7	11	1	12
1920-21	Cy Denneny, Ottawa	7	4	2	6
1919-20	Frank Nighbor, Ottawa	5	6	1	7
	Jack Darragh, Ottawa	5	5	2	7
1918-19	Newsy Lalonde, Montreal	10	17	2	19
1917-18	Alf Skinner, Toronto	7	8	3	11

Three-or-more-Goal Games, Playoffs 1918–2013

Player	Team	Date	City	Total Goals	Opposing Goaltender	Score
Wayne Gretzky (10)	Edm.	Apr. 11/81	Edm.	3	Richard Sevigny	Edm. 6 Mtl. 2
		Apr. 19/81	Edm.	3	Billy Smith	Edm. 5 NYI 2
		Apr. 6/83	Edm.	4	Brian Hayward	Edm. 6 Wpg. 3
		Apr. 17/83	Cgy.	4	Reggie Lemelin	Edm. 10 Cgy. 2
		Apr. 25/85	Wpg.	3	Brian Hayward (2)	
					Marc Behrend (1)	Edm. 8 Wpg. 3
		May 25/85	Edm.	3	Pelle Lindbergh	Edm. 4 Phi. 3
		Apr. 24/86	Cgy.	3	Mike Vernon	Edm. 7 Cgy. 4
	L.A.	May 29/93	Tor.	3	Felix Potvin	L.A. 5 Tor. 4
	NYR	Apr. 23/97	NYR	3	John Vanbiesbrouck	NYR 3 Fla. 2
		May 18/97	Phi.	3	Garth Snow	NYR 5 Phi. 4
Maurice Richard (7)	Mtl.	Mar. 23/44	Mtl.	5	Paul Bibeault	Mtl. 5 Tor. 1
		Apr. 6/44	Chi.	3	Mike Karakas	Mtl. 3 Chi. 1
		Mar. 29/45	Mtl.	4	Frank McCool	Mtl. 10 Tor. 3
		Apr. 14/53	Bos.	3	Gord Henry	Mtl. 7 Bos. 3
		Mar. 20/56	Mtl.	3	Gump Worsley	Mtl. 7 NYR 1
		Apr. 6/57	Mtl.	4	Don Simmons	Mtl. 5 Bos. 1
		Apr. 1/58	Det.	3	Terry Sawchuk	Mtl. 4 Det. 3
Jari Kurri (7)	Edm.	Apr. 4/84	Edm.	3	Doug Soetaert (1)	
					Mike Veisor (2)	Edm. 9 Wpg. 2
		Apr. 25/85	Wpg.	3	Brian Hayward (2)	
					Marc Behrend (1)	Edm. 8 Wpg. 3
		May 7/85	Edm.	3	Murray Bannerman	Edm. 7 Chi. 3
		May 14/85	Edm.	3	Murray Bannerman	Edm. 10 Chi. 5
		May 16/85	Chi.	4	Murray Bannerman	Edm. 8 Chi. 2
		Apr. 9/87	Edm.	4	Rollie Melanson (2)	
					Darren Eliot (2)	Edm. 13 L.A. 3
		May 18/90	Bos.	3	Andy Moog (2)	
					Reggie Lemelin (1)	Edm. 7 Bos. 2
Dino Ciccarelli (6)	Min.	May 5/81	Min.	3	Pat Riggin	Min. 7 Cgy. 4
		Apr. 10/82	Min.	3	Murray Bannerman	Min. 7 Chi. 1
	Wsh.	Apr. 5/90	N.J.	3	Sean Burke	Wsh. 5 N.J. 4
		Apr. 25/92	Pit.	4	Tom Barrasso (1)	
					Ken Wregget (3)	Wsh. 7 Pit. 2
	Det.	Apr. 29/93	Tor.	3	Felix Potvin (2)	
					Daren Puppa (1)	Det. 7 Tor. 3
		May 11/95	Dal.	3	Andy Moog (2)	
					Darcy Wakaluk (1)	Det. 5 Dal. 1
Mike Bossy (5)	NYI	Apr. 16/79	NYI	3	Tony Esposito	NYI 6 Chi. 2
		May 8/82	NYI	3	Richard Brodeur	NYI 6 Van. 5
		Apr. 10/83	Wsh.	3	Al Jensen	NYI 6 Wsh. 3
		May 3/83	NYI	3	Pete Peeters	NYI 8 Bos. 3
		May 7/83	NYI	4	Pete Peeters	NYI 8 Bos. 4
Phil Esposito (4)	Bos.	Apr. 2/69	Bos.	4	Bruce Gamble	Bos. 10 Tor. 0
		Apr. 8/70	Bos.	3	Ed Giacomin	Bos. 8 NYR 2
		Apr. 19/70	Chi.	3	Tony Esposito	Bos. 6 Chi. 3
		Apr. 8/75	Bos.	3	Tony Esposito (2)	
					Michel Dumas (1)	Bos. 8 Chi. 2
Mark Messier (4)	Edm.	Apr. 14/83	Edm.	4	Reggie Lemelin	Edm. 6 Cgy. 3
		Apr. 17/83	Cgy.	3	Reggie Lemelin (1)	Edm. 10 Cgy. 2
					Don Edwards (2)	
		Apr. 26/83	Edm.	3	Murray Bannerman	Edm. 8 Chi. 2
	NYR	May 25/94	N.J.	3	Martin Brodeur (2)	NYR 4 N.J. 2
					ENG (1)	
Steve Yzerman (4)	Det.	Apr. 6/89	Det.	3	Alain Chevrier	Chi. 5 Det. 4
		Apr. 4/91	St.L.	3	Vincent Riendeau (2)	Det. 6 St.L. 3
					Pat Jablonski (1)	
		May 8/96	St.L.	3	Jon Casey	St.L. 5 Det. 4
		Apr. 21/99	Det.	3	Guy Hebert (2)	Det. 5 Ana. 3
					Pat Jablonski (1)	
Bernie Geoffrion (3)	Mtl.	Mar. 27/52	Mtl.	3	Jim Henry	Mtl. 4 Bos. 0
		Apr. 7/55	Mtl.	3	Terry Sawchuk	Mtl. 4 Det. 2
		Mar. 30/57	Mtl.	3	Gump Worsley	Mtl. 8 NYR 3
Norm Ullman (3)	Det.	Mar. 29/64	Chi.	3	Glenn Hall	Det. 5 Chi. 4
		Apr. 7/64	Det.	3	Glenn Hall (2)	
					Denis DeJordy (1)	Det. 7 Chi. 2
		Apr. 11/65	Det.	3	Glenn Hall	Det. 4 Chi. 2
John Bucyk (3)	Bos.	May 3/70	St.L.	3	Jacques Plante (1)	
					Ernie Wakely (2)	Bos. 6 St.L. 1
		Apr. 20/72	Bos.	3	Jacques Caron (1)	
					Ernie Wakely (2)	Bos. 10 St.L. 2
		Apr. 21/74	Bos.	3	Tony Esposito	Bos. 8 Chi. 6
Rick MacLeish (3)	Phi.	Apr. 11/74	Phi.	3	Phil Myre	Phi. 5 Atl. 1
		Apr. 13/75	Phi.	3	Gord McRae	Phi. 6 Tor. 3
		May 13/75	Phi.	3	Glenn Resch	Phi. 4 NYI 1
Denis Savard (3)	Chi.	Apr. 19/82	Chi.	3	Mike Liut	Chi. 7 StL. 4
		Apr. 10/86	Chi.	4	Ken Wregget	Tor. 6 Chi. 4
		Apr. 9/88	St.L.	3	Greg Millen	Chi. 6 St.L. 3
Tim Kerr (3)	Phi.	Apr. 13/85	NYR	4	Glen Hanlon	Phi. 6 NYR 5
		Apr. 20/87	Phi.	3	Kelly Hrudey	Phi. 4 NYI 2
		Apr. 19/89	Pit.	3	Tom Barrasso	Phi. 4 Pit. 2
Cam Neely (3)	Bos.	Apr. 9/87	Mtl.	3	Patrick Roy	Mtl. 4 Bos. 3
		Apr. 5/91	Bos.	3	Peter Sidorkiewicz	Bos. 4 Hfd. 3
		Apr. 25/91	Bos.	3	Patrick Roy	Bos. 4 Mtl. 1
Petr Klima (3)	Det.	Apr. 7/88	Tor.	3	Allan Bester (2)	
					Ken Wregett (1)	Det. 6 Tor. 2
		Apr. 21/88	St.L.	3	Greg Millen	Det. 6 St.L. 0
	Edm.	May 4/91	Edm.	3	Jon Casey	Edm. 7 Min. 2

Player	Team	Date	City	Total Goals	Opposing Goaltender	Score
Esa Tikkanen (3)	Edm.	May 22/88	Edm.	3	Reggie Lemelin	Edm. 6 Bos. 3
		Apr. 16/91	Cgy.	3	Mike Vernon	Edm. 5 Cgy. 4
		Apr. 26/92	L.A.	3	Kelly Hrudey (2)	Edm. 5 L.A. 2
					Tom Askey (1)	
Mike Gartner (3)	NYR	Apr. 13/90	NYR	3	Mark Fitzpatrick (2)	
					Glenn Healy (1)	NYR 6 NYI 5
		Apr. 27/92	NYR	3	Chris Terreri	NYR 8 N.J. 5
	Tor.	Apr. 25/96	Tor.	3	Jon Casey	Tor. 5 St.L. 4
Mario Lemieux (3)	Pit.	Apr. 25/89	Pit.	5	Ron Hextall	Pit. 10 Phi. 7
		Apr. 23/92	Pit.	3	Don Beaupre	Pit. 6 Wsh. 4
		May 11/96	Pit.	3	Mike Richter	Pit. 7 NYR 3
Patrick Marleau (3)	S.J.	Apr. 10/04	S.J.	3	Chris Osgood	S.J. 3 St.L. 1
		Apr. 22/04	S.J.	3	David Aebischer	S.J. 5 Col. 2
		Apr. 27/06	S.J.	3	Chris Mason	Nsh. 4 S.J. 5
Johan Franzen (3)	Det.	Apr. 26/08	Det.	3	Jose Theodore (2)	
					Peter Budaj (1)	Det. 5 Col. 1
		May 1/08	Col.	3	Jose Theodore (1)	Det. 8 Col. 2
					Peter Budaj (2)	
		May 6/10	Det.	4	Evgeni Nabokov (3)	Det. 7 S.J. 1
					Thomas Greiss (1)	
Newsy Lalonde (2)	Mtl.	Mar. 1/19	Mtl.	5	Clint Benedict	Mtl. 6 Ott. 3
		Mar. 22/19	Sea.	4	Hap Holmes	Mtl. 4 Sea. 2
Howie Morenz (2)	Mtl.	Mar. 22/24	Mtl.	3	Charles Reid	Mtl. 6 Cgy.T. 1
		Mar. 27/25	Mtl.	3	Hap Holmes	Mtl. 4 Vic. 2
Doug Bentley (2)	Chi.	Mar. 28/44	Chi.	3	Connie Dion	Chi. 7 Det. 1
		Mar. 30/44	Det.	3	Connie Dion	Chi. 5 Det. 2
Toe Blake (2)	Mtl.	Mar. 22/38	Mtl.	3	Mike Karakas	Mtl. 6 Chi. 4
		Mar. 26/46	Chi.	3	Mike Karakas	Mtl. 7 Chi. 2
Ted Kennedy (2)	Tor.	Apr. 14/45	Tor.	3	Harry Lumley	Det. 5 Tor. 3
		Mar. 27/48	Tor.	4	Frank Brimsek	Tor. 5 Bos. 3
F. St. Marseille (2)	St.L.	Apr. 28/70	St.L.	3	Al Smith	St.L. 5 Pit. 0
		Apr. 6/72	Min.	3	Cesare Maniago	Min. 6 St.L. 5
Bobby Hull (2)	Chi.	Apr. 7/63	Det.	3	Terry Sawchuk	Det. 7 Chi. 4
		Apr. 9/72	Pit.	3	Jim Rutherford	Chi. 6 Pit. 5
Pit Martin (2)	Chi.	Apr. 4/73	Chi.	3	Wayne Stephenson	Chi. 7 St.L. 1
		May 10/73	Chi.	3	Ken Dryden	Mtl. 6 Chi. 4
Yvan Cournoyer (2)	Mtl.	Apr. 5/73	Mtl.	3	Dave Dryden	Mtl. 7 Buf. 3
		Apr. 11/74	Mtl.	3	Ed Giacomin	Mtl. 4 NYR 1
Guy Lafleur (2)	Mtl.	May 1/75	Mtl.	3	Roger Crozier (1)	
					Gerry Desjardins (2)	Mtl. 7 Buf. 0
		Apr. 11/77	Mtl.	3	Ed Staniowski	Mtl. 7 St.L. 2
Lanny McDonald (2)	Tor.	Apr. 9/77	Pit.	3	Denis Herron	Tor. 5 Pit. 2
		Apr. 17/77	Tor.	4	Wayne Stephenson	Phi. 6 Tor. 5
Bill Barber (2)	Phi.	May 4/80	Min.	4	Gilles Meloche	Phi. 5 Min. 3
		Apr. 9/81	Phi.	3	Dan Bouchard	Phi. 8 Que. 5
Bryan Trottier (2)	NYI	Apr. 8/80	NYI	3	Doug Keans	NYI 8 L.A. 1
		Apr. 9/81	NYI	3	Michel Larocque	NYI 5 Tor. 1
Butch Goring (2)	L.A.	Apr. 9/77	L.A.	3	Phil Myre	L.A. 4 Atl. 2
	NYI	May 17/81	Min.	3	Gilles Meloche	NYI 7 Min. 5
Paul Reinhart (2)	Cgy.	Apr. 14/83	Edm.	3	Andy Moog	Edm. 6 Cgy. 3
		Apr. 8/84	Van	3	Richard Brodeur	Cgy. 5 Van. 1
Brian Propp (2)	Phi.	Apr. 22/81	Phi.	3	Pat Riggin	Phi. 9 Cgy. 4
		Apr. 21/85	Phi.	3	Billy Smith	Phi. 5 NYI 2
Peter Stastny (2)	Que.	Apr. 5/83	Bos.	3	Pete Peeters	Bos. 4 Que. 3
		Apr. 11/87	Que.	3	Mike Liut (2)	
					Steve Weeks (1)	Que. 5 Hfd. 1
Michel Goulet (2)	Que.	Apr. 23/85	Que.	3	Steve Penney	Que. 7 Mtl. 6
		Apr. 12/87	Que.	3	Mike Liut	Que. 4 Hfd. 1
Glenn Anderson (2)	Edm.	Apr. 26/83	Edm.	4	Murray Bannerman	Edm. 8 Chi. 2
		Apr. 6/88	Wpg.	3	Daniel Berthiaume	Edm. 7 Wpg. 4
Peter Zezel (2)	Phi.	Apr. 13/86	NYR	3	John Vanbiesbrouck	Phi. 7 NYR 1
	St.L.	Apr. 11/89	St.L.	3	Jon Casey (2)	
					Kari Takko (1)	St.L. 6 Min. 1
Geoff Courtnall (2)	Van.	Apr. 4/91	L.A.	3	Kelly Hrudey	Van. 6 L.A. 5
		Apr. 30/92	Van.	3	Rick Tabaracci	Van. 5 Win. 0
Joe Sakic (2)	Que.	May 6/95	Que.	3	Mike Richter	Que. 5 NYR 4
	Col.	Apr. 25/96	Col.	3	Corey Hirsch	Col. 5 Van. 4
Daniel Alfredsson (2)	Ott.	Apr. 28/98	Ott.	3	Martin Brodeur	Ott. 4 N.J. 3
		May 11/98	Ott.	3	Olaf Kolzig	Ott. 4 Wsh. 3
David Krejci (2)	Bos.	May 25/11	T.B.	3	Dwayne Roloson	T.B. 5 Bos. 4
	Bos.	May 8/13	Tor.	3	James Reimer	Bos. 4 Tor. 3
Sidney Crosby (2)	Pit.	May 4/09	Wsh.	3	Semyon Varlamov	Wsh. 4 Pit. 3
	Pit.	May 24/13	Pit.	3	Craig Anderson	Pit. 6 Ott. 2
Patrick Kane (2)	Chi.	May 11/09	Chi.	3	Roberto Luongo	Chi. 7 Van. 5
	Chi.	June 8/13	Chi.	3	Jonathan Quick	Chi. 4 L.A. 2
Harry Meeking	Tor.	Mar. 11/18	Tor.	3	Georges Vezina	Tor. 7 Mtl. 3
Alf Skinner	Tor.	Mar. 23/18	Tor.	3	Hugh Lehman	Van.M. 6 Tor. 4
Joe Malone	Mtl.	Feb. 23/19	Mtl.	3	Clint Benedict	Mtl. 8 Ott. 4
Odie Cleghorn	Mtl.	Feb. 27/19	Ott.	3	Clint Benedict	Mtl. 5 Ott. 3
Jack Darragh	Ott.	Apr. 1/20	Tor.	3	Hap Holmes	Ott. 6 Sea. 1
George Boucher	Ott.	Mar. 10/21	Ott.	3	Jake Forbes	Ott. 5 Tor. 0
Babe Dye	Tor.	Mar. 28/22	Tor.	4	Hugh Lehman	Tor. 5 Van.M. 1
Percy Galbraith	Bos.	Mar. 31/27	Bos.	3	Hugh Lehman	Bos. 4 Chi. 4
Busher Jackson	Tor.	Apr. 5/32	NYR	3	John Ross Roach	Tor. 6 NYR 4
Frank Boucher	NYR	Apr. 9/32	Tor.	3	Lorne Chabot	Tor. 6 NYR 4
Charlie Conacher	Tor.	Mar. 26/36	Tor.	3	Tiny Thompson	Tor. 8 Bos. 3
Syd Howe	Det.	Mar. 23/39	Det.	3	Claude Bourque	Det. 7 Mtl. 3
Bryan Hextall	NYR	Apr. 3/40	NYR	3	Turk Broda	NYR 6 Tor. 2
Joe Benoit	Mtl.	Mar. 22/41	Mtl.	3	Sam LoPresti	Mtl. 4 Chi. 3
Syl Apps	Tor.	Mar. 25/41	Tor.	3	Frank Brimsek	Tor. 7 Bos. 2

Three-or-more-Goal Games, Playoffs *— continued*

Player	Team	Date	City	Total Goals	Opposing Goaltender	Score	
Jack McGill	Bos.	Mar. 29/42	Bos.	3	Johnny Mowers	Det. 6	Bos. 4
Don Metz	Tor.	Apr. 14/42	Tor.	3	Johnny Mowers	Tor. 9	Det. 3
Mud Bruneteau	Det.	Apr. 1/43	Det.	3	Frank Brimsek	Det. 6	Bos. 2
Don Grosso	Det.	Apr. 7/43	Bos.	3	Frank Brimsek	Det. 4	Bos. 0
Carl Liscombe	Det.	Apr. 3/45	Bos.	4	Paul Bibeault	Det. 5	Bos. 3
Billy Reay	Mtl.	Apr. 1/47	Bos.	4	Frank Brimsek	Mtl. 5	Bos. 1
Gerry Plamondon	Mtl.	Mar. 24/49	Det.	3	Harry Lumley	Mtl. 4	Det. 3
Sid Smith	Tor.	Apr. 10/49	Det.	3	Harry Lumley	Tor. 3	Det. 1
Pentti Lund	NYR	Apr. 2/50	NYR	3	Bill Durnan	NYR 4	Mtl. 1
Ted Lindsay	Det.	Apr. 5/55	Det.	4	Charlie Hodge (1)		
					Jacques Plante (3)	Det. 7	Mtl. 1
Gordie Howe	Det.	Apr. 10/55	Det.	3	Jacques Plante	Det. 5	Mtl. 1
Phil Goyette	Mtl.	Mar. 25/58	Mtl.	3	Terry Sawchuk	Mtl. 8	Det. 1
Jerry Toppazzini	Bos.	Apr. 5/58	Bos.	3	Gump Worsley	Bos. 8	NYR 2
Bob Pulford	Tor.	Apr. 19/62	Tor.	3	Glenn Hall	Tor. 8	Chi. 4
Dave Keon	Tor.	Apr. 9/64	Mtl.	3	Charlie Hodge (2)	Tor. 3	Mtl. 1
					ENG (1)		
Henri Richard	Mtl.	Apr. 20/67	Mtl.	3	Terry Sawchuk (2)		
					Johnny Bower (1)	Mtl. 6	Tor. 2
Rosaire Paiement	Phi.	Apr. 13/68	Phi.	3	Glenn Hall (1)		
					Seth Martin (2)	Phi. 6	St.L. 1
Jean Beliveau	Mtl.	Apr. 20/68	Mtl.	3	Denis DeJordy	Mtl. 4	Chi. 1
Red Berenson	St.L.	Apr. 15/69	St.L.	3	Gerry Desjardins	St.L. 4	L.A. 0
Ken Schinkel	Pit.	Apr. 11/70	Oak.	3	Gary Smith	Pit. 5	Oak. 2
Jim Pappin	Chi.	Apr. 11/71	Phi.	3	Bruce Gamble	Chi. 6	Phi. 2
Bobby Orr	Bos.	Apr. 11/71	Mtl.	3	Ken Dryden	Bos. 5	Mtl. 2
Jacques Lemaire	Mtl.	Apr. 20/71	Mtl.	3	Gump Worsley	Mtl. 7	Min. 2
Vic Hadfield	NYR	Apr. 22/71	NYR	3	Tony Esposito	NYR 4	Chi. 1
Fred Stanfield	Bos.	Apr. 18/72	Bos.	3	Jacques Caron	Bos. 6	St.L. 1
Ken Hodge	Bos.	Apr. 30/72	Bos.	3	Ed Giacomin	Bos. 6	NYR 5
Dick Redmond	Chi.	Apr. 4/73	Chi.	3	Wayne Stephenson	Chi. 7	St.L. 1
Steve Vickers	NYR	Apr. 10/73	Bos.	3	Ross Brooks (2)		
					Eddie Johnston (1)	NYR 6	Bos. 3
Tom Williams	L.A.	Apr. 14/74	L.A.	3	Mike Veisor	L.A. 5	Chi. 1
Marcel Dionne	L.A.	Apr. 15/76	L.A.	3	Gilles Gilbert	L.A. 6	Bos. 4
Don Saleski	Phi.	Apr. 20/76	Phi.	3	Wayne Thomas	Phi. 7	Tor. 1
Darryl Sittler	Tor.	Apr. 22/76	Tor.	5	Bernie Parent	Tor. 8	Phi. 5
Reggie Leach	Phi.	May 6/76	Phi.	5	Gilles Gilbert	Phi. 6	Bos. 3
Jim Lorentz	Buf.	Apr. 7/77	Min.	3	Pete LoPresti (2)		
					Gary Smith (1)	Buf. 7	Min. 1
Bobby Schmautz	Bos.	Apr. 11/77	Bos.	3	Rogie Vachon	Bos. 8	L.A. 3
Billy Harris	NYI	Apr. 23/77	Mtl.	3	Ken Dryden	Mtl. 4	NYI 3
George Ferguson	Tor.	Apr. 11/78	Tor.	3	Rogie Vachon	Tor. 7	L.A. 3
Jean Ratelle	Bos.	May 3/79	Bos.	3	Ken Dryden	Bos. 4	Mtl. 3
Stan Jonathan	Bos.	May 8/79	Bos.	3	Ken Dryden	Bos. 5	Mtl. 2
Ron Duguay	NYR	Apr. 20/80	NYR	3	Pete Peeters	NYR 4	Phi. 2
Steve Shutt	Mtl.	Apr. 22/80	Mtl.	3	Gilles Meloche	Mtl. 6	Min. 2
Gilbert Perreault	Buf.	May 6/80	NYI	3	Billy Smith (2)		
					ENG (1)	Buf. 7	NYI 4
Paul Holmgren	Phi.	May 15/80	Phi.	3	Billy Smith	Phi. 8	NYI 3
Steve Payne	Min.	Apr. 8/81	Bos.	3	Rogie Vachon	Min. 5	Bos. 4
Denis Potvin	NYI	Apr. 17/81	NYI	3	Andy Moog	NYI 6	Edm. 3
Barry Pederson	Bos.	Apr. 8/82	Bos.	3	Don Edwards	Bos. 7	Buf. 3
Duane Sutter	NYI	Apr. 15/83	NYI	3	Glen Hanlon	NYI 5	NYR 0
Doug Halward	Van.	Apr. 7/84	Van.	3	Reggie Lemelin (2)		
					Don Edwards (1)	Van. 7	Cgy. 0
Jorgen Pettersson	St.L.	Apr. 8/84	Det.	3	Eddie Mio	St.L. 3	Det. 2
Clark Gillies	NYI	May 12/84	NYI	3	Grant Fuhr	NYI 6	Edm. 1
Ken Linseman	Bos.	Apr. 14/85	Bos.	3	Steve Penney	Bos. 7	Mtl. 6
Dave Andreychuk	Buf.	Apr. 14/85	Buf.	3	Dan Bouchard	Buf. 7	Que. 4
Greg Paslawski	St.L.	Apr. 15/86	Min.	3	Don Beaupre	St.L. 6	Min. 3
Doug Risebrough	Cgy.	May 4/86	Cgy.	3	Rick Wamsley	Cgy. 8	St.L. 2
Mike McPhee	Mtl.	Apr. 11/87	Bos.	3	Doug Keans	Mtl. 5	Bos. 4
John Ogrodnick	Que.	Apr. 14/87	Hfd.	3	Mike Liut	Que. 7	Hfd. 5
Pelle Eklund	Phi.	May 10/87	Mtl.	3	Patrick Roy (1)		
					Brian Hayward (2)	Phi. 6	Mtl. 3
John Tucker	Buf.	Apr. 9/88	Bos.	4	Andy Moog	Buf. 6	Bos. 2
Tony Hrkac	St.L.	Apr. 10/88	St.L.	4	Darren Pang	St.L. 6	Chi. 5
Hakan Loob	Cgy.	Apr. 10/88	Cgy.	3	Glenn Healy	Cgy. 7	L.A. 3
Ed Olczyk	Tor.	Apr. 12/88	Tor.	3	Greg Stefan (2)		
					Glen Hanlon (1)	Tor. 6	Det. 5
Aaron Broten	N.J.	Apr. 20/88	N.J.	3	Pete Peeters	N.J. 5	Wsh. 2
Mark Johnson	N.J.	Apr. 22/88	Wsh.	4	Pete Peeters	N.J. 10	Wsh. 4
Patrik Sundstrom	N.J.	Apr. 22/88	Wsh.	3	Pete Peeters (2)		
					Clint Malarchuk (1)	N.J. 10	Wsh. 4
Bob Brooke	Min.	Apr. 5/89	St.L.	3	Greg Millen	St.L. 4	Min. 3
Chris Kontos	L.A.	Apr. 6/89	L.A.	3	Grant Fuhr	L.A. 5	Edm. 2
Wayne Presley	Chi.	Apr. 13/89	Chi.	3	Greg Stefan (1)		
					Glen Hanlon (2)	Chi. 7	Det. 1
Tony Granato	L.A.	Apr. 10/90	L.A.	3	Mike Vernon (1)		
					Rick Wamsley (2)	L.A. 12	Cgy. 4
Tomas Sandstrom	L.A.	Apr. 10/90	L.A.	3	Mike Vernon (1)		
					Rick Wamsley (2)	L.A. 12	Cgy. 4
Dave Taylor	L.A.	Apr. 10/90	L.A.	3	Mike Vernon (1)		
					Rick Wamsley (2)	L.A. 12	Cgy. 4
Bernie Nicholls	NYR	Apr. 19/90	NYR	3	Mike Liut	NYR 7	Wsh. 3
John Druce	Wsh.	Apr. 21/90	NYR	3	John Vanbiesbrouck	Wsh. 6	NYR 3
Adam Oates	St.L.	Apr. 12/91	St.L.	3	Tim Chevaldae	St.L. 6	Det. 1
Luc Robitaille	L.A.	Apr. 26/91	L.A.	3	Grant Fuhr	L.A. 5	Edm. 2
Ray Sheppard	Det.	Apr. 24/92	Min.	3	Jon Casey	Min. 5	Det. 2
Pavel Bure	Van.	Apr. 28/92	Wpg.	3	Rick Tabaracci	Van. 8	Wpg. 3
Joe Murphy	Edm.	May 6/92	Edm.	3	Kirk McLean	Edm. 5	Van. 2
Ron Francis	Pit.	May 9/92	Pit.	3	Mike Richter (2)		
					John V'brouck (1)	Pit. 5	NYR. 4
Kevin Stevens	Pit.	May 21/92	Bos.	4	Andy Moog	Pit. 5	Bos. 2
Dirk Graham	Chi.	Jun. 1/92	Chi.	3	Tom Barrasso	Pit. 6	Chi. 5
Brian Noonan	Chi.	Apr. 18/93	Chi.	3	Curtis Joseph	St.L. 4	Chi. 3
Dale Hunter	Wsh.	Apr. 20/93	Wsh.	3	Glenn Healy	NYI 5	Wsh. 4
Teemu Selanne	Wpg.	Apr. 23/93	Wpg.	3	Kirk McLean	Wpg. 5	Van. 4
Ray Ferraro	NYI	Apr. 26/93	Wsh.	4	Don Beaupre	Wsh. 6	NYI 4
Al Iafrate	Wsh.	Apr. 26/93	Wsh.	3	Glenn Healy (2)		
					Mark Fitzpatrick (1)	Wsh. 6	NYI 4
Paul DiPietro	Mtl.	Apr. 28/93	Mtl.	3	Ron Hextall	Mtl. 6	Que. 2
Wendel Clark	Tor.	May 27/93	L.A.	3	Kelly Hrudey	L.A. 5	Tor. 4
Eric Desjardins	Mtl.	Jun. 3/93	Mtl.	3	Kelly Hrudey	Mtl. 3	L.A. 2
Tony Amonte	Chi.	Apr. 23/94	Chi.	4	Felix Potvin	Chi. 5	Tor. 4
Gary Suter	Chi.	Apr. 24/94	Chi.	3	Felix Potvin	Chi. 4	Tor. 3
Ulf Dahlen	S.J.	May 6/94	S.J.	3	Felix Potvin	S.J. 5	Tor. 2
Mike Sullivan	Cgy.	May 11/95	S.J.	3	Arturs Irbe (2)		
					Wade Flaherty (1)	Cgy. 9	S.J. 2
Theoren Fleury	Cgy.	May 13/95	S.J.	4	Arturs Irbe (3)		
					ENG (1)	Cgy. 6	S.J. 4
Brendan Shanahan	St.L.	May 13/95	Van.	3	Kirk McLean	St.L. 5	Van. 2
John LeClair	Phi.	May 21/95	Phi.	3	Mike Richter	Phi. 5	NYR 4
Brian Leetch	NYR	May 22/95	Phi.	3	Ron Hextall	Phi. 4	NYR 3
Trevor Linden	Van.	Apr. 25/96	Col.	3	Patrick Roy	Col. 5	Van. 4
Jaromir Jagr	Pit.	May 11/96	Pit.	3	Mike Richter	Pit. 7	NYR 3
Peter Forsberg	Col.	Jun. 6/96	Col.	3	John Vanbiesbrouck	Col. 8	Fla. 1
Valeri Zelepukin	N.J.	Apr. 22/97	Mtl.	3	Jocelyn Thibault	N.J. 6	Mtl. 4
Valeri Kamensky	Col.	Apr. 24/97	Col.	3	Jeff Hackett (2)		
					Chris Terreri (1)	Col. 7	Chi. 0
Eric Lindros	Phi.	May 20/97	NYR	3	Mike Richter	Phi. 6	NYR 3
Matthew Barnaby	Buf.	May 10/98	Buf.	3	Andy Moog (2)	Buf. 6	Mtl. 3
					ENG (1)		
Martin Straka	Pit.	Apr. 25/99	Pit.	3	Martin Brodeur	Pit. 4	N.J. 2
Martin Lapointe	Det.	Apr. 15/00	Det.	3	Stephane Fiset (2)	Det. 8	L.A. 5
					Jamie Storr (1)		
Doug Weight	Edm.	Apr. 16/00	Edm.	3	Ed Belfour	Edm. 5	Dal. 2
Bill Guerin	Edm.	Apr. 18/00	Edm.	3	Ed Belfour	Dal. 4	Edm. 3
Scott Young	St.L.	Apr. 23/00	S.J.	3	Steve Shields	St.L. 6	S.J. 2
Andy Delmore	Phi.	May 7/00	Phi.	3	Ron Tugnutt (2)	Phi. 6	Pit. 3
					Peter Skudra (1)		
Brett Hull	Det.	Apr. 27/02	Van.	3	Peter Skudra	Det. 6	Van. 4
Keith Tkachuk	St.L.	May 7/02	St.L.	3	Dominik Hasek	St.L. 6	Det. 1
Darren McCarty	Det.	May 18/02	Det.	3	Patrick Roy	Det. 5	Col. 3
Alexander Mogilny	Tor.	Apr. 9/03	Phi.	3	Roman Cechmanek (2)	Tor. 5	Phi. 3
					ENG (1)		
Mike Sillinger	St.L.	Apr. 12/04	St.L.	3	Evgeni Nabokov (2)	St.L. 4	S.J. 1
					ENG (1)		
Keith Primeau	Phi.	May 2/04	Phi.	3	Ed Belfour (2)	Phi. 7	Tor. 2
					Trevor Kidd (1)		
J.P. Dumont	Buf.	Apr. 24/06	Buf.	3	Antero Niittymaki (1)	Phi. 2	Buf. 8
					Robert Esche (2)		
John Madden	N.J.	Apr. 24/06	N.J.	3	Kevin Weekes	NYR 1	N.J. 4
Jason Pominville	Buf.	Apr. 24/06	Buf.	3	Antero Niittymaki (2)	Phi. 2	Buf. 8
					Robert Esche (1)		
Joffrey Lupul	Ana.	May 9/06	Col.	4	Jose Theodore	Ana. 4	Col. 3
Michael Nylander	NYR	Apr. 17/07	NYR	3	Kari Lehtonen	NYR 7	Atl. 0
Andy McDonald	Ana.	Apr. 25/07	Ana.	3	Dany Sabourin (1)	Ana. 5	Van. 1
					Roberto Luongo (2)		
Pavel Datsyuk	Det.	May 12/08	Dal.	3	Marty Turco	Det. 5	Dal. 2
Alex Ovechkin	Wsh.	May 4/09	Wsh.	3	Marc-Andre Fleury	Wsh. 4	Pit. 3
Evgeni Malkin	Pit.	May 21/09	Pit.	3	Cam Ward	Pit. 7	Car. 4
Henrik Zetterberg	Det.	Apr. 16/10	Phx.	3	Ilya Bryzgalov	Det. 7	Phx. 4
Andrei Kostitsyn	Mtl.	Apr. 17/10	Wsh.	3	Jose Theodore (1)	Wsh. 6	Mtl. 5
					Semyon Varlamov (2)		
Nicklas Backstrom	Wsh.	Apr. 17/10	Wsh.	3	Jaroslav Halak	Wsh. 6	Mtl. 5
Dustin Byfuglien	Chi.	May 5/10	Van.	3	Roberto Luongo	Chi. 5	Van. 2
Jonathan Toews	Chi.	May 7/10	Van.	3	Roberto Luongo	Chi. 7	Van. 4
Devin Setoguchi	S.J.	May 4/11	Det.	3	Jimmy Howard	S.J. 4	Det. 3
Sean Couturier	Phi.	Apr. 13/12	Pit.	3	Marc-Andre Fleury	Phi. 8	Pit. 5
Claude Giroux	Phi.	Apr. 13/12	Pit.	3	Marc-Andre Fleury	Phi. 8	Pit. 5
Jordan Staal	Pit.	Apr. 18/12	Phi.	3	Ilya Bryzgalov (1)	Pit. 10	Phi. 3
					Sergei Bobrovsky (2)		
Jeff Carter	L.A.	May 15/12	Phx.	3	Mike Smith	L.A. 4	Phx. 0
Jean-Gabriel Pageau	Ott.	May 5/13	Ott.	3	Carey Price	Ott. 6	Mtl. 1
James Neal	Pit.	May 24/13	Pit.	3	Craig Anderson	Pit. 6	Ott. 2

Overtime Games since 1918

Abbreviations: Teams/Cities: — **Ana.** - Anaheim; **Atl.** - Atlanta; **Bos.** - Boston; **Buf.** - Buffalo; **Cgy.** - Calgary; **Cgy. T.** - Calgary Tigers (Western Canada Hockey League); **Car.** - Carolina; **Chi.** - Chicago; **Col.** - Colorado; **Dal.** - Dallas; **Det.** - Detroit; **Edm.** - Edmonton; **Edm. E.** - Edmonton Eskimos (WCHL); **Fla.** - Florida; **Hfd.** - Hartford; **L.A.** - Los Angeles; **Min.** - Minnesota; **Mtl.** - Montreal; **Mtl. M.** - Montreal Maroons; **Nsh.** - Nashville, **N.J.** - New Jersey; **NYA** - NY Americans; **NYI** - New York Islanders; **NYR** - New York Rangers; **Oak.** - Oakland; **Ott.** - Ottawa; **Phi.** - Philadelphia; **Phx.** - Phoenix; **Pit.** - Pittsburgh; **Que.** - Quebec; **St.L.** - St. Louis; **Sea.** - Seattle Metropolitans (Pacific Coast Hockey Association); **S.J.** - San Jose; **T.B.** - Tampa Bay; **Tor.** - Toronto; **Van.** - Vancouver; **Van. M.** - Vancouver Millionaires (PCHA); **Vic.** - Victoria Cougars (WCHL); **Wpg.** - Winnipeg; **Wsh.** - Washington.

SERIES — **CF** - conference final; **CQF** - conference quarter-final; **CSF** - conference semi-final; **DF** - division final; **DSF** - division semi-final; **F** - final; **PRE** - preliminary round; **QF** - quarter-final; **SF** - semi-final.

Date	City	Series	Score		Scorer	Overtime	Series Winner
Mar. 26/19	Sea.	F	Mtl. 0	Sea. 0	no scorer	20:00	....
Mar. 29/19	Sea.	F	Mtl. 4	Sea. 3	Jack McDonald	15:57	....
Mar. 21/22	Tor.	F	Tor. 2	Van. M. 1	Babe Dye	4:50	Tor.
Mar. 29/23	Van.	F	Ott. 2	Edm. E. 1	Cy Denneny	2:08	Ott.
Mar. 31/27	Mtl.	QF	Mtl. 1	Mtl. M. 0	Howie Morenz	12:05	Mtl.
Apr. 7/27	Bos.	F	Ott. 0	Bos. 0	no scorer	20:00	Ott.
Apr. 11/27	Ott.	F	Bos. 1	Ott. 1	no scorer	20:00	Ott.
Apr. 3/28	Mtl.	QF	Mtl. M. 1	Mtl. 0	Russell Oatman	8:20	Mtl. M.
Apr. 7/28	Mtl.	F	NYR 2	Mtl. M. 1	Frank Boucher	7:05	NYR
Mar. 21/29	NYR	QF	NYR 1	NYA 0	Butch Keeling	29:50	NYR
Mar. 26/29	Tor.	SF	NYR 2	Tor. 1	Frank Boucher	2:03	NYR
Mar. 20/30	Mtl.	SF	Bos. 2	Mtl. M. 1	Harry Oliver	45:35	Bos.
Mar. 25/30	Bos.	SF	Mtl. M. 1	Bos. 0	Archie Wilcox	26:27	Bos.
Mar. 26/30	Mtl.	QF	Chi. 2	Mtl. 2	Howie Morenz (Mtl.)	51:43	Mtl.
Mar. 28/30	Mtl.	SF	Mtl. 2	NYR 1	Gus Rivers	68:52	Mtl.
Mar. 24/31	Bos.	SF	Bos. 5	Mtl. 4	Cooney Weiland	18:56	Mtl.
Mar. 26/31	Chi.	QF	Chi. 2	Tor. 1	Stew Adams	19:20	Chi.
Mar. 28/31	Mtl.	SF	Mtl. 4	Bos. 3	Georges Mantha	5:10	Mtl.
Apr. 1/31	Mtl.	SF	Mtl. 3	Bos. 2	Wildor Larochelle	19:00	Mtl.
Apr. 5/31	Chi.	F	Chi. 2	Mtl. 1	Johnny Gottselig	24:50	Mtl.
Apr. 9/31	Mtl.	F	Chi. 3	Mtl. 2	Cy Wentworth	53:50	Mtl.
Mar. 26/32	Mtl.	SF	NYR 4	Mtl. 3	Fred Cook	59:32	NYR
Apr. 2/32	Tor.	SF	Tor. 3	Mtl. M. 2	Bob Gracie	17:59	Tor.
Mar. 25/33	Bos.	SF	Bos. 2	Tor. 1	Marty Barry	14:14	Tor.
Mar. 28/33	Bos.	SF	Tor. 1	Bos. 0	Busher Jackson	15:03	Tor.
Mar. 30/33	Tor.	SF	Bos. 2	Tor. 1	Eddie Shore	4:23	Tor.
Apr. 3/33	Tor.	SF	Tor. 1	Bos. 0	Ken Doraty	104:46	Tor.
Apr. 13/33	Tor.	F	NYR 1	Tor. 0	Bill Cook	7:33	NYR
Mar. 22/34	Tor.	SF	Det. 2	Tor. 1	Herbie Lewis	1:33	Det.
Mar. 25/34	Chi.	QF	Chi. 1	Mtl. 1	Mush March (Chi)	11:05	Chi.
Apr. 3/34	Det.	F	Chi. 2	Det. 1	Paul Thompson	21:10	Chi.
Apr. 10/34	Chi.	F	Chi. 1	Det. 0	Mush March	30:05	Chi.
Mar. 23/35	Bos.	SF	Bos. 1	Tor. 0	Dit Clapper	33:26	Tor.
Mar. 26/35	Chi.	QF	Mtl. M. 1	Chi. 0	Baldy Northcott	4:02	Mtl. M.
Mar. 30/35	Tor.	SF	Tor. 2	Bos. 1	Pep Kelly	1:36	Tor.
Apr. 4/35	Tor.	F	Mtl. M. 3	Tor. 2	Dave Trottier	5:28	Mtl. M.
Mar. 24/36	Mtl.	SF	Det. 1	Mtl. M. 0	Mud Bruneteau	116:30	Det.
Apr. 9/36	Tor.	F	Tor. 4	Det. 3	Buzz Boll	0:31	Det.
Mar. 25/37	NYR	QF	NYR 2	Tor. 1	Babe Pratt	13:05	NYR
Apr. 1/37	Mtl.	SF	Det. 2	Mtl. 1	Hec Kilrea	51:49	Det.
Mar. 22/38	NYR	QF	NYA 2	NYR 1	John Sorrell	21:25	NYA
Mar. 24/38	Tor.	SF	Tor. 1	Bos. 0	George Parsons	21:31	Tor.
Mar. 26/38	Mtl.	QF	Chi. 3	Mtl. 2	Paul Thompson	11:49	Chi.
Mar. 27/38	NYR	QF	NYA 3	NYR 2	Lorne Carr	60:40	NYA
Mar. 29/38	Bos.	SF	Tor. 3	Bos. 2	Gordie Drillon	10:04	Tor.
Mar. 31/38	Chi.	SF	Chi. 1	NYA 0	Cully Dahlstrom	33:01	Chi.
Mar. 21/39	NYR	SF	Bos. 2	NYR 1	Mel Hill	59:25	Bos.
Mar. 23/39	Bos.	SF	Bos. 3	NYR 2	Mel Hill	8:24	Bos.
Mar. 26/39	Det.	QF	Det. 1	Mtl. 0	Marty Barry	7:47	Det.
Mar. 30/39	Bos.	SF	NYR 2	Bos. 1	Clint Smith	17:19	Bos.
Apr. 1/39	Tor.	SF	Tor. 5	Det. 4	Gordie Drillon	5:42	Tor.
Apr. 2/39	Bos.	SF	Bos. 2	NYR 1	Mel Hill	48:00	Bos.
Apr. 9/39	Bos.	F	Tor. 3	Bos. 2	Doc Romnes	10:38	Bos.
Mar. 19/40	Det.	QF	Det. 2	NYA 1	Syd Howe	0:25	Det.
Mar. 19/40	Tor.	QF	Tor. 3	Chi. 2	Syl Apps	6:35	Tor.
Apr. 2/40	NYR	F	NYR 2	Tor. 1	Alf Pike	15:30	NYR
Apr. 11/40	Tor.	F	NYR 2	Tor. 1	Muzz Patrick	31:43	NYR
Apr. 13/40	Tor.	F	NYR 3	Tor. 2	Bryan Hextall	2:07	NYR
Mar. 20/41	Det.	QF	Det. 2	NYR 1	Syd Howe	12:01	Det.
Mar. 22/41	Mtl.	QF	Mtl. 4	Chi. 3	Charlie Sands	34:04	Chi.
Mar. 29/41	Bos.	SF	Tor. 2	Bos. 1	Pete Langelle	17:31	Bos.
Mar. 30/41	Chi.	SF	Det. 2	Chi. 1	Gus Giesebrecht	9:15	Det.
Mar. 22/42	Chi.	QF	Bos. 2	Chi. 1	Des Smith	6:51	Bos.
Mar. 21/43	Bos.	SF	Bos. 5	Mtl. 4	Don Gallinger	12:30	Bos.
Mar. 23/43	Det.	SF	Tor. 3	Det. 2	Jack McLean	70:18	Det.
Mar. 25/43	Mtl.	SF	Bos. 3	Mtl. 2	Busher Jackson	3:20	Bos.
Mar. 30/43	Tor.	SF	Det. 3	Tor. 2	Adam Brown	9:21	Det.
Mar. 30/43	Bos.	SF	Bos. 5	Mtl. 4	Ab DeMarco	3:41	Bos.
Apr. 13/44	Mtl.	F	Mtl. 5	Chi. 4	Toe Blake	9:12	Mtl.
Mar. 27/45	Tor.	SF	Tor. 4	Mtl. 3	Gus Bodnar	12:36	Tor.
Mar. 29/45	Det.	SF	Det. 3	Bos. 2	Mud Bruneteau	17:12	Det.
Apr. 21/45	Tor.	F	Det. 1	Tor. 0	Eddie Bruneteau	14:16	Tor.
Mar. 28/46	Bos.	SF	Bos. 4	Det. 3	Don Gallinger	9:51	Bos.
Mar. 30/46	Mtl.	F	Mtl. 4	Bos. 3	Maurice Richard	9:08	Mtl.
Apr. 2/46	Mtl.	F	Mtl. 3	Bos. 2	Jimmy Peters	16:55	Mtl.
Apr. 7/46	Bos.	F	Bos. 3	Mtl. 2	Terry Reardon	15:13	Mtl.
Mar. 26/47	Tor.	SF	Tor. 3	Det. 2	Howie Meeker	3:05	Tor.
Mar. 27/47	Mtl.	SF	Mtl. 2	Bos. 1	Ken Mosdell	5:38	Mtl.
Apr. 3/47	Mtl.	SF	Mtl. 4	Bos. 3	John Quilty	36:40	Mtl.
Apr. 15/47	Tor.	F	Tor. 2	Mtl. 1	Syl Apps	16:36	Tor.
Mar. 24/48	Tor.	SF	Tor. 5	Bos. 4	Nick Metz	17:03	Tor.
Mar. 22/49	Det.	SF	Det. 2	Mtl. 1	Max McNab	44:52	Det.
Mar. 24/49	Det.	SF	Mtl. 4	Det. 3	Gerry Plamondon	2:59	Det.
Mar. 26/49	Tor.	SF	Bos. 5	Tor. 4	Woody Dumart	16:14	Tor.
Apr. 8/49	Det.	F	Tor. 3	Det. 2	Joe Klukay	17:31	Tor.
Apr. 4/50	Tor.	SF	Det. 2	Tor. 1	Leo Reise Jr.	20:38	Det.
Apr. 4/50	Mtl.	SF	Mtl. 3	NYR 2	Elmer Lach	15:19	NYR
Apr. 9/50	Det.	SF	Det. 1	Tor. 0	Leo Reise Jr.	8:39	Det.
Apr. 18/50	Det.	F	NYR 4	Det. 3	Don Raleigh	8:34	Det.
Apr. 20/50	Det.	F	NYR 2	Det. 1	Don Raleigh	1:38	Det.
Apr. 23/50	Det.	F	Det. 4	NYR 3	Pete Babando	28:31	Det.
Mar. 27/51	Det.	SF	Mtl. 3	Det. 2	Maurice Richard	61:09	Mtl.
Mar. 29/51	Det.	SF	Mtl. 1	Det. 0	Maurice Richard	42:20	Mtl.
Mar. 31/51	Tor.	SF	Bos. 1	Tor. 1	no scorer	20:00	Tor.
Apr. 11/51	Tor.	F	Tor. 3	Mtl. 2	Sid Smith	5:51	Tor.
Apr. 14/51	Tor.	F	Mtl. 3	Tor. 2	Maurice Richard	2:55	Tor.
Apr. 17/51	Mtl.	F	Tor. 2	Mtl. 1	Ted Kennedy	4:47	Tor.
Apr. 19/51	Mtl.	F	Tor. 3	Mtl. 2	Harry Watson	5:15	Tor.
Apr. 21/51	Tor.	F	Tor. 3	Mtl. 2	Bill Barilko	2:53	Tor.
Apr. 6/52	Bos.	SF	Mtl. 3	Bos. 2	Paul Masnick	27:49	Mtl.
Mar. 29/53	Bos.	SF	Bos. 2	Det. 1	Jack McIntyre	12:29	Bos.
Mar. 29/53	Chi.	SF	Chi. 2	Mtl. 1	Al Dewsbury	5:18	Mtl.
Apr. 16/53	Mtl.	F	Mtl. 1	Bos. 0	Elmer Lach	1:22	Mtl.
Apr. 1/54	Det.	SF	Det. 4	Tor. 3	Ted Lindsay	21:01	Det.
Apr. 11/54	Det.	F	Mtl. 1	Det. 0	Ken Mosdell	5:45	Det.
Apr. 16/54	Det.	F	Det. 2	Mtl. 1	Tony Leswick	4:29	Det.
Mar. 29/55	Bos.	SF	Mtl. 4	Bos. 3	Don Marshall	3:05	Mtl.
Mar. 24/56	Tor.	SF	Det. 5	Tor. 4	Ted Lindsay	4:22	Det.
Mar. 28/57	NYR	SF	NYR 4	Mtl. 3	Andy Hebenton	13:38	Mtl.
Apr. 4/57	Mtl.	SF	Mtl. 4	NYR 3	Maurice Richard	1:11	Mtl.
Mar. 27/58	NYR	SF	Bos. 4	NYR 3	Jerry Toppazzini	4:46	Bos.
Mar. 30/58	Det.	SF	Mtl. 2	Det. 1	André Pronovost	11:52	Mtl.
Apr. 17/58	Mtl.	F	Mtl. 3	Bos. 2	Maurice Richard	5:45	Mtl.
Mar. 28/59	Tor.	SF	Tor. 3	Bos. 2	Gerry Ehman	5:02	Tor.
Mar. 31/59	Tor.	SF	Tor. 3	Bos. 2	Frank Mahovlich	11:21	Tor.
Apr. 14/59	Tor.	F	Tor. 3	Mtl. 2	Dick Duff	10:06	Mtl.
Mar. 26/60	Mtl.	SF	Mtl. 4	Chi. 3	Doug Harvey	8:38	Mtl.
Mar. 27/60	Det.	SF	Tor. 5	Det. 4	Frank Mahovlich	43:00	Tor.
Mar. 29/60	Det.	SF	Det. 2	Tor. 1	Gerry Melnyk	1:54	Tor.
Mar. 22/61	Tor.	SF	Tor. 3	Det. 2	George Armstrong	24:51	Det.
Mar. 26/61	Chi.	SF	Chi. 2	Mtl. 1	Murray Balfour	52:12	Chi.
Apr. 5/62	Tor.	SF	Tor. 3	NYR 2	Red Kelly	24:23	Tor.
Apr. 2/64	Det.	SF	Chi. 3	Det. 2	Murray Balfour	8:21	Det.
Apr. 14/64	Tor.	F	Det. 4	Tor. 3	Larry Jeffrey	7:52	Tor.
Apr. 23/64	Det.	F	Tor. 4	Det. 3	Bob Baun	1:43	Tor.
Apr. 6/65	Tor.	SF	Tor. 3	Mtl. 2	Dave Keon	4:17	Mtl.
Apr. 13/65	Tor.	SF	Mtl. 4	Tor. 3	Claude Provost	16:33	Mtl.
May 5/66	Det.	F	Mtl. 3	Det. 2	Henri Richard	2:20	Mtl.
Apr. 13/67	NYR	SF	Mtl. 2	NYR 1	John Ferguson	6:28	Mtl.
Apr. 25/67	Tor.	F	Tor. 3	Mtl. 2	Bob Pulford	28:26	Tor.
Apr. 10/68	St.L.	QF	St.L. 3	Phi. 2	Larry Keenan	24:10	St.L.
Apr. 16/68	St.L.	QF	Phi. 2	St.L. 1	Don Blackburn	31:18	St.L.
Apr. 16/68	Min.	QF	Min. 4	L.A. 3	Milan Marcetta	9:11	Min.
Apr. 22/68	Min.	SF	Min. 3	St.L. 2	Parker MacDonald	3:41	St.L.
Apr. 27/68	St.L.	SF	St.L. 4	Min. 3	Gary Sabourin	1:32	St.L.
Apr. 28/68	Mtl.	SF	Mtl. 4	Chi. 3	Jacques Lemaire	2:14	Mtl.
Apr. 29/68	St.L.	SF	St.L. 3	Min. 2	Bill McCreary	17:27	St.L.
May 3/68	St.L.	SF	St.L. 2	Min. 1	Ron Schock	22:50	St.L.
May 5/68	St.L.	F	Mtl. 3	St.L. 2	Jacques Lemaire	1:41	Mtl.
May 9/68	Mtl.	F	Mtl. 4	St.L. 3	Bobby Rousseau	1:13	Mtl.
Apr. 2/69	Oak.	QF	L.A. 5	Oak. 4	Ted Irvine	0:19	L.A.
Apr. 10/69	Mtl.	SF	Mtl. 3	Bos. 2	Ralph Backstrom	0:42	Mtl.
Apr. 13/69	Mtl.	SF	Mtl. 4	Bos. 3	Mickey Redmond	4:55	Mtl.
Apr. 24/69	Bos.	SF	Mtl. 2	Bos. 1	Jean Béliveau	31:28	Mtl.
Apr. 12/70	Oak.	QF	Pit. 3	Oak. 2	Michel Briere	8:28	Pit.
May 10/70	Bos.	F	Bos. 4	St.L. 3	Bobby Orr	0:40	Bos.
Apr. 15/71	Tor.	QF	NYR 2	Tor. 1	Bob Nevin	9:07	NYR
Apr. 18/71	Chi.	SF	NYR 2	Chi. 1	Pete Stemkowski	1:37	Chi.
Apr. 27/71	Chi.	SF	Chi. 3	NYR 2	Bobby Hull	6:35	Chi.
Apr. 29/71	NYR	SF	NYR 3	Chi. 2	Pete Stemkowski	41:29	Chi.
May 4/71	Chi.	F	Chi. 2	Mtl. 1	Jim Pappin	21:11	Mtl.
Apr. 6/72	Bos.	QF	Tor. 4	Bos. 3	Jim Harrison	2:58	Bos.
Apr. 6/72	Min.	QF	Min. 6	St.L. 5	Bill Goldsworthy	1:36	St.L.
Apr. 9/72	Pit.	QF	Chi. 6	Pit. 5	Pit Martin	0:12	Chi.
Apr. 16/72	Min.	QF	St.L. 2	Min. 1	Kevin O'Shea	10:07	St.L.
Apr. 1/73	Mtl.	QF	Buf. 3	Mtl. 2	René Robert	9:18	Mtl.
Apr. 10/73	Phi.	QF	Phi. 3	Min. 2	Gary Dornhoefer	8:35	Phi.
Apr. 14/73	Mtl.	SF	Phi. 5	Mtl. 4	Rick MacLeish	2:56	Mtl.
Apr. 17/73	Mtl.	SF	Mtl. 4	Phi. 3	Larry Robinson	6:45	Mtl.
Apr. 14/74	Tor.	QF	Bos. 4	Tor. 3	Ken Hodge	1:27	Bos.
Apr. 14/74	Atl.	QF	Phi. 4	Atl. 3	Dave Schultz	5:40	Phi.
Apr. 16/74	Mtl.	QF	NYR 3	Mtl. 2	Ron Harris	4:07	NYR
Apr. 23/74	Chi.	SF	Chi. 4	Bos. 3	Jim Pappin	3:48	Bos.
Apr. 28/74	NYR	SF	NYR 2	Phi. 1	Rod Gilbert	4:20	Phi.
May 9/74	Bos.	F	Phi. 3	Bos. 2	Bobby Clarke	12:01	Phi.
Apr. 8/75	L.A.	PRE	L.A. 3	Tor. 2	Mike Murphy	8:53	Tor.
Apr. 10/75	Tor.	PRE	Tor. 3	L.A. 2	Blaine Stoughton	10:19	Tor.
Apr. 10/75	Chi.	PRE	Chi. 4	Bos. 3	Ivan Boldirev	7:33	Chi.
Apr. 11/75	NYR	PRE	NYI 4	NYR 3	J.P. Parise	0:11	NYI
Apr. 17/75	Chi.	QF	Chi. 5	Buf. 4	Stan Mikita	2:31	Buf.
Apr. 19/75	Tor.	QF	Phi. 4	Tor. 3	André Dupont	1:45	Phi.
Apr. 22/75	Mtl.	QF	Mtl. 5	Van. 4	Guy Lafleur	17:06	Mtl.
Apr. 27/75	Buf.	SF	Buf. 6	Mtl. 5	Danny Gare	4:42	Buf.
May 1/75	Phi.	SF	Phi. 5	NYI 4	Bobby Clarke	2:56	Phi.
May 6/75	Buf.	SF	Buf. 5	Mtl. 4	René Robert	5:56	Buf.
May 7/75	NYI	SF	NYI 4	Phi. 3	Jude Drouin	1:53	Phi.
May 20/75	Buf.	F	Buf. 5	Phi. 4	René Robert	18:29	Phi.
Apr. 8/76	Buf.	PRE	Buf. 3	St.L. 2	Danny Gare	11:43	Buf.
Apr. 9/76	Buf.	PRE	Buf. 2	St.L. 1	Don Luce	14:27	Buf.
Apr. 13/76	Bos.	QF	L.A. 3	Bos. 2	Butch Goring	0:27	Bos.
Apr. 13/76	Buf.	QF	Buf. 3	NYI 2	Danny Gare	14:04	NYI
Apr. 22/76	L.A.	QF	L.A. 4	Bos. 3	Butch Goring	18:28	Bos.
Apr. 29/76	Phi.	SF	Phi. 2	Bos. 1	Reggie Leach	13:38	Phi.
Apr. 15/77	Tor.	QF	Phi. 4	Tor. 3	Rick MacLeish	2:55	Phi.
Apr. 17/77	Tor.	QF	Phi. 6	Tor. 5	Reggie Leach	19:10	Phi.
Apr. 24/77	Phi.	SF	Bos. 4	Phi. 3	Rick Middleton	2:57	Bos.
Apr. 26/77	Phi.	SF	Bos. 5	Phi. 4	Terry O'Reilly	30:07	Bos.

Overtime Games since 1918 *— continued*

Date	City	Series	Score		Scorer	Overtime	Series Winner
May 3/77	Mtl.	SF	NYI 4	Mtl. 3	Billy Harris	3:58	Mtl.
May 14/77	Bos.	F	Mtl. 2	Bos. 1	Jacques Lemaire	4:32	Mtl.
Apr. 11/78	Phi.	PRE	Phi. 3	Col. 2	Mel Bridgman	0:23	Phi.
Apr. 13/78	NYR	PRE	NYR 4	Buf. 3	Don Murdoch	1:37	Buf.
Apr. 19/78	Bos.	QF	Bos. 4	Chi. 3	Terry O'Reilly	1:50	Bos.
Apr. 19/78	NYI	QF	NYI 3	Tor. 2	Mike Bossy	2:50	Tor.
Apr. 21/78	Chi.	QF	Bos. 4	Chi. 3	Peter McNab	10:17	Bos.
Apr. 25/78	NYI	QF	NYI 2	Tor. 1	Bob Nystrom	8:02	Tor.
Apr. 29/78	NYI	QF	Tor. 2	NYI 1	Lanny McDonald	4:13	Tor.
May 2/78	Bos.	SF	Bos. 3	Phi. 2	Rick Middleton	1:43	Bos.
May 16/78	Mtl.	F	Mtl. 3	Bos. 2	Guy Lafleur	13:09	Mtl.
May 21/78	Bos.	F	Bos. 4	Mtl. 3	Bobby Schmautz	6:22	Mtl.
Apr. 12/79	L.A.	PRE	NYR 2	L.A. 1	Phil Esposito	6:11	NYR
Apr. 14/79	Buf.	PRE	Pit. 4	Buf. 3	George Ferguson	0:47	Pit.
Apr. 16/79	Phi.	QF	Phi. 3	NYR 2	Ken Linseman	0:44	NYR
Apr. 18/79	NYI	QF	NYI 1	Chi. 0	Mike Bossy	2:31	NYI
Apr. 21/79	Tor.	QF	Mtl. 4	Tor. 3	Cam Connor	25:25	Mtl.
Apr. 22/79	Tor.	QF	Mtl. 5	Tor. 4	Larry Robinson	4:14	Mtl.
Apr. 28/79	NYI	SF	NYI 4	NYR 3	Denis Potvin	8:02	NYR
May 3/79	NYR	SF	NYI 3	NYR 2	Bob Nystrom	3:40	NYR
May 3/79	Bos.	SF	Bos. 4	Mtl. 3	Jean Ratelle	3:46	Mtl.
May 10/79	Mtl.	SF	Mtl. 5	Bos. 4	Yvon Lambert	9:33	Mtl.
May 19/79	NYR	F	Mtl. 4	NYR 3	Serge Savard	7:25	Mtl.
Apr. 8/80	NYR	PRE	NYR 2	Atl. 1	Steve Vickers	0:33	NYR
Apr. 8/80	Phi.	PRE	Phi. 4	Edm. 3	Bobby Clarke	8:06	Phi.
Apr. 8/80	Chi.	PRE	Chi. 3	St.L. 2	Doug Lecuyer	12:34	Chi.
Apr. 11/80	Hfd.	PRE	Mtl. 4	Hfd. 3	Yvon Lambert	0:29	Mtl.
Apr. 11/80	Tor.	PRE	Min. 4	Tor. 3	Al MacAdam	0:32	Min.
Apr. 11/80	L.A.	PRE	NYI 4	L.A. 3	Ken Morrow	6:55	NYI
Apr. 11/80	Edm.	PRE	Phi. 3	Edm. 2	Ken Linseman	23:56	Phi.
Apr. 16/80	Bos.	QF	NYI 2	Bos. 1	Clark Gillies	1:02	NYI
Apr. 17/80	Bos.	QF	NYI 5	Bos. 4	Bob Bourne	1:24	NYI
Apr. 21/80	NYI	QF	Bos. 4	NYI 3	Terry O'Reilly	17:13	NYI
May 1/80	Buf.	SF	NYI 2	Buf. 1	Bob Nystrom	21:20	NYI
May 13/80	Phi.	F	NYI 4	Phi. 3	Denis Potvin	4:07	NYI
May 24/80	NYI	F	NYI 5	Phi. 4	Bob Nystrom	7:11	NYI
Apr. 8/81	Buf.	PRE	Buf. 3	Van. 2	Alan Haworth	5:00	Buf.
Apr. 8/81	Bos.	PRE	Min. 5	Bos. 4	Steve Payne	3:34	Min.
Apr. 11/81	Chi.	PRE	Cgy. 5	Chi. 4	Willi Plett	35:17	Cgy.
Apr. 12/81	Que.	PRE	Que. 4	Phi. 3	Dale Hunter	0:37	Phi.
Apr. 14/81	St.L.	PRE	St.L. 4	Pit. 3	Mike Crombeen	25:16	St.L.
Apr. 16/81	Buf.	QF	Min. 4	Buf. 3	Steve Payne	0:22	Min.
Apr. 20/81	Min.	QF	Buf. 5	Min. 4	Craig Ramsay	16:32	Min.
Apr. 20/81	Edm.	QF	NYI 5	Edm. 4	Ken Morrow	5:41	NYI
Apr. 7/82	Min.	DSF	Chi. 3	Min. 2	Greg Fox	3:34	Chi.
Apr. 8/82	Edm.	DSF	Edm. 3	L.A. 2	Wayne Gretzky	6:20	L.A.
Apr. 8/82	Van.	DSF	Van. 2	Cgy. 1	Tiger Williams	14:20	Van.
Apr. 10/82	Pit.	DSF	Pit. 2	NYI 1	Rick Kehoe	4:14	NYI
Apr. 10/82	L.A.	DSF	L.A. 6	Edm. 5	Daryl Evans	2:35	L.A.
Apr. 13/82	Mtl.	DSF	Que. 3	Mtl. 2	Dale Hunter	0:22	Que.
Apr. 13/82	NYI	DSF	NYI 4	Pit. 3	John Tonelli	6:19	NYI
Apr. 16/82	Van.	DF	L.A. 3	Van. 2	Steve Bozek	4:33	Van.
Apr. 18/82	Que.	DF	Que. 3	Bos. 2	Wilf Paiement	11:44	Que.
Apr. 18/82	NYR	DF	NYI 4	NYR 3	Bryan Trottier	3:00	NYI
Apr. 18/82	L.A.	DF	Van. 4	L.A. 3	Colin Campbell	1:23	Van.
Apr. 21/82	St.L.	DF	St.L. 3	Chi. 2	Bernie Federko	3:28	Chi.
Apr. 23/82	Que.	DF	Bos. 6	Que. 5	Peter McNab	10:54	Que.
Apr. 27/82	Chi.	CF	Van. 2	Chi. 1	Jim Nill	28:58	Van.
May 1/82	Que.	CF	NYI 5	Que. 4	Wayne Merrick	16:52	NYI
May 8/82	NYI	F	NYI 6	Van. 5	Mike Bossy	19:58	NYI
Apr. 5/83	Bos.	DSF	Bos. 4	Que. 3	Barry Pederson	1:46	Bos.
Apr. 6/83	Cgy.	DSF	Cgy. 4	Van. 3	Eddy Beers	12:27	Cgy.
Apr. 7/83	Min.	DSF	Min. 5	Tor. 4	Bobby Smith	5:03	Min.
Apr. 10/83	Tor.	DSF	Min. 5	Tor. 4	Dino Ciccarelli	8:05	Min.
Apr. 10/83	Van.	DSF	Cgy. 4	Van. 3	Greg Meredith	1:06	Cgy.
Apr. 18/83	Min.	DF	Chi. 4	Min. 3	Rich Preston	10:34	Chi.
Apr. 24/83	Bos.	DF	Bos. 3	Buf. 2	Brad Park	1:52	Bos.
Apr. 5/84	Edm.	DSF	Edm. 5	Wpg. 4	Randy Gregg	0:21	Edm.
Apr. 7/84	Det.	DSF	St.L. 4	Det. 3	Mark Reeds	37:07	St.L.
Apr. 8/84	Det.	DSF	St.L. 3	Det. 2	Jorgen Pettersson	2:42	St.L.
Apr. 10/84	NYI	DSF	NYI 3	NYR 2	Ken Morrow	8:56	NYI
Apr. 13/84	Min.	DF	St.L. 4	Min. 3	Doug Gilmour	16:16	Min.
Apr. 13/84	Edm.	DF	Cgy. 6	Edm. 5	Carey Wilson	3:42	Edm.
Apr. 13/84	NYI	DF	NYI 5	Wsh. 4	Anders Kallur	7:35	NYI
Apr. 16/84	Mtl.	DF	Que. 4	Mtl. 3	Bo Berglund	3:00	Mtl.
Apr. 20/84	Cgy.	DF	Cgy. 5	Edm. 4	Lanny McDonald	1:04	Edm.
Apr. 22/84	Min.	DF	Min. 4	St.L. 3	Steve Payne	6:00	Min.
Apr. 10/85	Phi.	DSF	Phi. 5	NYR 4	Mark Howe	8:01	Phi.
Apr. 10/85	Wsh.	DSF	Wsh. 4	NYI 3	Alan Haworth	2:28	NYI
Apr. 10/85	Edm.	DSF	Edm. 3	L.A. 2	Lee Fogolin	3:01	Edm.
Apr. 10/85	Wpg.	DSF	Wpg. 5	Cgy. 4	Brian Mullen	7:56	Wpg.
Apr. 11/85	Wsh.	DSF	Wsh. 2	NYI 1	Mike Gartner	21:23	NYI
Apr. 13/85	L.A.	DSF	Edm. 4	L.A. 3	Glenn Anderson	0:46	Edm.
Apr. 18/85	Mtl.	DF	Que. 2	Mtl. 1	Mark Kumpel	12:23	Que.
Apr. 23/85	Que.	DF	Que. 7	Mtl. 6	Dale Hunter	18:36	Que.
Apr. 25/85	Min.	DF	Chi. 7	Min. 6	Darryl Sutter	21:57	Chi.
Apr. 28/85	Chi.	DF	Min. 5	Chi. 4	Dennis Maruk	1:14	Chi.
Apr. 30/85	Min.	DF	Chi. 6	Min. 5	Darryl Sutter	15:41	Chi.
May 2/85	Mtl.	DF	Que. 3	Mtl. 2	Peter Stastny	2:22	Que.
May 5/85	Que.	CF	Que. 2	Phi. 1	Peter Stastny	6:20	Phi.
Apr. 9/86	Que.	DSF	Hfd. 3	Que. 2	Sylvain Turgeon	2:36	Hfd.
Apr. 12/86	Wpg.	DSF	Cgy. 4	Wpg. 3	Lanny McDonald	8:25	Cgy.
Apr. 17/86	Wsh.	DF	NYR 4	Wsh. 3	Brian MacLellan	1:16	NYR
Apr. 20/86	Edm.	DF	Edm. 6	Cgy. 5	Glenn Anderson	1:04	Cgy.
Apr. 23/86	Hfd.	DF	Hfd. 2	Mtl. 1	Kevin Dineen	1:07	Mtl.
Apr. 23/86	NYR	DF	NYR 6	Wsh. 5	Bob Brooke	2:40	NYR
Apr. 26/86	St L.	DF	St L. 4	Tor. 3	Mark Reeds	7:11	St L.
Apr. 29/86	Mtl.	DF	Mtl. 2	Hfd. 1	Claude Lemieux	5:55	Mtl.
May 5/86	NYR	CF	Mtl. 4	NYR 3	Claude Lemieux	9:41	Mtl.
May 12/86	St L.	CF	St L. 6	Cgy. 5	Doug Wickenheiser	7:30	Cgy.
May 18/86	Cgy.	F	Mtl. 3	Cgy. 2	Brian Skrudland	0:09	Mtl.
Apr. 8/87	Hfd.	DSF	Hfd. 3	Que. 2	Paul MacDermid	2:20	Que.
Apr. 9/87	Mtl.	DSF	Mtl. 4	Bos. 3	Mats Naslund	2:38	Mtl.
Apr. 9/87	St.L.	DSF	Tor. 3	St.L. 2	Rick Lanz	10:17	Tor.
Apr. 11/87	Wpg.	DSF	Cgy. 3	Wpg. 2	Mike Bullard	3:53	Wpg.
Apr. 11/87	Chi.	DSF	Det. 4	Chi. 3	Shawn Burr	4:51	Det.
Apr. 16/87	Que.	DSF	Que. 5	Hfd. 4	Peter Stastny	6:05	Que.
Apr. 18/87	Wsh.	DSF	NYI 3	Wsh. 2	Pat LaFontaine	68:47	NYI
Apr. 21/87	Edm.	DF	Edm. 3	Wpg. 2	Glenn Anderson	0:36	Edm.
Apr. 26/87	Que.	DF	Mtl. 3	Que. 2	Mats Naslund	5:30	Mtl.
Apr. 27/87	Tor.	DF	Tor. 3	Det. 2	Mike Allison	9:31	Det.
May 4/87	Phi.	CF	Phi. 4	Mtl. 3	Ilkka Sinisalo	9:11	Phi.
May 20/87	Edm.	F	Edm. 3	Phi. 2	Jari Kurri	6:50	Edm.
Apr. 6/88	NYI	DSF	NYI 4	N.J. 3	Pat LaFontaine	6:11	N.J.
Apr. 10/88	Phi.	DSF	Phi. 5	Wsh. 4	Murray Craven	1:18	Wsh.
Apr. 10/88	N.J.	DSF	NYI 5	N.J. 4	Brent Sutter	15:07	N.J.
Apr. 10/88	Buf.	DSF	Buf. 6	Bos. 5	John Tucker	5:32	Bos.
Apr. 12/88	Det.	DSF	Tor. 6	Det. 5	Ed Olczyk	0:34	Det.
Apr. 16/88	Wsh.	DSF	Wsh. 5	Phi. 4	Dale Hunter	5:57	Wsh.
Apr. 21/88	Cgy.	DF	Edm. 5	Cgy. 4	Wayne Gretzky	7:54	Edm.
May 4/88	Bos.	CF	N.J. 3	Bos. 2	Doug Brown	17:46	Bos.
May 9/88	Det.	CF	Edm. 4	Det. 3	Jari Kurri	11:02	Edm.
Apr. 5/89	St.L.	DSF	St.L. 4	Min. 3	Brett Hull	11:55	St.L.
Apr. 5/89	Cgy.	DSF	Van. 4	Cgy. 3	Paul Reinhart	2:47	Cgy.
Apr. 6/89	St.L.	DSF	St.L. 4	Min. 3	Rick Meagher	5:30	St.L.
Apr. 6/89	Det.	DSF	Chi. 5	Det. 4	Duane Sutter	14:36	Chi.
Apr. 8/89	Hfd.	DSF	Mtl. 5	Hfd. 4	Stephane Richer	5:01	Mtl.
Apr. 8/89	Phi.	DSF	Wsh. 4	Phi. 3	Kelly Miller	0:51	Phi.
Apr. 9/89	Hfd.	DSF	Mtl. 4	Hfd. 3	Russ Courtnall	15:12	Mtl.
Apr. 15/89	Cgy.	DSF	Cgy. 4	Van. 3	Joel Otto	19:21	Cgy.
Apr. 18/89	Cgy.	DF	Cgy. 4	L.A. 3	Doug Gilmour	7:47	Cgy.
Apr. 19/89	Mtl.	DF	Mtl. 3	Bos. 2	Bobby Smith	12:24	Mtl.
Apr. 20/89	St.L.	DF	St.L. 5	Chi. 4	Tony Hrkac	33:49	Chi.
Apr. 21/89	Phi.	DF	Pit. 4	Phi. 3	Phil Bourque	12:08	Phi.
May 8/89	Chi.	CF	Cgy. 2	Chi. 1	Al MacInnis	15:05	Cgy.
May 9/89	Mtl.	CF	Phi. 2	Mtl. 1	Dave Poulin	5:02	Mtl.
May 19/89	Mtl.	F	Mtl. 4	Cgy. 3	Ryan Walter	38:08	Cgy.
Apr. 5/90	N.J.	DSF	Wsh. 5	N.J. 4	Dino Ciccarelli	5:34	Wsh.
Apr. 6/90	Edm.	DSF	Edm. 3	Wpg. 2	Mark Lamb	4:21	Edm.
Apr. 8/90	Tor.	DSF	St.L. 6	Tor. 5	Sergio Momesso	6:04	St.L.
Apr. 8/90	L.A.	DSF	L.A. 2	Cgy. 1	Tony Granato	8:37	L.A.
Apr. 9/90	Mtl.	DSF	Mtl. 2	Buf. 1	Brian Skrudland	12:35	Mtl.
Apr. 9/90	NYI	DSF	NYI 4	NYR 3	Brent Sutter	20:59	NYR
Apr. 10/90	Wpg.	DSF	Wpg. 4	Edm. 3	Dave Ellett	21:08	Edm.
Apr. 14/90	L.A.	DSF	L.A. 4	Cgy. 3	Mike Krushelnyski	23:14	L.A.
Apr. 15/90	Hfd.	DSF	Hfd. 3	Bos. 2	Kevin Dineen	12:30	Bos.
Apr. 21/90	Bos.	DF	Bos. 5	Mtl. 4	Garry Galley	3:42	Bos.
Apr. 24/90	L.A.	DF	Edm. 6	L.A. 5	Joe Murphy	4:42	Edm.
Apr. 25/90	Wsh.	DF	Wsh. 4	NYR 3	Rod Langway	0:34	Wsh.
Apr. 27/90	NYR	DF	Wsh. 2	NYR 1	John Druce	6:48	Wsh.
May 15/90	Bos.	F	Edm. 3	Bos. 2	Petr Klima	55:13	Edm.
Apr. 4/91	Chi.	DSF	Min. 4	Chi. 3	Brian Propp	4:14	Min.
Apr. 5/91	Pit.	DSF	Pit. 5	N.J. 4	Jaromir Jagr	8:52	Pit.
Apr. 6/91	L.A.	DSF	L.A. 3	Van. 2	Wayne Gretzky	11:08	L.A.
Apr. 8/91	Van.	DSF	Van. 2	L.A. 1	Cliff Ronning	3:12	L.A.
Apr. 11/91	NYR	DSF	Wsh. 5	NYR 4	Dino Ciccarelli	6:44	Wsh.
Apr. 11/91	Mtl.	DSF	Mtl. 4	Buf. 3	Russ Courtnall	5:56	Mtl.
Apr. 14/91	Edm.	DSF	Cgy. 2	Edm. 1	Theoren Fleury	4:40	Edm.
Apr. 16/91	Cgy.	DSF	Edm. 5	Cgy. 4	Esa Tikkanen	6:58	Edm.
Apr. 18/91	L.A.	DF	L.A. 4	Edm. 3	Luc Robitaille	2:13	Edm.
Apr. 19/91	Bos.	DF	Mtl. 4	Bos. 3	Stephane Richer	0:27	Bos.
Apr. 19/91	Pit.	DF	Pit. 7	Wsh. 6	Kevin Stevens	8:10	Pit.
Apr. 20/91	L.A.	DF	Edm. 4	L.A. 3	Petr Klima	24:48	Edm.
Apr. 22/91	Edm.	DF	Edm. 4	L.A. 3	Esa Tikkanen	20:48	Edm.
Apr. 27/91	Mtl.	DF	Mtl. 3	Bos. 2	Shayne Corson	17:47	Bos.
Apr. 28/91	Edm.	DF	Edm. 4	L.A. 3	Craig MacTavish	16:57	Edm.
May 3/91	Bos.	CF	Bos. 5	Pit. 4	Vladimir Ruzicka	8:14	Pit.
Apr. 21/92	Bos.	DSF	Bos. 3	Buf. 2	Adam Oates	11:14	Bos.
Apr. 22/92	Min.	DSF	Det. 5	Min. 4	Yves Racine	1:15	Det.
Apr. 22/92	St.L.	DSF	St.L. 5	Chi. 4	Brett Hull	23:33	Chi.
Apr. 25/92	Buf.	DSF	Bos. 5	Buf. 4	Ted Donato	2:08	Bos.
Apr. 28/92	Min.	DSF	Det. 1	Min. 0	Sergei Fedorov	16:13	Det.
Apr. 29/92	Hfd.	DSF	Hfd. 2	Mtl. 1	Yvon Corriveau	0:24	Mtl.
May 1/92	Mtl.	DSF	Mtl. 3	Hfd. 2	Russ Courtnall	25:26	Mtl.
May 3/92	Van.	DF	Edm. 4	Van. 3	Joe Murphy	8:36	Edm.
May 5/92	Mtl.	DF	Bos. 3	Mtl. 2	Peter Douris	3:12	Bos.
May 7/92	Pit.	DF	NYR 6	Pit. 5	Kris King	1:29	Pit.
May 9/92	Pit.	DF	Pit. 5	NYR 4	Ron Francis	2:47	Pit.
May 17/92	Pit.	CF	Pit. 4	Bos. 3	Jaromir Jagr	9:44	Pit.
May 20/92	Edm.	CF	Chi. 4	Edm. 3	Jeremy Roenick	2:45	Chi.
Apr. 18/93	Bos.	DSF	Buf. 5	Bos. 4	Bob Sweeney	11:03	Buf.
Apr. 18/93	Que.	DSF	Que. 3	Mtl. 2	Scott Young	16:49	Mtl.
Apr. 20/93	Wsh.	DSF	NYI 5	Wsh. 4	Brian Mullen	34:50	NYI
Apr. 22/93	Mtl.	DSF	Mtl. 2	Que. 1	Vincent Damphousse	10:30	Mtl.
Apr. 22/93	Buf.	DSF	Buf. 4	Bos. 3	Yuri Khmylev	1:05	Buf.
Apr. 22/93	NYI	DSF	NYI 4	Wsh. 3	Ray Ferraro	4:46	NYI
Apr. 24/93	Buf.	DSF	Buf. 6	Bos. 5	Brad May	4:48	Buf.
Apr. 24/93	NYI	DSF	NYI 4	Wsh. 3	Ray Ferraro	25:40	NYI
Apr. 25/93	St.L.	DSF	St.L. 4	Chi. 3	Craig Janney	10:43	St.L.
Apr. 26/93	Que.	DSF	Mtl. 5	Que. 4	Kirk Muller	8:17	Mtl.
Apr. 27/93	Det.	DSF	Tor. 5	Det. 4	Mike Foligno	2:05	Tor.
Apr. 27/93	Van.	DSF	Wpg. 4	Van. 3	Teemu Selanne	6:18	Van.
Apr. 29/93	Wpg.	DSF	Van. 4	Wpg. 3	Greg Adams	4:30	Van.
May 1/93	Det.	DSF	Tor. 4	Det. 3	Nikolai Borschevsky	2:35	Tor.
May 3/93	Tor.	DF	Tor. 2	St.L. 1	Doug Gilmour	23:16	Tor.
May 4/93	Mtl.	DF	Mtl. 4	Buf. 3	Guy Carbonneau	2:50	Mtl.
May 5/93	Tor.	DF	St.L. 2	Tor. 1	Jeff Brown	23:03	Tor.
May 6/93	Buf.	DF	Mtl. 4	Buf. 3	Gilbert Dionne	8:28	Mtl.

Overtime Games since 1918 — *continued*

Date	City	Series	Score		Scorer	Overtime	Series Winner
May 8/93	Buf.	DF	Mtl. 4	Buf. 3	Kirk Muller	11:37	Mtl.
May 11/93	Van.	DF	L.A. 4	Van. 3	Gary Shuchuk	26:31	L.A.
May 14/93	Pit.	DF	NYI 4	Pit. 3	Dave Volek	5:16	NYI
May 18/93	Mtl.	CF	Mtl. 4	NYI 3	Stephan Lebeau	26:21	Mtl.
May 20/93	NYI	CF	Mtl. 2	NYI 1	Guy Carbonneau	12:34	Mtl.
May 25/93	Tor.	CF	Tor. 3	L.A. 2	Glenn Anderson	19:20	L.A.
May 27/93	L.A.	CF	L.A. 5	Tor. 4	Wayne Gretzky	1:41	L.A.
Jun. 3/93	Mtl.	F	Mtl. 3	L.A. 2	Eric Desjardins	0:51	Mtl.
Jun. 5/93	L.A.	F	Mtl. 4	L.A. 3	John LeClair	0:34	Mtl.
Jun. 7/93	L.A.	F	Mtl. 3	L.A. 2	John LeClair	14:37	Mtl.
Apr. 20/94	Tor.	CQF	Tor. 1	Chi. 0	Todd Gill	2:15	Tor.
Apr. 22/94	St.L.	CQF	Dal. 5	St.L. 4	Paul Cavallini	8:34	Dal.
Apr. 24/94	Chi.	CQF	Chi. 4	Tor. 3	Jeremy Roenick	1:23	Tor.
Apr. 25/94	Bos.	CQF	Mtl. 2	Bos. 1	Kirk Muller	17:18	Bos.
Apr. 26/94	Cgy.	CQF	Van. 2	Cgy. 1	Geoff Courtnall	7:15	Van.
Apr. 27/94	Buf.	CQF	Buf. 1	N.J. 0	Dave Hannan	65:43	N.J.
Apr. 28/94	Van.	CQF	Van. 3	Cgy. 2	Trevor Linden	16:43	Van.
Apr. 30/94	Cgy.	CQF	Van. 4	Cgy. 3	Pavel Bure	22:20	Van.
May 3/94	N.J.	CSF	Bos. 6	N.J. 5	Don Sweeney	9:08	N.J.
May 7/94	Bos.	CSF	N.J. 5	Bos. 4	Stephane Richer	14:19	N.J.
May 8/94	Van.	CSF	Van. 2	Dal. 1	Sergio Momesso	11:01	Van.
May 12/94	Tor.	CSF	Tor. 3	S.J. 2	Mike Gartner	8:53	Tor.
May 15/94	NYR	CF	N.J. 4	NYR 3	Stephane Richer	35:23	NYR
May 16/94	Tor.	CF	Tor. 3	Van. 2	Peter Zezel	16:55	Van.
May 19/94	N.J.	CF	NYR 3	N.J. 2	Stephane Matteau	26:13	NYR
May 24/94	Van.	CF	Van. 4	Tor. 3	Greg Adams	20:14	Van.
May 27/94	NYR	CF	NYR 2	N.J. 1	Stephane Matteau	24:24	NYR
May 31/94	NYR	F	Van. 3	NYR 2	Greg Adams	19:26	NYR
May 7/95	Phi.	CQF	Phi. 4	Buf. 3	Karl Dykhuis	10:06	Phi.
May 9/95	Cgy.	CQF	S.J. 5	Cgy. 4	Ulf Dahlen	12:21	S.J.
May 12/95	NYR	CQF	NYR 3	Que. 2	Steve Larmer	8:09	NYR
May 12/95	N.J.	CQF	N.J. 1	Bos. 0	Randy McKay	8:51	N.J.
May 14/95	Pit.	CQF	Pit. 6	Wsh. 5	Luc Robitaille	4:30	Pit.
May 15/95	St.L.	CQF	Van. 6	St.L. 5	Cliff Ronning	1:48	Van.
May 17/95	Tor.	CQF	Tor. 5	Chi. 4	Randy Wood	10:00	Chi.
May 19/95	Cgy.	CQF	S.J. 5	Cgy. 4	Ray Whitney	21:54	S.J.
May 21/95	Phi.	CSF	Phi. 5	NYR 4	Eric Desjardins	7:03	Phi.
May 21/95	Chi.	CSF	Chi. 2	Van. 1	Joe Murphy	9:04	Chi.
May 22/95	Phi.	CSF	Phi. 4	NYR 3	Kevin Haller	0:25	Phi.
May 25/95	Van.	CSF	Chi. 3	Van. 2	Chris Chelios	6:22	Chi.
May 26/95	N.J.	CSF	N.J. 2	Pit. 1	Neal Broten	18:36	N.J.
May 27/95	Van.	CSF	Chi. 4	Van. 3	Chris Chelios	5:35	Chi.
Jun. 1/95	Det.	CF	Det. 2	Chi. 1	Nicklas Lidstrom	1:01	Det.
Jun. 6/95	Chi.	CF	Det. 4	Chi. 3	Vladimir Konstantinov	29:25	Det.
Jun. 7/95	N.J.	CF	Phi. 3	N.J. 2	Eric Lindros	4:19	N.J.
Jun. 11/95	Det.	CF	Det. 2	Chi. 1	Vyacheslav Kozlov	22:25	Det.
Apr. 16/96	NYR	CQF	Mtl. 3	NYR 2	Vincent Damphousse	5:04	NYR
Apr. 18/96	Tor.	CQF	Tor. 5	St.L. 4	Mats Sundin	4:02	St.L.
Apr. 18/96	Phi.	CQF	T.B. 2	Phi. 1	Brian Bellows	9:05	Phi.
Apr. 21/96	St.L.	CQF	St.L. 3	Tor. 2	Glenn Anderson	1:24	St.L.
Apr. 21/96	T.B.	CQF	T.B. 5	Phi. 4	Alexander Selivanov	2:04	Phi.
Apr. 23/96	Cgy.	CQF	Chi. 2	Cgy. 1	Joe Murphy	50:02	Chi.
Apr. 24/96	Wsh.	CQF	Pit. 3	Wsh. 2	Petr Nedved	79:15	Pit.
Apr. 25/96	Col.	CQF	Col. 5	Van. 4	Joe Sakic	0:51	Col.
Apr. 25/96	Tor.	CQF	Tor. 5	St.L. 4	Mike Gartner	7:31	St.L.
May 2/96	Col.	CSF	Chi. 3	Col. 2	Jeremy Roenick	6:29	Col.
May 6/96	Chi.	CSF	Chi. 4	Col. 3	Sergei Krivokrasov	0:46	Col.
May 8/96	St.L.	CSF	St.L. 5	Det. 4	Igor Kravchuk	3:23	Det.
May 8/96	Chi.	CSF	Col. 3	Chi. 2	Joe Sakic	44:33	Col.
May 9/96	Fla.	CSF	Fla. 4	Phi. 3	Dave Lowry	4:06	Fla.
May 12/96	Phi.	CSF	Fla. 2	Phi. 1	Mike Hough	28:05	Fla.
May 13/96	Chi.	CSF	Col. 4	Chi. 3	Sandis Ozolinsh	25:18	Col.
May 16/96	Det.	CSF	Det. 1	St.L. 0	Steve Yzerman	21:15	Det.
May 19/96	Det.	CF	Col. 3	Det. 2	Mike Keane	17:31	Col.
Jun. 10/96	Fla.	F	Col. 1	Fla. 0	Uwe Krupp	44:31	Col.
Apr. 20/97	Chi.	CQF	Chi. 4	Col. 3	Sergei Krivokrasov	31:03	Col.
Apr. 20/97	Edm.	CQF	Edm. 4	Dal. 3	Kelly Buchberger	9:15	Edm.
Apr. 22/97	NYR	CQF	NYR 4	Fla. 3	Esa Tikkanen	16:29	NYR
Apr. 23/97	Ott.	CQF	Ott. 1	Buf. 0	Daniel Alfredsson	2:34	Buf.
Apr. 24/97	Mtl.	CQF	Mtl. 4	N.J. 3	Patrice Brisebois	47:37	N.J.
Apr. 25/97	Fla.	CQF	NYR 3	Fla. 2	Esa Tikkanen	12:02	NYR
Apr. 25/97	Dal.	CQF	Edm. 1	Dal. 0	Ryan Smyth	20:22	Edm.
Apr. 27/97	Phx.	CQF	Ana. 3	Phx. 2	Paul Kariya	7:29	Ana.
Apr. 29/97	Buf.	CQF	Buf. 3	Ott. 2	Derek Plante	5:24	Buf.
Apr. 29/97	Dal.	CQF	Edm. 4	Dal. 3	Todd Marchant	12:26	Edm.
May 2/97	Det.	CSF	Det. 2	Ana. 1	Martin Lapointe	0:59	Det.
May 4/97	Det.	CSF	Det. 3	Ana. 2	Vyacheslav Kozlov	41:31	Det.
May 8/97	Ana.	CSF	Det. 3	Ana. 2	Brendan Shanahan	37:03	Det.
May 9/97	Phi.	CSF	Buf. 5	Phi. 4	Ed Ronan	6:24	Phi.
May 9/97	Edm.	CSF	Col. 3	Edm. 2	Claude Lemieux	8:35	Col.
May 11/97	N.J.	CSF	NYR 2	N.J. 1	Adam Graves	14:08	NYR
Apr. 22/98	N.J.	CQF	Ott. 2	N.J. 1	Bruce Gardiner	5:58	Ott.
Apr. 23/98	Pit.	CQF	Mtl. 3	Pit. 2	Benoit Brunet	18:43	Mtl.
Apr. 24/98	Wsh.	CQF	Bos. 4	Wsh. 3	Darren Van Impe	20:54	Wsh.
Apr. 26/98	Ott.	CQF	Ott. 2	N.J. 1	Alexei Yashin	2:47	Ott.
Apr. 26/98	Bos.	CQF	Wsh. 3	Bos. 2	Joe Juneau	26:31	Wsh.
Apr. 26/98	Edm.	CQF	Col. 5	Edm. 4	Joe Sakic	15:25	Edm.
Apr. 28/98	S.J.	CQF	S.J. 1	Dal. 0	Andrei Zyuzin	6:31	Dal.
May 1/98	Phi.	CQF	Buf. 3	Phi. 2	Michal Grosek	5:40	Buf.
May 2/98	S.J.	CQF	Dal. 3	S.J. 2	Mike Keane	3:43	Dal.
May 3/98	Bos.	CQF	Wsh. 3	Bos. 2	Brian Bellows	15:24	Wsh.
May 3/98	Buf.	CSF	Buf. 3	Mtl. 2	Geoff Sanderson	2:37	Buf.
May 11/98	Edm.	CSF	Dal. 1	Edm. 0	Benoit Hogue	13:07	Dal.
May 12/98	Mtl.	CSF	Buf. 5	Mtl. 4	Michael Peca	21:24	Buf.
May 12/98	St.L.	CSF	Det. 3	St.L. 2	Brendan Shanahan	31:12	Det.
May 25/98	Wsh.	CF	Wsh. 3	Buf. 2	Todd Krygier	3:01	Wsh.
May 28/98	Buf.	CF	Wsh. 4	Buf. 3	Peter Bondra	9:37	Wsh.
Jun. 3/98	Dal.	CF	Dal. 3	Det. 2	Jamie Langenbrunner	0:46	Det.
Jun. 4/98	Buf.	CF	Wsh. 3	Buf. 2	Joe Juneau	6:24	Wsh.
Jun. 11/98	Det.	F	Det. 5	Wsh. 4	Kris Draper	15:24	Det.
Apr. 23/99	Ott.	CQF	Buf. 3	Ott. 2	Miroslav Satan	30:35	Buf.
Apr. 24/99	Car.	CQF	Car. 3	Bos. 2	Ray Sheppard	17:05	Bos.
Apr. 24/99	Phx.	CQF	Phx. 4	St.L. 3	Shane Doan	8:58	St.L.
Apr. 26/99	S.J.	CQF	Col. 2	S.J. 1	Milan Hejduk	7:53	Col.
Apr. 27/99	Edm.	CQF	Dal. 3	Edm. 2	Joe Nieuwendyk	57:34	Dal.
Apr. 30/99	Tor.	CQF	Tor. 2	Phi. 1	Yanic Perreault	11:51	Tor.
Apr. 30/99	Car.	CQF	Bos. 4	Car. 3	Anson Carter	34:45	Bos.
Apr. 30/99	Phx.	CQF	St.L. 2	Phx. 1	Scott Young	5:43	St.L.
May 2/99	Pit.	CQF	Pit. 3	N.J. 2	Jaromir Jagr	8:59	Pit.
May 3/99	S.J.	CQF	Col. 3	S.J. 2	Milan Hejduk	13:12	Col.
May 4/99	Phx.	CQF	St.L. 1	Phx. 0	Pierre Turgeon	17:59	St.L.
May 7/99	Col.	CSF	Det. 3	Col. 2	Kirk Maltby	4:18	Col.
May 8/99	Dal.	CSF	Dal. 5	St.L. 4	Joe Nieuwendyk	8:22	Dal.
May 10/99	St.L.	CSF	St.L. 3	Dal. 2	Pavol Demitra	2:43	Dal.
May 12/99	St.L.	CSF	St.L. 3	Dal. 2	Pierre Turgeon	5:52	Dal.
May 13/99	Pit.	CSF	Tor. 3	Pit. 2	Sergei Berezin	2:18	Tor.
May 17/99	Pit.	CSF	Tor. 4	Pit. 3	Garry Valk	1:57	Tor.
May 17/99	St.L.	CSF	Dal. 2	St.L. 1	Mike Modano	2:21	Dal.
May 28/99	Col.	CF	Col. 3	Dal. 2	Chris Drury	19:29	Dal.
Jun. 8/99	Dal.	F	Buf. 3	Dal. 2	Jason Woolley	15:30	Dal.
Jun. 19/99	Buf.	F	Dal. 2	Buf. 1	Brett Hull	54:51	Dal.
Apr. 15/00	Pit.	CQF	Pit. 2	Wsh. 1	Jaromir Jagr	5:49	Pit.
Apr. 18/00	Buf.	CQF	Buf. 3	Phi. 2	Stu Barnes	4:42	Phi.
Apr. 22/00	Tor.	CQF	Tor. 2	Ott. 1	Steve Thomas	14:47	Tor.
May 2/00	Pit.	CSF	Phi. 4	Pit. 3	Andy Delmore	11:01	Phi.
May 3/00	Det.	CSF	Col. 3	Det. 2	Chris Drury	10:21	Col.
May 4/00	Pit.	CSF	Phi. 2	Pit. 1	Keith Primeau	92:01	Phi.
May 23/00	Dal.	CF	Dal. 3	Col. 2	Joe Nieuwendyk	12:10	Dal.
Jun. 8/00	N.J.	F	Dal. 1	N.J. 0	Mike Modano	46:21	N.J.
Jun. 10/00	Dal.	F	N.J. 2	Dal. 1	Jason Arnott	28:20	N.J.
Apr. 11/01	Dal.	CQF	Dal. 2	Edm. 1	Jamie Langenbrunner	2:08	Dal.
Apr. 13/01	Ott.	CQF	Tor. 1	Ott. 0	Mats Sundin	10:49	Tor.
Apr. 14/01	Phi.	CQF	Buf. 4	Phi. 3	Jay McKee	18:02	Buf.
Apr. 15/01	Edm.	CQF	Dal. 3	Edm. 2	Benoit Hogue	19:48	Dal.
Apr. 16/01	Tor.	CQF	Tor. 3	Ott. 2	Cory Cross	2:16	Tor.
Apr. 16/01	Van.	CQF	Col. 4	Van. 3	Peter Forsberg	2:50	Col.
Apr. 17/01	Buf.	CQF	Buf. 4	Phi. 3	Curtis Brown	6:13	Buf.
Apr. 17/01	Edm.	CQF	Edm. 2	Dal. 1	Mike Comrie	17:19	Dal.
Apr. 18/01	Car.	CQF	Car. 3	N.J. 2	Rod Brind'Amour	:46	N.J.
Apr. 18/01	Pit.	CQF	Wsh. 4	Pit. 3	Jeff Halpern	4:01	Pit.
Apr. 18/01	L.A.	CQF	L.A. 4	Det. 3	Eric Belanger	2:36	L.A.
Apr. 19/01	Dal.	CQF	Dal. 4	Edm. 3	Kirk Muller	8:01	Dal.
Apr. 19/01	St.L.	CQF	St.L. 3	S.J. 2	Bryce Salvador	9:54	St.L.
Apr. 23/01	Pit.	CQF	Pit. 4	Wsh. 3	Martin Straka	13:04	Pit.
Apr. 23/01	L.A.	CQF	L.A. 3	Det. 2	Adam Deadmarsh	4:48	L.A.
Apr. 26/01	Col.	CSF	L.A. 4	Col. 3	Jaroslav Modry	14:23	Col.
Apr. 28/01	N.J.	CSF	N.J. 6	Tor. 5	Randy McKay	5:31	N.J.
May 1/01	Tor.	CSF	N.J. 3	Tor. 2	Brian Rafalski	7:00	N.J.
May 1/01	St.L.	CSF	St.L. 3	Dal. 2	Cory Stillman	29:26	St.L.
May 5/01	Buf.	CSF	Buf. 3	Pit. 2	Stu Barnes	8:34	Pit.
May 6/01	L.A.	CSF	L.A. 1	Col. 0	Glen Murray	22:41	Col.
May 8/01	Pit.	CSF	Pit. 3	Buf. 2	Martin Straka	11:29	Pit.
May 10/01	Buf.	CSF	Pit. 3	Buf. 2	Darius Kasparaitis	13:01	Pit.
May 16/01	St.L.	CF	St.L. 4	Col. 3	Scott Young	30:27	Col.
May 18/01	St.L.	CF	Col. 4	St.L. 3	Stephane Yelle	4:23	Col.
May 21/01	Col.	CF	Col. 2	St.L. 1	Joe Sakic	:24	Col.
Apr. 17/02	Phi.	CQF	Phi. 1	Ott. 0	Ruslan Fedotenko	7:47	Ott.
Apr. 17/02	Det.	CQF	Van. 4	Det. 3	Henrik Sedin	13:59	Det.
Apr. 19/02	Car.	CQF	Car. 2	N.J. 1	Bates Battaglia	15:26	Car.
Apr. 24/02	Car.	CQF	Car. 3	N.J. 2	Josef Vasicek	8:16	Car.
Apr. 25/02	Col.	CQF	L.A. 1	Col. 0	Craig Johnson	2:19	Col.
Apr. 26/02	Phi.	CQF	Ott. 2	Phi. 1	Martin Havlat	7:33	Ott.
May 4/02	Tor.	CSF	Tor. 3	Ott. 2	Gary Roberts	44:30	Tor.
May 7/02	Mtl.	CSF	Mtl. 2	Car. 1	Donald Audette	2:26	Car.
May 9/02	Mtl.	CSF	Car. 4	Mtl. 3	Niclas Wallin	3:14	Car.
May 13/02	S.J.	CSF	Col. 2	S.J. 1	Peter Forsberg	2:47	Col.
May 19/02	Car.	CF	Car. 2	Tor. 1	Niclas Wallin	13:42	Car.
May 20/02	Det.	CF	Col. 4	Det. 3	Chris Drury	2:17	Det.
May 21/02	Tor.	CF	Car. 2	Tor. 1	Jeff O'Neill	6:01	Car.
May 22/02	Col.	CF	Det. 2	Col. 1	Fredrik Olausson	12:44	Det.
May 27/02	Det.	CF	Col. 2	Det. 1	Peter Forsberg	6:24	Det.
May 28/02	Tor.	CF	Car. 2	Tor. 1	Martin Gelinas	8:05	Car.
Jun. 4/02	Det.	F	Car. 3	Det. 2	Ron Francis	:58	Det.
Jun. 8/02	Car.	F	Det. 3	Car. 2	Igor Larionov	54:47	Det.
Apr. 10/03	Det.	CQF	Ana. 2	Det. 1	Paul Kariya	43:18	Ana.
Apr. 14/03	NYI	CQF	Ott. 3	NYI 2	Todd White	22:25	Ott.
Apr. 14/03	Tor.	CQF	Tor. 4	Phi. 3	Tomas Kaberle	27:20	Phi.
Apr. 15/03	Wsh.	CQF	T.B. 4	Wsh. 3	Vincent Lecavalier	2:29	T.B.
Apr. 16/03	Tor.	CQF	Phi. 3	Tor. 2	Mark Recchi	53:54	Phi.
Apr. 16/03	Ana.	CQF	Ana. 3	Det. 2	Steve Rucchin	6:53	Ana.
Apr. 20/03	Wsh.	CQF	T.B. 2	Wsh. 1	Martin St. Louis	44:03	T.B.
Apr. 21/03	Tor.	CQF	Tor. 2	Phi. 1	Travis Green	30:51	Phi.
Apr. 21/03	Min.	CQF	Min. 3	Col. 2	Richard Park	4:22	Min.
Apr. 22/03	Col.	CQF	Min. 3	Col. 2	Andrew Brunette	3:25	Min.
Apr. 24/03	Dal.	CSF	Ana. 4	Dal. 3	Petr Sykora	80:48	Ana.
Apr. 25/03	Van.	CSF	Van. 4	Min. 3	Trent Klatt	3:42	Min.
Apr. 26/03	N.J.	CSF	N.J. 3	T.B. 2	Jamie Langenbrunner	2:09	N.J.
Apr. 26/03	Dal.	CSF	Ana. 3	Dal. 2	Mike Leclerc	1:44	Ana.
Apr. 29/03	Phi.	CSF	Ott. 3	Phi. 2	Wade Redden	6:43	Ott.
May 2/03	Min.	CSF	Van. 3	Min. 2	Brent Sopel	15:52	Min.
May 2/03	N.J.	CSF	N.J. 2	T.B. 1	Grant Marshall	51:12	N.J.
May 10/03	Min.	CF	Ana. 1	Min. 0	Petr Sykora	28:06	Ana.
May 10/03	Ott.	CF	Ott. 3	N.J. 2	Shaun Van Allen	3:08	N.J.
May 21/03	N.J.	CF	Ott. 2	N.J. 1	Chris Phillips	15:51	N.J.
May 31/03	Ana.	F	Ana. 3	N.J. 2	Ruslan Salei	6:59	N.J.
Jun. 2/03	Ana.	F	Ana. 1	N.J. 0	Steve Thomas	0:39	N.J.
Apr. 8/04	S.J.	CQF	S.J. 1	St.L. 0	Niko Dimitrakos	9:16	S.J.

Overtime Games since 1918 *— continued*

Date	City	Series	Score		Scorer	Overtime	Series Winner
Apr. 9/04	Bos.	CQF	Bos. 2	Mtl. 1	Patrice Bergeron	1:26	Mtl.
Apr. 12/04	Dal.	CQF	Dal. 4	Col. 3	Steve Ott	2:11	Col.
Apr. 13/04	Mtl.	CQF	Bos. 4	Mtl. 3	Glen Murray	29:27	Mtl.
Apr. 14/04	Dal.	CQF	Col. 3	Dal. 2	Marek Svatos	25:21	Col.
Apr. 16/04	T.B.	CQF	T.B. 3	NYI 2	Martin St. Louis	4:07	T.B.
Apr. 17/04	Cgy.	CQF	Van. 5	Cgy. 4	Brendan Morrison	42:28	Cgy.
Apr. 18/04	Ott.	CQF	Ott. 2	Tor. 1	Mike Fisher	21:47	Tor.
Apr. 19/04	Van.	CQF	Cgy. 3	Van. 2	Martin Gelinas	1:25	Cgy.
Apr. 22/04	Det.	CSF	Cgy. 2	Det. 1	Marcus Nilson	2:39	Cgy.
Apr. 27/04	Mtl.	CSF	T.B. 4	Mtl 3	Brad Richards	1:05	T.B.
Apr. 28/04	Col	CSF	Col. 1	S.J. 0	Joe Sakic	5:15	S.J.
May 1/04	S.J.	CSF	Col. 2	S.J. 1	Joe Sakic	1:54	S.J.
May 3/04	Cgy	CSF	Cgy. 1	Det. 0	Martin Gelinas	19:13	Cgy.
May 4/04	Phi.	CSF	Phi. 3	Tor. 2	Jeremy Roenick	7:39	Phi.
May 9/04	S.J.	CF	Cgy. 4	S.J. 3	Steve Montador	18:43	Cgy.
May 20/04	Phi.	CF	Phi. 5	T.B. 4	Simon Gagne	18:18	T.B.
Jun. 3/04	T.B.	F	Cgy. 3	T.B. 2	Oleg Saprykin	14:40	T.B.
Jun. 5/04	Cgy.	F	T.B. 3	Cgy. 2	Martin St. Louis	20:33	T.B.
Apr. 21/06	Det.	CQF	Det. 3	Edm. 2	Kirk Maltby	22:39	Edm.
Apr. 21/06	Cgy.	CQF	Cgy. 2	Ana. 1	Darren McCarty	9:45	Ana.
Apr. 22/06	Buf.	CQF	Buf. 3	Phi. 2	Daniel Briere	27:31	Buf.
Apr. 24/06	Car.	CQF	Mtl. 6	Car. 5	Michael Ryder	22:32	Car.
Apr. 24/06	Dal.	CQF	Col. 5	Dal. 4	Joe Sakic	4:36	Col.
Apr. 25/06	Edm.	CQF	Edm. 4	Det. 3	Jarret Stoll	28:44	Edm.
Apr. 26/06	Mtl.	CQF	Car. 2	Mtl. 1	Eric Staal	3:38	Car.
Apr. 26/06	Col.	CQF	Col. 4	Dal. 3	Alex Tanguay	1:09	Col.
Apr. 27/06	Ana.	CQF	Ana. 3	Cgy. 2	Sean O'Donnell	1:36	Ana.
Apr. 30/06	Dal.	CQF	Col. 3	Dal. 2	Andrew Brunette	13:55	Col.
May 2/06	Mtl.	CQF	Car. 2	Mtl. 1	Cory Stillman	1:19	Car.
May 5/06	Ott.	CSF	Buf. 7	Ott. 6	Chris Drury	0:18	Buf.
May 8/06	Car.	CSF	Car. 3	N.J. 2	Niclas Wallin	3:09	Car.
May 9/06	Col.	CSF	Ana. 4	Col. 3	Joffrey Lupul	16:30	Ana.
May 10/06	Buf.	CSF	Buf. 3	Ott. 2	J.P. Dumont	5:05	Buf.
May 10/06	Edm.	CSF	Edm. 3	S.J. 2	Shawn Horcoff	42:24	Edm.
May 13/06	Ott.	CSF	Buf. 3	Ott. 2	Jason Pominville	2:26	Buf.
May 28/06	Car.	CF	Car. 4	Buf. 3	Cory Stillman	8:46	Car.
May 30/06	Buf.	CF	Buf. 2	Car. 1	Daniel Briere	4:22	Car.
June 14/06	Car.	F	Edm. 4	Car. 3	Fernando Pisani	3:31	Car.
Apr. 11/07	Nsh.	CQF	S.J. 5	Nsh. 4	Patrick Rissmiller	28:14	S.J.
Apr. 11/07	Van.	CQF	Van. 5	Dal. 4	Henrik Sedin	78:06	Van.
Apr. 15/07	Dal.	CQF	Van. 2	Dal. 1	Taylor Pyatt	7:47	Van.
Apr. 18/07	T.B.	CQF	N.J. 4	T.B. 3	Scott Gomez	12:54	N.J.
Apr. 19/07	Van.	CQF	Dal. 1	Van. 0	Brenden Morrow	6:22	Van.
Apr. 22/07	Cgy.	CQF	Det. 2	Cgy. 1	Johan Franzen	24:23	Det.
Apr. 27/07	Ana.	CSF	Van. 2	Ana. 1	Jeff Cowan	27:49	Ana.
Apr. 28/07	N.J.	CSF	N.J. 3	Ott. 2	Jamie Langenbrunner	21:55	Ott.
Apr. 29/07	NYR	CSF	NYR 2	Buf. 1	Michal Rozsival	36:43	Buf.
May 1/07	Van.	CSF	Ana. 3	Van. 2	Travis Moen	2:07	Ana.
May 2/07	S.J.	CSF	Det. 3	S.J. 2	Mathieu Schnieder	16:04	Det.
May 3/07	Ana.	CSF	Ana. 2	Van. 1	Scott Niedermayer	24:30	Ana.
May 4/07	Buf.	CSF	Buf. 2	NYR 1	Maxim Afinogenov	4:39	Buf.
May 12/07	Buf.	CF	Ott. 4	Buf. 3	Joe Corvo	24:58	Ott.
May 13/07	Det.	CF	Ana. 4	Det. 3	Scott Niedermayer	14:17	Ana.
May 19/07	Buf.	CF	Ott. 3	Buf. 2	Daniel Alfredsson	9:32	Ott.
May 20/07	Det.	CF	Ana. 2	Det. 1	Teemu Selanne	11:57	Ana.
Apr. 9/08	Min.	CQF	Col. 3	Min. 2	Joe Sakic	11:11	Col.
Apr. 11/08	Min.	CQF	Min. 3	Col. 2	Keith Carney	1:14	Col.
Apr. 12/08	Mtl.	CQF	Mtl. 3	Bos. 2	Alex Kovalev	2:30	Mtl.
Apr. 13/08	Mtl.	CQF	Bos. 2	Mtl.1	Marc Savard	9:25	Mtl.
Apr. 13/08	NYR	CQF	N.J. 4	NYR 3	John Madden	6:01	NYR
Apr. 14/08	Col.	CQF	Min. 3	Col. 2	Pierre-Marc Bouchard	11:58	Col.
Apr. 17/08	Phi.	CQF	Phi. 4	Wsh. 3	Mike Knuble	26:40	Phi.
Apr. 18/08	Det.	CQF	Det. 2	Nsh. 1	Johan Franzen	1:48	Det.
Apr. 22/08	Wsh.	CQF	Phi. 3	Wsh. 2	Joffrey Lupul	6:06	Phi.
Apr. 24/08	Mtl.	CSF	Mtl. 4	Phi. 3	Tom Kostopoulos	0:48	Phi.
Apr. 25/08	S.J.	CSF	Dal. 3	S.J. 2	Brenden Morrow	4:39	Dal.
Apr. 29/08	Dal.	CSF	Dal. 2	S.J. 1	Mattias Norstrom	4:37	Dal.
May 2/08	S.J.	CSF	S.J. 3	Dal. 2	Joe Pavelski	1:05	Dal.
May 4/08	Pit.	CSF	Pit. 3	NYR 2	Marian Hossa	7:10	Pit.
May 4/08	Dal.	CSF	Dal. 2	S.J. 1	Brenden Morrow	69:03	Dal.
June 2/08	Det.	F	Pit. 3	Det. 2	Petr Sykora	49:57	Det.
Apr. 16/09	Chi.	CQF	Chi. 3	Cgy. 2	Martin Havlat	0:12	Chi.
Apr. 17/09	Pit.	CQF	Pit. 3	Phi. 2	Bill Guerin	18:29	Pit.
Apr. 17/09	N.J.	CQF	Car. 2	N.J. 1	Tim Gleason	2:40	Car.
Apr. 19/09	Car.	CQF	N.J. 3	Car. 2	Travis Zajac	4:58	Car.
Apr. 21/09	St.L.	CQF	Van. 3	St.L. 2	Alex Burrows	19:41	Van.
Apr. 25/09	S.J.	CQF	S.J. 3	Ana. 2	Patrick Marleau	6:02	Ana.
May 3/09	Det.	CSF	Ana. 4	Det. 3	Todd Marchant	41:15	Det.
May 6/09	Pit.	CSF	Pit. 3	Wsh. 2	Kris Letang	11:23	Pit.
May 6/09	Car.	CSF	Car. 3	Bos. 2	Jussi Jokinen	2:48	Car.
May 7/09	Chi.	CSF	Chi. 2	Van. 1	Andrew Ladd	2:52	Chi.
May 9/09	Wsh.	CSF	Pit. 4	Wsh. 3	Evgeni Malkin	3:28	Pit.
May 11/09	Pit.	CSF	Wsh. 5	Pit. 4	David Steckel	6:22	Pit.
May 14/09	Bos.	CSF	Car. 3	Bos. 2	Scott Walker	18:46	Car.
May 19/09	Det.	CF	Det. 3	Chi. 2	Mikael Samuelsson	5:14	Det.
May 22/09	Chi.	CF	Chi. 4	Det. 3	Patrick Sharp	1:52	Det.
May 27/09	Det.	CF	Det. 2	Chi. 1	Darren Helm	3:58	Det.
Apr. 15/10	Wsh.	CQF	Mtl. 3	Wsh. 2	Tomas Plekanec	13:19	Mtl.
Apr. 15/10	Van.	CQF	Van. 3	L.A. 2	Mikael Samuelsson	8:52	Van.
Apr. 16/10	S.J.	CQF	S.J. 6	Col. 5	Devin Setoguchi	5:22	S.J.
Apr. 17/10	Wsh.	CQF	Wsh. 6	Mtl. 5	Nicklas Backstrom	0:31	Mtl.
Apr. 17/10	Van.	CQF	L.A. 3	Van. 2	Anze Kopitar	7:28	Van.
Apr. 18/10	Phi.	CQF	Phi. 3	N.J. 2	Daniel Carcillo	3:35	Phi.
Apr. 18/10	Col.	CQF	Col. 1	S.J. 0	Ryan O'Reilly	0:51	S.J.
Apr. 20/10	Col.	CQF	S.J. 2	Col. 1	Joe Pavelski	10:24	S.J.
Apr. 21/10	Bos.	CQF	Bos. 3	Buf. 2	Miroslav Satan	27:41	Bos.
Apr. 22/10	Pit.	CQF	Ott. 4	Pit. 3	Matt Carkner	47:06	Pit.
Apr. 24/10	Chi.	CQF	Chi. 5	Nsh. 4	Marian Hossa	4:07	Chi.
Apr. 24/10	Ott.	CQF	Pit. 4	Ott. 3	Pascal Dupuis	9:56	Pit.
May 1/10	Bos.	CSF	Bos. 5	Phi. 4	Marc Savard	13:52	Phi.
May 4/10	Det.	CSF	S.J. 4	Det. 3	Patrick Marleau	7:07	S.J.
May 7/10	Phi.	CSF	Phi. 5	Bos. 4	Simon Gagne	14:40	Phi.
May 21/10	Chi.	CF	Chi. 3	S.J. 2	Dustin Byfuglien	12:24	Chi.
June 2/10	Phi.	F	Phi. 4	Chi. 3	Claude Giroux	5:59	Chi.
June 9/10	Phi.	F	Chi. 4	Phi. 3	Patrick Kane	4:06	Chi.
Apr. 13/11	Wsh.	CQF	Wsh. 2	NYR 1	Alexander Semin	18:24	Wsh.
Apr. 14/11	S.J.	CQF	S.J. 3	L.A. 2	Joe Pavelski	14:44	S.J.
Apr. 20/11	L.A.	CQF	S.J. 6	L.A. 5	Devin Setoguchi	3:09	S.J.
Apr. 20/11	NYR	CQF	Wsh. 4	NYR 3	Jason Chimera	32:36	Wsh.
Apr. 20/11	T.B.	CQF	Pit. 3	T.B. 2	James Neal	23:38	T.B.
Apr. 21/11	Mtl.	CQF	Bos. 5	Mtl. 4	Michael Ryder	1:59	Bos.
Apr. 22/11	Phi.	CQF	Buf. 4	Phi. 3	Tyler Ennis	5:31	Phi.
Apr. 22/11	Ana.	CQF	Nsh. 4	Ana. 3	Jerred Smithson	1:57	Nsh.
Apr. 23/11	Bos.	CQF	Bos. 2	Mtl. 1	Nathan Horton	29:03	Bos.
Apr. 24/11	Buf.	CQF	Phi. 5	Buf. 4	Ville Leino	4:43	Phi.
Apr. 24/11	Chi.	CQF	Chi. 4	Van. 3	Ben Smith	15:30	Van.
Apr. 25/11	L.A.	CQF	S.J. 4	L.A. 3	Joe Thornton	2:22	S.J.
Apr. 26/11	Van.	CQF	Van. 2	Chi. 3	Alexandre Burrows	5:22	Van.
Apr. 27/11	Bos.	CQF	Bos. 4	Mtl. 3	Nathan Horton	5:43	Bos.
Apr. 29/11	S.J.	CSF	S.J. 2	Det. 1	Benn Ferriero	7:03	S.J.
Apr. 30/11	Van.	CSF	Nsh. 2	Van. 1	Matt Halischuk	34:51	Van.
May 1/11	Wsh.	CSF	T.B. 3	Wsh. 2	Vincent Lecavalier	6:19	T.B.
May 2/11	Phi.	CSF	Bos. 3	Phi. 2	David Krejci	14:00	Bos.
May 3/11	Nsh.	CSF	Van. 3	Nsh. 2	Ryan Kesler	10:49	Van.
May 4/11	Det.	CSF	S.J. 4	Det. 3	Devin Setoguchi	9:21	S.J.
May 24/11	Van.	CF	Van. 3	S.J. 2	Kevin Bieksa	30:18	Van.
June 4/11	Van.	F	Van. 3	Bos. 2	Alexandre Burrows	0:11	Bos.
Apr. 11/12	Pit.	CQF	Phi. 4	Pit. 3	Jakub Voracek	2:23	Phi.
Apr. 12/12	Bos.	CQF	Bos. 1	Wsh. 0	Chris Kelly	1:18	Wsh.
Apr. 12/12	St. L.	CQF	S.J. 3	St. L. 2	Martin Havlat	23:34	St. L.
Apr. 12/12	Phx.	CQF	Phx. 3	Chi. 2	Martin Hanzal	9:29	Phx.
Apr. 14/12	Bos.	CQF	Wsh. 2	Bos. 1	Nicklas Backstrom	2:56	Wsh.
Apr. 14/12	NYR	CQF	Ott. 3	NYR 2	Chris Neil	1:17	NYR
Apr. 14/12	Phx.	CQF	Chi. 4	Phx. 3	Bryan Bickell	10:36	Phx.
Apr. 17/12	Chi.	CQF	Phx. 3	Chi. 2	Mikkel Boedker	13:15	Phx.
Apr. 18/12	Ott.	CQF	Ott. 3	NYR 2	Kyle Turris	2:42	NYR
Apr. 19/12	Chi.	CQF	Phx. 3	Chi. 2	Mikkel Boedker	2:15	Phx.
Apr. 21/12	Phx.	CQF	Chi. 2	Phx. 1	Jonathan Toews	2:44	Phx.
Apr. 22/12	Wsh.	CQF	Bos. 4	Wsh. 3	Tyler Seguin	3:17	Wsh.
Apr. 22/12	Van.	CQF	L.A. 2	Van. 1	Jarret Stoll	4:27	L.A.
Apr. 24/12	N.J.	CQF	N.J. 3	Fla. 2	Travis Zajac	5:39	N.J.
Apr. 25/12	Bos.	CQF	Wsh. 2	Bos. 1	Joel Ward	2:57	Wsh.
Apr. 26/12	Fla.	CQF	N.J. 3	Fla. 2	Adam Henrique	23:47	N.J.
Apr. 27/12	Phx.	CSF	Phx. 4	Nsh. 2	Ray Whitney	14:04	Phx.
Apr. 29/12	Phi.	CSF	Phi. 4	N.J. 3	Daniel Briere	4:36	N.J.
May 2/12	Wsh.	CSF	NYR 2	Wsh. 1	Marian Gaborik	54:41	NYR
May 3/12	N.J.	CSF	N.J. 4	Phi. 3	Alexei Ponikarovsky	17:21	N.J.
May 7/12	NYR	CSF	NYR 3	Wsh. 2	Marc Staal	1:35	NYR
May 22/12	Phx.	CF	L.A. 4	Phx. 3	Dustin Penner	17:42	L.A.
May 25/12	N.J.	CF	N.J. 2	NYR 1	Adam Henrique	1:03	N.J.
May 30/12	N.J.	F	L.A. 2	N.J. 1	Anze Kopitar	8:13	L.A.
June 2/12	N.J.	F	L.A. 2	N.J. 1	Jeff Carter	13:42	L.A.
Apr. 30/13	Chi.	CQF	Chi. 2	Min. 1	Bryan Bickell	16:35	Chi.
Apr. 30/13	St.L.	CQF	St.L. 2	L.A. 1	Alex Steen	13:26	L.A.
May 2/13	Ana.	CQF	Det. 5	Ana. 4	Gustav Nyquist	1:21	Det.
May 3/13	Van.	CQF	S.J. 3	Van. 2	RaffiTorres	5:31	S.J.
May 4/13	Wsh.	CQF	Wsh. 1	NYR 0	Mike Green	8:00	NYR
May 5/13	NYI	CQF	Pit. 5	NYI 4	Chris Kunitz	8:44	Pit.
May 5/13	Min.	CQF	Min. 3	Chi.2	Jason Zucker	2:15	Chi.
May 6/13	Det.	CQF	Det. 3	Ana. 2	Damien Brunner	15:10	Det.
May 7/13	Ott.	CQF	Ott. 3	Mtl. 2	Kyle Turris	2:32	Ott.
May 7/13	S.J.	CQF	S.J. 4	Van. 3	Patrick Marleau	13:18	S.J.
May 8/13	Tor.	CQF	Bos. 4	Tor. 3	David Krejci	13:06	Bos.
May 8/13	Ana.	CQF	Ana. 3	Det. 2	Nick Bonino	1:54	Det.
May 8/13	St.L.	CQF	L.A. 3	St.L. 2	Slava Voynov	8:00	L.A.
May 10/13	Wsh.	CQF	Wsh. 2	NYR 1	Mike Ribeiro	9:24	NYR
May 10/13	Det.	CQF	Det. 4	Ana. 3	Henrik Zetterberg	1:04	Det.
May 11/13	NYI	CQF	Pit. 4	NYI 3	Brooks Orpik	7:49	Pit.
May 13/13	Bos.	CQF	Bos. 5	Tor. 4	Patrice Bergeron	6:05	Bos.
May 16/13	Bos.	CSF	Bos. 3	NYR 2	Brad Marchand	15:40	Bos.
May 18/13	S.J.	CSF	S.J. 2	L.A. 1	Logan Couture	1:29	L.A.
May 19/13	Ott.	CSF	Ott. 2	Pit. 1	Colin Greening	27:39	Pit.
May 23/13	NYR	CSF	NYR 4	Bos. 3	Chris Kreider	7:03	Bos.
May 29/13	Chi.	CSF	Chi. 2	Det. 1	Brent Seabrook	3:35	Chi.
June 5/13	Bos.	CF	Bos.2	Pit. 1	Patrice Bergeron	35:19	Bos.
June 8/13	Chi.	CF	Chi. 4	L.A. 3	Patrick Kane	31:40	Chi.
June 12/13	Chi.	F	Chi. 4	Bos. 3	Andrew Shaw	52:08	Chi.
June 15/13	Chi.	F	Bos.2	Chi. 1	Daniel Paille	13:48	Chi.
June 19/13	Bos.	F	Chi. 6	Bos. 5	Brent Seabrook	9:51	Chi.

Ten Longest Overtime Games

Date	City	Series	Score		Scorer	Overtime	Series Winner
Mar. 24/36	Mtl.	SF	Det. 1	Mtl. M. 0	Mud Bruneteau	116:30	Det.
Apr. 3/33	Tor.	SF	Tor. 1	Bos. 0	Ken Doraty	104:46	Tor.
May 4/00	Pit.	CSF	Phi. 2	Pit. 1	Keith Primeau	92:01	Phi.
Apr. 24/03	Dal.	CSF	Ana. 4	Dal. 3	Petr Sykora	80:48	Ana.
Apr. 24/96	Wsh.	CQF	Pit. 3	Wsh. 2	Petr Nedved	79:15	Pit.
Apr. 11/07	Van.	CQF	Van. 5	Dal. 4	Henrik Sedin	78:06	Van.
Mar. 23/43	Det.	SF	Tor. 3	Det. 2	Jack McLean	70:18	Det.
May 4/08	Dal.	CSF	Dal. 2	S.J. 1	Brenden Morrow	69:03	Dal.
Mar. 28/30	Mtl.	SF	Mtl. 2	NYR 1	Gus Rivers	68:52	Mtl.
Apr. 18/87	Wsh.	DSF	NYI 3	Wsh. 2	Pat LaFontaine	68:47	NYI

Overtime Record of Current Teams

(Listed by number of OT games played)

	Overall				Home					Road				
Team	GP	W	L	T	GP	W	L	T	Last OT Game	GP	W	L	T	Last OT Game
Montreal	139	75	61	3	65	39	25	1	Apr. 21/11	74	36	36	2	May 7/13
Boston	125	54	68	3	59	30	28	1	June 19/13	66	24	40	2	June 15/13
Toronto	110	56	53	1	70	37	32	1	May 8/13	40	19	21	0	May 13/13
Detroit	97	43	54	0	57	22	35	0	May 10/13	40	21	19	0	May 29/13
Chicago	86	45	39	2	44	26	17	1	June 15/13	42	19	22	1	June 19/13
NY Rangers	78	34	44	0	33	15	18	0	May 23/13	45	19	26	0	May 16/13
Philadelphia	74	36	38	0	34	19	15	0	Apr. 29/12	40	17	23	0	May 3/12
Dallas[1]	65	29	36	0	32	13	19	0	May 4/08	33	16	17	0	May 2/08
Colorado[2]	62	35	27	0	26	12	14	0	Apr. 20/10	36	23	13	0	Apr. 16/10
Buffalo	59	32	27	0	33	20	13	0	Apr. 24/11	26	12	14	0	Apr. 22/11
St. Louis	56	29	27	0	32	21	11	0	May 8/13	24	8	16	0	Apr. 8/04
Vancouver	54	26	28	0	26	11	15	0	May 3/13	28	15	13	0	May 7/13
Washington	49	22	27	0	22	9	13	0	May 10/13	27	13	14	0	May 7/12
Los Angeles	48	23	25	0	21	11	10	0	Apr. 25/11	27	12	15	0	June 8/13
New Jersey[4]	47	18	29	0	21	9	12	0	June 2/12	26	9	17	0	Apr. 29/12
Pittsburgh	43	24	19	0	25	13	12	0	Apr. 11/12	18	11	7	0	June 5/13
NY Islanders	42	29	13	0	20	14	6	0	May 11/13	22	15	7	0	Apr. 16/04
Edmonton	42	24	18	0	23	13	10	0	May 10/06	19	11	8	0	June 14/06
Calgary[3]	41	17	24	0	19	6	13	0	Apr. 22/07	22	11	11	0	Apr. 16/09
San Jose	36	19	17	0	17	9	8	0	May 18/13	19	10	9	0	May 3/13
Carolina[5]	34	21	13	0	20	12	8	0	May 6/09	14	9	5	0	May 14/09
Ottawa	28	16	12	0	12	7	5	0	May 19/13	16	9	7	0	Apr. 14/12
Anaheim	26	16	10	0	10	6	4	0	May 8/13	16	10	6	0	May 10/13
Phoenix[6]	20	8	12	0	14	5	9	0	May 22/12	6	3	3	0	Apr. 19/12
Tampa Bay	14	8	6	0	5	2	3	0	Apr. 20/11	9	6	3	0	May 1/11
Minnesota	10	5	5	0	6	3	3	0	May 5/13	4	2	2	0	Apr. 30/13
Nashville	7	2	5	0	4	1	3	0	May 3/11	3	1	2	0	Apr. 27/12
Florida	7	2	5	0	2	0	2	0	Apr. 26/12	5	2	3	0	Apr. 24/12
Columbus	0	0	0	0	0	0	0	0		0	0	0	0	
Winnipeg[7]	0	0	0	0	0	0	0	0		0	0	0	0	

[1] Totals include those of Minnesota North Stars 1967-93.
[2] Totals include those of Quebec Nordiques 1979-95.
[3] Totals include those of Atlanta Flames 1972-80.
[4] Totals include those of Kansas City Scouts 1974-76 and Colorado Rockies 1977-82.
[5] Totals include those of Hartford Whalers 1979-97.
[6] Totals include those of Winnipeg Jets 1979-96.
[7] Totals include those of Atlanta Thrashers 1999-2011.

Patrick Kane (#88) and Andrew Shaw celebrate Shaw's goal at 12:08 of the third overtime period that gave Chicago a 4-3 win over Boston in game one of the 2013 Stanley Cup Final. Shaw's goal ended the longest game of the 2013 postseason which saw 27 games – the second most ever – decided in overtime.

Penalty Shots in Stanley Cup Playoff Games

Date	Player, Team	Goaltender, Team	Scored	Final Score				Series
Mar. 21/22	Babe Dye, Toronto	Hugh Lehman, Vancouver	No	Van.	1	at Tor.	2*	F
Mar. 25/37	Lionel Conacher, Mtl. Maroons	Tiny Thompson, Boston	No	Mtl. M.	0	at Bos.	4	QF
Apr. 15/37	Alex Shibicky, NY Rangers	Earl Robertson, Detroit	No	NYR	0	at Det.	3	F
Mar. 24/38	Mush March, Chicago	Wilf Cude, Montreal	No	Mtl.	0	at Chi.	4	QF
Mar. 29/38	Lorne Carr, NY Americans	Mike Karakas, Chicago	No	Chi.	1	at NYA	3	SF
Apr. 10/38	Art Wiebe, Chicago	Turk Broda, Toronto	No	Tor.	1	at Chi.	2	F
Mar. 24/42	Charlie Sands, Montreal	Johnny Mowers, Detroit	No	Det.	0	at Mtl.	5	QF
Apr. 13/44	Virgil Johnson, Chicago	Bill Durnan, Montreal	No	Chi.	4	at Mtl.	5*	F
Apr. 9/68	Wayne Connelly, Minnesota	Terry Sawchuk, Los Angeles	Yes	L.A.	5	at Min.	7	QF
Apr. 27/68	Jim Roberts, St. Louis	Cesare Maniago, Minnesota	No	St.L.	4	at Min.	3	SF
May 16/71	Frank Mahovlich, Montreal	Tony Esposito, Chicago	No	Chi.	3	at Mtl.	4	F
May 7/75	Bill Barber, Philadelphia	Glenn Resch, NY Islanders	No	Phi.	3	at NYI	4*	SF
Apr. 20/79	Mike Walton, Chicago	Glenn Resch, NY Islanders	No	NYI	4	at Chi.	0	QF
Apr. 9/81	Peter McNab, Boston	Don Beaupre, Minnesota	No	Min.	5	at Bos.	4*	PR
Apr. 17/81	Anders Hedberg, NY Rangers	Mike Liut, St. Louis	Yes	NYR	6	at St.L.	4	QF
Apr. 9/83	Denis Potvin, NY Islanders	Pat Riggin, Washington	No	NYI	6	at Wsh.	2	DSF
Apr. 28/84	Wayne Gretzky, Edmonton	Don Beaupre, Minnesota	Yes	Edm.	8	at Min.	5	CF
May 1/84	Mats Naslund, Montreal	Billy Smith, NY Islanders	No	Mtl.	1	at NYI	3	CF
Apr. 14/85	Bob Carpenter, Washington	Billy Smith, NY Islanders	No	Wsh.	4	at NYI.	6	DF
May 28/85	Ron Sutter, Philadelphia	Grant Fuhr, Edmonton	No	Phi.	3	at Edm.	5	F
May 30/85	Dave Poulin, Philadelphia	Grant Fuhr, Edmonton	No	Phi.	3	at Edm.	8	F
Apr. 9/88	John Tucker, Buffalo	Andy Moog, Boston	Yes	Bos.	2	at Buf.	6	DSF
Apr. 9/88	Petr Klima, Detroit	Allan Bester, Toronto	Yes	Det.	6	at Tor.	3	DSF
Apr. 8/89	Neal Broten, Minnesota	Greg Millen, St. Louis	Yes	St.L.	5	at Min.	3	DSF
Apr. 4/90	Al MacInnis, Calgary	Kelly Hrudey, Los Angeles	Yes	L.A.	5	at Cgy.	3	DSF
Apr. 5/90	Randy Wood, NY Islanders	Mike Richter, NY Rangers	No	NYI	1	at NYR	2	DSF
May 3/90	Kelly Miller, Washington	Andy Moog, Boston	No	Wsh.	3	at Bos.	5	CF
May 18/90	Petr Klima, Edmonton	Reggie Lemelin, Boston	No	Edm.	7	at Bos.	2	F
Apr. 6/91	Basil McRae, Minnesota	Ed Belfour, Chicago	Yes	Min.	2	at Chi.	5	DSF
Apr. 10/91	Steve Duchesne, Los Angeles	Kirk McLean, Vancouver	Yes	L.A.	6	at Van.	1	DSF
May 11/92	Jaromir Jagr, Pittsburgh	John Vanbiesbrouck, NYR	Yes	Pit.	3	at NYR	2	DF
May 13/92	Shawn McEachern, Pittsburgh	John Vanbiesbrouck, NYR	No	NYR	1	at Pit.	5	DF
June 7/94	Pavel Bure, Vancouver	Mike Richter, NYR	No	NYR	4	at Van.	2	F
May 9/95	Patrick Poulin, Chicago	Felix Potvin, Toronto	No	Tor.	3	at Chi.	0	CQF
May 10/95	Michal Pivonka, Washington	Tom Barrasso, Pittsburgh	No	Pit.	2	at Wsh.	6	CQF
Apr. 24/96	Joe Juneau, Washington	Ken Wregget, Pittsburgh	No	Pit.	3	at Wsh.	2**	CQF
May 11/97	Eric Lindros, Philadelphia	Steve Shields, Buffalo	Yes	Phi.	6	at Buf.	3	CSF
Apr. 23/98	Aleksey Morozov, Pittsburgh	Andy Moog, Montreal	No	Mtl.	3	at Pit.	2**	CQF
Apr. 22/99	Mats Sundin, Toronto	John Vanbiesbrouck, Phi.	No	Phi.	3	at Tor.	0	CQF
May 29/99	Mats Sundin, Toronto	Dominik Hasek, Buffalo	Yes	Tor.	2	at Buf.	5	CF
Apr. 16/00	Eric Desjardins, Philadelphia	Dominik Hasek, Buffalo	No	Phi.	2	at Buf.	0	CQF
Apr. 11/01	Mark Recchi, Philadelphia	Dominik Hasek, Buffalo	No	Buf.	2	at Phi.	1	CQF
May 2/01	Martin Straka, Pittsburgh	Dominik Hasek, Buffalo	No	Buf.	5	at Pit.	2	CSF
May 12/01	Joe Sakic, Colorado	Roman Turek, St. Louis	Yes	St.L.	1	at Col.	4	CF
Apr. 21/02	Todd Bertuzzi, Vancouver	Dominik Hasek, Detroit	No	Det.	3	at Van.	1	CQF
Apr. 24/02	Shawn Bates, NY Islanders	Curtis Joseph, Toronto	Yes	Tor.	3	at NYI	4	CQF
Apr. 26/02	Mike Johnson, Phoenix	Evgeni Nabokov, San Jose	Yes	Phx.	1	at S.J.	4	CQF
Apr. 15/03	Dainius Zubrus, Washington	Nikolai Khabibulin, Tampa Bay	No	T.B.	4	at Wsh.	3	CQF
Apr. 21/03	Robert Reichel, Toronto	Roman Cechmanek, Philadelphia	No	Phi.	1	at Tor.	2	CQF
Apr. 7/04	Steve Sullivan, Nashville	Manny Legace, Detroit	No	Nsh.	1	at Det.	3	CQF
Apr. 28/06	Derek Roy, Buffalo	Robert Esche, Philadelphia	No	Buf.	4	at Phi.	5	CQF
June 5/06	Chris Pronger, Edmonton***	Cam Ward, Carolina	Yes	Edm.	4	at Car.	5	F
Apr. 21/07	Daniel Cleary, Detroit	Miikka Kiprusoff, Calgary	Yes	Cgy.	1	at Det.	5	CQF
June 6/07	Antoine Vermette, Ottawa	J.S. Giguere, Anaheim	No	Ott.	2	at Ana.	6	F
Apr. 9/08	Ryan Smyth, Colorado	Niklas Backstrom, Minnesota	No	Col.	3	at Min.	2	CQF
Apr. 15/08	Mike Richards, Philadelphia	Cristobal Huet, Washington	Yes	Wsh.	3	at Phi.	6	CQF
Apr. 18/08	John Madden, New Jersey	Henrik Lundqvist, NY Rangers	No	NYR	5	at N.J.	3	CQF
Apr. 24/08	Andrei Kostitsyn, Montreal	Martin Biron, Philadelphia	No	Phi.	3	at Mtl.	4	CSF
Apr. 29/08	Niklas Hagman, Dallas	Evgeni Nabokov, San Jose	No	S.J.	1	at Dal.	2	CSF
May 1/08	Evgeni Malkin, Pittsburgh	Henrik Lundqvist, NY Rangers	No	Pit.	0	at NYR	3	CSF
Apr. 20/10	Martin Erat, Nashville	Antti Niemi, Chicago	Yes	Chi.	1	at Nsh.	4	CQF
May 4/10	Henrik Zetterberg, Detroit	Evgeni Nabokov, San Jose	No	S.J.	4	at Det.	3	CSF
May 8/10	Joe Pavelski, San Jose	Jimmy Howard, Detroit	No	S.J.	2	at Det.	1	CSF
May 12/10	Ville Leino, Philadelphia	Tuukka Rask, Boston	No	Phi.	2	at Bos.	1	CSF
Apr. 24/11	Michael Frolik, Chicago	Cory Schneider, Vancouver	Yes	Van.	3	at Chi.	4	CQF
Apr. 25/11	Chris Connor, Pittsburgh	Dwayne Roloson, Tampa Bay	No	Pit.	3	at T.B.	4	CQF
Apr. 26/11	Alexandre Burrows, Vancouver	Corey Crawford, Chicago	No	Chi.	1	at Van.	2	CQF
Apr. 18/12	Dustin Brown, Los Angeles	Cory Schneider, Vancouver	No	Van.	3	at L.A.	1	CQF
May 27/13	Michael Frolik, Chicago	Jimmy Howard, Detroit	Yes	Chi.	4	at Det.	3	CSF

* Game was decided in overtime, but shot taken during regulation time.
** Shot taken in overtime.
*** First penalty shot scored in Stanley Cup Final history

All-Time Playoff NHL Coaching Register

Playoffs, 1917-2013

Coach	Team	Games Coached	Wins	Losses	T	Years	Cup Wins	Career
Abel, Sid	Chicago	7	3	4		1		
	Detroit	69	29	40		8		
	Totals	76	32	44		9		1952-76
Adams, Jack	Detroit	105	52	52	1	15	3	1927-47
Allen, Keith	Philadelphia	11	3	8		2		1967-69
Arbour, Al	St. Louis	11	4	7		1		
	NY Islanders	198	119	79		15	4	
	Totals	209	123	86		16	4	1970-08
Babcock, Mike	Anaheim	21	15	6		1		
	Detroit	111	63	48		8	1	
	Totals	132	78	54		9	1	2002-13
Barber, Bill	Philadelphia	11	3	8		2		2000-02
Berenson, Red	St. Louis	14	5	9		2		1979-82
Bergeron, Michel	Quebec	68	31	37		7		1980-90
Berry, Bob	Los Angeles	10	2	8		3		
	Montreal	8	2	6		2		
	St. Louis	15	7	8		2		
	Totals	33	11	22		7		1978-94
Beverley, Nick	Toronto	6	2	4		1		1995-96
Blackburn, Don	Hartford	3	0	3		1		1979-81
Blair, Wren	Minnesota	14	7	7		1		1967-70
Blake, Toe	Montreal	119	82	37		13	8	1955-68
Boileau, Marc	Pittsburgh	9	5	4		1		1973-76
Boivin, Leo	St. Louis	3	1	2		1		1975-78
Boucher, Frank	NY Rangers	27	13	14		4	1	1939-54
Boucher, George	Mtl. Maroons	2	0	2	0	1		1930-50
Boucher, Guy	Tampa Bay	18	11	7		1		2010-13
Boudreau, Bruce	Washington	37	17	20		4		
	Anaheim	7	3	4		1		
	Totals	44	20	24		5		2007-13
Bowman, Scotty	St. Louis	52	26	26		4		
	Montreal	98	70	28		8	5	
	Buffalo	36	18	18		5		
	Pittsburgh	33	23	10		2	1	
	Detroit	134	86	48		9	3	
	Totals	353	223	130		28	9	1967-02
Bowness, Rick	Boston	15	8	7		1		1988-05
Brooks, Herb	NY Rangers	24	12	12		3		
	New Jersey	5	1	4		1		
	Pittsburgh	11	6	5		1		
	Totals	40	19	21		5		1981-00
Brophy, John	Toronto	19	9	10		2		1986-89
Burns, Charlie	Minnesota	6	2	4		1		1969-75
Burns, Pat	Montreal	56	30	26		4		
	Toronto	46	23	23		3		
	Boston	18	8	10		2		
	New Jersey	29	17	12		2	1	
	Totals	149	78	71		11	1	1988-05
Bylsma, Dan	Pittsburgh	65	36	29		5	1	2008-13
Campbell, Colin	NY Rangers	36	18	18		3		1994-98
Capuano, Jack	NY Islanders	6	2	4		1		2010-13
Carbonneau, Guy	Montreal	12	5	7		1		2006-09
Carlyle, Randy	Anaheim	62	36	26		5	1	
	Toronto	7	3	4		1		
	Totals	69	39	30		6	1	2005-13
Carpenter, Doug	Toronto	5	1	4		1		1984-91
Carroll, Dick	Toronto	2	1	1	0	1	1	1917-19
Carroll, Frank	Toronto	2	0	2	0	1		1920-21
Cassidy, Bruce	Washington	6	2	4		1		2002-04
Cheevers, Gerry	Boston	34	15	19		4		1980-85
Cherry, Don	Boston	55	31	24		5		1974-80
Clancy, King	Toronto	14	2	12		3		1937-56
Clapper, Dit	Boston	25	8	17		4		1945-49
Cleghorn, Odie	Pittsburgh	4	1	2	1	2		1925-29
Cleghorn, Sprague	Mtl. Maroons	4	1	1	2	1		1931-32
Clouston, Cory	Ottawa	6	2	4		1		2008-11
Constantine, Kevin	San Jose	25	11	14		2		
	Pittsburgh	19	8	11		2		
	New Jersey	6	2	4		1		
	Totals	50	21	29		5		1993-02
Crawford, Marc	Quebec	6	2	4		1		
	Colorado	46	29	17		3	1	
	Vancouver	27	12	15		3		
	Totals	79	43	36		7	1	1994-11
Creighton, Fred	Atlanta	9	2	7		4		1974-80
Crisp, Terry	Calgary	37	22	15		3	1	
	Tampa Bay	6	2	4		1		
	Totals	43	24	19		4	1	1987-98
Crozier, Joe	Buffalo	6	2	4		1		1971-81
Cunniff, John	New Jersey	6	2	4		1		1982-91
Curry, Alex	Ottawa	2	0	1	1	1		1925-26
Dandurand, Leo	Montreal	8	5	3	0	4	1	1921-35
Day, Hap	Toronto	80	49	31		9	5	1940-50
DeBoer, Peter	New Jersey	24	14	10		1		2008-13
Demers, Jacques	St. Louis	33	16	17		3		
	Detroit	38	20	18		3		
	Montreal	27	19	8		2	1	
	Totals	98	55	43		8	1	1979-99
Dineen, Kevin	Florida	7	3	4		1		2011-13
Dudley, Rick	Buffalo	12	4	8		2		1989-04
Dugal, Jules	Montreal	3	1	2		1		1938-39

Coach	Team	Games Coached	Wins	Losses	Ties	Years	Cup Wins	Career
Duncan, Art	Toronto	2	0	1	1	1		1926-32
Dutton, Red	NY Americans	11	4	7		3		1936-40
Esposito, Phil	NY Rangers	10	2	8		2		1986-89
Evans, Jack	Hartford	16	8	8		2		1975-88
Ferguson, John	Winnipeg	3	0	3		1		1975-86
Francis, Bob	Phoenix	10	2	8		2		1999-04
Francis, Emile	NY Rangers	75	34	41		9		
	St. Louis	14	5	9		2		
	Totals	89	39	50		11		1965-83
Ftorek, Robbie	Los Angeles	16	5	11		2		
	New Jersey	7	3	4		1		
	Boston	6	2	4		1		
	Totals	29	10	19		4		1987-03
Gainey, Bob	Minnesota	30	17	13		2		
	Dallas	14	6	8		2		
	Montreal	10	2	8		2		
	Totals	54	25	29		6		1990-09
Geoffrion, Bernie	Atlanta	4	0	4		1		1968-80
Gerard, Eddie	Mtl. Maroons	21	8	8	5	5	1	1917-35
Gill, David	Ottawa	8	3	2	3	2	1	1926-29
Glover, Fred	Oakland	11	3	8		2		1968-74
Gordon, Jackie	Minnesota	25	11	14		3		1970-75
Goring, Butch	Boston	3	0	3		1		1985-01
Gorman, Tommy	NY Americans	2	0	1	1	1		
	Chicago	8	6	1	1	1	1	
	Mtl. Maroons	15	7	6	2	3	1	
	Totals	25	13	8	4	5	2	1925-38
Gottselig, Johnny	Chicago	4	0	4		1		1944-48
Granato, Tony	Colorado	18	9	9		2		2002-09
Green, Pete	Ottawa	8	3	4	1	4	3	1919-25
Green, Ted	Edmonton	16	8	8		1		1991-94
Guidolin, Bep	Boston	21	11	10		2		1972-76
Harris, Ted	Minnesota	2	0	2		1		1975-78
Hart, Cecil	Montreal	37	16	17	4	8	2	1926-39
Hartley, Bob	Colorado	80	49	31		4	1	
	Atlanta	4	0	4		1		
	Totals	84	49	35		5	1	1998-13
Hartsburg, Craig	Chicago	16	8	8		2		
	Anaheim	4	0	4		1		
	Totals	20	8	12		3		1995-09
Harvey, Doug	NY Rangers	6	2	4		1		1961-62
Hay, Don	Phoenix	7	3	4		1		1996-01
Helmer, Rosie	NY Americans	5	2	3	0	1		1935-36
Henning, Lorne	Minnesota	5	2	3		1		1985-01
Hitchcock, Ken	Dallas	80	47	33		5	1	
	Philadelphia	37	19	18		3		
	Columbus	4	0	4		1		
	St. Louis	15	6	9		2		
	Totals	136	72	64		11	1	1995-13
Hlinka, Ivan	Pittsburgh	18	9	9		1		2000-02
Holmgren, Paul	Philadelphia	19	10	9		1		1988-96
Hunter, Dale	Washington	14	7	7		1		2011-12
Imlach, Punch	Toronto	92	44	48		11	4	1958-80
Inglis, Bill	Buffalo	3	1	2		1		1978-79
Irvin, Dick	Chicago	9	5	3	1	1		
	Toronto	66	33	32	1	9	1	
	Montreal	115	62	53		14	3	
	Totals	190	100	88	2	24	4	1928-56
Ivan, Tommy	Detroit	67	36	31		7	3	1947-58
Johnson, Bob	Calgary	52	25	27		5		
	Pittsburgh	24	16	8		1	1	
	Totals	76	41	35		6	1	1982-91
Johnson, Tom	Boston	22	15	7		2	1	1970-73
Johnston, Eddie	Chicago	7	3	4		1		
	Pittsburgh	46	22	24		5		
	Totals	53	25	28		6		1979-97
Julien, Claude	Montreal	11	4	7		1		
	Boston	85	50	35		6	1	
	Totals	96	54	42		7	1	2002-13
Kasper, Steve	Boston	5	1	4		1		1995-97
Keenan, Mike	Philadelphia	57	32	25		4		
	Chicago	60	33	27		4		
	NY Rangers	23	16	7		1	1	
	St. Louis	20	10	10		2		
	Calgary	13	5	8		2		
	Totals	173	96	77		13	1	1984-09
Kelly, Pat	Colorado	2	0	2		1		1977-79
Kelly, Red	Los Angeles	18	7	11		2		
	Pittsburgh	14	6	8		2		
	Toronto	30	11	19		4		
	Totals	62	24	38		8		1967-77
King, Dave	Calgary	20	8	12		3		1992-03
Kromm, Bobby	Detroit	7	3	4		1		1977-80
Lalonde, Newsy	Montreal	11	5	4	2	4		
	Ottawa	2	0	1	1	1		
	Totals	13	5	5	3	5		1917-35
Lamoriello, Lou	New Jersey	20	10	10		2		2005-07
Laviolette, Peter	NY Islanders	12	4	8		2		
	Carolina	25	16	9		1	1	
	Philadelphia	45	23	22		3		
	Totals	82	43	39		6	1	2001-13
Lemaire, Jacques	Montreal	27	15	12		2		
	New Jersey	61	35	26		5	1	
	Minnesota	29	11	18		3		
	Totals	117	61	56		10	1	1983-11
Lewis, Dave	Detroit	16	6	10		2		1998-07
Ley, Rick	Hartford	13	5	8		2		
	Vancouver	11	4	7		1		
	Totals	24	9	15		3		1989-96

Coach	Team	Games Coached	Wins	Losses	Ties	Years	Cup Wins	Career
Long, Barry	Winnipeg	11	3	8		2		1983-86
Loughlin, Clem	Chicago	4	1	2	1	2		1934-37
Low, Ron	Edmonton	28	10	18		3		1994-02
Lowe, Kevin	Edmonton	5	1	4		1		1999-00
MacLean, Doug	Florida	27	13	14		2		1995-04
MacLean, Paul	Ottawa	17	8	9		2		2011-13
MacNeil, Al	Montreal	20	12	8		1	1	
	Atlanta	4	1	3		1		
	Calgary	19	9	10		2		
	Totals	43	22	21		4	1	1970-03
MacTavish, Craig	Edmonton	36	19	17		3		2000-09
Magnuson, Keith	Chicago	3	0	3		1		1980-82
Mahoney, Bill	Minnesota	16	7	9		1		1983-85
Maloney, Dan	Toronto	10	6	4		1		
	Winnipeg	15	5	10		2		
	Totals	25	11	14		3		1984-89
Maloney, Phil	Vancouver	7	1	6		2		1973-77
Martin, Jacques	St. Louis	16	7	9		2		
	Ottawa	69	31	38		8		
	Montreal	26	12	14		2		
	Totals	111	50	61		12		1986-12
Maurice, Paul	Carolina	53	25	28		4		1995-12
McCammon, Bob	Philadelphia	10	1	9		3		
	Vancouver	7	3	4		1		
	Totals	17	4	13		4		1978-91
McLellan, John	Toronto	11	3	8		2		1969-73
McLellan, Todd	San Jose	55	27	28		5		2008-13
McVie, Tom	New Jersey	14	6	8		2		1975-92
Melrose, Barry	Los Angeles	24	13	11		1		1992-09
Milbury, Mike	Boston	40	23	17		2		1989-99
Muckler, John	Edmonton	40	25	15		2	1	
	Buffalo	27	11	16		4		
	Totals	67	36	31		6	1	1968-00
Muldoon, Pete	Chicago	2	0	1	1	1		1926-27
Munro, Dunc	Mtl. Maroons	4	1	3	0	1		1929-31
Murdoch, Bob	Chicago	5	1	4		1		
	Winnipeg	7	3	4		1		
	Totals	12	4	8		2		1987-91
Murphy, Mike	Los Angeles	5	1	4		1		1986-98
Murray, Andy	Los Angeles	24	10	14		3		
	St. Louis	4	0	4		1		
	Totals	28	10	18		4		1999-10
Murray, Bryan	Washington	53	24	29		7		
	Detroit	25	10	15		3		
	Ottawa	34	18	16		3		
	Totals	112	52	60		13		1981-08
Murray, Terry	Washington	39	18	21		4		
	Philadelphia	46	28	18		3		
	Florida	4	0	4		1		
	Los Angeles	12	4	8		2		
	Totals	101	50	51		10		1989-12
Neale, Harry	Vancouver	14	3	11		4		1978-86
Neilson, Roger	Toronto	19	8	11		2		
	Buffalo	8	4	4		1		
	Vancouver	21	12	9		2		
	NY Rangers	29	13	16		3		
	Philadelphia	29	14	15		3		
	Totals	106	51	55		11		1977-02
Nolan, Ted	Buffalo	12	5	7		1		
	NY Islanders	5	1	4		1		
	Totals	17	6	11		2		1995-08
Nykoluk, Mike	Toronto	7	1	6		2		1980-84
Oates, Adam	Washington	7	3	4		1		2012-13
O'Connell, Mike	Boston	5	1	4		1		2002-03
O'Donoghue, George	Toronto	2	1	0	1	1	1	1921-23
Oliver, Murray	Minnesota	9	4	5		1		1982-83
O'Reilly, Terry	Boston *	37	17	19	1	3		1986-89

* Playoff game May 24, 1988 suspended due to power failure. Score tied.

Coach	Team	Games Coached	Wins	Losses	Ties	Years	Cup Wins	Career
Paddock, John	Winnipeg	13	5	8		2		1991-08
Page, Pierre	Minnesota	12	4	8		2		
	Quebec	6	2	4		1		
	Calgary	4	0	4		1		
	Totals	22	6	16		4		1988-98
Patrick, Craig	NY Rangers	17	7	10		2		
	Pittsburgh	5	1	4		1		
	Totals	22	8	14		3		1980-97
Patrick, Frank	Boston	6	2	4	0	2		1934-36
Patrick, Lester	NY Rangers	65	32	26	7	12	2	1926-39
Patrick, Lynn	NY Rangers	12	7	5		1		
	Boston *	28	9	18	1	4		
	Totals	40	16	23	1	5		1948-76

* Playoff game March 31, 1951 suspended due to Toronto city curfew. Score tied.

Coach	Team	Games Coached	Wins	Losses	Ties	Years	Cup Wins	Career
Perron, Jean	Montreal	48	30	18		3	1	1985-89
Perry, Don	Los Angeles	10	4	6		1		1981-84
Pilous, Rudy	Chicago	41	19	22		5	1	1957-63
Plager, Barclay	St. Louis	4	1	3		1		1977-83
Playfair, Jim	Calgary	6	2	4		1		2006-07
Pleau, Larry	Hartford	10	2	8		2		1980-89
Polano, Nick	Detroit	7	1	6		2		1982-85
Powers, Eddie	Toronto	2	0	2	0	1		1924-26
Primeau, Joe	Toronto *	15	8	6	1	2	1	1950-53

* Playoff game March 31, 1951 suspended due to Toronto city curfew. Score tied.

Coach	Team	Games Coached	Wins	Losses	Ties	Years	Cup Wins	Career
Pronovost, Marcel	Buffalo	8	3	5		1		1977-79
Pulford, Bob	Los Angeles	26	10	16		4		
	Chicago	45	17	28		6		
	Totals	71	27	44		10		1972-00
Quenneville, Joel	St. Louis	68	34	34		7		
	Colorado	19	8	11		2		
	Chicago	75	46	29		5	2	
	Totals	162	88	74		14	2	1996-13
Quinn, Pat	Philadelphia	39	22	17		3		
	Los Angeles	3	0	3		1		
	Vancouver	61	31	30		5		
	Toronto	80	41	39		6		
	Totals	183	94	89		15		1978-10
Reay, Billy	Chicago	116	56	60		12		1957-77
Renney, Tom	NY Rangers	24	11	13		3		1996-12
Risebrough, Doug	Calgary	7	3	4		1		1990-92
Roberts, Jim	Hartford	7	3	4		1		1981-97
Robinson, Larry	Los Angeles	4	0	4		1		
	New Jersey	48	31	17		2	1	
	Totals	52	31	21		3	1	1995-06
Ross, Art	Boston	70	32	33	5	12	2	1917-45
Ruel, Claude	Montreal	27	18	9		3	1	1968-81
Ruff, Lindy	Buffalo	101	57	44		8		1997-13
Sacco, Joe	Colorado	6	2	4		1		2009-13
Sather, Glen	Edmonton *	127	89	37	1	10	4	1979-04

* Playoff game May 24, 1988 suspended due to power failure. Score tied.

Coach	Team	Games Coached	Wins	Losses	Ties	Years	Cup Wins	Career
Sator, Ted	NY Rangers	16	8	8		1		
	Buffalo	11	3	8		2		
	Totals	27	11	16		3		1985-89
Schinkel, Ken	Pittsburgh	6	2	4		2		1972-77
Schmidt, Milt	Boston	34	15	19		4		1954-76
Schoenfeld, Jim	New Jersey	20	11	9		1		
	Washington	24	10	14		3		
	Phoenix	13	5	8		2		
	Totals	57	26	31		6		1985-99
Shero, Fred	Philadelphia	83	48	35		6	2	
	NY Rangers	27	15	12		2		
	Totals	110	63	47		8	2	1971-81
Simpson, Terry	NY Islanders	20	9	11		2		
	Winnipeg	6	2	4		1		
	Totals	26	11	15		3		1986-96
Sinden, Harry	Boston	43	24	19		5	1	1966-85
Skinner, Jimmy	Detroit	26	14	12		3	1	1954-58
Smith, Alf	Ottawa	5	1	4	0	1		1918-19
Smith, Floyd	Buffalo	32	16	16		3		1971-80
Smythe, Conn	Toronto	4	2	2	0	1		1927-32
Sonmor, Glen	Minnesota	47	26	21		4		1978-87
Stasiuk, Vic	Philadelphia	4	0	4		1		1969-73
Stevens, John	Philadelphia	23	11	12		2		2006-12
Stewart, Bill	Chicago	10	7	3		1	1	1937-39
Stewart, Ron	Los Angeles	2	0	2		1		1975-78
Sutter, Brent	New Jersey	12	4	8		2		2007-12
Sutter, Brian	St. Louis	41	20	21		4		
	Boston	22	7	15		3		
	Chicago	5	1	4		1		
	Totals	68	28	40		8		1988-05
Sutter, Darryl	Chicago	26	11	15		3		
	San Jose	42	18	24		5		
	Calgary	33	18	15		2		
	Los Angeles	38	25	13		2	1	
	Totals	139	72	67		12	1	1992-13
Talbot, Jean-Guy	St. Louis	5	1	4		1		
	NY Rangers	3	1	2		1		
	Totals	8	2	6		2		1972-78
Tessier, Orval	Chicago	18	9	9		2		1982-85
Therrien, Michel	Montreal	17	7	10		2		
	Pittsburgh	25	15	10		2		
	Totals	42	22	20		4		2000-13
Thompson, Paul	Chicago	19	7	12		4		1938-45
Tippett, Dave	Dallas	47	21	26		5		
	Phoenix	27	12	15		3		
	Totals	74	33	41		8		2002-13
Tobin, Bill	Chicago	4	1	2	1	2		1929-32
Tortorella, John	NY Rangers	44	19	25		4		
	Tampa Bay	45	24	21		4	1	
	Totals	89	43	46		8	1	1999-13
Tremblay, Mario	Montreal	11	3	8		2		1995-97
Trotz, Barry	Nashville	50	19	31		7		1998-13
Ubriaco, Gene	Pittsburgh	11	7	4		1		1988-90
Vigneault, Alain	Montreal	10	4	6		1		
	Vancouver	68	33	35		6		
	Totals	78	37	41		7		1997-13
Watson, Phil	NY Rangers	16	4	12		3		1955-63
Watt, Tom	Winnipeg	7	1	6		2		
	Vancouver	3	0	3		1		
	Totals	10	1	9		3		1981-92
Webster, Tom	Los Angeles	28	12	16		3		1986-92
Weiland, Cooney	Boston	17	10	7		2	1	1939-41
White, Bill	Chicago	2	0	2		1		1976-77
Wilson, Johnny	Pittsburgh	12	4	8		2		1969-80
Wilson, Ron	Anaheim	11	4	7		1		
	Washington	32	15	17		3		
	San Jose	52	28	24		4		
	Totals	95	47	48		8		1993-12
Yeo, Mike	Minnesota	5	1	4		1		2011-13
Young, Garry	St. Louis	2	0	2		1		1972-76

Key to Prospect, NHL Player and Goaltender Registers

Demographics: Position, shooting side (catching hand for goaltenders), height, weight, place and date of birth as well as draft information, if any, is located on this line.

Major and tier-II junior, NCAA, minor pro, European and NHL clubs form a permanent part of each player's data panel. If a player sees action with more than one club in any of the above categories, a separate line is included for each one.

Olympic Team statistics are also listed.

Asterisks (*) indicates league leader in individual statistical categories.

Players' NHL organization as of August 12, 2013. This includes players under contract, unsigned draft choices and other players on reserve lists. Free agents as of this date show a blank here.

The complete career data panels of players with NHL experience who announced their retirement before the start of the 2012-13 season are included in the Player Register and Goaltender Register.

These newly-retired players also show a blank here.

Each NHL club's minor-pro affiliates are listed on page 14.

HOSSA, Marian (HOH-sa, MAIR-ee-uhn) **CHI**

Right wing. Shoots left. 6'1", 210 lbs. Born, Stara Lubovna, Czech., January 12, 1979. Ottawa's 1st choice, 12th overall, in 1997 Entry Draft.

			Regular Season														Playoffs								
Season	Club	League	GP	G	A	Pts	PIM	PP	SH	GW	S	%	+/-	TF	F%	Min	GP	G	A	Pts	PIM	PP	SH	GW	Min
1995-96	Dukla Trencin Jr.	Slovak-Jr.	53	42	49	91	26	....	....	....	....	....	....	....	....	....	....	....	....	....	....	....	....	....	....
1996-97	Dukla Trencin	Slovakia	46	25	19	44	33	....	....	....	....	....	....	....	....	....	7	5	5	10	....	....	....	....	....
1997-98	Portland	WHL	53	45	40	85	50	....	....	....	....	....	....	....	....	....	16	13	6	19	6	....	....	....	....
	Ottawa	**NHL**	**7**	**0**	**1**	**1**	**0**	**0**	[illegible]	**0**	**10**	**0.0**	**–1**	....	....	....	....	....	....	....	....	....	....	....	....
1998-99	**Ottawa**	**NHL**	**60**	**15**	**15**	**30**	[illegible]	**1**	**0**	**2**	**124**	**12.1**	**18**	**4**	**25.0**	**13:59**	**4**	**0**	**2**	**2**	**4**	**0**	**0**	**0**	**16:46**
99-2000	**Ottawa**	**NHL**	**78**	**29**	**27**	**56**	[illegible]	**5**	**0**	**4**	**240**	**12.1**	**5**	**7**	**57.1**	**17:12**	**6**	**0**	**0**	**0**	**2**	**0**	**0**	**0**	**15:22**
2000-01	**Ottawa**	**NHL**	**81**	**32**	**43**	**75**	[illegible]	**11**	**2**	**7**	**249**	**12.9**	**19**	**14**	**42.9**	**18:01**	**4**	**1**	**1**	**2**	**4**	**0**	**0**	**0**	**19:02**
2001-02	Dukla Trencin	Slovakia	8	3	4	7	[illegible]	....	....	....	....	....	....	....	....	....	....	....	....	....	....	....	....	....	....
	Ottawa	**NHL**	**80**	**31**	**35**	**66**	[illegible]	**9**	**1**	**4**	**278**	**11.2**	**11**	**12**	**33.3**	**18:29**	**12**	**4**	**6**	**10**	**2**	**1**	**0**	**0**	**19:04**
	Slovakia	Olympics	2	4	2	6	0	....	....	....	....	....	....	....	....	....	....	....	....	....	....	....	....	....	....
2002-03	**Ottawa**	**NHL**	**80**	**45**	**35**	**80**	**34**	**14**	**0**	**10**	**229**	**19.7**	**8**	**19**	**36.8**	**18:31**	**18**	**5**	**11**	**16**	**6**	**3**	**0**	**1**	**18:41**
2003-04	**Ottawa**	**NHL**	**81**	**36**	**46**	**82**	**46**	**14**	**1**	**5**	**233**	**15.5**	**4**	**25**	**40.0**	**18:37**	**7**	**3**	**1**	**4**	**0**	**1**	**0**	**2**	**21:24**
2004-05	Dukla Trencin	Slovakia	25	22	20	42	38	....	....	....	....	....	....	....	....	....	5	4	5	9	4	....	....	....	....
	Mora IK	Sweden	24	18	14	32	22	....	....	....	....	....	....	....	....	....	....	....	....	....	....	....	....	....	....
2005-06	**Atlanta**	**NHL**	**80**	**39**	**53**	**92**	**67**	**14**	***7**	**7**	**341**	**11.4**	**17**	**15**	**26.7**	**21:41**	....	....	....	....	....	....	....	....	....
	Slovakia	Olympics	6	5	5	10	4	....	....	....	....	....	....	....	....	....	....	....	....	....	....	....	....	....	....
2006-07	**Atlanta**	**NHL**	**82**	**43**	**57**	**100**	**49**	**17**	**3**	**5**	**340**	**12.6**	**18**	**18**	**22.2**	**21:41**	**4**	**0**	**1**	**1**	[illegible]	**0**	**0**	**0**	**18:55**
2007-08	**Atlanta**	**NHL**	**60**	**26**	**30**	[illegible]	**30**	**8**	**2**	**4**	**229**	**11.4**	**–14**	**14**	**28.6**	**21:55**	....	....	....	....	....	....	....	....	....
	Pittsburgh	**NHL**	**12**	**3**	**7**	[illegible]	**6**	**0**	**0**	**0**	**35**	**8.6**	**0**	**1**	**0.0**	**18:34**	**20**	**12**	**14**	**26**	[illegible]	**5**	**0**	**2**	**21:00**
2008-09	**Detroit**	**NHL**	**74**	**40**	**31**	[illegible]	**63**	**10**	**0**	**8**	**307**	**13.0**	**27**	**19**	**21.1**	**17:48**	**23**	**6**	**9**	**15**	[illegible]	**2**	**1**	**1**	**18:38**
2009-10 ♦	**Chicago**	**NHL**	**57**	**24**	**27**	[illegible]	**18**	**2**	**5**	**2**	**199**	**12.1**	**24**	**1**	**0.0**	**18:44**	**22**	**3**	**12**	**15**	[illegible]	**0**	**0**	**1**	**18:25**
	Slovakia	Olympics	7	3	6	[illegible]	6	....	....	....	....	....	....	....	....	....	....	....	....	....	....	....	....	....	....
2010-11	**Chicago**	**NHL**	**65**	**25**	**32**	**57**	**32**	**8**	**2**	**2**	**205**	**12.2**	**9**	**4**	**75.0**	**19:42**	**7**	**2**	**4**	**6**	[illegible]	**1**	**0**	**1**	**18:35**
2011-12	**Chicago**	**NHL**	**81**	**29**	**48**	**77**	**20**	**9**	**2**	**4**	**248**	**11.7**	**18**	**9**	**33.3**	**19:58**	**3**	**0**	**0**	**0**	[illegible]	**0**	**0**	**0**	**17:21**
2012-13 ♦	**Chicago**	**NHL**	**40**	**17**	**14**	**31**	**16**	**4**	**1**	**6**	**116**	**14.7**	**20**	**3**	**33.3**	**18:02**	**22**	**7**	**9**	**16**	[illegible]	**3**	**0**	**2**	**19:56**
	NHL Totals		**1018**	**434**	**501**	**935**	**544**	**126**	**26**	**70**	**3383**	**12.8**		**165**	**33.3**	**18:57**	**152**	**43**	**70**	**113**	**75**	**16**	**1**	**10**	**19:05**

L West First All-Star Team (1998) • WHL Rookie of the Year (1998) • Canadian Major Junior First All-Star Team (1998) • Memorial Cup All-Star Team (1998) • NHL All-Rookie Team (1999) • NHL Second Star Team (2009)

ed in NHL All-Star Game (2001, 2003, 2007, 2008, 2012)

ned as a free agent by **Trencin** (Slovakia), September 16, 2004. Signed as a free agent by **Mora** (Sweden), November 11, 2004. Signed as a free agent by **Trencin** (Slovakia), January 31, 2005. Traded to nta by **Ottawa** with Greg de Vries for Dany Heatley, August 23, 2005. Traded to **Pittsburgh** by **Atlanta** with Pascal Dupuis for Colby Armstrong, Erik Christensen, Angelo Esposito and Pittsburgh's 1st nd choice (Daulton Leveille) in 2008 Entry Draft , February 26, 2008. Signed as a free agent by **Detroit**, July 2, 2008. Signed as a free agent by **Chicago**, July 1, 2009.

Diamond (♦) indicates member of Stanley Cup-winning team.

"Did not play" Indicates that a player did not participate in a professional, junior or college league for an entire season.

Birthplace reflects the world map at the time a player was born. The Czech Republic and Slovakia became independent on January 1, 1993. Previously, players were born in Czechoslovakia. The Russian Republic was established on January 1, 1992. Previously, players were born in the USSR. Germany was unified on October 3, 1990. Previously, players were born in either East or West Germany. Former Soviet Republics (Belarus Estonia, Kazakhstan, Latvia, Lithuania, Ukraine) achieved independence between August 20 and December 25, 1991.

All trades, free agent signings and other transactions involving NHL clubs are listed here and are presented in chronological order. First draft selection for players who re-enter the NHL Entry Draft is noted here as well. Also listed are other special notes. These are highlighted with a bullet (•).

Dates for trades or free agent signings often differ depending upon source. Signings can be reported based on when contracts are filed with NHL Central Registry or on the date a club announces that it has made a trade or come to terms with a free agent.

All-Star Team selections and awards are listed below player's year-by-year data.

NHL All-Star Game appearances are listed above trade notes.

THIS 82ND EDITION OF THE *NHL Official Guide & Record Book* includes additional statistical categories for forwards and defensemen in the National Hockey League. These categories are, from left to right in the sample panel above, power-play goals (PP), shorthand goals (SH), game-winning goals (GW), shots on goal (S), percentage of shots that score (%), plus-minus rating (+/–), total faceoffs taken (TF), faceoff winning percentage (F%), and average time-on-ice per game played (Min).

To integrate this data, the Player Register is split into two sections. The Prospect Register presents data on players who have yet to play in the NHL. The NHL Player Register, containing more information and a photo of each player, lists all active players who have appeared in an NHL regular-season or playoff game at any time.

Goaltenders, whether prospects or active NHLers, are included in one register. With the addition of the shootout to NHL regular-season play, the column formerly used to record tie games for goaltenders has been renamed "O/T." For NHL goaltenders beginning in 2005-06, it lists overtime losses and shootout losses; previous to 2005-06, it lists tie games.

Registers (with their starting page) are presented in the following order: Prospects (281), NHL Players (348), Goaltenders (591), Retired Players (616) and Retired Goaltenders (659). League abbreviations, page 670. Late additions to the Registers, page 615.

Some information is unavailable at press time. Readers are encouraged to contribute. See page 5 for contact names and addresses.

Pronunciation of Player Names

United Press International phonetic style.

AY	long A as in mate
A	short A as in cat
AI	nasal A as on air
AH	short A as in father
AW	broad A as in talk
EE	long E as in meat
EH	short E as in get
UH	hollow E as in the
AY	French long E with acute accent as in Pathe
IH	middle E as in pretty
EW	EW dipthong as in few
IGH	long I as in time
EE	French long I as in machine
IH	short I as in pity
OH	long O as in note
AH	short O as in hot
AW	broad O as in fought
OI	OI dipthong as in noise
OO	long double OO as in fool
U	short double O as in foot
OW	OW dipthong as in how
EW	long U as in mule
OO	long U as in rule
U	middle U as in put
UH	short U as in shut or hurt
K	hard C as in cat
S	soft C as in cease
SH	soft CH as in machine
CH	hard CH or TCH as in catch
Z	hard S as in bells
S	soft S as in sun
G	hard G as in gang
J	soft G as in general
ZH	soft J as in French version of Joliet
KH	gutteral CH as in Scottish version of Loch

2013-14 Prospect Register

Note: The 2013-14 Prospect Register lists forwards and defensemen only. Goaltenders are listed separately. The Prospect Register lists every player drafted in the 2013 Entry Draft, players on NHL Reserve Lists and other players who have not yet played in the NHL. Trades and roster changes are current as of August 12, 2013.

Abbreviations: GP – games played; **G** – goals; **A** – assists; **Pts** – points; **PIM** – penalties in minutes; ***** – league-leading total.

NHL Player Register begins on page 348.
Goaltender Register begins on page 591.
Retired Player Index begins on page 616.
Retired Goaltender Index begins on page 659.
League Abbreviations are listed on page 670.

AALTONEN, Miro (AL-toh-nehn, MEE-roh) ANA

Center. Shoots left. 5'10", 172 lbs. Born, Joensuu, Finland, June 7, 1993.
(Anaheim's 5th choice, 177th overall, in 2013 Entry Draft).

			Regular Season					Playoffs				
Season	**Club**	**League**	**GP**	**G**	**A**	**Pts**	**PIM**	**GP**	**G**	**A**	**Pts**	**PIM**
2008-09	Jokipojat U18	Fin-U18	1	3	1	4	0	....	....	....	....	....
2009-10	Blues Espoo U18	Fin-U18	8	4	12	16	8	11	6	8	14	6
	Blues Espoo Jr.	Fin-Jr.	40	12	15	27	18	....	....	....	....	....
2010-11	Blues Espoo U18	Fin-U18	2	0	3	3	2	2	3	1	4	2
	Blues Espoo Jr.	Fin-Jr.	12	3	5	8	6	13	5	6	11	2
2011-12	Blues Espoo Jr.	Fin-Jr.	14	10	17	27	14	4	2	3	5	2
	Jokipojat Joensuu	Finland-2	4	2	3	5	0	....	....	....	....	....
	Blues Espoo	Finland	26	1	1	2	2	10	1	1	2	2
2012-13	Blues Espoo	Finland	32	11	5	16	22	....	....	....	....	....
	Blues Espoo Jr.	Fin-Jr.	....	....	....	....	....	8	4	9	13	4

ABBOTT, Spencer (A-buht, SPEHN-suhr) TOR

Right wing. Shoots right. 5'10", 175 lbs. Born, Hamilton, Ont., April 30, 1988.

			Regular Season					Playoffs				
Season	**Club**	**League**	**GP**	**G**	**A**	**Pts**	**PIM**	**GP**	**G**	**A**	**Pts**	**PIM**
2005-06	Sherwood Saints	High-ON		STATISTICS NOT AVAILABLE								
	Hamilton Reps	Minor-ON		STATISTICS NOT AVAILABLE								
	Hamilton	ON-Jr.A	11	1	0	1	0	1	0	0	0	0
2006-07	Hamilton	ON-Jr.A	49	32	43	75	22	19	4	5	9	12
2007-08	Hamilton	ON-Jr.A	48	42	41	83	42	5	2	4	6	2
2008-09	U. of Maine	H-East	38	7	9	16	8	....	....	....	....	....
2009-10	U. of Maine	H-East	38	9	19	28	6	....	....	....	....	....
2010-11	U. of Maine	H-East	36	17	23	40	16	....	....	....	....	....
2011-12	U. of Maine	H-East	39	21	41	62	34	....	....	....	....	....
	Toronto Marlies	AHL	3	0	1	1	0	5	0	0	0	0
2012-13	Toronto Marlies	AHL	55	13	20	33	10	5	2	3	5	2

Hockey East First All-Star Team (2012) • NCAA East First All-American Team (2012)

Signed as a free agent by **Toronto**, March 28, 2012.

ABELTSHAUSER, Konrad (ah-behlts-HAHW-zuhr, KAWN-rad) S.J.

Defense. Shoots left. 6'5", 225 lbs. Born, Bad Tolz, Germany, September 2, 1992.
(San Jose's 6th choice, 163rd overall, in 2010 Entry Draft).

			Regular Season					Playoffs				
Season	**Club**	**League**	**GP**	**G**	**A**	**Pts**	**PIM**	**GP**	**G**	**A**	**Pts**	**PIM**
2007-08	EC Bad Tolz Jr.	Ger-Jr.	36	1	10	11	32	8	0	6	6	2
2008-09	EC Bad Tolz Jr.	Ger-Jr.	36	16	28	44	26	4	1	0	1	0
2009-10	Halifax	QMJHL	48	5	20	25	28	....	....	....	....	....
2010-11	Halifax	QMJHL	58	8	19	27	47	4	3	0	3	0
2011-12	Halifax	QMJHL	57	8	36	44	30	15	5	11	16	16
2012-13	Halifax	QMJHL	56	7	47	54	22	17	7	13	20	12

QMJHL Second All-Star Team (2013) • Memorial Cup All-Star Team (2013)

ABERG, Pontus (AW-buhrg, PAWN-tuhs) NSH

Left wing. Shoots right. 5'11", 199 lbs. Born, Stockholm, Sweden, September 23, 1993.
(Nashville's 1st choice, 37th overall, in 2012 Entry Draft).

			Regular Season					Playoffs				
Season	**Club**	**League**	**GP**	**G**	**A**	**Pts**	**PIM**	**GP**	**G**	**A**	**Pts**	**PIM**
2008-09	Djurgarden U18	Swe-U18	27	6	3	9	8	....	....	....	....	....
2009-10	Djurgarden U18	Swe-U18	36	29	33	62	24	5	4	7	11	4
	Djurgarden Jr.	Swe-Jr.	11	0	1	1	4	....	....	....	....	....
2010-11	Djurgarden U18	Swe-U18	8	11	7	18	27	3	0	2	2	2
	Djurgarden Jr.	Swe-Jr.	41	13	17	30	16	4	2	3	5	2
	Djurgarden	Sweden	1	0	0	0	0	....	....	....	....	....
2011-12	Djurgarden Jr.	Swe-Jr.	6	4	2	6	0	1	1	0	1	0
	Djurgarden	Sweden	47	8	7	15	6	....	....	....	....	....
	Djurgarden	Sweden-Q	7	1	0	1	0	....	....	....	....	....
2012-13	Djurgarden	Sweden-2	58	15	29	44	8	....	....	....	....	....
	Djurgarden Jr.	Swe-Jr.	3	1	3	4	2	1	0	0	0	0

ABNEY, Cameron (AB-nee, KAM-ih-RUHN) EDM

Right wing. Shoots right. 6'5", 200 lbs. Born, Aldergrove, B.C., May 23, 1991.
(Edmonton's 4th choice, 82nd overall, in 2009 Entry Draft).

			Regular Season					Playoffs				
Season	**Club**	**League**	**GP**	**G**	**A**	**Pts**	**PIM**	**GP**	**G**	**A**	**Pts**	**PIM**
2007-08	North Delta Devils	PIJHL	42	12	14	26	110	5	1	0	1	27
	Everett Silvertips	WHL	4	0	0	0	0	....	....	....	....	....
2008-09	Everett Silvertips	WHL	48	1	3	4	103	5	0	0	0	2
2009-10	Everett Silvertips	WHL	34	3	3	6	60	....	....	....	....	....
	Edmonton	WHL	34	3	4	7	63	....	....	....	....	....
2010-11	Edmonton	WHL	60	7	13	20	72	4	1	0	1	6
2011-12	Oklahoma City	AHL	14	0	0	0	24	3	0	0	0	12
	Stockton Thunder	ECHL	29	2	3	5	132	....	....	....	....	....
2012-13	Oklahoma City	AHL	4	0	0	0	14	....	....	....	....	....
	Stockton Thunder	ECHL	36	5	3	8	58	6	0	0	0	8

ACOLATSE, Sena (ah-koh-LAWT-say, SEH-na) S.J.

Defense. Shoots right. 6', 210 lbs. Born, Hayward, CA, November 28, 1990.

			Regular Season					Playoffs				
Season	**Club**	**League**	**GP**	**G**	**A**	**Pts**	**PIM**	**GP**	**G**	**A**	**Pts**	**PIM**
2006-07	Seattle	WHL	45	0	4	4	61	11	0	0	0	8
2007-08	Seattle	WHL	71	7	24	31	107	12	1	2	3	12
2008-09	Seattle	WHL	70	7	14	21	143	5	1	1	2	0
2009-10	Seattle	WHL	39	13	9	22	35	....	....	....	....	....
	Saskatoon Blades	WHL	30	3	10	13	25	7	1	1	2	17
2010-11	Saskatoon Blades	WHL	1	0	0	0	2	....	....	....	....	....
	Prince George	WHL	66	15	48	63	128	4	3	4	7	4
	Worcester Sharks	AHL	1	0	0	0	0	....	....	....	....	....
2011-12	Worcester Sharks	AHL	65	8	13	21	89	....	....	....	....	....
2012-13	Worcester Sharks	AHL	50	4	17	21	62	....	....	....	....	....

Signed as a free agent by **San Jose**, March 4, 2011.

ACTON, Will (AK-tuhn, WIHL) EDM

Center. Shoots left. 6'2", 190 lbs. Born, Stouffville, Ont., July 16, 1987.

			Regular Season					Playoffs				
Season	**Club**	**League**	**GP**	**G**	**A**	**Pts**	**PIM**	**GP**	**G**	**A**	**Pts**	**PIM**
2004-05	Stouffville Spirit	ON-Jr.A	41	5	8	13	28	....	....	....	....	....
2005-06	Stouffville Spirit	ON-Jr.A	48	11	20	31	38	....	....	....	....	....
2006-07	Stouffville Spirit	ON-Jr.A	33	16	13	29	63	....	....	....	....	....
2007-08	Lake Superior	CCHA	36	6	7	13	22	....	....	....	....	....
2008-09	Lake Superior	CCHA	38	7	9	16	53	....	....	....	....	....
2009-10	Lake Superior	CCHA	36	10	14	24	39	....	....	....	....	....
2010-11	Lake Superior	CCHA	34	9	15	24	18	....	....	....	....	....
	Toronto Marlies	AHL	5	0	0	0	0	....	....	....	....	....
	Reading Royals	ECHL	1	0	0	0	0	....	....	....	....	....
2011-12	Toronto Marlies	AHL	69	7	9	16	58	17	1	1	2	9
2012-13	Toronto Marlies	AHL	67	8	11	19	60	9	4	2	6	12

Signed as a free agent by **Edmonton**, July 6, 2013.

ADAMS, Mark (A-duhmz, MAHRK) BUF

Defense. Shoots right. 6'1", 194 lbs. Born, Boston, MA, May 23, 1991.
(Buffalo's 4th choice, 134th overall, in 2009 Entry Draft).

			Regular Season					Playoffs				
Season	**Club**	**League**	**GP**	**G**	**A**	**Pts**	**PIM**	**GP**	**G**	**A**	**Pts**	**PIM**
2007-08	Malden Cath.	High-MA	23	4	13	17	....	....	....	....	....	....
2008-09	Malden Cath.	High-MA	23	6	23	29	....	....	....	....	....	....
	Bos. Jr. Bruins	EJHL	32	5	10	15	18	....	....	....	....	....
2009-10	Chicago Steel	USHL	53	4	10	14	85	....	....	....	....	....
2010-11	Providence College	H-East	33	0	3	3	22	....	....	....	....	....
2011-12	Providence College	H-East	19	0	1	1	12	....	....	....	....	....
2012-13	Providence College	H-East	7	0	0	0	6	....	....	....	....	....

AGOSTINO, Kenny (a-goh-STEE-noh, KEHN-nee) CGY

Left wing. Shoots left. 6'1", 200 lbs. Born, Morristown, NJ, April 30, 1992.
(Pittsburgh's 4th choice, 140th overall, in 2010 Entry Draft).

			Regular Season					Playoffs				
Season	Club	League	GP	G	A	Pts	PIM	GP	G	A	Pts	PIM
2007-08	Delbarton	High-NJ	....	24	48	72	....	....	....	....	....	....
2008-09	Delbarton	High-NJ	....	....	....	74	....	....	....	....	....	....
2009-10	Delbarton	High-NJ	27	50	33	83	40	....	....	....	....	....
	USNTDP	U-18	2	0	0	0	2	....	....	....	....	....
2010-11	Yale	ECAC	31	11	14	25	30	....	....	....	....	....
2011-12	Yale	ECAC	33	14	20	34	32	....	....	....	....	....
2012-13	Yale	ECAC	37	17	24	41	32	....	....	....	....	....

ECAC Second All-Star Team (2013)

Traded to **Calgary** by **Pittsburgh** with Ben Hanowski and Pittsburgh's 1st round choice (Morgan Klimchuk) in 2013 Entry Draft for Jarome Iginla, March 28, 2013.

AGOZZINO, Andrew (a-guh-ZEEN-oh, AN-droo) COL

Left wing. Shoots left. 5'9", 185 lbs. Born, Kleinburg, Ont., January 3, 1991.

			Regular Season					Playoffs				
Season	Club	League	GP	G	A	Pts	PIM	GP	G	A	Pts	PIM
2007-08	Niagara Ice Dogs	OHL	50	12	10	22	47	....	....	....	....	....
2008-09	Niagara Ice Dogs	OHL	67	27	29	56	88	12	6	5	11	24
2009-10	Niagara Ice Dogs	OHL	66	37	29	66	95	5	3	2	5	15
	Peoria Rivermen	AHL	2	0	0	0	0	....	....	....	....	....
2010-11	Niagara Ice Dogs	OHL	68	43	31	74	73	14	6	7	13	19
2011-12	Niagara Ice Dogs	OHL	67	40	48	88	67	20	11	7	18	16
2012-13	Lake Erie Monsters	AHL	76	20	32	52	73	....	....	....	....	....

Signed to a ATO (amateur tryout) contract by **Peoria** (AHL), April 8, 2010. Signed as a free agent by **Lake Erie** (AHL), August 28, 2012. Signed as a free agent by **Colorado**, March 22, 2013.

ALBERT, John (AL-buhrt, JAWN) WPG

Center. Shoots left. 5'11", 190 lbs. Born, Cleveland, OH, January 19, 1989.
(Atlanta's 3rd choice, 175th overall, in 2007 Entry Draft).

			Regular Season					Playoffs				
Season	Club	League	GP	G	A	Pts	PIM	GP	G	A	Pts	PIM
2004-05	Cleveland Barons	MWEHL	67	34	60	94	....	....	....	....	....	....
	Cleveland Barons	NAHL	3	0	0	0	0	....	....	....	....	....
2005-06	USNTDP	U-17	19	8	15	23	25	....	....	....	....	....
	USNTDP	NAHL	36	8	15	23	23	....	....	....	....	....
2006-07	USNTDP	U-18	41	8	16	24	10	....	....	....	....	....
	USNTDP	NAHL	15	4	9	13	4	....	....	....	....	....
2007-08	Ohio State	CCHA	41	4	17	21	10	....	....	....	....	....
2008-09	Ohio State	CCHA	42	11	28	39	20	....	....	....	....	....
2009-10	Ohio State	CCHA	39	6	24	30	20	....	....	....	....	....
2010-11	Ohio State	CCHA	37	12	22	34	18	....	....	....	....	....
2011-12	St. John's IceCaps	AHL	64	9	18	27	28	15	3	2	5	8
2012-13	St. John's IceCaps	AHL	24	3	2	5	10	....	....	....	....	....

• Transferred to **Winnipeg** after **Atlanta** franchise relocated, June 21, 2011.

ALDERSON, Brandon (AHL-duhr-suhn, BRAN-duhn) PHI

Right wing. Shoots right. 6'4", 195 lbs. Born, Oakville, Ont., January 22, 1992.

			Regular Season					Playoffs				
Season	Club	League	GP	G	A	Pts	PIM	GP	G	A	Pts	PIM
2007-08	Lon. Jr. Knights	Minor-ON	52	26	27	53	....	....	....	....	....	....
2008-09	Oakville Rangers	Minor-ON	STATISTICS NOT AVAILABLE									
	Oakville Blades	ON-Jr.A	1	1	1	2	0	....	....	....	....	....
2009-10	Sarnia Sting	OHL	67	13	11	24	30	....	....	....	....	....
2010-11	Sarnia Sting	OHL	68	11	19	30	63	....	....	....	....	....
2011-12	Sault Ste. Marie	OHL	65	17	22	39	81	....	....	....	....	....
2012-13	Sault Ste. Marie	OHL	67	28	36	64	64	6	1	3	4	4
	Adirondack	AHL	9	0	2	2	2	....	....	....	....	....

Signed as a free agent by **Philadelphia**, March 1, 2013.

ALLEN, Conor (AL-uhn, KAW-nuhr) NYR

Defense. Shoots left. 6'1", 210 lbs. Born, Chicago, IL, January 31, 1990.

			Regular Season					Playoffs				
Season	Club	League	GP	G	A	Pts	PIM	GP	G	A	Pts	PIM
2008-09	St. Louis Bandits	NAHL	46	5	10	15	48	....	....	....	....	....
2009-10	Sioux Falls	USHL	48	7	8	15	69	....	....	....	....	....
2010-11	Massachusetts	H-East	31	2	4	6	29	....	....	....	....	....
2011-12	Massachusetts	H-East	35	7	7	14	28	....	....	....	....	....
2012-13	Massachusetts	H-East	33	5	14	19	53	....	....	....	....	....
	Connecticut Whale	AHL	1	0	0	0	0	....	....	....	....	....

Signed as a free agent by **NY Rangers**, March 29, 2013.

ALMQVIST, Adam (AHLM-kwihst, A-duhm) DET

Defense. Shoots left. 5'11", 174 lbs. Born, Jonkoping, Sweden, February 27, 1991.
(Detroit's 7th choice, 210th overall, in 2009 Entry Draft).

			Regular Season					Playoffs				
Season	Club	League	GP	G	A	Pts	PIM	GP	G	A	Pts	PIM
2007-08	HV 71 U18	Swe-U18	18	8	12	20	28	....	....	....	....	....
	HV 71 Jr.	Swe-Jr.	23	1	6	7	12	3	0	0	0	4
2008-09	HV 71 Jr.	Swe-Jr.	41	8	28	36	44	....	....	....	....	....
2009-10	HV 71 Jonkoping	Sweden	28	2	6	8	10	16	1	10	11	8
	HV 71 Jr.	Swe-Jr.	15	5	29	34	14	....	....	....	....	....
2010-11	HV 71 Jonkoping	Sweden	52	0	16	16	32	2	0	0	0	0
	HV 71 Jr.	Swe-Jr.	....	....	....	....	....	5	2	0	2	4
2011-12	HV 71 Jonkoping	Sweden	42	3	8	11	26	3	0	1	1	4
	Grand Rapids	AHL	3	0	0	0	0	....	....	....	....	....
2012-13	Grand Rapids	AHL	68	10	21	31	34	21	3	7	10	12

ALT, Mark (AHLT, MAHRK) PHI

Defense. Shoots right. 6'4", 200 lbs. Born, Kansas City, MO, October 18, 1991.
(Carolina's 3rd choice, 53rd overall, in 2010 Entry Draft).

			Regular Season					Playoffs				
Season	Club	League	GP	G	A	Pts	PIM	GP	G	A	Pts	PIM
2007-08	Cretin-Derham	High-MN	17	1	5	6	4	....	....	....	....	....
2008-09	Cretin-Derham	High-MN	26	11	16	27	10	....	....	....	....	....
2009-10	Cretin-Derham	High-MN	24	6	14	20	....	....	....	....	....	....
	Team Northeast	UMHSEL	24	13	9	22	....	....	....	....	....	....
2010-11	U. of Minnesota	WCHA	35	2	8	10	22	....	....	....	....	....
2011-12	U. of Minnesota	WCHA	43	5	17	22	43	....	....	....	....	....
2012-13	U. of Minnesota	WCHA	39	0	7	7	20	....	....	....	....	....
	Adirondack	AHL	6	1	1	2	2	....	....	....	....	....

Traded to **Philadelphia** by **Carolina** with Brian Boucher for Luke Pither, January 13, 2013.

AMBROZ, Seth (AM-brohz, SEHTH) CBJ

Right wing. Shoots right. 6'2", 211 lbs. Born, New Prague, MN, April 3, 1993.
(Columbus' 4th choice, 128th overall, in 2011 Entry Draft).

			Regular Season					Playoffs				
Season	Club	League	GP	G	A	Pts	PIM	GP	G	A	Pts	PIM
2007-08	New Prague	High-MN	22	36	32	68	....	....	....	....	....	....
2008-09	Omaha Lancers	USHL	60	14	17	31	88	3	0	0	0	2
2009-10	Omaha Lancers	USHL	56	22	27	49	118	8	4	2	6	8
2010-11	Omaha Lancers	USHL	56	24	22	46	89	3	2	0	2	4
2011-12	U. of Minnesota	WCHA	41	5	3	8	53	....	....	....	....	....
2012-13	U. of Minnesota	WCHA	38	9	7	16	22	....	....	....	....	....

AMOROSA, Terrance (a-moh-ROH-suh, TAIR-uhns) PHI

Defense. Shoots left. 6'1", 185 lbs. Born, Kirkland, Que., November 13, 1994.
(Philadelphia's 4th choice, 132nd overall, in 2013 Entry Draft).

			Regular Season					Playoffs				
Season	Club	League	GP	G	A	Pts	PIM	GP	G	A	Pts	PIM
2010-11	West Island Royals	Minor-QU	31	5	15	20	6	....	....	....	....	....
2011-12	Holderness School	High-NH	29	6	9	15	....	....	....	....	....	....
2012-13	Holderness School	High-NH	27	9	13	22	....	....	....	....	....	....

• Signed Letter of Intent to attend **University of New Hampshire** (Hockey East) in fall of 2014.

ANDERSON, Josh (AN-duhr-suhn, JAWSH) CBJ

Right wing. Shoots right. 6'2", 189 lbs. Born, Burlington, Ont., May 7, 1994.
(Columbus' 4th choice, 95th overall, in 2012 Entry Draft).

			Regular Season					Playoffs				
Season	Club	League	GP	G	A	Pts	PIM	GP	G	A	Pts	PIM
2010-11	Burlington Eagles	Minor-ON	58	41	35	76	....	....	....	....	....	....
	Burlington	ON-Jr.A	4	0	2	2	0	1	0	0	0	0
2011-12	London Knights	OHL	64	12	10	22	34	19	2	3	5	4
2012-13	London Knights	OHL	68	23	26	49	77	19	1	2	3	23

ANDERSSON, Calle (AN-duhr-suhn, KAHL-leh) NYR

Defense. Shoots right. 6'2", 211 lbs. Born, Malmo, Sweden, May 16, 1994.
(NY Rangers' 3rd choice, 119th overall, in 2012 Entry Draft).

			Regular Season					Playoffs				
Season	Club	League	GP	G	A	Pts	PIM	GP	G	A	Pts	PIM
2009-10	Malmo U18	Swe-U18	29	1	2	3	34	....	....	....	....	....
2010-11	Malmo U18	Swe-U18	21	2	5	7	38	....	....	....	....	....
	Malmo Jr.	Swe-Jr.	25	2	4	6	24	....	....	....	....	....
2011-12	Farjestad U18	Swe-U18	10	3	6	9	0	1	0	1	1	2
	Farjestad Jr.	Swe-Jr.	49	12	24	36	56	6	2	3	5	2
2012-13	Malmo	Sweden-2	9	0	2	2	4	....	....	....	....	....
	Farjestad	Sweden	34	1	1	2	6	....	....	....	....	....
	Farjestad Jr.	Swe-Jr.	22	11	16	27	14	4	1	0	1	4

ANDERSSON, Peter (AN-duhr-suhn, PEE-tuhr) VAN

Defense. Shoots left. 6'3", 194 lbs. Born, Kvidinge, Sweden, April 13, 1991.
(Vancouver's 5th choice, 143rd overall, in 2009 Entry Draft).

			Regular Season					Playoffs				
Season	Club	League	GP	G	A	Pts	PIM	GP	G	A	Pts	PIM
2007-08	Frolunda U18	Swe-U18	12	2	3	5	18	5	0	1	1	14
	Frolunda Jr.	Swe-Jr.	8	0	2	2	4	1	0	0	0	0
	Frolunda	Sweden	1	0	0	0	0	....	....	....	....	....
2008-09	Frolunda U18	Swe-U18	5	0	1	1	4	5	1	1	2	2
	Frolunda Jr.	Swe-Jr.	36	3	5	8	42	4	0	1	1	0
2009-10	Frolunda Jr.	Swe-Jr.	1	1	0	1	0	....	....	....	....	....
	Frolunda	Sweden	21	1	4	5	4	....	....	....	....	....
	Boras HC	Sweden-2	10	2	4	6	12	....	....	....	....	....
2010-11	Frolunda	Sweden	27	0	0	0	8	....	....	....	....	....
	Boras HC	Sweden-2	30	2	2	4	24	....	....	....	....	....
	Frolunda Jr.	Swe-Jr.	....	....	....	....	....	7	1	3	4	2
2011-12	Orebro HK	Sweden-2	40	7	2	9	20	....	....	....	....	....
2012-13	Chicago Wolves	AHL	42	1	7	8	16	....	....	....	....	....

ANDREOFF, Andy (an-DRAY-awf, AN-dee) L.A.

Left wing. Shoots left. 6'1", 201 lbs. Born, Pickering, Ont., May 17, 1991.
(Los Angeles' 2nd choice, 80th overall, in 2011 Entry Draft).

			Regular Season					Playoffs				
Season	Club	League	GP	G	A	Pts	PIM	GP	G	A	Pts	PIM
2006-07	Ajax Pickering	Minor-ON	48	17	21	38	58	....	....	....	....	....
2007-08	Pickering Panthers	ON-Jr.A	40	12	15	27	58	....	....	....	....	....
	Oshawa Generals	OHL	25	0	1	1	8	9	0	0	0	2
2008-09	Oshawa Generals	OHL	66	11	14	25	37	....	....	....	....	....
2009-10	Oshawa Generals	OHL	67	15	33	48	70	....	....	....	....	....
2010-11	Oshawa Generals	OHL	66	33	42	75	109	10	3	8	11	16
2011-12	Oshawa Generals	OHL	57	22	36	58	88	6	1	3	4	4
	Manchester	AHL	5	1	0	1	4	4	2	0	2	2
2012-13	Manchester	AHL	69	13	13	26	111	4	0	3	3	0

ANDRIGHETTO, Sven (an-drih-GEH-toh, SVEHN) MTL

Right wing. Shoots left. 5'9", 182 lbs. Born, Zurich, Switz., March 21, 1993.
(Montreal's 6th choice, 86th overall, in 2013 Entry Draft).

			Regular Season					Playoffs				
Season	Club	League	GP	G	A	Pts	PIM	GP	G	A	Pts	PIM
2007-08	Zurich II U17	Swiss-U17	17	10	13	23	26	....	....	....	....	....
	Zurich U17	Swiss-U17	1	0	0	0	0	....	....	....	....	....
2008-09	Zurich U17	Swiss-U17	28	14	11	25	40	10	3	2	5	8
	EHC Dubendorf Jr.	Swiss-Jr.	4	1	4	5	0	....	....	....	....	....
2009-10	Zurich U17	Swiss-U17	22	24	31	55	14	10	16	8	24	18
	GCK Zurich Jr.	Swiss-Jr.	14	3	4	7	4	....	....	....	....	....
2010-11	GCK Lions Zurich	Swiss-2	36	11	12	23	20	....	....	....	....	....
	EHC Visp	Swiss-2	2	0	0	0	0	17	1	2	3	12
2011-12	Rouyn-Noranda	QMJHL	62	36	38	74	50	4	0	2	2	4
2012-13	Rouyn-Noranda	QMJHL	53	31	67	98	45	14	8	22	30	14

ANDRONOV, Sergei (an-DROH-nahv, SAIR-gay) **ST.L.**

Right wing. Shoots left. 6'2", 190 lbs. Born, Penza, USSR, July 19, 1989.
(St. Louis' 3rd choice, 78th overall, in 2009 Entry Draft).

			Regular Season					Playoffs				
Season	Club	League	GP	G	A	Pts	PIM	GP	G	A	Pts	PIM
2006-07	Lada Togliatti	Russia	3	0	0	0	2	....	....	....	....	....
2007-08	Lada Togliatti 2	Russia-3	16	10	2	12	16	8	7	2	9	0
	Lada Togliatti	Russia	38	2	5	7	2	4	1	0	1	6
2008-09	Lada Togliatti 2	Russia-3	7	5	2	7	6	3	0	2	2	32
	Lada Togliatti	KHL	47	9	5	14	22	5	0	1	1	8
2009-10	Lada Togliatti	KHL	33	5	9	14	20	....	....	....	....	....
	CSKA Moscow	KHL	19	5	3	8	6	3	0	0	0	0
2010-11	CSKA Moscow	KHL	53	5	2	7	14	....	....	....	....	....
	CSKA Jr.	Russia-Jr.	7	3	2	5	29	16	6	5	11	4
2011-12	CSKA Moscow	KHL	29	1	3	4	4	5	1	0	1	0
2012-13	Peoria Rivermen	AHL	59	8	11	19	32	....	....	....	....	....

ANTHONY, Steven (AN-thuh-nee, STEE-vehn) **VAN**

Left wing. Shoots left. 6'2", 195 lbs. Born, Halifax, N.S., March 21, 1991.
(Vancouver's 7th choice, 187th overall, in 2009 Entry Draft).

			Regular Season					Playoffs				
Season	Club	League	GP	G	A	Pts	PIM	GP	G	A	Pts	PIM
2006-07	Dartmouth	NSMHL	35	33	31	64	78	9	8	16	24	10
2007-08	Saint John	QMJHL	55	6	8	14	38	10	1	1	2	2
2008-09	Saint John	QMJHL	67	19	29	48	47	4	1	2	3	4
2009-10	Saint John	QMJHL	61	18	23	41	28	5	0	0	0	6
2010-11	Saint John	QMJHL	61	23	37	60	23	14	5	7	12	12
2011-12	Kalamazoo Wings	ECHL	34	8	12	20	28	....	....	....	....	....
2012-13	Kalamazoo Wings	ECHL	41	3	8	11	10	....	....	....	....	....

ARCHAMBAULT, Olivier (AHR-sham-boh, oh-lih-VEE-ay)

Left wing. Shoots left. 5'11", 184 lbs. Born, Le Gardeur, Que., February 16, 1993.
(Montreal's 7th choice, 108th overall, in 2011 Entry Draft).

			Regular Season					Playoffs				
Season	Club	League	GP	G	A	Pts	PIM	GP	G	A	Pts	PIM
2008-09	Esther-Blondin	QAAA	45	16	33	49	32	15	8	7	15	12
2009-10	Val-d'Or Foreurs	QMJHL	58	12	15	27	14	4	0	0	0	0
2010-11	Val-d'Or Foreurs	QMJHL	65	20	33	53	28	4	1	2	3	4
2011-12	Drummondville	QMJHL	45	17	22	39	24	4	1	2	3	0
2012-13	Drummondville	QMJHL	64	32	34	66	56	5	2	4	6	6
	Hamilton Bulldogs	AHL	10	1	1	2	10	....	....	....	....	....

ARCHIBALD, Darren (ahr-CHIH-bawld, DAIR-ehn) **VAN**

Left wing. Shoots left. 6'3", 210 lbs. Born, Newmarket, Ont., February 9, 1990.

			Regular Season					Playoffs				
Season	Club	League	GP	G	A	Pts	PIM	GP	G	A	Pts	PIM
2007-08	Stouffville Spirit	ON-Jr.A	49	21	27	48	46	15	9	9	18	35
2008-09	Barrie Colts	OHL	68	25	24	49	35	5	4	3	7	2
2009-10	Barrie Colts	OHL	57	26	33	59	62	16	5	5	10	16
2010-11	Barrie Colts	OHL	24	18	12	30	21	....	....	....	....	....
	Niagara Ice Dogs	OHL	37	23	13	36	30	14	10	4	14	6
2011-12	Chicago Wolves	AHL	20	1	0	1	10	....	....	....	....	....
	Kalamazoo Wings	ECHL	49	14	31	45	59	14	2	4	6	21
2012-13	Chicago Wolves	AHL	55	12	10	22	47	....	....	....	....	....
	Kalamazoo Wings	ECHL	18	6	7	13	29	....	....	....	....	....

Signed as a free agent by **Vancouver**, December 13, 2010.

ARCHIBALD, Josh (AHR-chih-bawld, JAWSH) **PIT**

Wing. Shoots right. 5'10", 181 lbs. Born, Regina, Sask., October 6, 1992.
(Pittsburgh's 4th choice, 174th overall, in 2011 Entry Draft).

			Regular Season					Playoffs				
Season	Club	League	GP	G	A	Pts	PIM	GP	G	A	Pts	PIM
2009-10	Brainerd	High-MN	25	20	30	50	72	2	2	5	7	2
2010-11	Team North	UMHSEL	21	8	7	15	49	3	0	2	2	6
	Brainerd	High-MN	25	27	46	73	40	2	3	2	5	0
2011-12	Nebraska-Omaha	WCHA	36	10	5	15	33	....	....	....	....	....
2012-13	Nebraska-Omaha	WCHA	39	19	17	36	34	....	....	....	....	....

ARMIA, Joel (AHR-mee-uh, JOHL) **BUF**

Right wing. Shoots right. 6'3", 192 lbs. Born, Pori, Finland, May 31, 1993.
(Buffalo's 1st choice, 16th overall, in 2011 Entry Draft).

			Regular Season					Playoffs				
Season	Club	League	GP	G	A	Pts	PIM	GP	G	A	Pts	PIM
2008-09	Assat Pori U18	Fin-U18	8	3	1	4	2	....	....	....	....	....
2009-10	Assat Pori U18	Fin-U18	9	7	9	16	31	6	6	3	9	8
	Assat Pori Jr.	Fin-Jr.	27	15	6	21	32	5	1	1	2	0
2010-11	Suomi U20	Finland-2	4	0	3	3	6	....	....	....	....	....
	Assat Pori	Finland	48	18	11	29	24	5	2	0	2	4
2011-12	Assat Pori	Finland	54	18	20	38	64	3	0	2	2	0
2012-13	Assat Pori	Finland	47	19	14	33	32	16	3	5	8	20

ARNESSON, Linus (AHR-neh-suhn, LEE-nuhs) **BOS**

Defense. Shoots left. 6'2", 187 lbs. Born, Stockholm, Sweden, September 21, 1994.
(Boston's 1st choice, 60th overall, in 2013 Entry Draft).

			Regular Season					Playoffs				
Season	Club	League	GP	G	A	Pts	PIM	GP	G	A	Pts	PIM
2009-10	Djurgarden U18	Swe-U18	22	2	6	8	14	....	....	....	....	....
2010-11	Djurgarden U18	Swe-U18	21	2	6	8	12	5	1	1	2	0
	Djurgarden Jr.	Swe-Jr.	8	0	0	0	2	....	....	....	....	....
2011-12	Djurgarden U18	Swe-U18	9	0	3	3	8	4	0	2	2	2
	Djurgarden Jr.	Swe-Jr.	40	2	13	15	20	3	0	1	1	2
	Djurgarden	Sweden	3	0	0	0	0	....	....	....	....	....
2012-13	Djurgarden Jr.	Swe-Jr.	13	1	3	4	22	1	0	0	0	0
	Djurgarden	Sweden-2	35	0	1	1	8	....	....	....	....	....

ARNOLD, Bill (AHR-nohld, BIHL) **CGY**

Center. Shoots right. 6', 215 lbs. Born, Boston, MA, May 13, 1992.
(Calgary's 4th choice, 108th overall, in 2010 Entry Draft).

			Regular Season					Playoffs				
Season	Club	League	GP	G	A	Pts	PIM	GP	G	A	Pts	PIM
2008-09	Nobles	High-MA	29	28	27	55	....	....	....	....	....	....
	Bos. Little Bruins	Minor-MA	33	26	21	47	24	....	....	....	....	....
2009-10	USNTDP	USHL	26	8	15	23	20	....	....	....	....	....
	USNTDP	U-18	38	12	16	28	30	....	....	....	....	....
2010-11	Boston College	H-East	39	10	10	20	38	....	....	....	....	....
2011-12	Boston College	H-East	42	17	19	36	46	....	....	....	....	....
2012-13	Boston College	H-East	38	17	18	35	40	....	....	....	....	....

Hockey East All-Rookie Team (2011)

ARONSON, Taylor (AIR-uhn-suhn, TAY-luhr) **NSH**

Defense. Shoots right. 6'1", 184 lbs. Born, Placentia, CA, December 30, 1991.
(Nashville's 2nd choice, 78th overall, in 2010 Entry Draft).

			Regular Season					Playoffs				
Season	Club	League	GP	G	A	Pts	PIM	GP	G	A	Pts	PIM
2008-09	L.A. Jr. Kings	T1EHL	45	9	16	25	68	....	....	....	....	....
2009-10	Portland	WHL	71	5	25	30	65	11	2	7	9	13
2010-11	Portland	WHL	71	5	32	37	81	21	0	2	2	20
2011-12	Milwaukee	AHL	14	0	1	1	8	....	....	....	....	....
	Cincinnati	ECHL	40	6	12	18	49	....	....	....	....	....
2012-13	Milwaukee	AHL	12	0	2	2	4	....	....	....	....	....
	Cincinnati	ECHL	38	1	12	13	12	2	0	0	0	0

ATHANASIOU, Andreas (ath-an-AYZH-yew, an–DRAY-uhs) **DET**

Center/Left wing. Shoots left. 6', 177 lbs. Born, London, Ont., August 6, 1994.
(Detroit's 3rd choice, 110th overall, in 2012 Entry Draft).

			Regular Season					Playoffs				
Season	Club	League	GP	G	A	Pts	PIM	GP	G	A	Pts	PIM
2009-10	Toronto Titans	GTHL	56	24	34	58	32	....	....	....	....	....
2010-11	London Knights	OHL	57	11	11	22	21	6	0	0	0	0
2011-12	London Knights	OHL	63	22	15	37	22	11	1	4	5	0
2012-13	Barrie Colts	OHL	66	29	38	67	30	22	12	13	25	11

AUBRY, Louis-Marc (AW-bree, LOO-ee-MAHRK) **DET**

Center. Shoots left. 6'4", 205 lbs. Born, Arthabaska, Que., November 11, 1991.
(Detroit's 3rd choice, 81st overall, in 2010 Entry Draft).

			Regular Season					Playoffs				
Season	Club	League	GP	G	A	Pts	PIM	GP	G	A	Pts	PIM
2007-08	Trois-Rivieres	QAAA	20	9	20	29	30	7	1	1	2	20
2008-09	Montreal	QMJHL	65	10	12	22	53	10	2	2	4	8
2009-10	Montreal	QMJHL	66	15	18	33	69	7	1	1	2	6
2010-11	Montreal	QMJHL	35	13	12	25	26	10	5	1	6	2
2011-12	Grand Rapids	AHL	62	5	11	16	39	....	....	....	....	....
2012-13	Grand Rapids	AHL	64	4	8	12	60	14	0	1	1	0

AUGER, Justin (AW-guhr, JUHS-tihn) **L.A.**

Right wing. Shoots right. 6'7", 215 lbs. Born, Kitchener, Ont., May 14, 1994.
(Los Angeles' 2nd choice, 103rd overall, in 2013 Entry Draft).

			Regular Season					Playoffs				
Season	Club	League	GP	G	A	Pts	PIM	GP	G	A	Pts	PIM
2010-11	Waterloo Siskins	ON-Jr.B	42	22	15	37	57	4	2	5	7	2
2011-12	Guelph Storm	OHL	58	7	7	14	39	6	0	0	0	0
2012-13	Guelph Storm	OHL	68	16	17	33	39	5	0	0	0	0

AUSMUS, Gage (AWZ-muhs, GAYJ) **S.J.**

Defense. Shoots left. 6'1", 210 lbs. Born, Billings, MT, April 22, 1995.
(San Jose's 5th choice, 151st overall, in 2013 Entry Draft).

			Regular Season					Playoffs				
Season	Club	League	GP	G	A	Pts	PIM	GP	G	A	Pts	PIM
2010-11	Team Great Plains	UMHSEL	14	2	0	2	10	1	0	0	0	0
	E. Grand Forks	High-MN	17	4	8	12	10	....	....	....	....	....
2011-12	USNTDP	USHL	36	2	3	5	42	1	0	0	0	0
	USNTDP	U-17	17	0	1	1	18	....	....	....	....	....
2012-13	USNTDP	USHL	26	2	5	7	20	....	....	....	....	....
	USNTDP	U-18	40	0	7	7	34	....	....	....	....	....

• Signed Letter of Intent to attend **University of North Dakota** (WCHA) in fall of 2013.

AUSTIN, Brady (AWZ-tihn, BRAY-dee) **BUF**

Defense. Shoots left. 6'3", 232 lbs. Born, Lindsay, Ont., June 16, 1993.
(Buffalo's 7th choice, 193rd overall, in 2012 Entry Draft).

			Regular Season					Playoffs				
Season	Club	League	GP	G	A	Pts	PIM	GP	G	A	Pts	PIM
2008-09	Cent. Ont. Wolves	Minor-ON	60	25	27	52	72	....	....	....	....	....
2009-10	Erie Otters	OHL	64	5	10	15	24	4	0	0	0	0
2010-11	Erie Otters	OHL	59	1	12	13	47	7	0	0	0	0
2011-12	Belleville Bulls	OHL	68	6	20	26	59	6	1	0	1	0
2012-13	Belleville Bulls	OHL	64	8	15	23	22	17	0	5	5	6

AZEVEDO, Justin (a-zeh-VAY-doh, JUHS-tihn) **L.A.**

Center. Shoots right. 5'7", 172 lbs. Born, West Lorne, Ont., April 1, 1988.
(Los Angeles' 8th choice, 153rd overall, in 2008 Entry Draft).

			Regular Season					Playoffs				
Season	Club	League	GP	G	A	Pts	PIM	GP	G	A	Pts	PIM
2004-05	Kitchener Rangers	OHL	58	18	21	39	34	15	3	1	4	14
2005-06	Kitchener Rangers	OHL	60	29	40	69	80	5	0	3	3	12
2006-07	Kitchener Rangers	OHL	50	17	39	56	42	9	4	11	15	22
2007-08	Kitchener Rangers	OHL	67	43	*81	*124	69	20	10	*26	*36	33
2008-09	Manchester	AHL	49	12	24	36	31	....	....	....	....	....
2009-10	Manchester	AHL	46	14	13	27	31	16	3	6	9	12
2010-11	Manchester	AHL	79	18	35	53	71	7	3	7	10	10
2011-12	Manchester	AHL	63	28	22	50	37	4	1	1	2	4
2012-13	Lukko Rauma	Finland	58	20	38	58	88	14	*10	8	*18	6

OHL First All-Star Team (2008) • Memorial Cup All-Star Team (2008) • Ed Chynoweth Trophy (Memorial Cup - Leading Scorer) (2008) • Canadian Major Junior First All-Star Team (2008) • Canadian Major Junior Player of the Year (2008)

Signed as a free agent by **Rauma** (Finland), June 7, 2012.

BACKMAN, Mattias (BAK-man, mah-TIGH-uhs) DET

Defense. Shoots left. 6'2", 169 lbs. Born, Linkoping, Sweden, October 3, 1992.
(Detroit's 7th choice, 146th overall, in 2011 Entry Draft).

			Regular Season					Playoffs				
Season	Club	League	GP	G	A	Pts	PIM	GP	G	A	Pts	PIM
2007-08	Linkopings HC U18	Swe-U18	21	0	2	2	14	....	....	....	....	....
2008-09	Linkopings HC U18	Swe-U18	30	5	8	13	16	1	0	1	1	0
	Linkopings HC Jr.	Swe-Jr.	2	0	0	0	2	....	....	....	....	....
2009-10	Linkopings HC	Sweden	5	0	0	0	2	....	....	....	....	....
	Linkopings HC U18	Swe-U18	2	2	1	3	4	3	0	0	0	2
	Linkopings HC Jr.	Swe-Jr.	33	4	5	9	38	6	1	0	1	10
	Linkopings HC	Sweden	5	0	0	0	2	....	....	....	....	....
2010-11	Linkopings HC Jr.	Swe-Jr.	27	2	18	20	34	3	0	2	2	4
	Linkopings HC	Sweden	6	0	0	0	4	....	....	....	....	....
	Mjolby HC	Sweden-3	2	1	2	3	2	....	....	....	....	....
2011-12	Linkopings HC	Sweden	42	1	7	8	14	....	....	....	....	....
	Linkopings HC Jr.	Swe-Jr.	6	1	1	2	0	6	2	6	8	4
2012-13	Linkopings HC	Sweden	52	2	24	26	34	10	2	4	6	4

BACKMAN, Sean (BAK-man, SHAWN)

Right wing. Shoots right. 5'9", 170 lbs. Born, Cos Cob, CT, April 29, 1986.

			Regular Season					Playoffs				
Season	Club	League	GP	G	A	Pts	PIM	GP	G	A	Pts	PIM
2006-07	Yale	ECAC	29	18	13	31	38	....	....	....	....	....
2007-08	Yale	ECAC	32	18	9	27	16	....	....	....	....	....
2008-09	Yale	ECAC	32	20	13	33	44	....	....	....	....	....
2009-10	Yale	ECAC	29	21	14	35	12	....	....	....	....	....
2010-11	Texas Stars	AHL	67	7	16	23	20	6	0	0	0	6
	Idaho Steelheads	ECHL	5	2	2	4	4	....	....	....	....	....
2011-12	Bridgeport	AHL	66	7	11	18	20	3	0	0	0	0
2012-13	Bridgeport	AHL	67	11	10	21	40	....	....	....	....	....

ECAC Second All-Star Team (2009) • ECAC First All-Star Team (2010) • NCAA East Second All-American Team (2010)

Signed as a free agent by **Dallas**, March 30, 2010. Signed as a free agent by **NY Islanders**, August 8, 2011.

BAILEY, Justin (BAY-lee, JUHS-tihn) BUF

Right wing. Shoots right. 6'3", 188 lbs. Born, Buffalo, NY, July 1, 1995.
(Buffalo's 5th choice, 52nd overall, in 2013 Entry Draft).

			Regular Season					Playoffs				
Season	Club	League	GP	G	A	Pts	PIM	GP	G	A	Pts	PIM
2010-11	Buffalo Regals	T1EHL	12	4	1	5	0	....	....	....	....	....
	Buffalo Regals	Minor-NY	10	5	12	17	12	....	....	....	....	....
2011-12	Long Island Royals	AYHL	22	21	13	34	52	....	....	....	....	....
	Indiana Ice	USHL	2	1	0	1	0	....	....	....	....	....
2012-13	Kitchener Rangers	OHL	57	17	19	36	34	10	1	2	3	4

BAILLARGEON, Robert (ba-LAIR-zhee-awn, RAW-buhrt) OTT

Center. Shoots right. 6', 175 lbs. Born, Springfield, MA, November 26, 1993.
(Ottawa's 5th choice, 136th overall, in 2012 Entry Draft).

			Regular Season					Playoffs				
Season	Club	League	GP	G	A	Pts	PIM	GP	G	A	Pts	PIM
2009-10	Cushing	High-MA	32	15	30	45	....	....	....	....	....	....
2010-11	Cushing	High-MA	32	30	34	64	....	....	....	....	....	....
2011-12	Indiana Ice	USHL	54	14	34	48	36	6	4	2	6	2
2012-13	Indiana Ice	USHL	25	6	9	15	30	....	....	....	....	....
	Omaha Lancers	USHL	30	12	14	26	18	....	....	....	....	....

• Signed Letter of Intent to attend **Boston University** (Hockey East) in fall of 2013.

BALISY, Chase (BAL-ih-see, CHAYS) NSH

Center. Shoots left. 5'10", 178 lbs. Born, Fullerton, CA, February 2, 1992.
(Nashville's 6th choice, 170th overall, in 2011 Entry Draft).

			Regular Season					Playoffs				
Season	Club	League	GP	G	A	Pts	PIM	GP	G	A	Pts	PIM
2007-08	Tor. Jr. Canadiens	GTHL	80	40	110	150	....	....	....	....	....	....
2008-09	USNTDP	NAHL	42	8	14	22	8	9	0	3	3	0
	USNTDP	U-17	16	4	10	14	6	....	....	....	....	....
2009-10	USNTDP	U-17	2	0	1	1	2	....	....	....	....	....
	USNTDP	USHL	28	5	6	11	8	....	....	....	....	....
	USNTDP	U-18	35	4	10	14	6	....	....	....	....	....
2010-11	Western Mich.	CCHA	42	12	18	30	12	....	....	....	....	....
2011-12	Western Mich.	CCHA	41	13	24	37	35	....	....	....	....	....
2012-13	Western Mich.	CCHA	38	11	14	25	12	....	....	....	....	....

CCHA All-Rookie Team (2011)

BAPTISTE, Nicholas (Bap-TEEST, NIH-koh-las) BUF

Right wing. Shoots right. 6', 191 lbs. Born, Ottawa, Ont., August 4, 1995.
(Buffalo's 6th choice, 69th overall, in 2013 Entry Draft).

			Regular Season					Playoffs				
Season	Club	League	GP	G	A	Pts	PIM	GP	G	A	Pts	PIM
2010-11	Ott. Senators M.M.	Minor-ON	24	22	33	55	26	....	....	....	....	....
	Ott. Senators M.M.	Exhib.	18	17	15	32	12	....	....	....	....	....
	Cumberland	ON-Jr.A	2	1	0	1	0	....	....	....	....	....
2011-12	Sudbury Wolves	OHL	64	8	19	27	42	4	0	0	0	2
2012-13	Sudbury Wolves	OHL	66	21	27	48	44	9	3	1	4	6

BARBER, Riley (BAHR-buhr, RIGH-lee) WSH

Right wing. Shoots right. 6', 194 lbs. Born, Livonia, MI, February 7, 1994.
(Washington's 7th choice, 167th overall, in 2012 Entry Draft).

			Regular Season					Playoffs				
Season	Club	League	GP	G	A	Pts	PIM	GP	G	A	Pts	PIM
2009-10	Det. Compuware	T1EHL	38	16	22	38	28	5	2	3	5	0
	Det. Compuware	Exhib.	6	1	4	5	8	....	....	....	....	....
2010-11	Dubuque	USHL	57	14	14	28	48	11	2	0	2	6
2011-12	USNTDP	USHL	24	5	6	11	59	....	....	....	....	....
	USNTDP	U-18	36	16	9	25	26	....	....	....	....	....
2012-13	Miami U.	CCHA	40	15	24	39	22	....	....	....	....	....

CCHA All-Rookie Team (2013) • CCHA Rookie of the Year (2013) • CCHA First All-Star Team (2013)

BARKOV, Aleksander (bar-KAWV, al-ehx-AN-duhr) FLA

Center. Shoots left. 6'3", 209 lbs. Born, Tampere, Finland, September 2, 1995.
(Florida's 1st choice, 2nd overall, in 2013 Entry Draft).

			Regular Season					Playoffs				
Season	Club	League	GP	G	A	Pts	PIM	GP	G	A	Pts	PIM
2010-11	Tappara U18	Fin-U18	11	7	8	15	8	2	3	0	3	0
	Tappara Jr.	Fin-Jr.	25	5	12	17	6	....	....	....	....	....
2011-12	Tappara Jr.	Fin-Jr.	5	2	3	5	2	....	....	....	....	....
	Tappara Tampere	Finland	32	7	9	16	4	....	....	....	....	....
2012-13	Tappara Tampere	Finland	53	21	27	48	8	5	0	5	5	2

BASARABA, Joe (ba-za-RA-bah, JOH) FLA

Right wing. Shoots right. 6'2", 195 lbs. Born, Fort Frances, Ont., May 2, 1992.
(Florida's 7th choice, 69th overall, in 2010 Entry Draft).

			Regular Season					Playoffs				
Season	Club	League	GP	G	A	Pts	PIM	GP	G	A	Pts	PIM
2008-09	Shat.-St. Mary's	High-MN	54	20	24	44	54	....	....	....	....	....
2009-10	Shat.-St. Mary's	High-MN	52	24	22	46	39	....	....	....	....	....
2010-11	U. Minn-Duluth	WCHA	36	3	2	5	20	....	....	....	....	....
2011-12	U. Minn-Duluth	WCHA	40	7	9	16	58	....	....	....	....	....
2012-13	U. Minn-Duluth	WCHA	37	10	7	17	40	....	....	....	....	....

BASHKIROV, Ruslan (bash-KIHR-ahv, roos-LAHN) OTT

Left wing. Shoots left. 5'11", 193 lbs. Born, Moscow, USSR, March 7, 1989.
(Ottawa's 2nd choice, 60th overall, in 2007 Entry Draft).

			Regular Season					Playoffs				
Season	Club	League	GP	G	A	Pts	PIM	GP	G	A	Pts	PIM
2005-06	Spartak Moscow 2	Russia-3	35	16	9	25	44	....	....	....	....	....
2006-07	Quebec Remparts	QMJHL	64	30	37	67	117	5	1	3	4	6
2007-08	Mytischi	Russia	4	0	0	0	0	....	....	....	....	....
	Kristall Elektrostal	Russia-2	12	4	0	4	22	....	....	....	....	....
2008-09	Lada Togliatti	KHL	2	0	0	0	2	....	....	....	....	....
	Rys Podolsk	Russia-2	48	9	8	17	20	3	1	3	4	2
2009-10	Perm	Russia-2	37	10	8	18	12	10	2	3	5	4
2010-11	Perm	Russia-2	8	1	0	1	2	....	....	....	....	....
	HK Ryazan	Russia-2	28	8	10	18	18	3	0	0	0	12
2011-12	HK Ryazan	Russia-2	20	5	5	10	14	....	....	....	....	....
2012-13	HK Ryazan	Russia-2	17	7	1	8	4	....	....	....	....	....

BEACH, Cody (BEECH, KOH-dee) ST.L.

Right wing. Shoots right. 6'5", 190 lbs. Born, Nanaimo, B.C., August 8, 1992.
(St. Louis' 6th choice, 134th overall, in 2010 Entry Draft).

			Regular Season					Playoffs				
Season	Club	League	GP	G	A	Pts	PIM	GP	G	A	Pts	PIM
2007-08	Okanagan Rockets	BCMML	37	8	17	25	68	6	1	3	4	16
2008-09	Calgary Hitmen	WHL	3	0	0	0	2	....	....	....	....	....
	Okanagan Rockets	BCMML	23	10	13	23	58	2	1	0	1	2
2009-10	Calgary Hitmen	WHL	51	3	11	14	157	19	1	7	8	34
2010-11	Calgary Hitmen	WHL	17	5	10	15	73	....	....	....	....	....
	Moose Jaw	WHL	40	6	28	34	163	....	....	....	....	....
2011-12	Moose Jaw	WHL	58	15	41	56	*229	13	4	6	10	29
2012-13	Peoria Rivermen	AHL	23	2	5	7	71	....	....	....	....	....
	Evansville IceMen	ECHL	24	2	7	9	81	....	....	....	....	....

BEACH, Kyle (BEECH, KIGH-uhl) CHI

Center. Shoots right. 6'3", 208 lbs. Born, Vancouver, B.C., January 13, 1990.
(Chicago's 1st choice, 11th overall, in 2008 Entry Draft).

			Regular Season					Playoffs				
Season	Club	League	GP	G	A	Pts	PIM	GP	G	A	Pts	PIM
2005-06	Okanagan Rockets	BCMML	25	23	18	41	220	....	....	....	....	....
	Everett Silvertips	WHL	4	2	1	3	4	9	1	3	4	31
2006-07	Everett Silvertips	WHL	65	29	32	61	196	11	5	6	11	19
2007-08	Everett Silvertips	WHL	60	27	33	60	222	4	0	0	0	4
2008-09	Everett Silvertips	WHL	30	9	21	30	106	....	....	....	....	....
	Lethbridge	WHL	24	15	18	33	59	10	1	1	2	31
	Rockford IceHogs	AHL	2	0	0	0	15	1	0	0	0	0
2009-10	Spokane Chiefs	WHL	68	*52	34	86	186	7	7	2	9	19
	Rockford IceHogs	AHL	4	0	0	0	0	4	3	0	3	6
2010-11	Rockford IceHogs	AHL	71	16	20	36	163	....	....	....	....	....
2011-12	Rockford IceHogs	AHL	19	5	5	10	30	....	....	....	....	....
2012-13	Rockford IceHogs	AHL	66	16	10	26	204	....	....	....	....	....

WHL Rookie of the Year (2007) • WHL West First All-Star Team (2010)

BEATTIE, Matthew (BAY-tee, MA-thew) VAN

Left wing. Shoots right. 6'3", 190 lbs. Born, Morristown, NJ, December 14, 1992.
(Vancouver's 5th choice, 207th overall, in 2012 Entry Draft).

			Regular Season					Playoffs				
Season	Club	League	GP	G	A	Pts	PIM	GP	G	A	Pts	PIM
2008-09	N.J. Rockets	AYHL	29	4	7	11	12	....	....	....	....	....
2009-10	Pingry Big Blue	High-NJ	25	33	34	67	10	....	....	....	....	....
	N.J. Renegades	MtJHL	38	4	10	14	60	4	2	0	2	0
2010-11	Pingry Big Blue	High-NJ	25	40	54	94	10	....	....	....	....	....
	N.J. Jr. Titans	MtJHL	38	23	24	47	34	2	2	0	2	0
2011-12	Exeter	High-NH	28	39	34	73	18	....	....	....	....	....
2012-13	Yale	ECAC	15	0	0	0	8	....	....	....	....	....

BEAUDOIN, Matt (boh-DWEH, MAT) **CHI**

Right wing. Shoots right. 5'11", 190 lbs. Born, Rock Forest, Que., April 6, 1984.

			Regular Season					Playoffs				
Season	Club	League	GP	G	A	Pts	PIM	GP	G	A	Pts	PIM
2003-04	Ohio State	CCHA	40	7	7	14	26	....	....	....	....	....
2004-05	Ohio State	CCHA	40	23	11	34	50	....	....	....	....	....
2005-06	Ohio State	CCHA	32	8	8	16	18	....	....	....	....	....
2006-07	Ohio State	CCHA	37	14	11	25	24	....	....	....	....	....
2007-08	Iowa Stars	AHL	3	0	0	0	0	....	....	....	....	....
	Rochester	AHL	1	0	0	0	0	....	....	....	....	....
	Hershey Bears	AHL	7	0	0	0	0	1	0	0	0	0
	Las Vegas	ECHL	1	0	1	1	0	....	....	....	....	....
	Dayton Bombers	ECHL	61	38	30	68	44	2	0	0	0	0
2008-09	San Antonio	AHL	1	0	1	1	2	....	....	....	....	....
	Milwaukee	AHL	2	0	0	0	0	....	....	....	....	....
	Houston Aeros	AHL	41	11	8	19	17	20	8	9	17	12
	Las Vegas	ECHL	15	10	6	16	10	....	....	....	....	....
2009-10	Texas Stars	AHL	72	19	25	44	22	22	4	3	7	4
2010-11	San Antonio	AHL	63	21	30	51	24	....	....	....	....	....
2011-12	Portland Pirates	AHL	47	5	17	22	14	....	....	....	....	....
2012-13	Hershey Bears	AHL	32	3	7	10	2	....	....	....	....	....
	Rockford IceHogs	AHL	21	1	3	4	8	....	....	....	....	....

Signed as a free agent by **Phoenix**, July 3, 2010.

BEAUPRE, Gabriel (boh-PRAY, gay-BREE-ehl) **COL**

Defense. Shoots left. 6'2", 180 lbs. Born, Levis, Que., November 23, 1992.
(Colorado's 5th choice, 153rd overall, in 2011 Entry Draft).

			Regular Season					Playoffs				
Season	Club	League	GP	G	A	Pts	PIM	GP	G	A	Pts	PIM
2007-08	Levis	QAAA	45	2	6	8	52	3	0	0	0	6
2008-09	Val-d'Or Foreurs	QMJHL	52	0	3	3	48	....	....	....	....	....
2009-10	Val-d'Or Foreurs	QMJHL	56	2	5	7	94	6	1	1	2	8
2010-11	Val-d'Or Foreurs	QMJHL	66	3	15	18	73	4	0	1	1	4
2011-12	Val-d'Or Foreurs	QMJHL	62	6	15	21	102	4	0	0	0	6
2012-13	Val-d'Or Foreurs	QMJHL	4	0	0	0	6	....	....	....	....	....
	Denver Cutthroats	CHL	28	3	5	8	23	....	....	....	....	....
	Lake Erie Monsters	AHL	43	1	4	5	67	....	....	....	....	....

BEAUVILLIER, Francis (boh-VIHL-yay, FRAN-sihs) **FLA**

Center/Left wing. Shoots left. 6'1", 181 lbs. Born, Sorel-Tracy, Que., October 22, 1993.
(Florida's 4th choice, 174th overall, in 2012 Entry Draft).

			Regular Season					Playoffs				
Season	Club	League	GP	G	A	Pts	PIM	GP	G	A	Pts	PIM
2008-09	Antoine-Girouard	QAAA	44	16	20	36	30	5	1	1	2	2
2009-10	Lewiston	QMJHL	61	12	14	26	46	4	0	0	0	0
2010-11	Lewiston	QMJHL	57	11	14	25	39	3	0	0	0	0
2011-12	Rimouski Oceanic	QMJHL	67	23	11	34	75	21	5	4	9	31
2012-13	Rimouski Oceanic	QMJHL	64	30	32	62	86	6	1	2	3	10
	San Antonio	AHL	8	0	2	2	4	....	....	....	....	....

BELL, Myles (BEHL, MIGH-uhz) **N.J.**

Right wing. Shoots right. 6', 210 lbs. Born, Calgary, Alta., August 19, 1993.
(New Jersey's 4th choice, 160th overall, in 2013 Entry Draft).

			Regular Season					Playoffs				
Season	Club	League	GP	G	A	Pts	PIM	GP	G	A	Pts	PIM
2008-09	Calgary Flames	AMHL	26	3	6	9	65	....	....	....	....	....
	Regina Pats	WHL	8	0	1	1	0	....	....	....	....	....
2009-10	Regina Pats	WHL	61	4	14	18	36	....	....	....	....	....
2010-11	Regina Pats	WHL	66	14	31	45	86	....	....	....	....	....
2011-12	Kelowna Rockets	WHL	54	15	26	41	55	4	1	1	2	0
2012-13	Kelowna Rockets	WHL	69	38	55	93	68	11	5	4	9	8

WHL West Second All-Star Team (2013)

BELOV, Anton (BEE-lawv, AN-tawn) **EDM**

Defense. Shoots left. 6'4", 219 lbs. Born, Ryazan, USSR, July 29, 1986.

			Regular Season					Playoffs				
Season	Club	League	GP	G	A	Pts	PIM	GP	G	A	Pts	PIM
2004-05	CSKA Moscow 2	Russia-3	20	1	7	8	14	....	....	....	....	....
	CSKA Moscow	Russia	31	0	0	0	14	....	....	....	....	....
2005-06	CSKA Moscow 2	Russia-3	6	1	2	3	2	....	....	....	....	....
	CSKA Moscow	Russia	18	0	2	2	35	1	0	0	0	0
2006-07	CSKA Moscow	Russia	49	4	4	8	42	12	1	3	4	8
2007-08	CSKA Moscow	Russia	54	1	4	5	69	6	1	1	2	16
2008-09	Omsk	KHL	38	1	4	5	71	5	1	0	1	4
2009-10	Omsk	KHL	39	1	10	11	48	....	....	....	....	....
2010-11	Omsk	KHL	54	4	12	16	26	8	1	2	3	4
2011-12	Omsk	KHL	50	0	6	6	30	18	1	2	3	12
2012-13	Omsk	KHL	46	9	17	26	30	12	1	3	4	24

Signed as a free agent by **Edmonton**, May 30, 2013.

BENNETT, Mac (BEHN-neht, MAK) **MTL**

Defense. Shoots left. 6', 195 lbs. Born, Narragansett, RI, March 25, 1991.
(Montreal's 3rd choice, 79th overall, in 2009 Entry Draft).

			Regular Season					Playoffs				
Season	Club	League	GP	G	A	Pts	PIM	GP	G	A	Pts	PIM
2006-07	Hotchkiss School	High-CT	25	7	6	13	....	....	....	....	....	....
2007-08	Hotchkiss School	High-CT	25	6	9	15	....	....	....	....	....	....
2008-09	Neponset Valley	Minor-MA	16	5	19	24	....	....	....	....	....	....
	Hotchkiss School	High-CT	15	4	11	15	....	....	....	....	....	....
2009-10	Cedar Rapids	USHL	53	9	15	24	34	2	1	0	1	0
2010-11	U. of Michigan	CCHA	32	2	10	12	21	....	....	....	....	....
2011-12	U. of Michigan	CCHA	41	4	17	21	18	....	....	....	....	....
2012-13	U. of Michigan	CCHA	32	6	12	18	4	....	....	....	....	....

USHL All-Rookie Team (2010)

BENNING, Matthew (BENH-ihng, MA-thew) **BOS**

Defense. Shoots right. 6', 202 lbs. Born, Edmonton, Alta., May 25, 1994.
(Boston's 5th choice, 175th overall, in 2012 Entry Draft).

			Regular Season					Playoffs				
Season	Club	League	GP	G	A	Pts	PIM	GP	G	A	Pts	PIM
2008-09	St. Albert Sabres	AMBHL	33	2	15	17	44	....	....	....	....	....
2009-10	St. Albert Raiders	AMHL	33	7	14	21	32	4	1	0	1	2
2010-11	Spruce Grove	AJHL	43	0	7	7	65	13	0	1	1	20
2011-12	Spruce Grove	AJHL	44	4	14	18	87	11	2	1	3	16
2012-13	Dubuque	USHL	57	10	16	26	73	10	1	1	2	6

• Signed Letter of Intent to attend **Northeastern University** (Hockey East) in fall of 2013.

BERTSCHY, Christoph (BAIRT-chee, KRIHS-tawf) **MIN**

Center. Shoots right. 5'10", 189 lbs. Born, Friburg, Switz., April 5, 1994.
(Minnesota's 6th choice, 158th overall, in 2012 Entry Draft).

			Regular Season					Playoffs				
Season	Club	League	GP	G	A	Pts	PIM	GP	G	A	Pts	PIM
2007-08	Fribourg U17	Swiss-U17	3	0	0	0	0	....	....	....	....	....
	Ecole U17	Swiss-U17	2	0	0	0	2	....	....	....	....	....
2008-09	Fribourg U17	Swiss-U17	34	3	4	7	50	....	....	....	....	....
2009-10	SC Bern Future Jr.	Swiss-Jr.	4	0	1	1	0	....	....	....	....	....
	SC Bern U17	Swiss-U17	29	25	15	40	46	9	4	7	11	10
2010-11	SC Bern Future Jr.	Swiss-Jr.	36	16	16	32	34	1	0	0	0	4
	SC Bern U17	Swiss-U17	4	7	4	11	2	9	8	15	23	10
2011-12	SC Bern Future Jr.	Swiss-Jr.	13	7	15	22	22	....	....	....	....	....
	SC Bern	Swiss	31	8	7	15	8	17	1	1	2	8
2012-13	SC Bern Future Jr.	Swiss-Jr.	2	2	1	3	2	....	....	....	....	....
	SC Bern	Swiss	41	4	2	6	18	20	2	1	3	2

BERTUZZI, Tyler (buhr-TOO-zee, TIGH-luhr) **DET**

Left wing. Shoots left. 6', 178 lbs. Born, Sudbury, Ont., February 24, 1995.
(Detroit's 3rd choice, 58th overall, in 2013 Entry Draft).

			Regular Season					Playoffs				
Season	Club	League	GP	G	A	Pts	PIM	GP	G	A	Pts	PIM
2010-11	Sud. Wolves M.M.	Minor-ON	32	20	45	65	58	....	....	....	....	....
	Sud. Wolves Mid.	Minor-ON	3	1	1	2	12	2	0	0	0	12
2011-12	Guelph Storm	OHL	61	6	11	17	117	6	0	2	2	7
2012-13	Guelph Storm	OHL	43	13	9	22	68	5	0	0	0	14

BESSE, Grant (BEH-see, GRANT) **ANA**

Right wing. Shoots left. 5'10", 177 lbs. Born, Edina, MN, July 14, 1994.
(Anaheim's 4th choice, 147th overall, in 2013 Entry Draft).

			Regular Season					Playoffs				
Season	Club	League	GP	G	A	Pts	PIM	GP	G	A	Pts	PIM
2009-10	Benilde	High-MN	25	27	19	46	12	2	3	1	4	0
2010-11	Team Northwest	UMHSEL	21	9	11	20	16	1	0	0	0	0
	Benilde	High-MN	25	19	19	38	16	2	4	1	5	2
2011-12	Team Northwest	UMHSEL	21	15	17	32	16	3	2	1	3	2
	Benilde	High-MN	25	40	35	75	20	3	4	3	7	2
2012-13	Team Northwest	UMHSEL	4	2	0	2	0	....	....	....	....	....
	Benilde	High-MN	28	48	28	76	16	....	....	....	....	....
	Omaha Lancers	USHL	7	4	0	4	0	....	....	....	....	....

BETKER, Ben (BEHT-kuhr, BEHN) **EDM**

Defense. Shoots left. 6'5", 200 lbs. Born, Cranbrook, B.C., September 29, 1994.
(Edmonton's 9th choice, 158th overall, in 2013 Entry Draft).

			Regular Season					Playoffs				
Season	Club	League	GP	G	A	Pts	PIM	GP	G	A	Pts	PIM
2010-11	Kootenay Ice	BCMML	38	1	12	13	56	....	....	....	....	....
2011-12	Westside Warriors	BCHL	59	5	13	18	52	....	....	....	....	....
	Portland	WHL	1	0	0	0	0	....	....	....	....	....
2012-13	Everett Silvertips	WHL	68	1	5	6	100	6	0	1	1	8

BIEGA, Alex (bee-AY-guh, AL-ehx) **VAN**

Defense. Shoots right. 5'11", 192 lbs. Born, Montreal, Que., April 4, 1988.
(Buffalo's 5th choice, 147th overall, in 2006 Entry Draft).

			Regular Season					Playoffs				
Season	Club	League	GP	G	A	Pts	PIM	GP	G	A	Pts	PIM
2004-05	Salisbury School	High-CT	27	9	22	31	45	....	....	....	....	....
2005-06	Salisbury School	High-CT	28	10	17	27	51	....	....	....	....	....
2006-07	Harvard Crimson	ECAC	33	6	12	18	36	....	....	....	....	....
2007-08	Harvard Crimson	ECAC	34	3	19	22	28	....	....	....	....	....
2008-09	Harvard Crimson	ECAC	31	4	16	20	46	....	....	....	....	....
2009-10	Harvard Crimson	ECAC	33	2	8	10	30	....	....	....	....	....
2010-11	Portland Pirates	AHL	61	3	15	18	52	12	1	1	2	6
2011-12	Rochester	AHL	65	5	18	23	47	2	0	2	2	6
2012-13	Rochester	AHL	72	5	20	25	59	3	0	2	2	2

ECAC All-Rookie Team (2007)

Signed as a free agent by **Vancouver**, July 6, 2013.

BIEGA, Danny (bee-AY-ga, DAN-ee) **CAR**

Defense. Shoots right. 6', 205 lbs. Born, Montreal, Que., September 29, 1991.
(Carolina's 4th choice, 67th overall, in 2010 Entry Draft).

			Regular Season					Playoffs				
Season	Club	League	GP	G	A	Pts	PIM	GP	G	A	Pts	PIM
2007-08	Salisbury School	High-CT	26	4	13	17	....	....	....	....	....	....
2008-09	Salisbury School	High-CT	29	8	14	22	....	....	....	....	....	....
2009-10	Harvard Crimson	ECAC	32	5	4	9	47	....	....	....	....	....
2010-11	Harvard Crimson	ECAC	34	11	19	30	34	....	....	....	....	....
2011-12	Harvard Crimson	ECAC	34	10	25	35	41	....	....	....	....	....
2012-13	Harvard Crimson	ECAC	32	2	9	11	43	....	....	....	....	....
	Charlotte	AHL	1	0	0	0	0	3	0	2	2	8

ECAC Second All-Star Team (2011) • ECAC First All-Star Team (2012) • NCAA East First All-American Team (2012)

BIGGS, Tyler (BIHGZ, TIGH-luhr) **TOR**

Right wing. Shoots right. 6'3", 224 lbs. Born, Binghamton, NY, April 30, 1993.
(Toronto's 1st choice, 22nd overall, in 2011 Entry Draft).

			Regular Season					Playoffs				
Season	Club	League	GP	G	A	Pts	PIM	GP	G	A	Pts	PIM
2008-09	Tor. Jr. Canadiens	GTHL	72	40	47	87	....	....	....	....	....	....
	Tor. Canadiens	ON-Jr.A	3	0	0	0	2	....	....	....	....	....
2009-10	USNTDP	USHL	24	6	5	11	54	....	....	....	....	....
	USNTDP	U-17	20	10	4	14	31	....	....	....	....	....
	USNTDP	U-18	9	0	0	0	6	....	....	....	....	....
2010-11	USNTDP	USHL	20	7	4	11	41	....	....	....	....	....
	USNTDP	U-18	35	12	8	20	120	....	....	....	....	....
2011-12	Miami U.	CCHA	37	9	8	17	63	....	....	....	....	....
2012-13	Oshawa Generals	OHL	60	26	27	53	55	9	0	1	1	13
	Toronto Marlies	AHL	4	1	0	1	0	1	0	0	0	0

BIGOS, Kyle (BEE-gohs, KIGHL) S.J.

Defense. Shoots right. 6'4", 235 lbs. Born, Upland, CA, May 12, 1989.
(Edmonton's 5th choice, 99th overall, in 2009 Entry Draft).

			Regular Season					Playoffs				
Season	Club	League	GP	G	A	Pts	PIM	GP	G	A	Pts	PIM
2006-07	Notre Dame	SMHL	39	12	24	36	165	....	....	....	....	....
	Notre Dame	SJHL	3	0	0	0	0	....	....	....	....	....
2007-08	Vernon Vipers	BCHL	58	2	15	17	152	10	0	2	2	28
2008-09	Vernon Vipers	BCHL	58	8	25	33	126	17	2	4	6	37
2009-10	Merrimack College	H-East	36	4	7	11	94	....	....	....	....	....
2010-11	Merrimack College	H-East	33	2	6	8	127	....	....	....	....	....
2011-12	Merrimack College	H-East	34	4	13	17	125	....	....	....	....	....
2012-13	Merrimack College	H-East	30	4	7	11	111	....	....	....	....	....

Traded to **San Jose** by **Edmonton** for Lee Moffie, July 6, 2013.

BIGRAS, Chris (bee-GRAH, KRIHS) COL

Defense. Shoots left. 6'1", 186 lbs. Born, Orillia, Ont., February 22, 1995.
(Colorado's 2nd choice, 32nd overall, in 2013 Entry Draft).

			Regular Season					Playoffs				
Season	Club	League	GP	G	A	Pts	PIM	GP	G	A	Pts	PIM
2010-11	Barrie Colts	Minor-ON	43	7	25	32	20	....	....	....	....	....
2011-12	Owen Sound	OHL	49	3	16	19	33	5	2	3	5	0
2012-13	Owen Sound	OHL	68	8	30	38	34	12	0	2	2	8

BILLINS, Chad (BIHL-uhns, CHAD) CGY

Defense. Shoots left. 5'10", 175 lbs. Born, Marysville, MI, May 26, 1989.

			Regular Season					Playoffs				
Season	Club	League	GP	G	A	Pts	PIM	GP	G	A	Pts	PIM
2005-06	Det. Caesers	MWEHL	22	1	4	5	18	3	0	1	1	6
	Alpena IceDiggers	NAHL	1	0	0	0	0	....	....	....	....	....
2006-07	Alpena IceDiggers	NAHL	61	7	18	25	98	....	....	....	....	....
2007-08	Waterloo	USHL	60	10	26	36	81	11	5	4	9	0
2008-09	Ferris State	CCHA	27	2	9	11	38	....	....	....	....	....
2009-10	Ferris State	CCHA	40	3	8	11	26	....	....	....	....	....
2010-11	Ferris State	CCHA	39	5	11	16	20	....	....	....	....	....
2011-12	Ferris State	CCHA	43	7	22	29	24	....	....	....	....	....
2012-13	Grand Rapids	AHL	76	10	27	37	40	24	2	12	14	12

NCAA West Second All-American Team (2012)

Signed as a free agent by **Calgary**, July 5, 2013.

BIRCH, Braden (BUHRCH, BRAY-duhn) CHI

Defense. Shoots left. 6'3", 192 lbs. Born, Hamilton, Ont., September 25, 1989.
(Chicago's 6th choice, 179th overall, in 2008 Entry Draft).

			Regular Season					Playoffs				
Season	Club	League	GP	G	A	Pts	PIM	GP	G	A	Pts	PIM
2006-07	Stoney Creek	ON-Jr.B	43	10	11	21	86	....	....	....	....	....
2007-08	Nanaimo Clippers	BCHL	19	0	2	2	15	....	....	....	....	....
	Oakville Blades	ON-Jr.A	13	1	4	5	6	19	0	2	2	4
2008-09	Oakville Blades	ON-Jr.A	35	7	18	25	46	27	4	6	10	20
2009-10	Cornell Big Red	ECAC	32	0	2	2	10	....	....	....	....	....
2010-11	Cornell Big Red	ECAC	30	2	6	8	46	....	....	....	....	....
2011-12	Cornell Big Red	ECAC	32	1	6	7	22	....	....	....	....	....
2012-13	Cornell Big Red	ECAC	34	2	2	4	14	....	....	....	....	....

BIRKS, Dane (BURKS, DAYN) PIT

Defense. Shoots right. 6'3", 190 lbs. Born, Merritt, B.C., August 29, 1995.
(Pittsburgh's 4th choice, 164th overall, in 2013 Entry Draft).

			Regular Season					Playoffs				
Season	Club	League	GP	G	A	Pts	PIM	GP	G	A	Pts	PIM
2010-11	Williams Lake	Minor-BC		STATISTICS NOT AVAILABLE								
2011-12	Creston Valley	KIJHL	47	3	21	24	72	6	0	1	1	20
	Trail Smoke Eaters	BCHL	10	0	0	0	12	....	....	....	....	....
2012-13	Merritt	BCHL	52	5	15	20	28	5	0	1	1	6

• Signed Letter of Intent to attend **Michigan Tech University** (WCHA) in fall of 2014.

BISCHOFF, Jake (BIHSH-awf, JAYK) NYI

Defense. Shoots left. 6', 185 lbs. Born, Cambridge, MN, July 25, 1994.
(NY Islanders' 7th choice, 185th overall, in 2012 Entry Draft).

			Regular Season					Playoffs				
Season	Club	League	GP	G	A	Pts	PIM	GP	G	A	Pts	PIM
2010-11	Grand Rapids	High-MN	27	5	24	29	14	....	....	....	....	....
2011-12	Team North	UMHSEL	24	5	8	13	4	....	....	....	....	....
	Grand Rapids	High-MN	25	11	29	40	17	....	....	....	....	....
	Omaha Lancers	USHL	10	0	1	1	2	....	....	....	....	....
2012-13	Omaha Lancers	USHL	12	0	2	2	0	....	....	....	....	....

• Signed Letter of Intent to attend **University of Minnesota** (WCHA) in fall of 2014.

BITETTO, Anthony (bih-TEH-toh, AN-thuh-nee) NSH

Defense. Shoots left. 6', 215 lbs. Born, Island Park, NY, July 15, 1990.
(Nashville's 4th choice, 168th overall, in 2010 Entry Draft).

			Regular Season					Playoffs				
Season	Club	League	GP	G	A	Pts	PIM	GP	G	A	Pts	PIM
2007-08	NY Apple Core	EmJHL	12	4	10	14	32	....	....	....	....	....
	NY Apple Core	EJHL	17	2	6	8	28	....	....	....	....	....
2008-09	NY Apple Core	EJHL	30	2	9	11	50	....	....	....	....	....
	Indiana Ice	USHL	24	1	3	4	29	13	0	3	3	6
2009-10	Indiana Ice	USHL	58	11	29	40	99	9	2	2	4	19
2010-11	Northeastern	H-East	38	3	17	20	66	....	....	....	....	....
2011-12	Northeastern	H-East	34	4	11	15	34	....	....	....	....	....
	Milwaukee	AHL	....	....	....	....	....	1	0	0	0	0
2012-13	Cincinnati	ECHL	23	1	2	3	16	....	....	....	....	....
	Milwaukee	AHL	34	1	5	6	35	....	....	....	....	....

USHL Second All-Star Team (2010) • Hockey East All-Rookie Team (2011)

BJORKSTRAND, Oliver (bih-YOHRK-strand, AWL-ih-vuhr) CBJ

Right wing. Shoots right. 5'11", 166 lbs. Born, Herning, Denmark, April 10, 1995.
(Columbus' 5th choice, 89th overall, in 2013 Entry Draft).

			Regular Season					Playoffs				
Season	Club	League	GP	G	A	Pts	PIM	GP	G	A	Pts	PIM
2009-10	Herning IK U17	Den-U17	10	7	9	16	2	....	....	....	....	....
2010-11	Herning IK U17	Den-U17	19	28	26	54	39	....	....	....	....	....
	Herning IK Jr.	Den-Jr.	11	13	6	19	2	6	1	7	8	0
	Herning IK II	Den-2	....	....	....	....	....	1	0	0	0	0
2011-12	Herning IK II	Den-2	5	1	2	3	0	....	....	....	....	....
	Herning Blue Fox	Denmark	36	13	13	26	10	10	1	2	3	4
2012-13	Portland	WHL	65	31	32	63	10	21	8	11	19	4

BLACK, Graham (BLAK, GRAY-uhm) N.J.

Center. Shoots left. 5'11", 175 lbs. Born, Regina, Sask., January 13, 1993.
(New Jersey's 5th choice, 135th overall, in 2012 Entry Draft).

			Regular Season					Playoffs				
Season	Club	League	GP	G	A	Pts	PIM	GP	G	A	Pts	PIM
2009-10	Reg. Pat Cdns.	SMHL	42	22	27	49	40	....	....	....	....	....
2010-11	Reg. Pat Cdns.	SMHL	43	*47	29	*76	48	5	7	3	10	20
	Swift Current	WHL	6	1	1	2	0	....	....	....	....	....
2011-12	Swift Current	WHL	71	17	33	50	49	....	....	....	....	....
2012-13	Swift Current	WHL	68	24	26	50	33	5	1	3	4	2

BLACKER, Jesse (BLA-kuhr, JEH-see) TOR

Defense. Shoots right. 6'2", 190 lbs. Born, Toronto, Ont., April 19, 1991.
(Toronto's 3rd choice, 58th overall, in 2009 Entry Draft).

			Regular Season					Playoffs				
Season	Club	League	GP	G	A	Pts	PIM	GP	G	A	Pts	PIM
2006-07	Tor. Red Wings	GTHL	43	9	25	34	86	....	....	....	....	....
2007-08	Chatham Maroons	ON-Jr.B	8	1	2	3	25	....	....	....	....	....
	Windsor Spitfires	OHL	17	0	4	4	6	5	0	1	1	2
2008-09	Windsor Spitfires	OHL	67	4	17	21	54	20	0	4	4	18
2009-10	Windsor Spitfires	OHL	9	0	3	3	12	....	....	....	....	....
	Owen Sound	OHL	48	6	24	30	62	....	....	....	....	....
	Toronto Marlies	AHL	6	0	1	1	0	....	....	....	....	....
2010-11	Owen Sound	OHL	62	10	44	54	83	22	5	11	16	14
2011-12	Toronto Marlies	AHL	58	1	15	16	73	6	0	1	1	4
2012-13	Toronto Marlies	AHL	61	4	7	11	33	4	0	1	1	0

BLACKWELL, Colin (BLAK-wehll, KAWL-ihn) S.J.

Center. Shoots right. 5'9", 190 lbs. Born, Lawrence, MA, March 28, 1993.
(San Jose's 6th choice, 194th overall, in 2011 Entry Draft).

			Regular Season					Playoffs				
Season	Club	League	GP	G	A	Pts	PIM	GP	G	A	Pts	PIM
2007-08	St. John's Prep	High-MA	....	2	0	2	....	....	....	....	....	....
2008-09	St. John's Prep	High-MA	....	18	10	28	....	....	....	....	....	....
2009-10	St. John's Prep	High-MA	....	17	19	36	....	....	....	....	....	....
2010-11	St. John's Prep	High-MA	25	33	33	66	....	....	....	....	....	....
2011-12	Harvard Crimson	ECAC	34	5	14	19	46	....	....	....	....	....
2012-13	Harvard Crimson	ECAC	21	3	11	14	10	....	....	....	....	....

BLAIN, Jeremie (BLAYN, JAIR-uh-mee) VAN

Defense. Shoots right. 6'2", 192 lbs. Born, Le Moyne, Que., March 19, 1992.
(Edmonton's 6th choice, 91st overall, in 2010 Entry Draft).

			Regular Season					Playoffs				
Season	Club	League	GP	G	A	Pts	PIM	GP	G	A	Pts	PIM
2007-08	C.C. Lemoyne	QAAA	45	2	21	23	16	8	4	3	7	2
2008-09	Victoriaville Tigres	QMJHL	27	1	3	4	0	....	....	....	....	....
	Acadie-Bathurst	QMJHL	22	0	3	3	6	5	0	2	2	4
2009-10	Acadie-Bathurst	QMJHL	64	4	34	38	72	5	2	2	4	10
2010-11	Acadie-Bathurst	QMJHL	40	2	35	37	48	4	2	2	4	4
2011-12	Acadie-Bathurst	QMJHL	29	6	18	24	54	....	....	....	....	....
	Victoriaville Tigres	QMJHL	29	3	23	26	38	4	0	2	2	6
2012-13	Chicago Wolves	AHL	25	0	4	4	40	....	....	....	....	....
	Idaho Steelheads	ECHL	47	7	24	31	58	....	....	....	....	....

Signed as a free agent by **Vancouver**, July 5, 2013.

BLANDISI, Joseph (blan-DEE-zee, JOH-sehf) COL

Center/Right wing. Shoots left. 5'11", 182 lbs. Born, Scarborough, Ont., July 18, 1994.
(Colorado's 4th choice, 162nd overall, in 2012 Entry Draft).

			Regular Season					Playoffs				
Season	Club	League	GP	G	A	Pts	PIM	GP	G	A	Pts	PIM
2010-11	Vaughan Kings	GTHL	41	51	41	92	....	....	....	....	....	....
	Vaughan Vipers	ON-Jr.A	7	2	0	2	14	....	....	....	....	....
2011-12	Owen Sound	OHL	68	17	14	31	72	5	0	1	1	8
2012-13	Owen Sound	OHL	37	7	18	25	49	....	....	....	....	....
	Ottawa 67's	OHL	26	8	18	26	68	....	....	....	....	....

BLIDH, Anton (BLIHD, AN-tawn) BOS

Left wing. Shoots left. 6', 184 lbs. Born, Molnlycke, Sweden, March 14, 1995.
(Boston's 5th choice, 180th overall, in 2013 Entry Draft).

			Regular Season					Playoffs				
Season	Club	League	GP	G	A	Pts	PIM	GP	G	A	Pts	PIM
2010-11	Frolunda U18	Swe-U18	12	2	1	3	8	1	0	0	0	25
2011-12	Frolunda U18	Swe-U18	38	13	19	32	28	4	2	0	2	4
2012-13	Frolunda U18	Swe-U18	8	5	2	7	14	3	1	3	4	0
	Frolunda Jr.	Swe-Jr.	43	17	10	27	80	6	1	2	3	0

BLOMQVIST, Anton (BLAWM-kvihst, AN-tawn) CBJ

Defense. Shoots left. 6'6", 206 lbs. Born, Kristianstad, Sweden, March 7, 1990.
(Columbus' 5th choice, 167th overall, in 2009 Entry Draft).

			Regular Season					Playoffs				
Season	Club	League	GP	G	A	Pts	PIM	GP	G	A	Pts	PIM
2005-06	Osby IK	Sweden-3	22	1	1	2	6	....	....	....	....	....
2006-07	Linkopings HC U18	Swe-U18	10	2	1	3	16	....	....	....	....	....
	Linkopings HC Jr.	Swe-Jr.	1	0	1	1	0	....	....	....	....	....
2007-08	Malmo U18	Swe-U18	20	2	2	4	57	2	0	0	0	2
	Malmo Jr.	Swe-Jr.	18	0	1	1	20	5	0	1	1	2
2008-09	Malmo Jr.	Swe-Jr.	31	2	14	16	73	....	....	....	....	....
	Malmo	Sweden-2	13	0	3	3	8	....	....	....	....	....
2009-10	Malmo	Sweden-2	49	3	2	5	55	5	0	0	0	10
	Malmo Jr.	Swe-Jr.	....	....	....	....	....	1	0	0	0	0
2010-11	Malmo	Sweden-2	27	0	1	1	14	....	....	....	....	....
	Springfield Falcons	AHL	5	0	1	1	21	....	....	....	....	....
2011-12	Springfield Falcons	AHL	24	0	0	0	19	....	....	....	....	....
2012-13	Evansville IceMen	ECHL	36	1	2	3	46	....	....	....	....	....

BLOMSTRAND, Ludwig (BLAWM-strand, LUHD-wihg) VAN

Left wing. Shoots left. 6'1", 198 lbs. Born, Uppsala, Sweden, March 8, 1993.
(Vancouver's 5th choice, 120th overall, in 2011 Entry Draft).

			Regular Season					Playoffs				
Season	Club	League	GP	G	A	Pts	PIM	GP	G	A	Pts	PIM
2008-09	Almtuna U18	Swe-U18	10	3	0	3	8	....	....	....	....	....
	Gimo IF Hockey	Sweden-4	26	17	10	27	18	....	....	....	....	....
2009-10	Djurgarden U18	Swe-U18	35	9	19	28	24	5	0	2	2	0
2010-11	Djurgarden U18	Swe-U18	9	2	11	13	4	5	1	3	4	10
	Djurgarden Jr.	Swe-Jr.	35	3	4	7	14	3	0	0	0	2
2011-12	Djurgarden Jr.	Swe-Jr.	41	16	15	31	62	....	....	....	....	....
	Djurgarden	Sweden	18	0	1	1	4	....	....	....	....	....
	Djurgarden	Sweden-Q	8	0	0	0	0	....	....	....	....	....
2012-13	Djurgarden Jr.	Swe-Jr.	7	2	1	3	0	....	....	....	....	....
	Djurgarden	Sweden-2	14	0	0	0	8	....	....	....	....	....
	Almtuna	Sweden-2	30	13	6	19	12	....	....	....	....	....
	Chicago Wolves	AHL	8	1	1	2	2	....	....	....	....	....

BLOOD, Ben (BLUHD, BEHN) OTT

Defense. Shoots left. 6'3", 223 lbs. Born, Plymouth, MN, March 15, 1989.
(Ottawa's 4th choice, 120th overall, in 2007 Entry Draft).

			Regular Season					Playoffs				
Season	Club	League	GP	G	A	Pts	PIM	GP	G	A	Pts	PIM
2005-06	Shat.-St. Mary's	High-MN	73	3	22	25	32	....	....	....	....	....
2006-07	Shat.-St. Mary's	High-MN	63	11	25	36	144	....	....	....	....	....
2007-08	Des Moines	USHL	11	0	7	7	17	....	....	....	....	....
	Indiana Ice	USHL	46	10	6	16	83	4	1	2	3	14
2008-09	North Dakota	WCHA	31	0	1	1	12	....	....	....	....	....
2009-10	North Dakota	WCHA	43	5	9	14	96	....	....	....	....	....
2010-11	North Dakota	WCHA	44	2	10	12	48	....	....	....	....	....
2011-12	North Dakota	WCHA	42	3	18	21	73	....	....	....	....	....
	Binghamton	AHL	4	0	0	0	17	....	....	....	....	....
2012-13	Binghamton	AHL	24	0	0	0	30	....	....	....	....	....
	Elmira Jackals	ECHL	32	1	1	2	23	6	0	1	1	9

BLUEGER, Teddy (BLEW-guhr, TEH-dee) PIT

Center. Shoots left. 6'1", 183 lbs. Born, Riga, Latvia, August 15, 1994.
(Pittsburgh's 3rd choice, 52nd overall, in 2012 Entry Draft).

			Regular Season					Playoffs				
Season	Club	League	GP	G	A	Pts	PIM	GP	G	A	Pts	PIM
2009-10	Shattuck Midget	High-MN	53	20	40	60	84	....	....	....	....	....
2010-11	Shattuck Midget	High-MN	54	24	42	66	32	....	....	....	....	....
2011-12	Shattuck	High-MN	51	24	64	88	63	....	....	....	....	....
2012-13	Minnesota State	WCHA	37	6	13	19	40	....	....	....	....	....

BLUJUS, Dylan (BLOO-juhs, DIH-luhn) T.B.

Defense. Shoots right. 6'3", 207 lbs. Born, Buffalo, NY, January 22, 1994.
(Tampa Bay's 3rd choice, 40th overall, in 2012 Entry Draft).

			Regular Season					Playoffs				
Season	Club	League	GP	G	A	Pts	PIM	GP	G	A	Pts	PIM
2009-10	Buffalo Regals	Minor-NY	47	5	17	22	36	....	....	....	....	....
2010-11	Brampton	OHL	67	4	22	26	26	4	0	0	0	0
2011-12	Brampton	OHL	66	7	27	34	38	8	1	4	5	4
2012-13	Brampton	OHL	68	2	27	29	57	5	2	2	4	2

BODIN, Rasmus (BOH-dihn, RAS-muhs) DET

Left wing. Shoots left. 6'6", 207 lbs. Born, Ostersund, Sweden, May 5, 1994.
(Detroit's 6th choice, 200th overall, in 2012 Entry Draft).

			Regular Season					Playoffs				
Season	Club	League	GP	G	A	Pts	PIM	GP	G	A	Pts	PIM
2010-11	Ostersunds IK U18	Swe-U18	29	5	3	8	60	....	....	....	....	....
2011-12	Ostersunds IK U18	Swe-U18	29	9	17	26	94	....	....	....	....	....
	Ostersunds IK	Sweden-3	20	3	7	10	18	....	....	....	....	....
2012-13	HV 71 Jr.	Swe-Jr.	18	0	1	1	10	....	....	....	....	....
	Tranas AIF IF	Sweden-3	6	0	3	3	0	....	....	....	....	....

BONNEAU, Jimmy (BAW-noh, JIHM-mee)

Left wing. Shoots left. 6'3", 228 lbs. Born, Baie-Comeau, Que., March 22, 1985.
(Montreal's 10th choice, 241st overall, in 2003 Entry Draft).

			Regular Season					Playoffs				
Season	Club	League	GP	G	A	Pts	PIM	GP	G	A	Pts	PIM
2001-02	Jonquiere Elites	QAAA	40	5	10	15	55	3	1	1	2	2
2002-03	Montreal Rocket	QMJHL	65	1	5	6	261	7	0	0	0	12
2003-04	P.E.I. Rocket	QMJHL	70	7	12	19	263	11	1	0	1	12
2004-05	P.E.I. Rocket	QMJHL	70	11	11	22	234	....	....	....	....	....
2005-06	Long Beach	ECHL	65	1	5	6	137	....	....	....	....	....
2006-07	Hamilton Bulldogs	AHL	9	0	0	0	59	....	....	....	....	....
	Cincinnati	ECHL	46	2	5	7	89	10	0	0	0	23
2007-08	Hamilton Bulldogs	AHL	6	1	0	1	5	....	....	....	....	....
	Cincinnati	ECHL	18	0	4	4	61	3	0	0	0	0
2008-09	Portland Pirates	AHL	46	0	6	6	122	....	....	....	....	....
2009-10	Rochester	AHL	57	4	2	6	187	....	....	....	....	....
2010-11	Hamilton Bulldogs	AHL	77	1	2	3	180	15	1	2	3	16
2011-12	Worcester Sharks	AHL	54	2	3	5	168	....	....	....	....	....
2012-13	Worcester Sharks	AHL	26	1	0	1	81	....	....	....	....	....

Signed as a free agent by **Buffalo**, August 13, 2008. Signed as a free agent by **Hamilton** (AHL), July 2, 2010. Signed as a free agent by **Worcester** (AHL), October 7, 2011.

BOUCHER, Reid (BOO-shay, REED) N.J.

Right wing. Shoots left. 5'11", 195 lbs. Born, Lansing, MI, September 8, 1993.
(New Jersey's 4th choice, 99th overall, in 2011 Entry Draft).

			Regular Season					Playoffs				
Season	Club	League	GP	G	A	Pts	PIM	GP	G	A	Pts	PIM
2008-09	Lansing Capitals	Minor-MI	64	79	41	120	119	....	....	....	....	....
2009-10	USNTDP	USHL	24	10	4	14	22	....	....	....	....	....
	USNTDP	U-17	17	7	9	16	16	....	....	....	....	....
	USNTDP	U-18	1	0	0	0	0	....	....	....	....	....
2010-11	USNTDP	USHL	24	14	6	20	13	....	....	....	....	....
	USNTDP	U-18	35	12	8	20	120	....	....	....	....	....
2011-12	Sarnia Sting	OHL	67	28	22	50	19	6	2	1	3	4
	Albany Devils	AHL	1	0	0	0	0	....	....	....	....	....
2012-13	Sarnia Sting	OHL	68	*62	33	95	53	4	2	3	5	4
	Albany Devils	AHL	11	3	2	5	6	....	....	....	....	....

OHL First All-Star Team (2013)

BOUDREAU, Gabryel (boo-DROH, gab-REE-ehl) S.J.

Left wing. Shoots left. 5'11", 170 lbs. Born, Beloeil, Que., February 21, 1995.
(San Jose's 2nd choice, 49th overall, in 2013 Entry Draft).

			Regular Season					Playoffs				
Season	Club	League	GP	G	A	Pts	PIM	GP	G	A	Pts	PIM
2010-11	Antoine-Girouard	Minor-QU	32	13	12	25	72	....	....	....	....	....
	Antoine-Girouard	QAAA	2	0	0	0	0	....	....	....	....	....
2011-12	Antoine-Girouard	QAAA	43	33	25	58	38	11	11	5	16	20
2012-13	Baie-Comeau	QMJHL	67	22	41	63	43	18	9	9	18	27

BOURKE, Troy (BOHRK, TROI) COL

Left wing. Shoots left. 5'10", 156 lbs. Born, Edmonton, Alta., March 30, 1994.
(Colorado's 2nd choice, 72nd overall, in 2012 Entry Draft).

			Regular Season					Playoffs				
Season	Club	League	GP	G	A	Pts	PIM	GP	G	A	Pts	PIM
2007-08	PAC Spruce Grove	AMBHL	33	13	15	28	26	2	0	0	0	0
2008-09	PAC Spruce Grove	AMBHL	33	*45	38	*83	38	7	5	6	11	10
2009-10	St. Albert Raiders	AMHL	34	27	26	53	24	5	2	0	2	4
	Prince George	WHL	5	3	0	3	4	....	....	....	....	....
2010-11	Prince George	WHL	68	19	23	42	20	4	0	1	1	0
2011-12	Prince George	WHL	71	18	38	56	56	....	....	....	....	....
2012-13	Prince George	WHL	63	15	35	50	37	....	....	....	....	....

BOURNIVAL, Michael (boor-nee-VAHL, MIGH-kuhl) MTL

Left wing. Shoots left. 5'11", 192 lbs. Born, Shawinigan, Que., May 31, 1992.
(Colorado's 3rd choice, 71st overall, in 2010 Entry Draft).

			Regular Season					Playoffs				
Season	Club	League	GP	G	A	Pts	PIM	GP	G	A	Pts	PIM
2007-08	Trois-Rivieres	QAAA	52	33	23	56	66	7	3	3	6	10
2008-09	Shawinigan	QMJHL	46	11	11	22	29	21	1	3	4	12
2009-10	Shawinigan	QMJHL	58	24	38	62	37	6	2	2	4	6
2010-11	Shawinigan	QMJHL	56	28	36	64	28	12	5	8	13	10
2011-12	Shawinigan	QMJHL	41	30	26	56	27	11	1	6	7	12
2012-13	Hamilton Bulldogs	AHL	69	10	20	30	26	....	....	....	....	....

Traded to **Montreal** by **Colorado** for Ryan O'Byrne, November 11, 2010.

BOURQUE, Ryan (BOHRK, RIGH-uhn) NYR

Center. Shoots left. 5'9", 170 lbs. Born, Boxford, MA, January 3, 1991.
(NY Rangers' 3rd choice, 80th overall, in 2009 Entry Draft).

			Regular Season					Playoffs				
Season	Club	League	GP	G	A	Pts	PIM	GP	G	A	Pts	PIM
2006-07	Cushing	High-MA	29	19	31	50	....	....	....	....	....	....
2007-08	USNTDP	NAHL	34	11	9	20	14	....	....	....	....	....
	USNTDP	U-17	7	4	3	7	10	....	....	....	....	....
	USNTDP	U-18	27	4	12	16	18	....	....	....	....	....
2008-09	USNTDP	NAHL	14	7	9	16	10	....	....	....	....	....
	USNTDP	U-18	43	14	24	38	48	....	....	....	....	....
2009-10	Quebec Remparts	QMJHL	44	19	24	43	20	9	3	7	10	6
2010-11	Quebec Remparts	QMJHL	49	26	33	59	22	18	5	11	16	8
2011-12	Connecticut Whale	AHL	69	6	8	14	10	9	2	1	3	4
2012-13	Connecticut Whale	AHL	53	8	7	15	11	....	....	....	....	....

BOWEY, Madison (BOW-ee, MA-dih-suhn) WSH

Defense. Shoots right. 6'1", 195 lbs. Born, Winnipeg, Man., April 22, 1995.
(Washington's 2nd choice, 53rd overall, in 2013 Entry Draft).

			Regular Season					Playoffs				
Season	Club	League	GP	G	A	Pts	PIM	GP	G	A	Pts	PIM
2010-11	Winnipeg Wild	MMHL	41	16	22	38	35	6	2	0	2	10
	Kelowna Rockets	WHL	3	0	1	1	4	1	0	0	0	0
2011-12	Kelowna Rockets	WHL	57	8	13	21	39	4	1	0	1	4
2012-13	Kelowna Rockets	WHL	69	12	18	30	75	11	0	4	4	14

BOYCHUK, Riley (BOY-chuhk, RIGH-lee) N.J.

Left wing. Shoots left. 6'5", 220 lbs. Born, Vancouver, B.C., February 20, 1991.
(Buffalo's 9th choice, 208th overall, in 2010 Entry Draft).

			Regular Season					Playoffs				
Season	Club	League	GP	G	A	Pts	PIM	GP	G	A	Pts	PIM
2006-07	Fraser Valley	BCMML	29	18	18	36	72	....	....	....	....	....
2007-08	Portland	WHL	5	0	1	1	0	....	....	....	....	....
2008-09	Portland	WHL	62	7	10	17	86	....	....	....	....	....
2009-10	Portland	WHL	66	14	16	30	157	13	2	1	3	24
2010-11	Portland	WHL	60	18	17	35	148	21	4	8	12	*50
2011-12	Gwinnett	ECHL	20	1	4	5	33	....	....	....	....	....
	Rochester	AHL	26	0	2	2	18	....	....	....	....	....
2012-13	Fort Worth	CHL	41	8	9	17	30	....	....	....	....	....

• Missed majority of 2007-08 due to surgeries on both hips. Traded to **New Jersey** by **Buffalo** for Henrik Tallinder, July 7, 2013.

BOYD, R.J. (BOID, AHR-JAY) FLA

Defense. Shoots left. 6'3", 201 lbs. Born, Sarasota, FL, February 7, 1991.
(Florida's 13th choice, 183rd overall, in 2010 Entry Draft).

			Regular Season					Playoffs				
Season	Club	League	GP	G	A	Pts	PIM	GP	G	A	Pts	PIM
2007-08	Cushing	High-MA	35	0	3	3	....	....	....	....	....	....
2008-09	Cushing	High-MA	35	2	11	13	35	....	....	....	....	....
2009-10	Cushing	High-MA	31	4	18	22	....	....	....	....	....	....
2010-11	Sacred Heart	AH	15	1	3	4	16	....	....	....	....	....
	Chicago Steel	USHL	33	2	0	2	42	....	....	....	....	....
2011-12	Indiana Ice	USHL	50	1	13	14	93	6	0	2	2	10
2012-13	Michigan State	CCHA	42	2	9	11	20	....	....	....	....	....

BOYD, Travis (BOID, TRA-vihs) WSH

Center. Shoots right. 5'11", 185 lbs. Born, Hopkins, MN, September 14, 1993.
(Washington's 3rd choice, 177th overall, in 2011 Entry Draft).

			Regular Season					Playoffs				
Season	Club	League	GP	G	A	Pts	PIM	GP	G	A	Pts	PIM
2008-09	Hopkins Royals	High-MN	26	26	25	51	....	....	....	....	....	....
2009-10	USNTDP	USHL	35	8	10	18	18	....	....	....	....	....
	USNTDP	U-17	17	2	4	6	4	....	....	....	....	....
	USNTDP	U-18	1	0	0	0	0	....	....	....	....	....
2010-11	USNTDP	USHL	24	5	13	18	10	....	....	....	....	....
	USNTDP	U-18	36	8	12	20	6	....	....	....	....	....
2011-12	U. of Minnesota	WCHA	35	1	8	9	4	....	....	....	....	....
2012-13	U. of Minnesota	WCHA	40	3	11	14	8	....	....	....	....	....

BOYLE, Timothy (BOIL, TIH-moh-thee) OTT

Defense. Shoots right. 6'2", 185 lbs. Born, Hingham, MA, March 21, 1993.
(Ottawa's 4th choice, 106th overall, in 2012 Entry Draft).

			Regular Season					Playoffs				
Season	Club	League	GP	G	A	Pts	PIM	GP	G	A	Pts	PIM
2010-11	Nobles	High-MA	27	3	25	28	20	....	....	....	....	....
2011-12	Cape Cod Whalers	Minor-MA	33	5	15	20	....	....	....	....	....	....
	Nobles	High-MA	24	6	12	18	10	....	....	....	....	....
2012-13	Union College	ECAC	15	0	2	2	25	....	....	....	....	....

BOZON, Tim (boh-ZAWN, TIHM) MTL

Left wing. Shoots left. 6'1", 192 lbs. Born, St. Louis, MO, March 24, 1994.
(Montreal's 4th choice, 64th overall, in 2012 Entry Draft).

			Regular Season					Playoffs				
Season	Club	League	GP	G	A	Pts	PIM	GP	G	A	Pts	PIM
2007-08	Geneve U17	Swiss-U17	4	4	2	6	0	....	....	....	....	....
2008-09	Geneve U17	Swiss-U17	29	15	8	23	18	....	....	....	....	....
2009-10	Kloten Flyers U17	Swiss-U17	30	26	29	55	22	10	2	4	6	10
	Kloten Flyers Jr.	Swiss-Jr.	3	2	0	2	4	....	....	....	....	....
2010-11	Kloten Flyers Jr.	Swiss-Jr.	3	1	0	1	0	....	....	....	....	....
	HC Lugano U17	Swiss-U17	8	8	9	17	18	5	2	1	3	22
	HC Lugano Jr.	Swiss-Jr.	27	16	13	29	24	3	1	1	2	2
2011-12	Kamloops Blazers	WHL	71	36	35	71	40	11	5	0	5	11
2012-13	Kamloops Blazers	WHL	69	36	55	91	58	8	4	2	6	10

BRASSARD, Austen (BRA-sahrd, AWS-tuhn) WPG

Right wing. Shoots right. 6'2", 203 lbs. Born, Windsor, Ont., January 14, 1993.
(Winnipeg's 5th choice, 149th overall, in 2011 Entry Draft).

			Regular Season					Playoffs				
Season	Club	League	GP	G	A	Pts	PIM	GP	G	A	Pts	PIM
2008-09	Wind. Jr. Spitfires	Minor-ON	69	55	66	121	111	....	....	....	....	....
2009-10	Windsor Spitfires	OHL	37	4	8	12	36	....	....	....	....	....
	Belleville Bulls	OHL	26	6	11	17	9	....	....	....	....	....
2010-11	Belleville Bulls	OHL	67	19	15	34	78	4	1	0	1	4
2011-12	Belleville Bulls	OHL	64	27	24	51	71	6	1	1	2	6
2012-13	Belleville Bulls	OHL	62	14	19	33	94	17	6	6	12	22

BREEN, Chris (BREEN, KRIHS) CGY

Defense. Shoots left. 6'7", 224 lbs. Born, Uxbridge, Ont., June 29, 1989.

			Regular Season					Playoffs				
Season	Club	League	GP	G	A	Pts	PIM	GP	G	A	Pts	PIM
2005-06	Mississauga	ON-Jr.A	33	1	6	7	10	....	....	....	....	....
	Saginaw Spirit	OHL	25	0	0	0	10	....	....	....	....	....
2006-07	Saginaw Spirit	OHL	39	1	2	3	32	2	0	0	0	2
2007-08	Saginaw Spirit	OHL	55	0	6	6	67	4	0	1	1	0
2008-09	Saginaw Spirit	OHL	6	0	1	1	9	....	....	....	....	....
	Erie Otters	OHL	59	0	12	12	31	5	0	1	1	7
2009-10	Erie Otters	OHL	12	0	2	2	11	....	....	....	....	....
	Peterborough	OHL	53	4	8	12	36	4	1	0	1	5
	Abbotsford Heat	AHL	1	0	1	1	4	....	....	....	....	....
2010-11	Abbotsford Heat	AHL	73	4	7	11	47	....	....	....	....	....
2011-12	Abbotsford Heat	AHL	70	1	6	7	37	8	1	0	1	0
2012-13	Abbotsford Heat	AHL	60	3	4	7	55	....	....	....	....	....

Signed to an ATO (amateur tryout) contract by **Abbotsford** (AHL), March 30, 2010. Signed as a free agent by **Calgary**, May 28, 2010.

BRICKLEY, Connor (BRIH-klee, KAW-nuhr) FLA

Center. Shoots left. 6'1", 195 lbs. Born, Malden, MA, February 25, 1992.
(Florida's 6th choice, 50th overall, in 2010 Entry Draft).

			Regular Season					Playoffs				
Season	Club	League	GP	G	A	Pts	PIM	GP	G	A	Pts	PIM
2008-09	Belmont Hill	High-MA	30	17	18	35	60	....	....	....	....	....
2009-10	Des Moines	USHL	52	22	21	43	68	....	....	....	....	....
	USNTDP	U-18	14	2	5	7	6	....	....	....	....	....
2010-11	U. of Vermont	H-East	35	4	9	13	33	....	....	....	....	....
2011-12	U. of Vermont	H-East	23	9	3	12	16	....	....	....	....	....
2012-13	U. of Vermont	H-East	24	3	5	8	31	....	....	....	....	....

BRISEBOIS, Mathieu (BREEZ-bwah, MA-tyew) PHX

Defense. Shoots right. 5'11", 200 lbs. Born, Mont St-Hilaire, Que., April 17, 1992.

			Regular Season					Playoffs				
Season	Club	League	GP	G	A	Pts	PIM	GP	G	A	Pts	PIM
2009-10	Sherbrooke	QJHL	32	7	9	16	32	....	....	....	....	....
	Lewiston	QMJHL	31	0	7	7	22	3	0	0	0	4
2010-11	Rouyn-Noranda	QMJHL	47	3	15	18	32	....	....	....	....	....
2011-12	Rouyn-Noranda	QMJHL	68	17	39	56	106	4	1	0	1	12
2012-13	Rouyn-Noranda	QMJHL	64	19	54	73	103	14	3	12	15	24

Signed as a free agent by **Phoenix**, March 6, 2013.

BRITTAIN, Josh (BRIH-tehn, JAWSH)

Left wing. Shoots left. 6'5", 226 lbs. Born, Milton, Ont., January 3, 1990.
(Anaheim's 5th choice, 71st overall, in 2008 Entry Draft).

			Regular Season					Playoffs				
Season	Club	League	GP	G	A	Pts	PIM	GP	G	A	Pts	PIM
2005-06	Tor. Jr. Canadiens	GTHL	33	19	21	40	47	....	....	....	....	....
2006-07	Kingston	OHL	54	5	12	17	38	2	0	0	0	0
2007-08	Kingston	OHL	68	28	23	51	106	....	....	....	....	....
2008-09	Kingston	OHL	27	17	7	24	31	....	....	....	....	....
	Barrie Colts	OHL	41	15	13	28	65	5	1	2	3	4
2009-10	Barrie Colts	OHL	12	3	5	8	29	....	....	....	....	....
	Plymouth Whalers	OHL	56	12	12	24	101	9	1	0	1	5
2010-11	Syracuse Crunch	AHL	13	0	1	1	48	....	....	....	....	....
	Elmira Jackals	ECHL	38	3	8	11	92	4	1	0	1	2
2011-12	Syracuse Crunch	AHL	38	2	4	6	37	....	....	....	....	....
	Elmira Jackals	ECHL	9	5	0	5	4	....	....	....	....	....
2012-13	Norfolk Admirals	AHL	43	11	8	19	69	....	....	....	....	....
	Fort Wayne	ECHL	31	13	14	27	34	....	....	....	....	....

BROADHURST, Alex (BRAWD-hurst, AL-ehx) CHI

Center. Shoots left. 5'11", 174 lbs. Born, Orland Park, IL, March 7, 1993.
(Chicago's 10th choice, 199th overall, in 2011 Entry Draft).

			Regular Season					Playoffs				
Season	Club	League	GP	G	A	Pts	PIM	GP	G	A	Pts	PIM
2006-07	Chicago Mission	MWEHL	31	20	29	49	10	....	....	....	....	....
2007-08	Chicago Fury	MWEHL	31	4	4	8	6	....	....	....	....	....
2008-09	Team Illinois	T1EHL	31	8	18	26	22	....	....	....	....	....
2009-10	Chicago Mission	T1EHL	48	16	29	45	26	....	....	....	....	....
2010-11	Green Bay	USHL	55	13	20	33	22	11	3	6	9	4
2011-12	Green Bay	USHL	53	26	47	73	40	7	7	6	13	4
2012-13	London Knights	OHL	65	23	40	63	36	21	10	18	28	22

USHL First All-Star Team (2012)

BROADHURST, Terry (BRAWD-hurst, TAIR-ee)

Left wing. Shoots left. 5'11", 162 lbs. Born, Orland Park, IL, November 30, 1988.

			Regular Season					Playoffs				
Season	Club	League	GP	G	A	Pts	PIM	GP	G	A	Pts	PIM
2007-08	Sioux Falls	USHL	56	7	16	23	12	3	2	1	3	0
2008-09	Sioux City	USHL	60	27	31	58	30	4	2	1	3	2
2009-10	Nebraska-Omaha	CCHA	42	13	11	24	10	....	....	....	....	....
2010-11	Nebraska-Omaha	WCHA	30	11	19	30	14	....	....	....	....	....
2011-12	Nebraska-Omaha	WCHA	38	16	20	36	6	....	....	....	....	....
	Rockford IceHogs	AHL	8	0	2	2	0	....	....	....	....	....
2012-13	Rockford IceHogs	AHL	31	5	8	13	12	....	....	....	....	....
	Toledo Walleye	ECHL	36	12	19	31	14	....	....	....	....	....

CCHA All-Rookie Team (2010)

Signed as a free agent by **Chicago**, March 19, 2012.

BRODEUR, Mathieu (broh-DUHR, MA-tyew) PHX

Defense. Shoots left. 6'6", 220 lbs. Born, Laval, Que., June 21, 1990.
(Phoenix's 5th choice, 76th overall, in 2008 Entry Draft).

			Regular Season					Playoffs				
Season	Club	League	GP	G	A	Pts	PIM	GP	G	A	Pts	PIM
2006-07	Laurentides	QAAA	44	5	7	12	58	15	2	4	6	18
2007-08	Cape Breton	QMJHL	69	1	6	7	27	11	0	0	0	6
2008-09	Cape Breton	QMJHL	61	3	12	15	15	11	1	3	4	4
2009-10	Cape Breton	QMJHL	65	4	25	29	31	5	0	0	0	9
	San Antonio	AHL	2	0	1	1	0	....	....	....	....	....
2010-11	San Antonio	AHL	4	0	0	0	2	....	....	....	....	....
	Las Vegas	ECHL	52	0	1	1	43	....	....	....	....	....
2011-12	Portland Pirates	AHL	43	2	4	6	29	....	....	....	....	....
2012-13	Portland Pirates	AHL	65	3	16	19	47	3	0	0	0	2

BRODZINSKI, Jonny (brawd-ZIHN-skee, JAW-nee) L.A.

Center. Shoots right. 6', 202 lbs. Born, Ham Lake, MN, June 19, 1993.
(Los Angeles' 5th choice, 148th overall, in 2013 Entry Draft).

			Regular Season					Playoffs				
Season	Club	League	GP	G	A	Pts	PIM	GP	G	A	Pts	PIM
2010-11	Fargo Force	USHL	10	2	3	5	2	2	0	0	0	0
2011-12	Fargo Force	USHL	58	10	12	22	18	6	1	1	2	0
2012-13	St. Cloud State	WCHA	42	22	11	33	10	....	....	....	....	....

BRODZINSKI, Michael (brawd-ZIHN-skee, MIGH-kuhl) S.J.

Defense. Shoots right. 5'11", 180 lbs. Born, Coon Rapids, MN, May 28, 1995.
(San Jose's 4th choice, 141st overall, in 2013 Entry Draft).

			Regular Season					Playoffs				
Season	Club	League	GP	G	A	Pts	PIM	GP	G	A	Pts	PIM
2009-10	Blaine Bengals	High-MN	29	3	3	6	12	....	....	....	....	....
2010-11	Team Northeast	UMHSEL	21	3	8	11	20	2	0	1	1	2
	Blaine Bengals	High-MN	30	14	17	31	22	....	....	....	....	....
2011-12	Team Northwest	UMHSEL	20	4	10	14	51	3	1	1	2	0
	Blaine Bengals	High-MN	28	16	20	36	43	....	....	....	....	....
	Muskegon	USHL	3	0	1	1	0	....	....	....	....	....
2012-13	Muskegon	USHL	61	16	17	33	47	3	0	1	1	0

USHL All-Rookie Team (2013) • USHL Second All-Star Team (2013)

• Signed Letter of Intent to attend **University of Minnesota** (WCHA) in fall of 2013.

BROLL, David (BROHL, DAY-vihd) TOR

Left wing. Shoots left. 6'3", 235 lbs. Born, Mississauga, Ont., January 4, 1993.
(Toronto's 6th choice, 152nd overall, in 2011 Entry Draft).

			Regular Season					Playoffs				
Season	Club	League	GP	G	A	Pts	PIM	GP	G	A	Pts	PIM
2008-09	Tor. Young Nats	GTHL	73	31	26	57	....	....	....	....	....	....
2009-10	Erie Otters	OHL	64	9	9	18	42	4	0	0	0	2
2010-11	Erie Otters	OHL	41	8	14	22	51	....	....	....	....	....
	Sault Ste. Marie	OHL	24	5	7	12	34	....	....	....	....	....
2011-12	Sault Ste. Marie	OHL	59	8	25	33	81	....	....	....	....	....
	Toronto Marlies	AHL	3	0	0	0	5	2	0	0	0	0
2012-13	Sault Ste. Marie	OHL	67	17	37	54	77	6	0	2	2	21
	Toronto Marlies	AHL	7	0	0	0	15	3	0	0	0	2

BROUILLETTE, Julien (BREE-eht, JOO-lee-ehn) WSH

Defense. Shoots left. 5'11", 185 lbs. Born, St. Esprit, Que., December 5, 1986.

			Regular Season					Playoffs				
Season	Club	League	GP	G	A	Pts	PIM	GP	G	A	Pts	PIM
2002-03	Cap-d-Madeleine	QAAA	41	8	20	28	26	....	....	....	....	....
2003-04	Trois-Rivieres	QAAA	13	5	15	20	16	....	....	....	....	....
	Chicoutimi	QMJHL	24	0	0	0	7	18	0	4	4	0
2004-05	Chicoutimi	QMJHL	65	7	11	18	61	17	4	4	8	23
2005-06	Chicoutimi	QMJHL	70	10	42	52	86	9	1	3	4	8
2006-07	Chicoutimi	QMJHL	68	10	43	53	52	4	1	2	3	8
2007-08	Columbia Inferno	ECHL	67	6	11	17	55	13	0	4	4	6
2008-09	Charlotte	ECHL	70	11	18	29	67	6	0	1	1	2
2009-10	Charlotte	ECHL	47	13	20	33	23	7	0	5	5	2
	Providence Bruins	AHL	3	0	1	1	0	....	....	....	....	....
	Hartford Wolf Pack	AHL	21	1	3	4	4	....	....	....	....	....
2010-11	Greenville	ECHL	25	11	12	23	8	1	0	0	0	0
	Charlotte	AHL	1	0	0	0	0	....	....	....	....	....
	Lake Erie Monsters	AHL	49	2	15	17	20	7	1	1	2	2
2011-12	Hershey Bears	AHL	74	7	14	21	24	3	0	1	1	4
2012-13	Hershey Bears	AHL	61	2	5	7	35	5	0	3	3	0
	Reading Royals	ECHL	1	0	0	0	2	....	....	....	....	....

Signed as a free agent by **Washington**, April 5, 2013.

BROWN, Connor (BROWN, KAW-nuhr) TOR

Right wing. Shoots right. 5'11", 170 lbs. Born, Etobicoke, Ont., January 14, 1994.
(Toronto's 4th choice, 156th overall, in 2012 Entry Draft).

			Regular Season					Playoffs				
Season	Club	League	GP	G	A	Pts	PIM	GP	G	A	Pts	PIM
2009-10	Toronto Marlboros	GTHL	80	25	44	69	16	....	....	....	....	....
2010-11	St. Michael's	ON-Jr.A	49	17	22	39	18	3	0	1	1	0
2011-12	Erie Otters	OHL	68	25	28	53	14	....	....	....	....	....
2012-13	Erie Otters	OHL	63	28	41	69	39	....	....	....	....	....

OHL All-Rookie Team (2012)

BROWN, Joshua (BROWN, JAW-shoo-wuh) FLA

Defense. Shoots right. 6'5", 213 lbs. Born, London, Ont., January 21, 1994.
(Florida's 7th choice, 152nd overall, in 2013 Entry Draft).

			Regular Season					Playoffs				
Season	Club	League	GP	G	A	Pts	PIM	GP	G	A	Pts	PIM
2010-11	Whitby Fury	ON-Jr.A	35	6	4	10	59	....	....	....	....	....
2011-12	Oshawa Generals	OHL	46	0	4	4	49	2	0	0	0	0
2012-13	Oshawa Generals	OHL	68	0	16	16	79	9	1	4	5	11

BROWN, Travis (BROWN, TRA-vihs) CHI

Defense. Shoots left. 6'2", 179 lbs. Born, Winnipeg, MB, March 15, 1994.
(Chicago's 5th choice, 149th overall, in 2012 Entry Draft).

			Regular Season					Playoffs				
Season	Club	League	GP	G	A	Pts	PIM	GP	G	A	Pts	PIM
2009-10	Wpg. Monarchs	Minor-MB	32	7	17	24	42	....	....	....	....	....
	Winnipeg Wild	MMHL	1	0	0	0	0	....	....	....	....	....
2010-11	Winnipeg Wild	MMHL	42	6	24	30	33	7	0	3	3	4
	Wpg. South Blues	MJHL	1	0	0	0	0	....	....	....	....	....
	Moose Jaw	WHL	3	0	1	1	0	3	0	0	0	0
2011-12	Moose Jaw	WHL	66	7	24	31	45	10	0	2	2	4
2012-13	Moose Jaw	WHL	70	9	30	39	54	....	....	....	....	....

BROWN, Tyler (BROWN, TIGH-luhr) PHI

Center. Shoots left. 6'1", 185 lbs. Born, Wasaga Beach, Ont., February 7, 1990.

			Regular Season					Playoffs				
Season	Club	League	GP	G	A	Pts	PIM	GP	G	A	Pts	PIM
2007-08	Plymouth Whalers	OHL	38	1	5	6	13	3	0	1	1	2
2008-09	Plymouth Whalers	OHL	49	8	13	21	18	11	1	2	3	0
2009-10	Plymouth Whalers	OHL	66	14	25	39	28	9	2	1	3	2
2010-11	Plymouth Whalers	OHL	67	25	34	59	44	11	3	11	14	8
2011-12	Adirondack	AHL	71	8	9	17	28	....	....	....	....	....
2012-13	Adirondack	AHL	55	3	3	6	30	....	....	....	....	....

Signed as a free agent by **Philadelphia**, March 2, 2011.

BRUTON, Chris (BRUH-tuhn, KRIHS) NYI

Right wing. Shoots right. 5'11", 195 lbs. Born, Calgary, Alta., January 23, 1987.

			Regular Season					Playoffs				
Season	Club	League	GP	G	A	Pts	PIM	GP	G	A	Pts	PIM
2004-05	Spokane Chiefs	WHL	62	11	17	28	55	....	....	....	....	....
2005-06	Spokane Chiefs	WHL	66	12	14	26	111	....	....	....	....	....
2006-07	Spokane Chiefs	WHL	63	9	12	21	103	6	1	1	2	6
2007-08	Spokane Chiefs	WHL	67	26	37	63	99	21	3	7	10	6
2008-09	Acadia University	AUAA	26	15	14	29	62	....	....	....	....	....
2009-10	Acadia University	AUAA	24	11	13	24	20	....	....	....	....	....
2010-11	Acadia University	AUAA	19	8	13	21	36	....	....	....	....	....
2011-12	Alaska Aces	ECHL	27	6	7	13	60	4	0	3	3	19
	Peoria Rivermen	AHL	38	2	3	5	66	....	....	....	....	....
2012-13	Peoria Rivermen	AHL	69	4	6	10	134	....	....	....	....	....

Signed as a free agent by **NY Islanders**, May 21, 2013.

BUCHNEVICH, Pavel (buhtch-NY'AY-vihch, PAH-vehl) NYR

Left wing. Shoots left. 6'1", 176 lbs. Born, Cherepovets, Russia, April 17, 1995.
(NY Rangers' 2nd choice, 75th overall, in 2013 Entry Draft).

			Regular Season					Playoffs				
Season	Club	League	GP	G	A	Pts	PIM	GP	G	A	Pts	PIM
2011-12	Cherepovets Jr.	Russia-Jr.	45	15	29	44	55	10	4	3	7	4
2012-13	Cherepovets Jr.	Russia-Jr.	24	8	15	23	36	3	1	4	5	12
	Cherepovets	KHL	12	1	1	2	0	6	0	0	0	0

BUCKLES, Matt (BUH-kuhlz, MAT) FLA

Center. Shoots right. 6'1", 205 lbs. Born, Toronto, Ont., May 5, 1995.
(Florida's 5th choice, 98th overall, in 2013 Entry Draft).

			Regular Season					Playoffs				
Season	Club	League	GP	G	A	Pts	PIM	GP	G	A	Pts	PIM
2010-11	Don Mills Flyers	GTHL	39	16	15	31	66	....	....	....	....	....
2011-12	Tor. Patriots	ON-Jr.A	46	15	21	36	76	21	5	6	11	20
2012-13	St. Michael's	ON-Jr.A	50	40	31	71	107	17	7	10	17	54

• Signed Letter of Intent to attend **Cornell University** (ECAC) in fall of 2013.

BUDISH, Zach (BOO-dihsh, ZAK) NSH

Right wing. Shoots right. 6'3", 218 lbs. Born, Edina, MN, May 9, 1991.
(Nashville's 2nd choice, 41st overall, in 2009 Entry Draft).

			Regular Season					Playoffs				
Season	Club	League	GP	G	A	Pts	PIM	GP	G	A	Pts	PIM
2006-07	Edina Hornets	High-MN	31	22	25	47	....	....	....	....	....	....
2007-08	Edina Hornets	High-MN	30	26	37	63	....	....	....	....	....	....
2008-09	Team Southwest	UMHSEL	15	14	13	27	12	....	....	....	....	....
	Edina Hornets	High-MN	DID NOT PLAY – INJURED									
2009-10	U. of Minnesota	WCHA	39	7	10	17	45	....	....	....	....	....
2010-11	U. of Minnesota	WCHA	7	2	4	6	2	....	....	....	....	....
2011-12	U. of Minnesota	WCHA	43	12	23	35	43	....	....	....	....	....
2012-13	U. of Minnesota	WCHA	40	14	22	36	14	....	....	....	....	....
	Milwaukee	AHL	9	1	3	4	0	3	0	0	0	2

• Missed majority of 2008-09 (High-MN) due to knee injury in football.

BURAKOVSKY, Andre (buhr-a-KAWV-skee, AHN-DRAY) WSH

Left wing. Shoots left. 6'1", 178 lbs. Born, Klagenfurt , Austria, February 9, 1995.
(Washington's 1st choice, 23rd overall, in 2013 Entry Draft).

			Regular Season					Playoffs				
Season	Club	League	GP	G	A	Pts	PIM	GP	G	A	Pts	PIM
2010-11	Malmo U18	Swe-U18	27	8	9	17	6	....	....	....	....	....
2011-12	Malmo U18	Swe-U18	9	6	8	14	14	4	2	4	6	0
	Malmo Jr.	Swe-Jr.	42	17	25	42	43	5	1	4	5	2
	Malmo	Sweden-2	10	0	1	1	0	3	0	0	0	0
2012-13	Malmo U18	Swe-U18	3	6	4	10	2	4	3	3	6	0
	Malmo Jr.	Swe-Jr.	13	3	4	7	8	3	1	2	3	8
	Malmo	Sweden-2	43	4	7	11	8	....	....	....	....	....

BURKE, Greg (BUHRK, GREHG) WSH

Left wing. Shoots left. 6'3", 205 lbs. Born, Portsmouth, NH, May 16, 1990.
(Washington's 7th choice, 174th overall, in 2008 Entry Draft).

			Regular Season					Playoffs				
Season	Club	League	GP	G	A	Pts	PIM	GP	G	A	Pts	PIM
2006-07	N.H. Jr. Monarchs	EJHL	34	6	12	18	22	....	....	....	....	....
2007-08	N.H. Jr. Monarchs	EJHL	40	21	25	46	46	6	5	4	9	6
2008-09	Cedar Rapids	USHL	8	2	0	2	8	....	....	....	....	....
2009-10	New Hampshire	H-East	32	2	8	10	18	....	....	....	....	....
2010-11	New Hampshire	H-East	18	2	1	3	12	....	....	....	....	....
2011-12	New Hampshire	H-East	34	6	5	11	36	....	....	....	....	....
2012-13	New Hampshire	H-East	13	3	2	5	21	....	....	....	....	....

• Missed majority of 2008-09, 2009-10 and 2012-13 due to recurring shoulder injury.

BURLON, Brandon (BUHR-lohn, BRAN-duhn) N.J.

Defense. Shoots left. 6', 195 lbs. Born, Nobleton, Ont., March 5, 1990.
(New Jersey's 2nd choice, 52nd overall, in 2008 Entry Draft).

			Regular Season					Playoffs				
Season	Club	League	GP	G	A	Pts	PIM	GP	G	A	Pts	PIM
2005-06	Vaughan Kings	GTHL	55	19	29	48	38	....	....	....	....	....
2006-07	St. Michael's	ON-Jr.A	45	4	19	23	46	4	0	1	1	4
2007-08	St. Michael's	ON-Jr.A	32	7	17	24	41	10	2	4	6	8
2008-09	U. of Michigan	CCHA	33	5	10	15	14	....	....	....	....	....
2009-10	U. of Michigan	CCHA	45	3	11	14	24	....	....	....	....	....
2010-11	U. of Michigan	CCHA	38	5	13	18	28	....	....	....	....	....
2011-12	Albany Devils	AHL	57	1	8	9	21	....	....	....	....	....
2012-13	Albany Devils	AHL	53	1	16	17	25	....	....	....	....	....

CCHA All-Rookie Team (2009)

BURROUGHS, Kyle (BUHR-ohz, KIGHL) NYI

Defense. Shoots right. 5'11", 189 lbs. Born, Vancouver, B.C., July 12, 1995.
(NY Islanders' 7th choice, 196th overall, in 2013 Entry Draft).

			Regular Season					Playoffs				
Season	Club	League	GP	G	A	Pts	PIM	GP	G	A	Pts	PIM
2010-11	Valley West Hawks	BCMML	36	11	25	36	58	4	0	4	4	2
	Aldergrove	PIJHL	4	0	1	1	18	....	....	....	....	....
	Regina Pats	WHL	1	0	0	0	0	....	....	....	....	....
2011-12	Regina Pats	WHL	55	2	6	8	54	5	1	1	2	0
2012-13	Regina Pats	WHL	70	5	28	33	91	....	....	....	....	....

BUSSIERES, Raphael (boo-SEE-air, ra-FIGH-ehl) MIN

Left wing. Shoots left. 6'2", 198 lbs. Born, Longueuil, Que., November 5, 1993.
(Minnesota's 2nd choice, 46th overall, in 2012 Entry Draft).

			Regular Season					Playoffs				
Season	Club	League	GP	G	A	Pts	PIM	GP	G	A	Pts	PIM
2008-09	C.C. Lemoyne	QAAA	41	12	11	23	22	16	7	7	14	2
2009-10	C.C. Lemoyne	QAAA	9	10	15	25	4	....	....	....	....	....
	Moncton Wildcats	QMJHL	20	1	2	3	8	....	....	....	....	....
	Baie-Comeau	QMJHL	24	6	8	14	13	....	....	....	....	....
2010-11	Baie-Comeau	QMJHL	66	17	22	39	39	....	....	....	....	....
2011-12	Baie-Comeau	QMJHL	56	21	23	44	60	5	3	5	8	11
2012-13	Baie-Comeau	QMJHL	60	29	39	68	43	19	4	12	16	18

BUTCHER, Will (BUH-chuhr, WIHL) COL

Defense. Shoots left. 5'10", 191 lbs. Born, Madison, WI, January 6, 1995.
(Colorado's 5th choice, 123rd overall, in 2013 Entry Draft).

			Regular Season					Playoffs				
Season	Club	League	GP	G	A	Pts	PIM	GP	G	A	Pts	PIM
2010-11	Madison Capitols	T1EHL	34	10	20	30	2	....	....	....	....	....
	Dubuque	USHL	2	0	2	2	0	....	....	....	....	....
2011-12	USNTDP	USHL	31	2	8	10	4	....	....	....	....	....
	USNTDP	U-17	17	6	17	23	4	....	....	....	....	....
	USNTDP	U-18	8	0	0	0	2	....	....	....	....	....
2012-13	USNTDP	USHL	26	3	10	13	2	....	....	....	....	....
	USNTDP	U-18	41	8	16	24	6	....	....	....	....	....

• Signed Letter of Intent to attend **University of Denver** (WCHA) in fall of 2013.

BUTTON, Ryan (BUH-tuhn, RIGH-uhn) DAL

Defense. Shoots left. 6'1", 190 lbs. Born, Edmonton, Alta., March 26, 1991.
(Boston's 2nd choice, 86th overall, in 2009 Entry Draft).

			Regular Season					Playoffs				
Season	Club	League	GP	G	A	Pts	PIM	GP	G	A	Pts	PIM
2006-07	Edmonton CAC	AMHL	28	2	6	8	74	....	....	....	....	....
2007-08	Prince Albert	WHL	58	0	8	8	30	....	....	....	....	....
2008-09	Prince Albert	WHL	70	5	32	37	43	....	....	....	....	....
2009-10	Prince Albert	WHL	67	6	27	33	46	....	....	....	....	....
2010-11	Prince Albert	WHL	44	3	20	23	31	....	....	....	....	....
	Seattle	WHL	25	2	10	12	18	....	....	....	....	....
	Providence Bruins	AHL	7	0	1	1	2	....	....	....	....	....
2011-12	Providence Bruins	AHL	28	0	2	2	16	....	....	....	....	....
	Reading Royals	ECHL	30	1	5	6	14	....	....	....	....	....
2012-13	South Carolina	ECHL	5	0	0	0	4	4	0	1	1	2
	Providence Bruins	AHL	25	0	0	0	15	6	0	0	0	4

Traded to **Dallas** by **Boston** with Tyler Seguin and Rich Peverley for Loui Eriksson, Joe Morrow, Reilly Smith and Matt Fraser, July 4, 2013.

BYRON, Blaine (BIGH-ruhn, BLAYN) PIT

Center. Shoots left. 5'11", 163 lbs. Born, Ottawa, Ont., February 21, 1995.
(Pittsburgh's 5th choice, 179th overall, in 2013 Entry Draft).

			Regular Season					Playoffs				
Season	Club	League	GP	G	A	Pts	PIM	GP	G	A	Pts	PIM
2009-10	U.C. Cyclones	Minor-ON	28	16	23	39	14	12	6	11	17	8
2010-11	U.C. Cyclones MM	Minor-ON	30	18	30	48	12	....	....	....	....	....
	U.C. Cyclones Mid.	Minor-ON	6	2	1	3	2	....	....	....	....	....
	Kemptville 73's	ON-Jr.A	9	1	1	2	2	....	....	....	....	....
2011-12	Kemptville 73's	ON-Jr.A	42	12	27	39	20	....	....	....	....	....
2012-13	Kemptville 73's	ON-Jr.A	24	7	16	23	8	....	....	....	....	....
	Smiths Falls Bears	ON-Jr.A	27	5	24	29	16	5	0	1	1	0

• Signed Letter of Intent to attend **University of Maine** (Hockey East) in fall of 2013 or 2014.

BYSTROM, Ludwig (B'YEW-struhm, LOOD-wihg) DAL

Defense. Shoots left. 6'1", 169 lbs. Born, Ornskoldsvik, Sweden, July 20, 1994.
(Dallas' 2nd choice, 43rd overall, in 2012 Entry Draft).

			Regular Season					Playoffs				
Season	Club	League	GP	G	A	Pts	PIM	GP	G	A	Pts	PIM
2009-10	MODO U18	Swe-U18	24	4	0	4	10	5	0	1	1	0
2010-11	MODO U18	Swe-U18	9	1	5	6	10	3	0	0	0	10
	MODO Jr.	Swe-Jr.	37	1	10	11	28	6	1	2	3	6
	MODO	Sweden	1	0	0	0	0	....	....	....	....	....
2011-12	MODO U18	Swe-U18	1	1	0	1	2	1	0	0	0	10
	MODO Jr.	Swe-Jr.	34	7	22	29	101	8	1	3	4	4
	MODO	Sweden	20	0	1	1	8	1	0	0	0	0
2012-13	MODO	Sweden	30	3	3	6	2	....	....	....	....	....
	Orebro HK	Sweden-2	9	0	0	0	2	....	....	....	....	....
	MODO Jr.	Swe-Jr.	8	1	2	3	4	7	1	5	6	4

CALLAHAN, Mitch (kal-AH-han, MIHCH) DET

Right wing. Shoots right. 6', 200 lbs. Born, Whittier, CA, August 17, 1991.
(Detroit's 6th choice, 180th overall, in 2009 Entry Draft).

			Regular Season					Playoffs				
Season	Club	League	GP	G	A	Pts	PIM	GP	G	A	Pts	PIM
2007-08	L.A. Jr. Kings	Minor-CA	52	32	37	69	62	....	....	....	....	....
2008-09	Kelowna Rockets	WHL	70	14	13	27	188	22	1	3	4	43
2009-10	Kelowna Rockets	WHL	72	20	27	47	165	12	2	4	6	10
2010-11	Kelowna Rockets	WHL	62	23	31	54	87	10	5	4	9	17
2011-12	Grand Rapids	AHL	48	6	3	9	103	....	....	....	....	....
2012-13	Grand Rapids	AHL	71	11	9	20	93	24	6	5	11	33

CALNAN, Chris (KAL-nan, KRIHS) CHI

Right wing. Shoots right. 6'2", 187 lbs. Born, Boston, MA, May 5, 1994.
(Chicago's 3rd choice, 79th overall, in 2012 Entry Draft).

			Regular Season					Playoffs				
Season	Club	League	GP	G	A	Pts	PIM	GP	G	A	Pts	PIM
2010-11	Neponset Valley	Minor-MA	11	7	11	18	28	....	....	....	....	....
	Nobles	High-MA	27	14	11	25	8	....	....	....	....	....
2011-12	Cape Cod Whalers	Minor-MA	32	21	28	49	....	....	....	....	....	....
	Nobles	High-MA	27	28	27	55	13	....	....	....	....	....
2012-13	South Shore Kings	EJHL	31	27	22	49	35	2	2	0	2	2

• Signed Letter of Intent to attend **Boston College** (Hockey East) in fall of 2013.

CAMARA, Anthony (kuh-MAR-uh, an-THUH-nee) BOS

Left wing. Shoots left. 6', 192 lbs. Born, Toronto, Ont., September 4, 1993.
(Boston's 3rd choice, 81st overall, in 2011 Entry Draft).

			Regular Season					Playoffs				
Season	Club	League	GP	G	A	Pts	PIM	GP	G	A	Pts	PIM
2008-09	Miss. Senators	GTHL	50	31	25	56	94	....	....	....	....	....
2009-10	Saginaw Spirit	OHL	65	6	6	12	96	6	1	1	2	5
2010-11	Saginaw Spirit	OHL	64	8	9	17	132	12	0	1	1	25
2011-12	Saginaw Spirit	OHL	35	7	12	19	76	....	....	....	....	....
	Barrie Colts	OHL	31	9	5	14	59	13	2	3	5	22
2012-13	Barrie Colts	OHL	50	36	24	60	91	16	9	7	16	*42

CAMERANESI, Tony (kam-uhr-ihn-EHS-ee, TOH-nee) TOR

Center. Shoots right. 5'10", 180 lbs. Born, Maple Grove, MN, August 12, 1993.
(Toronto's 5th choice, 130th overall, in 2011 Entry Draft).

			Regular Season					Playoffs				
Season	Club	League	GP	G	A	Pts	PIM	GP	G	A	Pts	PIM
2009-10	Wayzata	High-MN	25	16	29	45	6	2	2	1	3	0
2010-11	Team Northwest	UMHSEL	21	16	17	33	18	3	2	4	6	2
	Wayzata	High-MN	25	15	39	54	26	3	2	7	9	4
2011-12	Waterloo	USHL	55	18	24	42	47	10	1	5	6	4
2012-13	U. Minn-Duluth	WCHA	38	14	20	34	28	....	....	....	....	....

WCHA All-Rookie Team (2013)

CAMMARATA, Taylor (kam-a-RAT-ta, TAY-luhr) NYI

Center/Left wing. Shoots left. 5'7", 156 lbs. Born, Minneapolis, MN, May 13, 1995.
(NY Islanders' 3rd choice, 76th overall, in 2013 Entry Draft).

			Regular Season					Playoffs				
Season	Club	League	GP	G	A	Pts	PIM	GP	G	A	Pts	PIM
2009-10	Shattuck Bantam	High-MN	58	92	78	170	8	....	....	....	....	....
2010-11	Shattuck Midget	High-MN	54	71	68	139	6	....	....	....	....	....
2011-12	Waterloo	USHL	60	27	42	69	6	15	8	8	16	6
2012-13	Waterloo	USHL	59	*38	55	*93	49	5	2	3	5	0

USHL All-Rookie Team (2012) • USHL Second All-Star Team (2012) • USHL Rookie of the Year (2012) • USHL First All-Star Team (2013)

• Signed Letter of Intent to attend **University of Minnesota** (WCHA) in fall of 2013.

CAMPBELL, Andrew (KAM-buhl, AN-droo) L.A.

Defense. Shoots left. 6'3", 207 lbs. Born, Caledonia, Ont., February 4, 1988.
(Los Angeles' 5th choice, 74th overall, in 2008 Entry Draft).

			Regular Season					Playoffs				
Season	Club	League	GP	G	A	Pts	PIM	GP	G	A	Pts	PIM
2005-06	Sault Ste. Marie	OHL	31	1	3	4	23	3	0	0	0	4
2006-07	Sault Ste. Marie	OHL	63	4	14	18	75	13	0	1	1	6
2007-08	Sault Ste. Marie	OHL	68	13	22	35	64	14	2	3	5	13
2008-09	Manchester	AHL	72	3	5	8	72	....	....	....	....	....
2009-10	Manchester	AHL	74	2	9	11	68	16	1	4	5	6
2010-11	Manchester	AHL	76	1	11	12	68	7	0	0	0	0
2011-12	Manchester	AHL	76	2	17	19	54	4	0	0	0	9
2012-13	Manchester	AHL	47	2	9	11	40	4	0	0	0	2

CAMPBELL, Evan (KAM-behl, EH-vuhn) EDM

Left wing. Shoots left. 6'1", 175 lbs. Born, Port Coquitlam, B.C., March 1, 1993.
(Edmonton's 8th choice, 128th overall, in 2013 Entry Draft).

			Regular Season					Playoffs				
Season	Club	League	GP	G	A	Pts	PIM	GP	G	A	Pts	PIM
2009-10	Van. NE Chiefs	BCMML	39	14	14	28	64	4	1	1	2	2
2010-11	Kerry Park	VIJHL	41	14	22	36	28	5	2	1	3	4
	Cowichan Valley	BCHL	1	0	0	0	0	....	....	....	....	....
2011-12	Coquitlam Express	BCHL	17	1	1	2	17	....	....	....	....	....
	Langley Rivermen	BCHL	31	11	8	19	18	....	....	....	....	....
2012-13	Langley Rivermen	BCHL	51	20	46	66	46	4	2	0	2	6

• Signed Letter of Intent to attend **University of Massachusetts-Lowell** (Hockey East) in fall of 2013.

CANNONE, Pat (ka-NOHN, PAT) ST.L.

Right wing. Shoots right. 5'11", 204 lbs. Born, Bayport, NY, August 9, 1986.

			Regular Season					Playoffs				
Season	Club	League	GP	G	A	Pts	PIM	GP	G	A	Pts	PIM
2006-07	Cedar Rapids	USHL	59	18	37	55	46	6	1	7	8	6
2007-08	Miami U.	CCHA	42	6	24	30	20	....	....	....	....	....
2008-09	Miami U.	CCHA	41	11	24	35	16	....	....	....	....	....
2009-10	Miami U.	CCHA	44	14	17	31	22	....	....	....	....	....
2010-11	Miami U.	CCHA	39	14	23	37	25	....	....	....	....	....
	Binghamton	AHL	2	1	1	2	2	....	....	....	....	....
2011-12	Binghamton	AHL	76	19	24	43	32	....	....	....	....	....
2012-13	Binghamton	AHL	74	10	15	25	41	3	0	0	0	4

Signed as a free agent by **Ottawa**, April 8, 2011. Traded to **St. Louis** by **Ottawa** for future considerations, July 8, 2013.

CANTIN, Marc (KAN-tihn, MAHRK) NYI

Defense. Shoots left. 6'1", 204 lbs. Born, Omemee, Ont., March 27, 1990.

			Regular Season					Playoffs				
Season	Club	League	GP	G	A	Pts	PIM	GP	G	A	Pts	PIM
2006-07	Lindsay Muskies	ON-Jr.A	40	2	14	16	60	2	0	0	0	2
	Belleville Bulls	OHL	9	0	1	1	12	6	0	0	0	2
2007-08	Belleville Bulls	OHL	60	2	6	8	33	13	0	1	1	9
2008-09	Belleville Bulls	OHL	62	1	14	15	51	17	0	2	2	26
2009-10	Belleville Bulls	OHL	33	1	7	8	63	....	....	....	....	....
	Windsor Spitfires	OHL	24	2	5	7	41	19	3	3	6	21
2010-11	St. Michael's	OHL	61	10	31	41	78	20	0	6	6	18
2011-12	Providence Bruins	AHL	19	0	0	0	22	....	....	....	....	....
	Reading Royals	ECHL	25	2	7	9	34	5	0	2	2	0
	Bridgeport	AHL	2	0	0	0	4	....	....	....	....	....
2012-13	Bridgeport	AHL	22	0	1	1	48	....	....	....	....	....
	Las Vegas	ECHL	6	0	1	1	16	7	2	2	4	8

OHL Second All-Star Team (2011) • George Parsons Trophy (Memorial Cup - Most Sportsmanlike Player) (2011)

Signed as a free agent by **Boston**, March 23, 2011. Traded to **NY Islanders** by **Boston** with Yannick Riendeau for Brian Rolston and Mike Mottau, February 27, 2012.

CAREY, Paul (KAIR-ee, PAWL) COL

Center. Shoots left. 6'1", 196 lbs. Born, Boston, MA, September 24, 1988.
(Colorado's 7th choice, 135th overall, in 2007 Entry Draft).

			Regular Season					Playoffs				
Season	Club	League	GP	G	A	Pts	PIM	GP	G	A	Pts	PIM
2005-06	Salisbury School	High-CT	27	14	11	25	18	....	....	....	....	....
2006-07	Salisbury School	High-CT	24	16	11	27	16	....	....	....	....	....
2007-08	Indiana Ice	USHL	60	34	32	66	32	4	1	2	3	2
2008-09	Boston College	H-East	24	5	4	9	8	....	....	....	....	....
2009-10	Boston College	H-East	41	9	12	21	29	....	....	....	....	....
2010-11	Boston College	H-East	38	13	13	26	18	....	....	....	....	....
2011-12	Boston College	H-East	44	18	12	30	30	....	....	....	....	....
	Lake Erie Monsters	AHL	2	0	0	0	2	....	....	....	....	....
2012-13	Lake Erie Monsters	AHL	72	19	22	41	29	....	....	....	....	....

USHL All-Rookie Team (2008) • USHL Second All-Star Team (2008) • NCAA Championship All-Tournament Team (2012)

CARMAN, Mike (KAR-mahn, MIGHK)

Center. Shoots left. 6', 180 lbs. Born, Augusta, GA, April 14, 1988.
(Colorado's 4th choice, 81st overall, in 2006 Entry Draft).

			Regular Season					Playoffs				
Season	Club	League	GP	G	A	Pts	PIM	GP	G	A	Pts	PIM
2003-04	Holy Angels	High-MN	29	19	40	59	....	....	....	....	....	....
2004-05	USNTDP	U-17	14	2	9	11	40	....	....	....	....	....
	USNTDP	NAHL	39	12	15	27	38	10	2	4	6	10
2005-06	USNTDP	U-18	43	15	23	38	78	....	....	....	....	....
	USNTDP	NAHL	17	6	10	16	24	....	....	....	....	....
2006-07	U. of Minnesota	WCHA	41	9	11	20	55	....	....	....	....	....
2007-08	U. of Minnesota	WCHA	23	4	7	11	28	....	....	....	....	....
2008-09	U. of Minnesota	WCHA	32	8	9	17	32	....	....	....	....	....
2009-10	U. of Minnesota	WCHA	39	8	10	18	39	....	....	....	....	....
	Lake Erie Monsters	AHL	10	2	0	2	10	....	....	....	....	....
2010-11	Lake Erie Monsters	AHL	69	9	8	17	59	7	0	1	1	2
2011-12	Lake Erie Monsters	AHL	28	3	3	6	10	....	....	....	....	....
	Hershey Bears	AHL	32	7	5	12	31	5	1	0	1	0
2012-13	Hershey Bears	AHL	62	4	6	10	20	....	....	....	....	....

Traded to **Washington** by **Colorado** for Danny Richmond, February 2, 2012.

CARON, Josh (kah-ROHN, JAWSH) MIN

Defense. Shoots right. 6'4", 216 lbs. Born, Campbell River, B.C., February 10, 1991.

			Regular Season					Playoffs				
Season	Club	League	GP	G	A	Pts	PIM	GP	G	A	Pts	PIM
2007-08	Kamloops Storm	KIJHL	47	1	4	5	86	21	0	0	0	53
	Merritt	BCHL	5	0	0	0	0	....	....	....	....	....
2008-09	Kamloops Storm	KIJHL	29	4	8	12	182	....	....	....	....	....
	Kamloops Blazers	WHL	21	0	1	1	50	4	0	0	0	9
2009-10	Kamloops Blazers	WHL	60	1	5	6	190	4	0	1	1	10
2010-11	Kamloops Blazers	WHL	27	1	1	2	47	....	....	....	....	....
2011-12	Kamloops Blazers	WHL	20	0	6	6	88	....	....	....	....	....
	Everett Silvertips	WHL	43	1	6	7	71	4	1	0	1	4
2012-13	Houston Aeros	AHL	11	0	0	0	7	....	....	....	....	....
	Orlando	ECHL	25	1	1	2	41	....	....	....	....	....

Signed as a free agent by **Minnesota**, September 23, 2010.

CARRICK, Connor (KAIR-ihk, KAW-nuhr) **WSH**

Defense. Shoots right. 5'11", 185 lbs. Born, Orland Park, IL, April 13, 1994.
(Washington's 6th choice, 137th overall, in 2012 Entry Draft).

			Regular Season					Playoffs				
Season	**Club**	**League**	**GP**	**G**	**A**	**Pts**	**PIM**	**GP**	**G**	**A**	**Pts**	**PIM**
2009-10	Chicago Fury U18	T1EHL	22	2	4	6	2	....	....	....	....	....
	Chicago Fury	T1EHL	37	7	15	22	48	....	....	....	....	....
2010-11	USNTDP	USHL	36	1	6	7	42	2	0	0	0	2
	USNTDP	U-17	17	3	10	13	10	....	....	....	....	....
2011-12	USNTDP	USHL	21	1	4	5	30	....	....	....	....	....
	USNTDP	U-18	36	7	9	16	16	....	....	....	....	....
2012-13	Plymouth Whalers	OHL	68	12	32	44	79	15	2	16	18	6

CARRICK, Sam (KAIR-ihk, SAM) **TOR**

Center. Shoots right. 6', 207 lbs. Born, Stouffville, Ont., February 4, 1992.
(Toronto's 5th choice, 144th overall, in 2010 Entry Draft).

			Regular Season					Playoffs				
Season	**Club**	**League**	**GP**	**G**	**A**	**Pts**	**PIM**	**GP**	**G**	**A**	**Pts**	**PIM**
2007-08	Tor. Red Wings	GTHL	55	40	30	70	130	....	....	....	....	....
2008-09	Brampton	OHL	61	10	11	21	47	21	1	0	1	16
2009-10	Brampton	OHL	66	21	21	42	96	8	2	2	4	8
2010-11	Brampton	OHL	59	16	23	39	74	4	0	1	1	4
2011-12	Brampton	OHL	68	37	30	67	104	8	4	4	8	16
2012-13	Idaho Steelheads	ECHL	50	16	21	37	70	....	....	....	....	....
	Toronto Marlies	AHL	19	2	2	4	18	5	0	0	0	0

CARRICK, Trevor (KAIR-ihk, TREH-vuhr) **CAR**

Defense. Shoots left. 6'2", 180 lbs. Born, Stouffville, Ont., July 4, 1994.
(Carolina's 5th choice, 115th overall, in 2012 Entry Draft).

			Regular Season					Playoffs				
Season	**Club**	**League**	**GP**	**G**	**A**	**Pts**	**PIM**	**GP**	**G**	**A**	**Pts**	**PIM**
2009-10	Markham Majors	GTHL	49	6	23	29	48	....	....	....	....	....
	Upper Canada	ON-Jr.A	2	0	1	1	2	....	....	....	....	....
2010-11	Stouffville Spirit	ON-Jr.A	40	6	13	19	44	19	2	11	13	10
2011-12	St. Michael's	OHL	68	6	13	19	64	6	1	0	1	7
2012-13	Mississauga	OHL	56	10	21	31	56	6	0	2	2	11

CARRIER, William (kair-ree-AY, WIHL-yuhm) **ST.L.**

Left wing. Shoots left. 6'2", 198 lbs. Born, La Salle, Que., December 20, 1994.
(St. Louis' 2nd choice, 57th overall, in 2013 Entry Draft).

			Regular Season					Playoffs				
Season	**Club**	**League**	**GP**	**G**	**A**	**Pts**	**PIM**	**GP**	**G**	**A**	**Pts**	**PIM**
2009-10	Lac St-Louis Royals	Minor-QU	STATISTICS NOT AVAILABLE									
	Lac St-Louis Lions	QAAA	3	0	0	0	2	....	....	....	....	....
2010-11	Cape Breton	QMJHL	61	8	4	12	54	4	0	0	0	2
2011-12	Cape Breton	QMJHL	66	27	43	70	65	4	3	3	6	4
2012-13	Cape Breton	QMJHL	34	16	26	42	41	....	....	....	....	....

CASSELS, Cole (KA-suhlz, KOHL) **VAN**

Center. Shoots right. 6', 178 lbs. Born, Hartford, CT, May 4, 1995.
(Vancouver's 3rd choice, 85th overall, in 2013 Entry Draft).

			Regular Season					Playoffs				
Season	**Club**	**League**	**GP**	**G**	**A**	**Pts**	**PIM**	**GP**	**G**	**A**	**Pts**	**PIM**
2009-10	Cleveland Barons	T1EHL	31	6	22	28	46	....	....	....	....	....
2010-11	Ohio Blue Jackets	T1EHL	37	11	23	34	61	....	....	....	....	....
	Ohio Blue Jackets	Minor-OH	11	11	21	32	....	....	....	....	....	....
2011-12	Oshawa Generals	OHL	64	3	8	11	31	6	1	0	1	6
2012-13	Oshawa Generals	OHL	64	15	28	43	61	9	1	0	1	14

CASTO, Chris (KAS-toh, KRIHS) **BOS**

Defense. Shoots right. 6'1", 200 lbs. Born, Stillwater, MN, December 27, 1991.

			Regular Season					Playoffs				
Season	**Club**	**League**	**GP**	**G**	**A**	**Pts**	**PIM**	**GP**	**G**	**A**	**Pts**	**PIM**
2010-11	Lincoln Stars	USHL	58	6	19	25	40	2	0	0	0	0
2011-12	U. Minn-Duluth	WCHA	41	2	11	13	14	....	....	....	....	....
2012-13	U. Minn-Duluth	WCHA	36	3	6	9	16	....	....	....	....	....
	Providence Bruins	AHL	4	0	0	0	0	....	....	....	....	....

Signed as a free agent by **Boston**, March 26, 2013..

CATENACCI, Daniel (ka-tehn-AH-chee, DAN-yehl) **BUF**

Center. Shoots left. 5', 187 lbs. Born, Newmarket, Ont., March 9, 1993.
(Buffalo's 2nd choice, 77th overall, in 2011 Entry Draft).

			Regular Season					Playoffs				
Season	**Club**	**League**	**GP**	**G**	**A**	**Pts**	**PIM**	**GP**	**G**	**A**	**Pts**	**PIM**
2008-09	York Simcoe	Minor-ON	39	42	45	87	152	....	....	....	....	....
	Villanova Knights	ON-Jr.A	1	1	0	1	2	....	....	....	....	....
2009-10	Sault Ste. Marie	OHL	65	10	20	30	68	5	1	1	2	6
2010-11	Sault Ste. Marie	OHL	67	26	45	71	117	....	....	....	....	....
2011-12	Owen Sound	OHL	67	33	39	72	114	5	1	3	4	8
2012-13	Owen Sound	OHL	67	38	41	79	115	12	3	6	9	32

CECI, Cody (SEE-SEE, KOH-dee) **OTT**

Defense. Shoots right. 6'2", 210 lbs. Born, Ottawa, Ont., December 21, 1993.
(Ottawa's 1st choice, 15th overall, in 2012 Entry Draft).

			Regular Season					Playoffs				
Season	**Club**	**League**	**GP**	**G**	**A**	**Pts**	**PIM**	**GP**	**G**	**A**	**Pts**	**PIM**
2008-09	Peterborough	Minor-ON	57	24	48	72	26	....	....	....	....	....
2009-10	Ottawa 67's	OHL	64	4	8	12	12	12	0	3	3	0
2010-11	Ottawa 67's	OHL	68	9	25	34	28	4	0	2	2	4
2011-12	Ottawa 67's	OHL	64	17	43	60	14	18	2	13	15	4
2012-13	Ottawa 67's	OHL	42	11	29	40	10	....	....	....	....	....
	Owen Sound	OHL	27	8	16	24	2	12	1	9	10	0
	Binghamton	AHL	3	1	1	2	0	3	0	0	0	0

OHL Second All-Star Team (2012, 2013)

CEDERHOLM, Anton (SEH-duhr-holm, an-TAWN) **VAN**

Defense. Shoots left. 6'2", 204 lbs. Born, Helsingborg, Sweden, February 21, 1995.
(Vancouver's 5th choice, 145th overall, in 2013 Entry Draft).

			Regular Season					Playoffs				
Season	**Club**	**League**	**GP**	**G**	**A**	**Pts**	**PIM**	**GP**	**G**	**A**	**Pts**	**PIM**
2009-10	Jonstorps IF U18	Swe-U18	12	1	3	4	14	....	....	....	....	....
	Jonstorps IF Jr.	Swe-Jr.	3	0	0	0	4	....	....	....	....	....
2010-11	Rogle U18	Swe-U18	31	4	8	12	18	4	0	1	1	2
	Rogle Jr.	Swe-Jr.	2	0	0	0	0	....	....	....	....	....
2011-12	Rogle U18	Swe-U18	8	1	3	4	45	....	....	....	....	....
	Rogle Jr.	Swe-Jr.	41	3	5	8	71	....	....	....	....	....
2012-13	Rogle U18	Swe-U18	8	0	1	1	10	3	0	1	1	6
	Rogle Jr.	Swe-Jr.	36	5	8	13	64	2	0	0	0	0
	Rogle	Sweden	12	0	0	0	6	....	....	....	....	....

CEHLARIK, Peter (T'SECH-lahr-ihk, PEE-tuhr) **BOS**

Left wing. Shoots left. 6'2", 192 lbs. Born, Zilina, Slovakia, August 2, 1995.
(Boston's 2nd choice, 90th overall, in 2013 Entry Draft).

			Regular Season					Playoffs				
Season	**Club**	**League**	**GP**	**G**	**A**	**Pts**	**PIM**	**GP**	**G**	**A**	**Pts**	**PIM**
2008-09	MsHK Zilina U18	Svk-U18	1	0	0	0	0	....	....	....	....	....
2009-10	Zilina U18	Svk-U18	28	4	4	8	4	....	....	....	....	....
2010-11	MsHK Zilina U18	Svk-U18	40	15	18	33	8	....	....	....	....	....
2011-12	MsHK Zilina U18	Svk-U18	6	6	2	8	16	....	....	....	....	....
	MsHK Zilina Jr.	Slovak-Jr.	4	1	2	3	2	....	....	....	....	....
	Lulea HF U18	Swe-U18	24	15	15	30	0	4	2	0	2	0
	Lulea HF Jr.	Swe-Jr.	8	2	2	4	2	1	3	0	3	0
2012-13	Lulea HF U18	Swe-U18	10	8	9	17	0	....	....	....	....	....
	Lulea HF Jr.	Swe-Jr.	38	17	20	37	10	3	0	1	1	2
	Lulea HF	Sweden	8	3	3	6	0	6	1	0	1	0

CEHLIN, Patrick (seh-LIHN, PAHT-rihk) **NSH**

Right wing. Shoots right. 5'11", 177 lbs. Born, Huddinge, Sweden, July 27, 1991.
(Nashville's 3rd choice, 126th overall, in 2010 Entry Draft).

			Regular Season					Playoffs				
Season	**Club**	**League**	**GP**	**G**	**A**	**Pts**	**PIM**	**GP**	**G**	**A**	**Pts**	**PIM**
2006-07	Djurgarden U18	Swe-U18	27	10	18	28	49	3	1	2	3	0
2007-08	Djurgarden U18	Swe-U18	12	7	16	23	10	8	0	5	5	12
	Djurgarden Jr.	Swe-Jr.	22	5	3	8	8	4	0	1	1	4
2008-09	Djurgarden U18	Swe-U18	4	5	2	7	0	1	0	0	0	2
	Djurgarden Jr.	Swe-Jr.	36	10	25	35	110	6	1	2	3	6
	Djurgarden	Sweden	2	0	0	0	0	....	....	....	....	....
2009-10	Djurgarden Jr.	Swe-Jr.	9	3	3	6	4	....	....	....	....	....
	Djurgarden	Sweden	54	5	6	11	10	16	0	2	2	2
2010-11	Djurgarden	Sweden	48	4	12	16	14	7	1	0	1	2
	Djurgarden Jr.	Swe-Jr.	....	....	....	....	....	5	4	2	6	0
2011-12	Djurgarden	Sweden	48	10	4	14	20	....	....	....	....	....
	Djurgarden	Sweden-Q	8	0	0	0	2	....	....	....	....	....
2012-13	Milwaukee	AHL	70	9	23	32	28	4	1	0	1	0
	Cincinnati	ECHL	1	1	0	1	0	....	....	....	....	....

CERESNAK, Peter (CHUHR-ehsh-nak, PEE-tuhr)

Defense. Shoots right. 6'3", 209 lbs. Born, Trencin, Slovakia, January 26, 1993.
(NY Rangers' 6th choice, 172nd overall, in 2011 Entry Draft).

			Regular Season					Playoffs				
Season	**Club**	**League**	**GP**	**G**	**A**	**Pts**	**PIM**	**GP**	**G**	**A**	**Pts**	**PIM**
2007-08	Dukla Trencin U18	Svk-U18	10	0	2	2	10	....	....	....	....	....
2008-09	Dukla Trencin U18	Svk-U18	28	1	2	3	10	....	....	....	....	....
	Dukla Trencin Jr.	Slovak-Jr.	15	1	1	2	0	8	0	0	0	0
2009-10	Dukla Trencin U18	Svk-U18	2	1	2	3	0	....	....	....	....	....
	Dukla Trencin Jr.	Slovak-Jr.	40	4	17	21	30	7	0	1	1	8
2010-11	Slovakia U20	Slovakia	25	1	3	4	16	....	....	....	....	....
	Dukla Trencin Jr.	Slovak-Jr.	8	0	3	3	4	11	0	3	3	37
	Dukla Trencin	Slovakia	7	0	0	0	0	....	....	....	....	....
	Dukla Trencin U18	Svk-U18	....	....	....	....	....	3	2	2	4	4
2011-12	Peterborough	OHL	61	6	9	15	34	....	....	....	....	....
2012-13	Peterborough	OHL	56	3	9	12	24	....	....	....	....	....

CHAPUT, Michael (sha-PUT, MIGH-kuhl) **CBJ**

Center. Shoots left. 6'2", 194 lbs. Born, Ile Bizard, Que., April 9, 1992.
(Philadelphia's 1st choice, 89th overall, in 2010 Entry Draft).

			Regular Season					Playoffs				
Season	**Club**	**League**	**GP**	**G**	**A**	**Pts**	**PIM**	**GP**	**G**	**A**	**Pts**	**PIM**
2007-08	Lac St-Louis Royals	Minor-QU	STATISTICS NOT AVAILABLE									
	Lac St-Louis Lions	QAAA	4	0	0	0	0	....	....	....	....	....
2008-09	Lewiston	QMJHL	29	3	7	10	34	....	....	....	....	....
2009-10	Lewiston	QMJHL	68	28	27	55	60	4	0	1	1	2
2010-11	Lewiston	QMJHL	62	25	34	59	97	13	7	13	20	11
2011-12	Shawinigan	QMJHL	57	21	42	63	47	11	4	8	12	2
2012-13	Springfield Falcons	AHL	73	13	19	32	57	8	1	1	2	4

Memorial Cup All-Star Team (2012) • Ed Chynoweth Trophy (Memorial Cup - Leading Scorer) (2012) • Stafford Smythe Memorial Trophy (Memorial Cup - MVP) (2012)

• Missed majority of 2008-09 due to shoulder injury. Traded to **Columbus** by **Philadelphia** with Greg Moore for Tom Sestito, February 28, 2011.

CHASE, Gregory (CHAYS, GREH-goh-ree) **EDM**

Center/Right wing. Shoots right. 6', 195 lbs. Born, Sherwood Park, Alta., January 1, 1995.
(Edmonton's 10th choice, 188th overall, in 2013 Entry Draft).

			Regular Season					Playoffs				
Season	**Club**	**League**	**GP**	**G**	**A**	**Pts**	**PIM**	**GP**	**G**	**A**	**Pts**	**PIM**
2010-11	Sherwood Park	AMHL	30	24	15	39	64	12	7	3	10	36
	Calgary Hitmen	WHL	5	0	0	0	6	....	....	....	....	....
2011-12	Calgary Hitmen	WHL	60	6	22	28	41	5	1	1	2	11
2012-13	Calgary Hitmen	WHL	69	17	32	49	58	17	3	7	10	24

CHEEK, Trevor (CHEEK, TREH-vuhr) **COL**

Center. Shoots left. 6'2", 198 lbs. Born, Vancouver, WA, December 29, 1992.

			Regular Season					Playoffs				
Season	**Club**	**League**	**GP**	**G**	**A**	**Pts**	**PIM**	**GP**	**G**	**A**	**Pts**	**PIM**
2010-11	Calgary Hitmen	WHL	57	10	15	25	37	....	....	....	....	....
2011-12	Calgary Hitmen	WHL	67	23	26	49	75	5	3	1	4	4
2012-13	Calgary Hitmen	WHL	1	0	1	1	0	....	....	....	....	....
	Vancouver Giants	WHL	39	18	14	32	35	....	....	....	....	....
	Edmonton	WHL	31	14	13	27	22	15	8	8	16	14

Signed as a free agent by **Colorado**, April 1, 2013.

CHIAROT, Ben (CHAIR-awt, BEHN) WPG

Defense. Shoots left. 6'3", 224 lbs. Born, Hamilton, Ont., May 9, 1991.
(Atlanta's 5th choice, 120th overall, in 2009 Entry Draft).

			Regular Season					Playoffs				
Season	Club	League	GP	G	A	Pts	PIM	GP	G	A	Pts	PIM
2006-07	Mississauga Reps	GTHL	60	21	42	63	166	....	....	....	....	....
2007-08	Guelph Storm	OHL	31	0	0	0	14	....	....	....	....	....
2008-09	Guelph Storm	OHL	67	2	10	12	111	4	0	3	3	8
2009-10	Guelph Storm	OHL	41	4	9	13	106	....	....	....	....	....
	Sudbury Wolves	OHL	26	4	4	8	61	4	1	1	2	6
	Chicago Wolves	AHL	1	0	0	0	4	....	....	....	....	....
2010-11	Sudbury Wolves	OHL	25	5	8	13	62	....	....	....	....	....
	Saginaw Spirit	OHL	39	5	19	24	51	12	1	4	5	21
2011-12	St. John's IceCaps	AHL	18	1	1	2	19	....	....	....	....	....
	Colorado Eagles	ECHL	24	6	7	13	13	....	....	....	....	....
2012-13	St. John's IceCaps	AHL	61	1	11	12	81	....	....	....	....	....

• Transferred to **Winnipeg** after **Atlanta** franchise relocated, June 21, 2011.

CHUDINOV, Maxim (choo-DEE-nawf, max-EEM) BOS

Defense. Shoots right. 5'11", 187 lbs. Born, Cherepovets, USSR, March 25, 1990.
(Boston's 7th choice, 195th overall, in 2010 Entry Draft).

			Regular Season					Playoffs				
Season	Club	League	GP	G	A	Pts	PIM	GP	G	A	Pts	PIM
2006-07	Cherepovets	Russia	2	0	0	0	0	3	0	0	0	2
2007-08	Cherepovets 2	Russia-3	STATISTICS NOT AVAILABLE									
	Cherepovets	Russia	18	0	0	0	10	1	0	0	0	0
2008-09	Cherepovets	KHL	26	0	0	0	14	....	....	....	....	....
2009-10	Cherepovets Jr.	Russia-Jr.	4	1	0	1	12	2	0	1	1	4
	Cherepovets	KHL	47	6	8	14	30	....	....	....	....	....
2010-11	Cherepovets	KHL	52	8	15	23	30	6	0	2	2	4
	Cherepovets Jr.	Russia-Jr.	....	....	....	....	....	5	2	2	4	8
2011-12	Cherepovets	KHL	52	9	26	35	62	6	0	2	2	10
	Cherepovets Jr.	Russia-Jr.	....	....	....	....	....	5	0	0	0	8
2012-13	SKA St. Petersburg	KHL	47	2	8	10	46	12	1	1	2	6

CICHY, Michael (KEE-chee, MIGH-kuhl) MTL

Center. Shoots left. 5'11", 175 lbs. Born, New Britain, CT, July 8, 1990.
(Montreal's 7th choice, 199th overall, in 2009 Entry Draft).

			Regular Season					Playoffs				
Season	Club	League	GP	G	A	Pts	PIM	GP	G	A	Pts	PIM
2006-07	USNTDP	NAHL	32	2	8	10	35	....	....	....	....	....
	USNTDP	U-17	7	4	1	5	4	....	....	....	....	....
2007-08	Tri-City Storm	USHL	59	16	29	45	45	....	....	....	....	....
2008-09	Tri-City Storm	USHL	26	*10	19	29	11	....	....	....	....	....
	Indiana Ice	USHL	30	*24	23	47	12	13	6	*19	*25	6
2009-10	North Dakota	WCHA	23	2	2	4	6	....	....	....	....	....
2010-11	North Dakota	WCHA	25	3	4	7	6	....	....	....	....	....
2011-12			DID NOT PLAY – TRANSFERRED COLLEGES									
2012-13	Western Mich.	CCHA	37	4	14	18	14	....	....	....	....	....

USHL First All-Star Team (2009)

CISSE, Yasin (SIH-say, YA-sihn) WPG

Right wing. Shoots right. 6'3", 210 lbs. Born, Westmount, Que., March 11, 1992.
(Atlanta's 5th choice, 150th overall, in 2010 Entry Draft).

			Regular Season					Playoffs				
Season	Club	League	GP	G	A	Pts	PIM	GP	G	A	Pts	PIM
2007-08	Lac St-Louis Lions	QAAA	44	20	38	58	66	13	6	10	16	28
2008-09	Des Moines	USHL	31	2	6	8	46	....	....	....	....	....
2009-10	Des Moines	USHL	18	13	6	19	16	....	....	....	....	....
2010-11	Boston University	H-East	1	0	0	0	0	....	....	....	....	....
2011-12	Boston University	H-East	25	2	3	5	24	....	....	....	....	....
2012-13	Boston University	H-East	13	0	2	2	16	....	....	....	....	....
	Blainville-Bois.	QMJHL	27	8	6	14	27	12	1	5	6	19

• Missed majority of 2009-10 due to ankle injury. • Missed majority of 2010-11 due to ankle injury vs. Wisconsin (WCHA), October 8. 2010. • Transferred to **Winnipeg** after **Atlanta** franchise relocated, June 21, 2011.

CLAESSON, Fredrik (KLA-suhn, FREH-drihk) OTT

Defense. Shoots left. 6', 210 lbs. Born, Stockholm, Sweden, November 24, 1992.
(Ottawa's 6th choice, 126th overall, in 2011 Entry Draft).

			Regular Season					Playoffs				
Season	Club	League	GP	G	A	Pts	PIM	GP	G	A	Pts	PIM
2007-08	Hammarby U18	Swe-U18	15	1	2	3	29	....	....	....	....	....
	Hammarby	Sweden-2	2	0	0	0	2	....	....	....	....	....
2008-09	Djurgarden U18	Swe-U18	28	9	8	17	4	....	....	....	....	....
	Djurgarden Jr.	Swe-Jr.	7	0	0	0	0	....	....	....	....	....
2009-10	Djurgarden U18	Swe-U18	3	1	1	2	0	5	0	3	3	6
	Djurgarden Jr.	Swe-Jr.	22	0	4	4	18	....	....	....	....	....
2010-11	Djurgarden Jr.	Swe-Jr.	18	2	3	5	6	5	0	1	1	0
	Djurgarden	Sweden	35	2	0	2	6	7	0	1	1	0
2011-12	Djurgarden Jr.	Swe-Jr.	1	0	0	0	2	....	....	....	....	....
	Djurgarden	Sweden	47	1	6	7	8	....	....	....	....	....
	Djurgarden	Sweden-Q	10	1	1	2	0	....	....	....	....	....
2012-13	Binghamton	AHL	70	3	8	11	51	3	0	1	1	2

CLAPPERTON, Christopher (KLAP-uhr-yuhn, KRIHS-toh-fuhr) FLA

Left wing. Shoots left. 5'9", 174 lbs. Born, Chandler, Que., February 22, 1994.
(Florida's 6th choice, 122nd overall, in 2013 Entry Draft).

			Regular Season					Playoffs				
Season	Club	League	GP	G	A	Pts	PIM	GP	G	A	Pts	PIM
2009-10	Ecole Notre Dame	QAAA	42	7	23	30	16	8	6	1	7	6
2010-11	Ecole Notre Dame	QAAA	32	9	20	29	28	17	10	11	21	12
2011-12	Blainville-Bois.	QMJHL	56	18	37	55	40	11	3	6	9	8
2012-13	Blainville-Bois.	QMJHL	67	34	43	77	71	15	6	14	20	20

CLARK, Jason (KLARK, JAY-suhn) NYI

Center/Left wing. Shoots left. 6'2", 204 lbs. Born, Eden Prairie, MN, February 27, 1992.
(NY Islanders' 4th choice, 82nd overall, in 2010 Entry Draft).

			Regular Season					Playoffs				
Season	Club	League	GP	G	A	Pts	PIM	GP	G	A	Pts	PIM
2008-09	Shat.-St. Mary's	High-MN	52	18	26	44	68	....	....	....	....	....
2009-10	Shat.-St. Mary's	High-MN	54	23	23	46	80	....	....	....	....	....
2010-11	U. of Wisconsin	WCHA	14	0	1	1	6	....	....	....	....	....
2011-12	U. of Wisconsin	WCHA	21	0	1	1	8	....	....	....	....	....
2012-13	Bridgeport	AHL	8	0	2	2	13	....	....	....	....	....
	Gwinnett	ECHL	24	2	7	9	36	....	....	....	....	....

CLARKE, Michael (KLARK, MIGH-kuhl) COL

Center. Shoots left. 5'11", 184 lbs. Born, London, Ont., April 29, 1994.
(Colorado's 3rd choice, 132nd overall, in 2012 Entry Draft).

			Regular Season					Playoffs				
Season	Club	League	GP	G	A	Pts	PIM	GP	G	A	Pts	PIM
2008-09	Lon. Knights Bant.	Minor-ON	63	58	42	100	....	....	....	....	....	....
	Lon. Knights M.M.	Minor-ON	3	1	0	1	0	1	0	0	0	0
2009-10	Lon. Knights M.M.	Minor-ON	72	38	46	84	47	....	....	....	....	....
	Lon. Knights Mid.	Minor-ON	1	0	0	0	0	....	....	....	....	....
2010-11	London Nationals	ON-Jr.B	39	14	22	36	29	12	6	3	9	8
	Windsor Spitfires	OHL	8	0	0	0	0	1	0	0	0	0
2011-12	Windsor Spitfires	OHL	68	15	21	36	81	4	1	0	1	4
2012-13	Windsor Spitfires	OHL	34	8	11	19	28	....	....	....	....	....
	Peterborough	OHL	28	7	6	13	18	....	....	....	....	....

CLENDENING, Adam (klehn-DEHN-ihng, A-duhm) CHI

Defense. Shoots right. 5'11", 187 lbs. Born, Niagara Falls, NY, October 26, 1992.
(Chicago's 3rd choice, 36th overall, in 2011 Entry Draft).

			Regular Season					Playoffs				
Season	Club	League	GP	G	A	Pts	PIM	GP	G	A	Pts	PIM
2007-08	Toronto Marlboros	GTHL	60	8	42	50	116	....	....	....	....	....
2008-09	USNTDP	NAHL	34	0	9	9	38	....	....	....	....	....
	USNTDP	U-17	15	1	5	6	18	....	....	....	....	....
	USNTDP	U-18	13	1	5	6	14	....	....	....	....	....
2009-10	USNTDP	USHL	26	4	13	17	44	....	....	....	....	....
	USNTDP	U-18	39	10	22	32	76	....	....	....	....	....
2010-11	Boston University	H-East	39	5	21	26	80	....	....	....	....	....
2011-12	Boston University	H-East	38	4	29	33	64	....	....	....	....	....
2012-13	Rockford IceHogs	AHL	73	9	37	46	67	....	....	....	....	....

Hockey East All-Rookie Team (2011) • Hockey East First All-Star Team (2012) • AHL Second All-Star Team (2013)

CLIFTON, Connor (KLIHF-tuhn, KAW-nuhr) PHX

Defense. Shoots right. 5'11", 175 lbs. Born, Matawan, NJ, April 28, 1995.
(Phoenix's 4th choice, 133rd overall, in 2013 Entry Draft).

			Regular Season					Playoffs				
Season	Club	League	GP	G	A	Pts	PIM	GP	G	A	Pts	PIM
2010-11	Jersey Hitmen	EmJHL	36	4	14	18	95	7	2	2	4	10
2011-12	Jersey Hitmen	EmJHL	4	0	1	1	26	....	....	....	....	....
	Jersey Hitmen	EJHL	28	1	11	12	46	6	0	3	3	15
	USNTDP	USHL	8	1	0	1	16	....	....	....	....	....
	USNTDP	U-17	4	0	1	1	8	....	....	....	....	....
2012-13	USNTDP	USHL	25	3	6	9	90	....	....	....	....	....
	USNTDP	U-18	41	5	9	14	24	....	....	....	....	....

• Signed Letter of Intent to attend **Quinnipiac University** (ECAC) in fall of 2013.

COETZEE, Willie (KOHT-zee, WIHL-ee) DET

Right wing. Shoots right. 5'10", 188 lbs. Born, Maple Ridge, B.C., November 7, 1990.

			Regular Season					Playoffs				
Season	Club	League	GP	G	A	Pts	PIM	GP	G	A	Pts	PIM
2007-08	Cowichan Valley	BCHL	33	5	11	16	19	....	....	....	....	....
	Red Deer Rebels	WHL	23	2	0	2	14	....	....	....	....	....
2008-09	Red Deer Rebels	WHL	72	18	24	42	42	....	....	....	....	....
2009-10	Red Deer Rebels	WHL	72	29	52	81	32	4	1	0	1	0
	Grand Rapids	AHL	2	0	0	0	0	....	....	....	....	....
2010-11	Grand Rapids	AHL	25	0	5	5	8	....	....	....	....	....
	Toledo Walleye	ECHL	36	9	11	20	4	....	....	....	....	....
2011-12	Grand Rapids	AHL	61	11	11	22	25	....	....	....	....	....
2012-13	Toledo Walleye	ECHL	64	28	40	68	22	6	0	4	4	2
	Grand Rapids	AHL	1	0	0	0	0	....	....	....	....	....

Signed as a free agent by **Detroit**, September 18, 2009.

COLEMAN, Blake (KOHL-man, BLAYK) N.J.

Center. Shoots left. 5'10", 200 lbs. Born, Plano, TX, November 28, 1991.
(New Jersey's 3rd choice, 75th overall, in 2011 Entry Draft).

			Regular Season					Playoffs				
Season	Club	League	GP	G	A	Pts	PIM	GP	G	A	Pts	PIM
2009-10	Tri-City Storm	USHL	22	2	10	12	32	....	....	....	....	....
	Indiana Ice	USHL	36	8	8	16	24	9	0	2	2	13
2010-11	Indiana Ice	USHL	59	34	*58	*92	72	5	2	2	4	10
2011-12	Miami U.	CCHA	39	12	11	23	56	....	....	....	....	....
2012-13	Miami U.	CCHA	40	9	10	19	56	....	....	....	....	....

USHL First All-Star Team (2011) • USHL Player of the Year (2011)

COLLBERG, Sebastian (KOHL-buhrg, seh-BAS-t'yehn) MTL

Right wing. Shoots right. 5'11", 181 lbs. Born, Mariestad, Sweden, February 23, 1994.
(Montreal's 2nd choice, 33rd overall, in 2012 Entry Draft).

			Regular Season					Playoffs				
Season	Club	League	GP	G	A	Pts	PIM	GP	G	A	Pts	PIM
2008-09	Mariestad U18	Swe-U18	16	8	8	16	4	....	....	....	....	....
	Mariestad Jr.	Swe-Jr.	21	4	4	8	10	....	....	....	....	....
2009-10	Mariestad U18	Swe-U18	15	12	15	27	8	....	....	....	....	....
	Mariestad Jr.	Swe-Jr.	26	25	14	39	16	....	....	....	....	....
	Mariestads BoIS	Sweden-3	4	1	0	1	0	....	....	....	....	....
2010-11	Frolunda U18	Swe-U18	8	9	7	16	0	4	1	1	2	0
	Frolunda Jr.	Swe-Jr.	35	21	23	44	12	7	4	5	9	0
	Frolunda	Sweden	5	0	0	0	0	....	....	....	....	....
2011-12	Frolunda U18	Swe-U18	1	1	1	2	0	4	3	3	6	4
	Frolunda Jr.	Swe-Jr.	21	9	8	17	18	2	0	0	0	0
	Frolunda	Sweden	41	0	0	0	0	....	....	....	....	....
2012-13	Frolunda Jr.	Swe-Jr.	1	0	0	0	0	2	0	0	0	0
	Orebro HK	Sweden-2	15	6	2	8	2	....	....	....	....	....
	Mariestads BoIS HC	Sweden-3	1	1	1	2	0	....	....	....	....	....
	Frolunda	Sweden	35	6	3	9	6	5	0	2	2	0
	Hamilton Bulldogs	AHL	2	0	0	0	0	....	....	....	....	....

COLLIER, Brendan (kawl-EE-uhr, BREHN-duhn) CAR

Left wing. Shoots left. 5'9", 183 lbs. Born, Charlestown, MA, October 8, 1993.
(Carolina's 9th choice, 189th overall, in 2012 Entry Draft).

			Regular Season					Playoffs				
Season	Club	League	GP	G	A	Pts	PIM	GP	G	A	Pts	PIM
2009-10	Malden Catholic	High-MA	24	19	24	43	....	....	....	....	....	....
2010-11	Malden Catholic	High-MA	25	30	45	75	....	....	....	....	....	....
2011-12	Malden Catholic	High-MA	25	26	38	64	....	....	....	....	....	....
2012-13	Valley Junior	EJHL	43	14	28	42	27	6	1	5	6	4

• Signed Letter of Intent to attend **Boston University** (Hockey East) in fall of 2013.

COMPHER, J.T. (KAWM-fuhr, JAY-TEE) **BUF**

Left wing. Shoots right. 5'10", 182 lbs. Born, Northbrook, IL, April 8, 1995.
(Buffalo's 3rd choice, 35th overall, in 2013 Entry Draft).

			Regular Season					Playoffs				
Season	**Club**	**League**	**GP**	**G**	**A**	**Pts**	**PIM**	**GP**	**G**	**A**	**Pts**	**PIM**
2010-11	Team Illinois	T1EHL	34	17	22	39	56	....	....	....	....	....
2011-12	USNTDP	USHL	32	13	14	27	37	....	....	....	....	....
	USNTDP	U-17	17	8	15	23	18	....	....	....	....	....
	USNTDP	U-18	9	4	3	7	4	....	....	....	....	....
2012-13	USNTDP	USHL	21	7	17	24	23	....	....	....	....	....
	USNTDP	U-18	31	11	15	26	18	....	....	....	....	....

• Signed Letter of Intent to attend **University of Michigan** (CCHA) in fall of 2013.

COMRIE, Adam (KAWM-ree, A-duhm) **S.J.**

Defense. Shoots left. 6'4", 215 lbs. Born, Kanata, Ont., July 31, 1990.
(Florida's 3rd choice, 80th overall, in 2008 Entry Draft).

			Regular Season					Playoffs				
Season	**Club**	**League**	**GP**	**G**	**A**	**Pts**	**PIM**	**GP**	**G**	**A**	**Pts**	**PIM**
2006-07	Ohio	USHL	19	6	4	10	28	....	....	....	....	....
	Omaha Lancers	USHL	38	1	6	7	27	5	0	0	0	4
2007-08	Saginaw Spirit	OHL	58	10	18	28	90	4	0	0	0	4
2008-09	Saginaw Spirit	OHL	52	9	21	30	70	8	0	2	2	8
2009-10	Guelph Storm	OHL	68	14	26	40	79	5	1	2	3	4
2010-11	Rochester	AHL	44	0	5	5	18	....	....	....	....	....
	Cincinnati	ECHL	13	4	4	8	18	2	1	0	1	2
2011-12	Cincinnati	ECHL	4	3	3	6	2	....	....	....	....	....
	Greenville	ECHL	3	1	0	1	2	1	0	0	0	2
2012-13	Reading Royals	ECHL	45	17	16	33	106	....	....	....	....	....
	Worcester Sharks	AHL	24	3	12	15	24	....	....	....	....	....

Signed as a free agent by **Greenville** (ECHL), March 19, 2012. Signed as a free agent by **Worcester** (AHL), February 9, 2013. Signed as a free agent by **San Jose**, July 10, 2013.

CONDON, Nathan (KOHN-duhn, NAY-thun) **COL**

Center. Shoots left. 6', 198 lbs. Born, Wausau, WI, May 29, 1990.
(Colorado's 7th choice, 200th overall, in 2008 Entry Draft).

			Regular Season					Playoffs				
Season	**Club**	**League**	**GP**	**G**	**A**	**Pts**	**PIM**	**GP**	**G**	**A**	**Pts**	**PIM**
2004-05	Wausau West	High-WI	22	1	4	5	4	....	....	....	....	....
2005-06	Wausau West	High-WI	22	21	22	43	6	....	....	....	....	....
	Team Wisconsin	UMHSEL	24	16	13	29	10	....	....	....	....	....
2006-07	Wausau West	High-WI	21	21	27	48	10	....	....	....	....	....
	Team Wisconsin	UMHSEL	23	14	9	23	6	....	....	....	....	....
2007-08	Wausau West	High-WI	23	33	26	59	10	....	....	....	....	....
	Team Wisconsin	UMHSEL	24	20	25	45	6	....	....	....	....	....
2008-09	Fargo Force	USHL	58	11	18	29	20	10	1	5	6	2
2009-10	Fargo Force	USHL	60	23	28	51	20	13	3	2	5	6
2010-11	U. of Minnesota	WCHA	35	8	9	17	14	....	....	....	....	....
2011-12	U. of Minnesota	WCHA	43	11	19	30	25	....	....	....	....	....
2012-13	U. of Minnesota	WCHA	40	12	19	31	8	....	....	....	....	....

CONNAUTON, Kevin (kuh-NAW-tuhn, KEH-vihn) **DAL**

Defense. Shoots left. 6'1", 196 lbs. Born, Edmonton, Alta., February 23, 1990.
(Vancouver's 3rd choice, 83rd overall, in 2009 Entry Draft).

			Regular Season					Playoffs				
Season	**Club**	**League**	**GP**	**G**	**A**	**Pts**	**PIM**	**GP**	**G**	**A**	**Pts**	**PIM**
2007-08	Spruce Grove	AJHL	56	13	32	45	59	15	5	0	5	18
2008-09	Western Mich.	CCHA	40	7	11	18	44	....	....	....	....	....
2009-10	Vancouver Giants	WHL	69	24	48	72	107	16	3	10	13	21
2010-11	Manitoba Moose	AHL	73	11	12	23	51	6	1	0	1	0
2011-12	Chicago Wolves	AHL	73	13	20	33	58	5	0	1	1	8
2012-13	Chicago Wolves	AHL	60	7	18	25	67	....	....	....	....	....
	Texas Stars	AHL	9	2	4	6	6	9	2	3	5	6

WHL West First All-Star Team (2010) • Canadian Major Junior All-Rookie Team (2010)

Traded to **Dallas** by **Vancouver** with Vancouver's 2nd round choice (Philippe Desrosiers) in 2013 Entry Draft for Derek Roy, April 2, 2013.

CONNELLY, Brian (KAW-nuh-lee, BRIGH-uhn) **MIN**

Defense. Shoots left. 5'11", 185 lbs. Born, Bloomington, MN, June 10, 1986.

			Regular Season					Playoffs				
Season	**Club**	**League**	**GP**	**G**	**A**	**Pts**	**PIM**	**GP**	**G**	**A**	**Pts**	**PIM**
2004-05	Bloomington-Jeff.	High-MN	....	18	45	63	....	....	....	....	....	....
	Tri-City Storm	USHL	20	0	3	3	12	9	0	1	1	2
2005-06	Tri-City Storm	USHL	54	3	9	12	16	5	1	0	1	0
2006-07	Colorado College	WCHA	35	2	15	17	22	....	....	....	....	....
2007-08	Colorado College	WCHA	41	3	16	19	32	....	....	....	....	....
2008-09	Colorado College	WCHA	38	3	24	27	46	....	....	....	....	....
	Rockford IceHogs	AHL	9	1	2	3	6	3	0	0	0	2
2009-10	Rockford IceHogs	AHL	78	4	31	35	28	4	0	3	3	2
2010-11	Rockford IceHogs	AHL	80	11	41	52	39	....	....	....	....	....
2011-12	Rockford IceHogs	AHL	44	5	31	36	16	....	....	....	....	....
	Abbotsford Heat	AHL	28	1	15	16	10	8	0	2	2	8
2012-13	Houston Aeros	AHL	54	5	34	39	14	5	1	3	4	4

AHL Second All-Star Team (2012)

Signed as a free agent by **Chicago** , March 26, 2009. Traded to Calgary by **Chicago** for Brendan Morrison, January 27, 2012. Signed as a free agent by **Minnesota**, July 6, 2012.

COOPER, Brian (KOO-puhr, BRIGH-uhn) **ANA**

Defense. Shoots left. 5'10", 197 lbs. Born, Anchorage, AK, November 1, 1993.
(Anaheim's 6th choice, 127th overall, in 2012 Entry Draft).

			Regular Season					Playoffs				
Season	**Club**	**League**	**GP**	**G**	**A**	**Pts**	**PIM**	**GP**	**G**	**A**	**Pts**	**PIM**
2009-10	Fargo Force	USHL	55	3	10	13	69	13	0	4	4	22
2010-11	Fargo Force	USHL	51	11	22	33	132	5	2	0	2	18
2011-12	Fargo Force	USHL	55	6	18	24	92	6	1	2	3	8
2012-13	Nebraska-Omaha	WCHA	32	0	2	2	45	....	....	....	....	....

USHL Second All-Star Team (2011, 2012)

COPP, Andrew (KAWP, AN-droo) **WPG**

Center. Shoots left. 6'1", 200 lbs. Born, Ann Arbor, MI, July 8, 1994.
(Winnipeg's 6th choice, 104th overall, in 2013 Entry Draft).

			Regular Season					Playoffs				
Season	**Club**	**League**	**GP**	**G**	**A**	**Pts**	**PIM**	**GP**	**G**	**A**	**Pts**	**PIM**
2009-10	Det. Compuware	T1EHL	38	12	15	27	12	....	....	....	....	....
2010-11	Det. Compuware	T1EHL	17	2	7	9	6	....	....	....	....	....
	USNTDP	USHL	22	1	4	5	4	1	0	0	0	0
	USNTDP	U-17	3	1	0	1	0	....	....	....	....	....
	USNTDP	U-18	5	0	0	0	0	....	....	....	....	....
2011-12	USNTDP	USHL	18	3	7	10	2	....	....	....	....	....
	USNTDP	U-17	7	3	3	6	....	....	....	....	....	....
	USNTDP	U-18	7	0	1	1	2	....	....	....	....	....
2012-13	U. of Michigan	CCHA	38	11	10	21	12	....	....	....	....	....

COSTELLO, Jeff (kaw-STEHL-oh, JEHF) **OTT**

Left wing. Shoots left. 5'11", 212 lbs. Born, Milwaukee, WI, November 20, 1990.
(Ottawa's 6th choice, 146th overall, in 2009 Entry Draft).

			Regular Season					Playoffs				
Season	**Club**	**League**	**GP**	**G**	**A**	**Pts**	**PIM**	**GP**	**G**	**A**	**Pts**	**PIM**
2005-06	Catholic Memorial	High-WI	....	13	16	29	....	....	....	....	....	....
2006-07	Catholic Memorial	High-WI	....	34	20	54	....	....	....	....	....	....
2007-08	Catholic Memorial	High-WI	22	31	17	48	60	....	....	....	....	....
	Team Wisconsin	UMHSEL	....	18	18	36	....	....	....	....	....	....
2008-09	Cedar Rapids	USHL	54	24	9	33	73	5	0	2	2	0
2009-10	Cedar Rapids	USHL	54	29	19	48	149	5	2	3	5	8
2010-11	U. of Notre Dame	CCHA	44	12	6	18	56	....	....	....	....	....
2011-12	U. of Notre Dame	CCHA	28	5	7	12	58	....	....	....	....	....
2012-13	U. of Notre Dame	CCHA	33	11	19	30	52	....	....	....	....	....

• Re-assigned to **San Francisco** (ECHL) by **Toronto** (Toronto-AHL), November 9, 2012.

COUSINS, Nick (KUH-zihnz, NIHK) **PHI**

Center. Shoots left. 5'11", 177 lbs. Born, Belleville, Ont., July 20, 1993.
(Philadelphia's 2nd choice, 68th overall, in 2011 Entry Draft).

			Regular Season					Playoffs				
Season	**Club**	**League**	**GP**	**G**	**A**	**Pts**	**PIM**	**GP**	**G**	**A**	**Pts**	**PIM**
2008-09	Quinte Red Devils	Minor-ON	71	72	67	139	....	....	....	....	....	....
	Trenton Hercs	ON-Jr.A	5	0	1	1	2	....	....	....	....	....
2009-10	Sault Ste. Marie	OHL	67	11	21	32	34	5	0	1	1	2
2010-11	Sault Ste. Marie	OHL	68	29	39	68	56	....	....	....	....	....
2011-12	Sault Ste. Marie	OHL	65	35	53	88	88	....	....	....	....	....
	Adirondack	AHL	1	0	0	0	0	....	....	....	....	....
2012-13	Sault Ste. Marie	OHL	64	27	76	103	83	6	3	3	6	12
	Adirondack	AHL	7	0	1	1	2	....	....	....	....	....

COWICK, Corey (KOW-ihk, KOH-ree) **OTT**

Left wing. Shoots left. 6'3", 211 lbs. Born, Gloucester, Ont., August 1, 1989.
(Ottawa's 7th choice, 160th overall, in 2009 Entry Draft).

			Regular Season					Playoffs				
Season	**Club**	**League**	**GP**	**G**	**A**	**Pts**	**PIM**	**GP**	**G**	**A**	**Pts**	**PIM**
2006-07	Oshawa Generals	OHL	67	4	4	8	54	9	0	0	0	2
2007-08	Oshawa Generals	OHL	63	11	14	25	79	15	1	1	2	22
2008-09	Ottawa 67's	OHL	68	34	26	60	48	7	7	2	9	14
2009-10	Ottawa 67's	OHL	27	15	6	21	33	12	9	3	12	27
2010-11	Binghamton	AHL	30	1	3	4	20	....	....	....	....	....
	Elmira Jackals	ECHL	31	5	9	14	76	....	....	....	....	....
2011-12	Elmira Jackals	ECHL	22	8	5	13	20	8	2	0	2	26
	Binghamton	AHL	53	5	6	11	38	....	....	....	....	....
2012-13	Binghamton	AHL	72	16	19	35	85	3	0	0	0	2

• Missed majority of 2009-10 due to pre-season shoulder injury at Kingston (OHL), August 30, 2009.

CRAMAROSSA, Joseph (kra-ma-ROH-sa, JOH-sehf) **ANA**

Center. Shoots left. 6'1", 200 lbs. Born, Toronto, Ont., October 26, 1992.
(Anaheim's 4th choice, 65th overall, in 2011 Entry Draft).

			Regular Season					Playoffs				
Season	**Club**	**League**	**GP**	**G**	**A**	**Pts**	**PIM**	**GP**	**G**	**A**	**Pts**	**PIM**
2007-08	Markham Majors	GTHL	70	31	37	68	64	....	....	....	....	....
2008-09	Markham Waxers	ON-Jr.A	38	7	3	10	14	12	1	2	3	0
2009-10	St. Michael's	OHL	64	6	10	16	60	14	0	2	2	11
2010-11	St. Michael's	OHL	59	12	20	32	101	14	2	2	4	6
2011-12	St. Michael's	OHL	15	6	5	11	40	....	....	....	....	....
	Belleville Bulls	OHL	29	8	8	16	43	6	2	2	4	18
2012-13	Belleville Bulls	OHL	68	19	44	63	89	17	5	4	9	35

CRANE, Chris (KRAYN, KRIHS-tuh-fuhr) **S.J.**

Right wing. Shoots right. 6'1", 190 lbs. Born, Virginia Beach, VA, December 2, 1991.
(San Jose's 8th choice, 200th overall, in 2010 Entry Draft).

			Regular Season					Playoffs				
Season	**Club**	**League**	**GP**	**G**	**A**	**Pts**	**PIM**	**GP**	**G**	**A**	**Pts**	**PIM**
2008-09	Green Bay	USHL	48	10	9	19	120	5	2	1	3	2
2009-10	Green Bay	USHL	52	15	14	29	107	12	2	3	5	27
2010-11	Ohio State	CCHA	37	4	6	10	37	....	....	....	....	....
2011-12	Ohio State	CCHA	35	14	10	24	30	....	....	....	....	....
2012-13	Ohio State	CCHA	38	6	3	9	69	....	....	....	....	....
	Worcester Sharks	AHL	8	0	0	0	6	....	....	....	....	....

CRAWFORD, Nick (KRAW-fuhrd, NIHK) **BUF**

Defense. Shoots left. 6'1", 191 lbs. Born, Brampton, Ont., February 23, 1990.
(Buffalo's 8th choice, 164th overall, in 2008 Entry Draft).

			Regular Season					Playoffs				
Season	**Club**	**League**	**GP**	**G**	**A**	**Pts**	**PIM**	**GP**	**G**	**A**	**Pts**	**PIM**
2006-07	Saginaw Spirit	OHL	63	1	7	8	32	5	0	1	1	0
2007-08	Saginaw Spirit	OHL	68	4	16	20	58	4	1	1	2	2
2008-09	Saginaw Spirit	OHL	65	7	35	42	41	8	1	4	5	4
2009-10	Saginaw Spirit	OHL	19	4	17	21	4	....	....	....	....	....
	Barrie Colts	OHL	49	7	42	49	20	17	0	12	12	4
2010-11	Portland Pirates	AHL	76	7	24	31	27	12	0	2	2	4
2011-12	Rochester	AHL	70	6	16	22	26	3	0	1	1	0
2012-13	Rochester	AHL	53	5	14	19	18	1	0	0	0	0

OHL First All-Star Team (2010) • Canadian Major Junior Second All-Star Team (2010)

CRESCENZI, Andrew (kruh-SEHN-zee, AN-droo) TOR

Center. Shoots left. 6'5", 213 lbs. Born, Thornhill, Ont., July 29, 1992.

			Regular Season					Playoffs				
Season	Club	League	GP	G	A	Pts	PIM	GP	G	A	Pts	PIM
2008-09	Villanova Knights	ON-Jr.A	45	6	17	23	40	....	....	....	....	....
2009-10	Kitchener Rangers	OHL	68	8	4	12	42	20	1	2	3	11
2010-11	Kitchener Rangers	OHL	55	12	11	23	74	7	1	1	2	6
	Toronto Marlies	AHL	2	0	1	1	0	....	....	....	....	....
2011-12	Kitchener Rangers	OHL	52	24	23	47	74	15	4	7	11	20
2012-13	Toronto Marlies	AHL	15	1	1	2	17	....	....	....	....	....
	San Francisco Bulls	ECHL	23	3	11	14	28	....	....	....	....	....

Signed as a free agent by **Toronto**, September 24, 2010. • Re-assigned to **San Francisco** (ECHL) by **Toronto** (Toronto-AHL), November 9, 2012.

CRISP, Connor (KRIHSP, KAW-nuhr) MTL

Left wing. Shoots left. 6'3", 223 lbs. Born, Alliston, Ont., April 8, 1994.
(Montreal's 5th choice, 71st overall, in 2013 Entry Draft).

			Regular Season					Playoffs				
Season	Club	League	GP	G	A	Pts	PIM	GP	G	A	Pts	PIM
2009-10	York Simcoe	Minor-ON	60	31	37	68	126	....	....	....	....	....
2010-11	Erie Otters	OHL	48	5	0	5	45	7	0	0	0	4
2011-12	Erie Otters	OHL	6	0	1	1	4	....	....	....	....	....
2012-13	Erie Otters	OHL	63	22	14	36	139	....	....	....	....	....

• Missed majority of 2011-12 with shoulder injury. • Replaced goaltender Ramis Sadikov in a game vs. Niagara (OHL), March 4, 2012. Played 58:15 and allowed 13 goals on 45 shots. (Niagara 13, Erie 4).

CROSS, Tommy (KRAWS, TAW-mee) BOS

Defense. Shoots left. 6'3", 206 lbs. Born, Hartford, CT, September 12, 1989.
(Boston's 2nd choice, 35th overall, in 2007 Entry Draft).

			Regular Season					Playoffs				
Season	Club	League	GP	G	A	Pts	PIM	GP	G	A	Pts	PIM
2004-05	Simsbury	High-CT	23	5	40	45	18	....	....	....	....	....
2005-06	Simsbury	High-CT	22	15	35	50	....	....	....	....	....	....
2006-07	Westminster	High-CT	25	8	12	20	20	....	....	....	....	....
	USNTDP	NAHL	2	0	2	2	0	....	....	....	....	....
	USNTDP	U-18	11	0	1	1	8	....	....	....	....	....
2007-08	Westminster	High-CT	25	9	12	21	....	....	....	....	....	....
	Ohio	USHL	9	0	4	4	8	....	....	....	....	....
2008-09	Boston College	H-East	24	0	8	8	24	....	....	....	....	....
2009-10	Boston College	H-East	38	5	5	10	36	....	....	....	....	....
2010-11	Boston College	H-East	28	7	11	18	45	....	....	....	....	....
2011-12	Boston College	H-East	44	5	19	24	66	....	....	....	....	....
	Providence Bruins	AHL	2	0	0	0	2	....	....	....	....	....
2012-13	Providence Bruins	AHL	42	1	10	11	23	12	0	3	3	8
	South Carolina	ECHL	24	6	13	19	23	....	....	....	....	....

CRUSRYDBERG, Victor (KRUHS-RIGHD-buhrg, VIHK-tuhr) NYI

Center. Shoots right. 5'11", 190 lbs. Born, Vaxjo, Sweden, March 21, 1995.
(NY Islanders' 5th choice, 136th overall, in 2013 Entry Draft).

			Regular Season					Playoffs				
Season	Club	League	GP	G	A	Pts	PIM	GP	G	A	Pts	PIM
2009-10	Tingsryds AIF U18	Swe-U18	15	12	7	19	12	....	....	....	....	....
	Tingsryds AIF Jr.	Swe-Jr.	2	0	0	0	0	....	....	....	....	....
2010-11	Tingsryds AIF U18	Swe-U18	11	1	12	13	6	3	1	2	3	0
	Tingsryds AIF Jr.	Swe-Jr.	30	6	9	15	8	....	....	....	....	....
2011-12	Linkopings HC U18	Swe-U18	30	17	20	37	26	3	1	2	3	0
	Linkopings HC Jr.	Swe-Jr.	10	0	2	2	6	....	....	....	....	....
2012-13	Linkopings HC U18	Swe-U18	4	4	2	6	4	2	0	0	0	0
	Linkopings HC Jr.	Swe-Jr.	35	12	23	35	24	4	2	0	2	0
	Linkopings HC	Sweden	1	0	0	0	0	....	....	....	....	....

CULEK, Jakub (TSOO-lehk, YA-koob) OTT

Left wing. Shoots left. 6'3", 200 lbs. Born, Klatovy, Czech., September 7, 1992.
(Ottawa's 1st choice, 76th overall, in 2010 Entry Draft).

			Regular Season					Playoffs				
Season	Club	League	GP	G	A	Pts	PIM	GP	G	A	Pts	PIM
2006-07	HC Kladno U17	CzR-U17	5	1	0	1	0	....	....	....	....	....
2007-08	HC Plzen U17	CzR-U17	44	12	22	34	76	8	1	4	5	10
2008-09	HC Plzen U17	CzR-U17	29	15	16	31	98	1	0	0	0	0
	HC Plzen Jr.	CzRep-Jr.	12	3	2	5	10	5	3	0	3	0
2009-10	Rimouski Oceanic	QMJHL	63	13	34	47	54	12	6	3	9	4
2010-11	Rimouski Oceanic	QMJHL	55	7	15	22	37	5	0	2	2	2
2011-12	Rimouski Oceanic	QMJHL	55	13	27	40	58	21	4	7	11	28
2012-13	Cape Breton	QMJHL	9	4	3	7	5	....	....	....	....	....
	Binghamton	AHL	3	0	0	0	10	....	....	....	....	....

CULKIN, Ryan (KUHL-kin, RIGH-uhn) CGY

Defense. Shoots left. 6'1", 176 lbs. Born, Montreal, Que., December 15, 1993.
(Calgary's 5th choice, 124th overall, in 2012 Entry Draft).

			Regular Season					Playoffs				
Season	Club	League	GP	G	A	Pts	PIM	GP	G	A	Pts	PIM
2009-10	Deux Rives	Minor-QU	STATISTICS NOT AVAILABLE									
	Lac St-Louis Lions	QAAA	13	2	2	4	4	21	1	1	2	4
2010-11	Quebec Remparts	QMJHL	40	6	5	11	12	18	0	5	5	4
2011-12	Quebec Remparts	QMJHL	60	6	19	25	28	10	0	7	7	8
2012-13	Quebec Remparts	QMJHL	67	5	40	45	46	11	2	4	6	10

CUNNINGHAM, Craig (KUN-ihng-ham, KRAYG) BOS

Left wing. Shoots right. 5'10", 184 lbs. Born, Trail, B.C., September 13, 1990.
(Boston's 4th choice, 97th overall, in 2010 Entry Draft).

			Regular Season					Playoffs				
Season	Club	League	GP	G	A	Pts	PIM	GP	G	A	Pts	PIM
2005-06	Beaver Valley	KIJHL	47	19	25	44	22	16	4	5	9	29
2006-07	Vancouver Giants	WHL	48	0	5	5	38	15	0	1	1	15
2007-08	Vancouver Giants	WHL	67	11	14	25	72	10	1	2	3	6
2008-09	Vancouver Giants	WHL	72	28	22	50	62	17	5	9	14	12
2009-10	Vancouver Giants	WHL	72	37	60	97	44	16	12	12	24	12
2010-11	Vancouver Giants	WHL	36	10	35	45	31	....	....	....	....	....
	Portland	WHL	35	17	25	42	25	21	7	14	21	12
2011-12	Providence Bruins	AHL	76	20	16	36	20	....	....	....	....	....
2012-13	Providence Bruins	AHL	75	25	21	46	26	12	3	5	8	4

WHL West First All-Star Team (2010)

CURCURUTO, Gianluca (kuhr-kuhr-ROO-toh, GEE-an-LOO-kuh) CBJ

Defense. Shoots left. 6'1", 200 lbs. Born, Toronto, Ont., February 25, 1994.
(Columbus' 6th choice, 182nd overall, in 2012 Entry Draft).

			Regular Season					Playoffs				
Season	Club	League	GP	G	A	Pts	PIM	GP	G	A	Pts	PIM
2009-10	Mississauga Reps	GTHL	64	38	44	82	....	5	3	3	6	....
2010-11	Sault Ste. Marie	OHL	56	1	25	26	26	....	....	....	....	....
2011-12	Sault Ste. Marie	OHL	63	3	13	16	36	....	....	....	....	....
2012-13	Plymouth Whalers	OHL	67	9	38	47	32	11	2	7	9	7

CZARNIK, Robert (CHAHR-nihk, RAW-buhrt) L.A.

Center. Shoots right. 6'1", 188 lbs. Born, Detroit, MI, January 25, 1990.
(Los Angeles' 4th choice, 63rd overall, in 2008 Entry Draft).

			Regular Season					Playoffs				
Season	Club	League	GP	G	A	Pts	PIM	GP	G	A	Pts	PIM
2005-06	Det. Honeybaked	MWEHL	....	53	78	131	....	....	....	....	....	....
2006-07	USNTDP	U-17	19	10	2	12	22	....	....	....	....	....
	USNTDP	NAHL	46	7	10	17	46	....	....	....	....	....
2007-08	USNTDP	U-18	43	15	18	33	30	....	....	....	....	....
	USNTDP	NAHL	14	4	2	6	12	....	....	....	....	....
2008-09	U. of Michigan	CCHA	39	5	11	16	32	....	....	....	....	....
2009-10	U. of Michigan	CCHA	12	3	3	6	4	....	....	....	....	....
2010-11	Plymouth Whalers	OHL	61	33	44	77	46	11	4	5	9	6
2011-12	Manchester	AHL	49	8	15	23	32	4	2	0	2	2
2012-13	Manchester	AHL	51	4	2	6	22	1	0	0	0	0

D'AGOSTINO, Nick (DA-goh-STEE-noh, NIHK) PIT

Defense. Shoots left. 6'2", 197 lbs. Born, Mississauga, Ont., June 24, 1990.
(Pittsburgh's 4th choice, 210th overall, in 2008 Entry Draft).

			Regular Season					Playoffs				
Season	Club	League	GP	G	A	Pts	PIM	GP	G	A	Pts	PIM
2006-07	Tor. Young Nats	GTHL	30	5	21	26	....	5	0	4	4	....
	Young Nats	Exhib.	8	1	5	6	....	....	....	....	....	....
2007-08	St. Michael's	ON-Jr.A	46	5	18	23	22	12	0	3	3	8
2008-09	St. Michael's	ON-Jr.A	43	9	24	33	34	6	2	3	5	8
2009-10	Cornell Big Red	ECAC	32	4	14	18	6	....	....	....	....	....
2010-11	Cornell Big Red	ECAC	32	7	10	17	20	....	....	....	....	....
2011-12	Cornell Big Red	ECAC	34	8	12	20	24	....	....	....	....	....
2012-13	Cornell Big Red	ECAC	34	6	11	17	30	....	....	....	....	....

ECAC All-Rookie Team (2010) • ECAC Second All-Star Team (2012)

DAHLBECK, Klas (DAHL-behk, KLAHS) CHI

Defense. Shoots left. 6'2", 194 lbs. Born, Katrineholm, Sweden, July 6, 1991.
(Chicago's 6th choice, 79th overall, in 2011 Entry Draft).

			Regular Season					Playoffs				
Season	Club	League	GP	G	A	Pts	PIM	GP	G	A	Pts	PIM
2007-08	Vaxjo U18	Swe-U18	16	7	10	17	4	....	....	....	....	....
	Vaxjo Jr.	Swe-Jr.	22	3	4	7	14	....	....	....	....	....
2008-09	Vaxjo U18	Swe-U18	14	4	5	9	6	....	....	....	....	....
	Vaxjo Jr.	Swe-Jr.	15	4	6	10	8	....	....	....	....	....
2009-10	Linkopings HC Jr.	Swe-Jr.	39	4	7	11	8	6	1	1	2	4
	Mjolby HC	Sweden-3	2	0	0	0	0	....	....	....	....	....
	Linkopings HC	Sweden	6	0	0	0	0	3	0	0	0	0
2010-11	Linkopings HC	Sweden	47	0	8	8	12	7	0	0	0	0
2011-12	Linkopings HC	Sweden	55	2	2	4	20	....	....	....	....	....
2012-13	Rockford IceHogs	AHL	70	1	5	6	29	....	....	....	....	....

DAHLSTROM, Carl (DAL-struhm, KAHRL) CHI

Defense. Shoots left. 6'3", 211 lbs. Born, Stockholm, Sweden, January 28, 1995.
(Chicago's 2nd choice, 51st overall, in 2013 Entry Draft).

			Regular Season					Playoffs				
Season	Club	League	GP	G	A	Pts	PIM	GP	G	A	Pts	PIM
2010-11	Djurgarden U18	Swe-U18	1	0	0	0	0	....	....	....	....	....
2011-12	Djurgarden U18	Swe-U18	37	2	13	15	4	4	0	3	3	0
2012-13	Linkopings HC U18	Swe-U18	3	2	2	4	2	2	0	0	0	2
	Linkopings HC Jr.	Swe-Jr.	37	5	8	13	12	5	1	1	2	4

D'AMIGO, Jerry (dah-MEE-goh, JAIR-ree) TOR

Right wing. Shoots left. 5'11", 213 lbs. Born, Binghamton, NY, February 19, 1991.
(Toronto's 6th choice, 158th overall, in 2009 Entry Draft).

			Regular Season					Playoffs				
Season	Club	League	GP	G	A	Pts	PIM	GP	G	A	Pts	PIM
2007-08	USNTDP	NAHL	44	5	12	17	59	3	1	1	2	6
	USNTDP	U-17	17	5	4	9	10	....	....	....	....	....
2008-09	USNTDP	NAHL	11	8	6	14	4	....	....	....	....	....
	USNTDP	U-18	42	15	27	42	57	....	....	....	....	....
2009-10	RPI Engineers	ECAC	35	10	24	34	37	....	....	....	....	....
2010-11	Toronto Marlies	AHL	43	5	10	15	23	....	....	....	....	....
	Kitchener Rangers	OHL	21	12	16	28	12	7	6	3	9	0
2011-12	Toronto Marlies	AHL	76	15	26	41	39	17	8	5	13	12
2012-13	Toronto Marlies	AHL	70	17	12	29	40	9	1	8	9	10

ECAC All-Rookie Team (2010) • ECAC Rookie of the Year (2010)

• Loaned to **Kitchener** (OHL) by **Toronto** (Toronto-AHL), February 3, 2011.

DANAULT, Phillip (duh-NOH, FIHL-ihp) CHI

Left wing. Shoots left. 6', 184 lbs. Born, Victoriaville, Que., February 24, 1993.
(Chicago's 2nd choice, 26th overall, in 2011 Entry Draft).

			Regular Season					Playoffs				
Season	Club	League	GP	G	A	Pts	PIM	GP	G	A	Pts	PIM
2008-09	Trois-Rivieres	QAAA	44	8	19	27	39	19	4	11	15	8
2009-10	Victoriaville Tigres	QMJHL	61	10	18	28	54	16	0	1	1	8
2010-11	Victoriaville Tigres	QMJHL	64	23	44	67	59	9	5	10	15	6
2011-12	Victoriaville Tigres	QMJHL	62	18	53	71	61	4	0	3	3	4
	Rockford IceHogs	AHL	7	0	2	2	10	....	....	....	....	....
2012-13	Victoriaville Tigres	QMJHL	29	14	30	44	28	....	....	....	....	....
	Moncton Wildcats	QMJHL	27	9	32	41	22	4	1	3	4	0
	Rockford IceHogs	AHL	5	0	0	0	2	....	....	....	....	....

DANO, Marko (DA-NOH, MAHR-koh) CBJ

Center. Shoots left. 5'11", 183 lbs. Born, Eisenstadt , Austria, November 30, 1994.
(Columbus' 3rd choice, 27th overall, in 2013 Entry Draft).

				Regular Season					Playoffs			
Season	Club	League	GP	G	A	Pts	PIM	GP	G	A	Pts	PIM
2008-09	Dukla Trencin U18	Svk-U18	5	1	0	1	14	....	....	....	....	....
2009-10	Dukla Trencin U18	Svk-U18	36	13	12	25	77	....	....	....	....	....
2010-11	Dukla Trencin U18	Svk-U18	9	13	4	17	2	4	2	2	4	8
	Dukla Trencin Jr.	Slovak-Jr.	28	18	22	40	86	8	4	2	6	14
	Dukla Trencin	Slovakia	8	0	1	1	10	3	0	0	0	0
2011-12	Dukla Trencin Jr.	Slovak-Jr.	3	3	1	4	18	3	4	2	6	4
	Dukla Trencin	Slovakia	32	4	6	10	12	9	0	3	3	18
2012-13	Bratislava	KHL	37	3	4	7	26	4	0	0	0	4
	Dukla Trencin Jr.	Slovak-Jr.	....	....	....	....	....	2	0	0	0	0

DAUPHIN, Laurent (daw-PHEHN, LOHR-awnt) PHX

Center. Shoots left. 6', 165 lbs. Born, Repenigny, Que., March 27, 1995.
(Phoenix's 2nd choice, 39th overall, in 2013 Entry Draft).

				Regular Season					Playoffs			
Season	Club	League	GP	G	A	Pts	PIM	GP	G	A	Pts	PIM
2010-11	Esther-Blondin	QAAA	41	16	25	41	28	3	0	1	1	0
2011-12	Esther-Blondin	QAAA	40	17	45	62	48	13	12	14	*26	12
2012-13	Chicoutimi	QMJHL	62	25	32	57	50	6	2	2	4	8

DAVIDSON, Brandon (DAY-vihn-suhn, BRAN-duhn) EDM

Defense. Shoots left. 6'2", 194 lbs. Born, Lethbridge, Alta., August 21, 1991.
(Edmonton's 8th choice, 162nd overall, in 2010 Entry Draft).

				Regular Season					Playoffs			
Season	Club	League	GP	G	A	Pts	PIM	GP	G	A	Pts	PIM
2008-09	Lethbridge	AMHL	31	7	14	21	52	7	2	5	7	14
2009-10	Regina Pats	WHL	59	1	33	34	37	....	....	....	....	....
2010-11	Regina Pats	WHL	72	8	43	51	71	....	....	....	....	....
	Oklahoma City	AHL	1	0	0	0	0	1	0	0	0	0
2011-12	Regina Pats	WHL	69	13	36	49	83	4	0	1	1	6
2012-13	Oklahoma City	AHL	26	2	3	5	14	17	0	6	6	2
	Stockton Thunder	ECHL	11	7	5	12	4	....	....	....	....	....

WHL East Second All-Star Team (2012) • Fred T. Hunt Memorial Award (AHL – Sportsmanship) (2013)

DE HAAS, James (dih-HAHZ, JAYMZ) DET

Defense. Shoots left. 6'4", 210 lbs. Born, Mississauga, Ont., May 3, 1994.
(Detroit's 5th choice, 170th overall, in 2012 Entry Draft).

				Regular Season					Playoffs			
Season	Club	League	GP	G	A	Pts	PIM	GP	G	A	Pts	PIM
2010-11	Toronto Marlboros	GTHL	70	12	18	30	40	....	....	....	....	....
2011-12	Tor. Patriots	ON-Jr.A	45	10	19	29	32	21	5	7	12	10
2012-13	Penticton Vees	BCHL	53	5	19	24	19	15	3	6	9	8

• Signed Letter of Intent to attend **Clarkson College** (ECAC) in fall of 2013.

DE JONG, Nolan (deh JAWNG, NOH-luhn) MIN

Defense. Shoots left. 6'2", 186 lbs. Born, Victoria, B.C., April 25, 1995.
(Minnesota's 6th choice, 197th overall, in 2013 Entry Draft).

				Regular Season					Playoffs			
Season	Club	League	GP	G	A	Pts	PIM	GP	G	A	Pts	PIM
2009-10	Saanich Braves	Minor-BC		STATISTICS NOT AVAILABLE								
	South Island	BCMML	5	0	0	0	2	....	....	....	....	....
2010-11	South Island	BCMML	35	3	7	10	69	3	0	2	2	4
2011-12	Victoria Grizzlies	BCHL	56	2	15	17	20	....	....	....	....	....
2012-13	Victoria Grizzlies	BCHL	51	5	19	24	16	10	2	2	4	6

• Signed Letter of Intent to attend **University of Michigan** (CCHA) in fall of 2013.

DEBLOUW, Matthew (deh-BLOW, MA-thew) CGY

Center. Shoots left. 6', 179 lbs. Born, Chesterfield, MI, September 17, 1993.
(Calgary's 7th choice, 186th overall, in 2012 Entry Draft).

				Regular Season					Playoffs			
Season	Club	League	GP	G	A	Pts	PIM	GP	G	A	Pts	PIM
2008-09	Detroit Belle Tire	T1EHL	31	11	16	27	50	4	3	1	4	0
2009-10	Little Caesars	T1EHL	48	23	21	44	91	....	....	....	....	....
	Det. Little Ceasars	Exhib.	3	1	0	1	8	....	....	....	....	....
2010-11	Muskegon	USHL	33	2	4	6	51	6	3	5	8	6
2011-12	Muskegon	USHL	58	11	23	34	50	....	....	....	....	....
2012-13	Michigan State	CCHA	42	10	11	21	34	....	....	....	....	....

DEFAZIO, Brandon (deh-FAZ-ee-oh, BRAN-duhn) VAN

Left wing. Shoots left. 6'2", 215 lbs. Born, Etobicoke, Ont., September 13, 1988.

				Regular Season					Playoffs			
Season	Club	League	GP	G	A	Pts	PIM	GP	G	A	Pts	PIM
2005-06	Oakville Blades	ON-Jr.A	11	2	11	13	8	....	....	....	....	....
	Milton Icehawks	ON-Jr.A	36	10	6	16	38	....	....	....	....	....
2006-07	Oakville Blades	ON-Jr.A	46	12	33	45	135	....	....	....	....	....
2007-08	Clarkson Knights	ECAC	37	3	4	7	34	....	....	....	....	....
2008-09	Clarkson Knights	ECAC	33	7	11	18	28	....	....	....	....	....
2009-10	Clarkson Knights	ECAC	35	12	14	26	58	....	....	....	....	....
2010-11	Clarkson Knights	ECAC	36	14	12	26	56	....	....	....	....	....
	Wilkes-Barre	AHL	2	0	0	0	0	....	....	....	....	....
	Wheeling Nailers	ECHL	10	4	5	9	7	14	4	2	6	8
2011-12	Wilkes-Barre	AHL	66	11	5	16	104	12	0	0	0	6
2012-13	Bridgeport	AHL	69	11	14	25	139	....	....	....	....	....

Signed to an ATO (amateur tryout) contract by **Pittsburgh**, April 1, 2011. Signed as a free agent by **Pittsburgh**, October 7, 2011. Signed as a free agent by **NY Islanders**, July 2, 2012. Signed as a free agent by **Vancouver**, July 12, 2013.

DE LA ROSE, Jacob (deh la ROHZ, YA-kuhb) MTL

Left wing. Shoots left. 6'3", 187 lbs. Born, Arvika, Sweden, May 20, 1995.
(Montreal's 2nd choice, 34th overall, in 2013 Entry Draft).

				Regular Season					Playoffs			
Season	Club	League	GP	G	A	Pts	PIM	GP	G	A	Pts	PIM
2008-09	Nor U18	Swe-U18	11	3	14	17	4	....	....	....	....	....
2009-10	Farjestad U18	Swe-U18	6	0	0	0	2	7	0	0	0	0
2010-11	Leksands IF U18	Swe-U18	30	12	13	25	22	6	0	4	4	4
	Leksands IF Jr.	Swe-Jr.	2	1	0	1	0	....	....	....	....	....
2011-12	Leksands IF U18	Swe-U18	4	3	3	6	6	....	....	....	....	....
	Leksands IF Jr.	Swe-Jr.	28	4	9	13	24	....	....	....	....	....
	Leksands IF	Sweden-2	24	4	0	4	12	....	....	....	....	....
2012-13	Leksands IF Jr.	Swe-Jr.	4	1	4	5	0	....	....	....	....	....
	Leksands IF	Sweden-2	48	6	7	13	33	....	....	....	....	....

DELISLE, Dan (deh-LIGH-uhl, DAN) CHI

Center/Left wing. Shoots left. 6'4", 222 lbs. Born, Minneapolis, MN, September 24, 1990.
(Chicago's 3rd choice, 89th overall, in 2009 Entry Draft).

				Regular Season					Playoffs			
Season	Club	League	GP	G	A	Pts	PIM	GP	G	A	Pts	PIM
2006-07	Totino-Grace	High-MN	....	21	26	47	....	....	....	....	....	....
2007-08	Totino-Grace	High-MN	27	25	31	56	26	....	....	....	....	....
2008-09	Totino-Grace	High-MN	27	32	24	56	16	....	....	....	....	....
	Team Northeast	UMHSEL	24	12	11	23	....	....	....	....	....	....
2009-10	U. Minn-Duluth	WCHA	25	0	1	1	24	....	....	....	....	....
2010-11	U. Minn-Duluth	WCHA	31	4	2	6	12	....	....	....	....	....
2011-12	U. Minn-Duluth	WCHA	19	2	2	4	4	....	....	....	....	....
2012-13	U. Minn-Duluth	WCHA	28	3	2	5	40	....	....	....	....	....

DELNOV, Alexander (dehl-NAWV, al-ehx-AN-duhr) FLA

Left wing. Shoots left. 6', 187 lbs. Born, Moscow, Russia, January 14, 1994.
(Florida's 3rd choice, 114th overall, in 2012 Entry Draft).

				Regular Season					Playoffs			
Season	Club	League	GP	G	A	Pts	PIM	GP	G	A	Pts	PIM
2011-12	Mytischi Jr.	Russia-Jr.	47	11	11	22	16	5	0	0	0	2
2012-13	Seattle	WHL	69	20	29	49	33	7	2	2	4	0
	San Antonio	AHL	6	0	0	0	0	....	....	....	....	....

DEMELO, Dylan (dih-MEH-loh, DIH-luhn) S.J.

Defense. Shoots right. 6'1", 195 lbs. Born, London, Ont., May 1, 1993.
(San Jose's 5th choice, 179th overall, in 2011 Entry Draft).

				Regular Season					Playoffs			
Season	Club	League	GP	G	A	Pts	PIM	GP	G	A	Pts	PIM
2008-09	Lon. Jr. Knights	Minor-ON	74	11	34	45	46	....	....	....	....	....
2009-10	Mississauga	ON-Jr.A	36	9	20	29	24	....	....	....	....	....
	St. Michael's	OHL	20	0	1	1	12	....	....	....	....	....
2010-11	St. Michael's	OHL	67	3	24	27	70	20	1	4	5	15
2011-12	St. Michael's	OHL	67	7	40	47	70	6	1	1	2	13
	Worcester Sharks	AHL	4	0	1	1	2	....	....	....	....	....
2012-13	Mississauga	OHL	64	15	35	50	68	6	1	3	4	6
	Worcester Sharks	AHL	10	0	4	4	6	....	....	....	....	....

DEMPSEY, Mitchell (DEHMP-see, MIH-chuhl) BOS

Left wing. Shoots left. 6'3", 204 lbs. Born, Cambridge, Ont., February 27, 1995.
(Boston's 6th choice, 210th overall, in 2013 Entry Draft).

				Regular Season					Playoffs			
Season	Club	League	GP	G	A	Pts	PIM	GP	G	A	Pts	PIM
2010-11	Camb. Hawks MM	Minor-ON	29	17	27	44	38	7	6	0	6	8
	Camb. Hawks MM	Exhib.	19	15	7	22	30	....	....	....	....	....
	Camb. Hawks Mid.	Minor-ON	....	....	....	....	....	2	0	0	0	0
2011-12	Plymouth Whalers	OHL	34	1	4	5	29	5	0	0	0	0
2012-13	Sault Ste. Marie	OHL	36	1	4	5	17	....	....	....	....	....

DERLYUK, Roman (duhr-LYUHK, ROH-muhn) FLA

Defense. Shoots left. 6'3", 198 lbs. Born, Leningrad, USSR, October 27, 1986.
(Florida's 7th choice, 164th overall, in 2005 Entry Draft).

				Regular Season					Playoffs			
Season	Club	League	GP	G	A	Pts	PIM	GP	G	A	Pts	PIM
2003-04	Lokom. St. Pete.	Russia-3		STATISTICS NOT AVAILABLE								
2004-05	Spartak St. Pet.	Russia-2	51	0	3	3	74	....	....	....	....	....
2005-06	SKA St. Petersburg	Russia	32	0	3	3	63	2	1	0	1	0
	St. Petersburg 2	Russia-3	2	0	1	1	0	....	....	....	....	....
2006-07	SKA St. Petersburg	Russia	6	0	1	1	4	....	....	....	....	....
	St. Petersburg 2	Russia-3	6	1	4	5	6	....	....	....	....	....
	THK Tver	Russia-3	2	0	2	2	0	....	....	....	....	....
	MVD	Russia	19	0	3	3	14	1	0	0	0	0
2007-08	MVD 2	Russia-3	24	1	5	6	36	....	....	....	....	....
	MVD	Russia	26	3	3	6	26	3	0	0	0	2
2008-09	MVD	KHL	54	3	8	11	50	....	....	....	....	....
2009-10	MVD	KHL	25	2	7	9	34	15	1	3	4	16
2010-11	Dynamo Moscow	KHL	44	5	9	14	18	6	0	2	2	8
2011-12	San Antonio	AHL	69	2	9	11	31	10	1	0	1	6
2012-13	Dynamo Moscow	KHL	27	2	2	4	10	11	2	0	2	4

Signed as a free agent by **Dynamo Moscow** (KHL), June 18, 2012.

DeSANTIS, Jason (dih-SAN-this, JAY-suhn)

Defense. Shoots right. 5'11", 185 lbs. Born, Oxford, MI, March 9, 1986.

				Regular Season					Playoffs			
Season	Club	League	GP	G	A	Pts	PIM	GP	G	A	Pts	PIM
2002-03	USNTDP	NAHL	43	4	5	9	42	....	....	....	....	....
2003-04	USNTDP	NAHL	10	1	1	2	4	....	....	....	....	....
2004-05	Ohio State	CCHA	42	4	5	9	32	....	....	....	....	....
2005-06	Ohio State	CCHA	24	2	4	6	30	....	....	....	....	....
2006-07	Ohio State	CCHA	37	5	20	25	50	....	....	....	....	....
2007-08	Ohio State	CCHA	41	5	15	20	38	....	....	....	....	....
	Philadelphia	AHL	10	0	5	5	6	10	0	1	1	6
2008-09	Philadelphia	AHL	56	1	16	17	12	....	....	....	....	....
2009-10	Liberec	CzRep	14	2	3	5	10	....	....	....	....	....
2010-11	Wilkes-Barre	AHL	19	1	4	5	8	....	....	....	....	....
	Wheeling Nailers	ECHL	45	6	21	27	38	15	1	2	3	18
2011-12	St. John's IceCaps	AHL	66	11	32	43	58	10	0	3	3	8
2012-13	San Antonio	AHL	28	2	7	9	22	....	....	....	....	....
	Hamilton Bulldogs	AHL	27	2	3	5	18	....	....	....	....	....

Signed to an ATO (amateur tryout) contract by **Philadelphia** (AHL), March 15, 2008. Signed as a free agent by **Philadelphia** (AHL), October 8, 2008. Signed as a free agent by **Liberec** (CzRep), October 6, 2009. Signed as a free agent by **Wilkes-Barre** (AHL), August 18, 2010. Signed as a free agent by **Florida**, June 14, 2012. Traded to **Montreal** by **Florida** for Brenden Nash, January 14, 2013. Signed as a free agent by **HIFK Helsinki** (Finland), June 17, 2013.

DESCHAMPS, Nicolas (day-SHAWMP, NIHK-oh-las) **WSH**

Center. Shoots left. 6'1", 207 lbs. Born, Lasalle, Que., January 6, 1990.
(Anaheim's 2nd choice, 35th overall, in 2008 Entry Draft).

			Regular Season					Playoffs				
Season	**Club**	**League**	**GP**	**G**	**A**	**Pts**	**PIM**	**GP**	**G**	**A**	**Pts**	**PIM**
2005-06	C.C. Lemoyne	QAAA	23	5	4	9	14	8	0	0	0	12
2006-07	C.C. Lemoyne	QAAA	35	20	28	48	60	10	4	7	11	22
2007-08	Chicoutimi	QMJHL	70	24	43	67	63	6	2	3	5	6
2008-09	Chicoutimi	QMJHL	65	24	41	65	40	4	3	1	4	12
	Iowa Chops	AHL	2	0	1	1	0	....	....	....	....	....
2009-10	Chicoutimi	QMJHL	31	18	26	*44	20	....	....	....	....	....
	Moncton Wildcats	QMJHL	33	21	31	*52	20	15	5	9	14	10
2010-11	Syracuse Crunch	AHL	80	15	31	46	26	....	....	....	....	....
2011-12	Syracuse Crunch	AHL	31	5	2	7	10	....	....	....	....	....
	Toronto Marlies	AHL	40	7	23	30	14	17	3	9	12	8
2012-13	Toronto Marlies	AHL	50	7	9	16	26	....	....	....	....	....
	Hershey Bears	AHL	16	3	4	7	2	5	1	2	3	2

QMJHL All-Rookie Team (2008) • Canadian Major Junior All-Rookie Team (2008) • QMJHL Second All-Star Team (2010)

Traded to **Toronto** by **Anaheim** for Luca Caputi, January 3, 2012. Traded to **Washington** by **Toronto** for Kevin Marshall, March 14, 2013.

DESLAURIERS, Nicolas (duh-LOHR-ree-AY, NIH-koh-las) **L.A.**

Defense. Shoots left. 6'1", 214 lbs. Born, LaSalle, Que., February 22, 1991.
(Los Angeles' 3rd choice, 84th overall, in 2009 Entry Draft).

			Regular Season					Playoffs				
Season	**Club**	**League**	**GP**	**G**	**A**	**Pts**	**PIM**	**GP**	**G**	**A**	**Pts**	**PIM**
2006-07	Chateauguay	QAAA	43	2	10	12	28	3	1	0	1	4
2007-08	Rouyn-Noranda	QMJHL	42	2	7	9	38	4	0	0	0	0
2008-09	Rouyn-Noranda	QMJHL	68	11	19	30	80	6	2	2	4	8
2009-10	Rouyn-Noranda	QMJHL	65	9	36	45	72	11	2	6	8	2
2010-11	Gatineau	QMJHL	48	13	30	43	53	24	5	15	20	19
2011-12	Manchester	AHL	65	1	13	14	67	4	0	0	0	7
2012-13	Manchester	AHL	63	4	19	23	80	4	2	2	4	2

DEVANE, Jamie (deh-VAYN, JAY-mee) **TOR**

Left wing. Shoots left. 6'5", 220 lbs. Born, Mississauga, Ont., February 20, 1991.
(Toronto's 4th choice, 68th overall, in 2009 Entry Draft).

			Regular Season					Playoffs				
Season	**Club**	**League**	**GP**	**G**	**A**	**Pts**	**PIM**	**GP**	**G**	**A**	**Pts**	**PIM**
2007-08	Vaughan Kings	GTHL	15	4	11	15	24	....	....	....	....	....
	Vaughan Vipers	ON-Jr.A	19	2	0	2	17	1	0	0	0	0
2008-09	Plymouth Whalers	OHL	64	5	12	17	92	11	0	0	0	17
2009-10	Plymouth Whalers	OHL	51	6	8	14	84	9	0	1	1	12
	Toronto Marlies	AHL	2	0	0	0	4	....	....	....	....	....
2010-11	Plymouth Whalers	OHL	63	18	20	38	131	10	2	3	5	19
2011-12	Plymouth Whalers	OHL	59	23	22	45	104	13	2	1	3	19
2012-13	San Francisco Bulls	ECHL	12	1	0	1	45	....	....	....	....	....
	Toronto Marlies	AHL	22	2	3	5	41	....	....	....	....	....

DI GIUSEPPE, Phillip (DEE-joo-SEH-pee, FIHL-ihp) **CAR**

Left wing. Shoots left. 6', 197 lbs. Born, Toronto, Ont., October 9, 1993.
(Carolina's 1st choice, 38th overall, in 2012 Entry Draft).

			Regular Season					Playoffs				
Season	**Club**	**League**	**GP**	**G**	**A**	**Pts**	**PIM**	**GP**	**G**	**A**	**Pts**	**PIM**
2008-09	Vaughan Kings	GTHL	41	16	17	33	19	....	....	....	....	....
2009-10	Villanova Knights	ON-Jr.A	56	16	31	47	44	6	1	3	4	0
2010-11	Villanova Knights	ON-Jr.A	49	24	39	63	25	10	6	10	16	6
2011-12	U. of Michigan	CCHA	40	11	15	26	18	....	....	....	....	....
2012-13	U. of Michigan	CCHA	40	9	19	28	32	....	....	....	....	....

DI PAULI, Thomas (DEE-paw-LEE, TAW-muhs) **WSH**

Center. Shoots left. 5'11", 188 lbs. Born, Woodbridge, IL, April 29, 1994.
(Washington's 4th choice, 100th overall, in 2012 Entry Draft).

			Regular Season					Playoffs				
Season	**Club**	**League**	**GP**	**G**	**A**	**Pts**	**PIM**	**GP**	**G**	**A**	**Pts**	**PIM**
2009-10	Chicago Mission	T1EHL	30	18	15	33	10	....	....	....	....	....
	Chicago Mission	Exhib.	19	11	26	37	....	....	....	....	....	....
2010-11	USNTDP	USHL	32	4	11	15	16	2	0	1	1	0
	USNTDP	U-17	17	4	9	12	10	....	....	....	....	....
2011-12	USNTDP	USHL	21	6	5	11	6	....	....	....	....	....
	USNTDP	U-18	34	5	5	10	16	....	....	....	....	....
2012-13	U. of Notre Dame	CCHA	41	5	7	12	31	....	....	....	....	....

DIABY, Jonathan (dee-AH-bee, JAWN-ah-thuhn) **NSH**

Defense. Shoots left. 6'5", 223 lbs. Born, Montreal, Que., November 16, 1994.
(Nashville's 2nd choice, 64th overall, in 2013 Entry Draft).

			Regular Season					Playoffs				
Season	**Club**	**League**	**GP**	**G**	**A**	**Pts**	**PIM**	**GP**	**G**	**A**	**Pts**	**PIM**
2009-10	Esther-Blondin	QAAA	39	1	5	6	60	....	....	....	....	....
2010-11	Esther-Blondin	QAAA	30	2	9	11	79	....	....	....	....	....
	Victoriaville Tigres	QMJHL	19	0	0	0	19	3	0	0	0	0
2011-12	Victoriaville Tigres	QMJHL	51	1	8	9	64	4	0	0	0	11
2012-13	Victoriaville Tigres	QMJHL	67	4	22	26	117	9	0	1	1	20

DIAMOND, Joe (DIGH-muhnd, JOH) **NYI**

Right wing. Shoots left. 5'7", 175 lbs. Born, Long Beach, NY, June 16, 1989.

			Regular Season					Playoffs				
Season	**Club**	**League**	**GP**	**G**	**A**	**Pts**	**PIM**	**GP**	**G**	**A**	**Pts**	**PIM**
2007-08	Omaha Lancers	USHL	32	13	10	23	53	14	4	3	7	19
2008-09	Hamilton	ON-Jr.A	45	42	34	76	213	2	1	0	1	2
2009-10	U. of Maine	H-East	32	9	3	12	73	....	....	....	....	....
2010-11	U. of Maine	H-East	33	11	10	21	130	....	....	....	....	....
2011-12	U. of Maine	H-East	37	25	22	47	117	....	....	....	....	....
2012-13	U. of Maine	H-East	33	14	10	24	*147	....	....	....	....	....
	Bridgeport	AHL	10	2	3	5	27	....	....	....	....	....

Hockey East Second All-Star Team (2012)

Signed to an ATO (amateur tryout) contract by **Bridgeport** (AHL), March 22, 2013. Signed as a free agent by **NY Islanders**, April 30, 2013.

DICKINSON, Jason (DIH-kihn-suhn, JAY-suhn) **DAL**

Center. Shoots left. 6'1", 179 lbs. Born, Georgetown, Ont., July 4, 1995.
(Dallas' 2nd choice, 29th overall, in 2013 Entry Draft).

			Regular Season					Playoffs				
Season	**Club**	**League**	**GP**	**G**	**A**	**Pts**	**PIM**	**GP**	**G**	**A**	**Pts**	**PIM**
2010-11	Halton Hurricanes	Minor-ON	59	45	34	79	22	....	....	....	....	....
2011-12	Guelph Storm	OHL	63	13	22	35	24	6	3	2	5	6
2012-13	Guelph Storm	OHL	66	18	29	47	31	5	1	1	2	0

DIDIER, Josiah (DIH-dee-ay, joh-SIGH-uh) **MTL**

Defense. Shoots right. 6'3", 218 lbs. Born, Littleton, CO, April 8, 1993.
(Montreal's 2nd choice, 97th overall, in 2011 Entry Draft).

			Regular Season					Playoffs				
Season	**Club**	**League**	**GP**	**G**	**A**	**Pts**	**PIM**	**GP**	**G**	**A**	**Pts**	**PIM**
2009-10	Colorado T-birds	Minor-CO	19	3	15	18	12	....	....	....	....	....
	Colorado T-birds	Exhib.	9	5	2	7	12	....	....	....	....	....
2010-11	Cedar Rapids	USHL	58	8	13	21	81	8	0	2	2	7
2011-12	U. of Denver	WCHA	41	0	3	3	36	....	....	....	....	....
2012-13	U. of Denver	WCHA	31	0	7	7	48	....	....	....	....	....

DIETZ, Darren (DEETZ, DAIR-uhn) **MTL**

Defense. Shoots right. 6'1", 205 lbs. Born, Medicine Hat, Alta., July 17, 1993.
(Montreal's 4th choice, 138th overall, in 2011 Entry Draft).

			Regular Season					Playoffs				
Season	**Club**	**League**	**GP**	**G**	**A**	**Pts**	**PIM**	**GP**	**G**	**A**	**Pts**	**PIM**
2008-09	Medicine Hat	AMHL	34	0	4	4	62	....	....	....	....	....
2009-10	Lethbridge	AMHL	33	9	15	24	105	5	4	3	7	14
	Saskatoon Blades	WHL	8	1	1	2	4	3	0	0	0	2
2010-11	Saskatoon Blades	WHL	68	8	19	27	66	10	1	4	5	15
2011-12	Saskatoon Blades	WHL	72	15	29	44	118	3	0	1	1	5
2012-13	Saskatoon Blades	WHL	72	24	34	58	100	4	1	1	2	2

WHL East First All-Star Team (2013)

DJOOS, Christian (YEW-uhs, KRIHS-t'yehn) **WSH**

Defense. Shoots left. 5'11", 158 lbs. Born, Gothenburg, Sweden, August 6, 1994.
(Washington's 8th choice, 195th overall, in 2012 Entry Draft).

			Regular Season					Playoffs				
Season	**Club**	**League**	**GP**	**G**	**A**	**Pts**	**PIM**	**GP**	**G**	**A**	**Pts**	**PIM**
2009-10	Brynas U18	Swe-U18	35	4	12	16	66	4	1	1	2	4
2010-11	Brynas U18	Swe-U18	38	11	34	45	34	5	0	5	5	4
	Brynas IF Gavle Jr.	Swe-Jr.	11	0	1	1	0	....	....	....	....	....
2011-12	Brynas U18	Swe-U18	7	5	8	13	4	5	1	0	1	2
	Brynas IF Gavle Jr.	Swe-Jr.	40	3	21	24	22	2	0	0	0	0
	Brynas IF Gavle	Sweden	1	0	0	0	0	....	....	....	....	....
2012-13	Brynas IF Gavle Jr.	Swe-Jr.	2	0	2	2	2	....	....	....	....	....
	Brynas IF Gavle	Sweden	47	2	6	8	38	4	0	0	0	0

DOHERTY, Taylor (DOHR-eh-tee, TAY-luhr) **S.J.**

Defense. Shoots right. 6'7", 235 lbs. Born, Cambridge, Ont., March 2, 1991.
(San Jose's 2nd choice, 57th overall, in 2009 Entry Draft).

			Regular Season					Playoffs				
Season	**Club**	**League**	**GP**	**G**	**A**	**Pts**	**PIM**	**GP**	**G**	**A**	**Pts**	**PIM**
2006-07	Cambridge Hawks	Minor-ON	70	10	37	47	169	....	....	....	....	....
2007-08	Kingston	OHL	64	6	14	20	118	....	....	....	....	....
2008-09	Kingston	OHL	68	2	18	20	140	....	....	....	....	....
2009-10	Kingston	OHL	63	16	28	44	114	5	1	4	5	0
2010-11	Kingston	OHL	68	14	39	53	86	5	0	3	3	12
	Worcester Sharks	AHL	3	0	0	0	0	....	....	....	....	....
2011-12	Worcester Sharks	AHL	63	0	6	6	76	....	....	....	....	....
2012-13	Worcester Sharks	AHL	40	1	9	10	67	....	....	....	....	....

DOMI, Max (DOH-mee, MAX) **PHX**

Center/Left wing. Shoots left. 5'9", 195 lbs. Born, Winnipeg, Man., March 2, 1995.
(Phoenix's 1st choice, 12th overall, in 2013 Entry Draft).

			Regular Season					Playoffs				
Season	**Club**	**League**	**GP**	**G**	**A**	**Pts**	**PIM**	**GP**	**G**	**A**	**Pts**	**PIM**
2010-11	Don Mills Flyers	GTHL	30	27	30	57	45	....	....	....	....	....
	St. Michael's	ON-Jr.A	2	1	1	2	0	....	....	....	....	....
2011-12	London Knights	OHL	62	21	28	49	48	19	4	5	9	10
2012-13	London Knights	OHL	64	39	48	87	71	21	11	21	32	26

DONNAY, Troy (duh-NAY, TROI) **NYR**

Defense. Shoots right. 6'7", 185 lbs. Born, Flint, MI, February 18, 1994.

			Regular Season					Playoffs				
Season	**Club**	**League**	**GP**	**G**	**A**	**Pts**	**PIM**	**GP**	**G**	**A**	**Pts**	**PIM**
2009-10	Detroit Belle Tire	T1EHL	37	1	10	11	69	....	....	....	....	....
2010-11	London Knights	OHL	25	0	1	1	12	....	....	....	....	....
2011-12	London Knights	OHL	23	0	3	3	16	....	....	....	....	....
	Erie Otters	OHL	27	1	4	5	28	....	....	....	....	....
2012-13	Erie Otters	OHL	68	1	7	8	48	....	....	....	....	....

Signed as a free agent by **NY Rangers**, July 31, 2013.

DOTCHIN, Jake (DAW-CHIHN, JAYK) **T.B.**

Defense. Shoots right. 6'3", 212 lbs. Born, Cambridge, Ont., March 24, 1994.
(Tampa Bay's 7th choice, 161st overall, in 2012 Entry Draft).

			Regular Season					Playoffs				
Season	**Club**	**League**	**GP**	**G**	**A**	**Pts**	**PIM**	**GP**	**G**	**A**	**Pts**	**PIM**
2009-10	Cambridge Hawks	Minor-ON	30	8	19	27	60	11	4	6	10	26
	Cambridge Hawks	Exhib.	11	5	10	15	6	....	....	....	....	....
2010-11	Cambridge	ON-Jr.B	41	5	10	15	88	5	1	3	4	8
2011-12	Owen Sound	OHL	64	3	16	19	77	5	0	3	3	8
2012-13	Owen Sound	OHL	38	2	12	14	39	....	....	....	....	....
	Barrie Colts	OHL	28	2	6	8	42	17	1	4	5	25

DOWD, Nic (DOWD, NIHK) **L.A.**

Center. Shoots right. 6'2", 196 lbs. Born, Huntsville, AL, May 27, 1990.
(Los Angeles' 10th choice, 198th overall, in 2009 Entry Draft).

			Regular Season					Playoffs				
Season	**Club**	**League**	**GP**	**G**	**A**	**Pts**	**PIM**	**GP**	**G**	**A**	**Pts**	**PIM**
2007-08	Culver Academy	High-IN	45	15	31	46	38	....	....	....	....	....
2008-09	Wenatchee Wild	NAHL	43	16	33	49	71	13	8	*14	*22	34
2009-10	Indiana Ice	USHL	46	16	23	39	48	9	2	4	6	2
2010-11	St. Cloud State	WCHA	36	5	13	18	34	....	....	....	....	....
2011-12	St. Cloud State	WCHA	39	11	13	24	36	....	....	....	....	....
2012-13	St. Cloud State	WCHA	42	14	25	39	41	....	....	....	....	....

DOWNING, Michael (DOW-nihng, MIGH-kuhl) FLA

Defense. Shoots left. 6'3", 192 lbs. Born, Canton, MI, May 19, 1995.
(Florida's 4th choice, 97th overall, in 2013 Entry Draft).

			Regular Season					Playoffs				
Season	**Club**	**League**	**GP**	**G**	**A**	**Pts**	**PIM**	**GP**	**G**	**A**	**Pts**	**PIM**
2010-11	Catholic Central	High-MI	26	7	16	23	18	....	....	....	....	....
2011-12	USNTDP	U-17	7	0	1	1	0	....	....	....	....	....
	Dubuque	USHL	54	4	10	14	68	5	1	1	2	4
2012-13	Dubuque	USHL	52	3	20	23	107	11	0	3	3	6

• Signed Letter of Intent to attend **University of Michigan** (CCHA) in fall of 2013.

DRAEGER, John (DRAY-guhr, JAWN) MIN

Defense. Shoots right. 6'2", 188 lbs. Born, Edina, MN, December 2, 1993.
(Minnesota's 3rd choice, 68th overall, in 2012 Entry Draft).

			Regular Season					Playoffs				
Season	**Club**	**League**	**GP**	**G**	**A**	**Pts**	**PIM**	**GP**	**G**	**A**	**Pts**	**PIM**
2009-10	Shattuck U16	High-MN	53	1	9	10	57	....	....	....	....	....
2010-11	Shat.-St. Mary's	High-MN	54	3	8	11	18	....	....	....	....	....
2011-12	Shat.-St. Mary's	High-MN	57	11	30	41	36	....	....	....	....	....
2012-13	Michigan State	CCHA	42	1	9	10	22	....	....	....	....	....

DRAKE, David (DRAYK, DAY-vihd) PHI

Defense. Shoots left. 6'4", 170 lbs. Born, Naperville, IL, January 7, 1995.
(Philadelphia's 6th choice, 192nd overall, in 2013 Entry Draft).

			Regular Season					Playoffs				
Season	**Club**	**League**	**GP**	**G**	**A**	**Pts**	**PIM**	**GP**	**G**	**A**	**Pts**	**PIM**
2011-12	Indiana Jr. Ice	NAPHL	18	1	4	5	22	5	1	3	4	0
	Indiana Jr. Ice	HPHL	6	2	0	2	2	....	....	....	....	....
2012-13	Chicago Fury	T1EHL	40	2	4	6	16	2	0	0	0	0
	Des Moines	USHL	12	1	0	1	6	....	....	....	....	....

DROUIN, Jonathan (droo-EHN, JAWN-ah-thuhn) T.B.

Left wing. Shoots left. 5'11", 191 lbs. Born, Ste-Agathe, Que., March 28, 1995.
(Tampa Bay's 1st choice, 3rd overall, in 2013 Entry Draft).

			Regular Season					Playoffs				
Season	**Club**	**League**	**GP**	**G**	**A**	**Pts**	**PIM**	**GP**	**G**	**A**	**Pts**	**PIM**
2010-11	Lac St-Louis Lions	QAAA	38	22	36	58	38	15	11	17	28	18
2011-12	Lac St-Louis Lions	QAAA	21	21	29	50	35	....	....	....	....	....
	Halifax	QMJHL	33	7	22	29	12	17	9	17	26	4
2012-13	Halifax	QMJHL	49	41	64	105	32	17	12	*23	*35	14

QMJHL First All-Star Team (2013) • QMJHL Player of the Year (2013) • Canadian Major Junior Player of the Year (2013)

DUCLAIR, Anthony (doo-KLAIR, AN-thuh-nee) NYR

Left wing. Shoots left. 5'11", 177 lbs. Born, Pointe-Claire, Que., August 26, 1995.
(NY Rangers' 3rd choice, 80th overall, in 2013 Entry Draft).

			Regular Season					Playoffs				
Season	**Club**	**League**	**GP**	**G**	**A**	**Pts**	**PIM**	**GP**	**G**	**A**	**Pts**	**PIM**
2009-10	Laurentides	Minor-QU	59	81	47	128	32	....	....	....	....	....
2010-11	Lac St-Louis Lions	QAAA	34	25	32	57	36	14	9	14	23	20
2011-12	Quebec Remparts	QMJHL	63	31	35	66	50	11	3	5	8	8
2012-13	Quebec Remparts	QMJHL	55	20	30	50	22	11	3	5	8	12

DUMBA, Mathew (DUHM-ba, MA-thew) MIN

Defense. Shoots right. 6', 181 lbs. Born, Regina, Sask., July 25, 1994.
(Minnesota's 1st choice, 7th overall, in 2012 Entry Draft).

			Regular Season					Playoffs				
Season	**Club**	**League**	**GP**	**G**	**A**	**Pts**	**PIM**	**GP**	**G**	**A**	**Pts**	**PIM**
2007-08	Calgary Bronks	AMBHL	33	3	8	11	26	2	1	1	2	2
2008-09	Calgary Bronks	AMBHL	33	20	18	38	96	....	....	....	....	....
2009-10	Edge School	High-AB	41	16	28	44	47	....	....	....	....	....
	Red Deer Rebels	WHL	6	0	2	2	4	2	0	0	0	4
2010-11	Red Deer Rebels	WHL	62	15	11	26	83	9	2	0	2	20
2011-12	Red Deer Rebels	WHL	69	20	37	57	67	....	....	....	....	....
2012-13	Red Deer Rebels	WHL	62	16	26	42	80	9	2	2	4	14
	Houston Aeros	AHL	3	0	0	0	2	5	0	0	0	0

DUMOULIN, Brian (DOO-moh-lihn, BRIGH-uhn) PIT

Defense. Shoots left. 6'4", 219 lbs. Born, Biddeford, ME, September 6, 1991.
(Carolina's 2nd choice, 51st overall, in 2009 Entry Draft).

			Regular Season					Playoffs				
Season	**Club**	**League**	**GP**	**G**	**A**	**Pts**	**PIM**	**GP**	**G**	**A**	**Pts**	**PIM**
2007-08	Biddeford Tigers	High-ME	24	13	48	61	10	....	....	....	....	....
2008-09	N.H. Jr. Monarchs	EJHL	41	7	23	30	30	7	0	3	3	2
2009-10	Boston College	H-East	42	1	21	22	16	....	....	....	....	....
2010-11	Boston College	H-East	37	3	30	33	6	....	....	....	....	....
2011-12	Boston College	H-East	44	7	21	28	26	....	....	....	....	....
2012-13	Wilkes-Barre	AHL	73	6	18	24	18	15	2	6	8	6

Hockey East All-Rookie Team (2010) • NCAA Championship All-Tournament Team (2010, 2012) • Hockey East First All-Star Team (2011, 2012) • NCAA East First All-American Team (2011, 2012)

Traded to **Pittsburgh** by **Carolina** with Brandon Sutter and Carolina's 1st round choice (Derrick Pouliot) in 2012 Entry Draft for Jordan Staal, June 22, 2012.

DUNN, Vincent (DUHN, VIHN-sehnt) OTT

Center. Shoots left. 5'11", 183 lbs. Born, Hull, Que., September 14, 1995.
(Ottawa's 5th choice, 138th overall, in 2013 Entry Draft).

			Regular Season					Playoffs				
Season	**Club**	**League**	**GP**	**G**	**A**	**Pts**	**PIM**	**GP**	**G**	**A**	**Pts**	**PIM**
2010-11	Gatineau Intrepide	QAAA	41	22	26	48	122	3	1	1	2	6
2011-12	Val-d'Or Foreurs	QMJHL	56	5	8	13	94	3	1	0	1	5
2012-13	Val-d'Or Foreurs	QMJHL	53	25	27	52	98	10	0	3	3	19

DZINGEL, Ryan (ZIHN-guhl, RIGH-uhn) OTT

Center. Shoots left. 6', 188 lbs. Born, Wheaton, IL, March 9, 1992.
(Ottawa's 10th choice, 204th overall, in 2011 Entry Draft).

			Regular Season					Playoffs				
Season	**Club**	**League**	**GP**	**G**	**A**	**Pts**	**PIM**	**GP**	**G**	**A**	**Pts**	**PIM**
2006-07	Chicago Mission	MWEHL	31	12	8	20	26	....	....	....	....	....
2007-08	Team Illinois	MWEHL	31	6	14	20	20	....	....	....	....	....
2008-09	Team Illinois	T1EHL	31	18	15	33	30	....	....	....	....	....
2009-10	Team Illinois	T1EHL	31	19	27	46	28	....	....	....	....	....
2010-11	Lincoln Stars	USHL	54	23	44	67	8	2	1	0	1	2
2011-12	Ohio State	CCHA	33	7	17	24	32	....	....	....	....	....
2012-13	Ohio State	CCHA	40	16	22	38	22	....	....	....	....	....

DZIURZYNSKI, Darian (z'yuhr-ZIHN-skee, dair-EE-uhn) PHX

Left wing. Shoots left. 6'1", 204 lbs. Born, Prince Albert, Sask., March 30, 1991.
(Phoenix's 6th choice, 141st overall, in 2011 Entry Draft).

			Regular Season					Playoffs				
Season	**Club**	**League**	**GP**	**G**	**A**	**Pts**	**PIM**	**GP**	**G**	**A**	**Pts**	**PIM**
2007-08	Lloydminster	AMHL	26	20	15	35	98	....	....	....	....	....
	Saskatoon Blades	WHL	33	3	1	4	18	....	....	....	....	....
	Lloydminster	AJHL	2	0	0	0	0	....	....	....	....	....
2008-09	Saskatoon Blades	WHL	64	10	15	25	96	7	0	1	1	6
2009-10	Saskatoon Blades	WHL	70	14	15	29	156	7	3	6	9	9
2010-11	Saskatoon Blades	WHL	72	35	22	57	125	10	3	3	6	18
2011-12	Saskatoon Blades	WHL	4	3	0	3	4	....	....	....	....	....
	Brandon	WHL	61	27	16	43	106	9	2	2	4	16
2012-13	Portland Pirates	AHL	59	9	7	16	87	3	1	0	1	0

EBERT, Nick (EE-buhrt, NIHK) L.A.

Defense. Shoots right. 5'11", 205 lbs. Born, Livingston, NJ, May 11, 1994.
(Los Angeles' 6th choice, 211th overall, in 2012 Entry Draft).

			Regular Season					Playoffs				
Season	**Club**	**League**	**GP**	**G**	**A**	**Pts**	**PIM**	**GP**	**G**	**A**	**Pts**	**PIM**
2007-08	N. Jersey Bantams	AYHL	25	9	9	18	24	....	....	....	....	....
2008-09	N. Jersey Bantams	AYHL	2	0	0	0	0	....	....	....	....	....
	N. Jersey Midgets	AYHL	26	10	15	25	23	....	....	....	....	....
2009-10	Waterloo	USHL	53	6	12	18	26	3	1	0	1	0
2010-11	Windsor Spitfires	OHL	64	11	30	41	44	18	1	2	3	6
2011-12	Windsor Spitfires	OHL	66	6	33	39	58	4	0	2	2	8
2012-13	Windsor Spitfires	OHL	68	11	27	38	58	....	....	....	....	....
	Ontario Reign	ECHL	4	0	3	3	2	10	2	5	7	0

OHL All-Rookie Team (2011)

EDDY, Cullen (EH-dee, CUHL-ihn) PHI

Defense. Shoots right. 6', 195 lbs. Born, Hidden Valley, PA, November 18, 1988.

			Regular Season					Playoffs				
Season	**Club**	**League**	**GP**	**G**	**A**	**Pts**	**PIM**	**GP**	**G**	**A**	**Pts**	**PIM**
2006-07	Mercyhurst	AH	35	5	11	16	62	....	....	....	....	....
2007-08	Mercyhurst	AH	41	2	10	12	70	....	....	....	....	....
2008-09	Mercyhurst	AH	38	1	14	15	93	....	....	....	....	....
2009-10	Mercyhurst	AH	30	1	5	6	97	....	....	....	....	....
	Cincinnati	ECHL	7	0	1	1	6	8	0	0	0	6
2010-11	Adirondack	AHL	47	3	7	10	40	....	....	....	....	....
	Greenville	ECHL	16	1	3	4	26	....	....	....	....	....
2011-12	Adirondack	AHL	54	2	13	15	130	....	....	....	....	....
	Greenville	ECHL	15	4	10	14	21	....	....	....	....	....
2012-13	Adirondack	AHL	70	2	3	5	120	....	....	....	....	....

Signed as a free agent by **Cincinnati** (AHL), March 19, 2010. Signed as a free agent by **Philadelphia**, September 22, 2010.

EDDY, David (EH-dee, DAY-vihd) CGY

Right wing. Shoots right. 6', 187 lbs. Born, Woodbury, MN, December 10, 1989.

			Regular Season					Playoffs				
Season	**Club**	**League**	**GP**	**G**	**A**	**Pts**	**PIM**	**GP**	**G**	**A**	**Pts**	**PIM**
2008-09	Sioux Falls	USHL	60	21	35	56	52	3	0	3	3	14
2009-10	St. Cloud State	WCHA	35	12	11	23	12	....	....	....	....	....
2010-11	St. Cloud State	WCHA	18	9	8	17	17	....	....	....	....	....
2011-12	St. Cloud State	WCHA	39	9	16	25	52	....	....	....	....	....
	Abbotsford Heat	AHL	4	1	0	1	0	....	....	....	....	....
2012-13	Utah Grizzlies	ECHL	32	5	11	16	61	4	1	0	1	11
	Abbotsford Heat	AHL	10	0	0	0	7	....	....	....	....	....

Signed as a free agent by **Calgary**, March 20, 2012.

EDMUNDSON, Joel (EHD-muhnd-suhn, JOHL) ST.L.

Defense. Shoots left. 6'5", 190 lbs. Born, Brandon, MB, June 28, 1993.
(St. Louis' 3rd choice, 46th overall, in 2011 Entry Draft).

			Regular Season					Playoffs				
Season	**Club**	**League**	**GP**	**G**	**A**	**Pts**	**PIM**	**GP**	**G**	**A**	**Pts**	**PIM**
2008-09	Brandon	MMHL	41	5	18	23	58	6	2	4	6	4
2009-10	Brandon	MMHL	44	10	25	35	54	7	0	5	5	10
2010-11	Moose Jaw	WHL	71	2	18	20	95	6	0	0	0	2
2011-12	Moose Jaw	WHL	56	4	19	23	91	14	3	2	5	12
2012-13	Moose Jaw	WHL	29	2	6	8	70	....	....	....	....	....
	Kamloops Blazers	WHL	34	7	10	17	71	15	3	5	8	29

ELIE, Remi (EH-lee, REH-mee) DAL

Left wing. Shoots left. 6'1", 203 lbs. Born, Cornwall, Ont., April 16, 1995.
(Dallas' 3rd choice, 40th overall, in 2013 Entry Draft).

			Regular Season					Playoffs				
Season	**Club**	**League**	**GP**	**G**	**A**	**Pts**	**PIM**	**GP**	**G**	**A**	**Pts**	**PIM**
2010-11	E. Ont. Wild MM	Minor-ON	29	15	24	39	43	5	3	3	6	6
	E. Ont. Wild Mid.	Minor-ON	2	0	2	2	2	1	1	0	1	4
2011-12	Hawkesbury	ON-Jr.A	59	21	25	46	39	9	5	4	9	12
2012-13	London Knights	OHL	65	7	10	17	34	21	4	4	8	8

ELLIS, Morgan (EHL-ihs, MOHR-guhn) MTL

Defense. Shoots right. 6'1", 202 lbs. Born, Summerside, P.E.I., April 30, 1992.
(Montreal's 3rd choice, 117th overall, in 2010 Entry Draft).

			Regular Season					Playoffs				
Season	**Club**	**League**	**GP**	**G**	**A**	**Pts**	**PIM**	**GP**	**G**	**A**	**Pts**	**PIM**
2007-08	Charlottetown	NBPEI	33	3	4	7	28	7	0	2	2	10
	Charlottetown	Exhib.	16	2	6	8	16	....	....	....	....	....
2008-09	Cape Breton	QMJHL	52	0	6	6	45	10	0	1	1	4
2009-10	Cape Breton	QMJHL	60	4	25	29	56	5	1	0	1	10
2010-11	Cape Breton	QMJHL	65	8	28	36	65	4	0	0	0	8
2011-12	Cape Breton	QMJHL	34	7	18	25	18	....	....	....	....	....
	Shawinigan	QMJHL	26	8	19	27	38	11	4	7	11	6
2012-13	Hamilton Bulldogs	AHL	71	4	4	8	57	....	....	....	....	....

QMJHL Second All-Star Team (2012)

ELSON, Turner (EHL-suhn, TUHR-nuhr) CGY

Left wing. Shoots left. 5'11", 175 lbs. Born, St. Albert, Alta., September 13, 1992.

			Regular Season					Playoffs				
Season	Club	League	GP	G	A	Pts	PIM	GP	G	A	Pts	PIM
2008-09	St. Albert Raiders	AMHL	33	11	12	23	77	2	0	0	0	4
2009-10	Red Deer Rebels	WHL	66	9	8	17	94	4	0	0	0	4
2010-11	Red Deer Rebels	WHL	68	16	15	31	124	9	0	4	4	23
2011-12	Red Deer Rebels	WHL	55	21	25	46	59	....	....	....	....	....
	Abbotsford Heat	AHL	1	0	0	0	2	....	....	....	....	....
2012-13	Red Deer Rebels	WHL	64	26	31	57	60	9	5	4	9	6
	Abbotsford Heat	AHL	2	0	0	0	0	....	....	....	....	....

Signed as a free agent by **Calgary**, September 22, 2011.

EMANUELSSON, Petter (EE-man-yew EHL-suhn, PEH-tuhr) S.J.

Right wing. Shoots right. 6', 200 lbs. Born, Kiruna, Sweden, August 7, 1991.

			Regular Season					Playoffs				
Season	Club	League	GP	G	A	Pts	PIM	GP	G	A	Pts	PIM
2007-08	Skelleftea U18	Swe-U18	27	18	17	35	0	....	....	....	....	....
	Skelleftea Jr.	Swe-Jr.	2	0	0	0	0	2	0	0	0	0
2008-09	Skelleftea AIK U18	Swe-U18	9	5	9	14	2	8	5	3	8	4
	Skelleftea AIK Jr.	Swe-Jr.	36	7	12	19	4	5	2	2	4	4
2009-10	Skelleftea AIK Jr.	Swe-Jr.	22	5	9	14	2	....	....	....	....	....
	Skelleftea AIK	Sweden	1	0	1	1	0	....	....	....	....	....
2010-11	Skelleftea AIK	Sweden	4	0	0	0	0	....	....	....	....	....
	Sundsvall	Sweden-2	5	2	1	3	0	....	....	....	....	....
	Skelleftea AIK Jr.	Swe-Jr.	40	21	28	49	14	5	3	3	6	0
2011-12	Skelleftea AIK Jr.	Swe-Jr.	6	2	3	5	0	....	....	....	....	....
	Pitea HC	Sweden-3	27	16	9	25	10	....	....	....	....	....
	Skelleftea AIK	Sweden	17	1	0	1	4	....	....	....	....	....
2012-13	Skelleftea AIK	Sweden	54	9	9	18	8	13	6	2	8	0

Signed as a free agent by **San Jose**, June 11, 2013.

ERNE, Adam (UHR-nee, A-duhm) T.B.

Left wing. Shoots left. 6'1", 211 lbs. Born, New Haven, CT, April 20, 1995.
(Tampa Bay's 2nd choice, 33rd overall, in 2013 Entry Draft).

			Regular Season					Playoffs				
Season	Club	League	GP	G	A	Pts	PIM	GP	G	A	Pts	PIM
2009-10	L.A. Selects	Minor-CA	STATISTICS NOT AVAILABLE									
2010-11	Indiana Ice	USHL	45	10	8	18	49	3	0	1	1	0
2011-12	Quebec Remparts	QMJHL	64	28	27	55	32	11	2	4	6	10
2012-13	Quebec Remparts	QMJHL	68	28	44	72	67	11	5	5	10	19

EVERSON, Max (EHV-uhr-suhn, MAX) TOR

Defense. Shoots left. 6'1", 190 lbs. Born, Edina, MN, February 22, 1993.
(Toronto's 9th choice, 203rd overall, in 2011 Entry Draft).

			Regular Season					Playoffs				
Season	Club	League	GP	G	A	Pts	PIM	GP	G	A	Pts	PIM
2009-10	Edina Hornets	High-MN	21	2	8	10	10	6	1	1	2	2
2010-11	Team Southwest	UMHSEL	7	1	4	5	0	2	0	0	0	0
	Edina Hornets	High-MN	22	4	17	21	20	6	0	4	4	4
	USNTDP	USHL	5	1	1	2	2	....	....	....	....	....
	USNTDP	U-18	12	0	1	1	10	....	....	....	....	....
2011-12	Harvard Crimson	ECAC	34	0	4	4	12	....	....	....	....	....
2012-13	Harvard Crimson	ECAC	7	0	1	1	4	....	....	....	....	....
	Omaha Lancers	USHL	16	1	4	5	8	....	....	....	....	....

Signed as a free agent by **Omaha** (USHL), December 15, 2012.

EWANYK, Travis (ee-WAHN-ihk, TRA-vihs) EDM

Left wing. Shoots left. 6'2", 189 lbs. Born, North Vancouver, B.C., March 29, 1993.
(Edmonton's 5th choice, 74th overall, in 2011 Entry Draft).

			Regular Season					Playoffs				
Season	Club	League	GP	G	A	Pts	PIM	GP	G	A	Pts	PIM
2007-08	St. Albert Sabres	AMBHL	30	12	19	31	66	2	0	1	1	2
2008-09	St. Albert Raiders	AMHL	33	7	12	19	14	2	0	0	0	4
	Edmonton	WHL	2	0	0	0	0	3	0	0	0	0
2009-10	Edmonton	WHL	42	1	4	5	45	....	....	....	....	....
2010-11	Edmonton	WHL	72	16	11	27	126	4	0	0	0	13
2011-12	Edmonton	WHL	11	1	3	4	8	20	3	2	5	10
2012-13	Edmonton	WHL	58	8	15	23	119	22	6	4	10	26

FAKSA, Radek (FAK-suh, RA-dehk) DAL

Center. Shoots left. 6'3", 200 lbs. Born, Vitkov, Czech Rep., January 9, 1994.
(Dallas' 1st choice, 13th overall, in 2012 Entry Draft).

			Regular Season					Playoffs				
Season	Club	League	GP	G	A	Pts	PIM	GP	G	A	Pts	PIM
2007-08	HC Trinec U17	CzR-U17	2	0	1	1	0	1	0	0	0	0
2008-09	HC Trinec U17	CzR-U17	44	16	21	37	32	9	0	2	2	8
2009-10	HC Trinec U18	CzR-U18	36	19	19	38	52	....	....	....	....	....
	HC Trinec Jr.	CzRep-Jr.	3	0	0	0	2	....	....	....	....	....
2010-11	HC Trinec U18	CzR-U18	28	19	30	49	32	2	1	0	1	10
	HC Trinec Jr.	CzRep-Jr.	24	9	6	15	12	2	2	2	4	4
2011-12	Kitchener Rangers	OHL	62	29	37	66	47	13	2	4	6	10
2012-13	Kitchener Rangers	OHL	39	9	22	31	26	10	4	2	6	4
	Texas Stars	AHL	2	0	1	1	0	....	....	....	....	....

OHL All-Rookie Team (2012)

FALLSTROM, Alex (FAHL-struhm, al-EHX) BOS

Right wing. Shoots right. 6'2", 203 lbs. Born, Goteborg, Sweden, September 15, 1990.
(Minnesota's 4th choice, 116th overall, in 2009 Entry Draft).

			Regular Season					Playoffs				
Season	Club	League	GP	G	A	Pts	PIM	GP	G	A	Pts	PIM
2005-06	Djurgarden U18	Swe-U18	11	1	2	3	2	....	....	....	....	....
2006-07	Djurgarden U18	Swe-U18	33	22	15	37	52	3	2	1	3	2
	Djurgarden Jr.	Swe-Jr.	2	0	0	0	0	1	0	0	0	0
2007-08	Shat.-St. Mary's	High-MN	62	20	27	47	56	....	....	....	....	....
2008-09	Shat.-St. Mary's	High-MN	52	40	47	87	52	....	....	....	....	....
2009-10	Harvard Crimson	ECAC	32	4	8	12	23	....	....	....	....	....
2010-11	Harvard Crimson	ECAC	22	7	5	12	17	....	....	....	....	....
2011-12	Harvard Crimson	ECAC	28	13	12	25	10	....	....	....	....	....
2012-13	Harvard Crimson	ECAC	31	9	12	21	22	....	....	....	....	....

Traded to **Boston** by **Minnesota** with Craig Weller and Minnesota's 2nd round choice (Alexander Khokhlachev) in 2011 Entry Draft for Chuck Kobasew, October 18, 2009.

FARNHAM, Bobby (FAHRN-uhm, BAW-bee) PIT

Left wing. Shoots left. 5'10", 180 lbs. Born, North Andover, MA, January 21, 1989.

			Regular Season					Playoffs				
Season	Club	League	GP	G	A	Pts	PIM	GP	G	A	Pts	PIM
2008-09	Brown U.	ECAC	31	4	3	7	24	....	....	....	....	....
2009-10	Brown U.	ECAC	36	3	8	11	14	....	....	....	....	....
2010-11	Brown U.	ECAC	31	8	7	15	39	....	....	....	....	....
2011-12	Brown U.	ECAC	31	8	13	21	51	....	....	....	....	....
	Providence Bruins	AHL	3	0	0	0	4	....	....	....	....	....
	Worcester Sharks	AHL	3	0	0	0	2	....	....	....	....	....
2012-13	Wheeling Nailers	ECHL	9	3	1	4	46	....	....	....	....	....
	Wilkes-Barre	AHL	65	3	8	11	274	6	0	0	0	4

Signed as a free agent by **Pittsburgh**, July 6, 2013.

FASCHING, Hudson (FA-SHIHNG, HUHD-suhn) L.A.

Right wing. Shoots right. 6'2", 213 lbs. Born, Milwaukee, WI, July 28, 1995.
(Los Angeles' 3rd choice, 118th overall, in 2013 Entry Draft).

			Regular Season					Playoffs				
Season	Club	League	GP	G	A	Pts	PIM	GP	G	A	Pts	PIM
2009-10	Apple Valley	High-MN	31	24	18	42	12	....	....	....	....	....
2010-11	Team Southeast	UMHSEL	18	7	8	15	12	3	1	3	4	4
	Apple Valley	High-MN	28	18	32	50	16	....	....	....	....	....
2011-12	USNTDP	USHL	37	7	14	21	38	1	1	1	2	2
	USNTDP	U-17	16	8	5	13	12	....	....	....	....	....
	USNTDP	U-18	1	0	0	0	0	....	....	....	....	....
2012-13	USNTDP	USHL	25	4	7	11	8	....	....	....	....	....
	USNTDP	U-18	40	7	18	25	50	....	....	....	....	....

• Signed Letter of Intent to attend **University of Minnesota** (WCHA) in fall of 2013.

FAST, Jesper (FAHST, YEHS-puhr) NYR

Right wing. Shoots right. 5'11", 165 lbs. Born, Nassjo, Sweden, December 2, 1991.
(NY Rangers' 5th choice, 157th overall, in 2010 Entry Draft).

			Regular Season					Playoffs				
Season	Club	League	GP	G	A	Pts	PIM	GP	G	A	Pts	PIM
2007-08	HV 71 U18	Swe-U18	30	15	11	26	14	....	....	....	....	....
	HV 71 Jr.	Swe-Jr.	3	0	0	0	2	....	....	....	....	....
2008-09	HV 71 U18	Swe-U18	3	2	2	4	2	....	....	....	....	....
	HV 71 Jr.	Swe-Jr.	37	7	7	14	16	7	2	1	3	6
2009-10	HV 71 Jr.	Swe-Jr.	37	23	26	49	10	3	0	2	2	0
	HV 71 Jonkoping	Sweden	2	0	0	0	0	....	....	....	....	....
2010-11	HV 71 Jonkoping	Sweden	36	7	9	16	6	3	0	0	0	0
	HV 71 Jr.	Swe-Jr.	6	3	7	10	4	3	2	2	4	2
2011-12	HV 71 Jonkoping	Sweden	21	5	11	16	4	5	2	1	3	0
2012-13	HV 71 Jonkoping	Sweden	47	18	17	35	4	5	1	4	5	0
	Connecticut Whale	AHL	1	1	0	1	2	....	....	....	....	....

FAUST, Joe (FOWST, JOH) N.J.

Defense. Shoots right. 6', 205 lbs. Born, Edina, MN, November 15, 1991.
(New Jersey's 3rd choice, 114th overall, in 2010 Entry Draft).

			Regular Season					Playoffs				
Season	Club	League	GP	G	A	Pts	PIM	GP	G	A	Pts	PIM
2007-08	Bloomington-Jeff.	High-MN	28	4	14	18	10	....	....	....	....	....
2008-09	Bloomington-Jeff.	High-MN	28	14	26	40	12	....	....	....	....	....
2009-10	Team Southeast	UMHSEL	24	3	6	9		....	....	....	....	....
	Bloomington-Jeff.	High-MN	25	12	28	40	18	3	2	4	6	2
2010-11	U. of Wisconsin	WCHA	20	1	1	2	8	....	....	....	....	....
2011-12	U. of Wisconsin	WCHA	37	2	3	5	16	....	....	....	....	....
2012-13	U. of Wisconsin	WCHA	42	1	0	1	14	....	....	....	....	....

FEDUN, Taylor (fuh-DOON, TAY-luhr) EDM

Defense. Shoots right. 6', 190 lbs. Born, Edmonton, Alta., June 4, 1988.

			Regular Season					Playoffs				
Season	Club	League	GP	G	A	Pts	PIM	GP	G	A	Pts	PIM
2003-04	SSAC Thunder	Minor-AB	36	8	26	34	24	....	....	....	....	....
	SSAC Athletics	AMHL	1	0	0	0	0	....	....	....	....	....
2004-05	SSAC Athletics	AMHL	36	7	13	20	68	....	....	....	....	....
	Ft. Saskatchewan	AJHL	1	0	1	1	0	....	....	....	....	....
2005-06	Ft. Saskatchewan	AJHL	60	13	18	31	72	3	1	1	2	4
2006-07	Spruce Grove	AJHL	50	10	33	43	103	10	3	5	8	31
2007-08	Princeton	ECAC	32	4	10	14	32	....	....	....	....	....
2008-09	Princeton	ECAC	35	3	12	15	50	....	....	....	....	....
2009-10	Princeton	ECAC	31	3	14	17	34	....	....	....	....	....
2010-11	Princeton	ECAC	29	10	12	22	38	....	....	....	....	....
2011-12			DID NOT PLAY – INJURED									
2012-13	Oklahoma City	AHL	70	8	19	27	30	17	3	3	6	6

ECAC Second All-Star Team (2010) • ECAC First All-Star Team (2011) • NCAA East Second All-American Team (2011)

Signed as a free agent by **Edmonton**, March 8, 2011. • Missed 2011-12 due to leg injury in pre-season vs. **Minnesota**, September 30, 2011.

FEJES, Hunter (FAY-jihs, HUHN -tuhr) PHX

Left wing. Shoots left. 6'1", 190 lbs. Born, Anchorage, AK, May 31, 1994.
(Phoenix's 6th choice, 178th overall, in 2012 Entry Draft).

			Regular Season					Playoffs				
Season	Club	League	GP	G	A	Pts	PIM	GP	G	A	Pts	PIM
2010-11	Shat.-St. Mary's	High-MN	49	14	14	28	12	....	....	....	....	....
2011-12	Shat.-St. Mary's	High-MN	55	38	40	78	20	....	....	....	....	....
2012-13	Colorado College	WCHA	41	8	6	14	8	....	....	....	....	....

FERLAND, Michael (FAIR-land, MIGH-kuhl) CGY

Left wing. Shoots left. 6'2", 208 lbs. Born, Swan River, Man., April 20, 1992.
(Calgary's 5th choice, 133rd overall, in 2010 Entry Draft).

			Regular Season					Playoffs				
Season	Club	League	GP	G	A	Pts	PIM	GP	G	A	Pts	PIM
2007-08	Brandon	MMHL	40	12	8	20	20	6	3	2	5	4
2008-09	Brandon	MMHL	44	45	40	85	52	6	4	5	9	8
2009-10	Brandon	WHL	61	9	19	28	85	15	3	1	4	8
2010-11	Brandon	WHL	56	23	33	56	110	6	4	2	6	4
2011-12	Brandon	WHL	68	47	49	96	84	8	3	3	6	6
2012-13	Brandon	WHL	4	1	1	2	4	....	....	....	....	....
	Saskatoon Blades	WHL	26	8	21	29	18	4	0	0	0	2
	Abbotsford Heat	AHL	7	0	0	0	10	....	....	....	....	....
	Utah Grizzlies	ECHL	3	0	1	1	5	....	....	....	....	....

WHL East Second All-Star Team (2012)

FERLIN, Brian (FUHR-lihn, BRIGH-uhn) **BOS**

Right wing. Shoots right. 6'2", 209 lbs. Born, Jacksonville, FL, June 3, 1992.
(Boston's 4th choice, 121st overall, in 2011 Entry Draft).

			Regular Season					Playoffs				
Season	Club	League	GP	G	A	Pts	PIM	GP	G	A	Pts	PIM
2009-10	Indiana Ice	USHL	57	6	10	16	36	8	1	2	3	2
2010-11	Indiana Ice	USHL	55	25	48	73	26	5	1	4	5	4
2011-12	Cornell Big Red	ECAC	26	8	13	21	30	....	....	....	....	....
2012-13	Cornell Big Red	ECAC	34	10	14	24	55	....	....	....	....	....

ECAC All-Rookie Team (2012) • ECAC Rookie of the Year (2012)

FERNHOLM, Simon (FUHRN-hohlm, see-MOHN) **NSH**

Defense. Shoots left. 6'6", 197 lbs. Born, Stockholm, Sweden, March 6, 1994.
(Nashville's 7th choice, 164th overall, in 2012 Entry Draft).

			Regular Season					Playoffs				
Season	Club	League	GP	G	A	Pts	PIM	GP	G	A	Pts	PIM
2010-11	Huddinge IK U18	Swe-U18	35	0	10	10	16	....	....	....	....	....
	Huddinge IK Jr.	Swe-Jr.	2	0	0	0	0	....	....	....	....	....
2011-12	Huddinge IK U18	Swe-U18	5	0	1	1	0	2	0	1	1	0
	Huddinge IK Jr.	Swe-Jr.	47	3	12	15	12	....	....	....	....	....
2012-13	Frolunda	Sweden	5	0	1	1	0	....	....	....	....	....
	Frolunda Jr.	Swe-Jr.	41	0	10	10	10	4	0	1	1	2

FERRARO, Landon (fuh-RAHR-oh, LAN-duhn) **DET**

Center. Shoots right. 6', 174 lbs. Born, Trail, B.C., August 8, 1991.
(Detroit's 1st choice, 32nd overall, in 2009 Entry Draft).

			Regular Season					Playoffs				
Season	Club	League	GP	G	A	Pts	PIM	GP	G	A	Pts	PIM
2006-07	Van. NW Giants	BCMML	25	21	13	34	77	....	....	....	....	....
	Red Deer Rebels	WHL	4	0	0	0	0	1	0	0	0	0
2007-08	Red Deer Rebels	WHL	54	13	11	24	65	....	....	....	....	....
2008-09	Red Deer Rebels	WHL	68	37	18	55	99	....	....	....	....	....
2009-10	Red Deer Rebels	WHL	53	16	30	46	55	3	0	0	0	2
	Grand Rapids	AHL	2	0	0	0	0	....	....	....	....	....
2010-11	Everett Silvertips	WHL	41	10	17	27	51	4	0	3	3	13
2011-12	Grand Rapids	AHL	56	9	11	20	47	....	....	....	....	....
2012-13	Grand Rapids	AHL	72	24	23	47	44	24	5	11	16	11

FERRIERO, Cody (fair-ee-AIR-oh, KOH-dee) **S.J.**

Center. Shoots right. 5'11", 195 lbs. Born, Boston, MA, December 19, 1991.
(San Jose's 3rd choice, 127th overall, in 2010 Entry Draft).

			Regular Season					Playoffs				
Season	Club	League	GP	G	A	Pts	PIM	GP	G	A	Pts	PIM
2006-07	Gov. Academy	High-MA	27	6	3	9	26	....	....	....	....	....
2007-08	Gov. Academy	High-MA	25	13	9	22	26	....	....	....	....	....
2008-09	Gov. Academy	High-MA	27	10	10	20	87	....	....	....	....	....
2009-10	Gov. Academy	High-MA	27	21	19	40	112	....	....	....	....	....
2010-11	Northeastern	H-East	34	4	3	7	38	....	....	....	....	....
2011-12	Northeastern	H-East	17	9	6	15	34	....	....	....	....	....
2012-13	Northeastern	H-East	34	12	14	26	60	....	....	....	....	....

FIENHAGE, Corey (fihn-AH-gee, KOH-ree) **BUF**

Defense. Shoots right. 6'2", 215 lbs. Born, Topeka, KS, May 4, 1990.
(Buffalo's 4th choice, 81st overall, in 2008 Entry Draft).

			Regular Season					Playoffs				
Season	Club	League	GP	G	A	Pts	PIM	GP	G	A	Pts	PIM
2005-06	Eastview High	High-MN	25	1	6	7	32	....	....	....	....	....
2006-07	Eastview High	High-MN	20	4	11	15	....	....	....	....	....	....
	Team Southeast	UMWEHL	11	4	4	8	....	....	....	....	....	....
2007-08	Eastview High	High-MN	26	6	10	16	87	....	....	....	....	....
	Team Southeast	UMWEHL	12	2	4	6	....	....	....	....	....	....
	Indiana Ice	USHL	12	1	2	3	12	2	0	0	0	0
2008-09	North Dakota	WCHA	9	0	1	1	28	....	....	....	....	....
2009-10	North Dakota	WCHA	30	0	2	2	28	....	....	....	....	....
2010-11	Kamloops Blazers	WHL	70	4	10	14	96	....	....	....	....	....
	Portland Pirates	AHL	4	0	0	0	6	6	0	0	0	4
2011-12	Rochester	AHL	20	0	4	4	20	....	....	....	....	....
	Gwinnett	ECHL	32	5	8	13	28	....	....	....	....	....
2012-13	Gwinnett	ECHL	65	2	13	15	44	10	0	0	0	6
	Rochester	AHL	3	0	0	0	0	....	....	....	....	....

FINN, Matt (FIHN, MAT) **TOR**

Defense. Shoots left. 6', 207 lbs. Born, Toronto, Ont., February 24, 1994.
(Toronto's 2nd choice, 35th overall, in 2012 Entry Draft).

			Regular Season					Playoffs				
Season	Club	League	GP	G	A	Pts	PIM	GP	G	A	Pts	PIM
2009-10	Toronto Marlboros	GTHL	79	22	35	57	94	....	....	....	....	....
2010-11	Guelph Storm	OHL	60	3	18	21	23	5	0	3	3	0
2011-12	Guelph Storm	OHL	61	10	38	48	58	6	0	2	2	10
2012-13	Guelph Storm	OHL	41	11	20	31	24	....	....	....	....	....

FITZGERALD, Ryan (fihtz-JAIR-uhld, RIGH-uhn) **BOS**

Center. Shoots right. 5'10", 170 lbs. Born, Boca Raton, FL, October 19, 1994.
(Boston's 3rd choice, 120th overall, in 2013 Entry Draft).

			Regular Season					Playoffs				
Season	Club	League	GP	G	A	Pts	PIM	GP	G	A	Pts	PIM
2009-10	Malden Catholic	High-MA	24	17	30	47	....	....	....	....	....	....
2010-11	Malden Catholic	High-MA	24	28	44	72	....	....	....	....	....	....
2011-12	Malden Catholic	High-MA	19	31	20	51	....	....	....	....	....	....
2012-13	Valley Junior	EJHL	26	14	16	30	50	6	3	3	6	8
	USNTDP	U-18	5	1	0	1	8	....	....	....	....	....

• Signed Letter of Intent to attend **Boston College** (Hockey East) in fall of 2013.

FLANAGAN, Kyle (FLAN-uh-guhn, KIGHL) **PHI**

Center. Shoots left. 5'9", 179 lbs. Born, Canton, NY, December 30, 1988.

			Regular Season					Playoffs				
Season	Club	League	GP	G	A	Pts	PIM	GP	G	A	Pts	PIM
2006-07	Cornwall Colts	ON-Jr.A	44	18	24	42	70	....	....	....	....	....
2007-08	Cedar Rapids	USHL	57	12	24	36	40	3	0	0	0	0
2008-09	Cedar Rapids	USHL	60	17	40	57	24	5	6	1	7	8
2009-10	St. Lawrence	ECAC	32	5	23	28	26	....	....	....	....	....
2010-11	St. Lawrence	ECAC	39	12	23	35	38	....	....	....	....	....
2011-12	St. Lawrence	ECAC	28	14	23	37	22	....	....	....	....	....
2012-13	St. Lawrence	ECAC	35	15	32	47	42	....	....	....	....	....
	Adirondack	AHL	13	1	6	7	4	....	....	....	....	....

Signed as a free agent by **Philadelphia**, March 21, 2013.

FLEMMING, Brett (FLEH-mihng, BREHT) **WSH**

Defense. Shoots right. 5'11", 184 lbs. Born, Regina, Sask., February 26, 1991.
(Washington's 5th choice, 145th overall, in 2009 Entry Draft).

			Regular Season					Playoffs				
Season	Club	League	GP	G	A	Pts	PIM	GP	G	A	Pts	PIM
2006-07	Burlington Eagles	Minor-ON	67	15	36	51	130	....	....	....	....	....
2007-08	St. Michael's	OHL	47	1	9	10	30	4	0	0	0	6
2008-09	St. Michael's	OHL	64	3	25	28	89	10	1	3	4	2
2009-10	St. Michael's	OHL	68	1	23	24	90	16	0	5	5	10
2010-11	St. Michael's	OHL	68	4	39	43	79	20	1	12	13	28
2011-12	South Carolina	ECHL	41	3	10	13	55	9	2	3	5	8
	Hershey Bears	AHL	21	2	2	4	31	....	....	....	....	....
2012-13	Hershey Bears	AHL	11	0	1	1	2	....	....	....	....	....
	Reading Royals	ECHL	50	2	13	15	77	22	5	7	12	28

FLICK, Rob (FLIHK, RAWB) **BOS**

Center. Shoots left. 6'2", 208 lbs. Born, London, Ont., March 28, 1991.
(Chicago's 7th choice, 120th overall, in 2010 Entry Draft).

			Regular Season					Playoffs				
Season	Club	League	GP	G	A	Pts	PIM	GP	G	A	Pts	PIM
2007-08	Lon. Jr. Knights	Minor-ON	57	32	29	61	160	....	....	....	....	....
	London Nationals	ON-Jr.B	8	0	1	1	25	....	....	....	....	....
2008-09	St. Michael's	OHL	48	4	4	8	69	10	1	1	2	14
2009-10	St. Michael's	OHL	65	15	19	34	157	16	2	2	4	*44
2010-11	St. Michael's	OHL	68	27	30	57	167	20	8	8	16	34
2011-12	Rockford IceHogs	AHL	45	7	6	13	91	....	....	....	....	....
	Toledo Walleye	ECHL	17	4	6	10	43	....	....	....	....	....
2012-13	Rockford IceHogs	AHL	51	3	2	5	97	....	....	....	....	....
	Providence Bruins	AHL	5	0	0	0	7	....	....	....	....	....

Traded to **Boston** by **Chicago** for Max Sauve, April 3, 2013.

FLOREK, Justin (FLOHR-ehk, JUHS-tihn) **BOS**

Left wing. Shoots left. 6'4", 204 lbs. Born, Marquette, MI, May 18, 1990.
(Boston's 5th choice, 135th overall, in 2010 Entry Draft).

			Regular Season					Playoffs				
Season	Club	League	GP	G	A	Pts	PIM	GP	G	A	Pts	PIM
2006-07	USNTDP	NAHL	47	11	10	21	40	6	3	0	3	4
	USNTDP	U-17	13	6	1	7	8	....	....	....	....	....
2007-08	USNTDP	NAHL	13	3	3	6	8	....	....	....	....	....
	USNTDP	U-17	1	0	0	0	2	....	....	....	....	....
	USNTDP	U-18	41	5	5	10	20	....	....	....	....	....
2008-09	Northern Mich.	CCHA	40	9	8	17	6	....	....	....	....	....
2009-10	Northern Mich.	CCHA	41	12	23	35	22	....	....	....	....	....
2010-11	Northern Mich.	CCHA	39	13	15	28	14	....	....	....	....	....
2011-12	Northern Mich.	CCHA	37	19	17	36	18	....	....	....	....	....
	Providence Bruins	AHL	8	2	2	4	2	....	....	....	....	....
2012-13	Providence Bruins	AHL	71	11	16	27	37	12	1	2	3	4

CCHA Second All-Star Team (2012)

FLORENTINO, Anthony (flohr-ehn-TEE-noh, AN-thuh-nee) **BUF**

Defense. Shoots right. 6'1", 226 lbs. Born, Boston, MA, January 30, 1995.
(Buffalo's 9th choice, 143rd overall, in 2013 Entry Draft).

			Regular Season					Playoffs				
Season	Club	League	GP	G	A	Pts	PIM	GP	G	A	Pts	PIM
2010-11	South Shore Kings	EmJHL	7	0	1	1	26	....	....	....	....	....
	South Kent School	High-CT	24	5	10	15	....	....	....	....	....	....
2011-12	South Kent School	High-CT	36	5	14	19	....	....	....	....	....	....
	USNTDP	U-17	3	0	2	2	4	....	....	....	....	....
2012-13	South Kent	High-CT	62	21	32	53	68	....	....	....	....	....

• Signed Letter of Intent to attend **Providence College** (Hockey East) in fall of 2013.

FOGARTY, Steven (FOH-guhr-tee, STEE-vehn) **NYR**

Center. Shoots right. 6'2", 194 lbs. Born, Chambersburg, PA, April 19, 1993.
(NY Rangers' 2nd choice, 72nd overall, in 2011 Entry Draft).

			Regular Season					Playoffs				
Season	Club	League	GP	G	A	Pts	PIM	GP	G	A	Pts	PIM
2009-10	Edina Hornets	High-MN	25	18	12	30	4	6	3	7	10	2
2010-11	Team Southwest	UMHSEL	19	10	4	14	10	3	2	5	7	4
	Edina Hornets	High-MN	24	23	17	40	12	6	2	7	9	10
	Chicago Steel	USHL	6	2	0	2	2	....	....	....	....	....
2011-12	Penticton Vees	BCHL	60	33	48	81	32	15	4	4	8	12
2012-13	U. of Notre Dame	CCHA	41	5	5	10	4	....	....	....	....	....

FONTAINE, Justin (fawn-TAYN, JUHS-tihn) **MIN**

Right wing. Shoots right. 5'10", 175 lbs. Born, Bonnyville, Alta., November 6, 1987.

			Regular Season					Playoffs				
Season	Club	League	GP	G	A	Pts	PIM	GP	G	A	Pts	PIM
2004-05	N.E. Panthers	Minor-AB	STATISTICS NOT AVAILABLE									
	Bonnyville Pontiacs	AJHL	12	1	4	5	12	....	....	....	....	....
2005-06	Bonnyville Pontiacs	AJHL	50	26	55	81	36	9	1	6	7	4
2006-07	Bonnyville Pontiacs	AJHL	52	30	41	71	60	5	3	5	8	10
2007-08	U. Minn-Duluth	WCHA	35	4	8	12	8	....	....	....	....	....
2008-09	U. Minn-Duluth	WCHA	43	15	33	48	18	....	....	....	....	....
2009-10	U. Minn-Duluth	WCHA	39	21	25	46	22	....	....	....	....	....
2010-11	U. Minn-Duluth	WCHA	42	22	36	58	42	....	....	....	....	....
2011-12	Houston Aeros	AHL	73	16	39	55	32	4	0	0	0	0
2012-13	Houston Aeros	AHL	64	23	33	56	18	5	3	5	8	4

WCHA Second All-Star Team (2009, 2010, 2011)

Signed as a free agent by **Minnesota**, April 19, 2011.

FORBORT, Derek (FOHR-bohrt, DAIR-ihk) **L.A.**

Defense. Shoots left. 6'5", 207 lbs. Born, Duluth, MN, March 4, 1992.
(Los Angeles' 1st choice, 15th overall, in 2010 Entry Draft).

			Regular Season					Playoffs				
Season	Club	League	GP	G	A	Pts	PIM	GP	G	A	Pts	PIM
2008-09	Duluth East	High-MN	25	7	21	28	....	....	....	....	....	....
	USNTDP	NAHL	2	0	1	1	6	....	....	....	....	....
	USNTDP	U-17	7	1	4	5	4	....	....	....	....	....
2009-10	USNTDP	USHL	26	4	10	14	26	....	....	....	....	....
	USNTDP	U-18	39	1	13	14	20	....	....	....	....	....
2010-11	North Dakota	WCHA	38	0	15	15	26	....	....	....	....	....
2011-12	North Dakota	WCHA	35	2	11	13	28	....	....	....	....	....
2012-13	North Dakota	WCHA	42	4	13	17	22	....	....	....	....	....
	Manchester	AHL	6	0	1	1	0	4	0	0	0	4

FORD, Scott (FOHRD, SKAWT)

Defense. Shoots right. 6'3", 225 lbs. Born, Charlie Lake, B.C., December 24, 1979.

Season	Club	League	GP	G	A	Pts	PIM	GP	G	A	Pts	PIM
			Regular Season					Playoffs				
99-2000	Merritt	BCHL	42	1	14	15	90	....	....	....	....	....
2000-01	Brown U.	ECAC	23	2	6	8	18	....	....	....	....	....
2001-02	Brown U.	ECAC	31	1	6	7	38	....	....	....	....	....
2002-03	Brown U.	ECAC	33	6	11	17	44	....	....	....	....	....
2003-04	Brown U.	ECAC	31	6	9	15	30	....	....	....	....	....
2004-05	Cleveland Barons	AHL	1	0	0	0	2	....	....	....	....	....
	Fresno Falcons	ECHL	17	0	2	2	10	....	....	....	....	....
2005-06	Bridgeport	AHL	2	0	0	0	2	....	....	....	....	....
	Providence Bruins	AHL	44	1	6	7	72	....	....	....	....	....
	Trenton Titans	ECHL	22	1	4	5	35	....	....	....	....	....
2006-07	Dayton Bombers	ECHL	70	10	16	26	113	22	0	7	7	16
2007-08	Bridgeport	AHL	54	1	6	7	55	....	....	....	....	....
	Utah Grizzlies	ECHL	23	1	11	12	53	....	....	....	....	....
2008-09	Milwaukee	AHL	63	4	6	10	128	11	0	1	1	2
2009-10	Milwaukee	AHL	61	1	7	8	84	5	0	0	0	2
2010-11	Milwaukee	AHL	80	2	5	7	164	13	0	2	2	10
2011-12	Milwaukee	AHL	75	4	7	11	89	3	0	0	0	20
2012-13	Peoria Rivermen	AHL	43	2	4	6	54	....	....	....	....	....
	Milwaukee	AHL	21	0	1	1	15	4	0	0	0	6

Signed as a free agent by **San Jose**, June 27, 2004. • Missed majority of 2004-05 due to knee injury in training camp, September, 2004. Signed as a free agent by **Bridgeport** (AHL), December 21, 2005. Signed as a free agent by **Providence** (AHL), January 3, 2006. Signed as a free agent by **Milwaukee** (AHL), October 1, 2008. Signed as a free agent by **St. Louis**, July 1, 2012. Traded to **Nashville** by **St. Louis** for Jani Lajunen, February 19, 2013.

FOURNIER, Dillon (FOHR-n'yay, DIHL-uhn) CHI

Defense. Shoots left. 6'2", 173 lbs. Born, Montreal, Que., June 15, 1994.
(Chicago's 2nd choice, 48th overall, in 2012 Entry Draft).

Season	Club	League	GP	G	A	Pts	PIM	GP	G	A	Pts	PIM
			Regular Season					Playoffs				
2009-10	Lac St-Louis Lions	QAAA	39	0	12	12	24	21	0	3	3	40
2010-11	Lewiston	QMJHL	60	3	11	14	38	11	0	2	2	15
2011-12	Rouyn-Noranda	QMJHL	52	9	29	38	59	....	....	....	....	....
2012-13	Rouyn-Noranda	QMJHL	59	6	18	24	61	14	4	8	12	14

FOURNIER, Gleason (FOHR-n'yay, GLEE-suhn) DET

Defense. Shoots left. 6', 191 lbs. Born, Rimouski, Que., September 8, 1991.
(Detroit's 4th choice, 90th overall, in 2009 Entry Draft).

Season	Club	League	GP	G	A	Pts	PIM	GP	G	A	Pts	PIM
			Regular Season					Playoffs				
2006-07	Ecole Notre Dame	QAAA	44	3	17	20	32	13	0	2	2	30
2007-08	Rimouski Oceanic	QMJHL	56	3	8	11	26	3	0	0	0	0
2008-09	Rimouski Oceanic	QMJHL	66	3	25	28	64	4	0	0	0	0
2009-10	Rimouski Oceanic	QMJHL	58	13	37	50	76	12	2	10	12	10
2010-11	Rimouski Oceanic	QMJHL	57	12	32	44	58	4	1	1	2	12
2011-12	Grand Rapids	AHL	13	1	3	4	14	....	....	....	....	....
	Toledo Walleye	ECHL	55	2	16	18	32	....	....	....	....	....
2012-13	Grand Rapids	AHL	30	1	5	6	23	6	0	1	1	2
	Toledo Walleye	ECHL	15	1	0	1	12	....	....	....	....	....

FOURNIER, Stefan (FOHR-n'yay, STEH-fan) MTL

Right wing. Shoots right. 6'3", 212 lbs. Born, Dorval, Que., April 30, 1992.

Season	Club	League	GP	G	A	Pts	PIM	GP	G	A	Pts	PIM
			Regular Season					Playoffs				
2008-09	Acadie-Bathurst	QMJHL	40	2	1	3	18	....	....	....	....	....
2009-10	Lewiston	QMJHL	52	12	13	25	54	4	1	2	3	2
2010-11	Lewiston	QMJHL	67	20	27	47	69	15	4	6	10	22
2011-12	Victoriaville Tigres	QMJHL	64	32	33	65	96	4	1	1	2	2
2012-13	Halifax	QMJHL	66	35	37	72	100	17	*16	13	29	31

Signed as a free agent by **Montreal**, July 6, 2013.

FRIBERG, Max (FREE-buhrg, MAX) ANA

Left wing. Shoots right. 5'11", 203 lbs. Born, Skovde, Sweden, November 20, 1992.
(Anaheim's 6th choice, 143rd overall, in 2011 Entry Draft).

Season	Club	League	GP	G	A	Pts	PIM	GP	G	A	Pts	PIM
			Regular Season					Playoffs				
2007-08	Skovde IK U18	Swe-U18	24	6	3	9	44	....	....	....	....	....
	Skovde IK Jr.	Swe-Jr.	12	1	2	3	0	....	....	....	....	....
2008-09	Skovde IK U18	Swe-U18	10	14	18	32	4	....	....	....	....	....
	Skovde IK Jr.	Swe-Jr.	17	13	7	20	18	....	....	....	....	....
	Skovde IK	Sweden-3	24	1	3	4	2	....	....	....	....	....
2009-10	Skovde IK U18	Swe-U18	5	5	6	11	2	....	....	....	....	....
	Skovde IK Jr.	Swe-Jr.	1	0	3	3	0	....	....	....	....	....
	Skovde IK	Sweden-3	36	12	18	30	22	....	....	....	....	....
2010-11	Skovde IK Jr.	Swe-Jr.	2	1	3	4	2	....	....	....	....	....
	Skovde IK	Sweden-3	34	13	27	40	6	....	....	....	....	....
2011-12	Timra IK Jr.	Swe-Jr.	2	2	2	4	0	....	....	....	....	....
	Sundsvall	Sweden-2	1	0	0	0	0	....	....	....	....	....
	Timra IK	Sweden	48	5	5	10	8	....	....	....	....	....
	Timra IK	Sweden-Q	10	3	4	7	4	....	....	....	....	....
2012-13	Timra IK	Sweden	55	8	8	16	12	....	....	....	....	....
	Timra IK	Sweden-Q	10	4	2	6	0	....	....	....	....	....
	Norfolk Admirals	AHL	6	1	0	1	0	....	....	....	....	....

FRIESEN, Alex (FREE-zuhn, ALehx) VAN

Center. Shoots left. 5'10", 186 lbs. Born, Niagara-on-the-Lake, Ont., January 30, 1991.
(Vancouver's 3rd choice, 172nd overall, in 2010 Entry Draft).

Season	Club	League	GP	G	A	Pts	PIM	GP	G	A	Pts	PIM
			Regular Season					Playoffs				
2006-07	Niag. Falls Thunder	Minor-ON	69	45	67	112	66	....	....	....	....	....
2007-08	Niagara Ice Dogs	OHL	46	5	9	14	26	10	0	2	2	6
2008-09	Niagara Ice Dogs	OHL	64	11	22	33	94	12	3	7	10	25
2009-10	Niagara Ice Dogs	OHL	60	23	37	60	94	5	1	6	7	8
2010-11	Niagara Ice Dogs	OHL	60	26	40	66	61	14	2	8	10	19
2011-12	Niagara Ice Dogs	OHL	62	26	45	71	106	20	8	14	22	18
2012-13	Chicago Wolves	AHL	42	1	4	5	22	....	....	....	....	....
	Kalamazoo Wings	ECHL	10	0	4	4	2	....	....	....	....	....

FRITSCH, Andrew (FRIHTCH, AN-droo)

Right wing. Shoots right. 6', 180 lbs. Born, Brantford, Ont., March 24, 1993.
(Phoenix's 7th choice, 155th overall, in 2011 Entry Draft).

Season	Club	League	GP	G	A	Pts	PIM	GP	G	A	Pts	PIM
			Regular Season					Playoffs				
2008-09	Brantford 99s	Minor-ON	59	33	38	71	12	....	....	....	....	....
2009-10	Niagara Ice Dogs	OHL	62	11	7	18	13	5	1	0	1	0
2010-11	Niagara Ice Dogs	OHL	2	1	0	1	0	....	....	....	....	....
	Owen Sound	OHL	58	27	35	62	18	7	0	2	2	2
2011-12	Sault Ste. Marie	OHL	35	13	19	32	8	....	....	....	....	....
2012-13	Sault Ste. Marie	OHL	55	27	25	52	10	6	0	2	2	8

FRK, Martin (FRIHK, MAHR-tihn) DET

Right wing. Shoots right. 6', 193 lbs. Born, Pelhrimov, Czech Rep., October 5, 1993.
(Detroit's 1st choice, 49th overall, in 2012 Entry Draft).

Season	Club	League	GP	G	A	Pts	PIM	GP	G	A	Pts	PIM
			Regular Season					Playoffs				
2006-07	Karlovy Vary U17	CzR-U17	5	0	1	1	0	....	....	....	....	....
2007-08	Karlovy Vary U17	CzR-U17	44	25	17	42	56	2	1	0	1	4
2008-09	Karlovy Vary U17	CzR-U17	22	26	12	38	85	....	....	....	....	....
	Karlovy Vary Jr.	CzRep-Jr.	16	8	12	20	6	....	....	....	....	....
2009-10	Karlovy Vary U18	CzR-U18	8	9	4	13	41	....	....	....	....	....
	Karlovy Vary Jr.	CzRep-Jr.	41	28	30	58	186	6	2	3	5	4
2010-11	Halifax	QMJHL	62	22	28	50	75	4	0	2	2	8
2011-12	Halifax	QMJHL	34	16	13	29	41	17	5	6	11	26
2012-13	Halifax	QMJHL	56	35	49	84	84	17	13	20	33	32

Memorial Cup All-Star Team (2013)

FROESE, Byron (FRAYZ, BIGH-ruhn) CHI

Center. Shoots right. 6', 190 lbs. Born, Winkler, Man., March 12, 1991.
(Chicago's 4th choice, 119th overall, in 2009 Entry Draft).

Season	Club	League	GP	G	A	Pts	PIM	GP	G	A	Pts	PIM
			Regular Season					Playoffs				
2007-08	Pembina Valley	MMHL	23	14	20	34	8	11	7	7	14	8
2008-09	Everett Silvertips	WHL	72	19	38	57	30	5	0	3	3	4
2009-10	Everett Silvertips	WHL	70	29	32	61	37	7	3	2	5	0
2010-11	Red Deer Rebels	WHL	70	43	38	81	37	9	5	2	7	4
2011-12	Rockford IceHogs	AHL	57	4	6	10	17	....	....	....	....	....
	Toledo Walleye	ECHL	3	1	1	2	2	....	....	....	....	....
2012-13	Rockford IceHogs	AHL	9	0	2	2	4	....	....	....	....	....
	Toledo Walleye	ECHL	38	12	21	33	12	6	2	4	6	6

GABRIEL, Kurtis (GAY-bree-uhl, KUHR-tihs) MIN

Right wing. Shoots right. 6'5", 214 lbs. Born, Newmarket, Ont., April 20, 1993.
(Minnesota's 2nd choice, 81st overall, in 2013 Entry Draft).

Season	Club	League	GP	G	A	Pts	PIM	GP	G	A	Pts	PIM
			Regular Season					Playoffs				
2009-10	Markham Waxers	Minor-ON	50	16	23	39	....	....	....	....	....	....
2010-11	Owen Sound	OHL	40	1	3	4	20	....	....	....	....	....
2011-12	Owen Sound	OHL	65	4	13	17	72	3	0	0	0	0
2012-13	Owen Sound	OHL	67	13	15	28	100	12	3	2	5	34

GABRIEL, Oliver (gah-BREE-ehl, AWL-ih-vuhr) CBJ

Left wing. Shoots left. 6'2", 206 lbs. Born, Edmonton, Alta., May 13, 1991.

Season	Club	League	GP	G	A	Pts	PIM	GP	G	A	Pts	PIM
			Regular Season					Playoffs				
2006-07	CAC United Cycle	Minor-AB	31	11	17	28	71	....	....	....	....	....
2007-08	CAC B & P	Minor-AB	STATISTICS NOT AVAILABLE									
	Gregg Distributors	AMHL	1	1	0	1	0	....	....	....	....	....
2008-09	Portland	WHL	50	6	5	11	32	....	....	....	....	....
2009-10	Portland	WHL	41	10	14	24	28	13	2	4	6	9
2010-11	Portland	WHL	41	11	21	32	36	....	....	....	....	....
2011-12	Portland	WHL	39	20	22	42	32	17	6	3	9	12
	Springfield Falcons	AHL	11	1	0	1	0	....	....	....	....	....
2012-13	Evansville IceMen	ECHL	20	5	5	10	0	....	....	....	....	....

Signed as a free agent by **Columbus**, October 7, 2010.

GAEDE, Max (GAYD, MAX) S.J.

Right wing. Shoots right. 6'2", 205 lbs. Born, Maryland, MN, March 27, 1992.
(San Jose's 2nd choice, 88th overall, in 2010 Entry Draft).

Season	Club	League	GP	G	A	Pts	PIM	GP	G	A	Pts	PIM
			Regular Season					Playoffs				
2007-08	Woodbury	High-MN	26	5	11	16	2	....	....	....	....	....
2008-09	Woodbury	High-MN	27	16	28	44	66	....	....	....	....	....
2009-10	Team Southeast	UMHSEL	23	5	6	11	....	....	....	....	....	....
	Woodbury	High-MN	25	19	17	36	36	3	3	0	3	0
2010-11	Sioux City	USHL	54	10	18	28	57	3	0	0	0	2
2011-12	Minnesota State	WCHA	30	3	4	7	42	....	....	....	....	....
2012-13	Minnesota State	WCHA	41	1	10	11	11	....	....	....	....	....

GAGNE, Kevin (gahn-YAY, KEH-vihn) ANA

Defense. Shoots left. 5'8", 176 lbs. Born, Edmundston, N.B., April 14, 1992.

Season	Club	League	GP	G	A	Pts	PIM	GP	G	A	Pts	PIM
			Regular Season					Playoffs				
2008-09	Saint John	QMJHL	48	3	3	6	20	4	0	0	0	0
2009-10	Saint John	QMJHL	63	4	25	29	40	5	0	1	1	2
2010-11	Saint John	QMJHL	59	6	26	32	34	19	2	5	7	4
2011-12	Saint John	QMJHL	68	9	26	35	10	17	2	13	15	2
2012-13	Saint John	QMJHL	31	11	23	34	14	....	....	....	....	....
	Rimouski Oceanic	QMJHL	31	6	31	37	22	6	1	1	2	0
	Norfolk Admirals	AHL	5	0	1	1	0	....	....	....	....	....

QMJHL First All-Star Team (2013) • QMJHL Defenseman of the Year (2013)

Signed as a free agent by **Anaheim**, March 6, 2013.

GALIEV, Stanislav (gah-LEE-ehv, stan-ihs-LAHV) WSH

Right wing. Shoots right. 6'1", 188 lbs. Born, Moscow, Russia, January 17, 1992.
(Washington's 2nd choice, 86th overall, in 2010 Entry Draft).

Season	Club	League	GP	G	A	Pts	PIM	GP	G	A	Pts	PIM
			Regular Season					Playoffs				
2008-09	Indiana Ice	USHL	60	29	35	64	46	13	5	4	9	8
2009-10	Saint John	QMJHL	67	15	45	60	38	21	8	11	19	14
2010-11	Saint John	QMJHL	64	37	28	65	40	19	10	17	27	12
2011-12	Saint John	QMJHL	20	13	6	19	16	17	16	18	34	6
2012-13	Hershey Bears	AHL	17	0	1	1	8	....	....	....	....	....
	Reading Royals	ECHL	46	23	24	47	32	10	4	7	11	0

QMJHL All-Rookie Team (2010)

GALIMOV, Emil (ga-LEE-mawv, eh-MIHL) **S.J.**

Left wing. Shoots left. 6'1", 170 lbs. Born, Nizhnekamsk, Russia, May 9, 1992.
(San Jose's 7th choice, 207th overall, in 2013 Entry Draft).

			Regular Season					Playoffs				
Season	Club	League	GP	G	A	Pts	PIM	GP	G	A	Pts	PIM
2009-10	Nizhnekamsk Jr.	Russia-Jr.	32	6	4	10	69	1	0	1	1	0
2010-11	Nizhnekamsk Jr.	Russia-Jr.	27	11	7	18	34	5	3	0	3	27
	Nizhnekamsk	KHL	18	1	1	2	4	....	....	....	....	....
2011-12	Nizhnekamsk Jr.	Russia-Jr.	9	5	4	9	33	....	....	....	....	....
	Nizhnekamsk	KHL	8	0	0	0	2	....	....	....	....	....
	Loko Yaroslavl Jr.	Russia-Jr.	8	4	5	9	2	....	....	....	....	....
	Yaroslavl	Russia-2	17	9	4	13	12	10	2	3	5	10
2012-13	Loko Yaroslavl Jr.	Russia-Jr.	2	1	1	2	2	....	....	....	....	....
	Yaroslavl-VHL	Russia-2	5	4	1	5	4	....	....	....	....	....
	Yaroslavl	KHL	33	7	13	20	10	6	0	2	2	6

GALLACHER, Ben (gal-lah-CHUR, BEHN) **FLA**

Defense. Shoots left. 5'11", 185 lbs. Born, Calgary, Alta., September 11, 1992.
(Florida's 9th choice, 93rd overall, in 2010 Entry Draft).

			Regular Season					Playoffs				
Season	Club	League	GP	G	A	Pts	PIM	GP	G	A	Pts	PIM
2008-09	Camrose Kodiaks	AJHL	43	4	6	10	58	9	0	1	1	4
2009-10	Camrose Kodiaks	AJHL	34	3	19	22	61	11	1	1	2	43
2010-11	Camrose Kodiaks	AJHL	37	5	22	27	119	18	3	5	8	52
2011-12	Ohio State	CCHA	24	1	11	12	30	....	....	....	....	....
2012-13	Green Bay	USHL	42	4	15	19	72	3	0	0	0	0

• Signed Letter of Intent to attend **University of Massachusetts** (Hockey East) in fall of 2013.

GALLANT, Brett (guh-LANT, BREHT) **NYI**

Left wing. Shoots left. 6', 190 lbs. Born, Summerside, PEI, December 28, 1988.

			Regular Season					Playoffs				
Season	Club	League	GP	G	A	Pts	PIM	GP	G	A	Pts	PIM
2005-06	Saint John	QMJHL	26	0	1	1	72	....	....	....	....	....
	Summerside	MJrHL	9	0	2	2	148	....	....	....	....	....
2006-07	Saint John	QMJHL	48	5	1	6	192	....	....	....	....	....
2007-08	Saint John	QMJHL	57	3	2	5	175	11	1	0	1	15
2008-09	Summerside	MJrHL	50	24	49	73	235	....	....	....	....	....
2009-10	Elmira Jackals	ECHL	38	1	1	2	185	....	....	....	....	....
	Syracuse Crunch	AHL	1	0	0	0	5	....	....	....	....	....
2010-11	Elmira Jackals	ECHL	13	0	0	0	80	....	....	....	....	....
	Reading Royals	ECHL	12	1	2	3	52	....	....	....	....	....
	Bridgeport	AHL	17	1	0	1	73	....	....	....	....	....
2011-12	Bridgeport	AHL	25	2	1	3	80	....	....	....	....	....
2012-13	Bridgeport	AHL	42	0	0	0	202	....	....	....	....	....

• Missed majority of 2011-12 due to shoulder injury. Signed as a free agent by **NY Islanders**, February 5, 2013.

GANLY, Tyler (GAN-lee, TIGH-luhr) **CAR**

Defense. Shoots right. 6'1", 201 lbs. Born, Mississauga, Ont., March 22, 1995.
(Carolina's 4th choice, 156th overall, in 2013 Entry Draft).

			Regular Season					Playoffs				
Season	Club	League	GP	G	A	Pts	PIM	GP	G	A	Pts	PIM
2010-11	Tor. Jr. Canadiens	GTHL	84	14	30	44	44	....	....	....	....	....
	Tor. Canadiens	ON-Jr.A	2	0	1	1	0	....	....	....	....	....
2011-12	Tor. Jr. Canadiens	GTHL	39	9	15	24	60	10	2	4	6	4
	Tor. Jr. Canadiens	Exhib.	24	3	10	13	18	....	....	....	....	....
	Brampton Capitals	ON-Jr.A	7	0	1	1	0	....	....	....	....	....
2012-13	Sault Ste. Marie	OHL	62	0	17	17	64	6	0	0	0	0

GARDINER, Max (GAR-dih-nuhr, MAX) **ST.L.**

Center. Shoots left. 6'3", 187 lbs. Born, Edina, MN, May 7, 1992.
(St. Louis' 4th choice, 74th overall, in 2010 Entry Draft).

			Regular Season					Playoffs				
Season	Club	League	GP	G	A	Pts	PIM	GP	G	A	Pts	PIM
2007-08	Minnetonka High	High-MN	27	9	12	21	16	....	....	....	....	....
2008-09	Minnetonka High	High-MN	28	15	28	43	8	....	....	....	....	....
2009-10	Team Southwest	UMHSEL	22	6	6	12	....	....	....	....	....	....
	Minnetonka High	High-MN	17	17	26	43	14	6	5	6	11	0
2010-11	U. of Minnesota	WCHA	17	1	2	3	24	....	....	....	....	....
2011-12	Dubuque	USHL	50	12	14	26	29	5	1	3	4	2
2012-13	Penn State	NCAA	27	3	19	22	22	....	....	....	....	....

GAUDREAU, John (GAW-droh, JAWN) **CGY**

Left wing. Shoots left. 5'7", 150 lbs. Born, Salem, NJ, August 13, 1993.
(Calgary's 4th choice, 104th overall, in 2011 Entry Draft).

			Regular Season					Playoffs				
Season	Club	League	GP	G	A	Pts	PIM	GP	G	A	Pts	PIM
2009-10	Team Comcast	T1EHL	48	29	29	58	16	....	....	....	....	....
2010-11	Dubuque	USHL	60	36	36	72	36	11	5	6	11	6
2011-12	Boston College	H-East	44	21	23	44	10	....	....	....	....	....
2012-13	Boston College	H-East	35	21	30	*51	29	....	....	....	....	....

USHL All-Rookie Team (2011) • USHL Second All-Star Team (2011) • USHL Rookie of the Year (2011) • Hockey East All-Rookie Team (2012) • Hockey East First All-Star Team (2013) • Hockey East Player of the Year (2013) • NCAA East First All-American Team (2013)

GAUNCE, Brendan (GAWNS, BREHN-duhn) **VAN**

Center. Shoots left. 6'2", 207 lbs. Born, Sudbury, Ont., March 25, 1994.
(Vancouver's 1st choice, 26th overall, in 2012 Entry Draft).

			Regular Season					Playoffs				
Season	Club	League	GP	G	A	Pts	PIM	GP	G	A	Pts	PIM
2009-10	Markham Waxers	Minor-ON	86	55	93	*148	54	....	....	....	....	....
	Markham Waxers	ON-Jr.A	1	0	0	0	0	....	....	....	....	....
2010-11	Belleville Bulls	OHL	65	11	25	36	40	4	0	0	0	4
2011-12	Belleville Bulls	OHL	68	28	40	68	68	6	1	2	3	2
2012-13	Belleville Bulls	OHL	60	33	27	60	44	17	8	14	22	10

GAUTHIER, Danick (GOH-t'yay, DAN-ihk) **T.B.**

Right wing. Shoots left. 6'2", 212 lbs. Born, Repentigny, Que., October 24, 1991.

			Regular Season					Playoffs				
Season	Club	League	GP	G	A	Pts	PIM	GP	G	A	Pts	PIM
2008-09	Shawinigan	QMJHL	1	0	1	1	0	....	....	....	....	....
	Saint John	QMJHL	21	5	2	7	12	4	1	1	20	0
2009-10	Saint John	QMJHL	66	13	9	22	68	21	6	4	10	8
2010-11	Saint John	QMJHL	65	11	19	30	78	18	3	1	4	21
2011-12	Saint John	QMJHL	66	47	39	86	67	17	13	8	21	28
2012-13	Syracuse Crunch	AHL	38	5	5	10	32	....	....	....	....	....
	Florida Everblades	ECHL	5	3	3	6	0	....	....	....	....	....

Signed as a free agent by **Tampa Bay**, March 2, 2012.

GAUTHIER, Frederik (goh-T'YAY, FREHD-RIHK) **TOR**

Center. Shoots left. 6'5", 214 lbs. Born, St-Lin, Que., April 26, 1995.
(Toronto's 1st choice, 21st overall, in 2013 Entry Draft).

			Regular Season					Playoffs				
Season	Club	League	GP	G	A	Pts	PIM	GP	G	A	Pts	PIM
2010-11	Esther-Blondin	QAAA	37	7	14	21	6	3	0	0	0	0
2011-12	Esther-Blondin	QAAA	39	26	25	51	28	13	13	11	24	6
2012-13	Rimouski Oceanic	QMJHL	62	22	38	60	26	6	0	2	2	2

QMJHL All-Rookie Team (2013)

GAUTHIER-LEDUC, Jerome (GOH-t'yay-leh-DOOK, Jah-ROHM) **BUF**

Defense. Shoots right. 6'1", 190 lbs. Born, Quebec City, Que., July 30, 1992.
(Buffalo's 2nd choice, 68th overall, in 2010 Entry Draft).

			Regular Season					Playoffs				
Season	Club	League	GP	G	A	Pts	PIM	GP	G	A	Pts	PIM
2007-08	Sem. St-Francois	QAAA	43	10	12	22	10	17	2	6	8	26
2008-09	Rouyn-Noranda	QMJHL	52	1	16	17	8	6	0	2	2	5
2009-10	Rouyn-Noranda	QMJHL	68	20	26	46	16	11	2	4	6	2
2010-11	Rimouski Oceanic	QMJHL	61	18	38	56	26	5	1	2	3	6
2011-12	Rimouski Oceanic	QMJHL	62	28	46	74	41	21	9	10	19	12
2012-13	Rochester	AHL	48	3	4	7	8	3	0	0	0	0

QMJHL First All-Star Team (2012)

GAVRUS, Artur (GAV-ruhs, ahr-TUHR) **N.J.**

Center/Left wing. Shoots left. 5'10", 175 lbs. Born, Ratichi, Belarus, January 3, 1994.
(New Jersey's 7th choice, 180th overall, in 2012 Entry Draft).

			Regular Season					Playoffs				
Season	Club	League	GP	G	A	Pts	PIM	GP	G	A	Pts	PIM
2009-10	Neman Grodno 2	Belarus-2	41	14	12	26	22	....	....	....	....	....
2010-11	Neman Grodno 2	Belarus-2	19	4	4	8	18	....	....	....	....	....
2011-12	Owen Sound	OHL	45	15	22	37	18	1	0	0	0	0
2012-13	Neman Grodno	Belarus	15	5	7	12	0	....	....	....	....	....
	Neman Grodno 2	Belarus-2	2	0	3	3	0	....	....	....	....	....
	Owen Sound	OHL	21	8	6	14	11	12	3	5	8	2

GAZDIC, Luke (GAZ-dihk, LEWK) **DAL**

Left wing. Shoots left. 6'3", 228 lbs. Born, Toronto, Ont., July 25, 1989.
(Dallas' 8th choice, 172nd overall, in 2007 Entry Draft).

			Regular Season					Playoffs				
Season	Club	League	GP	G	A	Pts	PIM	GP	G	A	Pts	PIM
2004-05	North York	GTHL	38	13	16	29	24	....	....	....	....	....
2005-06	Wexford Raiders	ON-Jr.A	47	17	16	33	105	....	....	....	....	....
2006-07	Erie Otters	OHL	58	5	8	13	136	....	....	....	....	....
2007-08	Erie Otters	OHL	67	17	12	29	144	....	....	....	....	....
2008-09	Erie Otters	OHL	63	20	10	30	127	5	0	0	0	9
	Idaho Steelheads	ECHL	2	1	0	1	14	2	0	0	0	0
2009-10	Texas Stars	AHL	49	3	1	4	155	....	....	....	....	....
	Idaho Steelheads	ECHL	4	1	1	2	10	....	....	....	....	....
2010-11	Texas Stars	AHL	72	9	8	17	110	5	0	0	0	2
2011-12	Texas Stars	AHL	76	11	12	23	102	....	....	....	....	....
2012-13	Texas Stars	AHL	59	4	7	11	80	8	0	0	0	19

GEDIG, Curtis (GEH-dihg, KUHR-tihs) **N.J.**

Defense. Shoots left. 6'3", 195 lbs. Born, Penticton, B.C., September 14, 1991.
(New Jersey's 7th choice, 204th overall, in 2009 Entry Draft).

			Regular Season					Playoffs				
Season	Club	League	GP	G	A	Pts	PIM	GP	G	A	Pts	PIM
2007-08	Okanagan Rockets	BCMML	40	4	14	18	36	....	....	....	....	....
	Princeton Posse	KIJHL	9	0	2	2	4	1	0	0	0	0
2008-09	Merritt	BCHL	16	2	4	6	2	....	....	....	....	....
	Cowichan Valley	BCHL	30	2	10	12	16	10	0	3	3	2
2009-10	Cowichan Valley	BCHL	23	6	3	9	14	....	....	....	....	....
	Vernon Vipers	BCHL	30	5	7	12	6	19	1	5	6	10
2010-11	Ohio State	CCHA	34	0	12	12	6	....	....	....	....	....
2011-12	Ohio State	CCHA	34	2	12	14	10	....	....	....	....	....
2012-13	Ohio State	CCHA	32	3	12	15	6	....	....	....	....	....

GEERTSEN, Mason (GEERT-suhn, MAY-suhn) **COL**

Defense. Shoots left. 6'3", 199 lbs. Born, Drayton Valley, Alta., April 19, 1995.
(Colorado's 4th choice, 93rd overall, in 2013 Entry Draft).

			Regular Season					Playoffs				
Season	Club	League	GP	G	A	Pts	PIM	GP	G	A	Pts	PIM
2010-11	Sherwood Park	AMHL	31	3	7	10	84	10	1	2	3	24
	Edmonton	WHL	3	0	0	0	4	....	....	....	....	....
2011-12	Edmonton	WHL	34	0	3	3	70	....	....	....	....	....
2012-13	Edmonton	WHL	15	0	4	4	32	....	....	....	....	....
	Vancouver Giants	WHL	58	2	8	10	98	....	....	....	....	....

GERNAT, Martin (GAIR-naht, MAR-tihn) **EDM**

Defense. Shoots left. 6'5", 187 lbs. Born, Presov, Slovakia, April 11, 1993.
(Edmonton's 8th choice, 122nd overall, in 2011 Entry Draft).

			Regular Season					Playoffs				
Season	Club	League	GP	G	A	Pts	PIM	GP	G	A	Pts	PIM
2008-09	P.H.K. Presov U18	Svk-U18	41	6	28	34	36	....	....	....	....	....
2009-10	HC Kosice U18	Svk-U18	36	4	21	25	20	5	0	3	3	2
	HC Kosice Jr.	Slovak-Jr.	....	....	....	....	....	2	0	0	0	2
2010-11	HC Kosice U18	Svk-U18	8	3	4	7	22	1	0	0	0	2
	HC Kosice Jr.	Slovak-Jr.	28	3	15	18	20	12	3	3	6	10
2011-12	Edmonton	WHL	60	9	46	55	46	20	7	6	13	8
2012-13	Edmonton	WHL	23	3	10	13	14	22	6	11	17	6

GIBBONS, Brian (GIH-buhnz, BRIGH-uhn) PIT

Center. Shoots left. 5'8", 170 lbs. Born, Braintree, MA, February 26, 1988.

			Regular Season					Playoffs				
Season	**Club**	**League**	**GP**	**G**	**A**	**Pts**	**PIM**	**GP**	**G**	**A**	**Pts**	**PIM**
2006-07	Salisbury School	High-CT	25	8	19	27	....	....	....	....	....	....
2007-08	Boston College	H-East	43	13	22	35	32	....	....	....	....	....
2008-09	Boston College	H-East	36	9	19	28	52	....	....	....	....	....
2009-10	Boston College	H-East	42	16	34	50	78	....	....	....	....	....
2010-11	Boston College	H-East	39	18	*33	51	79	....	....	....	....	....
2011-12	Wilkes-Barre	AHL	70	11	19	30	26	9	0	0	0	8
2012-13	Wilkes-Barre	AHL	70	8	22	30	34	15	3	5	8	22

Hockey East First All-Star Team (2010) • Hockey East Second All-Star Team (2011)

Signed as a free agent by **Pittsburgh**, April 4, 2011.

GILBERT, David (zhihl-BAIR, DAY-vihd) CHI

Center. Shoots left. 6'2", 186 lbs. Born, Chateauguay, Que., February 9, 1991.
(Chicago's 8th choice, 209th overall, in 2009 Entry Draft).

			Regular Season					Playoffs				
Season	**Club**	**League**	**GP**	**G**	**A**	**Pts**	**PIM**	**GP**	**G**	**A**	**Pts**	**PIM**
2006-07	Antoine-Girouard	QAAA	44	19	26	45	10	4	2	1	3	2
2007-08	Antoine-Girouard	QAAA	29	29	24	53	54	....	....	....	....	....
	Quebec Remparts	QMJHL	28	7	7	14	12	11	1	0	1	2
2008-09	Quebec Remparts	QMJHL	67	11	32	43	24	17	6	2	8	11
2009-10	Quebec Remparts	QMJHL	31	6	12	18	15	....	....	....	....	....
	Acadie-Bathurst	QMJHL	31	18	12	30	22	5	5	2	7	6
	Rockford IceHogs	AHL	1	0	1	1	0	....	....	....	....	....
2010-11	Acadie-Bathurst	QMJHL	52	28	23	51	39	4	2	1	3	0
	Rockford IceHogs	AHL	5	2	1	3	2	....	....	....	....	....
2011-12	Rockford IceHogs	AHL	28	1	4	5	13	....	....	....	....	....
	Toledo Walleye	ECHL	29	6	12	18	18	....	....	....	....	....
2012-13	Rockford IceHogs	AHL	10	1	2	3	6	....	....	....	....	....

GILMOUR, Adam (GIHL-mohr, A-duhm) MIN

Center. Shoots right. 6'4", 192 lbs. Born, Albany, NY, January 29, 1994.
(Minnesota's 4th choice, 98th overall, in 2012 Entry Draft).

			Regular Season					Playoffs				
Season	**Club**	**League**	**GP**	**G**	**A**	**Pts**	**PIM**	**GP**	**G**	**A**	**Pts**	**PIM**
2010-11	Nobles	High-MA	27	11	16	27	8	....	....	....	....	....
2011-12	Cape Cod Whalers	Minor-MA	30	19	26	45	....	....	....	....	....	....
	Nobles	High-MA	26	26	30	56	28	....	....	....	....	....
2012-13	Muskegon	USHL	64	19	28	47	12	3	1	0	1	10

• Signed Letter of Intent to attend **Boston College** (Hockey East) in fall of 2013.

GILMOUR, John (GIHL-mohr, JAWN) CGY

Defense. Shoots left. 5'11", 173 lbs. Born, Montreal, Que., May 17, 1993.
(Calgary's 8th choice, 198th overall, in 2013 Entry Draft).

			Regular Season					Playoffs				
Season	**Club**	**League**	**GP**	**G**	**A**	**Pts**	**PIM**	**GP**	**G**	**A**	**Pts**	**PIM**
2010-11	Gilmour Acad.	MPHL	13	4	7	11	8	3	0	2	2	0
	Gilmour Acad.	High-OH	46	....	....	31	....	....	....	....	....	....
2011-12	Cedar Rapids	USHL	58	10	14	24	14	2	0	1	1	0
2012-13	Providence College	H-East	38	4	9	13	35	....	....	....	....	....

GIMAYEV, Sergei (gih-MIGH-ehv, SAIR-gay) OTT

Defense. Shoots left. 6'1", 183 lbs. Born, Moscow, USSR, February 16, 1984.
(Ottawa's 6th choice, 166th overall, in 2003 Entry Draft).

			Regular Season					Playoffs				
Season	**Club**	**League**	**GP**	**G**	**A**	**Pts**	**PIM**	**GP**	**G**	**A**	**Pts**	**PIM**
2001-02	CSKA Moscow 2	Russia-3	36	0	10	10	50	....	....	....	....	....
2002-03	Cherepovets	Russia	11	0	0	0	4	....	....	....	....	....
2003-04	Cherepovets	Russia	50	1	3	4	32	....	....	....	....	....
2004-05	Cherepovets	Russia	5	0	1	1	2	....	....	....	....	....
	Sibir Novosibirsk	Russia	31	1	6	7	34	....	....	....	....	....
2005-06	Dynamo Moscow	Russia	46	1	3	4	36	2	0	0	0	0
2006-07	Dynamo Moscow	Russia	23	0	2	2	28	2	0	0	0	6
2007-08	Cherepovets	Russia	39	1	0	1	30	8	1	1	2	4
2008-09	Barys Astana	KHL	45	0	2	2	79	....	....	....	....	....
2009-10	Barys Astana	KHL	54	6	6	12	73	3	0	0	0	8
2010-11	Barys Astana	KHL	52	5	3	8	44	4	0	0	0	4
2011-12	Ufa	KHL	43	1	4	5	27	3	0	0	0	0
2012-13	CSKA Moscow	KHL	43	1	0	1	22	2	0	0	0	2

GIRARD, Felix (zhih-RAHRD, FEE-lihx) NSH

Center. Shoots right. 5'11", 193 lbs. Born, Quebec, Que., May 9, 1994.
(Nashville's 3rd choice, 95th overall, in 2013 Entry Draft).

			Regular Season					Playoffs				
Season	**Club**	**League**	**GP**	**G**	**A**	**Pts**	**PIM**	**GP**	**G**	**A**	**Pts**	**PIM**
2009-10	St-Francois	QAAA	41	7	11	18	68	3	1	1	2	15
2010-11	Baie-Comeau	QMJHL	64	5	12	17	37	....	....	....	....	....
2011-12	Baie-Comeau	QMJHL	60	6	15	21	63	8	2	1	3	14
2012-13	Baie-Comeau	QMJHL	58	23	38	61	58	19	4	11	15	42

GIRGENSONS, Zemgus (GEER-gehn-suhn, ZEHM-guhz) BUF

Center. Shoots left. 6'1", 188 lbs. Born, Riga, Latvia, January 5, 1994.
(Buffalo's 2nd choice, 14th overall, in 2012 Entry Draft).

			Regular Season					Playoffs				
Season	**Club**	**League**	**GP**	**G**	**A**	**Pts**	**PIM**	**GP**	**G**	**A**	**Pts**	**PIM**
2009-10	Green Mountain	EmJHL	19	17	12	29	6	....	....	....	....	....
	Green Mountain	EJHL	23	11	17	28	13	2	0	2	2	0
2010-11	Dubuque	USHL	51	21	28	49	46	11	3	5	8	8
2011-12	Dubuque	USHL	49	24	31	55	69	2	2	2	4	0
2012-13	Rochester	AHL	61	6	11	17	28	3	3	0	3	0

USHL First All-Star Team (2012)

GLEASON, Joe (GLEE-suhn, JOH) CHI

Defense. Shoots right. 5'9", 171 lbs. Born, Edina, MN, March 30, 1990.
(Chicago's 7th choice, 192nd overall, in 2008 Entry Draft).

			Regular Season					Playoffs				
Season	**Club**	**League**	**GP**	**G**	**A**	**Pts**	**PIM**	**GP**	**G**	**A**	**Pts**	**PIM**
2006-07	Edina Hornets	High-MN	21	10	23	33	....	....	....	....	....	....
	Team Southwest	UMWEHL	11	4	6	10	....	....	....	....	....	....
2007-08	Edina Hornets	High-MN	23	9	33	42	....	....	....	....	....	....
	Team Southwest	UMWEHL	12	6	14	20	....	....	....	....	....	....
2008-09	Des Moines	USHL	59	5	16	21	40	....	....	....	....	....
2009-10	North Dakota	WCHA	39	0	9	9	31	....	....	....	....	....
2010-11	North Dakota	WCHA	22	1	3	4	19	....	....	....	....	....
2011-12	North Dakota	WCHA	41	0	15	15	14	....	....	....	....	....
2012-13	North Dakota	WCHA	41	5	13	18	18	....	....	....	....	....

GLENDENING, Luke (glehn-DEHN-ihng , LEWK) DET

Right wing. Shoots right. 5'11", 200 lbs. Born, Grand Rapids, MI, April 28, 1989.

			Regular Season					Playoffs				
Season	**Club**	**League**	**GP**	**G**	**A**	**Pts**	**PIM**	**GP**	**G**	**A**	**Pts**	**PIM**
2008-09	U. of Michigan	CCHA	35	6	4	10	33	....	....	....	....	....
2009-10	U. of Michigan	CCHA	45	7	14	21	39	....	....	....	....	....
2010-11	U. of Michigan	CCHA	44	8	10	18	26	....	....	....	....	....
2011-12	U. of Michigan	CCHA	41	10	11	21	24	....	....	....	....	....
	Providence Bruins	AHL	3	0	0	0	0	....	....	....	....	....
2012-13	Toledo Walleye	ECHL	27	14	7	21	27	....	....	....	....	....
	Grand Rapids	AHL	51	8	18	26	50	24	6	10	16	30

Signed as a free agent by **Detroit**, July 5, 2013.

GOGOL, Curt (GOH-guhl, KUHRT) S.J.

Left wing. Shoots left. 6'1", 190 lbs. Born, Calgary, Alta., September 21, 1991.

			Regular Season					Playoffs				
Season	**Club**	**League**	**GP**	**G**	**A**	**Pts**	**PIM**	**GP**	**G**	**A**	**Pts**	**PIM**
2007-08	Calgary Flames	AMHL	31	10	4	14	96	....	....	....	....	....
	Kelowna Rockets	WHL	1	0	0	0	0	....	....	....	....	....
2008-09	Kelowna Rockets	WHL	63	1	4	5	144	22	1	0	1	30
2009-10	Kelowna Rockets	WHL	35	0	6	6	120	....	....	....	....	....
	Saskatoon Blades	WHL	8	1	0	1	29	10	1	3	4	23
2010-11	Saskatoon Blades	WHL	15	1	1	2	59	....	....	....	....	....
	Chilliwack Bruins	WHL	47	4	8	12	142	5	0	1	1	6
2011-12	Worcester Sharks	AHL	53	6	4	10	167	....	....	....	....	....
2012-13	Worcester Sharks	AHL	38	4	2	6	139	....	....	....	....	....

Signed as a free agent by **San Jose**, September 21, 2010.

GOGULLA, Philip (GOH-goo-lah, FIHL-ihp) BUF

Right wing. Shoots left. 6'2", 182 lbs. Born, Dusseldorf, West Germany, July 31, 1987.
(Buffalo's 2nd choice, 48th overall, in 2005 Entry Draft).

			Regular Season					Playoffs				
Season	**Club**	**League**	**GP**	**G**	**A**	**Pts**	**PIM**	**GP**	**G**	**A**	**Pts**	**PIM**
2002-03	Krefelder EV Jr.	Ger-Jr.	32	11	23	34	42	2	0	0	0	2
2003-04	Krefelder EV Jr.	Ger-Jr.	35	35	44	79	22	2	0	2	2	27
2004-05	Essen	German-2	3	0	0	0	0	....	....	....	....	....
	Koln Jr.	Ger-Jr.	7	4	5	9	18	....	....	....	....	....
	Kolner Haie	Germany	47	1	1	2	14	7	0	0	0	2
2005-06	Kolner Haie	Germany	48	7	15	22	49	9	3	2	5	40
2006-07	Kolner Haie	Germany	44	8	13	21	26	7	0	0	0	8
2007-08	Kolner Haie	Germany	51	11	33	44	30	14	3	9	12	6
2008-09	Kolner Haie	Germany	48	17	21	38	58	....	....	....	....	....
	Germany	Oly-Q	3	1	1	2	2	....	....	....	....	....
2009-10	Portland Pirates	AHL	76	15	20	35	27	3	0	0	0	0
2010-11	Kolner Haie	Germany	52	13	33	46	50	5	2	2	4	0
2011-12	Kolner Haie	Germany	52	20	26	46	64	6	1	4	5	10
2012-13	Kolner Haie	Germany	46	11	21	32	14	12	4	5	9	8

GONCHAROV, Maxim (gohn-CHAR-ahv, mahx-EEM) PHX

Defense. Shoots right. 6'3", 215 lbs. Born, Moscow, USSR, June 15, 1989.
(Phoenix's 6th choice, 123rd overall, in 2007 Entry Draft).

			Regular Season					Playoffs				
Season	**Club**	**League**	**GP**	**G**	**A**	**Pts**	**PIM**	**GP**	**G**	**A**	**Pts**	**PIM**
2005-06	CSKA Moscow 2	Russia-3	STATISTICS NOT AVAILABLE									
2006-07	CSKA Moscow 2	Russia-3	STATISTICS NOT AVAILABLE									
	CSKA Moscow	Russia	18	0	0	0	10	5	0	0	0	2
2007-08	CSKA Moscow	Russia	47	3	2	5	38	6	0	2	2	0
	CSKA Moscow 2	Russia-3	4	0	2	2	35	3	0	0	0	8
2008-09	CSKA Moscow	KHL	47	7	8	15	50	7	0	0	0	4
2009-10	CSKA Moscow	KHL	51	4	13	17	52	3	1	0	1	2
2010-11	San Antonio	AHL	61	6	9	15	65	....	....	....	....	....
2011-12	Portland Pirates	AHL	45	1	3	4	37	....	....	....	....	....
2012-13	Portland Pirates	AHL	45	2	13	15	114	1	0	0	0	4

Signed as a free agent by **CSKA Moscow** (KHL), June 3, 2013.

GORDON, Coda (GOHR-duhn, KOH-duh) CGY

Left wing. Shoots left. 6'1", 176 lbs. Born, Calgary, Alta., August 4, 1994.
(Calgary's 6th choice, 165th overall, in 2012 Entry Draft).

			Regular Season					Playoffs				
Season	**Club**	**League**	**GP**	**G**	**A**	**Pts**	**PIM**	**GP**	**G**	**A**	**Pts**	**PIM**
2010-11	Edge School	High-AB	65	52	58	110	42	....	....	....	....	....
	Swift Current	WHL	1	0	0	0	0	....	....	....	....	....
2011-12	Swift Current	WHL	66	30	23	53	12	....	....	....	....	....
2012-13	Swift Current	WHL	70	17	42	59	21	5	2	2	4	4

GORMLEY, Brandon (GOHRM-lee, BRAN-duhn) PHX

Defense. Shoots left. 6'2", 205 lbs. Born, Murray River, P.E.I., February 18, 1992.
(Phoenix's 1st choice, 13th overall, in 2010 Entry Draft).

			Regular Season					Playoffs				
Season	**Club**	**League**	**GP**	**G**	**A**	**Pts**	**PIM**	**GP**	**G**	**A**	**Pts**	**PIM**
2007-08	Notre Dame	SMHL	42	23	33	56	63	9	1	6	7	18
2008-09	Moncton Wildcats	QMJHL	62	7	20	27	34	10	1	3	4	6
2009-10	Moncton Wildcats	QMJHL	58	9	34	43	54	21	2	15	17	10
2010-11	Moncton Wildcats	QMJHL	47	13	35	48	42	5	0	1	1	6
	San Antonio	AHL	4	1	0	1	0	....	....	....	....	....
2011-12	Moncton Wildcats	QMJHL	26	10	17	27	18	....	....	....	....	....
	Shawinigan	QMJHL	9	0	5	5	4	7	5	2	7	8
2012-13	Portland Pirates	AHL	68	5	24	29	44	3	1	2	3	0

QMJHL All-Rookie Team (2009) • QMJHL Second All-Star Team (2010, 2011) • Memorial Cup All-Star Team (2012)

GORTZ, Max (GUHRTS, MAX) NSH

Right wing. Shoots right. 6'3", 200 lbs. Born, Hoor, Sweden, January 28, 1993.
(Nashville's 8th choice, 172nd overall, in 2012 Entry Draft).

			Regular Season					Playoffs				
Season	Club	League	GP	G	A	Pts	PIM	GP	G	A	Pts	PIM
2008-09	Malmo U18	Swe-U18	10	2	0	2	2	....	....	....	....	....
2009-10	Malmo U18	Swe-U18	23	8	23	31	2	....	....	....	....	....
	Malmo Jr.	Swe-Jr.	26	1	3	4	6	....	....	....	....	....
2010-11	Malmo U18	Swe-U18	8	2	1	3	6	....	....	....	....	....
	Malmo Jr.	Swe-Jr.	40	9	9	18	14	5	2	0	2	2
2011-12	Farjestad Jr.	Swe-Jr.	28	17	18	35	6	6	4	3	7	0
	Farjestad	Sweden	18	2	3	5	0	2	0	0	0	2
2012-13	Farjestad Jr.	Swe-Jr.	8	7	1	8	0	4	2	3	5	0
	Farjestad	Sweden	50	9	6	15	4	9	0	2	2	0

GOSTISBEHERE, Shayne (gaws-TIHS-bair, SHAYN) PHI

Defense. Shoots left. 5'11", 170 lbs. Born, Pembroke Pines, FL, April 20, 1993.
(Philadelphia's 3rd choice, 78th overall, in 2012 Entry Draft).

			Regular Season					Playoffs				
Season	Club	League	GP	G	A	Pts	PIM	GP	G	A	Pts	PIM
2010-11	South Kent School	High-CT	24	7	29	36	32	....	....	....	....	....
2011-12	Union College	ECAC	41	5	17	22	20	....	....	....	....	....
2012-13	Union College	ECAC	36	8	18	26	39	....	....	....	....	....

ECAC All-Rookie Team (2012) • ECAC Second All-Star Team (2013) • NCAA East Second All-American Team (2013)

GOTOVETS, Kirill (goh-TOH-vets, kih-RIHL) CHI

Defense. Shoots left. 5'11", 175 lbs. Born, Minsk, USSR, June 25, 1991.
(Tampa Bay's 7th choice, 183rd overall, in 2009 Entry Draft).

			Regular Season					Playoffs				
Season	Club	League	GP	G	A	Pts	PIM	GP	G	A	Pts	PIM
2007-08	Yunior Minsk	Belarus-2	45	2	8	10	54	....	....	....	....	....
2008-09	Shat.-St. Mary's	High-MN	54	7	25	32	70	....	....	....	....	....
2009-10	Shat.-St. Mary's	High-MN	44	8	19	27	73	....	....	....	....	....
2010-11	Cornell Big Red	ECAC	34	1	6	7	32	....	....	....	....	....
2011-12	Cornell Big Red	ECAC	24	1	7	8	12	....	....	....	....	....
2012-13	Cornell Big Red	ECAC	22	0	0	0	12	....	....	....	....	....

• Rights traded to **Chicago** by **Tampa Bay** for Phillipe Paradis, April 2, 2013.

GOULBOURNE, Tyrell (GOHL-buhrn, tigh-REHL) PHI

Left wing. Shoots left. 5'11", 195 lbs. Born, Edmonton, Alta., January 26, 1994.
(Philadelphia's 3rd choice, 72nd overall, in 2013 Entry Draft).

			Regular Season					Playoffs				
Season	Club	League	GP	G	A	Pts	PIM	GP	G	A	Pts	PIM
2009-10	CAC Gregg's Dist.	AMHL	31	13	13	26	85	2	0	0	0	2
	Kelowna Rockets	WHL	5	0	1	1	0	....	....	....	....	....
2010-11	CAC Gregg's Dist.	AMHL	26	10	16	26	69	....	....	....	....	....
	Kelowna Rockets	WHL	13	1	0	1	27	6	0	0	0	6
2011-12	Kelowna Rockets	WHL	63	6	8	14	109	4	0	0	0	2
2012-13	Kelowna Rockets	WHL	64	14	13	27	135	11	1	2	3	15

GOULET, Alain (goo-LAY, AL-eh) BOS

Defense. Shoots right. 6'2", 186 lbs. Born, Kapuskasing, Ont., September 22, 1988.
(Boston's 4th choice, 159th overall, in 2007 Entry Draft).

			Regular Season					Playoffs				
Season	Club	League	GP	G	A	Pts	PIM	GP	G	A	Pts	PIM
2005-06	Ottawa Jr. Sens	ON-Jr.A	41	6	14	20	22	....	....	....	....	....
2006-07	Aurora Tigers	ON-Jr.A	43	10	32	42	34	25	5	16	21	32
2007-08	Nebraska-Omaha	CCHA	37	6	8	14	14	....	....	....	....	....
2008-09	Nebraska-Omaha	CCHA	17	2	3	5	21	....	....	....	....	....
	Gatineau	QMJHL	32	16	19	35	10	10	0	10	10	18
2009-10	Providence Bruins	AHL	71	3	15	18	28	....	....	....	....	....
2010-11	Providence Bruins	AHL	16	2	6	8	10	....	....	....	....	....
	Reading Royals	ECHL	43	4	14	18	29	6	0	1	1	2
2011-12	Bakersfield	ECHL	46	7	10	17	53	....	....	....	....	....
	Cincinnati	ECHL	16	1	8	9	4	....	....	....	....	....
2012-13	Alaska Aces	ECHL	28	1	4	5	10	....	....	....	....	....
	Orlando	ECHL	31	2	8	10	28	....	....	....	....	....

GRAHAM, Jesse (GRAY-uhm, JEH-see) NYI

Defense. Shoots right. 6', 173 lbs. Born, Oshawa, Ont., May 13, 1994.
(NY Islanders' 6th choice, 155th overall, in 2012 Entry Draft).

			Regular Season					Playoffs				
Season	Club	League	GP	G	A	Pts	PIM	GP	G	A	Pts	PIM
2009-10	Tor. Young Nats	GTHL	84	14	74	88	38	....	....	....	....	....
2010-11	Niagara Ice Dogs	OHL	63	1	17	18	22	14	1	8	9	8
2011-12	Niagara Ice Dogs	OHL	68	4	37	41	36	20	1	9	10	20
2012-13	Niagara Ice Dogs	OHL	68	4	35	39	48	5	0	3	3	6

OHL All-Rookie Team (2011)

GRANBERG, Petter (GRAN-buhrg, PEH-tuhr) TOR

Defense. Shoots right. 6'3", 205 lbs. Born, Gallivare, Sweden, August 27, 1992.
(Toronto's 4th choice, 116th overall, in 2010 Entry Draft).

			Regular Season					Playoffs				
Season	Club	League	GP	G	A	Pts	PIM	GP	G	A	Pts	PIM
2007-08	Skelleftea U18	Swe-U18	28	1	3	4	4	....	....	....	....	....
2008-09	Skelleftea AIK U18	Swe-U18	32	0	8	8	20	8	0	0	0	4
	Skelleftea AIK Jr.	Swe-Jr.	4	0	0	0	0	2	0	0	0	6
2009-10	Skelleftea AIK U18	Swe-U18	6	0	1	1	2	3	0	3	3	4
	Skelleftea AIK Jr.	Swe-Jr.	40	2	7	9	39	4	1	0	1	4
	Skelleftea AIK	Sweden	1	0	0	0	0	....	....	....	....	....
2010-11	Skelleftea AIK Jr.	Swe-Jr.	34	2	6	8	16	5	0	1	1	0
	Pitea HC	Sweden-3	1	0	0	0	0	....	....	....	....	....
	Skelleftea AIK	Sweden	23	0	1	1	6	11	0	1	1	2
2011-12	Skelleftea AIK Jr.	Swe-Jr.	5	2	4	6	6	....	....	....	....	....
	Sundsvall	Sweden-2	3	0	0	0	6	....	....	....	....	....
	Skelleftea AIK	Sweden	38	1	3	4	10	19	1	1	2	12
2012-13	Skelleftea AIK	Sweden	13	0	0	0	4	13	0	2	2	10
	Skelleftea AIK Jr.	Swe-Jr.	3	0	1	1	2	....	....	....	....	....

GRANLUND, Markus (GRAN-luhnd, mahr-KUHS) CGY

Center. Shoots left. 5'11", 166 lbs. Born, Oulu, Finland, April 16, 1993.
(Calgary's 2nd choice, 45th overall, in 2011 Entry Draft).

			Regular Season					Playoffs				
Season	Club	League	GP	G	A	Pts	PIM	GP	G	A	Pts	PIM
2008-09	Karpat Oulu U18	Fin-U18	4	1	3	4	0	....	....	....	....	....
2009-10	HIFK Helsinki U18	Fin-U18	11	9	20	29	6	....	....	....	....	....
	HIFK Helsinki Jr.	Fin-Jr.	37	17	25	42	38	14	2	11	13	18
2010-11	Suomi U20	Finland-2	6	3	3	6	6	....	....	....	....	....
	HIFK Helsinki	Finland	2	0	0	0	0	....	....	....	....	....
	HIFK Helsinki Jr.	Fin-Jr.	40	20	32	52	49	5	4	5	9	6
2011-12	Kiekko-Vantaa	Finland-2	7	2	5	7	6	....	....	....	....	....
	HIFK Helsinki	Finland	47	15	19	34	18	3	0	0	0	0
	HIFK Helsinki Jr.	Fin-Jr.	....	....	....	....	....	1	1	0	1	0
2012-13	HIFK Helsinki	Finland	50	10	20	30	18	5	1	2	3	4

GRANT, Alex (GRANT, AL-ehx) ANA

Defense. Shoots right. 6'2", 185 lbs. Born, Antigonish, N.S., January 20, 1989.
(Pittsburgh's 6th choice, 118th overall, in 2007 Entry Draft).

			Regular Season					Playoffs				
Season	Club	League	GP	G	A	Pts	PIM	GP	G	A	Pts	PIM
2004-05	Antigonish	MJrHL	50	7	9	16	36	3	1	1	2	2
2005-06	Saint John	QMJHL	47	4	9	13	58	....	....	....	....	....
2006-07	Saint John	QMJHL	68	12	20	32	108	....	....	....	....	....
2007-08	Saint John	QMJHL	70	15	33	48	96	14	3	11	14	12
2008-09	Saint John	QMJHL	37	9	22	31	51	....	....	....	....	....
	Shawinigan	QMJHL	23	4	15	19	11	21	4	5	9	18
2009-10	Wilkes-Barre	AHL	14	3	2	5	28	2	0	0	0	0
	Wheeling Nailers	ECHL	40	7	20	27	36	....	....	....	....	....
2010-11	Wilkes-Barre	AHL	4	0	0	0	0	....	....	....	....	....
	Wheeling Nailers	ECHL	14	3	2	5	6	17	2	0	2	13
2011-12	Wilkes-Barre	AHL	61	10	27	37	73	12	2	5	7	13
2012-13	Wilkes-Barre	AHL	46	4	16	20	73	13	2	2	4	27

• Missed majority of 2010-11 due to wrist injury. Traded to **Anaheim** by **Pittsburgh** for Harry Zolnierczyk, June 24, 2013.

GRANT, Tommy (GRANT, TAW-mee)

Left wing. Shoots left. 6'2", 195 lbs. Born, North Vancouver, B.C., August 29, 1986.

			Regular Season					Playoffs				
Season	Club	League	GP	G	A	Pts	PIM	GP	G	A	Pts	PIM
2004-05	Victoria Salsa	BCHL	51	11	8	19	47	5	1	1	2	6
2005-06	Victoria Salsa	BCHL	50	6	10	16	54	16	5	9	14	32
2006-07	Quesnel	BCHL	11	6	6	12	26	....	....	....	....	....
	Westside Warriors	BCHL	45	30	33	63	103	6	2	2	4	12
2007-08	Alaska-Anchorage	WCHA	31	5	2	7	26	....	....	....	....	....
2008-09	Alaska-Anchorage	WCHA	32	15	10	25	54	....	....	....	....	....
2009-10	Alaska-Anchorage	WCHA	34	9	17	26	42	....	....	....	....	....
2010-11	Alaska-Anchorage	WCHA	37	16	16	32	57	....	....	....	....	....
	Connecticut Whale	AHL	7	0	3	3	2	6	1	1	2	6
2011-12	Connecticut Whale	AHL	72	11	12	23	39	8	0	1	1	4
2012-13	Connecticut Whale	AHL	34	9	9	18	15	....	....	....	....	....
	Worcester Sharks	AHL	16	1	2	3	6	....	....	....	....	....
	San Francisco Bulls	ECHL	5	1	4	5	19	3	0	0	0	10

Signed as a free agent by **NY Rangers**, March 29, 2011. Traded to **San Jose** by **NY Rangers** with future considerations for Brandon Mashinter, January 16, 2013.

GRAOVAC, Tyler (GRAW-vak, TIGH-luhr) MIN

Center. Shoots left. 6'5", 196 lbs. Born, Brampton, Ont., April 27, 1993.
(Minnesota's 6th choice, 191st overall, in 2011 Entry Draft).

			Regular Season					Playoffs				
Season	Club	League	GP	G	A	Pts	PIM	GP	G	A	Pts	PIM
2008-09	Mississauga Reps	GTHL	26	13	18	31	12	....	....	....	....	....
2009-10	Ottawa 67's	OHL	52	2	7	9	17	12	0	0	0	2
2010-11	Ottawa 67's	OHL	66	10	11	21	10	....	....	....	....	....
2011-12	Ottawa 67's	OHL	50	8	19	27	31	18	4	6	10	12
2012-13	Ottawa 67's	OHL	30	21	14	35	8	....	....	....	....	....
	Belleville Bulls	OHL	30	17	21	38	10	15	6	16	22	17

Canadian Major Junior Sportsman of the Year (2013)

GRAVEL, Kevin (gra-VEHL, KEH-vihn) L.A.

Defense. Shoots left. 6'4", 198 lbs. Born, Kingsford, MI, March 6, 1992.
(Los Angeles' 4th choice, 148th overall, in 2010 Entry Draft).

			Regular Season					Playoffs				
Season	Club	League	GP	G	A	Pts	PIM	GP	G	A	Pts	PIM
2008-09	Marquette	NAHL	58	3	11	14	29	....	....	....	....	....
	USNTDP	U-17	3	0	1	1	4	....	....	....	....	....
2009-10	Sioux City	USHL	53	3	3	6	36	....	....	....	....	....
2010-11	St. Cloud State	WCHA	36	1	5	6	4	....	....	....	....	....
2011-12	St. Cloud State	WCHA	37	1	7	8	12	....	....	....	....	....
2012-13	St. Cloud State	WCHA	42	1	11	12	25	....	....	....	....	....

GRAVES, Ryan (GRAVZ, RIGH-uhn) NYR

Defense. Shoots left. 6'4", 220 lbs. Born, Yarmouth, N.S., May 21, 1995.
(NY Rangers' 4th choice, 110th overall, in 2013 Entry Draft).

			Regular Season					Playoffs				
Season	Club	League	GP	G	A	Pts	PIM	GP	G	A	Pts	PIM
2010-11	South Shore	NSMHL	32	5	7	12	58	5	0	6	6	8
	Yarmouth	MJrHL	1	0	0	0	2	3	0	0	0	2
2011-12	P.E.I. Rocket	QMJHL	62	2	7	9	34	....	....	....	....	....
2012-13	P.E.I. Rocket	QMJHL	68	3	13	16	90	6	0	0	0	6

GREGOIRE, Jason (GREHG-wahr, JAY-suhn)

Left wing. Shoots left. 6'1", 196 lbs. Born, Winnipeg, Man., February 24, 1989.
(NY Islanders' 2nd choice, 76th overall, in 2007 Entry Draft).

			Regular Season					Playoffs				
Season	Club	League	GP	G	A	Pts	PIM	GP	G	A	Pts	PIM
2005-06	Wpg. South Blues	MJHL	57	22	28	50	46	14	12	11	23	....
2006-07	Lincoln Stars	USHL	32	16	20	36	10	4	4	0	4	2
2007-08	Lincoln Stars	USHL	54	*37	32	69	41	8	3	9	*12	6
2008-09	North Dakota	WCHA	42	12	17	29	28	....	....	....	....	....
2009-10	North Dakota	WCHA	43	20	17	37	10	....	....	....	....	....
2010-11	North Dakota	WCHA	35	25	18	43	8	....	....	....	....	....
2011-12	St. John's IceCaps	AHL	44	6	8	14	13	....	....	....	....	....
2012-13	St. John's IceCaps	AHL	60	10	8	18	6	....	....	....	....	....

USHL First All-Star Team (2008) • USHL Player of the Year (2008)
Signed as a free agent by **Winnipeg**, July 7, 2011.

GREGOIRE, Jeremy (greh-G'WAHR, JAIR-ih-mee) MTL

Center. Shoots right. 6', 188 lbs. Born, Sherbrooke, Que., September 5, 1995.
(Montreal's 8th choice, 176th overall, in 2013 Entry Draft).

			Regular Season					Playoffs				
Season	Club	League	GP	G	A	Pts	PIM	GP	G	A	Pts	PIM
2009-10	Magog	QAAA	28	4	8	12	22	10	3	1	4	6
2010-11	Magog	QAAA	38	28	25	53	42	13	8	8	16	10
2011-12	Chicoutimi	QMJHL	61	15	15	30	59	18	2	4	6	14
2012-13	Chicoutimi	QMJHL	35	7	8	15	71	....	....	....	....	....
	Baie-Comeau	QMJHL	27	12	5	17	29	18	9	7	16	27

GRENIER, Alexandre (GREHN-yay, al-ehx-AHN-druh) VAN

Right wing. Shoots right. 6'5", 200 lbs. Born, Laval, Que., May 9, 1991.
(Vancouver's 3rd choice, 90th overall, in 2011 Entry Draft).

			Regular Season					Playoffs				
Season	Club	League	GP	G	A	Pts	PIM	GP	G	A	Pts	PIM
2009-10	St-Jerome	QJHL	51	26	28	54	63	7	1	3	4	2
2010-11	St-Jerome	QJHL	33	25	35	60	34	....	....	....	....	....
	Quebec Remparts	QMJHL	31	9	15	24	6	15	8	8	16	4
2011-12	Halifax	QMJHL	64	25	39	64	42	17	4	12	16	19
2012-13	Salzburg	Austria	25	5	8	13	21	....	....	....	....	....
	Chicago Wolves	AHL	4	0	0	0	2	....	....	....	....	....
	Kalamazoo Wings	ECHL	37	10	21	31	51	....	....	....	....	....

Signed as a free agent by **Salzburg** (Austria), June 1, 2012.

GRIFFITH, Seth (GRIH-fihth, SEHTH) BOS

Center. Shoots right. 5'9", 192 lbs. Born, Wallaceburg, Ont., January 4, 1993.
(Boston's 3rd choice, 131st overall, in 2012 Entry Draft).

			Regular Season					Playoffs				
Season	Club	League	GP	G	A	Pts	PIM	GP	G	A	Pts	PIM
2008-09	Chatham-Kent	Minor-ON	52	42	45	87	112	....	....	....	....	....
	Chatham Maroons	ON-Jr.B	1	0	0	0	0	....	....	....	....	....
2009-10	St. Mary's Lincolns	ON-Jr.B	49	43	35	78	56	5	6	3	9	4
	London Knights	OHL	17	2	1	3	2	10	4	3	7	2
2010-11	London Knights	OHL	68	22	40	62	28	6	3	4	7	6
2011-12	London Knights	OHL	68	45	40	85	49	19	10	13	23	12
2012-13	London Knights	OHL	54	33	48	81	52	21	9	16	25	14

OHL Second All-Star Team (2012) • OHL First All-Star Team (2013)

GRIMALDI, Rocco (grih-MAL-dee, RAW-koh) FLA

Center. Shoots right. 5'6", 165 lbs. Born, Anaheim, CA, February 8, 1993.
(Florida's 2nd choice, 33rd overall, in 2011 Entry Draft).

			Regular Season					Playoffs				
Season	Club	League	GP	G	A	Pts	PIM	GP	G	A	Pts	PIM
2008-09	Little Caesars	T1EHL	32	11	9	20	22	7	1	5	6	0
	Little Caesars	Exhib.	19	19	15	34	....	....	....	....	....	....
2009-10	USNTDP	USHL	32	11	9	20	22	....	....	....	....	....
	USNTDP	U-17	16	7	18	25	20	....	....	....	....	....
	USNTDP	U-18	14	3	15	18	12	....	....	....	....	....
2010-11	USNTDP	USHL	23	12	13	25	18	....	....	....	....	....
	USNTDP	U-18	35	27	21	48	47	....	....	....	....	....
2011-12	North Dakota	WCHA	4	1	1	2	2	....	....	....	....	....
2012-13	North Dakota	WCHA	40	13	23	36	18	....	....	....	....	....

WCHA All-Rookie Team (2013)
• Missed majority of 2011-12 due to training camp knee injury and resulting surgery.

GROULX, Danny (GROO, DA-nee)

Defense. Shoots left. 6', 205 lbs. Born, LaSalle, Que., June 23, 1981.

			Regular Season					Playoffs				
Season	Club	League	GP	G	A	Pts	PIM	GP	G	A	Pts	PIM
1996-97	C.C. Lemoyne	QAAA	40	2	26	28	....	15	3	15	18	....
1997-98	Val-d'Or Foreurs	QMJHL	63	4	16	20	61	19	1	4	5	18
1998-99	Val-d'Or Foreurs	QMJHL	36	3	26	29	55	....	....	....	....	....
	Acadie-Bathurst	QMJHL	36	2	15	17	51	18	0	2	2	6
99-2000	Victoriaville Tigres	QMJHL	66	12	55	67	131	6	0	4	4	14
2000-01	Victoriaville Tigres	QMJHL	72	16	71	87	164	13	2	19	21	46
2001-02	Victoriaville Tigres	QMJHL	68	29	83	112	165	22	9	*30	39	68
2002-03	Grand Rapids	AHL	71	3	7	10	52	7	0	1	1	7
2003-04	Grand Rapids	AHL	79	8	13	21	93	3	0	0	0	0
2004-05	Grand Rapids	AHL	53	1	11	12	90	....	....	....	....	....
	Manitoba Moose	AHL	16	2	6	8	16	13	1	3	4	14
2005-06	Kassel Huskies	Germany	51	2	11	13	93	5	0	1	1	6
2006-07	Hamilton Bulldogs	AHL	58	0	16	16	62	22	6	6	12	14
2007-08	Manitoba Moose	AHL	58	4	20	24	32	6	2	1	3	12
2008-09	Rockford IceHogs	AHL	80	6	34	40	58	4	0	2	2	2
2009-10	Worcester Sharks	AHL	80	14	52	66	80	10	1	6	7	6
2010-11	Nizhny Novgorod	KHL	38	2	23	25	50	....	....	....	....	....
2011-12	Dynamo Minsk	KHL	4	0	0	0	2	....	....	....	....	....
	Khanty-Mansiisk	KHL	20	0	2	2	20	1	0	0	0	0
2012-13	Worcester Sharks	AHL	33	4	12	16	24	....	....	....	....	....
	Chicago Wolves	AHL	13	2	4	6	4	....	....	....	....	....

QMJHL First All-Star Team (2001, 2002) • Canadian Major Junior First All-Star Team (2002) • Memorial Cup All-Star Team (2002) • Stafford Smythe Memorial Trophy (Memorial Cup – MVP) (2002) • AHL First All-Star Team (2010) • Eddie Shore Award (AHL – Outstanding Defenseman) (2010)

Signed as a free agent by **Detroit**, August 12, 2002. • Loaned to **Manitoba** (AHL) by **Detroit** (Grand Rapids-AHL) for cash, March 15, 2005. Signed as a free agent by **Kassel** (Germany), August 25, 2005. Signed as a free agent by **San Jose**, July 16, 2009. Signed as a free agent by **Nizhny Novgorod** (KHL), July 1, 2010. Signed as a free agent by **Minsk** (KHL), May 12, 2011. Signed as a free agent by **Kharity-Mansisk** (KHL), October 12, 2011. Signed as a free agent by **San Jose**, July 2, 2012.

GRZELCYK, Matthew (GRIHZ-lihk, MA-thew) BOS

Defense. Shoots left. 5'9", 171 lbs. Born, Charlestown, MA, January 5, 1994.
(Boston's 2nd choice, 85th overall, in 2012 Entry Draft).

			Regular Season					Playoffs				
Season	Club	League	GP	G	A	Pts	PIM	GP	G	A	Pts	PIM
2009-10	Belmont Hill	High-MA	31	2	18	20	30	....	....	....	....	....
2010-11	USNTDP	USHL	36	1	9	10	28	2	0	0	0	2
	USNTDP	U-17	17	1	7	8	10	....	....	....	....	....
2011-12	USNTDP	USHL	24	1	10	11	6	....	....	....	....	....
	USNTDP	U-18	36	2	19	21	16	....	....	....	....	....
2012-13	Boston University	H-East	38	3	20	23	26	....	....	....	....	....

Hockey East All-Rookie Team (2013)

GUENTZEL, Jake (GUHNT-zuhl, JAYK) PIT

Center. Shoots left. 5'10", 157 lbs. Born, Omaha, NE, October 6, 1994.
(Pittsburgh's 2nd choice, 77th overall, in 2013 Entry Draft).

			Regular Season					Playoffs				
Season	Club	League	GP	G	A	Pts	PIM	GP	G	A	Pts	PIM
2010-11	Team Northwest	UMHSEL	15	6	5	11	4	3	0	0	0	0
	Hill-Murray	High-MN	28	19	30	49	10	....	....	....	....	....
2011-12	Team Southeast	UMHSEL	21	14	27	41	8	3	0	3	3	0
	Hill-Murray	High-MN	31	23	52	75	16	....	....	....	....	....
2012-13	Sioux City	USHL	60	29	44	73	24	....	....	....	....	....

USHL All-Rookie Team (2013) • USHL Second All-Star Team (2013) • USHL Rookie of the Year (2013)
• Signed Letter of Intent to attend **University of Nebraska-Omaha** (WCHA) in fall of 2013.

GUNNARSSON, Daniel (GUHN-nuhr-suhn, DAN-yehl) MIN

Defense. Shoots right. 6'6", 205 lbs. Born, Koping, Sweden, April 15, 1992.
(Minnesota's 5th choice, 128th overall, in 2012 Entry Draft).

			Regular Season					Playoffs				
Season	Club	League	GP	G	A	Pts	PIM	GP	G	A	Pts	PIM
2006-07	Koping HC	Sweden-4	3	0	0	0	0	....	....	....	....	....
2007-08	Kopings HC	Sweden-4	STATISTICS NOT AVAILABLE									
2008-09	Leksands IF U18	Swe-U18	12	3	2	5	31	....	....	....	....	....
	Leksands IF Jr.	Swe-Jr.	33	1	5	6	26	3	0	1	1	0
2009-10	Leksands IF U18	Swe-U18	8	3	2	5	0	3	0	0	0	0
	Leksands IF Jr.	Swe-Jr.	14	2	3	5	6	....	....	....	....	....
	Leksands IF	Sweden-2	1	0	0	0	0	....	....	....	....	....
2010-11	Leksands IF Jr.	Swe-Jr.	38	3	13	16	51	....	....	....	....	....
	Leksands IF	Sweden-2	9	0	0	0	2	....	....	....	....	....
	Falu IF	Sweden-3	5	0	3	3	4	....	....	....	....	....
2011-12	Lulea HF Jr.	Swe-Jr.	6	2	1	3	8	....	....	....	....	....
	Lulea HF	Sweden	46	3	4	7	8	5	0	0	0	0
2012-13	Lulea HF	Sweden	53	6	11	17	20	15	3	2	5	2

GUPTILL, Alexander (GUP-tihl, al-ehx-AN-duhr) DAL

Left wing. Shoots left. 6'3", 189 lbs. Born, Burlington, Ont., March 5, 1992.
(Dallas' 3rd choice, 77th overall, in 2010 Entry Draft).

			Regular Season					Playoffs				
Season	Club	League	GP	G	A	Pts	PIM	GP	G	A	Pts	PIM
2008-09	Brampton Capitals	ON-Jr.A	49	30	34	64	28	3	0	1	1	0
2009-10	Brampton Capitals	ON-Jr.A	10	6	5	11	24	....	....	....	....	....
	Orangeville	ON-Jr.A	19	13	13	26	26	2	1	0	1	2
2010-11	Waterloo	USHL	43	13	12	25	53	2	0	0	0	0
2011-12	U. of Michigan	CCHA	41	16	17	33	48	....	....	....	....	....
2012-13	U. of Michigan	CCHA	38	16	20	36	32	....	....	....	....	....

CCHA All-Rookie Team (2012) • CCHA Rookie of the Year (2012)

GUSEV, Nikita (GOO-sehv, nih-KEE-tuh) T.B.

Left wing. Shoots right. 5'9", 173 lbs. Born, Moscow, Russia, July 8, 1992.
(Tampa Bay's 8th choice, 202nd overall, in 2012 Entry Draft).

			Regular Season					Playoffs				
Season	Club	League	GP	G	A	Pts	PIM	GP	G	A	Pts	PIM
2009-10	CSKA Jr.	Russia-Jr.	48	17	40	57	14	5	1	2	3	0
2010-11	CSKA Jr.	Russia-Jr.	38	22	37	59	14	16	17	10	27	6
	CSKA Moscow	KHL	18	1	0	1	2	....	....	....	....	....
2011-12	CSKA Jr.	Russia-Jr.	34	30	46	76	26	19	16	17	33	0
	CSKA Moscow	KHL	15	2	1	3	0	1	0	0	0	0
2012-13	CSKA Moscow	KHL	6	0	1	1	0	....	....	....	....	....
	THK Tver	Russia-2	15	7	6	13	2	....	....	....	....	....
	Amur Khabarovsk	KHL	24	4	8	12	6	12	1	4	5	6

GUSTAFSSON, Erik (GOOS-tahf-suhn, AIR-ihk) EDM

Defense. Shoots left. 6', 176 lbs. Born, Nynashamn, Sweden, March 14, 1992.
(Edmonton's 5th choice, 93rd overall, in 2012 Entry Draft).

			Regular Season					Playoffs				
Season	Club	League	GP	G	A	Pts	PIM	GP	G	A	Pts	PIM
2008-09	Djurgarden U18	Swe-U18	33	2	8	10	22	2	0	0	0	0
2009-10	Djurgarden Jr.	Swe-Jr.	24	0	8	8	26	....	....	....	....	....
	Djurgarden U18	Swe-U18	27	7	13	20	54	3	0	0	0	0
2010-11	Djurgarden Jr.	Swe-Jr.	38	2	21	23	104	4	0	1	1	6
2011-12	Djurgarden Jr.	Swe-Jr.	21	3	11	14	14	....	....	....	....	....
	Djurgarden	Sweden	41	3	4	7	16	....	....	....	....	....
	Djurgarden	Sweden-Q	10	0	1	1	6	....	....	....	....	....
2012-13	Djurgarden	Sweden-2	55	8	16	24	82	....	....	....	....	....

GYSBERS, Simon (GIGHZ-buhrz, SIGH-muhn)

Defense. Shoots right. 6'4", 200 lbs. Born, Richmond Hill, Ont., May 7, 1987.

			Regular Season					Playoffs				
Season	Club	League	GP	G	A	Pts	PIM	GP	G	A	Pts	PIM
2004-05	Stouffville Spirit	ON-Jr.A	46	11	23	34	32	....	....	....	....	....
2005-06	Stouffville Spirit	ON-Jr.A	46	8	24	32	94	31	1	9	10	40
2006-07	Lake Superior	CCHA	41	4	9	13	45	....	....	....	....	....
2007-08	Lake Superior	CCHA	37	6	13	19	46	....	....	....	....	....
2008-09	Lake Superior	CCHA	39	3	18	21	28	....	....	....	....	....
2009-10	Lake Superior	CCHA	38	6	9	15	46	....	....	....	....	....
	Toronto Marlies	AHL	14	0	1	1	2	....	....	....	....	....
2010-11	Toronto Marlies	AHL	60	7	25	32	32	....	....	....	....	....
2011-12	Toronto Marlies	AHL	68	5	24	29	20	17	1	1	2	8
2012-13	Toronto Marlies	AHL	54	4	15	19	36	....	....	....	....	....

Signed to an ATO (amateur tryout) contact by **Toronto** (AHL), March 10, 2010. Signed as a free agent by **Toronto**, March 13, 2010.

HAAR, Garrett (HAHR, GAIR-eht) WSH

Defense. Shoots left. 6', 190 lbs. Born, Huntington Beach, CA, August 16, 1993.
(Washington's 4th choice, 207th overall, in 2011 Entry Draft).

			Regular Season					Playoffs				
Season	Club	League	GP	G	A	Pts	PIM	GP	G	A	Pts	PIM
2008-09	L.A. Selects	Minor-CA	STATISTICS NOT AVAILABLE									
2009-10	Russell Stover	T1EHL	42	4	34	38	28	....	....	....	....	....
2010-11	Fargo Force	USHL	51	7	16	23	38	5	1	2	3	2
2011-12	Western Mich.	CCHA	36	1	7	8	32	....	....	....	....	....
2012-13	Western Mich.	CCHA	22	3	6	9	12	....	....	....	....	....

CCHA All-Rookie Team (2012)

HACHE, Justin (ha-SHAY, JUHS-tihn) PHX

Defense. Shoots left. 6'2", 195 lbs. Born, Petit-Rocher, NB, January 10, 1994.
(Phoenix's 8th choice, 208th overall, in 2012 Entry Draft).

			Regular Season					Playoffs				
Season	Club	League	GP	G	A	Pts	PIM	GP	G	A	Pts	PIM
2008-09	Miramichi	NBPEI	33	0	4	4	8	3	0	1	1	0
2009-10	Miramichi	NBPEI	31	6	16	22	31	9	0	5	5	4
2010-11	Shawinigan	QMJHL	37	3	12	15	17	10	0	2	2	4
2011-12	Shawinigan	QMJHL	60	2	16	18	46	11	1	0	1	2
2012-13	Cape Breton	QMJHL	68	7	26	33	61	....	....	....	....	....

HAGG, Robert (HAG, RAW-buhrt) PHI

Defense. Shoots left. 6'2", 204 lbs. Born, Uppsala, Sweden, February 8, 1995.
(Philadelphia's 2nd choice, 41st overall, in 2013 Entry Draft).

			Regular Season					Playoffs				
Season	Club	League	GP	G	A	Pts	PIM	GP	G	A	Pts	PIM
2008-09	Gimo IF Hockey	Sweden-4	23	0	0	0	6	....	....	....	....	....
2009-10	Gimo IF	Sweden-4	32	7	9	16	28	....	....	....	....	....
2010-11	Tierps HK	Sweden-3	30	2	9	11	30	....	....	....	....	....
	MODO U18	Swe-U18	2	0	0	0	2	....	....	....	....	....
2011-12	MODO U18	Swe-U18	5	1	4	5	10	1	0	0	0	0
	MODO Jr.	Swe-Jr.	44	4	13	17	46	8	1	1	2	2
2012-13	MODO Jr.	Swe-Jr.	28	11	13	24	24	7	1	1	2	4
	MODO	Sweden	27	0	1	1	2	1	0	0	0	0
	MODO U18	Swe-U18	....	....	....	....	....	2	1	1	2	0

HAKANPAA, Jani (HAHK-an-pah, YAH-nee) ST.L.

Defense. Shoots right. 6'5", 218 lbs. Born, Kirkkonummi, Finland, March 31, 1992.
(St. Louis' 5th choice, 104th overall, in 2010 Entry Draft).

			Regular Season					Playoffs				
Season	Club	League	GP	G	A	Pts	PIM	GP	G	A	Pts	PIM
2007-08	K-Vantaa U18	Fin-U18	2	0	1	1	2	2	0	0	0	0
2008-09	K-Vantaa U18	Fin-U18	10	3	4	7	14	....	....	....	....	....
2009-10	K-Vantaa U18	Fin-U18	32	3	16	19	69	6	0	2	2	6
2010-11	Suomi U20	Finland-2	8	1	2	3	31	....	....	....	....	....
	Blues Espoo Jr.	Fin-Jr.	36	3	20	23	61	12	3	2	5	10
2011-12	Blues Espoo Jr.	Fin-Jr.	5	0	4	4	0	....	....	....	....	....
	Blues Espoo	Finland	41	5	7	12	30	....	....	....	....	....
2012-13	Peoria Rivermen	AHL	14	1	3	4	6	....	....	....	....	....
	Blues Espoo	Finland	34	2	3	5	34	....	....	....	....	....

HALMO, Mike (HAL-moh, MIGHK) NYI

Left wing. Shoots left. 5'10", 197 lbs. Born, Waterloo, Ont., May 11, 1991.

			Regular Season					Playoffs				
Season	Club	League	GP	G	A	Pts	PIM	GP	G	A	Pts	PIM
2008-09	Owen Sound	OHL	62	5	3	8	90	4	0	1	1	2
2009-10	Owen Sound	OHL	60	11	18	29	121	....	....	....	....	....
2010-11	Owen Sound	OHL	59	20	23	43	121	22	5	10	15	36
2011-12	Owen Sound	OHL	66	40	45	85	162	....	....	....	....	....
	Bridgeport	AHL	5	1	0	1	5	....	....	....	....	....
2012-13	Bridgeport	AHL	46	5	9	14	46	....	....	....	....	....

Signed as a free agent by **NY Islanders**, March 10, 2012.

HAMBURG, Anthony (HAM-buhrg, AN-thuh-nee) MIN

Center. Shoots right. 6'1", 185 lbs. Born, Houston, TX, August 30, 1991.
(Minnesota's 8th choice, 193rd overall, in 2009 Entry Draft).

			Regular Season					Playoffs				
Season	Club	League	GP	G	A	Pts	PIM	GP	G	A	Pts	PIM
2007-08	Dallas Stars AAA	Exhib.	65	20	57	77	68	....	....	....	....	....
2008-09	Dallas Stars AAA	T1EHL	46	16	38	54	38	....	....	....	....	....
	Dallas Stars AAA	Exhib.	24	13	32	45	38	....	....	....	....	....
2009-10	Omaha Lancers	USHL	54	5	17	22	35	3	0	0	0	2
2010-11	Colgate	ECAC	7	0	3	3	4	....	....	....	....	....
	Omaha Lancers	USHL	31	6	15	21	15	3	1	1	2	0
2011-12	Omaha Lancers	USHL	55	13	25	38	65	4	0	2	2	0
2012-13	RIT Tigers	AH	33	4	7	11	12	....	....	....	....	....

HAMILTON, Curtis (HAM-ihl-tuhn, KUHR-tihs) EDM

Left wing. Shoots left. 6'3", 206 lbs. Born, Tacoma, WA, December 4, 1991.
(Edmonton's 4th choice, 48th overall, in 2010 Entry Draft).

			Regular Season					Playoffs				
Season	Club	League	GP	G	A	Pts	PIM	GP	G	A	Pts	PIM
2006-07	Okanagan Rockets	BCMML	37	26	27	53	68	....	....	....	....	....
	Saskatoon Blades	WHL	2	0	0	0	0	....	....	....	....	....
2007-08	Saskatoon Blades	WHL	68	14	13	27	43	....	....	....	....	....
2008-09	Saskatoon Blades	WHL	58	20	28	48	24	7	1	1	2	2
2009-10	Saskatoon Blades	WHL	26	7	9	16	6	5	2	1	3	6
2010-11	Saskatoon Blades	WHL	62	26	56	82	22	10	4	7	11	4
2011-12	Oklahoma City	AHL	41	5	6	11	8	2	0	0	0	2
2012-13	Oklahoma City	AHL	61	5	4	9	10	1	0	0	0	0

HAMILTON, Freddie (HAM-ihl-tuhn, FREH-dee) S.J.

Center. Shoots right. 6'1", 195 lbs. Born, Toronto, Ont., January 1, 1992.
(San Jose's 4th choice, 129th overall, in 2010 Entry Draft).

			Regular Season					Playoffs				
Season	Club	League	GP	G	A	Pts	PIM	GP	G	A	Pts	PIM
2007-08	Toronto Marlboros	GTHL	51	39	42	81	4	....	....	....	....	....
2008-09	Niagara Ice Dogs	OHL	65	10	18	28	8	12	2	2	4	4
2009-10	Niagara Ice Dogs	OHL	64	25	30	55	12	5	1	1	2	6
2010-11	Niagara Ice Dogs	OHL	68	38	45	83	20	14	4	10	14	4
2011-12	Niagara Ice Dogs	OHL	61	35	51	86	31	20	7	17	24	9
2012-13	Worcester Sharks	AHL	76	13	13	26	16	....	....	....	....	....

HAMILTON, Wacey (HAM-ihl-tuhn, WAY-see) OTT

Center. Shoots left. 5'11", 185 lbs. Born, Calgary, Alta., September 10, 1990.

			Regular Season					Playoffs				
Season	Club	League	GP	G	A	Pts	PIM	GP	G	A	Pts	PIM
2006-07	Camrose Kodiaks	AJHL	49	11	6	17	38	5	1	1	2	8
2007-08	Medicine Hat	WHL	63	13	19	32	95	5	1	0	1	6
2008-09	Medicine Hat	WHL	37	4	13	17	64	11	1	3	4	24
2009-10	Medicine Hat	WHL	67	24	47	71	100	12	3	5	8	23
2010-11	Medicine Hat	WHL	67	20	53	73	113	15	4	8	12	20
2011-12	Binghamton	AHL	74	5	6	11	46	....	....	....	....	....
	Elmira Jackals	ECHL	2	0	2	2	2	....	....	....	....	....
2012-13	Binghamton	AHL	38	4	4	8	17	3	0	0	0	4

Signed as a free agent by **Ottawa**, March 8, 2011.

HANSEN, Jake (HAHN-suhn, JAYK) CBJ

Wing. Shoots right. 6'2", 189 lbs. Born, St.Paul, MN, August 21, 1989.
(Columbus' 4th choice, 68th overall, in 2007 Entry Draft).

			Regular Season					Playoffs				
Season	Club	League	GP	G	A	Pts	PIM	GP	G	A	Pts	PIM
2005-06	White Bear Lake	High-MN	STATISTICS NOT AVAILABLE									
2006-07	White Bear Lake	High-MN	25	28	43	71	....	....	....	....	....	....
	Sioux Falls	USHL	15	4	4	8	14	7	0	2	2	6
2007-08	Sioux Falls	USHL	60	31	27	58	57	3	1	0	1	0
2008-09	U. of Minnesota	WCHA	33	2	5	7	38	....	....	....	....	....
2009-10	U. of Minnesota	WCHA	38	7	5	12	20	....	....	....	....	....
2010-11	U. of Minnesota	WCHA	35	11	9	20	49	....	....	....	....	....
2011-12	U. of Minnesota	WCHA	43	16	22	38	58	....	....	....	....	....
	Springfield Falcons	AHL	2	0	1	1	0	....	....	....	....	....
2012-13	Springfield Falcons	AHL	46	4	5	9	26	3	0	0	0	0

USHL Second All-Star Team (2008)

HANSSON, Niklas (HAN-suhn, NIHK-luhs) DAL

Defense. Shoots right. 6'1", 175 lbs. Born, Helsingborg, Sweden, January 8, 1995.
(Dallas' 5th choice, 68th overall, in 2013 Entry Draft).

			Regular Season					Playoffs				
Season	Club	League	GP	G	A	Pts	PIM	GP	G	A	Pts	PIM
2010-11	Jonstorps IF U18	Swe-U18	2	0	0	0	0	....	....	....	....	....
	Jonstorps IF Jr.	Swe-Jr.	1	0	0	0	0	....	....	....	....	....
	Jonstorps IF	Sweden-4	18	0	2	2	2	....	....	....	....	....
	Rogle U18	Swe-U18	5	0	0	0	0	....	....	....	....	....
2011-12	Rogle U18	Swe-U18	33	3	28	31	14	5	1	3	4	0
	Rogle Jr.	Swe-Jr.	18	2	1	3	6	7	0	2	2	0
2012-13	Rogle U18	Swe-U18	7	3	3	6	4	3	0	1	1	0
	Rogle Jr.	Swe-Jr.	39	3	20	23	47	2	0	0	0	0
	Rogle	Sweden	9	0	0	0	4	....	....	....	....	....
	Rogle	Sweden-Q	6	0	1	1	0	....	....	....	....	....

HARGROVE, Colton (HAHR-grohv, KOHL-tuhn) BOS

Left wing. Shoots left. 6'1", 211 lbs. Born, Dallas, TX, June 25, 1992.
(Boston's 6th choice, 205th overall, in 2012 Entry Draft).

			Regular Season					Playoffs				
Season	Club	League	GP	G	A	Pts	PIM	GP	G	A	Pts	PIM
2009-10	Dallas Stars	T1EHL	16	5	6	11	16	....	....	....	....	....
	St.L. Amateur Blues	T1EHL	30	14	10	24	72	....	....	....	....	....
2010-11	Fargo Force	USHL	56	13	14	27	109	5	0	3	3	2
2011-12	Fargo Force	USHL	54	16	22	38	140	6	0	0	0	10
2012-13	Western Mich.	CCHA	32	9	1	10	29	....	....	....	....	....

HARPUR, Ben (HAHR-puhr, BEHN) OTT

Defense. Shoots left. 6'6", 210 lbs. Born, Hamilton, Ont., January 12, 1995.
(Ottawa's 4th choice, 108th overall, in 2013 Entry Draft).

			Regular Season					Playoffs				
Season	Club	League	GP	G	A	Pts	PIM	GP	G	A	Pts	PIM
2010-11	N.F. Canucks	Minor-ON	43	6	12	18	111	....	....	....	....	....
2011-12	Guelph Storm	OHL	34	1	3	4	22	....	....	....	....	....
2012-13	Guelph Storm	OHL	67	3	12	15	59	5	0	0	0	2

HARRINGTON, Scott (HAIR-ihng-tuhn, SKAWT) PIT

Defense. Shoots left. 6'2", 205 lbs. Born, Kingston, Ont., March 10, 1993.
(Pittsburgh's 2nd choice, 54th overall, in 2011 Entry Draft).

			Regular Season					Playoffs				
Season	Club	League	GP	G	A	Pts	PIM	GP	G	A	Pts	PIM
2008-09	King. Jr. Front.	Minor-ON	66	19	48	67	46	....	....	....	....	....
	Kingston	ON-Jr.A	2	1	0	1	2	18	1	6	7	6
2009-10	London Knights	OHL	55	1	13	14	20	12	0	2	2	4
2010-11	London Knights	OHL	67	6	16	22	51	6	0	1	1	0
2011-12	London Knights	OHL	44	3	23	26	32	19	1	6	7	6
2012-13	London Knights	OHL	50	3	16	19	26	17	0	4	4	14
	Wilkes-Barre	AHL	....	....	....	....	....	2	1	0	1	0

OHL All-Rookie Team (2010) • OHL First All-Star Team (2012, 2013)

HARRISON, Tim (HAIR-ih-suhn, TIHM) CGY

Right wing. Shoots right. 6'3", 175 lbs. Born, Duxbury, MA, January 11, 1994.
(Calgary's 6th choice, 157th overall, in 2013 Entry Draft).

			Regular Season					Playoffs				
Season	Club	League	GP	G	A	Pts	PIM	GP	G	A	Pts	PIM
2009-10	Duxbury	High-MA	....	2	5	7	....	....	....	....	....	....
2010-11	Duxbury	High-MA	....	9	9	18	....	....	....	....	....	....
2011-12	Dexter School	High-MA	21	13	13	26	....	....	....	....	....	....
2012-13	Dexter School	High-MA	28	24	27	51	....	....	....	....	....	....

• Signed Letter of Intent to attend **Colgate Univerisy** (ECAC) in fall of 2013.

HARSTAD, Aaron (HAHR-stad, AIR-uhn) WPG

Defense. Shoots left. 6'1", 200 lbs. Born, Stevens Point, WI, April 27, 1992.
(Winnipeg's 7th choice, 187th overall, in 2011 Entry Draft).

			Regular Season					Playoffs				
Season	Club	League	GP	G	A	Pts	PIM	GP	G	A	Pts	PIM
2008-09	Team Wisconsin	UMHSEL	3	0	2	2	6	....	....	....	....	....
	Stevens Point High	High-WI	18	22	19	41	....	....	....	....	....	....
	Green Bay	USHL	10	0	0	0	2	5	0	0	0	6
2009-10	Green Bay	USHL	47	2	6	8	61	11	0	3	3	9
2010-11	Green Bay	USHL	51	7	14	21	73	11	2	2	4	26
2011-12	Colorado College	WCHA	29	0	6	6	27	....	....	....	....	....
2012-13	Colorado College	WCHA	31	2	4	6	10	....	....	....	....	....

HART, Brian (HAHRT, BRIGH-uhn) T.B.

Right wing. Shoots right. 6'3", 215 lbs. Born, Cumberland, ME, November 25, 1993.
(Tampa Bay's 4th choice, 53rd overall, in 2012 Entry Draft).

			Regular Season					Playoffs				
Season	Club	League	GP	G	A	Pts	PIM	GP	G	A	Pts	PIM
2008-09	Greely Rangers	High-ME	20	28	21	39	....	....	....	....	....	....
2009-10	Brewster Academy	High-NH	28	27	24	51	....	....	....	....	....	....
2010-11	Exeter	High-NH	27	29	32	61	12	....	....	....	....	....
2011-12	Exeter	High-NH	29	31	34	65	20	....	....	....	....	....
2012-13	Harvard Crimson	ECAC	30	5	13	18	10	....	....	....	....	....

HARTMAN, Ryan (HAHRT-man, RIGH-uhn) CHI

Right wing. Shoots right. 5'11", 181 lbs. Born, Hilton Head Island, SC, September 20, 1994.
(Chicago's 1st choice, 30th overall, in 2013 Entry Draft).

			Regular Season					Playoffs				
Season	Club	League	GP	G	A	Pts	PIM	GP	G	A	Pts	PIM
2009-10	Chicago Mission	T1EHL	38	25	19	44	64	....	....	....	....	....
	Chicago Mission	Exhib.	25	21	30	51	....	....	....	....	....	....
2010-11	USNTDP	USHL	35	12	8	20	59	2	1	0	1	17
	USNTDP	U-17	17	9	5	14	12	....	....	....	....	....
	USNTDP	U-18	2	0	0	0	4	....	....	....	....	....
2011-12	USNTDP	USHL	24	7	9	16	46	....	....	....	....	....
	USNTDP	U-18	35	9	16	25	90	....	....	....	....	....
2012-13	Plymouth Whalers	OHL	56	23	37	60	120	9	4	2	6	16

HAULA, Erik (HOW-la, AIR-ihk) MIN

Left wing. Shoots left. 5'11", 192 lbs. Born, Pori, Finland, March 23, 1991.
(Minnesota's 7th choice, 182nd overall, in 2009 Entry Draft).

			Regular Season					Playoffs				
Season	Club	League	GP	G	A	Pts	PIM	GP	G	A	Pts	PIM
2006-07	Assat Pori U18	Fin-U18	29	19	24	43	24	6	1	3	4	4
2007-08	Assat Pori U18	Fin-U18	3	1	1	2	0	2	4	2	6	14
	Assat Pori Jr.	Fin-Jr.	40	7	15	22	26	12	2	0	2	4
2008-09	Shat.-St. Mary's	High-MN	53	26	58	84	46	....	....	....	....	....
2009-10	Omaha Lancers	USHL	56	28	44	72	59	8	2	9	11	2
2010-11	U. of Minnesota	WCHA	34	6	18	24	22	....	....	....	....	....
2011-12	U. of Minnesota	WCHA	43	20	29	49	30	....	....	....	....	....
2012-13	U. of Minnesota	WCHA	37	16	35	51	14	....	....	....	....	....
	Houston Aeros	AHL	6	0	2	2	2	5	1	1	2	4

USHL All-Rookie Team (2010) • USHL Second All-Star Team (2010) • WCHA Second All-Star Team (2013)

HAYDEN, John (HAY-duhn, JAWN) CHI

Center. Shoots right. 6'3", 210 lbs. Born, Chicago, IL, February 14, 1995.
(Chicago's 3rd choice, 74th overall, in 2013 Entry Draft).

			Regular Season					Playoffs				
Season	Club	League	GP	G	A	Pts	PIM	GP	G	A	Pts	PIM
2010-11	Brunswick Bruins	High-CT	26	21	9	30	....	....	....	....	....	....
2011-12	USNTDP	USHL	36	8	7	15	51	2	0	2	2	2
	USNTDP	U-17	17	3	6	9	12	....	....	....	....	....
2012-13	USNTDP	USHL	24	11	9	20	51	....	....	....	....	....
	USNTDP	U-18	29	6	8	14	29	....	....	....	....	....

• Signed Letter of Intent to attend **Yale University** (ECAC) in fall of 2013.

HAYES, Eriah (HAYZ, ee-RIGH-uh) S.J.

Right wing. Shoots right. 6'4", 210 lbs. Born, La Crescent, MN, July 7, 1988.

			Regular Season					Playoffs				
Season	Club	League	GP	G	A	Pts	PIM	GP	G	A	Pts	PIM
2007-08	Topeka	NAHL	53	30	26	56	61	12	5	5	10	6
2008-09	Waterloo	USHL	59	27	18	45	81	3	1	0	1	4
2009-10	Minnesota State	WCHA	38	8	6	14	59	....	....	....	....	....
2010-11	Minnesota State	WCHA	38	11	11	22	52	....	....	....	....	....
2011-12	Minnesota State	WCHA	36	13	11	24	83	....	....	....	....	....
2012-13	Minnesota State	WCHA	41	20	16	36	51	....	....	....	....	....
	Worcester Sharks	AHL	7	3	1	4	4	....	....	....	....	....

Signed as a free agent by **San Jose**, April 5, 2013.

HAYES, Kevin (HAYZ, KEH-vihn) CHI

Right wing. Shoots left. 6'2", 201 lbs. Born, Boston, MA, May 8, 1992.
(Chicago's 1st choice, 24th overall, in 2010 Entry Draft).

			Regular Season					Playoffs				
Season	Club	League	GP	G	A	Pts	PIM	GP	G	A	Pts	PIM
2007-08	Nobles	High-MA	29	8	5	13	2	....	....	....	....	....
2008-09	Nobles	High-MA	23	28	27	55	15	....	....	....	....	....
2009-10	Cape Cod Whalers	Minor-MA	25	21	30	51	....	....	....	....	....	....
	Nobles	High-MA	29	25	44	69	8	....	....	....	....	....
	USNTDP	U-18	2	2	0	2	0	....	....	....	....	....
2010-11	Boston College	H-East	31	4	10	14	8	....	....	....	....	....
2011-12	Boston College	H-East	44	7	21	28	10	....	....	....	....	....
2012-13	Boston College	H-East	27	6	19	25	14	....	....	....	....	....

HAZEN, Jonathan (HAY-zuhn, JAWN-ah-thuhn) FLA

Right wing. Shoots right. 6', 168 lbs. Born, Val Belair, Que., June 18, 1990.

			Regular Season					Playoffs				
Season	Club	League	GP	G	A	Pts	PIM	GP	G	A	Pts	PIM
2007-08	Val-d'Or Foreurs	QMJHL	65	21	19	40	25	4	2	1	3	0
2008-09	Val-d'Or Foreurs	QMJHL	62	20	25	45	26	....	....	....	....	....
2009-10	Val-d'Or Foreurs	QMJHL	53	24	35	59	59	6	2	1	3	2
2010-11	Val-d'Or Foreurs	QMJHL	62	41	42	83	29	1	0	0	0	5
2011-12	Cincinnati	ECHL	48	12	19	31	30	....	....	....	....	....
	San Antonio	AHL	9	1	0	1	0	....	....	....	....	....
2012-13	San Antonio	AHL	48	2	14	16	14	....	....	....	....	....
	Cincinnati	ECHL	12	6	4	10	5	....	....	....	....	....

Signed as a free agent by **Florida**, March 19, 2011.

HEARD, Mitchell (HUHRD, MIH-chuhl) COL

Center. Shoots left. 6'1", 188 lbs. Born, Bowmanville, Ont., March 12, 1992.
(Colorado's 1st choice, 41st overall, in 2012 Entry Draft).

			Regular Season					Playoffs				
Season	Club	League	GP	G	A	Pts	PIM	GP	G	A	Pts	PIM
2008-09	Clarington Toros	Minor-ON	36	....	....	31	48	....	....	....	....	....
2009-10	Bowmanville	ON-Jr.A	22	17	13	30	24	22	6	13	19	34
	Plymouth Whalers	OHL	16	2	1	3	4	....	....	....	....	....
2010-11	Plymouth Whalers	OHL	66	20	30	50	67	11	1	2	3	10
2011-12	Plymouth Whalers	OHL	57	29	28	57	111	13	4	7	11	26
2012-13	Plymouth Whalers	OHL	32	17	19	36	34	14	8	5	13	37
	Lake Erie Monsters	AHL	23	1	3	4	72	....	....	....	....	....

HEATHERINGTON, Dillon (HEH-thuhr-ihng-tuhn, DIH-luhn) CBJ

Defense. Shoots left. 6'3", 196 lbs. Born, Calgary, Alta., May 9, 1995.
(Columbus' 4th choice, 50th overall, in 2013 Entry Draft).

			Regular Season					Playoffs				
Season	Club	League	GP	G	A	Pts	PIM	GP	G	A	Pts	PIM
2010-11	Calgary Flames	AMHL	31	0	11	11	44	4	0	0	0	2
	Swift Current	WHL	1	0	0	0	0	....	....	....	....	....
2011-12	Swift Current	WHL	57	2	8	10	63	....	....	....	....	....
2012-13	Swift Current	WHL	71	4	23	27	80	5	0	3	3	0

HEINRICH, Blake (HIGHN-rihch, BLAYK) WSH

Defense. Shoots left. 5'11", 194 lbs. Born, Cambridge, MN, February 17, 1995.
(Washington's 4th choice, 144th overall, in 2013 Entry Draft).

			Regular Season					Playoffs				
Season	Club	League	GP	G	A	Pts	PIM	GP	G	A	Pts	PIM
2010-11	Hill-Murray	High-MN	28	4	16	20	18	....	....	....	....	....
2011-12	Team Northeast	UMHSEL	21	2	6	8	34	3	2	2	4	0
	Hill-Murray	High-MN	31	11	24	35	32	....	....	....	....	....
	Sioux City	USHL	1	0	1	1	0	....	....	....	....	....
2012-13	Sioux City	USHL	42	3	17	20	110	....	....	....	....	....

• Signed Letter of Intent to attend **University of Minnesota-Duluth** (WCHA) in fall of 2013.

HELGESEN, Kenton (HEHL-geh-suhn, KEHN-tuhn) ANA

Defense. Shoots left. 6'3", 188 lbs. Born, Grand Prarie, Alta., March 19, 1994.
(Anaheim's 7th choice, 187th overall, in 2012 Entry Draft).

			Regular Season					Playoffs				
Season	Club	League	GP	G	A	Pts	PIM	GP	G	A	Pts	PIM
2008-09	Grand Prairie	AMBHL	33	10	14	24	82	....	....	....	....	....
2009-10	Grand Prairie	AMHL	35	0	9	9	54	....	....	....	....	....
2010-11	Grande Prairie	AJHL	42	1	5	6	39	2	0	0	0	0
2011-12	Calgary Hitmen	WHL	58	3	11	14	63	5	0	0	0	2
2012-13	Calgary Hitmen	WHL	70	0	20	20	116	3	0	1	1	0

HELGESON, Seth (HEHL-guh-suhn, SEHTH) N.J.

Defense. Shoots left. 6'5", 215 lbs. Born, Faribault, MN, October 8, 1990.
(New Jersey's 4th choice, 114th overall, in 2009 Entry Draft).

			Regular Season					Playoffs				
Season	Club	League	GP	G	A	Pts	PIM	GP	G	A	Pts	PIM
2006-07	Faribault Falcons	High-MN	27	19	17	36	....	....	....	....	....	....
2007-08	Sioux City	USHL	58	3	8	11	41	4	0	1	1	2
2008-09	Sioux City	USHL	58	4	12	16	64	....	....	....	....	....
2009-10	U. of Minnesota	WCHA	31	1	0	1	24	....	....	....	....	....
2010-11	U. of Minnesota	WCHA	36	1	6	7	66	....	....	....	....	....
2011-12	U. of Minnesota	WCHA	43	5	9	14	70	....	....	....	....	....
2012-13	U. of Minnesota	WCHA	40	0	5	5	62	....	....	....	....	....
	Albany Devils	AHL	4	0	0	0	2	....	....	....	....	....

HERBERT, Caleb (HUHR-buhrt, KAY-lehb) WSH

Center. Shoots right. 5'11", 195 lbs. Born, St. Paul, MN, October 12, 1991.
(Washington's 4th choice, 142nd overall, in 2010 Entry Draft).

			Regular Season					Playoffs				
Season	Club	League	GP	G	A	Pts	PIM	GP	G	A	Pts	PIM
2007-08	Bloomington-Jeff.	High-MN	6	4	3	7	6	....	....	....	....	....
2008-09	Bloomington-Jeff.	High-MN	27	29	24	53	36	....	....	....	....	....
2009-10	Team Southeast	UMHSEL	24	14	8	22	....	....	....	....	....	....
	Bloomington-Jeff.	High-MN	25	26	28	54	42	3	4	4	8	2
2010-11	Sioux City	USHL	51	23	27	50	61	3	0	0	0	4
2011-12	U. Minn-Duluth	WCHA	41	14	19	33	30	....	....	....	....	....
2012-13	U. Minn-Duluth	WCHA	35	6	19	25	53	....	....	....	....	....

HERTL, Tomas (HUHR-tuhl, TAW-muhsh) S.J.

Center. Shoots left. 6'2", 210 lbs. Born, Prague, Czech Rep., November 12, 1993.
(San Jose's 1st choice, 17th overall, in 2012 Entry Draft).

			Regular Season					Playoffs				
Season	Club	League	GP	G	A	Pts	PIM	GP	G	A	Pts	PIM
2007-08	Slavia U17	CzR-U17	22	7	6	13	4	5	1	0	1	2
2008-09	Slavia U17	CzR-U17	35	16	15	31	12	8	5	2	7	4
2009-10	Slavia U18	CzR-U18	7	13	10	23	8	5	5	6	11	31
	HC Slavia Praha Jr.	CzRep-Jr.	42	12	26	38	12	4	1	0	1	2
2010-11	Slavia U18	CzR-U18	4	2	6	8	0	....	....	....	....	....
	HC Slavia Praha Jr.	CzRep-Jr.	33	14	27	41	49	4	4	2	6	0
	HC Slavia Praha	CzRep	1	0	0	0	0	....	....	....	....	....
2011-12	HC Slavia Praha	CzRep	50	15	13	28	28	....	....	....	....	....
	Usti nad Labem	CzRep-2	....	....	....	....	....	3	2	0	2	2
2012-13	HC Slavia Praha	CzRep	43	18	12	30	16	11	3	5	8	0

HERZOG, Fabrice (HUHR-tsawg, fah-BREES) TOR

Right wing. Shoots left. 6'2", 176 lbs. Born, Frauenfeld, Switz., December 9, 1994.
(Toronto's 3rd choice, 142nd overall, in 2013 Entry Draft).

			Regular Season					Playoffs				
Season	Club	League	GP	G	A	Pts	PIM	GP	G	A	Pts	PIM
2007-08	Oberthurgau II U17	Swiss-U17	8	6	3	9	4	....	....	....	....	....
2008-09	Oberthurgau U17	Swiss-U17	17	1	1	2	0	2	0	0	0	0
	SC Herisau U17	Swiss-U17	5	0	0	0	2	....	....	....	....	....
2009-10	Oberthurgau U17	Swiss-U17	32	6	7	13	12	6	6	0	6	6
2010-11	Oberthurgau U17	Swiss-U17	27	22	14	36	14	6	6	3	9	0
	Oberthurgau	Swiss-3	2	0	0	0	0	....	....	....	....	....
	Oberthurgau II U17	Swiss-5	1	0	1	1	2	....	....	....	....	....
2011-12	EV Zug Jr.	Swiss-Jr.	35	18	14	32	45	10	6	2	8	6
2012-13	EV Zug Jr.	Swiss-Jr.	32	28	17	45	26	4	3	2	5	2
	EV Zug	Swiss	20	2	2	4	6	....	....	....	....	....

HEXTALL, Brett (HEHX-tahl, BREHT) PHX

Center. Shoots right. 5'10", 185 lbs. Born, Philadelphia, PA, April 2, 1988.
(Phoenix's 7th choice, 159th overall, in 2008 Entry Draft).

			Regular Season					Playoffs				
Season	Club	League	GP	G	A	Pts	PIM	GP	G	A	Pts	PIM
2006-07	Penticton Vees	BCHL	59	18	27	45	156	11	2	2	4	8
2007-08	Penticton Vees	BCHL	54	24	48	72	52	15	*12	3	15	12
2008-09	North Dakota	WCHA	42	12	24	36	91	....	....	....	....	....
2009-10	North Dakota	WCHA	34	14	12	26	88	....	....	....	....	....
2010-11	North Dakota	WCHA	39	13	16	29	63	....	....	....	....	....
2011-12	Portland Pirates	AHL	72	7	8	15	59	....	....	....	....	....
2012-13	Portland Pirates	AHL	66	9	6	15	79	3	0	0	0	4

HINOSTROZA, Vincent (hihn-oh-STROH-za, VIHN-sihnt) CHI

Center. Shoots right. 5'9", 158 lbs. Born, Chicago, IL, April 3, 1994.
(Chicago's 6th choice, 169th overall, in 2012 Entry Draft).

			Regular Season					Playoffs				
Season	Club	League	GP	G	A	Pts	PIM	GP	G	A	Pts	PIM
2009-10	Chicago Mission	T1EHL	34	13	21	34	38	....	....	....	....	....
2010-11	Waterloo	USHL	50	8	14	22	36	....	....	....	....	....
2011-12	Waterloo	USHL	55	20	24	44	56	1	0	0	0	0
2012-13	Waterloo	USHL	46	25	35	60	14	5	4	3	7	8

• Signed Letter of Intent to attend **University of Notre Dame** (CCHA) in fall of 2013.

HISHON, Joey (HIHS-hawn, JOH-ee) COL

Center. Shoots left. 5'10", 175 lbs. Born, Stratford, Ont., October 20, 1991.
(Colorado's 1st choice, 17th overall, in 2010 Entry Draft).

			Regular Season					Playoffs				
Season	Club	League	GP	G	A	Pts	PIM	GP	G	A	Pts	PIM
2006-07	Stratford Warriors	Minor-ON	50	44	42	86	114	....	....	....	....	....
2007-08	Owen Sound	OHL	63	20	27	47	38	....	....	....	....	....
2008-09	Owen Sound	OHL	65	37	44	81	34	4	4	3	7	6
2009-10	Owen Sound	OHL	36	16	24	40	26	....	....	....	....	....
2010-11	Owen Sound	OHL	50	37	50	87	64	22	5	*19	*24	32
2011-12			DID NOT PLAY – INJURED									
2012-13	Lake Erie Monsters	AHL	9	1	5	6	2	....	....	....	....	....

OHL First All-Star Team (2011)

• Missed 2011-12 and majority of 2012-13 due to head injury in 2011 Memorial Cup.

HODGES, Steven (HAW-juhz, STEE-vehn) FLA

Center. Shoots left. 5'11", 178 lbs. Born, Yellowknife, NT, May 5, 1994.
(Florida's 2nd choice, 84th overall, in 2012 Entry Draft).

			Regular Season					Playoffs				
Season	Club	League	GP	G	A	Pts	PIM	GP	G	A	Pts	PIM
2008-09	South Delta Storm	Minor-BC	60	62	80	142	....	....	....	....	....	....
	Greater Van.	BCMML	1	0	0	0	0	....	....	....	....	....
2009-10	Fraser Valley	BCMML	37	17	17	34	84	....	....	....	....	....
	Chilliwack Bruins	WHL	5	0	2	2	0	....	....	....	....	....
2010-11	Chilliwack Bruins	WHL	58	5	6	11	44	3	0	0	0	0
2011-12	Victoria Royals	WHL	72	21	25	46	62	4	0	4	4	4
2012-13	Victoria Royals	WHL	60	28	23	51	67	6	2	4	6	2

HOEFFEL, Mike (HOH-fuhl, MIGHK) N.J.

Left wing. Shoots left. 6'4", 205 lbs. Born, North Oaks, MN, April 9, 1989.
(New Jersey's 1st choice, 57th overall, in 2007 Entry Draft).

			Regular Season					Playoffs				
Season	Club	League	GP	G	A	Pts	PIM	GP	G	A	Pts	PIM
2004-05	Hill-Murray	High-MN	26	24	19	43	10	....	....	....	....	....
2005-06	Hill-Murray	High-MN	30	27	46	73	20	....	....	....	....	....
2006-07	USNTDP	U-18	33	10	2	12	18	....	....	....	....	....
	USNTDP	NAHL	11	6	5	11	10	....	....	....	....	....
2007-08	U. of Minnesota	WCHA	45	9	10	19	22	....	....	....	....	....
2008-09	U. of Minnesota	WCHA	35	12	8	20	38	....	....	....	....	....
2009-10	U. of Minnesota	WCHA	34	14	10	24	22	....	....	....	....	....
2010-11	U. of Minnesota	WCHA	35	13	11	24	24	....	....	....	....	....
	Albany Devils	AHL	10	2	0	2	6	....	....	....	....	....
2011-12	Albany Devils	AHL	50	5	4	9	28	....	....	....	....	....
2012-13	Albany Devils	AHL	52	5	5	10	37	....	....	....	....	....

HOEFFLIN, Mirko (HOHF-lihn, MIHR-koh) CHI

Center. Shoots left. 6', 174 lbs. Born, Freiburg, Germany, June 18, 1992.
(Chicago's 8th choice, 151st overall, in 2010 Entry Draft).

			Regular Season					Playoffs				
Season	Club	League	GP	G	A	Pts	PIM	GP	G	A	Pts	PIM
2007-08	Heil./Mann. Jr.	Ger-Jr.	34	8	7	15	28	8	0	2	2	4
2008-09	Heil./Mann. Jr.	Ger-Jr.	36	14	30	44	26	8	6	8	14	0
2009-10	Heil./Mann. Jr.	Ger-Jr.	24	32	35	67	20	8	5	9	14	2
	Heilbronner Falken	German-2	18	0	3	3	0	5	0	0	0	2
2010-11	Quebec Remparts	QMJHL	54	14	31	45	16	15	4	10	14	12
2011-12	Acadie-Bathurst	QMJHL	59	18	24	42	30	6	2	2	4	2
2012-13	Adler Mannheim	Germany	35	3	4	7	10	....	....	....	....	....

HOFMANN, Gregory (HAWF-man, GREH-goh-ree) CAR

Center. Shoots left. 6', 178 lbs. Born, Tramelan, Switz., November 13, 1992.
(Carolina's 4th choice, 103rd overall, in 2011 Entry Draft).

			Regular Season					Playoffs				
Season	Club	League	GP	G	A	Pts	PIM	GP	G	A	Pts	PIM
2006-07	Chaux-de-Fonds Jr.	Swiss-Jr.	2	0	0	0	0	....	....	....	....	....
2007-08	HC Luzern U17	Swiss-U17	6	2	5	7	14	....	....	....	....	....
	Ambri U17	Swiss-U17	22	14	11	25	64	5	4	3	7	20
	Ambri Jr.	Swiss-Jr.	11	4	1	5	6	8	0	0	0	2
2008-09	Ambri U17	Swiss-U17	20	9	16	25	42	....	....	....	....	....
	Ambri Jr.	Swiss-Jr.	22	10	7	17	26	2	0	0	0	2
2009-10	Ambri Jr.	Swiss-Jr.	34	25	30	55	20	3	1	2	3	6
	HC Ambri-Piotta	Swiss	1	0	0	0	0	1	0	0	0	0
2010-11	Ambri Jr.	Swiss-Jr.	2	2	0	2	2	....	....	....	....	....
	HC Ambri-Piotta	Swiss	41	3	9	12	2	12	0	2	2	2
	HC Ambri-Piotta	Swiss-Q	....	....	....	....	....	5	1	2	3	2
2011-12	HC Ambri-Piotta	Swiss	34	5	1	6	6	8	1	0	1	0
	HC Ambri-Piotta	Swiss-Q	....	....	....	....	....	4	1	1	2	2
	Ambri Jr.	Swiss-Jr.	7	3	1	4	2	2	2	0	2	0
2012-13	HC Davos	Swiss	49	16	11	27	20	7	0	2	2	0

HOLL, Justin (HOHL, JUHS-tihn) CHI

Defense. Shoots right. 6'2", 170 lbs. Born, Edina, MN, January 30, 1992.
(Chicago's 3rd choice, 54th overall, in 2010 Entry Draft).

			Regular Season					Playoffs				
Season	Club	League	GP	G	A	Pts	PIM	GP	G	A	Pts	PIM
2007-08	Minnetonka High	High-MN	24	0	1	1	0	....	....	....	....	....
2008-09	Minnetonka High	High-MN	28	1	6	7	4	....	....	....	....	....
2009-10	Team Southwest	UMHSEL	STATISTICS NOT AVAILABLE									
	Minnetonka High	High-MN	25	17	14	31	8	6	3	3	6	0
2010-11	U. of Minnesota	WCHA	25	1	6	7	12	....	....	....	....	....
2011-12	U. of Minnesota	WCHA	43	3	8	11	34	....	....	....	....	....
2012-13	U. of Minnesota	WCHA	35	3	4	7	10	....	....	....	....	....

HOLLAND, Patrick (HAW-luhnd, PAT-rihk) MTL

Right wing. Shoots right. 6', 179 lbs. Born, Lethbridge, Alta., January 7, 1992.
(Calgary's 6th choice, 193rd overall, in 2010 Entry Draft).

			Regular Season					Playoffs				
Season	Club	League	GP	G	A	Pts	PIM	GP	G	A	Pts	PIM
2007-08	Leth. Hurricanes	Minor-AB	32	33	21	54	34	....	....	....	....	....
2008-09	Lethbridge	AMHL	34	17	28	45	20	7	5	11	16	2
	Lethbridge	Exhib.	6	5	3	8	0	....	....	....	....	....
	Tri-City Americans	WHL	1	0	0	0	0	....	....	....	....	....
2009-10	Tri-City Americans	WHL	59	16	20	36	14	22	3	7	10	10
2010-11	Tri-City Americans	WHL	71	22	40	62	24	10	4	4	8	2
2011-12	Tri-City Americans	WHL	72	25	84	109	48	14	6	13	19	22
2012-13	Tri-City Americans	WHL	2	0	1	1	0	....	....	....	....	....
	Hamilton Bulldogs	AHL	69	10	18	28	8	....	....	....	....	....

WHL West Second All-Star Team (2012)

Traded to **Montreal** by **Calgary** with Rene Bourque and Calgary's 2nd round choice (Zachary Fucale) in 2013 Entry Draft for Mike Cammalleri, Karri Ramo and Montreal's 5th round choice (Ryan Culkin) in 2012 Entry Draft, January 12, 2012.

HOLLAND, Rhett (HAW-luhnd, REHT) PHX

Defense. Shoots right. 6'2", 220 lbs. Born, Calgary, Alta., September 25, 1993.
(Phoenix's 4th choice, 102nd overall, in 2012 Entry Draft).

			Regular Season					Playoffs				
Season	Club	League	GP	G	A	Pts	PIM	GP	G	A	Pts	PIM
2007-08	Calgary Royals	AMBHL	33	0	5	5	75	3	0	0	0	0
2008-09	Calgary Royals	AMHL	30	1	3	4	66	4	0	0	0	0
2009-10	Okotoks Oilers	AJHL	57	3	8	11	91	7	0	1	1	6
2010-11	Okotoks Oilers	AJHL	31	2	9	11	117	....	....	....	....	....
2011-12	Okotoks Oilers	AJHL	47	3	7	10	223	8	0	1	1	18
2012-13	Michigan State	CCHA	3	0	0	0	15	....	....	....	....	....

HOLLOWAY, Bud (HAHL-OH-way, BUHD) L.A.

Left wing. Shoots right. 6', 201 lbs. Born, Wapella, Sask., March 1, 1988.
(Los Angeles' 5th choice, 86th overall, in 2006 Entry Draft).

			Regular Season					Playoffs				
Season	Club	League	GP	G	A	Pts	PIM	GP	G	A	Pts	PIM
2003-04	Yorkton Harvest	SMHL	43	15	21	36	22	....	....	....	....	....
	Seattle	WHL	2	0	0	0	0	....	....	....	....	....
2004-05	Seattle	WHL	67	4	11	15	27	12	0	1	1	0
2005-06	Seattle	WHL	72	21	13	34	18	7	3	2	5	4
2006-07	Seattle	WHL	71	27	38	65	50	11	3	3	6	8
2007-08	Seattle	WHL	70	43	40	83	55	12	5	5	10	4
2008-09	Manchester	AHL	38	7	5	12	6	....	....	....	....	....
	Ontario Reign	ECHL	23	14	8	22	8	7	5	9	14	8
2009-10	Manchester	AHL	75	19	28	47	26	16	7	7	14	9
2010-11	Manchester	AHL	78	28	33	61	58	7	4	7	11	10
2011-12	Skelleftea AIK	Sweden	55	21	28	49	32	19	10	*13	*23	4
2012-13	Skelleftea AIK	Sweden	55	20	*51	*71	36	13	4	5	9	18

Signed as a free agent by **Skelleftea** (Sweden), July 25, 2011.

HOLZAPFEL, Riley (HOHL-za-fehl, RIGH-lee) PIT

Center. Shoots left. 6'3", 190 lbs. Born, Regina, Sask., August 18, 1988.
(Atlanta's 2nd choice, 43rd overall, in 2006 Entry Draft).

			Regular Season					Playoffs				
Season	Club	League	GP	G	A	Pts	PIM	GP	G	A	Pts	PIM
2004-05	Moose Jaw	WHL	63	15	13	28	32	5	1	2	3	8
2005-06	Moose Jaw	WHL	64	19	38	57	46	22	7	9	16	20
2006-07	Moose Jaw	WHL	72	39	43	82	94	....	....	....	....	....
2007-08	Moose Jaw	WHL	49	18	23	41	43	6	3	5	8	12
	Chicago Wolves	AHL	1	0	0	0	0	....	....	....	....	....
2008-09	Chicago Wolves	AHL	73	13	19	32	38	....	....	....	....	....
2009-10	Chicago Wolves	AHL	60	7	16	23	30	14	0	3	3	6
2010-11	Chicago Wolves	AHL	68	12	15	27	20	....	....	....	....	....
2011-12	St. John's IceCaps	AHL	29	8	7	15	8	....	....	....	....	....
	Syracuse Crunch	AHL	28	8	14	22	34	4	0	1	1	4
2012-13	Wilkes-Barre	AHL	76	21	30	51	93	15	4	6	10	8

WHL East First All-Star Team (2007)

• Transferred to **Winnipeg** after **Atlanta** franchise relocated, June 21, 2011. Traded to **Anaheim** by **Winnipeg** for Maxime Macenauer, February 13, 2012. Signed as a free agent by **Pittsburgh**, July 1, 2012. Signed as a free agent by **Jonkoping** (Sweden), July 4, 2013.

HORVAT, Bo (HOHR-vat, BOH) VAN

Center. Shoots left. 6', 206 lbs. Born, London, Ont., April 5, 1995.
(Vancouver's 1st choice, 9th overall, in 2013 Entry Draft).

			Regular Season					Playoffs				
Season	Club	League	GP	G	A	Pts	PIM	GP	G	A	Pts	PIM
2010-11	Elgin-Middlesex	Minor-ON	30	30	31	61	12	12	5	7	12	4
	Elgin-Middlesex	Exhib.	32	14	38	52	8	....	....	....	....	....
	St. Thomas Stars	ON-Jr.B	5	1	3	4	0	7	3	3	6	0
2011-12	London Knights	OHL	64	11	19	30	8	18	1	3	4	0
2012-13	London Knights	OHL	67	33	28	61	29	21	*16	7	23	10

HOSTETTER, Tyler (HAWS-the-tuhr, TIGH-luhr) PHI

Defense. Shoots right. 6', 197 lbs. Born, Lancaster, PA, January 30, 1991.

			Regular Season					Playoffs				
Season	Club	League	GP	G	A	Pts	PIM	GP	G	A	Pts	PIM
2007-08	Erie Otters	OHL	57	1	10	11	31	....	....	....	....	....
2008-09	Erie Otters	OHL	61	6	17	23	49	5	1	1	2	2
2009-10	Erie Otters	OHL	59	2	24	26	37	4	0	1	1	2
2010-11	Erie Otters	OHL	36	6	17	23	17	7	2	2	4	2
	Adirondack	AHL	3	0	0	0	0	....	....	....	....	....
2011-12	Adirondack	AHL	7	0	0	0	0	....	....	....	....	....
	Trenton Titans	ECHL	34	7	7	14	22	....	....	....	....	....
2012-13	Trenton Titans	ECHL	38	0	16	16	37	....	....	....	....	....

Signed as a free agent by **Philadelphia**, September 21, 2009.

HOUCK, Jackson (HOWK, JAHK-suhn) EDM

Right wing. Shoots right. 6', 186 lbs. Born, North Vancouver, B.C., February 27, 1995.
(Edmonton's 5th choice, 94th overall, in 2013 Entry Draft).

			Regular Season					Playoffs				
Season	Club	League	GP	G	A	Pts	PIM	GP	G	A	Pts	PIM
2010-11	Van. NW Giants	BCMML	31	20	18	38	72	5	1	1	2	6
2011-12	Vancouver Giants	WHL	53	8	12	20	39	6	0	4	4	2
2012-13	Vancouver Giants	WHL	69	23	34	57	68	....	....	....	....	....

HOUSE, Tanner (HOWS, TA-nuhr)

Center. Shoots right. 6'1", 195 lbs. Born, Cochrane, Alta., April 27, 1986.

			Regular Season					Playoffs				
Season	Club	League	GP	G	A	Pts	PIM	GP	G	A	Pts	PIM
2002-03	Bow Valley	Minor-AB	STATISTICS NOT AVAILABLE									
	Canmore Eagles	AJHL	2	0	0	0	0	....	....	....	....	....
2003-04	Canmore Eagles	AJHL	58	13	19	32	48	....	....	....	....	....
2004-05	Canmore Eagles	AJHL	58	11	18	29	119	....	....	....	....	....
2005-06	Canmore Eagles	AJHL	10	0	2	2	14	....	....	....	....	....
	Penticton Vees	BCHL	52	14	17	31	36	15	5	4	9	11
2006-07	Penticton Vees	BCHL	58	14	55	69	69	13	4	6	10	12
2007-08	U. of Maine	H-East	29	1	10	11	12	....	....	....	....	....
2008-09	U. of Maine	H-East	39	10	14	24	24	....	....	....	....	....
2009-10	U. of Maine	H-East	35	18	21	39	29	....	....	....	....	....
2010-11	U. of Maine	H-East	35	10	25	35	56	....	....	....	....	....
	Oklahoma City	AHL	6	1	4	5	0	1	0	0	0	0
2011-12	Oklahoma City	AHL	68	8	12	20	31	14	1	2	3	7
2012-13	Oklahoma City	AHL	55	7	2	9	43	9	0	1	1	4

Signed as a free agent by **Edmonton**, March 19, 2011.

HOWSE, Ryan (HOWS, RIGH-uhn) CGY

Left wing. Shoots left. 5'11", 195 lbs. Born, Prince George, B.C., July 6, 1991.
(Calgary's 2nd choice, 74th overall, in 2009 Entry Draft).

			Regular Season					Playoffs				
Season	Club	League	GP	G	A	Pts	PIM	GP	G	A	Pts	PIM
2006-07	Cariboo Cougars	BCMML	30	21	16	37	40	....	....	....	....	....
	Chilliwack Bruins	WHL	5	1	0	1	2	1	0	0	0	0
2007-08	Chilliwack Bruins	WHL	54	10	7	17	12	4	1	1	2	2
2008-09	Chilliwack Bruins	WHL	61	31	13	44	12	....	....	....	....	....
2009-10	Chilliwack Bruins	WHL	72	47	25	72	27	6	5	1	6	2
2010-11	Chilliwack Bruins	WHL	70	51	32	83	40	5	1	0	1	2
2011-12	Abbotsford Heat	AHL	39	6	3	9	10	1	0	0	0	0
2012-13	Abbotsford Heat	AHL	20	0	1	1	6	....	....	....	....	....
	Utah Grizzlies	ECHL	20	2	7	9	12	2	1	0	1	0

WHL West Second All-Star Team (2011)

HRABARENKA, Raman (h'rab-ah-REHN-kah, rah-MAHN) N.J.

Defense. Shoots right. 6'4", 235 lbs. Born, Mogilev, Belarus, August 24, 1992.

			Regular Season					Playoffs				
Season	Club	League	GP	G	A	Pts	PIM	GP	G	A	Pts	PIM
2009-10	Phi. Revolution	EJHL	32	4	5	9	59	....	....	....	....	....
2010-11	Cape Breton	QMJHL	50	2	7	9	68	4	0	0	0	8
2011-12	Cape Breton	QMJHL	30	1	5	6	26	....	....	....	....	....
	Drummondville	QMJHL	27	3	11	14	29	4	2	1	3	6
2012-13	Albany Devils	AHL	34	1	4	5	18	....	....	....	....	....

Signed as a free agent by **Albany** (AHL), October 7, 2012. • Missed majority of 2012-13 as a healthy reserve. Signed as a free agent by **New Jersey**, July 12, 2013.

HRIVIK, Marek (huh-RIHV-ihk, MAIR-ehk) NYR

Left wing. Shoots left. 6'1", 195 lbs. Born, Zilina, Slovakia, August 28, 1991.

			Regular Season					Playoffs				
Season	Club	League	GP	G	A	Pts	PIM	GP	G	A	Pts	PIM
2007-08	MsHK Zilina Jr.	Slovak-Jr.	47	17	17	34	24	....	....	....	....	....
2009-10	Moncton Wildcats	QMJHL	66	26	29	55	14	21	5	12	17	8
2010-11	Moncton Wildcats	QMJHL	59	38	41	79	18	4	0	6	6	11
2011-12	Moncton Wildcats	QMJHL	54	29	41	70	8	4	1	2	3	0
	Connecticut Whale	AHL	8	1	0	1	0	9	5	4	9	10
2012-13	Connecticut Whale	AHL	40	7	19	26	10	....	....	....	....	....

Signed as a free agent by **NY Rangers**, May 30, 2012.

HUDON, Charles (OO-dawn, CHAR-uhz) MTL

Left wing. Shoots left. 5'10", 179 lbs. Born, Alma, Que., June 23, 1994.
(Montreal's 6th choice, 122nd overall, in 2012 Entry Draft).

			Regular Season					Playoffs				
Season	Club	League	GP	G	A	Pts	PIM	GP	G	A	Pts	PIM
2009-10	Saint-Eustache	QAAA	40	23	24	47	32	6	4	5	9	4
2010-11	Chicoutimi	QMJHL	63	23	37	60	42	4	0	3	3	4
2011-12	Chicoutimi	QMJHL	59	25	41	66	50	18	6	5	11	16
2012-13	Chicoutimi	QMJHL	56	30	41	71	66	6	5	5	10	8
	Hamilton Bulldogs	AHL	9	1	2	3	4	....	....	....	....	....

QMJHL All-Rookie Team (2011) • QMJHL Rookie of the Year (2011)

HUDON, Philippe (hoo-DAWN, fihl-EEP) DET

Center/Right wing. Shoots right. 6', 197 lbs. Born, Montreal, Que., April 15, 1993.
(Detroit's 6th choice, 145th overall, in 2011 Entry Draft).

			Regular Season					Playoffs				
Season	Club	League	GP	G	A	Pts	PIM	GP	G	A	Pts	PIM
2008-09	Choate-Rosemary	High-CT	24	8	12	20	....	....	....	....	....	....
2009-10	Choate-Rosemary	High-CT	20	9	11	20	....	....	....	....	....	....
2010-11	Choate-Rosemary	High-CT	22	10	10	20	44	....	....	....	....	....
2011-12	Victoriaville Tigres	QMJHL	34	3	2	5	29	4	0	0	0	2
2012-13	Victoriaville Tigres	QMJHL	65	15	20	35	63	9	6	1	7	6

HUGHES, Tommy (HEWZ, TAW-mee) NYR

Defense. Shoots right. 6'2", 215 lbs. Born, London, Ont., April 7, 1992.

			Regular Season					Playoffs				
Season	Club	League	GP	G	A	Pts	PIM	GP	G	A	Pts	PIM
2009-10	Lon. Knights Mid.	Minor-ON	27	5	15	20	38	10	3	5	8	12
	London Nationals	ON-Jr.B	2	0	0	0	0	....	....	....	....	....
	London Knights	OHL	7	0	0	0	0	....	....	....	....	....
2010-11	London Nationals	ON-Jr.B	24	2	11	13	54	....	....	....	....	....
	London Knights	OHL	39	0	6	6	39	6	0	0	0	12
2011-12	London Knights	OHL	56	2	8	10	64	19	1	3	4	20
2012-13	London Knights	OHL	67	1	15	16	66	20	1	1	2	19

Signed as a free agent by **NY Rangers**, April 1, 2013.

HUNT, Brad (HUHNT, BRAD) EDM

Defense. Shoots left. 5'9", 188 lbs. Born, Ridge Meadows, BC, August 24, 1988.

			Regular Season					Playoffs				
Season	Club	League	GP	G	A	Pts	PIM	GP	G	A	Pts	PIM
2005-06	Ridge Meadow	PIJHL	STATISTICS NOT AVAILABLE									
	Burnaby Express	BCHL	3	0	0	0	0	2	0	0	0	0
2006-07	Burnaby Express	BCHL	60	4	34	38	65	14	2	6	8	16
2007-08	Burnaby Express	BCHL	60	16	39	55	53	....	....	....	....	....
2008-09	Bemidji State	CHA	37	9	23	32	24	....	....	....	....	....
2009-10	Bemidji State	CHA	37	7	26	33	35	....	....	....	....	....
2010-11	Bemidji State	WCHA	38	3	18	21	33	....	....	....	....	....
2011-12	Bemidji State	WCHA	38	5	21	26	8	....	....	....	....	....
	Chicago Wolves	AHL	14	1	4	5	8	5	1	3	4	0
2012-13	Chicago Wolves	AHL	65	4	29	33	22	....	....	....	....	....

Signed as a free agent by **Edmonton**, July 6, 2013.

HURLEY, Connor (HUHR-lee, KAW-nuhr) BUF

Center. Shoots left. 6'1", 172 lbs. Born, Eagan, MN, September 15, 1995.
(Buffalo's 4th choice, 38th overall, in 2013 Entry Draft).

			Regular Season					Playoffs				
Season	Club	League	GP	G	A	Pts	PIM	GP	G	A	Pts	PIM
2011-12	Edina Hornets	High-MN	25	22	26	48	10	4	3	6	9	2
2012-13	Edina Hornets	High-MN	25	15	28	43	8	....	....	....	....	....
	Team Southwest	UMHSEL	11	3	13	16	12	....	....	....	....	....
	Muskegon	USHL	11	1	7	8	4	3	0	1	1	4
	USNTDP	U-18	10	1	1	2	4	....	....	....	....	....

• Signed Letter of Intent to attend **University of Notre Dame** (CCHA) in fall of 2014.

HUTTON, Ben (HUH-tuhn, BEHN) VAN

Defense. Shoots left. 6'2", 192 lbs. Born, Brockville, Ont., April 20, 1993.
(Vancouver's 3rd choice, 147th overall, in 2012 Entry Draft).

			Regular Season					Playoffs				
Season	Club	League	GP	G	A	Pts	PIM	GP	G	A	Pts	PIM
2008-09	Upper Canada	Minor-ON	54	6	21	27	20	....	....	....	....	....
	Kemptville 73's	ON-Jr.A	4	0	0	0	2	....	....	....	....	....
2009-10	Kemptville 73's	ON-Jr.A	60	16	18	34	6	4	0	0	0	2
2010-11	Kemptville 73's	ON-Jr.A	61	8	27	35	28	....	....	....	....	....
2011-12	Kemptville 73's	ON-Jr.A	35	7	20	27	25	....	....	....	....	....
	Nepean Raiders	ON-Jr.A	22	4	12	16	6	18	5	8	13	6
2012-13	U. of Maine	H-East	34	4	11	15	18	....	....	....	....	....

HYKA, Tomas (HEE-kuh, TAW-muhsh) L.A.

Right wing. Shoots right. 5'11", 160 lbs. Born, Mlada Boleslav, Czech Rep., March 23, 1993.
(Los Angeles' 4th choice, 171st overall, in 2012 Entry Draft).

			Regular Season					Playoffs				
Season	Club	League	GP	G	A	Pts	PIM	GP	G	A	Pts	PIM
2007-08	Ml. Boleslav U17	CzR-U17	20	0	2	2	2	1	0	0	0	0
2008-09	Ml. Boleslav U17	CzR-U17	42	28	21	49	18	2	1	0	1	2
2009-10	Ml. Boleslav U18	CzR-U18	46	34	24	58	46	2	1	1	2	0
	Ml. Boleslav Jr.	CzRep-Jr.	2	0	1	1	0	....	....	....	....	....
2010-11	Ml. Boleslav U18	CzR-U18	8	3	9	12	6	....	....	....	....	....
	Ml. Boleslav Jr.	CzRep-Jr.	38	14	17	31	10	....	....	....	....	....
	BK Mlada Boleslav	CzRep	14	1	0	1	6	....	....	....	....	....
2011-12	Gatineau	QMJHL	50	20	44	64	30	4	1	1	2	0
2012-13	Gatineau	QMJHL	49	20	34	54	24	10	2	2	4	8

HYMAN, Zach (HIGH-muhn, ZAK) FLA

Center. Shoots right. 6', 195 lbs. Born, Toronto, Ont., June 9, 1992.
(Florida's 11th choice, 123rd overall, in 2010 Entry Draft).

			Regular Season					Playoffs				
Season	Club	League	GP	G	A	Pts	PIM	GP	G	A	Pts	PIM
2008-09	Hamilton	ON-Jr.A	49	13	24	37	24	5	2	2	4	4
2009-10	Hamilton	ON-Jr.A	49	35	40	75	30	11	7	9	16	4
2010-11	Hamilton	ON-Jr.A	43	42	60	102	24	7	3	5	8	6
2011-12	U. of Michigan	CCHA	41	2	7	9	12	....	....	....	....	....
2012-13	U. of Michigan	CCHA	38	4	5	9	8	....	....	....	....	....

CJHL Player of the Year (2011)

IKONEN, Henri (EEH-koh-nehn, AWN-ree) T.B.

Left wing. Shoots left. 5'11", 188 lbs. Born, Savonlinna, Finland, April 17, 1994.
(Tampa Bay's 4th choice, 154th overall, in 2013 Entry Draft).

			Regular Season					Playoffs				
Season	Club	League	GP	G	A	Pts	PIM	GP	G	A	Pts	PIM
2008-09	SaPKo U18	Fin-U18	3	1	2	3	0	....	....	....	....	....
2009-10	SaPKo U18	Fin-U18	5	6	4	10	12	....	....	....	....	....
	SapKo Jr.	Fin-Jr.	14	13	8	21	8	4	3	0	3	4
2010-11	KalPa Kuopio U18	Fin-U18	10	5	6	11	28	4	1	3	4	0
	KalPa Kuopio Jr.	Fin-Jr.	33	9	13	22	10	....	....	....	....	....
2011-12	KalPa Kuopio U18	Fin-U18	6	6	9	15	2	....	....	....	....	....
	KalPa Kuopio Jr.	Fin-Jr.	37	17	28	45	18	9	8	6	14	2
	KalPa Kuopio	Finland	8	0	1	1	4	....	....	....	....	....
2012-13	Kingston	OHL	61	22	29	51	30	4	1	0	1	4

ILLO, Radoslav (IHL-oh, RAD-oh-slav) ANA

Center. Shoots left. 6', 195 lbs. Born, Povazska Bystrica, Czech., January 21, 1990.
(Anaheim's 6th choice, 136th overall, in 2009 Entry Draft).

			Regular Season					Playoffs				
Season	Club	League	GP	G	A	Pts	PIM	GP	G	A	Pts	PIM
2005-06	P. Bystrica U18	Svk-U18	4	1	1	2	2	....	....	....	....	....
2006-07	Bratislava U18	Svk-U18	26	9	14	23	12	....	....	....	....	....
2007-08	Hampton Roads	MJHL	....	48	38	86	....	....	....	....	....	....
2008-09	Tri-City Storm	USHL	47	21	12	33	37	....	....	....	....	....
2009-10	Tri-City Storm	USHL	50	24	19	43	56	1	1	0	1	0
2010-11	Bemidji State	WCHA	37	4	2	6	20	....	....	....	....	....
2011-12	Bemidji State	WCHA	30	7	10	17	21	....	....	....	....	....
2012-13	Bemidji State	WCHA	34	4	10	14	16	....	....	....	....	....

ISACKSON, Christian (IGH-zak-suhn, KRIHS-ch'yehn) **BUF**

Right wing. Shoots right. 6'1", 190 lbs. Born, Pine City, MN, January 20, 1992.
(Buffalo's 8th choice, 203rd overall, in 2010 Entry Draft).

			Regular Season					Playoffs				
Season	Club	League	GP	G	A	Pts	PIM	GP	G	A	Pts	PIM
2006-07	Saint Thomas	High-MN	31	6	12	18	....	....	....	....	....	....
2007-08	Saint Thomas	High-MN	31	22	34	56	....	....	....	....	....	....
2008-09	Saint Thomas	High-MN	27	18	39	57	....	....	....	....	....	....
2009-10	Team Southeast	UMHSEL	24	11	11	22	....	....	....	....	....	....
	Saint Thomas	High-MN	25	24	33	57	26	3	1	2	3	0
2010-11	Sioux Falls	USHL	58	17	27	44	31	10	3	5	8	8
2011-12	U. of Minnesota	WCHA	11	0	0	0	2	....	....	....	....	....
2012-13	U. of Minnesota	WCHA	40	4	16	20	20	....	....	....	....	....

JACKSON, Jacob (JAK-suhn, JAY-kuhb) **S.J.**

Center. Shoots left. 5'11", 190 lbs. Born, Maplewood, MN, December 5, 1994.
(San Jose's 6th choice, 201st overall, in 2013 Entry Draft).

			Regular Season					Playoffs				
Season	Club	League	GP	G	A	Pts	PIM	GP	G	A	Pts	PIM
2010-11	Tartan School	High-MN	25	15	10	25	18	1	1	0	1	0
2011-12	Tartan School	High-MN	25	24	19	43	28	2	1	0	1	2
2012-13	Tartan School	High-MN	25	29	27	56	10	....	....	....	....	....
	Team Northeast	UMHSEL	21	10	4	14	10	....	....	....	....	....
	Waterloo	USHL	2	1	0	1	0	....	....	....	....	....

• Signed Letter of Intent to attend **Michigan Tech University** (WCHA) in fall of 2014.

JACOBS, Colin (JAY-kuhbz, KAWL-ihn) **BUF**

Center. Shoots right. 6'1", 211 lbs. Born, Coppell, TX, January 20, 1993.
(Buffalo's 3rd choice, 107th overall, in 2011 Entry Draft).

			Regular Season					Playoffs				
Season	Club	League	GP	G	A	Pts	PIM	GP	G	A	Pts	PIM
2007-08	Dallas Ice Jets	Minor-TX	51	61	50	111	88	....	....	....	....	....
2008-09	Dallas Stars U16	Minor-TX	50	36	36	72	147	....	....	....	....	....
	Seattle	WHL	2	0	0	0	0	4	2	1	3	0
2009-10	Seattle	WHL	72	13	13	26	119	....	....	....	....	....
2010-11	Seattle	WHL	68	22	22	44	69	....	....	....	....	....
2011-12	Seattle	WHL	44	9	10	19	46	....	....	....	....	....
2012-13	Prince George	WHL	66	25	28	53	98	....	....	....	....	....
	Rochester	AHL	11	1	2	3	0	....	....	....	....	....

JANKOWSKI, Mark (jan-KOW-skee, MAHRK) **CGY**

Center. Shoots left. 6'3", 168 lbs. Born, Hamilton, Ont., September 13, 1994.
(Calgary's 1st choice, 21st overall, in 2012 Entry Draft).

			Regular Season					Playoffs				
Season	Club	League	GP	G	A	Pts	PIM	GP	G	A	Pts	PIM
2009-10	St. Cath. Falcons	Minor-ON	33	11	14	25	14	....	....	....	....	....
2010-11	Stanstead Coll.	MPHL	13	5	4	9	10	2	2	1	3	2
	Stanstead Coll.	High-QU	50	24	37	61	10	....	....	....	....	....
2011-12	Stanstead Coll.	MPHL	13	*19	11	*30	12	3	3	*4	*7	0
	Stanstead Coll.	High-QU	41	31	26	57	22	....	....	....	....	....
2012-13	Providence College	H-East	34	7	11	18	10	....	....	....	....	....

JANMARK-NYLEN, Mattias (YAN-mahrk-NEW-lehn, mah-TEE-uhs) **DET**

Center. Shoots left. 6'1", 189 lbs. Born, Stockholm, Sweden, December 8, 1992.
(Detroit's 4th choice, 79th overall, in 2013 Entry Draft).

			Regular Season					Playoffs				
Season	Club	League	GP	G	A	Pts	PIM	GP	G	A	Pts	PIM
2007-08	SDE U18	Swe-U18	15	3	4	7	10	....	....	....	....	....
2008-09	SDE U18	Swe-U18	22	16	21	37	36	....	....	....	....	....
	AIK IF Solna U18	Swe-U18	12	2	6	8	4	7	5	5	10	2
2009-10	AIK IF Solna U18	Swe-U18	33	13	22	35	12	1	0	0	0	0
	AIK IF Solna Jr.	Swe-Jr.	13	4	7	11	6	4	0	1	1	0
2010-11	AIK IF Solna Jr.	Swe-Jr.	40	11	17	28	34	....	....	....	....	....
2011-12	AIK Solna Jr.	Swe-Jr.	40	23	38	61	30	3	0	0	0	4
	AIK Solna	Sweden	18	0	0	0	2	3	0	0	0	0
2012-13	AIK Solna	Sweden	55	14	17	31	32	....	....	....	....	....

JARDINE, Sam (jar-DEEN, SAM) **CHI**

Defense. Shoots left. 6'1", 190 lbs. Born, Lacombe, Alta., August 12, 1993.
(Chicago's 9th choice, 169th overall, in 2011 Entry Draft).

			Regular Season					Playoffs				
Season	Club	League	GP	G	A	Pts	PIM	GP	G	A	Pts	PIM
2008-09	Red Deer Chiefs	Minor-AB	32	6	21	27	36	....	....	....	....	....
	Red Deer	AMHL	4	0	1	1	0	....	....	....	....	....
2009-10	Red Deer	AMHL	34	9	15	24	18	....	....	....	....	....
	Camrose Kodiaks	AJHL	3	0	0	0	2	....	....	....	....	....
2010-11	Camrose Kodiaks	AJHL	50	6	16	22	56	23	4	7	11	24
2011-12	Camrose Kodiaks	AJHL	51	11	19	30	83	4	0	2	2	19
2012-13	Ohio State	CCHA	28	0	7	7	48	....	....	....	....	....

JARNKROK, Calle (YAHRN-krohk, KAHL-leh) **DET**

Center. Shoots right. 5'11", 156 lbs. Born, Gavle, Sweden, September 25, 1991.
(Detroit's 2nd choice, 51st overall, in 2010 Entry Draft).

			Regular Season					Playoffs				
Season	Club	League	GP	G	A	Pts	PIM	GP	G	A	Pts	PIM
2007-08	Brynas U18	Swe-U18	13	4	4	8	4	5	0	1	1	0
	Brynas IF Gavle Jr.	Swe-Jr.	2	0	0	0	2	....	....	....	....	....
2008-09	Brynas U18	Swe-U18	7	5	7	12	12	2	0	1	1	2
	Brynas IF Gavle Jr.	Swe-Jr.	41	8	18	26	37	7	4	3	7	2
2009-10	Brynas IF Gavle Jr.	Swe-Jr.	19	11	20	31	30	2	0	1	1	0
	Brynas IF Gavle	Sweden	33	4	6	10	2	5	1	1	2	0
2010-11	Brynas IF Gavle	Sweden	49	11	16	27	4	3	3	0	3	2
2011-12	Brynas IF Gavle	Sweden	50	16	23	39	22	16	4	12	16	12
2012-13	Brynas IF Gavle	Sweden	53	13	29	42	12	4	0	0	0	6
	Grand Rapids	AHL	9	0	3	3	0	....	....	....	....	....

JARVINEN, Joonas (yar-VIH-nehen, YOH-nuhs) **NSH**

Defense. Shoots left. 6'3", 234 lbs. Born, Turku, Finland, January 5, 1989.

			Regular Season					Playoffs				
Season	Club	League	GP	G	A	Pts	PIM	GP	G	A	Pts	PIM
2004-05	TPS Turku U18	Fin-U18	2	0	0	0	2	....	....	....	....	....
2005-06	TPS Turku U18	Fin-U18	34	2	4	6	50	....	....	....	....	....
	TPS Turku Jr.	Fin-Jr.	2	0	0	0	0	....	....	....	....	....
2006-07	TPS Turku U18	Fin-U18	4	0	1	1	6	6	3	3	6	5
	TPS Turku Jr.	Fin-Jr.	37	2	4	6	26	5	2	1	3	2
2007-08	Suomi U20	Finland-2	3	0	0	0	2	....	....	....	....	....
	TPS Turku Jr.	Fin-Jr.	10	5	1	6	12	....	....	....	....	....
	TPS Turku	Finland	50	1	3	4	14	2	0	1	1	0
2008-09	Suomi U20	Finland-2	3	1	0	1	10	....	....	....	....	....
	TPS Turku Jr.	Fin-Jr.	3	1	1	2	4	1	0	0	0	2
	TPS Turku	Finland	53	1	0	1	16	8	1	0	1	6
2009-10	TPS Turku	Finland	50	2	3	5	70	15	1	3	4	16
2010-11	TPS Turku	Finland	50	4	7	11	85	....	....	....	....	....
2011-12	Pelicans Lahti	Finland	57	5	18	23	125	17	3	3	6	16
2012-13	Milwaukee	AHL	75	2	9	11	124	4	0	0	0	2

Signed as a free agent by **Nashville**, May 30, 2012.

JEAN, Kyle (JEEN, KIGHL) **NYR**

Left wing. Shoots left. 6'4", 203 lbs. Born, Sault Ste. Marie, MI, March 1, 1990.

			Regular Season					Playoffs				
Season	Club	League	GP	G	A	Pts	PIM	GP	G	A	Pts	PIM
2007-08	Traverse City	NAHL	26	5	1	6	24	....	....	....	....	....
	Marquette	NAHL	16	2	3	5	6	....	....	....	....	....
2008-09	Traverse City	NAHL	58	22	21	43	77	....	....	....	....	....
2009-10	Traverse City	NAHL	34	15	11	26	47	....	....	....	....	....
2010-11	Lake Superior	CCHA	38	1	13	14	45	....	....	....	....	....
2011-12	Lake Superior	CCHA	39	12	12	24	54	....	....	....	....	....
2012-13	Connecticut Whale	AHL	73	9	14	23	47	....	....	....	....	....

Signed as a free agent by **NY Rangers**, July 5, 2012.

JENNER, Boone (JEH-nuhr, BOON) **CBJ**

Center. Shoots left. 6'2", 202 lbs. Born, Dorchester, Ont., June 15, 1993.
(Columbus' 1st choice, 37th overall, in 2011 Entry Draft).

			Regular Season					Playoffs				
Season	Club	League	GP	G	A	Pts	PIM	GP	G	A	Pts	PIM
2008-09	Elgin-Mid. Chiefs	Minor-ON	54	49	54	103	72	15	10	19	29	22
	St. Thomas Stars	ON-Jr.B	4	0	0	0	16	....	....	....	....	....
2009-10	Oshawa Generals	OHL	65	19	30	49	91	....	....	....	....	....
2010-11	Oshawa Generals	OHL	63	25	41	66	57	10	7	5	12	14
2011-12	Oshawa Generals	OHL	43	22	27	49	59	6	4	7	11	10
	Springfield Falcons	AHL	5	1	0	1	2	....	....	....	....	....
2012-13	Oshawa Generals	OHL	56	45	37	82	58	9	2	6	8	8
	Springfield Falcons	AHL	5	3	1	4	0	8	2	3	5	8

OHL All-Rookie Team (2010)

JENSEN, Nick (JEHN-suhn, NIHK) **DET**

Defense. Shoots right. 6'1", 187 lbs. Born, St. Paul, MN, September 21, 1990.
(Detroit's 5th choice, 150th overall, in 2009 Entry Draft).

			Regular Season					Playoffs				
Season	Club	League	GP	G	A	Pts	PIM	GP	G	A	Pts	PIM
2006-07	Rogers Royals	High-MN	21	20	17	37	....	....	....	....	....	....
2007-08	Rogers Royals	High-MN	14	14	13	27	....	....	....	....	....	....
2008-09	Green Bay	USHL	52	5	17	22	27	7	0	1	1	2
2009-10	Green Bay	USHL	53	6	21	27	35	12	2	6	8	6
2010-11	St. Cloud State	WCHA	38	5	18	23	18	....	....	....	....	....
2011-12	St. Cloud State	WCHA	39	6	26	32	4	....	....	....	....	....
2012-13	St. Cloud State	WCHA	42	4	27	31	14	....	....	....	....	....

WCHA First All-Star Team (2013) • NCAA West First All-American Team (2013)

JOBKE, Colton (JAWB-kee, KOHL-tuhn) **MIN**

Defense. Shoots left. 6'1", 190 lbs. Born, Vancouver, B.C., April 20, 1992.

			Regular Season					Playoffs				
Season	Club	League	GP	G	A	Pts	PIM	GP	G	A	Pts	PIM
2007-08	Greater Van.	BCMML	38	4	10	14	24	....	....	....	....	....
2008-09	Penticton Vees	BCHL	46	3	8	11	11	5	0	0	0	2
2009-10	Kelowna Rockets	WHL	69	0	8	8	71	12	0	4	4	14
2010-11	Kelowna Rockets	WHL	51	1	9	10	84	9	0	0	0	7
2011-12	Regina Pats	WHL	71	10	19	29	104	5	0	0	0	10
	Houston Aeros	AHL	2	0	0	0	0	....	....	....	....	....
2012-13	Regina Pats	WHL	31	3	15	18	58	....	....	....	....	....
	Orlando	ECHL	3	0	0	0	10	....	....	....	....	....

Signed as a free agent by **Minnesota**, September 23, 2010.

JOHNS, Stephen (JAWNZ, STEE-vehn) **CHI**

Defense. Shoots right. 6'3", 215 lbs. Born, Ellwood City, PA, April 18, 1992.
(Chicago's 5th choice, 60th overall, in 2010 Entry Draft).

			Regular Season					Playoffs				
Season	Club	League	GP	G	A	Pts	PIM	GP	G	A	Pts	PIM
2007-08	Pittsburgh Hornets	MWEHL	26	4	7	11	24	....	....	....	....	....
	Pittsburgh Hornets	Minor-PA	50	12	22	34	46	....	....	....	....	....
2008-09	USNTDP	NAHL	31	3	5	8	30	....	....	....	....	....
	USNTDP	U-17	16	2	6	8	20	....	....	....	....	....
2009-10	USNTDP	USHL	23	1	7	8	29	....	....	....	....	....
	USNTDP	U-18	39	2	9	11	38	....	....	....	....	....
2010-11	U. of Notre Dame	CCHA	44	2	11	13	*98	....	....	....	....	....
2011-12	U. of Notre Dame	CCHA	39	4	6	10	71	....	....	....	....	....
2012-13	U. of Notre Dame	CCHA	41	1	13	14	62	....	....	....	....	....

JOHNSON, Andreas (YAWN-suhn, ahn-DRAY-uhs) **TOR**

Left wing. Shoots left. 5'10", 172 lbs. Born, Gavle, Sweden, November 21, 1994.
(Toronto's 5th choice, 202nd overall, in 2013 Entry Draft).

			Regular Season					Playoffs				
Season	Club	League	GP	G	A	Pts	PIM	GP	G	A	Pts	PIM
2009-10	Frolunda U18	Swe-U18	5	1	1	2	0	....	....	....	....	....
2010-11	Frolunda U18	Swe-U18	27	23	22	45	26	5	3	1	4	2
	Frolunda Jr.	Swe-Jr.	30	9	5	14	4	3	0	1	1	0
2011-12	Frolunda U18	Swe-U18	6	9	5	14	4	4	2	4	6	4
	Frolunda Jr.	Swe-Jr.	42	19	13	32	75	2	0	0	0	0
2012-13	Frolunda Jr.	Swe-Jr.	42	23	31	54	54	4	1	1	2	12
	Frolunda	Sweden	7	1	0	1	0	5	0	0	0	0

JOHNSON, Ben (JAWN-suhn, BEHN) N.J.

Center/Left wing. Shoots left. 5'11", 190 lbs. Born, Hancock, MI, June 7, 1994.
(New Jersey's 3rd choice, 90th overall, in 2012 Entry Draft).

			Regular Season					Playoffs				
Season	**Club**	**League**	**GP**	**G**	**A**	**Pts**	**PIM**	**GP**	**G**	**A**	**Pts**	**PIM**
2009-10	Calumet High	High-MI	....	....	....	59	....	....	....	....	....	....
	Ojibway Eagles	Minor-MI	21	8	11	19	....	....	....	....	....	....
	Marquette	Minor-MI	2	0	1	1	2	....	....	....	....	....
2010-11	Calumet High	High-MI	30	37	40	77	....	....	....	....	....	....
	Little Caesars	T1EHL	13	3	2	5	16	....	....	....	....	....
	Det. Little Caesars	Exhib.	9	3	1	4	0	....	....	....	....	....
	Fargo Force	USHL	5	0	0	0	2	....	....	....	....	....
	USNTDP	USHL	2	1	0	1	0	....	....	....	....	....
	USNTDP	U-17	2	3	1	4	0	....	....	....	....	....
2011-12	Windsor Spitfires	OHL	68	18	20	38	44	4	0	2	2	0
2012-13	Windsor Spitfires	OHL	64	20	17	37	32	....	....	....	....	....

JOHNSON, Luke (JAWN-suhn, LOOK) CHI

Center. Shoots right. 5'11", 179 lbs. Born, Grand Forks, ND, September 19, 1994.
(Chicago's 6th choice, 134th overall, in 2013 Entry Draft).

			Regular Season					Playoffs				
Season	**Club**	**League**	**GP**	**G**	**A**	**Pts**	**PIM**	**GP**	**G**	**A**	**Pts**	**PIM**
2008-09	Gr. Forks R.R.R.	High-ND	27	9	17	26	....	....	....	....	....	....
2009-10	Grand Forks C.K.	High-ND	27	17	29	46	....	....	....	....	....	....
2010-11	Team Great Plains	UMHSEL	20	9	12	21	26	3	0	1	1	0
	Grand Forks C.K.	High-ND	25	17	25	42	....	....	....	....	....	....
2011-12	Lincoln Stars	USHL	55	20	35	55	52	8	1	1	2	2
2012-13	Lincoln Stars	USHL	57	19	27	46	32	5	0	0	0	0

• Signed Letter of Intent to attend **University of North Dakota** (WCHA) in fall of 2013.

JOHNSTON, Andrew (JAWN-stuhn, AN-droo) PHI

Left wing. Shoots left. 6'1", 178 lbs. Born, Saskatoon, Sask., July 6, 1991.

			Regular Season					Playoffs				
Season	**Club**	**League**	**GP**	**G**	**A**	**Pts**	**PIM**	**GP**	**G**	**A**	**Pts**	**PIM**
2007-08	Sask. Contacts	SMHL	40	10	9	19	42	3	1	1	2	0
	Flin Flon Bombers	SJHL	4	0	0	0	2	....	....	....	....	....
2008-09	Sask. Contacts	SMHL	43	13	26	39	48	10	15	10	25	8
2009-10	Flin Flon Bombers	SJHL	56	15	28	43	46	6	1	1	2	4
2010-11	Flin Flon Bombers	SJHL	57	34	32	66	61	9	6	3	9	8
2011-12	Humboldt Broncos	SJHL	58	29	52	81	39	16	10	4	14	28
2012-13	Adirondack	AHL	29	2	3	5	5	....	....	....	....	....
	Trenton Titans	ECHL	18	3	8	11	8	....	....	....	....	....

Signed as a free agent by **Philadelphia**, May 21, 2012.

JOKIPAKKA, Jyrki (yoh-kih-PA-ka, YUHR-kee) DAL

Defense. Shoots left. 6'3", 191 lbs. Born, Tampere, Finland, August 20, 1991.
(Dallas' 6th choice, 195th overall, in 2011 Entry Draft).

			Regular Season					Playoffs				
Season	**Club**	**League**	**GP**	**G**	**A**	**Pts**	**PIM**	**GP**	**G**	**A**	**Pts**	**PIM**
2007-08	Ilves Tampere U17	Fin-U17	24	6	15	21	26	2	1	1	2	0
2008-09	Ilves Tampere U18	Fin-U18	33	4	7	11	12	....	....	....	....	....
	Ilves Tampere Jr.	Fin-Jr.	4	0	0	0	2	....	....	....	....	....
2009-10	Ilves Tampere Jr.	Fin-Jr.	38	3	12	15	77	5	1	0	1	2
2010-11	Suomi U20	Finland-2	6	0	3	3	2	....	....	....	....	....
	Ilves Tampere Jr.	Fin-Jr.	3	0	0	0	6	2	0	0	0	2
	LeKi Lempaala	Finland-2	1	0	0	0	0	....	....	....	....	....
	Ilves Tampere	Finland	48	1	8	9	18	5	0	0	0	2
2011-12	Ilves Tampere Jr.	Fin-Jr.	1	0	1	1	2	....	....	....	....	....
	LeKi Lempaala	Finland-2	3	1	0	1	0	....	....	....	....	....
	Ilves Tampere	Finland	52	9	8	17	18	....	....	....	....	....
	Ilves Tampere	Finland-Q	....	....	....	....	....	5	0	2	2	2
2012-13	Ilves Tampere	Finland	59	5	13	18	20	....	....	....	....	....
	Ilves Tampere	Finland-Q	....	....	....	....	....	5	0	0	0	0

JONES, Kellen (JOHNZ, KEHL-ehn) EDM

Forward. Shoots left. 5'9", 164 lbs. Born, Montrose, B.C., August 16, 1990.
(Edmonton's 11th choice, 202nd overall, in 2010 Entry Draft).

			Regular Season					Playoffs				
Season	**Club**	**League**	**GP**	**G**	**A**	**Pts**	**PIM**	**GP**	**G**	**A**	**Pts**	**PIM**
2006-07	Beaver Valley	KIJHL	50	32	35	67	48	13	8	4	12	6
	Vernon Vipers	BCHL	2	0	1	1	0	16	3	5	8	8
2007-08	Vernon Vipers	BCHL	60	12	55	67	30	10	7	4	11	8
2008-09	Vernon Vipers	BCHL	51	15	37	52	16	17	6	12	18	8
2009-10	Vernon Vipers	BCHL	41	12	41	53	18	19	5	14	19	14
2010-11	Quinnipiac	ECAC	38	8	14	22	33	....	....	....	....	....
2011-12	Quinnipiac	ECAC	36	14	22	36	39	....	....	....	....	....
2012-13	Quinnipiac	ECAC	43	13	14	27	24	....	....	....	....	....

JONES, Seth (JOHNZ, SEHTH) NSH

Defense. Shoots right. 6'5", 210 lbs. Born, Arlington, TX, October 3, 1994.
(Nashville's 1st choice, 4th overall, in 2013 Entry Draft).

			Regular Season					Playoffs				
Season	**Club**	**League**	**GP**	**G**	**A**	**Pts**	**PIM**	**GP**	**G**	**A**	**Pts**	**PIM**
2009-10	Dallas Stars	T1EHL	42	5	13	18	20	....	....	....	....	....
2010-11	USNTDP	USHL	28	1	13	14	20	....	....	....	....	....
	USNTDP	U-17	17	3	7	10	8	....	....	....	....	....
	USNTDP	U-18	12	0	7	7	4	....	....	....	....	....
2011-12	USNTDP	USHL	20	4	8	12	6	....	....	....	....	....
	USNTDP	U-18	32	4	15	19	12	....	....	....	....	....
2012-13	Portland	WHL	61	14	42	56	33	21	5	10	15	4

WHL West First All-Star Team (2013) • WHL Rookie of the Year (2013) • Canadian Major Junior Top Prospect of the Year (2013)

JOORIS, Josh (JUHR-his, JAWSH) CGY

Right wing. Shoots right. 6'1", 190 lbs. Born, Burlington, Ont., July 14, 1990.

			Regular Season					Playoffs				
Season	**Club**	**League**	**GP**	**G**	**A**	**Pts**	**PIM**	**GP**	**G**	**A**	**Pts**	**PIM**
2008-09	Burlington	ON-Jr.A	42	8	26	34	36	8	1	7	8	12
2009-10	Burlington	ON-Jr.A	50	26	*90	*116	42	12	5	10	15	10
2010-11	Union College	ECAC	40	9	23	32	18	....	....	....	....	....
2011-12	Union College	ECAC	38	8	20	28	30	....	....	....	....	....
2012-13	Union College	ECAC	39	12	16	28	46	....	....	....	....	....

Signed as a free agent by **Calgary**, July 30, 2013.

JORG, Mauro (YOHRG, MAHW-roh) N.J.

Left wing. Shoots left. 6', 200 lbs. Born, Chur, Switz., April 29, 1990.
(New Jersey's 5th choice, 204th overall, in 2010 Entry Draft).

			Regular Season					Playoffs				
Season	**Club**	**League**	**GP**	**G**	**A**	**Pts**	**PIM**	**GP**	**G**	**A**	**Pts**	**PIM**
2006-07	HC Lugano Jr.	Swiss-Jr.	4	2	3	5	6	....	....	....	....	....
	EHC Arosa	Swiss-3	7	4	1	5	8	1	0	0	0	2
	EHC Chur	Swiss-2	20	1	1	2	0	....	....	....	....	....
2007-08	Switzerland U20	Swiss-2	1	0	0	0	0	....	....	....	....	....
	EHC Chur Jr.	Swiss-Jr.	4	4	1	5	18	....	....	....	....	....
	EHC Chur	Swiss-2	40	11	9	20	33	....	....	....	....	....
	HC Lugano Jr.	Swiss-Jr.	8	5	2	7	12	....	....	....	....	....
	HC Lugano	Swiss	....	....	....	....	....	1	0	0	0	0
2008-09	Switzerland U20	Swiss-2	5	1	0	1	0	....	....	....	....	....
	HC Lugano	Swiss	47	3	3	6	6	7	0	0	0	0
	HC Ceresio Lugano	Swiss-3	1	0	0	0	0	....	....	....	....	....
	HC Lugano Jr.	Swiss-Jr.	3	0	3	3	0	2	0	3	3	4
2009-10	HC Lugano	Swiss	44	1	7	8	14	4	0	0	0	0
	HC Lugano Jr.	Swiss-Jr.	1	0	0	0	0	....	....	....	....	....
	EHC Visp	Swiss-2	....	....	....	....	....	7	0	1	1	0
2010-11	HC Lugano	Swiss	50	3	9	12	26	4	0	0	0	2
2011-12	HC Lugano	Swiss	48	4	3	7	8	6	0	2	2	0
	Sierre	Swiss-2	2	3	1	4	2	....	....	....	....	....
2012-13	Rapperswil	Swiss	48	4	6	10	10	12	0	4	4	4

JOSEPHS, Troy (JOH-sehfs, TROI) PIT

Center. Shoots left. 5'11", 176 lbs. Born, Whitby, Ont., May 9, 1994.
(Pittsburgh's 6th choice, 209th overall, in 2013 Entry Draft).

			Regular Season					Playoffs				
Season	**Club**	**League**	**GP**	**G**	**A**	**Pts**	**PIM**	**GP**	**G**	**A**	**Pts**	**PIM**
2009-10	Whitby Wildcats	Minor-ON	70	27	25	52	52	4	0	0	0	6
2010-11	PEAC Panthers	High-ON	52	29	38	67	38	....	....	....	....	....
	Pickering Panthers	ON-Jr.A	7	4	1	5	4	....	....	....	....	....
2011-12	St. Michael's	ON-Jr.A	41	11	13	24	10	5	0	0	0	2
2012-13	St. Michael's	ON-Jr.A	42	17	20	37	64	24	7	13	20	38

• Signed Letter of Intent to attend **Clarkson University** (ECAC) in fall of 2013.

JURCO, Tomas (YUHR-koh, TAW-mahsh) DET

Right wing. Shoots left. 6'2", 193 lbs. Born, Kosice, Czech., December 28, 1992.
(Detroit's 1st choice, 35th overall, in 2011 Entry Draft).

			Regular Season					Playoffs				
Season	**Club**	**League**	**GP**	**G**	**A**	**Pts**	**PIM**	**GP**	**G**	**A**	**Pts**	**PIM**
2007-08	HC Kosice U18	Svk-U18	57	28	24	52	30	....	....	....	....	....
2008-09	HC Kosice U18	Svk-U18	5	8	5	13	2	....	....	....	....	....
	HC Kosice Jr.	Slovak-Jr.	48	19	30	49	20	3	5	0	5	0
2009-10	Saint John	QMJHL	64	26	25	51	24	21	7	10	17	8
2010-11	Saint John	QMJHL	60	31	25	56	17	19	6	12	18	8
2011-12	Saint John	QMJHL	48	30	38	68	37	16	13	16	29	12
2012-13	Grand Rapids	AHL	74	14	14	28	22	24	8	6	14	21

KABANOV, Kirill (kuh-BAH-nawf, kih-RIHL) NYI

Left wing. Shoots right. 6'2", 192 lbs. Born, Moscow, Russia, July 16, 1992.
(NY Islanders' 3rd choice, 65th overall, in 2010 Entry Draft).

			Regular Season					Playoffs				
Season	**Club**	**League**	**GP**	**G**	**A**	**Pts**	**PIM**	**GP**	**G**	**A**	**Pts**	**PIM**
2008-09	Spartak Moscow	KHL	6	0	0	0	2	5	0	0	0	0
	Spartak Moscow 2	Russia-3	STATISTICS NOT AVAILABLE									
2009-10	Moncton Wildcats	QMJHL	22	10	13	23	34	1	0	0	0	2
2010-11	Moncton Wildcats	QMJHL	2	0	0	0	6	....	....	....	....	....
	Lewiston	QMJHL	37	11	17	28	38	15	8	12	20	18
2011-12	Shawinigan	QMJHL	50	21	34	55	42	11	4	9	13	12
2012-13	Bridgeport	AHL	32	2	7	9	27	....	....	....	....	....

KANTOR, Michael (KAN-tohr, MIGH-kuhl) NYR

Right wing. Shoots right. 6'1", 196 lbs. Born, Lake Forest, IL, February 2, 1992.

			Regular Season					Playoffs				
Season	**Club**	**League**	**GP**	**G**	**A**	**Pts**	**PIM**	**GP**	**G**	**A**	**Pts**	**PIM**
2009-10	Albert Lea	NAHL	24	2	3	5	108	....	....	....	....	....
	Saginaw Spirit	OHL	29	4	8	12	71	6	0	0	0	10
2010-11	Saginaw Spirit	OHL	35	8	5	13	85	....	....	....	....	....
	Sault Ste. Marie	OHL	17	3	4	7	35	....	....	....	....	....
2011-12	Sault Ste. Marie	OHL	34	2	8	10	76	....	....	....	....	....
	Sudbury Wolves	OHL	26	6	13	19	60	....	....	....	....	....
2012-13	Sudbury Wolves	OHL	56	20	13	33	93	9	2	2	4	12

Signed to an ATO (amateur tryout) contract by **Connecticut** (AHL), April 16, 2013. Signed as a free agent by **NY Rangers**, April 20, 2013.

KANZIG, Keegan (KAN-zihg, KEE-guhn) CGY

Defense. Shoots left. 6'7", 241 lbs. Born, Athabasca, Alta., February 26, 1995.
(Calgary's 4th choice, 67th overall, in 2013 Entry Draft).

			Regular Season					Playoffs				
Season	**Club**	**League**	**GP**	**G**	**A**	**Pts**	**PIM**	**GP**	**G**	**A**	**Pts**	**PIM**
2010-11	Ft. Saskatchewan	AMHL	31	4	8	12	82	3	0	0	0	18
2011-12	Victoria Royals	WHL	63	0	2	2	66	4	0	0	0	8
2012-13	Victoria Royals	WHL	70	0	7	7	159	6	1	0	1	10

KARLSSON, Erik (KAHRL-suhn, AIR-ihk) CAR

Center/Left wing. Shoots left. 6', 170 lbs. Born, Lerum, Sweden, July 28, 1994.
(Carolina's 4th choice, 99th overall, in 2012 Entry Draft).

			Regular Season					Playoffs				
Season	**Club**	**League**	**GP**	**G**	**A**	**Pts**	**PIM**	**GP**	**G**	**A**	**Pts**	**PIM**
2009-10	Frolunda U18	Swe-U18	13	2	3	5	2	1	0	0	0	27
2010-11	Frolunda U18	Swe-U18	26	20	22	42	12	4	1	1	2	4
	Frolunda Jr.	Swe-Jr.	29	4	9	13	41	7	1	1	2	4
2011-12	Frolunda U18	Swe-U18	4	3	7	10	8	4	2	3	5	4
	Frolunda Jr.	Swe-Jr.	47	14	19	33	70	2	0	0	0	0
2012-13	Frolunda	Sweden	5	0	0	0	0	....	....	....	....	....
	Karlskrona HK	Sweden-2	2	0	1	1	0	....	....	....	....	....
	Frolunda Jr.	Swe-Jr.	40	10	25	35	48	6	1	5	6	0

KARLSSON, Ludwig (KAHRL-suhn, LOOD-wihg) OTT

Left wing. Shoots left. 6'3", 200 lbs. Born, Stockholm, Sweden, January 6, 1991.

			Regular Season					Playoffs				
Season	Club	League	GP	G	A	Pts	PIM	GP	G	A	Pts	PIM
2009-10	Green Bay	USHL	58	8	21	29	16	12	1	2	3	2
2010-11	Green Bay	USHL	56	13	25	38	14	11	2	3	5	0
2011-12	Northeastern	H-East	32	10	16	26	8	....	....	....	....	....
2012-13	Northeastern	H-East	17	5	3	8	4	....	....	....	....	....

Signed as a free agent by **Ottawa**, July 25, 2013.

KARLSSON, William (KARL-suhn, WIHL-yuhm) ANA

Center. Shoots left. 6'1", 179 lbs. Born, Marsta, Sweden, January 8, 1993.
(Anaheim's 3rd choice, 53rd overall, in 2011 Entry Draft).

			Regular Season					Playoffs				
Season	Club	League	GP	G	A	Pts	PIM	GP	G	A	Pts	PIM
2007-08	Arlanda U18	Swe-U18	5	2	7	9	4	....	....	....	....	....
2008-09	Arlanda U18	Swe-U18	33	10	18	28	16	....	....	....	....	....
2009-10	Vasteras U18	Swe-U18	39	23	21	44	62	....	....	....	....	....
	Vasteras Jr.	Swe-Jr.	6	0	1	1	2	2	0	1	1	0
2010-11	Vasteras U18	Swe-U18	11	5	9	14	10	6	7	8	15	2
	Vasteras Jr.	Swe-Jr.	38	20	34	54	45	....	....	....	....	....
	VIK Vasteras HK	Sweden-2	14	1	3	4	2	....	....	....	....	....
2011-12	VIK Vasteras HK	Sweden-2	52	13	34	47	6	....	....	....	....	....
	Vasteras Jr.	Swe-Jr.	....	....	....	....	....	5	2	2	4	2
2012-13	HV 71 Jonkoping	Sweden	50	4	24	28	12	5	0	2	2	0
	HV 71 Jr.	Swe-Jr.	....	....	....	....	....	2	2	2	4	2

KARLSTROM, Marcus (KAHRL-struhm, MAHR-kuhs) WPG

Defense. Shoots right. 6'3", 181 lbs. Born, Sweden, Sweden, January 6, 1995.
(Winnipeg's 10th choice, 194th overall, in 2013 Entry Draft).

			Regular Season					Playoffs				
Season	Club	League	GP	G	A	Pts	PIM	GP	G	A	Pts	PIM
2010-11	SDE U18	Swe-U18	3	0	1	1	2	....	....	....	....	....
2011-12	AIK Solna U18	Swe-U18	38	1	7	8	20	....	....	....	....	....
2012-13	AIK Solna U18	Swe-U18	40	14	30	44	38	5	0	1	1	2
	AIK Solna Jr.	Swe-Jr.	5	1	0	1	0	....	....	....	....	....

KEA, Justin (KEE-a, JUHS-tihn) BUF

Center. Shoots left. 6'4", 213 lbs. Born, Port Perry, Ont., February 7, 1994.
(Buffalo's 4th choice, 73rd overall, in 2012 Entry Draft).

			Regular Season					Playoffs				
Season	Club	League	GP	G	A	Pts	PIM	GP	G	A	Pts	PIM
2009-10	Cent. Ont. Wolves	Minor-ON	51	22	22	44	44	....	....	....	....	....
2010-11	Saginaw Spirit	OHL	62	4	2	6	49	10	0	1	1	0
2011-12	Saginaw Spirit	OHL	65	3	11	14	76	12	1	4	5	2
2012-13	Saginaw Spirit	OHL	68	22	26	48	102	4	1	0	1	7

KELLY, Dan (KEHL-lee, DAN) N.J.

Defense. Shoots left. 6'1", 205 lbs. Born, Morrisonville, NY, May 17, 1989.

			Regular Season					Playoffs				
Season	Club	League	GP	G	A	Pts	PIM	GP	G	A	Pts	PIM
2003-04	Beekmantown	High-NY	STATISTICS NOT AVAILABLE									
2004-05	Pembroke	ON-Jr.A	50	2	12	14	80	11	0	1	1	2
2005-06	Pembroke	ON-Jr.A	46	2	15	17	95	11	0	3	3	18
	Kitchener Rangers	OHL	9	0	3	3	8	....	....	....	....	....
2006-07	Kitchener Rangers	OHL	59	0	19	19	79	9	1	1	2	10
2007-08	Kitchener Rangers	OHL	65	1	17	18	61	8	0	2	2	4
2008-09	Kitchener Rangers	OHL	44	4	11	15	30	....	....	....	....	....
2009-10	Kitchener Rangers	OHL	58	6	21	27	99	20	4	9	13	23
2010-11	Albany Devils	AHL	61	2	5	7	71	....	....	....	....	....
2011-12	Albany Devils	AHL	54	2	4	6	93	....	....	....	....	....
2012-13	Albany Devils	AHL	47	2	6	8	62	....	....	....	....	....

Signed as a free agent by **New Jersey**, May 19, 2010.

KENINS, Ronalds (CHEHN-ihsh, RAWN-uhlds) VAN

Left wing. Shoots left. 6', 201 lbs. Born, Riga, Latvia, February 28, 1991.

			Regular Season					Playoffs				
Season	Club	League	GP	G	A	Pts	PIM	GP	G	A	Pts	PIM
2008-09	GC Kusnacht Jr.	Swiss-Jr.	6	6	6	12	6	....	....	....	....	....
	GCK Lions Zurich	Swiss-2	42	2	8	10	24	....	....	....	....	....
2009-10	GCK Zurich Jr.	Swiss-Jr.	30	13	18	31	38	9	0	4	4	10
	GCK Lions Zurich	Swiss-2	4	1	3	4	4	....	....	....	....	....
2010-11	GCK Zurich Jr.	Swiss-Jr.	18	7	14	21	45	11	7	13	20	24
	GCK Lions Zurich	Swiss-2	11	1	2	3	8	....	....	....	....	....
2011-12	ZSC Lions Zurich	Swiss	47	6	12	18	48	15	0	4	4	6
2012-13	ZSC Lions Zurich	Swiss	45	3	14	17	12	12	4	4	8	10

Signed as a free agent by **Vancouver**, July 30, 2013.

KERDILES, Nicolas (kair-DEE-lihs, NIH-koh-las) ANA

Left wing. Shoots left. 6'2", 200 lbs. Born, Lewisville, TX, January 11, 1994.
(Anaheim's 2nd choice, 36th overall, in 2012 Entry Draft).

			Regular Season					Playoffs				
Season	Club	League	GP	G	A	Pts	PIM	GP	G	A	Pts	PIM
2009-10	L.A. Selects	T1EHL	37	25	29	54	48	....	....	....	....	....
	L.A. Selects	Exhib.	31	40	27	67	30	....	....	....	....	....
2010-11	USNTDP	USHL	32	12	8	20	52	....	....	....	....	....
	USNTDP	U-17	14	7	5	12	12	....	....	....	....	....
	USNTDP	U-18	14	1	4	5	2	....	....	....	....	....
2011-12	USNTDP	USHL	18	4	9	13	18	....	....	....	....	....
	USNTDP	U-18	36	18	17	35	20	....	....	....	....	....
2012-13	U. of Wisconsin	WCHA	32	11	22	33	37	....	....	....	....	....

KERFOOT, Alexander (KUHR-fut, al-ehx-AN-duhr) N.J.

Center. Shoots left. 5'10", 155 lbs. Born, Vancouver, B.C., August 11, 1994.
(New Jersey's 6th choice, 150th overall, in 2012 Entry Draft).

			Regular Season					Playoffs				
Season	Club	League	GP	G	A	Pts	PIM	GP	G	A	Pts	PIM
2009-10	Van. NW Giants	BCMML	26	7	14	21	4	....	....	....	....	....
2010-11	Van. NW Giants	BCMML	38	36	*72	*108	58	5	6	6	*12	6
	Coquitlam Express	BCHL	5	0	0	0	0	1	0	0	0	0
2011-12	Coquitlam Express	BCHL	51	25	44	69	24	6	4	0	4	6
2012-13	Coquitlam Express	BCHL	16	8	11	19	16	....	....	....	....	....

KESSY, Kale (KEH-see, KAYL) EDM

Left wing. Shoots left. 6'2", 200 lbs. Born, Shaunavon, Sask., December 4, 1992.
(Phoenix's 5th choice, 111th overall, in 2011 Entry Draft).

			Regular Season					Playoffs				
Season	Club	League	GP	G	A	Pts	PIM	GP	G	A	Pts	PIM
2008-09	Medicine Hat	AMHL	33	17	12	29	42	....	....	....	....	....
	Medicine Hat	WHL	9	0	0	0	2	....	....	....	....	....
2009-10	Medicine Hat	WHL	70	11	18	29	123	12	1	3	4	10
2010-11	Medicine Hat	WHL	65	10	14	24	129	14	3	3	6	37
2011-12	Medicine Hat	WHL	49	4	12	16	151	2	0	1	1	2
2012-13	Medicine Hat	WHL	2	2	0	2	17	....	....	....	....	....
	Vancouver Giants	WHL	27	7	9	16	45	....	....	....	....	....
	Kamloops Blazers	WHL	31	12	13	25	44	15	11	3	14	21

Traded to **Edmonton** by **Phoenix** for Tobias Rieder, March 30, 2013.

KHAIRA, Jujhar (KAIR-a, JOO-jahr) EDM

Left wing. Shoots left. 6'3", 198 lbs. Born, Surrey, B.C., August 13, 1994.
(Edmonton's 3rd choice, 63rd overall, in 2012 Entry Draft).

			Regular Season					Playoffs				
Season	Club	League	GP	G	A	Pts	PIM	GP	G	A	Pts	PIM
2009-10	Cloverdale Colts	Minor-BC	STATISTICS NOT AVAILABLE									
2010-11	Prince George	BCHL	58	10	32	42	21	....	....	....	....	....
2011-12	Prince George	BCHL	54	29	50	79	69	4	0	2	2	2
2012-13	Michigan Tech	WCHA	37	6	19	25	49	....	....	....	....	....

KHOKHLACHEV, Alexander (khohkh-luh-CHAWV, al-ehx-AHN-duhr) BOS

Center. Shoots left. 5'11", 184 lbs. Born, Moscow, Russia, September 9, 1993.
(Boston's 2nd choice, 40th overall, in 2011 Entry Draft).

			Regular Season					Playoffs				
Season	Club	League	GP	G	A	Pts	PIM	GP	G	A	Pts	PIM
2009-10	Spartak Jr.	Russia-Jr.	51	15	25	40	22	....	....	....	....	....
2010-11	Windsor Spitfires	OHL	67	34	42	76	28	18	9	11	20	8
2011-12	Windsor Spitfires	OHL	56	25	44	69	32	....	....	....	....	....
2012-13	Spartak Moscow	KHL	26	2	5	7	20	....	....	....	....	....
	Windsor Spitfires	OHL	29	22	26	48	20	....	....	....	....	....
	Providence Bruins	AHL	11	2	1	3	8	....	....	....	....	....

Signed as a free agent by **Spartak Moscow** (KHL), July 1, 2012.

KICHTON, Brenden (KIHCH-tuhn, BREHN-duhn) WPG

Defense. Shoots right. 6', 189 lbs. Born, Edmonton, Alta., June 18, 1992.
(Winnipeg's 9th choice, 190th overall, in 2013 Entry Draft).

			Regular Season					Playoffs				
Season	Club	League	GP	G	A	Pts	PIM	GP	G	A	Pts	PIM
2007-08	St. Albert	AMHL	35	10	16	26	14	1	0	0	0	2
2008-09	Spokane Chiefs	WHL	57	1	8	9	12	8	0	0	0	0
2009-10	Spokane Chiefs	WHL	70	4	15	19	21	7	0	0	0	4
2010-11	Spokane Chiefs	WHL	64	23	58	81	31	17	1	10	11	2
2011-12	Spokane Chiefs	WHL	71	17	57	74	49	1	0	1	1	0
2012-13	Spokane Chiefs	WHL	71	22	63	85	30	9	2	5	7	6

• Re-entered NHL Entry Draft. Originally NY Islanders' 7th choice, 127th overall, in 2011 Entry Draft.

WHL West Second All-Star Team (2011) • WHL West First All-Star Team (2012, 2013)

KING, Tristan (KIHNG, TRIHS-tuhn) DAL

Center. Shoots right. 6', 183 lbs. Born, Elk River, MN, November 7, 1990.

			Regular Season					Playoffs				
Season	Club	League	GP	G	A	Pts	PIM	GP	G	A	Pts	PIM
2006-07	Portland	WHL	64	6	9	15	26	....	....	....	....	....
2007-08	Portland	WHL	69	9	16	25	39	....	....	....	....	....
2008-09	Medicine Hat	WHL	47	14	22	36	33	2	0	0	0	0
2009-10	Medicine Hat	WHL	70	21	44	65	65	12	3	3	6	12
2010-11	Texas Stars	AHL	11	2	2	4	6	....	....	....	....	....
	Idaho Steelheads	ECHL	24	3	10	13	13	6	2	1	3	0
2011-12	Idaho Steelheads	ECHL	4	1	0	1	2	....	....	....	....	....
	Greenville	ECHL	1	0	0	0	0	....	....	....	....	....
	Ontario Reign	ECHL	45	17	24	41	38	3	0	2	2	2
2012-13	Idaho Steelheads	ECHL	35	18	19	37	30	....	....	....	....	....
	San Francisco Bulls	ECHL	17	4	4	8	6	2	0	0	0	0

Signed as a free agent by **Dallas**, September 18, 2009.

KITSYN, Maxim (KIHT-sihn, max-EEM) L.A.

Left wing. Shoots right. 6'2", 194 lbs. Born, Novokuznetsk, USSR, December 24, 1991.
(Los Angeles' 5th choice, 158th overall, in 2010 Entry Draft).

			Regular Season					Playoffs				
Season	Club	League	GP	G	A	Pts	PIM	GP	G	A	Pts	PIM
2007-08	Novokuznetsk 2	Russia-3	4	1	0	1	0	....	....	....	....	....
2008-09	Novokuznetsk 2	Russia-3	STATISTICS NOT AVAILABLE									
	Novokuznetsk	KHL	31	5	2	7	26	....	....	....	....	....
2009-10	Novokuznetsk Jr.	Russia-Jr.	11	6	12	18	26	17	9	12	21	42
	Novokuznetsk	KHL	21	1	1	2	12	....	....	....	....	....
2010-11	Novokuznetsk Jr.	Russia-Jr.	3	1	1	2	2	....	....	....	....	....
	Novokuznetsk	KHL	18	3	4	7	8	....	....	....	....	....
	St. Michael's	OHL	32	9	17	26	24	20	10	9	19	14
2011-12	Novokuznetsk	KHL	32	1	2	3	13	....	....	....	....	....
	Yermak Angarsk	Russia-2	6	2	2	4	0	4	0	0	0	4
	Novokuznetsk Jr.	Russia-Jr.	10	7	1	8	10	7	3	3	6	8
2012-13	Nizhny Novgorod	KHL	8	0	0	0	4	1	0	0	0	2
	HK Sarov	Russia-2	29	9	3	12	63	5	1	1	2	4

KIVIHALME, Teemu (kih-vih-HAHL-meh, TEE-moo) NSH

Defense. Shoots left. 5'11", 158 lbs. Born, Cloquet, MN, June 17, 1995.
(Nashville's 6th choice, 140th overall, in 2013 Entry Draft).

			Regular Season					Playoffs				
Season	Club	League	GP	G	A	Pts	PIM	GP	G	A	Pts	PIM
2010-11	Burnsville Blaze	High-MN	27	3	11	14	12	2	0	0	0	0
	Team North	UMHSEL	5	0	0	0	2	....	....	....	....	....
2011-12	Burnsville Blaze	High-MN	25	8	21	29	25	3	1	1	2	0
	Team Southeast	UMHSEL	2	1	0	1	0	....	....	....	....	....
2012-13	Team Southeast	UMHSEL	20	3	4	7	8	....	....	....	....	....
	Burnsville Blaze	High-MN	25	9	21	30	22	....	....	....	....	....
	Fargo Force	USHL	4	0	1	1	0	....	....	....	....	....

• Signed Letter of Intent to attend **Colorado College** (WCHA) in fall of 2014.

KIVISTO, Tommi (K'VIHS-toh, TAW-mee) CAR

Defense. Shoots left. 6'2", 200 lbs. Born, Vantaa, Finland, June 7, 1991.
(Carolina's 6th choice, 208th overall, in 2009 Entry Draft).

			Regular Season					Playoffs				
Season	**Club**	**League**	**GP**	**G**	**A**	**Pts**	**PIM**	**GP**	**G**	**A**	**Pts**	**PIM**
2006-07	Jokerit U18	Fin-U18	24	0	2	2	10	....	....	....	....	....
2007-08	Jokerit U18	Fin-U18	26	6	10	16	50	4	0	3	3	4
	Jokerit Helsinki Jr.	Fin-Jr.	9	2	0	2	4	4	0	3	3	2
2008-09	Red Deer Rebels	WHL	65	1	21	22	49	....	....	....	....	....
2009-10	Suomi U20	Finland-2	2	0	0	0	2	....	....	....	....	....
	Jokerit Helsinki	Finland	22	0	2	2	12	3	0	0	0	0
	Kiekko-Vantaa	Finland-2	2	0	0	0	2	....	....	....	....	....
	Jokerit Helsinki Jr.	Fin-Jr.	18	2	5	7	58	2	0	0	0	0
2010-11	Suomi U20	Finland-2	4	0	1	1	0	....	....	....	....	....
	Jokerit Helsinki Jr.	Fin-Jr.	5	0	6	6	8	....	....	....	....	....
	Kiekko-Vantaa	Finland-2	5	1	2	3	0	....	....	....	....	....
	Jokerit Helsinki	Finland	38	0	5	5	22	7	0	0	0	16
2011-12	Jokerit Helsinki	Finland	26	0	4	4	8	....	....	....	....	....
	Kiekko-Vantaa	Finland-2	20	5	7	12	22	4	1	1	2	2
2012-13	Charlotte	AHL	17	0	2	2	12	....	....	....	....	....
	Florida Everblades	ECHL	48	4	11	15	59	12	1	5	6	18

KLEFBOM, Oscar (KLEHF-bawm, AWS-kuhr) EDM

Defense. Shoots left. 6'3", 204 lbs. Born, Karlstad, Sweden, July 20, 1993.
(Edmonton's 2nd choice, 19th overall, in 2011 Entry Draft).

			Regular Season					Playoffs				
Season	**Club**	**League**	**GP**	**G**	**A**	**Pts**	**PIM**	**GP**	**G**	**A**	**Pts**	**PIM**
2008-09	Farjestad U18	Swe-U18	15	2	2	4	4	4	0	1	1	2
2009-10	Farjestad U18	Swe-U18	31	10	18	28	37	6	0	0	0	0
	IFK Munkfors	Sweden-3	3	0	1	1	0	....	....	....	....	....
	Skare BK	Sweden-3	2	0	0	0	2	....	....	....	....	....
2010-11	Farjestad U18	Swe-U18	8	3	3	6	2	....	....	....	....	....
	Skare BK	Sweden-3	12	0	1	1	0	....	....	....	....	....
	Farjestad	Sweden	23	1	1	2	2	....	....	....	....	....
2011-12	Farjestad Jr.	Swe-Jr.	15	1	3	4	0	....	....	....	....	....
	Farjestad	Sweden	33	2	0	2	4	11	0	1	1	2
2012-13	Farjestad	Sweden	11	0	3	3	2	....	....	....	....	....

KLIMCHUK, Morgan (KLIHM-chuhk, MOHR-guhn) CGY

Left wing. Shoots left. 5'11", 180 lbs. Born, Regina, Sask., March 2, 1995.
(Calgary's 3rd choice, 28th overall, in 2013 Entry Draft).

			Regular Season					Playoffs				
Season	**Club**	**League**	**GP**	**G**	**A**	**Pts**	**PIM**	**GP**	**G**	**A**	**Pts**	**PIM**
2010-11	Calgary Buffaloes	AMHL	32	27	23	50	12	2	0	0	0	0
	Regina Pats	WHL	5	0	1	1	0	....	....	....	....	....
2011-12	Regina Pats	WHL	67	18	18	36	27	5	0	1	1	2
2012-13	Regina Pats	WHL	72	36	40	76	20	....	....	....	....	....

KLINGBERG, John (KLIHNG-buhrg, JAWN) DAL

Defense. Shoots right. 6', 158 lbs. Born, Lerum, Sweden, August 14, 1992.
(Dallas' 5th choice, 131st overall, in 2010 Entry Draft).

			Regular Season					Playoffs				
Season	**Club**	**League**	**GP**	**G**	**A**	**Pts**	**PIM**	**GP**	**G**	**A**	**Pts**	**PIM**
2008-09	Frolunda U18	Swe-U18	30	3	12	15	12	3	0	0	0	0
2009-10	Frolunda U18	Swe-U18	20	3	13	16	22	7	2	9	11	10
	Frolunda Jr.	Swe-Jr.	27	0	5	5	32	5	1	0	1	6
2010-11	Frolunda	Sweden	26	0	5	5	10	....	....	....	....	....
	Boras HC	Sweden-2	7	1	0	1	2	....	....	....	....	....
	Frolunda Jr.	Swe-Jr.	13	3	14	17	29	7	1	10	11	6
2011-12	Jokerit Helsinki	Finland	20	1	2	3	8	....	....	....	....	....
	Skelleftea AIK	Sweden	16	1	3	4	6	16	0	4	4	14
2012-13	Skelleftea AIK Jr.	Swe-Jr.	1	0	0	0	0	....	....	....	....	....
	Skelleftea AIK	Sweden	25	1	12	13	6	13	1	3	4	8
	Texas Stars	AHL	....	....	....	....	....	1	0	0	0	0

Signed as a free agent by **Frolunda** (Sweden), May 20, 2013.

KNIGHT, Corban (NIGHT, KOHR-buhn) CGY

Center. Shoots right. 6'2", 193 lbs. Born, Oliver, B.C., September 10, 1990.
(Florida's 5th choice, 135th overall, in 2009 Entry Draft).

			Regular Season					Playoffs				
Season	**Club**	**League**	**GP**	**G**	**A**	**Pts**	**PIM**	**GP**	**G**	**A**	**Pts**	**PIM**
2006-07	UFA Bisons	AMHL	36	6	18	24	44	8	2	4	6	16
2007-08	UFA Bisons	AMHL	36	29	36	65	64	6	5	4	9	10
	Okotoks Oilers	AJHL	4	1	0	1	0	7	0	0	0	0
2008-09	Okotoks Oilers	AJHL	61	34	38	72	55	9	10	2	12	12
2009-10	North Dakota	WCHA	37	6	7	13	35	....	....	....	....	....
2010-11	North Dakota	WCHA	44	14	30	44	34	....	....	....	....	....
2011-12	North Dakota	WCHA	39	16	24	40	36	....	....	....	....	....
2012-13	North Dakota	WCHA	41	16	33	49	40	....	....	....	....	....

WCHA Second All-Star Team (2013) • NCAA West Second All-American Team (2013)

Traded to **Calgary** by **Florida** for Calgary's 4th round choice (Michael Downing) in 2013 Entry Draft, June 18, 2013.

KNIGHT, Jared (NIGHT, JAIR-uhd) BOS

Center. Shoots right. 5'11", 203 lbs. Born, Battle Creek, MI, January 16, 1992.
(Boston's 2nd choice, 32nd overall, in 2010 Entry Draft).

			Regular Season					Playoffs				
Season	**Club**	**League**	**GP**	**G**	**A**	**Pts**	**PIM**	**GP**	**G**	**A**	**Pts**	**PIM**
2007-08	Det. Compuware	MWEHL	22	8	21	29	21	....	....	....	....	....
	Det. Compuware	Exhib.	5	1	2	3	8	....	....	....	....	....
2008-09	London Knights	OHL	67	15	15	30	60	14	3	0	3	2
2009-10	London Knights	OHL	63	36	21	57	39	12	10	7	17	12
2010-11	London Knights	OHL	68	25	45	70	39	6	4	2	6	2
	Providence Bruins	AHL	3	0	2	2	2	....	....	....	....	....
2011-12	London Knights	OHL	52	26	26	52	28	15	4	4	8	9
2012-13	Providence Bruins	AHL	10	1	2	3	8	6	1	1	2	6
	South Carolina	ECHL	2	0	0	0	0	....	....	....	....	....

KNODEL, Eric (NOH-dehl, AIR-ihk) TOR

Defense. Shoots left. 6'6", 225 lbs. Born, West Chester, PA, June 8, 1990.
(Toronto's 5th choice, 128th overall, in 2009 Entry Draft).

			Regular Season					Playoffs				
Season	**Club**	**League**	**GP**	**G**	**A**	**Pts**	**PIM**	**GP**	**G**	**A**	**Pts**	**PIM**
2007-08	Phi. Jr. Flyers	AYHL	16	5	6	11	6	....	....	....	....	....
	Phi. Jr. Flyers	Exhib.	35	11	17	28	30	....	....	....	....	....
2008-09	Phi. Jr. Flyers	AYHL	16	2	13	15	12	....	....	....	....	....
	Phi. Jr. Flyers	Exhib.	35	11	19	30	18	....	....	....	....	....
2009-10	Des Moines	USHL	50	3	17	20	37	....	....	....	....	....
2010-11	New Hampshire	H-East	DID NOT PLAY – FRESHMAN									
2011-12	New Hampshire	H-East	37	3	9	12	24	....	....	....	....	....
2012-13	New Hampshire	H-East	38	10	11	21	8	....	....	....	....	....

KOEKKOEK, Slater (KOO-KOO, SLAY-tuhr) T.B.

Defense. Shoots left. 6'2", 188 lbs. Born, Winchester, Ont., February 18, 1994.
(Tampa Bay's 1st choice, 10th overall, in 2012 Entry Draft).

			Regular Season					Playoffs				
Season	**Club**	**League**	**GP**	**G**	**A**	**Pts**	**PIM**	**GP**	**G**	**A**	**Pts**	**PIM**
2008-09	Notre Dame	Minor-SK	47	20	39	59	40	....	....	....	....	....
2009-10	Notre Dame	SMHL	44	16	27	43	91	13	3	4	7	6
2010-11	Peterborough	OHL	65	7	16	23	67	....	....	....	....	....
2011-12	Peterborough	OHL	26	5	13	18	17	....	....	....	....	....
2012-13	Peterborough	OHL	40	6	22	28	28	....	....	....	....	....
	Windsor Spitfires	OHL	2	0	1	1	0	....	....	....	....	....

• Missed majority of 2011-12 due to shoulder injury vs. Windsor (OHL), November 27, 2011.

KOLOMATIS, David (koh-loh-MA-tihs, DAY-vihd) WSH

Defense. Shoots right. 5'11", 196 lbs. Born, Livingston, NJ, February 25, 1989.
(Los Angeles' 6th choice, 126th overall, in 2009 Entry Draft).

			Regular Season					Playoffs				
Season	**Club**	**League**	**GP**	**G**	**A**	**Pts**	**PIM**	**GP**	**G**	**A**	**Pts**	**PIM**
2005-06	USNTDP	NAHL	16	1	0	1	4	....	....	....	....	....
	USNTDP	U-17	3	0	0	0	2	....	....	....	....	....
2006-07	Owen Sound	OHL	67	4	16	20	54	4	0	0	0	0
2007-08	Owen Sound	OHL	68	9	36	45	68	....	....	....	....	....
2008-09	Owen Sound	OHL	63	18	28	46	52	4	2	2	4	0
	Providence Bruins	AHL	4	0	0	0	0	16	0	1	1	2
2009-10	Manchester	AHL	76	8	21	29	30	15	0	1	1	2
2010-11	Manchester	AHL	70	8	20	28	58	7	2	2	4	2
2011-12	Manchester	AHL	58	5	20	25	12	4	0	1	1	4
2012-13	Manchester	AHL	46	8	20	28	18	4	0	0	0	6

Signed as a free agent by **Washington**, July 6, 2013.

KOROBOV, Dmitry (koh-roh-BAWF, dih-MEE-tree) T.B.

Defense. Shoots left. 6'3", 230 lbs. Born, Novopolotsk, USSR, March 12, 1989.

			Regular Season					Playoffs				
Season	**Club**	**League**	**GP**	**G**	**A**	**Pts**	**PIM**	**GP**	**G**	**A**	**Pts**	**PIM**
2004-05	HK Gomel 2	Belarus-2	44	0	9	9	20	....	....	....	....	....
2005-06	HK Gomel 2	Belarus-2	39	3	16	19	75	....	....	....	....	....
2006-07	HK Gomel 2	Belarus-2	2	0	0	0	0	....	....	....	....	....
	HK Gomel	Belarus	41	3	5	8	20	5	1	0	1	4
2007-08	HK Gomel 2	Belarus-2	15	1	2	3	20	....	....	....	....	....
	Keramin Minsk	Belarus	5	0	1	1	0	....	....	....	....	....
	HK Gomel	Belarus	47	3	7	10	36	....	....	....	....	....
2008-09	Shinnik Bobruisk	Belarus	24	1	10	11	32	....	....	....	....	....
	Keramin Minsk	Belarus	1	0	1	1	0	....	....	....	....	....
	Dynamo Minsk	KHL	12	0	2	2	6	....	....	....	....	....
2009-10	Shakhter Soligorsk	Belarus	4	0	0	0	4	....	....	....	....	....
2010-11	Dynamo Minsk	KHL	31	1	6	7	24	6	1	2	3	10
2011-12	HK Gomel	Belarus	2	0	0	0	0	....	....	....	....	....
	Dynamo Minsk	KHL	39	1	10	11	16	3	0	0	0	2
2012-13	Syracuse Crunch	AHL	65	3	19	22	34	17	1	1	2	9

Signed as a free agent by **Tampa Bay**, August 2, 2012.

KOSMACHUK, Scott (KAWZ-muh-chuk, SKAWT) WPG

Right wing. Shoots right. 6', 190 lbs. Born, Richmond Hill, Ont., January 24, 1994.
(Winnipeg's 3rd choice, 70th overall, in 2012 Entry Draft).

			Regular Season					Playoffs				
Season	**Club**	**League**	**GP**	**G**	**A**	**Pts**	**PIM**	**GP**	**G**	**A**	**Pts**	**PIM**
2009-10	Toronto Marlboros	GTHL	79	39	33	72	108	....	....	....	....	....
2010-11	Guelph Storm	OHL	68	6	15	21	25	6	1	0	1	5
2011-12	Guelph Storm	OHL	67	30	29	59	110	6	2	3	5	12
2012-13	Guelph Storm	OHL	68	35	30	65	105	5	1	0	1	13

KOSOV, Yaroslav (KAW-sawf, YAHR-oh-slahv) FLA

Center. Shoots left. 6'3", 220 lbs. Born, Magnitogorsk, Russia, July 5, 1993.
(Florida's 8th choice, 124th overall, in 2011 Entry Draft).

			Regular Season					Playoffs				
Season	**Club**	**League**	**GP**	**G**	**A**	**Pts**	**PIM**	**GP**	**G**	**A**	**Pts**	**PIM**
2010-11	Magnitogorsk Jr.	Russia-Jr.	42	11	10	21	22	17	6	1	7	0
2011-12	Magnitogorsk Jr.	Russia-Jr.	12	6	4	10	6	6	0	0	0	0
	Magnitogorsk	KHL	27	4	5	9	6	7	0	0	0	0
2012-13	Magnitogorsk	KHL	40	4	3	7	10	5	0	0	0	0
	Magnitogorsk Jr.	Russia-Jr.	....	....	....	....	....	3	0	1	1	0

KOSTALEK, Jan (kawsh-TAH-lehk, YAHN) WPG

Defense. Shoots right. 6'1", 181 lbs. Born, Prague, Czech Republic, February 17, 1995.
(Winnipeg's 7th choice, 114th overall, in 2013 Entry Draft).

			Regular Season					Playoffs				
Season	**Club**	**League**	**GP**	**G**	**A**	**Pts**	**PIM**	**GP**	**G**	**A**	**Pts**	**PIM**
2010-11	Sparta U18	CzR-U18	39	2	9	11	34	5	0	0	0	8
	Sparta Jr.	CzRep-Jr.	1	0	0	0	0	....	....	....	....	....
2011-12	Sparta U18	CzR-U18	7	0	13	13	12	3	1	3	4	2
	Sparta Jr.	CzRep-Jr.	32	3	4	7	30	4	0	0	0	2
	HC Sparta Praha	CzRep	10	0	0	0	4	....	....	....	....	....
2012-13	Rimouski Oceanic	QMJHL	48	5	13	18	53	6	0	1	1	2

QMJHL All-Rookie Team (2013)

KOUDYS, Patrick (KOO-dihs, PAT-rihk) **WSH**

Defense. Shoots left. 6'4", 210 lbs. Born, Hamilton, Ont., November 15, 1992.
(Washington's 2nd choice, 147th overall, in 2011 Entry Draft).

			Regular Season					Playoffs				
Season	Club	League	GP	G	A	Pts	PIM	GP	G	A	Pts	PIM
2008-09	Welland Tigers	Minor-ON	52	1	11	12	48	....	....	....	....	....
2009-10	Burlington	ON-Jr.A	50	5	28	33	42	12	0	1	1	16
2010-11	RPI Engineers	ECAC	31	1	2	3	14	....	....	....	....	....
2011-12	RPI Engineers	ECAC	27	1	1	2	22	....	....	....	....	....
2012-13	Muskegon	USHL	64	1	14	15	95	3	0	0	0	0

KOZUN, Brandon (KOH-zuhn, BRAN-duhn) **L.A.**

Right wing. Shoots right. 5'8", 162 lbs. Born, Los Angeles, CA, March 8, 1990.
(Los Angeles' 8th choice, 179th overall, in 2009 Entry Draft).

			Regular Season					Playoffs				
Season	Club	League	GP	G	A	Pts	PIM	GP	G	A	Pts	PIM
2006-07	Calgary Royals	AJHL	39	20	22	42	38	4	2	1	3	2
	Calgary Hitmen	WHL	11	1	1	2	4	....	....	....	....	....
2007-08	Calgary Hitmen	WHL	69	19	34	53	46	16	4	14	18	6
2008-09	Calgary Hitmen	WHL	72	40	68	108	58	18	7	12	19	8
2009-10	Calgary Hitmen	WHL	65	32	*75	*107	50	23	8	*22	*30	12
2010-11	Manchester	AHL	73	23	25	48	48	7	1	3	4	2
2011-12	Manchester	AHL	74	20	26	46	58	3	1	1	2	2
2012-13	Manchester	AHL	74	26	30	56	52	4	0	2	2	0

WHL East First All-Star Team (2009, 2010) • Canadian Major Junior First All-Star Team (2010)

KRAMER, Darren (KRAY-muhr, DAIR-uhn) **OTT**

Center. Shoots left. 6'1", 212 lbs. Born, Peace River, Alta., November 19, 1991.
(Ottawa's 7th choice, 156th overall, in 2011 Entry Draft).

			Regular Season					Playoffs				
Season	Club	League	GP	G	A	Pts	PIM	GP	G	A	Pts	PIM
2007-08	Peace River Royals	Minor-AB	30	26	22	48	58	9	9	8	17	18
	Peace River	NWJHL	1	0	0	0	0	....	....	....	....	....
2008-09	Grande Prairie	AJHL	38	4	0	4	220	14	1	0	1	45
2009-10	Grande Prairie	AJHL	58	19	11	30	*311	9	2	2	4	23
2010-11	Grande Prairie	AJHL	10	4	1	5	28	....	....	....	....	....
	Spokane Chiefs	WHL	68	7	7	14	*306	17	5	3	8	21
2011-12	Spokane Chiefs	WHL	71	22	18	40	200	12	3	3	6	20
2012-13	Binghamton	AHL	21	1	0	1	83	....	....	....	....	....
	Elmira Jackals	ECHL	19	3	7	10	127	....	....	....	....	....

KRISTO, Danny (KRIHS-toh, DAN-ee) **NYR**

Right wing. Shoots right. 5'11", 188 lbs. Born, Edina, MN, June 18, 1990.
(Montreal's 1st choice, 56th overall, in 2008 Entry Draft).

			Regular Season					Playoffs				
Season	Club	League	GP	G	A	Pts	PIM	GP	G	A	Pts	PIM
2006-07	USNTDP	U-17	14	4	5	9	0	....	....	....	....	....
	USNTDP	NAHL	39	8	10	18	34	6	0	1	1	2
2007-08	USNTDP	U-18	43	18	14	32	18	....	....	....	....	....
	USNTDP	NAHL	14	4	4	8	6	....	....	....	....	....
2008-09	Omaha Lancers	USHL	50	22	35	57	18	3	3	0	3	2
2009-10	North Dakota	WCHA	41	15	21	36	8	....	....	....	....	....
2010-11	North Dakota	WCHA	34	8	20	28	18	....	....	....	....	....
2011-12	North Dakota	WCHA	42	19	26	45	33	....	....	....	....	....
2012-13	North Dakota	WCHA	40	*26	26	52	24	....	....	....	....	....
	Hamilton Bulldogs	AHL	9	0	3	3	2	....	....	....	....	....

WCHA All-Rookie Team (2010) • WCHA Rookie of the Year (2010) • WCHA First All-Star Team (2013) • NCAA West First All-American Team (2013)

Traded to **NY Rangers** by **Montreal** for Christian Thomas, July 2, 2013.

KRUPP, Bjorn (KROOP, B'YOHRN) **MIN**

Defense. Shoots right. 6'3", 200 lbs. Born, Manhattan Beach, CA, March 6, 1991.

			Regular Season					Playoffs				
Season	Club	League	GP	G	A	Pts	PIM	GP	G	A	Pts	PIM
2007-08	USNTDP	NAHL	43	0	3	3	40	....	....	....	....	....
2008-09	Belleville Bulls	OHL	57	1	3	4	22	17	0	0	0	9
2009-10	Belleville Bulls	OHL	67	0	11	11	53	....	....	....	....	....
2010-11	Belleville Bulls	OHL	61	1	10	11	54	4	0	0	0	2
2011-12	Kolner Haie	Germany	48	0	8	8	70	4	0	0	0	2
2012-13	Kolner Haie	Germany	40	1	8	9	22	12	0	2	2	8

Signed as a free agent by **Minnesota**, September 18, 2009. Signed as a free agent by **Koln** (Germany), April 4, 2011.

KUBALIK, Dominik (koo-BAH-lihk, DOHM-ihn-ihk) **L.A.**

Left wing. Shoots left. 6'1", 181 lbs. Born, Plzen, Czech Republic, August 21, 1995.
(Los Angeles' 7th choice, 191st overall, in 2013 Entry Draft).

			Regular Season					Playoffs				
Season	Club	League	GP	G	A	Pts	PIM	GP	G	A	Pts	PIM
2010-11	HC Plzen U18	CzR-U18	42	38	21	59	32	6	4	2	6	2
2011-12	HC Plzen U18	CzR-U18	20	22	16	38	12	2	3	0	3	2
	HC Plzen Jr.	CzRep-Jr.	24	11	6	17	22	2	1	2	3	0
	HC Plzen 1929	CzRep	8	1	0	1	0	....	....	....	....	....
2012-13	Sudbury Wolves	OHL	67	17	17	34	25	9	3	3	6	4

KUCHEROV, Nikita (KOO-chuhr-awv, nih-KEE-tuh) **T.B.**

Left wing. Shoots left. 5'11", 174 lbs. Born, Maikop, Russia, June 17, 1993.
(Tampa Bay's 2nd choice, 58th overall, in 2011 Entry Draft).

			Regular Season					Playoffs				
Season	Club	League	GP	G	A	Pts	PIM	GP	G	A	Pts	PIM
2009-10	CSKA Jr.	Russia-Jr.	53	29	25	54	40	5	0	2	2	2
2010-11	CSKA Jr.	Russia-Jr.	41	27	31	58	81	10	5	8	13	16
	CSKA Moscow	KHL	8	0	2	2	0	....	....	....	....	....
2011-12	CSKA Jr.	Russia-Jr.	23	24	19	43	40	7	3	1	4	0
	CSKA Moscow	KHL	18	1	4	5	4	....	....	....	....	....
2012-13	Quebec Remparts	QMJHL	6	3	7	10	2	....	....	....	....	....
	Rouyn-Noranda	QMJHL	27	26	27	53	12	14	9	15	24	10

KUHNHACKL, Tom (koon-HAH-kuhl, TAWM) **PIT**

Center. Shoots left. 6'2", 172 lbs. Born, Landshut, Germany, January 21, 1992.
(Pittsburgh's 3rd choice, 110th overall, in 2010 Entry Draft).

			Regular Season					Playoffs				
Season	Club	League	GP	G	A	Pts	PIM	GP	G	A	Pts	PIM
2007-08	EV Landshut Jr.	Ger-Jr.	30	21	20	41	102	3	1	0	1	2
2008-09	EV Landshut Jr.	Ger-Jr.	6	4	3	7	31	7	5	5	10	27
	Landshut Cann.	German-2	42	11	10	21	34	6	1	0	1	6
2009-10	EV Landshut Jr.	Ger-Jr.	2	1	3	4	0	3	4	4	8	12
	Landshut Cann.	German-2	38	12	9	21	38	6	0	0	0	2
	Augsburg	Germany	4	0	0	0	0	....	....	....	....	....
2010-11	Windsor Spitfires	OHL	63	39	29	68	47	18	11	12	23	10
2011-12	Windsor Spitfires	OHL	4	1	3	4	6	....	....	....	....	....
	Niagara Ice Dogs	OHL	30	7	18	25	29	20	6	5	11	14
2012-13	Wheeling Nailers	ECHL	2	1	0	1	2	....	....	....	....	....
	Wilkes-Barre	AHL	11	2	2	4	6	....	....	....	....	....

KUJAWINSKI, Ryan (koo-juh-WIHN-skee, RIGH-uhn) **N.J.**

Center. Shoots left. 6'2", 205 lbs. Born, Kirkland Lake, Ont., March 30, 1995.
(New Jersey's 2nd choice, 73rd overall, in 2013 Entry Draft).

			Regular Season					Playoffs				
Season	Club	League	GP	G	A	Pts	PIM	GP	G	A	Pts	PIM
2010-11	Sud. Wolves M.M.	Minor-ON	24	35	21	56	24	....	....	....	....	....
	Sud. Wolves Mid.	Minor-ON	2	1	1	2	0	3	4	6	10	4
2011-12	Sarnia Sting	OHL	29	1	5	6	2	....	....	....	....	....
	Kingston	OHL	30	15	15	30	15	....	....	....	....	....
2012-13	Kingston	OHL	66	17	31	48	40	4	2	0	2	2

KULAK, Brett (koo-LAK, BREHT) **CGY**

Defense. Shoots left. 6'1", 181 lbs. Born, Edmonton, Alta., January 6, 1994.
(Calgary's 4th choice, 105th overall, in 2012 Entry Draft).

			Regular Season					Playoffs				
Season	Club	League	GP	G	A	Pts	PIM	GP	G	A	Pts	PIM
2008-09	PAC Spruce Grove	AMBHL	33	2	19	21	28	....	....	....	....	....
2009-10	PAC Spruce Grove	Minor-AB	32	4	34	38	42	10	2	8	10	14
2010-11	St. Albert Raiders	AMHL	31	9	18	27	71	5	1	1	2	0
	Vancouver Giants	WHL	3	0	0	0	0	....	....	....	....	....
2011-12	Vancouver Giants	WHL	72	9	15	24	22	6	0	4	4	2
2012-13	Vancouver Giants	WHL	72	12	32	44	34	....	....	....	....	....
	Abbotsford Heat	AHL	4	0	0	0	0	....	....	....	....	....

KULYASH, Denis (kuh-L'YASH, DEH-nihs) **NSH**

Defense. Shoots left. 6'3", 199 lbs. Born, Omsk, USSR, May 31, 1983.
(Nashville's 9th choice, 243rd overall, in 2004 Entry Draft).

			Regular Season					Playoffs				
Season	Club	League	GP	G	A	Pts	PIM	GP	G	A	Pts	PIM
2003-04	CSK VVS Samara 2	Russia-3	Statistics not available									
	CSKA Moscow	Russia	10	1	0	1	8	....	....	....	....	....
2004-05	CSKA Moscow	Russia	59	8	10	18	58	....	....	....	....	....
2005-06	Dynamo Moscow	Russia	44	12	5	17	117	4	0	2	2	6
2006-07	Dynamo Moscow	Russia	48	3	9	12	58	2	0	0	0	2
2007-08	CSKA Moscow	Russia	53	9	13	22	79	6	1	1	2	34
2008-09	CSKA Moscow	KHL	56	16	10	26	62	8	2	1	3	20
2009-10	CSKA Moscow	KHL	35	11	10	21	34	....	....	....	....	....
	Omsk	KHL	6	1	1	2	6	3	0	0	0	4
2010-11	Omsk	KHL	48	11	15	26	45	14	3	3	6	12
2011-12	Ak Bars Kazan	KHL	44	6	12	18	40	12	0	1	1	37
2012-13	Ak Bars Kazan	KHL	44	4	9	13	66	18	2	5	7	6

KURALY, Sean (KUH-ra-lee, SHAWN) **S.J.**

Center. Shoots left. 6'2", 205 lbs. Born, Lewiston, NY, January 20, 1993.
(San Jose's 3rd choice, 133rd overall, in 2011 Entry Draft).

			Regular Season					Playoffs				
Season	Club	League	GP	G	A	Pts	PIM	GP	G	A	Pts	PIM
2009-10	Ohio Blue Jackets	T1EHL	37	19	30	49	24	....	....	....	....	....
	Indiana Ice	USHL	5	1	2	3	0	....	....	....	....	....
2010-11	Indiana Ice	USHL	51	8	21	29	45	5	1	1	2	4
2011-12	Indiana Ice	USHL	54	32	38	70	48	6	3	3	6	4
2012-13	Miami U.	CCHA	40	6	6	12	41	....	....	....	....	....

USHL Second All-Star Team (2012)

KURKER, Sam (KUHR-kuhr, SAM) **ST.L.**

Right wing. Shoots right. 6'2", 201 lbs. Born, Boston, MA, April 8, 1994.
(St. Louis' 2nd choice, 56th overall, in 2012 Entry Draft).

			Regular Season					Playoffs				
Season	Club	League	GP	G	A	Pts	PIM	GP	G	A	Pts	PIM
2010-11	Bos. Little Bruins	Minor-MA	Statistics not available									
	St. John's Prep	High-MA	25	20	17	37	24	....	....	....	....	....
2011-12	Bos. Little Bruins	Minor-MA	Statistics not available									
	St. John's Prep	High-MA	24	32	28	60	23	....	....	....	....	....
	USNTDP	U-18	2	0	0	0	2	....	....	....	....	....
2012-13	Boston University	H-East	35	3	2	5	61	....	....	....	....	....

KURTZ, John (KUHRTZ, JAWN) **ANA**

Left wing. Shoots left. 6'2", 204 lbs. Born, Oakville, Ont., May 16, 1989.

			Regular Season					Playoffs				
Season	Club	League	GP	G	A	Pts	PIM	GP	G	A	Pts	PIM
2005-06	Burlington	ON-Jr.A	42	7	11	18	34	4	0	0	0	2
2006-07	Windsor Spitfires	OHL	58	8	7	15	31	....	....	....	....	....
2007-08	Sudbury Wolves	OHL	63	12	16	28	41	....	....	....	....	....
2008-09	Sudbury Wolves	OHL	68	21	33	54	44	6	1	1	2	2
2009-10	Sudbury Wolves	OHL	62	30	16	46	59	4	0	1	1	2
	Syracuse Crunch	AHL	6	1	0	1	7	....	....	....	....	....
2010-11	Syracuse Crunch	AHL	49	4	2	6	102	....	....	....	....	....
	Elmira Jackals	ECHL	8	1	2	3	0	....	....	....	....	....
2011-12	Syracuse Crunch	AHL	12	1	0	1	40	....	....	....	....	....
	Elmira Jackals	ECHL	19	3	5	8	30	....	....	....	....	....
2012-13	Norfolk Admirals	AHL	59	3	5	8	103	....	....	....	....	....

Signed as a free agent by **Anaheim**, April 10, 2013.

KUZNETSOV, Evgeny (kooz-neht-SAWF, ehv-GEH-nee) WSH

Center. Shoots left. 6', 172 lbs. Born, Chelyabinsk, Russia, May 19, 1992.
(Washington's 1st choice, 26th overall, in 2010 Entry Draft).

			Regular Season					Playoffs				
Season	Club	League	GP	G	A	Pts	PIM	GP	G	A	Pts	PIM
2007-08	Chelyabinsk 2	Russia-3	2	0	0	0	0	....	....	....	....	....
2008-09	Chelyabinsk 2	Russia-3	22	5	11	16	40	....	....	....	....	....
2009-10	Chelyabinsk Jr.	Russia-Jr.	9	4	12	16	8	2	1	2	3	4
	Chelyabinsk	KHL	35	2	6	8	10	4	1	0	1	0
2010-11	Chelyabinsk	KHL	44	17	15	32	30	....	....	....	....	....
	Chelyabinsk Jr.	Russia-Jr.	8	10	5	15	4	5	0	2	2	10
2011-12	Chelyabinsk	KHL	49	19	22	41	30	12	7	2	9	10
2012-13	Chelyabinsk	KHL	51	19	25	44	42	25	5	6	11	28

LABATE, Joseph (luh-BA-tay, JOH-sehf) VAN

Center. Shoots left. 6'4", 195 lbs. Born, Burnsville, MN, April 16, 1993.
(Vancouver's 4th choice, 101st overall, in 2011 Entry Draft).

			Regular Season					Playoffs				
Season	Club	League	GP	G	A	Pts	PIM	GP	G	A	Pts	PIM
2009-10	Holy Angels	High-MN	25	29	29	58	26	2	0	1	1	2
2010-11	Team Southeast	UMHSEL	5	2	6	8	2	3	4	2	6	0
	Holy Angels	High-MN	25	27	22	49	42	1	2	1	3	0
2011-12	U. of Wisconsin	WCHA	37	5	15	20	24	....	....	....	....	....
2012-13	U. of Wisconsin	WCHA	41	9	14	23	51	....	....	....	....	....

LABBE, Dylan (la-BAY, DIH-luhn) MIN

Defense. Shoots left. 6'2", 190 lbs. Born, St-George, Que., January 9, 1995.
(Minnesota's 3rd choice, 107th overall, in 2013 Entry Draft).

			Regular Season					Playoffs				
Season	Club	League	GP	G	A	Pts	PIM	GP	G	A	Pts	PIM
2011-12	Levis	QAAA	38	13	11	24	30	4	0	1	1	0
	Shawinigan	QMJHL	6	0	0	0	7	4	0	1	1	0
2012-13	Shawinigan	QMJHL	61	7	21	28	57	....	....	....	....	....

LABRIE, Hubert (la-BREE, hew-BAIR) DAL

Defense. Shoots left. 5'11", 190 lbs. Born, Victoriaville, Que., July 12, 1991.

			Regular Season					Playoffs				
Season	Club	League	GP	G	A	Pts	PIM	GP	G	A	Pts	PIM
2007-08	Gatineau	QMJHL	61	2	15	17	79	19	1	3	4	26
2008-09	Gatineau	QMJHL	55	1	3	4	82	5	0	0	0	14
2009-10	Gatineau	QMJHL	67	4	16	20	99	11	3	4	7	20
2010-11	Gatineau	QMJHL	9	3	4	7	8	24	4	8	12	30
2011-12	Texas Stars	AHL	33	2	1	3	18	....	....	....	....	....
	Idaho Steelheads	ECHL	8	1	4	5	0	6	0	0	0	4
2012-13	Texas Stars	AHL	27	0	3	3	45	....	....	....	....	....
	Idaho Steelheads	ECHL	22	2	3	5	46	17	0	1	1	21

Signed as a free agent by **Dallas**, September 18, 2009.

LADUE, Paul (la-DOO, PAWL) L.A.

Defense. Shoots right. 6'1", 186 lbs. Born, Grand Forks, ND, September 6, 1992.
(Los Angeles' 5th choice, 181st overall, in 2012 Entry Draft).

			Regular Season					Playoffs				
Season	Club	League	GP	G	A	Pts	PIM	GP	G	A	Pts	PIM
2009-10	Grand Forks C.K.	High-ND	25	....	....	....	30	....	....	....	....	....
2010-11	Alexandria Blizzard	NAHL	56	3	19	22	58	3	0	2	2	2
2011-12	Lincoln Stars	USHL	56	9	25	34	27	8	1	2	3	2
2012-13	Lincoln Stars	USHL	62	12	37	49	20	5	1	1	2	0

USHL First All-Star Team (2013)
• Signed Letter of Intent to attend **University of North Dakota** (WCHA) in fall of 2013.

LAGACE, Jacob (luh-ga-SEE, JAY-kawb) BUF

Left wing. Shoots left. 5'11", 199 lbs. Born, Beloeil, Que., January 9, 1990.
(Buffalo's 7th choice, 134th overall, in 2008 Entry Draft).

			Regular Season					Playoffs				
Season	Club	League	GP	G	A	Pts	PIM	GP	G	A	Pts	PIM
2005-06	Antoine-Girouard	QAAA	38	10	11	21	....	8	0	2	2	4
2006-07	Antoine-Girouard	QAAA	44	24	29	53	46	4	1	4	5	2
2007-08	Chicoutimi	QMJHL	67	23	39	62	40	6	3	2	5	7
2008-09	Chicoutimi	QMJHL	64	32	37	69	52	4	1	2	3	4
2009-10	Chicoutimi	QMJHL	35	30	23	53	20	....	....	....	....	....
	Cape Breton	QMJHL	25	5	15	20	32	5	0	3	3	4
	Portland Pirates	AHL	....	....	....	....	....	1	0	0	0	0
2010-11	Portland Pirates	AHL	58	10	13	23	34	3	0	0	0	0
	Greenville	ECHL	13	0	6	6	0	....	....	....	....	....
2011-12	Rochester	AHL	58	10	10	20	25	....	....	....	....	....
2012-13	Rochester	AHL	4	0	0	0	2	....	....	....	....	....
	Bakersfield	ECHL	57	16	20	36	68	....	....	....	....	....

QMJHL All-Rookie Team (2008)

LAGANIERE, Antoine (LA-GAH-n'yay, an-TWAHN) ANA

Center. Shoots left. 6'5", 207 lbs. Born, L'Ile-Cadieux, Que., July 5, 1990.

			Regular Season					Playoffs				
Season	Club	League	GP	G	A	Pts	PIM	GP	G	A	Pts	PIM
2007-08	Deerfield Academy	High-MA	25	8	30	38	14	....	....	....	....	....
2008-09	Deerfield Academy	High-MA	....	12	16	28	....	....	....	....	....	....
2009-10	Yale	ECAC	25	7	3	10	18	....	....	....	....	....
2010-11	Yale	ECAC	25	5	8	13	14	....	....	....	....	....
2011-12	Yale	ECAC	35	19	14	33	45	....	....	....	....	....
2012-13	Yale	ECAC	37	15	14	29	58	....	....	....	....	....

Signed as a free agent by **Anaheim**, April 16, 2013.

LAIN, Kellan (LANE, KEHL-uhn) VAN

Left wing. Shoots left. 6'6", 222 lbs. Born, Oakville, Ont., August 11, 1989.

			Regular Season					Playoffs				
Season	Club	League	GP	G	A	Pts	PIM	GP	G	A	Pts	PIM
2007-08	Orleans Blues	ON-Jr.A	31	9	13	22	51	21	11	4	15	60
2008-09	Oakville Blades	ON-Jr.A	47	19	23	42	74	18	10	6	16	22
2009-10	Oakville Blades	ON-Jr.A	16	8	9	17	16	17	5	17	22	22
2010-11	Lake Superior	CCHA	38	4	4	8	40	....	....	....	....	....
2011-12	Lake Superior	CCHA	38	9	6	15	59	....	....	....	....	....
2012-13	Lake Superior	CCHA	32	8	8	16	*111	....	....	....	....	....
	Chicago Wolves	AHL	13	0	0	0	6	....	....	....	....	....

Signed as a free agent by **Vancouver**, July 19, 2013.

LAJUNEN, Jani (LA-joo-nehn, YAH-nee)

Center. Shoots left. 6'1", 190 lbs. Born, Helsinki, Finland, June 16, 1990.
(Nashville's 6th choice, 201st overall, in 2008 Entry Draft).

			Regular Season					Playoffs				
Season	Club	League	GP	G	A	Pts	PIM	GP	G	A	Pts	PIM
2005-06	K-Vantaa U18	Fin-U18	2	0	0	0	0	....	....	....	....	....
2006-07	Blues Espoo U18	Fin-U18	28	5	12	17	20	6	1	1	2	4
2007-08	Blues Espoo U18	Fin-U18	1	1	0	1	2	4	2	2	4	0
	Blues Espoo Jr.	Fin-Jr.	25	4	10	14	14	3	0	0	0	0
	Blues Espoo	Finland	1	0	0	0	0	....	....	....	....	....
2008-09	Suomi U20	Finland-2	2	2	2	4	0	....	....	....	....	....
	Blues Espoo Jr.	Fin-Jr.	25	16	10	26	24	8	2	1	3	12
	Blues Espoo	Finland	25	1	1	2	4	2	0	0	0	0
2009-10	Blues Espoo Jr.	Fin-Jr.	4	1	1	2	0	....	....	....	....	....
	Suomi U20	Finland-2	2	0	0	0	0	....	....	....	....	....
	Blues Espoo	Finland	46	6	9	15	34	3	0	0	0	2
2010-11	Blues Espoo	Finland	60	10	12	22	46	18	3	4	7	12
2011-12	Milwaukee	AHL	75	5	11	16	18	3	1	0	1	0
2012-13	Milwaukee	AHL	40	1	4	5	14	....	....	....	....	....
	Peoria Rivermen	AHL	19	1	1	2	4	....	....	....	....	....

Traded to **St. Louis** by **Nashville** for Scott Ford, February 19, 2013. Signed as a free agent by **Vaxjo** (Sweden), May 7, 2013.

LALANCETTE, Christophe (la-lan-SEHT, KRIHS-tawf) S.J.

Right wing. Shoots right. 6', 180 lbs. Born, Roberval, Que., May 6, 1994.
(San Jose's 3rd choice, 109th overall, in 2012 Entry Draft).

			Regular Season					Playoffs				
Season	Club	League	GP	G	A	Pts	PIM	GP	G	A	Pts	PIM
2009-10	Quebec Cyclones	Minor-QU	STATISTICS NOT AVAILABLE									
	St-Francois	QAAA	9	0	4	4	0	....	....	....	....	....
2010-11	St-Francois	QAAA	40	10	25	35	22	4	1	0	1	2
	Acadie-Bathurst	QMJHL	3	0	0	0	0	....	....	....	....	....
2011-12	Acadie-Bathurst	QMJHL	63	16	31	47	35	6	1	1	2	2
2012-13	Acadie-Bathurst	QMJHL	62	18	37	55	36	5	4	3	7	0

LALEGGIA, Joey (lah-lehj-EE-a, JOH-ee) EDM

Defense. Shoots left. 5'9", 182 lbs. Born, Burnaby, B.C., June 24, 1992.
(Edmonton's 6th choice, 123rd overall, in 2012 Entry Draft).

			Regular Season					Playoffs				
Season	Club	League	GP	G	A	Pts	PIM	GP	G	A	Pts	PIM
2006-07	Burnaby W.C.	Minor-BC	65	7	37	44	58	....	....	....	....	....
2007-08	Van. NW Giants	BCMML	40	7	34	41	32	2	0	1	1	0
2008-09	Van. NW Giants	BCMML	40	15	39	54	67	5	2	4	6	0
	Penticton Vees	BCHL	2	0	0	0	0	....	....	....	....	....
2009-10	Penticton Vees	BCHL	54	13	52	65	19	16	2	10	12	8
2010-11	Penticton Vees	BCHL	58	20	62	82	47	9	1	9	10	12
2011-12	U. of Denver	WCHA	43	11	27	38	35	....	....	....	....	....
2012-13	U. of Denver	WCHA	39	11	18	29	31	....	....	....	....	....

WCHA All-Rookie Team (2012) • WCHA Rookie of the Year (2012) • WCHA Second All-Star Team (2013)

LAMARCHE, Maxim (la-MARSH, MAX-eem) PHI

Defense. Shoots right. 6'3", 218 lbs. Born, Laval, Que., July 11, 1992.

			Regular Season					Playoffs				
Season	Club	League	GP	G	A	Pts	PIM	GP	G	A	Pts	PIM
2009-10	Victoriaville Tigres	QMJHL	33	3	10	13	21	....	....	....	....	....
	Baie-Comeau	QMJHL	29	3	1	4	20	....	....	....	....	....
2010-11	Baie-Comeau	QMJHL	67	4	24	28	98	....	....	....	....	....
2011-12	Baie-Comeau	QMJHL	68	4	21	25	67	8	0	4	4	12
2012-13	Baie-Comeau	QMJHL	55	9	34	43	63	19	3	8	11	28

Signed as a free agent by **Philadelphia**, May 31, 2013.

LAMB, Brady (LAMB, BRAY-dee) CGY

Defense. Shoots right. 6'1", 215 lbs. Born, Calgary, Alta., August 15, 1988.

			Regular Season					Playoffs				
Season	Club	League	GP	G	A	Pts	PIM	GP	G	A	Pts	PIM
2005-06	Calgary Royals	AJHL	56	2	10	12	51	....	....	....	....	....
2006-07	Calgary Royals	AJHL	47	8	18	26	87	4	0	0	0	0
2007-08	Calgary Royals	AJHL	58	10	22	32	109	....	....	....	....	....
2008-09	U. Minn-Duluth	WCHA	21	1	1	2	13	....	....	....	....	....
2009-10	U. Minn-Duluth	WCHA	40	11	13	24	55	....	....	....	....	....
2010-11	U. Minn-Duluth	WCHA	37	1	9	10	42	....	....	....	....	....
2011-12	U. Minn-Duluth	WCHA	41	9	22	31	51	....	....	....	....	....
	Abbotsford Heat	AHL	1	0	0	0	2	....	....	....	....	....
2012-13	Abbotsford Heat	AHL	50	2	7	9	21	....	....	....	....	....

Signed as a free agent by **Calgary**, March 29, 2012.

LANDRY, Charles (LAN-dree, CHAR-uhlz) T.B.

Defense. Shoots right. 6'1", 198 lbs. Born, Napierville, Que., June 3, 1991.

			Regular Season					Playoffs				
Season	Club	League	GP	G	A	Pts	PIM	GP	G	A	Pts	PIM
2007-08	Drummondville	QMJHL	61	5	8	13	47	....	....	....	....	....
2008-09	Drummondville	QMJHL	48	0	13	13	41	19	2	2	4	8
2009-10	Drummondville	QMJHL	68	6	24	30	41	14	3	2	5	10
2010-11	Montreal	QMJHL	57	11	29	40	30	10	1	3	4	12
	Norfolk Admirals	AHL	....	....	....	....	....	1	0	0	0	0
2011-12	Norfolk Admirals	AHL	23	0	6	6	19	....	....	....	....	....
	Florida Everblades	ECHL	36	2	7	9	12	11	1	2	3	5
2012-13	Syracuse Crunch	AHL	9	0	0	0	4	....	....	....	....	....
	Florida Everblades	ECHL	51	4	12	16	33	13	0	1	1	11

Signed as a free agent by **Tampa Bay**, September 15, 2010.

LANDRY, Jon (LAN-dree, JAWN) MIN

Defense. Shoots left. 6'2", 201 lbs. Born, Montreal, Que., May 1, 1983.

			Regular Season					Playoffs				
Season	Club	League	GP	G	A	Pts	PIM	GP	G	A	Pts	PIM
2002-03	Bowdoin College	NCAA-3	23	11	14	25	14	....	....	....	....	....
2003-04	Bowdoin College	NCAA-3	24	13	20	33	20	....	....	....	....	....
2004-05	Bowdoin College	NCAA-3	24	11	14	25	16	....	....	....	....	....
2005-06	Bowdoin College	NCAA-3	27	16	22	38	37	....	....	....	....	....
	Portland Pirates	AHL	2	0	0	0	2	....	....	....	....	....
2006-07	Augusta Lynx	ECHL	2	1	0	1	2	....	....	....	....	....
	Arizona Sundogs	CHL	41	7	7	14	41	14	0	0	0	4
2007-08	Arizona Sundogs	CHL	60	9	33	42	70	17	3	6	9	14
2008-09	Arizona Sundogs	CHL	64	11	31	42	63	....	....	....	....	....
2009-10	Arizona Sundogs	CHL	38	9	22	31	54	....	....	....	....	....
	Kolner Haie	Germany	9	0	2	2	20	....	....	....	....	....
2010-11	Braehead Clan	Britain	54	18	40	58	67	....	....	....	....	....
2011-12	Colorado Eagles	ECHL	35	12	18	30	44	....	....	....	....	....
	Bridgeport	AHL	34	2	18	20	27	2	0	0	0	0
2012-13	Bridgeport	AHL	72	8	25	33	57	....	....	....	....	....

Signed as a free agent by **Koln** (Germany), January 29, 2010. Signed as a free agent by **Braehead** (Britain), July 13, 2010. Signed as a free agent by **Colorado** (ECHL), September 21, 2011. Signed to a PTO (professional tryout) contract by **Bridgeport** (AHL), January 12, 2012. Signed as a free agent by **Bridgeport** (AHL), February 24, 2012. Signed as a free agent by **NY Islanders**, July 1, 2012. Signed as a free agent by **Minnesota**, July 9, 2013.

LANE, Phil (LAYN, FIHL) PHX

Right wing. Shoots right. 6'2", 203 lbs. Born, Rochester, NY, May 29, 1992.
(Phoenix's 3rd choice, 52nd overall, in 2010 Entry Draft).

			Regular Season					Playoffs				
Season	Club	League	GP	G	A	Pts	PIM	GP	G	A	Pts	PIM
2008-09	Buffalo Jr. Sabres	ON-Jr.A	45	18	24	42	72	5	0	0	0	6
2009-10	Brampton	OHL	64	18	14	32	52	11	3	0	3	14
2010-11	Brampton	OHL	54	17	17	34	113	4	0	1	1	2
2011-12	Brampton	OHL	53	15	26	41	94	8	4	1	5	7
2012-13	Portland Pirates	AHL	70	14	8	22	61	3	0	1	1	9

LANE, Tanner (LAYN, TA-nuhr) WPG

Center. Shoots right. 6'2", 185 lbs. Born, Detroit Lakes, MN, August 13, 1992.
(Atlanta's 7th choice, 160th overall, in 2010 Entry Draft).

			Regular Season					Playoffs				
Season	Club	League	GP	G	A	Pts	PIM	GP	G	A	Pts	PIM
2007-08	Detroit Lakes	High-MN	26	24	20	44	28	....	....	....	....	....
2008-09	Detroit Lakes	High-MN	26	26	26	52	50	....	....	....	....	....
2009-10	Team Great Plains	UMHSEL	21	8	7	15	....	....	....	....	....	....
	Detroit Lakes	High-MN	25	49	41	*90	62	1	0	0	0	2
2010-11	Fargo Force	USHL	57	4	9	13	48	5	0	0	0	0
2011-12	Fargo Force	USHL	12	1	8	9	10	....	....	....	....	....
	Omaha Lancers	USHL	48	12	20	32	38	4	0	0	0	2
2012-13	Nebraska-Omaha	WCHA	31	2	4	6	8	....	....	....	....	....

• Transferred to **Winnipeg** after **Atlanta** franchise relocated, June 21, 2011.

LAPLANTE, Pavel (la-PLAHNT, PAH-vehl) PHX

Center. Shoots left. 6', 176 lbs. Born, Chateauguay, Que., April 23, 1995.
(Phoenix's 3rd choice, 62nd overall, in 2013 Entry Draft).

			Regular Season					Playoffs				
Season	Club	League	GP	G	A	Pts	PIM	GP	G	A	Pts	PIM
2010-11	Chateauguay	QAAA	25	6	8	14	42	8	4	1	5	8
2011-12	P.E.I. Rocket	QMJHL	57	6	15	21	33	....	....	....	....	....
2012-13	P.E.I. Rocket	QMJHL	18	5	8	13	12	6	3	2	5	4

• Missed majority of 2012-13 recovering from pre-season shoulder injury.

LARKIN, Thomas (LAHR-kihn, TAW-muhs) CBJ

Defense. Shoots right. 6'5", 223 lbs. Born, London, England, December 31, 1990.
(Columbus' 4th choice, 137th overall, in 2009 Entry Draft).

			Regular Season					Playoffs				
Season	Club	League	GP	G	A	Pts	PIM	GP	G	A	Pts	PIM
2006-07	Exeter	High-NH	28	1	7	8	5	....	....	....	....	....
2007-08	Exeter	High-NH	29	6	15	21	18	....	....	....	....	....
2008-09	Exeter	High-NH	35	14	38	52	30	....	....	....	....	....
	Bos. Little Bruins	Minor-MA	18	1	1	2	10	....	....	....	....	....
2009-10	Colgate	ECAC	33	3	16	19	32	....	....	....	....	....
2010-11	Colgate	ECAC	41	5	6	11	41	....	....	....	....	....
2011-12	Colgate	ECAC	37	4	10	14	48	....	....	....	....	....
2012-13	Colgate	ECAC	36	3	11	14	55	....	....	....	....	....
	Springfield Falcons	AHL	7	1	0	1	2	....	....	....	....	....

LARRAZA, Zac (Luh-RAZ-uh, ZAK) PHX

Left wing. Shoots left. 6'3", 195 lbs. Born, Scottsdale, AZ, February 25, 1993.
(Phoenix's 8th choice, 196th overall, in 2011 Entry Draft).

			Regular Season					Playoffs				
Season	Club	League	GP	G	A	Pts	PIM	GP	G	A	Pts	PIM
2008-09	P.F. Chang's	T1EHL	26	11	8	19	8	....	....	....	....	....
2009-10	USNTDP	USHL	30	6	5	11	26	....	....	....	....	....
	USNTDP	U-17	20	2	4	6	32	....	....	....	....	....
	USNTDP	U-18	1	0	1	1	0	....	....	....	....	....
2010-11	USNTDP	USHL	24	6	3	9	16	....	....	....	....	....
	USNTDP	U-18	33	3	6	9	10	....	....	....	....	....
2011-12	U. of Denver	WCHA	26	1	4	5	12	....	....	....	....	....
2012-13	U. of Denver	WCHA	36	12	9	21	48	....	....	....	....	....

LARSSON, Fredric (LAHR-suhn, FREHD-rihk) PHI

Defense. Shoots left. 6'3", 172 lbs. Born, Karlstad, Sweden, July 4, 1994.
(Philadelphia's 4th choice, 111th overall, in 2012 Entry Draft).

			Regular Season					Playoffs				
Season	Club	League	GP	G	A	Pts	PIM	GP	G	A	Pts	PIM
2009-10	Brynas U18	Swe-U18	9	0	0	0	6	....	....	....	....	....
2010-11	Brynas U18	Swe-U18	36	6	18	24	73	5	0	0	0	6
2011-12	Brynas U18	Swe-U18	35	3	12	15	158	5	1	0	1	8
	Brynas IF Gavle Jr.	Swe-Jr.	14	1	3	4	24	2	0	0	0	6
2012-13	Brynas IF Gavle Jr.	Swe-Jr.	41	4	6	10	134	....	....	....	....	....

LASCH, Ryan (LASH, RIGH-uhn)

Right wing. Shoots right. 5'9", 175 lbs. Born, Lake Forest, CA, January 22, 1987.

			Regular Season					Playoffs				
Season	Club	League	GP	G	A	Pts	PIM	GP	G	A	Pts	PIM
2006-07	St. Cloud State	WCHA	40	16	23	39	8	....	....	....	....	....
2007-08	St. Cloud State	WCHA	40	25	28	53	12	....	....	....	....	....
2008-09	St. Cloud State	WCHA	38	18	24	42	52	....	....	....	....	....
2009-10	St. Cloud State	WCHA	43	20	29	49	26	....	....	....	....	....
2010-11	Sodertalje SK	Sweden	55	12	18	30	40	....	....	....	....	....
	Sodertalje SK	Sweden-Q	10	4	5	9	6	....	....	....	....	....
2011-12	Pelicans Lahti	Finland	59	24	38	62	26	17	5	11	16	29
2012-13	Vaxjo Lakers HC	Sweden	10	0	5	5	4	....	....	....	....	....
	Fort Wayne	ECHL	12	6	9	15	2	....	....	....	....	....
	Norfolk Admirals	AHL	19	2	3	5	6	....	....	....	....	....
	Toronto Marlies	AHL	11	4	1	5	4	2	1	0	1	0

WCHA First All-Star Team (2008, 2009) • NCAA West Second All-American Team (2008) • WCHA Second All-Star Team (2010)

Signed as a free agent by **Anaheim**, May 31, 2012. Traded to **Toronto** by **Anaheim** with Anaheim's 7th round choice in 2014 Entry Draft for David Steckel, March 15, 2013.

LATTA, Michael (LA-tuh, MIGH-kuhl) WSH

Center. Shoots right. 6', 209 lbs. Born, Kitchener, Ont., May 25, 1991.
(Nashville's 5th choice, 72nd overall, in 2009 Entry Draft).

			Regular Season					Playoffs				
Season	Club	League	GP	G	A	Pts	PIM	GP	G	A	Pts	PIM
2006-07	Waterloo Wolves	Minor-ON	73	52	66	118	213	....	....	....	....	....
2007-08	Ottawa 67's	OHL	50	14	14	28	78	4	0	1	1	2
2008-09	Ottawa 67's	OHL	23	8	13	21	32	....	....	....	....	....
	Guelph Storm	OHL	42	14	22	36	60	4	0	2	2	12
2009-10	Guelph Storm	OHL	58	33	40	73	157	5	2	7	9	14
	Milwaukee	AHL	....	....	....	....	....	1	0	0	0	0
2010-11	Guelph Storm	OHL	68	34	55	89	158	6	5	5	10	11
	Milwaukee	AHL	4	0	1	1	2	7	0	0	0	12
2011-12	Milwaukee	AHL	51	14	13	27	100	3	0	1	1	2
2012-13	Milwaukee	AHL	67	9	26	35	184	....	....	....	....	....
	Hershey Bears	AHL	9	1	2	3	14	5	2	1	3	6

Traded to **Washington** by **Nashville** with Martin Erat for Filip Forsberg, April 3, 2013.

LAURIDSEN, Markus (LAWR-rihd-suhn, MAHR-kuhs) COL

Defense. Shoots left. 6'1", 205 lbs. Born, Gentofte, Denmark, February 28, 1991.

			Regular Season					Playoffs				
Season	Club	League	GP	G	A	Pts	PIM	GP	G	A	Pts	PIM
2010-11	Green Bay	USHL	44	5	5	10	16	11	0	4	4	0
2011-12	Green Bay	USHL	58	6	24	30	32	11	3	1	4	8
2012-13	Lake Erie Monsters	AHL	36	0	12	12	16	....	....	....	....	....
	Denver Cutthroats	CHL	30	6	9	15	14	....	....	....	....	....

Signed as a free agent by **Lake Erie** (AHL), September, 2012. Signed as a free agent by **Colorado**, March 22, 2013.

LAVIN, Joe (LA-vihn, JOH)

Defense. Shoots left. 6'2", 197 lbs. Born, Worcester, MA, July 17, 1989.
(Chicago's 6th choice, 126th overall, in 2007 Entry Draft).

			Regular Season					Playoffs				
Season	Club	League	GP	G	A	Pts	PIM	GP	G	A	Pts	PIM
2004-05	Junior Bruins	EmJHL	64	11	44	55	....	....	....	....	....	....
2005-06	USNTDP	U-17	19	2	1	3	30	....	....	....	....	....
	USNTDP	NAHL	37	8	10	18	16	12	3	2	5	4
2006-07	USNTDP	U-18	23	1	0	1	18	....	....	....	....	....
	USNTDP	NAHL	18	1	8	9	22	6	0	2	2	4
2007-08	Providence College	H-East	36	0	8	8	26	....	....	....	....	....
2008-09	Providence College	H-East	12	0	1	1	10	....	....	....	....	....
	Omaha Lancers	USHL	33	7	15	22	28	3	0	4	4	8
2009-10	Omaha Lancers	USHL	24	5	12	17	16	....	....	....	....	....
2010-11	U. of Notre Dame	CCHA	44	6	11	17	22	....	....	....	....	....
	Rockford IceHogs	AHL	2	0	1	1	4	....	....	....	....	....
2011-12	Rockford IceHogs	AHL	71	3	14	17	20	....	....	....	....	....
2012-13	Rockford IceHogs	AHL	39	1	8	9	16	....	....	....	....	....

Signed as a free agent by **Springfield** (AHL), July 15, 2013.

LAZAR, Curtis (lah-ZAHR, KUHR-tihs) OTT

Center/Right wing. Shoots right. 6', 196 lbs. Born, Salmon Arm, B.C., February 2, 1995.
(Ottawa's 1st choice, 17th overall, in 2013 Entry Draft).

			Regular Season					Playoffs				
Season	Club	League	GP	G	A	Pts	PIM	GP	G	A	Pts	PIM
2010-11	Okanagan H.A.	CSSHL	6	4	5	9	4	1	0	0	0	0
	Okanagan H.A.	High-BC	39	22	27	49	67	....	....	....	....	....
	Edmonton	WHL	6	0	1	1	0	4	1	0	1	0
2011-12	Edmonton	WHL	63	20	11	31	56	20	8	11	19	4
2012-13	Edmonton	WHL	72	38	23	61	47	22	9	2	11	20

LEBLANC, Chris (luh-BLAWNK, KRIHS) OTT

Right wing. Shoots right. 6'3", 199 lbs. Born, Winthrop, MA , September 12, 1993.
(Ottawa's 6th choice, 161st overall, in 2013 Entry Draft).

			Regular Season					Playoffs				
Season	Club	League	GP	G	A	Pts	PIM	GP	G	A	Pts	PIM
2008-09	Winthrop Vikings	High-MA	20	6	10	16	18	....	....	....	....	....
2009-10	Winthrop Vikings	High-MA	20	13	18	31	32	3	3	3	6	6
2010-11	Winthrop Vikings	High-MA	....	21	25	46	....	....	....	....	....	....
2011-12	Winthrop Vikings	High-MA	....	24	22	46	....	....	....	....	....	....
2012-13	South Shore Kings	EJHL	44	13	20	33	38	2	1	0	1	0

• Signed Letter of Intent to attend **Merrimack College** (Hockey East) in fall of 2013 or 2014.

LEBLANC, Peter (luh-BLAWNK, PEE-tuhr) WSH

Center. Shoots left. 5'10", 175 lbs. Born, Hamilton, Ont., February 3, 1988.
(Chicago's 9th choice, 186th overall, in 2006 Entry Draft).

			Regular Season					Playoffs				
Season	Club	League	GP	G	A	Pts	PIM	GP	G	A	Pts	PIM
2004-05	Hamilton	ON-Jr.A	49	14	22	36	....	....	....	....	....	....
2005-06	Hamilton	ON-Jr.A	21	10	12	22	25	14	8	8	16	8
2006-07	New Hampshire	H-East	39	1	4	5	4	....	....	....	....	....
2007-08	New Hampshire	H-East	37	5	10	15	37	....	....	....	....	....
2008-09	New Hampshire	H-East	38	14	16	30	8	....	....	....	....	....
2009-10	New Hampshire	H-East	39	14	21	35	24	....	....	....	....	....
2010-11	Rockford IceHogs	AHL	57	12	18	30	12	....	....	....	....	....
	Toledo Walleye	ECHL	22	8	14	22	6	....	....	....	....	....
2011-12	Rockford IceHogs	AHL	72	24	20	44	14	....	....	....	....	....
2012-13	Rockford IceHogs	AHL	34	4	8	12	15	....	....	....	....	....
	Hershey Bears	AHL	33	8	10	18	4	5	0	8	8	0

OPJHL Rookie of the Year (2005)

• Missed majority of 2005-06 due to mononucleosis. Signed as a free agent by **Rockford** (AHL), July 29, 2010. • Re-assigned to **Toledo** (ECHL) by **Chicago** (Rockford-AHL), October 13, 2010. Traded to **Washington** by **Chicago** for Mathieu Beaudoin, January 31, 2013.

LEDUC, Loic (luh-DOOK, LOYK) NYI

Defense. Shoots right. 6'6", 221 lbs. Born, Mercier, Que., June 14, 1994.
(NY Islanders' 4th choice, 103rd overall, in 2012 Entry Draft).

			Regular Season					Playoffs				
Season	Club	League	GP	G	A	Pts	PIM	GP	G	A	Pts	PIM
2009-10	Lac St-L. Patriotes	Minor-QU	STATISTICS NOT AVAILABLE									
	Chateauguay	QAAA	1	0	0	0	0	....	....	....	....	....
2010-11	Cape Breton	QMJHL	36	1	3	4	27	2	0	0	0	0
2011-12	Cape Breton	QMJHL	65	2	8	10	99	4	0	1	1	4
2012-13	Cape Breton	QMJHL	38	0	2	2	50	....	....	....	....	....

LEE, John (LEE, JAWN)

Defense. Shoots right. 6'2", 190 lbs. Born, Fargo, ND, January 16, 1989.
(Florida's 5th choice, 131st overall, in 2007 Entry Draft).

			Regular Season					Playoffs				
Season	Club	League	GP	G	A	Pts	PIM	GP	G	A	Pts	PIM
2004-05	Moorhead J.V.	High-MN	STATISTICS NOT AVAILABLE									
	Moorhead Spuds	High-MN	3	0	1	1	0	....	....	....	....	....
2005-06	Moorhead Spuds	High-MN	26	6	21	27	50	....	....	....	....	....
2006-07	Moorhead Spuds	High-MN	26	6	33	39	62	....	....	....	....	....
	Waterloo	USHL	27	2	7	9	56	9	0	3	3	4
2007-08	Waterloo	USHL	59	1	11	12	106	11	0	4	4	24
2008-09	U. of Denver	WCHA	39	0	5	5	38	....	....	....	....	....
2009-10	U. of Denver	WCHA	41	2	10	12	55	....	....	....	....	....
2010-11	U. of Denver	WCHA	39	3	9	12	32	....	....	....	....	....
2011-12	U. of Denver	WCHA	43	3	11	14	45	....	....	....	....	....
2012-13	San Antonio	AHL	50	1	6	7	40	....	....	....	....	....

LEFEBVRE, Philippe (luh-FAYV, fihl-EEP) FLA

Left wing. Shoots left. 5'11", 182 lbs. Born, Trois-Rivieres, Que., February 28, 1991.

			Regular Season					Playoffs				
Season	Club	League	GP	G	A	Pts	PIM	GP	G	A	Pts	PIM
2006-07	Trois-Rivieres	QAAA	43	25	23	48	56	8	3	6	9	6
2007-08	Drummondville	QMJHL	62	10	15	25	16	....	....	....	....	....
2008-09	Drummondville	QMJHL	68	21	27	48	38	19	3	5	8	2
2009-10	Drummondville	QMJHL	66	26	29	55	38	14	2	4	6	9
2010-11	Montreal	QMJHL	60	19	27	46	38	10	3	5	8	0
2011-12	Hamilton Bulldogs	AHL	69	5	6	11	10	....	....	....	....	....
2012-13	Hamilton Bulldogs	AHL	23	4	3	7	10	....	....	....	....	....
	Wheeling Nailers	ECHL	28	8	8	16	12	....	....	....	....	....

Signed as a free agent by **Montreal**, September 15, 2009. Traded to **Florida** by **Montreal** with Florida's 7th round choice (previously acquired) in 2014 Entry Draft for George Parros, July 5, 2013.

LEGAULT, Maxime (luh-GOH, max-EEM)

Right wing. Shoots right. 6'2", 195 lbs. Born, Ste. Agathe, Que., March 28, 1989.
(Buffalo's 6th choice, 194th overall, in 2009 Entry Draft).

			Regular Season					Playoffs				
Season	Club	League	GP	G	A	Pts	PIM	GP	G	A	Pts	PIM
2005-06	Laval-Laurentides	QAAA	36	13	15	28	138	4	2	1	3	21
2006-07	Shawinigan	QMJHL	55	7	12	19	98	4	0	0	0	4
2007-08	Shawinigan	QMJHL	31	6	4	10	61	....	....	....	....	....
2008-09	Shawinigan	QMJHL	63	28	16	44	66	21	10	3	13	23
2009-10	Shawinigan	QMJHL	22	10	10	20	29	....	....	....	....	....
	Cape Breton	QMJHL	21	7	12	19	25	5	1	0	1	4
	Portland Pirates	AHL	5	0	0	0	4	....	....	....	....	....
2010-11	Portland Pirates	AHL	67	12	12	24	83	9	1	1	2	8
2011-12	Rochester	AHL	62	8	9	17	19	3	0	1	1	2
2012-13	Rochester	AHL	60	11	7	18	26	1	0	0	0	0

LEGEIN, Stefan (LEE-gihn, STEH-fan)

Right wing. Shoots right. 5'10", 185 lbs. Born, Oakville, Ont., November 24, 1988.
(Columbus' 2nd choice, 37th overall, in 2007 Entry Draft).

			Regular Season					Playoffs				
Season	Club	League	GP	G	A	Pts	PIM	GP	G	A	Pts	PIM
2003-04	Tor. Red Wings	GTHL	33	19	14	33	63	....	....	....	....	....
2004-05	Milton Icehawks	ON-Jr.A	26	7	12	19	18	....	....	....	....	....
	Mississauga	OHL	49	3	5	8	37	5	0	1	1	0
2005-06	Mississauga	OHL	59	7	9	16	101	....	....	....	....	....
2006-07	Mississauga	OHL	64	43	32	75	115	5	3	2	5	0
2007-08	Niagara Ice Dogs	OHL	30	24	13	37	80	10	7	11	18	28
	Syracuse Crunch	AHL	....	....	....	....	....	2	0	0	0	0
2008-09	Syracuse Crunch	AHL	26	1	0	1	4	....	....	....	....	....
2009-10	Syracuse Crunch	AHL	6	2	1	3	0	....	....	....	....	....
	Adirondack	AHL	71	24	10	34	48	....	....	....	....	....
2010-11	Adirondack	AHL	41	5	12	17	24	....	....	....	....	....
	Greenville	ECHL	2	0	0	0	2	....	....	....	....	....
2011-12	Manchester	AHL	63	14	11	25	44	4	2	0	2	15
2012-13	Manchester	AHL	51	5	12	17	32	1	0	0	0	0

OHL Second All-Star Team (2008)

Traded to **Philadelphia** by **Columbus** for Michael Ratchuk, October 20, 2009. Traded to **Los Angeles** by **Philadelphia** with Philadelphia's 6th round choice (Tomas Hyka) in 2012 Entry Draft for futture considerations, October 12, 2011.

LEHKONEN, Artturi (lehch-KOH-nehn, AHR-tu-ree) MTL

Left wing. Shoots left. 5'11", 161 lbs. Born, Piikkio, Finland, April 7, 1995.
(Montreal's 4th choice, 55th overall, in 2013 Entry Draft).

			Regular Season					Playoffs				
Season	Club	League	GP	G	A	Pts	PIM	GP	G	A	Pts	PIM
2010-11	TPS Turku U18	Fin-U18	28	23	15	38	43	13	8	6	14	4
	TPS Turku Jr.	Fin-Jr.	2	0	1	1	0	....	....	....	....	....
2011-12	TPS Turku U18	Fin-U18	3	4	6	10	0	4	3	4	7	2
	TPS Turku Jr.	Fin-Jr.	40	28	26	54	54	....	....	....	....	....
	TPS Turku	Finland	18	2	2	4	8	2	0	0	0	0
2012-13	KalPa Kuopio	Finland	45	14	16	30	12	4	2	1	3	2

LEHTERA, Jori (LEH-tuhr-a, YOHR-ee) ST.L.

Center. Shoots left. 6'2", 191 lbs. Born, Helsinki, Finland, December 23, 1987.
(St. Louis' 4th choice, 65th overall, in 2008 Entry Draft).

			Regular Season					Playoffs				
Season	Club	League	GP	G	A	Pts	PIM	GP	G	A	Pts	PIM
2003-04	Jokerit U18	Fin-U18	19	0	6	6	2	5	3	1	4	0
2004-05	Jokerit U18	Fin-U18	30	13	37	50	24	7	6	5	11	2
2005-06	Suomi U20	Finland-2	2	0	0	0	0	....	....	....	....	....
	Jokerit Helsinki Jr.	Fin-Jr.	39	14	33	47	16	4	1	4	5	0
2006-07	Suomi U20	Finland-2	10	4	7	11	10	....	....	....	....	....
	Jokerit Helsinki Jr.	Fin-Jr.	24	18	48	66	20	5	1	7	8	2
	Jokerit Helsinki	Finland	28	6	6	12	14	....	....	....	....	....
2007-08	Tappara Tampere	Finland	54	13	29	42	32	11	4	2	6	8
2008-09	Tappara Tampere	Finland	58	9	38	47	34	3	4	5	9	4
	Peoria Rivermen	AHL	7	0	1	1	2	7	1	1	2	10
2009-10	Tappara Tampere	Finland	57	19	*50	*69	58	9	1	9	10	8
2010-11	Yaroslavl	KHL	53	16	21	37	38	18	0	3	3	14
2011-12	Sibir Novosibirsk	KHL	25	10	16	26	10	....	....	....	....	....
2012-13	Sibir Novosibirsk	KHL	52	17	29	46	46	3	0	2	2	0

LEIER, Taylor (LEER, TAY-luhr) PHI

Left wing. Shoots left. 5'10", 174 lbs. Born, Saskatoon, Sask., February 15, 1994.
(Philadelphia's 5th choice, 117th overall, in 2012 Entry Draft).

			Regular Season					Playoffs				
Season	Club	League	GP	G	A	Pts	PIM	GP	G	A	Pts	PIM
2008-09	Saskatoon Bobcats	Minor-SK	STATISTICS NOT AVAILABLE									
	Sask. Contacts	SMHL	2	2	0	2	0	....	....	....	....	....
2009-10	Sask. Contacts	SMHL	41	17	24	41	30	11	5	2	7	0
2010-11	Sask. Contacts	SMHL	44	31	43	74	32	9	7	6	13	8
2011-12	Portland	WHL	72	13	24	37	36	22	5	2	7	12
2012-13	Portland	WHL	64	27	35	62	63	21	9	7	16	12

LEIPSIC, Brendan (LIGHP-sihk, BREHN-duhn) NSH

Left wing. Shoots left. 5'9", 176 lbs. Born, Winnipeg, MB, May 19, 1994.
(Nashville's 4th choice, 89th overall, in 2012 Entry Draft).

			Regular Season					Playoffs				
Season	Club	League	GP	G	A	Pts	PIM	GP	G	A	Pts	PIM
2009-10	Winnipeg Wild	MMHL	40	23	40	63	36	7	2	2	4	17
2010-11	Portland	WHL	68	16	17	33	50	21	3	4	7	14
2011-12	Portland	WHL	65	28	30	58	82	20	7	8	15	28
2012-13	Portland	WHL	68	*49	71	*120	103	21	10	14	24	41

WHL West Second All-Star Team (2013)

LEIVO, Josh (LEE-voh, JAWSH) TOR

Left wing. Shoots right. 6'2", 195 lbs. Born, Innisfil, Ont., May 26, 1993.
(Toronto's 3rd choice, 86th overall, in 2011 Entry Draft).

			Regular Season					Playoffs				
Season	Club	League	GP	G	A	Pts	PIM	GP	G	A	Pts	PIM
2008-09	Barrie Colts	Minor-ON	71	31	35	66	65	....	....	....	....	....
2009-10	Barrie Colts	Minor-ON	52	27	41	68	59	....	....	....	....	....
2010-11	Sudbury Wolves	OHL	64	13	17	30	37	8	6	7	13	4
2011-12	Sudbury Wolves	OHL	66	32	41	73	61	4	2	1	3	6
	Toronto Marlies	AHL	1	0	0	0	0	....	....	....	....	....
2012-13	Sudbury Wolves	OHL	34	19	25	44	34	....	....	....	....	....
	Kitchener Rangers	OHL	29	10	19	29	18	10	3	9	12	8
	Toronto Marlies	AHL	4	0	2	2	2	3	0	1	1	0

LERG, Bryan (LEHRG, BRIGH-uhn) COL

Center. Shoots left. 5'10", 175 lbs. Born, Livonia, MI, January 20, 1986.

			Regular Season					Playoffs				
Season	Club	League	GP	G	A	Pts	PIM	GP	G	A	Pts	PIM
2002-03	USNTDP	U-17	19	11	6	17	5	....	....	....	....	....
	USNTDP	NAHL	46	10	12	22	32	....	....	....	....	....
2003-04	USNTDP	U-18	46	22	25	47	....	....	....	....	....	....
	USNTDP	NAHL	11	5	7	12	10	....	....	....	....	....
2004-05	Michigan State	CCHA	41	10	5	15	14	....	....	....	....	....
2005-06	Michigan State	CCHA	45	15	23	38	26	....	....	....	....	....
2006-07	Michigan State	CCHA	41	23	13	36	21	....	....	....	....	....
2007-08	Michigan State	CCHA	42	20	19	39	18	....	....	....	....	....
	Springfield Falcons	AHL	4	0	2	2	2	....	....	....	....	....
2008-09	Springfield Falcons	AHL	42	9	8	17	24	....	....	....	....	....
	Stockton Thunder	ECHL	7	2	8	10	4	....	....	....	....	....
2009-10	Springfield Falcons	AHL	36	4	3	7	11	....	....	....	....	....
2010-11	Geneve	Swiss	1	0	0	0	0	....	....	....	....	....
	Wilkes-Barre	AHL	65	15	17	32	21	9	1	2	3	4
2011-12	Wilkes-Barre	AHL	70	27	26	53	32	12	0	2	2	4
2012-13	Lake Erie Monsters	AHL	28	9	7	16	6	....	....	....	....	....

Signed as a free agent by **Edmonton**, April 2, 2008. Signed as a free agent by **Geneve** (Swiss), September 3, 2010. Signed as a free agent by **Wilkes-Barre** (AHL), December 8, 2010. Signed as a free agent by **Colorado**, July 13, 2012.

LESLIE, Zachary (LEHS-lee, za-KAH-ree) L.A.

Defense. Shoots left. 6', 168 lbs. Born, Ottawa, Ont., January 31, 1994.
(Los Angeles' 6th choice, 178th overall, in 2013 Entry Draft).

			Regular Season					Playoffs				
Season	Club	League	GP	G	A	Pts	PIM	GP	G	A	Pts	PIM
2009-10	Ott. Jr. 67's M.M.	Minor-ON	29	10	24	34	36	11	2	6	8	12
	Ott. Jr. 67's Mid.	Minor-ON	5	1	1	2	2	3	0	2	2	4
	Gloucester	ON-Jr.A	1	0	0	0	0	....	....	....	....	....
2010-11	Gloucester	ON-Jr.A	56	13	22	35	26	9	1	3	4	4
2011-12	Guelph Storm	OHL	65	2	15	17	54	5	0	0	0	4
2012-13	Guelph Storm	OHL	68	12	28	40	58	5	0	1	1	4

LESSIO, Lucas (LEH-see-oh, LOO-kuhs) **PHX**

Left wing. Shoots left. 6'1", 206 lbs. Born, Maple, Ont., January 23, 1993.
(Phoenix's 3rd choice, 56th overall, in 2011 Entry Draft).

			Regular Season					Playoffs				
Season	Club	League	GP	G	A	Pts	PIM	GP	G	A	Pts	PIM
2008-09	Toronto Marlboros	GTHL	72	53	60	113	126	....	....	....	....	....
2009-10	St. Michael's	ON-Jr.A	41	30	42	72	87	5	0	3	3	10
2010-11	Oshawa Generals	OHL	66	27	27	54	66	10	5	4	9	6
2011-12	Oshawa Generals	OHL	66	34	28	62	71	6	3	2	5	6
2012-13	Oshawa Generals	OHL	35	19	15	34	38	9	1	2	3	20
	Portland Pirates	AHL	5	1	1	2	4	3	0	2	2	0

OHL All-Rookie Team (2011)

LEVI, Austin (LEH-vee, AW-stuhn) **CAR**

Defense. Shoots left. 6'4", 212 lbs. Born, Columbus, OH, February 16, 1992.
(Carolina's 5th choice, 85th overall, in 2010 Entry Draft).

			Regular Season					Playoffs				
Season	Club	League	GP	G	A	Pts	PIM	GP	G	A	Pts	PIM
2007-08	Det. Compuware	MWEHL	22	0	5	5	33	....	....	....	....	....
2008-09	Plymouth Whalers	OHL	12	0	2	2	4	5	0	0	0	5
2009-10	Plymouth Whalers	OHL	68	3	9	12	116	9	0	0	0	8
2010-11	Plymouth Whalers	OHL	66	6	19	25	87	11	1	4	5	8
2011-12	Plymouth Whalers	OHL	64	5	25	30	46	13	2	8	10	10
2012-13	Plymouth Whalers	OHL	58	2	15	17	49	15	0	3	3	14

LEWINGTON, Tyler (LOO-ihng-tuhn, TIGH-luhr) **WSH**

Defense. Shoots right. 6'1", 189 lbs. Born, Edmonton, Alta., December 5, 1994.
(Washington's 6th choice, 204th overall, in 2013 Entry Draft).

			Regular Season					Playoffs				
Season	Club	League	GP	G	A	Pts	PIM	GP	G	A	Pts	PIM
2010-11	Sherwood Park	AMHL	34	4	22	26	46	13	1	8	9	4
2011-12	Medicine Hat	WHL	44	0	3	3	46	8	0	1	1	2
2012-13	Medicine Hat	WHL	69	2	24	26	131	8	1	0	1	14

LIBERATI, Miles (lih-biuhr-A-tee, MIGH-uhlz) **VAN**

Defense. Shoots left. 6', 195 lbs. Born, Pittsburgh, PA, June 21, 1995.
(Vancouver's 7th choice, 205th overall, in 2013 Entry Draft).

			Regular Season					Playoffs				
Season	Club	League	GP	G	A	Pts	PIM	GP	G	A	Pts	PIM
2010-11	Pit. V. Stars M.M.	Minor-PA	62	17	38	55	56	....	....	....	....	....
	Pit. Viper Stars	NAPHL	20	3	9	12	46	....	....	....	....	....
	Pit. V. Stars Mid.	Minor-PA	5	0	4	4	14	....	....	....	....	....
2011-12	The Hill Academy	High-ON	63	20	37	57		....	....	....	....	....
2012-13	London Knights	OHL	42	3	6	9	25	10	0	1	1	0

LIND, Kevin (LIHND, KEH-vihn) **ANA**

Defense. Shoots left. 6'3", 220 lbs. Born, Homer Glen, IL, March 31, 1992.
(Anaheim's 7th choice, 177th overall, in 2010 Entry Draft).

			Regular Season					Playoffs				
Season	Club	League	GP	G	A	Pts	PIM	GP	G	A	Pts	PIM
2008-09	Chicago Mission	T1EHL	25	3	0	3	16	....	....	....	....	....
	Chicago Steel	USHL	50	2	3	5	45	....	....	....	....	....
2009-10	Chicago Steel	USHL	55	6	10	16	76	....	....	....	....	....
2010-11	U. of Notre Dame	CCHA	32	1	10	11	24	....	....	....	....	....
2011-12	U. of Notre Dame	CCHA	39	1	2	3	22	....	....	....	....	....
2012-13	U. of Notre Dame	CCHA	40	2	3	5	33	....	....	....	....	....

LINDBERG, Oscar (LIHND-buhrg, AWS-kuhr) **NYR**

Center. Shoots left. 6'1", 190 lbs. Born, Skelleftea, Sweden, October 29, 1991.
(Phoenix's 4th choice, 57th overall, in 2010 Entry Draft).

			Regular Season					Playoffs				
Season	Club	League	GP	G	A	Pts	PIM	GP	G	A	Pts	PIM
2007-08	Skelleftea U18	Swe-U18	31	19	29	48	36	....	....	....	....	....
	Skelleftea Jr.	Swe-Jr.	1	0	0	0	2	2	0	1	1	0
2008-09	Skelleftea AIK U18	Swe-U18	6	8	10	18	14	7	4	5	9	8
	Skelleftea AIK Jr.	Swe-Jr.	38	14	19	33	54	5	0	1	1	4
2009-10	Skelleftea AIK Jr.	Swe-Jr.	30	14	23	37	44	1	1	1	2	12
	Skelleftea AIK	Sweden	36	1	1	2	35	10	2	0	2	2
2010-11	Skelleftea AIK Jr.	Swe-Jr.	9	8	4	12	8	....	....	....	....	....
	Skelleftea AIK	Sweden	41	5	9	14	31	18	3	4	7	4
2011-12	Skelleftea AIK Jr.	Swe-Jr.	2	1	3	4	2	....	....	....	....	....
	Sundsvall	Sweden-2	5	1	1	2	2	....	....	....	....	....
	Skelleftea AIK	Sweden	46	5	5	10	18	18	1	3	4	10
2012-13	Skelleftea AIK	Sweden	55	17	25	42	54	13	4	8	*12	16

Traded to **NY Rangers** by **Phoenix** for Ethan Werek, May 8, 2011.

LINDBERG, Tobias (LIHND-buhrg, toh-BEE-uhs) **OTT**

Right wing. Shoots left. 6'2", 201 lbs. Born, Stockholm, Sweden, July 22, 1995.
(Ottawa's 3rd choice, 102nd overall, in 2013 Entry Draft).

			Regular Season					Playoffs				
Season	Club	League	GP	G	A	Pts	PIM	GP	G	A	Pts	PIM
2010-11	SDE U18	Swe-U18	9	0	2	2	18	....	....	....	....	....
2011-12	Djurgarden U18	Swe-U18	39	19	20	39	42	4	2	0	2	20
	Djurgarden Jr.	Swe-Jr.	1	0	0	0	0	3	0	1	1	0
2012-13	Djurgarden U18	Swe-U18	14	9	12	21	6	9	4	10	14	24
	Djurgarden Jr.	Swe-Jr.	43	9	13	22	30	2	0	2	2	2
	Djurgarden	Sweden-2	6	0	1	1	4	....	....	....	....	....

LINDBLAD, Matt (LIHN-blad, MAT) **BOS**

Left wing. Shoots left. 5'11", 193 lbs. Born, Winnetka, IL, March 23, 1990.

			Regular Season					Playoffs				
Season	Club	League	GP	G	A	Pts	PIM	GP	G	A	Pts	PIM
2008-09	Chicago Steel	USHL	51	5	20	25	17	....	....	....	....	....
2009-10	Sioux Falls	USHL	57	24	46	70	20	3	1	2	3	2
2010-11	Dartmouth	ECAC	33	13	15	28	4	....	....	....	....	....
2011-12	Dartmouth	ECAC	26	6	18	24	2	....	....	....	....	....
2012-13	Dartmouth	ECAC	30	10	18	28	2	....	....	....	....	....
	Providence Bruins	AHL	4	1	4	5	0	....	....	....	....	....

Signed as a free agent by **Boston**, April 5, 2013.

LINDBOHM, Petteri (LIHND-bawm, PEH-tuh-ree) **ST.L.**

Defense. Shoots left. 6'3", 209 lbs. Born, Helsinki, Finland, September 23, 1993.
(St. Louis' 7th choice, 176th overall, in 2012 Entry Draft).

			Regular Season					Playoffs				
Season	Club	League	GP	G	A	Pts	PIM	GP	G	A	Pts	PIM
2009-10	K-Vantaa U18	Fin-U18	31	1	3	4	34	6	0	0	0	24
2010-11	Blues Espoo U18	Fin-U18	7	2	6	8	10	2	0	2	2	2
	Blues Espoo Jr.	Fin-Jr.	41	1	8	9	56	13	0	3	3	12
2011-12	Jokerit Helsinki Jr.	Fin-Jr.	41	3	7	10	98	12	0	3	3	12
	Kiekko-Vantaa	Finland-2	5	0	3	3	8	....	....	....	....	....
2012-13	Jokerit Helsinki Jr.	Fin-Jr.	2	0	1	1	2	....	....	....	....	....
	Kiekko-Vantaa	Finland-2	6	3	0	3	4	....	....	....	....	....
	Jokerit Helsinki	Finland	35	0	4	4	61	....	....	....	....	....

LINDELL, Esa (lihn-DEHL, EH-suh) **DAL**

Defense. Shoots left. 6'3", 187 lbs. Born, Vantaa, Finland, May 23, 1994.
(Dallas' 5th choice, 74th overall, in 2012 Entry Draft).

			Regular Season					Playoffs				
Season	Club	League	GP	G	A	Pts	PIM	GP	G	A	Pts	PIM
2009-10	Jokerit U18	Fin-U18	3	0	1	1	2	....	....	....	....	....
2010-11	Jokerit U18	Fin-U18	14	5	7	12	10	4	0	1	1	4
	Jokerit Helsinki Jr.	Fin-Jr.	....	....	....	....	....	3	1	1	2	2
2011-12	Jokerit Helsinki Jr.	Fin-Jr.	48	21	30	51	16	11	2	5	7	6
	Kiekko-Vantaa	Finland-2	2	0	0	0	0	....	....	....	....	....
2012-13	Jokerit Helsinki Jr.	Fin-Jr.	11	5	4	9	6	....	....	....	....	....
	Kiekko-Vantaa	Finland-2	22	4	6	10	16	....	....	....	....	....
	Jokerit Helsinki	Finland	19	0	0	0	4	....	....	....	....	....

LINDHOLM, Elias (LIHND-hohlm, uh-LIGH-uhs) **CAR**

Center. Shoots right. 6'1", 192 lbs. Born, Boden , Sweden, December 2, 1994.
(Carolina's 1st choice, 5th overall, in 2013 Entry Draft).

			Regular Season					Playoffs				
Season	Club	League	GP	G	A	Pts	PIM	GP	G	A	Pts	PIM
2009-10	Brynas U18	Swe-U18	9	4	6	10	0	....	....	....	....	....
2010-11	Brynas U18	Swe-U18	40	17	44	61	32	4	3	3	6	29
	Brynas IF Gavle Jr.	Swe-Jr.	2	0	0	0	0	2	0	1	1	0
2011-12	Brynas U18	Swe-U18	4	1	6	7	0	3	1	2	3	0
	Brynas IF Gavle Jr.	Swe-Jr.	36	14	35	49	45	2	1	1	2	16
	Brynas IF Gavle	Sweden	12	0	0	0	0	2	0	0	0	0
2012-13	Brynas IF Gavle	Sweden	48	11	19	30	2	4	0	0	0	4

LINDHOLM, Hampus (LIHND-hohlm, HAM-puhs) **ANA**

Defense. Shoots left. 6'3", 200 lbs. Born, Helsingborg, Sweden, January 20, 1994.
(Anaheim's 1st choice, 6th overall, in 2012 Entry Draft).

			Regular Season					Playoffs				
Season	Club	League	GP	G	A	Pts	PIM	GP	G	A	Pts	PIM
2008-09	Jonstorps IF U18	Swe-U18	1	0	0	0	0	....	....	....	....	....
2009-10	Jonstorps IF U18	Swe-U18	15	3	4	7	8	....	....	....	....	....
	Jonstorps IF Jr.	Swe-Jr.	3	1	2	3	0	....	....	....	....	....
2010-11	Rogle U18	Swe-U18	11	2	3	5	10	3	0	2	2	0
	Rogle Jr.	Swe-Jr.	39	0	4	4	34	3	0	0	0	0
2011-12	Rogle U18	Swe-U18	1	1	3	4	2	....	....	....	....	....
	Rogle Jr.	Swe-Jr.	28	5	12	17	16	....	....	....	....	....
	Rogle	Sweden-2	36	2	7	9	18	....	....	....	....	....
2012-13	Norfolk Admirals	AHL	44	1	10	11	16	....	....	....	....	....

LINDSTROM, Mattias (LIHND-struhm, ma-TEE-uhs) **FLA**

Left wing. Shoots left. 6'4", 205 lbs. Born, Lulea, Sweden, March 21, 1991.
(Carolina's 3rd choice, 88th overall, in 2009 Entry Draft).

			Regular Season					Playoffs				
Season	Club	League	GP	G	A	Pts	PIM	GP	G	A	Pts	PIM
2007-08	Skelleftea U18	Swe-U18	3	1	0	1	0	....	....	....	....	....
	Skelleftea Jr.	Swe-Jr.	21	5	1	6	40	....	....	....	....	....
2008-09	Skelleftea AIK U18	Swe-U18	2	0	0	0	6	5	0	1	1	10
	Skelleftea AIK Jr.	Swe-Jr.	31	8	5	13	46	5	2	0	2	0
	Skelleftea AIK	Sweden	7	1	0	1	0	7	1	0	1	0
2009-10	Skelleftea AIK Jr.	Swe-Jr.	1	0	0	0	0	....	....	....	....	....
2010-11	Skelleftea AIK Jr.	Swe-Jr.	28	3	8	11	38	5	0	2	2	4
	Bodens HF	Sweden-3	2	0	0	0	2	....	....	....	....	....
	Skelleftea AIK	Sweden	11	0	0	0	8	9	0	0	0	0
2011-12	Tingsryds AIF	Sweden-2	34	0	3	3	16	....	....	....	....	....
2012-13	Cincinnati	ECHL	49	4	9	13	54	13	0	1	1	8

• Missed majority of 2009-10 due to knee injury. Traded to **Florida** by **Carolina** with Jon Matsumoto for Evgeny Dadonov and A.J. Jenks, January 18, 2012.

LIPON, J.C. (lih-PAWN, JAY-SEE) **WPG**

Right wing. Shoots right. 6', 180 lbs. Born, Regina, Sask., July 10, 1993.
(Winnipeg's 5th choice, 91st overall, in 2013 Entry Draft).

			Regular Season					Playoffs				
Season	Club	League	GP	G	A	Pts	PIM	GP	G	A	Pts	PIM
2008-09	Reg. Pat Cdns.	SMHL	43	4	9	13	26	5	2	1	3	4
2009-10	Kamloops Blazers	WHL	53	3	10	13	38	3	0	0	0	0
2010-11	Kamloops Blazers	WHL	65	3	18	21	111	....	....	....	....	....
2011-12	Kamloops Blazers	WHL	69	19	46	65	111	10	2	7	9	20
2012-13	Kamloops Blazers	WHL	61	36	53	89	115	15	6	17	23	20

LIVINGSTON, James (LIH-vihng-stuhn, JAYMZ) **S.J.**

Right wing. Shoots right. 6'1", 210 lbs. Born, Halifax, N.S., March 8, 1990.
(St. Louis' 5th choice, 70th overall, in 2008 Entry Draft).

			Regular Season					Playoffs				
Season	Club	League	GP	G	A	Pts	PIM	GP	G	A	Pts	PIM
2005-06	York Simcoe	Minor-ON	51	25	32	57		....	....	....	....	....
2006-07	Sault Ste. Marie	OHL	60	2	5	7	95	13	1	0	1	15
2007-08	Sault Ste. Marie	OHL	68	21	23	44	135	14	2	3	5	14
2008-09	Sault Ste. Marie	OHL	66	20	17	37	98	....	....	....	....	....
2009-10	Sault Ste. Marie	OHL	36	14	12	26	47	....	....	....	....	....
	Plymouth Whalers	OHL	24	3	6	9	57	9	1	1	2	6
2010-11	Plymouth Whalers	OHL	62	22	27	49	52	11	4	1	5	8
2011-12	Worcester Sharks	AHL	68	6	14	20	47	....	....	....	....	....
2012-13	Worcester Sharks	AHL	67	7	14	21	78	....	....	....	....	....

Signed as a free agent by **San Jose**, March 11, 2011.

LOCKE, Eric (LAWK, AIR-ihk) BUF

Center. Shoots left. 5'10", 183 lbs. Born, Mount Holly, NJ, November 21, 1993.
(Buffalo's 11th choice, 189th overall, in 2013 Entry Draft).

			Regular Season					Playoffs				
Season	Club	League	GP	G	A	Pts	PIM	GP	G	A	Pts	PIM
2008-09	Mississauga Reps	GTHL	28	12	30	42	24	....	....	....	....	....
2009-10	Mississauga Reps	GTHL	29	13	27	40	20	10	12	7	19	4
2010-11	Windsor Spitfires	OHL	38	19	14	33	12	....	....	....	....	....
	Barrie Colts	OHL	27	7	14	21	18	....	....	....	....	....
2011-12	Barrie Colts	OHL	21	7	6	13	12	....	....	....	....	....
	Saginaw Spirit	OHL	31	13	14	27	22	12	2	2	4	14
2012-13	Saginaw Spirit	OHL	68	44	53	97	84	4	2	0	2	2

LODGE, Jimmy (LAWDG, JIHM-ee) WPG

Center. Shoots right. 6'1", 166 lbs. Born, West Chester, PA, March 5, 1995.
(Winnipeg's 4th choice, 84th overall, in 2013 Entry Draft).

			Regular Season					Playoffs				
Season	Club	League	GP	G	A	Pts	PIM	GP	G	A	Pts	PIM
2010-11	Toronto Titans	GTHL	29	18	25	43	44	....	....	....	....	....
2011-12	Saginaw Spirit	OHL	45	8	4	12	10	11	0	0	0	0
2012-13	Saginaw Spirit	OHL	64	28	39	67	28	4	1	2	3	7

LOOV, Viktor (LOHV, VIHK-tohr) TOR

Defense. Shoots left. 6'3", 190 lbs. Born, Sodertalje, Sweden, November 16, 1992.
(Toronto's 6th choice, 209th overall, in 2012 Entry Draft).

			Regular Season					Playoffs				
Season	Club	League	GP	G	A	Pts	PIM	GP	G	A	Pts	PIM
2008-09	Sodertalje SK U18	Swe-U18	17	0	3	3	8	4	0	1	1	6
2009-10	Sodertalje SK U18	Swe-U18	21	4	14	18	32	2	0	0	0	4
	Sodertalje SK Jr.	Swe-Jr.	12	0	4	4	8	....	....	....	....	....
2010-11	Sodertalje SK Jr.	Swe-Jr.	42	4	19	23	36	2	0	0	0	2
	Sodertalje SK	Sweden-Q	1	0	0	0	0	....	....	....	....	....
2011-12	Sodertalje SK Jr.	Swe-Jr.	5	0	3	3	2	4	2	0	2	2
	Sodertalje SK	Sweden-2	50	3	3	6	42	....	....	....	....	....
2012-13	Sodertalje SK	Sweden-2	50	2	9	11	57	....	....	....	....	....

LOUIS, Anthony (LOO-ihs, AN-thuh-nee) CHI

Center. Shoots left. 5'7", 145 lbs. Born, Wheaton, IL, February 10, 1995.
(Chicago's 7th choice, 181st overall, in 2013 Entry Draft).

			Regular Season					Playoffs				
Season	Club	League	GP	G	A	Pts	PIM	GP	G	A	Pts	PIM
2010-11	Team Illinois	T1EHL	35	33	27	60	18	....	....	....	....	....
2011-12	USNTDP	USHL	32	16	6	22	12	....	....	....	....	....
	USNTDP	U-17	17	12	8	20	6	....	....	....	....	....
	USNTDP	U-18	7	0	1	1	2	....	....	....	....	....
2012-13	USNTDP	USHL	24	10	15	25	10	....	....	....	....	....
	USNTDP	U-18	38	12	14	26	10	....	....	....	....	....

• Signed Letter of Intent to attend **Miami University** (CCHA) in fall of 2013.

LOUIS, Mark (LEW-ihs, MAHRK) PHX

Defense. Shoots right. 6'4", 225 lbs. Born, Ponoka, Alta., April 18, 1987.

			Regular Season					Playoffs				
Season	Club	League	GP	G	A	Pts	PIM	GP	G	A	Pts	PIM
2003-04	Brandon	WHL	39	0	1	1	18	....	....	....	....	....
2004-05	Brandon	WHL	66	2	10	12	94	12	0	2	2	12
2005-06	Brandon	WHL	58	1	7	8	61	6	0	0	0	4
2006-07	Brandon	WHL	72	2	6	8	113	11	0	0	0	8
2007-08	Brandon	WHL	6	0	2	2	15	....	....	....	....	....
	Red Deer Rebels	WHL	62	5	14	19	78	....	....	....	....	....
2008-09	St. FX University	AUAA	3	0	0	0	8	....	....	....	....	....
2009-10	St. FX University	AUAA	11	0	2	2	36	....	....	....	....	....
2010-11	St. FX University	AUAA	27	1	1	2	48	....	....	....	....	....
2011-12	Portland Pirates	AHL	23	0	4	4	72	....	....	....	....	....
2012-13	Portland Pirates	AHL	61	0	3	3	111	2	0	0	0	0

Signed as a free agent by **Phoenix**, April 30, 2012.

LOWE, Keegan (LOH, KEE-guhn) CAR

Defense. Shoots left. 6'2", 195 lbs. Born, Greenwich, CT, March 29, 1993.
(Carolina's 3rd choice, 73rd overall, in 2011 Entry Draft).

			Regular Season					Playoffs				
Season	Club	League	GP	G	A	Pts	PIM	GP	G	A	Pts	PIM
2008-09	Shattuck U16	High-MN	55	7	26	33	77	....	....	....	....	....
2009-10	Edmonton	WHL	69	2	12	14	60	....	....	....	....	....
2010-11	Edmonton	WHL	71	2	22	24	123	4	1	0	1	4
2011-12	Edmonton	WHL	72	3	20	23	139	20	3	4	7	44
2012-13	Edmonton	WHL	64	15	16	31	148	22	1	7	8	28

WHL East Second All-Star Team (2013)

LOWRY, Adam (LOW-ree, A-duhm) WPG

Left wing. Shoots left. 6'5", 210 lbs. Born, Calgary, Alta., March 29, 1993.
(Winnipeg's 2nd choice, 67th overall, in 2011 Entry Draft).

			Regular Season					Playoffs				
Season	Club	League	GP	G	A	Pts	PIM	GP	G	A	Pts	PIM
2007-08	Calgary Bisons	AMBHL	33	27	21	48	56	12	4	6	10	10
	Cgy. Blackhawks	Minor-AB	1	0	1	1	0	....	....	....	....	....
2008-09	Calgary Rangers	Minor-AB	29	29	25	54	51	....	....	....	....	....
2009-10	Swift Current	WHL	61	15	19	34	57	3	0	1	1	6
2010-11	Swift Current	WHL	66	18	27	45	84	....	....	....	....	....
2011-12	Swift Current	WHL	36	12	25	37	90	....	....	....	....	....
2012-13	Swift Current	WHL	72	45	43	88	102	5	3	2	5	4
	St. John's IceCaps	AHL	9	0	1	1	4	....	....	....	....	....

WHL East First All-Star Team (2013) • WHL Player of the Year (2013)

LOWRY, Joel (LOW-ree, JOHL) L.A.

Left wing. Shoots left. 6'2", 185 lbs. Born, Calgary, Alta., November 15, 1991.
(Los Angeles' 5th choice, 140th overall, in 2011 Entry Draft).

			Regular Season					Playoffs				
Season	Club	League	GP	G	A	Pts	PIM	GP	G	A	Pts	PIM
2008-09	Calgary Buffaloes	AMHL	32	14	16	30	32	15	5	6	11	20
	Okotoks Oilers	AJHL	3	0	0	0	0	....	....	....	....	....
2009-10	Victoria Grizzlies	BCHL	57	15	29	44	55	6	1	4	5	2
2010-11	Victoria Grizzlies	BCHL	42	24	43	67	35	12	5	12	17	6
2011-12	Cornell Big Red	ECAC	35	6	16	22	47	....	....	....	....	....
2012-13	Cornell Big Red	ECAC	33	12	11	23	55	....	....	....	....	....

LUCIA, Mario (LOO-chee-a, MAR-ee-oh) MIN

Left wing. Shoots left. 6'3", 195 lbs. Born, Fairbanks, AK, August 25, 1993.
(Minnesota's 3rd choice, 60th overall, in 2011 Entry Draft).

			Regular Season					Playoffs				
Season	Club	League	GP	G	A	Pts	PIM	GP	G	A	Pts	PIM
2009-10	Wayzata	High-MN	25	15	25	40	6	2	0	2	2	0
2010-11	Team Northwest	UMHSEL	10	6	6	12	4	1	0	0	0	0
	Wayzata	High-MN	24	25	22	47	14	3	5	2	7	2
	USNTDP	USHL	6	3	0	3	0	....	....	....	....	....
	USNTDP	U-18	9	1	1	2	0	....	....	....	....	....
2011-12	Penticton Vees	BCHL	56	42	51	93	42	15	6	10	16	2
2012-13	U. of Notre Dame	CCHA	32	12	11	23	18	....	....	....	....	....

CCHA All-Rookie Team (2013)

LUCIANI, Anthony (loo-chee-AN-ee, AN-thun-ee) FLA

Right wing. Shoots right. 5'8", 185 lbs. Born, Maple, Ont., May 13, 1990.

			Regular Season					Playoffs				
Season	Club	League	GP	G	A	Pts	PIM	GP	G	A	Pts	PIM
2005-06	Don Mills Flyers	GTHL	STATISTICS NOT AVAILABLE									
	Wexford Raiders	ON-Jr.A	2	0	0	0	2	....	....	....	....	....
2006-07	Huntsville	ON-Jr.A	42	6	8	14	35	5	0	0	0	0
2007-08	Georgetown	ON-Jr.A	13	7	7	14	19	7	1	3	4	17
2008-09	Erie Otters	OHL	59	6	8	14	84	4	0	1	1	5
2009-10	Erie Otters	OHL	68	38	30	68	67	3	2	1	3	7
2010-11	Erie Otters	OHL	54	29	49	78	30	7	7	3	10	12
	Rochester	AHL	3	2	1	3	2	....	....	....	....	....
2011-12	Cincinnati	ECHL	54	26	23	49	53	....	....	....	....	....
	San Antonio	AHL	2	0	0	0	0	....	....	....	....	....
2012-13	Cincinnati	ECHL	29	4	12	16	43	....	....	....	....	....
	San Antonio	AHL	5	1	0	1	6	....	....	....	....	....

Signed as a free agent by **Florida**, April 7, 2011.

LUNDEN, Josh (LUHN-dehn, JAWSH)

Left wing. Shoots left. 6'2", 202 lbs. Born, Burnaby, B.C., February 24, 1986.

			Regular Season					Playoffs				
Season	Club	League	GP	G	A	Pts	PIM	GP	G	A	Pts	PIM
2006-07	Alaska Anchorage	WCHA	31	11	9	20	36	....	....	....	....	....
2008-09	Alaska-Anchorage	WCHA	34	14	6	20	26	....	....	....	....	....
2009-10	Alaska-Anchorage	WCHA	25	8	9	17	22	....	....	....	....	....
	San Antonio	AHL	8	0	2	2	7	....	....	....	....	....
2010-11	San Antonio	AHL	12	0	0	0	6	....	....	....	....	....
	Las Vegas	ECHL	11	5	3	8	8	....	....	....	....	....
2011-12	Peoria Rivermen	AHL	1	0	0	0	0	....	....	....	....	....
	Las Vegas	ECHL	44	21	21	42	61	15	4	6	10	21
	Peoria Rivermen	AHL	1	0	0	0	0	....	....	....	....	....
	Houston Aeros	AHL	2	0	0	0	0	....	....	....	....	....
	St. John's IceCaps	AHL	11	0	1	1	7	....	....	....	....	....
	St. John's IceCaps	AHL	2	0	0	0	0	....	....	....	....	....
2012-13	Las Vegas	ECHL	24	7	12	19	44	....	....	....	....	....
	St. John's IceCaps	AHL	31	8	10	18	33	....	....	....	....	....

Signed as a free agent by **Phoenix**, March 19, 2010.

LUUKKO, Nick (LOO-koh, NIHK) PHI

Defense. Shoots right. 6'2", 210 lbs. Born, West Chester, PA, November 29, 1991.
(Philadelphia's 4th choice, 179th overall, in 2010 Entry Draft).

			Regular Season					Playoffs				
Season	Club	League	GP	G	A	Pts	PIM	GP	G	A	Pts	PIM
2008-09	Team Comcast	AYHL	3	0	1	1	2	....	....	....	....	....
	The Gunnery	High-CT	34	4	11	15		....	....	....	....	....
2009-10	The Gunnery	High-CT	....	3	22	25	....	....	....	....	....	....
2010-11	Dubuque	USHL	45	7	10	17	20	11	1	4	5	2
2011-12	U. of Vermont	H-East	17	0	3	3	4	....	....	....	....	....
2012-13	U. of Vermont	H-East	36	3	7	10	26	....	....	....	....	....

LYAMIN, Kirill (L'YAH-mihn, kih-RIHL) OTT

Defense. Shoots left. 6'2", 211 lbs. Born, Moscow, USSR, January 13, 1986.
(Ottawa's 2nd choice, 58th overall, in 2004 Entry Draft).

			Regular Season					Playoffs				
Season	Club	League	GP	G	A	Pts	PIM	GP	G	A	Pts	PIM
2001-02	Moscow 18	Exhib.	5	0	3	3	4	....	....	....	....	....
2002-03	CSKA Moscow 2	Russia-3	5	0	0	0	10	....	....	....	....	....
	Moscow 18	Exhib.	5	0	0	0	6	....	....	....	....	....
2003-04	CSKA Moscow 2	Russia-3	STATISTICS NOT AVAILABLE									
	CSKA Moscow	Russia	28	0	3	3	12	....	....	....	....	....
2004-05	CSKA Moscow 2	Russia-3	STATISTICS NOT AVAILABLE									
2005-06	CSKA Moscow	Russia	25	0	1	1	28	2	0	0	0	0
2006-07	CSKA Moscow	Russia	47	1	7	8	48	12	1	0	1	8
2007-08	Mytischi	Russia	40	1	6	7	77	3	0	0	0	0
2008-09	Spartak Moscow	KHL	54	1	7	8	82	6	0	0	0	4
2009-10	Spartak Moscow	KHL	48	3	9	12	52	9	0	1	1	8
2010-11	Cherepovets	KHL	49	3	9	12	66	6	1	2	3	8
2011-12	Omsk	KHL	49	1	4	5	53	19	0	5	5	12
2012-13	Omsk	KHL	37	3	1	4	32	12	1	0	1	6

MAATTA, Olli (MA-TA, OH-lee) PIT

Defense. Shoots left. 6'2", 206 lbs. Born, Jyvaskyla, Finland, August 22, 1994.
(Pittsburgh's 2nd choice, 22nd overall, in 2012 Entry Draft).

			Regular Season					Playoffs				
Season	Club	League	GP	G	A	Pts	PIM	GP	G	A	Pts	PIM
2009-10	JyP Jyvaskyla U18	Fin-U18	2	0	0	0	2	....	....	....	....	....
	JyP Jyvaskyla Jr.	Fin-Jr.	1	0	1	1	0	....	....	....	....	....
2010-11	Suomi U20	Finland-2	2	0	2	2	2	....	....	....	....	....
	JyP Jyvaskyla U18	Fin-U18	1	0	0	0	0	....	....	....	....	....
	D Team Jyvaskyla	Finland-2	23	1	5	6	6	....	....	....	....	....
	JyP Jyvaskyla Jr.	Fin-Jr.	19	2	6	8	8	12	1	4	5	6
2011-12	London Knights	OHL	58	5	27	32	25	19	6	17	23	2
2012-13	London Knights	OHL	57	8	30	38	30	21	4	10	14	8
	Wilkes-Barre	AHL	....	....	....	....	....	3	0	0	0	0

OHL All-Rookie Team (2012)

MacDERMID, Kurtis (mak-DUHR-mihd, KUHR-this) L.A.

Defense. Shoots left. 6'3", 186 lbs. Born, Quebec, Que., March 25, 1994.

			Regular Season					Playoffs				
Season	Club	League	GP	G	A	Pts	PIM	GP	G	A	Pts	PIM
2010-11	Owen Sound	ON-Jr.B	51	6	16	22	124	....	....	....	....	....
2011-12	Owen Sound	ON-Jr.B	20	3	6	9	80	....	....	....	....	....
	Owen Sound	OHL	9	0	2	2	7	....	....	....	....	....
2012-13	Owen Sound	OHL	65	1	7	8	110	12	0	3	3	11

Signed as a free agent by **Los Angeles**, September 12, 2012.

MACEACHERN, Mackenzie (MAK-EHK-uhrn, muh-KEHN-zee) ST.L.

Left wing. Shoots left. 6'3", 180 lbs. Born, Royal Oak, MI, March 9, 1994.
(St. Louis' 3rd choice, 67th overall, in 2012 Entry Draft).

			Regular Season					Playoffs				
Season	Club	League	GP	G	A	Pts	PIM	GP	G	A	Pts	PIM
2010-11	Brother Rice	High-MI	30	23	41	64	12	....	....	....	....	....
2011-12	Brother Rice	High-MI	29	42	48	90	16	....	....	....	....	....
	Michigan D.H.L.	Exhib.	18	7	8	15	8	....	....	....	....	....
2012-13	Chicago Steel	USHL	50	8	13	21	35	....	....	....	....	....

• Signed Letter of Intent to attend **Michigan State University** (CCHA) in fall of 2013.

MacKENZIE, Drew (muh-KEHN-zee , DROO)

Defense. Shoots left. 6'2", 195 lbs. Born, New Canaan, CT, December 17, 1988.
(Buffalo's 8th choice, 209th overall, in 2007 Entry Draft).

			Regular Season					Playoffs				
Season	Club	League	GP	G	A	Pts	PIM	GP	G	A	Pts	PIM
2004-05	Taft Rhinos	High-CT	....	0	1	1	....	....	....	....	....	....
2005-06	Taft Rhinos	High-CT	....	0	11	11	....	....	....	....	....	....
2006-07	Taft Rhinos	High-CT	24	3	10	13	10	....	....	....	....	....
2007-08	Waterloo	USHL	57	4	14	18	103	11	0	6	6	4
2008-09	U. of Vermont	H-East	31	1	9	10	14	....	....	....	....	....
2009-10	U. of Vermont	H-East	36	4	10	14	16	....	....	....	....	....
2010-11	U. of Vermont	H-East	34	5	12	17	16	....	....	....	....	....
2011-12	U. of Vermont	H-East	32	7	16	23	32	....	....	....	....	....
2012-13	Utah Grizzlies	ECHL	25	5	9	14	26	....	....	....	....	....
	Abbotsford Heat	AHL	27	1	8	9	14	....	....	....	....	....

MacKENZIE, Matt (muh-KEHN-zee, MAT) BUF

Defense. Shoots right. 6'1", 180 lbs. Born, New Westminster, B.C., October 15, 1991.
(Buffalo's 4th choice, 83rd overall, in 2010 Entry Draft).

			Regular Season					Playoffs				
Season	Club	League	GP	G	A	Pts	PIM	GP	G	A	Pts	PIM
2006-07	Van. NW Giants	BCMML	40	5	11	16	64	....	....	....	....	....
2007-08	Calgary Hitmen	WHL	39	2	6	8	8	6	1	2	3	2
2008-09	Calgary Hitmen	WHL	49	3	9	12	24	16	0	2	2	4
2009-10	Calgary Hitmen	WHL	64	6	34	40	62	23	6	10	16	31
2010-11	Calgary Hitmen	WHL	40	2	21	23	50	....	....	....	....	....
	Tri-City Americans	WHL	33	5	10	15	36	10	1	4	5	6
2011-12	Gwinnett	ECHL	5	0	2	2	11	....	....	....	....	....
	Rochester	AHL	20	0	4	4	16	....	....	....	....	....
2012-13	Rochester	AHL	30	0	4	4	66	2	0	1	1	2
	Greenville	ECHL	2	1	0	1	2	....	....	....	....	....

MacKINNON, Nathan (muh-KIH-nuhn, NAY-thuhn) COL

Center. Shoots right. 6', 182 lbs. Born, Halifax, N.S., September 1, 1995.
(Colorado's 1st choice, 1st overall, in 2013 Entry Draft).

			Regular Season					Playoffs				
Season	Club	League	GP	G	A	Pts	PIM	GP	G	A	Pts	PIM
2009-10	Shattuck Bantam	High-MN	58	54	47	101	56	....	....	....	....	....
2010-11	Shattuck Midget	High-MN	40	45	48	93	72	....	....	....	....	....
2011-12	Halifax	QMJHL	58	31	47	78	45	17	13	15	28	12
2012-13	Halifax	QMJHL	44	32	43	75	45	17	11	22	33	12

QMJHL Second All-Star Team (2013)

MacLEOD, Isaac (muh-KLOWD, IGH-zihk) S.J.

Defense. Shoots left. 6'4", 215 lbs. Born, Nelson, B.C., February 22, 1992.
(San Jose's 5th choice, 136th overall, in 2010 Entry Draft).

			Regular Season					Playoffs				
Season	Club	League	GP	G	A	Pts	PIM	GP	G	A	Pts	PIM
2008-09	Nelson Leafs	KIJHL	45	3	16	19	68	13	3	2	5	48
	Penticton Vees	BCHL	3	0	1	1	0	....	....	....	....	....
2009-10	Penticton Vees	BCHL	56	0	23	23	51	14	0	1	1	6
2010-11	Boston College	H-East	22	0	3	3	10	....	....	....	....	....
2011-12	Boston College	H-East	44	0	6	6	22	....	....	....	....	....
2012-13	Boston College	H-East	36	2	5	7	16	....	....	....	....	....

MacMILLAN, Mark (muhk-MIHL-uhn, MAHRK) MTL

Forward. Shoots left. 6', 171 lbs. Born, Penticton, B.C., January 23, 1992.
(Montreal's 2nd choice, 113th overall, in 2010 Entry Draft).

			Regular Season					Playoffs				
Season	Club	League	GP	G	A	Pts	PIM	GP	G	A	Pts	PIM
2008-09	Okanagan Prep	Minor-BC	50	16	21	37	34	....	....	....	....	....
2009-10	Alberni Valley	BCHL	59	26	54	80	44	13	5	9	14	16
2010-11	Penticton Vees	BCHL	40	21	36	57	43	3	0	5	5	6
2011-12	North Dakota	WCHA	42	7	16	23	26	....	....	....	....	....
2012-13	North Dakota	WCHA	42	13	12	25	28	....	....	....	....	....

MacWILLIAM, Andrew (MAK-WIHL-yuhm, AN-droo) TOR

Defense. Shoots left. 6'2", 230 lbs. Born, Calgary, Alta., March 25, 1990.
(Toronto's 8th choice, 188th overall, in 2008 Entry Draft).

			Regular Season					Playoffs				
Season	Club	League	GP	G	A	Pts	PIM	GP	G	A	Pts	PIM
2006-07	Calgary Royals	AMHL	35	5	13	18	125	....	....	....	....	....
	Camrose Kodiaks	AJHL	2	0	0	0	0	1	0	0	0	0
2007-08	Camrose Kodiaks	AJHL	54	0	13	13	130	18	0	5	5	49
2008-09	Camrose Kodiaks	AJHL	57	8	21	29	220	11	0	4	4	39
2009-10	North Dakota	WCHA	43	0	3	3	87	....	....	....	....	....
2010-11	North Dakota	WCHA	37	0	8	8	49	....	....	....	....	....
2011-12	North Dakota	WCHA	42	2	5	7	75	....	....	....	....	....
2012-13	North Dakota	WCHA	41	2	11	13	116	....	....	....	....	....
	Toronto Marlies	AHL	2	0	0	0	0	....	....	....	....	....

MADAISKY, Austin (muh-DAY-skee, AW-stuhn) CBJ

Defense. Shoots right. 6'2", 195 lbs. Born, Surrey, B.C., January 30, 1992.
(Columbus' 6th choice, 124th overall, in 2010 Entry Draft).

			Regular Season					Playoffs				
Season	Club	League	GP	G	A	Pts	PIM	GP	G	A	Pts	PIM
2007-08	Valley West Hawks	BCMML	35	6	23	29	38	....	....	....	....	....
2008-09	Calgary Hitmen	WHL	48	2	7	9	16	2	0	0	0	2
2009-10	Calgary Hitmen	WHL	39	5	13	18	46	....	....	....	....	....
	Kamloops Blazers	WHL	26	2	7	9	28	4	3	3	6	6
2010-11	Kamloops Blazers	WHL	55	7	20	27	104	....	....	....	....	....
2011-12	Kamloops Blazers	WHL	70	13	37	50	87	9	0	7	7	12
2012-13	Springfield Falcons	AHL	6	0	0	0	2	....	....	....	....	....
	Evansville IceMen	ECHL	11	2	4	6	2	....	....	....	....	....

WHL West Second All-Star Team (2012)

MAENALANEN, Saku (mai-NA-lah-nehn, SA-koo) NSH

Right wing. Shoots left. 6'3", 176 lbs. Born, Kemi, Finland, May 29, 1994.
(Nashville's 5th choice, 125th overall, in 2013 Entry Draft).

			Regular Season					Playoffs				
Season	Club	League	GP	G	A	Pts	PIM	GP	G	A	Pts	PIM
2010-11	Laser U18	Fin-U18	26	27	38	65	20	....	....	....	....	....
	Karpat Oulu U18	Fin-U18	1	0	0	0	2	....	....	....	....	....
2011-12	Karpat Oulu U18	Fin-U18	41	14	35	49	72	12	8	4	12	6
2012-13	Karpat Oulu Jr.	Fin-Jr.	45	23	35	58	43	5	5	2	7	18

MAIDENS, Jarrod (MAY-duhnz, JAIR-uhd) OTT

Center/Left wing. Shoots left. 6'1", 173 lbs. Born, Niagara Falls, Ont., March 4, 1994.
(Ottawa's 3rd choice, 82nd overall, in 2012 Entry Draft).

			Regular Season					Playoffs				
Season	Club	League	GP	G	A	Pts	PIM	GP	G	A	Pts	PIM
2009-10	Ham. Jr. Bulldogs	Minor-ON	57	63	41	104	59	....	....	....	....	....
2010-11	Owen Sound	OHL	47	10	11	21	11	22	6	4	10	13
2011-12	Owen Sound	OHL	28	12	11	23	4	....	....	....	....	....
2012-13			DID NOT PLAY – INJURED									

• Missed majority of 2011-12 and all of 2012-13 due to head injury.

MAKELA, Aleksi (ma-KIH-luh, A-LEHK-see) DAL

Defense. Shoots left. 6'1", 195 lbs. Born, Tampere, Finland, February 8, 1995.
(Dallas' 9th choice, 182nd overall, in 2013 Entry Draft).

			Regular Season					Playoffs				
Season	Club	League	GP	G	A	Pts	PIM	GP	G	A	Pts	PIM
2011-12	Ilves Tampere U17	Fin-U17	2	0	2	2	2	9	4	6	10	10
	Ilves Tampere U18	Fin-U18	35	4	10	14	10	3	1	0	1	2
	Ilves Tampere Jr.	Fin-Jr.	4	0	0	0	2	....	....	....	....	....
2012-13	Ilves Tampere U18	Fin-U18	8	0	9	9	4	....	....	....	....	....
	Ilves Tampere Jr.	Fin-Jr.	37	8	9	17	42	....	....	....	....	....
	Ilves Tampere	Finland	7	1	1	2	4	....	....	....	....	....
	Ilves Tampere	Finland-Q	....	....	....	....	....	3	0	1	1	0

MALLET, Alexandre (mah-LEHT, al-ehx-AN-druh) VAN

Left wing. Shoots right. 6'1", 195 lbs. Born, Amqui, Que., May 22, 1992.
(Vancouver's 2nd choice, 57th overall, in 2012 Entry Draft).

			Regular Season					Playoffs				
Season	Club	League	GP	G	A	Pts	PIM	GP	G	A	Pts	PIM
2007-08	Ecole Notre Dame	QAAA	33	11	10	21	50	3	0	0	0	4
2008-09	Ecole Notre Dame	QAAA	39	15	13	28	50	4	2	4	6	0
	Rouyn-Noranda	QMJHL	10	1	0	1	0	1	0	1	1	0
2009-10	Rouyn-Noranda	QMJHL	39	4	5	9	31	....	....	....	....	....
	Rimouski Oceanic	QMJHL	26	5	5	10	54	12	2	0	2	6
2010-11	Rimouski Oceanic	QMJHL	60	10	9	19	86	5	0	2	2	7
2011-12	Rimouski Oceanic	QMJHL	68	34	47	81	132	21	10	15	25	22
2012-13	Kalamazoo Wings	ECHL	44	10	19	29	48	....	....	....	....	....

MALONE, Sean (ma-LOHN, SHAWN) BUF

Center. Shoots left. 5'11", 186 lbs. Born, Buffalo, NY, April 30, 1995.
(Buffalo's 10th choice, 159th overall, in 2013 Entry Draft).

			Regular Season					Playoffs				
Season	Club	League	GP	G	A	Pts	PIM	GP	G	A	Pts	PIM
2010-11	Nichols	High-NY	14	3	9	12	4	3	3	3	6	0
	Buffalo Saints	Minor-NY	STATISTICS NOT AVAILABLE									
2011-12	Nichols	High-NY	15	17	18	35	6	1	0	1	1	0
	Nichols	Exhib.	16	17	17	34		....	....	....	....	....
	Buffalo Saints	Minor-NY	....	27	27	54		....	....	....	....	....
2012-13	USNTDP	USHL	15	5	8	13	17	....	....	....	....	....
	USNTDP	U-18	35	9	11	20	2	....	....	....	....	....

• Signed Letter of Intent to attend **Harvard University** (ECAC) in fall of 2014.

MANGENE, Matt (MAN-jeen, MAT) PHI

Right wing. Shoots right. 5'11", 190 lbs. Born, Manorville, NY, March 12, 1989.

			Regular Season					Playoffs				
Season	Club	League	GP	G	A	Pts	PIM	GP	G	A	Pts	PIM
2009-10	U. of Maine	H-East	29	1	10	11	10	....	....	....	....	....
2010-11	U. of Maine	H-East	36	3	7	10	42	....	....	....	....	....
2011-12	U. of Maine	H-East	40	16	18	34	58	....	....	....	....	....
	Adirondack	AHL	5	0	0	0	0	....	....	....	....	....
2012-13	Trenton Titans	ECHL	14	0	6	6	23	....	....	....	....	....
	Adirondack	AHL	36	5	6	11	8	....	....	....	....	....

Signed as a free agent by **Philadelphia**, April 2, 2012.

MANSON, Josh (MAN-suhn, JAWSH) ANA

Defense. Shoots right. 6'3", 223 lbs. Born, Prince Albert, Sask., October 7, 1991.
(Anaheim's 7th choice, 160th overall, in 2011 Entry Draft).

			Regular Season					Playoffs				
Season	Club	League	GP	G	A	Pts	PIM	GP	G	A	Pts	PIM
2008-09	Prince Albert	SMHL	40	19	16	35	64	3	1	0	1	4
2009-10	Salmon Arm	BCHL	54	10	14	24	75	6	1	0	1	15
2010-11	Salmon Arm	BCHL	57	12	35	47	80	14	2	7	9	15
2011-12	Northeastern	H-East	33	0	4	4	48	....	....	....	....	....
2012-13	Northeastern	H-East	33	3	4	7	45	....	....	....	....	....

MANTHA, Anthony (MAN-tha, AN-thuh-nee) **DET**

Right wing. Shoots left. 6'4", 190 lbs. Born, Longueuil, Que., September 16, 1994.
(Detroit's 1st choice, 20th overall, in 2013 Entry Draft).

			Regular Season					Playoffs				
Season	Club	League	GP	G	A	Pts	PIM	GP	G	A	Pts	PIM
2010-11	C.C. Lemoyne	QAAA	37	20	24	44	42	3	0	1	1	12
	Val-d'Or Foreurs	QMJHL	2	0	0	0	0	....	....	....	....	....
2011-12	Val-d'Or Foreurs	QMJHL	63	22	29	51	39	4	2	2	4	6
2012-13	Val-d'Or Foreurs	QMJHL	67	*50	39	89	71	9	5	7	12	13

QMJHL Second All-Star Team (2013)

MARCANTUONI, Matia (mark-an-tew-oh—nee, mah-TEE-ah) **PIT**

Center/Right wing. Shoots right. 6', 197 lbs. Born, Woodbridge, Ont., February 22, 1994.
(Pittsburgh's 6th choice, 92nd overall, in 2012 Entry Draft).

			Regular Season					Playoffs				
Season	Club	League	GP	G	A	Pts	PIM	GP	G	A	Pts	PIM
2009-10	Toronto Marlboros	GTHL	77	39	33	72	64	....	....	....	....	....
	St. Michael's	ON-Jr.A	2	2	0	2	2	....	....	....	....	....
2010-11	Kitchener Rangers	OHL	42	11	16	27	26	7	0	0	0	0
2011-12	Kitchener Rangers	OHL	24	9	5	14	10	....	....	....	....	....
2012-13	Kitchener Rangers	OHL	64	7	18	25	34	10	1	1	2	6

• Missed majority of 2011-12 due to shoulder injury vs. Erie (OHL), January 7, 2012.

MARCHENKO, Alexei (MAHR-chehn-koh, al-EHX-ay) **DET**

Defense. Shoots right. 6'2", 183 lbs. Born, Moscow, Russia, January 2, 1992.
(Detroit's 9th choice, 205th overall, in 2011 Entry Draft).

			Regular Season					Playoffs				
Season	Club	League	GP	G	A	Pts	PIM	GP	G	A	Pts	PIM
2009-10	CSKA Jr.	Russia-Jr.	43	11	23	34	59	2	0	0	0	4
	CSKA Moscow	KHL	10	0	0	0	0	....	....	....	....	....
2010-11	CSKA Jr.	Russia-Jr.	36	5	33	38	28	15	3	8	11	31
	CSKA Moscow	KHL	22	0	2	2	4	....	....	....	....	....
2011-12	CSKA Jr.	Russia-Jr.	5	2	4	6	10	19	4	14	18	18
	CSKA Moscow	KHL	6	0	0	0	2	5	0	1	1	4
2012-13	CSKA Moscow	KHL	44	4	5	9	6	7	0	0	0	0

MARCINKO, Tomas (mahr-TSIHN-koh, TAW-mahsh) **NYI**

Center. Shoots right. 6'4", 208 lbs. Born, Poprad, Czech., April 11, 1988.
(NY Islanders' 6th choice, 115th overall, in 2006 Entry Draft).

			Regular Season					Playoffs				
Season	Club	League	GP	G	A	Pts	PIM	GP	G	A	Pts	PIM
2003-04	HC Kosice U18	Svk-U18	42	19	23	42	60	2	0	0	0	4
	HC Kosice Jr.	Slovak-Jr.	7	0	2	2	4	3	0	1	1	0
2004-05	HC Kosice Jr.	Slovak-Jr.	38	11	18	29	28	8	1	2	3	6
	HC Kosice	Slovakia	6	0	0	0	0	....	....	....	....	....
	HC Kosice	Slovakia	6	0	0	0	0	....	....	....	....	....
2005-06	HC Kosice Jr.	Slovak-Jr.	35	26	21	47	50	3	1	0	1	4
	HKm Humenne	Slovak-2	9	3	5	8	10	....	....	....	....	....
	HC Kosice	Slovakia	18	2	0	2	2	5	0	0	0	0
2006-07	Barrie Colts	OHL	56	19	21	40	56	8	0	1	1	8
2007-08	Barrie Colts	OHL	48	19	26	45	54	9	4	3	7	14
2008-09	Bridgeport	AHL	58	4	7	11	30	4	0	0	0	0
2009-10	Bridgeport	AHL	54	4	2	6	27	5	0	1	1	2
2010-11	Bridgeport	AHL	66	4	7	11	56	....	....	....	....	....
2011-12	Bridgeport	AHL	65	8	13	21	78	2	0	0	0	0
2012-13	MODO	Sweden	4	0	1	1	2	....	....	....	....	....
	HC Kosice	Slovakia	38	11	20	31	48	17	2	3	5	*60

Signed as a free agent by **MODO** (Sweden), August 31, 2012. Signed as a free agent by **Kosice** (Slovakia), October 8, 2012.

MARINCIN, Martin (mah-RIHN-chihn, MAHR-tihn) **EDM**

Defense. Shoots left. 6'4", 187 lbs. Born, Kosice, Czech., February 18, 1992.
(Edmonton's 3rd choice, 46th overall, in 2010 Entry Draft).

			Regular Season					Playoffs				
Season	Club	League	GP	G	A	Pts	PIM	GP	G	A	Pts	PIM
2006-07	HC Kosice U18	Svk-U18	16	0	3	3	6	....	....	....	....	....
2007-08	HC Kosice U18	Svk-U18	59	3	29	32	36	....	....	....	....	....
2008-09	HC Kosice U18	Svk-U18	5	4	4	8	35	....	....	....	....	....
	HC Kosice Jr.	Slovak-Jr.	46	11	15	26	50	3	0	0	0	0
2009-10	Slovakia U20	Slovakia	35	2	4	6	71	....	....	....	....	....
	HC Kosice Jr.	Slovak-Jr.	....	....	....	....	....	2	0	0	0	0
2010-11	Prince George	WHL	67	14	42	56	65	4	1	4	5	6
	Oklahoma City	AHL	1	0	0	0	2	....	....	....	....	....
2011-12	Prince George	WHL	30	4	13	17	25	....	....	....	....	....
	Regina Pats	WHL	28	7	16	23	10	5	2	0	2	6
	Oklahoma City	AHL	6	0	1	1	2	....	....	....	....	....
2012-13	Oklahoma City	AHL	69	7	23	30	40	17	1	6	7	2

MARSHALL, Ben (MAR-shuhl, BEHN) **DET**

Defense. Shoots left. 5'9", 160 lbs. Born, St. Paul, MN, August 30, 1992.
(Detroit's 7th choice, 201st overall, in 2010 Entry Draft).

			Regular Season					Playoffs				
Season	Club	League	GP	G	A	Pts	PIM	GP	G	A	Pts	PIM
2007-08	Mahtomedi	High-MN	12	4	12	16	....	....	....	....	....	....
2008-09	Mahtomedi	High-MN	29	21	29	50	30	....	....	....	....	....
2009-10	Team Northeast	UMHSEL	16	1	3	4	....	....	....	....	....	....
	Minnetonka High	High-MN	23	18	30	48	40	6	2	10	12	10
2010-11	Omaha Lancers	USHL	56	11	21	32	34	3	0	1	1	0
2011-12	U. of Minnesota	WCHA	41	4	9	13	31	....	....	....	....	....
2012-13	U. of Minnesota	WCHA	40	8	11	19	20	....	....	....	....	....

USHL All-Rookie Team (2011) • USHL Second All-Star Team (2011)

MARTIN, James (MAHR-tihn, JAYMZ) **CGY**

Defense. Shoots left. 6'1", 200 lbs. Born, Winnipeg, Man., May 29, 1991.

			Regular Season					Playoffs				
Season	Club	League	GP	G	A	Pts	PIM	GP	G	A	Pts	PIM
2006-07	Winnipeg Wild	MMHL	36	3	17	20	54	....	....	....	....	....
2007-08	Winnipeg Wild	MMHL	36	9	22	31	72	....	....	....	....	....
	Wpg. South Blues	MJHL	1	0	0	0	0	....	....	....	....	....
	Swift Current	WHL	2	0	0	0	0	....	....	....	....	....
2008-09	Swift Current	WHL	31	0	4	4	14	....	....	....	....	....
	Kootenay Ice	WHL	25	0	0	0	25	4	0	0	0	4
2009-10	Kootenay Ice	WHL	66	8	11	19	31	6	1	1	2	2
2010-11	Kootenay Ice	WHL	65	11	18	29	68	19	0	6	6	21
2011-12	Abbotsford Heat	AHL	28	2	1	3	23	....	....	....	....	....
2012-13	Abbotsford Heat	AHL	5	0	1	1	7	....	....	....	....	....
	Utah Grizzlies	ECHL	44	3	10	13	54	4	0	0	0	2

Signed as a free agent by **Calgary**, September 22, 2011.

MARTINDALE, Ryan (MAHR-tihn-dayl, RIGH-uhn) **EDM**

Center. Shoots left. 6'3", 190 lbs. Born, Oshawa, Ont., October 27, 1991.
(Edmonton's 5th choice, 61st overall, in 2010 Entry Draft).

			Regular Season					Playoffs				
Season	Club	League	GP	G	A	Pts	PIM	GP	G	A	Pts	PIM
2006-07	Whitby Wildcats	Minor-ON	79	65	67	132	....	....	....	....	....	....
2007-08	Ottawa 67's	OHL	64	9	8	17	18	4	0	0	0	2
2008-09	Ottawa 67's	OHL	53	23	24	47	14	7	2	1	3	7
2009-10	Ottawa 67's	OHL	61	19	41	60	37	12	4	5	9	6
2010-11	Ottawa 67's	OHL	65	34	49	83	30	4	3	2	5	2
2011-12	Oklahoma City	AHL	16	0	2	2	4	....	....	....	....	....
	Stockton Thunder	ECHL	34	6	9	15	10	....	....	....	....	....
2012-13	Stockton Thunder	ECHL	5	2	0	2	0	....	....	....	....	....
	Oklahoma City	AHL	41	6	8	14	10	2	0	0	0	5

MARTINOOK, Jordan (mahr-TIHN-ook, JOHR-dahn) **PHX**

Left wing. Shoots left. 6'1", 210 lbs. Born, Brandon, MB, July 25, 1992.
(Phoenix's 2nd choice, 58th overall, in 2012 Entry Draft).

			Regular Season					Playoffs				
Season	Club	League	GP	G	A	Pts	PIM	GP	G	A	Pts	PIM
2006-07	Leduc Oil Kings	AMBHL	30	19	14	33	32	....	....	....	....	....
2007-08	Leduc Oil Kings	Minor-AB	STATISTICS NOT AVAILABLE									
	Leduc Oil Kings	AMHL	3	1	0	1	0	....	....	....	....	....
2008-09	Leduc Oil Kings	AMHL	33	7	13	20	38	....	....	....	....	....
	Drayton Valley	AJHL	2	0	0	0	0	....	....	....	....	....
2009-10	Drayton Valley	AJHL	59	21	19	40	48	....	....	....	....	....
2010-11	Vancouver Giants	WHL	72	11	17	28	67	4	1	0	1	8
2011-12	Vancouver Giants	WHL	72	40	24	64	80	6	3	6	9	2
2012-13	Portland Pirates	AHL	53	9	10	19	30	3	0	1	1	0

MATHERS, Derek (MA-thurz, DAIR-ihk) **PHI**

Right wing. Shoots right. 6'3", 226 lbs. Born, Strathroy, Ont., August 4, 1993.
(Philadelphia's 6th choice, 206th overall, in 2011 Entry Draft).

			Regular Season					Playoffs				
Season	Club	League	GP	G	A	Pts	PIM	GP	G	A	Pts	PIM
2008-09	Elgin-Mid. Chiefs	Minor-ON	30	2	5	7	60	....	....	....	....	....
2009-10	Strathroy Rockets	ON-Jr.B	43	2	5	7	53	5	0	3	3	4
2010-11	Peterborough	OHL	55	1	4	5	*171	....	....	....	....	....
2011-12	Peterborough	OHL	65	9	8	17	177	....	....	....	....	....
	Adirondack	AHL	9	0	0	0	26	....	....	....	....	....
2012-13	Peterborough	OHL	64	10	19	29	125	....	....	....	....	....
	Adirondack	AHL	12	1	0	1	24	....	....	....	....	....

MATHESON, Michael (MA-thuh-suhn, MIGH-kuhl) **FLA**

Defense. Shoots left. 6'2", 178 lbs. Born, Pointe-Claire, Que., February 27, 1994.
(Florida's 1st choice, 23rd overall, in 2012 Entry Draft).

			Regular Season					Playoffs				
Season	Club	League	GP	G	A	Pts	PIM	GP	G	A	Pts	PIM
2009-10	Lac St-Louis Lions	QAAA	30	5	6	11	33	17	6	7	13	10
2010-11	Lac St-Louis Lions	QAAA	35	14	24	38	72	15	7	18	25	16
2011-12	Dubuque	USHL	53	11	16	27	84	5	4	1	5	4
2012-13	Boston College	H-East	36	8	17	25	78	....	....	....	....	....

Hockey East All-Rookie Team (2013)

MATTSON, Nick (MAT-suhn, NIHK) **CHI**

Defense. Shoots left. 6'1", 189 lbs. Born, Salem, OR, October 25, 1991.
(Chicago's 9th choice, 180th overall, in 2010 Entry Draft).

			Regular Season					Playoffs				
Season	Club	League	GP	G	A	Pts	PIM	GP	G	A	Pts	PIM
2006-07	Chaska Hawks	High-MN	41	5	15	20	....	....	....	....	....	....
2007-08	USNTDP	NAHL	43	1	10	11	16	3	0	0	0	0
	USNTDP	U-17	17	0	9	9	....	....	....	....	....	....
2008-09	USNTDP	NAHL	16	1	5	6	4	....	....	....	....	....
	USNTDP	U-18	47	3	14	17	4	....	....	....	....	....
2009-10	Indiana Ice	USHL	51	5	14	19	14	9	0	6	6	2
2010-11	Indiana Ice	USHL	57	6	30	36	12	5	0	2	2	0
2011-12	North Dakota	WCHA	42	6	13	19	10	....	....	....	....	....
2012-13	North Dakota	WCHA	38	3	12	15	8	....	....	....	....	....

USHL First All-Star Team (2011)

MAYFIELD, Scott (MAY-feeld, SKAWT) **NYI**

Defense. Shoots right. 6'4", 209 lbs. Born, St. Louis, MO, October 14, 1992.
(NY Islanders' 2nd choice, 34th overall, in 2011 Entry Draft).

			Regular Season					Playoffs				
Season	Club	League	GP	G	A	Pts	PIM	GP	G	A	Pts	PIM
2008-09	St.L. AAA Blues	Minor-MO	62	10	20	30	84	....	....	....	....	....
2009-10	Youngstown	USHL	59	10	12	22	145	....	....	....	....	....
2010-11	Youngstown	USHL	52	7	9	16	159	....	....	....	....	....
2011-12	U. of Denver	WCHA	42	3	9	12	76	....	....	....	....	....
2012-13	U. of Denver	WCHA	39	4	13	17	112	....	....	....	....	....
	Bridgeport	AHL	6	0	0	0	2	....	....	....	....	....

McCABE, Jake (muh-KAYB, JAYK) BUF

Defense. Shoots left. 6'1", 210 lbs. Born, Eau Claire, WI, October 12, 1993.
(Buffalo's 3rd choice, 44th overall, in 2012 Entry Draft).

			Regular Season					Playoffs				
Season	**Club**	**League**	**GP**	**G**	**A**	**Pts**	**PIM**	**GP**	**G**	**A**	**Pts**	**PIM**
2008-09	Eau Claire Mem.	High-WI	23	2	20	22	16	....	....	....	....	....
	Team Wisconsin	UMHSEL	22	3	7	10	....	....	....	....	....	....
2009-10	USNTDP	USHL	35	0	5	5	34	....	....	....	....	....
	USNTDP	U-17	16	0	3	3	16	....	....	....	....	....
	USNTDP	U-18	1	0	0	0	2	....	....	....	....	....
2010-11	USNTDP	USHL	19	2	4	6	4	....	....	....	....	....
	USNTDP	U-18	27	2	8	10	10	....	....	....	....	....
2011-12	U. of Wisconsin	WCHA	26	3	9	12	12	....	....	....	....	....
2012-13	U. of Wisconsin	WCHA	38	3	18	21	50	....	....	....	....	....

MCCARRON, John (muh-KAIR-uhn, JAWN) EDM

Right wing. Shoots right. 6'3", 219 lbs. Born, Grosse Pointe, MI, April 16, 1992.
(Edmonton's 7th choice, 153rd overall, in 2012 Entry Draft).

			Regular Season					Playoffs				
Season	**Club**	**League**	**GP**	**G**	**A**	**Pts**	**PIM**	**GP**	**G**	**A**	**Pts**	**PIM**
2006-07	Det. Honeybaked	MWEHL	24	12	11	23	18	5	1	2	3	2
	Det. Honeybaked	Exhib.	32	9	21	30	8	....	....	....	....	....
2007-08	Det. Honeybaked	MWEHL	31	6	9	15	38	4	0	1	1	6
	Det. Honeybaked	Exhib.	29	3	15	18	....	....	....	....	....	....
2008-09	Lincoln Stars	USHL	19	2	0	2	11	7	0	2	2	4
	Motor City	NAHL	3	0	0	0	2	....	....	....	....	....
2009-10	Lincoln Stars	USHL	58	7	19	26	114	....	....	....	....	....
2010-11	Lincoln Stars	USHL	60	24	33	57	113	2	0	0	0	4
2011-12	Cornell Big Red	ECAC	35	6	13	19	61	....	....	....	....	....
2012-13	Cornell Big Red	ECAC	33	7	12	19	84	....	....	....	....	....

McCARRON, Michael (muh-KAIR-uhn, MIGH-kuhl) MTL

Right wing. Shoots right. 6'5", 237 lbs. Born, Gross Pointe, MI, March 7, 1995.
(Montreal's 1st choice, 25th overall, in 2013 Entry Draft).

			Regular Season					Playoffs				
Season	**Club**	**League**	**GP**	**G**	**A**	**Pts**	**PIM**	**GP**	**G**	**A**	**Pts**	**PIM**
2009-10	Det. Honeybaked	T1EHL	29	12	20	32	44	....	....	....	....	....
2010-11	Det. Honeybaked	T1EHL	38	6	12	18	88	....	....	....	....	....
2011-12	USNTDP	USHL	35	3	14	17	112	1	0	1	1	2
	USNTDP	U-17	17	3	6	9	14	....	....	....	....	....
2012-13	USNTDP	USHL	19	5	5	10	84	....	....	....	....	....
	USNTDP	U-18	40	11	16	27	98	....	....	....	....	....

MCCORMICK, Max (muh-KOHR-mihk, MAX) OTT

Left wing. Shoots left. 5'11", 185 lbs. Born, De Pere, WI, May 1, 1992.
(Ottawa's 8th choice, 171st overall, in 2011 Entry Draft).

			Regular Season					Playoffs				
Season	**Club**	**League**	**GP**	**G**	**A**	**Pts**	**PIM**	**GP**	**G**	**A**	**Pts**	**PIM**
2007-08	Notre Dame	High-WI	16	19	20	39	....	....	....	....	....	....
2008-09	Team Wisconsin	UMHSEL	STATISTICS NOT AVAILABLE									
	Notre Dame	High-WI	18	19	38	57	....	....	....	....	....	....
2009-10	Team Wisconsin	UMHSEL	24	....	....	24	....	....	....	....	....	....
	Notre Dame	High-WI	29	38	37	75	74	....	....	....	....	....
2010-11	Sioux City	USHL	55	21	21	42	102	3	1	2	3	4
2011-12	Ohio State	CCHA	27	10	12	22	31	....	....	....	....	....
2012-13	Ohio State	CCHA	40	15	16	31	26	....	....	....	....	....

CCHA All-Rookie Team (2012)

McCOSHEN, Ian (muh-KOH-shuhn, EE-uhn) FLA

Defense. Shoots left. 6'3", 205 lbs. Born, Anaheim, CA, August 5, 1995.
(Florida's 2nd choice, 31st overall, in 2013 Entry Draft).

			Regular Season					Playoffs				
Season	**Club**	**League**	**GP**	**G**	**A**	**Pts**	**PIM**	**GP**	**G**	**A**	**Pts**	**PIM**
2009-10	Shattuck Bantam	High-MN	58	21	35	56	46	....	....	....	....	....
2010-11	Waterloo	USHL	42	0	6	6	38	2	0	0	0	0
2011-12	Waterloo	USHL	55	8	12	20	43	15	4	3	7	6
2012-13	Waterloo	USHL	53	11	33	44	48	5	2	2	4	4

USHL First All-Star Team (2013)

• Signed Letter of Intent to attend **Boston College** (Hockey East) in fall of 2013.

McENENY, Evan (muhk-EHN-ehn-ee, EH-vuhn) VAN

Defense. Shoots left. 6'2", 205 lbs. Born, Hamilton, Ont., May 22, 1994.

			Regular Season					Playoffs				
Season	**Club**	**League**	**GP**	**G**	**A**	**Pts**	**PIM**	**GP**	**G**	**A**	**Pts**	**PIM**
2009-10	Ham. Jr. Bulldogs	Minor-ON	59	13	37	50	50	....	....	....	....	....
	Burlington	ON-Jr.A	4	0	1	1	0	....	....	....	....	....
2010-11	Kitchener Rangers	OHL	44	0	4	4	14	4	0	0	0	0
2011-12	Kitchener Rangers	OHL	2	0	2	2	4	....	....	....	....	....
2012-13	Kitchener Rangers	OHL	65	6	28	34	42	10	1	3	4	14

• Missed majority of 2011-12 due to knne injury at Sarnia (OHL), September 23, 2011. Signed as a free agent by **Vancouver**, September 13, 2012.

McFADDEN, Josh (muhk-FA-duhn, JAWSH) FLA

Defense. Shoots left. 6'1", 207 lbs. Born, Guelph, Ont., May 23, 1991.

			Regular Season					Playoffs				
Season	**Club**	**League**	**GP**	**G**	**A**	**Pts**	**PIM**	**GP**	**G**	**A**	**Pts**	**PIM**
2008-09	Mississauga	ON-Jr.A	7	3	1	4	32	....	....	....	....	....
	St. Michael's	OHL	47	1	6	7	8	6	1	0	1	6
2009-10	St. Michael's	OHL	16	2	4	6	2	....	....	....	....	....
	Sudbury Wolves	OHL	45	2	22	24	26	4	1	2	3	2
2010-11	Sudbury Wolves	OHL	67	19	53	72	74	8	4	2	6	8
2011-12	Sudbury Wolves	OHL	47	15	26	41	43	4	0	2	2	4
2012-13	San Antonio	AHL	9	0	0	0	2	....	....	....	....	....
	Cincinnati	ECHL	28	2	12	14	28	9	0	5	5	2

Signed as a free agent by **Florida**, July 11, 2012.

McFARLAND, John (muhk-FAHR-luhnd, JAWN) FLA

Left wing. Shoots right. 6'1", 205 lbs. Born, Richmond Hill, Ont., April 2, 1992.
(Florida's 4th choice, 33rd overall, in 2010 Entry Draft).

			Regular Season					Playoffs				
Season	**Club**	**League**	**GP**	**G**	**A**	**Pts**	**PIM**	**GP**	**G**	**A**	**Pts**	**PIM**
2007-08	Tor. Jr. Canadiens	GTHL	76	96	69	165	176	....	....	....	....	....
2008-09	Sudbury Wolves	OHL	58	21	31	52	36	6	1	3	4	2
2009-10	Sudbury Wolves	OHL	64	20	30	50	70	4	3	0	3	2
2010-11	Sudbury Wolves	OHL	12	6	4	10	13	....	....	....	....	....
	Saginaw Spirit	OHL	37	19	9	28	33	12	5	4	9	6
2011-12	Saginaw Spirit	OHL	36	20	21	41	18	....	....	....	....	....
	Ottawa 67's	OHL	12	4	5	9	10	....	....	....	....	....
2012-13	Cincinnati	ECHL	23	12	13	25	12	12	4	5	9	6
	San Antonio	AHL	43	5	9	14	10	....	....	....	....	....

MCGINN, Brock (muh-GIHN, BRAWK) CAR

Left wing. Shoots left. 5'11", 185 lbs. Born, Fergus, Ont., February 2, 1994.
(Carolina's 2nd choice, 47th overall, in 2012 Entry Draft).

			Regular Season					Playoffs				
Season	**Club**	**League**	**GP**	**G**	**A**	**Pts**	**PIM**	**GP**	**G**	**A**	**Pts**	**PIM**
2009-10	Guelph Jr. Storm	Minor-ON	STATISTICS NOT AVAILABLE									
	Orangeville	ON-Jr.A	3	0	0	0	0	1	0	0	0	0
2010-11	Guelph Storm	OHL	68	10	4	14	38	6	0	0	0	2
2011-12	Guelph Storm	OHL	33	12	7	19	25	6	1	1	2	8
2012-13	Guelph Storm	OHL	68	28	26	54	71	3	2	2	4	11
	Charlotte	AHL	4	0	0	0	0	2	0	0	0	2

McILRATH, Dylan (MAK-ihl-rayth, DIH-luhn) NYR

Defense. Shoots right. 6'5", 220 lbs. Born, Winnipeg, Man., April 20, 1992.
(NY Rangers' 1st choice, 10th overall, in 2010 Entry Draft).

			Regular Season					Playoffs				
Season	**Club**	**League**	**GP**	**G**	**A**	**Pts**	**PIM**	**GP**	**G**	**A**	**Pts**	**PIM**
2007-08	Winnipeg Warriors	Minor-MB	34	5	17	22	68	....	....	....	....	....
2008-09	Moose Jaw	WHL	53	1	3	4	102	....	....	....	....	....
2009-10	Moose Jaw	WHL	65	7	17	24	169	7	0	1	1	21
2010-11	Moose Jaw	WHL	62	5	18	23	153	6	0	0	0	15
	Connecticut Whale	AHL	2	0	0	0	7	....	....	....	....	....
2011-12	Moose Jaw	WHL	52	3	20	23	127	14	0	6	6	12
	Connecticut Whale	AHL	....	....	....	....	....	5	0	0	0	9
2012-13	Connecticut Whale	AHL	45	0	5	5	125	....	....	....	....	....

MCKEE, Michael (muh-KEE, MIGH-kuhl) DET

Defense. Shoots left. 6'5", 220 lbs. Born, Newmarket, Ont., August 17, 1993.
(Detroit's 4th choice, 140th overall, in 2012 Entry Draft).

			Regular Season					Playoffs				
Season	**Club**	**League**	**GP**	**G**	**A**	**Pts**	**PIM**	**GP**	**G**	**A**	**Pts**	**PIM**
2008-09	South Central	Minor-ON	25	8	6	14	74	....	....	....	....	....
2009-10	Kent Prep School	High-CT	26	3	8	11	22	....	....	....	....	....
2010-11	Kent Prep School	High-CT	27	8	14	22	50	....	....	....	....	....
2011-12	Lincoln Stars	USHL	59	2	17	19	237	8	0	0	0	44
2012-13	Lincoln Stars	USHL	42	3	18	21	292	5	0	4	4	18

• Signed Letter of Intent to attend **Western Michigan University** (CCHA) in fall of 2013.

McKEGG, Greg (muh-KEHG, GREHG) TOR

Center. Shoots left. 6', 200 lbs. Born, St.Thomas, Ont., June 17, 1992.
(Toronto's 2nd choice, 62nd overall, in 2010 Entry Draft).

			Regular Season					Playoffs				
Season	**Club**	**League**	**GP**	**G**	**A**	**Pts**	**PIM**	**GP**	**G**	**A**	**Pts**	**PIM**
2007-08	Elgin-Mid. Chiefs	Minor-ON	64	73	53	126	....	....	....	....	....	....
	St. Thomas Stars	ON-Jr.B	3	4	1	5	2	....	....	....	....	....
2008-09	Erie Otters	OHL	64	8	10	18	22	5	2	1	3	4
2009-10	Erie Otters	OHL	67	37	48	85	32	4	2	1	3	0
2010-11	Erie Otters	OHL	66	49	43	92	35	7	4	1	5	12
	Toronto Marlies	AHL	2	1	0	1	0	....	....	....	....	....
2011-12	Erie Otters	OHL	35	12	22	34	32	....	....	....	....	....
	London Knights	OHL	30	19	22	41	22	15	4	7	11	2
2012-13	Toronto Marlies	AHL	61	8	15	23	22	9	3	3	6	10

McKELVIE, Zach (muh-KEHL-vee, ZAK) CGY

Defense. Shoots left. 6'2", 200 lbs. Born, St. Paul, MN, February 22, 1985.

			Regular Season					Playoffs				
Season	**Club**	**League**	**GP**	**G**	**A**	**Pts**	**PIM**	**GP**	**G**	**A**	**Pts**	**PIM**
2004-05	Bozeman IceDogs	NAHL	53	0	6	6	108	....	....	....	....	....
2005-06	Army	AH	32	2	8	10	64	....	....	....	....	....
2006-07	Army	AH	34	3	9	12	48	....	....	....	....	....
2007-08	Army	AH	35	4	13	17	48	....	....	....	....	....
2008-09	Army	AH	33	5	12	17	48	....	....	....	....	....
2009-10	Army	AH	MILITARY SERVICE									
2010-11	Army	AH	MILITARY SERVICE									
2011-12	Providence Bruins	AHL	39	1	1	2	46	....	....	....	....	....
	Reading Royals	ECHL	7	1	0	1	7	5	0	2	2	6
2012-13	Abbotsford Heat	AHL	52	0	2	2	112	....	....	....	....	....

AH First All-Star Team (2009)

Signed as a free agent by **Boston**, July 13, 2009. • Missed 2009-10 and 2010-11 fulfilling his U.S. military service requirements as per his enrollment at West Point. Signed as a free agent by **Abbotsford** (AHL), July 1, 2012.

McKENZIE, Curtis (muh-KEHN-zee, KUHR-tihs) DAL

Left wing. Shoots left. 6'2", 207 lbs. Born, Golden, B.C., February 22, 1991.
(Dallas' 5th choice, 159th overall, in 2009 Entry Draft).

			Regular Season					Playoffs				
Season	**Club**	**League**	**GP**	**G**	**A**	**Pts**	**PIM**	**GP**	**G**	**A**	**Pts**	**PIM**
2007-08	Penticton Vees	BCHL	49	3	7	10	81	7	0	1	1	9
2008-09	Penticton Vees	BCHL	53	30	34	64	90	10	3	7	10	81
2009-10	Miami U.	CCHA	42	6	21	27	88	....	....	....	....	....
2010-11	Miami U.	CCHA	37	7	5	12	57	....	....	....	....	....
2011-12	Miami U.	CCHA	40	5	12	17	60	....	....	....	....	....
2012-13	Miami U.	CCHA	39	11	13	24	80	....	....	....	....	....
	Texas Stars	AHL	5	0	1	1	14	2	0	0	0	0

McNALLY, Patrick (muhk-NAL-ee, PAT-rihk) VAN

Defense. Shoots left. 6'2", 190 lbs. Born, Glen Head, NY, December 4, 1991.
(Vancouver's 1st choice, 115th overall, in 2010 Entry Draft).

			Regular Season					Playoffs				
Season	Club	League	GP	G	A	Pts	PIM	GP	G	A	Pts	PIM
2008-09	Suffolk PAL S.S.	MtJHL	52	25	41	66	72	....	....	....	....	....
2009-10	Milton Academy	High-MA	28	14	21	35	....	....	....	....	....	....
2010-11	Milton Academy	High-MA	28	22	29	51	....	....	....	....	....	....
2011-12	Harvard Crimson	ECAC	34	6	22	28	40	....	....	....	....	....
2012-13	Harvard Crimson	ECAC	7	1	2	3	6	....	....	....	....	....

ECAC All-Rookie Team (2012)

McNEILL, Mark (muhk-NEEL, MAHRK) CHI

Center. Shoots right. 6'1", 211 lbs. Born, Langley, B.C., February 22, 1993.
(Chicago's 1st choice, 18th overall, in 2011 Entry Draft).

			Regular Season					Playoffs				
Season	Club	League	GP	G	A	Pts	PIM	GP	G	A	Pts	PIM
2008-09	SSAC Athletics	AMHL	33	21	18	39	38	4	2	0	2	2
	Prince Albert	WHL	4	0	0	0	0	....	....	....	....	....
2009-10	Prince Albert	WHL	68	9	15	24	27	....	....	....	....	....
2010-11	Prince Albert	WHL	70	32	49	81	53	6	2	3	5	2
2011-12	Prince Albert	WHL	69	31	40	71	48	....	....	....	....	....
	Rockford IceHogs	AHL	7	0	0	0	12	....	....	....	....	....
2012-13	Prince Albert	WHL	65	25	42	67	43	4	1	3	4	4
	Rockford IceHogs	AHL	5	0	0	0	0	....	....	....	....	....

McNEILL, Patrick (muhk-NEEL, PAT-rihk) CBJ

Defense. Shoots left. 6', 198 lbs. Born, Strathroy, Ont., March 17, 1987.
(Washington's 4th choice, 118th overall, in 2005 Entry Draft).

			Regular Season					Playoffs				
Season	Club	League	GP	G	A	Pts	PIM	GP	G	A	Pts	PIM
2002-03	Strathroy Rockets	ON-Jr.B	45	6	13	19	53	....	....	....	....	....
2003-04	Saginaw Spirit	OHL	57	3	11	14	28	....	....	....	....	....
2004-05	Saginaw Spirit	OHL	66	7	26	33	31	....	....	....	....	....
2005-06	Saginaw Spirit	OHL	68	21	56	77	64	4	1	3	4	6
2006-07	Saginaw Spirit	OHL	58	22	36	58	49	6	3	2	5	6
2007-08	Hershey Bears	AHL	48	1	13	14	16	2	0	0	0	0
	South Carolina	ECHL	19	5	11	16	16	5	0	2	2	4
2008-09	Hershey Bears	AHL	46	3	15	18	20	10	0	3	3	4
2009-10	Hershey Bears	AHL	62	8	27	35	36	11	3	3	6	2
2010-11	Hershey Bears	AHL	51	7	20	27	30	6	1	2	3	4
2011-12	Hershey Bears	AHL	71	10	31	41	32	2	1	1	2	2
2012-13	Hershey Bears	AHL	47	4	13	17	16	....	....	....	....	....

OHL Second All-Star Team (2006)

Signed as a free agent by **Columbus**, July 6, 2013.

McNEILL, Reid (muhk-NEEL, REED) PIT

Defense. Shoots left. 6'4", 204 lbs. Born, London, Ont., April 29, 1992.
(Pittsburgh's 6th choice, 170th overall, in 2010 Entry Draft).

			Regular Season					Playoffs				
Season	Club	League	GP	G	A	Pts	PIM	GP	G	A	Pts	PIM
2008-09	Lambeth Lancers	ON-Jr.D	16	0	4	4	12	....	....	....	....	....
	Lucas High School	High-ON	STATISTICS NOT AVAILABLE									
2009-10	London Nationals	ON-Jr.B	20	0	7	7	6	....	....	....	....	....
	London Knights	OHL	53	2	3	5	32	12	0	1	1	0
2010-11	London Knights	OHL	62	2	4	6	70	6	0	0	0	4
2011-12	Barrie Colts	OHL	51	3	9	12	60	13	0	0	0	22
2012-13	Wheeling Nailers	ECHL	44	2	4	6	90	....	....	....	....	....
	Wilkes-Barre	AHL	3	0	0	0	0	12	0	1	1	12

McNULTY, Marc (muhk-NUHL-tee, MAHRK) DET

Defense. Shoots left. 6'6", 185 lbs. Born, Moose Jaw, Sask., April 5, 1995.
(Detroit's 7th choice, 169th overall, in 2013 Entry Draft).

			Regular Season					Playoffs				
Season	Club	League	GP	G	A	Pts	PIM	GP	G	A	Pts	PIM
2010-11	Medicine Hat	AMHL	25	2	2	4	26	....	....	....	....	....
2011-12	Medicine Hat	AMHL	19	4	8	12	28	....	....	....	....	....
	Lloydminster	AJHL	2	0	0	0	0	....	....	....	....	....
	Prince George	WHL	21	0	0	0	8	....	....	....	....	....
2012-13	Prince George	WHL	52	8	7	15	70	....	....	....	....	....

McPHERSON, Corbin (muhk-FUHR-suhn, KOHR-bihn) N.J.

Defense. Shoots right. 6'5", 220 lbs. Born, Folsom, CA, September 7, 1988.
(New Jersey's 3rd choice, 87th overall, in 2007 Entry Draft).

			Regular Season					Playoffs				
Season	Club	League	GP	G	A	Pts	PIM	GP	G	A	Pts	PIM
2005-06	San Jose Jr. Sharks	Minor-CA	59	5	16	21	45	....	....	....	....	....
2006-07	Cowichan Valley	BCHL	45	4	10	14	63	18	1	3	4	14
2007-08	Cowichan Valley	BCHL	55	3	14	17	84	....	....	....	....	....
2008-09	Colgate	ECAC	37	0	5	5	50	....	....	....	....	....
2009-10	Colgate	ECAC	35	2	6	8	20	....	....	....	....	....
2010-11	Colgate	ECAC	41	4	6	10	36	....	....	....	....	....
2011-12	Colgate	ECAC	39	4	6	10	28	....	....	....	....	....
	Albany Devils	AHL	9	0	1	1	2	....	....	....	....	....
2012-13	Albany Devils	AHL	72	2	5	7	43	....	....	....	....	....

MECKLER, David (MEHK-luhr, DAY-vihd)

Left wing. Shoots right. 6', 213 lbs. Born, Highland Park, IL, July 9, 1987.
(Los Angeles' 7th choice, 134th overall, in 2006 Entry Draft).

			Regular Season					Playoffs				
Season	Club	League	GP	G	A	Pts	PIM	GP	G	A	Pts	PIM
2004-05	Waterloo	USHL	60	30	15	45	32	5	3	2	5	2
2005-06	Yale	ECAC	31	7	3	10	28	....	....	....	....	....
2006-07	London Knights	OHL	67	38	35	73	53	16	*15	7	22	20
2007-08	Manchester	AHL	76	23	13	36	24	4	1	1	2	2
2008-09	Manchester	AHL	74	14	15	29	28	....	....	....	....	....
2009-10	Manchester	AHL	73	11	9	20	22	14	1	0	1	2
2010-11	Manchester	AHL	75	16	17	33	28	7	2	0	2	0
2011-12	Manchester	AHL	44	10	7	17	13	4	0	0	0	0
2012-13	Manchester	AHL	39	3	6	9	8	4	1	1	2	4

MEDVEC, Kyle (MEHD-vek, KIGHL) MIN

Defense. Shoots left. 6'6", 230 lbs. Born, Westminster, CO, June 16, 1988.
(Minnesota's 4th choice, 102nd overall, in 2006 Entry Draft).

			Regular Season					Playoffs				
Season	Club	League	GP	G	A	Pts	PIM	GP	G	A	Pts	PIM
2003-04	Apple Valley	High-MN	27	1	12	13	30	....	....	....	....	....
2004-05	Apple Valley	High-MN	23	4	16	20	18	....	....	....	....	....
2005-06	Apple Valley	High-MN	28	13	22	35	44	....	....	....	....	....
	Sioux City	USHL	3	0	0	0	0	....	....	....	....	....
2006-07	Sioux City	USHL	57	4	14	18	83	7	0	0	0	4
2007-08	U. of Vermont	H-East	30	1	4	5	18	....	....	....	....	....
2008-09	U. of Vermont	H-East	39	2	10	12	40	....	....	....	....	....
2009-10	U. of Vermont	H-East	39	5	10	15	50	....	....	....	....	....
2010-11	U. of Vermont	H-East	29	2	4	6	28	....	....	....	....	....
2011-12	Houston Aeros	AHL	56	1	3	4	33	....	....	....	....	....
2012-13	Houston Aeros	AHL	53	6	2	8	50	5	0	0	0	2
	Orlando	ECHL	12	3	4	7	16	....	....	....	....	....

MEGALINSKY, Dmitri (meh-gahl-IHN-skee, dih-MEE-tree) OTT

Defense. Shoots left. 6'2", 212 lbs. Born, Perm, USSR, April 15, 1985.
(Ottawa's 7th choice, 186th overall, in 2005 Entry Draft).

			Regular Season					Playoffs				
Season	Club	League	GP	G	A	Pts	PIM	GP	G	A	Pts	PIM
2003-04	HK Voronezh	Russia-2	42	4	8	12	159	....	....	....	....	....
	Yaroslavl	Russia	1	0	0	0	0	....	....	....	....	....
	Yaroslavl 2	Russia-3	11	0	4	4	16	....	....	....	....	....
2004-05	Yaroslavl	Russia	1	0	0	0	2	....	....	....	....	....
	Yaroslavl 2	Russia-3	30	6	12	18	82	....	....	....	....	....
2005-06	Yaroslavl 2	Russia-3	12	4	10	14	6	....	....	....	....	....
	Yaroslavl	Russia	20	0	1	1	8	8	0	0	0	6
2006-07	Khimik	Russia-2	33	4	7	11	34	7	0	1	1	16
2007-08	Vityaz Chekhov	Russia	25	2	7	9	20	....	....	....	....	....
2008-09	Vityaz Chekhov	KHL	52	2	5	7	72	....	....	....	....	....
2009-10	Vityaz Chekhov	KHL	52	4	16	20	98	....	....	....	....	....
2010-11	Vityaz Chekhov	KHL	27	0	3	3	18	....	....	....	....	....
2011-12	Novokuznetsk	KHL	46	2	11	13	34	....	....	....	....	....
2012-13	Novokuznetsk	KHL	38	5	9	14	18	....	....	....	....	....

MEGAN, Wade (MEE-guhn, WAYD)

Center. Shoots left. 6'1", 195 lbs. Born, Canton, NY, July 22, 1990.
(Florida's 6th choice, 138th overall, in 2009 Entry Draft).

			Regular Season					Playoffs				
Season	Club	League	GP	G	A	Pts	PIM	GP	G	A	Pts	PIM
2007-08	Kent Prep School	High-CT	34	24	29	53	....	....	....	....	....	....
2008-09	Kent Prep School	High-CT	32	27	36	63	18	....	....	....	....	....
	Neponset Valley	Minor-MA	16	8	8	16	....	....	....	....	....	....
2009-10	Boston University	H-East	35	5	7	12	22	....	....	....	....	....
2010-11	Boston University	H-East	39	8	5	13	32	....	....	....	....	....
2011-12	Boston University	H-East	39	20	9	29	57	....	....	....	....	....
2012-13	Boston University	H-East	38	16	13	29	50	....	....	....	....	....
	San Antonio	AHL	13	1	0	1	0	....	....	....	....	....

MEGNA, Jaycob (MEHG-na, JAY-kuhb) ANA

Defense. Shoots left. 6'6", 218 lbs. Born, Plantation, FL, December 10, 1992.
(Anaheim's 8th choice, 210th overall, in 2012 Entry Draft).

			Regular Season					Playoffs				
Season	Club	League	GP	G	A	Pts	PIM	GP	G	A	Pts	PIM
2009-10	Team Illinois	T1EHL	48	1	12	13	8	....	....	....	....	....
	Team Illinois	Exhib.	25	1	19	20	4	....	....	....	....	....
2010-11	Muskegon	USHL	55	1	17	18	24	6	0	3	3	0
2011-12	Nebraska-Omaha	WCHA	35	2	3	5	8	....	....	....	....	....
2012-13	Nebraska-Omaha	WCHA	38	2	5	7	14	....	....	....	....	....

WCHA All-Rookie Team (2012)

MEGNA, Jayson (MEHG-na, JAY-suhn) PIT

Right wing. Shoots right. 6'1", 195 lbs. Born, Northbrook, IL, February 1, 1990.

			Regular Season					Playoffs				
Season	Club	League	GP	G	A	Pts	PIM	GP	G	A	Pts	PIM
2009-10	Cedar Rapids	USHL	56	11	15	26	62	5	0	0	0	6
2010-11	Cedar Rapids	USHL	60	30	28	58	45	8	4	3	7	4
2011-12	Nebraska-Omaha	WCHA	38	13	18	31	27	....	....	....	....	....
2012-13	Wilkes-Barre	AHL	56	5	7	12	28	12	2	3	5	0

USHL First All-Star Team (2011)

Signed as a free agent by **Pittsburgh**, August 1, 2012.

MELART, Ilari (MEHL-art, ihl-AH-ree) CBJ

Defense. Shoots left. 6'4", 227 lbs. Born, Helsinki, Finland, February 11, 1989.

			Regular Season					Playoffs				
Season	Club	League	GP	G	A	Pts	PIM	GP	G	A	Pts	PIM
2008-09	HIFK Helsinki	Finland	27	1	1	2	62	....	....	....	....	....
2009-10	HIFK Helsinki	Finland	13	1	0	1	47	2	0	0	0	0
2010-11	HIFK Helsinki	Finland	20	1	1	2	94	....	....	....	....	....
2011-12	HIFK Helsinki	Finland	36	2	3	5	132	2	1	0	1	0
2012-13	HIFK Helsinki	Finland	50	7	11	18	80	7	0	0	0	29

Signed as a free agent by **Columbus**, May 24, 2013.

MELCHIORI, Julian (mehl-KEE-awr-ee, JOO-lee-ehn) WPG

Defense. Shoots left. 6'4", 200 lbs. Born, Richmond Hill, Ont., December 6, 1991.
(Atlanta's 2nd choice, 87th overall, in 2010 Entry Draft).

			Regular Season					Playoffs				
Season	Club	League	GP	G	A	Pts	PIM	GP	G	A	Pts	PIM
2007-08	Toronto Marlboros	GTHL	43	2	13	15	36	....	....	....	....	....
2008-09	Newmarket	ON-Jr.A	48	2	20	22	34	9	1	2	3	14
2009-10	Newmarket	ON-Jr.A	39	7	16	23	16	20	2	9	11	10
2010-11	Kitchener Rangers	OHL	63	1	18	19	55	3	0	0	0	0
2011-12	Kitchener Rangers	OHL	35	2	17	19	42	....	....	....	....	....
	Oshawa Generals	OHL	26	0	17	17	22	6	2	1	3	2
	St. John's IceCaps	AHL	1	0	0	0	0	....	....	....	....	....
2012-13	St. John's IceCaps	AHL	52	1	7	8	39	....	....	....	....	....

• Transferred to **Winnipeg** after **Atlanta** franchise relocated, June 21, 2011.

MELEN, Hampus (MEH-lehn, HAHM-puhs) **DET**

Right wing. Shoots left. 6'2", 165 lbs. Born, Karlskrona, Sweden, February 28, 1995.
(Detroit's 8th choice, 199th overall, in 2013 Entry Draft).

			Regular Season					Playoffs				
Season	Club	League	GP	G	A	Pts	PIM	GP	G	A	Pts	PIM
2010-11	Karlskrona HK U18	Swe-U18	6	3	8	11	4	....	....	....	....	....
	Karlskrona HK U20	Swe-Jr.	2	0	3	3	0	2	1	1	2	0
2011-12	Tingsryds AIF U18	Swe-U18	26	9	22	31	16	....	....	....	....	....
2012-13	Tingsryds AIF U18	Swe-U18	24	18	22	40	59	....	....	....	....	....
	Tingsryds AIF Jr.	Swe-Jr.	5	0	0	0	2	....	....	....	....	....

MELINDY, James (muh-LIHN-dee, JAYMZ) **PHX**

Defense. Shoots right. 6'3", 205 lbs. Born, Goulds, Nfld., December 11, 1993.
(Phoenix's 3rd choice, 88th overall, in 2012 Entry Draft).

			Regular Season					Playoffs				
Season	Club	League	GP	G	A	Pts	PIM	GP	G	A	Pts	PIM
2008-09	Notre Dame Argos	SMHL	40	1	8	9	32	....	....	....	....	....
2009-10	Notre Dame	SMHL	41	8	19	27	92	13	0	2	2	14
2010-11	Moncton Wildcats	QMJHL	40	4	1	5	17	5	0	0	0	0
2011-12	Moncton Wildcats	QMJHL	61	9	18	27	74	4	2	1	3	12
2012-13	Moncton Wildcats	QMJHL	67	4	20	24	90	5	0	0	0	4
	Portland Pirates	AHL	2	0	0	0	0	....	....	....	....	....

MERRILL, Jon (MAIR-ihl, JAWN) **N.J.**

Defense. Shoots left. 6'4", 205 lbs. Born, Oklahoma City, OK, February 3, 1992.
(New Jersey's 1st choice, 38th overall, in 2010 Entry Draft).

			Regular Season					Playoffs				
Season	Club	League	GP	G	A	Pts	PIM	GP	G	A	Pts	PIM
2007-08	Det. Caesars	MWEHL	25	2	9	11	26	....	....	....	....	....
	Little Caesars	Minor-MI	....	7	21	28	....	....	....	....	....	....
2008-09	USNTDP	NAHL	26	2	2	4	14	....	....	....	....	....
	USNTDP	U-17	8	0	1	1	6	....	....	....	....	....
	USNTDP	U-18	9	1	2	3	4	....	....	....	....	....
2009-10	USNTDP	USHL	22	1	8	9	12	....	....	....	....	....
	USNTDP	U-18	34	4	19	23	6	....	....	....	....	....
2010-11	U. of Michigan	CCHA	42	7	18	25	16	....	....	....	....	....
2011-12	U. of Michigan	CCHA	19	2	9	11	15	....	....	....	....	....
2012-13	U. of Michigan	CCHA	21	2	9	11	14	....	....	....	....	....
	Albany Devils	AHL	12	1	7	8	4	....	....	....	....	....

CCHA All-Rookie Team (2011) • CCHA Second All-Star Team (2011) • NCAA Championship All-Tournament Team (2011)

MERSCH, Michael (MUHRSH, MIGH-kuhl) **L.A.**

Left wing. Shoots left. 6'2", 210 lbs. Born, Park Ridge, IL, October 2, 1992.
(Los Angeles' 4th choice, 110th overall, in 2011 Entry Draft).

			Regular Season					Playoffs				
Season	Club	League	GP	G	A	Pts	PIM	GP	G	A	Pts	PIM
2007-08	Team Illinois	MWEHL	31	13	16	29	46	....	....	....	....	....
	Team Illinois	Exhib.	....	22	24	46	29	....	....	....	....	....
2008-09	USNTDP	NAHL	42	15	13	28	50	9	5	2	7	4
	USNTDP	U-17	14	7	4	11	4	....	....	....	....	....
2009-10	USNTDP	USHL	26	4	4	8	22	....	....	....	....	....
	USNTDP	U-18	23	0	6	6	8	....	....	....	....	....
2010-11	U. of Wisconsin	WCHA	41	8	11	19	32	....	....	....	....	....
2011-12	U. of Wisconsin	WCHA	37	14	16	30	37	....	....	....	....	....
2012-13	U. of Wisconsin	WCHA	42	23	13	36	22	....	....	....	....	....

MEURS, Garrett (MEWRZ, GAIR-eht) **COL**

Center. Shoots right. 5'11", 175 lbs. Born, Wingham, Ont., January 12, 1993.
(Colorado's 4th choice, 123rd overall, in 2011 Entry Draft).

			Regular Season					Playoffs				
Season	Club	League	GP	G	A	Pts	PIM	GP	G	A	Pts	PIM
2008-09	Huron-Perth	Minor-ON	67	52	43	95	67	....	....	....	....	....
2009-10	Plymouth Whalers	OHL	62	16	18	34	22	9	1	2	3	0
2010-11	Plymouth Whalers	OHL	68	10	31	41	61	11	1	2	3	8
2011-12	Plymouth Whalers	OHL	67	20	33	53	67	....	....	....	....	....
2012-13	Plymouth Whalers	OHL	68	32	33	65	66	15	7	7	14	22

MILAN, Daniel (mih-LAN, DAN-yehl) **T.B.**

Defense. Shoots left. 6'2", 210 lbs. Born, Detroit, MI, April 14, 1992.

			Regular Season					Playoffs				
Season	Club	League	GP	G	A	Pts	PIM	GP	G	A	Pts	PIM
2010-11	Moncton Wildcats	QMJHL	68	14	24	38	76	5	1	1	2	5
2011-12	Moncton Wildcats	QMJHL	33	0	5	5	31	....	....	....	....	....
	Victoriaville Tigres	QMJHL	29	2	4	6	42	3	0	0	0	2
2012-13	Florida Everblades	ECHL	43	2	7	9	56	....	....	....	....	....

Signed as a free agent by **Tampa Bay**, September 23, 2011.

MILLER, Andrew (MIH-luhr, AN-droo) **EDM**

Center. Shoots right. 5'10", 180 lbs. Born, Bloomfield Hills, MI, September 18, 1988.

			Regular Season					Playoffs				
Season	Club	League	GP	G	A	Pts	PIM	GP	G	A	Pts	PIM
2007-08	Chicago Steel	USHL	59	14	27	41	28	7	2	4	6	4
2008-09	Chicago Steel	USHL	58	32	50	82	76	....	....	....	....	....
2009-10	Yale	ECAC	34	5	29	34	12	....	....	....	....	....
2010-11	Yale	ECAC	36	12	33	45	18	....	....	....	....	....
2011-12	Yale	ECAC	34	7	29	36	8	....	....	....	....	....
2012-13	Yale	ECAC	37	18	23	41	15	....	....	....	....	....

USHL Player of the Year (2009) • ECAC First All-Star Team (2011, 2013) • NCAA East Second All-American Team (2013) • NCAA Championship All-Tournament Team (2013) • NCAA Championship Tournament MVP (2013)

Signed as a free agent by **Edmonton**, April 17, 2013.

MILLER, Colin (MIH-luhr, KAW-lihn) **L.A.**

Defense. Shoots right. 6'1", 175 lbs. Born, Sault Ste. Marie, Ont., October 29, 1992.
(Los Angeles' 3rd choice, 151st overall, in 2012 Entry Draft).

			Regular Season					Playoffs				
Season	Club	League	GP	G	A	Pts	PIM	GP	G	A	Pts	PIM
2008-09	Soo North Stars	Minor-ON	32	6	15	21	42	10	2	7	9	14
2009-10	Soo Thunderbirds	NOJHL	46	7	23	30	38	14	5	9	14	6
2010-11	Sault Ste. Marie	OHL	66	3	19	22	44	....	....	....	....	....
2011-12	Sault Ste. Marie	OHL	54	8	20	28	79	....	....	....	....	....
2012-13	Sault Ste. Marie	OHL	54	20	35	55	78	6	1	6	7	0

MILLER, Kevan (MIHL-luhr, KEH-vuhn) **BOS**

Defense. Shoots right. 6'2", 200 lbs. Born, Los Angeles, CA, November 15, 1987.

			Regular Season					Playoffs				
Season	Club	League	GP	G	A	Pts	PIM	GP	G	A	Pts	PIM
2007-08	U. of Vermont	H-East	39	2	5	7	12	....	....	....	....	....
2008-09	U. of Vermont	H-East	39	1	7	8	30	....	....	....	....	....
2009-10	U. of Vermont	H-East	39	1	10	11	26	....	....	....	....	....
2010-11	U. of Vermont	H-East	27	1	3	4	29	....	....	....	....	....
	Providence Bruins	AHL	6	0	0	0	9	....	....	....	....	....
2011-12	Providence Bruins	AHL	65	3	21	24	98	....	....	....	....	....
2012-13	Providence Bruins	AHL	64	2	14	16	71	9	0	5	5	10

Signed as a free agent by **Providence** (AHL), March 18, 2011. Signed as a free agent by **Boston**, October 21, 2011.

MISKOVIC, Zach (MIHS-koh-vihch, ZAK)

Defense. Shoots right. 6'1", 190 lbs. Born, River Forest, IL, May 8, 1985.

			Regular Season					Playoffs				
Season	Club	League	GP	G	A	Pts	PIM	GP	G	A	Pts	PIM
2002-03	Cedar Rapids	USHL	60	2	6	8	91	7	0	0	0	12
2003-04	Cedar Rapids	USHL	60	6	15	21	139	4	1	1	2	2
2004-05	Cedar Rapids	USHL	60	4	16	20	149	8	1	0	1	14
2005-06	St. Lawrence	ECAC	40	1	15	16	30	....	....	....	....	....
2006-07	St. Lawrence	ECAC	39	2	10	12	48	....	....	....	....	....
2007-08	St. Lawrence	ECAC	37	8	12	20	36	....	....	....	....	....
2008-09	St. Lawrence	ECAC	38	16	9	25	32	....	....	....	....	....
2009-10	Hershey Bears	AHL	59	6	20	26	25	6	1	1	2	0
2010-11	Hershey Bears	AHL	58	7	9	16	58	5	0	0	0	8
2011-12	Hershey Bears	AHL	35	0	3	3	26	3	0	2	2	0
2012-13	Chicago Wolves	AHL	15	2	1	3	9	....	....	....	....	....
	San Antonio	AHL	27	4	9	13	22	....	....	....	....	....

ECAC First All-Star Team (2009) • NCAA East First All-American Team (2009)

Signed as a free agent by **Washington**, March 25, 2009. Signed as a free agent by **Chicago** (AHL), August 13, 2012. Signed as a free agent by **San Antonio** (AHL), February 14, 2013.

MITCHELL, Garrett (MIH-chuhl, GAIR-reht) **WSH**

Right wing. Shoots right. 5'10", 180 lbs. Born, Regina, Sask., September 2, 1991.
(Washington's 6th choice, 175th overall, in 2009 Entry Draft).

			Regular Season					Playoffs				
Season	Club	League	GP	G	A	Pts	PIM	GP	G	A	Pts	PIM
2006-07	Reg. Pat Cdns.	SMHL	42	14	11	25	140	....	....	....	....	....
	Regina Pats	WHL	4	0	1	1	2	....	....	....	....	....
2007-08	Regina Pats	WHL	62	8	5	13	73	6	1	0	1	6
2008-09	Regina Pats	WHL	71	10	5	15	140	....	....	....	....	....
2009-10	Regina Pats	WHL	57	15	16	31	110	....	....	....	....	....
	Hershey Bears	AHL	1	0	0	0	0	....	....	....	....	....
2010-11	Regina Pats	WHL	70	18	34	52	140	....	....	....	....	....
	Hershey Bears	AHL	2	0	0	0	5	....	....	....	....	....
2011-12	Hershey Bears	AHL	65	6	9	15	85	5	1	0	1	0
	South Carolina	ECHL	2	0	0	0	7	....	....	....	....	....
2012-13	Hershey Bears	AHL	75	15	15	30	94	5	1	0	1	4

MITCHELL, John (MIH-chuhl, JAWN) **ANA**

Left wing. Shoots left. 6'5", 216 lbs. Born, Neenah, WI, July 10, 1986.

			Regular Season					Playoffs				
Season	Club	League	GP	G	A	Pts	PIM	GP	G	A	Pts	PIM
2004-05	Tri-City Storm	USHL	12	2	1	3	16	....	....	....	....	....
	Green Bay	USHL	42	6	5	11	22	....	....	....	....	....
2005-06	Green Bay	USHL	6	0	1	1	6	....	....	....	....	....
	Indiana Ice	USHL	14	1	1	2	4	....	....	....	....	....
2006-07	U. of Wisconsin	WCHA	18	1	2	3	21	....	....	....	....	....
2007-08	U. of Wisconsin	WCHA	40	8	5	13	49	....	....	....	....	....
2008-09	U. of Wisconsin	WCHA	40	15	11	26	118	....	....	....	....	....
2009-10	U. of Wisconsin	WCHA	41	8	11	19	54	....	....	....	....	....
2010-11	Syracuse Crunch	AHL	60	9	10	19	64	....	....	....	....	....
	Elmira Jackals	ECHL	3	1	1	2	0	....	....	....	....	....
2011-12	Syracuse Crunch	AHL	50	8	10	18	23	4	1	0	1	0
2012-13	Norfolk Admirals	AHL	61	10	4	14	48	....	....	....	....	....

Signed as a free agent by **Anaheim**, May 3, 2012.

MOFFATT, Luke (MAW-fuht, LEWK) **COL**

Center. Shoots right. 6', 198 lbs. Born, Scottsdale, AZ, June 11, 1992.
(Colorado's 8th choice, 197th overall, in 2010 Entry Draft).

			Regular Season					Playoffs				
Season	Club	League	GP	G	A	Pts	PIM	GP	G	A	Pts	PIM
2007-08	Det. Compuware	MWEHL	30	37	19	56	....	....	....	....	....	....
	Det. Compuware	Minor-MI	5	4	1	5	4	....	....	....	....	....
2008-09	USNTDP	NAHL	42	17	10	27	30	9	0	3	3	4
	USNTDP	U-17	16	4	7	11	2	....	....	....	....	....
2009-10	USNTDP	USHL	28	5	10	15	22	....	....	....	....	....
	USNTDP	U-18	37	13	9	22	14	....	....	....	....	....
2010-11	U. of Michigan	CCHA	36	5	8	13	12	....	....	....	....	....
2011-12	U. of Michigan	CCHA	40	6	10	16	29	....	....	....	....	....
2012-13	U. of Michigan	CCHA	38	8	13	21	14	....	....	....	....	....

MOFFIE, Lee (MAW-fee, LEE)

Defense. Shoots left. 6'1", 205 lbs. Born, Wallingford, CT, August 29, 1990.
(San Jose's 7th choice, 188th overall, in 2010 Entry Draft).

			Regular Season					Playoffs				
Season	Club	League	GP	G	A	Pts	PIM	GP	G	A	Pts	PIM
2008-09	Waterloo	USHL	55	9	35	44	97	3	0	0	0	6
2009-10	U. of Michigan	CCHA	29	4	8	12	27	....	....	....	....	....
2010-11	U. of Michigan	CCHA	32	8	9	17	16	....	....	....	....	....
2011-12	U. of Michigan	CCHA	41	7	25	32	26	....	....	....	....	....
2012-13	U. of Michigan	CCHA	40	3	10	13	46	....	....	....	....	....

Traded to **Edmonton** by **San Jose** for Kyle Bigos, July 6, 2013.

MOLIN, Emil (moh-LEEN, eh-MIHL) DAL

Right wing. Shoots left. 6', 170 lbs. Born, Gavle, Sweden, February 3, 1993.
(Dallas' 3rd choice, 105th overall, in 2011 Entry Draft).

			Regular Season					Playoffs				
Season	Club	League	GP	G	A	Pts	PIM	GP	G	A	Pts	PIM
2009-10	Brynas U18	Swe-U18	38	22	35	57	24	4	2	6	8	0
2010-11	Brynas U18	Swe-U18	36	31	50	81	60	5	3	5	8	0
	Brynas IF Gavle Jr.	Swe-Jr.	9	0	1	1	2	1	0	0	0	0
2011-12	Brynas IF Gavle Jr.	Swe-Jr.	29	15	27	42	45	1	0	1	1	0
	Brynas IF Gavle	Sweden	34	1	4	5	0	10	0	1	1	0
2012-13	Mora IK	Sweden-2	8	0	0	0	2	....	....	....	....	....
	Brynas IF Gavle Jr.	Swe-Jr.	15	5	6	11	37	2	0	1	1	0
	Brynas IF Gavle	Sweden	34	1	2	3	0	1	0	0	0	0

MONAHAN, Sean (MAWN-ah-han, SHAWN) CGY

Center. Shoots left. 6'2", 187 lbs. Born, Brampton, Ont., October 12, 1994.
(Calgary's 1st choice, 6th overall, in 2013 Entry Draft).

			Regular Season					Playoffs				
Season	Club	League	GP	G	A	Pts	PIM	GP	G	A	Pts	PIM
2009-10	Mississauga Rebels	GTHL	47	46	44	90	48	....	....	....	....	....
2010-11	Ottawa 67's	OHL	65	20	27	47	32	4	2	2	4	0
2011-12	Ottawa 67's	OHL	62	33	45	78	38	18	8	7	15	12
2012-13	Ottawa 67's	OHL	58	31	47	78	24	....	....	....	....	....

OHL Second All-Star Team (2012)

MORIN, Samuel (moh-REHN, sam-YUHL) PHI

Defense. Shoots left. 6'6", 202 lbs. Born, Lac-Beauport, Que., July 12, 1995.
(Philadelphia's 1st choice, 11th overall, in 2013 Entry Draft).

			Regular Season					Playoffs				
Season	Club	League	GP	G	A	Pts	PIM	GP	G	A	Pts	PIM
2010-11	Levis	QAAA	36	0	12	12	40	4	0	0	0	4
2011-12	Rimouski Oceanic	QMJHL	62	0	8	8	57	10	0	1	1	8
2012-13	Rimouski Oceanic	QMJHL	46	4	12	16	117	6	1	6	7	16

MOROZ, Mitchell (maw-RAWZ, MIH-chuhl) EDM

Left wing. Shoots left. 6'2", 208 lbs. Born, Edmonton, Alta., May 3, 1994.
(Edmonton's 2nd choice, 32nd overall, in 2012 Entry Draft).

			Regular Season					Playoffs				
Season	Club	League	GP	G	A	Pts	PIM	GP	G	A	Pts	PIM
2007-08	Cgy. N. Sabres	AMBHL	31	5	7	12	40	2	0	2	2	12
2008-09	Cgy. N. Sabres	AMBHL	31	20	16	36	50	....	....	....	....	....
2009-10	Edge School	High-AB	43	20	23	43	80	....	....	....	....	....
	Edmonton	WHL	7	0	1	1	2	....	....	....	....	....
2010-11	Calgary Northstars	AMHL	22	10	4	14	34	2	0	0	0	0
	Edmonton	WHL	1	0	0	0	0	....	....	....	....	....
2011-12	Edmonton	WHL	66	16	9	25	131	20	4	4	8	24
2012-13	Edmonton	WHL	69	13	21	34	140	22	2	5	7	41

MORRISSEY, Josh (MOHR-ih-see, JAWSH) WPG

Defense. Shoots left. 6', 186 lbs. Born, Calgary, Alta., March 28, 1995.
(Winnipeg's 1st choice, 13th overall, in 2013 Entry Draft).

			Regular Season					Playoffs				
Season	Club	League	GP	G	A	Pts	PIM	GP	G	A	Pts	PIM
2008-09	Calgary Royals	AMBHL	33	6	18	24	56	....	....	....	....	....
2009-10	Calgary Royals	AMBHL	32	21	28	49	108	....	....	....	....	....
2010-11	Calgary Royals	AMHL	30	17	22	39	11	6	1	3	4	10
	Prince Albert	WHL	5	0	0	0	4	....	....	....	....	....
2011-12	Prince Albert	WHL	68	10	28	38	60	....	....	....	....	....
2012-13	Prince Albert	WHL	70	15	32	47	91	4	0	1	1	9

Canadian Major Junior Scholastic Player of the Year (2013)

MORROW, Joe (MOH-row, JOH) BOS

Defense. Shoots left. 6'1", 204 lbs. Born, Edmonton, Alta., December 9, 1992.
(Pittsburgh's 1st choice, 23rd overall, in 2011 Entry Draft).

			Regular Season					Playoffs				
Season	Club	League	GP	G	A	Pts	PIM	GP	G	A	Pts	PIM
2006-07	Strathcona	AMBHL	32	16	16	32	75	4	2	3	5	8
2007-08	Sherwood Park	Minor-AB	24	7	11	18	57	....	....	....	....	....
	Portland	WHL	1	0	0	0	0	....	....	....	....	....
2008-09	Portland	WHL	41	0	7	7	26	....	....	....	....	....
2009-10	Portland	WHL	63	7	24	31	59	13	0	2	2	6
2010-11	Portland	WHL	60	9	40	49	67	21	6	14	20	27
2011-12	Portland	WHL	62	17	47	64	99	22	4	13	17	35
2012-13	Wilkes-Barre	AHL	57	4	11	15	35	....	....	....	....	....
	Texas Stars	AHL	9	1	3	4	4	8	2	1	3	8

WHL West First All-Star Team (2012)

Traded to **Dallas** by **Pittsburgh** with Pittsburgh's 5th round choce (Matej Paulovic) in 2013 Entry Draft for Brenden Morrow and Minnesota's 3rd round choice (previously acquired, Philadelphia selected Jake Guentzel) in 2013 Entry Draft, March 24, 2013. Traded to **Boston** by **Dallas** with Loui Eriksson, Reilly Smith and Matt Fraser for Tyler Seguin, Rich Peverley and Ryan Button, July 4, 2013.

MOTTE, Tyler (MAWT, TIGH-luhr) CHI

Center. Shoots left. 5'9", 190 lbs. Born, Port Huron, MI, March 10, 1995.
(Chicago's 5th choice, 121st overall, in 2013 Entry Draft).

			Regular Season					Playoffs				
Season	Club	League	GP	G	A	Pts	PIM	GP	G	A	Pts	PIM
2010-11	Det. Honeybaked	T1EHL	34	23	14	37	20	....	....	....	....	....
2011-12	USNTDP	USHL	36	15	13	28	32	2	2	0	2	0
	USNTDP	U-17	17	8	3	11	30	....	....	....	....	....
	USNTDP	U-18	2	1	0	1	0	....	....	....	....	....
2012-13	USNTDP	USHL	26	11	6	17	6	....	....	....	....	....
	USNTDP	U-18	41	15	13	28	44	....	....	....	....	....

• Signed Letter of Intent to attend **University of Michigan** (CCHA) in fall of 2013.

MOUTREY, Nick (MOO-tree, NIHK) CBJ

Center/Left wing. Shoots left. 6'2", 208 lbs. Born, Toronto, Ont., June 24, 1995.
(Columbus' 6th choice, 105th overall, in 2013 Entry Draft).

			Regular Season					Playoffs				
Season	Club	League	GP	G	A	Pts	PIM	GP	G	A	Pts	PIM
2010-11	York Simcoe	Minor-ON	69	43	46	89	46	....	....	....	....	....
2011-12	Saginaw Spirit	OHL	66	2	7	9	46	12	0	0	0	4
2012-13	Saginaw Spirit	OHL	65	16	27	43	44	4	0	0	0	12

MUELLER, Mirco (MEW-luhr, MIHR-koh) S.J.

Defense. Shoots left. 6'3", 184 lbs. Born, Winterthur, Switz., March 21, 1995.
(San Jose's 1st choice, 18th overall, in 2013 Entry Draft).

			Regular Season					Playoffs				
Season	Club	League	GP	G	A	Pts	PIM	GP	G	A	Pts	PIM
2009-10	Winterthur U17	Swiss-U17	12	0	4	4	0	....	....	....	....	....
2010-11	Kloten Flyers U17	Swiss-U17	32	12	19	31	14	10	0	6	6	12
	Kloten Flyers Jr.	Swiss-Jr.	1	0	0	0	0	....	....	....	....	....
2011-12	Kloten Flyers U17	Swiss-U17	4	1	3	4	0	....	....	....	....	....
	Kloten Flyers Jr.	Swiss-Jr.	26	3	3	6	8	4	1	2	3	2
	Kloten Flyers	Swiss	7	1	0	1	0	....	....	....	....	....
2012-13	Everett Silvertips	WHL	63	6	25	31	57	6	0	1	1	6

MUIR, Aidan (MEWR, AY-duhn) EDM

Wing. Shoots right. 6'3", 182 lbs. Born, Brampton, Ont., August 21, 1995.
(Edmonton's 7th choice, 113th overall, in 2013 Entry Draft).

			Regular Season					Playoffs				
Season	Club	League	GP	G	A	Pts	PIM	GP	G	A	Pts	PIM
2011-12	Det. Vic. Honda	T1EHL	40	13	7	20	8	4	3	4	7	8
2012-13	Det. Vic. Honda	T1EHL	37	17	23	40	41	3	0	1	1	0

MULLEN, Patrick (MUHL-uhn, PA-trihk) VAN

Defense. Shoots right. 5'11", 180 lbs. Born, Pittsburgh, PA, May 6, 1986.

			Regular Season					Playoffs				
Season	Club	League	GP	G	A	Pts	PIM	GP	G	A	Pts	PIM
2004-05	Sioux City	USHL	60	14	23	37	8	....	....	....	....	....
2005-06	U. of Denver	WCHA	37	7	10	17	24	....	....	....	....	....
2006-07	U. of Denver	WCHA	37	5	12	17	20	....	....	....	....	....
2007-08	U. of Denver	WCHA	40	4	18	22	65	....	....	....	....	....
2008-09	U. of Denver	WCHA	38	4	21	25	39	....	....	....	....	....
2009-10	Manchester	AHL	44	4	6	10	16	2	0	0	0	2
	Ontario Reign	ECHL	1	0	0	0	0	....	....	....	....	....
2010-11	Manchester	AHL	67	3	17	20	32	7	0	1	1	4
2011-12	Manchester	AHL	69	13	28	41	45	4	1	2	3	8
2012-13	Chicago Wolves	AHL	2	0	0	0	0	....	....	....	....	....

Signed as a free agent by **Los Angeles**, April 3, 2009. Signed as a free agent by **Vancouver**, July 5, 2012.

MULLIN, Jimmy (MUH-lihn, JIHM-ee) T.B.

Right wing. Shoots right. 5'11", 181 lbs. Born, Philadelphia, PA, February 24, 1992.
(Tampa Bay's 6th choice, 118th overall, in 2010 Entry Draft).

			Regular Season					Playoffs				
Season	Club	League	GP	G	A	Pts	PIM	GP	G	A	Pts	PIM
2006-07	Shattuck Bantam	High-MN	67	24	34	58	24	....	....	....	....	....
2007-08	Shattuck U16	High-MN	52	20	29	49	32	....	....	....	....	....
2008-09	Shattuck U16	High-MN	56	62	44	106	38	....	....	....	....	....
2009-10	Shat.-St. Mary's	High-MN	55	32	40	72	26	....	....	....	....	....
2010-11	Fargo Force	USHL	52	23	37	60	26	5	0	0	0	0
2011-12	Miami U.	CCHA	37	11	15	26	10	....	....	....	....	....
2012-13	Miami U.	CCHA	38	6	8	14	14	....	....	....	....	....

USHL All-Rookie Team (2011) • USHL First All-Star Team (2011)

MURPHY, Connor (MUHR-fee, KAW-nuhr) PHX

Defense. Shoots right. 6'4", 205 lbs. Born, Dublin, OH, March 26, 1993.
(Phoenix's 1st choice, 20th overall, in 2011 Entry Draft).

			Regular Season					Playoffs				
Season	Club	League	GP	G	A	Pts	PIM	GP	G	A	Pts	PIM
2008-09	Ohio Blue Jackets	Ind.	35	7	11	18	....	....	....	....	....	....
2009-10	USNTDP	USHL	2	0	0	0	2	....	....	....	....	....
	USNTDP	U-17	6	1	0	1	2	....	....	....	....	....
2010-11	USNTDP	USHL	9	3	1	4	6	....	....	....	....	....
	USNTDP	U-18	13	3	3	6	0	....	....	....	....	....
2011-12	Sarnia Sting	OHL	35	8	18	26	26	6	1	2	3	6
2012-13	Sarnia Sting	OHL	33	6	12	18	32	....	....	....	....	....

• Missed majority of 2009-10 and 2010-11 due to back injury.

MURPHY, Wade (MUHR-fee, WAYD) NSH

Right wing. Shoots right. 6', 176 lbs. Born, Victoria, B.C., October 22, 1993.
(Nashville's 9th choice, 185th overall, in 2013 Entry Draft).

			Regular Season					Playoffs				
Season	Club	League	GP	G	A	Pts	PIM	GP	G	A	Pts	PIM
2008-09	South Island	BCMML	39	9	9	18	40	4	0	0	0	2
2009-10	Saanich Braves	VIJHL	STATISTICS NOT AVAILABLE									
	Victoria Grizzlies	BCHL	6	3	1	4	2	....	....	....	....	....
2010-11	Victoria Grizzlies	BCHL	56	7	9	16	30	8	2	1	3	6
2011-12	Victoria Grizzlies	BCHL	38	22	40	62	58	....	....	....	....	....
	Penticton Vees	BCHL	22	14	15	29	8	15	*9	9	*18	6
2012-13	Penticton Vees	BCHL	50	23	47	70	50	15	5	6	11	12

• Signed Letter of Intent to attend **University of North Dakota** (WCHA) in fall of 2013.

MURRAY, Ryan (MUHR-ee, RIGH-uhn) CBJ

Defense. Shoots left. 6'1", 201 lbs. Born, Regina, Sask., September 27, 1993.
(Columbus' 1st choice, 2nd overall, in 2012 Entry Draft).

			Regular Season					Playoffs				
Season	Club	League	GP	G	A	Pts	PIM	GP	G	A	Pts	PIM
2007-08	Balgonie	SMBHL	25	11	31	42	26	....	....	....	....	....
	Balgonie	Minor-SK	10	2	5	7	....	....	....	....	....	....
2008-09	Moose Jaw	SMHL	41	12	26	38	12	5	1	6	7	6
	Everett Silvertips	WHL	....	....	....	....	....	5	0	1	1	2
2009-10	Everett Silvertips	WHL	52	5	22	27	31	7	2	5	7	2
2010-11	Everett Silvertips	WHL	70	6	40	46	45	4	1	2	3	4
2011-12	Everett Silvertips	WHL	46	9	22	31	31	4	3	2	5	0
2012-13	Everett Silvertips	WHL	23	2	15	17	14	....	....	....	....	....

WHL West Second All-Star Team (2011, 2012)

MUSIL, David (moo-SIHL, DAY-vihd) **EDM**

Defense. Shoots left. 6'3", 196 lbs. Born, Calgary, AB, Alta., April 9, 1993.
(Edmonton's 3rd choice, 31st overall, in 2011 Entry Draft).

			Regular Season					Playoffs				
Season	Club	League	GP	G	A	Pts	PIM	GP	G	A	Pts	PIM
2005-06	Jihlava U17	CzR-U17	5	0	0	0	0	....	....	....	....	....
2006-07	Jihlava U17	CzR-U17	36	7	23	30	42	....	....	....	....	....
	Trebic U17	CzR-U17	14	1	3	4	26	....	....	....	....	....
2007-08	Jihlava U17	CzR-U17	42	8	27	35	98	3	0	1	1	6
	Jihlava Jr.	CzRep-Jr.	9	0	5	5	6	....	....	....	....	....
2008-09	Jihlava U17	CzR-U17	9	3	3	6	46	....	....	....	....	....
	Jihlava Jr.	CzRep-Jr.	27	9	12	21	46	8	3	3	6	10
	HC Dukla Jihlava	CzRep-2	14	0	1	1	4	4	0	0	0	4
2009-10	Vancouver Giants	WHL	71	7	25	32	67	16	2	2	4	8
2010-11	Vancouver Giants	WHL	62	6	19	25	83	4	0	1	1	2
2011-12	Vancouver Giants	WHL	59	6	21	27	104	....	....	....	....	....
2012-13	Vancouver Giants	WHL	14	2	6	8	18	....	....	....	....	....
	Edmonton	WHL	48	7	16	23	56	22	0	6	6	26

MYRON, Wesley (MIGH-ruhn, WEHS-lee) **VAN**

Left wing. Shoots left. 6'2", 190 lbs. Born, Victoria, B.C., August 16, 1992.
(Vancouver's 4th choice, 177th overall, in 2012 Entry Draft).

			Regular Season					Playoffs				
Season	Club	League	GP	G	A	Pts	PIM	GP	G	A	Pts	PIM
2007-08	South Island	BCMML	38	4	9	13	22	....	....	....	....	....
2008-09	South Island	BCMML	36	19	23	42	42	4	0	3	3	10
	Saanich Braves	VIJHL	1	1	0	1	0	....	....	....	....	....
2009-10	Victoria Grizzlies	BCHL	46	13	15	28	13	6	0	1	1	0
2010-11	Victoria Grizzlies	BCHL	59	20	21	41	21	12	3	3	6	6
2011-12	Victoria Grizzlies	BCHL	26	17	25	42	18	....	....	....	....	....
2012-13	Boston University	H-East	21	2	1	3	8	....	....	....	....	....
	Kalamazoo Wings	ECHL	17	2	7	9	8	....	....	....	....	....

NAMESTNIKOV, Vladislav (nah-MEHST-nih-kawv, vla-dih-SLAHV) **T.B.**

Center. Shoots left. 6', 179 lbs. Born, Zhukovsky, Russia, November 22, 1992.
(Tampa Bay's 1st choice, 27th overall, in 2011 Entry Draft).

			Regular Season					Playoffs				
Season	Club	League	GP	G	A	Pts	PIM	GP	G	A	Pts	PIM
2009-10	Khimik	Russia-2	33	12	9	21	18	2	1	0	1	2
2010-11	London Knights	OHL	68	30	39	69	49	6	1	4	5	6
2011-12	London Knights	OHL	63	22	49	71	50	19	4	14	18	20
2012-13	Syracuse Crunch	AHL	44	7	14	21	32	18	2	5	7	10

NANNE, Louis (NA-nee, LOO-ee) **MIN**

Left wing. Shoots left. 5'10", 171 lbs. Born, Edina, MN, June 18, 1994.
(Minnesota's 7th choice, 188th overall, in 2012 Entry Draft).

			Regular Season					Playoffs				
Season	Club	League	GP	G	A	Pts	PIM	GP	G	A	Pts	PIM
2009-10	Edina Hornets	High-MN	26	4	1	5	6	....	....	....	....	....
2010-11	Edina Hornets	High-MN	27	13	16	29	12	....	....	....	....	....
2011-12	Team Southwest	UMHSEL	23	7	13	20	12	....	....	....	....	....
	Edina Hornets	High-MN	28	15	12	27	34	....	....	....	....	....
2012-13	Penticton Vees	BCHL	45	19	22	41	16	15	6	6	12	4

• Signed Letter of Intent to attend **University of Minnesota** (WCHA) in fall of 2013.

NASTASIUK, Zach (nas-TAYZ-ee-uhk, ZAK) **DET**

Right wing. Shoots right. 6'1", 190 lbs. Born, Barrie, Ont., March 30, 1995.
(Detroit's 2nd choice, 48th overall, in 2013 Entry Draft).

			Regular Season					Playoffs				
Season	Club	League	GP	G	A	Pts	PIM	GP	G	A	Pts	PIM
2010-11	Barrie Colts	Minor-ON	41	17	23	40	38	....	....	....	....	....
	Orangeville Flyers	ON-Jr.A	1	0	0	0	0	....	....	....	....	....
2011-12	Owen Sound	OHL	68	11	8	19	15	5	1	0	1	0
2012-13	Owen Sound	OHL	62	20	20	40	32	12	4	7	11	0

NATTINEN, Joonas (NA-tih-nuhn, YOH-nuhs) **MTL**

Center. Shoots right. 6'3", 197 lbs. Born, Jamsa, Finland, January 3, 1991.
(Montreal's 2nd choice, 65th overall, in 2009 Entry Draft).

			Regular Season					Playoffs				
Season	Club	League	GP	G	A	Pts	PIM	GP	G	A	Pts	PIM
2006-07	JyP Jyvaskyla U18	Fin-U18	30	10	25	35	22	8	5	7	12	0
2007-08	JyP Jyvaskyla U18	Fin-U18	34	14	34	48	22	2	0	0	0	0
	JyP Jyvaskyla Jr.	Fin-Jr.	8	0	2	2	2	3	0	2	2	2
2008-09	Suomi U20	Finland-2	5	2	2	4	0	....	....	....	....	....
	Blues Espoo Jr.	Fin-Jr.	30	9	29	38	6	10	3	10	13	4
	Blues Espoo	Finland	14	0	0	0	4	....	....	....	....	....
2009-10	Suomi U20	Finland-2	7	0	8	8	6	....	....	....	....	....
	Blues Espoo	Finland	23	0	3	3	4	1	0	0	0	0
	Hokki Kajaani	Finland-2	10	2	2	4	4	....	....	....	....	....
	Blues Espoo Jr.	Fin-Jr.	11	7	6	13	2	....	....	....	....	....
2010-11	Suomi U20	Finland-2	2	0	0	0	0	....	....	....	....	....
	Blues Espoo Jr.	Fin-Jr.	2	0	2	2	0	....	....	....	....	....
	Blues Espoo	Finland	11	0	0	0	6	....	....	....	....	....
	HPK Hameenlinna	Finland	10	0	2	2	6	1	0	1	1	0
2011-12	Hamilton Bulldogs	AHL	63	11	10	21	30	....	....	....	....	....
2012-13	Hamilton Bulldogs	AHL	24	5	4	9	8	....	....	....	....	....

• Missed majority of 2012-13 due to upper-body injury vs. St. Johns (AHL), December 28, 2012 and resulting surgery.

NAVIN, Brad (NAY-vihn, BRAD) **BUF**

Center. Shoots left. 6'2", 198 lbs. Born, Waupaca, WI, June 5, 1992.
(Buffalo's 6th choice, 197th overall, in 2011 Entry Draft).

			Regular Season					Playoffs				
Season	Club	League	GP	G	A	Pts	PIM	GP	G	A	Pts	PIM
2007-08	Waupaca Comets	High-WI	16	20	17	37	....					
2008-09	Waupaca Comets	High-WI	16	25	18	43	....					
2009-10	Waupaca Comets	High-WI	23	53	39	92	57					
2010-11	Waupaca Comets	High-WI	14	29	23	52	40					
2011-12	U. of Wisconsin	WCHA	36	3	3	6	16					
2012-13	U. of Wisconsin	WCHA	34	1	3	4	8					

NEDOMLEL, Richard (NEHD-oh-muh-lehl, rih-CHUHRD) **DET**

Defense. Shoots left. 6'4", 204 lbs. Born, Prague, Czech Rep., July 1, 1993.
(Detroit's 8th choice, 175th overall, in 2011 Entry Draft).

			Regular Season					Playoffs				
Season	Club	League	GP	G	A	Pts	PIM	GP	G	A	Pts	PIM
2008-09	Chomutov U17	CzR-U17	17	0	3	3	47	....	....	....	....	....
	Slavia U17	CzR-U17	25	0	4	4	18	9	1	1	2	4
2009-10	Slavia U18	CzR-U18	44	9	10	19	221	4	1	0	1	54
2010-11	Swift Current	WHL	66	0	10	10	107	....	....	....	....	....
2011-12	Swift Current	WHL	72	10	36	46	83	....	....	....	....	....
2012-13	Swift Current	WHL	72	7	21	28	105	5	0	1	1	2

NELSON, Logan (NEHL-suhn, LOH-guhn) **BUF**

Center. Shoots right. 6'1", 186 lbs. Born, Coon Rapids, MN, September 9, 1993.
(Buffalo's 5th choice, 133rd overall, in 2012 Entry Draft).

			Regular Season					Playoffs				
Season	Club	League	GP	G	A	Pts	PIM	GP	G	A	Pts	PIM
2009-10	Russell Stover	T1EHL	38	18	17	35	46	....	....	....	....	....
2010-11	Des Moines	USHL	41	6	3	9	69	....	....	....	....	....
2011-12	Victoria Royals	WHL	71	23	39	62	70	4	0	4	4	4
2012-13	Victoria Royals	WHL	49	14	29	43	41	6	2	4	6	8

NEMETH, Patrik (NEH-meht, PAHT-rihk) **DAL**

Defense. Shoots left. 6'3", 201 lbs. Born, Stockholm, Sweden, February 8, 1992.
(Dallas' 2nd choice, 41st overall, in 2010 Entry Draft).

			Regular Season					Playoffs				
Season	Club	League	GP	G	A	Pts	PIM	GP	G	A	Pts	PIM
2007-08	Hammarby U18	Swe-U18	13	1	3	4	12	....	....	....	....	....
2008-09	AIK IF Solna U18	Swe-U18	27	3	10	13	123	4	1	0	1	29
	AIK IF Solna Jr.	Swe-Jr.	19	0	0	0	43	....	....	....	....	....
	AIK IF Solna	Sweden-2	1	0	1	1	0	....	....	....	....	....
2009-10	AIK IF Solna U18	Swe-U18	3	0	1	1	4	1	0	1	1	0
	AIK IF Solna Jr.	Swe-Jr.	38	1	19	20	120	5	1	2	3	10
	AIK IF Solna	Sweden-2	19	0	3	3	8	....	....	....	....	....
2010-11	AIK IF Solna	Sweden	38	1	6	7	18	7	0	0	0	2
2011-12	AIK Solna	Sweden	46	0	3	3	55	11	0	1	1	8
2012-13	Texas Stars	AHL	47	1	11	12	40	....	....	....	....	....

NESTEROV, Nikita (NEHS-tehr-awf, nih-KEE-tuh) **T.B.**

Defense. Shoots left. 6', 191 lbs. Born, Chelyabinsk, Russia, March 28, 1993.
(Tampa Bay's 3rd choice, 148th overall, in 2011 Entry Draft).

			Regular Season					Playoffs				
Season	Club	League	GP	G	A	Pts	PIM	GP	G	A	Pts	PIM
2009-10	Chelyabinsk Jr.	Russia-Jr.	9	5	2	7	8	4	0	0	0	6
2010-11	Chelyabinsk Jr.	Russia-Jr.	46	5	14	19	72	5	0	0	0	6
2011-12	Chelyabinsk Jr.	Russia-Jr.	41	11	20	31	66	4	0	5	5	6
	Chelyabinsk	KHL	10	0	1	1	4	3	0	0	0	0
2012-13	Chelyabinsk Jr.	Russia-Jr.	2	0	1	1	2	4	2	1	3	0
	Chelyabinsk	KHL	35	0	0	0	14	19	0	4	4	6

NESTRASIL, Andrej (NEHS-tra-shihl, ahn-DRAY) **DET**

Right wing. Shoots left. 6'2", 210 lbs. Born, Prague, Czech., February 22, 1991.
(Detroit's 3rd choice, 75th overall, in 2009 Entry Draft).

			Regular Season					Playoffs				
Season	Club	League	GP	G	A	Pts	PIM	GP	G	A	Pts	PIM
2004-05	Slavia U17	CzR-U17	3	0	1	1	2	....	....	....	....	....
2005-06	Slavia U17	CzR-U17	41	6	12	18	18	....	....	....	....	....
2006-07	Slavia U17	CzR-U17	43	24	37	61	75	5	2	2	4	6
2007-08	Slavia U17	CzR-U17	....	....	....	....	....	2	1	0	1	2
	HC Slavia Praha Jr.	CzRep-Jr.	40	12	16	28	58	5	1	2	3	4
2008-09	Victoriaville Tigres	QMJHL	66	22	35	57	67	4	2	1	3	10
2009-10	Victoriaville Tigres	QMJHL	50	16	35	51	40	16	2	4	6	10
2010-11	P.E.I. Rocket	QMJHL	58	19	51	70	40	5	1	5	6	2
2011-12	Grand Rapids	AHL	25	3	1	4	6	....	....	....	....	....
	Toledo Walleye	ECHL	51	7	22	29	20	....	....	....	....	....
2012-13	Toledo Walleye	ECHL	40	11	30	41	26	4	1	2	3	0
	Grand Rapids	AHL	25	3	3	6	2	1	0	0	0	0

NICASTRO, Max (nih-KAS-troh, MAX) **DET**

Defense. Shoots right. 6'2", 189 lbs. Born, Thousand Oaks, CA, March 2, 1990.
(Detroit's 2nd choice, 91st overall, in 2008 Entry Draft).

			Regular Season					Playoffs				
Season	Club	League	GP	G	A	Pts	PIM	GP	G	A	Pts	PIM
2006-07	L.A. Jr. Kings	Minor-CA	48	17	19	36	44	....	....	....	....	....
2007-08	Chicago Steel	USHL	58	6	14	20	78	7	1	2	3	12
2008-09	Chicago Steel	USHL	57	9	22	31	84	....	....	....	....	....
2009-10	Boston University	H-East	37	3	12	15	26	....	....	....	....	....
2010-11	Boston University	H-East	38	5	4	9	59	....	....	....	....	....
2011-12	Boston University	H-East	27	3	6	9	32	....	....	....	....	....
2012-13	Grand Rapids	AHL	25	1	2	3	10	....	....	....	....	....
	Toledo Walleye	ECHL	9	2	3	5	4	4	1	0	1	0

Hockey East All-Rookie Team (2010)

NICHOLLS, Josh (NIH-kuhls, JAWSH) **NYR**

Right wing. Shoots right. 6'2", 196 lbs. Born, Tsawwassen, B.C., April 27, 1992.
(Toronto's 7th choice, 182nd overall, in 2010 Entry Draft).

			Regular Season					Playoffs				
Season	Club	League	GP	G	A	Pts	PIM	GP	G	A	Pts	PIM
2007-08	Greater Van.	BCMML	39	18	30	48	68	2	0	0	0	20
2008-09	Saskatoon Blades	WHL	63	9	16	25	37	7	2	0	2	4
2009-10	Saskatoon Blades	WHL	71	18	30	48	55	10	0	5	5	6
2010-11	Saskatoon Blades	WHL	71	34	53	87	47	10	4	2	6	6
2011-12	Saskatoon Blades	WHL	56	30	38	68	24	4	2	1	3	2
2012-13	Saskatoon Blades	WHL	71	47	38	85	43	4	0	1	1	9

Signed as a free agent by **NY Rangers**, March 5, 2013.

NICHUSHKIN, Valeri (nih-CHOOSH-kihn, val-AIR-ee) **DAL**

Right wing. Shoots left. 6'4", 202 lbs. Born, Chelyabinsk, Russia, March 4, 1995.
(Dallas' 1st choice, 10th overall, in 2013 Entry Draft).

			Regular Season					Playoffs				
Season	Club	League	GP	G	A	Pts	PIM	GP	G	A	Pts	PIM
2011-12	Chelyabinsk Jr.	Russia-Jr.	38	4	6	10	6	....	....	....	....	....
2012-13	Chelyabinsk Jr.	Russia-Jr.	9	4	4	8	0	....	....	....	....	....
	Chelmet	Russia-2	15	8	2	10	4	....	....	....	....	....
	Chelyabinsk	KHL	18	4	2	6	0	25	6	3	9	0

NIELSEN, Jonatan (NEEL-suhn, JAWN-ah-thuhn) **FLA**

Defense. Shoots right. 6'3", 183 lbs. Born, Anderstorp, Sweden, September 11, 1993.
(Florida's 5th choice, 194th overall, in 2012 Entry Draft).

			Regular Season					Playoffs				
Season	Club	League	GP	G	A	Pts	PIM	GP	G	A	Pts	PIM
2007-08	Tranas AIF U18	Swe-U18	10	9	4	13	8	....	....	....	....	....
2008-09	Tranas AIF U18	Swe-U18	13	8	5	13	32	....	....	....	....	....
	Tranas AIF Jr.	Swe-Jr.	22	4	7	11	8	....	....	....	....	....
	Tranas AIF	Sweden-3	3	0	0	0	0	....	....	....	....	....
2009-10	Linkopings HC U18	Swe-U18	34	7	8	15	16	2	0	0	0	0
2010-11	Linkopings HC U18	Swe-U18	12	3	7	10	6	5	1	1	2	2
	Linkopings HC Jr.	Swe-Jr.	29	2	1	3	6	3	0	0	0	0
2011-12	Linkopings HC Jr.	Swe-Jr.	38	5	4	9	24	6	1	3	4	0
	Linkopings HC	Sweden	1	0	0	0	0	....	....	....	....	....
2012-13	Linkopings HC Jr.	Swe-Jr.	13	4	4	8	10	....	....	....	....	....
	Linkopings HC	Sweden	6	0	0	0	0	....	....	....	....	....
	Sodertalje SK	Sweden-2	38	4	4	8	10	....	....	....	....	....

NIETO, Matthew (NEE-eh-toh, MA-thew) **S.J.**

Left wing. Shoots left. 5'11", 190 lbs. Born, Long Beach, CA, November 5, 1992.
(San Jose's 1st choice, 47th overall, in 2011 Entry Draft).

			Regular Season					Playoffs				
Season	Club	League	GP	G	A	Pts	PIM	GP	G	A	Pts	PIM
2007-08	Salisbury School	High-CT	23	8	10	18	....	....	....	....	....	....
2008-09	USNTDP	NAHL	38	11	24	35	14	....	....	....	....	....
	USNTDP	U-17	14	9	9	18	8	....	....	....	....	....
	USNTDP	U-18	13	6	8	14	14	....	....	....	....	....
2009-10	USNTDP	USHL	24	15	14	29	19	....	....	....	....	....
	USNTDP	U-18	30	13	12	25	12	....	....	....	....	....
2010-11	Boston University	H-East	39	10	13	23	16	....	....	....	....	....
2011-12	Boston University	H-East	37	16	26	42	26	....	....	....	....	....
2012-13	Boston University	H-East	39	18	19	37	24	....	....	....	....	....

NIEVES, Cristoval (noo-EH-vehz, KRIHS-TOH-vahl) **NYR**

Center. Shoots left. 6'3", 192 lbs. Born, Syracuse, NY, January 23, 1994.
(NY Rangers' 2nd choice, 59th overall, in 2012 Entry Draft).

			Regular Season					Playoffs				
Season	Club	League	GP	G	A	Pts	PIM	GP	G	A	Pts	PIM
2009-10	Syracuse Nationals	Minor-NY	60	30	42	72	....	....	....	....	....	....
2010-11	Kent Prep School	High-CT	22	11	28	39	6	....	....	....	....	....
2011-12	Kent Prep School	High-CT	26	7	32	39	24	....	....	....	....	....
	Indiana Ice	USHL	13	2	8	10	2	....	....	....	....	....
2012-13	U. of Michigan	CCHA	40	8	21	29	18	....	....	....	....	....

NIGRO, Anthony (NIGH-groh, AN-thuh-nee)

Center. Shoots left. 5'11", 185 lbs. Born, Vaughan, Ont., January 11, 1990.
(St. Louis' 9th choice, 155th overall, in 2008 Entry Draft).

			Regular Season					Playoffs				
Season	Club	League	GP	G	A	Pts	PIM	GP	G	A	Pts	PIM
2006-07	Guelph Storm	OHL	56	4	13	17	26	4	0	0	0	2
2007-08	Guelph Storm	OHL	67	24	24	48	65	10	2	3	5	7
2008-09	Guelph Storm	OHL	25	7	11	18	31	....	....	....	....	....
	Ottawa 67's	OHL	42	23	28	51	28	7	4	4	8	4
2009-10	Ottawa 67's	OHL	61	16	46	62	49	12	6	7	13	12
2010-11	Peoria Rivermen	AHL	54	9	6	15	22	4	0	0	0	4
2011-12	Peoria Rivermen	AHL	75	13	12	25	36	....	....	....	....	....
2012-13	Evansville IceMen	ECHL	19	3	5	8	6	....	....	....	....	....
	Peoria Rivermen	AHL	46	5	7	12	12	....	....	....	....	....

NILSSON, Tom (NIHL-suhn, TAWM) **TOR**

Defense. Shoots right. 6', 176 lbs. Born, Tyreso, Sweden, August 19, 1993.
(Toronto's 4th choice, 100th overall, in 2011 Entry Draft).

			Regular Season					Playoffs				
Season	Club	League	GP	G	A	Pts	PIM	GP	G	A	Pts	PIM
2009-10	Mora IK U18	Swe-U18	35	11	9	20	30	....	....	....	....	....
	Mora IK Jr.	Swe-Jr.	3	0	0	0	0	....	....	....	....	....
2010-11	Mora IK U18	Swe-U18	11	1	7	8	10	1	0	0	0	12
	Mora IK Jr.	Swe-Jr.	37	2	6	8	26	....	....	....	....	....
	Mora IK	Sweden-2	16	0	1	1	12	....	....	....	....	....
2011-12	Mora IK	Sweden-2	44	4	6	10	45	....	....	....	....	....
	Mora IK Jr.	Swe-Jr.	10	0	2	2	2	2	0	1	1	0
2012-13	Mora IK	Sweden-2	42	1	3	4	18	....	....	....	....	....
	Mora IK Jr.	Swe-Jr.	3	0	0	0	0	2	3	2	5	0

NOEBELS, Marcel (N'YOH-behlz, MAHR-sehl) **PHI**

Left wing. Shoots left. 6'3", 201 lbs. Born, Tönisvorst, Germany, March 14, 1992.
(Philadelphia's 4th choice, 118th overall, in 2011 Entry Draft).

			Regular Season					Playoffs				
Season	Club	League	GP	G	A	Pts	PIM	GP	G	A	Pts	PIM
2007-08	Heil./Mann. Jr.	Ger-Jr.	36	13	18	31	22	8	4	6	10	4
2008-09	Heil./Mann. Jr.	Ger-Jr.	36	23	27	50	26	7	6	11	17	6
2009-10	Krefelder EV Jr.	Ger-Jr.	25	17	36	53	52	5	3	3	6	31
	Krefeld Pinguine	Germany	33	1	2	3	29	....	....	....	....	....
2010-11	Seattle	WHL	66	28	26	54	23	....	....	....	....	....
2011-12	Seattle	WHL	31	10	14	24	18	....	....	....	....	....
	Portland	WHL	31	10	24	34	8	22	8	15	23	6
2012-13	Adirondack	AHL	43	13	10	23	6	....	....	....	....	....
	Trenton Titans	ECHL	31	11	19	30	14	....	....	....	....	....

NOESEN, Stefan (NAY-sehn, STEH-fan) **ANA**

Right wing. Shoots right. 6'1", 200 lbs. Born, Plano, TX, February 12, 1993.
(Ottawa's 2nd choice, 21st overall, in 2011 Entry Draft).

			Regular Season					Playoffs				
Season	Club	League	GP	G	A	Pts	PIM	GP	G	A	Pts	PIM
2006-07	Dallas Ice Jets	Minor-TX	52	78	60	138	78	....	....	....	....	....
2007-08	Det. Compuware	MWEHL	31	31	14	45	54	....	....	....	....	....
	Det. Compuware	Exhib.	4	3	2	5	4	....	....	....	....	....
2008-09	Det. Compuware	T1EHL	28	14	9	23	67	5	4	5	9	0
	Det. Compuware	Exhib.	20	6	10	16	....	....	....	....	....	....
2009-10	Plymouth Whalers	OHL	33	3	5	8	4	....	....	....	....	....
2010-11	Plymouth Whalers	OHL	68	33	44	77	80	11	6	5	11	16
2011-12	Plymouth Whalers	OHL	63	38	44	82	74	7	7	8	15	4
2012-13	Plymouth Whalers	OHL	51	25	28	53	43	15	7	12	19	24

Traded to **Anaheim** by **Ottawa** wirh Jakob Silfverberg and Ottawa's 1st round choice in 2014 Entry Draft for Bobby Ryan, July 5, 2013.

NOONAN, Garrett (NOO-nuhn, GAIR-eht) **NSH**

Defense. Shoots left. 6', 214 lbs. Born, Norfolk, MA, January 28, 1991.
(Nashville's 4th choice, 112th overall, in 2011 Entry Draft).

			Regular Season					Playoffs				
Season	Club	League	GP	G	A	Pts	PIM	GP	G	A	Pts	PIM
2008-09	Catholic Memorial	High-MA	30	12	22	34	....	....	....	....	....	....
2009-10	Vernon Vipers	BCHL	58	2	16	18	60	19	3	3	6	16
2010-11	Boston University	H-East	38	4	11	15	89	....	....	....	....	....
2011-12	Boston University	H-East	38	16	11	27	64	....	....	....	....	....
2012-13	Boston University	H-East	34	6	13	19	94	....	....	....	....	....

Hockey East Second All-Star Team (2012)

NORDSTROM, Joakim (NOHRD-stuhm, YOH-a-kihm) **CHI**

Center. Shoots left. 6'1", 160 lbs. Born, Tyreso, Sweden, February 25, 1992.
(Chicago's 6th choice, 90th overall, in 2010 Entry Draft).

			Regular Season					Playoffs				
Season	Club	League	GP	G	A	Pts	PIM	GP	G	A	Pts	PIM
2008-09	AIK IF Solna U18	Swe-U18	35	8	16	24	32	7	2	2	4	2
	AIK IF Solna Jr.	Swe-Jr.	4	2	0	2	2	....	....	....	....	....
2009-10	AIK IF Solna U18	Swe-U18	2	1	1	2	0	3	1	2	3	4
	AIK IF Solna Jr.	Swe-Jr.	28	6	9	15	53	....	....	....	....	....
	AIK IF Solna	Sweden-2	2	0	0	0	0	....	....	....	....	....
2010-11	AIK IF Solna Jr.	Swe-Jr.	25	9	11	20	36	....	....	....	....	....
	Almtuna	Sweden-2	12	0	1	1	4	....	....	....	....	....
	AIK IF Solna	Sweden	11	0	1	1	0	1	0	0	0	0
2011-12	AIK Solna	Sweden	47	3	3	6	4	10	1	2	3	2
2012-13	AIK Solna	Sweden	43	5	4	9	29	....	....	....	....	....
	Rockford IceHogs	AHL	11	0	3	3	12	....	....	....	....	....

NOREAU, Samuel (noh-ROH, SAM-ew-l) **NYR**

Defense. Shoots right. 6'5", 215 lbs. Born, Montreal, Que., January 31, 1993.
(NY Rangers' 5th choice, 136th overall, in 2011 Entry Draft).

			Regular Season					Playoffs				
Season	Club	League	GP	G	A	Pts	PIM	GP	G	A	Pts	PIM
2008-09	Lac St-Louis Tigres	Minor-QU	33	5	20	25	8	....	....	....	....	....
2009-10	Baie-Comeau	QMJHL	34	1	3	4	17	....	....	....	....	....
2010-11	Baie-Comeau	QMJHL	67	5	5	10	141	....	....	....	....	....
2011-12	Baie-Comeau	QMJHL	58	5	12	17	92	8	0	0	0	18
2012-13	Baie-Comeau	QMJHL	66	7	25	32	64	15	2	1	3	12

NORELL, Robin (NOH-REHL, RAW-bihn) **CHI**

Defense. Shoots left. 5'11", 189 lbs. Born, Stockholm, Sweden, February 18, 1995.
(Chicago's 4th choice, 111th overall, in 2013 Entry Draft).

			Regular Season					Playoffs				
Season	Club	League	GP	G	A	Pts	PIM	GP	G	A	Pts	PIM
2010-11	Djurgarden U18	Swe-U18	4	0	0	0	0	....	....	....	....	....
2011-12	Djurgarden U18	Swe-U18	37	2	9	11	24	4	0	0	0	2
	Djurgarden Jr.	Swe-Jr.	....	....	....	....	....	1	0	0	0	0
2012-13	Djurgarden U18	Swe-U18	30	10	7	17	16	9	2	1	3	6
	Djurgarden Jr.	Swe-Jr.	33	1	4	5	4	2	0	0	0	2

NURSE, Darnell (NUHRS, dahr-NEHL) **EDM**

Defense. Shoots left. 6'4", 185 lbs. Born, Hamilton, Ont., February 4, 1995.
(Edmonton's 1st choice, 7th overall, in 2013 Entry Draft).

			Regular Season					Playoffs				
Season	Club	League	GP	G	A	Pts	PIM	GP	G	A	Pts	PIM
2010-11	Don Mills Flyers	GTHL	38	11	18	29	72	....	....	....	....	....
	St. Michael's	ON-Jr.A	2	0	0	0	4	....	....	....	....	....
2011-12	Sault Ste. Marie	OHL	53	1	9	10	61	....	....	....	....	....
2012-13	Sault Ste. Marie	OHL	68	12	29	41	116	6	1	3	4	6

NYGREN, Magnus (NEW-grihn, MAG-nuhs) **MTL**

Defense. Shoots right. 6'1", 193 lbs. Born, Karlstad, Sweden, June 7, 1990.
(Montreal's 3rd choice, 113th overall, in 2011 Entry Draft).

			Regular Season					Playoffs				
Season	Club	League	GP	G	A	Pts	PIM	GP	G	A	Pts	PIM
2006-07	Farjestad U18	Swe-U18	7	0	4	4	4	8	1	2	3	6
2007-08	Farjestad U18	Swe-U18	31	9	19	28	61	8	2	6	8	12
2008-09	Skare Jr.	Swe-Jr.	2	2	3	5	0	....	....	....	....	....
	Skare BK Karlstad	Sweden-3	41	7	21	28	32	3	1	0	1	2
2009-10	Skare BK	Sweden-3	24	9	18	27	10	....	....	....	....	....
	Farjestad	Sweden	9	0	0	0	4	....	....	....	....	....
	Mora IK	Sweden-2	21	2	5	7	10	2	0	1	1	2
2010-11	Bofors	Sweden-2	35	5	6	11	10	....	....	....	....	....
	Farjestad	Sweden	22	4	11	15	4	14	3	7	10	6
2011-12	Farjestad Jr.	Swe-Jr.	1	1	0	1	2	....	....	....	....	....
	Bofors	Sweden-2	3	1	1	2	4	....	....	....	....	....
	Farjestad	Sweden	50	7	11	18	6	10	2	0	2	0
2012-13	Farjestad	Sweden	51	13	19	32	49	10	1	3	4	10

NYSTROM, Erik (NIGH-struhm, AIR-ihk) **MTL**

Left wing. Shoots left. 5'11", 180 lbs. Born, Stockholm, Sweden, October 30, 1993.
(Montreal's 7th choice, 154th overall, in 2012 Entry Draft).

			Regular Season					Playoffs				
Season	Club	League	GP	G	A	Pts	PIM	GP	G	A	Pts	PIM
2008-09	Nacka HK U18	Swe-U18	13	5	12	17	....	....	....	....	....	....
2009-10	MODO Jr.	Swe-Jr.	4	0	2	2	0	....	....	....	....	....
	MODO U18	Swe-U18	40	24	33	57	6	1	0	0	0	0
2010-11	MODO U18	Swe-U18	14	10	17	27	2	3	0	4	4	0
	MODO Jr.	Swe-Jr.	39	6	13	19	8	6	2	1	3	0
2011-12	MODO Jr.	Swe-Jr.	32	9	19	28	16	8	5	4	9	0
	MODO	Sweden	19	0	2	2	0	....	....	....	....	....
2012-13	MODO Jr.	Swe-Jr.	22	8	16	24	32	....	....	....	....	....
	Karlskrona HK	Sweden-2	28	5	8	13	6	....	....	....	....	....

O'BRIEN, Andrew (oh-BRIGH-uhn, an-DROO) **ANA**

Defense. Shoots left. 6'4", 214 lbs. Born, Hamilton, Ont., November 21, 1992.
(Anaheim's 5th choice, 108th overall, in 2012 Entry Draft).

			Regular Season					Playoffs				
Season	Club	League	GP	G	A	Pts	PIM	GP	G	A	Pts	PIM
2008-09	Humber Valley	Minor-ON	STATISTICS NOT AVAILABLE									
	Milton Icehawks	ON-Jr.A	2	0	0	0	0	....	....	....	....	....
2009-10	Dixie Beehives	ON-Jr.A	44	3	4	7	45	....	....	....	....	....
2010-11	Chicoutimi	QMJHL	55	1	9	10	33	4	1	1	2	6
2011-12	Chicoutimi	QMJHL	68	8	21	29	95	18	1	9	10	31
2012-13	Rouyn-Noranda	QMJHL	67	2	16	18	113	14	0	4	4	22

O'DELL, Eric (OH-DEHL, AIR-ihk) **WPG**

Center. Shoots right. 6'1", 181 lbs. Born, Ottawa, Ont., June 21, 1990.
(Anaheim's 3rd choice, 39th overall, in 2008 Entry Draft).

			Regular Season					Playoffs				
Season	Club	League	GP	G	A	Pts	PIM	GP	G	A	Pts	PIM
2006-07	Ottawa West	ON-Jr.B	40	28	20	48	45	....	....	....	....	....
	Ottawa Jr. Sens	ON-Jr.A	2	1	0	1	0	....	....	....	....	....
2007-08	Cumberland	ON-Jr.A	34	23	33	56	12	....	....	....	....	....
	Sudbury Wolves	OHL	26	14	18	32	19	....	....	....	....	....
2008-09	Sudbury Wolves	OHL	65	33	30	63	55	6	0	4	4	4
2009-10	Sudbury Wolves	OHL	68	33	35	68	63	4	0	2	2	7
	Chicago Wolves	AHL	3	0	0	0	0	....	....	....	....	....
2010-11	Sudbury Wolves	OHL	39	20	24	44	34	8	7	5	12	15
2011-12	St. John's IceCaps	AHL	39	12	10	22	27	3	0	0	0	2
2012-13	St. John's IceCaps	AHL	59	29	26	55	26	....	....	....	....	....

Traded to **Atlanta** by **Anaheim** for Erik Christensen, March 4, 2009. • Transferred to **Winnipeg** after **Atlanta** franchise relocated, June 21, 2011.

O'DONNELL, Brendan (OH'DAW-nuhl, BREHN-duhn) **T.B.**

Center. Shoots left. 6'1", 188 lbs. Born, Flin Flon, Man., June 25, 1992.
(Tampa Bay's 7th choice, 156th overall, in 2010 Entry Draft).

			Regular Season					Playoffs				
Season	Club	League	GP	G	A	Pts	PIM	GP	G	A	Pts	PIM
2008-09	Winnipeg Wild	MMHL	38	....	....	83	....	10	....	....	20	....
2009-10	Wpg. South Blues	MJHL	53	29	32	61	55	4	2	1	3	4
2010-11	Penticton Vees	BCHL	58	29	43	72	28	6	1	5	6	9
2011-12	North Dakota	WCHA	17	5	1	6	0	....	....	....	....	....
2012-13	North Dakota	WCHA	29	2	8	10	20	....	....	....	....	....

O'GARA, Rob (OH-GAR-uh, RAWB) **BOS**

Defense. Shoots left. 6'4", 206 lbs. Born, Massapequa, NY, July 6, 1993.
(Boston's 5th choice, 151st overall, in 2011 Entry Draft).

			Regular Season					Playoffs				
Season	Club	League	GP	G	A	Pts	PIM	GP	G	A	Pts	PIM
2007-08	Long Island	AYHL	27	1	6	7	22	....	....	....	....	....
2008-09	Long Island	AYHL	17	1	4	5	16	....	....	....	....	....
2009-10	Long Island	AYHL	33	8	17	25	48	....	....	....	....	....
2010-11	Milton Academy	High-MA	30	2	7	9	22	....	....	....	....	....
2011-12	Milton Academy	High-MA	STATISTICS NOT AVAILABLE									
2012-13	Yale	ECAC	37	0	7	7	32	....	....	....	....	....

OLEKSUK, Travis (oh-LEHK-suhk, TRA-vihs) **S.J.**

Center. Shoots left. 6', 200 lbs. Born, Thunder Bay, Ont., February 3, 1989.

			Regular Season					Playoffs				
Season	Club	League	GP	G	A	Pts	PIM	GP	G	A	Pts	PIM
2006-07	Sioux City	USHL	56	6	16	22	35	7	0	2	2	0
2007-08	Sioux City	USHL	60	14	30	44	27	4	1	2	3	2
2008-09	U. Minn-Duluth	WCHA	18	0	5	5	10	....	....	....	....	....
2009-10	U. Minn-Duluth	WCHA	33	10	14	24	24	....	....	....	....	....
2010-11	U. Minn-Duluth	WCHA	42	14	19	33	33	....	....	....	....	....
2011-12	U. Minn-Duluth	WCHA	41	21	32	53	6	....	....	....	....	....
2012-13	Worcester Sharks	AHL	60	3	10	13	12	....	....	....	....	....

Signed as a free agent by **San Jose**, March 30, 2012.

OLIVER, Nick (aw-LIH-vuhr, NIHK) **NSH**

Center/Left wing. Shoots left. 6'1", 194 lbs. Born, Grand Forks, ND, May 4, 1991.
(Nashville's 8th choice, 110th overall, in 2009 Entry Draft).

			Regular Season					Playoffs				
Season	Club	League	GP	G	A	Pts	PIM	GP	G	A	Pts	PIM
2006-07	Roseau Rams	High-MN	31	12	14	26	51	....	....	....	....	....
2007-08	Roseau Rams	High-MN	30	17	25	42	45	....	....	....	....	....
2008-09	Roseau Rams	High-MN	11	5	11	16	8	....	....	....	....	....
	Fargo Force	USHL	12	1	1	2	11	1	0	0	0	0
2009-10	Fargo Force	USHL	53	5	13	18	95	13	1	1	2	4
2010-11	Fargo Force	USHL	56	7	10	17	64	5	0	0	0	6
2011-12	St. Cloud State	WCHA	34	2	2	4	33	....	....	....	....	....
2012-13	St. Cloud State	WCHA	34	1	5	6	22	....	....	....	....	....

OLOFSSON, Gustav (OH-lawf-suhn, GOO-stahv) **MIN**

Defense. Shoots left. 6'4", 191 lbs. Born, Boras, Sweden, December 1, 1994.
(Minnesota's 1st choice, 46th overall, in 2013 Entry Draft).

			Regular Season					Playoffs				
Season	Club	League	GP	G	A	Pts	PIM	GP	G	A	Pts	PIM
2010-11	Col. T-birds U16	T1EHL	35	5	10	15	18	....	....	....	....	....
2011-12	Col. T-birds U18	T1EHL	38	5	25	30	10	....	....	....	....	....
	Green Bay	USHL	3	0	1	1	0	....	....	....	....	....
2012-13	Green Bay	USHL	63	2	21	23	59	4	0	0	0	0

USHL All-Rookie Team (2013)

• Signed Letter of Intent to attend **Colorado College** (WCHA) in fall of 2013 or 2014..

OLSEN, Ryan (OHL-suhn, RIGH-uhn) **WPG**

Center. Shoots right. 6'2", 190 lbs. Born, Delta, B.C., March 25, 1994.
(Winnipeg's 5th choice, 160th overall, in 2012 Entry Draft).

			Regular Season					Playoffs				
Season	Club	League	GP	G	A	Pts	PIM	GP	G	A	Pts	PIM
2008-09	South Delta Storm	Minor-BC	60	65	67	132	....	....	....	....	....	....
2009-10	Greater Van.	BCMML	38	24	23	47	32	5	2	1	3	20
	Saskatoon Blades	WHL	5	0	0	0	2	....	....	....	....	....
2010-11	Saskatoon Blades	WHL	63	7	7	14	39	3	0	0	0	4
2011-12	Saskatoon Blades	WHL	67	15	17	32	64	4	0	0	0	4
2012-13	Kelowna Rockets	WHL	69	32	24	56	87	11	1	5	6	14

OLSON, Drew (OHL-suhn, DROO) **T.B.**

Forward. Shoots left. 6', 213 lbs. Born, Brainerd, MN, April 4, 1990.
(Columbus' 4th choice, 118th overall, in 2008 Entry Draft).

			Regular Season					Playoffs				
Season	Club	League	GP	G	A	Pts	PIM	GP	G	A	Pts	PIM
2006-07	Brainerd	High-MN	STATISTICS NOT AVAILABLE									
	Team North	UMWEHL	11	2	4	6	....	....	....	....	....	....
2007-08	Brainerd	High-MN	27	20	16	36	....	....	....	....	....	....
	Team North	UMWEHL	11	3	4	7	....	....	....	....	....	....
2008-09	Omaha Lancers	USHL	39	2	6	8	43	....	....	....	....	....
2009-10	U. Minn-Duluth	WCHA	34	0	2	2	12	....	....	....	....	....
2010-11	U. Minn-Duluth	WCHA	34	1	3	4	18	....	....	....	....	....
2011-12	U. Minn-Duluth	WCHA	41	1	7	8	51	....	....	....	....	....
2012-13	U. Minn-Duluth	WCHA	38	1	6	7	28	....	....	....	....	....
	Peoria Rivermen	AHL	5	0	1	1	2	....	....	....	....	....

Traded to **Tampa Bay** by **Columbus** for future considerations, July 2, 2013.

O'NEILL, Will (oh-NEEL, WIHL) **WPG**

Defense. Shoots left. 6'1", 200 lbs. Born, Boston, MA, April 28, 1988.
(Atlanta's 8th choice, 210th overall, in 2006 Entry Draft).

			Regular Season					Playoffs				
Season	Club	League	GP	G	A	Pts	PIM	GP	G	A	Pts	PIM
2004-05	Tabor	High-MA	....	1	16	17	....	....	....	....	....	....
2005-06	Tabor	High-MA	28	5	25	30	38	....	....	....	....	....
2006-07	Omaha Lancers	USHL	57	4	9	13	73	5	0	0	0	8
2007-08	Omaha Lancers	USHL	58	5	19	24	95	14	1	6	7	38
2008-09	U. of Maine	H-East	34	4	12	16	82	....	....	....	....	....
2009-10	U. of Maine	H-East	39	8	23	31	69	....	....	....	....	....
2010-11	U. of Maine	H-East	28	4	17	21	44	....	....	....	....	....
2011-12	U. of Maine	H-East	40	3	30	33	68	....	....	....	....	....
	St. John's IceCaps	AHL	7	1	2	3	9	....	....	....	....	....
2012-13	St. John's IceCaps	AHL	59	3	18	21	32	....	....	....	....	....

• Transferred to **Winnipeg** after **Atlanta** franchise relocated, June 21, 2011

O'NEILL, Brian (oh-NEEL, BRIG-uhn) **L.A.**

Right wing. Shoots right. 5'9", 170 lbs. Born, Yardley, PA, June 1, 1988.

			Regular Season					Playoffs				
Season	Club	League	GP	G	A	Pts	PIM	GP	G	A	Pts	PIM
2007-08	Chicago Steel	USHL	60	23	38	61	40	7	3	2	5	10
2008-09	Yale	ECAC	30	12	14	26	37	....	....	....	....	....
2009-10	Yale	ECAC	34	16	29	45	20	....	....	....	....	....
2010-11	Yale	ECAC	36	20	26	46	39	....	....	....	....	....
2011-12	Yale	ECAC	35	21	25	46	26	....	....	....	....	....
	Manchester	AHL	12	1	1	2	4	4	0	1	1	6
2012-13	Manchester	AHL	49	3	12	15	18	4	1	0	1	2

ECAC All-Rookie Team (2009) • ECAC First All-Star Team (2011, 2012) • NCAA East Second All-American Team (2012)

Signed as a free agent by **Los Angeles**, March 15, 2012.

O'REGAN, Daniel (oh-REE-guhn, DAN-yehl) **S.J.**

Center. Shoots right. 5'9", 175 lbs. Born, Berlin, Germany, January 30, 1994.
(San Jose's 4th choice, 138th overall, in 2012 Entry Draft).

			Regular Season					Playoffs				
Season	Club	League	GP	G	A	Pts	PIM	GP	G	A	Pts	PIM
2010-11	Cape Cod U-16	Minor-MA	22	16	16	32	....	....	....	....	....	....
	St. Sebastian's	High-MA	27	25	25	50	10	....	....	....	....	....
2011-12	Cape Cod Whalers	Minor-MA	19	15	18	33	....	....	....	....	....	....
	St. Sebastian's	High-MA	27	21	35	56	8	....	....	....	....	....
	USNTDP	USHL	7	3	2	5	0	....	....	....	....	....
	USNTDP	U-18	7	1	4	5	2	....	....	....	....	....
2012-13	Boston University	H-East	39	16	22	38	16	....	....	....	....	....

Hockey East All-Rookie Team (2013)

OUELLET, Xavier (OO-leht, ehx-AV-ee-ay) **DET**

Defense. Shoots left. 6'1", 190 lbs. Born, Bayonne, France, July 29, 1993.
(Detroit's 2nd choice, 48th overall, in 2011 Entry Draft).

			Regular Season					Playoffs				
Season	Club	League	GP	G	A	Pts	PIM	GP	G	A	Pts	PIM
2008-09	Esther-Blondin	QAAA	41	2	9	11	49	14	1	3	4	24
2009-10	Montreal	QMJHL	43	2	14	16	22	7	0	3	3	12
2010-11	Montreal	QMJHL	67	8	35	43	44	10	0	8	8	6
2011-12	Blainville-Bois.	QMJHL	63	21	39	60	67	11	3	7	10	14
2012-13	Blainville-Bois.	QMJHL	50	10	31	41	44	15	7	9	16	22

QMJHL All-Rookie Team (2010) • QMJHL First All-Star Team (2012, 2013)

PALIOTTA, Michael (pal-ee-AW-tuh, MIGH-kuhl) **CHI**

Defense. Shoots right. 6'3", 198 lbs. Born, Westport, CT, April 6, 1993.
(Chicago's 5th choice, 70th overall, in 2011 Entry Draft).

			Regular Season					Playoffs				
Season	Club	League	GP	G	A	Pts	PIM	GP	G	A	Pts	PIM
2008-09	Choate-Rosemary	High-CT	24	1	14	15	....	....	....	....	....	....
2009-10	USNTDP	USHL	32	1	6	7	43	....	....	....	....	....
	USNTDP	U-17	18	1	6	7	10	....	....	....	....	....
2010-11	USNTDP	USHL	24	0	5	5	35	....	....	....	....	....
	USNTDP	U-18	36	1	9	10	42	....	....	....	....	....
2011-12	U. of Vermont	H-East	30	4	6	10	44	....	....	....	....	....
2012-13	U. of Vermont	H-East	35	1	9	10	50	....	....	....	....	....

PAQUETTE, Cedric (pah-KEHT, SEH-drihk) **T.B.**

Center. Shoots left. 6'1", 187 lbs. Born, Gaspe, Que., August 13, 1993.
(Tampa Bay's 6th choice, 101st overall, in 2012 Entry Draft).

			Regular Season					Playoffs				
Season	Club	League	GP	G	A	Pts	PIM	GP	G	A	Pts	PIM
2008-09	Ecole Notre Dame	QAAA	45	12	6	18	34	4	0	0	0	4
2009-10	Ecole Notre Dame	QAAA	32	10	18	28	83	8	5	2	7	24
2010-11	Ecole Notre Dame	QAAA	34	28	27	55	102	17	5	11	16	36
2011-12	Blainville-Bois.	QMJHL	63	31	17	48	88	11	7	10	17	22
2012-13	Blainville-Bois.	QMJHL	63	27	56	83	103	15	7	5	12	33
	Syracuse Crunch	AHL	....	....	....	....	....	3	0	0	0	0

PAQUETTE, Danick (pa-KETT, DA-nihk) WSH

Right wing. Shoots right. 6'1", 210 lbs. Born, Montreal, Que., July 17, 1990.
(Atlanta's 3rd choice, 64th overall, in 2008 Entry Draft).

			Regular Season					Playoffs				
Season	Club	League	GP	G	A	Pts	PIM	GP	G	A	Pts	PIM
2005-06	Ecole Montpetit	QAAA	36	17	16	33	191	3	0	1	1	6
2006-07	Lewiston	QMJHL	63	4	14	18	112	14	0	0	0	18
2007-08	Lewiston	QMJHL	63	29	13	42	213	5	1	2	3	30
2008-09	Lewiston	QMJHL	61	25	25	50	230	2	1	2	3	25
	Chicago Wolves	AHL	4	0	0	0	12					
2009-10	Quebec Remparts	QMJHL	64	36	29	65	136	5	1	3	4	21
2010-11	Gwinnett	ECHL	59	13	7	20	179					
2011-12	South Carolina	ECHL	31	6	11	17	118					
	Utah Grizzlies	ECHL	9	0	0	0	64					
	Chicago Express	ECHL	13	7	4	11	27					
2012-13	Hershey Bears	AHL	2	0	0	0	5					
	Reading Royals	ECHL	19	2	5	7	78					

• Transferred to **Winnipeg** after **Atlanta** franchise relocated, June 21, 2011. Traded to **Washington** by **Winnipeg** with Winnipeg's 4th round choice (Thomas Di Pauli) in 2012 Entry Draft for Eric Fehr, July 8, 2011.

PARADIS, Philippe (PAIR-a-dee, fihl-EEP) T.B.

Center. Shoots left. 6'2", 205 lbs. Born, Dolbeau, Que., January 2, 1991.
(Carolina's 1st choice, 27th overall, in 2009 Entry Draft).

			Regular Season					Playoffs				
Season	Club	League	GP	G	A	Pts	PIM	GP	G	A	Pts	PIM
2006-07	Jonquiere Elites	QAAA	38	5	12	17	76	3	1	1	2	6
2007-08	Shawinigan	QMJHL	45	11	12	23	44	3	0	0	0	0
2008-09	Shawinigan	QMJHL	66	19	31	50	74	21	6	6	12	20
2009-10	Shawinigan	QMJHL	63	24	20	44	104	6	2	1	3	4
	Toronto Marlies	AHL	4	0	2	2	0					
2010-11	P.E.I. Rocket	QMJHL	59	23	30	53	85	5	1	1	2	8
	Rockford IceHogs	AHL	4	1	0	1	2					
2011-12	Rockford IceHogs	AHL	58	5	11	16	39					
2012-13	Rockford IceHogs	AHL	36	1	7	8	100					
	Toledo Walleye	ECHL	5	0	0	0	9					
	Syracuse Crunch	AHL	8	0	1	1	11	18	3	1	4	23

Traded to **Toronto** by **Carolina** for Jiri Tlusty, December 3, 2009. Traded to **Chicago** by **Toronto** with Viktor Stalberg and Chris Didomenico for Kris Versteeg and Bill Sweatt, June 30, 2010. Traded to **Tampa Bay** by **Chicago** for the rights to Kirill Gotovets, April 2, 2013.

PARAYKO, Colton (pa-RAY-koh, KOHL-tuhn) ST.L.

Defense. Shoots right. 6'5", 191 lbs. Born, St. Albert, Alta., May 12, 1993.
(St. Louis' 4th choice, 86th overall, in 2012 Entry Draft).

			Regular Season					Playoffs				
Season	Club	League	GP	G	A	Pts	PIM	GP	G	A	Pts	PIM
2008-09	St. Albert Flyers	Minor-AB	33	1	16	17	10	2	0	2	2	0
2009-10	St. Albert	Minor-AB	33	5	8	13	10					
2010-11	Fort McMurray	AJHL	42	3	9	12	12	12	2	1	3	2
2011-12	Fort McMurray	AJHL	53	9	33	42	65	21	3	9	12	14
2012-13	Alaska	CCHA	33	4	13	17	23					

PARE, Francis (pa-RAY, FRAN-sihs)

Right wing. Shoots right. 5'10", 190 lbs. Born, Lemoyne, Que., June 30, 1987.

			Regular Season					Playoffs				
Season	Club	League	GP	G	A	Pts	PIM	GP	G	A	Pts	PIM
2003-04	C.C. Lemoyne	QAAA	38	*52	30	82	38	15	*15	9	*24	50
	Shawinigan	QMJHL	5	2	0	2	2					
2004-05	Shawinigan	QMJHL	70	24	23	47	52	4	0	3	3	4
2005-06	Shawinigan	QMJHL	50	26	48	74	66	5	1	3	4	4
2006-07	Shawinigan	QMJHL	68	29	44	73	37	4	1	1	2	8
2007-08	Chicoutimi	QMJHL	69	54	48	102	54	6	5	3	8	4
2008-09	Grand Rapids	AHL	63	24	24	48	14	10	2	2	4	2
2009-10	Grand Rapids	AHL	77	16	23	39	20					
2010-11	Grand Rapids	AHL	80	24	30	54	49					
2011-12	Grand Rapids	AHL	75	16	36	52	18					
2012-13	Grand Rapids	AHL	68	22	22	44	37	24	3	9	12	12

QMJHL First All-Star Team (2008) • Canadian Major Junior Second All-Star Team (2008)

Signed as a free agent by **Grand Rapids** (AHL), June 13, 2008. Signed as a free agent by **Detroit**, April 7, 2009. Signed as a free agent by **TPS Turku** (Finland), July 9, 2013.

PARKER, Jonathan (PAR-kuhr, JAWN-ah-thuhn) BUF

Right wing. Shoots right. 6'1", 192 lbs. Born, Solana Beach, CA, September 25, 1991.

			Regular Season					Playoffs				
Season	Club	League	GP	G	A	Pts	PIM	GP	G	A	Pts	PIM
2008-09	Seattle	WHL	65	17	22	39	55	5	0	0	0	0
2009-10	Seattle	WHL	40	13	13	26	16					
	Prince Albert	WHL	29	2	2	4	24					
2010-11	Prince Albert	WHL	71	45	41	86	45	6	0	3	3	4
2011-12	Rochester	AHL	37	3	3	6	6					
	Gwinnett	ECHL	19	4	7	11	10					
2012-13	Rochester	AHL	28	3	2	5	11					

Signed as a free agent by **Buffalo**, October 6, 2011.

PARKES, Trevor (PAHRKS, TREH-vuhr) DET

Right wing. Shoots right. 6'2", 188 lbs. Born, Fort Erie, Ont., May 13, 1991.

			Regular Season					Playoffs				
Season	Club	League	GP	G	A	Pts	PIM	GP	G	A	Pts	PIM
2008-09	Fort Erie Meteors	ON-Jr.B	52	23	20	43	34	5	0	1	1	2
2009-10	Montreal	QMJHL	66	27	20	47	34					
2010-11	Montreal	QMJHL	60	33	29	62	32	10	6	2	8	12
2011-12	Grand Rapids	AHL	44	2	6	8	23					
	Toledo Walleye	ECHL	4	4	0	4	2					
2012-13	Toledo Walleye	ECHL	19	14	16	30	6	6	3	2	5	6
	Grand Rapids	AHL	36	3	6	9	35					

Signed as a free agent by **Detroit**, September 23, 2010.

PARKS, Michael (PARKS, MIGH-kuhl) PHI

Right wing. Shoots right. 5'11", 188 lbs. Born, O'Fallon, MO, February 15, 1992.
(Philadelphia's 3rd choice, 149th overall, in 2010 Entry Draft).

			Regular Season					Playoffs				
Season	Club	League	GP	G	A	Pts	PIM	GP	G	A	Pts	PIM
2008-09	St. Louis Selects	Exhib.	46	38	47	85	26					
2009-10	Cedar Rapids	USHL	51	11	11	22	57	5	0	1	1	0
2010-11	Cedar Rapids	USHL	56	25	17	42	42	8	3	1	4	6
2011-12	North Dakota	WCHA	42	12	10	22	38					
2012-13	North Dakota	WCHA	25	7	1	8	31					

PARLETT, Blake (pahr-LET, BLAYK) CBJ

Defense. Shoots right. 6'1", 205 lbs. Born, Bracebridge, Ont., May 13, 1989.

			Regular Season					Playoffs				
Season	Club	League	GP	G	A	Pts	PIM	GP	G	A	Pts	PIM
2004-05	Huntsville	ON-Jr.A	48	4	12	16	56					
2005-06	Barrie Colts	OHL	38	0	2	2	39	14	0	2	2	6
2006-07	Barrie Colts	OHL	36	1	5	6	47					
	Windsor Spitfires	OHL	30	5	10	15	30					
2007-08	Windsor Spitfires	OHL	33	3	3	6	10					
	St. Michael's	OHL	28	0	7	7	53	4	0	0	0	8
2008-09	St. Michael's	OHL	68	8	26	34	74	10	0	2	2	13
2009-10	St. Michael's	OHL	68	11	35	46	108	16	1	4	5	18
2010-11	Connecticut Whale	AHL	24	2	10	12	17	6	1	2	3	2
	Greenville	ECHL	46	7	25	32	40	2	0	1	1	2
2011-12	Connecticut Whale	AHL	55	4	10	14	38					
	Greenville	ECHL	12	1	6	7	17	3	0	1	1	4
2012-13	Connecticut Whale	AHL	67	6	22	28	85					
	Springfield Falcons	AHL	9	2	2	4	8	7	2	1	3	4

Signed as a free agent by **Connecticut** (AHL), July 28, 2010. • Assigned to **Greenville** (ECHL) by **Connecticut** (AHL), October 6, 2010. Signed as a free agent by **NY Rangers**, June 2, 2011. Traded to **Columbus** by **NY Rangers** with Marian Gaborik and Steven Delisle for Derek Dorsett, Derick Brassard, John Moore and Columbus' 6th round choice in 2014 Entry Draft, April 3, 2013.

PASHNIN, Mikhail (pahsh-NIHN, mih-KHIGH-eel) NYR

Defense. Shoots left. 6'1", 191 lbs. Born, Chelyabinsk, USSR, May 11, 1989.
(NY Rangers' 7th choice, 200th overall, in 2009 Entry Draft).

			Regular Season					Playoffs				
Season	Club	League	GP	G	A	Pts	PIM	GP	G	A	Pts	PIM
2005-06	Mechel 2	Russia-3	25	0	5	5	30					
2006-07	Mechel 2	Russia-3	12	1	3	4	26					
	Mechel	Russia-2	41	0	2	2	40	4	0	0	0	8
2007-08	Mechel 2	Russia-3	8	4	1	5	12					
	Mechel	Russia-2	49	2	5	7	58					
2008-09	Mechel 2	Russia-3	3	0	1	1	4					
	Mechel	Russia-2	35	2	4	6	40	7	0	2	2	8
2009-10	CSKA Moscow	KHL	44	1	4	5	52	1	0	0	0	0
	CSKA Jr.	Russia-Jr.	4	0	3	3	2	4	1	1	2	20
2010-11	CSKA Moscow	KHL	42	2	2	4	38					
	CSKA Jr.	Russia-Jr.	10	2	2	4	14	16	1	4	5	60
2011-12	CSKA Moscow	KHL	50	3	2	5	68	5	0	1	1	20
2012-13	Yaroslavl	KHL	32	1	1	2	75	6	0	0	0	6

PATTERSON, Gaelan (PA-tuhr-suhn, GAY-luhn)

Center. Shoots left. 6', 204 lbs. Born, La Ronge, Sask., August 22, 1990.
(Calgary's 6th choice, 201st overall, in 2009 Entry Draft).

			Regular Season					Playoffs				
Season	Club	League	GP	G	A	Pts	PIM	GP	G	A	Pts	PIM
2005-06	Beardy's	SMHL	38	7	10	17	16					
2006-07	Saskatoon Blades	WHL	53	3	1	4	24					
2007-08	Saskatoon Blades	WHL	51	4	6	10	38					
2008-09	Saskatoon Blades	WHL	71	22	35	57	41	7	1	1	2	2
2009-10	Saskatoon Blades	WHL	71	26	33	59	31	10	4	6	10	6
	Abbotsford Heat	AHL						3	1	0	1	0
2010-11	Abbotsford Heat	AHL	61	7	14	21	15					
2011-12	Abbotsford Heat	AHL	56	1	5	6	14					
	Utah Grizzlies	ECHL	5	2	1	3	0	3	0	1	1	0
2012-13	Utah Grizzlies	ECHL	64	6	21	27	31	2	0	0	0	0

PAUL, Nicholas (PAWL, NIH-koh-las) DAL

Left wing. Shoots left. 6'2", 202 lbs. Born, Mississauga, Ont., March 20, 1995.
(Dallas' 6th choice, 101st overall, in 2013 Entry Draft).

			Regular Season					Playoffs				
Season	Club	League	GP	G	A	Pts	PIM	GP	G	A	Pts	PIM
2010-11	Miss. Senators	GTHL	37	14	11	25	12					
2011-12	Mississauga Reps	GTHL	33	25	32	57						
	Mississauga Reps	Exhib.	30	23	28	51						
	Mississauga	ON-Jr.A	9	3	2	5	4					
2012-13	Brampton	OHL	66	12	16	28	21	5	0	1	1	0

PAULOVIC, Matej (PAWL-oh-vihch, mah-TAY) DAL

Left wing. Shoots right. 6'3", 187 lbs. Born, Slovakia, Slovakia, January 13, 1995.
(Dallas' 8th choice, 149th overall, in 2013 Entry Draft).

			Regular Season					Playoffs				
Season	Club	League	GP	G	A	Pts	PIM	GP	G	A	Pts	PIM
2009-10	HC Topolcany U18	Svk-U18	39	17	16	33	26					
2010-11	HC Topolcany U18	Svk-U18	42	33	29	62	34					
	HK Nitra Jr.	Slovak-Jr.	2	0	0	0	0					
2011-12	Farjestad U18	Swe-U18	33	17	23	40	51	6	2	1	3	2
	Farjestad Jr.	Swe-Jr.	12	2	1	3	6					
2012-13	Farjestad U18	Swe-U18	8	3	4	7	8					
	Farjestad Jr.	Swe-Jr.	34	5	12	17	6	7	1	1	2	6

PAYERL, Adam (PAIR-uhl, A-duhm) PIT

Center. Shoots right. 6'3", 218 lbs. Born, Kitchener, Ont., March 4, 1991.

			Regular Season					Playoffs				
Season	Club	League	GP	G	A	Pts	PIM	GP	G	A	Pts	PIM
2007-08	Barrie Colts	OHL	47	4	3	7	20	1	0	0	0	0
2008-09	Barrie Colts	OHL	68	7	10	17	59	5	0	1	1	8
2009-10	Belleville Bulls	OHL	67	17	26	43	39					
2010-11	Belleville Bulls	OHL	63	10	19	29	79	4	0	0	0	0
2011-12	Belleville Bulls	OHL	61	22	25	47	106	6	1	2	3	9
	Wilkes-Barre	AHL	2	0	1	1	2					
2012-13	Wilkes-Barre	AHL	44	3	7	10	53	15	2	1	3	13
	Wheeling Nailers	ECHL	4	1	0	1	15					

Signed as a free agent by **Pittsburgh**, March 1, 2012.

PAYNE, Cody (PAYN, KOH-dee) DAL

Right wing. Shoots right. 6'2", 201 lbs. Born, London, England, January 14, 1994.
(Boston's 4th choice, 145th overall, in 2012 Entry Draft).

			Regular Season					Playoffs				
Season	Club	League	GP	G	A	Pts	PIM	GP	G	A	Pts	PIM
2009-10	Mississauga Reps	GTHL	64	39	26	65						
2010-11	Oshawa Generals	OHL	50	1	12	13	35	2	1	0	1	0
2011-12	Oshawa Generals	OHL	10	2	0	2	12					
	Plymouth Whalers	OHL	50	3	11	14	95	9	0	1	1	9
2012-13	Plymouth Whalers	OHL	66	24	21	45	75	15	1	1	2	15

Traded to **Dallas** by **Boston** with Lane MacDermid and Boston's 1st round choice (Jason Dickinson) in 2013 Entry Draft for Jaromir Jagr, April 2, 2013.

PECA, Matthew (PEH-kuh, MA-thew) T.B.

Center. Shoots left. 5'9", 172 lbs. Born, Petawawa, Ont., April 27, 1993.
(Tampa Bay's 5th choice, 201st overall, in 2011 Entry Draft).

			Regular Season					Playoffs				
Season	**Club**	**League**	**GP**	**G**	**A**	**Pts**	**PIM**	**GP**	**G**	**A**	**Pts**	**PIM**
2008-09	Ott. Valley Titans	Minor-ON	23	10	17	27	12	6	2	3	5	2
	Ottawa Valley	Exhib.	12	7	13	20	6	....	....	....	....	....
2009-10	Pembroke	ON-Jr.A	60	21	26	47	10	15	3	3	6	6
2010-11	Pembroke	ON-Jr.A	50	26	46	72	14	14	11	10	21	6
2011-12	Quinnipiac	ECAC	39	8	31	39	12	....	....	....	....	....
2012-13	Quinnipiac	ECAC	39	15	15	30	36	....	....	....	....	....

ECAC All-Rookie Team (2012)

PEDAN, Andrey (peh-DAHN, AWN-dray) NYI

Defense. Shoots left. 6'4", 207 lbs. Born, Kaunas, Lithuania, July 3, 1993.
(NY Islanders' 4th choice, 63rd overall, in 2011 Entry Draft).

			Regular Season					Playoffs				
Season	**Club**	**League**	**GP**	**G**	**A**	**Pts**	**PIM**	**GP**	**G**	**A**	**Pts**	**PIM**
2009-10	Dyn.Moscow U18	Rus-U18	3	2	1	3	12	....	....	....	....	....
2010-11	Guelph Storm	OHL	51	2	10	12	89	6	0	8	8	8
2011-12	Guelph Storm	OHL	63	10	30	40	152	6	1	2	3	14
2012-13	Guelph Storm	OHL	60	14	30	44	*145	5	3	1	4	16
	Bridgeport	AHL	8	0	2	2	7	....	....	....	....	....

PEDERSEN, Brent (PEE-duhr-suhn, BREHNT) CAR

Left wing. Shoots left. 6'2", 205 lbs. Born, Kitchener, Ont., July 5, 1995.
(Carolina's 3rd choice, 126th overall, in 2013 Entry Draft).

			Regular Season					Playoffs				
Season	**Club**	**League**	**GP**	**G**	**A**	**Pts**	**PIM**	**GP**	**G**	**A**	**Pts**	**PIM**
2010-11	Wat. Wolves M.M.	Minor-ON	29	24	11	35	4	13	9	8	17	2
	Wat. Wolves Mid.	Minor-ON	4	1	1	2	4	....	....	....	....	....
	Waterloo Siskins	ON-Jr.B	2	1	0	1	0	....	....	....	....	....
2011-12	Kitchener Rangers	OHL	65	9	5	14	12	16	0	1	1	0
2012-13	Kitchener Rangers	OHL	67	14	16	30	52	8	0	0	0	2

PELECH, Adam (PEHL-ehk, A-duhm) NYI

Defense. Shoots left. 6'2", 215 lbs. Born, Toronto, Ont., August 16, 1994.
(NY Islanders' 3rd choice, 65th overall, in 2012 Entry Draft).

			Regular Season					Playoffs				
Season	**Club**	**League**	**GP**	**G**	**A**	**Pts**	**PIM**	**GP**	**G**	**A**	**Pts**	**PIM**
2009-10	Toronto Marlboros	GTHL	69	6	28	34	40	....	....	....	....	....
2010-11	Erie Otters	OHL	65	1	13	14	27	7	0	2	2	2
2011-12	Erie Otters	OHL	44	2	18	20	52	....	....	....	....	....
2012-13	Erie Otters	OHL	59	8	32	40	98	....	....	....	....	....

PERCY, Stuart (PUHR-see, STEW-uhrt) TOR

Defense. Shoots left. 6'1", 195 lbs. Born, Oakville, Ont., May 18, 1993.
(Toronto's 2nd choice, 25th overall, in 2011 Entry Draft).

			Regular Season					Playoffs				
Season	**Club**	**League**	**GP**	**G**	**A**	**Pts**	**PIM**	**GP**	**G**	**A**	**Pts**	**PIM**
2008-09	Toronto Marlboros	GTHL	79	13	44	57	42	....	....	....	....	....
2009-10	St. Michael's	OHL	52	3	15	18	40	16	0	1	1	12
2010-11	St. Michael's	OHL	64	4	30	34	50	20	2	10	12	14
2011-12	St. Michael's	OHL	34	5	20	25	41	6	1	1	2	4
	Toronto Marlies	AHL	1	0	1	1	0	3	0	0	0	0
2012-13	Mississauga	OHL	68	13	32	45	44	6	0	2	2	4
	Toronto Marlies	AHL	4	1	2	3	2	....	....	....	....	....

Memorial Cup All-Star Team (2011)

PERSSON, Dennis (PAIR-suhn, DEH-nihs) BUF

Defense. Shoots left. 6'1", 192 lbs. Born, Nykoping, Sweden, June 2, 1988.
(Buffalo's 1st choice, 24th overall, in 2006 Entry Draft).

			Regular Season					Playoffs				
Season	**Club**	**League**	**GP**	**G**	**A**	**Pts**	**PIM**	**GP**	**G**	**A**	**Pts**	**PIM**
2004-05	Vasteras U18	Swe-U18	3	0	1	1	2	4	0	1	1	0
	Vasteras Jr.	Swe-Jr.	27	3	3	6	24	....	....	....	....	....
2005-06	Vasteras Jr.	Swe-Jr.	28	11	15	26	22	....	....	....	....	....
	VIK Vasteras HK	Sweden-2	19	0	2	2	6	....	....	....	....	....
2006-07	Djurgarden	Sweden	9	0	0	0	2	....	....	....	....	....
	Almtuna	Sweden-2	3	0	0	0	2	....	....	....	....	....
	Nykoping	Sweden-2	29	4	4	8	38	....	....	....	....	....
	Djurgarden Jr.	Swe-Jr.	11	1	3	4	8	5	2	3	5	2
2007-08	Djurgarden Jr.	Swe-Jr.	4	0	0	0	10	....	....	....	....	....
	Djurgarden	Sweden	21	0	1	1	6	....	....	....	....	....
	Nykoping	Sweden-2	21	1	3	4	14	....	....	....	....	....
2008-09	Timra IK	Sweden	46	1	5	6	24	7	0	0	0	0
	Timra IK Jr.	Swe-Jr.	1	0	0	0	0	....	....	....	....	....
	Portland Pirates	AHL	8	0	2	2	6	3	0	0	0	0
2009-10	Portland Pirates	AHL	60	1	6	7	16	....	....	....	....	....
2010-11	Portland Pirates	AHL	64	4	13	17	18	11	0	4	4	0
2011-12	Rochester	AHL	39	3	4	7	10	....	....	....	....	....
2012-13	Brynas IF Gavle	Sweden	16	1	3	4	6	3	0	0	0	4

Signed as a free agent by **Gavle** (Sweden), June 13, 2012.

PERSSON, John (PAIR-suhn, JAWN) NYI

Left wing. Shoots left. 6'2", 209 lbs. Born, Ostersund, Sweden, May 18, 1992.
(NY Islanders' 6th choice, 125th overall, in 2011 Entry Draft).

			Regular Season					Playoffs				
Season	**Club**	**League**	**GP**	**G**	**A**	**Pts**	**PIM**	**GP**	**G**	**A**	**Pts**	**PIM**
2008-09	Mora IK U18	Swe-U18	24	18	12	30	6	....	....	....	....	....
	Mora IK Jr.	Swe-Jr.	12	4	2	6	12	....	....	....	....	....
2009-10	Red Deer Rebels	WHL	62	7	4	11	12	2	0	0	0	2
2010-11	Red Deer Rebels	WHL	68	33	28	61	34	9	2	3	5	4
2011-12	Red Deer Rebels	WHL	70	23	35	58	56	....	....	....	....	....
	Bridgeport	AHL	12	4	4	8	0	2	0	0	0	0
2012-13	Bridgeport	AHL	65	17	12	29	25	....	....	....	....	....

PERVYSHIN, Andrei (pair-VIHSH-ihn, AWN-dray) ST.L.

Defense. Shoots left. 5'8", 165 lbs. Born, Arkhangelsk, USSR, February 2, 1985.
(St. Louis' 11th choice, 253rd overall, in 2003 Entry Draft).

			Regular Season					Playoffs				
Season	**Club**	**League**	**GP**	**G**	**A**	**Pts**	**PIM**	**GP**	**G**	**A**	**Pts**	**PIM**
2003-04	Spartak Moscow	Russia-2	59	3	6	9	14	13	0	1	1	4
2004-05	Ak Bars Kazan 2	Russia-3	....	0	1	1	....	....	....	....	....	....
	Ak Bars Kazan	Russia	52	0	3	3	10	2	0	0	0	0
2005-06	Ak Bars Kazan	Russia	48	3	7	10	22	13	0	3	3	14
2006-07	Ak Bars Kazan	Russia	45	5	8	13	71	12	2	3	5	8
2007-08	Ak Bars Kazan	Russia	55	7	8	15	40	10	1	1	2	2
2008-09	Ak Bars Kazan	KHL	54	6	21	27	28	21	1	9	10	10
2009-10	Ak Bars Kazan	KHL	53	5	15	20	26	17	0	2	2	6
2010-11	Omsk	KHL	52	5	19	24	28	14	2	3	5	10
2011-12	Omsk	KHL	23	1	1	2	16	....	....	....	....	....
	SKA St. Petersburg	KHL	23	1	7	8	10	15	2	4	6	4
2012-13	SKA St. Petersburg	KHL	21	0	2	2	11	8	1	1	2	0

PESCE, Brett (PEH-SHEE, BREHT) CAR

Defense. Shoots right. 6'3", 190 lbs. Born, Tarrytown, NY, November 15, 1994.
(Carolina's 2nd choice, 66th overall, in 2013 Entry Draft).

			Regular Season					Playoffs				
Season	**Club**	**League**	**GP**	**G**	**A**	**Pts**	**PIM**	**GP**	**G**	**A**	**Pts**	**PIM**
2011-12	Jersey Hitmen	EJHL	17	1	5	6	18	....	....	....	....	....
	USNTDP	U-18	6	0	0	0	2	....	....	....	....	....
2012-13	New Hampshire	H-East	38	1	5	6	10	....	....	....	....	....

PETAN, Nic (peh-TAN, NIHK) WPG

Center. Shoots left. 5'9", 170 lbs. Born, Delta, B.C., March 22, 1995.
(Winnipeg's 2nd choice, 43rd overall, in 2013 Entry Draft).

			Regular Season					Playoffs				
Season	**Club**	**League**	**GP**	**G**	**A**	**Pts**	**PIM**	**GP**	**G**	**A**	**Pts**	**PIM**
2010-11	Greater Van.	BCMML	35	19	30	49	36	6	3	3	6	18
	Portland	WHL	3	0	1	1	0	7	0	0	0	0
2011-12	Portland	WHL	61	14	21	35	22	22	0	0	0	4
2012-13	Portland	WHL	71	46	*74	*120	43	21	9	*19	28	16

WHL West First All-Star Team (2013)

PETERS, Taylor (PEE-tuhrs, TAY-luhr) DAL

Center. Shoots left. 6'3", 212 lbs. Born, Delta, B.C., January 24, 1992.

			Regular Season					Playoffs				
Season	**Club**	**League**	**GP**	**G**	**A**	**Pts**	**PIM**	**GP**	**G**	**A**	**Pts**	**PIM**
2007-08	Greater Van.	BCMML	39	10	14	24	66	2	1	0	1	2
	Portland	WHL	5	2	0	2	0	....	....	....	....	....
2008-09	Portland	WHL	70	4	4	8	41	....	....	....	....	....
2009-10	Penticton Vees	BCHL	22	3	5	8	16	....	....	....	....	....
	Portland	WHL	32	4	3	7	15	2	0	0	0	0
2010-11	Portland	WHL	72	8	11	19	47	21	3	5	8	8
2011-12	Portland	WHL	72	12	26	38	60	22	1	7	8	12
2012-13	Portland	WHL	68	15	27	42	61	21	1	9	10	19

Signed as a free agent by **Dallas**, March 4, 2013.

PETERSON, Avery (PEE-tuhr-suhn, AY-vuhr-ee) MIN

Center. Shoots left. 6'3", 200 lbs. Born, Grand Rapids, MN, June 20, 1995.
(Minnesota's 5th choice, 167th overall, in 2013 Entry Draft).

			Regular Season					Playoffs				
Season	**Club**	**League**	**GP**	**G**	**A**	**Pts**	**PIM**	**GP**	**G**	**A**	**Pts**	**PIM**
2010-11	Grand Rapids	High-MN	25	7	15	22	20	....	....	....	....	....
2011-12	Grand Rapids	High-MN	26	14	34	48	46	....	....	....	....	....
2012-13	Grand Rapids	High-MN	26	27	35	62	2	....	....	....	....	....
	Team North	UMHSEL	21	5	10	15	19	....	....	....	....	....
	Sioux City	USHL	8	1	3	4	7	....	....	....	....	....

PETERSON, Judd (PEE-tuhr-suhn, JUHD) BUF

Center/Right wing. Shoots right. 6', 189 lbs. Born, Duluth, MN, September 27, 1993.
(Buffalo's 8th choice, 204th overall, in 2012 Entry Draft).

			Regular Season					Playoffs				
Season	**Club**	**League**	**GP**	**G**	**A**	**Pts**	**PIM**	**GP**	**G**	**A**	**Pts**	**PIM**
2009-10	Duluth Marshall	High-MN	25	16	14	30	24	....	....	....	....	....
2010-11	Team North	UMHSEL	24	8	3	11	22	....	....	....	....	....
	Duluth Marshall	High-MN	27	25	21	46	40	....	....	....	....	....
2011-12	Team North	UMHSEL	16	4	2	6	22	....	....	....	....	....
	Duluth Marshall	High-MN	30	47	36	83	32	....	....	....	....	....
2012-13	Cedar Rapids	USHL	46	11	15	26	38	....	....	....	....	....

• Signed Letter of Intent to attend **St. Cloud State University** (WCHA) in fall of 2013.

PETROV, Kirill (peh-TRAWF, kih-RIHL) NYI

Right wing. Shoots left. 6'3", 198 lbs. Born, Kazan, USSR, April 13, 1990.
(NY Islanders' 7th choice, 73rd overall, in 2008 Entry Draft).

			Regular Season					Playoffs				
Season	**Club**	**League**	**GP**	**G**	**A**	**Pts**	**PIM**	**GP**	**G**	**A**	**Pts**	**PIM**
2005-06	Ak Bars Kazan 2	Russia-3	STATISTICS NOT AVAILABLE									
2006-07	Ak Bars Kazan 2	Russia-3	STATISTICS NOT AVAILABLE									
	Ak Bars Kazan	Russia	9	1	1	2	8	3	0	0	0	2
2007-08	Ak Bars Kazan	Russia	47	4	6	10	54	8	1	1	2	0
2008-09	Ak Bars Kazan 2	Russia-3	9	4	10	14	26	....	....	....	....	....
	Ak Bars Kazan	KHL	6	1	0	1	2	....	....	....	....	....
2009-10	Ak Bars Kazan	KHL	8	0	0	0	4	3	0	1	1	0
	Bars Kazan Jr.	Russia-Jr.	4	2	1	3	4	....	....	....	....	....
	Almetjevsk	Russia-2	22	7	13	20	48	13	12	7	19	24
2010-11	Ak Bars Kazan	KHL	2	0	0	0	0	....	....	....	....	....
	Bars Kazan Jr.	Russia-Jr.	3	1	1	2	4	....	....	....	....	....
	Khanty-Mansiisk	KHL	47	8	11	19	20	6	2	2	4	8
2011-12	Ak Bars Kazan	KHL	52	16	13	29	8	12	3	2	5	8
2012-13	Ak Bars Kazan	KHL	47	12	8	20	26	18	4	1	5	6

PETTERSSON, Emil (PEH-tuhr-suhn, eh-MIHL) **NSH**

Center. Shoots left. 6'2", 178 lbs. Born, Sundsvall, Sweden, January 14, 1994.
(Nashville's 7th choice, 155th overall, in 2013 Entry Draft).

			Regular Season					Playoffs				
Season	Club	League	GP	G	A	Pts	PIM	GP	G	A	Pts	PIM
2010-11	Timra IK U18	Swe-U18	34	10	16	26	26	5	0	1	1	0
2011-12	Timra IK U18	Swe-U18	31	19	22	41	94	3	1	4	5	10
	Timra IK Jr.	Swe-Jr.	17	4	2	6	10	3	1	1	2	2
2012-13	Timra IK Jr.	Swe-Jr.	44	13	31	44	38	2	0	0	0	2
	Timra IK	Sweden	2	0	0	0	0	....	....	....	....	....
	Timra IK	Sweden-Q	2	1	0	1	0	....	....	....	....	....

PHILLIPS, Paul (FIHL-ihps, PAWL) **CHI**

Defense. Shoots left. 6'1", 195 lbs. Born, Darien, IL, July 16, 1991.
(Chicago's 7th choice, 195th overall, in 2009 Entry Draft).

			Regular Season					Playoffs				
Season	Club	League	GP	G	A	Pts	PIM	GP	G	A	Pts	PIM
2006-07	Chicago Fury	MWEHL	26	7	5	12	40	....	....	....	....	....
2007-08	Cedar Rapids	USHL	43	1	2	3	25	3	0	0	0	4
2008-09	Cedar Rapids	USHL	60	8	25	33	56	5	0	0	0	6
2009-10	U. of Denver	WCHA	31	0	4	4	16	....	....	....	....	....
2010-11	U. of Denver	WCHA	38	0	4	4	22	....	....	....	....	....
2011-12	U. of Denver	WCHA	40	1	8	9	22	....	....	....	....	....
2012-13	U. of Denver	WCHA	39	1	10	11	24	....	....	....	....	....

PHILLIPS, Zack (FIHL-ihps, ZAK) **MIN**

Center. Shoots right. 6', 196 lbs. Born, Fredericton, NB, October 28, 1992.
(Minnesota's 2nd choice, 28th overall, in 2011 Entry Draft).

			Regular Season					Playoffs				
Season	Club	League	GP	G	A	Pts	PIM	GP	G	A	Pts	PIM
2008-09	Lawrence	High-MA	30	19	29	48	....	....	....	....	....	....
2009-10	Saint John	QMJHL	65	16	28	44	31	21	2	4	6	4
2010-11	Saint John	QMJHL	67	38	57	95	16	17	9	15	24	8
2011-12	Saint John	QMJHL	60	30	50	80	32	17	9	23	32	4
2012-13	Houston Aeros	AHL	71	8	19	27	10	5	0	1	1	2

George Parsons Trophy (Memorial Cup – Most Sportsmanlike Player) (2012)

PIETILA, Blake (pee-EH-tihl-a, BLAYK) **N.J.**

Left wing. Shoots left. 6', 195 lbs. Born, Milford, MI, February 20, 1993.
(New Jersey's 5th choice, 129th overall, in 2011 Entry Draft).

			Regular Season					Playoffs				
Season	Club	League	GP	G	A	Pts	PIM	GP	G	A	Pts	PIM
2008-09	Det. Compuware	T1EHL	31	8	11	19	8	5	1	5	6	0
2009-10	USNTDP	USHL	28	5	3	8	27	....	....	....	....	....
	USNTDP	U-17	18	1	6	7	10	....	....	....	....	....
	USNTDP	U-18	1	0	0	0	0	....	....	....	....	....
2010-11	USNTDP	USHL	24	4	5	9	20	....	....	....	....	....
	USNTDP	U-18	13	10	4	14	33	....	....	....	....	....
2011-12	Michigan Tech	WCHA	39	10	14	24	46	....	....	....	....	....
2012-13	Michigan Tech	WCHA	35	14	10	24	44	....	....	....	....	....

PINHO, Brian (PIHN-oh, BRIGH-uhn) **WSH**

Center. Shoots right. 6', 173 lbs. Born, Beverly, MA, May 11, 1995.
(Washington's 5th choice, 174th overall, in 2013 Entry Draft).

			Regular Season					Playoffs				
Season	Club	League	GP	G	A	Pts	PIM	GP	G	A	Pts	PIM
2011-12	St. John's Prep	High-MA	24	20	37	57	....	....	....	....	....	....
	Valley Jr. Warriors	Minor-MA	10	0	10	10	2	....	....	....	....	....
2012-13	St. John's Prep	High-MA	24	15	27	42	....	....	....	....	....	....

• Signed Letter of Intent to attend **Providence College** (Hockey East) in fall of 2014.

PITLICK, Tyler (PIHT-lihk, TIGH-luhr) **EDM**

Center. Shoots right. 6'2", 195 lbs. Born, Minneapolis, MN, November 1, 1991.
(Edmonton's 2nd choice, 31st overall, in 2010 Entry Draft).

			Regular Season					Playoffs				
Season	Club	League	GP	G	A	Pts	PIM	GP	G	A	Pts	PIM
2007-08	Centennial	High-MN	....	25	34	59	....	....	....	....	....	....
2008-09	Centennial	High-MN	25	31	33	64	....	....	....	....	....	....
2009-10	Minnesota State	WCHA	38	11	8	19	27	....	....	....	....	....
2010-11	Medicine Hat	WHL	56	27	35	62	31	....	....	....	....	....
2011-12	Oklahoma City	AHL	62	7	16	23	28	13	2	5	7	2
2012-13	Oklahoma City	AHL	44	3	7	10	10	16	2	4	6	8

PLACEK, Petr (PLAH-chehk, PEH-tuhr) **PHI**

Right wing. Shoots right. 6'4", 215 lbs. Born, Slany, Czech., December 28, 1992.
(Philadelphia's 5th choice, 176th overall, in 2011 Entry Draft).

			Regular Season					Playoffs				
Season	Club	League	GP	G	A	Pts	PIM	GP	G	A	Pts	PIM
2006-07	HC Kladno U17	CzR-U17	3	1	0	1	4	....	....	....	....	....
2007-08	HC Kladno U17	CzR-U17	46	10	12	22	10	3	0	1	1	0
2008-09	Hotchkiss School	High-CT	21	7	8	15	....	....	....	....	....	....
2009-10	Hotchkiss School	High-CT	22	16	16	32	....	....	....	....	....	....
2010-11	Junior Bobcats	Indep.	STATISTICS NOT AVAILABLE									
	Hotchkiss School	High-CT	8	7	6	13	10	....	....	....	....	....
2011-12	Harvard Crimson	ECAC	16	0	1	1	6	....	....	....	....	....
2012-13	Harvard Crimson	ECAC	29	2	0	2	16	....	....	....	....	....

• Missed majority of 2008-09 due to knee and ankle injuries. • Missed majority of 2010-11 due to knee surgery.

PLATZER, Kyle (PLAT-zuhr, KIGHL) **EDM**

Center. Shoots right. 5'11", 185 lbs. Born, Waterloo, Ont., March 4, 1995.
(Edmonton's 6th choice, 96th overall, in 2013 Entry Draft).

			Regular Season					Playoffs				
Season	Club	League	GP	G	A	Pts	PIM	GP	G	A	Pts	PIM
2010-11	Wat. Wolves M.M.	Minor-ON	30	20	22	42	20	13	6	7	13	16
	Wat. Wolves Mid.	Minor-ON	8	2	2	4	8	....	....	....	....	....
	Waterloo Siskins	ON-Jr.B	2	0	0	0	0	....	....	....	....	....
2011-12	Waterloo Siskins	ON-Jr.B	50	31	24	55	70	6	4	6	10	6
	London Knights	OHL	4	0	1	1	0	....	....	....	....	....
2012-13	London Knights	OHL	65	5	17	22	15	21	2	4	6	8

POCHIRO, Zach (puh-CHUHR-oh, ZAK) **ST.L.**

Left wing. Shoots right. 6'1", 159 lbs. Born, St. Louis, MO, March 6, 1994.
(St. Louis' 3rd choice, 112th overall, in 2013 Entry Draft).

			Regular Season					Playoffs				
Season	Club	League	GP	G	A	Pts	PIM	GP	G	A	Pts	PIM
2010-11	L.A. Jr. Kings	T1EHL	31	22	12	34	128	....	....	....	....	....
2011-12	Wichita Falls	NAHL	52	18	16	34	154	....	....	....	....	....
2012-13	Prince George	WHL	65	15	24	39	105	....	....	....	....	....

POIRIER, Emile (p'wah-REE-ay, eh-MEEL) **CGY**

Left wing. Shoots left. 6'1", 183 lbs. Born, Montreal, Que., December 14, 1994.
(Calgary's 2nd choice, 22nd overall, in 2013 Entry Draft).

			Regular Season					Playoffs				
Season	Club	League	GP	G	A	Pts	PIM	GP	G	A	Pts	PIM
2010-11	Laval-Montreal	QAAA	42	27	24	51	30	5	1	2	3	4
2011-12	Gatineau	QMJHL	67	15	25	40	53	4	1	0	1	8
2012-13	Gatineau	QMJHL	65	32	38	70	101	10	6	4	10	14

POKKA, Ville (POH-ka, VIHL-ee) **NYI**

Defense. Shoots right. 6', 206 lbs. Born, Tornio, Finland, June 3, 1994.
(NY Islanders' 2nd choice, 34th overall, in 2012 Entry Draft).

			Regular Season					Playoffs				
Season	Club	League	GP	G	A	Pts	PIM	GP	G	A	Pts	PIM
2009-10	Karpat Oulu U18	Fin-U18	25	0	7	7	10	5	0	0	0	4
2010-11	Karpat Oulu Jr.	Fin-Jr.	33	6	16	22	18	....	....	....	....	....
	Karpat Oulu	Finland	2	0	0	0	2	....	....	....	....	....
	Kiekko-Laser Oulu	Finland-2	3	0	3	3	0	....	....	....	....	....
	Karpat Oulu U18	Fin-U18	3	0	2	2	0	9	0	7	7	8
2011-12	Karpat Oulu Jr.	Fin-Jr.	4	3	4	7	2	....	....	....	....	....
	Karpat Oulu	Finland	35	0	3	3	12	9	0	3	3	2
2012-13	Karpat Oulu Jr.	Fin-Jr.	3	0	0	0	4	....	....	....	....	....
	Karpat Oulu	Finland	47	6	6	12	8	3	0	2	2	0

POLASEK, Adam (poh-LAH-shehk, A-duhm) **VAN**

Defense. Shoots left. 6'3", 207 lbs. Born, Ostrava, Czech., July 12, 1991.
(Vancouver's 2nd choice, 145th overall, in 2010 Entry Draft).

			Regular Season					Playoffs				
Season	Club	League	GP	G	A	Pts	PIM	GP	G	A	Pts	PIM
2005-06	HC Vitkovice U17	CzR-U17	17	1	0	1	2	....	....	....	....	....
2006-07	HC Vitkovice U17	CzR-U17	43	6	13	19	83	9	0	1	1	12
	HC Vitkovice Jr.	CzRep-Jr.	1	0	0	0	2	....	....	....	....	....
2007-08	HC Vitkovice U17	CzR-U17	18	3	2	5	50	2	0	0	0	0
	HC Vitkovice Jr.	CzRep-Jr.	23	0	3	3	16	2	0	1	1	0
2008-09	HC Vitkovice Jr.	CzRep-Jr.	38	7	13	20	68	9	0	9	9	18
2009-10	P.E.I. Rocket	QMJHL	66	13	28	41	91	5	0	0	0	2
2010-11	P.E.I. Rocket	QMJHL	61	7	32	39	59	5	0	0	0	8
2011-12	Chicago Wolves	AHL	46	1	8	9	27	....	....	....	....	....
2012-13	Chicago Wolves	AHL	24	1	7	8	27	....	....	....	....	....
	Kalamazoo Wings	ECHL	34	4	4	8	37	....	....	....	....	....

QMJHL All-Rookie Team (2010) • Canadian Major Junior All-Rookie Team (2010)

PONICH, Brett (PAW-nihch, BREHT) **ST.L.**

Defense. Shoots left. 6'7", 220 lbs. Born, Edmonton, Alta., February 22, 1991.
(St. Louis' 2nd choice, 48th overall, in 2009 Entry Draft).

			Regular Season					Playoffs				
Season	Club	League	GP	G	A	Pts	PIM	GP	G	A	Pts	PIM
2006-07	Leduc Oil Kings	AMHL	35	1	10	11	64	13	1	6	7	24
	Portland	WHL	2	0	0	0	0	....	....	....	....	....
2007-08	Portland	WHL	64	0	3	3	63	....	....	....	....	....
2008-09	Portland	WHL	72	1	17	18	117	....	....	....	....	....
2009-10	Portland	WHL	66	1	13	14	87	13	1	2	3	13
2010-11	Portland	WHL	45	0	12	12	60	....	....	....	....	....
2011-12	Peoria Rivermen	AHL	61	0	5	5	47	....	....	....	....	....
2012-13	Peoria Rivermen	AHL	26	0	0	0	38	....	....	....	....	....
	Evansville IceMen	ECHL	13	1	2	3	26	....	....	....	....	....
	Alaska Aces	ECHL	5	0	0	0	11	11	0	3	3	9

POOLMAN, Tucker (POOL-MAN, TUH-kuhr) **WPG**

Defense. Shoots right. 6'2", 199 lbs. Born, Dubuque, IA, June 8, 1993.
(Winnipeg's 8th choice, 127th overall, in 2013 Entry Draft).

			Regular Season					Playoffs				
Season	Club	League	GP	G	A	Pts	PIM	GP	G	A	Pts	PIM
2008-09	E. Grand Forks	High-MN	25	3	4	7	2	....	....	....	....	....
2009-10	E. Grand Forks	High-MN	27	3	9	12	10	....	....	....	....	....
2010-11	Team Great Plains	UMHSEL	16	2	3	5	4	3	0	2	2	0
	E. Grand Forks	High-MN	25	5	17	22	13	....	....	....	....	....
2011-12	Wichita Falls	NAHL	59	7	22	29	29	....	....	....	....	....
2012-13	Omaha Lancers	USHL	64	14	14	28	49	....	....	....	....	....

• Signed Letter of Intent to attend **University of North Dakota** (WCHA) in fall of 2013.

POPE, David (POHP, DAY-vihd) **DET**

Left wing. Shoots left. 6'2", 187 lbs. Born, Edmonton, Alta., September 27, 1994.
(Detroit's 5th choice, 109th overall, in 2013 Entry Draft).

			Regular Season					Playoffs				
Season	Club	League	GP	G	A	Pts	PIM	GP	G	A	Pts	PIM
2009-10	K of C Pats	AMHL	27	2	8	10	12	....	....	....	....	....
2010-11	Pursuit of Ex. H.A.	High-BC	STATISTICS NOT AVAILABLE									
	Pursuit of Ex. H.A.	CSSHL	10	8	8	16	2	5	4	4	8	2
2011-12	Cowichan Valley	BCHL	24	2	5	7	12	....	....	....	....	....
	Westside Warriors	BCHL	20	6	12	18	19	....	....	....	....	....
2012-13	West Kelowna	BCHL	42	17	22	39	20	....	....	....	....	....

• Signed Letter of Intent to attend **University of Nebraska-Omaha** (WCHA) in fall of 2014.

POSSLER, Gustav (POHS-luhr, GOO-stahv) **BUF**

Right wing. Shoots left. 6', 182 lbs. Born, Sodertalje, Sweden, November 11, 1994.
(Buffalo's 8th choice, 130th overall, in 2013 Entry Draft).

			Regular Season					Playoffs				
Season	**Club**	**League**	**GP**	**G**	**A**	**Pts**	**PIM**	**GP**	**G**	**A**	**Pts**	**PIM**
2009-10	Bjorkloven U18	Swe-U18	25	9	16	25	24	....	....	....	....	....
2010-11	Lulea HF U18	Swe-U18	18	21	15	36	16	....	....	....	....	....
	Lulea HF Jr.	Swe-Jr.	4	0	0	0	0	....	....	....	....	....
	MODO U18	Swe-U18	13	6	7	13	2	3	2	2	4	4
	MODO Jr.	Swe-Jr.	1	1	1	2	0	3	0	0	0	0
2011-12	MODO U18	Swe-U18	10	9	4	13	6	1	0	0	0	0
	MODO Jr.	Swe-Jr.	37	23	17	40	14	8	2	1	3	4
	MODO	Sweden	2	1	0	1	0	....	....	....	....	....
2012-13	MODO Jr.	Swe-Jr.	36	19	21	40	28	7	4	4	8	4
	MODO	Sweden	7	1	0	1	2	....	....	....	....	....
	Mora IK	Sweden-2	3	0	0	0	0	....	....	....	....	....

POULIOT, Derrick (POO-lee-oh, DAIR-ihk) **PIT**

Defense. Shoots left. 5'11", 195 lbs. Born, Estevan, Sask., January 16, 1994.
(Pittsburgh's 1st choice, 8th overall, in 2012 Entry Draft).

			Regular Season					Playoffs				
Season	**Club**	**League**	**GP**	**G**	**A**	**Pts**	**PIM**	**GP**	**G**	**A**	**Pts**	**PIM**
2008-09	Weyburn Wings	Minor-SK	26	25	38	63	24	5	5	1	6	....
	Moose Jaw	SMHL	5	1	1	2	0	....	....	....	....	....
2009-10	Moose Jaw	SMHL	43	14	29	43	38	4	0	2	2	4
	Portland	WHL	7	0	1	1	0	....	....	....	....	....
2010-11	Portland	WHL	66	5	25	30	38	21	1	3	4	16
2011-12	Portland	WHL	72	11	48	59	79	22	3	14	17	18
2012-13	Portland	WHL	44	9	36	45	60	21	4	16	20	12
	Wilkes-Barre	AHL	....	....	....	....	....	1	0	0	0	0

Memorial Cup All-Star Team (2013)

PRESS, Robin (PREHS, RAW-bihn) **CHI**

Defense. Shoots right. 6'2", 187 lbs. Born, , Sweden, December 21, 1994.
(Chicago's 8th choice, 211th overall, in 2013 Entry Draft).

			Regular Season					Playoffs				
Season	**Club**	**League**	**GP**	**G**	**A**	**Pts**	**PIM**	**GP**	**G**	**A**	**Pts**	**PIM**
2010-11	Almtuna U18	Swe-U18	31	7	6	13	8	....	....	....	....	....
2011-12	Almtuna U18	Swe-U18	28	8	16	24	52	....	....	....	....	....
	Almtuna Jr.	Swe-Jr.	24	15	20	35	26	....	....	....	....	....
	Almtuna	Sweden-2	9	0	1	1	4	....	....	....	....	....
2012-13	Sodertalje SK Jr.	Swe-Jr.	26	7	9	16	16	3	0	2	2	0
	Sodertalje SK	Sweden-2	49	2	3	5	14	....	....	....	....	....

PRICE, Jeremy (PRIGHS, JAIR-eh-mee) **VAN**

Defense. Shoots right. 6'1", 190 lbs. Born, Milton, Ont., September 26, 1990.
(Vancouver's 4th choice, 113th overall, in 2009 Entry Draft).

			Regular Season					Playoffs				
Season	**Club**	**League**	**GP**	**G**	**A**	**Pts**	**PIM**	**GP**	**G**	**A**	**Pts**	**PIM**
2006-07	Milton Icehawks	ON-Jr.A	37	1	6	7	51	5	2	1	3	9
2007-08	Milton Icehawks	ON-Jr.A	44	10	22	32	28	10	0	6	6	4
2008-09	Nepean Raiders	ON-Jr.A	55	12	29	41	50	14	2	4	6	14
2009-10	Colgate	ECAC	35	6	8	14	32	....	....	....	....	....
2010-11	Colgate	ECAC	42	5	14	19	28	....	....	....	....	....
2011-12	Colgate	ECAC	36	2	21	23	33	....	....	....	....	....
2012-13	Colgate	ECAC	36	6	14	20	12	....	....	....	....	....
	Chicago Wolves	AHL	5	0	1	1	4	....	....	....	....	....

PRINCE, Shane (PRIHNS, SHAYN) **OTT**

Center. Shoots left. 5'11", 186 lbs. Born, Rochester, NY, November 16, 1992.
(Ottawa's 4th choice, 61st overall, in 2011 Entry Draft).

			Regular Season					Playoffs				
Season	**Club**	**League**	**GP**	**G**	**A**	**Pts**	**PIM**	**GP**	**G**	**A**	**Pts**	**PIM**
2007-08	Maksymum	EmJHL	34	15	31	46	10	....	....	....	....	....
	Maksymum	Exhib.	10	3	4	7	4	....	....	....	....	....
	Rochester	EJHL	11	3	3	6	4	....	....	....	....	....
2008-09	Kitchener Rangers	OHL	63	3	9	12	34	....	....	....	....	....
2009-10	Kitchener Rangers	OHL	39	8	9	17	32	....	....	....	....	....
	Ottawa 67's	OHL	26	7	6	13	13	12	2	2	4	4
2010-11	Ottawa 67's	OHL	59	25	63	88	18	3	1	0	1	0
2011-12	Ottawa 67's	OHL	57	43	47	90	12	18	7	9	16	6
2012-13	Binghamton	AHL	65	18	17	35	24	3	1	0	1	0

PROKHORKIN, Nikolay (proh-KHOHR-kihn, nih-koh-LIGH) **L.A.**

Left wing. Shoots left. 6'2", 191 lbs. Born, Chelyabinsk, Russia, September 17, 1993.
(Los Angeles' 2nd choice, 121st overall, in 2012 Entry Draft).

			Regular Season					Playoffs				
Season	**Club**	**League**	**GP**	**G**	**A**	**Pts**	**PIM**	**GP**	**G**	**A**	**Pts**	**PIM**
2010-11	CSKA Jr.	Russia-Jr.	46	23	17	40	42	16	3	5	8	10
	CSKA Moscow	KHL	6	0	0	0	0	....	....	....	....	....
2011-12	CSKA Jr.	Russia-Jr.	15	9	17	26	47	16	2	9	11	14
	CSKA Moscow	KHL	15	1	1	2	4	4	0	1	1	2
2012-13	Manchester	AHL	8	0	1	1	6	....	....	....	....	....
	THK Tver	Russia-2	5	2	2	4	4	....	....	....	....	....
	CSKA Moscow	KHL	14	2	1	3	10	9	3	1	4	0

PUEMPEL, Matt (PUHM-puhl, MAT) **OTT**

Left wing. Shoots left. 6'1", 207 lbs. Born, Windsor, Ont., January 24, 1993.
(Ottawa's 3rd choice, 24th overall, in 2011 Entry Draft).

			Regular Season					Playoffs				
Season	**Club**	**League**	**GP**	**G**	**A**	**Pts**	**PIM**	**GP**	**G**	**A**	**Pts**	**PIM**
2008-09	Sun County	Minor-ON	76	88	56	144	....	....	....	....	....	....
	Leamington Flyers	ON-Jr.B	1	2	0	2	0	....	....	....	....	....
2009-10	Peterborough	OHL	59	33	31	64	43	4	1	1	2	6
2010-11	Peterborough	OHL	55	34	35	69	49	....	....	....	....	....
2011-12	Peterborough	OHL	30	17	16	33	31	....	....	....	....	....
	Binghamton	AHL	9	1	0	1	2	....	....	....	....	....
2012-13	Kitchener Rangers	OHL	51	35	12	47	43	10	3	4	7	10
	Binghamton	AHL	2	0	0	0	0	3	2	0	2	0

OHL All-Rookie Team (2010) • OHL Rookie of the Year (2010) • Canadian Major Junior All-Rookie Team (2010) • Canadian Major Junior Rookie of the Year (2010)

PULKKINEN, Teemu (PUHL-kih-nuhn, TEE-moo) **DET**

Left wing. Shoots right. 5'11", 183 lbs. Born, Vantaa, Finland, January 2, 1992.
(Detroit's 4th choice, 111th overall, in 2010 Entry Draft).

			Regular Season					Playoffs				
Season	**Club**	**League**	**GP**	**G**	**A**	**Pts**	**PIM**	**GP**	**G**	**A**	**Pts**	**PIM**
2007-08	Jokerit U18	Fin-U18	32	36	24	60	8	6	11	6	17	6
2008-09	Suomi U20	Finland-2	1	0	0	0	0	....	....	....	....	....
	Jokerit U18	Fin-U18	9	16	19	35	4	....	....	....	....	....
	Jokerit Helsinki Jr.	Fin-Jr.	24	15	13	28	12	....	....	....	....	....
	Jokerit Helsinki	Finland	3	0	0	0	6	....	....	....	....	....
2009-10	Jokerit Helsinki Jr.	Fin-Jr.	17	20	21	41	41	4	3	3	6	0
	Jokerit Helsinki	Finland	12	1	2	3	6	....	....	....	....	....
2010-11	Suomi U20	Finland-2	1	1	0	1	0	....	....	....	....	....
	Jokerit Helsinki	Finland	55	18	36	54	32	3	0	1	1	0
2011-12	Jokerit Helsinki	Finland	56	16	21	37	41	4	0	1	1	2
2012-13	Jokerit Helsinki	Finland	59	14	20	34	49	6	2	3	5	22
	Grand Rapids	AHL	2	0	1	1	2	14	3	2	5	10

PULOCK, Ryan (POO-lawk, RIGH-uhn) **NYI**

Defense. Shoots right. 6'1", 213 lbs. Born, Dauphin, Man., October 6, 1994.
(NY Islanders' 1st choice, 15th overall, in 2013 Entry Draft).

			Regular Season					Playoffs				
Season	**Club**	**League**	**GP**	**G**	**A**	**Pts**	**PIM**	**GP**	**G**	**A**	**Pts**	**PIM**
2009-10	Parkland Rangers	MMHL	39	9	10	19	8	3	0	1	1	0
2010-11	Brandon	WHL	63	8	34	42	4	6	2	4	6	2
2011-12	Brandon	WHL	71	19	41	60	20	9	3	2	5	0
2012-13	Brandon	WHL	61	14	31	45	22	....	....	....	....	....

WHL East First All-Star Team (2012)

PUUSTINEN, Juuso (POOS-tih-nehn, YUH-soh) **NSH**

Right wing. Shoots right. 6'2", 190 lbs. Born, Kuopio, Finland, April 5, 1988.
(Calgary's 5th choice, 149th overall, in 2006 Entry Draft).

			Regular Season					Playoffs				
Season	**Club**	**League**	**GP**	**G**	**A**	**Pts**	**PIM**	**GP**	**G**	**A**	**Pts**	**PIM**
2004-05	KalPa Kuopio U18	Fin-U18	26	14	15	29	81	6	1	2	3	4
	KalPa Kuopio Jr.	Fin-Jr.	1	0	0	0	0	....	....	....	....	....
2005-06	KalPa Kuopio U18	Fin-U18	7	8	7	15	18	1	0	0	0	2
	KalPa Kuopio Jr.	Fin-Jr.	29	9	5	14	46	5	0	0	0	0
2006-07	Suomi U20	Finland-2	2	0	1	1	2	....	....	....	....	....
	Kamloops Blazers	WHL	64	32	39	71	52	4	0	3	3	4
2007-08	Kamloops Blazers	WHL	60	27	26	53	26	4	1	1	2	2
2008-09	Blues Espoo	Finland	53	13	20	33	14	14	1	1	2	4
2009-10	Blues Espoo	Finland	54	8	13	21	64	2	0	1	1	0
2010-11	HPK Hameenlinna	Finland	59	26	12	38	46	2	1	0	1	4
2011-12	Milwaukee	AHL	55	16	16	32	8	....	....	....	....	....
2012-13	Milwaukee	AHL	73	15	16	31	14	4	0	0	0	4

Signed as a free agent by **Nashville**, June 16, 2011. Signed as a free agent by **HIFK Helsinki** (Finland), May 22, 2013.

PYETT, Logan (PIGH-eht, LOH-guhn)

Defense. Shoots right. 5'10", 199 lbs. Born, Regina, Sask., May 26, 1988.
(Detroit's 7th choice, 212th overall, in 2006 Entry Draft).

			Regular Season					Playoffs				
Season	**Club**	**League**	**GP**	**G**	**A**	**Pts**	**PIM**	**GP**	**G**	**A**	**Pts**	**PIM**
2002-03	Balgonie	SSMHL	35	27	46	73	40	....	....	....	....	....
2003-04	Reg. Pat Cdns.	SMHL	44	18	27	45	34	....	....	....	....	....
	Regina Pats	WHL	2	0	1	1	0	3	0	0	0	0
2004-05	Regina Pats	WHL	67	5	19	24	67	....	....	....	....	....
2005-06	Regina Pats	WHL	71	10	35	45	89	6	1	6	7	12
2006-07	Regina Pats	WHL	71	14	48	62	84	10	3	6	9	4
2007-08	Regina Pats	WHL	62	20	34	54	54	6	1	3	4	0
2008-09	Grand Rapids	AHL	61	3	11	14	12	1	0	0	0	0
2009-10	Grand Rapids	AHL	80	9	21	30	41	....	....	....	....	....
2010-11	Grand Rapids	AHL	74	9	13	22	38	....	....	....	....	....
2011-12	Grand Rapids	AHL	73	2	25	27	54	....	....	....	....	....
2012-13	Connecticut Whale	AHL	74	7	32	39	35	....	....	....	....	....

WHL East First All-Star Team (2008) • Canadian Major Junior Second All-Star Team (2008)

Signed as a free agent by **NY Rangers**, July 10, 2012. Signed as a free agent by **Podolsk** (KHL), June 10, 2013.

QUAILER, Steve (KWAY-luhr, STEEV) **MTL**

Left wing. Shoots left. 6'4", 209 lbs. Born, Arvada, CO, August 5, 1989.
(Montreal's 2nd choice, 86th overall, in 2008 Entry Draft).

			Regular Season					Playoffs				
Season	**Club**	**League**	**GP**	**G**	**A**	**Pts**	**PIM**	**GP**	**G**	**A**	**Pts**	**PIM**
2006-07	Rocky Mountain	Minor-CO	53	14	23	37	25	....	....	....	....	....
2007-08	Sioux City	USHL	60	19	30	49	55	4	1	2	3	4
2008-09	Northeastern	H-East	41	10	15	25	12	....	....	....	....	....
2009-10	Northeastern	H-East	DID NOT PLAY – INJURED									
2010-11	Northeastern	H-East	38	3	10	13	39	....	....	....	....	....
2011-12	Northeastern	H-East	26	8	17	25	34	....	....	....	....	....
2012-13	Hamilton Bulldogs	AHL	64	6	4	10	54	....	....	....	....	....

USHL All-Rookie Team (2008) • Hockey East All-Rookie Team (2009)

• Missed 2009-10 due to knee injury in pre-season vs. St. Thomas University (MIAC), October 3, 2009.

QUENNEVILLE, Peter (KWEHN-vihl, PEE-tuhr) **CBJ**

Center/Right wing. Shoots right. 5'11", 183 lbs. Born, Edmonton, Alta., March 9, 1994.
(Columbus' 8th choice, 195th overall, in 2013 Entry Draft).

			Regular Season					Playoffs				
Season	**Club**	**League**	**GP**	**G**	**A**	**Pts**	**PIM**	**GP**	**G**	**A**	**Pts**	**PIM**
2009-10	Edmonton MLAC	AMHL	33	13	11	24	10	....	....	....	....	....
2010-11	Sherwood Park	AJHL	54	6	16	22	8	3	0	0	0	0
2011-12	Sherwood Park	AJHL	53	31	50	81	22	10	4	4	8	10
2012-13	Dubuque	USHL	63	33	37	70	18	9	6	3	9	2

USHL Second All-Star Team (2013)

• Signed Letter of Intent to attend **Quinnipiac University** (ECAC) in fall of 2013.

QUINE, Alan (KWIH-nee, AL-uhn) NYI

Center. Shoots left. 5'11", 191 lbs. Born, Belleville, Ont., February 25, 1993.
(NY Islanders' 6th choice, 166th overall, in 2013 Entry Draft).

			Regular Season					Playoffs				
Season	Club	League	GP	G	A	Pts	PIM	GP	G	A	Pts	PIM
2008-09	Tor. Jr. Canadiens	GTHL	35	26	26	52	8	....	....	....	....	....
	Tor. Canadiens	ON-Jr.A	2	1	1	2	0	....	....	....	....	....
2009-10	Kingston	OHL	64	11	17	28	8	7	1	2	3	0
2010-11	Kingston	OHL	17	4	7	11	2	....	....	....	....	....
	Peterborough	OHL	52	22	20	42	6	....	....	....	....	....
2011-12	Peterborough	OHL	65	30	40	70	21	....	....	....	....	....
	Grand Rapids	AHL	3	0	1	1	0	....	....	....	....	....
2012-13	Peterborough	OHL	26	9	17	26	14	....	....	....	....	....
	Belleville Bulls	OHL	28	14	27	41	6	17	8	7	15	6

• Re-entered NHL Entry Draft. Originally Detroit's 4th choice, 85th overall, in 2011 Entry Draft.

RACINE, Jonathan (RAY-seen, JAWN-ah-thuhn) FLA

Defense. Shoots left. 6'2", 189 lbs. Born, Montreal, Que., May 28, 1993.
(Florida's 6th choice, 87th overall, in 2011 Entry Draft).

			Regular Season					Playoffs				
Season	Club	League	GP	G	A	Pts	PIM	GP	G	A	Pts	PIM
2008-09	Saint-Eustache	QAAA	45	5	7	12	74	8	0	2	2	12
2009-10	Shawinigan	QMJHL	55	0	4	4	43	6	0	0	0	0
2010-11	Shawinigan	QMJHL	68	2	5	7	86	12	0	1	1	22
2011-12	Shawinigan	QMJHL	61	3	10	13	107	11	1	5	6	22
2012-13	Moncton Wildcats	QMJHL	61	8	13	21	138	5	0	0	0	7
	San Antonio	AHL	8	0	0	0	4	....	....	....	....	....

RAEDEKE, Brent (RAD-kee, BREHNT)

Left wing. Shoots left. 6', 200 lbs. Born, Regina, Sask., May 29, 1990.

			Regular Season					Playoffs				
Season	Club	League	GP	G	A	Pts	PIM	GP	G	A	Pts	PIM
2005-06	Regina Pat Cdns.	SAHA	41	7	7	14	36	2	0	0	0	0
2006-07	Regina Pat Cdns.	SAHA	40	16	20	36	74	1	1	0	1	0
2007-08	Edmonton	WHL	72	15	16	31	62	....	....	....	....	....
2008-09	Edmonton	WHL	70	19	36	55	80	4	1	1	2	6
	Grand Rapids	AHL	2	0	0	0	0	....	....	....	....	....
2009-10	Edmonton	WHL	39	16	15	31	60	....	....	....	....	....
	Brandon	WHL	33	7	18	25	35	15	5	7	12	16
2010-11	Grand Rapids	AHL	67	8	5	13	17	....	....	....	....	....
2011-12	Grand Rapids	AHL	64	11	10	21	33	....	....	....	....	....
2012-13	Grand Rapids	AHL	38	3	6	9	43	....	....	....	....	....
	Toledo Walleye	ECHL	2	1	0	1	0	....	....	....	....	....

Signed as a free agent by **Detroit**, October 1, 2008. Signed as a free agent by **Iserlohn** (Germany), July 24, 2013.

RAFFL, Michael (RA-fuhl, mi-KHIGH-ehl) PHI

Left wing. Shoots left. 6', 192 lbs. Born, Villach, Austria, December 1, 1988.

			Regular Season					Playoffs				
Season	Club	League	GP	G	A	Pts	PIM	GP	G	A	Pts	PIM
2005-06	EC VSV Villach Jr.	Austria-Jr.	26	11	27	38	91	4	6	6	12	10
	EC VSV Villach	Austria	5	0	0	0	0	3	0	0	0	0
2006-07	EC VSV Villach Jr.	Austria-Jr.	21	23	24	47	82	....	....	....	....	....
	EC VSV Villach	Austria	43	4	2	6	22	4	0	0	0	0
2007-08	EC VSV Villach Jr.	Austria-Jr.	6	5	7	12	28	....	....	....	....	....
	EC VSV Villach	Austria	40	3	6	9	24	5	2	0	2	2
2008-09	EC VSV Villach	Austria	49	9	10	19	77	6	0	2	2	12
2009-10	EC VSV Villach	Austria	42	25	18	43	54	5	1	0	1	14
2010-11	EC VSV Villach	Austria	50	26	29	55	62	8	5	4	9	20
2011-12	Leksands IF	Sweden-2	45	10	14	24	26	....	....	....	....	....
2012-13	Leksands IF	Sweden-2	59	27	25	52	44	....	....	....	....	....

Signed as a free agent by **Philadelphia**, May 31, 2013.

RAFIKOV, Rushan (ra-FIH-kawv, roo-SHAN) CGY

Defense. Shoots left. 6'2", 181 lbs. Born, Saratov, Russia, May 15, 1995.
(Calgary's 7th choice, 187th overall, in 2013 Entry Draft).

			Regular Season					Playoffs				
Season	Club	League	GP	G	A	Pts	PIM	GP	G	A	Pts	PIM
2011-12	Loko Yaroslavl Jr.	Russia-Jr.	24	4	2	6	14	3	0	1	1	25
2012-13	Loko Yaroslavl Jr.	Russia-Jr.	53	1	9	10	38	....	....	....	....	....

RAMAGE, John (RAM-ihj, JAWN) CGY

Defense. Shoots right. 6', 201 lbs. Born, Mississauga, Ont., February 7, 1991.
(Calgary's 3rd choice, 103rd overall, in 2010 Entry Draft).

			Regular Season					Playoffs				
Season	Club	League	GP	G	A	Pts	PIM	GP	G	A	Pts	PIM
2007-08	St. Louis Bandits	NAHL	45	4	5	9	75	11	0	2	2	2
	USNTDP	U-17	3	0	0	0	0	....	....	....	....	....
2008-09	USNTDP	NAHL	14	1	4	5	12	....	....	....	....	....
	USNTDP	U-18	40	1	4	5	32	....	....	....	....	....
2009-10	U. of Wisconsin	WCHA	41	2	10	12	51	....	....	....	....	....
2010-11	U. of Wisconsin	WCHA	37	1	10	11	59	....	....	....	....	....
2011-12	U. of Wisconsin	WCHA	37	3	7	10	62	....	....	....	....	....
2012-13	U. of Wisconsin	WCHA	42	8	12	20	65	....	....	....	....	....

RANDELL, Tyler (RAN-duhl, TIGH-luhr) BOS

Right wing. Shoots right. 6'1", 197 lbs. Born, Scarborough, Ont., June 15, 1991.
(Boston's 4th choice, 176th overall, in 2009 Entry Draft).

			Regular Season					Playoffs				
Season	Club	League	GP	G	A	Pts	PIM	GP	G	A	Pts	PIM
2006-07	Brampton	Minor-ON	63	53	38	91	81	....	....	....	....	....
2007-08	Belleville Bulls	OHL	62	5	6	11	24	19	0	0	0	0
2008-09	Belleville Bulls	OHL	36	10	5	15	60	....	....	....	....	....
	Kitchener Rangers	OHL	37	14	8	22	39	....	....	....	....	....
2009-10	Kitchener Rangers	OHL	47	9	12	21	88	20	1	4	5	19
2010-11	Kitchener Rangers	OHL	68	20	12	32	160	7	0	0	0	7
2011-12	Kitchener Rangers	OHL	17	9	1	10	21	6	7	1	8	14
	Providence Bruins	AHL	30	2	0	2	45	....	....	....	....	....
2012-13	Providence Bruins	AHL	23	0	0	0	56	....	....	....	....	....
	South Carolina	ECHL	22	2	2	4	46	....	....	....	....	....

RANFORD, Brendan (RAN-fohrd, BREHN-duhn)

Left wing. Shoots left. 5'10", 186 lbs. Born, Edmonton, Alta., May 3, 1992.
(Philadelphia's 6th choice, 209th overall, in 2010 Entry Draft).

			Regular Season					Playoffs				
Season	Club	League	GP	G	A	Pts	PIM	GP	G	A	Pts	PIM
2007-08	Gregg Distributors	AMHL	35	*33	46	*79	58	12	10	5	15	6
	Kamloops Blazers	WHL	3	0	0	0	0	....	....	....	....	....
2008-09	Kamloops Blazers	WHL	66	13	14	27	46	4	0	3	3	2
2009-10	Kamloops Blazers	WHL	72	29	36	65	83	4	2	3	5	4
2010-11	Kamloops Blazers	WHL	68	33	53	86	68	....	....	....	....	....
2011-12	Kamloops Blazers	WHL	69	40	52	92	73	11	5	9	14	8
2012-13	Kamloops Blazers	WHL	70	22	65	87	28	15	5	15	20	0

WHL West Second All-Star Team (2011)

Signed as a free agent by **Texas** (AHL), May 24, 2013.

RASK, Victor (RASK, VIHK-tohr) CAR

Center. Shoots left. 6'2", 200 lbs. Born, Leksand, Sweden, March 1, 1993.
(Carolina's 2nd choice, 42nd overall, in 2011 Entry Draft).

			Regular Season					Playoffs				
Season	Club	League	GP	G	A	Pts	PIM	GP	G	A	Pts	PIM
2007-08	Leksands IF U18	Swe-U18	8	0	2	2	2	2	0	0	0	0
2008-09	Leksands IF U18	Swe-U18	26	9	6	15	8	....	....	....	....	....
2009-10	Leksands IF U18	Swe-U18	10	6	3	9	4	4	4	3	7	2
	Leksands IF Jr.	Swe-Jr.	39	22	19	41	35	5	3	2	5	2
	Leksands IF	Sweden-2	8	0	0	0	0	....	....	....	....	....
2010-11	Leksands IF U18	Swe-U18	4	4	4	8	0	6	3	2	5	6
	Leksands IF Jr.	Swe-Jr.	13	3	9	12	2	....	....	....	....	....
	Leksands IF	Sweden-2	37	5	6	11	8	....	....	....	....	....
2011-12	Calgary Hitmen	WHL	64	33	30	63	21	....	....	....	....	....
2012-13	Calgary Hitmen	WHL	37	14	27	41	16	17	6	10	16	10
	Charlotte	AHL	10	1	4	5	0	....	....	....	....	....

RATTIE, Ty (RA-tee, TIGH) ST.L.

Right wing. Shoots right. 6', 176 lbs. Born, Calgary, Alta., February 5, 1993.
(St. Louis' 1st choice, 32nd overall, in 2011 Entry Draft).

			Regular Season					Playoffs				
Season	Club	League	GP	G	A	Pts	PIM	GP	G	A	Pts	PIM
2007-08	Airdrie Xtreme	AMBHL	33	*75	56	*131	24	10	12	*11	*23	16
2008-09	UFA Bisons	AMHL	34	29	25	54	12	3	1	4	5	2
	Portland	WHL	10	1	0	1	0	....	....	....	....	....
	Brooks Bandits	AJHL	2	0	0	0	0	2	0	1	1	0
2009-10	Portland	WHL	61	17	20	37	38	13	2	2	4	12
2010-11	Portland	WHL	67	28	51	79	55	21	9	13	22	22
2011-12	Portland	WHL	69	57	64	121	54	21	19	14	33	12
2012-13	Portland	WHL	62	48	62	110	27	21	*20	16	*36	17

WHL West First All-Star Team (2012) • WHL West Second All-Star Team (2013) • Memorial Cup All-Star Team (2013)

RAU, Kyle (ROW, KIGHL) FLA

Center. Shoots left. 5'8", 172 lbs. Born, Hoffman Estates, IL, October 24, 1992.
(Florida's 7th choice, 91st overall, in 2011 Entry Draft).

			Regular Season					Playoffs				
Season	Club	League	GP	G	A	Pts	PIM	GP	G	A	Pts	PIM
2009-10	Eden Prairie Eagles	High-MN	25	38	39	77	12	3	2	2	4	0
2010-11	Team Southwest	UMHSEL	19	16	7	23	14	3	0	0	0	0
	Eden Prairie Eagles	High-MN	25	33	36	69	16	6	8	4	12	2
	Sioux Falls	USHL	11	4	6	10	15	10	*7	5	*12	4
2011-12	U. of Minnesota	WCHA	40	18	25	43	29	....	....	....	....	....
2012-13	U. of Minnesota	WCHA	40	15	25	40	22	....	....	....	....	....

WCHA All-Rookie Team (2012)

REID, Brodie (REED, BROH-dee) S.J.

Right wing. Shoots right. 6'1", 190 lbs. Born, Delta, B.C., August 25, 1989.

			Regular Season					Playoffs				
Season	Club	League	GP	G	A	Pts	PIM	GP	G	A	Pts	PIM
2005-06	Greater Van.	BCMML	33	16	22	38	36	....	....	....	....	....
	Surrey Eagles	BCHL	7	1	0	1	0	....	....	....	....	....
2006-07	Surrey Eagles	BCHL	50	4	6	10	17	4	0	0	0	0
2007-08	Burnaby Express	BCHL	60	*52	35	87	37	5	3	4	7	9
2008-09	Burnaby Express	BCHL	9	4	7	11	15	....	....	....	....	....
	Penticton Vees	BCHL	31	13	15	28	10	10	1	5	6	2
2009-10	Lincoln Stars	USHL	46	16	20	36	46	....	....	....	....	....
2010-11	Northeastern	H-East	37	11	17	28	18	....	....	....	....	....
2011-12	Worcester Sharks	AHL	66	10	15	25	17	....	....	....	....	....
2012-13	Worcester Sharks	AHL	34	10	11	21	19	....	....	....	....	....

Hockey East All-Rookie Team (2011)

Signed as a free agent by **San Jose**, April 15, 2011.

REID, Cam (REED, KAM)

Center. Shoots left. 6'2", 200 lbs. Born, Delta, B.C., August 25, 1991.
(Nashville's 10th choice, 192nd overall, in 2009 Entry Draft).

			Regular Season					Playoffs				
Season	Club	League	GP	G	A	Pts	PIM	GP	G	A	Pts	PIM
2007-08	Victoria Grizzlies	BCHL	55	10	16	26	25	11	2	3	5	4
2008-09	Victoria Grizzlies	BCHL	41	6	17	23	32	....	....	....	....	....
	Westside Warriors	BCHL	17	6	11	17	10	8	4	3	7	0
2009-10	Westside Warriors	BCHL	54	27	45	72	70	11	2	6	8	16
2010-11	St. Cloud State	WCHA	37	8	21	29	27	....	....	....	....	....
2011-12	St. Cloud State	WCHA	22	6	9	15	31	....	....	....	....	....
	Portland	WHL	31	13	19	32	14	22	5	6	11	32
2012-13	Peoria Rivermen	AHL	1	0	0	0	0	....	....	....	....	....
	Cincinnati	ECHL	11	2	6	8	6	....	....	....	....	....
	Milwaukee	AHL	54	3	16	19	13	3	0	0	0	0

REILLY, Mike (RIGH-lee, MIGHK) CBJ

Defense. Shoots left. 6'1", 170 lbs. Born, Chicago, IL, July 13, 1993.
(Columbus' 3rd choice, 98th overall, in 2011 Entry Draft).

			Regular Season					Playoffs				
Season	Club	League	GP	G	A	Pts	PIM	GP	G	A	Pts	PIM
2009-10	Holy Angels	High-MN	24	4	29	33	19	2	3	2	5	0
2010-11	Shat.-St. Mary's	High-MN	54	14	34	48	30	....	....	....	....	....
2011-12	Penticton Vees	BCHL	51	24	59	83	42	15	1	8	9	10
2012-13	U. of Minnesota	WCHA	37	3	11	14	14	....	....	....	....	....

REINHART, Griffin (RIGHN-hart, GRIHF-uhn) **NYI**

Defense. Shoots left. 6'4", 202 lbs. Born, North Vancouver, B.C., January 24, 1994.
(NY Islanders' 1st choice, 4th overall, in 2012 Entry Draft).

			Regular Season					Playoffs				
Season	Club	League	GP	G	A	Pts	PIM	GP	G	A	Pts	PIM
2008-09	Hollyburn Huskies	Minor-BC	STATISTICS NOT AVAILABLE									
	Van. NW Giants	BCMML	3	1	3	4	0	2	0	0	0	0
2009-10	Van. NW Giants	BCMML	32	9	25	34	24	5	3	5	8	14
	Edmonton	WHL	2	0	0	0	0	....	....	....	....	....
2010-11	Edmonton	WHL	45	6	19	25	36	4	0	0	0	6
2011-12	Edmonton	WHL	58	12	24	36	38	20	2	6	8	20
2012-13	Edmonton	WHL	59	8	21	29	35	12	3	4	7	12

RENSFELDT, Ludvig (REHNS-fehldt, LOOD-vihg) **CHI**

Left wing. Shoots left. 6'3", 192 lbs. Born, Gavle, Sweden, January 29, 1992.
(Chicago's 2nd choice, 35th overall, in 2010 Entry Draft).

			Regular Season					Playoffs				
Season	Club	League	GP	G	A	Pts	PIM	GP	G	A	Pts	PIM
2007-08	Brynas U18	Swe-U18	5	1	2	3	0	....	....	....	....	....
2008-09	Brynas U18	Swe-U18	31	13	23	36	14	3	0	1	1	0
	Brynas IF Gavle Jr.	Swe-Jr.	2	0	0	0	2	1	0	0	0	0
2009-10	Brynas U18	Swe-U18	6	5	7	12	16	4	3	5	8	0
	Brynas IF Gavle Jr.	Swe-Jr.	39	21	29	50	37	5	3	0	3	0
2010-11	Brynas IF Gavle Jr.	Swe-Jr.	26	17	19	36	12	1	0	0	0	0
	Bofors	Sweden-2	11	5	2	7	4	....	....	....	....	....
	Brynas IF Gavle	Sweden	16	0	1	1	0	5	0	0	0	2
2011-12	Sarnia Sting	OHL	58	22	21	43	18	6	2	3	5	2
2012-13	Malmo	Sweden-2	52	9	30	39	32	....	....	....	....	....

Signed as a free agent by **Malmo** (Sweden-2), June 6, 2012.

REWAY, Martin (rih-VIGH, MAR-tihn) **MTL**

Left wing. Shoots left. 5'8", 158 lbs. Born, Prague, Czech Republic, January 24, 1995.
(Montreal's 7th choice, 116th overall, in 2013 Entry Draft).

			Regular Season					Playoffs				
Season	Club	League	GP	G	A	Pts	PIM	GP	G	A	Pts	PIM
2008-09	Dolny Kubin U18	Svk-U18	13	8	12	20	10	....	....	....	....	....
	MHC Martin U18	Svk-U18	2	0	0	0	0	....	....	....	....	....
2009-10	Dolny Kubin U18	Svk-U18	26	32	38	70	24	....	....	....	....	....
2010-11	MHC Martin U18	Svk-U18	20	13	22	35	65	....	....	....	....	....
	MHC Martin Jr.	Slovak-Jr.	10	5	5	10	0	....	....	....	....	....
2011-12	Sparta U18	CzR-U18	25	21	39	60	42	9	8	16	24	12
	Sparta Jr.	CzRep-Jr.	5	2	4	6	2	....	....	....	....	....
2012-13	Gatineau	QMJHL	47	22	28	50	56	10	1	11	12	20

RICHARD, Tanner (Rih-SHARD, TA-nuhr) **T.B.**

Center. Shoots left. 5'11", 184 lbs. Born, Markham, Ont., April 6, 1993.
(Tampa Bay's 5th choice, 71st overall, in 2012 Entry Draft).

			Regular Season					Playoffs				
Season	Club	League	GP	G	A	Pts	PIM	GP	G	A	Pts	PIM
2010-11	Rapperswil	Swiss	4	0	0	0	0	4	0	1	1	0
2011-12	Guelph Storm	OHL	43	13	35	48	46	6	1	4	5	6
2012-13	Guelph Storm	OHL	52	11	51	62	94	5	0	3	3	6
	Syracuse Crunch	AHL	8	0	3	3	6	....	....	....	....	....

RIEDER, Tobias (REE-duhr, TOH-bee-uhs) **PHX**

Center. Shoots left. 5'11", 190 lbs. Born, Landshut, Germany, January 10, 1993.
(Edmonton's 7th choice, 114th overall, in 2011 Entry Draft).

			Regular Season					Playoffs				
Season	Club	League	GP	G	A	Pts	PIM	GP	G	A	Pts	PIM
2008-09	EV Landshut Jr.	Ger-Jr.	36	27	24	51	18	9	6	8	14	10
2009-10	EV Landshut Jr.	Ger-Jr.	5	6	3	9	25	4	5	1	6	2
	Landshut Cann.	German-2	45	10	13	23	28	6	0	0	0	0
2010-11	Kitchener Rangers	OHL	65	23	26	49	35	7	0	2	2	4
2011-12	Kitchener Rangers	OHL	60	42	43	85	25	16	13	14	27	4
2012-13	Kitchener Rangers	OHL	52	27	29	56	12	9	2	10	12	4

Traded to **Phoenix** by **Edmonton** for Kale Kessy, March 30, 2013.

RIELLY, Morgan (RIGH-lee, MOHR-guhn) **TOR**

Defense. Shoots left. 6'1", 205 lbs. Born, Vancouver, B.C., March 9, 1994.
(Toronto's 1st choice, 5th overall, in 2012 Entry Draft).

			Regular Season					Playoffs				
Season	Club	League	GP	G	A	Pts	PIM	GP	G	A	Pts	PIM
2008-09	Notre Dame	Minor-SK	43	41	43	84	10	....	....	....	....	....
2009-10	Notre Dame	SMHL	43	18	37	55	20	13	7	2	9	0
2010-11	Moose Jaw	WHL	65	6	22	28	21	6	0	6	6	0
2011-12	Moose Jaw	WHL	18	3	15	18	2	5	0	3	3	0
2012-13	Moose Jaw	WHL	60	12	42	54	19	....	....	....	....	....
	Toronto Marlies	AHL	14	1	2	3	0	8	1	0	1	0

WHL East First All-Star Team (2013)

• Missed majority of 2011-12 due to knee injury vs. Calgary (WHL), November 6, 2011.

RILEY, Blair (RIGH-lee, BLAIR)

Left wing. Shoots right. 6', 217 lbs. Born, Kamloops, B.C., November 1, 1985.

			Regular Season					Playoffs				
Season	Club	League	GP	G	A	Pts	PIM	GP	G	A	Pts	PIM
2002-03	Merritt	BCHL	19	9	4	13	17	....	....	....	....	....
2003-04	Merritt	BCHL	60	22	42	64	214	5	2	0	2	10
2004-05	Nanaimo Clippers	BCHL	61	41	26	67	91	13	6	9	15	45
2005-06	Nanaimo Clippers	BCHL	59	41	38	79	79	5	1	1	2	7
2006-07	Ferris State	CCHA	34	3	6	9	44	....	....	....	....	....
2007-08	Ferris State	CCHA	36	14	10	24	90	....	....	....	....	....
2008-09	Ferris State	CCHA	37	7	9	16	70	....	....	....	....	....
2009-10	Ferris State	CCHA	40	18	20	38	58	....	....	....	....	....
	Springfield Falcons	AHL	3	0	0	0	2	....	....	....	....	....
2010-11	San Antonio	AHL	4	1	0	1	0	....	....	....	....	....
	Peoria Rivermen	AHL	8	0	2	2	7	....	....	....	....	....
	Las Vegas	ECHL	59	20	20	40	114	5	4	1	5	0
2011-12	Chicago Express	ECHL	15	7	9	16	8	....	....	....	....	....
	Bridgeport	AHL	55	7	4	11	77	3	0	0	0	2
2012-13	Bridgeport	AHL	74	7	8	15	165	....	....	....	....	....

Signed as a free agent by **NY Islanders**, June 1, 2012. Signed as a free agent by **St. John's** (AHL), July 16, 2013.

RISSANEN, Rasmus (RIH-sa-nehn, RAS-mus) **CAR**

Defense. Shoots left. 6'3", 217 lbs. Born, Kuopio, Finland, July 13, 1991.
(Carolina's 5th choice, 178th overall, in 2009 Entry Draft).

			Regular Season					Playoffs				
Season	Club	League	GP	G	A	Pts	PIM	GP	G	A	Pts	PIM
2006-07	KalPa Kuopio U18	Fin-U18	9	1	1	2	28	3	0	1	1	8
2007-08	KalPa Kuopio U18	Fin-U18	29	7	9	16	99	2	0	0	0	8
	KalPa Kuopio Jr.	Fin-Jr.	5	0	0	0	10	....	....	....	....	....
2008-09	KalPa Kuopio Jr.	Fin-Jr.	29	1	8	9	56	4	0	1	1	6
2009-10	Everett Silvertips	WHL	71	4	11	15	103	7	0	1	1	8
2010-11	Everett Silvertips	WHL	68	1	11	12	89	4	2	0	2	8
	Charlotte	AHL	1	0	0	0	0	....	....	....	....	....
2011-12	Charlotte	AHL	64	3	3	6	57	....	....	....	....	....
2012-13	Charlotte	AHL	61	0	9	9	84	5	0	0	0	10

RISSLING, Jaynen (RIHZ-lihng, JAY-nehn) **WSH**

Defense. Shoots left. 6'4", 223 lbs. Born, Edmonton, Alta., September 21, 1993.
(Washington's 9th choice, 197th overall, in 2012 Entry Draft).

			Regular Season					Playoffs				
Season	Club	League	GP	G	A	Pts	PIM	GP	G	A	Pts	PIM
2007-08	CAC Lehigh	AMBHL	33	7	13	20	54	2	0	2	2	2
2008-09	CAC Gregg's Dist.	AMHL	33	3	11	14	68	5	0	0	0	22
2009-10	Calgary Hitmen	WHL	36	0	8	8	19	9	1	2	3	4
2010-11	Calgary Hitmen	WHL	67	5	16	21	95	....	....	....	....	....
2011-12	Calgary Hitmen	WHL	55	5	18	23	124	5	0	0	0	0
2012-13	Calgary Hitmen	WHL	61	5	23	28	122	17	0	6	6	18

RISTOLAINEN, Rasmus (rihs-toh-LIGH-nehn, RAZ-muhs) **BUF**

Defense. Shoots right. 6'4", 224 lbs. Born, Turku, Finland, October 27, 1994.
(Buffalo's 1st choice, 8th overall, in 2013 Entry Draft).

			Regular Season					Playoffs				
Season	Club	League	GP	G	A	Pts	PIM	GP	G	A	Pts	PIM
2009-10	TPS Turku U18	Fin-U18	32	3	7	10	28	3	1	0	1	4
	TPS Turku Jr.	Fin-Jr.	5	1	1	2	0	....	....	....	....	....
2010-11	TPS Turku U18	Fin-U18	2	1	2	3	0	13	5	3	8	8
	TPS Turku Jr.	Fin-Jr.	27	0	12	12	30	....	....	....	....	....
	TPS Turku	Finland	1	0	0	0	0	....	....	....	....	....
2011-12	TPS Turku Jr.	Fin-Jr.	8	0	4	4	6	....	....	....	....	....
	TPS Turku	Finland	40	3	5	8	78	2	0	0	0	0
2012-13	TPS Turku	Finland	52	3	12	15	32	....	....	....	....	....
	TPS Turku Jr.	Fin-Jr.	....	....	....	....	....	5	2	1	3	2

RITCHIE, Brett (RIH-chee, BREHT) **DAL**

Right wing. Shoots right. 6'3", 209 lbs. Born, Orangeville, Ont., July 1, 1993.
(Dallas' 2nd choice, 44th overall, in 2011 Entry Draft).

			Regular Season					Playoffs				
Season	Club	League	GP	G	A	Pts	PIM	GP	G	A	Pts	PIM
2008-09	Toronto Marlboros	GTHL	71	36	33	69	67	....	....	....	....	....
2009-10	Sarnia Sting	OHL	65	13	16	29	35	....	....	....	....	....
2010-11	Sarnia Sting	OHL	49	21	20	41	47	....	....	....	....	....
2011-12	Sarnia Sting	OHL	23	8	7	15	30	....	....	....	....	....
	Niagara Ice Dogs	OHL	30	16	14	30	24	20	3	8	11	14
2012-13	Niagara Ice Dogs	OHL	53	41	35	76	40	4	1	3	4	9
	Texas Stars	AHL	5	3	1	4	0	9	2	0	2	2

OHL Second All-Star Team (2013)

ROACH, Alex (ROHCH, AL-ehx) **L.A.**

Defense. Shoots left. 6'4", 227 lbs. Born, Quesnel, B.C., April 19, 1993.

			Regular Season					Playoffs				
Season	Club	League	GP	G	A	Pts	PIM	GP	G	A	Pts	PIM
2009-10	Cariboo Cougars	BCMML	40	6	15	21	68	4	0	2	2	16
	Quesnel	BCHL	4	0	0	0	2	....	....	....	....	....
2010-11	Calgary Hitmen	WHL	61	4	12	16	77	....	....	....	....	....
2011-12	Calgary Hitmen	WHL	61	4	14	18	78	5	1	2	3	2
2012-13	Calgary Hitmen	WHL	62	15	34	49	72	17	2	4	6	12

WHL East Second All-Star Team (2013)

Signed as a free agent by **Los Angeles**, September 26, 2011.

ROBERTSON, Dennis (RAW-buhrt-suhn, DEH-nihs) **TOR**

Defense. Shoots left. 6'1", 210 lbs. Born, Fort St. John, B.C., May 24, 1991.
(Toronto's 7th choice, 173rd overall, in 2011 Entry Draft).

			Regular Season					Playoffs				
Season	Club	League	GP	G	A	Pts	PIM	GP	G	A	Pts	PIM
2006-07	Okanagan Prep	Minor-BC	62	15	15	30	78	....	....	....	....	....
2007-08	Summerland Sting	KIJHL	50	9	18	27	66	4	2	1	3	12
2008-09	Langley Chiefs	BCHL	55	1	11	12	64	4	0	1	1	4
2009-10	Langley Chiefs	BCHL	53	9	25	34	83	10	2	2	4	14
2010-11	Brown U.	ECAC	30	6	11	17	48	....	....	....	....	....
2011-12	Brown U.	ECAC	32	2	14	16	72	....	....	....	....	....
2012-13	Brown U.	ECAC	36	3	17	20	69	....	....	....	....	....

ECAC All-Rookie Team (2011)

ROBINS, Bobby (RAW-bihns, BAW-bee) BOS

Right wing. Shoots right. 6'1", 220 lbs. Born, Peshtigo, WI, October 17, 1981.

			Regular Season					Playoffs				
Season	Club	League	GP	G	A	Pts	PIM	GP	G	A	Pts	PIM
2001-02	Tri-City Storm	USHL	60	16	14	30	176	....	....	....	....	....
2002-03	U. Mass-Lowell	H-East	26	5	3	8	24	....	....	....	....	....
2003-04	U. Mass-Lowell	H-East	32	5	7	12	49	....	....	....	....	....
2004-05	U. Mass-Lowell	H-East	34	9	9	18	86	....	....	....	....	....
2005-06	U. Mass-Lowell	H-East	35	13	18	31	*94	....	....	....	....	....
	Binghamton	AHL	16	4	3	7	19	....	....	....	....	....
2006-07	Binghamton	AHL	80	7	8	15	110	....	....	....	....	....
2007-08	Rochester	AHL	5	0	0	0	13	....	....	....	....	....
	Elmira Jackals	ECHL	68	18	17	35	151	6	2	3	5	8
	Albany River Rats	AHL	1	0	0	0	0	....	....	....	....	....
	Syracuse Crunch	AHL	1	0	0	0	2	....	....	....	....	....
2008-09	Belfast Giants	Britain	43	21	25	46	79	2	1	0	1	4
2009-10	HK Acroni Jesenice	Austria	34	3	4	7	178	....	....	....	....	....
	HK Acroni Jesenice	Slovenia	4	0	0	0	4	6	1	0	1	27
2010-11	Bakersfield	ECHL	46	14	13	27	186	4	0	1	1	11
2011-12	Chicago Express	ECHL	28	7	8	15	123	....	....	....	....	....
	Abbotsford Heat	AHL	2	0	0	0	0	....	....	....	....	....
	Providence Bruins	AHL	33	2	10	12	150	....	....	....	....	....
2012-13	Providence Bruins	AHL	74	4	7	11	316	12	1	1	2	69

Signed as a free agent by **Ottawa**, July 13, 2006. Signed to PTO (professional tryout) contract by **Abbotsford** (AHL), December 20, 2011. Signed to PTO (professional tryout) contract by **Providence** (AHL), December 28, 2011. Signed as a free agent by **Boston**, July 6, 2013.

ROBINSON, Buddy (RAW-bihn-suhn, BUH-dee) OTT

Right wing. Shoots right. 6'5", 236 lbs. Born, Bellmawr, NJ, September 30, 1991.

			Regular Season					Playoffs				
Season	Club	League	GP	G	A	Pts	PIM	GP	G	A	Pts	PIM
2009-10	Hamilton	ON-Jr.A	49	11	12	23	62	....	....	....	....	....
2010-11	Hamilton	ON-Jr.A	32	15	23	38	39	....	....	....	....	....
	Nepean Raiders	ON-Jr.A	19	5	19	24	20	....	....	....	....	....
2011-12	Lake Superior	CCHA	39	5	5	10	37	....	....	....	....	....
2012-13	Lake Superior	CCHA	38	8	8	16	48	....	....	....	....	....
	Binghamton	AHL	6	2	2	4	8	2	0	0	0	0

Signed as a free agent by **Ottawa**, March 25, 2013.

RODWELL, Derek (RAWD-wehl, DAIR-ihk) N.J.

Left wing. Shoots right. 6'2", 200 lbs. Born, Taber, Alta., July 8, 1990.
(New Jersey's 5th choice, 144th overall, in 2009 Entry Draft).

			Regular Season					Playoffs				
Season	Club	League	GP	G	A	Pts	PIM	GP	G	A	Pts	PIM
2007-08	Okotoks Oilers	AJHL	62	9	10	19	69	9	0	3	3	6
2008-09	Okotoks Oilers	AJHL	41	17	12	29	69	9	1	2	3	6
2009-10	Okotoks Oilers	AJHL	55	18	35	53	38	11	6	3	9	20
2010-11	North Dakota	WCHA	39	5	4	9	20	....	....	....	....	....
2011-12	North Dakota	WCHA	19	1	1	2	2	....	....	....	....	....
2012-13	North Dakota	WCHA	32	2	1	3	34	....	....	....	....	....

ROE, Garrett (ROH, GAIR-eht)

Left wing. Shoots left. 5'8", 162 lbs. Born, Vienna, VA, February 22, 1988.
(Los Angeles' 9th choice, 183rd overall, in 2008 Entry Draft).

			Regular Season					Playoffs				
Season	Club	League	GP	G	A	Pts	PIM	GP	G	A	Pts	PIM
2004-05	Indiana Ice	USHL	49	6	15	21	62	3	0	3	3	4
2005-06	Indiana Ice	USHL	49	21	32	53	93	2	3	0	3	0
2006-07	Indiana Ice	USHL	57	24	39	63	143	6	3	10	13	8
2007-08	St. Cloud State	WCHA	39	18	27	45	55	....	....	....	....	....
2008-09	St. Cloud State	WCHA	38	17	31	48	72	....	....	....	....	....
2009-10	St. Cloud State	WCHA	41	20	29	49	65	....	....	....	....	....
2010-11	St. Cloud State	WCHA	38	10	26	36	48	....	....	....	....	....
2011-12	Adirondack	AHL	72	8	32	40	44	....	....	....	....	....
2012-13	Adirondack	AHL	57	12	14	26	41	....	....	....	....	....

WCHA All-Rookie Team (2008)

Signed as a free agent by **Adirondack** (AHL), July 3, 2011. Signed as a free agent by **Salzburg** (Austria), July 15, 2013.

ROSS, Brad (RAWS, BRAD) TOR

Left wing. Shoots left. 6'1", 183 lbs. Born, Lethbridge, Alta., May 28, 1992.
(Toronto's 1st choice, 43rd overall, in 2010 Entry Draft).

			Regular Season					Playoffs				
Season	Club	League	GP	G	A	Pts	PIM	GP	G	A	Pts	PIM
2007-08	Lethbridge	AMHL	35	10	14	24	82	6	6	5	11	22
	Portland	WHL	3	0	0	0	0	....	....	....	....	....
2008-09	Portland	WHL	61	9	17	26	119	....	....	....	....	....
2009-10	Portland	WHL	71	27	41	68	*203	13	2	7	9	36
2010-11	Portland	WHL	67	31	38	69	171	16	4	2	6	33
2011-12	Portland	WHL	68	42	40	82	163	22	12	10	22	57
2012-13	Toronto Marlies	AHL	40	8	3	11	29	7	0	1	1	6
	Idaho Steelheads	ECHL	5	1	2	3	2	....	....	....	....	....

ROSS, Garret (RAWS, GAIR-eht) CHI

Left wing. Shoots left. 6', 180 lbs. Born, Dearborn Heights, MI, May 26, 1992.
(Chicago's 4th choice, 139th overall, in 2012 Entry Draft).

			Regular Season					Playoffs				
Season	Club	League	GP	G	A	Pts	PIM	GP	G	A	Pts	PIM
2007-08	Det. Honda U-18	MWEHL	16	18	8	26	6	....	....	....	....	....
	Det. Belle Tire U-16	MWEHL	30	7	13	20	32	....	....	....	....	....
	Det. Belle Tire U-16	Exhib.	4	1	1	2	6	....	....	....	....	....
2008-09	Det. Vic. Honda	T1EHL	46	28	28	56	40	4	2	3	5	0
2009-10	Saginaw Spirit	OHL	43	7	4	11	103	6	0	0	0	12
2010-11	Saginaw Spirit	OHL	53	6	9	15	111	12	3	1	4	8
2011-12	Saginaw Spirit	OHL	60	25	29	54	93	12	6	4	10	23
2012-13	Saginaw Spirit	OHL	61	44	46	90	114	4	0	3	3	8
	Rockford IceHogs	AHL	2	0	0	0	5	....	....	....	....	....

OHL Second All-Star Team (2013)

ROUSSEL, Charles-Olivier (roo-SEHL, CHAR-uhlz-OH-lihv-ee-ay) NSH

Defense. Shoots right. 6'1", 205 lbs. Born, St. Eustache, Que., September 13, 1991.
(Nashville's 3rd choice, 42nd overall, in 2009 Entry Draft).

			Regular Season					Playoffs				
Season	Club	League	GP	G	A	Pts	PIM	GP	G	A	Pts	PIM
2006-07	Laurentides	QAAA	44	8	24	32	90	15	2	9	11	24
2007-08	Shawinigan	QMJHL	50	3	13	16	28	5	1	2	3	2
2008-09	Shawinigan	QMJHL	68	11	33	44	77	21	5	13	18	14
2009-10	Shawinigan	QMJHL	64	15	36	51	70	6	0	1	1	4
2010-11	Montreal	QMJHL	59	5	25	30	46	10	1	3	4	10
2011-12	Saint John	QMJHL	58	13	27	40	65	17	3	12	15	23
2012-13	Milwaukee	AHL	17	0	1	1	15	....	....	....	....	....
	Cincinnati	ECHL	40	6	11	17	42	17	1	4	5	12

QMJHL Second All-Star Team (2009)

ROY, Eric (ROI, AIR-ihk) CGY

Defense. Shoots left. 6'3", 180 lbs. Born, Meadow Lake, Sask., October 24, 1994.
(Calgary's 5th choice, 135th overall, in 2013 Entry Draft).

			Regular Season					Playoffs				
Season	Club	League	GP	G	A	Pts	PIM	GP	G	A	Pts	PIM
2009-10	Prince Albert	SMHL	40	9	25	34	30	8	5	3	8	8
2010-11	Brandon	WHL	49	4	15	19	15	6	0	3	3	0
2011-12	Brandon	WHL	69	11	42	53	55	9	1	2	3	9
2012-13	Brandon	WHL	72	17	22	39	37	....	....	....	....	....

ROY, Kevin (ROY, KEH-vihn) ANA

Center. Shoots left. 5'9", 174 lbs. Born, Greenfield Park, Que., May 20, 1993.
(Anaheim's 4th choice, 97th overall, in 2012 Entry Draft).

			Regular Season					Playoffs				
Season	Club	League	GP	G	A	Pts	PIM	GP	G	A	Pts	PIM
2009-10	Deerfield Academy	High-MA	27	12	16	28	....	....	....	....	....	....
2010-11	Deerfield Academy	High-MA	18	19	15	34	6	....	....	....	....	....
2011-12	Lincoln Stars	USHL	59	54	50	104	50	8	7	3	10	4
2012-13	Northeastern	H-East	29	17	17	34	24	....	....	....	....	....

USHL All-Rookie Team (2012) • USHL First All-Star Team (2012) • USHL Player of the Year (2012) • Hockey East All-Rookie Team (2013)

ROY, Marc-Olivier (WAH, MAHRK-oh-LIHV-y'ay) EDM

Center. Shoots left. 6', 175 lbs. Born, Ste-Foy, Que., November 5, 1994.
(Edmonton's 2nd choice, 56th overall, in 2013 Entry Draft).

			Regular Season					Playoffs				
Season	Club	League	GP	G	A	Pts	PIM	GP	G	A	Pts	PIM
2009-10	Saint-Eustache	QAAA	42	9	14	23	6	6	1	4	5	2
2010-11	Saint-Eustache	QAAA	38	22	25	47	67	10	11	14	25	10
	Montreal	QMJHL	3	0	1	1	0	....	....	....	....	....
2011-12	Blainville-Bois.	QMJHL	63	17	22	39	29	11	6	8	14	14
2012-13	Blainville-Bois.	QMJHL	65	29	38	67	68	15	6	13	19	10

RUOPP, Harrison (ROO-awp, HAIR-ih-suhn) PIT

Defense. Shoots right. 6'3", 205 lbs. Born, Zehner, Sask., March 17, 1993.
(Phoenix's 4th choice, 84th overall, in 2011 Entry Draft).

			Regular Season					Playoffs				
Season	Club	League	GP	G	A	Pts	PIM	GP	G	A	Pts	PIM
2007-08	Balgonie	Minor-SK	26	9	11	20	37	7	0	3	3	4
2008-09	Reg. Pat Cdns.	SMHL	36	0	1	1	46	5	0	1	1	4
2009-10	Prince Albert	WHL	33	0	0	0	38	....	....	....	....	....
2010-11	Prince Albert	WHL	54	0	9	9	98	6	0	0	0	9
2011-12	Prince Albert	WHL	62	2	7	9	127	....	....	....	....	....
2012-13	Prince Albert	WHL	65	1	15	16	132	4	0	0	0	4

Traded to **Pittsburgh** by **Phoenix** with Marc Cheverie and Philadelphia's 3rd round choice (previously acquired, Pittsburgh selected Oskar Sundqvist) in 2012 Entry Draft for Zbynek Michalek, June 22, 2012.

RUPERT, Ryan (ROO-puhrt, RIGH-uhn) TOR

Center. Shoots left. 5'9", 186 lbs. Born, Grand Bend, Ont., June 2, 1994.
(Toronto's 5th choice, 157th overall, in 2012 Entry Draft).

			Regular Season					Playoffs				
Season	Club	League	GP	G	A	Pts	PIM	GP	G	A	Pts	PIM
2008-09	Lambton Jr. Sting	Minor-ON	27	21	20	41	53	11	3	3	6	14
2009-10	Elgin-Mid. Chiefs	Minor-ON	30	22	27	49	40	15	11	10	21	22
	Elgin-Mid. Chiefs	Exhib.	11	3	11	14	38	....	....	....	....	....
	Lambton Shores	ON-Jr.B	4	0	2	2	12	....	....	....	....	....
2010-11	Lambton Shores	ON-Jr.B	25	15	21	36	107	....	....	....	....	....
	London Knights	OHL	39	9	18	27	30	6	2	1	3	6
2011-12	London Knights	OHL	63	17	31	48	120	19	9	6	15	31
2012-13	London Knights	OHL	54	11	35	46	75	21	11	9	20	12

RUSSO, Robbie (ROO-soh, RAW-bee) NYI

Defense. Shoots right. 6', 189 lbs. Born, Westmount, IL, February 15, 1993.
(NY Islanders' 5th choice, 95th overall, in 2011 Entry Draft).

			Regular Season					Playoffs				
Season	Club	League	GP	G	A	Pts	PIM	GP	G	A	Pts	PIM
2008-09	Chicago Mission	T1EHL	46	5	17	22	10	....	....	....	....	....
	Chicago Mission	Exhib.	....	5	3	8	10	....	....	....	....	....
2009-10	USNTDP	USHL	34	3	17	20	36	....	....	....	....	....
	USNTDP	U-17	18	4	7	11	22	....	....	....	....	....
2010-11	USNTDP	USHL	24	0	6	6	11	....	....	....	....	....
	USNTDP	U-18	36	4	20	24	16	....	....	....	....	....
2011-12	U. of Notre Dame	CCHA	40	4	11	15	14	....	....	....	....	....
2012-13	U. of Notre Dame	CCHA	41	5	18	23	40	....	....	....	....	....

CCHA All-Rookie Team (2012)

RUST, Bryan (RUHST, BRIGH-uhn) **PIT**

Right wing. Shoots right. 6', 191 lbs. Born, Pontiac, MI, May 11, 1992.
(Pittsburgh's 2nd choice, 80th overall, in 2010 Entry Draft).

			Regular Season					Playoffs				
Season	Club	League	GP	G	A	Pts	PIM	GP	G	A	Pts	PIM
2007-08	Det. Honeybaked	MWEHL	31	17	28	45	6	....	....	....	....	....
	Det. Honeybaked	Minor-MI	37	27	20	47	....	....	....	....	....	....
2008-09	USNTDP	NAHL	42	6	9	15	18	9	0	2	2	4
	USNTDP	U-17	16	3	2	5	4	....	....	....	....	....
2009-10	USNTDP	USHL	27	10	13	23	6	....	....	....	....	....
	USNTDP	U-17	1	0	0	0	0	....	....	....	....	....
	USNTDP	U-18	38	16	13	29	18	....	....	....	....	....
2010-11	U. of Notre Dame	CCHA	40	6	13	19	4	....	....	....	....	....
2011-12	U. of Notre Dame	CCHA	40	5	6	11	14	....	....	....	....	....
2012-13	U. of Notre Dame	CCHA	41	15	19	34	4	....	....	....	....	....

RUTKOWSKI, Troy (ruht-KOW-skee, TROI) **OTT**

Defense. Shoots right. 6'2", 195 lbs. Born, Edmonton, Alta., April 29, 1992.
(Colorado's 6th choice, 137th overall, in 2010 Entry Draft).

			Regular Season					Playoffs				
Season	Club	League	GP	G	A	Pts	PIM	GP	G	A	Pts	PIM
2007-08	SSAC Athletics	AMHL	36	6	16	22	28	....	....	....	....	....
2008-09	Portland	WHL	64	6	9	15	34	....	....	....	....	....
2009-10	Portland	WHL	71	12	31	43	70	13	4	3	7	8
2010-11	Portland	WHL	72	10	37	47	65	21	4	9	13	16
2011-12	Portland	WHL	72	13	32	45	37	22	1	9	10	10
2012-13	Portland	WHL	72	20	46	66	43	21	4	10	14	14

WHL West Second All-Star Team (2013)

Signed as a free agent by **Ottawa**, March 14, 2013.

RYAN, Ben (RIGH-uhn, BEHN)

Center. Shoots right. 5'11", 193 lbs. Born, Detroit, MI, October 16, 1988.
(Nashville's 5th choice, 114th overall, in 2007 Entry Draft).

			Regular Season					Playoffs				
Season	Club	League	GP	G	A	Pts	PIM	GP	G	A	Pts	PIM
2005-06	Des Moines	USHL	60	14	23	37	38	11	4	1	5	4
2006-07	Des Moines	USHL	59	22	42	64	66	8	3	5	8	8
2007-08	U. of Notre Dame	CCHA	47	10	16	26	22	....	....	....	....	....
2008-09	U. of Notre Dame	CCHA	39	12	15	27	30	....	....	....	....	....
2009-10	U. of Notre Dame	CCHA	29	7	12	19	24	....	....	....	....	....
2010-11	U. of Notre Dame	CCHA	44	6	19	25	37	....	....	....	....	....
	Milwaukee	AHL	2	0	1	1	0	6	0	0	0	2
2011-12	Milwaukee	AHL	23	3	3	6	6	2	0	0	0	0
	Cincinnati	ECHL	7	2	2	4	0	....	....	....	....	....
2012-13	Milwaukee	AHL	36	1	3	4	16	....	....	....	....	....

RYAN, Joakim (RIGHN, YOH-ah-kihm) **S.J.**

Defense. Shoots left. 5'11", 185 lbs. Born, Rumson, NJ, June 17, 1993.
(San Jose's 6th choice, 198th overall, in 2012 Entry Draft).

			Regular Season					Playoffs				
Season	Club	League	GP	G	A	Pts	PIM	GP	G	A	Pts	PIM
2009-10	N.J. Devils Youth	AYHL	32	13	23	36	34	....	....	....	....	....
2010-11	Dubuque	USHL	53	3	29	32	26	11	2	3	5	2
2011-12	Cornell Big Red	ECAC	34	7	10	17	20	....	....	....	....	....
2012-13	Cornell Big Red	ECAC	34	3	20	23	12	....	....	....	....	....

RYAN, Kenny (RIGH-uhn, KEHN-nee) **TOR**

Right wing. Shoots right. 6', 200 lbs. Born, Franklin Village, MI, July 10, 1991.
(Toronto's 2nd choice, 50th overall, in 2009 Entry Draft).

			Regular Season					Playoffs				
Season	Club	League	GP	G	A	Pts	PIM	GP	G	A	Pts	PIM
2006-07	Det. Honeybaked	MWEHL	31	16	17	33	34	....	....	....	....	....
	Det. Honeybaked	Exhib.	34	17	24	41	....	....	....	....	....	....
2007-08	USNTDP	NAHL	36	10	8	18	53	....	....	....	....	....
	USNTDP	U-17	13	0	5	5	12	....	....	....	....	....
2008-09	USNTDP	NAHL	16	4	9	13	12	....	....	....	....	....
	USNTDP	U-18	46	23	13	36	38	....	....	....	....	....
2009-10	Windsor Spitfires	OHL	52	14	21	35	33	19	3	2	5	14
2010-11	Windsor Spitfires	OHL	63	21	37	58	42	18	4	8	12	25
2011-12	Toronto Marlies	AHL	16	1	0	1	9	....	....	....	....	....
	Reading Royals	ECHL	32	13	10	23	18	5	3	2	5	27
2012-13	Toronto Marlies	AHL	59	9	12	21	38	9	0	0	0	13

RYCHEL, Kerby (RIGH-kuhl, KUHR-bee) **CBJ**

Left wing. Shoots left. 6'1", 205 lbs. Born, Torrance, CA, October 7, 1994.
(Columbus' 2nd choice, 19th overall, in 2013 Entry Draft).

			Regular Season					Playoffs				
Season	Club	League	GP	G	A	Pts	PIM	GP	G	A	Pts	PIM
2008-09	Sun County	Minor-ON	26	11	17	28	24	12	8	5	13	2
2009-10	Detroit Belle Tire	T1EHL	29	13	10	23	29	....	....	....	....	....
	Detroit Belle Tire	Exhib.	26	17	9	26	29	....	....	....	....	....
2010-11	St. Michael's	OHL	30	2	6	8	47	....	....	....	....	....
	Windsor Spitfires	OHL	32	5	8	13	26	18	2	4	6	14
2011-12	Windsor Spitfires	OHL	68	41	33	74	54	4	2	0	2	5
2012-13	Windsor Spitfires	OHL	68	40	47	87	94	....	....	....	....	....

SAARI, Santeri (sah-AH-RI, SAHN-tair-ee) **ST.L.**

Defense. Shoots left. 6'1", 191 lbs. Born, Helsinki, Finland, October 18, 1994.
(St. Louis' 4th choice, 173rd overall, in 2013 Entry Draft).

			Regular Season					Playoffs				
Season	Club	League	GP	G	A	Pts	PIM	GP	G	A	Pts	PIM
2009-10	Jokerit U18	Fin-U18	1	0	0	0	0	....	....	....	....	....
2010-11	Jokerit U18	Fin-U18	14	0	1	1	24	9	0	2	2	4
	Jokerit Helsinki Jr.	Fin-Jr.	3	0	0	0	2	....	....	....	....	....
2011-12	Jokerit U18	Fin-U18	33	7	17	24	48	11	3	2	5	2
	Jokerit Helsinki Jr.	Fin-Jr.	13	2	2	4	10	....	....	....	....	....
2012-13	Jokerit Helsinki Jr.	Fin-Jr.	46	5	18	23	34	....	....	....	....	....
	Jokerit Helsinki	Finland	2	0	0	0	0	....	....	....	....	....
	Kiekko-Vantaa	Finland-2	7	0	0	0	6	....	....	....	....	....

ST. CROIX, Michael (SAYNT KR'WAH, MIGH-kuhl) **NYR**

Center. Shoots right. 5'11", 179 lbs. Born, Winnipeg, MB, April 10, 1993.
(NY Rangers' 3rd choice, 106th overall, in 2011 Entry Draft).

			Regular Season					Playoffs				
Season	Club	League	GP	G	A	Pts	PIM	GP	G	A	Pts	PIM
2008-09	Winnipeg Wild	MMHL	41	*56	47	*103	10	9	8	12	20	4
	Edmonton	WHL	2	1	1	2	0	....	....	....	....	....
2009-10	Edmonton	WHL	66	18	28	46	30	....	....	....	....	....
2010-11	Edmonton	WHL	68	27	48	75	48	4	1	0	1	9
2011-12	Edmonton	WHL	72	45	60	105	49	20	7	12	19	6
2012-13	Edmonton	WHL	72	37	55	92	36	22	13	13	26	14

WHL East Second All-Star Team (2012) • WHL East First All-Star Team (2013)

SALMINEN, Saku (SAL-mih-nehn, SA-koo) **T.B.**

Center. Shoots left. 6'3", 202 lbs. Born, Helsinki, Finland, October 20, 1994.
(Tampa Bay's 5th choice, 184th overall, in 2013 Entry Draft).

			Regular Season					Playoffs				
Season	Club	League	GP	G	A	Pts	PIM	GP	G	A	Pts	PIM
2009-10	HIFK Helsinki U18	Fin-U18	25	8	10	18	22	11	4	1	5	2
2010-11	HIFK Helsinki U18	Fin-U18	16	7	9	16	30	4	0	1	1	6
	HIFK Helsinki Jr.	Fin-Jr.	13	2	2	4	2	....	....	....	....	....
2011-12	Jokerit U18	Fin-U18	2	1	1	2	2	2	0	0	0	2
	Jokerit Helsinki Jr.	Fin-Jr.	44	9	17	26	16	12	0	1	1	2
2012-13	Jokerit Helsinki Jr.	Fin-Jr.	4	1	2	3	2	....	....	....	....	....
	Jokerit Helsinki	Finland	13	1	1	2	12	....	....	....	....	....
	Kiekko-Vantaa	Finland-2	12	1	4	5	0	4	1	5	6	2

SALOMAKI, Miikka (sa-loh-MYA-kee, MEEKA) **NSH**

Right wing. Shoots left. 5'11", 203 lbs. Born, Raahe, Finland, March 9, 1993.
(Nashville's 2nd choice, 52nd overall, in 2011 Entry Draft).

			Regular Season					Playoffs				
Season	Club	League	GP	G	A	Pts	PIM	GP	G	A	Pts	PIM
2008-09	Laser HT U18	Fin-U18	23	13	30	43	71	....	....	....	....	....
2009-10	Karpat Oulu U18	Fin-U18	3	4	2	6	4	....	....	....	....	....
	Karpat Oulu Jr.	Fin-Jr.	37	18	25	43	93	....	....	....	....	....
2010-11	Suomi U20	Finland-2	3	1	1	2	27	....	....	....	....	....
	Karpat Oulu	Finland	40	4	6	10	53	3	0	1	1	27
	Karpat Oulu U18	Fin-U18	....	....	....	....	....	2	0	1	1	2
2011-12	Karpat Oulu	Finland	40	12	9	21	56	7	1	0	1	56
2012-13	Karpat Oulu	Finland	42	9	10	19	44	3	2	0	2	14

SAMUELSSON, Henrik (SAM-yuhl-suhn, HEHN-rihk) **PHX**

Center/Right wing. Shoots right. 6'3", 211 lbs. Born, Pittsburgh, PA, February 7, 1994.
(Phoenix's 1st choice, 27th overall, in 2012 Entry Draft).

			Regular Season					Playoffs				
Season	Club	League	GP	G	A	Pts	PIM	GP	G	A	Pts	PIM
2009-10	P.F. Chang's	T1EHL	37	12	23	35	73	....	....	....	....	....
	P.F. Chang's	Exhib.	11	15	13	28	....	....	....	....	....	....
	P.F. Chang's U18	T1EHL	8	2	6	8	25	....	....	....	....	....
2010-11	USNTDP	USHL	27	4	7	11	78	....	....	....	....	....
	USNTDP	U-17	17	8	10	18	24	....	....	....	....	....
	USNTDP	U-18	10	3	3	6	10	....	....	....	....	....
2011-12	MODO U18	Swe-U18	3	4	1	5	8	....	....	....	....	....
	MODO Jr.	Swe-Jr.	16	4	5	9	22	....	....	....	....	....
	MODO	Sweden	15	0	2	2	12	....	....	....	....	....
	Edmonton	WHL	28	7	16	23	42	17	4	10	14	20
2012-13	Edmonton	WHL	69	33	47	80	97	22	11	8	19	*43

Memorial Cup All-Star Team (2012)

SAMUELSSON, Philip (SAM-yuhl-suhn, FIHL-ihp) **PIT**

Defense. Shoots left. 6'2", 194 lbs. Born, Leksand, Sweden, July 26, 1991.
(Pittsburgh's 2nd choice, 61st overall, in 2009 Entry Draft).

			Regular Season					Playoffs				
Season	Club	League	GP	G	A	Pts	PIM	GP	G	A	Pts	PIM
2006-07	P.F. Chang's	Minor-AZ	54	9	31	40	70	....	....	....	....	....
2007-08	P.F. Chang's	Minor-AZ	41	8	25	33	48	....	....	....	....	....
2008-09	Chicago Steel	USHL	54	0	22	22	60	....	....	....	....	....
	USNTDP	U-18	4	0	0	0	6	....	....	....	....	....
2010-11	Boston College	H-East	39	4	12	16	72	....	....	....	....	....
2011-12	Wilkes-Barre	AHL	46	1	8	9	26	10	0	1	1	18
	Wheeling Nailers	ECHL	5	0	1	1	11	3	1	0	1	0
2012-13	Wilkes-Barre	AHL	65	2	8	10	70	15	0	2	2	8

SAMUELS-THOMAS, Jordan (SAM-yewlz-TAW-muhs, JOHR-dahn) **WPG**

Left wing. Shoots left. 6'3", 198 lbs. Born, Hartford, CT, May 28, 1990.
(Atlanta's 9th choice, 203rd overall, in 2009 Entry Draft).

			Regular Season					Playoffs				
Season	Club	League	GP	G	A	Pts	PIM	GP	G	A	Pts	PIM
2006-07	Hartford	AtJHL	43	21	37	58	44	....	....	....	....	....
2007-08	Waterloo	USHL	56	8	3	11	65	11	0	2	2	10
2008-09	Waterloo	USHL	59	32	22	54	59	3	2	1	3	2
2009-10	Bowling Green	CCHA	35	11	14	25	30	....	....	....	....	....
2010-11	Bowling Green	CCHA	36	9	12	21	46	....	....	....	....	....
2011-12	Quinnipiac	ECAC	DID NOT PLAY – TRANSFERRED COLLEGES									
2012-13	Quinnipiac	ECAC	43	17	12	29	40	....	....	....	....	....

NCAA Championship All-Tournament Team (2013)

• Transferred to **Winnipeg** after **Atlanta** franchise relocated, June 21, 2011.

SANFORD, Zachary (SAN-fohrd, za-KAH-ree) **WSH**

Left wing. Shoots left. 6'3", 185 lbs. Born, Salem, MA, November 9, 1994.
(Washington's 3rd choice, 61st overall, in 2013 Entry Draft).

			Regular Season					Playoffs				
Season	Club	League	GP	G	A	Pts	PIM	GP	G	A	Pts	PIM
2011-12	Pinkerton	High-NH	21	36	33	69	40	....	....	....	....	....
2012-13	Islanders H.C.	EJHL	37	12	24	36	22	7	4	4	8	8

• Signed Letter of Intent to attend **Boston College** (Hockey East) in fall of 2014.

SANTINI, Steven (san-TEE-nee, STEE-vehn) N.J.

Defense. Shoots right. 6'2", 205 lbs. Born, Bronxville, NY, March 7, 1995.
(New Jersey's 1st choice, 42nd overall, in 2013 Entry Draft).

			Regular Season					Playoffs				
Season	Club	League	GP	G	A	Pts	PIM	GP	G	A	Pts	PIM
2010-11	NY Apple Core	EJHL	44	3	14	17	26	5	0	1	1	0
2011-12	USNTDP	USHL	36	1	4	5	41	2	0	1	1	0
	USNTDP	U-17	17	1	3	4	28	....	....	....	....	....
2012-13	USNTDP	USHL	25	0	5	5	6	....	....	....	....	....
	USNTDP	U-18	41	0	10	10	38	....	....	....	....	....

• Signed Letter of Intent to attend **Boston College** (Hockey East) in fall of 2013.

SAPONARI, Vinny (sa-pawn-AIR-ee, VIH-nee)

Right wing. Shoots right. 6', 197 lbs. Born, Powder Springs, GA, February 15, 1990.
(Atlanta's 4th choice, 94th overall, in 2008 Entry Draft).

			Regular Season					Playoffs				
Season	Club	League	GP	G	A	Pts	PIM	GP	G	A	Pts	PIM
2006-07	USNTDP	U-17	4	11	6	17	....	....	....	....	....	....
	USNTDP	U-18	21	4	3	7	6	....	....	....	....	....
	USNTDP	NAHL	35	9	10	19	43	....	....	....	....	....
2007-08	USNTDP	U-18	42	12	16	28	42	....	....	....	....	....
	USNTDP	NAHL	15	1	7	8	0	....	....	....	....	....
2008-09	Boston University	H-East	44	8	9	17	39	....	....	....	....	....
2009-10	Boston University	H-East	38	12	18	30	32	....	....	....	....	....
2010-11	Dubuque	USHL	56	18	46	64	35	11	5	4	9	6
2011-12	Northeastern	H-East	34	7	16	23	14	....	....	....	....	....
2012-13	Northeastern	H-East	34	7	22	29	24	....	....	....	....	....
	St. John's IceCaps	AHL	7	1	1	2	0	....	....	....	....	....

USHL Second All-Star Team (2011)

• Transferred to **Winnipeg** after **Atlanta** franchise relocated, June 21, 2011.

SARAULT, Charles (sah-ROH, CHAR-uhlz) ANA

Center. Shoots left. 5'11", 188 lbs. Born, Ottawa, Ont., February 20, 1992.

			Regular Season					Playoffs				
Season	Club	League	GP	G	A	Pts	PIM	GP	G	A	Pts	PIM
2008-09	Kingston	OHL	68	2	7	9	22	....	....	....	....	....
2009-10	Kingston	OHL	62	4	12	16	31	6	1	3	4	4
2010-11	Kingston	OHL	68	13	25	38	32	5	1	1	2	0
2011-12	Sarnia Sting	OHL	68	20	67	87	32	6	0	4	4	4
2012-13	Sarnia Sting	OHL	68	22	*86	108	28	4	1	3	4	4
	Norfolk Admirals	AHL	11	0	6	6	0	....	....	....	....	....

OHL Second All-Star Team (2013)

Signed as a free agent by **Anaheim**, March 5, 2013.

SCARLETT, Reece (SKAR-leht, REES) N.J.

Defense. Shoots right. 6'1", 175 lbs. Born, Edmonton, Alta., March 31, 1993.
(New Jersey's 6th choice, 159th overall, in 2011 Entry Draft).

			Regular Season					Playoffs				
Season	Club	League	GP	G	A	Pts	PIM	GP	G	A	Pts	PIM
2007-08	Sherwood Park	AMBHL	33	14	16	30	48	12	4	5	9	26
	Sherwood Park	Minor-AB	3	1	0	1	4	....	....	....	....	....
2008-09	Sherwood Park	AMHL	34	4	13	17	60	11	2	6	8	4
	Swift Current	WHL	1	0	0	0	0	....	....	....	....	....
2009-10	Swift Current	WHL	65	1	9	10	49	4	0	2	2	4
2010-11	Swift Current	WHL	72	6	18	24	59	....	....	....	....	....
2011-12	Swift Current	WHL	71	9	40	49	74	....	....	....	....	....
2012-13	Swift Current	WHL	67	9	40	49	66	5	0	3	3	10

SCHALLER, Tim (SHAL-uhr, TIHM) BUF

Left wing. Shoots left. 6'2", 213 lbs. Born, Merrimack, NH, November 16, 1990.

			Regular Season					Playoffs				
Season	Club	League	GP	G	A	Pts	PIM	GP	G	A	Pts	PIM
2007-08	N.E. Jr. Huskies	EJHL	44	8	25	33	29	....	....	....	....	....
2008-09	Islanders H.C.	EJHL	45	16	23	39	54	2	0	1	1	0
2009-10	Providence College	H-East	33	2	3	5	40	....	....	....	....	....
2010-11	Providence College	H-East	34	5	14	19	36	....	....	....	....	....
2011-12	Providence College	H-East	26	14	7	21	24	....	....	....	....	....
2012-13	Providence College	H-East	38	8	15	23	61	....	....	....	....	....

Signed as a free agent by **Buffalo**, April 2, 2013.

SCHIESTEL, Drew (SHIHS-tuhl, DROO)

Defense. Shoots right. 6'1", 197 lbs. Born, Hamilton, Ont., March 9, 1989.
(Buffalo's 2nd choice, 59th overall, in 2007 Entry Draft).

			Regular Season					Playoffs				
Season	Club	League	GP	G	A	Pts	PIM	GP	G	A	Pts	PIM
2004-05	Hamilton Reps	Minor-ON	68	21	27	46	....	....	....	....	....	....
2005-06	Mississauga	OHL	40	1	4	5	42	....	....	....	....	....
2006-07	Mississauga	OHL	66	6	15	21	40	5	0	6	6	2
2007-08	Niagara Ice Dogs	OHL	68	8	29	37	40	10	1	6	7	10
2008-09	Niagara Ice Dogs	OHL	63	10	38	48	75	12	2	6	8	14
2009-10	Portland Pirates	AHL	52	1	11	12	19	4	0	0	0	0
2010-11	Portland Pirates	AHL	45	5	18	23	32	....	....	....	....	....
2011-12	Rochester	AHL	43	2	10	12	12	....	....	....	....	....
	Texas Stars	AHL	16	0	5	5	8	....	....	....	....	....
2012-13	Rochester	AHL	35	1	2	3	16	3	0	0	0	2
	Greenville	ECHL	3	0	0	0	0	....	....	....	....	....

Signed as a free agent by **Hamilton** (AHL), July 29, 2013.

SCHMALTZ, Jordan (SHMAHLTZ, JOHR-dahn) ST.L.

Defense. Shoots right. 6'2", 180 lbs. Born, Madison, WI, October 8, 1993.
(St. Louis' 1st choice, 25th overall, in 2012 Entry Draft).

			Regular Season					Playoffs				
Season	Club	League	GP	G	A	Pts	PIM	GP	G	A	Pts	PIM
2008-09	Chi. Mission U16	T1EHL	25	3	10	13	33	....	....	....	....	....
2009-10	Chicago Mission	T1EHL	39	10	21	31	30	....	....	....	....	....
2010-11	Sioux City	USHL	53	13	31	44	22	3	0	1	1	4
2011-12	Sioux City	USHL	9	3	3	6	9	....	....	....	....	....
	Green Bay	USHL	46	7	28	35	20	12	2	5	7	8
2012-13	North Dakota	WCHA	42	3	9	12	31	....	....	....	....	....

USHL All-Rookie Team (2011) • USHL First All-Star Team (2011, 2012)

SCHMIDT, Nate (SHMIHT, NAYT) WSH

Defense. Shoots left. 6', 194 lbs. Born, St. Cloud, MN, July 16, 1991.

			Regular Season					Playoffs				
Season	Club	League	GP	G	A	Pts	PIM	GP	G	A	Pts	PIM
2009-10	Fargo Force	USHL	57	14	23	37	81	13	0	6	6	2
2010-11	U. of Minnesota	WCHA	13	0	1	1	6	....	....	....	....	....
2011-12	U. of Minnesota	WCHA	43	3	38	41	14	....	....	....	....	....
2012-13	U. of Minnesota	WCHA	40	9	23	32	16	....	....	....	....	....
	Hershey Bears	AHL	8	1	3	4	2	5	0	2	2	0

WCHA Second All-Star Team (2012) • WCHA First All-Star Team (2013) • NCAA West Second All-American Team (2013)

Signed as a free agent by **Washington**, April 3, 2013.

SCHMITZ, Beau (SHMIHTZ, BOH) CAR

Defense. Shoots right. 5'10", 195 lbs. Born, Howell, MI, March 26, 1991.

			Regular Season					Playoffs				
Season	Club	League	GP	G	A	Pts	PIM	GP	G	A	Pts	PIM
2007-08	USNTDP	NAHL	41	5	7	12	84	....	....	....	....	....
2008-09	Plymouth Whalers	OHL	66	6	31	37	97	11	2	2	4	14
2009-10	Plymouth Whalers	OHL	68	8	22	30	97	9	0	2	2	10
2010-11	Plymouth Whalers	OHL	48	7	24	31	65	11	2	5	7	18
2011-12	Plymouth Whalers	OHL	62	14	40	54	91	7	0	0	0	6
2012-13	Charlotte	AHL	21	4	6	10	18	1	0	0	0	0
	Florida Everblades	ECHL	50	0	8	8	31	....	....	....	....	....

Signed as a free agent by **Carolina**, April 23, 2012.

SCHNEIDER, Cole (SHNIGH-duhr, KOHL) OTT

Left wing. Shoots left. 6'1", 197 lbs. Born, Williamsville, NY, August 26, 1990.

			Regular Season					Playoffs				
Season	Club	League	GP	G	A	Pts	PIM	GP	G	A	Pts	PIM
2008-09	Mahoning Valley	NAHL	42	17	16	33	12	14	3	7	10	2
2009-10	Topeka	NAHL	29	25	14	39	18	9	7	4	11	20
2010-11	U. of Connecticut	AH	37	13	20	33	30	....	....	....	....	....
2011-12	U. of Connecticut	AH	38	23	22	45	35	....	....	....	....	....
	Binghamton	AHL	11	0	2	2	0	....	....	....	....	....
2012-13	Binghamton	AHL	60	17	18	35	37	3	0	0	0	0

Signed as a free agent by **Ottawa**, March 14, 2012.

SCHNEIDER, Stefan (SHNIGH-duhr, STEH-fan)

Center. Shoots right. 6'4", 199 lbs. Born, Vernon, B.C., December 13, 1989.

			Regular Season					Playoffs				
Season	Club	League	GP	G	A	Pts	PIM	GP	G	A	Pts	PIM
2006-07	Beaver Valley	KIJHL	57	9	23	32	40	....	....	....	....	....
2007-08	Vancouver Giants	WHL	36	0	4	4	36	4	0	0	0	0
2008-09	Vancouver Giants	WHL	67	11	5	16	45	....	....	....	....	....
2009-10	Portland	WHL	72	12	11	23	42	13	3	2	5	10
2010-11	Manitoba Moose	AHL	47	2	2	4	9	3	0	0	0	0
2011-12	Chicago Wolves	AHL	46	4	5	9	6	3	0	0	0	0
2012-13	Chicago Wolves	AHL	32	2	5	7	12	....	....	....	....	....
	Kalamazoo Wings	ECHL	8	1	1	2	9	....	....	....	....	....
	Peoria Rivermen	AHL	2	0	0	0	0	....	....	....	....	....

Signed as a free agent by **Vancouver**, March 29, 2010.

SCHUMACHER, Michael (SHOO-mah-kuhr, MIGH-kuhl)

Left wing. Shoots left. 6'5", 203 lbs. Born, Ornskoldsvik, Sweden, August 25, 1993.
(Los Angeles' 6th choice, 200th overall, in 2011 Entry Draft).

			Regular Season					Playoffs				
Season	Club	League	GP	G	A	Pts	PIM	GP	G	A	Pts	PIM
2007-08	Stenungsund U18	Swe-U18	3	2	1	3	....					
2008-09	Stenungsund U18	Swe-U18	STATISTICS NOT AVAILABLE									
2009-10	Frolunda U18	Swe-U18	38	21	8	29	14	8	6	2	8	20
	Frolunda Jr.	Swe-Jr.	1	0	0	0	0	....	....	....	....	....
2010-11	Frolunda U18	Swe-U18	25	18	14	32	18	5	1	3	4	12
	Frolunda Jr.	Swe-Jr.	22	4	3	7	28	....	....	....	....	....
2011-12	Sault Ste. Marie	OHL	65	26	24	50	41	....	....	....	....	....
2012-13	Sault Ste. Marie	OHL	65	20	30	50	50	6	4	2	6	0

SCHWARTZ, Rylan (SHWOHRTZ, RIGH-luhn) S.J.

Center. Shoots left. 5'10", 200 lbs. Born, Wilcox, Sask., January 8, 1990.

			Regular Season					Playoffs				
Season	Club	League	GP	G	A	Pts	PIM	GP	G	A	Pts	PIM
2005-06	Notre Dame	SMHL	40	18	26	44	26	....	....	....	....	....
2006-07	Notre Dame	SMHL	41	30	53	83	44	11	9	12	21	10
	Notre Dame	SJHL	9	6	4	10	0	....	....	....	....	....
2007-08	Notre Dame	SJHL	56	29	34	62	83	....	....	....	....	....
2008-09	Notre Dame	SJHL	48	39	49	*88	54	....	....	....	....	....
2009-10	Colorado College	WCHA	39	6	22	28	24	....	....	....	....	....
2010-11	Colorado College	WCHA	41	10	28	38	61	....	....	....	....	....
2011-12	Colorado College	WCHA	35	23	17	40	47	....	....	....	....	....
2012-13	Colorado College	WCHA	41	20	33	*53	35	....	....	....	....	....
	Worcester Sharks	AHL	7	1	3	4	6	....	....	....	....	....

WCHA All-Rookie Team (2010) • WCHA Second All-Star Team (2013)

Signed as a free agent by **San Jose**, April 5, 2013.

SCOTT, Greg (SKAWT, GREHG)

Right wing. Shoots right. 6', 193 lbs. Born, Victoria, B.C., June 3, 1988.

			Regular Season					Playoffs				
Season	Club	League	GP	G	A	Pts	PIM	GP	G	A	Pts	PIM
2004-05	Peninsula Panthers	VIJHL	48	34	40	74	65	....	....	....	....	....
	Victoria Salsa	BCHL	7	1	1	2	0	....	....	....	....	....
2005-06	Seattle	WHL	69	8	14	22	37	7	1	3	4	4
2006-07	Seattle	WHL	72	18	14	32	62	11	0	2	2	2
2007-08	Seattle	WHL	72	38	37	75	56	12	5	4	9	9
2008-09	Seattle	WHL	65	32	44	76	39	5	0	6	6	2
2009-10	Toronto Marlies	AHL	71	10	22	32	28	....	....	....	....	....
	Reading Royals	ECHL	5	1	1	2	2	13	1	9	10	0
2010-11	Toronto Marlies	AHL	55	10	21	31	30	....	....	....	....	....
2011-12	Toronto Marlies	AHL	75	21	23	44	30	17	3	2	5	21
2012-13	Toronto Marlies	AHL	69	13	18	31	43	9	7	2	9	2

Signed as a free agent by **Toronto**, July 3, 2008. Signed as a free agent by **Gavle** (Sweden), May 29, 2013.

SDAO, Michael (S'DAY-oh, MIGH-kuhl) OTT

Defense. Shoots left. 6'4", 207 lbs. Born, Bloomington, MN, July 3, 1989.
(Ottawa's 9th choice, 191st overall, in 2009 Entry Draft).

			Regular Season					Playoffs				
Season	Club	League	GP	G	A	Pts	PIM	GP	G	A	Pts	PIM
2005-06	Culver Academy	High-IN	40	1	6	7	38	....	....	....	....	....
2006-07	Culver Academy	High-IN	43	1	6	7	85	....	....	....	....	....
2007-08	Lincoln Stars	USHL	53	3	6	9	178	8	0	1	1	20
2008-09	Lincoln Stars	USHL	51	3	7	10	162	7	0	0	0	*33
2009-10	Princeton	ECAC	30	5	4	9	48	....	....	....	....	....
2010-11	Princeton	ECAC	27	3	7	10	65	....	....	....	....	....
2011-12	Princeton	ECAC	30	10	10	20	87	....	....	....	....	....
2012-13	Princeton	ECAC	31	8	7	15	36	....	....	....	....	....
	Binghamton	AHL	12	1	0	1	23	....	....	....	....	....

ECAC Second All-Star Team (2012)

SEDLAK, Lukas (SEHD-lak, LOO-kuhsh) CBJ

Center. Shoots left. 6', 201 lbs. Born, Ceske Budejovice, Czech Rep., February 25, 1993.
(Columbus' 5th choice, 158th overall, in 2011 Entry Draft).

			Regular Season					Playoffs				
Season	Club	League	GP	G	A	Pts	PIM	GP	G	A	Pts	PIM
2007-08	C. Budejovice U17	CzR-U17	6	0	2	2	4	2	0	0	0	2
2008-09	C. Budejovice U17	CzR-U17	44	12	17	29	14	4	0	0	0	4
2009-10	C. Budejovice U18	CzR-U18	37	29	27	56	76	4	5	1	6	39
	C. Budejovice Jr.	CzRep-Jr.	11	4	8	12	4	....	....	....	....	....
2010-11	C. Budejovice Jr.	CzRep-Jr.	47	14	13	27	65	....	....	....	....	....
	C. Budejovice U18	CzR-U18	....	....	....	....	....	1	0	1	1	0
2011-12	Chicoutimi	QMJHL	50	17	28	45	57	18	5	3	8	18
2012-13	Chicoutimi	QMJHL	48	15	19	34	64	6	1	4	5	8

SEELER, Nick (SEE-luhr, NIHK) MIN

Defense. Shoots left. 6'2", 200 lbs. Born, Eden Prairie, MN, June 3, 1993.
(Minnesota's 4th choice, 131st overall, in 2011 Entry Draft).

			Regular Season					Playoffs				
Season	Club	League	GP	G	A	Pts	PIM	GP	G	A	Pts	PIM
2009-10	Eden Prairie Eagles	High-MN	25	3	14	17	12	3	1	3	4	0
2010-11	Team Southwest	UMHSEL	21	3	7	10	32	3	0	3	3	16
	Eden Prairie Eagles	High-MN	22	7	27	34	38	6	2	7	9	10
2011-12	Muskegon	USHL	32	2	13	15	32	....	....	....	....	....
	Des Moines	USHL	26	2	11	13	33	....	....	....	....	....
2012-13	Nebraska-Omaha	WCHA	34	2	7	9	55	....	....	....	....	....

USHL All-Rookie Team (2012)

SEGALLA, Ryan (seh-GAL-ah, RIGH-uhn) PIT

Defense. Shoots left. 6'1", 190 lbs. Born, Boston, MA, December 29, 1994.
(Pittsburgh's 3rd choice, 119th overall, in 2013 Entry Draft).

			Regular Season					Playoffs				
Season	Club	League	GP	G	A	Pts	PIM	GP	G	A	Pts	PIM
2010-11	Salisbury School	High-CT	26	3	10	13	30	....	....	....	....	....
	South Shore	Minor-CT	11	1	0	1	4	4	0	0	0	6
2011-12	Salisbury School	High-CT	28	6	6	12	36	....	....	....	....	....
2012-13	Salisbury School	High-CT	28	10	8	18	28	....	....	....	....	....
	Mid Fairfield Blues	Minor-CT	STATISTICS NOT AVAILABLE									

• Signed Letter of Intent to attend **University of Connecticut** (Atlantic Hockey) in fall of 2014.

SERGEEV, Artem (sair-GAY-ehv, AHR-tehm) T.B.

Defense. Shoots right. 6'1", 213 lbs. Born, Moscow, Russia, April 20, 1993.

			Regular Season					Playoffs				
Season	Club	League	GP	G	A	Pts	PIM	GP	G	A	Pts	PIM
2009-10	Chi. Americans	T1EHL	35	9	29	38	68	....	....	....	....	....
2010-11	Val-d'Or Foreurs	QMJHL	64	5	22	27	40	4	0	1	1	0
2011-12	Val-d'Or Foreurs	QMJHL	46	7	13	20	46	3	0	0	0	9
2012-13	Val-d'Or Foreurs	QMJHL	55	6	33	39	65	10	3	3	6	12
	Syracuse Crunch	AHL	1	0	0	0	0	....	....	....	....	....

Signed as a free agent by **Tampa Bay**, July 1, 2012.

SERVILLE, Brennan (SUHR-vihl, BREH-nuhn) WPG

Defense. Shoots right. 6'3", 194 lbs. Born, Scarborough, Ont., June 2, 1993.
(Winnipeg's 3rd choice, 78th overall, in 2011 Entry Draft).

			Regular Season					Playoffs				
Season	Club	League	GP	G	A	Pts	PIM	GP	G	A	Pts	PIM
2008-09	Ajax Pickering	Minor-ON	56	4	15	19	28	....	....	....	....	....
2009-10	Stouffville Spirit	ON-Jr.A	43	3	12	15	26	4	1	2	3	0
2010-11	Stouffville Spirit	ON-Jr.A	36	3	27	30	29	19	2	10	12	20
2011-12	U. of Michigan	CCHA	34	0	8	8	4	....	....	....	....	....
2012-13	U. of Michigan	CCHA	29	1	2	3	16	....	....	....	....	....

SEVERSON, Damon (seh-VUHR-suhn, DAY-muhn) N.J.

Defense. Shoots right. 6'2", 195 lbs. Born, Brandon, Man., August 7, 1994.
(New Jersey's 2nd choice, 60th overall, in 2012 Entry Draft).

			Regular Season					Playoffs				
Season	Club	League	GP	G	A	Pts	PIM	GP	G	A	Pts	PIM
2009-10	Yorkton Harvest	SMHL	44	9	25	34	53	4	1	1	2	18
	Melville	SJHL	1	0	1	1	2	....	....	....	....	....
	Kelowna Rockets	WHL	5	0	0	0	0	....	....	....	....	....
2010-11	Kelowna Rockets	WHL	64	4	13	17	53	10	2	0	2	13
2011-12	Kelowna Rockets	WHL	56	7	30	37	80	4	2	0	2	2
2012-13	Kelowna Rockets	WHL	71	10	42	52	74	11	1	9	10	18
	Albany Devils	AHL	2	0	2	2	0	....	....	....	....	....

SEXTON, Ben (SEHKS-tuhn, BEHN) BOS

Center. Shoots right. 5'11", 200 lbs. Born, Ottawa, Ont., June 6, 1991.
(Boston's 5th choice, 206th overall, in 2009 Entry Draft).

			Regular Season					Playoffs				
Season	Club	League	GP	G	A	Pts	PIM	GP	G	A	Pts	PIM
2007-08	Nepean Raiders	ON-Jr.A	48	15	15	30	71	6	1	5	6	4
2008-09	Nepean Raiders	ON-Jr.A	38	14	21	35	54	11	3	9	12	22
2009-10	Penticton Vees	BCHL	50	13	29	42	83	5	1	2	3	4
2010-11	Clarkson Knights	ECAC	12	5	3	8	12	....	....	....	....	....
2011-12	Clarkson Knights	ECAC	27	8	21	29	44	....	....	....	....	....
2012-13	Clarkson Knights	ECAC	28	5	15	20	70	....	....	....	....	....

• Missed majority of 2010-11 due to arm injury vs. Colgate (ECAC), November 5, 2010.

SEYMOUR, Clark (SEE-mohr, KLAHRK) PIT

Defense. Shoots right. 6'4", 202 lbs. Born, Brockville, Ont., May 18, 1993.
(Pittsburgh's 8th choice, 143rd overall, in 2012 Entry Draft).

			Regular Season					Playoffs				
Season	Club	League	GP	G	A	Pts	PIM	GP	G	A	Pts	PIM
2008-09	Upper Canada	Minor-ON	53	3	28	31	97	....	....	....	....	....
	Brockville Braves	ON-Jr.A	4	0	0	0	4	12	0	0	0	6
2009-10	Kingston	OHL	60	1	5	6	58	5	0	0	0	2
2010-11	Kingston	OHL	18	2	2	4	14	....	....	....	....	....
	Peterborough	OHL	40	1	2	3	45	....	....	....	....	....
2011-12	Peterborough	OHL	47	0	8	8	96	....	....	....	....	....
2012-13	Peterborough	OHL	62	3	10	13	61	....	....	....	....	....

SHALLA, Josh (SHAL-uh, JAWSH) NSH

Left wing. Shoots left. 6'2", 208 lbs. Born, Whitby, Ont., September 25, 1991.
(Nashville's 3rd choice, 94th overall, in 2011 Entry Draft).

			Regular Season					Playoffs				
Season	Club	League	GP	G	A	Pts	PIM	GP	G	A	Pts	PIM
2006-07	Whitby Wildcats	Minor-ON	80	56	60	116	....	....	....	....	....	....
2007-08	Bowmanville	ON-Jr.A	49	26	11	37	20	7	5	2	7	6
	Brampton	OHL	6	0	0	0	0	....	....	....	....	....
2008-09	Brampton	OHL	37	11	4	15	12	....	....	....	....	....
	Guelph Storm	OHL	24	3	2	5	16	4	0	0	0	0
2009-10	Saginaw Spirit	OHL	68	32	33	65	62	6	0	1	1	2
2010-11	Saginaw Spirit	OHL	68	47	25	72	62	12	8	7	15	8
2011-12	Saginaw Spirit	OHL	53	40	36	76	27	12	4	10	14	2
2012-13	Cincinnati	ECHL	37	21	7	28	18	7	1	3	4	4
	Milwaukee	AHL	32	3	9	12	4	2	0	1	1	0

SHALUNOV, Maxim (shal-oo-NAWV, max-EEM) CHI

Right wing. Shoots left. 6'3", 185 lbs. Born, Chelyabinsk, Russia, January 31, 1993.
(Chicago's 7th choice, 109th overall, in 2011 Entry Draft).

			Regular Season					Playoffs				
Season	Club	League	GP	G	A	Pts	PIM	GP	G	A	Pts	PIM
2009-10	Chelyabinsk Jr.	Russia-Jr.	3	2	3	5	12	4	6	1	7	6
2010-11	Chelyabinsk Jr.	Russia-Jr.	39	22	14	36	30	5	1	6	7	2
	Chelyabinsk	KHL	6	0	1	1	0	....	....	....	....	....
2011-12	Chelyabinsk Jr.	Russia-Jr.	48	30	30	60	60	6	3	5	8	8
2012-13	Chelyabinsk Jr.	Russia-Jr.	7	3	7	10	6	....	....	....	....	....
	Chelmet	Russia-2	19	2	7	9	10	....	....	....	....	....
	Chelyabinsk	KHL	1	0	0	0	0	....	....	....	....	....

SHATTOCK, Tyler (SHA-tuhk, TIGH-luhr) ST.L.

Right wing. Shoots right. 6'2", 205 lbs. Born, Vernon, B.C., February 10, 1990.
(St. Louis' 4th choice, 108th overall, in 2009 Entry Draft).

			Regular Season					Playoffs				
Season	Club	League	GP	G	A	Pts	PIM	GP	G	A	Pts	PIM
2005-06	Thompson Blazers	BCMML	STATISTICS NOT AVAILABLE									
	Kamloops Blazers	WHL	2	0	1	1	2	....	....	....	....	....
2006-07	Kamloops Blazers	WHL	58	7	9	16	51	4	0	0	0	0
2007-08	Kamloops Blazers	WHL	48	9	14	23	45	4	1	1	2	4
2008-09	Kamloops Blazers	WHL	68	30	39	69	82	4	0	1	1	6
2009-10	Kamloops Blazers	WHL	42	22	28	50	65	....	....	....	....	....
	Calgary Hitmen	WHL	30	8	20	28	26	21	5	12	17	24
2010-11	Peoria Rivermen	AHL	67	3	12	15	60	4	0	0	0	4
2011-12	Peoria Rivermen	AHL	65	7	8	15	20	....	....	....	....	....
2012-13	Evansville IceMen	ECHL	3	3	2	5	2	....	....	....	....	....
	Peoria Rivermen	AHL	62	4	8	12	23	....	....	....	....	....

SHAW, Logan (SHAW, LOH-guhn) FLA

Right wing. Shoots right. 6'3", 193 lbs. Born, Glace Bay, N.S., October 5, 1992.
(Florida's 5th choice, 76th overall, in 2011 Entry Draft).

			Regular Season					Playoffs				
Season	Club	League	GP	G	A	Pts	PIM	GP	G	A	Pts	PIM
2007-08	Cape Breton	NSMHL	34	17	22	39	55	10	3	9	12	8
	Cape Breton	Exhib.	2	1	0	1	0	....	....	....	....	....
2008-09	Cape Breton	QMJHL	49	5	3	8	22	8	0	0	0	0
2009-10	Cape Breton	QMJHL	67	9	15	24	31	5	0	0	0	4
2010-11	Cape Breton	QMJHL	68	26	20	46	37	4	0	1	1	4
2011-12	Cape Breton	QMJHL	37	14	12	26	27	....	....	....	....	....
	Quebec Remparts	QMJHL	23	6	9	15	19	11	6	5	11	12
2012-13	Quebec Remparts	QMJHL	67	26	42	68	37	11	3	5	8	8

SHERMAN, Wiley (SHUHR-man, WIGH-lee) BOS

Defense. Shoots left. 6'6", 206 lbs. Born, Greenwich, CT, May 24, 1995.
(Boston's 4th choice, 150th overall, in 2013 Entry Draft).

			Regular Season					Playoffs				
Season	Club	League	GP	G	A	Pts	PIM	GP	G	A	Pts	PIM
2010-11	Hotchkiss School	High-CT	23	0	4	4	....	....	....	....	....	....
2011-12	Hotchkiss School	High-CT	24	2	5	7	....	....	....	....	....	....
2012-13	Hotchkiss School	High-CT	26	4	6	10	32	....	....	....	....	....
	Mid Fairfield Blues	Minor-CT	STATISTICS NOT AVAILABLE									

• Signed Letter of Intent to attend **Harvard University** (ECAC) in fall of 2014.

SHIELDS, David (SHEELDZ, DAY-vihd) ST.L.

Defense. Shoots right. 6'3", 204 lbs. Born, Buffalo, NY, January 27, 1991.
(St. Louis' 5th choice, 168th overall, in 2009 Entry Draft).

			Regular Season					Playoffs				
Season	Club	League	GP	G	A	Pts	PIM	GP	G	A	Pts	PIM
2006-07	Maksymum	Minor-NY	37	4	16	20	60	....	....	....	....	....
2007-08	Erie Otters	OHL	60	1	3	4	31	....	....	....	....	....
2008-09	Erie Otters	OHL	61	1	16	17	28	5	0	0	0	5
2009-10	Erie Otters	OHL	68	7	12	19	42	4	0	0	0	12
2010-11	Erie Otters	OHL	61	6	21	27	48	7	1	4	5	4
2011-12	Peoria Rivermen	AHL	48	0	4	4	10	....	....	....	....	....
	Alaska Aces	ECHL	12	1	5	6	2	3	0	2	2	0
2012-13	Peoria Rivermen	AHL	59	0	5	5	41	....	....	....	....	....

SHINKARUK, Hunter (shinh-KA-ruhk, HUHN-tuhr) VAN

Center/Left wing. Shoots left. 5'10", 181 lbs. Born, Calgary, Alta., October 13, 1994.
(Vancouver's 2nd choice, 24th overall, in 2013 Entry Draft).

			Regular Season					Playoffs				
Season	Club	League	GP	G	A	Pts	PIM	GP	G	A	Pts	PIM
2008-09	Calgary Royals	AMBHL	27	32	31	63	10	10	11	11	22	6
2009-10	Calgary Royals	AMHL	3	0	1	1	0	....	....	....	....	....
2010-11	Medicine Hat	WHL	63	14	28	42	24	14	4	5	9	0
2011-12	Medicine Hat	WHL	66	49	42	91	38	8	2	9	11	6
2012-13	Medicine Hat	WHL	64	37	49	86	44	8	3	3	6	8

WHL East Second All-Star Team (2013)

• Missed majority of 2009-10 season due to leg injury.

SHINNIMIN, Brendan (SHIHN-ih-mihm, BREHN-duhn) PHX

Center. Shoots left. 5'10", 185 lbs. Born, Winnipeg, Man., January 7, 1991.

			Regular Season					Playoffs				
Season	Club	League	GP	G	A	Pts	PIM	GP	G	A	Pts	PIM
2007-08	Selkirk Steelers	MJHL	51	7	19	26	38	....	....	....	....	....
	Tri-City Americans	WHL	4	0	0	0	0	....	....	....	....	....
2008-09	Tri-City Americans	WHL	64	12	13	25	69	11	0	5	5	16
2009-10	Tri-City Americans	WHL	70	27	55	82	82	22	8	17	25	29
2010-11	Tri-City Americans	WHL	60	34	62	96	84	10	4	7	11	16
2011-12	Tri-City Americans	WHL	69	58	76	*134	82	15	7	16	23	28
2012-13	Portland Pirates	AHL	74	12	21	33	77	1	0	1	1	0

WHL West Second All-Star Team (2011) • WHL West First All-Star Team (2012) • WHL Player of the Year (2012) • Canadian Major Junior Player of the Year (2012)

Signed as a free agent by **Phoenix**, March 2, 2012.

SHORE, Devin (SHOHR, DEH-vihn) DAL

Center. Shoots left. 6'1", 185 lbs. Born, Ajax, Ont., July 19, 1994.
(Dallas' 4th choice, 61st overall, in 2012 Entry Draft).

			Regular Season					Playoffs				
Season	Club	League	GP	G	A	Pts	PIM	GP	G	A	Pts	PIM
2009-10	Ajax-Pickering	Minor-ON	68	40	48	88	35	....	....	....	....	....
2010-11	The Hill Academy	High-ON	61	33	62	95	18	....	....	....	....	....
2011-12	Whitby Fury	ON-Jr.A	41	29	29	58	26	23	7	25	32	10
2012-13	U. of Maine	H-East	38	6	20	26	10	....	....	....	....	....

SHORE, Nick (SHOHR, NIHK) L.A.

Center. Shoots right. 6', 190 lbs. Born, Denver, CO, September 26, 1992.
(Los Angeles' 3rd choice, 82nd overall, in 2011 Entry Draft).

			Regular Season					Playoffs				
Season	Club	League	GP	G	A	Pts	PIM	GP	G	A	Pts	PIM
2007-08	Colorado T-birds	Minor-CO	....	64	71	135	....	....	....	....	....	....
2008-09	USNTDP	NAHL	42	10	11	21	30	9	2	2	4	6
	USNTDP	U-17	16	7	6	13	18	....	....	....	....	....
2009-10	USNTDP	USHL	26	6	14	20	10	....	....	....	....	....
	USNTDP	U-18	39	13	24	37	30	....	....	....	....	....
2010-11	U. of Denver	WCHA	33	7	11	18	37	....	....	....	....	....
2011-12	U. of Denver	WCHA	43	13	28	41	16	....	....	....	....	....
2012-13	U. of Denver	WCHA	39	14	20	34	47	....	....	....	....	....

SHORE, Quentin (SHOHR, KWEHN-tihn) OTT

Center. Shoots right. 6'2", 183 lbs. Born, Denver, CO, May 25, 1994.
(Ottawa's 7th choice, 168th overall, in 2013 Entry Draft).

			Regular Season					Playoffs				
Season	Club	League	GP	G	A	Pts	PIM	GP	G	A	Pts	PIM
2009-10	Col. Thunderbirds	T1EHL	33	13	13	26	10	....	....	....	....	....
2010-11	USNTDP	USHL	33	3	6	9	14	2	0	0	0	0
	USNTDP	U-17	17	1	8	9	14	....	....	....	....	....
2011-12	USNTDP	USHL	24	8	2	10	15	....	....	....	....	....
	USNTDP	U-18	36	9	8	17	16	....	....	....	....	....
2012-13	U. of Denver	WCHA	39	10	9	22	1	....	....	....	....	....

SHUGG, Justin (SHUHG, JUHS-tihn) CAR

Left wing. Shoots right. 5'11", 185 lbs. Born, Niagara Falls, Ont., December 24, 1991.
(Carolina's 6th choice, 105th overall, in 2010 Entry Draft).

			Regular Season					Playoffs				
Season	Club	League	GP	G	A	Pts	PIM	GP	G	A	Pts	PIM
2006-07	Niag. Falls Thunder	Minor-ON	70	65	46	111	42	....	....	....	....	....
2007-08	Oshawa Generals	OHL	38	4	10	14	10	....	....	....	....	....
	Windsor Spitfires	OHL	23	0	3	3	2	3	0	0	0	0
2008-09	Windsor Spitfires	OHL	68	17	16	33	48	20	5	4	9	16
2009-10	Windsor Spitfires	OHL	67	39	40	79	43	18	5	10	15	10
2010-11	St. Michael's	OHL	66	41	45	86	43	20	10	9	19	14
2011-12	Charlotte	AHL	33	5	8	13	12	....	....	....	....	....
	Florida Everblades	ECHL	11	4	8	12	8	11	7	5	12	8
2012-13	Charlotte	AHL	39	7	14	21	10	4	2	0	2	0
	Florida Everblades	ECHL	19	11	11	22	20	....	....	....	....	....

SIELOFF, Patrick (SEE-lawf, PAT-rihk) CGY

Defense. Shoots left. 6', 192 lbs. Born, Ann Arbor, MI, May 15, 1994.
(Calgary's 2nd choice, 42nd overall, in 2012 Entry Draft).

			Regular Season					Playoffs				
Season	Club	League	GP	G	A	Pts	PIM	GP	G	A	Pts	PIM
2009-10	Det. Compuware	T1EHL	37	2	8	10	52	5	0	3	3	0
	Det. Compuware	Exhib.	6	0	3	3	2	....	....	....	....	....
2010-11	USNTDP	USHL	36	1	3	4	66	2	0	0	0	2
	USNTDP	U-17	17	2	3	5	10	....	....	....	....	....
2011-12	USNTDP	USHL	24	0	2	2	55	....	....	....	....	....
	USNTDP	U-18	36	3	5	8	58	....	....	....	....	....
2012-13	Windsor Spitfires	OHL	45	3	8	11	85	....	....	....	....	....

SIEMENS, Duncan (SEE-muhns, DUHN-kuhn) COL

Defense. Shoots left. 6'4", 209 lbs. Born, Edmonton, Alta., September 7, 1993.
(Colorado's 2nd choice, 11th overall, in 2011 Entry Draft).

			Regular Season					Playoffs				
Season	Club	League	GP	G	A	Pts	PIM	GP	G	A	Pts	PIM
2007-08	Sherwood Park	AMBHL	32	14	22	36	54	12	5	7	12	32
2008-09	Sherwood Park	AMHL	34	5	13	18	68	11	2	6	8	24
	Saskatoon Blades	WHL	2	0	1	1	2	....	....	....	....	....
2009-10	Saskatoon Blades	WHL	57	3	17	20	89	7	0	0	0	11
2010-11	Saskatoon Blades	WHL	72	5	38	43	121	10	1	3	4	15
2011-12	Saskatoon Blades	WHL	57	6	22	28	91	4	1	1	2	10
	Lake Erie Monsters	AHL	3	0	0	0	2	....	....	....	....	....
2012-13	Saskatoon Blades	WHL	70	3	29	32	109	4	0	1	1	2

WHL East Second All-Star Team (2011)

SILL, Zach (SIHL, ZAK) PIT

Center. Shoots left. 6', 202 lbs. Born, Truro, N.S., May 4, 1988.

			Regular Season					Playoffs				
Season	Club	League	GP	G	A	Pts	PIM	GP	G	A	Pts	PIM
2005-06	Truro Bearcats	MJrHL	48	12	8	20	68	2	0	0	0	0
2006-07	U. of Maine	H-East	6	1	1	2	2	....	....	....	....	....
	Truro Bearcats	MJrHL	6	1	0	1	18	13	5	5	10	31
2007-08	Moncton Wildcats	QMJHL	66	18	8	26	95	....	....	....	....	....
2008-09	Moncton Wildcats	QMJHL	58	9	15	24	78	10	4	1	5	10
2009-10	Moncton Wildcats	QMJHL	54	5	6	11	48	4	0	0	0	2
	Wheeling Nailers	ECHL	6	1	2	3	15	....	....	....	....	....
2010-11	Wilkes-Barre	AHL	80	11	19	30	85	12	1	2	3	6
2011-12	Wilkes-Barre	AHL	68	10	7	17	40	12	3	1	4	0
2012-13	Wilkes-Barre	AHL	57	4	5	9	108	15	2	2	4	6

Signed as a free agent by **Pittsburgh**, May 16, 2011.

SIMPSON, Dillon (SIHMP-suhn, DIH-luhn) EDM

Defense. Shoots left. 6'2", 191 lbs. Born, Edmonton, Alta., February 10, 1993.
(Edmonton's 6th choice, 92nd overall, in 2011 Entry Draft).

			Regular Season					Playoffs				
Season	Club	League	GP	G	A	Pts	PIM	GP	G	A	Pts	PIM
2007-08	Southgate	AMBHL	33	7	31	38	32	4	4	2	6	2
2008-09	SSAC Athletics	AMHL	34	3	12	15	8	4	0	0	0	0
	Spruce Grove	AJHL	1	0	0	0	0	1	0	0	0	2
2009-10	Spruce Grove	AJHL	58	12	29	41	19	16	0	6	6	6
2010-11	North Dakota	WCHA	30	2	8	10	8	....	....	....	....	....
2011-12	North Dakota	WCHA	42	2	16	18	8	....	....	....	....	....
2012-13	North Dakota	WCHA	42	5	19	24	12	....	....	....	....	....

SINITSYN, Dmitry (sih-NIHT-sihn, dih-MEE-tree) DAL

Defense. Shoots left. 6'2", 200 lbs. Born, Moscow, Russia, June 17, 1994.
(Dallas' 9th choice, 183rd overall, in 2012 Entry Draft).

			Regular Season					Playoffs				
Season	Club	League	GP	G	A	Pts	PIM	GP	G	A	Pts	PIM
2010-11	Dallas Stars U16	T1EHL	36	11	20	31	18	....	....	....	....	....
	Dallas Stars U-16	Exhib.	21	13	8	21	26	....	....	....	....	....
2011-12	Zelenograd Jr.	Russia-Jr. B	7	0	0	0	10	....	....	....	....	....
	U. Mass-Lowell	H-East	DID NOT PLAY – FRESHMAN									
2012-13	U. Mass-Lowell	H-East	13	2	0	2	4	....	....	....	....	....

SISLO, Mike (SIHS-loh, MIGHK) N.J.

Right wing. Shoots right. 6', 195 lbs. Born, Superior, WI, January 20, 1988.

			Regular Season					Playoffs				
Season	Club	League	GP	G	A	Pts	PIM	GP	G	A	Pts	PIM
2005-06	Green Bay	USHL	57	3	3	6	36	3	0	0	0	5
2006-07	Green Bay	USHL	60	23	26	49	28	4	3	1	4	2
2007-08	New Hampshire	H-East	38	3	5	8	12	....	....	....	....	....
2008-09	New Hampshire	H-East	38	19	12	31	12	....	....	....	....	....
2009-10	New Hampshire	H-East	39	14	15	29	20	....	....	....	....	....
2010-11	New Hampshire	H-East	39	15	*33	48	38	....	....	....	....	....
	Albany Devils	AHL	3	0	0	0	0	....	....	....	....	....
2011-12	Albany Devils	AHL	59	9	18	27	20	....	....	....	....	....
2012-13	Albany Devils	AHL	61	13	13	26	46	....	....	....	....	....

Signed as a free agent by **New Jersey**, April 5, 2011.

SISSONS, Colton (SIH-suhnz, KOHL-tuhn) NSH

Center. Shoots right. 6'1", 189 lbs. Born, North Vancouver, B.C., November 5, 1993.
(Nashville's 2nd choice, 50th overall, in 2012 Entry Draft).

			Regular Season					Playoffs				
Season	Club	League	GP	G	A	Pts	PIM	GP	G	A	Pts	PIM
2008-09	Van. NW Giants	BCMML	39	30	24	54	44	....	....	....	....	....
2009-10	Westside Warriors	BCHL	58	6	16	22	29	11	1	1	2	4
2010-11	Kelowna Rockets	WHL	63	17	24	41	46	10	3	3	6	6
2011-12	Kelowna Rockets	WHL	58	26	15	41	62	4	1	1	2	2
2012-13	Kelowna Rockets	WHL	61	28	39	67	54	....	....	....	....	....

SKJEI, Brady (SHAY, BRAY-dee) NYR

Defense. Shoots left. 6'2", 196 lbs. Born, Lakevill, MN, March 26, 1994.
(NY Rangers' 1st choice, 28th overall, in 2012 Entry Draft).

			Regular Season					Playoffs				
Season	Club	League	GP	G	A	Pts	PIM	GP	G	A	Pts	PIM
2009-10	Lakeville North	High-MN	30	11	18	29	20	....	....	....	....	....
2010-11	USNTDP	USHL	36	1	5	6	14	2	0	0	0	0
	USNTDP	U-17	17	4	9	13	10	....	....	....	....	....
2011-12	USNTDP	USHL	24	3	9	12	12	....	....	....	....	....
	USNTDP	U-18	36	1	10	11	24	....	....	....	....	....
2012-13	U. of Minnesota	WCHA	36	1	2	3	14	....	....	....	....	....

SLAVIN, Jaccob (SLA-vihn, JAY-kuhb) CAR

Defense. Shoots left. 6'1", 180 lbs. Born, Denver, CO, May 1, 1994.
(Carolina's 6th choice, 120th overall, in 2012 Entry Draft).

			Regular Season					Playoffs				
Season	Club	League	GP	G	A	Pts	PIM	GP	G	A	Pts	PIM
2010-11	Col. Thunderbirds	T1EHL	34	5	21	26	12	....	....	....	....	....
	Chicago Steel	USHL	17	1	0	1	10	....	....	....	....	....
2011-12	Chicago Steel	USHL	60	3	27	30	12	....	....	....	....	....
2012-13	Chicago Steel	USHL	62	5	28	33	6	....	....	....	....	....

• Signed Letter of Intent to attend **Colorado College** (WCHA) in fall of 2013.

SLEPYSHEV, Anton (SLEHP-ih-shehv, an-TAWN) **EDM**

Left wing. Shoots left. 6'2", 194 lbs. Born, Penza, Russia, May 13, 1994.
(Edmonton's 4th choice, 88th overall, in 2013 Entry Draft).

			Regular Season					Playoffs				
Season	**Club**	**League**	**GP**	**G**	**A**	**Pts**	**PIM**	**GP**	**G**	**A**	**Pts**	**PIM**
2009-10	Dizel Penza 2	Russia-3	39	12	9	21	10	4	1	1	2	4
2010-11	Dizel Penza 2	Russia-3	20	8	4	12	10	....	....	....	....	....
2011-12	Novokuznetsk Jr.	Russia-Jr.	13	7	2	9	6	3	1	0	1	0
	Novokuznetsk	KHL	39	4	3	7	2	....	....	....	....	....
2012-13	Novokuznetsk Jr.	Russia-Jr.	1	0	0	0	0	....	....	....	....	....
	Novokuznetsk	KHL	15	3	0	3	2	....	....	....	....	....
	Ufa	KHL	11	4	2	6	2	14	0	0	0	0
	Tolpar Ufa Jr.	Russia-Jr.	....	....	....	....	....	3	0	1	1	12

SMITH, Austin (SMIHTH, AUZ-tihn) **DAL**

Right wing. Shoots right. 5'11", 180 lbs. Born, Dallas, TX, November 7, 1988.
(Dallas' 4th choice, 128th overall, in 2007 Entry Draft).

			Regular Season					Playoffs				
Season	**Club**	**League**	**GP**	**G**	**A**	**Pts**	**PIM**	**GP**	**G**	**A**	**Pts**	**PIM**
2003-04	Dallas Jesuit Prep	High-TX	STATISTICS NOT AVAILABLE									
2004-05	Dallas Jesuit Prep	High-TX	STATISTICS NOT AVAILABLE									
	Alliance Bulldogs	NTHL	53	29	46	75	24	....	....	....	....	....
2005-06	The Gunnery	High-CT	31	23	20	43	22	....	....	....	....	....
2006-07	The Gunnery	High-CT	30	25	38	63	36	....	....	....	....	....
2007-08	Penticton Vees	BCHL	60	32	35	67	42	15	11	11	22	12
2008-09	Colgate	ECAC	37	17	14	31	24	....	....	....	....	....
2009-10	Colgate	ECAC	36	16	25	41	20	....	....	....	....	....
2010-11	Colgate	ECAC	41	10	21	31	36	....	....	....	....	....
2011-12	Colgate	ECAC	39	36	21	57	30	....	....	....	....	....
	Texas Stars	AHL	12	0	3	3	8	....	....	....	....	....
2012-13	Idaho Steelheads	ECHL	38	27	23	50	15	17	7	5	12	12
	Texas Stars	AHL	16	2	1	3	6	....	....	....	....	....

ECAC First All-Star Team (2012) • ECAC Player of the Year (2012) • NCAA East First All-American Team (2012)

SMITH, Colin (SMIHTH, KAW-lihn) **COL**

Center. Shoots right. 5'10", 162 lbs. Born, Edmonton, Alta., June 20, 1993.
(Colorado's 5th choice, 192nd overall, in 2012 Entry Draft).

			Regular Season					Playoffs				
Season	**Club**	**League**	**GP**	**G**	**A**	**Pts**	**PIM**	**GP**	**G**	**A**	**Pts**	**PIM**
2006-07	CAC Lehigh	AMBHL	30	24	37	61	8	....	....	....	....	....
2007-08	CAC Lehigh	AMBHL	33	36	*70	106	28	2	2	1	3	0
2008-09	CAC Gregg's Dist.	AMHL	34	23	32	55	10	5	3	4	7	2
	Kamloops Blazers	WHL	8	0	4	4	4	4	1	0	1	0
2009-10	Kamloops Blazers	WHL	48	5	21	26	46	4	2	2	4	2
2010-11	Kamloops Blazers	WHL	72	21	29	50	61	....	....	....	....	....
2011-12	Kamloops Blazers	WHL	72	35	50	85	51	11	3	7	10	12
2012-13	Kamloops Blazers	WHL	72	41	65	106	72	12	2	12	14	2

WHL West First All-Star Team (2013)

SMITH, Dalton (SMIHTH, DAHL-tuhn) **CBJ**

Left wing. Shoots left. 6'2", 206 lbs. Born, Markham, Ont., June 30, 1992.
(Columbus' 2nd choice, 34th overall, in 2010 Entry Draft).

			Regular Season					Playoffs				
Season	**Club**	**League**	**GP**	**G**	**A**	**Pts**	**PIM**	**GP**	**G**	**A**	**Pts**	**PIM**
2007-08	Osh. Generals	Minor-ON	62	22	38	60	192	....	....	....	....	....
2008-09	Whitby Fury	ON-Jr.A	40	10	13	23	109	4	2	1	3	12
	Ottawa 67's	OHL	17	2	5	7	8	7	0	0	0	0
2009-10	Ottawa 67's	OHL	62	21	23	44	129	12	3	3	6	27
2010-11	Ottawa 67's	OHL	64	12	17	29	124	4	2	2	4	12
2011-12	Ottawa 67's	OHL	53	15	10	25	67	18	4	4	8	46
2012-13	Springfield Falcons	AHL	67	3	6	9	128	1	0	0	0	12

SMITH, Gemel (SMIHTH, juh-MEHL) **DAL**

Center. Shoots left. 5'10", 164 lbs. Born, Toronto, Ont., April 16, 1994.
(Dallas' 6th choice, 104th overall, in 2012 Entry Draft).

			Regular Season					Playoffs				
Season	**Club**	**League**	**GP**	**G**	**A**	**Pts**	**PIM**	**GP**	**G**	**A**	**Pts**	**PIM**
2009-10	North York	GTHL	52	31	51	82	....	....	....	....	....	....
2010-11	Owen Sound	OHL	66	8	8	16	14	21	1	2	3	2
2011-12	Owen Sound	OHL	68	21	39	60	51	5	1	2	3	10
2012-13	Owen Sound	OHL	61	23	29	52	54	12	7	3	10	10

SOBERG, Markus (SHOH-buhrg, MAHR-kuhs) **CBJ**

Right wing. Shoots right. 6', 187 lbs. Born, Oslo, Norway, April 22, 1995.
(Columbus' 7th choice, 165th overall, in 2013 Entry Draft).

			Regular Season					Playoffs				
Season	**Club**	**League**	**GP**	**G**	**A**	**Pts**	**PIM**	**GP**	**G**	**A**	**Pts**	**PIM**
2009-10	Manglerud U17	Nor-U17	8	10	8	18	14	2	2	1	3	10
2010-11	MODO U18	Swe-U18	10	7	7	14	18	....	....	....	....	....
	Manglerud U17	Nor-U17	13	22	20	42	106	7	9	7	16	6
	Manglerud Jr.	Nor-U19	14	21	15	36	22	3	4	0	4	4
2011-12	Frolunda U18	Swe-U18	27	26	16	42	26	4	1	2	3	6
	Frolunda Jr.	Swe-Jr.	25	5	5	10	14	....	....	....	....	....
2012-13	Frolunda U18	Swe-U18	7	4	1	5	10	2	3	4	7	0
	Frolunda Jr.	Swe-Jr.	36	10	16	26	20	6	5	1	6	4

SOL, Cody (SAWL, KOH-dee) **WPG**

Defense. Shoots left. 6'6", 235 lbs. Born, Woodstock, Ont., February 11, 1991.
(Atlanta's 6th choice, 125th overall, in 2009 Entry Draft).

			Regular Season					Playoffs				
Season	**Club**	**League**	**GP**	**G**	**A**	**Pts**	**PIM**	**GP**	**G**	**A**	**Pts**	**PIM**
2007-08	St. Mary's Lincolns	ON-Jr.B	20	2	2	4	30	....	....	....	....	....
	Saginaw Spirit	OHL	12	0	0	0	4	1	0	0	0	0
2008-09	Saginaw Spirit	OHL	66	1	6	7	128	8	0	2	2	14
2009-10	Saginaw Spirit	OHL	55	7	8	15	151	6	0	0	0	8
	Chicago Wolves	AHL	1	0	0	0	0	....	....	....	....	....
2010-11	Kitchener Rangers	OHL	60	4	12	16	114	7	0	3	3	10
2011-12	Kitchener Rangers	OHL	62	15	23	38	178	16	4	8	12	29
2012-13	Colorado Eagles	ECHL	25	5	3	8	109	....	....	....	....	....
	St. John's IceCaps	AHL	26	1	3	4	63	....	....	....	....	....

• Transferred to **Winnipeg** after **Atlanta** franchise relocated, June 21, 2011.

SOLEWAY, Jedd (SOHL-way, JEHD) **PHX**

Center. Shoots right. 6'2", 207 lbs. Born, Vernon, B.C., May 12, 1994.
(Phoenix's 6th choice, 193rd overall, in 2013 Entry Draft).

			Regular Season					Playoffs				
Season	**Club**	**League**	**GP**	**G**	**A**	**Pts**	**PIM**	**GP**	**G**	**A**	**Pts**	**PIM**
2010-11	Okanagan Rockets	BCMML	40	16	17	33	97	....	....	....	....	....
2011-12	Vernon Vipers	BCHL	58	13	12	25	50	....	....	....	....	....
2012-13	Vernon Vipers	BCHL	26	5	12	17	29	....	....	....	....	....
	Penticton Vees	BCHL	22	14	15	29	33	....	....	....	....	....

• Signed Letter of Intent to attend **University of Wisconsin** (WCHA) in fall of 2014.

SOMERBY, Doyle (SUH-muhr-bee, DOIL) **NYI**

Defense. Shoots left. 6'6", 233 lbs. Born, Marblehead, MA, July 4, 1994.
(NY Islanders' 5th choice, 125th overall, in 2012 Entry Draft).

			Regular Season					Playoffs				
Season	**Club**	**League**	**GP**	**G**	**A**	**Pts**	**PIM**	**GP**	**G**	**A**	**Pts**	**PIM**
2009-10	St. Mary's High	High-MA	24	2	3	5	....	....	....	....	....	....
2010-11	Kimball Union	High-NH	32	2	5	7	18	....	....	....	....	....
2011-12	Kimball Union	High-NH	34	4	20	24	26	....	....	....	....	....
2012-13	Muskegon	USHL	10	2	0	2	6	....	....	....	....	....

• Signed Letter of Intent to attend **Boston University** (Hockey East) in fall of 2013.

SONNE, Brett (SOHNE, BREHT)

Center/Left wing. Shoots left. 6', 195 lbs. Born, Chilliwack, B.C., May 16, 1989.
(St. Louis' 6th choice, 85th overall, in 2007 Entry Draft).

			Regular Season					Playoffs				
Season	**Club**	**League**	**GP**	**G**	**A**	**Pts**	**PIM**	**GP**	**G**	**A**	**Pts**	**PIM**
2004-05	Port Coquitlam	PIJHL	47	21	34	55	125	....	....	....	....	....
	Calgary Hitmen	WHL	6	0	0	0	2	....	....	....	....	....
2005-06	Calgary Hitmen	WHL	64	12	9	21	38	13	1	2	3	8
2006-07	Calgary Hitmen	WHL	71	21	9	30	65	18	5	1	6	22
2007-08	Calgary Hitmen	WHL	29	8	12	20	12	16	3	1	4	14
2008-09	Calgary Hitmen	WHL	62	48	52	100	58	14	7	9	16	18
2009-10	Peoria Rivermen	AHL	77	11	13	24	33	....	....	....	....	....
2010-11	Peoria Rivermen	AHL	62	5	4	9	45	4	0	0	0	2
2011-12	Peoria Rivermen	AHL	70	8	9	17	40	....	....	....	....	....
2012-13	Evansville IceMen	ECHL	7	3	4	7	2	....	....	....	....	....
	Peoria Rivermen	AHL	56	7	8	15	14	....	....	....	....	....
	Texas Stars	AHL	6	1	2	3	2	2	0	1	1	0

WHL East First All-Star Team (2009) • WHL Player of the Year (2009) • Canadian Major Junior Second All-Star Team (2009)

SORENSEN, Nick (SOHR-ehn-sehn, NIHK) **ANA**

Right wing. Shoots right. 6'1", 181 lbs. Born, Holback, Denmark, October 23, 1994.
(Anaheim's 2nd choice, 45th overall, in 2013 Entry Draft).

			Regular Season					Playoffs				
Season	**Club**	**League**	**GP**	**G**	**A**	**Pts**	**PIM**	**GP**	**G**	**A**	**Pts**	**PIM**
2009-10	Rogle U18	Swe-U18	30	22	17	39	22	2	0	0	0	0
2010-11	Rogle U18	Swe-U18	6	7	3	10	4	4	1	0	1	2
	Rogle Jr.	Swe-Jr.	30	18	11	29	34	....	....	....	....	....
	Rogle	Sweden-2	6	0	0	0	2	....	....	....	....	....
2011-12	Quebec Remparts	QMJHL	8	5	4	9	2	....	....	....	....	....
2012-13	Quebec Remparts	QMJHL	46	20	27	47	18	8	7	3	10	10

SOUCY, Carson (SOO-SEE, KAR-suhn) **MIN**

Defense. Shoots left. 6'5", 200 lbs. Born, Viking, Alta., July 27, 1994.
(Minnesota's 4th choice, 137th overall, in 2013 Entry Draft).

			Regular Season					Playoffs				
Season	**Club**	**League**	**GP**	**G**	**A**	**Pts**	**PIM**	**GP**	**G**	**A**	**Pts**	**PIM**
2009-10	Lloydminster	Minor-AB	34	1	7	8	58	....	....	....	....	....
2010-11	Lloydminster	AMHL	34	3	8	11	20	2	0	0	0	2
2011-12	Lloydminster	AMHL	30	9	20	29	100	3	0	4	4	10
	Spruce Grove	AJHL	7	0	0	0	4	....	....	....	....	....
2012-13	Spruce Grove	AJHL	35	5	10	15	71	16	1	1	2	30

• Signed Letter of Intent to attend **University of Minnesota-Duluth** (WCHA) in fall of 2014.

SPELLING, Thomas (SPEHL-ihng, TAW-muhs) **NYR**

Right wing. Shoots left. 6'1", 176 lbs. Born, Herning, Denmark, February 9, 1993.
(NY Rangers' 4th choice, 142nd overall, in 2012 Entry Draft).

			Regular Season					Playoffs				
Season	**Club**	**League**	**GP**	**G**	**A**	**Pts**	**PIM**	**GP**	**G**	**A**	**Pts**	**PIM**
2008-09	Herning IK II	Den-2	7	3	2	5	0	....	....	....	....	....
	Herning IK Jr.	Den-Jr.	26	21	15	36	12	2	0	0	0	0
2009-10	Herning Blue Fox	Denmark	32	5	9	14	6	10	2	0	2	6
2010-11	Herning Blue Fox	Denmark	43	20	14	34	16	7	1	1	2	0
2011-12	Herning Blue Fox	Denmark	33	21	16	37	6	17	10	10	20	14
2012-13	Rogle	Sweden	7	0	0	0	0	....	....	....	....	....
	IK Oskarshamn	Sweden-2	4	0	0	0	0	....	....	....	....	....
	Rogle Jr.	Swe-Jr.	36	19	30	49	6	2	0	1	1	0

SPROUL, Ryan (SPROHL, RIGH-uhn) **DET**

Defense. Shoots right. 6'3", 185 lbs. Born, Mississauga, Ont., January 13, 1993.
(Detroit's 3rd choice, 55th overall, in 2011 Entry Draft).

			Regular Season					Playoffs				
Season	**Club**	**League**	**GP**	**G**	**A**	**Pts**	**PIM**	**GP**	**G**	**A**	**Pts**	**PIM**
2008-09	Vaughan Kings	GTHL	31	2	7	9	14	....	....	....	....	....
2009-10	Bramalea Blues	ON-Jr.A	6	0	1	1	6	....	....	....	....	....
	Vaughan Vipers	ON-Jr.A	8	1	1	2	0	2	0	0	0	0
2010-11	Vaughan Vipers	ON-Jr.A	3	1	2	3	4	....	....	....	....	....
	Sault Ste. Marie	OHL	61	14	19	33	36	....	....	....	....	....
2011-12	Sault Ste. Marie	OHL	61	23	31	54	53	....	....	....	....	....
2012-13	Sault Ste. Marie	OHL	50	20	46	66	45	6	2	3	5	0
	Grand Rapids	AHL	2	0	0	0	2	....	....	....	....	....

OHL First All-Star Team (2013) • Canadian Major Junior Defenseman of the Year (2013)

STALBERG, Sebastian (STAHL-buhrg. suh-BAZ-t'yehn) **S.J.**

Right wing. Shoots right. 6'1", 185 lbs. Born, Gothenburg, Sweden, June 30, 1990.

			Regular Season					Playoffs				
Season	Club	League	GP	G	A	Pts	PIM	GP	G	A	Pts	PIM
2009-10	U. of Vermont	H-East	36	6	13	19	14	....	....	....	....	....
2010-11	U. of Vermont	H-East	36	9	19	28	10	....	....	....	....	....
2011-12	U. of Vermont	H-East	34	12	19	31	22	....	....	....	....	....
	Worcester Sharks	AHL	13	3	2	5	4	....	....	....	....	....
2012-13	Worcester Sharks	AHL	66	10	8	18	10	....	....	....	....	....

Hockey East All-Rookie Team (2010)

Signed as a free agent by **San Jose**, March 14, 2012.

STEPAN, Zach (steh-PAHN, ZAK) **NSH**

Center. Shoots left. 6', 176 lbs. Born, Faribault, MN, January 6, 1994.
(Nashville's 5th choice, 112th overall, in 2012 Entry Draft).

			Regular Season					Playoffs				
Season	Club	League	GP	G	A	Pts	PIM	GP	G	A	Pts	PIM
2009-10	Shattuck U16	High-MN	40	19	23	42	20	....	....	....	....	....
2010-11	Shat.-St. Mary's	High-MN	54	25	39	64	20	....	....	....	....	....
2011-12	Shat.-St. Mary's	High-MN	50	22	43	65	20	....	....	....	....	....
2012-13	Waterloo	USHL	56	32	46	78	50	5	3	1	4	0

• Signed Letter of Intent to attend **Minnesota State University** (CCHA) in fall of 2013.

STEPHENSON, Chandler (STEE-vehn-suhn, CHAND-luhr) **WSH**

Center/Left wing. Shoots left. 5'11", 190 lbs. Born, Saskatoon, Sask., April 22, 1994.
(Washington's 3rd choice, 77th overall, in 2012 Entry Draft).

			Regular Season					Playoffs				
Season	Club	League	GP	G	A	Pts	PIM	GP	G	A	Pts	PIM
2008-09	Sask. Generals	Minor-SK	46	49	61	110	72	....	....	....	....	....
	Saskatoon Blazers	SMHL	9	2	1	3	2	....	....	....	....	....
2009-10	Sask. Contacts	SMHL	42	17	37	54	34	11	5	14	19	4
2010-11	Regina Pats	WHL	60	7	12	19	6	....	....	....	....	....
2011-12	Regina Pats	WHL	55	22	20	42	24	5	1	3	4	0
2012-13	Regina Pats	WHL	46	14	31	45	37	....	....	....	....	....

STOLLERY, Karl (STAW-luh-ree, KAHRL) **COL**

Defense. Shoots left. 5'11", 165 lbs. Born, Camrose, Alta., November 21, 1987.

			Regular Season					Playoffs				
Season	Club	League	GP	G	A	Pts	PIM	GP	G	A	Pts	PIM
2004-05	Camrose AA	Minor-AB		STATISTICS NOT AVAILABLE								
	Camrose Kodiaks	AJHL	4	0	0	0	0	....	....	....	....	....
2005-06	Camrose Kodiaks	AJHL	42	1	5	6	40	....	....	....	....	....
2006-07	Camrose Kodiaks	AJHL	59	11	24	35	57	17	2	7	9	26
2007-08	Camrose Kodiaks	AJHL	52	3	24	27	40	18	5	10	15	18
2008-09	Merrimack College	H-East	34	5	11	16	26	....	....	....	....	....
2009-10	Merrimack College	H-East	35	4	15	19	42	....	....	....	....	....
2010-11	Merrimack College	H-East	39	6	21	27	48	....	....	....	....	....
2011-12	Merrimack College	H-East	37	7	14	21	58	....	....	....	....	....
	Lake Erie Monsters	AHL	9	2	5	7	4	....	....	....	....	....
2012-13	Lake Erie Monsters	AHL	72	5	29	34	62	....	....	....	....	....

Hockey East All-Rookie Team (2009) • Hockey East Second All-Star Team (2012)

Signed to a ATO (amateur tryout) contract by **Lake Erie** (AHL), March 23, 2012. Signed as a free agent by **Colorado**, May 2, 2013.

STORM, Ben (STOHRM, BEHN) **COL**

Defense. Shoots left. 6'6", 216 lbs. Born, Hancock, MI, March 30, 1994.
(Colorado's 6th choice, 153rd overall, in 2013 Entry Draft).

			Regular Season					Playoffs				
Season	Club	League	GP	G	A	Pts	PIM	GP	G	A	Pts	PIM
2009-10	Calumet High	High-MI	29	13	14	27	35	....	....	....	....	....
2010-11	Calumet High	High-MI	30	11	19	30	34	....	....	....	....	....
2011-12	Calumet High	High-MI	26	15	20	35	24	....	....	....	....	....
2012-13	Muskegon	USHL	52	2	10	12	82	3	0	0	0	2

• Signed Letter of Intent to attend **St. Cloud State University** (WCHA) in fall of 2013.

STOYKEWYCH, Peter (STOY-kuh-wihch, PEE-tuhr) **WPG**

Defense. Shoots left. 6'3", 200 lbs. Born, Winnipeg, Man., July 14, 1992.
(Atlanta's 9th choice, 199th overall, in 2010 Entry Draft).

			Regular Season					Playoffs				
Season	Club	League	GP	G	A	Pts	PIM	GP	G	A	Pts	PIM
2007-08	Winnipeg Wild	MMHL	39	1	21	22	22	....	....	....	....	....
2008-09	Wpg. South Blues	MJHL	28	2	7	9	....	....	....	....	....	....
2009-10	Wpg. South Blues	MJHL	56	6	25	31	63	4	1	0	1	16
2010-11	Des Moines	USHL	58	5	10	15	77	....	....	....	....	....
2011-12	Colorado College	WCHA	26	0	3	3	14	....	....	....	....	....
2012-13	Colorado College	WCHA	42	2	9	11	20	....	....	....	....	....

• Transferred to **Winnipeg** after **Atlanta** franchise relocated, June 21, 2011.

STRAKA, Petr (STRAH-kuh, PEH-tuhr) **PHI**

Right wing. Shoots left. 6'1", 181 lbs. Born, Plzen, Czech., June 15, 1992.
(Columbus' 3rd choice, 55th overall, in 2010 Entry Draft).

			Regular Season					Playoffs				
Season	Club	League	GP	G	A	Pts	PIM	GP	G	A	Pts	PIM
2006-07	HC Plzen U17	CzR-U17	22	5	6	11	14	7	0	0	0	0
2007-08	HC Plzen U17	CzR-U17	46	40	34	74	42	8	5	9	14	4
2008-09	HC Plzen U17	CzR-U17	1	1	2	3	4	1	0	2	2	2
	HC Plzen Jr.	CzRep-Jr.	27	13	10	23	6	5	3	1	4	2
2009-10	Rimouski Oceanic	QMJHL	62	28	36	64	54	12	5	9	14	10
2010-11	Rimouski Oceanic	QMJHL	41	10	15	25	33	5	2	2	4	0
2011-12	Rimouski Oceanic	QMJHL	54	18	19	37	41	21	10	12	22	6
2012-13	Baie-Comeau	QMJHL	55	41	41	82	34	19	11	14	25	12

QMJHL All-Rookie Team (2010) • Canadian Major Junior All-Rookie Team (2010)

Signed as a free agent by **Philadelphia**, April 24, 2013.

STRANSKY, Matej (STRAHN-skee, MAH-tay) **DAL**

Right wing. Shoots right. 6'3", 215 lbs. Born, Ostrava, Czech Republic, July 11, 1993.
(Dallas' 5th choice, 165th overall, in 2011 Entry Draft).

			Regular Season					Playoffs				
Season	Club	League	GP	G	A	Pts	PIM	GP	G	A	Pts	PIM
2006-07	HC Vitkovice U17	CzR-U17	1	0	0	0	0	....	....	....	....	....
2007-08	HC Vitkovice U17	CzR-U17	43	5	14	19	22	3	1	1	2	2
2008-09	HC Vitkovice U17	CzR-U17	46	40	23	63	68	7	5	5	10	6
2009-10	HC Vitkovice U18	CzR-U18	43	17	33	50	112	2	1	2	3	4
	HC Vitkovice Jr.	CzRep-Jr.	11	2	1	3	4	....	....	....	....	....
2010-11	Saskatoon Blades	WHL	71	14	12	26	53	10	3	6	9	8
2011-12	Saskatoon Blades	WHL	70	39	42	81	75	4	1	1	2	2
2012-13	Saskatoon Blades	WHL	72	40	45	85	88	4	0	0	0	4

STROME, Ryan (STROHM, RIGH-uhn) **NYI**

Center. Shoots right. 6'1", 188 lbs. Born, Mississauga, Ont., July 11, 1993.
(NY Islanders' 1st choice, 5th overall, in 2011 Entry Draft).

			Regular Season					Playoffs				
Season	Club	League	GP	G	A	Pts	PIM	GP	G	A	Pts	PIM
2008-09	Toronto Marlboros	GTHL	76	41	63	104	86	....	....	....	....	....
2009-10	Barrie Colts	OHL	34	5	9	14	35	....	....	....	....	....
	Niagara Ice Dogs	OHL	27	3	10	13	26	5	0	3	3	0
2010-11	Niagara Ice Dogs	OHL	65	33	73	106	82	14	6	6	12	19
2011-12	Niagara Ice Dogs	OHL	46	30	38	68	47	20	7	16	23	31
2012-13	Niagara Ice Dogs	OHL	53	34	60	94	59	5	2	1	3	8
	Bridgeport	AHL	10	2	5	7	4	....	....	....	....	....

OHL Second All-Star Team (2011)

SUBBAN, Jordan (soo-BAN, JOHR-duhn) **VAN**

Defense. Shoots right. 5'9", 175 lbs. Born, Toronto, Ont., March 3, 1995.
(Vancouver's 4th choice, 115th overall, in 2013 Entry Draft).

			Regular Season					Playoffs				
Season	Club	League	GP	G	A	Pts	PIM	GP	G	A	Pts	PIM
2010-11	Toronto Marlboros	GTHL	68	21	43	64	64	....	....	....	....	....
2011-12	Belleville Bulls	OHL	56	5	15	20	31	5	0	0	0	4
2012-13	Belleville Bulls	OHL	68	15	36	51	47	17	2	3	5	20

SULLIVAN, Colin (SUHL-ih-vuhn, KAWL-ihn) **MTL**

Defense. Shoots right. 6'1", 197 lbs. Born, Milford, CT, March 26, 1993.
(Montreal's 6th choice, 198th overall, in 2011 Entry Draft).

			Regular Season					Playoffs				
Season	Club	League	GP	G	A	Pts	PIM	GP	G	A	Pts	PIM
2009-10	Avon Old Farms	High-CT	29	1	8	9	16	....	....	....	....	....
2010-11	Avon Old Farms	High-CT	27	3	12	15	14	....	....	....	....	....
2011-12	Avon Old Farms	High-CT	24	7	9	16	24	....	....	....	....	....
2012-13	Boston College	H-East	32	0	1	1	6	....	....	....	....	....

SUNDHER, Kevin (SUHND-hurh, KEH-vihn) **BUF**

Center. Shoots left. 6', 181 lbs. Born, Surrey, B.C., January 18, 1992.
(Buffalo's 3rd choice, 75th overall, in 2010 Entry Draft).

			Regular Season					Playoffs				
Season	Club	League	GP	G	A	Pts	PIM	GP	G	A	Pts	PIM
2007-08	Valley West Hawks	BCMML	40	20	34	54	86	....	....	....	....	....
	Chilliwack Bruins	WHL	6	0	1	1	2	....	....	....	....	....
2008-09	Chilliwack Bruins	WHL	67	19	20	39	68	....	....	....	....	....
2009-10	Chilliwack Bruins	WHL	72	25	36	61	101	6	3	2	5	4
2010-11	Chilliwack Bruins	WHL	70	24	52	76	93	5	3	4	7	6
2011-12	Victoria Royals	WHL	40	22	42	64	51	....	....	....	....	....
	Brandon	WHL	18	4	7	11	12	9	1	2	3	9
2012-13	Rochester	AHL	38	4	9	13	26	....	....	....	....	....

SUNDQVIST, Oskar (SUHND-qvihst, AWS-kuhr) **PIT**

Center. Shoots right. 6'3", 182 lbs. Born, Boden, Sweden, March 23, 1994.
(Pittsburgh's 4th choice, 81st overall, in 2012 Entry Draft).

			Regular Season					Playoffs				
Season	Club	League	GP	G	A	Pts	PIM	GP	G	A	Pts	PIM
2010-11	Skelleftea AIK Jr.	Swe-Jr.	1	0	0	0	0	....	....	....	....	....
	Skelleftea AIK U18	Swe-U18	38	19	16	35	100	8	1	0	1	29
2011-12	Skelleftea AIK Jr.	Swe-Jr.	2	1	0	1	0	....	....	....	....	....
	Skelleftea AIK U18	Swe-U18	39	21	32	53	129	7	5	5	10	14
2012-13	Skelleftea AIK	Sweden	14	1	0	1	8	....	....	....	....	....
	Skelleftea AIK Jr.	Swe-Jr.	38	17	16	33	48	5	3	2	5	4

SUNDSTROM, Johan (SOOND-struhm, YOH-han) **NYI**

Center. Shoots right. 6'3", 201 lbs. Born, Gothenburg, Sweden, September 21, 1992.
(NY Islanders' 3rd choice, 50th overall, in 2011 Entry Draft).

			Regular Season					Playoffs				
Season	Club	League	GP	G	A	Pts	PIM	GP	G	A	Pts	PIM
2008-09	Frolunda U18	Swe-U18	22	6	7	13	4	7	0	2	2	0
2009-10	Frolunda U18	Swe-U18	5	6	4	10	6	1	0	0	0	0
	Frolunda Jr.	Swe-Jr.	37	13	17	30	14	1	0	0	0	0
	Frolunda	Sweden	1	0	0	0	0	....	....	....	....	....
2010-11	Frolunda Jr.	Swe-Jr.	15	10	9	19	4	7	8	7	15	2
	Boras HC	Sweden-2	1	0	0	0	0	....	....	....	....	....
	Frolunda	Sweden	41	1	0	1	10	....	....	....	....	....
2011-12	Frolunda	Sweden	49	6	5	11	8	6	0	0	0	2
2012-13	Bridgeport	AHL	59	11	21	32	30	....	....	....	....	....

SUTTER, Brody (SUH-tuhr, BROH-dee) **CAR**

Center. Shoots right. 6'4", 203 lbs. Born, Viking, Alta., September 26, 1991.
(Carolina's 6th choice, 193rd overall, in 2011 Entry Draft).

			Regular Season					Playoffs				
Season	Club	League	GP	G	A	Pts	PIM	GP	G	A	Pts	PIM
2007-08	Calgary Buffaloes	AMHL	32	8	11	19	24	12	4	6	10	4
2008-09	Saskatoon Blades	WHL	18	0	2	2	4	....	....	....	....	....
	Lethbridge	WHL	30	4	3	7	7	10	0	0	0	2
2009-10	Lethbridge	WHL	72	5	9	14	42	....	....	....	....	....
2010-11	Lethbridge	WHL	46	18	24	42	35	....	....	....	....	....
2011-12	Lethbridge	WHL	65	30	30	60	49	....	....	....	....	....
	Charlotte	AHL	4	1	0	1	0	....	....	....	....	....
2012-13	Charlotte	AHL	23	3	2	5	13	5	2	3	5	2
	Florida Everblades	ECHL	37	8	8	16	13	....	....	....	....	....

SUTTER, Lukas (suh-TUHR, LOO-kuhs) **WPG**

Center. Shoots left. 6'1", 214 lbs. Born, St. Louis, MO, October 4, 1993.
(Winnipeg's 2nd choice, 39th overall, in 2012 Entry Draft).

			Regular Season					Playoffs				
Season	Club	League	GP	G	A	Pts	PIM	GP	G	A	Pts	PIM
2007-08	Lethbridge	AMBHL	33	14	28	42	110	5	1	4	5	6
2008-09	Lethbridge	AMHL	33	6	5	11	83	6	2	1	3	31
	Okotoks Oilers	AJHL	2	0	0	0	0	....	....	....	....	....
2009-10	Lethbridge	AMHL	13	6	6	12	16	5	2	1	3	4
	Saskatoon Blades	WHL	7	0	1	1	8	5	0	0	0	2
2010-11	Saskatoon Blades	WHL	71	4	15	19	179	10	0	0	0	6
2011-12	Saskatoon Blades	WHL	70	28	31	59	165	4	0	2	2	14
2012-13	Saskatoon Blades	WHL	72	13	11	24	168	4	2	0	2	6

SZWARZ, Jordan (SWAWRZ, JOHR-dahn) **PHX**

Right wing. Shoots right. 5'11", 196 lbs. Born, Burlington, Ont., May 14, 1991.
(Phoenix's 4th choice, 97th overall, in 2009 Entry Draft).

			Regular Season					Playoffs				
Season	Club	League	GP	G	A	Pts	PIM	GP	G	A	Pts	PIM
2006-07	Burlington Eagles	Minor-ON	66	56	54	110	88	....	....	....	....	....
2007-08	Saginaw Spirit	OHL	65	12	21	33	56	4	0	0	0	2
2008-09	Saginaw Spirit	OHL	67	17	34	51	76	8	1	5	6	10
2009-10	Saginaw Spirit	OHL	65	26	28	54	82	6	1	2	3	0
	San Antonio	AHL	1	0	0	0	0	....	....	....	....	....
2010-11	Saginaw Spirit	OHL	65	27	39	66	90	12	4	9	13	8
2011-12	Portland Pirates	AHL	58	7	13	20	28	....	....	....	....	....
2012-13	Portland Pirates	AHL	60	11	22	33	31	....	....	....	....	....

SZYDLOWSKI, Shawn (sihd-LOW-skee, SHAWN) **BUF**

Right wing. Shoots right. 6', 206 lbs. Born, St. Clair Shores, MI, August 5, 1990.

			Regular Season					Playoffs				
Season	Club	League	GP	G	A	Pts	PIM	GP	G	A	Pts	PIM
2007-08	Erie Otters	OHL	66	9	16	25	57	....	....	....	....	....
2008-09	Erie Otters	OHL	61	23	23	46	80	5	3	0	3	14
2009-10	Erie Otters	OHL	65	21	27	48	90	4	1	4	5	2
2010-11	Erie Otters	OHL	66	41	37	78	79	7	2	5	7	14
	Portland Pirates	AHL	2	0	0	0	0	....	....	....	....	....
2011-12	Gwinnett	ECHL	6	1	2	3	0	....	....	....	....	....
	Rochester	AHL	53	0	8	8	21	....	....	....	....	....
2012-13	Rochester	AHL	7	0	0	0	4	....	....	....	....	....

Signed as a free agent by **Buffalo**, April 8, 2011.

TAMBELLINI, Adam (tam-buh-LEE-nee, A-duhm) **NYR**

Center. Shoots left. 6'2", 169 lbs. Born, Port Moody, B.C., November 1, 1994.
(NY Rangers' 1st choice, 65th overall, in 2013 Entry Draft).

			Regular Season					Playoffs				
Season	Club	League	GP	G	A	Pts	PIM	GP	G	A	Pts	PIM
2009-10	SSAC Bulldogs	Minor-AB	34	27	24	51	20	6	6	4	10	10
2010-11	SSAC Athletics	AMHL	33	22	25	47	4	5	4	2	6	0
	Sherwood Park	AJHL	3	1	0	1	0	....	....	....	....	....
2011-12	Vernon Vipers	BCHL	55	27	29	56	28	....	....	....	....	....
2012-13	Vernon Vipers	BCHL	36	22	17	39	18	....	....	....	....	....
	Surrey Eagles	BCHL	16	14	12	26	8	17	*10	8	*18	6

• Signed Letter of Intent to attend **University of North Dakota** (WCHA) in fall of 2013.

TARDY, Max (TAHR-dee, MAX) **ST.L.**

Center. Shoots right. 6', 185 lbs. Born, Duluth, MN, October 27, 1990.
(St. Louis' 6th choice, 202nd overall, in 2009 Entry Draft).

			Regular Season					Playoffs				
Season	Club	League	GP	G	A	Pts	PIM	GP	G	A	Pts	PIM
2006-07	Duluth East	High-MN	....	12	12	24	....	....	....	....	....	....
2007-08	Duluth East	High-MN	....	14	27	41	....	....	....	....	....	....
2008-09	Team North	UMHSEL	24	19	20	39	....	....	....	....	....	....
	Duluth East	High-MN	30	35	26	61	24	....	....	....	....	....
2009-10	Tri-City Storm	USHL	52	12	24	36	34	3	0	1	1	4
2010-11	U. Minn-Duluth	WCHA	26	1	2	3	14	....	....	....	....	....
2011-12	U. Minn-Duluth	WCHA	41	2	5	7	6	....	....	....	....	....
2012-13	U. Minn-Duluth	WCHA	14	0	1	1	6	....	....	....	....	....

TELEGIN, Ivan (tuh-LEH-gihn, ih-VUHN) **WPG**

Left wing. Shoots left. 6'4", 185 lbs. Born, Novokuznetsk, Russia, February 28, 1992.
(Atlanta's 3rd choice, 101st overall, in 2010 Entry Draft).

			Regular Season					Playoffs				
Season	Club	League	GP	G	A	Pts	PIM	GP	G	A	Pts	PIM
2008-09	Novokuznetsk 2	Russia-3	STATISTICS NOT AVAILABLE									
2009-10	Saginaw Spirit	OHL	51	26	18	44	20	6	1	1	2	6
2010-11	Saginaw Spirit	OHL	59	20	41	61	35	12	2	8	10	8
2011-12	Barrie Colts	OHL	46	35	29	64	26	13	5	9	14	6
2012-13	St. John's IceCaps	AHL	34	3	7	10	8	....	....	....	....	....

• Transferred to **Winnipeg** after **Atlanta** franchise relocated, June 21, 2011.

TERAVAINEN, Teuvo (tehr-a-VIGH-nuhn, TEW-voh) **CHI**

Left wing. Shoots left. 5'11", 169 lbs. Born, Helsinki, Finland, September 11, 1994.
(Chicago's 1st choice, 18th overall, in 2012 Entry Draft).

			Regular Season					Playoffs				
Season	Club	League	GP	G	A	Pts	PIM	GP	G	A	Pts	PIM
2009-10	Jokerit U18	Fin-U18	29	16	14	30	6	4	0	4	4	0
2010-11	Jokerit U18	Fin-U18	4	1	3	4	2	1	0	1	1	25
	Jokerit Helsinki Jr.	Fin-Jr.	26	3	17	20	8	8	1	4	5	4
2011-12	Jokerit Helsinki Jr.	Fin-Jr.	11	12	8	20	4	2	1	1	2	0
	Kiekko-Vantaa	Finland-2	3	1	2	3	0	....	....	....	....	....
	Jokerit Helsinki	Finland	40	11	7	18	6	9	2	4	6	0
2012-13	Kiekko-Vantaa	Finland-2	1	0	1	1	0	....	....	....	....	....
	Jokerit Helsinki	Finland	44	13	18	31	6	6	1	1	2	0

TESINK, Ryan (TEH-sihnk, RIGH-uhn) **ST.L.**

Center. Shoots left. 6', 165 lbs. Born, Saint John, N.B., May 21, 1993.
(St. Louis' 7th choice, 162nd overall, in 2011 Entry Draft).

			Regular Season					Playoffs				
Season	Club	League	GP	G	A	Pts	PIM	GP	G	A	Pts	PIM
2008-09	Holderness School	High-NH	28	4	13	17	....	....	....	....	....	....
2009-10	Woodstock	MJrHL	44	10	19	29	96	14	4	6	10	12
2010-11	Saint John	QMJHL	59	8	27	35	38	19	3	2	5	10
2011-12	Saint John	QMJHL	36	13	27	40	54	17	7	6	13	24
2012-13	Saint John	QMJHL	35	16	21	37	75	....	....	....	....	....
	Blainville-Bois.	QMJHL	6	1	3	4	6	4	1	0	1	23

TESTWUIDE, Mike (TEHST-wud, MIGHK)

Right wing. Shoots right. 6'3", 210 lbs. Born, Vail, CO, February 5, 1987.

			Regular Season					Playoffs				
Season	Club	League	GP	G	A	Pts	PIM	GP	G	A	Pts	PIM
2004-05	Waterloo	USHL	46	2	8	10	43	4	0	1	1	4
2005-06	Waterloo	USHL	54	18	13	31	88	....	....	....	....	....
2006-07	Colorado College	WCHA	29	8	2	10	25	....	....	....	....	....
2007-08	Colorado College	WCHA	33	11	10	21	31	....	....	....	....	....
2008-09	Colorado College	WCHA	36	4	5	9	20	....	....	....	....	....
2009-10	Colorado College	WCHA	36	21	10	31	26	....	....	....	....	....
2010-11	Adirondack	AHL	76	18	21	39	62	....	....	....	....	....
2011-12	Adirondack	AHL	66	12	17	29	79	....	....	....	....	....
2012-13	Adirondack	AHL	19	2	0	2	27	....	....	....	....	....
	Abbotsford Heat	AHL	9	2	1	3	28	....	....	....	....	....

Signed as a free agent by **Philadelphia**, March 19, 2010. Traded to **Calgary** by **Philadelphia** for Mitch Wahl, February 26, 2013.

THEODORE, Shea (THEE-oh-dohr, SHAY) **ANA**

Defense. Shoots left. 6'1", 173 lbs. Born, Langley, B.C., August 3, 1995.
(Anaheim's 1st choice, 26th overall, in 2013 Entry Draft).

			Regular Season					Playoffs				
Season	Club	League	GP	G	A	Pts	PIM	GP	G	A	Pts	PIM
2010-11	Fraser Valley	BCMML	35	5	24	29	28	....	....	....	....	....
	Seattle	WHL	4	0	0	0	2	....	....	....	....	....
2011-12	Seattle	WHL	69	4	31	35	30	....	....	....	....	....
2012-13	Seattle	WHL	71	19	31	50	32	7	0	2	2	4

THOMPSON, Keaton (TAWM-suhn, KEE-tuhn) **ANA**

Defense. Shoots left. 6', 182 lbs. Born, Edina, MN, September 14, 1995.
(Anaheim's 3rd choice, 87th overall, in 2013 Entry Draft).

			Regular Season					Playoffs				
Season	Club	League	GP	G	A	Pts	PIM	GP	G	A	Pts	PIM
2010-11	Fargo Force	USHL	13	0	0	0	4	2	0	0	0	5
	Team Great Plains	UMHSEL	16	0	1	1	12	3	0	2	2	4
2011-12	USNTDP	USHL	35	4	9	13	17	2	0	0	0	2
	USNTDP	U-17	17	1	8	9	14	....	....	....	....	....
2012-13	USNTDP	USHL	26	3	6	9	18	....	....	....	....	....
	USNTDP	U-18	41	1	12	13	22	....	....	....	....	....

• Signed Letter of Intent to attend **University of North Dakota** (WCHA) in fall of 2014.

THOMPSON, Paul (TAWM-suhn, PAWL) **PIT**

Right wing. Shoots right. 6'1", 198 lbs. Born, Melrose, MA, November 30, 1988.

			Regular Season					Playoffs				
Season	Club	League	GP	G	A	Pts	PIM	GP	G	A	Pts	PIM
2005-06	N.H. Jr. Monarchs	EJHL	38	13	17	30	20	....	....	....	....	....
2006-07	N.H. Jr. Monarchs	EJHL	44	45	38	83	56	....	....	....	....	....
2007-08	New Hampshire	H-East	35	6	6	12	22	....	....	....	....	....
2008-09	New Hampshire	H-East	27	4	5	9	22	....	....	....	....	....
2009-10	New Hampshire	H-East	39	19	20	39	24	....	....	....	....	....
2010-11	New Hampshire	H-East	39	28	24	*52	30	....	....	....	....	....
	Wilkes-Barre	AHL	6	1	2	3	2	4	0	1	1	2
2011-12	Wilkes-Barre	AHL	67	10	15	25	37	12	2	1	3	2
	Wheeling Nailers	ECHL	1	1	1	2	0	....	....	....	....	....
2012-13	Wilkes-Barre	AHL	58	20	9	29	84	15	3	3	6	21

Hockey East First All-Star Team (2011) • NCAA East First All-American Team (2011) • Hockey East Player of the Year (2011)

Signed as a free agent by **Pittsburgh**, March 28, 2011.

THOMSON, Ben (TAWM-suhn, BEHN) **N.J.**

Left wing. Shoots left. 6'3", 205 lbs. Born, Brampton, Ont., January 16, 1993.
(New Jersey's 4th choice, 96th overall, in 2012 Entry Draft).

			Regular Season					Playoffs				
Season	Club	League	GP	G	A	Pts	PIM	GP	G	A	Pts	PIM
2008-09	Mississauga Reps	GTHL	20	13	25	38	88	....	....	....	....	....
2009-10	Kitchener Rangers	OHL	46	6	6	12	30	11	0	1	1	6
2010-11	Kitchener Rangers	OHL	68	6	13	19	107	7	0	1	1	0
2011-12	Kitchener Rangers	OHL	67	11	31	42	137	16	5	5	10	36
2012-13	Kitchener Rangers	OHL	67	15	17	32	119	10	1	2	3	18

THROWER, Dalton (THROW-uhr, DAHL-tuhn) **MTL**

Defense. Shoots right. 6', 203 lbs. Born, Squamish, B.C., December 20, 1993.
(Montreal's 3rd choice, 51st overall, in 2012 Entry Draft).

			Regular Season					Playoffs				
Season	Club	League	GP	G	A	Pts	PIM	GP	G	A	Pts	PIM
2008-09	Van. NW Giants	BCMML	31	8	11	19	72	5	1	0	1	6
2009-10	Saskatoon Blades	WHL	55	0	7	7	61	8	0	1	1	2
2010-11	Saskatoon Blades	WHL	68	6	14	20	91	10	2	1	3	11
2011-12	Saskatoon Blades	WHL	66	18	36	54	103	4	0	1	1	4
2012-13	Saskatoon Blades	WHL	54	6	21	27	89	4	0	0	0	6

TIERNEY, Chris (TEER-nee, KRIHS) **S.J.**

Center. Shoots left. 6', 195 lbs. Born, Keswick, Ont., July 1, 1994.
(San Jose's 2nd choice, 55th overall, in 2012 Entry Draft).

			Regular Season					Playoffs				
Season	Club	League	GP	G	A	Pts	PIM	GP	G	A	Pts	PIM
2009-10	York Simcoe	Minor-ON	57	35	55	90	28	....	....	....	....	....
	York Simcoe	Exhib.	6	2	1	3	0	....	....	....	....	....
2010-11	London Knights	OHL	47	3	8	11	12	4	0	1	1	0
2011-12	London Knights	OHL	65	11	23	34	20	19	5	2	7	4
2012-13	London Knights	OHL	68	18	39	57	12	21	6	15	21	6

TIKKINEN, Niklas (TIHK-ih-nehn, NIHK-luhs) **PHX**

Defense. Shoots left. 5'11", 172 lbs. Born, Espoo, Finland, June 1, 1994.
(Phoenix's 5th choice, 148th overall, in 2012 Entry Draft).

			Regular Season					Playoffs				
Season	Club	League	GP	G	A	Pts	PIM	GP	G	A	Pts	PIM
2009-10	Blues Espoo U18	Fin-U18	15	3	1	4	8	1	0	1	1	0
2010-11	Blues Espoo U18	Fin-U18	34	8	23	31	8	13	3	4	7	6
	Blues Espoo Jr.	Fin-Jr.	1	0	0	0	0	....	....	....	....	....
2011-12	Blues Espoo Jr.	Fin-Jr.	39	8	15	23	14	4	0	1	1	4
	Blues Espoo U18	Fin-U18	7	3	9	12	32	9	2	8	10	12
2012-13	Blues Espoo	Finland	25	1	7	8	12	....	....	....	....	....
	HCK	Finland-2	5	1	2	3	0	....	....	....	....	....
	LeKi Lempaala	Finland-2	2	0	3	3	0	....	....	....	....	....
	Blues Espoo Jr.	Fin-Jr.	14	3	15	18	6	12	5	4	9	16

TOCHKIN, Kellan (TAWCH-kihn, KEHL-uhn) VAN

Right wing. Shoots right. 5'10", 172 lbs. Born, Abbotsford, B.C., February 15, 1991.

			Regular Season					Playoffs				
Season	Club	League	GP	G	A	Pts	PIM	GP	G	A	Pts	PIM
2006-07	Fraser Valley	BCMML	37	34	34	68	48	....	....	....	....	....
	Everett Silvertips	WHL	3	0	0	0	2	....	....	....	....	....
2007-08	Ridge Meadow	PIJHL	32	24	35	59	56	10	3	8	11	2
	Langley Chiefs	BCHL	1	0	1	1	0	....	....	....	....	....
2008-09	Everett Silvertips	WHL	72	20	54	74	37	2	1	0	1	2
2009-10	Everett Silvertips	WHL	72	28	40	68	64	7	1	1	2	11
2010-11	Everett Silvertips	WHL	38	17	19	36	30	....	....	....	....	....
	Medicine Hat	WHL	32	12	16	28	38	15	5	7	12	20
2011-12	Medicine Hat	WHL	10	0	8	8	16	....	....	....	....	....
	Prince Albert	WHL	29	14	15	29	30	....	....	....	....	....
2012-13	Missouri Mavericks	CHL	56	15	29	44	61	12	8	9	17	10

Signed as a free agent by **Vancouver**, July 27, 2009.

TOMMERNES, Henrik (TOHM-uhr-nehs, HEHN-rihk) VAN

Defense. Shoots left. 6'1", 176 lbs. Born, Karlstad, Sweden, August 28, 1990.
(Vancouver's 8th choice, 210th overall, in 2011 Entry Draft).

			Regular Season					Playoffs				
Season	Club	League	GP	G	A	Pts	PIM	GP	G	A	Pts	PIM
2006-07	Farjestad U18	Swe-U18	14	3	6	9	32	8	3	4	7	4
2007-08	Farjestad U18	Swe-U18	22	4	16	20	10	8	0	3	3	10
2008-09	Frolunda Jr.	Swe-Jr.	40	10	22	32	52	5	2	6	8	8
	Frolunda	Sweden	11	0	0	0	0	....	....	....	....	....
2009-10	Frolunda Jr.	Swe-Jr.	4	1	1	2	4	....	....	....	....	....
	Boras HC	Sweden-2	23	5	9	14	43	....	....	....	....	....
	Frolunda	Sweden	27	0	3	3	10	7	0	1	1	2
2010-11	Frolunda	Sweden	47	3	17	20	24	....	....	....	....	....
2011-12	Frolunda	Sweden	44	5	9	14	36	6	1	3	4	4
2012-13	Frolunda	Sweden	54	5	11	16	28	6	1	4	5	6

TONINATO, Dominic (toh-nee-NAH-toh, DOHM-ihn-ihk) TOR

Center. Shoots left. 6'1", 165 lbs. Born, Duluth, MN, March 9, 1994.
(Toronto's 3rd choice, 126th overall, in 2012 Entry Draft).

			Regular Season					Playoffs				
Season	Club	League	GP	G	A	Pts	PIM	GP	G	A	Pts	PIM
2009-10	Duluth East	High-MN	31	8	11	19	12	....	....	....	....	....
2010-11	Team North	UMHSEL	24	11	8	19	12	....	....	....	....	....
	Duluth East	High-MN	29	28	33	61	12	....	....	....	....	....
2011-12	Team North	UMHSEL	24	10	15	25	30	....	....	....	....	....
	Duluth East	High-MN	31	33	40	73	32	....	....	....	....	....
	Fargo Force	USHL	4	1	0	1	2	....	....	....	....	....
2012-13	Fargo Force	USHL	64	29	41	70	50	12	3	3	6	6

USHL Second All-Star Team (2013)

• Signed Letter of Intent to attend **University of Minnesota-Duluth** (WCHA) in fall of 2013.

TROCHECK, Vincent (TROH-chehk, VOHN-sihnt) FLA

Center. Shoots right. 5'11", 190 lbs. Born, Pittsburgh, PA, July 11, 1993.
(Florida's 4th choice, 64th overall, in 2011 Entry Draft).

			Regular Season					Playoffs				
Season	Club	League	GP	G	A	Pts	PIM	GP	G	A	Pts	PIM
2008-09	Little Caesars	T1EHL	44	27	19	46	32	7	1	4	5	0
2009-10	Saginaw Spirit	OHL	68	15	28	43	56	6	2	2	4	2
2010-11	Saginaw Spirit	OHL	68	26	36	62	60	12	6	5	11	4
2011-12	Saginaw Spirit	OHL	65	29	56	85	65	12	5	6	11	10
2012-13	Saginaw Spirit	OHL	35	24	26	*50	34	....	....	....	....	....
	Plymouth Whalers	OHL	28	26	33	*59	24	15	10	14	24	8

OHL First All-Star Team (2013) • OHL Player of the Year (2013)

TROOCK, Branden (TROOK, BRAN-duhn) DAL

Right wing. Shoots right. 6'3", 194 lbs. Born, Edmonton, Alta., March 20, 1994.
(Dallas' 7th choice, 134th overall, in 2012 Entry Draft).

			Regular Season					Playoffs				
Season	Club	League	GP	G	A	Pts	PIM	GP	G	A	Pts	PIM
2008-09	CAC Lehigh	AMBHL	32	21	28	49	82	....	....	....	....	....
2009-10	CAC Gregg's Dist.	AMHL	27	19	18	37	38	2	0	3	3	2
	Seattle	WHL	9	2	4	6	4	....	....	....	....	....
2010-11			DID NOT PLAY – INJURED									
2011-12	Seattle	WHL	58	14	12	26	83	....	....	....	....	....
2012-13	Seattle	WHL	19	5	6	11	19	....	....	....	....	....

• Missed remainder of 2009-10 and all of 2010-11 due to head injury, playing for Team Alberta, in Western Canada Under-16 Challenge Tournament, October 31, 2009. • Missed majority of 2012-13 due to shoulder injury vs. Lethbridge (WHL), January 20, 2013.

TROTMAN, Zach (TRAWT-muhn, ZAK) BOS

Defense. Shoots right. 6'3", 216 lbs. Born, Novi, MI, August 26, 1990.
(Boston's 8th choice, 210th overall, in 2010 Entry Draft).

			Regular Season					Playoffs				
Season	Club	League	GP	G	A	Pts	PIM	GP	G	A	Pts	PIM
2008-09	Wichita Falls	NAHL	47	2	4	6	79	5	0	1	1	8
2009-10	Lake Superior	CCHA	36	2	6	8	18	....	....	....	....	....
2010-11	Lake Superior	CCHA	38	6	14	20	12	....	....	....	....	....
2011-12	Lake Superior	CCHA	40	11	10	21	12	....	....	....	....	....
	Providence Bruins	AHL	9	1	2	3	2	....	....	....	....	....
2012-13	Providence Bruins	AHL	48	2	14	16	19	4	0	0	0	0

TROUBA, Jacob (TROO-buh, JAY-kuhb) WPG

Defense. Shoots right. 6'2", 196 lbs. Born, Rochester, MI, February 26, 1994.
(Winnipeg's 1st choice, 9th overall, in 2012 Entry Draft).

			Regular Season					Playoffs				
Season	Club	League	GP	G	A	Pts	PIM	GP	G	A	Pts	PIM
2009-10	Det. Compuware	T1EHL	38	14	14	28	40	....	....	....	....	....
	Det. Compuware	Exhib.	6	3	5	8	12	....	....	....	....	....
	Det. Comp. U18	T1EHL	3	3	0	3	2	....	....	....	....	....
2010-11	USNTDP	USHL	31	3	4	7	31	....	....	....	....	....
	USNTDP	U-17	17	4	12	16	18	....	....	....	....	....
	USNTDP	U-18	10	1	2	3	10	....	....	....	....	....
2011-12	USNTDP	USHL	22	4	14	18	35	....	....	....	....	....
	USNTDP	U-18	32	5	9	14	36	....	....	....	....	....
2012-13	U. of Michigan	CCHA	37	12	17	29	88	....	....	....	....	....

CCHA All-Rookie Team (2013) • CCHA First All-Star Team (2013) • NCAA West First All-American Team (2013)

TVRDON, Marek (T'VAIR-doin, MAIR-ehk) DET

Right wing. Shoots left. 6'2", 210 lbs. Born, Nitra, Slovakia, January 31, 1993.
(Detroit's 5th choice, 115th overall, in 2011 Entry Draft).

			Regular Season					Playoffs				
Season	Club	League	GP	G	A	Pts	PIM	GP	G	A	Pts	PIM
2007-08	HK Ardo Nitra U18	Svk-U18	20	5	4	9	10	....	....	....	....	....
2008-09	HK Nitra U18	Svk-U18	58	50	33	83	113	....	....	....	....	....
	HK Nitra Jr.	Slovak-Jr.	....	....	....	....	....	1	0	0	0	0
2009-10	HK Nitra Jr.	Slovak-Jr.	45	25	31	56	90	....	....	....	....	....
	HK Nitra	Slovakia	6	0	0	0	2	1	0	0	0	0
2010-11	Vancouver Giants	WHL	12	6	5	11	14	....	....	....	....	....
2011-12	Vancouver Giants	WHL	60	31	43	74	62	6	3	3	6	0
2012-13	Vancouver Giants	WHL	18	8	14	22	16	....	....	....	....	....

TYNAN, T.J. (TIGH-nuhn, TAW-muhs) CBJ

Center. Shoots right. 5'8", 165 lbs. Born, Orland Park, IL, February 25, 1992.
(Columbus' 2nd choice, 66th overall, in 2011 Entry Draft).

			Regular Season					Playoffs				
Season	Club	League	GP	G	A	Pts	PIM	GP	G	A	Pts	PIM
2009-10	Des Moines	USHL	60	17	*55	72	55	....	....	....	....	....
2010-11	U. of Notre Dame	CCHA	44	23	31	54	36	....	....	....	....	....
2011-12	U. of Notre Dame	CCHA	39	13	28	41	38	....	....	....	....	....
2012-13	U. of Notre Dame	CCHA	41	10	18	28	28	....	....	....	....	....

USHL All-Rookie Team (2010) • CCHA All-Rookie Team (2011) • CCHA Second All-Star Team (2011) • CCHA Rookie of the Year (2011) • CCHA First All-Star Team (2012)

TYRVAINEN, Antti (TUHR-va-nihn, AHN-tee) EDM

Left wing. Shoots left. 5'11", 200 lbs. Born, Seinajoki, Finland, April 3, 1989.

			Regular Season					Playoffs				
Season	Club	League	GP	G	A	Pts	PIM	GP	G	A	Pts	PIM
2006-07	Pelicans Lahti Jr.	Fin-Jr.	19	1	4	5	51	....	....	....	....	....
2007-08	Pelicans Lahti Jr.	Fin-Jr.	41	5	13	18	56	....	....	....	....	....
2008-09	Pelicans Lahti Jr.	Fin-Jr.	27	9	9	18	104	....	....	....	....	....
	HeKi Heinola	Finland-2	3	0	0	0	25	....	....	....	....	....
	Pelicans Lahti	Finland	5	0	0	0	0	1	0	0	0	0
2009-10	Pelicans Lahti	Finland	32	8	3	11	85	....	....	....	....	....
2010-11	Pelicans Lahti	Finland	52	14	9	23	186	....	....	....	....	....
	Pelicans Lahti	Finland-Q	....	....	....	....	....	4	3	2	5	24
2011-12	Oklahoma City	AHL	55	6	13	19	71	14	0	1	1	20
2012-13	Oklahoma City	AHL	32	3	2	5	65	16	3	3	6	28

Signed as a free agent by **Edmonton**, June 15, 2011. Signed as a free agent by **Jokerit Helsinki** (Finland), June 6, 2013.

UHER, Dominik (YEW-air, DOHM-ih-NIHK) PIT

Center. Shoots left. 6'1", 199 lbs. Born, Frydek-Mistek, Czech., December 31, 1992.
(Pittsburgh's 3rd choice, 144th overall, in 2011 Entry Draft).

			Regular Season					Playoffs				
Season	Club	League	GP	G	A	Pts	PIM	GP	G	A	Pts	PIM
2006-07	HC Trinec U17	CzR-U17	6	1	1	2	2	3	1	0	1	0
2007-08	HC Trinec U17	CzR-U17	44	5	11	16	44	5	1	0	1	4
2008-09	HC Trinec U17	CzR-U17	38	19	27	46	46	9	5	6	11	6
	HC Trinec Jr.	CzRep-Jr.	2	0	1	1	2	....	....	....	....	....
2009-10	Spokane Chiefs	WHL	53	4	12	16	45	6	0	0	0	2
2010-11	Spokane Chiefs	WHL	65	21	39	60	60	17	2	9	11	18
2011-12	Spokane Chiefs	WHL	63	33	35	68	60	13	5	4	9	6
2012-13	Wilkes-Barre	AHL	53	4	3	7	61	8	0	3	3	4
	Wheeling Nailers	ECHL	3	0	1	1	0	....	....	....	....	....

ULLY, Cole (YEW-lee, KOHL) DAL

Left wing. Shoots left. 5'11", 164 lbs. Born, Calgary, Alta., February 20, 1995.
(Dallas' 7th choice, 131st overall, in 2013 Entry Draft).

			Regular Season					Playoffs				
Season	Club	League	GP	G	A	Pts	PIM	GP	G	A	Pts	PIM
2010-11	Calgary Flames	AMHL	32	17	17	34	20	2	0	0	0	0
	Kamloops Blazers	WHL	1	0	1	1	0	....	....	....	....	....
2011-12	Kamloops Blazers	WHL	55	9	11	20	2	6	1	1	2	2
2012-13	Kamloops Blazers	WHL	62	22	28	50	37	15	1	7	8	4

VAIL, Brady (VAYL, BRAY-dee) MTL

Center. Shoots left. 6', 198 lbs. Born, Hendersonville, NC, March 11, 1994.
(Montreal's 5th choice, 94th overall, in 2012 Entry Draft).

			Regular Season					Playoffs				
Season	Club	League	GP	G	A	Pts	PIM	GP	G	A	Pts	PIM
2007-08	Det. Compuware	MWEHL	31	21	9	30	28	....	....	....	....	....
	Det. Compuware	Exhib.	4	3	0	3	2	....	....	....	....	....
2008-09	Det. Compuware	T1EHL	31	11	11	22	36	5	3	0	3	0
2009-10	Waterloo	USHL	48	4	4	8	40	2	0	0	0	0
2010-11	Windsor Spitfires	OHL	61	3	7	10	27	16	4	0	4	4
2011-12	Windsor Spitfires	OHL	68	22	30	52	55	4	0	0	0	4
2012-13	Windsor Spitfires	OHL	68	20	35	55	47	....	....	....	....	....
	Hamilton Bulldogs	AHL	12	1	3	4	4	....	....	....	....	....

VAINONEN, Mikko (VIGH-noh-nehn, MEE-koh) NSH

Defense. Shoots left. 6'2", 210 lbs. Born, Helsinki, Finland, April 11, 1994.
(Nashville's 6th choice, 118th overall, in 2012 Entry Draft).

			Regular Season					Playoffs				
Season	Club	League	GP	G	A	Pts	PIM	GP	G	A	Pts	PIM
2009-10	HIFK Helsinki U18	Fin-U18	1	0	1	1	0	....	....	....	....	....
2010-11	HIFK Helsinki U18	Fin-U18	24	4	10	14	24	1	0	0	0	0
	HIFK Helsinki Jr.	Fin-Jr.	8	1	2	3	12	4	0	0	0	6
2011-12	HIFK Helsinki U18	Fin-U18	2	0	1	1	8	1	0	0	0	2
	HIFK Helsinki Jr.	Fin-Jr.	38	7	11	18	44	10	0	1	1	12
	HIFK Helsinki	Finland	8	0	0	0	2	....	....	....	....	....
2012-13	Kingston	OHL	55	4	18	22	42	4	2	1	3	2

VALENTENKO, Pavel (val-ehn-TEHN-koh, PAH-vehl) NYR

Defense. Shoots left. 6'2", 219 lbs. Born, Nizhnekamsk, USSR, October 20, 1987.
(Montreal's 5th choice, 139th overall, in 2006 Entry Draft).

			Regular Season					Playoffs				
Season	Club	League	GP	G	A	Pts	PIM	GP	G	A	Pts	PIM
2002-03	Lada Togliatti 2	Russia-3	6	0	0	0	4	....	....	....	....	....
2003-04	Nizhnekamsk 2	Russia-3	26	0	1	1	28	....	....	....	....	....
2004-05	Nizhnekamsk 2	Russia-3	STATISTICS NOT AVAILABLE									
2005-06	Nizhnekamsk 2	Russia-3	STATISTICS NOT AVAILABLE									
	Nizhnekamsk	Russia	2	0	0	0	2	....	....	....	....	....
2006-07	Nizhnekamsk	Russia	50	0	2	2	62	4	0	0	0	2
2007-08	Hamilton Bulldogs	AHL	57	1	15	16	58	....	....	....	....	....
2008-09	Hamilton Bulldogs	AHL	4	0	2	2	2	....	....	....	....	....
	Dynamo Moscow	KHL	8	0	1	1	8	1	0	0	0	2
2009-10	Dynamo Moscow	KHL	7	0	0	0	2	....	....	....	....	....
2010-11	Connecticut Whale	AHL	79	5	12	17	38	6	0	0	0	12
2011-12	Connecticut Whale	AHL	60	5	16	21	53	9	0	3	3	6
2012-13	Omsk	KHL	39	1	2	3	48	11	2	0	2	2

• Missed majority of 2008-09 for personal reasons. Signed as a free agent by **Dynamo Moscow** (KHL), October 31, 2008. Traded to **NY Rangers** by **Montreal** with Chris Higgins and Ryan McDonagh for Scott Gomez, Tom Pyatt and Michael Busto, June 30, 2009. • Missed majority of 2009-10 due to shoulder injury. Signed as a free agent by **Omsk** (KHL), May 17, 2012.

VALENTINE, Scott (VAL-ehn-tighn, SKAWT) NSH

Defense. Shoots left. 6'1", 213 lbs. Born, Ottawa, Ont., May 2, 1991.
(Anaheim's 7th choice, 166th overall, in 2009 Entry Draft).

			Regular Season					Playoffs				
Season	Club	League	GP	G	A	Pts	PIM	GP	G	A	Pts	PIM
2007-08	Hawkesbury	ON-Jr.A	51	2	15	17	81	11	3	4	7	18
	London Knights	OHL	3	0	0	0	2	....	....	....	....	....
2008-09	London Knights	OHL	17	0	0	0	20	....	....	....	....	....
	Oshawa Generals	OHL	26	1	8	9	51	....	....	....	....	....
2009-10	Oshawa Generals	OHL	63	5	14	19	82	....	....	....	....	....
2010-11	Oshawa Generals	OHL	62	4	32	36	106	9	1	1	2	28
2011-12	Milwaukee	AHL	63	2	10	12	69	2	0	0	0	0
2012-13	Milwaukee	AHL	64	6	4	10	74	2	0	0	0	2

Signed as a free agent by **Nashville**, September 30. 2011.

VANCE, Troy (VANS, TROI) DAL

Defense. Shoots right. 6'6", 200 lbs. Born, Goshen, NY, August 2, 1993.
(Dallas' 4th choice, 135th overall, in 2011 Entry Draft).

			Regular Season					Playoffs				
Season	Club	League	GP	G	A	Pts	PIM	GP	G	A	Pts	PIM
2010-11	Phi. Revolution	EmJHL	9	1	9	10	10	....	....	....	....	....
	Phi. Revolution	EJHL	18	1	2	3	33	....	....	....	....	....
	Victoriaville Tigres	QMJHL	23	1	3	4	21	9	1	3	4	4
2011-12	Victoriaville Tigres	QMJHL	57	4	20	24	45	4	0	2	2	4
2012-13	Victoriaville Tigres	QMJHL	39	3	15	18	41	....	....	....	....	....
	P.E.I. Rocket	QMJHL	28	1	7	8	16	6	0	2	2	2

VAN GUILDER, Mark (VAN GIHL-duhr, MAHRK) NSH

Right wing. Shoots right. 6'2", 205 lbs. Born, Roseville, MN, January 17, 1984.

			Regular Season					Playoffs				
Season	Club	League	GP	G	A	Pts	PIM	GP	G	A	Pts	PIM
2002-03	Tri-City Storm	USHL	59	11	8	19	23	3	0	0	0	14
2003-04	Tri-City Storm	USHL	60	17	22	39	23	11	3	2	5	18
2004-05	U. of Notre Dame	CCHA	38	3	5	8	16	....	....	....	....	....
2005-06	U. of Notre Dame	CCHA	36	8	18	26	6	....	....	....	....	....
2006-07	U. of Notre Dame	CCHA	42	18	16	34	26	....	....	....	....	....
2007-08	U. of Notre Dame	CCHA	47	13	17	30	28	....	....	....	....	....
2008-09	Milwaukee	AHL	5	0	0	0	0	....	....	....	....	....
	Cincinnati	ECHL	65	26	44	70	18	15	3	4	7	8
	Hamilton Bulldogs	AHL	3	0	1	1	0	....	....	....	....	....
2009-10	Milwaukee	AHL	28	0	7	7	8	7	0	0	0	2
	Cincinnati	ECHL	15	6	5	11	21	14	5	10	15	2
2010-11	Milwaukee	AHL	62	10	7	17	10	13	3	3	6	2
2011-12	Milwaukee	AHL	70	12	15	27	14	3	1	0	1	0
2012-13	Milwaukee	AHL	73	14	18	32	9	4	0	0	0	0

Signed as a free agent by **Nashville**, May 20, 2013.

VANNELLI, Thomas (vuh-NEHL-ee, TAW-muhs) ST.L.

Defense. Shoots right. 6'2", 165 lbs. Born, Minneapolis, MN, January 26, 1995.
(St. Louis' 1st choice, 47th overall, in 2013 Entry Draft).

			Regular Season					Playoffs				
Season	Club	League	GP	G	A	Pts	PIM	GP	G	A	Pts	PIM
2011-12	Minnetonka High	High-MN	28	7	18	25	8	....	....	....	....	....
2012-13	Team Northwest	UMHSEL	20	4	10	14	16	3	0	0	0	0
	Minnetonka High	High-MN	27	10	25	35	14	....	....	....	....	....
	USNTDP	USHL	11	1	1	2	4	....	....	....	....	....
	USNTDP	U-18	9	2	1	3	0	....	....	....	....	....

• Signed Letter of Intent to attend **University of Minnesota** (WCHA) in fall of 2013.

VARONE, Phil (vah-RUHN, FIHL) BUF

Center. Shoots left. 5'10", 190 lbs. Born, Vaughan, Ont., December 4, 1990.
(San Jose's 3rd choice, 147th overall, in 2009 Entry Draft).

			Regular Season					Playoffs				
Season	Club	League	GP	G	A	Pts	PIM	GP	G	A	Pts	PIM
2005-06	Vaughan M.M.	GTHL	49	34	29	63	....	....	....	....	....	....
	Vaughan Midgets	GTHL	4	6	1	7	2	....	....	....	....	....
2006-07	Kitchener	ON-Jr.B	20	10	11	21	21	....	....	....	....	....
	Kitchener Rangers	OHL	13	1	3	4	2	....	....	....	....	....
2007-08	Kitchener Rangers	OHL	35	5	20	25	12	....	....	....	....	....
	London Knights	OHL	31	10	26	36	14	5	1	1	2	7
2008-09	London Knights	OHL	58	19	33	52	32	14	10	9	19	19
2009-10	London Knights	OHL	31	9	22	31	17	....	....	....	....	....
2010-11	London Knights	OHL	4	1	0	1	2	....	....	....	....	....
	Erie Otters	OHL	55	33	48	81	30	7	3	10	13	4
2011-12	Rochester	AHL	76	11	41	52	42	3	2	1	3	0
2012-13	Rochester	AHL	62	11	24	35	42	3	0	0	0	2

Signed as a free agent by **Rochester** (AHL), September 27, 2011. Signed as a free agent by **Buffalo**, March 19. 2012.

VASILIEV, Valeri (va-sihl-EE-ehv, val-AIR-ee) PHI

Defense. Shoots left. 6'1", 203 lbs. Born, Moscow, Russia, May 31, 1994.
(Philadelphia's 7th choice, 201st overall, in 2012 Entry Draft).

			Regular Season					Playoffs				
Season	Club	League	GP	G	A	Pts	PIM	GP	G	A	Pts	PIM
2011-12	Spartak Jr.	Russia-Jr.	18	1	1	2	24	....	....	....	....	....
2012-13	Spartak Moscow	KHL	11	0	1	1	4	5	1	1	2	2
	Spartak Jr.	Russia-Jr.	33	2	4	6	57	20	1	1	2	30

VEILLEUX, Tommy (VAY-yew, TAW-mee) NSH

Left wing. Shoots left. 5'11", 186 lbs. Born, St.-George, Que., May 7, 1995.
(Nashville's 8th choice, 171st overall, in 2013 Entry Draft).

			Regular Season					Playoffs				
Season	Club	League	GP	G	A	Pts	PIM	GP	G	A	Pts	PIM
2010-11	Beauce-Amiante	Minor-QU	22	12	8	20	40	....	....	....	....	....
	Levis	QAAA	9	1	0	1	14	....	....	....	....	....
2011-12	Victoriaville Tigres	QMJHL	38	1	4	5	71	1	0	0	0	2
2012-13	Victoriaville Tigres	QMJHL	66	11	17	28	129	8	1	2	3	29

VEILLEUX, Yannick (VAY-yew, YA-nihk) ST.L.

Left wing. Shoots left. 6'2", 195 lbs. Born, Saint-Hippolyte, Que., February 22, 1993.
(St. Louis' 5th choice, 102nd overall, in 2011 Entry Draft).

			Regular Season					Playoffs				
Season	Club	League	GP	G	A	Pts	PIM	GP	G	A	Pts	PIM
2008-09	Saint-Eustache	QAAA	43	21	13	34	44	5	1	4	5	23
2009-10	Shawinigan	QMJHL	55	3	6	9	17	6	0	0	0	6
2010-11	Shawinigan	QMJHL	68	19	29	48	40	12	2	5	7	14
2011-12	Shawinigan	QMJHL	59	27	31	58	69	11	5	6	11	17
2012-13	Moncton Wildcats	QMJHL	65	34	39	73	102	4	2	0	2	10
	Peoria Rivermen	AHL	8	2	1	3	0	....	....	....	....	....

VERHAEGHE, Carter (vuhr-HAYG, KAR-tuhr) TOR

Center. Shoots left. 6'1", 181 lbs. Born, Waterdown, Ont., August 14, 1995.
(Toronto's 2nd choice, 82nd overall, in 2013 Entry Draft).

			Regular Season					Playoffs				
Season	Club	League	GP	G	A	Pts	PIM	GP	G	A	Pts	PIM
2010-11	Ham. Jr. Bulldogs	Minor-ON	45	34	30	64	28	....	....	....	....	....
2011-12	Niagara Ice Dogs	OHL	62	4	12	16	10	19	1	2	3	2
2012-13	Niagara Ice Dogs	OHL	67	18	26	44	22	5	2	2	4	6

VERMIN, Joel (VAIR-mihn, JOHL) T.B.

Right wing. Shoots left. 5'10", 187 lbs. Born, Bern, Switz., February 5, 1992.
(Tampa Bay's 6th choice, 186th overall, in 2013 Entry Draft).

			Regular Season					Playoffs				
Season	Club	League	GP	G	A	Pts	PIM	GP	G	A	Pts	PIM
2007-08	SC Bern U17	Swiss-U17	32	24	21	45	22	13	2	8	10	2
	SC Bern Future Jr.	Swiss-Jr.	4	0	0	0	6	....	....	....	....	....
2008-09	SC Bern U17	Swiss-U17	28	29	25	54	50	8	7	9	16	12
	SC Bern Future Jr.	Swiss-Jr.	13	3	5	8	2	....	....	....	....	....
2009-10	SC Bern Future Jr.	Swiss-Jr.	34	28	27	55	59	7	3	8	11	2
	SC Bern	Swiss	12	0	0	0	0	....	....	....	....	....
2010-11	SC Bern Future Jr.	Swiss-Jr.	6	4	6	10	2	....	....	....	....	....
	SC Bern	Swiss	36	1	7	8	6	11	3	3	6	0
2011-12	SC Bern	Swiss	33	11	10	21	0	17	2	3	5	2
2012-13	SC Bern	Swiss	47	13	22	35	14	19	3	6	9	8

VESEY, Jimmy (VEE-ZEE, JIHM-mee) NSH

Left wing. Shoots left. 6'1", 205 lbs. Born, North Reading, MA, May 26, 1993.
(Nashville's 3rd choice, 66th overall, in 2012 Entry Draft).

			Regular Season					Playoffs				
Season	Club	League	GP	G	A	Pts	PIM	GP	G	A	Pts	PIM
2009-10	Belmont Hill	High-MA	30	13	17	30	....	....	....	....	....	....
2010-11	Belmont Hill	High-MA	23	23	12	35	90	....	....	....	....	....
2011-12	South Shore Kings	EJHL	45	*48	43	*91	52	6	5	3	8	2
2012-13	Harvard Crimson	ECAC	27	11	7	18	25	....	....	....	....	....

ECAC All-Rookie Team (2013)

VEY, Linden (VAY, LIHN-duhn) L.A.

Right wing. Shoots right. 6', 183 lbs. Born, Wakaw, Sask., July 17, 1991.
(Los Angeles' 5th choice, 96th overall, in 2009 Entry Draft).

			Regular Season					Playoffs				
Season	Club	League	GP	G	A	Pts	PIM	GP	G	A	Pts	PIM
2006-07	Beardy's	SMHL	44	28	44	72	26	....	....	....	....	....
	Medicine Hat	WHL	2	0	0	0	2	....	....	....	....	....
2007-08	Medicine Hat	WHL	48	8	9	17	21	5	0	1	1	2
2008-09	Medicine Hat	WHL	71	24	48	72	20	11	2	5	7	2
2009-10	Medicine Hat	WHL	72	24	51	75	34	12	2	6	8	8
2010-11	Medicine Hat	WHL	69	46	70	*116	36	15	12	13	25	8
2011-12	Manchester	AHL	74	19	24	43	16	4	2	4	6	0
2012-13	Manchester	AHL	74	22	45	67	32	4	2	0	2	4

WHL East First All-Star Team (2011)

VIEDENSKY, Marek (vee-ehd-EHN-skee, MAR-ehk) S.J.

Center. Shoots right. 6'3", 210 lbs. Born, Handlova, Czech., August 18, 1990.
(San Jose's 4th choice, 189th overall, in 2009 Entry Draft).

			Regular Season					Playoffs				
Season	Club	League	GP	G	A	Pts	PIM	GP	G	A	Pts	PIM
2004-05	Prievidza U18	Svk-U18	10	2	1	3	2	....	....	....	....	....
2005-06	Prievidza U18	Svk-U18	31	18	18	36	18	....	....	....	....	....
2006-07	Dukla Trencin U18	Svk-U18	12	6	12	18	6	....	....	....	....	....
	Dukla Trencin Jr.	Slovak-Jr.	30	5	3	8	8	7	1	1	2	16
2007-08	Dukla Trencin U18	Svk-U18	2	0	1	1	0	....	....	....	....	....
	Dukla Trencin Jr.	Slovak-Jr.	33	11	15	26	24	7	1	1	2	6
2008-09	Prince George	WHL	59	16	24	40	34	4	2	0	2	2
2009-10	Prince George	WHL	31	4	21	25	37	....	....	....	....	....
	Saskatoon Blades	WHL	30	16	18	34	27	10	7	3	10	0
2010-11	Saskatoon Blades	WHL	63	36	52	88	52	10	1	5	6	4
2011-12	Worcester Sharks	AHL	52	5	6	11	14	....	....	....	....	....
2012-13	Worcester Sharks	AHL	14	4	2	6	4	....	....	....	....	....
	San Francisco Bulls	ECHL	20	8	11	19	22	....	....	....	....	....

WAGNER, Chris (WAG-nuhr, KRIHS) ANA

Center. Shoots right. 5'11", 201 lbs. Born, Wellesley, MA, May 27, 1991.
(Anaheim's 4th choice, 122nd overall, in 2010 Entry Draft).

Season	Club	League	Regular Season GP	G	A	Pts	PIM	Playoffs GP	G	A	Pts	PIM
2008-09	South Shore Kings	EJHL	38	20	14	34	72	2	2	0	2	0
2009-10	South Shore Kings	EJHL	44	34	49	*83	70	4	3	6	9	8
2010-11	Colgate	ECAC	41	9	10	19	26					
2011-12	Colgate	ECAC	38	17	34	51	69					
2012-13	Norfolk Admirals	AHL	70	8	13	21	65					

ECAC Second All-Star Team (2012)

WAHL, Mitch (WAWL, MIHTCH)

Center. Shoots right. 6', 175 lbs. Born, Long Beach, CA, January 22, 1990.
(Calgary's 2nd choice, 48th overall, in 2008 Entry Draft).

Season	Club	League	Regular Season GP	G	A	Pts	PIM	Playoffs GP	G	A	Pts	PIM
2005-06	L.A. Jr. Kings	Minor-CA	64	40	50	90	95					
	Spokane Chiefs	WHL	2	0	0	0	0					
2006-07	Spokane Chiefs	WHL	69	16	32	48	50	4	0	1	1	5
2007-08	Spokane Chiefs	WHL	67	20	53	73	63	21	6	8	14	20
2008-09	Spokane Chiefs	WHL	63	32	35	67	78	12	2	11	13	6
2009-10	Spokane Chiefs	WHL	72	30	66	96	96	7	4	5	9	8
	Abbotsford Heat	AHL	4	1	3	4	0	12	2	4	6	4
2010-11	Abbotsford Heat	AHL	17	1	4	5	8					
2011-12	Abbotsford Heat	AHL	5	0	0	0	0					
	Hamilton Bulldogs	AHL	22	2	3	5	6					
	Utah Grizzlies	ECHL	38	20	20	40	95	3	0	0	0	2
2012-13	Abbotsford Heat	AHL	6	1	0	1	4					
	Utah Grizzlies	ECHL	45	19	40	59	115	4	0	2	2	2
	Adirondack	AHL	15	1	3	4	6					

Memorial Cup All-Star Team (2008) • WHL West First All-Star Team (2010)

Traded to **Philadelphia** by **Calgary** for Mike Testwuide, February 26, 2013.

WALKER, Geoff (WAW-kuhr, JEHF) T.B.

Right wing. Shoots right. 6'3", 225 lbs. Born, Charlottetown, P.E.I., December 9, 1987.

Season	Club	League	Regular Season GP	G	A	Pts	PIM	Playoffs GP	G	A	Pts	PIM
2004-05	Gatineau	QMJHL	45	11	6	17	27					
2005-06	Gatineau	QMJHL	15	0	2	2	18					
	P.E.I. Rocket	QMJHL	34	15	11	26	49	6	2	1	3	6
2006-07	P.E.I. Rocket	QMJHL	65	30	50	80	105	7	4	5	9	6
2007-08	P.E.I. Rocket	QMJHL	69	38	52	90	59	4	4	3	7	4
	Texas Brahmas	CHL						5	0	0	0	9
2008-09	Ontario Reign	ECHL	68	21	27	48	39	7	3	5	8	0
2009-10	Manchester	AHL	37	5	9	14	55					
	Ontario Reign	ECHL	26	7	16	23	20					
2010-11	Wilkes-Barre	AHL	70	11	19	30	102	12	1	3	4	8
2011-12	Wilkes-Barre	AHL	68	18	26	44	114	12	1	4	5	4
2012-13	Lake Erie Monsters	AHL	51	5	15	20	55					

Signed as a free agent by **Wilkes-Barre** (AHL), September 3, 2010. Signed as a free agent by **Colorado**, July 1, 2012. Signed as a free agent by **Tampa Bay**, July 5, 2013.

WALKER, Luke (WAW-kuhr, LEWK) COL

Right wing. Shoots right. 6'1", 175 lbs. Born, New Haven, CT, February 19, 1990.
(Colorado's 7th choice, 139th overall, in 2010 Entry Draft).

Season	Club	League	Regular Season GP	G	A	Pts	PIM	Playoffs GP	G	A	Pts	PIM
2006-07	Okanagan Prep	Minor-BC	52	50	42	92	87					
2007-08	Portland	WHL	70	9	12	21	84					
2008-09	Portland	WHL	71	29	23	52	84					
2009-10	Portland	WHL	61	27	30	57	103	13	6	4	10	17
2010-11	Lake Erie Monsters	AHL	75	10	8	18	40	5	1	1	2	0
2011-12	Lake Erie Monsters	AHL	61	9	18	27	26					
2012-13	Lake Erie Monsters	AHL	47	12	13	25	51					

WALSH, Dustin (WAWLSH, DUHS-tihn) MTL

Center. Shoots left. 6'4", 190 lbs. Born, Shannonville, Ont., March 20, 1991.
(Montreal's 6th choice, 169th overall, in 2009 Entry Draft).

Season	Club	League	Regular Season GP	G	A	Pts	PIM	Playoffs GP	G	A	Pts	PIM
2007-08	Trenton Hercs	ON-Jr.A	22	11	7	18	10					
2008-09	Trenton Hercs	ON-Jr.A	32	22	20	42	20					
	Kingston	ON-Jr.A	12	10	11	21	8	25	13	11	24	10
2009-10	Dartmouth	ECAC	22	8	2	10	6					
2010-11	Dartmouth	ECAC	34	10	10	20	8					
2011-12	Dartmouth	ECAC	8	3	7	10	2					
2012-13	Dartmouth	ECAC	29	11	11	22	18					

WALTERS, Nicholas (WAHL-tuhrz, NIH-koh-las) ST.L.

Defense. Shoots left. 6'2", 200 lbs. Born, Edmonton, Alta., April 11, 1994.
(St. Louis' 5th choice, 116th overall, in 2012 Entry Draft).

Season	Club	League	Regular Season GP	G	A	Pts	PIM	Playoffs GP	G	A	Pts	PIM
2008-09	St. Albert Sabres	AMBHL	32	4	24	28	68					
2009-10	St. Albert Raiders	AMHL	30	5	13	18	89	5	1	1	2	16
2010-11	Everett Silvertips	WHL	48	0	4	4	4	1	0	0	0	2
2011-12	Everett Silvertips	WHL	62	6	12	18	95	1	0	0	0	5
2012-13	Everett Silvertips	WHL	35	1	9	10	70					
	Brandon	WHL	29	0	9	9	36					

WANNSTROM, Sebastian (VAN-strohm, seh-BAS-t'yehn) ST.L.

Right wing. Shoots right. 6'1", 180 lbs. Born, Gavle, Sweden, March 3, 1991.
(St. Louis' 3rd choice, 44th overall, in 2010 Entry Draft).

Season	Club	League	Regular Season GP	G	A	Pts	PIM	Playoffs GP	G	A	Pts	PIM
2006-07	Brynas U18	Swe-U18	11	0	4	4	4	3	0	0	0	4
2007-08	Brynas U18	Swe-U18	5	0	1	1	4	5	1	3	4	2
	Brynas IF Gavle Jr.	Swe-Jr.	15	0	4	4	8					
2008-09	Brynas U18	Swe-U18	9	6	12	18	12	2	0	3	3	0
	Brynas IF Gavle Jr.	Swe-Jr.	32	11	9	20	4	6	0	0	0	0
2009-10	Brynas IF Gavle Jr.	Swe-Jr.	35	30	27	57	55	5	2	3	5	0
	Brynas IF Gavle	Sweden	18	0	0	0	2	1	0	0	0	0
2010-11	Brynas IF Gavle Jr.	Swe-Jr.	7	5	4	9	0	1	0	0	0	10
	Leksands IF	Sweden-2	2	0	0	0	0					
	Brynas IF Gavle	Sweden	45	0	2	2	6	5	0	0	0	0
2011-12	Brynas IF Gavle Jr.	Swe-Jr.	5	2	1	3	2					
	Brynas IF Gavle	Sweden	43	8	7	15	20	17	2	5	7	4
2012-13	Peoria Rivermen	AHL	16	1	2	3	4					
	Evansville IceMen	ECHL	14	6	1	7	12					
	Brynas IF Gavle	Sweden	9	0	0	0	8	4	0	0	0	2

WARG, Stefan (WAHRG, STEH-fan) ANA

Defense. Shoots right. 6'2", 187 lbs. Born, Stockholm, Sweden, February 6, 1990.
(Anaheim's 9th choice, 143rd overall, in 2008 Entry Draft).

Season	Club	League	Regular Season GP	G	A	Pts	PIM	Playoffs GP	G	A	Pts	PIM
2006-07	Vasteras U18	Swe-U18	14	0	6	6	14	5	0	0	0	6
2007-08	Vasteras U18	Swe-U18	1	0	0	0	12					
	Vasteras Jr.	Swe-Jr.	33	2	6	8	61	3	0	0	0	14
	VIK Vasteras HK	Sweden-2	3	0	0	0	0					
2008-09	Seattle	WHL	70	1	16	17	80	5	0	0	0	2
2009-10	Seattle	WHL	37	0	13	13	53					
	Prince Albert	WHL	27	0	7	7	42					
2010-11	Orebro HK	Sweden-2	60	1	7	8	166					
2011-12	Orebro HK	Sweden-2	61	2	3	5	56					
2012-13	VIK Vasteras HK	Sweden-2	62	5	16	21	42					

WARSOFSKY, David (wawr-SAWF-skee, DAY-vihd) BOS

Defense. Shoots left. 5'8", 160 lbs. Born, Marshfield, MA, May 30, 1990.
(St. Louis' 7th choice, 95th overall, in 2008 Entry Draft).

Season	Club	League	Regular Season GP	G	A	Pts	PIM	Playoffs GP	G	A	Pts	PIM
2005-06	Cushing	High-MA	....	8	26	34	....					
2006-07	Cushing	High-MA	29	15	34	49	55					
2007-08	USNTDP	U-18	41	5	29	34	26					
	USNTDP	NAHL	15	4	2	6	8					
2008-09	Boston University	H-East	45	3	20	23	28					
2009-10	Boston University	H-East	34	12	11	23	48					
2010-11	Boston University	H-East	34	7	15	22	46					
	Providence Bruins	AHL	10	0	3	3	6					
2011-12	Providence Bruins	AHL	66	5	24	29	18					
2012-13	Providence Bruins	AHL	58	3	13	16	17	12	0	3	3	0

Hockey East Second All-Star Team (2011)

Traded to **Boston** by **St. Louis** for Vladimir Sobotka, June 26, 2010.

WATSON, Clifford (WAWT-suhn, KLIHF-uhrd) S.J.

Defense. Shoots left. 6'2", 185 lbs. Born, Sheboygan, WI, December 21, 1993.
(San Jose's 5th choice, 168th overall, in 2012 Entry Draft).

Season	Club	League	Regular Season GP	G	A	Pts	PIM	Playoffs GP	G	A	Pts	PIM
2009-10	Appleton United	High-WI	23	5	12	17	34					
2010-11	Team Wisconsin	UMHSEL	24	1	15	16	28					
	Appleton United	High-WI	22	18	22	40	44					
2011-12	Sioux City	USHL	58	0	8	8	53	2	0	0	0	0
2012-13	Sioux City	USHL	62	3	8	11	65					

• Signed Letter of Intent to attend **Ohio State University** (CCHA) in fall of 2013.

WEAL, Jordan (WEEL, JOHR-dahn) L.A.

Center. Shoots right. 5'9", 173 lbs. Born, North Vancouver, B.C., April 15, 1992.
(Los Angeles' 3rd choice, 70th overall, in 2010 Entry Draft).

Season	Club	League	Regular Season GP	G	A	Pts	PIM	Playoffs GP	G	A	Pts	PIM
2007-08	Van. NW Giants	BCMML	40	*39	*61	*100	44	2	0	2	2	2
	Regina Pats	WHL	3	0	1	1	0	4	0	0	0	0
2008-09	Regina Pats	WHL	65	16	54	70	26					
2009-10	Regina Pats	WHL	72	35	67	102	54					
2010-11	Regina Pats	WHL	72	43	53	96	70					
	Manchester	AHL	7	0	1	1	0					
2011-12	Regina Pats	WHL	70	41	75	116	36	5	1	4	5	0
	Manchester	AHL	2	0	0	0	0					
2012-13	Manchester	AHL	63	15	18	33	38	4	0	2	2	4

WHL East First All-Star Team (2012)

WEBER, Will (WEH-buhr, WIHL) CBJ

Defense. Shoots left. 6'4", 219 lbs. Born, Gaylord, MI, October 28, 1988.
(Columbus' 3rd choice, 53rd overall, in 2007 Entry Draft).

Season	Club	League	Regular Season GP	G	A	Pts	PIM	Playoffs GP	G	A	Pts	PIM
2003-04	Gaylord	High-MI	STATISTICS NOT AVAILABLE									
2004-05	Gaylord	High-MI	STATISTICS NOT AVAILABLE									
2005-06	Gaylord	High-MI	STATISTICS NOT AVAILABLE									
2006-07	Gaylord	High-MI	25	18	20	38	104					
2007-08	Chicago Steel	USHL	46	8	10	18	137					
2008-09	Miami U.	CCHA	38	3	2	5	75					
2009-10	Miami U.	CCHA	43	1	9	10	62					
2010-11	Miami U.	CCHA	33	1	10	11	57					
2011-12	Miami U.	CCHA	40	0	4	4	69					
	Springfield Falcons	AHL	2	0	0	0	0					
2012-13	Springfield Falcons	AHL	58	2	3	5	82	8	0	0	0	6
	Evansville IceMen	ECHL	8	0	0	0	14					

WEEGAR, MacKenzie (WEE-guhr, muh-KEHN-zee) FLA

Defense. Shoots right. 6', 183 lbs. Born, Ottawa, Ont., January 7, 1994.
(Florida's 8th choice, 206th overall, in 2013 Entry Draft).

			Regular Season					Playoffs				
Season	Club	League	GP	G	A	Pts	PIM	GP	G	A	Pts	PIM
2010-11	Winchester Hawks	ON-Jr.B	40	10	23	33	94	13	3	6	9	83
	Nepean Raiders	ON-Jr.A	5	0	2	2	0	....	....	....	....	....
2011-12	Nepean Raiders	ON-Jr.A	53	13	37	50	61	18	2	4	6	24
2012-13	Halifax	QMJHL	62	8	36	44	58	17	0	5	5	10

QMJHL All-Rookie Team (2013)

WELINSKI, Andy (wehl-IHN-skee, AN-dee) ANA

Defense. Shoots right. 6'1", 196 lbs. Born, Duluth, MN, April 27, 1993.
(Anaheim's 5th choice, 83rd overall, in 2011 Entry Draft).

			Regular Season					Playoffs				
Season	Club	League	GP	G	A	Pts	PIM	GP	G	A	Pts	PIM
2009-10	Duluth East	High-MN	19	3	12	15	16	6	2	7	9	2
2010-11	Green Bay	USHL	51	6	8	14	14	11	2	0	2	4
2011-12	Green Bay	USHL	54	15	22	37	37	7	1	1	2	4
2012-13	U. Minn-Duluth	WCHA	38	4	14	18	24	....	....	....	....	....

USHL First All-Star Team (2012) • WCHA All-Rookie Team (2013)

WELLER, Justin (WEHL-uhr, JUHS-tihn) PHX

Defense. Shoots right. 6'3", 211 lbs. Born, Daysland, Alta., July 26, 1991.
(Phoenix's 5th choice, 105th overall, in 2009 Entry Draft).

			Regular Season					Playoffs				
Season	Club	League	GP	G	A	Pts	PIM	GP	G	A	Pts	PIM
2006-07	Sherwood Park	AMHL	35	0	8	8	46	9	3	2	5	10
2007-08	Red Deer Rebels	WHL	49	0	3	3	40	....	....	....	....	....
2008-09	Red Deer Rebels	WHL	32	0	4	4	30	....	....	....	....	....
2009-10	Red Deer Rebels	WHL	71	2	7	9	88	4	0	1	1	16
2010-11	Red Deer Rebels	WHL	68	4	13	17	104	9	2	1	3	10
2011-12	Red Deer Rebels	WHL	39	3	5	8	43	....	....	....	....	....
2012-13	Gwinnett	ECHL	65	2	9	11	43	10	1	1	2	8

WENNBERG, Alexander (VEHN-buhrg, al-ehx-AN-duhr) CBJ

Center. Shoots left. 6'1", 190 lbs. Born, Stockholm, Sweden, September 22, 1994.
(Columbus' 1st choice, 14th overall, in 2013 Entry Draft).

			Regular Season					Playoffs				
Season	Club	League	GP	G	A	Pts	PIM	GP	G	A	Pts	PIM
2010-11	Djurgarden U18	Swe-U18	40	11	23	34	6	5	1	2	3	2
2011-12	Djurgarden U18	Swe-U18	10	4	2	6	4	2	0	1	1	0
	Djurgarden Jr.	Swe-Jr.	42	1	18	19	6	3	0	1	1	0
	Djurgarden	Sweden	1	0	0	0	0	....	....	....	....	....
2012-13	Djurgarden Jr.	Swe-Jr.	2	1	1	2	0	1	0	1	1	0
	Djurgarden	Sweden-2	46	14	18	32	14	3	0	3	3	0

WEREK, Ethan (WAIR-ehk, EE-thuhn) PHX

Center. Shoots left. 6'2", 205 lbs. Born, Markham, Ont., June 7, 1991.
(NY Rangers' 2nd choice, 47th overall, in 2009 Entry Draft).

			Regular Season					Playoffs				
Season	Club	League	GP	G	A	Pts	PIM	GP	G	A	Pts	PIM
2006-07	Toronto Marlboros	GTHL	55	59	69	128	72					
2007-08	Stouffville Spirit	ON-Jr.A	37	29	41	70	76	15	6	13	19	44
2008-09	Kingston	OHL	66	32	32	64	83	....	....	....	....	....
2009-10	Kingston	OHL	57	30	34	64	68	6	3	2	5	9
2010-11	Kingston	OHL	47	24	28	52	51	3	0	3	3	12
2011-12	Portland Pirates	AHL	67	10	9	19	53	....	....	....	....	....
2012-13	Portland Pirates	AHL	67	11	14	25	43	1	0	1	1	0

Traded to **Phoenix** by **NY Rangers** for Oscar Lindberg, May 8, 2011.

WESTLUND, Wilhelm (WEHST-luhnd, WIHL-hehlm) COL

Defense. Shoots left. 5'11", 184 lbs. Born, Stockholm, Sweden, March 15, 1995.
(Colorado's 7th choice, 183rd overall, in 2013 Entry Draft).

			Regular Season					Playoffs				
Season	Club	League	GP	G	A	Pts	PIM	GP	G	A	Pts	PIM
2009-10	SDE U18	Swe-U18	2	0	1	1	0	....	....	....	....	....
2010-11	Farjestad U18	Swe-U18	35	2	11	13	18	....	....	....	....	....
2011-12	Farjestad U18	Swe-U18	13	4	5	9	8	2	1	0	1	2
	Farjestad Jr.	Swe-Jr.	33	3	4	7	12	6	0	0	0	0
2012-13	Farjestad U18	Swe-U18	1	0	0	0	0	....	....	....	....	....
	Farjestad Jr.	Swe-Jr.	33	3	12	15	76	5	0	3	3	2
	Farjestad	Sweden	26	1	0	1	0	6	0	0	0	0

WEY, Patrick (WAY, PAT-rihk) WSH

Defense. Shoots right. 6'3", 210 lbs. Born, Pittsburgh, PA, March 21, 1991.
(Washington's 4th choice, 115th overall, in 2009 Entry Draft).

			Regular Season					Playoffs				
Season	Club	League	GP	G	A	Pts	PIM	GP	G	A	Pts	PIM
2006-07	Pittsburgh Hornets	MWEHL	18	0	5	5	14	....	....	....	....	....
2007-08	Waterloo	USHL	35	1	5	6	30	8	1	0	1	2
2008-09	Waterloo	USHL	58	7	27	34	75	3	0	0	0	0
2009-10	Boston College	H-East	27	0	5	5	24	....	....	....	....	....
2010-11	Boston College	H-East	37	1	7	8	45	....	....	....	....	....
2011-12	Boston College	H-East	32	2	5	7	24	....	....	....	....	....
2012-13	Boston College	H-East	37	1	12	13	54	....	....	....	....	....

Hockey East Second All-Star Team (2013)

WHEATON, Mitchell (WHEE-tuhn, MIH-chuhl) DET

Defense. Shoots left. 6'4", 228 lbs. Born, Sherwood Park, Alta., February 6, 1995.
(Detroit's 6th choice, 139th overall, in 2013 Entry Draft).

			Regular Season					Playoffs				
Season	Club	League	GP	G	A	Pts	PIM	GP	G	A	Pts	PIM
2010-11	Sherwood Park	AMHL	31	0	8	8	55	10	1	0	1	16
2011-12	Spruce Grove	AJHL	45	7	7	14	62	11	1	2	3	17
2012-13	Spruce Grove	AJHL	1	0	0	0	2	....	....	....	....	....
	Kelowna Rockets	WHL	39	1	7	8	27	4	0	0	0	4

WHITNEY, Joe (WHIHT-nee, JOH) N.J.

Right wing. Shoots left. 5'6", 170 lbs. Born, Reading, MA, February 6, 1988.

			Regular Season					Playoffs				
Season	Club	League	GP	G	A	Pts	PIM	GP	G	A	Pts	PIM
2007-08	Boston College	H-East	41	11	40	51	50	....	....	....	....	....
2008-09	Boston College	H-East	36	7	8	15	36	....	....	....	....	....
2009-10	Boston College	H-East	42	17	28	45	61	....	....	....	....	....
2010-11	Boston College	H-East	39	5	26	31	60	....	....	....	....	....
	Portland Pirates	AHL	1	0	1	1	0	....	....	....	....	....
2011-12	Albany Devils	AHL	72	15	29	44	36	....	....	....	....	....
2012-13	Albany Devils	AHL	66	26	25	51	32	....	....	....	....	....

NCAA Championship All-Tournament Team (2010)

Signed as a free agent by **Albany** (AHL), July 28, 2011. Signed as a free agent by **New Jersey**, May 2, 2013.

WHITNEY, Steven (WHIHT-nee, STEE-vehn) ANA

Center. Shoots right. 5'7", 164 lbs. Born, Reading, MA, February 18, 1991.

			Regular Season					Playoffs				
Season	Club	League	GP	G	A	Pts	PIM	GP	G	A	Pts	PIM
2005-06	Lawrence	High-MA	20	8	10	18	....	....	....	....	....	....
2006-07	Lawrence	High-MA	29	23	30	53	....	....	....	....	....	....
2007-08	Lawrence	High-MA	25	15	22	37	50	....	....	....	....	....
2008-09	Lawrence	High-MA	28	21	34	55	....	....	....	....	....	....
	Omaha Lancers	USHL	12	4	11	15	10	3	0	1	1	6
2009-10	Boston College	H-East	42	7	21	28	28	....	....	....	....	....
2010-11	Boston College	H-East	36	6	10	16	56	....	....	....	....	....
2011-12	Boston College	H-East	44	16	23	39	65	....	....	....	....	....
2012-13	Boston College	H-East	38	*26	19	45	54	....	....	....	....	....
	Norfolk Admirals	AHL	8	3	1	4	2	....	....	....	....	....

Hockey East First All-Star Team (2013) • NCAA East First All-American Team (2013)

Signed as a free agent by **Anaheim**, April 4, 2013.

WIDEMAN, Chris (WIGHD-muhn, KRIHS) OTT

Defense. Shoots right. 5'10", 180 lbs. Born, St. Louis, MO, January 7, 1990.
(Ottawa's 4th choice, 100th overall, in 2009 Entry Draft).

			Regular Season					Playoffs				
Season	Club	League	GP	G	A	Pts	PIM	GP	G	A	Pts	PIM
2006-07	St.L. AAA Blues	Minor-MO	62	9	21	30	122	....	....	....	....	....
	St. Louis Bandits	NAHL	1	0	0	0	0	7	0	1	1	4
2007-08	Cedar Rapids	USHL	53	2	12	14	51	1	0	0	0	0
2008-09	Miami U.	CCHA	39	0	26	26	56	....	....	....	....	....
2009-10	Miami U.	CCHA	44	5	17	22	63	....	....	....	....	....
2010-11	Miami U.	CCHA	39	3	20	23	32	....	....	....	....	....
2011-12	Miami U.	CCHA	41	4	20	24	40	....	....	....	....	....
2012-13	Binghamton	AHL	60	2	16	18	46	3	1	2	3	2
	Elmira Jackals	ECHL	5	0	5	5	7	....	....	....	....	....

CCHA All-Rookie Team (2009) • CCHA Second All-Star Team (2011)

WIKSTRAND, Mikael (VIHK-strand, mih-kigh-EHL) OTT

Defense. Shoots left. 6'1", 183 lbs. Born, Karlstad, Sweden, November 5, 1993.
(Ottawa's 7th choice, 196th overall, in 2012 Entry Draft).

			Regular Season					Playoffs				
Season	Club	League	GP	G	A	Pts	PIM	GP	G	A	Pts	PIM
2007-08	Ore U18	Swe-U18	14	0	4	4	6	....	....	....	....	....
2008-09	Ore U18	Swe-U18	9	0	2	2	31	1	1	1	2	....
	IFK Ore Furudal	Sweden-5	3	0	0	0	....	....	....	....	....	....
2009-10	Mora IK U18	Swe-U18	23	10	11	21	26	....	....	....	....	....
	Mora IK Jr.	Swe-Jr.	14	1	2	3	8	....	....	....	....	....
2010-11	Mora IK U18	Swe-U18	4	1	2	3	6	3	1	3	4	4
	Mora IK Jr.	Swe-Jr.	16	3	5	8	6	....	....	....	....	....
	Mora IK	Sweden-2	37	0	1	1	8	....	....	....	....	....
2011-12	Mora IK Jr.	Swe-Jr.	11	3	4	7	2	2	1	3	4	2
	Mora IK	Sweden-2	47	2	1	3	14	....	....	....	....	....
2012-13	Mora IK Jr.	Swe-Jr.	2	0	1	1	0	....	....	....	....	....
	Mora IK	Sweden-2	45	11	14	25	35	....	....	....	....	....

WILLCOX, Reece (WIHL-cawx, REES) PHI

Defense. Shoots right. 6'3", 184 lbs. Born, Surrey, B.C., March 20, 1994.
(Philadelphia's 6th choice, 141st overall, in 2012 Entry Draft).

			Regular Season					Playoffs				
Season	Club	League	GP	G	A	Pts	PIM	GP	G	A	Pts	PIM
2009-10	Surrey Thunder	Minor-BC	STATISTICS NOT AVAILABLE									
	West Valley Hawks	BCMML	9	1	3	4	0	....	....	....	....	....
2010-11	Merritt	BCHL	53	5	9	14	16	4	1	2	3	0
2011-12	Merritt	BCHL	52	5	18	23	26	9	2	2	4	6
2012-13	Cornell Big Red	ECAC	34	0	5	5	8	....	....	....	....	....

WILLIAMSON, Mike (WIHL-yuhm-suhn, MIGHK) VAN

Defense. Shoots left. 6'3", 187 lbs. Born, Leduc, Alta., September 5, 1993.
(Vancouver's 6th choice, 175th overall, in 2013 Entry Draft).

			Regular Season					Playoffs				
Season	Club	League	GP	G	A	Pts	PIM	GP	G	A	Pts	PIM
2008-09	Leduc Oil Kings	Minor-AB	27	6	18	24	36	....	....	....	....	....
2009-10	Leduc Oil Kings	AMHL	31	7	3	10	72	10	0	3	3	8
	Drayton Valley	AJHL	4	0	0	0	0	....	....	....	....	....
2010-11	Leduc Oil Kings	AMHL	32	6	13	19	70	15	3	1	4	33
	Spruce Grove	AJHL	1	0	0	0	2	....	....	....	....	....
2011-12	Spruce Grove	AJHL	41	9	9	18	73	11	4	2	6	14
2012-13	Spruce Grove	AJHL	23	1	10	11	35	15	1	3	4	21

• Signed Letter of Intent to attend **Penn State University** (NCAA) in fall of 2013.

WILSON, Garrett (WIHL-suhn, GAIR-reht) FLA

Left wing. Shoots left. 6'3", 206 lbs. Born, Barrie, Ont., March 16, 1991.
(Florida's 4th choice, 107th overall, in 2009 Entry Draft).

			Regular Season					Playoffs				
Season	Club	League	GP	G	A	Pts	PIM	GP	G	A	Pts	PIM
2007-08	Tecumseh Chiefs	ON-Jr.B	46	11	26	37	40	14	13	8	21	22
	Windsor Spitfires	OHL	7	1	0	1	2	3	0	0	0	0
2008-09	Owen Sound	OHL	53	17	18	35	44	4	1	3	4	7
2009-10	Owen Sound	OHL	65	36	26	62	80	....	....	....	....	....
2010-11	Owen Sound	OHL	66	40	46	86	114	22	11	10	21	28
2011-12	San Antonio	AHL	11	1	0	1	2	....	....	....	....	....
	Cincinnati	ECHL	63	17	18	35	50	....	....	....	....	....
2012-13	Cincinnati	ECHL	38	19	10	29	56	15	4	1	5	17
	San Antonio	AHL	26	3	2	5	19	....	....	....	....	....

OHL First All-Star Team (2011)

WILSON, Jason (WIHL-suhn, JAY-suhn) NYR

Left wing. Shoots left. 6'2", 205 lbs. Born, Toronto, Ont., April 15, 1990.
(NY Rangers' 4th choice, 130th overall, in 2010 Entry Draft).

			Regular Season					Playoffs				
Season	Club	League	GP	G	A	Pts	PIM	GP	G	A	Pts	PIM
2007-08	Tor. Canadiens	ON-Jr.A	37	7	10	17	69	11	1	1	2	4
2008-09	London Knights	OHL	52	12	5	17	104	14	0	2	2	8
2009-10	Owen Sound	OHL	46	17	18	35	101	....	....	....	....	....
2010-11	Niagara Ice Dogs	OHL	64	18	25	43	94	14	5	7	12	19
2011-12	Greenville	ECHL	56	4	10	14	102	1	0	0	0	0
2012-13	Connecticut Whale	AHL	17	1	0	1	30	....	....	....	....	....
	Greenville	ECHL	23	1	4	5	75	4	1	0	1	6

WILSON, Scott (WIHL-suhn, SKAWT) PIT

Center/Left wing. Shoots left. 5'11", 184 lbs. Born, Oakville, Ont., April 24, 1992.
(Pittsburgh's 5th choice, 209th overall, in 2011 Entry Draft).

			Regular Season					Playoffs				
Season	Club	League	GP	G	A	Pts	PIM	GP	G	A	Pts	PIM
2008-09	Oakville Rangers	Minor-ON	STATISTICS NOT AVAILABLE									
	Georgetown	ON-Jr.A	6	0	1	1	2	1	0	0	0	0
2009-10	Georgetown	ON-Jr.A	56	24	43	67	28	11	9	8	17	2
2010-11	Georgetown	ON-Jr.A	42	20	41	61	59	4	1	2	3	8
2011-12	U. Mass-Lowell	H-East	37	16	22	38	26	....	....	....	....	....
2012-13	U. Mass-Lowell	H-East	41	16	22	38	32	....	....	....	....	....

Hockey East All-Rookie Team (2012)

WINTHER, Mike (WIHN-thur, MIGHK) DAL

Center. Shoots left. 6', 181 lbs. Born, Olds, Alta., January 9, 1994.
(Dallas' 3rd choice, 54th overall, in 2012 Entry Draft).

			Regular Season					Playoffs				
Season	Club	League	GP	G	A	Pts	PIM	GP	G	A	Pts	PIM
2008-09	Airdrie Xtreme	AMBHL	32	40	23	63	48	14	*13	9	*22	20
2009-10	UFA Bisons	AMHL	28	14	16	30	77	2	0	0	0	2
2010-11	Prince Albert	WHL	61	9	1	10	18	4	0	0	0	2
2011-12	Prince Albert	WHL	71	32	24	56	59	....	....	....	....	....
2012-13	Prince Albert	WHL	68	22	28	50	61	4	1	0	1	6

WITKOWSKI, Luke (wiht-KOW-skee, LEWK) T.B.

Defense. Shoots right. 6'2", 200 lbs. Born, Holland, MI, April 14, 1990.
(Tampa Bay's 6th choice, 160th overall, in 2008 Entry Draft).

			Regular Season					Playoffs				
Season	Club	League	GP	G	A	Pts	PIM	GP	G	A	Pts	PIM
2006-07	Team nXi Majors	Minor-MI	59	18	22	40	172	....	....	....	....	....
2007-08	Ohio	USHL	58	3	10	13	139	....	....	....	....	....
2008-09	Fargo Force	USHL	55	6	16	22	118	10	2	1	3	29
2009-10	Western Mich.	CCHA	32	2	4	6	67	....	....	....	....	....
2010-11	Western Mich.	CCHA	42	1	8	9	56	....	....	....	....	....
2011-12	Western Mich.	CCHA	40	2	11	13	66	....	....	....	....	....
2012-13	Western Mich.	CCHA	38	2	8	10	46	....	....	....	....	....
	Syracuse Crunch	AHL	3	0	0	0	4	....	....	....	....	....

CCHA Second All-Star Team (2013)

WITTCHOW, Eddie (WIHT-chow, EH-dee) FLA

Defense. Shoots left. 6'4", 200 lbs. Born, Burnsville, MN, October 31, 1992.
(Florida's 9th choice, 154th overall, in 2011 Entry Draft).

			Regular Season					Playoffs				
Season	Club	League	GP	G	A	Pts	PIM	GP	G	A	Pts	PIM
2009-10	Burnsville Blaze	High-MN	25	2	5	7	20	2	0	1	1	0
2010-11	Burnsville Blaze	High-MN	25	9	14	23	28	3	2	1	3	2
2011-12	Waterloo	USHL	60	5	13	18	74	7	0	4	4	4
2012-13	U. of Wisconsin	WCHA	29	0	3	3	28	....	....	....	....	....

USHL All-Rookie Team (2012)

WOHLBERG, David (WOHL-buhrg, DAY-vihd) N.J.

Center. Shoots left. 6'1", 200 lbs. Born, Southfield, MI, July 18, 1990.
(New Jersey's 7th choice, 172nd overall, in 2008 Entry Draft).

			Regular Season					Playoffs				
Season	Club	League	GP	G	A	Pts	PIM	GP	G	A	Pts	PIM
2006-07	USNTDP	U-17	12	2	6	8	42	....	....	....	....	....
	USNTDP	NAHL	45	10	10	20	99	6	1	4	5	22
2007-08	USNTDP	U-18	37	9	7	16	48	....	....	....	....	....
	USNTDP	NAHL	22	10	5	15	27	....	....	....	....	....
2008-09	U. of Michigan	CCHA	40	15	15	30	51	....	....	....	....	....
2009-10	U. of Michigan	CCHA	44	10	17	27	76	....	....	....	....	....
2010-11	U. of Michigan	CCHA	37	15	6	21	42	....	....	....	....	....
2011-12	U. of Michigan	CCHA	41	16	17	33	30	....	....	....	....	....
	Albany Devils	AHL	6	1	0	1	0	....	....	....	....	....
2012-13	Albany Devils	AHL	36	4	5	9	26	....	....	....	....	....

CCHA All-Rookie Team (2009) • CCHA Rookie of the Year (2009)

WOOD, Miles (WUD, MIGH-uhlz) N.J.

Left wing. Shoots left. 6'1", 185 lbs. Born, Buffalo, NY, September 13, 1995.
(New Jersey's 3rd choice, 100th overall, in 2013 Entry Draft).

			Regular Season					Playoffs				
Season	Club	League	GP	G	A	Pts	PIM	GP	G	A	Pts	PIM
2010-11	Salem Ice Dogs	EmJHL	13	4	5	9	8	2	0	0	0	0
2011-12	Salem Ice Dogs	EmJHL	14	8	1	9	28	....	....	....	....	....
2012-13	Nobles	High-MA	15	8	10	18	18	....	....	....	....	....

WOODS, Brendan (WOODZ, BREHN-duhn) CAR

Left wing. Shoots left. 6'3", 215 lbs. Born, Humboldt, Sask., June 11, 1992.
(Carolina's 7th choice, 129th overall, in 2012 Entry Draft).

			Regular Season					Playoffs				
Season	Club	League	GP	G	A	Pts	PIM	GP	G	A	Pts	PIM
2008-09	Williston North.	High-MA	29	8	11	19	28	....	....	....	....	....
2009-10	Chicago Steel	USHL	34	6	4	10	32	....	....	....	....	....
2010-11	Muskegon	USHL	57	14	12	26	86	6	1	1	2	14
2011-12	U. of Wisconsin	WCHA	34	5	5	10	67	....	....	....	....	....
2012-13	U. of Wisconsin	WCHA	41	5	7	12	47	....	....	....	....	....
	Charlotte	AHL	2	0	0	0	2	....	....	....	....	....

WOTHERSPOON, Tyler (WUH-thuhr-spoon, TIGH-luhr) CGY

Defense. Shoots left. 6'1", 196 lbs. Born, Burnaby, B.C., March 12, 1993.
(Calgary's 3rd choice, 57th overall, in 2011 Entry Draft).

			Regular Season					Playoffs				
Season	Club	League	GP	G	A	Pts	PIM	GP	G	A	Pts	PIM
2008-09	Valley West Hawks	BCMML	37	11	13	24	85	....	....	....	....	....
	Portland	WHL	4	0	0	0	0	....	....	....	....	....
2009-10	Portland	WHL	43	1	4	5	21	2	0	0	0	0
2010-11	Portland	WHL	64	2	10	12	73	20	3	1	4	10
2011-12	Portland	WHL	67	7	21	28	42	22	1	6	7	6
2012-13	Portland	WHL	61	7	30	37	30	21	2	8	10	20

WHL West Second All-Star Team (2013)

WRENN, William (REHN, WILL-yuhm)

Defense. Shoots right. 6', 205 lbs. Born, Anchorage, AK, March 16, 1991.
(San Jose's 1st choice, 43rd overall, in 2009 Entry Draft).

			Regular Season					Playoffs				
Season	Club	League	GP	G	A	Pts	PIM	GP	G	A	Pts	PIM
2007-08	USNTDP	NAHL	43	0	5	5	36	3	0	0	0	15
	USNTDP	U-17	17	0	2	2	14	....	....	....	....	....
2008-09	USNTDP	NAHL	13	1	4	5	37	....	....	....	....	....
	USNTDP	U-18	47	5	7	12	46	....	....	....	....	....
2009-10	U. of Denver	WCHA	23	0	7	7	36	....	....	....	....	....
2010-11	U. of Denver	WCHA	18	0	1	1	2	....	....	....	....	....
	Portland	WHL	29	2	11	13	17	21	1	4	5	10
2011-12	Portland	WHL	60	3	13	16	27	22	0	4	4	10
2012-13	Alaska Aces	ECHL	51	5	16	21	21	....	....	....	....	....
	Worcester Sharks	AHL	3	0	0	0	0	....	....	....	....	....
	Texas Stars	AHL	19	2	5	7	21	....	....	....	....	....

WUTHRICH, Austin (wuhth-RIHCH, AW-stuhn) WSH

Right wing. Shoots right. 6'1", 190 lbs. Born, Bakersfield, CA, August 11, 1993.
(Washington's 5th choice, 107th overall, in 2012 Entry Draft).

			Regular Season					Playoffs				
Season	Club	League	GP	G	A	Pts	PIM	GP	G	A	Pts	PIM
2008-09	South Anchorage	High-AK	26	15	12	27	12	....	....	....	....	....
2009-10	Team Illinois	T1EHL	31	9	8	17	22	....	....	....	....	....
	USNTDP	USHL	15	2	2	4	10	....	....	....	....	....
	USNTDP	U-17	10	0	1	1	6	....	....	....	....	....
2010-11	USNTDP	USHL	16	3	4	7	38	2	0	0	0	17
	USNTDP	U-18	2	0	1	1	2	....	....	....	....	....
2011-12	U. of Notre Dame	CCHA	36	7	10	17	34	....	....	....	....	....
2012-13	U. of Notre Dame	CCHA	33	5	4	9	18	....	....	....	....	....

YAKIMOV, Bogdan (ya-KIH-mawv, bawg-DAHN) EDM

Center. Shoots left. 6'5", 202 lbs. Born, Nizhnekamsk, Russia, October 4, 1994.
(Edmonton's 3rd choice, 83rd overall, in 2013 Entry Draft).

			Regular Season					Playoffs				
Season	Club	League	GP	G	A	Pts	PIM	GP	G	A	Pts	PIM
2011-12	Nizhnekamsk Jr.	Russia-Jr.	46	15	10	25	10	2	2	1	3	0
2012-13	Dizel Penza	Russia-2	21	3	6	9	12	....	....	....	....	....
	Izhstal Izhevsk	Russia-2	16	5	8	13	4	....	....	....	....	....
	Nizhnekamsk Jr.	Russia-Jr.	11	6	7	13	2	....	....	....	....	....

YOGAN, Andrew (YOH-guhn, an-DROO) NYR

Center/Left wing. Shoots left. 6'3", 201 lbs. Born, Coral Springs, FL, December 4, 1991.
(NY Rangers' 3rd choice, 100th overall, in 2010 Entry Draft).

			Regular Season					Playoffs				
Season	Club	League	GP	G	A	Pts	PIM	GP	G	A	Pts	PIM
2006-07	Fla. Jr. Panthers	Minor-FL	52	45	36	81	34	....	....	....	....	....
2007-08	Windsor Spitfires	OHL	50	5	2	7	32	5	0	0	0	6
2008-09	Windsor Spitfires	OHL	16	5	3	8	24	....	....	....	....	....
	Erie Otters	OHL	35	17	17	34	32	....	....	....	....	....
2009-10	Erie Otters	OHL	63	25	30	55	97	....	....	....	....	....
2010-11	Erie Otters	OHL	10	3	1	4	6	3	0	2	2	4
	Connecticut Whale	AHL	2	2	1	3	0	....	....	....	....	....
2011-12	Peterborough	OHL	66	41	37	78	96	....	....	....	....	....
	Connecticut Whale	AHL	4	0	0	0	15	....	....	....	....	....
2012-13	Connecticut Whale	AHL	43	7	12	19	35	....	....	....	....	....
	Greenville	ECHL	15	9	3	12	14	....	....	....	....	....

YOUNG, Gus (YUHNG, GUHS) COL

Defense. Shoots left. 6'2", 200 lbs. Born, Dedham, MA, July 10, 1991.
(Colorado's 7th choice, 184th overall, in 2009 Entry Draft).

			Regular Season					Playoffs				
Season	Club	League	GP	G	A	Pts	PIM	GP	G	A	Pts	PIM
2006-07	Nobles	High-MA	31	3	10	13	14	....	....	....	....	....
2007-08	Bos. Little Bruins	Minor-MA	11	0	6	6		....	....	....	....	....
	Nobles	High-MA	29	6	9	15		....	....	....	....	....
2008-09	Cape Cod Whalers	Minor-MA	14	3	11	14		....	....	....	....	....
	Nobles	High-MA	29	5	29	34	16	....	....	....	....	....
2009-10	Cape Cod Whalers	Minor-MA	33	13	27	40		....	....	....	....	....
	Nobles	High-MA	29	12	26	38	10	....	....	....	....	....
2010-11	Yale	ECAC	5	0	1	1	4	....	....	....	....	....
2011-12	Yale	ECAC	35	3	9	12	36	....	....	....	....	....
2012-13	Yale	ECAC	37	2	7	9	58	....	....	....	....	....

NCAA Championship All-Tournament Team (2013)

• Missed majority of 2010-11 as a healthy reserve.

YOUNG, Harry (YUHNG, HAIR-ee) N.J.

Defense. Shoots left. 6'5", 230 lbs. Born, Windsor, Ont., November 12, 1989.
(New Jersey's 8th choice, 202nd overall, in 2008 Entry Draft).

			Regular Season					Playoffs				
Season	Club	League	GP	G	A	Pts	PIM	GP	G	A	Pts	PIM
2005-06	Guelph Storm	OHL	44	0	4	4	20	....	....	....	....	....
2006-07	Guelph Storm	OHL	7	0	2	2	11	....	....	....	....	....
	Windsor Spitfires	OHL	47	0	3	3	72	....	....	....	....	....
2007-08	Windsor Spitfires	OHL	68	2	12	14	155	5	0	1	1	8
2008-09	Windsor Spitfires	OHL	46	8	4	12	138	20	1	4	5	*41
2009-10	Windsor Spitfires	OHL	65	9	11	20	153	19	0	1	1	24
2010-11	Albany Devils	AHL	52	1	4	5	142	....	....	....	....	....
	Trenton Devils	ECHL	3	0	1	1	12	....	....	....	....	....
2011-12	Kalamazoo Wings	ECHL	32	3	7	10	55	14	0	2	2	29
	Albany Devils	AHL	11	0	0	0	21	....	....	....	....	....
2012-13	Trenton Titans	ECHL	4	0	0	0	5	....	....	....	....	....
	Kalamazoo Wings	ECHL	33	0	1	1	52	....	....	....	....	....
	Albany Devils	AHL	4	0	0	0	7	....	....	....	....	....

YUEN, Zachary
(YEW-ehn, ZA-kuh-ree)

Defense. Shoots left. 6'1", 200 lbs. Born, Vancouver, B.C., March 3, 1993.
(Winnipeg's 4th choice, 119th overall, in 2011 Entry Draft).

			Regular Season					Playoffs				
Season	**Club**	**League**	**GP**	**G**	**A**	**Pts**	**PIM**	**GP**	**G**	**A**	**Pts**	**PIM**
2008-09	Greater Van.	BCMML	35	6	13	19	60	6	0	3	3	2
	Tri-City Americans	WHL	4	0	0	0	0	7	1	0	1	2
2009-10	Tri-City Americans	WHL	42	1	3	4	19	22	1	1	2	12
2010-11	Tri-City Americans	WHL	72	8	24	32	65	10	0	3	3	12
2011-12	Tri-City Americans	WHL	66	12	26	38	46	15	1	4	5	18
2012-13	Tri-City Americans	WHL	71	9	35	44	58	5	0	1	1	10

ZAAR, Daniel
(ZAHR, DAN-yehl) **CBJ**

Right wing. Shoots right. 5'11", 172 lbs. Born, Helsingborg, Sweden, April 24, 1994.
(Columbus' 5th choice, 152nd overall, in 2012 Entry Draft).

			Regular Season					Playoffs				
Season	**Club**	**League**	**GP**	**G**	**A**	**Pts**	**PIM**	**GP**	**G**	**A**	**Pts**	**PIM**
2009-10	Jonstorps IF U18	Swe-U18	17	12	11	23	10	....	....	....	....	....
	Jonstorps IF Jr.	Swe-Jr.	4	3	3	6	4	....	....	....	....	....
	Jonstorps IF	Sweden-4	....	....	....	....	....	4	1	1	2	0
2010-11	Rogle U18	Swe-U18	23	16	18	34	4	4	0	4	4	4
	Rogle Jr.	Swe-Jr.	26	3	3	6	14	3	0	0	0	0
2011-12	Rogle U18	Swe-U18	7	6	6	12	0	5	5	4	9	6
	Rogle Jr.	Swe-Jr.	44	14	24	38	28	7	5	3	8	8
2012-13	Rogle Jr.	Swe-Jr.	17	11	8	19	6	1	0	0	0	2
	Bofors	Sweden-2	21	2	8	10	4	....	....	....	....	....
	Rogle	Sweden	25	2	1	3	0	....	....	....	....	....
	Rogle	Sweden-Q	7	1	0	1	2	....	....	....	....	....

ZADOROV, Nikita
(za-DOHR-awv, nih-KEE-tuh) **BUF**

Defense. Shoots left. 6'5", 219 lbs. Born, Moscow, Russia, April 16, 1995.
(Buffalo's 2nd choice, 16th overall, in 2013 Entry Draft).

			Regular Season					Playoffs				
Season	**Club**	**League**	**GP**	**G**	**A**	**Pts**	**PIM**	**GP**	**G**	**A**	**Pts**	**PIM**
2011-12	CSKA Jr.	Russia-Jr.	41	2	4	6	63	8	0	0	0	8
2012-13	London Knights	OHL	63	6	19	25	54	20	2	4	6	36

OHL All-Rookie Team (2013)

ZAJAC, Darcy
(ZAY-jak, DAHR-see) **N.J.**

Center. Shoots right. 6'1", 205 lbs. Born, Winnipeg, Man., September 23, 1986.

			Regular Season					Playoffs				
Season	**Club**	**League**	**GP**	**G**	**A**	**Pts**	**PIM**	**GP**	**G**	**A**	**Pts**	**PIM**
2004-05	Salmon Arm	BCHL	60	12	21	33	75	....	....	....	....	....
2005-06	Salmon Arm	BCHL	57	37	43	80	76	....	....	....	....	....
2006-07	North Dakota	WCHA	41	8	2	10	18	....	....	....	....	....
2007-08	North Dakota	WCHA	41	3	5	8	46	....	....	....	....	....
2008-09	North Dakota	WCHA	43	5	12	17	32	....	....	....	....	....
2009-10	North Dakota	WCHA	41	8	11	19	49	....	....	....	....	....
	Adirondack	AHL	2	0	0	0	4	....	....	....	....	....
2010-11	Albany Devils	AHL	40	4	5	9	60	....	....	....	....	....
	Trenton Devils	ECHL	32	6	17	23	35	....	....	....	....	....
2011-12	Albany Devils	AHL	66	8	16	24	86	....	....	....	....	....
2012-13	Albany Devils	AHL	67	9	8	17	86	....	....	....	....	....

Signed as a free agent by **Adirondack** (AHL), April 8, 2010. Signed as a free agent by **Albany** (AHL), June 26, 2010. Signed as a free agent by **New Jersey**, July 6, 2013.

ZHARKOV, Daniil
(zharh-KAWV, da-NEEL) **EDM**

Left wing. Shoots left. 6'4", 208 lbs. Born, St. Petersburg, Russia, February 6, 1994.
(Edmonton's 4th choice, 91st overall, in 2012 Entry Draft).

			Regular Season					Playoffs				
Season	**Club**	**League**	**GP**	**G**	**A**	**Pts**	**PIM**	**GP**	**G**	**A**	**Pts**	**PIM**
2010-11	Ser. Ljvy Jr.	Russia-Jr.	12	1	2	3	16	....	....	....	....	....
	Tri-City Storm	USHL	36	8	3	11	27	....	....	....	....	....
2011-12	Belleville Bulls	OHL	50	23	13	36	25	6	1	2	3	2
2012-13	Belleville Bulls	OHL	59	25	18	43	24	17	4	8	12	21

ZLOBIN, Anton
(ZLOH-bihn, an-TAWN) **PIT**

Right wing. Shoots right. 5'11", 189 lbs. Born, Moscow, Russia, February 22, 1993.
(Pittsburgh's 9th choice, 173rd overall, in 2012 Entry Draft).

			Regular Season					Playoffs				
Season	**Club**	**League**	**GP**	**G**	**A**	**Pts**	**PIM**	**GP**	**G**	**A**	**Pts**	**PIM**
2010-11	Shawinigan	QMJHL	59	23	22	45	28	12	5	1	6	2
2011-12	Shawinigan	QMJHL	66	40	36	76	50	11	3	7	10	2
2012-13	Val-d'Or Foreurs	QMJHL	61	29	62	91	43	10	2	8	10	4

ZYKOV, Valentin
(ZIH-kawv, val-ehn-TEEN) **L.A.**

Left wing. Shoots right. 5'11", 209 lbs. Born, St. Petersburg, Russia, May 15, 1995.
(Los Angeles' 1st choice, 37th overall, in 2013 Entry Draft).

			Regular Season					Playoffs				
Season	**Club**	**League**	**GP**	**G**	**A**	**Pts**	**PIM**	**GP**	**G**	**A**	**Pts**	**PIM**
2011-12	CSKA Jr.	Russia-Jr.	52	5	6	11	105	18	0	2	2	4
2012-13	Baie-Comeau	QMJHL	67	40	35	75	60	19	10	9	19	18

QMJHL All-Rookie Team (2013) • QMJHL Rookie of the Year (2013) • Canadian Major Junior Rookie of the Year (2013)

2013-14 NHL Player Register

Note: The 2013-14 NHL Player Register lists forwards and defensemen only. Goaltenders are listed separately. The NHL Player Register lists every active skater who played in the NHL in 2012-13 plus additional players with NHL experience. Trades and roster changes are current as of August 12, 2013.

Abbreviations: GP – games played; **G** – goals; **A** – assists; **Pts** – points; **PIM** – penalties in minutes; **PP** – power-play goals; **SH** – shorthanded goals; **GW** – game-winning goals; **S** – shots; **%** – shooting percentage; **+/–** – plus/minus; **TF** – total faceoffs taken; **F%** – faceoff winning percentage; **Min** – average time on ice per game; ***** – league-leading total
♦ – member of Stanley Cup-winning team.

Prospect Register begins on page 281.
Goaltender Register begins on page 591.
Retired Player Index begins on page 616.
Retired Goaltender Index begins on page 659.
League abbreviations are listed on page 670.

ABDELKADER, Justin
(abdehl-KAY-duhr, JUHS-tihn) **DET**

Left wing. Shoots left. 6'1", 219 lbs. Born, Muskegon, MI, February 25, 1987. Detroit's 2nd choice, 42nd overall, in 2005 Entry Draft.

			Regular Season														Playoffs								
Season	Club	League	GP	G	A	Pts	PIM	PP	SH	GW	S	%	+/-	TF	F%	Min	GP	G	A	Pts	PIM	PP	SH	GW	Min
2003-04	Muskegon M.S.	High-MI	28	37	43	80	....	....	....	....	....	....	....	....	....	....	....	....	....	....	....	....	....	....	....
2004-05	Cedar Rapids	USHL	60	27	25	52	86	....	....	....	....	....	....	....	....	....	11	0	4	4	8	....	....	....	....
2005-06	Michigan State	CCHA	44	10	12	22	83	....	....	....	....	....	....	....	....	....	....	....	....	....	....	....	....	....	....
2006-07	Michigan State	CCHA	38	15	18	33	91	....	....	....	....	....	....	....	....	....	....	....	....	....	....	....	....	....	....
2007-08	Michigan State	CCHA	42	19	21	40	107	....	....	....	....	....	....	....	....	....	....	....	....	....	....	....	....	....	....
	Detroit	**NHL**	**2**	**0**	**0**	**0**	**2**	**0**	**0**	**0**	**6**	**0.0**	**0**	**12**	**41.7**	**12:13**	....	....	....	....	....	....	....	....	....
2008-09	**Detroit**	**NHL**	**2**	**0**	**0**	**0**	**0**	**0**	**0**	**0**	**2**	**0.0**	**0**	**7**	**57.1**	**9:18**	**10**	**2**	**1**	**3**	**0**	**0**	**0**	**0**	**6:58**
	Grand Rapids	AHL	76	24	28	52	102	....	....	....	....	....	....	....	....	....	10	6	2	8	23	....	....	....	....
2009-10	**Detroit**	**NHL**	**50**	**3**	**3**	**6**	**35**	**0**	**0**	**0**	**79**	**3.8**	**–11**	**318**	**46.5**	**10:35**	**11**	**1**	**1**	**2**	***36**	**0**	**0**	**0**	**7:30**
	Grand Rapids	AHL	33	11	13	24	86	....	....	....	....	....	....	....	....	....	....	....	....	....	....	....	....	....	....
2010-11	**Detroit**	**NHL**	**74**	**7**	**12**	**19**	**61**	**0**	**0**	**1**	**129**	**5.4**	**15**	**430**	**52.8**	**12:18**	**11**	**0**	**0**	**0**	**22**	**0**	**0**	**0**	**13:27**
2011-12	**Detroit**	**NHL**	**81**	**8**	**14**	**22**	**62**	**0**	**0**	**1**	**121**	**6.6**	**4**	**452**	**52.9**	**12:19**	**5**	**0**	**0**	**0**	**2**	**0**	**0**	**0**	**12:31**
2012-13	**Detroit**	**NHL**	**48**	**10**	**3**	**13**	**34**	**0**	**0**	**0**	**96**	**10.4**	**6**	**125**	**52.0**	**14:49**	**12**	**2**	**1**	**3**	**33**	**0**	**1**	**0**	**16:57**
	NHL Totals		**257**	**28**	**32**	**60**	**194**	**0**	**0**	**2**	**433**	**6.5**		**1344**	**51.2**	**12:25**	**49**	**5**	**3**	**8**	**93**	**0**	**1**	**0**	**11:33**

NCAA Championship All-Tournament Team (2007) • NCAA Championship Tournament MVP (2007) • AHL All-Rookie Team (2009)

ADAM, Luke
(A-duhm, LEWK) **BUF**

Center. Shoots left. 6'2", 216 lbs. Born, St. John's, Nfld., June 18, 1990. Buffalo's 3rd choice, 44th overall, in 2008 Entry Draft.

			Regular Season														Playoffs								
Season	Club	League	GP	G	A	Pts	PIM	PP	SH	GW	S	%	+/-	TF	F%	Min	GP	G	A	Pts	PIM	PP	SH	GW	Min
2006-07	St. John's	QMJHL	63	6	9	15	51	....	....	....	....	....	....	....	....	....	4	0	2	2	4	....	....	....	....
2007-08	St. John's	QMJHL	70	36	30	66	72	....	....	....	....	....	....	....	....	....	6	3	5	8	8	....	....	....	....
2008-09	Montreal	QMJHL	47	22	27	49	59	....	....	....	....	....	....	....	....	....	....	....	....	....	....	....	....	....	....
2009-10	Cape Breton	QMJHL	56	49	41	90	75	....	....	....	....	....	....	....	....	....	5	3	1	4	2	....	....	....	....
	Portland Pirates	AHL	....	....	....	....	....	....	....	....	....	....	....	....	....	....	3	0	2	2	0	....	....	....	....
2010-11	**Buffalo**	**NHL**	**19**	**3**	**1**	**4**	**12**	**0**	**0**	**1**	**31**	**9.7**	**–6**	**119**	**34.5**	**11:13**	....	....	....	....	....	....	....	....	....
	Portland Pirates	AHL	57	29	33	62	46	....	....	....	....	....	....	....	....	....	12	4	3	7	14	....	....	....	....
2011-12	**Buffalo**	**NHL**	**52**	**10**	**10**	**20**	**14**	**0**	**0**	**0**	**89**	**11.2**	**–6**	**259**	**44.0**	**12:24**	....	....	....	....	....	....	....	....	....
	Rochester	AHL	27	4	9	13	18	....	....	....	....	....	....	....	....	....	3	0	1	1	4	....	....	....	....
2012-13	Rochester	AHL	67	15	22	37	57	....	....	....	....	....	....	....	....	....	3	0	0	0	2	....	....	....	....
	Buffalo	**NHL**	**4**	**1**	**0**	**1**	**2**	**0**	**0**	**0**	**2**	**50.0**	**1**	**1**	**100.0**	**9:48**	....	....	....	....	....	....	....	....	....
	NHL Totals		**75**	**14**	**11**	**25**	**28**	**0**	**0**	**1**	**122**	**11.5**		**379**	**41.2**	**11:58**	....	....	....	....	....	....	....	....	....

QMJHL First All-Star Team (2010) • AHL All-Rookie Team (2011) • Dudley "Red" Garrett Memorial Award (AHL – Rookie of the Year) (2011)

ADAMS, Craig
(A-duhmz, KRAYG) **PIT**

Right wing. Shoots right. 6', 197 lbs. Born, Seria, Brunei, April 26, 1977. Hartford's 9th choice, 223rd overall, in 1996 Entry Draft.

			Regular Season														Playoffs								
Season	Club	League	GP	G	A	Pts	PIM	PP	SH	GW	S	%	+/-	TF	F%	Min	GP	G	A	Pts	PIM	PP	SH	GW	Min
1995-96	Harvard Crimson	ECAC	34	8	9	17	56	....	....	....	....	....	....	....	....	....	....	....	....	....	....	....	....	....	....
1996-97	Harvard Crimson	ECAC	32	6	4	10	36	....	....	....	....	....	....	....	....	....	....	....	....	....	....	....	....	....	....
1997-98	Harvard Crimson	ECAC	12	6	6	12	12	....	....	....	....	....	....	....	....	....	....	....	....	....	....	....	....	....	....
1998-99	Harvard Crimson	ECAC	31	9	14	23	53	....	....	....	....	....	....	....	....	....	....	....	....	....	....	....	....	....	....
99-2000	Cincinnati	IHL	73	12	12	24	124	....	....	....	....	....	....	....	....	....	8	0	1	1	14	....	....	....	....
2000-01	**Carolina**	**NHL**	**44**	**1**	**0**	**1**	**20**	**0**	**0**	**0**	**15**	**6.7**	**–7**	**4**	**25.0**	**4:30**	**3**	**0**	**0**	**0**	**0**	**0**	**0**	**0**	**3:45**
	Cincinnati	IHL	4	0	1	1	9	....	....	....	....	....	....	....	....	....	1	0	0	0	2	....	....	....	....
2001-02	**Carolina**	**NHL**	**33**	**0**	**1**	**1**	**38**	**0**	**0**	**0**	**17**	**0.0**	**2**	**9**	**33.3**	**5:54**	**1**	**0**	**0**	**0**	**0**	**0**	**0**	**0**	**7:41**
	Lowell	AHL	22	5	4	9	51	....	....	....	....	....	....	....	....	....	....	....	....	....	....	....	....	....	....
2002-03	**Carolina**	**NHL**	**81**	**6**	**12**	**18**	**71**	**1**	**0**	**1**	**107**	**5.6**	**–11**	**20**	**35.0**	**12:12**	....	....	....	....	....	....	....	....	....
2003-04	**Carolina**	**NHL**	**80**	**7**	**10**	**17**	**69**	**0**	**1**	**0**	**110**	**6.4**	**–5**	**20**	**45.0**	**13:41**	....	....	....	....	....	....	....	....	....
2004-05	HC Milano	Italy	30	15	14	29	57	....	....	....	....	....	....	....	....	....	15	4	7	11	26	....	....	....	....
2005-06 ♦	**Carolina**	**NHL**	**67**	**10**	**11**	**21**	**51**	**1**	**1**	**2**	**68**	**14.7**	**1**	**13**	**53.9**	**12:18**	**25**	**0**	**0**	**0**	**10**	**0**	**0**	**0**	**8:16**
	Lowell	AHL	13	4	3	7	20	....	....	....	....	....	....	....	....	....	....	....	....	....	....	....	....	....	....
2006-07	**Carolina**	**NHL**	**82**	**7**	**7**	**14**	**54**	**0**	**1**	**1**	**71**	**9.9**	**–9**	**36**	**30.6**	**10:04**	....	....	....	....	....	....	....	....	....
2007-08	**Carolina**	**NHL**	**40**	**2**	**3**	**5**	**34**	**0**	**0**	**0**	**31**	**6.5**	**–8**	**11**	**27.3**	**9:48**	....	....	....	....	....	....	....	....	....
	Chicago	**NHL**	**35**	**2**	**4**	**6**	**24**	**0**	**1**	**1**	**32**	**6.3**	**–8**	**30**	**53.3**	**11:56**	....	....	....	....	....	....	....	....	....
2008-09	**Chicago**	**NHL**	**36**	**2**	**4**	**6**	**22**	**1**	**0**	**0**	**38**	**5.3**	**–3**	**16**	**37.5**	**8:43**	....	....	....	....	....	....	....	....	....
	♦ **Pittsburgh**	**NHL**	**9**	**0**	**1**	**1**	**0**	**0**	**0**	**0**	**9**	**0.0**	**0**	**5**	**40.0**	**8:34**	**24**	**3**	**2**	**5**	**16**	**0**	**0**	**0**	**9:45**
2009-10	**Pittsburgh**	**NHL**	**82**	**0**	**10**	**10**	**72**	**0**	**0**	**0**	**84**	**0.0**	**–5**	**562**	**43.8**	**11:06**	**13**	**2**	**1**	**3**	**15**	**0**	**0**	**1**	**10:38**
2010-11	**Pittsburgh**	**NHL**	**80**	**4**	**11**	**15**	**76**	**0**	**2**	**1**	**90**	**4.4**	**–5**	**465**	**41.7**	**12:11**	**7**	**1**	**0**	**1**	**2**	**0**	**0**	**0**	**13:06**
2011-12	**Pittsburgh**	**NHL**	**82**	**5**	**13**	**18**	**34**	**0**	**0**	**0**	**76**	**6.6**	**–6**	**292**	**45.2**	**11:17**	**5**	**0**	**0**	**0**	**19**	**0**	**0**	**0**	**8:39**
2012-13	**Pittsburgh**	**NHL**	**48**	**3**	**6**	**9**	**28**	**0**	**1**	**0**	**46**	**6.5**	**–1**	**98**	**52.0**	**11:10**	**15**	**0**	**1**	**1**	**10**	**0**	**0**	**0**	**12:02**
	NHL Totals		**799**	**49**	**93**	**142**	**593**	**3**	**7**	**6**	**794**	**6.2**		**1581**	**43.5**	**10:51**	**93**	**6**	**4**	**10**	**72**	**0**	**0**	**1**	**9:49**

• Rights transferred to **Carolina** after **Hartford** franchise relocated, June 25, 1997. • Missed majority of 1997-98 due to shoulder injury vs. University of Wisconsin (WCHA), December 27, 1997. Signed as a free agent by **Milano**, (Italy), July 28, 2004. Signed as a free agent by **Anaheim**, August 25, 2005. Traded to **Carolina** by **Anaheim** for Bruno St. Jacques, October 3, 2005. Traded to **Chicago** by **Carolina** for future considerations, January 17, 2008. Claimed on waivers by **Pittsburgh** from **Chicago**, March 4, 2009.

AKESON, Jason
(AK-uh-suhn, JAY-suhn) **PHI**

Right wing. Shoots right. 5'10", 190 lbs. Born, Orleans, Ont., June 3, 1990.

			Regular Season														Playoffs								
Season	Club	League	GP	G	A	Pts	PIM	PP	SH	GW	S	%	+/-	TF	F%	Min	GP	G	A	Pts	PIM	PP	SH	GW	Min
2006-07	Cumberland	ON-Jr.A	54	17	36	53	40	....	....	....	....	....	....	....	....	....	....	....	....	....	....	....	....	....	....
2007-08	Cumberland	ON-Jr.A	34	18	43	61	14	....	....	....	....	....	....	....	....	....	....	....	....	....	....	....	....	....	....
	Kitchener Rangers	OHL	13	0	2	2	4	....	....	....	....	....	....	....	....	....	16	0	1	1	0	....	....	....	....
2008-09	Kitchener Rangers	OHL	56	20	44	64	16	....	....	....	....	....	....	....	....	....	....	....	....	....	....	....	....	....	....
2009-10	Kitchener Rangers	OHL	65	24	56	80	24	....	....	....	....	....	....	....	....	....	20	8	11	19	14	....	....	....	....
2010-11	Kitchener Rangers	OHL	67	24	*84	*108	23	....	....	....	....	....	....	....	....	....	7	3	6	9	0	....	....	....	....
2011-12	Adirondack	AHL	76	14	41	55	26	....	....	....	....	....	....	....	....	....	....	....	....	....	....	....	....	....	....
2012-13	Adirondack	AHL	62	20	33	53	27	....	....	....	....	....	....	....	....	....	....	....	....	....	....	....	....	....	....
	Trenton Titans	ECHL	14	2	8	10	7	....	....	....	....	....	....	....	....	....	....	....	....	....	....	....	....	....	....
	Philadelphia	**NHL**	**1**	**1**	**0**	**1**	**0**	**0**	**0**	**0**	**2**	**50.0**	**2**	**0**	**0.0**	**12:23**	....	....	....	....	....	....	....	....	....
	NHL Totals		**1**	**1**	**0**	**1**	**0**	**0**	**0**	**0**	**2**	**50.0**		**0**	**0.0**	**12:23**	....	....	....	....	....	....	....	....	....

OHL Second All-Star Team (2011)

Signed as a free agent by **Philadelphia**, March 2, 2011.

ALBERTS, Andrew
(AL-buhrts, AN-droo) **VAN**

Defense. Shoots left. 6'5", 206 lbs. Born, Minneapolis, MN, June 30, 1981. Boston's 5th choice, 179th overall, in 2001 Entry Draft.

Season	Club	League	GP	G	A	Pts	PIM	PP	SH	GW	S	%	+/-	TF	F%	Min	GP	G	A	Pts	PIM	PP	SH	GW	Min
1998-99	Benilde	High-MN	26	10	25	35	....	....	....	....	....	....	....	....	....	....	....	....	....	....	....	....	....	....	....
99-2000	Waterloo	USHL	49	2	2	4	55	....	....	....	....	....	....	....	....	....	4	0	0	0	12	....	....	....	....
2000-01	Waterloo	USHL	54	4	10	14	128	....	....	....	....	....	....	....	....	....	....	....	....	....	....	....	....	....	....
2001-02	Boston College	H-East	38	2	10	12	52	....	....	....	....	....	....	....	....	....	....	....	....	....	....	....	....	....	....
2002-03	Boston College	H-East	39	6	16	22	60	....	....	....	....	....	....	....	....	....	....	....	....	....	....	....	....	....	....
2003-04	Boston College	H-East	42	4	12	16	64	....	....	....	....	....	....	....	....	....	....	....	....	....	....	....	....	....	....
2004-05	Boston College	H-East	30	4	12	16	67	....	....	....	....	....	....	....	....	....	....	....	....	....	....	....	....	....	....
	Providence Bruins	AHL	8	0	0	0	16	....	....	....	....	....	....	....	....	....	16	1	4	5	40	....	....	....	....
2005-06	**Boston**	**NHL**	**73**	**1**	**6**	**7**	**68**	**0**	**1**	**0**	**30**	**3.3**	**3**	**2**	**50.0**	**12:50**	....	....	....	....	....	....	....	....	....
	Providence Bruins	AHL	6	0	1	1	7	....	....	....	....	....	....	....	....	....	....	....	....	....	....	....	....	....	....
2006-07	**Boston**	**NHL**	**76**	**0**	**10**	**10**	**124**	**0**	**0**	**0**	**41**	**0.0**	**–15**	**1**	**0.0**	**19:40**	....	....	....	....	....	....	....	....	....
2007-08	**Boston**	**NHL**	**35**	**0**	**2**	**2**	**39**	**0**	**0**	**0**	**25**	**0.0**	**4**	**2**	**50.0**	**20:37**	**2**	**0**	**0**	**0**	**0**	**0**	**0**	**0**	**11:07**
2008-09	**Philadelphia**	**NHL**	**79**	**1**	**12**	**13**	**61**	**0**	**0**	**0**	**46**	**2.2**	**6**	**0**	**0.0**	**15:48**	**6**	**0**	**1**	**1**	**10**	**0**	**0**	**0**	**13:40**
2009-10	**Carolina**	**NHL**	**62**	**2**	**8**	**10**	**74**	**0**	**0**	**0**	**38**	**5.3**	**7**	**0**	**0.0**	**15:04**	....	....	....	....	....	....	....	....	....
	Vancouver	**NHL**	**14**	**1**	**1**	**2**	**13**	**0**	**0**	**0**	**12**	**8.3**	**–1**	**1**	**0.0**	**16:45**	**10**	**0**	**1**	**1**	**27**	**0**	**0**	**0**	**12:27**
2010-11	**Vancouver**	**NHL**	**42**	**1**	**6**	**7**	**41**	**0**	**0**	**0**	**21**	**4.8**	**0**	**0**	**0.0**	**15:10**	**9**	**0**	**0**	**0**	**6**	**0**	**0**	**0**	**12:48**
2011-12	**Vancouver**	**NHL**	**44**	**2**	**1**	**3**	**40**	**0**	**0**	**2**	**19**	**10.5**	**4**	**0**	**0.0**	**14:18**	....	....	....	....	....	....	....	....	....
2012-13	**Vancouver**	**NHL**	**24**	**0**	**1**	**1**	**32**	**0**	**0**	**0**	**15**	**0.0**	**–7**	**0**	**0.0**	**15:11**	**4**	**0**	**0**	**0**	**2**	**0**	**0**	**0**	**13:05**
	NHL Totals		**449**	**8**	**47**	**55**	**492**	**0**	**1**	**2**	**247**	**3.2**		**6**	**33.3**	**16:02**	**31**	**0**	**2**	**2**	**45**	**0**	**0**	**0**	**12:47**

Hockey East Second All-Star Team (2004) • NCAA East First All-American Team (2004, 2005) • Hockey East First All-Star Team (2005)

• Missed majority of 2007-08 due to post-concussion syndrome. Traded to **Philadelphia** by **Boston** for Ned Lukacevic and Philadelphia's 4th round choice (Lane MacDermid) in 2009 Entry Draft, October 14, 2008. Signed as a free agent by **Carolina**, July 15, 2009. Traded to **Vancouver** by **Carolina** for Vancouver's 3rd round choice (Austin Levi) in 2010 Entry Draft, March 3, 2010. • Missed majority of 2012-13 as a healthy reserve.

ALFREDSSON, Daniel
(AHL-frehd-suhn, DAN-yehl) **DET**

Right wing. Shoots right. 5'11", 196 lbs. Born, Gothenburg, Sweden, December 11, 1972. Ottawa's 5th choice, 133rd overall, in 1994 Entry Draft.

Season	Club	League	GP	G	A	Pts	PIM	PP	SH	GW	S	%	+/-	TF	F%	Min	GP	G	A	Pts	PIM	PP	SH	GW	Min
1990-91	Molndal Hockey	Sweden-2	3	0	0	0	2	....	....	....	....	....	....	....	....	....	8	4	4	8	4	....	....	....	....
1991-92	Molndal	Sweden-2	32	12	8	20	43	....	....	....	....	....	....	....	....	....	....	....	....	....	....	....	....	....	....
1992-93	V.Frolunda	Sweden	20	1	5	6	8	....	....	....	....	....	....	....	....	....	....	....	....	....	....	....	....	....	....
1993-94	V.Frolunda	Sweden	39	20	10	30	18	....	....	....	....	....	....	....	....	....	4	1	1	2	....	....	....	....	....
1994-95	V.Frolunda	Sweden	22	7	11	18	22	....	....	....	....	....	....	....	....	....	....	....	....	....	....	....	....	....	....
1995-96	**Ottawa**	**NHL**	**82**	**26**	**35**	**61**	**28**	**8**	**2**	**3**	**212**	**12.3**	**–18**	....	....	....	....	....	....	....	....	....	....	....	....
1996-97	**Ottawa**	**NHL**	**76**	**24**	**47**	**71**	**30**	**11**	**1**	**1**	**247**	**9.7**	**5**	....	....	....	**7**	**5**	**2**	**7**	**6**	**3**	**0**	**2**	....
1997-98	**Ottawa**	**NHL**	**55**	**17**	**28**	**45**	**18**	**7**	**0**	**7**	**149**	**11.4**	**7**	....	....	....	**11**	**7**	**2**	**9**	**20**	**2**	**1**	**1**	....
	Sweden	Olympics	4	2	3	5	2	....	....	....	....	....	....	....	....	....	....	....	....	....	....	....	....	....	....
1998-99	**Ottawa**	**NHL**	**58**	**11**	**22**	**33**	**14**	**3**	**0**	**5**	**163**	**6.7**	**8**	**7**	**57.1**	**17:22**	**4**	**1**	**2**	**3**	**4**	**1**	**0**	**0**	**22:23**
99-2000	**Ottawa**	**NHL**	**57**	**21**	**38**	**59**	**28**	**4**	**2**	**0**	**164**	**12.8**	**11**	**3**	**66.7**	**18:45**	**6**	**1**	**3**	**4**	**2**	**1**	**0**	**0**	**20:22**
2000-01	**Ottawa**	**NHL**	**68**	**24**	**46**	**70**	**30**	**10**	**0**	**3**	**206**	**11.7**	**11**	**8**	**50.0**	**18:47**	**4**	**1**	**0**	**1**	**2**	**0**	**0**	**0**	**21:20**
2001-02	**Ottawa**	**NHL**	**78**	**37**	**34**	**71**	**45**	**9**	**1**	**4**	**243**	**15.2**	**3**	**30**	**30.0**	**20:19**	**12**	**7**	**6**	**13**	**4**	**3**	**0**	**3**	**21:43**
	Sweden	Olympics	4	1	4	5	2	....	....	....	....	....	....	....	....	....	....	....	....	....	....	....	....	....	....
2002-03	**Ottawa**	**NHL**	**78**	**27**	**51**	**78**	**42**	**9**	**0**	**6**	**240**	**11.3**	**15**	**40**	**40.0**	**19:32**	**18**	**4**	**4**	**8**	**12**	**4**	**0**	**1**	**18:00**
2003-04	**Ottawa**	**NHL**	**77**	**32**	**48**	**80**	**24**	**9**	**0**	**5**	**230**	**13.9**	**12**	**33**	**24.2**	**19:24**	**7**	**1**	**2**	**3**	**2**	**0**	**0**	**0**	**20:03**
2004-05	Frolunda	Sweden	15	8	9	17	10	....	....	....	....	....	....	....	....	....	14	*12	6	*18	8	....	....	....	....
2005-06	**Ottawa**	**NHL**	**77**	**43**	**60**	**103**	**50**	**16**	**5**	**8**	**249**	**17.3**	**29**	**44**	**20.5**	**21:41**	**10**	**2**	**8**	**10**	**4**	**1**	**0**	**0**	**21:10**
	Sweden	Olympics	8	5	5	10	4	....	....	....	....	....	....	....	....	....	....	....	....	....	....	....	....	....	....
2006-07	**Ottawa**	**NHL**	**77**	**29**	**58**	**87**	**42**	**7**	**2**	**7**	**240**	**12.1**	**42**	**43**	**34.9**	**21:35**	**20**	***14**	**8**	***22**	**10**	***6**	**1**	***4**	**23:20**
2007-08	**Ottawa**	**NHL**	**70**	**40**	**49**	**89**	**34**	**9**	***7**	**5**	**217**	**18.4**	**15**	**39**	**53.9**	**22:17**	**2**	**0**	**0**	**0**	**0**	**0**	**0**	**0**	**19:20**
2008-09	**Ottawa**	**NHL**	**79**	**24**	**50**	**74**	**24**	**8**	**1**	**3**	**204**	**11.8**	**7**	**17**	**23.5**	**20:53**	....	....	....	....	....	....	....	....	....
2009-10	**Ottawa**	**NHL**	**70**	**20**	**51**	**71**	**22**	**4**	**1**	**5**	**168**	**11.9**	**8**	**40**	**35.0**	**19:40**	**6**	**2**	**6**	**8**	**2**	**0**	**0**	**0**	**22:54**
	Sweden	Olympics	4	3	0	3	0	....	....	....	....	....	....	....	....	....	....	....	....	....	....	....	....	....	....
2010-11	**Ottawa**	**NHL**	**54**	**14**	**17**	**31**	**18**	**7**	**0**	**1**	**96**	**14.6**	**–19**	**12**	**16.7**	**19:17**	....	....	....	....	....	....	....	....	....
2011-12	**Ottawa**	**NHL**	**75**	**27**	**32**	**59**	**18**	**7**	**3**	**4**	**191**	**14.1**	**16**	**46**	**43.5**	**18:57**	**4**	**2**	**0**	**2**	**0**	**1**	**0**	**0**	**17:58**
2012-13	**Ottawa**	**NHL**	**47**	**10**	**16**	**26**	**33**	**3**	**0**	**2**	**101**	**9.9**	**1**	**38**	**42.1**	**19:21**	**10**	**4**	**6**	**10**	**6**	**3**	**1**	**0**	**19:10**
	NHL Totals		**1178**	**426**	**682**	**1108**	**500**	**131**	**25**	**69**	**3320**	**12.8**		**400**	**36.0**	**19:56**	**121**	**51**	**49**	**100**	**74**	**25**	**3**	**11**	**20:46**

NHL All-Rookie Team (1996) • Calder Memorial Trophy (1996) • NHL Second All-Star Team (2006) • King Clancy Memorial Trophy (2012) • Mark Messier NHL Leadership Award (2013)

Played in NHL All-Star Game (1996, 1997, 1998, 2004, 2008, 2012)

Signed as a free agent by **Frolunda** (Sweden), November 10, 2004. Signed as a free agent by **Detroit**, July 5, 2013.

ALIU, Akim
(ah-lee-OO, a-KEEM)

Right wing. Shoots right. 6'4", 225 lbs. Born, Okene, Nigeria, April 24, 1989. Chicago's 3rd choice, 56th overall, in 2007 Entry Draft.

Season	Club	League	GP	G	A	Pts	PIM	PP	SH	GW	S	%	+/-	TF	F%	Min	GP	G	A	Pts	PIM	PP	SH	GW	Min
2004-05	Tor. Marlboros	GTHL	68	35	50	85	197	....	....	....	....	....	....	....	....	....	....	....	....	....	....	....	....	....	....
2005-06	Windsor Spitfires	OHL	18	3	4	7	25	....	....	....	....	....	....	....	....	....	....	....	....	....	....	....	....	....	....
	Sudbury Wolves	OHL	29	7	6	13	54	....	....	....	....	....	....	....	....	....	6	0	1	1	7	....	....	....	....
2006-07	Sudbury Wolves	OHL	53	20	22	42	104	....	....	....	....	....	....	....	....	....	21	1	5	6	50	....	....	....	....
2007-08	London Knights	OHL	60	28	33	61	133	....	....	....	....	....	....	....	....	....	5	2	1	3	15	....	....	....	....
	Rockford IceHogs	AHL	2	0	0	0	2	....	....	....	....	....	....	....	....	....	....	....	....	....	....	....	....	....	....
2008-09	London Knights	OHL	16	8	10	18	30	....	....	....	....	....	....	....	....	....	....	....	....	....	....	....	....	....	....
	Sudbury Wolves	OHL	29	10	16	26	61	....	....	....	....	....	....	....	....	....	6	2	1	3	14	....	....	....	....
	Rockford IceHogs	AHL	5	2	0	2	14	....	....	....	....	....	....	....	....	....	1	1	0	1	0	....	....	....	....
2009-10	Rockford IceHogs	AHL	48	11	6	17	69	....	....	....	....	....	....	....	....	....	....	....	....	....	....	....	....	....	....
	Toledo Walleye	ECHL	13	5	9	14	18	....	....	....	....	....	....	....	....	....	2	1	1	2	16	....	....	....	....
2010-11	Chicago Wolves	AHL	43	4	5	9	53	....	....	....	....	....	....	....	....	....	....	....	....	....	....	....	....	....	....
	Gwinnett	ECHL	16	12	8	20	22	....	....	....	....	....	....	....	....	....	....	....	....	....	....	....	....	....	....
	Peoria Rivermen	AHL	16	5	4	9	20	....	....	....	....	....	....	....	....	....	2	1	0	1	6	....	....	....	....
2011-12	Colorado Eagles	ECHL	10	2	4	6	28	....	....	....	....	....	....	....	....	....	....	....	....	....	....	....	....	....	....
	Calgary	**NHL**	**2**	**2**	**1**	**3**	**12**	**0**	**0**	**0**	**3**	**66.7**	**3**	**0**	**0.0**	**11:02**	....	....	....	....	....	....	....	....	....
	Abbotsford Heat	AHL	42	10	4	14	59	....	....	....	....	....	....	....	....	....	5	0	1	1	28	....	....	....	....
2012-13	Abbotsford Heat	AHL	42	4	7	11	111	....	....	....	....	....	....	....	....	....	....	....	....	....	....	....	....	....	....
	Calgary	**NHL**	**5**	**0**	**0**	**0**	**14**	**0**	**0**	**0**	**2**	**0.0**	**–2**	**0**	**0.0**	**10:52**	....	....	....	....	....	....	....	....	....
	NHL Totals		**7**	**2**	**1**	**3**	**26**	**0**	**0**	**0**	**5**	**40.0**		**0**	**0.0**	**10:55**	....	....	....	....	....	....	....	....	....

Traded to **Atlanta** by **Chicago** with Brent Sopel, Dustin Byfuglien and Ben Eager for Marty Reasoner, Joey Crabb, Jeremy Morin and New Jersey's 1st (previously acquired, Chicago selected Kevin Hayes) and 2nd (previously acquired, Chicago selected Justin Holl) round choices in 2010 Entry Draft, June 24, 2010. • Transferred to **Winnipeg** after **Atlanta** franchise relocated, June 21, 2011. Traded to **Calgary** by **Winnipeg** for John Negrin, January 29, 2012.

ALLEN, Bryan (AHL-lehn, BRIGH-uhn) ANA

Defense. Shoots left. 6'5", 229 lbs. Born, Kingston, Ont., August 21, 1980. Vancouver's 1st choice, 4th overall, in 1998 Entry Draft.

Season	Club	League	GP	G	A	Pts	PIM	PP	SH	GW	S	%	+/-	TF	F%	Min	Playoffs GP	G	A	Pts	PIM	PP	SH	GW	Min
1995-96	Ernestown Jets	ON-Jr.C	36	1	16	17	71																		
1996-97	Oshawa Generals	OHL	60	2	4	6	76										18	1	3	4	26				
1997-98	Oshawa Generals	OHL	48	6	13	19	126										5	0	5	5	18				
1998-99	Oshawa Generals	OHL	37	7	15	22	77										15	0	3	3	26				
99-2000	Oshawa Generals	OHL	3	0	2	2	12										3	0	0	0	13				
	Syracuse Crunch	AHL	9	1	1	2	11										2	0	0	0	2				
2000-01	**Vancouver**	**NHL**	**6**	**0**	**0**	**0**	**0**	**0**	**0**	**0**	**2**	**0.0**	**0**	**0**	**0.0**	**9:20**	**2**	**0**	**0**	**0**	**2**	**0**	**0**	**0**	**13:47**
	Kansas City	IHL	75	5	20	25	99																		
2001-02	**Vancouver**	**NHL**	**11**	**0**	**0**	**0**	**6**	**0**	**0**	**0**	**4**	**0.0**	**1**	**0**	**0.0**	**10:47**									
	Manitoba Moose	AHL	68	7	18	25	121										5	0	1	1	8				
2002-03	**Vancouver**	**NHL**	**48**	**5**	**3**	**8**	**73**	**0**	**0**	**1**	**43**	**11.6**	**8**	**0**	**0.0**	**12:56**	**1**	**0**	**0**	**0**	**2**	**0**	**0**	**0**	**10:35**
	Manitoba Moose	AHL	7	0	1	1	4																		
2003-04	**Vancouver**	**NHL**	**74**	**2**	**5**	**7**	**94**	**0**	**0**	**0**	**70**	**2.9**	**–10**	**0**	**0.0**	**16:51**	**4**	**0**	**0**	**0**	**2**	**0**	**0**	**0**	**14:37**
2004-05	Voskresensk	Russia	19	0	3	3	34																		
2005-06	**Vancouver**	**NHL**	**77**	**7**	**10**	**17**	**115**	**1**	**0**	**0**	**88**	**8.0**	**4**	**0**	**0.0**	**20:27**									
2006-07	**Florida**	**NHL**	**82**	**4**	**21**	**25**	**112**	**0**	**0**	**0**	**99**	**4.0**	**7**	**1**	**0.0**	**21:36**									
2007-08	**Florida**	**NHL**	**73**	**2**	**14**	**16**	**67**	**0**	**0**	**0**	**67**	**3.0**	**5**	**0**	**0.0**	**21:17**									
2008-09	**Florida**	**NHL**	**2**	**0**	**1**	**1**	**0**	**0**	**0**	**0**	**5**	**0.0**	**2**	**0**	**0.0**	**27:11**									
2009-10	**Florida**	**NHL**	**74**	**4**	**9**	**13**	**99**	**0**	**1**	**2**	**78**	**5.1**	**–8**	**0**	**0.0**	**19:10**									
2010-11	**Florida**	**NHL**	**53**	**4**	**8**	**12**	**63**	**0**	**0**	**1**	**50**	**8.0**	**–5**	**0**	**0.0**	**19:13**									
	Carolina	**NHL**	**19**	**0**	**5**	**5**	**19**	**0**	**0**	**0**	**8**	**0.0**	**4**	**0**	**0.0**	**15:51**									
2011-12	**Carolina**	**NHL**	**82**	**1**	**13**	**14**	**76**	**0**	**0**	**1**	**87**	**1.1**	**–1**	**0**	**0.0**	**19:10**									
2012-13	**Anaheim**	**NHL**	**41**	**0**	**6**	**6**	**34**	**0**	**0**	**0**	**25**	**0.0**	**1**	**0**	**0.0**	**18:44**	**7**	**0**	**1**	**1**	**2**	**0**	**0**	**0**	**17:22**
	NHL Totals		**642**	**29**	**95**	**124**	**758**	**1**	**1**	**5**	**626**	**4.6**		**1**	**0.0**	**18:48**	**14**	**0**	**1**	**1**	**8**	**0**	**0**	**0**	**15:35**

OHL First All-Star Team (1999)

• Missed majority of 1999-2000 due to knee injury in training camp, September 21, 1999. Signed as a free agent by **Voskresensk** (Russia), December 20, 2004. Traded to **Florida** by **Vancouver** with Todd Bertuzzi and Alex Auld for Roberto Luongo, Lukas Krajicek and Florida's 6th round choice (Sergei Shirokov) in 2006 Entry Draft, June 23, 2006. • Missed majority of 2008-09 due to off-season arthroscopic knee surgery and follow-up cartilage surgery, October 27, 2008. Traded to **Carolina** by **Florida** for Sergei Samsonov, February 28, 2011. Signed as a free agent by **Anaheim**, July 1, 2012.

ALMOND, Cody (al-MUHND, KOH-dee) MIN

Center. Shoots left. 6'2", 209 lbs. Born, Calgary, Alta., July 24, 1989. Minnesota's 3rd choice, 140th overall, in 2007 Entry Draft.

Season	Club	League	GP	G	A	Pts	PIM	PP	SH	GW	S	%	+/-	TF	F%	Min	Playoffs GP	G	A	Pts	PIM	PP	SH	GW	Min
2004-05	Cgy. Stampeders	SAMHL	30	28	15	43	108																		
2005-06	Kelowna Rockets	WHL	23	2	1	3	7										8	0	0	0	0				
2006-07	Kelowna Rockets	WHL	68	15	28	43	72																		
2007-08	Kelowna Rockets	WHL	69	22	34	56	114										7	1	2	3	2				
2008-09	Kelowna Rockets	WHL	70	33	33	66	105										22	10	17	27	*51				
2009-10	**Minnesota**	**NHL**	**7**	**1**	**0**	**1**	**9**	**0**	**0**	**0**	**6**	**16.7**	**–3**	**30**	**60.0**	**7:45**									
	Houston Aeros	AHL	48	7	11	18	77																		
2010-11	**Minnesota**	**NHL**	**8**	**0**	**0**	**0**	**2**	**0**	**0**	**0**	**3**	**0.0**	**0**	**32**	**40.6**	**7:02**									
	Houston Aeros	AHL	65	15	19	34	124										22	0	6	6	20				
2011-12	**Minnesota**	**NHL**	**10**	**1**	**0**	**1**	**15**	**0**	**0**	**0**	**7**	**14.3**	**–5**	**58**	**43.1**	**10:13**									
	Houston Aeros	AHL	46	7	8	15	91										4	1	1	2	6				
2012-13	Geneve	Swiss	39	8	22	30	56										7	0	2	2	18				
	NHL Totals		**25**	**2**	**0**	**2**	**26**	**0**	**0**	**0**	**16**	**12.5**		**120**	**46.7**	**8:30**									

Signed as a free agent by **Geneve** (Swiss), June 20, 2012.

ALZNER, Karl (ALZ-nuhr, KARL) WSH

Defense. Shoots left. 6'3", 213 lbs. Born, Burnaby, B.C., September 24, 1988. Washington's 1st choice, 5th overall, in 2007 Entry Draft.

Season	Club	League	GP	G	A	Pts	PIM	PP	SH	GW	S	%	+/-	TF	F%	Min	Playoffs GP	G	A	Pts	PIM	PP	SH	GW	Min
2002-03	Burnaby W.C.	Minor-BC	64	17	31	48	24																		
2003-04	Richmond	PIJHL	41	3	9	12	8										13	0	2	2	0				
	Calgary Hitmen	WHL	1	0	0	0	0																		
2004-05	Calgary Hitmen	WHL	66	0	10	10	19										12	0	3	3	9				
2005-06	Calgary Hitmen	WHL	70	4	20	24	28										13	1	3	4	4				
2006-07	Calgary Hitmen	WHL	63	8	39	47	32										18	1	12	13	4				
2007-08	Calgary Hitmen	WHL	60	7	29	36	15										16	6	2	8	4				
2008-09	**Washington**	**NHL**	**30**	**1**	**4**	**5**	**2**	**0**	**0**	**0**	**31**	**3.2**	**–1**	**0**	**0.0**	**19:25**									
	Hershey Bears	AHL	48	4	16	20	10										10	0	2	2	2				
2009-10	**Washington**	**NHL**	**21**	**0**	**5**	**5**	**8**	**0**	**0**	**0**	**16**	**0.0**	**–2**	**0**	**0.0**	**16:24**	**1**	**0**	**0**	**0**	**0**	**0**	**0**	**0**	**15:09**
	Hershey Bears	AHL	56	3	18	21	10										20	3	7	10	4				
2010-11	**Washington**	**NHL**	**82**	**2**	**10**	**12**	**24**	**0**	**0**	**0**	**64**	**3.1**	**14**	**0**	**0.0**	**20:01**	**9**	**0**	**1**	**1**	**0**	**0**	**0**	**0**	**22:44**
2011-12	**Washington**	**NHL**	**82**	**1**	**16**	**17**	**29**	**0**	**0**	**0**	**56**	**1.8**	**12**	**0**	**0.0**	**20:52**	**14**	**0**	**2**	**2**	**0**	**0**	**0**	**0**	**24:53**
2012-13	**Washington**	**NHL**	**48**	**1**	**4**	**5**	**14**	**0**	**0**	**0**	**39**	**2.6**	**–6**	**0**	**0.0**	**20:57**	**7**	**1**	**1**	**2**	**2**	**0**	**0**	**0**	**22:18**
	NHL Totals		**263**	**5**	**39**	**44**	**77**	**0**	**0**	**0**	**206**	**2.4**		**0**	**0.0**	**20:06**	**31**	**1**	**4**	**5**	**2**	**0**	**0**	**0**	**23:22**

WHL East Second All-Star Team (2007) • Canadian Major Junior Second All-Star Team (2007) • WHL East First All-Star Team (2008) • WHL Defenseman of the Year (2008) • WHL Player of the Year (2008) • Canadian Major Junior First All-Star Team (2008) • Canadian Major Junior Defenseman of the Year (2008)

ANDERSON, Matt (AN-duhr-suhn, MAT)

Right wing. Shoots right. 5'11", 195 lbs. Born, West Islip, NY, October 31, 1982.

Season	Club	League	GP	G	A	Pts	PIM	PP	SH	GW	S	%	+/-	TF	F%	Min	Playoffs GP	G	A	Pts	PIM	PP	SH	GW	Min
2002-03	Massachusetts	H-East	36	10	21	31	34																		
2003-04	Massachusetts	H-East	DID NOT PLAY – INJURED																						
2004-05	Massachusetts	H-East	18	7	13	20	34																		
2005-06	Massachusetts	H-East	36	7	13	20	30																		
2006-07	Massachusetts	H-East	38	10	10	20	32																		
	Chicago Wolves	AHL															13	1	1	2	6				
2007-08	Chicago Wolves	AHL	14	1	1	2	8										10	1	1	2	4				
	Gwinnett	ECHL	37	14	14	28	28										8	3	2	5	0				
2008-09	Chicago Wolves	AHL	66	13	18	31	32																		
2009-10	Chicago Wolves	AHL	63	16	29	45	18										14	0	12	12	4				
2010-11	Albany Devils	AHL	76	23	32	55	49																		
2011-12	Albany Devils	AHL	56	10	21	31	30																		
2012-13	Albany Devils	AHL	67	13	30	43	42																		
	New Jersey	**NHL**	**2**	**0**	**1**	**1**	**0**	**0**	**0**	**0**	**0**	**0.0**	**1**	**0**	**0.0**	**5:47**									
	NHL Totals		**2**	**0**	**1**	**1**	**0**	**0**	**0**	**0**	**0**	**0.0**		**0**	**0.0**	**5:47**									

• Missed 2003-04 due to shoulder injury. • Missed majority of 2004-05 due to broken ankle. Signed as a free agent by **Chicago** (AHL), March 30, 2007. Signed as a free agent by **Albany** (AHL), July 21, 2010. Signed as a free agent by **New Jersey**, July 1, 2011. Signed as a free agent by **Spartak Moscow** (KHL), May 5, 2013.

ANDERSSON, Joakim (AN-duhr-suhn, YOH-ah-kihm) DET

Center. Shoots left. 6'2", 206 lbs. Born, Munkedal, Sweden, February 5, 1989. Detroit's 2nd choice, 88th overall, in 2007 Entry Draft.

Season	Club	League	GP	G	A	Pts	PIM	PP	SH	GW	S	%	+/-	TF	F%	Min	Playoffs GP	G	A	Pts	PIM	PP	SH	GW	Min
2004-05	Munkedals BK	Sweden-5	STATISTICS NOT AVAILABLE																						
2005-06	Frolunda U18	Swe-U18	1	0	0	0	0										2	0	1	1	0				
	Frolunda Jr.	Swe-Jr.	35	9	11	20	10										7	2	5	7	4				
2006-07	Frolunda U18	Swe-U18	2	1	2	3	2										6	3	2	5	28				
	Frolunda Jr.	Swe-Jr.	41	20	26	46	60										8	0	7	7	4				
	Frolunda	Sweden	1	0	0	0	0																		
2007-08	Boras HC	Sweden-2	33	6	17	23	26																		
	Frolunda Jr.	Swe-Jr.	6	8	2	10	30										5	6	3	9	4				
	Frolunda	Sweden	9	1	0	1	2										4	1	1	2	0				
2008-09	Boras HC	Sweden-2	4	2	2	4	2																		
	Frolunda	Sweden	49	6	6	12	22										11	0	0	0	4				
	Grand Rapids	AHL	1	0	1	1	2										10	1	2	3	4				
2009-10	Frolunda	Sweden	55	6	12	18	42										7	1	2	3	0				
2010-11	Grand Rapids	AHL	79	7	15	22	30																		
2011-12	**Detroit**	**NHL**	**5**	**0**	**0**	**0**	**0**	**0**	**0**	**0**	**3**	**0.0**	**1**	**6**	**83.3**	**6:40**									
	Grand Rapids	AHL	73	21	30	51	34																		

			Regular Season														Playoffs								
Season	Club	League	GP	G	A	Pts	PIM	PP	SH	GW	S	%	+/-	TF	F%	Min	GP	G	A	Pts	PIM	PP	SH	GW	Min
2012-13	Grand Rapids	AHL	36	10	17	27	55	....	....	....	....	....	....	....	....	....	10	3	5	8	0	....	....	....	....
	Detroit	NHL	38	3	5	8	8	0	0	0	43	7.0	2	310	46.5	12:05	14	1	4	5	10	0	0	0	13:20
	NHL Totals		43	3	5	8	8	0	0	0	46	6.5		316	47.2	11:27	14	1	4	5	10	0	0	0	13:20

ANGELIDIS, Mike

(AN-gehl-EE-dihs, MIGHK) **T.B.**

Left wing. Shoots left. 6'1", 212 lbs. Born, Woodbridge, Ont., June 27, 1985.

2002-03	Owen Sound	OHL	65	7	10	17	81	....	....	....	....	....	....	....	....	....	4	1	1	2	0	....	....	....	....
2003-04	Owen Sound	OHL	66	9	9	18	118	....	....	....	....	....	....	....	....	....	7	4	1	5	4	....	....	....	....
2004-05	Owen Sound	OHL	41	9	10	19	126	....	....	....	....	....	....	....	....	....	8	3	2	5	10	....	....	....	....
2005-06	Owen Sound	OHL	68	53	25	78	167	....	....	....	....	....	....	....	....	....	11	5	9	14	38	....	....	....	....
2006-07	Albany River Rats	AHL	27	4	5	9	44	....	....	....	....	....	....	....	....	....	4	0	0	0	10	....	....	....	....
	Florida Everblades	ECHL	24	10	8	18	54	....	....	....	....	....	....	....	....	....	....	....	....	....	....	....	....	....	....
2007-08	Albany River Rats	AHL	74	11	16	27	151	....	....	....	....	....	....	....	....	....	7	0	2	2	6	....	....	....	....
2008-09	Albany River Rats	AHL	67	15	10	25	142	....	....	....	....	....	....	....	....	....	....	....	....	....	....	....	....	....	....
2009-10	Albany River Rats	AHL	67	12	12	24	119	....	....	....	....	....	....	....	....	....	8	2	4	6	12	....	....	....	....
2010-11	Norfolk Admirals	AHL	80	20	18	38	169	....	....	....	....	....	....	....	....	....	3	0	0	0	2	....	....	....	....
2011-12	Tampa Bay	NHL	6	1	0	1	5	0	0	0	8	12.5	–1	7	57.1	6:30	....	....	....	....	....	....	....	....	....
	Norfolk Admirals	AHL	54	14	13	27	135	....	....	....	....	....	....	....	....	....	18	1	5	6	35	....	....	....	....
2012-13	Syracuse Crunch	AHL	71	11	13	24	158	....	....	....	....	....	....	....	....	....	18	2	4	6	49	....	....	....	....
	Tampa Bay	NHL	1	0	0	0	0	0	0	0	0	0.0	0	7	42.9	7:22	....	....	....	....	....	....	....	....	....
	NHL Totals		7	1	0	1	5	0	0	0	8	12.5		14	50.0	6:37	....	....	....	....	....	....	....	....	....

OHL First All-Star Team (2006) • Canadian Major Junior Humanitarian Player of the Year (2006)

Signed as a free agent by **Carolina**, July 27, 2006. Signed as a free agent by **Tampa Bay**, August 3, 2010.

ANISIMOV, Artem

(a-NEE-see-mawv, AHR-tehm) **CBJ**

Center. Shoots left. 6'4", 200 lbs. Born, Yaroslavl, USSR, May 24, 1988. NY Rangers' 2nd choice, 54th overall, in 2006 Entry Draft.

2004-05	Yaroslavl 2	Russia-3	24	3	5	8	10	....	....	....	....	....	....	....	....	....	....	....	....	....	....	....	....	....	....
2005-06	Yaroslavl 2	Russia-3	32	15	12	27	28	....	....	....	....	....	....	....	....	....	....	....	....	....	....	....	....	....	....
	Yaroslavl	Russia	10	0	1	1	4	....	....	....	....	....	....	....	....	....	....	....	....	....	....	....	....	....	....
2006-07	Yaroslavl 2	Russia-3	2	2	0	2	0	....	....	....	....	....	....	....	....	....	....	....	....	....	....	....	....	....	....
	Yaroslavl	Russia	39	2	8	10	26	....	....	....	....	....	....	....	....	....	7	3	2	5	4	....	....	....	....
2007-08	Hartford	AHL	74	16	27	43	30	....	....	....	....	....	....	....	....	....	5	1	0	1	2	....	....	....	....
2008-09	NY Rangers	NHL	1	0	0	0	0	0	0	0	1	0.0	0	5	40.0	9:27	1	0	0	0	0	0	0	0	5:35
	Hartford	AHL	80	37	44	81	50	....	....	....	....	....	....	....	....	....	6	2	0	2	0	....	....	....	....
2009-10	NY Rangers	NHL	82	12	16	28	32	1	0	2	124	9.7	–2	690	44.9	12:54	....	....	....	....	....	....	....	....	....
2010-11	NY Rangers	NHL	82	18	26	44	20	3	0	2	190	9.5	3	688	44.5	16:12	5	1	0	1	0	0	0	0	15:10
2011-12	NY Rangers	NHL	79	16	20	36	34	4	1	1	132	12.1	12	345	46.7	15:24	20	3	7	10	4	0	0	0	13:52
2012-13	Yaroslavl	KHL	36	12	17	29	22	....	....	....	....	....	....	....	....	....	....	....	....	....	....	....	....	....	....
	Columbus	NHL	35	11	7	18	12	1	0	3	68	16.2	–6	509	48.9	16:25	....	....	....	....	....	....	....	....	....
	NHL Totals		279	57	69	126	98	9	1	8	515	11.1		2237	46.0	15:01	26	4	7	11	4	0	0	0	13:48

Traded to **Columbus** by **NY Rangers** with Brandon Dubinsky, Tim Erixon and NY Rangers' 1st round choice (Kerby Rychel) in 2013 Entry Draft for Rick Nash, Steven Delisle and Columbus' 3rd round choice (Pavel Buchnevich) in 2013 Entry Draft, July 23, 2012. Signed as a free agent by **Yaroslavl** (KHL), September 20, 2012.

ANTROPOV, Nik

(an-TROH-pahv, NIHK)

Center. Shoots left. 6'6", 245 lbs. Born, Ust-Kamenogorsk, USSR, February 18, 1980. Toronto's 1st choice, 10th overall, in 1998 Entry Draft.

1996-97	Ust-Kamenogorsk	Russia-2	8	2	1	3	6	....	....	....	....	....	....	....	....	....	....	....	....	....	....	....	....	....	....
1997-98	Ust-Kamenogorsk	Russia-2	42	15	24	39	62	....	....	....	....	....	....	....	....	....	....	....	....	....	....	....	....	....	....
1998-99	Dynamo Moscow	Russia	30	5	9	14	30	....	....	....	....	....	....	....	....	....	11	0	1	1	4	....	....	....	....
99-2000	Toronto	NHL	66	12	18	30	41	0	0	2	89	13.5	14	501	46.3	12:48	3	0	0	0	4	0	0	0	10:14
	St. John's	AHL	2	0	0	0	4	....	....	....	....	....	....	....	....	....	....	....	....	....	....	....	....	....	....
2000-01	Toronto	NHL	52	6	11	17	30	0	0	1	71	8.5	5	431	44.3	10:02	9	2	1	3	12	1	0	1	11:04
2001-02	Toronto	NHL	11	1	1	2	4	0	0	0	12	8.3	–1	31	38.7	8:57	....	....	....	....	....	....	....	....	....
	St. John's	AHL	34	11	24	35	47	....	....	....	....	....	....	....	....	....	....	....	....	....	....	....	....	....	....
2002-03	Toronto	NHL	72	16	29	45	124	2	1	6	102	15.7	11	621	40.1	15:00	3	0	0	0	0	0	0	0	19:17
2003-04	Toronto	NHL	62	13	18	31	62	1	1	2	89	14.6	7	309	40.8	15:18	13	0	2	2	18	0	0	0	15:56
2004-05	Ak Bars Kazan	Russia	10	2	3	5	6	....	....	....	....	....	....	....	....	....	....	....	....	....	....	....	....	....	....
	Yaroslavl	Russia	26	4	15	19	44	....	....	....	....	....	....	....	....	....	9	3	4	7	18	....	....	....	....
2005-06	Toronto	NHL	57	12	19	31	56	2	1	0	113	10.6	13	172	34.3	15:34	....	....	....	....	....	....	....	....	....
	Kazakhstan	Olympics	5	1	0	1	4	....	....	....	....	....	....	....	....	....	....	....	....	....	....	....	....	....	....
2006-07	Toronto	NHL	54	18	15	33	44	4	0	4	125	14.4	8	34	35.3	16:36	....	....	....	....	....	....	....	....	....
2007-08	Toronto	NHL	72	26	30	56	92	12	0	5	165	15.8	10	271	42.1	20:07	....	....	....	....	....	....	....	....	....
2008-09	Toronto	NHL	63	21	25	46	24	6	0	2	171	12.3	–13	195	41.0	17:13	....	....	....	....	....	....	....	....	....
	NY Rangers	NHL	18	7	6	13	6	2	0	2	53	13.2	–1	4	0.0	17:05	7	2	1	3	6	1	0	0	16:42
2009-10	Atlanta	NHL	76	24	43	67	44	8	0	4	126	19.0	13	1108	43.4	18:14	....	....	....	....	....	....	....	....	....
2010-11	Atlanta	NHL	76	16	25	41	42	5	0	2	105	15.2	–17	534	48.7	15:39	....	....	....	....	....	....	....	....	....
2011-12	Winnipeg	NHL	69	15	20	35	42	4	0	0	95	15.8	0	652	43.4	16:31	....	....	....	....	....	....	....	....	....
2012-13	Barys Astana	KHL	26	3	14	17	39	....	....	....	....	....	....	....	....	....	....	....	....	....	....	....	....	....	....
	Winnipeg	NHL	40	6	12	18	16	2	0	0	56	10.7	6	304	42.1	15:57	....	....	....	....	....	....	....	....	....
	NHL Totals		788	193	272	465	627	48	3	30	1372	14.1		5167	43.1	15:49	35	4	4	8	40	2	0	1	14:38

Signed as a free agent by **Kazan** (Russia), October 27, 2004. Signed as a free agent by **Yaroslavl** (Russia), December 20, 2004. Traded to **NY Rangers** by **Toronto** for NY Ranger's 2nd round choice (Kenny Ryan) in 2009 Entry Draft, March 4, 2009. Signed as a free agent by **Atlanta**, July 2, 2009. • Transferred to **Winnipeg** after **Atlanta** franchise relocated, June 21, 2011. Signed as a free agent by **Astana** (KHL), September 23, 2012. Signed as a free agent by **Astana** (KHL), August 8, 2013.

ARCOBELLO, Mark

(ahr-koh-BEHL-oh, MAHRK) **EDM**

Right wing. Shoots right. 5'10", 185 lbs. Born, Milford, CT, August 12, 1988.

2006-07	Yale	ECAC	29	10	14	24	49	....	....	....	....	....	....	....	....	....	....	....	....	....	....	....	....	....	....
2007-08	Yale	ECAC	34	7	14	21	40	....	....	....	....	....	....	....	....	....	....	....	....	....	....	....	....	....	....
2008-09	Yale	ECAC	34	17	18	35	68	....	....	....	....	....	....	....	....	....	....	....	....	....	....	....	....	....	....
2009-10	Yale	ECAC	34	15	21	36	46	....	....	....	....	....	....	....	....	....	....	....	....	....	....	....	....	....	....
2010-11	Stockton Thunder	ECHL	33	7	13	20	10	....	....	....	....	....	....	....	....	....	....	....	....	....	....	....	....	....	....
	Oklahoma City	AHL	26	11	11	22	4	....	....	....	....	....	....	....	....	....	6	1	1	2	0	....	....	....	....
2011-12	Oklahoma City	AHL	73	17	26	43	28	....	....	....	....	....	....	....	....	....	14	5	8	13	6	....	....	....	....
2012-13	Oklahoma City	AHL	74	22	46	68	48	....	....	....	....	....	....	....	....	....	17	12	8	20	14	....	....	....	....
	Edmonton	NHL	1	0	0	0	0	0	0	0	0	0.0	0	10	30.0	18:15	....	....	....	....	....	....	....	....	....
	NHL Totals		1	0	0	0	0	0	0	0	0	0.0		10	30.0	18:15	....	....	....	....	....	....	....	....	....

ECAC First All-Star Team (2009) • NCAA East Second All-American Team (2009)

Signed as a free agent by **Oklahoma City** (AHL), September 27, 2010. • Assigned to **Stockton** (ECHL) by **Oklahoma City** (AHL), October 13, 2010. Signed as a free agent by **Edmonton**, April 1, 2011.

ARMSTRONG, Colby

(AHRM-strawng, KOHL-bee)

Right wing. Shoots right. 6'2", 195 lbs. Born, Lloydminster, Sask., November 23, 1982. Pittsburgh's 1st choice, 21st overall, in 2001 Entry Draft.

1998-99	Sask. Contacts	SMHL	33	21	19	40	103	....	....	....	....	....	....	....	....	....	....	....	....	....	....	....	....	....	....
	Red Deer Rebels	WHL	1	0	1	1	0	....	....	....	....	....	....	....	....	....	....	....	....	....	....	....	....	....	....
99-2000	Red Deer Rebels	WHL	68	13	25	38	122	....	....	....	....	....	....	....	....	....	2	0	1	1	11	....	....	....	....
2000-01	Red Deer Rebels	WHL	72	36	42	78	156	....	....	....	....	....	....	....	....	....	21	6	6	12	39	....	....	....	....
2001-02	Red Deer Rebels	WHL	64	27	41	68	115	....	....	....	....	....	....	....	....	....	23	6	10	16	32	....	....	....	....
2002-03	Wilkes-Barre	AHL	73	7	11	18	76	....	....	....	....	....	....	....	....	....	3	0	0	0	4	....	....	....	....
2003-04	Wilkes-Barre	AHL	67	10	17	27	71	....	....	....	....	....	....	....	....	....	24	3	1	4	45	....	....	....	....
2004-05	Wilkes-Barre	AHL	80	18	37	55	89	....	....	....	....	....	....	....	....	....	10	4	2	6	14	....	....	....	....
2005-06	Pittsburgh	NHL	47	16	24	40	58	7	2	3	86	18.6	15	44	27.3	19:04	....	....	....	....	....	....	....	....	....
	Wilkes-Barre	AHL	31	11	18	29	44	....	....	....	....	....	....	....	....	....	....	....	....	....	....	....	....	....	....
2006-07	Pittsburgh	NHL	80	12	22	34	67	1	1	3	145	8.3	2	13	15.4	16:50	5	0	1	1	11	0	0	0	15:18
2007-08	Pittsburgh	NHL	54	9	15	24	50	0	0	2	84	10.7	6	12	25.0	15:24	....	....	....	....	....	....	....	....	....
	Atlanta	NHL	18	4	7	11	6	1	0	1	29	13.8	–2	3	0.0	18:02	....	....	....	....	....	....	....	....	....
2008-09	Atlanta	NHL	82	22	18	40	75	3	0	2	141	15.6	5	28	28.6	15:09	....	....	....	....	....	....	....	....	....
2009-10	Atlanta	NHL	79	15	14	29	61	0	1	1	101	14.9	6	20	50.0	14:48	....	....	....	....	....	....	....	....	....

			Regular Season														Playoffs								
Season	Club	League	GP	G	A	Pts	PIM	PP	SH	GW	S	%	+/-	TF	F%	Min	GP	G	A	Pts	PIM	PP	SH	GW	Min
2010-11	**Toronto**	**NHL**	**50**	**8**	**15**	**23**	**38**	**0**	**0**	**0**	**69**	**11.6**	**–1**	**8**	**37.5**	**16:07**	....	....	....	....	....	....	....	....	....
2011-12	**Toronto**	**NHL**	**29**	**1**	**2**	**3**	**9**	**0**	**0**	**0**	**14**	**7.1**	**–8**	**18**	**38.9**	**9:19**	....	....	....	....	....	....	....	....	....
2012-13	**Montreal**	**NHL**	**37**	**2**	**3**	**5**	**12**	**0**	**0**	**0**	**33**	**6.1**	**1**	**21**	**42.9**	**11:12**	**4**	**0**	**0**	**0**	**15**	**0**	**0**	**0**	**11:31**
	NHL Totals		**476**	**89**	**120**	**209**	**376**	**12**	**4**	**12**	**702**	**12.7**		**167**	**32.3**	**15:20**	**9**	**0**	**1**	**1**	**26**	**0**	**0**	**0**	**13:37**

Traded to **Atlanta** by **Pittsburgh** with Erik Christensen, Angelo Esposito and Pittsburgh's 1st round choice (Daultan Leveille) in 2008 Entry Draft for Marian Hossa and Pascal Dupuis, February 26, 2008. Signed as a free agent by **Toronto**, July 1, 2010. Signed as a free agent by **Montreal**, July 1, 2012. • Missed majority of 2011-12 due to ankle (October 17, 2011 vs. Colorado) and foot (December 17, 2011 vs. Vancouver) injuries and as a healthy reserve. Signed as a free agent by **Vaxjo** (Sweden), July 27, 2013.

ARNIEL, Jamie

(ahr-NEEL, JAY-mee)

Center. Shoots right. 5'11", 183 lbs. Born, Kingston, Ont., November 16, 1989. Boston's 4th choice, 97th overall, in 2008 Entry Draft.

2005-06	Guelph Storm	OHL	61	11	8	19	30	....	....	....	....	....	....	....	....	....	15	2	0	2	4	....	....	....	....
2006-07	Guelph Storm	OHL	68	31	31	62	51	....	....	....	....	....	....	....	....	....	4	2	2	4	0	....	....	....	....
2007-08	Guelph Storm	OHL	20	9	4	13	16	....	....	....	....	....	....	....	....	....	....	....	....	....	....	....	....	....	....
	Sarnia Sting	OHL	40	18	16	34	22	....	....	....	....	....	....	....	....	....	9	2	2	4	6	....	....	....	....
2008-09	Sarnia Sting	OHL	63	32	36	68	28	....	....	....	....	....	....	....	....	....	5	1	2	3	4	....	....	....	....
	Providence Bruins	AHL	....	....	....	....	....	....	....	....	....	....	....	....	....	....	8	1	0	1	0	....	....	....	....
2009-10	Providence Bruins	AHL	67	12	16	28	16	....	....	....	....	....	....	....	....	....	....	....	....	....	....	....	....	....	....
2010-11	**Boston**	**NHL**	**1**	**0**	**0**	**0**	**0**	**0**	**0**	**0**	**3**	**0.0**	**–1**	**0**	**0.0**	**12:26**	....	....	....	....	....	....	....	....	....
	Providence Bruins	AHL	78	23	27	50	26	....	....	....	....	....	....	....	....	....	....	....	....	....	....	....	....	....	....
2011-12	Providence Bruins	AHL	74	7	17	24	26	....	....	....	....	....	....	....	....	....	....	....	....	....	....	....	....	....	....
2012-13	Eisbaren Berlin	Germany	50	8	9	17	4	....	....	....	....	....	....	....	....	....	13	0	5	5	16	....	....	....	....
	NHL Totals		**1**	**0**	**0**	**0**	**0**	**0**	**0**	**0**	**3**	**0.0**		**0**	**0.0**	**12:26**	....	....	....	....	....	....	....	....	....

Signed as a free agent by **Berlin** (Germany), August 20, 2012,

ARSENE, Dean

(ahr-SEH-nee, DEEN)

Defense. Shoots left. 6'2", 195 lbs. Born, Abbotsford, B.C., July 20, 1980.

1995-96	Abbotsford	Minor-BC	40	25	35	60	70	....	....	....	....	....	....	....	....	....	....	....	....	....	....	....	....	....	....
1996-97	Regina Pats	WHL	62	0	8	8	53	....	....	....	....	....	....	....	....	....	3	0	0	0	2	....	....	....	....
1997-98	Regina Pats	WHL	31	2	7	9	47	....	....	....	....	....	....	....	....	....	....	....	....	....	....	....	....	....	....
	Edmonton Ice	WHL	43	0	12	12	90	....	....	....	....	....	....	....	....	....	....	....	....	....	....	....	....	....	....
1998-99	Kootenay Ice	WHL	68	1	4	5	111	....	....	....	....	....	....	....	....	....	4	0	0	0	4	....	....	....	....
99-2000	Kootenay Ice	WHL	66	4	7	11	150	....	....	....	....	....	....	....	....	....	21	1	2	3	59	....	....	....	....
2000-01	Kootenay Ice	WHL	68	1	10	11	178	....	....	....	....	....	....	....	....	....	11	0	1	1	34	....	....	....	....
2001-02	Charlotte	ECHL	63	3	10	13	101	....	....	....	....	....	....	....	....	....	5	0	2	2	16	....	....	....	....
2002-03	Hartford	AHL	50	1	3	4	94	....	....	....	....	....	....	....	....	....	....	....	....	....	....	....	....	....	....
2003-04	Hershey Bears	AHL	22	0	2	2	44	....	....	....	....	....	....	....	....	....	....	....	....	....	....	....	....	....	....
	Reading Royals	ECHL	46	0	6	6	118	....	....	....	....	....	....	....	....	....	15	1	5	6	34	....	....	....	....
2004-05	Hershey Bears	AHL	56	1	5	6	140	....	....	....	....	....	....	....	....	....	....	....	....	....	....	....	....	....	....
2005-06	Hershey Bears	AHL	68	2	5	7	181	....	....	....	....	....	....	....	....	....	21	0	1	1	29	....	....	....	....
2006-07	Hershey Bears	AHL	61	3	12	15	187	....	....	....	....	....	....	....	....	....	6	0	2	2	8	....	....	....	....
2007-08	Hershey Bears	AHL	14	0	2	2	23	....	....	....	....	....	....	....	....	....	....	....	....	....	....	....	....	....	....
2008-09	Hershey Bears	AHL	46	1	10	11	99	....	....	....	....	....	....	....	....	....	22	0	2	2	14	....	....	....	....
2009-10	**Edmonton**	**NHL**	**13**	**0**	**0**	**0**	**41**	**0**	**0**	**0**	**4**	**0.0**	**–3**	**0**	**0.0**	**12:57**	....	....	....	....	....	....	....	....	....
	Springfield	AHL	56	2	9	11	100	....	....	....	....	....	....	....	....	....	....	....	....	....	....	....	....	....	....
2010-11	Peoria Rivermen	AHL	77	1	10	11	137	....	....	....	....	....	....	....	....	....	4	0	0	0	6	....	....	....	....
2011-12	Portland Pirates	AHL	63	2	8	10	110	....	....	....	....	....	....	....	....	....	....	....	....	....	....	....	....	....	....
2012-13	St. John's IceCaps	AHL	69	1	10	11	98	....	....	....	....	....	....	....	....	....	....	....	....	....	....	....	....	....	....
	NHL Totals		**13**	**0**	**0**	**0**	**41**	**0**	**0**	**0**	**4**	**0.0**		**0**	**0.0**	**12:57**	....	....	....	....	....	....	....	....	....

Signed as a free agent by **Washington**, July 26, 2006. Signed as a free agent by **Edmonton**, July 16, 2009. Signed as a free agent by **St. Louis**, August 11, 2010. Signed as a free agent by **Phoenix**, July 6, 2011. Signed as a free agent by **St. John's** (AHL), August 9, 2012.

ASHAM, Arron

(ASH-uhm, AIR-ruhn) **NYR**

Right wing. Shoots right. 5'11", 205 lbs. Born, Portage La Prairie, Man., April 13, 1978. Montreal's 3rd choice, 71st overall, in 1996 Entry Draft.

1993-94	Portage	MAHA	21	18	19	37	82	....	....	....	....	....	....	....	....	....	....	....	....	....	....	....	....	....	....
1994-95	Red Deer Rebels	WHL	62	11	16	27	126	....	....	....	....	....	....	....	....	....	....	....	....	....	....	....	....	....	....
1995-96	Red Deer Rebels	WHL	70	32	45	77	174	....	....	....	....	....	....	....	....	....	10	6	3	9	20	....	....	....	....
1996-97	Red Deer Rebels	WHL	67	45	51	96	149	....	....	....	....	....	....	....	....	....	16	12	14	26	36	....	....	....	....
1997-98	Red Deer Rebels	WHL	67	43	49	92	153	....	....	....	....	....	....	....	....	....	5	0	2	2	8	....	....	....	....
	Fredericton	AHL	2	1	1	2	0	....	....	....	....	....	....	....	....	....	2	0	1	1	0	....	....	....	....
1998-99	**Montreal**	**NHL**	**7**	**0**	**0**	**0**	**0**	**0**	**0**	**0**	**5**	**0.0**	**–4**	**0**	**0.0**	**7:27**	....	....	....	....	....	....	....	....	....
	Fredericton	AHL	60	16	18	34	118	....	....	....	....	....	....	....	....	....	13	8	6	14	11	....	....	....	....
99-2000	**Montreal**	**NHL**	**33**	**4**	**2**	**6**	**24**	**0**	**1**	**1**	**29**	**13.8**	**–7**	**1**	**0.0**	**10:14**	....	....	....	....	....	....	....	....	....
	Quebec Citadelles	AHL	13	4	5	9	32	....	....	....	....	....	....	....	....	....	2	0	0	0	2	....	....	....	....
2000-01	**Montreal**	**NHL**	**46**	**2**	**3**	**5**	**59**	**0**	**0**	**0**	**32**	**6.3**	**–9**	**3**	**100.0**	**8:28**	....	....	....	....	....	....	....	....	....
	Quebec Citadelles	AHL	15	7	9	16	51	....	....	....	....	....	....	....	....	....	7	1	2	3	2	....	....	....	....
2001-02	**Montreal**	**NHL**	**35**	**5**	**4**	**9**	**55**	**0**	**0**	**0**	**30**	**16.7**	**7**	**4**	**25.0**	**8:13**	**3**	**0**	**1**	**1**	**0**	**0**	**0**	**0**	**5:39**
	Quebec Citadelles	AHL	24	9	14	23	35	....	....	....	....	....	....	....	....	....	....	....	....	....	....	....	....	....	....
2002-03	**NY Islanders**	**NHL**	**78**	**15**	**19**	**34**	**57**	**4**	**0**	**1**	**114**	**13.2**	**1**	**17**	**41.2**	**12:13**	**5**	**0**	**0**	**0**	**16**	**0**	**0**	**0**	**15:09**
2003-04	**NY Islanders**	**NHL**	**79**	**12**	**12**	**24**	**92**	**1**	**0**	**0**	**108**	**11.1**	**–12**	**23**	**34.8**	**13:13**	**5**	**0**	**1**	**1**	**4**	**0**	**0**	**0**	**8:44**
2004-05	EHC Visp	Swiss-2	5	2	4	6	6	....	....	....	....	....	....	....	....	....	4	1	1	2	8	....	....	....	....
2005-06	**NY Islanders**	**NHL**	**63**	**9**	**15**	**24**	**103**	**2**	**1**	**0**	**99**	**9.1**	**–5**	**63**	**41.3**	**13:33**	....	....	....	....	....	....	....	....	....
2006-07	**NY Islanders**	**NHL**	**80**	**11**	**12**	**23**	**63**	**0**	**0**	**2**	**85**	**12.9**	**3**	**10**	**60.0**	**9:20**	**5**	**1**	**0**	**1**	**0**	**0**	**0**	**0**	**10:08**
2007-08	**New Jersey**	**NHL**	**77**	**6**	**4**	**10**	**84**	**0**	**0**	**2**	**68**	**8.8**	**–6**	**3**	**0.0**	**8:33**	**5**	**0**	**1**	**1**	**2**	**0**	**0**	**0**	**5:04**
2008-09	**Philadelphia**	**NHL**	**78**	**8**	**12**	**20**	**155**	**0**	**0**	**1**	**74**	**10.8**	**0**	**15**	**46.7**	**8:45**	**6**	**1**	**1**	**2**	**6**	**0**	**0**	**1**	**7:55**
2009-10	**Philadelphia**	**NHL**	**72**	**10**	**14**	**24**	**126**	**0**	**0**	**2**	**91**	**11.0**	**–2**	**13**	**15.4**	**10:04**	**23**	**4**	**3**	**7**	**10**	**0**	**0**	**0**	**11:14**
2010-11	**Pittsburgh**	**NHL**	**44**	**5**	**6**	**11**	**46**	**0**	**0**	**0**	**60**	**8.3**	**0**	**9**	**33.3**	**9:33**	**7**	**3**	**1**	**4**	**2**	**0**	**0**	**0**	**10:00**
2011-12	**Pittsburgh**	**NHL**	**64**	**5**	**11**	**16**	**76**	**0**	**0**	**0**	**49**	**10.2**	**–5**	**11**	**54.6**	**9:14**	**3**	**0**	**0**	**0**	**10**	**0**	**0**	**0**	**3:59**
2012-13	**NY Rangers**	**NHL**	**27**	**2**	**0**	**2**	**50**	**0**	**0**	**0**	**14**	**14.3**	**2**	**10**	**50.0**	**6:38**	**10**	**2**	**0**	**2**	**6**	**0**	**0**	**1**	**6:40**
	NHL Totals		**783**	**94**	**114**	**208**	**990**	**7**	**2**	**9**	**858**	**11.0**		**182**	**40.7**	**10:07**	**72**	**11**	**8**	**19**	**56**	**0**	**0**	**2**	**9:16**

Traded to **NY Islanders** by **Montreal** with Montreal's 5th round choice (Marcus Paulsson) in 2002 Entry Draft for Mariusz Czerkawski, June 22, 2002. Signed as a free agent by **Visp** (Swiss-2), January 19, 2005. Signed as a free agent by **New Jersey**, August 7, 2007. Signed as a free agent by **Philadelphia**, July 7, 2008. Signed as a free agent by **Pittsburgh**, August 20, 2010. Signed as a free agent by **NY Rangers**, July 1. 2012.

ASHTON, Carter

(ASH-tuhn, KAHR-tuhr) **TOR**

Right wing. Shoots left. 6'3", 215 lbs. Born, Winnipeg, Man., April 1, 1991. Tampa Bay's 2nd choice, 29th overall, in 2009 Entry Draft.

2006-07	Sask. Contacts	SMHL	41	28	38	66	99	....	....	....	....	....	....	....	....	....	....	....	....	....	....	....	....	....	....
	Lethbridge	WHL	2	0	0	0	0	....	....	....	....	....	....	....	....	....	....	....	....	....	....	....	....	....	....
2007-08	Lethbridge	WHL	40	5	4	9	21	....	....	....	....	....	....	....	....	....	19	0	1	1	12	....	....	....	....
2008-09	Lethbridge	WHL	70	30	20	50	93	....	....	....	....	....	....	....	....	....	11	1	2	3	15	....	....	....	....
2009-10	Lethbridge	WHL	28	13	13	26	52	....	....	....	....	....	....	....	....	....	....	....	....	....	....	....	....	....	....
	Regina Pats	WHL	37	11	14	25	57	....	....	....	....	....	....	....	....	....	....	....	....	....	....	....	....	....	....
	Norfolk Admirals	AHL	11	1	0	1	6	....	....	....	....	....	....	....	....	....	....	....	....	....	....	....	....	....	....
2010-11	Regina Pats	WHL	29	16	11	27	44	....	....	....	....	....	....	....	....	....	....	....	....	....	....	....	....	....	....
	Tri-City	WHL	33	17	27	44	62	....	....	....	....	....	....	....	....	....	10	3	5	8	4	....	....	....	....
	Norfolk Admirals	AHL	....	....	....	....	....	....	....	....	....	....	....	....	....	....	2	0	0	0	0	....	....	....	....
2011-12	Norfolk Admirals	AHL	56	19	16	35	58	....	....	....	....	....	....	....	....	....	....	....	....	....	....	....	....	....	....
	Toronto	**NHL**	**15**	**0**	**0**	**0**	**13**	**0**	**0**	**0**	**22**	**0.0**	**–10**	**2**	**50.0**	**10:25**	....	....	....	....	....	....	....	....	....
	Toronto Marlies	AHL	7	2	1	3	8	....	....	....	....	....	....	....	....	....	6	1	2	3	8	....	....	....	....
2012-13	Toronto Marlies	AHL	53	11	8	19	67	....	....	....	....	....	....	....	....	....	9	3	2	5	4	....	....	....	....
	NHL Totals		**15**	**0**	**0**	**0**	**13**	**0**	**0**	**0**	**22**	**0.0**		**2**	**50.0**	**10:25**	....	....	....	....	....	....	....	....	....

Traded to **Toronto** by **Tampa Bay** for Keith Aulie, February 27, 2012.

ATKINSON, Cam

(AT-kihn-suhn, KAM) **CBJ**

Right wing. Shoots right. 5'7", 173 lbs. Born, Riverside, CT, June 5, 1989. Columbus' 8th choice, 157th overall, in 2008 Entry Draft.

			Regular Season														Playoffs								
Season	Club	League	GP	G	A	Pts	PIM	PP	SH	GW	S	%	+/-	TF	F%	Min	GP	G	A	Pts	PIM	PP	SH	GW	Min
2005-06	Avon Old Farms	High-CT	25	15	20	35	16	....	....	....	....	....	....	....	....	....	....	....	....	....	....	....	....	....	....
2006-07	Avon Old Farms	High-CT	27	28	24	52	12	....	....	....	....	....	....	....	....	....	....	....	....	....	....	....	....	....	....
2007-08	Avon Old Farms	High-CT	28	26	37	63	10	....	....	....	....	....	....	....	....	....	....	....	....	....	....	....	....	....	....
2008-09	Boston College	H-East	36	7	12	19	28	....	....	....	....	....	....	....	....	....	....	....	....	....	....	....	....	....	....
2009-10	Boston College	H-East	42	*30	23	53	30	....	....	....	....	....	....	....	....	....	....	....	....	....	....	....	....	....	....
2010-11	Boston College	H-East	39	*31	21	*52	28	....	....	....	....	....	....	....	....	....	....	....	....	....	....	....	....	....	....
	Springfield	AHL	5	3	2	5	0	....	....	....	....	....	....	....	....	....	....	....	....	....	....	....	....	....	....
2011-12	**Columbus**	**NHL**	**27**	**7**	**7**	**14**	**14**	**1**	**0**	**0**	**66**	**10.6**	**1**	**1**	**0.0**	**15:23**	....	....	....	....	....	....	....	....	....
	Springfield	AHL	51	29	15	44	31	....	....	....	....	....	....	....	....	....	....	....	....	....	....	....	....	....	....
2012-13	Springfield	AHL	33	17	21	38	14	....	....	....	....	....	....	....	....	....	....	....	....	....	....	....	....	....	....
	Columbus	**NHL**	**35**	**9**	**9**	**18**	**4**	**1**	**0**	**1**	**91**	**9.9**	**9**	**0**	**0.0**	**15:35**	....	....	....	....	....	....	....	....	....
	NHL Totals		**62**	**16**	**16**	**32**	**18**	**2**	**0**	**1**	**157**	**10.2**		**1**	**0.0**	**15:30**	....	....	....	....	....	....	....	....	....

Hockey East Second All-Star Team (2010) • NCAA Championship All-Tournament Team (2010) • Hockey East First All-Star Team (2011) • NCAA East First All-American Team (2011)

AUCOIN, Adrian

(oh-KOIN, AY-dree-uhn)

Defense. Shoots right. 6'2", 215 lbs. Born, Ottawa, Ont., July 3, 1973. Vancouver's 7th choice, 117th overall, in 1992 Entry Draft.

			Regular Season														Playoffs								
Season	Club	League	GP	G	A	Pts	PIM	PP	SH	GW	S	%	+/-	TF	F%	Min	GP	G	A	Pts	PIM	PP	SH	GW	Min
1989-90	Nepean Raiders	ON-Jr.A	54	2	14	16	95	....	....	....	....	....	....	....	....	....	4	0	1	1	....	....	....	....	....
1990-91	Nepean Raiders	ON-Jr.A	56	17	33	50	125	....	....	....	....	....	....	....	....	....	....	....	....	....	....	....	....	....	....
1991-92	Boston University	H-East	32	2	10	12	60	....	....	....	....	....	....	....	....	....	....	....	....	....	....	....	....	....	....
1992-93	Canada	Nat-Tm	42	8	10	18	71	....	....	....	....	....	....	....	....	....	....	....	....	....	....	....	....	....	....
1993-94	Canada	Nat-Tm	59	5	12	17	80	....	....	....	....	....	....	....	....	....	....	....	....	....	....	....	....	....	....
	Canada	Olympics	4	0	0	0	2	....	....	....	....	....	....	....	....	....	....	....	....	....	....	....	....	....	....
	Hamilton	AHL	13	1	2	3	19	....	....	....	....	....	....	....	....	....	4	0	2	2	6	....	....	....	....
1994-95	Syracuse Crunch	AHL	71	13	18	31	52	....	....	....	....	....	....	....	....	....	....	....	....	....	....	....	....	....	....
	Vancouver	**NHL**	**1**	**1**	**0**	**1**	**0**	**0**	**0**	**0**	**2**	**50.0**	**1**	....	....	....	**4**	**1**	**0**	**1**	**0**	**1**	**0**	**0**	....
1995-96	**Vancouver**	**NHL**	**49**	**4**	**14**	**18**	**34**	**2**	**0**	**0**	**85**	**4.7**	**8**	....	....	....	**6**	**0**	**0**	**0**	**2**	**0**	**0**	**0**	....
	Syracuse Crunch	AHL	29	5	13	18	47	....	....	....	....	....	....	....	....	....	....	....	....	....	....	....	....	....	....
1996-97	**Vancouver**	**NHL**	**70**	**5**	**16**	**21**	**63**	**1**	**0**	**0**	**116**	**4.3**	**0**	....	....	....	....	....	....	....	....	....	....	....	....
1997-98	**Vancouver**	**NHL**	**35**	**3**	**3**	**6**	**21**	**1**	**0**	**1**	**44**	**6.8**	**–4**	....	....	....	....	....	....	....	....	....	....	....	....
1998-99	**Vancouver**	**NHL**	**82**	**23**	**11**	**34**	**77**	**18**	**2**	**3**	**174**	**13.2**	**–14**	**1**	**100.0**	**23:52**	....	....	....	....	....	....	....	....	....
99-2000	**Vancouver**	**NHL**	**57**	**10**	**14**	**24**	**30**	**4**	**0**	**1**	**126**	**7.9**	**7**	**0**	**0.0**	**23:06**	....	....	....	....	....	....	....	....	....
2000-01	**Vancouver**	**NHL**	**47**	**3**	**13**	**16**	**20**	**1**	**0**	**0**	**99**	**3.0**	**13**	**0**	**0.0**	**18:21**	....	....	....	....	....	....	....	....	....
	Tampa Bay	**NHL**	**26**	**1**	**11**	**12**	**25**	**1**	**0**	**0**	**60**	**1.7**	**–8**	**0**	**0.0**	**23:34**	....	....	....	....	....	....	....	....	....
2001-02	**NY Islanders**	**NHL**	**81**	**12**	**22**	**34**	**62**	**7**	**0**	**1**	**232**	**5.2**	**23**	**0**	**0.0**	**28:54**	**7**	**2**	**5**	**7**	**4**	**2**	**0**	**0**	**32:19**
2002-03	**NY Islanders**	**NHL**	**73**	**8**	**27**	**35**	**70**	**5**	**0**	**1**	**175**	**4.6**	**–5**	**0**	**0.0**	**29:01**	**5**	**1**	**2**	**3**	**4**	**0**	**0**	**0**	**31:43**
2003-04	**NY Islanders**	**NHL**	**81**	**13**	**31**	**44**	**54**	**4**	**0**	**2**	**213**	**6.1**	**29**	**0**	**0.0**	**26:38**	**5**	**0**	**0**	**0**	**6**	**0**	**0**	**0**	**28:21**
2004-05	MODO	Sweden	14	2	4	6	32	....	....	....	....	....	....	....	....	....	6	1	0	1	16	....	....	....	....
2005-06	**Chicago**	**NHL**	**33**	**1**	**5**	**6**	**38**	**1**	**0**	**0**	**59**	**1.7**	**–13**	**0**	**0.0**	**22:58**	....	....	....	....	....	....	....	....	....
2006-07	**Chicago**	**NHL**	**59**	**4**	**12**	**16**	**50**	**2**	**0**	**3**	**96**	**4.2**	**–22**	**0**	**0.0**	**20:50**	....	....	....	....	....	....	....	....	....
2007-08	**Calgary**	**NHL**	**76**	**10**	**25**	**35**	**37**	**5**	**0**	**1**	**121**	**8.3**	**13**	**0**	**0.0**	**20:58**	**7**	**0**	**3**	**3**	**4**	**0**	**0**	**0**	**18:13**
2008-09	**Calgary**	**NHL**	**81**	**10**	**24**	**34**	**46**	**3**	**0**	**3**	**126**	**7.9**	**–8**	**0**	**0.0**	**22:18**	**6**	**2**	**1**	**3**	**2**	**0**	**0**	**0**	**21:10**
2009-10	**Phoenix**	**NHL**	**82**	**8**	**20**	**28**	**56**	**1**	**0**	**2**	**144**	**5.6**	**2**	**1**	**100.0**	**22:33**	**7**	**0**	**2**	**2**	**10**	**0**	**0**	**0**	**21:16**
2010-11	**Phoenix**	**NHL**	**75**	**3**	**19**	**22**	**52**	**0**	**0**	**0**	**99**	**3.0**	**18**	**1**	**100.0**	**21:40**	**4**	**0**	**0**	**0**	**2**	**0**	**0**	**0**	**19:17**
2011-12	**Phoenix**	**NHL**	**64**	**2**	**7**	**9**	**42**	**1**	**0**	**0**	**92**	**2.2**	**14**	**0**	**0.0**	**20:15**	**11**	**0**	**2**	**2**	**10**	**0**	**0**	**0**	**18:03**
2012-13	**Columbus**	**NHL**	**36**	**0**	**4**	**4**	**16**	**0**	**0**	**0**	**26**	**0.0**	**–8**	**0**	**0.0**	**16:20**	....	....	....	....	....	....	....	....	....
	NHL Totals		**1108**	**121**	**278**	**399**	**793**	**57**	**2**	**18**	**2089**	**5.8**		**3**	**100.0**	**23:12**	**62**	**6**	**15**	**21**	**44**	**3**	**0**	**0**	**23:11**

Played in NHL All-Star Game (2004)

• Missed majority of 1997-98 due to ankle (October 4, 1997 vs. Anaheim) and groin (November 1, 1997 vs. Pittsburgh) injuries. Traded to **Tampa Bay** by **Vancouver** with Vancouver's 2nd round choice (Alexander Polushin) in 2001 Entry Draft for Dan Cloutier, February 7, 2001. Traded to **NY Islanders** by **Tampa Bay** with Alexander Kharitonov for Mathieu Biron and NY Islanders' 2nd round choice (later traded to Washington, later traded to Vancouver – Vancouver selected Denis Grot) in 2002 Entry Draft, June 22, 2001. Signed as a free agent by **MODO** (Sweden), December 21, 2004. Signed as a free agent by **Chicago**, August 2, 2005. Traded to **Calgary** by **Chicago** with Chicago's 7th round choice (C.J. Severyn) in 2007 Entry Draft for Andrei Zyuzin and Steve Marr, June 22, 2007. Signed as a free agent by **Phoenix**, July 2, 2009. Signed as a free agent by **Columbus**, July 1, 2012.

AUCOIN, Keith

(oh-KOIN, KEETH) **ST.L.**

Center. Shoots right. 5'8", 171 lbs. Born, Waltham, MA, November 6, 1978.

			Regular Season														Playoffs								
Season	Club	League	GP	G	A	Pts	PIM	PP	SH	GW	S	%	+/-	TF	F%	Min	GP	G	A	Pts	PIM	PP	SH	GW	Min
1997-98	Norwich U.	ECAC-3	26	19	14	33	....	....	....	....	....	....	....	....	....	....	....	....	....	....	....	....	....	....	....
1998-99	Norwich U.	ECAC-3	31	33	39	72	....	....	....	....	....	....	....	....	....	....	....	....	....	....	....	....	....	....	....
99-2000	Norwich U.	ECAC-3	31	36	41	77	14	....	....	....	....	....	....	....	....	....	....	....	....	....	....	....	....	....	....
2000-01	Norwich U.	ECAC-3	28	26	30	56	26	....	....	....	....	....	....	....	....	....	....	....	....	....	....	....	....	....	....
2001-02	Lowell	AHL	30	6	10	16	8	....	....	....	....	....	....	....	....	....	....	....	....	....	....	....	....	....	....
	Florida Everblades	ECHL	1	0	2	2	0	....	....	....	....	....	....	....	....	....	....	....	....	....	....	....	....	....	....
	BC Icemen	UHL	44	23	35	58	42	....	....	....	....	....	....	....	....	....	10	3	5	8	4	....	....	....	....
2002-03	Providence Bruins	AHL	78	25	49	74	71	....	....	....	....	....	....	....	....	....	4	0	1	1	6	....	....	....	....
2003-04	Cincinnati	AHL	80	18	30	48	64	....	....	....	....	....	....	....	....	....	9	0	3	3	4	....	....	....	....
2004-05	Memphis	CHL	5	4	5	9	10	....	....	....	....	....	....	....	....	....	....	....	....	....	....	....	....	....	....
	Providence Bruins	AHL	72	21	45	66	49	....	....	....	....	....	....	....	....	....	17	4	*14	18	18	....	....	....	....
2005-06	**Carolina**	**NHL**	**7**	**0**	**1**	**1**	**4**	**0**	**0**	**0**	**3**	**0.0**	**–4**	**4**	**100.0**	**5:19**	....	....	....	....	....	....	....	....	....
	Lowell	AHL	72	29	56	85	68	....	....	....	....	....	....	....	....	....	....	....	....	....	....	....	....	....	....
2006-07	**Carolina**	**NHL**	**8**	**0**	**1**	**1**	**0**	**0**	**0**	**0**	**6**	**0.0**	**1**	**29**	**65.5**	**6:17**	....	....	....	....	....	....	....	....	....
	Albany River Rats	AHL	65	27	72	99	108	....	....	....	....	....	....	....	....	....	5	1	3	4	7	....	....	....	....
2007-08	**Carolina**	**NHL**	**38**	**5**	**8**	**13**	**10**	**0**	**0**	**0**	**65**	**7.7**	**3**	**327**	**37.9**	**13:28**	....	....	....	....	....	....	....	....	....
	Albany River Rats	AHL	38	8	37	45	38	....	....	....	....	....	....	....	....	....	....	....	....	....	....	....	....	....	....
2008-09	**Washington**	**NHL**	**12**	**2**	**4**	**6**	**4**	**1**	**0**	**0**	**15**	**13.3**	**5**	**83**	**39.8**	**10:19**	....	....	....	....	....	....	....	....	....
	Hershey Bears	AHL	70	25	*71	96	73	....	....	....	....	....	....	....	....	....	21	5	*18	23	16	....	....	....	....
2009-10	**Washington**	**NHL**	**9**	**1**	**4**	**5**	**0**	**0**	**0**	**0**	**4**	**25.0**	**–2**	**56**	**55.4**	**8:48**	....	....	....	....	....	....	....	....	....
	Hershey Bears	AHL	72	35	*71	*106	49	....	....	....	....	....	....	....	....	....	21	2	*23	25	2	....	....	....	....
2010-11	**Washington**	**NHL**	**1**	**0**	**0**	**0**	**0**	**0**	**0**	**0**	**0**	**0.0**	**0**	**3**	**33.3**	**11:47**	....	....	....	....	....	....	....	....	....
	Hershey Bears	AHL	53	18	54	72	49	....	....	....	....	....	....	....	....	....	6	2	6	8	2	....	....	....	....
2011-12	**Washington**	**NHL**	**27**	**3**	**8**	**11**	**0**	**0**	**0**	**1**	**21**	**14.3**	**4**	**121**	**47.1**	**11:04**	**14**	**0**	**2**	**2**	**2**	**0**	**0**	**0**	**10:21**
	Hershey Bears	AHL	43	11	59	70	34	....	....	....	....	....	....	....	....	....	....	....	....	....	....	....	....	....	....
2012-13	Toronto Marlies	AHL	34	10	27	37	40	....	....	....	....	....	....	....	....	....	....	....	....	....	....	....	....	....	....
	NY Islanders	**NHL**	**41**	**6**	**6**	**12**	**4**	**1**	**0**	**1**	**50**	**12.0**	**–1**	**344**	**48.6**	**12:30**	**6**	**0**	**3**	**3**	**10**	**0**	**0**	**0**	**12:19**
	NHL Totals		**143**	**17**	**32**	**49**	**22**	**2**	**0**	**2**	**164**	**10.4**		**967**	**45.1**	**11:22**	**20**	**0**	**5**	**5**	**12**	**0**	**0**	**0**	**10:56**

ECAC-3 First All-Star Team (2000, 2001) • ECAC-3 Player of the Year (2000, 2001) • AHL Second All-Star Team (2006, 2007, 2011) • AHL First All-Star Team (2009, 2010, 2012) • John B. Sollenberger Trophy (AHL – Leading Scorer) (2010) • Les Cunningham Award (AHL – MVP) (2010)

Signed as a free agent by **Lowell** (AHL), June 19, 2001. Signed as a free agent by **Providence** (AHL), August 2, 2002. Signed as a free agent by **Anaheim**, August 29, 2003. Signed to a PTO (professional tryout) contract by **Providence** (AHL), November 4, 2004, Signed as a free agent by **Providence** (AHL), December 9, 2004. Signed as a free agent by **Carolina**, August 4, 2005. Signed as a free agent by **Washington**, July 3, 2008. Signed as a free agent by **Toronto**, July 24, 2012. Claimed on waivers by **NY Islanders** from **Toronto**, January 17, 2013. Signed as a free agent by **St. Louis**, July 5, 2013.

AUDY-MARCHESSAULT, Jon

(OH-dee-mahr-SHUH-sohn, JAWN) **CBJ**

Center. Shoots right. 5'9", 175 lbs. Born, Cap-Rouge, Que., December 27, 1990.

			Regular Season														Playoffs								
Season	Club	League	GP	G	A	Pts	PIM	PP	SH	GW	S	%	+/-	TF	F%	Min	GP	G	A	Pts	PIM	PP	SH	GW	Min
2007-08	Quebec Remparts	QMJHL	56	10	10	20	18	....	....	....	....	....	....	....	....	....	11	1	0	1	6	....	....	....	....
2008-09	Quebec Remparts	QMJHL	62	18	35	53	75	....	....	....	....	....	....	....	....	....	14	2	4	6	10	....	....	....	....
2009-10	Quebec Remparts	QMJHL	68	30	41	71	54	....	....	....	....	....	....	....	....	....	9	3	11	14	14	....	....	....	....
2010-11	Quebec Remparts	QMJHL	68	40	55	95	41	....	....	....	....	....	....	....	....	....	18	11	22	33	12	....	....	....	....
2011-12	Connecticut	AHL	76	24	40	64	50	....	....	....	....	....	....	....	....	....	9	4	0	4	26	....	....	....	....
2012-13	Springfield	AHL	74	21	46	67	65	....	....	....	....	....	....	....	....	....	8	0	3	3	8	....	....	....	....
	Columbus	**NHL**	**2**	**0**	**0**	**0**	**0**	**0**	**0**	**0**	**0**	**0.0**	**–1**	**0**	**0.0**	**10:57**	....	....	....	....	....	....	....	....	....
	NHL Totals		**2**	**0**	**0**	**0**	**0**	**0**	**0**	**0**	**0**	**0.0**		**0**	**0.0**	**10:57**	....	....	....	....	....	....	....	....	....

QMJHL First All-Star Team (2011) • AHL First All-Star Team (2013)

Signed as a free agent by **Columbus**, July 1, 2012.

			Regular Season														Playoffs								
Season	Club	League	GP	G	A	Pts	PIM	PP	SH	GW	S	%	+/-	TF	F%	Min	GP	G	A	Pts	PIM	PP	SH	GW	Min

AULIE, Keith

(AW-lee, KEETH) **T.B.**

Defense. Shoots left. 6'6", 228 lbs. Born, Rouleau, Sask., June 11, 1989. Calgary's 3rd choice, 116th overall, in 2007 Entry Draft.

Season	Club	League	GP	G	A	Pts	PIM	PP	SH	GW	S	%	+/-	TF	F%	Min	GP	G	A	Pts	PIM	PP	SH	GW	Min
2004-05	Notre Dame	SMHL	38	2	7	9	53	....	....	....	....	....	....	....	....	....	....	....	....	....	....	....	....	....	....
2005-06	Brandon	WHL	38	0	2	2	32	....	....	....	....	....	....	....	....	....	4	0	0	0	4	....	....	....	....
2006-07	Brandon	WHL	66	1	8	9	82	....	....	....	....	....	....	....	....	....	11	0	2	2	14	....	....	....	....
2007-08	Brandon	WHL	72	5	12	17	81	....	....	....	....	....	....	....	....	....	6	0	3	3	11	....	....	....	....
2008-09	Brandon	WHL	58	6	27	33	83	....	....	....	....	....	....	....	....	....	12	2	7	9	12	....	....	....	....
2009-10	Abbotsford Heat	AHL	43	2	4	6	32	....	....	....	....	....	....	....	....	....	....	....	....	....	....	....	....	....	....
	Toronto Marlies	AHL	5	0	0	0	6	....	....	....	....	....	....	....	....	....	....	....	....	....	....	....	....	....	....
2010-11	**Toronto**	**NHL**	**40**	**2**	**0**	**2**	**32**	**0**	**0**	**0**	**32**	**6.3**	**–1**	**0**	**0.0**	**19:08**	....	....	....	....	....	....	....	....	....
	Toronto Marlies	AHL	36	3	6	9	61	....	....	....	....	....	....	....	....	....	....	....	....	....	....	....	....	....	....
2011-12	**Toronto**	**NHL**	**17**	**0**	**2**	**2**	**16**	**0**	**0**	**0**	**14**	**0.0**	**–2**	**0**	**0.0**	**16:07**	....	....	....	....	....	....	....	....	....
	Toronto Marlies	AHL	23	0	1	1	30	....	....	....	....	....	....	....	....	....	....	....	....	....	....	....	....	....	....
	Tampa Bay	**NHL**	**19**	**0**	**1**	**1**	**13**	**0**	**0**	**0**	**4**	**0.0**	**–5**	**0**	**0.0**	**11:02**	....	....	....	....	....	....	....	....	....
	Norfolk Admirals	AHL	3	0	2	2	0	....	....	....	....	....	....	....	....	....	18	1	5	6	10	....	....	....	....
2012-13	Syracuse Crunch	AHL	20	3	3	6	34	....	....	....	....	....	....	....	....	....	....	....	....	....	....	....	....	....	....
	Tampa Bay	**NHL**	**45**	**2**	**5**	**7**	**60**	**0**	**0**	**0**	**37**	**5.4**	**1**	**0**	**0.0**	**12:49**	....	....	....	....	....	....	....	....	....
	NHL Totals		**121**	**4**	**8**	**12**	**121**	**0**	**0**	**0**	**87**	**4.6**		**0**	**0.0**	**15:05**	....	....	....	....	....	....	....	....	....

WHL East First All-Star Team (2009)

Traded to **Toronto** by **Calgary** with Dion Phaneuf and Fredrik Sjostrom for Matt Stajan, Niklas Hagman, Jamal Mayers and Ian White, January 31, 2010. Traded to **Tampa Bay** by **Toronto** for Carter Ashton, February 27, 2012.

BABCHUK, Anton

(bab-CHUHK, AN-tawn)

Defense. Shoots right. 6'5", 200 lbs. Born, Kiev, USSR, May 6, 1984. Chicago's 1st choice, 21st overall, in 2002 Entry Draft.

Season	Club	League	GP	G	A	Pts	PIM	PP	SH	GW	S	%	+/-	TF	F%	Min	GP	G	A	Pts	PIM	PP	SH	GW	Min
99-2000	Elektrostal 2	Russia-3	6	0	0	0	8	....	....	....	....	....	....	....	....	....	....	....	....	....	....	....	....	....	....
	Elektrostal 2	Russia-3	18	0	1	1	18	....	....	....	....	....	....	....	....	....	....	....	....	....	....	....	....	....	....
2000-01	Elektrostal	Russia-2	7	0	0	0	12	....	....	....	....	....	....	....	....	....	....	....	....	....	....	....	....	....	....
	Russia 17	Nat-Tm	15	1	3	4	12	....	....	....	....	....	....	....	....	....	....	....	....	....	....	....	....	....	....
2001-02	Elektrostal	Russia-2	40	7	8	15	90	....	....	....	....	....	....	....	....	....	....	....	....	....	....	....	....	....	....
	Elektrostal 2	Russia-3	3	0	0	0	8	....	....	....	....	....	....	....	....	....	....	....	....	....	....	....	....	....	....
2002-03	Ak Bars Kazan	Russia	10	0	0	0	4	....	....	....	....	....	....	....	....	....	....	....	....	....	....	....	....	....	....
	St. Petersburg	Russia	20	3	0	3	10	....	....	....	....	....	....	....	....	....	....	....	....	....	....	....	....	....	....
	Spartak St. Pet.	Russia-2	1	1	0	1	0	....	....	....	....	....	....	....	....	....	....	....	....	....	....	....	....	....	....
2003-04	**Chicago**	**NHL**	**5**	**0**	**2**	**2**	**2**	**0**	**0**	**0**	**11**	**0.0**	**–1**	**0**	**0.0**	**12:43**	....	....	....	....	....	....	....	....	....
	Norfolk Admirals	AHL	73	8	14	22	89	....	....	....	....	....	....	....	....	....	8	0	2	2	6	....	....	....	....
2004-05	Norfolk Admirals	AHL	66	8	16	24	88	....	....	....	....	....	....	....	....	....	2	0	0	0	2	....	....	....	....
2005-06	**Chicago**	**NHL**	**17**	**2**	**3**	**5**	**16**	**1**	**0**	**0**	**24**	**8.3**	**–5**	**0**	**0.0**	**16:38**	....	....	....	....	....	....	....	....	....
	Norfolk Admirals	AHL	24	5	7	12	22	....	....	....	....	....	....	....	....	....	....	....	....	....	....	....	....	....	....
	♦ **Carolina**	**NHL**	**22**	**3**	**2**	**5**	**6**	**2**	**0**	**0**	**32**	**9.4**	**–2**	**0**	**0.0**	**13:22**	....	....	....	....	....	....	....	....	....
	Lowell	AHL	5	1	3	4	0	....	....	....	....	....	....	....	....	....	....	....	....	....	....	....	....	....	....
2006-07	**Carolina**	**NHL**	**52**	**2**	**12**	**14**	**30**	**0**	**0**	**2**	**63**	**3.2**	**–6**	**0**	**0.0**	**17:26**	....	....	....	....	....	....	....	....	....
	Albany River Rats	AHL	9	1	6	7	2	....	....	....	....	....	....	....	....	....	....	....	....	....	....	....	....	....	....
2007-08	Avangard Omsk	Russia	57	9	17	26	30	....	....	....	....	....	....	....	....	....	4	1	1	2	6	....	....	....	....
2008-09	**Carolina**	**NHL**	**72**	**16**	**19**	**35**	**16**	**9**	**0**	**4**	**127**	**12.6**	**13**	**0**	**0.0**	**18:04**	**13**	**0**	**1**	**1**	**10**	**0**	**0**	**0**	**16:03**
2009-10	Omsk	KHL	49	9	13	22	36	....	....	....	....	....	....	....	....	....	2	0	0	0	0	....	....	....	....
2010-11	**Carolina**	**NHL**	**17**	**3**	**5**	**8**	**12**	**1**	**0**	**1**	**45**	**6.7**	**–4**	**0**	**0.0**	**19:07**	....	....	....	....	....	....	....	....	....
	Calgary	**NHL**	**65**	**8**	**19**	**27**	**20**	**5**	**1**	**1**	**87**	**9.2**	**18**	**0**	**0.0**	**15:37**	....	....	....	....	....	....	....	....	....
2011-12	**Calgary**	**NHL**	**32**	**2**	**8**	**10**	**6**	**1**	**0**	**1**	**48**	**4.2**	**2**	**0**	**0.0**	**14:29**	....	....	....	....	....	....	....	....	....
2012-13	Donetsk	KHL	31	1	2	3	22	....	....	....	....	....	....	....	....	....	....	....	....	....	....	....	....	....	....
	Calgary	**NHL**	**7**	**0**	**1**	**1**	**0**	**0**	**0**	**0**	**5**	**0.0**	**–1**	**0**	**0.0**	**11:51**	....	....	....	....	....	....	....	....	....
	NHL Totals		**289**	**36**	**71**	**107**	**108**	**19**	**1**	**9**	**442**	**8.1**		**0**	**0.0**	**16:23**	**13**	**0**	**1**	**1**	**10**	**0**	**0**	**0**	**16:03**

Traded to **Carolina** by **Chicago** for Danny Richmond and Columbus' 4th round choice (previously acquired, later traded to Toronto - Toronto selected James Reimer) in 2006 Entry Draft, January 20, 2006. Signed as a free agent by **Omsk** (KHL), September 20, 2009. Traded to **Calgary** by **Carolina** with Tom Kostopoulos for Ian White and Brett Sutter, November 17, 2010. • Missed majority of 2011-12 due to hand injury vs. Minnesota, November 8, 2011. Signed as a free agent by **Donetsk** (KHL), September 27, 2012. Signed as a free agent by **Ufa** (KHL), May 28, 2013.

BACKES, David

(BA-kuhs, DAY-vihd) **ST.L.**

Center. Shoots right. 6'3", 221 lbs. Born, Blaine, MN, May 1, 1984. St. Louis' 2nd choice, 62nd overall, in 2003 Entry Draft.

Season	Club	League	GP	G	A	Pts	PIM	PP	SH	GW	S	%	+/-	TF	F%	Min	GP	G	A	Pts	PIM	PP	SH	GW	Min
99-2000	Spring Lake Park	High-MN	24	17	20	37	....	....	....	....	....	....	....	....	....	....	....	....	....	....	....	....	....	....	....
2000-01	Spring Lake Park	High-MN	24	29	46	75	....	....	....	....	....	....	....	....	....	....	....	....	....	....	....	....	....	....	....
2001-02	Chicago Steel	USHL	25	31	36	67	....	....	....	....	....	....	....	....	....	....	2	1	1	2	....	....	....	....	....
	Lincoln Stars	USHL	30	11	10	21	54	....	....	....	....	....	....	....	....	....	3	0	0	0	2	....	....	....	....
2002-03	Lincoln Stars	USHL	57	28	41	69	126	....	....	....	....	....	....	....	....	....	7	4	1	5	17	....	....	....	....
2003-04	Minnesota State	WCHA	39	16	21	37	66	....	....	....	....	....	....	....	....	....	....	....	....	....	....	....	....	....	....
2004-05	Minnesota State	WCHA	38	17	23	40	55	....	....	....	....	....	....	....	....	....	....	....	....	....	....	....	....	....	....
2005-06	Minnesota State	WCHA	38	13	29	42	91	....	....	....	....	....	....	....	....	....	....	....	....	....	....	....	....	....	....
	Peoria Rivermen	AHL	12	5	5	10	10	....	....	....	....	....	....	....	....	....	3	1	1	2	8	....	....	....	....
2006-07	**St. Louis**	**NHL**	**49**	**10**	**13**	**23**	**37**	**2**	**0**	**2**	**89**	**11.2**	**6**	**26**	**46.2**	**13:25**	....	....	....	....	....	....	....	....	....
	Peoria Rivermen	AHL	31	10	3	13	47	....	....	....	....	....	....	....	....	....	....	....	....	....	....	....	....	....	....
2007-08	**St. Louis**	**NHL**	**72**	**13**	**18**	**31**	**99**	**3**	**0**	**2**	**129**	**10.1**	**–11**	**67**	**44.8**	**14:41**	....	....	....	....	....	....	....	....	....
2008-09	**St. Louis**	**NHL**	**82**	**31**	**23**	**54**	**165**	**6**	**2**	**1**	**208**	**14.9**	**–3**	**477**	**44.4**	**17:41**	**4**	**1**	**2**	**3**	**10**	**0**	**0**	**0**	**22:56**
2009-10	**St. Louis**	**NHL**	**79**	**17**	**31**	**48**	**106**	**5**	**0**	**3**	**163**	**10.4**	**–4**	**1065**	**47.3**	**18:18**	....	....	....	....	....	....	....	....	....
	United States	Olympics	6	1	2	3	2	....	....	....	....	....	....	....	....	....	....	....	....	....	....	....	....	....	....
2010-11	**St. Louis**	**NHL**	**82**	**31**	**31**	**62**	**93**	**5**	**0**	**2**	**211**	**14.7**	**32**	**1138**	**44.5**	**19:42**	....	....	....	....	....	....	....	....	....
2011-12	**St. Louis**	**NHL**	**82**	**24**	**30**	**54**	**101**	**8**	**2**	**4**	**234**	**10.3**	**15**	**1353**	**48.6**	**20:00**	**9**	**2**	**2**	**4**	**18**	**0**	**0**	**0**	**20:19**
2012-13	**St. Louis**	**NHL**	**48**	**6**	**22**	**28**	**62**	**1**	**0**	**1**	**100**	**6.0**	**5**	**912**	**52.3**	**19:37**	**6**	**1**	**2**	**3**	**0**	**0**	**0**	**0**	**20:32**
	NHL Totals		**494**	**132**	**168**	**300**	**663**	**30**	**4**	**15**	**1134**	**11.6**		**5038**	**47.6**	**17:50**	**19**	**4**	**6**	**10**	**28**	**0**	**0**	**0**	**20:56**

USHL First All-Star Team (2003) • WCHA All-Rookie Team (2004) • WCHA Second All-Star Team (2006) • NCAA West Second All-American Team (2006)

Played in NHL All-Star Game (2011)

BACKLUND, Mikael

(BAHK-luhnd, mih-KIGH-ehl) **CGY**

Center. Shoots left. 6', 198 lbs. Born, Vasteras, Sweden, March 17, 1989. Calgary's 1st choice, 24th overall, in 2007 Entry Draft.

Season	Club	League	GP	G	A	Pts	PIM	PP	SH	GW	S	%	+/-	TF	F%	Min	GP	G	A	Pts	PIM	PP	SH	GW	Min
2004-05	Vasteras U18	Swe-U18	14	5	6	11	14	....	....	....	....	....	....	....	....	....	4	2	1	3	2	....	....	....	....
2005-06	Vasteras Jr.	Swe-Jr.	25	15	16	31	30	....	....	....	....	....	....	....	....	....	....	....	....	....	....	....	....	....	....
	VIK Vasteras HK	Sweden-2	12	2	2	4	14	....	....	....	....	....	....	....	....	....	....	....	....	....	....	....	....	....	....
2006-07	Vasteras U18	Swe-U18	2	2	1	3	2	....	....	....	....	....	....	....	....	....	1	0	0	0	10	....	....	....	....
	Vasteras Jr.	Swe-Jr.	7	5	4	9	8	....	....	....	....	....	....	....	....	....	5	1	0	1	4	....	....	....	....
	VIK Vasteras HK	Sweden-2	18	1	2	3	14	....	....	....	....	....	....	....	....	....	....	....	....	....	....	....	....	....	....
2007-08	Vasteras Jr.	Swe-Jr.	9	7	6	13	20	....	....	....	....	....	....	....	....	....	....	....	....	....	....	....	....	....	....
	VIK Vasteras HK	Sweden-2	46	11	4	15	28	....	....	....	....	....	....	....	....	....	5	4	3	7	0	....	....	....	....
2008-09	Vasteras Jr.	Swe-Jr.	2	3	2	5	0	....	....	....	....	....	....	....	....	....	....	....	....	....	....	....	....	....	....
	VIK Vasteras HK	Sweden-2	17	4	4	8	39	....	....	....	....	....	....	....	....	....	....	....	....	....	....	....	....	....	....
	Calgary	**NHL**	**1**	**0**	**0**	**0**	**0**	**0**	**0**	**0**	**1**	**0.0**	**0**	**7**	**28.6**	**10:44**	....	....	....	....	....	....	....	....	....
	Kelowna Rockets	WHL	28	12	18	30	26	....	....	....	....	....	....	....	....	....	19	*13	10	23	26	....	....	....	....
2009-10	**Calgary**	**NHL**	**23**	**1**	**9**	**10**	**6**	**0**	**0**	**0**	**47**	**2.1**	**5**	**191**	**53.4**	**12:36**	....	....	....	....	....	....	....	....	....
	Abbotsford Heat	AHL	54	15	17	32	26	....	....	....	....	....	....	....	....	....	13	1	8	9	14	....	....	....	....
2010-11	**Calgary**	**NHL**	**73**	**10**	**15**	**25**	**18**	**2**	**0**	**1**	**144**	**6.9**	**4**	**664**	**48.0**	**12:05**	....	....	....	....	....	....	....	....	....
	Abbotsford Heat	AHL	1	0	0	0	0	....	....	....	....	....	....	....	....	....	....	....	....	....	....	....	....	....	....
2011-12	**Calgary**	**NHL**	**41**	**4**	**7**	**11**	**16**	**2**	**0**	**2**	**85**	**4.7**	**–13**	**496**	**45.4**	**15:23**	....	....	....	....	....	....	....	....	....
2012-13	VIK Vasteras HK	Sweden-2	23	12	18	30	22	....	....	....	....	....	....	....	....	....	....	....	....	....	....	....	....	....	....
	Calgary	**NHL**	**32**	**8**	**8**	**16**	**29**	**2**	**0**	**1**	**88**	**9.1**	**–6**	**407**	**47.7**	**15:07**	....	....	....	....	....	....	....	....	....
	NHL Totals		**170**	**23**	**39**	**62**	**69**	**6**	**0**	**4**	**365**	**6.3**		**1765**	**47.7**	**13:31**	....	....	....	....	....	....	....	....	....

Signed as a free agent by **Vasteras** (Sweden-2), October 4, 2012.

BACKSTROM, Nicklas

(BAK-struhm, NIHK-luhs) **WSH**

Center. Shoots left. 6'1", 213 lbs. Born, Gavle, Sweden, November 23, 1987. Washington's 1st choice, 4th overall, in 2006 Entry Draft.

			Regular Season														Playoffs								
Season	Club	League	GP	G	A	Pts	PIM	PP	SH	GW	S	%	+/-	TF	F%	Min	GP	G	A	Pts	PIM	PP	SH	GW	Min
2001-02	Brynas U18	Swe-U18	2	0	0	0	0																		
2002-03	Brynas U18	Swe-U18	STATISTICS NOT AVAILABLE																						
2003-04	Brynas U18	Swe-U18	6	9	5	14	4																		
	Brynas IF Gavle Jr.	Swe-Jr.	21	2	6	8	2										3	0	3	3	0				
2004-05	Brynas IF Gavle Jr.	Swe-Jr.	29	17	17	34	24										5	0	0	0	4				
	Brynas IF Gavle	Sweden	19	0	0	0	2																		
2005-06	Brynas IF Gavle	Sweden	46	10	16	26	30										4	1	0	1	2				
	Brynas IF Gavle Jr.	Swe-Jr.															1	0	0	0	2				
2006-07	Brynas IF Gavle	Sweden	45	12	28	40	46										7	3	3	6	6				
2007-08	**Washington**	**NHL**	**82**	**14**	**55**	**69**	**24**	**3**	**0**	**4**	**153**	**9.2**	**13**	**874**	**46.3**	**19:00**	**7**	**4**	**2**	**6**	**2**	**3**	**0**	**0**	**20:26**
2008-09	**Washington**	**NHL**	**82**	**22**	**66**	**88**	**46**	**14**	**0**	**1**	**174**	**12.6**	**16**	**1171**	**48.7**	**19:57**	**14**	**3**	**12**	**15**	**8**	**2**	**0**	**0**	**21:40**
2009-10	**Washington**	**NHL**	**82**	**33**	**68**	**101**	**50**	**11**	**0**	**4**	**222**	**14.9**	**37**	**1336**	**49.9**	**20:27**	**7**	**5**	**4**	**9**	**4**	**0**	**0**	**1**	**21:03**
	Sweden	Olympics	4	1	5	6	0																		
2010-11	**Washington**	**NHL**	**77**	**18**	**47**	**65**	**40**	**4**	**1**	**2**	**202**	**8.9**	**24**	**1315**	**52.5**	**20:36**	**9**	**0**	**2**	**2**	**4**	**0**	**0**	**0**	**23:18**
2011-12	**Washington**	**NHL**	**42**	**14**	**30**	**44**	**24**	**3**	**0**	**4**	**95**	**14.7**	**–4**	**691**	**51.1**	**19:10**	**13**	**2**	**6**	**8**	**18**	**0**	**0**	**1**	**21:31**
2012-13	Dynamo Moscow	KHL	19	10	15	25	10																		
	Washington	**NHL**	**48**	**8**	**40**	**48**	**20**	**3**	**0**	**1**	**82**	**9.8**	**8**	**840**	**51.4**	**19:54**	**7**	**1**	**2**	**3**	**0**	**0**	**0**	**0**	**19:47**
	NHL Totals		**413**	**109**	**306**	**415**	**204**	**38**	**1**	**16**	**928**	**11.7**		**6227**	**50.1**	**19:54**	**57**	**15**	**28**	**43**	**36**	**5**	**0**	**2**	**21:26**

NHL All-Rookie Team (2008)

Signed as a free agent by **Dynamo Moscow** (KHL), October 18, 2012.

BAERTSCHI, Sven

(BEHR-chee, SVEHN) **CGY**

Left wing. Shoots left. 5'11", 187 lbs. Born, Langenthal, Switzerland, October 5, 1992. Calgary's 1st choice, 13th overall, in 2011 Entry Draft.

Season	Club	League	GP	G	A	Pts	PIM	PP	SH	GW	S	%	+/-	TF	F%	Min	GP	G	A	Pts	PIM	PP	SH	GW	Min
2006-07	Langenthal U17	Swiss-U17	13	15	23	38	16																		
2007-08	Langenthal U17	Swiss-U17	17	16	22	38	22																		
	SC Langenthal Jr.	Swiss-Jr.	18	3	3	6	4										7	1	2	3	4				
2008-09	Langenthal U17	Swiss-U17	3	4	4	8	0																		
	SC Langenthal Jr.	Swiss-Jr.	37	21	32	53	40										6	4	3	7	35				
	SC Langenthal	Swiss-2	2	0	0	0	0																		
2009-10	SC Langenthal Jr.	Swiss-Jr.	2	3	0	3	2																		
	EV Zug Jr.	Swiss-Jr.	9	10	13	23	4										2	3	1	4	2				
	SC Langenthal	Swiss-2	37	6	6	12	8										7	0	3	3	4				
2010-11	Portland	WHL	66	34	51	85	74										21	10	17	27	16				
2011-12	**Calgary**	**NHL**	**5**	**3**	**0**	**3**	**4**	**0**	**0**	**0**	**10**	**30.0**	**2**	**0**	**0.0**	**11:08**									
	Portland	WHL	47	33	61	94	36										22	14	20	34	10				
2012-13	**Calgary**	**NHL**	**20**	**3**	**7**	**10**	**6**	**0**	**0**	**0**	**28**	**10.7**	**0**	**1**	**100.0**	**13:24**									
	Abbotsford Heat	AHL	32	10	16	26	16																		
	NHL Totals		**25**	**6**	**7**	**13**	**10**	**0**	**0**	**0**	**38**	**15.8**		**1**	**100.0**	**12:57**									

WHL West Second All-Star Team (2012)

BAGNALL, Drew

(BAG-nuhl, DROO)

Defense. Shoots left. 6'3", 220 lbs. Born, Oakbank, Man., October 26, 1983. Dallas' 9th choice, 195th overall, in 2003 Entry Draft.

Season	Club	League	GP	G	A	Pts	PIM	PP	SH	GW	S	%	+/-	TF	F%	Min	GP	G	A	Pts	PIM	PP	SH	GW	Min
2000-01	Battlefords	SJHL	58	7	20	27	205																		
2001-02	Battlefords	SJHL	60	16	23	39	247																		
2002-03	Battlefords	SJHL	55	17	46	63	248										4	0	1	1	4				
2003-04	St. Lawrence	ECAC	40	5	13	18	61																		
2004-05	St. Lawrence	ECAC	37	7	12	19	68																		
2005-06	St. Lawrence	ECAC	24	1	9	10	32																		
2006-07	St. Lawrence	ECAC	39	6	19	25	74																		
2007-08	Manchester	AHL	54	1	11	12	115										4	0	0	0	4				
	Reading Royals	ECHL	10	1	2	3	32																		
2008-09	Manchester	AHL	79	0	6	6	150																		
2009-10	Manchester	AHL	58	2	10	12	113										16	0	3	3	21				
2010-11	**Minnesota**	**NHL**	**2**	**0**	**0**	**0**	**4**	**0**	**0**	**0**	**1**	**0.0**	**–2**	**0**	**0.0**	**13:00**									
	Houston Aeros	AHL	72	0	2	2	112										24	1	1	2	22				
2011-12	Houston Aeros	AHL	72	2	12	14	98										4	0	0	0	8				
2012-13	Houston Aeros	AHL	47	1	5	6	88										5	0	0	0	6				
	NHL Totals		**2**	**0**	**0**	**0**	**4**	**0**	**0**	**0**	**1**	**0.0**		**0**	**0.0**	**13:00**									

Traded to **Florida** by **Dallas** with Dallas' 2nd round compensatory choice (later traded to Phoenix – Phoenix selected Enver Lisin) in 2004 Entry Draft for Valeri Bure, March 8, 2004. Signed as a free agent by **Los Angeles**, August 23, 2007. Signed as a free agent by **Minnesota**, July 2, 2010.

BAILEY, Josh

(BAY-lee, JAWSH) **NYI**

Center. Shoots left. 6'1", 190 lbs. Born, Bowmanville, Ont., October 2, 1989. NY Islanders' 1st choice, 9th overall, in 2008 Entry Draft.

Season	Club	League	GP	G	A	Pts	PIM	PP	SH	GW	S	%	+/-	TF	F%	Min	GP	G	A	Pts	PIM	PP	SH	GW	Min
2004-05	Clarington Toros	Minor-ON	69	53	59	112	38																		
2005-06	Owen Sound	OHL	55	7	19	26	8										11	0	0	0	0				
2006-07	Owen Sound	OHL	27	11	15	26	8																		
	Windsor Spitfires	OHL	42	11	24	35	16																		
2007-08	Windsor Spitfires	OHL	67	29	67	96	32										5	1	5	6	2				
2008-09	**NY Islanders**	**NHL**	**68**	**7**	**18**	**25**	**16**	**3**	**0**	**0**	**74**	**9.5**	**–14**	**807**	**41.1**	**15:29**									
2009-10	**NY Islanders**	**NHL**	**73**	**16**	**19**	**35**	**18**	**3**	**1**	**2**	**112**	**14.3**	**5**	**426**	**40.1**	**15:09**									
2010-11	**NY Islanders**	**NHL**	**70**	**11**	**17**	**28**	**37**	**5**	**0**	**2**	**102**	**10.8**	**–13**	**615**	**44.4**	**17:50**									
	Bridgeport	AHL	11	6	11	17	4																		
2011-12	**NY Islanders**	**NHL**	**80**	**13**	**19**	**32**	**32**	**1**	**3**	**1**	**104**	**12.5**	**–10**	**736**	**43.9**	**15:13**									
2012-13	Bietigheim	German-2	6	3	8	11	16																		
	NY Islanders	**NHL**	**38**	**11**	**8**	**19**	**6**	**0**	**0**	**1**	**76**	**14.5**	**7**	**75**	**46.7**	**16:23**	**6**	**0**	**3**	**3**	**0**	**0**	**0**	**0**	**20:14**
	NHL Totals		**329**	**58**	**81**	**139**	**109**	**12**	**4**	**6**	**468**	**12.4**		**2659**	**42.6**	**15:57**	**6**	**0**	**3**	**3**	**0**	**0**	**0**	**0**	**20:14**

Signed as a free agent by **Bietigheim-Bissingen** (German-2), November 9, 2012.

BALLARD, Keith

(BAL-uhrd, KEETH) **MIN**

Defense. Shoots left. 5'11", 208 lbs. Born, Baudette, MN, November 26, 1982. Buffalo's 1st choice, 11th overall, in 2002 Entry Draft.

Season	Club	League	GP	G	A	Pts	PIM	PP	SH	GW	S	%	+/-	TF	F%	Min	GP	G	A	Pts	PIM	PP	SH	GW	Min
99-2000	USNTDP	U-18	6	1	1	2	4																		
	USNTDP	USHL	58	12	21	33	119																		
2000-01	Omaha Lancers	USHL	56	22	29	51	168										10	1	6	7	8				
2001-02	U. of Minnesota	WCHA	41	10	13	23	42																		
2002-03	U. of Minnesota	WCHA	41	12	29	41	78																		
2003-04	U. of Minnesota	WCHA	37	11	25	36	83																		
2004-05	Utah Grizzlies	AHL	60	2	18	20	88																		
2005-06	**Phoenix**	**NHL**	**82**	**8**	**31**	**39**	**99**	**1**	**3**	**1**	**102**	**7.8**	**–18**	**0**	**0.0**	**19:59**									
2006-07	**Phoenix**	**NHL**	**69**	**5**	**22**	**27**	**59**	**2**	**0**	**0**	**79**	**6.3**	**–7**	**0**	**0.0**	**22:00**									
2007-08	**Phoenix**	**NHL**	**82**	**6**	**15**	**21**	**85**	**2**	**1**	**1**	**105**	**5.7**	**7**	**0**	**0.0**	**21:16**									
2008-09	**Florida**	**NHL**	**82**	**6**	**28**	**34**	**72**	**1**	**0**	**1**	**106**	**5.7**	**14**	**1**	**0.0**	**22:23**									
2009-10	**Florida**	**NHL**	**82**	**8**	**20**	**28**	**88**	**1**	**0**	**1**	**90**	**8.9**	**–7**	**0**	**0.0**	**22:24**									
2010-11	**Vancouver**	**NHL**	**65**	**2**	**5**	**7**	**53**	**0**	**0**	**0**	**53**	**3.8**	**10**	**0**	**0.0**	**15:54**	**10**	**0**	**0**	**0**	**6**	**0**	**0**	**0**	**14:14**
2011-12	**Vancouver**	**NHL**	**47**	**1**	**6**	**7**	**64**	**0**	**0**	**0**	**41**	**2.4**	**0**	**0**	**0.0**	**15:33**	**4**	**0**	**1**	**1**	**2**	**0**	**0**	**0**	**14:40**
2012-13	**Vancouver**	**NHL**	**36**	**0**	**2**	**2**	**29**	**0**	**0**	**0**	**35**	**0.0**	**–2**	**0**	**0.0**	**15:28**									
	NHL Totals		**545**	**36**	**129**	**165**	**549**	**7**	**4**	**4**	**611**	**5.9**		**1**	**0.0**	**19:59**	**14**	**0**	**1**	**1**	**8**	**0**	**0**	**0**	**14:22**

USHL First All-Star Team (2001) • WCHA All-Rookie Team (2002) • WCHA First All-Star Team (2003, 2004) • NCAA West First All-American Team (2004)

Traded to **Colorado** by **Buffalo** for Steve Reinprecht, July 3, 2003. Traded to **Phoenix** by **Colorado** with Derek Morris for Ossi Vaananen, Chris Gratton and Phoenix's 2nd round choice (Paul Stastny) in 2005 Entry Draft, March 9, 2004. Traded to **Florida** by **Phoenix** with Nick Boynton and Ottawa's 2nd round choice (previously acquired, later traded back to Phoenix - Phoenix selected Jared Staal) in 2008 Entry Draft for Olli Jokinen, June 20, 2008. Traded to **Vancouver** by **Florida** with Victor Oreskovich for Steve Bernier, Michael Grabner and Vancouver's 1st round choice (Quinton Howden) in 2010 Entry Draft, June 25, 2010. Signed as a free agent by **Minnesota**, July 5, 2013.

BANCKS, Carter
(BANKS, KAHR-tuhr) **CGY**

Left wing. Shoots left. 5'11", 180 lbs. Born, Marysville, B.C., August 9, 1989.

Season	Club	League	GP	G	A	Pts	PIM	PP	SH	GW	S	%	+/-	TF	F%	Min	GP	G	A	Pts	PIM	PP	SH	GW	Min
			Regular Season														Playoffs								
2004-05	Kimberley	KIJHL	11	1	5	6	10	....	....	....	....	....	....	....	....	....	....	....	....	....	....	....	....	....	....
2005-06	Kimberley	KIJHL	50	24	49	73	57	....	....	....	....	....	....	....	....	....	13	5	7	12	6	....	....	....	....
	Lethbridge	WHL	2	0	0	0	0	....	....	....	....	....	....	....	....	....	6	0	0	0	4	....	....	....	....
2006-07	Lethbridge	WHL	67	11	20	31	64	....	....	....	....	....	....	....	....	....	....	....	....	....	....	....	....	....	....
2007-08	Lethbridge	WHL	70	15	30	45	56	....	....	....	....	....	....	....	....	....	19	6	4	10	19	....	....	....	....
2008-09	Lethbridge	WHL	53	13	34	47	68	....	....	....	....	....	....	....	....	....	3	0	0	0	4	....	....	....	....
2009-10	Lethbridge	WHL	70	19	36	55	96	....	....	....	....	....	....	....	....	....	....	....	....	....	....	....	....	....	....
	Abbotsford Heat	AHL	9	0	0	0	0	....	....	....	....	....	....	....	....	....	13	0	1	1	7	....	....	....	....
2010-11	Abbotsford Heat	AHL	29	5	14	19	16	....	....	....	....	....	....	....	....	....	....	....	....	....	....	....	....	....	....
2011-12	Abbotsford Heat	AHL	55	2	8	10	57	....	....	....	....	....	....	....	....	....	8	0	0	0	14	....	....	....	....
2012-13	Abbotsford Heat	AHL	59	5	7	12	53	....	....	....	....	....	....	....	....	....	....	....	....	....	....	....	....	....	....
	Calgary	**NHL**	**2**	**0**	**0**	**0**	**0**	**0**	**0**	**0**	**0**	**0.0**	**0**	**0**	**0.0**	**14:41**	....	....	....	....	....	....	....	....	....
	NHL Totals		**2**	**0**	**0**	**0**	**0**	**0**	**0**	**0**	**0**	**0.0**		**0**	**0.0**	**14:41**	....	....	....	....	....	....	....	....	....

• Missed majority of 2004-05 due to leg injury. Signed to a ATO (amateur tryout) contract by **Abbotsford** (AHL), March 18, 2010. Signed as a free agent by **Calgary**, July 1, 2011.

BANG, Daniel
(BANG, DAN-yehl) **NSH**

Wing. Shoots left. 6'3", 205 lbs. Born, Kista, Sweden, April 19, 1987.

Season	Club	League	GP	G	A	Pts	PIM	PP	SH	GW	S	%	+/-	TF	F%	Min	GP	G	A	Pts	PIM	PP	SH	GW	Min
2004-05	AIK Solna Jr.	Swe-Jr.	22	0	4	4	12	....	....	....	....	....	....	....	....	....	....	....	....	....	....	....	....	....	....
2005-06	AIK Solna Jr.	Swe-Jr.	26	1	3	4	78	....	....	....	....	....	....	....	....	....	....	....	....	....	....	....	....	....	....
	AIK Solna	Sweden-2	1	0	0	0	0	....	....	....	....	....	....	....	....	....	....	....	....	....	....	....	....	....	....
2006-07	AIK IF Solna Jr.	Swe-Jr.	6	2	0	2	22	....	....	....	....	....	....	....	....	....	....	....	....	....	....	....	....	....	....
	AIK IF Solna	Sweden-2	44	6	11	17	50	....	....	....	....	....	....	....	....	....	....	....	....	....	....	....	....	....	....
2007-08	AIK IF Solna Jr.	Swe-Jr.	2	0	2	2	31	....	....	....	....	....	....	....	....	....	....	....	....	....	....	....	....	....	....
	AIK IF Solna	Sweden-2	37	7	7	14	26	....	....	....	....	....	....	....	....	....	....	....	....	....	....	....	....	....	....
2008-09	AIK IF Solna	Sweden-2	38	20	9	29	65	....	....	....	....	....	....	....	....	....	9	3	0	3	27	....	....	....	....
2009-10	AIK IF Solna	Sweden-2	48	14	17	31	86	....	....	....	....	....	....	....	....	....	6	2	2	4	0	....	....	....	....
2010-11	AIK IF Solna	Sweden	40	5	7	12	82	....	....	....	....	....	....	....	....	....	6	2	2	4	0	....	....	....	....
2011-12	AIK Solna	Sweden	50	8	10	18	30	....	....	....	....	....	....	....	....	....	12	3	3	6	0	....	....	....	....
2012-13	Milwaukee	AHL	53	9	13	22	21	....	....	....	....	....	....	....	....	....	3	0	0	0	0	....	....	....	....
	Nashville	**NHL**	**8**	**0**	**2**	**2**	**0**	**0**	**0**	**0**	**13**	**0.0**	**–2**	**0**	**0.0**	**12:54**	....	....	....	....	....	....	....	....	....
	NHL Totals		**8**	**0**	**2**	**2**	**0**	**0**	**0**	**0**	**13**	**0.0**		**0**	**0.0**	**12:54**	....	....	....	....	....	....	....	....	....

Signed as a free agent by **Nashville**, June 1, 2012.

BARBERIO, Mark
(bahr-BAIR-ee-oh, MAHRK) **T.B.**

Defense. Shoots left. 6'1", 185 lbs. Born, Montreal, Que., March 23, 1990. Tampa Bay's 5th choice, 152nd overall, in 2008 Entry Draft.

Season	Club	League	GP	G	A	Pts	PIM	PP	SH	GW	S	%	+/-	TF	F%	Min	GP	G	A	Pts	PIM	PP	SH	GW	Min
2005-06	Lac St-Louis Lions	QAAA	43	2	12	14	80	....	....	....	....	....	....	....	....	....	10	1	7	8	26	....	....	....	....
2006-07	Cape Breton	QMJHL	41	2	8	10	42	....	....	....	....	....	....	....	....	....	....	....	....	....	....	....	....	....	....
	Moncton Wildcats	QMJHL	19	1	6	7	21	....	....	....	....	....	....	....	....	....	7	0	2	2	8	....	....	....	....
2007-08	Moncton Wildcats	QMJHL	70	11	35	46	75	....	....	....	....	....	....	....	....	....	....	....	....	....	....	....	....	....	....
2008-09	Moncton Wildcats	QMJHL	66	15	30	45	42	....	....	....	....	....	....	....	....	....	10	0	4	4	8	....	....	....	....
2009-10	Moncton Wildcats	QMJHL	65	17	43	60	72	....	....	....	....	....	....	....	....	....	21	5	17	22	12	....	....	....	....
2010-11	Norfolk Admirals	AHL	68	9	22	31	28	....	....	....	....	....	....	....	....	....	6	1	0	1	4	....	....	....	....
2011-12	Norfolk Admirals	AHL	74	13	48	61	39	....	....	....	....	....	....	....	....	....	18	2	7	9	12	....	....	....	....
2012-13	Syracuse Crunch	AHL	73	8	34	42	44	....	....	....	....	....	....	....	....	....	18	3	12	15	18	....	....	....	....
	Tampa Bay	**NHL**	**2**	**0**	**0**	**0**	**0**	**0**	**0**	**0**	**1**	**0.0**	**–2**	**0**	**0.0**	**15:30**	....	....	....	....	....	....	....	....	....
	NHL Totals		**2**	**0**	**0**	**0**	**0**	**0**	**0**	**0**	**1**	**0.0**		**0**	**0.0**	**15:30**	....	....	....	....	....	....	....	....	....

QMJHL All-Rookie Team (2007) • QMJHL Second All-Star Team (2010) • AHL First All-Star Team (2012) • Eddie Shore Award (AHL - Outstanding Defenseman) (2012) • AHL Second All-Star Team (2013)

BARCH, Krys
(BAHRCH, KRIHS) **N.J.**

Left wing. Shoots left. 6'1", 220 lbs. Born, Hamilton, Ont., March 26, 1980. Washington's 3rd choice, 106th overall, in 1998 Entry Draft.

Season	Club	League	GP	G	A	Pts	PIM	PP	SH	GW	S	%	+/-	TF	F%	Min	GP	G	A	Pts	PIM	PP	SH	GW	Min
1995-96	Georgetown	ON-Jr.A	41	6	8	14	10	....	....	....	....	....	....	....	....	....	....	....	....	....	....	....	....	....	....
1996-97	Georgetown	ON-Jr.A	51	18	26	44	58	....	....	....	....	....	....	....	....	....	....	....	....	....	....	....	....	....	....
1997-98	London Knights	OHL	65	9	27	36	62	....	....	....	....	....	....	....	....	....	16	4	3	7	16	....	....	....	....
1998-99	London Knights	OHL	66	18	20	38	66	....	....	....	....	....	....	....	....	....	25	9	17	26	15	....	....	....	....
99-2000	London Knights	OHL	56	23	26	49	78	....	....	....	....	....	....	....	....	....	....	....	....	....	....	....	....	....	....
	Portland Pirates	AHL	....	....	....	....	....	....	....	....	....	....	....	....	....	....	4	0	2	2	2	....	....	....	....
2000-01	Portland Pirates	AHL	76	10	15	25	91	....	....	....	....	....	....	....	....	....	2	0	0	0	0	....	....	....	....
2001-02	Portland Pirates	AHL	29	3	8	11	28	....	....	....	....	....	....	....	....	....	....	....	....	....	....	....	....	....	....
	Richmond	ECHL	25	6	4	10	43	....	....	....	....	....	....	....	....	....	....	....	....	....	....	....	....	....	....
2002-03	Portland Pirates	AHL	36	1	7	8	49	....	....	....	....	....	....	....	....	....	....	....	....	....	....	....	....	....	....
2003-04			DID NOT PLAY																						
2004-05	Norfolk Admirals	AHL	9	1	0	1	37	....	....	....	....	....	....	....	....	....	....	....	....	....	....	....	....	....	....
	Greenville	ECHL	55	11	19	30	154	....	....	....	....	....	....	....	....	....	3	0	0	0	36	....	....	....	....
2005-06	Iowa Stars	AHL	43	7	6	13	129	....	....	....	....	....	....	....	....	....	7	0	1	1	37	....	....	....	....
	Greenville	ECHL	14	10	4	14	75	....	....	....	....	....	....	....	....	....	....	....	....	....	....	....	....	....	....
2006-07	**Dallas**	**NHL**	**26**	**3**	**2**	**5**	**107**	**0**	**0**	**2**	**12**	**25.0**	**2**	**1**	**0.0**	**5:38**	....	....	....	....	....	....	....	....	....
	Iowa Stars	AHL	31	3	5	8	110	....	....	....	....	....	....	....	....	....	....	....	....	....	....	....	....	....	....
2007-08	**Dallas**	**NHL**	**48**	**1**	**2**	**3**	**105**	**0**	**0**	**0**	**23**	**4.3**	**–3**	**2**	**0.0**	**6:30**	**3**	**0**	**0**	**0**	**2**	**0**	**0**	**0**	**2:21**
2008-09	**Dallas**	**NHL**	**72**	**4**	**5**	**9**	**133**	**0**	**0**	**1**	**27**	**14.8**	**1**	**7**	**28.6**	**6:27**	....	....	....	....	....	....	....	....	....
2009-10	**Dallas**	**NHL**	**63**	**0**	**6**	**6**	**130**	**0**	**0**	**0**	**29**	**0.0**	**0**	**3**	**0.0**	**7:03**	....	....	....	....	....	....	....	....	....
2010-11	**Dallas**	**NHL**	**44**	**2**	**1**	**3**	**80**	**0**	**0**	**0**	**16**	**12.5**	**–7**	**4**	**50.0**	**5:13**	....	....	....	....	....	....	....	....	....
2011-12	**Dallas**	**NHL**	**10**	**0**	**0**	**0**	**23**	**0**	**0**	**0**	**2**	**0.0**	**–2**	**0**	**0.0**	**6:43**	....	....	....	....	....	....	....	....	....
	Florida	**NHL**	**41**	**2**	**3**	**5**	**91**	**0**	**0**	**0**	**22**	**9.1**	**2**	**7**	**28.6**	**7:30**	....	....	....	....	....	....	....	....	....
2012-13	**New Jersey**	**NHL**	**22**	**0**	**0**	**0**	**44**	**0**	**0**	**0**	**4**	**0.0**	**1**	**2**	**50.0**	**5:51**	....	....	....	....	....	....	....	....	....
	NHL Totals		**326**	**12**	**19**	**31**	**713**	**0**	**0**	**3**	**135**	**8.9**		**26**	**26.9**	**6:27**	**3**	**0**	**0**	**0**	**2**	**0**	**0**	**0**	**2:21**

Signed as a free agent by **Dallas**, July 18, 2006. Traded to **Florida** by **Dallas** with Dallas's 6th round choice (later traded to Nashville – Nashville selected Simon Fernholm) in 2012 Entry Draft for Jake Hauswirth and Florida's 5th round choice (Henri Kiviaho) in 2012 Entry Draft, December 7, 2011. Signed as a free agent by **New Jersey**, July 10, 2012. • Missed majority of 2012-13 as a healthy reserve.

BARKER, Cam
(BAR-kuhr, KAM)

Defense. Shoots left. 6'3", 223 lbs. Born, Winnipeg, Man., April 4, 1986. Chicago's 1st choice, 3rd overall, in 2004 Entry Draft.

Season	Club	League	GP	G	A	Pts	PIM	PP	SH	GW	S	%	+/-	TF	F%	Min	GP	G	A	Pts	PIM	PP	SH	GW	Min
2001-02	Gloucester	ON-Jr.A	32	1	8	9	77	....	....	....	....	....	....	....	....	....	....	....	....	....	....	....	....	....	....
	Cornwall Colts	ON-Jr.A	18	3	13	16	66	....	....	....	....	....	....	....	....	....	13	0	2	2	26	....	....	....	....
	Medicine Hat	WHL	3	0	1	1	0	....	....	....	....	....	....	....	....	....	....	....	....	....	....	....	....	....	....
2002-03	Medicine Hat	WHL	64	10	37	47	79	....	....	....	....	....	....	....	....	....	11	3	4	7	17	....	....	....	....
2003-04	Medicine Hat	WHL	69	21	44	65	105	....	....	....	....	....	....	....	....	....	20	3	9	12	18	....	....	....	....
2004-05	Medicine Hat	WHL	52	15	33	48	99	....	....	....	....	....	....	....	....	....	12	3	3	6	16	....	....	....	....
2005-06	**Chicago**	**NHL**	**1**	**0**	**0**	**0**	**0**	**0**	**0**	**0**	**1**	**0.0**	**0**	**0**	**0.0**	**11:02**	....	....	....	....	....	....	....	....	....
	Medicine Hat	WHL	26	5	13	18	63	....	....	....	....	....	....	....	....	....	13	4	8	12	*59	....	....	....	....
2006-07	**Chicago**	**NHL**	**35**	**1**	**7**	**8**	**44**	**1**	**0**	**0**	**38**	**2.6**	**–12**	**0**	**0.0**	**19:19**	....	....	....	....	....	....	....	....	....
	Norfolk Admirals	AHL	34	5	10	15	53	....	....	....	....	....	....	....	....	....	6	1	3	4	13	....	....	....	....
2007-08	**Chicago**	**NHL**	**45**	**6**	**12**	**18**	**52**	**2**	**0**	**0**	**42**	**14.3**	**–3**	**0**	**0.0**	**17:12**	....	....	....	....	....	....	....	....	....
	Rockford IceHogs	AHL	29	8	11	19	67	....	....	....	....	....	....	....	....	....	....	....	....	....	....	....	....	....	....
2008-09	**Chicago**	**NHL**	**68**	**6**	**34**	**40**	**65**	**5**	**0**	**1**	**101**	**5.9**	**–6**	**1**	**0.0**	**18:20**	**17**	**3**	**6**	**9**	**2**	**0**	**0**	**0**	**16:39**
	Rockford IceHogs	AHL	7	3	2	5	6	....	....	....	....	....	....	....	....	....	....	....	....	....	....	....	....	....	....
2009-10	**Chicago**	**NHL**	**51**	**4**	**10**	**14**	**58**	**3**	**0**	**1**	**74**	**5.4**	**7**	**0**	**0.0**	**13:06**	....	....	....	....	....	....	....	....	....
	Minnesota	**NHL**	**19**	**1**	**6**	**7**	**10**	**1**	**0**	**0**	**31**	**3.2**	**–2**	**0**	**0.0**	**22:02**	....	....	....	....	....	....	....	....	....
2010-11	**Minnesota**	**NHL**	**52**	**1**	**4**	**5**	**34**	**0**	**0**	**1**	**44**	**2.3**	**–10**	**0**	**0.0**	**16:24**	....	....	....	....	....	....	....	....	....
2011-12	**Edmonton**	**NHL**	**25**	**2**	**0**	**2**	**23**	**1**	**0**	**1**	**35**	**5.7**	**0**	**0**	**0.0**	**18:22**	....	....	....	....	....	....	....	....	....
2012-13	Texas Stars	AHL	23	3	5	8	24	....	....	....	....	....	....	....	....	....	....	....	....	....	....	....	....	....	....
	Vancouver	**NHL**	**14**	**0**	**2**	**2**	**4**	**0**	**0**	**0**	**19**	**0.0**	**–3**	**0**	**0.0**	**14:12**	....	....	....	....	....	....	....	....	....
	NHL Totals		**310**	**21**	**75**	**96**	**290**	**13**	**0**	**4**	**385**	**5.5**		**1**	**0.0**	**17:07**	**17**	**3**	**6**	**9**	**2**	**0**	**0**	**0**	**16:39**

Traded to **Minnesota** by **Chicago** for Kim Johnsson and Nick Leddy, February 12, 2010. Signed as a free agent by **Edmonton**, July 1, 2011. • Missed majority of 2011-12 due to ankle injury at Boston, November 11, 2011. Signed as a free agent by **Texas** (AHL), September 28, 2012. Signed as a free agent by **Vancouver**, January 13, 2012. • Missed majority of 2012-13 a a healthy reserve.

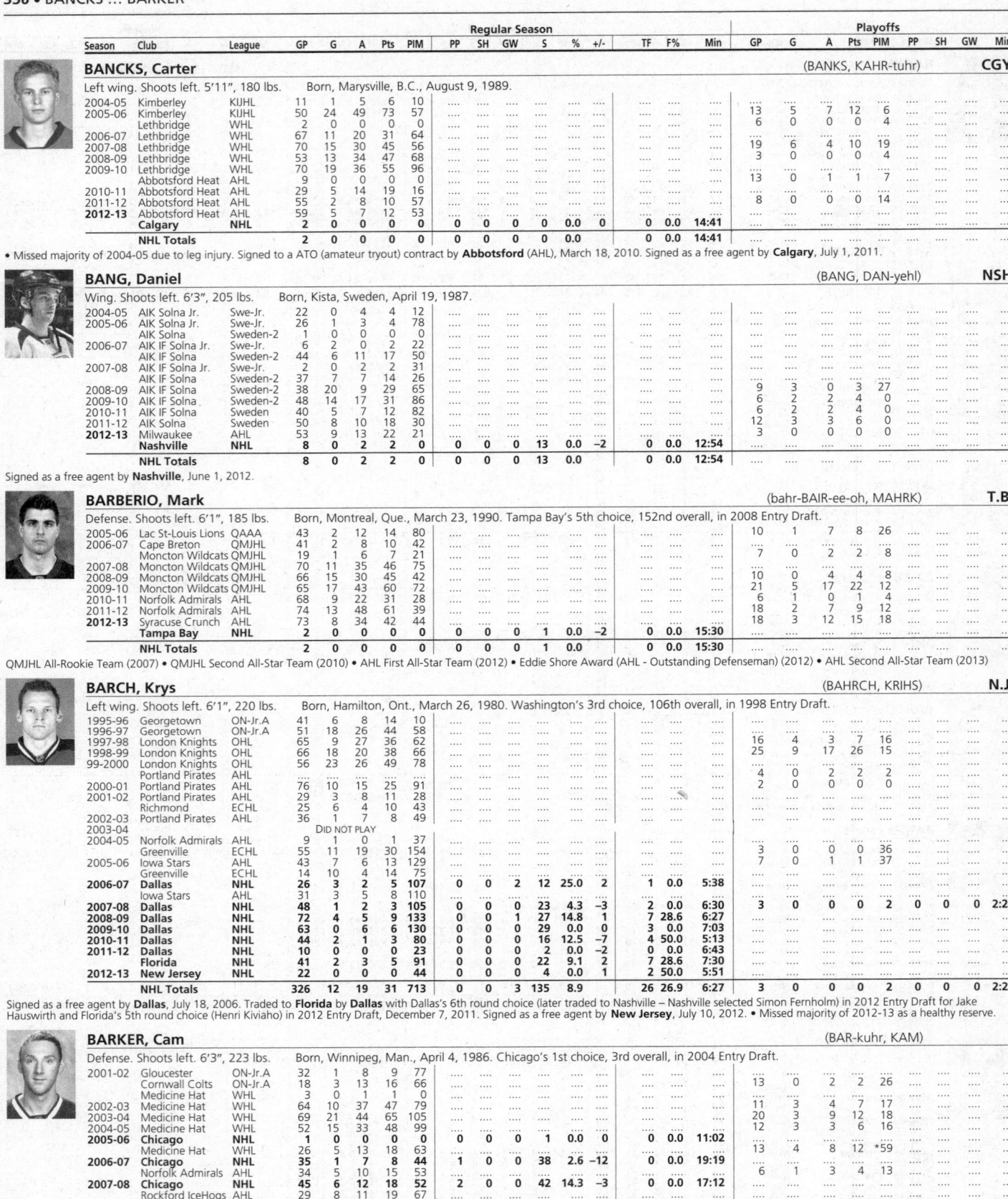

BARRIE, Tyson — (BAIR-ree, TIGH-suhn) — COL

Defense. Shoots right. 5'10", 191 lbs. Born, Victoria, B.C., July 26, 1991. Colorado's 4th choice, 64th overall, in 2009 Entry Draft.

			Regular Season														Playoffs								
Season	Club	League	GP	G	A	Pts	PIM	PP	SH	GW	S	%	+/-	TF	F%	Min	GP	G	A	Pts	PIM	PP	SH	GW	Min
2006-07	Juan de Fuca	Minor-BC	72	43	87	130	....	....	....	....	....	....	....	....	....	....	....	....	....	....	....	....	....	....	....
	Kelowna Rockets	WHL	7	0	3	3	2	....	....	....	....	....	....	....	....	....	....	....	....	....	....	....	....	....	....
2007-08	Kelowna Rockets	WHL	64	9	34	43	32	....	....	....	....	....	....	....	....	....	7	1	3	4	0	....	....	....	....
2008-09	Kelowna Rockets	WHL	68	12	40	52	31	....	....	....	....	....	....	....	....	....	22	4	14	18	12	....	....	....	....
2009-10	Kelowna Rockets	WHL	63	19	53	72	31	....	....	....	....	....	....	....	....	....	12	3	8	11	6	....	....	....	....
2010-11	Kelowna Rockets	WHL	54	11	47	58	34	....	....	....	....	....	....	....	....	....	10	2	9	11	8	....	....	....	....
2011-12	**Colorado**	**NHL**	**10**	**0**	**0**	**0**	**0**	**0**	**0**	**0**	**15**	**0.0**	**–2**	**0**	**0.0**	**17:39**	....	....	....	....	....	....	....	....	....
	Lake Erie	AHL	49	5	27	32	24	....	....	....	....	....	....	....	....	....	....	....	....	....	....	....	....	....	....
2012-13	Lake Erie	AHL	38	7	22	29	7	....	....	....	....	....	....	....	....	....	....	....	....	....	....	....	....	....	....
	Colorado	**NHL**	**32**	**2**	**11**	**13**	**10**	**1**	**0**	**1**	**58**	**3.4**	**–11**	**0**	**0.0**	**21:35**	....	....	....	....	....	....	....	....	....
	NHL Totals		**42**	**2**	**11**	**13**	**10**	**1**	**0**	**1**	**73**	**2.7**		**0**	**0.0**	**20:39**	....	....	....	....	....	....	....	....	....

Canadian Major Junior All-Rookie Team (2008) • WHL West First All-Star Team (2010, 2011) • WHL Defenseman of the Year (2010) • Canadian Major Junior Second All-Star Team (2010)

BARTKOWSKI, Matt — (bahrt-KOW-skee, MATT) — BOS

Defense. Shoots left. 6'1", 196 lbs. Born, Pittsburgh, PA, June 4, 1988. Florida's 5th choice, 190th overall, in 2008 Entry Draft.

Season	Club	League	GP	G	A	Pts	PIM	PP	SH	GW	S	%	+/-	TF	F%	Min	GP	G	A	Pts	PIM	PP	SH	GW	Min
2006-07	Lincoln Stars	USHL	57	3	6	9	95	....	....	....	....	....	....	....	....	....	3	0	0	0	2	....	....	....	....
2007-08	Lincoln Stars	USHL	60	4	37	41	135	....	....	....	....	....	....	....	....	....	8	1	4	5	10	....	....	....	....
2008-09	Ohio State	CCHA	41	5	15	20	46	....	....	....	....	....	....	....	....	....	....	....	....	....	....	....	....	....	....
2009-10	Ohio State	CCHA	39	6	12	18	*99	....	....	....	....	....	....	....	....	....	....	....	....	....	....	....	....	....	....
2010-11	**Boston**	**NHL**	**6**	**0**	**0**	**0**	**4**	**0**	**0**	**0**	**2**	**0.0**	**–1**	**0**	**0.0**	**9:10**	....	....	....	....	....	....	....	....	....
	Providence Bruins	AHL	69	5	18	23	42	....	....	....	....	....	....	....	....	....	....	....	....	....	....	....	....	....	....
2011-12	**Boston**	**NHL**	**3**	**0**	**0**	**0**	**0**	**0**	**0**	**0**	**0**	**0.0**	**–2**	**0**	**0.0**	**6:08**	....	....	....	....	....	....	....	....	....
	Providence Bruins	AHL	50	3	19	22	38	....	....	....	....	....	....	....	....	....	....	....	....	....	....	....	....	....	....
2012-13	Providence Bruins	AHL	56	3	21	24	56	....	....	....	....	....	....	....	....	....	5	0	5	5	4	....	....	....	....
	Boston	**NHL**	**11**	**0**	**2**	**2**	**6**	**0**	**0**	**0**	**9**	**0.0**	**0**	**0**	**0.0**	**13:29**	**7**	**1**	**1**	**2**	**4**	**0**	**0**	**0**	**19:47**
	NHL Totals		**20**	**0**	**2**	**2**	**10**	**0**	**0**	**0**	**11**	**0.0**		**0**	**0.0**	**11:05**	**7**	**1**	**1**	**2**	**4**	**0**	**0**	**0**	**19:47**

CCHA All-Rookie Team (2009) • USHL First All-Star Team (2008)

Traded to **Boston** by **Florida** with Dennis Seidenberg for Byron Bitz, Craig Weller and Tampa Bay's 2nd round choice (previously acquired, Florida selected Alexander Petrovic) in 2010 Entry Draft, March 3, 2010.

BARTLEY, Victor — (BAR-tlee, WAYD) — NSH

Defense. Shoots left. 6', 212 lbs. Born, Maple Ridge, B.C., February 17, 1988.

Season	Club	League	GP	G	A	Pts	PIM	PP	SH	GW	S	%	+/-	TF	F%	Min	GP	G	A	Pts	PIM	PP	SH	GW	Min
2003-04	Delta Ice Hawks	PIJHL	42	2	25	27	66	....	....	....	....	....	....	....	....	....	....	....	....	....	....	....	....	....	....
	Kamloops Blazers	WHL	3	0	0	0	0	....	....	....	....	....	....	....	....	....	....	....	....	....	....	....	....	....	....
2004-05	Kamloops Blazers	WHL	68	4	6	10	58	....	....	....	....	....	....	....	....	....	5	0	3	3	4	....	....	....	....
2005-06	Kamloops Blazers	WHL	65	3	24	27	114	....	....	....	....	....	....	....	....	....	....	....	....	....	....	....	....	....	....
2006-07	Kamloops Blazers	WHL	67	4	39	43	104	....	....	....	....	....	....	....	....	....	4	0	2	2	8	....	....	....	....
2007-08	Kamloops Blazers	WHL	36	3	15	18	51	....	....	....	....	....	....	....	....	....	....	....	....	....	....	....	....	....	....
	Regina Pats	WHL	25	7	17	24	42	....	....	....	....	....	....	....	....	....	6	1	3	4	8	....	....	....	....
2008-09	Regina Pats	WHL	72	15	31	46	97	....	....	....	....	....	....	....	....	....	....	....	....	....	....	....	....	....	....
	Providence Bruins	AHL	10	0	0	0	6	....	....	....	....	....	....	....	....	....	....	....	....	....	....	....	....	....	....
2009-10	Bridgeport	AHL	8	2	0	2	6	....	....	....	....	....	....	....	....	....	....	....	....	....	....	....	....	....	....
	Utah Grizzlies	ECHL	21	2	11	13	21	....	....	....	....	....	....	....	....	....	....	....	....	....	....	....	....	....	....
2010-11	Rogle	Sweden-2	52	11	23	34	56	....	....	....	....	....	....	....	....	....	....	....	....	....	....	....	....	....	....
2011-12	Milwaukee	AHL	76	9	30	39	64	....	....	....	....	....	....	....	....	....	1	1	0	1	0	....	....	....	....
2012-13	Milwaukee	AHL	54	7	19	26	35	....	....	....	....	....	....	....	....	....	2	0	1	1	0	....	....	....	....
	Nashville	**NHL**	**24**	**0**	**7**	**7**	**6**	**0**	**0**	**0**	**19**	**0.0**	**2**	**0**	**0.0**	**19:33**	....	....	....	....	....	....	....	....	....
	NHL Totals		**24**	**0**	**7**	**7**	**6**	**0**	**0**	**0**	**19**	**0.0**		**0**	**0.0**	**19:33**	....	....	....	....	....	....	....	....	....

Signed as a free agent by **Rogle** (Sweden-2), May 26, 2010. Signed as a free agent by **Nashville**, May 24, 2011.

BARTULIS, Oskars — (bahr-TEW-lihs, AWZ-kahrz)

Defense. Shoots left. 6'2", 184 lbs. Born, Ogre, Latvia, January 21, 1987. Philadelphia's 2nd choice, 91st overall, in 2005 Entry Draft.

Season	Club	League	GP	G	A	Pts	PIM	PP	SH	GW	S	%	+/-	TF	F%	Min	GP	G	A	Pts	PIM	PP	SH	GW	Min
2001-02	Prizma '83 Riga	EEHL-B	3	1	0	1	2	....	....	....	....	....	....	....	....	....	....	....	....	....	....	....	....	....	....
	Prizma '83 Riga	Latvia	6	0	1	1	2	....	....	....	....	....	....	....	....	....	....	....	....	....	....	....	....	....	....
2002-03	Prizma '83 Riga	EEHL-B	12	5	5	10	12	....	....	....	....	....	....	....	....	....	....	....	....	....	....	....	....	....	....
	Vilki Riga	Latvia	....	0	1	1	12	....	....	....	....	....	....	....	....	....	....	....	....	....	....	....	....	....	....
2003-04	CSKA Moscow 2	Russia-3	65	3	9	12	....	....	....	....	....	....	....	....	....	....	....	....	....	....	....	....	....	....	....
2004-05	Moncton Wildcats	QMJHL	62	5	19	24	55	....	....	....	....	....	....	....	....	....	12	1	1	2	16	....	....	....	....
2005-06	Moncton Wildcats	QMJHL	54	6	25	31	84	....	....	....	....	....	....	....	....	....	21	1	9	10	22	....	....	....	....
2006-07	Cape Breton	QMJHL	55	13	35	48	52	....	....	....	....	....	....	....	....	....	16	3	9	12	24	....	....	....	....
2007-08	Philadelphia	AHL	57	1	20	21	42	....	....	....	....	....	....	....	....	....	....	....	....	....	....	....	....	....	....
2008-09	Philadelphia	AHL	80	2	11	13	59	....	....	....	....	....	....	....	....	....	4	0	0	0	4	....	....	....	....
2009-10	**Philadelphia**	**NHL**	**53**	**1**	**8**	**9**	**28**	**0**	**0**	**0**	**26**	**3.8**	**–12**	**0**	**0.0**	**13:59**	**7**	**0**	**0**	**0**	**4**	**0**	**0**	**0**	**6:44**
	Adirondack	AHL	12	2	2	4	14	....	....	....	....	....	....	....	....	....	....	....	....	....	....	....	....	....	....
	Latvia	Olympics	4	0	0	0	2	....	....	....	....	....	....	....	....	....	....	....	....	....	....	....	....	....	....
2010-11	**Philadelphia**	**NHL**	**13**	**0**	**0**	**0**	**4**	**0**	**0**	**0**	**7**	**0.0**	**–4**	**0**	**0.0**	**13:01**	....	....	....	....	....	....	....	....	....
	Adirondack	AHL	4	0	1	1	2	....	....	....	....	....	....	....	....	....	....	....	....	....	....	....	....	....	....
2011-12	Adirondack	AHL	36	1	10	11	20	....	....	....	....	....	....	....	....	....	....	....	....	....	....	....	....	....	....
2012-13	Donetsk	KHL	40	3	4	7	88	....	....	....	....	....	....	....	....	....	4	0	0	0	4	....	....	....	....
	NHL Totals		**66**	**1**	**8**	**9**	**32**	**0**	**0**	**0**	**33**	**3.0**		**0**	**0.0**	**13:48**	**7**	**0**	**0**	**0**	**4**	**0**	**0**	**0**	**6:44**

QMJHL All-Rookie Team (2005) • Canadian Major Junior All-Rookie Team (2005) • QMJHL Second All-Star Team (2007)

• Missed majority of 2010-11 and 2011-12 due to recurring shoulder injury and as a healthy reserve. Signed as a free agent by **Donetsk** (KHL), August 29, 2012.

BASS, Cody — (BAS, KOH-dee) — CBJ

Center. Shoots right. 6', 205 lbs. Born, Owen Sound, Ont., January 7, 1987. Ottawa's 3rd choice, 95th overall, in 2005 Entry Draft.

Season	Club	League	GP	G	A	Pts	PIM	PP	SH	GW	S	%	+/-	TF	F%	Min	GP	G	A	Pts	PIM	PP	SH	GW	Min
2003-04	Mississauga	OHL	61	3	7	10	30	....	....	....	....	....	....	....	....	....	24	2	3	5	21	....	....	....	....
2004-05	Mississauga	OHL	66	11	17	28	103	....	....	....	....	....	....	....	....	....	5	1	1	2	8	....	....	....	....
2005-06	Mississauga	OHL	67	16	25	41	152	....	....	....	....	....	....	....	....	....	....	....	....	....	....	....	....	....	....
	Binghamton	AHL	9	1	0	1	2	....	....	....	....	....	....	....	....	....	....	....	....	....	....	....	....	....	....
2006-07	Mississauga	OHL	23	5	11	16	37	....	....	....	....	....	....	....	....	....	....	....	....	....	....	....	....	....	....
	Saginaw Spirit	OHL	30	5	24	29	49	....	....	....	....	....	....	....	....	....	6	1	2	3	10	....	....	....	....
	Binghamton	AHL	5	0	2	2	9	....	....	....	....	....	....	....	....	....	....	....	....	....	....	....	....	....	....
2007-08	**Ottawa**	**NHL**	**21**	**2**	**2**	**4**	**19**	**0**	**1**	**1**	**12**	**16.7**	**–1**	**73**	**43.8**	**5:19**	**4**	**1**	**0**	**1**	**6**	**0**	**0**	**0**	**8:21**
	Binghamton	AHL	24	3	5	8	44	....	....	....	....	....	....	....	....	....	....	....	....	....	....	....	....	....	....
2008-09	**Ottawa**	**NHL**	**12**	**0**	**0**	**0**	**15**	**0**	**0**	**0**	**5**	**0.0**	**–2**	**50**	**42.0**	**5:41**	....	....	....	....	....	....	....	....	....
	Binghamton	AHL	18	1	1	2	41	....	....	....	....	....	....	....	....	....	....	....	....	....	....	....	....	....	....
2009-10	Binghamton	AHL	57	5	6	11	109	....	....	....	....	....	....	....	....	....	....	....	....	....	....	....	....	....	....
2010-11	**Ottawa**	**NHL**	**1**	**0**	**0**	**0**	**0**	**0**	**0**	**0**	**0**	**0.0**	**0**	**0**	**0.0**	**7:09**	....	....	....	....	....	....	....	....	....
	Binghamton	AHL	58	6	9	15	111	....	....	....	....	....	....	....	....	....	18	2	2	4	24	....	....	....	....
2011-12	**Columbus**	**NHL**	**14**	**0**	**1**	**1**	**32**	**0**	**0**	**0**	**13**	**0.0**	**0**	**8**	**62.5**	**9:05**	....	....	....	....	....	....	....	....	....
	Springfield	AHL	23	5	6	11	43	....	....	....	....	....	....	....	....	....	....	....	....	....	....	....	....	....	....
2012-13	Springfield	AHL	18	2	5	7	54	....	....	....	....	....	....	....	....	....	8	2	2	4	26	....	....	....	....
	NHL Totals		**48**	**2**	**3**	**5**	**66**	**0**	**1**	**1**	**30**	**6.7**		**131**	**44.3**	**6:33**	**4**	**1**	**0**	**1**	**6**	**0**	**0**	**0**	**8:21**

Yanick Dupre Memorial Award (AHL - Outstanding Humanitarian Contribution) (2011)

• Missed remainder of 2008-09 due to shoulder injury at Calgary, December 27, 2008. Signed as a free agent by **Columbus**. July 13, 2011. • Missed majority of 2011-12 due to shoulder injury at Springfield (AHL) practice, December 19, 2011. • Missed majority of 2012-13 due to injury vs. Portland (AHL), October 28, 2012.

BEAGLE, Jay
(BEE-guhl, JAY) **WSH**

Right wing. Shoots right. 6'3", 215 lbs. Born, Calgary, Alta., October 16, 1985.

			Regular Season														Playoffs								
Season	Club	League	GP	G	A	Pts	PIM	PP	SH	GW	S	%	+/-	TF	F%	Min	GP	G	A	Pts	PIM	PP	SH	GW	Min
2003-04	Calgary Royals	AJHL	58	10	27	37	100	....	....	....	....	....	....	....	....	....	....	....	....	....	....	....	....	....	....
2004-05	Calgary Royals	AJHL	64	28	42	70	114	....	....	....	....	....	....	....	....	....	....	....	....	....	....	....	....	....	....
2005-06	Alaska Anchorage	WCHA	31	4	6	10	40	....	....	....	....	....	....	....	....	....	....	....	....	....	....	....	....	....	....
2006-07	Alaska Anchorage	WCHA	36	10	10	20	93	....	....	....	....	....	....	....	....	....	....	....	....	....	....	....	....	....	....
	Idaho Steelheads	ECHL	8	2	8	10	4	....	....	....	....	....	....	....	....	....	18	1	2	3	22	....	....	....	....
2007-08	Hershey Bears	AHL	64	19	18	37	41	....	....	....	....	....	....	....	....	....	5	0	1	1	2	....	....	....	....
2008-09	**Washington**	**NHL**	**3**	**0**	**0**	**0**	**2**	**0**	**0**	**0**	**5**	**0.0**	**–3**	**13**	**38.5**	**7:36**	**4**	**0**	**0**	**0**	**0**	**0**	**0**	**0**	**3:33**
	Hershey Bears	AHL	47	4	5	9	37	....	....	....	....	....	....	....	....	....	18	1	3	4	16	....	....	....	....
2009-10	**Washington**	**NHL**	**7**	**1**	**1**	**2**	**2**	**0**	**0**	**0**	**10**	**10.0**	**–1**	**31**	**54.8**	**9:16**	....	....	....	....	....	....	....	....	....
	Hershey Bears	AHL	66	16	19	35	25	....	....	....	....	....	....	....	....	....	21	2	6	8	0	....	....	....	....
2010-11	**Washington**	**NHL**	**31**	**2**	**1**	**3**	**8**	**0**	**0**	**2**	**27**	**7.4**	**–2**	**105**	**55.2**	**10:30**	....	....	....	....	....	....	....	....	....
	Hershey Bears	AHL	34	8	6	14	26	....	....	....	....	....	....	....	....	....	....	....	....	....	....	....	....	....	....
2011-12	**Washington**	**NHL**	**41**	**4**	**1**	**5**	**23**	**0**	**0**	**0**	**49**	**8.2**	**–2**	**215**	**57.7**	**11:51**	**12**	**1**	**1**	**2**	**4**	**0**	**0**	**0**	**18:26**
2012-13	**Washington**	**NHL**	**48**	**2**	**6**	**8**	**14**	**0**	**0**	**1**	**56**	**3.6**	**–1**	**444**	**56.1**	**12:06**	**7**	**1**	**0**	**1**	**4**	**0**	**0**	**0**	**9:39**
	NHL Totals		**130**	**9**	**9**	**18**	**49**	**0**	**0**	**3**	**147**	**6.1**		**808**	**56.1**	**11:23**	**23**	**2**	**1**	**3**	**8**	**0**	**0**	**0**	**13:10**

Signed as a free agent by **Washington**, March 26, 2008.

BEAUCHEMIN, Francois
(boh-sheh-MEH, frahn-SWUH) **ANA**

Defense. Shoots left. 6'1", 207 lbs. Born, Sorel, Que., June 4, 1980. Montreal's 3rd choice, 75th overall, in 1998 Entry Draft.

Season	Club	League	GP	G	A	Pts	PIM	PP	SH	GW	S	%	+/-	TF	F%	Min	GP	G	A	Pts	PIM	PP	SH	GW	Min
1995-96	Richelieu Riverains	QAAA	40	9	23	32	59	....	....	....	....	....	....	....	....	....	....	....	....	....	....	....	....	....	....
1996-97	Laval Titan	QMJHL	66	7	20	27	112	....	....	....	....	....	....	....	....	....	3	0	0	0	2	....	....	....	....
1997-98	Laval Titan	QMJHL	70	12	35	47	132	....	....	....	....	....	....	....	....	....	16	1	3	4	23	....	....	....	....
1998-99	Acadie-Bathurst	QMJHL	31	4	17	21	53	....	....	....	....	....	....	....	....	....	23	2	16	18	55	....	....	....	....
99-2000	Acadie-Bathurst	QMJHL	38	11	36	47	64	....	....	....	....	....	....	....	....	....	....	....	....	....	....	....	....	....	....
	Moncton Wildcats	QMJHL	33	8	31	39	35	....	....	....	....	....	....	....	....	....	16	2	11	13	14	....	....	....	....
2000-01	Quebec Citadelles	AHL	56	3	6	9	44	....	....	....	....	....	....	....	....	....	....	....	....	....	....	....	....	....	....
2001-02	Quebec Citadelles	AHL	56	8	11	19	88	....	....	....	....	....	....	....	....	....	3	0	1	1	0	....	....	....	....
	Mississippi	ECHL	7	1	3	4	2	....	....	....	....	....	....	....	....	....	....	....	....	....	....	....	....	....	....
2002-03	**Montreal**	**NHL**	**1**	**0**	**0**	**0**	**0**	**0**	**0**	**0**	**1**	**0.0**	**–1**	**0**	**0.0**	**17:11**	....	....	....	....	....	....	....	....	....
	Hamilton	AHL	75	7	21	28	92	....	....	....	....	....	....	....	....	....	23	1	9	10	16	....	....	....	....
2003-04	Hamilton	AHL	77	9	27	36	57	....	....	....	....	....	....	....	....	....	10	2	4	6	18	....	....	....	....
2004-05	Syracuse Crunch	AHL	72	3	27	30	55	....	....	....	....	....	....	....	....	....	....	....	....	....	....	....	....	....	....
2005-06	**Columbus**	**NHL**	**11**	**0**	**2**	**2**	**11**	**0**	**0**	**0**	**16**	**0.0**	**–6**	**0**	**0.0**	**17:16**	....	....	....	....	....	....	....	....	....
	Anaheim	**NHL**	**61**	**8**	**26**	**34**	**41**	**4**	**0**	**3**	**121**	**6.6**	**8**	**1**	**0.0**	**24:14**	**16**	**3**	**6**	**9**	**11**	**3**	**0**	**0**	**27:26**
2006-07♦	**Anaheim**	**NHL**	**71**	**7**	**21**	**28**	**49**	**2**	**0**	**0**	**128**	**5.5**	**7**	**1**	**0.0**	**25:28**	**20**	**4**	**4**	**8**	**16**	**4**	**0**	**0**	**30:33**
2007-08	**Anaheim**	**NHL**	**82**	**2**	**19**	**21**	**59**	**0**	**0**	**2**	**144**	**1.4**	**–9**	**1**	**0.0**	**25:32**	**6**	**0**	**0**	**0**	**26**	**0**	**0**	**0**	**21:02**
2008-09	**Anaheim**	**NHL**	**20**	**4**	**1**	**5**	**12**	**0**	**0**	**2**	**45**	**8.9**	**–3**	**0**	**0.0**	**24:54**	**13**	**1**	**0**	**1**	**15**	**0**	**0**	**0**	**21:25**
2009-10	**Toronto**	**NHL**	**82**	**5**	**21**	**26**	**33**	**4**	**0**	**1**	**170**	**2.9**	**–13**	**4**	**75.0**	**25:28**	....	....	....	....	....	....	....	....	....
2010-11	**Toronto**	**NHL**	**54**	**2**	**10**	**12**	**16**	**0**	**0**	**0**	**76**	**2.6**	**–4**	**0**	**0.0**	**23:45**	....	....	....	....	....	....	....	....	....
	Anaheim	**NHL**	**27**	**3**	**2**	**5**	**16**	**1**	**0**	**0**	**30**	**10.0**	**–4**	**1**	**0.0**	**21:42**	**6**	**0**	**2**	**2**	**2**	**0**	**0**	**0**	**23:32**
2011-12	**Anaheim**	**NHL**	**82**	**8**	**14**	**22**	**48**	**3**	**0**	**1**	**139**	**5.8**	**–14**	**2**	**50.0**	**25:33**	....	....	....	....	....	....	....	....	....
2012-13	**Anaheim**	**NHL**	**48**	**6**	**18**	**24**	**22**	**1**	**0**	**0**	**74**	**8.1**	**19**	**0**	**0.0**	**23:27**	**7**	**2**	**4**	**6**	**4**	**1**	**0**	**0**	**25:22**
	NHL Totals		**539**	**45**	**134**	**179**	**307**	**15**	**0**	**9**	**944**	**4.8**		**10**	**40.0**	**24:36**	**68**	**10**	**16**	**26**	**74**	**8**	**0**	**0**	**26:05**

QMJHL All-Rookie Team (1997) • QMJHL Second All-Star Team (2000) • NHL Second All-Star Team (2013)

Claimed on waivers by **Columbus** from **Montreal**, September 15, 2004. Traded to **Anaheim** by **Columbus** with Tyler Wright for Sergei Fedorov and Anaheim's 5th round choice (Maxime Frechette) in 2006 Entry Draft, November 15, 2005. • Missed remainder of 2008-09 due to knee injury vs. Nashville, November 14, 2008. Signed as a free agent by **Toronto**, July 6, 2009. Traded to **Anaheim** by **Toronto** for Joffrey Lupul, Jake Gardiner and Anaheim's 4th round choice (later traded to San Jose – San Jose selected Fredrik Bergvik) in 2013 Entry Draft, February 9, 2011.

BEAULIEU, Nathan
(BOI-loh, NAY-thun) **MTL**

Defense. Shoots left. 6'2", 191 lbs. Born, Strathroy, Ont., December 5, 1992. Montreal's 1st choice, 17th overall, in 2011 Entry Draft.

Season	Club	League	GP	G	A	Pts	PIM	PP	SH	GW	S	%	+/-	TF	F%	Min	GP	G	A	Pts	PIM	PP	SH	GW	Min
2007-08	Saint John Vito's	NBPEI	33	1	14	15	45	....	....	....	....	....	....	....	....	....	4	1	2	3	6	....	....	....	....
2008-09	Saint John	QMJHL	49	2	8	10	14	....	....	....	....	....	....	....	....	....	4	0	0	0	2	....	....	....	....
2009-10	Saint John	QMJHL	66	12	33	45	40	....	....	....	....	....	....	....	....	....	21	4	12	16	22	....	....	....	....
2010-11	Saint John	QMJHL	65	12	33	45	52	....	....	....	....	....	....	....	....	....	19	4	13	17	26	....	....	....	....
2011-12	Saint John	QMJHL	53	11	41	52	100	....	....	....	....	....	....	....	....	....	17	4	11	15	32	....	....	....	....
2012-13	Hamilton	AHL	67	7	24	31	63	....	....	....	....	....	....	....	....	....	....	....	....	....	....	....	....	....	....
	Montreal	**NHL**	**6**	**0**	**2**	**2**	**0**	**0**	**0**	**0**	**8**	**0.0**	**5**	**0**	**0.0**	**15:22**	....	....	....	....	....	....	....	....	....
	NHL Totals		**6**	**0**	**2**	**2**	**0**	**0**	**0**	**0**	**8**	**0.0**		**0**	**0.0**	**15:22**	....	....	....	....	....	....	....	....	....

Memorial Cup All-Star Team (2011)

BECK, Taylor
(BEHK, TAY-luhr) **NSH**

Right wing. Shoots right. 6'2", 208 lbs. Born, St. Catharines, Ont., May 13, 1991. Nashville's 4th choice, 70th overall, in 2009 Entry Draft.

Season	Club	League	GP	G	A	Pts	PIM	PP	SH	GW	S	%	+/-	TF	F%	Min	GP	G	A	Pts	PIM	PP	SH	GW	Min
2006-07	Niag. Falls Thunder	Minor-ON	69	64	75	139	76	....	....	....	....	....	....	....	....	....	....	....	....	....	....	....	....	....	....
2007-08	Guelph Storm	OHL	56	7	14	21	43	....	....	....	....	....	....	....	....	....	7	0	0	0	4	....	....	....	....
2008-09	Guelph Storm	OHL	67	22	36	58	36	....	....	....	....	....	....	....	....	....	4	0	0	0	2	....	....	....	....
2009-10	Guelph Storm	OHL	61	39	54	93	54	....	....	....	....	....	....	....	....	....	5	3	3	6	2	....	....	....	....
2010-11	Guelph Storm	OHL	62	42	53	95	60	....	....	....	....	....	....	....	....	....	6	3	5	8	10	....	....	....	....
	Milwaukee	AHL	4	0	1	1	0	....	....	....	....	....	....	....	....	....	8	2	0	2	2	....	....	....	....
2011-12	Milwaukee	AHL	74	16	24	40	32	....	....	....	....	....	....	....	....	....	3	0	1	1	2	....	....	....	....
2012-13	Milwaukee	AHL	50	11	30	41	28	....	....	....	....	....	....	....	....	....	2	0	1	1	2	....	....	....	....
	Nashville	**NHL**	**16**	**3**	**4**	**7**	**2**	**1**	**0**	**0**	**39**	**7.7**	**0**	**9**	**66.7**	**16:06**	....	....	....	....	....	....	....	....	....
	NHL Totals		**16**	**3**	**4**	**7**	**2**	**1**	**0**	**0**	**39**	**7.7**		**9**	**66.7**	**16:06**	....	....	....	....	....	....	....	....	....

OHL Second All-Star Team (2010)

BEGIN, Steve
(bay-ZHIN, STEEV) **CGY**

Center. Shoots left. 6', 192 lbs. Born, Trois-Rivieres, Que., June 14, 1978. Calgary's 3rd choice, 40th overall, in 1996 Entry Draft.

Season	Club	League	GP	G	A	Pts	PIM	PP	SH	GW	S	%	+/-	TF	F%	Min	GP	G	A	Pts	PIM	PP	SH	GW	Min
1993-94	Cap-d-Madelaine	QAAA	8	0	1	1	6	....	....	....	....	....	....	....	....	....	2	0	0	0	0	....	....	....	....
1994-95	Cap-d-Madelaine	QAAA	35	9	15	24	48	....	....	....	....	....	....	....	....	....	3	0	0	0	2	....	....	....	....
1995-96	Val-d'Or Foreurs	QMJHL	64	13	23	36	218	....	....	....	....	....	....	....	....	....	13	1	3	4	33	....	....	....	....
1996-97	Val-d'Or Foreurs	QMJHL	58	13	33	46	207	....	....	....	....	....	....	....	....	....	10	0	3	3	8	....	....	....	....
	Saint John Flames	AHL	....	....	....	....	....	....	....	....	....	....	....	....	....	....	4	0	2	2	6	....	....	....	....
1997-98	**Calgary**	**NHL**	**5**	**0**	**0**	**0**	**23**	**0**	**0**	**0**	**2**	**0.0**	**0**				....	....	....	....	....	....	....	....	....
	Val-d'Or Foreurs	QMJHL	35	18	17	35	73	....	....	....	....	....	....	....	....	....	15	2	12	14	34	....	....	....	....
1998-99	Saint John Flames	AHL	73	11	9	20	156	....	....	....	....	....	....	....	....	....	7	2	0	2	18	....	....	....	....
99-2000	**Calgary**	**NHL**	**13**	**1**	**1**	**2**	**18**	**0**	**0**	**0**	**3**	**33.3**	**–3**	**19**	**47.4**	**7:13**	....	....	....	....	....	....	....	....	....
	Saint John Flames	AHL	47	13	12	25	99	....	....	....	....	....	....	....	....	....	....	....	....	....	....	....	....	....	....
2000-01	**Calgary**	**NHL**	**4**	**0**	**0**	**0**	**21**	**0**	**0**	**0**	**3**	**0.0**	**0**	**0**	**0.0**	**6:04**	....	....	....	....	....	....	....	....	....
	Saint John Flames	AHL	58	14	14	28	109	....	....	....	....	....	....	....	....	....	19	10	7	17	18	....	....	....	....
2001-02	**Calgary**	**NHL**	**51**	**7**	**5**	**12**	**79**	**1**	**0**	**0**	**65**	**10.8**	**–3**	**129**	**53.5**	**9:25**	....	....	....	....	....	....	....	....	....
2002-03	**Calgary**	**NHL**	**50**	**3**	**1**	**4**	**51**	**0**	**0**	**1**	**59**	**5.1**	**–7**	**50**	**60.0**	**9:13**	....	....	....	....	....	....	....	....	....
2003-04	**Montreal**	**NHL**	**52**	**10**	**5**	**15**	**41**	**0**	**1**	**1**	**91**	**11.0**	**6**	**436**	**48.6**	**12:32**	**9**	**0**	**1**	**1**	**10**	**0**	**0**	**0**	**12:26**
2004-05	Hamilton	AHL	21	10	3	13	20	....	....	....	....	....	....	....	....	....	4	0	2	2	8	....	....	....	....
2005-06	**Montreal**	**NHL**	**76**	**11**	**12**	**23**	**113**	**1**	**2**	**2**	**134**	**8.2**	**9**	**573**	**50.1**	**14:19**	**2**	**0**	**0**	**0**	**2**	**0**	**0**	**0**	**13:42**
2006-07	**Montreal**	**NHL**	**52**	**5**	**5**	**10**	**46**	**0**	**0**	**0**	**64**	**7.8**	**–6**	**159**	**49.7**	**11:55**	....	....	....	....	....	....	....	....	....
2007-08	**Montreal**	**NHL**	**44**	**3**	**5**	**8**	**48**	**0**	**0**	**0**	**67**	**4.5**	**0**	**69**	**34.8**	**11:38**	**12**	**0**	**3**	**3**	**8**	**0**	**0**	**0**	**12:45**
2008-09	**Montreal**	**NHL**	**42**	**6**	**4**	**10**	**27**	**0**	**0**	**1**	**65**	**9.2**	**–5**	**78**	**53.9**	**10:51**	....	....	....	....	....	....	....	....	....
	Dallas	**NHL**	**20**	**1**	**1**	**2**	**15**	**0**	**0**	**0**	**25**	**4.0**	**–1**	**55**	**41.8**	**10:26**	....	....	....	....	....	....	....	....	....
2009-10	**Boston**	**NHL**	**77**	**5**	**9**	**14**	**53**	**0**	**1**	**2**	**110**	**4.5**	**–7**	**694**	**53.5**	**12:50**	**13**	**1**	**0**	**1**	**10**	**0**	**0**	**0**	**11:57**
2010-11	**Nashville**	**NHL**	**2**	**0**	**0**	**0**	**4**	**0**	**0**	**0**	**2**	**0.0**	**–2**	**0**	**0.0**	**9:48**	....	....	....	....	....	....	....	....	....
	Milwaukee	AHL	36	3	3	6	30	....	....	....	....	....	....	....	....	....	13	3	4	7	12	....	....	....	....

			Regular Season														Playoffs								
Season	Club	League	GP	G	A	Pts	PIM	PP	SH	GW	S	%	+/-	TF	F%	Min	GP	G	A	Pts	PIM	PP	SH	GW	Min
2011-12			DID NOT PLAY – INJURED																						
2012-13	**Calgary**	**NHL**	36	4	4	8	22	0	1	2	31	12.9	–2	117	48.7	8:00	....	....	....	....	....	....	....	....	....
	NHL Totals		524	56	52	108	561	2	5	9	721	7.8		2379	50.6	11:21	36	1	4	5	30	0	0	0	12:26

Jack A. Butterfield Trophy (AHL – Playoff MVP) (2001)

Traded to **Buffalo** by **Calgary** with Chris Drury for Steve Reinprecht and Rhett Warrener, July 3, 2003. Claimed by **Montreal** from **Buffalo** in Waiver Draft, October 3, 2003. Traded to **Dallas** by **Montreal** for Doug Janik, February 26, 2009. Signed as a free agent by **Boston**, July 1, 2009. Signed as a free agent by **Nashville**, October 20, 2010. • Missed majority of 2010-11 and all of 2011-12 due to various injuries. Signed as a free agent by **Calgary**, January 18, 2013.

BELANGER, Eric

(buh-LAWN-zhay, AIR-ihk)

Center. Shoots left. 5'11", 185 lbs. Born, Sherbrooke, Que., December 16, 1977. Los Angeles' 5th choice, 96th overall, in 1996 Entry Draft.

Season	Club	League	GP	G	A	Pts	PIM	PP	SH	GW	S	%	+/-	TF	F%	Min	GP	G	A	Pts	PIM	PP	SH	GW	Min
1993-94	Magog	QAAA	32	19	24	43	24	....	....	....	....	....	....	....	....	....	13	5	6	11	36	....	....	....	....
1994-95	Beauport	QMJHL	71	12	28	40	24	....	....	....	....	....	....	....	....	....	18	5	9	14	25	....	....	....	....
1995-96	Beauport	QMJHL	59	35	48	83	18	....	....	....	....	....	....	....	....	....	20	13	14	27	6	....	....	....	....
1996-97	Beauport	QMJHL	33	16	37	53	32	....	....	....	....	....	....	....	....	....	....	....	....	....	....	....	....	....	....
	Rimouski Oceanic	QMJHL	29	23	41	64	34	....	....	....	....	....	....	....	....	....	4	2	3	5	10	....	....	....	....
1997-98	Fredericton	AHL	56	17	34	51	28	....	....	....	....	....	....	....	....	....	4	2	1	3	2	....	....	....	....
1998-99	Springfield	AHL	33	8	18	26	10	....	....	....	....	....	....	....	....	....	3	0	1	1	2	....	....	....	....
	Long Beach	IHL	1	0	0	0	0	....	....	....	....	....	....	....	....	....	....	....	....	....	....	....	....	....	....
99-2000	Lowell	AHL	65	15	25	40	20	....	....	....	....	....	....	....	....	....	7	3	3	6	2	....	....	....	....
2000-01	**Los Angeles**	**NHL**	62	9	12	21	16	1	2	1	80	11.3	14	849	56.4	13:25	13	1	4	5	2	0	0	1	13:47
	Lowell	AHL	13	8	10	18	4	....	....	....	....	....	....	....	....	....	....	....	....	....	....	....	....	....	....
2001-02	**Los Angeles**	**NHL**	53	8	16	24	21	2	1	1	67	11.9	2	882	57.7	14:33	7	0	0	0	4	0	0	0	12:57
2002-03	**Los Angeles**	**NHL**	62	16	19	35	26	0	3	1	114	14.0	–5	1143	51.8	17:42	....	....	....	....	....	....	....	....	....
2003-04	**Los Angeles**	**NHL**	81	13	20	33	44	0	1	2	132	9.8	–16	1418	53.7	17:01	....	....	....	....	....	....	....	....	....
2004-05	HC Forst Bolzano	Italy	12	13	10	23	20	....	....	....	....	....	....	....	....	....	9	3	7	10	33	....	....	....	....
2005-06	**Los Angeles**	**NHL**	65	17	20	37	62	5	0	1	119	14.3	–5	1179	49.0	17:33	....	....	....	....	....	....	....	....	....
2006-07	**Carolina**	**NHL**	56	8	12	20	14	3	0	1	100	8.0	–2	689	53.4	14:51	....	....	....	....	....	....	....	....	....
	Atlanta	**NHL**	24	9	6	15	12	1	0	0	49	18.4	0	517	52.6	19:29	4	1	0	1	12	1	0	0	16:47
2007-08	**Minnesota**	**NHL**	75	13	24	37	30	7	1	3	115	11.3	–6	1195	49.1	17:13	6	0	0	0	4	0	0	0	18:34
2008-09	**Minnesota**	**NHL**	79	13	23	36	26	4	0	4	147	8.8	–5	1205	52.0	17:50	....	....	....	....	....	....	....	....	....
2009-10	**Minnesota**	**NHL**	60	13	22	35	28	3	0	3	120	10.8	–1	722	57.6	15:45	....	....	....	....	....	....	....	....	....
	Washington	**NHL**	17	2	4	6	4	0	0	0	31	6.5	3	202	52.0	14:40	7	0	1	1	4	0	0	0	14:05
2010-11	**Phoenix**	**NHL**	82	13	27	40	36	1	1	2	127	10.2	11	1297	55.3	17:21	4	0	0	0	2	0	0	0	15:57
2011-12	**Edmonton**	**NHL**	78	4	12	16	32	1	1	0	118	3.4	–13	1007	55.3	14:44	....	....	....	....	....	....	....	....	....
2012-13	**Edmonton**	**NHL**	26	0	3	3	10	0	0	0	31	0.0	–1	378	53.7	14:07	....	....	....	....	....	....	....	....	....
	NHL Totals		820	138	220	358	361	28	10	19	1350	10.2		12683	53.4	16:17	41	2	5	7	28	1	0	1	14:54

Signed as a free agent by **Bolzano** (Italy), December 22, 2004. Traded to **Carolina** by **Los Angeles** with Tim Gleason for Oleg Tverdovsky and Jack Johnson, September 29, 2006. Traded to **Nashville** by **Carolina** for Josef Vasicek, February 9, 2007. Traded to **Atlanta** by **Nashville** for Vitaly Vishnevski, February 10, 2007. Signed as a free agent by **Minnesota**, July 3, 2007. Traded to **Washington** by **Minnesota** for Washington's 2nd round choice (Johan Larsson) in 2010 Entry Draft, March 3, 2010. Signed as a free agent by **Phoenix**, September 14, 2010. Signed as a free agent by **Edmonton**, July 1, 2011. Signed as a free agent by **Yekaterinburg** (KHL), July 15, 2013.

BELESKEY, Matt

(beh-LEH-skee, MAT) **ANA**

Left wing. Shoots left. 6', 198 lbs. Born, Windsor, Ont., June 7, 1988. Anaheim's 4th choice, 112th overall, in 2006 Entry Draft.

Season	Club	League	GP	G	A	Pts	PIM	PP	SH	GW	S	%	+/-	TF	F%	Min	GP	G	A	Pts	PIM	PP	SH	GW	Min
2003-04	Collingwood	ON-Jr.A	46	8	13	21	110	....	....	....	....	....	....	....	....	....	8	1	7	8	18	....	....	....	....
2004-05	Belleville Bulls	OHL	68	10	13	23	118	....	....	....	....	....	....	....	....	....	5	0	0	0	18	....	....	....	....
2005-06	Belleville Bulls	OHL	61	20	20	40	119	....	....	....	....	....	....	....	....	....	6	1	2	3	10	....	....	....	....
2006-07	Belleville Bulls	OHL	66	27	41	68	124	....	....	....	....	....	....	....	....	....	15	4	10	14	18	....	....	....	....
2007-08	Belleville Bulls	OHL	62	41	49	90	106	....	....	....	....	....	....	....	....	....	21	12	21	33	23	....	....	....	....
2008-09	**Anaheim**	**NHL**	2	0	0	0	0	0	0	0	0	0.0	0	2	0.0	11:10	....	....	....	....	....	....	....	....	....
	Iowa Chops	AHL	58	11	24	35	58	....	....	....	....	....	....	....	....	....	....	....	....	....	....	....	....	....	....
2009-10	**Anaheim**	**NHL**	60	11	7	18	35	0	0	3	123	8.9	–10	20	40.0	13:59	....	....	....	....	....	....	....	....	....
	San Antonio	AHL	12	1	4	5	19	....	....	....	....	....	....	....	....	....	....	....	....	....	....	....	....	....	....
	Toronto Marlies	AHL	3	1	1	2	2	....	....	....	....	....	....	....	....	....	....	....	....	....	....	....	....	....	....
2010-11	**Anaheim**	**NHL**	35	3	7	10	36	0	0	0	58	5.2	–10	8	37.5	12:59	6	1	0	1	4	0	0	0	11:14
	Syracuse Crunch	AHL	27	11	13	24	39	....	....	....	....	....	....	....	....	....	....	....	....	....	....	....	....	....	....
2011-12	**Anaheim**	**NHL**	70	4	11	15	72	0	0	0	75	5.3	–2	26	42.3	10:16	....	....	....	....	....	....	....	....	....
2012-13	Coventry Blaze	Britain	26	12	21	33	39	....	....	....	....	....	....	....	....	....	....	....	....	....	....	....	....	....	....
	Anaheim	**NHL**	42	8	5	13	56	2	0	1	61	13.1	2	19	31.6	12:01	7	2	1	3	2	1	0	0	11:01
	NHL Totals		209	26	30	56	199	2	0	4	317	8.2		75	37.3	12:09	13	3	1	4	6	1	0	0	11:08

Signed as a free agent by **Coventry** (Britain), October 9, 2012.

BELL, Brendan

(BEHL, BREHN-duhn)

Defense. Shoots left. 6'2", 211 lbs. Born, Ottawa, Ont., March 31, 1983. Toronto's 3rd choice, 65th overall, in 2001 Entry Draft.

Season	Club	League	GP	G	A	Pts	PIM	PP	SH	GW	S	%	+/-	TF	F%	Min	GP	G	A	Pts	PIM	PP	SH	GW	Min
1998-99	Ott. Jr. Senators	ON-Jr.A	54	7	20	27	46	....	....	....	....	....	....	....	....	....	....	....	....	....	....	....	....	....	....
99-2000	Ottawa 67's	OHL	48	1	32	33	34	....	....	....	....	....	....	....	....	....	5	0	1	1	4	....	....	....	....
2000-01	Ottawa 67's	OHL	68	7	32	39	59	....	....	....	....	....	....	....	....	....	20	1	11	12	22	....	....	....	....
2001-02	Ottawa 67's	OHL	67	10	36	46	56	....	....	....	....	....	....	....	....	....	13	2	5	7	25	....	....	....	....
2002-03	Ottawa 67's	OHL	55	14	39	53	46	....	....	....	....	....	....	....	....	....	23	8	19	27	25	....	....	....	....
2003-04	St. John's	AHL	74	7	18	25	72	....	....	....	....	....	....	....	....	....	....	....	....	....	....	....	....	....	....
2004-05	St. John's	AHL	75	6	25	31	57	....	....	....	....	....	....	....	....	....	5	0	1	1	2	....	....	....	....
2005-06	**Toronto**	**NHL**	1	0	0	0	0	0	0	0	2	0.0	0	0	0.0	14:00	....	....	....	....	....	....	....	....	....
	Toronto Marlies	AHL	70	6	37	43	99	....	....	....	....	....	....	....	....	....	5	0	4	4	10	....	....	....	....
2006-07	**Toronto**	**NHL**	31	1	4	5	19	1	0	0	29	3.4	–3	1	0.0	12:08	....	....	....	....	....	....	....	....	....
	Phoenix	**NHL**	14	0	2	2	8	0	0	0	18	0.0	–8	0	0.0	17:07	....	....	....	....	....	....	....	....	....
2007-08	**Phoenix**	**NHL**	2	0	0	0	0	0	0	0	0	0.0	–2	0	0.0	14:49	....	....	....	....	....	....	....	....	....
	San Antonio	AHL	69	7	24	31	80	....	....	....	....	....	....	....	....	....	7	2	5	7	10	....	....	....	....
2008-09	**Ottawa**	**NHL**	53	6	15	21	24	5	0	1	76	7.9	–5	0	0.0	17:44	....	....	....	....	....	....	....	....	....
	Binghamton	AHL	15	6	9	15	12	....	....	....	....	....	....	....	....	....	....	....	....	....	....	....	....	....	....
2009-10	Peoria Rivermen	AHL	22	4	13	17	26	....	....	....	....	....	....	....	....	....	....	....	....	....	....	....	....	....	....
	Syracuse Crunch	AHL	49	10	25	35	30	....	....	....	....	....	....	....	....	....	....	....	....	....	....	....	....	....	....
2010-11	Omsk	KHL	1	0	2	2	0	....	....	....	....	....	....	....	....	....	....	....	....	....	....	....	....	....	....
	EHC Biel-Bienne	Swiss	29	2	9	11	14	....	....	....	....	....	....	....	....	....	6	0	4	4	10	....	....	....	....
2011-12	**NY Rangers**	**NHL**	1	0	0	0	0	0	0	0	2	0.0	–1	0	0.0	11:26	....	....	....	....	....	....	....	....	....
	Connecticut	AHL	65	7	26	33	68	....	....	....	....	....	....	....	....	....	5	0	1	1	4	....	....	....	....
2012-13	Frolunda	Sweden	21	1	9	10	8	....	....	....	....	....	....	....	....	....	6	1	0	1	6	....	....	....	....
	NHL Totals		102	7	21	28	51	6	0	1	127	5.5		1	0.0	15:47	....	....	....	....	....	....	....	....	....

OHL First All-Star Team (2003) • Canadian Major Junior First All-Star Team (2003) • Canadian Major Junior Defenseman of the Year (2003)

Traded to **Phoenix** by **Toronto** with Toronto's 2nd round choice (later traded to Nashville - Nashville selected Roman Josi) in 2008 Entry Draft for Yanic Perreault and Phoenix's 5th round choice (Joel Champagne) in 2008 Entry Draft, February 27, 2007. Signed as a free agent by **Ottawa**, July 11, 2008. Signed as a free agent by **St. Louis**, July 31, 2009. Traded to **Columbus** by **St. Louis** with Tomas Kana for Pascal Pelletier, December 8, 2009. Signed as a free agent by **Omsk** (KHL), May 20, 2010. Signed as a free agent by **Biel-Bienne** (Swiss), October 24, 2010. Signed as a free agent by **NY Rangers**, August 9, 2011. Signed as a free agent by **Frolunda** (Sweden), December 13, 2012.

BELL, Mark

(BEHL, MAHRK)

Center. Shoots left. 6'3", 220 lbs. Born, St. Pauls, Ont., August 5, 1980. Chicago's 1st choice, 8th overall, in 1998 Entry Draft.

Season	Club	League	GP	G	A	Pts	PIM	PP	SH	GW	S	%	+/-	TF	F%	Min	GP	G	A	Pts	PIM	PP	SH	GW	Min
1995-96	Stratford Cullitons	ON-Jr.B	47	8	15	23	32	....	....	....	....	....	....	....	....	....	....	....	....	....	....	....	....	....	....
1996-97	Ottawa 67's	OHL	65	8	12	20	40	....	....	....	....	....	....	....	....	....	24	4	7	11	13	....	....	....	....
1997-98	Ottawa 67's	OHL	55	34	26	60	87	....	....	....	....	....	....	....	....	....	13	6	5	11	14	....	....	....	....
1998-99	Ottawa 67's	OHL	44	29	26	55	69	....	....	....	....	....	....	....	....	....	9	6	5	11	8	....	....	....	....
99-2000	Ottawa 67's	OHL	48	34	38	72	95	....	....	....	....	....	....	....	....	....	2	0	1	1	0	....	....	....	....
2000-01	**Chicago**	**NHL**	13	0	1	1	4	0	0	0	14	0.0	0	141	48.9	12:00	....	....	....	....	....	....	....	....	....
	Norfolk Admirals	AHL	61	15	27	42	126	....	....	....	....	....	....	....	....	....	9	4	3	7	10	....	....	....	....
2001-02	**Chicago**	**NHL**	80	12	16	28	124	1	0	1	120	10.0	–6	47	42.6	12:39	5	0	0	0	8	0	0	0	9:18
2002-03	**Chicago**	**NHL**	82	14	15	29	113	0	2	0	127	11.0	0	377	52.5	14:04	....	....	....	....	....	....	....	....	....
2003-04	**Chicago**	**NHL**	82	21	24	45	106	2	0	1	202	10.4	–14	387	48.3	17:37	....	....	....	....	....	....	....	....	....
2004-05	Trondheim IK	Norway	25	10	17	27	87	....	....	....	....	....	....	....	....	....	11	6	6	12	44	....	....	....	....
2005-06	**Chicago**	**NHL**	82	25	23	48	107	11	1	1	227	11.0	–14	1034	48.5	17:37	....	....	....	....	....	....	....	....	....
2006-07	**San Jose**	**NHL**	71	11	10	21	83	3	0	2	116	9.5	–9	108	48.2	12:57	4	0	0	0	2	0	0	0	10:16

			Regular Season														Playoffs								
Season	Club	League	GP	G	A	Pts	PIM	PP	SH	GW	S	%	+/-	TF	F%	Min	GP	G	A	Pts	PIM	PP	SH	GW	Min
2007-08	**Toronto**	**NHL**	**35**	**4**	**6**	**10**	**60**	**0**	**0**	**0**	**42**	**9.5**	**–2**	**179**	**41.3**	**9:45**	....	....	....	....	....	....	....	....	....
2008-09	Toronto Marlies	AHL	56	12	15	27	34	....	....	....	....	....	....	....	....	....	....	....	....	....	....	....	....	....	....
	Hartford	AHL	18	6	8	14	31	....	....	....	....	....	....	....	....	....	5	1	0	1	4	....	....	....	....
2009-10	Kloten Flyers	Swiss	39	13	14	27	69	....	....	....	....	....	....	....	....	....	10	1	4	5	29	....	....	....	....
2010-11	Kloten Flyers	Swiss	41	16	10	26	58	....	....	....	....	....	....	....	....	....	18	6	3	9	*60	....	....	....	....
2011-12	**Anaheim**	**NHL**	**5**	**0**	**0**	**0**	**5**	**0**	**0**	**0**	**0**	**0.0**	**0**	**22**	**54.6**	**6:26**	....	....	....	....	....	....	....	....	....
	Syracuse Crunch	AHL	39	7	10	17	41	....	....	....	....	....	....	....	....	....	4	3	1	4	0	....	....	....	....
2012-13	Iserlohn Roosters	Germany	43	13	15	28	122	....	....	....	....	....	....	....	....	....	....	....	....	....	....	....	....	....	....
	NHL Totals		**450**	**87**	**95**	**182**	**602**	**17**	**3**	**5**	**848**	**10.3**		**2295**	**48.5**	**14:27**	**9**	**0**	**0**	**0**	**10**	**0**	**0**	**0**	**9:44**

Signed as a free agent by **Trondheim** (Norway), November 6, 2004. Traded to **San Jose** by **Chicago** for Tom Preissing and Josh Hennessy, July 10, 2006. Traded to **Toronto** by **San Jose** with Vesa Toskala for Toronto's 1st (later traded to St. Louis – St. Louis selected Lars Eller) and 2nd (later traded to St. Louis – St. Louis selected Aaron Palushaj) round choices in 2007 Entry Draft and Toronto's 4th round choice (later traded to Nashville – Nashville selected Craig Smith) in 2009 Entry Draft, June 22, 2007. • Suspended by NHL for 15 games for substance abuse violations. • Missed majority of 2007-08 due to facial injury at Pittsburgh, January 3, 2008. Claimed on waivers by **NY Rangers** from **Toronto**, February 25, 2009. Signed as a free agent by **Kloten** (Swiss), October 6, 2009. Signed as a free agent by **Anaheim**, July 20, 2011. Signed as a free agent by **Iserlohn** (Germany), September 19, 2012.

BELLE, Shawn
(BEHL, SHAWN)

Defense. Shoots left. 6'1", 235 lbs. Born, Edmonton, Alta., January 3, 1985. St. Louis' 1st choice, 30th overall, in 2003 Entry Draft.

Season	Club	League	GP	G	A	Pts	PIM	PP	SH	GW	S	%	+/-	TF	F%	Min	GP	G	A	Pts	PIM	PP	SH	GW	Min
99-2000	K of C Squires	AMBHL	34	7	20	27	36	....	....	....	....	....	....	....	....	....	....	....	....	....	....	....	....	....	....
2000-01	K of C Squires	AMBHL	39	18	30	48	69	....	....	....	....	....	....	....	....	....	....	....	....	....	....	....	....	....	....
	Regina Pats	WHL	4	0	3	3	0	....	....	....	....	....	....	....	....	....	....	....	....	....	....	....	....	....	....
	Tri-City	WHL	2	0	1	1	0	....	....	....	....	....	....	....	....	....	....	....	....	....	....	....	....	....	....
2001-02	Tri-City	WHL	64	1	17	18	51	....	....	....	....	....	....	....	....	....	5	2	1	3	2	....	....	....	....
2002-03	Tri-City	WHL	66	7	14	21	77	....	....	....	....	....	....	....	....	....	....	....	....	....	....	....	....	....	....
2003-04	Tri-City	WHL	55	9	20	29	68	....	....	....	....	....	....	....	....	....	11	3	5	8	15	....	....	....	....
2004-05	Tri-City	WHL	62	13	32	45	76	....	....	....	....	....	....	....	....	....	5	1	1	2	6	....	....	....	....
2005-06	Iowa Stars	AHL	45	1	2	3	63	....	....	....	....	....	....	....	....	....	....	....	....	....	....	....	....	....	....
	Houston Aeros	AHL	16	1	1	2	18	....	....	....	....	....	....	....	....	....	8	1	0	1	4	....	....	....	....
2006-07	**Minnesota**	**NHL**	**9**	**0**	**1**	**1**	**0**	**0**	**0**	**0**	**3**	**0.0**	**4**	**0**	**0.0**	**9:56**	....	....	....	....	....	....	....	....	....
	Houston Aeros	AHL	57	4	14	18	73	....	....	....	....	....	....	....	....	....	....	....	....	....	....	....	....	....	....
2007-08	Houston Aeros	AHL	63	1	2	3	74	....	....	....	....	....	....	....	....	....	3	0	0	0	2	....	....	....	....
2008-09	Hamilton	AHL	60	3	10	13	93	....	....	....	....	....	....	....	....	....	6	1	0	1	16	....	....	....	....
2009-10	**Montreal**	**NHL**	**2**	**0**	**0**	**0**	**0**	**0**	**0**	**0**	**1**	**0.0**	**–2**	**0**	**0.0**	**10:38**	....	....	....	....	....	....	....	....	....
	Hamilton	AHL	70	3	16	19	69	....	....	....	....	....	....	....	....	....	19	1	6	7	20	....	....	....	....
2010-11	**Edmonton**	**NHL**	**5**	**0**	**0**	**0**	**0**	**0**	**0**	**0**	**7**	**0.0**	**–2**	**0**	**0.0**	**16:26**	....	....	....	....	....	....	....	....	....
	Oklahoma City	AHL	39	3	17	20	61	....	....	....	....	....	....	....	....	....	....	....	....	....	....	....	....	....	....
	Colorado	**NHL**	**4**	**0**	**0**	**0**	**2**	**0**	**0**	**0**	**1**	**0.0**	**1**	**0**	**0.0**	**18:02**	....	....	....	....	....	....	....	....	....
	Lake Erie	AHL	12	3	3	6	8	....	....	....	....	....	....	....	....	....	7	0	3	3	8	....	....	....	....
2011-12	Adler Mannheim	Germany	46	3	5	8	87	....	....	....	....	....	....	....	....	....	14	1	3	4	14	....	....	....	....
2012-13	Adler Mannheim	Germany	42	2	7	9	68	....	....	....	....	....	....	....	....	....	3	0	1	1	2	....	....	....	....
	NHL Totals		**20**	**0**	**1**	**1**	**2**	**0**	**0**	**0**	**12**	**0.0**		**0**	**0.0**	**13:15**	....	....	....	....	....	....	....	....	....

• Rights traded to **Dallas** by **St. Louis** for Jason Bacashihua, June 25, 2004. Traded to **Minnesota** by **Dallas** with Martin Skoula for Willie Mitchell and Minnesota's 2nd round choice (Nico Saccheti) in 2007 Entry Draft, March 9, 2006. Traded to **Montreal** by **Minnesota** for Cory Locke, July 11, 2008. Signed as a free agent by **Edmonton**, July 13, 2010. Traded to **Colorado** by **Edmonton** for Kevin Montgomery, February 28, 2011. Signed as a free agent by **Mannheim** (Germany), September 10, 2011.

BELLEMORE, Brett
(BEHL-mohr, BREHT) **CAR**

Defense. Shoots right. 6'4", 225 lbs. Born, Windsor, Ont., June 25, 1988. Carolina's 5th choice, 162nd overall, in 2007 Entry Draft.

Season	Club	League	GP	G	A	Pts	PIM	PP	SH	GW	S	%	+/-	TF	F%	Min	GP	G	A	Pts	PIM	PP	SH	GW	Min
2005-06	Plymouth Whalers	OHL	46	0	0	0	16	....	....	....	....	....	....	....	....	....	10	0	0	0	0	....	....	....	....
2006-07	Plymouth Whalers	OHL	50	0	12	12	50	....	....	....	....	....	....	....	....	....	20	0	5	5	28	....	....	....	....
2007-08	Plymouth Whalers	OHL	56	6	18	24	70	....	....	....	....	....	....	....	....	....	4	0	2	2	8	....	....	....	....
	Albany River Rats	AHL	4	0	0	0	6	....	....	....	....	....	....	....	....	....	5	0	0	0	6	....	....	....	....
2008-09	Plymouth Whalers	OHL	29	2	10	12	39	....	....	....	....	....	....	....	....	....	11	1	2	3	16	....	....	....	....
	Albany River Rats	AHL	6	0	0	0	4	....	....	....	....	....	....	....	....	....	....	....	....	....	....	....	....	....	....
2009-10	Albany River Rats	AHL	75	1	6	7	81	....	....	....	....	....	....	....	....	....	8	0	1	1	2	....	....	....	....
2010-11	Charlotte	AHL	71	2	8	10	74	....	....	....	....	....	....	....	....	....	16	1	1	2	12	....	....	....	....
2011-12	Charlotte	AHL	76	1	9	10	60	....	....	....	....	....	....	....	....	....	....	....	....	....	....	....	....	....	....
2012-13	Charlotte	AHL	68	2	11	13	87	....	....	....	....	....	....	....	....	....	5	0	1	1	6	....	....	....	....
	Carolina	**NHL**	**8**	**0**	**2**	**2**	**7**	**0**	**0**	**0**	**3**	**0.0**	**–2**	**0**	**0.0**	**13:46**	....	....	....	....	....	....	....	....	....
	NHL Totals		**8**	**0**	**2**	**2**	**7**	**0**	**0**	**0**	**3**	**0.0**		**0**	**0.0**	**13:46**	....	....	....	....	....	....	....	....	....

BENN, Jamie
(BEHN, JAY-mee) **DAL**

Left wing. Shoots left. 6'2", 205 lbs. Born, Victoria, B.C., July 18, 1989. Dallas' 5th choice, 129th overall, in 2007 Entry Draft.

Season	Club	League	GP	G	A	Pts	PIM	PP	SH	GW	S	%	+/-	TF	F%	Min	GP	G	A	Pts	PIM	PP	SH	GW	Min
2004-05	Peninsula Eagles	Minor-BC	STATISTICS NOT AVAILABLE																						
	Peninsula	VIJHL	4	1	2	3	2	....	....	....	....	....	....	....	....	....	2	0	0	0	0	....	....	....	....
2005-06	Peninsula	VIJHL	38	31	24	55	92	....	....	....	....	....	....	....	....	....	7	5	7	10	20	....	....	....	....
	Victoria Salsa	BCHL	6	0	0	0	0	....	....	....	....	....	....	....	....	....	....	....	....	....	....	....	....	....	....
2006-07	Victoria Grizzlies	BCHL	53	42	23	65	78	....	....	....	....	....	....	....	....	....	11	5	4	9	12	....	....	....	....
2007-08	Victoria Grizzlies	BCHL	2	0	0	0	2	....	....	....	....	....	....	....	....	....	....	....	....	....	....	....	....	....	....
	Kelowna Rockets	WHL	51	33	32	65	68	....	....	....	....	....	....	....	....	....	7	3	8	11	4	....	....	....	....
2008-09	Kelowna Rockets	WHL	56	46	36	82	71	....	....	....	....	....	....	....	....	....	19	*13	*20	*33	18	....	....	....	....
2009-10	**Dallas**	**NHL**	**82**	**22**	**19**	**41**	**45**	**2**	**0**	**3**	**182**	**12.1**	**–1**	**236**	**46.2**	**14:42**	....	....	....	....	....	....	....	....	....
	Texas Stars	AHL	....	....	....	....	....	....	....	....	....	....	....	....	....	....	24	*14	12	26	22	....	....	....	....
2010-11	**Dallas**	**NHL**	**69**	**22**	**34**	**56**	**52**	**6**	**4**	**3**	**177**	**12.4**	**–5**	**195**	**43.1**	**18:01**	....	....	....	....	....	....	....	....	....
2011-12	**Dallas**	**NHL**	**71**	**26**	**37**	**63**	**55**	**2**	**1**	**7**	**203**	**12.8**	**15**	**751**	**46.2**	**18:04**	....	....	....	....	....	....	....	....	....
2012-13	Hamburg Freezers	Germany	19	7	13	20	30	....	....	....	....	....	....	....	....	....	....	....	....	....	....	....	....	....	....
	Dallas	**NHL**	**41**	**12**	**21**	**33**	**40**	**3**	**0**	**3**	**110**	**10.9**	**–12**	**709**	**46.1**	**19:55**	....	....	....	....	....	....	....	....	....
	NHL Totals		**263**	**82**	**111**	**193**	**192**	**13**	**5**	**16**	**672**	**12.2**		**1891**	**45.8**	**17:18**	....	....	....	....	....	....	....	....	....

WHL West First All-Star Team (2009)
Played in NHL All-Star Game (2012)
Signed as a free agent by **Hamburg** (Germany), October 3, 2012.

BENN, Jordie
(BEHN, JOHR-dee) **DAL**

Defense. Shoots left. 6'1", 200 lbs. Born, Victoria, B.C., July 26, 1987.

Season	Club	League	GP	G	A	Pts	PIM	PP	SH	GW	S	%	+/-	TF	F%	Min	GP	G	A	Pts	PIM	PP	SH	GW	Min
2004-05	Victoria Salsa	BCHL	4	0	1	1	6	....	....	....	....	....	....	....	....	....	1	0	0	0	2	....	....	....	....
2005-06	Victoria Salsa	BCHL	55	5	20	25	61	....	....	....	....	....	....	....	....	....	16	1	5	6	6	....	....	....	....
2006-07	Victoria Grizzlies	BCHL	53	4	37	41	62	....	....	....	....	....	....	....	....	....	11	1	7	8	22	....	....	....	....
2007-08	Victoria Grizzlies	BCHL	60	15	32	47	78	....	....	....	....	....	....	....	....	....	11	2	8	10	8	....	....	....	....
2008-09	Victoria	ECHL	55	1	11	12	26	....	....	....	....	....	....	....	....	....	3	0	0	0	0	....	....	....	....
2009-10	Allen Americans	CHL	45	9	9	18	55	....	....	....	....	....	....	....	....	....	20	2	9	11	12	....	....	....	....
2010-11	Texas Stars	AHL	60	2	10	12	39	....	....	....	....	....	....	....	....	....	1	0	0	0	0	....	....	....	....
2011-12	**Dallas**	**NHL**	**3**	**0**	**2**	**2**	**0**	**0**	**0**	**0**	**1**	**0.0**	**1**	**0**	**0.0**	**13:57**	....	....	....	....	....	....	....	....	....
	Texas Stars	AHL	62	9	23	32	33	....	....	....	....	....	....	....	....	....	....	....	....	....	....	....	....	....	....
2012-13	Texas Stars	AHL	43	7	14	21	33	....	....	....	....	....	....	....	....	....	7	0	2	2	10	....	....	....	....
	Dallas	**NHL**	**26**	**1**	**5**	**6**	**10**	**1**	**0**	**0**	**31**	**3.2**	**–4**	**0**	**0.0**	**17:19**	....	....	....	....	....	....	....	....	....
	NHL Totals		**29**	**1**	**7**	**8**	**10**	**1**	**0**	**0**	**32**	**3.1**		**0**	**0.0**	**16:58**	....	....	....	....	....	....	....	....	....

Signed as a free agent by **Texas** (AHL), October 8, 2010. Signed as a free agent by **Dallas**, July 1, 2011.

BENNETT, Beau
(BEH-neht, BOH) **PIT**

Right wing. Shoots right. 6'2", 207 lbs. Born, Gardena, CA, November 27, 1991. Pittsburgh's 1st choice, 20th overall, in 2010 Entry Draft.

Season	Club	League	GP	G	A	Pts	PIM	PP	SH	GW	S	%	+/-	TF	F%	Min	GP	G	A	Pts	PIM	PP	SH	GW	Min
2008-09	L.A. Jr. Kings	T1EHL	46	25	33	58	10	....	....	....	....	....	....	....	....	....	....	....	....	....	....	....	....	....	....
2009-10	Penticton Vees	BCHL	56	41	79	*120	20	....	....	....	....	....	....	....	....	....	15	5	9	14	6	....	....	....	....
2010-11	U. of Denver	WCHA	37	9	16	25	18	....	....	....	....	....	....	....	....	....	....	....	....	....	....	....	....	....	....
2011-12	U. of Denver	WCHA	10	4	9	13	25	....	....	....	....	....	....	....	....	....	....	....	....	....	....	....	....	....	....
2012-13	Wilkes-Barre	AHL	39	7	21	28	18	....	....	....	....	....	....	....	....	....	....	....	....	....	....	....	....	....	....
	Pittsburgh	**NHL**	**26**	**3**	**11**	**14**	**6**	**1**	**0**	**2**	**30**	**10.0**	**7**	**4**	**25.0**	**12:18**	**6**	**1**	**0**	**1**	**0**	**1**	**0**	**1**	**11:05**
	NHL Totals		**26**	**3**	**11**	**14**	**6**	**1**	**0**	**2**	**30**	**10.0**		**4**	**25.0**	**12:18**	**6**	**1**	**0**	**1**	**0**	**1**	**0**	**1**	**11:05**

BENOIT, Andre

(behn-WAH, AWN-dray) **COL**

Defense. Shoots left. 5'11", 186 lbs. Born, St. Albert, Ont., January 6, 1984.

			Regular Season														Playoffs								
Season	Club	League	GP	G	A	Pts	PIM	PP	SH	GW	S	%	+/-	TF	F%	Min	GP	G	A	Pts	PIM	PP	SH	GW	Min
2000-01	Kitchener Rangers	OHL	65	16	19	35	37	....	....	....	....	....	....	....	....	....	....	....	....	....	....	....	....	....	....
2001-02	Kitchener Rangers	OHL	62	13	32	45	77	....	....	....	....	....	....	....	....	....	4	1	0	1	8	....	....	....	....
2002-03	Kitchener Rangers	OHL	65	22	45	67	77	....	....	....	....	....	....	....	....	....	21	1	16	17	16	....	....	....	....
2003-04	Kitchener Rangers	OHL	65	24	51	75	67	....	....	....	....	....	....	....	....	....	5	1	1	2	6	....	....	....	....
2004-05	Kitchener Rangers	OHL	67	24	53	77	72	....	....	....	....	....	....	....	....	....	15	5	13	18	6	....	....	....	....
2005-06	Hamilton	AHL	70	7	19	26	60	....	....	....	....	....	....	....	....	....	....	....	....	....	....	....	....	....	....
2006-07	Hamilton	AHL	64	10	21	31	41	....	....	....	....	....	....	....	....	....	22	2	11	13	22	....	....	....	....
2007-08	Tappara Tampere	Finland	54	12	26	38	96	....	....	....	....	....	....	....	....	....	11	2	3	5	10	....	....	....	....
2008-09	Sodertalje SK	Sweden	54	4	16	20	34	....	....	....	....	....	....	....	....	....	....	....	....	....	....	....	....	....	....
	Sodertalje SK	Sweden-Q	10	0	2	2	10	....	....	....	....	....	....	....	....	....	....	....	....	....	....	....	....	....	....
2009-10	Hamilton	AHL	78	6	30	36	63	....	....	....	....	....	....	....	....	....	19	3	11	14	8	....	....	....	....
2010-11	**Ottawa**	**NHL**	**8**	**0**	**1**	**1**	**6**	**0**	**0**	**0**	**17**	**0.0**	**–1**	**0**	**0.0**	**16:50**	....	....	....	....	....	....	....	....	....
	Binghamton	AHL	73	11	44	55	53	....	....	....	....	....	....	....	....	....	23	3	*15	18	14	....	....	....	....
2011-12	Spartak Moscow	KHL	53	5	12	17	34	....	....	....	....	....	....	....	....	....	....	....	....	....	....	....	....	....	....
2012-13	Binghamton	AHL	34	9	16	25	28	....	....	....	....	....	....	....	....	....	....	....	....	....	....	....	....	....	....
	Ottawa	**NHL**	**33**	**3**	**7**	**10**	**8**	**1**	**0**	**2**	**50**	**6.0**	**–3**	**0**	**0.0**	**16:25**	**5**	**0**	**3**	**3**	**0**	**0**	**0**	**0**	**15:28**
	NHL Totals		**41**	**3**	**8**	**11**	**14**	**1**	**0**	**2**	**67**	**4.5**		**0**	**0.0**	**16:30**	**5**	**0**	**3**	**3**	**0**	**0**	**0**	**0**	**15:28**

AHL Second All-Star Team (2011)

Signed as a free agent by **Montreal**, January 9, 2006. Signed as a free agent by **Tappara Tampere** (Finland), June 21, 2007. Signed as a free agent by **Sodertalje** (Sweden), April 7, 2008. Signed as a free agent by **Montreal**, May 13, 2009. Signed as a free agent by **Ottawa**, August 6, 2010. Signed as a free agent by **Spartak Moscow** (KHL), August 11, 2011. Signed as a free agent by **Ottawa**, July 2, 2012. Signed as a free agent by **Colorado**, July 5, 2013.

BERGENHEIM, Sean

(BUHR-gehn-highm, SHAWN) **FLA**

Left wing. Shoots left. 5'10", 205 lbs. Born, Helsinki, Finland, February 8, 1984. NY Islanders' 1st choice, 22nd overall, in 2002 Entry Draft.

			Regular Season														Playoffs								
Season	Club	League	GP	G	A	Pts	PIM	PP	SH	GW	S	%	+/-	TF	F%	Min	GP	G	A	Pts	PIM	PP	SH	GW	Min
99-2000	Jokerit U18	Fin-U18	30	22	11	33	34	....	....	....	....	....	....	....	....	....	3	1	0	1	0	....	....	....	....
	Jokerit U18	Fin-U18	17	10	8	18	14	....	....	....	....	....	....	....	....	....	3	1	0	1	2	....	....	....	....
2000-01	Jokerit U18	Fin-U18	1	1	0	1	4	....	....	....	....	....	....	....	....	....	6	9	5	14	8	....	....	....	....
	Jokerit Helsinki Jr.	Fin-Jr.	18	6	4	10	26	....	....	....	....	....	....	....	....	....	2	0	0	0	4	....	....	....	....
2001-02	Jokerit U18	Fin-U18	....	....	....	....	....	....	....	....	....	....	....	....	....	....	5	6	2	8	18	....	....	....	....
	Jokerit Helsinki Jr.	Fin-Jr.	23	11	19	30	36	....	....	....	....	....	....	....	....	....	1	0	0	0	2	....	....	....	....
	Kiekko-Vantaa	Finland-2	4	0	0	0	52	....	....	....	....	....	....	....	....	....	....	....	....	....	....	....	....	....	....
	Jokerit Helsinki	Finland	28	2	2	4	4	....	....	....	....	....	....	....	....	....	....	....	....	....	....	....	....	....	....
2002-03	Jokerit Helsinki Jr.	Fin-Jr.	2	3	0	3	2	....	....	....	....	....	....	....	....	....	....	....	....	....	....	....	....	....	....
	Jokerit Helsinki	Finland	38	3	3	6	4	....	....	....	....	....	....	....	....	....	2	0	0	0	0	....	....	....	....
2003-04	**NY Islanders**	**NHL**	**18**	**1**	**1**	**2**	**4**	**0**	**1**	**0**	**12**	**8.3**	**–4**	**2**	**50.0**	**8:55**	....	....	....	....	....	....	....	....	....
	Jokerit Helsinki	Finland	20	2	2	4	18	....	....	....	....	....	....	....	....	....	3	1	1	2	0	....	....	....	....
	Bridgeport	AHL	....	....	....	....	....	....	....	....	....	....	....	....	....	....	7	2	3	5	10	....	....	....	....
2004-05	Bridgeport	AHL	61	15	14	29	69	....	....	....	....	....	....	....	....	....	....	....	....	....	....	....	....	....	....
2005-06	**NY Islanders**	**NHL**	**28**	**4**	**5**	**9**	**20**	**0**	**0**	**1**	**63**	**6.3**	**–11**	**14**	**28.6**	**13:17**	....	....	....	....	....	....	....	....	....
	Bridgeport	AHL	55	25	22	47	112	....	....	....	....	....	....	....	....	....	7	0	2	2	24	....	....	....	....
2006-07	Yaroslavl	Russia	9	1	4	5	26	....	....	....	....	....	....	....	....	....	....	....	....	....	....	....	....	....	....
	Frolunda	Sweden	36	16	17	33	80	....	....	....	....	....	....	....	....	....	....	....	....	....	....	....	....	....	....
2007-08	**NY Islanders**	**NHL**	**78**	**10**	**12**	**22**	**62**	**1**	**0**	**1**	**155**	**6.5**	**–3**	**15**	**60.0**	**11:15**	....	....	....	....	....	....	....	....	....
2008-09	**NY Islanders**	**NHL**	**59**	**15**	**9**	**24**	**64**	**0**	**4**	**5**	**152**	**9.9**	**–2**	**22**	**40.9**	**14:15**	....	....	....	....	....	....	....	....	....
2009-10	**NY Islanders**	**NHL**	**63**	**10**	**13**	**23**	**45**	**0**	**2**	**0**	**133**	**7.5**	**1**	**17**	**29.4**	**14:04**	....	....	....	....	....	....	....	....	....
2010-11	**Tampa Bay**	**NHL**	**80**	**14**	**15**	**29**	**56**	**2**	**0**	**1**	**182**	**7.7**	**0**	**51**	**49.0**	**13:59**	**16**	**9**	**2**	**11**	**8**	**0**	**0**	**1**	**14:09**
2011-12	**Florida**	**NHL**	**62**	**17**	**6**	**23**	**48**	**5**	**1**	**2**	**185**	**9.2**	**–5**	**11**	**27.3**	**16:25**	**7**	**3**	**3**	**6**	**4**	**1**	**0**	**0**	**16:14**
2012-13	HIFK Helsinki	Finland	2	1	0	1	0	....	....	....	....	....	....	....	....	....	....	....	....	....	....	....	....	....	....
	NHL Totals		**388**	**71**	**61**	**132**	**299**	**8**	**8**	**10**	**882**	**8.0**		**132**	**42.4**	**13:35**	**23**	**12**	**5**	**17**	**12**	**1**	**0**	**1**	**14:47**

Signed as a free agent by **Yaroslavl** (Russia), August 5, 2006. Signed as a free agent by **Frolunda** (Sweden), November 3, 2006. Signed as a free agent by **Tampa Bay**, August 17, 2010. Signed as a free agent by **Florida**, July 1, 2011. Signed as a free agent by **HIFK Helsinki** (Finland), September 25, 2012. • Suspended by the Florida Panthers after sustaining hip injury during lockout, January 16, 2013.

BERGERON, Marc-Andre

(BAIR-zhur-uhn, MAHRK-AWN-dray)

Defense. Shoots left. 5'9", 198 lbs. Born, St-Louis-de-France, Que., October 13, 1980.

			Regular Season														Playoffs								
Season	Club	League	GP	G	A	Pts	PIM	PP	SH	GW	S	%	+/-	TF	F%	Min	GP	G	A	Pts	PIM	PP	SH	GW	Min
1996-97	Cap-d-Madeleine	QAAA	4	0	1	1	0	....	....	....	....	....	....	....	....	....	2	0	0	0	0	....	....	....	....
1997-98	Baie-Comeau	QMJHL	40	6	14	20	48	....	....	....	....	....	....	....	....	....	....	....	....	....	....	....	....	....	....
1998-99	Baie-Comeau	QMJHL	47	9	14	23	57	....	....	....	....	....	....	....	....	....	....	....	....	....	....	....	....	....	....
	Shawinigan	QMJHL	23	5	7	12	66	....	....	....	....	....	....	....	....	....	5	2	2	4	24	....	....	....	....
99-2000	Shawinigan	QMJHL	70	24	50	74	173	....	....	....	....	....	....	....	....	....	13	4	7	11	45	....	....	....	....
2000-01	Shawinigan	QMJHL	69	42	59	101	185	....	....	....	....	....	....	....	....	....	10	4	11	15	24	....	....	....	....
2001-02	Hamilton	AHL	50	2	13	15	61	....	....	....	....	....	....	....	....	....	9	1	4	5	8	....	....	....	....
2002-03	**Edmonton**	**NHL**	**5**	**1**	**1**	**2**	**9**	**0**	**0**	**0**	**5**	**20.0**	**2**	**0**	**0.0**	**16:30**	**1**	**0**	**1**	**1**	**0**	**0**	**0**	**0**	**19:20**
	Hamilton	AHL	66	8	31	39	73	....	....	....	....	....	....	....	....	....	20	0	7	7	25	....	....	....	....
2003-04	**Edmonton**	**NHL**	**54**	**9**	**17**	**26**	**26**	**3**	**0**	**0**	**105**	**8.6**	**13**	**0**	**0.0**	**17:39**	....	....	....	....	....	....	....	....	....
	Toronto	AHL	17	4	3	7	23	....	....	....	....	....	....	....	....	....	....	....	....	....	....	....	....	....	....
2004-05	Brynas IF Gavle	Sweden	10	3	2	5	72	....	....	....	....	....	....	....	....	....	....	....	....	....	....	....	....	....	....
	Brynas IF Gavle	Sweden-Q	9	1	2	3	8	....	....	....	....	....	....	....	....	....	....	....	....	....	....	....	....	....	....
2005-06	**Edmonton**	**NHL**	**75**	**15**	**20**	**35**	**38**	**8**	**0**	**1**	**144**	**10.4**	**3**	**0**	**0.0**	**21:14**	**18**	**2**	**1**	**3**	**14**	**2**	**0**	**0**	**14:56**
2006-07	**Edmonton**	**NHL**	**55**	**8**	**17**	**25**	**28**	**6**	**0**	**3**	**111**	**7.2**	**–9**	**0**	**0.0**	**17:27**	....	....	....	....	....	....	....	....	....
	NY Islanders	**NHL**	**23**	**6**	**15**	**21**	**10**	**4**	**0**	**1**	**55**	**10.9**	**5**	**0**	**0.0**	**23:07**	**5**	**1**	**1**	**2**	**6**	**1**	**0**	**1**	**27:21**
2007-08	**NY Islanders**	**NHL**	**46**	**9**	**9**	**18**	**16**	**8**	**0**	**1**	**96**	**9.4**	**–14**	**0**	**0.0**	**18:17**	....	....	....	....	....	....	....	....	....
	Anaheim	**NHL**	**9**	**0**	**1**	**1**	**4**	**0**	**0**	**0**	**12**	**0.0**	**–2**	**0**	**0.0**	**12:50**	....	....	....	....	....	....	....	....	....
2008-09	**Minnesota**	**NHL**	**72**	**14**	**18**	**32**	**30**	**7**	**0**	**3**	**140**	**10.0**	**5**	**0**	**0.0**	**16:54**	....	....	....	....	....	....	....	....	....
2009-10	**Montreal**	**NHL**	**60**	**13**	**21**	**34**	**16**	**7**	**0**	**4**	**123**	**10.6**	**–7**	**0**	**0.0**	**15:04**	**19**	**2**	**4**	**6**	**10**	**2**	**0**	**0**	**16:27**
	Hamilton	AHL	3	0	6	6	0	....	....	....	....	....	....	....	....	....	....	....	....	....	....	....	....	....	....
2010-11	**Tampa Bay**	**NHL**	**23**	**2**	**6**	**8**	**8**	**0**	**0**	**1**	**37**	**5.4**	**–10**	**0**	**0.0**	**14:19**	**14**	**2**	**1**	**3**	**9**	**2**	**0**	**1**	**12:58**
	Norfolk Admirals	AHL	13	2	6	8	6	....	....	....	....	....	....	....	....	....	....	....	....	....	....	....	....	....	....
2011-12	**Tampa Bay**	**NHL**	**43**	**4**	**20**	**24**	**20**	**1**	**0**	**0**	**80**	**5.0**	**6**	**0**	**0.0**	**19:21**	....	....	....	....	....	....	....	....	....
2012-13	**Tampa Bay**	**NHL**	**12**	**1**	**4**	**5**	**4**	**0**	**0**	**0**	**22**	**4.5**	**3**	**0**	**0.0**	**12:22**	....	....	....	....	....	....	....	....	....
	Carolina	**NHL**	**13**	**0**	**4**	**4**	**5**	**0**	**0**	**0**	**21**	**0.0**	**–7**	**0**	**0.0**	**15:04**	....	....	....	....	....	....	....	....	....
	NHL Totals		**490**	**82**	**153**	**235**	**214**	**44**	**0**	**14**	**951**	**8.6**		**0**	**0.0**	**17:46**	**57**	**7**	**8**	**15**	**39**	**7**	**0**	**2**	**16:07**

QMJHL First All-Star Team (2001) • Canadian Major Junior First All-Star Team (2001) • Canadian Major Junior Defenseman of the Year (2001) • AHL Second All-Star Team (2003)

Signed as a free agent by **Edmonton**, July 20, 2001. Signed as a free agent by **Gavle** (Sweden), January 23, 2005. Traded to **NY Islanders** by **Edmonton** with Edmonton's 3rd round choice (later traded back to Edmonton, later traded to Anaheim, later traded back to NY Islanders – NY Islanders selected Kirill Petrov) in 2008 Entry Draft for Denis Grebeshkov, February 18, 2007. Traded to **Anaheim** by **NY Islanders** for Edmonton's 3rd round choice (previously acquired, NY Islanders selected Kirill Petrov) in 2008 Entry Draft, February 26, 2008. Traded to **Minnesota** by **Anaheim** for Minnesota's 3rd round choice (Brandon McMillan) in 2008 Entry Draft, June 10, 2008. Signed as a free agent by **Montreal**, October 6, 2009. Signed as a free agent by **Tampa Bay**, January 4, 2011. Traded to **Carolina** by **Tampa Bay** for Adam Hall and Carolina's 7th round choice (Joel Vermin) in 2013 Entry Draft, April 2, 2013. Signed as a free agent by **Zurich** (Swiss), July 18, 2013.

BERGERON, Patrice

(BUHR-zhuhr-uhn, pa-TREES) **BOS**

Center. Shoots right. 6'2", 194 lbs. Born, Ancienne-Lorette, Que., July 24, 1985. Boston's 2nd choice, 45th overall, in 2003 Entry Draft.

			Regular Season														Playoffs								
Season	Club	League	GP	G	A	Pts	PIM	PP	SH	GW	S	%	+/-	TF	F%	Min	GP	G	A	Pts	PIM	PP	SH	GW	Min
2000-01	Ste-Foy	QAAA	5	1	2	3	0	....	....	....	....	....	....	....	....	....	....	....	....	....	....	....	....	....	....
2001-02	St-Francois	QAAA	38	25	37	62	18	....	....	....	....	....	....	....	....	....	8	6	4	10	10	....	....	....	....
	Acadie-Bathurst	QMJHL	4	0	1	1	0	....	....	....	....	....	....	....	....	....	....	....	....	....	....	....	....	....	....
2002-03	Acadie-Bathurst	QMJHL	70	23	50	73	62	....	....	....	....	....	....	....	....	....	11	6	9	15	6	....	....	....	....
2003-04	**Boston**	**NHL**	**71**	**16**	**23**	**39**	**22**	**7**	**0**	**2**	**133**	**12.0**	**5**	**699**	**49.4**	**16:21**	**7**	**1**	**3**	**4**	**0**	**0**	**0**	**1**	**17:13**
2004-05	Providence Bruins	AHL	68	21	40	61	59	....	....	....	....	....	....	....	....	....	16	5	7	12	4	....	....	....	....
2005-06	**Boston**	**NHL**	**81**	**31**	**42**	**73**	**22**	**12**	**1**	**6**	**310**	**10.0**	**3**	**1447**	**54.7**	**20:36**	....	....	....	....	....	....	....	....	....
2006-07	**Boston**	**NHL**	**77**	**22**	**48**	**70**	**26**	**14**	**0**	**6**	**224**	**9.8**	**–28**	**1560**	**51.2**	**20:49**	....	....	....	....	....	....	....	....	....
2007-08	**Boston**	**NHL**	**10**	**3**	**4**	**7**	**2**	**2**	**0**	**0**	**24**	**12.5**	**2**	**175**	**50.3**	**18:10**	....	....	....	....	....	....	....	....	....
2008-09	**Boston**	**NHL**	**64**	**8**	**31**	**39**	**16**	**1**	**1**	**1**	**155**	**5.2**	**2**	**1025**	**54.5**	**17:59**	**11**	**0**	**5**	**5**	**11**	**0**	**0**	**0**	**17:56**
2009-10	**Boston**	**NHL**	**73**	**19**	**33**	**52**	**28**	**0**	**1**	**4**	**184**	**10.3**	**6**	**1342**	**58.0**	**18:54**	**13**	**4**	**7**	**11**	**2**	**0**	**0**	**1**	**20:23**
	Canada	Olympics	7	0	1	1	2	....	....	....	....	....	....	....	....	....	....	....	....	....	....	....	....	....	....
2010-11 ♦	**Boston**	**NHL**	**80**	**22**	**35**	**57**	**26**	**3**	**2**	**4**	**211**	**10.4**	**20**	**1439**	**56.6**	**17:53**	**23**	**6**	**14**	**20**	**28**	**0**	***2**	**1**	**18:42**
2011-12	**Boston**	**NHL**	**81**	**22**	**42**	**64**	**20**	**5**	**2**	**3**	**191**	**11.5**	**36**	**1641**	**59.3**	**18:35**	**7**	**0**	**2**	**2**	**8**	**0**	**0**	**0**	**19:38**

			Regular Season														Playoffs								
Season	Club	League	GP	G	A	Pts	PIM	PP	SH	GW	S	%	+/-	TF	F%	Min	GP	G	A	Pts	PIM	PP	SH	GW	Min
2012-13	HC Lugano	Swiss	21	11	18	29	8	....	....	....	....	....	....	....	....	....	....	....	....	....	....	....	....	....	....
	Boston	**NHL**	42	10	22	32	18	2	0	3	125	8.0	24	884	62.1	19:18	22	9	6	15	13	4	0	2	20:44
	NHL Totals		579	153	280	433	180	46	7	29	1557	9.8		10212	55.8	18:49	83	20	37	57	62	4	2	5	19:21

QAAA Second All-Star Team (2002) • Frank J. Selke Trophy (2012) • King Clancy Memorial Trophy (2013)
• Missed majority of 2007-08 due to head injury vs. Philadelphia, October 27, 2007. Signed as a free agent by **Lugano** (Swiss), October 2, 2012.

BERGLUND, Patrik
(BUHRG-luhnd, PAT-rihk) **ST.L.**

Center. Shoots left. 6'3", 217 lbs. Born, Vasteras, Sweden, June 2, 1988. St. Louis' 2nd choice, 25th overall, in 2006 Entry Draft.

Season	Club	League	GP	G	A	Pts	PIM	PP	SH	GW	S	%	+/-	TF	F%	Min	GP	G	A	Pts	PIM	PP	SH	GW	Min
2002-03	Vasteras U18	Swe-U18	1	0	1	1	0	....	....	....	....	....	....	....	....	....	....	....	....	....	....	....	....	....	....
2003-04	Vasteras U18	Swe-U18	10	4	1	5	18	....	....	....	....	....	....	....	....	....	....	....	....	....	....	....	....	....	....
2004-05	Vasteras U18	Swe-U18	5	2	1	3	4	....	....	....	....	....	....	....	....	....	3	0	1	1	6	....	....	....	....
	Vasteras Jr.	Swe-Jr.	25	5	5	10	14	....	....	....	....	....	....	....	....	....	....	....	....	....	....	....	....	....	....
2005-06	Vasteras Jr.	Swe-Jr.	27	17	12	29	38	....	....	....	....	....	....	....	....	....	....	....	....	....	....	....	....	....	....
	VIK Vasteras HK	Sweden-2	21	3	1	4	4	....	....	....	....	....	....	....	....	....	....	....	....	....	....	....	....	....	....
2006-07	VIK Vasteras HK	Sweden-2	35	21	27	48	30	....	....	....	....	....	....	....	....	....	1	0	0	0	2	....	....	....	....
	Vasteras Jr.	Swe-Jr.	....	....	....	....	....	....	....	....	....	....	....	....	....	....	5	4	5	9	6	....	....	....	....
2007-08	VIK Vasteras HK	Sweden-2	46	22	32	54	26	....	....	....	....	....	....	....	....	....	5	1	2	3	6	....	....	....	....
2008-09	**St. Louis**	**NHL**	76	21	26	47	16	7	0	1	143	14.7	19	540	39.8	14:43	4	0	0	0	2	0	0	0	10:11
2009-10	**St. Louis**	**NHL**	71	13	13	26	16	6	0	4	129	10.1	–5	504	43.7	13:30	....	....	....	....	....	....	....	....	....
2010-11	**St. Louis**	**NHL**	81	22	30	52	26	8	0	1	175	12.6	–3	974	46.2	17:11	....	....	....	....	....	....	....	....	....
2011-12	**St. Louis**	**NHL**	82	19	19	38	30	0	2	3	188	10.1	4	1168	48.5	17:58	9	3	4	7	6	2	0	0	20:08
2012-13	VIK Vasteras HK	Sweden-2	30	20	12	32	20	....	....	....	....	....	....	....	....	....	....	....	....	....	....	....	....	....	....
	St. Louis	**NHL**	48	17	8	25	12	5	2	3	74	23.0	–2	603	46.3	16:50	6	1	1	2	2	0	0	0	17:46
	NHL Totals		358	92	96	188	100	26	4	12	709	13.0		3789	45.7	16:04	19	4	5	9	10	2	0	0	17:18

NHL All-Rookie Team (2009)
Signed as a free agent by **Vasteras** (Sweden-2), September 18, 2012.

BERNIER, Steve
(BAIRN-yay, STEEV) **N.J.**

Right wing. Shoots right. 6'3", 220 lbs. Born, Quebec City, Que., March 31, 1985. San Jose's 2nd choice, 16th overall, in 2003 Entry Draft.

Season	Club	League	GP	G	A	Pts	PIM	PP	SH	GW	S	%	+/-	TF	F%	Min	GP	G	A	Pts	PIM	PP	SH	GW	Min
1998-99	Quebec AA Aces	QAHA	28	33	23	56	24	....	....	....	....	....	....	....	....	....	....	....	....	....	....	....	....	....	....
99-2000	Quebec AA Aces	QAHA	26	12	23	35	42	....	....	....	....	....	....	....	....	....	....	....	....	....	....	....	....	....	....
2000-01	Ste-Foy	QAAA	39	17	35	52	48	....	....	....	....	....	....	....	....	....	16	9	17	26	8	....	....	....	....
2001-02	Moncton Wildcats	QMJHL	66	31	28	59	51	....	....	....	....	....	....	....	....	....	....	....	....	....	....	....	....	....	....
2002-03	Moncton Wildcats	QMJHL	71	49	52	101	90	....	....	....	....	....	....	....	....	....	2	1	0	1	2	....	....	....	....
2003-04	Moncton Wildcats	QMJHL	66	36	46	82	80	....	....	....	....	....	....	....	....	....	20	7	10	17	17	....	....	....	....
2004-05	Moncton Wildcats	QMJHL	68	35	36	71	114	....	....	....	....	....	....	....	....	....	12	6	13	19	22	....	....	....	....
2005-06	**San Jose**	**NHL**	39	14	13	27	35	2	1	1	75	18.7	4	8	62.5	14:08	11	1	5	6	8	1	0	1	15:17
	Cleveland Barons	AHL	49	20	23	43	33	....	....	....	....	....	....	....	....	....	....	....	....	....	....	....	....	....	....
2006-07	**San Jose**	**NHL**	62	15	16	31	29	6	0	4	104	14.4	5	18	27.8	13:35	11	0	1	1	2	0	0	0	10:39
	Worcester Sharks	AHL	10	3	4	7	2	....	....	....	....	....	....	....	....	....	....	....	....	....	....	....	....	....	....
2007-08	**San Jose**	**NHL**	59	13	10	23	62	4	0	0	96	13.5	–2	10	50.0	13:07	....	....	....	....	....	....	....	....	....
	Buffalo	**NHL**	17	3	6	9	2	0	0	0	35	8.6	1	5	20.0	14:06	....	....	....	....	....	....	....	....	....
2008-09	**Vancouver**	**NHL**	81	15	17	32	27	2	0	4	137	10.9	4	21	23.8	13:50	10	2	2	4	7	2	0	2	15:00
2009-10	**Vancouver**	**NHL**	59	11	11	22	21	3	0	0	95	11.6	0	34	20.6	14:10	12	4	1	5	0	2	0	0	9:59
2010-11	**Florida**	**NHL**	68	5	10	15	21	3	0	0	97	5.2	–14	17	23.5	13:02	....	....	....	....	....	....	....	....	....
2011-12	Albany Devils	AHL	17	3	3	6	8	....	....	....	....	....	....	....	....	....	....	....	....	....	....	....	....	....	....
	New Jersey	**NHL**	32	1	5	6	16	0	0	0	23	4.3	6	15	20.0	11:58	24	2	5	7	27	0	0	0	10:21
2012-13	**New Jersey**	**NHL**	47	8	7	15	17	2	0	1	88	9.1	–7	10	50.0	13:46	....	....	....	....	....	....	....	....	....
	NHL Totals		464	85	95	180	230	22	1	10	750	11.3		138	29.0	13:32	68	9	14	23	44	5	0	3	11:49

QMJHL All-Rookie Team (2002) • QMJHL Second All-Star Team (2003, 2004) • Canadian Major Junior Second All-Star Team (2003)
Traded to **Buffalo** by **San Jose** with San Jose's 1st round choice (Tyler Ennis) in 2008 Entry Draft for Brian Campbell and Buffalo's 7th round choice (Drew Daniels) in 2008 Entry Draft, February 26, 2008. Traded to **Vancouver** by **Buffalo** for Los Angeles' 3rd round choice (previously acquired, Buffalo selected Brayden McNabb) in 2009 Entry Draft and Vancouver's 2nd round choice (later traded to Columbus – Columbus selected Petr Straka) in 2010 Entry Draft, July 4, 2008. Traded to **Florida** by **Vancouver** with Michael Grabner and Vancouver's 1st round choice (Quinton Howden) in 2010 Entry Draft for Keith Ballard and Victor Oreskovich, June 25, 2010. Signed as a free agent by **Albany** (AHL), October 26, 2011. Signed as a free agent by **New Jersey**, January 30, 2012.

BERTUZZI, Todd
(buhr-TOO-zee, TAWD) **DET**

Right wing. Shoots left. 6'3", 229 lbs. Born, Sudbury, Ont., February 2, 1975. NY Islanders' 1st choice, 23rd overall, in 1993 Entry Draft.

Season	Club	League	GP	G	A	Pts	PIM	PP	SH	GW	S	%	+/-	TF	F%	Min	GP	G	A	Pts	PIM	PP	SH	GW	Min
1990-91	Sudbury Legion	NOHA	48	25	46	71	247	....	....	....	....	....	....	....	....	....	....	....	....	....	....	....	....	....	....
	Sudbury Cubs	NOJHA	3	3	2	5	10	....	....	....	....	....	....	....	....	....	....	....	....	....	....	....	....	....	....
1991-92	Guelph Storm	OHL	47	7	14	21	145	....	....	....	....	....	....	....	....	....	....	....	....	....	....	....	....	....	....
1992-93	Guelph Storm	OHL	59	27	32	59	164	....	....	....	....	....	....	....	....	....	5	2	2	4	6	....	....	....	....
1993-94	Guelph Storm	OHL	61	28	54	82	165	....	....	....	....	....	....	....	....	....	9	2	6	8	30	....	....	....	....
1994-95	Guelph Storm	OHL	62	54	65	119	58	....	....	....	....	....	....	....	....	....	14	*15	18	33	41	....	....	....	....
1995-96	**NY Islanders**	**NHL**	76	18	21	39	83	4	0	2	127	14.2	–14	....	....	....	....	....	....	....	....	....	....	....	....
1996-97	**NY Islanders**	**NHL**	64	10	13	23	68	3	0	1	79	12.7	–3	....	....	....	....	....	....	....	....	....	....	....	....
	Utah Grizzlies	IHL	13	5	5	10	16	....	....	....	....	....	....	....	....	....	....	....	....	....	....	....	....	....	....
1997-98	**NY Islanders**	**NHL**	52	7	11	18	58	1	0	1	63	11.1	–19	....	....	....	....	....	....	....	....	....	....	....	....
	Vancouver	**NHL**	22	6	9	15	63	1	1	1	39	15.4	2	....	....	....	....	....	....	....	....	....	....	....	....
1998-99	**Vancouver**	**NHL**	32	8	8	16	44	1	0	3	72	11.1	–6	191	43.5	18:28	....	....	....	....	....	....	....	....	....
99-2000	**Vancouver**	**NHL**	80	25	25	50	126	4	0	2	173	14.5	–2	476	46.6	15:24	....	....	....	....	....	....	....	....	....
2000-01	**Vancouver**	**NHL**	79	25	30	55	93	14	0	3	203	12.3	–18	84	45.2	17:13	4	2	2	4	8	0	0	0	19:01
2001-02	**Vancouver**	**NHL**	72	36	49	85	110	14	0	3	203	17.7	21	151	49.0	19:40	6	2	2	4	14	1	0	0	21:50
2002-03	**Vancouver**	**NHL**	82	46	51	97	144	*25	0	7	243	18.9	2	208	47.1	20:34	14	2	4	6	*60	0	0	0	21:05
2003-04	**Vancouver**	**NHL**	69	17	43	60	122	8	0	2	156	10.9	21	111	45.1	21:00	....	....	....	....	....	....	....	....	....
2004-05			DID NOT PLAY – SUSPENDED																						
2005-06	**Vancouver**	**NHL**	82	25	46	71	120	12	0	3	200	12.5	–17	363	43.8	19:08	....	....	....	....	....	....	....	....	....
	Canada	Olympics	6	0	3	3	6	....	....	....	....	....	....	....	....	....	....	....	....	....	....	....	....	....	....
2006-07	**Florida**	**NHL**	7	1	6	7	13	1	0	0	8	12.5	–4	0	0.0	16:32	....	....	....	....	....	....	....	....	....
	Detroit	**NHL**	8	2	2	4	6	0	0	0	15	13.3	3	2	50.0	15:32	16	3	4	7	15	1	0	0	14:25
2007-08	**Anaheim**	**NHL**	68	14	26	40	97	4	0	2	121	11.6	8	110	45.5	16:27	6	0	2	2	14	0	0	0	14:15
2008-09	**Calgary**	**NHL**	66	15	29	44	74	6	0	4	127	11.8	–13	45	46.7	18:36	6	1	1	2	8	0	0	0	17:25
2009-10	**Detroit**	**NHL**	82	18	26	44	80	4	0	4	216	8.3	–7	23	47.8	16:46	12	2	9	11	12	1	0	0	17:08
2010-11	**Detroit**	**NHL**	81	16	29	45	71	2	0	2	138	11.6	–7	40	45.0	15:57	11	2	4	6	15	0	0	0	13:42
2011-12	**Detroit**	**NHL**	71	14	24	38	64	0	0	1	118	11.9	23	13	38.5	15:33	5	0	0	0	9	0	0	0	12:19
2012-13	**Detroit**	**NHL**	7	2	1	3	2	0	0	0	10	20.0	3	0	0.0	15:31	6	0	0	0	2	0	0	0	9:39
	NHL Totals		1100	305	449	754	1438	104	1	41	2311	13.2		1817	45.7	17:48	86	14	28	42	157	3	0	0	16:16

OHL Second All-Star Team (1995) • NHL First All-Star Team (2003)
Played in NHL All-Star Game (2003, 2004)
Traded to **Vancouver** by **NY Islanders** with Bryan McCabe and NY Islanders' 3rd round choice (Jarkko Ruutu) in 1998 Entry Draft for Trevor Linden, February 6, 1998. • Missed majority of 1998-99 due to leg injury vs. Washington, November 1, 1998. • Suspended indefinitely by NHL for deliberate injury to Steve Moore in game vs. Colorado, March 8, 2004. • Reinstated by NHL on August 8, 2005. Traded to **Florida** by **Vancouver** with Bryan Allen and Alex Auld for Roberto Luongo, Lukas Krajicek and Florida's 6th round choice (Sergei Shirokov) in 2006 Entry Draft, June 23, 2006. Traded to **Detroit** by **Florida** for Shawn Matthias and Detroit's 2nd round choice (later traded to Nashville - Nashville selected Nick Spaling) in 2007 Entry Draft, February 27, 2007. • Missed majority of 2006-07 due to back injury. Signed as a free agent by **Anaheim**, July 2, 2007. Signed as a free agent by **Calgary**, July 7, 2008. Signed as a free agent by **Detroit**, August 18, 2009. • Missed majority of 2012-13 due to back injury at St. Louis, February 7, 2013.

BICKEL, Stu
(BIH-kuhl, STEW) **NYR**

Defense. Shoots right. 6'4", 207 lbs. Born, Chanhassen, MN, October 2, 1986.

Season	Club	League	GP	G	A	Pts	PIM	PP	SH	GW	S	%	+/-	TF	F%	Min	GP	G	A	Pts	PIM	PP	SH	GW	Min
2004-05	Green Bay	USHL	13	0	0	0	20	....	....	....	....	....	....	....	....	....	....	....	....	....	....	....	....	....	....
2005-06	Green Bay	USHL	14	0	0	0	25	....	....	....	....	....	....	....	....	....	....	....	....	....	....	....	....	....	....
2006-07	Sioux Falls	USHL	57	2	11	13	*215	....	....	....	....	....	....	....	....	....	8	0	3	3	29	....	....	....	....
2007-08	U. of Minnesota	WCHA	45	1	6	7	*92	....	....	....	....	....	....	....	....	....	....	....	....	....	....	....	....	....	....
2008-09	Iowa Chops	AHL	21	0	1	1	51	....	....	....	....	....	....	....	....	....	....	....	....	....	....	....	....	....	....
2009-10	San Antonio	AHL	36	2	2	4	38	....	....	....	....	....	....	....	....	....	....	....	....	....	....	....	....	....	....
	Bakersfield	ECHL	24	1	12	13	50	....	....	....	....	....	....	....	....	....	9	0	2	2	14	....	....	....	....

			Regular Season														Playoffs								
Season	Club	League	GP	G	A	Pts	PIM	PP	SH	GW	S	%	+/-	TF	F%	Min	GP	G	A	Pts	PIM	PP	SH	GW	Min
2010-11	Syracuse Crunch	AHL	6	0	3	3	14	....	....	....	....	....	....	....	....	....	....	....	....	....	....	....	....	....	....
	Elmira Jackals	ECHL	1	0	0	0	0	....	....	....	....	....	....	....	....	....	....	....	....	....	....	....	....	....	....
	Connecticut	AHL	54	2	7	9	135	....	....	....	....	....	....	....	....	....	6	0	1	1	6	....	....	....	....
2011-12	**NY Rangers**	**NHL**	**51**	**0**	**9**	**9**	**108**	**0**	**0**	**0**	**22**	**0.0**	**2**	**1**	**100.0**	**10:26**	**18**	**0**	**0**	**0**	**16**	**0**	**0**	**0**	**5:10**
	Connecticut	AHL	27	1	3	4	80	....	....	....	....	....	....	....	....	....	....	....	....	....	....	....	....	....	....
2012-13	Connecticut	AHL	10	0	1	1	18	....	....	....	....	....	....	....	....	....	....	....	....	....	....	....	....	....	....
	NY Rangers	**NHL**	**16**	**0**	**0**	**0**	**49**	**0**	**0**	**0**	**2**	**0.0**	**–2**	**0**	**0.0**	**5:31**	....	....	....	....	....	....	....	....	....
	NHL Totals		**67**	**0**	**9**	**9**	**157**	**0**	**0**	**0**	**24**	**0.0**		**1**	**100.0**	**9:16**	**18**	**0**	**0**	**0**	**16**	**0**	**0**	**0**	**5:10**

Signed as a free agent by **Anaheim**, July 2, 2008. Traded to **NY Rangers** by **Anaheim** for Nigel Williams, November 23, 2010. • Missed majority of 2012-13 as a healthy reserve.

BICKELL, Bryan

(BIH-kuhl, BRIGH-uhn) **CHI**

Left wing. Shoots left. 6'4", 233 lbs. Born, Bowmanville, Ont., March 9, 1986. Chicago's 3rd choice, 41st overall, in 2004 Entry Draft.

2000-01	Tor. Red Wings	GTHL	68	24	26	50	20	....	....	....	....	....	....	....	....	....	5	3	1	4	4	....	....	....	....
2001-02	Tor. Red Wings	GTHL	65	31	41	72	76	....	....	....	....	....	....	....	....	....	2	2	2	4	0	....	....	....	....
2002-03	Ottawa 67's	OHL	50	7	10	17	4	....	....	....	....	....	....	....	....	....	20	5	3	8	12	....	....	....	....
2003-04	Ottawa 67's	OHL	59	20	16	36	76	....	....	....	....	....	....	....	....	....	7	3	0	3	11	....	....	....	....
2004-05	Ottawa 67's	OHL	66	22	32	54	95	....	....	....	....	....	....	....	....	....	21	5	12	17	32	....	....	....	....
2005-06	Ottawa 67's	OHL	41	28	22	50	41	....	....	....	....	....	....	....	....	....	....	....	....	....	....	....	....	....	....
	Windsor Spitfires	OHL	26	17	16	33	19	....	....	....	....	....	....	....	....	....	7	5	5	10	10	....	....	....	....
2006-07	**Chicago**	**NHL**	**3**	**2**	**0**	**2**	**0**	**0**	**0**	**0**	**10**	**20.0**	**1**	**0**	**0.0**	**11:49**	....	....	....	....	....	....	....	....	....
	Norfolk Admirals	AHL	48	10	15	25	66	....	....	....	....	....	....	....	....	....	2	0	0	0	0	....	....	....	....
2007-08	**Chicago**	**NHL**	**4**	**0**	**0**	**0**	**2**	**0**	**0**	**0**	**3**	**0.0**	**–1**	**0**	**0.0**	**9:08**	....	....	....	....	....	....	....	....	....
	Rockford IceHogs	AHL	73	19	20	39	52	....	....	....	....	....	....	....	....	....	12	2	3	5	11	....	....	....	....
2008-09	Rockford IceHogs	AHL	42	6	8	14	60	....	....	....	....	....	....	....	....	....	4	0	2	2	4	....	....	....	....
2009-10	**Chicago**	**NHL**	**16**	**3**	**1**	**4**	**5**	**0**	**0**	**1**	**20**	**15.0**	**4**	**2**	**0.0**	**9:36**	**4**	**0**	**1**	**1**	**2**	**0**	**0**	**0**	**13:14**
	Rockford IceHogs	AHL	65	16	15	31	58	....	....	....	....	....	....	....	....	....	....	....	....	....	....	....	....	....	....
2010-11	**Chicago**	**NHL**	**78**	**17**	**20**	**37**	**40**	**2**	**0**	**2**	**130**	**13.1**	**6**	**12**	**25.0**	**13:50**	**5**	**2**	**2**	**4**	**0**	**0**	**0**	**0**	**13:05**
2011-12	**Chicago**	**NHL**	**71**	**9**	**15**	**24**	**48**	**0**	**0**	**0**	**84**	**10.7**	**–3**	**1**	**0.0**	**12:08**	**6**	**2**	**0**	**2**	**4**	**1**	**0**	**1**	**16:46**
2012-13	Orli Znojmo	Austria	28	9	18	27	14	....	....	....	....	....	....	....	....	....	....	....	....	....	....	....	....	....	....
	♦ Chicago	**NHL**	**48**	**9**	**14**	**23**	**25**	**0**	**0**	**2**	**82**	**11.0**	**12**	**6**	**33.3**	**12:48**	**23**	**9**	**8**	**17**	**14**	**1**	**0**	**2**	**15:22**
	NHL Totals		**220**	**40**	**50**	**90**	**120**	**2**	**0**	**5**	**329**	**12.2**		**21**	**23.8**	**12:39**	**38**	**13**	**11**	**24**	**20**	**2**	**0**	**3**	**15:04**

Signed as a free agent by **Znojmo** (Austria), October 3, 2012.

BIEKSA, Kevin

(BEE-ehks-ah, KEH-vihn) **VAN**

Defense. Shoots right. 6'1", 206 lbs. Born, Grimsby, Ont., June 16, 1981. Vancouver's 4th choice, 151st overall, in 2001 Entry Draft.

1997-98	Stoney Creek	ON-Jr.B	STATISTICS NOT AVAILABLE																						
	Burlington	ON-Jr.A	27	0	3	3	10	....	....	....	....	....	....	....	....	....	....	....	....	....	....	....	....	....	....
1998-99	Burlington	ON-Jr.A	49	8	29	37	83	....	....	....	....	....	....	....	....	....	....	....	....	....	....	....	....	....	....
99-2000	Burlington	ON-Jr.A	49	6	27	33	139	....	....	....	....	....	....	....	....	....	....	....	....	....	....	....	....	....	....
2000-01	Bowling Green	CCHA	35	4	9	13	90	....	....	....	....	....	....	....	....	....	....	....	....	....	....	....	....	....	....
2001-02	Bowling Green	CCHA	40	5	10	15	68	....	....	....	....	....	....	....	....	....	....	....	....	....	....	....	....	....	....
2002-03	Bowling Green	CCHA	34	8	17	25	92	....	....	....	....	....	....	....	....	....	....	....	....	....	....	....	....	....	....
2003-04	Bowling Green	CCHA	38	7	15	22	66	....	....	....	....	....	....	....	....	....	....	....	....	....	....	....	....	....	....
	Manitoba Moose	AHL	4	0	2	2	2	....	....	....	....	....	....	....	....	....	....	....	....	....	....	....	....	....	....
2004-05	Manitoba Moose	AHL	80	12	27	39	192	....	....	....	....	....	....	....	....	....	14	1	1	2	52	....	....	....	....
2005-06	**Vancouver**	**NHL**	**39**	**0**	**6**	**6**	**77**	**0**	**0**	**0**	**38**	**0.0**	**–1**	**0**	**0.0**	**16:06**	....	....	....	....	....	....	....	....	....
	Manitoba Moose	AHL	23	3	17	20	71	....	....	....	....	....	....	....	....	....	13	0	10	10	38	....	....	....	....
2006-07	**Vancouver**	**NHL**	**81**	**12**	**30**	**42**	**134**	**6**	**0**	**2**	**203**	**5.9**	**1**	**0**	**0.0**	**24:16**	**9**	**0**	**0**	**0**	**20**	**0**	**0**	**0**	**28:01**
2007-08	**Vancouver**	**NHL**	**34**	**2**	**10**	**12**	**90**	**1**	**0**	**1**	**64**	**3.1**	**–11**	**0**	**0.0**	**23:24**	....	....	....	....	....	....	....	....	....
	Manitoba Moose	AHL	1	0	1	1	2	....	....	....	....	....	....	....	....	....	....	....	....	....	....	....	....	....	....
2008-09	**Vancouver**	**NHL**	**72**	**11**	**32**	**43**	**97**	**5**	**0**	**2**	**153**	**7.2**	**–4**	**0**	**0.0**	**23:29**	**10**	**0**	**5**	**5**	**14**	**0**	**0**	**0**	**24:08**
2009-10	**Vancouver**	**NHL**	**55**	**3**	**19**	**22**	**85**	**1**	**0**	**0**	**95**	**3.2**	**–5**	**0**	**0.0**	**21:49**	**12**	**3**	**5**	**8**	**14**	**1**	**0**	**1**	**22:37**
2010-11	**Vancouver**	**NHL**	**66**	**6**	**16**	**22**	**73**	**1**	**0**	**2**	**105**	**5.7**	**32**	**0**	**0.0**	**22:28**	**25**	**5**	**5**	**10**	**51**	**1**	**0**	**1**	**25:40**
2011-12	**Vancouver**	**NHL**	**78**	**8**	**36**	**44**	**94**	**2**	**0**	**2**	**166**	**4.8**	**12**	**1**	**0.0**	**23:38**	**5**	**1**	**0**	**1**	**6**	**0**	**0**	**1**	**24:46**
2012-13	**Vancouver**	**NHL**	**36**	**6**	**6**	**12**	**48**	**2**	**0**	**1**	**77**	**7.8**	**6**	**0**	**0.0**	**21:56**	**4**	**1**	**0**	**1**	**8**	**0**	**0**	**0**	**25:51**
	NHL Totals		**461**	**48**	**155**	**203**	**698**	**18**	**0**	**10**	**901**	**5.3**		**1**	**0.0**	**22:33**	**65**	**10**	**15**	**25**	**113**	**2**	**0**	**3**	**25:08**

AHL All-Rookie Team (2005)

BISSONNETTE, Paul

(bih-sawn-EHT, PAWL) **PHX**

Left wing. Shoots left. 6'2", 216 lbs. Born, Welland, Ont., March 11, 1985. Pittsburgh's 5th choice, 121st overall, in 2003 Entry Draft.

2001-02	North Bay	OHL	57	3	3	6	21	....	....	....	....	....	....	....	....	....	5	0	0	0	2	....	....	....	....
2002-03	Saginaw Spirit	OHL	67	7	16	23	57	....	....	....	....	....	....	....	....	....	....	....	....	....	....	....	....	....	....
2003-04	Saginaw Spirit	OHL	67	5	14	19	96	....	....	....	....	....	....	....	....	....	....	....	....	....	....	....	....	....	....
2004-05	Saginaw Spirit	OHL	28	1	6	7	46	....	....	....	....	....	....	....	....	....	....	....	....	....	....	....	....	....	....
	Owen Sound	OHL	35	2	11	13	46	....	....	....	....	....	....	....	....	....	8	1	3	4	2	....	....	....	....
2005-06	Wilkes-Barre	AHL	55	1	5	6	60	....	....	....	....	....	....	....	....	....	11	0	1	1	4	....	....	....	....
	Wheeling Nailers	ECHL	14	3	7	10	4	....	....	....	....	....	....	....	....	....	....	....	....	....	....	....	....	....	....
2006-07	Wilkes-Barre	AHL	3	0	0	0	6	....	....	....	....	....	....	....	....	....	....	....	....	....	....	....	....	....	....
	Wheeling Nailers	ECHL	65	10	32	42	115	....	....	....	....	....	....	....	....	....	....	....	....	....	....	....	....	....	....
2007-08	Wilkes-Barre	AHL	46	3	5	8	145	....	....	....	....	....	....	....	....	....	7	0	0	0	11	....	....	....	....
	Wheeling Nailers	ECHL	22	3	14	17	43	....	....	....	....	....	....	....	....	....	....	....	....	....	....	....	....	....	....
2008-09	**Pittsburgh**	**NHL**	**15**	**0**	**1**	**1**	**22**	**0**	**0**	**0**	**4**	**0.0**	**–1**	**0**	**0.0**	**3:31**	....	....	....	....	....	....	....	....	....
	Wilkes-Barre	AHL	57	9	7	16	176	....	....	....	....	....	....	....	....	....	8	0	2	2	9	....	....	....	....
2009-10	**Phoenix**	**NHL**	**41**	**3**	**2**	**5**	**117**	**0**	**0**	**1**	**25**	**12.0**	**–2**	**0**	**0.0**	**5:52**	....	....	....	....	....	....	....	....	....
2010-11	**Phoenix**	**NHL**	**48**	**1**	**0**	**1**	**71**	**0**	**0**	**0**	**18**	**5.6**	**6**	**3**	**66.7**	**5:15**	**1**	**0**	**0**	**0**	**0**	**0**	**0**	**0**	**4:05**
2011-12	**Phoenix**	**NHL**	**31**	**1**	**0**	**1**	**41**	**0**	**0**	**1**	**15**	**6.7**	**–4**	**1**	**0.0**	**6:04**	**3**	**0**	**0**	**0**	**15**	**0**	**0**	**0**	**2:41**
2012-13	Cardiff Devils	Britain	11	6	15	21	8	....	....	....	....	....	....	....	....	....	....	....	....	....	....	....	....	....	....
	Phoenix	**NHL**	**28**	**0**	**6**	**6**	**36**	**0**	**0**	**0**	**13**	**0.0**	**2**	**0**	**0.0**	**5:25**	....	....	....	....	....	....	....	....	....
	NHL Totals		**163**	**5**	**9**	**14**	**287**	**0**	**0**	**2**	**75**	**6.7**		**4**	**50.0**	**5:26**	**4**	**0**	**0**	**0**	**15**	**0**	**0**	**0**	**3:02**

Claimed on waivers by **Phoenix** from **Pittsburgh**, September 30, 2009. • Missed majority of 2011-12 as a healthy reserve. Signed as a free agent by **Cardiff** (Britain), November 1, 2012.

BITZ, Byron

(BIHTZ, BIGH-ruhn)

Right wing. Shoots right. 6'5", 215 lbs. Born, Saskatoon, Sask., July 21, 1984. Boston's 4th choice, 107th overall, in 2003 Entry Draft.

2000-01	Saskatoon	SMBHL	40	17	35	52	....	....	....	....	....	....	....	....	....	....	....	....	....	....	....	....	....	....	....
2001-02	Sask. Contacts	SMHL	41	25	48	73	69	....	....	....	....	....	....	....	....	....	11	12	10	22	9	....	....	....	....
2002-03	Nanaimo Clippers	BCHL	58	27	46	73	59	....	....	....	....	....	....	....	....	....	....	....	....	....	....	....	....	....	....
2003-04	Cornell Big Red	ECAC	31	5	16	21	36	....	....	....	....	....	....	....	....	....	....	....	....	....	....	....	....	....	....
2004-05	Cornell Big Red	ECAC	29	5	10	15	20	....	....	....	....	....	....	....	....	....	....	....	....	....	....	....	....	....	....
2005-06	Cornell Big Red	ECAC	35	10	18	28	52	....	....	....	....	....	....	....	....	....	....	....	....	....	....	....	....	....	....
2006-07	Cornell Big Red	ECAC	29	8	16	24	49	....	....	....	....	....	....	....	....	....	....	....	....	....	....	....	....	....	....
2007-08	Providence Bruins	AHL	61	13	14	27	70	....	....	....	....	....	....	....	....	....	10	1	1	2	6	....	....	....	....
2008-09	**Boston**	**NHL**	**35**	**4**	**3**	**7**	**18**	**0**	**0**	**0**	**31**	**12.9**	**0**	**50**	**42.0**	**10:22**	**5**	**1**	**1**	**2**	**2**	**0**	**0**	**0**	**11:27**
	Providence Bruins	AHL	37	3	7	10	68	....	....	....	....	....	....	....	....	....	....	....	....	....	....	....	....	....	....
2009-10	**Boston**	**NHL**	**45**	**4**	**5**	**9**	**31**	**0**	**0**	**2**	**51**	**7.8**	**–9**	**17**	**41.2**	**10:57**	....	....	....	....	....	....	....	....	....
	Florida	**NHL**	**7**	**1**	**1**	**2**	**2**	**0**	**0**	**0**	**7**	**14.3**	**1**	**1**	**0.0**	**11:37**	....	....	....	....	....	....	....	....	....
2010-11			DID NOT PLAY – INJURED																						
2011-12	**Vancouver**	**NHL**	**10**	**1**	**3**	**4**	**14**	**0**	**0**	**0**	**6**	**16.7**	**2**	**3**	**0.0**	**10:30**	**1**	**0**	**0**	**0**	**15**	**0**	**0**	**0**	**2:51**
	Chicago Wolves	AHL	24	2	7	9	11	....	....	....	....	....	....	....	....	....	3	0	1	1	2	....	....	....	....
2012-13			DID NOT PLAY – INJURED																						
	NHL Totals		**97**	**10**	**12**	**22**	**65**	**0**	**0**	**2**	**95**	**10.5**		**71**	**39.4**	**10:44**	**6**	**1**	**1**	**2**	**17**	**0**	**0**	**0**	**10:01**

Traded to **Florida** by **Boston** with Craig Weller and Tampa Bay's 2nd round choice (previously acquired, Florida selected Alexander Petrovic) in 2010 Entry Draft for Dennis Seidenberg and Matt Bartkowski, March 3, 2010. • Missed 2010-11 due to hernia surgery. Signed as a free agent by **Vancouver**, July 26, 2011. • Missed majority of 2011-12 and all of 2012-13 due to sports hernia injury and resulting surgery.

BJUGSTAD, Nick
(BYOOG-stad, NIHK) **FLA**

Center. Shoots right. 6'5", 211 lbs. Born, Minneapolis, MN, July 17, 1992. Florida's 2nd choice, 19th overall, in 2010 Entry Draft.

			Regular Season														Playoffs								
Season	Club	League	GP	G	A	Pts	PIM	PP	SH	GW	S	%	+/-	TF	F%	Min	GP	G	A	Pts	PIM	PP	SH	GW	Min
2007-08	Blaine Bengals	High-MN	24	6	14	20	10	....	....	....	....	....	....	....	....	....	....	....	....	....	....	....	....	....	....
2008-09	Blaine Bengals	High-MN	25	26	25	51	20	....	....	....	....	....	....	....	....	....	....	....	....	....	....	....	....	....	....
2009-10	Team Northwest	UMHSEL	23	13	8	21	18	....	....	....	....	....	....	....	....	....	....	....	....	....	....	....	....	....	....
	Blaine Bengals	High-MN	30	35	34	69	26	....	....	....	....	....	....	....	....	....	....	....	....	....	....	....	....	....	....
	USNTDP	U-18	4	0	0	0	0	....	....	....	....	....	....	....	....	....	....	....	....	....	....	....	....	....	....
2010-11	U. of Minnesota	WCHA	29	8	12	20	51	....	....	....	....	....	....	....	....	....	....	....	....	....	....	....	....	....	....
2011-12	U. of Minnesota	WCHA	40	25	17	42	28	....	....	....	....	....	....	....	....	....	....	....	....	....	....	....	....	....	....
2012-13	U. of Minnesota	WCHA	40	21	15	36	28	....	....	....	....	....	....	....	....	....	....	....	....	....	....	....	....	....	....
	Florida	**NHL**	**11**	**1**	**0**	**1**	**2**	**0**	**0**	**0**	**17**	**5.9**	**–8**	**132**	**40.2**	**15:13**	....	....	....	....	....	....	....	....	....
	NHL Totals		**11**	**1**	**0**	**1**	**2**	**0**	**0**	**0**	**17**	**5.9**		**132**	**40.2**	**15:13**	....	....	....	....	....	....	....	....	....

WCHA First All-Star Team (2012) • NCAA West Second All-American Team (2012)

BLANCHARD, Nicolas
(BLAN-shard, NIHK-oh-las) **CAR**

Left wing. Shoots left. 6'3", 205 lbs. Born, Granby, Que., May 31, 1987. Carolina's 8th choice, 192nd overall, in 2005 Entry Draft.

			Regular Season														Playoffs								
Season	Club	League	GP	G	A	Pts	PIM	PP	SH	GW	S	%	+/-	TF	F%	Min	GP	G	A	Pts	PIM	PP	SH	GW	Min
2003-04	Antoine-Girouard	QAAA	42	24	28	52	28	....	....	....	....	....	....	....	....	....	13	9	6	15	4	....	....	....	....
2004-05	Chicoutimi	QMJHL	69	13	26	39	31	....	....	....	....	....	....	....	....	....	17	2	2	4	10	....	....	....	....
2005-06	Chicoutimi	QMJHL	60	15	29	44	51	....	....	....	....	....	....	....	....	....	9	1	2	3	4	....	....	....	....
2006-07	Chicoutimi	QMJHL	62	22	35	57	41	....	....	....	....	....	....	....	....	....	4	0	2	2	8	....	....	....	....
	Albany River Rats	AHL	7	1	2	3	2	....	....	....	....	....	....	....	....	....	5	0	0	0	2	....	....	....	....
2007-08	Albany River Rats	AHL	64	11	12	23	70	....	....	....	....	....	....	....	....	....	7	0	2	2	2	....	....	....	....
2008-09	Albany River Rats	AHL	55	7	12	19	132	....	....	....	....	....	....	....	....	....	....	....	....	....	....	....	....	....	....
2009-10	Albany River Rats	AHL	76	14	8	22	171	....	....	....	....	....	....	....	....	....	8	0	0	0	13	....	....	....	....
2010-11	Charlotte	AHL	72	8	10	18	101	....	....	....	....	....	....	....	....	....	16	2	3	5	16	....	....	....	....
2011-12	Charlotte	AHL	68	9	12	21	103	....	....	....	....	....	....	....	....	....	....	....	....	....	....	....	....	....	....
2012-13	Charlotte	AHL	61	4	5	9	124	....	....	....	....	....	....	....	....	....	3	0	1	1	7	....	....	....	....
	Carolina	**NHL**	**9**	**0**	**0**	**0**	**20**	**0**	**0**	**0**	**6**	**0.0**	**–2**	**1**	**100.0**	**8:41**	....	....	....	....	....	....	....	....	....
	NHL Totals		**9**	**0**	**0**	**0**	**20**	**0**	**0**	**0**	**6**	**0.0**		**1**	**100.0**	**8:41**	....	....	....	....	....	....	....	....	....

BLUM, Jonathon
(BLUHM, JAWN-ah-thuhn) **MIN**

Defense. Shoots right. 6'1", 186 lbs. Born, Long Beach, CA, January 30, 1989. Nashville's 1st choice, 23rd overall, in 2007 Entry Draft.

			Regular Season														Playoffs								
Season	Club	League	GP	G	A	Pts	PIM	PP	SH	GW	S	%	+/-	TF	F%	Min	GP	G	A	Pts	PIM	PP	SH	GW	Min
2004-05	California Wave	Minor-CA	55	15	50	65	65	....	....	....	....	....	....	....	....	....	....	....	....	....	....	....	....	....	....
2005-06	Vancouver Giants	WHL	61	7	17	24	25	....	....	....	....	....	....	....	....	....	18	1	7	8	16	....	....	....	....
2006-07	Vancouver Giants	WHL	72	8	43	51	48	....	....	....	....	....	....	....	....	....	22	3	6	9	8	....	....	....	....
2007-08	Vancouver Giants	WHL	64	18	45	63	44	....	....	....	....	....	....	....	....	....	10	3	4	7	10	....	....	....	....
2008-09	Vancouver Giants	WHL	51	16	50	66	30	....	....	....	....	....	....	....	....	....	17	7	11	18	6	....	....	....	....
	Milwaukee	AHL	....	....	....	....	....	....	....	....	....	....	....	....	....	....	5	0	0	0	0	....	....	....	....
2009-10	Milwaukee	AHL	80	11	30	41	32	....	....	....	....	....	....	....	....	....	7	1	7	8	0	....	....	....	....
2010-11	**Nashville**	**NHL**	**23**	**3**	**5**	**8**	**8**	**1**	**0**	**1**	**18**	**16.7**	**8**	**0**	**0.0**	**17:45**	**12**	**0**	**2**	**2**	**0**	**0**	**0**	**0**	**18:51**
	Milwaukee	AHL	54	7	27	34	20	....	....	....	....	....	....	....	....	....	1	0	0	0	0	....	....	....	....
2011-12	**Nashville**	**NHL**	**33**	**3**	**4**	**7**	**6**	**0**	**0**	**1**	**25**	**12.0**	**–14**	**0**	**0.0**	**17:56**	....	....	....	....	....	....	....	....	....
	Milwaukee	AHL	48	4	22	26	36	....	....	....	....	....	....	....	....	....	3	0	1	1	4	....	....	....	....
2012-13	Milwaukee	AHL	34	1	11	12	16	....	....	....	....	....	....	....	....	....	....	....	....	....	....	....	....	....	....
	Nashville	**NHL**	**35**	**1**	**6**	**7**	**6**	**0**	**0**	**0**	**26**	**3.8**	**–1**	**0**	**0.0**	**14:18**	....	....	....	....	....	....	....	....	....
	NHL Totals		**91**	**7**	**15**	**22**	**20**	**1**	**0**	**2**	**69**	**10.1**		**0**	**0.0**	**16:30**	**12**	**0**	**2**	**2**	**0**	**0**	**0**	**0**	**18:51**

WHL West Second All-Star Team (2008) • WHL West First All-Star Team (2009) • WHL Defenseman of the Year (2009) • Canadian Major Junior First All-Star Team (2009) • Canadian Major Junior Defenseman of the Year (2009)

Signed as a free agent by **Minnesota**, July 12, 2013.

BLUNDEN, Mike
(BLUHN-dehn, MIGHK) **MTL**

Right wing. Shoots right. 6'4", 211 lbs. Born, Toronto, Ont., December 15, 1986. Chicago's 2nd choice, 43rd overall, in 2005 Entry Draft.

			Regular Season														Playoffs								
Season	Club	League	GP	G	A	Pts	PIM	PP	SH	GW	S	%	+/-	TF	F%	Min	GP	G	A	Pts	PIM	PP	SH	GW	Min
2001-02	Gloucester	Minor-ON	32	23	12	35	52	....	....	....	....	....	....	....	....	....	....	....	....	....	....	....	....	....	....
	Gloucester	ON-Jr.A	2	0	0	0	2	....	....	....	....	....	....	....	....	....	....	....	....	....	....	....	....	....	....
2002-03	Erie Otters	OHL	63	10	7	17	55	....	....	....	....	....	....	....	....	....	....	....	....	....	....	....	....	....	....
2003-04	Erie Otters	OHL	52	22	17	39	53	....	....	....	....	....	....	....	....	....	3	0	0	0	0	....	....	....	....
2004-05	Erie Otters	OHL	61	22	19	41	75	....	....	....	....	....	....	....	....	....	2	0	0	0	2	....	....	....	....
2005-06	Erie Otters	OHL	60	46	38	84	63	....	....	....	....	....	....	....	....	....	....	....	....	....	....	....	....	....	....
	Norfolk Admirals	AHL	11	1	5	6	2	....	....	....	....	....	....	....	....	....	1	0	0	0	0	....	....	....	....
2006-07	**Chicago**	**NHL**	**9**	**0**	**0**	**0**	**10**	**0**	**0**	**0**	**10**	**0.0**	**–5**	**1**	**0.0**	**11:23**	....	....	....	....	....	....	....	....	....
	Norfolk Admirals	AHL	17	4	5	9	15	....	....	....	....	....	....	....	....	....	....	....	....	....	....	....	....	....	....
2007-08	**Chicago**	**NHL**	**1**	**0**	**0**	**0**	**0**	**0**	**0**	**0**	**1**	**0.0**	**–1**	**0**	**0.0**	**7:51**	....	....	....	....	....	....	....	....	....
	Rockford IceHogs	AHL	74	16	21	37	83	....	....	....	....	....	....	....	....	....	12	1	3	4	35	....	....	....	....
2008-09	Rockford IceHogs	AHL	37	3	7	10	42	....	....	....	....	....	....	....	....	....	....	....	....	....	....	....	....	....	....
	Syracuse Crunch	AHL	39	9	12	21	68	....	....	....	....	....	....	....	....	....	....	....	....	....	....	....	....	....	....
2009-10	**Columbus**	**NHL**	**40**	**2**	**2**	**4**	**59**	**0**	**0**	**0**	**40**	**5.0**	**3**	**90**	**32.2**	**8:07**	....	....	....	....	....	....	....	....	....
	Syracuse Crunch	AHL	25	7	9	16	43	....	....	....	....	....	....	....	....	....	....	....	....	....	....	....	....	....	....
2010-11	**Columbus**	**NHL**	**1**	**0**	**0**	**0**	**0**	**0**	**0**	**0**	**2**	**0.0**	**–1**	**10**	**50.0**	**10:31**	....	....	....	....	....	....	....	....	....
	Springfield	AHL	37	12	9	21	41	....	....	....	....	....	....	....	....	....	....	....	....	....	....	....	....	....	....
2011-12	**Montreal**	**NHL**	**39**	**2**	**2**	**4**	**27**	**0**	**0**	**0**	**34**	**5.9**	**–1**	**5**	**40.0**	**9:22**	....	....	....	....	....	....	....	....	....
	Hamilton	AHL	17	3	5	8	12	....	....	....	....	....	....	....	....	....	....	....	....	....	....	....	....	....	....
2012-13	Hamilton	AHL	54	10	12	22	76	....	....	....	....	....	....	....	....	....	....	....	....	....	....	....	....	....	....
	Montreal	**NHL**	**5**	**0**	**0**	**0**	**4**	**0**	**0**	**0**	**5**	**0.0**	**–1**	**0**	**0.0**	**8:21**	**1**	**0**	**0**	**0**	**10**	**0**	**0**	**0**	**8:12**
	NHL Totals		**95**	**4**	**4**	**8**	**100**	**0**	**0**	**0**	**92**	**4.3**		**106**	**34.0**	**8:58**	**1**	**0**	**0**	**0**	**10**	**0**	**0**	**0**	**8:12**

• Missed majority of 2006-07 due to shoulder injury vs. Hershey (AHL), December 10, 2006. Traded to **Columbus** by **Chicago** for Adam Pineault, January 10, 2008. • Missed remainder of 2010-11 due to shoulder injury vs. Worcester (AHL), January 14, 2011. Traded to **Montreal** by **Columbus** for Ryan Russell, July 7, 2011.

BODIE, Troy
(BOH-dee, TROI) **TOR**

Right wing. Shoots right. 6'4", 220 lbs. Born, Portage La Prairie, Man., January 25, 1985. Edmonton's 12th choice, 278th overall, in 2003 Entry Draft.

			Regular Season														Playoffs								
Season	Club	League	GP	G	A	Pts	PIM	PP	SH	GW	S	%	+/-	TF	F%	Min	GP	G	A	Pts	PIM	PP	SH	GW	Min
2001-02	Central Plains	MMMHL	40	22	21	43	10	....	....	....	....	....	....	....	....	....	....	....	....	....	....	....	....	....	....
2002-03	Kelowna Rockets	WHL	35	4	4	8	36	....	....	....	....	....	....	....	....	....	11	1	1	2	2	....	....	....	....
2003-04	Kelowna Rockets	WHL	71	8	12	20	112	....	....	....	....	....	....	....	....	....	17	7	3	10	6	....	....	....	....
2004-05	Kelowna Rockets	WHL	72	24	24	48	96	....	....	....	....	....	....	....	....	....	24	4	13	17	26	....	....	....	....
2005-06	Kelowna Rockets	WHL	72	28	25	53	117	....	....	....	....	....	....	....	....	....	12	5	4	9	8	....	....	....	....
2006-07	Hamilton	AHL	20	0	1	1	29	....	....	....	....	....	....	....	....	....	....	....	....	....	....	....	....	....	....
	Stockton Thunder	ECHL	46	21	17	38	80	....	....	....	....	....	....	....	....	....	6	0	2	2	6	....	....	....	....
2007-08	Springfield	AHL	62	9	6	15	108	....	....	....	....	....	....	....	....	....	....	....	....	....	....	....	....	....	....
2008-09	**Anaheim**	**NHL**	**4**	**0**	**0**	**0**	**0**	**0**	**0**	**0**	**5**	**0.0**	**0**	**2**	**50.0**	**8:09**	....	....	....	....	....	....	....	....	....
	Iowa Chops	AHL	71	15	12	27	105	....	....	....	....	....	....	....	....	....	....	....	....	....	....	....	....	....	....
2009-10	**Anaheim**	**NHL**	**44**	**5**	**2**	**7**	**80**	**0**	**1**	**1**	**58**	**8.6**	**–8**	**1**	**0.0**	**11:15**	....	....	....	....	....	....	....	....	....
	San Antonio	AHL	16	2	1	3	43	....	....	....	....	....	....	....	....	....	....	....	....	....	....	....	....	....	....
	Toronto Marlies	AHL	16	6	4	10	13	....	....	....	....	....	....	....	....	....	....	....	....	....	....	....	....	....	....
2010-11	**Anaheim**	**NHL**	**9**	**0**	**1**	**1**	**7**	**0**	**0**	**0**	**5**	**0.0**	**–3**	**0**	**0.0**	**9:43**	....	....	....	....	....	....	....	....	....
	Carolina	**NHL**	**50**	**1**	**2**	**3**	**54**	**0**	**0**	**0**	**39**	**2.6**	**–4**	**1**	**0.0**	**6:19**	....	....	....	....	....	....	....	....	....
2011-12	Syracuse Crunch	AHL	69	5	10	15	119	....	....	....	....	....	....	....	....	....	4	0	0	0	0	....	....	....	....
2012-13	Norfolk Admirals	AHL	47	4	8	12	111	....	....	....	....	....	....	....	....	....	....	....	....	....	....	....	....	....	....
	Portland Pirates	AHL	5	3	1	4	7	....	....	....	....	....	....	....	....	....	2	0	0	0	2	....	....	....	....
	NHL Totals		**107**	**6**	**5**	**11**	**141**	**0**	**1**	**1**	**107**	**5.6**		**4**	**25.0**	**8:42**	....	....	....	....	....	....	....	....	....

Signed as a free agent by **Anaheim**, July 22, 2008. Claimed on waivers by **Carolina** from **Anaheim**, November 16, 2010. Signed as a free agent by **Anaheim**, October 12, 2011. Signed as a free agent by **Norfolk** (AHL), September 21, 2012. • Loaned to **Portland** (AHL) by **Norfolk** (AHL), April 10, 2013. Signed as a free agent by **Toronto**, July 10, 2013.

BODNARCHUK, Andrew

(BAWD-nahr-chuhk, AN-droo) **L.A.**

Defense. Shoots left. 5'11", 190 lbs. Born, Drumheller, Alta., July 11, 1988. Boston's 5th choice, 128th overall, in 2006 Entry Draft.

			Regular Season														Playoffs								
Season	Club	League	GP	G	A	Pts	PIM	PP	SH	GW	S	%	+/-	TF	F%	Min	GP	G	A	Pts	PIM	PP	SH	GW	Min
2003-04	Dartmouth	NSMHL	58	16	23	39	81	....	....	....	....	....	....	....	....	....	....	....	....	....	....	....	....	....	....
2004-05	St. Paul's School	High-NH	36	3	15	18	....	....	....	....	....	....	....	....	....	....	....	....	....	....	....	....	....	....	....
2005-06	Halifax	QMJHL	68	6	17	23	136	....	....	....	....	....	....	....	....	....	11	0	2	2	22	....	....	....	....
2006-07	Halifax	QMJHL	63	16	41	57	96	....	....	....	....	....	....	....	....	....	12	1	10	11	25	....	....	....	....
	Providence Bruins	AHL	....	....	....	....	....	....	....	....	....	....	....	....	....	....	1	0	0	0	0	....	....	....	....
2007-08	Halifax	QMJHL	65	10	33	43	89	....	....	....	....	....	....	....	....	....	14	0	9	9	16	....	....	....	....
2008-09	Providence Bruins	AHL	62	1	8	9	33	....	....	....	....	....	....	....	....	....	15	0	2	2	22	....	....	....	....
2009-10	**Boston**	**NHL**	**5**	**0**	**0**	**0**	**2**	**0**	**0**	**0**	**0**	**0.0**	**–2**	**0**	**0.0**	**7:19**	....	....	....	....	....	....	....	....	....
	Providence Bruins	AHL	70	5	10	15	51	....	....	....	....	....	....	....	....	....	....	....	....	....	....	....	....	....	....
2010-11	Providence Bruins	AHL	75	1	15	16	91	....	....	....	....	....	....	....	....	....	....	....	....	....	....	....	....	....	....
2011-12	Providence Bruins	AHL	63	5	12	17	44	....	....	....	....	....	....	....	....	....	....	....	....	....	....	....	....	....	....
2012-13	Manchester	AHL	69	5	15	20	77	....	....	....	....	....	....	....	....	....	4	0	0	0	0	....	....	....	....
	NHL Totals		**5**	**0**	**0**	**0**	**2**	**0**	**0**	**0**	**0**	**0.0**		**0**	**0.0**	**7:19**	....	....	....	....	....	....	....	....	....

QMJHL All-Rookie Team (2006)

Signed as a free agent by **Los Angeles**, July 6, 2012.

BOEDKER, Mikkel

(BAWD-kuhr, MIH-kehl) **PHX**

Right wing. Shoots left. 6', 211 lbs. Born, Brondby, Denmark, December 16, 1989. Phoenix's 1st choice, 8th overall, in 2008 Entry Draft.

Season	Club	League	GP	G	A	Pts	PIM	PP	SH	GW	S	%	+/-	TF	F%	Min	GP	G	A	Pts	PIM	PP	SH	GW	Min
2004-05	Rodovre IK	Den-2	1	0	1	1	0	....	....	....	....	....	....	....	....	....	....	....	....	....	....	....	....	....	....
2005-06	Frolunda U18	Swe-U18	5	2	0	2	0	....	....	....	....	....	....	....	....	....	....	....	....	....	....	....	....	....	....
	Frolunda Jr.	Swe-Jr.	37	9	8	17	22	....	....	....	....	....	....	....	....	....	2	0	1	1	0	....	....	....	....
2006-07	Frolunda U18	Swe-U18	3	3	2	5	2	....	....	....	....	....	....	....	....	....	2	1	2	3	0	....	....	....	....
	Frolunda Jr.	Swe-Jr.	39	19	30	49	14	....	....	....	....	....	....	....	....	....	6	5	4	9	2	....	....	....	....
	Frolunda	Sweden	2	0	0	0	0	....	....	....	....	....	....	....	....	....	8	6	5	11	6	....	....	....	....
2007-08	Kitchener Rangers	OHL	62	29	44	73	14	....	....	....	....	....	....	....	....	....	20	9	*26	35	2	....	....	....	....
2008-09	**Phoenix**	**NHL**	**78**	**11**	**17**	**28**	**18**	**2**	**0**	**3**	**116**	**9.5**	**–6**	**8**	**12.5**	**15:32**	....	....	....	....	....	....	....	....	....
2009-10	**Phoenix**	**NHL**	**14**	**1**	**2**	**3**	**0**	**0**	**0**	**0**	**7**	**14.3**	**2**	**0**	**0.0**	**8:43**	....	....	....	....	....	....	....	....	....
	San Antonio	AHL	64	11	27	38	4	....	....	....	....	....	....	....	....	....	....	....	....	....	....	....	....	....	....
2010-11	**Phoenix**	**NHL**	**34**	**4**	**10**	**14**	**8**	**0**	**0**	**0**	**39**	**10.3**	**11**	**5**	**60.0**	**10:54**	**4**	**0**	**1**	**1**	**2**	**0**	**0**	**0**	**8:58**
	San Antonio	AHL	36	12	22	34	8	....	....	....	....	....	....	....	....	....	....	....	....	....	....	....	....	....	....
2011-12	**Phoenix**	**NHL**	**82**	**11**	**13**	**24**	**12**	**0**	**0**	**2**	**86**	**12.8**	**–2**	**2**	**50.0**	**13:38**	**16**	**4**	**4**	**8**	**0**	**0**	**0**	**2**	**16:56**
2012-13	Lukko Rauma	Finland	29	21	12	33	10	....	....	....	....	....	....	....	....	....	....	....	....	....	....	....	....	....	....
	Phoenix	**NHL**	**48**	**7**	**19**	**26**	**12**	**3**	**0**	**2**	**83**	**8.4**	**0**	**11**	**9.1**	**18:29**	....	....	....	....	....	....	....	....	....
	NHL Totals		**256**	**34**	**61**	**95**	**50**	**5**	**0**	**7**	**331**	**10.3**		**26**	**23.1**	**14:30**	**20**	**4**	**5**	**9**	**2**	**0**	**0**	**2**	**15:20**

Signed as a free agent by **Rauma** (Finland), September 27, 2012.

BOGOSIAN, Zach

(buh-GOH-zhuhn, ZAK) **WPG**

Defense. Shoots right. 6'3", 215 lbs. Born, Massena, NY, July 15, 1990. Atlanta's 1st choice, 3rd overall, in 2008 Entry Draft.

Season	Club	League	GP	G	A	Pts	PIM	PP	SH	GW	S	%	+/-	TF	F%	Min	GP	G	A	Pts	PIM	PP	SH	GW	Min
2005-06	Cushing	High-MA	36	1	16	17	....	....	....	....	....	....	....	....	....	....	....	....	....	....	....	....	....	....	....
2006-07	Peterborough	OHL	67	7	26	33	63	....	....	....	....	....	....	....	....	....	....	....	....	....	....	....	....	....	....
2007-08	Peterborough	OHL	60	11	50	61	72	....	....	....	....	....	....	....	....	....	5	0	3	3	8	....	....	....	....
2008-09	**Atlanta**	**NHL**	**47**	**9**	**10**	**19**	**47**	**2**	**1**	**1**	**90**	**10.0**	**11**	**0**	**0.0**	**18:06**	....	....	....	....	....	....	....	....	....
	Chicago Wolves	AHL	5	1	0	1	0	....	....	....	....	....	....	....	....	....	....	....	....	....	....	....	....	....	....
2009-10	**Atlanta**	**NHL**	**81**	**10**	**13**	**23**	**61**	**3**	**1**	**0**	**155**	**6.5**	**–18**	**0**	**0.0**	**21:25**	....	....	....	....	....	....	....	....	....
2010-11	**Atlanta**	**NHL**	**71**	**5**	**12**	**17**	**29**	**0**	**0**	**1**	**155**	**3.2**	**–27**	**0**	**0.0**	**22:24**	....	....	....	....	....	....	....	....	....
2011-12	**Winnipeg**	**NHL**	**65**	**5**	**25**	**30**	**71**	**1**	**0**	**0**	**150**	**3.3**	**–3**	**0**	**0.0**	**23:19**	....	....	....	....	....	....	....	....	....
2012-13	**Winnipeg**	**NHL**	**33**	**5**	**9**	**14**	**29**	**0**	**0**	**0**	**85**	**5.9**	**–5**	**0**	**0.0**	**23:07**	....	....	....	....	....	....	....	....	....
	NHL Totals		**297**	**34**	**69**	**103**	**237**	**6**	**2**	**2**	**635**	**5.4**		**0**	**0.0**	**21:44**	....	....	....	....	....	....	....	....	....

OHL First All-Star Team (2008)

• Transferred to **Winnipeg** after **Atlanta** franchise relocated, June 21, 2011.

BOLDUC, Alexandre

(bohl-DUHK, ahl-ehx-AHN-druh) **ST.L.**

Center. Shoots left. 6'3", 208 lbs. Born, Montreal, Que., June 26, 1985. St. Louis' 6th choice, 127th overall, in 2003 Entry Draft.

Season	Club	League	GP	G	A	Pts	PIM	PP	SH	GW	S	%	+/-	TF	F%	Min	GP	G	A	Pts	PIM	PP	SH	GW	Min
2000-01	Notre Dame	SMHL	61	17	35	52	....	....	....	....	....	....	....	....	....	....	....	....	....	....	....	....	....	....	....
2001-02	Rouyn-Noranda	QMJHL	64	6	14	20	69	....	....	....	....	....	....	....	....	....	4	1	1	2	4	....	....	....	....
2002-03	Rouyn-Noranda	QMJHL	66	14	29	43	131	....	....	....	....	....	....	....	....	....	4	0	2	2	2	....	....	....	....
2003-04	Rouyn-Noranda	QMJHL	65	23	35	58	115	....	....	....	....	....	....	....	....	....	11	3	4	7	18	....	....	....	....
2004-05	Rouyn-Noranda	QMJHL	33	7	10	17	46	....	....	....	....	....	....	....	....	....	....	....	....	....	....	....	....	....	....
	Shawinigan	QMJHL	29	7	11	18	14	....	....	....	....	....	....	....	....	....	3	0	0	0	0	....	....	....	....
2005-06	Manitoba Moose	AHL	29	3	7	10	35	....	....	....	....	....	....	....	....	....	....	....	....	....	....	....	....	....	....
	Bakersfield	ECHL	24	10	6	16	56	....	....	....	....	....	....	....	....	....	11	4	4	8	28	....	....	....	....
2006-07	Manitoba Moose	AHL	32	4	5	9	35	....	....	....	....	....	....	....	....	....	5	0	0	0	8	....	....	....	....
	Bakersfield	ECHL	16	7	17	24	42	....	....	....	....	....	....	....	....	....	6	2	4	6	9	....	....	....	....
2007-08	Manitoba Moose	AHL	70	18	19	37	93	....	....	....	....	....	....	....	....	....	6	1	0	1	6	....	....	....	....
2008-09	**Vancouver**	**NHL**	**7**	**0**	**1**	**1**	**4**	**0**	**0**	**0**	**7**	**0.0**	**1**	**13**	**38.5**	**7:20**	....	....	....	....	....	....	....	....	....
	Manitoba Moose	AHL	63	12	21	33	116	....	....	....	....	....	....	....	....	....	13	5	4	9	14	....	....	....	....
2009-10	**Vancouver**	**NHL**	**15**	**0**	**0**	**0**	**13**	**0**	**0**	**0**	**14**	**0.0**	**–3**	**87**	**54.0**	**9:58**	....	....	....	....	....	....	....	....	....
	Manitoba Moose	AHL	13	2	1	3	20	....	....	....	....	....	....	....	....	....	....	....	....	....	....	....	....	....	....
2010-11	**Vancouver**	**NHL**	**24**	**2**	**2**	**4**	**21**	**0**	**0**	**1**	**21**	**9.5**	**1**	**97**	**45.4**	**7:26**	**3**	**0**	**0**	**0**	**0**	**0**	**0**	**0**	**3:38**
	Manitoba Moose	AHL	26	6	9	15	28	....	....	....	....	....	....	....	....	....	14	4	0	4	20	....	....	....	....
2011-12	**Phoenix**	**NHL**	**2**	**0**	**0**	**0**	**2**	**0**	**0**	**0**	**1**	**0.0**	**–1**	**1**	**100.0**	**7:10**	....	....	....	....	....	....	....	....	....
	Portland Pirates	AHL	23	3	12	15	30	....	....	....	....	....	....	....	....	....	....	....	....	....	....	....	....	....	....
2012-13	Portland Pirates	AHL	56	24	27	51	90	....	....	....	....	....	....	....	....	....	1	1	1	2	2	....	....	....	....
	Phoenix	**NHL**	**14**	**0**	**0**	**0**	**2**	**0**	**0**	**0**	**17**	**0.0**	**–4**	**21**	**33.3**	**7:38**	....	....	....	....	....	....	....	....	....
	NHL Totals		**62**	**2**	**3**	**5**	**42**	**0**	**0**	**1**	**60**	**3.3**		**219**	**47.5**	**8:04**	**3**	**0**	**0**	**0**	**0**	**0**	**0**	**0**	**3:39**

Signed as a free agent by **Vancouver**, July 2, 2008. • Missed majority of 2009-10 due to shoulder injury at Los Angeles, October 29, 2009. Signed as a free agent by **Phoenix**, July 2, 2011. • Missed majority of 2011-12 due to upper body injury. Signed as a free agent by **St. Louis**, July 6, 2013.

BOLL, Jared

(BOWL, JAIR-ehd) **CBJ**

Right wing. Shoots right. 6'2", 219 lbs. Born, Charlotte, NC, May 13, 1986. Columbus' 4th choice, 101st overall, in 2005 Entry Draft.

Season	Club	League	GP	G	A	Pts	PIM	PP	SH	GW	S	%	+/-	TF	F%	Min	GP	G	A	Pts	PIM	PP	SH	GW	Min
2003-04	Lincoln Stars	USHL	57	6	8	14	*176	....	....	....	....	....	....	....	....	....	....	....	....	....	....	....	....	....	....
2004-05	Lincoln Stars	USHL	59	23	24	47	*294	....	....	....	....	....	....	....	....	....	4	1	3	4	25	....	....	....	....
2005-06	Plymouth Whalers	OHL	65	19	22	41	205	....	....	....	....	....	....	....	....	....	13	2	4	6	21	....	....	....	....
2006-07	Plymouth Whalers	OHL	66	28	27	55	198	....	....	....	....	....	....	....	....	....	20	6	4	10	*66	....	....	....	....
2007-08	**Columbus**	**NHL**	**75**	**5**	**5**	**10**	**226**	**0**	**0**	**3**	**63**	**7.9**	**–4**	**6**	**33.3**	**8:01**	....	....	....	....	....	....	....	....	....
2008-09	**Columbus**	**NHL**	**75**	**4**	**10**	**14**	**180**	**1**	**0**	**0**	**73**	**5.5**	**–6**	**4**	**0.0**	**8:54**	**1**	**0**	**0**	**0**	**0**	**0**	**0**	**0**	**5:17**
2009-10	**Columbus**	**NHL**	**68**	**4**	**3**	**7**	**149**	**0**	**0**	**0**	**56**	**7.1**	**–8**	**3**	**0.0**	**7:12**	....	....	....	....	....	....	....	....	....
2010-11	**Columbus**	**NHL**	**73**	**7**	**5**	**12**	**182**	**0**	**0**	**2**	**66**	**10.6**	**–2**	**6**	**0.0**	**7:40**	....	....	....	....	....	....	....	....	....
2011-12	**Columbus**	**NHL**	**54**	**2**	**1**	**3**	**126**	**0**	**0**	**0**	**35**	**5.7**	**–8**	**5**	**60.0**	**8:07**	....	....	....	....	....	....	....	....	....
2012-13	TuTo Turku	Finland-2	5	2	1	3	31	....	....	....	....	....	....	....	....	....	....	....	....	....	....	....	....	....	....
	Columbus	**NHL**	**43**	**2**	**4**	**6**	**100**	**0**	**0**	**0**	**19**	**10.5**	**1**	**9**	**44.4**	**8:05**	....	....	....	....	....	....	....	....	....
	NHL Totals		**388**	**24**	**28**	**52**	**963**	**1**	**0**	**5**	**312**	**7.7**		**33**	**27.3**	**8:00**	**1**	**0**	**0**	**0**	**0**	**0**	**0**	**0**	**5:17**

Signed as a free agent by **TuTo Turku** (Finland-2), November 15, 2012.

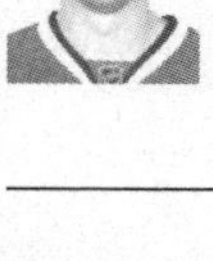

BOLLAND, Dave

(BOHL-uhnd, DAYV) **TOR**

Center. Shoots right. 6', 184 lbs. Born, Mimico, Ont., June 5, 1986. Chicago's 2nd choice, 32nd overall, in 2004 Entry Draft.

Season	Club	League	GP	G	A	Pts	PIM	PP	SH	GW	S	%	+/-	TF	F%	Min	GP	G	A	Pts	PIM	PP	SH	GW	Min
2000-01	Tor. Red Wings	GTHL	95	79	67	146	....	....	....	....	....	....	....	....	....	....	....	....	....	....	....	....	....	....	....
2001-02	Tor. Red Wings	GTHL	36	35	35	70	40	....	....	....	....	....	....	....	....	....	....	....	....	....	....	....	....	....	....
2002-03	London Knights	OHL	64	7	10	17	21	....	....	....	....	....	....	....	....	....	14	2	1	3	2	....	....	....	....
2003-04	London Knights	OHL	65	37	30	67	58	....	....	....	....	....	....	....	....	....	15	3	10	13	18	....	....	....	....
2004-05	London Knights	OHL	66	34	51	85	97	....	....	....	....	....	....	....	....	....	18	11	14	25	30	....	....	....	....
2005-06	London Knights	OHL	59	*57	73	130	104	....	....	....	....	....	....	....	....	....	15	*15	9	24	41	....	....	....	....

			Regular Season														Playoffs								
Season	Club	League	GP	G	A	Pts	PIM	PP	SH	GW	S	%	+/-	TF	F%	Min	GP	G	A	Pts	PIM	PP	SH	GW	Min
2006-07	**Chicago**	**NHL**	**1**	**0**	**0**	**0**	**0**	**0**	**0**	**0**	**1**	**0.0**	**-1**	**11**	**36.4**	**11:17**	....	....	....	....	....	....	....	....	....
	Norfolk Admirals	AHL	65	17	32	49	53	....	....	....	....	....	....	....	....	....	6	0	4	4	17	....	....	....	....
2007-08	**Chicago**	**NHL**	**39**	**4**	**13**	**17**	**28**	**0**	**0**	**0**	**49**	**8.2**	**6**	**385**	**46.5**	**13:43**	....	....	....	....	....	....	....	....	....
	Rockford IceHogs	AHL	16	6	4	10	22	....	....	....	....	....	....	....	....	....	7	0	0	0	8	....	....	....	....
2008-09	**Chicago**	**NHL**	**81**	**19**	**28**	**47**	**52**	**2**	**2**	**4**	**111**	**17.1**	**19**	**1177**	**44.4**	**16:27**	**17**	**4**	**8**	**12**	**24**	**1**	**1**	**1**	**18:43**
2009-10♦	**Chicago**	**NHL**	**39**	**6**	**10**	**16**	**28**	**1**	**0**	**0**	**52**	**11.5**	**5**	**555**	**49.4**	**17:22**	**22**	**8**	**8**	**16**	**30**	**2**	**2**	**1**	**18:40**
2010-11	**Chicago**	**NHL**	**61**	**15**	**22**	**37**	**34**	**4**	**0**	**1**	**102**	**14.7**	**11**	**1008**	**45.1**	**17:39**	**4**	**2**	**4**	**6**	**4**	**0**	**0**	**0**	**19:58**
2011-12	**Chicago**	**NHL**	**76**	**19**	**18**	**37**	**47**	**7**	**3**	**2**	**126**	**15.1**	**0**	**1203**	**48.4**	**16:30**	**6**	**0**	**3**	**3**	**2**	**0**	**0**	**0**	**19:30**
2012-13♦	**Chicago**	**NHL**	**35**	**7**	**7**	**14**	**22**	**1**	**0**	**1**	**46**	**15.2**	**-7**	**518**	**46.1**	**16:20**	**18**	**3**	**3**	**6**	**24**	**0**	**0**	**1**	**13:31**
	NHL Totals		**332**	**70**	**98**	**168**	**211**	**15**	**5**	**8**	**487**	**14.4**		**4857**	**46.4**	**16:26**	**67**	**17**	**26**	**43**	**84**	**3**	**3**	**3**	**17:27**

OHL First All-Star Team (2006) • Canadian Major Junior First All-Star Team (2006)

• Missed majority of 2009-10 due to back injury and resulting surgery. Traded to **Toronto** by **Chicago** for Toronto's 2nd round choice (Carl Dahlstrom) in 2013 Entry Draft, Anaheim's 4th round choice (previously acquired, later traded to San Jose – San Jose selected Fredrik Bergvik) in 2013 Entry Draft and a 4th round choice in 2014 Entry Draft, June 30, 2013.

BOLLIG, Brandon

(BOH-lihg, BRAN-duhn) **CHI**

Left wing. Shoots left. 6'2", 223 lbs. Born, St. Charles, MO, January 31, 1987.

Season	Club	League	GP	G	A	Pts	PIM	PP	SH	GW	S	%	+/-	TF	F%	Min	GP	G	A	Pts	PIM	PP	SH	GW	Min
2005-06	Lincoln Stars	USHL	58	8	8	16	175	....	....	....	....	....	....	....	....	....	9	1	2	3	12	....	....	....	....
2006-07	Lincoln Stars	USHL	57	14	12	26	207	....	....	....	....	....	....	....	....	....	4	0	2	2	2	....	....	....	....
2007-08	Lincoln Stars	USHL	58	15	16	31	211	....	....	....	....	....	....	....	....	....	8	2	4	6	40	....	....	....	....
2008-09	St. Lawrence	ECAC	36	6	7	13	51	....	....	....	....	....	....	....	....	....	....	....	....	....	....	....	....	....	....
2009-10	St. Lawrence	ECAC	42	7	18	25	83	....	....	....	....	....	....	....	....	....	....	....	....	....	....	....	....	....	....
	Rockford IceHogs	AHL	3	1	1	2	7	....	....	....	....	....	....	....	....	....	....	....	....	....	....	....	....	....	....
2010-11	Rockford IceHogs	AHL	55	4	0	4	115	....	....	....	....	....	....	....	....	....	....	....	....	....	....	....	....	....	....
2011-12	**Chicago**	**NHL**	**18**	**0**	**0**	**0**	**58**	**0**	**0**	**0**	**16**	**0.0**	**-2**	**0**	**0.0**	**5:53**	**4**	**1**	**0**	**1**	**19**	**0**	**0**	**0**	**6:01**
	Rockford IceHogs	AHL	53	3	6	9	163	....	....	....	....	....	....	....	....	....	....	....	....	....	....	....	....	....	....
2012-13	Rockford IceHogs	AHL	35	5	4	9	157	....	....	....	....	....	....	....	....	....	....	....	....	....	....	....	....	....	....
	♦ Chicago	**NHL**	**25**	**0**	**0**	**0**	**51**	**0**	**0**	**0**	**34**	**0.0**	**-1**	**3**	**0.0**	**8:01**	**5**	**0**	**0**	**0**	**2**	**0**	**0**	**0**	**8:51**
	NHL Totals		**43**	**0**	**0**	**0**	**109**	**0**	**0**	**0**	**50**	**0.0**		**3**	**0.0**	**7:07**	**9**	**1**	**0**	**1**	**21**	**0**	**0**	**0**	**7:36**

Signed as a free agent by **Chicago**, April 3, 2010.

BONINO, Nick

(boh-NEE-noh, NIHK) **ANA**

Center. Shoots left. 6'1", 194 lbs. Born, Hartford, CT, April 20, 1988. San Jose's 6th choice, 173rd overall, in 2007 Entry Draft.

Season	Club	League	GP	G	A	Pts	PIM	PP	SH	GW	S	%	+/-	TF	F%	Min	GP	G	A	Pts	PIM	PP	SH	GW	Min
2003-04	Farmington	High-CT	24	44	23	67	10	....	....	....	....	....	....	....	....	....	....	....	....	....	....	....	....	....	....
2004-05	Farmington	High-CT	24	68	23	91	12	....	....	....	....	....	....	....	....	....	....	....	....	....	....	....	....	....	....
2005-06	Avon Old Farms	High-CT	25	26	30	56	10	....	....	....	....	....	....	....	....	....	....	....	....	....	....	....	....	....	....
2006-07	Avon Old Farms	High-CT	26	24	42	66	14	....	....	....	....	....	....	....	....	....	....	....	....	....	....	....	....	....	....
2007-08	Boston University	H-East	39	16	13	29	10	....	....	....	....	....	....	....	....	....	....	....	....	....	....	....	....	....	....
2008-09	Boston University	H-East	44	18	32	50	30	....	....	....	....	....	....	....	....	....	....	....	....	....	....	....	....	....	....
2009-10	Boston University	H-East	33	11	27	38	12	....	....	....	....	....	....	....	....	....	....	....	....	....	....	....	....	....	....
	Anaheim	**NHL**	**9**	**1**	**1**	**2**	**6**	**1**	**0**	**0**	**14**	**7.1**	**0**	**78**	**43.6**	**14:13**	....	....	....	....	....	....	....	....	....
2010-11	**Anaheim**	**NHL**	**26**	**0**	**0**	**0**	**4**	**0**	**0**	**0**	**23**	**0.0**	**-3**	**166**	**47.0**	**9:48**	**4**	**0**	**0**	**0**	**2**	**0**	**0**	**0**	**11:36**
	Syracuse Crunch	AHL	50	12	33	45	32	....	....	....	....	....	....	....	....	....	....	....	....	....	....	....	....	....	....
2011-12	**Anaheim**	**NHL**	**50**	**5**	**13**	**18**	**8**	**0**	**0**	**0**	**63**	**7.9**	**1**	**454**	**43.0**	**12:29**	....	....	....	....	....	....	....	....	....
	Syracuse Crunch	AHL	19	6	16	22	2	....	....	....	....	....	....	....	....	....	....	....	....	....	....	....	....	....	....
2012-13	Neumarkt/Egna	Italy-2	19	26	26	52	14	....	....	....	....	....	....	....	....	....	....	....	....	....	....	....	....	....	....
	Anaheim	**NHL**	**27**	**5**	**8**	**13**	**8**	**1**	**0**	**0**	**37**	**13.5**	**-3**	**295**	**46.8**	**15:53**	**7**	**3**	**1**	**4**	**4**	**2**	**0**	**2**	**16:38**
	NHL Totals		**112**	**11**	**22**	**33**	**26**	**2**	**0**	**0**	**137**	**8.0**		**993**	**44.8**	**12:49**	**11**	**3**	**1**	**4**	**6**	**2**	**0**	**2**	**14:48**

NCAA Championship All-Tournament Team (2009)

Traded to **Anaheim** by **San Jose** with Timo Pielmeier and San Jose's 4th round choice (Andrew O'Brien) in 2012 Entry Draft for Travis Moen and Kent Huskins, March 4, 2009. Signed as a free agent by **Neumarkt/Egna** (Italy-2), October 16, 2012.

BOOTH, David

(BOOTH, DAY-vihd) **VAN**

Left wing. Shoots left. 6', 212 lbs. Born, Detroit, MI, November 24, 1984. Florida's 3rd choice, 53rd overall, in 2004 Entry Draft.

Season	Club	League	GP	G	A	Pts	PIM	PP	SH	GW	S	%	+/-	TF	F%	Min	GP	G	A	Pts	PIM	PP	SH	GW	Min
2000-01	Det. Compuware	NAHL	42	17	13	30	44	....	....	....	....	....	....	....	....	....	2	1	0	1	2	....	....	....	....
2001-02	USNTDP	U-18	40	12	6	18	17	....	....	....	....	....	....	....	....	....	....	....	....	....	....	....	....	....	....
	USNTDP	USHL	12	4	3	7	6	....	....	....	....	....	....	....	....	....	....	....	....	....	....	....	....	....	....
	USNTDP	NAHL	6	1	3	4	18	....	....	....	....	....	....	....	....	....	....	....	....	....	....	....	....	....	....
2002-03	Michigan State	CCHA	39	17	19	36	53	....	....	....	....	....	....	....	....	....	....	....	....	....	....	....	....	....	....
2003-04	Michigan State	CCHA	30	8	10	18	30	....	....	....	....	....	....	....	....	....	....	....	....	....	....	....	....	....	....
2004-05	Michigan State	CCHA	29	7	9	16	30	....	....	....	....	....	....	....	....	....	....	....	....	....	....	....	....	....	....
2005-06	Michigan State	CCHA	37	13	22	35	50	....	....	....	....	....	....	....	....	....	....	....	....	....	....	....	....	....	....
2006-07	**Florida**	**NHL**	**48**	**3**	**7**	**10**	**12**	**0**	**0**	**1**	**86**	**3.5**	**0**	**11**	**36.4**	**9:34**	....	....	....	....	....	....	....	....	....
	Rochester	AHL	25	7	7	14	26	....	....	....	....	....	....	....	....	....	6	0	2	2	4	....	....	....	....
2007-08	**Florida**	**NHL**	**73**	**22**	**18**	**40**	**26**	**1**	**0**	**6**	**228**	**9.6**	**13**	**38**	**34.2**	**16:10**	....	....	....	....	....	....	....	....	....
2008-09	**Florida**	**NHL**	**72**	**31**	**29**	**60**	**38**	**11**	**0**	**5**	**246**	**12.6**	**10**	**17**	**41.2**	**17:05**	....	....	....	....	....	....	....	....	....
2009-10	**Florida**	**NHL**	**28**	**8**	**8**	**16**	**23**	**0**	**0**	**1**	**95**	**8.4**	**-3**	**10**	**20.0**	**18:08**	....	....	....	....	....	....	....	....	....
2010-11	**Florida**	**NHL**	**82**	**23**	**17**	**40**	**26**	**8**	**0**	**3**	**280**	**8.2**	**-31**	**48**	**50.0**	**18:54**	....	....	....	....	....	....	....	....	....
2011-12	**Florida**	**NHL**	**6**	**0**	**1**	**1**	**2**	**0**	**0**	**0**	**14**	**0.0**	**-6**	**0**	**0.0**	**15:30**	....	....	....	....	....	....	....	....	....
	Vancouver	**NHL**	**56**	**16**	**13**	**29**	**32**	**3**	**0**	**1**	**145**	**11.0**	**1**	**18**	**50.0**	**14:52**	**5**	**0**	**1**	**1**	**0**	**0**	**0**	**0**	**16:07**
2012-13	**Vancouver**	**NHL**	**12**	**1**	**2**	**3**	**4**	**0**	**0**	**0**	**27**	**3.7**	**-3**	**1**	**100.0**	**12:45**	....	....	....	....	....	....	....	....	....
	NHL Totals		**377**	**104**	**95**	**199**	**163**	**23**	**0**	**17**	**1121**	**9.3**		**143**	**42.0**	**15:56**	**5**	**0**	**1**	**1**	**0**	**0**	**0**	**0**	**16:07**

CCHA All-Rookie Team (2003)

• Missed majority of 2009-10 due to head injury at Philadelphia, October 24, 2009. Traded to **Vancouver** by **Florida** with Steve Reinprecht and Vancouver's 3rd round choice (previously acquired, Vancouver selected Cole Cassels) in 2013 Entry Draft for Mikael Samuelsson and Marco Sturm, October 22, 2011. • Missed majority of 2012-13 due to recurring groin injury and ankle injury vs. Detroit, March 16, 2013.

BORDELEAU, Patrick

(BOHR-duh-loh, PAT-rihk) **COL**

Left wing. Shoots left. 6'6", 225 lbs. Born, Montreal, Que., March 23, 1986. Minnesota's 6th choice, 114th overall, in 2004 Entry Draft.

Season	Club	League	GP	G	A	Pts	PIM	PP	SH	GW	S	%	+/-	TF	F%	Min	GP	G	A	Pts	PIM	PP	SH	GW	Min
2002-03	Gatineau	QAAA	39	8	13	21	50	....	....	....	....	....	....	....	....	....	....	....	....	....	....	....	....	....	....
2003-04	Val-d'Or Foreurs	QMJHL	68	7	11	18	97	....	....	....	....	....	....	....	....	....	7	1	1	2	8	....	....	....	....
2004-05	Val-d'Or Foreurs	QMJHL	63	14	24	38	51	....	....	....	....	....	....	....	....	....	....	....	....	....	....	....	....	....	....
2005-06	Val-d'Or Foreurs	QMJHL	67	23	33	56	87	....	....	....	....	....	....	....	....	....	5	1	0	1	7	....	....	....	....
2006-07	Drummondville	QMJHL	3	0	2	2	6	....	....	....	....	....	....	....	....	....	....	....	....	....	....	....	....	....	....
	Acadie-Bathurst	QMJHL	17	7	12	19	26	....	....	....	....	....	....	....	....	....	....	....	....	....	....	....	....	....	....
2007-08	Charlotte	ECHL	10	1	2	3	11	....	....	....	....	....	....	....	....	....	....	....	....	....	....	....	....	....	....
	Wheeling Nailers	ECHL	3	0	1	1	0	....	....	....	....	....	....	....	....	....	....	....	....	....	....	....	....	....	....
	Pensacola	ECHL	38	7	11	18	60	....	....	....	....	....	....	....	....	....	....	....	....	....	....	....	....	....	....
2008-09	Augusta Lynx	ECHL	18	4	6	10	57	....	....	....	....	....	....	....	....	....	....	....	....	....	....	....	....	....	....
	Albany River Rats	AHL	6	0	2	2	21	....	....	....	....	....	....	....	....	....	....	....	....	....	....	....	....	....	....
	Florida Everblades	ECHL	29	4	9	13	81	....	....	....	....	....	....	....	....	....	....	....	....	....	....	....	....	....	....
	Springfield	AHL	4	0	0	0	4	....	....	....	....	....	....	....	....	....	....	....	....	....	....	....	....	....	....
	Lake Erie	AHL	3	0	1	1	17	....	....	....	....	....	....	....	....	....	....	....	....	....	....	....	....	....	....
	Milwaukee	AHL	2	0	0	0	0	....	....	....	....	....	....	....	....	....	....	....	....	....	....	....	....	....	....
2009-10	Lake Erie	AHL	60	1	2	3	106	....	....	....	....	....	....	....	....	....	....	....	....	....	....	....	....	....	....
2010-11	Lake Erie	AHL	72	2	10	12	125	....	....	....	....	....	....	....	....	....	7	0	0	0	6	....	....	....	....
2011-12	Lake Erie	AHL	52	4	4	8	96	....	....	....	....	....	....	....	....	....	....	....	....	....	....	....	....	....	....
2012-13	Lake Erie	AHL	29	2	5	7	91	....	....	....	....	....	....	....	....	....	....	....	....	....	....	....	....	....	....
	Colorado	**NHL**	**46**	**2**	**3**	**5**	**70**	**0**	**0**	**0**	**24**	**8.3**	**-7**	**2**	**0.0**	**6:13**	....	....	....	....	....	....	....	....	....
	NHL Totals		**46**	**2**	**3**	**5**	**70**	**0**	**0**	**0**	**24**	**8.3**		**2**	**0.0**	**6:13**									

Signed to a PTO (professional tryout) contract by **Albany** (AHL), December 5, 2008. Signed to a PTO (professional tryout) contract by **Springfield** (AHL), January 5, 2009. Signed to a PTO (professional tryout) contract by **Lake Erie** (AHL), March 31, 2009. Signed to a PTO (professional tryout) contract by **Milwaukee** (AHL), April 6, 2009. Signed as a free agent by **Colorado**, July 1, 2011.

BOROWIECKI, Mark

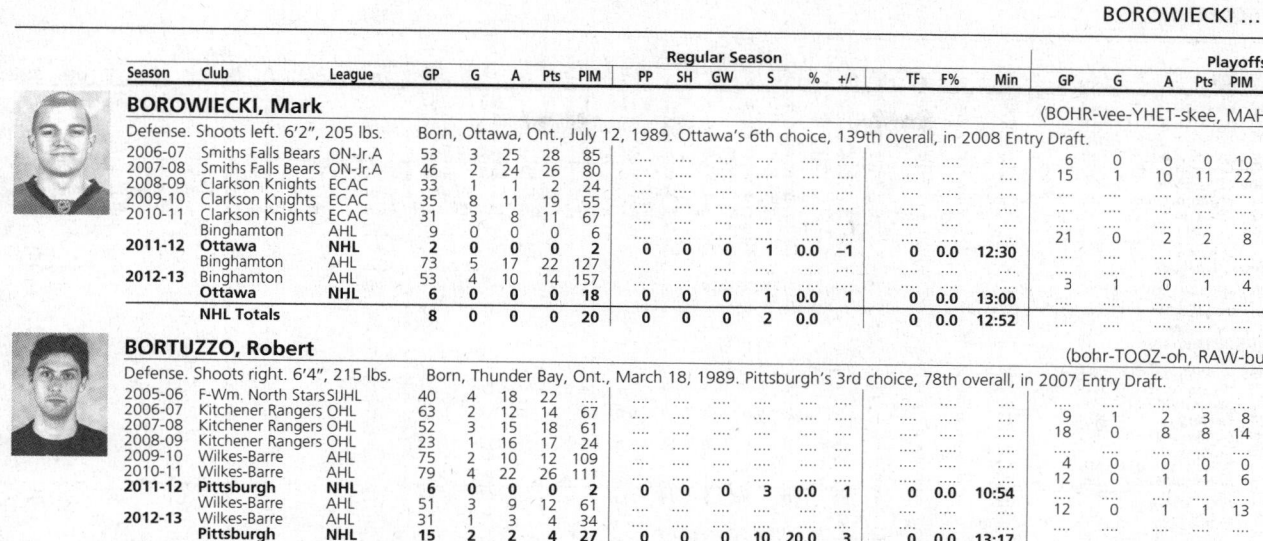

(BOHR-vee-YHET-skee, MAHRK) **OTT**

Defense. Shoots left. 6'2", 205 lbs. Born, Ottawa, Ont., July 12, 1989. Ottawa's 6th choice, 139th overall, in 2008 Entry Draft.

			Regular Season														Playoffs								
Season	Club	League	GP	G	A	Pts	PIM	PP	SH	GW	S	%	+/-	TF	F%	Min	GP	G	A	Pts	PIM	PP	SH	GW	Min
2006-07	Smiths Falls Bears	ON-Jr.A	53	3	25	28	85	....	....	....	....	....	....	....	....	....	6	0	0	0	10	....	....	....	....
2007-08	Smiths Falls Bears	ON-Jr.A	46	2	24	26	80	....	....	....	....	....	....	....	....	....	15	1	10	11	22	....	....	....	....
2008-09	Clarkson Knights	ECAC	33	1	1	2	24	....	....	....	....	....	....	....	....	....	....	....	....	....	....	....	....	....	....
2009-10	Clarkson Knights	ECAC	35	8	11	19	55	....	....	....	....	....	....	....	....	....	....	....	....	....	....	....	....	....	....
2010-11	Clarkson Knights	ECAC	31	3	8	11	67	....	....	....	....	....	....	....	....	....	....	....	....	....	....	....	....	....	....
	Binghamton	AHL	9	0	0	0	6	....	....	....	....	....	....	....	....	....	21	0	2	2	8	....	....	....	....
2011-12	**Ottawa**	**NHL**	**2**	**0**	**0**	**0**	**2**	**0**	**0**	**0**	**1**	**0.0**	**–1**	**0**	**0.0**	**12:30**	....	....	....	....	....	....	....	....	....
	Binghamton	AHL	73	5	17	22	127	....	....	....	....	....	....	....	....	....	....	....	....	....	....	....	....	....	....
2012-13	Binghamton	AHL	53	4	10	14	157	....	....	....	....	....	....	....	....	....	3	1	0	1	4	....	....	....	....
	Ottawa	**NHL**	**6**	**0**	**0**	**0**	**18**	**0**	**0**	**0**	**1**	**0.0**	**1**	**0**	**0.0**	**13:00**	....	....	....	....	....	....	....	....	....
	NHL Totals		**8**	**0**	**0**	**0**	**20**	**0**	**0**	**0**	**2**	**0.0**		**0**	**0.0**	**12:52**	....	....	....	....	....	....	....	....	....

BORTUZZO, Robert

(bohr-TOOZ-oh, RAW-buhrt) **PIT**

Defense. Shoots right. 6'4", 215 lbs. Born, Thunder Bay, Ont., March 18, 1989. Pittsburgh's 3rd choice, 78th overall, in 2007 Entry Draft.

2005-06	F-Wm. North Stars	SIJHL	40	4	18	22	....	....	....	....	....	....	....	....	....	....	....	....	....	....	....	....	....	....	....
2006-07	Kitchener Rangers	OHL	63	2	12	14	67	....	....	....	....	....	....	....	....	....	9	1	2	3	8	....	....	....	....
2007-08	Kitchener Rangers	OHL	52	3	15	18	61	....	....	....	....	....	....	....	....	....	18	0	8	8	14	....	....	....	....
2008-09	Kitchener Rangers	OHL	23	1	16	17	24	....	....	....	....	....	....	....	....	....	....	....	....	....	....	....	....	....	....
2009-10	Wilkes-Barre	AHL	75	2	10	12	109	....	....	....	....	....	....	....	....	....	4	0	0	0	0	....	....	....	....
2010-11	Wilkes-Barre	AHL	79	4	22	26	111	....	....	....	....	....	....	....	....	....	12	0	1	1	6	....	....	....	....
2011-12	**Pittsburgh**	**NHL**	**6**	**0**	**0**	**0**	**2**	**0**	**0**	**0**	**3**	**0.0**	**1**	**0**	**0.0**	**10:54**	....	....	....	....	....	....	....	....	....
	Wilkes-Barre	AHL	51	3	9	12	61	....	....	....	....	....	....	....	....	....	12	0	1	1	13	....	....	....	....
2012-13	Wilkes-Barre	AHL	31	1	3	4	34	....	....	....	....	....	....	....	....	....	....	....	....	....	....	....	....	....	....
	Pittsburgh	**NHL**	**15**	**2**	**2**	**4**	**27**	**0**	**0**	**0**	**10**	**20.0**	**3**	**0**	**0.0**	**13:17**	....	....	....	....	....	....	....	....	....
	NHL Totals		**21**	**2**	**2**	**4**	**29**	**0**	**0**	**0**	**13**	**15.4**		**0**	**0.0**	**12:36**	....	....	....	....	....	....	....	....	....

BOUCHARD, Pierre-Marc

(BOO-shahrd, PEE-air- MAHRK) **NYI**

Center. Shoots left. 5'11", 171 lbs. Born, Sherbrooke, Que., April 27, 1984. Minnesota's 1st choice, 8th overall, in 2002 Entry Draft.

1998-99	Mtl.-Bourassa	QAHA	28	23	41	64	....	....	....	....	....	....	....	....	....	....	....	....	....	....	....	....	....	....	....
99-2000	C.C. Lemoyne	QAAA	42	28	*45	*74	20	....	....	....	....	....	....	....	....	....	9	4	8	12	6	....	....	....	....
2000-01	Chicoutimi	QMJHL	67	38	57	95	20	....	....	....	....	....	....	....	....	....	6	5	8	13	0	....	....	....	....
2001-02	Chicoutimi	QMJHL	69	46	*94	*140	54	....	....	....	....	....	....	....	....	....	4	2	3	5	4	....	....	....	....
2002-03	**Minnesota**	**NHL**	**50**	**7**	**13**	**20**	**18**	**5**	**0**	**1**	**53**	**13.2**	**1**	**474**	**40.7**	**13:16**	**5**	**0**	**1**	**1**	**2**	**0**	**0**	**0**	**13:15**
2003-04	**Minnesota**	**NHL**	**61**	**4**	**18**	**22**	**22**	**2**	**0**	**0**	**60**	**6.7**	**–7**	**60**	**50.0**	**14:00**	....	....	....	....	....	....	....	....	....
2004-05	Houston Aeros	AHL	67	12	42	54	46	....	....	....	....	....	....	....	....	....	5	0	1	1	0	....	....	....	....
2005-06	**Minnesota**	**NHL**	**80**	**17**	**42**	**59**	**28**	**7**	**0**	**3**	**118**	**14.4**	**3**	**15**	**46.7**	**15:15**	....	....	....	....	....	....	....	....	....
2006-07	**Minnesota**	**NHL**	**82**	**20**	**37**	**57**	**14**	**5**	**0**	**3**	**173**	**11.6**	**13**	**18**	**33.3**	**15:59**	**5**	**1**	**1**	**2**	**0**	**0**	**0**	**0**	**14:48**
2007-08	**Minnesota**	**NHL**	**81**	**13**	**50**	**63**	**34**	**6**	**0**	**4**	**129**	**10.1**	**11**	**10**	**40.0**	**16:51**	**6**	**2**	**2**	**4**	**2**	**1**	**0**	**1**	**17:47**
2008-09	**Minnesota**	**NHL**	**71**	**16**	**30**	**46**	**20**	**2**	**0**	**1**	**142**	**11.3**	**–5**	**19**	**57.9**	**16:59**	....	....	....	....	....	....	....	....	....
2009-10	**Minnesota**	**NHL**	**1**	**0**	**0**	**0**	**2**	**0**	**0**	**0**	**0**	**0.0**	**0**	**3**	**33.3**	**10:44**	....	....	....	....	....	....	....	....	....
2010-11	**Minnesota**	**NHL**	**59**	**12**	**26**	**38**	**14**	**0**	**0**	**2**	**98**	**12.2**	**–3**	**43**	**39.5**	**15:43**	....	....	....	....	....	....	....	....	....
2011-12	**Minnesota**	**NHL**	**37**	**9**	**13**	**22**	**18**	**2**	**0**	**3**	**84**	**10.7**	**–1**	**16**	**25.0**	**16:19**	....	....	....	....	....	....	....	....	....
2012-13	**Minnesota**	**NHL**	**43**	**8**	**12**	**20**	**8**	**0**	**0**	**2**	**71**	**11.3**	**3**	**7**	**14.3**	**13:57**	**5**	**1**	**1**	**2**	**0**	**0**	**0**	**0**	**14:36**
	NHL Totals		**565**	**106**	**241**	**347**	**178**	**29**	**0**	**19**	**928**	**11.4**		**665**	**41.2**	**15:30**	**21**	**4**	**5**	**9**	**4**	**1**	**0**	**1**	**15:14**

QMJHL Rookie of the Year (2001) • QMJHL First All-Star Team (2002) • Canadian Major Junior First All-Star Team (2002) • Canadian Major Junior Player of the Year (2002)
• Missed majority of 2009-10 due to post-concussion syndrome. Signed as a free agent by **NY Islanders**, July 5, 2013.

BOUILLON, Francis

(BOO-liawn, FRAN-sihs) **MTL**

Defense. Shoots left. 5'8", 198 lbs. Born, New York, NY, October 17, 1975.

1991-92	Mtl-Bourassa	QAAA	42	2	5	7	28	....	....	....	....	....	....	....	....	....	9	1	0	1	6	....	....	....	....
1992-93	Laval Titan	QMJHL	45	0	6	6	45	....	....	....	....	....	....	....	....	....	....	....	....	....	....	....	....	....	....
1993-94	Laval Titan	QMJHL	68	3	14	17	131	....	....	....	....	....	....	....	....	....	19	2	9	11	48	....	....	....	....
1994-95	Laval Titan	QMJHL	72	8	25	33	115	....	....	....	....	....	....	....	....	....	20	3	11	14	21	....	....	....	....
1995-96	Granby	QMJHL	68	11	35	46	156	....	....	....	....	....	....	....	....	....	21	2	12	14	30	....	....	....	....
1996-97	Wheeling Nailers	ECHL	69	10	32	42	77	....	....	....	....	....	....	....	....	....	3	0	2	2	10	....	....	....	....
1997-98	Quebec Rafales	IHL	71	8	27	35	76	....	....	....	....	....	....	....	....	....	....	....	....	....	....	....	....	....	....
1998-99	Fredericton	AHL	79	19	36	55	174	....	....	....	....	....	....	....	....	....	5	2	1	3	0	....	....	....	....
99-2000	**Montreal**	**NHL**	**74**	**3**	**13**	**16**	**38**	**2**	**0**	**1**	**76**	**3.9**	**–7**	**1**	**0.0**	**15:52**	....	....	....	....	....	....	....	....	....
2000-01	**Montreal**	**NHL**	**29**	**0**	**6**	**6**	**26**	**0**	**0**	**0**	**24**	**0.0**	**3**	**0**	**0.0**	**13:24**	....	....	....	....	....	....	....	....	....
	Quebec Citadelles	AHL	4	0	0	0	0	....	....	....	....	....	....	....	....	....	....	....	....	....	....	....	....	....	....
2001-02	**Montreal**	**NHL**	**28**	**0**	**5**	**5**	**33**	**0**	**0**	**0**	**24**	**0.0**	**–5**	**0**	**0.0**	**18:47**	....	....	....	....	....	....	....	....	....
	Quebec Citadelles	AHL	38	8	14	22	30	....	....	....	....	....	....	....	....	....	....	....	....	....	....	....	....	....	....
2002-03	**Nashville**	**NHL**	**4**	**0**	**0**	**0**	**2**	**0**	**0**	**0**	**0**	**0.0**	**–1**	**0**	**0.0**	**12:52**	....	....	....	....	....	....	....	....	....
	Montreal	**NHL**	**20**	**3**	**1**	**4**	**2**	**0**	**1**	**0**	**30**	**10.0**	**–1**	**0**	**0.0**	**20:24**	....	....	....	....	....	....	....	....	....
	Hamilton	AHL	29	1	12	13	31	....	....	....	....	....	....	....	....	....	....	....	....	....	....	....	....	....	....
2003-04	**Montreal**	**NHL**	**73**	**2**	**16**	**18**	**70**	**0**	**0**	**0**	**86**	**2.3**	**1**	**0**	**0.0**	**19:39**	**11**	**0**	**0**	**0**	**7**	**0**	**0**	**0**	**18:00**
2004-05	Leksands IF	Sweden-2	31	10	21	31	46	....	....	....	....	....	....	....	....	....	....	....	....	....	....	....	....	....	....
2005-06	**Montreal**	**NHL**	**67**	**3**	**19**	**22**	**34**	**3**	**0**	**1**	**75**	**4.0**	**–6**	**0**	**0.0**	**20:47**	**6**	**1**	**2**	**3**	**10**	**1**	**0**	**0**	**22:24**
2006-07	**Montreal**	**NHL**	**62**	**3**	**11**	**14**	**52**	**1**	**0**	**1**	**56**	**5.4**	**–10**	**0**	**0.0**	**18:19**	....	....	....	....	....	....	....	....	....
2007-08	**Montreal**	**NHL**	**74**	**2**	**6**	**8**	**61**	**0**	**0**	**0**	**60**	**3.3**	**9**	**0**	**0.0**	**17:22**	**7**	**1**	**2**	**3**	**4**	**0**	**0**	**0**	**15:55**
2008-09	**Montreal**	**NHL**	**54**	**5**	**4**	**9**	**53**	**0**	**0**	**1**	**51**	**9.8**	**–7**	**0**	**0.0**	**16:30**	**1**	**0**	**0**	**0**	**0**	**0**	**0**	**0**	**1:46**
2009-10	**Nashville**	**NHL**	**81**	**3**	**8**	**11**	**50**	**1**	**0**	**1**	**86**	**3.5**	**5**	**0**	**0.0**	**19:18**	**6**	**0**	**0**	**0**	**6**	**0**	**0**	**0**	**19:37**
2010-11	**Nashville**	**NHL**	**44**	**1**	**9**	**10**	**27**	**0**	**0**	**0**	**47**	**2.1**	**–3**	**0**	**0.0**	**20:14**	....	....	....	....	....	....	....	....	....
2011-12	**Nashville**	**NHL**	**66**	**4**	**7**	**11**	**33**	**0**	**0**	**2**	**38**	**10.5**	**–4**	**0**	**0.0**	**17:33**	**10**	**0**	**3**	**3**	**2**	**0**	**0**	**0**	**14:58**
2012-13	**Montreal**	**NHL**	**48**	**1**	**8**	**9**	**21**	**0**	**0**	**0**	**46**	**2.2**	**4**	**0**	**0.0**	**18:05**	**5**	**0**	**0**	**0**	**17**	**0**	**0**	**0**	**16:02**
	NHL Totals		**724**	**30**	**113**	**143**	**502**	**7**	**1**	**7**	**699**	**4.3**		**1**	**0.0**	**18:11**	**46**	**2**	**7**	**9**	**46**	**1**	**0**	**0**	**17:14**

Signed as a free agent by **Montreal**, August 18, 1998. • Missed majority of 2000-01 due to ankle injury vs. Calgary, December 31, 2000. Claimed by **Nashville** from **Montreal** in Waiver Draft, October 4, 2002. Claimed on waivers by **Montreal** from **Nashville**, October 25, 2002. Signed as a free agent by **Leksands** (Sweden-2), November 15, 2004. Signed as a free agent by **Nashville**, September 30, 2009. Signed as a free agent by **Montreal**, July 1, 2012.

BOULTON, Eric

(BOHL-tuhn, AIR-ihk) **NYI**

Left wing. Shoots left. 6', 224 lbs. Born, Halifax, N.S., August 17, 1976. NY Rangers' 12th choice, 234th overall, in 1994 Entry Draft.

1992-93	Cole Harbour	MJrHL	44	12	15	27	212	....	....	....	....	....	....	....	....	....	....	....	....	....	....	....	....	....	....
1993-94	Oshawa Generals	OHL	45	4	3	7	149	....	....	....	....	....	....	....	....	....	5	0	0	0	16	....	....	....	....
1994-95	Oshawa Generals	OHL	27	7	5	12	125	....	....	....	....	....	....	....	....	....	....	....	....	....	....	....	....	....	....
	Sarnia Sting	OHL	24	3	7	10	134	....	....	....	....	....	....	....	....	....	4	0	1	1	10	....	....	....	....
1995-96	Sarnia Sting	OHL	66	14	29	43	243	....	....	....	....	....	....	....	....	....	9	0	3	3	29	....	....	....	....
1996-97	Binghamton	AHL	23	2	3	5	67	....	....	....	....	....	....	....	....	....	3	0	0	0	4	....	....	....	....
	Charlotte	ECHL	44	14	11	25	325	....	....	....	....	....	....	....	....	....	3	0	1	1	6	....	....	....	....
1997-98	Charlotte	ECHL	53	11	16	27	202	....	....	....	....	....	....	....	....	....	4	1	0	1	0	....	....	....	....
	Fort Wayne	IHL	8	0	2	2	42	....	....	....	....	....	....	....	....	....	....	....	....	....	....	....	....	....	....
1998-99	Kentucky	AHL	34	3	3	6	154	....	....	....	....	....	....	....	....	....	10	0	1	1	36	....	....	....	....
	Florida Everblades	ECHL	26	9	13	22	143	....	....	....	....	....	....	....	....	....	....	....	....	....	....	....	....	....	....
	Houston Aeros	IHL	7	1	0	1	41	....	....	....	....	....	....	....	....	....	....	....	....	....	....	....	....	....	....
99-2000	Rochester	AHL	76	2	2	4	276	....	....	....	....	....	....	....	....	....	18	2	1	3	53	....	....	....	....
2000-01	**Buffalo**	**NHL**	**35**	**1**	**2**	**3**	**94**	**0**	**0**	**0**	**20**	**5.0**	**–1**	**2**	**0.0**	**5:42**	....	....	....	....	....	....	....	....	....
2001-02	**Buffalo**	**NHL**	**35**	**2**	**3**	**5**	**129**	**0**	**0**	**1**	**21**	**9.5**	**–1**	**0**	**0.0**	**6:08**	....	....	....	....	....	....	....	....	....
2002-03	**Buffalo**	**NHL**	**58**	**1**	**5**	**6**	**178**	**0**	**0**	**0**	**33**	**3.0**	**1**	**6**	**33.3**	**6:35**	....	....	....	....	....	....	....	....	....
2003-04	**Buffalo**	**NHL**	**44**	**1**	**2**	**3**	**110**	**0**	**0**	**0**	**20**	**5.0**	**–2**	**1**	**0.0**	**4:52**	....	....	....	....	....	....	....	....	....
2004-05	Columbia Inferno	ECHL	48	23	16	39	124	....	....	....	....	....	....	....	....	....	4	2	3	5	8	....	....	....	....
2005-06	**Atlanta**	**NHL**	**51**	**4**	**5**	**9**	**87**	**0**	**0**	**0**	**28**	**14.3**	**–4**	**2**	**50.0**	**4:54**	....	....	....	....	....	....	....	....	....
2006-07	**Atlanta**	**NHL**	**45**	**3**	**4**	**7**	**49**	**0**	**0**	**0**	**42**	**7.1**	**2**	**2**	**50.0**	**6:16**	**4**	**0**	**0**	**0**	**24**	**0**	**0**	**0**	**5:04**
2007-08	**Atlanta**	**NHL**	**74**	**4**	**5**	**9**	**127**	**0**	**0**	**0**	**64**	**6.3**	**–10**	**4**	**25.0**	**7:27**	....	....	....	....	....	....	....	....	....
2008-09	**Atlanta**	**NHL**	**76**	**3**	**10**	**13**	**176**	**0**	**0**	**0**	**71**	**4.2**	**–3**	**4**	**25.0**	**7:33**	....	....	....	....	....	....	....	....	....
2009-10	**Atlanta**	**NHL**	**62**	**2**	**6**	**8**	**113**	**1**	**0**	**0**	**39**	**5.1**	**–1**	**4**	**50.0**	**6:51**	....	....	....	....	....	....	....	....	....

			Regular Season														Playoffs								
Season	Club	League	GP	G	A	Pts	PIM	PP	SH	GW	S	%	+/-	TF	F%	Min	GP	G	A	Pts	PIM	PP	SH	GW	Min
2010-11	**Atlanta**	**NHL**	**69**	**6**	**4**	**10**	**87**	**0**	**0**	**1**	**51**	**11.8**	**1**	**3**	**0.0**	**8:57**	....	....	....	....	....	....	....	....	....
2011-12	**New Jersey**	**NHL**	**51**	**0**	**0**	**0**	**115**	**0**	**0**	**0**	**25**	**0.0**	**–12**	**3**	**33.3**	**6:35**	....	....	....	....	....	....	....	....	....
	Albany Devils	AHL	2	0	0	0	0	....	....	....	....	....	....	....	....	....	....	....	....	....	....	....	....	....	....
2012-13	**NY Islanders**	**NHL**	**15**	**0**	**0**	**0**	**36**	**0**	**0**	**0**	**5**	**0.0**	**–4**	**0**	**0.0**	**5:40**	....	....	....	....	....	....	....	....	....
	NHL Totals		**615**	**27**	**46**	**73**	**1301**	**1**	**0**	**2**	**419**	**6.4**		**31**	**29.0**	**6:43**	**4**	**0**	**0**	**0**	**24**	**0**	**0**	**0**	**5:04**

Signed as a free agent by **Buffalo**, September 14, 1999. Signed as a free agent by **Columbia** (ECHL), November 24, 2004. Signed as a free agent by **Atlanta**, August 8, 2005. • Transferred to **Winnipeg** after **Atlanta** franchise relocated, June 21, 2011. Signed as a free agent by **New Jersey**, July 15, 2011. Signed as a free agent by **NY Islanders**, July 2, 2012. • Missed majority of 2012-13 as a healthy reserve.

BOUMA, Lance (BOW-ma, LANTZ) CGY

Center. Shoots left. 6'1", 210 lbs. Born, Provost, Alta., March 25, 1990. Calgary's 3rd choice, 78th overall, in 2008 Entry Draft.

Season	Club	League	GP	G	A	Pts	PIM	PP	SH	GW	S	%	+/-	TF	F%	Min	GP	G	A	Pts	PIM	PP	SH	GW	Min
2005-06	Wainwright	RAMHL	37	21	29	50	....	....	....	....	....	....	....	....	....	....	....	....	....	....	....	....	....	....	....
	Vancouver Giants	WHL	5	1	3	4	0	....	....	....	....	....	....	....	....	....	....	....	....	....	....	....	....	....	....
2006-07	Vancouver Giants	WHL	49	3	5	8	31	....	....	....	....	....	....	....	....	....	22	3	3	6	12	....	....	....	....
2007-08	Vancouver Giants	WHL	71	12	23	35	93	....	....	....	....	....	....	....	....	....	10	0	1	1	8	....	....	....	....
2008-09	Vancouver Giants	WHL	48	9	16	25	116	....	....	....	....	....	....	....	....	....	17	7	5	12	30	....	....	....	....
2009-10	Vancouver Giants	WHL	57	14	29	43	134	....	....	....	....	....	....	....	....	....	16	4	13	17	*47	....	....	....	....
	Abbotsford Heat	AHL	....	....	....	....	....	....	....	....	....	....	....	....	....	....	5	1	0	1	2	....	....	....	....
2010-11	**Calgary**	**NHL**	**16**	**0**	**1**	**1**	**2**	**0**	**0**	**0**	**9**	**0.0**	**–1**	**3**	**0.0**	**5:52**	....	....	....	....	....	....	....	....	....
	Abbotsford Heat	AHL	61	12	8	20	53	....	....	....	....	....	....	....	....	....	....	....	....	....	....	....	....	....	....
2011-12	**Calgary**	**NHL**	**27**	**1**	**2**	**3**	**11**	**0**	**0**	**0**	**26**	**3.8**	**–5**	**22**	**50.0**	**10:10**	....	....	....	....	....	....	....	....	....
	Abbotsford Heat	AHL	31	3	3	6	53	....	....	....	....	....	....	....	....	....	....	....	....	....	....	....	....	....	....
2012-13	Abbotsford Heat	AHL	3	1	0	1	2	....	....	....	....	....	....	....	....	....	....	....	....	....	....	....	....	....	....
	NHL Totals		**43**	**1**	**3**	**4**	**13**	**0**	**0**	**0**	**35**	**2.9**		**25**	**44.0**	**8:34**	....	....	....	....	....	....	....	....	....

• Missed majority of 2012-13 due to knee injury vs. Chicago (AHL), October 19, 2012..

BOURDON, Marc-Andre (boor-DOHN, MAHRK-AHN-dray) PHI

Defense. Shoots left. 6', 206 lbs. Born, St-Hyacinthe, Que., September 17, 1989. Philadelphia's 2nd choice, 67th overall, in 2008 Entry Draft.

Season	Club	League	GP	G	A	Pts	PIM	PP	SH	GW	S	%	+/-	TF	F%	Min	GP	G	A	Pts	PIM	PP	SH	GW	Min
2006-07	Rouyn-Noranda	QMJHL	63	2	26	28	80	....	....	....	....	....	....	....	....	....	16	0	4	4	21	....	....	....	....
2007-08	Rouyn-Noranda	QMJHL	69	12	47	59	114	....	....	....	....	....	....	....	....	....	17	2	16	18	25	....	....	....	....
2008-09	Rouyn-Noranda	QMJHL	37	11	27	38	89	....	....	....	....	....	....	....	....	....	....	....	....	....	....	....	....	....	....
	Rimouski Oceanic	QMJHL	17	7	15	22	23	....	....	....	....	....	....	....	....	....	13	1	12	13	25	....	....	....	....
2009-10	Adirondack	AHL	61	2	17	19	53	....	....	....	....	....	....	....	....	....	....	....	....	....	....	....	....	....	....
2010-11	Adirondack	AHL	46	1	9	10	84	....	....	....	....	....	....	....	....	....	....	....	....	....	....	....	....	....	....
	Greenville	ECHL	5	0	2	2	14	....	....	....	....	....	....	....	....	....	10	0	3	3	16	....	....	....	....
2011-12	**Philadelphia**	**NHL**	**45**	**4**	**3**	**7**	**52**	**0**	**0**	**2**	**45**	**8.9**	**4**	**0**	**0.0**	**16:11**	**1**	**0**	**0**	**0**	**0**	**0**	**0**	**0**	**11:14**
	Adirondack	AHL	18	1	3	4	31	....	....	....	....	....	....	....	....	....	....	....	....	....	....	....	....	....	....
2012-13	Adirondack	AHL	17	1	3	4	59	....	....	....	....	....	....	....	....	....	....	....	....	....	....	....	....	....	....
	NHL Totals		**45**	**4**	**3**	**7**	**52**	**0**	**0**	**2**	**45**	**8.9**		**0**	**0.0**	**16:11**	**1**	**0**	**0**	**0**	**0**	**0**	**0**	**0**	**11:14**

QMJHL First All-Star Team (2008, 2009) • Canadian Major Junior Second All-Star Team (2008)

BOURQUE, Chris (BOHRK, KRIHS)

Center. Shoots left. 5'8", 180 lbs. Born, Boston, MA, January 29, 1986. Washington's 4th choice, 33rd overall, in 2004 Entry Draft.

Season	Club	League	GP	G	A	Pts	PIM	PP	SH	GW	S	%	+/-	TF	F%	Min	GP	G	A	Pts	PIM	PP	SH	GW	Min
2002-03	Cushing	High-MA	28	31	26	57	49	....	....	....	....	....	....	....	....	....	....	....	....	....	....	....	....	....	....
2003-04	Cushing	High-MA	31	37	53	90	96	....	....	....	....	....	....	....	....	....	....	....	....	....	....	....	....	....	....
2004-05	Boston University	H-East	35	10	13	23	50	....	....	....	....	....	....	....	....	....	....	....	....	....	....	....	....	....	....
	Portland Pirates	AHL	6	1	1	2	2	....	....	....	....	....	....	....	....	....	....	....	....	....	....	....	....	....	....
2005-06	Hershey Bears	AHL	52	8	28	36	40	....	....	....	....	....	....	....	....	....	1	0	0	0	0	....	....	....	....
2006-07	Hershey Bears	AHL	76	25	33	58	49	....	....	....	....	....	....	....	....	....	19	2	6	8	18	....	....	....	....
2007-08	**Washington**	**NHL**	**4**	**0**	**0**	**0**	**2**	**0**	**0**	**0**	**4**	**0.0**	**0**	**1**	**0.0**	**8:42**	....	....	....	....	....	....	....	....	....
	Hershey Bears	AHL	73	28	35	63	56	....	....	....	....	....	....	....	....	....	5	1	3	4	8	....	....	....	....
2008-09	**Washington**	**NHL**	**8**	**1**	**0**	**1**	**0**	**0**	**0**	**0**	**11**	**9.1**	**0**	**0**	**0.0**	**9:46**	....	....	....	....	....	....	....	....	....
	Hershey Bears	AHL	69	21	52	73	57	....	....	....	....	....	....	....	....	....	22	5	16	21	30	....	....	....	....
2009-10	**Pittsburgh**	**NHL**	**20**	**0**	**3**	**3**	**10**	**0**	**0**	**0**	**20**	**0.0**	**–4**	**0**	**0.0**	**9:35**	....	....	....	....	....	....	....	....	....
	Washington	**NHL**	**1**	**0**	**0**	**0**	**0**	**0**	**0**	**0**	**1**	**0.0**	**–2**	**0**	**0.0**	**9:37**	....	....	....	....	....	....	....	....	....
	Hershey Bears	AHL	49	22	48	70	26	....	....	....	....	....	....	....	....	....	21	7	20	*27	10	....	....	....	....
2010-11	Mytischi	KHL	8	1	0	1	0	....	....	....	....	....	....	....	....	....	....	....	....	....	....	....	....	....	....
	HC Lugano	Swiss	39	14	19	33	24	....	....	....	....	....	....	....	....	....	2	1	4	5	0	....	....	....	....
2011-12	Hershey Bears	AHL	73	27	*66	*93	42	....	....	....	....	....	....	....	....	....	5	1	3	4	0	....	....	....	....
2012-13	Providence Bruins	AHL	39	10	28	38	34	....	....	....	....	....	....	....	....	....	12	5	9	14	14	....	....	....	....
	Boston	**NHL**	**18**	**1**	**3**	**4**	**6**	**0**	**0**	**1**	**24**	**4.2**	**–6**	**1**	**0.0**	**12:05**	....	....	....	....	....	....	....	....	....
	NHL Totals		**51**	**2**	**6**	**8**	**18**	**0**	**0**	**1**	**60**	**3.3**		**2**	**0.0**	**10:25**	....	....	....	....	....	....	....	....	....

Hockey East All-Rookie Team (2005) • Jack A. Butterfield Trophy (AHL – Playoff MVP) (2010) • AHL First All-Star Team (2012) • John P. Sollenberger Trophy (AHL - Top Scorer) (2012)

Claimed on waivers by **Pittsburgh** from **Washington**, September 30, 2009. Claimed on waivers by **Washington** from **Pittsburgh**, December 5, 2009. Signed as a free agent by **Mytischi** (KHL), June 23, 2010. Signed as a free agent by **Lugano** (Swiss), October 4, 2010. Traded to **Boston** by **Washington** for Zach Hamill, May 26, 2012. Signed as a free agent by **Kazan** (KHL), June 17, 2013.

BOURQUE, Gabriel (BOHRK, gah-BREE-ehl) NSH

Left wing. Shoots left. 5'10", 192 lbs. Born, Rimouski, Que., September 23, 1990. Nashville's 9th choice, 132nd overall, in 2009 Entry Draft.

Season	Club	League	GP	G	A	Pts	PIM	PP	SH	GW	S	%	+/-	TF	F%	Min	GP	G	A	Pts	PIM	PP	SH	GW	Min
2006-07	Ecole Notre Dame	QAAA	43	15	35	50	115	....	....	....	....	....	....	....	....	....	13	8	16	24	14	....	....	....	....
2007-08	Baie-Comeau	QMJHL	65	10	18	28	38	....	....	....	....	....	....	....	....	....	5	0	0	0	0	....	....	....	....
2008-09	Baie-Comeau	QMJHL	60	22	39	61	82	....	....	....	....	....	....	....	....	....	5	0	2	2	16	....	....	....	....
2009-10	Baie-Comeau	QMJHL	30	13	25	38	61	....	....	....	....	....	....	....	....	....	....	....	....	....	....	....	....	....	....
	Moncton Wildcats	QMJHL	25	3	11	14	37	....	....	....	....	....	....	....	....	....	21	19	10	29	18	....	....	....	....
2010-11	Milwaukee	AHL	78	18	18	36	19	....	....	....	....	....	....	....	....	....	13	7	6	13	4	....	....	....	....
2011-12	**Nashville**	**NHL**	**43**	**7**	**12**	**19**	**6**	**0**	**0**	**1**	**59**	**11.9**	**–2**	**1**	**0.0**	**12:47**	**10**	**3**	**2**	**5**	**4**	**0**	**0**	**1**	**13:00**
	Milwaukee	AHL	25	2	14	16	23	....	....	....	....	....	....	....	....	....	....	....	....	....	....	....	....	....	....
2012-13	Milwaukee	AHL	15	7	5	12	4	....	....	....	....	....	....	....	....	....	....	....	....	....	....	....	....	....	....
	Nashville	**NHL**	**34**	**11**	**5**	**16**	**4**	**3**	**1**	**2**	**50**	**22.0**	**6**	**6**	**66.7**	**15:50**	....	....	....	....	....	....	....	....	....
	NHL Totals		**77**	**18**	**17**	**35**	**10**	**3**	**1**	**3**	**109**	**16.5**		**7**	**57.1**	**14:08**	**10**	**3**	**2**	**5**	**4**	**0**	**0**	**1**	**13:00**

BOURQUE, Rene (BOHRK, reh-NAY) MTL

Right wing. Shoots left. 6'2", 211 lbs. Born, Lac La Biche, Alta., December 10, 1981.

Season	Club	League	GP	G	A	Pts	PIM	PP	SH	GW	S	%	+/-	TF	F%	Min	GP	G	A	Pts	PIM	PP	SH	GW	Min
1998-99	Notre Dame	SMHL	42	22	19	41	84	....	....	....	....	....	....	....	....	....	3	1	0	1	6	....	....	....	....
	Notre Dame	SJHL	5	1	0	0	0	....	....	....	....	....	....	....	....	....	1	0	0	0	0	....	....	....	....
2000-01	U. of Wisconsin	WCHA	32	10	5	15	18	....	....	....	....	....	....	....	....	....	....	....	....	....	....	....	....	....	....
2001-02	U. of Wisconsin	WCHA	38	12	7	19	26	....	....	....	....	....	....	....	....	....	....	....	....	....	....	....	....	....	....
2002-03	U. of Wisconsin	WCHA	40	19	8	27	54	....	....	....	....	....	....	....	....	....	....	....	....	....	....	....	....	....	....
2003-04	U. of Wisconsin	WCHA	42	16	20	36	74	....	....	....	....	....	....	....	....	....	....	....	....	....	....	....	....	....	....
2004-05	Norfolk Admirals	AHL	78	33	27	60	105	....	....	....	....	....	....	....	....	....	6	1	0	1	8	....	....	....	....
2005-06	**Chicago**	**NHL**	**77**	**16**	**18**	**34**	**56**	**4**	**0**	**2**	**180**	**8.9**	**3**	**11**	**36.4**	**15:20**	....	....	....	....	....	....	....	....	....
2006-07	**Chicago**	**NHL**	**44**	**7**	**10**	**17**	**38**	**2**	**1**	**1**	**82**	**8.5**	**–4**	**9**	**22.2**	**16:01**	....	....	....	....	....	....	....	....	....
	Norfolk Admirals	AHL	1	0	0	0	0	....	....	....	....	....	....	....	....	....	....	....	....	....	....	....	....	....	....
2007-08	**Chicago**	**NHL**	**62**	**10**	**14**	**24**	**42**	**0**	**5**	**2**	**103**	**9.7**	**6**	**8**	**25.0**	**15:16**	....	....	....	....	....	....	....	....	....
2008-09	**Calgary**	**NHL**	**58**	**21**	**19**	**40**	**70**	**0**	**1**	**0**	**149**	**14.1**	**18**	**18**	**50.0**	**16:05**	**5**	**1**	**0**	**1**	**22**	**0**	**0**	**0**	**17:06**
2009-10	**Calgary**	**NHL**	**73**	**27**	**31**	**58**	**88**	**6**	**4**	**5**	**215**	**12.6**	**7**	**25**	**32.0**	**18:19**	....	....	....	....	....	....	....	....	....
2010-11	**Calgary**	**NHL**	**80**	**27**	**23**	**50**	**42**	**6**	**1**	**6**	**218**	**12.4**	**–17**	**24**	**29.2**	**17:45**	....	....	....	....	....	....	....	....	....
2011-12	**Calgary**	**NHL**	**38**	**13**	**3**	**16**	**41**	**3**	**0**	**1**	**91**	**14.3**	**–3**	**13**	**69.2**	**17:10**	....	....	....	....	....	....	....	....	....
	Montreal	**NHL**	**38**	**5**	**3**	**8**	**27**	**0**	**1**	**0**	**67**	**7.5**	**–16**	**7**	**42.9**	**18:29**	....	....	....	....	....	....	....	....	....
2012-13	**Montreal**	**NHL**	**27**	**7**	**6**	**13**	**32**	**2**	**0**	**1**	**63**	**11.1**	**–1**	**1**	**0.0**	**16:20**	**5**	**2**	**1**	**3**	**10**	**1**	**0**	**0**	**16:08**
	NHL Totals		**497**	**133**	**127**	**260**	**436**	**23**	**13**	**18**	**1168**	**11.4**		**116**	**37.9**	**16:44**	**10**	**3**	**1**	**4**	**32**	**1**	**0**	**0**	**16:37**

AHL All-Rookie Team (2005) • Dudley "Red" Garrett Memorial Trophy (AHL - Top Rookie) (2005)

Signed as a free agent by **Chicago**, July 29, 2004. Traded to **Calgary** by **Chicago** for Calgary's 2nd round choice (later traded to Toronto – Toronto selected Brad Ross) in 2010 Entry Draft, July 1, 2008. Traded to **Montreal** by **Calgary** with Patrick Holland and Calgary's 2nd round choice (Zachary Fucale) in 2013 Entry Draft for Mike Cammalleri, Karri Ramo and Montreal's 5th round choice (Ryan Culkin) in 2012 Entry Draft, January 12, 2012.

BOUWMEESTER, Jay

(BOW-mee-stuhr, JAY) **ST.L.**

Defense. Shoots left. 6'4", 212 lbs. Born, Edmonton, Alta., September 27, 1983. Florida's 1st choice, 3rd overall, in 2002 Entry Draft.

			Regular Season														Playoffs								
Season	Club	League	GP	G	A	Pts	PIM	PP	SH	GW	S	%	+/-	TF	F%	Min	GP	G	A	Pts	PIM	PP	SH	GW	Min
1998-99	Edmonton SSAC	AMHL	32	14	29	43	36	....	....	....	....	....	....	....	....	....	....	....	....	....	....	....	....	....	....
	Medicine Hat	WHL	8	2	1	3	2	....	....	....	....	....	....	....	....	....	....	....	....	....	....	....	....	....	....
99-2000	Medicine Hat	WHL	64	13	21	34	26	....	....	....	....	....	....	....	....	....	....	....	....	....	....	....	....	....	....
2000-01	Medicine Hat	WHL	61	14	39	53	44	....	....	....	....	....	....	....	....	....	....	....	....	....	....	....	....	....	....
2001-02	Medicine Hat	WHL	61	11	50	61	42	....	....	....	....	....	....	....	....	....	....	....	....	....	....	....	....	....	....
2002-03	**Florida**	**NHL**	**82**	**4**	**12**	**16**	**14**	**2**	**0**	**0**	**110**	**3.6**	**-29**	**0**	**0.0**	**20:09**	....	....	....	....	....	....	....	....	....
2003-04	**Florida**	**NHL**	**61**	**2**	**18**	**20**	**30**	**0**	**0**	**0**	**85**	**2.4**	**-15**	**0**	**0.0**	**23:02**	....	....	....	....	....	....	....	....	....
	San Antonio	AHL	2	0	1	1	2	....	....	....	....	....	....	....	....	....	....	....	....	....	....	....	....	....	....
2004-05	San Antonio	AHL	64	4	13	17	50	....	....	....	....	....	....	....	....	....	....	....	....	....	....	....	....	....	....
	Chicago Wolves	AHL	18	6	3	9	12	....	....	....	....	....	....	....	....	....	18	0	0	0	14	....	....	....	....
2005-06	**Florida**	**NHL**	**82**	**5**	**41**	**46**	**79**	**0**	**0**	**0**	**189**	**2.6**	**1**	**1**	**0.0**	**25:29**	....	....	....	....	....	....	....	....	....
	Canada	Olympics	6	0	0	0	0	....	....	....	....	....	....	....	....	....	....	....	....	....	....	....	....	....	....
2006-07	**Florida**	**NHL**	**82**	**12**	**30**	**42**	**66**	**3**	**0**	**3**	**174**	**6.9**	**23**	**0**	**0.0**	**26:09**	....	....	....	....	....	....	....	....	....
2007-08	**Florida**	**NHL**	**82**	**15**	**22**	**37**	**72**	**4**	**0**	**0**	**182**	**8.2**	**-5**	**0**	**0.0**	**27:28**	....	....	....	....	....	....	....	....	....
2008-09	**Florida**	**NHL**	**82**	**15**	**27**	**42**	**68**	**9**	**0**	**2**	**182**	**8.2**	**-2**	**0**	**0.0**	**26:59**	....	....	....	....	....	....	....	....	....
2009-10	**Calgary**	**NHL**	**82**	**3**	**26**	**29**	**48**	**1**	**0**	**0**	**130**	**2.3**	**-4**	**0**	**0.0**	**25:55**	....	....	....	....	....	....	....	....	....
2010-11	**Calgary**	**NHL**	**82**	**4**	**20**	**24**	**44**	**1**	**0**	**1**	**121**	**3.3**	**-2**	**0**	**0.0**	**25:59**	....	....	....	....	....	....	....	....	....
2011-12	**Calgary**	**NHL**	**82**	**5**	**24**	**29**	**26**	**2**	**0**	**1**	**107**	**4.7**	**-21**	**0**	**0.0**	**25:57**	....	....	....	....	....	....	....	....	....
2012-13	**Calgary**	**NHL**	**33**	**6**	**9**	**15**	**16**	**1**	**0**	**0**	**55**	**10.9**	**-11**	**0**	**0.0**	**25:10**	....	....	....	....	....	....	....	....	....
	St. Louis	**NHL**	**14**	**1**	**6**	**7**	**6**	**0**	**0**	**0**	**24**	**4.2**	**5**	**0**	**0.0**	**23:24**	**6**	**0**	**1**	**1**	**0**	**0**	**0**	**0**	**25:08**
	NHL Totals		**764**	**72**	**235**	**307**	**469**	**23**	**0**	**7**	**1359**	**5.3**		**1**	**0.0**	**25:16**	**6**	**0**	**1**	**1**	**0**	**0**	**0**	**0**	**25:08**

WHL East First All-Star Team (2002) • NHL All-Rookie Team (2003)

Played in NHL All-Star Game (2007, 2009)

• Loaned to **Chicago** (AHL) by **Florida** (San Antonio-AHL) for cash, March 8, 2005. Traded to **Calgary** by **Florida** for Jordan Leopold and Phoenix's 3rd round choice (previously acquired, Florida selected Josh Birkholz) in 2009 Entry Draft, June 27, 2009. Traded to **St. Louis** by **Calgary** for Mark Cundari, Reto Berra and St. Louis' 1st round choice (Emile Poirier) in 2013 Entry Draft, April 1, 2013.

BOWMAN, Drayson

(BOH-muhn, DRAY-suhn) **CAR**

Center/Left wing. Shoots left. 6'1", 195 lbs. Born, Grand Rapids, MI, March 8, 1989. Carolina's 2nd choice, 72nd overall, in 2007 Entry Draft.

Season	Club	League	GP	G	A	Pts	PIM	PP	SH	GW	S	%	+/-	TF	F%	Min	GP	G	A	Pts	PIM	PP	SH	GW	Min
2004-05	Kimberley	KIJHL	47	29	30	59	108	....	....	....	....	....	....	....	....	....	....	....	....	....	....	....	....	....	....
	Spokane Chiefs	WHL	4	0	0	0	0	....	....	....	....	....	....	....	....	....	....	....	....	....	....	....	....	....	....
2005-06	Spokane Chiefs	WHL	72	17	17	34	51	....	....	....	....	....	....	....	....	....	....	....	....	....	....	....	....	....	....
2006-07	Spokane Chiefs	WHL	61	24	19	43	55	....	....	....	....	....	....	....	....	....	6	2	5	7	4	....	....	....	....
2007-08	Spokane Chiefs	WHL	66	42	40	82	62	....	....	....	....	....	....	....	....	....	21	11	9	20	8	....	....	....	....
2008-09	Spokane Chiefs	WHL	62	47	36	83	107	....	....	....	....	....	....	....	....	....	12	8	5	13	8	....	....	....	....
2009-10	**Carolina**	**NHL**	**9**	**2**	**0**	**2**	**4**	**1**	**0**	**0**	**17**	**11.8**	**-1**	**0**	**0.0**	**12:01**	....	....	....	....	....	....	....	....	....
	Albany River Rats	AHL	56	17	15	32	29	....	....	....	....	....	....	....	....	....	8	3	6	9	12	....	....	....	....
2010-11	**Carolina**	**NHL**	**23**	**0**	**1**	**1**	**12**	**0**	**0**	**0**	**28**	**0.0**	**0**	**0**	**0.0**	**9:49**	....	....	....	....	....	....	....	....	....
	Charlotte	AHL	51	12	18	30	53	....	....	....	....	....	....	....	....	....	15	2	6	8	6	....	....	....	....
2011-12	**Carolina**	**NHL**	**37**	**6**	**7**	**13**	**4**	**0**	**0**	**0**	**70**	**8.6**	**2**	**0**	**0.0**	**13:21**	....	....	....	....	....	....	....	....	....
	Charlotte	AHL	42	13	13	26	45	....	....	....	....	....	....	....	....	....	....	....	....	....	....	....	....	....	....
2012-13	Charlotte	AHL	37	14	8	22	21	....	....	....	....	....	....	....	....	....	....	....	....	....	....	....	....	....	....
	Carolina	**NHL**	**37**	**3**	**2**	**5**	**17**	**0**	**0**	**0**	**68**	**4.4**	**-7**	**10**	**40.0**	**11:42**	....	....	....	....	....	....	....	....	....
	NHL Totals		**106**	**11**	**10**	**21**	**37**	**1**	**0**	**0**	**183**	**6.0**		**10**	**40.0**	**11:54**	....	....	....	....	....	....	....	....	....

WHL West Second All-Star Team (2008, 2009) • Memorial Cup All-Star Team (2008)

BOYCE, Darryl

(BOIS, DAIR-uhl)

Center. Shoots left. 6', 200 lbs. Born, Summerside, P.E.I., July 7, 1984.

Season	Club	League	GP	G	A	Pts	PIM	PP	SH	GW	S	%	+/-	TF	F%	Min	GP	G	A	Pts	PIM	PP	SH	GW	Min
2001-02	St. Michael's	OHL	67	10	11	21	71	....	....	....	....	....	....	....	....	....	15	2	5	7	46	....	....	....	....
2002-03	St. Michael's	OHL	64	16	21	37	119	....	....	....	....	....	....	....	....	....	19	1	3	4	28	....	....	....	....
2003-04	St. Michael's	OHL	64	13	24	37	110	....	....	....	....	....	....	....	....	....	18	1	3	4	23	....	....	....	....
2004-05	St. Michael's	OHL	67	15	35	50	152	....	....	....	....	....	....	....	....	....	10	2	5	7	28	....	....	....	....
2005-06	New Brunswick	AUAA	28	15	17	32	50	....	....	....	....	....	....	....	....	....	....	....	....	....	....	....	....	....	....
2006-07	New Brunswick	AUAA	25	14	19	33	63	....	....	....	....	....	....	....	....	....	....	....	....	....	....	....	....	....	....
2007-08	Toronto Marlies	AHL	41	8	16	24	71	....	....	....	....	....	....	....	....	....	....	....	....	....	....	....	....	....	....
	Toronto	**NHL**	**1**	**0**	**0**	**0**	**0**	**0**	**0**	**0**	**0**	**0.0**	**0**	**2**	**100.0**	**3:20**	....	....	....	....	....	....	....	....	....
2008-09	Toronto Marlies	AHL	73	12	18	30	131	....	....	....	....	....	....	....	....	....	6	2	0	2	27	....	....	....	....
2009-10	Toronto Marlies	AHL	20	2	9	11	48	....	....	....	....	....	....	....	....	....	....	....	....	....	....	....	....	....	....
2010-11	**Toronto**	**NHL**	**46**	**5**	**8**	**13**	**33**	**0**	**0**	**1**	**27**	**18.5**	**8**	**457**	**46.4**	**11:23**	....	....	....	....	....	....	....	....	....
	Toronto Marlies	AHL	35	6	10	16	48	....	....	....	....	....	....	....	....	....	....	....	....	....	....	....	....	....	....
2011-12	**Toronto**	**NHL**	**17**	**1**	**1**	**2**	**16**	**0**	**0**	**1**	**12**	**8.3**	**-3**	**15**	**53.3**	**10:04**	....	....	....	....	....	....	....	....	....
	Toronto Marlies	AHL	22	4	6	10	22	....	....	....	....	....	....	....	....	....	....	....	....	....	....	....	....	....	....
	Columbus	**NHL**	**20**	**0**	**3**	**3**	**19**	**0**	**0**	**0**	**13**	**0.0**	**-5**	**148**	**51.4**	**9:55**	....	....	....	....	....	....	....	....	....
2012-13	Hamilton	AHL	22	1	6	7	27	....	....	....	....	....	....	....	....	....	....	....	....	....	....	....	....	....	....
	JYP Jyvaskyla	Finland	14	1	3	4	22	....	....	....	....	....	....	....	....	....	11	3	0	3	31	....	....	....	....
	NHL Totals		**84**	**6**	**12**	**18**	**68**	**0**	**0**	**2**	**52**	**11.5**		**622**	**47.9**	**10:40**	....	....	....	....	....	....	....	....	....

Signed as a free agent by **Toronto** (AHL), April, 2007. Signed as a free agent by **Toronto**, January 1, 2008. • Missed majority of 2009-10 due to various injuries. Claimed on waivers by **Columbus** from **Toronto**, February 25, 2012. Signed to a PTO (professional tryout) contract by **Hamilton** (AHL), October 5, 2012. Signed as a free agent by **Jyvaskyla** (Finland), January 29, 2013.

BOYCHUK, Johnny

(BOY-chuhk, JAW-nee) **BOS**

Defense. Shoots right. 6'2", 225 lbs. Born, Edmonton, Alta., January 19, 1984. Colorado's 2nd choice, 61st overall, in 2002 Entry Draft.

Season	Club	League	GP	G	A	Pts	PIM	PP	SH	GW	S	%	+/-	TF	F%	Min	GP	G	A	Pts	PIM	PP	SH	GW	Min
1998-99	Edm. Cycle	AMBHL	36	8	20	28	59	....	....	....	....	....	....	....	....	....	....	....	....	....	....	....	....	....	....
99-2000	Edm. Cycle	AMHL	35	6	17	23	59	....	....	....	....	....	....	....	....	....	....	....	....	....	....	....	....	....	....
	Calgary Hitmen	WHL	1	0	0	0	0	....	....	....	....	....	....	....	....	....	....	....	....	....	....	....	....	....	....
2000-01	Calgary Hitmen	WHL	66	4	8	12	61	....	....	....	....	....	....	....	....	....	12	1	1	2	17	....	....	....	....
2001-02	Calgary Hitmen	WHL	70	8	32	40	85	....	....	....	....	....	....	....	....	....	7	1	1	2	6	....	....	....	....
2002-03	Calgary Hitmen	WHL	40	8	18	26	58	....	....	....	....	....	....	....	....	....	....	....	....	....	....	....	....	....	....
	Moose Jaw	WHL	27	5	17	22	32	....	....	....	....	....	....	....	....	....	13	2	6	8	29	....	....	....	....
2003-04	Moose Jaw	WHL	62	13	20	33	71	....	....	....	....	....	....	....	....	....	10	1	9	10	9	....	....	....	....
2004-05	Hershey Bears	AHL	80	3	12	15	69	....	....	....	....	....	....	....	....	....	....	....	....	....	....	....	....	....	....
2005-06	Lowell	AHL	74	6	26	32	73	....	....	....	....	....	....	....	....	....	....	....	....	....	....	....	....	....	....
2006-07	Albany River Rats	AHL	80	10	18	28	125	....	....	....	....	....	....	....	....	....	5	1	1	2	4	....	....	....	....
2007-08	**Colorado**	**NHL**	**4**	**0**	**0**	**0**	**0**	**0**	**0**	**0**	**3**	**0.0**	**1**	**1**	**0.0**	**8:57**	....	....	....	....	....	....	....	....	....
	Lake Erie	AHL	60	8	18	26	63	....	....	....	....	....	....	....	....	....	....	....	....	....	....	....	....	....	....
2008-09	**Boston**	**NHL**	**1**	**0**	**0**	**0**	**0**	**0**	**0**	**0**	**0**	**0.0**	**0**	**0**	**0.0**	**14:48**	....	....	....	....	....	....	....	....	....
	Providence Bruins	AHL	78	20	46	66	61	....	....	....	....	....	....	....	....	....	16	3	5	8	19	....	....	....	....
2009-10	**Boston**	**NHL**	**51**	**5**	**10**	**15**	**43**	**0**	**0**	**0**	**96**	**5.2**	**10**	**0**	**0.0**	**17:39**	**13**	**2**	**4**	**6**	**6**	**1**	**0**	**0**	**26:10**
	Providence Bruins	AHL	2	1	0	1	0	....	....	....	....	....	....	....	....	....	....	....	....	....	....	....	....	....	....
2010-11 ♦	**Boston**	**NHL**	**69**	**3**	**13**	**16**	**45**	**1**	**0**	**1**	**154**	**1.9**	**15**	**0**	**0.0**	**20:30**	**25**	**3**	**6**	**9**	**12**	**0**	**0**	**1**	**20:38**
2011-12	**Boston**	**NHL**	**77**	**5**	**10**	**15**	**53**	**0**	**0**	**2**	**171**	**2.9**	**27**	**0**	**0.0**	**20:37**	**7**	**1**	**2**	**3**	**4**	**1**	**0**	**0**	**22:16**
2012-13	Salzburg	Austria	15	2	6	8	2	....	....	....	....	....	....	....	....	....	....	....	....	....	....	....	....	....	....
	Boston	**NHL**	**44**	**1**	**5**	**6**	**12**	**0**	**0**	**0**	**75**	**1.3**	**5**	**0**	**0.0**	**20:24**	**22**	**6**	**1**	**7**	**10**	**0**	**0**	**1**	**23:56**
	NHL Totals		**246**	**14**	**38**	**52**	**153**	**1**	**0**	**3**	**499**	**2.8**		**1**	**0.0**	**19:43**	**67**	**12**	**13**	**25**	**32**	**2**	**0**	**2**	**22:58**

AHL First All-Star Team (2009) • Eddie Shore Award (AHL – Outstanding Defenseman) (2009)

Traded to **Boston** by **Colorado** for Matt Hendricks, June 24, 2008. Signed as a free agent by **Salzburg** (Austria), November 16, 2012.

BOYCHUK, Zach

(BOY-chuhk, ZAK)

Center. Shoots left. 5'10", 185 lbs. Born, Airdrie, Alta., October 4, 1989. Carolina's 1st choice, 14th overall, in 2008 Entry Draft.

Season	Club	League	GP	G	A	Pts	PIM	PP	SH	GW	S	%	+/-	TF	F%	Min	GP	G	A	Pts	PIM	PP	SH	GW	Min
2004-05	UFA Bisons	AMHL	36	13	14	27	18	....	....	....	....	....	....	....	....	....	16	10	5	15	....	....	....	....	....
2005-06	Lethbridge	WHL	64	18	33	51	30	....	....	....	....	....	....	....	....	....	6	0	5	5	2	....	....	....	....
2006-07	Lethbridge	WHL	69	31	60	91	52	....	....	....	....	....	....	....	....	....	....	....	....	....	....	....	....	....	....
2007-08	Lethbridge	WHL	61	33	39	72	80	....	....	....	....	....	....	....	....	....	18	*13	8	21	6	....	....	....	....

			Regular Season														Playoffs								
Season	Club	League	GP	G	A	Pts	PIM	PP	SH	GW	S	%	+/-	TF	F%	Min	GP	G	A	Pts	PIM	PP	SH	GW	Min
2008-09	Carolina	NHL	2	0	0	0	0	0	0	0	0	0.0	0	1	0.0	12:03	....	....	....	....	....	....	....	....	....
	Lethbridge	WHL	43	28	29	57	22	....	....	....	....	....	....	....	....	....	11	7	6	13	12	....	....	....	....
	Albany River Rats	AHL	2	0	1	1	2	....	....	....	....	....	....	....	....	....	....	....	....	....	....	....	....	....	....
2009-10	Carolina	NHL	31	3	6	9	2	0	0	0	37	8.1	1	9	55.6	10:45	....	....	....	....	....	....	....	....	....
	Albany River Rats	AHL	52	15	21	36	24	....	....	....	....	....	....	....	....	....	8	2	3	5	4	....	....	....	....
2010-11	Carolina	NHL	23	4	3	7	4	1	0	1	44	9.1	–2	5	20.0	10:43	....	....	....	....	....	....	....	....	....
	Charlotte	AHL	60	22	43	65	48	....	....	....	....	....	....	....	....	....	16	3	6	9	14	....	....	....	....
2011-12	Carolina	NHL	16	0	2	2	0	0	0	0	10	0.0	–3	4	50.0	8:55	....	....	....	....	....	....	....	....	....
	Charlotte	AHL	64	21	23	44	46	....	....	....	....	....	....	....	....	....	....	....	....	....	....	....	....	....	....
2012-13	Charlotte	AHL	49	23	20	43	16	....	....	....	....	....	....	....	....	....	5	3	3	6	4	....	....	....	....
	Carolina	NHL	1	0	0	0	0	0	0	0	0	0.0	0	0	0.0	10:13	....	....	....	....	....	....	....	....	....
	Pittsburgh	NHL	7	0	0	0	2	0	0	0	6	0.0	–2	0	0.0	11:37	....	....	....	....	....	....	....	....	....
	Nashville	NHL	5	1	1	2	4	0	0	0	8	12.5	1	0	0.0	13:42	....	....	....	....	....	....	....	....	....
	NHL Totals		85	8	12	20	12	1	0	1	105	7.6		19	42.1	10:40	....	....	....	....	....	....	....	....	....

WHL East Second All-Star Team (2007, 2008)

Claimed on waivers by **Pittsburgh** from **Carolina**, January 29, 2013. Claimed on waivers by **Nashville** from **Pittsburgh**, March 5, 2013.

BOYES, Brad

(BOIZ, BRAD)

Right wing. Shoots right. 6', 195 lbs. Born, Mississauga, Ont., April 17, 1982. Toronto's 1st choice, 24th overall, in 2000 Entry Draft.

Season	Club	League	GP	G	A	Pts	PIM	PP	SH	GW	S	%	+/-	TF	F%	Min	GP	G	A	Pts	PIM	PP	SH	GW	Min
1997-98	Mississauga Reps	MTHL	44	27	50	77	....	....	....	....	....	....	....	....	....	....	....	....	....	....	....	....	....	....	....
1998-99	Erie Otters	OHL	59	24	36	60	30	....	....	....	....	....	....	....	....	....	5	1	2	3	10	....	....	....	....
99-2000	Erie Otters	OHL	68	36	46	82	38	....	....	....	....	....	....	....	....	....	13	6	8	14	10	....	....	....	....
2000-01	Erie Otters	OHL	59	45	45	90	42	....	....	....	....	....	....	....	....	....	15	10	13	23	8	....	....	....	....
2001-02	Erie Otters	OHL	47	36	41	77	42	....	....	....	....	....	....	....	....	....	21	22	*19	41	27	....	....	....	....
2002-03	St. John's	AHL	65	23	28	51	45	....	....	....	....	....	....	....	....	....	....	....	....	....	....	....	....	....	....
	Cleveland Barons	AHL	15	7	6	13	21	....	....	....	....	....	....	....	....	....	....	....	....	....	....	....	....	....	....
2003-04	San Jose	NHL	1	0	0	0	2	0	0	0	0	0.0	–2	0	0.0	13:03	....	....	....	....	....	....	....	....	....
	Cleveland Barons	AHL	61	25	35	60	38	....	....	....	....	....	....	....	....	....	....	....	....	....	....	....	....	....	....
	Providence Bruins	AHL	17	6	6	12	13	....	....	....	....	....	....	....	....	....	2	1	0	1	0	....	....	....	....
2004-05	Providence Bruins	AHL	80	33	42	75	58	....	....	....	....	....	....	....	....	....	16	8	7	15	23	....	....	....	....
2005-06	Boston	NHL	82	26	43	69	30	8	0	3	203	12.8	11	265	53.6	15:46	....	....	....	....	....	....	....	....	....
2006-07	Boston	NHL	62	13	21	34	25	1	1	1	139	9.4	–17	220	44.1	16:04	....	....	....	....	....	....	....	....	....
	St. Louis	NHL	19	4	8	12	4	0	0	1	43	9.3	0	93	58.1	17:25	....	....	....	....	....	....	....	....	....
2007-08	St. Louis	NHL	82	43	22	65	20	11	0	9	207	20.8	1	236	44.5	17:57	....	....	....	....	....	....	....	....	....
2008-09	St. Louis	NHL	82	33	39	72	26	16	0	11	220	15.0	–20	315	49.2	19:08	4	2	1	3	0	1	0	0	21:34
2009-10	St. Louis	NHL	82	14	28	42	26	2	0	3	197	7.1	1	311	44.4	16:47	....	....	....	....	....	....	....	....	....
2010-11	St. Louis	NHL	62	12	29	41	30	4	0	2	132	9.1	11	135	41.5	17:10	....	....	....	....	....	....	....	....	....
	Buffalo	NHL	21	5	9	14	6	2	0	1	46	10.9	2	185	43.2	16:28	7	1	0	1	0	1	0	0	14:23
2011-12	Buffalo	NHL	65	8	15	23	6	2	0	0	100	8.0	2	267	47.2	13:10	....	....	....	....	....	....	....	....	....
2012-13	NY Islanders	NHL	48	10	25	35	16	1	0	1	97	10.3	–6	16	25.0	18:13	6	0	3	3	2	0	0	0	19:06
	NHL Totals		606	168	239	407	191	47	1	32	1384	12.1		2043	46.8	16:49	17	3	4	7	2	2	0	0	17:44

Canadian Major Junior Scholastic Player of the Year (2000) • OHL Second All-Star Team (2001) • OHL First All-Star Team (2002) • Canadian Major Junior Second All-Star Team (2002) • Canadian Major Junior Sportsman of the Year (2002) • AHL All-Rookie Team (2003) • AHL Second All-Star Team (2004) • NHL All-Rookie Team (2006)

Traded to **San Jose** by **Toronto** with Alyn McCauley and Toronto's 1st round choice (later traded to Boston – Boston selected Mark Stuart) in 2003 Entry Draft for Owen Nolan, March 5, 2003. Traded to **Boston** by **San Jose** for Jeff Jillson, March 9, 2004. Traded to **St. Louis** by **Boston** for Dennis Wideman, February 27, 2007. Traded to **Buffalo** by **St. Louis** for Buffalo's 2nd round choice (Joel Edmundson) in 2011 Entry Draft, February 27, 2011. Signed as a free agent by **NY Islanders**, July 1, 2012.

BOYLE, Brian

(BOIL, BRIGH-uhn) **NYR**

Center. Shoots left. 6'7", 244 lbs. Born, Hingham, MA, December 18, 1984. Los Angeles' 2nd choice, 26th overall, in 2003 Entry Draft.

Season	Club	League	GP	G	A	Pts	PIM	PP	SH	GW	S	%	+/-	TF	F%	Min	GP	G	A	Pts	PIM	PP	SH	GW	Min
2000-01	St. Sebastian's	High-MA	25	20	19	39	23	....	....	....	....	....	....	....	....	....	....	....	....	....	....	....	....	....	....
2001-02	St. Sebastian's	High-MA	28	21	26	47	22	....	....	....	....	....	....	....	....	....	....	....	....	....	....	....	....	....	....
2002-03	St. Sebastian's	High-MA	31	32	31	62	46	....	....	....	....	....	....	....	....	....	....	....	....	....	....	....	....	....	....
2003-04	Boston College	H-East	35	5	3	8	36	....	....	....	....	....	....	....	....	....	....	....	....	....	....	....	....	....	....
2004-05	Boston College	H-East	40	19	8	27	64	....	....	....	....	....	....	....	....	....	....	....	....	....	....	....	....	....	....
2005-06	Boston College	H-East	42	22	*30	52	90	....	....	....	....	....	....	....	....	....	....	....	....	....	....	....	....	....	....
2006-07	Boston College	H-East	42	19	*34	*53	*104	....	....	....	....	....	....	....	....	....	....	....	....	....	....	....	....	....	....
	Manchester	AHL	2	0	0	0	2	....	....	....	....	....	....	....	....	....	16	3	5	8	13	....	....	....	....
2007-08	Los Angeles	NHL	8	4	1	5	4	0	0	0	19	21.1	4	80	46.3	13:38	....	....	....	....	....	....	....	....	....
	Manchester	AHL	70	31	31	62	87	....	....	....	....	....	....	....	....	....	....	....	....	....	....	....	....	....	....
2008-09	Los Angeles	NHL	28	4	1	5	42	0	0	1	36	11.1	–9	225	45.3	10:08	....	....	....	....	....	....	....	....	....
	Manchester	AHL	42	10	11	21	73	....	....	....	....	....	....	....	....	....	....	....	....	....	....	....	....	....	....
2009-10	NY Rangers	NHL	71	4	2	6	47	0	0	1	73	5.5	–6	323	38.7	8:25	....	....	....	....	....	....	....	....	....
2010-11	NY Rangers	NHL	82	21	14	35	74	4	1	2	218	9.6	2	1101	48.5	15:44	5	0	0	0	6	0	0	0	21:30
2011-12	NY Rangers	NHL	82	11	15	26	59	0	0	2	165	6.7	2	1215	51.8	15:14	17	3	3	6	15	0	0	2	16:44
2012-13	NY Rangers	NHL	38	2	3	5	29	0	0	1	56	3.6	–13	381	56.4	14:13	11	3	2	5	2	1	0	0	18:50
	NHL Totals		309	46	36	82	255	4	1	7	567	8.1		3325	49.4	13:11	33	6	5	11	23	1	0	2	18:09

Hockey East First All-Star Team (2006, 2007) • NCAA East Second All-American Team (2006) • NCAA East First All-American Team (2007) • NCAA Championship All-Tournament Team (2007) • AHL All-Rookie Team (2008)

Traded to **NY Rangers** by **Los Angeles** for NY Rangers' 3rd round choice (Jordan Weal) in 2010 Entry Draft, June 27, 2009.

BOYLE, Dan

(BOIL, DAN) **S.J.**

Defense. Shoots right. 5'11", 190 lbs. Born, Ottawa, Ont., July 12, 1976.

Season	Club	League	GP	G	A	Pts	PIM	PP	SH	GW	S	%	+/-	TF	F%	Min	GP	G	A	Pts	PIM	PP	SH	GW	Min
1992-93	Gloucester	ON-Jr.A	55	22	51	73	60	....	....	....	....	....	....	....	....	....	5	0	4	4	12	....	....	....	....
1993-94	Gloucester	ON-Jr.A	53	27	54	81	155	....	....	....	....	....	....	....	....	....	15	9	17	26	36	....	....	....	....
1994-95	Miami U.	CCHA	35	8	18	26	24	....	....	....	....	....	....	....	....	....	....	....	....	....	....	....	....	....	....
1995-96	Miami U.	CCHA	36	7	20	27	70	....	....	....	....	....	....	....	....	....	....	....	....	....	....	....	....	....	....
1996-97	Miami U.	CCHA	40	11	43	54	52	....	....	....	....	....	....	....	....	....	....	....	....	....	....	....	....	....	....
1997-98	Miami U.	CCHA	37	14	26	40	58	....	....	....	....	....	....	....	....	....	....	....	....	....	....	....	....	....	....
1998-99	Florida	NHL	22	3	5	8	6	1	0	1	31	9.7	0	1	100.0	18:50	....	....	....	....	....	....	....	....	....
	Kentucky	AHL	53	8	34	42	87	....	....	....	....	....	....	....	....	....	12	3	5	8	16	....	....	....	....
99-2000	Florida	NHL	13	0	3	3	4	0	0	0	9	0.0	–2	0	0.0	16:57	....	....	....	....	....	....	....	....	....
	Louisville Panthers	AHL	58	14	38	52	75	....	....	....	....	....	....	....	....	....	4	0	2	2	8	....	....	....	....
2000-01	Florida	NHL	69	4	18	22	28	1	0	0	83	4.8	–14	0	0.0	16:56	....	....	....	....	....	....	....	....	....
	Louisville Panthers	AHL	6	0	5	5	12	....	....	....	....	....	....	....	....	....	....	....	....	....	....	....	....	....	....
2001-02	Florida	NHL	25	3	3	6	12	1	0	0	31	9.7	–1	2	50.0	15:40	....	....	....	....	....	....	....	....	....
	Tampa Bay	NHL	41	5	15	20	27	2	0	1	68	7.4	–15	0	0.0	22:28	....	....	....	....	....	....	....	....	....
2002-03	Tampa Bay	NHL	77	13	40	53	44	8	0	1	136	9.6	9	2	0.0	24:31	11	0	7	7	6	0	0	0	27:45
2003-04♦	Tampa Bay	NHL	78	9	30	39	60	3	0	2	137	6.6	23	0	0.0	22:46	23	2	8	10	16	1	0	0	21:27
2004-05	Djurgarden	Sweden	32	9	9	18	47	....	....	....	....	....	....	....	....	....	12	2	3	5	26	....	....	....	....
2005-06	Tampa Bay	NHL	79	15	38	53	38	6	0	4	153	9.8	–8	1	0.0	23:26	5	1	3	4	6	0	0	0	25:54
	Canada	Olympics	DID NOT PLAY																						
2006-07	Tampa Bay	NHL	82	20	43	63	62	10	1	4	203	9.9	–5	1	0.0	27:03	6	0	1	1	2	0	0	0	28:03
2007-08	Tampa Bay	NHL	37	4	21	25	57	2	0	1	74	5.4	–29	0	0.0	27:24	....	....	....	....	....	....	....	....	....
2008-09	San Jose	NHL	77	16	41	57	52	8	0	4	213	7.5	6	1	0.0	24:46	6	2	2	4	8	1	0	0	23:17
2009-10	San Jose	NHL	76	15	43	58	70	6	0	3	180	8.3	6	3	0.0	26:13	15	2	12	14	8	1	0	0	27:11
	Canada	Olympics	7	1	5	6	2	....	....	....	....	....	....	....	....	....	....	....	....	....	....	....	....	....	....
2010-11	San Jose	NHL	76	9	41	50	67	4	0	2	199	4.5	2	2	0.0	26:14	18	4	12	16	8	2	0	1	26:10
2011-12	San Jose	NHL	81	9	39	48	57	3	0	2	252	3.6	10	0	0.0	25:35	5	0	2	2	4	0	0	0	28:23
2012-13	San Jose	NHL	46	7	13	20	27	5	0	0	97	7.2	3	0	0.0	22:48	11	3	5	8	2	1	0	1	22:12
	NHL Totals		879	132	393	525	611	60	1	25	1866	7.1		13	15.4	23:45	100	14	52	66	60	6	0	2	25:01

CCHA First All-Star Team (1997, 1998) • NCAA West First All-American Team (1997, 1998) • AHL All-Rookie Team (1999) • AHL Second All-Star Team (1999, 2000) • NHL Second All-Star Team (2007, 2009)

Played in NHL All-Star Game (2009, 2011)

Signed as a free agent by **Florida**, March 30, 1998. Traded to **Tampa Bay** by **Florida** for Tampa Bay's 5th round choice (Martin Tuma) in 2003 Entry Draft, January 7, 2002. Signed as a free agent by **Djurgarden** (Sweden), November 14, 2004. • Missed majority of 2007-08 due to off-ice wrist injury, September 22, 2007 and resulting surgery, November 6, 2007. Traded to **San Jose** by **Tampa Bay** with Brad Lukowich for Matt Carle, Ty Wishart, San Jose's 1st round choice (later traded to Ottawa, later traded to NY Islanders, later traded to Columbus, later traded to Anaheim - Anaheim selected Kyle Palmieri) in 2009 Entry Draft and San Jose's 4th round choice (James Mullin) in 2010 Entry Draft, July 4, 2008.

			Regular Season														Playoffs								
Season	Club	League	GP	G	A	Pts	PIM	PP	SH	GW	S	%	+/-	TF	F%	Min	GP	G	A	Pts	PIM	PP	SH	GW	Min

BOZAK, Tyler

(BOH-zak, TIGH-luhr) **TOR**

Center. Shoots right. 6'1", 195 lbs. Born, Regina, Sask., March 19, 1986.

Season	Club	League	GP	G	A	Pts	PIM	PP	SH	GW	S	%	+/-	TF	F%	Min	GP	G	A	Pts	PIM	PP	SH	GW	Min
2003-04	Reg. Pat Cdns.	SMHL	42	17	19	36	40	....	....	....	....	....	....	....	....	....	....	....	....	....	....	....	....	....	....
2004-05	Victoria Salsa	BCHL	55	15	16	31	24	....	....	....	....	....	....	....	....	....	....	....	....	....	....	....	....	....	....
2005-06	Victoria Salsa	BCHL	56	31	38	69	26	....	....	....	....	....	....	....	....	....	5	0	2	2	2	....	....	....	....
2006-07	Victoria Grizzlies	BCHL	59	45	83	128	45	....	....	....	....	....	....	....	....	....	16	8	8	16	14	....	....	....	....
2007-08	U. of Denver	WCHA	41	18	16	34	22	....	....	....	....	....	....	....	....	....	11	4	9	13	6	....	....	....	....
2008-09	U. of Denver	WCHA	19	8	15	23	10	....	....	....	....	....	....	....	....	....	....	....	....	....	....	....	....	....	....
2009-10	**Toronto**	**NHL**	**37**	**8**	**19**	**27**	**6**	**2**	**0**	**1**	**51**	**15.7**	**–5**	**648**	**55.3**	**19:14**	....	....	....	....	....	....	....	....	....
	Toronto Marlies	AHL	32	4	16	20	6	....	....	....	....	....	....	....	....	....	....	....	....	....	....	....	....	....	....
2010-11	**Toronto**	**NHL**	**82**	**15**	**17**	**32**	**14**	**6**	**1**	**4**	**120**	**12.5**	**–29**	**1441**	**54.6**	**19:17**	....	....	....	....	....	....	....	....	....
2011-12	**Toronto**	**NHL**	**73**	**18**	**29**	**47**	**22**	**4**	**0**	**1**	**109**	**16.5**	**–7**	**1198**	**52.7**	**18:51**	....	....	....	....	....	....	....	....	....
2012-13	**Toronto**	**NHL**	**46**	**12**	**16**	**28**	**6**	**4**	**1**	**3**	**61**	**19.7**	**–1**	**1063**	**52.6**	**20:19**	**5**	**1**	**1**	**2**	**4**	**0**	**1**	**0**	**21:44**
	NHL Totals		**238**	**53**	**81**	**134**	**48**	**16**	**2**	**9**	**341**	**15.5**		**4350**	**53.7**	**19:20**	**5**	**1**	**1**	**2**	**4**	**0**	**1**	**0**	**21:44**

WCHA All-Rookie Team (2008)

Signed as a free agent by **Toronto**, April 3, 2009.

BRADLEY, Matt

(BRAD-lee, MAT)

Right wing. Shoots right. 6'3", 200 lbs. Born, Stittsville, Ont., June 13, 1978. San Jose's 4th choice, 102nd overall, in 1996 Entry Draft.

Season	Club	League	GP	G	A	Pts	PIM	PP	SH	GW	S	%	+/-	TF	F%	Min	GP	G	A	Pts	PIM	PP	SH	GW	Min
1994-95	Cumberland	ON-Jr.A	49	13	20	33	18	....	....	....	....	....	....	....	....	....	....	....	....	....	....	....	....	....	....
1995-96	Kingston	OHL	55	10	14	24	17	....	....	....	....	....	....	....	....	....	6	0	1	1	6	....	....	....	....
1996-97	Kingston	OHL	65	24	24	48	41	....	....	....	....	....	....	....	....	....	5	0	4	4	2	....	....	....	....
	Kentucky	AHL	1	0	1	1	0	....	....	....	....	....	....	....	....	....	....	....	....	....	....	....	....	....	....
1997-98	Kingston	OHL	55	33	50	83	24	....	....	....	....	....	....	....	....	....	8	3	4	7	7	....	....	....	....
1998-99	Kentucky	AHL	79	23	20	43	57	....	....	....	....	....	....	....	....	....	10	1	4	5	4	....	....	....	....
99-2000	Kentucky	AHL	80	22	19	41	81	....	....	....	....	....	....	....	....	....	9	6	3	9	9	....	....	....	....
2000-01	**San Jose**	**NHL**	**21**	**1**	**1**	**2**	**19**	**0**	**0**	**0**	**16**	**6.3**	**0**	**0**	**0.0**	**6:58**	....	....	....	....	....	....	....	....	....
	Kentucky	AHL	22	5	8	13	16	....	....	....	....	....	....	....	....	....	1	1	0	1	5	....	....	....	....
2001-02	**San Jose**	**NHL**	**54**	**9**	**13**	**22**	**43**	**0**	**0**	**2**	**63**	**14.3**	**22**	**2**	**0.0**	**8:27**	**10**	**0**	**0**	**0**	**0**	**0**	**0**	**0**	**5:16**
2002-03	**San Jose**	**NHL**	**46**	**2**	**3**	**5**	**37**	**0**	**0**	**0**	**21**	**9.5**	**–1**	**1**	**0.0**	**7:54**	....	....	....	....	....	....	....	....	....
2003-04	**Pittsburgh**	**NHL**	**82**	**7**	**9**	**16**	**65**	**0**	**0**	**1**	**85**	**8.2**	**–27**	**29**	**41.4**	**12:48**	....	....	....	....	....	....	....	....	....
2004-05	Dornbirn	Austria-2	6	5	2	7	18	....	....	....	....	....	....	....	....	....	....	....	....	....	....	....	....	....	....
2005-06	**Washington**	**NHL**	**74**	**7**	**12**	**19**	**72**	**0**	**0**	**1**	**87**	**8.0**	**–8**	**25**	**52.0**	**12:36**	....	....	....	....	....	....	....	....	....
2006-07	**Washington**	**NHL**	**57**	**4**	**9**	**13**	**47**	**0**	**0**	**0**	**77**	**5.2**	**–5**	**20**	**45.0**	**11:55**	....	....	....	....	....	....	....	....	....
2007-08	**Washington**	**NHL**	**77**	**7**	**11**	**18**	**74**	**1**	**1**	**2**	**111**	**6.3**	**1**	**32**	**43.8**	**10:00**	**7**	**0**	**2**	**2**	**2**	**0**	**0**	**0**	**11:40**
2008-09	**Washington**	**NHL**	**81**	**5**	**6**	**11**	**59**	**0**	**0**	**1**	**98**	**5.1**	**–1**	**24**	**41.7**	**10:37**	**14**	**2**	**4**	**6**	**0**	**0**	**1**	**1**	**12:45**
2009-10	**Washington**	**NHL**	**77**	**10**	**14**	**24**	**47**	**0**	**1**	**5**	**98**	**10.2**	**6**	**28**	**39.3**	**11:02**	**7**	**1**	**2**	**3**	**2**	**0**	**0**	**0**	**10:36**
2010-11	**Washington**	**NHL**	**61**	**4**	**7**	**11**	**68**	**0**	**0**	**0**	**58**	**6.9**	**–3**	**11**	**36.4**	**10:29**	**9**	**0**	**0**	**0**	**4**	**0**	**0**	**0**	**8:48**
2011-12	**Florida**	**NHL**	**45**	**3**	**5**	**8**	**31**	**0**	**0**	**0**	**35**	**8.6**	**–3**	**28**	**42.9**	**10:52**	....	....	....	....	....	....	....	....	....
2012-13	TuTo Turku	Finland-2	1	0	1	1	0	....	....	....	....	....	....	....	....	....	....	....	....	....	....	....	....	....	....
	NHL Totals		**675**	**59**	**90**	**149**	**562**	**1**	**2**	**12**	**749**	**7.9**		**200**	**42.5**	**10:43**	**47**	**3**	**8**	**11**	**8**	**0**	**1**	**1**	**9:55**

Traded to **Pittsburgh** by **San Jose** for Wayne Primeau, March 11, 2003. Signed as a free agent by **Dornbirn** (Austria-2), November 14, 2004. Signed as a free agent by **Washington**, August 18, 2005. Signed as a free agent by **Florida**, July 2, 2011. Signed as a free agent by **TuTo Turku** (Finland-2), October 29, 2012. • Missed majority of 2012-13 due to injury, November 1, 2012 and resulting surgery.

BRASSARD, Derick

(bruh-SAHRD, DAIR-ihk) **NYR**

Center. Shoots left. 6'1", 202 lbs. Born, Hull, Que., September 22, 1987. Columbus' 1st choice, 6th overall, in 2006 Entry Draft.

Season	Club	League	GP	G	A	Pts	PIM	PP	SH	GW	S	%	+/-	TF	F%	Min	GP	G	A	Pts	PIM	PP	SH	GW	Min
2003-04	Drummondville	QMJHL	10	0	1	1	0	....	....	....	....	....	....	....	....	....	7	0	0	0	0	....	....	....	....
2004-05	Drummondville	QMJHL	69	25	51	76	25	....	....	....	....	....	....	....	....	....	6	1	5	6	6	....	....	....	....
2005-06	Drummondville	QMJHL	58	44	72	116	92	....	....	....	....	....	....	....	....	....	7	5	4	9	10	....	....	....	....
2006-07	Drummondville	QMJHL	14	6	19	25	24	....	....	....	....	....	....	....	....	....	12	9	15	24	12	....	....	....	....
2007-08	**Columbus**	**NHL**	**17**	**1**	**1**	**2**	**6**	**0**	**0**	**0**	**13**	**7.7**	**–4**	**80**	**42.5**	**9:03**	....	....	....	....	....	....	....	....	....
	Syracuse Crunch	AHL	42	15	36	51	51	....	....	....	....	....	....	....	....	....	13	4	9	13	10	....	....	....	....
2008-09	**Columbus**	**NHL**	**31**	**10**	**15**	**25**	**17**	**3**	**0**	**1**	**59**	**16.9**	**12**	**332**	**48.5**	**14:25**	....	....	....	....	....	....	....	....	....
2009-10	**Columbus**	**NHL**	**79**	**9**	**27**	**36**	**48**	**4**	**0**	**0**	**125**	**7.2**	**–17**	**503**	**41.8**	**14:57**	....	....	....	....	....	....	....	....	....
2010-11	**Columbus**	**NHL**	**74**	**17**	**30**	**47**	**55**	**6**	**0**	**3**	**183**	**9.3**	**–11**	**888**	**46.6**	**17:02**	....	....	....	....	....	....	....	....	....
2011-12	**Columbus**	**NHL**	**74**	**14**	**27**	**41**	**42**	**5**	**0**	**3**	**125**	**11.2**	**–20**	**617**	**45.1**	**16:20**	....	....	....	....	....	....	....	....	....
2012-13	Salzburg	Austria	6	4	1	5	6	....	....	....	....	....	....	....	....	....	....	....	....	....	....	....	....	....	....
	Columbus	**NHL**	**34**	**7**	**11**	**18**	**16**	**1**	**0**	**1**	**63**	**11.1**	**–2**	**283**	**45.6**	**16:32**	....	....	....	....	....	....	....	....	....
	NY Rangers	**NHL**	**13**	**5**	**6**	**11**	**0**	**2**	**0**	**0**	**25**	**20.0**	**3**	**163**	**52.8**	**16:38**	**12**	**2**	**10**	**12**	**2**	**1**	**0**	**1**	**18:55**
	NHL Totals		**322**	**63**	**117**	**180**	**184**	**21**	**0**	**8**	**593**	**10.6**		**2866**	**45.8**	**15:37**	**12**	**2**	**10**	**12**	**2**	**1**	**0**	**1**	**18:55**

QMJHL First All-Star Team (2006) • Canadian Major Junior Second All-Star Team (2006)

• Missed majority of 2006-07 due to pre-season shoulder injury. • Missed majority of 2008-09 due to shoulder injury at Dallas, December 18, 2008. Signed as a free agent by **Salzburg** (Austria), November 26, 2012. Traded to **NY Rangers** by **Columbus** with Derek Dorsett, John Moore and Columbus' 6th round choice in 2014 Entry Draft for Marian Gaborik, Blake Parlett and Steven Delisle, April 3, 2013.

BRAUN, Justin

(BRAWN, JUHS-tihn) **S.J.**

Defense. Shoots right. 6'2", 205 lbs. Born, St. Paul, MN, February 10, 1987. San Jose's 7th choice, 201st overall, in 2007 Entry Draft.

Season	Club	League	GP	G	A	Pts	PIM	PP	SH	GW	S	%	+/-	TF	F%	Min	GP	G	A	Pts	PIM	PP	SH	GW	Min
2004-05	White Bear Lake	High-MN	STATISTICS NOT AVAILABLE																						
	Green Bay	USHL	10	0	0	0	2	....	....	....	....	....	....	....	....	....	....	....	....	....	....	....	....	....	....
2005-06	Green Bay	USHL	59	2	11	13	69	....	....	....	....	....	....	....	....	....	3	0	0	0	2	....	....	....	....
2006-07	Massachusetts	H-East	39	4	10	14	20	....	....	....	....	....	....	....	....	....	....	....	....	....	....	....	....	....	....
2007-08	Massachusetts	H-East	36	4	16	20	20	....	....	....	....	....	....	....	....	....	....	....	....	....	....	....	....	....	....
2008-09	Massachusetts	H-East	39	7	16	23	50	....	....	....	....	....	....	....	....	....	....	....	....	....	....	....	....	....	....
2009-10	Massachusetts	H-East	36	8	23	31	30	....	....	....	....	....	....	....	....	....	....	....	....	....	....	....	....	....	....
	Worcester Sharks	AHL	3	0	3	3	0	....	....	....	....	....	....	....	....	....	11	0	3	3	4	....	....	....	....
2010-11	**San Jose**	**NHL**	**28**	**2**	**9**	**11**	**2**	**2**	**0**	**0**	**44**	**4.5**	**–1**	**0**	**0.0**	**16:30**	**1**	**0**	**0**	**0**	**0**	**0**	**0**	**0**	**15:32**
	Worcester Sharks	AHL	34	5	18	23	8	....	....	....	....	....	....	....	....	....	....	....	....	....	....	....	....	....	....
2011-12	**San Jose**	**NHL**	**66**	**2**	**9**	**11**	**23**	**1**	**0**	**0**	**113**	**1.8**	**–2**	**0**	**0.0**	**16:33**	**5**	**0**	**0**	**0**	**15**	**0**	**0**	**0**	**17:55**
	Worcester Sharks	AHL	6	0	3	3	0	....	....	....	....	....	....	....	....	....	....	....	....	....	....	....	....	....	....
2012-13	Tappara Tampere	Finland	6	0	3	3	2	....	....	....	....	....	....	....	....	....	....	....	....	....	....	....	....	....	....
	San Jose	**NHL**	**41**	**0**	**7**	**7**	**6**	**0**	**0**	**0**	**48**	**0.0**	**–5**	**0**	**0.0**	**18:48**	**11**	**0**	**1**	**1**	**0**	**0**	**0**	**0**	**19:38**
	NHL Totals		**135**	**4**	**25**	**29**	**31**	**3**	**0**	**0**	**205**	**2.0**		**0**	**0.0**	**17:13**	**17**	**0**	**1**	**1**	**15**	**0**	**0**	**0**	**18:53**

Hockey East All-Rookie Team (2007) • Hockey East Second All-Star Team (2009) • Hockey East First All-Star Team (2010) • NCAA East Second All-American Team (2010)

Signed as a free agent by **Tappara Tampere** (Finland), November 23, 2012.

BRENNAN, T.J.

(BREH-nan, TEE-JAY) **TOR**

Defense. Shoots left. 6'1", 213 lbs. Born, Willingboro, NJ, April 3, 1989. Buffalo's 1st choice, 31st overall, in 2007 Entry Draft.

Season	Club	League	GP	G	A	Pts	PIM	PP	SH	GW	S	%	+/-	TF	F%	Min	GP	G	A	Pts	PIM	PP	SH	GW	Min
2005-06	Phi. Little Flyers	AtJHL	42	9	23	32	....	....	....	....	....	....	....	....	....	....	....	....	....	....	....	....	....	....	....
2006-07	St. John's	QMJHL	68	16	25	41	79	....	....	....	....	....	....	....	....	....	4	1	1	2	4	....	....	....	....
2007-08	St. John's	QMJHL	65	16	25	41	92	....	....	....	....	....	....	....	....	....	6	2	4	6	12	....	....	....	....
2008-09	Montreal	QMJHL	59	5	29	34	63	....	....	....	....	....	....	....	....	....	10	4	8	12	34	....	....	....	....
2009-10	Portland Pirates	AHL	65	6	17	23	64	....	....	....	....	....	....	....	....	....	4	0	1	1	2	....	....	....	....
2010-11	Portland Pirates	AHL	72	15	24	39	49	....	....	....	....	....	....	....	....	....	4	0	1	1	6	....	....	....	....
2011-12	**Buffalo**	**NHL**	**11**	**1**	**0**	**1**	**6**	**0**	**0**	**0**	**14**	**7.1**	**0**	**0**	**0.0**	**14:07**	....	....	....	....	....	....	....	....	....
	Rochester	AHL	52	16	14	30	39	....	....	....	....	....	....	....	....	....	3	2	0	2	6	....	....	....	....
2012-13	Rochester	AHL	36	14	21	35	57	....	....	....	....	....	....	....	....	....	....	....	....	....	....	....	....	....	....
	Buffalo	**NHL**	**10**	**1**	**0**	**1**	**6**	**1**	**0**	**0**	**18**	**5.6**	**–1**	**0**	**0.0**	**14:49**	....	....	....	....	....	....	....	....	....
	Florida	**NHL**	**19**	**2**	**7**	**9**	**2**	**0**	**0**	**0**	**24**	**8.3**	**–8**	**0**	**0.0**	**17:41**	....	....	....	....	....	....	....	....	....
	NHL Totals		**40**	**4**	**7**	**11**	**14**	**1**	**0**	**0**	**56**	**7.1**		**0**	**0.0**	**15:59**	....	....	....	....	....	....	....	....	....

Traded to **Florida** by **Buffalo** for New Jersey's 5th round choice (previously acqured, later traded to Buffalo – Buffalo selected Gustav Possler) in 2013 Entry Draft, March 15, 2013. Traded to **Nashville** by **Florida** for Bobby Butler, June 14, 2013. Signed as a free agent by **Toronto**, July 5, 2013.

			Regular Season														Playoffs								
Season	Club	League	GP	G	A	Pts	PIM	PP	SH	GW	S	%	+/-	TF	F%	Min	GP	G	A	Pts	PIM	PP	SH	GW	Min

BRENT, Tim

(BREHNT, TIHM)

Center. Shoots right. 6', 188 lbs. Born, Cambridge, Ont., March 10, 1984. Anaheim's 3rd choice, 75th overall, in 2004 Entry Draft.

Season	Club	League	GP	G	A	Pts	PIM	PP	SH	GW	S	%	+/-	TF	F%	Min	GP	G	A	Pts	PIM	PP	SH	GW	Min
99-2000	Cambridge	ON-Jr.B	40	19	16	35	42	....	....	....	....	....	....	....	....	....	....	....	....	....	....	....	....	....	....
2000-01	St. Michael's	OHL	64	9	19	28	31	....	....	....	....	....	....	....	....	....	18	2	8	10	6	....	....	....	....
2001-02	St. Michael's	OHL	61	19	40	59	52	....	....	....	....	....	....	....	....	....	14	7	12	19	20	....	....	....	....
2002-03	St. Michael's	OHL	60	24	42	66	74	....	....	....	....	....	....	....	....	....	19	7	17	24	14	....	....	....	....
2003-04	St. Michael's	OHL	53	26	41	67	105	....	....	....	....	....	....	....	....	....	18	4	13	17	24	....	....	....	....
2004-05	Cincinnati	AHL	46	5	13	18	42	....	....	....	....	....	....	....	....	....	12	0	1	1	6	....	....	....	....
2005-06	Portland Pirates	AHL	37	15	9	24	32	....	....	....	....	....	....	....	....	....	15	4	4	8	16	....	....	....	....
2006-07	**Anaheim**	**NHL**	**15**	**1**	**0**	**1**	**6**	**0**	**0**	**0**	**14**	**7.1**	**–5**	**86**	**48.8**	**6:55**	....	....	....	....	....	....	....	....	....
	Portland Pirates	AHL	48	16	14	30	40	....	....	....	....	....	....	....	....	....	....	....	....	....	....	....	....	....	....
2007-08	**Pittsburgh**	**NHL**	**1**	**0**	**0**	**0**	**0**	**0**	**0**	**0**	**0**	**0.0**	**–1**	**5**	**60.0**	**4:34**	....	....	....	....	....	....	....	....	....
	Wilkes-Barre	AHL	74	18	43	61	79	....	....	....	....	....	....	....	....	....	23	*12	15	27	10	....	....	....	....
2008-09	**Chicago**	**NHL**	**2**	**0**	**0**	**0**	**2**	**0**	**0**	**0**	**0**	**0.0**	**0**	**10**	**50.0**	**8:21**	....	....	....	....	....	....	....	....	....
	Rockford IceHogs	AHL	64	20	42	62	59	....	....	....	....	....	....	....	....	....	4	0	1	1	2	....	....	....	....
2009-10	**Toronto**	**NHL**	**1**	**0**	**0**	**0**	**0**	**0**	**0**	**0**	**3**	**0.0**	**0**	**8**	**50.0**	**13:21**	....	....	....	....	....	....	....	....	....
	Toronto Marlies	AHL	33	13	15	28	19	....	....	....	....	....	....	....	....	....	....	....	....	....	....	....	....	....	....
2010-11	**Toronto**	**NHL**	**79**	**8**	**12**	**20**	**33**	**0**	**1**	**1**	**60**	**13.3**	**–4**	**788**	**52.0**	**11:39**	....	....	....	....	....	....	....	....	....
2011-12	**Carolina**	**NHL**	**79**	**12**	**12**	**24**	**27**	**3**	**1**	**3**	**71**	**16.9**	**–8**	**571**	**48.7**	**10:53**	....	....	....	....	....	....	....	....	....
2012-13	**Carolina**	**NHL**	**30**	**0**	**3**	**3**	**8**	**0**	**0**	**0**	**23**	**0.0**	**–3**	**240**	**51.7**	**9:48**	....	....	....	....	....	....	....	....	....
	NHL Totals		**207**	**21**	**27**	**48**	**76**	**3**	**2**	**4**	**171**	**12.3**		**1708**	**50.7**	**10:41**	....	....	....	....	....	....	....	....	....

• Re-entered NHL Entry Draft. Originally Anaheim's 2nd choice, 37th overall, in 2002 Entry Draft.

Traded to **Pittsburgh** by **Anaheim** for Stephen Dixon, June 23, 2007. Traded to **Chicago** by **Pittsburgh** for Danny Richmond, July 17, 2008. Signed as a free agent by **Toronto**, July 6, 2009. • Missed majority of 2009-10 due to chest injury. Signed as a free agent by **Carolina**, July 1, 2011.

BREWER, Eric

(BREW-uhr, AIR-ihk) **T.B.**

Defense. Shoots left. 6'4", 216 lbs. Born, Vernon, B.C., April 17, 1979. NY Islanders' 2nd choice, 5th overall, in 1997 Entry Draft.

Season	Club	League	GP	G	A	Pts	PIM	PP	SH	GW	S	%	+/-	TF	F%	Min	GP	G	A	Pts	PIM	PP	SH	GW	Min
1994-95	Kamloops	Minor-BC	40	19	19	38	62	....	....	....	....	....	....	....	....	....	....	....	....	....	....	....	....	....	....
1995-96	Prince George	WHL	63	4	10	14	25	....	....	....	....	....	....	....	....	....	....	....	....	....	....	....	....	....	....
1996-97	Prince George	WHL	71	5	24	29	81	....	....	....	....	....	....	....	....	....	15	2	4	6	16	....	....	....	....
1997-98	Prince George	WHL	34	5	28	33	45	....	....	....	....	....	....	....	....	....	11	4	2	6	19	....	....	....	....
1998-99	**NY Islanders**	**NHL**	**63**	**5**	**6**	**11**	**32**	**2**	**0**	**0**	**63**	**7.9**	**–14**	**0**	**0.0**	**15:28**	....	....	....	....	....	....	....	....	....
99-2000	**NY Islanders**	**NHL**	**26**	**0**	**2**	**2**	**20**	**0**	**0**	**0**	**30**	**0.0**	**–11**	**0**	**0.0**	**18:33**	....	....	....	....	....	....	....	....	....
	Lowell	AHL	25	2	2	4	26	....	....	....	....	....	....	....	....	....	7	0	0	0	0	....	....	....	....
2000-01	**Edmonton**	**NHL**	**77**	**7**	**14**	**21**	**53**	**2**	**0**	**2**	**91**	**7.7**	**15**	**0**	**0.0**	**18:31**	**6**	**1**	**5**	**6**	**2**	**1**	**0**	**0**	**28:12**
2001-02	**Edmonton**	**NHL**	**81**	**7**	**18**	**25**	**45**	**6**	**0**	**2**	**165**	**4.2**	**–5**	**0**	**0.0**	**23:56**	....	....	....	....	....	....	....	....	....
	Canada	Olympics	6	2	0	2	0	....	....	....	....	....	....	....	....	....	....	....	....	....	....	....	....	....	....
2002-03	**Edmonton**	**NHL**	**80**	**8**	**21**	**29**	**45**	**1**	**0**	**1**	**147**	**5.4**	**–11**	**1**	**100.0**	**24:56**	**6**	**1**	**3**	**4**	**6**	**0**	**0**	**0**	**25:31**
2003-04	**Edmonton**	**NHL**	**77**	**7**	**18**	**25**	**67**	**3**	**0**	**1**	**135**	**5.2**	**–6**	**0**	**0.0**	**24:40**	....	....	....	....	....	....	....	....	....
2004-05			DID NOT PLAY																						
2005-06	**St. Louis**	**NHL**	**32**	**6**	**3**	**9**	**45**	**1**	**0**	**1**	**64**	**9.4**	**–17**	**0**	**0.0**	**23:28**	....	....	....	....	....	....	....	....	....
2006-07	**St. Louis**	**NHL**	**82**	**6**	**23**	**29**	**69**	**2**	**0**	**1**	**111**	**5.4**	**–10**	**0**	**0.0**	**24:32**	....	....	....	....	....	....	....	....	....
2007-08	**St. Louis**	**NHL**	**77**	**1**	**21**	**22**	**91**	**0**	**0**	**0**	**101**	**1.0**	**–18**	**0**	**0.0**	**24:38**	....	....	....	....	....	....	....	....	....
2008-09	**St. Louis**	**NHL**	**28**	**1**	**5**	**6**	**24**	**1**	**0**	**0**	**49**	**2.0**	**–14**	**0**	**0.0**	**25:07**	....	....	....	....	....	....	....	....	....
2009-10	**St. Louis**	**NHL**	**59**	**8**	**7**	**15**	**46**	**0**	**0**	**0**	**84**	**9.5**	**–17**	**0**	**0.0**	**21:27**	....	....	....	....	....	....	....	....	....
2010-11	**St. Louis**	**NHL**	**54**	**8**	**6**	**14**	**57**	**0**	**0**	**1**	**86**	**9.3**	**1**	**0**	**0.0**	**22:14**	....	....	....	....	....	....	....	....	....
	Tampa Bay	**NHL**	**22**	**1**	**1**	**2**	**24**	**0**	**0**	**0**	**24**	**4.2**	**5**	**0**	**0.0**	**21:34**	**18**	**1**	**6**	**7**	**14**	**0**	**0**	**0**	**25:36**
2011-12	**Tampa Bay**	**NHL**	**82**	**1**	**20**	**21**	**49**	**0**	**0**	**0**	**83**	**1.2**	**–5**	**0**	**0.0**	**23:16**	....	....	....	....	....	....	....	....	....
2012-13	**Tampa Bay**	**NHL**	**48**	**4**	**8**	**12**	**30**	**1**	**0**	**1**	**56**	**7.1**	**3**	**0**	**0.0**	**20:31**	....	....	....	....	....	....	....	....	....
	NHL Totals		**888**	**70**	**173**	**243**	**697**	**19**	**0**	**10**	**1289**	**5.4**		**1**	**100.0**	**22:25**	**30**	**3**	**14**	**17**	**22**	**1**	**0**	**0**	**26:07**

WHL West Second All-Star Team (1998)

Played in NHL All-Star Game (2003)

Traded to **Edmonton** by **NY Islanders** with Josh Green and NY Islanders' 2nd round choice (Brad Winchester) in 2000 Entry Draft for Roman Hamrlik, June 24, 2000. Traded to **St. Louis** by **Edmonton** with Doug Lynch and Jeff Woywitka for Chris Pronger, August 2, 2005. • Missed majority of 2005-06 due to shoulder injuries at Columbus (November 16, 2005) and Atlanta (January 13, 2006). • Missed majority of 2008-09 due to back injury at Los Angeles, December 11, 2008. Traded to **Tampa Bay** by **St. Louis** for Brock Beukeboom and Tampa Bay's 3rd round choice (Jordan Binnington) in 2011 Entry Draft, February 18, 2011.

BRIERE, Daniel

(bree-AIR, DAN-yehl) **MTL**

Center. Shoots right. 5'10", 179 lbs. Born, Gatineau, Que., October 6, 1977. Phoenix's 2nd choice, 24th overall, in 1996 Entry Draft.

Season	Club	League	GP	G	A	Pts	PIM	PP	SH	GW	S	%	+/-	TF	F%	Min	GP	G	A	Pts	PIM	PP	SH	GW	Min
1992-93	Abitibi Regents	QAAA	42	24	30	54	28	....	....	....	....	....	....	....	....	....	3	0	3	3	8	....	....	....	....
1993-94	Gatineau	QAAA	44	56	47	103	56	....	....	....	....	....	....	....	....	....	....	....	....	....	....	....	....	....	....
1994-95	Drummondville	QMJHL	72	51	72	123	54	....	....	....	....	....	....	....	....	....	4	2	3	5	2	....	....	....	....
1995-96	Drummondville	QMJHL	67	*67	*96	*163	84	....	....	....	....	....	....	....	....	....	6	6	12	18	8	....	....	....	....
1996-97	Drummondville	QMJHL	59	52	78	130	86	....	....	....	....	....	....	....	....	....	8	7	7	14	14	....	....	....	....
1997-98	**Phoenix**	**NHL**	**5**	**1**	**0**	**1**	**2**	**0**	**0**	**0**	**4**	**25.0**	**1**	....	....	....	....	....	....	....	....	....	....	....	....
	Springfield	AHL	68	36	56	92	42	....	....	....	....	....	....	....	....	....	4	1	2	3	4	....	....	....	....
1998-99	**Phoenix**	**NHL**	**64**	**8**	**14**	**22**	**30**	**2**	**0**	**2**	**90**	**8.9**	**–3**	**484**	**47.5**	**11:13**	....	....	....	....	....	....	....	....	....
	Las Vegas	IHL	1	1	1	2	0	....	....	....	....	....	....	....	....	....	....	....	....	....	....	....	....	....	....
	Springfield	AHL	13	2	6	8	20	....	....	....	....	....	....	....	....	....	3	0	1	1	2	....	....	....	....
99-2000	**Phoenix**	**NHL**	**13**	**1**	**1**	**2**	**0**	**0**	**0**	**0**	**9**	**11.1**	**0**	**65**	**49.2**	**7:41**	**1**	**0**	**0**	**0**	**0**	**0**	**0**	**0**	**6:16**
	Springfield	AHL	58	29	42	71	56	....	....	....	....	....	....	....	....	....	....	....	....	....	....	....	....	....	....
2000-01	**Phoenix**	**NHL**	**30**	**11**	**4**	**15**	**12**	**9**	**0**	**1**	**43**	**25.6**	**–2**	**210**	**50.0**	**10:50**	....	....	....	....	....	....	....	....	....
	Springfield	AHL	30	21	25	46	30	....	....	....	....	....	....	....	....	....	....	....	....	....	....	....	....	....	....
2001-02	**Phoenix**	**NHL**	**78**	**32**	**28**	**60**	**52**	**12**	**0**	**5**	**149**	**21.5**	**6**	**951**	**51.8**	**15:44**	**5**	**2**	**1**	**3**	**2**	**1**	**0**	**1**	**16:25**
2002-03	**Phoenix**	**NHL**	**68**	**17**	**29**	**46**	**50**	**4**	**0**	**3**	**142**	**12.0**	**–21**	**1108**	**52.5**	**17:02**	....	....	....	....	....	....	....	....	....
	Buffalo	**NHL**	**14**	**7**	**5**	**12**	**12**	**5**	**0**	**1**	**39**	**17.9**	**1**	**206**	**50.0**	**17:49**	....	....	....	....	....	....	....	....	....
2003-04	**Buffalo**	**NHL**	**82**	**28**	**37**	**65**	**70**	**11**	**0**	**3**	**194**	**14.4**	**–7**	**1066**	**47.1**	**18:20**	....	....	....	....	....	....	....	....	....
2004-05	SC Bern	Swiss	36	16	29	45	26	....	....	....	....	....	....	....	....	....	11	1	6	7	2	....	....	....	....
2005-06	**Buffalo**	**NHL**	**48**	**25**	**33**	**58**	**48**	**11**	**0**	**4**	**147**	**17.0**	**3**	**517**	**50.7**	**19:04**	**18**	**8**	**11**	**19**	**12**	**3**	**0**	**2**	**18:48**
2006-07	**Buffalo**	**NHL**	**81**	**32**	**63**	**95**	**89**	**9**	**0**	**6**	**234**	**13.7**	**17**	**1089**	**49.6**	**19:19**	**16**	**3**	**12**	**15**	**16**	**2**	**0**	**1**	**20:53**
2007-08	**Philadelphia**	**NHL**	**79**	**31**	**41**	**72**	**68**	**14**	**0**	**3**	**182**	**17.0**	**–22**	**1250**	**50.5**	**18:52**	**17**	**9**	**7**	**16**	**20**	***6**	**0**	**3**	**18:26**
2008-09	**Philadelphia**	**NHL**	**29**	**11**	**14**	**25**	**26**	**4**	**0**	**0**	**54**	**20.4**	**–1**	**147**	**46.3**	**15:39**	**6**	**1**	**3**	**4**	**8**	**1**	**0**	**0**	**16:41**
2009-10	**Philadelphia**	**NHL**	**75**	**26**	**27**	**53**	**71**	**8**	**0**	**1**	**193**	**13.5**	**–2**	**120**	**44.2**	**16:35**	**23**	**12**	**18**	***30**	**18**	**4**	**0**	**4**	**19:37**
2010-11	**Philadelphia**	**NHL**	**77**	**34**	**34**	**68**	**87**	**6**	**0**	**6**	**246**	**13.8**	**20**	**820**	**48.2**	**18:19**	**11**	**7**	**2**	**9**	**14**	**2**	**0**	**1**	**19:56**
2011-12	**Philadelphia**	**NHL**	**70**	**16**	**33**	**49**	**69**	**4**	**0**	**3**	**174**	**9.2**	**5**	**831**	**48.9**	**17:22**	**11**	***8**	**5**	**13**	**4**	**1**	**0**	**1**	**17:44**
2012-13	Eisbaren Berlin	Germany	21	10	24	34	24	....	....	....	....	....	....	....	....	....	....	....	....	....	....	....	....	....	....
	Philadelphia	**NHL**	**34**	**6**	**10**	**16**	**10**	**3**	**0**	**1**	**87**	**6.9**	**–13**	**135**	**45.9**	**16:04**	....	....	....	....	....	....	....	....	....
	NHL Totals		**847**	**286**	**373**	**659**	**696**	**102**	**0**	**39**	**1987**	**14.4**		**8999**	**49.6**	**16:46**	**108**	**50**	**59**	**109**	**94**	**20**	**0**	**13**	**18:53**

QMJHL All-Rookie Team (1995) • QMJHL Offensive Rookie of the Year (1995) • QMJHL Second All-Star Team (1996, 1997) • AHL All-Rookie Team (1998) • AHL First All-Star Team (1998) • Dudley "Red" Garrett Memorial Award (AHL – Rookie of the Year) (1998)

Played in NHL All-Star Game (2007, 2011)

Traded to **Buffalo** by **Phoenix** with Phoenix's 3rd round choice (Andrej Sekera) in 2004 Entry Draft for Chris Gratton and Buffalo's 4th round choice (later traded to Edmonton – Edmonton selected Liam Reddox) in 2004 Entry Draft, March 10, 2003. Signed as a free agent by **Bern** (Swiss), September 28, 2004. Signed as a free agent by **Philadelphia**, July 1, 2007. • Missed majority of 2008-09 due to abdominal surgery (October 25, 2008) and groin surgery (January 22, 2009). Signed as a free agent by **Berlin** (Germany), October 4, 2012. Signed as a free agent by **Montreal**, July 4, 2013.

BRODIE, T.J.

(BROH-dee, TEE-JAY) **CGY**

Defense. Shoots left. 6'1", 182 lbs. Born, Chatham, Ont., June 7, 1990. Calgary's 5th choice, 114th overall, in 2008 Entry Draft.

Season	Club	League	GP	G	A	Pts	PIM	PP	SH	GW	S	%	+/-	TF	F%	Min	GP	G	A	Pts	PIM	PP	SH	GW	Min
2006-07	Leamington Flyers	ON-Jr.B	43	8	38	46	104	....	....	....	....	....	....	....	....	....	5	1	2	3	12	....	....	....	....
	Saginaw Spirit	OHL	20	0	4	4	23	....	....	....	....	....	....	....	....	....	3	0	1	1	2	....	....	....	....
2007-08	Saginaw Spirit	OHL	68	4	26	30	73	....	....	....	....	....	....	....	....	....	4	0	3	3	2	....	....	....	....
2008-09	Saginaw Spirit	OHL	63	12	38	50	67	....	....	....	....	....	....	....	....	....	8	3	6	9	8	....	....	....	....
2009-10	Saginaw Spirit	OHL	19	4	19	23	20	....	....	....	....	....	....	....	....	....	....	....	....	....	....	....	....	....	....
	Barrie Colts	OHL	46	3	30	33	38	....	....	....	....	....	....	....	....	....	17	1	14	15	14	....	....	....	....
2010-11	**Calgary**	**NHL**	**3**	**0**	**0**	**0**	**2**	**0**	**0**	**0**	**1**	**0.0**	**–3**	**0**	**0.0**	**16:00**	....	....	....	....	....	....	....	....	....
	Abbotsford Heat	AHL	68	5	29	34	32	....	....	....	....	....	....	....	....	....	....	....	....	....	....	....	....	....	....

			Regular Season														Playoffs								
Season	Club	League	GP	G	A	Pts	PIM	PP	SH	GW	S	%	+/-	TF	F%	Min	GP	G	A	Pts	PIM	PP	SH	GW	Min
2011-12	Calgary	NHL	54	2	12	14	14	1	0	2	44	4.5	3	0	0.0	16:29	....	....	....	....	....	....	....	....	....
	Abbotsford Heat	AHL	12	1	2	3	10	....	....	....	....	....	....	....	....	....	....	....	....	....	....	....	....	....	....
2012-13	Calgary	NHL	47	2	12	14	8	0	0	0	44	4.5	–9	0	0.0	20:13	....	....	....	....	....	....	....	....	....
	NHL Totals		104	4	24	28	24	1	0	2	89	4.5		0	0.0	18:09	....	....	....	....	....	....	....	....	....

BRODIN, Jonas

(BROH-deen, YOH-nuhs) **MIN**

Defense. Shoots left. 6'1", 180 lbs. Born, Karlstad, Sweden, July 12, 1993. Minnesota's 1st choice, 10th overall, in 2011 Entry Draft.

Season	Club	League	GP	G	A	Pts	PIM	PP	SH	GW	S	%	+/-	TF	F%	Min	GP	G	A	Pts	PIM	PP	SH	GW	Min
2008-09	Farjestad U18	Swe-U18	22	3	8	11	10	....	....	....	....	....	....	....	....	....	4	1	1	2	4	....	....	....	....
2009-10	Skare BK Jr.	Swe-Jr.	2	0	1	1	2	....	....	....	....	....	....	....	....	....	....	....	....	....	....	....	....	....	....
	Skare BK	Sweden-3	21	1	6	7	10	....	....	....	....	....	....	....	....	....	....	....	....	....	....	....	....	....	....
	Farjestad	Sweden	3	0	0	0	2	....	....	....	....	....	....	....	....	....	....	....	....	....	....	....	....	....	....
	Farjestad U18	Swe-U18	19	6	11	17	6	....	....	....	....	....	....	....	....	....	7	3	8	11	8	....	....	....	....
2010-11	Farjestad U18	Swe-U18	2	0	1	1	2	....	....	....	....	....	....	....	....	....	....	....	....	....	....	....	....	....	....
	Farjestad	Sweden	42	0	4	4	12	....	....	....	....	....	....	....	....	....	14	2	0	2	2	....	....	....	....
2011-12	Farjestad Jr.	Swe-Jr.	1	0	0	0	0	....	....	....	....	....	....	....	....	....	....	....	....	....	....	....	....	....	....
	Farjestad	Sweden	49	0	8	8	14	....	....	....	....	....	....	....	....	....	11	2	0	2	6	....	....	....	....
2012-13	Houston Aeros	AHL	9	2	2	4	4	....	....	....	....	....	....	....	....	....	....	....	....	....	....	....	....	....	....
	Minnesota	NHL	45	2	9	11	10	1	0	0	51	3.9	3	0	0.0	23:13	5	0	0	0	0	0	0	0	26:23
	NHL Totals		45	2	9	11	10	1	0	0	51	3.9		0	0.0	23:13	5	0	0	0	0	0	0	0	26:23

NHL All-Rookie Team (2013)

BRODZIAK, Kyle

(brohd-ZEE-ak, KIGHL) **MIN**

Center. Shoots right. 6'2", 209 lbs. Born, St. Paul, Alta., May 25, 1984. Edmonton's 9th choice, 214th overall, in 2003 Entry Draft.

Season	Club	League	GP	G	A	Pts	PIM	PP	SH	GW	S	%	+/-	TF	F%	Min	GP	G	A	Pts	PIM	PP	SH	GW	Min
99-2000	Ft. Saskatchewan	AMBHL	36	23	33	56	57	....	....	....	....	....	....	....	....	....	....	....	....	....	....	....	....	....	....
	Moose Jaw	WHL	2	0	0	0	0	....	....	....	....	....	....	....	....	....	....	....	....	....	....	....	....	....	....
2000-01	Moose Jaw	WHL	57	2	8	10	47	....	....	....	....	....	....	....	....	....	3	0	0	0	0	....	....	....	....
2001-02	Moose Jaw	WHL	72	8	12	20	56	....	....	....	....	....	....	....	....	....	12	0	3	3	11	....	....	....	....
2002-03	Moose Jaw	WHL	72	32	30	62	84	....	....	....	....	....	....	....	....	....	13	5	3	8	16	....	....	....	....
2003-04	Moose Jaw	WHL	70	39	54	93	58	....	....	....	....	....	....	....	....	....	10	5	4	9	10	....	....	....	....
2004-05	Edmonton	AHL	56	6	26	32	49	....	....	....	....	....	....	....	....	....	....	....	....	....	....	....	....	....	....
2005-06	Edmonton	NHL	10	0	0	0	4	0	0	0	7	0.0	–4	75	52.0	11:02	....	....	....	....	....	....	....	....	....
	Iowa Stars	AHL	55	12	19	31	41	....	....	....	....	....	....	....	....	....	7	1	3	4	2	....	....	....	....
2006-07	Edmonton	NHL	6	1	0	1	2	0	0	0	11	9.1	0	48	52.1	17:08	....	....	....	....	....	....	....	....	....
	Wilkes-Barre	AHL	62	24	32	56	44	....	....	....	....	....	....	....	....	....	11	1	5	6	14	....	....	....	....
2007-08	Edmonton	NHL	80	14	17	31	33	0	1	3	125	11.2	–6	297	51.5	12:55	....	....	....	....	....	....	....	....	....
2008-09	Edmonton	NHL	79	11	16	27	21	1	1	3	99	11.1	4	947	51.6	12:43	....	....	....	....	....	....	....	....	....
2009-10	Minnesota	NHL	82	9	23	32	22	0	0	3	140	6.4	–3	1001	48.4	15:20	....	....	....	....	....	....	....	....	....
2010-11	Minnesota	NHL	80	16	21	37	56	2	1	1	126	12.7	–4	1088	48.9	15:47	....	....	....	....	....	....	....	....	....
2011-12	Minnesota	NHL	82	22	22	44	66	5	0	0	160	13.8	–15	1429	49.5	19:04	....	....	....	....	....	....	....	....	....
2012-13	Minnesota	NHL	48	8	4	12	20	1	1	1	88	9.1	–18	763	49.4	17:21	5	0	2	2	4	0	0	0	20:41
	NHL Totals		467	81	103	184	224	9	4	11	756	10.7		5648	49.7	15:21	5	0	2	2	4	0	0	0	20:41

WHL East First All-Star Team (2004) • Canadian Major Junior Second All-Star Team (2004)

Traded to **Minnesota** by **Edmonton** with Edmonton's 6th round choice (Darcy Kuemper) in 2009 Entry Draft for Dallas's 4th round choice (previously acquired, Edmonton selected Kyle Bigos) in 2009 Entry Draft and Minnesota's 5th round choice (Olivier Roy) in 2009 Entry Draft, June 27, 2009.

BROOKBANK, Sheldon

(BRUK-bank, SHEHL-duhn) **CHI**

Defense. Shoots right. 6'1", 202 lbs. Born, Lanigan, Sask., October 3, 1980.

Season	Club	League	GP	G	A	Pts	PIM	PP	SH	GW	S	%	+/-	TF	F%	Min	GP	G	A	Pts	PIM	PP	SH	GW	Min
2000-01	Humboldt	SJHL	59	14	35	49	281	....	....	....	....	....	....	....	....	....	....	....	....	....	....	....	....	....	....
2001-02	Grand Rapids	AHL	6	0	1	1	24	....	....	....	....	....	....	....	....	....	....	....	....	....	....	....	....	....	....
	Mississippi	ECHL	62	8	21	29	137	....	....	....	....	....	....	....	....	....	10	1	4	5	27	....	....	....	....
2002-03	Grand Rapids	AHL	69	2	11	13	136	....	....	....	....	....	....	....	....	....	15	1	3	4	28	....	....	....	....
2003-04	Cincinnati	AHL	74	2	9	11	216	....	....	....	....	....	....	....	....	....	9	0	2	2	20	....	....	....	....
2004-05	Cincinnati	AHL	60	1	11	12	181	....	....	....	....	....	....	....	....	....	11	0	0	0	40	....	....	....	....
2005-06	Milwaukee	AHL	73	9	26	35	232	....	....	....	....	....	....	....	....	....	21	1	8	9	49	....	....	....	....
2006-07	Nashville	NHL	3	0	1	1	12	0	0	0	3	0.0	0	0	0.0	8:16	....	....	....	....	....	....	....	....	....
	Milwaukee	AHL	78	15	38	53	176	....	....	....	....	....	....	....	....	....	4	0	0	0	6	....	....	....	....
2007-08	New Jersey	NHL	44	0	8	8	63	0	0	0	43	0.0	0	0	0.0	15:08	....	....	....	....	....	....	....	....	....
	Lowell Devils	AHL	1	0	0	0	5	....	....	....	....	....	....	....	....	....	....	....	....	....	....	....	....	....	....
2008-09	New Jersey	NHL	15	0	0	0	25	0	0	0	6	0.0	1	0	0.0	8:51	....	....	....	....	....	....	....	....	....
	Anaheim	NHL	29	1	3	4	51	0	0	0	24	4.2	3	0	0.0	13:50	13	0	0	0	18	0	0	0	11:13
2009-10	Anaheim	NHL	66	0	9	9	114	0	0	0	60	0.0	10	0	0.0	14:58	....	....	....	....	....	....	....	....	....
2010-11	Anaheim	NHL	40	0	0	0	63	0	0	0	29	0.0	–8	0	0.0	13:20	4	0	0	0	14	0	0	0	14:35
2011-12	Anaheim	NHL	80	3	11	14	72	0	0	1	49	6.1	11	0	0.0	15:36	....	....	....	....	....	....	....	....	....
2012-13 ♦	Chicago	NHL	26	1	0	1	21	0	1	0	25	4.0	–2	1	0.0	12:45	1	0	0	0	0	0	0	0	6:50
	NHL Totals		303	5	32	37	421	0	1	1	239	2.1		1	0.0	14:16	18	0	0	0	32	0	0	0	11:43

AHL First All-Star Team (2007) • Eddie Shore Award (AHL - Outstanding Defenseman) (2007)

Signed as a free agent by **Anaheim**, July 21, 2003. Signed as a free agent by **Nashville**, August 4, 2005. Signed as a free agent by **Columbus**, July 1, 2007. Claimed on waivers by **New Jersey** from **Columbus**, October 2, 2007. Traded to **Anaheim** by **New Jersey** for David McIntyre, February 3, 2009. Signed as a free agent by **Chicago**, July 1. 2012.

BROUWER, Troy

(BROW-uhr, TROI) **WSH**

Right wing. Shoots right. 6'3", 213 lbs. Born, Vancouver, B.C., August 17, 1985. Chicago's 13th choice, 214th overall, in 2004 Entry Draft.

Season	Club	League	GP	G	A	Pts	PIM	PP	SH	GW	S	%	+/-	TF	F%	Min	GP	G	A	Pts	PIM	PP	SH	GW	Min
2001-02	Moose Jaw	WHL	13	0	0	0	7	....	....	....	....	....	....	....	....	....	....	....	....	....	....	....	....	....	....
2002-03	Moose Jaw	WHL	59	9	12	21	54	....	....	....	....	....	....	....	....	....	13	1	2	3	14	....	....	....	....
2003-04	Moose Jaw	WHL	72	23	26	49	111	....	....	....	....	....	....	....	....	....	10	3	0	3	12	....	....	....	....
2004-05	Moose Jaw	WHL	71	22	25	47	132	....	....	....	....	....	....	....	....	....	5	1	2	3	8	....	....	....	....
2005-06	Moose Jaw	WHL	72	49	53	*102	122	....	....	....	....	....	....	....	....	....	17	10	4	14	34	....	....	....	....
2006-07	Chicago	NHL	10	0	0	0	7	0	0	0	7	0.0	–7	0	0.0	9:55	....	....	....	....	....	....	....	....	....
	Norfolk Admirals	AHL	66	41	38	79	70	....	....	....	....	....	....	....	....	....	6	1	0	1	4	....	....	....	....
2007-08	Chicago	NHL	2	0	1	1	0	0	0	0	0	0.0	1	0	0.0	11:56	....	....	....	....	....	....	....	....	....
	Rockford IceHogs	AHL	75	35	19	54	154	....	....	....	....	....	....	....	....	....	12	5	4	9	16	....	....	....	....
2008-09	Chicago	NHL	69	10	16	26	50	4	1	0	126	7.9	7	20	45.0	15:05	17	0	2	2	12	0	0	0	11:51
	Rockford IceHogs	AHL	5	2	6	8	20	....	....	....	....	....	....	....	....	....	....	....	....	....	....	....	....	....	....
2009-10 ♦	Chicago	NHL	78	22	18	40	66	7	1	7	116	19.0	9	9	55.6	16:22	19	4	4	8	8	0	0	0	11:01
2010-11	Chicago	NHL	79	17	19	36	38	7	0	5	122	13.9	–2	25	48.0	15:06	7	0	0	0	11	0	0	0	14:25
2011-12	Washington	NHL	82	18	15	33	61	3	0	5	133	13.5	–15	83	45.8	17:11	14	2	2	4	8	1	0	1	19:01
2012-13	Washington	NHL	47	19	14	33	28	7	1	5	111	17.1	–5	232	47.8	18:32	7	1	1	2	10	0	0	0	19:34
	NHL Totals		367	86	83	169	250	28	3	22	615	14.0		369	47.4	16:07	64	7	9	16	49	1	0	1	14:18

WHL East First All-Star Team (2006) • Canadian Major Junior Second All-Star Team (2006) • AHL All-Rookie Team (2007) • AHL Second All-Star Team (2007)

Traded to **Washington** by **Chicago** for Washington's 1st round choice (Phillip Danault) in 2011 Entry Draft, June 24, 2011.

BROWN, Chris

(BROWN, KRIHS) **PHX**

Center. Shoots right. 6'2", 210 lbs. Born, Flower Mound, TX, February 3, 1991. Phoenix's 2nd choice, 36th overall, in 2009 Entry Draft.

Season	Club	League	GP	G	A	Pts	PIM	PP	SH	GW	S	%	+/-	TF	F%	Min	GP	G	A	Pts	PIM	PP	SH	GW	Min
2007-08	USNTDP	NAHL	43	8	6	14	66	....	....	....	....	....	....	....	....	....	3	0	0	0	0	....	....	....	....
	USNTDP	U-17	17	5	1	6	8	....	....	....	....	....	....	....	....	....	....	....	....	....	....	....	....	....	....
2008-09	USNTDP	NAHL	15	6	2	8	37	....	....	....	....	....	....	....	....	....	....	....	....	....	....	....	....	....	....
	USNTDP	U-18	47	14	16	30	83	....	....	....	....	....	....	....	....	....	....	....	....	....	....	....	....	....	....
2009-10	U. of Michigan	CCHA	45	13	15	28	58	....	....	....	....	....	....	....	....	....	....	....	....	....	....	....	....	....	....
2010-11	U. of Michigan	CCHA	42	9	14	23	59	....	....	....	....	....	....	....	....	....	....	....	....	....	....	....	....	....	....
2011-12	U. of Michigan	CCHA	38	12	17	29	66	....	....	....	....	....	....	....	....	....	....	....	....	....	....	....	....	....	....
2012-13	Portland Pirates	AHL	68	29	18	47	98	....	....	....	....	....	....	....	....	....	3	1	1	2	6	....	....	....	....
	Phoenix	NHL	5	0	0	0	2	0	0	0	6	0.0	0	0	0.0	7:38	....	....	....	....	....	....	....	....	....
	NHL Totals		5	0	0	0	2	0	0	0	6	0.0		0	0.0	7:38	....	....	....	....	....	....	....	....	....

CCHA All-Rookie Team (2010)

BROWN, Dustin

(BROWN, DUHS-tihn) **L.A.**

Right wing. Shoots right. 6', 212 lbs. Born, Ithaca, NY, November 4, 1984. Los Angeles' 1st choice, 13th overall, in 2003 Entry Draft.

			Regular Season														Playoffs								
Season	Club	League	GP	G	A	Pts	PIM	PP	SH	GW	S	%	+/-	TF	F%	Min	GP	G	A	Pts	PIM	PP	SH	GW	Min
1998-99	Ithaca	High-NY	18	4	13	17	....	....	....	....	....	....	....	....	....	....	....	....	....	....	....	....	....	....	....
99-2000	Ithaca	High-NY	24	33	21	54	....	....	....	....	....	....	....	....	....	....	....	....	....	....	....	....	....	....	....
2000-01	Guelph Storm	OHL	53	23	22	45	45	....	....	....	....	....	....	....	....	....	4	0	0	0	10	....	....	....	....
2001-02	Guelph Storm	OHL	63	41	32	73	56	....	....	....	....	....	....	....	....	....	9	8	5	13	14	....	....	....	....
2002-03	Guelph Storm	OHL	58	34	42	76	89	....	....	....	....	....	....	....	....	....	11	7	8	15	6	....	....	....	....
2003-04	**Los Angeles**	**NHL**	**31**	**1**	**4**	**5**	**16**	**0**	**0**	**0**	**40**	**2.5**	**0**	**1**	**0.0**	**10:29**	....	....	....	....	....	....	....	....	....
2004-05	Manchester	AHL	79	29	45	74	96	....	....	....	....	....	....	....	....	....	6	5	2	7	10	....	....	....	....
2005-06	**Los Angeles**	**NHL**	**79**	**14**	**14**	**28**	**80**	**6**	**0**	**2**	**159**	**8.8**	**-10**	**15**	**66.7**	**13:59**	....	....	....	....	....	....	....	....	....
2006-07	**Los Angeles**	**NHL**	**81**	**17**	**29**	**46**	**54**	**13**	**0**	**1**	**195**	**8.7**	**-21**	**77**	**49.4**	**18:43**	....	....	....	....	....	....	....	....	....
2007-08	**Los Angeles**	**NHL**	**78**	**33**	**27**	**60**	**55**	**12**	**2**	**4**	**219**	**15.1**	**-13**	**40**	**50.0**	**20:18**	....	....	....	....	....	....	....	....	....
2008-09	**Los Angeles**	**NHL**	**80**	**24**	**29**	**53**	**64**	**7**	**0**	**6**	**292**	**8.2**	**-15**	**54**	**46.3**	**19:24**	....	....	....	....	....	....	....	....	....
2009-10	**Los Angeles**	**NHL**	**82**	**24**	**32**	**56**	**41**	**7**	**0**	**3**	**248**	**9.7**	**-6**	**39**	**43.6**	**19:15**	**6**	**1**	**4**	**5**	**6**	**1**	**0**	**0**	**18:53**
	United States	Olympics	6	0	0	0	0	....	....	....	....	....	....	....	....	....	....	....	....	....	....	....	....	....	....
2010-11	**Los Angeles**	**NHL**	**82**	**28**	**29**	**57**	**67**	**7**	**0**	**2**	**228**	**12.3**	**17**	**37**	**48.7**	**19:22**	**6**	**1**	**1**	**2**	**6**	**1**	**0**	**0**	**20:00**
2011-12◆	**Los Angeles**	**NHL**	**82**	**22**	**32**	**54**	**53**	**9**	**1**	**6**	**214**	**10.3**	**18**	**39**	**43.6**	**20:10**	**20**	***8**	***12**	***20**	**34**	**1**	***2**	**3**	**20:44**
2012-13	ZSC Lions Zurich	Swiss	16	8	5	13	26	....	....	....	....	....	....	....	....	....	....	....	....	....	....	....	....	....	....
	Los Angeles	**NHL**	**46**	**18**	**11**	**29**	**22**	**8**	**0**	**1**	**142**	**12.7**	**6**	**41**	**36.6**	**19:30**	**18**	**3**	**1**	**4**	**8**	**2**	**0**	**0**	**18:47**
	NHL Totals		**641**	**181**	**207**	**388**	**452**	**69**	**3**	**25**	**1737**	**10.4**		**343**	**46.6**	**18:24**	**50**	**13**	**18**	**31**	**54**	**5**	**2**	**3**	**19:43**

OHL All-Rookie Team (2001) • Canadian Major Junior Scholastic Player of the Year (2003) • NHL Foundation Player Award (2011)
Played in NHL All-Star Game (2009)
• Missed majority of 2003-04 due to ankle injury vs. Chicago, November 29, 2003. Signed as a free agent by **Zurich** (Swiss), November 1, 2012.

BROWN, J.T.

(BROWN, JAY-TEE) **T.B.**

Right wing. Shoots right. 5'11", 177 lbs. Born, High Point, NC, July 2, 1990.

			Regular Season														Playoffs								
Season	Club	League	GP	G	A	Pts	PIM	PP	SH	GW	S	%	+/-	TF	F%	Min	GP	G	A	Pts	PIM	PP	SH	GW	Min
2008-09	Waterloo	USHL	36	14	22	36	28	....	....	....	....	....	....	....	....	....	3	1	0	1	4	....	....	....	....
2009-10	Waterloo	USHL	60	34	43	77	64	....	....	....	....	....	....	....	....	....	3	1	0	1	0	....	....	....	....
2010-11	U. Minn-Duluth	WCHA	42	16	21	37	50	....	....	....	....	....	....	....	....	....	....	....	....	....	....	....	....	....	....
2011-12	U. Minn-Duluth	WCHA	39	24	23	47	59	....	....	....	....	....	....	....	....	....	....	....	....	....	....	....	....	....	....
	Tampa Bay	**NHL**	**5**	**0**	**1**	**1**	**0**	**0**	**0**	**0**	**13**	**0.0**	**2**	**0**	**0.0**	**13:51**	....	....	....	....	....	....	....	....	....
2012-13	Syracuse Crunch	AHL	51	10	18	28	27	....	....	....	....	....	....	....	....	....	18	4	5	9	18	....	....	....	....
	NHL Totals		**5**	**0**	**1**	**1**	**0**	**0**	**0**	**0**	**13**	**0.0**		**0**	**0.0**	**13:51**	....	....	....	....	....	....	....	....	....

USHL Second All-Star Team (2010) • WCHA All-Rookie Team (2011) • NCAA Championship All-Tournament Team (2011) • NCAA Championship Tournament MVP (2011) • WCHA First All-Star Team (2012) • NCAA West Second All-American Team (2012)
Signed as a free agent by **Tampa Bay**, March 28, 2012.

BROWN, Mike

(BROWN, MIGHK) **EDM**

Right wing. Shoots right. 5'11", 205 lbs. Born, Chicago, IL, June 24, 1985. Vancouver's 4th choice, 159th overall, in 2004 Entry Draft.

			Regular Season														Playoffs								
Season	Club	League	GP	G	A	Pts	PIM	PP	SH	GW	S	%	+/-	TF	F%	Min	GP	G	A	Pts	PIM	PP	SH	GW	Min
2000-01	Chicago Chill	USAHA	66	27	23	50	....	....	....	....	....	....	....	....	....	....	....	....	....	....	....	....	....	....	....
2001-02	USNTDP	U-17	17	6	4	10	13	....	....	....	....	....	....	....	....	....	....	....	....	....	....	....	....	....	....
	USNTDP	NAHL	46	5	11	16	56	....	....	....	....	....	....	....	....	....	....	....	....	....	....	....	....	....	....
2002-03	USNTDP	U-18	34	5	3	8	16	....	....	....	....	....	....	....	....	....	....	....	....	....	....	....	....	....	....
	USNTDP	NAHL	9	0	3	3	29	....	....	....	....	....	....	....	....	....	....	....	....	....	....	....	....	....	....
2003-04	U. of Michigan	CCHA	42	8	5	13	51	....	....	....	....	....	....	....	....	....	....	....	....	....	....	....	....	....	....
2004-05	U. of Michigan	CCHA	35	3	5	8	95	....	....	....	....	....	....	....	....	....	....	....	....	....	....	....	....	....	....
2005-06	Manitoba Moose	AHL	73	7	8	15	139	....	....	....	....	....	....	....	....	....	13	1	2	3	17	....	....	....	....
2006-07	Manitoba Moose	AHL	62	3	0	3	194	....	....	....	....	....	....	....	....	....	13	0	2	2	16	....	....	....	....
2007-08	**Vancouver**	**NHL**	**19**	**1**	**0**	**1**	**55**	**0**	**0**	**0**	**9**	**11.1**	**-2**	**0**	**0.0**	**6:19**	....	....	....	....	....	....	....	....	....
	Manitoba Moose	AHL	54	10	3	13	201	....	....	....	....	....	....	....	....	....	6	2	0	2	11	....	....	....	....
2008-09	**Vancouver**	**NHL**	**20**	**0**	**1**	**1**	**85**	**0**	**0**	**0**	**6**	**0.0**	**-5**	**2**	**0.0**	**5:29**	....	....	....	....	....	....	....	....	....
	Anaheim	**NHL**	**28**	**2**	**1**	**3**	**60**	**0**	**0**	**2**	**38**	**5.3**	**-2**	**4**	**0.0**	**10:02**	**13**	**0**	**2**	**2**	**25**	**0**	**0**	**0**	**8:28**
2009-10	**Anaheim**	**NHL**	**75**	**6**	**1**	**7**	**106**	**0**	**1**	**2**	**82**	**7.3**	**1**	**7**	**0.0**	**8:21**	....	....	....	....	....	....	....	....	....
2010-11	**Toronto**	**NHL**	**50**	**3**	**5**	**8**	**69**	**1**	**0**	**0**	**59**	**5.1**	**1**	**15**	**26.7**	**10:06**	....	....	....	....	....	....	....	....	....
2011-12	**Toronto**	**NHL**	**50**	**2**	**2**	**4**	**74**	**0**	**0**	**0**	**56**	**3.6**	**-8**	**1**	**0.0**	**9:17**	....	....	....	....	....	....	....	....	....
2012-13	**Toronto**	**NHL**	**12**	**0**	**1**	**1**	**70**	**0**	**0**	**0**	**2**	**0.0**	**1**	**1**	**0.0**	**4:39**	....	....	....	....	....	....	....	....	....
	Edmonton	**NHL**	**27**	**1**	**0**	**1**	**53**	**0**	**0**	**0**	**16**	**6.3**	**-8**	**7**	**71.4**	**8:48**	....	....	....	....	....	....	....	....	....
	NHL Totals		**281**	**15**	**11**	**26**	**572**	**1**	**1**	**4**	**268**	**5.6**		**37**	**24.3**	**8:32**	**13**	**0**	**2**	**2**	**25**	**0**	**0**	**0**	**8:28**

Traded to **Anaheim** by **Vancouver** for Nathan McIver, February 4, 2009. Traded to **Toronto** by **Anaheim** for Toronto's 5th round choice (Chris Wagner) in 2010 Entry Draft, June 25, 2010. Traded to **Edmonton** by **Toronto** for future considerations, March 6, 2013.

BRULE, Gilbert

(broo-LAY, zhihl-BAIR)

Center. Shoots right. 5'11", 187 lbs. Born, Edmonton, Alta., January 1, 1987. Columbus' 1st choice, 6th overall, in 2005 Entry Draft.

			Regular Season														Playoffs								
Season	Club	League	GP	G	A	Pts	PIM	PP	SH	GW	S	%	+/-	TF	F%	Min	GP	G	A	Pts	PIM	PP	SH	GW	Min
2001-02	North Shore	Minor-BC	56	97	55	152	....	....	....	....	....	....	....	....	....	....	7	*13	7	*20	14	....	....	....	....
2002-03	Quesnel	BCHL	48	32	25	57	71	....	....	....	....	....	....	....	....	....	....	....	....	....	....	....	....	....	....
	Vancouver Giants	WHL	1	0	0	0	0	....	....	....	....	....	....	....	....	....	4	1	0	1	0	....	....	....	....
2003-04	Vancouver Giants	WHL	67	25	35	60	100	....	....	....	....	....	....	....	....	....	11	4	5	9	10	....	....	....	....
2004-05	Vancouver Giants	WHL	70	39	48	87	169	....	....	....	....	....	....	....	....	....	6	1	3	4	8	....	....	....	....
2005-06	**Columbus**	**NHL**	**7**	**2**	**2**	**4**	**0**	**0**	**0**	**0**	**11**	**18.2**	**-2**	**60**	**43.3**	**13:11**	....	....	....	....	....	....	....	....	....
	Vancouver Giants	WHL	27	23	15	38	40	....	....	....	....	....	....	....	....	....	18	*16	14	*30	44	....	....	....	....
2006-07	**Columbus**	**NHL**	**78**	**9**	**10**	**19**	**28**	**3**	**0**	**0**	**98**	**9.2**	**-21**	**268**	**45.9**	**10:39**	....	....	....	....	....	....	....	....	....
2007-08	**Columbus**	**NHL**	**61**	**1**	**8**	**9**	**24**	**0**	**0**	**1**	**74**	**1.4**	**-4**	**78**	**51.3**	**9:54**	....	....	....	....	....	....	....	....	....
	Syracuse Crunch	AHL	16	5	5	10	44	....	....	....	....	....	....	....	....	....	13	2	3	5	16	....	....	....	....
2008-09	**Edmonton**	**NHL**	**11**	**2**	**1**	**3**	**12**	**0**	**0**	**1**	**13**	**15.4**	**-3**	**5**	**80.0**	**9:52**	....	....	....	....	....	....	....	....	....
	Springfield	AHL	39	13	11	24	58	....	....	....	....	....	....	....	....	....	....	....	....	....	....	....	....	....	....
2009-10	**Edmonton**	**NHL**	**65**	**17**	**20**	**37**	**38**	**2**	**0**	**3**	**121**	**14.0**	**-8**	**274**	**52.6**	**14:14**	....	....	....	....	....	....	....	....	....
2010-11	**Edmonton**	**NHL**	**41**	**7**	**2**	**9**	**41**	**1**	**0**	**1**	**72**	**9.7**	**-7**	**199**	**53.3**	**13:48**	....	....	....	....	....	....	....	....	....
2011-12	Oklahoma City	AHL	27	8	10	18	31	....	....	....	....	....	....	....	....	....	....	....	....	....	....	....	....	....	....
	Phoenix	**NHL**	**33**	**5**	**9**	**14**	**11**	**1**	**0**	**0**	**56**	**8.9**	**7**	**21**	**38.1**	**11:34**	**12**	**2**	**1**	**3**	**0**	**0**	**0**	**0**	**7:55**
2012-13	ZSC Lions Zurich	Swiss	14	0	6	6	4	....	....	....	....	....	....	....	....	....	....	....	....	....	....	....	....	....	....
	NHL Totals		**296**	**43**	**52**	**95**	**154**	**7**	**0**	**6**	**445**	**9.7**		**905**	**49.8**	**11:51**	**12**	**2**	**1**	**3**	**0**	**0**	**0**	**0**	**7:55**

WHL West First All-Star Team (2005) • Canadian Major Junior Second All-Star Team (2005) • Canadian Major Junior Scholastic Player of the Year (2005) • WHL West Second All-Star Team (2006) • Memorial Cup All-Star Team (2006) • Ed Chynoweth Trophy (Memorial Cup - Leading Scorer) (2006)
• Missed majority of 2005-06 due to sternum (October 7, 2005 vs. Calgary) and leg (November 30, 2005 at Minnesota) injuries. Traded to **Edmonton** by **Columbus** for Raffi Torres, July 1, 2008. Claimed on waivers by **Phoenix** from **Edmonton**, January 10, 2012. Signed as a free agent by **Zurich** (Swiss), August 13, 2012.

BRUNNER, Damien

(BROO-nuhr, DAY-mee-uhn)

Right wing. Shoots right. 5'10", 184 lbs. Born, Oberfunkhofen, Switz., March 9, 1986.

			Regular Season														Playoffs								
Season	Club	League	GP	G	A	Pts	PIM	PP	SH	GW	S	%	+/-	TF	F%	Min	GP	G	A	Pts	PIM	PP	SH	GW	Min
2006-07	Kloten Flyers	Swiss	42	9	9	18	22	....	....	....	....	....	....	....	....	....	11	1	0	1	4	....	....	....	....
2007-08	Kloten Flyers	Swiss	50	5	2	7	8	....	....	....	....	....	....	....	....	....	5	0	0	0	0	....	....	....	....
2008-09	Kloten Flyers	Swiss	12	0	0	0	2	....	....	....	....	....	....	....	....	....	....	....	....	....	....	....	....	....	....
	HC Thurgau	Swiss-2	3	1	3	4	4	....	....	....	....	....	....	....	....	....	....	....	....	....	....	....	....	....	....
	EV Zug	Swiss	36	12	14	26	16	....	....	....	....	....	....	....	....	....	10	3	2	5	4	....	....	....	....
2009-10	EV Zug	Swiss	47	23	35	58	22	....	....	....	....	....	....	....	....	....	13	5	5	10	6	....	....	....	....
2010-11	EV Zug	Swiss	40	19	27	46	34	....	....	....	....	....	....	....	....	....	8	4	4	8	2	....	....	....	....
2011-12	EV Zug	Swiss	45	24	36	60	48	....	....	....	....	....	....	....	....	....	9	3	11	14	6	....	....	....	....
2012-13	EV Zug	Swiss	33	25	32	57	49	....	....	....	....	....	....	....	....	....	....	....	....	....	....	....	....	....	....
	Detroit	**NHL**	**44**	**12**	**14**	**26**	**12**	**3**	**0**	**1**	**123**	**9.8**	**-6**	**5**	**40.0**	**15:35**	**14**	**5**	**4**	**9**	**4**	**0**	**0**	**1**	**13:07**
	NHL Totals		**44**	**12**	**14**	**26**	**12**	**3**	**0**	**1**	**123**	**9.8**		**5**	**40.0**	**15:35**	**14**	**5**	**4**	**9**	**4**	**0**	**0**	**1**	**13:07**

Signed as a free agent by **Detroit**, July 1, 2012. Signed as a free agent by **Zug** (Swiss), September 17, 2012.

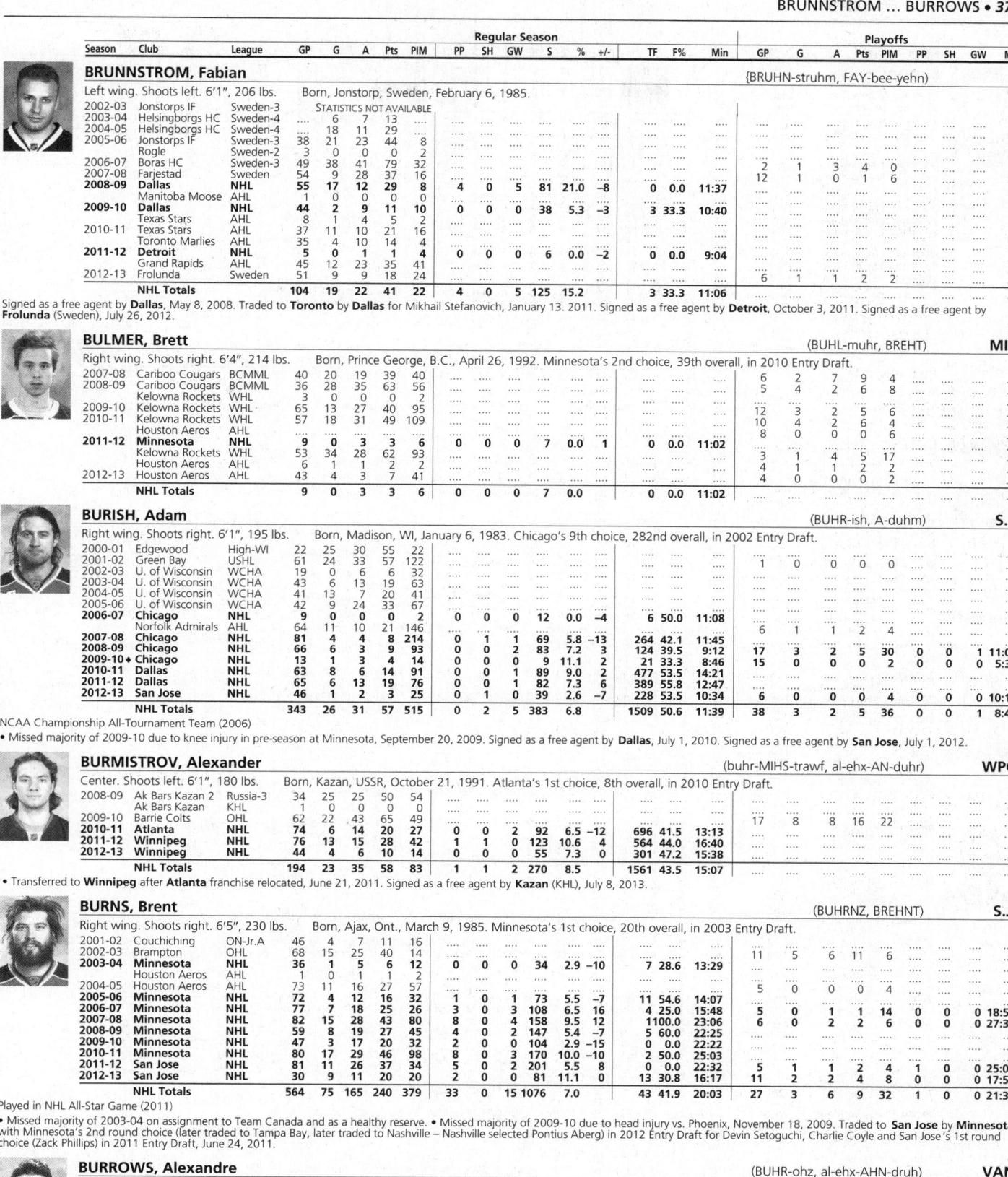

BRUNNSTROM, Fabian

(BRUHN-struhm, FAY-bee-yehn)

Left wing. Shoots left. 6'1", 206 lbs. Born, Jonstorp, Sweden, February 6, 1985.

			Regular Season														Playoffs								
Season	Club	League	GP	G	A	Pts	PIM	PP	SH	GW	S	%	+/-	TF	F%	Min	GP	G	A	Pts	PIM	PP	SH	GW	Min
2002-03	Jonstorps IF	Sweden-3	STATISTICS NOT AVAILABLE																						
2003-04	Helsingborgs HC	Sweden-4	....	6	7	13	....	....	....	....	....	....	....	....	....	....	....	....	....	....	....	....	....	....	....
2004-05	Helsingborgs HC	Sweden-4	....	18	11	29	....	....	....	....	....	....	....	....	....	....	....	....	....	....	....	....	....	....	....
2005-06	Jonstorps IF	Sweden-3	38	21	23	44	8	....	....	....	....	....	....	....	....	....	....	....	....	....	....	....	....	....	....
	Rogle	Sweden-2	3	0	0	0	2	....	....	....	....	....	....	....	....	....	....	....	....	....	....	....	....	....	....
2006-07	Boras HC	Sweden-3	49	38	41	79	32	....	....	....	....	....	....	....	....	....	2	1	3	4	0	....	....	....	....
2007-08	Farjestad	Sweden	54	9	28	37	16	....	....	....	....	....	....	....	....	....	12	1	0	1	6	....	....	....	....
2008-09	**Dallas**	**NHL**	**55**	**17**	**12**	**29**	**8**	**4**	**0**	**5**	**81**	**21.0**	**−8**	**0**	**0.0**	**11:37**	....	....	....	....	....	....	....	....	....
	Manitoba Moose	AHL	1	0	0	0	0	....	....	....	....	....	....	....	....	....	....	....	....	....	....	....	....	....	....
2009-10	**Dallas**	**NHL**	**44**	**2**	**9**	**11**	**10**	**0**	**0**	**0**	**38**	**5.3**	**−3**	**3**	**33.3**	**10:40**	....	....	....	....	....	....	....	....	....
	Texas Stars	AHL	8	1	4	5	2	....	....	....	....	....	....	....	....	....	....	....	....	....	....	....	....	....	....
2010-11	Texas Stars	AHL	37	11	10	21	16	....	....	....	....	....	....	....	....	....	....	....	....	....	....	....	....	....	....
	Toronto Marlies	AHL	35	4	10	14	4	....	....	....	....	....	....	....	....	....	....	....	....	....	....	....	....	....	....
2011-12	**Detroit**	**NHL**	**5**	**0**	**1**	**1**	**4**	**0**	**0**	**0**	**6**	**0.0**	**−2**	**0**	**0.0**	**9:04**	....	....	....	....	....	....	....	....	....
	Grand Rapids	AHL	45	12	23	35	41	....	....	....	....	....	....	....	....	....	....	....	....	....	....	....	....	....	....
2012-13	Frolunda	Sweden	51	9	9	18	24	....	....	....	....	....	....	....	....	....	6	1	1	2	2	....	....	....	....
	NHL Totals		**104**	**19**	**22**	**41**	**22**	**4**	**0**	**5**	**125**	**15.2**		**3**	**33.3**	**11:06**	....	....	....	....	....	....	....	....	....

Signed as a free agent by **Dallas**, May 8, 2008. Traded to **Toronto** by **Dallas** for Mikhail Stefanovich, January 13. 2011. Signed as a free agent by **Detroit**, October 3, 2011. Signed as a free agent by **Frolunda** (Sweden), July 26, 2012.

BULMER, Brett

(BUHL-muhr, BREHT) **MIN**

Right wing. Shoots right. 6'4", 214 lbs. Born, Prince George, B.C., April 26, 1992. Minnesota's 2nd choice, 39th overall, in 2010 Entry Draft.

Season	Club	League	GP	G	A	Pts	PIM	PP	SH	GW	S	%	+/-	TF	F%	Min	GP	G	A	Pts	PIM	PP	SH	GW	Min
2007-08	Cariboo Cougars	BCMML	40	20	19	39	40	....	....	....	....	....	....	....	....	....	6	2	7	9	4	....	....	....	....
2008-09	Cariboo Cougars	BCMML	36	28	35	63	56	....	....	....	....	....	....	....	....	....	5	4	2	6	8	....	....	....	....
	Kelowna Rockets	WHL	3	0	0	0	2	....	....	....	....	....	....	....	....	....	....	....	....	....	....	....	....	....	....
2009-10	Kelowna Rockets	WHL	65	13	27	40	95	....	....	....	....	....	....	....	....	....	12	3	2	5	6	....	....	....	....
2010-11	Kelowna Rockets	WHL	57	18	31	49	109	....	....	....	....	....	....	....	....	....	10	4	2	6	4	....	....	....	....
	Houston Aeros	AHL	....	....	....	....	....	....	....	....	....	....	....	....	....	....	8	0	0	0	6	....	....	....	....
2011-12	**Minnesota**	**NHL**	**9**	**0**	**3**	**3**	**6**	**0**	**0**	**0**	**7**	**0.0**	**1**	**0**	**0.0**	**11:02**	....	....	....	....	....	....	....	....	....
	Kelowna Rockets	WHL	53	34	28	62	93	....	....	....	....	....	....	....	....	....	3	1	4	5	17	....	....	....	....
	Houston Aeros	AHL	6	1	1	2	2	....	....	....	....	....	....	....	....	....	4	1	1	2	2	....	....	....	....
2012-13	Houston Aeros	AHL	43	4	3	7	41	....	....	....	....	....	....	....	....	....	4	0	0	0	2	....	....	....	....
	NHL Totals		**9**	**0**	**3**	**3**	**6**	**0**	**0**	**0**	**7**	**0.0**		**0**	**0.0**	**11:02**	....	....	....	....	....	....	....	....	....

BURISH, Adam

(BUHR-ish, A-duhm) **S.J.**

Right wing. Shoots right. 6'1", 195 lbs. Born, Madison, WI, January 6, 1983. Chicago's 9th choice, 282nd overall, in 2002 Entry Draft.

Season	Club	League	GP	G	A	Pts	PIM	PP	SH	GW	S	%	+/-	TF	F%	Min	GP	G	A	Pts	PIM	PP	SH	GW	Min
2000-01	Edgewood	High-WI	22	25	30	55	22	....	....	....	....	....	....	....	....	....	....	....	....	....	....	....	....	....	....
2001-02	Green Bay	USHL	61	24	33	57	122	....	....	....	....	....	....	....	....	....	1	0	0	0	0	....	....	....	....
2002-03	U. of Wisconsin	WCHA	19	0	6	6	32	....	....	....	....	....	....	....	....	....	....	....	....	....	....	....	....	....	....
2003-04	U. of Wisconsin	WCHA	43	6	13	19	63	....	....	....	....	....	....	....	....	....	....	....	....	....	....	....	....	....	....
2004-05	U. of Wisconsin	WCHA	41	13	7	20	41	....	....	....	....	....	....	....	....	....	....	....	....	....	....	....	....	....	....
2005-06	U. of Wisconsin	WCHA	42	9	24	33	67	....	....	....	....	....	....	....	....	....	....	....	....	....	....	....	....	....	....
2006-07	**Chicago**	**NHL**	**9**	**0**	**0**	**0**	**2**	**0**	**0**	**0**	**12**	**0.0**	**−4**	**6**	**50.0**	**11:08**	....	....	....	....	....	....	....	....	....
	Norfolk Admirals	AHL	64	11	10	21	146	....	....	....	....	....	....	....	....	....	6	1	1	2	4	....	....	....	....
2007-08	**Chicago**	**NHL**	**81**	**4**	**4**	**8**	**214**	**0**	**1**	**1**	**69**	**5.8**	**−13**	**264**	**42.1**	**11:45**	....	....	....	....	....	....	....	....	....
2008-09	**Chicago**	**NHL**	**66**	**6**	**3**	**9**	**93**	**0**	**0**	**2**	**83**	**7.2**	**3**	**124**	**39.5**	**9:12**	**17**	**3**	**2**	**5**	**30**	**0**	**0**	**1**	**11:02**
2009-10◆	**Chicago**	**NHL**	**13**	**1**	**3**	**4**	**14**	**0**	**0**	**0**	**9**	**11.1**	**2**	**21**	**33.3**	**8:46**	**15**	**0**	**0**	**0**	**2**	**0**	**0**	**0**	**5:35**
2010-11	**Dallas**	**NHL**	**63**	**8**	**6**	**14**	**91**	**0**	**0**	**1**	**89**	**9.0**	**2**	**477**	**53.5**	**14:21**	....	....	....	....	....	....	....	....	....
2011-12	**Dallas**	**NHL**	**65**	**6**	**13**	**19**	**76**	**0**	**0**	**1**	**82**	**7.3**	**6**	**389**	**55.8**	**12:47**	....	....	....	....	....	....	....	....	....
2012-13	**San Jose**	**NHL**	**46**	**1**	**2**	**3**	**25**	**0**	**1**	**0**	**39**	**2.6**	**−7**	**228**	**53.5**	**10:34**	**6**	**0**	**0**	**0**	**4**	**0**	**0**	**0**	**10:15**
	NHL Totals		**343**	**26**	**31**	**57**	**515**	**0**	**2**	**5**	**383**	**6.8**		**1509**	**50.6**	**11:39**	**38**	**3**	**2**	**5**	**36**	**0**	**0**	**1**	**8:45**

NCAA Championship All-Tournament Team (2006)

• Missed majority of 2009-10 due to knee injury in pre-season at Minnesota, September 20, 2009. Signed as a free agent by **Dallas**, July 1, 2010. Signed as a free agent by **San Jose**, July 1, 2012.

BURMISTROV, Alexander

(buhr-MIHS-trawf, al-ehx-AN-duhr) **WPG**

Center. Shoots left. 6'1", 180 lbs. Born, Kazan, USSR, October 21, 1991. Atlanta's 1st choice, 8th overall, in 2010 Entry Draft.

Season	Club	League	GP	G	A	Pts	PIM	PP	SH	GW	S	%	+/-	TF	F%	Min	GP	G	A	Pts	PIM	PP	SH	GW	Min
2008-09	Ak Bars Kazan 2	Russia-3	34	25	25	50	54	....	....	....	....	....	....	....	....	....	....	....	....	....	....	....	....	....	....
	Ak Bars Kazan	KHL	1	0	0	0	0	....	....	....	....	....	....	....	....	....	....	....	....	....	....	....	....	....	....
2009-10	Barrie Colts	OHL	62	22	43	65	49	....	....	....	....	....	....	....	....	....	17	8	8	16	22	....	....	....	....
2010-11	**Atlanta**	**NHL**	**74**	**6**	**14**	**20**	**27**	**0**	**0**	**2**	**92**	**6.5**	**−12**	**696**	**41.5**	**13:13**	....	....	....	....	....	....	....	....	....
2011-12	**Winnipeg**	**NHL**	**76**	**13**	**15**	**28**	**42**	**1**	**1**	**0**	**123**	**10.6**	**4**	**564**	**44.0**	**16:40**	....	....	....	....	....	....	....	....	....
2012-13	**Winnipeg**	**NHL**	**44**	**4**	**6**	**10**	**14**	**0**	**0**	**0**	**55**	**7.3**	**0**	**301**	**47.2**	**15:38**	....	....	....	....	....	....	....	....	....
	NHL Totals		**194**	**23**	**35**	**58**	**83**	**1**	**1**	**2**	**270**	**8.5**		**1561**	**43.5**	**15:07**	....	....	....	....	....	....	....	....	....

• Transferred to **Winnipeg** after **Atlanta** franchise relocated, June 21, 2011. Signed as a free agent by **Kazan** (KHL), July 8, 2013.

BURNS, Brent

(BUHRNZ, BREHNT) **S.J.**

Right wing. Shoots right. 6'5", 230 lbs. Born, Ajax, Ont., March 9, 1985. Minnesota's 1st choice, 20th overall, in 2003 Entry Draft.

Season	Club	League	GP	G	A	Pts	PIM	PP	SH	GW	S	%	+/-	TF	F%	Min	GP	G	A	Pts	PIM	PP	SH	GW	Min
2001-02	Couchiching	ON-Jr.A	46	4	7	11	16	....	....	....	....	....	....	....	....	....	....	....	....	....	....	....	....	....	....
2002-03	Brampton	OHL	68	15	25	40	14	....	....	....	....	....	....	....	....	....	11	5	6	11	6	....	....	....	....
2003-04	**Minnesota**	**NHL**	**36**	**1**	**5**	**6**	**12**	**0**	**0**	**0**	**34**	**2.9**	**−10**	**7**	**28.6**	**13:29**	....	....	....	....	....	....	....	....	....
	Houston Aeros	AHL	1	0	1	1	2	....	....	....	....	....	....	....	....	....	....	....	....	....	....	....	....	....	....
2004-05	Houston Aeros	AHL	73	11	16	27	57	....	....	....	....	....	....	....	....	....	5	0	0	0	4	....	....	....	....
2005-06	**Minnesota**	**NHL**	**72**	**4**	**12**	**16**	**32**	**1**	**0**	**1**	**73**	**5.5**	**−7**	**11**	**54.6**	**14:07**	....	....	....	....	....	....	....	....	....
2006-07	**Minnesota**	**NHL**	**77**	**7**	**18**	**25**	**26**	**3**	**0**	**3**	**108**	**6.5**	**16**	**4**	**25.0**	**15:48**	**5**	**0**	**1**	**1**	**14**	**0**	**0**	**0**	**18:59**
2007-08	**Minnesota**	**NHL**	**82**	**15**	**28**	**43**	**80**	**8**	**0**	**4**	**158**	**9.5**	**12**	**1**	**100.0**	**23:06**	**6**	**0**	**2**	**2**	**6**	**0**	**0**	**0**	**27:35**
2008-09	**Minnesota**	**NHL**	**59**	**8**	**19**	**27**	**45**	**4**	**0**	**2**	**147**	**5.4**	**−7**	**5**	**60.0**	**22:25**	....	....	....	....	....	....	....	....	....
2009-10	**Minnesota**	**NHL**	**47**	**3**	**17**	**20**	**32**	**2**	**0**	**0**	**104**	**2.9**	**−15**	**0**	**0.0**	**22:22**	....	....	....	....	....	....	....	....	....
2010-11	**Minnesota**	**NHL**	**80**	**17**	**29**	**46**	**98**	**8**	**0**	**3**	**170**	**10.0**	**−10**	**2**	**50.0**	**25:03**	....	....	....	....	....	....	....	....	....
2011-12	**San Jose**	**NHL**	**81**	**11**	**26**	**37**	**34**	**5**	**0**	**2**	**201**	**5.5**	**8**	**0**	**0.0**	**22:32**	**5**	**1**	**1**	**2**	**4**	**1**	**0**	**0**	**25:07**
2012-13	**San Jose**	**NHL**	**30**	**9**	**11**	**20**	**20**	**2**	**0**	**0**	**81**	**11.1**	**0**	**13**	**30.8**	**16:17**	**11**	**2**	**2**	**4**	**8**	**0**	**0**	**0**	**17:50**
	NHL Totals		**564**	**75**	**165**	**240**	**379**	**33**	**0**	**15**	**1076**	**7.0**		**43**	**41.9**	**20:03**	**27**	**3**	**6**	**9**	**32**	**1**	**0**	**0**	**21:34**

Played in NHL All-Star Game (2011)

• Missed majority of 2003-04 on assignment to Team Canada and as a healthy reserve. • Missed majority of 2009-10 due to head injury vs. Phoenix, November 18, 2009. Traded to **San Jose** by **Minnesota** with Minnesota's 2nd round choice (later traded to Tampa Bay, later traded to Nashville – Nashville selected Pontius Aberg) in 2012 Entry Draft for Devin Setoguchi, Charlie Coyle and San Jose's 1st round choice (Zack Phillips) in 2011 Entry Draft, June 24, 2011.

BURROWS, Alexandre

(BUHR-ohz, al-ehx-AHN-druh) **VAN**

Left wing. Shoots left. 6'1", 195 lbs. Born, Pincourt, Que., April 11, 1981.

Season	Club	League	GP	G	A	Pts	PIM	PP	SH	GW	S	%	+/-	TF	F%	Min	GP	G	A	Pts	PIM	PP	SH	GW	Min
99-2000	Kahnawake	QJHL	53	24	45	69	223	....	....	....	....	....	....	....	....	....	....	....	....	....	....	....	....	....	....
2000-01	Shawinigan	QMJHL	63	16	14	30	105	....	....	....	....	....	....	....	....	....	10	2	1	3	8	....	....	....	....
2001-02	Shawinigan	QMJHL	64	35	35	70	184	....	....	....	....	....	....	....	....	....	12	9	11	20	34	....	....	....	....
2002-03	Greenville	ECHL	53	9	17	26	201	....	....	....	....	....	....	....	....	....	....	....	....	....	....	....	....	....	....
	Baton Rouge	ECHL	13	4	2	6	64	....	....	....	....	....	....	....	....	....	....	....	....	....	....	....	....	....	....
2003-04	Manitoba Moose	AHL	2	0	0	0	0	....	....	....	....	....	....	....	....	....	....	....	....	....	....	....	....	....	....
	Columbia Inferno	ECHL	64	29	44	73	194	....	....	....	....	....	....	....	....	....	4	2	0	2	28	....	....	....	....
2004-05	Manitoba Moose	AHL	72	9	17	26	107	....	....	....	....	....	....	....	....	....	14	0	3	3	37	....	....	....	....
	Columbia Inferno	ECHL	4	5	1	6	4	....	....	....	....	....	....	....	....	....	....	....	....	....	....	....	....	....	....
2005-06	**Vancouver**	**NHL**	**43**	**7**	**5**	**12**	**61**	**0**	**1**	**1**	**49**	**14.3**	**5**	**19**	**47.4**	**10:24**	....	....	....	....	....	....	....	....	....
	Manitoba Moose	AHL	33	12	18	30	57	....	....	....	....	....	....	....	....	....	13	6	7	13	27	....	....	....	....
2006-07	**Vancouver**	**NHL**	**81**	**3**	**6**	**9**	**93**	**0**	**0**	**1**	**70**	**4.3**	**−7**	**16**	**43.8**	**11:26**	**11**	**1**	**0**	**1**	**14**	**0**	**0**	**0**	**10:34**
2007-08	**Vancouver**	**NHL**	**82**	**12**	**19**	**31**	**179**	**1**	**3**	**3**	**126**	**9.5**	**11**	**37**	**35.1**	**15:06**	....	....	....	....	....	....	....	....	....
2008-09	**Vancouver**	**NHL**	**82**	**28**	**23**	**51**	**150**	**0**	**4**	**3**	**175**	**16.0**	**23**	**80**	**46.3**	**16:51**	**10**	**3**	**1**	**4**	**20**	**0**	**0**	**1**	**18:48**

			Regular Season														Playoffs								
Season	Club	League	GP	G	A	Pts	PIM	PP	SH	GW	S	%	+/-	TF	F%	Min	GP	G	A	Pts	PIM	PP	SH	GW	Min
2009-10	Vancouver	NHL	82	35	32	67	121	4	5	3	209	16.7	34	34	41.2	17:52	12	3	3	6	22	0	0	0	18:51
2010-11	Vancouver	NHL	72	26	22	48	77	1	1	4	152	17.1	26	14	42.9	17:02	25	9	8	17	34	1	1	2	20:40
2011-12	Vancouver	NHL	80	28	24	52	90	3	2	7	198	14.1	24	20	35.0	18:28	5	1	0	1	7	0	0	0	18:50
2012-13	Vancouver	NHL	47	13	11	24	54	1	0	2	140	9.3	15	108	44.4	18:54	4	2	1	3	6	1	0	0	20:36
	NHL Totals		569	152	142	294	825	10	16	24	1119	13.6		328	43.0	15:54	67	19	13	32	103	2	1	3	18:16

Signed as a free agent by **Manitoba** (AHL), October 21, 2003. Signed as a free agent by **Vancouver**, November 8, 2005.

BUTLER, Bobby

(BUHT-luhr, BAW-bee) **FLA**

Right wing. Shoots right. 6', 189 lbs. Born, Marlborough, MA, April 26, 1987.

2002-03	Bos. Little Bruins	Minor-MA	35	21	27	48	12	....	....	....	....	....	....	....	....	....	....	....	....	....	....	....	....	....	....
	Bos. Jr. Bruins	EJHL	13	1	3	4	0	....	....	....	....	....	....	....	....	....	....	....	....	....	....	....	....	....	....
2003-04	Bos. Jr. Bruins	EJHL	59	15	18	33	28	....	....	....	....	....	....	....	....	....	....	....	....	....	....	....	....	....	....
2004-05	Bos. Jr. Bruins	EJHL	56	19	20	39	20	....	....	....	....	....	....	....	....	....	....	....	....	....	....	....	....	....	....
2005-06	Bos. Jr. Bruins	EJHL	61	28	30	58	48	....	....	....	....	....	....	....	....	....	....	....	....	....	....	....	....	....	....
2006-07	New Hampshire	H-East	38	9	3	12	12	....	....	....	....	....	....	....	....	....	....	....	....	....	....	....	....	....	....
2007-08	New Hampshire	H-East	38	14	12	26	20	....	....	....	....	....	....	....	....	....	....	....	....	....	....	....	....	....	....
2008-09	New Hampshire	H-East	38	9	21	30	36	....	....	....	....	....	....	....	....	....	....	....	....	....	....	....	....	....	....
2009-10	New Hampshire	H-East	39	29	24	53	20	....	....	....	....	....	....	....	....	....	....	....	....	....	....	....	....	....	....
	Ottawa	**NHL**	**2**	**0**	**0**	**0**	**0**	0	0	0	2	0.0	–1	0	0.0	8:21	....	....	....	....	....	....	....	....	....
2010-11	**Ottawa**	**NHL**	**36**	**10**	**11**	**21**	**10**	1	0	3	73	13.7	–16	2	0.0	15:26	....	....	....	....	....	....	....	....	....
	Binghamton	AHL	47	22	11	33	35	....	....	....	....	....	....	....	....	....	23	13	4	17	6	....	....	....	....
2011-12	**Ottawa**	**NHL**	**56**	**6**	**10**	**16**	**12**	0	0	4	86	7.0	8	3	100.0	11:29	3	0	0	0	0	0	0	0	12:44
2012-13	Albany Devils	AHL	37	16	11	27	8	....	....	....	....	....	....	....	....	....	....	....	....	....	....	....	....	....	....
	New Jersey	**NHL**	**14**	**1**	**1**	**2**	**0**	1	0	0	13	7.7	–6	4	50.0	9:59	....	....	....	....	....	....	....	....	....
	Nashville	**NHL**	**20**	**3**	**6**	**9**	**4**	0	0	0	28	10.7	–2	1	0.0	11:23	....	....	....	....	....	....	....	....	....
	NHL Totals		**128**	**20**	**28**	**48**	**26**	2	0	7	202	9.9		10	50.0	12:22	3	0	0	0	0	0	0	0	12:44

Hockey East First All-Star Team (2010) • Hockey East Player of the Year (2010) • NCAA East First All-American Team (2010)

Signed as a free agent by **Ottawa**, March 29, 2010. Signed as a free agent by **New Jersey**, August 9, 2012. Claimed on waivers by **Nashville** from **New Jersey**, March 4, 2013. Traded to **Florida** by **Nashville** for T.J. Brennan, June 14, 2013.

BUTLER, Chris

(BUHT-luhr, KRIHS) **CGY**

Defense. Shoots left. 6'1", 196 lbs. Born, St. Louis, MO, October 27, 1986. Buffalo's 4th choice, 96th overall, in 2005 Entry Draft.

2003-04	Sioux City	USHL	55	3	6	9	37	....	....	....	....	....	....	....	....	....	7	0	1	1	6	....	....	....	....
2004-05	Sioux City	USHL	60	6	22	28	90	....	....	....	....	....	....	....	....	....	13	1	6	7	10	....	....	....	....
2005-06	U. of Denver	WCHA	35	7	15	22	28	....	....	....	....	....	....	....	....	....	....	....	....	....	....	....	....	....	....
2006-07	U. of Denver	WCHA	39	10	17	27	42	....	....	....	....	....	....	....	....	....	....	....	....	....	....	....	....	....	....
2007-08	U. of Denver	WCHA	41	3	14	17	38	....	....	....	....	....	....	....	....	....	....	....	....	....	....	....	....	....	....
2008-09	**Buffalo**	**NHL**	**47**	**2**	**4**	**6**	**18**	0	0	1	36	5.6	11	0	0.0	16:43	....	....	....	....	....	....	....	....	....
	Portland Pirates	AHL	27	2	10	12	14	....	....	....	....	....	....	....	....	....	4	0	0	0	0	....	....	....	....
2009-10	**Buffalo**	**NHL**	**59**	**1**	**20**	**21**	**22**	0	0	0	61	1.6	–15	0	0.0	20:01	....	....	....	....	....	....	....	....	....
2010-11	**Buffalo**	**NHL**	**49**	**2**	**7**	**9**	**26**	0	0	0	52	3.8	8	0	0.0	18:10	7	0	1	1	10	0	0	0	22:59
2011-12	**Calgary**	**NHL**	**68**	**2**	**13**	**15**	**34**	0	0	0	62	3.2	–9	0	0.0	21:36	....	....	....	....	....	....	....	....	....
2012-13	Karlskrona HK	Sweden-2	5	0	0	0	8	....	....	....	....	....	....	....	....	....	....	....	....	....	....	....	....	....	....
	Calgary	**NHL**	**44**	**1**	**7**	**8**	**19**	0	1	0	40	2.5	–10	0	0.0	17:02	....	....	....	....	....	....	....	....	....
	NHL Totals		**267**	**8**	**51**	**59**	**119**	0	1	1	251	3.2		0	0.0	19:01	7	0	1	1	10	0	0	0	23:00

USHL First All-Star Team (2005) • WCHA All-Rookie Team (2006) • WCHA Second All-Star Team (2008) • NCAA West Second All-American Team (2008)

Traded to **Calgary** by **Buffalo** with Paul Byron for Robyn Regehr, Ales Kotalik and Calgary's 2nd round choice (Jake McCabe) in 2012 Entry Draft, June 25, 2011. Signed as a free agent by **Karlskrona** (Sweden-2), November 27, 2012.

BYERS, Dane

(BIGH-uhrs, DAYN)

Left wing. Shoots left. 6'3", 204 lbs. Born, Nipawin, Sask., February 21, 1986. NY Rangers' 4th choice, 48th overall, in 2004 Entry Draft.

2001-02	Prince Albert	SMMHL	43	5	15	20	67	....	....	....	....	....	....	....	....	....	3	2	3	5	9	....	....	....	....
2002-03	Prince Albert	WHL	49	8	6	14	46	....	....	....	....	....	....	....	....	....	....	....	....	....	....	....	....	....	....
2003-04	Prince Albert	WHL	51	9	8	17	134	....	....	....	....	....	....	....	....	....	6	1	2	3	17	....	....	....	....
2004-05	Prince Albert	WHL	65	11	9	20	181	....	....	....	....	....	....	....	....	....	17	4	6	10	18	....	....	....	....
2005-06	Prince Albert	WHL	71	21	27	48	157	....	....	....	....	....	....	....	....	....	....	....	....	....	....	....	....	....	....
	Hartford	AHL	5	0	2	2	6	....	....	....	....	....	....	....	....	....	....	....	....	....	....	....	....	....	....
2006-07	Hartford	AHL	78	17	30	47	213	....	....	....	....	....	....	....	....	....	7	2	0	2	16	....	....	....	....
2007-08	**NY Rangers**	**NHL**	**1**	**0**	**0**	**0**	**0**	0	0	0	0	0.0	–1	0	0.0	5:05	....	....	....	....	....	....	....	....	....
	Hartford	AHL	73	23	23	46	184	....	....	....	....	....	....	....	....	....	5	2	1	3	2	....	....	....	....
2008-09	Hartford	AHL	9	4	3	7	18	....	....	....	....	....	....	....	....	....	6	3	1	4	7	....	....	....	....
2009-10	**NY Rangers**	**NHL**	**5**	**1**	**0**	**1**	**31**	0	0	0	3	33.3	1	0	0.0	6:21	....	....	....	....	....	....	....	....	....
	Hartford	AHL	74	25	27	52	100	....	....	....	....	....	....	....	....	....	....	....	....	....	....	....	....	....	....
2010-11	Connecticut	AHL	16	3	6	9	25	....	....	....	....	....	....	....	....	....	....	....	....	....	....	....	....	....	....
	Springfield	AHL	48	9	16	25	95	....	....	....	....	....	....	....	....	....	....	....	....	....	....	....	....	....	....
	San Antonio	AHL	21	3	9	12	41	....	....	....	....	....	....	....	....	....	....	....	....	....	....	....	....	....	....
2011-12	**Columbus**	**NHL**	**8**	**0**	**0**	**0**	**29**	0	0	0	8	0.0	0	0	0.0	8:05	....	....	....	....	....	....	....	....	....
	Springfield	AHL	61	16	23	39	108	....	....	....	....	....	....	....	....	....	....	....	....	....	....	....	....	....	....
2012-13	Oklahoma City	AHL	58	6	4	10	144	....	....	....	....	....	....	....	....	....	....	....	....	....	....	....	....	....	....
	Hershey Bears	AHL	5	0	0	0	11	....	....	....	....	....	....	....	....	....	1	0	1	1	0	....	....	....	....
	NHL Totals		**14**	**1**	**0**	**1**	**60**	0	0	0	11	9.1		0	0.0	7:15	....	....	....	....	....	....	....	....	....

• Missed majority of 2008-09 due to knee injury vs. Worcester (AHL), October 31, 2008. Traded to **Columbus** by **NY Rangers** for Chad Kolarik, November 11, 2010. Traded to **Phoenix** by **Columbus** with Rostislav Klesla for Scottie Upshall and Sami Lepisto, February 28, 2011. Signed as a free agent by **Columbus**. July 11, 2011. Signed as a free agent by **Edmonton**, July 5, 2012. Traded to **Washington** by **Edmonton** for Garrett Stafford, April 2, 2013.

BYFUGLIEN, Dustin

(BUHF-lihn, DUHS-tihn) **WPG**

Defense. Shoots right. 6'5", 265 lbs. Born, Minneapolis, MN, March 27, 1985. Chicago's 8th choice, 245th overall, in 2003 Entry Draft.

2001-02	Chicago Mission	MAHL	52	32	30	62	40	....	....	....	....	....	....	....	....	....	....	....	....	....	....	....	....	....	....
	Brandon	WHL	3	0	0	0	0	....	....	....	....	....	....	....	....	....	....	....	....	....	....	....	....	....	....
2002-03	Brandon	WHL	8	1	1	2	4	....	....	....	....	....	....	....	....	....	....	....	....	....	....	....	....	....	....
	Prince George	WHL	48	9	28	37	74	....	....	....	....	....	....	....	....	....	5	1	3	4	12	....	....	....	....
2003-04	Prince George	WHL	66	16	29	45	137	....	....	....	....	....	....	....	....	....	....	....	....	....	....	....	....	....	....
2004-05	Prince George	WHL	64	22	36	58	184	....	....	....	....	....	....	....	....	....	....	....	....	....	....	....	....	....	....
2005-06	**Chicago**	**NHL**	**25**	**3**	**2**	**5**	**24**	0	0	1	45	6.7	–6	0	0.0	17:19	....	....	....	....	....	....	....	....	....
	Norfolk Admirals	AHL	53	8	15	23	75	....	....	....	....	....	....	....	....	....	4	1	2	3	4	....	....	....	....
2006-07	**Chicago**	**NHL**	**9**	**1**	**2**	**3**	**10**	0	0	0	18	5.6	–2	0	0.0	17:18	....	....	....	....	....	....	....	....	....
	Norfolk Admirals	AHL	63	16	28	44	146	....	....	....	....	....	....	....	....	....	6	0	2	2	18	....	....	....	....
2007-08	**Chicago**	**NHL**	**67**	**19**	**17**	**36**	**59**	7	0	4	163	11.7	–7	1	0.0	17:02	....	....	....	....	....	....	....	....	....
	Rockford IceHogs	AHL	8	2	5	7	25	....	....	....	....	....	....	....	....	....	....	....	....	....	....	....	....	....	....
2008-09	**Chicago**	**NHL**	**77**	**15**	**16**	**31**	**81**	3	0	4	202	7.4	7	11	18.2	14:52	17	3	6	9	26	1	0	0	17:11
2009-10♦	**Chicago**	**NHL**	**82**	**17**	**17**	**34**	**94**	6	0	3	211	8.1	–7	2	50.0	16:25	22	11	5	16	20	5	0	5	16:16
2010-11	**Atlanta**	**NHL**	**81**	**20**	**33**	**53**	**93**	8	0	6	347	5.8	–2	0	0.0	23:18	....	....	....	....	....	....	....	....	....
2011-12	**Winnipeg**	**NHL**	**66**	**12**	**41**	**53**	**72**	4	0	3	223	5.4	–8	0	0.0	24:07	....	....	....	....	....	....	....	....	....
2012-13	**Winnipeg**	**NHL**	**43**	**8**	**20**	**28**	**34**	4	0	2	142	5.6	–1	0	0.0	24:24	....	....	....	....	....	....	....	....	....
	NHL Totals		**450**	**95**	**148**	**243**	**467**	32	0	23	1351	7.0		14	21.4	19:27	39	14	11	25	46	6	0	5	16:40

AHL Second All-Star Team (2007)

Played in NHL All-Star Game (2011)

Traded to **Atlanta** by **Chicago** with Brent Sopel, Ben Eager and Akim Aliu for Marty Reasoner, Joey Crabb, Jeremy Morin and New Jersey's 1st (previously acquired, Chicago selected Kevin Hayes) and 2nd (previously acquired, Chicago selected Justin Holl) round choices in 2010 Entry Draft, June 24, 2010. • Transferred to **Winnipeg** after **Atlanta** franchise relocated, June 21, 2011.

BYRON, Paul

(BIGH-ruhn, PAWL) **CGY**

Center. Shoots left. 5'9", 144 lbs. Born, Ottawa, Ont., April 27, 1989. Buffalo's 6th choice, 179th overall, in 2007 Entry Draft.

Season	Club	League	GP	G	A	Pts	PIM	PP	SH	GW	S	%	+/-	TF	F%	Min	GP	G	A	Pts	PIM	PP	SH	GW	Min
			Regular Season														Playoffs								
2005-06	Ottawa West	ON-Jr.B	33	20	23	43	33	....	....	....	....	....	....	....	....	....	7	3	8	11	4	....	....	....	....
2006-07	Gatineau	QMJHL	68	21	23	44	46	....	....	....	....	....	....	....	....	....	5	5	1	6	2	....	....	....	....
2007-08	Gatineau	QMJHL	52	37	31	68	25	....	....	....	....	....	....	....	....	....	19	*21	11	32	12	....	....	....	....
2008-09	Gatineau	QMJHL	64	33	66	99	32	....	....	....	....	....	....	....	....	....	10	2	14	16	4	....	....	....	....
2009-10	Portland Pirates	AHL	57	14	19	33	59	....	....	....	....	....	....	....	....	....	4	0	0	0	0	....	....	....	....
2010-11	**Buffalo**	**NHL**	**8**	**1**	**1**	**2**	**2**	**0**	**0**	**0**	**5**	**20.0**	**0**	**71**	**40.9**	**10:57**	....	....	....	....	....	....	....	....	....
	Portland Pirates	AHL	67	26	27	53	52	....	....	....	....	....	....	....	....	....	12	2	5	7	6	....	....	....	....
2011-12	**Calgary**	**NHL**	**22**	**3**	**2**	**5**	**2**	**0**	**0**	**1**	**13**	**23.1**	**3**	**22**	**36.4**	**10:14**	....	....	....	....	....	....	....	....	....
	Abbotsford Heat	AHL	39	7	14	21	40	....	....	....	....	....	....	....	....	....	8	1	3	4	2	....	....	....	....
2012-13	**Calgary**	**NHL**	**4**	**0**	**1**	**1**	**2**	**0**	**0**	**0**	**1**	**0.0**	**-2**	**17**	**41.2**	**10:27**	....	....	....	....	....	....	....	....	....
	Abbotsford Heat	AHL	38	6	9	15	38	....	....	....	....	....	....	....	....	....	....	....	....	....	....	....	....	....	....
	NHL Totals		**34**	**4**	**4**	**8**	**6**	**0**	**0**	**1**	**19**	**21.1**		**110**	**40.0**	**10:26**	....	....	....	....	....	....	....	....	....

QMJHL Second All-Star Team (2009)

Traded to **Calgary** by **Buffalo** with Chris Butler for Robyn Regehr, Ales Kotalik and Calgary's 2nd round choice (Jake McCabe) in 2012 Entry Draft, June 25, 2011.

CALLAHAN, Joe

(kal-AH-han, JOH)

Defense. Shoots right. 6'3", 220 lbs. Born, Brockton, MA, December 20, 1982. Phoenix's 4th choice, 70th overall, in 2002 Entry Draft.

Season	Club	League	GP	G	A	Pts	PIM	PP	SH	GW	S	%	+/-	TF	F%	Min	GP	G	A	Pts	PIM	PP	SH	GW	Min
2001-02	Yale	ECAC	31	3	8	11	20	....	....	....	....	....	....	....	....	....	....	....	....	....	....	....	....	....	....
2002-03	Yale	ECAC	32	2	11	13	38	....	....	....	....	....	....	....	....	....	....	....	....	....	....	....	....	....	....
2003-04	Yale	ECAC	31	6	14	20	38	....	....	....	....	....	....	....	....	....	....	....	....	....	....	....	....	....	....
	Springfield	AHL	13	0	4	4	12	....	....	....	....	....	....	....	....	....	....	....	....	....	....	....	....	....	....
2004-05	Utah Grizzlies	AHL	75	4	7	11	66	....	....	....	....	....	....	....	....	....	....	....	....	....	....	....	....	....	....
2005-06	San Antonio	AHL	80	1	5	6	88	....	....	....	....	....	....	....	....	....	....	....	....	....	....	....	....	....	....
2006-07	San Antonio	AHL	78	1	13	14	65	....	....	....	....	....	....	....	....	....	....	....	....	....	....	....	....	....	....
2007-08	Portland Pirates	AHL	65	1	23	24	59	....	....	....	....	....	....	....	....	....	18	1	11	12	25	....	....	....	....
2008-09	**NY Islanders**	**NHL**	**18**	**0**	**2**	**2**	**4**	**0**	**0**	**0**	**6**	**0.0**	**5**	**1**	**0.0**	**15:00**	....	....	....	....	....	....	....	....	....
	Bridgeport	AHL	56	4	9	13	38	....	....	....	....	....	....	....	....	....	5	1	2	3	4	....	....	....	....
2009-10	**San Jose**	**NHL**	**1**	**0**	**1**	**1**	**0**	**0**	**0**	**0**	**0**	**0.0**	**1**	**0**	**0.0**	**9:34**	....	....	....	....	....	....	....	....	....
	Worcester Sharks	AHL	35	4	11	15	19	....	....	....	....	....	....	....	....	....	2	0	0	0	2	....	....	....	....
2010-11	**Florida**	**NHL**	**27**	**0**	**1**	**1**	**12**	**0**	**0**	**0**	**21**	**0.0**	**-1**	**0**	**0.0**	**15:53**	....	....	....	....	....	....	....	....	....
	Rochester	AHL	48	4	9	13	12	....	....	....	....	....	....	....	....	....	....	....	....	....	....	....	....	....	....
2011-12	Hamilton	AHL	60	3	17	20	50	....	....	....	....	....	....	....	....	....	....	....	....	....	....	....	....	....	....
2012-13	Abbotsford Heat	AHL	64	0	10	10	44	....	....	....	....	....	....	....	....	....	....	....	....	....	....	....	....	....	....
	NHL Totals		**46**	**0**	**4**	**4**	**16**	**0**	**0**	**0**	**27**	**0.0**		**1**	**0.0**	**15:24**	....	....	....	....	....	....	....	....	....

Signed as a free agent by **Anaheim**, July 12, 2007. Signed as a free agent by **NY Islanders**, July 8, 2008. Signed as a free agent by **San Jose**, July 16, 2009. • Missed majority of 2009-10 due to upper-body injury, February 11, 2010. Signed as a free agent by **Florida**, August 3, 2010. Signed as a free agent by **Montreal**, October 7, 2011. Signed as a free agent by **Abbotsford** (AHL), July 24, 2012.

CALLAHAN, Ryan

(kal-AH-han, RIGH-uhn) **NYR**

Right wing. Shoots right. 5'11", 190 lbs. Born, Rochester, NY, March 21, 1985. NY Rangers' 9th choice, 127th overall, in 2004 Entry Draft.

Season	Club	League	GP	G	A	Pts	PIM	PP	SH	GW	S	%	+/-	TF	F%	Min	GP	G	A	Pts	PIM	PP	SH	GW	Min
2002-03	Guelph Storm	OHL	59	14	17	31	47	....	....	....	....	....	....	....	....	....	11	0	3	3	2	....	....	....	....
2003-04	Guelph Storm	OHL	68	36	32	68	86	....	....	....	....	....	....	....	....	....	22	*13	8	21	20	....	....	....	....
2004-05	Guelph Storm	OHL	60	28	26	54	108	....	....	....	....	....	....	....	....	....	4	1	1	2	6	....	....	....	....
2005-06	Guelph Storm	OHL	62	52	32	84	126	....	....	....	....	....	....	....	....	....	13	7	17	24	20	....	....	....	....
2006-07	**NY Rangers**	**NHL**	**14**	**4**	**2**	**6**	**9**	**0**	**0**	**1**	**40**	**10.0**	**5**	**3**	**66.7**	**10:31**	**10**	**2**	**1**	**3**	**6**	**1**	**0**	**0**	**12:19**
	Hartford	AHL	60	35	20	55	74	....	....	....	....	....	....	....	....	....	....	....	....	....	....	....	....	....	....
2007-08	**NY Rangers**	**NHL**	**52**	**8**	**5**	**13**	**31**	**0**	**1**	**1**	**92**	**8.7**	**7**	**5**	**20.0**	**12:22**	**10**	**2**	**2**	**4**	**10**	**0**	**1**	**1**	**15:55**
	Hartford	AHL	11	7	8	15	27	....	....	....	....	....	....	....	....	....	....	....	....	....	....	....	....	....	....
2008-09	**NY Rangers**	**NHL**	**81**	**22**	**18**	**40**	**45**	**2**	**1**	**1**	**237**	**9.3**	**7**	**10**	**70.0**	**17:04**	**7**	**2**	**0**	**2**	**4**	**1**	**0**	**1**	**19:44**
2009-10	**NY Rangers**	**NHL**	**77**	**19**	**18**	**37**	**48**	**9**	**0**	**3**	**204**	**9.3**	**-12**	**35**	**48.6**	**19:24**	....	....	....	....	....	....	....	....	....
	United States	Olympics	6	0	1	1	2	....	....	....	....	....	....	....	....	....	....	....	....	....	....	....	....	....	....
2010-11	**NY Rangers**	**NHL**	**60**	**23**	**25**	**48**	**46**	**10**	**0**	**5**	**179**	**12.8**	**-7**	**17**	**11.8**	**19:54**	....	....	....	....	....	....	....	....	....
2011-12	**NY Rangers**	**NHL**	**76**	**29**	**25**	**54**	**61**	**13**	**1**	**9**	**235**	**12.3**	**-8**	**20**	**50.0**	**21:02**	**20**	**6**	**4**	**10**	**12**	**2**	**0**	**0**	**23:32**
2012-13	**NY Rangers**	**NHL**	**45**	**16**	**15**	**31**	**12**	**6**	**2**	**4**	**144**	**11.1**	**9**	**30**	**46.7**	**21:31**	**12**	**2**	**3**	**5**	**6**	**0**	**0**	**0**	**23:22**
	NHL Totals		**405**	**121**	**108**	**229**	**252**	**40**	**5**	**24**	**1131**	**10.7**		**120**	**44.2**	**18:20**	**59**	**14**	**10**	**24**	**38**	**4**	**1**	**2**	**19:51**

OHL Second All-Star Team (2006) • AHL All-Rookie Team (2007)

CALVERT, Matt

(KAL-vuhrt, MAT) **CBJ**

Left wing. Shoots left. 5'10", 187 lbs. Born, Brandon, Man., December 24, 1989. Columbus' 5th choice, 127th overall, in 2008 Entry Draft.

Season	Club	League	GP	G	A	Pts	PIM	PP	SH	GW	S	%	+/-	TF	F%	Min	GP	G	A	Pts	PIM	PP	SH	GW	Min
2005-06	Brandon	MMHL	38	24	30	54	48	....	....	....	....	....	....	....	....	....	6	3	6	9	18	....	....	....	....
2006-07	Brandon	MMHL	30	28	55	83	46	....	....	....	....	....	....	....	....	....	16	5	13	18	16	....	....	....	....
	Winkler Flyers	MJHL	1	0	0	0	15	....	....	....	....	....	....	....	....	....	....	....	....	....	....	....	....	....	....
2007-08	Brandon	WHL	72	24	40	64	53	....	....	....	....	....	....	....	....	....	6	1	2	3	2	....	....	....	....
2008-09	Brandon	WHL	58	28	39	67	58	....	....	....	....	....	....	....	....	....	12	9	8	17	22	....	....	....	....
2009-10	Brandon	WHL	68	47	52	99	70	....	....	....	....	....	....	....	....	....	15	9	7	16	15	....	....	....	....
2010-11	**Columbus**	**NHL**	**42**	**11**	**9**	**20**	**12**	**3**	**0**	**1**	**50**	**22.0**	**3**	**9**	**33.3**	**11:06**	....	....	....	....	....	....	....	....	....
	Springfield	AHL	38	13	12	25	12	....	....	....	....	....	....	....	....	....	....	....	....	....	....	....	....	....	....
2011-12	**Columbus**	**NHL**	**13**	**0**	**3**	**3**	**16**	**0**	**0**	**0**	**4**	**0.0**	**-5**	**0**	**0.0**	**9:08**	....	....	....	....	....	....	....	....	....
	Springfield	AHL	56	17	19	36	52	....	....	....	....	....	....	....	....	....	....	....	....	....	....	....	....	....	....
2012-13	Springfield	AHL	34	10	11	21	39	....	....	....	....	....	....	....	....	....	....	....	....	....	....	....	....	....	....
	Columbus	**NHL**	**42**	**9**	**7**	**16**	**32**	**0**	**1**	**2**	**63**	**14.3**	**-9**	**6**	**33.3**	**14:11**	....	....	....	....	....	....	....	....	....
	NHL Totals		**97**	**20**	**19**	**39**	**60**	**3**	**1**	**3**	**117**	**17.1**		**15**	**33.3**	**12:10**	....	....	....	....	....	....	....	....	....

WHL East Second All-Star Team (2010) • Memorial Cup All-Star Team (2010)

CAMMALLERI, Mike

(kam-UH-LAIR-ee, MIGHK) **CGY**

Center/Wing. Shoots left. 5'9", 190 lbs. Born, Richmond Hill, Ont., June 8, 1982. Los Angeles' 3rd choice, 49th overall, in 2001 Entry Draft.

Season	Club	League	GP	G	A	Pts	PIM	PP	SH	GW	S	%	+/-	TF	F%	Min	GP	G	A	Pts	PIM	PP	SH	GW	Min
1997-98	Bramalea Blues	ON-Jr.A	46	36	52	88	30	....	....	....	....	....	....	....	....	....	....	....	....	....	....	....	....	....	....
1998-99	Bramalea Blues	ON-Jr.A	41	31	72	103	51	....	....	....	....	....	....	....	....	....	....	....	....	....	....	....	....	....	....
99-2000	U. of Michigan	CCHA	39	13	13	26	32	....	....	....	....	....	....	....	....	....	....	....	....	....	....	....	....	....	....
2000-01	U. of Michigan	CCHA	42	*29	32	61	24	....	....	....	....	....	....	....	....	....	....	....	....	....	....	....	....	....	....
2001-02	U. of Michigan	CCHA	29	23	21	44	28	....	....	....	....	....	....	....	....	....	....	....	....	....	....	....	....	....	....
2002-03	**Los Angeles**	**NHL**	**28**	**5**	**3**	**8**	**22**	**2**	**0**	**2**	**40**	**12.5**	**-4**	**253**	**51.4**	**14:05**	....	....	....	....	....	....	....	....	....
	Manchester	AHL	13	5	15	20	12	....	....	....	....	....	....	....	....	....	....	....	....	....	....	....	....	....	....
2003-04	**Los Angeles**	**NHL**	**31**	**9**	**6**	**15**	**20**	**2**	**0**	**2**	**53**	**17.0**	**1**	**280**	**53.6**	**13:18**	....	....	....	....	....	....	....	....	....
	Manchester	AHL	41	20	19	39	28	....	....	....	....	....	....	....	....	....	1	0	1	1	0	....	....	....	....
2004-05	Manchester	AHL	79	*46	63	109	60	....	....	....	....	....	....	....	....	....	6	1	5	6	0	....	....	....	....
2005-06	**Los Angeles**	**NHL**	**80**	**26**	**29**	**55**	**50**	**15**	**0**	**4**	**206**	**12.6**	**-14**	**578**	**53.5**	**16:45**	....	....	....	....	....	....	....	....	....
2006-07	**Los Angeles**	**NHL**	**81**	**34**	**46**	**80**	**48**	**16**	**0**	**5**	**299**	**11.4**	**5**	**301**	**54.2**	**18:03**	....	....	....	....	....	....	....	....	....
2007-08	**Los Angeles**	**NHL**	**63**	**19**	**28**	**47**	**30**	**10**	**0**	**1**	**210**	**9.0**	**-16**	**380**	**54.2**	**18:35**	....	....	....	....	....	....	....	....	....
2008-09	**Calgary**	**NHL**	**81**	**39**	**43**	**82**	**44**	**19**	**0**	**6**	**255**	**15.3**	**-2**	**368**	**60.3**	**17:33**	**6**	**1**	**2**	**3**	**2**	**0**	**0**	**0**	**18:02**
2009-10	**Montreal**	**NHL**	**65**	**26**	**24**	**50**	**16**	**4**	**0**	**4**	**218**	**11.9**	**7**	**51**	**51.0**	**19:31**	**19**	***13**	**6**	**19**	**6**	**4**	**0**	**3**	**20:40**
2010-11	**Montreal**	**NHL**	**67**	**19**	**28**	**47**	**33**	**7**	**0**	**2**	**193**	**9.8**	**2**	**74**	**44.6**	**18:29**	**7**	**3**	**7**	**10**	**0**	**1**	**0**	**0**	**23:35**
2011-12	**Montreal**	**NHL**	**38**	**9**	**13**	**22**	**10**	**1**	**0**	**2**	**111**	**8.1**	**-6**	**29**	**34.5**	**17:49**	....	....	....	....	....	....	....	....	....
	Calgary	**NHL**	**28**	**11**	**8**	**19**	**16**	**2**	**0**	**2**	**64**	**17.2**	**-4**	**199**	**47.2**	**18:30**	....	....	....	....	....	....	....	....	....
2012-13	**Calgary**	**NHL**	**44**	**13**	**19**	**32**	**25**	**5**	**0**	**3**	**102**	**12.7**	**-15**	**496**	**51.0**	**18:03**	....	....	....	....	....	....	....	....	....
	NHL Totals		**606**	**210**	**247**	**457**	**314**	**83**	**0**	**33**	**1751**	**12.0**		**3009**	**53.0**	**17:39**	**32**	**17**	**15**	**32**	**8**	**5**	**0**	**3**	**20:49**

CCHA First All-Star Team (2001) • NCAA West Second All-American Team (2001) • CCHA Second All-Star Team (2002) • NCAA West First All-American Team (2002) • AHL Second All-Star Team (2005) • Willie Marshall Award (AHL - Top Goal-scorer) (2005)

• Missed majority of 2002-03 due to head injury vs. San Jose, January 28, 2003. Traded to **Calgary** by **Los Angeles** with Calgary's 2nd round choice (previously acquired, Calgary selected Mitch Wahl) in 2008 Entry Draft for Calgary's 1st round choice (later traded to Anaheim – Anaheim selected Jake Gardiner) in 2008 Entry Draft and Calgary's 2nd round choice (later traded to Carolina – Carolina selected Brian Dumoulin) in 2009 Entry Draft, June 20, 2008. Signed as a free agent by **Montreal**, July 1, 2009. Traded to **Calgary** by **Montreal** with Karri Ramo and Montreal's 5th round choice (Ryan Culkin) in 2012 Entry Draft for Rene Bourque, Patrick Holland and Calgary's 2nd round choice (Zachary Fucale) in 2013 Entry Draft, January 12, 2012.

CAMPBELL, Brian (KAM-behl, BRIGH-uhn) FLA

Defense. Shoots left. 5'10", 190 lbs. Born, Strathroy, Ont., May 23, 1979. Buffalo's 7th choice, 156th overall, in 1997 Entry Draft.

			Regular Season														Playoffs								
Season	Club	League	GP	G	A	Pts	PIM	PP	SH	GW	S	%	+/-	TF	F%	Min	GP	G	A	Pts	PIM	PP	SH	GW	Min
1994-95	Petrolia Oil Barons	ON-Jr.B	49	11	27	38	43	....	....	....	....	....	....	....	....	....	....	....	....	....	....	....	....	....	....
1995-96	Ottawa 67's	OHL	66	5	22	27	23	....	....	....	....	....	....	....	....	....	4	0	1	1	2	....	....	....	....
1996-97	Ottawa 67's	OHL	66	7	36	43	12	....	....	....	....	....	....	....	....	....	24	2	11	13	8	....	....	....	....
1997-98	Ottawa 67's	OHL	66	14	39	53	31	....	....	....	....	....	....	....	....	....	13	1	14	15	0	....	....	....	....
1998-99	Ottawa 67's	OHL	62	12	75	87	27	....	....	....	....	....	....	....	....	....	9	2	10	12	6	....	....	....	....
	Rochester	AHL	....	....	....	....	....	....	....	....	....	....	....	....	....	....	2	0	0	0	0	....	....	....	....
99-2000	Buffalo	NHL	12	1	4	5	4	0	0	0	10	10.0	-2	0	0.0	15:48	....	....	....	....	....	....	....	....	....
	Rochester	AHL	67	2	24	26	22	....	....	....	....	....	....	....	....	....	21	0	3	3	0	....	....	....	....
2000-01	Buffalo	NHL	8	0	0	0	2	0	0	0	7	0.0	-2	0	0.0	15:40	....	....	....	....	....	....	....	....	....
	Rochester	AHL	65	7	25	32	24	....	....	....	....	....	....	....	....	....	4	0	1	1	0	....	....	....	....
2001-02	Buffalo	NHL	29	3	3	6	12	0	0	0	30	10.0	0	1	0.0	15:18	....	....	....	....	....	....	....	....	....
	Rochester	AHL	45	2	35	37	13	....	....	....	....	....	....	....	....	....	....	....	....	....	....	....	....	....	....
2002-03	Buffalo	NHL	65	2	17	19	20	0	0	1	90	2.2	-8	1	0.0	18:40	....	....	....	....	....	....	....	....	....
2003-04	Buffalo	NHL	53	3	8	11	12	0	0	0	45	6.7	-8	0	0.0	16:02	....	....	....	....	....	....	....	....	....
2004-05	Jokerit Helsinki	Finland	44	12	13	25	12	....	....	....	....	....	....	....	....	....	12	3	4	7	6	....	....	....	....
2005-06	Buffalo	NHL	79	12	32	44	16	5	0	5	105	11.4	-14	0	0.0	17:43	18	0	6	6	12	0	0	0	20:29
2006-07	Buffalo	NHL	82	6	42	48	35	1	0	1	92	6.5	28	0	0.0	21:53	16	3	4	7	14	2	0	0	21:39
2007-08	Buffalo	NHL	63	5	38	43	12	3	0	0	102	4.9	-1	0	0.0	25:06	....	....	....	....	....	....	....	....	....
	San Jose	NHL	20	3	16	19	8	2	0	0	40	7.5	9	0	0.0	25:07	13	1	6	7	4	0	0	0	29:19
2008-09	Chicago	NHL	82	7	45	52	22	4	0	1	108	6.5	5	0	0.0	22:34	17	2	8	10	0	2	0	0	20:29
2009-10 ♦	Chicago	NHL	68	7	31	38	18	3	0	2	131	5.3	18	0	0.0	23:13	19	1	4	5	2	0	0	0	19:35
2010-11	Chicago	NHL	65	5	22	27	6	2	0	1	84	6.0	28	0	0.0	22:59	7	1	2	3	6	0	0	0	26:26
2011-12	Florida	NHL	82	4	49	53	6	1	0	0	131	3.1	-9	0	0.0	26:54	7	1	4	5	2	1	0	1	28:00
2012-13	Florida	NHL	48	8	19	27	12	6	0	2	70	11.4	-22	0	0.0	26:25	....	....	....	....	....	....	....	....	....
	NHL Totals		756	66	326	392	185	27	0	13	1045	6.3		2	0.0	21:49	97	9	34	43	40	5	0	1	22:39

OHL First All-Star Team (1999) • OHL MVP (1999) • Canadian Major Junior First All-Star Team (1999) • Canadian Major Junior Player of the Year (1999) • George Parsons Trophy (Memorial Cup - Most Sportsmanlike Player) (1999) • NHL Second All-Star Team (2008) • Lady Byng Trophy (2012)

Played in NHL All-Star Game (2007, 2008, 2009, 2012)

Signed as a free agent by **Jokerit Helsinki** (Finland), October 19, 2004. Traded to **San Jose** by **Buffalo** with Buffalo's 7th round choice (Drew Daniels) in 2008 Entry Draft for Steve Bernier and San Jose's 1st round choice (Tyler Ennis) in 2008 Entry Draft, February 26, 2008. Signed as a free agent by **Chicago**, July 1, 2008. Traded to **Florida** by **Chicago** for Rostislav Olesz, June 25, 2011.

CAMPBELL, Gregory (KAM-behl, GREH-goh-ree) BOS

Left wing. Shoots left. 6', 197 lbs. Born, London, Ont., December 17, 1983. Florida's 4th choice, 67th overall, in 2002 Entry Draft.

Season	Club	League	GP	G	A	Pts	PIM	PP	SH	GW	S	%	+/-	TF	F%	Min	GP	G	A	Pts	PIM	PP	SH	GW	Min
1998-99	Aylmer Aces	ON-Jr.B	49	5	9	14	44	....	....	....	....	....	....	....	....	....	....	....	....	....	....	....	....	....	....
99-2000	St. Thomas Stars	ON-Jr.B	51	12	8	20	51	....	....	....	....	....	....	....	....	....	....	....	....	....	....	....	....	....	....
2000-01	Plymouth Whalers	OHL	65	2	12	14	40	....	....	....	....	....	....	....	....	....	10	0	0	0	7	....	....	....	....
2001-02	Plymouth Whalers	OHL	65	17	36	53	105	....	....	....	....	....	....	....	....	....	6	0	2	2	13	....	....	....	....
2002-03	Kitchener Rangers	OHL	55	23	33	56	116	....	....	....	....	....	....	....	....	....	21	15	4	19	34	....	....	....	....
2003-04	Florida	NHL	2	0	0	0	5	0	0	0	0	0.0	-1	1	0.0	9:09	....	....	....	....	....	....	....	....	....
	San Antonio	AHL	76	13	16	29	73	....	....	....	....	....	....	....	....	....	....	....	....	....	....	....	....	....	....
2004-05	San Antonio	AHL	70	12	16	28	113	....	....	....	....	....	....	....	....	....	....	....	....	....	....	....	....	....	....
2005-06	Florida	NHL	64	3	6	9	40	0	0	0	59	5.1	-11	38	34.2	8:38	....	....	....	....	....	....	....	....	....
	Rochester	AHL	11	3	3	6	30	....	....	....	....	....	....	....	....	....	....	....	....	....	....	....	....	....	....
2006-07	Florida	NHL	79	6	3	9	66	0	1	0	103	5.8	-10	588	45.2	10:34	....	....	....	....	....	....	....	....	....
2007-08	Florida	NHL	81	5	13	18	72	0	2	1	113	4.4	-12	460	51.1	12:27	....	....	....	....	....	....	....	....	....
2008-09	Florida	NHL	77	13	19	32	76	1	0	1	135	9.6	0	1018	50.0	16:47	....	....	....	....	....	....	....	....	....
2009-10	Florida	NHL	60	2	15	17	53	0	0	1	84	2.4	-5	341	46.3	15:24	....	....	....	....	....	....	....	....	....
2010-11 ♦	Boston	NHL	80	13	16	29	93	1	1	1	98	13.3	11	832	51.7	13:26	25	1	3	4	4	0	0	0	10:59
2011-12	Boston	NHL	78	8	8	16	80	0	0	0	74	10.8	-3	678	50.7	12:48	7	0	2	2	0	0	0	0	10:51
2012-13	Boston	NHL	48	4	9	13	41	0	1	0	52	7.7	2	401	47.1	13:43	15	3	4	7	11	0	0	1	11:35
	NHL Totals		569	54	89	143	526	2	5	4	718	7.5		4357	49.2	12:56	47	4	9	13	15	0	0	1	11:10

Memorial Cup All-Star Team (2003) • George Parsons Trophy (Memorial Cup - Most Sportsmanlike Player) (2003) • Ed Chynoweth Trophy (Memorial Cup - Leading Scorer) (2003)

Traded to **Boston** by **Florida** with Nathan Horton for Dennis Wideman, Boston's 1st round choice (later traded to Los Angeles – Los Angeles selected Derek Forbert) in 2010 Entry Draft and Boston's 3rd round choice (Kyle Rau) in 2011 Entry Draft, June 22, 2010.

CAMPER, Carter (KAM-puhr, KAR-tuhr) BOS

Right wing. Shoots right. 5'9", 176 lbs. Born, Rocky River, OH, July 6, 1988.

Season	Club	League	GP	G	A	Pts	PIM	PP	SH	GW	S	%	+/-	TF	F%	Min	GP	G	A	Pts	PIM	PP	SH	GW	Min
2004-05	Cleveland Barons	NAHL	54	14	23	37	12	....	....	....	....	....	....	....	....	....	....	....	....	....	....	....	....	....	....
2005-06	Cleveland Barons	NAHL	57	31	51	82	26	....	....	....	....	....	....	....	....	....	14	6	15	21	4	....	....	....	....
2006-07	Lincoln Stars	USHL	56	23	48	71	40	....	....	....	....	....	....	....	....	....	4	1	1	2	2	....	....	....	....
2007-08	Miami U.	CCHA	33	15	26	41	20	....	....	....	....	....	....	....	....	....	....	....	....	....	....	....	....	....	....
2008-09	Miami U.	CCHA	40	20	22	42	24	....	....	....	....	....	....	....	....	....	....	....	....	....	....	....	....	....	....
2009-10	Miami U.	CCHA	44	15	28	43	14	....	....	....	....	....	....	....	....	....	....	....	....	....	....	....	....	....	....
2010-11	Miami U.	CCHA	39	19	38	57	27	....	....	....	....	....	....	....	....	....	....	....	....	....	....	....	....	....	....
	Providence Bruins	AHL	3	1	1	2	2	....	....	....	....	....	....	....	....	....	....	....	....	....	....	....	....	....	....
2011-12	Boston	NHL	3	1	0	1	0	0	0	0	1	100.0	1	14	42.9	6:42	....	....	....	....	....	....	....	....	....
	Providence Bruins	AHL	69	18	30	48	18	....	....	....	....	....	....	....	....	....	....	....	....	....	....	....	....	....	....
2012-13	Providence Bruins	AHL	57	10	37	47	6	....	....	....	....	....	....	....	....	....	12	8	5	13	0	....	....	....	....
	NHL Totals		3	1	0	1	0	0	0	0	1	100.0		14	42.9	6:42	....	....	....	....	....	....	....	....	....

CCHA All-Rookie Team (2008) • CCHA First All-Star Team (2009, 2011) • NCAA West Second All-American Team (2009, 2011)

Signed as a free agent by **Boston**, April 7, 2011.

CAMPOLI, Chris (kam-POH-lee, KRIHS)

Defense. Shoots left. 6', 200 lbs. Born, North York, Ont., July 9, 1984. NY Islanders' 8th choice, 227th overall, in 2004 Entry Draft.

Season	Club	League	GP	G	A	Pts	PIM	PP	SH	GW	S	%	+/-	TF	F%	Min	GP	G	A	Pts	PIM	PP	SH	GW	Min
2000-01	Erie Otters	OHL	52	1	9	10	47	....	....	....	....	....	....	....	....	....	15	0	0	0	4	....	....	....	....
2001-02	Erie Otters	OHL	68	2	24	26	117	....	....	....	....	....	....	....	....	....	20	0	5	5	18	....	....	....	....
2002-03	Erie Otters	OHL	60	8	40	48	82	....	....	....	....	....	....	....	....	....	....	....	....	....	....	....	....	....	....
2003-04	Erie Otters	OHL	67	20	46	66	66	....	....	....	....	....	....	....	....	....	8	0	6	6	16	....	....	....	....
2004-05	Bridgeport	AHL	79	15	34	49	78	....	....	....	....	....	....	....	....	....	....	....	....	....	....	....	....	....	....
2005-06	NY Islanders	NHL	80	9	25	34	46	2	0	2	123	7.3	-16	0	0.0	18:32	....	....	....	....	....	....	....	....	....
2006-07	NY Islanders	NHL	51	1	13	14	23	0	0	0	41	2.4	-3	0	0.0	14:50	5	1	1	2	2	0	0	0	13:30
	Bridgeport	AHL	15	3	3	6	8	....	....	....	....	....	....	....	....	....	....	....	....	....	....	....	....	....	....
2007-08	NY Islanders	NHL	46	4	14	18	16	2	1	0	68	5.9	-1	0	0.0	19:09	....	....	....	....	....	....	....	....	....
2008-09	NY Islanders	NHL	51	6	11	17	43	0	1	2	53	11.3	-20	0	0.0	19:50	....	....	....	....	....	....	....	....	....
	Ottawa	NHL	25	5	8	13	12	2	0	2	38	13.2	4	0	0.0	18:58	....	....	....	....	....	....	....	....	....
2009-10	Ottawa	NHL	67	4	14	18	16	1	0	1	71	5.6	-3	1	0.0	17:51	6	0	2	2	4	0	0	0	19:48
2010-11	Ottawa	NHL	58	3	11	14	34	0	0	0	59	5.1	-3	0	0.0	18:49	....	....	....	....	....	....	....	....	....
	Chicago	NHL	19	1	6	7	2	1	0	1	25	4.0	3	0	0.0	20:08	7	0	1	1	2	0	0	0	18:56
2011-12	Montreal	NHL	43	2	9	11	8	0	0	0	43	4.7	-3	0	0.0	17:12	....	....	....	....	....	....	....	....	....
2012-13	EHC Biel-Bienne	Swiss	4	0	3	3	2	....	....	....	....	....	....	....	....	....	6	1	5	6	4	....	....	....	....
	NHL Totals		440	35	111	146	200	8	2	8	521	6.7		1	0.0	18:13	18	1	4	5	8	0	0	0	17:43

OHL Humanitarian Player of the Year (2004) • Canadian Major Junior Humanitarian Player of the Year (2004) • AHL All-Rookie Team (2005)

Traded to **Ottawa** by **NY Islanders** with Mike Comrie for Dean McAmmond and San Jose's 1st round choice (previously acquired, later traded to Columbus, later traded to Anahaim – Anaheim selected Kyle Palmieri) in 2009 Entry Draft, February 20, 2009. Traded to **Chicago** by **Ottawa** with future considerations for Ryan Potulny and Chicago's 2nd round choice (later traded to Detroit – Detroit selected Xavier Ouellet) in 2011 Entry Draft, February 28, 2011. Signed as a free agent by **Montreal**, September 26, 2011. Signed as a free agent by **Biel-Bienne** (Swiss), February 13, 2013. Signed as a free agent by **Lugano** (Swiss), July 29, 2013.

CAPUTI, Luca
(ka-POO-tee, LOO-ka)

Left wing. Shoots left. 6'3", 200 lbs. Born, Toronto, Ont., October 1, 1988. Pittsburgh's 5th choice, 111th overall, in 2007 Entry Draft.

			Regular Season														Playoffs								
Season	Club	League	GP	G	A	Pts	PIM	PP	SH	GW	S	%	+/-	TF	F%	Min	GP	G	A	Pts	PIM	PP	SH	GW	Min
2003-04	Tor. Jr. Canadiens	GTHL	53	52	55	107	127	....	....	....	....	....	....	....	....	....	....	....	....	....	....	....	....	....	....
2004-05	Mississauga	OHL	48	5	1	6	25	....	....	....	....	....	....	....	....	....	....	....	....	....	....	....	....	....	....
2005-06	Mississauga	OHL	32	3	0	3	43	....	....	....	....	....	....	....	....	....	....	....	....	....	....	....	....	....	....
2006-07	Mississauga	OHL	68	27	38	65	66	....	....	....	....	....	....	....	....	....	5	2	1	3	0	....	....	....	....
2007-08	Niagara Ice Dogs	OHL	66	51	60	111	107	....	....	....	....	....	....	....	....	....	10	8	9	17	14	....	....	....	....
	Wilkes-Barre	AHL	....	....	....	....	....	....	....	....	....	....	....	....	....	....	19	4	4	8	8	....	....	....	....
2008-09	**Pittsburgh**	**NHL**	**5**	**1**	**0**	**1**	**4**	**0**	**0**	**0**	**7**	**14.3**	**–1**	**0**	**0.0**	**10:16**	....	....	....	....	....	....	....	....	....
	Wilkes-Barre	AHL	66	18	27	45	45	....	....	....	....	....	....	....	....	....	12	3	5	8	10	....	....	....	....
	Wheeling Nailers	ECHL	3	2	1	3	0	....	....	....	....	....	....	....	....	....	....	....	....	....	....	....	....	....	....
2009-10	**Pittsburgh**	**NHL**	**4**	**1**	**1**	**2**	**2**	**0**	**0**	**0**	**4**	**25.0**	**–1**	**0**	**0.0**	**11:46**	....	....	....	....	....	....	....	....	....
	Wilkes-Barre	AHL	54	23	24	47	61	....	....	....	....	....	....	....	....	....	....	....	....	....	....	....	....	....	....
	Toronto	**NHL**	**19**	**1**	**5**	**6**	**10**	**0**	**0**	**0**	**32**	**3.1**	**0**	**23**	**43.5**	**14:38**	....	....	....	....	....	....	....	....	....
2010-11	**Toronto**	**NHL**	**7**	**0**	**0**	**0**	**4**	**0**	**0**	**0**	**8**	**0.0**	**–2**	**6**	**33.3**	**11:04**	....	....	....	....	....	....	....	....	....
	Toronto Marlies	AHL	13	1	4	5	30	....	....	....	....	....	....	....	....	....	....	....	....	....	....	....	....	....	....
2011-12	Toronto Marlies	AHL	21	2	1	3	10	....	....	....	....	....	....	....	....	....	....	....	....	....	....	....	....	....	....
	Syracuse Crunch	AHL	39	10	12	22	19	....	....	....	....	....	....	....	....	....	....	....	....	....	....	....	....	....	....
2012-13	Norfolk Admirals	AHL	35	3	15	18	23	....	....	....	....	....	....	....	....	....	....	....	....	....	....	....	....	....	....
	Fort Wayne	ECHL	15	6	8	14	17	....	....	....	....	....	....	....	....	....	....	....	....	....	....	....	....	....	....
	NHL Totals		**35**	**3**	**6**	**9**	**20**	**0**	**0**	**0**	**51**	**5.9**		**29**	**41.4**	**12:58**	....	....	....	....	....	....	....	....	....

OHL Second All-Star Team (2008)

Traded to **Toronto** by **Pittsburgh** with Martin Skoula for Alexei Ponikarovsky, March 2, 2010. • Missed majority of 2010-11 due to sports hernia surgery. Traded to **Anaheim** by **Toronto** for Nicolas Deschamps, January 3, 2012. • Loaned to **Fort Wayne** (ECHL) by **Anaheim** (Norfolk-AHL), November 27, 2012.

CARCILLO, Daniel
(KAR-sihl-oh, DAN-yuhl) **L.A.**

Left wing. Shoots left. 6', 203 lbs. Born, King City, Ont., January 28, 1985. Pittsburgh's 4th choice, 73rd overall, in 2003 Entry Draft.

			Regular Season														Playoffs								
Season	Club	League	GP	G	A	Pts	PIM	PP	SH	GW	S	%	+/-	TF	F%	Min	GP	G	A	Pts	PIM	PP	SH	GW	Min
2001-02	Milton Merchants	ON-Jr.B	47	15	16	31	162	....	....	....	....	....	....	....	....	....	....	....	....	....	....	....	....	....	....
2002-03	Sarnia Sting	OHL	68	29	37	66	157	....	....	....	....	....	....	....	....	....	6	0	4	4	14	....	....	....	....
2003-04	Sarnia Sting	OHL	61	30	29	59	148	....	....	....	....	....	....	....	....	....	4	1	2	3	12	....	....	....	....
2004-05	Sarnia Sting	OHL	12	2	7	9	40	....	....	....	....	....	....	....	....	....	....	....	....	....	....	....	....	....	....
	Mississauga	OHL	20	8	10	18	75	....	....	....	....	....	....	....	....	....	5	3	1	4	18	....	....	....	....
2005-06	Wilkes-Barre	AHL	51	11	13	24	311	....	....	....	....	....	....	....	....	....	11	1	0	1	47	....	....	....	....
	Wheeling Nailers	ECHL	6	3	2	5	32	....	....	....	....	....	....	....	....	....	....	....	....	....	....	....	....	....	....
2006-07	Wilkes-Barre	AHL	52	21	9	30	183	....	....	....	....	....	....	....	....	....	....	....	....	....	....	....	....	....	....
	Phoenix	**NHL**	**18**	**4**	**3**	**7**	**74**	**3**	**0**	**0**	**32**	**12.5**	**–7**	**0**	**0.0**	**14:56**	....	....	....	....	....	....	....	....	....
2007-08	**Phoenix**	**NHL**	**57**	**13**	**11**	**24**	***324**	**3**	**0**	**1**	**106**	**12.3**	**1**	**5**	**80.0**	**12:43**	....	....	....	....	....	....	....	....	....
	San Antonio	AHL	5	2	1	3	16	....	....	....	....	....	....	....	....	....	....	....	....	....	....	....	....	....	....
2008-09	**Phoenix**	**NHL**	**54**	**3**	**7**	**10**	***174**	**2**	**0**	**0**	**95**	**3.2**	**–13**	**18**	**55.6**	**11:59**	....	....	....	....	....	....	....	....	....
	Philadelphia	**NHL**	**20**	**0**	**4**	**4**	***80**	**0**	**0**	**0**	**35**	**0.0**	**–2**	**2**	**100.0**	**10:16**	**5**	**1**	**1**	**2**	**5**	**0**	**0**	**0**	**8:11**
2009-10	**Philadelphia**	**NHL**	**76**	**12**	**10**	**22**	**207**	**1**	**0**	**1**	**105**	**11.4**	**5**	**3**	**33.3**	**11:15**	**17**	**2**	**4**	**6**	**34**	**0**	**0**	**1**	**10:32**
2010-11	**Philadelphia**	**NHL**	**57**	**4**	**2**	**6**	**127**	**0**	**0**	**2**	**56**	**7.1**	**–14**	**2**	**50.0**	**7:46**	**11**	**2**	**1**	**3**	**30**	**0**	**0**	**0**	**8:25**
2011-12	**Chicago**	**NHL**	**28**	**2**	**9**	**11**	**82**	**0**	**0**	**0**	**27**	**7.4**	**10**	**4**	**50.0**	**11:24**	....	....	....	....	....	....	....	....	....
2012-13	**Chicago**	**NHL**	**23**	**2**	**1**	**3**	**11**	**0**	**0**	**1**	**23**	**8.7**	**1**	**1**	**0.0**	**9:00**	**4**	**0**	**1**	**1**	**6**	**0**	**0**	**0**	**6:41**
	NHL Totals		**333**	**40**	**47**	**87**	**1079**	**9**	**0**	**5**	**479**	**8.4**		**35**	**57.1**	**11:01**	**37**	**5**	**7**	**12**	**75**	**0**	**0**	**1**	**9:10**

Traded to **Phoenix** by **Pittsburgh** with Pittsburgh's 3rd round choice (later traded to NY Rangers - NY Rangers selected Tomas Kundratek) in 2008 Entry Draft for Georges Laraque, February 27, 2007. Traded to **Philadelphia** by **Phoenix** for Scottie Upshall and Philadelphia's 2nd round choice (Lucas Lessio) in 2011 Entry Draft, March 4, 2009. Signed as a free agent by **Chicago**, July 1, 2011. • Missed majority of 2011-12 due to knee injury vs. Edmonton, January 2, 2012. Traded to **Los Angeles** by **Chicago** for future considerations, July 16, 2013.

CARKNER, Matt
(KARK-nehr, MAT) **NYI**

Defense. Shoots right. 6'4", 227 lbs. Born, Winchester, Ont., November 3, 1980. Montreal's 2nd choice, 58th overall, in 1999 Entry Draft.

			Regular Season														Playoffs								
Season	Club	League	GP	G	A	Pts	PIM	PP	SH	GW	S	%	+/-	TF	F%	Min	GP	G	A	Pts	PIM	PP	SH	GW	Min
1996-97	Winchester	ON-Jr.B	29	1	18	19	....	....	....	....	....	....	....	....	....	....	....	....	....	....	....	....	....	....	....
	Brockville Braves	ON-Jr.A	7	0	0	0	37	....	....	....	....	....	....	....	....	....	9	0	1	1	6	....	....	....	....
1997-98	Peterborough	OHL	57	0	6	6	121	....	....	....	....	....	....	....	....	....	4	0	0	0	2	....	....	....	....
1998-99	Peterborough	OHL	60	2	16	18	173	....	....	....	....	....	....	....	....	....	5	0	0	0	20	....	....	....	....
99-2000	Peterborough	OHL	62	3	13	16	177	....	....	....	....	....	....	....	....	....	5	0	1	1	6	....	....	....	....
2000-01	Peterborough	OHL	53	8	8	16	128	....	....	....	....	....	....	....	....	....	7	0	3	3	25	....	....	....	....
2001-02	Cleveland Barons	AHL	74	0	3	3	335	....	....	....	....	....	....	....	....	....	....	....	....	....	....	....	....	....	....
2002-03	Cleveland Barons	AHL	39	1	4	5	104	....	....	....	....	....	....	....	....	....	....	....	....	....	....	....	....	....	....
2003-04	Cleveland Barons	AHL	60	2	11	13	115	....	....	....	....	....	....	....	....	....	9	0	3	3	39	....	....	....	....
2004-05	Cleveland Barons	AHL	73	0	10	10	192	....	....	....	....	....	....	....	....	....	....	....	....	....	....	....	....	....	....
2005-06	**San Jose**	**NHL**	**1**	**0**	**1**	**1**	**2**	**0**	**0**	**0**	**0**	**0.0**	**0**	**0**	**0.0**	**6:01**	....	....	....	....	....	....	....	....	....
	Cleveland Barons	AHL	69	10	21	31	202	....	....	....	....	....	....	....	....	....	....	....	....	....	....	....	....	....	....
2006-07	Wilkes-Barre	AHL	75	6	24	30	167	....	....	....	....	....	....	....	....	....	8	1	0	1	19	....	....	....	....
2007-08	Binghamton	AHL	67	10	15	25	218	....	....	....	....	....	....	....	....	....	....	....	....	....	....	....	....	....	....
2008-09	**Ottawa**	**NHL**	**1**	**0**	**0**	**0**	**0**	**0**	**0**	**0**	**0**	**0.0**	**0**	**0**	**0.0**	**4:08**	....	....	....	....	....	....	....	....	....
	Binghamton	AHL	67	3	18	21	210	....	....	....	....	....	....	....	....	....	....	....	....	....	....	....	....	....	....
2009-10	**Ottawa**	**NHL**	**81**	**2**	**9**	**11**	**190**	**0**	**0**	**0**	**87**	**2.3**	**0**	**0**	**0.0**	**16:55**	**6**	**1**	**0**	**1**	**12**	**0**	**0**	**1**	**18:38**
2010-11	**Ottawa**	**NHL**	**50**	**1**	**6**	**7**	**136**	**0**	**0**	**0**	**40**	**2.5**	**0**	**0**	**0.0**	**14:53**	....	....	....	....	....	....	....	....	....
2011-12	**Ottawa**	**NHL**	**29**	**1**	**2**	**3**	**33**	**0**	**0**	**0**	**17**	**5.9**	**0**	**0**	**0.0**	**11:55**	**4**	**0**	**1**	**1**	**21**	**0**	**0**	**0**	**7:02**
	Binghamton	AHL	3	0	1	1	11	....	....	....	....	....	....	....	....	....	....	....	....	....	....	....	....	....	....
2012-13	**NY Islanders**	**NHL**	**22**	**0**	**2**	**2**	**46**	**0**	**0**	**0**	**19**	**0.0**	**–2**	**0**	**0.0**	**12:35**	**4**	**0**	**1**	**1**	**2**	**0**	**0**	**0**	**12:41**
	NHL Totals		**184**	**4**	**20**	**24**	**407**	**0**	**0**	**0**	**163**	**2.5**		**0**	**0.0**	**14:56**	**14**	**1**	**2**	**3**	**35**	**0**	**0**	**1**	**13:37**

Yanick Dupre Memorial Award (AHL - Outstanding Humanitarian Contribution) (2007)

Signed as a free agent by **San Jose**, June 6, 2001. • Missed majority of 2002-03 due to knee injury vs. Utah (AHL), January 4, 2003. Signed as a free agent by **Pittsburgh**, July 23, 2006. Signed as a free agent by **Ottawa**, July 3, 2007. Signed as a free agent by **NY Islanders**, July 1. 2012. • Missed majority of 2011-12 due to knee surgery, October 3, 2011 and as a healthy reserve. • Missed majority of 2012-13 due to wrist injury vs. Pittsburgh, February 5, 2013 and as a healthy reserve.

CARLE, Mathieu
(KAHRL, MA-tyew) **ANA**

Defense. Shoots right. 6', 201 lbs. Born, Gatineau, Que., September 30, 1987. Montreal's 3rd choice, 53rd overall, in 2006 Entry Draft.

			Regular Season														Playoffs								
Season	Club	League	GP	G	A	Pts	PIM	PP	SH	GW	S	%	+/-	TF	F%	Min	GP	G	A	Pts	PIM	PP	SH	GW	Min
2003-04	Acadie-Bathurst	QMJHL	59	11	12	23	57	....	....	....	....	....	....	....	....	....	....	....	....	....	....	....	....	....	....
2004-05	Acadie-Bathurst	QMJHL	69	4	29	33	53	....	....	....	....	....	....	....	....	....	....	....	....	....	....	....	....	....	....
2005-06	Acadie-Bathurst	QMJHL	67	18	51	69	122	....	....	....	....	....	....	....	....	....	17	1	14	15	29	....	....	....	....
2006-07	Acadie-Bathurst	QMJHL	38	12	39	51	52	....	....	....	....	....	....	....	....	....	....	....	....	....	....	....	....	....	....
	Rouyn-Noranda	QMJHL	25	4	15	19	27	....	....	....	....	....	....	....	....	....	16	6	10	16	16	....	....	....	....
2007-08	Hamilton	AHL	64	7	17	24	43	....	....	....	....	....	....	....	....	....	....	....	....	....	....	....	....	....	....
2008-09	Hamilton	AHL	59	7	22	29	43	....	....	....	....	....	....	....	....	....	6	0	2	2	4	....	....	....	....
2009-10	**Montreal**	**NHL**	**3**	**0**	**0**	**0**	**4**	**0**	**0**	**0**	**2**	**0.0**	**1**	**0**	**0.0**	**14:28**	....	....	....	....	....	....	....	....	....
	Hamilton	AHL	31	5	10	15	26	....	....	....	....	....	....	....	....	....	1	0	0	0	0	....	....	....	....
2010-11	Hamilton	AHL	68	11	18	29	44	....	....	....	....	....	....	....	....	....	19	3	9	12	8	....	....	....	....
2011-12	Syracuse Crunch	AHL	72	6	31	37	41	....	....	....	....	....	....	....	....	....	4	0	3	3	0	....	....	....	....
2012-13	Dynamo Riga	KHL	35	3	2	5	39	....	....	....	....	....	....	....	....	....	....	....	....	....	....	....	....	....	....
	Geneve	Swiss	12	0	1	1	2	....	....	....	....	....	....	....	....	....	7	0	3	3	14	....	....	....	....
	NHL Totals		**3**	**0**	**0**	**0**	**4**	**0**	**0**	**0**	**2**	**0.0**		**0**	**0.0**	**14:28**	....	....	....	....	....	....	....	....	....

QMJHL All-Rookie Team (2004)

• Missed majority of 2009-10 due to head injury in pre-season vs. Chicago, September 24, 2009. Traded to **Anaheim** by **Montreal** for Mark Mitera, July 15, 2011. Signed as a free agent by **Riga** (KHL), May 2, 2012. Signed as a free agent by **Geneve** (Swiss), January 15, 2013.

			Regular Season														Playoffs								
Season	Club	League	GP	G	A	Pts	PIM	PP	SH	GW	S	%	+/-	TF	F%	Min	GP	G	A	Pts	PIM	PP	SH	GW	Min

CARLE, Matt

(KAHRL, MAT) **T.B.**

Defense. Shoots left. 6', 205 lbs. Born, Anchorage, AK, September 25, 1984. San Jose's 4th choice, 47th overall, in 2003 Entry Draft.

99-2000	Alaska All-Stars	AASHA	42	14	28	42	....	....	....	....	....	....	....	....	....	....	....	....	....	....	....	....	....	....	....
2000-01	USNTDP	U-17	13	0	1	1	....	....	....	....	....	....	....	....	....	....	....	....	....	....	....	....	....	....	....
	USNTDP	NAHL	55	1	4	5	33	....	....	....	....	....	....	....	....	....	....	....	....	....	....	....	....	....	....
2001-02	USNTDP	U-18	45	3	13	16	30	....	....	....	....	....	....	....	....	....	....	....	....	....	....	....	....	....	....
	USNTDP	NAHL	7	1	2	3	0	....	....	....	....	....	....	....	....	....	....	....	....	....	....	....	....	....	....
	USNTDP	USHL	12	0	0	0	21	....	....	....	....	....	....	....	....	....	....	....	....	....	....	....	....	....	....
2002-03	River City Lancers	USHL	59	12	30	42	98	....	....	....	....	....	....	....	....	....	11	2	2	4	20	....	....	....	....
2003-04	U. of Denver	WCHA	30	5	20	25	33	....	....	....	....	....	....	....	....	....	....	....	....	....	....	....	....	....	....
2004-05	U. of Denver	WCHA	43	13	31	44	68	....	....	....	....	....	....	....	....	....	....	....	....	....	....	....	....	....	....
2005-06	U. of Denver	WCHA	39	11	*42	53	58	....	....	....	....	....	....	....	....	....	....	....	....	....	....	....	....	....	....
	San Jose	**NHL**	**12**	**3**	**3**	**6**	**14**	**2**	**0**	**1**	**11**	**27.3**	**-2**	**0**	**0.0**	**16:07**	**11**	**0**	**3**	**3**	**4**	**0**	**0**	**0**	**15:17**
2006-07	**San Jose**	**NHL**	**77**	**11**	**31**	**42**	**30**	**8**	**0**	**1**	**111**	**9.9**	**9**	**1**	**0.0**	**18:08**	**11**	**2**	**3**	**5**	**0**	**1**	**0**	**1**	**14:51**
	Worcester Sharks	AHL	3	0	2	2	0	....	....	....	....	....	....	....	....	....	....	....	....	....	....	....	....	....	....
2007-08	**San Jose**	**NHL**	**62**	**2**	**13**	**15**	**26**	**2**	**0**	**1**	**63**	**3.2**	**-8**	**1**	**100.0**	**16:33**	**11**	**0**	**1**	**1**	**4**	**0**	**0**	**0**	**13:56**
2008-09	**Tampa Bay**	**NHL**	**12**	**1**	**1**	**2**	**6**	**0**	**0**	**0**	**13**	**7.7**	**1**	**0**	**0.0**	**21:58**	....	....	....	....	....	....	....	....	....
	Philadelphia	**NHL**	**64**	**4**	**20**	**24**	**16**	**0**	**0**	**2**	**72**	**5.6**	**2**	**0**	**0.0**	**21:17**	**6**	**0**	**3**	**3**	**4**	**0**	**0**	**0**	**22:15**
2009-10	**Philadelphia**	**NHL**	**80**	**6**	**29**	**35**	**16**	**2**	**0**	**1**	**137**	**4.4**	**19**	**0**	**0.0**	**23:23**	**23**	**1**	**12**	**13**	**8**	**0**	**0**	**0**	**25:54**
2010-11	**Philadelphia**	**NHL**	**82**	**1**	**39**	**40**	**23**	**0**	**0**	**0**	**117**	**0.9**	**30**	**0**	**0.0**	**21:59**	**11**	**0**	**4**	**4**	**2**	**0**	**0**	**0**	**23:24**
2011-12	**Philadelphia**	**NHL**	**82**	**4**	**34**	**38**	**36**	**3**	**0**	**0**	**132**	**3.0**	**4**	**0**	**0.0**	**23:01**	**11**	**2**	**4**	**6**	**6**	**1**	**0**	**0**	**25:19**
2012-13	**Tampa Bay**	**NHL**	**48**	**5**	**17**	**22**	**4**	**2**	**0**	**0**	**66**	**7.6**	**1**	**0**	**0.0**	**23:45**	....	....	....	....	....	....	....	....	....
	NHL Totals		**519**	**37**	**187**	**224**	**171**	**19**	**0**	**6**	**722**	**5.1**		**2**	**50.0**	**21:05**	**84**	**5**	**30**	**35**	**28**	**2**	**0**	**1**	**20:50**

USHL First All-Star Team (2003) • USHL Defenseman of the Year (2003) • WCHA All-Rookie Team (2004) • WCHA First All-Star Team (2005, 2006) • NCAA West First All-American Team (2005, 2006) • NCAA Championship All-Tournament Team (2005) • WCHA Player of the Year (2006) • Hobey Baker Memorial Award (Top U.S. Collegiate Player) (2006) • NHL All-Rookie Team (2007)

Traded to **Tampa Bay** by **San Jose** with Ty Wishart, San Jose's 1st round choice (later traded to Ottawa, later traded to NY Islanders, later traded to Columbus, later traded to Anaheim – Anaheim selected Kyle Palmieri) in 2009 Entry Draft and San Jose's 4th round choice (James Mullin) in 2010 Entry Draft for Dan Boyle and Brad Lukowich, July 4, 2008. Traded to **Philadelphia** by **Tampa Bay** with San Jose's 3rd round choice (previously acquired, Philadelphia selected Simon Bertilsson) in 2009 Entry Draft for Steve Eminger, Steve Downie and Tampa Bay's 4th round choice (previously acquired, Tampa Bay selected Alex Hutchings) in 2009 Entry Draft, November 7, 2008. Signed as a free agent by **Tampa Bay**, July 4, 2012.

CARLSON, John

(KAHRL-suhn, JAWN) **WSH**

Defense. Shoots right. 6'3", 212 lbs. Born, Natick, MA, January 10, 1990. Washington's 2nd choice, 27th overall, in 2008 Entry Draft.

2005-06	N.J. Rockets	AtJHL	38	2	10	12	42	....	....	....	....	....	....	....	....	....	....	....	....	....	....	....	....	....	....
2006-07	N.J. Rockets	AtJHL	44	12	38	50	96	....	....	....	....	....	....	....	....	....	....	....	....	....	....	....	....	....	....
	Indiana Ice	USHL	2	0	0	0	6	....	....	....	....	....	....	....	....	....	....	....	....	....	....	....	....	....	....
2007-08	Indiana Ice	USHL	59	12	31	43	72	....	....	....	....	....	....	....	....	....	4	1	0	1	0	....	....	....	....
2008-09	London Knights	OHL	59	16	60	76	65	....	....	....	....	....	....	....	....	....	14	7	15	22	16	....	....	....	....
	Hershey Bears	AHL	....	....	....	....	....	....	....	....	....	....	....	....	....	....	16	2	1	3	0	....	....	....	....
2009-10	**Washington**	**NHL**	**22**	**1**	**5**	**6**	**8**	**0**	**0**	**0**	**21**	**4.8**	**11**	**0**	**0.0**	**15:15**	**7**	**1**	**3**	**4**	**0**	**0**	**0**	**0**	**20:14**
	Hershey Bears	AHL	48	4	35	39	26	....	....	....	....	....	....	....	....	....	13	2	4	6	8	....	....	....	....
2010-11	**Washington**	**NHL**	**82**	**7**	**30**	**37**	**44**	**1**	**0**	**3**	**144**	**4.9**	**21**	**0**	**0.0**	**22:39**	**9**	**2**	**1**	**3**	**4**	**0**	**0**	**0**	**24:23**
2011-12	**Washington**	**NHL**	**82**	**9**	**23**	**32**	**22**	**4**	**0**	**0**	**152**	**5.9**	**-15**	**1**	**0.0**	**21:52**	**14**	**2**	**3**	**5**	**8**	**1**	**0**	**0**	**24:02**
2012-13	**Washington**	**NHL**	**48**	**6**	**16**	**22**	**18**	**0**	**0**	**0**	**97**	**6.2**	**11**	**1**	**100.0**	**23:01**	**7**	**0**	**1**	**1**	**4**	**0**	**0**	**0**	**22:29**
	NHL Totals		**234**	**23**	**74**	**97**	**92**	**5**	**0**	**3**	**414**	**5.6**		**2**	**50.0**	**21:45**	**37**	**5**	**8**	**13**	**16**	**1**	**0**	**0**	**23:07**

USHL All-Rookie Team (2008) • USHL Second All-Star Team (2008) • OHL Second All-Star Team (2009) • Canadian Major Junior All-Rookie Team (2009) • AHL All-Rookie Team (2010) • NHL All-Rookie Team (2011)

CARON, Jordan

(kuh-RAWN, JOHR-dihn) **BOS**

Right wing. Shoots left. 6'2", 202 lbs. Born, Sayabec, Que., November 2, 1990. Boston's 1st choice, 25th overall, in 2009 Entry Draft.

2005-06	Notre Dame	SMHL	35	8	16	24	32	....	....	....	....	....	....	....	....	....	....	....	....	....	....	....	....	....	....
2006-07	Rimouski Oceanic	QMJHL	59	18	22	40	41	....	....	....	....	....	....	....	....	....	....	....	....	....	....	....	....	....	....
2007-08	Rimouski Oceanic	QMJHL	46	20	23	43	42	....	....	....	....	....	....	....	....	....	9	3	1	4	18	....	....	....	....
2008-09	Rimouski Oceanic	QMJHL	56	36	31	67	66	....	....	....	....	....	....	....	....	....	13	6	5	11	16	....	....	....	....
2009-10	Rimouski Oceanic	QMJHL	20	9	11	20	8	....	....	....	....	....	....	....	....	....	....	....	....	....	....	....	....	....	....
	Rouyn-Noranda	QMJHL	23	17	16	33	16	....	....	....	....	....	....	....	....	....	11	7	11	18	15	....	....	....	....
2010-11	**Boston**	**NHL**	**23**	**3**	**4**	**7**	**6**	**0**	**0**	**1**	**27**	**11.1**	**3**	**7**	**14.3**	**12:40**	....	....	....	....	....	....	....	....	....
	Providence Bruins	AHL	47	12	16	28	16	....	....	....	....	....	....	....	....	....	....	....	....	....	....	....	....	....	....
2011-12	**Boston**	**NHL**	**48**	**7**	**8**	**15**	**14**	**0**	**0**	**0**	**57**	**12.3**	**0**	**2**	**50.0**	**11:32**	**2**	**0**	**0**	**0**	**0**	**0**	**0**	**0**	**6:41**
	Providence Bruins	AHL	17	4	9	13	10	....	....	....	....	....	....	....	....	....	....	....	....	....	....	....	....	....	....
2012-13	Providence Bruins	AHL	47	11	7	18	38	....	....	....	....	....	....	....	....	....	12	2	7	9	10	....	....	....	....
	Boston	**NHL**	**17**	**1**	**2**	**3**	**4**	**0**	**0**	**0**	**20**	**5.0**	**1**	**0**	**0.0**	**9:24**	....	....	....	....	....	....	....	....	....
	NHL Totals		**88**	**11**	**14**	**25**	**24**	**0**	**0**	**1**	**104**	**10.6**		**9**	**22.2**	**11:25**	**2**	**0**	**0**	**0**	**0**	**0**	**0**	**0**	**6:41**

CARSON, Brett

(KAR-suhn, BREHT) **CGY**

Defense. Shoots right. 6'4", 220 lbs. Born, Regina, Sask., November 29, 1985. Carolina's 4th choice, 109th overall, in 2004 Entry Draft.

2000-01	Pipestone Valley	SSMHL	31	5	17	22	20	....	....	....	....	....	....	....	....	....	....	....	....	....	....	....	....	....	....
2001-02	Yorkton Terriers	SMHL	41	16	37	53	32	....	....	....	....	....	....	....	....	....	....	....	....	....	....	....	....	....	....
	Moose Jaw	WHL	6	0	0	0	0	....	....	....	....	....	....	....	....	....	12	2	0	2	0	....	....	....	....
2002-03	Moose Jaw	WHL	28	1	4	5	28	....	....	....	....	....	....	....	....	....	....	....	....	....	....	....	....	....	....
	Calgary Hitmen	WHL	30	3	6	9	4	....	....	....	....	....	....	....	....	....	5	2	1	3	0	....	....	....	....
2003-04	Calgary Hitmen	WHL	71	5	27	32	49	....	....	....	....	....	....	....	....	....	7	0	0	0	6	....	....	....	....
2004-05	Calgary Hitmen	WHL	61	8	16	24	61	....	....	....	....	....	....	....	....	....	8	2	2	4	8	....	....	....	....
2005-06	Calgary Hitmen	WHL	72	11	29	40	62	....	....	....	....	....	....	....	....	....	13	1	6	7	20	....	....	....	....
2006-07	Albany River Rats	AHL	63	2	16	18	26	....	....	....	....	....	....	....	....	....	5	0	2	2	0	....	....	....	....
	Florida Everblades	ECHL	3	1	1	2	0	....	....	....	....	....	....	....	....	....	....	....	....	....	....	....	....	....	....
2007-08	Albany River Rats	AHL	77	2	22	24	32	....	....	....	....	....	....	....	....	....	7	1	3	4	11	....	....	....	....
2008-09	**Carolina**	**NHL**	**5**	**0**	**0**	**0**	**4**	**0**	**0**	**0**	**2**	**0.0**	**-3**	**0**	**0.0**	**15:44**	....	....	....	....	....	....	....	....	....
	Albany River Rats	AHL	69	6	29	35	34	....	....	....	....	....	....	....	....	....	....	....	....	....	....	....	....	....	....
2009-10	**Carolina**	**NHL**	**54**	**2**	**10**	**12**	**12**	**0**	**0**	**0**	**42**	**4.8**	**5**	**0**	**0.0**	**17:22**	....	....	....	....	....	....	....	....	....
	Albany River Rats	AHL	14	3	8	11	0	....	....	....	....	....	....	....	....	....	....	....	....	....	....	....	....	....	....
2010-11	**Carolina**	**NHL**	**13**	**0**	**0**	**0**	**4**	**0**	**0**	**0**	**8**	**0.0**	**7**	**0**	**0.0**	**10:50**	....	....	....	....	....	....	....	....	....
	Charlotte	AHL	38	4	16	20	14	....	....	....	....	....	....	....	....	....	....	....	....	....	....	....	....	....	....
	Calgary	**NHL**	**6**	**0**	**0**	**0**	**0**	**0**	**0**	**0**	**4**	**0.0**	**2**	**0**	**0.0**	**12:46**	....	....	....	....	....	....	....	....	....
2011-12	**Calgary**	**NHL**	**2**	**0**	**0**	**0**	**0**	**0**	**0**	**0**	**1**	**0.0**	**-2**	**0**	**0.0**	**11:22**	....	....	....	....	....	....	....	....	....
	Abbotsford Heat	AHL	34	2	6	8	10	....	....	....	....	....	....	....	....	....	3	0	0	0	2	....	....	....	....
2012-13	Abbotsford Heat	AHL	26	6	5	11	16	....	....	....	....	....	....	....	....	....	....	....	....	....	....	....	....	....	....
	Calgary	**NHL**	**10**	**0**	**1**	**1**	**0**	**0**	**0**	**0**	**8**	**0.0**	**-1**	**0**	**0.0**	**10:56**	....	....	....	....	....	....	....	....	....
	NHL Totals		**90**	**2**	**11**	**13**	**20**	**0**	**0**	**0**	**65**	**3.1**		**0**	**0.0**	**15:11**	....	....	....	....	....	....	....	....	....

WHL East First All-Star Team (2006)

Claimed on waivers by **Calgary** from **Carolina**, February 28, 2011. • Missed majority of 2011-12 due to back injury in pre-season training .

CARTER, Jeff

(KAHR-tuhr, JEHF) **L.A.**

Center. Shoots right. 6'4", 210 lbs. Born, London, Ont., January 1, 1985. Philadelphia's 1st choice, 11th overall, in 2003 Entry Draft.

2000-01	Strathroy Rockets	ON-Jr.B	49	27	20	47	10	....	....	....	....	....	....	....	....	....	....	....	....	....	....	....	....	....	....
2001-02	Sault Ste. Marie	OHL	63	18	17	35	12	....	....	....	....	....	....	....	....	....	4	0	0	0	2	....	....	....	....
2002-03	Sault Ste. Marie	OHL	61	35	36	71	55	....	....	....	....	....	....	....	....	....	4	0	2	2	2	....	....	....	....
2003-04	Sault Ste. Marie	OHL	57	36	30	66	26	....	....	....	....	....	....	....	....	....	....	....	....	....	....	....	....	....	....
	Philadelphia	AHL	....	....	....	....	....	....	....	....	....	....	....	....	....	....	12	4	1	5	0	....	....	....	....
2004-05	Sault Ste. Marie	OHL	55	34	40	74	40	....	....	....	....	....	....	....	....	....	7	5	5	10	6	....	....	....	....
	Philadelphia	AHL	3	0	1	1	4	....	....	....	....	....	....	....	....	....	21	12	11	23	12	....	....	....	....
2005-06	**Philadelphia**	**NHL**	**81**	**23**	**19**	**42**	**40**	**6**	**2**	**7**	**189**	**12.2**	**10**	**683**	**48.2**	**12:04**	**6**	**0**	**0**	**0**	**10**	**0**	**0**	**0**	**13:04**
2006-07	**Philadelphia**	**NHL**	**62**	**14**	**23**	**37**	**48**	**3**	**2**	**1**	**215**	**6.5**	**-17**	**1062**	**45.4**	**19:00**	....	....	....	....	....	....	....	....	....
2007-08	**Philadelphia**	**NHL**	**82**	**29**	**24**	**53**	**55**	**7**	**2**	**5**	**260**	**11.2**	**6**	**1378**	**47.7**	**18:51**	**17**	**6**	**5**	**11**	**12**	**3**	**0**	**1**	**20:08**
2008-09	**Philadelphia**	**NHL**	**82**	**46**	**38**	**84**	**68**	**13**	**4**	***12**	**342**	**13.5**	**23**	**1725**	**48.3**	**20:57**	**6**	**1**	**0**	**1**	**8**	**0**	**0**	**0**	**20:21**
2009-10	**Philadelphia**	**NHL**	**74**	**33**	**28**	**61**	**38**	**11**	**2**	**6**	**319**	**10.3**	**2**	**1314**	**52.4**	**19:18**	**12**	**5**	**2**	**7**	**2**	**2**	**0**	**1**	**17:57**
2010-11	**Philadelphia**	**NHL**	**80**	**36**	**30**	**66**	**39**	**8**	**0**	**7**	**335**	**10.7**	**27**	**605**	**54.7**	**18:15**	**6**	**1**	**1**	**2**	**2**	**1**	**0**	**0**	**15:15**

Season	Club	League	Regular Season														Playoffs								
			GP	G	A	Pts	PIM	PP	SH	GW	S	%	+/-	TF	F%	Min	GP	G	A	Pts	PIM	PP	SH	GW	Min
2011-12	Columbus	NHL	39	15	10	25	14	8	0	1	130	11.5	-11	740	51.0	19:38	....	....	....	....	....	....	....	....	....
	♦ Los Angeles	NHL	16	6	3	9	2	2	0	1	54	11.1	-1	34	47.1	18:06	20	*8	5	13	4	4	0	*3	18:02
2012-13	Los Angeles	NHL	48	26	7	33	16	8	0	8	133	19.5	0	384	52.6	17:35	18	6	7	13	14	1	0	0	19:37
	NHL Totals		564	228	182	410	320	66	12	48	1977	11.5		7925	49.4	18:06	85	27	20	47	52	11	0	5	18:24

OHL Second All-Star Team (2004) • OHL First All-Star Team (2005) • Canadian Major Junior Sportsman of the Year (2005) • Canadian Major Junior First All-Star Team (2005)

Played in NHL All-Star Game (2009)

Traded to **Columbus** by **Philadelphia** for Jakub Voracek and Columbus's 1st (Sean Couturier) and 3rd (Nick Cousins) round choices in 2011 Entry Draft, June 23, 2011. Traded to **Los Angeles** by **Columbus** for Jack Johnson and Los Angeles' 1st round choice (Marko Dano) in 2013 Entry Draft, February 23, 2012.

CARTER, Ryan
(KAHR-tuhr, RIGH-uhn) **N.J.**

Left wing. Shoots left. 6'1", 205 lbs. Born, White Bear Lake, MN, August 3, 1983.

2002-03	Green Bay	USHL	55	19	17	36	94	....	....	....	....	....	....	....	....	....	....	....	....	....	....	....	....	....	....
2003-04	Green Bay	USHL	59	22	23	45	131	....	....	....	....	....	....	....	....	....	....	....	....	....	....	....	....	....	....
2004-05	Minnesota State	WCHA	37	15	8	23	44	....	....	....	....	....	....	....	....	....	....	....	....	....	....	....	....	....	....
2005-06	Minnesota State	WCHA	39	19	16	35	71	....	....	....	....	....	....	....	....	....	....	....	....	....	....	....	....	....	....
2006-07	Portland Pirates	AHL	76	16	20	36	85	....	....	....	....	....	....	....	....	....	....	....	....	....	....	....	....	....	....
	♦ Anaheim	**NHL**	....	....	....	....	....	....	....	....	....	....	....	....	....	....	4	0	0	0	0	0	0	0	3:12
2007-08	**Anaheim**	**NHL**	34	4	4	8	36	0	0	1	56	7.1	-2	299	61.5	10:29	6	0	0	0	6	0	0	0	11:03
	Portland Pirates	AHL	13	3	2	5	38	....	....	....	....	....	....	....	....	....	....	....	....	....	....	....	....	....	....
2008-09	**Anaheim**	**NHL**	48	3	6	9	52	0	0	1	40	7.5	3	304	48.0	9:06	10	2	3	5	0	1	0	0	12:14
2009-10	**Anaheim**	**NHL**	38	4	5	9	31	0	0	1	38	10.5	0	221	52.5	9:51	....	....	....	....	....	....	....	....	....
2010-11	**Anaheim**	**NHL**	18	1	2	3	22	0	0	0	23	4.3	-4	171	50.3	10:44	....	....	....	....	....	....	....	....	....
	Carolina	**NHL**	32	0	3	3	22	0	0	0	26	0.0	0	208	50.5	8:18	....	....	....	....	....	....	....	....	....
	Florida	**NHL**	12	2	1	3	22	0	0	0	14	14.3	3	99	51.5	13:30	....	....	....	....	....	....	....	....	....
2011-12	**Florida**	**NHL**	7	0	0	0	6	0	0	0	3	0.0	-1	39	46.2	9:19	....	....	....	....	....	....	....	....	....
	New Jersey	**NHL**	65	4	4	8	84	0	0	0	47	8.5	-12	393	50.1	10:28	23	5	2	7	32	0	0	2	8:43
2012-13	**New Jersey**	**NHL**	44	6	9	15	31	0	1	1	63	9.5	-2	83	51.8	13:03	....	....	....	....	....	....	....	....	....
	NHL Totals		**298**	**24**	**34**	**58**	**306**	**0**	**1**	**4**	**310**	**7.7**		**1817**	**52.1**	**10:26**	**43**	**7**	**5**	**12**	**38**	**1**	**0**	**2**	**9:21**

Signed as a free agent by **Anaheim**, July 12, 2006. • Missed majority of 2009-10 due to foot injury in pre-game skate at Columbus, November 13, 2009. Traded to **Carolina** by **Anaheim** for Stefan Chaput and Matt Kennedy, November 23, 2010. Traded to **Florida** by **Carolina** with Carolina's 5th round choice (later traded to Atlanta, later traded to San Jose – San Jose selected Sean Kuraly) in 2011 Entry Draft for Cory Stillman, February 24, 2011. Claimed on waivers by **New Jersey** from **Florida**, October 26, 2011.

CARUSO, Michael
(kah-ROO-soh, MIGH-kuhl) **FLA**

Defense. Shoots left. 6'2", 191 lbs. Born, Mississauga, Ont., July 5, 1988. Florida's 3rd choice, 103rd overall, in 2006 Entry Draft.

2004-05	Guelph Storm	OHL	56	0	3	3	31	....	....	....	....	....	....	....	....	....	4	0	0	0	2	....	....	....	....
2005-06	Guelph Storm	OHL	66	1	15	16	85	....	....	....	....	....	....	....	....	....	15	1	2	3	24	....	....	....	....
2006-07	Guelph Storm	OHL	64	4	16	20	119	....	....	....	....	....	....	....	....	....	4	0	0	0	8	....	....	....	....
2007-08	Guelph Storm	OHL	62	10	24	34	103	....	....	....	....	....	....	....	....	....	10	2	6	8	22	....	....	....	....
2008-09	Rochester	AHL	73	1	9	10	66	....	....	....	....	....	....	....	....	....	....	....	....	....	....	....	....	....	....
2009-10	Rochester	AHL	67	1	10	11	42	....	....	....	....	....	....	....	....	....	....	....	....	....	....	....	....	....	....
2010-11	Rochester	AHL	75	5	4	9	77	....	....	....	....	....	....	....	....	....	....	....	....	....	....	....	....	....	....
2011-12	San Antonio	AHL	68	5	8	13	63	....	....	....	....	....	....	....	....	....	10	0	4	4	4	....	....	....	....
2012-13	San Antonio	AHL	35	1	3	4	22	....	....	....	....	....	....	....	....	....	....	....	....	....	....	....	....	....	....
	Florida	**NHL**	2	0	0	0	0	0	0	0	0	0.0	-1	0	0.0	7:55	....	....	....	....	....	....	....	....	....
	NHL Totals		**2**	**0**	**0**	**0**	**0**	**0**	**0**	**0**	**0**	**0.0**		**0**	**0.0**	**7:55**	....	....	....	....	....	....	....	....	....

CERVENKA, Roman
(chuhr-VEHN-ka, ROH-man)

Center. Shoots left. 5'11", 201 lbs. Born, Prague, Czech., December 10, 1985.

2003-04	HC Slavia Praha	CzRep	15	0	1	1	2	....	....	....	....	....	....	....	....	....	8	0	0	0	2	....	....	....	....
2004-05	Hr. Kralove	CzRep-2	23	15	8	23	28	....	....	....	....	....	....	....	....	....	....	....	....	....	....	....	....	....	....
	Havl. Brod	CzRep-3	1	0	1	1	0	....	....	....	....	....	....	....	....	....	19	9	3	12	48	....	....	....	....
2005-06	HC Slavia Praha	CzRep	22	0	0	0	12	....	....	....	....	....	....	....	....	....	....	....	....	....	....	....	....	....	....
2006-07	HC Slavia Praha	CzRep	51	6	6	12	54	....	....	....	....	....	....	....	....	....	6	3	1	4	6	....	....	....	....
2007-08	HC Slavia Praha	CzRep	40	19	11	30	72	....	....	....	....	....	....	....	....	....	14	4	4	8	20	....	....	....	....
2008-09	HC Slavia Praha	CzRep	51	28	31	59	56	....	....	....	....	....	....	....	....	....	18	13	11	24	20	....	....	....	....
2009-10	HC Slavia Praha	CzRep	50	30	43	73	56	....	....	....	....	....	....	....	....	....	....	....	....	....	....	....	....	....	....
2010-11	Omsk	KHL	51	31	30	61	56	....	....	....	....	....	....	....	....	....	12	5	4	9	4	....	....	....	....
2011-12	Omsk	KHL	54	23	16	39	18	....	....	....	....	....	....	....	....	....	20	11	10	21	4	....	....	....	....
2012-13	HC Slavia Praha	CzRep	9	5	8	13	14	....	....	....	....	....	....	....	....	....	....	....	....	....	....	....	....	....	....
	HC Lev Praha	KHL	5	1	2	3	2	....	....	....	....	....	....	....	....	....	....	....	....	....	....	....	....	....	....
	Calgary	**NHL**	39	9	8	17	14	1	0	0	51	17.6	-13	125	46.4	13:08	....	....	....	....	....	....	....	....	....
	NHL Totals		**39**	**9**	**8**	**17**	**14**	**1**	**0**	**0**	**51**	**17.6**		**125**	**46.4**	**13:08**	....	....	....	....	....	....	....	....	....

Signed as a free agent by **Calgary**, May 2, 2012. Signed as a free agent by **Slavia Praha** (CzRep), September 17, 2012. Signed as a free agent by **Lev Praha** (KHL), November 12, 2012. Signed as a free agent by **St. Petersburg** (KHL), May 15, 2013.

CHARA, Zdeno
(CHAH-rah, z'DEHN-oh) **BOS**

Defense. Shoots left. 6'9", 255 lbs. Born, Trencin, Czechoslovakia, March 18, 1977. NY Islanders' 3rd choice, 56th overall, in 1996 Entry Draft.

1994-95	Dukla Trencin U18	Svk-U18	30	22	22	44	113	....	....	....	....	....	....	....	....	....	....	....	....	....	....	....	....	....	....
	Dukla Trencin Jr.	Slovak-Jr.	2	0	0	0	0	....	....	....	....	....	....	....	....	....	....	....	....	....	....	....	....	....	....
1995-96	Dukla Trencin Jr.	Slovak-Jr.	22	1	13	14	80	....	....	....	....	....	....	....	....	....	....	....	....	....	....	....	....	....	....
	HK VTJ Piestany	Slovak-2	10	1	3	4	10	....	....	....	....	....	....	....	....	....	....	....	....	....	....	....	....	....	....
	Sparta Jr.	CzRep-Jr.	15	1	2	3	42	....	....	....	....	....	....	....	....	....	....	....	....	....	....	....	....	....	....
	HC Sparta Praha	CzRep	1	0	0	0	0	....	....	....	....	....	....	....	....	....	....	....	....	....	....	....	....	....	....
1996-97	Prince George	WHL	49	3	19	22	120	....	....	....	....	....	....	....	....	....	15	1	7	8	45	....	....	....	....
1997-98	**NY Islanders**	**NHL**	25	0	1	1	50	0	0	0	10	0.0	1				....	....	....	....	....	....	....	....	....
	Kentucky	AHL	48	4	9	13	125	....	....	....	....	....	....	....	....	....	1	0	0	0	4	....	....	....	....
1998-99	**NY Islanders**	**NHL**	59	2	6	8	83	0	1	0	56	3.6	-8	0	0.0	18:54	....	....	....	....	....	....	....	....	....
	Lowell	AHL	23	2	2	4	47	....	....	....	....	....	....	....	....	....	....	....	....	....	....	....	....	....	....
99-2000	**NY Islanders**	**NHL**	65	2	9	11	57	0	0	1	47	4.3	-27	0	0.0	22:52	....	....	....	....	....	....	....	....	....
2000-01	**NY Islanders**	**NHL**	82	2	7	9	157	0	1	0	83	2.4	-27	0	0.0	22:20	....	....	....	....	....	....	....	....	....
2001-02	Dukla Trencin	Slovakia	8	2	2	4	32	....	....	....	....	....	....	....	....	....	....	....	....	....	....	....	....	....	....
	Ottawa	**NHL**	75	10	13	23	156	4	1	2	105	9.5	30	0	0.0	22:16	10	0	1	1	12	0	0	0	26:07
2002-03	**Ottawa**	**NHL**	74	9	30	39	116	3	0	2	168	5.4	29	0	0.0	24:57	18	1	6	7	14	0	0	0	25:07
2003-04	**Ottawa**	**NHL**	79	16	25	41	147	7	0	3	185	8.6	33	0	0.0	24:38	7	1	1	2	8	0	0	0	24:38
2004-05	Farjestad	Sweden	33	10	15	25	132	....	....	....	....	....	....	....	....	....	13	3	5	8	82	....	....	....	....
2005-06	**Ottawa**	**NHL**	71	16	27	43	135	10	1	3	212	7.5	17	24	41.7	27:11	10	1	3	4	23	1	0	0	27:32
	Slovakia	Olympics	6	1	1	2	2	....	....	....	....	....	....	....	....	....	....	....	....	....	....	....	....	....	....
2006-07	**Boston**	**NHL**	80	11	32	43	100	9	0	3	204	5.4	-21	1	0.0	27:58	....	....	....	....	....	....	....	....	....
2007-08	**Boston**	**NHL**	77	17	34	51	114	9	1	0	207	8.2	14	0	0.0	26:50	7	1	1	2	12	1	0	0	25:52
2008-09	**Boston**	**NHL**	80	19	31	50	95	11	0	3	216	8.8	23	4	25.0	26:04	11	1	3	4	12	1	0	1	25:11
2009-10	**Boston**	**NHL**	80	7	37	44	87	4	0	1	242	2.9	19	2	50.0	25:22	13	2	5	7	29	0	0	1	28:08
	Slovakia	Olympics	7	0	3	3	6	....	....	....	....	....	....	....	....	....	....	....	....	....	....	....	....	....	....
2010-11	**♦ Boston**	**NHL**	81	14	30	44	88	8	1	2	264	5.3	*33	0	0.0	25:26	24	2	7	9	34	1	0	0	27:39
2011-12	**Boston**	**NHL**	79	12	40	52	86	8	0	0	224	5.4	33	1	0.0	25:00	7	1	2	3	8	0	0	1	27:21
2012-13	HC Lev Praha	KHL	25	4	6	10	24	....	....	....	....	....	....	....	....	....	....	....	....	....	....	....	....	....	....
	Boston	**NHL**	48	7	12	19	70	3	0	2	119	5.9	14	1	0.0	24:56	22	3	12	15	20	0	0	0	29:32
	NHL Totals		**1055**	**144**	**334**	**478**	**1541**	**76**	**6**	**22**	**2342**	**6.1**		**33**	**36.4**	**24:44**	**129**	**13**	**41**	**54**	**172**	**4**	**0**	**3**	**27:03**

AHL All-Rookie Team (1998) • NHL First All-Star Team (2004, 2009) • NHL Second All-Star Team (2006, 2008, 2011, 2012) • James Norris Memorial Trophy (2009) • Mark Messier NHL Leadership Award (2011)

Played in NHL All-Star Game (2003, 2007, 2008, 2009, 2011, 2012)

Traded to **Ottawa** by **NY Islanders** with Bill Muckalt and NY Islanders' 1st round choice (Jason Spezza) in 2001 Entry Draft for Alexei Yashin, June 23, 2001. Signed as a free agent by **Farjestad** (Sweden), September 24, 2004. Signed as a free agent by **Boston**, July 1, 2006. Signed as a free agent by **Lev Praha** (KHL), October 2, 2012.

CHIASSON, Alex (CHAY-sahn, Al-ehx) DAL

Right wing. Shoots right. 6'3", 202 lbs. Born, Montreal, Que., October 1, 1990. Dallas' 2nd choice, 38th overall, in 2009 Entry Draft.

Season	Club	League	GP	G	A	Pts	PIM	PP	SH	GW	S	%	+/-	TF	F%	Min	Playoffs GP	G	A	Pts	PIM	PP	SH	GW	Min
2007-08	Northwood	High-NY	45	35	46	81	....	....	....	....	....	....	....	....	....	....	....	....	....	....	....	....	....	....	....
2008-09	Des Moines	USHL	56	17	33	50	101	....	....	....	....	....	....	....	....	....	....	....	....	....	....	....	....	....	....
2009-10	Boston University	H-East	35	7	12	19	44	....	....	....	....	....	....	....	....	....	....	....	....	....	....	....	....	....	....
2010-11	Boston University	H-East	35	14	20	34	75	....	....	....	....	....	....	....	....	....	....	....	....	....	....	....	....	....	....
2011-12	Boston University	H-East	38	15	31	46	67	....	....	....	....	....	....	....	....	....	....	....	....	....	....	....	....	....	....
	Texas Stars	AHL	9	1	4	5	9	....	....	....	....	....	....	....	....	....	....	....	....	....	....	....	....	....	....
2012-13	Texas Stars	AHL	57	13	22	35	43	....	....	....	....	....	....	....	....	....	7	2	1	3	4	....	....	....	....
	Dallas	**NHL**	**7**	**6**	**1**	**7**	**0**	**1**	**0**	**1**	**13**	**46.2**	**3**	**18**	**27.8**	**14:05**	....	....	....	....	....	....	....	....	....
	NHL Totals		**7**	**6**	**1**	**7**	**0**	**1**	**0**	**1**	**13**	**46.2**		**18**	**27.8**	**14:05**	....	....	....	....	....	....	....	....	....

CHIMERA, Jason (shih-MAIR-uh, JAY-suhn) WSH

Left wing. Shoots left. 6'3", 213 lbs. Born, Edmonton, Alta., May 2, 1979. Edmonton's 5th choice, 121st overall, in 1997 Entry Draft.

Season	Club	League	GP	G	A	Pts	PIM	PP	SH	GW	S	%	+/-	TF	F%	Min	Playoffs GP	G	A	Pts	PIM	PP	SH	GW	Min
1994-95	Edmonton Pats	AMHL	33	27	31	58	42	....	....	....	....	....	....	....	....	....	....	....	....	....	....	....	....	....	....
1995-96	Edmonton Pats	AMHL	34	23	24	47	44	....	....	....	....	....	....	....	....	....	....	....	....	....	....	....	....	....	....
1996-97	Medicine Hat	WHL	71	16	23	39	54	....	....	....	....	....	....	....	....	....	4	0	1	1	4	....	....	....	....
1997-98	Medicine Hat	WHL	72	34	32	66	93	....	....	....	....	....	....	....	....	....	....	....	....	....	....	....	....	....	....
	Hamilton	AHL	4	0	0	0	8	....	....	....	....	....	....	....	....	....	....	....	....	....	....	....	....	....	....
1998-99	Medicine Hat	WHL	37	18	22	40	84	....	....	....	....	....	....	....	....	....	....	....	....	....	....	....	....	....	....
	Brandon	WHL	21	14	12	26	32	....	....	....	....	....	....	....	....	....	5	4	1	5	8	....	....	....	....
99-2000	Hamilton	AHL	78	15	13	28	77	....	....	....	....	....	....	....	....	....	10	0	2	2	12	....	....	....	....
2000-01	**Edmonton**	**NHL**	**1**	**0**	**0**	**0**	**0**	**0**	**0**	**0**	**0**	**0.0**	**0**	**0**	**0.0**	**6:58**	....	....	....	....	....	....	....	....	....
	Hamilton	AHL	78	29	25	54	93	....	....	....	....	....	....	....	....	....	....	....	....	....	....	....	....	....	....
2001-02	**Edmonton**	**NHL**	**3**	**1**	**0**	**1**	**0**	**0**	**0**	**0**	**3**	**33.3**	**–3**	**0**	**0.0**	**12:44**	....	....	....	....	....	....	....	....	....
	Hamilton	AHL	77	26	51	77	158	....	....	....	....	....	....	....	....	....	15	4	6	10	10	....	....	....	....
2002-03	**Edmonton**	**NHL**	**66**	**14**	**9**	**23**	**36**	**0**	**1**	**4**	**90**	**15.6**	**–2**	**11**	**54.6**	**10:46**	**2**	**0**	**2**	**2**	**0**	**0**	**0**	**0**	**10:55**
2003-04	**Edmonton**	**NHL**	**60**	**4**	**8**	**12**	**57**	**0**	**0**	**1**	**79**	**5.1**	**–1**	**22**	**31.8**	**10:07**	....	....	....	....	....	....	....	....	....
2004-05	AS Varese Hockey	Italy	15	7	3	10	34	....	....	....	....	....	....	....	....	....	5	2	1	3	31	....	....	....	....
2005-06	**Columbus**	**NHL**	**80**	**17**	**13**	**30**	**95**	**1**	**1**	**5**	**127**	**13.4**	**–10**	**16**	**50.0**	**12:41**	....	....	....	....	....	....	....	....	....
2006-07	**Columbus**	**NHL**	**82**	**15**	**21**	**36**	**91**	**2**	**2**	**2**	**151**	**9.9**	**2**	**38**	**36.8**	**15:22**	....	....	....	....	....	....	....	....	....
2007-08	**Columbus**	**NHL**	**81**	**14**	**17**	**31**	**98**	**1**	**1**	**3**	**198**	**7.1**	**–5**	**35**	**45.7**	**17:30**	....	....	....	....	....	....	....	....	....
2008-09	**Columbus**	**NHL**	**49**	**8**	**14**	**22**	**41**	**1**	**0**	**1**	**115**	**7.0**	**8**	**42**	**42.9**	**16:15**	**4**	**0**	**1**	**1**	**2**	**0**	**0**	**0**	**13:21**
2009-10	**Columbus**	**NHL**	**39**	**8**	**9**	**17**	**47**	**1**	**0**	**1**	**92**	**8.7**	**–7**	**23**	**65.2**	**14:47**	....	....	....	....	....	....	....	....	....
	Washington	**NHL**	**39**	**7**	**10**	**17**	**51**	**0**	**0**	**0**	**68**	**10.3**	**6**	**17**	**41.2**	**12:36**	**7**	**1**	**2**	**3**	**2**	**0**	**0**	**1**	**11:46**
2010-11	**Washington**	**NHL**	**81**	**10**	**16**	**26**	**64**	**2**	**0**	**1**	**162**	**6.2**	**–10**	**39**	**51.3**	**13:15**	**9**	**2**	**2**	**4**	**2**	**0**	**0**	**2**	**12:53**
2011-12	**Washington**	**NHL**	**82**	**20**	**19**	**39**	**78**	**1**	**2**	**5**	**205**	**9.8**	**4**	**62**	**48.4**	**14:26**	**14**	**4**	**3**	**7**	**6**	**0**	**0**	**1**	**13:42**
2012-13	Pirati Chomutov	CzRep	5	1	0	1	10	....	....	....	....	....	....	....	....	....	....	....	....	....	....	....	....	....	....
	Washington	**NHL**	**47**	**3**	**11**	**14**	**48**	**0**	**0**	**0**	**92**	**3.3**	**–5**	**36**	**58.3**	**12:40**	**7**	**1**	**2**	**3**	**4**	**0**	**0**	**0**	**13:40**
	NHL Totals		**710**	**121**	**147**	**268**	**706**	**9**	**7**	**23**	**1382**	**8.8**		**341**	**47.5**	**13:46**	**43**	**8**	**12**	**20**	**16**	**0**	**0**	**4**	**13:03**

AHL First All-Star Team (2002)

Traded to **Phoenix** by **Edmonton** with Edmonton's 3rd round choice (later traded to Carolina, later traded to NY Rangers – NY Rangers selected Billy Ryan) in 2004 Entry Draft for New Jersey's 2nd round choice (previously acquired, Edmonton selected Geoff Paukovich) in 2004 Entry Draft and Buffalo's 4th round choice (previously acquired, Edmonton selected Liam Reddox) in 2004 Entry Draft, June 26, 2004. Signed as a free agent by **Varese** (Italy), December 15, 2004. Traded to **Columbus** by **Phoenix** with Cale Hulse and Mike Rupp for Geoff Sanderson and Tim Jackman, October 8, 2005. Traded to **Washington** by **Columbus** for Chris Clark and Milan Jurcina, December 28, 2009. Signed as a free agent by **Chomutov** (CzRep), November 14, 2012.

CHIPCHURA, Kyle (chip-CHUHR-a, KIGHL) PHX

Center. Shoots left. 6'2", 203 lbs. Born, Westlock, Alta., February 19, 1986. Montreal's 1st choice, 18th overall, in 2004 Entry Draft.

Season	Club	League	GP	G	A	Pts	PIM	PP	SH	GW	S	%	+/-	TF	F%	Min	Playoffs GP	G	A	Pts	PIM	PP	SH	GW	Min
2000-01	Spruce Grove	AMBHL	36	26	34	60	48	....	....	....	....	....	....	....	....	....	....	....	....	....	....	....	....	....	....
2001-02	Ft. Saskatchewan	AMHL	33	15	36	51	78	....	....	....	....	....	....	....	....	....	17	16	20	36	....	....	....	....	....
	Prince Albert	WHL	2	0	0	0	0	....	....	....	....	....	....	....	....	....	....	....	....	....	....	....	....	....	....
2002-03	Prince Albert	WHL	63	9	21	30	89	....	....	....	....	....	....	....	....	....	....	....	....	....	....	....	....	....	....
2003-04	Prince Albert	WHL	64	15	33	48	118	....	....	....	....	....	....	....	....	....	6	2	4	6	12	....	....	....	....
2004-05	Prince Albert	WHL	28	14	18	32	32	....	....	....	....	....	....	....	....	....	14	4	7	11	25	....	....	....	....
2005-06	Prince Albert	WHL	59	21	34	55	81	....	....	....	....	....	....	....	....	....	....	....	....	....	....	....	....	....	....
	Hamilton	AHL	8	1	2	3	6	....	....	....	....	....	....	....	....	....	....	....	....	....	....	....	....	....	....
2006-07	Hamilton	AHL	80	12	27	39	56	....	....	....	....	....	....	....	....	....	22	6	7	13	20	....	....	....	....
2007-08	**Montreal**	**NHL**	**36**	**4**	**7**	**11**	**10**	**0**	**0**	**0**	**36**	**11.1**	**–1**	**317**	**43.9**	**11:22**	....	....	....	....	....	....	....	....	....
	Hamilton	AHL	39	10	11	21	27	....	....	....	....	....	....	....	....	....	....	....	....	....	....	....	....	....	....
2008-09	**Montreal**	**NHL**	**13**	**0**	**3**	**3**	**5**	**0**	**0**	**0**	**5**	**0.0**	**–6**	**107**	**43.9**	**10:18**	....	....	....	....	....	....	....	....	....
	Hamilton	AHL	51	14	21	35	65	....	....	....	....	....	....	....	....	....	6	3	0	3	2	....	....	....	....
2009-10	**Montreal**	**NHL**	**19**	**0**	**0**	**0**	**16**	**0**	**0**	**0**	**11**	**0.0**	**–10**	**106**	**53.8**	**8:38**	....	....	....	....	....	....	....	....	....
	Anaheim	**NHL**	**55**	**6**	**6**	**12**	**56**	**0**	**1**	**1**	**43**	**14.0**	**–2**	**670**	**47.9**	**12:29**	....	....	....	....	....	....	....	....	....
2010-11	**Anaheim**	**NHL**	**40**	**0**	**2**	**2**	**32**	**0**	**0**	**0**	**23**	**0.0**	**1**	**283**	**46.6**	**8:00**	....	....	....	....	....	....	....	....	....
2011-12	**Phoenix**	**NHL**	**53**	**3**	**13**	**16**	**42**	**0**	**0**	**0**	**43**	**7.0**	**2**	**364**	**47.8**	**10:32**	**15**	**1**	**3**	**4**	**7**	**0**	**0**	**0**	**7:46**
	Portland Pirates	AHL	8	4	2	6	4	....	....	....	....	....	....	....	....	....	....	....	....	....	....	....	....	....	....
2012-13	Arizona Sundogs	CHL	10	2	11	13	4	....	....	....	....	....	....	....	....	....	....	....	....	....	....	....	....	....	....
	Phoenix	**NHL**	**46**	**5**	**9**	**14**	**50**	**0**	**0**	**0**	**37**	**13.5**	**1**	**261**	**48.3**	**9:42**	....	....	....	....	....	....	....	....	....
	NHL Totals		**262**	**18**	**40**	**58**	**211**	**0**	**1**	**1**	**198**	**9.1**		**2108**	**47.2**	**10:22**	**15**	**1**	**3**	**4**	**7**	**0**	**0**	**0**	**7:46**

WHL East Second All-Star Team (2006)

Traded to **Anaheim** by **Montreal** for Anaheim's 4th round choice (Magnus Nygren) in 2011 Entry Draft, December 1, 2009. • Missed majority of 2010-11 due to head injury at San Jose, October 30, 2010, and as a healthy reserve. Signed as a free agent by **Phoenix**, July 19, 2011. Signed as a free agent by **Arizona** (CHL), October 16, 2012.

CHORNEY, Taylor (CHOHR-nee, TAY-luhr) ST.L.

Defense. Shoots left. 6'1", 189 lbs. Born, Thunder Bay, Ont., April 27, 1987. Edmonton's 2nd choice, 36th overall, in 2005 Entry Draft.

Season	Club	League	GP	G	A	Pts	PIM	PP	SH	GW	S	%	+/-	TF	F%	Min	Playoffs GP	G	A	Pts	PIM	PP	SH	GW	Min
2003-04	Shat.-St. Mary's	High-MN	74	12	44	56	58	....	....	....	....	....	....	....	....	....	....	....	....	....	....	....	....	....	....
2004-05	Shat.-St. Mary's	High-MN	50	4	30	34	52	....	....	....	....	....	....	....	....	....	....	....	....	....	....	....	....	....	....
2005-06	North Dakota	WCHA	44	3	15	18	54	....	....	....	....	....	....	....	....	....	....	....	....	....	....	....	....	....	....
2006-07	North Dakota	WCHA	39	8	23	31	48	....	....	....	....	....	....	....	....	....	....	....	....	....	....	....	....	....	....
2007-08	North Dakota	WCHA	43	3	21	24	24	....	....	....	....	....	....	....	....	....	....	....	....	....	....	....	....	....	....
2008-09	**Edmonton**	**NHL**	**2**	**0**	**0**	**0**	**0**	**0**	**0**	**0**	**0**	**0.0**	**–4**	**0**	**0.0**	**15:43**	....	....	....	....	....	....	....	....	....
	Springfield	AHL	68	5	16	21	22	....	....	....	....	....	....	....	....	....	....	....	....	....	....	....	....	....	....
2009-10	**Edmonton**	**NHL**	**42**	**0**	**3**	**3**	**12**	**0**	**0**	**0**	**35**	**0.0**	**–21**	**0**	**0.0**	**17:24**	....	....	....	....	....	....	....	....	....
	Springfield	AHL	32	4	9	13	14	....	....	....	....	....	....	....	....	....	....	....	....	....	....	....	....	....	....
2010-11	**Edmonton**	**NHL**	**12**	**1**	**3**	**4**	**4**	**1**	**0**	**1**	**13**	**7.7**	**–5**	**0**	**0.0**	**15:59**	....	....	....	....	....	....	....	....	....
	Oklahoma City	AHL	46	3	13	16	22	....	....	....	....	....	....	....	....	....	....	....	....	....	....	....	....	....	....
2011-12	**St. Louis**	**NHL**	**2**	**0**	**0**	**0**	**0**	**0**	**0**	**0**	**1**	**0.0**	**0**	**0**	**0.0**	**11:40**	....	....	....	....	....	....	....	....	....
	Edmonton	**NHL**	**3**	**0**	**0**	**0**	**0**	**0**	**0**	**0**	**1**	**0.0**	**–1**	**0**	**0.0**	**15:48**	....	....	....	....	....	....	....	....	....
	Oklahoma City	AHL	50	6	18	24	29	....	....	....	....	....	....	....	....	....	10	0	1	1	6	....	....	....	....
2012-13	Peoria Rivermen	AHL	73	4	20	24	37	....	....	....	....	....	....	....	....	....	....	....	....	....	....	....	....	....	....
	NHL Totals		**61**	**1**	**6**	**7**	**16**	**1**	**0**	**1**	**50**	**2.0**		**0**	**0.0**	**16:48**	....	....	....	....	....	....	....	....	....

WCHA Second All-Star Team (2007) • NCAA West Second All-American Team (2007) • WCHA First All-Star Team (2008)

Claimed on waivers by **St. Louis** from **Edmonton** October 11, 2011. Claimed on waivers by **Edmonton** from **St. Louis** November 10, 2011. Signed as a free agent by **St. Louis**, July 1, 2012.

CHRISTENSEN, Erik (KRIHS-tehn-suhn, AIR-ihk)

Center. Shoots left. 6'1", 200 lbs. Born, Edmonton, Alta., December 17, 1983. Pittsburgh's 3rd choice, 69th overall, in 2002 Entry Draft.

Season	Club	League	GP	G	A	Pts	PIM	PP	SH	GW	S	%	+/-	TF	F%	Min	Playoffs GP	G	A	Pts	PIM	PP	SH	GW	Min
1998-99	Leduc Oil Kings	AMBHL	36	34	42	76	70	....	....	....	....	....	....	....	....	....	....	....	....	....	....	....	....	....	....
99-2000	Kamloops Blazers	WHL	66	9	5	14	39	....	....	....	....	....	....	....	....	....	4	0	0	0	2	....	....	....	....
2000-01	Kamloops Blazers	WHL	72	21	23	44	36	....	....	....	....	....	....	....	....	....	4	1	1	2	0	....	....	....	....
2001-02	Kamloops Blazers	WHL	70	22	36	58	68	....	....	....	....	....	....	....	....	....	4	0	0	0	4	....	....	....	....
2002-03	Kamloops Blazers	WHL	67	*54	54	*108	60	....	....	....	....	....	....	....	....	....	6	1	7	8	14	....	....	....	....
2003-04	Kamloops Blazers	WHL	29	10	14	24	40	....	....	....	....	....	....	....	....	....	....	....	....	....	....	....	....	....	....
	Brandon	WHL	34	17	21	38	20	....	....	....	....	....	....	....	....	....	11	8	4	12	8	....	....	....	....
2004-05	Wilkes-Barre	AHL	77	14	13	27	33	....	....	....	....	....	....	....	....	....	11	1	6	7	4	....	....	....	....
2005-06	**Pittsburgh**	**NHL**	**33**	**6**	**7**	**13**	**34**	**2**	**0**	**0**	**85**	**7.1**	**–3**	**381**	**53.0**	**14:17**	....	....	....	....	....	....	....	....	....
	Wilkes-Barre	AHL	48	24	22	46	50	....	....	....	....	....	....	....	....	....	11	2	2	4	2	....	....	....	....

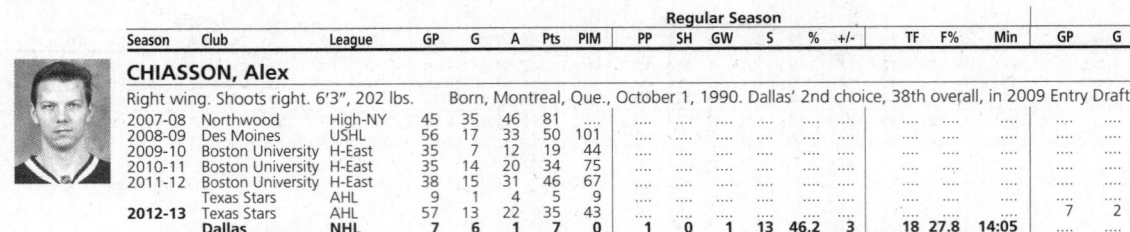

Season	Club	League	GP	G	A	Pts	PIM	PP	SH	GW	S	%	+/-	TF	F%	Min	GP	G	A	Pts	PIM	PP	SH	GW	Min
			Regular Season														Playoffs								
2006-07	**Pittsburgh**	**NHL**	**61**	**18**	**15**	**33**	**26**	**6**	**0**	**1**	**133**	**13.5**	**-3**	**240**	**56.3**	**11:38**	**4**	**0**	**0**	**0**	**6**	**0**	**0**	**0**	**8:15**
	Wilkes-Barre	AHL	16	12	12	24	8																		
2007-08	**Pittsburgh**	**NHL**	**49**	**9**	**11**	**20**	**28**	**2**	**0**	**0**	**109**	**8.3**	**-3**	**314**	**58.6**	**12:37**									
	Atlanta	**NHL**	**10**	**2**	**2**	**4**	**2**	**0**	**0**	**0**	**23**	**8.7**	**-7**	**160**	**58.1**	**16:57**									
2008-09	**Atlanta**	**NHL**	**47**	**5**	**14**	**19**	**14**	**1**	**0**	**0**	**90**	**5.6**	**-7**	**427**	**54.6**	**14:16**									
	Anaheim	**NHL**	**17**	**2**	**7**	**9**	**6**	**1**	**0**	**0**	**32**	**6.3**	**-2**	**70**	**62.9**	**11:55**	**8**	**0**	**2**	**2**	**0**	**0**	**0**	**0**	**10:37**
2009-10	**Anaheim**	**NHL**	**9**	**0**	**0**	**0**	**2**	**0**	**0**	**0**	**9**	**0.0**	**-3**	**51**	**41.2**	**11:27**									
	Manitoba Moose	AHL	6	2	0	2	0																		
	NY Rangers	**NHL**	**49**	**8**	**18**	**26**	**24**	**1**	**0**	**1**	**77**	**10.4**	**14**	**623**	**49.4**	**15:28**									
2010-11	**NY Rangers**	**NHL**	**63**	**11**	**16**	**27**	**18**	**4**	**0**	**1**	**86**	**12.8**	**3**	**639**	**49.5**	**12:46**	**5**	**1**	**0**	**1**	**2**	**1**	**0**	**0**	**13:04**
2011-12	**NY Rangers**	**NHL**	**20**	**1**	**4**	**5**	**2**	**1**	**0**	**0**	**10**	**10.0**	**0**	**114**	**53.5**	**8:07**									
	Connecticut	AHL	5	2	1	3	8																		
	Minnesota	**NHL**	**29**	**6**	**1**	**7**	**6**	**2**	**0**	**1**	**34**	**17.6**	**-13**	**188**	**52.1**	**11:59**									
2012-13	HC Lev Praha	KHL	41	11	10	21	18																		
	NHL Totals		**387**	**68**	**95**	**163**	**162**	**20**	**0**	**4**	**688**	**9.9**		**3207**	**52.9**	**12:58**	**17**	**1**	**2**	**3**	**8**	**1**	**0**	**0**	**10:47**

WHL West First All-Star Team (2003) • Canadian Major Junior Second All-Star Team (2003)

Traded to **Atlanta** by **Pittsburgh** with Colby Armstrong, Angelo Esposito and Pittsburgh's 1st round choice (Daultan Leveille) in 2008 Entry Draft for Marian Hossa and Pascal Dupuis, February 26, 2008. Traded to **Anaheim** by **Atlanta** for Eric O'Dell, March 4, 2009. Claimed on waivers by **NY Rangers** from **Anaheim**, December 2, 2009. Traded to **Minnesota** by **NY Rangers** with NY Rangers' 7th round choice (Alexandre Belanger) in 2013 Entry Draft for Casey Wellman, February 3. 2012. Signed as a free agent by **Lev Praha** (KHL), June 5, 2012.

CIZIKAS, Casey

(sih-ZEE-kuhs, KAY-see) **NYI**

Center. Shoots left. 5'11", 187 lbs. Born, Toronto, Ont., February 27, 1991. NY Islanders' 5th choice, 92nd overall, in 2009 Entry Draft.

Season	Club	League	GP	G	A	Pts	PIM	PP	SH	GW	S	%	+/-	TF	F%	Min	GP	G	A	Pts	PIM	PP	SH	GW	Min
2006-07	Mississauga Reps	GTHL	77	46	60	106	88																		
2007-08	St. Michael's	OHL	62	18	23	41	41										4	1	2	3	6				
2008-09	St. Michael's	OHL	55	16	20	36	39										11	5	4	9	11				
2009-10	St. Michael's	OHL	68	25	37	62	77										16	7	7	14	16				
2010-11	St. Michael's	OHL	52	29	35	64	40										16	5	14	19	14				
2011-12	**NY Islanders**	**NHL**	**15**	**0**	**4**	**4**	**6**	**0**	**0**	**0**	**12**	**0.0**	**1**	**115**	**40.9**	**10:36**									
	Bridgeport	AHL	52	15	30	45	30										3	0	0	0	20				
2012-13	Bridgeport	AHL	31	10	11	21	35																		
	NY Islanders	**NHL**	**45**	**6**	**9**	**15**	**14**	**0**	**0**	**1**	**45**	**13.3**	**0**	**276**	**52.2**	**10:47**	**6**	**2**	**2**	**4**	**12**	**0**	**0**	**0**	**10:46**
	NHL Totals		**60**	**6**	**13**	**19**	**20**	**0**	**0**	**1**	**57**	**10.5**		**391**	**48.8**	**10:44**	**6**	**2**	**2**	**4**	**12**	**0**	**0**	**0**	**10:46**

CLARK, Brett

(KLAHRK, BREHT)

Defense. Shoots left. 6', 194 lbs. Born, Wapella, Sask., December 23, 1976. Montreal's 7th choice, 154th overall, in 1996 Entry Draft.

Season	Club	League	GP	G	A	Pts	PIM	PP	SH	GW	S	%	+/-	TF	F%	Min	GP	G	A	Pts	PIM	PP	SH	GW	Min
1994-95	Melville	SJHL	62	19	32	51	77																		
1995-96	U. of Maine	H-East	39	7	31	38	22																		
1996-97	Canada	Nat-Tm	57	6	21	27	52																		
1997-98	**Montreal**	**NHL**	**41**	**1**	**0**	**1**	**20**	**0**	**0**	**0**	**26**	**3.8**	**-3**												
	Fredericton	AHL	20	0	6	6	6										4	0	1	1	17				
1998-99	**Montreal**	**NHL**	**61**	**2**	**2**	**4**	**16**	**0**	**0**	**0**	**36**	**5.6**	**-3**	**0**	**0.0**	**13:11**									
	Fredericton	AHL	3	1	0	1	0																		
99-2000	**Atlanta**	**NHL**	**14**	**0**	**1**	**1**	**4**	**0**	**0**	**0**	**13**	**0.0**	**-12**	**0**	**0.0**	**16:51**									
	Orlando	IHL	63	9	17	26	31										6	0	1	1	0				
2000-01	**Atlanta**	**NHL**	**28**	**1**	**2**	**3**	**14**	**0**	**0**	**0**	**35**	**2.9**	**-12**	**0**	**0.0**	**18:02**									
	Orlando	IHL	43	2	9	11	32										15	1	6	7	2				
2001-02	**Atlanta**	**NHL**	**2**	**0**	**0**	**0**	**0**	**0**	**0**	**0**	**0**	**0.0**	**-3**	**1**	**100.0**	**15:32**									
	Chicago Wolves	AHL	42	3	17	20	18																		
	Hershey Bears	AHL	32	7	9	16	12										8	0	2	2	6				
2002-03	Hershey Bears	AHL	80	8	27	35	26										5	0	4	4	4				
2003-04	**Colorado**	**NHL**	**12**	**1**	**1**	**2**	**6**	**0**	**0**	**0**	**14**	**7.1**	**3**	**0**	**0.0**	**10:26**									
	Hershey Bears	AHL	64	11	21	32	37																		
2004-05	Hershey Bears	AHL	67	7	37	44	54																		
2005-06	**Colorado**	**NHL**	**80**	**9**	**27**	**36**	**56**	**4**	**0**	**1**	**148**	**6.1**	**3**	**1**	**0.0**	**19:39**	**9**	**2**	**2**	**4**	**2**	**0**	**1**	**0**	**24:17**
2006-07	**Colorado**	**NHL**	**82**	**10**	**29**	**39**	**50**	**4**	**0**	**1**	**140**	**7.1**	**5**	**1**	**100.0**	**23:41**									
2007-08	**Colorado**	**NHL**	**57**	**5**	**16**	**21**	**33**	**1**	**0**	**0**	**87**	**5.7**	**5**	**0**	**0.0**	**23:09**									
2008-09	**Colorado**	**NHL**	**76**	**2**	**10**	**12**	**32**	**0**	**0**	**1**	**97**	**2.1**	**-16**	**0**	**0.0**	**22:20**									
2009-10	**Colorado**	**NHL**	**64**	**3**	**17**	**20**	**28**	**2**	**0**	**1**	**75**	**4.0**	**6**	**0**	**0.0**	**19:08**	**1**	**0**	**0**	**0**	**0**	**0**	**0**	**0**	**17:55**
2010-11	**Tampa Bay**	**NHL**	**82**	**9**	**22**	**31**	**14**	**6**	**0**	**1**	**87**	**10.3**	**2**	**0**	**0.0**	**18:53**	**18**	**1**	**2**	**3**	**8**	**0**	**0**	**0**	**17:35**
2011-12	**Tampa Bay**	**NHL**	**82**	**2**	**13**	**15**	**20**	**0**	**0**	**0**	**61**	**3.3**	**-26**	**0**	**0.0**	**18:23**									
2012-13	Oklahoma City	AHL	18	1	16	17	10																		
	Minnesota	**NHL**	**8**	**0**	**1**	**1**	**0**	**0**	**0**	**0**	**6**	**0.0**	**-9**	**0**	**0.0**	**14:04**									
	NHL Totals		**689**	**45**	**141**	**186**	**293**	**17**	**0**	**5**	**825**	**5.5**		**3**	**66.7**	**19:29**	**28**	**3**	**4**	**7**	**10**	**0**	**1**	**0**	**19:45**

Claimed by **Atlanta** from **Montreal** in Expansion Draft, June 25, 1999. Traded to **Colorado** by **Atlanta** for Frederic Cassivi, January 24, 2002. Signed as a free agent by **Tampa Bay**, July 5, 2010. Signed as a free agent by **Oklahoma City** (AHL), January 21, 2013. Signed as a free agent by **Minnesota**, July 13, 2013. • Missed majority of 2012-13 as a healthy reserve.

CLARK, Mat

(KLAHRK, MAT) **ANA**

Defense. Shoots right. 6'3", 225 lbs. Born, Wheat Ridge, CO, October 17, 1990. Anaheim's 3rd choice, 37th overall, in 2009 Entry Draft.

Season	Club	League	GP	G	A	Pts	PIM	PP	SH	GW	S	%	+/-	TF	F%	Min	GP	G	A	Pts	PIM	PP	SH	GW	Min
2006-07	Brampton	ON-Jr.A	47	2	7	9	50										8	1	1	2	19				
2007-08	Brampton	ON-Jr.A	46	6	11	17	64										8	1	4	5	45				
2008-09	Brampton	OHL	63	3	20	23	91										21	0	5	5	37				
2009-10	Brampton	OHL	66	7	16	23	88										7	2	4	6	9				
	Manitoba Moose	AHL	1	0	0	0	0										6	0	0	0	2				
2010-11	Syracuse Crunch	AHL	80	2	14	16	128																		
2011-12	**Anaheim**	**NHL**	**2**	**0**	**0**	**0**	**0**	**0**	**0**	**0**	**2**	**0.0**	**-2**	**0**	**0.0**	**11:02**									
	Syracuse Crunch	AHL	62	1	11	12	72										4	1	1	2	11				
2012-13	Norfolk Admirals	AHL	71	1	9	10	79																		
	NHL Totals		**2**	**0**	**0**	**0**	**0**	**0**	**0**	**0**	**2**	**0.0**		**0**	**0.0**	**11:02**									

CLARKSON, David

(KLAHRK-suhn, DAYV-ihd) **TOR**

Right wing. Shoots right. 6'1", 200 lbs. Born, Toronto, Ont., March 31, 1984.

Season	Club	League	GP	G	A	Pts	PIM	PP	SH	GW	S	%	+/-	TF	F%	Min	GP	G	A	Pts	PIM	PP	SH	GW	Min
2000-01	Port Hope	ON-Jr.A	47	18	14	32	118																		
2001-02	Aurora Tigers	ON-Jr.A	37	26	21	47	141																		
	Belleville Bulls	OHL	22	2	7	9	34										8	1	1	2	6				
2002-03	Belleville Bulls	OHL	3	0	0	0	11																		
	Kitchener Rangers	OHL	54	17	11	28	122										21	4	3	7	23				
2003-04	Kitchener Rangers	OHL	55	22	17	39	173																		
2004-05	Kitchener Rangers	OHL	51	33	21	54	145										15	6	2	8	40				
2005-06	Albany River Rats	AHL	56	13	21	34	233																		
2006-07	**New Jersey**	**NHL**	**7**	**3**	**1**	**4**	**6**	**2**	**0**	**1**	**18**	**16.7**	**-1**	**1**	**0.0**	**17:02**	**3**	**0**	**0**	**0**	**2**	**0**	**0**	**0**	**6:42**
	Lowell Devils	AHL	67	20	18	38	150																		
2007-08	**New Jersey**	**NHL**	**81**	**9**	**13**	**22**	**183**	**0**	**0**	**1**	**151**	**6.0**	**1**	**15**	**40.0**	**12:02**	**5**	**0**	**0**	**0**	**4**	**0**	**0**	**0**	**12:20**
2008-09	**New Jersey**	**NHL**	**82**	**17**	**15**	**32**	**164**	**4**	**0**	**3**	**158**	**10.8**	**-1**	**7**	**28.6**	**12:03**	**7**	**2**	**0**	**2**	**19**	**1**	**0**	**1**	**8:32**
2009-10	**New Jersey**	**NHL**	**46**	**11**	**13**	**24**	**85**	**3**	**0**	**2**	**106**	**10.4**	**3**	**20**	**30.0**	**14:27**	**5**	**0**	**0**	**0**	**22**	**0**	**0**	**0**	**12:28**
2010-11	**New Jersey**	**NHL**	**82**	**12**	**6**	**18**	**116**	**1**	**0**	**1**	**192**	**6.3**	**-20**	**45**	**42.2**	**13:37**									
2011-12	**New Jersey**	**NHL**	**80**	**30**	**16**	**46**	**138**	**8**	**0**	**7**	**228**	**13.2**	**-8**	**243**	**42.0**	**16:22**	**24**	**3**	**9**	**12**	**32**	**0**	**0**	***3**	**14:52**
2012-13	Salzburg	Austria	5	2	1	3	18																		
	New Jersey	**NHL**	**48**	**15**	**9**	**24**	**78**	**6**	**0**	**5**	**180**	**8.3**	**-6**	**25**	**24.0**	**17:36**									
	NHL Totals		**426**	**97**	**73**	**170**	**770**	**24**	**0**	**20**	**1033**	**9.4**		**356**	**39.6**	**14:07**	**44**	**5**	**9**	**14**	**79**	**1**	**0**	**4**	**12:44**

Signed as a free agent by **New Jersey**, August 12, 2005. Signed as a free agent by **Salzburg** (Austria), October 24, 2012. Signed as a free agent by **Toronto**, July 5, 2013.

CLEARY, Dan
(KLIH-ree, DAN) **DET**

Right wing. Shoots left. 6', 208 lbs. Born, Carbonear, Nfld., December 18, 1978. Chicago's 1st choice, 13th overall, in 1997 Entry Draft.

Season	Club	League	GP	G	A	Pts	PIM	PP	SH	GW	S	%	+/-	TF	F%	Min	GP	G	A	Pts	PIM	PP	SH	GW	Min
			Regular Season														Playoffs								
1993-94	Kingston	ON-Jr.A	41	18	28	46	33	....	....	....	....	....	....	....	....	....	2	0	1	1	0	....	....	....	....
1994-95	Belleville Bulls	OHL	62	26	55	81	62	....	....	....	....	....	....	....	....	....	16	7	10	17	23	....	....	....	....
1995-96	Belleville Bulls	OHL	64	53	62	115	74	....	....	....	....	....	....	....	....	....	14	10	17	27	40	....	....	....	....
1996-97	Belleville Bulls	OHL	64	32	48	80	88	....	....	....	....	....	....	....	....	....	6	3	4	7	6	....	....	....	....
1997-98	**Chicago**	**NHL**	**6**	**0**	**0**	**0**	**0**	**0**	**0**	**0**	**4**	**0.0**	**−2**	....	....	....	....	....	....	....	....	....	....	....	....
	Belleville Bulls	OHL	30	16	31	47	14	....	....	....	....	....	....	....	....	....	10	6	*17	*23	10	....	....	....	....
	Indianapolis Ice	IHL	4	2	1	3	6	....	....	....	....	....	....	....	....	....	....	....	....	....	....	....	....	....	....
1998-99	**Chicago**	**NHL**	**35**	**4**	**5**	**9**	**24**	**0**	**0**	**0**	**49**	**8.2**	**−1**	**13**	**46.2**	**14:21**	....	....	....	....	....	....	....	....	....
	Portland Pirates	AHL	30	9	17	26	74	....	....	....	....	....	....	....	....	....	....	....	....	....	....	....	....	....	....
	Hamilton	AHL	9	0	1	1	7	....	....	....	....	....	....	....	....	....	3	0	0	0	0	....	....	....	....
99-2000	**Edmonton**	**NHL**	**17**	**3**	**2**	**5**	**8**	**0**	**0**	**1**	**18**	**16.7**	**−1**	**1**	**100.0**	**9:44**	**4**	**0**	**1**	**1**	**2**	**0**	**0**	**0**	**8:40**
	Hamilton	AHL	58	22	52	74	108	....	....	....	....	....	....	....	....	....	5	2	3	5	18	....	....	....	....
2000-01	**Edmonton**	**NHL**	**81**	**14**	**21**	**35**	**37**	**2**	**0**	**2**	**107**	**13.1**	**5**	**13**	**23.1**	**12:58**	**6**	**1**	**1**	**2**	**8**	**1**	**0**	**0**	**14:09**
2001-02	**Edmonton**	**NHL**	**65**	**10**	**19**	**29**	**51**	**2**	**1**	**1**	**75**	**13.3**	**−1**	**5**	**60.0**	**12:43**	....	....	....	....	....	....	....	....	....
2002-03	**Edmonton**	**NHL**	**57**	**4**	**13**	**17**	**31**	**0**	**0**	**1**	**89**	**4.5**	**5**	**5**	**40.0**	**11:58**	....	....	....	....	....	....	....	....	....
2003-04	**Phoenix**	**NHL**	**68**	**6**	**11**	**17**	**42**	**0**	**3**	**0**	**83**	**7.2**	**−8**	**51**	**39.2**	**13:12**	....	....	....	....	....	....	....	....	....
2004-05	Mora IK	Sweden	47	11	26	37	138	....	....	....	....	....	....	....	....	....	....	....	....	....	....	....	....	....	....
2005-06	**Detroit**	**NHL**	**77**	**3**	**12**	**15**	**40**	**0**	**0**	**1**	**106**	**2.8**	**5**	**286**	**45.8**	**10:30**	**6**	**0**	**1**	**1**	**6**	**0**	**0**	**0**	**10:44**
2006-07	**Detroit**	**NHL**	**71**	**20**	**20**	**40**	**24**	**6**	**2**	**5**	**135**	**14.8**	**6**	**411**	**51.1**	**15:28**	**18**	**4**	**8**	**12**	**30**	**1**	***2**	**0**	**16:28**
2007-08♦	**Detroit**	**NHL**	**63**	**20**	**22**	**42**	**33**	**5**	**0**	**3**	**177**	**11.3**	**21**	**110**	**50.9**	**17:23**	**22**	**2**	**1**	**3**	**4**	**0**	**1**	**0**	**17:50**
2008-09	**Detroit**	**NHL**	**74**	**14**	**26**	**40**	**46**	**3**	**0**	**3**	**163**	**8.6**	**0**	**121**	**55.4**	**16:56**	**23**	**9**	**6**	**15**	**12**	**0**	**0**	***3**	**16:55**
2009-10	**Detroit**	**NHL**	**64**	**15**	**19**	**34**	**29**	**2**	**0**	**2**	**140**	**10.7**	**−3**	**119**	**49.6**	**17:14**	**12**	**2**	**0**	**2**	**4**	**0**	**0**	**0**	**14:47**
2010-11	**Detroit**	**NHL**	**68**	**26**	**20**	**46**	**20**	**5**	**0**	**8**	**192**	**13.5**	**−1**	**91**	**38.5**	**16:38**	**11**	**2**	**4**	**6**	**6**	**0**	**0**	**1**	**17:09**
2011-12	**Detroit**	**NHL**	**75**	**12**	**21**	**33**	**30**	**2**	**0**	**0**	**199**	**6.0**	**2**	**51**	**41.2**	**15:59**	**5**	**0**	**0**	**0**	**2**	**0**	**0**	**0**	**15:11**
2012-13	**Detroit**	**NHL**	**48**	**9**	**6**	**15**	**40**	**5**	**1**	**0**	**93**	**9.7**	**−6**	**23**	**47.8**	**16:27**	**14**	**4**	**6**	**10**	**2**	**1**	**0**	**0**	**16:47**
	NHL Totals		**869**	**160**	**217**	**377**	**455**	**32**	**7**	**27**	**1630**	**9.8**		**1300**	**48.1**	**14:36**	**121**	**24**	**28**	**52**	**76**	**3**	**3**	**4**	**16:01**

OHL All-Rookie Team (1995) • OHL First All-Star Team (1996, 1997) • AHL Second All-Star Team (2000)

Traded to **Edmonton** by **Chicago** with Chad Kilger, Ethan Moreau and Christian Laflamme for Boris Mironov, Dean McAmmond and Jonas Elofsson, March 20, 1999. Signed as a free agent by **Phoenix**, July 15, 2003. Signed as a free agent by **Mora** (Sweden), September 6, 2004. Signed as a free agent by **Detroit**, October 4, 2005.

CLICHE, Marc-Andre
(KLEESH, MAHRK-AWN-dray) **L.A.**

Center. Shoots right. 6', 203 lbs. Born, Rouyn-Noranda, Que., March 23, 1987. NY Rangers' 3rd choice, 56th overall, in 2005 Entry Draft.

Season	Club	League	GP	G	A	Pts	PIM	PP	SH	GW	S	%	+/-	TF	F%	Min	GP	G	A	Pts	PIM	PP	SH	GW	Min
2003-04	Lewiston	QMJHL	52	8	10	18	17	....	....	....	....	....	....	....	....	....	7	1	2	3	0	....	....	....	....
2004-05	Lewiston	QMJHL	19	4	4	8	8	....	....	....	....	....	....	....	....	....	....	....	....	....	....	....	....	....	....
2005-06	Lewiston	QMJHL	66	37	45	82	60	....	....	....	....	....	....	....	....	....	6	2	2	4	0	....	....	....	....
2006-07	Lewiston	QMJHL	52	24	30	54	42	....	....	....	....	....	....	....	....	....	16	6	16	22	10	....	....	....	....
2007-08	Manchester	AHL	52	11	10	21	25	....	....	....	....	....	....	....	....	....	4	0	1	1	2	....	....	....	....
2008-09	Manchester	AHL	31	5	4	9	19	....	....	....	....	....	....	....	....	....	....	....	....	....	....	....	....	....	....
2009-10	**Los Angeles**	**NHL**	**1**	**0**	**0**	**0**	**0**	**0**	**0**	**0**	**0**	**0.0**	**1**	**6**	**66.7**	**7:23**	....	....	....	....	....	....	....	....	....
	Manchester	AHL	66	11	14	25	45	....	....	....	....	....	....	....	....	....	12	1	1	2	8	....	....	....	....
2010-11	Manchester	AHL	63	14	21	35	35	....	....	....	....	....	....	....	....	....	....	....	....	....	....	....	....	....	....
2011-12	Manchester	AHL	72	17	24	41	35	....	....	....	....	....	....	....	....	....	4	1	0	1	6	....	....	....	....
2012-13	Manchester	AHL	57	10	10	20	46	....	....	....	....	....	....	....	....	....	3	0	0	0	4	....	....	....	....
	NHL Totals		**1**	**0**	**0**	**0**	**0**	**0**	**0**	**0**	**0**	**0.0**		**6**	**66.7**	**7:23**	....	....	....	....	....	....	....	....	....

• Missed majority of 2004-05 due to shoulder injury. Traded to **Los Angeles** by **NY Rangers** with Jason Ward, Jan Marek and NY Rangers' 3rd round choice (later traded to Buffalo - Buffalo selected Corey Fienhage) in 2008 Entry Draft for Sean Avery and John Seymour, February 5, 2007. • Missed majority of 2008-09 due to shoulder injury in training camp.

CLIFFORD, Kyle
(KLIHF-fuhrd, KIGHL) **L.A.**

Left wing. Shoots left. 6'2", 209 lbs. Born, Ayr, Ont., January 13, 1991. Los Angeles' 2nd choice, 35th overall, in 2009 Entry Draft.

Season	Club	League	GP	G	A	Pts	PIM	PP	SH	GW	S	%	+/-	TF	F%	Min	GP	G	A	Pts	PIM	PP	SH	GW	Min
2006-07	Cambridge	Minor-ON	70	31	49	80	119	....	....	....	....	....	....	....	....	....	....	....	....	....	....	....	....	....	....
2007-08	Barrie Colts	OHL	66	1	14	15	83	....	....	....	....	....	....	....	....	....	9	0	1	1	4	....	....	....	....
2008-09	Barrie Colts	OHL	60	16	12	28	133	....	....	....	....	....	....	....	....	....	5	0	0	0	13	....	....	....	....
2009-10	Barrie Colts	OHL	58	28	29	57	111	....	....	....	....	....	....	....	....	....	17	5	9	14	28	....	....	....	....
	Manchester	AHL	....	....	....	....	....	....	....	....	....	....	....	....	....	....	7	0	2	2	12	....	....	....	....
2010-11	**Los Angeles**	**NHL**	**76**	**7**	**7**	**14**	**141**	**0**	**0**	**0**	**69**	**10.1**	**−10**	**15**	**53.3**	**9:30**	**6**	**3**	**2**	**5**	**7**	**0**	**0**	**1**	**13:17**
2011-12♦	**Los Angeles**	**NHL**	**81**	**5**	**7**	**12**	**123**	**0**	**0**	**2**	**88**	**5.7**	**−5**	**8**	**12.5**	**9:24**	**3**	**0**	**0**	**0**	**2**	**0**	**0**	**0**	**5:01**
2012-13	Ontario Reign	ECHL	9	4	3	7	2	....	....	....	....	....	....	....	....	....	....	....	....	....	....	....	....	....	....
	Los Angeles	**NHL**	**48**	**7**	**7**	**14**	**51**	**0**	**0**	**1**	**56**	**12.5**	**1**	**9**	**11.1**	**10:36**	**14**	**0**	**2**	**2**	**8**	**0**	**0**	**0**	**10:21**
	NHL Totals		**205**	**19**	**21**	**40**	**315**	**0**	**0**	**3**	**213**	**8.9**		**32**	**31.3**	**9:43**	**23**	**3**	**4**	**7**	**17**	**0**	**0**	**1**	**10:26**

Signed as a free agent by **Ontario** (ECHL), November 20, 2012.

CLITSOME, Grant
(KLIHT-suhm, GRANT) **WPG**

Defense. Shoots left. 5'11", 215 lbs. Born, Gloucester, Ont., April 14, 1985. Columbus' 12th choice, 271st overall, in 2004 Entry Draft.

Season	Club	League	GP	G	A	Pts	PIM	PP	SH	GW	S	%	+/-	TF	F%	Min	GP	G	A	Pts	PIM	PP	SH	GW	Min
2001-02	Nepean Raiders	ON-Jr.A	43	1	6	7	20	....	....	....	....	....	....	....	....	....	1	0	0	0	....	....	....	....	....
2002-03	Nepean Raiders	ON-Jr.A	54	4	12	16	46	....	....	....	....	....	....	....	....	....	17	5	10	15	18	....	....	....	....
2003-04	Nepean Raiders	ON-Jr.A	55	13	26	39	67	....	....	....	....	....	....	....	....	....	17	1	10	11	6	....	....	....	....
2004-05	Clarkson Knights	ECAC	39	2	11	13	36	....	....	....	....	....	....	....	....	....	....	....	....	....	....	....	....	....	....
2005-06	Clarkson Knights	ECAC	34	2	17	19	20	....	....	....	....	....	....	....	....	....	....	....	....	....	....	....	....	....	....
2006-07	Clarkson Knights	ECAC	38	7	12	19	38	....	....	....	....	....	....	....	....	....	....	....	....	....	....	....	....	....	....
2007-08	Clarkson Knights	ECAC	39	5	17	22	28	....	....	....	....	....	....	....	....	....	....	....	....	....	....	....	....	....	....
	Syracuse Crunch	AHL	....	....	....	....	....	....	....	....	....	....	....	....	....	....	1	0	0	0	0	....	....	....	....
2008-09	Syracuse Crunch	AHL	73	4	15	19	74	....	....	....	....	....	....	....	....	....	....	....	....	....	....	....	....	....	....
2009-10	**Columbus**	**NHL**	**11**	**1**	**2**	**3**	**6**	**0**	**0**	**0**	**7**	**14.3**	**0**	**0**	**0.0**	**14:44**	....	....	....	....	....	....	....	....	....
	Syracuse Crunch	AHL	64	5	15	20	42	....	....	....	....	....	....	....	....	....	....	....	....	....	....	....	....	....	....
2010-11	**Columbus**	**NHL**	**31**	**4**	**15**	**19**	**16**	**2**	**0**	**0**	**50**	**8.0**	**2**	**0**	**0.0**	**21:16**	....	....	....	....	....	....	....	....	....
	Springfield	AHL	32	5	10	15	22	....	....	....	....	....	....	....	....	....	....	....	....	....	....	....	....	....	....
2011-12	**Columbus**	**NHL**	**51**	**4**	**10**	**14**	**24**	**1**	**0**	**1**	**74**	**5.4**	**−6**	**1**	**0.0**	**17:02**	....	....	....	....	....	....	....	....	....
	Winnipeg	**NHL**	**12**	**0**	**3**	**3**	**8**	**0**	**0**	**0**	**13**	**0.0**	**−3**	**0**	**0.0**	**16:54**	....	....	....	....	....	....	....	....	....
2012-13	**Winnipeg**	**NHL**	**44**	**4**	**12**	**16**	**18**	**2**	**0**	**0**	**56**	**7.1**	**10**	**0**	**0.0**	**18:50**	....	....	....	....	....	....	....	....	....
	NHL Totals		**149**	**13**	**42**	**55**	**72**	**5**	**0**	**1**	**200**	**6.5**		**1**	**0.0**	**18:16**	....	....	....	....	....	....	....	....	....

ECAC First All-Star Team (2008) • NCAA East Second All-American Team (2008)

Claimed on waivers by **Winnipeg** from **Columbus**, February 27, 2012.

CLOWE, Ryane
(KLOH, RIGH-uhn) **N.J.**

Left wing. Shoots left. 6'2", 225 lbs. Born, St. John's, Nfld., September 30, 1982. San Jose's 5th choice, 175th overall, in 2001 Entry Draft.

Season	Club	League	GP	G	A	Pts	PIM	PP	SH	GW	S	%	+/-	TF	F%	Min	GP	G	A	Pts	PIM	PP	SH	GW	Min
2000-01	Rimouski Oceanic	QMJHL	32	15	10	25	43	....	....	....	....	....	....	....	....	....	11	8	1	9	12	....	....	....	....
2001-02	Rimouski Oceanic	QMJHL	53	28	45	73	120	....	....	....	....	....	....	....	....	....	7	1	6	7	2	....	....	....	....
2002-03	Rimouski Oceanic	QMJHL	17	8	19	27	44	....	....	....	....	....	....	....	....	....	....	....	....	....	....	....	....	....	....
	Montreal Rocket	QMJHL	43	18	30	48	60	....	....	....	....	....	....	....	....	....	7	3	7	10	6	....	....	....	....
2003-04	Cleveland Barons	AHL	72	11	29	40	97	....	....	....	....	....	....	....	....	....	8	3	1	4	9	....	....	....	....
2004-05	Cleveland Barons	AHL	74	27	35	62	101	....	....	....	....	....	....	....	....	....	....	....	....	....	....	....	....	....	....
2005-06	**San Jose**	**NHL**	**18**	**0**	**2**	**2**	**9**	**0**	**0**	**0**	**14**	**0.0**	**−2**	**2**	**0.0**	**9:40**	**1**	**0**	**0**	**0**	**0**	**0**	**0**	**0**	**5:06**
	Cleveland Barons	AHL	35	13	21	34	35	....	....	....	....	....	....	....	....	....	....	....	....	....	....	....	....	....	....
2006-07	**San Jose**	**NHL**	**58**	**16**	**18**	**34**	**78**	**4**	**0**	**3**	**93**	**17.2**	**4**	**5**	**60.0**	**13:11**	**11**	**4**	**2**	**6**	**17**	**0**	**0**	**1**	**15:19**
2007-08	**San Jose**	**NHL**	**15**	**3**	**5**	**8**	**22**	**2**	**0**	**0**	**22**	**13.6**	**−1**	**14**	**35.7**	**14:17**	**13**	**5**	**4**	**9**	**12**	**2**	**0**	**0**	**19:00**
2008-09	**San Jose**	**NHL**	**71**	**22**	**30**	**52**	**51**	**11**	**0**	**1**	**161**	**13.7**	**8**	**120**	**40.8**	**17:47**	**6**	**1**	**1**	**2**	**8**	**0**	**0**	**0**	**18:22**
2009-10	**San Jose**	**NHL**	**82**	**19**	**38**	**57**	**131**	**2**	**0**	**2**	**189**	**10.1**	**0**	**73**	**48.0**	**17:10**	**15**	**2**	**8**	**10**	**28**	**0**	**0**	**0**	**20:11**
2010-11	**San Jose**	**NHL**	**75**	**24**	**38**	**62**	**100**	**5**	**0**	**2**	**185**	**13.0**	**13**	**41**	**41.5**	**17:58**	**17**	**6**	**9**	**15**	**32**	**3**	**0**	**0**	**19:27**
2011-12	**San Jose**	**NHL**	**76**	**17**	**28**	**45**	**97**	**4**	**0**	**2**	**180**	**9.4**	**−5**	**20**	**30.0**	**17:52**	**5**	**0**	**3**	**3**	**0**	**0**	**0**	**0**	**19:25**

			Regular Season														Playoffs								
Season	Club	League	GP	G	A	Pts	PIM	PP	SH	GW	S	%	+/-	TF	F%	Min	GP	G	A	Pts	PIM	PP	SH	GW	Min
2012-13	San Jose	NHL	28	0	11	11	79	0	0	0	65	0.0	-4	12	33.3	16:28	....	....	....	....	....	....	....	....	....
	NY Rangers	NHL	12	3	5	8	14	1	0	0	22	13.6	5	3	33.3	17:02	2	0	1	1	0	0	0	0	7:07
	NHL Totals		435	104	175	279	581	29	0	10	931	11.2		290	41.4	16:32	70	18	28	46	97	5	0	1	18:13

• Missed majority of 2007-08 due to knee injury at Columbus, October 27, 2007. Traded to **NY Rangers** by **San Jose** for NY Rangers' 2nd round choice (Gabryel Boudreau) in 2013 Entry Draft, Florida's 3rd round choice (previously acquired, later traded to Phoenix – Phoenix selected Pavel Laplante) in 2013 Entry Draft and NY Rangers' 5th round choice in 2014 Entry Draft, April 2, 2013. Signed as a free agent by **New Jersey**, July 5, 2013.

CLUNE, Rich
(KLOON, RITCH) **NSH**

Left wing. Shoots left. 5'10", 207 lbs. Born, Toronto, Ont., April 25, 1987. Dallas' 3rd choice, 71st overall, in 2005 Entry Draft.

2003-04	Sarnia Sting	OHL	58	3	13	16	72	....	....	....	....	....	....	....	....	....	5	0	1	1	0	....	....	....	....
2004-05	Sarnia Sting	OHL	68	21	13	34	103	....	....	....	....	....	....	....	....	....	....	....	....	....	....	....	....	....	....
2005-06	Sarnia Sting	OHL	61	20	32	52	126	....	....	....	....	....	....	....	....	....	....	....	....	....	....	....	....	....	....
2006-07	Barrie Colts	OHL	67	32	46	78	151	....	....	....	....	....	....	....	....	....	8	3	4	7	8	....	....	....	....
	Iowa Stars	AHL	1	0	0	0	2	....	....	....	....	....	....	....	....	....	....	....	....	....	....	....	....	....	....
2007-08	Iowa Stars	AHL	38	3	5	8	137	....	....	....	....	....	....	....	....	....	....	....	....	....	....	....	....	....	....
	Idaho Steelheads	ECHL	19	1	9	10	41	....	....	....	....	....	....	....	....	....	....	....	....	....	....	....	....	....	....
2008-09	Manchester	AHL	35	3	6	9	87	....	....	....	....	....	....	....	....	....	....	....	....	....	....	....	....	....	....
2009-10	Los Angeles	NHL	14	0	2	2	26	0	0	0	7	0.0	1	5	40.0	7:17	4	0	0	0	5	0	0	0	5:12
	Manchester	AHL	44	4	10	14	126	....	....	....	....	....	....	....	....	....	....	....	....	....	....	....	....	....	....
2010-11	Manchester	AHL	66	8	14	22	222	....	....	....	....	....	....	....	....	....	7	0	3	3	6	....	....	....	....
2011-12	Manchester	AHL	56	6	9	15	253	....	....	....	....	....	....	....	....	....	4	0	0	0	14	....	....	....	....
2012-13	Manchester	AHL	35	2	5	7	98	....	....	....	....	....	....	....	....	....	....	....	....	....	....	....	....	....	....
	Nashville	NHL	47	4	5	9	113	0	0	1	46	8.7	3	2	0.0	9:24	....	....	....	....	....	....	....	....	....
	NHL Totals		61	4	7	11	139	0	0	1	53	7.5		7	28.6	8:55	4	0	0	0	5	0	0	0	5:12

Traded to **Los Angeles** by **Dallas** for Lauri Tukonen, July 21, 2008. Claimed on waivers by **Nashville** from **Los Angeles**, January 15, 2013.

CLUTTERBUCK, Cal
(KLUH-tuhr-buhck, KAL) **NYI**

Right wing. Shoots right. 5'11", 213 lbs. Born, Welland, Ont., November 18, 1987. Minnesota's 3rd choice, 72nd overall, in 2006 Entry Draft.

2004-05	St. Michael's	OHL	38	10	6	16	55	....	....	....	....	....	....	....	....	....	....	....	....	....	....	....	....	....	....
	Oshawa Generals	OHL	27	9	9	18	42	....	....	....	....	....	....	....	....	....	....	....	....	....	....	....	....	....	....
2005-06	Oshawa Generals	OHL	66	35	33	68	139	....	....	....	....	....	....	....	....	....	....	....	....	....	....	....	....	....	....
2006-07	Oshawa Generals	OHL	65	35	54	89	153	....	....	....	....	....	....	....	....	....	9	8	5	13	21	....	....	....	....
2007-08	Minnesota	NHL	2	0	0	0	0	0	0	0	0	0.0	0	1	100.0	7:05	....	....	....	....	....	....	....	....	....
	Houston Aeros	AHL	73	11	13	24	97	....	....	....	....	....	....	....	....	....	5	0	0	0	14	....	....	....	....
2008-09	Minnesota	NHL	78	11	7	18	76	1	0	1	136	8.1	-5	17	11.8	13:00	....	....	....	....	....	....	....	....	....
	Houston Aeros	AHL	2	0	0	0	0	....	....	....	....	....	....	....	....	....	....	....	....	....	....	....	....	....	....
2009-10	Minnesota	NHL	74	13	8	21	52	1	2	1	136	9.6	-8	10	30.0	14:17	....	....	....	....	....	....	....	....	....
2010-11	Minnesota	NHL	76	19	15	34	79	4	0	3	191	9.9	-5	11	27.3	15:51	....	....	....	....	....	....	....	....	....
2011-12	Minnesota	NHL	74	15	12	27	103	3	*4	2	161	9.3	-4	15	33.3	16:21	....	....	....	....	....	....	....	....	....
2012-13	Minnesota	NHL	42	4	6	10	27	0	0	1	87	4.6	-5	2	50.0	13:44	5	1	1	2	4	0	0	0	15:51
	NHL Totals		346	62	48	110	337	9	6	8	711	8.7		56	26.8	14:40	5	1	1	2	4	0	0	0	15:51

Traded to **NY Islanders** by **Minnesota** with New Jersey's 3rd round choice (previously acquired, NY Islanders selected Eamon McAdam) in 2013 Entry Draft for Nino Niederreiter, June 30, 2013.

COBURN, Braydon
(KOH-buhrn, BRAY-duhn) **PHI**

Defense. Shoots left. 6'5", 220 lbs. Born, Calgary, Alta., February 27, 1985. Atlanta's 1st choice, 8th overall, in 2003 Entry Draft.

2000-01	Notre Dame	SMHL	32	3	19	22	70	....	....	....	....	....	....	....	....	....	....	....	....	....	....	....	....	....	....
	Portland	WHL	2	0	1	1	0	....	....	....	....	....	....	....	....	....	14	0	4	4	2	....	....	....	....
2001-02	Portland	WHL	68	4	33	37	100	....	....	....	....	....	....	....	....	....	7	1	1	2	9	....	....	....	....
2002-03	Portland	WHL	53	3	16	19	147	....	....	....	....	....	....	....	....	....	7	0	1	1	8	....	....	....	....
2003-04	Portland	WHL	55	10	20	30	92	....	....	....	....	....	....	....	....	....	5	0	1	1	10	....	....	....	....
2004-05	Portland	WHL	60	12	32	44	144	....	....	....	....	....	....	....	....	....	7	1	5	6	6	....	....	....	....
	Chicago Wolves	AHL	3	0	1	1	5	....	....	....	....	....	....	....	....	....	18	0	1	1	36	....	....	....	....
2005-06	Atlanta	NHL	9	0	1	1	4	0	0	0	4	0.0	-2	0	0.0	7:43	....	....	....	....	....	....	....	....	....
	Chicago Wolves	AHL	73	6	20	26	134	....	....	....	....	....	....	....	....	....	....	....	....	....	....	....	....	....	....
2006-07	Atlanta	NHL	29	0	4	4	30	0	0	0	21	0.0	1	0	0.0	11:41	....	....	....	....	....	....	....	....	....
	Chicago Wolves	AHL	15	1	10	11	36	....	....	....	....	....	....	....	....	....	....	....	....	....	....	....	....	....	....
	Philadelphia	NHL	20	3	4	7	16	1	0	0	33	9.1	-2	0	0.0	20:58	....	....	....	....	....	....	....	....	....
2007-08	Philadelphia	NHL	78	9	27	36	74	5	0	2	113	8.0	17	0	0.0	21:14	14	0	6	6	14	0	0	0	22:25
2008-09	Philadelphia	NHL	80	7	21	28	97	3	0	0	130	5.4	7	0	0.0	24:37	6	0	3	3	7	0	0	0	26:29
2009-10	Philadelphia	NHL	81	5	14	19	54	1	0	0	122	4.1	-6	0	0.0	21:08	23	1	3	4	22	1	0	1	25:09
2010-11	Philadelphia	NHL	82	2	14	16	53	0	0	0	114	1.8	15	0	0.0	21:04	11	1	2	3	6	0	0	0	24:07
2011-12	Philadelphia	NHL	81	4	20	24	56	0	0	0	113	3.5	10	1	0.0	22:03	11	0	4	4	8	0	0	0	27:10
2012-13	Philadelphia	NHL	33	1	4	5	41	0	0	0	38	2.6	-10	0	0.0	22:37	....	....	....	....	....	....	....	....	....
	NHL Totals		493	31	109	140	425	10	0	2	688	4.5		1	0.0	21:09	65	2	18	20	57	1	0	1	24:51

WHL Rookie of the Year (2002) • WHL West First All-Star Team (2004, 2005) • Canadian Major Junior Second All-Star Team (2005)
Traded to **Philadelphia** by **Atlanta** for Alexei Zhitnik, February 24, 2007.

COGLIANO, Andrew
(kawg-lee-A-noh, AN-droo) **ANA**

Center. Shoots left. 5'10", 180 lbs. Born, Toronto, Ont., June 14, 1987. Edmonton's 1st choice, 25th overall, in 2005 Entry Draft.

2002-03	Vaughan Kings	GTHL	58	39	54	93	122	....	....	....	....	....	....	....	....	....	....	....	....	....	....	....	....	....	....
2003-04	St. Mike's B's	ON-Jr.A	36	26	47	73	14	....	....	....	....	....	....	....	....	....	24	11	20	31	12	....	....	....	....
2004-05	St. Mike's B's	ON-Jr.A	49	36	*66	*102	33	....	....	....	....	....	....	....	....	....	25	*22	*24	*46	20	....	....	....	....
2005-06	U. of Michigan	CCHA	39	12	16	28	38	....	....	....	....	....	....	....	....	....	....	....	....	....	....	....	....	....	....
2006-07	U. of Michigan	CCHA	38	24	26	50	12	....	....	....	....	....	....	....	....	....	....	....	....	....	....	....	....	....	....
2007-08	Edmonton	NHL	82	18	27	45	20	1	2	5	98	18.4	1	542	39.5	13:40	....	....	....	....	....	....	....	....	....
2008-09	Edmonton	NHL	82	18	20	38	22	4	0	4	116	15.5	-6	702	37.2	14:24	....	....	....	....	....	....	....	....	....
2009-10	Edmonton	NHL	82	10	18	28	31	1	0	1	139	7.2	-5	379	43.0	14:11	....	....	....	....	....	....	....	....	....
2010-11	Edmonton	NHL	82	11	24	35	64	0	1	3	129	8.5	-12	1108	41.6	17:15	....	....	....	....	....	....	....	....	....
2011-12	Anaheim	NHL	82	13	13	26	15	2	0	2	115	11.3	-4	386	42.0	14:42	....	....	....	....	....	....	....	....	....
2012-13	Klagenfurter AC	Austria	7	2	4	6	2	....	....	....	....	....	....	....	....	....	....	....	....	....	....	....	....	....	....
	Anaheim	NHL	48	13	10	23	6	0	2	1	79	16.5	14	92	34.8	15:22	7	0	1	1	4	0	0	0	15:47
	NHL Totals		458	83	112	195	158	8	5	16	676	12.3		3209	40.3	14:54	7	0	1	1	4	0	0	0	15:47

CCHA All-Rookie Team (2006)
Traded to **Anaheim** by **Edmonton** for Anaheim's 2nd round choice (Marc-Olivier Roy) in 2013 Entry Draft, July 12, 2011. Signed as a free agent by **Klagenfurt** (Austria), November 17, 2012.

COLAIACOVO, Carlo
(koh-lee-A-KOH-voh, KAHR-loh)

Defense. Shoots left. 6'1", 200 lbs. Born, Toronto, Ont., January 27, 1983. Toronto's 1st choice, 17th overall, in 2001 Entry Draft.

1998-99	Mississauga Reps	GTHL	44	10	12	23	28	....	....	....	....	....	....	....	....	....	....	....	....	....	....	....	....	....	....
99-2000	Erie Otters	OHL	52	4	18	22	12	....	....	....	....	....	....	....	....	....	13	2	4	6	9	....	....	....	....
2000-01	Erie Otters	OHL	62	12	27	39	59	....	....	....	....	....	....	....	....	....	14	4	7	11	16	....	....	....	....
2001-02	Erie Otters	OHL	60	13	27	40	49	....	....	....	....	....	....	....	....	....	21	7	10	17	20	....	....	....	....
2002-03	Toronto	NHL	2	0	1	1	0	0	0	0	1	0.0	0	0	0.0	13:43	....	....	....	....	....	....	....	....	....
	Erie Otters	OHL	35	14	21	35	12	....	....	....	....	....	....	....	....	....	....	....	....	....	....	....	....	....	....
2003-04	Toronto	NHL	2	0	1	1	2	0	0	0	0	0.0	1	0	0.0	13:56	....	....	....	....	....	....	....	....	....
	St. John's	AHL	62	6	25	31	50	....	....	....	....	....	....	....	....	....	....	....	....	....	....	....	....	....	....
2004-05	St. John's	AHL	49	4	20	24	59	....	....	....	....	....	....	....	....	....	5	0	1	1	2	....	....	....	....
2005-06	Toronto	NHL	21	2	5	7	17	1	0	0	21	9.5	0	1	0.0	15:26	....	....	....	....	....	....	....	....	....
	Toronto Marlies	AHL	14	5	6	11	14	....	....	....	....	....	....	....	....	....	....	....	....	....	....	....	....	....	....
2006-07	Toronto	NHL	48	8	9	17	22	0	0	1	60	13.3	5	0	0.0	17:57	....	....	....	....	....	....	....	....	....
	Toronto Marlies	AHL	5	1	5	6	4	....	....	....	....	....	....	....	....	....	....	....	....	....	....	....	....	....	....
2007-08	Toronto	NHL	28	2	4	6	10	0	0	1	30	6.7	-4	0	0.0	17:26	....	....	....	....	....	....	....	....	....
	Toronto Marlies	AHL	2	0	0	0	0	....	....	....	....	....	....	....	....	....	....	....	....	....	....	....	....	....	....
2008-09	Toronto	NHL	10	0	1	1	6	0	0	0	9	0.0	-2	0	0.0	16:52	....	....	....	....	....	....	....	....	....
	St. Louis	NHL	63	3	26	29	29	0	0	0	78	3.8	2	0	0.0	18:29	4	0	0	0	2	0	0	0	22:19
2009-10	St. Louis	NHL	67	7	25	32	60	4	1	1	74	9.5	8	1	100.0	17:18	....	....	....	....	....	....	....	....	....

			Regular Season														Playoffs								
Season	Club	League	GP	G	A	Pts	PIM	PP	SH	GW	S	%	+/-	TF	F%	Min	GP	G	A	Pts	PIM	PP	SH	GW	Min
2010-11	**St. Louis**	**NHL**	**65**	**6**	**20**	**26**	**23**	**1**	**0**	**1**	**81**	**7.4**	**–4**	**0**	**0.0**	**18:08**	....	....	....	....	....	....	....	....	....
2011-12	**St. Louis**	**NHL**	**64**	**2**	**17**	**19**	**22**	**0**	**0**	**2**	**68**	**2.9**	**7**	**0**	**0.0**	**19:00**	**7**	**0**	**3**	**3**	**16**	**0**	**0**	**0**	**17:55**
2012-13	Grand Rapids	AHL	2	0	0	0	0	....	....	....	....	....	....	....	....	....	....	....	....	....	....	....	....	....	....
	Detroit	**NHL**	**6**	**0**	**1**	**1**	**2**	**0**	**0**	**0**	**12**	**0.0**	**–4**	**0**	**0.0**	**18:55**	**9**	**0**	**1**	**1**	**2**	**0**	**0**	**0**	**15:14**
	NHL Totals		**376**	**30**	**110**	**140**	**193**	**6**	**1**	**6**	**434**	**6.9**		**2**	**50.0**	**17:54**	**20**	**0**	**4**	**4**	**20**	**0**	**0**	**0**	**17:35**

OHL Second All-Star Team (2002, 2003)

• Missed remainder of 2005-06 due to head injury at Ottawa, January 23, 2006. • Missed majority of 2007-08 due to knee surgery, April 29, 2007. Traded to **St. Louis** by **Toronto** with Alex Steen for Lee Stempniak, November 24, 2008. Signed as a free agent by **Detroit**, September 14, 2012. • Missed majority of 2012-13 due to recurring shoullder injury and as a healthy reserve.

COLBORNE, Joe

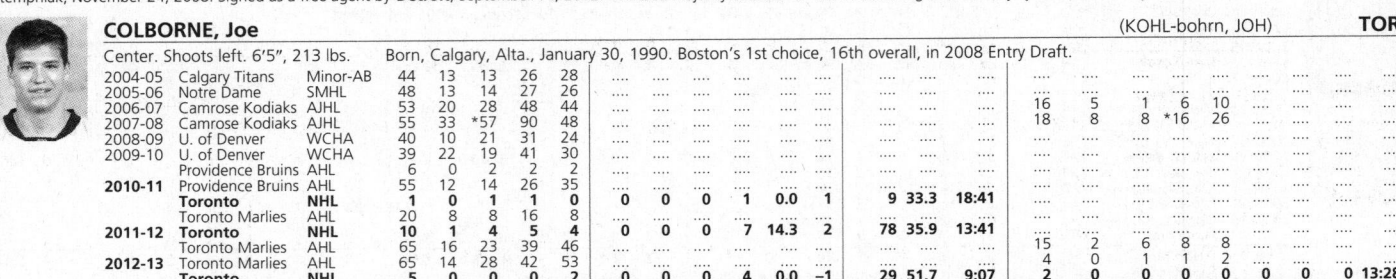

(KOHL-bohrn, JOH) **TOR**

Center. Shoots left. 6'5", 213 lbs. Born, Calgary, Alta., January 30, 1990. Boston's 1st choice, 16th overall, in 2008 Entry Draft.

Season	Club	League	GP	G	A	Pts	PIM	PP	SH	GW	S	%	+/-	TF	F%	Min	GP	G	A	Pts	PIM	PP	SH	GW	Min
2004-05	Calgary Titans	Minor-AB	44	13	13	26	28	....	....	....	....	....	....	....	....	....	....	....	....	....	....	....	....	....	....
2005-06	Notre Dame	SMHL	48	13	14	27	26	....	....	....	....	....	....	....	....	....	....	....	....	....	....	....	....	....	....
2006-07	Camrose Kodiaks	AJHL	53	20	28	48	44	....	....	....	....	....	....	....	....	....	16	5	1	6	10	....	....	....	....
2007-08	Camrose Kodiaks	AJHL	55	33	*57	90	48	....	....	....	....	....	....	....	....	....	18	8	8	*16	26	....	....	....	....
2008-09	U. of Denver	WCHA	40	10	21	31	24	....	....	....	....	....	....	....	....	....	....	....	....	....	....	....	....	....	....
2009-10	U. of Denver	WCHA	39	22	19	41	30	....	....	....	....	....	....	....	....	....	....	....	....	....	....	....	....	....	....
	Providence Bruins	AHL	6	0	2	2	2	....	....	....	....	....	....	....	....	....	....	....	....	....	....	....	....	....	....
2010-11	Providence Bruins	AHL	55	12	14	26	35	....	....	....	....	....	....	....	....	....	....	....	....	....	....	....	....	....	....
	Toronto	**NHL**	**1**	**0**	**1**	**1**	**0**	**0**	**0**	**0**	**1**	**0.0**	**1**	**9**	**33.3**	**18:41**	....	....	....	....	....	....	....	....	....
	Toronto Marlies	AHL	20	8	8	16	8	....	....	....	....	....	....	....	....	....	....	....	....	....	....	....	....	....	....
2011-12	**Toronto**	**NHL**	**10**	**1**	**4**	**5**	**4**	**0**	**0**	**0**	**7**	**14.3**	**2**	**78**	**35.9**	**13:41**	....	....	....	....	....	....	....	....	....
	Toronto Marlies	AHL	65	16	23	39	46	....	....	....	....	....	....	....	....	....	15	2	6	8	8	....	....	....	....
2012-13	Toronto Marlies	AHL	65	14	28	42	53	....	....	....	....	....	....	....	....	....	4	0	1	1	2	....	....	....	....
	Toronto	**NHL**	**5**	**0**	**0**	**0**	**2**	**0**	**0**	**0**	**4**	**0.0**	**–1**	**29**	**51.7**	**9:07**	**2**	**0**	**0**	**0**	**0**	**0**	**0**	**0**	**13:28**
	NHL Totals		**16**	**1**	**5**	**6**	**6**	**0**	**0**	**0**	**12**	**8.3**		**116**	**39.7**	**12:34**	**2**	**0**	**0**	**0**	**0**	**0**	**0**	**0**	**13:28**

WCHA All-Rookie Team (2009)

Traded to **Toronto** by **Boston** with Boston's 1st round choice (later traded to Anaheim – Anaheim selected Rickard Rakell) in 2011 Entry Draft and Boston's 2nd round choice (later traded to Colorado, later traded to Washington, later traded to Dallas – Dallas selected Mke Winther) in 2012 Entry Draft for Tomas Kaberle, February 18, 2011.

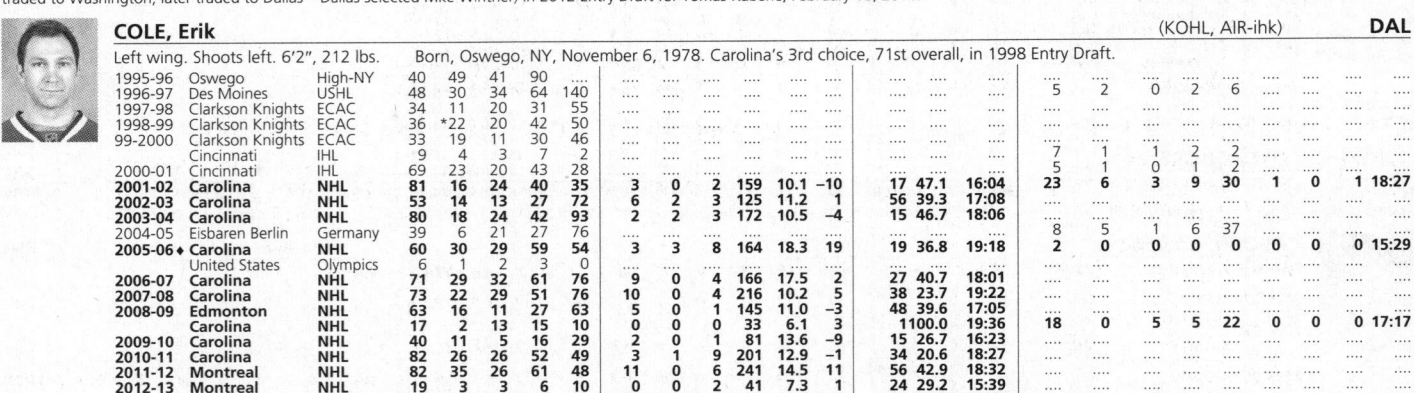

COLE, Erik

(KOHL, AIR-ihk) **DAL**

Left wing. Shoots left. 6'2", 212 lbs. Born, Oswego, NY, November 6, 1978. Carolina's 3rd choice, 71st overall, in 1998 Entry Draft.

Season	Club	League	GP	G	A	Pts	PIM	PP	SH	GW	S	%	+/-	TF	F%	Min	GP	G	A	Pts	PIM	PP	SH	GW	Min
1995-96	Oswego	High-NY	40	49	41	90	....	....	....	....	....	....	....	....	....	....	....	....	....	....	....	....	....	....	....
1996-97	Des Moines	USHL	48	30	34	64	140	....	....	....	....	....	....	....	....	....	5	2	0	2	6	....	....	....	....
1997-98	Clarkson Knights	ECAC	34	11	20	31	55	....	....	....	....	....	....	....	....	....	....	....	....	....	....	....	....	....	....
1998-99	Clarkson Knights	ECAC	36	*22	20	42	50	....	....	....	....	....	....	....	....	....	....	....	....	....	....	....	....	....	....
99-2000	Clarkson Knights	ECAC	33	19	11	30	46	....	....	....	....	....	....	....	....	....	....	....	....	....	....	....	....	....	....
	Cincinnati	IHL	9	4	3	7	2	....	....	....	....	....	....	....	....	....	7	1	1	2	2	....	....	....	....
2000-01	Cincinnati	IHL	69	23	20	43	28	....	....	....	....	....	....	....	....	....	5	1	0	1	2	....	....	....	....
2001-02	**Carolina**	**NHL**	**81**	**16**	**24**	**40**	**35**	**3**	**0**	**2**	**159**	**10.1**	**–10**	**17**	**47.1**	**16:04**	**23**	**6**	**3**	**9**	**30**	**1**	**0**	**1**	**18:27**
2002-03	**Carolina**	**NHL**	**53**	**14**	**13**	**27**	**72**	**6**	**2**	**3**	**125**	**11.2**	**1**	**56**	**39.3**	**17:08**	....	....	....	....	....	....	....	....	....
2003-04	**Carolina**	**NHL**	**80**	**18**	**24**	**42**	**93**	**2**	**2**	**3**	**172**	**10.5**	**–4**	**15**	**46.7**	**18:06**	....	....	....	....	....	....	....	....	....
2004-05	Eisbaren Berlin	Germany	39	6	21	27	76	....	....	....	....	....	....	....	....	....	8	5	1	6	37	....	....	....	....
2005-06 ♦	**Carolina**	**NHL**	**60**	**30**	**29**	**59**	**54**	**3**	**3**	**8**	**164**	**18.3**	**19**	**19**	**36.8**	**19:18**	**2**	**0**	**0**	**0**	**0**	**0**	**0**	**0**	**15:29**
	United States	Olympics	6	1	2	3	0	....	....	....	....	....	....	....	....	....	....	....	....	....	....	....	....	....	....
2006-07	**Carolina**	**NHL**	**71**	**29**	**32**	**61**	**76**	**9**	**0**	**4**	**166**	**17.5**	**2**	**27**	**40.7**	**18:01**	....	....	....	....	....	....	....	....	....
2007-08	**Carolina**	**NHL**	**73**	**22**	**29**	**51**	**76**	**10**	**0**	**4**	**216**	**10.2**	**5**	**38**	**23.7**	**19:22**	....	....	....	....	....	....	....	....	....
2008-09	**Edmonton**	**NHL**	**63**	**16**	**11**	**27**	**63**	**5**	**0**	**1**	**145**	**11.0**	**–3**	**48**	**39.6**	**17:05**	....	....	....	....	....	....	....	....	....
	Carolina	**NHL**	**17**	**2**	**13**	**15**	**10**	**0**	**0**	**0**	**33**	**6.1**	**3**	**1**	**100.0**	**19:36**	**18**	**0**	**5**	**5**	**22**	**0**	**0**	**0**	**17:17**
2009-10	**Carolina**	**NHL**	**40**	**11**	**5**	**16**	**29**	**2**	**0**	**1**	**81**	**13.6**	**–9**	**15**	**26.7**	**16:23**	....	....	....	....	....	....	....	....	....
2010-11	**Carolina**	**NHL**	**82**	**26**	**26**	**52**	**49**	**3**	**1**	**9**	**201**	**12.9**	**–1**	**34**	**20.6**	**18:27**	....	....	....	....	....	....	....	....	....
2011-12	**Montreal**	**NHL**	**82**	**35**	**26**	**61**	**48**	**11**	**0**	**6**	**241**	**14.5**	**11**	**56**	**42.9**	**18:32**	....	....	....	....	....	....	....	....	....
2012-13	**Montreal**	**NHL**	**19**	**3**	**3**	**6**	**10**	**0**	**0**	**2**	**41**	**7.3**	**1**	**24**	**29.2**	**15:39**	....	....	....	....	....	....	....	....	....
	Dallas	**NHL**	**28**	**6**	**1**	**7**	**10**	**1**	**0**	**0**	**45**	**13.3**	**–7**	**43**	**34.9**	**16:54**	....	....	....	....	....	....	....	....	....
	NHL Totals		**749**	**228**	**236**	**464**	**625**	**55**	**8**	**43**	**1789**	**12.7**		**393**	**35.9**	**17:51**	**43**	**6**	**8**	**14**	**52**	**1**	**0**	**1**	**17:50**

USHL Second All-Star Team (1997) • ECAC Rookie of the Year (1998) (co-winner - Willie Mitchell) • ECAC First All-Star Team (1999) • NCAA East Second All-American Team (1999) • ECAC Second All-Star Team (2000)

Signed as a free agent by **Berlin** (Germany), October 24, 2004. Traded to **Edmonton** by **Carolina** for Joni Pitkanen, July 1, 2008. Traded to **Carolina** by **Edmonton** with Edmonton's 5th round choice (Matt Kennedy) in 2009 Entry Draft for Patrick O'Sullivan and Carolina's 2nd round choice (later traded to Buffalo, later traded to Toronto – Toronto selected Jesse Blacker) in 2009 Entry Draft, March 4, 2009. • Missed majority of 2009-10 due to leg and upper-body injuries. Signed as a free agent by **Montreal**, July 1, 2011. Traded to **Dallas** by **Montreal** for Michael Ryder and Dallas' 3rd round choice (Connor Crisp) in 2013 Entry Draft, February 26, 2013.

COLE, Ian

(KOHL, EE-an) **ST.L.**

Defense. Shoots left. 6'1", 219 lbs. Born, Ann Arbour, MI, February 21, 1989. St. Louis' 2nd choice, 18th overall, in 2007 Entry Draft.

Season	Club	League	GP	G	A	Pts	PIM	PP	SH	GW	S	%	+/-	TF	F%	Min	GP	G	A	Pts	PIM	PP	SH	GW	Min
2004-05	Det. Vic. Honda	MWEHL	60	15	25	40	....	....	....	....	....	....	....	....	....	....	....	....	....	....	....	....	....	....	....
2005-06	USNTDP	U-17	18	2	1	3	14	....	....	....	....	....	....	....	....	....	....	....	....	....	....	....	....	....	....
	USNTDP	NAHL	40	2	8	10	75	....	....	....	....	....	....	....	....	....	12	0	3	3	14	....	....	....	....
2006-07	USNTDP	U-18	42	6	11	17	36	....	....	....	....	....	....	....	....	....	....	....	....	....	....	....	....	....	....
	USNTDP	NAHL	16	2	7	9	28	....	....	....	....	....	....	....	....	....	....	....	....	....	....	....	....	....	....
2007-08	U. of Notre Dame	CCHA	43	8	12	20	40	....	....	....	....	....	....	....	....	....	....	....	....	....	....	....	....	....	....
2008-09	U. of Notre Dame	CCHA	38	6	20	26	58	....	....	....	....	....	....	....	....	....	....	....	....	....	....	....	....	....	....
2009-10	U. of Notre Dame	CCHA	30	3	16	19	55	....	....	....	....	....	....	....	....	....	....	....	....	....	....	....	....	....	....
	Peoria Rivermen	AHL	9	1	4	5	4	....	....	....	....	....	....	....	....	....	....	....	....	....	....	....	....	....	....
2010-11	**St. Louis**	**NHL**	**26**	**1**	**3**	**4**	**35**	**0**	**0**	**0**	**22**	**4.5**	**6**	**0**	**0.0**	**17:36**	....	....	....	....	....	....	....	....	....
	Peoria Rivermen	AHL	44	5	10	15	63	....	....	....	....	....	....	....	....	....	....	....	....	....	....	....	....	....	....
2011-12	**St. Louis**	**NHL**	**26**	**1**	**5**	**6**	**22**	**0**	**0**	**0**	**18**	**5.6**	**7**	**0**	**0.0**	**15:55**	**2**	**0**	**0**	**0**	**0**	**0**	**0**	**0**	**10:26**
	Peoria Rivermen	AHL	22	1	3	4	26	....	....	....	....	....	....	....	....	....	....	....	....	....	....	....	....	....	....
2012-13	Peoria Rivermen	AHL	34	3	11	14	43	....	....	....	....	....	....	....	....	....	....	....	....	....	....	....	....	....	....
	St. Louis	**NHL**	**15**	**0**	**1**	**1**	**10**	**0**	**0**	**0**	**10**	**0.0**	**–4**	**0**	**0.0**	**17:45**	....	....	....	....	....	....	....	....	....
	NHL Totals		**67**	**2**	**9**	**11**	**67**	**0**	**0**	**0**	**50**	**4.0**		**0**	**0.0**	**16:59**	**2**	**0**	**0**	**0**	**0**	**0**	**0**	**0**	**10:26**

CCHA First All-Star Team (2009) • NCAA West First All-American Team (2009)

COLLINS, Sean

(KAW-lihnz, SHAWN)

Defense. Shoots right. 6'1", 205 lbs. Born, Troy, MI, October 30, 1983.

Season	Club	League	GP	G	A	Pts	PIM	PP	SH	GW	S	%	+/-	TF	F%	Min	GP	G	A	Pts	PIM	PP	SH	GW	Min
2002-03	Sioux City	USHL	59	6	22	28	89	....	....	....	....	....	....	....	....	....	4	0	1	1	2	....	....	....	....
2003-04	Ohio State	CCHA	41	3	12	15	57	....	....	....	....	....	....	....	....	....	....	....	....	....	....	....	....	....	....
2004-05	Ohio State	CCHA	40	9	17	26	40	....	....	....	....	....	....	....	....	....	....	....	....	....	....	....	....	....	....
2005-06	Ohio State	CCHA	39	7	11	18	63	....	....	....	....	....	....	....	....	....	....	....	....	....	....	....	....	....	....
2006-07	Ohio State	CCHA	37	9	19	28	50	....	....	....	....	....	....	....	....	....	....	....	....	....	....	....	....	....	....
	Hershey Bears	AHL	3	0	0	0	2	....	....	....	....	....	....	....	....	....	....	....	....	....	....	....	....	....	....
2007-08	Hershey Bears	AHL	12	0	0	0	11	....	....	....	....	....	....	....	....	....	....	....	....	....	....	....	....	....	....
	South Carolina	ECHL	31	1	13	14	16	....	....	....	....	....	....	....	....	....	20	1	8	9	24	....	....	....	....
2008-09	**Washington**	**NHL**	**15**	**1**	**1**	**2**	**12**	**0**	**0**	**0**	**14**	**7.1**	**1**	**0**	**0.0**	**14:32**	....	....	....	....	....	....	....	....	....
	Hershey Bears	AHL	39	1	7	8	38	....	....	....	....	....	....	....	....	....	6	0	2	2	2	....	....	....	....
2009-10	Hershey Bears	AHL	63	1	17	18	55	....	....	....	....	....	....	....	....	....	15	1	2	3	16	....	....	....	....
2010-11	**Washington**	**NHL**	**4**	**1**	**0**	**1**	**0**	**0**	**0**	**1**	**4**	**25.0**	**2**	**0**	**0.0**	**14:44**	**1**	**0**	**0**	**0**	**0**	**0**	**0**	**0**	**6:10**
	Hershey Bears	AHL	73	4	16	20	78	....	....	....	....	....	....	....	....	....	....	....	....	....	....	....	....	....	....
2011-12	**Washington**	**NHL**	**2**	**0**	**0**	**0**	**0**	**0**	**0**	**0**	**3**	**0.0**	**–1**	**0**	**0.0**	**10:56**	....	....	....	....	....	....	....	....	....
	Hershey Bears	AHL	65	2	8	10	45	....	....	....	....	....	....	....	....	....	5	0	0	0	4	....	....	....	....
2012-13	Connecticut	AHL	76	0	13	13	46	....	....	....	....	....	....	....	....	....	....	....	....	....	....	....	....	....	....
	NHL Totals		**21**	**2**	**1**	**3**	**12**	**0**	**0**	**1**	**21**	**9.5**		**0**	**0.0**	**14:14**	**1**	**0**	**0**	**0**	**0**	**0**	**0**	**0**	**6:10**

Signed as a free agent by **Washington**, March 19, 2007. Signed as a free agent by **NY Rangers**, July 12, 2012.

			Regular Season														Playoffs								
Season	Club	League	GP	G	A	Pts	PIM	PP	SH	GW	S	%	+/-	TF	F%	Min	GP	G	A	Pts	PIM	PP	SH	GW	Min

COLLINS, Sean
(KAW-lihnz, SHAWN) **CBJ**

Center. Shoots left. 6'3", 205 lbs. Born, Saskatoon, Sask., December 29, 1988. Columbus' 9th choice, 187th overall, in 2008 Entry Draft.

2006-07	Waywayseecappo	MJHL	70	20	69	89	34	....	....	....	....	....	....	....	....	....	....	....	....	....	....	....	....	....	....
2007-08	Waywayseecappo	MJHL	60	51	64	115	34	....	....	....	....	....	....	....	....	....	7	9	4	13	10	....	....	....	....
2008-09	Cornell Big Red	ECAC	33	3	3	6	16	....	....	....	....	....	....	....	....	....	....	....	....	....	....	....	....	....	....
2009-10	Cornell Big Red	ECAC	34	7	3	10	12	....	....	....	....	....	....	....	....	....	....	....	....	....	....	....	....	....	....
2010-11	Cornell Big Red	ECAC	34	7	8	15	20	....	....	....	....	....	....	....	....	....	....	....	....	....	....	....	....	....	....
2011-12	Cornell Big Red	ECAC	35	13	13	26	14	....	....	....	....	....	....	....	....	....	....	....	....	....	....	....	....	....	....
	Springfield	AHL	8	1	4	5	0	....	....	....	....	....	....	....	....	....	....	....	....	....	....	....	....	....	....
2012-13	Springfield	AHL	64	11	20	31	24	....	....	....	....	....	....	....	....	....	8	0	0	0	4	....	....	....	....
	Columbus	**NHL**	**5**	**0**	**0**	**0**	**6**	**0**	**0**	**0**	**0**	**0.0**	**−2**	**5**	**20.0**	**12:30**	....	....	....	....	....	....	....	....	....
	NHL Totals		**5**	**0**	**0**	**0**	**6**	**0**	**0**	**0**	**0**	**0.0**		**5**	**20.0**	**12:30**	....	....	....	....	....	....	....	....	....

COMEAU, Blake
(KOH-moh, BLAYK) **CBJ**

Right wing. Shoots right. 6', 195 lbs. Born, Meadow Lake, Sask., February 18, 1986. NY Islanders' 2nd choice, 47th overall, in 2004 Entry Draft.

2001-02	Sask. Contacts	SMHL	42	27	33	60	72	....	....	....	....	....	....	....	....	....	....	....	....	....	....	....	....	....	....
	Kelowna Rockets	WHL	3	0	0	0	4	....	....	....	....	....	....	....	....	....	....	....	....	....	....	....	....	....	....
2002-03	Kelowna Rockets	WHL	54	5	18	23	77	....	....	....	....	....	....	....	....	....	19	2	1	3	20	....	....	....	....
2003-04	Kelowna Rockets	WHL	71	10	23	33	123	....	....	....	....	....	....	....	....	....	17	4	2	6	23	....	....	....	....
2004-05	Kelowna Rockets	WHL	65	24	23	47	108	....	....	....	....	....	....	....	....	....	24	6	12	18	34	....	....	....	....
2005-06	Kelowna Rockets	WHL	60	21	53	74	85	....	....	....	....	....	....	....	....	....	12	4	9	13	22	....	....	....	....
	Bridgeport	AHL	....	....	....	....	....	....	....	....	....	....	....	....	....	....	7	0	3	3	0	....	....	....	....
2006-07	**NY Islanders**	**NHL**	**3**	**0**	**0**	**0**	**0**	**0**	**0**	**0**	**1**	**0.0**	**0**	**0**	**0.0**	**9:25**	....	....	....	....	....	....	....	....	....
	Bridgeport	AHL	61	12	31	43	46	....	....	....	....	....	....	....	....	....	....	....	....	....	....	....	....	....	....
2007-08	**NY Islanders**	**NHL**	**51**	**8**	**7**	**15**	**22**	**1**	**0**	**1**	**67**	**11.9**	**1**	**27**	**29.6**	**11:40**	....	....	....	....	....	....	....	....	....
	Bridgeport	AHL	31	4	15	19	30	....	....	....	....	....	....	....	....	....	....	....	....	....	....	....	....	....	....
2008-09	**NY Islanders**	**NHL**	**53**	**7**	**18**	**25**	**32**	**2**	**0**	**0**	**78**	**9.0**	**−17**	**45**	**31.1**	**16:17**	....	....	....	....	....	....	....	....	....
	Bridgeport	AHL	19	4	15	19	22	....	....	....	....	....	....	....	....	....	2	0	0	0	0	....	....	....	....
2009-10	**NY Islanders**	**NHL**	**61**	**17**	**18**	**35**	**40**	**0**	**1**	**2**	**133**	**12.8**	**−2**	**21**	**47.6**	**15:25**	....	....	....	....	....	....	....	....	....
2010-11	**NY Islanders**	**NHL**	**77**	**24**	**22**	**46**	**43**	**5**	**1**	**3**	**182**	**13.2**	**−17**	**112**	**31.3**	**18:41**	....	....	....	....	....	....	....	....	....
2011-12	**NY Islanders**	**NHL**	**16**	**0**	**0**	**0**	**6**	**0**	**0**	**0**	**20**	**0.0**	**−11**	**8**	**25.0**	**13:04**	....	....	....	....	....	....	....	....	....
	Calgary	**NHL**	**58**	**5**	**10**	**15**	**24**	**0**	**0**	**0**	**117**	**4.3**	**0**	**83**	**32.5**	**16:06**	....	....	....	....	....	....	....	....	....
2012-13	**Calgary**	**NHL**	**33**	**4**	**3**	**7**	**14**	**0**	**1**	**1**	**44**	**9.1**	**−9**	**81**	**45.7**	**12:17**	....	....	....	....	....	....	....	....	....
	Columbus	**NHL**	**9**	**2**	**3**	**5**	**6**	**0**	**0**	**0**	**4**	**50.0**	**5**	**5**	**60.0**	**11:41**	....	....	....	....	....	....	....	....	....
	NHL Totals		**361**	**67**	**81**	**148**	**187**	**8**	**3**	**7**	**646**	**10.4**		**382**	**35.6**	**15:17**	....	....	....	....	....	....	....	....	....

WHL West First All-Star Team (2006)

Claimed on waivers by **Calgary** from **NY Islanders**, November 25, 2011. Traded to **Columbus** by **Calgary** for Columbus' 5th round choice (Eric Roy) in 2013 Entry Draft, April 3, 2013.

COMMODORE, Mike
(KAWM-uh-dohr, MIGHK)

Defense. Shoots right. 6'4", 227 lbs. Born, Fort Saskatchewan, Alta., November 7, 1979. New Jersey's 2nd choice, 42nd overall, in 1999 Entry Draft.

1996-97	Ft. Saskatchewan	AJHL	51	3	8	11	244	....	....	....	....	....	....	....	....	....	....	....	....	....	....	....	....	....	....
1997-98	North Dakota	WCHA	29	0	5	5	74	....	....	....	....	....	....	....	....	....	....	....	....	....	....	....	....	....	....
1998-99	North Dakota	WCHA	39	5	8	13	154	....	....	....	....	....	....	....	....	....	....	....	....	....	....	....	....	....	....
99-2000	North Dakota	WCHA	38	5	7	12	*154	....	....	....	....	....	....	....	....	....	....	....	....	....	....	....	....	....	....
2000-01	**New Jersey**	**NHL**	**20**	**1**	**4**	**5**	**14**	**0**	**0**	**0**	**11**	**9.1**	**5**	**0**	**0.0**	**12:46**	....	....	....	....	....	....	....	....	....
	Albany River Rats	AHL	41	2	5	7	59	....	....	....	....	....	....	....	....	....	....	....	....	....	....	....	....	....	....
2001-02	**New Jersey**	**NHL**	**37**	**0**	**1**	**1**	**30**	**0**	**0**	**0**	**22**	**0.0**	**−12**	**0**	**0.0**	**12:37**	....	....	....	....	....	....	....	....	....
	Albany River Rats	AHL	14	0	3	3	31	....	....	....	....	....	....	....	....	....	....	....	....	....	....	....	....	....	....
2002-03	Cincinnati	AHL	61	2	9	11	210	....	....	....	....	....	....	....	....	....	....	....	....	....	....	....	....	....	....
	Calgary	**NHL**	**6**	**0**	**1**	**1**	**19**	**0**	**0**	**0**	**5**	**0.0**	**2**	**0**	**0.0**	**11:35**	....	....	....	....	....	....	....	....	....
	Saint John Flames	AHL	7	0	3	3	18	....	....	....	....	....	....	....	....	....	....	....	....	....	....	....	....	....	....
2003-04	**Calgary**	**NHL**	**12**	**0**	**0**	**0**	**25**	**0**	**0**	**0**	**10**	**0.0**	**−4**	**0**	**0.0**	**15:17**	**20**	**0**	**2**	**2**	**19**	**0**	**0**	**0**	**11:34**
	Lowell	AHL	37	5	11	16	75	....	....	....	....	....	....	....	....	....	....	....	....	....	....	....	....	....	....
2004-05	Lowell	AHL	73	6	29	35	175	....	....	....	....	....	....	....	....	....	11	1	2	3	18	....	....	....	....
2005-06 ♦	**Carolina**	**NHL**	**72**	**3**	**10**	**13**	**138**	**0**	**0**	**2**	**72**	**4.2**	**12**	**1**	**0.0**	**15:30**	**25**	**2**	**2**	**4**	**33**	**0**	**1**	**0**	**19:27**
2006-07	**Carolina**	**NHL**	**82**	**7**	**22**	**29**	**113**	**0**	**2**	**1**	**136**	**5.1**	**0**	**0**	**0.0**	**19:54**	....	....	....	....	....	....	....	....	....
2007-08	**Carolina**	**NHL**	**41**	**3**	**9**	**12**	**74**	**0**	**0**	**0**	**67**	**4.5**	**2**	**0**	**0.0**	**19:16**	....	....	....	....	....	....	....	....	....
	Ottawa	**NHL**	**26**	**0**	**2**	**2**	**26**	**0**	**0**	**0**	**30**	**0.0**	**−9**	**0**	**0.0**	**16:33**	**4**	**0**	**2**	**2**	**0**	**0**	**0**	**0**	**20:14**
2008-09	**Columbus**	**NHL**	**81**	**5**	**19**	**24**	**100**	**0**	**0**	**0**	**103**	**4.9**	**11**	**3**	**66.7**	**22:54**	**4**	**0**	**0**	**0**	**18**	**0**	**0**	**0**	**21:32**
2009-10	**Columbus**	**NHL**	**57**	**2**	**9**	**11**	**62**	**0**	**0**	**1**	**54**	**3.7**	**−9**	**0**	**0.0**	**19:00**	....	....	....	....	....	....	....	....	....
2010-11	**Columbus**	**NHL**	**20**	**2**	**4**	**6**	**44**	**0**	**0**	**2**	**32**	**6.3**	**−8**	**1**	**0.0**	**18:34**	....	....	....	....	....	....	....	....	....
	Springfield	AHL	11	0	2	2	20	....	....	....	....	....	....	....	....	....	....	....	....	....	....	....	....	....	....
2011-12	**Detroit**	**NHL**	**17**	**0**	**2**	**2**	**21**	**0**	**0**	**0**	**16**	**0.0**	**3**	**0**	**0.0**	**11:30**	....	....	....	....	....	....	....	....	....
	Tampa Bay	**NHL**	**13**	**0**	**0**	**0**	**17**	**0**	**0**	**0**	**7**	**0.0**	**4**	**0**	**0.0**	**14:03**	....	....	....	....	....	....	....	....	....
2012-13	Hamilton	AHL	17	0	2	2	26	....	....	....	....	....	....	....	....	....	....	....	....	....	....	....	....	....	....
	Texas Stars	AHL	5	2	0	2	4	....	....	....	....	....	....	....	....	....	1	0	0	0	0	....	....	....	....
	NHL Totals		**484**	**23**	**83**	**106**	**683**	**0**	**2**	**6**	**565**	**4.1**		**5**	**40.0**	**17:50**	**53**	**2**	**6**	**8**	**70**	**0**	**1**	**0**	**16:42**

NCAA Championship All-Tournament Team (2000)

Traded to **Anaheim** by **New Jersey** with Petr Sykora, Jean-Francois Damphousse and Igor Pohanka for Jeff Friesen, Oleg Tverdovsky and Maxim Balmochnykh, July 6, 2002. Traded to **Calgary** by **Anaheim** with Jean-Francois Damphousse for Rob Niedermayer, March 11, 2003. Traded to **Carolina** by **Calgary** for Atlanta's 3rd round choice (previously acquired, Calgary selected Gord Baldwin) in 2005 Entry Draft, July 29, 2005. Traded to **Ottawa** by **Carolina** with Cory Stillman for Joe Corvo and Patrick Eaves, February 11, 2008. Signed as a free agent by **Columbus**, July 1, 2008. • Missed majority of 2010-11 due to hand injury and as a healthy reserve. Signed as a free agent by **Detroit**, July 1, 2011. Traded to **Tampa Bay** by **Detroit** for future considerations, February 27, 2012. • Missed majority of 2011-12 as a healthy reserve. Signed as a free agent by **Hamilton** (AHL), November 21, 2012. Signed as a free agent by **Texas** (AHL), March 19, 2013.

CONACHER, Cory
(KAW-nuh-kuhr, KOHR-ee) **OTT**

Left wing. Shoots left. 5'8", 179 lbs. Born, Burlington, Ont., December 14, 1989.

2006-07	Burlington	ON-Jr.A	48	22	40	62	62	....	....	....	....	....	....	....	....	....	6	3	3	6	8	....	....	....	....
2007-08	Canisius College	AH	20	7	10	17	24	....	....	....	....	....	....	....	....	....	....	....	....	....	....	....	....	....	....
2008-09	Canisius College	AH	37	12	23	35	40	....	....	....	....	....	....	....	....	....	....	....	....	....	....	....	....	....	....
2009-10	Canisius College	AH	35	20	33	53	36	....	....	....	....	....	....	....	....	....	....	....	....	....	....	....	....	....	....
2010-11	Canisius College	AH	37	23	19	42	54	....	....	....	....	....	....	....	....	....	....	....	....	....	....	....	....	....	....
	Rochester	AHL	2	1	0	1	2	....	....	....	....	....	....	....	....	....	....	....	....	....	....	....	....	....	....
	Cincinnati	ECHL	3	5	2	7	0	....	....	....	....	....	....	....	....	....	....	....	....	....	....	....	....	....	....
	Milwaukee	AHL	5	3	2	5	2	....	....	....	....	....	....	....	....	....	7	0	1	1	6	....	....	....	....
2011-12	Norfolk Admirals	AHL	75	*39	41	80	114	....	....	....	....	....	....	....	....	....	18	2	13	15	28	....	....	....	....
2012-13	**Tampa Bay**	**NHL**	**35**	**9**	**15**	**24**	**16**	**1**	**0**	**2**	**53**	**17.0**	**−3**	**3**	**0.0**	**14:22**	....	....	....	....	....	....	....	....	....
	Syracuse Crunch	AHL	36	12	16	28	56	....	....	....	....	....	....	....	....	....	....	....	....	....	....	....	....	....	....
	Ottawa	**NHL**	**12**	**2**	**3**	**5**	**4**	**0**	**0**	**1**	**14**	**14.3**	**6**	**12**	**33.3**	**12:51**	**8**	**3**	**0**	**3**	**31**	**1**	**0**	**1**	**11:57**
	NHL Totals		**47**	**11**	**18**	**29**	**20**	**1**	**0**	**3**	**67**	**16.4**		**15**	**26.7**	**13:58**	**8**	**3**	**0**	**3**	**31**	**1**	**0**	**1**	**11:57**

AHL All-Rookie Team (2012) • AHL Second All-Star Team (2012) • Dudley "Red" Garrett Memorial Trophy (AHL - Top Rookie) (2012) • Willie Marshall Award (AHL - Top Goal-scorer) (2012) • Les Cunningham Award (AHL - MVP) (2012)

Signed to an ATO (amateur tryout) contract by **Rochester** (AHL), March 24, 2011. • Assigned to **Cincinatti** (ECHL) by **Rochester** (AHL), March 27, 2010. Signed to an ATO (amateur tryout) contract by **Milwaukee** (AHL), April 12, 2011. Signed as a free agent by **Norfolk** (AHL), July 5, 2011. Signed as a free agent by **Tampa Bay**, March 1, 2012. Traded to **Ottawa** by **Tampa Bay** with Philadelphia's 4th round choice (previously acquired, Ottawa selected Tobias Lindberg) in 2013 Entry Draft for Ben Bishop, April 3, 2013.

CONDRA, Erik
(KAWN-druh, AIR-ihk) **OTT**

Right wing. Shoots right. 6', 190 lbs. Born, Trenton, MI, August 6, 1986. Ottawa's 7th choice, 211th overall, in 2006 Entry Draft.

2004-05	Lincoln Stars	USHL	60	30	30	60	56	....	....	....	....	....	....	....	....	....	4	0	2	2	4	....	....	....	....
2005-06	U. of Notre Dame	CCHA	36	6	28	34	32	....	....	....	....	....	....	....	....	....	....	....	....	....	....	....	....	....	....
2006-07	U. of Notre Dame	CCHA	42	14	34	48	18	....	....	....	....	....	....	....	....	....	....	....	....	....	....	....	....	....	....
2007-08	U. of Notre Dame	CCHA	41	15	23	38	26	....	....	....	....	....	....	....	....	....	....	....	....	....	....	....	....	....	....
2008-09	U. of Notre Dame	CCHA	40	13	25	38	34	....	....	....	....	....	....	....	....	....	....	....	....	....	....	....	....	....	....
2009-10	Binghamton	AHL	80	11	27	38	61	....	....	....	....	....	....	....	....	....	....	....	....	....	....	....	....	....	....
2010-11	**Ottawa**	**NHL**	**26**	**6**	**5**	**11**	**12**	**1**	**0**	**2**	**48**	**12.5**	**−1**	**4**	**50.0**	**15:52**	....	....	....	....	....	....	....	....	....
	Binghamton	AHL	55	17	30	47	28	....	....	....	....	....	....	....	....	....	23	5	12	17	8	....	....	....	....
2011-12	**Ottawa**	**NHL**	**81**	**8**	**17**	**25**	**30**	**0**	**2**	**1**	**140**	**5.7**	**11**	**27**	**40.7**	**14:10**	**7**	**1**	**0**	**1**	**0**	**0**	**0**	**0**	**11:41**

			Regular Season														Playoffs								
Season	Club	League	GP	G	A	Pts	PIM	PP	SH	GW	S	%	+/-	TF	F%	Min	GP	G	A	Pts	PIM	PP	SH	GW	Min
2012-13	EV Fussen	German-3	7	8	11	19	2	....	....	....	....	....	....	....	....	....	....	....	....	....	....	....	....	....	....
	Riessersee	German-2	10	10	5	15	8	....	....	....	....	....	....	....	....	....	....	....	....	....	....	....	....	....	....
	Ottawa	**NHL**	**48**	**4**	**8**	**12**	**34**	**0**	**0**	**0**	**73**	**5.5**	**3**	**21**	**38.1**	**13:10**	**10**	**1**	**6**	**7**	**2**	**1**	**0**	**0**	**13:36**
	NHL Totals		**155**	**18**	**30**	**48**	**76**	**1**	**2**	**3**	**261**	**6.9**		**52**	**40.4**	**14:09**	**17**	**2**	**6**	**8**	**2**	**1**	**0**	**0**	**12:49**

CCHA All-Rookie Team (2006) • CCHA Second All-Star Team (2009) • NCAA West Second All-American Team (2009)

Signed as a free agent by **Fussen** (German-3), October 16, 2012. Signed as a free agent by **Riessersee** (German-2), November 12, 2012.

CONNER, Chris

(KAWN-uhr, KRIHS) **PIT**

Right wing. Shoots left. 5'8", 180 lbs. Born, Westland, MI, December 23, 1983.

2002-03	Michigan Tech	WCHA	38	13	24	37	8	....	....	....	....	....	....	....	....	....	....	....	....	....	....	....	....	....	....
2003-04	Michigan Tech	WCHA	38	25	14	39	12	....	....	....	....	....	....	....	....	....	....	....	....	....	....	....	....	....	....
2004-05	Michigan Tech	WCHA	37	14	10	24	6	....	....	....	....	....	....	....	....	....	....	....	....	....	....	....	....	....	....
2005-06	Michigan Tech	WCHA	38	17	12	29	18	....	....	....	....	....	....	....	....	....	....	....	....	....	....	....	....	....	....
	Iowa Stars	AHL	15	2	3	5	0	....	....	....	....	....	....	....	....	....	7	1	1	2	2	....	....	....	....
2006-07	**Dallas**	**NHL**	**11**	**1**	**2**	**3**	**4**	**0**	**0**	**0**	**18**	**5.6**	**-3**	**1**	**100.0**	**11:15**	....	....	....	....	....	....	....	....	....
	Iowa Stars	AHL	48	19	18	37	24	....	....	....	....	....	....	....	....	....	12	2	5	7	2	....	....	....	....
2007-08	**Dallas**	**NHL**	**22**	**3**	**2**	**5**	**6**	**0**	**0**	**0**	**27**	**11.1**	**0**	**1**	**100.0**	**12:00**	**1**	**0**	**0**	**0**	**0**	**0**	**0**	**0**	**4:17**
	Iowa Stars	AHL	55	13	26	39	17	....	....	....	....	....	....	....	....	....	....	....	....	....	....	....	....	....	....
2008-09	**Dallas**	**NHL**	**38**	**3**	**10**	**13**	**10**	**0**	**0**	**1**	**34**	**8.8**	**-5**	**1**	**0.0**	**10:56**	....	....	....	....	....	....	....	....	....
	Peoria Rivermen	AHL	30	16	12	28	10	....	....	....	....	....	....	....	....	....	....	....	....	....	....	....	....	....	....
2009-10	**Pittsburgh**	**NHL**	**8**	**2**	**1**	**3**	**0**	**0**	**0**	**1**	**11**	**18.2**	**-1**	**1**	**0.0**	**9:36**	**1**	**0**	**0**	**0**	**0**	**0**	**0**	**0**	**11:03**
	Wilkes-Barre	AHL	59	19	37	56	21	....	....	....	....	....	....	....	....	....	4	2	2	4	2	....	....	....	....
2010-11	**Pittsburgh**	**NHL**	**60**	**7**	**9**	**16**	**10**	**0**	**0**	**3**	**91**	**7.7**	**5**	**4**	**25.0**	**11:49**	**7**	**1**	**0**	**1**	**0**	**0**	**0**	**0**	**12:22**
	Wilkes-Barre	AHL	11	3	6	9	2	....	....	....	....	....	....	....	....	....	....	....	....	....	....	....	....	....	....
2011-12	**Detroit**	**NHL**	**8**	**1**	**2**	**3**	**0**	**0**	**0**	**0**	**10**	**10.0**	**2**	**0**	**0.0**	**10:34**	....	....	....	....	....	....	....	....	....
	Grand Rapids	AHL	57	16	37	53	22	....	....	....	....	....	....	....	....	....	....	....	....	....	....	....	....	....	....
2012-13	Portland Pirates	AHL	60	13	27	40	28	....	....	....	....	....	....	....	....	....	1	0	1	1	2	....	....	....	....
	Phoenix	**NHL**	**12**	**1**	**1**	**2**	**2**	**0**	**0**	**0**	**15**	**6.7**	**3**	**2**	**0.0**	**11:23**	....	....	....	....	....	....	....	....	....
	NHL Totals		**159**	**18**	**27**	**45**	**32**	**0**	**0**	**5**	**206**	**8.7**		**10**	**30.0**	**11:23**	**9**	**1**	**0**	**1**	**0**	**0**	**0**	**0**	**11:20**

WCHA Second All-Star Team (2004)

Signed as a free agent by **Dallas**, July 13, 2006. Signed as a free agent by **Pittsburgh**, July 5. 2009. Signed as a free agent by **Detroit**, July 5, 2011. Signed as a free agent by **Phoenix**, July 2, 2012. Signed as a free agent by **Pittsburgh**, July 6, 2013.

CONNOLLY, Brett

(KAW-nuh-lee, BREHT) **T.B.**

Right wing. Shoots right. 6'2", 200 lbs. Born, Prince George, B.C., May 2, 1992. Tampa Bay's 1st choice, 6th overall, in 2010 Entry Draft.

2007-08	Cariboo Cougars	BCMML	38	16	16	32	80	....	....	....	....	....	....	....	....	....	6	4	1	5	10	....	....	....	....
	Prince George	WHL	4	0	0	0	0	....	....	....	....	....	....	....	....	....	....	....	....	....	....	....	....	....	....
2008-09	Prince George	WHL	65	30	30	60	38	....	....	....	....	....	....	....	....	....	4	0	2	2	6	....	....	....	....
2009-10	Prince George	WHL	16	10	9	19	8	....	....	....	....	....	....	....	....	....	....	....	....	....	....	....	....	....	....
2010-11	Prince George	WHL	59	46	27	73	26	....	....	....	....	....	....	....	....	....	1	0	0	0	0	....	....	....	....
2011-12	**Tampa Bay**	**NHL**	**68**	**4**	**11**	**15**	**30**	**1**	**0**	**2**	**94**	**4.3**	**-9**	**52**	**38.5**	**11:28**	....	....	....	....	....	....	....	....	....
2012-13	Syracuse Crunch	AHL	71	31	32	63	53	....	....	....	....	....	....	....	....	....	18	6	5	11	12	....	....	....	....
	Tampa Bay	**NHL**	**5**	**1**	**0**	**1**	**0**	**1**	**0**	**0**	**10**	**10.0**	**-3**	**5**	**80.0**	**10:16**	....	....	....	....	....	....	....	....	....
	NHL Totals		**73**	**5**	**11**	**16**	**30**	**2**	**0**	**2**	**104**	**4.8**		**57**	**42.1**	**11:23**	....	....	....	....	....	....	....	....	....

WHL Rookie of the Year (2009) • Canadian Major Junior All-Rookie Team (2009) • Canadian Major Junior Rookie of the Year (2009) • AHL Second All-Star Team (2013)

• Missed majority of 2009-10 due to pre-season hip injury..

CONNOLLY, Tim

(KAW-nuhl-lee, TIHM)

Center. Shoots right. 6'1", 190 lbs. Born, Syracuse, NY, May 7, 1981. NY Islanders' 1st choice, 5th overall, in 1999 Entry Draft.

1996-97	Syracuse	ON-Jr.A	50	42	62	104	34	....	....	....	....	....	....	....	....	....	....	....	....	....	....	....	....	....	....
1997-98	Erie Otters	OHL	59	30	32	62	32	....	....	....	....	....	....	....	....	....	7	1	6	7	6	....	....	....	....
1998-99	Erie Otters	OHL	46	34	34	68	50	....	....	....	....	....	....	....	....	....	....	....	....	....	....	....	....	....	....
99-2000	**NY Islanders**	**NHL**	**81**	**14**	**20**	**34**	**44**	**2**	**1**	**1**	**114**	**12.3**	**-25**	**786**	**36.3**	**16:18**	....	....	....	....	....	....	....	....	....
2000-01	**NY Islanders**	**NHL**	**82**	**10**	**31**	**41**	**42**	**5**	**0**	**0**	**171**	**5.8**	**-14**	**989**	**41.7**	**20:02**	....	....	....	....	....	....	....	....	....
2001-02	**Buffalo**	**NHL**	**82**	**10**	**35**	**45**	**34**	**3**	**0**	**3**	**126**	**7.9**	**4**	**1074**	**39.6**	**16:58**	....	....	....	....	....	....	....	....	....
2002-03	**Buffalo**	**NHL**	**80**	**12**	**13**	**25**	**32**	**6**	**0**	**2**	**159**	**7.5**	**-28**	**845**	**42.8**	**16:00**	....	....	....	....	....	....	....	....	....
2003-04	**Buffalo**	**NHL**	DID NOT PLAY – INJURED																						
2004-05	Langnau	Swiss	16	7	3	10	14	....	....	....	....	....	....	....	....	....	....	....	....	....	....	....	....	....	....
2005-06	**Buffalo**	**NHL**	**63**	**16**	**39**	**55**	**28**	**7**	**0**	**3**	**99**	**16.2**	**5**	**844**	**42.5**	**18:00**	**8**	**5**	**6**	**11**	**0**	**1**	**1**	**1**	**17:29**
2006-07	**Buffalo**	**NHL**	**2**	**1**	**0**	**1**	**2**	**0**	**0**	**0**	**2**	**50.0**	**1**	**13**	**53.9**	**13:07**	**16**	**0**	**9**	**9**	**4**	**0**	**0**	**0**	**16:56**
2007-08	**Buffalo**	**NHL**	**48**	**7**	**33**	**40**	**8**	**3**	**1**	**3**	**111**	**6.3**	**4**	**463**	**48.0**	**18:41**	....	....	....	....	....	....	....	....	....
2008-09	**Buffalo**	**NHL**	**48**	**18**	**29**	**47**	**22**	**5**	**1**	**5**	**126**	**14.3**	**12**	**544**	**42.1**	**19:07**	....	....	....	....	....	....	....	....	....
2009-10	**Buffalo**	**NHL**	**73**	**17**	**48**	**65**	**28**	**7**	**1**	**5**	**206**	**8.3**	**10**	**764**	**46.9**	**18:37**	**6**	**0**	**1**	**1**	**2**	**0**	**0**	**0**	**17:49**
2010-11	**Buffalo**	**NHL**	**68**	**13**	**29**	**42**	**20**	**6**	**0**	**3**	**151**	**8.6**	**-10**	**969**	**45.9**	**16:55**	**6**	**0**	**2**	**2**	**2**	**0**	**0**	**0**	**19:04**
2011-12	**Toronto**	**NHL**	**70**	**13**	**23**	**36**	**40**	**2**	**0**	**3**	**104**	**12.5**	**-14**	**786**	**48.7**	**17:00**	....	....	....	....	....	....	....	....	....
2012-13	Toronto Marlies	AHL	28	5	7	12	23	....	....	....	....	....	....	....	....	....	6	0	1	1	8	....	....	....	....
	NHL Totals		**697**	**131**	**300**	**431**	**300**	**46**	**4**	**28**	**1369**	**9.6**		**8077**	**43.2**	**17:39**	**36**	**5**	**18**	**23**	**8**	**1**	**1**	**1**	**17:34**

Traded to **Buffalo** by **NY Islanders** with Taylor Pyatt for Michael Peca, June 24, 2001. • Missed entire 2003-04 due to head injury in pre-season vs. Chicago, October 2, 2003. Signed as a free agent by **Langnau** (Swiss), October 10, 2004. • Missed majority of 2006-07 due to head injury in playoff game vs. Ottawa, May 8, 2006. Signed as a free agent by **Toronto**, July 2, 2011.

COOKE, Matt

(KUK, MAT) **MIN**

Center. Shoots left. 5'11", 205 lbs. Born, Belleville, Ont., September 7, 1978. Vancouver's 8th choice, 144th overall, in 1997 Entry Draft.

1994-95	Wellington Dukes	ON-Jr.A	46	9	23	32	62	....	....	....	....	....	....	....	....	....	....	....	....	....	....	....	....	....	....
1995-96	Windsor Spitfires	OHL	61	8	11	19	102	....	....	....	....	....	....	....	....	....	7	1	3	4	6	....	....	....	....
1996-97	Windsor Spitfires	OHL	65	45	50	95	146	....	....	....	....	....	....	....	....	....	5	5	5	10	10	....	....	....	....
1997-98	Windsor Spitfires	OHL	23	14	19	33	50	....	....	....	....	....	....	....	....	....	....	....	....	....	....	....	....	....	....
	Kingston	OHL	25	8	13	21	49	....	....	....	....	....	....	....	....	....	12	8	8	16	20	....	....	....	....
1998-99	**Vancouver**	**NHL**	**30**	**0**	**2**	**2**	**27**	**0**	**0**	**0**	**22**	**0.0**	**-12**	**189**	**40.2**	**8:07**	....	....	....	....	....	....	....	....	....
	Syracuse Crunch	AHL	37	15	18	33	119	....	....	....	....	....	....	....	....	....	....	....	....	....	....	....	....	....	....
99-2000	**Vancouver**	**NHL**	**51**	**5**	**7**	**12**	**39**	**0**	**1**	**1**	**58**	**8.6**	**3**	**71**	**39.4**	**11:48**	....	....	....	....	....	....	....	....	....
	Syracuse Crunch	AHL	18	5	8	13	27	....	....	....	....	....	....	....	....	....	....	....	....	....	....	....	....	....	....
2000-01	**Vancouver**	**NHL**	**81**	**14**	**13**	**27**	**94**	**0**	**2**	**0**	**121**	**11.6**	**5**	**321**	**43.0**	**14:35**	**4**	**0**	**0**	**0**	**4**	**0**	**0**	**0**	**12:04**
2001-02	**Vancouver**	**NHL**	**82**	**13**	**20**	**33**	**111**	**1**	**0**	**2**	**103**	**12.6**	**4**	**28**	**32.1**	**14:03**	**6**	**3**	**2**	**5**	**0**	**1**	**0**	**0**	**15:09**
2002-03	**Vancouver**	**NHL**	**82**	**15**	**27**	**42**	**82**	**1**	**4**	**0**	**118**	**12.7**	**21**	**31**	**35.5**	**13:24**	**14**	**2**	**1**	**3**	**12**	**0**	**0**	**0**	**14:07**
2003-04	**Vancouver**	**NHL**	**53**	**11**	**12**	**23**	**73**	**1**	**1**	**4**	**79**	**13.9**	**5**	**34**	**52.9**	**14:06**	**7**	**3**	**1**	**4**	**12**	**0**	**0**	**1**	**18:23**
2004-05			DID NOT PLAY																						
2005-06	**Vancouver**	**NHL**	**45**	**8**	**10**	**18**	**71**	**0**	**0**	**2**	**67**	**11.9**	**-8**	**25**	**24.0**	**13:57**	....	....	....	....	....	....	....	....	....
2006-07	**Vancouver**	**NHL**	**81**	**10**	**20**	**30**	**64**	**1**	**0**	**3**	**133**	**7.5**	**0**	**19**	**47.4**	**15:37**	**1**	**0**	**0**	**0**	**2**	**0**	**0**	**0**	**9:51**
2007-08	**Vancouver**	**NHL**	**61**	**7**	**9**	**16**	**64**	**0**	**0**	**1**	**68**	**10.3**	**-4**	**26**	**42.3**	**13:24**	....	....	....	....	....	....	....	....	....
	Washington	**NHL**	**17**	**3**	**4**	**7**	**27**	**0**	**1**	**0**	**18**	**16.7**	**5**	**2**	**50.0**	**12:19**	**7**	**0**	**0**	**0**	**4**	**0**	**0**	**0**	**13:55**
2008-09♦	**Pittsburgh**	**NHL**	**76**	**13**	**18**	**31**	**101**	**0**	**0**	**1**	**86**	**15.1**	**0**	**19**	**36.8**	**14:13**	**24**	**1**	**6**	**7**	**22**	**0**	**0**	**0**	**15:09**
2009-10	**Pittsburgh**	**NHL**	**79**	**15**	**15**	**30**	**106**	**2**	**0**	**1**	**105**	**14.3**	**17**	**24**	**54.2**	**14:47**	**13**	**4**	**2**	**6**	**22**	**0**	**0**	**0**	**15:11**
2010-11	**Pittsburgh**	**NHL**	**67**	**12**	**18**	**30**	**129**	**0**	**3**	**2**	**95**	**12.6**	**14**	**29**	**27.6**	**15:38**	....	....	....	....	....	....	....	....	....
2011-12	**Pittsburgh**	**NHL**	**82**	**19**	**19**	**38**	**44**	**1**	**2**	**4**	**147**	**12.9**	**5**	**33**	**54.6**	**15:41**	**6**	**0**	**4**	**4**	**16**	**0**	**0**	**0**	**16:13**
2012-13	**Pittsburgh**	**NHL**	**48**	**8**	**13**	**21**	**36**	**0**	**0**	**1**	**61**	**13.1**	**-2**	**14**	**21.4**	**14:43**	**15**	**0**	**4**	**4**	**35**	**0**	**0**	**0**	**15:08**
	NHL Totals		**935**	**153**	**207**	**360**	**1068**	**7**	**14**	**22**	**1281**	**11.9**		**865**	**41.2**	**14:09**	**97**	**13**	**20**	**33**	**129**	**1**	**0**	**1**	**15:02**

Traded to **Washington** by **Vancouver** for Matt Pettinger, February 26, 2008. Signed as a free agent by **Pittsburgh**, July 6, 2008. Signed as a free agent by **Minnesota**, July 5, 2013.

CORMIER, Patrice
(KOHR-mee-ay, pa-TREEZ) **WPG**

Center. Shoots left. 6'2", 215 lbs. Born, Moncton, N.B., June 14, 1990. New Jersey's 3rd choice, 54th overall, in 2008 Entry Draft.

Season	Club	League	Regular Season GP	G	A	Pts	PIM	PP	SH	GW	S	%	+/-	TF	F%	Min	Playoffs GP	G	A	Pts	PIM	PP	SH	GW	Min
2005-06	Dieppe	MJrHL	43	21	27	48	41	....	....	....	....	....	....	....	....	....	6	2	2	4	6	....	....	....	....
2006-07	Rimouski Oceanic	QMJHL	53	11	10	21	73	....	....	....	....	....	....	....	....	....	....	....	....	....	....	....	....	....	....
2007-08	Rimouski Oceanic	QMJHL	51	18	23	41	84	....	....	....	....	....	....	....	....	....	9	4	5	9	10	....	....	....	....
2008-09	Rimouski Oceanic	QMJHL	54	23	28	51	118	....	....	....	....	....	....	....	....	....	13	4	6	10	30	....	....	....	....
2009-10	Rimouski Oceanic	QMJHL	28	11	15	26	57	....	....	....	....	....	....	....	....	....	....	....	....	....	....	....	....	....	....
	Rouyn-Noranda	QMJHL	3	0	5	5	7	....	....	....	....	....	....	....	....	....	....	....	....	....	....	....	....	....	....
	Chicago Wolves	AHL	....	....	....	....	....	....	....	....	....	....	....	....	....	....	9	0	0	0	8	....	....	....	....
2010-11	**Atlanta**	**NHL**	**21**	**1**	**1**	**2**	**4**	**0**	**0**	**0**	**27**	**3.7**	**–5**	**67**	**58.2**	**9:39**	....	....	....	....	....	....	....	....	....
	Chicago Wolves	AHL	11	2	3	5	14	....	....	....	....	....	....	....	....	....	....	....	....	....	....	....	....	....	....
2011-12	**Winnipeg**	**NHL**	**9**	**0**	**0**	**0**	**0**	**0**	**0**	**0**	**8**	**0.0**	**1**	**30**	**73.3**	**6:22**	....	....	....	....	....	....	....	....	....
	St. John's IceCaps	AHL	56	18	15	33	75	....	....	....	....	....	....	....	....	....	15	3	0	3	12	....	....	....	....
2012-13	St. John's IceCaps	AHL	35	7	4	11	69	....	....	....	....	....	....	....	....	....	....	....	....	....	....	....	....	....	....
	Winnipeg	**NHL**	**10**	**0**	**0**	**0**	**7**	**0**	**0**	**0**	**4**	**0.0**	**–3**	**6**	**16.7**	**3:53**	....	....	....	....	....	....	....	....	....
	NHL Totals		**40**	**1**	**1**	**2**	**11**	**0**	**0**	**0**	**39**	**2.6**		**103**	**60.2**	**7:28**	....	....	....	....	....	....	....	....	....

Traded to **Atlanta** by **New Jersey** with Johnny Oduya, Niclas Bergfors and New Jersey's 1st (later traded to Chicago - Chicago selected Kevin Hayes) and 2nd (later traded to Chicago - Chicago selected Justin Holl) round choices in 2010 Entry Draft for Ilya Kovalchuk, Anssi Salmela and Atlanta's 2nd round choice (Jonathon Merrill) in 2010 Entry Draft, February 4, 2010. • Missed majority of 2010-11 due to foot injury in training camp and upper-body injury at Phoenix, February 17, 2011. • Transferred to **Winnipeg** after **Atlanta** franchise relocated, June 21, 2011.

CORNET, Philippe
(kohr-NAY, fih-LEEP) **EDM**

Left wing. Shoots left. 6', 196 lbs. Born, Val-Senneville, Que., March 28, 1990. Edmonton's 3rd choice, 133rd overall, in 2008 Entry Draft.

2006-07	Rimouski Oceanic	QMJHL	46	7	14	21	8	....	....	....	....	....	....	....	....	....	....	....	....	....	....	....	....	....	....
2007-08	Rimouski Oceanic	QMJHL	61	23	26	49	24	....	....	....	....	....	....	....	....	....	9	3	3	6	6	....	....	....	....
2008-09	Rimouski Oceanic	QMJHL	63	29	48	77	34	....	....	....	....	....	....	....	....	....	13	4	11	15	14	....	....	....	....
2009-10	Rouyn-Noranda	QMJHL	65	28	49	77	32	....	....	....	....	....	....	....	....	....	11	5	6	11	6	....	....	....	....
2010-11	Oklahoma City	AHL	60	7	16	23	8	....	....	....	....	....	....	....	....	....	....	....	....	....	....	....	....	....	....
2011-12	**Edmonton**	**NHL**	**2**	**0**	**1**	**1**	**0**	**0**	**0**	**0**	**0**	**0.0**	**0**	**0**	**0.0**	**10:35**	....	....	....	....	....	....	....	....	....
	Oklahoma City	AHL	67	24	13	37	26	....	....	....	....	....	....	....	....	....	14	2	5	7	2	....	....	....	....
2012-13	Oklahoma City	AHL	46	15	18	33	18	....	....	....	....	....	....	....	....	....	17	2	7	9	0	....	....	....	....
	Stockton Thunder	ECHL	18	9	14	23	2	....	....	....	....	....	....	....	....	....	....	....	....	....	....	....	....	....	....
	NHL Totals		**2**	**0**	**1**	**1**	**0**	**0**	**0**	**0**	**0**	**0.0**		**0**	**0.0**	**10:35**	....	....	....	....	....	....	....	....	....

CORRADO, Frank
(koh-RA-doh, FRANK) **VAN**

Defense. Shoots right. 6'2", 191 lbs. Born, Woodbridge, Ont., March 26, 1993. Vancouver's 6th choice, 150th overall, in 2011 Entry Draft.

2008-09	Vaughan Kings	GTHL	62	15	33	48	136	....	....	....	....	....	....	....	....	....	....	....	....	....	....	....	....	....	....
2009-10	Sudbury Wolves	OHL	63	1	8	9	46	....	....	....	....	....	....	....	....	....	4	0	1	1	0	....	....	....	....
2010-11	Sudbury Wolves	OHL	67	4	26	30	94	....	....	....	....	....	....	....	....	....	8	1	4	5	8	....	....	....	....
2011-12	Sudbury Wolves	OHL	60	3	23	26	81	....	....	....	....	....	....	....	....	....	4	0	0	0	12	....	....	....	....
	Chicago Wolves	AHL	4	0	1	1	0	....	....	....	....	....	....	....	....	....	2	0	0	0	0	....	....	....	....
2012-13	Sudbury Wolves	OHL	41	6	21	27	44	....	....	....	....	....	....	....	....	....	....	....	....	....	....	....	....	....	....
	Kitchener Rangers	OHL	28	1	17	18	45	....	....	....	....	....	....	....	....	....	10	1	1	2	6	....	....	....	....
	Chicago Wolves	AHL	3	0	2	2	0	....	....	....	....	....	....	....	....	....	....	....	....	....	....	....	....	....	....
	Vancouver	**NHL**	**3**	**0**	**0**	**0**	**0**	**0**	**0**	**0**	**4**	**0.0**	**–1**	**0**	**0.0**	**19:24**	**4**	**0**	**0**	**0**	**0**	**0**	**0**	**0**	**12:19**
	NHL Totals		**3**	**0**	**0**	**0**	**0**	**0**	**0**	**0**	**4**	**0.0**		**0**	**0.0**	**19:24**	**4**	**0**	**0**	**0**	**0**	**0**	**0**	**0**	**12:19**

CORRENTE, Matthew
(kohr-REHN-tay, MA-thew)

Defense. Shoots right. 6', 205 lbs. Born, Mississauga, Ont., March 17, 1988. New Jersey's 1st choice, 30th overall, in 2006 Entry Draft.

2004-05	Saginaw Spirit	OHL	62	6	9	15	89	....	....	....	....	....	....	....	....	....	....	....	....	....	....	....	....	....	....
2005-06	Saginaw Spirit	OHL	61	6	24	30	172	....	....	....	....	....	....	....	....	....	4	1	1	2	8	....	....	....	....
2006-07	Saginaw Spirit	OHL	29	2	13	15	67	....	....	....	....	....	....	....	....	....	....	....	....	....	....	....	....	....	....
	Mississauga	OHL	14	1	10	11	27	....	....	....	....	....	....	....	....	....	5	0	1	1	8	....	....	....	....
2007-08	Niagara Ice Dogs	OHL	21	2	13	15	64	....	....	....	....	....	....	....	....	....	10	0	5	5	33	....	....	....	....
2008-09	Lowell Devils	AHL	67	6	12	18	161	....	....	....	....	....	....	....	....	....	....	....	....	....	....	....	....	....	....
2009-10	**New Jersey**	**NHL**	**12**	**0**	**0**	**0**	**24**	**0**	**0**	**0**	**6**	**0.0**	**0**	**0**	**0.0**	**8:51**	**2**	**0**	**0**	**0**	**2**	**0**	**0**	**0**	**5:51**
	Lowell Devils	AHL	43	5	15	20	74	....	....	....	....	....	....	....	....	....	....	....	....	....	....	....	....	....	....
2010-11	**New Jersey**	**NHL**	**22**	**0**	**6**	**6**	**44**	**0**	**0**	**0**	**21**	**0.0**	**–5**	**0**	**0.0**	**13:36**	....	....	....	....	....	....	....	....	....
	Albany Devils	AHL	3	0	1	1	10	....	....	....	....	....	....	....	....	....	....	....	....	....	....	....	....	....	....
2011-12	Albany Devils	AHL	39	2	6	8	73	....	....	....	....	....	....	....	....	....	....	....	....	....	....	....	....	....	....
2012-13	Albany Devils	AHL	11	0	2	2	32	....	....	....	....	....	....	....	....	....	....	....	....	....	....	....	....	....	....
	NHL Totals		**34**	**0**	**6**	**6**	**68**	**0**	**0**	**0**	**27**	**0.0**		**0**	**0.0**	**11:56**	**2**	**0**	**0**	**0**	**2**	**0**	**0**	**0**	**5:51**

• Missed majority of 2010-11 due to shoulder injury at Tampa Bay, January 14, 2011. • Missed majority of 2011-12 due to various injuries. • Missed majority of 2012-13 due to recurring shoulder injury and resulting surgery.

CORVO, Joe
(KOHR-voh, JOH) **OTT**

Defense. Shoots right. 6', 204 lbs. Born, Oak Park, IL, June 20, 1977. Los Angeles' 4th choice, 83rd overall, in 1997 Entry Draft.

1995-96	Western Mich.	CCHA	41	5	25	30	38	....	....	....	....	....	....	....	....	....	....	....	....	....	....	....	....	....	....
1996-97	Western Mich.	CCHA	32	12	21	33	85	....	....	....	....	....	....	....	....	....	....	....	....	....	....	....	....	....	....
1997-98	Western Mich.	CCHA	32	5	12	17	93	....	....	....	....	....	....	....	....	....	....	....	....	....	....	....	....	....	....
1998-99	Springfield	AHL	50	5	15	20	32	....	....	....	....	....	....	....	....	....	....	....	....	....	....	....	....	....	....
	Hampton Roads	ECHL	5	0	0	0	15	....	....	....	....	....	....	....	....	....	4	0	1	1	0	....	....	....	....
99-2000			DID NOT PLAY																						
2000-01	Lowell	AHL	77	10	23	33	31	....	....	....	....	....	....	....	....	....	4	3	1	4	0	....	....	....	....
2001-02	Manchester	AHL	80	13	37	50	30	....	....	....	....	....	....	....	....	....	5	0	5	5	0	....	....	....	....
2002-03	**Los Angeles**	**NHL**	**50**	**5**	**7**	**12**	**14**	**2**	**0**	**0**	**84**	**6.0**	**2**	**0**	**0.0**	**18:37**	....	....	....	....	....	....	....	....	....
	Manchester	AHL	26	8	18	26	8	....	....	....	....	....	....	....	....	....	3	0	0	0	0	....	....	....	....
2003-04	**Los Angeles**	**NHL**	**72**	**8**	**17**	**25**	**36**	**0**	**0**	**3**	**150**	**5.3**	**7**	**1**	**0.0**	**21:09**	....	....	....	....	....	....	....	....	....
2004-05	Chicago Wolves	AHL	23	7	7	14	14	....	....	....	....	....	....	....	....	....	18	4	5	9	12	....	....	....	....
2005-06	**Los Angeles**	**NHL**	**81**	**14**	**26**	**40**	**38**	**7**	**0**	**3**	**190**	**7.4**	**16**	**0**	**0.0**	**19:59**	....	....	....	....	....	....	....	....	....
2006-07	**Ottawa**	**NHL**	**76**	**8**	**29**	**37**	**42**	**3**	**0**	**2**	**160**	**5.0**	**8**	**0**	**0.0**	**18:04**	**20**	**2**	**7**	**9**	**6**	**1**	**0**	**1**	**17:18**
2007-08	**Ottawa**	**NHL**	**51**	**6**	**21**	**27**	**18**	**1**	**0**	**1**	**111**	**5.4**	**13**	**0**	**0.0**	**17:41**	....	....	....	....	....	....	....	....	....
	Carolina	**NHL**	**23**	**7**	**14**	**21**	**8**	**5**	**0**	**2**	**56**	**12.5**	**4**	**0**	**0.0**	**20:46**	....	....	....	....	....	....	....	....	....
2008-09	**Carolina**	**NHL**	**81**	**14**	**24**	**38**	**18**	**8**	**1**	**6**	**213**	**6.6**	**–1**	**0**	**0.0**	**24:19**	**18**	**2**	**5**	**7**	**4**	**1**	**0**	**1**	**25:27**
2009-10	**Carolina**	**NHL**	**34**	**4**	**8**	**12**	**10**	**4**	**0**	**0**	**76**	**5.3**	**–6**	**0**	**0.0**	**25:13**	....	....	....	....	....	....	....	....	....
	Washington	**NHL**	**18**	**2**	**4**	**6**	**2**	**1**	**0**	**0**	**23**	**8.7**	**–4**	**0**	**0.0**	**19:41**	**7**	**1**	**1**	**2**	**4**	**0**	**0**	**0**	**16:53**
2010-11	**Carolina**	**NHL**	**82**	**11**	**29**	**40**	**18**	**5**	**1**	**1**	**191**	**5.8**	**–14**	**1**	**0.0**	**24:47**	....	....	....	....	....	....	....	....	....
2011-12	**Boston**	**NHL**	**75**	**4**	**21**	**25**	**13**	**1**	**0**	**1**	**168**	**2.4**	**10**	**0**	**0.0**	**18:49**	**5**	**0**	**0**	**0**	**0**	**0**	**0**	**0**	**14:54**
2012-13	**Carolina**	**NHL**	**40**	**6**	**11**	**17**	**14**	**3**	**0**	**2**	**71**	**8.5**	**–3**	**0**	**0.0**	**18:46**	....	....	....	....	....	....	....	....	....
	NHL Totals		**683**	**89**	**211**	**300**	**231**	**40**	**2**	**21**	**1493**	**6.0**		**2**	**0.0**	**20:47**	**50**	**5**	**13**	**18**	**14**	**2**	**0**	**2**	**19:56**

CCHA All-Rookie Team (1996) • CCHA Second All-Star Team (1997)

• Missed 1999-2000 after failing to come to contract terms with **Los Angeles.** Signed as a free agent by **Chicago** (AHL), February 24, 2005. Signed as a free agent by **Ottawa**, July 1, 2006. Traded to **Carolina** by **Ottawa** with Patrick Eaves for Cory Stillman and Mike Commodore, February 11, 2008. • Missed majority of 2009-10 due to leg injury vs. Washington, November 30, 2009. Traded to **Washington** by **Carolina** for Brian Pothier, Oskar Osala and Washington's 2nd round choice (later traded to NY Rangers, later traded to Calgary – Calgary selected Tyler Wotherspoon) in 2011 Entry Draft, March 3, 2010. Signed as a free agent by **Carolina**, July 7, 2010. Traded to **Boston** by **Carolina** for Boston's 4th round choice (Trevor Carrick) in 2012 Entry Draft, July 5, 2011. Signed as a free agent by **Carolina**, July 1, 2012. Signed as a free agent by **Ottawa**, July 8, 2013.

COUTURE, Logan
(koh-TYOOR, LOH-guhn) **S.J.**

Center. Shoots left. 6'1", 200 lbs. Born, Guelph, Ont., March 28, 1989. San Jose's 1st choice, 9th overall, in 2007 Entry Draft.

2004-05	St. Thomas Stars	ON-Jr.B	48	24	22	46	....	....	....	....	....	....	....	....	....	....	....	....	....	....	....	....	....	....	....
2005-06	Ottawa 67's	OHL	65	25	39	64	52	....	....	....	....	....	....	....	....	....	6	3	4	7	0	....	....	....	....
2006-07	Ottawa 67's	OHL	54	26	52	78	24	....	....	....	....	....	....	....	....	....	5	1	7	8	4	....	....	....	....
2007-08	Ottawa 67's	OHL	51	21	37	58	37	....	....	....	....	....	....	....	....	....	4	2	1	3	0	....	....	....	....
2008-09	Ottawa 67's	OHL	62	39	48	87	46	....	....	....	....	....	....	....	....	....	7	3	7	10	6	....	....	....	....
	Worcester Sharks	AHL	4	0	0	0	7	....	....	....	....	....	....	....	....	....	12	2	1	3	11	....	....	....	....

			Regular Season														Playoffs								
Season	Club	League	GP	G	A	Pts	PIM	PP	SH	GW	S	%	+/-	TF	F%	Min	GP	G	A	Pts	PIM	PP	SH	GW	Min
2009-10	San Jose	NHL	25	5	4	9	6	1	0	1	42	11.9	4	143	52.5	10:16	15	4	0	4	4	0	0	1	11:23
	Worcester Sharks	AHL	42	20	33	53	12	....	....	....	....	....	....	....	....	....	....	....	....	....	....	....	....	....	....
2010-11	San Jose	NHL	79	32	24	56	41	10	0	8	253	12.6	18	888	53.4	17:49	18	7	7	14	2	1	0	0	19:23
2011-12	San Jose	NHL	80	31	34	65	16	11	2	5	245	12.7	2	910	51.4	18:34	5	1	3	4	0	0	0	0	19:54
2012-13	Geneve	Swiss	22	7	16	23	10	....	....	....	....	....	....	....	....	....	....	....	....	....	....	....	....	....	....
	San Jose	NHL	48	21	16	37	4	7	0	5	151	13.9	7	489	51.5	18:06	11	5	6	11	0	5	0	3	20:31
	NHL Totals		232	89	78	167	67	29	2	19	691	12.9		2430	52.2	17:19	49	17	16	33	6	6	0	4	17:15

AHL All-Rookie Team (2010) • NHL All-Rookie Team (2011)
Played in NHL All-Star Game (2012)
Signed as a free agent by **Geneve** (Swiss), September 18, 2012.

COUTURIER, Sean
(koo-TOO-ree-ay, SHAWN) **PHI**

Center. Shoots left. 6'3", 197 lbs. Born, Phoenix, AZ, December 7, 1992. Philadelphia's 1st choice, 8th overall, in 2011 Entry Draft.

2007-08	Notre Dame	SMHL	40	19	37	56	32	....	....	....	....	....	....	....	....	....	10	3	8	11	10	....	....	....	....
2008-09	Drummondville	QMJHL	58	9	22	31	14	....	....	....	....	....	....	....	....	....	19	1	7	8	8	....	....	....	....
2009-10	Drummondville	QMJHL	68	41	55	*96	47	....	....	....	....	....	....	....	....	....	14	10	8	18	18	....	....	....	....
2010-11	Drummondville	QMJHL	58	36	60	96	36	....	....	....	....	....	....	....	....	....	10	6	5	11	14	....	....	....	....
2011-12	Philadelphia	NHL	77	13	14	27	14	0	2	4	116	11.2	18	804	47.0	14:08	11	3	1	4	2	0	0	0	14:30
2012-13	Adirondack	AHL	31	10	18	28	16	....	....	....	....	....	....	....	....	....	....	....	....	....	....	....	....	....	....
	Philadelphia	NHL	46	4	11	15	10	0	0	0	75	5.3	–8	553	43.9	15:53	....	....	....	....	....	....	....	....	....
	NHL Totals		123	17	25	42	24	0	2	4	191	8.9		1357	45.8	14:48	11	3	1	4	2	0	0	0	14:30

QMJHL Second All-Star Team (2010) • QMJHL First All-Star Team (2011) • QMJHL Player of the Year (2011)

COWEN, Jared
(KOW-ehn, JAIR-ehd) **OTT**

Defense. Shoots left. 6'5", 230 lbs. Born, Saskatoon, Sask., January 25, 1991. Ottawa's 1st choice, 9th overall, in 2009 Entry Draft.

2006-07	Sask. Contacts	SMHL	41	6	22	28	103	....	....	....	....	....	....	....	....	....	....	....	....	....	....	....	....	....	....
	Spokane Chiefs	WHL	6	0	2	2	2	....	....	....	....	....	....	....	....	....	6	0	1	1	6	....	....	....	....
2007-08	Spokane Chiefs	WHL	68	4	14	18	62	....	....	....	....	....	....	....	....	....	21	1	3	4	17	....	....	....	....
2008-09	Spokane Chiefs	WHL	48	7	14	21	45	....	....	....	....	....	....	....	....	....	....	....	....	....	....	....	....	....	....
2009-10	Spokane Chiefs	WHL	59	8	22	30	74	....	....	....	....	....	....	....	....	....	7	1	1	2	8	....	....	....	....
	Ottawa	NHL	1	0	0	0	2	0	0	0	0	0.0	0	0	0.0	6:46	....	....	....	....	....	....	....	....	....
2010-11	Spokane Chiefs	WHL	58	18	30	48	91	....	....	....	....	....	....	....	....	....	17	2	12	14	16	....	....	....	....
	Binghamton	AHL	....	....	....	....	....	....	....	....	....	....	....	....	....	....	10	0	4	4	0	....	....	....	....
2011-12	Ottawa	NHL	82	5	12	17	56	0	0	1	58	8.6	–4	0	0.0	18:54	7	0	1	1	4	0	0	0	17:02
2012-13	Binghamton	AHL	3	0	3	3	2	....	....	....	....	....	....	....	....	....	....	....	....	....	....	....	....	....	....
	Ottawa	NHL	7	1	0	1	10	0	0	0	8	12.5	1	0	0.0	20:17	10	0	3	3	21	0	0	0	18:34
	NHL Totals		90	6	12	18	68	0	0	1	66	9.1		0	0.0	18:52	17	0	4	4	25	0	0	0	17:56

WHL West Second All-Star Team (2010) • WHL West First All-Star Team (2011)
• Missed majority of 2012-13 due to hip injury vs. Albany (AHL), October 6, 2012.

COYLE, Charlie
(KOYL, CHAR-lee) **MIN**

Center/Right wing. Shoots right. 6'3", 222 lbs. Born, E. Weymouth, MA, March 2, 1992. San Jose's 1st choice, 28th overall, in 2010 Entry Draft.

2007-08	Thayer Academy	High-MA	....	14	23	37	....	....	....	....	....	....	....	....	....	....	....	....	....	....	....	....	....	....	....
2008-09	Thayer Academy	High-MA	26	20	28	48	4	....	....	....	....	....	....	....	....	....	....	....	....	....	....	....	....	....	....
2009-10	South Shore	EJHL	42	21	42	63	50	....	....	....	....	....	....	....	....	....	....	....	....	....	....	....	....	....	....
	USNTDP	U-18	4	1	0	1	2	....	....	....	....	....	....	....	....	....	....	....	....	....	....	....	....	....	....
2010-11	Boston University	H-East	37	7	19	26	34	....	....	....	....	....	....	....	....	....	....	....	....	....	....	....	....	....	....
2011-12	Boston University	H-East	16	3	11	14	20	....	....	....	....	....	....	....	....	....	....	....	....	....	....	....	....	....	....
	Saint John	QMJHL	23	15	23	38	8	....	....	....	....	....	....	....	....	....	17	15	19	34	8	....	....	....	....
2012-13	Houston Aeros	AHL	47	14	11	25	22	....	....	....	....	....	....	....	....	....	....	....	....	....	....	....	....	....	....
	Minnesota	NHL	37	8	6	14	28	1	0	2	50	16.0	3	26	34.6	15:04	5	0	2	2	2	0	0	0	18:10
	NHL Totals		37	8	6	14	28	1	0	2	50	16.0		26	34.6	15:04	5	0	2	2	2	0	0	0	18:10

Hockey East All-Rookie Team (2011) • Hockey East Rookie of the Year (2011)
Traded to **Minnesota** by **San Jose** with Devin Setoguchi and San Jose's 1st round choice (Zack Phillips) in 2011 Entry Draft for Brent Burns and Minnesota's 2nd round choice (later traded to Tampa Bay – later traded to Nashville – Nashville selected Pontius Aberg) in 2012 Entry Draft, June 24, 2011.

CRABB, Joey
(KRAB, JOH-ee) **FLA**

Right wing. Shoots right. 6'1", 190 lbs. Born, Anchorage, AK, April 3, 1983. NY Rangers' 7th choice, 226th overall, in 2002 Entry Draft.

99-2000	USNTDP	NAHL	55	13	10	23	69	....	....	....	....	....	....	....	....	....	3	1	0	1	4	....	....	....	....
2000-01	USNTDP	U-18	39	10	10	20	22	....	....	....	....	....	....	....	....	....	....	....	....	....	....	....	....	....	....
	USNTDP	USHL	21	2	3	5	18	....	....	....	....	....	....	....	....	....	....	....	....	....	....	....	....	....	....
2001-02	Green Bay	USHL	61	15	27	42	94	....	....	....	....	....	....	....	....	....	7	4	8	12	21	....	....	....	....
2002-03	Colorado College	WCHA	35	4	4	8	40	....	....	....	....	....	....	....	....	....	....	....	....	....	....	....	....	....	....
2003-04	Colorado College	WCHA	39	15	12	27	20	....	....	....	....	....	....	....	....	....	....	....	....	....	....	....	....	....	....
2004-05	Colorado College	WCHA	43	16	16	32	44	....	....	....	....	....	....	....	....	....	....	....	....	....	....	....	....	....	....
2005-06	Colorado College	WCHA	42	18	25	43	45	....	....	....	....	....	....	....	....	....	....	....	....	....	....	....	....	....	....
2006-07	Chicago Wolves	AHL	63	7	15	22	25	....	....	....	....	....	....	....	....	....	6	0	0	0	0	....	....	....	....
2007-08	Chicago Wolves	AHL	72	9	26	35	78	....	....	....	....	....	....	....	....	....	24	1	4	5	20	....	....	....	....
2008-09	Atlanta	NHL	29	4	5	9	28	0	1	1	33	12.1	–2	33	39.4	12:13	....	....	....	....	....	....	....	....	....
	Chicago Wolves	AHL	42	15	14	29	62	....	....	....	....	....	....	....	....	....	....	....	....	....	....	....	....	....	....
2009-10	Chicago Wolves	AHL	79	24	29	53	59	....	....	....	....	....	....	....	....	....	14	6	5	11	12	....	....	....	....
2010-11	Toronto	NHL	48	3	12	15	24	0	1	2	51	5.9	–1	22	22.7	12:59	....	....	....	....	....	....	....	....	....
	Toronto Marlies	AHL	34	11	7	18	31	....	....	....	....	....	....	....	....	....	....	....	....	....	....	....	....	....	....
2011-12	Toronto	NHL	67	11	15	26	33	0	2	4	75	14.7	1	10	10.0	13:27	....	....	....	....	....	....	....	....	....
	Toronto Marlies	AHL	9	7	8	15	7	....	....	....	....	....	....	....	....	....	....	....	....	....	....	....	....	....	....
2012-13	Alaska Aces	ECHL	35	17	21	38	56	....	....	....	....	....	....	....	....	....	....	....	....	....	....	....	....	....	....
	Hershey Bears	AHL	12	6	6	12	6	....	....	....	....	....	....	....	....	....	5	5	0	5	2	....	....	....	....
	Washington	NHL	26	2	0	2	8	0	0	0	20	10.0	–1	34	20.6	9:25	....	....	....	....	....	....	....	....	....
	NHL Totals		170	20	32	52	93	0	4	7	179	11.2		99	26.3	12:29	....	....	....	....	....	....	....	....	....

Signed as a free agent by **Atlanta**, August 31, 2006. Traded to **Chicago** by **Atlanta** with Marty Reasoner, Jeremy Morin and New Jersey's 1st (previously acquired, Chicago selected Kevin Hayes) and 2nd (previously acquired, Chicago selected Justin Holl) round choices in 2010 Entry Draft for Brent Sopel, Dustin Byfuglien, Ben Eager and Akim Aliu, June 24, 2010. Signed as a free agent by **Toronto**, July 15, 2010. Signed as a free agent by **Washington**, July 2, 2012. Signed as a free agent by **Alaska** (ECHL), September 28, 2012. Signed as a free agent by **Florida**, July 5, 2013.

CRACKNELL, Adam
(krak-NEHL, A-duhm) **ST.L.**

Right wing. Shoots right. 6'2", 210 lbs. Born, Prince Albert, Sask., July 15, 1985. Calgary's 10th choice, 279th overall, in 2004 Entry Draft.

2002-03	Kootenay Ice	WHL	67	7	4	11	37	....	....	....	....	....	....	....	....	....	11	0	0	0	2	....	....	....	....
2003-04	Kootenay Ice	WHL	72	26	35	61	63	....	....	....	....	....	....	....	....	....	4	1	1	2	2	....	....	....	....
2004-05	Kootenay Ice	WHL	72	19	29	48	65	....	....	....	....	....	....	....	....	....	16	8	8	16	6	....	....	....	....
2005-06	Kootenay Ice	WHL	72	42	51	93	85	....	....	....	....	....	....	....	....	....	6	1	4	5	6	....	....	....	....
	Omaha	AHL	6	1	2	3	2	....	....	....	....	....	....	....	....	....	....	....	....	....	....	....	....	....	....
2006-07	Las Vegas	ECHL	31	8	14	22	35	....	....	....	....	....	....	....	....	....	8	3	3	6	6	....	....	....	....
2007-08	Quad City Flames	AHL	4	1	0	1	0	....	....	....	....	....	....	....	....	....	....	....	....	....	....	....	....	....	....
	Las Vegas	ECHL	61	29	30	59	47	....	....	....	....	....	....	....	....	....	21	9	13	22	4	....	....	....	....
2008-09	Quad City Flames	AHL	79	10	16	26	36	....	....	....	....	....	....	....	....	....	....	....	....	....	....	....	....	....	....
2009-10	Peoria Rivermen	AHL	76	17	21	38	40	....	....	....	....	....	....	....	....	....	....	....	....	....	....	....	....	....	....
2010-11	St. Louis	NHL	24	3	4	7	8	0	0	0	26	11.5	1	118	39.0	8:55	....	....	....	....	....	....	....	....	....
	Peoria Rivermen	AHL	61	6	19	25	54	....	....	....	....	....	....	....	....	....	4	2	0	2	0	....	....	....	....
2011-12	St. Louis	NHL	2	1	0	1	0	0	0	0	1	100.0	1	1	0.0	7:39	....	....	....	....	....	....	....	....	....
	Peoria Rivermen	AHL	72	23	26	49	54	....	....	....	....	....	....	....	....	....	....	....	....	....	....	....	....	....	....

			Regular Season														Playoffs								
Season	Club	League	GP	G	A	Pts	PIM	PP	SH	GW	S	%	+/-	TF	F%	Min	GP	G	A	Pts	PIM	PP	SH	GW	Min
2012-13	Peoria Rivermen	AHL	49	17	16	33	26	....	....	....	....	....	....	....	....	....	....	....	....	....	....	....	....	....	....
	St. Louis	**NHL**	**20**	**2**	**4**	**6**	**4**	**0**	**0**	**0**	**21**	**9.5**	**3**	**25**	**24.0**	**8:37**	**5**	**0**	**0**	**0**	**0**	**0**	**0**	**0**	**7:59**
	NHL Totals		**46**	**6**	**8**	**14**	**12**	**0**	**0**	**0**	**48**	**12.5**		**144**	**36.1**	**8:44**	**5**	**0**	**0**	**0**	**0**	**0**	**0**	**0**	**7:59**

WHL West Second All-Star Team (2006)

Signed as a free agent by **St. Louis**, July 23, 2009.

CRAIG, Ryan

(KRAIG, RIGH-uhn) **CBJ**

Center. Shoots left. 6'2", 221 lbs. Born, Abbotsford, B.C., January 6, 1982. Tampa Bay's 10th choice, 255th overall, in 2002 Entry Draft.

Season	Club	League	GP	G	A	Pts	PIM	PP	SH	GW	S	%	+/-	TF	F%	Min	GP	G	A	Pts	PIM	PP	SH	GW	Min
1997-98	Abbotsford	Minor-BC	80	118	120	238	110	....	....	....	....	....	....	....	....	....	....	....	....	....	....	....	....	....	....
	Brandon	WHL	1	0	0	0	0	....	....	....	....	....	....	....	....	....	....	....	....	....	....	....	....	....	....
1998-99	Brandon	WHL	54	11	12	23	46	....	....	....	....	....	....	....	....	....	5	0	0	0	4	....	....	....	....
99-2000	Brandon	WHL	65	17	19	36	40	....	....	....	....	....	....	....	....	....	....	....	....	....	....	....	....	....	....
2000-01	Brandon	WHL	70	38	33	71	49	....	....	....	....	....	....	....	....	....	6	3	0	3	7	....	....	....	....
2001-02	Brandon	WHL	52	29	35	64	52	....	....	....	....	....	....	....	....	....	19	11	10	21	13	....	....	....	....
2002-03	Brandon	WHL	60	42	32	74	69	....	....	....	....	....	....	....	....	....	17	5	8	13	29	....	....	....	....
2003-04	Hershey Bears	AHL	61	4	8	12	24	....	....	....	....	....	....	....	....	....	....	....	....	....	....	....	....	....	....
	Pensacola	ECHL	5	3	5	8	0	....	....	....	....	....	....	....	....	....	2	0	1	1	0	....	....	....	....
2004-05	Springfield	AHL	80	27	14	41	50	....	....	....	....	....	....	....	....	....	....	....	....	....	....	....	....	....	....
2005-06	**Tampa Bay**	**NHL**	**48**	**15**	**13**	**28**	**6**	**6**	**0**	**0**	**81**	**18.5**	**–4**	**95**	**46.3**	**15:21**	**5**	**0**	**0**	**0**	**10**	**0**	**0**	**0**	**12:59**
	Springfield	AHL	28	12	10	22	14	....	....	....	....	....	....	....	....	....	....	....	....	....	....	....	....	....	....
2006-07	**Tampa Bay**	**NHL**	**72**	**14**	**13**	**27**	**55**	**4**	**0**	**2**	**130**	**10.8**	**–11**	**110**	**40.0**	**15:20**	**6**	**0**	**0**	**0**	**12**	**0**	**0**	**0**	**7:02**
2007-08	**Tampa Bay**	**NHL**	**7**	**1**	**1**	**2**	**0**	**1**	**0**	**0**	**8**	**12.5**	**–1**	**1**	**100.0**	**13:04**	....	....	....	....	....	....	....	....	....
	Norfolk Admirals	AHL	2	1	2	3	2	....	....	....	....	....	....	....	....	....	....	....	....	....	....	....	....	....	....
2008-09	**Tampa Bay**	**NHL**	**54**	**2**	**4**	**6**	**60**	**0**	**0**	**0**	**64**	**3.1**	**–7**	**222**	**49.6**	**10:16**	....	....	....	....	....	....	....	....	....
2009-10	**Tampa Bay**	**NHL**	**3**	**0**	**0**	**0**	**5**	**0**	**0**	**0**	**5**	**0.0**	**0**	**1**	**0.0**	**9:47**	....	....	....	....	....	....	....	....	....
	Norfolk Admirals	AHL	73	23	22	45	64	....	....	....	....	....	....	....	....	....	....	....	....	....	....	....	....	....	....
2010-11	**Pittsburgh**	**NHL**	**6**	**0**	**0**	**0**	**22**	**0**	**0**	**0**	**7**	**0.0**	**–3**	**5**	**60.0**	**9:49**	....	....	....	....	....	....	....	....	....
	Wilkes-Barre	AHL	71	19	29	48	84	....	....	....	....	....	....	....	....	....	12	3	4	7	12	....	....	....	....
2011-12	Wilkes-Barre	AHL	68	11	19	30	70	....	....	....	....	....	....	....	....	....	12	1	3	4	2	....	....	....	....
2012-13	Springfield	AHL	75	20	27	47	71	....	....	....	....	....	....	....	....	....	8	2	2	4	7	....	....	....	....
	NHL Totals		**190**	**32**	**31**	**63**	**148**	**11**	**0**	**2**	**295**	**10.8**		**434**	**46.5**	**13:33**	**11**	**0**	**0**	**0**	**22**	**0**	**0**	**0**	**9:44**

WHL East First All-Star Team (2003) • Canadian Major Junior Humanitarian Player of the Year (2003)

• Missed majority of 2007-08 due to back and knee injuries. Signed as a free agent by **Pittsburgh**, July 2, 2010. Signed as a free agent by **Springfield** (AHL), July 19, 2012. Signed as a free agent by **Columbus**, July 6, 2013.

CROMBEEN, B.J.

(KRAWM-been, BEE-JAY) **T.B.**

Right wing. Shoots right. 6'2", 209 lbs. Born, Denver, CO, July 10, 1985. Dallas' 3rd choice, 54th overall, in 2003 Entry Draft.

Season	Club	League	GP	G	A	Pts	PIM	PP	SH	GW	S	%	+/-	TF	F%	Min	GP	G	A	Pts	PIM	PP	SH	GW	Min
2000-01	Newmarket	ON-Jr.A	35	14	14	28	63	....	....	....	....	....	....	....	....	....	....	....	....	....	....	....	....	....	....
2001-02	Barrie Colts	OHL	60	12	13	25	118	....	....	....	....	....	....	....	....	....	20	1	1	2	31	....	....	....	....
2002-03	Barrie Colts	OHL	63	22	24	46	133	....	....	....	....	....	....	....	....	....	6	1	0	1	8	....	....	....	....
2003-04	Barrie Colts	OHL	62	21	29	50	154	....	....	....	....	....	....	....	....	....	12	5	7	12	35	....	....	....	....
2004-05	Barrie Colts	OHL	63	31	18	49	111	....	....	....	....	....	....	....	....	....	6	2	4	6	35	....	....	....	....
2005-06	Iowa Stars	AHL	52	5	7	12	97	....	....	....	....	....	....	....	....	....	5	1	0	1	9	....	....	....	....
	Idaho Steelheads	ECHL	8	5	3	8	5	....	....	....	....	....	....	....	....	....	....	....	....	....	....	....	....	....	....
2006-07	Assat Pori	Finland	55	13	9	22	152	....	....	....	....	....	....	....	....	....	....	....	....	....	....	....	....	....	....
	Idaho Steelheads	ECHL	13	7	4	11	43	....	....	....	....	....	....	....	....	....	22	5	5	10	45	....	....	....	....
2007-08	**Dallas**	**NHL**	**8**	**0**	**2**	**2**	**39**	**0**	**0**	**0**	**9**	**0.0**	**1**	**1**	**0.0**	**6:38**	**5**	**0**	**0**	**0**	**0**	**0**	**0**	**0**	**4:16**
	Iowa Stars	AHL	65	14	14	28	158	....	....	....	....	....	....	....	....	....	....	....	....	....	....	....	....	....	....
2008-09	**Dallas**	**NHL**	**15**	**1**	**4**	**5**	**26**	**0**	**0**	**0**	**12**	**8.3**	**–1**	**0**	**0.0**	**8:14**	....	....	....	....	....	....	....	....	....
	St. Louis	**NHL**	**66**	**11**	**6**	**17**	**122**	**0**	**1**	**3**	**112**	**9.8**	**–8**	**7**	**42.9**	**13:45**	**4**	**0**	**0**	**0**	**12**	**0**	**0**	**0**	**9:46**
2009-10	**St. Louis**	**NHL**	**79**	**7**	**8**	**15**	**168**	**0**	**1**	**1**	**120**	**5.8**	**–5**	**51**	**35.3**	**13:05**	....	....	....	....	....	....	....	....	....
2010-11	**St. Louis**	**NHL**	**80**	**7**	**7**	**14**	**154**	**0**	**1**	**0**	**113**	**6.2**	**–18**	**64**	**29.7**	**12:48**	....	....	....	....	....	....	....	....	....
2011-12	**St. Louis**	**NHL**	**40**	**1**	**2**	**3**	**71**	**0**	**0**	**0**	**50**	**2.0**	**–2**	**12**	**25.0**	**8:18**	**7**	**1**	**0**	**1**	**31**	**0**	**0**	**0**	**8:27**
2012-13	Orlando	ECHL	2	0	0	0	2	....	....	....	....	....	....	....	....	....	....	....	....	....	....	....	....	....	....
	Tampa Bay	**NHL**	**44**	**1**	**7**	**8**	**112**	**0**	**0**	**0**	**50**	**2.0**	**4**	**20**	**20.0**	**11:05**	....	....	....	....	....	....	....	....	....
	NHL Totals		**332**	**28**	**36**	**64**	**692**	**0**	**3**	**4**	**466**	**6.0**		**155**	**30.3**	**11:56**	**16**	**1**	**0**	**1**	**43**	**0**	**0**	**0**	**7:28**

Signed as a free agent by **Pori** (Finland), August 2, 2006. Claimed on waivers by **St. Louis** from **Dallas**, November 18, 2008. Traded to **Tampa Bay** by **St. Louis** with St. Louis's 5th round choice in 2014 Entry Draft for Tampa Bay's 4th round choice (later traded to Edmonton – Edmonton selected Jackson Houck) in 2013 Entry Draft and Tampa Bay's 4th round choice in 2014 Entry Draft, July 10, 2012. Signed as a free agent by **Orlando** (ECHL), November 16, 2012.

CROSBY, Sidney

(KRAWZ-bee, SIHD-nee) **PIT**

Center. Shoots left. 5'11", 200 lbs. Born, Cole Harbour, N.S., August 7, 1987. Pittsburgh's 1st choice, 1st overall, in 2005 Entry Draft.

Season	Club	League	GP	G	A	Pts	PIM	PP	SH	GW	S	%	+/-	TF	F%	Min	GP	G	A	Pts	PIM	PP	SH	GW	Min
2001-02	Dartmouth	NSMHL	74	95	98	193	114	....	....	....	....	....	....	....	....	....	....	....	....	....	....	....	....	....	....
2002-03	Shat.-St. Mary's	High-MN	57	72	90	162	....	....	....	....	....	....	....	....	....	....	....	....	....	....	....	....	....	....	....
2003-04	Rimouski Oceanic	QMJHL	59	54	*81	*135	74	....	....	....	....	....	....	....	....	....	9	7	9	16	10	....	....	....	....
2004-05	Rimouski Oceanic	QMJHL	62	*66	*102	*168	84	....	....	....	....	....	....	....	....	....	13	*14	*17	*31	16	....	....	....	....
2005-06	**Pittsburgh**	**NHL**	**81**	**39**	**63**	**102**	**110**	**16**	**0**	**5**	**278**	**14.0**	**–1**	**1174**	**45.5**	**20:08**	....	....	....	....	....	....	....	....	....
2006-07	**Pittsburgh**	**NHL**	**79**	**36**	**84**	***120**	**60**	**13**	**0**	**4**	**250**	**14.4**	**10**	**1686**	**49.8**	**20:46**	**5**	**3**	**2**	**5**	**4**	**1**	**0**	**1**	**21:40**
2007-08	**Pittsburgh**	**NHL**	**53**	**24**	**48**	**72**	**39**	**6**	**0**	**4**	**173**	**13.9**	**18**	**1103**	**51.4**	**20:51**	**20**	**6**	***21**	***27**	**12**	**2**	**0**	**1**	**20:42**
2008-09 ♦	**Pittsburgh**	**NHL**	**77**	**33**	**70**	**103**	**76**	**7**	**0**	**3**	**238**	**13.9**	**3**	**1615**	**51.3**	**21:57**	**24**	***15**	**16**	**31**	**14**	**5**	**0**	**2**	**20:49**
2009-10	**Pittsburgh**	**NHL**	**81**	***51**	**58**	**109**	**71**	**13**	**2**	**6**	**298**	**17.1**	**15**	**1791**	**55.9**	**21:57**	**13**	**6**	**13**	**19**	**6**	**1**	**0**	**1**	**23:32**
	Canada	Olympics	7	4	3	7	4	....	....	....	....	....	....	....	....	....	....	....	....	....	....	....	....	....	....
2010-11	**Pittsburgh**	**NHL**	**41**	**32**	**34**	**66**	**31**	**10**	**1**	**3**	**161**	**19.9**	**20**	**981**	**55.7**	**21:55**	....	....	....	....	....	....	....	....	....
2011-12	**Pittsburgh**	**NHL**	**22**	**8**	**29**	**37**	**14**	**2**	**0**	**3**	**75**	**10.7**	**15**	**453**	**50.1**	**18:28**	**6**	**3**	**5**	**8**	**9**	**0**	**0**	**0**	**20:37**
2012-13	**Pittsburgh**	**NHL**	**36**	**15**	**41**	**56**	**16**	**3**	**0**	**1**	**124**	**12.1**	**26**	**834**	**54.3**	**21:06**	**14**	**7**	**8**	**15**	**8**	**2**	**0**	**0**	**23:05**
	NHL Totals		**470**	**238**	**427**	**665**	**417**	**70**	**3**	**29**	**1597**	**14.9**		**9637**	**51.8**	**21:05**	**82**	**40**	**65**	**105**	**53**	**11**	**0**	**5**	**21:38**

QMJHL All-Rookie Team (2004) • QMJHL First All-Star Team (2004, 2005) • QMJHL Player of the Year (2004, 2005) • Canadian Major Junior First All-Star Team (2004, 2005) • Canadian Major Junior Rookie of the Year (2004) • Canadian Major Junior Player of the Year (2004, 2005) • Memorial Cup All-Star Team (2005) • Ed Chynoweth Trophy (Memorial Cup - Leading Scorer) (2005) • NHL All-Rookie Team (2006) • NHL First All-Star Team (2007, 2013) • Art Ross Trophy (2007) • Lester B. Pearson Award (2007) • Hart Memorial Trophy (2007) • NHL Second All-Star Team (2010) • Mark Messier NHL Leadership Award (2010) • Maurice "Rocket" Richard Trophy (2010) (tied with Steven Stamkos) • Ted Lindsay Award (2013)

Played in NHL All-Star Game (2007)

• Missed majority of 2010-11 and 2011-12 due to post-concussion syndrome.

CULLEN, Mark

(KUH-lehn, MAHRK)

Center. Shoots left. 5'11", 182 lbs. Born, Moorhead, MN, October 28, 1978.

Season	Club	League	GP	G	A	Pts	PIM	PP	SH	GW	S	%	+/-	TF	F%	Min	GP	G	A	Pts	PIM	PP	SH	GW	Min
1996-97	Fargo High	High-ND	30	20	45	65	....	....	....	....	....	....	....	....	....	....	....	....	....	....	....	....	....	....	....
1997-98	Fargo-Moorhead	USHL	30	17	37	54	16	....	....	....	....	....	....	....	....	....	4	3	0	3	25	....	....	....	....
1998-99	Colorado College	WCHA	42	8	25	33	22	....	....	....	....	....	....	....	....	....	....	....	....	....	....	....	....	....	....
99-2000	Colorado College	WCHA	37	11	20	31	22	....	....	....	....	....	....	....	....	....	....	....	....	....	....	....	....	....	....
2000-01	Colorado College	WCHA	31	20	33	53	26	....	....	....	....	....	....	....	....	....	....	....	....	....	....	....	....	....	....
2001-02	Colorado College	WCHA	43	14	36	50	14	....	....	....	....	....	....	....	....	....	....	....	....	....	....	....	....	....	....
2002-03	Houston Aeros	AHL	72	22	25	47	20	....	....	....	....	....	....	....	....	....	15	3	7	10	4	....	....	....	....
2003-04	Houston Aeros	AHL	53	10	28	38	28	....	....	....	....	....	....	....	....	....	2	0	0	0	0	....	....	....	....
2004-05	Houston Aeros	AHL	64	10	24	34	26	....	....	....	....	....	....	....	....	....	5	1	1	2	0	....	....	....	....
2005-06	**Chicago**	**NHL**	**29**	**7**	**9**	**16**	**2**	**0**	**0**	**0**	**45**	**15.6**	**7**	**281**	**48.8**	**13:15**	....	....	....	....	....	....	....	....	....
	Norfolk Admirals	AHL	54	29	39	68	48	....	....	....	....	....	....	....	....	....	4	2	2	4	0	....	....	....	....
2006-07	**Philadelphia**	**NHL**	**3**	**0**	**0**	**0**	**0**	**0**	**0**	**0**	**4**	**0.0**	**–3**	**14**	**50.0**	**6:15**	....	....	....	....	....	....	....	....	....
	Philadelphia	AHL	56	16	36	52	34	....	....	....	....	....	....	....	....	....	....	....	....	....	....	....	....	....	....
2007-08	Grand Rapids	AHL	59	16	31	47	61	....	....	....	....	....	....	....	....	....	....	....	....	....	....	....	....	....	....
2008-09	Manitoba Moose	AHL	56	14	25	39	22	....	....	....	....	....	....	....	....	....	20	4	9	13	0	....	....	....	....
2009-10	Rockford IceHogs	AHL	62	21	32	53	16	....	....	....	....	....	....	....	....	....	4	0	2	2	2	....	....	....	....
2010-11	Rochester	AHL	28	5	9	14	6	....	....	....	....	....	....	....	....	....	....	....	....	....	....	....	....	....	....
2011-12	**Florida**	**NHL**	**6**	**0**	**1**	**1**	**2**	**0**	**0**	**0**	**1**	**0.0**	**2**	**27**	**55.6**	**8:00**	....	....	....	....	....	....	....	....	....
	San Antonio	AHL	58	10	37	47	30	....	....	....	....	....	....	....	....	....	10	4	6	10	2	....	....	....	....

							Regular Season										Playoffs								
Season	Club	League	GP	G	A	Pts	PIM	PP	SH	GW	S	%	+/-	TF	F%	Min	GP	G	A	Pts	PIM	PP	SH	GW	Min
2012-13	Vityaz Chekhov	KHL	23	0	1	1	8	....	....	....	....	....	....	....	....	....	....	....	....	....	....	....	....	....	....
	Salzburg	Austria	19	7	10	17	4	....	....	....	....	....	....	....	....	....	12	1	6	7	4	....	....	....	....
	NHL Totals		**38**	**7**	**10**	**17**	**4**	**0**	**0**	**0**	**50**	**14.0**		**322**	**49.4**	**11:52**	....	....	....	....	....	....	....	....	....

USHL All-Rookie Team (1998) • USHL Rookie of the Year (1998) • WCHA First All-Star Team (2001, 2002) • NCAA West Second All-American Team (2001) • Fred Hunt Memorial Trophy (AHL - Sportsmanship) (2006)

Signed as a free agent by **Minnesota**, April 8, 2002. Signed as a free agent by **Chicago**, August 4, 2005. Signed as a free agent by **Philadelphia**, July 5, 2006. Signed as a free agent by **Detroit**, July 16, 2007. Signed as a free agent by **Vancouver**, July 4, 2008. Signed as a free agent by **Chicago**, July 13, 2009. Signed as a free agent by **Florida**, July 24, 2010. Signed as a free agent by **Chekhov** (KHL), August 8, 2012. Signed as a free agent by **Salzburg** (Austria), December 16, 2012.

CULLEN, Matt

(KUH-lehn, MAT) **NSH**

Center. Shoots left. 6', 200 lbs. Born, Virginia, MN, November 2, 1976. Anaheim's 2nd choice, 35th overall, in 1996 Entry Draft.

Season	Club	League	GP	G	A	Pts	PIM	PP	SH	GW	S	%	+/-	TF	F%	Min	GP	G	A	Pts	PIM	PP	SH	GW	Min
1993-94	Moorhead Spuds	High-MN	STATISTICS NOT AVAILABLE																						
1994-95	Moorhead Spuds	High-MN	28	47	42	89	78	....	....	....	....	....	....	....	....	....	....	....	....	....	....	....	....	....	....
1995-96	St. Cloud State	WCHA	39	12	29	41	28	....	....	....	....	....	....	....	....	....	....	....	....	....	....	....	....	....	....
1996-97	St. Cloud State	WCHA	36	15	30	45	70	....	....	....	....	....	....	....	....	....	....	....	....	....	....	....	....	....	....
	Baltimore Bandits	AHL	6	3	3	6	7	....	....	....	....	....	....	....	....	....	3	0	2	2	0	....	....	....	....
1997-98	**Anaheim**	**NHL**	**61**	**6**	**21**	**27**	**23**	**2**	**0**	**0**	**75**	**8.0**	**–4**	....	....	....	....	....	....	....	....	....	....	....	....
	Cincinnati	AHL	18	15	12	27	2	....	....	....	....	....	....	....	....	....	....	....	....	....	....	....	....	....	....
1998-99	**Anaheim**	**NHL**	**75**	**11**	**14**	**25**	**47**	**5**	**1**	**1**	**112**	**9.8**	**–12**	**1047**	**47.7**	**15:31**	**4**	**0**	**0**	**0**	**0**	**0**	**0**	**0**	**15:30**
	Cincinnati	AHL	3	1	2	3	8	....	....	....	....	....	....	....	....	....	....	....	....	....	....	....	....	....	....
99-2000	**Anaheim**	**NHL**	**80**	**13**	**26**	**39**	**24**	**1**	**0**	**1**	**137**	**9.5**	**5**	**1247**	**44.6**	**16:54**	....	....	....	....	....	....	....	....	....
2000-01	**Anaheim**	**NHL**	**82**	**10**	**30**	**40**	**38**	**4**	**0**	**1**	**159**	**6.3**	**–23**	**1478**	**48.0**	**18:15**	....	....	....	....	....	....	....	....	....
2001-02	**Anaheim**	**NHL**	**79**	**18**	**30**	**48**	**24**	**3**	**1**	**4**	**164**	**11.0**	**–1**	**1283**	**51.4**	**17:01**	....	....	....	....	....	....	....	....	....
2002-03	**Anaheim**	**NHL**	**50**	**7**	**14**	**21**	**12**	**1**	**0**	**1**	**77**	**9.1**	**–4**	**271**	**50.6**	**14:18**	....	....	....	....	....	....	....	....	....
	Florida	**NHL**	**30**	**6**	**6**	**12**	**22**	**2**	**1**	**1**	**54**	**11.1**	**–4**	**423**	**47.3**	**14:43**	....	....	....	....	....	....	....	....	....
2003-04	**Florida**	**NHL**	**56**	**6**	**13**	**19**	**24**	**1**	**0**	**2**	**75**	**8.0**	**–2**	**735**	**50.6**	**14:12**	....	....	....	....	....	....	....	....	....
2004-05	SG Cortina	Italy	36	*27	33	60	64	....	....	....	....	....	....	....	....	....	18	8	14	22	32	....	....	....	....
2005-06♦	**Carolina**	**NHL**	**78**	**25**	**24**	**49**	**40**	**8**	**0**	**5**	**214**	**11.7**	**4**	**583**	**52.1**	**16:26**	**25**	**4**	**14**	**18**	**12**	**2**	**0**	**1**	**15:37**
2006-07	**NY Rangers**	**NHL**	**80**	**16**	**25**	**41**	**52**	**2**	**3**	**2**	**217**	**7.4**	**0**	**1134**	**54.6**	**17:10**	**10**	**1**	**3**	**4**	**6**	**0**	**0**	**1**	**16:55**
2007-08	**Carolina**	**NHL**	**59**	**13**	**36**	**49**	**32**	**8**	**0**	**1**	**137**	**9.5**	**2**	**649**	**56.1**	**16:52**	....	....	....	....	....	....	....	....	....
2008-09	**Carolina**	**NHL**	**69**	**22**	**21**	**43**	**20**	**4**	**2**	**2**	**139**	**15.8**	**11**	**884**	**51.7**	**16:48**	**18**	**3**	**3**	**6**	**14**	**0**	**1**	**0**	**16:41**
2009-10	**Carolina**	**NHL**	**60**	**12**	**28**	**40**	**26**	**1**	**2**	**1**	**137**	**8.8**	**0**	**898**	**49.1**	**19:02**	....	....	....	....	....	....	....	....	....
	Ottawa	**NHL**	**21**	**4**	**4**	**8**	**8**	**1**	**0**	**1**	**58**	**6.9**	**–7**	**223**	**58.7**	**17:59**	**6**	**3**	**5**	**8**	**0**	**2**	**0**	**0**	**23:14**
2010-11	**Minnesota**	**NHL**	**78**	**12**	**27**	**39**	**34**	**5**	**4**	**2**	**150**	**8.0**	**–14**	**843**	**56.1**	**18:02**	....	....	....	....	....	....	....	....	....
2011-12	**Minnesota**	**NHL**	**73**	**14**	**21**	**35**	**24**	**4**	**0**	**0**	**164**	**8.5**	**–10**	**1178**	**53.2**	**18:56**	....	....	....	....	....	....	....	....	....
2012-13	**Minnesota**	**NHL**	**42**	**7**	**20**	**27**	**10**	**0**	**0**	**0**	**79**	**8.9**	**9**	**448**	**54.7**	**15:53**	**5**	**0**	**3**	**3**	**2**	**0**	**0**	**0**	**19:08**
	NHL Totals		**1073**	**202**	**360**	**562**	**460**	**52**	**14**	**25**	**2148**	**9.4**		**13324**	**51.0**	**16:53**	**68**	**11**	**28**	**39**	**34**	**4**	**1**	**2**	**17:01**

WCHA Second All-Star Team (1997)

Traded to **Florida** by **Anaheim** with Pavel Trnka and Anaheim's 4th round choice (James Pemberton) in 2003 Entry Draft for Sandis Ozolinsh and Lance Ward, January 30, 2003. Signed as a free agent by **Carolina**, August 5, 2004. Signed as a free agent by **Cortina** (Italy), September 18, 2004. Signed as a free agent by **NY Rangers**, July 1, 2006. Traded to **Carolina** by **NY Rangers** for Andrew Hutchinson, Joe Barnes and Carolina's 3rd round choice (Evgeny Grachev) in 2008 Entry Draft, July 17, 2007. Traded to **Ottawa** by **Carolina** for Alexandre Picard and Ottawa's 2nd round choice (later traded to Edmonton – Edmonton selected Martin Marincin) in 2010 Entry Draft, February 12, 2010. Signed as a free agent by **Minnesota**, July 1, 2010. Signed as a free agent by **Nashville**, July 5, 2013.

CUMA, Tyler

(KOO-ma, TIGH-luhr) **MIN**

Defense. Shoots left. 6'2", 196 lbs. Born, Toronto, Ont., January 19, 1990. Minnesota's 1st choice, 23rd overall, in 2008 Entry Draft.

Season	Club	League	GP	G	A	Pts	PIM	PP	SH	GW	S	%	+/-	TF	F%	Min	GP	G	A	Pts	PIM	PP	SH	GW	Min
2005-06	Mississauga Reps	GTHL	40	15	20	35	52	....	....	....	....	....	....	....	....	....	....	....	....	....	....	....	....	....	....
2006-07	Ottawa 67's	OHL	63	3	16	19	55	....	....	....	....	....	....	....	....	....	5	0	2	2	6	....	....	....	....
2007-08	Ottawa 67's	OHL	59	4	28	32	69	....	....	....	....	....	....	....	....	....	4	1	1	2	2	....	....	....	....
2008-09	Ottawa 67's	OHL	21	1	8	9	27	....	....	....	....	....	....	....	....	....	....	....	....	....	....	....	....	....	....
2009-10	Ottawa 67's	OHL	52	5	17	22	73	....	....	....	....	....	....	....	....	....	12	0	5	5	20	....	....	....	....
2010-11	Houston Aeros	AHL	31	1	3	4	15	....	....	....	....	....	....	....	....	....	....	....	....	....	....	....	....	....	....
2011-12	**Minnesota**	**NHL**	**1**	**0**	**0**	**0**	**2**	**0**	**0**	**0**	**0**	**0.0**	**0**	**0**	**0.0**	**11:09**	....	....	....	....	....	....	....	....	....
	Houston Aeros	AHL	73	0	9	9	48	....	....	....	....	....	....	....	....	....	2	0	0	0	0	....	....	....	....
2012-13	Houston Aeros	AHL	42	1	11	12	14	....	....	....	....	....	....	....	....	....	1	0	0	0	0	....	....	....	....
	NHL Totals		**1**	**0**	**0**	**0**	**2**	**0**	**0**	**0**	**0**	**0.0**		**0**	**0.0**	**11:09**	....	....	....	....	....	....	....	....	....

• Missed majority of 2008-09 due to knee injury in Team Canada Jr. training camp, December 12, 2008.

CUMISKEY, Kyle

(kuh-MIHS-kee, KIGHL) **ANA**

Defense. Shoots left. 5'10", 185 lbs. Born, Abbotsford, B.C., December 2, 1986. Colorado's 9th choice, 222nd overall, in 2005 Entry Draft.

Season	Club	League	GP	G	A	Pts	PIM	PP	SH	GW	S	%	+/-	TF	F%	Min	GP	G	A	Pts	PIM	PP	SH	GW	Min
2002-03	Penticton	BCHL	59	10	11	21	36	....	....	....	....	....	....	....	....	....	....	....	....	....	....	....	....	....	....
2003-04	Kelowna Rockets	WHL	54	2	7	9	20	....	....	....	....	....	....	....	....	....	17	0	0	0	0	....	....	....	....
2004-05	Kelowna Rockets	WHL	72	4	36	40	47	....	....	....	....	....	....	....	....	....	24	0	13	13	12	....	....	....	....
2005-06	Kelowna Rockets	WHL	51	6	24	30	52	....	....	....	....	....	....	....	....	....	12	0	6	6	8	....	....	....	....
2006-07	**Colorado**	**NHL**	**9**	**1**	**1**	**2**	**2**	**0**	**0**	**0**	**8**	**12.5**	**0**	**0**	**0.0**	**13:28**	....	....	....	....	....	....	....	....	....
	Albany River Rats	AHL	63	7	26	33	32	....	....	....	....	....	....	....	....	....	5	0	2	2	6	....	....	....	....
2007-08	**Colorado**	**NHL**	**38**	**0**	**5**	**5**	**16**	**0**	**0**	**0**	**19**	**0.0**	**–3**	**0**	**0.0**	**12:08**	....	....	....	....	....	....	....	....	....
	Lake Erie	AHL	5	1	1	2	4	....	....	....	....	....	....	....	....	....	....	....	....	....	....	....	....	....	....
2008-09	**Colorado**	**NHL**	**6**	**0**	**0**	**0**	**0**	**0**	**0**	**0**	**2**	**0.0**	**–2**	**0**	**0.0**	**8:32**	....	....	....	....	....	....	....	....	....
	Lake Erie	AHL	28	5	12	17	16	....	....	....	....	....	....	....	....	....	....	....	....	....	....	....	....	....	....
2009-10	**Colorado**	**NHL**	**61**	**7**	**13**	**20**	**20**	**2**	**0**	**1**	**74**	**9.5**	**0**	**0**	**0.0**	**19:48**	**6**	**1**	**1**	**2**	**2**	**0**	**0**	**0**	**22:37**
2010-11	**Colorado**	**NHL**	**18**	**1**	**7**	**8**	**10**	**0**	**0**	**0**	**21**	**4.8**	**–3**	**0**	**0.0**	**19:40**	....	....	....	....	....	....	....	....	....
2011-12	Syracuse Crunch	AHL	57	6	23	29	44	....	....	....	....	....	....	....	....	....	4	0	1	1	0	....	....	....	....
2012-13	MODO	Sweden	46	7	25	32	30	....	....	....	....	....	....	....	....	....	5	1	4	5	0	....	....	....	....
	NHL Totals		**132**	**9**	**26**	**35**	**48**	**2**	**0**	**1**	**124**	**7.3**		**0**	**0.0**	**16:38**	**6**	**1**	**1**	**2**	**2**	**0**	**0**	**0**	**22:37**

• Missed majority of 2010-11 due to post-concussion syndrome. Traded to **Anaheim** by **Colorado** for Jake Newton and Anaheim's 7th round choice (later traded to San Jose – San Jose selected Emil Galimov) in 2013 Entry Draft, October 8, 2011. Signed as a free agent by **MODO** (Sweden), July 9, 2012.

CUNDARI, Mark

(kuhn-DAHR-ee, MAHRK) **CGY**

Defense. Shoots left. 5'9", 200 lbs. Born, Woodbridge, Ont., April 23, 1990.

Season	Club	League	GP	G	A	Pts	PIM	PP	SH	GW	S	%	+/-	TF	F%	Min	GP	G	A	Pts	PIM	PP	SH	GW	Min
2005-06	Vaughan Kings	GTHL	STATISTICS NOT AVAILABLE																						
	Vaughan Vipers	ON-Jr.A	2	0	0	0	0	....	....	....	....	....	....	....	....	....	....	....	....	....	....	....	....	....	....
2006-07	Windsor Spitfires	OHL	62	6	16	22	130	....	....	....	....	....	....	....	....	....	....	....	....	....	....	....	....	....	....
2007-08	Windsor Spitfires	OHL	63	6	17	23	141	....	....	....	....	....	....	....	....	....	3	0	0	0	10	....	....	....	....
2008-09	Windsor Spitfires	OHL	60	10	22	32	143	....	....	....	....	....	....	....	....	....	20	1	8	9	38	....	....	....	....
2009-10	Windsor Spitfires	OHL	63	8	46	54	139	....	....	....	....	....	....	....	....	....	19	3	15	18	42	....	....	....	....
2010-11	Peoria Rivermen	AHL	69	10	20	30	106	....	....	....	....	....	....	....	....	....	3	0	1	1	4	....	....	....	....
2011-12	Peoria Rivermen	AHL	48	3	12	15	62	....	....	....	....	....	....	....	....	....	....	....	....	....	....	....	....	....	....
2012-13	Peoria Rivermen	AHL	56	7	18	25	80	....	....	....	....	....	....	....	....	....	....	....	....	....	....	....	....	....	....
	Calgary	**NHL**	**4**	**1**	**2**	**3**	**2**	**1**	**0**	**0**	**8**	**12.5**	**–2**	**0**	**0.0**	**19:46**	....	....	....	....	....	....	....	....	....
	Abbotsford Heat	AHL	2	0	3	3	13	....	....	....	....	....	....	....	....	....	....	....	....	....	....	....	....	....	....
	NHL Totals		**4**	**1**	**2**	**3**	**2**	**1**	**0**	**0**	**8**	**12.5**		**0**	**0.0**	**19:46**	....	....	....	....	....	....	....	....	....

Signed as a free agent by **St. Louis**, September 24, 2008. Traded to **Calgary** by **St. Louis** with Reto Berra and St. Louis' 1st round choice (Emile Poirier) in 2013 Entry Draft for Jay Bouwmeester, April 1, 2013.

DA COSTA, Stephane

(DA-KAWS-tuh, steh-FAN) **OTT**

Center. Shoots right. 5'11", 183 lbs. Born, Paris, France, July 11, 1989.

Season	Club	League	GP	G	A	Pts	PIM	PP	SH	GW	S	%	+/-	TF	F%	Min	GP	G	A	Pts	PIM	PP	SH	GW	Min
2006-07	Texas Tornado	NAHL	50	23	17	40	31	....	....	....	....	....	....	....	....	....	10	4	3	7	6	....	....	....	....
2007-08	Sioux City	USHL	51	12	25	37	22	....	....	....	....	....	....	....	....	....	4	1	2	3	8	....	....	....	....
2008-09	Sioux City	USHL	48	31	36	67	23	....	....	....	....	....	....	....	....	....	....	....	....	....	....	....	....	....	....
2009-10	Merrimack	H-East	34	16	29	45	41	....	....	....	....	....	....	....	....	....	....	....	....	....	....	....	....	....	....
2010-11	Merrimack	H-East	33	14	31	45	42	....	....	....	....	....	....	....	....	....	....	....	....	....	....	....	....	....	....
	Ottawa	**NHL**	**4**	**0**	**0**	**0**	**0**	**0**	**0**	**0**	**9**	**0.0**	**–1**	**21**	**28.6**	**11:25**	....	....	....	....	....	....	....	....	....
2011-12	**Ottawa**	**NHL**	**22**	**3**	**2**	**5**	**8**	**0**	**0**	**0**	**31**	**9.7**	**–9**	**177**	**36.7**	**12:10**	....	....	....	....	....	....	....	....	....
	Binghamton	AHL	46	13	23	36	12	....	....	....	....	....	....	....	....	....	....	....	....	....	....	....	....	....	....

			Regular Season														Playoffs								
Season	Club	League	GP	G	A	Pts	PIM	PP	SH	GW	S	%	+/-	TF	F%	Min	GP	G	A	Pts	PIM	PP	SH	GW	Min
2012-13	Binghamton	AHL	57	13	25	38	26										3	0	1	1	0				
	Ottawa	**NHL**	9	1	1	2	0	0	0	0	15	6.7	–3	64	60.9	11:52									
	NHL Totals		35	4	3	7	8	0	0	0	55	7.3		262	42.0	12:00									

Hockey East All-Rookie Team (2010) • Hockey East Second All-Star Team (2010, 2011) • Hockey East Rookie of the Year (2010) • NCAA Rookie of the Year (2010) • NCAA East Second All-American Team (2011)

Signed as a free agent by **Ottawa**. March 31, 2011.

DADONOV, Evgeni

(do-DON-nauv, ehv-GEH-nee) **CAR**

Right wing. Shoots left. 5'11", 184 lbs. Born, Chelyabinsk, USSR, March 12, 1989. Florida's 3rd choice, 71st overall, in 2007 Entry Draft.

2005-06	Chelyabinsk 2	Russia-3	12	1	4	5	2																		
	Chelyabinsk	Russia-2															1	0	0	0	0				
2006-07	Chelyabinsk 2	Russia-3	4	2	0	2	14																		
	Chelyabinsk	Russia	24	1	1	2	8																		
2007-08	Chelyabinsk 2	Russia-3	12	4	7	11	32																		
	Chelyabinsk	Russia	43	7	13	20	20										2	0	0	0	0				
2008-09	Chelyabinsk	KHL	40	11	4	15	8										3	0	0	0	2				
2009-10	**Florida**	**NHL**	4	0	0	0	0	0	0	0	4	0.0	–1	0	0.0	13:14									
	Rochester	AHL	76	17	23	40	36										7	0	1	1	0				
2010-11	**Florida**	**NHL**	36	8	9	17	14	1	0	0	60	13.3	0	5	20.0	14:15									
	Rochester	AHL	24	8	8	16	4																		
2011-12	**Florida**	**NHL**	15	2	1	3	2	0	0	0	21	9.5	–4	6	0.0	10:03									
	San Antonio	AHL	20	5	4	9	4																		
	Charlotte	AHL	35	3	16	19	6																		
2012-13	Donetsk	KHL	54	14	24	38	12																		
	NHL Totals		55	10	10	20	16	1	0	0	85	11.8		11	9.1	13:02									

Traded to **Carolina** by **Florida** with A.J. Jenks for Jon Matsumoto and Mattias Lindstrom, January 18, 2012. Signed as a free agent by **Donetsk** (KHL), July 4, 2012.

D'AGOSTINI, Matt

(DAG-uh-stee-noh, MAT) **PIT**

Right wing. Shoots right. 6', 198 lbs. Born, Sault Ste. Marie, Ont., October 23, 1986. Montreal's 5th choice, 190th overall, in 2005 Entry Draft.

2003-04	Soo North Stars	GNML	36	36	23	59	41																		
2004-05	Guelph Storm	OHL	59	24	22	46	29										4	0	2	2	8				
2005-06	Guelph Storm	OHL	66	25	54	79	81										15	8	20	28	16				
2006-07	Hamilton	AHL	63	21	28	49	33										22	4	9	13	18				
2007-08	**Montreal**	**NHL**	1	0	0	0	2	0	0	0	0	0.0	0	0	0.0	8:49									
	Hamilton	AHL	76	23	30	53	38																		
2008-09	**Montreal**	**NHL**	53	12	9	21	16	3	0	1	116	10.3	–17	9	33.3	13:25	3	0	0	0	0	0	0	0	11:49
	Hamilton	AHL	20	14	11	25	16																		
2009-10	**Montreal**	**NHL**	40	2	2	4	26	0	0	0	48	4.2	–12	3	66.7	9:53									
	Hamilton	AHL	3	0	1	1	2																		
	St. Louis	**NHL**	7	0	0	0	2	0	0	0	6	0.0	–3	7	71.4	9:13									
2010-11	**St. Louis**	**NHL**	82	21	25	46	40	6	0	5	163	12.9	8	55	38.2	14:46									
2011-12	**St. Louis**	**NHL**	55	9	9	18	27	3	0	3	101	8.9	12	29	27.6	14:01	4	1	0	1	4	0	0	0	12:16
2012-13	Riessersee	German-2	10	2	6	8	6																		
	St. Louis	**NHL**	16	1	1	2	2	0	0	0	19	5.3	–4	14	28.6	11:52									
	New Jersey	**NHL**	13	2	2	4	6	0	0	0	14	14.3	–1	4	25.0	12:51									
	NHL Totals		267	47	48	95	121	12	0	9	467	10.1		121	36.4	13:11	7	1	0	1	4	0	0	0	12:04

Traded to **St. Louis** by **Montreal** for Aaron Palushaj, March 2, 2010. Signed as a free agent by **Riessersee** (German-2), October 8, 2012. Traded to **New Jersey** by **St. Louis** with future considerations for future considerations, March 22, 2013. Signed as a free agent by **Pittsburgh**, July 10, 2013.

DALEY, Trevor

(DAY-lee, TREH-vuhr) **DAL**

Defense. Shoots left. 5'11", 198 lbs. Born, Toronto, Ont., October 9, 1983. Dallas' 5th choice, 43rd overall, in 2002 Entry Draft.

1998-99	Vaughan Vipers	ON-Jr.A	44	10	36	46	79																		
99-2000	Sault Ste. Marie	OHL	54	16	30	46	77										15	3	7	10	12				
2000-01	Sault Ste. Marie	OHL	58	14	27	41	105																		
2001-02	Sault Ste. Marie	OHL	47	9	39	48	38										6	2	2	4	4				
2002-03	Sault Ste. Marie	OHL	57	20	33	53	128										1	0	0	0	2				
2003-04	**Dallas**	**NHL**	27	1	5	6	14	1	0	0	34	2.9	–6	0	0.0	16:02	1	0	0	0	0	0	0	0	10:21
	Utah Grizzlies	AHL	40	8	6	14	76																		
2004-05	Hamilton	AHL	78	7	27	34	109										4	0	1	1	2				
2005-06	**Dallas**	**NHL**	81	3	11	14	87	0	0	1	91	3.3	–2	0	0.0	18:40	3	0	0	0	0	0	0	0	11:30
2006-07	**Dallas**	**NHL**	74	4	8	12	63	0	0	1	68	5.9	2	0	0.0	19:23	7	1	0	1	4	0	0	0	22:26
2007-08	**Dallas**	**NHL**	82	5	19	24	85	0	0	1	87	5.7	–1	1	100.0	19:48	18	1	0	1	20	0	0	0	18:52
2008-09	**Dallas**	**NHL**	75	7	18	25	73	0	0	2	104	6.7	2	1	0.0	22:00									
2009-10	**Dallas**	**NHL**	77	6	16	22	25	2	0	2	107	5.6	3	0	0.0	22:11									
2010-11	**Dallas**	**NHL**	82	8	19	27	34	2	0	1	131	6.1	7	0	0.0	22:29									
2011-12	**Dallas**	**NHL**	79	4	21	25	42	1	0	2	134	3.0	3	0	0.0	21:39									
2012-13	**Dallas**	**NHL**	44	4	9	13	14	2	0	0	58	6.9	1	0	0.0	21:25									
	NHL Totals		621	42	126	168	437	8	0	10	814	5.2		2	50.0	20:42	29	2	0	2	24	0	0	0	18:40

DALPE, Zac

(DAL-pee, ZAK) **CAR**

Right wing. Shoots right. 6'1", 195 lbs. Born, Paris, Ont., November 1, 1989. Carolina's 2nd choice, 45th overall, in 2008 Entry Draft.

2006-07	Stratford Cullitons	ON-Jr.B	52	30	43	73	68																		
2007-08	Penticton Vees	BCHL	46	27	36	63	14										15	8	9	17	4				
2008-09	Ohio State	CCHA	37	13	12	25	25																		
2009-10	Ohio State	CCHA	39	*21	24	45	19																		
	Albany River Rats	AHL	9	6	2	8	0										8	3	3	6	0				
2010-11	**Carolina**	**NHL**	15	3	1	4	0	0	0	1	16	18.8	0	26	26.9	7:56									
	Charlotte	AHL	61	23	34	57	21										16	6	7	13	6				
2011-12	**Carolina**	**NHL**	16	1	2	3	4	0	0	0	20	5.0	–3	11	45.5	9:35									
	Charlotte	AHL	56	18	14	32	17																		
2012-13	Charlotte	AHL	54	21	21	42	12										5	0	0	0	4				
	Carolina	**NHL**	10	1	2	3	0	0	0	0	18	5.6	–7	3	33.3	12:18									
	NHL Totals		41	5	5	10	4	0	0	1	54	9.3		40	32.5	9:39									

CCHA All-Rookie Team (2009) • CCHA First All-Star Team (2010) • NCAA West Second All-American Team (2010) • AHL All-Rookie Team (2011)

DATSYUK, Pavel

(daht-SOOK, PAH-vehl) **DET**

Center. Shoots left. 5'11", 198 lbs. Born, Sverdlovsk, USSR, July 20, 1978. Detroit's 8th choice, 171st overall, in 1998 Entry Draft.

1996-97	Yekaterinburg 2	Russia-3	18	2	2	4	4																		
	Yekaterinburg	Russia	36	12	10	22	12																		
1997-98	Yekaterinburg	Russia	24	3	5	8	4																		
	Yekaterinburg 2	Russia-3	22	7	8	15	4																		
1998-99	Yekaterinburg 2	Russia-4	10	14	14	28	4																		
	Yekaterinburg	Russia-2	35	21	23	44	14																		
99-2000	Yekaterinburg	Russia	15	1	3	4	4										9	3	7	10	10				
2000-01	Ak Bars Kazan	Russia	42	9	18	27	10										4	0	1	1	2				
2001-02♦	**Detroit**	**NHL**	70	11	24	35	4	2	0	1	79	13.9	4	794	47.7	13:39	21	3	3	6	2	1	0	1	10:40
	Russia	Olympics	6	1	2	3	0																		
2002-03	**Detroit**	**NHL**	64	12	39	51	16	1	0	1	82	14.6	20	778	48.2	15:28	4	0	0	0	0	0	0	0	18:48
2003-04	**Detroit**	**NHL**	75	30	38	68	35	8	1	4	136	22.1	–2	1314	54.0	18:16	12	0	6	6	2	0	0	0	17:23
2004-05	Dynamo Moscow	Russia	47	15	17	32	16										10	*6	3	9	4				
2005-06	**Detroit**	**NHL**	75	28	59	87	22	11	0	4	145	19.3	26	1059	53.1	17:53	5	0	3	3	0	0	0	0	20:05
	Russia	Olympics	8	1	7	8	10																		
2006-07	**Detroit**	**NHL**	79	27	60	87	20	5	2	5	207	13.0	36	845	56.2	19:57	18	8	8	16	8	4	0	2	22:03
2007-08♦	**Detroit**	**NHL**	82	31	66	97	20	10	1	6	264	11.7	*41	833	54.4	21:23	22	10	13	23	6	4	0	1	21:40
2008-09	**Detroit**	**NHL**	81	32	65	97	22	11	1	3	248	12.9	34	1135	56.0	19:13	16	1	8	9	9	1	0	0	20:05

			Regular Season														Playoffs								
Season	Club	League	GP	G	A	Pts	PIM	PP	SH	GW	S	%	+/-	TF	F%	Min	GP	G	A	Pts	PIM	PP	SH	GW	Min
2009-10	**Detroit**	**NHL**	**80**	**27**	**43**	**70**	**18**	**9**	**0**	**3**	**203**	**13.3**	**17**	**1070**	**55.1**	**20:21**	**12**	**6**	**7**	**13**	**8**	**1**	**0**	**1**	**18:49**
	Russia	Olympics	4	1	2	3	2	....	....	....	....	....	....	....	....	....	....	....	....	....	....	....	....	....	....
2010-11	**Detroit**	**NHL**	**56**	**23**	**36**	**59**	**15**	**6**	**1**	**5**	**137**	**16.8**	**11**	**785**	**54.7**	**19:19**	**11**	**4**	**11**	**15**	**8**	**2**	**0**	**0**	**21:09**
2011-12	**Detroit**	**NHL**	**70**	**19**	**48**	**67**	**14**	**4**	**0**	**5**	**164**	**11.6**	**21**	**1249**	**56.2**	**19:34**	**5**	**1**	**2**	**3**	**2**	**0**	**0**	**0**	**21:17**
2012-13	CSKA Moscow	KHL	31	11	25	36	4	....	....	....	....	....	....	....	....	....	....	....	....	....	....	....	....	....	....
	Detroit	**NHL**	**47**	**15**	**34**	**49**	**14**	**8**	**0**	**6**	**107**	**14.0**	**21**	**887**	**55.0**	**20:11**	**14**	**3**	**6**	**9**	**4**	**0**	**0**	**0**	**20:59**
	NHL Totals		**779**	**255**	**512**	**767**	**200**	**75**	**6**	**43**	**1772**	**14.4**		**10749**	**53.9**	**18:42**	**140**	**36**	**67**	**103**	**49**	**13**	**0**	**5**	**19:01**

Lady Byng Memorial Trophy (2006, 2007, 2008, 2009) • Frank J. Selke Trophy (2008, 2009, 2010) • NHL Second All-Star Team (2009)
Played in NHL All-Star Game (2004, 2008, 2012)
• Spent majority of 1999-2000 on **Kazan** (Russia) reserve squad. Signed as a free agent by **Dynamo Moscow** (Russia), June 19, 2004. Signed as a free agent by **CSKA Moscow** (KHL), September 22, 2012.

DAUGAVINS, Kaspars

(DAH-gah-vihnsh, KAS-purz)

Left wing. Shoots left. 6'1", 204 lbs. Born, Riga, Latvia, May 18, 1988. Ottawa's 3rd choice, 91st overall, in 2006 Entry Draft.

2003-04	HK Riga 2000	EEHL	2	0	1	1	0	....	....	....	....	....	....	....	....	....	....	....	....	....	....	....	....	....	....
	Prizma/Riga 86	Latvia	14	6	6	12	10	....	....	....	....	....	....	....	....	....	2	1	1	2	4	....	....	....	....
2004-05	CSKA Moscow 2	Russia-3	STATISTICS NOT AVAILABLE																						
2005-06	HK Riga 2000	Latvia	....	4	6	10	16	....	....	....	....	....	....	....	....	....	....	....	....	....	....	....	....	....	....
	HK Riga 2000	BelOpen	45	4	11	15	16	....	....	....	....	....	....	....	....	....	....	....	....	....	....	....	....	....	....
2006-07	St. Michael's	OHL	61	18	42	60	64	....	....	....	....	....	....	....	....	....	....	....	....	....	....	....	....	....	....
	Binghamton	AHL	11	2	0	2	9	....	....	....	....	....	....	....	....	....	....	....	....	....	....	....	....	....	....
2007-08	St. Michael's	OHL	62	40	34	74	42	....	....	....	....	....	....	....	....	....	4	2	1	3	4	....	....	....	....
	Binghamton	AHL	3	0	1	1	0	....	....	....	....	....	....	....	....	....	....	....	....	....	....	....	....	....	....
2008-09	Binghamton	AHL	23	2	1	3	9	....	....	....	....	....	....	....	....	....	....	....	....	....	....	....	....	....	....
	St. Michael's	OHL	30	11	17	28	35	....	....	....	....	....	....	....	....	....	11	2	7	9	14	....	....	....	....
2009-10	**Ottawa**	**NHL**	**1**	**0**	**0**	**0**	**0**	**0**	**0**	**0**	**2**	**0.0**	**0**	**0**	**0.0**	**8:26**	....	....	....	....	....	....	....	....	....
	Binghamton	AHL	72	21	25	46	16	....	....	....	....	....	....	....	....	....	....	....	....	....	....	....	....	....	....
	Latvia	Olympics	4	0	0	0	2	....	....	....	....	....	....	....	....	....	....	....	....	....	....	....	....	....	....
2010-11	Binghamton	AHL	73	19	35	54	34	....	....	....	....	....	....	....	....	....	23	10	10	20	8	....	....	....	....
2011-12	**Ottawa**	**NHL**	**65**	**5**	**6**	**11**	**12**	**0**	**0**	**1**	**77**	**6.5**	**–2**	**60**	**38.3**	**11:20**	**1**	**0**	**0**	**0**	**0**	**0**	**0**	**0**	**10:30**
	Binghamton	AHL	7	4	2	6	0	....	....	....	....	....	....	....	....	....	....	....	....	....	....	....	....	....	....
2012-13	Dynamo Riga	KHL	35	5	9	14	26	....	....	....	....	....	....	....	....	....	....	....	....	....	....	....	....	....	....
	Ottawa	**NHL**	**19**	**1**	**2**	**3**	**9**	**0**	**0**	**0**	**23**	**4.3**	**–7**	**18**	**50.0**	**11:26**	....	....	....	....	....	....	....	....	....
	Boston	**NHL**	**6**	**0**	**1**	**1**	**0**	**0**	**0**	**0**	**13**	**0.0**	**–1**	**0**	**0.0**	**9:43**	**6**	**0**	**0**	**0**	**2**	**0**	**0**	**0**	**8:47**
	NHL Totals		**91**	**6**	**9**	**15**	**21**	**0**	**0**	**1**	**115**	**5.2**		**78**	**41.0**	**11:13**	**7**	**0**	**0**	**0**	**2**	**0**	**0**	**0**	**9:02**

OHL All-Rookie Team (2007)
Signed as a free agent by **Riga** (KHL), September 16, 2012. Claimed on waiver by **Boston** from **Ottawa**, March 27, 2013.

DAVISON, Rob

(DAY-vihs-ohn, RAWB) **S.J.**

Defense. Shoots left. 6'2", 215 lbs. Born, St. Catharines, Ont., May 1, 1980. San Jose's 4th choice, 98th overall, in 1998 Entry Draft.

1996-97	St. Mike's B's	ON-Jr.A	45	2	6	8	93	....	....	....	....	....	....	....	....	....	6	0	0	0	9	....	....	....	....
1997-98	North Bay	OHL	59	0	11	11	200	....	....	....	....	....	....	....	....	....	....	....	....	....	....	....	....	....	....
1998-99	North Bay	OHL	59	2	17	19	150	....	....	....	....	....	....	....	....	....	4	0	1	1	12	....	....	....	....
99-2000	North Bay	OHL	67	4	6	10	194	....	....	....	....	....	....	....	....	....	6	0	1	1	8	....	....	....	....
2000-01	Kentucky	AHL	72	0	4	4	230	....	....	....	....	....	....	....	....	....	3	0	0	0	0	....	....	....	....
2001-02	Cleveland Barons	AHL	70	1	3	4	206	....	....	....	....	....	....	....	....	....	....	....	....	....	....	....	....	....	....
2002-03	**San Jose**	**NHL**	**15**	**1**	**2**	**3**	**22**	**0**	**0**	**0**	**15**	**6.7**	**4**	**0**	**0.0**	**17:53**	....	....	....	....	....	....	....	....	....
	Cleveland Barons	AHL	42	1	3	4	82	....	....	....	....	....	....	....	....	....	....	....	....	....	....	....	....	....	....
2003-04	**San Jose**	**NHL**	**55**	**0**	**3**	**3**	**92**	**0**	**0**	**0**	**33**	**0.0**	**–3**	**0**	**0.0**	**14:22**	**5**	**0**	**2**	**2**	**4**	**0**	**0**	**0**	**9:01**
2004-05	Cardiff Devils	Britain	24	2	3	5	114	....	....	....	....	....	....	....	....	....	8	0	1	1	12	....	....	....	....
2005-06	**San Jose**	**NHL**	**69**	**1**	**5**	**6**	**76**	**0**	**0**	**0**	**36**	**2.8**	**6**	**0**	**0.0**	**13:50**	**1**	**0**	**0**	**0**	**0**	**0**	**0**	**0**	**8:00**
2006-07	**San Jose**	**NHL**	**22**	**0**	**2**	**2**	**27**	**0**	**0**	**0**	**14**	**0.0**	**–2**	**0**	**0.0**	**9:19**	....	....	....	....	....	....	....	....	....
2007-08	**San Jose**	**NHL**	**15**	**0**	**0**	**0**	**21**	**0**	**0**	**0**	**10**	**0.0**	**–3**	**0**	**0.0**	**7:47**	....	....	....	....	....	....	....	....	....
	NY Islanders	**NHL**	**19**	**1**	**1**	**2**	**32**	**0**	**1**	**0**	**22**	**4.5**	**–3**	**0**	**0.0**	**18:40**	....	....	....	....	....	....	....	....	....
2008-09	**Vancouver**	**NHL**	**23**	**0**	**2**	**2**	**51**	**0**	**0**	**0**	**15**	**0.0**	**–4**	**0**	**0.0**	**10:05**	....	....	....	....	....	....	....	....	....
2009-10	**New Jersey**	**NHL**	**1**	**0**	**0**	**0**	**0**	**0**	**0**	**0**	**0**	**0.0**	**0**	**0**	**0.0**	**3:59**	....	....	....	....	....	....	....	....	....
	Lowell Devils	AHL	70	4	13	17	182	....	....	....	....	....	....	....	....	....	5	0	1	1	12	....	....	....	....
2010-11	Albany Devils	AHL	63	4	14	18	151	....	....	....	....	....	....	....	....	....	....	....	....	....	....	....	....	....	....
2011-12	HC Ocelari Trinec	CzRep	19	1	2	3	12	....	....	....	....	....	....	....	....	....	....	....	....	....	....	....	....	....	....
	Salzburg	Austria	14	0	4	4	35	....	....	....	....	....	....	....	....	....	3	0	1	1	14	....	....	....	....
2012-13	Salzburg	Austria	53	3	6	9	54	....	....	....	....	....	....	....	....	....	8	0	1	1	24	....	....	....	....
	NHL Totals		**219**	**3**	**15**	**18**	**321**	**0**	**1**	**0**	**145**	**2.1**		**0**	**0.0**	**13:22**	**6**	**0**	**2**	**2**	**4**	**0**	**0**	**0**	**8:51**

Signed as a free agent by **Cardiff** (Britain), October 5, 2004. Traded to **NY Islanders** by **San Jose** for NY Islanders' 7th round choice (Jason Demers) in 2008 Entry Draft, February 26, 2008. Signed as a free agent by **Vancouver**, July 10, 2008. • Missed majority of 2006-07, 2007-08 and 2008-09 due to various injuries and as a healthy reserve. Signed as a free agent by **New Jersey**, July 31, 2009. Signed as a free agent by **Trinec** (CzRep), September 20, 2011. Signed as a free agent by **Salzburg** (Austria), November 23, 2011. Signed as a free agent by **San Jose**, August, 2013.

de HAAN, Calvin

(DUH HAWN, CAL-vihn) **NYI**

Defense. Shoots left. 6'1", 187 lbs. Born, Carp, Ont., May 9, 1991. NY Islanders' 2nd choice, 12th overall, in 2009 Entry Draft.

2006-07	Ott. Valley Titans	Minor-ON	32	4	22	26	20	....	....	....	....	....	....	....	....	....	....	....	....	....	....	....	....	....	....
2007-08	Kemptville 73's	ON-Jr.A	58	3	39	42	14	....	....	....	....	....	....	....	....	....	....	....	....	....	....	....	....	....	....
2008-09	Oshawa Generals	OHL	68	8	55	63	40	....	....	....	....	....	....	....	....	....	....	....	....	....	....	....	....	....	....
2009-10	Oshawa Generals	OHL	34	5	19	24	14	....	....	....	....	....	....	....	....	....	....	....	....	....	....	....	....	....	....
2010-11	Oshawa Generals	OHL	55	6	42	48	48	....	....	....	....	....	....	....	....	....	10	1	11	12	6	....	....	....	....
2011-12	**NY Islanders**	**NHL**	**1**	**0**	**0**	**0**	**0**	**0**	**0**	**0**	**2**	**0.0**	**1**	**0**	**0.0**	**13:01**	....	....	....	....	....	....	....	....	....
	Bridgeport	AHL	56	2	14	16	24	....	....	....	....	....	....	....	....	....	3	0	2	2	2	....	....	....	....
2012-13	Bridgeport	AHL	3	0	2	2	4	....	....	....	....	....	....	....	....	....	....	....	....	....	....	....	....	....	....
	NHL Totals		**1**	**0**	**0**	**0**	**0**	**0**	**0**	**0**	**2**	**0.0**		**0**	**0.0**	**13:01**	....	....	....	....	....	....	....	....	....

• Missed remainder of 2012-13 due to shoulder injury at Wilkes-Barre (AHL), October 20, 2012.

DeKEYSER, Danny

(duh-KIGH-zuhr, DAN-ee) **DET**

Defense. Shoots left. 6'3", 190 lbs. Born, Detroit, MI, March 7, 1990.

2008-09	Trail	BCHL	58	8	17	25	12	....	....	....	....	....	....	....	....	....	3	1	0	1	4	....	....	....	....
2009-10	Sioux City	USHL	41	1	10	11	12	....	....	....	....	....	....	....	....	....	....	....	....	....	....	....	....	....	....
2010-11	Western Mich.	CCHA	42	5	12	17	43	....	....	....	....	....	....	....	....	....	....	....	....	....	....	....	....	....	....
2011-12	Western Mich.	CCHA	41	5	12	17	42	....	....	....	....	....	....	....	....	....	....	....	....	....	....	....	....	....	....
2012-13	Western Mich.	CCHA	35	2	13	15	22	....	....	....	....	....	....	....	....	....	....	....	....	....	....	....	....	....	....
	Detroit	**NHL**	**11**	**0**	**1**	**1**	**2**	**0**	**0**	**0**	**15**	**0.0**	**4**	**0**	**0.0**	**18:03**	**2**	**0**	**0**	**0**	**0**	**0**	**0**	**0**	**17:53**
	Grand Rapids	AHL	....	....	....	....	....	....	....	....	....	....	....	....	....	....	6	0	1	1	8	....	....	....	....
	NHL Totals		**11**	**0**	**1**	**1**	**2**	**0**	**0**	**0**	**15**	**0.0**		**0**	**0.0**	**18:03**	**2**	**0**	**0**	**0**	**0**	**0**	**0**	**0**	**17:53**

CCHA All-Rookie Team (2011) • CCHA Second All-Star Team (2012) • CCHA First All-Star Team (2013) • NCAA West Second All-American Team (2012, 2013)
Signed as a free agent by **Detroit**, March 29, 2013.

DEL ZOTTO, Michael

(DEHL ZAW-toh, MIGH-kuhl) **NYR**

Defense. Shoots left. 6', 195 lbs. Born, Stouffville, Ont., June 24, 1990. NY Rangers' 1st choice, 20th overall, in 2008 Entry Draft.

2005-06	Markham Waxers	Minor-ON	73	30	90	120	90	....	....	....	....	....	....	....	....	....	....	....	....	....	....	....	....	....	....
2006-07	Oshawa Generals	OHL	64	10	47	57	78	....	....	....	....	....	....	....	....	....	9	3	9	12	14	....	....	....	....
2007-08	Oshawa Generals	OHL	64	16	47	63	82	....	....	....	....	....	....	....	....	....	15	2	6	8	38	....	....	....	....
2008-09	Oshawa Generals	OHL	34	7	26	33	48	....	....	....	....	....	....	....	....	....	....	....	....	....	....	....	....	....	....
	London Knights	OHL	28	6	24	30	30	....	....	....	....	....	....	....	....	....	14	3	16	19	18	....	....	....	....
2009-10	**NY Rangers**	**NHL**	**80**	**9**	**28**	**37**	**32**	**4**	**0**	**1**	**81**	**11.1**	**–20**	**0**	**0.0**	**18:58**	....	....	....	....	....	....	....	....	....
2010-11	**NY Rangers**	**NHL**	**47**	**2**	**9**	**11**	**20**	**2**	**0**	**0**	**58**	**3.4**	**–5**	**0**	**0.0**	**19:29**	....	....	....	....	....	....	....	....	....
	Connecticut	AHL	11	0	7	7	8	....	....	....	....	....	....	....	....	....	....	....	....	....	....	....	....	....	....
2011-12	**NY Rangers**	**NHL**	**77**	**10**	**31**	**41**	**36**	**1**	**1**	**2**	**113**	**8.8**	**20**	**0**	**0.0**	**22:26**	**20**	**2**	**8**	**10**	**12**	**1**	**0**	**1**	**21:39**

			Regular Season														Playoffs								
Season	Club	League	GP	G	A	Pts	PIM	PP	SH	GW	S	%	+/-	TF	F%	Min	GP	G	A	Pts	PIM	PP	SH	GW	Min
2012-13	Rapperswil	Swiss	9	2	5	7	10	....	....	....	....	....	....	....	....	....	....	....	....	....	....	....	....	....	....
	NY Rangers	**NHL**	46	3	18	21	18	0	1	0	81	3.7	6	0	0.0	23:10	12	1	1	2	8	0	0	0	21:10
	NHL Totals		250	24	86	110	106	7	2	3	333	7.2		0	0.0	20:55	32	3	9	12	20	1	0	1	21:28

NHL All-Rookie Team (2010)

Signed as a free agent by **Rapperswil** (Swiss), October 31, 2012.

DELLA ROVERE, Stefan

(DEHL-ah ROH-vair, STEH-fan)

Left wing. Shoots left. 5'11", 205 lbs. Born, Richmond Hill, Ont., February 25, 1990. Washington's 8th choice, 204th overall, in 2008 Entry Draft.

Season	Club	League	GP	G	A	Pts	PIM	PP	SH	GW	S	%	+/-	TF	F%	Min	GP	G	A	Pts	PIM	PP	SH	GW	Min
2005-06	Tor. Jr. Canadiens	GTHL	47	25	31	56	69	....	....	....	....	....	....	....	....	....	....	....	....	....	....	....	....	....	....
2006-07	Barrie Colts	OHL	48	7	7	14	37	....	....	....	....	....	....	....	....	....	6	0	0	0	0	....	....	....	....
2007-08	Barrie Colts	OHL	68	13	19	32	171	....	....	....	....	....	....	....	....	....	9	1	2	3	16	....	....	....	....
2008-09	Barrie Colts	OHL	57	27	24	51	146	....	....	....	....	....	....	....	....	....	5	2	2	4	19	....	....	....	....
	South Carolina	ECHL	2	0	1	1	6	....	....	....	....	....	....	....	....	....	....	....	....	....	....	....	....	....	....
2009-10	Barrie Colts	OHL	57	18	23	41	125	....	....	....	....	....	....	....	....	....	17	8	1	9	29	....	....	....	....
	Hershey Bears	AHL	....	....	....	....	....	....	....	....	....	....	....	....	....	....	2	0	0	0	0	....	....	....	....
2010-11	**St. Louis**	**NHL**	7	0	0	0	11	0	0	0	4	0.0	0	4	75.0	6:05	....	....	....	....	....	....	....	....	....
	Peoria Rivermen	AHL	66	8	8	16	110	....	....	....	....	....	....	....	....	....	1	0	0	0	0	....	....	....	....
2011-12	Peoria Rivermen	AHL	69	4	6	10	116	....	....	....	....	....	....	....	....	....	....	....	....	....	....	....	....	....	....
2012-13	Peoria Rivermen	AHL	33	1	1	2	43	....	....	....	....	....	....	....	....	....	....	....	....	....	....	....	....	....	....
	Evansville IceMen	ECHL	12	2	5	7	36	....	....	....	....	....	....	....	....	....	....	....	....	....	....	....	....	....	....
	NHL Totals		7	0	0	0	11	0	0	0	4	0.0		4	75.0	6:05	....	....	....	....	....	....	....	....	....

Traded to **St. Louis** by **Washington** for D.J. King, July 28, 2010.

DEMERS, Jason

(duh-MAIRZ, JAY-suhn) **S.J.**

Defense. Shoots right. 6'1", 195 lbs. Born, Dorval, Que., June 9, 1988. San Jose's 6th choice, 186th overall, in 2008 Entry Draft.

Season	Club	League	GP	G	A	Pts	PIM	PP	SH	GW	S	%	+/-	TF	F%	Min	GP	G	A	Pts	PIM	PP	SH	GW	Min
2004-05	Moncton Wildcats	QMJHL	25	0	1	1	10	....	....	....	....	....	....	....	....	....	....	....	....	....	....	....	....	....	....
2005-06	Moncton Wildcats	QMJHL	21	1	3	4	15	....	....	....	....	....	....	....	....	....	....	....	....	....	....	....	....	....	....
	Victoriaville Tigres	QMJHL	33	2	13	15	58	....	....	....	....	....	....	....	....	....	5	0	2	2	10	....	....	....	....
2006-07	Victoriaville Tigres	QMJHL	69	5	19	24	98	....	....	....	....	....	....	....	....	....	6	0	0	0	2	....	....	....	....
2007-08	Victoriaville Tigres	QMJHL	67	9	55	64	91	....	....	....	....	....	....	....	....	....	6	1	5	6	6	....	....	....	....
2008-09	Worcester Sharks	AHL	78	2	31	33	54	....	....	....	....	....	....	....	....	....	12	0	4	4	6	....	....	....	....
2009-10	**San Jose**	**NHL**	51	4	17	21	21	3	0	1	52	7.7	5	0	0.0	15:26	15	1	4	5	8	1	0	0	11:10
	Worcester Sharks	AHL	25	4	13	17	24	....	....	....	....	....	....	....	....	....	....	....	....	....	....	....	....	....	....
2010-11	**San Jose**	**NHL**	75	2	22	24	28	0	0	0	105	1.9	19	0	0.0	19:30	13	2	1	3	8	0	0	0	19:56
2011-12	**San Jose**	**NHL**	57	4	9	13	22	2	0	1	73	5.5	–8	0	0.0	16:51	3	0	0	0	2	0	0	0	15:28
2012-13	Karpat Oulu	Finland	30	5	16	21	18	....	....	....	....	....	....	....	....	....	....	....	....	....	....	....	....	....	....
	San Jose	**NHL**	22	1	2	3	10	0	0	0	27	3.7	–4	0	0.0	18:38	1	0	0	0	2	0	0	0	3:47
	NHL Totals		205	11	50	61	81	5	0	2	257	4.3		0	0.0	17:39	32	3	5	8	20	1	0	0	14:54

Signed as a free agent by **Oulu** (Finland), September 15, 2012.

DESBIENS, Guillaume

(deh-BYEHN, GEE-OHM) **COL**

Right wing. Shoots right. 6'3", 216 lbs. Born, Alma, Que., April 20, 1985. Atlanta's 3rd choice, 116th overall, in 2003 Entry Draft.

Season	Club	League	GP	G	A	Pts	PIM	PP	SH	GW	S	%	+/-	TF	F%	Min	GP	G	A	Pts	PIM	PP	SH	GW	Min
2001-02	Rouyn-Noranda	QMJHL	65	14	10	24	115	....	....	....	....	....	....	....	....	....	4	1	1	2	9	....	....	....	....
2002-03	Rouyn-Noranda	QMJHL	64	15	18	33	233	....	....	....	....	....	....	....	....	....	4	0	0	0	4	....	....	....	....
2003-04	Rouyn-Noranda	QMJHL	58	20	21	41	199	....	....	....	....	....	....	....	....	....	11	2	2	4	24	....	....	....	....
2004-05	Rouyn-Noranda	QMJHL	56	27	16	43	206	....	....	....	....	....	....	....	....	....	10	1	4	5	25	....	....	....	....
2005-06	Chicago Wolves	AHL	3	0	0	0	7	....	....	....	....	....	....	....	....	....	....	....	....	....	....	....	....	....	....
	Gwinnett	ECHL	65	33	27	60	187	....	....	....	....	....	....	....	....	....	17	10	6	16	38	....	....	....	....
2006-07	Chicago Wolves	AHL	54	3	6	9	118	....	....	....	....	....	....	....	....	....	6	0	1	1	2	....	....	....	....
2007-08	Chicago Wolves	AHL	23	2	1	3	30	....	....	....	....	....	....	....	....	....	1	0	1	1	0	....	....	....	....
	Gwinnett	ECHL	10	2	5	7	46	....	....	....	....	....	....	....	....	....	8	3	6	9	10	....	....	....	....
2008-09	Manitoba Moose	AHL	78	21	26	47	158	....	....	....	....	....	....	....	....	....	22	4	8	12	18	....	....	....	....
2009-10	**Vancouver**	**NHL**	1	0	0	0	2	0	0	0	0	0.0	0	0	0.0	9:25	....	....	....	....	....	....	....	....	....
	Manitoba Moose	AHL	67	19	15	34	144	....	....	....	....	....	....	....	....	....	6	3	6	9	17	....	....	....	....
2010-11	**Vancouver**	**NHL**	12	0	0	0	10	0	0	0	4	0.0	–3	1	100.0	7:21	....	....	....	....	....	....	....	....	....
	Manitoba Moose	AHL	53	11	16	27	104	....	....	....	....	....	....	....	....	....	13	1	3	4	31	....	....	....	....
2011-12	**Calgary**	**NHL**	10	0	0	0	25	0	0	0	2	0.0	–1	2	50.0	7:07	....	....	....	....	....	....	....	....	....
	Abbotsford Heat	AHL	59	3	11	14	114	....	....	....	....	....	....	....	....	....	7	1	0	1	21	....	....	....	....
2012-13	Chicago Wolves	AHL	52	4	4	8	118	....	....	....	....	....	....	....	....	....	....	....	....	....	....	....	....	....	....
	NHL Totals		23	0	0	0	37	0	0	0	6	0.0		3	66.7	7:20	....	....	....	....	....	....	....	....	....

Signed as a free agent by **Manitoba** (AHL), December 15, 2008. Signed as a free agent by **Vancouver**, July 22, 2009. Signed as a free agent by **Calgary**, July 4, 2011. Signed as a free agent by **Vancouver**, July 30, 2012. Signed as a free agent by **Colorado**, July 6, 2013.

DESHARNAIS, David

(day-hahr-NAY, DAY-vihd) **MTL**

Center. Shoots left. 5'7", 177 lbs. Born, Laurier-Station, Que., September 14, 1986.

Season	Club	League	GP	G	A	Pts	PIM	PP	SH	GW	S	%	+/-	TF	F%	Min	GP	G	A	Pts	PIM	PP	SH	GW	Min
2003-04	Chicoutimi	QMJHL	70	23	28	51	12	....	....	....	....	....	....	....	....	....	18	4	7	11	8	....	....	....	....
2004-05	Chicoutimi	QMJHL	68	32	65	97	39	....	....	....	....	....	....	....	....	....	17	5	10	15	8	....	....	....	....
2005-06	Chicoutimi	QMJHL	63	33	85	118	44	....	....	....	....	....	....	....	....	....	9	2	9	11	4	....	....	....	....
2006-07	Chicoutimi	QMJHL	61	38	70	108	32	....	....	....	....	....	....	....	....	....	4	1	5	6	2	....	....	....	....
	Bridgeport	AHL	7	1	1	2	4	....	....	....	....	....	....	....	....	....	....	....	....	....	....	....	....	....	....
2007-08	Hamilton	AHL	4	0	1	1	6	....	....	....	....	....	....	....	....	....	....	....	....	....	....	....	....	....	....
	Cincinnati	ECHL	68	29	*77	*106	18	....	....	....	....	....	....	....	....	....	22	9	*24	*33	18	....	....	....	....
2008-09	Hamilton	AHL	77	24	34	58	20	....	....	....	....	....	....	....	....	....	6	1	3	4	4	....	....	....	....
2009-10	**Montreal**	**NHL**	6	0	1	1	0	0	0	0	2	0.0	–1	28	57.1	8:27	....	....	....	....	....	....	....	....	....
	Hamilton	AHL	60	27	51	78	34	....	....	....	....	....	....	....	....	....	19	10	13	23	16	....	....	....	....
2010-11	**Montreal**	**NHL**	43	8	14	22	12	4	0	0	55	14.5	–3	445	49.7	12:52	5	0	1	1	2	0	0	0	11:03
	Hamilton	AHL	35	10	35	45	24	....	....	....	....	....	....	....	....	....	....	....	....	....	....	....	....	....	....
2011-12	**Montreal**	**NHL**	81	16	44	60	24	3	0	2	98	16.3	10	1371	49.5	18:24	....	....	....	....	....	....	....	....	....
2012-13	Fribourg	Swiss	16	4	12	16	12	....	....	....	....	....	....	....	....	....	....	....	....	....	....	....	....	....	....
	Montreal	**NHL**	48	10	18	28	26	2	0	3	66	15.2	–2	764	50.0	16:28	5	0	1	1	2	0	0	0	17:14
	NHL Totals		178	34	77	111	62	9	0	5	221	15.4		2608	49.7	16:12	10	0	2	2	4	0	0	0	14:09

ECHL Rookie of the Year (2008) • ECHL Leading Scorer (2008) • ECHL MVP (2008)

Signed as a free agent by **Montreal**, November 5, 2008. Signed as a free agent by **Fribourg** (Swiss), November 2, 2012.

DESJARDINS, Andrew

(deh-ZHAHR-dai, AN-droo) **S.J.**

Center. Shoots right. 6'1", 195 lbs. Born, Lively, Ont., July 27, 1986.

Season	Club	League	GP	G	A	Pts	PIM	PP	SH	GW	S	%	+/-	TF	F%	Min	GP	G	A	Pts	PIM	PP	SH	GW	Min
2003-04	Sault Ste. Marie	OHL	55	3	6	9	41	....	....	....	....	....	....	....	....	....	....	....	....	....	....	....	....	....	....
2004-05	Sault Ste. Marie	OHL	68	17	17	34	49	....	....	....	....	....	....	....	....	....	7	0	0	0	2	....	....	....	....
2005-06	Sault Ste. Marie	OHL	6	12	16	28	78	....	....	....	....	....	....	....	....	....	4	2	3	5	10	....	....	....	....
2006-07	Sault Ste. Marie	OHL	65	16	26	42	96	....	....	....	....	....	....	....	....	....	13	2	5	7	18	....	....	....	....
2007-08	Laredo Bucks	CHL	64	22	37	59	112	....	....	....	....	....	....	....	....	....	11	2	4	6	21	....	....	....	....
2008-09	Phoenix	ECHL	5	2	0	2	6	....	....	....	....	....	....	....	....	....	....	....	....	....	....	....	....	....	....
	Worcester Sharks	AHL	74	8	14	22	99	....	....	....	....	....	....	....	....	....	12	4	2	6	13	....	....	....	....
2009-10	Worcester Sharks	AHL	80	19	27	46	126	....	....	....	....	....	....	....	....	....	11	2	2	4	32	....	....	....	....
2010-11	**San Jose**	**NHL**	17	1	2	3	4	0	0	0	12	8.3	–1	56	55.4	7:08	3	1	0	1	4	0	0	0	6:48
	Worcester Sharks	AHL	58	12	17	29	69	....	....	....	....	....	....	....	....	....	....	....	....	....	....	....	....	....	....
2011-12	**San Jose**	**NHL**	76	4	13	17	47	0	0	3	80	5.0	4	362	53.0	9:35	5	1	0	1	2	0	0	0	11:32
2012-13	**San Jose**	**NHL**	42	2	1	3	61	0	0	0	51	3.9	–6	72	54.2	10:07	11	0	0	0	6	0	0	0	10:58
	NHL Totals		135	7	16	23	112	0	0	3	143	4.9		490	53.5	9:27	19	2	0	2	12	0	0	0	10:27

Signed as a free agent by **Worcester** (AHL), October, 2008. Signed as a free agent by **San Jose**, June 26, 2010.

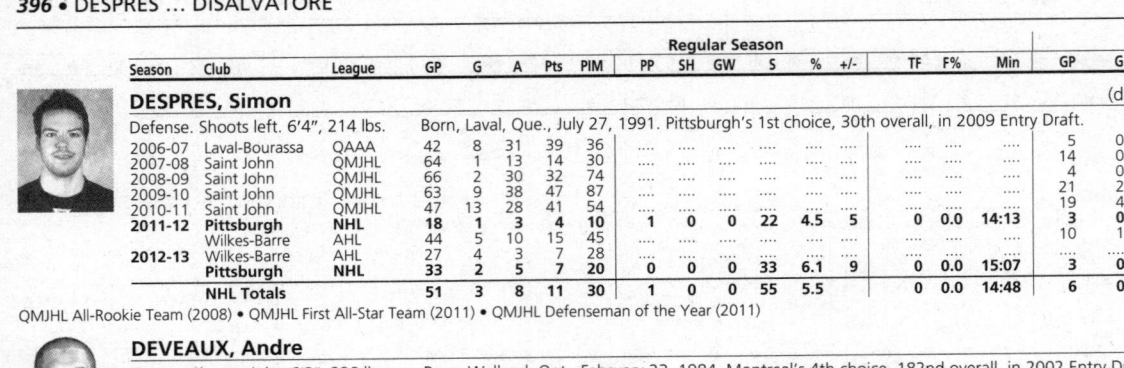

DESPRES, Simon (duh-PRAY, see-MOHN) PIT

Defense. Shoots left. 6'4", 214 lbs. Born, Laval, Que., July 27, 1991. Pittsburgh's 1st choice, 30th overall, in 2009 Entry Draft.

Season	Club	League	GP	G	A	Pts	PIM	PP	SH	GW	S	%	+/-	TF	F%	Min	Playoffs GP	G	A	Pts	PIM	PP	SH	GW	Min
2006-07	Laval-Bourassa	QAAA	42	8	31	39	36	....	....	....	....	....	....	....	....	....	5	0	2	2	8	....	....	....	....
2007-08	Saint John	QMJHL	64	1	13	14	30	....	....	....	....	....	....	....	....	....	14	0	4	4	18	....	....	....	....
2008-09	Saint John	QMJHL	66	2	30	32	74	....	....	....	....	....	....	....	....	....	4	0	4	4	2	....	....	....	....
2009-10	Saint John	QMJHL	63	9	38	47	87	....	....	....	....	....	....	....	....	....	21	2	17	19	18	....	....	....	....
2010-11	Saint John	QMJHL	47	13	28	41	54	....	....	....	....	....	....	....	....	....	19	4	8	12	16	....	....	....	....
2011-12	**Pittsburgh**	**NHL**	**18**	**1**	**3**	**4**	**10**	**1**	**0**	**0**	**22**	**4.5**	**5**	**0**	**0.0**	**14:13**	**3**	**0**	**0**	**0**	**2**	**0**	**0**	**0**	**9:18**
	Wilkes-Barre	AHL	44	5	10	15	45	....	....	....	....	....	....	....	....	....	10	1	1	2	2	....	....	....	....
2012-13	Wilkes-Barre	AHL	27	4	3	7	28	....	....	....	....	....	....	....	....	....	....	....	....	....	....	....	....	....	....
	Pittsburgh	**NHL**	**33**	**2**	**5**	**7**	**20**	**0**	**0**	**0**	**33**	**6.1**	**9**	**0**	**0.0**	**15:07**	**3**	**0**	**0**	**0**	**0**	**0**	**0**	**0**	**11:07**
	NHL Totals		**51**	**3**	**8**	**11**	**30**	**1**	**0**	**0**	**55**	**5.5**		**0**	**0.0**	**14:48**	**6**	**0**	**0**	**0**	**2**	**0**	**0**	**0**	**10:13**

QMJHL All-Rookie Team (2008) • QMJHL First All-Star Team (2011) • QMJHL Defenseman of the Year (2011)

DEVEAUX, Andre (de-VOH, AWN-dray)

Center. Shoots right. 6'3", 220 lbs. Born, Welland, Ont., February 23, 1984. Montreal's 4th choice, 182nd overall, in 2002 Entry Draft.

Season	Club	League	GP	G	A	Pts	PIM	PP	SH	GW	S	%	+/-	TF	F%	Min	Playoffs GP	G	A	Pts	PIM	PP	SH	GW	Min
2000-01	Belleville Bulls	OHL	58	3	6	9	65	....	....	....	....	....	....	....	....	....	10	3	6	9	6	....	....	....	....
2001-02	Belleville Bulls	OHL	64	8	13	21	89	....	....	....	....	....	....	....	....	....	11	1	2	3	30	....	....	....	....
2002-03	Belleville Bulls	OHL	34	6	12	18	93	....	....	....	....	....	....	....	....	....	....	....	....	....	....	....	....	....	....
	Owen Sound	OHL	29	9	10	19	33	....	....	....	....	....	....	....	....	....	4	2	2	4	6	....	....	....	....
2003-04	Owen Sound	OHL	64	16	30	46	151	....	....	....	....	....	....	....	....	....	7	3	3	6	21	....	....	....	....
2004-05	Springfield	AHL	73	4	8	12	210	....	....	....	....	....	....	....	....	....	....	....	....	....	....	....	....	....	....
2005-06	Springfield	AHL	59	6	5	11	135	....	....	....	....	....	....	....	....	....	....	....	....	....	....	....	....	....	....
	Johnstown Chiefs	ECHL	11	4	7	11	36	....	....	....	....	....	....	....	....	....	5	1	1	2	2	....	....	....	....
2006-07	Springfield	AHL	8	1	2	3	8	....	....	....	....	....	....	....	....	....	....	....	....	....	....	....	....	....	....
	Johnstown Chiefs	ECHL	21	6	8	14	51	....	....	....	....	....	....	....	....	....	....	....	....	....	....	....	....	....	....
	Chicago Wolves	AHL	28	4	4	8	105	....	....	....	....	....	....	....	....	....	14	3	2	5	48	....	....	....	....
2007-08	Chicago Wolves	AHL	66	7	11	18	232	....	....	....	....	....	....	....	....	....	24	0	2	2	67	....	....	....	....
2008-09	**Toronto**	**NHL**	**21**	**0**	**1**	**1**	**75**	**0**	**0**	**0**	**15**	**0.0**	**–3**	**7**	**28.6**	**7:14**	....	....	....	....	....	....	....	....	....
	Toronto Marlies	AHL	38	14	11	25	114	....	....	....	....	....	....	....	....	....	6	0	3	3	14	....	....	....	....
2009-10	**Toronto**	**NHL**	**1**	**0**	**0**	**0**	**0**	**0**	**0**	**0**	**1**	**0.0**	**–1**	**1**	**100.0**	**6:09**	....	....	....	....	....	....	....	....	....
	Toronto Marlies	AHL	72	16	25	41	216	....	....	....	....	....	....	....	....	....	....	....	....	....	....	....	....	....	....
2010-11	Chicago Wolves	AHL	73	23	23	46	194	....	....	....	....	....	....	....	....	....	....	....	....	....	....	....	....	....	....
2011-12	**NY Rangers**	**NHL**	**9**	**0**	**1**	**1**	**29**	**0**	**0**	**0**	**2**	**0.0**	**3**	**1**	**100.0**	**5:23**	....	....	....	....	....	....	....	....	....
	Connecticut	AHL	59	20	20	40	157	....	....	....	....	....	....	....	....	....	9	2	2	4	47	....	....	....	....
2012-13	San Antonio	AHL	46	7	7	14	56	....	....	....	....	....	....	....	....	....	....	....	....	....	....	....	....	....	....
	NHL Totals		**31**	**0**	**2**	**2**	**104**	**0**	**0**	**0**	**18**	**0.0**		**9**	**44.4**	**6:40**	....	....	....	....	....	....	....	....	....

Signed as a free agent by **Tampa Bay**, September 15, 2004. Traded to **Atlanta** by **Tampa Bay** with Andy Delmore for and Stephen Baby and Kyle Wanvig, February 1, 2007. Signed as a free agent by **Toronto**, July 21, 2008. Signed as a free agent by **Chicago** (AHL), August 25, 2010. Signed as a free agent by **NY Rangers**, August 16, 2011. Signed as a free agent by **Florida**, July 9, 2012.

DIAZ, Raphael (DEE-az, ra-FIGH-ehl) MTL

Defense. Shoots right. 5'11", 194 lbs. Born, Baar, Switz., January 9, 1986.

Season	Club	League	GP	G	A	Pts	PIM	PP	SH	GW	S	%	+/-	TF	F%	Min	Playoffs GP	G	A	Pts	PIM	PP	SH	GW	Min
2001-02	EV Zug Jr.	Swiss-Jr.	4	0	1	1	0	....	....	....	....	....	....	....	....	....	....	....	....	....	....	....	....	....	....
2002-03	EV Zug Jr.	Swiss-Jr.	30	7	10	17	32	....	....	....	....	....	....	....	....	....	7	1	1	2	12	....	....	....	....
2003-04	EV Zug Jr.	Swiss-Jr.	15	6	5	11	22	....	....	....	....	....	....	....	....	....	....	....	....	....	....	....	....	....	....
	EV Zug	Swiss	38	2	1	3	16	....	....	....	....	....	....	....	....	....	5	0	0	0	2	....	....	....	....
2004-05	EV Zug	Swiss	41	1	4	5	12	....	....	....	....	....	....	....	....	....	9	0	0	0	4	....	....	....	....
2005-06	EV Zug	Swiss	35	5	2	7	34	....	....	....	....	....	....	....	....	....	7	0	0	0	4	....	....	....	....
2006-07	EV Zug	Swiss	44	2	4	6	22	....	....	....	....	....	....	....	....	....	12	0	1	1	6	....	....	....	....
2007-08	EV Zug	Swiss	50	3	11	14	44	....	....	....	....	....	....	....	....	....	7	0	0	0	4	....	....	....	....
2008-09	EV Zug	Swiss	50	4	9	13	36	....	....	....	....	....	....	....	....	....	10	1	1	2	4	....	....	....	....
2009-10	EV Zug	Swiss	49	4	27	31	22	....	....	....	....	....	....	....	....	....	13	1	5	6	10	....	....	....	....
	Switzerland	Olympics	5	0	0	0	4	....	....	....	....	....	....	....	....	....	....	....	....	....	....	....	....	....	....
2010-11	EV Zug	Swiss	45	12	27	39	26	....	....	....	....	....	....	....	....	....	10	2	4	6	4	....	....	....	....
2011-12	**Montreal**	**NHL**	**59**	**3**	**13**	**16**	**30**	**0**	**0**	**1**	**61**	**4.9**	**–7**	**2**	**50.0**	**18:00**	....	....	....	....	....	....	....	....	....
2012-13	EV Zug	Swiss	32	7	22	29	12	....	....	....	....	....	....	....	....	....	....	....	....	....	....	....	....	....	....
	Montreal	**NHL**	**23**	**1**	**13**	**14**	**6**	**0**	**0**	**0**	**34**	**2.9**	**4**	**0**	**0.0**	**20:33**	**5**	**0**	**0**	**0**	**0**	**0**	**0**	**0**	**22:22**
	NHL Totals		**82**	**4**	**26**	**30**	**36**	**0**	**0**	**1**	**95**	**4.2**		**2**	**50.0**	**18:43**	**5**	**0**	**0**	**0**	**0**	**0**	**0**	**0**	**22:22**

Signed as a free agent by **Montreal**, May 13, 2011. Signed as a free agent by **Zug** (Swiss), September 15, 2012.

DiBENEDETTO, Justin (dih-behn-ih-DEH-toh, JUHS-tihn) NYI

Center. Shoots left. 6', 198 lbs. Born, Maple, Ont., August 25, 1988. NY Islanders' 13th choice, 175th overall, in 2008 Entry Draft.

Season	Club	League	GP	G	A	Pts	PIM	PP	SH	GW	S	%	+/-	TF	F%	Min	Playoffs GP	G	A	Pts	PIM	PP	SH	GW	Min
2004-05	St. Michael's	OHL	64	3	6	9	37	....	....	....	....	....	....	....	....	....	9	0	0	0	0	....	....	....	....
2005-06	St. Michael's	OHL	61	17	13	30	58	....	....	....	....	....	....	....	....	....	4	1	0	1	11	....	....	....	....
2006-07	Sarnia Sting	OHL	58	28	35	63	46	....	....	....	....	....	....	....	....	....	4	2	1	3	4	....	....	....	....
2007-08	Sarnia Sting	OHL	58	39	54	93	61	....	....	....	....	....	....	....	....	....	9	3	7	10	12	....	....	....	....
2008-09	Sarnia Sting	OHL	62	45	48	93	85	....	....	....	....	....	....	....	....	....	5	0	3	3	12	....	....	....	....
	Bridgeport	AHL	....	....	....	....	....	....	....	....	....	....	....	....	....	....	3	1	0	1	4	....	....	....	....
2009-10	Bridgeport	AHL	67	6	8	14	62	....	....	....	....	....	....	....	....	....	....	....	....	....	....	....	....	....	....
2010-11	**NY Islanders**	**NHL**	**8**	**0**	**1**	**1**	**2**	**0**	**0**	**0**	**6**	**0.0**	**–2**	**0**	**0.0**	**9:04**	....	....	....	....	....	....	....	....	....
	Bridgeport	AHL	51	19	11	30	45	....	....	....	....	....	....	....	....	....	....	....	....	....	....	....	....	....	....
2011-12	Bridgeport	AHL	55	20	21	41	73	....	....	....	....	....	....	....	....	....	3	1	1	2	16	....	....	....	....
2012-13	Salzburg	Austria	47	19	25	44	36	....	....	....	....	....	....	....	....	....	12	3	5	8	12	....	....	....	....
	NHL Totals		**8**	**0**	**1**	**1**	**2**	**0**	**0**	**0**	**6**	**0.0**		**0**	**0.0**	**9:04**	....	....	....	....	....	....	....	....	....

OHL Second All-Star Team (2009)

Signed as a free agent by **Salzburg** (Austria), June 20, 2012.

DILLON, Brenden (DIHL-uhn, BREHN-duhn) DAL

Defense. Shoots left. 6'3", 209 lbs. Born, Surrey, B.C., November 13, 1990.

Season	Club	League	GP	G	A	Pts	PIM	PP	SH	GW	S	%	+/-	TF	F%	Min	Playoffs GP	G	A	Pts	PIM	PP	SH	GW	Min
2007-08	Seattle	WHL	71	1	10	11	54	....	....	....	....	....	....	....	....	....	12	0	2	2	21	....	....	....	....
2008-09	Seattle	WHL	70	0	10	10	68	....	....	....	....	....	....	....	....	....	5	0	1	1	6	....	....	....	....
2009-10	Seattle	WHL	67	2	12	14	101	....	....	....	....	....	....	....	....	....	....	....	....	....	....	....	....	....	....
2010-11	Seattle	WHL	72	8	51	59	139	....	....	....	....	....	....	....	....	....	....	....	....	....	....	....	....	....	....
	Texas Stars	AHL	10	0	0	0	8	....	....	....	....	....	....	....	....	....	6	0	2	2	7	....	....	....	....
2011-12	**Dallas**	**NHL**	**1**	**0**	**0**	**0**	**0**	**0**	**0**	**0**	**6**	**0.0**	**0**	**0**	**0.0**	**19:59**	....	....	....	....	....	....	....	....	....
	Texas Stars	AHL	76	6	23	29	97	....	....	....	....	....	....	....	....	....	....	....	....	....	....	....	....	....	....
2012-13	**Dallas**	**NHL**	**48**	**3**	**5**	**8**	**65**	**0**	**0**	**1**	**75**	**4.0**	**1**	**0**	**0.0**	**21:23**	....	....	....	....	....	....	....	....	....
	Texas Stars	AHL	37	3	11	14	45	....	....	....	....	....	....	....	....	....	....	....	....	....	....	....	....	....	....
	NHL Totals		**49**	**3**	**5**	**8**	**65**	**0**	**0**	**1**	**81**	**3.7**		**0**	**0.0**	**21:21**	....	....	....	....	....	....	....	....	....

Signed as a free agent by **Dallas**, March 1, 2011.

DiSALVATORE, Jon (dih-SAL-vuh-tohr, JAWN)

Right wing. Shoots right. 6'1", 200 lbs. Born, Bangor, ME, March 30, 1981. San Jose's 2nd choice, 104th overall, in 2000 Entry Draft.

Season	Club	League	GP	G	A	Pts	PIM	PP	SH	GW	S	%	+/-	TF	F%	Min	Playoffs GP	G	A	Pts	PIM	PP	SH	GW	Min
1997-98	N.E. Jr. Coyotes	EJHL	38	24	41	65	....	....	....	....	....	....	....	....	....	....	....	....	....	....	....	....	....	....	....
1998-99	N.E. Jr. Coyotes	EJHL	48	44	76	*120	38	....	....	....	....	....	....	....	....	....	....	....	....	....	....	....	....	....	....
99-2000	Providence	H-East	38	15	12	27	12	....	....	....	....	....	....	....	....	....	....	....	....	....	....	....	....	....	....
2000-01	Providence	H-East	36	9	16	25	29	....	....	....	....	....	....	....	....	....	....	....	....	....	....	....	....	....	....
2001-02	Providence	H-East	38	16	26	42	6	....	....	....	....	....	....	....	....	....	....	....	....	....	....	....	....	....	....
2002-03	Providence	H-East	36	19	29	48	12	....	....	....	....	....	....	....	....	....	....	....	....	....	....	....	....	....	....
2003-04	Cleveland Barons	AHL	74	22	24	46	30	....	....	....	....	....	....	....	....	....	8	1	1	2	2	....	....	....	....
2004-05	Worcester IceCats	AHL	79	22	23	45	42	....	....	....	....	....	....	....	....	....	....	....	....	....	....	....	....	....	....
2005-06	**St. Louis**	**NHL**	**5**	**0**	**0**	**0**	**2**	**0**	**0**	**0**	**3**	**0.0**	**–1**	**0**	**0.0**	**8:27**	....	....	....	....	....	....	....	....	....
	Peoria Rivermen	AHL	72	22	45	67	42	....	....	....	....	....	....	....	....	....	4	0	0	0	0	....	....	....	....
2006-07	Peoria Rivermen	AHL	76	21	39	60	50	....	....	....	....	....	....	....	....	....	....	....	....	....	....	....	....	....	....

			Regular Season														Playoffs								
Season	Club	League	GP	G	A	Pts	PIM	PP	SH	GW	S	%	+/-	TF	F%	Min	GP	G	A	Pts	PIM	PP	SH	GW	Min
2007-08	San Antonio	AHL	66	22	24	46	46	....	....	....	....	....	....	....	....	....	7	2	1	3	9	....	....	....	....
2008-09	Lowell Devils	AHL	76	20	33	53	32	....	....	....	....	....	....	....	....	....	....	....	....	....	....	....	....	....	....
2009-10	Houston Aeros	AHL	79	21	31	52	28	....	....	....	....	....	....	....	....	....	....	....	....	....	....	....	....	....	....
2010-11	Houston Aeros	AHL	80	28	33	61	57	....	....	....	....	....	....	....	....	....	24	7	5	12	12	....	....	....	....
2011-12	**Minnesota**	**NHL**	**1**	**0**	**0**	**0**	**2**	**0**	**0**	**0**	**2**	**0.0**	**0**	**0**	**0.0**	**14:27**	....	....	....	....	....	....	....	....	....
	Houston Aeros	AHL	76	28	33	61	22	....	....	....	....	....	....	....	....	....	4	0	0	0	2	....	....	....	....
2012-13	Hershey Bears	AHL	68	18	31	49	24	....	....	....	....	....	....	....	....	....	4	2	0	2	2	....	....	....	....
	NHL Totals		**6**	**0**	**0**	**0**	**4**	**0**	**0**	**0**	**5**	**0.0**		**0**	**0.0**	**9:27**	....	....	....	....	....	....	....	....	....

EJHL First All-Star Team (1999) • EJHL MVP (1999) • AHL Second All-Star Team (2012)

Signed as a free agent by **St. Louis**, June 30, 2004. Signed as a free agent by **Phoenix**, July 9, 2007. Signed as a free agent by **New Jersey**, July 17, 2008. Signed as a free agent by **Minnesota**, July 17, 2009. Signed as a free agent by **Hershey** (AHL), July 2, 2012. Signed as a free agent by **Munchen** (Germany), July 22, 2013.

DOAN, Shane

(DOHN, SHAYN) **PHX**

Right wing. Shoots right. 6'1", 223 lbs. Born, Halkirk, Alta., October 10, 1976. Winnipeg's 1st choice, 7th overall, in 1995 Entry Draft.

Season	Club	League	GP	G	A	Pts	PIM	PP	SH	GW	S	%	+/-	TF	F%	Min	GP	G	A	Pts	PIM	PP	SH	GW	Min
1991-92	Killam Selects	AAHA	56	80	84	164	74	....	....	....	....	....	....	....	....	....	....	....	....	....	....	....	....	....	....
1992-93	Kamloops Blazers	WHL	51	7	12	19	65	....	....	....	....	....	....	....	....	....	13	0	1	1	8	....	....	....	....
1993-94	Kamloops Blazers	WHL	52	24	24	48	88	....	....	....	....	....	....	....	....	....	....	....	....	....	....	....	....	....	....
1994-95	Kamloops Blazers	WHL	71	37	57	94	106	....	....	....	....	....	....	....	....	....	21	6	10	16	16	....	....	....	....
1995-96	**Winnipeg**	**NHL**	**74**	**7**	**10**	**17**	**101**	**1**	**0**	**3**	**106**	**6.6**	**-9**	....	....	....	**6**	**0**	**0**	**0**	**6**	**0**	**0**	**0**	....
1996-97	**Phoenix**	**NHL**	**63**	**4**	**8**	**12**	**49**	**0**	**0**	**0**	**100**	**4.0**	**-3**	....	....	....	**4**	**0**	**0**	**0**	**2**	**0**	**0**	**0**	....
1997-98	**Phoenix**	**NHL**	**33**	**5**	**6**	**11**	**35**	**0**	**0**	**3**	**42**	**11.9**	**-3**	....	....	....	**6**	**1**	**0**	**1**	**6**	**0**	**0**	**0**	....
	Springfield	AHL	39	21	21	42	64	....	....	....	....	....	....	....	....	....	....	....	....	....	....	....	....	....	....
1998-99	**Phoenix**	**NHL**	**79**	**6**	**16**	**22**	**54**	**0**	**0**	**0**	**156**	**3.8**	**-5**	**6**	**16.7**	**12:42**	**7**	**2**	**2**	**4**	**6**	**0**	**0**	**2**	**17:58**
99-2000	**Phoenix**	**NHL**	**81**	**26**	**25**	**51**	**66**	**1**	**1**	**4**	**221**	**11.8**	**6**	**25**	**36.0**	**16:51**	**4**	**1**	**2**	**3**	**8**	**1**	**0**	**0**	**18:11**
2000-01	**Phoenix**	**NHL**	**76**	**26**	**37**	**63**	**89**	**6**	**1**	**6**	**220**	**11.8**	**0**	**15**	**40.0**	**19:32**	....	....	....	....	....	....	....	....	....
2001-02	**Phoenix**	**NHL**	**81**	**20**	**29**	**49**	**61**	**6**	**0**	**2**	**205**	**9.8**	**11**	**52**	**44.2**	**18:10**	**5**	**2**	**2**	**4**	**6**	**0**	**0**	**0**	**17:21**
2002-03	**Phoenix**	**NHL**	**82**	**21**	**37**	**58**	**86**	**7**	**0**	**2**	**225**	**9.3**	**3**	**623**	**39.8**	**18:47**	....	....	....	....	....	....	....	....	....
2003-04	**Phoenix**	**NHL**	**79**	**27**	**41**	**68**	**47**	**9**	**2**	**1**	**254**	**10.6**	**-11**	**55**	**40.0**	**21:46**	....	....	....	....	....	....	....	....	....
2004-05			DID NOT PLAY																						
2005-06	**Phoenix**	**NHL**	**82**	**30**	**36**	**66**	**123**	**17**	**0**	**7**	**254**	**11.8**	**-9**	**126**	**43.7**	**19:08**	....	....	....	....	....	....	....	....	....
	Canada	Olympics	6	2	1	3	2	....	....	....	....	....	....	....	....	....	....	....	....	....	....	....	....	....	....
2006-07	**Phoenix**	**NHL**	**73**	**27**	**28**	**55**	**73**	**11**	**0**	**7**	**209**	**12.9**	**-14**	**174**	**39.1**	**20:27**	....	....	....	....	....	....	....	....	....
2007-08	**Phoenix**	**NHL**	**80**	**28**	**50**	**78**	**59**	**9**	**2**	**5**	**243**	**11.5**	**4**	**187**	**41.2**	**20:46**	....	....	....	....	....	....	....	....	....
2008-09	**Phoenix**	**NHL**	**82**	**31**	**42**	**73**	**72**	**10**	**0**	**4**	**230**	**13.5**	**5**	**362**	**44.2**	**20:15**	....	....	....	....	....	....	....	....	....
2009-10	**Phoenix**	**NHL**	**82**	**18**	**37**	**55**	**41**	**5**	**0**	**4**	**234**	**7.7**	**3**	**153**	**45.8**	**19:10**	**3**	**1**	**1**	**2**	**4**	**0**	**0**	**0**	**13:22**
2010-11	**Phoenix**	**NHL**	**72**	**20**	**40**	**60**	**67**	**11**	**0**	**6**	**221**	**9.0**	**5**	**159**	**45.9**	**19:17**	**4**	**3**	**2**	**5**	**6**	**2**	**0**	**0**	**21:42**
2011-12	**Phoenix**	**NHL**	**79**	**22**	**28**	**50**	**48**	**5**	**0**	**5**	**226**	**9.7**	**-8**	**59**	**55.9**	**19:36**	**16**	**5**	**4**	**9**	**41**	**1**	**0**	**2**	**20:47**
2012-13	**Phoenix**	**NHL**	**48**	**13**	**14**	**27**	**37**	**0**	**0**	**2**	**129**	**10.1**	**6**	**15**	**26.7**	**18:03**	....	....	....	....	....	....	....	....	....
	NHL Totals		**1246**	**331**	**484**	**815**	**1108**	**98**	**6**	**61**	**3275**	**10.1**		**2011**	**42.2**	**18:54**	**55**	**15**	**13**	**28**	**85**	**4**	**0**	**4**	**19:06**

Memorial Cup All-Star Team (1995) • Stafford Smythe Memorial Trophy (Memorial Cup - MVP) (1995) • King Clancy Memorial Trophy (2010) • Mark Messier NHL Leadership Award (2012)
Played in NHL All-Star Game (2004, 2009)

• Transferred to **Phoenix** after **Winnipeg** franchise relocated, July 1, 1996.

DONOVAN, Matt

(DAWN-uh-vuhn, MAT) **NYI**

Defense. Shoots left. 6', 195 lbs. Born, Edmond, OK, May 9, 1990. NY Islanders' 8th choice, 96th overall, in 2008 Entry Draft.

Season	Club	League	GP	G	A	Pts	PIM	PP	SH	GW	S	%	+/-	TF	F%	Min	GP	G	A	Pts	PIM	PP	SH	GW	Min
2006-07	Dallas Stars AAA	NTHL	....	22	46	68	54	....	....	....	....	....	....	....	....	....	....	....	....	....	....	....	....	....	....
2007-08	Cedar Rapids	USHL	59	12	18	30	41	....	....	....	....	....	....	....	....	....	3	0	1	1	4	....	....	....	....
2008-09	Cedar Rapids	USHL	57	19	32	51	43	....	....	....	....	....	....	....	....	....	5	0	4	4	2	....	....	....	....
2009-10	U. of Denver	WCHA	36	7	14	21	50	....	....	....	....	....	....	....	....	....	....	....	....	....	....	....	....	....	....
2010-11	U. of Denver	WCHA	42	9	23	32	64	....	....	....	....	....	....	....	....	....	....	....	....	....	....	....	....	....	....
	Bridgeport	AHL	6	1	4	5	10	....	....	....	....	....	....	....	....	....	....	....	....	....	....	....	....	....	....
2011-12	**NY Islanders**	**NHL**	**3**	**0**	**0**	**0**	**0**	**0**	**0**	**0**	**6**	**0.0**	**-3**	**0**	**0.0**	**18:34**	....	....	....	....	....	....	....	....	....
	Bridgeport	AHL	72	10	35	45	63	....	....	....	....	....	....	....	....	....	3	0	1	1	6	....	....	....	....
2012-13	Bridgeport	AHL	75	14	34	48	112	....	....	....	....	....	....	....	....	....	....	....	....	....	....	....	....	....	....
	NHL Totals		**3**	**0**	**0**	**0**	**0**	**0**	**0**	**0**	**6**	**0.0**		**0**	**0.0**	**18:34**	....	....	....	....	....	....	....	....	....

USHL All-Rookie Team (2008) • USHL First All-Star Team (2009) • WCHA All-Rookie Team (2010) • WCHA Second All-Star Team (2011) • AHL All-Rookie Team (2012)

DORSETT, Derek

(DOHRS-iht, DAIR-ihk) **NYR**

Right wing. Shoots right. 6', 192 lbs. Born, Kindersley, Sask., December 20, 1986. Columbus' 9th choice, 189th overall, in 2006 Entry Draft.

Season	Club	League	GP	G	A	Pts	PIM	PP	SH	GW	S	%	+/-	TF	F%	Min	GP	G	A	Pts	PIM	PP	SH	GW	Min
2004-05	Medicine Hat	WHL	51	5	11	16	108	....	....	....	....	....	....	....	....	....	13	5	1	6	35	....	....	....	....
2005-06	Medicine Hat	WHL	68	25	23	48	*279	....	....	....	....	....	....	....	....	....	13	8	4	12	53	....	....	....	....
2006-07	Medicine Hat	WHL	61	19	45	64	206	....	....	....	....	....	....	....	....	....	17	8	8	16	56	....	....	....	....
2007-08	Syracuse Crunch	AHL	64	10	8	18	289	....	....	....	....	....	....	....	....	....	12	0	1	1	56	....	....	....	....
2008-09	**Columbus**	**NHL**	**52**	**4**	**1**	**5**	**150**	**0**	**0**	**1**	**59**	**6.8**	**-1**	**9**	**44.4**	**8:53**	**3**	**0**	**0**	**0**	**2**	**0**	**0**	**0**	**9:11**
	Syracuse Crunch	AHL	7	1	5	6	35	....	....	....	....	....	....	....	....	....	....	....	....	....	....	....	....	....	....
2009-10	**Columbus**	**NHL**	**51**	**4**	**10**	**14**	**105**	**0**	**0**	**0**	**57**	**7.0**	**6**	**33**	**27.3**	**10:53**	....	....	....	....	....	....	....	....	....
2010-11	**Columbus**	**NHL**	**76**	**4**	**13**	**17**	**184**	**0**	**0**	**0**	**112**	**3.6**	**-15**	**51**	**37.3**	**13:12**	....	....	....	....	....	....	....	....	....
2011-12	**Columbus**	**NHL**	**77**	**12**	**8**	**20**	***235**	**2**	**1**	**1**	**137**	**8.8**	**-11**	**28**	**50.0**	**14:42**	....	....	....	....	....	....	....	....	....
2012-13	Salzburg	Austria	4	0	1	1	25	....	....	....	....	....	....	....	....	....	....	....	....	....	....	....	....	....	....
	Columbus	**NHL**	**24**	**3**	**6**	**9**	**53**	**0**	**0**	**0**	**38**	**7.9**	**-11**	**23**	**56.5**	**15:59**	....	....	....	....	....	....	....	....	....
	NY Rangers	**NHL**	....	....	....	....	....	....	....	....	....	....	....	....	....	....	**11**	**0**	**1**	**1**	**28**	**0**	**0**	**0**	**10:46**
	NHL Totals		**280**	**27**	**38**	**65**	**727**	**2**	**1**	**2**	**403**	**6.7**		**144**	**41.0**	**12:38**	**14**	**0**	**1**	**1**	**30**	**0**	**0**	**0**	**10:26**

Signed as a free agent by **Salzburg** (Austria), November 26, 2012. Traded to **NY Rangers** by **Columbus** with Derick Brassard, John Moore and Columbus' 6th round choice in 2014 Entry Draft for Marian Gaborik, Blake Parlett and Steven Delisle, April 3, 2013.

DOUGHTY, Drew

(DOW-tee, DROO) **L.A.**

Defense. Shoots right. 6'1", 208 lbs. Born, London, Ont., December 8, 1989. Los Angeles' 1st choice, 2nd overall, in 2008 Entry Draft.

Season	Club	League	GP	G	A	Pts	PIM	PP	SH	GW	S	%	+/-	TF	F%	Min	GP	G	A	Pts	PIM	PP	SH	GW	Min
2004-05	Lon. Jr. Knights	Minor-ON	55	19	30	49	31	....	....	....	....	....	....	....	....	....	....	....	....	....	....	....	....	....	....
2005-06	Guelph Storm	OHL	65	5	28	33	40	....	....	....	....	....	....	....	....	....	14	0	13	13	18	....	....	....	....
2006-07	Guelph Storm	OHL	67	21	53	74	76	....	....	....	....	....	....	....	....	....	4	2	3	5	8	....	....	....	....
2007-08	Guelph Storm	OHL	58	13	37	50	68	....	....	....	....	....	....	....	....	....	10	3	6	9	14	....	....	....	....
2008-09	**Los Angeles**	**NHL**	**81**	**6**	**21**	**27**	**56**	**3**	**0**	**1**	**126**	**4.8**	**-17**	**0**	**0.0**	**23:50**	....	....	....	....	....	....	....	....	....
2009-10	**Los Angeles**	**NHL**	**82**	**16**	**43**	**59**	**54**	**9**	**0**	**5**	**142**	**11.3**	**20**	**0**	**0.0**	**24:59**	**6**	**3**	**4**	**7**	**4**	**2**	**0**	**0**	**27:26**
	Canada	Olympics	7	0	2	2	2	....	....	....	....	....	....	....	....	....	....	....	....	....	....	....	....	....	....
2010-11	**Los Angeles**	**NHL**	**76**	**11**	**29**	**40**	**68**	**5**	**0**	**3**	**139**	**7.9**	**13**	**0**	**0.0**	**25:39**	**6**	**2**	**2**	**4**	**8**	**1**	**0**	**0**	**27:08**
2011-12 ◆	**Los Angeles**	**NHL**	**77**	**10**	**26**	**36**	**69**	**3**	**0**	**3**	**168**	**6.0**	**-2**	**0**	**0.0**	**24:54**	**20**	**4**	**12**	**16**	**14**	**1**	**0**	**0**	**26:09**
2012-13	**Los Angeles**	**NHL**	**48**	**6**	**16**	**22**	**36**	**3**	**0**	**0**	**114**	**5.3**	**4**	**0**	**0.0**	**26:24**	**18**	**2**	**3**	**5**	**8**	**1**	**0**	**0**	**27:57**
	NHL Totals		**364**	**49**	**135**	**184**	**283**	**23**	**0**	**12**	**689**	**7.1**		**0**	**0.0**	**25:02**	**50**	**11**	**21**	**32**	**34**	**5**	**0**	**0**	**27:04**

OHL All-Rookie Team (2006) • OHL First All-Star Team (2007, 2008) • Canadian Major Junior First All-Star Team (2008) • NHL All-Rookie Team (2009) • NHL Second All-Star Team (2010)

DOWELL, Jake

(DOW-uhl, JAYK) **MIN**

Center. Shoots left. 6', 202 lbs. Born, Eau Claire, WI, March 4, 1985. Chicago's 10th choice, 140th overall, in 2004 Entry Draft.

Season	Club	League	GP	G	A	Pts	PIM	PP	SH	GW	S	%	+/-	TF	F%	Min	GP	G	A	Pts	PIM	PP	SH	GW	Min
2000-01	Eau Claire Mem.	High-WI	24	25	30	55	....	....	....	....	....	....	....	....	....	....	....	....	....	....	....	....	....	....	....
2001-02	USNTDP	U-17	11	5	1	6	14	....	....	....	....	....	....	....	....	....	....	....	....	....	....	....	....	....	....
	USNTDP	NAHL	44	5	12	17	51	....	....	....	....	....	....	....	....	....	....	....	....	....	....	....	....	....	....
2002-03	USNTDP	U-18	54	8	17	25	54	....	....	....	....	....	....	....	....	....	....	....	....	....	....	....	....	....	....
	USNTDP	NAHL	9	2	2	4	13	....	....	....	....	....	....	....	....	....	....	....	....	....	....	....	....	....	....
2003-04	U. of Wisconsin	WCHA	37	6	13	19	48	....	....	....	....	....	....	....	....	....	....	....	....	....	....	....	....	....	....
2004-05	U. of Wisconsin	WCHA	38	12	14	26	74	....	....	....	....	....	....	....	....	....	....	....	....	....	....	....	....	....	....
2005-06	U. of Wisconsin	WCHA	43	5	15	20	42	....	....	....	....	....	....	....	....	....	....	....	....	....	....	....	....	....	....
2006-07	U. of Wisconsin	WCHA	41	19	6	25	54	....	....	....	....	....	....	....	....	....	....	....	....	....	....	....	....	....	....
	Norfolk Admirals	AHL	9	2	3	5	8	....	....	....	....	....	....	....	....	....	6	0	3	3	4	....	....	....	....
2007-08	**Chicago**	**NHL**	**19**	**2**	**1**	**3**	**10**	**0**	**1**	**0**	**19**	**10.5**	**1**	**170**	**46.5**	**11:56**	....	....	....	....	....	....	....	....	....
	Rockford IceHogs	AHL	49	7	10	17	64	....	....	....	....	....	....	....	....	....	12	1	1	2	6	....	....	....	....

			Regular Season														Playoffs								
Season	Club	League	GP	G	A	Pts	PIM	PP	SH	GW	S	%	+/-	TF	F%	Min	GP	G	A	Pts	PIM	PP	SH	GW	Min
2008-09	**Chicago**	**NHL**	**1**	**0**	**0**	**0**	**2**	**0**	**0**	**0**	**0**	**0.0**	**1**	**12**	**66.7**	**13:37**	....	....	....	....	....	....	....	....	....
	Rockford IceHogs	AHL	75	6	14	20	128	....	....	....	....	....	....	....	....	....	4	0	0	0	0	....	....	....	....
2009-10	**Chicago**	**NHL**	**3**	**1**	**1**	**2**	**5**	**0**	**0**	**0**	**4**	**25.0**	**1**	**4**	**50.0**	**6:56**	....	....	....	....	....	....	....	....	....
	Rockford IceHogs	AHL	78	7	16	23	96	....	....	....	....	....	....	....	....	....	4	0	0	0	0	....	....	....	....
2010-11	**Chicago**	**NHL**	**79**	**6**	**15**	**21**	**63**	**0**	**0**	**0**	**74**	**8.1**	**5**	**652**	**48.9**	**11:49**	**2**	**0**	**0**	**0**	**0**	**0**	**0**	**0**	**8:23**
2011-12	**Dallas**	**NHL**	**52**	**2**	**5**	**7**	**53**	**0**	**0**	**0**	**39**	**5.1**	**–3**	**197**	**47.7**	**7:38**	....	....	....	....	....	....	....	....	....
2012-13	Houston Aeros	AHL	37	4	5	9	34	....	....	....	....	....	....	....	....	....	4	0	1	1	4	....	....	....	....
	Minnesota	**NHL**	**2**	**0**	**0**	**0**	**0**	**0**	**0**	**0**	**3**	**0.0**	**0**	**3**	**66.7**	**8:33**	....	....	....	....	....	....	....	....	....
	NHL Totals		**156**	**11**	**22**	**33**	**133**	**0**	**1**	**0**	**139**	**7.9**		**1038**	**48.6**	**10:19**	**2**	**0**	**0**	**0**	**0**	**0**	**0**	**0**	**8:23**

Signed as a free agent by **Dallas**, July 1, 2011. Signed as a free agent by **Minnesota**, July 4, 2012.

DOWNIE, Steve

(DOW-nee, STEEV) **COL**

Right wing. Shoots right. 5'11", 191 lbs. Born, Newmarket, Ont., April 3, 1987. Philadelphia's 1st choice, 29th overall, in 2005 Entry Draft.

2002-03	Aurora Tigers	ON-Jr.A	34	12	13	25	55	....	....	....	....	....	....	....	....	....	....	....	....	....	....	....	....	....	....
2003-04	Windsor Spitfires	OHL	49	7	9	16	90	....	....	....	....	....	....	....	....	....	4	0	1	1	27	....	....	....	....
2004-05	Windsor Spitfires	OHL	61	21	52	73	179	....	....	....	....	....	....	....	....	....	11	4	5	9	49	....	....	....	....
2005-06	Windsor Spitfires	OHL	1	3	0	3	4	....	....	....	....	....	....	....	....	....	....	....	....	....	....	....	....	....	....
	Peterborough	OHL	34	16	34	50	109	....	....	....	....	....	....	....	....	....	19	6	15	21	38	....	....	....	....
2006-07	Peterborough	OHL	28	23	36	59	92	....	....	....	....	....	....	....	....	....	....	....	....	....	....	....	....	....	....
	Kitchener Rangers	OHL	17	12	21	33	32	....	....	....	....	....	....	....	....	....	9	8	14	22	15	....	....	....	....
	Philadelphia	AHL	1	0	0	0	0	....	....	....	....	....	....	....	....	....	....	....	....	....	....	....	....	....	....
2007-08	**Philadelphia**	**NHL**	**32**	**6**	**6**	**12**	**73**	**0**	**1**	**1**	**25**	**24.0**	**2**	**15**	**33.3**	**9:51**	**6**	**0**	**1**	**1**	**10**	**0**	**0**	**0**	**6:04**
	Philadelphia	AHL	21	5	12	17	114	....	....	....	....	....	....	....	....	....	....	....	....	....	....	....	....	....	....
2008-09	**Philadelphia**	**NHL**	**6**	**0**	**0**	**0**	**11**	**0**	**0**	**0**	**1**	**0.0**	**–4**	**13**	**15.4**	**5:57**	....	....	....	....	....	....	....	....	....
	Philadelphia	AHL	4	1	7	8	23	....	....	....	....	....	....	....	....	....	....	....	....	....	....	....	....	....	....
	Tampa Bay	**NHL**	**23**	**3**	**3**	**6**	**54**	**0**	**0**	**1**	**25**	**12.0**	**2**	**7**	**42.9**	**9:04**	....	....	....	....	....	....	....	....	....
	Norfolk Admirals	AHL	23	8	17	25	107	....	....	....	....	....	....	....	....	....	....	....	....	....	....	....	....	....	....
2009-10	**Tampa Bay**	**NHL**	**79**	**22**	**24**	**46**	**208**	**7**	**0**	**1**	**116**	**19.0**	**14**	**34**	**50.0**	**14:43**	....	....	....	....	....	....	....	....	....
2010-11	**Tampa Bay**	**NHL**	**57**	**10**	**22**	**32**	**171**	**2**	**0**	**1**	**83**	**12.0**	**8**	**96**	**44.8**	**14:31**	**17**	**2**	**12**	**14**	**40**	**0**	**0**	**1**	**12:35**
2011-12	**Tampa Bay**	**NHL**	**55**	**12**	**16**	**28**	**121**	**2**	**0**	**1**	**99**	**12.1**	**–15**	**77**	**45.5**	**15:30**	....	....	....	....	....	....	....	....	....
	Colorado	**NHL**	**20**	**2**	**11**	**13**	**16**	**0**	**0**	**1**	**41**	**4.9**	**9**	**10**	**50.0**	**17:06**	....	....	....	....	....	....	....	....	....
2012-13	**Colorado**	**NHL**	**2**	**0**	**1**	**1**	**6**	**0**	**0**	**0**	**2**	**0.0**	**1**	**1**	**100.0**	**8:54**	....	....	....	....	....	....	....	....	....
	NHL Totals		**274**	**55**	**83**	**138**	**660**	**11**	**1**	**6**	**392**	**14.0**		**253**	**43.9**	**13:44**	**23**	**2**	**13**	**15**	**50**	**0**	**0**	**1**	**10:54**

Traded to **Tampa Bay** by **Philadelphia** with Steve Eminger and Tampa Bay's 4th round choice (previously acquired, Tampa Bay selected Alex Hutchings) in 2009 Entry Draft for Matt Carle and San Jose's 3rd round choice (previously acquired, Philadelphia selected Simon Bertilsson) in 2009 Entry Draft, November 7, 2008. Traded to **Colorado** by **Tampa Bay** for Kyle Quincey, February 21, 2012. • Missed majority of 2012-13 due to knee injury vs. Los Angeles, January 22, 2013.

DRAZENOVIC, Nick

(DRAY-zehn-oh-vihk, NIHK) **PIT**

Center. Shoots left. 6', 192 lbs. Born, Prince George, B.C., January 14, 1987. St. Louis' 6th choice, 171st overall, in 2005 Entry Draft.

2002-03	Prince George	WHL	15	4	4	8	....	....	....	....	....	....	....	....	....	....	4	0	0	0	....	....	....	....	....
2003-04	Prince George	WHL	65	7	30	37	38	....	....	....	....	....	....	....	....	....	....	....	....	....	....	....	....	....	....
2004-05	Prince George	WHL	72	18	38	56	24	....	....	....	....	....	....	....	....	....	....	....	....	....	....	....	....	....	....
2005-06	Prince George	WHL	71	30	33	63	51	....	....	....	....	....	....	....	....	....	5	0	0	0	4	....	....	....	....
2006-07	Prince George	WHL	58	18	32	50	63	....	....	....	....	....	....	....	....	....	15	9	10	19	6	....	....	....	....
2007-08	Peoria Rivermen	AHL	69	16	26	42	38	....	....	....	....	....	....	....	....	....	....	....	....	....	....	....	....	....	....
2008-09	Peoria Rivermen	AHL	76	12	21	33	43	....	....	....	....	....	....	....	....	....	5	1	0	1	2	....	....	....	....
2009-10	Peoria Rivermen	AHL	58	19	20	39	40	....	....	....	....	....	....	....	....	....	....	....	....	....	....	....	....	....	....
2010-11	**St. Louis**	**NHL**	**3**	**0**	**0**	**0**	**0**	**0**	**0**	**0**	**2**	**0.0**	**–3**	**11**	**54.6**	**8:59**	....	....	....	....	....	....	....	....	....
	Peoria Rivermen	AHL	75	23	23	46	24	....	....	....	....	....	....	....	....	....	4	0	1	1	2	....	....	....	....
2011-12	Springfield	AHL	41	13	28	41	16	....	....	....	....	....	....	....	....	....	....	....	....	....	....	....	....	....	....
2012-13	Springfield	AHL	62	17	36	53	30	....	....	....	....	....	....	....	....	....	8	2	2	4	2	....	....	....	....
	Columbus	**NHL**	**8**	**0**	**0**	**0**	**4**	**0**	**0**	**0**	**5**	**0.0**	**–2**	**54**	**53.7**	**9:56**	....	....	....	....	....	....	....	....	....
	NHL Totals		**11**	**0**	**0**	**0**	**4**	**0**	**0**	**0**	**7**	**0.0**		**65**	**53.8**	**9:40**	....	....	....	....	....	....	....	....	....

Signed as a free agent by **Columbus**, July 1, 2011. Signed as a free agent by **Pittsburgh**, July 6, 2013.

DREWISKE, Davis

(droo-WIHS-kee, DAY-vihs) **MTL**

Defense. Shoots left. 6'1", 220 lbs. Born, Hudson, WI, November 22, 1984.

2003-04	Des Moines	USHL	60	4	19	23	63	....	....	....	....	....	....	....	....	....	3	0	0	0	4	....	....	....	....
2004-05	U. of Wisconsin	WCHA	34	1	5	6	20	....	....	....	....	....	....	....	....	....	....	....	....	....	....	....	....	....	....
2005-06	U. of Wisconsin	WCHA	35	2	2	4	22	....	....	....	....	....	....	....	....	....	....	....	....	....	....	....	....	....	....
2006-07	U. of Wisconsin	WCHA	41	4	6	10	46	....	....	....	....	....	....	....	....	....	....	....	....	....	....	....	....	....	....
2007-08	U. of Wisconsin	WCHA	40	5	16	21	46	....	....	....	....	....	....	....	....	....	....	....	....	....	....	....	....	....	....
	Manchester	AHL	5	0	0	0	6	....	....	....	....	....	....	....	....	....	4	0	1	1	6	....	....	....	....
2008-09	**Los Angeles**	**NHL**	**17**	**0**	**3**	**3**	**18**	**0**	**0**	**0**	**21**	**0.0**	**1**	**0**	**0.0**	**17:19**	....	....	....	....	....	....	....	....	....
	Manchester	AHL	61	1	13	14	95	....	....	....	....	....	....	....	....	....	....	....	....	....	....	....	....	....	....
2009-10	**Los Angeles**	**NHL**	**42**	**1**	**7**	**8**	**14**	**0**	**0**	**0**	**32**	**3.1**	**–4**	**0**	**0.0**	**15:15**	....	....	....	....	....	....	....	....	....
2010-11	**Los Angeles**	**NHL**	**38**	**0**	**5**	**5**	**19**	**0**	**0**	**0**	**27**	**0.0**	**–1**	**0**	**0.0**	**14:21**	....	....	....	....	....	....	....	....	....
2011-12♦	**Los Angeles**	**NHL**	**9**	**2**	**0**	**2**	**2**	**0**	**0**	**0**	**11**	**18.2**	**0**	**0**	**0.0**	**12:34**	....	....	....	....	....	....	....	....	....
2012-13	**Los Angeles**	**NHL**	**20**	**1**	**3**	**4**	**14**	**1**	**0**	**0**	**20**	**5.0**	**3**	**1**	**100.0**	**14:28**	....	....	....	....	....	....	....	....	....
	Montreal	**NHL**	**9**	**1**	**2**	**3**	**0**	**0**	**0**	**0**	**8**	**12.5**	**0**	**0**	**0.0**	**16:50**	....	....	....	....	....	....	....	....	....
	NHL Totals		**135**	**5**	**20**	**25**	**67**	**1**	**0**	**0**	**119**	**4.2**		**1**	**100.0**	**15:04**	....	....	....	....	....	....	....	....	....

Signed as a free agent by **Los Angeles**, April 1, 2008. • Missed majority of 2010-11 and 2011-12 as a healthy reserve. Traded to **Montreal** by **Los Angeles** for Montreal's 5th round choice (Patrik Bartosak) in 2013 Entry Draft, April 2, 2013.

DUBINSKY, Brandon

(DOO-bihn-skee, BRAN-duhn) **CBJ**

Center. Shoots left. 6'1", 210 lbs. Born, Anchorage, AK, April 29, 1986. NY Rangers' 6th choice, 60th overall, in 2004 Entry Draft.

2001-02	Alaska All-Stars	AASHA	37	14	24	38	....	....	....	....	....	....	....	....	....	....	....	....	....	....	....	....	....	....	....
2002-03	Portland	WHL	44	8	18	26	35	....	....	....	....	....	....	....	....	....	7	2	2	4	10	....	....	....	....
2003-04	Portland	WHL	71	30	48	78	137	....	....	....	....	....	....	....	....	....	5	0	2	2	6	....	....	....	....
2004-05	Portland	WHL	68	23	36	59	160	....	....	....	....	....	....	....	....	....	7	4	5	9	8	....	....	....	....
2005-06	Portland	WHL	51	21	46	67	98	....	....	....	....	....	....	....	....	....	12	5	10	15	24	....	....	....	....
	Hartford	AHL	....	....	....	....	....	....	....	....	....	....	....	....	....	....	11	5	5	10	14	....	....	....	....
2006-07	**NY Rangers**	**NHL**	**6**	**0**	**0**	**0**	**2**	**0**	**0**	**0**	**9**	**0.0**	**0**	**26**	**46.2**	**8:10**	....	....	....	....	....	....	....	....	....
	Hartford	AHL	71	21	22	43	115	....	....	....	....	....	....	....	....	....	7	1	3	4	12	....	....	....	....
2007-08	**NY Rangers**	**NHL**	**82**	**14**	**26**	**40**	**79**	**1**	**0**	**0**	**157**	**8.9**	**8**	**995**	**51.5**	**14:30**	**10**	**4**	**4**	**8**	**12**	**2**	**0**	**0**	**18:59**
2008-09	**NY Rangers**	**NHL**	**82**	**13**	**28**	**41**	**112**	**3**	**1**	**7**	**188**	**6.9**	**–6**	**870**	**53.6**	**16:38**	**7**	**1**	**3**	**4**	**18**	**0**	**0**	**1**	**18:14**
2009-10	**NY Rangers**	**NHL**	**69**	**20**	**24**	**44**	**54**	**6**	**2**	**5**	**165**	**12.1**	**9**	**675**	**51.4**	**19:33**	....	....	....	....	....	....	....	....	....
2010-11	**NY Rangers**	**NHL**	**77**	**24**	**30**	**54**	**100**	**4**	**2**	**2**	**202**	**11.9**	**–3**	**875**	**52.5**	**20:14**	**5**	**2**	**1**	**3**	**2**	**0**	**0**	**1**	**24:56**
2011-12	**NY Rangers**	**NHL**	**77**	**10**	**24**	**34**	**110**	**0**	**1**	**1**	**140**	**7.1**	**16**	**395**	**51.9**	**16:16**	**9**	**0**	**2**	**2**	**14**	**0**	**0**	**0**	**14:27**
2012-13	Alaska Aces	ECHL	17	9	7	16	22	....	....	....	....	....	....	....	....	....	....	....	....	....	....	....	....	....	....
	Columbus	**NHL**	**29**	**2**	**18**	**20**	**76**	**1**	**0**	**0**	**50**	**4.0**	**2**	**439**	**58.3**	**18:24**	....	....	....	....	....	....	....	....	....
	NHL Totals		**422**	**83**	**150**	**233**	**533**	**15**	**6**	**15**	**911**	**9.1**		**4275**	**52.8**	**17:17**	**31**	**7**	**10**	**17**	**46**	**2**	**0**	**2**	**18:28**

WHL West Second All-Star Team (2004, 2006)

Traded to **Columbus** by **NY Rangers** with Artem Anisimov, Tim Erixon and NY Rangers' 1st round choice (Kerby Rychel) in 2013 Entry Draft for Rick Nash, Steven Delisle and Columbus' 3rd round choice (Pavel Buchnevich) in 2013 Entry Draft, July 23, 2012. Signed as a free agent by **Alaska** (ECHL), October 1, 2012.

DUCHENE, Matt

(DOO-shayn, MAT) **COL**

Center. Shoots left. 5'11", 200 lbs. Born, Haliburton, Ont., January 16, 1991. Colorado's 1st choice, 3rd overall, in 2009 Entry Draft.

2006-07	Cent. Ont. Wolves	Minor-ON	52	69	37	106	36	....	....	....	....	....	....	....	....	....	....	....	....	....	....	....	....	....	....
2007-08	Brampton	OHL	64	30	20	50	22	....	....	....	....	....	....	....	....	....	5	1	1	2	10	....	....	....	....
2008-09	Brampton	OHL	57	31	48	79	42	....	....	....	....	....	....	....	....	....	21	14	12	26	21	....	....	....	....
2009-10	**Colorado**	**NHL**	**81**	**24**	**31**	**55**	**16**	**10**	**1**	**2**	**180**	**13.3**	**1**	**1088**	**44.0**	**17:44**	**6**	**0**	**3**	**3**	**0**	**0**	**0**	**0**	**19:20**
2010-11	**Colorado**	**NHL**	**80**	**27**	**40**	**67**	**33**	**3**	**0**	**2**	**202**	**13.4**	**–8**	**1246**	**50.4**	**18:57**	....	....	....	....	....	....	....	....	....
2011-12	**Colorado**	**NHL**	**58**	**14**	**14**	**28**	**8**	**5**	**0**	**2**	**132**	**10.6**	**–11**	**391**	**51.2**	**16:17**	....	....	....	....	....	....	....	....	....

			Regular Season														Playoffs								
Season	Club	League	GP	G	A	Pts	PIM	PP	SH	GW	S	%	+/-	TF	F%	Min	GP	G	A	Pts	PIM	PP	SH	GW	Min
2012-13	Frolunda	Sweden	19	4	10	14	12	....	....	....	....	....	....	....	....	....	....	....	....	....	....	....	....	....	....
	HC Ambri-Piotta	Swiss	4	2	3	5	2	....	....	....	....	....	....	....	....	....	....	....	....	....	....	....	....	....	....
	Colorado	**NHL**	**47**	**17**	**26**	**43**	**12**	**2**	**0**	**3**	**132**	**12.9**	**–12**	**893**	**54.7**	**20:55**	....	....	....	....	....	....	....	....	....
	NHL Totals		**266**	**82**	**111**	**193**	**69**	**20**	**1**	**9**	**646**	**12.7**		**3618**	**49.6**	**18:21**	**6**	**0**	**3**	**3**	**0**	**0**	**0**	**0**	**19:20**

NHL All-Rookie Team (2010)
Played in NHL All-Star Game (2011)
Signed as a free agent by **Frolunda** (Sweden), October 2, 2012. Signed as a free agent by **Ambri-Piotta** (Swiss), December 9, 2012.

DUCO, Mike

(DOO-koh, MIGHK)

Left wing. Shoots left. 5'10", 200 lbs. Born, Toronto, Ont., July 8, 1987.

Season	Club	League	GP	G	A	Pts	PIM	PP	SH	GW	S	%	+/-	TF	F%	Min	GP	G	A	Pts	PIM	PP	SH	GW	Min
2003-04	Kitchener Rangers	OHL	5	1	2	3	4	....	....	....	....	....	....	....	....	....	4	0	1	1	4	....	....	....	....
2004-05	Kitchener Rangers	OHL	62	24	26	50	78	....	....	....	....	....	....	....	....	....	15	0	0	0	11	....	....	....	....
2005-06	Kitchener Rangers	OHL	59	22	22	44	113	....	....	....	....	....	....	....	....	....	5	2	1	3	10	....	....	....	....
2006-07	Kitchener Rangers	OHL	54	20	20	40	121	....	....	....	....	....	....	....	....	....	9	1	1	2	12	....	....	....	....
2007-08	Kitchener Rangers	OHL	62	32	22	54	173	....	....	....	....	....	....	....	....	....	20	*16	6	22	37	....	....	....	....
2008-09	Rochester	AHL	68	14	14	28	147	....	....	....	....	....	....	....	....	....	....	....	....	....	....	....	....	....	....
2009-10	**Florida**	**NHL**	**10**	**0**	**0**	**0**	**50**	**0**	**0**	**0**	**6**	**0.0**	**–3**	**0**	**0.0**	**7:43**	....	....	....	....	....	....	....	....	....
	Rochester	AHL	59	9	10	19	111	....	....	....	....	....	....	....	....	....	7	1	0	1	18	....	....	....	....
2010-11	**Florida**	**NHL**	**2**	**0**	**0**	**0**	**10**	**0**	**0**	**0**	**0**	**0.0**	**–1**	**0**	**0.0**	**8:33**	....	....	....	....	....	....	....	....	....
	Rochester	AHL	67	20	11	31	126	....	....	....	....	....	....	....	....	....	....	....	....	....	....	....	....	....	....
2011-12	Chicago Wolves	AHL	56	11	13	24	59	....	....	....	....	....	....	....	....	....	5	0	0	0	2	....	....	....	....
	Vancouver	**NHL**	**6**	**0**	**2**	**2**	**5**	**0**	**0**	**0**	**4**	**0.0**	**1**	**0**	**0.0**	**8:03**	....	....	....	....	....	....	....	....	....
2012-13	Salzburg	Austria	15	4	2	6	7	....	....	....	....	....	....	....	....	....	6	2	0	2	4	....	....	....	....
	NHL Totals		**18**	**0**	**2**	**2**	**65**	**0**	**0**	**0**	**10**	**0.0**		**0**	**0.0**	**7:56**	....	....	....	....	....	....	....	....	....

Signed as a free agent by **Florida**, October 8, 2007. Traded to **Vancouver** by **Florida** for Sergei Shirokov, July 8, 2011. Signed as a free agent by **Salzburg** (Austria), December 9, 2012.

DUMONT, Gabriel

(doo-MAWNT, gah-BREE-ehl) **MTL**

Center. Shoots right. 5'10", 189 lbs. Born, Ville Degelis, Que., October 6, 1990. Montreal's 5th choice, 139th overall, in 2009 Entry Draft.

Season	Club	League	GP	G	A	Pts	PIM	PP	SH	GW	S	%	+/-	TF	F%	Min	GP	G	A	Pts	PIM	PP	SH	GW	Min
2006-07	Ecole Notre Dame	QAAA	39	30	42	72	127	....	....	....	....	....	....	....	....	....	13	11	12	23	20	....	....	....	....
	Drummondville	QMJHL	8	1	1	2	6	....	....	....	....	....	....	....	....	....	6	0	2	2	0	....	....	....	....
2007-08	Drummondville	QMJHL	59	11	14	25	103	....	....	....	....	....	....	....	....	....	....	....	....	....	....	....	....	....	....
2008-09	Drummondville	QMJHL	51	28	21	49	63	....	....	....	....	....	....	....	....	....	19	6	13	19	32	....	....	....	....
2009-10	Drummondville	QMJHL	62	*51	42	93	127	....	....	....	....	....	....	....	....	....	14	*11	10	21	19	....	....	....	....
	Hamilton	AHL	....	....	....	....	....	....	....	....	....	....	....	....	....	....	11	2	0	2	12	....	....	....	....
2010-11	Hamilton	AHL	64	5	13	18	79	....	....	....	....	....	....	....	....	....	20	6	3	9	6	....	....	....	....
2011-12	**Montreal**	**NHL**	**3**	**0**	**0**	**0**	**0**	**0**	**0**	**0**	**1**	**0.0**	**–1**	**18**	**16.7**	**8:34**	....	....	....	....	....	....	....	....	....
	Hamilton	AHL	59	13	11	24	55	....	....	....	....	....	....	....	....	....	....	....	....	....	....	....	....	....	....
2012-13	Hamilton	AHL	55	16	15	31	83	....	....	....	....	....	....	....	....	....	....	....	....	....	....	....	....	....	....
	Montreal	**NHL**	**10**	**1**	**2**	**3**	**13**	**0**	**0**	**0**	**20**	**5.0**	**1**	**46**	**63.0**	**9:41**	**3**	**0**	**0**	**0**	**12**	**0**	**0**	**0**	**6:21**
	NHL Totals		**13**	**1**	**2**	**3**	**13**	**0**	**0**	**0**	**21**	**4.8**		**64**	**50.0**	**9:25**	**3**	**0**	**0**	**0**	**12**	**0**	**0**	**0**	**6:21**

QMJHL First All-Star Team (2010) • Canadian Major Junior Second All-Star Team (2010)

DUPUIS, Pascal

(doo-PWEE, pas-KAL) **PIT**

Left wing. Shoots left. 6'1", 205 lbs. Born, Laval, Que., April 7, 1979.

Season	Club	League	GP	G	A	Pts	PIM	PP	SH	GW	S	%	+/-	TF	F%	Min	GP	G	A	Pts	PIM	PP	SH	GW	Min
1995-96	Laval-Laurentides	QAAA	41	10	15	25	....	....	....	....	....	....	....	....	....	....	14	11	11	22	....	....	....	....	....
1996-97	Rouyn-Noranda	QMJHL	44	9	15	24	20	....	....	....	....	....	....	....	....	....	....	....	....	....	....	....	....	....	....
1997-98	Rouyn-Noranda	QMJHL	42	10	19	29	36	....	....	....	....	....	....	....	....	....	....	....	....	....	....	....	....	....	....
	Shawinigan	QMJHL	25	6	11	17	10	....	....	....	....	....	....	....	....	....	6	2	0	2	4	....	....	....	....
1998-99	Shawinigan	QMJHL	57	30	42	72	118	....	....	....	....	....	....	....	....	....	6	1	8	9	18	....	....	....	....
99-2000	Shawinigan	QMJHL	61	50	55	105	164	....	....	....	....	....	....	....	....	....	13	*15	7	22	4	....	....	....	....
2000-01	**Minnesota**	**NHL**	**4**	**1**	**0**	**1**	**4**	**1**	**0**	**0**	**8**	**12.5**	**0**	**0**	**0.0**	**15:36**	....	....	....	....	....	....	....	....	....
	Cleveland	IHL	70	19	24	43	37	....	....	....	....	....	....	....	....	....	4	0	0	0	0	....	....	....	....
2001-02	**Minnesota**	**NHL**	**76**	**15**	**12**	**27**	**16**	**3**	**2**	**0**	**154**	**9.7**	**–10**	**40**	**32.5**	**15:08**	....	....	....	....	....	....	....	....	....
2002-03	**Minnesota**	**NHL**	**80**	**20**	**28**	**48**	**44**	**6**	**0**	**4**	**183**	**10.9**	**17**	**186**	**40.9**	**17:30**	**16**	**4**	**4**	**8**	**8**	**2**	**0**	**1**	**16:58**
2003-04	**Minnesota**	**NHL**	**59**	**11**	**15**	**26**	**20**	**2**	**0**	**1**	**127**	**8.7**	**5**	**129**	**45.7**	**15:48**	....	....	....	....	....	....	....	....	....
2004-05	HC Ajoie	Swiss-2	8	5	5	10	26	....	....	....	....	....	....	....	....	....	6	6	8	14	8	....	....	....	....
2005-06	**Minnesota**	**NHL**	**67**	**10**	**16**	**26**	**40**	**4**	**0**	**2**	**151**	**6.6**	**–10**	**93**	**29.0**	**16:30**	....	....	....	....	....	....	....	....	....
2006-07	**Minnesota**	**NHL**	**48**	**10**	**3**	**13**	**38**	**2**	**2**	**0**	**106**	**9.4**	**–7**	**110**	**27.3**	**15:07**	....	....	....	....	....	....	....	....	....
	NY Rangers	**NHL**	**6**	**1**	**0**	**1**	**0**	**0**	**0**	**0**	**10**	**10.0**	**–4**	**2**	**50.0**	**15:30**	....	....	....	....	....	....	....	....	....
	Atlanta	**NHL**	**17**	**3**	**2**	**5**	**4**	**0**	**0**	**1**	**40**	**7.5**	**–6**	**19**	**52.6**	**16:44**	**4**	**1**	**2**	**3**	**4**	**0**	**0**	**0**	**20:28**
2007-08	**Atlanta**	**NHL**	**62**	**10**	**5**	**15**	**24**	**0**	**3**	**1**	**111**	**9.0**	**–4**	**13**	**38.5**	**14:46**	....	....	....	....	....	....	....	....	....
	Pittsburgh	**NHL**	**16**	**2**	**10**	**12**	**8**	**0**	**0**	**0**	**32**	**6.3**	**4**	**3**	**0.0**	**16:50**	**20**	**2**	**5**	**7**	**18**	**0**	**0**	**0**	**16:14**
2008-09♦	**Pittsburgh**	**NHL**	**71**	**12**	**16**	**28**	**30**	**0**	**0**	**2**	**145**	**8.3**	**1**	**16**	**18.8**	**14:13**	**16**	**0**	**0**	**0**	**8**	**0**	**0**	**0**	**8:23**
2009-10	**Pittsburgh**	**NHL**	**81**	**18**	**20**	**38**	**16**	**0**	**0**	**5**	**157**	**11.5**	**5**	**33**	**39.4**	**14:11**	**13**	**2**	**6**	**8**	**4**	**0**	**0**	**1**	**16:51**
2010-11	**Pittsburgh**	**NHL**	**81**	**17**	**20**	**37**	**59**	**0**	**4**	**3**	**171**	**9.9**	**16**	**28**	**21.4**	**16:52**	**7**	**1**	**0**	**1**	**2**	**0**	**0**	**0**	**16:36**
2011-12	**Pittsburgh**	**NHL**	**82**	**25**	**34**	**59**	**34**	**0**	**3**	**8**	**214**	**11.7**	**18**	**115**	**44.4**	**16:56**	**6**	**2**	**4**	**6**	**0**	**0**	**0**	**0**	**17:08**
2012-13	**Pittsburgh**	**NHL**	**48**	**20**	**18**	**38**	**26**	**2**	**1**	**2**	**140**	**14.3**	**31**	**57**	**47.4**	**17:30**	**15**	**7**	**4**	**11**	**12**	**0**	**2**	**0**	**18:52**
	NHL Totals		**798**	**175**	**199**	**374**	**363**	**20**	**15**	**29**	**1749**	**10.0**		**844**	**38.0**	**15:54**	**97**	**19**	**25**	**44**	**56**	**2**	**2**	**2**	**15:48**

Signed as a free agent by **Minnesota**, August 18, 2000. Signed as a free agent by **Ajoie** (Swiss-2), January 14, 2005. Traded to **NY Rangers** by **Minnesota** for Adam Hall, February 9, 2007. Traded to **Atlanta** by **NY Rangers** with NY Rangers' 3rd round choice (later traded to Pittsburgh - Pittsburgh selected Robert Bortuzzo) in 2007 Entry Draft for Alex Bourret, February 27, 2007. Traded to **Pittsburgh** by **Atlanta** with Marian Hossa for Colby Armstrong, Erik Christensen, Angelo Esposito and Pittsburgh's 1st round choice (Daulton Leveille) in 2008 Entry Draft, February 26, 2008.

DUPUIS, Philippe

(doo-PWEE, fihl-EEP)

Center. Shoots right. 6', 196 lbs. Born, Laval, Que., April 24, 1985. Columbus' 5th choice, 104th overall, in 2003 Entry Draft.

Season	Club	League	GP	G	A	Pts	PIM	PP	SH	GW	S	%	+/-	TF	F%	Min	GP	G	A	Pts	PIM	PP	SH	GW	Min
2000-01	Laval-Laurentides	QAAA	46	16	27	43	74	....	....	....	....	....	....	....	....	....	8	1	5	6	30	....	....	....	....
2001-02	Hull Olympiques	QMJHL	67	7	14	21	59	....	....	....	....	....	....	....	....	....	12	6	5	11	14	....	....	....	....
2002-03	Hull Olympiques	QMJHL	68	22	34	56	89	....	....	....	....	....	....	....	....	....	20	2	4	6	22	....	....	....	....
2003-04	Gatineau	QMJHL	60	18	37	55	77	....	....	....	....	....	....	....	....	....	15	6	10	16	14	....	....	....	....
2004-05	Rouyn-Noranda	QMJHL	62	34	50	84	60	....	....	....	....	....	....	....	....	....	10	5	3	8	8	....	....	....	....
2005-06	Moncton Wildcats	QMJHL	56	32	76	108	52	....	....	....	....	....	....	....	....	....	19	14	18	32	14	....	....	....	....
2006-07	Syracuse Crunch	AHL	51	11	11	22	18	....	....	....	....	....	....	....	....	....	....	....	....	....	....	....	....	....	....
	Dayton Bombers	ECHL	8	3	2	5	8	....	....	....	....	....	....	....	....	....	19	6	9	15	28	....	....	....	....
2007-08	Syracuse Crunch	AHL	29	7	4	11	2	....	....	....	....	....	....	....	....	....	....	....	....	....	....	....	....	....	....
	Lake Erie	AHL	17	5	3	8	12	....	....	....	....	....	....	....	....	....	....	....	....	....	....	....	....	....	....
2008-09	**Colorado**	**NHL**	**8**	**0**	**0**	**0**	**4**	**0**	**0**	**0**	**11**	**0.0**	**–1**	**50**	**52.0**	**9:34**	....	....	....	....	....	....	....	....	....
	Lake Erie	AHL	67	17	29	46	42	....	....	....	....	....	....	....	....	....	....	....	....	....	....	....	....	....	....
2009-10	**Colorado**	**NHL**	**4**	**0**	**1**	**1**	**2**	**0**	**0**	**0**	**4**	**0.0**	**1**	**20**	**45.0**	**8:14**	....	....	....	....	....	....	....	....	....
	Lake Erie	AHL	68	16	19	35	47	....	....	....	....	....	....	....	....	....	....	....	....	....	....	....	....	....	....
2010-11	**Colorado**	**NHL**	**74**	**6**	**11**	**17**	**40**	**0**	**1**	**0**	**101**	**5.9**	**–4**	**331**	**46.2**	**9:07**	....	....	....	....	....	....	....	....	....
2011-12	**Toronto**	**NHL**	**30**	**0**	**0**	**0**	**16**	**0**	**0**	**0**	**30**	**0.0**	**–2**	**58**	**50.0**	**10:30**	....	....	....	....	....	....	....	....	....
	Toronto Marlies	AHL	42	15	16	31	8	....	....	....	....	....	....	....	....	....	17	4	10	14	20	....	....	....	....
2012-13	Wilkes-Barre	AHL	34	2	9	11	14	....	....	....	....	....	....	....	....	....	....	....	....	....	....	....	....	....	....
	NHL Totals		**116**	**6**	**12**	**18**	**62**	**0**	**1**	**0**	**146**	**4.1**		**459**	**47.3**	**9:28**	....	....	....	....	....	....	....	....	....

Traded to **Colorado** by **Columbus** with Darcy Campbell for Mark Rycroft, January 22, 2008. Signed as a free agent by **Toronto**, July 7, 2011. Signed as a free agent by **Pittsburgh**, July 5, 2012. Signed as a free agent by **Hamburg** (Germany), June 27, 2013.

DVORAK, Radek

(duh-VOHR-ak, RA-dehk)

Right wing. Shoots right. 6'2", 195 lbs. Born, Tabor, Czech., March 9, 1977. Florida's 1st choice, 10th overall, in 1995 Entry Draft.

Season	Club	League	GP	G	A	Pts	PIM	PP	SH	GW	S	%	+/-	TF	F%	Min	GP	G	A	Pts	PIM	PP	SH	GW	Min
1992-93	C. Budejovice Jr.	Czech-Jr.	35	44	46	90	....	....	....	....	....	....	....	....	....	....	....	....	....	....	....	....	....	....	....
1993-94	C. Budejovice Jr.	CzRep-Jr.	20	17	18	35	....	....	....	....	....	....	....	....	....	....	....	....	....	....	....	....	....	....	....
	C. Budejovice	CzRep	8	0	0	0	0	....	....	....	....	....	....	....	....	....	....	....	....	....	....	....	....	....	....
1994-95	C. Budejovice	CzRep	10	3	5	8	2	....	....	....	....	....	....	....	....	....	9	5	1	6	....	....	....	....	....
1995-96	**Florida**	**NHL**	**77**	**13**	**14**	**27**	**20**	**0**	**0**	**4**	**126**	**10.3**	**5**	....	....	....	**16**	**1**	**3**	**4**	**0**	**0**	**0**	**0**	
1996-97	**Florida**	**NHL**	**78**	**18**	**21**	**39**	**30**	**2**	**0**	**1**	**139**	**12.9**	**–2**	....	....	....	**3**	**0**	**0**	**0**	**0**	**0**	**0**	**0**	....
1997-98	**Florida**	**NHL**	**64**	**12**	**24**	**36**	**33**	**2**	**3**	**0**	**112**	**10.7**	**–1**	....	....	....	....	....	....	....	....	....	....	....	....

			Regular Season														Playoffs								
Season	Club	League	GP	G	A	Pts	PIM	PP	SH	GW	S	%	+/-	TF	F%	Min	GP	G	A	Pts	PIM	PP	SH	GW	Min
1998-99	Florida	NHL	82	19	24	43	29	0	4	0	182	10.4	7	98	46.9	16:13	....	....	....	....	....	....	....	....	....
99-2000	Florida	NHL	35	7	10	17	6	0	0	1	67	10.4	5	16	37.5	15:25	....	....	....	....	....	....	....	....	....
	NY Rangers	NHL	46	11	22	33	10	2	1	0	90	12.2	0	34	35.3	18:24	....	....	....	....	....	....	....	....	....
2000-01	NY Rangers	NHL	82	31	36	67	20	5	2	3	230	13.5	9	20	30.0	19:04	....	....	....	....	....	....	....	....	....
2001-02	NY Rangers	NHL	65	17	20	37	14	3	3	1	210	8.1	–20	5	0.0	19:44	....	....	....	....	....	....	....	....	....
	Czech Republic	Olympics	4	0	0	0	0	....	....	....	....	....	....	....	....	....	....	....	....	....	....	....	....	....	....
2002-03	NY Rangers	NHL	63	6	21	27	16	2	0	0	134	4.5	–3	9	44.4	15:42	....	....	....	....	....	....	....	....	....
	Edmonton	NHL	12	4	4	8	14	1	0	0	32	12.5	–3	1	0.0	16:07	4	1	0	1	0	0	0	1	15:05
2003-04	Edmonton	NHL	78	15	35	50	26	6	0	0	188	8.0	18	24	29.2	16:56	....	....	....	....	....	....	....	....	....
2004-05	C. Budejovice	CzRep-2	32	23	35	58	18	....	....	....	....	....	....	....	....	....	16	5	13	18	20	....	....	....	....
2005-06	Edmonton	NHL	64	8	20	28	26	2	0	2	131	6.1	–2	14	28.6	16:34	16	0	2	2	4	0	0	0	13:29
2006-07	St. Louis	NHL	82	10	27	37	48	1	1	1	139	7.2	–6	26	38.5	15:38	....	....	....	....	....	....	....	....	....
2007-08	Florida	NHL	67	8	9	17	16	0	1	1	146	5.5	–1	12	16.7	15:07	....	....	....	....	....	....	....	....	....
2008-09	Florida	NHL	81	15	21	36	42	0	4	3	136	11.0	0	17	35.3	16:26	....	....	....	....	....	....	....	....	....
2009-10	Florida	NHL	76	14	18	32	20	1	3	1	140	10.0	–7	17	17.7	17:26	....	....	....	....	....	....	....	....	....
2010-11	Florida	NHL	53	7	14	21	20	0	1	3	89	7.9	2	10	20.0	16:33	....	....	....	....	....	....	....	....	....
	Atlanta	NHL	13	0	1	1	4	0	0	0	20	0.0	0	9	55.6	14:08	....	....	....	....	....	....	....	....	....
2011-12	Dallas	NHL	73	4	17	21	12	0	1	0	83	4.8	–16	25	40.0	14:17	....	....	....	....	....	....	....	....	....
2012-13	HC Davos	Swiss	7	3	4	7	2	....	....	....	....	....	....	....	....	....	7	1	1	2	2	....	....	....	....
	Anaheim	NHL	9	4	0	4	2	0	0	1	17	23.5	2	2	0.0	13:08	....	....	....	....	....	....	....	....	....
	NHL Totals		1200	223	358	581	408	27	24	22	2411	9.2		339	36.3	16:37	39	2	5	7	4	0	0	1	13:48

Traded to **San Jose** by **Florida** for Mike Vernon and San Jose's 3rd round choice (Sean O'Connor) in 2000 Entry Draft, December 30, 1999. Traded to **NY Rangers** by **San Jose** for Todd Harvey and NY Rangers' 4th round choice (Dimitri Patzold) in 2001 Entry Draft, December 30, 1999. Traded to **Edmonton** by **NY Rangers** with Cory Cross for Anson Carter and Ales Pisa, March 11, 2003. Signed as a free agent by **Ceske Budejovice** (CzRep-2), September 15, 2004. Signed as a free agent by **St. Louis**, September 14, 2006. Signed as a free agent by **Florida**, July 1, 2007. Traded to **Atlanta** by **Florida** with Carolina's 5th round choice (previously acquired, later traded to San Jose – San Jose selected Sean Kuraly) in 2011 Entry Draft for Niclas Bergfors and Patrick Rissmiller, February 28, 2011. • Transferred to **Winnipeg** after **Atlanta** franchise relocated, June 21, 2011. Signed as a free agent by **Dallas**, July 1, 2011. Signed as a free agent by **Davos** (Swiss), January 31, 2013. Signed as a free agent by **Anaheim**, March 24, 2013.

DWYER, Patrick

(DWIGH-uhr, PAT-rihk) **CAR**

Right wing. Shoots right. 5'11", 175 lbs. Born, Spokane, WA, June 22, 1983. Atlanta's 3rd choice, 116th overall, in 2002 Entry Draft.

Season	Club	League	GP	G	A	Pts	PIM	PP	SH	GW	S	%	+/-	TF	F%	Min	GP	G	A	Pts	PIM	PP	SH	GW	Min
2000-01	Great Falls	NWJHL	40	33	57	90	106	....	....	....	....	....	....	....	....	....	12	10	12	22	....	....	....	....	....
2001-02	Western Mich.	CCHA	38	17	17	34	26	....	....	....	....	....	....	....	....	....	....	....	....	....	....	....	....	....	....
2002-03	Western Mich.	CCHA	33	9	10	19	20	....	....	....	....	....	....	....	....	....	....	....	....	....	....	....	....	....	....
2003-04	Western Mich.	CCHA	35	13	13	26	22	....	....	....	....	....	....	....	....	....	....	....	....	....	....	....	....	....	....
2004-05	Western Mich.	CCHA	36	6	16	22	56	....	....	....	....	....	....	....	....	....	....	....	....	....	....	....	....	....	....
2005-06	Chicago Wolves	AHL	73	16	29	45	49	....	....	....	....	....	....	....	....	....	....	....	....	....	....	....	....	....	....
2006-07	Albany River Rats	AHL	79	16	25	41	39	....	....	....	....	....	....	....	....	....	5	0	1	1	5	....	....	....	....
2007-08	Albany River Rats	AHL	59	13	12	25	29	....	....	....	....	....	....	....	....	....	7	0	2	2	0	....	....	....	....
2008-09	Carolina	NHL	13	1	0	1	0	0	0	0	9	11.1	–2	12	41.7	8:34	2	0	1	1	0	0	0	0	4:48
	Albany River Rats	AHL	62	24	16	40	29	....	....	....	....	....	....	....	....	....	....	....	....	....	....	....	....	....	....
2009-10	Carolina	NHL	58	7	5	12	6	0	0	2	80	8.8	–3	224	34.8	12:30	....	....	....	....	....	....	....	....	....
2010-11	Carolina	NHL	80	8	10	18	12	0	1	2	104	7.7	–6	238	33.6	12:35	....	....	....	....	....	....	....	....	....
2011-12	Carolina	NHL	73	5	7	12	23	0	2	0	120	4.2	0	29	51.7	15:22	....	....	....	....	....	....	....	....	....
2012-13	Carolina	NHL	46	8	8	16	12	1	1	0	93	8.6	–7	47	36.2	15:26	....	....	....	....	....	....	....	....	....
	NHL Totals		270	29	30	59	53	1	4	4	406	7.1		550	35.5	13:37	2	0	1	1	0	0	0	0	4:48

CCHA All-Rookie Team (2002) • CCHA Rookie of the Year (2002)

Signed as a free agent by **Carolina**, July 7, 2006.

DZIURZYNSKI, David

(z'yuhr-IHN-skee, DAY-vihd) **OTT**

Center. Shoots left. 6'3", 214 lbs. Born, Lloydminster, Alta., October 6, 1989.

Season	Club	League	GP	G	A	Pts	PIM	PP	SH	GW	S	%	+/-	TF	F%	Min	GP	G	A	Pts	PIM	PP	SH	GW	Min
2007-08	Lloydminster	AJHL	52	8	12	20	82	....	....	....	....	....	....	....	....	....	3	0	0	0	4	....	....	....	....
2008-09	Lloydminster	AJHL	54	12	25	37	185	....	....	....	....	....	....	....	....	....	4	0	1	1	2	....	....	....	....
2009-10	Alberni Valley	BCHL	57	21	53	74	79	....	....	....	....	....	....	....	....	....	13	9	10	19	8	....	....	....	....
2010-11	Binghamton	AHL	75	6	14	20	57	....	....	....	....	....	....	....	....	....	14	0	3	3	4	....	....	....	....
2011-12	Binghamton	AHL	72	11	17	28	92	....	....	....	....	....	....	....	....	....	....	....	....	....	....	....	....	....	....
2012-13	Binghamton	AHL	54	4	16	20	110	....	....	....	....	....	....	....	....	....	3	0	1	1	4	....	....	....	....
	Ottawa	NHL	12	2	0	2	13	0	0	0	20	10.0	–1	4	75.0	12:33	....	....	....	....	....	....	....	....	....
	NHL Totals		12	2	0	2	13	0	0	0	20	10.0		4	75.0	12:33	....	....	....	....	....	....	....	....	....

Signed as a free agent by **Ottawa**, April 6, 2010.

EAGER, Ben

(EE-guhr, BEHN) **EDM**

Left wing. Shoots left. 6'2", 240 lbs. Born, Ottawa, Ont., January 22, 1984. Phoenix's 2nd choice, 23rd overall, in 2002 Entry Draft.

Season	Club	League	GP	G	A	Pts	PIM	PP	SH	GW	S	%	+/-	TF	F%	Min	GP	G	A	Pts	PIM	PP	SH	GW	Min
99-2000	Ott. Jr. Senators	ON-Jr.A	50	8	11	19	119	....	....	....	....	....	....	....	....	....	....	....	....	....	....	....	....	....	....
2000-01	Oshawa Generals	OHL	61	4	6	10	120	....	....	....	....	....	....	....	....	....	....	....	....	....	....	....	....	....	....
2001-02	Oshawa Generals	OHL	63	14	23	37	255	....	....	....	....	....	....	....	....	....	5	0	1	1	13	....	....	....	....
2002-03	Oshawa Generals	OHL	58	16	24	40	216	....	....	....	....	....	....	....	....	....	8	0	4	4	8	....	....	....	....
2003-04	Oshawa Generals	OHL	61	25	27	52	204	....	....	....	....	....	....	....	....	....	7	2	3	5	31	....	....	....	....
	Philadelphia	AHL	5	0	0	0	0	....	....	....	....	....	....	....	....	....	3	0	1	1	8	....	....	....	....
2004-05	Philadelphia	AHL	66	7	10	17	232	....	....	....	....	....	....	....	....	....	16	1	1	2	71	....	....	....	....
2005-06	Philadelphia	NHL	25	3	5	8	18	0	0	0	21	14.3	0	0	0.0	7:24	2	0	0	0	26	0	0	0	7:06
	Philadelphia	AHL	49	6	12	18	256	....	....	....	....	....	....	....	....	....	....	....	....	....	....	....	....	....	....
2006-07	Philadelphia	NHL	63	6	5	11	*233	0	0	0	48	12.5	–13	1	100.0	8:14	....	....	....	....	....	....	....	....	....
	Philadelphia	AHL	3	0	0	0	21	....	....	....	....	....	....	....	....	....	....	....	....	....	....	....	....	....	....
2007-08	Philadelphia	NHL	23	0	0	0	62	0	0	0	11	0.0	–8	5	20.0	5:29	....	....	....	....	....	....	....	....	....
	Chicago	NHL	9	0	2	2	27	0	0	0	5	0.0	–1	0	0.0	6:37	....	....	....	....	....	....	....	....	....
2008-09	Chicago	NHL	75	11	4	15	161	0	0	0	80	13.8	1	0	0.0	8:31	17	1	1	2	*61	0	0	1	8:32
2009-10 ♦	Chicago	NHL	60	7	9	16	120	0	0	2	68	10.3	9	1	0.0	8:20	18	1	2	3	20	0	0	1	6:02
2010-11	Atlanta	NHL	34	3	7	10	77	0	0	1	41	7.3	4	2	0.0	12:15	....	....	....	....	....	....	....	....	....
	San Jose	NHL	34	4	3	7	43	0	0	0	43	9.3	0	0	0.0	9:02	10	1	0	1	41	0	0	0	4:53
2011-12	Edmonton	NHL	63	8	5	13	107	0	0	3	69	11.6	–1	2	0.0	8:32	....	....	....	....	....	....	....	....	....
2012-13	Oklahoma City	AHL	9	0	2	2	13	....	....	....	....	....	....	....	....	....	13	1	4	5	64	....	....	....	....
	Edmonton	NHL	14	1	1	2	25	0	0	0	14	7.1	–4	0	0.0	9:40	....	....	....	....	....	....	....	....	....
	NHL Totals		400	43	41	84	873	0	0	6	400	10.8		11	18.2	8:34	47	3	3	6	148	0	0	2	6:44

Traded to **Philadelphia** by **Phoenix** with Sean Burke and Branko Radivojevic for Mike Comrie, February 9, 2004. Traded to **Chicago** by **Philadelphia** for Jim Vandermeer, December 18, 2007. Traded to **Atlanta** by **Chicago** with Brent Sopel, Dustin Byfuglien and Akim Aliu for Marty Reasoner, Joey Crabb, Jeremy Morin and New Jersey's 1st (previously acquired, Chicago selected Kevin Hayes) and 2nd (previously acquired, Chicago selected Justin Holl) round choices in 2010 Entry Draft, June 24, 2010. Traded to **San Jose** by **Atlanta** for San Jose's 5th round choice (Austen Brassard) in 2011 Entry Draft, January 18, 2011. Signed as a free agent by **Edmonton**, July 1, 2011. • Missed majority of 2012-13 due to head injury at Vancouver, January 20, 2013.

EAKIN, Cody

(EE-kihn, KOH-dee) **DAL**

Center. Shoots left. 6', 190 lbs. Born, Winnipeg, Man., May 24, 1991. Washington's 3rd choice, 85th overall, in 2009 Entry Draft.

Season	Club	League	GP	G	A	Pts	PIM	PP	SH	GW	S	%	+/-	TF	F%	Min	GP	G	A	Pts	PIM	PP	SH	GW	Min
2006-07	Winnipeg Wild	MMHL	38	29	35	64	62	....	....	....	....	....	....	....	....	....	7	5	4	9	10	....	....	....	....
	Swift Current	WHL	3	0	0	0	0	....	....	....	....	....	....	....	....	....	....	....	....	....	....	....	....	....	....
2007-08	Swift Current	WHL	55	11	6	17	52	....	....	....	....	....	....	....	....	....	12	3	4	7	6	....	....	....	....
2008-09	Swift Current	WHL	54	24	24	48	42	....	....	....	....	....	....	....	....	....	7	3	0	3	10	....	....	....	....
2009-10	Swift Current	WHL	70	47	44	91	71	....	....	....	....	....	....	....	....	....	4	1	1	2	2	....	....	....	....
	Hershey Bears	AHL	4	2	0	2	2	....	....	....	....	....	....	....	....	....	5	0	0	0	2	....	....	....	....
2010-11	Swift Current	WHL	30	18	21	39	24	....	....	....	....	....	....	....	....	....	....	....	....	....	....	....	....	....	....
	Kootenay Ice	WHL	26	18	26	44	19	....	....	....	....	....	....	....	....	....	19	11	16	27	14	....	....	....	....
2011-12	Washington	NHL	30	4	4	8	4	0	0	0	31	12.9	2	40	52.5	9:17	....	....	....	....	....	....	....	....	....
	Hershey Bears	AHL	43	13	14	27	10	....	....	....	....	....	....	....	....	....	5	0	1	1	0	....	....	....	....
2012-13	Texas Stars	AHL	35	12	12	24	14	....	....	....	....	....	....	....	....	....	....	....	....	....	....	....	....	....	....
	Dallas	NHL	48	7	17	24	31	3	0	1	67	10.4	1	626	48.6	15:05	....	....	....	....	....	....	....	....	....
	NHL Totals		78	11	21	32	35	3	0	1	98	11.2		666	48.8	12:51	....	....	....	....	....	....	....	....	....

WHL East Second All-Star Team (2010, 2011)

Traded to **Dallas** by **Washington** with Boston's 2nd round choice (previously acquired, Dallas selected Mike Winther) in 2012 Entry Draft for Mike Ribeiro. June 22, 2012.

EATON, Mark

(EE-tohn, MAHRK)

Defense. Shoots left. 6'1", 215 lbs. Born, Wilmington, DE, May 6, 1977.

Season	Club	League	GP	G	A	Pts	PIM	PP	SH	GW	S	%	+/-	TF	F%	Min	GP	G	A	Pts	PIM	PP	SH	GW	Min
			Regular Season														Playoffs								
1995-96	Waterloo	USHL	50	4	21	25	....	....	....	....	....	....	....	....	....	....	....	....	....	....	....	....	....	....	....
1996-97	Waterloo	USHL	50	6	32	38	62	....	....	....	....	....	....	....	....	....	....	....	....	....	....	....	....	....	....
1997-98	U. of Notre Dame	CCHA	41	12	17	29	32	....	....	....	....	....	....	....	....	....	....	....	....	....	....	....	....	....	....
1998-99	Philadelphia	AHL	74	9	27	36	38	....	....	....	....	....	....	....	....	....	16	4	8	12	0	....	....	....	....
99-2000	**Philadelphia**	**NHL**	**27**	**1**	**1**	**2**	**8**	**0**	**0**	**1**	**25**	**4.0**	**1**	**0**	**0.0**	**18:17**	**7**	**0**	**0**	**0**	**0**	**0**	**0**	**0**	**13:36**
	Philadelphia	AHL	47	9	17	26	6	....	....	....	....	....	....	....	....	....	....	....	....	....	....	....	....	....	....
2000-01	**Nashville**	**NHL**	**34**	**3**	**8**	**11**	**14**	**1**	**0**	**1**	**32**	**9.4**	**7**	**0**	**0.0**	**17:13**	....	....	....	....	....	....	....	....	....
	Milwaukee	IHL	34	3	12	15	27	....	....	....	....	....	....	....	....	....	....	....	....	....	....	....	....	....	....
2001-02	**Nashville**	**NHL**	**58**	**3**	**5**	**8**	**24**	**0**	**0**	**0**	**52**	**5.8**	**–12**	**0**	**0.0**	**17:12**	....	....	....	....	....	....	....	....	....
2002-03	**Nashville**	**NHL**	**50**	**2**	**7**	**9**	**22**	**0**	**0**	**0**	**52**	**3.8**	**1**	**0**	**0.0**	**15:45**	....	....	....	....	....	....	....	....	....
	Milwaukee	AHL	3	1	0	1	2	....	....	....	....	....	....	....	....	....	....	....	....	....	....	....	....	....	....
2003-04	**Nashville**	**NHL**	**75**	**4**	**9**	**13**	**26**	**0**	**0**	**1**	**82**	**4.9**	**16**	**0**	**0.0**	**20:56**	**6**	**0**	**0**	**0**	**2**	**0**	**0**	**0**	**19:51**
2004-05	Grand Rapids	AHL	29	3	3	6	21	....	....	....	....	....	....	....	....	....	....	....	....	....	....	....	....	....	....
2005-06	**Nashville**	**NHL**	**69**	**3**	**1**	**4**	**44**	**0**	**0**	**0**	**28**	**10.7**	**–2**	**0**	**0.0**	**19:43**	**5**	**0**	**0**	**0**	**8**	**0**	**0**	**0**	**17:49**
2006-07	**Pittsburgh**	**NHL**	**35**	**0**	**3**	**3**	**16**	**0**	**0**	**0**	**22**	**0.0**	**–6**	**0**	**0.0**	**19:12**	**5**	**0**	**0**	**0**	**0**	**0**	**0**	**0**	**18:31**
2007-08	**Pittsburgh**	**NHL**	**36**	**0**	**3**	**3**	**4**	**0**	**0**	**0**	**28**	**0.0**	**6**	**0**	**0.0**	**19:40**	....	....	....	....	....	....	....	....	....
2008-09 ◆	**Pittsburgh**	**NHL**	**68**	**4**	**5**	**9**	**36**	**1**	**0**	**0**	**34**	**11.8**	**3**	**1**	**100.0**	**17:46**	**24**	**4**	**3**	**7**	**10**	**1**	**0**	**0**	**18:07**
2009-10	**Pittsburgh**	**NHL**	**79**	**3**	**13**	**16**	**26**	**0**	**0**	**1**	**65**	**4.6**	**5**	**0**	**0.0**	**19:45**	**13**	**0**	**3**	**3**	**4**	**0**	**0**	**0**	**20:43**
2010-11	**NY Islanders**	**NHL**	**34**	**0**	**3**	**3**	**8**	**0**	**0**	**0**	**29**	**0.0**	**–2**	**0**	**0.0**	**20:22**	....	....	....	....	....	....	....	....	....
2011-12	**NY Islanders**	**NHL**	**62**	**1**	**3**	**4**	**10**	**0**	**0**	**1**	**44**	**2.3**	**–17**	**0**	**0.0**	**16:03**	....	....	....	....	....	....	....	....	....
2012-13	Wilkes-Barre	AHL	6	0	1	1	4	....	....	....	....	....	....	....	....	....	....	....	....	....	....	....	....	....	....
	Pittsburgh	**NHL**	**23**	**0**	**0**	**0**	**4**	**0**	**0**	**0**	**8**	**0.0**	**9**	**0**	**0.0**	**17:59**	**8**	**0**	**3**	**3**	**0**	**0**	**0**	**0**	**17:16**
	NHL Totals		**650**	**24**	**61**	**85**	**242**	**2**	**0**	**5**	**501**	**4.8**		**1**	**100.0**	**18:32**	**68**	**4**	**9**	**13**	**24**	**1**	**0**	**0**	**18:13**

USHL Second All-Star Team (1997) • Curt Hammer Award (USHL – Most Gentlemanly Player) (1997) • CCHA Rookie of the Year (1998)

Signed as a free agent by **Philadelphia**, August 4, 1998. Traded to **Nashville** by **Philadelphia** for Detroit's 3rd round choice (previously acquired, Philadelphia selected Patrick Sharp) in 2001 Entry Draft, September 29, 2000. Signed as a free agent by **Grand Rapids** (AHL), February 16, 2005. Signed as a free agent by **Pittsburgh**, July 3, 2006. Signed as a free agent by **NY Islanders**, July 2, 2010. • Missed majority of 2010-11 due to hip injury at Calgary, January 3, 2011. Signed as a free agent by **Wilkes-Barre** (AHL), January 23, 2013. Signed as a free agent by **Pittsburgh**, February 25, 2013.

EAVES, Patrick

(EEVZ, PAT-rihk) **DET**

Right wing. Shoots right. 6', 187 lbs. Born, Calgary, Alta., May 1, 1984. Ottawa's 1st choice, 29th overall, in 2003 Entry Draft.

Season	Club	League	GP	G	A	Pts	PIM	PP	SH	GW	S	%	+/-	TF	F%	Min	GP	G	A	Pts	PIM	PP	SH	GW	Min
99-2000	Shat.-St. Mary's	High-MN	50	23	24	47	....	....	....	....	....	....	....	....	....	....	....	....	....	....	....	....	....	....	....
2000-01	USNTDP	U-17	13	7	8	15	3	....	....	....	....	....	....	....	....	....	....	....	....	....	....	....	....	....	....
	USNTDP	NAHL	34	12	11	23	75	....	....	....	....	....	....	....	....	....	....	....	....	....	....	....	....	....	....
2001-02	USNTDP	U-18	32	19	21	40	87	....	....	....	....	....	....	....	....	....	....	....	....	....	....	....	....	....	....
	USNTDP	USHL	9	1	4	5	18	....	....	....	....	....	....	....	....	....	....	....	....	....	....	....	....	....	....
	USNTDP	NAHL	8	5	3	8	37	....	....	....	....	....	....	....	....	....	....	....	....	....	....	....	....	....	....
2002-03	Boston College	H-East	14	10	8	18	61	....	....	....	....	....	....	....	....	....	....	....	....	....	....	....	....	....	....
2003-04	Boston College	H-East	34	18	23	41	66	....	....	....	....	....	....	....	....	....	....	....	....	....	....	....	....	....	....
2004-05	Boston College	H-East	36	19	29	48	36	....	....	....	....	....	....	....	....	....	....	....	....	....	....	....	....	....	....
2005-06	**Ottawa**	**NHL**	**58**	**20**	**9**	**29**	**22**	**5**	**1**	**4**	**100**	**20.0**	**7**	**14**	**21.4**	**12:29**	**10**	**1**	**0**	**1**	**10**	**0**	**0**	**0**	**11:40**
	Binghamton	AHL	18	5	8	13	10	....	....	....	....	....	....	....	....	....	....	....	....	....	....	....	....	....	....
2006-07	**Ottawa**	**NHL**	**73**	**14**	**18**	**32**	**36**	**3**	**1**	**1**	**130**	**10.8**	**1**	**9**	**11.1**	**12:13**	**7**	**0**	**2**	**2**	**2**	**0**	**0**	**0**	**7:23**
2007-08	**Ottawa**	**NHL**	**26**	**4**	**6**	**10**	**6**	**1**	**0**	**1**	**59**	**6.8**	**0**	**1**	**100.0**	**12:44**	....	....	....	....	....	....	....	....	....
	Carolina	**NHL**	**11**	**1**	**4**	**5**	**4**	**1**	**0**	**0**	**22**	**4.5**	**–2**	**2**	**0.0**	**12:51**	....	....	....	....	....	....	....	....	....
2008-09	**Carolina**	**NHL**	**74**	**6**	**8**	**14**	**31**	**1**	**1**	**1**	**115**	**5.2**	**7**	**12**	**41.7**	**11:15**	**18**	**1**	**2**	**3**	**13**	**0**	**0**	**0**	**9:29**
2009-10	**Detroit**	**NHL**	**65**	**12**	**10**	**22**	**26**	**0**	**1**	**1**	**120**	**10.0**	**0**	**14**	**28.6**	**13:26**	**8**	**0**	**0**	**0**	**2**	**0**	**0**	**0**	**11:58**
2010-11	**Detroit**	**NHL**	**63**	**13**	**7**	**20**	**14**	**2**	**1**	**1**	**108**	**12.0**	**–2**	**10**	**30.0**	**12:42**	**11**	**3**	**1**	**4**	**6**	**0**	**0**	**0**	**11:24**
2011-12	**Detroit**	**NHL**	**10**	**0**	**1**	**1**	**2**	**0**	**0**	**0**	**24**	**0.0**	**0**	**5**	**40.0**	**11:03**	....	....	....	....	....	....	....	....	....
2012-13	**Detroit**	**NHL**	**34**	**2**	**6**	**8**	**4**	**0**	**0**	**1**	**42**	**4.8**	**–1**	**11**	**63.6**	**10:35**	**13**	**1**	**2**	**3**	**4**	**0**	**0**	**0**	**10:00**
	NHL Totals		**414**	**72**	**69**	**141**	**145**	**13**	**5**	**10**	**720**	**10.0**		**78**	**33.3**	**12:14**	**67**	**6**	**7**	**13**	**37**	**0**	**0**	**0**	**10:18**

Hockey East Second All-Star Team (2004) • NCAA East Second All-American Team (2004) • Hockey East First All-Star Team (2005) • NCAA East First All-American Team (2005)

• Missed majority of 2002-03 due to neck injury vs. University of Maine (Hockey East), December 7, 2002. Traded to **Carolina** by **Ottawa** with Joe Corvo for Cory Stillman and Mike Commodore, February 11, 2008. • Missed majority of 2007-08 due to shoulder injury at Buffalo, November 21, 2007. Traded to **Boston** by **Carolina** with Carolina's 4th round choice (Craig Cunningham) in 2010 Entry Draft for Aaron Ward, July 24, 2009. Signed as a free agent by **Detroit**, August 4, 2009. • Missed majority of 2011-12 due to head injury vs. Nashville, November 26, 2012.

EBBETT, Andrew

(EH-beht, AN-droo) **PIT**

Center. Shoots left. 5'9", 174 lbs. Born, Calgary, Alta., January 2, 1983.

Season	Club	League	GP	G	A	Pts	PIM	PP	SH	GW	S	%	+/-	TF	F%	Min	GP	G	A	Pts	PIM	PP	SH	GW	Min
2002-03	U. of Michigan	CCHA	43	9	18	27	22	....	....	....	....	....	....	....	....	....	....	....	....	....	....	....	....	....	....
2003-04	U. of Michigan	CCHA	43	9	28	37	56	....	....	....	....	....	....	....	....	....	....	....	....	....	....	....	....	....	....
2004-05	U. of Michigan	CCHA	40	6	31	37	28	....	....	....	....	....	....	....	....	....	....	....	....	....	....	....	....	....	....
2005-06	U. of Michigan	CCHA	41	14	28	42	25	....	....	....	....	....	....	....	....	....	....	....	....	....	....	....	....	....	....
2006-07	Binghamton	AHL	71	26	39	65	44	....	....	....	....	....	....	....	....	....	....	....	....	....	....	....	....	....	....
2007-08	**Anaheim**	**NHL**	**3**	**0**	**0**	**0**	**2**	**0**	**0**	**0**	**3**	**0.0**	**3**	**29**	**58.6**	**13:18**	....	....	....	....	....	....	....	....	....
	Portland Pirates	AHL	74	18	54	72	66	....	....	....	....	....	....	....	....	....	18	6	11	17	4	....	....	....	....
2008-09	**Anaheim**	**NHL**	**48**	**8**	**24**	**32**	**24**	**6**	**0**	**0**	**100**	**8.0**	**8**	**455**	**48.6**	**13:52**	**13**	**1**	**2**	**3**	**8**	**0**	**0**	**0**	**13:11**
	Iowa Chops	AHL	28	10	19	29	6	....	....	....	....	....	....	....	....	....	....	....	....	....	....	....	....	....	....
2009-10	**Anaheim**	**NHL**	**2**	**0**	**0**	**0**	**0**	**0**	**0**	**0**	**1**	**0.0**	**–1**	**17**	**35.3**	**12:55**	....	....	....	....	....	....	....	....	....
	Chicago	**NHL**	**10**	**1**	**0**	**1**	**2**	**0**	**0**	**0**	**14**	**7.1**	**1**	**72**	**50.0**	**10:43**	....	....	....	....	....	....	....	....	....
	Minnesota	**NHL**	**49**	**8**	**6**	**14**	**6**	**2**	**0**	**2**	**57**	**14.0**	**–8**	**464**	**50.0**	**13:06**	....	....	....	....	....	....	....	....	....
2010-11	**Phoenix**	**NHL**	**33**	**2**	**3**	**5**	**4**	**0**	**1**	**1**	**23**	**8.7**	**–1**	**229**	**45.4**	**10:01**	**3**	**0**	**0**	**0**	**0**	**0**	**0**	**0**	**7:58**
	San Antonio	AHL	37	11	27	38	12	....	....	....	....	....	....	....	....	....	....	....	....	....	....	....	....	....	....
2011-12	**Vancouver**	**NHL**	**18**	**5**	**1**	**6**	**6**	**1**	**0**	**2**	**27**	**18.5**	**2**	**28**	**53.6**	**9:35**	**1**	**0**	**0**	**0**	**0**	**0**	**0**	**0**	**10:21**
2012-13	Chicago Wolves	AHL	37	11	21	32	10	....	....	....	....	....	....	....	....	....	....	....	....	....	....	....	....	....	....
	Vancouver	**NHL**	**28**	**1**	**5**	**6**	**4**	**0**	**0**	**0**	**23**	**4.3**	**–1**	**267**	**39.7**	**12:19**	**2**	**0**	**0**	**0**	**0**	**0**	**0**	**0**	**4:30**
	NHL Totals		**191**	**25**	**39**	**64**	**48**	**9**	**1**	**5**	**248**	**10.1**		**1561**	**47.2**	**12:11**	**19**	**1**	**2**	**3**	**8**	**0**	**0**	**0**	**11:18**

Signed as a free agent by **Anaheim**, May 16, 2007. Claimed on waivers by **Chicago** from **Anaheim**, October 17, 2009. Claimed on waivers by **Minnesota** from **Chicago**, November 21, 2009. Signed as a free agent by **Phoenix**, July 2, 2010. Signed as a free agent by **Vancouver**, July 5, 2011. • Missed majority of 2011-12 due to foot (November 11, 2011 at Anaheim) and collarbone (January 9, 2012 at Florida) injuries. Signed as a free agent by **Pittsburgh**, July 6, 2013.

EBERLE, Jordan

(EH-buhr-lee, JOHR-dahn) **EDM**

Center. Shoots right. 5'11", 184 lbs. Born, Regina, Sask., May 15, 1990. Edmonton's 1st choice, 22nd overall, in 2008 Entry Draft.

Season	Club	League	GP	G	A	Pts	PIM	PP	SH	GW	S	%	+/-	TF	F%	Min	GP	G	A	Pts	PIM	PP	SH	GW	Min
2005-06	Calgary Buffaloes	AMHL	31	14	20	34	6	....	....	....	....	....	....	....	....	....	11	7	1	8	8	....	....	....	....
2006-07	Regina Pats	WHL	66	28	27	55	32	....	....	....	....	....	....	....	....	....	6	2	5	7	2	....	....	....	....
2007-08	Regina Pats	WHL	70	42	33	75	20	....	....	....	....	....	....	....	....	....	5	2	4	6	7	....	....	....	....
2008-09	Regina Pats	WHL	61	35	39	74	20	....	....	....	....	....	....	....	....	....	....	....	....	....	....	....	....	....	....
	Springfield	AHL	9	3	6	9	4	....	....	....	....	....	....	....	....	....	....	....	....	....	....	....	....	....	....
2009-10	Regina Pats	WHL	57	50	56	106	32	....	....	....	....	....	....	....	....	....	....	....	....	....	....	....	....	....	....
	Springfield	AHL	11	6	8	14	0	....	....	....	....	....	....	....	....	....	....	....	....	....	....	....	....	....	....
2010-11	**Edmonton**	**NHL**	**69**	**18**	**25**	**43**	**22**	**4**	**2**	**5**	**158**	**11.4**	**–12**	**26**	**42.3**	**17:41**	....	....	....	....	....	....	....	....	....
2011-12	**Edmonton**	**NHL**	**78**	**34**	**42**	**76**	**10**	**10**	**0**	**4**	**180**	**18.9**	**4**	**27**	**44.4**	**17:36**	....	....	....	....	....	....	....	....	....
2012-13	Oklahoma City	AHL	34	25	26	51	10	....	....	....	....	....	....	....	....	....	....	....	....	....	....	....	....	....	....
	Edmonton	**NHL**	**48**	**16**	**21**	**37**	**16**	**3**	**0**	**3**	**133**	**12.0**	**–4**	**19**	**42.1**	**19:00**	....	....	....	....	....	....	....	....	....
	NHL Totals		**195**	**68**	**88**	**156**	**48**	**17**	**2**	**12**	**471**	**14.4**		**72**	**43.1**	**17:58**	....	....	....	....	....	....	....	....	....

WHL East First All-Star Team (2008, 2010) • WHL Player of the Year (2010) • Canadian Major Junior First All-Star Team (2010) • Canadian Major Junior Player of the Year (2010)

Played in NHL All-Star Game (2012)

ECKFORD, Tyler
(EHK-fuhrd, TIGH-luhr) **OTT**

Defense. Shoots left. 6'1", 205 lbs. Born, Vancouver, B.C., September 8, 1985. New Jersey's 5th choice, 217th overall, in 2004 Entry Draft.

			Regular Season														Playoffs								
Season	Club	League	GP	G	A	Pts	PIM	PP	SH	GW	S	%	+/-	TF	F%	Min	GP	G	A	Pts	PIM	PP	SH	GW	Min
2003-04	Surrey Eagles	BCHL	58	7	30	37	101										13	2	8	10	34				
2004-05	Surrey Eagles	BCHL	60	22	43	65	93										25	4	15	19	46				
2005-06	Alaska	CCHA	38	3	15	18	43																		
2006-07	Alaska	CCHA	39	5	17	22	54																		
2007-08	Alaska	CCHA	35	8	23	31	55																		
2008-09	Lowell Devils	AHL	72	2	25	27	59																		
2009-10	**New Jersey**	**NHL**	**3**	**0**	**1**	**1**	**4**	**0**	**0**	**0**	**1**	**0.0**	**0**	**0**	**0.0**	**7:23**									
	Lowell Devils	AHL	61	8	23	31	26										5	1	0	1	2				
2010-11	**New Jersey**	**NHL**	**4**	**0**	**0**	**0**	**0**	**0**	**0**	**0**	**1**	**0.0**	**–1**	**0**	**0.0**	**8:43**									
	Albany Devils	AHL	37	2	10	12	12																		
2011-12	Portland Pirates	AHL	75	10	15	25	37																		
2012-13	Binghamton	AHL	59	7	6	13	49										2	0	0	0	0				
	NHL Totals		**7**	**0**	**1**	**1**	**4**	**0**	**0**	**0**	**2**	**0.0**		**0**	**0.0**	**8:09**									

CCHA All-Rookie Team (2006) • CCHA First All-Star Team (2008) • NCAA West First All-American Team (2008)

Signed as a free agent by **Phoenix**, July 4, 2011. Signed as a free agent by **Ottawa**, July 10, 2012.

EDLER, Alexander
(EHD-luhr, al-EHX-AN-duhr) **VAN**

Defense. Shoots left. 6'4", 220 lbs. Born, Ostersund, Sweden, April 21, 1986. Vancouver's 2nd choice, 91st overall, in 2004 Entry Draft.

Season	Club	League	GP	G	A	Pts	PIM	PP	SH	GW	S	%	+/-	TF	F%	Min	GP	G	A	Pts	PIM	PP	SH	GW	Min
2001-02	Jamtland	Exhib.	8	0	1	1	2																		
2002-03	Jamtland	Exhib.	8	2	1	3	0																		
2003-04	Jamtland Jr.	Swe-Jr.	6	0	3	3	6																		
	Jamtland	Sweden-3	24	3	6	9	20																		
2004-05	MODO Jr.	Swe-Jr.	33	8	15	23	40										5	1	0	1	6				
2005-06	Kelowna Rockets	WHL	62	13	40	53	44										12	3	5	8	12				
2006-07	**Vancouver**	**NHL**	**22**	**1**	**2**	**3**	**6**	**0**	**0**	**0**	**10**	**10.0**	**3**	**0**	**0.0**	**11:27**	**3**	**0**	**0**	**0**	**2**	**0**	**0**	**0**	**11:51**
	Manitoba Moose	AHL	49	5	21	26	28										8	0	0	0	2				
2007-08	**Vancouver**	**NHL**	**75**	**8**	**12**	**20**	**42**	**4**	**0**	**0**	**124**	**6.5**	**6**	**1**	**100.0**	**21:20**									
	Manitoba Moose	AHL	2	0	1	1	0																		
2008-09	**Vancouver**	**NHL**	**80**	**10**	**27**	**37**	**54**	**5**	**0**	**1**	**145**	**6.9**	**11**	**1**	**100.0**	**21:08**	**10**	**1**	**7**	**8**	**6**	**1**	**0**	**0**	**22:09**
2009-10	**Vancouver**	**NHL**	**76**	**5**	**37**	**42**	**40**	**2**	**0**	**0**	**161**	**3.1**	**0**	**2**	**0.0**	**22:39**	**12**	**2**	**4**	**6**	**10**	**1**	**0**	**0**	**23:07**
2010-11	**Vancouver**	**NHL**	**51**	**8**	**25**	**33**	**24**	**5**	**0**	**1**	**121**	**6.6**	**13**	**2**	**0.0**	**24:17**	**25**	**2**	**9**	**11**	**8**	**0**	**0**	**0**	**24:46**
2011-12	**Vancouver**	**NHL**	**82**	**11**	**38**	**49**	**34**	**5**	**1**	**0**	**228**	**4.8**	**0**	**3**	**0.0**	**23:52**	**5**	**2**	**0**	**2**	**8**	**1**	**0**	**0**	**24:17**
2012-13	**Vancouver**	**NHL**	**45**	**8**	**14**	**22**	**37**	**5**	**0**	**0**	**113**	**7.1**	**–5**	**1**	**100.0**	**23:51**	**4**	**1**	**0**	**1**	**2**	**0**	**0**	**0**	**26:57**
	NHL Totals		**431**	**51**	**155**	**206**	**237**	**26**	**1**	**2**	**902**	**5.7**		**10**	**30.0**	**22:07**	**59**	**8**	**20**	**28**	**36**	**3**	**0**	**0**	**23:26**

Played in NHL All-Star Game (2012)

EHRHOFF, Christian
(AIR-hawf, KRIHS-tyehn) **BUF**

Defense. Shoots left. 6'2", 203 lbs. Born, Moers, West Germany, July 6, 1982. San Jose's 2nd choice, 106th overall, in 2001 Entry Draft.

Season	Club	League	GP	G	A	Pts	PIM	PP	SH	GW	S	%	+/-	TF	F%	Min	GP	G	A	Pts	PIM	PP	SH	GW	Min
1998-99	Krefelder EV Jr.	Ger-Jr.	22	10	14	24	46																		
99-2000	EV Duisburg	German-3	41	3	12	15	50																		
	Krefeld Pinguine	Germany	9	1	0	1	6										3	0	0	0	0				
2000-01	EV Duisburg	German-3	6	1	2	3	12																		
	Krefeld Pinguine	Germany	58	3	11	14	73																		
2001-02	Krefeld Pinguine	Germany	46	7	17	24	81										3	0	0	0	2				
	Germany	Olympics	7	0	0	0	8																		
2002-03	Krefeld Pinguine	Germany	48	10	17	27	54										14	3	6	9	24				
2003-04	**San Jose**	**NHL**	**41**	**1**	**11**	**12**	**14**	**0**	**0**	**1**	**58**	**1.7**	**4**	**0**	**0.0**	**15:23**									
	Cleveland Barons	AHL	27	4	10	14	43										9	2	6	8	11				
2004-05	Cleveland Barons	AHL	79	12	23	35	103																		
2005-06	**San Jose**	**NHL**	**64**	**5**	**18**	**23**	**32**	**2**	**0**	**2**	**124**	**4.0**	**10**	**0**	**0.0**	**17:48**	**11**	**2**	**6**	**8**	**18**	**1**	**0**	**1**	**19:47**
	Germany	Olympics	5	1	1	2	4																		
2006-07	**San Jose**	**NHL**	**82**	**10**	**23**	**33**	**63**	**6**	**0**	**2**	**164**	**6.1**	**8**	**1**	**0.0**	**18:34**	**11**	**0**	**2**	**2**	**6**	**0**	**0**	**0**	**17:47**
2007-08	**San Jose**	**NHL**	**77**	**1**	**21**	**22**	**72**	**1**	**0**	**1**	**97**	**1.0**	**9**	**0**	**0.0**	**21:44**	**10**	**0**	**5**	**5**	**14**	**0**	**0**	**0**	**23:04**
2008-09	**San Jose**	**NHL**	**77**	**8**	**34**	**42**	**63**	**5**	**0**	**2**	**165**	**4.8**	**–12**	**0**	**0.0**	**21:14**	**6**	**0**	**0**	**0**	**2**	**0**	**0**	**0**	**24:47**
2009-10	**Vancouver**	**NHL**	**80**	**14**	**30**	**44**	**42**	**6**	**0**	**3**	**181**	**7.7**	**36**	**0**	**0.0**	**22:47**	**12**	**3**	**4**	**7**	**8**	**1**	**0**	**0**	**24:09**
	Germany	Olympics	4	0	0	0	4																		
2010-11	**Vancouver**	**NHL**	**79**	**14**	**36**	**50**	**52**	**6**	**0**	**3**	**209**	**6.7**	**19**	**0**	**0.0**	**23:59**	**23**	**2**	**10**	**12**	**16**	**1**	**0**	**0**	**22:26**
2011-12	**Buffalo**	**NHL**	**66**	**5**	**27**	**32**	**47**	**1**	**0**	**3**	**136**	**3.7**	**–2**	**0**	**0.0**	**23:03**									
2012-13	Krefeld Pinguine	Germany	32	8	18	26	52																		
	Buffalo	**NHL**	**47**	**5**	**17**	**22**	**34**	**1**	**0**	**2**	**102**	**4.9**	**6**	**0**	**0.0**	**25:11**									
	NHL Totals		**613**	**63**	**217**	**280**	**419**	**28**	**0**	**19**	**1236**	**5.1**		**1**	**0.0**	**21:15**	**73**	**7**	**27**	**34**	**64**	**3**	**0**	**1**	**21:54**

Traded to **Vancouver** by **San Jose** with Brad Lukowich for Patrick White and Daniel Rahimi, August 28, 2009. Traded to **NY Islanders** by **Vancouver** for NY Islanders' 4th round choice (later traded to Columbus – Columbus selected Josh Anderson) in 2012 Entry Draft, June 28, 2011. Traded to **Buffalo** by **NY Islanders** for Buffalo's 4th round choice (Loic Leduc) in 2012 Entry Draft, June 29, 2011. Signed as a free agent by **Krefeld** (Germany), September 17, 2012.

EKHOLM, Mattias
(EHK-hohlm, ma-TEE-uhs) **NSH**

Defense. Shoots left. 6'4", 202 lbs. Born, Borlange, Sweden, May 24, 1990. Nashville's 7th choice, 102nd overall, in 2009 Entry Draft.

Season	Club	League	GP	G	A	Pts	PIM	PP	SH	GW	S	%	+/-	TF	F%	Min	GP	G	A	Pts	PIM	PP	SH	GW	Min
2006-07	Mora IK U18	Swe-U18	5	2	2	4	6																		
	Mora IK Jr.	Swe-Jr.	36	0	4	4	28										2	0	0	0	0				
2007-08	Mora IK U18	Swe-U18	9	4	5	9	12																		
	Mora IK Jr.	Swe-Jr.	37	5	7	12	54																		
	Mora IK	Sweden	1	0	0	0	0																		
	Mora IK	Sweden-Q	6	0	0	0	2																		
2008-09	Mora IK Jr.	Swe-Jr.	21	3	5	8	32																		
	Mora IK	Sweden-2	38	2	11	13	12										3	0	0	0	4				
2009-10	Mora IK	Sweden-2	41	1	21	22	54										2	0	0	0	6				
2010-11	Brynas IF Gavle	Sweden	55	10	23	33	38										5	0	4	4	10				
2011-12	**Nashville**	**NHL**	**2**	**0**	**0**	**0**	**0**	**0**	**0**	**0**	**1**	**0.0**	**–1**	**0**	**0.0**	**12:25**									
	Brynas IF Gavle	Sweden	41	9	8	17	55										17	1	8	9	12				
2012-13	Milwaukee	AHL	59	10	22	32	30										4	0	1	1	0				
	Nashville	**NHL**	**1**	**0**	**0**	**0**	**0**	**0**	**0**	**0**	**0**	**0.0**	**–1**	**0**	**0.0**	**16:05**									
	NHL Totals		**3**	**0**	**0**	**0**	**0**	**0**	**0**	**0**	**1**	**0.0**		**0**	**0.0**	**13:38**									

EKMAN-LARSSON, Oliver
(EHK-man-LAHR-suhn, AW-lih-vuhr) **PHX**

Defense. Shoots left. 6'2", 190 lbs. Born, Karlskrona, Sweden, July 17, 1991. Phoenix's 1st choice, 6th overall, in 2009 Entry Draft.

Season	Club	League	GP	G	A	Pts	PIM	PP	SH	GW	S	%	+/-	TF	F%	Min	GP	G	A	Pts	PIM	PP	SH	GW	Min
2005-06	Tingsryds AIF Jr.	Swe-Jr.	1	0	0	0	2																		
2006-07	Tingsryds AIF U18	Swe-U18	23	0	3	3	28																		
2007-08	Tingsryds AIF U18	Swe-U18	12	2	3	5	57																		
	Tingsryds AIF Jr.	Swe-Jr.	7	2	4	6	16																		
	Tingsryds AIF	Sweden-3	27	3	5	8	10																		
2008-09	Leksands IF	Sweden-2	47	5	16	21	38																		
2009-10	Leksands IF	Sweden-2	52	11	22	33	106																		
2010-11	**Phoenix**	**NHL**	**48**	**1**	**10**	**11**	**24**	**0**	**0**	**0**	**50**	**2.0**	**3**	**0**	**0.0**	**15:02**									
	San Antonio	AHL	15	3	7	10	16																		
2011-12	**Phoenix**	**NHL**	**82**	**13**	**19**	**32**	**32**	**2**	**1**	**2**	**147**	**8.8**	**0**	**0**	**0.0**	**22:07**	**16**	**1**	**3**	**4**	**8**	**1**	**0**	**1**	**25:47**
2012-13	Portland Pirates	AHL	20	7	14	21	28																		
	Phoenix	**NHL**	**48**	**3**	**21**	**24**	**26**	**0**	**0**	**1**	**101**	**3.0**	**5**	**0**	**0.0**	**25:06**									
	NHL Totals		**178**	**17**	**50**	**67**	**82**	**2**	**1**	**3**	**298**	**5.7**		**0**	**0.0**	**21:00**	**16**	**1**	**3**	**4**	**8**	**1**	**0**	**1**	**25:47**

ELIAS, Patrik

(ehl-EE-ahsh, PAT-rihk) **N.J.**

Left wing. Shoots left. 6'1", 195 lbs. Born, Trebic, Czech., April 13, 1976. New Jersey's 2nd choice, 51st overall, in 1994 Entry Draft.

			Regular Season														Playoffs								
Season	Club	League	GP	G	A	Pts	PIM	PP	SH	GW	S	%	+/-	TF	F%	Min	GP	G	A	Pts	PIM	PP	SH	GW	Min
1992-93	Poldi Kladno	Czech	2	0	0	0	....	....	....	....	....	....	....	....	....	....	....	....	....	....	....	....	....	....	....
1993-94	HC Kladno	CzRep	15	1	2	3	....	....	....	....	....	....	....	....	....	....	11	2	2	4	....	....	....	....	....
1994-95	HC Kladno	CzRep	28	4	3	7	37	....	....	....	....	....	....	....	....	....	7	1	2	3	12	....	....	....	....
1995-96	**New Jersey**	**NHL**	1	0	0	0	0	0	0	0	2	0.0	–1	....	....	....	....	....	....	....	....	....	....	....	....
	Albany River Rats	AHL	74	27	36	63	83	....	....	....	....	....	....	....	....	....	4	1	1	2	2	....	....	....	....
1996-97	**New Jersey**	**NHL**	17	2	3	5	2	0	0	0	23	8.7	–4	....	....	....	8	2	3	5	4	1	0	0	....
	Albany River Rats	AHL	57	24	43	67	76	....	....	....	....	....	....	....	....	....	6	1	2	3	8	....	....	....	....
1997-98	**New Jersey**	**NHL**	74	18	19	37	28	5	0	6	147	12.2	18	....	....	....	4	0	1	1	0	0	0	0	....
	Albany River Rats	AHL	3	3	0	3	2	....	....	....	....	....	....	....	....	....	....	....	....	....	....	....	....	....	....
1998-99	**New Jersey**	**NHL**	74	17	33	50	34	3	0	2	157	10.8	19	99	38.4	15:50	7	0	5	5	6	0	0	0	18:07
99-2000	Trebic	CzRep-2	2	2	1	3	2	....	....	....	....	....	....	....	....	....	....	....	....	....	....	....	....	....	....
	Pardubice	CzRep	5	1	4	5	31	....	....	....	....	....	....	....	....	....	....	....	....	....	....	....	....	....	....
	◆ New Jersey	**NHL**	72	35	37	72	58	9	0	9	183	19.1	16	134	45.5	17:28	23	7	*13	20	9	2	1	1	17:44
2000-01	**New Jersey**	**NHL**	82	40	56	96	51	8	3	6	220	18.2	*45	155	41.3	18:44	25	9	14	23	10	3	1	2	18:14
2001-02	**New Jersey**	**NHL**	75	29	32	61	36	8	1	8	199	14.6	4	128	45.3	18:57	6	2	4	6	6	2	0	0	20:33
	Czech Republic	Olympics	4	1	1	2	0	....	....	....	....	....	....	....	....	....	....	....	....	....	....	....	....	....	....
2002-03◆	**New Jersey**	**NHL**	81	28	29	57	22	6	0	4	255	11.0	17	427	43.8	18:05	24	5	8	13	26	2	0	2	17:14
2003-04	**New Jersey**	**NHL**	82	38	43	81	44	9	3	9	300	12.7	26	49	36.7	18:46	5	3	2	5	2	1	0	1	18:59
2004-05	Znojmo	CzRep	28	8	20	28	65	....	....	....	....	....	....	....	....	....	....	....	....	....	....	....	....	....	....
	Magnitogorsk	Russia	17	5	9	14	28	....	....	....	....	....	....	....	....	....	....	....	....	....	....	....	....	....	....
2005-06	**New Jersey**	**NHL**	38	16	29	45	20	6	0	3	142	11.3	11	10	20.0	18:34	9	6	10	16	4	4	0	0	18:43
	Czech Republic	Olympics	1	0	0	0	2	....	....	....	....	....	....	....	....	....	....	....	....	....	....	....	....	....	....
2006-07	**New Jersey**	**NHL**	75	21	48	69	38	8	0	5	267	7.9	1	18	38.9	18:37	10	1	9	10	4	1	0	0	19:13
2007-08	**New Jersey**	**NHL**	74	20	35	55	38	7	0	8	263	7.6	10	776	45.6	18:28	5	4	2	6	4	3	0	0	20:30
2008-09	**New Jersey**	**NHL**	77	31	47	78	32	12	2	6	247	12.6	18	87	29.9	18:34	7	1	2	3	2	0	0	0	17:53
2009-10	**New Jersey**	**NHL**	58	19	29	48	40	3	1	4	145	13.1	18	457	44.9	17:37	5	0	4	4	2	0	0	0	18:41
	Czech Republic	Olympics	5	2	2	4	2	....	....	....	....	....	....	....	....	....	....	....	....	....	....	....	....	....	....
2010-11	**New Jersey**	**NHL**	81	21	41	62	16	7	1	5	204	10.3	–4	498	45.0	18:38	....	....	....	....	....	....	....	....	....
2011-12	**New Jersey**	**NHL**	81	26	52	78	16	8	2	3	164	15.9	–8	1369	44.1	19:51	24	5	3	8	10	2	0	0	18:30
2012-13	**New Jersey**	**NHL**	48	14	22	36	22	5	1	0	118	11.9	5	163	43.6	18:43	....	....	....	....	....	....	....	....	....
	NHL Totals		1090	375	555	930	497	104	14	78	3036	12.4		4370	43.9	18:22	162	45	80	125	89	21	2	6	18:19

NHL All-Rookie Team (1998) • NHL First All-Star Team (2001) • Bud Light Plus/Minus Award (2001) (tied with Joe Sakic)

Played in NHL All-Star Game (2000, 2002, 2011)

Signed as a free agent by **Znojmo** (CzRep), September 6, 2004. Signed as a free agent by **Magnitogorsk** (Russia), December 9, 2004. • Missed majority of 2005-06 due to hepatitis-A virus.

ELKINS, Corey

(EHL-kihns, KOH-ree)

Left wing. Shoots left. 6'2", 214 lbs. Born, West Bloomfield, MI, February 23, 1985.

Season	Club	League	GP	G	A	Pts	PIM	PP	SH	GW	S	%	+/-	TF	F%	Min	GP	G	A	Pts	PIM	PP	SH	GW	Min
2002-03	Det. Compuware	NAHL	49	8	11	19	37	....	....	....	....	....	....	....	....	....	....	....	....	....	....	....	....	....	....
2003-04	St. Louis	USHL	57	12	17	29	36	....	....	....	....	....	....	....	....	....	....	....	....	....	....	....	....	....	....
2004-05	Sioux City	USHL	58	19	23	42	27	....	....	....	....	....	....	....	....	....	13	4	1	5	8	....	....	....	....
2005-06	Ohio State	CCHA	9	0	0	0	0	....	....	....	....	....	....	....	....	....	....	....	....	....	....	....	....	....	....
2006-07	Ohio State	CCHA	26	7	7	14	10	....	....	....	....	....	....	....	....	....	....	....	....	....	....	....	....	....	....
2007-08	Ohio State	CCHA	25	2	3	5	12	....	....	....	....	....	....	....	....	....	....	....	....	....	....	....	....	....	....
2008-09	Ohio State	CCHA	42	18	23	41	18	....	....	....	....	....	....	....	....	....	....	....	....	....	....	....	....	....	....
2009-10	**Los Angeles**	**NHL**	3	1	0	1	0	0	0	0	5	20.0	–2	18	33.3	11:54	....	....	....	....	....	....	....	....	....
	Manchester	AHL	73	21	22	43	24	....	....	....	....	....	....	....	....	....	14	3	5	8	0	....	....	....	....
2010-11	Manchester	AHL	76	18	26	44	29	....	....	....	....	....	....	....	....	....	7	2	3	5	2	....	....	....	....
2011-12	Pardubice	CzRep	26	6	7	13	24	....	....	....	....	....	....	....	....	....	5	2	2	4	0	....	....	....	....
2012-13	Norfolk Admirals	AHL	24	3	1	4	4	....	....	....	....	....	....	....	....	....	....	....	....	....	....	....	....	....	....
	Fort Wayne	ECHL	4	3	3	6	0	....	....	....	....	....	....	....	....	....	....	....	....	....	....	....	....	....	....
	HIFK Helsinki	Finland	10	3	2	5	2	....	....	....	....	....	....	....	....	....	8	3	2	5	4	....	....	....	....
	NHL Totals		3	1	0	1	0	0	0	0	5	20.0		18	33.3	11:54	....	....	....	....	....	....	....	....	....

Signed as a free agent by **Los Angeles**, March 31, 2009. Signed as a free agent by **Pardubice** (CzRep), July 18, 2011. Signed as a free agent by **Anaheim**, July 9, 2012. Signed as a free agent by **Fort Wayne** (ECHL), January 1, 2013. Signed as a free agent by **HIFK Helsinki** (Finland), January 5, 2013.

ELLER, Lars

(EHL-uhr, LARZ) **MTL**

Center. Shoots left. 6'2", 201 lbs. Born, Rodovre, Denmark, May 8, 1989. St. Louis' 1st choice, 13th overall, in 2007 Entry Draft.

Season	Club	League	GP	G	A	Pts	PIM	PP	SH	GW	S	%	+/-	TF	F%	Min	GP	G	A	Pts	PIM	PP	SH	GW	Min
2004-05	Rodovre IK Jr.	Den-Jr.	28	21	26	47	20	....	....	....	....	....	....	....	....	....	....	....	....	....	....	....	....	....	....
	Rodovre	Denmark	1	3	1	4	0	....	....	....	....	....	....	....	....	....	....	....	....	....	....	....	....	....	....
2005-06	Frolunda U18	Swe-U18	8	2	4	6	10	....	....	....	....	....	....	....	....	....	2	0	0	0	0	....	....	....	....
	Frolunda Jr.	Swe-Jr.	36	7	7	14	6	....	....	....	....	....	....	....	....	....	2	0	0	0	0	....	....	....	....
2006-07	Frolunda U18	Swe-U18	3	1	4	5	6	....	....	....	....	....	....	....	....	....	6	3	2	5	8	....	....	....	....
	Frolunda Jr.	Swe-Jr.	39	18	37	55	58	....	....	....	....	....	....	....	....	....	8	4	1	5	24	....	....	....	....
2007-08	Boras HC	Sweden-2	19	2	6	8	8	....	....	....	....	....	....	....	....	....	....	....	....	....	....	....	....	....	....
	Frolunda Jr.	Swe-Jr.	9	4	4	8	10	....	....	....	....	....	....	....	....	....	7	5	6	11	14	....	....	....	....
	Frolunda	Sweden	14	0	2	2	4	....	....	....	....	....	....	....	....	....	7	0	1	1	2	....	....	....	....
2008-09	Frolunda	Sweden	48	12	17	29	28	....	....	....	....	....	....	....	....	....	10	3	1	4	12	....	....	....	....
	Denmark	Oly-Q	3	1	1	2	8	....	....	....	....	....	....	....	....	....	....	....	....	....	....	....	....	....	....
2009-10	**St. Louis**	**NHL**	7	2	0	2	4	1	0	0	8	25.0	2	19	47.4	10:49	....	....	....	....	....	....	....	....	....
	Peoria Rivermen	AHL	70	18	39	57	84	....	....	....	....	....	....	....	....	....	....	....	....	....	....	....	....	....	....
2010-11	**Montreal**	**NHL**	77	7	10	17	48	0	0	2	79	8.9	–4	431	42.5	11:08	7	0	2	2	4	0	0	0	13:04
2011-12	**Montreal**	**NHL**	79	16	12	28	66	2	2	2	129	12.4	–5	685	46.6	15:19	....	....	....	....	....	....	....	....	....
2012-13	JYP Jyvaskyla	Finland	15	5	10	15	18	....	....	....	....	....	....	....	....	....	....	....	....	....	....	....	....	....	....
	Montreal	**NHL**	46	8	22	30	45	1	0	1	84	9.5	8	542	49.3	14:50	1	0	0	0	0	0	0	0	8:43
	NHL Totals		209	33	44	77	163	4	2	5	300	11.0		1677	46.4	13:31	8	0	2	2	4	0	0	0	12:32

AHL All-Rookie Team (2010)

Traded to **Montreal** by **St. Louis** with Ian Schultz for Jaroslav Halak, June 17, 2010. Signed as a free agent by **Jyvaskyla** (Finland), October 28, 2012.

ELLERBY, Keaton

(EHL-uhr-bee, KEE-tuhn) **L.A.**

Defense. Shoots left. 6'5", 221 lbs. Born, Strathmore, Alta., November 5, 1988. Florida's 1st choice, 10th overall, in 2007 Entry Draft.

Season	Club	League	GP	G	A	Pts	PIM	PP	SH	GW	S	%	+/-	TF	F%	Min	GP	G	A	Pts	PIM	PP	SH	GW	Min
2003-04	Okotoks Oilers	AMHA	30	7	32	39	69	....	....	....	....	....	....	....	....	....	....	....	....	....	....	....	....	....	....
2004-05	Kamloops Blazers	WHL	60	0	1	1	77	....	....	....	....	....	....	....	....	....	6	0	0	0	16	....	....	....	....
2005-06	Kamloops Blazers	WHL	68	2	6	8	121	....	....	....	....	....	....	....	....	....	....	....	....	....	....	....	....	....	....
2006-07	Kamloops Blazers	WHL	69	2	23	25	120	....	....	....	....	....	....	....	....	....	4	1	2	3	12	....	....	....	....
2007-08	Kamloops Blazers	WHL	16	0	3	3	29	....	....	....	....	....	....	....	....	....	....	....	....	....	....	....	....	....	....
	Moose Jaw	WHL	53	2	21	23	81	....	....	....	....	....	....	....	....	....	5	0	2	2	15	....	....	....	....
2008-09	Rochester	AHL	75	3	20	23	44	....	....	....	....	....	....	....	....	....	....	....	....	....	....	....	....	....	....
2009-10	**Florida**	**NHL**	22	0	0	0	2	0	0	0	5	0.0	–1	0	0.0	5:26	....	....	....	....	....	....	....	....	....
	Rochester	AHL	58	6	13	19	34	....	....	....	....	....	....	....	....	....	7	1	0	1	4	....	....	....	....
2010-11	**Florida**	**NHL**	54	2	10	12	22	0	0	0	56	3.6	–15	0	0.0	16:06	....	....	....	....	....	....	....	....	....
	Rochester	AHL	17	2	3	5	8	....	....	....	....	....	....	....	....	....	....	....	....	....	....	....	....	....	....
2011-12	**Florida**	**NHL**	40	0	5	5	10	0	0	0	45	0.0	–3	0	0.0	15:23	1	0	0	0	2	0	0	0	8:42
2012-13	**Florida**	**NHL**	9	0	0	0	36	0	0	0	8	0.0	–2	0	0.0	15:11	....	....	....	....	....	....	....	....	....
	Los Angeles	**NHL**	35	0	3	3	16	0	0	0	15	0.0	5	0	0.0	14:17	5	0	0	0	0	0	0	0	10:43
	NHL Totals		160	2	18	20	86	0	0	0	129	1.6		0	0.0	14:00	6	0	0	0	2	0	0	0	10:23

• Missed majority of 2011-12 as a healthy reserve. Traded to **Los Angeles** by **Florida** for New Jersey's 5th round choice (previously acquired, later traded to Buffalo – Buffalo selected Gustav Possler) in 2013 Entry Draft, February 8, 2013.

ELLIOTT, Stefan
(ehl-LEE-awt, STEH-fan) **COL**

Defense. Shoots right. 6'1", 192 lbs. Born, Vancouver, B.C., January 30, 1991. Colorado's 3rd choice, 49th overall, in 2009 Entry Draft.

Season	Club	League	GP	G	A	Pts	PIM	PP	SH	GW	S	%	+/-	TF	F%	Min	Playoffs GP	G	A	Pts	PIM	PP	SH	GW	Min
2006-07	Van. NW Giants	BCMML	36	12	19	31	18	....	....	....	....	....	....	....	....	....	....	....	....	....	....	....	....	....	....
	Saskatoon Blades	WHL	1	0	0	0	0	....	....	....	....	....	....	....	....	....	....	....	....	....	....	....	....	....	....
2007-08	Saskatoon Blades	WHL	67	9	31	40	17	....	....	....	....	....	....	....	....	....	....	....	....	....	....	....	....	....	....
2008-09	Saskatoon Blades	WHL	71	16	39	55	26	....	....	....	....	....	....	....	....	....	7	1	3	4	4	....	....	....	....
2009-10	Saskatoon Blades	WHL	72	26	39	65	24	....	....	....	....	....	....	....	....	....	10	3	5	8	4	....	....	....	....
2010-11	Saskatoon Blades	WHL	71	31	50	81	14	....	....	....	....	....	....	....	....	....	10	3	5	8	0	....	....	....	....
	Lake Erie	AHL	....	....	....	....	....	....	....	....	....	....	....	....	....	....	5	0	2	2	0	....	....	....	....
2011-12	**Colorado**	**NHL**	**39**	**4**	**9**	**13**	**8**	**0**	**0**	**1**	**84**	**4.8**	**2**	**0**	**0.0**	**17:09**	....	....	....	....	....	....	....	....	....
	Lake Erie	AHL	30	5	9	14	4	....	....	....	....	....	....	....	....	....	....	....	....	....	....	....	....	....	....
2012-13	Lake Erie	AHL	44	5	8	13	6	....	....	....	....	....	....	....	....	....	....	....	....	....	....	....	....	....	....
	Colorado	**NHL**	**18**	**1**	**3**	**4**	**2**	**0**	**0**	**0**	**35**	**2.9**	**–3**	**0**	**0.0**	**17:30**	....	....	....	....	....	....	....	....	....
	NHL Totals		**57**	**5**	**12**	**17**	**10**	**0**	**0**	**1**	**119**	**4.2**		**0**	**0.0**	**17:15**	....	....	....	....	....	....	....	....	....

Canadian Major Junior Scholastic Player of the Year (2009) • WHL East First All-Star Team (2011)

ELLIS, Matt
(EHL-ihs, MAT) **BUF**

Left wing. Shoots left. 6', 212 lbs. Born, Welland, Ont., August 31, 1981.

Season	Club	League	GP	G	A	Pts	PIM	PP	SH	GW	S	%	+/-	TF	F%	Min	Playoffs GP	G	A	Pts	PIM	PP	SH	GW	Min
1998-99	St. Michael's	OHL	47	10	8	18	6	....	....	....	....	....	....	....	....	....	....	....	....	....	....	....	....	....	....
99-2000	St. Michael's	OHL	59	15	20	35	20	....	....	....	....	....	....	....	....	....	....	....	....	....	....	....	....	....	....
2000-01	St. Michael's	OHL	68	21	24	45	19	....	....	....	....	....	....	....	....	....	18	4	8	12	6	....	....	....	....
2001-02	St. Michael's	OHL	66	38	51	89	20	....	....	....	....	....	....	....	....	....	15	8	6	14	6	....	....	....	....
2002-03	Toledo Storm	ECHL	71	27	32	59	34	....	....	....	....	....	....	....	....	....	7	3	5	8	0	....	....	....	....
2003-04	Grand Rapids	AHL	64	5	10	15	23	....	....	....	....	....	....	....	....	....	4	0	0	0	2	....	....	....	....
2004-05	Grand Rapids	AHL	79	18	23	41	59	....	....	....	....	....	....	....	....	....	....	....	....	....	....	....	....	....	....
2005-06	Grand Rapids	AHL	74	20	28	48	61	....	....	....	....	....	....	....	....	....	16	4	1	5	20	....	....	....	....
2006-07	**Detroit**	**NHL**	**16**	**0**	**0**	**0**	**6**	**0**	**0**	**0**	**22**	**0.0**	**–1**	**48**	**47.9**	**5:35**	....	....	....	....	....	....	....	....	....
	Grand Rapids	AHL	65	26	23	49	44	....	....	....	....	....	....	....	....	....	7	4	3	7	4	....	....	....	....
2007-08	**Detroit**	**NHL**	**35**	**2**	**4**	**6**	**12**	**0**	**0**	**1**	**28**	**7.1**	**1**	**87**	**49.4**	**5:23**	....	....	....	....	....	....	....	....	....
	Los Angeles	**NHL**	**19**	**1**	**1**	**2**	**14**	**0**	**1**	**0**	**38**	**2.6**	**2**	**27**	**37.0**	**12:41**	....	....	....	....	....	....	....	....	....
2008-09	**Buffalo**	**NHL**	**45**	**7**	**5**	**12**	**12**	**0**	**0**	**2**	**73**	**9.6**	**4**	**239**	**46.9**	**8:50**	....	....	....	....	....	....	....	....	....
	Portland Pirates	AHL	12	2	2	4	4	....	....	....	....	....	....	....	....	....	....	....	....	....	....	....	....	....	....
2009-10	**Buffalo**	**NHL**	**72**	**3**	**10**	**13**	**12**	**0**	**0**	**1**	**112**	**2.7**	**–1**	**282**	**50.0**	**9:03**	**3**	**1**	**0**	**1**	**0**	**0**	**0**	**0**	**9:44**
2010-11	**Buffalo**	**NHL**	**14**	**0**	**0**	**0**	**0**	**0**	**0**	**0**	**20**	**0.0**	**–4**	**58**	**48.3**	**10:03**	**1**	**0**	**0**	**0**	**0**	**0**	**0**	**0**	**11:32**
	Portland Pirates	AHL	52	10	21	31	12	....	....	....	....	....	....	....	....	....	11	1	5	6	4	....	....	....	....
2011-12	**Buffalo**	**NHL**	**60**	**3**	**5**	**8**	**25**	**0**	**0**	**1**	**85**	**3.5**	**–3**	**244**	**48.0**	**9:43**	....	....	....	....	....	....	....	....	....
2012-13	Rochester	AHL	32	7	5	12	6	....	....	....	....	....	....	....	....	....	3	0	0	0	2	....	....	....	....
	Buffalo	**NHL**	**6**	**0**	**0**	**0**	**0**	**0**	**0**	**0**	**8**	**0.0**	**0**	**36**	**41.7**	**6:12**	....	....	....	....	....	....	....	....	....
	NHL Totals		**267**	**16**	**25**	**41**	**81**	**0**	**1**	**5**	**386**	**4.1**		**1021**	**47.9**	**8:43**	**4**	**1**	**0**	**1**	**0**	**0**	**0**	**0**	**10:11**

Signed as a free agent by **Detroit**, May 10, 2002. Claimed on waivers by **Los Angeles** from **Detroit**, February 21, 2008. Claimed on waivers by **Buffalo** from **Los Angeles**, October 1, 2008.

ELLIS, Ryan
(EHL-ihs, RIGH-uhn) **NSH**

Defense. Shoots right. 5'10", 179 lbs. Born, Hamilton, Ont., January 3, 1991. Nashville's 1st choice, 11th overall, in 2009 Entry Draft.

Season	Club	League	GP	G	A	Pts	PIM	PP	SH	GW	S	%	+/-	TF	F%	Min	Playoffs GP	G	A	Pts	PIM	PP	SH	GW	Min
2006-07	Cambridge	Minor-ON	75	37	56	93	151	....	....	....	....	....	....	....	....	....	....	....	....	....	....	....	....	....	....
2007-08	Windsor Spitfires	OHL	63	15	48	63	51	....	....	....	....	....	....	....	....	....	5	2	3	5	2	....	....	....	....
2008-09	Windsor Spitfires	OHL	57	22	*67	89	57	....	....	....	....	....	....	....	....	....	20	8	*23	31	20	....	....	....	....
2009-10	Windsor Spitfires	OHL	48	12	49	61	38	....	....	....	....	....	....	....	....	....	19	3	*30	33	14	....	....	....	....
2010-11	Windsor Spitfires	OHL	58	24	77	101	61	....	....	....	....	....	....	....	....	....	18	6	13	19	12	....	....	....	....
	Milwaukee	AHL	....	....	....	....	....	....	....	....	....	....	....	....	....	....	7	1	1	2	2	....	....	....	....
2011-12	**Nashville**	**NHL**	**32**	**3**	**8**	**11**	**4**	**2**	**0**	**2**	**34**	**8.8**	**5**	**0**	**0.0**	**14:50**	**3**	**0**	**0**	**0**	**0**	**0**	**0**	**0**	**6:54**
	Milwaukee	AHL	29	4	14	18	8	....	....	....	....	....	....	....	....	....	....	....	....	....	....	....	....	....	....
2012-13	Milwaukee	AHL	32	5	9	14	18	....	....	....	....	....	....	....	....	....	4	0	0	0	0	....	....	....	....
	Nashville	**NHL**	**32**	**2**	**4**	**6**	**15**	**2**	**0**	**0**	**48**	**4.2**	**–2**	**0**	**0.0**	**16:23**	....	....	....	....	....	....	....	....	....
	NHL Totals		**64**	**5**	**12**	**17**	**19**	**4**	**0**	**2**	**82**	**6.1**		**0**	**0.0**	**15:36**	**3**	**0**	**0**	**0**	**0**	**0**	**0**	**0**	**6:54**

Canadian Major Junior All-Rookie Team (2008) • OHL First All-Star Team (2009, 2011) • Canadian Major Junior First All-Star Team (2009) • Memorial Cup All-Star Team (2009, 2010) • OHL Second All-Star Team (2010) • Canadian Major Junior Defenseman of the Year (2011) • Canadian Major Junior Player of the Year (2011)

EMELIN, Alexei
(eh-MUH-lehn, al-EHX-ay) **MTL**

Defense. Shoots left. 6'2", 219 lbs. Born, Togliatti, USSR, April 25, 1986. Montreal's 2nd choice, 84th overall, in 2004 Entry Draft.

Season	Club	League	GP	G	A	Pts	PIM	PP	SH	GW	S	%	+/-	TF	F%	Min	Playoffs GP	G	A	Pts	PIM	PP	SH	GW	Min
2002-03	Lada Togliatti 2	Russia-3	31	1	1	2	20	....	....	....	....	....	....	....	....	....	....	....	....	....	....	....	....	....	....
2003-04	Lada Togliatti 2	Russia-3	2	0	0	0	10	....	....	....	....	....	....	....	....	....	....	....	....	....	....	....	....	....	....
	CSK VVS Samara	Russia-2	52	2	4	6	180	....	....	....	....	....	....	....	....	....	1	0	0	0	18	....	....	....	....
2004-05	Lada Togliatti	Russia	12	0	1	1	24	....	....	....	....	....	....	....	....	....	2	0	0	0	2	....	....	....	....
2005-06	Lada Togliatti	Russia	44	6	6	12	131	....	....	....	....	....	....	....	....	....	6	0	1	1	*47	....	....	....	....
2006-07	Lada Togliatti	Russia	43	2	5	7	74	....	....	....	....	....	....	....	....	....	3	0	0	0	4	....	....	....	....
2007-08	Ak Bars Kazan	Russia	56	0	5	5	123	....	....	....	....	....	....	....	....	....	10	0	1	1	10	....	....	....	....
2008-09	Ak Bars Kazan	KHL	51	0	3	3	58	....	....	....	....	....	....	....	....	....	7	1	0	1	20	....	....	....	....
2009-10	Ak Bars Kazan	KHL	46	1	6	7	50	....	....	....	....	....	....	....	....	....	22	5	8	13	24	....	....	....	....
2010-11	Ak Bars Kazan	KHL	52	11	16	27	92	....	....	....	....	....	....	....	....	....	9	0	0	0	4	....	....	....	....
2011-12	**Montreal**	**NHL**	**67**	**3**	**4**	**7**	**30**	**0**	**1**	**0**	**62**	**4.8**	**–18**	**0**	**0.0**	**17:18**	....	....	....	....	....	....	....	....	....
2012-13	Ak Bars Kazan	KHL	24	2	7	9	40	....	....	....	....	....	....	....	....	....	....	....	....	....	....	....	....	....	....
	Montreal	**NHL**	**38**	**3**	**9**	**12**	**33**	**0**	**0**	**0**	**33**	**9.1**	**2**	**0**	**0.0**	**19:40**	....	....	....	....	....	....	....	....	....
	NHL Totals		**105**	**6**	**13**	**19**	**63**	**0**	**1**	**0**	**95**	**6.3**		**0**	**0.0**	**18:09**	....	....	....	....	....	....	....	....	....

Signed as a free agent by **Kazan** (KHL), October 13, 2012.

EMINGER, Steve
(EH-mihn-juhr, STEEV)

Defense. Shoots right. 6'2", 207 lbs. Born, Woodbridge, Ont., October 31, 1983. Washington's 1st choice, 12th overall, in 2002 Entry Draft.

Season	Club	League	GP	G	A	Pts	PIM	PP	SH	GW	S	%	+/-	TF	F%	Min	Playoffs GP	G	A	Pts	PIM	PP	SH	GW	Min
1998-99	Bramalea Blues	ON-Jr.A	47	6	9	15	81	....	....	....	....	....	....	....	....	....	....	....	....	....	....	....	....	....	....
99-2000	Kitchener Rangers	OHL	50	2	14	16	74	....	....	....	....	....	....	....	....	....	5	0	0	0	0	....	....	....	....
2000-01	Kitchener Rangers	OHL	54	6	26	32	66	....	....	....	....	....	....	....	....	....	....	....	....	....	....	....	....	....	....
2001-02	Kitchener Rangers	OHL	64	19	39	58	93	....	....	....	....	....	....	....	....	....	4	0	2	2	10	....	....	....	....
2002-03	**Washington**	**NHL**	**17**	**0**	**2**	**2**	**24**	**0**	**0**	**0**	**6**	**0.0**	**–3**	**0**	**0.0**	**10:08**	....	....	....	....	....	....	....	....	....
	Kitchener Rangers	OHL	23	2	27	29	40	....	....	....	....	....	....	....	....	....	21	3	8	11	44	....	....	....	....
2003-04	**Washington**	**NHL**	**41**	**0**	**4**	**4**	**45**	**0**	**0**	**0**	**12**	**0.0**	**–11**	**0**	**0.0**	**17:32**	....	....	....	....	....	....	....	....	....
	Portland Pirates	AHL	41	0	4	4	40	....	....	....	....	....	....	....	....	....	7	0	1	1	2	....	....	....	....
2004-05	Portland Pirates	AHL	62	3	17	20	40	....	....	....	....	....	....	....	....	....	....	....	....	....	....	....	....	....	....
2005-06	**Washington**	**NHL**	**66**	**5**	**13**	**18**	**81**	**1**	**0**	**0**	**50**	**10.0**	**–12**	**1**	**100.0**	**21:21**	....	....	....	....	....	....	....	....	....
2006-07	**Washington**	**NHL**	**68**	**1**	**16**	**17**	**63**	**0**	**0**	**0**	**27**	**3.7**	**–14**	**1**	**100.0**	**18:56**	....	....	....	....	....	....	....	....	....
2007-08	**Washington**	**NHL**	**20**	**0**	**2**	**2**	**8**	**0**	**0**	**0**	**14**	**0.0**	**–4**	**0**	**0.0**	**11:08**	**5**	**1**	**0**	**1**	**2**	**0**	**0**	**0**	**16:06**
2008-09	**Philadelphia**	**NHL**	**12**	**0**	**2**	**2**	**8**	**0**	**0**	**0**	**9**	**0.0**	**0**	**0**	**0.0**	**17:53**	....	....	....	....	....	....	....	....	....
	Tampa Bay	**NHL**	**50**	**4**	**19**	**23**	**36**	**2**	**0**	**0**	**63**	**6.3**	**–4**	**1**	**0.0**	**23:33**	....	....	....	....	....	....	....	....	....
	Florida	**NHL**	**9**	**1**	**0**	**1**	**6**	**0**	**0**	**1**	**13**	**7.7**	**1**	**0**	**0.0**	**15:49**	....	....	....	....	....	....	....	....	....
2009-10	**Anaheim**	**NHL**	**63**	**4**	**12**	**16**	**30**	**0**	**0**	**1**	**45**	**8.9**	**1**	**0**	**0.0**	**19:29**	....	....	....	....	....	....	....	....	....
2010-11	**NY Rangers**	**NHL**	**65**	**2**	**4**	**6**	**22**	**0**	**0**	**1**	**23**	**8.7**	**–5**	**0**	**0.0**	**15:51**	....	....	....	....	....	....	....	....	....
2011-12	**NY Rangers**	**NHL**	**42**	**2**	**3**	**5**	**28**	**0**	**0**	**0**	**19**	**10.5**	**0**	**0**	**0.0**	**13:17**	**4**	**0**	**0**	**0**	**0**	**0**	**0**	**0**	**6:49**
2012-13	**NY Rangers**	**NHL**	**35**	**0**	**3**	**3**	**8**	**0**	**0**	**0**	**22**	**0.0**	**9**	**0**	**0.0**	**13:02**	**11**	**0**	**2**	**2**	**4**	**0**	**0**	**0**	**12:45**
	Connecticut	AHL	4	1	0	1	0	....	....	....	....	....	....	....	....	....	....	....	....	....	....	....	....	....	....
	NHL Totals		**488**	**19**	**80**	**99**	**359**	**3**	**0**	**3**	**303**	**6.3**		**3**	**66.7**	**17:39**	**20**	**1**	**2**	**3**	**6**	**0**	**0**	**0**	**12:24**

OHL Second All-Star Team (2002, 2003) • Canadian Major Junior Second All-Star Team (2002) • Memorial Cup All-Star Team (2003)

Traded to **Philadelphia** by **Washington** with Washington's 3rd round choice (Jacob Deserres) in 2008 Entry Draft for Philadelphia's 1st round choice (John Carlson) in 2008 Entry Draft, June 20, 2008. Traded to **Tampa Bay** by **Philadelphia** with Steve Downie and Tampa Bay's 4th round choice (previously acquired, Tampa Bay selected Alex Hutchings) in 2009 Entry Draft for Matt Carle and San Jose's 3rd round choice (previously acquired, Philadelphia selected Simon Bertilsson) in 2009 Entry Draft, November 7, 2008. Traded to **Florida** by **Tampa Bay** for Noah Welch and Florida's 3rd round choice (later traded to Detroit – Detroit selected Andrej Nestrasil) in 2009 Entry Draft, March 4, 2009. Signed as a free agent by **Anaheim**, September 4, 2009. Traded to **NY Rangers** by **Anaheim** for Aaron Voros and Ryan Hillier, July 9, 2010.

EMMERTON, Cory

(EHM-uhr-tuhn, KOH-ree) **DET**

Center. Shoots left. 6', 191 lbs. Born, St. Thomas, Ont., June 1, 1988. Detroit's 1st choice, 41st overall, in 2006 Entry Draft.

			Regular Season														Playoffs								
Season	Club	League	GP	G	A	Pts	PIM	PP	SH	GW	S	%	+/-	TF	F%	Min	GP	G	A	Pts	PIM	PP	SH	GW	Min
2003-04	Elgin-Mid. Chiefs	Minor-ON	32	33	24	57	26	....	....	....	....	....	....	....	....	....	....	....	....	....	....	....	....	....	....
2004-05	Kingston	OHL	58	17	21	38	8	....	....	....	....	....	....	....	....	....	....	....	....	....	....	....	....	....	....
2005-06	Kingston	OHL	66	26	64	90	32	....	....	....	....	....	....	....	....	....	6	2	0	2	6	....	....	....	....
2006-07	Kingston	OHL	40	29	37	66	22	....	....	....	....	....	....	....	....	....	5	5	2	7	2	....	....	....	....
	Grand Rapids	AHL	....	....	....	....	....	....	....	....	....	....	....	....	....	....	2	0	0	0	0	....	....	....	....
2007-08	Kingston	OHL	24	13	18	31	6	....	....	....	....	....	....	....	....	....	....	....	....	....	....	....	....	....	....
	Brampton	OHL	30	12	18	30	10	....	....	....	....	....	....	....	....	....	5	0	2	2	2	....	....	....	....
	Grand Rapids	AHL	7	0	1	1	0	....	....	....	....	....	....	....	....	....	....	....	....	....	....	....	....	....	....
2008-09	Grand Rapids	AHL	69	10	25	35	18	....	....	....	....	....	....	....	....	....	9	1	0	1	2	....	....	....	....
2009-10	Grand Rapids	AHL	76	12	25	37	22	....	....	....	....	....	....	....	....	....	....	....	....	....	....	....	....	....	....
2010-11	**Detroit**	**NHL**	**2**	**1**	**0**	**1**	**0**	**0**	**0**	**0**	**3**	**33.3**	**1**	**1**	**0.0**	**8:20**	....	....	....	....	....	....	....	....	....
	Grand Rapids	AHL	65	12	26	38	26	....	....	....	....	....	....	....	....	....	....	....	....	....	....	....	....	....	....
2011-12	**Detroit**	**NHL**	**71**	**6**	**4**	**10**	**14**	**0**	**0**	**0**	**63**	**9.5**	**1**	**313**	**48.2**	**8:06**	**5**	**1**	**0**	**1**	**2**	**0**	**0**	**0**	**5:10**
2012-13	SaiPa	Finland	1	0	0	0	0	....	....	....	....	....	....	....	....	....	....	....	....	....	....	....	....	....	....
	Detroit	**NHL**	**48**	**5**	**3**	**8**	**4**	**0**	**0**	**0**	**55**	**9.1**	**–1**	**413**	**45.3**	**10:49**	**13**	**0**	**1**	**1**	**4**	**0**	**0**	**0**	**10:26**
	NHL Totals		**121**	**12**	**7**	**19**	**18**	**0**	**0**	**0**	**121**	**9.9**		**727**	**46.5**	**9:11**	**18**	**1**	**1**	**2**	**6**	**0**	**0**	**0**	**8:58**

Signed as a free agent by **SaiPa Lappeenranta** (Finland), October 10, 2012.

ENGELLAND, Deryk

(ehn-GUHL-uhnd, DEH-rihk) **PIT**

Defense. Shoots right. 6'2", 202 lbs. Born, Edmonton, Alta., April 5, 1982. New Jersey's 11th choice, 194th overall, in 2000 Entry Draft.

Season	Club	League	GP	G	A	Pts	PIM	PP	SH	GW	S	%	+/-	TF	F%	Min	GP	G	A	Pts	PIM	PP	SH	GW	Min
1998-99	Moose Jaw	WHL	2	0	0	0	0	....	....	....	....	....	....	....	....	....	....	....	....	....	....	....	....	....	....
99-2000	Moose Jaw	WHL	55	0	5	5	62	....	....	....	....	....	....	....	....	....	4	0	0	0	0	....	....	....	....
2000-01	Moose Jaw	WHL	65	4	11	15	157	....	....	....	....	....	....	....	....	....	4	0	0	0	10	....	....	....	....
2001-02	Moose Jaw	WHL	56	7	10	17	102	....	....	....	....	....	....	....	....	....	12	0	2	2	27	....	....	....	....
2002-03	Moose Jaw	WHL	65	3	8	11	199	....	....	....	....	....	....	....	....	....	13	1	1	2	20	....	....	....	....
2003-04	Lowell	AHL	26	0	0	0	34	....	....	....	....	....	....	....	....	....	....	....	....	....	....	....	....	....	....
	Las Vegas	ECHL	35	2	11	13	63	....	....	....	....	....	....	....	....	....	2	0	0	0	0	....	....	....	....
2004-05	Las Vegas	ECHL	72	5	16	21	138	....	....	....	....	....	....	....	....	....	....	....	....	....	....	....	....	....	....
2005-06	Hershey Bears	AHL	37	0	4	4	77	....	....	....	....	....	....	....	....	....	1	0	0	0	0	....	....	....	....
	South Carolina	ECHL	35	3	13	16	20	....	....	....	....	....	....	....	....	....	....	....	....	....	....	....	....	....	....
2006-07	Hershey Bears	AHL	44	4	6	10	95	....	....	....	....	....	....	....	....	....	14	0	0	0	14	....	....	....	....
	Reading Royals	ECHL	6	0	3	3	8	....	....	....	....	....	....	....	....	....	....	....	....	....	....	....	....	....	....
2007-08	Wilkes-Barre	AHL	80	2	15	17	141	....	....	....	....	....	....	....	....	....	23	1	3	4	14	....	....	....	....
2008-09	Wilkes-Barre	AHL	80	3	11	14	143	....	....	....	....	....	....	....	....	....	12	0	2	2	6	....	....	....	....
2009-10	**Pittsburgh**	**NHL**	**9**	**0**	**2**	**2**	**17**	**0**	**0**	**0**	**4**	**0.0**	**–2**	**0**	**0.0**	**16:08**	....	....	....	....	....	....	....	....	....
	Wilkes-Barre	AHL	71	5	6	11	121	....	....	....	....	....	....	....	....	....	4	0	1	1	7	....	....	....	....
2010-11	**Pittsburgh**	**NHL**	**63**	**3**	**7**	**10**	**123**	**0**	**0**	**0**	**49**	**6.1**	**–5**	**0**	**0.0**	**13:20**	....	....	....	....	....	....	....	....	....
2011-12	**Pittsburgh**	**NHL**	**73**	**4**	**13**	**17**	**56**	**0**	**0**	**1**	**86**	**4.7**	**10**	**0**	**0.0**	**16:09**	**6**	**0**	**1**	**1**	**14**	**0**	**0**	**0**	**11:30**
2012-13	Rosenborg Elite	Norway	15	1	8	9	43	....	....	....	....	....	....	....	....	....	....	....	....	....	....	....	....	....	....
	Pittsburgh	**NHL**	**42**	**0**	**6**	**6**	**54**	**0**	**0**	**0**	**31**	**0.0**	**5**	**0**	**0.0**	**13:55**	**7**	**0**	**0**	**0**	**8**	**0**	**0**	**0**	**15:28**
	NHL Totals		**187**	**7**	**28**	**35**	**250**	**0**	**0**	**1**	**170**	**4.1**		**0**	**0.0**	**14:42**	**13**	**0**	**1**	**1**	**22**	**0**	**0**	**0**	**13:38**

Signed as a free agent by **Calgary**, July, 2003. Signed as a free agent by **Pittsburgh**, July 16, 2007. Signed as a free agent by **Rosenborg** (Norway), October 12, 2012.

ENGQVIST, Andreas

(ENG-kvihst, awn-DRAY-uhs)

Center. Shoots right. 6'4", 199 lbs. Born, Stockholm, Sweden, December 23, 1987.

Season	Club	League	GP	G	A	Pts	PIM	PP	SH	GW	S	%	+/-	TF	F%	Min	GP	G	A	Pts	PIM	PP	SH	GW	Min
2004-05	Spanga U18	Swe-U18	6	3	6	9	6	....	....	....	....	....	....	....	....	....	....	....	....	....	....	....	....	....	....
	Spanga Jr.	Swe-Jr.	13	15	9	24	12	....	....	....	....	....	....	....	....	....	....	....	....	....	....	....	....	....	....
2005-06	Djurgarden Jr.	Swe-Jr.	26	6	13	19	6	....	....	....	....	....	....	....	....	....	4	1	1	2	2	....	....	....	....
	Djurgarden	Sweden	1	0	0	0	0	....	....	....	....	....	....	....	....	....	....	....	....	....	....	....	....	....	....
2006-07	Djurgarden Jr.	Swe-Jr.	5	1	3	4	4	....	....	....	....	....	....	....	....	....	7	3	4	7	10	....	....	....	....
	Djurgarden	Sweden	43	1	3	4	16	....	....	....	....	....	....	....	....	....	....	....	....	....	....	....	....	....	....
2007-08	Djurgarden Jr.	Swe-Jr.	1	1	0	1	0	....	....	....	....	....	....	....	....	....	....	....	....	....	....	....	....	....	....
	Djurgarden	Sweden	51	5	7	12	16	....	....	....	....	....	....	....	....	....	5	0	0	0	0	....	....	....	....
2008-09	Djurgarden	Sweden	31	9	7	16	12	....	....	....	....	....	....	....	....	....	....	....	....	....	....	....	....	....	....
2009-10	Djurgarden	Sweden	55	14	12	26	30	....	....	....	....	....	....	....	....	....	16	5	8	13	10	....	....	....	....
2010-11	**Montreal**	**NHL**	**3**	**0**	**0**	**0**	**0**	**0**	**0**	**0**	**1**	**0.0**	**0**	**19**	**36.8**	**8:46**	....	....	....	....	....	....	....	....	....
	Hamilton	AHL	71	10	15	25	18	....	....	....	....	....	....	....	....	....	20	4	5	9	0	....	....	....	....
2011-12	**Montreal**	**NHL**	**12**	**0**	**0**	**0**	**4**	**0**	**0**	**0**	**3**	**0.0**	**–1**	**60**	**40.0**	**6:36**	....	....	....	....	....	....	....	....	....
	Hamilton	AHL	60	20	23	43	36	....	....	....	....	....	....	....	....	....	....	....	....	....	....	....	....	....	....
2012-13	Mytischi	KHL	48	12	24	36	22	....	....	....	....	....	....	....	....	....	4	1	0	1	0	....	....	....	....
	NHL Totals		**15**	**0**	**0**	**0**	**4**	**0**	**0**	**0**	**4**	**0.0**		**79**	**39.2**	**7:02**	....	....	....	....	....	....	....	....	....

Signed as a free agent by **Montreal**, July 13, 2009. Signed as a free agent by **Mytischi** (KHL), June 27, 2012.

ENNIS, Tyler

(EH-nihs, TIGH-luhr) **BUF**

Center. Shoots left. 5'9", 157 lbs. Born, Edmonton, Alta., October 6, 1989. Buffalo's 2nd choice, 26th overall, in 2008 Entry Draft.

Season	Club	League	GP	G	A	Pts	PIM	PP	SH	GW	S	%	+/-	TF	F%	Min	GP	G	A	Pts	PIM	PP	SH	GW	Min
2004-05	K of C Pats	AMHL	36	15	17	32	10	....	....	....	....	....	....	....	....	....	....	....	....	....	....	....	....	....	....
2005-06	Medicine Hat	WHL	43	3	7	10	10	....	....	....	....	....	....	....	....	....	7	0	0	0	0	....	....	....	....
2006-07	Medicine Hat	WHL	71	26	24	50	30	....	....	....	....	....	....	....	....	....	22	8	4	12	6	....	....	....	....
2007-08	Medicine Hat	WHL	70	43	48	91	42	....	....	....	....	....	....	....	....	....	5	0	4	4	6	....	....	....	....
2008-09	Medicine Hat	WHL	61	43	42	85	21	....	....	....	....	....	....	....	....	....	11	8	11	19	10	....	....	....	....
2009-10	**Buffalo**	**NHL**	**10**	**3**	**6**	**9**	**6**	**0**	**0**	**0**	**23**	**13.0**	**1**	**31**	**41.9**	**15:20**	**6**	**1**	**3**	**4**	**0**	**0**	**0**	**0**	**17:09**
	Portland Pirates	AHL	69	23	42	65	12	....	....	....	....	....	....	....	....	....	....	....	....	....	....	....	....	....	....
2010-11	**Buffalo**	**NHL**	**82**	**20**	**29**	**49**	**30**	**5**	**0**	**1**	**210**	**9.5**	**0**	**9**	**22.2**	**15:40**	**7**	**2**	**2**	**4**	**4**	**0**	**0**	**1**	**16:38**
2011-12	**Buffalo**	**NHL**	**48**	**15**	**19**	**34**	**14**	**2**	**0**	**1**	**82**	**18.3**	**11**	**316**	**45.9**	**16:10**	....	....	....	....	....	....	....	....	....
2012-13	Langnau	Swiss	9	3	5	8	0	....	....	....	....	....	....	....	....	....	....	....	....	....	....	....	....	....	....
	Buffalo	**NHL**	**47**	**10**	**21**	**31**	**16**	**2**	**0**	**0**	**108**	**9.3**	**–14**	**377**	**41.9**	**17:53**	....	....	....	....	....	....	....	....	....
	NHL Totals		**187**	**48**	**75**	**123**	**66**	**9**	**0**	**2**	**423**	**11.3**		**733**	**43.4**	**16:20**	**13**	**3**	**5**	**8**	**4**	**0**	**0**	**1**	**16:52**

WHL East First All-Star Team (2008, 2009) • AHL All-Rookie Team (2010) • Dudley "Red" Garrett Memorial Award (AHL – Rookie of the Year) (2010)

Signed as a free agent by **Langnau** (Swiss), September 21, 2012.

ENSTROM, Toby

(EHN-struhm, toh-BEE) **WPG**

Defense. Shoots left. 5'10", 180 lbs. Born, Nordingra, Sweden, November 5, 1984. Atlanta's 8th choice, 239th overall, in 2003 Entry Draft.

Season	Club	League	GP	G	A	Pts	PIM	PP	SH	GW	S	%	+/-	TF	F%	Min	GP	G	A	Pts	PIM	PP	SH	GW	Min
99-2000	MoDo U18	Swe-U18	3	0	0	0	0	....	....	....	....	....	....	....	....	....	....	....	....	....	....	....	....	....	....
2000-01	MoDo U18	Swe-U18	16	7	6	13	18	....	....	....	....	....	....	....	....	....	....	....	....	....	....	....	....	....	....
	MoDo Jr.	Swe-Jr.	1	0	0	0	0	....	....	....	....	....	....	....	....	....	....	....	....	....	....	....	....	....	....
2001-02	MODO Jr.	Swe-Jr.	21	1	7	8	10	....	....	....	....	....	....	....	....	....	2	1	1	2	2	....	....	....	....
2002-03	MODO Jr.	Swe-Jr.	7	4	6	10	31	....	....	....	....	....	....	....	....	....	....	....	....	....	....	....	....	....	....
	MODO	Sweden	42	1	5	6	16	....	....	....	....	....	....	....	....	....	6	0	1	1	4	....	....	....	....
2003-04	MODO	Sweden	33	1	4	5	6	....	....	....	....	....	....	....	....	....	6	1	1	2	2	....	....	....	....
2004-05	MODO	Sweden	49	4	10	14	24	....	....	....	....	....	....	....	....	....	2	0	0	0	0	....	....	....	....
2005-06	MODO	Sweden	47	4	7	11	48	....	....	....	....	....	....	....	....	....	4	0	1	1	25	....	....	....	....
2006-07	MODO	Sweden	55	7	21	28	52	....	....	....	....	....	....	....	....	....	20	1	11	12	37	....	....	....	....
2007-08	**Atlanta**	**NHL**	**82**	**5**	**33**	**38**	**42**	**4**	**0**	**0**	**105**	**4.8**	**–5**	**0**	**0.0**	**24:28**	....	....	....	....	....	....	....	....	....
2008-09	**Atlanta**	**NHL**	**82**	**5**	**27**	**32**	**52**	**2**	**1**	**1**	**86**	**5.8**	**14**	**2**	**50.0**	**23:32**	....	....	....	....	....	....	....	....	....
2009-10	**Atlanta**	**NHL**	**82**	**6**	**44**	**50**	**30**	**2**	**0**	**0**	**109**	**5.5**	**–5**	**0**	**0.0**	**22:16**	....	....	....	....	....	....	....	....	....
	Sweden	Olympics	4	0	2	2	4	....	....	....	....	....	....	....	....	....	....	....	....	....	....	....	....	....	....
2010-11	**Atlanta**	**NHL**	**72**	**10**	**41**	**51**	**54**	**6**	**0**	**0**	**113**	**8.8**	**–10**	**0**	**0.0**	**23:41**	....	....	....	....	....	....	....	....	....
2011-12	**Winnipeg**	**NHL**	**62**	**6**	**27**	**33**	**38**	**2**	**0**	**1**	**94**	**6.4**	**6**	**0**	**0.0**	**23:51**	....	....	....	....	....	....	....	....	....

			Regular Season														Playoffs								
Season	Club	League	GP	G	A	Pts	PIM	PP	SH	GW	S	%	+/-	TF	F%	Min	GP	G	A	Pts	PIM	PP	SH	GW	Min
2012-13	Salzburg	Austria	5	1	0	1	4																		
	Winnipeg	**NHL**	**22**	**4**	**11**	**15**	**8**	**1**	**0**	**2**	**21**	**19.0**	**–8**	**0**	**0.0**	**22:31**									
	NHL Totals		**402**	**36**	**183**	**219**	**224**	**17**	**1**	**4**	**528**	**6.8**		**2**	**50.0**	**23:29**									

NHL All-Rookie Team (2008)

• Transferred to **Winnipeg** after **Atlanta** franchise relocated, June 21, 2011. Signed as a free agent by **Salzburg** (Austria), October 22, 2012. • Missed majority of 2012-13 due to shoulder (February 15, 2013 vs. Pittsburgh) and back (April 9, 2013 vs. Buffalo) injuries.

ERAT, Martin (EE-rat, MAHR-tihn) WSH

Right wing. Shoots left. 6', 200 lbs. Born, Trebic, Czech., August 29, 1981. Nashville's 12th choice, 191st overall, in 1999 Entry Draft.

1997-98	HC ZPS Zlin Jr.	CzRep-Jr.	46	35	30	65																			
1998-99	HC ZPS Zlin Jr.	CzRep-Jr.	35	21	23	44																			
	Zlin	CzRep	5	0	0	0	2																		
99-2000	Saskatoon Blades	WHL	66	27	26	53	82										11	4	8	12	16				
2000-01	Saskatoon Blades	WHL	31	19	35	54	48																		
	Red Deer Rebels	WHL	17	4	24	28	24										22	*15	*21	*36	32				
2001-02	**Nashville**	**NHL**	**80**	**9**	**24**	**33**	**32**	**2**	**0**	**2**	**84**	**10.7**	**–11**	**3**	**66.7**	**13:10**									
2002-03	**Nashville**	**NHL**	**27**	**1**	**7**	**8**	**14**	**1**	**0**	**0**	**39**	**2.6**	**–9**	**1**	**0.0**	**12:47**									
	Milwaukee	AHL	45	10	22	32	41										6	5	4	9	4				
2003-04	**Nashville**	**NHL**	**76**	**16**	**33**	**49**	**38**	**4**	**0**	**2**	**137**	**11.7**	**10**	**31**	**29.0**	**15:00**	**6**	**0**	**1**	**1**	**6**	**0**	**0**	**0**	**14:09**
2004-05	HC Hame Zlin	CzRep	48	20	23	43	129										16	*7	5	12	12				
2005-06	**Nashville**	**NHL**	**80**	**20**	**29**	**49**	**76**	**5**	**0**	**1**	**143**	**14.0**	**0**	**25**	**16.0**	**14:45**	**5**	**1**	**1**	**2**	**6**	**1**	**0**	**0**	**19:31**
	Czech Republic	Olympics	8	1	1	2	4																		
2006-07	**Nashville**	**NHL**	**68**	**16**	**41**	**57**	**50**	**5**	**1**	**3**	**132**	**12.1**	**13**	**43**	**44.2**	**18:59**	**3**	**0**	**1**	**1**	**0**	**0**	**0**	**0**	**14:13**
2007-08	**Nashville**	**NHL**	**76**	**23**	**34**	**57**	**40**	**4**	**0**	**6**	**163**	**14.1**	**–3**	**41**	**36.6**	**18:39**	**6**	**1**	**3**	**4**	**8**	**0**	**0**	**0**	**20:56**
2008-09	**Nashville**	**NHL**	**71**	**17**	**33**	**50**	**48**	**3**	**0**	**3**	**149**	**11.4**	**–7**	**38**	**29.0**	**18:34**									
2009-10	**Nashville**	**NHL**	**74**	**21**	**28**	**49**	**50**	**5**	**0**	**2**	**168**	**12.5**	**–7**	**73**	**32.9**	**17:59**	**6**	**4**	**1**	**5**	**4**	**0**	**0**	**0**	**18:56**
	Czech Republic	Olympics	5	0	1	1	2																		
2010-11	**Nashville**	**NHL**	**64**	**17**	**33**	**50**	**22**	**7**	**0**	**3**	**135**	**12.6**	**14**	**44**	**43.2**	**18:06**	**10**	**1**	**5**	**6**	**6**	**1**	**0**	**0**	**19:15**
2011-12	**Nashville**	**NHL**	**71**	**19**	**39**	**58**	**30**	**5**	**1**	**3**	**107**	**17.8**	**12**	**126**	**47.6**	**18:29**	**10**	**1**	**3**	**4**	**6**	**1**	**0**	**0**	**18:51**
2012-13	**Nashville**	**NHL**	**36**	**4**	**17**	**21**	**26**	**1**	**0**	**1**	**60**	**6.7**	**–7**	**60**	**51.7**	**18:55**									
	Washington	**NHL**	**9**	**1**	**2**	**3**	**4**	**0**	**0**	**1**	**9**	**11.1**	**0**	**2**	**50.0**	**13:55**	**4**	**0**	**0**	**0**	**4**	**0**	**0**	**0**	**14:32**
	NHL Totals		**732**	**164**	**320**	**484**	**430**	**42**	**2**	**27**	**1326**	**12.4**		**487**	**40.0**	**16:53**	**50**	**8**	**15**	**23**	**40**	**3**	**0**	**0**	**18:04**

Signed as a free agent by **Zlin** (CzRep), September 5, 2004. Traded to **Washington** by **Nashville** with Michael Latta for Filip Forsberg, April 3, 2013.

ERICSSON, Jonathan (AIR-ihk-suhn, JAWN-ah-thuhn) DET

Defense. Shoots left. 6'4", 221 lbs. Born, Karlskrona, Sweden, March 2, 1984. Detroit's 10th choice, 291st overall, in 2002 Entry Draft.

2001-02	Hasten Jr.	Swe-Jr.	STATISTICS NOT AVAILABLE																						
2002-03	Vita Hasten	Sweden-3	40	2	4	6	36																		
2003-04	Sodertalje SK	Sweden	42	1	0	1	12																		
2004-05	Sodertalje SK	Sweden	15	0	0	0	4										1	0	0	0	0				
2005-06	Sodertalje SK Jr.	Swe-Jr.	1	0	0	0	2																		
	Almtuna	Sweden-2	19	2	3	5	44																		
	Sodertalje SK	Sweden	24	0	0	0	20																		
	Sodertalje SK	Sweden-Q	7	0	1	1	4																		
2006-07	Grand Rapids	AHL	67	5	24	29	102										7	0	0	0	8				
2007-08	**Detroit**	**NHL**	**8**	**1**	**0**	**1**	**4**	**1**	**0**	**0**	**19**	**5.3**	**–3**	**0**	**0.0**	**15:58**									
	Grand Rapids	AHL	69	10	24	34	83																		
2008-09	**Detroit**	**NHL**	**19**	**1**	**3**	**4**	**15**	**0**	**0**	**0**	**25**	**4.0**	**–1**	**0**	**0.0**	**17:40**	**22**	**4**	**4**	**8**	**25**	**0**	**0**	**1**	**18:44**
	Grand Rapids	AHL	40	2	13	15	48																		
2009-10	**Detroit**	**NHL**	**62**	**4**	**9**	**13**	**44**	**0**	**1**	**1**	**55**	**7.3**	**–15**	**0**	**0.0**	**16:42**	**12**	**0**	**2**	**2**	**8**	**0**	**0**	**0**	**14:17**
2010-11	**Detroit**	**NHL**	**74**	**3**	**12**	**15**	**87**	**1**	**0**	**0**	**89**	**3.4**	**8**	**0**	**0.0**	**18:50**	**11**	**1**	**2**	**3**	**4**	**0**	**0**	**0**	**18:47**
2011-12	**Detroit**	**NHL**	**69**	**1**	**10**	**11**	**47**	**0**	**0**	**0**	**63**	**1.6**	**16**	**0**	**0.0**	**17:05**	**5**	**0**	**0**	**0**	**6**	**0**	**0**	**0**	**19:49**
2012-13	Vita Hasten	Sweden-3	3	0	3	3	4																		
	Sodertalje SK	Sweden-2	4	0	1	1	6																		
	Detroit	**NHL**	**45**	**3**	**10**	**13**	**29**	**0**	**0**	**1**	**34**	**8.8**	**6**	**0**	**0.0**	**21:19**	**14**	**0**	**3**	**3**	**2**	**0**	**0**	**0**	**22:33**
	NHL Totals		**277**	**13**	**44**	**57**	**226**	**2**	**1**	**2**	**285**	**4.6**		**0**	**0.0**	**18:10**	**64**	**5**	**11**	**16**	**45**	**0**	**0**	**1**	**18:50**

Signed as a free agent by **Vita Hasten** (Sweden-3). October 7, 2012. Signed as a free agent by **Sodertalje** (Sweden-2), October 26, 2012.

ERIKSSON, Loui (AIR-ihk-suhn, LOO-ee) BOS

Left wing. Shoots left. 6'2", 196 lbs. Born, Goteborg, Sweden, July 17, 1985. Dallas' 1st choice, 33rd overall, in 2003 Entry Draft.

2000-01	V.Frolunda U18	Swe-U18	9	5	3	8	4																		
	V.Frolunda Jr.	Swe-Jr.	1	0	0	0	0																		
2001-02	V.Frolunda U18	Swe-U18	1	1	0	1	0																		
	V.Frolunda Jr.	Swe-Jr.	35	7	15	22	2										8	2	3	5	2				
2002-03	V.Frolunda Jr.	Swe-Jr.	30	16	15	31	10										8	4	6	10	4				
2003-04	V.Frolunda	Sweden	46	8	5	13	4										10	1	5	6	0				
2004-05	Frolunda	Sweden	39	5	9	14	4										12	0	0	0	0				
2005-06	Iowa Stars	AHL	78	31	29	60	27										7	2	5	7	0				
2006-07	**Dallas**	**NHL**	**59**	**6**	**13**	**19**	**18**	**2**	**0**	**0**	**78**	**7.7**	**–3**	**9**	**44.4**	**13:11**	**4**	**0**	**1**	**1**	**0**	**0**	**0**	**0**	**15:47**
	Iowa Stars	AHL	15	5	3	8	13										9	2	5	7	0				
2007-08	**Dallas**	**NHL**	**69**	**14**	**17**	**31**	**28**	**4**	**0**	**0**	**120**	**11.7**	**5**	**13**	**15.4**	**14:02**	**18**	**4**	**4**	**8**	**8**	**1**	**0**	**0**	**18:12**
	Iowa Stars	AHL	2	1	2	3	2																		
2008-09	**Dallas**	**NHL**	**82**	**36**	**27**	**63**	**14**	**7**	**1**	**4**	**178**	**20.2**	**14**	**11**	**18.2**	**19:50**									
2009-10	**Dallas**	**NHL**	**82**	**29**	**42**	**71**	**26**	**6**	**2**	**4**	**214**	**13.6**	**–4**	**11**	**36.4**	**19:46**									
	Sweden	Olympics	4	3	1	4	0																		
2010-11	**Dallas**	**NHL**	**79**	**27**	**46**	**73**	**8**	**10**	**1**	**6**	**179**	**15.1**	**10**	**4**	**25.0**	**20:34**									
2011-12	**Dallas**	**NHL**	**82**	**26**	**45**	**71**	**12**	**5**	**2**	**3**	**187**	**13.9**	**18**	**16**	**43.8**	**19:46**									
2012-13	HC Davos	Swiss	7	3	3	6	0																		
	Dallas	**NHL**	**48**	**12**	**17**	**29**	**8**	**2**	**1**	**3**	**104**	**11.5**	**–9**	**34**	**26.5**	**20:07**									
	NHL Totals		**501**	**150**	**207**	**357**	**114**	**36**	**7**	**20**	**1060**	**14.2**		**98**	**29.6**	**18:22**	**22**	**4**	**5**	**9**	**8**	**1**	**0**	**0**	**17:46**

Played in NHL All-Star Game (2011)

Signed as a free agent by **Davos** (Swiss), December 4, 2012. Traded to **Boston** by **Dallas** with Joseph Morrow, Reilly Smith and Matt Fraser for Tyler Seguin, Rich Peverley and Ryan Button, July 4, 2013.

ERIXON, Tim (AIR-ihx-uhn, TIHM) CBJ

Defense. Shoots left. 6'2", 190 lbs. Born, Port Chester, NY, February 24, 1991. Calgary's 1st choice, 23rd overall, in 2009 Entry Draft.

2005-06	Skelleftea U18	Swe-U18	9	0	2	2	4																		
2006-07	Skelleftea U18	Swe-U18	8	2	2	4	20																		
	Skelleftea Jr.	Swe-Jr.	8	0	2	2	2										2	0	0	0	4				
2007-08	Skelleftea U18	Swe-U18	4	0	1	1	10																		
	Skelleftea Jr.	Swe-Jr.	28	3	11	14	78										1	0	1	1	4				
	Skelleftea AIK HK	Sweden	2	0	0	0	0																		
2008-09	Skelleftea AIK U18	Swe-U18	1	0	2	2	10										5	1	5	6	14				
	Skelleftea AIK Jr.	Swe-Jr.	9	2	12	14	10										5	1	2	3	4				
	Malmo	Sweden-2	3	0	2	2	0																		
	Skelleftea AIK	Sweden	45	2	5	7	12										9	0	0	0	4				
2009-10	Skelleftea AIK	Sweden	45	7	6	13	44										12	1	0	1	8				
2010-11	Skelleftea AIK	Sweden	48	5	19	24	40										18	3	5	8	12				
2011-12	**NY Rangers**	**NHL**	**18**	**0**	**2**	**2**	**8**	**0**	**0**	**0**	**9**	**0.0**	**–2**	**0**	**0.0**	**13:00**									
	Connecticut	AHL	52	3	30	33	42										9	0	4	4	8				
2012-13	Springfield	AHL	40	5	24	29	38																		
	Columbus	**NHL**	**31**	**0**	**5**	**5**	**14**	**0**	**0**	**0**	**21**	**0.0**	**4**	**0**	**0.0**	**15:42**									
	NHL Totals		**49**	**0**	**7**	**7**	**22**	**0**	**0**	**0**	**30**	**0.0**		**0**	**0.0**	**14:42**									

Traded to **NY Rangers** by **Calgary** with Calgary's 5th round choice (Shane McColgan) in 2011 Entry Draft for Roman Horak, NY Rangers' 2nd round choice (Markus Granlund) in 2011 Entry Draft and Pittsburgh's 2nd round choice (previously acquired, Calgary selected Tyler Wotherspoon) in 2011 Entry Draft, June 1, 2011. Traded to **Columbus** by **NY Rangers** with Brandon Dubinsky, Artem Anisimov and NY Rangers' 1st round choice (Kerby Rychel) in 2013 Entry Draft for Rick Nash, Steven Delisle and Columbus' 3rd round choice (Pavel Buchnevich) in 2013 Entry Draft, July 23, 2012.

ERSKINE, John
(UHR-skihn, JAWN) **WSH**

Defense. Shoots left. 6'4", 220 lbs. Born, Kingston, Ont., June 26, 1980. Dallas' 1st choice, 39th overall, in 1998 Entry Draft.

			Regular Season														Playoffs								
Season	Club	League	GP	G	A	Pts	PIM	PP	SH	GW	S	%	+/-	TF	F%	Min	GP	G	A	Pts	PIM	PP	SH	GW	Min
1996-97	Quinte Hawks	ON-Jr.A	48	4	16	20	241	....	....	....	....	....	....	....	....	....	....	....	....	....	....	....	....	....	....
1997-98	London Knights	OHL	55	0	9	9	205	....	....	....	....	....	....	....	....	....	16	0	5	5	25	....	....	....	....
1998-99	London Knights	OHL	57	8	12	20	208	....	....	....	....	....	....	....	....	....	25	5	10	15	38	....	....	....	....
99-2000	London Knights	OHL	58	12	31	43	177	....	....	....	....	....	....	....	....	....	....	....	....	....	....	....	....	....	....
2000-01	Utah Grizzlies	IHL	77	1	8	9	284	....	....	....	....	....	....	....	....	....	....	....	....	....	....	....	....	....	....
2001-02	**Dallas**	**NHL**	**33**	**0**	**1**	**1**	**62**	**0**	**0**	**0**	**16**	**0.0**	**–8**	**0**	**0.0**	**10:44**	....	....	....	....	....	....	....	....	....
	Utah Grizzlies	AHL	39	2	6	8	118	....	....	....	....	....	....	....	....	....	3	0	0	0	10	....	....	....	....
2002-03	**Dallas**	**NHL**	**16**	**2**	**0**	**2**	**29**	**0**	**0**	**0**	**12**	**16.7**	**1**	**0**	**0.0**	**10:45**	....	....	....	....	....	....	....	....	....
	Utah Grizzlies	AHL	52	2	8	10	274	....	....	....	....	....	....	....	....	....	1	0	1	1	15	....	....	....	....
2003-04	**Dallas**	**NHL**	**32**	**0**	**1**	**1**	**84**	**0**	**0**	**0**	**23**	**0.0**	**–9**	**0**	**0.0**	**12:36**	....	....	....	....	....	....	....	....	....
	Utah Grizzlies	AHL	5	0	0	0	18	....	....	....	....	....	....	....	....	....	....	....	....	....	....	....	....	....	....
2004-05	Houston Aeros	AHL	61	3	7	10	238	....	....	....	....	....	....	....	....	....	5	0	1	1	20	....	....	....	....
2005-06	**Dallas**	**NHL**	**26**	**0**	**0**	**0**	**62**	**0**	**0**	**0**	**9**	**0.0**	**–3**	**0**	**0.0**	**11:00**	....	....	....	....	....	....	....	....	....
	Iowa Stars	AHL	3	0	0	0	6	....	....	....	....	....	....	....	....	....	....	....	....	....	....	....	....	....	....
	NY Islanders	**NHL**	**34**	**1**	**0**	**1**	**99**	**0**	**0**	**0**	**23**	**4.3**	**–12**	**0**	**0.0**	**14:37**	....	....	....	....	....	....	....	....	....
2006-07	**Washington**	**NHL**	**29**	**1**	**6**	**7**	**69**	**0**	**0**	**0**	**14**	**7.1**	**–13**	**0**	**0.0**	**18:03**	....	....	....	....	....	....	....	....	....
	Hershey Bears	AHL	4	0	2	2	9	....	....	....	....	....	....	....	....	....	....	....	....	....	....	....	....	....	....
2007-08	**Washington**	**NHL**	**51**	**2**	**7**	**9**	**96**	**0**	**0**	**1**	**48**	**4.2**	**1**	**0**	**0.0**	**15:43**	**7**	**0**	**2**	**2**	**6**	**0**	**0**	**0**	**17:07**
2008-09	**Washington**	**NHL**	**52**	**0**	**4**	**4**	**63**	**0**	**0**	**0**	**50**	**0.0**	**1**	**0**	**0.0**	**16:48**	**12**	**0**	**1**	**1**	**16**	**0**	**0**	**0**	**19:06**
2009-10	**Washington**	**NHL**	**50**	**1**	**5**	**6**	**66**	**0**	**0**	**0**	**50**	**2.0**	**16**	**0**	**0.0**	**15:59**	....	....	....	....	....	....	....	....	....
2010-11	**Washington**	**NHL**	**73**	**4**	**7**	**11**	**94**	**0**	**0**	**1**	**58**	**6.9**	**1**	**0**	**0.0**	**14:50**	**9**	**1**	**1**	**2**	**6**	**0**	**0**	**0**	**13:26**
2011-12	**Washington**	**NHL**	**28**	**0**	**2**	**2**	**51**	**0**	**0**	**0**	**20**	**0.0**	**3**	**0**	**0.0**	**12:06**	**4**	**0**	**1**	**1**	**0**	**0**	**0**	**0**	**9:26**
2012-13	**Washington**	**NHL**	**30**	**3**	**3**	**6**	**34**	**0**	**0**	**0**	**32**	**9.4**	**10**	**0**	**0.0**	**18:28**	**7**	**0**	**1**	**1**	**4**	**0**	**0**	**0**	**19:27**
	NHL Totals		**454**	**14**	**36**	**50**	**809**	**0**	**0**	**2**	**355**	**3.9**		**0**	**0.0**	**14:43**	**39**	**1**	**6**	**7**	**32**	**0**	**0**	**0**	**16:31**

OHL First All-Star Team (2000)

• Missed majority of 2003-04 due to ankle (December 27, 2003 vs. Columbus) and hernia (January 24, 2004 vs. St. Louis) injuries. Traded to **NY Islanders** by **Dallas** with Dallas' 2nd round choice (Jesse Joensuu) in 2006 Entry Draft for Janne Niinimaa and NY Islanders' 5th round choice (Ondrej Roman) in 2007 Entry Draft, January 10, 2005. Signed as a free agent by **Washington**, September 14, 2006. • Missed majority of 2006-07 due to foot (December 16, 2006 vs. Philadelphia) and thumb (March 9, 2007 vs. Carolina) injuries. • Missed majority of 2011-12 due to various injuries and as a healthy reserve.

ETEM, Emerson
(EE-tehm, EHM-ur-suhn) **ANA**

Right wing. Shoots left. 6'1", 210 lbs. Born, Long Beach, CA, June 16, 1992. Anaheim's 2nd choice, 29th overall, in 2010 Entry Draft.

			Regular Season														Playoffs								
Season	Club	League	GP	G	A	Pts	PIM	PP	SH	GW	S	%	+/-	TF	F%	Min	GP	G	A	Pts	PIM	PP	SH	GW	Min
2007-08	Shat.-St. Mary's	High-MN	58	13	15	28	20	....	....	....	....	....	....	....	....	....	....	....	....	....	....	....	....	....	....
2008-09	USNTDP	NAHL	40	19	14	33	16	....	....	....	....	....	....	....	....	....	9	4	4	8	4	....	....	....	....
	USNTDP	U-17	13	6	7	13	0	....	....	....	....	....	....	....	....	....	....	....	....	....	....	....	....	....	....
2009-10	Medicine Hat	WHL	72	37	28	65	26	....	....	....	....	....	....	....	....	....	12	7	3	10	0	....	....	....	....
2010-11	Medicine Hat	WHL	65	45	35	80	24	....	....	....	....	....	....	....	....	....	15	10	11	21	7	....	....	....	....
2011-12	Medicine Hat	WHL	65	*61	46	107	34	....	....	....	....	....	....	....	....	....	7	7	6	13	13	....	....	....	....
	Syracuse Crunch	AHL	2	1	0	1	2	....	....	....	....	....	....	....	....	....	4	2	0	2	0	....	....	....	....
2012-13	Norfolk Admirals	AHL	45	13	3	16	12	....	....	....	....	....	....	....	....	....	....	....	....	....	....	....	....	....	....
	Anaheim	**NHL**	**38**	**3**	**7**	**10**	**9**	**0**	**0**	**0**	**48**	**6.3**	**7**	**5**	**40.0**	**11:28**	**7**	**3**	**2**	**5**	**2**	**0**	**0**	**0**	**12:50**
	NHL Totals		**38**	**3**	**7**	**10**	**9**	**0**	**0**	**0**	**48**	**6.3**		**5**	**40.0**	**11:28**	**7**	**3**	**2**	**5**	**2**	**0**	**0**	**0**	**12:50**

WHL East First All-Star Team (2012)

EVANS, Brennan
(EH-vans, BREH-nuhn) **DET**

Defense. Shoots left. 6'4", 225 lbs. Born, North Battleford, Sask., January 6, 1982.

			Regular Season														Playoffs								
Season	Club	League	GP	G	A	Pts	PIM	PP	SH	GW	S	%	+/-	TF	F%	Min	GP	G	A	Pts	PIM	PP	SH	GW	Min
1998-99	Camrose Kodiaks	AJHL	47	1	6	7	98	....	....	....	....	....	....	....	....	....	5	0	2	2	0	....	....	....	....
	Seattle	WHL	....	....	....	....	....	....	....	....	....	....	....	....	....	....	1	0	0	0	0	....	....	....	....
99-2000	Seattle	WHL	52	1	2	3	40	....	....	....	....	....	....	....	....	....	1	0	0	0	0	....	....	....	....
2000-01	Seattle	WHL	11	1	0	1	25	....	....	....	....	....	....	....	....	....	....	....	....	....	....	....	....	....	....
	Kootenay Ice	WHL	55	2	7	9	105	....	....	....	....	....	....	....	....	....	11	0	0	0	25	....	....	....	....
2001-02	Kootenay Ice	WHL	72	2	3	5	121	....	....	....	....	....	....	....	....	....	22	0	6	6	38	....	....	....	....
2002-03	Kootenay Ice	WHL	67	6	17	23	182	....	....	....	....	....	....	....	....	....	11	1	1	2	24	....	....	....	....
2003-04	Lowell	AHL	64	1	9	10	65	....	....	....	....	....	....	....	....	....	....	....	....	....	....	....	....	....	....
	Calgary	**NHL**	....	....	....	....	....	....	....	....	....	....	....	....	....	....	**2**	**0**	**0**	**0**	**0**	**0**	**0**	**0**	**2:52**
2004-05	Lowell	AHL	51	0	7	7	79	....	....	....	....	....	....	....	....	....	5	0	0	0	2	....	....	....	....
2005-06	Binghamton	AHL	70	3	6	9	198	....	....	....	....	....	....	....	....	....	....	....	....	....	....	....	....	....	....
2006-07	Worcester Sharks	AHL	75	2	14	16	170	....	....	....	....	....	....	....	....	....	5	0	1	1	21	....	....	....	....
2007-08	Worcester Sharks	AHL	80	1	13	14	211	....	....	....	....	....	....	....	....	....	....	....	....	....	....	....	....	....	....
2008-09	Iowa Chops	AHL	75	1	14	15	189	....	....	....	....	....	....	....	....	....	....	....	....	....	....	....	....	....	....
2009-10	Toronto Marlies	AHL	79	1	7	8	199	....	....	....	....	....	....	....	....	....	....	....	....	....	....	....	....	....	....
2010-11	Peoria Rivermen	AHL	66	3	11	14	113	....	....	....	....	....	....	....	....	....	4	0	0	0	6	....	....	....	....
2011-12	Peoria Rivermen	AHL	76	2	5	7	125	....	....	....	....	....	....	....	....	....	....	....	....	....	....	....	....	....	....
2012-13	Grand Rapids	AHL	76	0	7	7	148	....	....	....	....	....	....	....	....	....	24	2	6	8	36	....	....	....	....
	NHL Totals		....	....	....	....	....	....	....	....	....	....	....	....	....	....	**2**	**0**	**0**	**0**	**0**	**0**	**0**	**0**	**2:52**

Signed as a free agent by **Calgary**, September 30, 2003. Signed as a free agent by **San Jose**, July 18, 2007. Signed as a free agent by **Anaheim**, July 11, 2008. • Re-assigned to **Toronto** (AHL) by **Anaheim** (Iowa-AHL), October 2, 2009. Signed as a free agent by **St. Louis**, July 12, 2010. Signed as a free agent by **Grand Rapids** (AHL), July 24, 2012.

EXELBY, Garnet
(EHX-uhl-bee, GAHR-neht)

Defense. Shoots left. 6'1", 215 lbs. Born, Craik, Sask., August 16, 1981. Atlanta's 9th choice, 217th overall, in 1999 Entry Draft.

			Regular Season														Playoffs								
Season	Club	League	GP	G	A	Pts	PIM	PP	SH	GW	S	%	+/-	TF	F%	Min	GP	G	A	Pts	PIM	PP	SH	GW	Min
1997-98	Wpg. South Blues	MJHL	46	5	11	16	110	....	....	....	....	....	....	....	....	....	....	....	....	....	....	....	....	....	....
1998-99	Saskatoon Blades	WHL	61	5	3	8	91	....	....	....	....	....	....	....	....	....	....	....	....	....	....	....	....	....	....
99-2000	Saskatoon Blades	WHL	63	1	8	9	79	....	....	....	....	....	....	....	....	....	11	0	2	2	21	....	....	....	....
2000-01	Saskatoon Blades	WHL	43	5	10	15	110	....	....	....	....	....	....	....	....	....	....	....	....	....	....	....	....	....	....
	Regina Pats	WHL	22	2	8	10	51	....	....	....	....	....	....	....	....	....	6	0	2	2	2	....	....	....	....
2001-02	Chicago Wolves	AHL	75	3	4	7	257	....	....	....	....	....	....	....	....	....	25	0	4	4	49	....	....	....	....
2002-03	**Atlanta**	**NHL**	**15**	**0**	**2**	**2**	**41**	**0**	**0**	**0**	**9**	**0.0**	**0**	**0**	**0.0**	**18:04**	....	....	....	....	....	....	....	....	....
	Chicago Wolves	AHL	53	3	6	9	140	....	....	....	....	....	....	....	....	....	9	0	1	1	27	....	....	....	....
2003-04	**Atlanta**	**NHL**	**71**	**1**	**9**	**10**	**134**	**0**	**0**	**0**	**42**	**2.4**	**–10**	**0**	**0.0**	**19:32**	....	....	....	....	....	....	....	....	....
2004-05			DID NOT PLAY																						
2005-06	**Atlanta**	**NHL**	**75**	**1**	**9**	**10**	**75**	**0**	**0**	**0**	**44**	**2.3**	**11**	**0**	**0.0**	**15:41**	....	....	....	....	....	....	....	....	....
2006-07	**Atlanta**	**NHL**	**58**	**2**	**8**	**10**	**56**	**0**	**1**	**0**	**57**	**3.5**	**2**	**0**	**0.0**	**18:00**	**4**	**0**	**0**	**0**	**6**	**0**	**0**	**0**	**15:38**
2007-08	**Atlanta**	**NHL**	**79**	**2**	**5**	**7**	**85**	**0**	**0**	**0**	**37**	**5.4**	**–21**	**0**	**0.0**	**18:53**	....	....	....	....	....	....	....	....	....
2008-09	**Atlanta**	**NHL**	**59**	**0**	**7**	**7**	**120**	**0**	**0**	**0**	**42**	**0.0**	**–2**	**0**	**0.0**	**16:43**	....	....	....	....	....	....	....	....	....
2009-10	**Toronto**	**NHL**	**51**	**1**	**3**	**4**	**73**	**0**	**0**	**0**	**14**	**7.1**	**–8**	**0**	**0.0**	**10:06**	....	....	....	....	....	....	....	....	....
2010-11	Rockford IceHogs	AHL	77	3	10	13	128	....	....	....	....	....	....	....	....	....	....	....	....	....	....	....	....	....	....
2011-12	Grand Rapids	AHL	75	7	14	21	177	....	....	....	....	....	....	....	....	....	....	....	....	....	....	....	....	....	....
2012-13	Providence Bruins	AHL	52	2	7	9	95	....	....	....	....	....	....	....	....	....	12	0	2	2	31	....	....	....	....
	NHL Totals		**408**	**7**	**43**	**50**	**584**	**0**	**1**	**0**	**245**	**2.9**		**0**	**0.0**	**16:51**	**4**	**0**	**0**	**0**	**6**	**0**	**0**	**0**	**15:38**

Traded to **Toronto** by **Atlanta** with Colin Stuart for Pavel Kubina and Tim Stapleton, July 1, 2009. Signed to a PTO (professional tryout) contract by **Rockford** (AHL), October 9, 2010. Signed as a free agent by **Chicago**, November 26, 2010. Signed as a free agent by **Detroit**, July 5, 2011. Signed as a free agent by **Boston**, July 11, 2012.

FAIRCHILD, Cade
(FAIR-chighld, KAYD) **ST.L.**

Defense. Shoots left. 5'11", 175 lbs. Born, Duluth, MN, January 15, 1989. St. Louis' 7th choice, 96th overall, in 2007 Entry Draft.

			Regular Season														Playoffs								
Season	Club	League	GP	G	A	Pts	PIM	PP	SH	GW	S	%	+/-	TF	F%	Min	GP	G	A	Pts	PIM	PP	SH	GW	Min
2004-05	Duluth East	High-MN	29	10	32	42	....	....	....	....	....	....	....	....	....	....	....	....	....	....	....	....	....	....	....
2005-06	USNTDP	U-17	18	2	7	9	4	....	....	....	....	....	....	....	....	....	....	....	....	....	....	....	....	....	....
	USNTDP	NAHL	36	8	9	17	10	....	....	....	....	....	....	....	....	....	2	0	0	0	0	....	....	....	....
2006-07	USNTDP	U-18	36	3	16	19	34	....	....	....	....	....	....	....	....	....	....	....	....	....	....	....	....	....	....
	USNTDP	NAHL	13	1	6	7	16	....	....	....	....	....	....	....	....	....	....	....	....	....	....	....	....	....	....
2007-08	U. of Minnesota	WCHA	40	2	13	15	22	....	....	....	....	....	....	....	....	....	....	....	....	....	....	....	....	....	....
2008-09	U. of Minnesota	WCHA	35	9	24	33	52	....	....	....	....	....	....	....	....	....	....	....	....	....	....	....	....	....	....
2009-10	U. of Minnesota	WCHA	39	4	17	21	36	....	....	....	....	....	....	....	....	....	....	....	....	....	....	....	....	....	....
2010-11	U. of Minnesota	WCHA	35	6	18	24	12	....	....	....	....	....	....	....	....	....	....	....	....	....	....	....	....	....	....

			Regular Season														Playoffs								
Season	Club	League	GP	G	A	Pts	PIM	PP	SH	GW	S	%	+/-	TF	F%	Min	GP	G	A	Pts	PIM	PP	SH	GW	Min
2011-12	**St. Louis**	**NHL**	**5**	**0**	**1**	**1**	**0**	**0**	**0**	**0**	**1**	**0.0**	**–1**	**0**	**0.0**	**9:39**									
	Peoria Rivermen	AHL	68	8	26	34	32																		
2012-13	Peoria Rivermen	AHL	43	0	8	8	16																		
	NHL Totals		**5**	**0**	**1**	**1**	**0**	**0**	**0**	**0**	**1**	**0.0**		**0**	**0.0**	**9:39**									

WCHA All-Rookie Team (2008) • AHL All-Rookie Team (2012)

FALK, Justin

(FAWLK, JUHS-tihn) **NYR**

Defense. Shoots left. 6'5", 215 lbs. Born, Snowflake, Man., October 11, 1988. Minnesota's 2nd choice, 110th overall, in 2007 Entry Draft.

Season	Club	League	GP	G	A	Pts	PIM	PP	SH	GW	S	%	+/-	TF	F%	Min	GP	G	A	Pts	PIM	PP	SH	GW	Min
2004-05	Swan Valley	MJHL	56	0	8	8	46																		
	Calgary Hitmen	WHL	4	0	0	0	2										5	0	0	0	0				
2005-06	Calgary Hitmen	WHL	5	0	2	2	0																		
	Spokane Chiefs	WHL	48	0	8	8	35																		
2006-07	Spokane Chiefs	WHL	62	3	12	15	88										6	0	0	0	8				
2007-08	Spokane Chiefs	WHL	72	4	22	26	98										21	1	4	5	12				
2008-09	Houston Aeros	AHL	65	0	3	3	44										20	0	2	2	4				
2009-10	**Minnesota**	**NHL**	**3**	**0**	**0**	**0**	**0**	**0**	**0**	**0**	**1**	**0.0**	**–2**	**0**	**0.0**	**7:33**									
	Houston Aeros	AHL	69	3	6	9	87																		
2010-11	**Minnesota**	**NHL**	**22**	**0**	**3**	**3**	**6**	**0**	**0**	**0**	**7**	**0.0**	**–4**	**0**	**0.0**	**14:09**									
	Houston Aeros	AHL	55	3	11	14	41										24	0	5	5	33				
2011-12	**Minnesota**	**NHL**	**47**	**1**	**8**	**9**	**54**	**1**	**0**	**0**	**46**	**2.2**	**–13**	**0**	**0.0**	**19:30**									
2012-13	**Minnesota**	**NHL**	**36**	**0**	**3**	**3**	**40**	**0**	**0**	**0**	**27**	**0.0**	**–9**	**0**	**0.0**	**13:13**	**4**	**0**	**0**	**0**	**2**	**0**	**0**	**0**	**11:33**
	NHL Totals		**108**	**1**	**14**	**15**	**100**	**1**	**0**	**0**	**81**	**1.2**		**0**	**0.0**	**15:59**	**4**	**0**	**0**	**0**	**2**	**0**	**0**	**0**	**11:33**

Memorial Cup All-Star Team (2008)

Traded to **NY Rangers** by **Minnesota** for Benn Ferriero and Columbus' 6th round choice (previously acquired) in 2014 Entry Draft, June 30, 2013.

FAULK, Justin

(FAWLK, JUHS-tihn) **CAR**

Defense. Shoots right. 6', 215 lbs. Born, South St. Paul, MN, March 20, 1992. Carolina's 2nd choice, 37th overall, in 2010 Entry Draft.

Season	Club	League	GP	G	A	Pts	PIM	PP	SH	GW	S	%	+/-	TF	F%	Min	GP	G	A	Pts	PIM	PP	SH	GW	Min
2007-08	South St. Paul	High-MN	26	6	15	21	32																		
2008-09	USNTDP	NAHL	38	3	9	12	20										9	3	3	6	6				
	USNTDP	U-17	17	7	9	16	35																		
	USNTDP	U-18	1	0	0	0	0																		
2009-10	USNTDP	USHL	21	9	3	12	46																		
	USNTDP	U-18	39	12	9	21	20																		
2010-11	U. Minn-Duluth	WCHA	39	8	25	33	47																		
	Charlotte	AHL															13	0	2	2	2				
2011-12	**Carolina**	**NHL**	**66**	**8**	**14**	**22**	**29**	**5**	**0**	**2**	**101**	**7.9**	**–16**	**0**	**0.0**	**22:51**									
	Charlotte	AHL	12	2	4	6	11																		
2012-13	Charlotte	AHL	31	5	19	24	16																		
	Carolina	**NHL**	**38**	**5**	**10**	**15**	**15**	**1**	**1**	**0**	**76**	**6.6**	**1**	**0**	**0.0**	**24:00**									
	NHL Totals		**104**	**13**	**24**	**37**	**44**	**6**	**1**	**2**	**177**	**7.3**		**0**	**0.0**	**23:16**									

WCHA All-Rookie Team (2011) • NCAA Championship All-Tournament Team (2011) • NHL All-Rookie Team (2012)

FAYNE, Mark

(FAYN, MAHRK) **N.J.**

Defense. Shoots right. 6'3", 215 lbs. Born, Nashua, NH, May 15, 1987. New Jersey's 5th choice, 155th overall, in 2005 Entry Draft.

Season	Club	League	GP	G	A	Pts	PIM	PP	SH	GW	S	%	+/-	TF	F%	Min	GP	G	A	Pts	PIM	PP	SH	GW	Min
2003-04	Nobles	High-MA	20	3	5	8	14																		
2004-05	Nobles	High-MA	24	1	17	18	16																		
2005-06	Nobles	High-MA	29	10	24	34																			
2006-07	Providence	H-East	36	5	7	12	43																		
2007-08	Providence	H-East	36	2	4	6	18																		
2008-09	Providence	H-East	33	4	5	9	30																		
2009-10	Providence	H-East	34	5	17	22	14																		
2010-11	**New Jersey**	**NHL**	**57**	**4**	**10**	**14**	**27**	**0**	**0**	**0**	**77**	**5.2**	**10**	**0**	**0.0**	**17:50**									
	Albany Devils	AHL	19	1	3	4	6																		
2011-12	**New Jersey**	**NHL**	**82**	**4**	**13**	**17**	**26**	**0**	**0**	**1**	**94**	**4.3**	**–4**	**0**	**0.0**	**20:11**	**24**	**0**	**3**	**3**	**6**	**0**	**0**	**0**	**20:19**
2012-13	**New Jersey**	**NHL**	**31**	**1**	**5**	**6**	**16**	**0**	**1**	**0**	**34**	**2.9**	**6**	**0**	**0.0**	**18:06**									
	NHL Totals		**170**	**9**	**28**	**37**	**69**	**0**	**1**	**1**	**205**	**4.4**		**0**	**0.0**	**19:01**	**24**	**0**	**3**	**3**	**6**	**0**	**0**	**0**	**20:19**

FEDOTENKO, Ruslan

(feh-doh-TEHN-koh, roos-LAHN)

Left wing. Shoots left. 6'1", 200 lbs. Born, Kiev, USSR, January 18, 1979.

Season	Club	League	GP	G	A	Pts	PIM	PP	SH	GW	S	%	+/-	TF	F%	Min	GP	G	A	Pts	PIM	PP	SH	GW	Min
1995-96	Kiev 2	EEHL	33	9	11	20	12																		
	Sokol Kiev	CIS	2	0	0	0	0																		
1996-97	TPS Turku U18	Fin-U18	3	3	2	5	2																		
	TPS Turku Jr.	Fin-Jr.	11	1	1	2	2																		
	Kiekko-67 Turku	Finland-2	22	4	3	7	16																		
	Kiekko Turku	Finland-3															3	1	0	1	2				
1997-98	Melfort Mustangs	SJHL	68	35	31	66	55																		
1998-99	Sioux City	USHL	55	43	34	77	139										5	5	1	6	9				
99-2000	Trenton Titans	ECHL	8	5	3	8	9																		
	Philadelphia	AHL	67	16	34	50	42										2	0	0	0	0				
2000-01	**Philadelphia**	**NHL**	**74**	**16**	**20**	**36**	**72**	**3**	**0**	**4**	**119**	**13.4**	**8**	**7**	**71.4**	**14:38**	**6**	**0**	**1**	**1**	**4**	**0**	**0**	**0**	**11:18**
	Philadelphia	AHL	8	1	0	1	8																		
2001-02	**Philadelphia**	**NHL**	**78**	**17**	**9**	**26**	**43**	**0**	**1**	**3**	**121**	**14.0**	**15**	**41**	**43.9**	**13:56**	**5**	**1**	**0**	**1**	**2**	**0**	**0**	**1**	**14:11**
	Ukraine	Olympics	1	1	0	1	4																		
2002-03	**Tampa Bay**	**NHL**	**76**	**19**	**13**	**32**	**44**	**6**	**0**	**6**	**114**	**16.7**	**–7**	**90**	**48.9**	**16:01**	**11**	**0**	**1**	**1**	**2**	**0**	**0**	**0**	**13:58**
2003-04 ♦	**Tampa Bay**	**NHL**	**77**	**17**	**22**	**39**	**30**	**0**	**0**	**3**	**116**	**14.7**	**14**	**58**	**55.2**	**14:39**	**22**	**12**	**2**	**14**	**14**	**5**	**0**	**3**	**16:40**
2004-05			DID NOT PLAY																						
2005-06	**Tampa Bay**	**NHL**	**80**	**26**	**15**	**41**	**44**	**4**	**0**	**6**	**164**	**15.9**	**–4**	**28**	**42.9**	**15:21**	**5**	**0**	**0**	**0**	**20**	**0**	**0**	**0**	**14:38**
2006-07	**Tampa Bay**	**NHL**	**80**	**12**	**20**	**32**	**52**	**2**	**0**	**1**	**154**	**7.8**	**–3**	**8**	**25.0**	**16:15**	**4**	**0**	**0**	**0**	**4**	**0**	**0**	**0**	**17:27**
2007-08	**NY Islanders**	**NHL**	**67**	**16**	**17**	**33**	**40**	**8**	**0**	**2**	**121**	**13.2**	**–9**	**28**	**39.3**	**16:42**									
2008-09 ♦	**Pittsburgh**	**NHL**	**65**	**16**	**23**	**39**	**44**	**1**	**0**	**3**	**117**	**13.7**	**18**	**18**	**22.2**	**14:06**	**24**	**7**	**7**	**14**	**4**	**0**	**0**	**0**	**14:31**
2009-10	**Pittsburgh**	**NHL**	**80**	**11**	**19**	**30**	**50**	**3**	**0**	**3**	**158**	**7.0**	**–17**	**28**	**35.7**	**14:39**	**6**	**0**	**0**	**0**	**4**	**0**	**0**	**0**	**12:31**
2010-11	**NY Rangers**	**NHL**	**66**	**10**	**15**	**25**	**25**	**0**	**1**	**0**	**120**	**8.3**	**9**	**32**	**37.5**	**15:00**	**5**	**0**	**2**	**2**	**4**	**0**	**0**	**0**	**20:55**
2011-12	**NY Rangers**	**NHL**	**73**	**9**	**11**	**20**	**16**	**1**	**0**	**1**	**94**	**9.6**	**–7**	**34**	**47.1**	**13:36**	**20**	**2**	**5**	**7**	**8**	**0**	**0**	**0**	**15:17**
2012-13	Donetsk	KHL	33	8	10	18	22																		
	Philadelphia	**NHL**	**47**	**4**	**9**	**13**	**12**	**0**	**0**	**1**	**43**	**9.3**	**8**	**186**	**36.0**	**12:34**									
	NHL Totals		**863**	**173**	**193**	**366**	**472**	**28**	**2**	**33**	**1441**	**12.0**		**558**	**41.8**	**14:52**	**108**	**22**	**18**	**40**	**66**	**5**	**0**	**4**	**15:09**

USHL First All-Star Team (1999)

Signed as a free agent by **Philadelphia**, August 3, 1999. Traded to **Tampa Bay** by **Philadelphia** with Tampa Bay's 2nd round choice (previously acquired, later traded to Dallas – Dallas selected Tobias Stephan) in 2002 Entry Draft and Phoenix's 2nd round choice (previously acquired, later traded to San Jose – San Jose selected Dan Spang) in 2002 Entry Draft for Tampa Bay's 1st round choice (Joni Pitkanen) in 2002 Entry Draft, June 21, 2002. Signed as a free agent by **NY Islanders**, July 4, 2007. Signed as a free agent by **Pittsburgh**, July 3, 2008. Signed as a free agent by **NY Rangers**, October 4, 2010. Signed as a free agent by **Philadelphia**, July 5, 2012. Signed as a free agent by **Donetsk** (KHL), September 16, 2012.

FEHR, Eric

(FAIR, AIR-ihk) **WSH**

Right wing. Shoots right. 6'4", 212 lbs. Born, Winkler, Man., September 7, 1985. Washington's 1st choice, 18th overall, in 2003 Entry Draft.

Season	Club	League	GP	G	A	Pts	PIM	PP	SH	GW	S	%	+/-	TF	F%	Min	GP	G	A	Pts	PIM	PP	SH	GW	Min
2000-01	Pembina Valley	MMMHL	36	45	13	58	30																		
	Brandon	WHL	4	0	0	0	0																		
2001-02	Brandon	WHL	63	11	16	27	29										12	1	1	2	0				
2002-03	Brandon	WHL	70	26	29	55	76										17	4	8	12	26				
2003-04	Brandon	WHL	71	50	34	84	129										7	5	0	5	16				
2004-05	Brandon	WHL	71	*59	52	*111	91										24	16	16	*32	47				
2005-06	**Washington**	**NHL**	**11**	**0**	**0**	**0**	**2**	**0**	**0**	**0**	**10**	**0.0**	**0**	**4**	**25.0**	**5:45**									
	Hershey Bears	AHL	70	25	28	53	70										19	8	3	11	8				
2006-07	**Washington**	**NHL**	**14**	**2**	**1**	**3**	**8**	**0**	**0**	**1**	**25**	**8.0**	**3**	**6**	**16.7**	**10:43**									
	Hershey Bears	AHL	40	22	19	41	63																		

			Regular Season														Playoffs								
Season	Club	League	GP	G	A	Pts	PIM	PP	SH	GW	S	%	+/-	TF	F%	Min	GP	G	A	Pts	PIM	PP	SH	GW	Min
2007-08	**Washington**	**NHL**	23	1	5	6	6	0	0	0	40	2.5	4	2	0.0	10:31	5	1	0	1	0	0	0	0	9:41
	Hershey Bears	AHL	11	3	4	7	4	....	....	....	....	....	....	....	....	....	2	1	3	4	2	....	....	....	....
2008-09	**Washington**	**NHL**	61	12	13	25	22	1	0	2	134	9.0	8	3	33.3	11:15	9	0	0	0	0	0	0	0	7:22
2009-10	**Washington**	**NHL**	69	21	18	39	24	3	0	3	145	14.5	18	2	50.0	12:08	7	3	1	4	4	0	0	0	11:24
2010-11	**Washington**	**NHL**	52	10	10	20	16	3	0	1	120	8.3	0	1	0.0	12:35	5	1	0	1	0	0	0	0	13:28
2011-12	**Winnipeg**	**NHL**	35	2	1	3	12	0	0	1	54	3.7	–6	0	0.0	9:42	....	....	....	....	....	....	....	....	....
2012-13	HPK Hameenlinna	Finland	21	13	12	25	22	....	....	....	....	....	....	....	....	....	....	....	....	....	....	....	....	....	....
	Washington	**NHL**	41	9	8	17	10	2	1	2	72	12.5	14	4	0.0	13:22	7	0	0	0	6	0	0	0	15:52
	NHL Totals		306	57	56	113	100	9	1	10	600	9.5		22	18.2	11:30	33	5	1	6	10	0	0	0	11:18

WHL East First All-Star Team (2005) • WHL Player of the Year (2005) • Canadian Major Junior Second All-Star Team (2005)

• Missed majority of 2011-12 due to shoulder surgery and as a healthy reserve. Traded to **Winnipeg** by **Washington** for Danick Paquette and Winnipeg's 4th round choice (Thomas Di Pauli) in 2012 Entry Draft, July 8, 2011. Signed as a free agent by **Hameenlinna** (Finland), October 23, 2012. Signed as a free agent by **Washington**, Janiuary 12, 2013.

FERENCE, Andrew

(FAIR-ehns, AN-droo) **EDM**

Defense. Shoots left. 5'11", 189 lbs. Born, Edmonton, Alta., March 17, 1979. Pittsburgh's 8th choice, 208th overall, in 1997 Entry Draft.

Season	Club	League	GP	G	A	Pts	PIM	PP	SH	GW	S	%	+/-	TF	F%	Min	GP	G	A	Pts	PIM	PP	SH	GW	Min
1994-95	Sherwood Park	AMHL	31	4	14	18	74	....	....	....	....	....	....	....	....	....	....	....	....	....	....	....	....	....	....
	Portland	WHL	2	0	0	0	4	....	....	....	....	....	....	....	....	....	....	....	....	....	....	....	....	....	....
1995-96	Portland	WHL	72	9	31	40	159	....	....	....	....	....	....	....	....	....	7	1	3	4	12	....	....	....	....
1996-97	Portland	WHL	72	12	32	44	149	....	....	....	....	....	....	....	....	....	6	1	2	3	12	....	....	....	....
1997-98	Portland	WHL	72	11	57	68	142	....	....	....	....	....	....	....	....	....	16	2	18	20	28	....	....	....	....
1998-99	Portland	WHL	40	11	21	32	104	....	....	....	....	....	....	....	....	....	4	1	4	5	10	....	....	....	....
	Kansas City	IHL	5	1	2	3	4	....	....	....	....	....	....	....	....	....	3	0	0	0	9	....	....	....	....
99-2000	**Pittsburgh**	**NHL**	30	2	4	6	20	0	0	1	26	7.7	3	0	0.0	16:19	....	....	....	....	....	....	....	....	....
	Wilkes-Barre	AHL	44	8	20	28	58	....	....	....	....	....	....	....	....	....	....	....	....	....	....	....	....	....	....
2000-01	**Pittsburgh**	**NHL**	36	4	11	15	28	1	0	1	47	8.5	6	0	0.0	18:51	18	3	7	10	16	1	0	1	22:02
	Wilkes-Barre	AHL	43	6	18	24	95	....	....	....	....	....	....	....	....	....	3	1	0	1	12	....	....	....	....
2001-02	**Pittsburgh**	**NHL**	75	4	7	11	73	1	0	0	82	4.9	–12	2	0.0	18:34	....	....	....	....	....	....	....	....	....
2002-03	**Pittsburgh**	**NHL**	22	1	3	4	36	1	0	0	22	4.5	–16	1	100.0	19:33	....	....	....	....	....	....	....	....	....
	Wilkes-Barre	AHL	1	0	0	0	2	....	....	....	....	....	....	....	....	....	....	....	....	....	....	....	....	....	....
	Calgary	**NHL**	16	0	4	4	6	0	0	0	17	0.0	1	0	0.0	17:38	....	....	....	....	....	....	....	....	....
2003-04	**Calgary**	**NHL**	72	4	12	16	53	1	0	0	86	4.7	5	0	0.0	18:40	26	0	3	3	25	0	0	0	24:13
2004-05	C. Budejovice	CzRep-2	19	5	6	11	45	....	....	....	....	....	....	....	....	....	12	2	7	9	10	....	....	....	....
2005-06	**Calgary**	**NHL**	82	4	27	31	85	2	0	0	111	3.6	–12	1	0.0	20:08	7	0	4	4	12	0	0	0	23:09
2006-07	**Calgary**	**NHL**	54	2	10	12	66	1	0	0	51	3.9	7	3	33.3	18:29	....	....	....	....	....	....	....	....	....
	Boston	**NHL**	26	1	2	3	31	0	0	0	29	3.4	–2	0	0.0	22:22	....	....	....	....	....	....	....	....	....
2007-08	**Boston**	**NHL**	59	1	14	15	50	0	0	0	71	1.4	–14	1	100.0	22:15	7	0	4	4	6	0	0	0	21:39
2008-09	**Boston**	**NHL**	47	1	15	16	40	1	0	0	72	1.4	7	0	0.0	21:32	3	0	0	0	4	0	0	0	15:30
2009-10	**Boston**	**NHL**	51	0	8	8	16	0	0	0	60	0.0	–7	0	0.0	19:42	13	0	1	1	18	0	0	0	14:58
2010-11 ♦	**Boston**	**NHL**	70	3	12	15	60	0	0	0	78	3.8	22	0	0.0	17:59	25	4	6	10	37	1	0	1	20:36
2011-12	**Boston**	**NHL**	72	6	18	24	46	0	0	1	107	5.6	9	1	100.0	18:53	7	1	3	4	0	0	0	0	21:34
2012-13	C. Budejovice	CzRep	21	2	5	7	24	....	....	....	....	....	....	....	....	....	....	....	....	....	....	....	....	....	....
	Boston	**NHL**	48	4	9	13	35	0	0	0	66	6.1	9	0	0.0	19:29	14	0	2	2	4	0	0	0	24:31
	NHL Totals		760	37	156	193	645	8	0	3	925	4.0		9	44.4	19:23	120	8	30	38	122	2	0	2	21:35

WHL West First All-Star Team (1998) • WHL West Second All-Star Team (1999)

• Missed majority of 2002-03 due to groin (November 18, 2002 vs. Montreal) and ankle (March 20, 2003 vs. Los Angeles) injuries. Traded to **Calgary** by **Pittsburgh** for Calgary's 3rd round choice (Brian Gifford) in 2004 Entry Draft, February 9, 2003. Signed as a free agent by **Ceske Budejovice** (CzRep-2), December 1, 2004. Traded to **Boston** by **Calgary** with Chuck Kobasew for Brad Stuart, Wayne Primeau and Washington's 4th round choice (previously acquired, Calgary selected T.J. Brodie) in 2008 Entry Draft, February 10, 2007. Signed as a free agent by **Ceske Budejovice** (CzRep), September 19, 2012. Signed as a free agent by **Edmonton**, July 5, 2013.

FERRIERO, Benn

(fuh-RAIR-oh, BEHN) **VAN**

Center. Shoots right. 5'11", 195 lbs. Born, Boston, MA, April 29, 1987. Phoenix's 8th choice, 196th overall, in 2006 Entry Draft.

Season	Club	League	GP	G	A	Pts	PIM	PP	SH	GW	S	%	+/-	TF	F%	Min	GP	G	A	Pts	PIM	PP	SH	GW	Min
2001-02	Gov. Dummer	High-MA	STATISTICS NOT AVAILABLE																						
2002-03	Gov. Dummer	High-MA	....	8	10	18	....	....	....	....	....	....	....	....	....	....	....	....	....	....	....	....	....	....	....
2003-04	Gov. Dummer	High-MA	28	19	24	43	....	....	....	....	....	....	....	....	....	....	....	....	....	....	....	....	....	....	....
2004-05	Gov. Dummer	High-MA	28	15	27	42	....	....	....	....	....	....	....	....	....	....	....	....	....	....	....	....	....	....	....
2005-06	Boston College	H-East	42	16	9	25	36	....	....	....	....	....	....	....	....	....	....	....	....	....	....	....	....	....	....
2006-07	Boston College	H-East	42	23	23	46	43	....	....	....	....	....	....	....	....	....	....	....	....	....	....	....	....	....	....
2007-08	Boston College	H-East	44	17	25	42	71	....	....	....	....	....	....	....	....	....	....	....	....	....	....	....	....	....	....
2008-09	Boston College	H-East	37	8	18	26	44	....	....	....	....	....	....	....	....	....	....	....	....	....	....	....	....	....	....
2009-10	**San Jose**	**NHL**	24	2	3	5	8	0	0	0	42	4.8	4	4	75.0	11:08	....	....	....	....	....	....	....	....	....
	Worcester Sharks	AHL	58	19	31	50	20	....	....	....	....	....	....	....	....	....	11	4	2	6	4	....	....	....	....
2010-11	**San Jose**	**NHL**	33	5	4	9	9	1	0	1	56	8.9	8	11	18.2	13:05	8	1	0	1	6	0	0	1	6:54
	Worcester Sharks	AHL	43	16	17	33	16	....	....	....	....	....	....	....	....	....	....	....	....	....	....	....	....	....	....
2011-12	**San Jose**	**NHL**	35	7	1	8	8	0	0	4	68	10.3	0	12	25.0	12:03	....	....	....	....	....	....	....	....	....
	Worcester Sharks	AHL	20	9	11	20	18	....	....	....	....	....	....	....	....	....	....	....	....	....	....	....	....	....	....
2012-13	Wilkes-Barre	AHL	34	4	14	18	14	....	....	....	....	....	....	....	....	....	....	....	....	....	....	....	....	....	....
	Connecticut	AHL	23	4	8	12	17	....	....	....	....	....	....	....	....	....	....	....	....	....	....	....	....	....	....
	NY Rangers	**NHL**	4	0	1	1	0	0	0	0	4	0.0	0	9	22.2	9:37	....	....	....	....	....	....	....	....	....
	NHL Totals		96	14	9	23	25	1	0	5	170	8.2		36	27.8	12:05	8	1	0	1	6	0	0	1	6:54

Hockey East All-Rookie Team (2006)

Signed as a free agent by **San Jose**, August 23, 2009. Signed as a free agent by **Pittsburgh**, July 13, 2012. Traded to **NY Rangers** by **Pittsburgh** for Chad Kolarik, January 24, 2013. Traded to **Minnesota** by **NY Rangers** with Columbus' 6th round choice (previously acquired) in 2014 Entry Draft for Justin Falk, June 30, 2013. Signed as a free agent by **Vancouver**, July 12, 2013.

FESTERLING, Brett

(FEHS-tuhr-lihng, BREHT)

Defense. Shoots left. 6'1", 210 lbs. Born, Quesnel, B.C., March 3, 1986.

Season	Club	League	GP	G	A	Pts	PIM	PP	SH	GW	S	%	+/-	TF	F%	Min	GP	G	A	Pts	PIM	PP	SH	GW	Min
2001-02	Quesnel Thunder	Minor-BC	40	18	26	44	44	....	....	....	....	....	....	....	....	....	....	....	....	....	....	....	....	....	....
	Quesnel	BCHL	7	0	0	0	0	....	....	....	....	....	....	....	....	....	....	....	....	....	....	....	....	....	....
	Tri-City	WHL	3	0	0	0	0	....	....	....	....	....	....	....	....	....	....	....	....	....	....	....	....	....	....
2002-03	Tri-City	WHL	55	3	8	11	26	....	....	....	....	....	....	....	....	....	....	....	....	....	....	....	....	....	....
2003-04	Tri-City	WHL	54	1	9	10	34	....	....	....	....	....	....	....	....	....	11	1	1	2	2	....	....	....	....
2004-05	Tri-City	WHL	33	3	11	14	20	....	....	....	....	....	....	....	....	....	....	....	....	....	....	....	....	....	....
	Vancouver Giants	WHL	32	2	4	6	10	....	....	....	....	....	....	....	....	....	5	0	0	0	6	....	....	....	....
2005-06	Vancouver Giants	WHL	67	1	6	7	35	....	....	....	....	....	....	....	....	....	18	0	1	1	10	....	....	....	....
2006-07	Vancouver Giants	WHL	70	5	16	21	80	....	....	....	....	....	....	....	....	....	22	1	6	7	24	....	....	....	....
2007-08	Portland Pirates	AHL	74	3	11	14	64	....	....	....	....	....	....	....	....	....	15	1	3	4	6	....	....	....	....
2008-09	**Anaheim**	**NHL**	40	0	5	5	18	0	0	0	15	0.0	5	0	0.0	16:40	1	0	0	0	0	0	0	0	14:34
	Iowa Chops	AHL	34	0	7	7	31	....	....	....	....	....	....	....	....	....	....	....	....	....	....	....	....	....	....
2009-10	**Anaheim**	**NHL**	42	0	3	3	15	0	0	0	25	0.0	1	0	0.0	12:30	....	....	....	....	....	....	....	....	....
	San Antonio	AHL	17	0	1	1	19	....	....	....	....	....	....	....	....	....	....	....	....	....	....	....	....	....	....
	Toronto Marlies	AHL	11	0	4	4	8	....	....	....	....	....	....	....	....	....	....	....	....	....	....	....	....	....	....
2010-11	**Anaheim**	**NHL**	1	0	0	0	0	0	0	0	0	0.0	–2	0	0.0	14:53	....	....	....	....	....	....	....	....	....
	Syracuse Crunch	AHL	32	3	9	12	41	....	....	....	....	....	....	....	....	....	....	....	....	....	....	....	....	....	....
	Hamilton	AHL	16	0	4	4	15	....	....	....	....	....	....	....	....	....	....	....	....	....	....	....	....	....	....
	Chicago Wolves	AHL	5	0	0	0	0	....	....	....	....	....	....	....	....	....	....	....	....	....	....	....	....	....	....
2011-12	**Winnipeg**	**NHL**	5	0	0	0	2	0	0	0	2	0.0	–1	0	0.0	13:07	....	....	....	....	....	....	....	....	....
	St. John's IceCaps	AHL	52	3	15	18	50	....	....	....	....	....	....	....	....	....	14	0	2	2	10	....	....	....	....
2012-13	Nurnberg	Germany	41	1	8	9	50	....	....	....	....	....	....	....	....	....	3	0	0	0	10	....	....	....	....
	NHL Totals		88	0	8	8	35	0	0	0	42	0.0		0	0.0	14:28	1	0	0	0	0	0	0	0	14:34

Signed as a free agent by **Anaheim**, September 14, 2005. Traded to **Montreal** by **Anaheim** with Anaheim's 5th round choice (later traded back to Anaheim – Anaheim selkected Brian Cooper) in 2012 Entry Draft for Maxim Lapierre, December 31, 2010. Traded to **Atlanta** by **Montreal** for Drew MacIntyre, February 28, 2011. • Transferred to **Winnipeg** after **Atlanta** franchise relocated, June 21, 2011. Signed as a free agent by **Nurnberg** (Germany), July 24, 2012.

FIDDLER, Vernon
(FIHD-luhr, VUHR-nuhn) **DAL**

Center. Shoots left. 5'11", 197 lbs. Born, Edmonton, Alta., May 9, 1980.

			Regular Season														Playoffs								
Season	Club	League	GP	G	A	Pts	PIM	PP	SH	GW	S	%	+/-	TF	F%	Min	GP	G	A	Pts	PIM	PP	SH	GW	Min
1997-98	Kelowna Rockets	WHL	65	10	11	21	31	....	....	....	....	....	....	....	....	....	7	0	1	1	4	....	....	....	....
1998-99	Kelowna Rockets	WHL	68	22	21	43	82	....	....	....	....	....	....	....	....	....	6	2	0	2	8	....	....	....	....
99-2000	Kelowna Rockets	WHL	64	20	28	48	60	....	....	....	....	....	....	....	....	....	5	1	3	4	4	....	....	....	....
2000-01	Kelowna Rockets	WHL	3	0	2	2	0	....	....	....	....	....	....	....	....	....	....	....	....	....	....	....	....	....	....
	Medicine Hat	WHL	67	33	38	71	100	....	....	....	....	....	....	....	....	....	....	....	....	....	....	....	....	....	....
	Arkansas	ECHL	3	0	1	1	2	....	....	....	....	....	....	....	....	....	5	3	0	3	5	....	....	....	....
2001-02	Roanoke Express	ECHL	44	27	28	55	71	....	....	....	....	....	....	....	....	....	....	....	....	....	....	....	....	....	....
	Norfolk Admirals	AHL	38	8	5	13	28	....	....	....	....	....	....	....	....	....	4	1	3	4	2	....	....	....	....
2002-03	**Nashville**	**NHL**	**19**	**4**	**2**	**6**	**14**	**0**	**0**	**1**	**20**	**20.0**	**2**	**171**	**53.8**	**9:40**	....	....	....	....	....	....	....	....	....
	Milwaukee	AHL	54	8	16	24	70	....	....	....	....	....	....	....	....	....	6	1	2	3	14	....	....	....	....
2003-04	**Nashville**	**NHL**	**17**	**0**	**0**	**0**	**23**	**0**	**0**	**0**	**8**	**0.0**	**–6**	**123**	**49.6**	**8:06**	....	....	....	....	....	....	....	....	....
	Milwaukee	AHL	47	9	15	24	72	....	....	....	....	....	....	....	....	....	22	5	3	8	36	....	....	....	....
2004-05	Milwaukee	AHL	73	20	22	42	70	....	....	....	....	....	....	....	....	....	7	0	0	0	18	....	....	....	....
2005-06	**Nashville**	**NHL**	**40**	**8**	**4**	**12**	**42**	**3**	**0**	**2**	**46**	**17.4**	**–2**	**464**	**52.6**	**13:49**	**2**	**0**	**1**	**1**	**0**	**0**	**0**	**0**	**8:48**
	Milwaukee	AHL	11	1	6	7	20	....	....	....	....	....	....	....	....	....	....	....	....	....	....	....	....	....	....
2006-07	**Nashville**	**NHL**	**72**	**11**	**15**	**26**	**40**	**0**	**1**	**1**	**90**	**12.2**	**11**	**680**	**51.6**	**13:38**	**5**	**1**	**1**	**2**	**4**	**0**	**0**	**0**	**12:21**
2007-08	**Nashville**	**NHL**	**79**	**11**	**21**	**32**	**47**	**2**	**1**	**1**	**97**	**11.3**	**–4**	**384**	**50.3**	**13:56**	**6**	**0**	**0**	**0**	**0**	**0**	**0**	**0**	**16:48**
2008-09	**Nashville**	**NHL**	**78**	**11**	**6**	**17**	**24**	**1**	**2**	**2**	**114**	**9.6**	**–13**	**612**	**54.1**	**13:58**	....	....	....	....	....	....	....	....	....
2009-10	**Phoenix**	**NHL**	**76**	**8**	**22**	**30**	**46**	**0**	**3**	**1**	**119**	**6.7**	**13**	**1121**	**52.5**	**14:21**	**6**	**1**	**1**	**2**	**14**	**0**	**0**	**0**	**14:04**
2010-11	**Phoenix**	**NHL**	**71**	**6**	**16**	**22**	**46**	**0**	**1**	**2**	**97**	**6.2**	**3**	**1224**	**53.9**	**15:33**	**4**	**0**	**0**	**0**	**0**	**0**	**0**	**0**	**9:57**
2011-12	**Dallas**	**NHL**	**82**	**8**	**13**	**21**	**60**	**0**	**0**	**1**	**123**	**6.5**	**–13**	**1049**	**50.9**	**13:59**	....	....	....	....	....	....	....	....	....
2012-13	**Dallas**	**NHL**	**46**	**4**	**13**	**17**	**48**	**1**	**0**	**0**	**56**	**7.1**	**3**	**619**	**51.5**	**12:51**	....	....	....	....	....	....	....	....	....
	NHL Totals		**580**	**71**	**112**	**183**	**390**	**7**	**8**	**11**	**770**	**9.2**		**6447**	**52.3**	**13:45**	**23**	**2**	**3**	**5**	**18**	**0**	**0**	**0**	**13:14**

ECHL All-Rookie Team (2002)

Signed as a free agent by **Arkansas** (ECHL), March 31, 2001. Traded to **Roanoke** (ECHL) by **Arkansas** (ECHL) for Calvin Elfring, August 11, 2001. Signed as a free agent by **Nashville**, May 6, 2002. Signed as a free agent by **Phoenix**, July 1, 2009. Signed as a free agent by **Dallas**, July 1, 2011.

FILATOV, Nikita
(FIHL-uh-tawf, nih-KEE-ta) **OTT**

Left wing. Shoots right. 6', 190 lbs. Born, Moscow, USSR, May 25, 1990. Columbus' 1st choice, 6th overall, in 2008 Entry Draft.

Season	Club	League	GP	G	A	Pts	PIM	PP	SH	GW	S	%	+/-	TF	F%	Min	GP	G	A	Pts	PIM	PP	SH	GW	Min
2005-06	CSKA Moscow 2	Russia-3	Statistics Not Available																						
2006-07	CSKA Moscow 2	Russia-3	Statistics Not Available																						
2007-08	CSKA Moscow 2	Russia-3	23	24	23	47	62	....	....	....	....	....	....	....	....	....	11	14	9	23	28	....	....	....	....
	CSKA Moscow	Russia	5	0	0	0	0	....	....	....	....	....	....	....	....	....	....	....	....	....	....	....	....	....	....
2008-09	**Columbus**	**NHL**	**8**	**4**	**0**	**4**	**0**	**0**	**0**	**1**	**10**	**40.0**	**3**	**0**	**0.0**	**8:08**	....	....	....	....	....	....	....	....	....
	Syracuse Crunch	AHL	39	16	16	32	24	....	....	....	....	....	....	....	....	....	....	....	....	....	....	....	....	....	....
2009-10	**Columbus**	**NHL**	**13**	**2**	**0**	**2**	**8**	**0**	**0**	**1**	**11**	**18.2**	**0**	**3**	**66.7**	**8:07**	....	....	....	....	....	....	....	....	....
	CSKA Moscow	KHL	26	9	13	22	16	....	....	....	....	....	....	....	....	....	3	0	1	1	4	....	....	....	....
2010-11	**Columbus**	**NHL**	**23**	**0**	**7**	**7**	**8**	**0**	**0**	**0**	**31**	**0.0**	**3**	**0**	**0.0**	**12:19**	....	....	....	....	....	....	....	....	....
	Springfield	AHL	36	9	11	20	20	....	....	....	....	....	....	....	....	....	....	....	....	....	....	....	....	....	....
2011-12	**Ottawa**	**NHL**	**9**	**0**	**1**	**1**	**4**	**0**	**0**	**0**	**6**	**0.0**	**1**	**1**	**0.0**	**9:49**	....	....	....	....	....	....	....	....	....
	Binghamton	AHL	15	7	5	12	12	....	....	....	....	....	....	....	....	....	....	....	....	....	....	....	....	....	....
	CSKA Moscow	KHL	18	4	4	8	12	....	....	....	....	....	....	....	....	....	5	0	1	1	4	....	....	....	....
2012-13	Ufa	KHL	47	10	11	21	24	....	....	....	....	....	....	....	....	....	13	3	3	6	6	....	....	....	....
	NHL Totals		**53**	**6**	**8**	**14**	**20**	**0**	**0**	**2**	**58**	**10.3**		**4**	**50.0**	**10:14**	....	....	....	....	....	....	....	....	....

• Loaned to **CSKA Moscow** (KHL) by **Columbus** for remainder of 2009-10 season, November 17, 2009. Traded to **Ottawa** by **Columbus** for Ottawa's 3rd round choice (Thomas Tynan) in 2011 Entry Draft, June 25, 2011. • Loaned to **CSKA Moscow** (KHL) by **Ottawa** (Binghamton-AHL) for remainder of 2011-12 season, December 12, 2011. Signed as a free agent by **Ufa** (KHL), May 14, 2012.

FILPPULA, Valtteri
(FIHL-poo-luh, VAL-tuhr-ee) **T.B.**

Center. Shoots left. 6', 195 lbs. Born, Vantaa, Finland, March 20, 1984. Detroit's 3rd choice, 95th overall, in 2002 Entry Draft.

Season	Club	League	GP	G	A	Pts	PIM	PP	SH	GW	S	%	+/-	TF	F%	Min	GP	G	A	Pts	PIM	PP	SH	GW	Min
2000-01	Jokerit U18	Fin-U18	31	18	29	47	4	....	....	....	....	....	....	....	....	....	6	4	4	8	0	....	....	....	....
	Jokerit Helsinki Jr.	Fin-Jr.	1	0	1	1	0	....	....	....	....	....	....	....	....	....	....	....	....	....	....	....	....	....	....
2001-02	Jokerit U18	Fin-U18	1	0	1	1	0	....	....	....	....	....	....	....	....	....	8	4	9	13	2	....	....	....	....
	Jokerit Helsinki Jr.	Fin-Jr.	40	8	15	23	14	....	....	....	....	....	....	....	....	....	1	0	0	0	0	....	....	....	....
2002-03	Jokerit Helsinki Jr.	Fin-Jr.	35	16	37	53	14	....	....	....	....	....	....	....	....	....	11	4	10	14	4	....	....	....	....
2003-04	Suomi U20	Finland-2	1	0	0	0	2	....	....	....	....	....	....	....	....	....	....	....	....	....	....	....	....	....	....
	Jokerit Helsinki	Finland	49	5	13	18	6	....	....	....	....	....	....	....	....	....	....	....	....	....	....	....	....	....	....
2004-05	Jokerit Helsinki	Finland	55	10	20	30	20	....	....	....	....	....	....	....	....	....	12	5	6	11	2	....	....	....	....
2005-06	**Detroit**	**NHL**	**4**	**0**	**1**	**1**	**2**	**0**	**0**	**0**	**1**	**0.0**	**1**	**21**	**47.6**	**7:19**	....	....	....	....	....	....	....	....	....
	Grand Rapids	AHL	74	20	51	71	30	....	....	....	....	....	....	....	....	....	16	7	9	16	4	....	....	....	....
2006-07	**Detroit**	**NHL**	**73**	**10**	**7**	**17**	**20**	**0**	**0**	**1**	**76**	**13.2**	**8**	**267**	**55.8**	**11:16**	**18**	**3**	**2**	**5**	**2**	**0**	**0**	**0**	**12:12**
	Grand Rapids	AHL	3	2	2	4	2	....	....	....	....	....	....	....	....	....	....	....	....	....	....	....	....	....	....
2007-08 ♦	**Detroit**	**NHL**	**78**	**19**	**17**	**36**	**28**	**3**	**0**	**3**	**122**	**15.6**	**16**	**621**	**50.6**	**16:58**	**22**	**5**	**6**	**11**	**2**	**0**	**0**	**0**	**16:40**
2008-09	**Detroit**	**NHL**	**80**	**12**	**28**	**40**	**42**	**1**	**0**	**1**	**129**	**9.3**	**9**	**785**	**52.1**	**16:06**	**23**	**3**	**13**	**16**	**8**	**1**	**0**	**1**	**17:38**
2009-10	**Detroit**	**NHL**	**55**	**11**	**24**	**35**	**24**	**1**	**1**	**1**	**114**	**9.6**	**–4**	**573**	**51.7**	**18:14**	**12**	**4**	**5**	**9**	**6**	**2**	**0**	**0**	**18:34**
	Finland	Olympics	6	3	0	3	0	....	....	....	....	....	....	....	....	....	....	....	....	....	....	....	....	....	....
2010-11	**Detroit**	**NHL**	**71**	**16**	**23**	**39**	**22**	**4**	**0**	**5**	**115**	**13.9**	**–1**	**928**	**51.5**	**16:43**	**11**	**2**	**6**	**8**	**6**	**0**	**0**	**2**	**17:47**
2011-12	**Detroit**	**NHL**	**81**	**23**	**43**	**66**	**14**	**3**	**1**	**1**	**144**	**16.0**	**18**	**373**	**51.7**	**18:16**	**5**	**0**	**2**	**2**	**2**	**0**	**0**	**0**	**19:20**
2012-13	Jokerit Helsinki	Finland	16	6	9	15	6	....	....	....	....	....	....	....	....	....	....	....	....	....	....	....	....	....	....
	Detroit	**NHL**	**41**	**9**	**8**	**17**	**6**	**3**	**0**	**0**	**78**	**11.5**	**–4**	**323**	**55.4**	**17:47**	**14**	**2**	**4**	**6**	**4**	**0**	**0**	**1**	**16:36**
	NHL Totals		**483**	**100**	**151**	**251**	**158**	**15**	**2**	**12**	**779**	**12.8**		**3891**	**52.1**	**16:16**	**105**	**19**	**38**	**57**	**30**	**3**	**0**	**4**	**16:34**

Signed as a free agent by **Jokerit Helsinki** (Finland), September 21, 2012. Signed as a free agent by **Tampa Bay**, July 5, 2013.

FINLEY, Joe
(FIHN-lee, JOH) **NYI**

Defense. Shoots left. 6'8", 249 lbs. Born, Edina, MN, June 29, 1987. Washington's 2nd choice, 27th overall, in 2005 Entry Draft.

Season	Club	League	GP	G	A	Pts	PIM	PP	SH	GW	S	%	+/-	TF	F%	Min	GP	G	A	Pts	PIM	PP	SH	GW	Min
2004-05	Sioux Falls	USHL	55	3	10	13	181	....	....	....	....	....	....	....	....	....	....	....	....	....	....	....	....	....	....
2005-06	North Dakota	WCHA	43	0	3	3	96	....	....	....	....	....	....	....	....	....	....	....	....	....	....	....	....	....	....
2006-07	North Dakota	WCHA	41	1	6	7	72	....	....	....	....	....	....	....	....	....	....	....	....	....	....	....	....	....	....
2007-08	North Dakota	WCHA	43	4	11	15	79	....	....	....	....	....	....	....	....	....	....	....	....	....	....	....	....	....	....
2008-09	North Dakota	WCHA	27	2	8	10	56	....	....	....	....	....	....	....	....	....	....	....	....	....	....	....	....	....	....
	Hershey Bears	AHL	1	0	0	0	7	....	....	....	....	....	....	....	....	....	....	....	....	....	....	....	....	....	....
2009-10	South Carolina	ECHL	17	1	3	4	43	....	....	....	....	....	....	....	....	....	....	....	....	....	....	....	....	....	....
2010-11	Hershey Bears	AHL	7	0	1	1	15	....	....	....	....	....	....	....	....	....	....	....	....	....	....	....	....	....	....
	South Carolina	ECHL	26	1	7	8	73	....	....	....	....	....	....	....	....	....	4	0	0	0	10	....	....	....	....
2011-12	Rochester	AHL	57	1	5	6	143	....	....	....	....	....	....	....	....	....	3	0	0	0	0	....	....	....	....
	Buffalo	**NHL**	**5**	**0**	**0**	**0**	**12**	**0**	**0**	**0**	**1**	**0.0**	**–3**	**0**	**0.0**	**7:48**	....	....	....	....	....	....	....	....	....
2012-13	Rochester	AHL	36	1	4	5	81	....	....	....	....	....	....	....	....	....	....	....	....	....	....	....	....	....	....
	NY Islanders	**NHL**	**16**	**0**	**1**	**1**	**20**	**0**	**0**	**0**	**2**	**0.0**	**–5**	**1**	**0.0**	**11:57**	....	....	....	....	....	....	....	....	....
	NHL Totals		**21**	**0**	**1**	**1**	**32**	**0**	**0**	**0**	**3**	**0.0**		**1**	**0.0**	**10:58**	....	....	....	....	....	....	....	....	....

• Missed majority of 2009-10 due to recurring hand injury. Signed as a free agent by **Rochester**, September 18, 2011. Signed as a free agent by **Buffalo**, November 28, 2011. Claimed on waivers by **NY Islanders** from **Buffalo**, January 14, 2013.

FISHER, Mike
(FIH-shuhr, MIGHK) **NSH**

Center. Shoots right. 6'1", 208 lbs. Born, Peterborough, Ont., June 5, 1980. Ottawa's 2nd choice, 44th overall, in 1998 Entry Draft.

Season	Club	League	GP	G	A	Pts	PIM	PP	SH	GW	S	%	+/-	TF	F%	Min	GP	G	A	Pts	PIM	PP	SH	GW	Min
1996-97	Peterborough	ON-Jr.A	51	26	30	56	35	....	....	....	....	....	....	....	....	....	....	....	....	....	....	....	....	....	....
1997-98	Sudbury Wolves	OHL	66	24	25	49	65	....	....	....	....	....	....	....	....	....	9	2	2	4	13	....	....	....	....
1998-99	Sudbury Wolves	OHL	68	41	65	106	55	....	....	....	....	....	....	....	....	....	4	2	1	3	4	....	....	....	....
99-2000	**Ottawa**	**NHL**	**32**	**4**	**5**	**9**	**15**	**0**	**0**	**1**	**49**	**8.2**	**–6**	**356**	**47.8**	**12:57**	....	....	....	....	....	....	....	....	....
2000-01	**Ottawa**	**NHL**	**60**	**7**	**12**	**19**	**46**	**0**	**0**	**3**	**83**	**8.4**	**–1**	**709**	**50.2**	**11:38**	**4**	**0**	**1**	**1**	**4**	**0**	**0**	**0**	**13:41**
2001-02	**Ottawa**	**NHL**	**58**	**15**	**9**	**24**	**55**	**0**	**3**	**4**	**123**	**12.2**	**8**	**848**	**48.7**	**14:05**	**10**	**2**	**1**	**3**	**0**	**0**	**0**	**0**	**16:17**
2002-03	**Ottawa**	**NHL**	**74**	**18**	**20**	**38**	**54**	**5**	**1**	**3**	**142**	**12.7**	**13**	**1077**	**48.1**	**15:59**	**18**	**2**	**2**	**4**	**16**	**0**	**1**	**1**	**16:58**
2003-04	**Ottawa**	**NHL**	**24**	**4**	**6**	**10**	**39**	**1**	**0**	**0**	**47**	**8.5**	**–3**	**357**	**42.0**	**17:26**	**7**	**1**	**0**	**1**	**4**	**0**	**0**	**1**	**16:11**
2004-05	EV Zug	Swiss	21	9	18	27	34	....	....	....	....	....	....	....	....	....	9	2	3	5	10	....	....	....	....
2005-06	**Ottawa**	**NHL**	**68**	**22**	**22**	**44**	**64**	**2**	**4**	**3**	**150**	**14.7**	**23**	**883**	**50.3**	**17:09**	**10**	**2**	**2**	**4**	**12**	**0**	**1**	**0**	**18:50**
2006-07	**Ottawa**	**NHL**	**68**	**22**	**26**	**48**	**41**	**7**	**2**	**3**	**193**	**11.4**	**15**	**1191**	**52.1**	**18:25**	**20**	**5**	**5**	**10**	**24**	**2**	**1**	**1**	**17:43**

			Regular Season														Playoffs								
Season	Club	League	GP	G	A	Pts	PIM	PP	SH	GW	S	%	+/-	TF	F%	Min	GP	G	A	Pts	PIM	PP	SH	GW	Min
2007-08	**Ottawa**	**NHL**	**79**	**23**	**24**	**47**	**82**	**6**	**2**	**4**	**215**	**10.7**	**-10**	**1230**	**50.2**	**19:46**	....	....	....	....	....	....	....	....	....
2008-09	**Ottawa**	**NHL**	**78**	**13**	**19**	**32**	**66**	**1**	**2**	**3**	**182**	**7.1**	**0**	**1044**	**51.3**	**18:30**	....	....	....	....	....	....	....	....	....
2009-10	**Ottawa**	**NHL**	**79**	**25**	**28**	**53**	**59**	**10**	**0**	**6**	**212**	**11.8**	**1**	**1307**	**52.0**	**18:58**	**6**	**2**	**3**	**5**	**6**	**2**	**0**	**0**	**23:04**
2010-11	**Ottawa**	**NHL**	**55**	**14**	**10**	**24**	**33**	**3**	**0**	**1**	**132**	**10.6**	**-19**	**825**	**48.4**	**18:25**	....	....	....	....	....	....	....	....	....
	Nashville	**NHL**	**27**	**5**	**7**	**12**	**10**	**1**	**0**	**1**	**60**	**8.3**	**2**	**421**	**48.2**	**18:15**	**12**	**3**	**4**	**7**	**11**	**0**	**0**	**1**	**20:43**
2011-12	**Nashville**	**NHL**	**72**	**24**	**27**	**51**	**33**	**5**	**0**	**7**	**157**	**15.3**	**11**	**1217**	**48.3**	**19:18**	**10**	**1**	**3**	**4**	**8**	**0**	**0**	**0**	**20:44**
2012-13	**Nashville**	**NHL**	**38**	**10**	**11**	**21**	**27**	**1**	**0**	**0**	**68**	**14.7**	**6**	**563**	**48.9**	**19:28**	....	....	....	....	....	....	....	....	....
	NHL Totals		**812**	**206**	**226**	**432**	**624**	**42**	**14**	**39**	**1813**	**11.4**		**12028**	**49.6**	**17:21**	**97**	**18**	**21**	**39**	**85**	**4**	**3**	**4**	**18:17**

NHL Foundation Player Award (2012)

• Missed majority of 1999-2000 due to knee injury vs. Boston, December 30, 1999. • Missed majority of 2003-04 due to elbow injury in practice, October 4, 2003. Signed as a free agent by **Zug** (Swiss), November 1, 2004. Traded to **Nashville** by **Ottawa** for Nashville's 1st round choice (Stefan Noesen) in 2011 Entry Draft and Nashville's 3rd round choice (Jarrod Maidens) in 2012 Entry Draft , February 10, 2011.

FISTRIC, Mark

(FIHST-rihc, MAHRK)

Defense. Shoots left. 6'2", 233 lbs. Born, Edmonton, Alta., June 1, 1986. Dallas' 1st choice, 28th overall, in 2004 Entry Draft.

2000-01	Edmonton MLAC	AMBHL	34	13	13	26	144	....	....	....	....	....	....	....	....	....	....	....	....	....	....	....	....	....	....
2001-02	Edmonton MLAC	AMHL	30	8	10	18	85	....	....	....	....	....	....	....	....	....	....	....	....	....	....	....	....	....	....
	Vancouver Giants	WHL	4	0	2	2	0	....	....	....	....	....	....	....	....	....	....	....	....	....	....	....	....	....	....
2002-03	Vancouver Giants	WHL	63	2	7	9	81	....	....	....	....	....	....	....	....	....	4	0	0	0	8	....	....	....	....
2003-04	Vancouver Giants	WHL	72	1	11	12	192	....	....	....	....	....	....	....	....	....	11	0	2	2	10	....	....	....	....
2004-05	Vancouver Giants	WHL	15	1	5	6	32	....	....	....	....	....	....	....	....	....	6	1	1	2	16	....	....	....	....
2005-06	Vancouver Giants	WHL	60	7	22	29	148	....	....	....	....	....	....	....	....	....	18	1	9	10	30	....	....	....	....
2006-07	Iowa Stars	AHL	80	2	22	24	83	....	....	....	....	....	....	....	....	....	12	0	0	0	16	....	....	....	....
2007-08	**Dallas**	**NHL**	**37**	**0**	**2**	**2**	**24**	**0**	**0**	**0**	**17**	**0.0**	**3**	**0**	**0.0**	**12:44**	**9**	**0**	**0**	**0**	**6**	**0**	**0**	**0**	**14:51**
	Iowa Stars	AHL	30	1	4	5	48	....	....	....	....	....	....	....	....	....	....	....	....	....	....	....	....	....	....
2008-09	**Dallas**	**NHL**	**36**	**0**	**4**	**4**	**42**	**0**	**0**	**0**	**35**	**0.0**	**-1**	**0**	**0.0**	**15:57**	....	....	....	....	....	....	....	....	....
	Manitoba Moose	AHL	35	0	8	8	26	....	....	....	....	....	....	....	....	....	22	2	5	7	26	....	....	....	....
2009-10	**Dallas**	**NHL**	**67**	**1**	**9**	**10**	**69**	**0**	**0**	**0**	**46**	**2.2**	**27**	**0**	**0.0**	**14:56**	....	....	....	....	....	....	....	....	....
2010-11	**Dallas**	**NHL**	**57**	**2**	**3**	**5**	**44**	**0**	**0**	**1**	**26**	**7.7**	**-10**	**0**	**0.0**	**14:23**	....	....	....	....	....	....	....	....	....
	Texas Stars	AHL	3	0	0	0	2	....	....	....	....	....	....	....	....	....	....	....	....	....	....	....	....	....	....
2011-12	**Dallas**	**NHL**	**60**	**0**	**2**	**2**	**41**	**0**	**0**	**0**	**30**	**0.0**	**-3**	**1**	**100.0**	**16:31**	....	....	....	....	....	....	....	....	....
2012-13	**Edmonton**	**NHL**	**25**	**0**	**6**	**6**	**32**	**0**	**0**	**0**	**9**	**0.0**	**6**	**0**	**0.0**	**15:20**	....	....	....	....	....	....	....	....	....
	NHL Totals		**282**	**3**	**26**	**29**	**252**	**0**	**0**	**1**	**163**	**1.8**		**1**	**100.0**	**15:02**	**9**	**0**	**0**	**0**	**6**	**0**	**0**	**0**	**14:51**

Traded to **Edmonton** by **Dallas** for Edmonton's 3rd round choice (Niklas Hansson) in 2013 Entry Draft, January 14, 2013.

FITZGERALD, Zack

(fihtz-JAIR-uhld, ZAK)

Defense. Shoots left. 6'2", 205 lbs. Born, Two Harbors, MN, June 16, 1985. St. Louis' 4th choice, 88th overall, in 2003 Entry Draft.

2000-01	Duluth East	High-MN	26	1	7	8	44	....	....	....	....	....	....	....	....	....	....	....	....	....	....	....	....	....	....
2001-02	Seattle	WHL	61	3	7	10	214	....	....	....	....	....	....	....	....	....	10	0	2	2	19	....	....	....	....
2002-03	Seattle	WHL	64	8	14	22	232	....	....	....	....	....	....	....	....	....	15	0	4	4	33	....	....	....	....
2003-04	Seattle	WHL	58	4	15	19	163	....	....	....	....	....	....	....	....	....	....	....	....	....	....	....	....	....	....
2004-05	Seattle	WHL	65	7	18	25	*244	....	....	....	....	....	....	....	....	....	9	0	3	3	24	....	....	....	....
2005-06	Peoria Rivermen	AHL	13	1	1	2	47	....	....	....	....	....	....	....	....	....	....	....	....	....	....	....	....	....	....
	Alaska Aces	ECHL	12	1	1	2	108	....	....	....	....	....	....	....	....	....	....	....	....	....	....	....	....	....	....
2006-07	Peoria Rivermen	AHL	29	0	2	2	86	....	....	....	....	....	....	....	....	....	....	....	....	....	....	....	....	....	....
	Alaska Aces	ECHL	10	0	1	1	48	....	....	....	....	....	....	....	....	....	14	2	3	5	*82	....	....	....	....
2007-08	**Vancouver**	**NHL**	**1**	**0**	**0**	**0**	**0**	**0**	**0**	**0**	**1**	**0.0**	**0**	**0**	**0.0**	**13:20**	....	....	....	....	....	....	....	....	....
	Manitoba Moose	AHL	48	5	3	8	158	....	....	....	....	....	....	....	....	....	3	0	0	0	14	....	....	....	....
2008-09	Manitoba Moose	AHL	56	0	8	8	209	....	....	....	....	....	....	....	....	....	16	0	1	1	14	....	....	....	....
2009-10	Albany River Rats	AHL	77	2	12	14	*311	....	....	....	....	....	....	....	....	....	2	0	0	0	0	....	....	....	....
2010-11	Charlotte	AHL	76	0	8	8	229	....	....	....	....	....	....	....	....	....	10	0	1	1	32	....	....	....	....
2011-12	Hamilton	AHL	74	2	3	5	*268	....	....	....	....	....	....	....	....	....	....	....	....	....	....	....	....	....	....
2012-13	Adirondack	AHL	36	1	0	1	202	....	....	....	....	....	....	....	....	....	....	....	....	....	....	....	....	....	....
	NHL Totals		**1**	**0**	**0**	**0**	**0**	**0**	**0**	**0**	**1**	**0.0**		**0**	**0.0**	**13:20**	....	....	....	....	....	....	....	....	....

Traded to **Vancouver** by **St. Louis** for Francois-Pierre Guenette, August 1, 2007. Signed as a free agent by **Carolina**, July 15, 2009. Signed as a free agent b **Hamilton** (AHL), Septemeber 10, 2011. Signed as a free agent by **Adirondack** (AHL), July 3, 2012.

FLEISCHMANN, Tomas

(FLIGHSH-muhn, TAW-mahsh) **FLA**

Left wing. Shoots left. 6'1", 192 lbs. Born, Koprivnice, Czech., May 16, 1984. Detroit's 2nd choice, 63rd overall, in 2002 Entry Draft.

99-2000	HC Vitkovice Jr.	CzRep-Jr.	46	9	13	22	6	....	....	....	....	....	....	....	....	....	....	....	....	....	....	....	....	....	....
2000-01	HC Vitkovice U17	CzR-U17	30	28	34	62	8	....	....	....	....	....	....	....	....	....	....	....	....	....	....	....	....	....	....
	HC Vitkovice Jr.	CzRep-Jr.	21	4	9	13	8	....	....	....	....	....	....	....	....	....	....	....	....	....	....	....	....	....	....
2001-02	HC Vitkovice Jr.	CzRep-Jr.	46	26	35	51	16	....	....	....	....	....	....	....	....	....	....	....	....	....	....	....	....	....	....
	TJ Novy Jicin	CzRep-3	8	3	2	5	8	....	....	....	....	....	....	....	....	....	7	3	4	7	35	....	....	....	....
2002-03	Moose Jaw	WHL	65	21	50	71	36	....	....	....	....	....	....	....	....	....	12	4	11	15	6	....	....	....	....
2003-04	Moose Jaw	WHL	60	33	42	75	32	....	....	....	....	....	....	....	....	....	10	3	4	7	10	....	....	....	....
2004-05	Portland Pirates	AHL	53	7	12	19	14	....	....	....	....	....	....	....	....	....	....	....	....	....	....	....	....	....	....
2005-06	**Washington**	**NHL**	**14**	**0**	**2**	**2**	**0**	**0**	**0**	**0**	**11**	**0.0**	**-7**	**5**	**40.0**	**6:45**	....	....	....	....	....	....	....	....	....
	Hershey Bears	AHL	57	30	33	63	32	....	....	....	....	....	....	....	....	....	20	11	*21	32	15	....	....	....	....
2006-07	**Washington**	**NHL**	**29**	**4**	**4**	**8**	**8**	**1**	**0**	**1**	**52**	**7.7**	**-6**	**14**	**35.7**	**11:38**	....	....	....	....	....	....	....	....	....
	Hershey Bears	AHL	45	22	29	51	22	....	....	....	....	....	....	....	....	....	19	5	16	21	10	....	....	....	....
2007-08	**Washington**	**NHL**	**75**	**10**	**20**	**30**	**18**	**1**	**0**	**1**	**107**	**9.3**	**-7**	**30**	**50.0**	**12:37**	**2**	**0**	**0**	**0**	**0**	**0**	**0**	**0**	**9:49**
2008-09	**Washington**	**NHL**	**73**	**19**	**18**	**37**	**20**	**7**	**0**	**4**	**131**	**14.5**	**-3**	**34**	**26.5**	**15:05**	**14**	**3**	**1**	**4**	**4**	**1**	**0**	**1**	**14:19**
2009-10	**Washington**	**NHL**	**69**	**23**	**28**	**51**	**28**	**7**	**0**	**4**	**121**	**19.0**	**9**	**371**	**43.1**	**16:02**	**6**	**0**	**1**	**1**	**6**	**0**	**0**	**0**	**13:21**
	Hershey Bears	AHL	2	0	1	1	0	....	....	....	....	....	....	....	....	....	....	....	....	....	....	....	....	....	....
	Czech Republic	Olympics	5	1	2	3	2	....	....	....	....	....	....	....	....	....	....	....	....	....	....	....	....	....	....
2010-11	**Washington**	**NHL**	**23**	**4**	**6**	**10**	**10**	**0**	**0**	**1**	**44**	**9.1**	**3**	**225**	**43.1**	**14:20**	....	....	....	....	....	....	....	....	....
	Colorado	**NHL**	**22**	**8**	**13**	**21**	**8**	**3**	**0**	**1**	**54**	**14.8**	**-1**	**11**	**18.2**	**18:28**	....	....	....	....	....	....	....	....	....
2011-12	**Florida**	**NHL**	**82**	**27**	**34**	**61**	**26**	**6**	**0**	**4**	**217**	**12.4**	**-7**	**27**	**51.9**	**19:06**	**7**	**1**	**2**	**3**	**2**	**0**	**0**	**0**	**18:44**
2012-13	**Florida**	**NHL**	**48**	**12**	**23**	**35**	**16**	**2**	**1**	**2**	**121**	**9.9**	**-10**	**20**	**50.0**	**18:44**	....	....	....	....	....	....	....	....	....
	NHL Totals		**435**	**107**	**148**	**255**	**134**	**27**	**1**	**18**	**858**	**12.5**		**737**	**42.6**	**15:36**	**29**	**4**	**4**	**8**	**12**	**1**	**0**	**1**	**14:53**

WHL East Second All-Star Team (2004)

Traded to **Washington** by **Detroit** with Detroit's 1st round choice (Mike Green) in 2004 Entry Draft and Detroit's 4th round choice (Luke Lynes) in 2006 Entry Draft for Robert Lang, February 27, 2004. Traded to **Colorado** by **Washington** for Scott Hannan, November 30, 2010. Signed as a free agent by **Florida**, July 1, 2011.

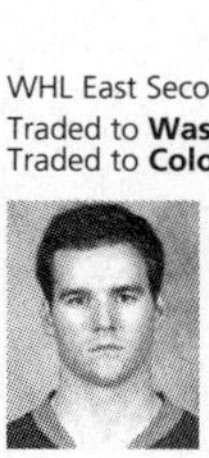

FLOOD, Mark

(FLUD, MAHRK) **CAR**

Defense. Shoots right. 6'1", 195 lbs. Born, Charlottetown, P.E.I., September 29, 1984. Montreal's 8th choice, 188th overall, in 2003 Entry Draft.

2000-01	Charlotwn AAA	PEIHA	STATISTICS NOT AVAILABLE																						
	Charlotwn Abbies	MJrHL	11	0	2	2	2	....	....	....	....	....	....	....	....	....	....	....	....	....	....	....	....	....	....
2001-02	Peterborough	OHL	57	1	4	5	21	....	....	....	....	....	....	....	....	....	6	0	0	0	2	....	....	....	....
2002-03	Peterborough	OHL	68	5	24	29	18	....	....	....	....	....	....	....	....	....	7	1	2	3	0	....	....	....	....
2003-04	Peterborough	OHL	68	15	29	44	30	....	....	....	....	....	....	....	....	....	....	....	....	....	....	....	....	....	....
2004-05	Peterborough	OHL	60	4	38	42	14	....	....	....	....	....	....	....	....	....	14	2	7	9	0	....	....	....	....
2005-06	Syracuse Crunch	AHL	9	1	1	2	2	....	....	....	....	....	....	....	....	....	....	....	....	....	....	....	....	....	....
	Dayton Bombers	ECHL	50	11	14	25	20	....	....	....	....	....	....	....	....	....	....	....	....	....	....	....	....	....	....
2006-07	Syracuse Crunch	AHL	8	1	1	2	2	....	....	....	....	....	....	....	....	....	....	....	....	....	....	....	....	....	....
	Albany River Rats	AHL	36	3	7	10	20	....	....	....	....	....	....	....	....	....	....	....	....	....	....	....	....	....	....
2007-08	Albany River Rats	AHL	53	10	12	22	18	....	....	....	....	....	....	....	....	....	....	....	....	....	....	....	....	....	....
2008-09	Albany River Rats	AHL	76	6	25	31	27	....	....	....	....	....	....	....	....	....	....	....	....	....	....	....	....	....	....
2009-10	**NY Islanders**	**NHL**	**6**	**0**	**1**	**1**	**0**	**0**	**0**	**0**	**5**	**0.0**	**-4**	**0**	**0.0**	**12:43**	....	....	....	....	....	....	....	....	....
	Bridgeport	AHL	61	10	23	33	39	....	....	....	....	....	....	....	....	....	5	0	2	2	6	....	....	....	....
2010-11	Manitoba Moose	AHL	63	11	29	40	29	....	....	....	....	....	....	....	....	....	14	0	6	6	2	....	....	....	....

			Regular Season														Playoffs								
Season	Club	League	GP	G	A	Pts	PIM	PP	SH	GW	S	%	+/-	TF	F%	Min	GP	G	A	Pts	PIM	PP	SH	GW	Min
2011-12	Winnipeg	NHL	33	3	4	7	10	1	0	1	30	10.0	–1	0	0.0	15:21									
	St. John's IceCaps	AHL	11	1	5	6	4																		
2012-13	Yaroslavl	KHL	52	1	5	6	25										6	0	0	0	2				
	NHL Totals		39	3	5	8	10	1	0	1	35	8.6		0	0.0	14:57									

Signed as a free agent by **Columbus**, August 22, 2005. Traded to **Carolina** by **Columbus** for Derrick Walser, November 29, 2006. Signed as a free agent by **NY Islanders**, July 6, 2009. Signed as a free agent by **Manitoba** (AHL), September 8, 2010. Signed as a free agent by **Winnipeg**, July 3. 2011. Signed as a free agent by **Yaroslavl** (KHL), July 22, 2012.

FLYNN, Brian

(FLIHN, BRIGH-uhn) **BUF**

Right wing. Shoots right. 6'1", 185 lbs. Born, Lynnfield, MA, July 26, 1988.

2008-09	U. of Maine	H-East	38	12	13	25	10																		
2009-10	U. of Maine	H-East	39	19	28	47	12																		
2010-11	U. of Maine	H-East	36	20	16	36	8																		
2011-12	U. of Maine	H-East	40	18	30	48	37																		
	Rochester	AHL	5	0	1	1	2																		
2012-13	Rochester	AHL	45	16	16	32	18										3	0	0	0	4				
	Buffalo	NHL	26	6	5	11	0	0	1	1	49	12.2	6	60	40.0	14:41									
	NHL Totals		26	6	5	11	0	0	1	1	49	12.2		60	40.0	14:41									

Hockey East First All-Star Team (2012)

Signed as a free agent by **Buffalo**, March 29, 2012.

FOLIGNO, Marcus

(foh-LEE-noh, MAHR-kuhs) **BUF**

Left wing. Shoots left. 6'2", 215 lbs. Born, Buffalo, NY, August 10, 1991. Buffalo's 3rd choice, 104th overall, in 2009 Entry Draft.

2006-07	Sud. Nickel Cap's	Minor-ON	30	21	15	36	70																		
2007-08	Sudbury Wolves	OHL	66	5	6	11	38																		
2008-09	Sudbury Wolves	OHL	65	12	18	30	96										6	1	2	3	9				
2009-10	Sudbury Wolves	OHL	67	14	25	39	156										4	1	1	2	6				
2010-11	Sudbury Wolves	OHL	47	23	36	59	92										8	2	1	3	24				
2011-12	Buffalo	NHL	14	6	7	13	9	2	0	1	23	26.1	6	3	0.0	15:49									
	Rochester	AHL	60	16	23	39	78										3	2	1	3	4				
2012-13	Rochester	AHL	33	10	17	27	38																		
	Buffalo	NHL	47	5	13	18	41	1	0	0	55	9.1	–4	75	60.0	13:38									
	NHL Totals		61	11	20	31	50	3	0	1	78	14.1		78	57.7	14:08									

OHL Second All-Star Team (2011)

FOLIGNO, Nick

(foh-LEE-noh, NIHK) **CBJ**

Left wing. Shoots left. 6', 210 lbs. Born, Buffalo, NY, October 31, 1987. Ottawa's 1st choice, 28th overall, in 2006 Entry Draft.

2003-04	USNTDP	U-17	18	7	9	16	28																		
	USNTDP	NAHL	43	8	12	20	44										7	2	1	3	8				
2004-05	USNTDP	U-18	4	2	1	3	0																		
	Sudbury Wolves	OHL	65	10	28	38	111										12	5	5	10	16				
2005-06	Sudbury Wolves	OHL	65	24	46	70	146										10	1	3	4	28				
2006-07	Sudbury Wolves	OHL	66	31	57	88	135										21	12	17	29	36				
2007-08	Ottawa	NHL	45	6	3	9	20	0	0	0	44	13.6	0	49	44.9	9:10	4	1	0	1	2	0	0	0	12:50
	Binghamton	AHL	28	6	13	19	16																		
2008-09	Ottawa	NHL	81	17	15	32	59	7	0	2	145	11.7	–10	47	44.7	13:41									
2009-10	Ottawa	NHL	61	9	17	26	53	2	0	2	83	10.8	6	50	34.0	14:19	6	0	1	1	2	0	0	0	17:07
2010-11	Ottawa	NHL	82	14	20	34	43	5	0	3	149	9.4	–19	138	47.1	15:35									
2011-12	Ottawa	NHL	82	15	32	47	124	1	0	3	153	9.8	2	149	41.6	14:39	7	1	3	4	8	0	0	0	15:10
2012-13	Columbus	NHL	45	6	13	19	28	1	0	2	69	8.7	6	9	33.3	16:31									
	NHL Totals		396	67	100	167	327	16	0	12	643	10.4		442	43.0	14:11	17	2	4	6	12	0	0	0	15:18

Traded to **Columbus** by **Ottawa** for Marc Methot, July 1, 2012.

FORSBERG, Filip

(FOHRZ-buhrg, FIHL-ihp) **NSH**

Center. Shoots right. 6'1", 194 lbs. Born, Ostervala, Sweden, August 13, 1994. Washington's 1st choice, 11th overall, in 2012 Entry Draft.

2008-09	Leksands IF U18 2	Swe-U18	15	12	9	21	14																		
2009-10	Leksands IF U18	Swe-U18	31	21	16	37	22										4	5	3	8	0				
	Leksands IF Jr.	Swe-Jr.															5	0	0	0	0				
2010-11	Leksands IF U18	Swe-U18	3	1	5	6	4										6	2	2	4	2				
	Leksands IF Jr.	Swe-Jr.	36	21	19	40	22																		
	Leksands IF	Sweden-2	16	1	1	2	0																		
2011-12	Leksands IF U18	Swe-U18	1	0	2	2	0																		
	Leksands IF Jr.	Swe-Jr.	6	0	1	1	2																		
	Leksands IF	Sweden-2	53	10	10	20	33																		
2012-13	Leksands IF	Sweden-2	47	20	22	42	22																		
	Nashville	NHL	5	0	1	1	0	0	0	0	14	0.0	–5	1	0.0	15:29									
	NHL Totals		5	0	1	1	0	0	0	0	14	0.0		1	0.0	15:29									

Traded to **Nashville** by **Washington** for Martin Erat and Michael Latta, April 3, 2013.

FORTUNUS, Maxime

(fohr-TOON-uhs, MAX-eem)

Defense. Shoots right. 6'1", 198 lbs. Born, Longueil, Que., July 28, 1983.

99-2000	Baie-Comeau	QMJHL	68	6	15	21	36										6	0	0	0	2				
2000-01	Baie-Comeau	QMJHL	71	10	31	41	106										11	2	4	6	6				
2001-02	Baie-Comeau	QMJHL	72	11	30	41	76										5	0	1	1	2				
2002-03	Baie-Comeau	QMJHL	69	12	32	44	44										12	2	4	6	6				
2003-04	Baie-Comeau	QMJHL	5	1	0	1	15																		
	Houston Aeros	AHL	12	0	2	2	2										1	0	0	0	0				
	Louisiana	ECHL	64	3	15	18	27										4	1	1	2	0				
2004-05	Houston Aeros	AHL	13	0	0	0	4																		
	Louisiana	ECHL	59	8	16	24	26																		
2005-06	Manitoba Moose	AHL	76	3	10	13	36										13	0	0	0	10				
2006-07	Manitoba Moose	AHL	72	2	18	20	64										13	1	4	5	10				
2007-08	Manitoba Moose	AHL	65	8	13	21	28										6	0	1	1	4				
2008-09	Manitoba Moose	AHL	58	7	12	19	18										22	3	7	10	2				
2009-10	Dallas	NHL	8	0	0	0	4	0	0	0	5	0.0	–6	0	0.0	15:09									
	Texas Stars	AHL	72	11	12	23	28										24	2	7	9	14				
2010-11	Texas Stars	AHL	73	5	29	34	20										6	0	1	1	2				
2011-12	Texas Stars	AHL	60	6	14	20	18																		
2012-13	Texas Stars	AHL	67	7	21	28	16										9	0	1	1	2				
	NHL Totals		8	0	0	0	4	0	0	0	5	0.0		0	0.0	15:09									

Signed as a free agent by **Dallas**, July 3, 2008. Signed as a free agent by **Texas** (AHL), July 16, 2013.

FOSTER, Kurtis

(FAW-stuhr, KUHR-this)

Defense. Shoots right. 6'5", 225 lbs. Born, Carp, Ont., November 24, 1981. Calgary's 2nd choice, 40th overall, in 2000 Entry Draft.

1996-97	Ottawa Valley	ODMHA	36	7	18	25	88																		
1997-98	Peterborough	OHL	39	1	1	2	45										4	0	0	0	2				
1998-99	Peterborough	OHL	54	2	13	15	59										5	0	0	0	6				
99-2000	Peterborough	OHL	68	6	18	24	116										5	1	2	3	4				
2000-01	Peterborough	OHL	62	17	24	41	78										7	1	1	2	10				
2001-02	Peterborough	OHL	33	10	4	14	58																		
	Chicago Wolves	AHL	39	6	9	15	59										14	1	1	2	21				
2002-03	Atlanta	NHL	2	0	0	0	0	0	0	0	1	0.0	–2	0	0.0	11:06									
	Chicago Wolves	AHL	75	15	27	42	159										9	1	3	4	14				

			Regular Season														Playoffs								
Season	Club	League	GP	G	A	Pts	PIM	PP	SH	GW	S	%	+/-	TF	F%	Min	GP	G	A	Pts	PIM	PP	SH	GW	Min
2003-04	**Atlanta**	**NHL**	**3**	**0**	**1**	**1**	**0**	**0**	**0**	**0**	**1**	**0.0**	**0**	**0**	**0.0**	**6:58**	....	....	....	....	....	....	....	....	....
	Chicago Wolves	AHL	67	11	19	30	95	....	....	....	....	....	....	....	....	....	10	0	3	3	12	....	....	....	....
2004-05	Cincinnati	AHL	78	17	25	42	71	....	....	....	....	....	....	....	....	....	9	2	3	5	28	....	....	....	....
2005-06	**Minnesota**	**NHL**	**58**	**10**	**18**	**28**	**60**	**6**	**0**	**2**	**124**	**8.1**	**–3**	**0**	**0.0**	**19:13**	....	....	....	....	....	....	....	....	....
	Houston Aeros	AHL	19	4	11	15	32	....	....	....	....	....	....	....	....	....	....	....	....	....	....	....	....	....	....
2006-07	**Minnesota**	**NHL**	**57**	**3**	**20**	**23**	**52**	**0**	**0**	**0**	**135**	**2.2**	**–3**	**1**	**100.0**	**17:59**	**3**	**0**	**2**	**2**	**0**	**0**	**0**	**0**	**18:38**
2007-08	**Minnesota**	**NHL**	**56**	**7**	**12**	**19**	**37**	**3**	**0**	**2**	**118**	**5.9**	**0**	**3**	**66.7**	**16:24**	....	....	....	....	....	....	....	....	....
2008-09	**Minnesota**	**NHL**	**10**	**1**	**5**	**6**	**6**	**0**	**0**	**0**	**10**	**10.0**	**7**	**0**	**0.0**	**13:35**	....	....	....	....	....	....	....	....	....
	Houston Aeros	AHL	6	1	5	6	6	....	....	....	....	....	....	....	....	....	....	....	....	....	....	....	....	....	....
2009-10	**Tampa Bay**	**NHL**	**71**	**8**	**34**	**42**	**48**	**3**	**0**	**1**	**165**	**4.8**	**–5**	**0**	**0.0**	**17:11**	....	....	....	....	....	....	....	....	....
2010-11	**Edmonton**	**NHL**	**74**	**8**	**14**	**22**	**45**	**5**	**0**	**0**	**182**	**4.4**	**–12**	**0**	**0.0**	**17:40**	....	....	....	....	....	....	....	....	....
2011-12	**Anaheim**	**NHL**	**9**	**1**	**1**	**2**	**8**	**0**	**0**	**0**	**16**	**6.3**	**–5**	**0**	**0.0**	**15:07**	....	....	....	....	....	....	....	....	....
	Syracuse Crunch	AHL	2	0	1	1	4	....	....	....	....	....	....	....	....	....	....	....	....	....	....	....	....	....	....
	New Jersey	**NHL**	**28**	**3**	**9**	**12**	**23**	**2**	**0**	**0**	**54**	**5.6**	**–9**	**0**	**0.0**	**17:09**	....	....	....	....	....	....	....	....	....
	Minnesota	**NHL**	**14**	**0**	**0**	**0**	**4**	**0**	**0**	**0**	**15**	**0.0**	**1**	**0**	**0.0**	**13:52**	....	....	....	....	....	....	....	....	....
2012-13	Tappara Tampere	Finland	13	3	3	6	78	....	....	....	....	....	....	....	....	....	....	....	....	....	....	....	....	....	....
	Philadelphia	**NHL**	**23**	**1**	**4**	**5**	**25**	**1**	**0**	**0**	**21**	**4.8**	**0**	**0**	**0.0**	**13:05**	....	....	....	....	....	....	....	....	....
	NHL Totals		**405**	**42**	**118**	**160**	**308**	**20**	**0**	**5**	**842**	**5.0**		**4**	**75.0**	**16:59**	**3**	**0**	**2**	**2**	**0**	**0**	**0**	**0**	**18:38**

Yanick Dupre Memorial Award (AHL - Outstanding Humanitarian Contribution) (2004)

• Rights traded to **Atlanta** by **Calgary** with Jeff Cowan for Petr Buzek and Atlanta's 6th round choice (Adam Pardy) in 2004 Entry Draft, December 18, 2001. Traded to **Anaheim** by **Atlanta** for Niclas Havelid, June 26, 2004. Signed as a free agent by **Minnesota**, August 4, 2005. • Missed majority of 2008-09 due to leg injury vs. San Jose, March 20, 2008. Signed as a free agent by **Tampa Bay**, July 8, 2009. Signed as a free agent by **Edmonton**, July 1, 2010. Traded to **Anaheim** by **Edmonton** for Andy Sutton, July 1, 2011. Traded to **New Jersey** by **Anaheim** with Timo Pielmeier for Rod Pelley, Mark Fraser and New Jersey's 7th round choice (Jaycob Megna) in 2012 Entry Draft, December 12, 2011. Traded to **Minnesota** by **New Jersey** with Nick Palmieri, Stephane Veilleux, Washington's 2nd round choice (previously acquired, Minnesota selected Raphael Bussieres) in 2012 Entry Draft and New Jerszey's 3rd round choice ((later traded to NY Islanders – NY Islanders selected Eamon McAdam) in 2013 Entry Draft for Marek Zidlicky, February 24, 2012. Signed as a free agent by **Tappara Tampere** (Finland), October 23, 2012.

FOUCAULT, Kris

(foo-KOH, KRIHS) **MIN**

Left wing. Shoots left. 6'1", 206 lbs. Born, Calgary, Alta., December 12, 1990. Minnesota's 3rd choice, 103rd overall, in 2009 Entry Draft.

Season	Club	League	GP	G	A	Pts	PIM	PP	SH	GW	S	%	+/-	TF	F%	Min	GP	G	A	Pts	PIM	PP	SH	GW	Min
2006-07	Calgary Buffaloes	AMHL	35	7	6	13	46	....	....	....	....	....	....	....	....	....	....	....	....	....	....	....	....	....	....
	Swift Current	WHL	3	0	0	0	0	....	....	....	....	....	....	....	....	....	....	....	....	....	....	....	....	....	....
2007-08	Kootenay Ice	WHL	33	0	3	3	12	....	....	....	....	....	....	....	....	....	8	2	1	3	2	....	....	....	....
2008-09	Kootenay Ice	WHL	4	0	1	1	4	....	....	....	....	....	....	....	....	....	....	....	....	....	....	....	....	....	....
	Canmore Eagles	AJHL	32	18	23	41	84	....	....	....	....	....	....	....	....	....	....	....	....	....	....	....	....	....	....
	Calgary Hitmen	WHL	22	9	7	16	12	....	....	....	....	....	....	....	....	....	18	11	5	16	10	....	....	....	....
2009-10	Calgary Hitmen	WHL	68	22	21	43	31	....	....	....	....	....	....	....	....	....	23	9	7	16	21	....	....	....	....
2010-11	Calgary Hitmen	WHL	65	25	23	48	60	....	....	....	....	....	....	....	....	....	....	....	....	....	....	....	....	....	....
	Houston Aeros	AHL	1	0	0	0	0	....	....	....	....	....	....	....	....	....	....	....	....	....	....	....	....	....	....
2011-12	**Minnesota**	**NHL**	**1**	**0**	**0**	**0**	**0**	**0**	**0**	**0**	**0**	**0.0**	**0**	**0**	**0.0**	**8:50**	....	....	....	....	....	....	....	....	....
	Houston Aeros	AHL	70	14	18	32	44	....	....	....	....	....	....	....	....	....	4	1	0	1	0	....	....	....	....
2012-13	Houston Aeros	AHL	28	5	6	11	4	....	....	....	....	....	....	....	....	....	4	0	0	0	0	....	....	....	....
	NHL Totals		**1**	**0**	**0**	**0**	**0**	**0**	**0**	**0**	**0**	**0.0**		**0**	**0.0**	**8:50**	....	....	....	....	....	....	....	....	....

FOWLER, Cam

(FOW-luhr, KAM) **ANA**

Defense. Shoots left. 6'1", 196 lbs. Born, Windsor, Ont., December 5, 1991. Anaheim's 1st choice, 12th overall, in 2010 Entry Draft.

Season	Club	League	GP	G	A	Pts	PIM	PP	SH	GW	S	%	+/-	TF	F%	Min	GP	G	A	Pts	PIM	PP	SH	GW	Min
2006-07	Det. Honeybaked	MWEHL	21	5	13	18	18	....	....	....	....	....	....	....	....	....	....	....	....	....	....	....	....	....	....
	Det. Honeybaked	Minor-MI	31	3	7	10	....	....	....	....	....	....	....	....	....	....	....	....	....	....	....	....	....	....	....
2007-08	USNTDP	NAHL	38	3	10	13	2	....	....	....	....	....	....	....	....	....	3	0	0	0	2	....	....	....	....
	USNTDP	U-17	18	0	2	2	8	....	....	....	....	....	....	....	....	....	....	....	....	....	....	....	....	....	....
	USNTDP	U-18	1	0	0	0	0	....	....	....	....	....	....	....	....	....	....	....	....	....	....	....	....	....	....
2008-09	USNTDP	NAHL	14	2	7	9	12	....	....	....	....	....	....	....	....	....	....	....	....	....	....	....	....	....	....
	USNTDP	U-18	33	6	25	31	32	....	....	....	....	....	....	....	....	....	....	....	....	....	....	....	....	....	....
2009-10	Windsor Spitfires	OHL	55	8	47	55	14	....	....	....	....	....	....	....	....	....	19	3	11	14	10	....	....	....	....
2010-11	**Anaheim**	**NHL**	**76**	**10**	**30**	**40**	**20**	**6**	**0**	**3**	**123**	**8.1**	**–25**	**0**	**0.0**	**22:08**	**6**	**1**	**3**	**4**	**2**	**1**	**0**	**0**	**22:13**
2011-12	**Anaheim**	**NHL**	**82**	**5**	**24**	**29**	**18**	**2**	**0**	**0**	**123**	**4.1**	**–28**	**1**	**100.0**	**23:16**	....	....	....	....	....	....	....	....	....
2012-13	Sodertalje SK	Sweden-2	14	2	5	7	14	....	....	....	....	....	....	....	....	....	....	....	....	....	....	....	....	....	....
	Anaheim	**NHL**	**37**	**1**	**10**	**11**	**4**	**1**	**0**	**0**	**50**	**2.0**	**–4**	**0**	**0.0**	**20:26**	**7**	**0**	**3**	**3**	**0**	**0**	**0**	**0**	**22:45**
	NHL Totals		**195**	**16**	**64**	**80**	**42**	**9**	**0**	**3**	**296**	**5.4**		**1**	**100.0**	**22:17**	**13**	**1**	**6**	**7**	**2**	**1**	**0**	**0**	**22:30**

Memorial Cup All-Star Team (2010)

Signed as a free agent by **Sodertalje** (Sweden-2), November 14, 2012.

FRANSON, Cody

(FRAN-suhn, KOH-dee) **TOR**

Defense. Shoots right. 6'5", 213 lbs. Born, Sicamous, B.C., August 8, 1987. Nashville's 3rd choice, 79th overall, in 2005 Entry Draft.

Season	Club	League	GP	G	A	Pts	PIM	PP	SH	GW	S	%	+/-	TF	F%	Min	GP	G	A	Pts	PIM	PP	SH	GW	Min
2002-03	Sicamous	Minor-BC	65	44	82	126	42	....	....	....	....	....	....	....	....	....	....	....	....	....	....	....	....	....	....
	Vancouver Giants	WHL	3	0	0	0	2	....	....	....	....	....	....	....	....	....	....	....	....	....	....	....	....	....	....
2003-04	Beaver Valley	KIJHL	48	10	22	32	70	....	....	....	....	....	....	....	....	....	....	....	....	....	....	....	....	....	....
	Trail	BCHL	2	0	1	1	0	....	....	....	....	....	....	....	....	....	....	....	....	....	....	....	....	....	....
	Vancouver Giants	WHL	2	0	0	0	0	....	....	....	....	....	....	....	....	....	....	....	....	....	....	....	....	....	....
2004-05	Vancouver Giants	WHL	64	2	11	13	44	....	....	....	....	....	....	....	....	....	4	0	1	1	0	....	....	....	....
2005-06	Vancouver Giants	WHL	71	15	40	55	61	....	....	....	....	....	....	....	....	....	18	5	15	20	12	....	....	....	....
2006-07	Vancouver Giants	WHL	59	17	34	51	88	....	....	....	....	....	....	....	....	....	19	3	4	7	10	....	....	....	....
2007-08	Milwaukee	AHL	76	11	25	36	40	....	....	....	....	....	....	....	....	....	6	0	2	2	2	....	....	....	....
2008-09	Milwaukee	AHL	76	11	41	52	47	....	....	....	....	....	....	....	....	....	11	3	5	8	8	....	....	....	....
2009-10	**Nashville**	**NHL**	**61**	**6**	**15**	**21**	**16**	**1**	**0**	**3**	**90**	**6.7**	**15**	**0**	**0.0**	**14:12**	**4**	**0**	**1**	**1**	**2**	**0**	**0**	**0**	**9:02**
	Milwaukee	AHL	6	2	5	7	4	....	....	....	....	....	....	....	....	....	....	....	....	....	....	....	....	....	....
2010-11	**Nashville**	**NHL**	**80**	**8**	**21**	**29**	**30**	**2**	**0**	**2**	**156**	**5.1**	**10**	**0**	**0.0**	**15:10**	**12**	**1**	**5**	**6**	**0**	**0**	**0**	**0**	**15:19**
2011-12	**Toronto**	**NHL**	**57**	**5**	**16**	**21**	**22**	**2**	**0**	**0**	**65**	**7.7**	**–1**	**0**	**0.0**	**16:11**	....	....	....	....	....	....	....	....	....
2012-13	Brynas IF Gavle	Sweden	26	3	4	7	10	....	....	....	....	....	....	....	....	....	....	....	....	....	....	....	....	....	....
	Toronto	**NHL**	**45**	**4**	**25**	**29**	**8**	**3**	**0**	**0**	**70**	**5.7**	**4**	**0**	**0.0**	**18:47**	**7**	**3**	**3**	**6**	**0**	**1**	**0**	**0**	**22:49**
	NHL Totals		**243**	**23**	**77**	**100**	**76**	**8**	**0**	**5**	**381**	**6.0**		**0**	**0.0**	**15:50**	**23**	**4**	**9**	**13**	**2**	**1**	**0**	**0**	**16:31**

WHL West Second All-Star Team (2006) • WHL West First All-Star Team (2007) • Memorial Cup All-Star Team (2007) • AHL All-Rookie Team (2008) • AHL Second All-Star Team (2009)

Traded to **Toronto** by **Nashville** with Matthew Lombardi for Robert Slaney, Brett Lebda and Toronto's 4th round choice (later traded to St. Louis – St. Louis selected Zachary Pochiro) in 2013 Entry Draft, July 3, 2011. Signed as a free agent by **Gavle** (Sweden), October 1, 2012.

FRANZEN, Johan

(FRAN-zehn, YOH-han) **DET**

Left wing. Shoots left. 6'3", 223 lbs. Born, Landsbro, Sweden, December 23, 1979. Detroit's 1st choice, 97th overall, in 2004 Entry Draft.

Season	Club	League	GP	G	A	Pts	PIM	PP	SH	GW	S	%	+/-	TF	F%	Min	GP	G	A	Pts	PIM	PP	SH	GW	Min
2001-02	Linkopings HC	Sweden	36	2	6	8	64	....	....	....	....	....	....	....	....	....	....	....	....	....	....	....	....	....	....
2002-03	Linkopings HC	Sweden	37	2	4	6	14	....	....	....	....	....	....	....	....	....	....	....	....	....	....	....	....	....	....
2003-04	Linkopings HC	Sweden	49	12	18	30	26	....	....	....	....	....	....	....	....	....	5	0	1	1	8	....	....	....	....
2004-05	Linkopings HC	Sweden	43	7	7	14	45	....	....	....	....	....	....	....	....	....	6	2	0	2	16	....	....	....	....
2005-06	**Detroit**	**NHL**	**80**	**12**	**4**	**16**	**36**	**0**	**2**	**2**	**119**	**10.1**	**4**	**171**	**41.5**	**12:27**	**6**	**1**	**2**	**3**	**4**	**0**	**0**	**0**	**12:00**
2006-07	**Detroit**	**NHL**	**69**	**10**	**20**	**30**	**37**	**0**	**1**	**2**	**151**	**6.6**	**20**	**45**	**40.0**	**15:35**	**18**	**3**	**4**	**7**	**10**	**0**	**0**	**2**	**16:47**
2007-08♦	**Detroit**	**NHL**	**72**	**27**	**11**	**38**	**51**	**14**	**0**	**8**	**199**	**13.6**	**12**	**390**	**48.5**	**17:44**	**16**	***13**	**5**	**18**	**14**	***6**	***2**	***5**	**18:49**
2008-09	**Detroit**	**NHL**	**71**	**34**	**25**	**59**	**44**	**11**	**1**	**8**	**246**	**13.8**	**21**	**241**	**56.0**	**18:06**	**23**	**12**	**11**	**23**	**12**	**4**	**0**	**3**	**19:41**
2009-10	**Detroit**	**NHL**	**27**	**10**	**11**	**21**	**22**	**6**	**0**	**1**	**91**	**11.0**	**1**	**27**	**55.6**	**18:42**	**12**	**6**	**12**	**18**	**16**	**1**	**0**	**1**	**17:34**
	Sweden	Olympics	4	1	1	2	2	....	....	....	....	....	....	....	....	....	....	....	....	....	....	....	....	....	....
2010-11	**Detroit**	**NHL**	**76**	**28**	**27**	**55**	**58**	**10**	**0**	**5**	**248**	**11.3**	**5**	**147**	**50.3**	**17:26**	**8**	**2**	**1**	**3**	**6**	**0**	**0**	**0**	**15:47**
2011-12	**Detroit**	**NHL**	**77**	**29**	**27**	**56**	**40**	**11**	**0**	**10**	**211**	**13.7**	**23**	**179**	**44.1**	**17:42**	**5**	**1**	**0**	**1**	**8**	**0**	**0**	**1**	**16:07**
2012-13	**Detroit**	**NHL**	**41**	**14**	**17**	**31**	**41**	**6**	**0**	**1**	**116**	**12.1**	**13**	**62**	**48.4**	**18:05**	**14**	**4**	**2**	**6**	**8**	**3**	**0**	**0**	**19:30**
	NHL Totals		**513**	**164**	**142**	**306**	**329**	**58**	**4**	**37**	**1381**	**11.9**		**1262**	**48.4**	**16:42**	**102**	**42**	**37**	**79**	**78**	**14**	**2**	**12**	**17:50**

• Missed majority of 2009-10 due to knee injury vs. Chicago, October 8, 2009.

FRASER, Colin

(FRAY-zuhr, KAW-lihn) **L.A.**

Center. Shoots left. 6'1", 189 lbs. Born, Sicamous, B.C., January 28, 1985. Philadelphia's 3rd choice, 69th overall, in 2003 Entry Draft.

			Regular Season														Playoffs								
Season	Club	League	GP	G	A	Pts	PIM	PP	SH	GW	S	%	+/-	TF	F%	Min	GP	G	A	Pts	PIM	PP	SH	GW	Min
2000-01	Port Coquitlam	PIJHL	38	16	24	40	90	....	....	....	....	....	....	....	....	....	8	2	2	4	21	....	....	....	....
2001-02	Red Deer Rebels	WHL	67	11	31	42	126	....	....	....	....	....	....	....	....	....	23	2	1	3	39	....	....	....	....
2002-03	Red Deer Rebels	WHL	69	15	37	52	192	....	....	....	....	....	....	....	....	....	22	7	6	13	40	....	....	....	....
2003-04	Red Deer Rebels	WHL	70	24	29	53	174	....	....	....	....	....	....	....	....	....	19	5	9	14	24	....	....	....	....
2004-05	Red Deer Rebels	WHL	63	24	43	67	148	....	....	....	....	....	....	....	....	....	7	2	5	7	8	....	....	....	....
	Norfolk Admirals	AHL	3	0	0	0	20	....	....	....	....	....	....	....	....	....	6	1	0	1	2	....	....	....	....
2005-06	Norfolk Admirals	AHL	75	12	13	25	145	....	....	....	....	....	....	....	....	....	4	0	0	0	7	....	....	....	....
2006-07	**Chicago**	**NHL**	**1**	**0**	**0**	**0**	**2**	**0**	**0**	**0**	**0**	**0.0**	**–1**	**2**	**0.0**	**3:18**	....	....	....	....	....	....	....	....	....
	Norfolk Admirals	AHL	67	12	24	36	158	....	....	....	....	....	....	....	....	....	6	1	0	1	21	....	....	....	....
2007-08	**Chicago**	**NHL**	**5**	**0**	**0**	**0**	**7**	**0**	**0**	**0**	**4**	**0.0**	**–2**	**38**	**36.8**	**10:19**	....	....	....	....	....	....	....	....	....
	Rockford IceHogs	AHL	75	17	24	41	165	....	....	....	....	....	....	....	....	....	12	1	2	3	28	....	....	....	....
2008-09	**Chicago**	**NHL**	**81**	**6**	**11**	**17**	**55**	**0**	**1**	**0**	**67**	**9.0**	**3**	**787**	**47.8**	**10:54**	**2**	**0**	**0**	**0**	**2**	**0**	**0**	**0**	**11:31**
2009-10♦	**Chicago**	**NHL**	**70**	**7**	**12**	**19**	**44**	**0**	**0**	**0**	**92**	**7.6**	**6**	**445**	**48.8**	**9:36**	**3**	**0**	**0**	**0**	**0**	**0**	**0**	**0**	**8:24**
2010-11	**Edmonton**	**NHL**	**67**	**3**	**2**	**5**	**60**	**0**	**1**	**0**	**57**	**5.3**	**–2**	**552**	**44.6**	**10:17**	....	....	....	....	....	....	....	....	....
2011-12♦	**Los Angeles**	**NHL**	**67**	**2**	**6**	**8**	**67**	**0**	**0**	**0**	**54**	**3.7**	**–2**	**370**	**47.3**	**9:44**	**18**	**1**	**1**	**2**	**4**	**0**	**0**	**0**	**8:34**
2012-13	**Los Angeles**	**NHL**	**34**	**2**	**5**	**7**	**25**	**0**	**0**	**0**	**19**	**10.5**	**–4**	**168**	**46.4**	**9:22**	**16**	**0**	**2**	**2**	**10**	**0**	**0**	**0**	**8:27**
	NHL Totals		**325**	**20**	**36**	**56**	**260**	**0**	**2**	**0**	**293**	**6.8**		**2362**	**46.8**	**10:04**	**39**	**1**	**3**	**4**	**16**	**0**	**0**	**0**	**8:40**

Canadian Major Junior Humanitarian Player of the Year (2005)

Traded to **Chicago** by **Philadelphia** with Jim Vandermeer and Los Angeles' 2nd round choice (previously acquired, Chicago selected Bryan Bickell) in 2004 Entry Draft for Alex Zhamnov and Washington's 4th round choice (previously acquired, Philadelphia selected R.J. Anderson) in 2004 Entry Draft, February 19, 2004. Traded to **Edmonton** by **Chicago** for Edmonton's 6th round choice (Mirko Hoefflin) in 2010 Entry Draft, June 24, 2010. Traded to **Los Angeles** by **Edmonton** with Edmonron's 7th round choice (later traded to Dallas – Dallas selected Dmitri Sinitsyn) in 2012 Entry Draft for Ryan Smyth, June 26, 2011.

FRASER, Mark

(FRAY-zuhr, MAHRK) **TOR**

Defense. Shoots left. 6'4", 220 lbs. Born, Ottawa, Ont., September 29, 1986. New Jersey's 3rd choice, 84th overall, in 2005 Entry Draft.

Season	Club	League	GP	G	A	Pts	PIM	PP	SH	GW	S	%	+/-	TF	F%	Min	GP	G	A	Pts	PIM	PP	SH	GW	Min
2002-03	Clarence Beavers	ON-Jr.B	Statistics not available																						
	Gloucester	ON-Jr.A	5	0	0	0	4	....	....	....	....	....	....	....	....	....	3	0	0	0	0	....	....	....	....
2003-04	Gloucester	ON-Jr.A	52	0	11	11	107	....	....	....	....	....	....	....	....	....	20	0	3	3	32	....	....	....	....
2004-05	Gloucester	ON-Jr.A	11	0	5	5	22	....	....	....	....	....	....	....	....	....	....	....	....	....	....	....	....	....	....
	Kitchener Rangers	OHL	58	0	8	8	96	....	....	....	....	....	....	....	....	....	15	0	3	3	26	....	....	....	....
2005-06	Kitchener Rangers	OHL	59	0	5	5	129	....	....	....	....	....	....	....	....	....	5	0	1	1	4	....	....	....	....
	Albany River Rats	AHL	4	0	0	0	2	....	....	....	....	....	....	....	....	....	....	....	....	....	....	....	....	....	....
2006-07	**New Jersey**	**NHL**	**7**	**0**	**0**	**0**	**7**	**0**	**0**	**0**	**1**	**0.0**	**–1**	**0**	**0.0**	**3:34**	....	....	....	....	....	....	....	....	....
	Lowell Devils	AHL	71	1	8	9	73	....	....	....	....	....	....	....	....	....	....	....	....	....	....	....	....	....	....
2007-08	Lowell Devils	AHL	79	1	17	18	96	....	....	....	....	....	....	....	....	....	....	....	....	....	....	....	....	....	....
2008-09	Lowell Devils	AHL	74	3	14	17	152	....	....	....	....	....	....	....	....	....	....	....	....	....	....	....	....	....	....
2009-10	**New Jersey**	**NHL**	**61**	**3**	**3**	**6**	**36**	**0**	**0**	**0**	**24**	**12.5**	**3**	**0**	**0.0**	**12:23**	**1**	**0**	**0**	**0**	**0**	**0**	**0**	**0**	**5:52**
2010-11	**New Jersey**	**NHL**	**26**	**0**	**2**	**2**	**29**	**0**	**0**	**0**	**16**	**0.0**	**2**	**0**	**0.0**	**13:59**	....	....	....	....	....	....	....	....	....
	Albany Devils	AHL	5	0	1	1	0	....	....	....	....	....	....	....	....	....	....	....	....	....	....	....	....	....	....
2011-12	**New Jersey**	**NHL**	**4**	**0**	**0**	**0**	**14**	**0**	**0**	**0**	**0**	**0.0**	**–2**	**0**	**0.0**	**14:20**	....	....	....	....	....	....	....	....	....
	Syracuse Crunch	AHL	25	0	5	5	35	....	....	....	....	....	....	....	....	....	....	....	....	....	....	....	....	....	....
	Toronto Marlies	AHL	20	0	2	2	32	....	....	....	....	....	....	....	....	....	17	0	3	3	31	....	....	....	....
2012-13	Toronto Marlies	AHL	30	2	3	5	114	....	....	....	....	....	....	....	....	....	....	....	....	....	....	....	....	....	....
	Toronto	**NHL**	**45**	**0**	**8**	**8**	**85**	**0**	**0**	**0**	**33**	**0.0**	**18**	**0**	**0.0**	**16:57**	**4**	**0**	**1**	**1**	**7**	**0**	**0**	**0**	**18:26**
	NHL Totals		**143**	**3**	**13**	**16**	**171**	**0**	**0**	**0**	**74**	**4.1**		**0**	**0.0**	**13:44**	**5**	**0**	**1**	**1**	**7**	**0**	**0**	**0**	**15:55**

• Missed majority of 2010-11 due to hand injury at Buffalo, October 13. 2010 and as a healthy reserve. Traded to **Anaheim** by **New Jersey** with Rod Pelley and New Jersey's 7th round choice (Jaycob Megna) in 2012 Entry Draft for Kurtis Foster and Timo Pielmeier, December 12, 2011. Traded to **Toronto** by **Anaheim** for Dale Mitchell, February 27, 2012.

FRASER, Matt

(FRAY-zuhr, MAT) **BOS**

Left wing. Shoots left. 6'1", 204 lbs. Born, Red Deer, Alta., May 20, 1990.

Season	Club	League	GP	G	A	Pts	PIM	PP	SH	GW	S	%	+/-	TF	F%	Min	GP	G	A	Pts	PIM	PP	SH	GW	Min
2005-06	Red Deer Chiefs	Minor-AB	33	31	23	54	62	....	....	....	....	....	....	....	....	....	....	....	....	....	....	....	....	....	....
	Red Deer	AMHL	1	0	1	1	0	....	....	....	....	....	....	....	....	....	....	....	....	....	....	....	....	....	....
2006-07	Red Deer	AMHL	23	8	17	25	47	....	....	....	....	....	....	....	....	....	10	1	6	7	4	....	....	....	....
	Red Deer Rebels	WHL	3	0	0	0	2	....	....	....	....	....	....	....	....	....	1	0	0	0	0	....	....	....	....
2007-08	Red Deer Rebels	WHL	5	0	0	0	2	....	....	....	....	....	....	....	....	....	....	....	....	....	....	....	....	....	....
	Kootenay Ice	WHL	63	9	11	20	48	....	....	....	....	....	....	....	....	....	8	1	1	2	0	....	....	....	....
2008-09	Kootenay Ice	WHL	63	10	14	24	123	....	....	....	....	....	....	....	....	....	4	0	2	2	12	....	....	....	....
2009-10	Kootenay Ice	WHL	65	32	24	56	117	....	....	....	....	....	....	....	....	....	6	1	1	2	12	....	....	....	....
	Peoria Rivermen	AHL	2	0	0	0	0	....	....	....	....	....	....	....	....	....	....	....	....	....	....	....	....	....	....
2010-11	Kootenay Ice	WHL	66	36	38	74	115	....	....	....	....	....	....	....	....	....	19	*17	10	27	18	....	....	....	....
2011-12	**Dallas**	**NHL**	**1**	**0**	**0**	**0**	**0**	**0**	**0**	**0**	**1**	**0.0**	**0**	**0**	**0.0**	**3:57**	....	....	....	....	....	....	....	....	....
	Texas Stars	AHL	73	37	18	55	45	....	....	....	....	....	....	....	....	....	....	....	....	....	....	....	....	....	....
2012-13	Texas Stars	AHL	62	33	13	46	26	....	....	....	....	....	....	....	....	....	9	2	0	2	2	....	....	....	....
	Dallas	**NHL**	**12**	**1**	**2**	**3**	**0**	**0**	**0**	**0**	**17**	**5.9**	**0**	**0**	**0.0**	**11:48**	....	....	....	....	....	....	....	....	....
	NHL Totals		**13**	**1**	**2**	**3**	**0**	**0**	**0**	**0**	**18**	**5.6**		**0**	**0.0**	**11:11**	....	....	....	....	....	....	....	....	....

AHL Second All-Star Team (2013)

Signed as a free agent by **Dallas**, November 18, 2010. Traded to **Boston** by **Dallas** with Loui Eriksson, Joe Morrow and Reilly Smith for Tyler Seguin, Rich Peverley and Ryan Button, July 4, 2013.

FRATTIN, Matt

(FRA-tihn, MAT) **L.A.**

Right wing. Shoots right. 6', 200 lbs. Born, Edmonton, Alta., January 3, 1988. Toronto's 2nd choice, 99th overall, in 2007 Entry Draft.

Season	Club	League	GP	G	A	Pts	PIM	PP	SH	GW	S	%	+/-	TF	F%	Min	GP	G	A	Pts	PIM	PP	SH	GW	Min
2004-05	Gregg Distributors	AMHL	34	12	13	25	14	....	....	....	....	....	....	....	....	....	....	....	....	....	....	....	....	....	....
2005-06	Gregg Distributors	AMHL	34	20	17	37	48	....	....	....	....	....	....	....	....	....	6	5	1	6	4	....	....	....	....
	Ft. Saskatchewan	AJHL	3	2	0	2	0	....	....	....	....	....	....	....	....	....	....	....	....	....	....	....	....	....	....
2006-07	Ft. Saskatchewan	AJHL	58	49	34	83	75	....	....	....	....	....	....	....	....	....	15	5	6	11	10	....	....	....	....
2007-08	North Dakota	WCHA	43	4	11	15	18	....	....	....	....	....	....	....	....	....	....	....	....	....	....	....	....	....	....
2008-09	North Dakota	WCHA	42	13	12	25	48	....	....	....	....	....	....	....	....	....	....	....	....	....	....	....	....	....	....
2009-10	North Dakota	WCHA	24	11	8	19	21	....	....	....	....	....	....	....	....	....	....	....	....	....	....	....	....	....	....
2010-11	North Dakota	WCHA	44	*36	24	*60	42	....	....	....	....	....	....	....	....	....	....	....	....	....	....	....	....	....	....
	Toronto	**NHL**	**1**	**0**	**0**	**0**	**0**	**0**	**0**	**0**	**5**	**0.0**	**–1**	**0**	**0.0**	**15:34**	....	....	....	....	....	....	....	....	....
2011-12	**Toronto**	**NHL**	**56**	**8**	**7**	**15**	**25**	**0**	**0**	**2**	**92**	**8.7**	**–4**	**8**	**25.0**	**13:10**	....	....	....	....	....	....	....	....	....
	Toronto Marlies	AHL	23	14	4	18	20	....	....	....	....	....	....	....	....	....	13	10	3	13	6	....	....	....	....
2012-13	Toronto Marlies	AHL	21	9	8	17	14	....	....	....	....	....	....	....	....	....	....	....	....	....	....	....	....	....	....
	Toronto	**NHL**	**25**	**7**	**6**	**13**	**4**	**0**	**0**	**3**	**42**	**16.7**	**6**	**8**	**62.5**	**13:14**	**6**	**0**	**2**	**2**	**0**	**0**	**0**	**0**	**13:47**
	NHL Totals		**82**	**15**	**13**	**28**	**29**	**0**	**0**	**5**	**139**	**10.8**		**16**	**43.8**	**13:13**	**6**	**0**	**2**	**2**	**0**	**0**	**0**	**0**	**13:47**

WCHA First All-Star Team (2011) • NCAA West First All-American Team (2011) • WCHA Player of the Year (2011)

Traded to **Los Angeles** by **Toronto** with Ben Scrivens and Toronto's 2nd round choice in 2014 or 2015 Entry Draft for Jonathan Bernier, June 23, 2013.

FREDHEIM, Kris

(FREHD-highm, KRIHS)

Defense. Shoots right. 6'2", 195 lbs. Born, Campbell River, B.C., February 23, 1987. Vancouver's 5th choice, 185th overall, in 2005 Entry Draft.

Season	Club	League	GP	G	A	Pts	PIM	PP	SH	GW	S	%	+/-	TF	F%	Min	GP	G	A	Pts	PIM	PP	SH	GW	Min
2003-04	Notre Dame	SMHL	41	9	21	30	38	....	....	....	....	....	....	....	....	....	....	....	....	....	....	....	....	....	....
2004-05	Notre Dame	SJHL	50	2	15	17	28	....	....	....	....	....	....	....	....	....	....	....	....	....	....	....	....	....	....
2005-06	Notre Dame	SJHL	52	12	23	35	75	....	....	....	....	....	....	....	....	....	11	2	9	11	15	....	....	....	....
2006-07	Colorado College	WCHA	23	1	3	4	16	....	....	....	....	....	....	....	....	....	....	....	....	....	....	....	....	....	....
2007-08	Colorado College	WCHA	34	1	4	5	24	....	....	....	....	....	....	....	....	....	....	....	....	....	....	....	....	....	....
2008-09	Colorado College	WCHA	32	2	5	7	40	....	....	....	....	....	....	....	....	....	....	....	....	....	....	....	....	....	....
2009-10	Colorado College	WCHA	36	4	12	16	46	....	....	....	....	....	....	....	....	....	....	....	....	....	....	....	....	....	....
	Victoria	ECHL	....	....	....	....	....	....	....	....	....	....	....	....	....	....	5	0	1	1	0	....	....	....	....
2010-11	Houston Aeros	AHL	66	3	6	9	24	....	....	....	....	....	....	....	....	....	....	....	....	....	....	....	....	....	....

			Regular Season														Playoffs								
Season	Club	League	GP	G	A	Pts	PIM	PP	SH	GW	S	%	+/-	TF	F%	Min	GP	G	A	Pts	PIM	PP	SH	GW	Min
2011-12	Minnesota	NHL	3	0	0	0	2	0	0	0	0	0.0	–2	0	0.0	11:59									
	Houston Aeros	AHL	73	3	9	12	29										4	0	0	0	2				
2012-13	Houston Aeros	AHL	52	1	6	7	20																		
	NHL Totals		3	0	0	0	2	0	0	0	0	0.0		0	0.0	11:59									

Signed as a free agent by **Houston** (AHL), November 4, 2010. Signed as a free agent by **Minnesota**, November 16, 2011.

FROLIK, Michael

(FROH-lihk, MIGH-kuhl) **WPG**

Left wing. Shoots left. 6'1", 198 lbs. Born, Kladno, Czech., February 17, 1988. Florida's 1st choice, 10th overall, in 2006 Entry Draft.

Season	Club	League	GP	G	A	Pts	PIM	PP	SH	GW	S	%	+/-	TF	F%	Min	GP	G	A	Pts	PIM	PP	SH	GW	Min
2002-03	HC Kladno U17	CzR-U17	46	37	21	58	36										9	9	1	10	18				
	HC Kladno Jr.	CzRep-Jr.															1	0	0	0	2				
2003-04	HC Kladno U17	CzR-U17	1	0	1	1	2																		
	HC Kladno Jr.	CzRep-Jr.	53	21	23	44	22										7	3	1	4	6				
2004-05	HC Kladno U17	CzR-U17															1	1	0	1	0				
	HC Kladno Jr.	CzRep-Jr.	15	9	11	20	18										5	1	0	1	0				
	HC Rabat Kladno	CzRep	27	3	1	4	6										1	0	0	0	0				
2005-06	HC Kladno Jr.	CzRep-Jr.	3	1	2	3	0										6	3	9	12	6				
	HC Rabat Kladno	CzRep	48	2	7	9	32																		
2006-07	Rimouski Oceanic	QMJHL	52	31	42	73	40																		
2007-08	Rimouski Oceanic	QMJHL	45	24	41	65	22										9	2	4	6	12				
2008-09	Florida	NHL	79	21	24	45	22	1	0	2	158	13.3	10	67	40.3	14:48									
2009-10	Florida	NHL	82	21	22	43	43	5	0	1	219	9.6	–4	35	37.1	17:29									
2010-11	Florida	NHL	52	8	21	29	16	1	0	1	158	5.1	2	12	41.7	16:02									
	Chicago	NHL	28	3	6	9	14	0	0	0	93	3.2	0	107	40.2	14:46	7	2	3	5	2	0	0	0	17:28
2011-12	Chicago	NHL	63	5	10	15	22	0	0	0	117	4.3	–10	48	33.3	12:52	4	2	1	3	0	0	0	0	17:23
2012-13	Pirati Chomutov	CzRep	32	14	10	24	22																		
	♦ Chicago	NHL	45	3	7	10	8	0	0	1	98	3.1	5	40	37.5	12:31	23	3	7	10	6	0	1	1	13:09
	NHL Totals		349	61	90	151	125	7	0	5	843	7.2		309	38.5	14:58	34	7	11	18	8	0	1	1	14:32

QMJHL All-Rookie Team (2007)

Traded to **Chicago** by **Florida** with Alexander Salak for Jack Skille, Hugh Jessiman and David Pacan, February 9, 2011. Signed as a free agent by **Chomutov** (CzRep), September 22, 2012. Traded to **Winnipeg** by **Chicago** for Winnipeg's 3rd (John Hayden) and 5th (Luke Johnson) round choices in 2013 Entry Draft, June 30, 2013.

GABORIK, Marian

(GAB-uhr-ihk, MAIR-ee-uhn) **CBJ**

Right wing. Shoots left. 6'1", 204 lbs. Born, Trencin, Czech., February 14, 1982. Minnesota's 1st choice, 3rd overall, in 2000 Entry Draft.

Season	Club	League	GP	G	A	Pts	PIM	PP	SH	GW	S	%	+/-	TF	F%	Min	GP	G	A	Pts	PIM	PP	SH	GW	Min
1997-98	Dukla Trencin Jr.	Slovak-Jr.	36	37	22	59	28																		
	Dukla Trencin	Slovakia	1	1	0	1	0																		
1998-99	Dukla Trencin	Slovakia	33	11	9	20	6										3	1	0	1	2				
99-2000	Dukla Trencin	Slovakia	50	25	21	46	34										5	1	2	3	2				
2000-01	Minnesota	NHL	71	18	18	36	32	6	0	3	179	10.1	–6	3	33.3	15:26									
2001-02	Minnesota	NHL	78	30	37	67	34	10	0	4	221	13.6	0	4	25.0	16:47									
2002-03	Minnesota	NHL	81	30	35	65	46	5	1	8	280	10.7	12	16	25.0	17:24	18	9	8	17	6	4	0	0	18:12
2003-04	Dukla Trencin	Slovakia	9	10	3	13	10																		
	Minnesota	NHL	65	18	22	40	20	3	0	4	220	8.2	10	11	45.5	18:17									
2004-05	Dukla Trencin	Slovakia	29	25	27	52	46										12	8	9	17	26				
	Farjestad	Sweden	12	6	4	10	45																		
2005-06	Minnesota	NHL	65	38	28	66	64	10	2	7	252	15.1	6	11	27.3	18:26									
	Slovakia	Olympics	6	3	4	7	4																		
2006-07	Minnesota	NHL	48	30	27	57	40	12	1	7	196	15.3	12	4	0.0	19:38	5	3	1	4	8	1	1	1	19:32
2007-08	Minnesota	NHL	77	42	41	83	63	11	1	8	278	15.1	17	21	28.6	19:36	6	0	1	1	4	0	0	0	21:51
2008-09	Minnesota	NHL	17	13	10	23	2	2	1	2	68	19.1	3	5	0.0	20:00									
2009-10	NY Rangers	NHL	76	42	44	86	37	14	1	4	272	15.4	15	7	28.6	21:15									
	Slovakia	Olympics	7	4	1	5	6																		
2010-11	NY Rangers	NHL	62	22	26	48	18	7	0	4	192	11.5	8	0	0.0	18:05	5	1	1	2	2	0	0	0	23:55
2011-12	NY Rangers	NHL	82	41	35	76	34	10	0	7	276	14.9	15	2	0.0	19:31	20	5	6	11	2	0	0	1	19:56
2012-13	NY Rangers	NHL	35	9	10	19	8	1	0	4	113	8.0	–8	2	0.0	18:40									
	Columbus	NHL	12	3	5	8	6	0	0	1	38	7.9	5	1	100.0	18:05									
	NHL Totals		769	336	338	674	404	91	7	63	2585	13.0		87	26.4	18:28	54	18	17	35	22	5	1	2	19:54

NHL Second All-Star Team (2012)

Played in NHL All-Star Game (2003, 2008, 2012)

Signed as a free agent by **Trencin** (Slovakia), July 5, 2004. Signed as a free agent by **Farjestad** (Sweden), December 21, 2004. • Missed majority of 2008-09 due to hip surgery, January 5, 2009. Signed as a free agent by **NY Rangers**, July 1, 2009. Traded to **Columbus** by **NY Rangers** with Blake Parlett and Steven Delisle for Derek Dorsett, Derick Brassard, John Moore and Columbus' 6th round choice in 2014 Entry Draft, April 3, 2013.

GAGNE, Simon

(gah-N'YAY, see-MOHN)

Left wing. Shoots left. 6'1", 195 lbs. Born, Ste-Foy, Que., February 29, 1980. Philadelphia's 1st choice, 22nd overall, in 1998 Entry Draft.

Season	Club	League	GP	G	A	Pts	PIM	PP	SH	GW	S	%	+/-	TF	F%	Min	GP	G	A	Pts	PIM	PP	SH	GW	Min
1995-96	Ste-Foy	QAAA	27	13	9	22	18										15	7	8	15	8				
1996-97	Beauport	QMJHL	51	9	22	31	39																		
1997-98	Quebec Remparts	QMJHL	53	30	39	69	26										12	11	5	16	23				
1998-99	Quebec Remparts	QMJHL	61	50	*70	*120	42										13	9	8	17	4				
99-2000	Philadelphia	NHL	80	20	28	48	22	8	1	4	159	12.6	11	443	42.2	14:59	17	5	5	10	2	2	0	1	16:46
2000-01	Philadelphia	NHL	69	27	32	59	18	6	0	7	191	14.1	24	21	28.6	18:05	6	3	0	3	0	2	0	0	19:09
2001-02	Philadelphia	NHL	79	33	33	66	32	4	1	7	199	16.6	31	6	83.3	18:09	5	0	0	0	2	0	0	0	19:16
	Canada	Olympics	6	1	3	4	0																		
2002-03	Philadelphia	NHL	46	9	18	27	16	1	1	3	115	7.8	20	70	42.9	17:24	13	4	1	5	6	0	1	1	18:13
2003-04	Philadelphia	NHL	80	24	21	45	29	6	0	6	211	11.4	12	104	39.4	16:27	18	5	4	9	12	0	0	1	16:48
2004-05			DID NOT PLAY																						
2005-06	Philadelphia	NHL	72	47	32	79	38	12	2	7	334	14.1	31	18	38.9	20:46	6	3	1	4	2	1	0	0	21:45
	Canada	Olympics	6	1	2	3	6																		
2006-07	Philadelphia	NHL	76	41	27	68	30	13	2	4	291	14.1	2	49	42.9	21:02									
2007-08	Philadelphia	NHL	25	7	11	18	4	5	0	2	76	9.2	–8	2	50.0	18:09									
2008-09	Philadelphia	NHL	79	34	40	74	42	12	4	3	221	15.4	21	10	30.0	19:01	6	3	1	4	2	1	1	1	20:29
2009-10	Philadelphia	NHL	58	17	23	40	47	5	0	4	183	9.3	–1	4	25.0	18:37	19	9	3	12	0	5	0	2	17:35
2010-11	Tampa Bay	NHL	63	17	23	40	20	7	0	3	154	11.0	–12	16	37.5	16:53	15	5	7	12	4	0	0	1	15:52
2011-12	♦ Los Angeles	NHL	34	7	10	17	18	0	1	2	75	9.3	–1	7	28.6	17:59	4	0	0	0	2	0	0	0	8:04
2012-13	Los Angeles	NHL	11	0	5	5	2	0	0	0	20	0.0	2	0	0.0	13:46									
	Philadelphia	NHL	27	5	6	11	6	2	0	0	56	8.9	–3	2	100.0	14:17									
	NHL Totals		799	288	309	597	324	81	12	52	2285	12.6		752	41.5	17:57	109	37	22	59	32	11	2	7	17:22

QMJHL Second All-Star Team (1999) • NHL All-Rookie Team (2000)

Played in NHL ALL-Star Game (2001, 2007)

• Missed majority of 2007-08 due to head injury at Pittsburgh, February 10, 2008. Traded to **Tampa Bay** by **Philadelphia** for Matt Walker and Tampa Bay's 4th round choice (Marcel Noebels) in 2011 Entry Draft, July 19, 2010. Signed as a free agent by **Los Angeles**, July 2, 2011. • Missed majority of 2011-12 due to head injury vs. Phoenix, December 26, 2011. Traded to **Philadelphia** by **Los Angeles** for Phoenix's 4th round choice (previously acquired, Los Angeles selected Justin Auger) in 2013 Entry Draft, February 26, 2013.

GAGNER, Sam

(GAH-n'yay, SAM) **EDM**

Center. Shoots right. 5'11", 195 lbs. Born, London, Ont., August 10, 1989. Edmonton's 1st choice, 6th overall, in 2007 Entry Draft.

Season	Club	League	GP	G	A	Pts	PIM	PP	SH	GW	S	%	+/-	TF	F%	Min	GP	G	A	Pts	PIM	PP	SH	GW	Min
2001-02	Tor. Marlboros	GTHL	68	56	61	117	42																		
2002-03	Tor. Marlboros	GTHL	72	68	86	154	35																		
2003-04	Tor. Marlboros	GTHL	85	64	108	171	36																		
2004-05	Tor. Marlboros	GTHL	70	62	118	180	56																		
	Milton Icehawks	ON-Jr.A	13	5	10	15	10																		
2005-06	Sioux City	USHL	56	11	35	46	60																		
2006-07	London Knights	OHL	53	35	83	118	36										16	7	*22	29	22				
2007-08	Edmonton	NHL	79	13	36	49	23	4	0	1	135	9.6	–21	299	41.8	15:41									
2008-09	Edmonton	NHL	76	16	25	41	51	6	0	1	156	10.3	–1	690	42.0	16:46									
2009-10	Edmonton	NHL	68	15	26	41	33	6	0	1	170	8.8	–8	709	47.4	16:17									
2010-11	Edmonton	NHL	68	15	27	42	37	3	1	2	138	10.9	–17	935	43.9	17:45									
2011-12	Edmonton	NHL	75	18	29	47	36	6	0	0	149	12.1	5	701	47.7	17:11									

Season	Club	League	GP	G	A	Pts	PIM	PP	SH	GW	S	%	+/-	TF	F%	Min	GP	G	A	Pts	PIM	PP	SH	GW	Min
								Regular Season									Playoffs								
2012-13	Klagenfurter AC	Austria	21	10	10	20	8	....	....	....	....	....	....	....	....	....	....	....	....	....	....	....	....	....	....
	Edmonton	**NHL**	**48**	**14**	**24**	**38**	**23**	**4**	**0**	**1**	**113**	**12.4**	**–6**	**741**	**43.9**	**19:25**	....	....	....	....	....	....	....	....	....
	NHL Totals		**414**	**91**	**167**	**258**	**203**	**29**	**1**	**6**	**861**	**10.6**		**4075**	**44.7**	**17:01**	....	....	....	....	....	....	....	....	....

USHL All-Rookie Team (2006) • OHL All-Rookie Team (2007)
Signed as a free agent by **Klagenfurt** (Austria), October 15, 2012.

GAGNON, Aaron

(GAN-YAWN, AIR-ruhn)

Center. Shoots right. 5'10", 185 lbs. Born, Quesnel, B.C., April 24, 1986. Phoenix's 8th choice, 240th overall, in 2004 Entry Draft.

Season	Club	League	GP	G	A	Pts	PIM	PP	SH	GW	S	%	+/-	TF	F%	Min	GP	G	A	Pts	PIM	PP	SH	GW	Min
2001-02	N. Okanagan	Minor-BC	41	59	59	118	60	....	....	....	....	....	....	....	....	....	....	....	....	....	....	....	....	....	....
	Seattle	WHL	2	0	0	0	0	....	....	....	....	....	....	....	....	....	....	....	....	....	....	....	....	....	....
2002-03	Seattle	WHL	60	5	13	18	14	....	....	....	....	....	....	....	....	....	15	3	2	5	4	....	....	....	....
2003-04	Seattle	WHL	63	21	15	36	29	....	....	....	....	....	....	....	....	....	....	....	....	....	....	....	....	....	....
2004-05	Seattle	WHL	72	31	34	65	29	....	....	....	....	....	....	....	....	....	12	4	5	9	16	....	....	....	....
2005-06	Seattle	WHL	62	24	21	45	40	....	....	....	....	....	....	....	....	....	7	5	3	8	6	....	....	....	....
2006-07	Seattle	WHL	59	42	38	80	58	....	....	....	....	....	....	....	....	....	11	6	2	8	10	....	....	....	....
2007-08	Iowa Stars	AHL	25	0	1	1	8	....	....	....	....	....	....	....	....	....	....	....	....	....	....	....	....	....	....
	Idaho Steelheads	ECHL	22	7	14	21	4	....	....	....	....	....	....	....	....	....	4	1	1	2	2	....	....	....	....
2008-09	Grand Rapids	AHL	61	8	11	19	28	....	....	....	....	....	....	....	....	....	10	1	2	3	2	....	....	....	....
2009-10	**Dallas**	**NHL**	**2**	**0**	**0**	**0**	**0**	**0**	**0**	**0**	**2**	**0.0**	**0**	**11**	**72.7**	**8:49**	....	....	....	....	....	....	....	....	....
	Texas Stars	AHL	78	27	31	58	42	....	....	....	....	....	....	....	....	....	24	8	4	12	18	....	....	....	....
2010-11	**Dallas**	**NHL**	**19**	**0**	**2**	**2**	**0**	**0**	**0**	**0**	**9**	**0.0**	**–3**	**55**	**54.6**	**8:04**	....	....	....	....	....	....	....	....	....
	Texas Stars	AHL	58	14	22	36	24	....	....	....	....	....	....	....	....	....	6	2	2	4	4	....	....	....	....
2011-12	**Winnipeg**	**NHL**	**7**	**0**	**0**	**0**	**0**	**0**	**0**	**0**	**6**	**0.0**	**–1**	**40**	**45.0**	**9:27**	....	....	....	....	....	....	....	....	....
	St. John's IceCaps	AHL	63	14	20	34	14	....	....	....	....	....	....	....	....	....	15	5	4	9	6	....	....	....	....
2012-13	St. John's IceCaps	AHL	43	11	13	24	18	....	....	....	....	....	....	....	....	....	....	....	....	....	....	....	....	....	....
	Winnipeg	**NHL**	**10**	**3**	**0**	**3**	**2**	**0**	**0**	**1**	**11**	**27.3**	**2**	**57**	**52.6**	**8:09**	....	....	....	....	....	....	....	....	....
	NHL Totals		**38**	**3**	**2**	**5**	**2**	**0**	**0**	**1**	**28**	**10.7**		**163**	**52.8**	**8:23**	....	....	....	....	....	....	....	....	....

WHL West First All-Star Team (2005, 2007)
Signed as a free agent by **Dallas**, February 2, 2007. Signed as a free agent by **Winnipeg**, July 4, 2011.

GALCHENYUK, Alex

(gal-CHEHN-yuhk, AL-ehx) **MTL**

Center. Shoots left. 6'1", 194 lbs. Born, Milwaukee, WI, February 12, 1994. Montreal's 1st choice, 3rd overall, in 2012 Entry Draft.

Season	Club	League	GP	G	A	Pts	PIM	PP	SH	GW	S	%	+/-	TF	F%	Min	GP	G	A	Pts	PIM	PP	SH	GW	Min
2009-10	Chi. Americans	T1EHL	38	44	43	87	56	....	....	....	....	....	....	....	....	....	....	....	....	....	....	....	....	....	....
2010-11	Sarnia Sting	OHL	68	31	52	83	52	....	....	....	....	....	....	....	....	....	....	....	....	....	....	....	....	....	....
2011-12	Sarnia Sting	OHL	2	0	0	0	0	....	....	....	....	....	....	....	....	....	6	2	2	4	4	....	....	....	....
2012-13	Sarnia Sting	OHL	33	27	34	61	22	....	....	....	....	....	....	....	....	....	....	....	....	....	....	....	....	....	....
	Montreal	**NHL**	**48**	**9**	**18**	**27**	**20**	**0**	**0**	**2**	**79**	**11.4**	**14**	**138**	**42.8**	**12:19**	**5**	**1**	**2**	**3**	**0**	**0**	**0**	**0**	**13:00**
	NHL Totals		**48**	**9**	**18**	**27**	**20**	**0**	**0**	**2**	**79**	**11.4**		**138**	**42.8**	**12:19**	**5**	**1**	**2**	**3**	**0**	**0**	**0**	**0**	**13:00**

OHL All-Rookie Team (2011)
• Missed majority of 2011-12 due to knee injury in pre-season vs. Windsor (OHL), September 16, 2011.

GALIARDI, T.J.

(gal-ee-AR-dee, TEE-JAY) **CGY**

Left wing. Shoots left. 6'2", 195 lbs. Born, Calgary, Alta., April 22, 1988. Colorado's 4th choice, 55th overall, in 2007 Entry Draft.

Season	Club	League	GP	G	A	Pts	PIM	PP	SH	GW	S	%	+/-	TF	F%	Min	GP	G	A	Pts	PIM	PP	SH	GW	Min
2004-05	Cgy. North Stars	AMHL	36	14	16	30	32	....	....	....	....	....	....	....	....	....	....	....	....	....	....	....	....	....	....
2005-06	Calgary Royals	AJHL	56	19	37	56	60	....	....	....	....	....	....	....	....	....	....	....	....	....	....	....	....	....	....
2006-07	Dartmouth	ECAC	33	14	17	31	30	....	....	....	....	....	....	....	....	....	....	....	....	....	....	....	....	....	....
2007-08	Calgary Hitmen	WHL	72	18	52	70	77	....	....	....	....	....	....	....	....	....	16	5	*19	*24	20	....	....	....	....
2008-09	**Colorado**	**NHL**	**11**	**3**	**1**	**4**	**6**	**0**	**0**	**0**	**14**	**21.4**	**–4**	**133**	**42.1**	**16:21**	....	....	....	....	....	....	....	....	....
	Lake Erie	AHL	66	10	17	27	32	....	....	....	....	....	....	....	....	....	....	....	....	....	....	....	....	....	....
2009-10	**Colorado**	**NHL**	**70**	**15**	**24**	**39**	**28**	**2**	**1**	**3**	**120**	**12.5**	**6**	**327**	**50.5**	**18:11**	**6**	**0**	**2**	**2**	**6**	**0**	**0**	**0**	**20:50**
2010-11	**Colorado**	**NHL**	**35**	**7**	**8**	**15**	**12**	**0**	**0**	**1**	**62**	**11.3**	**–6**	**134**	**46.3**	**16:12**	....	....	....	....	....	....	....	....	....
	Lake Erie	AHL	1	0	1	1	0	....	....	....	....	....	....	....	....	....	....	....	....	....	....	....	....	....	....
2011-12	**Colorado**	**NHL**	**55**	**8**	**6**	**14**	**47**	**0**	**1**	**2**	**101**	**7.9**	**–6**	**162**	**45.1**	**13:33**	....	....	....	....	....	....	....	....	....
	San Jose	**NHL**	**14**	**1**	**0**	**1**	**6**	**0**	**0**	**0**	**12**	**8.3**	**–2**	**5**	**40.0**	**11:04**	**3**	**0**	**0**	**0**	**6**	**0**	**0**	**0**	**12:37**
2012-13	Bietigheim	German-2	7	3	3	6	8	....	....	....	....	....	....	....	....	....	....	....	....	....	....	....	....	....	....
	San Jose	**NHL**	**36**	**5**	**9**	**14**	**14**	**1**	**0**	**0**	**68**	**7.4**	**1**	**19**	**26.3**	**13:52**	**11**	**1**	**1**	**2**	**6**	**0**	**0**	**1**	**16:50**
	NHL Totals		**221**	**39**	**48**	**87**	**113**	**3**	**2**	**6**	**377**	**10.3**		**780**	**46.5**	**15:28**	**20**	**1**	**3**	**4**	**18**	**0**	**0**	**1**	**17:24**

ECAC All-Rookie Team (2007)
• Missed majority of 2010-11 due to wrist injury vs. Calgary, November 9. 2010. Traded to **San Jose** by **Colorado** with Daniel Winnik and Anaheim's 7th round choice (previously acquired, San Jose selected Emil Galimov) in 2013 Entry Draft for Jamie McGinn, Michael Sgarbossa and Mike Connolly, February 27, 2012. Signed as a free agent by **Bietigheim** (German-2), October 4, 2012. Traded to **Calgary** by **San Jose** for Calgary's 4th round choice in 2015 Entry Draft, July 2, 2013.

GALLAGHER, Brendan

(gal-lah-GUR, BREHN-duhn) **MTL**

Right wing. Shoots right. 5'8", 175 lbs. Born, Edmonton, Alta., May 6, 1992. Montreal's 4th choice, 147th overall, in 2010 Entry Draft.

Season	Club	League	GP	G	A	Pts	PIM	PP	SH	GW	S	%	+/-	TF	F%	Min	GP	G	A	Pts	PIM	PP	SH	GW	Min
2007-08	Greater Van.	BCMML	39	23	33	56	66	....	....	....	....	....	....	....	....	....	2	0	1	1	0	....	....	....	....
2008-09	Vancouver Giants	WHL	52	10	21	31	61	....	....	....	....	....	....	....	....	....	16	1	2	3	10	....	....	....	....
2009-10	Vancouver Giants	WHL	72	41	40	81	111	....	....	....	....	....	....	....	....	....	16	11	10	21	14	....	....	....	....
2010-11	Vancouver Giants	WHL	66	44	47	91	108	....	....	....	....	....	....	....	....	....	4	2	0	2	16	....	....	....	....
2011-12	Vancouver Giants	WHL	54	41	36	77	79	....	....	....	....	....	....	....	....	....	6	5	5	10	16	....	....	....	....
2012-13	Hamilton	AHL	36	10	10	20	61	....	....	....	....	....	....	....	....	....	....	....	....	....	....	....	....	....	....
	Montreal	**NHL**	**44**	**15**	**13**	**28**	**33**	**3**	**0**	**3**	**117**	**12.8**	**10**	**25**	**32.0**	**13:52**	**5**	**2**	**0**	**2**	**5**	**1**	**0**	**1**	**14:26**
	NHL Totals		**44**	**15**	**13**	**28**	**33**	**3**	**0**	**3**	**117**	**12.8**		**25**	**32.0**	**13:52**	**5**	**2**	**0**	**2**	**5**	**1**	**0**	**1**	**14:26**

WHL West First All-Star Team (2011, 2012) • NHL All-Rookie Team (2013)

GARBUTT, Ryan

(GAHR-buht, RIGH-uhn) **DAL**

Center. Shoots left. 6', 190 lbs. Born, Winnipeg, Man., August 12, 1985.

Season	Club	League	GP	G	A	Pts	PIM	PP	SH	GW	S	%	+/-	TF	F%	Min	GP	G	A	Pts	PIM	PP	SH	GW	Min
2003-04	Wpg. South Blues	MJHL	60	23	25	48	143	....	....	....	....	....	....	....	....	....	....	....	....	....	....	....	....	....	....
2004-05	Wpg. South Blues	MJHL	63	47	34	81	303	....	....	....	....	....	....	....	....	....	....	....	....	....	....	....	....	....	....
2005-06	Brown U.	ECAC	28	2	4	6	61	....	....	....	....	....	....	....	....	....	....	....	....	....	....	....	....	....	....
2006-07	Brown U.	ECAC	29	9	4	13	30	....	....	....	....	....	....	....	....	....	....	....	....	....	....	....	....	....	....
2007-08	Brown U.	ECAC	29	12	11	23	56	....	....	....	....	....	....	....	....	....	....	....	....	....	....	....	....	....	....
2008-09	Brown U.	ECAC	30	6	10	16	56	....	....	....	....	....	....	....	....	....	....	....	....	....	....	....	....	....	....
2009-10	Corpus Christi	CHL	64	22	28	50	204	....	....	....	....	....	....	....	....	....	1	0	0	0	2	....	....	....	....
2010-11	Gwinnett	ECHL	10	10	7	17	24	....	....	....	....	....	....	....	....	....	....	....	....	....	....	....	....	....	....
	Chicago Wolves	AHL	65	19	18	37	118	....	....	....	....	....	....	....	....	....	....	....	....	....	....	....	....	....	....
2011-12	**Dallas**	**NHL**	**20**	**2**	**1**	**3**	**22**	**0**	**0**	**1**	**28**	**7.1**	**–1**	**27**	**44.4**	**8:17**	....	....	....	....	....	....	....	....	....
	Texas Stars	AHL	50	16	17	33	96	....	....	....	....	....	....	....	....	....	....	....	....	....	....	....	....	....	....
2012-13	**Dallas**	**NHL**	**36**	**3**	**7**	**10**	**32**	**0**	**0**	**0**	**59**	**5.1**	**1**	**17**	**41.2**	**9:55**	....	....	....	....	....	....	....	....	....
	NHL Totals		**56**	**5**	**8**	**13**	**54**	**0**	**0**	**1**	**87**	**5.7**		**44**	**43.2**	**9:20**	....	....	....	....	....	....	....	....	....

Signed as a free agent by **Corpus Christi** (CHL), September, 2009. Signed as a free agent by **Gwinnett** (ECHL), September 21, 2010. Signed as a free agent by **Chicago** (AHL), November 11, 2010. Signed as a free agent by **Dallas**, July 1, 2011.

GARDINER, Jake

(GAHR-dih-nuhr, JAYK) **TOR**

Defense. Shoots left. 6'2", 184 lbs. Born, Minnetonka, MN, July 4, 1990. Anaheim's 1st choice, 17th overall, in 2008 Entry Draft.

Season	Club	League	GP	G	A	Pts	PIM	PP	SH	GW	S	%	+/-	TF	F%	Min	GP	G	A	Pts	PIM	PP	SH	GW	Min
2005-06	Minnetonka High	High-MN	21	2	14	16	6	....	....	....	....	....	....	....	....	....	....	....	....	....	....	....	....	....	....
2006-07	Minnetonka High	High-MN	19	10	22	32	20	....	....	....	....	....	....	....	....	....	....	....	....	....	....	....	....	....	....
	Team Southwest	UMWEHL	11	4	3	7	....	....	....	....	....	....	....	....	....	....	....	....	....	....	....	....	....	....	....
2007-08	Minnetonka High	High-MN	24	20	28	48	14	....	....	....	....	....	....	....	....	....	....	....	....	....	....	....	....	....	....
	Team Southwest	UMWEHL	11	8	7	15	....	....	....	....	....	....	....	....	....	....	....	....	....	....	....	....	....	....	....
2008-09	U. of Wisconsin	WCHA	39	3	18	21	16	....	....	....	....	....	....	....	....	....	....	....	....	....	....	....	....	....	....
2009-10	U. of Wisconsin	WCHA	41	6	7	13	20	....	....	....	....	....	....	....	....	....	....	....	....	....	....	....	....	....	....

Season	Club	League	Regular Season GP	G	A	Pts	PIM	PP	SH	GW	S	%	+/-	TF	F%	Min	Playoffs GP	G	A	Pts	PIM	PP	SH	GW	Min
2010-11	U. of Wisconsin	WCHA	41	10	31	41	24	....	....	....	....	....	....	....	....	....	....	....	....	....	....	....	....	....	....
	Toronto Marlies	AHL	10	0	3	3	4	....	....	....	....	....	....	....	....	....	....	....	....	....	....	....	....	....	....
2011-12	**Toronto**	**NHL**	**75**	**7**	**23**	**30**	**18**	**1**	**0**	**0**	**79**	**8.9**	**–2**	**0**	**0.0**	**21:35**	....	....	....	....	....	....	....	....	....
	Toronto Marlies	AHL	4	0	2	2	2	....	....	....	....	....	....	....	....	....	17	2	9	11	10	....	....	....	....
2012-13	Toronto Marlies	AHL	43	10	21	31	12	....	....	....	....	....	....	....	....	....	....	....	....	....	....	....	....	....	....
	Toronto	**NHL**	**12**	**0**	**4**	**4**	**0**	**0**	**0**	**0**	**12**	**0.0**	**0**	**0**	**0.0**	**20:29**	**6**	**1**	**4**	**5**	**0**	**1**	**0**	**0**	**23:01**
	NHL Totals		**87**	**7**	**27**	**34**	**18**	**1**	**0**	**0**	**91**	**7.7**		**0**	**0.0**	**21:26**	**6**	**1**	**4**	**5**	**0**	**1**	**0**	**0**	**23:01**

WCHA All-Rookie Team (2009) • WCHA Second All-Star Team (2011) • NCAA West Second All-American Team (2011) • NHL All-Rookie Team (2012)

Traded to **Toronto** by **Anaheim** with Joffrey Lupul and Anaheim's 4th round choice (later traded to San Jose – San Jose selected Fredrik Bergvik) in 2013 Entry Draft for Francois Beauchemin, February 9, 2011.

GARRISON, Jason

(GAIR-ih-suhn, JAY-suhn) **VAN**

Defense. Shoots left. 6'2", 218 lbs. Born, White Rock, B.C., November 13, 1984.

2003-04	Nanaimo Clippers	BCHL	52	7	20	27	31	....	....	....	....	....	....	....	....	....	24	3	10	13	12	....	....	....	....
2004-05	Nanaimo Clippers	BCHL	57	22	40	62	42	....	....	....	....	....	....	....	....	....	....	....	....	....	....	....	....	....	....
2005-06	U. Minn-Duluth	WCHA	40	3	9	12	26	....	....	....	....	....	....	....	....	....	....	....	....	....	....	....	....	....	....
2006-07	U. Minn-Duluth	WCHA	21	1	2	3	16	....	....	....	....	....	....	....	....	....	....	....	....	....	....	....	....	....	....
2007-08	U. Minn-Duluth	WCHA	26	5	9	14	26	....	....	....	....	....	....	....	....	....	....	....	....	....	....	....	....	....	....
2008-09	**Florida**	**NHL**	**1**	**0**	**0**	**0**	**0**	**0**	**0**	**0**	**0**	**0.0**	**0**	**0**	**0.0**	**11:57**	....	....	....	....	....	....	....	....	....
	Rochester	AHL	75	8	27	35	68	....	....	....	....	....	....	....	....	....	....	....	....	....	....	....	....	....	....
2009-10	**Florida**	**NHL**	**39**	**2**	**6**	**8**	**23**	**0**	**0**	**0**	**24**	**8.3**	**5**	**0**	**0.0**	**15:08**	....	....	....	....	....	....	....	....	....
	Rochester	AHL	38	3	16	19	33	....	....	....	....	....	....	....	....	....	7	2	7	9	0	....	....	....	....
2010-11	**Florida**	**NHL**	**73**	**5**	**13**	**18**	**26**	**0**	**0**	**3**	**116**	**4.3**	**–2**	**0**	**0.0**	**22:18**	....	....	....	....	....	....	....	....	....
2011-12	**Florida**	**NHL**	**77**	**16**	**17**	**33**	**32**	**9**	**0**	**3**	**168**	**9.5**	**6**	**2**	**50.0**	**23:42**	**4**	**1**	**2**	**3**	**0**	**1**	**0**	**0**	**25:11**
2012-13	**Vancouver**	**NHL**	**47**	**8**	**8**	**16**	**28**	**3**	**0**	**2**	**94**	**8.5**	**18**	**0**	**0.0**	**21:41**	**4**	**0**	**0**	**0**	**2**	**0**	**0**	**0**	**23:44**
	NHL Totals		**237**	**31**	**44**	**75**	**109**	**12**	**0**	**8**	**402**	**7.7**		**2**	**50.0**	**21:25**	**8**	**1**	**2**	**3**	**2**	**1**	**0**	**0**	**24:27**

Signed as a free agent by **Florida**, April 2, 2008. Signed as a free agent by **Vancouver**, July 1, 2012.

GAUNCE, Cameron

(GAWNS, KAM-ih-RUHN) **DAL**

Defense. Shoots left. 6'1", 203 lbs. Born, Sudbury, Ont., March 19, 1990. Colorado's 1st choice, 50th overall, in 2008 Entry Draft.

2005-06	Markham Waxers	Minor-ON	72	11	60	71	122	....	....	....	....	....	....	....	....	....	....	....	....	....	....	....	....	....	....
2006-07	Markham Waxers	ON-Jr.A	45	2	12	14	68	....	....	....	....	....	....	....	....	....	11	0	3	3	26	....	....	....	....
2007-08	St. Michael's	OHL	63	10	30	40	99	....	....	....	....	....	....	....	....	....	4	0	1	1	6	....	....	....	....
2008-09	St. Michael's	OHL	67	17	47	64	110	....	....	....	....	....	....	....	....	....	11	4	6	10	20	....	....	....	....
2009-10	St. Michael's	OHL	55	6	31	37	112	....	....	....	....	....	....	....	....	....	16	0	13	13	34	....	....	....	....
2010-11	**Colorado**	**NHL**	**11**	**1**	**0**	**1**	**16**	**0**	**0**	**0**	**4**	**25.0**	**–3**	**0**	**0.0**	**12:44**	....	....	....	....	....	....	....	....	....
	Lake Erie	AHL	61	2	20	22	84	....	....	....	....	....	....	....	....	....	....	....	....	....	....	....	....	....	....
2011-12	Lake Erie	AHL	75	6	21	27	90	....	....	....	....	....	....	....	....	....	....	....	....	....	....	....	....	....	....
2012-13	Lake Erie	AHL	61	1	10	11	98	....	....	....	....	....	....	....	....	....	....	....	....	....	....	....	....	....	....
	Texas Stars	AHL	9	1	4	5	0	....	....	....	....	....	....	....	....	....	9	0	0	0	0	....	....	....	....
	NHL Totals		**11**	**1**	**0**	**1**	**16**	**0**	**0**	**0**	**4**	**25.0**		**0**	**0.0**	**12:44**	....	....	....	....	....	....	....	....	....

OHL Second All-Star Team (2009, 2010)

Traded to **Dallas** by **Colorado** for Tomas Vincour, April 2, 2013.

GAUSTAD, Paul

(GAW-stad, PAWL) **NSH**

Center. Shoots left. 6'5", 220 lbs. Born, Fargo, ND, February 3, 1982. Buffalo's 6th choice, 220th overall, in 2000 Entry Draft.

1998-99	Portland Hawks	USAHA	45	47	53	100	81	....	....	....	....	....	....	....	....	....	....	....	....	....	....	....	....	....	....
99-2000	Portland	WHL	56	6	8	14	110	....	....	....	....	....	....	....	....	....	....	....	....	....	....	....	....	....	....
2000-01	Portland	WHL	70	11	30	41	168	....	....	....	....	....	....	....	....	....	16	10	6	16	59	....	....	....	....
2001-02	Portland	WHL	72	36	44	80	202	....	....	....	....	....	....	....	....	....	6	3	1	4	16	....	....	....	....
2002-03	**Buffalo**	**NHL**	**1**	**0**	**0**	**0**	**0**	**0**	**0**	**0**	**0**	**0.0**	**0**	**7**	**42.9**	**5:48**	....	....	....	....	....	....	....	....	....
	Rochester	AHL	80	14	39	53	137	....	....	....	....	....	....	....	....	....	3	0	0	0	4	....	....	....	....
2003-04	Rochester	AHL	78	9	22	31	169	....	....	....	....	....	....	....	....	....	16	3	10	13	30	....	....	....	....
2004-05	Rochester	AHL	76	18	25	43	192	....	....	....	....	....	....	....	....	....	9	6	5	11	16	....	....	....	....
2005-06	**Buffalo**	**NHL**	**78**	**9**	**15**	**24**	**65**	**0**	**0**	**0**	**113**	**8.0**	**4**	**829**	**52.2**	**12:08**	**18**	**0**	**4**	**4**	**14**	**0**	**0**	**0**	**12:21**
2006-07	**Buffalo**	**NHL**	**54**	**9**	**13**	**22**	**74**	**3**	**0**	**0**	**75**	**12.0**	**11**	**386**	**52.9**	**13:19**	**7**	**0**	**1**	**1**	**2**	**0**	**0**	**0**	**11:00**
2007-08	**Buffalo**	**NHL**	**82**	**10**	**26**	**36**	**85**	**5**	**0**	**2**	**136**	**7.4**	**–4**	**1165**	**54.9**	**17:10**	....	....	....	....	....	....	....	....	....
2008-09	**Buffalo**	**NHL**	**62**	**12**	**17**	**29**	**108**	**3**	**1**	**1**	**122**	**9.8**	**4**	**858**	**52.7**	**16:06**	....	....	....	....	....	....	....	....	....
2009-10	**Buffalo**	**NHL**	**65**	**12**	**10**	**22**	**82**	**3**	**0**	**1**	**111**	**10.8**	**–7**	**1043**	**57.4**	**15:45**	**6**	**0**	**1**	**1**	**8**	**0**	**0**	**0**	**18:40**
2010-11	**Buffalo**	**NHL**	**81**	**12**	**19**	**31**	**101**	**1**	**0**	**3**	**117**	**10.3**	**7**	**1158**	**59.8**	**15:08**	**7**	**0**	**2**	**2**	**13**	**0**	**0**	**0**	**19:19**
2011-12	**Buffalo**	**NHL**	**56**	**7**	**10**	**17**	**70**	**0**	**0**	**3**	**62**	**11.3**	**–1**	**871**	**56.8**	**15:05**	....	....	....	....	....	....	....	....	....
	Nashville	**NHL**	**14**	**0**	**4**	**4**	**6**	**0**	**0**	**0**	**13**	**0.0**	**0**	**279**	**58.8**	**13:31**	**10**	**1**	**1**	**2**	**5**	**0**	**0**	**0**	**11:36**
2012-13	**Nashville**	**NHL**	**23**	**2**	**3**	**5**	**20**	**0**	**0**	**0**	**35**	**5.7**	**–1**	**449**	**59.7**	**15:13**	....	....	....	....	....	....	....	....	....
	NHL Totals		**516**	**73**	**117**	**190**	**611**	**15**	**1**	**10**	**784**	**9.3**		**7045**	**56.1**	**14:56**	**48**	**1**	**9**	**10**	**42**	**0**	**0**	**0**	**13:48**

Traded to **Nashville** by **Buffalo** with Buffalo's 4th round choice (Juuse Saros) in 2013 Entry Draft for Nashville's 1st round choice (later traded to Calgary – Calgary selected Mark Jankowski) in 2012 Entry Draft, February 27, 2012.

GELINAS, Eric

(ZHEHL-ih-nuh, AIR-ihk) **N.J.**

Defense. Shoots left. 6'4", 210 lbs. Born, Vanier, Ont., May 8, 1991. New Jersey's 2nd choice, 54th overall, in 2009 Entry Draft.

2006-07	C.C. Lemoyne	QAAA	44	5	14	19	50	....	....	....	....	....	....	....	....	....	10	1	4	5	14	....	....	....	....
2007-08	Lewiston	QMJHL	54	3	16	19	34	....	....	....	....	....	....	....	....	....	5	0	0	0	2	....	....	....	....
2008-09	Lewiston	QMJHL	67	10	29	39	80	....	....	....	....	....	....	....	....	....	4	0	1	1	12	....	....	....	....
2009-10	Lewiston	QMJHL	33	3	16	19	33	....	....	....	....	....	....	....	....	....	....	....	....	....	....	....	....	....	....
	Chicoutimi	QMJHL	28	3	9	12	26	....	....	....	....	....	....	....	....	....	6	1	4	5	6	....	....	....	....
2010-11	Chicoutimi	QMJHL	35	9	15	24	41	....	....	....	....	....	....	....	....	....	....	....	....	....	....	....	....	....	....
	Saint John	QMJHL	27	3	17	20	26	....	....	....	....	....	....	....	....	....	19	5	8	13	25	....	....	....	....
2011-12	Albany Devils	AHL	75	16	21	37	55	....	....	....	....	....	....	....	....	....	....	....	....	....	....	....	....	....	....
2012-13	Albany Devils	AHL	57	6	16	22	46	....	....	....	....	....	....	....	....	....	....	....	....	....	....	....	....	....	....
	New Jersey	**NHL**	**1**	**0**	**0**	**0**	**0**	**0**	**0**	**0**	**1**	**0.0**	**–1**	**0**	**0.0**	**15:59**	....	....	....	....	....	....	....	....	....
	NHL Totals		**1**	**0**	**0**	**0**	**0**	**0**	**0**	**0**	**1**	**0.0**		**0**	**0.0**	**15:59**	....	....	....	....	....	....	....	....	....

GENOWAY, Chay

(GEHN-oh-way, CHAY) **WSH**

Defense. Shoots left. 5'9", 177 lbs. Born, Swan River, Man., December 20, 1986.

2005-06	Vernon Vipers	BCHL	56	17	32	49	71	....	....	....	....	....	....	....	....	....	10	0	8	8	9	....	....	....	....
2006-07	North Dakota	WCHA	43	5	14	19	42	....	....	....	....	....	....	....	....	....	....	....	....	....	....	....	....	....	....
2007-08	North Dakota	WCHA	38	8	21	29	46	....	....	....	....	....	....	....	....	....	....	....	....	....	....	....	....	....	....
2008-09	North Dakota	WCHA	42	3	29	32	46	....	....	....	....	....	....	....	....	....	....	....	....	....	....	....	....	....	....
2009-10	North Dakota	WCHA	9	4	6	10	6	....	....	....	....	....	....	....	....	....	....	....	....	....	....	....	....	....	....
2010-11	North Dakota	WCHA	36	6	31	37	26	....	....	....	....	....	....	....	....	....	....	....	....	....	....	....	....	....	....
2011-12	**Minnesota**	**NHL**	**1**	**0**	**1**	**1**	**0**	**0**	**0**	**0**	**1**	**0.0**	**0**	**0**	**0.0**	**18:16**	....	....	....	....	....	....	....	....	....
	Houston Aeros	AHL	72	7	29	36	29	....	....	....	....	....	....	....	....	....	4	0	0	0	4	....	....	....	....
2012-13	Houston Aeros	AHL	53	4	15	19	41	....	....	....	....	....	....	....	....	....	....	....	....	....	....	....	....	....	....
	Hershey Bears	AHL	12	1	5	6	8	....	....	....	....	....	....	....	....	....	1	0	0	0	4	....	....	....	....
	NHL Totals		**1**	**0**	**1**	**1**	**0**	**0**	**0**	**0**	**1**	**0.0**		**0**	**0.0**	**18:16**	....	....	....	....	....	....	....	....	....

WCHA First All-Star Team (2009, 2011) • NCAA West Second All-American Team (2009) • NCAA West First All-American Team (2011)

• Missed majority of 2009-10 due to head injury vs. St. Cloud State (WCHA), November 13, 2009. Signed as a free agent by **Minnesota**, April 12, 2011. Traded to **Washington** by **Minnesota** for future considerations, March 14, 2013.

GERBE, Nathan (GUHR-bee, NAY-thuhn) CAR

Center. Shoots left. 5'5", 178 lbs. Born, Oxford, MI, July 24, 1987. Buffalo's 5th choice, 142nd overall, in 2005 Entry Draft.

			Regular Season														Playoffs								
Season	Club	League	GP	G	A	Pts	PIM	PP	SH	GW	S	%	+/-	TF	F%	Min	GP	G	A	Pts	PIM	PP	SH	GW	Min
2002-03	River City Lancers	USHL	25	3	3	6	49	....	....	....	....	....	....	....	....	....	7	1	1	2	2	....	....	....	....
2003-04	USNTDP	U-17	32	14	12	26	66	....	....	....	....	....	....	....	....	....	....	....	....	....	....	....	....	....	....
	USNTDP	NAHL	26	11	7	18	87	....	....	....	....	....	....	....	....	....	....	....	....	....	....	....	....	....	....
2004-05	USNTDP	U-18	26	6	11	17	48	....	....	....	....	....	....	....	....	....	....	....	....	....	....	....	....	....	....
	USNTDP	NAHL	12	7	5	12	25	....	....	....	....	....	....	....	....	....	....	....	....	....	....	....	....	....	....
2005-06	Boston College	H-East	39	11	7	18	75	....	....	....	....	....	....	....	....	....	....	....	....	....	....	....	....	....	....
2006-07	Boston College	H-East	41	*25	22	47	76	....	....	....	....	....	....	....	....	....	....	....	....	....	....	....	....	....	....
2007-08	Boston College	H-East	43	*35	33	*68	65	....	....	....	....	....	....	....	....	....	....	....	....	....	....	....	....	....	....
2008-09	**Buffalo**	**NHL**	**10**	**0**	**1**	**1**	**4**	**0**	**0**	**0**	**24**	**0.0**	**3**	**1**	**100.0**	**13:37**	....	....	....	....	....	....	....	....	....
	Portland Pirates	AHL	57	30	26	56	63	....	....	....	....	....	....	....	....	....	5	0	0	0	4	....	....	....	....
2009-10	**Buffalo**	**NHL**	**10**	**2**	**3**	**5**	**4**	**2**	**0**	**1**	**29**	**6.9**	**1**	**3**	**33.3**	**14:39**	**2**	**1**	**1**	**2**	**0**	**0**	**0**	**0**	**14:38**
	Portland Pirates	AHL	44	11	27	38	46	....	....	....	....	....	....	....	....	....	4	1	1	2	4	....	....	....	....
2010-11	**Buffalo**	**NHL**	**64**	**16**	**15**	**31**	**34**	**2**	**0**	**3**	**171**	**9.4**	**11**	**17**	**23.5**	**13:20**	**7**	**2**	**0**	**2**	**18**	**0**	**0**	**0**	**13:20**
2011-12	**Buffalo**	**NHL**	**62**	**6**	**19**	**25**	**32**	**0**	**0**	**2**	**137**	**4.4**	**2**	**19**	**36.8**	**14:12**	....	....	....	....	....	....	....	....	....
2012-13	**Buffalo**	**NHL**	**42**	**5**	**5**	**10**	**14**	**0**	**1**	**0**	**64**	**7.8**	**-3**	**1**	**0.0**	**12:30**	....	....	....	....	....	....	....	....	....
	NHL Totals		**188**	**29**	**43**	**72**	**88**	**4**	**1**	**6**	**425**	**6.8**		**41**	**31.7**	**13:31**	**9**	**3**	**1**	**4**	**18**	**0**	**0**	**0**	**13:38**

Hockey East Second Alll-Star Team (2007) • NCAA Championship All-Tournament Team (2007, 2008) • Hockey East First All-Star Team (2008) • NCAA East First All-American Team (2008) • NCAA Championship Tournament MVP (2008) • AHL All-Rookie Team (2009) • Dudley "Red" Garrett Memorial Award (AHL – Rookie of the Year) (2009)

Signed as a free agent by **Carolina**, July 26, 2013.

GERVAIS, Bruno (ZHUR-vay, BROO-noh) PHI

Defense. Shoots right. 6'1", 200 lbs. Born, Longueuil, Que., October 3, 1984. NY Islanders' 6th choice, 182nd overall, in 2003 Entry Draft.

			Regular Season														Playoffs								
Season	Club	League	GP	G	A	Pts	PIM	PP	SH	GW	S	%	+/-	TF	F%	Min	GP	G	A	Pts	PIM	PP	SH	GW	Min
99-2000	Antoine-Girouard	QAAA	6	0	0	0	0	....	....	....	....	....	....	....	....	....	4	0	0	0	0	....	....	....	....
2000-01	Antoine-Girouard	QAAA	40	8	27	35	46	....	....	....	....	....	....	....	....	....	7	4	2	6	8	....	....	....	....
2001-02	Acadie-Bathurst	QMJHL	65	4	12	16	42	....	....	....	....	....	....	....	....	....	16	3	2	5	8	....	....	....	....
2002-03	Acadie-Bathurst	QMJHL	72	22	28	50	73	....	....	....	....	....	....	....	....	....	11	3	5	8	14	....	....	....	....
2003-04	Acadie-Bathurst	QMJHL	23	4	6	10	28	....	....	....	....	....	....	....	....	....	....	....	....	....	....	....	....	....	....
2004-05	Bridgeport	AHL	76	8	22	30	58	....	....	....	....	....	....	....	....	....	....	....	....	....	....	....	....	....	....
2005-06	**NY Islanders**	**NHL**	**27**	**3**	**4**	**7**	**8**	**1**	**0**	**0**	**21**	**14.3**	**-1**	**0**	**0.0**	**16:47**	....	....	....	....	....	....	....	....	....
	Bridgeport	AHL	55	16	25	41	70	....	....	....	....	....	....	....	....	....	7	1	2	3	0	....	....	....	....
2006-07	**NY Islanders**	**NHL**	**51**	**0**	**6**	**6**	**28**	**0**	**0**	**0**	**47**	**0.0**	**-10**	**0**	**0.0**	**15:23**	**5**	**1**	**1**	**2**	**2**	**0**	**0**	**0**	**15:36**
	Bridgeport	AHL	3	0	0	0	6	....	....	....	....	....	....	....	....	....	....	....	....	....	....	....	....	....	....
2007-08	**NY Islanders**	**NHL**	**60**	**0**	**13**	**13**	**34**	**0**	**0**	**0**	**59**	**0.0**	**-5**	**0**	**0.0**	**20:00**	....	....	....	....	....	....	....	....	....
2008-09	**NY Islanders**	**NHL**	**69**	**3**	**16**	**19**	**33**	**0**	**0**	**1**	**82**	**3.7**	**-15**	**1**	**0.0**	**21:36**	....	....	....	....	....	....	....	....	....
2009-10	**NY Islanders**	**NHL**	**71**	**3**	**14**	**17**	**31**	**1**	**0**	**1**	**83**	**3.6**	**-15**	**0**	**0.0**	**20:01**	....	....	....	....	....	....	....	....	....
2010-11	**NY Islanders**	**NHL**	**53**	**0**	**6**	**6**	**30**	**0**	**0**	**0**	**43**	**0.0**	**-14**	**0**	**0.0**	**15:41**	....	....	....	....	....	....	....	....	....
2011-12	**Tampa Bay**	**NHL**	**50**	**6**	**7**	**13**	**8**	**1**	**0**	**0**	**57**	**10.5**	**-4**	**0**	**0.0**	**14:16**	....	....	....	....	....	....	....	....	....
2012-13	Heilbronn	German-2	9	0	3	3	18	....	....	....	....	....	....	....	....	....	....	....	....	....	....	....	....	....	....
	Philadelphia	**NHL**	**37**	**1**	**5**	**6**	**10**	**0**	**0**	**0**	**49**	**2.0**	**-17**	**0**	**0.0**	**17:08**	....	....	....	....	....	....	....	....	....
	NHL Totals		**418**	**16**	**71**	**87**	**182**	**3**	**0**	**2**	**441**	**3.6**		**1**	**0.0**	**18:00**	**5**	**1**	**1**	**2**	**2**	**0**	**0**	**0**	**15:36**

QMJHL Second All-Star Team (2003)

• Missed majority of 2003-04 due to knee injury in Team Canada Jr. training camp, December 12, 2003. Traded to **Tampa Bay** by **NY Islanders** for future considerations, June 25, 2011. Signed as a free agent by **Philadelphia**, July 5, 2012. Signed as a free agent by **Heilbronn** (German-2), November 14, 2012.

GETZLAF, Ryan (GEHTZ-laf, RIGH-uhn) ANA

Center. Shoots right. 6'4", 221 lbs. Born, Regina, Sask., May 10, 1985. Anaheim's 1st choice, 19th overall, in 2003 Entry Draft.

			Regular Season														Playoffs								
Season	Club	League	GP	G	A	Pts	PIM	PP	SH	GW	S	%	+/-	TF	F%	Min	GP	G	A	Pts	PIM	PP	SH	GW	Min
2000-01	Regina Rangers	SBHL	41	33	41	74	189	....	....	....	....	....	....	....	....	....	....	....	....	....	....	....	....	....	....
	Reg. Pat Cdns.	SMHL	8	4	3	7	8	....	....	....	....	....	....	....	....	....	....	....	....	....	....	....	....	....	....
2001-02	Calgary Hitmen	WHL	63	9	9	18	34	....	....	....	....	....	....	....	....	....	7	2	1	3	4	....	....	....	....
2002-03	Calgary Hitmen	WHL	70	29	39	68	121	....	....	....	....	....	....	....	....	....	5	1	1	2	6	....	....	....	....
2003-04	Calgary Hitmen	WHL	49	28	47	75	97	....	....	....	....	....	....	....	....	....	7	5	1	6	12	....	....	....	....
2004-05	Calgary Hitmen	WHL	51	29	25	54	102	....	....	....	....	....	....	....	....	....	12	4	13	17	18	....	....	....	....
	Cincinnati	AHL	....	....	....	....	....	....	....	....	....	....	....	....	....	....	10	1	4	5	4	....	....	....	....
2005-06	**Anaheim**	**NHL**	**57**	**14**	**25**	**39**	**22**	**10**	**0**	**1**	**116**	**12.1**	**6**	**534**	**44.0**	**12:35**	**16**	**3**	**4**	**7**	**13**	**2**	**0**	**1**	**15:49**
	Portland Pirates	AHL	17	8	25	33	36	....	....	....	....	....	....	....	....	....	1	0	0	0	4	....	....	....	....
2006-07♦	**Anaheim**	**NHL**	**82**	**25**	**33**	**58**	**66**	**11**	**1**	**6**	**203**	**12.3**	**17**	**888**	**49.4**	**15:04**	**21**	**7**	**10**	**17**	**32**	**3**	**1**	**3**	**21:43**
2007-08	**Anaheim**	**NHL**	**77**	**24**	**58**	**82**	**94**	**4**	**1**	**2**	**185**	**13.0**	**32**	**1152**	**47.3**	**19:39**	**6**	**2**	**3**	**5**	**6**	**1**	**0**	**0**	**20:29**
2008-09	**Anaheim**	**NHL**	**81**	**25**	**66**	**91**	**121**	**9**	**0**	**2**	**227**	**11.0**	**5**	**1128**	**50.2**	**20:08**	**13**	**4**	**14**	**18**	**25**	**1**	**0**	**0**	**24:08**
2009-10	**Anaheim**	**NHL**	**66**	**19**	**50**	**69**	**79**	**8**	**0**	**5**	**149**	**12.8**	**4**	**1124**	**47.4**	**21:40**	....	....	....	....	....	....	....	....	....
	Canada	Olympics	7	3	4	7	2	....	....	....	....	....	....	....	....	....	....	....	....	....	....	....	....	....	....
2010-11	**Anaheim**	**NHL**	**67**	**19**	**57**	**76**	**35**	**7**	**0**	**4**	**117**	**16.2**	**14**	**1183**	**45.8**	**21:51**	**6**	**2**	**4**	**6**	**9**	**0**	**0**	**1**	**24:01**
2011-12	**Anaheim**	**NHL**	**82**	**11**	**46**	**57**	**75**	**4**	**0**	**4**	**185**	**5.9**	**-11**	**1354**	**47.2**	**21:36**	....	....	....	....	....	....	....	....	....
2012-13	**Anaheim**	**NHL**	**44**	**15**	**34**	**49**	**41**	**4**	**3**	**3**	**99**	**15.2**	**14**	**739**	**48.0**	**20:12**	**7**	**3**	**3**	**6**	**6**	**1**	**1**	**0**	**21:28**
	NHL Totals		**556**	**152**	**369**	**521**	**533**	**57**	**5**	**27**	**1281**	**11.9**		**8102**	**47.6**	**19:09**	**69**	**21**	**38**	**59**	**91**	**8**	**2**	**5**	**20:53**

WHL East First All-Star Team (2004) • WHL East Second All-Star Team (2005)

Played in NHL All-Star Game (2008, 2009)

GILBERT, Tom (GIHL-buhrt, TAWM)

Defense. Shoots right. 6'2", 206 lbs. Born, Bloomington, MN, January 10, 1983. Colorado's 5th choice, 129th overall, in 2002 Entry Draft.

			Regular Season														Playoffs								
Season	Club	League	GP	G	A	Pts	PIM	PP	SH	GW	S	%	+/-	TF	F%	Min	GP	G	A	Pts	PIM	PP	SH	GW	Min
99-2000	Bloomington-Jeff.	High-MN	18	7	18	25	....	....	....	....	....	....	....	....	....	....	....	....	....	....	....	....	....	....	....
2000-01	Bloomington-Jeff.	High-MN	23	20	18	38	....	....	....	....	....	....	....	....	....	....	....	....	....	....	....	....	....	....	....
	Chicago Steel	USHL	1	0	0	0	0	....	....	....	....	....	....	....	....	....	....	....	....	....	....	....	....	....	....
2001-02	Chicago Steel	USHL	57	13	15	28	62	....	....	....	....	....	....	....	....	....	4	0	0	0	4	....	....	....	....
2002-03	U. of Wisconsin	WCHA	39	7	13	20	36	....	....	....	....	....	....	....	....	....	....	....	....	....	....	....	....	....	....
2003-04	U. of Wisconsin	WCHA	39	6	15	21	36	....	....	....	....	....	....	....	....	....	....	....	....	....	....	....	....	....	....
2004-05	U. of Wisconsin	WCHA	41	8	9	17	48	....	....	....	....	....	....	....	....	....	....	....	....	....	....	....	....	....	....
2005-06	U. of Wisconsin	WCHA	43	12	19	31	32	....	....	....	....	....	....	....	....	....	....	....	....	....	....	....	....	....	....
2006-07	**Edmonton**	**NHL**	**12**	**1**	**5**	**6**	**0**	**0**	**0**	**0**	**13**	**7.7**	**-1**	**0**	**0.0**	**20:05**	....	....	....	....	....	....	....	....	....
	Wilkes-Barre	AHL	48	4	26	30	32	....	....	....	....	....	....	....	....	....	10	1	7	8	10	....	....	....	....
2007-08	**Edmonton**	**NHL**	**82**	**13**	**20**	**33**	**20**	**3**	**0**	**1**	**98**	**13.3**	**-6**	**0**	**0.0**	**22:12**	....	....	....	....	....	....	....	....	....
2008-09	**Edmonton**	**NHL**	**82**	**5**	**40**	**45**	**26**	**2**	**0**	**1**	**107**	**4.7**	**6**	**0**	**0.0**	**21:58**	....	....	....	....	....	....	....	....	....
2009-10	**Edmonton**	**NHL**	**82**	**5**	**26**	**31**	**16**	**1**	**1**	**0**	**98**	**5.1**	**-10**	**0**	**0.0**	**22:25**	....	....	....	....	....	....	....	....	....
2010-11	**Edmonton**	**NHL**	**79**	**6**	**20**	**26**	**32**	**3**	**0**	**0**	**106**	**5.7**	**-14**	**0**	**0.0**	**24:30**	....	....	....	....	....	....	....	....	....
2011-12	**Edmonton**	**NHL**	**47**	**3**	**14**	**17**	**12**	**2**	**0**	**1**	**50**	**6.0**	**-3**	**0**	**0.0**	**22:49**	....	....	....	....	....	....	....	....	....
	Minnesota	**NHL**	**20**	**0**	**5**	**5**	**8**	**0**	**0**	**0**	**22**	**0.0**	**-5**	**0**	**0.0**	**27:01**	....	....	....	....	....	....	....	....	....
2012-13	**Minnesota**	**NHL**	**43**	**3**	**10**	**13**	**18**	**1**	**0**	**0**	**36**	**8.3**	**-11**	**0**	**0.0**	**19:19**	**5**	**0**	**0**	**0**	**2**	**0**	**0**	**0**	**16:16**
	NHL Totals		**447**	**36**	**140**	**176**	**132**	**12**	**1**	**3**	**530**	**6.8**		**0**	**0.0**	**22:33**	**5**	**0**	**0**	**0**	**2**	**0**	**0**	**0**	**16:16**

WCHA First All-Star Team (2006) • NCAA West Second All-American Team (2006) • NCAA Championship All-Tournament Team (2006) • NHL All-Rookie Team (2008)

Traded to **Edmonton** by **Colorado** for Tommy Salo and Edmonton's 6th round choice (Justin Mercier) in 2005 Entry Draft, March 8, 2004. Traded to **Minnesota** by **Edmonton** for Nick Schultz, February 27, 2012.

GILL, Hal (GIHL, HAL)

Defense. Shoots left. 6'7", 243 lbs. Born, Concord, MA, April 6, 1975. Boston's 8th choice, 207th overall, in 1993 Entry Draft.

			Regular Season														Playoffs								
Season	Club	League	GP	G	A	Pts	PIM	PP	SH	GW	S	%	+/-	TF	F%	Min	GP	G	A	Pts	PIM	PP	SH	GW	Min
1992-93	Nashoba	High-MA	20	25	25	50	....	....	....	....	....	....	....	....	....	....	....	....	....	....	....	....	....	....	....
1993-94	Providence	H-East	31	1	2	3	26	....	....	....	....	....	....	....	....	....	....	....	....	....	....	....	....	....	....
1994-95	Providence	H-East	26	1	3	4	22	....	....	....	....	....	....	....	....	....	....	....	....	....	....	....	....	....	....
1995-96	Providence	H-East	39	5	12	17	54	....	....	....	....	....	....	....	....	....	....	....	....	....	....	....	....	....	....
1996-97	Providence	H-East	35	5	16	21	52	....	....	....	....	....	....	....	....	....	....	....	....	....	....	....	....	....	....
1997-98	**Boston**	**NHL**	**68**	**2**	**4**	**6**	**47**	**0**	**0**	**0**	**56**	**3.6**	**4**	....	....	....	**6**	**0**	**0**	**0**	**4**	**0**	**0**	**0**	....
	Providence Bruins	AHL	4	1	0	1	23	....	....	....	....	....	....	....	....	....	....	....	....	....	....	....	....	....	....
1998-99	**Boston**	**NHL**	**80**	**3**	**7**	**10**	**63**	**0**	**0**	**2**	**102**	**2.9**	**-10**	**1**	**100.0**	**20:54**	**12**	**0**	**0**	**0**	**14**	**0**	**0**	**0**	**20:41**
99-2000	**Boston**	**NHL**	**81**	**3**	**9**	**12**	**51**	**0**	**0**	**0**	**120**	**2.5**	**0**	**0**	**0.0**	**17:15**	....	....	....	....	....	....	....	....	....
2000-01	**Boston**	**NHL**	**80**	**1**	**10**	**11**	**71**	**0**	**0**	**0**	**79**	**1.3**	**-2**	**0**	**0.0**	**18:21**	....	....	....	....	....	....	....	....	....

			Regular Season														Playoffs								
Season	Club	League	GP	G	A	Pts	PIM	PP	SH	GW	S	%	+/-	TF	F%	Min	GP	G	A	Pts	PIM	PP	SH	GW	Min
2001-02	Boston	NHL	79	4	18	22	77	0	0	0	137	2.9	16	0	0.0	24:13	6	0	1	1	2	0	0	0	23:04
2002-03	Boston	NHL	76	4	13	17	56	0	0	0	114	3.5	21	0	0.0	20:42	5	0	0	0	4	0	0	0	20:19
2003-04	Boston	NHL	82	2	7	9	99	0	0	0	104	1.9	16	0	0.0	18:24	7	0	1	1	4	0	0	0	19:03
2004-05	Lukko Rauma	Finland	31	2	8	10	110	....	....	....	....	....	....	....	....	....	8	0	0	0	*57	....	....	....	....
2005-06	Boston	NHL	80	1	9	10	124	0	0	0	68	1.5	–4	0	0.0	18:37	....	....	....	....	....	....	....	....	....
2006-07	Toronto	NHL	82	6	14	20	91	0	0	1	79	7.6	11	1	0.0	18:53	....	....	....	....	....	....	....	....	....
2007-08	Toronto	NHL	63	2	18	20	52	0	0	0	69	2.9	0	0	0.0	20:42	....	....	....	....	....	....	....	....	....
	Pittsburgh	NHL	18	1	3	4	16	0	0	0	17	5.9	6	0	0.0	17:31	20	0	1	1	12	0	0	0	19:17
2008-09♦	Pittsburgh	NHL	62	2	8	10	53	0	0	0	40	5.0	11	0	0.0	17:54	24	0	2	2	6	0	0	0	19:26
2009-10	Montreal	NHL	68	2	9	11	68	0	0	0	41	4.9	–10	1	0.0	18:21	18	0	1	1	20	0	0	0	19:54
2010-11	Montreal	NHL	75	2	7	9	43	0	0	1	62	3.2	–9	0	0.0	19:49	7	0	0	0	2	0	0	0	23:21
2011-12	Montreal	NHL	53	1	7	8	29	0	0	0	33	3.0	–7	0	0.0	16:44	....	....	....	....	....	....	....	....	....
	Nashville	NHL	23	0	5	5	8	0	0	0	16	0.0	4	0	0.0	18:03	5	0	0	0	0	0	0	0	15:07
2012-13	Nashville	NHL	32	0	0	0	12	0	0	0	8	0.0	–3	0	0.0	13:23	....	....	....	....	....	....	....	....	....
	NHL Totals		1102	36	148	184	960	0	0	4	1145	3.1		3	33.3	19:07	110	0	6	6	68	0	0	0	19:55

Signed as a free agent by **Rauma** (Finland), November 25, 2004. Signed as a free agent by **Toronto**, July 1, 2006. Traded to **Pittsburgh** by **Toronto** for Pittsburgh's 2nd round choice (Jimmy Hayes) in 2008 Entry Draft and Pittsburgh's 5th round choice (later traded to NY Rangers, later traded back to Pittsburgh – Pittsburgh selected Andy Bathgate) in 2009 Entry Draft, February 26, 2008. Signed as a free agent by **Montreal**, July 1, 2009. Traded to **Nashville** by **Montreal** with Montreal's 5th round choice (later traded back to Montreal, later traded to Los Angeles – Los Angeles selected Patrik Bartosak) in 2013 Entry Draft for Blake Geoffrion, Robert Slaney and Nashville's 2nd round choice (Dalton Thrower) in 2012 Entry Draft, February 17, 2012.

GILLIES, Colton

(GIHL-eez, KOHL-tuhn)

Left wing. Shoots left. 6'4", 208 lbs. Born, White Rock, B.C., February 12, 1989. Minnesota's 1st choice, 16th overall, in 2007 Entry Draft.

Season	Club	League	GP	G	A	Pts	PIM	PP	SH	GW	S	%	+/-	TF	F%	Min	GP	G	A	Pts	PIM	PP	SH	GW	Min
2004-05	North Delta Flyers	PIJHL	44	9	17	26	....	....	....	....	....	....	....	....	....	....	6	2	1	3	....	....	....	....	....
	Surrey Eagles	BCHL	3	1	0	1	0	....	....	....	....	....	....	....	....	....	....	....	....	....	....	....	....	....	....
	Saskatoon Blades	WHL	9	1	1	2	8	....	....	....	....	....	....	....	....	....	2	0	0	0	0	....	....	....	....
2005-06	Saskatoon Blades	WHL	63	6	6	12	57	....	....	....	....	....	....	....	....	....	8	0	0	0	4	....	....	....	....
2006-07	Saskatoon Blades	WHL	65	13	17	30	148	....	....	....	....	....	....	....	....	....	....	....	....	....	....	....	....	....	....
2007-08	Saskatoon Blades	WHL	58	24	23	47	97	....	....	....	....	....	....	....	....	....	....	....	....	....	....	....	....	....	....
	Houston Aeros	AHL	11	1	7	8	4	....	....	....	....	....	....	....	....	....	5	0	0	0	2	....	....	....	....
2008-09	Minnesota	NHL	45	2	5	7	18	0	0	1	22	9.1	–2	2	50.0	8:14	....	....	....	....	....	....	....	....	....
2009-10	Houston Aeros	AHL	72	7	13	20	73	....	....	....	....	....	....	....	....	....	....	....	....	....	....	....	....	....	....
2010-11	Minnesota	NHL	7	1	0	1	2	0	0	0	3	33.3	–2	2	50.0	10:22	....	....	....	....	....	....	....	....	....
	Houston Aeros	AHL	64	11	15	26	82	....	....	....	....	....	....	....	....	....	24	7	5	12	32	....	....	....	....
2011-12	Minnesota	NHL	37	0	2	2	10	0	0	0	24	0.0	–5	4	75.0	9:10	....	....	....	....	....	....	....	....	....
	Columbus	NHL	38	2	4	6	25	0	0	0	24	8.3	–4	13	30.8	10:59	....	....	....	....	....	....	....	....	....
2012-13	Columbus	NHL	27	1	1	2	17	0	0	0	17	5.9	1	2	0.0	8:18	....	....	....	....	....	....	....	....	....
	NHL Totals		154	6	12	18	72	0	0	1	90	6.7		23	39.1	9:15	....	....	....	....	....	....	....	....	....

Claimed on waivers by **Columbus** from **Minnesota**, January 14, 2012.

GILLIES, Trevor

(GIHL-eez, TREH-vuhr)

Left wing. Shoots left. 6'3", 227 lbs. Born, Cambridge, Ont., January 30, 1979.

Season	Club	League	GP	G	A	Pts	PIM	PP	SH	GW	S	%	+/-	TF	F%	Min	GP	G	A	Pts	PIM	PP	SH	GW	Min
1996-97	North Bay	OHL	26	0	3	3	72	....	....	....	....	....	....	....	....	....	....	....	....	....	....	....	....	....	....
1997-98	North Bay	OHL	2	0	0	0	4	....	....	....	....	....	....	....	....	....	....	....	....	....	....	....	....	....	....
	Sarnia Sting	OHL	17	0	1	1	33	....	....	....	....	....	....	....	....	....	....	....	....	....	....	....	....	....	....
	Oshawa Generals	OHL	45	1	2	3	184	....	....	....	....	....	....	....	....	....	7	0	1	1	12	....	....	....	....
1998-99	Oshawa Generals	OHL	66	6	9	15	270	....	....	....	....	....	....	....	....	....	11	0	2	2	28	....	....	....	....
99-2000	Lowell	AHL	8	0	0	0	38	....	....	....	....	....	....	....	....	....	....	....	....	....	....	....	....	....	....
	Mississippi	ECHL	53	0	6	6	202	....	....	....	....	....	....	....	....	....	....	....	....	....	....	....	....	....	....
2000-01	Greensboro	ECHL	63	1	6	7	303	....	....	....	....	....	....	....	....	....	....	....	....	....	....	....	....	....	....
	Worcester IceCats	AHL	....	....	....	....	....	....	....	....	....	....	....	....	....	....	6	0	0	0	24	....	....	....	....
2001-02	Providence Bruins	AHL	5	0	0	0	21	....	....	....	....	....	....	....	....	....	....	....	....	....	....	....	....	....	....
	Augusta Lynx	ECHL	46	0	1	1	*269	....	....	....	....	....	....	....	....	....	....	....	....	....	....	....	....	....	....
	Richmond	ECHL	18	0	1	1	*51	....	....	....	....	....	....	....	....	....	....	....	....	....	....	....	....	....	....
2002-03	Lowell	AHL	25	0	1	1	132	....	....	....	....	....	....	....	....	....	....	....	....	....	....	....	....	....	....
	Richmond	ECHL	6	0	0	0	20	....	....	....	....	....	....	....	....	....	....	....	....	....	....	....	....	....	....
	Peoria Rivermen	ECHL	24	0	1	1	180	....	....	....	....	....	....	....	....	....	....	....	....	....	....	....	....	....	....
2003-04	Springfield	AHL	61	2	1	3	277	....	....	....	....	....	....	....	....	....	....	....	....	....	....	....	....	....	....
2004-05	Hartford	AHL	49	0	2	2	277	....	....	....	....	....	....	....	....	....	....	....	....	....	....	....	....	....	....
2005-06	Anaheim	NHL	1	0	0	0	21	0	0	0	1	0.0	0	0	0.0	2:40	....	....	....	....	....	....	....	....	....
	Portland Pirates	AHL	50	2	3	5	169	....	....	....	....	....	....	....	....	....	4	0	0	0	0	....	....	....	....
2006-07	Portland Pirates	AHL	51	1	6	7	151	....	....	....	....	....	....	....	....	....	....	....	....	....	....	....	....	....	....
	Augusta Lynx	ECHL	7	0	2	2	23	....	....	....	....	....	....	....	....	....	....	....	....	....	....	....	....	....	....
2007-08	Albany River Rats	AHL	51	1	1	2	112	....	....	....	....	....	....	....	....	....	7	0	0	0	19	....	....	....	....
2008-09	Albany River Rats	AHL	30	0	0	0	125	....	....	....	....	....	....	....	....	....	....	....	....	....	....	....	....	....	....
2009-10	Bridgeport	AHL	24	1	0	1	169	....	....	....	....	....	....	....	....	....	....	....	....	....	....	....	....	....	....
	NY Islanders	NHL	14	0	1	1	75	0	0	0	6	0.0	–2	0	0.0	3:49	....	....	....	....	....	....	....	....	....
2010-11	NY Islanders	NHL	39	2	0	2	165	0	0	0	9	22.2	–3	1	0.0	3:04	....	....	....	....	....	....	....	....	....
2011-12	NY Islanders	NHL	3	0	0	0	0	0	0	0	1	0.0	–1	0	0.0	2:52	....	....	....	....	....	....	....	....	....
	Bridgeport	AHL	26	1	0	1	65	....	....	....	....	....	....	....	....	....	....	....	....	....	....	....	....	....	....
2012-13	Vityaz Chekhov	KHL	24	0	0	0	95	....	....	....	....	....	....	....	....	....	2	0	0	0	0	....	....	....	....
	NHL Totals		57	2	1	3	261	0	0	0	17	11.8		1	0.0	3:14	....	....	....	....	....	....	....	....	....

Signed as a free agent by **NY Rangers**, July 20, 2004. Traded to **Anaheim** by **NY Rangers** with NY Rangers' 4th round choice (later traded back to NY Rangers, later traded to Washington - Washington selected Brett Bruneteau) in 2007 Entry Draft for Steve Rucchin, August 23, 2005. Signed as a free agent by **Carolina**, July 2, 2007. • Missed majority of 2008-09 due to injury at Wilkes-Barre (AHL), December 20, 2008. Signed as a free agent by **Bridgeport** (AHL), October 2, 2009. Signed as a free agent by **NY Islanders**, January 29, 2010. • Suspended nine games by NHL for deliberate attempt to injure Eric Tangradi in game vs, Pittsburgh, February 11, 2011 and suspended an additional ten games for deliberate attempt to injure Cal Clutterbuck in game vs. Minnesota, March 2, 2011. • Missed majority of 2010-11 as a healthy reserve. • Missed majority of 2011-12 due to recurring groin injury and as a healthy reserve. Signed as a free agent by **Chekhov** (KHL), June 19, 2012.

GILROY, Matt

(GIHL-roy, MAT) **FLA**

Defense. Shoots right. 6'1", 199 lbs. Born, North Bellmore, NY, July 30, 1984.

Season	Club	League	GP	G	A	Pts	PIM	PP	SH	GW	S	%	+/-	TF	F%	Min	GP	G	A	Pts	PIM	PP	SH	GW	Min
2000-01	St. Mary's Gaels	High-NY	STATISTICS NOT AVAILABLE																						
2001-02	St. Mary's Gaels	High-NY	STATISTICS NOT AVAILABLE																						
2002-03	St. Mary's Gaels	High-NY	STATISTICS NOT AVAILABLE																						
2003-04	NY Apple Core	EJHL	STATISTICS NOT AVAILABLE																						
2004-05	Walpole Stars	EJHL	55	24	29	53	20	....	....	....	....	....	....	....	....	....	....	....	....	....	....	....	....	....	....
2005-06	Boston University	H-East	36	2	6	8	10	....	....	....	....	....	....	....	....	....	....	....	....	....	....	....	....	....	....
2006-07	Boston University	H-East	39	9	17	26	14	....	....	....	....	....	....	....	....	....	....	....	....	....	....	....	....	....	....
2007-08	Boston University	H-East	40	6	15	21	12	....	....	....	....	....	....	....	....	....	....	....	....	....	....	....	....	....	....
2008-09	Boston University	H-East	45	8	29	37	12	....	....	....	....	....	....	....	....	....	....	....	....	....	....	....	....	....	....
2009-10	NY Rangers	NHL	69	4	11	15	23	0	0	1	82	4.9	0	1	100.0	16:19	....	....	....	....	....	....	....	....	....
	Hartford	AHL	5	0	4	4	4	....	....	....	....	....	....	....	....	....	....	....	....	....	....	....	....	....	....
2010-11	NY Rangers	NHL	58	3	8	11	14	0	0	1	75	4.0	5	0	0.0	14:11	5	1	0	1	2	0	0	0	15:40
2011-12	Tampa Bay	NHL	53	2	15	17	16	0	0	0	60	3.3	2	0	0.0	17:36	....	....	....	....	....	....	....	....	....
	Ottawa	NHL	14	1	2	3	2	0	0	0	20	5.0	0	0	0.0	17:08	3	0	0	0	0	0	0	0	12:55
2012-13	Connecticut	AHL	34	6	9	15	14	....	....	....	....	....	....	....	....	....	....	....	....	....	....	....	....	....	....
	NY Rangers	NHL	15	0	0	0	6	0	0	0	14	0.0	–3	0	0.0	9:33	....	....	....	....	....	....	....	....	....
	NHL Totals		209	10	36	46	61	0	0	2	251	4.0		1	100.0	15:37	8	1	0	1	2	0	0	0	14:38

Hockey East First All-Star Team (2008, 2009) • NCAA East First All-American Team (2008, 2009) • Hobey Baker Memorial Award (Top U.S. Collegiate Player) (2009)

Signed as a free agent by **NY Rangers**, April 17, 2009. Signed as a free agent by **Tampa Bay**, July 2, 2011. Traded to **Ottawa** by **Tampa Bay** for Brian Lee, February 27, 2012. Signed as a free agent by **Connecticut** (AHL), October 7, 2012. Signed as a free agent by **Florida**, July 8, 2013.

GIONTA, Brian
(jee-OHN-tuh, BRIGH-uhn) **MTL**

Right wing. Shoots right. 5'7", 175 lbs. Born, Rochester, NY, January 18, 1979. New Jersey's 4th choice, 82nd overall, in 1998 Entry Draft.

			Regular Season														Playoffs								
Season	Club	League	GP	G	A	Pts	PIM	PP	SH	GW	S	%	+/-	TF	F%	Min	GP	G	A	Pts	PIM	PP	SH	GW	Min
1994-95	Rochester	EmJHL	28	*52	37	*89	....	....	....	....	....	....	....	....	....	....	....	....	....	....	....	....	....	....	....
1995-96	Niagara Scenic	ON-Jr.A	51	47	44	91	59	....	....	....	....	....	....	....	....	....	....	....	....	....	....	....	....	....	....
1996-97	Niagara Scenic	ON-Jr.A	50	57	70	127	101	....	....	....	....	....	....	....	....	....	6	6	11	17	21	....	....	....	....
1997-98	Boston College	H-East	40	30	32	62	44	....	....	....	....	....	....	....	....	....	....	....	....	....	....	....	....	....	....
1998-99	Boston College	H-East	39	27	33	60	46	....	....	....	....	....	....	....	....	....	....	....	....	....	....	....	....	....	....
99-2000	Boston College	H-East	42	*33	23	56	66	....	....	....	....	....	....	....	....	....	....	....	....	....	....	....	....	....	....
2000-01	Boston College	H-East	43	*33	21	*54	47	....	....	....	....	....	....	....	....	....	....	....	....	....	....	....	....	....	....
2001-02	**New Jersey**	**NHL**	**33**	**4**	**7**	**11**	**8**	**0**	**0**	**0**	**58**	**6.9**	**10**	**36**	**44.4**	**13:25**	**6**	**2**	**2**	**4**	**0**	**0**	**1**	**2**	**17:08**
	Albany River Rats	AHL	37	9	16	25	18	....	....	....	....	....	....	....	....	....	....	....	....	....	....	....	....	....	....
2002-03♦	**New Jersey**	**NHL**	**58**	**12**	**13**	**25**	**23**	**2**	**0**	**3**	**129**	**9.3**	**5**	**14**	**57.1**	**14:48**	**24**	**1**	**8**	**9**	**6**	**0**	**0**	**0**	**14:31**
2003-04	**New Jersey**	**NHL**	**75**	**21**	**8**	**29**	**36**	**0**	**0**	**8**	**174**	**12.1**	**19**	**60**	**58.3**	**14:44**	**5**	**2**	**3**	**5**	**0**	**1**	**0**	**0**	**15:41**
2004-05	Albany River Rats	AHL	15	5	7	12	10	....	....	....	....	....	....	....	....	....	....	....	....	....	....	....	....	....	....
2005-06	**New Jersey**	**NHL**	**82**	**48**	**41**	**89**	**46**	**24**	**1**	**10**	**291**	**16.5**	**18**	**73**	**38.4**	**19:49**	**9**	**3**	**4**	**7**	**2**	**1**	**1**	**2**	**20:06**
	United States	Olympics	6	4	0	4	2	....	....	....	....	....	....	....	....	....	....	....	....	....	....	....	....	....	....
2006-07	**New Jersey**	**NHL**	**62**	**25**	**20**	**45**	**36**	**11**	**0**	**4**	**194**	**12.9**	**–3**	**31**	**38.7**	**18:49**	**11**	**8**	**1**	**9**	**4**	**3**	**0**	**1**	**19:15**
2007-08	**New Jersey**	**NHL**	**82**	**22**	**31**	**53**	**46**	**8**	**1**	**4**	**257**	**8.6**	**1**	**55**	**54.6**	**18:16**	**5**	**1**	**0**	**1**	**2**	**0**	**0**	**0**	**17:52**
2008-09	**New Jersey**	**NHL**	**81**	**20**	**40**	**60**	**32**	**3**	**3**	**1**	**248**	**8.1**	**12**	**132**	**38.6**	**16:58**	**7**	**2**	**3**	**5**	**4**	**0**	**0**	**0**	**17:49**
2009-10	**Montreal**	**NHL**	**61**	**28**	**18**	**46**	**26**	**10**	**0**	**3**	**237**	**11.8**	**3**	**13**	**53.9**	**20:45**	**19**	**9**	**6**	**15**	**14**	**4**	**0**	**1**	**22:11**
2010-11	**Montreal**	**NHL**	**82**	**29**	**17**	**46**	**24**	**7**	**2**	**6**	**298**	**9.7**	**3**	**59**	**32.2**	**19:37**	**7**	**3**	**2**	**5**	**0**	**1**	**0**	**2**	**22:35**
2011-12	**Montreal**	**NHL**	**31**	**8**	**7**	**15**	**16**	**2**	**0**	**0**	**75**	**10.7**	**–7**	**33**	**42.4**	**19:26**	....	....	....	....	....	....	....	....	....
2012-13	**Montreal**	**NHL**	**48**	**14**	**12**	**26**	**8**	**5**	**0**	**3**	**112**	**12.5**	**3**	**42**	**33.3**	**18:07**	**2**	**0**	**1**	**1**	**0**	**0**	**0**	**0**	**17:10**
	NHL Totals		**695**	**231**	**214**	**445**	**301**	**72**	**7**	**42**	**2073**	**11.1**		**548**	**42.7**	**17:52**	**95**	**31**	**30**	**61**	**32**	**10**	**2**	**8**	**18:26**

Hockey East Rookie of the Year (1998) • Hockey East Second All-Star Team (1998) • NCAA East Second All-American Team (1998) • Hockey East First All-Star Team (1999, 2000, 2001) • NCAA East First All-American Team (1999, 2000, 2001) • Hockey East Player of the Year (2001)

Signed as a free agent by **Montreal**, July 1, 2009. • Missed majority of 2011-12 due to arm injury vs. St. Louis, January 10, 2012.

GIONTA, Stephen
(jee-OHN-tuh, STEE-vehn) **N.J.**

Center. Shoots right. 5'7", 185 lbs. Born, Rochester, NY, October 9, 1983.

Season	Club	League	GP	G	A	Pts	PIM	PP	SH	GW	S	%	+/-	TF	F%	Min	GP	G	A	Pts	PIM	PP	SH	GW	Min
99-2000	Rochester	NAHL	41	11	15	26	56	....	....	....	....	....	....	....	....	....	....	....	....	....	....	....	....	....	....
2000-01	USNTDP	USHL	16	1	2	3	12	....	....	....	....	....	....	....	....	....	....	....	....	....	....	....	....	....	....
	USNTDP	NAHL	1	0	0	0	0	....	....	....	....	....	....	....	....	....	....	....	....	....	....	....	....	....	....
2001-02	USNTDP	NAHL	22	2	5	7	33	....	....	....	....	....	....	....	....	....	....	....	....	....	....	....	....	....	....
2002-03	Boston College	H-East	33	5	10	15	36	....	....	....	....	....	....	....	....	....	....	....	....	....	....	....	....	....	....
2003-04	Boston College	H-East	41	9	15	24	36	....	....	....	....	....	....	....	....	....	....	....	....	....	....	....	....	....	....
2004-05	Boston College	H-East	38	8	11	19	44	....	....	....	....	....	....	....	....	....	....	....	....	....	....	....	....	....	....
2005-06	Boston College	H-East	37	11	21	32	66	....	....	....	....	....	....	....	....	....	....	....	....	....	....	....	....	....	....
	Albany River Rats	AHL	3	5	1	6	2	....	....	....	....	....	....	....	....	....	....	....	....	....	....	....	....	....	....
2006-07	Lowell Devils	AHL	67	7	8	15	15	....	....	....	....	....	....	....	....	....	....	....	....	....	....	....	....	....	....
2007-08	Lowell Devils	AHL	63	16	13	29	33	....	....	....	....	....	....	....	....	....	....	....	....	....	....	....	....	....	....
2008-09	Lowell Devils	AHL	52	2	9	11	30	....	....	....	....	....	....	....	....	....	....	....	....	....	....	....	....	....	....
2009-10	Lowell Devils	AHL	68	15	19	34	26	....	....	....	....	....	....	....	....	....	5	0	1	1	0	....	....	....	....
2010-11	**New Jersey**	**NHL**	**12**	**0**	**0**	**0**	**6**	**0**	**0**	**0**	**13**	**0.0**	**–3**	**0**	**0.0**	**9:00**	....	....	....	....	....	....	....	....	....
	Albany Devils	AHL	54	10	20	30	21	....	....	....	....	....	....	....	....	....	....	....	....	....	....	....	....	....	....
2011-12	**New Jersey**	**NHL**	**1**	**1**	**0**	**1**	**0**	**0**	**0**	**1**	**2**	**50.0**	**1**	**8**	**62.5**	**10:37**	**24**	**3**	**4**	**7**	**4**	**0**	**0**	**0**	**9:14**
	Albany Devils	AHL	56	6	10	16	40	....	....	....	....	....	....	....	....	....	....	....	....	....	....	....	....	....	....
2012-13	Albany Devils	AHL	11	2	3	5	4	....	....	....	....	....	....	....	....	....	....	....	....	....	....	....	....	....	....
	New Jersey	**NHL**	**48**	**4**	**10**	**14**	**14**	**0**	**0**	**0**	**58**	**6.9**	**2**	**390**	**35.1**	**13:02**	....	....	....	....	....	....	....	....	....
	NHL Totals		**61**	**5**	**10**	**15**	**20**	**0**	**0**	**1**	**73**	**6.8**		**398**	**35.7**	**12:12**	**24**	**3**	**4**	**7**	**4**	**0**	**0**	**0**	**9:14**

Signed to an ATO (amateur tryout) contract by **Albany** (AHL), April 12, 2006. Signed as a free agent by **New Jersey**, August 26, 2010.

GIORDANO, Mark
(jee-ohr-DAN-oh, MAHRK) **CGY**

Defense. Shoots left. 6', 200 lbs. Born, Toronto, Ont., October 3, 1983.

Season	Club	League	GP	G	A	Pts	PIM	PP	SH	GW	S	%	+/-	TF	F%	Min	GP	G	A	Pts	PIM	PP	SH	GW	Min
2002-03	Owen Sound	OHL	68	18	30	48	109	....	....	....	....	....	....	....	....	....	4	1	3	4	2	....	....	....	....
2003-04	Owen Sound	OHL	65	14	35	49	72	....	....	....	....	....	....	....	....	....	7	1	3	4	5	....	....	....	....
2004-05	Lowell	AHL	66	6	10	16	85	....	....	....	....	....	....	....	....	....	11	0	1	1	41	....	....	....	....
2005-06	**Calgary**	**NHL**	**7**	**0**	**1**	**1**	**8**	**0**	**0**	**0**	**5**	**0.0**	**2**	**0**	**0.0**	**12:05**	....	....	....	....	....	....	....	....	....
	Omaha	AHL	73	16	42	58	141	....	....	....	....	....	....	....	....	....	....	....	....	....	....	....	....	....	....
2006-07	**Calgary**	**NHL**	**48**	**7**	**8**	**15**	**36**	**3**	**0**	**2**	**49**	**14.3**	**7**	**0**	**0.0**	**13:27**	**4**	**1**	**0**	**1**	**0**	**1**	**0**	**0**	**12:16**
	Omaha	AHL	5	0	2	2	8	....	....	....	....	....	....	....	....	....	3	0	1	1	2	....	....	....	....
2007-08	Dynamo Moscow	Russia	50	4	8	12	89	....	....	....	....	....	....	....	....	....	9	1	5	6	35	....	....	....	....
2008-09	**Calgary**	**NHL**	**58**	**2**	**17**	**19**	**59**	**2**	**0**	**0**	**82**	**2.4**	**2**	**0**	**0.0**	**16:13**	....	....	....	....	....	....	....	....	....
2009-10	**Calgary**	**NHL**	**82**	**11**	**19**	**30**	**81**	**5**	**0**	**1**	**111**	**9.9**	**17**	**0**	**0.0**	**20:50**	....	....	....	....	....	....	....	....	....
2010-11	**Calgary**	**NHL**	**82**	**8**	**35**	**43**	**67**	**5**	**0**	**1**	**165**	**4.8**	**–8**	**0**	**0.0**	**23:08**	....	....	....	....	....	....	....	....	....
2011-12	**Calgary**	**NHL**	**61**	**9**	**18**	**27**	**75**	**5**	**0**	**0**	**125**	**7.2**	**0**	**0**	**0.0**	**23:01**	....	....	....	....	....	....	....	....	....
2012-13	**Calgary**	**NHL**	**47**	**4**	**11**	**15**	**40**	**1**	**1**	**1**	**58**	**6.9**	**–7**	**0**	**0.0**	**23:10**	....	....	....	....	....	....	....	....	....
	NHL Totals		**385**	**41**	**109**	**150**	**366**	**21**	**1**	**5**	**595**	**6.9**		**0**	**0.0**	**20:11**	**4**	**1**	**0**	**1**	**0**	**1**	**0**	**0**	**12:16**

Signed as a free agent by **Calgary**, July 6, 2004. Signed as a free agent by **Dynamo Moscow** (Russia) August 28, 2007. Signed as a free agent by **Calgary**, July 1, 2008.

GIRARDI, Dan
(jih-RAHR-dee, DAN) **NYR**

Defense. Shoots right. 6'1", 203 lbs. Born, Welland, Ont., April 29, 1984.

Season	Club	League	GP	G	A	Pts	PIM	PP	SH	GW	S	%	+/-	TF	F%	Min	GP	G	A	Pts	PIM	PP	SH	GW	Min
2000-01	Barrie Colts	OHL	6	0	0	0	0	....	....	....	....	....	....	....	....	....	....	....	....	....	....	....	....	....	....
2001-02	Barrie Colts	OHL	21	0	1	1	0	....	....	....	....	....	....	....	....	....	20	0	0	0	0	....	....	....	....
2002-03	Barrie Colts	OHL	31	3	13	16	24	....	....	....	....	....	....	....	....	....	....	....	....	....	....	....	....	....	....
	Guelph Storm	OHL	36	1	13	14	20	....	....	....	....	....	....	....	....	....	11	0	9	9	14	....	....	....	....
2003-04	Guelph Storm	OHL	68	8	39	47	55	....	....	....	....	....	....	....	....	....	22	2	17	19	10	....	....	....	....
2004-05	Guelph Storm	OHL	38	5	20	25	24	....	....	....	....	....	....	....	....	....	....	....	....	....	....	....	....	....	....
	London Knights	OHL	31	4	10	14	14	....	....	....	....	....	....	....	....	....	18	0	6	6	10	....	....	....	....
2005-06	Hartford	AHL	66	8	31	39	44	....	....	....	....	....	....	....	....	....	13	4	5	9	8	....	....	....	....
	Charlotte	ECHL	7	1	4	5	6	....	....	....	....	....	....	....	....	....	....	....	....	....	....	....	....	....	....
2006-07	**NY Rangers**	**NHL**	**34**	**0**	**6**	**6**	**8**	**0**	**0**	**0**	**33**	**0.0**	**7**	**0**	**0.0**	**15:50**	**10**	**0**	**0**	**0**	**4**	**0**	**0**	**0**	**19:52**
	Hartford	AHL	45	2	22	24	16	....	....	....	....	....	....	....	....	....	....	....	....	....	....	....	....	....	....
2007-08	**NY Rangers**	**NHL**	**82**	**10**	**18**	**28**	**14**	**5**	**0**	**1**	**147**	**6.8**	**0**	**1**	**0.0**	**21:12**	**10**	**0**	**3**	**3**	**6**	**0**	**0**	**0**	**20:42**
2008-09	**NY Rangers**	**NHL**	**82**	**4**	**18**	**22**	**53**	**2**	**0**	**1**	**122**	**3.3**	**–14**	**0**	**0.0**	**21:32**	**7**	**0**	**0**	**0**	**6**	**0**	**0**	**0**	**21:04**
2009-10	**NY Rangers**	**NHL**	**82**	**6**	**18**	**24**	**53**	**1**	**1**	**1**	**108**	**5.6**	**–2**	**0**	**0.0**	**21:29**	....	....	....	....	....	....	....	....	....
2010-11	**NY Rangers**	**NHL**	**80**	**4**	**27**	**31**	**37**	**2**	**0**	**1**	**110**	**3.6**	**7**	**0**	**0.0**	**24:35**	**5**	**0**	**0**	**0**	**0**	**0**	**0**	**0**	**27:01**
2011-12	**NY Rangers**	**NHL**	**82**	**5**	**24**	**29**	**20**	**1**	**0**	**2**	**122**	**4.1**	**13**	**0**	**0.0**	**26:15**	**20**	**3**	**9**	**12**	**2**	**1**	**0**	***3**	**26:52**
2012-13	**NY Rangers**	**NHL**	**46**	**2**	**12**	**14**	**16**	**0**	**0**	**1**	**81**	**2.5**	**–1**	**0**	**0.0**	**25:25**	**12**	**2**	**2**	**4**	**2**	**2**	**0**	**0**	**25:59**
	NHL Totals		**488**	**31**	**123**	**154**	**201**	**11**	**1**	**7**	**723**	**4.3**		**1**	**0.0**	**22:44**	**64**	**5**	**14**	**19**	**20**	**3**	**0**	**3**	**24:01**

AHL All-Rookie Team (2006)

Played in NHL All-Star Game (2012)

Signed as a free agent by **NY Rangers**, July 1, 2006.

GIROUX, Claude
(zhih-ROO, KLOHD) **PHI**

Right wing. Shoots right. 5'11", 172 lbs. Born, Hearst, Ont., January 12, 1988. Philadelphia's 1st choice, 22nd overall, in 2006 Entry Draft.

Season	Club	League	GP	G	A	Pts	PIM	PP	SH	GW	S	%	+/-	TF	F%	Min	GP	G	A	Pts	PIM	PP	SH	GW	Min
2004-05	Cumberland	ON-Jr.A	48	13	27	40	30	....	....	....	....	....	....	....	....	....	....	....	....	....	....	....	....	....	....
2005-06	Gatineau	QMJHL	69	39	64	103	64	....	....	....	....	....	....	....	....	....	17	5	15	20	24	....	....	....	....
2006-07	Gatineau	QMJHL	63	48	64	112	49	....	....	....	....	....	....	....	....	....	5	2	5	7	2	....	....	....	....
	Philadelphia	AHL	5	1	1	2	6	....	....	....	....	....	....	....	....	....	....	....	....	....	....	....	....	....	....
2007-08	**Philadelphia**	**NHL**	**2**	**0**	**0**	**0**	**0**	**0**	**0**	**0**	**2**	**0.0**	**–2**	**0**	**0.0**	**9:35**	....	....	....	....	....	....	....	....	....
	Gatineau	QMJHL	55	38	68	106	37	....	....	....	....	....	....	....	....	....	19	17	*34	*51	6	....	....	....	....
2008-09	**Philadelphia**	**NHL**	**42**	**9**	**18**	**27**	**14**	**2**	**0**	**0**	**67**	**13.4**	**10**	**309**	**47.3**	**15:10**	**6**	**2**	**3**	**5**	**6**	**0**	**0**	**0**	**15:57**
	Philadelphia	AHL	33	17	17	34	22	....	....	....	....	....	....	....	....	....	....	....	....	....	....	....	....	....	....
2009-10	**Philadelphia**	**NHL**	**82**	**16**	**31**	**47**	**23**	**8**	**0**	**2**	**145**	**11.0**	**–9**	**600**	**49.5**	**16:37**	**23**	**10**	**11**	**21**	**4**	**3**	**0**	**2**	**18:45**

			Regular Season														Playoffs								
Season	Club	League	GP	G	A	Pts	PIM	PP	SH	GW	S	%	+/-	TF	F%	Min	GP	G	A	Pts	PIM	PP	SH	GW	Min
2010-11	Philadelphia	NHL	82	25	51	76	47	8	3	5	169	14.8	20	1095	50.1	19:24	11	1	11	12	8	0	0	0	21:57
2011-12	Philadelphia	NHL	77	28	65	93	29	6	0	5	242	11.6	6	1543	53.7	21:33	10	*8	9	17	13	3	*2	0	22:43
2012-13	Eisbaren Berlin	Germany	9	4	15	19	6	....	....	....	....	....	....	....	....	....	....	....	....	....	....	....	....	....	....
	Philadelphia	NHL	48	13	35	48	22	6	1	2	137	9.5	–7	1182	54.5	21:10	....	....	....	....	....	....	....	....	....
	NHL Totals		333	91	200	291	135	30	4	14	762	11.9		4729	52.1	18:52	50	21	34	55	31	6	2	2	19:55

QMJHL All-Rookie Team (2006) • QMJHL First All-Star Team (2008) • Canadian Major Junior First All-Star Team (2008)
Played in NHL All-Star Game (2011, 2012)
Signed as a free agent by **Berlin** (Germany), October 4, 2012.

GLASS, Tanner (GLAS, TA-nuhr) PIT

Left wing. Shoots left. 6'1", 210 lbs. Born, Regina, Sask., November 29, 1983. Florida's 13th choice, 265th overall, in 2003 Entry Draft.

Season	Club	League	GP	G	A	Pts	PIM	PP	SH	GW	S	%	+/-	TF	F%	Min	GP	G	A	Pts	PIM	PP	SH	GW	Min
2000-01	Yorkton Mallers	SMHL	39	31	29	60	120	....	....	....	....	....	....	....	....	....	4	3	1	4	10	....	....	....	....
2001-02	Penticton	BCHL	57	11	28	39	171	....	....	....	....	....	....	....	....	....	....	....	....	....	....	....	....	....	....
2002-03	Penticton	BCHL	32	15	25	40	108	....	....	....	....	....	....	....	....	....	....	....	....	....	....	....	....	....	....
	Nanaimo Clippers	BCHL	18	8	14	22	46	....	....	....	....	....	....	....	....	....	....	....	....	....	....	....	....	....	....
2003-04	Dartmouth	ECAC	26	4	7	11	18	....	....	....	....	....	....	....	....	....	....	....	....	....	....	....	....	....	....
2004-05	Dartmouth	ECAC	33	7	8	15	32	....	....	....	....	....	....	....	....	....	....	....	....	....	....	....	....	....	....
2005-06	Dartmouth	ECAC	33	12	16	28	56	....	....	....	....	....	....	....	....	....	....	....	....	....	....	....	....	....	....
2006-07	Dartmouth	ECAC	32	8	20	28	92	....	....	....	....	....	....	....	....	....	....	....	....	....	....	....	....	....	....
	Rochester	AHL	4	0	1	1	5	....	....	....	....	....	....	....	....	....	....	....	....	....	....	....	....	....	....
2007-08	Florida	NHL	41	1	1	2	39	0	0	0	11	9.1	–5	2	0.0	4:25	....	....	....	....	....	....	....	....	....
	Rochester	AHL	43	6	5	11	84	....	....	....	....	....	....	....	....	....	....	....	....	....	....	....	....	....	....
2008-09	Florida	NHL	3	0	0	0	7	0	0	0	1	0.0	0	1	100.0	6:45	....	....	....	....	....	....	....	....	....
	Rochester	AHL	44	4	9	13	100	....	....	....	....	....	....	....	....	....	....	....	....	....	....	....	....	....	....
2009-10	Vancouver	NHL	67	4	7	11	115	0	0	0	52	7.7	5	18	16.7	10:28	4	0	0	0	0	0	0	0	3:08
2010-11	Vancouver	NHL	73	3	7	10	72	0	0	1	45	6.7	–5	62	40.3	8:56	20	0	0	0	18	0	0	0	7:28
2011-12	Winnipeg	NHL	78	5	11	16	73	0	0	1	86	5.8	–12	73	39.7	13:25	....	....	....	....	....	....	....	....	....
2012-13	B. Bystrica	Slovakia	6	0	1	1	75	....	....	....	....	....	....	....	....	....	....	....	....	....	....	....	....	....	....
	Pittsburgh	NHL	48	1	1	2	62	1	0	0	38	2.6	–11	51	43.1	10:04	5	1	0	1	4	0	0	0	8:13
	NHL Totals		310	14	27	41	368	1	0	2	233	6.0		207	38.6	9:57	29	1	0	1	22	0	0	0	7:00

Signed as a free aget by **Vancouver**, July 22, 2009. Signed as a free agent by **Winnipeg**, July 2, 2011. Signed as a free agent by **Pittsburgh**, July 1, 2012. Signed as a free agent by **Banska Bystrica** (Slovakia), December 4, 2012.

GLEASON, Tim (GLEE-suhn, TIHM) CAR

Defense. Shoots left. 6', 217 lbs. Born, Clawson, MI, January 29, 1983. Ottawa's 2nd choice, 23rd overall, in 2001 Entry Draft.

Season	Club	League	GP	G	A	Pts	PIM	PP	SH	GW	S	%	+/-	TF	F%	Min	GP	G	A	Pts	PIM	PP	SH	GW	Min
1998-99	Leamington Flyers	ON-Jr.B	52	5	26	31	76	....	....	....	....	....	....	....	....	....	....	....	....	....	....	....	....	....	....
99-2000	Windsor Spitfires	OHL	55	5	13	18	101	....	....	....	....	....	....	....	....	....	12	2	4	6	14	....	....	....	....
2000-01	Windsor Spitfires	OHL	47	8	28	36	124	....	....	....	....	....	....	....	....	....	9	1	2	3	23	....	....	....	....
2001-02	Windsor Spitfires	OHL	67	17	42	59	109	....	....	....	....	....	....	....	....	....	16	7	13	20	40	....	....	....	....
2002-03	Windsor Spitfires	OHL	45	7	31	38	75	....	....	....	....	....	....	....	....	....	7	5	2	7	17	....	....	....	....
2003-04	Los Angeles	NHL	47	0	7	7	21	0	0	0	45	0.0	1	0	0.0	14:59	....	....	....	....	....	....	....	....	....
	Manchester	AHL	22	0	8	8	19	....	....	....	....	....	....	....	....	....	6	0	1	1	4	....	....	....	....
2004-05	Manchester	AHL	67	10	14	24	112	....	....	....	....	....	....	....	....	....	5	0	0	0	4	....	....	....	....
2005-06	Los Angeles	NHL	78	2	19	21	77	0	0	0	72	2.8	0	0	0.0	17:41	....	....	....	....	....	....	....	....	....
2006-07	Carolina	NHL	57	2	4	6	57	1	0	0	72	2.8	–10	0	0.0	18:53	....	....	....	....	....	....	....	....	....
2007-08	Carolina	NHL	80	3	16	19	84	0	0	0	98	3.1	5	0	0.0	18:38	....	....	....	....	....	....	....	....	....
2008-09	Carolina	NHL	70	0	12	12	68	0	0	0	61	0.0	3	0	0.0	20:40	18	1	4	5	32	0	0	1	20:29
2009-10	Carolina	NHL	61	5	14	19	78	1	1	0	76	6.6	0	0	0.0	21:12	....	....	....	....	....	....	....	....	....
	United States	Olympics	6	0	0	0	0	....	....	....	....	....	....	....	....	....	....	....	....	....	....	....	....	....	....
2010-11	Carolina	NHL	82	2	14	16	85	0	0	0	84	2.4	–11	0	0.0	20:58	....	....	....	....	....	....	....	....	....
2011-12	Carolina	NHL	82	1	17	18	71	0	0	0	65	1.5	12	0	0.0	20:43	....	....	....	....	....	....	....	....	....
2012-13	Carolina	NHL	42	0	9	9	40	0	0	0	36	0.0	–3	0	0.0	19:34	....	....	....	....	....	....	....	....	....
	NHL Totals		599	15	112	127	581	2	1	0	609	2.5		0	0.0	19:25	18	1	4	5	32	0	0	1	20:29

• Rights traded to **Los Angeles** by **Ottawa** for Bryan Smolinski, March 11, 2003. Traded to **Carolina** by **Los Angeles** with Eric Belanger for Oleg Tverdovsky and Jack Johnson, September 29, 2006.

GLENCROSS, Curtis (GLEHN-kraws, KUHR-tihs) CGY

Center. Shoots left. 6'1", 197 lbs. Born, Kindersley, Sask., December 28, 1982.

Season	Club	League	GP	G	A	Pts	PIM	PP	SH	GW	S	%	+/-	TF	F%	Min	GP	G	A	Pts	PIM	PP	SH	GW	Min
2001-02	Brooks Bandits	AJHL	....	42	26	68	....	....	....	....	....	....	....	....	....	....	....	....	....	....	....	....	....	....	....
2002-03	Alaska Anchorage	WCHA	35	11	12	23	79	....	....	....	....	....	....	....	....	....	....	....	....	....	....	....	....	....	....
2003-04	Alaska Anchorage	WCHA	37	21	13	34	79	....	....	....	....	....	....	....	....	....	....	....	....	....	....	....	....	....	....
	Cincinnati	AHL	7	2	1	3	6	....	....	....	....	....	....	....	....	....	9	1	6	7	10	....	....	....	....
2004-05	Cincinnati	AHL	51	6	3	9	63	....	....	....	....	....	....	....	....	....	12	2	0	2	10	....	....	....	....
2005-06	Portland Pirates	AHL	41	15	10	25	85	....	....	....	....	....	....	....	....	....	19	4	6	10	37	....	....	....	....
2006-07	Anaheim	NHL	2	1	0	1	2	0	0	0	5	20.0	–1	0	0.0	10:43	....	....	....	....	....	....	....	....	....
	Portland Pirates	AHL	31	6	10	16	74	....	....	....	....	....	....	....	....	....	....	....	....	....	....	....	....	....	....
	Columbus	NHL	7	0	0	0	0	0	0	0	3	0.0	–4	2	0.0	8:43	....	....	....	....	....	....	....	....	....
	Syracuse Crunch	AHL	29	19	16	35	53	....	....	....	....	....	....	....	....	....	....	....	....	....	....	....	....	....	....
2007-08	Columbus	NHL	36	6	6	12	25	1	0	1	63	9.5	3	14	57.1	12:07	....	....	....	....	....	....	....	....	....
	Edmonton	NHL	26	9	4	13	28	0	0	0	41	22.0	5	11	45.5	10:19	....	....	....	....	....	....	....	....	....
2008-09	Calgary	NHL	74	13	27	40	42	1	1	3	152	8.6	14	62	48.4	14:41	6	0	3	3	12	0	0	0	15:00
2009-10	Calgary	NHL	67	15	18	33	58	2	3	2	117	12.8	11	24	37.5	15:43	....	....	....	....	....	....	....	....	....
2010-11	Calgary	NHL	79	24	19	43	59	3	2	4	149	16.1	6	141	40.4	16:15	....	....	....	....	....	....	....	....	....
2011-12	Calgary	NHL	67	26	22	48	62	8	1	3	110	23.6	–13	82	50.0	18:01	....	....	....	....	....	....	....	....	....
2012-13	Calgary	NHL	40	15	11	26	18	3	1	3	92	16.3	–8	46	43.5	18:14	....	....	....	....	....	....	....	....	....
	NHL Totals		398	109	107	216	294	18	8	16	732	14.9		382	44.5	15:27	6	0	3	3	12	0	0	0	15:00

Signed as a free agent by **Anaheim**, March 25, 2004. Traded to **Columbus** by **Anaheim** with Zenon Konopka and Anaheim's 7th round choice (Trent Vogelhuber) in 2007 Entry Draft for Mark Hartigan, Joe Motzko and Columbus' 4th round choice (Sebastian Stefaniszin) in 2007 Entry Draft, January 26, 2007. Traded to **Edmonton** by **Columbus** for Dick Tarnstrom, February 1, 2008. Signed as a free agent by **Calgary**, July 2, 2008.

GLENNIE, Scott (GLEH-nee, SKAWT) DAL

Right wing. Shoots right. 6'1", 180 lbs. Born, Winnipeg, Man., February 22, 1991. Dallas' 1st choice, 8th overall, in 2009 Entry Draft.

Season	Club	League	GP	G	A	Pts	PIM	PP	SH	GW	S	%	+/-	TF	F%	Min	GP	G	A	Pts	PIM	PP	SH	GW	Min
2006-07	Winnipeg Wild	MMHL	38	31	37	68	64	....	....	....	....	....	....	....	....	....	7	3	3	6	16	....	....	....	....
2007-08	Brandon	WHL	61	26	32	58	50	....	....	....	....	....	....	....	....	....	6	1	0	1	7	....	....	....	....
2008-09	Brandon	WHL	55	28	42	70	25	....	....	....	....	....	....	....	....	....	12	3	15	18	11	....	....	....	....
2009-10	Brandon	WHL	66	32	57	89	50	....	....	....	....	....	....	....	....	....	15	3	7	10	14	....	....	....	....
2010-11	Brandon	WHL	70	35	56	91	58	....	....	....	....	....	....	....	....	....	6	3	7	10	6	....	....	....	....
	Texas Stars	AHL	4	0	0	0	2	....	....	....	....	....	....	....	....	....	6	1	0	1	2	....	....	....	....
2011-12	Dallas	NHL	1	0	0	0	2	0	0	0	0	0.0	0	0	0.0	9:35	....	....	....	....	....	....	....	....	....
	Texas Stars	AHL	70	12	25	37	26	....	....	....	....	....	....	....	....	....	....	....	....	....	....	....	....	....	....
2012-13	Texas Stars	AHL	37	5	9	14	10	....	....	....	....	....	....	....	....	....	9	0	0	0	8	....	....	....	....
	NHL Totals		1	0	0	0	2	0	0	0	0	0.0		0	0.0	9:35	....	....	....	....	....	....	....	....	....

GOC, Marcel (GAWCH, MAHR-sehl) FLA

Center. Shoots left. 6'1", 197 lbs. Born, Calw, West Germany, August 24, 1983. San Jose's 1st choice, 20th overall, in 2001 Entry Draft.

Season	Club	League	GP	G	A	Pts	PIM	PP	SH	GW	S	%	+/-	TF	F%	Min	GP	G	A	Pts	PIM	PP	SH	GW	Min
1998-99	Schwenningen Jr.	Ger-Jr.	12	23	10	33	12	....	....	....	....	....	....	....	....	....	....	....	....	....	....	....	....	....	....
99-2000	Schwenningen	Germany	51	0	3	3	4	....	....	....	....	....	....	....	....	....	11	1	1	2	2	....	....	....	....
2000-01	Schwenningen	Germany	58	13	28	41	12	....	....	....	....	....	....	....	....	....	....	....	....	....	....	....	....	....	....
	Germany	Oly-Q	3	0	0	0	0	....	....	....	....	....	....	....	....	....	....	....	....	....	....	....	....	....	....
2001-02	Schwenningen	Germany	45	8	9	17	24	....	....	....	....	....	....	....	....	....	....	....	....	....	....	....	....	....	....
	Adler Mannheim	Germany	8	0	2	2	0	....	....	....	....	....	....	....	....	....	....	....	....	....	....	....	....	....	....
2002-03	Adler Mannheim	Germany	36	6	14	20	16	....	....	....	....	....	....	....	....	....	8	1	2	3	0	....	....	....	....
2003-04	Cleveland Barons	AHL	78	16	21	37	24	....	....	....	....	....	....	....	....	....	....	....	....	....	....	....	....	....	....
	San Jose	NHL	....	....	....	....	....	....	....	....	....	....	....	....	....	....	5	1	1	2	0	0	0	1	7:08
2004-05	Cleveland Barons	AHL	76	16	34	50	28	....	....	....	....	....	....	....	....	....	....	....	....	....	....	....	....	....	....

			Regular Season														Playoffs								
Season	Club	League	GP	G	A	Pts	PIM	PP	SH	GW	S	%	+/-	TF	F%	Min	GP	G	A	Pts	PIM	PP	SH	GW	Min
2005-06	San Jose	NHL	81	8	14	22	22	2	0	2	96	8.3	–7	808	47.9	11:42	11	0	3	3	0	0	0	0	12:38
	Germany	Olympics	5	1	0	1	0	....	....	....	....	....	....	....	....	....	....	....	....	....	....	....	....	....	....
2006-07	San Jose	NHL	78	5	8	13	24	0	1	0	96	5.2	–2	659	55.2	12:01	11	2	1	3	4	0	0	0	14:49
2007-08	San Jose	NHL	51	5	3	8	12	0	0	0	87	5.7	–15	208	51.4	10:41	4	0	0	0	2	0	0	0	8:03
2008-09	San Jose	NHL	55	2	9	11	18	0	0	1	104	1.9	–6	570	58.3	13:55	6	0	0	0	2	0	0	0	10:33
2009-10	Nashville	NHL	73	12	18	30	14	0	0	1	118	10.2	10	912	52.1	14:41	6	0	1	1	2	0	0	0	16:07
	Germany	Olympics	4	2	1	3	0	....	....	....	....	....	....	....	....	....	....	....	....	....	....	....	....	....	....
2010-11	Nashville	NHL	51	9	15	24	6	0	1	2	111	8.1	10	693	49.9	16:02	....	....	....	....	....	....	....	....	....
2011-12	Florida	NHL	57	11	16	27	10	3	0	1	97	11.3	5	978	51.6	17:37	7	2	3	5	0	1	0	1	18:11
2012-13	Adler Mannheim	Germany	18	4	15	19	8	....	....	....	....	....	....	....	....	....	....	....	....	....	....	....	....	....	....
	Florida	NHL	42	9	10	19	8	4	0	1	92	9.8	–6	786	52.2	18:16	....	....	....	....	....	....	....	....	....
	NHL Totals		488	61	93	154	114	9	2	8	801	7.6		5614	52.1	14:03	50	5	9	14	10	1	0	2	13:08

Signed as a free agent by **Nashville**, August 21, 2009. Signed as a free agent by **Florida**, July 1, 2011. Signed as a free agent by **Mannheim** (Germany). September 21, 2012.

GOLIGOSKI, Alex

(goh-lih-GAW-skee, AL-ehx) **DAL**

Defense. Shoots left. 5'11", 181 lbs. Born, Grand Rapids, MN, July 30, 1985. Pittsburgh's 3rd choice, 61st overall, in 2004 Entry Draft.

Season	Club	League	GP	G	A	Pts	PIM	PP	SH	GW	S	%	+/-	TF	F%	Min	GP	G	A	Pts	PIM	PP	SH	GW	Min
2002-03	Grand Rapids	High-MN	28	14	20	34	22	....	....	....	....	....	....	....	....	....	....	....	....	....	....	....	....	....	....
2003-04	Grand Rapids	High-MN	26	25	31	56	16	....	....	....	....	....	....	....	....	....	....	....	....	....	....	....	....	....	....
	Sioux Falls	USHL	10	0	2	2	6	....	....	....	....	....	....	....	....	....	....	....	....	....	....	....	....	....	....
2004-05	U. of Minnesota	WCHA	33	5	15	20	44	....	....	....	....	....	....	....	....	....	....	....	....	....	....	....	....	....	....
2005-06	U. of Minnesota	WCHA	41	11	28	39	63	....	....	....	....	....	....	....	....	....	....	....	....	....	....	....	....	....	....
2006-07	U. of Minnesota	WCHA	44	9	30	39	51	....	....	....	....	....	....	....	....	....	....	....	....	....	....	....	....	....	....
2007-08	Pittsburgh	NHL	3	0	2	2	2	0	0	0	2	0.0	2	0	0.0	13:56	....	....	....	....	....	....	....	....	....
	Wilkes-Barre	AHL	70	10	28	38	53	....	....	....	....	....	....	....	....	....	23	4	24	28	18	....	....	....	....
2008-09 ♦	Pittsburgh	NHL	45	6	14	20	16	4	0	0	61	9.8	5	0	0.0	18:18	2	0	1	1	0	0	0	0	10:22
	Wilkes-Barre	AHL	26	2	16	18	16	....	....	....	....	....	....	....	....	....	9	1	5	6	10	....	....	....	....
2009-10	Pittsburgh	NHL	69	8	29	37	22	2	0	0	98	8.2	7	0	0.0	21:25	13	2	7	9	2	1	0	0	20:34
2010-11	Pittsburgh	NHL	60	9	22	31	28	4	0	4	101	8.9	20	0	0.0	20:46	....	....	....	....	....	....	....	....	....
	Dallas	NHL	23	5	10	15	12	3	0	0	61	8.2	0	0	0.0	26:04	....	....	....	....	....	....	....	....	....
2011-12	Dallas	NHL	71	9	21	30	16	2	0	1	140	6.4	0	0	0.0	22:46	....	....	....	....	....	....	....	....	....
2012-13	Dallas	NHL	47	3	24	27	18	0	0	0	80	3.8	4	0	0.0	22:23	....	....	....	....	....	....	....	....	....
	NHL Totals		318	40	122	162	114	15	0	5	543	7.4		0	0.0	21:34	15	2	8	10	2	1	0	0	19:13

WCHA All-Rookie Team (2005) • WCHA Second All-Star Team (2006) • WCHA First All-Star Team (2007) • NCAA West First All-American Team (2007) • AHL All-Rookie Team (2008)

Traded to **Dallas** by **Pittsburgh** for James Neal and Matt Niskanen, February 21, 2011.

GOLOUBEF, Cody

(GOH-luh-behf, KOH-dee) **CBJ**

Defense. Shoots right. 6'1", 190 lbs. Born, Mississauga, Ont., November 30, 1989. Columbus' 2nd choice, 37th overall, in 2008 Entry Draft.

Season	Club	League	GP	G	A	Pts	PIM	PP	SH	GW	S	%	+/-	TF	F%	Min	GP	G	A	Pts	PIM	PP	SH	GW	Min
2003-04	Tor. Marlboros	GTHL	89	10	27	37	44	....	....	....	....	....	....	....	....	....	....	....	....	....	....	....	....	....	....
2004-05	Tor. Marlboros	GTHL	69	14	47	61	56	....	....	....	....	....	....	....	....	....	....	....	....	....	....	....	....	....	....
2005-06	Milton Icehawks	ON-Jr.A	42	9	29	38	38	....	....	....	....	....	....	....	....	....	7	1	3	4	10	....	....	....	....
2006-07	Oakville Blades	ON-Jr.A	9	5	5	10	46	....	....	....	....	....	....	....	....	....	10	2	10	12	18	....	....	....	....
2007-08	U. of Wisconsin	WCHA	40	4	6	10	36	....	....	....	....	....	....	....	....	....	....	....	....	....	....	....	....	....	....
2008-09	U. of Wisconsin	WCHA	36	5	8	13	38	....	....	....	....	....	....	....	....	....	....	....	....	....	....	....	....	....	....
2009-10	U. of Wisconsin	WCHA	42	3	11	14	64	....	....	....	....	....	....	....	....	....	....	....	....	....	....	....	....	....	....
2010-11	Springfield	AHL	50	5	12	17	42	....	....	....	....	....	....	....	....	....	....	....	....	....	....	....	....	....	....
2011-12	Columbus	NHL	1	0	0	0	0	0	0	0	0	0.0	1	0	0.0	6:00	....	....	....	....	....	....	....	....	....
	Springfield	AHL	48	1	11	12	43	....	....	....	....	....	....	....	....	....	....	....	....	....	....	....	....	....	....
2012-13	Springfield	AHL	38	5	8	13	49	....	....	....	....	....	....	....	....	....	7	0	2	2	10	....	....	....	....
	Columbus	NHL	11	1	0	1	0	0	0	1	14	7.1	–3	0	0.0	14:49	....	....	....	....	....	....	....	....	....
	NHL Totals		12	1	0	1	0	0	0	1	14	7.1		0	0.0	14:05	....	....	....	....	....	....	....	....	....

• Missed majority of 2006-07 due to various injuries.

GOMEZ, Scott

(GOH-mehz, SKAWT) **FLA**

Center. Shoots left. 5'11", 198 lbs. Born, Anchorage, AK, December 23, 1979. New Jersey's 2nd choice, 27th overall, in 1998 Entry Draft.

Season	Club	League	GP	G	A	Pts	PIM	PP	SH	GW	S	%	+/-	TF	F%	Min	GP	G	A	Pts	PIM	PP	SH	GW	Min
1994-95	East High	High-AK	28	30	48	78	....	....	....	....	....	....	....	....	....	....	....	....	....	....	....	....	....	....	....
1995-96	East High	High-AK	27	*56	49	*101	....	....	....	....	....	....	....	....	....	....	....	....	....	....	....	....	....	....	....
	Anchorage	AAHL	40	*70	*67	*137	44	....	....	....	....	....	....	....	....	....	....	....	....	....	....	....	....	....	....
1996-97	South Surrey	BCHL	56	48	76	124	94	....	....	....	....	....	....	....	....	....	21	18	23	41	57	....	....	....	....
1997-98	Tri-City	WHL	45	12	37	49	57	....	....	....	....	....	....	....	....	....	....	....	....	....	....	....	....	....	....
1998-99	Tri-City	WHL	58	30	*78	108	55	....	....	....	....	....	....	....	....	....	10	6	13	19	31	....	....	....	....
99-2000 ♦	New Jersey	NHL	82	19	51	70	78	7	0	1	204	9.3	14	341	44.6	16:21	23	4	6	10	4	1	0	2	14:08
2000-01	New Jersey	NHL	76	14	49	63	46	2	0	4	155	9.0	–1	1010	44.6	15:46	25	5	9	14	24	0	0	0	16:06
2001-02	New Jersey	NHL	76	10	38	48	36	1	0	1	156	6.4	–4	628	48.7	16:46	....	....	....	....	....	....	....	....	....
2002-03 ♦	New Jersey	NHL	80	13	42	55	48	2	0	4	205	6.3	17	864	47.5	16:01	24	3	9	12	2	0	0	0	13:45
2003-04	New Jersey	NHL	80	14	*56	70	70	3	0	1	189	7.4	18	1129	46.2	16:00	5	0	6	6	0	0	0	0	17:14
2004-05	Alaska Aces	ECHL	61	13	*73	*86	69	....	....	....	....	....	....	....	....	....	4	1	3	4	4	....	....	....	....
2005-06	New Jersey	NHL	82	33	51	84	42	9	0	5	244	13.5	8	1434	52.6	18:47	9	5	4	9	6	4	0	1	18:14
	United States	Olympics	6	1	4	5	10	....	....	....	....	....	....	....	....	....	....	....	....	....	....	....	....	....	....
2006-07	New Jersey	NHL	72	13	47	60	42	4	0	1	248	5.2	7	1204	52.2	18:56	11	4	10	14	14	0	0	1	20:01
2007-08	NY Rangers	NHL	81	16	54	70	36	7	0	3	242	6.6	3	1165	52.5	19:54	10	4	7	11	8	1	0	0	20:53
2008-09	NY Rangers	NHL	77	16	42	58	60	3	1	7	271	5.9	–2	1312	52.4	21:04	7	2	3	5	4	1	0	0	19:58
2009-10	Montreal	NHL	78	12	47	59	60	5	0	1	180	6.7	1	1375	50.8	19:56	19	2	12	14	25	0	0	0	21:10
2010-11	Montreal	NHL	80	7	31	38	48	3	0	2	157	4.5	–15	1197	48.0	18:34	7	0	4	4	2	0	0	0	19:42
2011-12	Montreal	NHL	38	2	9	11	14	2	0	1	59	3.4	–9	333	49.6	14:08	....	....	....	....	....	....	....	....	....
2012-13	Alaska Aces	ECHL	11	6	7	13	12	....	....	....	....	....	....	....	....	....	....	....	....	....	....	....	....	....	....
	San Jose	NHL	39	2	13	15	22	0	0	0	58	3.4	–10	324	55.9	13:32	9	0	2	2	6	0	0	0	15:01
	NHL Totals		941	171	530	701	602	48	1	31	2368	7.2		12316	49.8	17:39	149	29	72	101	95	7	0	4	17:08

WHL West First All-Star Team (1999) • NHL All-Rookie Team (2000) • Calder Memorial Trophy (2000) • ECHL First All-Star Team (2005) • ECHL Leading Scorer (2005) • ECHL MVP (2005)

Played in NHL All-Star Game (2000, 2008)

Signed as a free agent by **Alaska** (ECHL), October 25, 2004. Signed as a free agent by **NY Rangers**, July 1, 2007. Traded to **Montreal** by **NY Rangers** with Tom Pyatt and Michael Busto for Chris Higgins, Ryan McDonagh and Pavel Valentenko, June 30, 2009. • Missed majority of 2011-12 due to upper body, groin and head ijuries. Signed to a PTO (professional tryout) contract by **Alaska** (ECHL), September 28, 2012. Signed as a free agent by **San Jose**, January 23, 2013. Signed as a free agent by **Florida**, July 31, 2013.

GONCHAR, Sergei

(gohn-CHAR, SAIR-gay) **DAL**

Defense. Shoots left. 6'2", 212 lbs. Born, Chelyabinsk, USSR, April 13, 1974. Washington's 1st choice, 14th overall, in 1992 Entry Draft.

Season	Club	League	GP	G	A	Pts	PIM	PP	SH	GW	S	%	+/-	TF	F%	Min	GP	G	A	Pts	PIM	PP	SH	GW	Min
1990-91	Mechel	USSR-2	2	0	0	0	0	....	....	....	....	....	....	....	....	....	....	....	....	....	....	....	....	....	....
	Chelyabinsk	USSR-Q	11	0	0	0	4	....	....	....	....	....	....	....	....	....	....	....	....	....	....	....	....	....	....
1991-92	Chelyabinsk	CIS	31	1	0	1	6	....	....	....	....	....	....	....	....	....	....	....	....	....	....	....	....	....	....
1992-93	Dynamo Moscow	CIS	31	1	3	4	70	....	....	....	....	....	....	....	....	....	10	0	0	0	12	....	....	....	....
1993-94	Dynamo Moscow	CIS	44	4	5	9	36	....	....	....	....	....	....	....	....	....	....	....	....	....	....	....	....	....	....
	Portland Pirates	AHL	....	....	....	....	....	....	....	....	....	....	....	....	....	....	2	0	0	0	0	....	....	....	....
1994-95	Portland Pirates	AHL	61	10	32	42	67	....	....	....	....	....	....	....	....	....	....	....	....	....	....	....	....	....	....
	Washington	NHL	31	2	5	7	22	0	0	0	38	5.3	4	....	....	....	7	2	2	4	2	0	0	1	....
1995-96	Washington	NHL	78	15	26	41	60	4	0	4	139	10.8	25	....	....	....	6	2	4	6	4	1	0	0	....
1996-97	Washington	NHL	57	13	17	30	36	3	0	3	129	10.1	–11	....	....	....	....	....	....	....	....	....	....	....	....
1997-98	Lada Togliatti	Russia	7	3	2	5	4	....	....	....	....	....	....	....	....	....	....	....	....	....	....	....	....	....	....
	Washington	NHL	72	5	16	21	66	2	0	0	134	3.7	2	....	....	....	21	7	4	11	30	3	1	2	....
	Russia	Olympics	6	0	2	2	0	....	....	....	....	....	....	....	....	....	....	....	....	....	....	....	....	....	....
1998-99	Washington	NHL	53	21	10	31	57	13	1	3	180	11.7	1	0	0.0	23:55	....	....	....	....	....	....	....	....	....
99-2000	Washington	NHL	73	18	36	54	52	5	0	3	181	9.9	26	0	0.0	21:46	5	1	0	1	6	0	0	0	19:58
2000-01	Washington	NHL	76	19	38	57	70	8	0	2	241	7.9	12	1	100.0	22:26	6	1	3	4	2	1	0	0	19:45
2001-02	Washington	NHL	76	26	33	59	58	7	0	2	216	12.0	–1	1	100.0	23:51	....	....	....	....	....	....	....	....	....
	Russia	Olympics	6	0	0	0	2	....	....	....	....	....	....	....	....	....	....	....	....	....	....	....	....	....	....
2002-03	Washington	NHL	82	18	49	67	52	7	0	2	224	8.0	13	0	0.0	26:35	6	0	5	5	4	0	0	0	29:00
2003-04	Washington	NHL	56	7	42	49	44	4	0	0	127	5.5	–20	0	0.0	27:57	....	....	....	....	....	....	....	....	....
	Boston	NHL	15	4	5	9	12	2	0	0	34	11.8	6	0	0.0	25:32	7	1	4	5	4	1	0	1	27:51
2004-05	Magnitogorsk	Russia	40	2	17	19	54	....	....	....	....	....	....	....	....	....	4	1	1	2	6	....	....	....	....

			Regular Season														Playoffs								
Season	Club	League	GP	G	A	Pts	PIM	PP	SH	GW	S	%	+/-	TF	F%	Min	GP	G	A	Pts	PIM	PP	SH	GW	Min
2005-06	**Pittsburgh**	**NHL**	**75**	**12**	**46**	**58**	**100**	**8**	**0**	**2**	**192**	**6.3**	**–13**	**0**	**0.0**	**24:40**	....	....	....	....	....	....	....	....	....
	Russia	Olympics	8	0	2	2	8	....	....	....	....	....	....	....	....	....	....	....	....	....	....	....	....	....	....
2006-07	**Pittsburgh**	**NHL**	**82**	**13**	**54**	**67**	**72**	**10**	**1**	**3**	**191**	**6.8**	**–5**	**0**	**0.0**	**26:34**	**5**	**1**	**3**	**4**	**2**	**1**	**0**	**0**	**26:53**
2007-08	**Pittsburgh**	**NHL**	**78**	**12**	**53**	**65**	**66**	**8**	**0**	**2**	**173**	**6.9**	**13**	**0**	**0.0**	**25:55**	**20**	**1**	**13**	**14**	**8**	**1**	**0**	**0**	**25:13**
2008-09 ♦	**Pittsburgh**	**NHL**	**25**	**6**	**13**	**19**	**26**	**5**	**0**	**1**	**71**	**8.5**	**6**	**0**	**0.0**	**25:11**	**22**	**3**	**11**	**14**	**12**	**2**	**0**	**2**	**23:03**
2009-10	**Pittsburgh**	**NHL**	**62**	**11**	**39**	**50**	**49**	**6**	**0**	**3**	**138**	**8.0**	**–4**	**0**	**0.0**	**24:24**	**13**	**2**	**10**	**12**	**4**	**1**	**0**	**1**	**26:27**
	Russia	Olympics	4	1	0	1	2	....	....	....	....	....	....	....	....	....	....	....	....	....	....	....	....	....	....
2010-11	**Ottawa**	**NHL**	**67**	**7**	**20**	**27**	**20**	**5**	**0**	**0**	**107**	**6.5**	**–15**	**0**	**0.0**	**23:12**	....	....	....	....	....	....	....	....	....
2011-12	**Ottawa**	**NHL**	**74**	**5**	**32**	**37**	**55**	**2**	**0**	**1**	**131**	**3.8**	**–4**	**0**	**0.0**	**22:15**	**7**	**1**	**3**	**4**	**6**	**1**	**0**	**0**	**24:35**
2012-13	Magnitogorsk	KHL	37	3	26	29	40	....	....	....	....	....	....	....	....	....	....	....	....	....	....	....	....	....	....
	Ottawa	**NHL**	**45**	**3**	**24**	**27**	**26**	**2**	**0**	**3**	**85**	**3.5**	**4**	**0**	**0.0**	**24:00**	**10**	**0**	**6**	**6**	**14**	**0**	**0**	**0**	**23:55**
	NHL Totals		**1177**	**217**	**558**	**775**	**943**	**101**	**2**	**34**	**2731**	**7.9**		**2**	**100.0**	**24:28**	**135**	**22**	**68**	**90**	**98**	**12**	**1**	**7**	**24:38**

NHL Second All-Star Team (2002, 2003)

Played in NHL All-Star Game (2001, 2002, 2003, 2008)

Traded to **Boston** by **Washington** for Shaonne Morrisonn and Boston's 1st (Jeff Schultz) and 2nd (Michail Yunkov) round choices in 2004 Entry Draft, March 3, 2004. Signed as a free agent by **Magnitogorsk** (Russia), September 21, 2004. Signed as a free agent by **Pittsburgh**, August 3, 2005. Signed as a free agent by **Ottawa**, July 1, 2010. Signed as a free agent by **Magnitogorsk** (KHL), September 16, 2012. Traded to **Dallas** by **Ottawa** for Dallas' 6th round choice (Chris LeBlanc) in 2013 Entry Draft, June 7, 2013.

GORDON, Andrew

(GOHR-duhn, AN-droo) **WPG**

Right wing. Shoots right. 6', 194 lbs. Born, Halifax, N.S., December 13, 1985. Washington's 11th choice, 197th overall, in 2004 Entry Draft.

Season	Club	League	GP	G	A	Pts	PIM	PP	SH	GW	S	%	+/-	TF	F%	Min	GP	G	A	Pts	PIM	PP	SH	GW	Min
2002-03	Notre Dame	SJHL	58	20	27	47	12	....	....	....	....	....	....	....	....	....	....	....	....	....	....	....	....	....	....
2003-04	Notre Dame	SJHL	55	20	44	64	12	....	....	....	....	....	....	....	....	....	....	....	....	....	....	....	....	....	....
2004-05	St. Cloud State	WCHA	38	9	8	17	6	....	....	....	....	....	....	....	....	....	....	....	....	....	....	....	....	....	....
2005-06	St. Cloud State	WCHA	42	20	20	40	22	....	....	....	....	....	....	....	....	....	....	....	....	....	....	....	....	....	....
2006-07	St. Cloud State	WCHA	40	22	23	45	16	....	....	....	....	....	....	....	....	....	....	....	....	....	....	....	....	....	....
2007-08	Hershey Bears	AHL	58	16	35	51	39	....	....	....	....	....	....	....	....	....	5	3	2	5	2	....	....	....	....
	South Carolina	ECHL	11	8	6	14	6	....	....	....	....	....	....	....	....	....	9	5	3	8	8	....	....	....	....
2008-09	**Washington**	**NHL**	**1**	**0**	**0**	**0**	**0**	**0**	**0**	**0**	**1**	**0.0**	**0**	**0**	**0.0**	**7:12**	....	....	....	....	....	....	....	....	....
	Hershey Bears	AHL	80	21	24	45	47	....	....	....	....	....	....	....	....	....	22	6	4	10	6	....	....	....	....
2009-10	**Washington**	**NHL**	**2**	**0**	**0**	**0**	**0**	**0**	**0**	**0**	**0**	**0.0**	**–2**	**0**	**0.0**	**6:41**	....	....	....	....	....	....	....	....	....
	Hershey Bears	AHL	79	37	34	71	57	....	....	....	....	....	....	....	....	....	17	13	7	20	2	....	....	....	....
2010-11	**Washington**	**NHL**	**9**	**1**	**1**	**2**	**0**	**0**	**0**	**0**	**5**	**20.0**	**–2**	**0**	**0.0**	**8:40**	....	....	....	....	....	....	....	....	....
	Hershey Bears	AHL	50	28	29	57	24	....	....	....	....	....	....	....	....	....	2	0	1	1	6	....	....	....	....
2011-12	**Anaheim**	**NHL**	**37**	**2**	**3**	**5**	**6**	**0**	**0**	**0**	**38**	**5.3**	**–10**	**5**	**0.0**	**10:51**	....	....	....	....	....	....	....	....	....
	Syracuse Crunch	AHL	19	3	5	8	10	....	....	....	....	....	....	....	....	....	....	....	....	....	....	....	....	....	....
	Chicago Wolves	AHL	10	2	1	3	10	....	....	....	....	....	....	....	....	....	....	....	....	....	....	....	....	....	....
2012-13	Chicago Wolves	AHL	54	19	13	32	49	....	....	....	....	....	....	....	....	....	....	....	....	....	....	....	....	....	....
	Vancouver	**NHL**	**6**	**0**	**0**	**0**	**0**	**0**	**0**	**0**	**2**	**0.0**	**–1**	**5**	**40.0**	**8:25**	....	....	....	....	....	....	....	....	....
	NHL Totals		**55**	**3**	**4**	**7**	**6**	**0**	**0**	**0**	**46**	**6.5**		**10**	**20.0**	**10:01**	....	....	....	....	....	....	....	....	....

WCHA First All-Star Team (2007) • AHL Second All-Star Team (2010)

Signed as a free agent by **Anaheim**, July 2, 2011. Traded to **Vancouver** by **Anaheim** for Sebastian Erixon, February 27, 2012. Signed as a free agent by **Winnipeg**, July 6, 2013.

GORDON, Boyd

(GOHR-duhn, BOID) **EDM**

Center. Shoots right. 6', 200 lbs. Born, Unity, Sask., October 19, 1983. Washington's 3rd choice, 17th overall, in 2002 Entry Draft.

Season	Club	League	GP	G	A	Pts	PIM	PP	SH	GW	S	%	+/-	TF	F%	Min	GP	G	A	Pts	PIM	PP	SH	GW	Min
1998-99	Regina Rangers	SMBHL	60	70	102	172	53	....	....	....	....	....	....	....	....	....	....	....	....	....	....	....	....	....	....
99-2000	Red Deer Rebels	WHL	66	10	26	36	24	....	....	....	....	....	....	....	....	....	4	0	1	1	16	....	....	....	....
2000-01	Red Deer Rebels	WHL	72	12	27	39	39	....	....	....	....	....	....	....	....	....	22	3	6	9	2	....	....	....	....
2001-02	Red Deer Rebels	WHL	66	22	29	51	19	....	....	....	....	....	....	....	....	....	23	10	12	22	8	....	....	....	....
2002-03	Red Deer Rebels	WHL	56	33	48	81	28	....	....	....	....	....	....	....	....	....	23	8	12	20	14	....	....	....	....
2003-04	**Washington**	**NHL**	**41**	**1**	**5**	**6**	**8**	**0**	**0**	**0**	**42**	**2.4**	**–9**	**328**	**43.0**	**13:11**	....	....	....	....	....	....	....	....	....
	Portland Pirates	AHL	43	5	17	22	16	....	....	....	....	....	....	....	....	....	7	2	1	3	0	....	....	....	....
2004-05	Portland Pirates	AHL	80	17	22	39	35	....	....	....	....	....	....	....	....	....	....	....	....	....	....	....	....	....	....
2005-06	**Washington**	**NHL**	**25**	**0**	**1**	**1**	**4**	**0**	**0**	**0**	**12**	**0.0**	**–4**	**216**	**46.3**	**11:40**	....	....	....	....	....	....	....	....	....
	Hershey Bears	AHL	58	16	22	38	23	....	....	....	....	....	....	....	....	....	21	3	5	8	10	....	....	....	....
2006-07	**Washington**	**NHL**	**71**	**7**	**22**	**29**	**14**	**0**	**2**	**0**	**104**	**6.7**	**10**	**1214**	**52.1**	**15:53**	....	....	....	....	....	....	....	....	....
2007-08	**Washington**	**NHL**	**67**	**7**	**9**	**16**	**12**	**0**	**1**	**0**	**100**	**7.0**	**5**	**904**	**55.8**	**15:44**	**7**	**0**	**0**	**0**	**0**	**0**	**0**	**0**	**13:23**
2008-09	**Washington**	**NHL**	**63**	**5**	**9**	**14**	**16**	**0**	**1**	**2**	**69**	**7.2**	**–4**	**667**	**56.1**	**13:28**	**14**	**0**	**3**	**3**	**4**	**0**	**0**	**0**	**11:17**
2009-10	**Washington**	**NHL**	**36**	**4**	**6**	**10**	**12**	**0**	**0**	**0**	**40**	**10.0**	**4**	**205**	**61.0**	**10:17**	**6**	**1**	**1**	**2**	**0**	**0**	**1**	**0**	**11:02**
	Hershey Bears	AHL	2	0	2	2	0	....	....	....	....	....	....	....	....	....	....	....	....	....	....	....	....	....	....
2010-11	**Washington**	**NHL**	**60**	**3**	**6**	**9**	**16**	**0**	**1**	**1**	**77**	**3.9**	**–5**	**719**	**58.0**	**13:03**	**9**	**0**	**0**	**0**	**6**	**0**	**0**	**0**	**12:54**
2011-12	**Phoenix**	**NHL**	**75**	**8**	**15**	**23**	**10**	**0**	**1**	**2**	**114**	**7.0**	**9**	**1177**	**56.8**	**15:56**	**16**	**0**	**2**	**2**	**6**	**0**	**0**	**0**	**17:49**
2012-13	**Phoenix**	**NHL**	**48**	**4**	**10**	**14**	**8**	**0**	**0**	**0**	**59**	**6.8**	**0**	**789**	**57.3**	**15:01**	....	....	....	....	....	....	....	....	....
	NHL Totals		**486**	**39**	**83**	**122**	**100**	**0**	**6**	**5**	**617**	**6.3**		**6219**	**54.9**	**14:16**	**52**	**1**	**6**	**7**	**16**	**0**	**1**	**0**	**13:50**

WHL East First All-Star Team (2003)

• Missed majority of 2009-10 due to back injury. Signed as a free agent by **Phoeniix**, July 1, 2011. Signed as a free agent by **Edmonton**, July 5, 2013.

GORGES, Josh

(GOHR-juhz, JAWSH) **MTL**

Defense. Shoots left. 6'1", 201 lbs. Born, Kelowna, B.C., August 14, 1984.

Season	Club	League	GP	G	A	Pts	PIM	PP	SH	GW	S	%	+/-	TF	F%	Min	GP	G	A	Pts	PIM	PP	SH	GW	Min
2000-01	Kelowna Rockets	WHL	57	4	6	10	24	....	....	....	....	....	....	....	....	....	6	1	1	2	4	....	....	....	....
2001-02	Kelowna Rockets	WHL	72	7	34	41	74	....	....	....	....	....	....	....	....	....	15	1	7	8	8	....	....	....	....
2002-03	Kelowna Rockets	WHL	54	11	48	59	76	....	....	....	....	....	....	....	....	....	19	3	17	20	16	....	....	....	....
2003-04	Kelowna Rockets	WHL	62	11	31	42	38	....	....	....	....	....	....	....	....	....	17	2	13	15	6	....	....	....	....
2004-05	Cleveland Barons	AHL	74	4	8	12	37	....	....	....	....	....	....	....	....	....	....	....	....	....	....	....	....	....	....
2005-06	**San Jose**	**NHL**	**49**	**0**	**6**	**6**	**31**	**0**	**0**	**0**	**25**	**0.0**	**5**	**0**	**0.0**	**17:38**	**11**	**0**	**1**	**1**	**4**	**0**	**0**	**0**	**18:56**
	Cleveland Barons	AHL	18	2	3	5	12	....	....	....	....	....	....	....	....	....	....	....	....	....	....	....	....	....	....
2006-07	**San Jose**	**NHL**	**47**	**1**	**3**	**4**	**26**	**0**	**0**	**0**	**37**	**2.7**	**–3**	**0**	**0.0**	**17:48**	....	....	....	....	....	....	....	....	....
	Worcester Sharks	AHL	7	0	1	1	2	....	....	....	....	....	....	....	....	....	....	....	....	....	....	....	....	....	....
	Montreal	**NHL**	**7**	**0**	**0**	**0**	**0**	**0**	**0**	**0**	**3**	**0.0**	**–1**	**0**	**0.0**	**12:28**	....	....	....	....	....	....	....	....	....
2007-08	**Montreal**	**NHL**	**62**	**0**	**9**	**9**	**32**	**0**	**0**	**0**	**41**	**0.0**	**0**	**0**	**0.0**	**16:20**	**12**	**0**	**3**	**3**	**0**	**0**	**0**	**0**	**18:20**
2008-09	**Montreal**	**NHL**	**81**	**4**	**19**	**23**	**37**	**2**	**0**	**0**	**63**	**6.3**	**12**	**1**	**0.0**	**20:08**	**4**	**0**	**1**	**1**	**7**	**0**	**0**	**0**	**23:46**
2009-10	**Montreal**	**NHL**	**82**	**3**	**7**	**10**	**39**	**0**	**0**	**1**	**52**	**5.8**	**2**	**0**	**0.0**	**21:01**	**19**	**0**	**2**	**2**	**14**	**0**	**0**	**0**	**22:42**
2010-11	**Montreal**	**NHL**	**36**	**1**	**6**	**7**	**18**	**1**	**0**	**1**	**20**	**5.0**	**–3**	**0**	**0.0**	**21:10**	....	....	....	....	....	....	....	....	....
2011-12	**Montreal**	**NHL**	**82**	**2**	**14**	**16**	**39**	**0**	**0**	**1**	**59**	**3.4**	**14**	**0**	**0.0**	**22:38**	....	....	....	....	....	....	....	....	....
2012-13	**Montreal**	**NHL**	**48**	**2**	**7**	**9**	**15**	**0**	**0**	**0**	**40**	**5.0**	**4**	**0**	**0.0**	**21:23**	**5**	**0**	**0**	**0**	**4**	**0**	**0**	**0**	**21:18**
	NHL Totals		**494**	**13**	**71**	**84**	**237**	**3**	**0**	**3**	**340**	**3.8**		**1**	**0.0**	**19:50**	**51**	**0**	**7**	**7**	**29**	**0**	**0**	**0**	**20:48**

WHL West Second All-Star Team (2003) • WHL West First All-Star Team (2004) • George Parsons Trophy (Memorial Cup - Most Sportsmanlike Player) (2004)

Signed as a free agent by **San Jose**, September 20, 2002. Traded to **Montreal** by **San Jose** with San Jose's 1st round choice (Max Pacioretty) in 2007 Entry Draft for Craig Rivet and Montreal's 5th round choice (Julien Demers) in 2008 Entry Draft, February 25, 2007. • Missed majority of 2010-11 due to knee injury at NY Islanders, December 26, 2010.

GRABNER, Michael

(GRAB-nuhr, MIGH-kuhl) **NYI**

Right wing. Shoots left. 6'1", 186 lbs. Born, Villach, Austria, October 5, 1987. Vancouver's 1st choice, 14th overall, in 2006 Entry Draft.

Season	Club	League	GP	G	A	Pts	PIM	PP	SH	GW	S	%	+/-	TF	F%	Min	GP	G	A	Pts	PIM	PP	SH	GW	Min
2002-03	EC VSV Villach Jr.	Austria-Jr.	13	6	4	10	4	....	....	....	....	....	....	....	....	....	....	....	....	....	....	....	....	....	....
2003-04	EC VSV Villach Jr.	Austria-Jr.	23	32	5	37	58	....	....	....	....	....	....	....	....	....	....	....	....	....	....	....	....	....	....
	EC VSV Villach	Austria	18	2	1	3	0	....	....	....	....	....	....	....	....	....	....	....	....	....	....	....	....	....	....
	Austria	WJ18-B	5	3	1	4	4	....	....	....	....	....	....	....	....	....	....	....	....	....	....	....	....	....	....
2004-05	Spokane Chiefs	WHL	58	13	11	24	18	....	....	....	....	....	....	....	....	....	....	....	....	....	....	....	....	....	....
2005-06	Spokane Chiefs	WHL	67	36	14	50	28	....	....	....	....	....	....	....	....	....	....	....	....	....	....	....	....	....	....
2006-07	Spokane Chiefs	WHL	55	39	16	55	34	....	....	....	....	....	....	....	....	....	6	0	1	1	2	....	....	....	....
	Manitoba Moose	AHL	2	1	1	2	0	....	....	....	....	....	....	....	....	....	6	0	0	0	0	....	....	....	....
2007-08	Manitoba Moose	AHL	74	22	22	44	8	....	....	....	....	....	....	....	....	....	6	3	0	3	2	....	....	....	....
2008-09	Manitoba Moose	AHL	66	30	18	48	20	....	....	....	....	....	....	....	....	....	20	10	7	17	2	....	....	....	....
	Austria	Oly-Q	3	5	0	5	0	....	....	....	....	....	....	....	....	....	....	....	....	....	....	....	....	....	....
2009-10	**Vancouver**	**NHL**	**20**	**5**	**6**	**11**	**8**	**2**	**0**	**1**	**63**	**7.9**	**2**	**2**	**50.0**	**13:54**	**9**	**1**	**0**	**1**	**0**	**0**	**0**	**0**	**9:06**
	Manitoba Moose	AHL	38	15	11	26	6	....	....	....	....	....	....	....	....	....	....	....	....	....	....	....	....	....	....
2010-11	**NY Islanders**	**NHL**	**76**	**34**	**18**	**52**	**10**	**2**	**6**	**3**	**228**	**14.9**	**13**	**6**	**33.3**	**15:05**	....	....	....	....	....	....	....	....	....
2011-12	**NY Islanders**	**NHL**	**78**	**20**	**12**	**32**	**12**	**1**	**1**	**3**	**174**	**11.5**	**–18**	**5**	**60.0**	**15:33**	....	....	....	....	....	....	....	....	....

			Regular Season														Playoffs								
Season	Club	League	GP	G	A	Pts	PIM	PP	SH	GW	S	%	+/-	TF	F%	Min	GP	G	A	Pts	PIM	PP	SH	GW	Min
2012-13	EC VSV Villach	Austria	17	10	9	19	2	....	....	....	....	....	....	....	....	....	....	....	....	....	....	....	....	....	....
	NY Islanders	**NHL**	**45**	**16**	**5**	**21**	**12**	**2**	**1**	**3**	**108**	**14.8**	**4**	**22**	**45.5**	**14:48**	**6**	**1**	**3**	**4**	**0**	**0**	**0**	**0**	**12:30**
	NHL Totals		**219**	**75**	**41**	**116**	**42**	**7**	**8**	**10**	**573**	**13.1**		**35**	**45.7**	**15:05**	**15**	**2**	**3**	**5**	**0**	**0**	**0**	**0**	**10:28**

NHL All-Rookie Team (2011)

Traded to **Florida** by **Vancouver** with Steve Bernier and Vancouver's 1st round choice (Quinton Howden) in 2010 Entry Draft for Keith Ballard and Victor Oreskovich, June 25, 2010. Claimed on waivers by **NY Islanders** from **Florida**, October 5, 2010. Signed as a free agent by **Villach** (Austria), October 4, 2012.

GRABOVSKI, Mikhail
(gra-BAWV-skee, mih-kigh-EHL)

Center. Shoots left. 5'11", 183 lbs. Born, Potsdam, East Germany, January 31, 1984. Montreal's 4th choice, 150th overall, in 2004 Entry Draft.

Season	Club	League	GP	G	A	Pts	PIM	PP	SH	GW	S	%	+/-	TF	F%	Min	GP	G	A	Pts	PIM	PP	SH	GW	Min
2001-02	HC Minsk	Belarus	26	10	7	17	16	....	....	....	....	....	....	....	....	....	....	....	....	....	....	....	....	....	....
	Belarus	WJC-A	6	0	1	1	2	....	....	....	....	....	....	....	....	....	....	....	....	....	....	....	....	....	....
2002-03	HC Minsk	Belarus	STATISTICS NOT AVAILABLE																						
2003-04	Nizhnekamsk	Russia	45	6	11	17	26	....	....	....	....	....	....	....	....	....	5	0	0	0	4	....	....	....	....
2004-05	Nizhnekamsk	Russia	60	16	20	36	32	....	....	....	....	....	....	....	....	....	3	2	0	2	2	....	....	....	....
	Belarus	Oly-Q	3	4	3	7	10	....	....	....	....	....	....	....	....	....	....	....	....	....	....	....	....	....	....
	Yunost-Minsk	BelOpen	....	....	....	....	....	....	....	....	....	....	....	....	....	....	5	2	4	6	6	....	....	....	....
2005-06	Dynamo Moscow	Russia	48	10	17	27	28	....	....	....	....	....	....	....	....	....	4	0	0	0	4	....	....	....	....
	Yunost-Minsk	BelOpen	8	6	8	14	10	....	....	....	....	....	....	....	....	....	....	....	....	....	....	....	....	....	....
2006-07	**Montreal**	**NHL**	**3**	**0**	**0**	**0**	**0**	**0**	**0**	**0**	**5**	**0.0**	**–2**	**31**	**41.9**	**13:18**	....	....	....	....	....	....	....	....	....
	Hamilton	AHL	66	17	37	54	34	....	....	....	....	....	....	....	....	....	20	4	7	11	21	....	....	....	....
2007-08	**Montreal**	**NHL**	**24**	**3**	**6**	**9**	**8**	**0**	**0**	**1**	**23**	**13.0**	**–4**	**154**	**33.1**	**11:14**	....	....	....	....	....	....	....	....	....
	Hamilton	AHL	12	8	12	20	6	....	....	....	....	....	....	....	....	....	....	....	....	....	....	....	....	....	....
2008-09	**Toronto**	**NHL**	**78**	**20**	**28**	**48**	**92**	**6**	**0**	**2**	**120**	**16.7**	**–8**	**957**	**44.5**	**16:13**	....	....	....	....	....	....	....	....	....
2009-10	**Toronto**	**NHL**	**59**	**10**	**25**	**35**	**10**	**2**	**1**	**3**	**126**	**7.9**	**3**	**735**	**49.8**	**16:48**	....	....	....	....	....	....	....	....	....
2010-11	**Toronto**	**NHL**	**81**	**29**	**29**	**58**	**60**	**10**	**0**	**4**	**239**	**12.1**	**14**	**1326**	**48.4**	**19:22**	....	....	....	....	....	....	....	....	....
2011-12	**Toronto**	**NHL**	**74**	**23**	**28**	**51**	**51**	**5**	**0**	**2**	**163**	**14.1**	**0**	**905**	**51.5**	**17:36**	....	....	....	....	....	....	....	....	....
2012-13	CSKA Moscow	KHL	29	12	12	24	10	....	....	....	....	....	....	....	....	....	....	....	....	....	....	....	....	....	....
	Toronto	**NHL**	**48**	**9**	**7**	**16**	**24**	**0**	**0**	**1**	**80**	**11.3**	**–10**	**638**	**50.6**	**15:34**	**7**	**0**	**2**	**2**	**2**	**0**	**0**	**0**	**19:06**
	NHL Totals		**367**	**94**	**123**	**217**	**245**	**23**	**1**	**13**	**756**	**12.4**		**4746**	**48.2**	**16:51**	**7**	**0**	**2**	**2**	**2**	**0**	**0**	**0**	**19:06**

Traded to **Toronto** by **Montreal** for Greg Pateryn and Toronto's 2nd round choice (later traded to Chicago, later traded back to Toronto, later traded to Boston - Boston selected Jared Knight) in 2010 Entry Draft, July 3, 2008. Signed as a free agent by **CSKA Moscow** (KHL), September 25, 2012.

GRACHEV, Evgeny
(gra-CHAWF, ehv-GEH-nee) **ST.L.**

Center. Shoots left. 6'4", 225 lbs. Born, Khabarovsk, USSR, February 21, 1990. NY Rangers' 3rd choice, 75th overall, in 2008 Entry Draft.

Season	Club	League	GP	G	A	Pts	PIM	PP	SH	GW	S	%	+/-	TF	F%	Min	GP	G	A	Pts	PIM	PP	SH	GW	Min
2005-06	Yaroslavl 2	Russia-3	1	0	0	0	2	....	....	....	....	....	....	....	....	....	....	....	....	....	....	....	....	....	....
2006-07	Yaroslavl 2	Russia-3	28	7	6	13	6	....	....	....	....	....	....	....	....	....	....	....	....	....	....	....	....	....	....
2007-08	Yaroslavl 2	Russia-3	34	17	20	37	18	....	....	....	....	....	....	....	....	....	....	....	....	....	....	....	....	....	....
	Yaroslavl	Russia	1	0	0	0	0	....	....	....	....	....	....	....	....	....	....	....	....	....	....	....	....	....	....
2008-09	Brampton	OHL	60	40	40	80	22	....	....	....	....	....	....	....	....	....	19	11	14	25	4	....	....	....	....
2009-10	Hartford	AHL	80	12	16	28	14	....	....	....	....	....	....	....	....	....	....	....	....	....	....	....	....	....	....
2010-11	**NY Rangers**	**NHL**	**8**	**0**	**0**	**0**	**0**	**0**	**0**	**0**	**3**	**0.0**	**–3**	**1**	**0.0**	**7:42**	....	....	....	....	....	....	....	....	....
	Connecticut	AHL	73	16	22	38	24	....	....	....	....	....	....	....	....	....	6	0	2	2	4	....	....	....	....
2011-12	**St. Louis**	**NHL**	**26**	**1**	**3**	**4**	**2**	**0**	**0**	**1**	**14**	**7.1**	**–4**	**5**	**20.0**	**9:20**	....	....	....	....	....	....	....	....	....
	Peoria Rivermen	AHL	39	3	7	10	18	....	....	....	....	....	....	....	....	....	....	....	....	....	....	....	....	....	....
2012-13	Peoria Rivermen	AHL	76	11	15	26	40	....	....	....	....	....	....	....	....	....	....	....	....	....	....	....	....	....	....
	NHL Totals		**34**	**1**	**3**	**4**	**2**	**0**	**0**	**1**	**17**	**5.9**		**6**	**16.7**	**8:57**	....	....	....	....	....	....	....	....	....

OHL Rookie of the Year (2009) • Canadian Major Junior All-Rookie Team (2009)

Traded to **St. Louis** by **NY Rangers** for St. Louis' 3rd round choice (Steven Fogarty) in 2011 Entry Draft, June 25, 2011.

GRAGNANI, Marc-Andre
(GRUH-na-nee, MAHRK-AWN-dray)

Defense. Shoots left. 6'2", 201 lbs. Born, Montreal, Que., March 11, 1987. Buffalo's 3rd choice, 87th overall, in 2005 Entry Draft.

Season	Club	League	GP	G	A	Pts	PIM	PP	SH	GW	S	%	+/-	TF	F%	Min	GP	G	A	Pts	PIM	PP	SH	GW	Min
2002-03	West Island Lions	QAAA	34	3	15	18	22	....	....	....	....	....	....	....	....	....	....	....	....	....	....	....	....	....	....
2003-04	P.E.I. Rocket	QMJHL	61	2	13	15	42	....	....	....	....	....	....	....	....	....	11	0	0	0	4	....	....	....	....
2004-05	P.E.I. Rocket	QMJHL	68	10	29	39	48	....	....	....	....	....	....	....	....	....	....	....	....	....	....	....	....	....	....
2005-06	P.E.I. Rocket	QMJHL	62	16	55	71	75	....	....	....	....	....	....	....	....	....	6	1	4	5	14	....	....	....	....
2006-07	P.E.I. Rocket	QMJHL	65	22	46	68	58	....	....	....	....	....	....	....	....	....	7	5	8	13	4	....	....	....	....
2007-08	**Buffalo**	**NHL**	**2**	**0**	**0**	**0**	**4**	**0**	**0**	**0**	**1**	**0.0**	**–2**	**0**	**0.0**	**6:18**	....	....	....	....	....	....	....	....	....
	Rochester	AHL	78	14	38	52	38	....	....	....	....	....	....	....	....	....	....	....	....	....	....	....	....	....	....
2008-09	**Buffalo**	**NHL**	**4**	**0**	**0**	**0**	**2**	**0**	**0**	**0**	**3**	**0.0**	**2**	**0**	**0.0**	**15:23**	....	....	....	....	....	....	....	....	....
	Portland Pirates	AHL	76	9	42	51	59	....	....	....	....	....	....	....	....	....	5	0	2	2	4	....	....	....	....
2009-10	Portland Pirates	AHL	66	12	31	43	37	....	....	....	....	....	....	....	....	....	4	0	2	2	0	....	....	....	....
2010-11	**Buffalo**	**NHL**	**9**	**1**	**2**	**3**	**2**	**0**	**0**	**1**	**11**	**9.1**	**0**	**0**	**0.0**	**15:17**	**7**	**1**	**6**	**7**	**4**	**1**	**0**	**0**	**21:53**
	Portland Pirates	AHL	63	12	48	60	51	....	....	....	....	....	....	....	....	....	....	....	....	....	....	....	....	....	....
2011-12	**Buffalo**	**NHL**	**44**	**1**	**11**	**12**	**20**	**1**	**0**	**0**	**35**	**2.9**	**10**	**1**	**100.0**	**16:23**	....	....	....	....	....	....	....	....	....
	Vancouver	**NHL**	**14**	**1**	**2**	**3**	**6**	**0**	**0**	**0**	**12**	**8.3**	**–4**	**0**	**0.0**	**15:25**	....	....	....	....	....	....	....	....	....
2012-13	Charlotte	AHL	42	3	25	28	29	....	....	....	....	....	....	....	....	....	....	....	....	....	....	....	....	....	....
	Carolina	**NHL**	**1**	**0**	**0**	**0**	**0**	**0**	**0**	**0**	**0**	**0.0**	**0**	**0**	**0.0**	**7:53**	....	....	....	....	....	....	....	....	....
	NHL Totals		**74**	**3**	**15**	**18**	**34**	**1**	**0**	**1**	**62**	**4.8**		**1**	**100.0**	**15:37**	**7**	**1**	**6**	**7**	**4**	**1**	**0**	**0**	**21:54**

AHL First All-Star Team (2011) • Eddie Shore Award (AHL – Outstanding Defenseman) (2011)

Traded to **Vancouver** by **Buffalo** for Alexander Sulzer, February 27, 2012. Signed as a free agent by **Carolina**, July 11, 2012. Signed as a free agent by **Lev Praha** (KHL), May 22, 2013.

GRANLUND, Mikael
(GRAHN-lund, mih-kigh-EHL) **MIN**

Center. Shoots left. 5'10", 186 lbs. Born, Oulu, Finland, February 26, 1992. Minnesota's 1st choice, 9th overall, in 2010 Entry Draft.

Season	Club	League	GP	G	A	Pts	PIM	PP	SH	GW	S	%	+/-	TF	F%	Min	GP	G	A	Pts	PIM	PP	SH	GW	Min
2007-08	Karpat Oulu U18	Fin-U18	31	22	27	49	20	....	....	....	....	....	....	....	....	....	5	3	5	8	0	....	....	....	....
2008-09	Suomi U20	Finland-2	6	4	3	7	0	....	....	....	....	....	....	....	....	....	....	....	....	....	....	....	....	....	....
	Karpat Oulu Jr.	Fin-Jr.	38	22	44	66	45	....	....	....	....	....	....	....	....	....	....	....	....	....	....	....	....	....	....
	Karpat Oulu	Finland	2	0	0	0	0	....	....	....	....	....	....	....	....	....	....	....	....	....	....	....	....	....	....
	Karpat Oulu U18	Fin-U18	....	....	....	....	....	....	....	....	....	....	....	....	....	....	3	2	4	6	2	....	....	....	....
2009-10	Suomi U20	Finland-2	1	0	0	0	0	....	....	....	....	....	....	....	....	....	....	....	....	....	....	....	....	....	....
	HIFK Helsinki	Finland	43	13	27	40	2	....	....	....	....	....	....	....	....	....	6	1	5	6	0	....	....	....	....
2010-11	HIFK Helsinki	Finland	39	8	28	36	14	....	....	....	....	....	....	....	....	....	15	5	*11	*16	4	....	....	....	....
2011-12	HIFK Helsinki	Finland	45	20	31	51	18	....	....	....	....	....	....	....	....	....	4	0	2	2	0	....	....	....	....
2012-13	Houston Aeros	AHL	29	10	18	28	8	....	....	....	....	....	....	....	....	....	5	1	1	2	4	....	....	....	....
	Minnesota	**NHL**	**27**	**2**	**6**	**8**	**6**	**0**	**0**	**0**	**36**	**5.6**	**–4**	**206**	**47.1**	**13:11**	....	....	....	....	....	....	....	....	....
	NHL Totals		**27**	**2**	**6**	**8**	**6**	**0**	**0**	**0**	**36**	**5.6**		**206**	**47.1**	**13:11**	....	....	....	....	....	....	....	....	....

GRANT, Derek
(GRANT, DAIR-ihk) **OTT**

Center. Shoots left. 6'3", 203 lbs. Born, Abbotsford, B.C., April 20, 1990. Ottawa's 5th choice, 119th overall, in 2008 Entry Draft.

Season	Club	League	GP	G	A	Pts	PIM	PP	SH	GW	S	%	+/-	TF	F%	Min	GP	G	A	Pts	PIM	PP	SH	GW	Min
2006-07	Abbotsford Pilots	PIJHL	47	31	20	51	42	....	....	....	....	....	....	....	....	....	11	6	5	11	20	....	....	....	....
2007-08	Langley Chiefs	BCHL	57	24	39	63	44	....	....	....	....	....	....	....	....	....	12	5	5	10	15	....	....	....	....
2008-09	Langley Chiefs	BCHL	35	25	35	60	22	....	....	....	....	....	....	....	....	....	4	2	1	3	2	....	....	....	....
2009-10	Michigan State	CCHA	38	12	18	30	10	....	....	....	....	....	....	....	....	....	....	....	....	....	....	....	....	....	....
2010-11	Michigan State	CCHA	38	8	25	33	44	....	....	....	....	....	....	....	....	....	....	....	....	....	....	....	....	....	....
	Binghamton	AHL	14	1	5	6	0	....	....	....	....	....	....	....	....	....	7	1	1	2	2	....	....	....	....
2011-12	Binghamton	AHL	60	8	15	23	26	....	....	....	....	....	....	....	....	....	....	....	....	....	....	....	....	....	....
2012-13	Binghamton	AHL	63	19	9	28	37	....	....	....	....	....	....	....	....	....	3	0	0	0	6	....	....	....	....
	Ottawa	**NHL**	**5**	**0**	**0**	**0**	**0**	**0**	**0**	**0**	**5**	**0.0**	**–1**	**31**	**54.8**	**8:40**	....	....	....	....	....	....	....	....	....
	NHL Totals		**5**	**0**	**0**	**0**	**0**	**0**	**0**	**0**	**5**	**0.0**		**31**	**54.8**	**8:40**	....	....	....	....	....	....	....	....	....

GRANT, Triston

(GRANT, TRIHS-tuhn) **DET**

Left wing. Shoots left. 6'2", 215 lbs. Born, Neepawa, Man., February 2, 1984. Philadelphia's 10th choice, 286th overall, in 2004 Entry Draft.

			Regular Season														Playoffs								
Season	Club	League	GP	G	A	Pts	PIM	PP	SH	GW	S	%	+/-	TF	F%	Min	GP	G	A	Pts	PIM	PP	SH	GW	Min
2000-01	Neepawa Natives	MJHL	STATISTICS NOT AVAILABLE																						
	Lethbridge	WHL	23	2	0	2	75	....	....	....	....	....	....	....	....	....	5	0	0	0	11	....	....	....	....
2001-02	Lethbridge	WHL	36	8	1	9	110	....	....	....	....	....	....	....	....	....	....	....	....	....	....	....	....	....	....
	Vancouver Giants	WHL	21	2	4	6	53	....	....	....	....	....	....	....	....	....	....	....	....	....	....	....	....	....	....
2002-03	Vancouver Giants	WHL	72	10	10	20	200	....	....	....	....	....	....	....	....	....	4	0	0	0	10	....	....	....	....
2003-04	Vancouver Giants	WHL	69	10	8	18	267	....	....	....	....	....	....	....	....	....	11	1	1	2	33	....	....	....	....
2004-05	Vancouver Giants	WHL	70	20	12	32	193	....	....	....	....	....	....	....	....	....	6	1	0	1	8	....	....	....	....
2005-06	Philadelphia	AHL	64	2	3	5	190	....	....	....	....	....	....	....	....	....	....	....	....	....	....	....	....	....	....
2006-07	**Philadelphia**	**NHL**	**8**	**0**	**1**	**1**	**10**	**0**	**0**	**0**	**3**	**0.0**	**–1**	**0**	**0.0**	**4:32**	....	....	....	....	....	....	....	....	....
	Philadelphia	AHL	61	5	6	11	199	....	....	....	....	....	....	....	....	....	....	....	....	....	....	....	....	....	....
2007-08	Philadelphia	AHL	72	10	11	21	181	....	....	....	....	....	....	....	....	....	12	0	2	2	34	....	....	....	....
2008-09	Milwaukee	AHL	55	3	8	11	153	....	....	....	....	....	....	....	....	....	11	1	1	2	12	....	....	....	....
2009-10	**Nashville**	**NHL**	**3**	**0**	**0**	**0**	**9**	**0**	**0**	**0**	**2**	**0.0**	**–1**	**0**	**0.0**	**7:14**	....	....	....	....	....	....	....	....	....
	Milwaukee	AHL	74	12	13	25	236	....	....	....	....	....	....	....	....	....	5	0	2	2	16	....	....	....	....
2010-11	Rochester	AHL	56	7	6	13	144	....	....	....	....	....	....	....	....	....	....	....	....	....	....	....	....	....	....
2011-12	Oklahoma City	AHL	53	11	4	15	163	....	....	....	....	....	....	....	....	....	7	0	0	0	29	....	....	....	....
2012-13	Grand Rapids	AHL	75	4	6	10	196	....	....	....	....	....	....	....	....	....	24	2	2	4	26	....	....	....	....
	NHL Totals		**11**	**0**	**1**	**1**	**19**	**0**	**0**	**0**	**5**	**0.0**		**0**	**0.0**	**5:16**	....	....	....	....	....	....	....	....	....

Traded to **Nashville** by **Phladelphia** with Philadelphia's 7th round choice (later traded to St. Louis – St. Louis selected Maxwell Tardy) in 2009 Entry Draft for Janne Niskala, June 24, 2008. Signed as a free agent by **Florida**, July 2, 2010. Signed as a free agent by **Grand Rapids** (AHL), July 9, 2012.

GREBESHKOV, Denis

(greh-behsh-KAHV, DEH-nihs) **EDM**

Defense. Shoots left. 6', 209 lbs. Born, Yaroslavl, USSR, October 11, 1983. Los Angeles' 1st choice, 18th overall, in 2002 Entry Draft.

			Regular Season														Playoffs								
Season	Club	League	GP	G	A	Pts	PIM	PP	SH	GW	S	%	+/-	TF	F%	Min	GP	G	A	Pts	PIM	PP	SH	GW	Min
99-2000	Yaroslavl 2	Russia-3	42	2	1	3	12	....	....	....	....	....	....	....	....	....	6	0	0	0	2	....	....	....	....
2000-01	Yaroslavl 2	Russia-3	34	7	2	9	20	....	....	....	....	....	....	....	....	....	....	....	....	....	....	....	....	....	....
2001-02	Yaroslavl 2	Russia-3	7	1	1	2	2	....	....	....	....	....	....	....	....	....	....	....	....	....	....	....	....	....	....
	Yaroslavl	Russia	27	1	2	3	10	....	....	....	....	....	....	....	....	....	....	....	....	....	....	....	....	....	....
2002-03	Yaroslavl	Russia	48	0	7	7	26	....	....	....	....	....	....	....	....	....	10	0	1	1	2	....	....	....	....
2003-04	**Los Angeles**	**NHL**	**4**	**0**	**1**	**1**	**0**	**0**	**0**	**0**	**5**	**0.0**	**–4**	**0**	**0.0**	**18:29**	....	....	....	....	....	....	....	....	....
	Manchester	AHL	43	2	7	9	34	....	....	....	....	....	....	....	....	....	6	0	1	1	6	....	....	....	....
2004-05	Manchester	AHL	75	5	44	49	87	....	....	....	....	....	....	....	....	....	6	0	4	4	2	....	....	....	....
2005-06	**Los Angeles**	**NHL**	**8**	**0**	**2**	**2**	**12**	**0**	**0**	**0**	**10**	**0.0**	**–4**	**0**	**0.0**	**15:16**	....	....	....	....	....	....	....	....	....
	Manchester	AHL	48	2	25	27	59	....	....	....	....	....	....	....	....	....	....	....	....	....	....	....	....	....	....
	NY Islanders	**NHL**	**21**	**0**	**3**	**3**	**8**	**0**	**0**	**0**	**14**	**0.0**	**–8**	**0**	**0.0**	**17:11**	....	....	....	....	....	....	....	....	....
	Bridgeport	AHL	....	....	....	....	....	....	....	....	....	....	....	....	....	....	7	1	1	2	8	....	....	....	....
2006-07	Yaroslavl	Russia	47	8	9	17	79	....	....	....	....	....	....	....	....	....	7	0	2	2	6	....	....	....	....
2007-08	**Edmonton**	**NHL**	**71**	**3**	**15**	**18**	**22**	**1**	**0**	**0**	**34**	**8.8**	**2**	**0**	**0.0**	**16:53**	....	....	....	....	....	....	....	....	....
2008-09	**Edmonton**	**NHL**	**72**	**7**	**32**	**39**	**38**	**2**	**0**	**0**	**62**	**11.3**	**12**	**0**	**0.0**	**21:10**	....	....	....	....	....	....	....	....	....
2009-10	**Edmonton**	**NHL**	**47**	**6**	**13**	**19**	**26**	**1**	**0**	**0**	**43**	**14.0**	**–16**	**1**	**100.0**	**21:49**	....	....	....	....	....	....	....	....	....
	Russia	Olympics	4	0	1	1	2	....	....	....	....	....	....	....	....	....	....	....	....	....	....	....	....	....	....
	Nashville	**NHL**	**4**	**1**	**1**	**2**	**6**	**0**	**0**	**0**	**4**	**25.0**	**0**	**0**	**0.0**	**16:28**	**2**	**0**	**2**	**2**	**0**	**0**	**0**	**0**	**11:22**
2010-11	St. Petersburg	KHL	54	8	9	17	44	....	....	....	....	....	....	....	....	....	11	0	5	5	12	....	....	....	....
2011-12	St. Petersburg	KHL	46	0	8	8	51	....	....	....	....	....	....	....	....	....	6	0	2	2	2	....	....	....	....
2012-13	St. Petersburg	KHL	14	0	1	1	8	....	....	....	....	....	....	....	....	....	....	....	....	....	....	....	....	....	....
	Khanty-Mansiisk	KHL	30	0	8	8	14	....	....	....	....	....	....	....	....	....	4	0	0	0	4	....	....	....	....
	NHL Totals		**227**	**17**	**67**	**84**	**112**	**4**	**0**	**0**	**172**	**9.9**		**1**	**100.0**	**19:15**	**2**	**0**	**2**	**2**	**0**	**0**	**0**	**0**	**11:22**

Traded to **NY Islanders** by **Los Angeles** with Jeff Tambellini for Mark Parrish and Brent Sopel, March 8, 2006. Signed as a free agent by **Yaroslavl** (Russia), July 10, 2006. Traded to **Edmonton** by **NY Islanders** for Marc-Andre Bergeron and Edmonton's 3rd round choice (later traded back to Edmonton, later traded to Anaheim, later traded back to NY Islanders - NY Islanders selected Kirill Petrov) in 2008 Entry Draft, February 18, 2007. Traded to **Nashville** by **Edmonton** for Nashville's 2nd round choice (Curtis Hamilton) in 2010 Entry Draft, March 1, 2010. Signed as a free agent by **St. Petersburg** (KHL), July 28, 2010. Signed as a free agent by **Khanty-Mansiisk** (KHL), October 30, 2013. Signed as a free agent b y **Edmonton**, July 19, 2013.

GREEN, Josh

(GREEN, JAWSH)

Left wing. Shoots left. 6'4", 225 lbs. Born, Camrose, Alta., November 16, 1977. Los Angeles' 1st choice, 30th overall, in 1996 Entry Draft.

			Regular Season														Playoffs								
Season	Club	League	GP	G	A	Pts	PIM	PP	SH	GW	S	%	+/-	TF	F%	Min	GP	G	A	Pts	PIM	PP	SH	GW	Min
1992-93	Camrose Kodiaks	Minor-AB	60	55	45	100	80	....	....	....	....	....	....	....	....	....	....	....	....	....	....	....	....	....	....
1993-94	Medicine Hat	WHL	63	22	22	44	43	....	....	....	....	....	....	....	....	....	3	0	0	0	4	....	....	....	....
1994-95	Medicine Hat	WHL	68	32	23	55	64	....	....	....	....	....	....	....	....	....	5	5	1	6	2	....	....	....	....
1995-96	Medicine Hat	WHL	46	18	25	43	55	....	....	....	....	....	....	....	....	....	5	2	2	4	4	....	....	....	....
1996-97	Medicine Hat	WHL	51	25	32	57	61	....	....	....	....	....	....	....	....	....	....	....	....	....	....	....	....	....	....
	Swift Current	WHL	23	10	15	25	33	....	....	....	....	....	....	....	....	....	10	9	7	16	19	....	....	....	....
1997-98	Swift Current	WHL	5	9	1	10	9	....	....	....	....	....	....	....	....	....	....	....	....	....	....	....	....	....	....
	Portland	WHL	26	26	18	44	27	....	....	....	....	....	....	....	....	....	....	....	....	....	....	....	....	....	....
	Fredericton	AHL	43	16	15	31	14	....	....	....	....	....	....	....	....	....	4	1	3	4	6	....	....	....	....
1998-99	**Los Angeles**	**NHL**	**27**	**1**	**3**	**4**	**8**	**1**	**0**	**0**	**35**	**2.9**	**–5**	**2**	**50.0**	**11:44**	....	....	....	....	....	....	....	....	....
	Springfield	AHL	41	15	15	30	29	....	....	....	....	....	....	....	....	....	....	....	....	....	....	....	....	....	....
99-2000	**NY Islanders**	**NHL**	**49**	**12**	**14**	**26**	**41**	**2**	**0**	**3**	**109**	**11.0**	**–7**	**12**	**50.0**	**13:36**	....	....	....	....	....	....	....	....	....
	Lowell	AHL	17	6	2	8	19	....	....	....	....	....	....	....	....	....	....	....	....	....	....	....	....	....	....
2000-01	Hamilton	AHL	2	2	0	2	2	....	....	....	....	....	....	....	....	....	....	....	....	....	....	....	....	....	....
	Edmonton	**NHL**	....	....	....	....	....	....	....	....	....	....	....	....	....	....	**3**	**0**	**0**	**0**	**0**	**0**	**0**	**0**	**7:55**
2001-02	**Edmonton**	**NHL**	**61**	**10**	**5**	**15**	**52**	**1**	**0**	**1**	**78**	**12.8**	**9**	**18**	**38.9**	**10:05**	....	....	....	....	....	....	....	....	....
2002-03	**Edmonton**	**NHL**	**20**	**0**	**2**	**2**	**12**	**0**	**0**	**0**	**20**	**0.0**	**–3**	**5**	**0.0**	**10:22**	....	....	....	....	....	....	....	....	....
	NY Rangers	**NHL**	**4**	**0**	**0**	**0**	**2**	**0**	**0**	**0**	**3**	**0.0**	**–1**	**0**	**0.0**	**9:07**	....	....	....	....	....	....	....	....	....
	Washington	**NHL**	**21**	**1**	**2**	**3**	**7**	**0**	**0**	**0**	**20**	**5.0**	**1**	**3**	**0.0**	**8:07**	....	....	....	....	....	....	....	....	....
2003-04	**Calgary**	**NHL**	**36**	**2**	**4**	**6**	**24**	**0**	**0**	**0**	**47**	**4.3**	**–3**	**39**	**30.8**	**11:18**	....	....	....	....	....	....	....	....	....
	Lowell	AHL	22	6	9	15	46	....	....	....	....	....	....	....	....	....	....	....	....	....	....	....	....	....	....
	NY Rangers	**NHL**	**14**	**3**	**2**	**5**	**8**	**0**	**0**	**1**	**29**	**10.3**	**0**	**9**	**55.6**	**14:16**	....	....	....	....	....	....	....	....	....
2004-05	Manitoba Moose	AHL	67	21	19	40	72	....	....	....	....	....	....	....	....	....	14	9	5	14	26	....	....	....	....
2005-06	**Vancouver**	**NHL**	**33**	**4**	**2**	**6**	**14**	**0**	**0**	**0**	**35**	**11.4**	**2**	**146**	**40.4**	**8:35**	....	....	....	....	....	....	....	....	....
	Manitoba Moose	AHL	35	7	24	31	33	....	....	....	....	....	....	....	....	....	10	5	5	10	23	....	....	....	....
2006-07	**Vancouver**	**NHL**	**57**	**2**	**5**	**7**	**25**	**0**	**0**	**2**	**74**	**2.7**	**0**	**266**	**40.6**	**11:25**	**9**	**0**	**1**	**1**	**12**	**0**	**0**	**0**	**10:13**
2007-08	Salzburg	Austria	43	20	22	42	100	....	....	....	....	....	....	....	....	....	....	....	....	....	....	....	....	....	....
2008-09	Iowa Chops	AHL	39	10	14	24	52	....	....	....	....	....	....	....	....	....	....	....	....	....	....	....	....	....	....
	Anaheim	**NHL**	....	....	....	....	....	....	....	....	....	....	....	....	....	....	**5**	**0**	**0**	**0**	**0**	**0**	**0**	**0**	**5:53**
2009-10	MODO	Sweden	47	12	8	20	79	....	....	....	....	....	....	....	....	....	....	....	....	....	....	....	....	....	....
2010-11	**Anaheim**	**NHL**	**12**	**0**	**0**	**0**	**6**	**0**	**0**	**0**	**10**	**0.0**	**–3**	**7**	**42.9**	**10:00**	....	....	....	....	....	....	....	....	....
	Syracuse Crunch	AHL	69	15	31	46	74	....	....	....	....	....	....	....	....	....	....	....	....	....	....	....	....	....	....
2011-12	**Edmonton**	**NHL**	**7**	**1**	**1**	**2**	**7**	**1**	**0**	**0**	**14**	**7.1**	**–6**	**37**	**43.2**	**11:49**	....	....	....	....	....	....	....	....	....
	Oklahoma City	AHL	51	16	21	37	39	....	....	....	....	....	....	....	....	....	9	4	2	6	4	....	....	....	....
2012-13	Oklahoma City	AHL	49	9	15	24	25	....	....	....	....	....	....	....	....	....	17	4	8	12	6	....	....	....	....
	NHL Totals		**341**	**36**	**40**	**76**	**206**	**5**	**0**	**7**	**474**	**7.6**		**544**	**39.9**	**11:01**	**17**	**0**	**1**	**1**	**12**	**0**	**0**	**0**	**8:32**

Traded to **NY Islanders** by **Los Angeles** with Olli Jokinen, Mathieu Biron and Los Angeles' 1st round choice (Taylor Pyatt) in 1999 Entry Draft for Ziggy Palffy, Brian Smolinski, Marcel Cousineau and New Jersey's 4th round choice (previously acquired, Los Angeles selected Daniel Johansson) in 1999 Entry Draft, June 20, 1999. Traded to **Edmonton** by **NY Islanders** with Eric Brewer and NY Islanders' 2nd round choice (Brad Winchester) in 2000 Entry Draft for Roman Hamrlik, June 24, 2000. • Missed majority of 2000-01 due to shoulder injury vs. Detroit, October 10, 2000. Traded to **NY Rangers** by **Edmonton** for future considerations, December 12, 2002. Claimed on waivers by **Washington** from **NY Rangers**, January 15, 2003. Signed as a free agent by **Calgary**, July 17, 2003. Claimed on waivers by **NY Rangers** from **Calgary**, March 6, 2004. Signed to a PTO (professional tryout) contract by **Manitoba** (AHL), September 27, 2004. Signed as a free agent by **Vancouver**, August 23, 2005. Signed as a free agent by **Salzburg** (Austria), July 30, 2007. Signed as a free agent by **Anaheim**, July 22, 2008. • Missed majority of 2008-09 due to various injuries. Signed as a free agent by **MODO** (Sweden). July 9, 2009. Signed as a free agent by **Anaheim**, July 12, 2010. Signed as a free agent by **Edmonton**, July 3, 2011. Signed as a free agent by **Oklahoma City** (AHL), July 20, 2012.

GREEN, Mike

(GREEN, MIGHK) **WSH**

Defense. Shoots right. 6'1", 207 lbs. Born, Calgary, Alta., October 12, 1985. Washington's 3rd choice, 29th overall, in 2004 Entry Draft.

			Regular Season														Playoffs								
Season	Club	League	GP	G	A	Pts	PIM	PP	SH	GW	S	%	+/-	TF	F%	Min	GP	G	A	Pts	PIM	PP	SH	GW	Min
2000-01	Cgy. North Stars	AMHL	36	4	23	27	34	....	....	....	....	....	....	....	....	....	....	....	....	....	....	....	....	....	....
	Saskatoon Blades	WHL	5	0	2	2	0	....	....	....	....	....	....	....	....	....	....	....	....	....	....	....	....	....	....
2001-02	Saskatoon Blades	WHL	62	3	20	23	57	....	....	....	....	....	....	....	....	....	7	0	1	1	2	....	....	....	....
2002-03	Saskatoon Blades	WHL	72	6	36	42	70	....	....	....	....	....	....	....	....	....	6	0	2	2	6	....	....	....	....
2003-04	Saskatoon Blades	WHL	59	14	25	39	92	....	....	....	....	....	....	....	....	....	....	....	....	....	....	....	....	....	....
2004-05	Saskatoon Blades	WHL	67	14	52	66	105	....	....	....	....	....	....	....	....	....	4	0	0	0	6	....	....	....	....

			Regular Season														Playoffs								
Season	Club	League	GP	G	A	Pts	PIM	PP	SH	GW	S	%	+/-	TF	F%	Min	GP	G	A	Pts	PIM	PP	SH	GW	Min
2005-06	Washington	NHL	22	1	2	3	18	0	0	0	13	7.7	–8	0	0.0	14:54	....	....	....	....	....	....	....	....	....
	Hershey Bears	AHL	56	9	34	43	79	....	....	....	....	....	....	....	....	....	21	3	15	18	30	....	....	....	....
2006-07	Washington	NHL	70	2	10	12	36	0	0	0	68	2.9	–10	0	0.0	15:29	....	....	....	....	....	....	....	....	....
2007-08	Washington	NHL	82	18	38	56	62	8	0	4	234	7.7	6	1	0.0	23:38	7	3	4	7	15	2	0	0	26:59
2008-09	Washington	NHL	68	31	42	73	68	18	1	4	243	12.8	24	0	0.0	25:46	14	1	8	9	12	1	0	0	24:59
2009-10	Washington	NHL	75	19	57	76	54	10	0	4	205	9.3	39	0	0.0	25:29	7	0	3	3	12	0	0	0	26:01
2010-11	Washington	NHL	49	8	16	24	48	5	0	1	115	7.0	6	0	0.0	25:12	8	1	5	6	8	1	0	0	21:27
2011-12	Washington	NHL	32	3	4	7	12	3	0	1	64	4.7	5	0	0.0	21:03	14	2	2	4	10	1	0	1	23:45
2012-13	Washington	NHL	35	12	14	26	20	4	0	2	96	12.5	–3	0	0.0	24:51	7	2	2	4	4	1	0	1	25:32
	NHL Totals		433	94	183	277	318	48	1	16	1038	9.1		1	0.0	22:37	57	9	24	33	61	6	0	2	24:38

WHL East First All-Star Team (2005) • AHL All-Rookie Team (2006) • NHL First All-Star Team (2009, 2010)
Played in NHL All-Star Game (2011)

GREENE, Andy
(GREEN, AN-dee) **N.J.**

Defense. Shoots left. 5'11", 190 lbs. Born, Trenton, MI, October 30, 1982.

2002-03	Miami U.	CCHA	41	4	19	23	64	....	....	....	....	....	....	....	....	....	....	....	....	....	....	....	....	....	....
2003-04	Miami U.	CCHA	41	7	19	26	78	....	....	....	....	....	....	....	....	....	....	....	....	....	....	....	....	....	....
2004-05	Miami U.	CCHA	38	7	27	34	66	....	....	....	....	....	....	....	....	....	....	....	....	....	....	....	....	....	....
2005-06	Miami U.	CCHA	39	9	22	31	48	....	....	....	....	....	....	....	....	....	....	....	....	....	....	....	....	....	....
2006-07	New Jersey	NHL	23	1	5	6	6	1	0	0	23	4.3	–1	0	0.0	14:15	11	2	1	3	2	0	0	1	17:04
	Lowell Devils	AHL	52	5	16	21	28	....	....	....	....	....	....	....	....	....	....	....	....	....	....	....	....	....	....
2007-08	New Jersey	NHL	59	2	8	10	22	2	0	0	50	4.0	0	0	0.0	19:30	2	0	0	0	0	0	0	0	15:11
2008-09	New Jersey	NHL	49	2	7	9	22	0	0	0	38	5.3	3	0	0.0	16:17	3	0	1	1	0	0	0	0	15:18
2009-10	New Jersey	NHL	78	6	31	37	14	4	0	4	86	7.0	9	0	0.0	23:32	5	1	1	2	6	1	0	0	19:42
2010-11	New Jersey	NHL	82	4	19	23	22	1	0	1	91	4.4	–23	0	0.0	22:22	....	....	....	....	....	....	....	....	....
2011-12	New Jersey	NHL	56	1	15	16	16	0	0	0	53	1.9	3	0	0.0	19:30	24	0	1	1	8	0	0	0	22:02
2012-13	New Jersey	NHL	48	4	12	16	20	2	1	1	63	6.3	12	0	0.0	23:02	....	....	....	....	....	....	....	....	....
	NHL Totals		395	20	97	117	122	10	1	6	404	5.0		0	0.0	20:37	45	3	4	7	16	1	0	1	19:48

CCHA All-Rookie Team (2003) • CCHA First All-Star Team (2004, 2005, 2006) • NCAA West First All-American Team (2006)
Signed as a free agent by **New Jersey**, April 4, 2006.

GREENE, Matt
(GREEN, MAT) **L.A.**

Defense. Shoots right. 6'3", 232 lbs. Born, Grand Ledge, MI, May 13, 1983. Edmonton's 4th choice, 44th overall, in 2002 Entry Draft.

2000-01	USNTDP	U-18	34	0	9	9	8	....	....	....	....	....	....	....	....	....	....	....	....	....	....	....	....	....	....
	USNTDP	USHL	20	0	1	1	51	....	....	....	....	....	....	....	....	....	....	....	....	....	....	....	....	....	....
2001-02	Green Bay	USHL	55	4	20	24	150	....	....	....	....	....	....	....	....	....	7	0	1	1	31	....	....	....	....
2002-03	North Dakota	WCHA	39	0	4	4	*135	....	....	....	....	....	....	....	....	....	....	....	....	....	....	....	....	....	....
2003-04	North Dakota	WCHA	40	1	16	17	86	....	....	....	....	....	....	....	....	....	....	....	....	....	....	....	....	....	....
2004-05	North Dakota	WCHA	43	2	8	10	*126	....	....	....	....	....	....	....	....	....	....	....	....	....	....	....	....	....	....
2005-06	Edmonton	NHL	27	0	2	2	43	0	0	0	10	0.0	–6	0	0.0	11:13	18	0	1	1	34	0	0	0	10:03
	Iowa Stars	AHL	26	2	5	7	47	....	....	....	....	....	....	....	....	....	....	....	....	....	....	....	....	....	....
2006-07	Edmonton	NHL	78	1	9	10	109	0	0	0	52	1.9	–22	0	0.0	17:36	....	....	....	....	....	....	....	....	....
2007-08	Edmonton	NHL	46	0	1	1	53	0	0	0	28	0.0	–3	0	0.0	16:42	....	....	....	....	....	....	....	....	....
	Springfield	AHL	1	0	0	0	0	....	....	....	....	....	....	....	....	....	....	....	....	....	....	....	....	....	....
2008-09	Los Angeles	NHL	82	2	12	14	111	0	0	0	76	2.6	1	1	100.0	19:44	....	....	....	....	....	....	....	....	....
2009-10	Los Angeles	NHL	75	2	7	9	83	0	0	1	57	3.5	4	0	0.0	17:29	6	0	1	1	0	0	0	0	18:45
2010-11	Los Angeles	NHL	71	2	9	11	70	0	0	1	50	4.0	3	0	0.0	16:59	6	0	0	0	14	0	0	0	16:44
2011-12 ♦	Los Angeles	NHL	82	4	11	15	58	0	0	2	76	5.3	4	0	0.0	16:40	20	2	4	6	12	0	1	1	16:06
2012-13	Los Angeles	NHL	5	0	1	1	8	0	0	0	3	0.0	–1	0	0.0	15:17	9	0	2	2	6	0	0	0	15:29
	NHL Totals		466	11	52	63	535	0	0	4	352	3.1		1	100.0	17:13	59	2	8	10	66	0	1	1	14:30

USHL Second All-Star Team (2002)
Traded to **Los Angeles** by **Edmonton** with Jarret Stoll for Lubomir Visnovsky, June 29, 2008. • Missed majority of 2012-13 due to back injury vs. Chicago, January 19, 2013.

GREENING, Colin
(GREEN-ihng, KAW-lihn) **OTT**

Center/Left wing. Shoots left. 6'3", 212 lbs. Born, St. John's, Nfld., March 9, 1986. Ottawa's 8th choice, 204th overall, in 2005 Entry Draft.

2002-03	St. John's	NFAHA	60	24	34	58	48	....	....	....	....	....	....	....	....	....	....	....	....	....	....	....	....	....	....
2003-04	Upper Canada	High-ON	53	30	43	73	40	....	....	....	....	....	....	....	....	....	....	....	....	....	....	....	....	....	....
2004-05	Upper Canada	High-ON	35	24	22	46	24	....	....	....	....	....	....	....	....	....	....	....	....	....	....	....	....	....	....
2005-06	Nanaimo Clippers	BCHL	56	27	35	62	46	....	....	....	....	....	....	....	....	....	5	3	0	3	2	....	....	....	....
2006-07	Cornell Big Red	ECAC	31	11	8	19	26	....	....	....	....	....	....	....	....	....	....	....	....	....	....	....	....	....	....
2007-08	Cornell Big Red	ECAC	36	14	19	33	41	....	....	....	....	....	....	....	....	....	....	....	....	....	....	....	....	....	....
2008-09	Cornell Big Red	ECAC	36	15	16	31	28	....	....	....	....	....	....	....	....	....	....	....	....	....	....	....	....	....	....
2009-10	Cornell Big Red	ECAC	34	15	20	35	31	....	....	....	....	....	....	....	....	....	....	....	....	....	....	....	....	....	....
2010-11	Ottawa	NHL	24	6	7	13	10	0	0	2	57	10.5	2	24	45.8	15:05	....	....	....	....	....	....	....	....	....
	Binghamton	AHL	59	15	25	40	41	....	....	....	....	....	....	....	....	....	23	1	4	5	13	....	....	....	....
2011-12	Ottawa	NHL	82	17	20	37	46	4	0	0	184	9.2	–4	62	41.9	15:35	7	0	1	1	0	0	0	0	13:59
2012-13	Aalborg Pirates	Denmark	17	13	12	25	12	....	....	....	....	....	....	....	....	....	....	....	....	....	....	....	....	....	....
	Ottawa	NHL	47	8	11	19	11	2	0	2	80	10.0	5	47	46.8	14:44	10	3	1	4	2	0	0	1	15:57
	NHL Totals		153	31	38	69	67	6	0	4	321	9.7		133	44.4	15:15	17	3	2	5	2	0	0	1	15:08

ECAC Second All-Star Team (2008, 2009, 2010)
Signed as a free agent by **Aalborg** (Denmark), October 21, 2012.

GRIGORENKO, Mikhail
(grih-gohr-EHN-koh, mih-khigh-IHL) **BUF**

Center. Shoots left. 6'3", 215 lbs. Born, Khabarovsk, Russia, May 16, 1994. Buffalo's 1st choice, 12th overall, in 2012 Entry Draft.

2010-11	CSKA Jr.	Russia-Jr.	43	17	18	35	22	....	....	....	....	....	....	....	....	....	10	1	4	5	4	....	....	....	....
2011-12	Quebec Remparts	QMJHL	59	40	45	85	12	....	....	....	....	....	....	....	....	....	11	3	7	10	4	....	....	....	....
2012-13	Quebec Remparts	QMJHL	33	30	24	54	8	....	....	....	....	....	....	....	....	....	11	5	9	14	0	....	....	....	....
	Buffalo	NHL	25	1	4	5	0	0	0	0	31	3.2	–1	149	38.3	10:14	....	....	....	....	....	....	....	....	....
	Rochester	AHL	....	....	....	....	....	....	....	....	....	....	....	....	....	....	2	0	0	0	0	....	....	....	....
	NHL Totals		25	1	4	5	0	0	0	0	31	3.2		149	38.3	10:14	....	....	....	....	....	....	....	....	....

QMJHL All-Rookie Team (2012) • QMJHL First All-Star Team (2012) • Canadian Major Junior Rookie of the Year (2012)

GROSSMANN, Nicklas
(GROHS-man, NIHK-luhs) **PHI**

Defense. Shoots left. 6'4", 230 lbs. Born, Stockholm, Sweden, January 22, 1985. Dallas' 4th choice, 56th overall, in 2004 Entry Draft.

2002-03	Sodertalje SK Jr.	Swe-Jr.	34	1	1	2	32	....	....	....	....	....	....	....	....	....	....	....	....	....	....	....	....	....	....
2003-04	Sodertalje SK Jr.	Swe-Jr.	33	1	2	3	32	....	....	....	....	....	....	....	....	....	2	0	0	0	0	....	....	....	....
	Sodertalje SK	Sweden	1	0	0	0	0	....	....	....	....	....	....	....	....	....	....	....	....	....	....	....	....	....	....
2004-05	Sodertalje SK Jr.	Swe-Jr.	12	3	6	9	8	....	....	....	....	....	....	....	....	....	1	0	0	0	0	....	....	....	....
	Sodertalje SK	Sweden	31	0	2	2	14	....	....	....	....	....	....	....	....	....	9	0	0	0	0	....	....	....	....
2005-06	Iowa Stars	AHL	61	2	3	5	49	....	....	....	....	....	....	....	....	....	7	0	1	1	4	....	....	....	....
2006-07	Dallas	NHL	8	0	0	0	4	0	0	0	8	0.0	–1	0	0.0	12:49	....	....	....	....	....	....	....	....	....
	Iowa Stars	AHL	67	2	8	10	40	....	....	....	....	....	....	....	....	....	8	0	0	0	10	....	....	....	....
2007-08	Dallas	NHL	62	0	7	7	22	0	0	0	34	0.0	10	0	0.0	15:33	18	1	1	2	6	0	0	0	18:37
	Iowa Stars	AHL	10	0	0	0	10	....	....	....	....	....	....	....	....	....	....	....	....	....	....	....	....	....	....
2008-09	Dallas	NHL	81	2	10	12	51	0	0	1	60	3.3	–8	0	0.0	17:39	....	....	....	....	....	....	....	....	....
2009-10	Dallas	NHL	71	0	7	7	32	0	0	0	58	0.0	–3	1	0.0	19:11	....	....	....	....	....	....	....	....	....
2010-11	Dallas	NHL	59	1	9	10	35	0	0	0	38	2.6	7	0	0.0	18:12	....	....	....	....	....	....	....	....	....
2011-12	Dallas	NHL	52	0	5	5	26	0	0	0	38	0.0	0	0	0.0	18:59	....	....	....	....	....	....	....	....	....
	Philadelphia	NHL	22	0	6	6	10	0	0	0	18	0.0	5	0	0.0	18:25	9	0	1	1	8	0	0	0	18:55
2012-13	Sodertalje SK	Sweden-2	4	0	1	1	4	....	....	....	....	....	....	....	....	....	....	....	....	....	....	....	....	....	....
	Philadelphia	NHL	30	1	3	4	21	0	0	0	21	4.8	–1	0	0.0	18:20	....	....	....	....	....	....	....	....	....
	NHL Totals		385	4	47	51	201	0	0	1	275	1.5		1	0.0	17:51	27	1	2	3	14	0	0	0	18:43

Traded to **Philadelphia** by **Dallas** for Los Angeles' 2nd round choice (previously acquired, Dallas selected Devin Shore) in 2012 Entry Draft and Minnesota's 3rd round choice (previously acquired, later traded to Pittsburgh – Pittsburgh selected Jake Guentzel) in 2013 Entry Draft, February 16, 2012. Signed as a free agent by **Sodertalje** (Sweden-2), November 14, 2012.

GRYBA, Eric

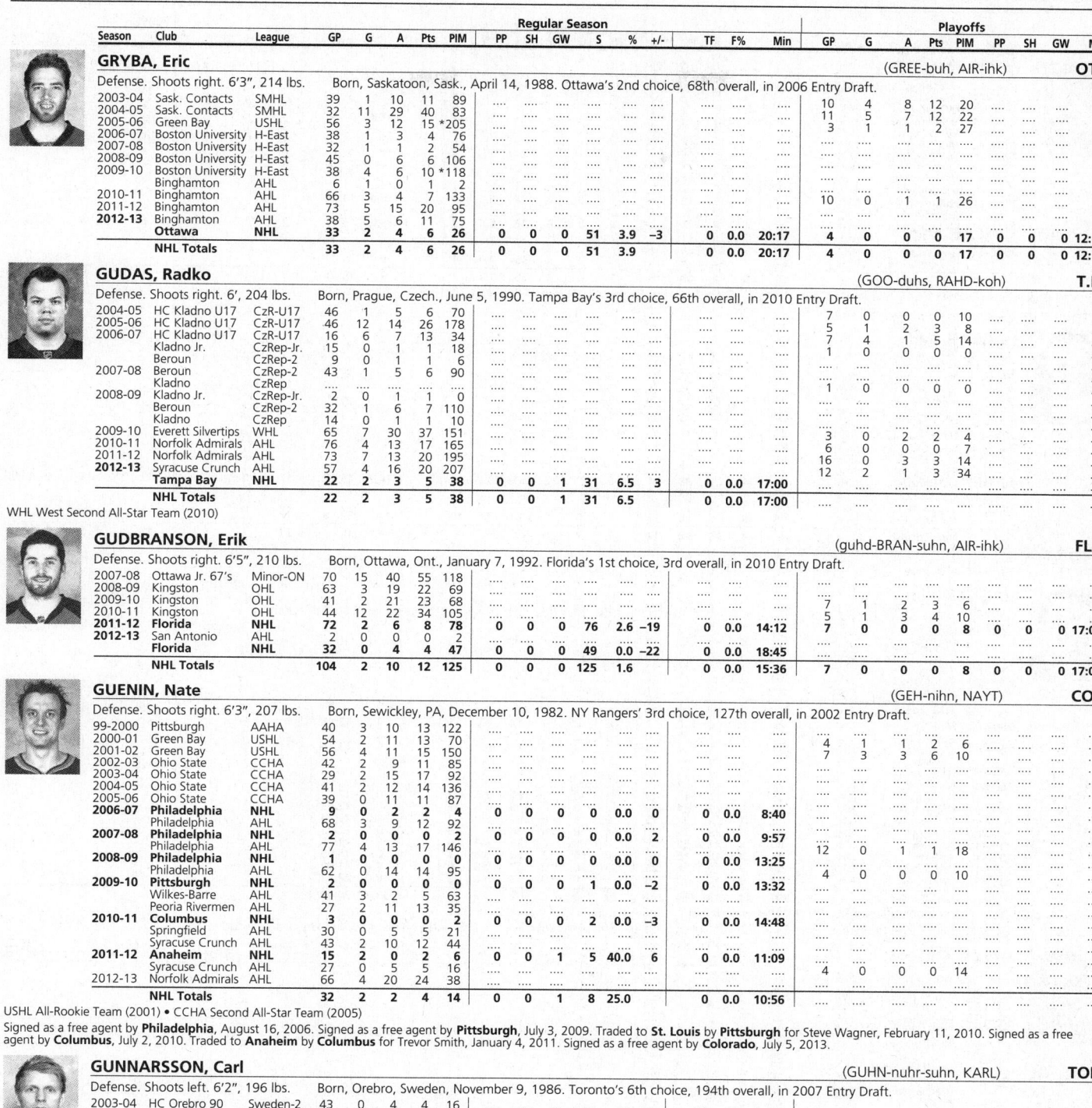

(GREE-buh, AIR-ihk) **OTT**

Defense. Shoots right. 6'3", 214 lbs. Born, Saskatoon, Sask., April 14, 1988. Ottawa's 2nd choice, 68th overall, in 2006 Entry Draft.

			Regular Season														Playoffs								
Season	Club	League	GP	G	A	Pts	PIM	PP	SH	GW	S	%	+/-	TF	F%	Min	GP	G	A	Pts	PIM	PP	SH	GW	Min
2003-04	Sask. Contacts	SMHL	39	1	10	11	89										10	4	8	12	20				
2004-05	Sask. Contacts	SMHL	32	11	29	40	83										11	5	7	12	22				
2005-06	Green Bay	USHL	56	3	12	15	*205										3	1	1	2	27				
2006-07	Boston University	H-East	38	1	3	4	76																		
2007-08	Boston University	H-East	32	1	1	2	54																		
2008-09	Boston University	H-East	45	0	6	6	106																		
2009-10	Boston University	H-East	38	4	6	10	*118																		
	Binghamton	AHL	6	1	0	1	2																		
2010-11	Binghamton	AHL	66	3	4	7	133										10	0	1	1	26				
2011-12	Binghamton	AHL	73	5	15	20	95																		
2012-13	Binghamton	AHL	38	5	6	11	75																		
	Ottawa	**NHL**	**33**	**2**	**4**	**6**	**26**	**0**	**0**	**0**	**51**	**3.9**	**–3**	**0**	**0.0**	**20:17**	**4**	**0**	**0**	**0**	**17**	**0**	**0**	**0**	**12:12**
	NHL Totals		**33**	**2**	**4**	**6**	**26**	**0**	**0**	**0**	**51**	**3.9**		**0**	**0.0**	**20:17**	**4**	**0**	**0**	**0**	**17**	**0**	**0**	**0**	**12:12**

GUDAS, Radko

(GOO-duhs, RAHD-koh) **T.B.**

Defense. Shoots right. 6', 204 lbs. Born, Prague, Czech., June 5, 1990. Tampa Bay's 3rd choice, 66th overall, in 2010 Entry Draft.

Season	Club	League	GP	G	A	Pts	PIM	PP	SH	GW	S	%	+/-	TF	F%	Min	GP	G	A	Pts	PIM	PP	SH	GW	Min
2004-05	HC Kladno U17	CzR-U17	46	1	5	6	70										7	0	0	0	10				
2005-06	HC Kladno U17	CzR-U17	46	12	14	26	178										5	1	2	3	8				
2006-07	HC Kladno U17	CzR-U17	16	6	7	13	34										7	4	1	5	14				
	Kladno Jr.	CzRep-Jr.	15	0	1	1	18										1	0	0	0	0				
	Beroun	CzRep-2	9	0	1	1	6																		
2007-08	Beroun	CzRep-2	43	1	5	6	90																		
	Kladno	CzRep															1	0	0	0	0				
2008-09	Kladno Jr.	CzRep-Jr.	2	0	1	1	0																		
	Beroun	CzRep-2	32	1	6	7	110																		
	Kladno	CzRep	14	0	1	1	10																		
2009-10	Everett Silvertips	WHL	65	7	30	37	151										3	0	2	2	4				
2010-11	Norfolk Admirals	AHL	76	4	13	17	165										6	0	0	0	7				
2011-12	Norfolk Admirals	AHL	73	7	13	20	195										16	0	3	3	14				
2012-13	Syracuse Crunch	AHL	57	4	16	20	207										12	2	1	3	34				
	Tampa Bay	**NHL**	**22**	**2**	**3**	**5**	**38**	**0**	**0**	**1**	**31**	**6.5**	**3**	**0**	**0.0**	**17:00**									
	NHL Totals		**22**	**2**	**3**	**5**	**38**	**0**	**0**	**1**	**31**	**6.5**		**0**	**0.0**	**17:00**									

WHL West Second All-Star Team (2010)

GUDBRANSON, Erik

(guhd-BRAN-suhn, AIR-ihk) **FLA**

Defense. Shoots right. 6'5", 210 lbs. Born, Ottawa, Ont., January 7, 1992. Florida's 1st choice, 3rd overall, in 2010 Entry Draft.

Season	Club	League	GP	G	A	Pts	PIM	PP	SH	GW	S	%	+/-	TF	F%	Min	GP	G	A	Pts	PIM	PP	SH	GW	Min
2007-08	Ottawa Jr. 67's	Minor-ON	70	15	40	55	118																		
2008-09	Kingston	OHL	63	3	19	22	69																		
2009-10	Kingston	OHL	41	2	21	23	68										7	1	2	3	6				
2010-11	Kingston	OHL	44	12	22	34	105										5	1	3	4	10				
2011-12	**Florida**	**NHL**	**72**	**2**	**6**	**8**	**78**	**0**	**0**	**0**	**76**	**2.6**	**–19**	**0**	**0.0**	**14:12**	**7**	**0**	**0**	**0**	**8**	**0**	**0**	**0**	**17:07**
2012-13	San Antonio	AHL	2	0	0	0	2																		
	Florida	**NHL**	**32**	**0**	**4**	**4**	**47**	**0**	**0**	**0**	**49**	**0.0**	**–22**	**0**	**0.0**	**18:45**									
	NHL Totals		**104**	**2**	**10**	**12**	**125**	**0**	**0**	**0**	**125**	**1.6**		**0**	**0.0**	**15:36**	**7**	**0**	**0**	**0**	**8**	**0**	**0**	**0**	**17:07**

GUENIN, Nate

(GEH-nihn, NAYT) **COL**

Defense. Shoots right. 6'3", 207 lbs. Born, Sewickley, PA, December 10, 1982. NY Rangers' 3rd choice, 127th overall, in 2002 Entry Draft.

Season	Club	League	GP	G	A	Pts	PIM	PP	SH	GW	S	%	+/-	TF	F%	Min	GP	G	A	Pts	PIM	PP	SH	GW	Min
99-2000	Pittsburgh	AAHA	40	3	10	13	122																		
2000-01	Green Bay	USHL	54	2	11	13	70										4	1	1	2	6				
2001-02	Green Bay	USHL	56	4	11	15	150										7	3	3	6	10				
2002-03	Ohio State	CCHA	42	2	9	11	85																		
2003-04	Ohio State	CCHA	29	2	15	17	92																		
2004-05	Ohio State	CCHA	41	2	12	14	136																		
2005-06	Ohio State	CCHA	39	0	11	11	87																		
2006-07	**Philadelphia**	**NHL**	**9**	**0**	**2**	**2**	**4**	**0**	**0**	**0**	**0**	**0.0**	**0**	**0**	**0.0**	**8:40**									
	Philadelphia	AHL	68	3	9	12	92																		
2007-08	**Philadelphia**	**NHL**	**2**	**0**	**0**	**0**	**2**	**0**	**0**	**0**	**0**	**0.0**	**2**	**0**	**0.0**	**9:57**									
	Philadelphia	AHL	77	4	13	17	146										12	0	1	1	18				
2008-09	**Philadelphia**	**NHL**	**1**	**0**	**0**	**0**	**0**	**0**	**0**	**0**	**0**	**0.0**	**0**	**0**	**0.0**	**13:25**									
	Philadelphia	AHL	62	0	14	14	95										4	0	0	0	10				
2009-10	**Pittsburgh**	**NHL**	**2**	**0**	**0**	**0**	**0**	**0**	**0**	**0**	**1**	**0.0**	**–2**	**0**	**0.0**	**13:32**									
	Wilkes-Barre	AHL	41	3	2	5	63																		
	Peoria Rivermen	AHL	27	2	11	13	35																		
2010-11	**Columbus**	**NHL**	**3**	**0**	**0**	**0**	**2**	**0**	**0**	**0**	**2**	**0.0**	**–3**	**0**	**0.0**	**14:48**									
	Springfield	AHL	30	0	5	5	21																		
	Syracuse Crunch	AHL	43	2	10	12	44																		
2011-12	**Anaheim**	**NHL**	**15**	**2**	**0**	**2**	**6**	**0**	**0**	**1**	**5**	**40.0**	**6**	**0**	**0.0**	**11:09**									
	Syracuse Crunch	AHL	27	0	5	5	16										4	0	0	0	14				
2012-13	Norfolk Admirals	AHL	66	4	20	24	38																		
	NHL Totals		**32**	**2**	**2**	**4**	**14**	**0**	**0**	**1**	**8**	**25.0**		**0**	**0.0**	**10:56**									

USHL All-Rookie Team (2001) • CCHA Second All-Star Team (2005)

Signed as a free agent by **Philadelphia**, August 16, 2006. Signed as a free agent by **Pittsburgh**, July 3, 2009. Traded to **St. Louis** by **Pittsburgh** for Steve Wagner, February 11, 2010. Signed as a free agent by **Columbus**, July 2, 2010. Traded to **Anaheim** by **Columbus** for Trevor Smith, January 4, 2011. Signed as a free agent by **Colorado**, July 5, 2013.

GUNNARSSON, Carl

(GUHN-nuhr-suhn, KARL) **TOR**

Defense. Shoots left. 6'2", 196 lbs. Born, Orebro, Sweden, November 9, 1986. Toronto's 6th choice, 194th overall, in 2007 Entry Draft.

Season	Club	League	GP	G	A	Pts	PIM	PP	SH	GW	S	%	+/-	TF	F%	Min	GP	G	A	Pts	PIM	PP	SH	GW	Min
2003-04	HC Orebro 90	Sweden-2	43	0	4	4	16																		
2004-05	Linkoping U18	Swe-U18	1	0	1	1	2																		
	Linkopings HC Jr.	Swe-Jr.	22	2	5	7	24																		
2005-06	Linkopings HC Jr.	Swe-Jr.	30	7	6	13	26										4	1	0	1	4				
	IFK Arboga IK	Sweden-2	12	1	5	6	8																		
	Linkopings HC	Sweden	14	0	0	0	0																		
2006-07	Linkopings HC Jr.	Swe-Jr.	6	0	5	5	6																		
	VIK Vasteras HK	Sweden-2	15	2	3	5	14																		
	Linkopings HC	Sweden	30	2	2	4	8										15	0	4	4	4				
2007-08	Linkopings HC	Sweden	53	2	7	9	26										16	0	4	4	10				
2008-09	Linkopings HC	Sweden	53	6	10	16	26										7	0	1	1	2				
2009-10	**Toronto**	**NHL**	**43**	**3**	**12**	**15**	**10**	**0**	**0**	**0**	**45**	**6.7**	**8**	**1**	**0.0**	**21:26**									
	Toronto Marlies	AHL	12	0	2	2	2																		
2010-11	**Toronto**	**NHL**	**68**	**4**	**16**	**20**	**14**	**1**	**0**	**1**	**69**	**5.8**	**–2**	**0**	**0.0**	**18:15**									
2011-12	**Toronto**	**NHL**	**76**	**4**	**15**	**19**	**20**	**0**	**0**	**0**	**89**	**4.5**	**–9**	**1**	**0.0**	**21:42**									
2012-13	Orebro HK	Sweden-2	10	0	4	4	2																		
	Toronto	**NHL**	**37**	**1**	**14**	**15**	**14**	**0**	**0**	**0**	**28**	**3.6**	**5**	**0**	**0.0**	**21:17**	**7**	**0**	**1**	**1**	**0**	**0**	**0**	**0**	**22:05**
	NHL Totals		**224**	**12**	**57**	**69**	**58**	**1**	**0**	**1**	**231**	**5.2**		**2**	**0.0**	**20:32**	**7**	**0**	**1**	**1**	**0**	**0**	**0**	**0**	**22:05**

Signed as a free agent by **Orebro** (Sweden-2), November 12, 2012.

GUSTAFSSON, Erik
(GOOS-tahf-suhn, AIR-ihk) **PHI**

Defense. Shoots left. 5'10", 180 lbs. Born, Kvissleby, Sweden, December 15, 1988.

			Regular Season														Playoffs								
Season	Club	League	GP	G	A	Pts	PIM	PP	SH	GW	S	%	+/-	TF	F%	Min	GP	G	A	Pts	PIM	PP	SH	GW	Min
2004-05	Timra IK U18	Swe-U18	14	4	2	6	12	....	....	....	....	....	....	....	....	....	3	0	0	0	0	....	....	....	....
2005-06	Timra IK U18	Swe-U18	8	2	1	3	8	....	....	....	....	....	....	....	....	....	....	....	....	....	....	....	....	....	....
	Timra IK Jr.	Swe-Jr.	38	3	4	7	26	....	....	....	....	....	....	....	....	....	1	0	0	0	0	....	....	....	....
2006-07	Timra IK Jr.	Swe-Jr.	41	7	13	20	93	....	....	....	....	....	....	....	....	....	3	0	0	0	14	....	....	....	....
2007-08	Northern Mich.	CCHA	44	0	27	27	12	....	....	....	....	....	....	....	....	....	....	....	....	....	....	....	....	....	....
2008-09	Northern Mich.	CCHA	40	4	30	34	10	....	....	....	....	....	....	....	....	....	....	....	....	....	....	....	....	....	....
2009-10	Northern Mich.	CCHA	39	3	29	32	26	....	....	....	....	....	....	....	....	....	....	....	....	....	....	....	....	....	....
	Adirondack	AHL	5	2	5	7	0	....	....	....	....	....	....	....	....	....	....	....	....	....	....	....	....	....	....
2010-11	**Philadelphia**	**NHL**	**3**	**0**	**0**	**0**	**4**	**0**	**0**	**0**	**2**	**0.0**	**–1**	**0**	**0.0**	**10:57**	....	....	....	....	....	....	....	....	....
	Adirondack	AHL	72	5	44	49	14	....	....	....	....	....	....	....	....	....	....	....	....	....	....	....	....	....	....
2011-12	**Philadelphia**	**NHL**	**30**	**1**	**4**	**5**	**2**	**0**	**0**	**0**	**18**	**5.6**	**12**	**0**	**0.0**	**16:48**	**7**	**1**	**1**	**2**	**2**	**0**	**0**	**0**	**15:13**
	Adirondack	AHL	28	1	16	17	14	....	....	....	....	....	....	....	....	....	....	....	....	....	....	....	....	....	....
2012-13	Adirondack	AHL	39	5	17	22	37	....	....	....	....	....	....	....	....	....	....	....	....	....	....	....	....	....	....
	Philadelphia	**NHL**	**27**	**3**	**5**	**8**	**2**	**0**	**0**	**1**	**36**	**8.3**	**–1**	**1**	**0.0**	**20:09**	....	....	....	....	....	....	....	....	....
	NHL Totals		**60**	**4**	**9**	**13**	**8**	**0**	**0**	**1**	**56**	**7.1**		**1**	**0.0**	**18:01**	**7**	**1**	**1**	**2**	**2**	**0**	**0**	**0**	**15:13**

CCHA All-Rookie Team (2008) • CCHA First All-Star Team (2009, 2010) • NCAA West Second All-American Team (2009, 2010) • AHL All-Rookie Team (2011)

Signed as a free agent by **Philadelphia**, March 31, 2010.

HAGELIN, Carl
(HAG-eh-lihn, KARL) **NYR**

Left wing. Shoots left. 5'11", 186 lbs. Born, Sodertalje, Sweden, August 23, 1988. NY Rangers' 4th choice, 168th overall, in 2007 Entry Draft.

Season	Club	League	GP	G	A	Pts	PIM	PP	SH	GW	S	%	+/-	TF	F%	Min	GP	G	A	Pts	PIM	PP	SH	GW	Min
2004-05	Sodertalje SK U18	Swe-U18	14	10	7	17	16	....	....	....	....	....	....	....	....	....	2	0	2	2	0	....	....	....	....
2005-06	Sodertalje SK U18	Swe-U18	7	4	8	12	2	....	....	....	....	....	....	....	....	....	....	....	....	....	....	....	....	....	....
	Sodertalje SK Jr.	Swe-Jr.	41	20	20	40	42	....	....	....	....	....	....	....	....	....	4	1	2	3	22	....	....	....	....
2006-07	Sodertalje SK Jr.	Swe-Jr.	40	24	31	55	42	....	....	....	....	....	....	....	....	....	3	1	5	6	20	....	....	....	....
2007-08	U. of Michigan	CCHA	41	11	11	22	28	....	....	....	....	....	....	....	....	....	....	....	....	....	....	....	....	....	....
2008-09	U. of Michigan	CCHA	41	13	18	31	32	....	....	....	....	....	....	....	....	....	....	....	....	....	....	....	....	....	....
2009-10	U. of Michigan	CCHA	45	19	*31	*50	34	....	....	....	....	....	....	....	....	....	....	....	....	....	....	....	....	....	....
2010-11	U. of Michigan	CCHA	44	18	31	49	39	....	....	....	....	....	....	....	....	....	....	....	....	....	....	....	....	....	....
	Connecticut	AHL	....	....	....	....	....	....	....	....	....	....	....	....	....	....	5	1	1	2	4	....	....	....	....
2011-12	**NY Rangers**	**NHL**	**64**	**14**	**24**	**38**	**24**	**0**	**2**	**2**	**131**	**10.7**	**21**	**6**	**16.7**	**15:03**	**17**	**0**	**3**	**3**	**17**	**0**	**0**	**0**	**16:45**
	Connecticut	AHL	17	7	6	13	6	....	....	....	....	....	....	....	....	....	....	....	....	....	....	....	....	....	....
2012-13	Sodertalje SK	Sweden-2	8	5	6	11	0	....	....	....	....	....	....	....	....	....	....	....	....	....	....	....	....	....	....
	NY Rangers	**NHL**	**48**	**10**	**14**	**24**	**18**	**1**	**0**	**1**	**132**	**7.6**	**10**	**17**	**41.2**	**17:18**	**12**	**3**	**3**	**6**	**0**	**0**	**0**	**0**	**18:06**
	NHL Totals		**112**	**24**	**38**	**62**	**42**	**1**	**2**	**3**	**263**	**9.1**		**23**	**34.8**	**16:01**	**29**	**3**	**6**	**9**	**17**	**0**	**0**	**0**	**17:19**

CCHA First All-Star Team (2011) • NCAA West Second All-American Team (2011)

Signed as a free agent by **Sodertalje** (Sweden-2), September 28, 2012.

HAINSEY, Ron
(HAYN-zee, RAWN)

Defense. Shoots left. 6'3", 210 lbs. Born, Bolton, CT, March 24, 1981. Montreal's 1st choice, 13th overall, in 2000 Entry Draft.

Season	Club	League	GP	G	A	Pts	PIM	PP	SH	GW	S	%	+/-	TF	F%	Min	GP	G	A	Pts	PIM	PP	SH	GW	Min
1997-98	USNTDP	U-17	18	2	7	9	28	....	....	....	....	....	....	....	....	....	....	....	....	....	....	....	....	....	....
	USNTDP	USHL	3	0	0	0	0	....	....	....	....	....	....	....	....	....	....	....	....	....	....	....	....	....	....
	USNTDP	NAHL	40	4	7	11	16	....	....	....	....	....	....	....	....	....	5	0	1	1	0	....	....	....	....
1998-99	USNTDP	USHL	48	5	12	17	45	....	....	....	....	....	....	....	....	....	....	....	....	....	....	....	....	....	....
99-2000	U. Mass-Lowell	H-East	30	3	8	11	20	....	....	....	....	....	....	....	....	....	....	....	....	....	....	....	....	....	....
2000-01	U. Mass-Lowell	H-East	33	10	26	36	51	....	....	....	....	....	....	....	....	....	....	....	....	....	....	....	....	....	....
	Quebec Citadelles	AHL	4	1	0	1	0	....	....	....	....	....	....	....	....	....	1	0	0	0	0	....	....	....	....
2001-02	Quebec Citadelles	AHL	63	7	24	31	26	....	....	....	....	....	....	....	....	....	3	0	0	0	0	....	....	....	....
2002-03	**Montreal**	**NHL**	**21**	**0**	**0**	**0**	**2**	**0**	**0**	**0**	**12**	**0.0**	**–1**	**0**	**0.0**	**12:25**	....	....	....	....	....	....	....	....	....
	Hamilton	AHL	33	2	11	13	26	....	....	....	....	....	....	....	....	....	23	1	10	11	20	....	....	....	....
2003-04	**Montreal**	**NHL**	**11**	**1**	**1**	**2**	**4**	**0**	**0**	**0**	**11**	**9.1**	**3**	**0**	**0.0**	**13:15**	....	....	....	....	....	....	....	....	....
	Hamilton	AHL	54	7	24	31	35	....	....	....	....	....	....	....	....	....	10	0	5	5	6	....	....	....	....
2004-05	Hamilton	AHL	68	9	14	23	45	....	....	....	....	....	....	....	....	....	4	1	1	2	0	....	....	....	....
2005-06	Hamilton	AHL	22	3	14	17	19	....	....	....	....	....	....	....	....	....	....	....	....	....	....	....	....	....	....
	Columbus	**NHL**	**55**	**2**	**15**	**17**	**43**	**1**	**0**	**0**	**81**	**2.5**	**13**	**1**	**0.0**	**17:47**	....	....	....	....	....	....	....	....	....
2006-07	**Columbus**	**NHL**	**80**	**9**	**25**	**34**	**69**	**7**	**0**	**0**	**136**	**6.6**	**–19**	**2**	**50.0**	**22:53**	....	....	....	....	....	....	....	....	....
2007-08	**Columbus**	**NHL**	**78**	**8**	**24**	**32**	**25**	**8**	**0**	**0**	**161**	**5.0**	**–7**	**0**	**0.0**	**22:34**	....	....	....	....	....	....	....	....	....
2008-09	**Atlanta**	**NHL**	**81**	**6**	**33**	**39**	**32**	**4**	**0**	**0**	**148**	**4.1**	**–16**	**0**	**0.0**	**22:22**	....	....	....	....	....	....	....	....	....
2009-10	**Atlanta**	**NHL**	**80**	**5**	**21**	**26**	**39**	**0**	**0**	**0**	**121**	**4.1**	**–6**	**0**	**0.0**	**22:08**	....	....	....	....	....	....	....	....	....
2010-11	**Atlanta**	**NHL**	**82**	**3**	**16**	**19**	**24**	**0**	**0**	**2**	**83**	**3.6**	**3**	**0**	**0.0**	**18:05**	....	....	....	....	....	....	....	....	....
2011-12	**Winnipeg**	**NHL**	**56**	**0**	**10**	**10**	**23**	**0**	**0**	**0**	**57**	**0.0**	**9**	**0**	**0.0**	**21:06**	....	....	....	....	....	....	....	....	....
2012-13	**Winnipeg**	**NHL**	**47**	**0**	**13**	**13**	**10**	**0**	**0**	**0**	**52**	**0.0**	**–8**	**0**	**0.0**	**22:52**	....	....	....	....	....	....	....	....	....
	NHL Totals		**591**	**34**	**158**	**192**	**271**	**20**	**0**	**2**	**862**	**3.9**		**3**	**33.3**	**20:49**	....	....	....	....	....	....	....	....	....

Hockey East First All-Star Team (2001) • NCAA East Second All-American Team (2001) • AHL All-Rookie Team (2002)

Claimed on waivers by **Columbus** from **Montreal**, November 29, 2005. Signed as a free agent by **Atlanta**, July 2, 2008. • Transferred to **Winnipeg** after **Atlanta** franchise relocated, June 21, 2011.

HALEY, Micheal
(HAY-lee, MIGH-kuhl) **NYR**

Center. Shoots left. 5'10", 204 lbs. Born, Guelph, Ont., March 30, 1986.

Season	Club	League	GP	G	A	Pts	PIM	PP	SH	GW	S	%	+/-	TF	F%	Min	GP	G	A	Pts	PIM	PP	SH	GW	Min
2002-03	Sarnia Sting	OHL	43	3	3	6	32	....	....	....	....	....	....	....	....	....	6	0	0	0	2	....	....	....	....
2003-04	Sarnia Sting	OHL	51	8	8	16	69	....	....	....	....	....	....	....	....	....	....	....	....	....	....	....	....	....	....
2004-05	Sarnia Sting	OHL	61	14	16	30	122	....	....	....	....	....	....	....	....	....	....	....	....	....	....	....	....	....	....
2005-06	Sarnia Sting	OHL	23	2	6	8	83	....	....	....	....	....	....	....	....	....	....	....	....	....	....	....	....	....	....
	St. Michael's	OHL	30	12	0	12	78	....	....	....	....	....	....	....	....	....	4	0	1	1	11	....	....	....	....
2006-07	St. Michael's	OHL	68	30	24	54	174	....	....	....	....	....	....	....	....	....	....	....	....	....	....	....	....	....	....
	South Carolina	ECHL	7	5	1	6	13	....	....	....	....	....	....	....	....	....	....	....	....	....	....	....	....	....	....
2007-08	Bridgeport	AHL	36	2	2	4	75	....	....	....	....	....	....	....	....	....	....	....	....	....	....	....	....	....	....
	Utah Grizzlies	ECHL	28	11	8	19	115	....	....	....	....	....	....	....	....	....	14	7	6	13	49	....	....	....	....
2008-09	Bridgeport	AHL	45	5	3	8	99	....	....	....	....	....	....	....	....	....	5	1	0	1	10	....	....	....	....
2009-10	**NY Islanders**	**NHL**	**2**	**0**	**0**	**0**	**9**	**0**	**0**	**0**	**0**	**0.0**	**–3**	**5**	**20.0**	**7:37**	....	....	....	....	....	....	....	....	....
	Bridgeport	AHL	65	6	8	14	196	....	....	....	....	....	....	....	....	....	3	0	0	0	4	....	....	....	....
2010-11	**NY Islanders**	**NHL**	**27**	**2**	**1**	**3**	**85**	**0**	**0**	**0**	**13**	**15.4**	**–4**	**20**	**35.0**	**8:02**	....	....	....	....	....	....	....	....	....
	Bridgeport	AHL	50	12	10	22	144	....	....	....	....	....	....	....	....	....	....	....	....	....	....	....	....	....	....
2011-12	**NY Islanders**	**NHL**	**14**	**0**	**0**	**0**	**57**	**0**	**0**	**0**	**13**	**0.0**	**–1**	**2**	**50.0**	**7:57**	....	....	....	....	....	....	....	....	....
	Bridgeport	AHL	51	15	10	25	125	....	....	....	....	....	....	....	....	....	3	0	0	0	2	....	....	....	....
2012-13	Connecticut	AHL	69	10	13	23	170	....	....	....	....	....	....	....	....	....	....	....	....	....	....	....	....	....	....
	NY Rangers	**NHL**	**9**	**0**	**0**	**0**	**12**	**0**	**0**	**0**	**4**	**0.0**	**–1**	**3**	**66.7**	**6:38**	**2**	**0**	**0**	**0**	**0**	**0**	**0**	**0**	**6:02**
	NHL Totals		**52**	**2**	**1**	**3**	**163**	**0**	**0**	**0**	**30**	**6.7**		**30**	**36.7**	**7:45**	**2**	**0**	**0**	**0**	**0**	**0**	**0**	**0**	**6:02**

Signed as a free agent by **NY Islanders**, May 19, 2008. Signed as a free agent by **NY Rangers**, July 1. 2012.

HALISCHUK, Matt
(ha-LIHS-chuhk, MAT) **WPG**

Right wing. Shoots right. 5'11", 187 lbs. Born, Toronto, Ont., June 1, 1988. New Jersey's 4th choice, 117th overall, in 2007 Entry Draft.

Season	Club	League	GP	G	A	Pts	PIM	PP	SH	GW	S	%	+/-	TF	F%	Min	GP	G	A	Pts	PIM	PP	SH	GW	Min
2003-04	Tor. Jr. Canadiens	GTHL	53	37	48	85	27	....	....	....	....	....	....	....	....	....	....	....	....	....	....	....	....	....	....
2004-05	St. Michael's	OHL	30	3	3	6	4	....	....	....	....	....	....	....	....	....	....	....	....	....	....	....	....	....	....
	St. Mike's B's	ON-Jr.A	17	5	11	16	8	....	....	....	....	....	....	....	....	....	32	10	15	25	4	....	....	....	....
2005-06	St. Michael's	OHL	61	13	18	31	16	....	....	....	....	....	....	....	....	....	4	1	1	2	0	....	....	....	....
2006-07	Kitchener Rangers	OHL	67	33	33	66	20	....	....	....	....	....	....	....	....	....	9	4	1	5	10	....	....	....	....
2007-08	Kitchener Rangers	OHL	40	13	46	59	16	....	....	....	....	....	....	....	....	....	20	*16	16	32	0	....	....	....	....
2008-09	**New Jersey**	**NHL**	**1**	**0**	**1**	**1**	**0**	**0**	**0**	**0**	**0**	**0.0**	**–1**	**0**	**0.0**	**9:47**	....	....	....	....	....	....	....	....	....
	Lowell Devils	AHL	47	14	15	29	10	....	....	....	....	....	....	....	....	....	....	....	....	....	....	....	....	....	....
2009-10	**New Jersey**	**NHL**	**20**	**1**	**1**	**2**	**2**	**0**	**0**	**0**	**22**	**4.5**	**–4**	**4**	**25.0**	**11:18**	....	....	....	....	....	....	....	....	....
	Lowell Devils	AHL	32	11	11	22	2	....	....	....	....	....	....	....	....	....	1	0	0	0	0	....	....	....	....
2010-11	**Nashville**	**NHL**	**27**	**4**	**8**	**12**	**2**	**0**	**0**	**1**	**29**	**13.8**	**5**	**4**	**0.0**	**10:08**	**12**	**2**	**0**	**2**	**0**	**0**	**0**	**1**	**11:45**
	Milwaukee	AHL	37	11	12	23	12	....	....	....	....	....	....	....	....	....	1	1	1	2	0	....	....	....	....
2011-12	**Nashville**	**NHL**	**73**	**15**	**13**	**28**	**27**	**0**	**0**	**2**	**96**	**15.6**	**9**	**30**	**36.7**	**11:15**	**5**	**0**	**1**	**1**	**4**	**0**	**0**	**0**	**7:01**

			Regular Season														Playoffs								
Season	Club	League	GP	G	A	Pts	PIM	PP	SH	GW	S	%	+/-	TF	F%	Min	GP	G	A	Pts	PIM	PP	SH	GW	Min
2012-13	Nashville	NHL	36	5	6	11	10	0	0	1	51	9.8	1	6	33.3	11:57	....	....	....	....	....	....	....	....	....
	Milwaukee	AHL	2	2	1	3	0	....	....	....	....	....	....	....	....	....	....	....	....	....	....	....	....	....	....
	NHL Totals		157	25	29	54	41	0	0	4	198	12.6		44	31.8	11:13	17	2	1	3	4	0	0	1	10:21

OHL First All-Star Team (2008) • George Parsons Trophy (Memorial Cup - Most Sportsmanlike Player) (2008)

Traded to **Nashville** by **New Jersey** with New Jersey's 2nd round choice (Magnus Hellberg) in 2011 Entry Draft for Jason Arnott, June 19, 2010. Signed as a free agent by **Winnipeg**, July 11, 2013.

HALL, Adam

(HAWL, A-duhm) **PHI**

Right wing. Shoots right. 6'2", 212 lbs. Born, Kalamazoo, MI, August 14, 1980. Nashville's 3rd choice, 52nd overall, in 1999 Entry Draft.

Season	Club	League	GP	G	A	Pts	PIM	PP	SH	GW	S	%	+/-	TF	F%	Min	GP	G	A	Pts	PIM	PP	SH	GW	Min
1996-97	Bramalea Blues	ON-Jr.A	43	9	14	23	92	....	....	....	....	....	....	....	....	....	....	....	....	....	....	....	....	....	....
1997-98	USNTDP	U-18	29	18	9	27	19	....	....	....	....	....	....	....	....	....	....	....	....	....	....	....	....	....	....
	USNTDP	USHL	21	9	11	20	20	....	....	....	....	....	....	....	....	....	....	....	....	....	....	....	....	....	....
	USNTDP	NAHL	15	12	1	13	20	....	....	....	....	....	....	....	....	....	6	3	2	5	4	....	....	....	....
1998-99	Michigan State	CCHA	36	16	7	23	74	....	....	....	....	....	....	....	....	....	....	....	....	....	....	....	....	....	....
99-2000	Michigan State	CCHA	40	*26	13	39	38	....	....	....	....	....	....	....	....	....	....	....	....	....	....	....	....	....	....
2000-01	Michigan State	CCHA	42	18	12	30	42	....	....	....	....	....	....	....	....	....	....	....	....	....	....	....	....	....	....
2001-02	Michigan State	CCHA	41	19	15	34	36	....	....	....	....	....	....	....	....	....	....	....	....	....	....	....	....	....	....
	Nashville	NHL	1	0	1	1	0	0	0	0	2	0.0	0	0	0.0	14:04	....	....	....	....	....	....	....	....	....
	Milwaukee	AHL	6	2	2	4	4	....	....	....	....	....	....	....	....	....	....	....	....	....	....	....	....	....	....
2002-03	Nashville	NHL	79	16	12	28	31	8	0	2	146	11.0	–8	17	52.9	14:09	....	....	....	....	....	....	....	....	....
	Milwaukee	AHL	1	0	0	0	2	....	....	....	....	....	....	....	....	....	....	....	....	....	....	....	....	....	....
2003-04	Nashville	NHL	79	13	14	27	37	6	0	1	151	8.6	–8	348	56.3	16:14	6	2	1	3	2	0	0	1	18:29
2004-05	KalPa Kuopio	Finland-2	36	23	17	40	28	....	....	....	....	....	....	....	....	....	9	2	3	5	4	....	....	....	....
2005-06	Nashville	NHL	75	14	15	29	40	10	0	5	122	11.5	0	470	48.9	16:47	5	1	0	1	0	1	0	1	12:10
2006-07	NY Rangers	NHL	49	4	8	12	18	3	0	0	61	6.6	–13	59	45.8	12:27	....	....	....	....	....	....	....	....	....
	Minnesota	NHL	23	2	3	5	8	0	0	0	42	4.8	2	11	72.7	12:13	3	0	0	0	7	0	0	0	10:06
2007-08	Pittsburgh	NHL	46	2	4	6	24	0	0	0	39	5.1	–2	290	50.3	11:52	17	3	1	4	8	0	0	1	10:59
2008-09	Tampa Bay	NHL	74	5	5	10	29	1	0	0	90	5.6	–9	338	50.0	11:12	....	....	....	....	....	....	....	....	....
2009-10	Norfolk Admirals	AHL	79	16	25	41	47	....	....	....	....	....	....	....	....	....	....	....	....	....	....	....	....	....	....
2010-11	Tampa Bay	NHL	82	7	11	18	32	0	0	1	167	4.2	–12	655	55.0	14:51	18	1	4	5	8	0	0	0	13:53
2011-12	Tampa Bay	NHL	57	2	5	7	17	0	0	1	63	3.2	–11	464	59.5	11:52	....	....	....	....	....	....	....	....	....
2012-13	Ravensburg	German-2	17	11	4	15	39	....	....	....	....	....	....	....	....	....	....	....	....	....	....	....	....	....	....
	Tampa Bay	NHL	20	0	4	4	23	0	0	0	16	0.0	3	165	56.4	10:18	....	....	....	....	....	....	....	....	....
	Carolina	NHL	6	0	0	0	0	0	0	0	3	0.0	–2	8	25.0	10:31	....	....	....	....	....	....	....	....	....
	Philadelphia	NHL	11	0	0	0	0	0	0	0	15	0.0	–1	78	59.0	10:59	....	....	....	....	....	....	....	....	....
	NHL Totals		602	65	82	147	259	28	0	10	917	7.1		2903	53.8	13:39	49	7	6	13	25	1	0	3	13:02

CCHA Second All-Star Team (2000)

Signed as a free agent by **Kuopio** (Finland-2), October 11, 2004. Traded to **NY Rangers** by **Nashville** for Dominic Moore, July 19, 2006. Traded to **Minnesota** by **NY Rangers** for Pascal Dupuis, February 9, 2007. Signed as a free agent by **Pittsburgh**, October 1, 2007. Signed as a free agent by **Tampa Bay**, July 1, 2008. Signed as a free agent by **Ravensburg** (German-2), October 11, 2012. Claimed on waivers by **Carolina** from **Tampa Bay**, March 16, 2013. Traded to **Tampa Bay** by **Carolina** with Carolina's 7th round choice (Joel Vermin) in 2013 Entry Draft for Marc-Andre Bergeron, April 2, 2013. Claimed on waivers by **Philadelphia** from **Tampa Bay**, April 3, 2013.

HALL, Taylor

(HAWL, TAY-luhr) **EDM**

Left wing. Shoots left. 6'1", 194 lbs. Born, Calgary, Alta., November 14, 1991. Edmonton's 1st choice, 1st overall, in 2010 Entry Draft.

Season	Club	League	GP	G	A	Pts	PIM	PP	SH	GW	S	%	+/-	TF	F%	Min	GP	G	A	Pts	PIM	PP	SH	GW	Min
2006-07	King. Jr. Front.	Minor-ON	29	44	41	85	10	....	....	....	....	....	....	....	....	....	....	....	....	....	....	....	....	....	....
2007-08	Windsor Spitfires	OHL	63	45	39	84	22	....	....	....	....	....	....	....	....	....	5	2	3	5	2	....	....	....	....
2008-09	Windsor Spitfires	OHL	63	38	52	90	60	....	....	....	....	....	....	....	....	....	20	*16	20	*36	12	....	....	....	....
2009-10	Windsor Spitfires	OHL	57	40	*66	*106	56	....	....	....	....	....	....	....	....	....	19	17	18	*35	32	....	....	....	....
2010-11	Edmonton	NHL	65	22	20	42	27	8	0	4	186	11.8	–9	105	40.0	18:13	....	....	....	....	....	....	....	....	....
2011-12	Edmonton	NHL	61	27	26	53	36	13	0	7	207	13.0	–3	57	40.4	18:13	....	....	....	....	....	....	....	....	....
2012-13	Oklahoma City	AHL	26	14	20	34	33	....	....	....	....	....	....	....	....	....	....	....	....	....	....	....	....	....	....
	Edmonton	NHL	45	16	34	50	33	4	0	4	154	10.4	5	53	54.7	18:37	....	....	....	....	....	....	....	....	....
	NHL Totals		171	65	80	145	96	25	0	15	547	11.9		215	43.7	18:19	....	....	....	....	....	....	....	....	....

Canadian Major Junior All-Rookie Team (2008) • Canadian Major Junior Rookie of the Year (2008) • OHL First All-Star Team (2009, 2010) • Canadian Major Junior Second All-Star Team (2010) • Memorial Cup All-Star Team (2009, 2010) • Ed Chynoweth Trophy (Memorial Cup - Leading Scorer) (2010) • Stafford Smythe Memorial Trophy (Memorial Cup - MVP) (2009, 2010)

HALPERN, Jeff

(HAL-pehrn, JEHF)

Center. Shoots right. 6', 200 lbs. Born, Washington, DC, May 3, 1976.

Season	Club	League	GP	G	A	Pts	PIM	PP	SH	GW	S	%	+/-	TF	F%	Min	GP	G	A	Pts	PIM	PP	SH	GW	Min
1994-95	Stratford Cullitons	ON-Jr.B	44	29	54	83	43	....	....	....	....	....	....	....	....	....	....	....	....	....	....	....	....	....	....
1995-96	Princeton	ECAC	29	3	11	14	30	....	....	....	....	....	....	....	....	....	....	....	....	....	....	....	....	....	....
1996-97	Princeton	ECAC	33	7	24	31	35	....	....	....	....	....	....	....	....	....	....	....	....	....	....	....	....	....	....
1997-98	Princeton	ECAC	36	*28	25	*53	46	....	....	....	....	....	....	....	....	....	....	....	....	....	....	....	....	....	....
1998-99	Princeton	ECAC	33	*22	22	44	32	....	....	....	....	....	....	....	....	....	....	....	....	....	....	....	....	....	....
	Portland Pirates	AHL	6	2	1	3	4	....	....	....	....	....	....	....	....	....	....	....	....	....	....	....	....	....	....
99-2000	Washington	NHL	79	18	11	29	39	4	4	1	108	16.7	21	812	51.1	13:14	5	2	1	3	0	1	0	1	15:16
2000-01	Washington	NHL	80	21	21	42	60	2	1	5	110	19.1	13	1293	52.4	16:08	6	2	3	5	17	1	0	1	20:02
2001-02	Washington	NHL	48	5	14	19	29	0	0	4	74	6.8	–9	661	56.0	15:19	....	....	....	....	....	....	....	....	....
2002-03	Washington	NHL	82	13	21	34	88	1	2	2	126	10.3	6	1492	54.1	17:25	6	0	1	1	2	0	0	0	19:59
2003-04	Washington	NHL	79	19	27	46	56	7	0	2	114	16.7	–21	1509	54.3	19:03	....	....	....	....	....	....	....	....	....
2004-05	HC Ajoie	Swiss-2	15	5	12	17	52	....	....	....	....	....	....	....	....	....	....	....	....	....	....	....	....	....	....
	Kloten Flyers	Swiss	9	7	4	11	6	....	....	....	....	....	....	....	....	....	....	....	....	....	....	....	....	....	....
2005-06	Washington	NHL	70	11	33	44	79	6	0	1	151	7.3	–8	1454	55.2	20:00	....	....	....	....	....	....	....	....	....
2006-07	Dallas	NHL	76	8	17	25	78	1	0	4	106	7.5	–7	1135	51.8	16:48	7	2	1	3	4	0	0	1	18:57
2007-08	Dallas	NHL	64	10	14	24	40	1	1	0	86	11.6	–2	548	54.0	16:21	....	....	....	....	....	....	....	....	....
	Tampa Bay	NHL	19	10	8	18	14	3	0	2	46	21.7	2	185	46.0	18:12	....	....	....	....	....	....	....	....	....
2008-09	Tampa Bay	NHL	52	7	9	16	32	1	1	1	60	11.7	–13	822	52.8	17:01	....	....	....	....	....	....	....	....	....
2009-10	Tampa Bay	NHL	55	9	8	17	27	2	0	1	65	13.8	–13	479	52.0	15:39	....	....	....	....	....	....	....	....	....
	Los Angeles	NHL	16	0	2	2	12	0	0	0	6	0.0	–1	91	49.5	10:41	6	0	0	0	4	0	0	0	10:12
2010-11	Montreal	NHL	72	11	15	26	29	0	1	3	62	17.7	6	594	56.9	12:44	4	1	0	1	0	0	0	0	17:46
2011-12	Washington	NHL	69	4	12	16	24	0	0	1	63	6.3	–1	625	58.4	12:36	2	0	0	0	4	0	0	0	8:04
2012-13	NY Rangers	NHL	30	0	1	1	8	0	0	0	13	0.0	–5	164	56.7	9:10	....	....	....	....	....	....	....	....	....
	Montreal	NHL	16	1	1	2	2	0	0	1	13	7.7	–3	207	55.6	12:06	3	0	1	1	0	0	0	0	14:25
	NHL Totals		907	147	214	361	617	28	10	28	1203	12.2		12071	53.8	15:42	39	7	7	14	31	2	0	3	16:26

ECAC Second All-Star Team (1998, 1999)

Signed as a free agent by **Washington**, March 29, 1999. Signed as a free agent by **Ajoie** (Swiss-2), October 8, 2004. Signed as a free agent by **Kloten** (Swiss), December 30, 2004. Signed as a free agent by **Dallas**, July 5, 2006. Traded to **Tampa Bay** by **Dallas** with Jussi Jokinen, Mike Smith and Dallas' 4th round choice (later traded to Minnesota, later traded to Edmonton – Edmonton selected Kyle Bigos) in 2009 Entry Draft for Brad Richards and Johan Holmqvist, February 26, 2008. Traded to **Los Angeles** by **Tampa Bay** for Teddy Purcell and Florida's 3rd round choice (previously acquired, Tampa Bay selected Brock Beukeboom) in 2010 Entry Draft, March 3, 2010. Signed as a free agent by **Montreal**, September 7, 2010. Signed as a free agent by **Washington**, July 1, 2011. Signed as a free agent by **NY Rangers**, July 10, 2012. Claimed on waivers by **Montreal** from **NY Rangers**, March 23, 2013.

HAMHUIS, Dan

(HAM-HOOS, DAN) **VAN**

Defense. Shoots left. 6'1", 202 lbs. Born, Smithers, B.C., December 13, 1982. Nashville's 1st choice, 12th overall, in 2001 Entry Draft.

Season	Club	League	GP	G	A	Pts	PIM	PP	SH	GW	S	%	+/-	TF	F%	Min	GP	G	A	Pts	PIM	PP	SH	GW	Min
1997-98	Smithers A's	Minor-BC	59	59	72	131	59	....	....	....	....	....	....	....	....	....	....	....	....	....	....	....	....	....	....
1998-99	Prince George	WHL	56	1	3	4	45	....	....	....	....	....	....	....	....	....	7	1	2	3	8	....	....	....	....
99-2000	Prince George	WHL	70	10	23	33	140	....	....	....	....	....	....	....	....	....	13	2	3	5	35	....	....	....	....
2000-01	Prince George	WHL	62	13	47	60	125	....	....	....	....	....	....	....	....	....	6	2	3	5	15	....	....	....	....
2001-02	Prince George	WHL	59	10	50	60	135	....	....	....	....	....	....	....	....	....	7	0	5	5	16	....	....	....	....
2002-03	Milwaukee	AHL	68	6	21	27	81	....	....	....	....	....	....	....	....	....	6	0	3	3	2	....	....	....	....
2003-04	Nashville	NHL	80	7	19	26	57	2	0	4	115	6.1	–12	0	0.0	22:08	6	0	2	2	6	0	0	0	20:29
2004-05	Milwaukee	AHL	76	13	38	51	85	....	....	....	....	....	....	....	....	....	7	0	2	2	10	....	....	....	....
2005-06	Nashville	NHL	82	7	31	38	70	4	1	1	135	5.2	11	0	0.0	22:34	5	0	2	2	2	0	0	0	19:41
2006-07	Nashville	NHL	81	6	14	20	66	0	0	1	84	7.1	8	1	0.0	21:20	5	0	1	1	2	0	0	0	21:36
2007-08	Nashville	NHL	80	4	23	27	66	1	0	1	127	3.1	–4	0	0.0	22:44	6	1	1	2	6	1	0	0	22:47
2008-09	Nashville	NHL	82	3	23	26	67	1	1	1	135	2.2	–4	0	0.0	22:50	....	....	....	....	....	....	....	....	....
2009-10	Nashville	NHL	78	5	19	24	49	0	0	0	115	4.3	4	0	0.0	21:15	6	0	2	2	2	0	0	0	22:25
2010-11	Vancouver	NHL	64	6	17	23	34	2	0	1	109	5.5	29	0	0.0	22:41	19	1	5	6	6	1	0	0	24:50

			Regular Season														Playoffs								
Season	Club	League	GP	G	A	Pts	PIM	PP	SH	GW	S	%	+/-	TF	F%	Min	GP	G	A	Pts	PIM	PP	SH	GW	Min
2011-12	**Vancouver**	**NHL**	**82**	**4**	**33**	**37**	**46**	**1**	**0**	**0**	**140**	**2.9**	**29**	**0**	**0.0**	**23:26**	**5**	**0**	**3**	**3**	**6**	**0**	**0**	**0**	**24:23**
2012-13	**Vancouver**	**NHL**	**47**	**4**	**20**	**24**	**12**	**0**	**1**	**0**	**61**	**6.6**	**9**	**0**	**0.0**	**23:23**	**4**	**1**	**1**	**2**	**8**	**0**	**0**	**0**	**25:14**
	NHL Totals		**676**	**46**	**199**	**245**	**467**	**11**	**3**	**9**	**1021**	**4.5**		**1**	**0.0**	**22:26**	**56**	**3**	**17**	**20**	**38**	**2**	**0**	**0**	**23:08**

WHL West First All-Star Team (2001, 2002) • WHL Player of the Year (2002) • Canadian Major Junior First All-Star Team (2002) • Canadian Major Junior Defenseman of the Year (2002) • AHL Second All-Star Team (2005)

Traded to **Philadelphia** by **Nashville** for Ryan Parent and future considerations, June 19, 2010. Traded to **Pittsburgh** by **Philadelphia** for Pittsburgh's 3rd round choice (later traded to Phoenix – Phoenix selected Harrison Ruopp) in 2011 Entry Draft, June 25, 2010. Signed as a free agent by **Vancouver**, July 1, 2010.

HAMILL, Zach

(HA-mihl, ZAK) **VAN**

Center. Shoots right. 5'11", 180 lbs. Born, Vancouver, B.C., September 23, 1988. Boston's 1st choice, 8th overall, in 2007 Entry Draft.

Season	Club	League	GP	G	A	Pts	PIM	PP	SH	GW	S	%	+/-	TF	F%	Min	GP	G	A	Pts	PIM	PP	SH	GW	Min
2002-03	Port Coquitlam	Minor-BC	61	120	83	203	....	....	....	....	....	....	....	....	....	....	....	....	....	....	....	....	....	....	....
2003-04	Port Coquitlam	PIJHL	39	30	31	51	50	....	....	....	....	....	....	....	....	....	....	....	....	....	....	....	....	....	....
	Everett Silvertips	WHL	4	0	2	2	0	....	....	....	....	....	....	....	....	....	20	3	2	5	2	....	....	....	....
2004-05	Everett Silvertips	WHL	57	8	25	33	29	....	....	....	....	....	....	....	....	....	11	2	3	5	8	....	....	....	....
2005-06	Everett Silvertips	WHL	53	21	38	59	28	....	....	....	....	....	....	....	....	....	15	3	11	14	4	....	....	....	....
2006-07	Everett Silvertips	WHL	69	32	*61	*93	90	....	....	....	....	....	....	....	....	....	12	2	8	10	16	....	....	....	....
2007-08	Everett Silvertips	WHL	67	26	49	75	88	....	....	....	....	....	....	....	....	....	4	0	3	3	2	....	....	....	....
	Providence Bruins	AHL	7	0	5	5	6	....	....	....	....	....	....	....	....	....	9	1	3	4	0	....	....	....	....
2008-09	Providence Bruins	AHL	65	13	13	26	40	....	....	....	....	....	....	....	....	....	16	1	5	6	4	....	....	....	....
2009-10	**Boston**	**NHL**	**1**	**0**	**1**	**1**	**0**	**0**	**0**	**0**	**1**	**0.0**	**1**	**4**	**25.0**	**12:08**	....	....	....	....	....	....	....	....	....
	Providence Bruins	AHL	75	14	30	44	24	....	....	....	....	....	....	....	....	....	....	....	....	....	....	....	....	....	....
2010-11	**Boston**	**NHL**	**3**	**0**	**1**	**1**	**0**	**0**	**0**	**0**	**1**	**0.0**	**1**	**16**	**31.3**	**10:28**	....	....	....	....	....	....	....	....	....
	Providence Bruins	AHL	68	9	34	43	66	....	....	....	....	....	....	....	....	....	....	....	....	....	....	....	....	....	....
2011-12	**Boston**	**NHL**	**16**	**0**	**2**	**2**	**4**	**0**	**0**	**0**	**13**	**0.0**	**3**	**31**	**48.4**	**10:59**	....	....	....	....	....	....	....	....	....
	Providence Bruins	AHL	41	8	13	21	24	....	....	....	....	....	....	....	....	....	....	....	....	....	....	....	....	....	....
2012-13	Hershey Bears	AHL	40	11	11	22	34	....	....	....	....	....	....	....	....	....	....	....	....	....	....	....	....	....	....
	San Antonio	AHL	26	5	13	18	20	....	....	....	....	....	....	....	....	....	....	....	....	....	....	....	....	....	....
	Milwaukee	AHL	6	3	1	4	0	....	....	....	....	....	....	....	....	....	4	1	1	2	2	....	....	....	....
	NHL Totals		**20**	**0**	**4**	**4**	**4**	**0**	**0**	**0**	**15**	**0.0**		**51**	**41.2**	**10:58**	....	....	....	....	....	....	....	....	....

WHL West First All-Star Team (2007) • Canadian Major Junior First All-Star Team (2007)

Traded to **Washington** by **Boston** for Chris Bourque, May 26, 2012. Traded to **Florida** by **Washington** for Casey Wellman, January 31, 2013. • Loaned to **Milwaukee** (AHL) by **Florida** (San Antonio-AHL), April 11, 2013. Signed as a free agent by **Vancouver**, July 25, 2013.

HAMILTON, Dougie

(HAM-ihl-tuhn, DUH-gee) **BOS**

Defense. Shoots right. 6'5", 199 lbs. Born, Toronto, Ont., June 17, 1993. Boston's 1st choice, 9th overall, in 2011 Entry Draft.

Season	Club	League	GP	G	A	Pts	PIM	PP	SH	GW	S	%	+/-	TF	F%	Min	GP	G	A	Pts	PIM	PP	SH	GW	Min
2008-09	St. Cath. Falcons	Minor-ON	67	20	33	53	26	....	....	....	....	....	....	....	....	....	....	....	....	....	....	....	....	....	....
2009-10	Niagara Ice Dogs	OHL	64	3	13	16	36	....	....	....	....	....	....	....	....	....	5	0	1	1	4	....	....	....	....
2010-11	Niagara Ice Dogs	OHL	67	12	46	58	77	....	....	....	....	....	....	....	....	....	14	4	12	16	16	....	....	....	....
2011-12	Niagara Ice Dogs	OHL	50	17	55	72	47	....	....	....	....	....	....	....	....	....	20	5	18	23	16	....	....	....	....
2012-13	**Boston**	**NHL**	**42**	**5**	**11**	**16**	**14**	**2**	**0**	**0**	**83**	**6.0**	**4**	**0**	**0.0**	**17:08**	**7**	**0**	**3**	**3**	**0**	**0**	**0**	**0**	**15:47**
	NHL Totals		**42**	**5**	**11**	**16**	**14**	**2**	**0**	**0**	**83**	**6.0**		**0**	**0.0**	**17:08**	**7**	**0**	**3**	**3**	**0**	**0**	**0**	**0**	**15:47**

OHL Second All-Star Team (2011) • Canadian Major Junior Scholastic Player of the Year (2011) • OHL First All-Star Team (2012) • Canadian Major Junior Defenseman of the Year (2012)

HAMILTON, Ryan

(HAM-ihl-tuhn, RIGH-uhn) **EDM**

Left wing. Shoots left. 6'2", 230 lbs. Born, Oshawa, Ont., April 15, 1985.

Season	Club	League	GP	G	A	Pts	PIM	PP	SH	GW	S	%	+/-	TF	F%	Min	GP	G	A	Pts	PIM	PP	SH	GW	Min
2002-03	Couchiching	ON-Jr.A	11	5	8	13	2	....	....	....	....	....	....	....	....	....	....	....	....	....	....	....	....	....	....
	Peterborough	ON-Jr.A	27	3	10	13	43	....	....	....	....	....	....	....	....	....	....	....	....	....	....	....	....	....	....
	Trenton Sting	ON-Jr.A	17	3	8	11	24	....	....	....	....	....	....	....	....	....	....	....	....	....	....	....	....	....	....
	Barrie Colts	OHL	24	3	2	5	10	....	....	....	....	....	....	....	....	....	6	1	0	1	0	....	....	....	....
2003-04	Kingston	ON-Jr.A	14	1	5	6	23	....	....	....	....	....	....	....	....	....	....	....	....	....	....	....	....	....	....
	Barrie Colts	OHL	46	17	10	27	21	....	....	....	....	....	....	....	....	....	7	0	1	1	8	....	....	....	....
2004-05	Barrie Colts	OHL	37	13	11	24	6	....	....	....	....	....	....	....	....	....	6	2	0	2	2	....	....	....	....
2005-06	Barrie Colts	OHL	63	46	26	72	58	....	....	....	....	....	....	....	....	....	14	8	9	17	11	....	....	....	....
	Houston Aeros	AHL	....	....	....	....	....	....	....	....	....	....	....	....	....	....	1	0	0	0	0	....	....	....	....
2006-07	Houston Aeros	AHL	62	7	9	16	36	....	....	....	....	....	....	....	....	....	....	....	....	....	....	....	....	....	....
2007-08	Houston Aeros	AHL	72	20	19	39	38	....	....	....	....	....	....	....	....	....	2	1	0	1	0	....	....	....	....
2008-09	Houston Aeros	AHL	29	8	4	12	24	....	....	....	....	....	....	....	....	....	....	....	....	....	....	....	....	....	....
	Toronto Marlies	AHL	36	7	6	13	33	....	....	....	....	....	....	....	....	....	6	1	2	3	4	....	....	....	....
2009-10	Toronto Marlies	AHL	47	16	9	25	37	....	....	....	....	....	....	....	....	....	....	....	....	....	....	....	....	....	....
2010-11	Toronto Marlies	AHL	45	16	13	29	21	....	....	....	....	....	....	....	....	....	....	....	....	....	....	....	....	....	....
2011-12	**Toronto**	**NHL**	**2**	**0**	**1**	**1**	**2**	**0**	**0**	**0**	**1**	**0.0**	**–1**	**0**	**0.0**	**13:08**	....	....	....	....	....	....	....	....	....
	Toronto Marlies	AHL	74	25	26	51	36	....	....	....	....	....	....	....	....	....	17	2	3	5	6	....	....	....	....
2012-13	Toronto Marlies	AHL	56	30	18	48	31	....	....	....	....	....	....	....	....	....	4	1	1	2	0	....	....	....	....
	Toronto	**NHL**	**10**	**0**	**2**	**2**	**0**	**0**	**0**	**0**	**6**	**0.0**	**1**	**18**	**22.2**	**10:51**	**2**	**0**	**1**	**1**	**0**	**0**	**0**	**0**	**8:08**
	NHL Totals		**12**	**0**	**3**	**3**	**2**	**0**	**0**	**0**	**7**	**0.0**		**18**	**22.2**	**11:14**	**2**	**0**	**1**	**1**	**0**	**0**	**0**	**0**	**8:08**

Signed as a free agent by **Minnesota**, July 5, 2006. Traded to **Toronto** by **Minnesota** for Robbie Earl, January 21, 2009. Signed as a free agent by **Edmointon**, July 5, 2013.

HAMONIC, Travis

(HA-mohn-ihk, TRA-vihs) **NYI**

Defense. Shoots right. 6'1", 206 lbs. Born, St. Malo, Man., August 16, 1990. NY Islanders' 4th choice, 53rd overall, in 2008 Entry Draft.

Season	Club	League	GP	G	A	Pts	PIM	PP	SH	GW	S	%	+/-	TF	F%	Min	GP	G	A	Pts	PIM	PP	SH	GW	Min
2006-07	Winnipeg Saints	MJHL	....	2	13	15	....	....	....	....	....	....	....	....	....	....	....	....	....	....	....	....	....	....	....
	Moose Jaw	WHL	22	0	3	3	30	....	....	....	....	....	....	....	....	....	....	....	....	....	....	....	....	....	....
2007-08	Moose Jaw	WHL	61	5	17	22	101	....	....	....	....	....	....	....	....	....	6	0	1	1	6	....	....	....	....
2008-09	Moose Jaw	WHL	57	13	27	40	126	....	....	....	....	....	....	....	....	....	....	....	....	....	....	....	....	....	....
2009-10	Moose Jaw	WHL	31	10	29	39	48	....	....	....	....	....	....	....	....	....	....	....	....	....	....	....	....	....	....
	Brandon	WHL	10	1	4	5	17	....	....	....	....	....	....	....	....	....	15	4	7	11	23	....	....	....	....
2010-11	**NY Islanders**	**NHL**	**62**	**5**	**21**	**26**	**103**	**1**	**0**	**0**	**118**	**4.2**	**4**	**0**	**0.0**	**21:34**	....	....	....	....	....	....	....	....	....
	Bridgeport	AHL	19	2	5	7	45	....	....	....	....	....	....	....	....	....	....	....	....	....	....	....	....	....	....
2011-12	**NY Islanders**	**NHL**	**73**	**2**	**22**	**24**	**73**	**1**	**0**	**0**	**124**	**1.6**	**6**	**0**	**0.0**	**22:26**	....	....	....	....	....	....	....	....	....
2012-13	Bridgeport	AHL	21	4	6	10	37	....	....	....	....	....	....	....	....	....	....	....	....	....	....	....	....	....	....
	NY Islanders	**NHL**	**48**	**3**	**7**	**10**	**28**	**1**	**0**	**1**	**83**	**3.6**	**–8**	**0**	**0.0**	**22:48**	**6**	**0**	**1**	**1**	**23**	**0**	**0**	**0**	**24:59**
	NHL Totals		**183**	**10**	**50**	**60**	**204**	**3**	**0**	**1**	**325**	**3.1**		**0**	**0.0**	**22:14**	**6**	**0**	**1**	**1**	**23**	**0**	**0**	**0**	**24:59**

WHL East Second All-Star Team (2010) • Memorial Cup All-Star Team (2010)

HAMRLIK, Roman

(HAHM-reh-lik, ROH-muhn)

Defense. Shoots left. 6'2", 206 lbs. Born, Zlin, Czech., April 12, 1974. Tampa Bay's 1st choice, 1st overall, in 1992 Entry Draft.

Season	Club	League	GP	G	A	Pts	PIM	PP	SH	GW	S	%	+/-	TF	F%	Min	GP	G	A	Pts	PIM	PP	SH	GW	Min
1990-91	AC ZPS Zlin	Czech	14	2	2	4	18	....	....	....	....	....	....	....	....	....	....	....	....	....	....	....	....	....	....
1991-92	AC ZPS Zlin	Czech	34	5	5	10	50	....	....	....	....	....	....	....	....	....	....	....	....	....	....	....	....	....	....
1992-93	**Tampa Bay**	**NHL**	**67**	**6**	**15**	**21**	**71**	**1**	**0**	**1**	**113**	**5.3**	**–21**	....	....	....	....	....	....	....	....	....	....	....	....
	Atlanta Knights	IHL	2	1	1	2	2	....	....	....	....	....	....	....	....	....	....	....	....	....	....	....	....	....	....
1993-94	**Tampa Bay**	**NHL**	**64**	**3**	**18**	**21**	**135**	**0**	**0**	**0**	**158**	**1.9**	**–14**	....	....	....	....	....	....	....	....	....	....	....	....
1994-95	AC ZPS Zlin	CzRep	2	1	0	1	10	....	....	....	....	....	....	....	....	....	....	....	....	....	....	....	....	....	....
	Tampa Bay	**NHL**	**48**	**12**	**11**	**23**	**86**	**7**	**1**	**2**	**134**	**9.0**	**–18**	....	....	....	....	....	....	....	....	....	....	....	....
1995-96	**Tampa Bay**	**NHL**	**82**	**16**	**49**	**65**	**103**	**12**	**0**	**2**	**281**	**5.7**	**–24**	....	....	....	**5**	**0**	**1**	**1**	**4**	**0**	**0**	**0**	....
1996-97	**Tampa Bay**	**NHL**	**79**	**12**	**28**	**40**	**57**	**6**	**0**	**0**	**238**	**5.0**	**–29**	....	....	....	....	....	....	....	....	....	....	....	....
1997-98	**Tampa Bay**	**NHL**	**37**	**3**	**12**	**15**	**22**	**1**	**0**	**0**	**86**	**3.5**	**–18**	....	....	....	....	....	....	....	....	....	....	....	....
	Edmonton	**NHL**	**41**	**6**	**20**	**26**	**48**	**4**	**1**	**3**	**112**	**5.4**	**3**	....	....	....	**12**	**0**	**6**	**6**	**12**	**0**	**0**	**0**	....
	Czech Republic	Olympics	6	1	0	1	2	....	....	....	....	....	....	....	....	....	....	....	....	....	....	....	....	....	....
1998-99	**Edmonton**	**NHL**	**75**	**8**	**24**	**32**	**70**	**3**	**0**	**0**	**172**	**4.7**	**9**	**0**	**0.0**	**23:49**	**3**	**0**	**0**	**0**	**2**	**0**	**0**	**0**	**16:23**
99-2000	Zlin	CzRep	6	0	3	3	4	....	....	....	....	....	....	....	....	....	....	....	....	....	....	....	....	....	....
	Edmonton	**NHL**	**80**	**8**	**37**	**45**	**68**	**5**	**0**	**0**	**180**	**4.4**	**1**	**0**	**0.0**	**25:18**	**5**	**0**	**1**	**1**	**4**	**0**	**0**	**0**	**24:44**
2000-01	**NY Islanders**	**NHL**	**76**	**16**	**30**	**46**	**92**	**5**	**1**	**4**	**232**	**6.9**	**–20**	**1**	**100.0**	**25:12**	....	....	....	....	....	....	....	....	....
2001-02	**NY Islanders**	**NHL**	**70**	**11**	**26**	**37**	**78**	**4**	**1**	**1**	**169**	**6.5**	**7**	**1**	**0.0**	**25:32**	**7**	**1**	**6**	**7**	**6**	**0**	**0**	**0**	**29:09**
	Czech Republic	Olympics	4	0	1	1	2	....	....	....	....	....	....	....	....	....	....	....	....	....	....	....	....	....	....
2002-03	**NY Islanders**	**NHL**	**73**	**9**	**32**	**41**	**87**	**3**	**0**	**2**	**151**	**6.0**	**21**	**0**	**0.0**	**26:34**	**5**	**0**	**2**	**2**	**2**	**0**	**0**	**0**	**29:24**
2003-04	**NY Islanders**	**NHL**	**81**	**7**	**22**	**29**	**68**	**2**	**0**	**2**	**182**	**3.8**	**2**	**0**	**0.0**	**24:35**	**5**	**0**	**1**	**1**	**2**	**0**	**0**	**0**	**25:30**

Season	Club	League	GP	G	A	Pts	PIM	PP	SH	GW	S	%	+/-	TF	F%	Min	GP	G	A	Pts	PIM	PP	SH	GW	Min
			Regular Season														Playoffs								
2004-05	HC Hame Zlin	CzRep	45	2	14	16	70										17	1	3	4	24				
2005-06	**Calgary**	**NHL**	**51**	**7**	**19**	**26**	**56**	**1**	**1**	**0**	**89**	**7.9**	**8**	**0**	**0.0**	**21:51**	**7**	**0**	**2**	**2**	**2**	**0**	**0**	**0**	**19:44**
2006-07	**Calgary**	**NHL**	**75**	**7**	**31**	**38**	**88**	**1**	**0**	**1**	**125**	**5.6**	**22**	**0**	**0.0**	**24:52**	**6**	**0**	**1**	**1**	**8**	**0**	**0**	**0**	**26:53**
2007-08	**Montreal**	**NHL**	**77**	**5**	**21**	**26**	**38**	**3**	**0**	**3**	**129**	**3.9**	**7**	**0**	**0.0**	**23:08**	**12**	**1**	**2**	**3**	**8**	**0**	**0**	**0**	**22:55**
2008-09	**Montreal**	**NHL**	**81**	**6**	**27**	**33**	**62**	**0**	**0**	**0**	**143**	**4.2**	**4**	**0**	**0.0**	**21:55**	**4**	**0**	**0**	**0**	**2**	**0**	**0**	**0**	**25:19**
2009-10	**Montreal**	**NHL**	**75**	**6**	**20**	**26**	**56**	**2**	**0**	**1**	**100**	**6.0**	**–2**	**0**	**0.0**	**23:26**	**19**	**0**	**9**	**9**	**15**	**0**	**0**	**0**	**20:08**
2010-11	**Montreal**	**NHL**	**79**	**5**	**29**	**34**	**81**	**2**	**0**	**0**	**129**	**3.9**	**6**	**0**	**0.0**	**22:17**	**7**	**0**	**3**	**3**	**6**	**0**	**0**	**0**	**23:20**
2011-12	**Washington**	**NHL**	**68**	**2**	**11**	**13**	**34**	**0**	**0**	**1**	**58**	**3.4**	**11**	**0**	**0.0**	**19:13**	**14**	**1**	**3**	**4**	**12**	**0**	**0**	**0**	**22:17**
2012-13	**Washington**	**NHL**	**4**	**0**	**1**	**1**	**2**	**0**	**0**	**0**	**2**	**0.0**	**–1**	**0**	**0.0**	**15:36**									
	NY Rangers	**NHL**	**12**	**0**	**0**	**0**	**6**	**0**	**0**	**0**	**5**	**0.0**	**–3**	**0**	**0.0**	**10:06**	**2**	**0**	**1**	**1**	**2**	**0**	**0**	**0**	**7:16**
	NHL Totals		**1395**	**155**	**483**	**638**	**1408**	**62**	**5**	**23**	**2988**	**5.2**		**2**	**50.0**	**23:32**	**113**	**3**	**38**	**41**	**87**	**0**	**0**	**0**	**22:55**

Played in NHL All-Star Game (1996, 1999, 2003)

Traded to **Edmonton** by **Tampa Bay** with Paul Comrie for Bryan Marchment, Steve Kelly and Jason Bonsignore, December 30, 1997. Traded to **NY Islanders** by **Edmonton** for Eric Brewer, Josh Green and NY Islanders' 2nd round choice (Brad Winchester) in 2000 Entry Draft, June 24, 2000. Signed as a free agent by **Zlin** (CzRep), August 4, 2004. Signed as a free agent by **Calgary**, August 14, 2005 Signed as a free agent by **Montreal**, July 2, 2007. Signed as a free agent by **Washington**, July 1, 2011. Claimed on waivers by **NY Rangers** from **Washington**, March 6, 2013. • Missed majority of 2012-13 as a healthy reserve.

HANDZUS, Michal

(HAHND-zoos, MIGH-kuhl) **CHI**

Center. Shoots left. 6'5", 215 lbs. Born, Banska Bystrica, Czech., March 11, 1977. St. Louis' 3rd choice, 101st overall, in 1995 Entry Draft.

Season	Club	League	GP	G	A	Pts	PIM	PP	SH	GW	S	%	+/-	TF	F%	Min	GP	G	A	Pts	PIM	PP	SH	GW	Min
1993-94	B. Bystrica Jr.	Slovak-Jr.	40	23	36	59																			
1994-95	B. Bystrica	Slovak-2	22	15	14	29	10																		
1995-96	B. Bystrica	Slovakia	19	3	1	4	8																		
1996-97	HC SKP PS Poprad	Slovakia	44	15	18	33																			
1997-98	Worcester IceCats	AHL	69	27	36	63	54										11	2	6	8	10				
1998-99	**St. Louis**	**NHL**	**66**	**4**	**12**	**16**	**30**	**0**	**0**	**0**	**78**	**5.1**	**–9**	**794**	**49.9**	**14:48**	**11**	**0**	**2**	**2**	**8**	**0**	**0**	**0**	**16:52**
99-2000	**St. Louis**	**NHL**	**81**	**25**	**28**	**53**	**44**	**3**	**4**	**5**	**166**	**15.1**	**19**	**1243**	**51.5**	**17:43**	**7**	**0**	**3**	**3**	**6**	**0**	**0**	**0**	**16:35**
2000-01	**St. Louis**	**NHL**	**36**	**10**	**14**	**24**	**12**	**3**	**2**	**2**	**58**	**17.2**	**11**	**581**	**50.6**	**18:00**									
	Phoenix	**NHL**	**10**	**4**	**4**	**8**	**21**	**0**	**1**	**0**	**14**	**28.6**	**5**	**111**	**60.4**	**15:26**									
2001-02	**Phoenix**	**NHL**	**79**	**15**	**30**	**45**	**34**	**3**	**1**	**1**	**94**	**16.0**	**–8**	**1227**	**48.7**	**16:09**	**5**	**0**	**0**	**0**	**2**	**0**	**0**	**0**	**15:01**
	Slovakia	Olympics	2	1	0	1	6																		
2002-03	**Philadelphia**	**NHL**	**82**	**23**	**21**	**44**	**46**	**1**	**1**	**9**	**133**	**17.3**	**13**	**1350**	**52.3**	**17:33**	**13**	**2**	**6**	**8**	**6**	**0**	**0**	**1**	**18:23**
2003-04	**Philadelphia**	**NHL**	**82**	**20**	**38**	**58**	**82**	**7**	**1**	**2**	**135**	**14.8**	**18**	**1457**	**49.9**	**18:43**	**18**	**5**	**5**	**10**	**10**	**0**	**0**	**0**	**18:33**
2004-05	HKm Zvolen	Slovakia	33	14	24	38	34										17	5	10	15	6				
2005-06	**Philadelphia**	**NHL**	**73**	**11**	**33**	**44**	**38**	**2**	**1**	**1**	**113**	**9.7**	**–2**	**1143**	**53.2**	**18:28**	**6**	**0**	**2**	**2**	**2**	**0**	**0**	**0**	**15:56**
2006-07	**Chicago**	**NHL**	**8**	**3**	**5**	**8**	**6**	**1**	**0**	**0**	**9**	**33.3**	**4**	**173**	**51.5**	**20:59**									
2007-08	**Los Angeles**	**NHL**	**82**	**7**	**14**	**21**	**45**	**0**	**3**	**0**	**89**	**7.9**	**–21**	**1167**	**45.6**	**15:14**									
2008-09	**Los Angeles**	**NHL**	**82**	**18**	**24**	**42**	**32**	**7**	**1**	**4**	**143**	**12.6**	**–7**	**1320**	**54.5**	**18:54**									
2009-10	**Los Angeles**	**NHL**	**81**	**20**	**22**	**42**	**38**	**5**	**1**	**6**	**117**	**17.1**	**4**	**1363**	**50.9**	**18:18**	**6**	**3**	**2**	**5**	**4**	**3**	**0**	**0**	**19:31**
	Slovakia	Olympics	7	3	3	6	0																		
2010-11	**Los Angeles**	**NHL**	**82**	**12**	**18**	**30**	**20**	**4**	**0**	**3**	**94**	**12.8**	**–5**	**1312**	**51.7**	**17:21**	**6**	**1**	**1**	**2**	**0**	**0**	**0**	**0**	**20:21**
2011-12	**San Jose**	**NHL**	**67**	**7**	**17**	**24**	**18**	**2**	**0**	**0**	**81**	**8.6**	**–6**	**815**	**50.7**	**14:27**	**2**	**0**	**0**	**0**	**0**	**0**	**0**	**0**	**10:58**
2012-13	B. Bystrica	Slovakia	15	9	10	19	22																		
	San Jose	**NHL**	**28**	**1**	**1**	**2**	**12**	**0**	**0**	**0**	**31**	**3.2**	**–9**	**297**	**55.6**	**13:32**									
	♦ Chicago	**NHL**	**11**	**1**	**5**	**6**	**4**	**0**	**0**	**0**	**10**	**10.0**	**7**	**129**	**55.0**	**12:07**	**23**	**3**	**8**	**11**	**6**	**0**	**1**	**0**	**16:03**
	NHL Totals		**950**	**181**	**286**	**467**	**482**	**38**	**16**	**33**	**1365**	**13.3**		**14482**	**51.1**	**17:01**	**97**	**14**	**29**	**43**	**44**	**3**	**1**	**1**	**17:16**

Traded to **Phoenix** by **St. Louis** with Ladislav Nagy, the rights to Jeff Taffe and St. Louis' 1st round choice (Ben Eager) in 2002 Entry Draft for Keith Tkachuk, March 13, 2001. Traded to **Philadelphia** by **Phoenix** with Robert Esche for Brian Boucher and Nashville's 3rd round choice (previously acquired, Phoenix selected Joe Callahan) in 2002 Entry Draft, June 12, 2002. Signed as a free agent by **Zvolen** (Slovakia), October 27, 2004. Traded to **Chicago** by **Philadelphia** for Kyle Calder, August 4, 2006. • Missed remainder of 2006-07 due to knee injury vs. St. Louis, October 21, 2006. Signed as a free agent by **Los Angeles**, July 2, 2007. Signed as a free agent by **San Jose**, July 1, 2011. Signed as a free agent by **Banska-Bystrica** (Slovakia), November 13, 2012. Traded to **Chicago** by **San Jose** for Anaheim's 4th round choice (previously acquired, San Jose selected Fredrik Bergvik) in 2013 Entry Draft, April 2, 2013.

HANNAN, Scott

(HAN-nan, SKAWT) **S.J.**

Defense. Shoots left. 6'1", 215 lbs. Born, Richmond, B.C., January 23, 1979. San Jose's 2nd choice, 23rd overall, in 1997 Entry Draft.

Season	Club	League	GP	G	A	Pts	PIM	PP	SH	GW	S	%	+/-	TF	F%	Min	GP	G	A	Pts	PIM	PP	SH	GW	Min
1994-95	Surrey Wolves	Minor-BC	70	54	54	108	200																		
	Tacoma Rockets	WHL	2	0	0	0	0																		
1995-96	Kelowna Rockets	WHL	69	4	5	9	76										6	0	1	1	4				
1996-97	Kelowna Rockets	WHL	70	17	26	43	84										6	0	0	0	8				
1997-98	Kelowna Rockets	WHL	47	10	30	40	70										7	2	7	9	14				
1998-99	**San Jose**	**NHL**	**5**	**0**	**2**	**2**	**6**	**0**	**0**	**0**	**4**	**0.0**	**0**	**0**	**0.0**	**7:15**									
	Kelowna Rockets	WHL	47	15	30	45	92										6	1	2	3	14				
	Kentucky	AHL	2	0	0	0	2										12	0	2	2	10				
99-2000	**San Jose**	**NHL**	**30**	**1**	**2**	**3**	**10**	**0**	**0**	**0**	**28**	**3.6**	**7**	**1**	**0.0**	**17:09**	**1**	**0**	**1**	**1**	**0**	**0**	**0**	**0**	**18:14**
	Kentucky	AHL	41	5	12	17	40																		
2000-01	**San Jose**	**NHL**	**75**	**3**	**14**	**17**	**51**	**0**	**0**	**1**	**96**	**3.1**	**10**	**0**	**0.0**	**19:02**	**6**	**0**	**1**	**1**	**6**	**0**	**0**	**0**	**25:10**
2001-02	**San Jose**	**NHL**	**75**	**2**	**12**	**14**	**57**	**0**	**0**	**1**	**68**	**2.9**	**10**	**1**	**100.0**	**20:19**	**12**	**0**	**2**	**2**	**12**	**0**	**0**	**0**	**20:46**
2002-03	**San Jose**	**NHL**	**81**	**3**	**19**	**22**	**61**	**1**	**0**	**0**	**103**	**2.9**	**0**	**3**	**33.3**	**24:16**									
2003-04	**San Jose**	**NHL**	**82**	**6**	**15**	**21**	**48**	**0**	**0**	**0**	**114**	**5.3**	**10**	**0**	**0.0**	**23:41**	**17**	**1**	**5**	**6**	**22**	**1**	**0**	**1**	**26:38**
2004-05			DID NOT PLAY																						
2005-06	**San Jose**	**NHL**	**81**	**6**	**18**	**24**	**58**	**2**	**0**	**1**	**104**	**5.8**	**7**	**0**	**0.0**	**24:34**	**11**	**0**	**1**	**1**	**6**	**0**	**0**	**0**	**25:16**
2006-07	**San Jose**	**NHL**	**79**	**4**	**20**	**24**	**38**	**0**	**1**	**1**	**79**	**5.1**	**1**	**0**	**0.0**	**22:49**	**11**	**0**	**2**	**2**	**33**	**0**	**0**	**0**	**21:42**
2007-08	**Colorado**	**NHL**	**82**	**2**	**19**	**21**	**55**	**0**	**0**	**0**	**79**	**2.5**	**–5**	**1**	**100.0**	**22:41**	**9**	**0**	**1**	**1**	**4**	**0**	**0**	**0**	**19:15**
2008-09	**Colorado**	**NHL**	**81**	**1**	**9**	**10**	**26**	**0**	**0**	**0**	**70**	**1.4**	**–21**	**1**	**0.0**	**22:22**									
2009-10	**Colorado**	**NHL**	**81**	**2**	**14**	**16**	**40**	**0**	**0**	**0**	**53**	**3.8**	**2**	**2**	**100.0**	**21:56**	**6**	**0**	**0**	**0**	**4**	**0**	**0**	**0**	**22:33**
2010-11	**Colorado**	**NHL**	**23**	**0**	**6**	**6**	**6**	**0**	**0**	**0**	**21**	**0.0**	**1**	**0**	**0.0**	**18:38**									
	Washington	**NHL**	**55**	**1**	**4**	**5**	**28**	**0**	**0**	**0**	**35**	**2.9**	**3**	**0**	**0.0**	**20:16**	**9**	**0**	**1**	**1**	**2**	**0**	**0**	**0**	**23:37**
2011-12	**Calgary**	**NHL**	**78**	**2**	**10**	**12**	**38**	**0**	**0**	**0**	**49**	**4.1**	**–10**	**1**	**100.0**	**20:21**									
2012-13	**Nashville**	**NHL**	**29**	**0**	**1**	**1**	**20**	**0**	**0**	**0**	**20**	**0.0**	**–11**	**0**	**0.0**	**19:30**									
	San Jose	**NHL**	**4**	**0**	**0**	**0**	**2**	**0**	**0**	**0**	**5**	**0.0**	**–3**	**0**	**0.0**	**18:17**	**11**	**0**	**4**	**4**	**4**	**0**	**0**	**0**	**17:18**
	NHL Totals		**941**	**33**	**165**	**198**	**544**	**3**	**1**	**4**	**928**	**3.6**		**10**	**60.0**	**21:42**	**93**	**1**	**18**	**19**	**93**	**1**	**0**	**1**	**22:34**

WHL West First All-Star Team (1999)

Signed as a free agent by **Colorado**, July 1, 2007. Traded to **Washington** by **Colorado** for Tomas Fleischmann, November 30, 2010. Signed as a free agent by **Calgary**, August 13, 2011. Signed as a free agent by **Nashville**, August 17, 2012. Traded to **San Jose** by **Nashville** for San Jose's 6th round choice (Tommy Veilleux) in 2013 Entry Draft, April 3, 2013.

HANOWSKI, Ben

(ha-NOW-skee, BEHN) **CGY**

Wing. Shoots left. 6'2", 195 lbs. Born, Little Falls, MN, October 18, 1990. Pittsburgh's 3rd choice, 63rd overall, in 2009 Entry Draft.

Season	Club	League	GP	G	A	Pts	PIM	PP	SH	GW	S	%	+/-	TF	F%	Min	GP	G	A	Pts	PIM	PP	SH	GW	Min
2005-06	Little Falls Flyers	High-MN	31	35	29	64																			
2006-07	Little Falls Flyers	High-MN	29	40	71	111																			
2007-08	Little Falls Flyers	High-MN	26	48	47	95																			
	Team North	UMHSEL		17	16	33																			
2008-09	Little Falls Flyers	High-MN	31	73	62	135	16																		
	Team North	UMHSEL	19	14	8	22																			
2009-10	St. Cloud State	WCHA	43	9	10	19	19																		
2010-11	St. Cloud State	WCHA	37	13	7	20	18																		
2011-12	St. Cloud State	WCHA	39	23	20	43	25																		
2012-13	St. Cloud State	WCHA	37	17	14	31	18																		
	Calgary	**NHL**	**5**	**1**	**0**	**1**	**0**	**0**	**0**	**0**	**4**	**25.0**	**0**	**2**	**0.0**	**13:18**									
	NHL Totals		**5**	**1**	**0**	**1**	**0**	**0**	**0**	**0**	**4**	**25.0**		**2**	**0.0**	**13:18**									

Traded to **Calgary** by **Pittsburgh** with Kenny Agostino and Pittsburgh's 1st round choice (Morgan Klimchuk) in 2013 Entry Draft for Jarome Iginla., March 28, 2013.

HANSEN, Jannik

(HAHN-suhn, YAH-nihk) **VAN**

Left wing. Shoots right. 6'1", 195 lbs. Born, Herlev, Denmark, March 15, 1986. Vancouver's 7th choice, 287th overall, in 2004 Entry Draft.

Season	Club	League	GP	G	A	Pts	PIM	PP	SH	GW	S	%	+/-	TF	F%	Min	GP	G	A	Pts	PIM	PP	SH	GW	Min
2002-03	Rodovre	Denmark	15	0	0	0	0																		
	Malmo U18	Swe-U18	12	8	7	15	2										3	2	0	2	0				
	Denmark	WJ18-B	5	2	5	7	14																		
2003-04	Rodovre	Denmark	35	12	7	19	48																		
	Denmark	WJC-B	3	0	1	1	12																		
	Denmark	WJ18-B	6	3	4	7	32																		

			Regular Season														Playoffs								
Season	Club	League	GP	G	A	Pts	PIM	PP	SH	GW	S	%	+/-	TF	F%	Min	GP	G	A	Pts	PIM	PP	SH	GW	Min
2004-05	Rodovre	Denmark	32	17	17	34	40	....	....	....	....	....	....	....	....	....	5	3	1	4	24	....	....	....	....
	Denmark	Oly-Q	3	0	1	1	4	....	....	....	....	....	....	....	....	....	....	....	....	....	....	....	....	....	....
2005-06	Portland	WHL	64	24	40	64	67	....	....	....	....	....	....	....	....	....	12	7	6	13	16	....	....	....	....
2006-07	Manitoba Moose	AHL	72	12	22	34	38	....	....	....	....	....	....	....	....	....	6	0	0	0	2	....	....	....	....
	Vancouver	NHL	....	....	....	....	....	....	....	....	....	....	....	....	....	....	10	0	1	1	4	0	0	0	12:41
2007-08	Vancouver	NHL	5	0	0	0	2	0	0	0	3	0.0	0	1	100.0	11:34	....	....	....	....	....	....	....	....	....
	Manitoba Moose	AHL	50	21	22	43	22	....	....	....	....	....	....	....	....	....	6	2	2	4	0	....	....	....	....
2008-09	Vancouver	NHL	55	6	15	21	37	0	0	1	64	9.4	5	12	16.7	12:31	2	0	0	0	0	0	0	0	10:16
	Manitoba Moose	AHL	2	1	0	1	2	....	....	....	....	....	....	....	....	....	....	....	....	....	....	....	....	....	....
2009-10	Vancouver	NHL	47	9	6	15	18	0	1	3	67	13.4	–5	14	42.9	12:20	12	1	2	3	4	0	0	0	10:05
	Manitoba Moose	AHL	5	0	2	2	5	....	....	....	....	....	....	....	....	....	....	....	....	....	....	....	....	....	....
2010-11	Vancouver	NHL	82	9	20	29	32	0	0	2	113	8.0	13	19	42.1	14:43	25	3	6	9	18	0	0	0	15:50
2011-12	Vancouver	NHL	82	16	23	39	34	0	1	1	137	11.7	18	29	41.4	14:54	5	1	0	1	14	0	0	0	16:26
2012-13	Tappara Tampere	Finland	20	7	10	17	43	....	....	....	....	....	....	....	....	....	....	....	....	....	....	....	....	....	....
	Vancouver	NHL	47	10	17	27	8	1	0	2	99	10.1	12	31	9.7	17:33	4	0	0	0	2	0	0	0	18:12
	NHL Totals		318	50	81	131	131	1	2	9	483	10.4		106	30.2	14:24	58	5	9	14	42	0	0	0	14:07

Signed as a free agent by **Tappara Tampere** (Finland), October 30, 2012.

HANSON, Christian

(HAN-suhn, KRIHST-chehn)

Center. Shoots right. 6'4", 228 lbs. Born, Venetia, PA, March 10, 1986.

Season	Club	League	GP	G	A	Pts	PIM	PP	SH	GW	S	%	+/-	TF	F%	Min	GP	G	A	Pts	PIM	PP	SH	GW	Min
2003-04	Tri-City Storm	USHL	58	11	8	19	35	....	....	....	....	....	....	....	....	....	11	2	2	4	4	....	....	....	....
2004-05	Tri-City Storm	USHL	60	19	33	52	23	....	....	....	....	....	....	....	....	....	9	1	2	3	8	....	....	....	....
2005-06	U. of Notre Dame	CCHA	23	1	2	3	14	....	....	....	....	....	....	....	....	....	....	....	....	....	....	....	....	....	....
2006-07	U. of Notre Dame	CCHA	33	6	2	8	24	....	....	....	....	....	....	....	....	....	....	....	....	....	....	....	....	....	....
2007-08	U. of Notre Dame	CCHA	47	13	9	22	57	....	....	....	....	....	....	....	....	....	....	....	....	....	....	....	....	....	....
2008-09	U. of Notre Dame	CCHA	37	16	15	31	28	....	....	....	....	....	....	....	....	....	....	....	....	....	....	....	....	....	....
	Toronto	NHL	5	1	1	2	2	0	0	0	9	11.1	–1	4	25.0	16:19	....	....	....	....	....	....	....	....	....
2009-10	Toronto	NHL	31	2	5	7	16	0	1	0	45	4.4	–2	177	55.4	13:22	....	....	....	....	....	....	....	....	....
	Toronto Marlies	AHL	38	12	19	31	35	....	....	....	....	....	....	....	....	....	....	....	....	....	....	....	....	....	....
2010-11	Toronto	NHL	6	0	0	0	4	0	0	0	2	0.0	0	17	41.2	8:26	....	....	....	....	....	....	....	....	....
	Toronto Marlies	AHL	58	13	21	34	51	....	....	....	....	....	....	....	....	....	....	....	....	....	....	....	....	....	....
2011-12	Hershey Bears	AHL	52	10	11	21	42	....	....	....	....	....	....	....	....	....	....	....	....	....	....	....	....	....	....
2012-13	Providence Bruins	AHL	67	12	17	29	53	....	....	....	....	....	....	....	....	....	12	1	2	3	8	....	....	....	....
	NHL Totals		42	3	6	9	22	0	1	0	56	5.4		198	53.5	13:01	....	....	....	....	....	....	....	....	....

CCHA Second All-Star Team (2009)

Signed as a free agent by **Toronto**, March 31, 2009. Signed as a free agent by **Washington**, July 11, 2011. Signed as a free agent by **Boston**, July 9, 2012.

HANZAL, Martin

(HAHN-zuhl, MAHR-tihn) **PHX**

Center. Shoots left. 6'6", 236 lbs. Born, Pisek, Czech., February 20, 1987. Phoenix's 1st choice, 17th overall, in 2005 Entry Draft.

Season	Club	League	GP	G	A	Pts	PIM	PP	SH	GW	S	%	+/-	TF	F%	Min	GP	G	A	Pts	PIM	PP	SH	GW	Min
2002-03	C. Budejovice U17	CzR-U17	47	24	30	54	28	....	....	....	....	....	....	....	....	....	7	1	3	4	25	....	....	....	....
2003-04	C. Budejovice U17	CzR-U17	2	0	2	2	2	....	....	....	....	....	....	....	....	....	2	1	0	1	4	....	....	....	....
	C. Budejovice Jr.	CzRep-Jr.	53	15	7	22	32	....	....	....	....	....	....	....	....	....	....	....	....	....	....	....	....	....	....
2004-05	C. Budejovice Jr.	CzRep-Jr.	37	22	22	44	80	....	....	....	....	....	....	....	....	....	2	1	2	3	2	....	....	....	....
	C. Budejovice	CzRep-2	15	1	2	3	2	....	....	....	....	....	....	....	....	....	6	0	0	0	6	....	....	....	....
2005-06	C. Budejovice Jr.	CzRep-Jr.	7	3	5	8	20	....	....	....	....	....	....	....	....	....	....	....	....	....	....	....	....	....	....
	C. Budejovice	CzRep	19	0	1	1	10	....	....	....	....	....	....	....	....	....	....	....	....	....	....	....	....	....	....
	BK Mlada Boleslav	CzRep-2	5	2	0	2	0	....	....	....	....	....	....	....	....	....	....	....	....	....	....	....	....	....	....
	Omaha Lancers	USHL	19	4	15	19	30	....	....	....	....	....	....	....	....	....	5	1	0	1	4	....	....	....	....
2006-07	Red Deer Rebels	WHL	60	26	59	85	94	....	....	....	....	....	....	....	....	....	6	2	7	9	19	....	....	....	....
2007-08	Phoenix	NHL	72	8	27	35	28	1	1	3	111	7.2	–7	1019	46.1	16:45	....	....	....	....	....	....	....	....	....
2008-09	Phoenix	NHL	74	11	20	31	40	0	2	2	97	11.3	–4	1078	48.3	16:21	....	....	....	....	....	....	....	....	....
2009-10	Phoenix	NHL	81	11	22	33	104	2	0	0	147	7.5	0	1104	50.6	18:29	7	0	3	3	10	0	0	0	18:58
2010-11	Phoenix	NHL	61	16	10	26	54	7	0	5	149	10.7	4	1029	50.3	19:30	4	1	2	3	8	1	0	0	19:50
2011-12	Phoenix	NHL	64	8	26	34	63	3	0	2	145	5.5	12	1097	52.1	18:27	12	3	3	6	29	0	0	2	16:35
2012-13	C. Budejovice	CzRep	18	8	11	19	73	....	....	....	....	....	....	....	....	....	....	....	....	....	....	....	....	....	....
	Phoenix	NHL	39	11	12	23	24	4	0	2	93	11.8	2	637	46.8	18:32	....	....	....	....	....	....	....	....	....
	NHL Totals		391	65	117	182	313	17	3	14	742	8.8		5964	49.2	17:55	23	4	8	12	47	1	0	2	17:52

WHL East Second All-Star Team (2007)

Signed as a free agent by **Ceske Budejovice** (CzRep), October 28, 2012.

HARRISON, Jay

(HAIR-ih-suhn, JAY) **CAR**

Defense. Shoots left. 6'4", 220 lbs. Born, Oshawa, Ont., November 3, 1982. Toronto's 4th choice, 82nd overall, in 2001 Entry Draft.

Season	Club	League	GP	G	A	Pts	PIM	PP	SH	GW	S	%	+/-	TF	F%	Min	GP	G	A	Pts	PIM	PP	SH	GW	Min
1997-98	Oshawa	ON-Jr.A	42	1	11	12	143	....	....	....	....	....	....	....	....	....	....	....	....	....	....	....	....	....	....
1998-99	Brampton	OHL	63	1	14	15	108	....	....	....	....	....	....	....	....	....	....	....	....	....	....	....	....	....	....
99-2000	Brampton	OHL	68	2	18	20	139	....	....	....	....	....	....	....	....	....	6	0	2	2	15	....	....	....	....
2000-01	Brampton	OHL	53	4	15	19	112	....	....	....	....	....	....	....	....	....	9	1	1	2	17	....	....	....	....
2001-02	Brampton	OHL	61	12	31	43	116	....	....	....	....	....	....	....	....	....	....	....	....	....	....	....	....	....	....
	St. John's	AHL	7	0	1	1	2	....	....	....	....	....	....	....	....	....	10	0	0	0	4	....	....	....	....
	Memphis	CHL	....	....	....	....	....	....	....	....	....	....	....	....	....	....	1	0	0	0	2	....	....	....	....
2002-03	St. John's	AHL	72	2	8	10	72	....	....	....	....	....	....	....	....	....	....	....	....	....	....	....	....	....	....
2003-04	St. John's	AHL	70	4	5	9	141	....	....	....	....	....	....	....	....	....	....	....	....	....	....	....	....	....	....
2004-05	St. John's	AHL	60	0	4	4	108	....	....	....	....	....	....	....	....	....	4	0	1	1	14	....	....	....	....
2005-06	Toronto	NHL	8	0	1	1	2	0	0	0	7	0.0	5	0	0.0	18:50	....	....	....	....	....	....	....	....	....
	Toronto Marlies	AHL	57	9	20	29	100	....	....	....	....	....	....	....	....	....	5	1	3	4	8	....	....	....	....
2006-07	Toronto	NHL	5	0	0	0	6	0	0	0	3	0.0	–5	0	0.0	8:22	....	....	....	....	....	....	....	....	....
	Toronto Marlies	AHL	41	4	14	18	68	....	....	....	....	....	....	....	....	....	....	....	....	....	....	....	....	....	....
2007-08	Toronto Marlies	AHL	69	13	14	27	73	....	....	....	....	....	....	....	....	....	18	2	10	12	35	....	....	....	....
2008-09	EV Zug	Swiss	41	6	9	15	96	....	....	....	....	....	....	....	....	....	7	1	2	3	33	....	....	....	....
	Toronto	NHL	7	0	1	1	10	0	0	0	6	0.0	–2	0	0.0	17:16	....	....	....	....	....	....	....	....	....
2009-10	Carolina	NHL	38	1	5	6	50	0	0	0	30	3.3	–8	0	0.0	14:43	....	....	....	....	....	....	....	....	....
	Albany River Rats	AHL	32	2	12	14	22	....	....	....	....	....	....	....	....	....	8	0	3	3	23	....	....	....	....
2010-11	Carolina	NHL	72	3	7	10	72	0	0	0	49	6.1	5	0	0.0	15:16	....	....	....	....	....	....	....	....	....
2011-12	Carolina	NHL	72	9	14	23	60	2	0	2	128	7.0	–10	0	0.0	20:33	....	....	....	....	....	....	....	....	....
2012-13	Carolina	NHL	47	3	7	10	51	0	0	2	54	5.6	–10	0	0.0	19:54	....	....	....	....	....	....	....	....	....
	NHL Totals		249	16	35	51	251	2	0	4	277	5.8		0	0.0	17:37	....	....	....	....	....	....	....	....	....

OHL All-Rookie Team (1999)

Signed as a free agent by **Zug** (Swiss), June 16, 2008. Signed as a free agent by **Toronto**, March 27, 2009. Signed as a free agent by **Carolina**, July 9, 2009.

HARROLD, Peter

(HAIR-ohld, PEE-tuhr) **N.J.**

Defense. Shoots right. 6', 185 lbs. Born, Kirtland Hills, OH, June 8, 1983.

Season	Club	League	GP	G	A	Pts	PIM	PP	SH	GW	S	%	+/-	TF	F%	Min	GP	G	A	Pts	PIM	PP	SH	GW	Min
2003-04	Boston College	H-East	40	2	12	14	12	....	....	....	....	....	....	....	....	....	....	....	....	....	....	....	....	....	....
2004-05	Boston College	H-East	35	4	10	14	22	....	....	....	....	....	....	....	....	....	....	....	....	....	....	....	....	....	....
2005-06	Boston College	H-East	42	7	23	30	32	....	....	....	....	....	....	....	....	....	....	....	....	....	....	....	....	....	....
2006-07	Los Angeles	NHL	12	0	2	2	8	0	0	0	11	0.0	0	1	0.0	15:12	....	....	....	....	....	....	....	....	....
	Manchester	AHL	62	7	27	34	43	....	....	....	....	....	....	....	....	....	16	3	8	11	18	....	....	....	....
2007-08	Los Angeles	NHL	25	2	3	5	2	0	0	0	16	12.5	3	2	50.0	16:23	....	....	....	....	....	....	....	....	....
	Manchester	AHL	49	7	36	43	25	....	....	....	....	....	....	....	....	....	4	0	1	1	4	....	....	....	....
2008-09	Los Angeles	NHL	69	4	8	12	28	1	0	1	95	4.2	–13	16	37.5	13:10	....	....	....	....	....	....	....	....	....
2009-10	Los Angeles	NHL	39	1	2	3	8	0	0	0	23	4.3	–2	14	14.3	9:15	2	0	0	0	0	0	0	0	11:58
2010-11	Los Angeles	NHL	19	1	3	4	4	0	0	0	12	8.3	3	0	0.0	12:15	....	....	....	....	....	....	....	....	....

			Regular Season														Playoffs								
Season	Club	League	GP	G	A	Pts	PIM	PP	SH	GW	S	%	+/-	TF	F%	Min	GP	G	A	Pts	PIM	PP	SH	GW	Min
2011-12	**New Jersey**	**NHL**	**11**	**0**	**2**	**2**	**0**	**0**	**0**	**0**	**11**	**0.0**	**0**	**0**	**0.0**	**14:36**	**17**	**0**	**4**	**4**	**6**	**0**	**0**	**0**	**15:31**
	Albany Devils	AHL	61	5	21	26	36	....	....	....	....	....	....	....	....	....	....	....	....	....	....	....	....	....	....
2012-13	**New Jersey**	**NHL**	**23**	**2**	**3**	**5**	**6**	**1**	**0**	**0**	**36**	**5.6**	**–8**	**0**	**0.0**	**17:38**	....	....	....	....	....	....	....	....	....
	NHL Totals		**198**	**10**	**23**	**33**	**56**	**2**	**0**	**1**	**204**	**4.9**		**33**	**27.3**	**13:26**	**19**	**0**	**4**	**4**	**6**	**0**	**0**	**0**	**15:09**

Hockey East First All-Star Team (2006) • NCAA East First All-American Team (2006)

Signed as a free agent by **Los Angeles**, April 12, 2006. • Missed majority of 2009-10 and 2010-11 as a healthy reserve. Signed as a free agent by **New Jersey**, August 22, 2011. • Missed majority of 2012-13 as a healthy reserve.

HARTIKAINEN, Teemu

(har-tih-KIGH-nehn, TEE-moo) **EDM**

Center. Shoots left. 6'1", 215 lbs. Born, Kuopio, Finland, May 3, 1990. Edmonton's 4th choice, 163rd overall, in 2008 Entry Draft.

Season	Club	League	GP	G	A	Pts	PIM	PP	SH	GW	S	%	+/-	TF	F%	Min	GP	G	A	Pts	PIM	PP	SH	GW	Min
2006-07	KalPa Kuopio U18	Fin-U18	19	24	13	37	51	....	....	....	....	....	....	....	....	....	....	....	....	....	....	....	....	....	....
	KalPa Kuopio Jr.	Fin-Jr.	11	2	1	3	0	....	....	....	....	....	....	....	....	....	3	0	0	0	4	....	....	....	....
2007-08	KalPa Kuopio U18	Fin-U18	7	9	6	15	6	....	....	....	....	....	....	....	....	....	....	....	....	....	....	....	....	....	....
	KalPa Kuopio Jr.	Fin-Jr.	37	10	7	17	24	....	....	....	....	....	....	....	....	....	11	1	4	5	6	....	....	....	....
	KalPa Kuopio	Finland	1	0	0	0	0	....	....	....	....	....	....	....	....	....	....	....	....	....	....	....	....	....	....
2008-09	Suomi U20	Finland-2	3	0	2	2	8	....	....	....	....	....	....	....	....	....	....	....	....	....	....	....	....	....	....
	KalPa Kuopio	Finland	51	17	6	23	12	....	....	....	....	....	....	....	....	....	12	3	0	3	0	....	....	....	....
2009-10	KalPa Kuopio	Finland	53	15	18	33	22	....	....	....	....	....	....	....	....	....	13	6	1	7	28	....	....	....	....
	Suomi U20	Finland-2	1	0	0	0	0	....	....	....	....	....	....	....	....	....	....	....	....	....	....	....	....	....	....
2010-11	**Edmonton**	**NHL**	**12**	**3**	**2**	**5**	**4**	**1**	**0**	**0**	**21**	**14.3**	**–3**	**18**	**33.3**	**17:25**	....	....	....	....	....	....	....	....	....
	Oklahoma City	AHL	66	17	25	42	27	....	....	....	....	....	....	....	....	....	6	0	1	1	4	....	....	....	....
2011-12	**Edmonton**	**NHL**	**17**	**2**	**3**	**5**	**6**	**0**	**0**	**1**	**24**	**8.3**	**1**	**12**	**33.3**	**13:01**	....	....	....	....	....	....	....	....	....
	Oklahoma City	AHL	51	14	18	32	19	....	....	....	....	....	....	....	....	....	14	4	4	8	4	....	....	....	....
2012-13	Oklahoma City	AHL	47	14	23	37	23	....	....	....	....	....	....	....	....	....	17	7	8	15	6	....	....	....	....
	Edmonton	**NHL**	**23**	**1**	**2**	**3**	**6**	**1**	**0**	**0**	**21**	**4.8**	**–8**	**4**	**25.0**	**10:34**	....	....	....	....	....	....	....	....	....
	NHL Totals		**52**	**6**	**7**	**13**	**16**	**2**	**0**	**1**	**66**	**9.1**		**34**	**32.4**	**12:57**	....	....	....	....	....	....	....	....	....

Signed as a free agent by **Ufa** (KHL), June 11, 2013.

HARTNELL, Scott

(HAHRT-nuhl, SKAWT) **PHI**

Left wing. Shoots left. 6'2", 210 lbs. Born, Regina, Sask., April 18, 1982. Nashville's 1st choice, 6th overall, in 2000 Entry Draft.

Season	Club	League	GP	G	A	Pts	PIM	PP	SH	GW	S	%	+/-	TF	F%	Min	GP	G	A	Pts	PIM	PP	SH	GW	Min
1997-98	Lloydminster	AJHL	56	9	25	34	82	....	....	....	....	....	....	....	....	....	4	2	1	3	8	....	....	....	....
	Prince Albert	WHL	1	0	1	1	2	....	....	....	....	....	....	....	....	....	....	....	....	....	....	....	....	....	....
1998-99	Prince Albert	WHL	65	10	34	44	104	....	....	....	....	....	....	....	....	....	14	0	5	5	22	....	....	....	....
99-2000	Prince Albert	WHL	62	27	55	82	124	....	....	....	....	....	....	....	....	....	6	3	2	5	6	....	....	....	....
2000-01	**Nashville**	**NHL**	**75**	**2**	**14**	**16**	**48**	**0**	**0**	**0**	**92**	**2.2**	**–8**	**3**	**33.3**	**10:54**	....	....	....	....	....	....	....	....	....
2001-02	**Nashville**	**NHL**	**75**	**14**	**27**	**41**	**111**	**3**	**0**	**4**	**162**	**8.6**	**5**	**12**	**25.0**	**16:58**	....	....	....	....	....	....	....	....	....
2002-03	**Nashville**	**NHL**	**82**	**12**	**22**	**34**	**101**	**2**	**0**	**2**	**221**	**5.4**	**–3**	**23**	**30.4**	**15:17**	....	....	....	....	....	....	....	....	....
2003-04	**Nashville**	**NHL**	**59**	**18**	**15**	**33**	**87**	**5**	**0**	**3**	**154**	**11.7**	**–5**	**48**	**37.5**	**16:16**	**6**	**1**	**2**	**3**	**2**	**0**	**0**	**0**	**15:37**
2004-05	Valerengen	Norway	28	17	12	29	103	....	....	....	....	....	....	....	....	....	11	12	7	19	24	....	....	....	....
2005-06	**Nashville**	**NHL**	**81**	**25**	**23**	**48**	**101**	**10**	**2**	**8**	**211**	**11.8**	**8**	**58**	**37.9**	**16:05**	**5**	**1**	**0**	**1**	**4**	**0**	**0**	**0**	**12:12**
2006-07	**Nashville**	**NHL**	**64**	**22**	**17**	**39**	**96**	**10**	**0**	**2**	**150**	**14.7**	**19**	**134**	**47.0**	**15:43**	**5**	**1**	**1**	**2**	**28**	**1**	**0**	**0**	**14:23**
2007-08	**Philadelphia**	**NHL**	**80**	**24**	**19**	**43**	**159**	**10**	**1**	**6**	**176**	**13.6**	**2**	**32**	**40.6**	**16:11**	**17**	**3**	**4**	**7**	**20**	**0**	**0**	**0**	**15:28**
2008-09	**Philadelphia**	**NHL**	**82**	**30**	**30**	**60**	**143**	**6**	**1**	**5**	**210**	**14.3**	**14**	**36**	**50.0**	**17:48**	**6**	**1**	**1**	**2**	**23**	**1**	**0**	**0**	**18:36**
2009-10	**Philadelphia**	**NHL**	**81**	**14**	**30**	**44**	**155**	**8**	**0**	**4**	**171**	**8.2**	**–6**	**5**	**20.0**	**15:43**	**23**	**8**	**9**	**17**	**25**	**3**	**0**	**0**	**16:14**
2010-11	**Philadelphia**	**NHL**	**82**	**24**	**25**	**49**	**142**	**4**	**0**	**4**	**177**	**13.6**	**14**	**10**	**50.0**	**16:36**	**11**	**1**	**3**	**4**	**23**	**0**	**0**	**0**	**16:18**
2011-12	**Philadelphia**	**NHL**	**82**	**37**	**30**	**67**	**136**	**16**	**0**	**6**	**232**	**15.9**	**19**	**63**	**31.8**	**17:47**	**11**	**3**	**5**	**8**	**15**	**3**	**0**	**1**	**17:29**
2012-13	**Philadelphia**	**NHL**	**32**	**8**	**3**	**11**	**70**	**4**	**0**	**1**	**74**	**10.8**	**–5**	**4**	**75.0**	**15:52**	....	....	....	....	....	....	....	....	....
	NHL Totals		**875**	**230**	**255**	**485**	**1349**	**78**	**4**	**45**	**2030**	**11.3**		**428**	**40.7**	**15:58**	**84**	**19**	**25**	**44**	**140**	**8**	**0**	**1**	**16:02**

Played in NHL All-Star Game (2012)

Signed as a free agent by **Oslo** (Norway), October 21, 2004. Traded to **Philadelphia** by **Nashville** with Kimmo Timmonen for Nashville's 1st round choice (previously acquired, Nashville selected Jonathon Blum) in 2007 Entry Draft, June 18, 2007.

HAVLAT, Martin

(HAV-lat, MAHR-tihn) **S.J.**

Right wing. Shoots left. 6'2", 210 lbs. Born, Mlada Boleslav, Czech., April 19, 1981. Ottawa's 1st choice, 26th overall, in 1999 Entry Draft.

Season	Club	League	GP	G	A	Pts	PIM	PP	SH	GW	S	%	+/-	TF	F%	Min	GP	G	A	Pts	PIM	PP	SH	GW	Min
1997-98	Ytong Brno Jr.	CzRep-Jr.	32	38	29	67	....	....	....	....	....	....	....	....	....	....	....	....	....	....	....	....	....	....	....
1998-99	HC Trinec Jr.	CzRep-Jr.	31	28	23	51	....	....	....	....	....	....	....	....	....	....	....	....	....	....	....	....	....	....	....
	Trinec	CzRep	24	2	3	5	4	....	....	....	....	....	....	....	....	....	8	0	0	0	....	....	....	....	....
99-2000	HC Ocelari Trinec	CzRep	46	13	29	42	42	....	....	....	....	....	....	....	....	....	4	0	2	2	8	....	....	....	....
2000-01	**Ottawa**	**NHL**	**73**	**19**	**23**	**42**	**20**	**7**	**0**	**5**	**133**	**14.3**	**8**	**40**	**30.0**	**13:47**	**4**	**0**	**0**	**0**	**2**	**0**	**0**	**0**	**14:04**
2001-02	**Ottawa**	**NHL**	**72**	**22**	**28**	**50**	**66**	**9**	**0**	**6**	**145**	**15.2**	**–7**	**15**	**40.0**	**14:46**	**12**	**2**	**5**	**7**	**14**	**2**	**0**	**2**	**16:19**
	Czech Republic	Olympics	4	3	1	4	27	....	....	....	....	....	....	....	....	....	....	....	....	....	....	....	....	....	....
2002-03	**Ottawa**	**NHL**	**67**	**24**	**35**	**59**	**30**	**9**	**0**	**4**	**179**	**13.4**	**20**	**7**	**14.3**	**16:27**	**18**	**5**	**6**	**11**	**14**	**1**	**0**	**2**	**16:27**
2003-04	HC Sparta Praha	CzRep	5	1	3	4	8	....	....	....	....	....	....	....	....	....	....	....	....	....	....	....	....	....	....
	Ottawa	**NHL**	**68**	**31**	**37**	**68**	**46**	**13**	**0**	**7**	**175**	**17.7**	**12**	**11**	**36.4**	**16:44**	**7**	**0**	**3**	**3**	**2**	**0**	**0**	**0**	**16:10**
2004-05	Znojmo	CzRep	12	10	4	14	16	....	....	....	....	....	....	....	....	....	....	....	....	....	....	....	....	....	....
	Dynamo Moscow	Russia	10	2	0	2	14	....	....	....	....	....	....	....	....	....	....	....	....	....	....	....	....	....	....
	HC Sparta Praha	CzRep	9	5	4	9	37	....	....	....	....	....	....	....	....	....	5	0	0	0	20	....	....	....	....
2005-06	**Ottawa**	**NHL**	**18**	**9**	**7**	**16**	**4**	**2**	**1**	**1**	**57**	**15.8**	**6**	**25**	**36.0**	**18:11**	**10**	**7**	**6**	**13**	**4**	**3**	**0**	**1**	**17:13**
2006-07	**Chicago**	**NHL**	**56**	**25**	**32**	**57**	**28**	**5**	**0**	**1**	**176**	**14.2**	**15**	**12**	**33.3**	**21:24**	....	....	....	....	....	....	....	....	....
2007-08	**Chicago**	**NHL**	**35**	**10**	**17**	**27**	**22**	**3**	**0**	**2**	**87**	**11.5**	**4**	**3**	**0.0**	**18:35**	....	....	....	....	....	....	....	....	....
2008-09	**Chicago**	**NHL**	**81**	**29**	**48**	**77**	**30**	**5**	**0**	**5**	**249**	**11.6**	**29**	**8**	**25.0**	**17:25**	**16**	**5**	**10**	**15**	**8**	**0**	**0**	**1**	**15:34**
2009-10	**Minnesota**	**NHL**	**73**	**18**	**36**	**54**	**34**	**4**	**0**	**3**	**169**	**10.7**	**–19**	**12**	**50.0**	**17:56**	....	....	....	....	....	....	....	....	....
	Czech Republic	Olympics	5	0	2	2	0	....	....	....	....	....	....	....	....	....	....	....	....	....	....	....	....	....	....
2010-11	**Minnesota**	**NHL**	**78**	**22**	**40**	**62**	**52**	**3**	**0**	**4**	**229**	**9.6**	**–10**	**10**	**30.0**	**18:21**	....	....	....	....	....	....	....	....	....
2011-12	**San Jose**	**NHL**	**39**	**7**	**20**	**27**	**22**	**4**	**0**	**1**	**96**	**7.3**	**10**	**7**	**0.0**	**17:37**	**5**	**2**	**1**	**3**	**8**	**1**	**0**	**1**	**19:01**
2012-13	**San Jose**	**NHL**	**40**	**8**	**10**	**18**	**30**	**1**	**0**	**1**	**89**	**9.0**	**7**	**6**	**16.7**	**15:51**	**2**	**0**	**0**	**0**	**0**	**0**	**0**	**0**	**4:04**
	NHL Totals		**700**	**224**	**333**	**557**	**384**	**65**	**1**	**40**	**1784**	**12.6**		**156**	**30.8**	**17:05**	**74**	**21**	**31**	**52**	**52**	**7**	**0**	**7**	**16:02**

NHL All-Rookie Team (2001)

Played in NHL All-Star Game (2007, 2011)

Signed as a free agent by **Znojmo** (CzRep), September 24, 2004. Signed as a free agent by **Dynamo Moscow** (Russia), November 10, 2004. Signed as a free agent by **Sparta Praha** (CzRep), January 31, 2005. • Missed majority of 2005-06 due to shoulder injury vs. Montreal, November 29, 2005. Traded to **Chicago** by **Ottawa** with Bryan Smolinski for Tom Preissing, Josh Hennessy, Michal Barinka and Chicago's 2nd round choice (Patrick Wiercioch) in 2008 Entry Draft, July 10, 2006. • Missed majority of 2007-08 due to shoulder (October 4, 2007 at Minnesota) and groin (December 22, 2007 at Ottawa) injuries. Signed as a free agent by **Minnesota**, July 1, 2009. Traded to **San Jose** by **Minnesota** for Dany Heatley, July 3, 2011. • Missed majority of 2011-12 due to lower-body injury vs. Edmonton, December 17, 2011.

HAYDAR, Darren

(HAY-duhr, DAIR-ehn)

Right wing. Shoots right. 5'9", 170 lbs. Born, Toronto, Ont., October 22, 1979. Nashville's 15th choice, 248th overall, in 1999 Entry Draft.

Season	Club	League	GP	G	A	Pts	PIM	PP	SH	GW	S	%	+/-	TF	F%	Min	GP	G	A	Pts	PIM	PP	SH	GW	Min
1995-96	Milton Merchants	ON-Jr.A	6	1	2	3	4	....	....	....	....	....	....	....	....	....	....	....	....	....	....	....	....	....	....
1996-97	Milton Merchants	ON-Jr.A	51	32	68	100	68	....	....	....	....	....	....	....	....	....	....	....	....	....	....	....	....	....	....
1997-98	Milton Merchants	ON-Jr.A	51	*71	*69	*140	65	....	....	....	....	....	....	....	....	....	....	....	....	....	....	....	....	....	....
1998-99	New Hampshire	H-East	41	31	30	61	34	....	....	....	....	....	....	....	....	....	....	....	....	....	....	....	....	....	....
99-2000	New Hampshire	H-East	38	22	19	41	42	....	....	....	....	....	....	....	....	....	....	....	....	....	....	....	....	....	....
2000-01	New Hampshire	H-East	39	18	23	41	38	....	....	....	....	....	....	....	....	....	....	....	....	....	....	....	....	....	....
2001-02	New Hampshire	H-East	40	31	*45	*76	28	....	....	....	....	....	....	....	....	....	....	....	....	....	....	....	....	....	....
2002-03	**Nashville**	**NHL**	**2**	**0**	**0**	**0**	**0**	**0**	**0**	**0**	**1**	**0.0**	**–1**	**0**	**0.0**	**8:54**	....	....	....	....	....	....	....	....	....
	Milwaukee	AHL	75	29	46	75	36	....	....	....	....	....	....	....	....	....	6	1	4	5	2	....	....	....	....
2003-04	Milwaukee	AHL	79	22	37	59	35	....	....	....	....	....	....	....	....	....	22	*11	15	*26	10	....	....	....	....
2004-05	Milwaukee	AHL	59	24	26	50	42	....	....	....	....	....	....	....	....	....	7	3	4	7	14	....	....	....	....
2005-06	Milwaukee	AHL	80	35	57	92	50	....	....	....	....	....	....	....	....	....	21	*18	17	*35	18	....	....	....	....
2006-07	**Atlanta**	**NHL**	**4**	**0**	**0**	**0**	**0**	**0**	**0**	**0**	**4**	**0.0**	**0**	**3**	**66.7**	**8:01**	....	....	....	....	....	....	....	....	....
	Chicago Wolves	AHL	73	41	*81	*122	55	....	....	....	....	....	....	....	....	....	15	*10	*14	*24	14	....	....	....	....
2007-08	**Atlanta**	**NHL**	**16**	**1**	**7**	**8**	**2**	**0**	**0**	**0**	**14**	**7.1**	**4**	**2**	**0.0**	**11:46**	....	....	....	....	....	....	....	....	....
	Chicago Wolves	AHL	51	19	39	58	52	....	....	....	....	....	....	....	....	....	24	*12	15	27	8	....	....	....	....
2008-09	Grand Rapids	AHL	79	31	49	80	26	....	....	....	....	....	....	....	....	....	10	4	7	11	4	....	....	....	....
2009-10	**Colorado**	**NHL**	**1**	**0**	**0**	**0**	**0**	**0**	**0**	**0**	**2**	**0.0**	**0**	**0**	**0.0**	**5:22**	....	....	....	....	....	....	....	....	....
	Lake Erie	AHL	66	23	41	64	60	....	....	....	....	....	....	....	....	....	....	....	....	....	....	....	....	....	....

			Regular Season														Playoffs								
Season	Club	League	GP	G	A	Pts	PIM	PP	SH	GW	S	%	+/-	TF	F%	Min	GP	G	A	Pts	PIM	PP	SH	GW	Min
2010-11	Chicago Wolves	AHL	77	27	47	74	60	....	....	....	....	....	....	....	....	....	....	....	....	....	....	....	....	....	....
2011-12	Chicago Wolves	AHL	70	21	36	57	32	....	....	....	....	....	....	....	....	....	5	4	4	8	0	....	....	....	....
2012-13	Chicago Wolves	AHL	71	20	37	57	58	....	....	....	....	....	....	....	....	....	....	....	....	....	....	....	....	....	....
	NHL Totals		**23**	**1**	**7**	**8**	**2**	**0**	**0**	**0**	**21**	**4.8**		**5**	**40.0**	**10:35**	....	....	....	....	....	....	....	....	....

Hockey East Second All-Star Team (1999, 2000) • Hockey East Rookie of the Year (1999) • Hockey East First All-Star Team (2002) • Hockey East Player of the Year (2002) • AHL All-Rookie Team (2003) • Dudley "Red" Garrett Memorial Award (AHL – Rookie of the Year) (2003) • AHL First All-Star Team (2007) • John P. Sollenberger Trophy (AHL – Top Scorer) (2007) • Les Cunningham Award (AHL – MVP) (2007) • AHL Second All-Star Team (2009, 2011)

Signed as a free agent by **Atlanta**, July 4, 2006. Signed as a free agent by **Detroit**, July 23, 2008. Signed as a free agent by **Colorado**, July 6, 2009. Signed as a free agent by **Chicago** (AHL), July 29, 2010.

HAYES, Jimmy

(HAYZ, JIH-mee) **CHI**

Right wing. Shoots right. 6'6", 221 lbs. Born, Boston, MA, November 21, 1989. Toronto's 2nd choice, 60th overall, in 2008 Entry Draft.

Season	Club	League	GP	G	A	Pts	PIM	PP	SH	GW	S	%	+/-	TF	F%	Min	GP	G	A	Pts	PIM	PP	SH	GW	Min
2006-07	USNTDP	U-17	42	17	14	31	37	....	....	....	....	....	....	....	....	....	....	....	....	....	....	....	....	....	....
	USNTDP	NAHL	14	6	8	14	4	....	....	....	....	....	....	....	....	....	....	....	....	....	....	....	....	....	....
2007-08	USNTDP	U-18	18	2	5	7	6	....	....	....	....	....	....	....	....	....	....	....	....	....	....	....	....	....	....
	USNTDP	NAHL	19	2	8	10	6	....	....	....	....	....	....	....	....	....	....	....	....	....	....	....	....	....	....
	Lincoln Stars	USHL	21	4	11	15	18	....	....	....	....	....	....	....	....	....	8	4	5	9	8	....	....	....	....
2008-09	Boston College	H-East	36	8	5	13	22	....	....	....	....	....	....	....	....	....	....	....	....	....	....	....	....	....	....
2009-10	Boston College	H-East	42	13	22	35	14	....	....	....	....	....	....	....	....	....	....	....	....	....	....	....	....	....	....
2010-11	Boston College	H-East	39	21	12	33	24	....	....	....	....	....	....	....	....	....	....	....	....	....	....	....	....	....	....
	Rockford IceHogs	AHL	7	0	0	0	2	....	....	....	....	....	....	....	....	....	....	....	....	....	....	....	....	....	....
2011-12	**Chicago**	**NHL**	**31**	**5**	**4**	**9**	**16**	**1**	**0**	**0**	**41**	**12.2**	**–3**	**10**	**50.0**	**10:15**	**2**	**0**	**0**	**0**	**15**	**0**	**0**	**0**	**10:08**
	Rockford IceHogs	AHL	33	7	16	23	11	....	....	....	....	....	....	....	....	....	....	....	....	....	....	....	....	....	....
2012-13	Rockford IceHogs	AHL	67	25	20	45	23	....	....	....	....	....	....	....	....	....	....	....	....	....	....	....	....	....	....
	Chicago	**NHL**	**10**	**1**	**3**	**4**	**0**	**0**	**0**	**0**	**13**	**7.7**	**0**	**7**	**57.1**	**14:20**	....	....	....	....	....	....	....	....	....
	NHL Totals		**41**	**6**	**7**	**13**	**16**	**1**	**0**	**0**	**54**	**11.1**		**17**	**52.9**	**11:15**	**2**	**0**	**0**	**0**	**15**	**0**	**0**	**0**	**10:08**

Traded to **Chicago** by **Toronto** for Calgary's 2nd round choice (previously acquired, Toronto selected Brad Ross) in 2010 Entry Draft, June 25, 2010.

HEATLEY, Dany

(HEET-lee, DA-nee) **MIN**

Left wing. Shoots left. 6'4", 220 lbs. Born, Freiburg, West Germany, January 21, 1981. Atlanta's 1st choice, 2nd overall, in 2000 Entry Draft.

Season	Club	League	GP	G	A	Pts	PIM	PP	SH	GW	S	%	+/-	TF	F%	Min	GP	G	A	Pts	PIM	PP	SH	GW	Min
1996-97	Calgary Blazers	AMHL	25	30	42	72	26	....	....	....	....	....	....	....	....	....	....	....	....	....	....	....	....	....	....
1997-98	Calgary Buffaloes	AMHL	36	39	52	*91	34	....	....	....	....	....	....	....	....	....	10	10	12	*22	30	....	....	....	....
1998-99	Calgary Canucks	AJHL	60	*70	56	*126	91	....	....	....	....	....	....	....	....	....	13	*22	13	*35	6	....	....	....	....
99-2000	U. of Wisconsin	WCHA	38	28	28	56	32	....	....	....	....	....	....	....	....	....	....	....	....	....	....	....	....	....	....
2000-01	U. of Wisconsin	WCHA	39	24	33	57	74	....	....	....	....	....	....	....	....	....	....	....	....	....	....	....	....	....	....
2001-02	**Atlanta**	**NHL**	**82**	**26**	**41**	**67**	**56**	**7**	**0**	**4**	**202**	**12.9**	**–19**	**116**	**32.8**	**19:53**	....	....	....	....	....	....	....	....	....
2002-03	**Atlanta**	**NHL**	**77**	**41**	**48**	**89**	**58**	**19**	**1**	**6**	**252**	**16.3**	**–8**	**49**	**36.7**	**21:57**	....	....	....	....	....	....	....	....	....
2003-04	**Atlanta**	**NHL**	**31**	**13**	**12**	**25**	**18**	**5**	**0**	**3**	**83**	**15.7**	**–8**	**41**	**24.4**	**19:53**	....	....	....	....	....	....	....	....	....
2004-05	SC Bern	Swiss	16	14	10	24	58	....	....	....	....	....	....	....	....	....	....	....	....	....	....	....	....	....	....
	Ak Bars Kazan	Russia	11	3	1	4	22	....	....	....	....	....	....	....	....	....	4	2	1	3	4	....	....	....	....
2005-06	**Ottawa**	**NHL**	**82**	**50**	**53**	**103**	**86**	**23**	**2**	**7**	**300**	**16.7**	**29**	**166**	**53.6**	**21:09**	**10**	**3**	**9**	**12**	**11**	**3**	**0**	**1**	**18:56**
	Canada	Olympics	6	2	1	3	8	....	....	....	....	....	....	....	....	....	....	....	....	....	....	....	....	....	....
2006-07	**Ottawa**	**NHL**	**82**	**50**	**55**	**105**	**74**	**17**	**3**	***10**	**310**	**16.1**	**31**	**60**	**38.3**	**21:02**	**20**	**7**	***15**	***22**	**14**	**2**	**0**	**2**	**21:18**
2007-08	**Ottawa**	**NHL**	**71**	**41**	**41**	**82**	**76**	**13**	**0**	**8**	**224**	**18.3**	**33**	**26**	**57.7**	**21:44**	**4**	**0**	**1**	**1**	**6**	**0**	**0**	**0**	**21:41**
2008-09	**Ottawa**	**NHL**	**82**	**39**	**33**	**72**	**88**	**15**	**0**	**6**	**258**	**15.1**	**–11**	**30**	**46.7**	**20:07**	....	....	....	....	....	....	....	....	....
2009-10	**San Jose**	**NHL**	**82**	**39**	**43**	**82**	**54**	**18**	**1**	**9**	**280**	**13.9**	**14**	**35**	**40.0**	**20:14**	**14**	**2**	**11**	**13**	**16**	**1**	**0**	**0**	**20:41**
	Canada	Olympics	7	4	3	7	4	....	....	....	....	....	....	....	....	....	....	....	....	....	....	....	....	....	....
2010-11	**San Jose**	**NHL**	**80**	**26**	**38**	**64**	**56**	**11**	**1**	**5**	**217**	**12.0**	**8**	**20**	**45.0**	**19:39**	**18**	**3**	**6**	**9**	**12**	**0**	**0**	**0**	**18:56**
2011-12	**Minnesota**	**NHL**	**82**	**24**	**29**	**53**	**28**	**8**	**0**	**3**	**238**	**10.1**	**2**	**67**	**53.7**	**20:57**	....	....	....	....	....	....	....	....	....
2012-13	**Minnesota**	**NHL**	**36**	**11**	**10**	**21**	**8**	**3**	**0**	**1**	**83**	**13.3**	**–12**	**31**	**38.7**	**18:32**	....	....	....	....	....	....	....	....	....
	NHL Totals		**787**	**360**	**403**	**763**	**602**	**139**	**8**	**62**	**2447**	**14.7**		**641**	**43.4**	**20:35**	**66**	**15**	**42**	**57**	**59**	**6**	**0**	**3**	**20:12**

WCHA First All-Star Team (2000) • WCHA Rookie of the Year (2000) • NCAA West Second All-American Team (2000) • WCHA Second All-Star Team (2001) • NCAA West First All-American Team (2001) • NHL All-Rookie Team (2002) • Calder Memorial Trophy (2002) • NHL Second All-Star Team (2006) • NHL First All-Star Team (2007)

Played in NHL All-Star Game (2003, 2007, 2009)

• Missed majority of 2003-04 due to automobile accident, September 29, 2003. Signed as a free agent by **Bern** (Swiss), October 13, 2004. Signed as a free agent by **Kazan** (Russia), February 9, 2005. Traded to **Ottawa** by **Atlanta** for Marian Hossa and Greg de Vries, August 23, 2005. Traded to **San Jose** by **Ottawa** with Ottawa's 5th round choice (Isaac MacLeod) in 2010 Entry Draft for Milan Michalek, Jonathan Cheechoo and San Jose's 2nd round choice (later traded to NY Islanders, later traded to Chicago – Chicago selected Kent Simpson) in 2010 Entry Draft, September 12, 2009. Traded to **Minnesota** by **San Jose** for Martin Havlat, July 3, 2011.

HECHT, Jochen

(HEHSHT, YOH-khehn)

Left wing. Shoots left. 6'1", 198 lbs. Born, Mannheim, West Germany, June 21, 1977. St. Louis' 1st choice, 49th overall, in 1995 Entry Draft.

Season	Club	League	GP	G	A	Pts	PIM	PP	SH	GW	S	%	+/-	TF	F%	Min	GP	G	A	Pts	PIM	PP	SH	GW	Min
1993-94	Mannheim Jr.	Ger-Jr.	28	27	13	40	103	....	....	....	....	....	....	....	....	....	....	....	....	....	....	....	....	....	....
1994-95	Adler Mannheim	Germany	43	11	12	23	68	....	....	....	....	....	....	....	....	....	10	5	4	9	12	....	....	....	....
1995-96	Adler Mannheim	Germany	44	12	16	28	68	....	....	....	....	....	....	....	....	....	8	3	2	5	6	....	....	....	....
1996-97	Adler Mannheim	Germany	46	21	21	42	36	....	....	....	....	....	....	....	....	....	9	3	3	6	4	....	....	....	....
1997-98	Adler Mannheim	Germany	44	7	19	26	42	....	....	....	....	....	....	....	....	....	10	1	1	2	14	....	....	....	....
	Adler Mannheim	EuroHL	5	0	4	4	8	....	....	....	....	....	....	....	....	....	....	....	....	....	....	....	....	....	....
	Germany	Olympics	4	1	0	1	6	....	....	....	....	....	....	....	....	....	....	....	....	....	....	....	....	....	....
1998-99	**St. Louis**	**NHL**	**3**	**0**	**0**	**0**	**0**	**0**	**0**	**0**	**4**	**0.0**	**–2**	**19**	**21.1**	**13:16**	**5**	**2**	**0**	**2**	**0**	**0**	**0**	**0**	**16:40**
	Worcester IceCats	AHL	74	21	35	56	48	....	....	....	....	....	....	....	....	....	4	1	1	2	2	....	....	....	....
99-2000	**St. Louis**	**NHL**	**63**	**13**	**21**	**34**	**28**	**5**	**0**	**1**	**140**	**9.3**	**20**	**75**	**49.3**	**15:25**	**7**	**4**	**6**	**10**	**2**	**1**	**0**	**1**	**17:02**
2000-01	**St. Louis**	**NHL**	**72**	**19**	**25**	**44**	**48**	**8**	**3**	**1**	**208**	**9.1**	**11**	**160**	**43.8**	**17:56**	**15**	**2**	**4**	**6**	**4**	**0**	**0**	**0**	**17:19**
2001-02	**Edmonton**	**NHL**	**82**	**16**	**24**	**40**	**60**	**5**	**0**	**3**	**211**	**7.6**	**4**	**26**	**53.9**	**15:00**	....	....	....	....	....	....	....	....	....
	Germany	Olympics	4	1	1	2	2	....	....	....	....	....	....	....	....	....	....	....	....	....	....	....	....	....	....
2002-03	**Buffalo**	**NHL**	**49**	**10**	**16**	**26**	**30**	**2**	**0**	**2**	**145**	**6.9**	**4**	**33**	**30.3**	**17:55**	....	....	....	....	....	....	....	....	....
2003-04	**Buffalo**	**NHL**	**64**	**15**	**37**	**52**	**49**	**2**	**1**	**0**	**174**	**8.6**	**17**	**141**	**43.3**	**19:00**	....	....	....	....	....	....	....	....	....
2004-05	Adler Mannheim	Germany	48	16	34	50	151	....	....	....	....	....	....	....	....	....	14	10	10	*20	14	....	....	....	....
2005-06	**Buffalo**	**NHL**	**64**	**18**	**24**	**42**	**34**	**4**	**2**	**4**	**179**	**10.1**	**10**	**156**	**39.7**	**18:07**	**15**	**2**	**6**	**8**	**8**	**0**	**0**	**1**	**17:29**
2006-07	**Buffalo**	**NHL**	**76**	**19**	**37**	**56**	**39**	**3**	**0**	**1**	**197**	**9.6**	**19**	**145**	**39.3**	**18:51**	**16**	**4**	**1**	**5**	**10**	**0**	**0**	**1**	**17:41**
2007-08	**Buffalo**	**NHL**	**75**	**22**	**27**	**49**	**38**	**3**	**1**	**2**	**229**	**9.6**	**1**	**905**	**42.0**	**19:19**	....	....	....	....	....	....	....	....	....
2008-09	**Buffalo**	**NHL**	**70**	**12**	**15**	**27**	**33**	**3**	**1**	**1**	**173**	**6.9**	**–9**	**538**	**43.7**	**17:24**	....	....	....	....	....	....	....	....	....
2009-10	**Buffalo**	**NHL**	**79**	**21**	**21**	**42**	**35**	**3**	**0**	**2**	**224**	**9.4**	**14**	**322**	**45.3**	**17:11**	....	....	....	....	....	....	....	....	....
	Germany	Olympics	4	0	1	1	2	....	....	....	....	....	....	....	....	....	....	....	....	....	....	....	....	....	....
2010-11	**Buffalo**	**NHL**	**67**	**12**	**17**	**29**	**40**	**0**	**0**	**4**	**172**	**7.0**	**4**	**729**	**43.1**	**17:05**	**1**	**0**	**1**	**1**	**0**	**0**	**0**	**0**	**15:22**
2011-12	**Buffalo**	**NHL**	**22**	**4**	**4**	**8**	**6**	**0**	**1**	**0**	**40**	**10.0**	**1**	**300**	**45.3**	**16:50**	....	....	....	....	....	....	....	....	....
2012-13	Adler Mannheim	Germany	6	5	8	13	8	....	....	....	....	....	....	....	....	....	....	....	....	....	....	....	....	....	....
	Buffalo	**NHL**	**47**	**5**	**9**	**14**	**18**	**0**	**1**	**1**	**69**	**7.2**	**6**	**353**	**41.6**	**13:42**	....	....	....	....	....	....	....	....	....
	NHL Totals		**833**	**186**	**277**	**463**	**458**	**38**	**10**	**22**	**2165**	**8.6**		**3902**	**42.9**	**17:17**	**59**	**14**	**18**	**32**	**24**	**1**	**0**	**3**	**17:20**

Traded to **Edmonton** by **St. Louis** with Marty Reasoner and Jan Horacek for Doug Weight and Michel Riesen, July 1, 2001. Traded to **Buffalo** by **Edmonton** for Atlanta's 2nd round choice (previously acquired, Edmonton selected Jeff Deslauriers) in 2002 Entry Draft and Nashville's 2nd round choice (previously acquired, Edmonton selected Jarret Stoll) in 2002 Entry Draft, June 22, 2002. Signed as a free agent by **Mannheim** (Germany), August 2, 2004. • Missed majority of 2011-12 due to recurring head injury. Signed as a free agent by **Manheim** (Germany), December 11, 2012.. • Officially announced his retirement, April 26, 2013.

HEDMAN, Victor

(HEHD-muhn, VIHK-tohr) **T.B.**

Defense. Shoots left. 6'6", 233 lbs. Born, Ornskoldsvik, Sweden, December 18, 1990. Tampa Bay's 1st choice, 2nd overall, in 2009 Entry Draft.

Season	Club	League	GP	G	A	Pts	PIM	PP	SH	GW	S	%	+/-	TF	F%	Min	GP	G	A	Pts	PIM	PP	SH	GW	Min
2005-06	MODO U18	Swe-U18	8	3	3	6	14	....	....	....	....	....	....	....	....	....	2	0	0	0	0	....	....	....	....
	MODO Jr.	Swe-Jr.	10	0	1	1	8	....	....	....	....	....	....	....	....	....	....	....	....	....	....	....	....	....	....
2006-07	MODO U18	Swe-U18	3	3	0	3	29	....	....	....	....	....	....	....	....	....	....	....	....	....	....	....	....	....	....
	MODO Jr.	Swe-Jr.	34	13	12	25	30	....	....	....	....	....	....	....	....	....	5	1	1	2	44	....	....	....	....
2007-08	MODO Jr.	Swe-Jr.	6	2	1	3	26	....	....	....	....	....	....	....	....	....	3	2	0	2	4	....	....	....	....
	MODO	Sweden	39	2	2	4	44	....	....	....	....	....	....	....	....	....	5	1	0	1	4	....	....	....	....
2008-09	MODO Jr.	Swe-Jr.	2	0	2	2	10	....	....	....	....	....	....	....	....	....	5	0	1	1	2	....	....	....	....
	MODO	Sweden	43	7	14	21	52	....	....	....	....	....	....	....	....	....	....	....	....	....	....	....	....	....	....
2009-10	**Tampa Bay**	**NHL**	**74**	**4**	**16**	**20**	**79**	**0**	**0**	**0**	**90**	**4.4**	**–3**	**0**	**0.0**	**20:51**	....	....	....	....	....	....	....	....	....
2010-11	**Tampa Bay**	**NHL**	**79**	**3**	**23**	**26**	**70**	**0**	**0**	**0**	**101**	**3.0**	**3**	**0**	**0.0**	**21:01**	**18**	**0**	**6**	**6**	**8**	**0**	**0**	**0**	**22:16**
2011-12	**Tampa Bay**	**NHL**	**61**	**5**	**18**	**23**	**65**	**0**	**0**	**0**	**82**	**6.1**	**–9**	**0**	**0.0**	**23:06**	....	....	....	....	....	....	....	....	....

			Regular Season														Playoffs								
Season	Club	League	GP	G	A	Pts	PIM	PP	SH	GW	S	%	+/-	TF	F%	Min	GP	G	A	Pts	PIM	PP	SH	GW	Min
2012-13	Barys Astana	KHL	26	1	21	22	70	....	....	....	....	....	....	....	....	....	....	....	....	....	....	....	....	....	....
	Tampa Bay	NHL	44	4	16	20	31	0	0	0	76	5.3	1	0	0.0	22:40	....	....	....	....	....	....	....	....	....
	NHL Totals		258	16	73	89	245	0	0	0	349	4.6		0	0.0	21:44	18	0	6	6	8	0	0	0	22:16

Signed as a free agent by **Astana** (KHL), September 25, 2012.

HEJDA, Jan

(HAY-dah, YAHN) **COL**

Defense. Shoots left. 6'4", 237 lbs. Born, Prague, Czech., June 18, 1978. Buffalo's 4th choice, 106th overall, in 2003 Entry Draft.

Season	Club	League	GP	G	A	Pts	PIM	PP	SH	GW	S	%	+/-	TF	F%	Min	GP	G	A	Pts	PIM	PP	SH	GW	Min
1997-98	HC Slavia Praha	CzRep	44	2	5	7	51	....	....	....	....	....	....	....	....	....	5	0	0	0	6	....	....	....	....
1998-99	HC Slavia Praha	CzRep	34	1	2	3	38	....	....	....	....	....	....	....	....	....	....	....	....	....	....	....	....	....	....
99-2000	HC Slavia Praha	CzRep	26	1	2	3	14	....	....	....	....	....	....	....	....	....	....	....	....	....	....	....	....	....	....
	HC Femax Havirov	CzRep	7	0	2	2	6	....	....	....	....	....	....	....	....	....	....	....	....	....	....	....	....	....	....
	Liberec	CzRep-2	1	0	0	0	4	....	....	....	....	....	....	....	....	....	....	....	....	....	....	....	....	....	....
2000-01	HC Slavia Praha	CzRep	38	2	6	8	70	....	....	....	....	....	....	....	....	....	11	3	0	3	12	....	....	....	....
	SK Kadan	CzRep-2	8	1	0	1	6	....	....	....	....	....	....	....	....	....	....	....	....	....	....	....	....	....	....
2001-02	HC Slavia Praha	CzRep	42	9	8	17	52	....	....	....	....	....	....	....	....	....	9	1	1	2	14	....	....	....	....
2002-03	HC Slavia Praha	CzRep	52	6	11	17	44	....	....	....	....	....	....	....	....	....	17	5	8	13	12	....	....	....	....
2003-04	CSKA Moscow	Russia	60	1	5	6	26	....	....	....	....	....	....	....	....	....	....	....	....	....	....	....	....	....	....
2004-05	CSKA Moscow	Russia	60	2	11	13	59	....	....	....	....	....	....	....	....	....	....	....	....	....	....	....	....	....	....
2005-06	Mytischi	Russia	50	3	12	15	56	....	....	....	....	....	....	....	....	....	9	2	3	5	24	....	....	....	....
2006-07	**Edmonton**	**NHL**	**39**	**1**	**8**	**9**	**20**	0	0	1	33	3.0	-6	0	0.0	20:23	....	....	....	....	....	....	....	....	....
	Hamilton	AHL	5	0	3	3	21	....	....	....	....	....	....	....	....	....	....	....	....	....	....	....	....	....	....
2007-08	**Columbus**	**NHL**	**81**	**0**	**13**	**13**	**61**	0	0	0	71	0.0	20	0	0.0	21:08	....	....	....	....	....	....	....	....	....
2008-09	**Columbus**	**NHL**	**82**	**3**	**18**	**21**	**38**	0	0	1	66	4.5	23	1	0.0	22:23	....	....	....	....	....	....	....	....	....
2009-10	**Columbus**	**NHL**	**62**	**3**	**10**	**13**	**36**	1	0	0	63	4.8	-14	2	50.0	20:39	3	0	0	0	2	0	0	0	16:53
	Czech Republic	Olympics	5	0	0	0	4	....	....	....	....	....	....	....	....	....	....	....	....	....	....	....	....	....	....
2010-11	**Columbus**	**NHL**	**77**	**5**	**15**	**20**	**28**	0	0	0	79	6.3	-6	1	100.0	21:07	....	....	....	....	....	....	....	....	....
2011-12	**Colorado**	**NHL**	**81**	**5**	**14**	**19**	**24**	0	0	1	78	6.4	-17	1	100.0	20:41	....	....	....	....	....	....	....	....	....
2012-13	**Colorado**	**NHL**	**46**	**1**	**9**	**10**	**28**	0	0	1	50	2.0	-3	1	0.0	19:42	....	....	....	....	....	....	....	....	....
	NHL Totals		**468**	**18**	**87**	**105**	**235**	**1**	**0**	**4**	**440**	**4.1**		**6**	**50.0**	**21:00**	**3**	**0**	**0**	**0**	**2**	**0**	**0**	**0**	**16:53**

• Rights traded to **Edmonton** by **Buffalo** for Edmonton's 7th round choice (Nick Eno) in 2007 Entry Draft, July 10, 2006. Signed as a free agent by **Columbus**, July 5, 2007. Signed as a free agent by **Colorado**, July 1, 2011.

HEJDUK, Milan

(HAY-dook, MEE-lan)

Right wing. Shoots right. 6', 190 lbs. Born, Usti nad Labem, Czech., February 14, 1976. Quebec's 6th choice, 87th overall, in 1994 Entry Draft.

Season	Club	League	GP	G	A	Pts	PIM	PP	SH	GW	S	%	+/-	TF	F%	Min	GP	G	A	Pts	PIM	PP	SH	GW	Min
1993-94	HC Pardubice	CzRep	22	6	3	9	....	....	....	....	....	....	....	....	....	....	10	5	1	6	....	....	....	....	....
1994-95	HC Pardubice	CzRep	43	11	13	24	6	....	....	....	....	....	....	....	....	....	6	3	1	4	0	....	....	....	....
1995-96	Pardubice	CzRep	37	13	7	20	....	....	....	....	....	....	....	....	....	....	....	....	....	....	....	....	....	....	....
1996-97	Pardubice	CzRep	51	27	11	38	10	....	....	....	....	....	....	....	....	....	10	6	0	6	27	....	....	....	....
1997-98	Pardubice	CzRep	48	26	19	45	20	....	....	....	....	....	....	....	....	....	3	0	0	0	2	....	....	....	....
	Czech Republic	Olympics	4	0	0	0	2	....	....	....	....	....	....	....	....	....	....	....	....	....	....	....	....	....	....
1998-99	**Colorado**	**NHL**	**82**	**14**	**34**	**48**	**26**	4	0	5	178	7.9	8	2	50.0	15:45	16	6	6	12	4	1	0	3	15:53
99-2000	**Colorado**	**NHL**	**82**	**36**	**36**	**72**	**16**	13	0	9	228	15.8	14	3	100.0	19:58	17	5	4	9	6	3	0	1	19:56
2000-01♦	**Colorado**	**NHL**	**80**	**41**	**38**	**79**	**36**	12	1	9	213	19.2	32	3	33.3	19:52	23	7	*16	23	6	4	0	1	21:33
2001-02	**Colorado**	**NHL**	**62**	**21**	**23**	**44**	**24**	7	1	5	139	15.1	0	5	40.0	20:11	16	3	3	6	4	1	0	0	18:24
	Czech Republic	Olympics	4	1	0	1	0	....	....	....	....	....	....	....	....	....	....	....	....	....	....	....	....	....	....
2002-03	**Colorado**	**NHL**	**82**	***50**	**48**	**98**	**32**	18	0	4	244	20.5	*52	43	44.2	19:50	7	2	2	4	2	1	0	0	20:42
2003-04	**Colorado**	**NHL**	**82**	**35**	**40**	**75**	**20**	16	0	6	237	14.8	19	69	47.8	18:46	11	5	2	7	0	2	0	0	18:40
2004-05	Pardubice	CzRep	48	25	26	51	14	....	....	....	....	....	....	....	....	....	16	6	2	8	6	....	....	....	....
2005-06	**Colorado**	**NHL**	**74**	**24**	**34**	**58**	**24**	14	1	2	221	10.9	13	23	17.4	18:33	9	2	6	8	2	0	0	0	20:56
	Czech Republic	Olympics	8	2	1	3	2	....	....	....	....	....	....	....	....	....	....	....	....	....	....	....	....	....	....
2006-07	**Colorado**	**NHL**	**80**	**35**	**35**	**70**	**44**	12	1	6	257	13.6	10	109	45.0	17:53	....	....	....	....	....	....	....	....	....
2007-08	**Colorado**	**NHL**	**77**	**29**	**25**	**54**	**36**	8	1	4	205	14.1	8	136	39.7	19:21	10	3	3	6	4	2	0	0	19:05
2008-09	**Colorado**	**NHL**	**82**	**27**	**32**	**59**	**16**	10	1	2	211	12.8	-19	160	45.0	19:56	....	....	....	....	....	....	....	....	....
2009-10	**Colorado**	**NHL**	**56**	**23**	**21**	**44**	**10**	8	0	4	153	15.0	6	14	28.6	19:01	3	1	0	1	0	0	0	0	12:58
2010-11	**Colorado**	**NHL**	**71**	**22**	**34**	**56**	**18**	10	0	2	170	12.9	-23	5	40.0	17:55	....	....	....	....	....	....	....	....	....
2011-12	**Colorado**	**NHL**	**81**	**14**	**23**	**37**	**14**	6	0	1	170	8.2	-12	8	25.0	17:01	....	....	....	....	....	....	....	....	....
2012-13	**Colorado**	**NHL**	**29**	**4**	**7**	**11**	**0**	2	0	0	41	9.8	-7	6	33.3	13:09	....	....	....	....	....	....	....	....	....
	NHL Totals		**1020**	**375**	**430**	**805**	**316**	**140**	**6**	**59**	**2667**	**14.1**		**586**	**42.3**	**18:35**	**112**	**34**	**42**	**76**	**28**	**14**	**0**	**5**	**19:13**

NHL All-Rookie Team (1999) • NHL Second All-Star Team (2003) • Bud Light Plus/Minus Award (2003) (tied with Peter Forsberg) • Maurice "Rocket" Richard Trophy (2003)
Played in NHL All-Star Game (2000, 2001, 2009)

• Rights transferred to **Colorado** after **Quebec** franchise relocated, June 21, 1995. Signed as a free agent by **Pardubice** (CzRep), September 18, 2004.

HELM, Darren

(HEHLM, DAIR-ehn) **DET**

Center/Left wing. Shoots left. 5'11", 192 lbs. Born, Winnipeg, Man., January 21, 1987. Detroit's 5th choice, 132nd overall, in 2005 Entry Draft.

Season	Club	League	GP	G	A	Pts	PIM	PP	SH	GW	S	%	+/-	TF	F%	Min	GP	G	A	Pts	PIM	PP	SH	GW	Min
2003-04	Selkirk Fishermen	MJBHL	34	39	32	71	34	....	....	....	....	....	....	....	....	....	....	....	....	....	....	....	....	....	....
2004-05	Medicine Hat	WHL	72	10	14	24	27	....	....	....	....	....	....	....	....	....	13	2	6	8	10	....	....	....	....
2005-06	Medicine Hat	WHL	70	41	38	79	37	....	....	....	....	....	....	....	....	....	13	5	4	9	2	....	....	....	....
2006-07	Medicine Hat	WHL	59	25	39	64	53	....	....	....	....	....	....	....	....	....	23	10	12	22	14	....	....	....	....
2007-08♦	**Detroit**	**NHL**	**7**	**0**	**0**	**0**	**2**	0	0	0	7	0.0	-2	23	21.7	7:00	18	2	2	4	2	0	0	0	7:30
	Grand Rapids	AHL	67	16	15	31	30	....	....	....	....	....	....	....	....	....	....	....	....	....	....	....	....	....	....
2008-09	**Detroit**	**NHL**	**16**	**0**	**1**	**1**	**4**	0	0	0	29	0.0	-7	132	56.1	12:26	23	4	1	5	4	0	0	1	12:06
	Grand Rapids	AHL	55	13	24	37	24	....	....	....	....	....	....	....	....	....	....	....	....	....	....	....	....	....	....
2009-10	**Detroit**	**NHL**	**75**	**11**	**13**	**24**	**18**	0	3	3	165	6.7	-2	875	51.1	14:30	12	1	0	1	4	0	0	0	13:56
2010-11	**Detroit**	**NHL**	**82**	**12**	**20**	**32**	**16**	0	2	2	177	6.8	9	938	52.6	13:18	11	3	3	6	8	0	0	1	13:28
2011-12	**Detroit**	**NHL**	**68**	**9**	**17**	**26**	**12**	0	0	2	124	7.3	5	777	51.9	14:31	1	0	0	0	0	0	0	0	3:08
2012-13	**Detroit**	**NHL**	**1**	**0**	**0**	**0**	**2**	0	0	0	1	0.0	0	14	42.9	12:27	....	....	....	....	....	....	....	....	....
	NHL Totals		**249**	**32**	**51**	**83**	**54**	**0**	**5**	**7**	**503**	**6.4**		**2759**	**51.8**	**13:45**	**65**	**10**	**6**	**16**	**18**	**0**	**0**	**2**	**11:16**

WHL East First All-Star Team (2006) • WHL East Second All-Star Team (2007) • Memorial Cup All-Star Team (2007)

• Missed majority of 2012-13 due to recurring back injury.

HEMSKY, Ales

(HEHM-skee, ahl-EHSH) **EDM**

Right wing. Shoots right. 6', 185 lbs. Born, Pardubice, Czech., August 13, 1983. Edmonton's 1st choice, 13th overall, in 2001 Entry Draft.

Season	Club	League	GP	G	A	Pts	PIM	PP	SH	GW	S	%	+/-	TF	F%	Min	GP	G	A	Pts	PIM	PP	SH	GW	Min
99-2000	HC Pardubice Jr.	CzRep-Jr.	45	20	36	56	54	....	....	....	....	....	....	....	....	....	7	4	14	18	36	....	....	....	....
	Pardubice	CzRep	4	0	1	1	0	....	....	....	....	....	....	....	....	....	....	....	....	....	....	....	....	....	....
2000-01	Hull Olympiques	QMJHL	68	36	64	100	67	....	....	....	....	....	....	....	....	....	5	2	3	5	2	....	....	....	....
2001-02	Hull Olympiques	QMJHL	53	27	70	97	86	....	....	....	....	....	....	....	....	....	10	6	10	16	6	....	....	....	....
2002-03	**Edmonton**	**NHL**	**59**	**6**	**24**	**30**	**14**	0	0	1	50	12.0	5	3	33.3	12:04	6	0	0	0	0	0	0	0	12:46
2003-04	**Edmonton**	**NHL**	**71**	**12**	**22**	**34**	**14**	4	0	3	87	13.8	-7	3	33.3	14:26	....	....	....	....	....	....	....	....	....
2004-05	Pardubice	CzRep	47	13	18	31	28	....	....	....	....	....	....	....	....	....	16	4	*10	*14	26	....	....	....	....
2005-06	**Edmonton**	**NHL**	**81**	**19**	**58**	**77**	**64**	7	1	4	178	10.7	-5	7	42.9	16:59	24	6	11	17	14	4	0	2	16:06
	Czech Republic	Olympics	8	1	2	3	2	....	....	....	....	....	....	....	....	....	....	....	....	....	....	....	....	....	....
2006-07	**Edmonton**	**NHL**	**64**	**13**	**40**	**53**	**40**	5	0	1	122	10.7	-7	10	30.0	16:59	....	....	....	....	....	....	....	....	....
2007-08	**Edmonton**	**NHL**	**74**	**20**	**51**	**71**	**34**	8	0	2	184	10.9	-9	5	20.0	18:35	....	....	....	....	....	....	....	....	....
2008-09	**Edmonton**	**NHL**	**72**	**23**	**43**	**66**	**32**	4	0	2	185	12.4	1	4	0.0	18:39	....	....	....	....	....	....	....	....	....
2009-10	**Edmonton**	**NHL**	**22**	**7**	**15**	**22**	**8**	3	0	0	57	12.3	7	1	100.0	17:56	....	....	....	....	....	....	....	....	....
2010-11	**Edmonton**	**NHL**	**47**	**14**	**28**	**42**	**18**	1	1	1	100	14.0	3	7	14.3	18:17	....	....	....	....	....	....	....	....	....
2011-12	**Edmonton**	**NHL**	**69**	**10**	**26**	**36**	**43**	1	0	1	137	7.3	-13	6	33.3	17:36	....	....	....	....	....	....	....	....	....
2012-13	Pardubice	CzRep	27	14	18	32	52	....	....	....	....	....	....	....	....	....	....	....	....	....	....	....	....	....	....
	Edmonton	**NHL**	**38**	**9**	**11**	**20**	**16**	5	0	1	82	11.0	-6	24	50.0	15:42	....	....	....	....	....	....	....	....	....
	NHL Totals		**597**	**133**	**318**	**451**	**283**	**38**	**2**	**16**	**1182**	**11.3**		**70**	**35.7**	**16:43**	**30**	**6**	**11**	**17**	**14**	**4**	**0**	**2**	**15:26**

QMJHL Second All-Star Team (2002)

Signed as a free agent by **Pardubice** (CzRep), September 18, 2004. • Missed majority of 2009-10 due to shoulder injury vs. Los Angeles, November 25, 2009. Signed as a free agent by **Pardubice** (CzRep), September 17, 2012.

HENDERSON, Kevin
(HEHN-duhr-SOHN, KEH-vihn) **NSH**

Left wing. Shoots left. 6'3", 210 lbs. Born, Toronto, Ont., December 3, 1986.

			Regular Season														Playoffs								
Season	Club	League	GP	G	A	Pts	PIM	PP	SH	GW	S	%	+/-	TF	F%	Min	GP	G	A	Pts	PIM	PP	SH	GW	Min
2003-04	Thornhill Rattlers	ON-Jr.A	47	11	23	34	44	....	....	....	....	....	....	....	....	....	....	....	....	....	....	....	....	....	....
2004-05	Kitchener Rangers	OHL	47	5	8	13	46	....	....	....	....	....	....	....	....	....	15	0	3	3	8	....	....	....	....
	Thornhill	ON-Jr.A	11	5	9	14	33	....	....	....	....	....	....	....	....	....	....	....	....	....	....	....	....	....	....
2005-06	Kitchener Rangers	OHL	63	6	11	17	66	....	....	....	....	....	....	....	....	....	2	1	0	1	0	....	....	....	....
2006-07	Kitchener Rangers	OHL	56	33	15	48	69	....	....	....	....	....	....	....	....	....	9	4	6	10	13	....	....	....	....
2007-08	New Brunswick	AUAA	27	5	10	15	22	....	....	....	....	....	....	....	....	....	....	....	....	....	....	....	....	....	....
2008-09	New Brunswick	AUAA	28	19	31	50	28	....	....	....	....	....	....	....	....	....	....	....	....	....	....	....	....	....	....
2009-10	Worcester Sharks	AHL	64	2	13	15	45	....	....	....	....	....	....	....	....	....	11	0	1	1	4	....	....	....	....
2010-11	Worcester Sharks	AHL	73	8	13	21	45	....	....	....	....	....	....	....	....	....	....	....	....	....	....	....	....	....	....
2011-12	Cincinnati	ECHL	2	0	0	0	4	....	....	....	....	....	....	....	....	....	....	....	....	....	....	....	....	....	....
	Milwaukee	AHL	30	4	7	11	12	....	....	....	....	....	....	....	....	....	3	0	0	0	2	....	....	....	....
2012-13	Milwaukee	AHL	67	17	12	29	24	....	....	....	....	....	....	....	....	....	3	1	0	1	2	....	....	....	....
	Nashville	**NHL**	**4**	**1**	**0**	**1**	**0**	**0**	**0**	**0**	**3**	**33.3**	**–1**	**0**	**0.0**	**14:42**	....	....	....	....	....	....	....	....	....
	NHL Totals		**4**	**1**	**0**	**1**	**0**	**0**	**0**	**0**	**3**	**33.3**		**0**	**0.0**	**14:42**	....	....	....	....	....	....	....	....	....

Signed as a free agent by **San Jose**, April 22, 2009. Signed as a free agent by **Nashville**, July 1, 2012.

HENDRICKS, Matt
(HEHN-drihks, MAT) **NSH**

Center. Shoots left. 6', 211 lbs. Born, Blaine, MN, June 17, 1981. Nashville's 5th choice, 131st overall, in 2000 Entry Draft.

			Regular Season														Playoffs								
Season	Club	League	GP	G	A	Pts	PIM	PP	SH	GW	S	%	+/-	TF	F%	Min	GP	G	A	Pts	PIM	PP	SH	GW	Min
1998-99	Blaine Bengals	High-MN	22	23	34	57	42	....	....	....	....	....	....	....	....	....	....	....	....	....	....	....	....	....	....
99-2000	Blaine Bengals	High-MN	21	23	30	53	28	....	....	....	....	....	....	....	....	....	....	....	....	....	....	....	....	....	....
2000-01	St. Cloud State	WCHA	37	3	9	12	23	....	....	....	....	....	....	....	....	....	....	....	....	....	....	....	....	....	....
2001-02	St. Cloud State	WCHA	42	19	20	39	74	....	....	....	....	....	....	....	....	....	....	....	....	....	....	....	....	....	....
2002-03	St. Cloud State	WCHA	37	18	18	36	64	....	....	....	....	....	....	....	....	....	....	....	....	....	....	....	....	....	....
2003-04	St. Cloud State	WCHA	37	14	11	25	32	....	....	....	....	....	....	....	....	....	....	....	....	....	....	....	....	....	....
	Milwaukee	AHL	1	0	0	0	2	....	....	....	....	....	....	....	....	....	....	....	....	....	....	....	....	....	....
2004-05	Lowell	AHL	15	1	2	3	10	....	....	....	....	....	....	....	....	....	....	....	....	....	....	....	....	....	....
	Florida Everblades	ECHL	54	24	26	50	94	....	....	....	....	....	....	....	....	....	4	0	0	0	4	....	....	....	....
2005-06	Rochester	AHL	56	13	14	27	84	....	....	....	....	....	....	....	....	....	....	....	....	....	....	....	....	....	....
2006-07	Hershey Bears	AHL	65	18	26	44	105	....	....	....	....	....	....	....	....	....	19	8	4	12	18	....	....	....	....
2007-08	Providence Bruins	AHL	67	22	30	52	121	....	....	....	....	....	....	....	....	....	10	0	3	3	6	....	....	....	....
2008-09	**Colorado**	**NHL**	**4**	**0**	**0**	**0**	**13**	**0**	**0**	**0**	**5**	**0.0**	**1**	**1**	**0.0**	**8:30**	....	....	....	....	....	....	....	....	....
	Lake Erie	AHL	43	14	15	29	71	....	....	....	....	....	....	....	....	....	....	....	....	....	....	....	....	....	....
2009-10	**Colorado**	**NHL**	**56**	**9**	**7**	**16**	**74**	**0**	**1**	**1**	**63**	**14.3**	**1**	**83**	**39.8**	**9:16**	**6**	**0**	**0**	**0**	**0**	**0**	**0**	**0**	**9:52**
2010-11	**Washington**	**NHL**	**77**	**9**	**16**	**25**	**110**	**1**	**0**	**3**	**113**	**8.0**	**–2**	**98**	**53.1**	**11:28**	**7**	**0**	**0**	**0**	**4**	**0**	**0**	**0**	**9:08**
2011-12	**Washington**	**NHL**	**78**	**4**	**5**	**9**	**95**	**0**	**0**	**0**	**97**	**4.1**	**–6**	**265**	**53.6**	**12:07**	**14**	**1**	**1**	**2**	**6**	**0**	**0**	**0**	**16:05**
2012-13	**Washington**	**NHL**	**48**	**5**	**3**	**8**	**73**	**0**	**0**	**1**	**54**	**9.3**	**–6**	**259**	**56.8**	**11:43**	**7**	**0**	**0**	**0**	**0**	**0**	**0**	**0**	**10:32**
	NHL Totals		**263**	**27**	**31**	**58**	**365**	**1**	**1**	**5**	**332**	**8.1**		**706**	**53.0**	**11:11**	**34**	**1**	**1**	**2**	**10**	**0**	**0**	**0**	**12:25**

Signed as a free agent by **Boston**, July 9, 2007. Traded to **Colorado** by **Boston** for Johnny Boychuk, June 24, 2008. Signed as a free agent by **Washington**, September 27, 2010. Signed as a free agent by **Nashville**, July 5, 2013.

HENDRY, Jordan
(HEHN-dree, JOHR-dahn)

Defense. Shoots left. 6', 197 lbs. Born, Nokomis, Sask., February 23, 1984.

			Regular Season														Playoffs								
Season	Club	League	GP	G	A	Pts	PIM	PP	SH	GW	S	%	+/-	TF	F%	Min	GP	G	A	Pts	PIM	PP	SH	GW	Min
2002-03	Alaska	CCHA	35	3	5	8	10	....	....	....	....	....	....	....	....	....	....	....	....	....	....	....	....	....	....
2003-04	Alaska	CCHA	36	4	9	13	38	....	....	....	....	....	....	....	....	....	....	....	....	....	....	....	....	....	....
2004-05	Alaska	CCHA	3	0	1	1	21	....	....	....	....	....	....	....	....	....	....	....	....	....	....	....	....	....	....
2005-06	Alaska	CCHA	38	4	10	14	74	....	....	....	....	....	....	....	....	....	....	....	....	....	....	....	....	....	....
	Norfolk Admirals	AHL	13	1	4	5	13	....	....	....	....	....	....	....	....	....	3	0	0	0	2	....	....	....	....
2006-07	Norfolk Admirals	AHL	80	4	12	16	84	....	....	....	....	....	....	....	....	....	6	0	2	2	6	....	....	....	....
2007-08	**Chicago**	**NHL**	**40**	**1**	**3**	**4**	**22**	**0**	**0**	**0**	**32**	**3.1**	**0**	**0**	**0.0**	**17:13**	....	....	....	....	....	....	....	....	....
	Rockford IceHogs	AHL	45	3	4	7	58	....	....	....	....	....	....	....	....	....	1	0	0	0	2	....	....	....	....
2008-09	**Chicago**	**NHL**	**9**	**0**	**0**	**0**	**4**	**0**	**0**	**0**	**1**	**0.0**	**–1**	**0**	**0.0**	**10:06**	....	....	....	....	....	....	....	....	....
	Rockford IceHogs	AHL	53	3	6	9	45	....	....	....	....	....	....	....	....	....	4	0	0	0	2	....	....	....	....
2009-10 ♦	**Chicago**	**NHL**	**43**	**2**	**6**	**8**	**10**	**0**	**0**	**1**	**42**	**4.8**	**5**	**0**	**0.0**	**11:51**	**15**	**0**	**0**	**0**	**2**	**0**	**0**	**0**	**8:09**
2010-11	**Chicago**	**NHL**	**37**	**1**	**0**	**1**	**4**	**0**	**0**	**0**	**35**	**2.9**	**–2**	**1**	**0.0**	**10:42**	....	....	....	....	....	....	....	....	....
2011-12	Houston Aeros	AHL	10	0	2	2	10	....	....	....	....	....	....	....	....	....	....	....	....	....	....	....	....	....	....
	HC Lugano	Swiss	29	1	9	10	18	....	....	....	....	....	....	....	....	....	5	0	0	0	2	....	....	....	....
2012-13	Norfolk Admirals	AHL	62	2	9	11	63	....	....	....	....	....	....	....	....	....	....	....	....	....	....	....	....	....	....
	Anaheim	**NHL**	**2**	**0**	**0**	**0**	**0**	**0**	**0**	**0**	**0**	**0.0**	**0**	**0**	**0.0**	**17:35**	....	....	....	....	....	....	....	....	....
	NHL Totals		**131**	**4**	**9**	**13**	**40**	**0**	**0**	**1**	**110**	**3.6**		**1**	**0.0**	**13:08**	**15**	**0**	**0**	**0**	**2**	**0**	**0**	**0**	**8:09**

Signed as a free agent by **Chicago**, July 17, 2006. • Missed majority of 2010-11 due to knee injury and as a healthy reserve. Signed as a free agent by **Houston** (AHL), October 5, 2011. Signed as a free agent by **Lugano** (Swiss), November 1, 2011. Signed as a free agent by **Anaheim**, July 1, 2012.

HENNESSY, Josh
(HEHN-eh-see, JAWSH)

Center. Shoots left. 6', 192 lbs. Born, Brockton, MA, February 7, 1985. San Jose's 3rd choice, 43rd overall, in 2003 Entry Draft.

			Regular Season														Playoffs								
Season	Club	League	GP	G	A	Pts	PIM	PP	SH	GW	S	%	+/-	TF	F%	Min	GP	G	A	Pts	PIM	PP	SH	GW	Min
2000-01	Milton Academy	High-MA	28	20	30	50	20	....	....	....	....	....	....	....	....	....	....	....	....	....	....	....	....	....	....
2001-02	Quebec Remparts	QMJHL	70	20	20	40	24	....	....	....	....	....	....	....	....	....	9	3	9	12	8	....	....	....	....
2002-03	Quebec Remparts	QMJHL	72	33	51	84	44	....	....	....	....	....	....	....	....	....	11	6	9	15	10	....	....	....	....
2003-04	Quebec Remparts	QMJHL	59	40	42	82	55	....	....	....	....	....	....	....	....	....	....	....	....	....	....	....	....	....	....
2004-05	Quebec Remparts	QMJHL	68	35	50	85	39	....	....	....	....	....	....	....	....	....	13	2	9	11	6	....	....	....	....
2005-06	Cleveland Barons	AHL	80	24	39	63	60	....	....	....	....	....	....	....	....	....	....	....	....	....	....	....	....	....	....
2006-07	**Ottawa**	**NHL**	**10**	**1**	**0**	**1**	**4**	**0**	**0**	**0**	**6**	**16.7**	**0**	**43**	**37.2**	**5:39**	....	....	....	....	....	....	....	....	....
	Binghamton	AHL	76	27	30	57	54	....	....	....	....	....	....	....	....	....	....	....	....	....	....	....	....	....	....
2007-08	**Ottawa**	**NHL**	**5**	**0**	**0**	**0**	**0**	**0**	**0**	**0**	**2**	**0.0**	**–1**	**12**	**41.7**	**3:46**	....	....	....	....	....	....	....	....	....
	Binghamton	AHL	76	22	29	51	49	....	....	....	....	....	....	....	....	....	....	....	....	....	....	....	....	....	....
2008-09	**Ottawa**	**NHL**	**1**	**0**	**0**	**0**	**0**	**0**	**0**	**0**	**0**	**0.0**	**0**	**7**	**28.6**	**13:40**	....	....	....	....	....	....	....	....	....
	Binghamton	AHL	59	20	17	37	26	....	....	....	....	....	....	....	....	....	....	....	....	....	....	....	....	....	....
2009-10	**Ottawa**	**NHL**	**4**	**0**	**0**	**0**	**0**	**0**	**0**	**0**	**2**	**0.0**	**–1**	**13**	**61.5**	**5:59**	....	....	....	....	....	....	....	....	....
	Binghamton	AHL	78	30	38	68	26	....	....	....	....	....	....	....	....	....	....	....	....	....	....	....	....	....	....
2010-11	HC Lugano	Swiss	36	9	10	19	22	....	....	....	....	....	....	....	....	....	1	0	0	0	0	....	....	....	....
2011-12	**Boston**	**NHL**	**3**	**0**	**0**	**0**	**2**	**0**	**0**	**0**	**2**	**0.0**	**1**	**13**	**61.5**	**6:46**	....	....	....	....	....	....	....	....	....
	Providence Bruins	AHL	69	19	22	41	22	....	....	....	....	....	....	....	....	....	....	....	....	....	....	....	....	....	....
2012-13	Vityaz Chekhov	KHL	48	11	14	25	53	....	....	....	....	....	....	....	....	....	2	0	0	0	4	....	....	....	....
	NHL Totals		**23**	**1**	**0**	**1**	**6**	**0**	**0**	**0**	**12**	**8.3**		**88**	**44.3**	**5:47**	....	....	....	....	....	....	....	....	....

Traded to **Chicago** by **San Jose** with Tom Preissing for Mark Bell, July 9, 2006. Traded to **Ottawa** by **Chicago** with Tom Preissing, Michal Barinka and Chicago's 2nd round choice (Patrick Wiercioch) in 2008 Entry Draft for Martin Havlat and Bryan Smolinski, July 10, 2006. Signed as a free agent by **Lugano** (Swiss), May 6, 2010. Signed as a free agent by **Boston**, July 5, 2011. Signed as a free agent by **Chekhov** (KHL), August 3, 2012.

HENRIQUE, Adam
(HEHN-reek, A-duhm) **N.J.**

Center. Shoots left. 6', 195 lbs. Born, Brantford, Ont., February 6, 1990. New Jersey's 4th choice, 82nd overall, in 2008 Entry Draft.

			Regular Season														Playoffs								
Season	Club	League	GP	G	A	Pts	PIM	PP	SH	GW	S	%	+/-	TF	F%	Min	GP	G	A	Pts	PIM	PP	SH	GW	Min
2006-07	Windsor Spitfires	OHL	62	23	21	44	20	....	....	....	....	....	....	....	....	....	....	....	....	....	....	....	....	....	....
2007-08	Windsor Spitfires	OHL	66	20	24	44	28	....	....	....	....	....	....	....	....	....	5	2	3	5	4	....	....	....	....
2008-09	Windsor Spitfires	OHL	56	30	33	63	47	....	....	....	....	....	....	....	....	....	20	8	9	17	19	....	....	....	....
2009-10	Windsor Spitfires	OHL	54	38	39	77	57	....	....	....	....	....	....	....	....	....	19	*20	5	25	12	....	....	....	....
2010-11	**New Jersey**	**NHL**	**1**	**0**	**0**	**0**	**0**	**0**	**0**	**0**	**3**	**0.0**	**1**	**1**	**0.0**	**13:21**	....	....	....	....	....	....	....	....	....
	Albany Devils	AHL	73	25	25	50	26	....	....	....	....	....	....	....	....	....	....	....	....	....	....	....	....	....	....
2011-12	**New Jersey**	**NHL**	**74**	**16**	**35**	**51**	**7**	**0**	***4**	**3**	**130**	**12.3**	**8**	**1026**	**48.8**	**18:10**	**24**	**5**	**8**	**13**	**11**	**0**	**0**	***3**	**17:15**
	Albany Devils	AHL	3	0	1	1	2	....	....	....	....	....	....	....	....	....	....	....	....	....	....	....	....	....	....
2012-13	Albany Devils	AHL	16	5	3	8	12	....	....	....	....	....	....	....	....	....	....	....	....	....	....	....	....	....	....
	New Jersey	**NHL**	**42**	**11**	**5**	**16**	**16**	**3**	**2**	**2**	**78**	**14.1**	**–3**	**680**	**49.0**	**18:19**	....	....	....	....	....	....	....	....	....
	NHL Totals		**117**	**27**	**40**	**67**	**23**	**3**	**6**	**5**	**211**	**12.8**		**1707**	**48.9**	**18:11**	**24**	**5**	**8**	**13**	**11**	**0**	**0**	**3**	**17:15**

NHL All-Rookie Team (2012)

								Regular Season									Playoffs								
Season	Club	League	GP	G	A	Pts	PIM	PP	SH	GW	S	%	+/-	TF	F%	Min	GP	G	A	Pts	PIM	PP	SH	GW	Min

HENSICK, T.J.

(HEHN-sihk, TEE-JAY)

Center. Shoots right. 5'10", 190 lbs. Born, Lansing, MI, December 10, 1985. Colorado's 5th choice, 88th overall, in 2005 Entry Draft.

2001-02	USNTDP	U-17	17	10	5	15	....	....	....	....	....	....	....	....	....	....	....	....	....	....	....	....	....	....	....
	USNTDP	NAHL	46	15	25	40	10	....	....	....	....	....	....	....	....	....	....	....	....	....	....	....	....	....	....
2002-03	USNTDP	U-18	48	24	24	48	11	....	....	....	....	....	....	....	....	....	....	....	....	....	....	....	....	....	....
	USNTDP	NAHL	10	6	7	13	0	....	....	....	....	....	....	....	....	....	....	....	....	....	....	....	....	....	....
2003-04	U. of Michigan	CCHA	43	12	*34	46	38	....	....	....	....	....	....	....	....	....	....	....	....	....	....	....	....	....	....
2004-05	U. of Michigan	CCHA	39	23	32	55	24	....	....	....	....	....	....	....	....	....	....	....	....	....	....	....	....	....	....
2005-06	U. of Michigan	CCHA	41	17	35	52	44	....	....	....	....	....	....	....	....	....	....	....	....	....	....	....	....	....	....
2006-07	U. of Michigan	CCHA	41	23	*46	*69	38	....	....	....	....	....	....	....	....	....	....	....	....	....	....	....	....	....	....
2007-08	**Colorado**	**NHL**	**31**	**6**	**5**	**11**	**2**	**4**	**0**	**1**	**52**	**11.5**	**–4**	**256**	**42.2**	**11:59**	**2**	**0**	**1**	**1**	**0**	**0**	**0**	**0**	**15:29**
	Lake Erie	AHL	50	12	33	45	18	....	....	....	....	....	....	....	....	....	....	....	....	....	....	....	....	....	....
2008-09	**Colorado**	**NHL**	**61**	**4**	**17**	**21**	**14**	**1**	**0**	**0**	**116**	**3.4**	**–7**	**510**	**47.3**	**12:54**	....	....	....	....	....	....	....	....	....
	Lake Erie	AHL	12	7	9	16	2	....	....	....	....	....	....	....	....	....	....	....	....	....	....	....	....	....	....
2009-10	**Colorado**	**NHL**	**7**	**1**	**2**	**3**	**0**	**0**	**0**	**0**	**13**	**7.7**	**0**	**14**	**42.9**	**9:27**	....	....	....	....	....	....	....	....	....
	Lake Erie	AHL	58	20	50	70	25	....	....	....	....	....	....	....	....	....	....	....	....	....	....	....	....	....	....
2010-11	**St. Louis**	**NHL**	**13**	**1**	**2**	**3**	**2**	**0**	**0**	**0**	**12**	**8.3**	**–5**	**29**	**37.9**	**9:05**	....	....	....	....	....	....	....	....	....
	Peoria Rivermen	AHL	59	21	48	69	27	....	....	....	....	....	....	....	....	....	4	2	1	3	2	....	....	....	....
2011-12	Peoria Rivermen	AHL	66	21	49	70	20	....	....	....	....	....	....	....	....	....	....	....	....	....	....	....	....	....	....
2012-13	Peoria Rivermen	AHL	76	19	48	67	50	....	....	....	....	....	....	....	....	....	....	....	....	....	....	....	....	....	....
	NHL Totals		**112**	**12**	**26**	**38**	**18**	**5**	**0**	**1**	**193**	**6.2**		**809**	**45.2**	**11:59**	**2**	**0**	**1**	**1**	**0**	**0**	**0**	**0**	**15:29**

CCHA All-Rookie Team (2004) • CCHA First All-Star Team (2004, 2005, 2007) • CCHA Rookie of the Year (2004) • NCAA West First All-American Team (2005, 2007) • CCHA Second All-Star Team (2006) • AHL Second All-Star Team (2012)

Traded to **St. Louis** by **Colorado** for Julian Talbot, June 17, 2010.

HICKEY, Thomas

(HIH-kee, TAW-muhs) **NYI**

Defense. Shoots left. 5'11", 190 lbs. Born, Calgary, Alta., February 8, 1989. Los Angeles' 1st choice, 4th overall, in 2007 Entry Draft.

2003-04	Calgary Royals	CBHL	32	13	25	38	51	....	....	....	....	....	....	....	....	....	....	....	....	....	....	....	....	....	....
2004-05	Calgary Royals	AMHL	33	9	13	22	36	....	....	....	....	....	....	....	....	....	....	....	....	....	....	....	....	....	....
	Seattle	WHL	5	2	1	3	6	....	....	....	....	....	....	....	....	....	....	....	....	....	....	....	....	....	....
2005-06	Seattle	WHL	69	1	27	28	53	....	....	....	....	....	....	....	....	....	7	1	3	4	10	....	....	....	....
2006-07	Seattle	WHL	68	9	41	50	70	....	....	....	....	....	....	....	....	....	11	3	4	7	4	....	....	....	....
2007-08	Seattle	WHL	63	11	34	45	49	....	....	....	....	....	....	....	....	....	9	1	9	10	4	....	....	....	....
2008-09	Seattle	WHL	57	16	35	51	30	....	....	....	....	....	....	....	....	....	5	2	1	3	4	....	....	....	....
	Manchester	AHL	7	1	6	7	2	....	....	....	....	....	....	....	....	....	....	....	....	....	....	....	....	....	....
2009-10	Manchester	AHL	19	1	5	6	12	....	....	....	....	....	....	....	....	....	4	0	3	3	0	....	....	....	....
2010-11	Manchester	AHL	77	6	18	24	38	....	....	....	....	....	....	....	....	....	7	0	2	2	0	....	....	....	....
2011-12	Manchester	AHL	76	3	23	26	36	....	....	....	....	....	....	....	....	....	4	0	4	4	2	....	....	....	....
2012-13	Manchester	AHL	33	3	9	12	12	....	....	....	....	....	....	....	....	....	....	....	....	....	....	....	....	....	....
	NY Islanders	**NHL**	**39**	**1**	**3**	**4**	**8**	**0**	**0**	**1**	**40**	**2.5**	**9**	**0**	**0.0**	**16:52**	**2**	**0**	**0**	**0**	**2**	**0**	**0**	**0**	**18:17**
	NHL Totals		**39**	**1**	**3**	**4**	**8**	**0**	**0**	**1**	**40**	**2.5**		**0**	**0.0**	**16:52**	**2**	**0**	**0**	**0**	**2**	**0**	**0**	**0**	**18:17**

WHL West Second All-Star Team (2007) • WHL West First All-Star Team (2008, 2009)

• Missed majority of 2009-10 due to shoulder injury. Claimed on waivers by **NY Islanders** from **Los Angeles**, January 15, 2013.

HIGGINS, Chris

(HIH-gihns, KRIHS) **VAN**

Left wing. Shoots left. 6', 193 lbs. Born, Smithtown, NY, June 2, 1983. Montreal's 1st choice, 14th overall, in 2002 Entry Draft.

99-2000	Avon Old Farms	High-CT	27	19	20	39	10	....	....	....	....	....	....	....	....	....	....	....	....	....	....	....	....	....	....
2000-01	Avon Old Farms	High-CT	24	22	14	36	29	....	....	....	....	....	....	....	....	....	....	....	....	....	....	....	....	....	....
2001-02	Yale	ECAC	27	14	17	31	32	....	....	....	....	....	....	....	....	....	....	....	....	....	....	....	....	....	....
2002-03	Yale	ECAC	28	20	21	41	41	....	....	....	....	....	....	....	....	....	....	....	....	....	....	....	....	....	....
2003-04	**Montreal**	**NHL**	**2**	**0**	**0**	**0**	**0**	**0**	**0**	**0**	**0**	**0.0**	**0**	**9**	**22.2**	**6:18**	....	....	....	....	....	....	....	....	....
	Hamilton	AHL	67	21	27	48	18	....	....	....	....	....	....	....	....	....	10	3	2	5	0	....	....	....	....
2004-05	Hamilton	AHL	76	28	23	51	33	....	....	....	....	....	....	....	....	....	4	3	3	6	4	....	....	....	....
2005-06	**Montreal**	**NHL**	**80**	**23**	**15**	**38**	**26**	**7**	**3**	**3**	**148**	**15.5**	**–1**	**45**	**51.1**	**14:25**	**6**	**1**	**3**	**4**	**0**	**0**	**0**	**0**	**17:04**
2006-07	**Montreal**	**NHL**	**61**	**22**	**16**	**38**	**26**	**8**	**3**	**3**	**159**	**13.8**	**–11**	**53**	**34.0**	**17:54**	....	....	....	....	....	....	....	....	....
2007-08	**Montreal**	**NHL**	**82**	**27**	**25**	**52**	**22**	**12**	**0**	**5**	**241**	**11.2**	**0**	**62**	**35.5**	**17:57**	**12**	**3**	**2**	**5**	**2**	**0**	**0**	**0**	**18:27**
2008-09	**Montreal**	**NHL**	**57**	**12**	**11**	**23**	**22**	**2**	**2**	**1**	**151**	**7.9**	**–1**	**57**	**50.9**	**17:00**	**4**	**2**	**0**	**2**	**2**	**0**	**0**	**0**	**17:35**
2009-10	**NY Rangers**	**NHL**	**55**	**6**	**8**	**14**	**32**	**0**	**0**	**1**	**137**	**4.4**	**–9**	**63**	**41.3**	**17:55**	....	....	....	....	....	....	....	....	....
	Calgary	**NHL**	**12**	**2**	**1**	**3**	**0**	**0**	**0**	**0**	**28**	**7.1**	**0**	**7**	**28.6**	**15:52**	....	....	....	....	....	....	....	....	....
2010-11	**Florida**	**NHL**	**48**	**11**	**12**	**23**	**10**	**0**	**0**	**0**	**126**	**8.7**	**5**	**65**	**46.2**	**16:39**	....	....	....	....	....	....	....	....	....
	Vancouver	**NHL**	**14**	**2**	**3**	**5**	**6**	**1**	**0**	**0**	**34**	**5.9**	**0**	**20**	**55.0**	**15:07**	**25**	**4**	**4**	**8**	**2**	**1**	**0**	**3**	**17:08**
2011-12	**Vancouver**	**NHL**	**71**	**18**	**25**	**43**	**16**	**1**	**1**	**4**	**165**	**10.9**	**11**	**30**	**40.0**	**16:19**	**5**	**0**	**0**	**0**	**2**	**0**	**0**	**0**	**15:34**
2012-13	**Vancouver**	**NHL**	**41**	**10**	**5**	**15**	**10**	**0**	**0**	**1**	**77**	**13.0**	**–4**	**91**	**36.3**	**16:25**	**4**	**0**	**0**	**0**	**0**	**0**	**0**	**0**	**16:41**
	NHL Totals		**523**	**133**	**121**	**254**	**170**	**31**	**9**	**18**	**1266**	**10.5**		**502**	**41.4**	**16:40**	**56**	**10**	**9**	**19**	**8**	**1**	**0**	**3**	**17:16**

ECAC All-Rookie Team (2002) • ECAC Second All-Star Team (2002) • ECAC Rookie of the Year (2002) • ECAC First All-Star Team (2003) • ECAC Player of the Year (2003) (co-winner - David LeNeveu) • NCAA East First All-American Team (2003)

Traded to **NY Rangers** by **Montreal** with Ryan McDonagh and Pavel Valentenko for Scott Gomez, Tom Pyatt and Michael Busto, June 30, 2009. Traded to **Calgary** by **NY Rangers** with Ales Kotalik for Olli Jokinen and Brandon Prust, February 2, 2010. Signed as a free agent by **Florida**, July 2, 2010. Traded to **Vancouver** by **Florida** for Evan Oberg and Vancouver's 3rd round choice (later traded back to Vancouver – Vancouver selected Cole Cassels) in 2013 Entry Draft, February 28, 2011.

HILLEN, Jack

(HIHL-uhn, JAK) **WSH**

Defense. Shoots left. 5'10", 190 lbs. Born, Minnetonka, MN, January 24, 1986.

2003-04	Tri-City Storm	USHL	21	2	2	4	16	....	....	....	....	....	....	....	....	....	8	0	1	1	4	....	....	....	....
2004-05	Colorado College	WCHA	30	2	9	11	20	....	....	....	....	....	....	....	....	....	....	....	....	....	....	....	....	....	....
2005-06	Colorado College	WCHA	42	4	9	13	48	....	....	....	....	....	....	....	....	....	....	....	....	....	....	....	....	....	....
2006-07	Colorado College	WCHA	38	7	8	15	38	....	....	....	....	....	....	....	....	....	....	....	....	....	....	....	....	....	....
2007-08	Colorado College	WCHA	41	6	*31	37	60	....	....	....	....	....	....	....	....	....	....	....	....	....	....	....	....	....	....
	NY Islanders	**NHL**	**2**	**0**	**1**	**1**	**4**	**0**	**0**	**0**	**3**	**0.0**	**1**	**0**	**0.0**	**15:32**	....	....	....	....	....	....	....	....	....
2008-09	**NY Islanders**	**NHL**	**40**	**1**	**5**	**6**	**16**	**0**	**0**	**0**	**47**	**2.1**	**–9**	**0**	**0.0**	**15:13**	....	....	....	....	....	....	....	....	....
	Bridgeport	AHL	33	4	13	17	31	....	....	....	....	....	....	....	....	....	5	0	2	2	2	....	....	....	....
2009-10	**NY Islanders**	**NHL**	**69**	**3**	**18**	**21**	**44**	**1**	**0**	**0**	**78**	**3.8**	**–5**	**1**	**100.0**	**20:42**	....	....	....	....	....	....	....	....	....
2010-11	**NY Islanders**	**NHL**	**64**	**4**	**18**	**22**	**45**	**0**	**0**	**1**	**81**	**4.9**	**–5**	**0**	**0.0**	**18:49**	....	....	....	....	....	....	....	....	....
2011-12	**Nashville**	**NHL**	**55**	**2**	**4**	**6**	**20**	**0**	**0**	**0**	**51**	**3.9**	**6**	**0**	**0.0**	**14:04**	**2**	**0**	**0**	**0**	**2**	**0**	**0**	**0**	**7:54**
2012-13	**Washington**	**NHL**	**23**	**3**	**6**	**9**	**14**	**0**	**0**	**1**	**28**	**10.7**	**9**	**0**	**0.0**	**17:37**	**7**	**0**	**1**	**1**	**6**	**0**	**0**	**0**	**16:37**
	NHL Totals		**253**	**13**	**52**	**65**	**143**	**1**	**0**	**2**	**288**	**4.5**		**1**	**100.0**	**17:35**	**9**	**0**	**1**	**1**	**8**	**0**	**0**	**0**	**14:41**

WCHA First All-Star Team (2008) • NCAA West First All-American Team (2008)

Signed as a free agent by **NY Islanders**, April 1, 2008. Signed as a free agent by **Nashville**, August 8, 2011. Signed as a free agent by **Washington**, July 3, 2012. • Missed majority of 2012-13 due to upper-body injury at Tampa Bay, January 19, 2013.

HJALMARSSON, Niklas

(JAHL-muhr-suhn, NIHK-luhs) **CHI**

Defense. Shoots left. 6'3", 207 lbs. Born, Eksjo, Sweden, June 6, 1987. Chicago's 5th choice, 108th overall, in 2005 Entry Draft.

2003-04	HV 71 Jr.	Swe-Jr.	15	1	3	4	14	....	....	....	....	....	....	....	....	....	2	0	0	0	8	....	....	....	....
2004-05	HV 71 U18	Swe-U18	3	0	2	2	4	....	....	....	....	....	....	....	....	....	....	....	....	....	....	....	....	....	....
	HV 71 Jr.	Swe-Jr.	31	4	11	15	87	....	....	....	....	....	....	....	....	....	....	....	....	....	....	....	....	....	....
	HV 71 Jonkoping	Sweden	14	0	0	0	0	....	....	....	....	....	....	....	....	....	....	....	....	....	....	....	....	....	....
2005-06	HV 71 Jr.	Swe-Jr.	7	3	2	5	12	....	....	....	....	....	....	....	....	....	....	....	....	....	....	....	....	....	....
	HV 71 Jonkoping	Sweden	4	1	2	3	0	....	....	....	....	....	....	....	....	....	12	0	1	1	4	....	....	....	....
2006-07	HV 71 Jonkoping	Sweden	37	2	0	2	24	....	....	....	....	....	....	....	....	....	14	1	1	2	0	....	....	....	....
	HV 71 Jr.	Swe-Jr.	7	0	2	2	14	....	....	....	....	....	....	....	....	....	....	....	....	....	....	....	....	....	....
	IK Oskarshamn	Sweden-2	8	1	2	3	6	....	....	....	....	....	....	....	....	....	....	....	....	....	....	....	....	....	....
2007-08	**Chicago**	**NHL**	**13**	**0**	**1**	**1**	**13**	**0**	**0**	**0**	**5**	**0.0**	**–2**	**0**	**0.0**	**13:37**	....	....	....	....	....	....	....	....	....
	Rockford IceHogs	AHL	47	4	9	13	31	....	....	....	....	....	....	....	....	....	12	0	4	4	8	....	....	....	....
2008-09	**Chicago**	**NHL**	**21**	**1**	**2**	**3**	**0**	**0**	**0**	**0**	**15**	**6.7**	**4**	**0**	**0.0**	**14:59**	**17**	**0**	**1**	**1**	**6**	**0**	**0**	**0**	**16:37**
	Rockford IceHogs	AHL	52	2	16	18	53	....	....	....	....	....	....	....	....	....	....	....	....	....	....	....	....	....	....
2009-10 ♦	**Chicago**	**NHL**	**77**	**2**	**15**	**17**	**20**	**0**	**0**	**1**	**62**	**3.2**	**9**	**0**	**0.0**	**19:40**	**22**	**1**	**7**	**8**	**6**	**0**	**0**	**0**	**21:01**

			Regular Season														Playoffs								
Season	Club	League	GP	G	A	Pts	PIM	PP	SH	GW	S	%	+/-	TF	F%	Min	GP	G	A	Pts	PIM	PP	SH	GW	Min
2010-11	**Chicago**	**NHL**	**80**	**3**	**7**	**10**	**39**	**0**	**0**	**0**	**64**	**4.7**	**13**	**0**	**0.0**	**18:29**	**7**	**0**	**2**	**2**	**2**	**0**	**0**	**0**	**18:55**
2011-12	**Chicago**	**NHL**	**69**	**1**	**14**	**15**	**14**	**0**	**0**	**0**	**65**	**1.5**	**9**	**0**	**0.0**	**20:11**	**6**	**0**	**1**	**1**	**4**	**0**	**0**	**0**	**18:10**
2012-13	HC Bolzano Foxes	Italy	18	6	16	22	8	....	....	....	....	....	....	....	....	....	....	....	....	....	....	....	....	....	....
	♦ Chicago	**NHL**	**46**	**2**	**8**	**10**	**22**	**0**	**0**	**0**	**43**	**4.7**	**15**	**0**	**0.0**	**20:54**	**23**	**0**	**5**	**5**	**4**	**0**	**0**	**0**	**23:15**
	NHL Totals		**306**	**9**	**47**	**56**	**108**	**0**	**0**	**1**	**254**	**3.5**		**0**	**0.0**	**19:05**	**75**	**1**	**16**	**17**	**22**	**0**	**0**	**0**	**20:17**

Signed as a free agent by **Bolzano** (Italy), November 8, 2012.

HODGSON, Cody

(HAWD-suhn, KOH-dee) **BUF**

Center. Shoots right. 6', 185 lbs. Born, Toronto, Ont., February 18, 1990. Vancouver's 1st choice, 10th overall, in 2008 Entry Draft.

2005-06	Markham Waxers	Minor-ON	30	27	24	51	22	....	....	....	....	....	....	....	....	....	15	13	14	27	8	....	....	....	....
2006-07	Brampton	OHL	63	23	23	46	24	....	....	....	....	....	....	....	....	....	4	1	3	4	0	....	....	....	....
2007-08	Brampton	OHL	68	40	45	85	36	....	....	....	....	....	....	....	....	....	5	5	0	5	2	....	....	....	....
2008-09	Brampton	OHL	53	43	49	92	33	....	....	....	....	....	....	....	....	....	21	11	20	31	18	....	....	....	....
	Manitoba Moose	AHL	....	....	....	....	....	....	....	....	....	....	....	....	....	....	11	2	4	6	4	....	....	....	....
2009-10	Brampton	OHL	13	8	12	20	9	....	....	....	....	....	....	....	....	....	11	3	7	10	4	....	....	....	....
2010-11	**Vancouver**	**NHL**	**8**	**1**	**1**	**2**	**0**	**0**	**0**	**0**	**9**	**11.1**	**1**	**42**	**38.1**	**7:44**	**12**	**0**	**1**	**1**	**2**	**0**	**0**	**0**	**6:45**
	Manitoba Moose	AHL	52	17	13	30	14	....	....	....	....	....	....	....	....	....	....	....	....	....	....	....	....	....	....
2011-12	**Vancouver**	**NHL**	**63**	**16**	**17**	**33**	**8**	**5**	**0**	**2**	**103**	**15.5**	**8**	**414**	**42.8**	**12:44**	....	....	....	....	....	....	....	....	....
	Buffalo	**NHL**	**20**	**3**	**5**	**8**	**2**	**2**	**0**	**1**	**51**	**5.9**	**–7**	**296**	**51.4**	**17:16**	....	....	....	....	....	....	....	....	....
2012-13	Rochester	AHL	19	5	14	19	10	....	....	....	....	....	....	....	....	....	....	....	....	....	....	....	....	....	....
	Buffalo	**NHL**	**48**	**15**	**19**	**34**	**20**	**3**	**1**	**1**	**114**	**13.2**	**–4**	**812**	**46.8**	**18:24**	....	....	....	....	....	....	....	....	....
	NHL Totals		**139**	**35**	**42**	**77**	**30**	**10**	**1**	**4**	**277**	**12.6**		**1564**	**46.4**	**15:03**	**12**	**0**	**1**	**1**	**2**	**0**	**0**	**0**	**6:46**

OHL First All-Star Team (2009) • OHL Player of the Year (2009) • Canadian Major Junior First All-Star Team (2009) • Canadian Major Junior Player of the Year (2009)

Traded to **Buffalo** by **Vancouver** for Zack Kassian, February 27, 2012.

HOFFMAN, Mike

(HAWF-muhn, MIGHK) **OTT**

Center/Left wing. Shoots left. 6', 185 lbs. Born, Kitchener, Ont., November 24, 1989. Ottawa's 5th choice, 130th overall, in 2009 Entry Draft.

2006-07	Kitchener	ON-Jr.B	47	28	29	57	70	....	....	....	....	....	....	....	....	....	6	3	5	8	6	....	....	....	....
	Kitchener Rangers	OHL	2	0	0	0	2	....	....	....	....	....	....	....	....	....	4	0	0	0	0	....	....	....	....
2007-08	Gatineau	QMJHL	19	5	7	12	16	....	....	....	....	....	....	....	....	....	....	....	....	....	....	....	....	....	....
	Drummondville	QMJHL	43	19	17	36	77	....	....	....	....	....	....	....	....	....	....	....	....	....	....	....	....	....	....
2008-09	Drummondville	QMJHL	62	52	42	94	86	....	....	....	....	....	....	....	....	....	19	21	13	34	26	....	....	....	....
2009-10	Saint John	QMJHL	56	46	39	85	38	....	....	....	....	....	....	....	....	....	21	11	13	24	23	....	....	....	....
2010-11	Binghamton	AHL	74	7	18	25	16	....	....	....	....	....	....	....	....	....	19	1	8	9	16	....	....	....	....
	Elmira Jackals	ECHL	4	0	3	3	0	....	....	....	....	....	....	....	....	....	....	....	....	....	....	....	....	....	....
2011-12	**Ottawa**	**NHL**	**1**	**0**	**0**	**0**	**0**	**0**	**0**	**0**	**0**	**0.0**	**–1**	**0**	**0.0**	**9:01**	....	....	....	....	....	....	....	....	....
	Binghamton	AHL	76	21	28	49	44	....	....	....	....	....	....	....	....	....	....	....	....	....	....	....	....	....	....
2012-13	Binghamton	AHL	41	13	15	28	38	....	....	....	....	....	....	....	....	....	....	....	....	....	....	....	....	....	....
	Ottawa	**NHL**	**3**	**0**	**0**	**0**	**2**	**0**	**0**	**0**	**6**	**0.0**	**–1**	**2**	**100.0**	**12:19**	....	....	....	....	....	....	....	....	....
	NHL Totals		**4**	**0**	**0**	**0**	**2**	**0**	**0**	**0**	**6**	**0.0**		**2**	**100.0**	**11:30**	....	....	....	....	....	....	....	....	....

QMJHL First All-Star Team (2009, 2010) • QMJHL Player of the Year (2010) • Canadian Major Junior Second All-Star Team (2010)

HOGGAN, Jeff

(HOH-guhn, JEHF)

Left wing. Shoots left. 6'1", 193 lbs. Born, Hope, B.C., February 1, 1978.

1998-99	Powell River Kings	BCHL	STATISTICS NOT AVAILABLE																						
99-2000	Nebraska-Omaha	CCHA	34	16	9	25	82	....	....	....	....	....	....	....	....	....	....	....	....	....	....	....	....	....	....
2000-01	Nebraska-Omaha	CCHA	42	12	17	29	78	....	....	....	....	....	....	....	....	....	....	....	....	....	....	....	....	....	....
2001-02	Nebraska-Omaha	CCHA	41	24	21	45	92	....	....	....	....	....	....	....	....	....	....	....	....	....	....	....	....	....	....
	Houston Aeros	AHL	....	....	....	....	....	....	....	....	....	....	....	....	....	....	4	0	0	0	2	....	....	....	....
2002-03	Houston Aeros	AHL	65	6	5	11	45	....	....	....	....	....	....	....	....	....	14	1	2	3	23	....	....	....	....
2003-04	Houston Aeros	AHL	77	21	15	36	88	....	....	....	....	....	....	....	....	....	2	0	1	1	4	....	....	....	....
2004-05	Worcester IceCats	AHL	47	16	9	25	55	....	....	....	....	....	....	....	....	....	....	....	....	....	....	....	....	....	....
2005-06	**St. Louis**	**NHL**	**52**	**2**	**6**	**8**	**34**	**0**	**0**	**0**	**60**	**3.3**	**–16**	**4**	**25.0**	**8:47**	....	....	....	....	....	....	....	....	....
2006-07	**Boston**	**NHL**	**46**	**0**	**2**	**2**	**33**	**0**	**0**	**0**	**53**	**0.0**	**–8**	**3**	**33.3**	**7:04**	....	....	....	....	....	....	....	....	....
	Providence Bruins	AHL	22	4	7	11	27	....	....	....	....	....	....	....	....	....	13	4	3	7	17	....	....	....	....
2007-08	**Boston**	**NHL**	**1**	**0**	**0**	**0**	**0**	**0**	**0**	**0**	**0**	**0.0**	**0**	**0**	**0.0**	**7:57**	....	....	....	....	....	....	....	....	....
	Providence Bruins	AHL	71	29	31	60	59	....	....	....	....	....	....	....	....	....	5	3	4	7	4	....	....	....	....
2008-09	**Phoenix**	**NHL**	**4**	**0**	**1**	**1**	**7**	**0**	**0**	**0**	**7**	**0.0**	**–1**	**2**	**0.0**	**12:00**	....	....	....	....	....	....	....	....	....
	San Antonio	AHL	60	22	13	35	64	....	....	....	....	....	....	....	....	....	....	....	....	....	....	....	....	....	....
2009-10	**Phoenix**	**NHL**	**4**	**0**	**0**	**0**	**2**	**0**	**0**	**0**	**5**	**0.0**	**–1**	**2**	**0.0**	**7:07**	....	....	....	....	....	....	....	....	....
	San Antonio	AHL	70	13	20	33	44	....	....	....	....	....	....	....	....	....	....	....	....	....	....	....	....	....	....
2010-11	Wolfsburg	Germany	38	11	10	21	63	....	....	....	....	....	....	....	....	....	2	0	0	0	2	....	....	....	....
2011-12	Hannover Scorp.	Germany	43	14	14	28	14	....	....	....	....	....	....	....	....	....	....	....	....	....	....	....	....	....	....
2012-13	Grand Rapids	AHL	76	20	25	45	31	....	....	....	....	....	....	....	....	....	24	5	7	12	14	....	....	....	....
	NHL Totals		**107**	**2**	**9**	**11**	**76**	**0**	**0**	**0**	**125**	**1.6**		**11**	**18.2**	**8:06**	....	....	....	....	....	....	....	....	....

CCHA First All-Star Team (2002) • NCAA West Second All-American Team (2002)

Signed to a PTO (professional tryout) contract by **Houston** (AHL), April 4, 2002. Signed as a free agent by **Minnesota**, August 20, 2002. Signed as a free agent by **Worcester** (AHL), September, 2004. Signed as a free agent by **St. Louis**, August 2, 2005. Signed as a free agent by **Boston**, July 21, 2006. Signed as a free agent by **Phoenix**, July 15, 2008. Signed as a free agent by **Wolfsburg** (Germany), July 29, 2010. Signed as a free agent by **Hannover** (Germany), June 14, 2011. Signed as a free agent by **Grand Rapids** (AHL), September 28, 2012.

HOLDEN, Nick

(HOHL-dehn, NIHK) **COL**

Defense. Shoots left. 6'4", 207 lbs. Born, St. Albert, Alta., May 15, 1987.

2004-05	Camrose Kodiaks	AJHL	4	0	0	0	0	....	....	....	....	....	....	....	....	....	....	....	....	....	....	....	....	....	....
2005-06	Camrose Kodiaks	AJHL	29	5	8	13	27	....	....	....	....	....	....	....	....	....	....	....	....	....	....	....	....	....	....
	Sherwood Park	AJHL	28	2	15	17	19	....	....	....	....	....	....	....	....	....	....	....	....	....	....	....	....	....	....
2006-07	Chilliwack Bruins	WHL	67	8	23	31	62	....	....	....	....	....	....	....	....	....	5	1	1	2	6	....	....	....	....
2007-08	Chilliwack Bruins	WHL	70	22	38	60	54	....	....	....	....	....	....	....	....	....	4	1	3	4	0	....	....	....	....
	Syracuse Crunch	AHL	1	0	0	0	2	....	....	....	....	....	....	....	....	....	....	....	....	....	....	....	....	....	....
2008-09	Syracuse Crunch	AHL	61	4	18	22	46	....	....	....	....	....	....	....	....	....	....	....	....	....	....	....	....	....	....
2009-10	Syracuse Crunch	AHL	68	6	17	23	52	....	....	....	....	....	....	....	....	....	....	....	....	....	....	....	....	....	....
2010-11	**Columbus**	**NHL**	**5**	**0**	**0**	**0**	**0**	**0**	**0**	**0**	**6**	**0.0**	**0**	**0**	**0.0**	**17:11**	....	....	....	....	....	....	....	....	....
	Springfield	AHL	67	4	21	25	63	....	....	....	....	....	....	....	....	....	....	....	....	....	....	....	....	....	....
2011-12	Springfield	AHL	25	3	6	9	14	....	....	....	....	....	....	....	....	....	....	....	....	....	....	....	....	....	....
2012-13	Springfield	AHL	73	9	30	39	58	....	....	....	....	....	....	....	....	....	8	0	3	3	6	....	....	....	....
	Columbus	**NHL**	**2**	**0**	**0**	**0**	**0**	**0**	**0**	**0**	**2**	**0.0**	**1**	**0**	**0.0**	**8:35**	....	....	....	....	....	....	....	....	....
	NHL Totals		**7**	**0**	**0**	**0**	**0**	**0**	**0**	**0**	**8**	**0.0**		**0**	**0.0**	**14:44**	....	....	....	....	....	....	....	....	....

Signed as a free agent by **Columbus**, March 28, 2008. • Missed majority of 2011-12 due to shoulder injury vs. Portland (AHL), January 13, 2012. Signed as a free agent by **Colorado**, July 6, 2013.

HOLLAND, Peter

(HAW-luhnd, PEE-tuhr) **ANA**

Center. Shoots left. 6'2", 195 lbs. Born, Toronto, Ont., January 14, 1991. Anaheim's 1st choice, 15th overall, in 2009 Entry Draft.

2006-07	Brampton	Minor-ON	60	59	60	119	107	....	....	....	....	....	....	....	....	....	....	....	....	....	....	....	....	....	....
2007-08	Guelph Storm	OHL	62	8	15	23	31	....	....	....	....	....	....	....	....	....	10	0	1	1	4	....	....	....	....
2008-09	Guelph Storm	OHL	68	28	39	67	42	....	....	....	....	....	....	....	....	....	4	4	0	4	2	....	....	....	....
2009-10	Guelph Storm	OHL	59	30	50	80	40	....	....	....	....	....	....	....	....	....	5	3	5	8	12	....	....	....	....
2010-11	Guelph Storm	OHL	67	37	51	88	57	....	....	....	....	....	....	....	....	....	6	3	6	9	4	....	....	....	....
	Syracuse Crunch	AHL	3	3	3	6	0	....	....	....	....	....	....	....	....	....	....	....	....	....	....	....	....	....	....
2011-12	**Anaheim**	**NHL**	**4**	**1**	**0**	**1**	**2**	**0**	**0**	**1**	**1**	**100.0**	**0**	**18**	**38.9**	**7:42**	....	....	....	....	....	....	....	....	....
	Syracuse Crunch	AHL	71	23	37	60	59	....	....	....	....	....	....	....	....	....	....	....	....	....	....	....	....	....	....
2012-13	Norfolk Admirals	AHL	45	19	20	39	68	....	....	....	....	....	....	....	....	....	....	....	....	....	....	....	....	....	....
	Anaheim	**NHL**	**21**	**3**	**2**	**5**	**4**	**1**	**0**	**0**	**26**	**11.5**	**4**	**203**	**43.8**	**11:35**	....	....	....	....	....	....	....	....	....
	NHL Totals		**25**	**4**	**2**	**6**	**6**	**1**	**0**	**1**	**27**	**14.8**		**221**	**43.4**	**10:58**	....	....	....	....	....	....	....	....	....

Season	Club	League	GP	G	A	Pts	PIM	PP	SH	GW	S	%	+/-	TF	F%	Min	Playoffs GP	G	A	Pts	PIM	PP	SH	GW	Min

HOLMSTROM, Ben

(HOHLM-struhm, BEHN) **PHI**

Right wing. Shoots right. 6'1", 197 lbs. Born, Colorado Springs, CO, April 9, 1987.

Season	Club	League	GP	G	A	Pts	PIM	PP	SH	GW	S	%	+/-	TF	F%	Min	Playoffs GP	G	A	Pts	PIM	PP	SH	GW	Min
2006-07	U. Mass-Lowell	H-East	30	4	9	13	18																		
2007-08	U. Mass-Lowell	H-East	37	7	20	27	62																		
2008-09	U. Mass-Lowell	H-East	38	6	15	21	52																		
2009-10	U. Mass-Lowell	H-East	39	9	14	23	69																		
	Adirondack	AHL	13	3	0	3	9																		
2010-11	**Philadelphia**	**NHL**	**2**	**0**	**0**	**0**	**5**	**0**	**0**	**0**	**0**	**0.0**	**-1**	**16**	**31.3**	**9:04**									
	Adirondack	AHL	79	16	22	38	75																		
2011-12	**Philadelphia**	**NHL**	**5**	**0**	**0**	**0**	**2**	**0**	**0**	**0**	**3**	**0.0**	**0**	**30**	**50.0**	**6:43**									
	Adirondack	AHL	67	15	26	41	134																		
2012-13	Adirondack	AHL	22	2	6	8	29																		
	NHL Totals		**7**	**0**	**0**	**0**	**7**	**0**	**0**	**0**	**3**	**0.0**		**46**	**43.5**	**7:24**									

Signed as a free agent by **Philadelphia**, March 17, 2010. • Missed majority of 2012-13 due to knee injury vs. Syracuse (AHL), December 8, 2012.

HOLOS, Jonas

(hoh-LAWS, YOH-nuhs) **COL**

Defense. Shoots right. 5'11", 196 lbs. Born, Sarpsborg, Norway, August 27, 1987. Colorado's 6th choice, 170th overall, in 2008 Entry Draft.

Season	Club	League	GP	G	A	Pts	PIM	PP	SH	GW	S	%	+/-	TF	F%	Min	Playoffs GP	G	A	Pts	PIM	PP	SH	GW	Min
2002-03	Sarpsborg Jr.	Nor-Jr.	20	1	1	2	0																		
2003-04	Sarpsborg Jr.	Nor-Jr.	35	10	7	17	24										1	0	1	1	2				
	Sarpsborg	Norway	1	0	0	0	0																		
2004-05	Sarpsborg Jr.	Nor-Jr.	1	1	1	2	0										1	0	0	0	0				
	Sarpsborg	Norway	41	3	2	5	18										4	0	0	0	2				
2005-06	Sarpsborg	Norway	26	3	4	7	14										6	0	0	0	0				
2006-07	Sarpsborg 2	Norway-2	1	2	0	2	0																		
	Sarpsborg	Norway	40	11	19	30	32										13	2	2	4	18				
2007-08	Sarpsborg	Norway	40	2	20	22	67										6	1	0	1	2				
2008-09	Farjestad	Sweden	55	8	8	16	12										13	3	3	6	8				
2009-10	Farjestad	Sweden	51	1	13	14	24										7	0	0	0	2				
	Norway	Olympics	4	0	1	1	2																		
2010-11	**Colorado**	**NHL**	**39**	**0**	**6**	**6**	**10**	**0**	**0**	**0**	**36**	**0.0**	**-3**	**0**	**0.0**	**18:03**									
	Lake Erie	AHL	17	0	6	6	8										7	1	1	2	8				
2011-12	Vaxjo Lakers HC	Sweden	41	2	7	9	8																		
2012-13	Vaxjo Lakers HC	Sweden	55	4	13	17	10																		
	NHL Totals		**39**	**0**	**6**	**6**	**10**	**0**	**0**	**0**	**36**	**0.0**		**0**	**0.0**	**18:03**									

• Re-assigned to **Vaxjo** (Sweden) by **Colorado**, October 16. 2011.

HOLZER, Korbinian

(HOHL-zuhr, kohr-BEEHN-yuhn) **TOR**

Defense. Shoots right. 6'3", 205 lbs. Born, Munich, West Germany, February 16, 1988. Toronto's 4th choice, 111th overall, in 2006 Entry Draft.

Season	Club	League	GP	G	A	Pts	PIM	PP	SH	GW	S	%	+/-	TF	F%	Min	Playoffs GP	G	A	Pts	PIM	PP	SH	GW	Min
2004-05	EC Bad Tolz Jr.	Ger-Jr.	34	7	11	18	66										5	0	2	2	2				
2005-06	EC Bad Tolz Jr.	Ger-Jr.	2	1	1	2	6																		
	Tolzer Lowen	German-2	46	3	3	6	94																		
2006-07	Regensburg	German-2	42	2	6	8	68										4	0	0	0	2				
2007-08	Dusseldorf	Germany	35	2	5	7	66										13	0	2	2	20				
2008-09	Dusseldorf	Germany	38	4	5	9	89										16	0	1	1	18				
2009-10	Dusseldorf	Germany	52	6	16	22	96										3	0	0	0	4				
	Germany	Olympics	4	0	0	0	2																		
2010-11	**Toronto**	**NHL**	**2**	**0**	**0**	**0**	**2**	**0**	**0**	**0**	**1**	**0.0**	**-1**	**0**	**0.0**	**13:01**									
	Toronto Marlies	AHL	73	3	10	13	88																		
2011-12	Toronto Marlies	AHL	67	1	19	20	68										17	1	4	5	39				
2012-13	Toronto Marlies	AHL	46	1	10	11	46										8	0	1	1	24				
	Toronto	**NHL**	**22**	**2**	**1**	**3**	**28**	**0**	**0**	**1**	**16**	**12.5**	**-12**	**0**	**0.0**	**18:30**									
	NHL Totals		**24**	**2**	**1**	**3**	**30**	**0**	**0**	**1**	**17**	**11.8**		**0**	**0.0**	**18:03**									

HORAK, Roman

(HOH-rak, ROH-muhn) **CGY**

Center. Shoots left. 6', 170 lbs. Born, Ceske Budejovice, Czech., May 21, 1991. NY Rangers' 4th choice, 127th overall, in 2009 Entry Draft.

Season	Club	League	GP	G	A	Pts	PIM	PP	SH	GW	S	%	+/-	TF	F%	Min	Playoffs GP	G	A	Pts	PIM	PP	SH	GW	Min
2004-05	C. Budejovice U17	CzR-U17	2	0	0	0	0																		
2005-06	C. Budejovice U17	CzR-U17	34	5	3	8	10										3	0	0	0	4				
2006-07	C. Budejovice U17	CzR-U17	24	22	16	38	38										2	1	0	1	4				
	C. Budejovice Jr.	CzRep-Jr.	16	1	4	5	6										1	0	0	0	0				
2007-08	C. Budejovice U17	CzR-U17	2	3	2	5	0																		
	C. Budejovice Jr.	CzRep-Jr.	34	17	11	28	14										3	0	1	1	0				
	C. Budejovice	CzRep	1	0	0	0	0																		
2008-09	C. Budejovice Jr.	CzRep-Jr.	31	16	17	33	14										2	0	0	0	0				
	C. Budejovice	CzRep	17	1	0	1	0																		
2009-10	Chilliwack Bruins	WHL	66	21	26	47	39										6	2	4	6	4				
2010-11	Chilliwack Bruins	WHL	64	26	52	78	60										5	1	2	3	0				
2011-12	**Calgary**	**NHL**	**61**	**3**	**8**	**11**	**14**	**0**	**0**	**1**	**53**	**5.7**	**3**	**441**	**41.5**	**10:12**									
	Abbotsford Heat	AHL	14	2	2	4	6										8	0	3	3	2				
2012-13	Abbotsford Heat	AHL	59	16	14	30	24																		
	Calgary	**NHL**	**20**	**2**	**5**	**7**	**2**	**0**	**0**	**0**	**28**	**7.1**	**-5**	**205**	**45.4**	**14:32**									
	NHL Totals		**81**	**5**	**13**	**18**	**16**	**0**	**0**	**1**	**81**	**6.2**		**646**	**42.7**	**11:16**									

Traded to **Calgary** by **NY Rangers** with NY Rangers' 2nd round choice (Markus Granlund) in 2011 Entry Draft and Pittsburgh's 2nd round choice (previously acquired, Calgary selected Tyler Wotherspoon) in 2011 Entry Draft for Tim Erixon and Calgary's 5th round choice (Shane McColgan) in 2011 Entry Draft, June 1, 2011.

HORCOFF, Shawn

(hohr-KAWF, SHAWN) **DAL**

Center. Shoots left. 6'1", 208 lbs. Born, Trail, B.C., September 17, 1978. Edmonton's 3rd choice, 99th overall, in 1998 Entry Draft.

Season	Club	League	GP	G	A	Pts	PIM	PP	SH	GW	S	%	+/-	TF	F%	Min	Playoffs GP	G	A	Pts	PIM	PP	SH	GW	Min
1994-95	Trail Smokies	RMJHL	47	50	46	96	26																		
1995-96	Chilliwack Chiefs	BCHL	58	49	96	*145	44										9	5	19	24	12				
1996-97	Michigan State	CCHA	40	10	13	23	20																		
1997-98	Michigan State	CCHA	34	14	13	27	50																		
1998-99	Michigan State	CCHA	39	12	25	37	70																		
99-2000	Michigan State	CCHA	42	14	*51	*65	50																		
2000-01	**Edmonton**	**NHL**	**49**	**9**	**7**	**16**	**10**	**0**	**0**	**2**	**42**	**21.4**	**8**	**122**	**41.8**	**9:14**	**5**	**0**	**0**	**0**	**0**	**0**	**0**	**0**	**6:31**
	Hamilton	AHL	24	10	18	28	19																		
2001-02	**Edmonton**	**NHL**	**61**	**8**	**14**	**22**	**18**	**0**	**0**	**0**	**57**	**14.0**	**3**	**454**	**46.3**	**11:20**									
	Hamilton	AHL	2	1	2	3	6																		
2002-03	**Edmonton**	**NHL**	**78**	**12**	**21**	**33**	**55**	**2**	**0**	**3**	**98**	**12.2**	**10**	**301**	**42.9**	**13:30**	**6**	**3**	**1**	**4**	**6**	**0**	**0**	**1**	**15:27**
2003-04	**Edmonton**	**NHL**	**80**	**15**	**25**	**40**	**73**	**0**	**2**	**3**	**110**	**13.6**	**0**	**1378**	**50.7**	**17:31**									
2004-05	Mora IK	Sweden	50	19	27	46	117																		
2005-06	**Edmonton**	**NHL**	**79**	**22**	**51**	**73**	**85**	**3**	**3**	**5**	**167**	**13.2**	**0**	**1421**	**52.7**	**19:59**	**24**	**7**	**12**	**19**	**12**	**1**	**1**	**2**	**21:37**
2006-07	**Edmonton**	**NHL**	**80**	**16**	**35**	**51**	**56**	**5**	**0**	**5**	**168**	**9.5**	**-22**	**1422**	**50.6**	**20:50**									
2007-08	**Edmonton**	**NHL**	**53**	**21**	**29**	**50**	**30**	**6**	**0**	**2**	**115**	**18.3**	**1**	**963**	**50.6**	**22:13**									
2008-09	**Edmonton**	**NHL**	**80**	**17**	**36**	**53**	**39**	**8**	**0**	**2**	**178**	**9.6**	**7**	**1756**	**53.9**	**21:22**									
2009-10	**Edmonton**	**NHL**	**77**	**13**	**23**	**36**	**51**	**4**	**0**	**1**	**123**	**10.6**	**-29**	**1337**	**46.5**	**19:26**									
2010-11	**Edmonton**	**NHL**	**47**	**9**	**18**	**27**	**46**	**5**	**0**	**1**	**78**	**11.5**	**-1**	**813**	**48.3**	**18:41**									
2011-12	**Edmonton**	**NHL**	**81**	**13**	**21**	**34**	**24**	**5**	**0**	**0**	**123**	**10.6**	**-23**	**1475**	**49.4**	**19:35**									
2012-13	**Edmonton**	**NHL**	**31**	**7**	**5**	**12**	**24**	**3**	**0**	**1**	**41**	**17.1**	**8**	**500**	**49.0**	**16:51**									
	NHL Totals		**796**	**162**	**285**	**447**	**511**	**41**	**5**	**25**	**1300**	**12.5**		**11942**	**50.1**	**17:51**	**35**	**10**	**13**	**23**	**18**	**1**	**1**	**3**	**18:24**

CCHA First All-Star Team (2000) • CCHA Player of the Year (2000) • NCAA West First All-American Team (2000)

Played in NHL All-Star Game (2008)

Signed as a free agent by **Mora** (Sweden), September 6, 2004. Traded to **Dallas** by **Edmonton** for Phillip Larsen and Dallas' 7th round choice in 2016 Entry Draft, July 5, 2013.

HORDICHUK, Darcy

(HOHR-dih-chuhk, DAHR-see)

Left wing. Shoots left. 6'1", 212 lbs. Born, Kamsack, Sask., August 10, 1980. Atlanta's 9th choice, 180th overall, in 2000 Entry Draft.

			Regular Season														Playoffs								
Season	Club	League	GP	G	A	Pts	PIM	PP	SH	GW	S	%	+/-	TF	F%	Min	GP	G	A	Pts	PIM	PP	SH	GW	Min
1996-97	Yorkton Mallers	SMHL	57	6	15	21	230	....	....	....	....	....	....	....	....	....	....	....	....	....	....	....	....	....	....
	Calgary Hitmen	WHL	3	0	0	0	2	....	....	....	....	....	....	....	....	....	....	....	....	....	....	....	....	....	....
1997-98	Dauphin Kings	MJHL	58	12	21	33	279	....	....	....	....	....	....	....	....	....	....	....	....	....	....	....	....	....	....
1998-99	Saskatoon Blades	WHL	66	3	2	5	246	....	....	....	....	....	....	....	....	....	....	....	....	....	....	....	....	....	....
99-2000	Saskatoon Blades	WHL	63	6	8	14	269	....	....	....	....	....	....	....	....	....	11	4	2	6	43	....	....	....	....
2000-01	**Atlanta**	**NHL**	**11**	**0**	**0**	**0**	**38**	**0**	**0**	**0**	**6**	**0.0**	**-3**	**0**	**0.0**	**7:18**	....	....	....	....	....	....	....	....	....
	Orlando	IHL	69	7	3	10	*369	....	....	....	....	....	....	....	....	....	16	3	3	6	*41	....	....	....	....
2001-02	**Atlanta**	**NHL**	**33**	**1**	**1**	**2**	**127**	**0**	**0**	**0**	**8**	**12.5**	**-5**	**4**	**25.0**	**6:03**	....	....	....	....	....	....	....	....	....
	Chicago Wolves	AHL	34	5	4	9	127	....	....	....	....	....	....	....	....	....	....	....	....	....	....	....	....	....	....
	Phoenix	**NHL**	**1**	**0**	**0**	**0**	**14**	**0**	**0**	**0**	**0**	**0.0**	**0**	**0**	**0.0**	**7:18**	....	....	....	....	....	....	....	....	....
2002-03	**Phoenix**	**NHL**	**25**	**0**	**0**	**0**	**82**	**0**	**0**	**0**	**5**	**0.0**	**-1**	**0**	**0.0**	**4:47**	....	....	....	....	....	....	....	....	....
	Springfield	AHL	22	1	3	4	38	....	....	....	....	....	....	....	....	....	....	....	....	....	....	....	....	....	....
	Florida	**NHL**	**3**	**0**	**0**	**0**	**15**	**0**	**0**	**0**	**2**	**0.0**	**-1**	**0**	**0.0**	**9:45**	....	....	....	....	....	....	....	....	....
2003-04	**Florida**	**NHL**	**57**	**3**	**1**	**4**	**158**	**0**	**0**	**1**	**27**	**11.1**	**-10**	**4**	**50.0**	**6:46**	....	....	....	....	....	....	....	....	....
2004-05			DID NOT PLAY																						
2005-06	**Nashville**	**NHL**	**74**	**7**	**6**	**13**	**163**	**0**	**0**	**1**	**52**	**13.5**	**9**	**1**	**0.0**	**6:09**	....	....	....	....	....	....	....	....	....
2006-07	**Nashville**	**NHL**	**53**	**1**	**3**	**4**	**90**	**0**	**0**	**0**	**22**	**4.5**	**-2**	**0**	**0.0**	**4:48**	**2**	**0**	**0**	**0**	**0**	**0**	**0**	**0**	**3:38**
2007-08	**Nashville**	**NHL**	**45**	**1**	**2**	**3**	**60**	**0**	**0**	**1**	**18**	**5.6**	**-1**	**0**	**0.0**	**5:09**	**5**	**0**	**0**	**0**	**2**	**0**	**0**	**0**	**3:32**
2008-09	**Vancouver**	**NHL**	**73**	**4**	**1**	**5**	**109**	**0**	**0**	**0**	**26**	**15.4**	**1**	**1**	**100.0**	**5:32**	**10**	**1**	**0**	**1**	**14**	**0**	**0**	**0**	**5:20**
2009-10	**Vancouver**	**NHL**	**56**	**1**	**1**	**2**	**142**	**0**	**0**	**0**	**21**	**4.8**	**-7**	**1**	**0.0**	**6:02**	....	....	....	....	....	....	....	....	....
2010-11	**Florida**	**NHL**	**64**	**1**	**4**	**5**	**76**	**0**	**0**	**0**	**32**	**3.1**	**-1**	**0**	**0.0**	**5:04**	....	....	....	....	....	....	....	....	....
2011-12	**Edmonton**	**NHL**	**43**	**1**	**2**	**3**	**64**	**0**	**0**	**0**	**27**	**3.7**	**-3**	**1**	**0.0**	**4:21**	....	....	....	....	....	....	....	....	....
2012-13	Oklahoma City	AHL	22	0	1	1	12	....	....	....	....	....	....	....	....	....	3	0	0	0	2	....	....	....	....
	Edmonton	**NHL**	**4**	**0**	**0**	**0**	**2**	**0**	**0**	**0**	**0**	**0.0**	**-1**	**0**	**0.0**	**2:02**	....	....	....	....	....	....	....	....	....
	NHL Totals		**542**	**20**	**21**	**41**	**1140**	**0**	**0**	**3**	**246**	**8.1**		**12**	**33.3**	**5:35**	**17**	**1**	**0**	**1**	**16**	**0**	**0**	**0**	**4:36**

Traded to **Phoenix** by **Atlanta** with Atlanta's 4th (Lance Monych) and 5th (John Zeiler) round choices in 2002 Entry Draft for Kiril Safronov, the rights to Ruslan Zainullin and Phoenix's 4th round choice (Patrick Dwyer) in 2002 Entry Draft, March 19, 2002. Traded to **Florida** by **Phoenix** with Phoenix's 2nd round choice (later traded to Tampa Bay – Tampa Bay selected Matt Smaby) in 2003 Entry Draft for Brad Ference, March 8, 2003. Traded to **Nashville** by **Florida** for Nashville's 4th round choice (Matt Duffy) in 2005 Entry Draft, July 27, 2005. Traded to **Carolina** by **Nashville** with Nashville's 5th round choice (later traded to Phoenix – Phoenix selected Louis Domingue) in 2010 Entry Draft for Carolina's 5th round choice (later traded to Tampa Bay – Tampa Bay selected Michael Zador) in 2009 Entry Draft, June 19, 2008. Signed as a free agent by **Vancouver**, July 1, 2008. Traded to **Florida** by **Vancouver** for Andrew Peters, October 6, 2010. Signed as a free agent by **Edmonton**, July 1, 2011.

HORNQVIST, Patric

(HOHRN-kwihst, PAT-rihk) **NSH**

Right wing. Shoots right. 6', 190 lbs. Born, Sollentuna, Sweden, January 1, 1987. Nashville's 7th choice, 230th overall, in 2005 Entry Draft.

			Regular Season														Playoffs								
Season	Club	League	GP	G	A	Pts	PIM	PP	SH	GW	S	%	+/-	TF	F%	Min	GP	G	A	Pts	PIM	PP	SH	GW	Min
2003-04	Vasby Jr.	Swe-Jr.	10	7	10	17	30	....	....	....	....	....	....	....	....	....	....	....	....	....	....	....	....	....	....
	Vasby	Sweden-3	32	8	5	13	26	....	....	....	....	....	....	....	....	....	....	....	....	....	....	....	....	....	....
2004-05	Vasby	Sweden-3	28	12	12	24	36	....	....	....	....	....	....	....	....	....	....	....	....	....	....	....	....	....	....
	Djurgarden Jr.	Swe-Jr.	5	3	0	3	2	....	....	....	....	....	....	....	....	....	....	....	....	....	....	....	....	....	....
2005-06	Djurgarden Jr.	Swe-Jr.	4	2	1	3	2	....	....	....	....	....	....	....	....	....	4	1	2	3	2	....	....	....	....
	Djurgarden	Sweden	47	5	2	7	36	....	....	....	....	....	....	....	....	....	....	....	....	....	....	....	....	....	....
2006-07	Djurgarden	Sweden	49	23	11	34	38	....	....	....	....	....	....	....	....	....	....	....	....	....	....	....	....	....	....
	Djurgarden Jr.	Swe-Jr.	....	....	....	....	....	....	....	....	....	....	....	....	....	....	7	2	5	7	14	....	....	....	....
2007-08	Djurgarden	Sweden	53	18	12	30	58	....	....	....	....	....	....	....	....	....	5	0	1	1	6	....	....	....	....
2008-09	**Nashville**	**NHL**	**28**	**2**	**5**	**7**	**16**	**0**	**0**	**0**	**54**	**3.7**	**-3**	**5**	**20.0**	**11:24**	....	....	....	....	....	....	....	....	....
	Milwaukee	AHL	49	17	18	35	44	....	....	....	....	....	....	....	....	....	11	4	4	8	6	....	....	....	....
2009-10	**Nashville**	**NHL**	**80**	**30**	**21**	**51**	**40**	**10**	**0**	**8**	**275**	**10.9**	**18**	**18**	**27.8**	**15:41**	**2**	**0**	**1**	**1**	**4**	**0**	**0**	**0**	**13:10**
	Sweden	Olympics	4	1	0	1	4	....	....	....	....	....	....	....	....	....	....	....	....	....	....	....	....	....	....
2010-11	**Nashville**	**NHL**	**79**	**21**	**27**	**48**	**47**	**6**	**0**	**5**	**265**	**7.9**	**11**	**45**	**48.9**	**15:44**	**12**	**2**	**1**	**3**	**6**	**1**	**0**	**0**	**15:16**
2011-12	**Nashville**	**NHL**	**76**	**27**	**16**	**43**	**28**	**8**	**0**	**3**	**230**	**11.7**	**9**	**9**	**66.7**	**15:20**	**10**	**1**	**3**	**4**	**2**	**1**	**0**	**0**	**15:25**
2012-13	Martigny	Swiss-2	9	7	7	14	8	....	....	....	....	....	....	....	....	....	....	....	....	....	....	....	....	....	....
	Djurgarden	Sweden-2	10	2	3	5	6	....	....	....	....	....	....	....	....	....	....	....	....	....	....	....	....	....	....
	Nashville	**NHL**	**24**	**4**	**10**	**14**	**14**	**4**	**0**	**1**	**87**	**4.6**	**-1**	**2**	**50.0**	**16:14**	....	....	....	....	....	....	....	....	....
	NHL Totals		**287**	**84**	**79**	**163**	**145**	**28**	**0**	**17**	**911**	**9.2**		**79**	**44.3**	**15:14**	**24**	**3**	**5**	**8**	**12**	**2**	**0**	**0**	**15:09**

Signed as a free agent by **Martigny** (Swiss-2), October 2, 2012. Signed as a free agent by **Djurgarden** (Sweden-2), November 12, 2012.

HORTON, Nathan

(HOHR-tuhn, NAY-thuhn) **CBJ**

Right wing. Shoots right. 6'2", 229 lbs. Born, Welland, Ont., May 29, 1985. Florida's 1st choice, 3rd overall, in 2003 Entry Draft.

			Regular Season														Playoffs								
Season	Club	League	GP	G	A	Pts	PIM	PP	SH	GW	S	%	+/-	TF	F%	Min	GP	G	A	Pts	PIM	PP	SH	GW	Min
2000-01	Thorold	ON-Jr.B	41	16	31	47	75	....	....	....	....	....	....	....	....	....	....	....	....	....	....	....	....	....	....
2001-02	Oshawa Generals	OHL	64	31	36	67	84	....	....	....	....	....	....	....	....	....	5	1	2	3	10	....	....	....	....
2002-03	Oshawa Generals	OHL	54	33	35	68	111	....	....	....	....	....	....	....	....	....	13	9	6	15	10	....	....	....	....
2003-04	**Florida**	**NHL**	**55**	**14**	**8**	**22**	**57**	**6**	**1**	**0**	**81**	**17.3**	**-5**	**270**	**41.9**	**13:20**	....	....	....	....	....	....	....	....	....
2004-05	San Antonio	AHL	21	5	4	9	21	....	....	....	....	....	....	....	....	....	....	....	....	....	....	....	....	....	....
2005-06	**Florida**	**NHL**	**71**	**28**	**19**	**47**	**89**	**3**	**0**	**1**	**162**	**17.3**	**8**	**24**	**45.8**	**16:53**	....	....	....	....	....	....	....	....	....
2006-07	**Florida**	**NHL**	**82**	**31**	**31**	**62**	**61**	**7**	**1**	**3**	**217**	**14.3**	**15**	**31**	**48.4**	**18:04**	....	....	....	....	....	....	....	....	....
2007-08	**Florida**	**NHL**	**82**	**27**	**35**	**62**	**85**	**9**	**0**	**3**	**212**	**12.7**	**15**	**73**	**39.7**	**18:44**	....	....	....	....	....	....	....	....	....
2008-09	**Florida**	**NHL**	**67**	**22**	**23**	**45**	**48**	**5**	**1**	**5**	**131**	**16.8**	**-5**	**863**	**43.7**	**17:51**	....	....	....	....	....	....	....	....	....
2009-10	**Florida**	**NHL**	**65**	**20**	**37**	**57**	**42**	**7**	**2**	**4**	**159**	**12.6**	**-1**	**85**	**56.5**	**20:53**	....	....	....	....	....	....	....	....	....
2010-11♦	**Boston**	**NHL**	**80**	**26**	**27**	**53**	**85**	**6**	**0**	**2**	**188**	**13.8**	**29**	**19**	**42.1**	**16:17**	**21**	**8**	**9**	**17**	**35**	**1**	**0**	**3**	**16:54**
2011-12	**Boston**	**NHL**	**46**	**17**	**15**	**32**	**54**	**6**	**0**	**3**	**90**	**18.9**	**0**	**3**	**66.7**	**15:56**	....	....	....	....	....	....	....	....	....
2012-13	**Boston**	**NHL**	**43**	**13**	**9**	**22**	**22**	**0**	**0**	**1**	**114**	**11.4**	**1**	**10**	**50.0**	**16:51**	**22**	**7**	**12**	**19**	**14**	**2**	**0**	**3**	**18:29**
	NHL Totals		**591**	**198**	**204**	**402**	**543**	**49**	**5**	**22**	**1354**	**14.6**		**1378**	**44.1**	**17:22**	**43**	**15**	**21**	**36**	**49**	**3**	**0**	**6**	**17:43**

OHL All-Rookie Team (2002)

Signed as a free agent by **San Antonio** (AHL), October 28, 2004. Traded to **Boston** by **Florida** with Gregory Campbell for Dennis Wideman, Boston's 1st round choice (later traded to Los Angeles – Los Angeles selected Derek Forbort) in 2010 Entry Draft and Boston's 3rd round choice (Kyle Rau) in 2011 Entry Draft, June 22, 2010. Signed as a free agent by **Columbus**, July 5, 2013.

HOSSA, Marian

(HOH-sa, MAIR-ee-uhn) **CHI**

Right wing. Shoots left. 6'1", 210 lbs. Born, Stara Lubovna, Czech., January 12, 1979. Ottawa's 1st choice, 12th overall, in 1997 Entry Draft.

			Regular Season														Playoffs								
Season	Club	League	GP	G	A	Pts	PIM	PP	SH	GW	S	%	+/-	TF	F%	Min	GP	G	A	Pts	PIM	PP	SH	GW	Min
1995-96	Dukla Trencin Jr.	Slovak-Jr.	53	42	49	91	26	....	....	....	....	....	....	....	....	....	....	....	....	....	....	....	....	....	....
1996-97	Dukla Trencin	Slovakia	46	25	19	44	33	....	....	....	....	....	....	....	....	....	7	5	5	10	....	....	....	....	....
1997-98	Portland	WHL	53	45	40	85	50	....	....	....	....	....	....	....	....	....	16	13	6	19	6	....	....	....	....
	Ottawa	**NHL**	**7**	**0**	**1**	**1**	**0**	**0**	**0**	**0**	**10**	**0.0**	**-1**	....	....	....	....	....	....	....	....	....	....	....	....
1998-99	**Ottawa**	**NHL**	**60**	**15**	**15**	**30**	**37**	**1**	**0**	**2**	**124**	**12.1**	**18**	**4**	**25.0**	**13:59**	**4**	**0**	**2**	**2**	**4**	**0**	**0**	**0**	**16:46**
99-2000	**Ottawa**	**NHL**	**78**	**29**	**27**	**56**	**32**	**5**	**0**	**4**	**240**	**12.1**	**5**	**7**	**57.1**	**17:12**	**6**	**0**	**0**	**0**	**2**	**0**	**0**	**0**	**15:22**
2000-01	**Ottawa**	**NHL**	**81**	**32**	**43**	**75**	**44**	**11**	**2**	**7**	**249**	**12.9**	**19**	**14**	**42.9**	**18:01**	**4**	**1**	**1**	**2**	**4**	**0**	**0**	**0**	**19:02**
2001-02	Dukla Trencin	Slovakia	8	3	4	7	16	....	....	....	....	....	....	....	....	....	....	....	....	....	....	....	....	....	....
	Ottawa	**NHL**	**80**	**31**	**35**	**66**	**50**	**9**	**1**	**4**	**278**	**11.2**	**11**	**12**	**33.3**	**18:29**	**12**	**4**	**6**	**10**	**2**	**1**	**0**	**0**	**19:04**
	Slovakia	Olympics	2	4	2	6	0	....	....	....	....	....	....	....	....	....	....	....	....	....	....	....	....	....	....
2002-03	**Ottawa**	**NHL**	**80**	**45**	**35**	**80**	**34**	**14**	**0**	**10**	**229**	**19.7**	**8**	**19**	**36.8**	**18:31**	**18**	**5**	**11**	**16**	**6**	**3**	**0**	**1**	**18:41**
2003-04	**Ottawa**	**NHL**	**81**	**36**	**46**	**82**	**46**	**14**	**1**	**5**	**233**	**15.5**	**4**	**25**	**40.0**	**18:37**	**7**	**3**	**1**	**4**	**0**	**1**	**0**	**2**	**21:24**
2004-05	Dukla Trencin	Slovakia	25	22	20	42	38	....	....	....	....	....	....	....	....	....	5	4	5	9	14	....	....	....	....
	Mora IK	Sweden	24	18	14	32	22	....	....	....	....	....	....	....	....	....	....	....	....	....	....	....	....	....	....
2005-06	**Atlanta**	**NHL**	**80**	**39**	**53**	**92**	**67**	**14**	***7**	**7**	**341**	**11.4**	**17**	**15**	**26.7**	**21:41**	....	....	....	....	....	....	....	....	....
	Slovakia	Olympics	6	5	5	10	4	....	....	....	....	....	....	....	....	....	....	....	....	....	....	....	....	....	....
2006-07	**Atlanta**	**NHL**	**82**	**43**	**57**	**100**	**49**	**17**	**3**	**5**	**340**	**12.6**	**18**	**18**	**22.2**	**21:41**	**4**	**0**	**1**	**1**	**6**	**0**	**0**	**0**	**18:55**
2007-08	**Atlanta**	**NHL**	**60**	**26**	**30**	**56**	**30**	**8**	**2**	**4**	**229**	**11.4**	**-14**	**14**	**28.6**	**21:55**	....	....	....	....	....	....	....	....	....
	Pittsburgh	**NHL**	**12**	**3**	**7**	**10**	**6**	**0**	**0**	**0**	**35**	**8.6**	**0**	**1**	**0.0**	**18:34**	**20**	**12**	**14**	**26**	**12**	**5**	**0**	**2**	**21:00**
2008-09	**Detroit**	**NHL**	**74**	**40**	**31**	**71**	**63**	**10**	**0**	**8**	**307**	**13.0**	**27**	**19**	**21.1**	**17:48**	**23**	**6**	**9**	**15**	**10**	**2**	**1**	**1**	**18:38**
2009-10♦	**Chicago**	**NHL**	**57**	**24**	**27**	**51**	**18**	**2**	**5**	**2**	**199**	**12.1**	**24**	**1**	**0.0**	**18:44**	**22**	**3**	**12**	**15**	**25**	**0**	**0**	**1**	**18:25**
	Slovakia	Olympics	7	3	6	9	6	....	....	....	....	....	....	....	....	....	....	....	....	....	....	....	....	....	....
2010-11	**Chicago**	**NHL**	**65**	**25**	**32**	**57**	**32**	**8**	**2**	**2**	**205**	**12.2**	**9**	**4**	**75.0**	**19:42**	**7**	**2**	**4**	**6**	**2**	**1**	**0**	**1**	**18:35**

Season	Club	League	Regular Season														Playoffs								
			GP	G	A	Pts	PIM	PP	SH	GW	S	%	+/-	TF	F%	Min	GP	G	A	Pts	PIM	PP	SH	GW	Min
2011-12	**Chicago**	**NHL**	**81**	**29**	**48**	**77**	**20**	**9**	**2**	**4**	**248**	**11.7**	**18**	**9**	**33.3**	**19:58**	**3**	**0**	**0**	**0**	**0**	**0**	**0**	**0**	**17:21**
2012-13♦	**Chicago**	**NHL**	**40**	**17**	**14**	**31**	**16**	**4**	**1**	**6**	**116**	**14.7**	**20**	**3**	**33.3**	**18:02**	**22**	**7**	**9**	**16**	**2**	**3**	**0**	**2**	**19:57**
	NHL Totals		**1018**	**434**	**501**	**935**	**544**	**126**	**26**	**70**	**3383**	**12.8**		**165**	**33.3**	**18:57**	**152**	**43**	**70**	**113**	**75**	**16**	**1**	**10**	**19:05**

WHL West First All-Star Team (1998) • WHL Rookie of the Year (1998) • Canadian Major Junior First All-Star Team (1998) • Memorial Cup All-Star Team (1998) • NHL All-Rookie Team (1999) • NHL Second All-Star Team (2009)

Played in NHL All-Star Game (2001, 2003, 2007, 2008, 2012)

Signed as a free agent by **Trencin** (Slovakia), September 16, 2004. Signed as a free agent by **Mora** (Sweden), November 11, 2004. Signed as a free agent by **Trencin** (Slovakia), January 31, 2005. Traded to **Atlanta** by **Ottawa** with Greg de Vries for Dany Heatley, August 23, 2005. Traded to **Pittsburgh** by **Atlanta** with Pascal Dupuis for Colby Armstrong, Erik Christensen, Angelo Esposito and Pittsburgh's 1st round choice (Daulton Leveille) in 2008 Entry Draft , February 26, 2008. Signed as a free agent by **Detroit**, July 2, 2008. Signed as a free agent by **Chicago**, July 1, 2009.

HOWDEN, Quinton (HOW-duhn, KWIHN-tuhn) FLA

Center. Shoots left. 6'3", 183 lbs. Born, Winnipeg, Man., January 21, 1992. Florida's 3rd choice, 25th overall, in 2010 Entry Draft.

Season	Club	League	GP	G	A	Pts	PIM	PP	SH	GW	S	%	+/-	TF	F%	Min	GP	G	A	Pts	PIM	PP	SH	GW	Min
2007-08	Eastman Selects	MMHL	37	23	27	50	36	....	....	....	....	....	....	....	....	....	....	....	....	....	....	....	....	....	....
	Moose Jaw	WHL	5	0	0	0	0	....	....	....	....	....	....	....	....	....	....	....	....	....	....	....	....	....	....
2008-09	Moose Jaw	WHL	62	13	17	30	22	....	....	....	....	....	....	....	....	....	....	....	....	....	....	....	....	....	....
2009-10	Moose Jaw	WHL	65	28	37	65	44	....	....	....	....	....	....	....	....	....	2	0	2	2	2	....	....	....	....
2010-11	Moose Jaw	WHL	60	40	39	79	43	....	....	....	....	....	....	....	....	....	6	5	2	7	2	....	....	....	....
2011-12	Moose Jaw	WHL	52	30	35	65	16	....	....	....	....	....	....	....	....	....	14	5	10	15	6	....	....	....	....
	San Antonio	AHL	....	....	....	....	....	....	....	....	....	....	....	....	....	....	4	0	0	0	2	....	....	....	....
2012-13	San Antonio	AHL	57	13	17	30	24	....	....	....	....	....	....	....	....	....	....	....	....	....	....	....	....	....	....
	Florida	**NHL**	**18**	**0**	**0**	**0**	**2**	**0**	**0**	**0**	**22**	**0.0**	**–11**	**4**	**25.0**	**10:27**	....	....	....	....	....	....	....	....	....
	NHL Totals		**18**	**0**	**0**	**0**	**2**	**0**	**0**	**0**	**22**	**0.0**		**4**	**25.0**	**10:27**	....	....	....	....	....	....	....	....	....

WHL East Second All-Star Team (2011)

HUBERDEAU, Jonathan (hoo-BAIR-doh, JAWN-ah-thuhn) FLA

Center. Shoots left. 6'1", 171 lbs. Born, Saint-Jerome, Que., June 4, 1993. Florida's 1st choice, 3rd overall, in 2011 Entry Draft.

Season	Club	League	GP	G	A	Pts	PIM	PP	SH	GW	S	%	+/-	TF	F%	Min	GP	G	A	Pts	PIM	PP	SH	GW	Min
2008-09	Saint-Eustache	QAAA	43	20	30	50	60	....	....	....	....	....	....	....	....	....	8	2	7	9	18	....	....	....	....
2009-10	Saint John	QMJHL	61	15	20	35	43	....	....	....	....	....	....	....	....	....	21	11	7	18	22	....	....	....	....
2010-11	Saint John	QMJHL	67	43	62	105	88	....	....	....	....	....	....	....	....	....	19	*16	14	30	16	....	....	....	....
2011-12	Saint John	QMJHL	37	30	42	72	50	....	....	....	....	....	....	....	....	....	15	10	11	21	18	....	....	....	....
2012-13	Saint John	QMJHL	30	16	29	45	48	....	....	....	....	....	....	....	....	....	....	....	....	....	....	....	....	....	....
	Florida	**NHL**	**48**	**14**	**17**	**31**	**18**	**2**	**0**	**1**	**112**	**12.5**	**–15**	**33**	**33.3**	**16:56**	....	....	....	....	....	....	....	....	....
	NHL Totals		**48**	**14**	**17**	**31**	**18**	**2**	**0**	**1**	**112**	**12.5**		**33**	**33.3**	**16:56**	....	....	....	....	....	....	....	....	....

QMJHL First All-Star Team (2011) • Memorial Cup All-Star Team (2011) • Stafford Smythe Memorial Trophy (Memorial Cup – MVP) (2011) • QMJHL Second All-Star Team (2012) • NHL All-Rookie Team (2013) • Calder Memorial Trophy (2013)

HUDLER, Jiri (HOOD-luhr, YIH-ree) CGY

Center. Shoots left. 5'10", 186 lbs. Born, Olomouc, Czech., January 4, 1984. Detroit's 1st choice, 58th overall, in 2002 Entry Draft.

Season	Club	League	GP	G	A	Pts	PIM	PP	SH	GW	S	%	+/-	TF	F%	Min	GP	G	A	Pts	PIM	PP	SH	GW	Min
1998-99	HC Vsetin U17	CzR-U17	46	57	57	114	....	....	....	....	....	....	....	....	....	....	....	....	....	....	....	....	....	....	....
99-2000	HC Vsetin Jr.	CzRep-Jr.	53	29	31	60	75	....	....	....	....	....	....	....	....	....	....	....	....	....	....	....	....	....	....
	Vsetin	CzRep	2	0	1	1	0	....	....	....	....	....	....	....	....	....	....	....	....	....	....	....	....	....	....
2000-01	HC Vsetin Jr.	CzRep-Jr.	16	8	14	22	16	....	....	....	....	....	....	....	....	....	....	....	....	....	....	....	....	....	....
	HC Slovnaft Vsetin	CzRep	22	1	4	5	10	....	....	....	....	....	....	....	....	....	....	....	....	....	....	....	....	....	....
	HC Femax Havirov	CzRep	15	5	1	6	12	....	....	....	....	....	....	....	....	....	....	....	....	....	....	....	....	....	....
2001-02	HC Vsetin	CzRep	46	15	31	46	54	....	....	....	....	....	....	....	....	....	....	....	....	....	....	....	....	....	....
	Liberec	CzRep-2	13	9	7	16	10	....	....	....	....	....	....	....	....	....	....	....	....	....	....	....	....	....	....
	HC Olomouc	CzRep-3	1	0	2	2	4	....	....	....	....	....	....	....	....	....	....	....	....	....	....	....	....	....	....
2002-03	HC Vsetin	CzRep	30	19	27	46	22	....	....	....	....	....	....	....	....	....	....	....	....	....	....	....	....	....	....
	Ak Bars Kazan	Russia	11	1	5	6	12	....	....	....	....	....	....	....	....	....	1	0	0	0	0	....	....	....	....
2003-04	**Detroit**	**NHL**	**12**	**1**	**2**	**3**	**10**	**1**	**0**	**0**	**8**	**12.5**	**–1**	**50**	**30.0**	**8:10**	....	....	....	....	....	....	....	....	....
	Grand Rapids	AHL	57	17	32	49	46	....	....	....	....	....	....	....	....	....	4	1	5	6	2	....	....	....	....
2004-05	Grand Rapids	AHL	52	12	22	34	10	....	....	....	....	....	....	....	....	....	....	....	....	....	....	....	....	....	....
	HC Vsetin	CzRep	7	5	2	7	10	....	....	....	....	....	....	....	....	....	....	....	....	....	....	....	....	....	....
2005-06	**Detroit**	**NHL**	**4**	**0**	**0**	**0**	**2**	**0**	**0**	**0**	**3**	**0.0**	**0**	**0**	**0.0**	**7:13**	....	....	....	....	....	....	....	....	....
	Grand Rapids	AHL	76	36	61	97	56	....	....	....	....	....	....	....	....	....	16	6	16	22	20	....	....	....	....
2006-07	**Detroit**	**NHL**	**76**	**15**	**10**	**25**	**36**	**3**	**0**	**4**	**107**	**14.0**	**16**	**20**	**30.0**	**10:02**	**6**	**0**	**2**	**2**	**4**	**0**	**0**	**0**	**9:09**
2007-08♦	**Detroit**	**NHL**	**81**	**13**	**29**	**42**	**26**	**3**	**0**	**2**	**131**	**9.9**	**11**	**26**	**38.5**	**13:10**	**22**	**5**	**9**	**14**	**14**	**2**	**0**	**2**	**11:36**
2008-09	**Detroit**	**NHL**	**82**	**23**	**34**	**57**	**16**	**6**	**0**	**2**	**155**	**14.8**	**7**	**29**	**44.8**	**13:39**	**23**	**4**	**8**	**12**	**6**	**2**	**0**	**1**	**13:28**
2009-10	Dynamo Moscow	KHL	54	19	35	54	18	....	....	....	....	....	....	....	....	....	4	0	1	1	4	....	....	....	....
2010-11	**Detroit**	**NHL**	**73**	**10**	**27**	**37**	**28**	**3**	**0**	**2**	**105**	**9.5**	**–7**	**70**	**44.3**	**13:40**	**10**	**1**	**2**	**3**	**6**	**0**	**0**	**0**	**11:57**
2011-12	**Detroit**	**NHL**	**81**	**25**	**25**	**50**	**42**	**2**	**0**	**2**	**127**	**19.7**	**10**	**7**	**28.6**	**15:40**	**5**	**2**	**0**	**2**	**4**	**1**	**0**	**0**	**16:53**
2012-13	HC Lev Praha	KHL	4	0	1	1	2	....	....	....	....	....	....	....	....	....	....	....	....	....	....	....	....	....	....
	HC Ocelari Trinec	CzRep	4	3	2	5	4	....	....	....	....	....	....	....	....	....	....	....	....	....	....	....	....	....	....
	Calgary	**NHL**	**42**	**10**	**17**	**27**	**22**	**5**	**0**	**0**	**56**	**17.9**	**–13**	**31**	**32.3**	**17:10**	....	....	....	....	....	....	....	....	....
	NHL Totals		**451**	**97**	**144**	**241**	**182**	**23**	**0**	**12**	**692**	**14.0**		**233**	**37.3**	**13:27**	**66**	**12**	**21**	**33**	**34**	**5**	**0**	**3**	**12:29**

AHL Second All-Star Team (2006)

Signed as a free agent by **Vsetin** (CzRep), December 2, 2004. Signed as a free agent by **Dynamo Moscow** (KHL), July 10, 2009. Signed as a free agent by **Detroit**, May 24, 2010. Signed as a free agent by **Calgary**, July 2, 2012. Signed as a free agent by **Lev Praha** (KHL), September 20, 2012. Signed as a free agent by **Trinec** (CzRep), December 19, 2012.

HUNWICK, Matt (HUHN-wihk, MAT) COL

Defense. Shoots left. 5'11", 190 lbs. Born, Warren, MI, May 21, 1985. Boston's 6th choice, 224th overall, in 2004 Entry Draft.

Season	Club	League	GP	G	A	Pts	PIM	PP	SH	GW	S	%	+/-	TF	F%	Min	GP	G	A	Pts	PIM	PP	SH	GW	Min
2001-02	USNTDP	U-17	14	3	4	7	6	....	....	....	....	....	....	....	....	....	....	....	....	....	....	....	....	....	....
	USNTDP	NAHL	29	2	1	3	30	....	....	....	....	....	....	....	....	....	....	....	....	....	....	....	....	....	....
2002-03	USNTDP	U-18	40	6	16	22	40	....	....	....	....	....	....	....	....	....	....	....	....	....	....	....	....	....	....
	USNTDP	NAHL	8	2	2	4	23	....	....	....	....	....	....	....	....	....	....	....	....	....	....	....	....	....	....
2003-04	U. of Michigan	CCHA	41	1	14	15	62	....	....	....	....	....	....	....	....	....	....	....	....	....	....	....	....	....	....
2004-05	U. of Michigan	CCHA	40	6	19	25	60	....	....	....	....	....	....	....	....	....	....	....	....	....	....	....	....	....	....
2005-06	U. of Michigan	CCHA	41	11	19	30	70	....	....	....	....	....	....	....	....	....	....	....	....	....	....	....	....	....	....
2006-07	U. of Michigan	CCHA	41	6	21	27	64	....	....	....	....	....	....	....	....	....	....	....	....	....	....	....	....	....	....
2007-08	**Boston**	**NHL**	**13**	**0**	**1**	**1**	**4**	**0**	**0**	**0**	**6**	**0.0**	**–1**	**0**	**0.0**	**10:36**	....	....	....	....	....	....	....	....	....
	Providence Bruins	AHL	55	2	21	23	49	....	....	....	....	....	....	....	....	....	10	0	5	5	8	....	....	....	....
2008-09	**Boston**	**NHL**	**53**	**6**	**21**	**27**	**31**	**0**	**0**	**1**	**58**	**10.3**	**15**	**0**	**0.0**	**16:59**	**1**	**0**	**0**	**0**	**0**	**0**	**0**	**0**	**15:59**
	Providence Bruins	AHL	3	0	3	3	0	....	....	....	....	....	....	....	....	....	....	....	....	....	....	....	....	....	....
2009-10	**Boston**	**NHL**	**76**	**6**	**8**	**14**	**32**	**1**	**1**	**1**	**60**	**10.0**	**–16**	**1**	**0.0**	**17:58**	**13**	**0**	**6**	**6**	**2**	**0**	**0**	**0**	**21:57**
2010-11	**Boston**	**NHL**	**22**	**1**	**2**	**3**	**9**	**0**	**0**	**0**	**26**	**3.8**	**4**	**0**	**0.0**	**16:13**	....	....	....	....	....	....	....	....	....
	Colorado	**NHL**	**51**	**0**	**10**	**10**	**16**	**0**	**0**	**0**	**74**	**0.0**	**–19**	**0**	**0.0**	**19:30**	....	....	....	....	....	....	....	....	....
2011-12	**Colorado**	**NHL**	**33**	**3**	**3**	**6**	**8**	**0**	**0**	**0**	**40**	**7.5**	**–3**	**1**	**0.0**	**18:04**	....	....	....	....	....	....	....	....	....
2012-13	**Colorado**	**NHL**	**43**	**0**	**6**	**6**	**16**	**0**	**0**	**0**	**57**	**0.0**	**4**	**0**	**0.0**	**21:31**	....	....	....	....	....	....	....	....	....
	NHL Totals		**291**	**16**	**51**	**67**	**116**	**1**	**1**	**2**	**321**	**5.0**		**2**	**0.0**	**18:08**	**14**	**0**	**6**	**6**	**2**	**0**	**0**	**0**	**21:31**

CCHA All-Rookie Team (2004) • CCHA Second All-Star Team (2005, 2006) • CCHA First All-Star Team (2007) • NCAA West Second All-American Team (2007)

Traded to **Colorado** by **Boston** for Colby Cohen, November 29, 2010. • Missed majority of 2011-12 as a healthy reserve.

HUSKINS, Kent (HUHS-kihnz, KEHNT)

Defense. Shoots left. 6'4", 210 lbs. Born, Ottawa, Ont., May 4, 1979. Chicago's 3rd choice, 156th overall, in 1998 Entry Draft.

Season	Club	League	GP	G	A	Pts	PIM	PP	SH	GW	S	%	+/-	TF	F%	Min	GP	G	A	Pts	PIM	PP	SH	GW	Min
1995-96	Kanata Valley	ON-Jr.A	49	6	21	27	18	....	....	....	....	....	....	....	....	....	5	0	1	1	10	....	....	....	....
1996-97	Kanata Valley	ON-Jr.A	53	11	36	47	89	....	....	....	....	....	....	....	....	....	14	4	4	8	18	....	....	....	....
1997-98	Clarkson Knights	ECAC	35	2	8	10	46	....	....	....	....	....	....	....	....	....	....	....	....	....	....	....	....	....	....
1998-99	Clarkson Knights	ECAC	37	5	11	16	28	....	....	....	....	....	....	....	....	....	....	....	....	....	....	....	....	....	....
99-2000	Clarkson Knights	ECAC	28	2	16	18	30	....	....	....	....	....	....	....	....	....	....	....	....	....	....	....	....	....	....
2000-01	Clarkson Knights	ECAC	35	6	28	34	22	....	....	....	....	....	....	....	....	....	....	....	....	....	....	....	....	....	....
2001-02	Norfolk Admirals	AHL	65	4	11	15	44	....	....	....	....	....	....	....	....	....	4	0	1	1	0	....	....	....	....
2002-03	Norfolk Admirals	AHL	80	5	22	27	48	....	....	....	....	....	....	....	....	....	9	2	2	4	4	....	....	....	....
2003-04	San Antonio	AHL	79	5	14	19	42	....	....	....	....	....	....	....	....	....	....	....	....	....	....	....	....	....	....
2004-05	Manitoba Moose	AHL	65	5	11	16	41	....	....	....	....	....	....	....	....	....	14	0	2	2	12	....	....	....	....

			Regular Season														Playoffs								
Season	Club	League	GP	G	A	Pts	PIM	PP	SH	GW	S	%	+/-	TF	F%	Min	GP	G	A	Pts	PIM	PP	SH	GW	Min
2005-06	Portland Pirates	AHL	80	8	23	31	64	....	....	....	....	....	....	....	....	....	18	3	6	9	14	....	....	....	....
2006-07 ♦	**Anaheim**	**NHL**	**33**	**0**	**3**	**3**	**14**	**0**	**0**	**0**	**16**	**0.0**	**–3**	**0**	**0.0**	**14:04**	**21**	**0**	**1**	**1**	**11**	**0**	**0**	**0**	**11:45**
	Portland Pirates	AHL	39	3	12	15	23	....	....	....	....	....	....	....	....	....	....	....	....	....	....	....	....	....	....
2007-08	**Anaheim**	**NHL**	**76**	**4**	**15**	**19**	**59**	**1**	**0**	**2**	**46**	**8.7**	**23**	**0**	**0.0**	**16:05**	**6**	**0**	**1**	**1**	**2**	**0**	**0**	**0**	**14:35**
2008-09	**Anaheim**	**NHL**	**33**	**2**	**4**	**6**	**27**	**0**	**0**	**0**	**20**	**10.0**	**6**	**1**	**0.0**	**18:47**	....	....	....	....	....	....	....	....	....
2009-10	**San Jose**	**NHL**	**82**	**3**	**19**	**22**	**47**	**0**	**0**	**0**	**47**	**6.4**	**6**	**0**	**0.0**	**17:29**	**15**	**0**	**0**	**0**	**6**	**0**	**0**	**0**	**12:48**
2010-11	**San Jose**	**NHL**	**50**	**2**	**8**	**10**	**12**	**0**	**0**	**0**	**38**	**5.3**	**8**	**0**	**0.0**	**16:37**	**5**	**0**	**1**	**1**	**2**	**0**	**0**	**0**	**18:48**
2011-12	**St. Louis**	**NHL**	**25**	**2**	**5**	**7**	**10**	**0**	**0**	**0**	**16**	**12.5**	**9**	**0**	**0.0**	**15:28**	**1**	**0**	**0**	**0**	**2**	**0**	**0**	**0**	**24:29**
2012-13	Norfolk Admirals	AHL	2	0	1	1	2	....	....	....	....	....	....	....	....	....	....	....	....	....	....	....	....	....	....
	Detroit	**NHL**	**11**	**0**	**0**	**0**	**4**	**0**	**0**	**0**	**2**	**0.0**	**–3**	**0**	**0.0**	**15:21**	....	....	....	....	....	....	....	....	....
	Philadelphia	**NHL**	**8**	**0**	**1**	**1**	**0**	**0**	**0**	**0**	**2**	**0.0**	**0**	**0**	**0.0**	**16:06**	....	....	....	....	....	....	....	....	....
	NHL Totals		**318**	**13**	**55**	**68**	**173**	**1**	**0**	**2**	**187**	**7.0**		**1**	**0.0**	**16:32**	**48**	**0**	**3**	**3**	**23**	**0**	**0**	**0**	**13:26**

ECAC First All-Star Team (2000, 2001) • NCAA East First All-American Team (2001)

Signed as a free agent by **Florida**, August 14, 2003. Signed as a free agent by **Manitoba** (AHL), September 16, 2004. Signed as a free agent by **Anaheim**, August 30, 2005. Traded to **San Jose** by **Anaheim** with Travis Moen for Timo Pielmeier, Nick Bonino and San Jose's 4th round choice (Andrew O'Brien) iun 2012 Entry Draft, March 4, 2009. Signed as a free agent by **St. Louis**, July 2, 2011. • Missed majority of 2011-12 due to ankle injury at Calgary, October 28, 2011. Signed as a free agent by **Norfolk** (AHL), January 17, 2013. Signed as a free agent by **Detroit**, January 22, 2013. Traded to **Philadelphia** by **Detroit** for future considerations, March 30, 2013.

IGINLA, Jarome

(ih-GIHN-lah, jah-ROHM) **BOS**

Right wing. Shoots right. 6'1", 210 lbs. Born, Edmonton, Alta., July 1, 1977. Dallas' 1st choice, 11th overall, in 1995 Entry Draft.

Season	Club	League	GP	G	A	Pts	PIM	PP	SH	GW	S	%	+/-	TF	F%	Min	GP	G	A	Pts	PIM	PP	SH	GW	Min
1991-92	St. Albert Raiders	AMHL	36	26	30	56	22	....	....	....	....	....	....	....	....	....	....	....	....	....	....	....	....	....	....
1992-93	St. Albert Raiders	AMHL	36	34	53	*87	20	....	....	....	....	....	....	....	....	....	....	....	....	....	....	....	....	....	....
1993-94	Kamloops Blazers	WHL	48	6	23	29	33	....	....	....	....	....	....	....	....	....	19	3	6	9	10	....	....	....	....
1994-95	Kamloops Blazers	WHL	72	33	38	71	111	....	....	....	....	....	....	....	....	....	21	7	11	18	34	....	....	....	....
1995-96	Kamloops Blazers	WHL	63	63	73	136	120	....	....	....	....	....	....	....	....	....	16	16	13	29	44	....	....	....	....
	Calgary	**NHL**	....	....	....	....	....	....	....	....	....	....	....	....	....	....	**2**	**1**	**1**	**2**	**0**	**0**	**0**	**0**	....
1996-97	**Calgary**	**NHL**	**82**	**21**	**29**	**50**	**37**	**8**	**1**	**3**	**169**	**12.4**	**–4**	....	....	....	....	....	....	....	....	....	....	....	....
1997-98	**Calgary**	**NHL**	**70**	**13**	**19**	**32**	**29**	**0**	**2**	**1**	**154**	**8.4**	**–10**	....	....	....	....	....	....	....	....	....	....	....	....
1998-99	**Calgary**	**NHL**	**82**	**28**	**23**	**51**	**58**	**7**	**0**	**4**	**211**	**13.3**	**1**	**111**	**51.4**	**16:30**	....	....	....	....	....	....	....	....	....
99-2000	**Calgary**	**NHL**	**77**	**29**	**34**	**63**	**26**	**12**	**0**	**4**	**256**	**11.3**	**0**	**278**	**52.9**	**18:24**	....	....	....	....	....	....	....	....	....
2000-01	**Calgary**	**NHL**	**77**	**31**	**40**	**71**	**62**	**10**	**0**	**4**	**229**	**13.5**	**–2**	**638**	**51.7**	**19:58**	....	....	....	....	....	....	....	....	....
2001-02	**Calgary**	**NHL**	**82**	***52**	**44**	***96**	**77**	**16**	**1**	**7**	**311**	**16.7**	**27**	**308**	**55.2**	**22:22**	....	....	....	....	....	....	....	....	....
	Canada	Olympics	6	3	1	4	0	....	....	....	....	....	....	....	....	....	....	....	....	....	....	....	....	....	....
2002-03	**Calgary**	**NHL**	**75**	**35**	**32**	**67**	**49**	**11**	**3**	**6**	**316**	**11.1**	**–10**	**90**	**43.3**	**21:26**	....	....	....	....	....	....	....	....	....
2003-04	**Calgary**	**NHL**	**81**	***41**	**32**	**73**	**84**	**8**	**4**	***10**	**265**	**15.5**	**21**	**305**	**54.4**	**21:18**	**26**	***13**	**9**	**22**	**45**	**4**	***2**	**3**	**23:18**
2004-05			DID NOT PLAY																						
2005-06	**Calgary**	**NHL**	**82**	**35**	**32**	**67**	**86**	**17**	**1**	**6**	**293**	**11.9**	**5**	**541**	**54.2**	**21:42**	**7**	**5**	**3**	**8**	**11**	**1**	**1**	**1**	**24:14**
	Canada	Olympics	6	2	1	3	4	....	....	....	....	....	....	....	....	....	....	....	....	....	....	....	....	....	....
2006-07	**Calgary**	**NHL**	**70**	**39**	**55**	**94**	**40**	**13**	**1**	**7**	**264**	**14.8**	**12**	**406**	**53.0**	**22:04**	**6**	**2**	**2**	**4**	**12**	**0**	**0**	**1**	**23:45**
2007-08	**Calgary**	**NHL**	**82**	**50**	**48**	**98**	**83**	**15**	**0**	**9**	**338**	**14.8**	**27**	**445**	**55.1**	**21:26**	**7**	**4**	**5**	**9**	**2**	**3**	**0**	**0**	**22:43**
2008-09	**Calgary**	**NHL**	**82**	**35**	**54**	**89**	**37**	**10**	**0**	**4**	**289**	**12.1**	**–2**	**501**	**52.5**	**21:37**	**6**	**3**	**1**	**4**	**0**	**2**	**0**	**0**	**20:56**
2009-10	**Calgary**	**NHL**	**82**	**32**	**37**	**69**	**58**	**10**	**0**	**5**	**257**	**12.5**	**–2**	**323**	**47.1**	**20:36**	....	....	....	....	....	....	....	....	....
	Canada	Olympics	7	*5	2	7	0	....	....	....	....	....	....	....	....	....	....	....	....	....	....	....	....	....	....
2010-11	**Calgary**	**NHL**	**82**	**43**	**43**	**86**	**40**	**14**	**0**	**6**	**289**	**14.9**	**0**	**420**	**54.1**	**20:56**	....	....	....	....	....	....	....	....	....
2011-12	**Calgary**	**NHL**	**82**	**32**	**35**	**67**	**43**	**8**	**0**	**5**	**251**	**12.7**	**–10**	**426**	**50.2**	**20:36**	....	....	....	....	....	....	....	....	....
2012-13	**Calgary**	**NHL**	**31**	**9**	**13**	**22**	**22**	**2**	**0**	**2**	**100**	**9.0**	**–7**	**237**	**50.2**	**19:18**	....	....	....	....	....	....	....	....	....
	Pittsburgh	**NHL**	**13**	**5**	**6**	**11**	**9**	**4**	**0**	**1**	**34**	**14.7**	**2**	**10**	**40.0**	**17:40**	**15**	**4**	**8**	**12**	**16**	**2**	**0**	**0**	**15:45**
	NHL Totals		**1232**	**530**	**576**	**1106**	**840**	**165**	**13**	**84**	**4026**	**13.2**		**5039**	**52.4**	**20:36**	**69**	**32**	**29**	**61**	**86**	**12**	**3**	**5**	**21:29**

George Parsons Trophy (Memorial Cup - Most Sportsmanlike Player) (1995) • WHL West First All-Star Team (1996) • WHL Player of the Year (1996) • Canadian Major Junior First All-Star Team (1996) • NHL All-Rookie Team (1997) • NHL First All-Star Team (2002, 2008, 2009) • Maurice "Rocket" Richard Trophy (2002) • Art Ross Trophy (2002) • Lester B. Pearson Award (2002) • NHL Second All-Star Team (2004) • NHL Foundation Player Award (2004) • King Clancy Memorial Trophy (2004) • Maurice "Rocket" Richard Trophy (2004) (tied with Ilya Kovalchuk and Rick Nash) • Mark Messier NHL Leadership Award (2009)

Played in NHL All-Star Game (2002, 2003, 2004, 2008, 2009, 2012)

Traded to **Calgary** by **Dallas** with Corey Millen for Joe Nieuwendyk, December 19, 1995. Traded to **Pittsburgh** by **Calgary** for Kenny Agostino, Ben Hanowski and Pittsburgh's 1st round choice (Morgan Klimchuk) in 2013 Entry Draft, March 28, 2013. Signed as a free agent by **Boston**, July 5, 2013.

IRWIN, Matt

(UHR-wihn, MAT) **S.J.**

Defense. Shoots left. 6'2", 210 lbs. Born, Brentwood Bay, B.C., November 29, 1987.

Season	Club	League	GP	G	A	Pts	PIM	PP	SH	GW	S	%	+/-	TF	F%	Min	GP	G	A	Pts	PIM	PP	SH	GW	Min
2004-05	Saanich Braves	VIJHL	STATISTICS NOT AVAILABLE																						
	Nanaimo Clippers	BCHL	3	0	0	0	2	....	....	....	....	....	....	....	....	....	....	....	....	....	....	....	....	....	....
2005-06	Nanaimo Clippers	BCHL	56	3	6	9	41	....	....	....	....	....	....	....	....	....	5	0	1	1	4	....	....	....	....
2006-07	Nanaimo Clippers	BCHL	60	22	27	49	67	....	....	....	....	....	....	....	....	....	24	10	4	14	18	....	....	....	....
2007-08	Nanaimo Clippers	BCHL	59	16	37	53	40	....	....	....	....	....	....	....	....	....	14	6	7	13	22	....	....	....	....
2008-09	Massachusetts	H-East	31	7	11	18	8	....	....	....	....	....	....	....	....	....	....	....	....	....	....	....	....	....	....
2009-10	Massachusetts	H-East	36	7	17	24	16	....	....	....	....	....	....	....	....	....	....	....	....	....	....	....	....	....	....
	Worcester Sharks	AHL	3	0	0	0	2	....	....	....	....	....	....	....	....	....	1	0	0	0	0	....	....	....	....
2010-11	Worcester Sharks	AHL	72	10	21	31	43	....	....	....	....	....	....	....	....	....	....	....	....	....	....	....	....	....	....
2011-12	Worcester Sharks	AHL	71	11	31	42	48	....	....	....	....	....	....	....	....	....	....	....	....	....	....	....	....	....	....
2012-13	Worcester Sharks	AHL	35	1	14	15	26	....	....	....	....	....	....	....	....	....	....	....	....	....	....	....	....	....	....
	San Jose	**NHL**	**38**	**6**	**6**	**12**	**10**	**4**	**0**	**0**	**79**	**7.6**	**–1**	**0**	**0.0**	**19:06**	**11**	**0**	**1**	**1**	**4**	**0**	**0**	**0**	**17:47**
	NHL Totals		**38**	**6**	**6**	**12**	**10**	**4**	**0**	**0**	**79**	**7.6**		**0**	**0.0**	**19:06**	**11**	**0**	**1**	**1**	**4**	**0**	**0**	**0**	**17:47**

Signed as a free agent by **San Jose**, March 23, 2010.

JACKMAN, Barret

(JAK-man, BAIR-reht) **ST.L.**

Defense. Shoots left. 6', 203 lbs. Born, Trail, B.C., March 5, 1981. St. Louis' 1st choice, 17th overall, in 1999 Entry Draft.

Season	Club	League	GP	G	A	Pts	PIM	PP	SH	GW	S	%	+/-	TF	F%	Min	GP	G	A	Pts	PIM	PP	SH	GW	Min
1996-97	Beaver Valley	VIJHL	32	22	25	47	180	....	....	....	....	....	....	....	....	....	....	....	....	....	....	....	....	....	....
1997-98	Regina Pats	WHL	68	2	11	13	224	....	....	....	....	....	....	....	....	....	9	0	3	3	32	....	....	....	....
1998-99	Regina Pats	WHL	70	8	36	44	259	....	....	....	....	....	....	....	....	....	....	....	....	....	....	....	....	....	....
99-2000	Regina Pats	WHL	53	9	37	46	175	....	....	....	....	....	....	....	....	....	6	1	1	2	19	....	....	....	....
	Worcester IceCats	AHL	....	....	....	....	....	....	....	....	....	....	....	....	....	....	2	0	0	0	13	....	....	....	....
2000-01	Regina Pats	WHL	43	9	27	36	138	....	....	....	....	....	....	....	....	....	6	0	3	3	8	....	....	....	....
2001-02	**St. Louis**	**NHL**	**1**	**0**	**0**	**0**	**0**	**0**	**0**	**0**	**1**	**0.0**	**0**	**0**	**0.0**	**18:56**	**1**	**0**	**0**	**0**	**2**	**0**	**0**	**0**	**18:24**
	Worcester IceCats	AHL	75	2	12	14	266	....	....	....	....	....	....	....	....	....	3	0	1	1	4	....	....	....	....
2002-03	**St. Louis**	**NHL**	**82**	**3**	**16**	**19**	**190**	**0**	**0**	**0**	**66**	**4.5**	**23**	**0**	**0.0**	**20:03**	**7**	**0**	**0**	**0**	**14**	**0**	**0**	**0**	**21:59**
2003-04	**St. Louis**	**NHL**	**15**	**1**	**2**	**3**	**41**	**0**	**0**	**0**	**11**	**9.1**	**–1**	**0**	**0.0**	**18:16**	....	....	....	....	....	....	....	....	....
2004-05	Missouri	UHL	28	3	17	20	61	....	....	....	....	....	....	....	....	....	3	0	0	0	4	....	....	....	....
2005-06	**St. Louis**	**NHL**	**63**	**4**	**6**	**10**	**156**	**0**	**0**	**2**	**56**	**7.1**	**–6**	**0**	**0.0**	**18:46**	....	....	....	....	....	....	....	....	....
2006-07	**St. Louis**	**NHL**	**70**	**3**	**24**	**27**	**82**	**1**	**0**	**1**	**86**	**3.5**	**20**	**0**	**0.0**	**21:30**	....	....	....	....	....	....	....	....	....
	Peoria Rivermen	AHL	1	0	0	0	0	....	....	....	....	....	....	....	....	....	....	....	....	....	....	....	....	....	....
2007-08	**St. Louis**	**NHL**	**78**	**2**	**14**	**16**	**93**	**1**	**0**	**0**	**80**	**2.5**	**–12**	**0**	**0.0**	**22:24**	....	....	....	....	....	....	....	....	....
2008-09	**St. Louis**	**NHL**	**82**	**4**	**17**	**21**	**86**	**1**	**1**	**0**	**89**	**4.5**	**–17**	**0**	**0.0**	**23:26**	**4**	**0**	**1**	**1**	**5**	**0**	**0**	**0**	**25:18**
2009-10	**St. Louis**	**NHL**	**66**	**2**	**15**	**17**	**81**	**0**	**1**	**0**	**73**	**2.7**	**3**	**1**	**0.0**	**22:41**	....	....	....	....	....	....	....	....	....
2010-11	**St. Louis**	**NHL**	**60**	**0**	**13**	**13**	**57**	**0**	**0**	**0**	**65**	**0.0**	**3**	**0**	**0.0**	**20:48**	....	....	....	....	....	....	....	....	....
2011-12	**St. Louis**	**NHL**	**81**	**1**	**12**	**13**	**57**	**0**	**0**	**0**	**82**	**1.2**	**20**	**0**	**0.0**	**20:41**	**9**	**0**	**1**	**1**	**21**	**0**	**0**	**0**	**18:54**
2012-13	**St. Louis**	**NHL**	**46**	**3**	**9**	**12**	**39**	**0**	**0**	**0**	**39**	**7.7**	**6**	**0**	**0.0**	**19:19**	**6**	**1**	**1**	**2**	**10**	**0**	**0**	**1**	**20:12**
	NHL Totals		**644**	**23**	**128**	**151**	**882**	**3**	**2**	**3**	**648**	**3.5**		**1**	**0.0**	**21:07**	**27**	**1**	**3**	**4**	**52**	**0**	**0**	**1**	**20:55**

WHL East Second All-Star Team (2000) • AHL All-Rookie Team (2002) • NHL All-Rookie Team (2003) • Calder Memorial Trophy (2003)

• Missed majority of 2003-04 due to shoulder injury vs. Vancouver, October 22, 2003. Signed as a free agent by **Missouri** (UHL), February 3, 2005.

JACKMAN, Tim

(JAK-man, TIHM) **CGY**

Right wing. Shoots right. 6'2", 225 lbs. Born, Minot, ND, November 14, 1981. Columbus' 2nd choice, 38th overall, in 2001 Entry Draft.

			Regular Season														Playoffs								
Season	Club	League	GP	G	A	Pts	PIM	PP	SH	GW	S	%	+/-	TF	F%	Min	GP	G	A	Pts	PIM	PP	SH	GW	Min
1998-99	Park Center	High-MN	22	22	22	44																			
99-2000	Park Center	High-MN	19	34	22	56																			
	Twin Cities	USHL	25	11	9	20	58										13	8	5	13	12				
2000-01	Minnesota State	WCHA	37	11	14	25	92																		
2001-02	Minnesota State	WCHA	36	14	14	28	86																		
2002-03	Syracuse Crunch	AHL	77	9	7	16	48																		
2003-04	**Columbus**	**NHL**	**19**	**1**	**2**	**3**	**16**	**0**	**0**	**0**	**18**	**5.6**	**–7**	**1**	**100.0**	**9:56**									
	Syracuse Crunch	AHL	64	23	13	36	61										7	2	3	5	12				
2004-05	Syracuse Crunch	AHL	73	14	21	35	98																		
2005-06	**Phoenix**	**NHL**	**8**	**0**	**0**	**0**	**21**	**0**	**0**	**0**	**4**	**0.0**	**1**	**1**	**0.0**	**7:13**									
	San Antonio	AHL	50	7	13	20	127																		
	Manchester	AHL	18	2	3	5	33										7	0	3	3	20				
2006-07	**Los Angeles**	**NHL**	**5**	**0**	**0**	**0**	**10**	**0**	**0**	**0**	**3**	**0.0**	**–1**	**0**	**0.0**	**6:36**									
	Manchester	AHL	69	19	14	33	143										16	3	3	6	26				
2007-08	**NY Islanders**	**NHL**	**36**	**1**	**3**	**4**	**57**	**0**	**0**	**0**	**36**	**2.8**	**–3**	**2**	**100.0**	**6:37**									
	Bridgeport	AHL	44	15	21	36	67																		
2008-09	**NY Islanders**	**NHL**	**69**	**5**	**7**	**12**	**155**	**0**	**1**	**0**	**99**	**5.1**	**–17**	**22**	**31.8**	**11:45**									
	Bridgeport	AHL	12	6	1	7	35																		
2009-10	**NY Islanders**	**NHL**	**54**	**4**	**5**	**9**	**98**	**0**	**0**	**0**	**51**	**7.8**	**–4**	**7**	**42.9**	**9:39**									
2010-11	**Calgary**	**NHL**	**82**	**10**	**13**	**23**	**86**	**1**	**0**	**1**	**131**	**7.6**	**4**	**16**	**37.5**	**9:49**									
2011-12	**Calgary**	**NHL**	**75**	**1**	**6**	**7**	**94**	**0**	**0**	**0**	**103**	**1.0**	**–21**	**34**	**44.1**	**9:07**									
2012-13	**Calgary**	**NHL**	**42**	**1**	**4**	**5**	**76**	**0**	**0**	**0**	**42**	**2.4**	**–9**	**24**	**45.8**	**7:36**									
	NHL Totals		**390**	**23**	**40**	**63**	**613**	**1**	**1**	**1**	**487**	**4.7**		**107**	**42.1**	**9:23**									

Traded to **Phoenix** by **Columbus** with Geoff Sanderson for Cale Hulse, Mike Rupp and Jason Chimera, October 8, 2005. Traded to **Los Angeles** by **Phoenix** for Yanick Lehoux, March 9, 2006. Signed as a free agent by **NY Islanders**, July 5, 2007. Signed as a free agent by **Calgary**, July 2, 2010.

JACQUES, Jean-Francois

(ZHAWK, ZHAWN-fran-SWUH)

Left wing. Shoots left. 6'4", 217 lbs. Born, Montreal, Que., April 29, 1985. Edmonton's 3rd choice, 68th overall, in 2003 Entry Draft.

Season	Club	League	GP	G	A	Pts	PIM	PP	SH	GW	S	%	+/-	TF	F%	Min	GP	G	A	Pts	PIM	PP	SH	GW	Min
2000-01	Cap-d-Madeleine	QAAA	39	22	13	35	28										10	5	8	13	14				
2001-02	Baie-Comeau	QMJHL	66	10	14	24	136										5	1	0	1	2				
2002-03	Baie-Comeau	QMJHL	67	12	21	33	123										12	4	2	6	13				
2003-04	Baie-Comeau	QMJHL	59	20	24	44	70										4	1	0	1	4				
2004-05	Baie-Comeau	QMJHL	69	36	42	78	56										6	3	5	8	6				
	Edmonton	AHL	6	0	0	0	5																		
2005-06	**Edmonton**	**NHL**	**7**	**0**	**0**	**0**	**0**	**0**	**0**	**0**	**8**	**0.0**	**–3**	**0**	**0.0**	**6:43**									
	Hamilton	AHL	65	24	19	43	131																		
2006-07	**Edmonton**	**NHL**	**37**	**0**	**0**	**0**	**33**	**0**	**0**	**0**	**23**	**0.0**	**–11**	**2**	**0.0**	**7:55**									
	Wilkes-Barre	AHL	29	10	17	27	53										11	1	2	3	43				
2007-08	**Edmonton**	**NHL**	**9**	**0**	**0**	**0**	**2**	**0**	**0**	**0**	**2**	**0.0**	**–3**	**0**	**0.0**	**6:10**									
	Springfield	AHL	38	11	14	25	63																		
2008-09	**Edmonton**	**NHL**	**7**	**1**	**0**	**1**	**9**	**0**	**0**	**0**	**3**	**33.3**	**0**	**0**	**0.0**	**7:22**									
	Springfield	AHL	8	1	5	6	13																		
2009-10	**Edmonton**	**NHL**	**49**	**4**	**7**	**11**	**78**	**0**	**0**	**0**	**49**	**8.2**	**–15**	**5**	**40.0**	**11:12**									
2010-11	**Edmonton**	**NHL**	**51**	**4**	**1**	**5**	**63**	**0**	**0**	**0**	**28**	**14.3**	**–6**	**16**	**31.3**	**7:04**									
	Oklahoma City	AHL	4	1	0	1	15																		
2011-12	**Anaheim**	**NHL**	**6**	**0**	**0**	**0**	**12**	**0**	**0**	**0**	**7**	**0.0**	**2**	**0**	**0.0**	**6:37**									
	Syracuse Crunch	AHL	65	21	19	40	95										4	0	0	0	2				
2012-13	San Antonio	AHL	24	5	2	7	37																		
	Syracuse Crunch	AHL	24	1	4	5	24																		
	NHL Totals		**166**	**9**	**8**	**17**	**197**	**0**	**0**	**0**	**120**	**7.5**		**23**	**30.4**	**8:25**									

• Missed majority of 2008-09 due to off-season back surgery. Signed as a free agent by **Anaheim**, July 6, 2011. Signed as a free agent by **Florida**, July 5, 2012. Traded to **Tampa Bay** by **Florida** for future considerations, January 21, 2013.

JAFFRAY, Jason

(JAF-ray, JAY-suhn)

Left wing. Shoots left. 6'1", 195 lbs. Born, Olds, Alta., June 30, 1981.

Season	Club	League	GP	G	A	Pts	PIM	PP	SH	GW	S	%	+/-	TF	F%	Min	GP	G	A	Pts	PIM	PP	SH	GW	Min
1997-98	Edmonton Ice	WHL	6	0	1	1	0																		
1998-99	Kootenay Ice	WHL	57	14	12	26	50										7	1	2	3	6				
99-2000	Kootenay Ice	WHL	71	24	28	52	102										21	10	9	19	17				
2000-01	Kootenay Ice	WHL	70	31	42	73	108										11	5	7	12	10				
2001-02	Kootenay Ice	WHL	32	15	19	34	38																		
	Swift Current	WHL	41	23	26	49	44										12	4	5	9	25				
2002-03	Norfolk Admirals	AHL	2	0	0	0	0																		
	Roanoke Express	ECHL	64	34	51	85	89										4	0	3	3	4				
2003-04	Wilkes-Barre	AHL	5	0	1	1	0																		
	Wheeling Nailers	ECHL	54	37	37	74	81										2	1	1	2	2				
2004-05	Cleveland Barons	AHL	30	10	6	16	23																		
	Manitoba Moose	AHL	14	4	4	8	6										1	0	0	0	0				
	Wheeling Nailers	ECHL	23	6	6	12	22																		
2005-06	Manitoba Moose	AHL	73	12	35	47	58										13	6	1	7	11				
2006-07	Manitoba Moose	AHL	77	35	46	81	75										13	6	7	13	6				
2007-08	**Vancouver**	**NHL**	**19**	**2**	**4**	**6**	**19**	**1**	**0**	**1**	**15**	**13.3**	**4**	**176**	**47.7**	**12:35**									
	Manitoba Moose	AHL	43	21	27	48	51										3	1	4	5	0				
2008-09	**Vancouver**	**NHL**	**14**	**2**	**2**	**4**	**14**	**0**	**0**	**2**	**11**	**18.2**	**–2**	**65**	**47.7**	**9:04**									
	Manitoba Moose	AHL	56	23	26	49	52										22	9	10	19	12				
2009-10	**Calgary**	**NHL**	**3**	**0**	**0**	**0**	**0**	**0**	**0**	**0**	**4**	**0.0**	**–1**	**14**	**35.7**	**6:39**									
	Abbotsford Heat	AHL	72	25	29	54	70										9	2	1	3	8				
2010-11	Manitoba Moose	AHL	6	1	1	2	2										14	3	6	9	6				
2011-12	**Winnipeg**	**NHL**	**13**	**0**	**1**	**1**	**7**	**0**	**0**	**0**	**10**	**0.0**	**–1**	**15**	**53.3**	**6:30**									
	St. John's IceCaps	AHL	47	17	21	38	30																		
2012-13	St. John's IceCaps	AHL	65	15	33	48	55																		
	NHL Totals		**49**	**4**	**7**	**11**	**40**	**1**	**0**	**3**	**40**	**10.0**		**270**	**47.4**	**9:36**									

ECHL Rookie of the Year (2003) • AHL Second All-Star Team (2007)

Signed as a free agent by **Vancouver**, July 3, 2007. Signed as a free agent by **Calgary**, July 7, 2009. Traded to **Anaheim** by **Calgary** with future considerations for Logan MacMillan and future considerations, June 30, 2010. Signed as a free agent by **Winnipeg**, July 19, 2011.

JAGR, Jaromir

(YAH-guhr, YAIR-oh-MEER) **N.J.**

Right wing. Shoots left. 6'3", 240 lbs. Born, Kladno, Czech., February 15, 1972. Pittsburgh's 1st choice, 5th overall, in 1990 Entry Draft.

Season	Club	League	GP	G	A	Pts	PIM	PP	SH	GW	S	%	+/-	TF	F%	Min	GP	G	A	Pts	PIM	PP	SH	GW	Min
1984-85	Kladno Jr.	Czech-Jr.	34	24	17	41																			
1985-86	Kladno Jr.	Czech-Jr.	36	41	29	70																			
1986-87	Kladno Jr.	Czech-Jr.	30	35	35	70																			
1987-88	Kladno Jr.	Czech-Jr.	35	57	27	84																			
1988-89	Kladno	Czech	29	3	3	6	4										10	5	7	12	0				
1989-90	Poldi Kladno	Czech	42	22	28	50											9	*8	2	10					
1990-91 ♦	**Pittsburgh**	**NHL**	**80**	**27**	**30**	**57**	**42**	**7**	**0**	**4**	**136**	**19.9**	**–4**				**24**	**3**	**10**	**13**	**6**	**1**	**0**	**1**	
1991-92 ♦	**Pittsburgh**	**NHL**	**70**	**32**	**37**	**69**	**34**	**4**	**0**	**4**	**194**	**16.5**	**12**				**21**	**11**	**13**	**24**	**6**	**2**	**0**	**4**	
1992-93	**Pittsburgh**	**NHL**	**81**	**34**	**60**	**94**	**61**	**10**	**1**	**9**	**242**	**14.0**	**30**				**12**	**5**	**4**	**9**	**23**	**1**	**0**	**1**	
1993-94	**Pittsburgh**	**NHL**	**80**	**32**	**67**	**99**	**61**	**9**	**0**	**6**	**298**	**10.7**	**15**				**6**	**2**	**4**	**6**	**16**	**0**	**0**	**1**	
1994-95	HC Kladno	CzRep	11	8	14	22	10																		
	HC Bolzano	Euroliga	5	8	8	16	4																		
	HC Bolzano	Italy	1	0	0	0	0																		
	Schalke	German-2	1	1	10	11	0																		
	Pittsburgh	**NHL**	**48**	**32**	**38**	***70**	**37**	**8**	**3**	**7**	**192**	**16.7**	**23**				**12**	**10**	**5**	**15**	**6**	**2**	**1**	**1**	
1995-96	**Pittsburgh**	**NHL**	**82**	**62**	**87**	**149**	**96**	**20**	**1**	***12**	**403**	**15.4**	**31**				**18**	**11**	**12**	**23**	**18**	**5**	**1**	**1**	
1996-97	**Pittsburgh**	**NHL**	**63**	**47**	**48**	**95**	**40**	**11**	**2**	**6**	**234**	**20.1**	**22**				**5**	**4**	**4**	**8**	**4**	**2**	**0**	**0**	
1997-98	**Pittsburgh**	**NHL**	**77**	**35**	***67**	***102**	**64**	**7**	**0**	**8**	**262**	**13.4**	**17**				**6**	**4**	**5**	**9**	**2**	**1**	**0**	**0**	
	Czech Republic	Olympics	6	1	4	5	2																		

			Regular Season														Playoffs								
Season	Club	League	GP	G	A	Pts	PIM	PP	SH	GW	S	%	+/-	TF	F%	Min	GP	G	A	Pts	PIM	PP	SH	GW	Min
1998-99	Pittsburgh	NHL	81	44	*83	*127	66	10	1	7	343	12.8	17	4	50.0	25:51	9	5	7	12	16	1	0	1	25:32
99-2000	Pittsburgh	NHL	63	42	54	*96	50	10	0	5	290	14.5	25	9	22.2	23:12	11	8	8	16	6	2	0	*4	24:32
2000-01	Pittsburgh	NHL	81	52	*69	*121	42	14	1	10	317	16.4	19	2	0.0	23:19	16	2	10	12	18	2	0	0	22:15
2001-02	Washington	NHL	69	31	48	79	30	10	0	3	197	15.7	0	2	50.0	21:43									
	Czech Republic	Olympics	4	2	3	5	4																		
2002-03	Washington	NHL	75	36	41	77	38	13	2	9	290	12.4	5	5	20.0	21:18	6	2	5	7	2	1	0	0	25:13
2003-04	Washington	NHL	46	16	29	45	26	6	0	1	159	10.1	–4	1	0.0	21:05									
	NY Rangers	NHL	31	15	14	29	12	4	0	2	98	15.3	–1	0	0.0	20:45									
2004-05	HC Rabat Kladno	CzRep	17	11	17	28	16																		
	Avangard Omsk	Russia	32	16	22	38	63										11	4	*10	*14	22				
2005-06	NY Rangers	NHL	82	54	69	123	72	24	0	9	368	14.7	34	6	16.7	22:05	3	0	1	1	2	0	0	0	13:47
	Czech Republic	Olympics	8	2	5	7	6																		
2006-07	NY Rangers	NHL	82	30	66	96	78	7	0	5	324	9.3	26	6	16.7	21:46	10	5	6	11	12	2	0	0	22:07
2007-08	NY Rangers	NHL	82	25	46	71	58	7	0	5	249	10.0	8	3	33.3	20:28	10	5	10	15	12	2	0	1	19:54
2008-09	Omsk	KHL	55	25	28	53	62										9	4	5	9	4				
2009-10	Omsk	KHL	51	22	20	42	50										3	1	1	2	0				
	Czech Republic	Olympics	5	2	1	3	6																		
2010-11	Omsk	KHL	49	19	31	50	48										14	2	7	9	8				
2011-12	Philadelphia	NHL	73	19	35	54	30	8	0	2	170	11.2	5	1	0.0	16:20	11	1	7	8	2	0	0	1	15:00
2012-13	Rytiri Kladno	CzRep	34	24	33	57	28																		
	Dallas	NHL	34	14	12	26	20	6	0	2	87	16.1	–5	1	0.0	18:18									
	Boston	NHL	11	2	7	9	2	0	0	2	28	7.1	3	0	0.0	18:27	22	0	10	10	8	0	0	0	17:55
	NHL Totals		1391	681	1007	1688	959	195	11	118	4881	14.0		40	22.5	21:32	202	78	121	199	159	24	2	16	20:42

NHL All-Rookie Team (1991) • NHL First All-Star Team (1995, 1996, 1998, 1999, 2000, 2001, 2006) • Art Ross Trophy (1995, 1998, 1999, 2000, 2001) • NHL Second All-Star Team (1997) • Lester B. Pearson Award (1999, 2000, 2006) • Hart Memorial Trophy (1999)

Played in NHL All-Star Game (1992, 1993, 1996, 1998, 1999, 2000, 2002, 2003, 2004)

Traded to **Washington** by **Pittsburgh** with Frantisek Kucera for Kris Beech, Michal Sivek, Ross Lupaschuk and future considerations, July 11, 2001. Traded to **NY Rangers** by **Washington** for Anson Carter, January 23, 2004. Signed as a free agent by **Kladno** (CzRep), September 17, 2004. Signed as a free agent by **Omsk** (Russia), November 7, 2004. Signed as a free agent by **Omsk** (KHL), July 4, 2008. Signed as a free agent by **Philadelphia**, July 1, 2011. Signed as a free agent by **Dallas**, July 3, 2012. Signed as a free agent by **Kladno** (CzRep), September 16, 2012. Traded to **Boston** by **Dallas** for Lane MacDermid, Cody Payne and Boston's 1st round choice (Jason Dickinson) in 2013 Entry Draft, April 2, 2013. Signed as a free agent by **New Jersey**, July 23, 2013.

JANIK, Doug

(JAN-nihk, DUHG)

Defense. Shoots left. 6'2", 211 lbs. Born, Agawam, MA, March 26, 1980. Buffalo's 3rd choice, 55th overall, in 1999 Entry Draft.

1995-96	N.E. Jr. Whalers	EJHL	48	16	38	54	....																		
1996-97	N.E. Jr. Whalers	EJHL	39	12	24	36	22										11	5	9	14	10				
1997-98	USNTDP	U-18	29	6	13	19	43																		
	USNTDP	USHL	19	1	6	7	34																		
	USNTDP	NAHL	10	0	4	4	10										7	1	3	4	18				
1998-99	U. of Maine	H-East	35	3	13	16	44																		
99-2000	U. of Maine	H-East	36	6	14	20	54																		
2000-01	U. of Maine	H-East	39	3	15	18	52																		
2001-02	Rochester	AHL	80	6	17	23	100										2	0	0	0	0				
2002-03	Buffalo	NHL	6	0	0	0	2	0	0	0	1	0.0	1	0	0.0	7:42									
	Rochester	AHL	75	3	13	16	120										3	0	0	0	6				
2003-04	Buffalo	NHL	4	0	0	0	19	0	0	0	3	0.0	0	0	0.0	8:26									
	Rochester	AHL	74	2	14	16	109										16	1	2	3	22				
2004-05	Rochester	AHL	76	2	10	12	196										9	0	2	2	10				
2005-06	Rochester	AHL	71	5	19	24	161																		
	Buffalo	NHL															5	1	0	1	2	0	0	0	10:30
2006-07	Tampa Bay	NHL	75	2	9	11	53	0	0	0	49	4.1	–11	0	0.0	14:28	1	0	0	0	0	0	0	0	3:42
2007-08	Tampa Bay	NHL	61	1	3	4	45	0	0	0	23	4.3	–3	0	0.0	9:20									
2008-09	Dallas	NHL	13	0	1	1	2	0	0	0	1	0.0	–2	0	0.0	9:45									
	Rockford IceHogs	AHL	4	0	2	2	4																		
	Montreal	NHL	2	0	0	0	2	0	0	0	0	0.0	–1	0	0.0	13:54									
	Hamilton	AHL	18	0	5	5	10										6	0	0	0	7				
2009-10	Detroit	NHL	13	0	2	2	18	0	0	0	5	0.0	–3	0	0.0	13:28									
	Grand Rapids	AHL	66	6	31	37	84																		
2010-11	Detroit	NHL	7	0	0	0	7	0	0	0	8	0.0	–2	0	0.0	13:13									
	Grand Rapids	AHL	60	5	17	22	77																		
2011-12	Detroit	NHL	9	0	1	1	6	0	0	0	6	0.0	2	0	0.0	14:30									
	Grand Rapids	AHL	67	10	23	33	74																		
2012-13	Adler Mannheim	Germany	40	3	7	10	54										6	0	2	2	2				
	NHL Totals		190	3	16	19	154	0	0	0	96	3.1		0	0.0	12:02	6	1	0	1	2	0	0	0	9:22

Signed as a free agent by **Tampa Bay**, July 6, 2006. Signed as a free agent by **Chicago**, July 15, 2008. Claimed on waivers by **Dallas** from **Chicago**, October 2, 2008. Claimed on waivers by **Chicago** from **Dallas**, October 8, 2008. Traded to **Dallas** by **Chicago** for Dallas's 7th round choice (Mac Carruth) in 2010 Entry Draft, October 8, 2008. Traded to **Montreal** by **Dallas** for Steve Begin, February 26, 2009. Signed as a free agent by **Detroit**, July 8, 2009. Signed as a free agent by **Mannheim** (Germany), July 12, 2012.

JANSSEN, Cam

(JAN-suhn, KAM) **N.J.**

Right wing. Shoots right. 6', 215 lbs. Born, St. Louis, MO, April 15, 1984. New Jersey's 6th choice, 117th overall, in 2002 Entry Draft.

2000-01	St. Louis Jr. Blues	CSJHL	45	1	2	3	244																		
2001-02	Windsor Spitfires	OHL	64	5	17	22	*268										10	0	0	0	13				
2002-03	Windsor Spitfires	OHL	50	1	12	13	211										7	0	1	1	22				
2003-04	Windsor Spitfires	OHL	35	4	9	13	144																		
	Guelph Storm	OHL	29	7	4	11	125										22	3	3	6	49				
2004-05	Albany River Rats	AHL	70	1	3	4	337																		
2005-06	New Jersey	NHL	47	0	0	0	91	0	0	0	10	0.0	–3	2	100.0	4:44	9	0	0	0	26	0	0	0	3:43
	Albany River Rats	AHL	26	1	3	4	117																		
2006-07	New Jersey	NHL	48	1	0	1	114	0	0	0	9	11.1	–2	1	100.0	4:06									
	Lowell Devils	AHL	9	0	1	1	29																		
2007-08	St. Louis	NHL	12	0	1	1	18	0	0	0	9	0.0	–1	0	0.0	7:07									
	Lowell Devils	AHL	3	0	0	0	4																		
2008-09	St. Louis	NHL	56	1	3	4	131	0	0	0	22	4.5	–5	2	0.0	5:01	1	0	0	0	0	0	0	0	3:59
2009-10	St. Louis	NHL	43	0	0	0	190	0	0	0	11	0.0	–3	1	0.0	4:43									
2010-11	St. Louis	NHL	54	1	3	4	131	0	0	0	16	6.3	–6	0	0.0	4:53									
2011-12	New Jersey	NHL	48	0	1	1	75	0	0	0	17	0.0	–8	5	40.0	4:41									
2012-13	Albany Devils	AHL	36	1	4	5	65																		
	New Jersey	NHL	4	0	0	0	2	0	0	0	0	0.0	–1	0	0.0	3:58									
	NHL Totals		312	3	8	11	752	0	0	0	94	3.2		11	45.5	4:47	10	0	0	0	26	0	0	0	3:45

Traded to **St. Louis** by **New Jersey** for Bryce Salvador, February 26, 2008. Signed as a free agent by **New Jersey**, July 14, 2011.

JASKIN, Dmitrij

(YASH-kihn, dih-MEE-tree) **ST.L.**

Right wing. Shoots left. 6'2", 196 lbs. Born, Omsk, Russia, March 23, 1993. St. Louis' 2nd choice, 41st overall, in 2011 Entry Draft.

2006-07	HC Vsetin U17	CzR-U17	4	1	0	1	0																		
2007-08	HC Vsetin U17	CzR-U17	40	15	25	40	72										2	2	0	2	6				
2008-09	Slavia U17	CzR-U17	46	28	19	47	34										9	6	2	8	8				
2009-10	Slavia U18	CzR-U18	12	15	12	27	36										2	1	3	4	4				
	Slavia Jr.	CzRep-Jr.	40	13	10	23	67										7	2	5	7	26				
2010-11	Slavia Jr.	CzRep-Jr.	1	0	0	0	0										2	2	3	5	2				
	HC Slavia Praha	CzRep	33	3	7	10	16										17	2	1	3	31				
2011-12	HC Slavia Praha	CzRep	37	4	2	6	18																		
	Beroun	CzRep-2	10	2	6	8	16																		
	Slavia Jr.	CzRep-Jr.	10	6	11	17	12										2	1	3	4	14				
2012-13	Moncton Wildcats	QMJHL	51	46	53	99	73										5	1	2	3	16				
	St. Louis	NHL	2	0	0	0	0	0	0	0	2	0.0	–1	0	0.0	7:30									
	NHL Totals		2	0	0	0	0	0	0	0	2	0.0		0	0.0	7:30									

QMJHL First All-Star Team (2013)

			Regular Season														Playoffs								
Season	Club	League	GP	G	A	Pts	PIM	PP	SH	GW	S	%	+/-	TF	F%	Min	GP	G	A	Pts	PIM	PP	SH	GW	Min

JEFFREY, Dustin

(JEHF-ree, DUHS-tihn) **PIT**

Center. Shoots left. 6'1", 205 lbs. Born, Sarnia, Ont., February 27, 1988. Pittsburgh's 8th choice, 171st overall, in 2007 Entry Draft.

2003-04	Lambton Sting	Minor-ON	40	44	23	67	22	....	....	....	....	....	....	....	....	....	....	....	....	....	....	....	....	....	....
2004-05	Mississauga	OHL	53	10	15	25	20	....	....	....	....	....	....	....	....	....	....	....	....	....	....	....	....	....	....
2005-06	Mississauga	OHL	30	6	9	15	26	....	....	....	....	....	....	....	....	....	....	....	....	....	....	....	....	....	....
	Sault Ste. Marie	OHL	39	12	11	23	10	....	....	....	....	....	....	....	....	....	4	1	2	3	2	....	....	....	....
2006-07	Sault Ste. Marie	OHL	68	34	58	92	40	....	....	....	....	....	....	....	....	....	13	6	12	18	11	....	....	....	....
2007-08	Sault Ste. Marie	OHL	56	38	59	97	30	....	....	....	....	....	....	....	....	....	14	3	8	11	12	....	....	....	....
	Wilkes-Barre	AHL	....	....	....	....	....	....	....	....	....	....	....	....	....	....	15	2	1	3	4	....	....	....	....
2008-09	**Pittsburgh**	**NHL**	**14**	**1**	**2**	**3**	**0**	**0**	**0**	**0**	**18**	**5.6**	**4**	**103**	**41.8**	**10:47**	....	....	....	....	....	....	....	....	....
	Wilkes-Barre	AHL	63	11	26	37	31	....	....	....	....	....	....	....	....	....	12	5	5	10	8	....	....	....	....
2009-10	**Pittsburgh**	**NHL**	**1**	**0**	**0**	**0**	**0**	**0**	**0**	**0**	**0**	**0.0**	**0**	**0**	**0.0**	**8:35**	....	....	....	....	....	....	....	....	....
	Wilkes-Barre	AHL	77	24	47	71	16	....	....	....	....	....	....	....	....	....	4	0	1	1	6	....	....	....	....
2010-11	**Pittsburgh**	**NHL**	**25**	**7**	**5**	**12**	**4**	**1**	**0**	**1**	**39**	**17.9**	**5**	**247**	**44.1**	**12:58**	....	....	....	....	....	....	....	....	....
	Wilkes-Barre	AHL	40	17	28	45	8	....	....	....	....	....	....	....	....	....	....	....	....	....	....	....	....	....	....
2011-12	**Pittsburgh**	**NHL**	**26**	**4**	**2**	**6**	**2**	**0**	**1**	**0**	**33**	**12.1**	**–4**	**225**	**48.4**	**12:06**	....	....	....	....	....	....	....	....	....
	Wilkes-Barre	AHL	2	0	1	1	0	....	....	....	....	....	....	....	....	....	....	....	....	....	....	....	....	....	....
2012-13	Zagreb	Austria	20	11	12	23	20	....	....	....	....	....	....	....	....	....	....	....	....	....	....	....	....	....	....
	Pittsburgh	**NHL**	**24**	**3**	**3**	**6**	**2**	**0**	**0**	**0**	**26**	**11.5**	**1**	**200**	**47.0**	**11:31**	....	....	....	....	....	....	....	....	....
	NHL Totals		**90**	**15**	**12**	**27**	**8**	**1**	**1**	**1**	**116**	**12.9**		**775**	**45.8**	**11:57**	....	....	....	....	....	....	....	....	....

• Missed majority of 2011-12 due to recurring knee injury and as a healthy reserve. Signed as a free agent by **Zagreb** (Austria), October 10, 2012.

JENSEN, Nicklas

(YEHN-suhn, NIHK-luhs) **VAN**

Left wing. Shoots left. 6'3", 187 lbs. Born, Herning, Denmark, March 6, 1993. Vancouver's 1st choice, 29th overall, in 2011 Entry Draft.

2008-09	Herning IK Jr.	Den-Jr.	28	28	15	43	30	....	....	....	....	....	....	....	....	....	....	....	....	....	....	....	....	....	....
	Herning IK II	Den-2	4	3	0	3	0	....	....	....	....	....	....	....	....	....	....	....	....	....	....	....	....	....	....
2009-10	Herning Blue Fox	Denmark	34	12	14	26	28	....	....	....	....	....	....	....	....	....	10	6	4	10	8	....	....	....	....
2010-11	Oshawa Generals	OHL	61	29	29	58	42	....	....	....	....	....	....	....	....	....	10	7	4	11	2	....	....	....	....
2011-12	Oshawa Generals	OHL	57	25	33	58	29	....	....	....	....	....	....	....	....	....	6	1	4	5	0	....	....	....	....
	Chicago Wolves	AHL	6	4	0	4	6	....	....	....	....	....	....	....	....	....	2	2	0	2	0	....	....	....	....
2012-13	AIK Solna	Sweden	50	17	6	23	16	....	....	....	....	....	....	....	....	....	....	....	....	....	....	....	....	....	....
	Chicago Wolves	AHL	20	2	2	4	8	....	....	....	....	....	....	....	....	....	....	....	....	....	....	....	....	....	....
	Vancouver	**NHL**	**2**	**0**	**0**	**0**	**0**	**0**	**0**	**0**	**0**	**0.0**	**–1**	**0**	**0.0**	**13:51**	....	....	....	....	....	....	....	....	....
	NHL Totals		**2**	**0**	**0**	**0**	**0**	**0**	**0**	**0**	**0**	**0.0**		**0**	**0.0**	**13:51**	....	....	....	....	....	....	....	....	....

• Loaned to **Solna** (Sweden) by **Vancouver** (Chicago-AHL), August 28, 2012.

JOENSUU, Jesse

(YOH-ehn-soo, JEH-see) **EDM**

Left wing. Shoots left. 6'4", 209 lbs. Born, Pori, Finland, October 5, 1987. NY Islanders' 2nd choice, 60th overall, in 2006 Entry Draft.

2002-03	Assat Pori U18	Fin-U18	26	8	10	18	53	....	....	....	....	....	....	....	....	....	3	1	2	3	0	....	....	....	....
	Assat Pori Jr.	Fin-Jr.	3	0	1	1	2	....	....	....	....	....	....	....	....	....	....	....	....	....	....	....	....	....	....
2003-04	Assat Pori U18	Fin-U18	6	7	2	9	8	....	....	....	....	....	....	....	....	....	....	....	....	....	....	....	....	....	....
	Assat Pori Jr.	Fin-Jr.	28	7	9	16	18	....	....	....	....	....	....	....	....	....	3	0	1	1	2	....	....	....	....
	Assat Pori	Finland	6	0	0	0	0	....	....	....	....	....	....	....	....	....	....	....	....	....	....	....	....	....	....
2004-05	Assat Pori Jr.	Fin-Jr.	17	7	13	20	20	....	....	....	....	....	....	....	....	....	2	1	1	2	2	....	....	....	....
	Assat Pori	Finland	39	1	1	2	4	....	....	....	....	....	....	....	....	....	....	....	....	....	....	....	....	....	....
2005-06	Assat Pori	Finland	51	4	8	12	57	....	....	....	....	....	....	....	....	....	14	0	2	2	12	....	....	....	....
	Suomi U20	Finland-2	2	1	0	1	12	....	....	....	....	....	....	....	....	....	....	....	....	....	....	....	....	....	....
2006-07	Assat Pori Jr.	Fin-Jr.	5	2	1	3	6	....	....	....	....	....	....	....	....	....	....	....	....	....	....	....	....	....	....
	Suomi U20	Finland-2	2	0	2	2	6	....	....	....	....	....	....	....	....	....	....	....	....	....	....	....	....	....	....
	Assat Pori	Finland	52	9	17	26	74	....	....	....	....	....	....	....	....	....	....	....	....	....	....	....	....	....	....
2007-08	Assat Pori	Finland	56	17	18	35	89	....	....	....	....	....	....	....	....	....	....	....	....	....	....	....	....	....	....
	Bridgeport	AHL	1	0	0	0	0	....	....	....	....	....	....	....	....	....	....	....	....	....	....	....	....	....	....
2008-09	**NY Islanders**	**NHL**	**7**	**1**	**2**	**3**	**4**	**0**	**0**	**0**	**9**	**11.1**	**–1**	**0**	**0.0**	**12:06**	....	....	....	....	....	....	....	....	....
	Bridgeport	AHL	71	20	19	39	58	....	....	....	....	....	....	....	....	....	5	2	1	3	4	....	....	....	....
2009-10	**NY Islanders**	**NHL**	**11**	**1**	**0**	**1**	**4**	**0**	**0**	**0**	**13**	**7.7**	**4**	**1**	**0.0**	**11:09**	....	....	....	....	....	....	....	....	....
	Bridgeport	AHL	70	14	34	48	66	....	....	....	....	....	....	....	....	....	5	0	2	2	6	....	....	....	....
2010-11	**NY Islanders**	**NHL**	**42**	**6**	**3**	**9**	**33**	**0**	**0**	**2**	**41**	**14.6**	**–6**	**9**	**55.6**	**11:35**	....	....	....	....	....	....	....	....	....
	Bridgeport	AHL	35	8	16	24	31	....	....	....	....	....	....	....	....	....	....	....	....	....	....	....	....	....	....
2011-12	HV 71 Jonkoping	Sweden	50	13	16	29	58	....	....	....	....	....	....	....	....	....	6	2	1	3	37	....	....	....	....
2012-13	Assat Pori	Finland	24	11	14	25	83	....	....	....	....	....	....	....	....	....	....	....	....	....	....	....	....	....	....
	NY Islanders	**NHL**	**7**	**0**	**2**	**2**	**6**	**0**	**0**	**0**	**15**	**0.0**	**2**	**0**	**0.0**	**10:08**	**1**	**0**	**0**	**0**	**0**	**0**	**0**	**0**	**8:26**
	NHL Totals		**67**	**8**	**7**	**15**	**47**	**0**	**0**	**2**	**78**	**10.3**		**10**	**50.0**	**11:25**	**1**	**0**	**0**	**0**	**0**	**0**	**0**	**0**	**8:26**

Signed as a free agent by **Jonkoping** (Sweden), July 1, 2011. Signed as a free agent by **Assat Pori** (Finland), September 18, 2012. • Missed majority of 2012-13 due to sports hernia surgery and as a healthy reserve. Signed as a free agent by **Edmonton**, July 5, 2013.

JOHANSEN, Ryan

(joh-HAN-suhn, RIGH-uhn) **CBJ**

Center. Shoots right. 6'3", 205 lbs. Born, Port Moody, B.C., July 31, 1992. Columbus' 1st choice, 4th overall, in 2010 Entry Draft.

2007-08	Van. NE Chiefs	BCMML	41	18	30	48	26	....	....	....	....	....	....	....	....	....	....	....	....	....	....	....	....	....	....
2008-09	Penticton Vees	BCHL	47	5	12	17	21	....	....	....	....	....	....	....	....	....	10	4	3	7	2	....	....	....	....
2009-10	Portland	WHL	71	25	44	69	53	....	....	....	....	....	....	....	....	....	13	6	12	18	18	....	....	....	....
2010-11	Portland	WHL	63	40	52	92	64	....	....	....	....	....	....	....	....	....	21	13	15	*28	6	....	....	....	....
2011-12	**Columbus**	**NHL**	**67**	**9**	**12**	**21**	**24**	**3**	**0**	**3**	**99**	**9.1**	**–2**	**215**	**45.1**	**12:44**	....	....	....	....	....	....	....	....	....
2012-13	Springfield	AHL	40	17	16	33	20	....	....	....	....	....	....	....	....	....	5	0	1	1	2	....	....	....	....
	Columbus	**NHL**	**40**	**5**	**7**	**12**	**12**	**0**	**0**	**2**	**84**	**6.0**	**–7**	**529**	**51.4**	**16:05**	....	....	....	....	....	....	....	....	....
	NHL Totals		**107**	**14**	**19**	**33**	**36**	**3**	**0**	**5**	**183**	**7.7**		**744**	**49.6**	**13:59**	....	....	....	....	....	....	....	....	....

WHL West First All-Star Team (2011)

JOHANSSON, Marcus

(yoh-HAHN-suhn, MAHR-kuhs) **WSH**

Center/Wing. Shoots left. 6'1", 205 lbs. Born, Landskrona, Sweden, October 6, 1990. Washington's 1st choice, 24th overall, in 2009 Entry Draft.

2005-06	Malmo U18	Swe-U18	12	0	7	7	0	....	....	....	....	....	....	....	....	....	6	0	4	4	0	....	....	....	....
2006-07	Farjestad U18	Swe-U18	12	5	9	14	8	....	....	....	....	....	....	....	....	....	8	7	3	10	2	....	....	....	....
2007-08	Farjestad U18	Swe-U18	24	12	26	38	16	....	....	....	....	....	....	....	....	....	8	4	8	12	0	....	....	....	....
	Skare BK	Sweden-3	19	2	10	12	10	....	....	....	....	....	....	....	....	....	....	....	....	....	....	....	....	....	....
	Farjestad	Sweden	....	....	....	....	....	....	....	....	....	....	....	....	....	....	3	0	0	0	0	....	....	....	....
2008-09	Farjestad U18	Swe-U18	2	2	0	2	0	....	....	....	....	....	....	....	....	....	....	....	....	....	....	....	....	....	....
	Skare BK Karlstad	Sweden-3	5	5	5	10	0	....	....	....	....	....	....	....	....	....	....	....	....	....	....	....	....	....	....
	Farjestad	Sweden	45	5	5	10	10	....	....	....	....	....	....	....	....	....	6	0	0	0	0	....	....	....	....
2009-10	Farjestad	Sweden	42	10	10	20	10	....	....	....	....	....	....	....	....	....	7	0	5	5	2	....	....	....	....
2010-11	**Washington**	**NHL**	**69**	**13**	**14**	**27**	**10**	**2**	**1**	**2**	**102**	**12.7**	**2**	**669**	**40.5**	**14:43**	**9**	**2**	**4**	**6**	**0**	**0**	**0**	**0**	**18:22**
	Hershey Bears	AHL	2	0	0	0	0	....	....	....	....	....	....	....	....	....	....	....	....	....	....	....	....	....	....
2011-12	**Washington**	**NHL**	**80**	**14**	**32**	**46**	**8**	**1**	**0**	**3**	**90**	**15.6**	**–5**	**710**	**43.2**	**16:48**	**14**	**1**	**2**	**3**	**0**	**0**	**0**	**0**	**19:35**
2012-13	Bofors	Sweden-2	16	8	10	18	8	....	....	....	....	....	....	....	....	....	....	....	....	....	....	....	....	....	....
	Washington	**NHL**	**34**	**6**	**16**	**22**	**4**	**3**	**0**	**1**	**40**	**15.0**	**3**	**87**	**46.0**	**16:35**	**7**	**1**	**1**	**2**	**0**	**0**	**0**	**1**	**16:59**
	NHL Totals		**183**	**33**	**62**	**95**	**22**	**6**	**1**	**6**	**232**	**14.2**		**1466**	**42.2**	**15:59**	**30**	**4**	**7**	**11**	**0**	**0**	**0**	**1**	**18:37**

Signed as a free agent by **Karlskoga Bofors** (Sweden-2), October 30, 2012.

JOHNSON, Aaron

(JAWN-suhn, AIR-ruhn) **NYR**

Defense. Shoots left. 6'2", 211 lbs. Born, Port Hawkesbury, N.S., April 30, 1983. Columbus' 4th choice, 85th overall, in 2001 Entry Draft.

1998-99	Cape Breton	NSAHA	56	28	42	70	98	....	....	....	....	....	....	....	....	....	....	....	....	....	....	....	....	....	....
99-2000	Rimouski Oceanic	QMJHL	63	1	14	15	57	....	....	....	....	....	....	....	....	....	8	0	0	0	0	....	....	....	....
2000-01	Rimouski Oceanic	QMJHL	64	12	41	53	128	....	....	....	....	....	....	....	....	....	11	2	4	6	35	....	....	....	....
2001-02	Rimouski Oceanic	QMJHL	68	17	49	66	172	....	....	....	....	....	....	....	....	....	7	1	2	3	12	....	....	....	....
2002-03	Rimouski Oceanic	QMJHL	25	4	20	24	41	....	....	....	....	....	....	....	....	....	....	....	....	....	....	....	....	....	....
	Quebec Remparts	QMJHL	32	6	31	37	41	....	....	....	....	....	....	....	....	....	11	4	4	8	25	....	....	....	....

			Regular Season														Playoffs								
Season	Club	League	GP	G	A	Pts	PIM	PP	SH	GW	S	%	+/-	TF	F%	Min	GP	G	A	Pts	PIM	PP	SH	GW	Min
2003-04	**Columbus**	**NHL**	**29**	**2**	**6**	**8**	**32**	**0**	**0**	**1**	**33**	**6.1**	**–2**	**0**	**0.0**	**15:02**	....	....	....	....	....	....	....	....	....
	Syracuse Crunch	AHL	49	6	15	21	83	....	....	....	....	....	....	....	....	....	7	2	3	5	27	....	....	....	....
2004-05	Syracuse Crunch	AHL	77	6	17	23	140	....	....	....	....	....	....	....	....	....	....	....	....	....	....	....	....	....	....
2005-06	**Columbus**	**NHL**	**26**	**2**	**6**	**8**	**23**	**1**	**0**	**1**	**28**	**7.1**	**9**	**0**	**0.0**	**14:12**	....	....	....	....	....	....	....	....	....
	Syracuse Crunch	AHL	49	5	24	29	122	....	....	....	....	....	....	....	....	....	6	1	3	4	19	....	....	....	....
2006-07	**Columbus**	**NHL**	**61**	**3**	**7**	**10**	**38**	**0**	**0**	**0**	**52**	**5.8**	**–9**	**0**	**0.0**	**12:44**	....	....	....	....	....	....	....	....	....
2007-08	**NY Islanders**	**NHL**	**30**	**0**	**2**	**2**	**30**	**0**	**0**	**0**	**16**	**0.0**	**2**	**0**	**0.0**	**13:52**	....	....	....	....	....	....	....	....	....
	Bridgeport	AHL	2	0	0	0	0	....	....	....	....	....	....	....	....	....	....	....	....	....	....	....	....	....	....
2008-09	**Chicago**	**NHL**	**38**	**3**	**5**	**8**	**33**	**0**	**0**	**1**	**27**	**11.1**	**19**	**0**	**0.0**	**14:09**	....	....	....	....	....	....	....	....	....
	Rockford IceHogs	AHL	2	0	1	1	4	....	....	....	....	....	....	....	....	....	....	....	....	....	....	....	....	....	....
2009-10	**Calgary**	**NHL**	**22**	**1**	**2**	**3**	**19**	**0**	**0**	**0**	**13**	**7.7**	**0**	**0**	**0.0**	**12:11**	....	....	....	....	....	....	....	....	....
	Edmonton	**NHL**	**19**	**3**	**4**	**7**	**16**	**1**	**0**	**0**	**23**	**13.0**	**–6**	**0**	**0.0**	**19:40**	....	....	....	....	....	....	....	....	....
2010-11	Milwaukee	AHL	72	9	26	35	70	....	....	....	....	....	....	....	....	....	13	1	2	3	16	....	....	....	....
2011-12	**Columbus**	**NHL**	**56**	**3**	**13**	**16**	**26**	**1**	**0**	**0**	**63**	**4.8**	**–12**	**0**	**0.0**	**16:30**	....	....	....	....	....	....	....	....	....
2012-13	Providence Bruins	AHL	2	0	1	1	2	....	....	....	....	....	....	....	....	....	....	....	....	....	....	....	....	....	....
	Boston	**NHL**	**10**	**0**	**0**	**0**	**10**	**0**	**0**	**0**	**8**	**0.0**	**0**	**0**	**0.0**	**14:52**	....	....	....	....	....	....	....	....	....
	NHL Totals		**291**	**17**	**45**	**62**	**227**	**3**	**0**	**3**	**263**	**6.5**		**0**	**0.0**	**14:36**	....	....	....	....	....	....	....	....	....

Signed as a free agent by **NY Islanders**, July 12, 2007. • Missed majority of 2007-08 due to knee injury and as a healthy reserve. Signed as a free agent by **Chicago**, July 15, 2008. Traded to **Calgary** by **Chicago** for Kyle Greentree, October 7, 2009. Traded to **Edmonton** by **Calgary** with Calgary's 3rd round choice (Travis Ewanyk) in 2011 Entry Draft for Steve Staios, March 3, 2010. Signed as a free agent by **Nashville**, August 31, 2010. Signed as a free agent by **Columbus**, July 5, 2011. Signed as a free agent by **Boston**, July 18. 2012. • Missed majority of 2012-13 as a healthy reserve. Signed as a free agent by **NY Rangersr**, July 5, 2013.

JOHNSON, Erik

(JAWN-suhn, AIR-ihk) **COL**

Defense. Shoots right. 6'4", 232 lbs. Born, Bloomington, MN, March 21, 1988. St. Louis' 1st choice, 1st overall, in 2006 Entry Draft.

			Regular Season														Playoffs								
Season	Club	League	GP	G	A	Pts	PIM	PP	SH	GW	S	%	+/-	TF	F%	Min	GP	G	A	Pts	PIM	PP	SH	GW	Min
2003-04	Holy Angels	High-MN	31	13	21	34	....	....	....	....	....	....	....	....	....	....	....	....	....	....	....	....	....	....	....
2004-05	USNTDP	U-17	26	5	9	14	14	....	....	....	....	....	....	....	....	....	....	....	....	....	....	....	....	....	....
	USNTDP	NAHL	31	6	6	12	12	....	....	....	....	....	....	....	....	....	....	....	....	....	....	....	....	....	....
2005-06	USNTDP	U-18	36	12	22	34	78	....	....	....	....	....	....	....	....	....	....	....	....	....	....	....	....	....	....
	USNTDP	NAHL	11	4	11	15	10	....	....	....	....	....	....	....	....	....	....	....	....	....	....	....	....	....	....
2006-07	U. of Minnesota	WCHA	41	4	20	24	50	....	....	....	....	....	....	....	....	....	....	....	....	....	....	....	....	....	....
2007-08	**St. Louis**	**NHL**	**69**	**5**	**28**	**33**	**28**	**4**	**0**	**3**	**105**	**4.8**	**–9**	**1**	**0.0**	**18:11**	....	....	....	....	....	....	....	....	....
	Peoria Rivermen	AHL	1	0	0	0	2	....	....	....	....	....	....	....	....	....	....	....	....	....	....	....	....	....	....
2008-09	**St. Louis**	**NHL**	DID NOT PLAY – INJURED														....	....	....	....	....	....	....	....	....
2009-10	**St. Louis**	**NHL**	**79**	**10**	**29**	**39**	**79**	**6**	**0**	**2**	**186**	**5.4**	**1**	**0**	**0.0**	**21:27**	....	....	....	....	....	....	....	....	....
	United States	Olympics	6	1	0	1	4	....	....	....	....	....	....	....	....	....	....	....	....	....	....	....	....	....	....
2010-11	**St. Louis**	**NHL**	**55**	**5**	**14**	**19**	**37**	**1**	**1**	**2**	**108**	**4.6**	**–8**	**0**	**0.0**	**22:08**	....	....	....	....	....	....	....	....	....
	Colorado	**NHL**	**22**	**3**	**7**	**10**	**19**	**2**	**0**	**0**	**53**	**5.7**	**–5**	**0**	**0.0**	**24:33**	....	....	....	....	....	....	....	....	....
2011-12	**Colorado**	**NHL**	**73**	**4**	**22**	**26**	**26**	**1**	**0**	**1**	**155**	**2.6**	**–7**	**0**	**0.0**	**20:50**	....	....	....	....	....	....	....	....	....
2012-13	**Colorado**	**NHL**	**31**	**0**	**4**	**4**	**18**	**0**	**0**	**0**	**64**	**0.0**	**–3**	**0**	**0.0**	**20:45**	....	....	....	....	....	....	....	....	....
	NHL Totals		**329**	**27**	**104**	**131**	**207**	**14**	**1**	**8**	**671**	**4.0**		**1**	**0.0**	**20:53**	....	....	....	....	....	....	....	....	....

WCHA All-Rookie Team (2007)

• Missed 2008-09 due to off-ice knee injury, September 16, 2008 and resulting surgery, November 20, 2008. Traded to **Colorado** by **St. Louis** with Jay McClement and St. Louis's 1st round choice (Duncan Siemens) in 2011 Entry Draft for Kevin Shattenkirk, Chris Stewart and Colorado's 2nd round choice (Ty Rattie) in 2011 Entry Draft, February 19, 2011.

JOHNSON, Jack

(JAHN-suhn, JAK) **CBJ**

Defense. Shoots left. 6'1", 231 lbs. Born, Indianapolis, IN, January 13, 1987. Carolina's 1st choice, 3rd overall, in 2005 Entry Draft.

			Regular Season														Playoffs								
Season	Club	League	GP	G	A	Pts	PIM	PP	SH	GW	S	%	+/-	TF	F%	Min	GP	G	A	Pts	PIM	PP	SH	GW	Min
2002-03	Shat.-St. Mary's	High-MN	48	15	27	42	....	....	....	....	....	....	....	....	....	....	....	....	....	....	....	....	....	....	....
2003-04	USNTDP	U-17	31	12	9	21	78	....	....	....	....	....	....	....	....	....	....	....	....	....	....	....	....	....	....
	USNTDP	NAHL	29	3	12	15	93	....	....	....	....	....	....	....	....	....	....	....	....	....	....	....	....	....	....
2004-05	USNTDP	U-18	26	5	9	14	86	....	....	....	....	....	....	....	....	....	....	....	....	....	....	....	....	....	....
	USNTDP	NAHL	12	7	10	17	57	....	....	....	....	....	....	....	....	....	....	....	....	....	....	....	....	....	....
2005-06	U. of Michigan	CCHA	38	10	22	32	*149	....	....	....	....	....	....	....	....	....	....	....	....	....	....	....	....	....	....
2006-07	U. of Michigan	CCHA	36	16	23	39	87	....	....	....	....	....	....	....	....	....	....	....	....	....	....	....	....	....	....
	Los Angeles	**NHL**	**5**	**0**	**0**	**0**	**18**	**0**	**0**	**0**	**5**	**0.0**	**–5**	**0**	**0.0**	**21:23**	....	....	....	....	....	....	....	....	....
2007-08	**Los Angeles**	**NHL**	**74**	**3**	**8**	**11**	**76**	**0**	**0**	**0**	**81**	**3.7**	**–19**	**5**	**60.0**	**21:42**	....	....	....	....	....	....	....	....	....
2008-09	**Los Angeles**	**NHL**	**41**	**6**	**5**	**11**	**46**	**3**	**0**	**0**	**50**	**12.0**	**–18**	**0**	**0.0**	**20:17**	....	....	....	....	....	....	....	....	....
2009-10	**Los Angeles**	**NHL**	**80**	**8**	**28**	**36**	**48**	**3**	**0**	**0**	**130**	**6.2**	**–15**	**0**	**0.0**	**22:37**	**6**	**0**	**7**	**7**	**6**	**0**	**0**	**0**	**23:42**
	United States	Olympics	6	0	1	1	2	....	....	....	....	....	....	....	....	....	....	....	....	....	....	....	....	....	....
2010-11	**Los Angeles**	**NHL**	**82**	**5**	**37**	**42**	**44**	**3**	**0**	**0**	**153**	**3.3**	**–21**	**0**	**0.0**	**23:12**	**6**	**1**	**4**	**5**	**0**	**1**	**0**	**1**	**22:48**
2011-12	**Los Angeles**	**NHL**	**61**	**8**	**16**	**24**	**24**	**5**	**0**	**4**	**120**	**6.7**	**–12**	**0**	**0.0**	**22:31**	....	....	....	....	....	....	....	....	....
	Columbus	**NHL**	**21**	**4**	**10**	**14**	**15**	**0**	**0**	**1**	**56**	**7.1**	**5**	**0**	**0.0**	**27:25**	....	....	....	....	....	....	....	....	....
2012-13	**Columbus**	**NHL**	**44**	**5**	**14**	**19**	**12**	**3**	**0**	**1**	**96**	**5.2**	**–5**	**0**	**0.0**	**25:58**	....	....	....	....	....	....	....	....	....
	NHL Totals		**408**	**39**	**118**	**157**	**283**	**17**	**0**	**6**	**691**	**5.6**		**5**	**60.0**	**22:55**	**12**	**1**	**11**	**12**	**6**	**1**	**0**	**1**	**23:15**

CCHA All-Rookie Team (2006) • CCHA First All-Star Team (2007) • NCAA West First All-American Team (2007)

Traded to **Los Angeles** by **Carolina** with Oleg Tverdovsky for Eric Belanger and Tim Gleason, September 29, 2006. Traded to **Columbus** by **Los Angeles** with Los Angeles' 1st round choice (Marko Dano) in 2013 Entry Draft for Jeff Carter, February 23, 2012.

JOHNSON, Nick

(JAWN-suhn, NIHK) **BOS**

Right wing. Shoots right. 6'2", 200 lbs. Born, Calgary, Alta., December 24, 1985. Pittsburgh's 4th choice, 67th overall, in 2004 Entry Draft.

			Regular Season														Playoffs								
Season	Club	League	GP	G	A	Pts	PIM	PP	SH	GW	S	%	+/-	TF	F%	Min	GP	G	A	Pts	PIM	PP	SH	GW	Min
2002-03	St. Albert Saints	AJHL	60	21	30	51	10	....	....	....	....	....	....	....	....	....	....	....	....	....	....	....	....	....	....
2003-04	St. Albert Saints	AJHL	51	35	36	71	33	....	....	....	....	....	....	....	....	....	4	0	2	2	0	....	....	....	....
2004-05	Dartmouth	ECAC	35	18	17	35	16	....	....	....	....	....	....	....	....	....	....	....	....	....	....	....	....	....	....
2005-06	Dartmouth	ECAC	33	15	10	25	24	....	....	....	....	....	....	....	....	....	....	....	....	....	....	....	....	....	....
2006-07	Dartmouth	ECAC	33	14	16	30	46	....	....	....	....	....	....	....	....	....	....	....	....	....	....	....	....	....	....
2007-08	Dartmouth	ECAC	32	10	25	35	20	....	....	....	....	....	....	....	....	....	....	....	....	....	....	....	....	....	....
	Wilkes-Barre	AHL	4	0	1	1	0	....	....	....	....	....	....	....	....	....	10	0	1	1	2	....	....	....	....
2008-09	Wilkes-Barre	AHL	56	14	17	31	30	....	....	....	....	....	....	....	....	....	12	4	6	10	8	....	....	....	....
	Wheeling Nailers	ECHL	18	14	10	24	19	....	....	....	....	....	....	....	....	....	....	....	....	....	....	....	....	....	....
2009-10	**Pittsburgh**	**NHL**	**6**	**1**	**1**	**2**	**2**	**0**	**0**	**0**	**7**	**14.3**	**–2**	**1**	**100.0**	**10:06**	....	....	....	....	....	....	....	....	....
	Wilkes-Barre	AHL	61	16	27	43	50	....	....	....	....	....	....	....	....	....	4	4	0	4	2	....	....	....	....
2010-11	**Pittsburgh**	**NHL**	**4**	**1**	**2**	**3**	**5**	**0**	**0**	**0**	**10**	**10.0**	**1**	**0**	**0.0**	**16:44**	....	....	....	....	....	....	....	....	....
	Wilkes-Barre	AHL	48	20	19	39	49	....	....	....	....	....	....	....	....	....	....	....	....	....	....	....	....	....	....
2011-12	**Minnesota**	**NHL**	**77**	**8**	**18**	**26**	**45**	**0**	**0**	**1**	**146**	**5.5**	**–6**	**13**	**23.1**	**14:27**	....	....	....	....	....	....	....	....	....
2012-13	Idaho Steelheads	ECHL	5	0	1	1	0	....	....	....	....	....	....	....	....	....	....	....	....	....	....	....	....	....	....
	Portland Pirates	AHL	14	3	6	9	13	....	....	....	....	....	....	....	....	....	3	2	1	3	9	....	....	....	....
	Phoenix	**NHL**	**17**	**4**	**2**	**6**	**0**	**1**	**0**	**1**	**23**	**17.4**	**3**	**3**	**0.0**	**9:57**	....	....	....	....	....	....	....	....	....
	NHL Totals		**104**	**14**	**23**	**37**	**52**	**1**	**0**	**2**	**186**	**7.5**		**17**	**23.5**	**13:33**	....	....	....	....	....	....	....	....	....

ECAC All-Rookie Team (2005) • ECAC First All-Star Team (2008) • NCAA East Second All-American Team (2008)

Claimed on waivers by **Minnesota** from **Pittsburgh**, September 29, 2011. Signed as a free agent by **Phoenix**, July 12, 2012. Signed as a free agent by **Idaho** (ECHL), December 11, 2012. Signed as a free agent by **Boston**, July 5, 2013.

JOHNSON, Tyler

(JAWN-suhn, TIGH-luhr) **T.B.**

Center. Shoots right. 5'9", 182 lbs. Born, Spokane, WA, July 29, 1990.

			Regular Season														Playoffs								
Season	Club	League	GP	G	A	Pts	PIM	PP	SH	GW	S	%	+/-	TF	F%	Min	GP	G	A	Pts	PIM	PP	SH	GW	Min
2007-08	Spokane Chiefs	WHL	69	13	22	35	34	....	....	....	....	....	....	....	....	....	21	5	3	8	24	....	....	....	....
2008-09	Spokane Chiefs	WHL	62	26	35	61	52	....	....	....	....	....	....	....	....	....	12	5	3	8	8	....	....	....	....
2009-10	Spokane Chiefs	WHL	64	36	35	71	32	....	....	....	....	....	....	....	....	....	7	3	5	8	0	....	....	....	....
2010-11	Spokane Chiefs	WHL	71	*53	62	115	48	....	....	....	....	....	....	....	....	....	14	7	7	14	9	....	....	....	....
2011-12	Norfolk Admirals	AHL	75	31	37	68	28	....	....	....	....	....	....	....	....	....	14	6	8	14	6	....	....	....	....
2012-13	Syracuse Crunch	AHL	62	*37	28	65	34	....	....	....	....	....	....	....	....	....	18	10	11	21	18	....	....	....	....
	Tampa Bay	**NHL**	**14**	**3**	**3**	**6**	**4**	**0**	**0**	**0**	**11**	**27.3**	**3**	**121**	**59.5**	**13:04**	....	....	....	....	....	....	....	....	....
	NHL Totals		**14**	**3**	**3**	**6**	**4**	**0**	**0**	**0**	**11**	**27.3**		**121**	**59.5**	**13:04**	....	....	....	....	....	....	....	....	....

WHL West First All-Star Team (2011) • AHL All-Rookie Team (2012) • Willie Marshall Award (AHL – Top Goal-scorer) (2013) • Les Cunningham Award (AHL – MVP) (2013)

Signed as a free agent by **Tampa Bay**, March 7, 2011.

JOKINEN, Jussi

(YOH-kih-nihn, YEW-see) **PIT**

Center. Shoots left. 5'11", 198 lbs. Born, Kalajoki, Finland, April 1, 1983. Dallas' 7th choice, 192nd overall, in 2001 Entry Draft.

			Regular Season														Playoffs								
Season	Club	League	GP	G	A	Pts	PIM	PP	SH	GW	S	%	+/-	TF	F%	Min	GP	G	A	Pts	PIM	PP	SH	GW	Min
99-2000	Karpat Oulu U18	Fin-U18	15	6	25	31	14	....	....	....	....	....	....	....	....	....	6	2	3	5	0	....	....	....	....
	Karpat Oulu Jr.	Fin-Jr.	28	4	7	11	14	....	....	....	....	....	....	....	....	....	....	....	....	....	....	....	....	....	....
2000-01	Karpat Oulu U18	Fin-U18	1	2	1	3	0	....	....	....	....	....	....	....	....	....	....	....	....	....	....	....	....	....	....
	Karpat Oulu Jr.	Fin-Jr.	41	18	31	49	69	....	....	....	....	....	....	....	....	....	6	2	1	3	0	....	....	....	....
2001-02	Karpat Oulu Jr.	Fin-Jr.	2	4	1	5	2	....	....	....	....	....	....	....	....	....	1	1	1	2	0	....	....	....	....
	Karpat Oulu	Finland	54	10	6	16	38	....	....	....	....	....	....	....	....	....	4	1	0	1	0	....	....	....	....
2002-03	Karpat Oulu	Finland	51	14	23	37	10	....	....	....	....	....	....	....	....	....	15	2	1	3	33	....	....	....	....
2003-04	Karpat Oulu	Finland	55	15	23	38	20	....	....	....	....	....	....	....	....	....	15	3	4	7	6	....	....	....	....
2004-05	Karpat Oulu	Finland	56	23	24	47	24	....	....	....	....	....	....	....	....	....	12	3	4	7	2	....	....	....	....
2005-06	**Dallas**	**NHL**	**81**	**17**	**38**	**55**	**30**	**8**	**0**	**2**	**107**	**15.9**	**2**	**23**	**30.4**	**13:34**	**5**	**2**	**1**	**3**	**0**	**1**	**0**	**0**	**13:40**
	Finland	Olympics	8	1	3	4	2	....	....	....	....	....	....	....	....	....	....	....	....	....	....	....	....	....	....
2006-07	**Dallas**	**NHL**	**82**	**14**	**34**	**48**	**18**	**6**	**0**	**1**	**121**	**11.6**	**8**	**278**	**52.2**	**13:54**	**4**	**0**	**1**	**1**	**0**	**0**	**0**	**0**	**13:22**
2007-08	**Dallas**	**NHL**	**52**	**14**	**14**	**28**	**14**	**5**	**0**	**2**	**93**	**15.1**	**2**	**295**	**53.2**	**12:44**	....	....	....	....	....	....	....	....	....
	Tampa Bay	**NHL**	**20**	**2**	**12**	**14**	**4**	**1**	**0**	**0**	**38**	**5.3**	**-16**	**46**	**45.7**	**18:57**	....	....	....	....	....	....	....	....	....
2008-09	**Tampa Bay**	**NHL**	**46**	**6**	**10**	**16**	**16**	**2**	**0**	**0**	**64**	**9.4**	**-8**	**510**	**52.2**	**15:38**	....	....	....	....	....	....	....	....	....
	Carolina	**NHL**	**25**	**1**	**10**	**11**	**12**	**0**	**0**	**1**	**37**	**2.7**	**-2**	**163**	**58.3**	**14:43**	**18**	**7**	**4**	**11**	**2**	**2**	**0**	***3**	**15:35**
2009-10	**Carolina**	**NHL**	**81**	**30**	**35**	**65**	**36**	**10**	**0**	**6**	**160**	**18.8**	**3**	**265**	**51.3**	**16:49**	....	....	....	....	....	....	....	....	....
2010-11	**Carolina**	**NHL**	**70**	**19**	**33**	**52**	**24**	**8**	**0**	**1**	**136**	**14.0**	**3**	**320**	**52.8**	**17:13**	....	....	....	....	....	....	....	....	....
2011-12	**Carolina**	**NHL**	**79**	**12**	**34**	**46**	**54**	**3**	**2**	**3**	**118**	**10.2**	**-2**	**833**	**55.1**	**17:40**	....	....	....	....	....	....	....	....	....
2012-13	Karpat Oulu	Finland	21	7	14	21	10	....	....	....	....	....	....	....	....	....	....	....	....	....	....	....	....	....	....
	Carolina	**NHL**	**33**	**6**	**5**	**11**	**18**	**2**	**0**	**3**	**61**	**9.8**	**-8**	**283**	**59.4**	**15:35**	....	....	....	....	....	....	....	....	....
	Pittsburgh	**NHL**	**10**	**7**	**4**	**11**	**6**	**1**	**0**	**0**	**13**	**53.8**	**3**	**149**	**55.0**	**14:55**	**8**	**0**	**3**	**3**	**4**	**0**	**0**	**0**	**11:01**
	NHL Totals		**579**	**128**	**229**	**357**	**232**	**46**	**2**	**19**	**948**	**13.5**		**3165**	**53.9**	**15:32**	**35**	**9**	**9**	**18**	**6**	**3**	**0**	**3**	**14:01**

Traded to **Tampa Bay** by **Dallas** with Jeff Halpern, Mike Smith and Dallas' 4th round choice (later traded to Minnesota, later traded to Edmonton – Edmonton selected Kyle Bigos) in 2009 Entry Draft for Brad Richards and Johan Holmqvist, February 26, 2008. Traded to **Carolina** by **Tampa Bay** for Wade Brookbank, Josef Melichar and future considerations, February 7, 2009. Signed as a free agent by **Oulu** (Finland), September 17, 2012. Traded to **Pittsburgh** by **Carolina** for future considerations, April 3, 2013.

JOKINEN, Olli

(YOH-kih-nihn, OH-lee) **WPG**

Center. Shoots left. 6'2", 210 lbs. Born, Kuopio, Finland, December 5, 1978. Los Angeles' 1st choice, 3rd overall, in 1997 Entry Draft.

			Regular Season														Playoffs								
Season	Club	League	GP	G	A	Pts	PIM	PP	SH	GW	S	%	+/-	TF	F%	Min	GP	G	A	Pts	PIM	PP	SH	GW	Min
1994-95	KalPa Kuopio U18	Fin-U18	30	22	28	50	92	....	....	....	....	....	....	....	....	....	....	....	....	....	....	....	....	....	....
	KalPa Kuopio Jr.	Fin-Jr.	6	0	1	1	6	....	....	....	....	....	....	....	....	....	....	....	....	....	....	....	....	....	....
1995-96	KalPa Kuopio U18	Fin-U18	9	9	13	22	4	....	....	....	....	....	....	....	....	....	....	....	....	....	....	....	....	....	....
	KalPa Kuopio Jr.	Fin-Jr.	25	20	14	34	47	....	....	....	....	....	....	....	....	....	7	4	4	8	20	....	....	....	....
	KalPa Kuopio	Finland	15	1	1	2	2	....	....	....	....	....	....	....	....	....	....	....	....	....	....	....	....	....	....
1996-97	HIFK Helsinki Jr.	Fin-Jr.	2	1	0	1	6	....	....	....	....	....	....	....	....	....	....	....	....	....	....	....	....	....	....
	HIFK Helsinki	Finland	50	14	27	41	88	....	....	....	....	....	....	....	....	....	....	....	....	....	....	....	....	....	....
1997-98	**Los Angeles**	**NHL**	**8**	**0**	**0**	**0**	**6**	**0**	**0**	**0**	**12**	**0.0**	**-5**	....	....	....	....	....	....	....	....	....	....	....	....
	HIFK Helsinki	Finland	30	11	28	39	32	....	....	....	....	....	....	....	....	....	9	7	2	9	2	....	....	....	....
1998-99	**Los Angeles**	**NHL**	**66**	**9**	**12**	**21**	**44**	**3**	**1**	**1**	**87**	**10.3**	**-10**	**779**	**43.9**	**14:42**	....	....	....	....	....	....	....	....	....
	Springfield	AHL	9	3	6	9	6	....	....	....	....	....	....	....	....	....	....	....	....	....	....	....	....	....	....
99-2000	**NY Islanders**	**NHL**	**82**	**11**	**10**	**21**	**80**	**1**	**2**	**3**	**138**	**8.0**	**0**	**841**	**46.1**	**16:15**	....	....	....	....	....	....	....	....	....
2000-01	**Florida**	**NHL**	**78**	**6**	**10**	**16**	**106**	**0**	**0**	**0**	**121**	**5.0**	**-22**	**638**	**42.3**	**13:23**	....	....	....	....	....	....	....	....	....
2001-02	**Florida**	**NHL**	**80**	**9**	**20**	**29**	**98**	**3**	**1**	**0**	**153**	**5.9**	**-16**	**1222**	**45.2**	**18:05**	....	....	....	....	....	....	....	....	....
	Finland	Olympics	4	2	1	3	0	....	....	....	....	....	....	....	....	....	....	....	....	....	....	....	....	....	....
2002-03	**Florida**	**NHL**	**81**	**36**	**29**	**65**	**79**	**13**	**3**	**6**	**240**	**15.0**	**-17**	**1925**	**46.7**	**22:02**	....	....	....	....	....	....	....	....	....
2003-04	**Florida**	**NHL**	**82**	**26**	**32**	**58**	**81**	**8**	**2**	**8**	**280**	**9.3**	**-16**	**1986**	**47.1**	**22:35**	....	....	....	....	....	....	....	....	....
2004-05	Kloten Flyers	Swiss	8	6	1	7	14	....	....	....	....	....	....	....	....	....	....	....	....	....	....	....	....	....	....
	Sodertalje SK	Sweden	23	13	9	22	52	....	....	....	....	....	....	....	....	....	....	....	....	....	....	....	....	....	....
	HIFK Helsinki	Finland	14	9	8	17	10	....	....	....	....	....	....	....	....	....	5	2	0	2	24	....	....	....	....
2005-06	**Florida**	**NHL**	**82**	**38**	**51**	**89**	**88**	**14**	**1**	**9**	**351**	**10.8**	**14**	**955**	**46.9**	**20:29**	....	....	....	....	....	....	....	....	....
	Finland	Olympics	8	6	2	8	2	....	....	....	....	....	....	....	....	....	....	....	....	....	....	....	....	....	....
2006-07	**Florida**	**NHL**	**82**	**39**	**52**	**91**	**78**	**9**	**1**	**8**	**351**	**11.1**	**18**	**1074**	**44.3**	**20:32**	....	....	....	....	....	....	....	....	....
2007-08	**Florida**	**NHL**	**82**	**34**	**37**	**71**	**67**	**18**	**0**	**5**	**341**	**10.0**	**-19**	**938**	**43.1**	**19:54**	....	....	....	....	....	....	....	....	....
2008-09	**Phoenix**	**NHL**	**57**	**21**	**21**	**42**	**49**	**6**	**2**	**2**	**169**	**12.4**	**-5**	**737**	**42.2**	**18:10**	....	....	....	....	....	....	....	....	....
	Calgary	**NHL**	**19**	**8**	**7**	**15**	**18**	**3**	**0**	**1**	**67**	**11.9**	**-7**	**215**	**47.4**	**21:03**	**6**	**2**	**3**	**5**	**4**	**0**	**0**	**0**	**19:24**
2009-10	**Calgary**	**NHL**	**56**	**11**	**24**	**35**	**53**	**2**	**0**	**2**	**162**	**6.8**	**2**	**739**	**49.3**	**18:30**	....	....	....	....	....	....	....	....	....
	NY Rangers	**NHL**	**26**	**4**	**11**	**15**	**22**	**1**	**0**	**1**	**74**	**5.4**	**1**	**234**	**49.6**	**16:29**	....	....	....	....	....	....	....	....	....
	Finland	Olympics	6	3	1	4	2	....	....	....	....	....	....	....	....	....	....	....	....	....	....	....	....	....	....
2010-11	**Calgary**	**NHL**	**79**	**17**	**37**	**54**	**44**	**5**	**0**	**1**	**208**	**8.2**	**-17**	**1165**	**47.4**	**17:47**	....	....	....	....	....	....	....	....	....
2011-12	**Calgary**	**NHL**	**82**	**23**	**38**	**61**	**54**	**9**	**0**	**5**	**223**	**10.3**	**-12**	**1333**	**46.5**	**18:58**	....	....	....	....	....	....	....	....	....
2012-13	**Winnipeg**	**NHL**	**45**	**7**	**7**	**14**	**14**	**0**	**0**	**0**	**85**	**8.2**	**-19**	**630**	**47.6**	**17:08**	....	....	....	....	....	....	....	....	....
	NHL Totals		**1087**	**299**	**398**	**697**	**981**	**95**	**13**	**52**	**3062**	**9.8**		**15411**	**45.9**	**18:35**	**6**	**2**	**3**	**5**	**4**	**0**	**0**	**0**	**19:24**

Played in NHL All-Star Game (2003)

Traded to **NY Islanders** by **Los Angeles** with Josh Green, Mathieu Biron and Los Angeles' 1st round choice (Taylor Pyatt) in 1999 Entry Draft for Ziggy Palffy, Bryan Smolinski, Marcel Cousineau and New Jersey's 4th round choice (previously acquired, Los Angeles selected Daniel Johansson) in 1999 Entry Draft, June 20, 1999. Traded to **Florida** by **NY Islanders** with Roberto Luongo for Mark Parrish and Oleg Kvasha, June 24, 2000. Signed as a free agent by **Kloten** (Swiss), September 15, 2004. Signed as a free agent by **Sodertalje** (Sweden), November, 2004. Signed as a free agent by **HIFK Helsinki** (Finland), January 30, 2005.Traded to **Phoenix** by **Florida** for Keith Ballard, Nick Boynton and Ottawa's 2nd round choice (previously acquired, later traded back to Phoenix - Phoenix selected Jared Staal) in 2008 Entry Draft, June 20, 2008. Traded to **Calgary** by **Phoenix** with Phoenix's 3rd round choice (later traded to Florida – Florida selected Josh Birkholz) in 2009 Entry Draft for Matthew Lombardi, Brandon Prust and Calgary's 1st round choice (Brandon Gormley) in 2010 Entry Draft, March 4, 2009. Traded to **NY Rangers** by **Calgary** with Brandon Prust for Chris Higgins and Ales Kotalik, February 2, 2010. Signed as a free agent by **Calgary**, July 1, 2010. Signed as a free agent by **Winnipeg**, July 2, 2012.

JONES, Blair

(JOHNZ, BLAYR) **CGY**

Center. Shoots right. 6'2", 216 lbs. Born, Central Butte, Sask., September 27, 1986. Tampa Bay's 5th choice, 102nd overall, in 2005 Entry Draft.

			Regular Season														Playoffs								
Season	Club	League	GP	G	A	Pts	PIM	PP	SH	GW	S	%	+/-	TF	F%	Min	GP	G	A	Pts	PIM	PP	SH	GW	Min
2002-03	Bethune	SBHL	STATISTICS NOT AVAILABLE																						
	Red Deer Rebels	WHL	37	3	4	7	17	....	....	....	....	....	....	....	....	....	10	1	0	1	0	....	....	....	....
2003-04	Red Deer Rebels	WHL	72	9	22	31	55	....	....	....	....	....	....	....	....	....	19	1	5	6	24	....	....	....	....
2004-05	Red Deer Rebels	WHL	39	7	18	25	48	....	....	....	....	....	....	....	....	....	....	....	....	....	....	....	....	....	....
	Moose Jaw	WHL	29	7	18	25	30	....	....	....	....	....	....	....	....	....	5	2	5	7	8	....	....	....	....
2005-06	Moose Jaw	WHL	72	35	50	85	85	....	....	....	....	....	....	....	....	....	22	9	12	21	45	....	....	....	....
2006-07	**Tampa Bay**	**NHL**	**20**	**1**	**2**	**3**	**2**	**0**	**0**	**0**	**6**	**16.7**	**0**	**65**	**41.5**	**5:46**	....	....	....	....	....	....	....	....	....
	Springfield	AHL	45	5	16	21	36	....	....	....	....	....	....	....	....	....	....	....	....	....	....	....	....	....	....
2007-08	**Tampa Bay**	**NHL**	**4**	**0**	**0**	**0**	**0**	**0**	**0**	**0**	**1**	**0.0**	**0**	**8**	**12.5**	**1:55**	....	....	....	....	....	....	....	....	....
	Norfolk Admirals	AHL	75	14	28	42	50	....	....	....	....	....	....	....	....	....	....	....	....	....	....	....	....	....	....
2008-09	Norfolk Admirals	AHL	80	20	34	54	61	....	....	....	....	....	....	....	....	....	....	....	....	....	....	....	....	....	....
2009-10	**Tampa Bay**	**NHL**	**14**	**0**	**0**	**0**	**10**	**0**	**0**	**0**	**26**	**0.0**	**-5**	**28**	**53.6**	**12:50**	....	....	....	....	....	....	....	....	....
	Norfolk Admirals	AHL	63	9	21	30	27	....	....	....	....	....	....	....	....	....	....	....	....	....	....	....	....	....	....
2010-11	**Tampa Bay**	**NHL**	**18**	**1**	**2**	**3**	**2**	**0**	**0**	**0**	**20**	**5.0**	**-2**	**86**	**53.5**	**8:01**	**7**	**0**	**0**	**0**	**2**	**0**	**0**	**0**	**6:24**
	Norfolk Admirals	AHL	56	24	31	55	75	....	....	....	....	....	....	....	....	....	4	1	0	1	8	....	....	....	....
2011-12	**Tampa Bay**	**NHL**	**22**	**2**	**2**	**4**	**10**	**0**	**0**	**0**	**21**	**9.5**	**-3**	**67**	**40.3**	**8:26**	....	....	....	....	....	....	....	....	....
	Norfolk Admirals	AHL	5	2	2	4	16	....	....	....	....	....	....	....	....	....	....	....	....	....	....	....	....	....	....
	Calgary	**NHL**	**21**	**1**	**3**	**4**	**8**	**0**	**0**	**1**	**37**	**2.7**	**2**	**235**	**43.0**	**14:25**	....	....	....	....	....	....	....	....	....
2012-13	Abbotsford Heat	AHL	21	3	4	7	23	....	....	....	....	....	....	....	....	....	....	....	....	....	....	....	....	....	....
	Calgary	**NHL**	**15**	**0**	**1**	**1**	**10**	**0**	**0**	**0**	**22**	**0.0**	**-6**	**109**	**53.2**	**10:45**	....	....	....	....	....	....	....	....	....
	NHL Totals		**114**	**5**	**10**	**15**	**42**	**0**	**0**	**1**	**133**	**3.8**		**598**	**46.0**	**9:37**	**7**	**0**	**0**	**0**	**2**	**0**	**0**	**0**	**6:24**

WHL East Second All-Star Team (2006)

Traded to **Calgary** by **Tampa Bay** for Brendan Mikkelson, January 6, 2012.

JONES, David

(JOHNZ, DAY-vihd) **CGY**

Right wing. Shoots right. 6'2", 210 lbs. Born, Guelph, Ont., August 10, 1984. Colorado's 8th choice, 288th overall, in 2003 Entry Draft.

			Regular Season														Playoffs								
Season	Club	League	GP	G	A	Pts	PIM	PP	SH	GW	S	%	+/-	TF	F%	Min	GP	G	A	Pts	PIM	PP	SH	GW	Min
2000-01	Port Coquitlam	PIJHL	40	18	11	29	33	....	....	....	....	....	....	....	....	....	....	....	....	....	....	....	....	....	....
2001-02	Coquitlam	BCHL	59	19	32	51	62	....	....	....	....	....	....	....	....	....	....	....	....	....	....	....	....	....	....
2002-03	Coquitlam	BCHL	35	9	19	28	55	....	....	....	....	....	....	....	....	....	7	2	6	8	8	....	....	....	....
2003-04	Coquitlam	BCHL	53	33	60	93	78	....	....	....	....	....	....	....	....	....	7	3	6	9	4	....	....	....	....
2004-05	Dartmouth	ECAC	34	9	5	14	26	....	....	....	....	....	....	....	....	....	....	....	....	....	....	....	....	....	....
2005-06	Dartmouth	ECAC	33	17	17	34	38	....	....	....	....	....	....	....	....	....	....	....	....	....	....	....	....	....	....
2006-07	Dartmouth	ECAC	33	18	26	*44	22	....	....	....	....	....	....	....	....	....	....	....	....	....	....	....	....	....	....

			Regular Season														Playoffs								
Season	Club	League	GP	G	A	Pts	PIM	PP	SH	GW	S	%	+/-	TF	F%	Min	GP	G	A	Pts	PIM	PP	SH	GW	Min
2007-08	Colorado	NHL	27	2	4	6	8	1	0	0	37	5.4	–5	8	37.5	11:22	10	0	1	1	6	0	0	0	11:50
	Lake Erie	AHL	45	14	16	30	16	....	....	....	....	....	....	....	....	....	....	....	....	....	....	....	....	....	....
2008-09	Colorado	NHL	40	8	5	13	8	1	0	1	47	17.0	–8	8	50.0	12:44	....	....	....	....	....	....	....	....	....
2009-10	Colorado	NHL	23	10	6	16	2	1	2	3	39	25.6	1	7	28.6	17:56	....	....	....	....	....	....	....	....	....
2010-11	Colorado	NHL	77	27	18	45	28	6	0	4	153	17.6	–2	21	47.6	17:41	....	....	....	....	....	....	....	....	....
2011-12	Colorado	NHL	72	20	17	37	32	3	1	5	136	14.7	–8	34	47.1	15:45	....	....	....	....	....	....	....	....	....
2012-13	Colorado	NHL	33	3	6	9	6	1	0	2	62	4.8	–11	21	28.6	16:49	....	....	....	....	....	....	....	....	....
	NHL Totals		272	70	56	126	84	13	3	15	474	14.8		99	41.4	15:44	10	0	1	1	6	0	0	0	11:50

ECAC Second All-Star Team (2006) • ECAC First All-Star Tearm (2007) • NCAA East First All-American Team (2007)

• Missed majority of 2008-09 due to shoulder injury vs. San Jose, January 27, 2009. • Missed remainder of 2009-10 due to knee injury vs. Minnesota, November 28, 2009. Traded to **Calgary** by **Colorado** with Shane O'Brien for Alex Tanguay and Cory Sarich. June 27, 2013.

JONES, Randy

(JOHNZ, RAN-dee)

Defense. Shoots left. 6'2", 210 lbs. Born, Quispamsis, N.B., July 23, 1981.

Season	Club	League	GP	G	A	Pts	PIM	PP	SH	GW	S	%	+/-	TF	F%	Min	GP	G	A	Pts	PIM	PP	SH	GW	Min
99-2000	Cobourg Cougars	ON-Jr.A	44	20	36	56	51	....	....	....	....	....	....	....	....	....	....	....	....	....	....	....	....	....	....
2000-01	Cobourg Cougars	ON-Jr.A	28	15	21	36	46	....	....	....	....	....	....	....	....	....	....	....	....	....	....	....	....	....	....
2001-02	Clarkson Knights	ECAC	34	9	11	20	32	....	....	....	....	....	....	....	....	....	....	....	....	....	....	....	....	....	....
2002-03	Clarkson Knights	ECAC	33	13	20	33	65	....	....	....	....	....	....	....	....	....	....	....	....	....	....	....	....	....	....
2003-04	Philadelphia	NHL	5	0	0	0	0	0	0	0	5	0.0	1	0	0.0	12:00	....	....	....	....	....	....	....	....	....
	Philadelphia	AHL	55	8	24	32	63	....	....	....	....	....	....	....	....	....	12	0	1	1	17	....	....	....	....
2004-05	Philadelphia	AHL	69	5	19	24	32	....	....	....	....	....	....	....	....	....	18	0	5	5	10	....	....	....	....
2005-06	Philadelphia	NHL	28	0	8	8	16	0	0	0	21	0.0	–6	1	100.0	14:58	....	....	....	....	....	....	....	....	....
	Philadelphia	AHL	21	2	3	5	53	....	....	....	....	....	....	....	....	....	....	....	....	....	....	....	....	....	....
2006-07	Philadelphia	NHL	66	4	18	22	38	0	0	0	67	6.0	–14	1	0.0	16:06	....	....	....	....	....	....	....	....	....
2007-08	Philadelphia	NHL	71	5	26	31	58	1	0	0	103	4.9	8	0	0.0	19:24	16	0	2	2	4	0	0	0	21:24
2008-09	Philadelphia	NHL	47	4	4	8	22	1	0	2	45	8.9	8	0	0.0	19:07	6	0	1	1	0	0	0	0	14:38
	Philadelphia	AHL	2	0	2	2	0	....	....	....	....	....	....	....	....	....	....	....	....	....	....	....	....	....	....
2009-10	Adirondack	AHL	6	0	1	1	6	....	....	....	....	....	....	....	....	....	....	....	....	....	....	....	....	....	....
	Los Angeles	NHL	48	5	16	21	28	1	1	1	54	9.3	–3	0	0.0	18:10	4	0	0	0	2	0	0	0	17:42
2010-11	Tampa Bay	NHL	61	1	12	13	15	0	0	0	52	1.9	–4	0	0.0	17:03	5	0	1	1	2	0	0	0	6:58
2011-12	Winnipeg	NHL	39	1	1	2	8	0	0	0	24	4.2	4	0	0.0	14:49	....	....	....	....	....	....	....	....	....
2012-13	Oklahoma City	AHL	18	0	2	2	31	....	....	....	....	....	....	....	....	....	17	1	4	5	6	....	....	....	....
	NHL Totals		365	20	85	105	185	3	1	3	371	5.4		2	50.0	17:17	31	0	4	4	8	0	0	0	17:17

ECAC First All-Star Team (2003)

Signed as a free agent by **Philadelphia**, July 24, 2003. Claimed on waivers by **Los Angeles** from **Philadelphia**, October 29, 2009. Signed as a free agent by **Tampa Bay**, August 25, 2010. Signed as a free agent by **Winnipeg**, July 4, 2011. • Missed majority of 2011-12 due to various injuries and as a healthy reserve. Signed to a PTO (professional tryout) contract by **Oklahoma City** (AHL), February 3, 2013.

JONES, Ryan

(JOHNZ, RIGH-uhn) **EDM**

Right wing. Shoots left. 6'1", 205 lbs. Born, Chatham, Ont., June 14, 1984. Minnesota's 5th choice, 111th overall, in 2004 Entry Draft.

Season	Club	League	GP	G	A	Pts	PIM	PP	SH	GW	S	%	+/-	TF	F%	Min	GP	G	A	Pts	PIM	PP	SH	GW	Min
2002-03	Chatham	ON-Jr.B	38	12	11	23	42	....	....	....	....	....	....	....	....	....	....	....	....	....	....	....	....	....	....
2003-04	Chatham	ON-Jr.B	46	39	30	69	64	....	....	....	....	....	....	....	....	....	17	17	9	26	25	....	....	....	....
2004-05	Miami U.	CCHA	38	8	7	15	79	....	....	....	....	....	....	....	....	....	....	....	....	....	....	....	....	....	....
2005-06	Miami U.	CCHA	39	22	13	35	72	....	....	....	....	....	....	....	....	....	....	....	....	....	....	....	....	....	....
2006-07	Miami U.	CCHA	42	29	19	48	88	....	....	....	....	....	....	....	....	....	....	....	....	....	....	....	....	....	....
2007-08	Miami U.	CCHA	42	31	18	49	83	....	....	....	....	....	....	....	....	....	....	....	....	....	....	....	....	....	....
	Houston Aeros	AHL	4	0	0	0	2	....	....	....	....	....	....	....	....	....	4	1	1	2	2	....	....	....	....
2008-09	Nashville	NHL	46	7	10	17	22	2	0	1	63	11.1	1	10	10.0	11:26	....	....	....	....	....	....	....	....	....
	Milwaukee	AHL	25	13	9	22	30	....	....	....	....	....	....	....	....	....	11	4	3	7	10	....	....	....	....
2009-10	Nashville	NHL	41	7	4	11	18	2	0	0	53	13.2	3	1	0.0	10:43	....	....	....	....	....	....	....	....	....
	Milwaukee	AHL	15	4	1	5	15	....	....	....	....	....	....	....	....	....	....	....	....	....	....	....	....	....	....
	Edmonton	NHL	8	1	0	1	8	0	0	0	9	11.1	–3	0	0.0	10:21	....	....	....	....	....	....	....	....	....
2010-11	Edmonton	NHL	81	18	7	25	34	2	1	2	126	14.3	–5	29	34.5	13:50	....	....	....	....	....	....	....	....	....
2011-12	Edmonton	NHL	79	17	16	33	42	3	2	2	137	12.4	–7	15	20.0	15:26	....	....	....	....	....	....	....	....	....
2012-13	Edmonton	NHL	27	2	5	7	17	0	0	0	38	5.3	0	9	22.2	12:59	....	....	....	....	....	....	....	....	....
	NHL Totals		282	52	42	94	141	9	3	5	426	12.2		64	25.0	13:15	....	....	....	....	....	....	....	....	....

CCHA Second All-Star Team (2006, 2007) • CCHA First All-Star Team (2008) • NCAA West First All-American Team (2008)

Traded to **Nashville** by **Minnesota** with Minnesota's 2nd round choice (Charles-Olivier Roussel) in 2009 Entry Draft for Marek Zidlicky, July 1, 2008. Claimed on waivers by **Edmonton** from **Nashville**, March 3, 2010.

JORDAN, Michal

(yohr-DAHN, MIH-kahl) **CAR**

Defense. Shoots left. 6'1", 195 lbs. Born, Zlin, Czech., July 17, 1990. Carolina's 3rd choice, 105th overall, in 2008 Entry Draft.

Season	Club	League	GP	G	A	Pts	PIM	PP	SH	GW	S	%	+/-	TF	F%	Min	GP	G	A	Pts	PIM	PP	SH	GW	Min
2005-06	HC Zlin U17	CzR-U17	43	7	15	22	12	....	....	....	....	....	....	....	....	....	5	0	1	1	2	....	....	....	....
2006-07	HC Zlin U17	CzR-U17	1	0	0	0	4	....	....	....	....	....	....	....	....	....	....	....	....	....	....	....	....	....	....
	HC Zlin Jr.	CzRep-Jr.	40	7	11	18	20	....	....	....	....	....	....	....	....	....	12	1	5	6	12	....	....	....	....
2007-08	Windsor Spitfires	OHL	22	1	5	6	12	....	....	....	....	....	....	....	....	....	....	....	....	....	....	....	....	....	....
	Plymouth Whalers	OHL	39	5	17	22	32	....	....	....	....	....	....	....	....	....	4	0	3	3	6	....	....	....	....
2008-09	Plymouth Whalers	OHL	58	12	30	42	39	....	....	....	....	....	....	....	....	....	11	0	3	3	12	....	....	....	....
2009-10	Plymouth Whalers	OHL	41	13	19	32	18	....	....	....	....	....	....	....	....	....	9	0	5	5	8	....	....	....	....
2010-11	Charlotte	AHL	67	4	14	18	35	....	....	....	....	....	....	....	....	....	16	0	2	2	0	....	....	....	....
2011-12	Charlotte	AHL	76	4	18	22	43	....	....	....	....	....	....	....	....	....	....	....	....	....	....	....	....	....	....
2012-13	Charlotte	AHL	54	6	10	16	22	....	....	....	....	....	....	....	....	....	1	0	1	1	0	....	....	....	....
	Carolina	NHL	5	0	0	0	2	0	0	0	2	0.0	–2	0	0.0	10:41	....	....	....	....	....	....	....	....	....
	NHL Totals		5	0	0	0	2	0	0	0	2	0.0		0	0.0	10:41	....	....	....	....	....	....	....	....	....

JOSEFSON, Jacob

(JOH-sehf-suhn, YA-kuhb) **N.J.**

Center. Shoots left. 6'1", 190 lbs. Born, Stockholm, Sweden, March 2, 1991. New Jersey's 1st choice, 20th overall, in 2009 Entry Draft.

Season	Club	League	GP	G	A	Pts	PIM	PP	SH	GW	S	%	+/-	TF	F%	Min	GP	G	A	Pts	PIM	PP	SH	GW	Min
2005-06	Djurgarden U18	Swe-U18	5	1	1	2	0	....	....	....	....	....	....	....	....	....	....	....	....	....	....	....	....	....	....
2006-07	Djurgarden U18	Swe-U18	25	14	17	31	22	....	....	....	....	....	....	....	....	....	3	0	0	0	0	....	....	....	....
2007-08	Djurgarden U18	Swe-U18	4	1	2	3	12	....	....	....	....	....	....	....	....	....	6	0	6	6	4	....	....	....	....
	Djurgarden Jr.	Swe-Jr.	34	14	17	31	22	....	....	....	....	....	....	....	....	....	7	2	3	5	8	....	....	....	....
	Djurgarden	Sweden	1	0	0	0	0	....	....	....	....	....	....	....	....	....	....	....	....	....	....	....	....	....	....
2008-09	Djurgarden Jr.	Swe-Jr.	5	1	2	3	8	....	....	....	....	....	....	....	....	....	6	1	3	4	4	....	....	....	....
	Djurgarden	Sweden	50	5	11	16	14	....	....	....	....	....	....	....	....	....	....	....	....	....	....	....	....	....	....
	Djurgarden U18	Swe-U18	....	....	....	....	....	....	....	....	....	....	....	....	....	....	1	0	0	0	0	....	....	....	....
2009-10	Djurgarden	Sweden	43	8	12	20	20	....	....	....	....	....	....	....	....	....	14	3	2	5	4	....	....	....	....
2010-11	New Jersey	NHL	28	3	7	10	6	0	0	1	31	9.7	5	202	47.0	13:14	....	....	....	....	....	....	....	....	....
	Albany Devils	AHL	18	3	9	12	4	....	....	....	....	....	....	....	....	....	....	....	....	....	....	....	....	....	....
2011-12	New Jersey	NHL	41	2	7	9	6	0	0	0	37	5.4	10	354	51.1	12:06	6	0	1	1	0	0	0	0	13:41
	Albany Devils	AHL	4	2	1	3	2	....	....	....	....	....	....	....	....	....	....	....	....	....	....	....	....	....	....
2012-13	Albany Devils	AHL	38	10	15	25	29	....	....	....	....	....	....	....	....	....	....	....	....	....	....	....	....	....	....
	New Jersey	NHL	22	1	2	3	2	0	0	0	20	5.0	–10	236	48.3	12:59	....	....	....	....	....	....	....	....	....
	NHL Totals		91	6	16	22	14	0	0	1	88	6.8		792	49.2	12:40	6	0	1	1	0	0	0	0	13:41

JOSI, Roman

(YOH-see, ROH-man) **NSH**

Defense. Shoots left. 6'1", 198 lbs. Born, Bern, Switzerland, June 1, 1990. Nashville's 3rd choice, 38th overall, in 2008 Entry Draft.

Season	Club	League	GP	G	A	Pts	PIM	PP	SH	GW	S	%	+/-	TF	F%	Min	GP	G	A	Pts	PIM	PP	SH	GW	Min
2005-06	SC Bern Future Jr.	Swiss-Jr.	5	0	0	0	0	....	....	....	....	....	....	....	....	....	....	....	....	....	....	....	....	....	....
2006-07	SC Bern Future Jr.	Swiss-Jr.	33	14	16	30	28	....	....	....	....	....	....	....	....	....	14	1	3	4	2	....	....	....	....
	Switzerland U20	Swiss-2	5	1	1	2	2	....	....	....	....	....	....	....	....	....	....	....	....	....	....	....	....	....	....
	SC Bern	Swiss	3	0	1	1	0	....	....	....	....	....	....	....	....	....	....	....	....	....	....	....	....	....	....
2007-08	Switzerland U20	Swiss-2	2	0	1	1	0	....	....	....	....	....	....	....	....	....	....	....	....	....	....	....	....	....	....
	HC Neuchatel	Swiss-2	3	2	0	2	4	....	....	....	....	....	....	....	....	....	....	....	....	....	....	....	....	....	....
	SC Bern	Swiss	35	2	6	8	10	....	....	....	....	....	....	....	....	....	6	0	0	0	0	....	....	....	....
2008-09	SC Bern	Swiss	42	7	17	24	16	....	....	....	....	....	....	....	....	....	6	0	0	0	2	....	....	....	....
2009-10	SC Bern	Swiss	26	9	12	21	12	....	....	....	....	....	....	....	....	....	15	6	7	13	8	....	....	....	....
2010-11	Milwaukee	AHL	69	6	34	40	22	....	....	....	....	....	....	....	....	....	13	1	6	7	8	....	....	....	....

Season	Club	League	GP	G	A	Pts	PIM	PP	SH	GW	S	%	+/-	TF	F%	Min	GP	G	A	Pts	PIM	PP	SH	GW	Min
			Regular Season														Playoffs								
2011-12	Nashville	NHL	52	5	11	16	14	1	0	0	64	7.8	1	0	0.0	18:23	10	0	0	0	10	0	0	0	18:48
	Milwaukee	AHL	5	1	3	4	0	....	....	....	....	....	....	....	....	....	....	....	....	....	....	....	....	....	....
2012-13	SC Bern	Swiss	26	6	11	17	14	....	....	....	....	....	....	....	....	....	....	....	....	....	....	....	....	....	....
	Nashville	NHL	48	5	13	18	8	1	0	1	96	5.2	–7	0	0.0	23:32	....	....	....	....	....	....	....	....	....
	NHL Totals		100	10	24	34	22	2	0	1	160	6.3		0	0.0	20:51	10	0	0	0	10	0	0	0	18:48

Signed as a free agent by **Bern** (Swiss), September 20, 2012.

JOSLIN, Derek

(JAWS-lihn, DAIR-ihk)

Defense. Shoots left. 6'1", 210 lbs. Born, Richmond Hill, Ont., March 17, 1987. San Jose's 5th choice, 149th overall, in 2005 Entry Draft.

Season	Club	League	GP	G	A	Pts	PIM	PP	SH	GW	S	%	+/-	TF	F%	Min	GP	G	A	Pts	PIM	PP	SH	GW	Min
2002-03	Vaughan Kings	GTHL	60	9	18	27	72	....	....	....	....	....	....	....	....	....	....	....	....	....	....	....	....	....	....
2003-04	Aurora Tigers	ON-Jr.A	36	4	12	16	....	....	....	....	....	....	....	....	....	....	....	....	....	....	....	....	....	....	....
	Ottawa 67's	OHL	7	0	0	0	4	....	....	....	....	....	....	....	....	....	....	....	....	....	....	....	....	....	....
2004-05	Ottawa 67's	OHL	68	6	24	30	44	....	....	....	....	....	....	....	....	....	21	0	3	3	24	....	....	....	....
2005-06	Ottawa 67's	OHL	68	11	37	48	40	....	....	....	....	....	....	....	....	....	6	1	5	6	10	....	....	....	....
	Cleveland Barons	AHL	2	0	0	0	0	....	....	....	....	....	....	....	....	....	....	....	....	....	....	....	....	....	....
2006-07	Ottawa 67's	OHL	68	11	38	49	66	....	....	....	....	....	....	....	....	....	5	1	4	5	4	....	....	....	....
	Worcester Sharks	AHL	3	0	0	0	0	....	....	....	....	....	....	....	....	....	4	0	0	0	2	....	....	....	....
2007-08	Worcester Sharks	AHL	80	10	24	34	44	....	....	....	....	....	....	....	....	....	....	....	....	....	....	....	....	....	....
2008-09	San Jose	NHL	12	0	0	0	6	0	0	0	9	0.0	–3	0	0.0	11:22	....	....	....	....	....	....	....	....	....
	Worcester Sharks	AHL	63	11	19	30	40	....	....	....	....	....	....	....	....	....	12	0	2	2	8	....	....	....	....
2009-10	San Jose	NHL	24	0	3	3	12	0	0	0	19	0.0	1	0	0.0	13:53	....	....	....	....	....	....	....	....	....
	Worcester Sharks	AHL	55	5	27	32	29	....	....	....	....	....	....	....	....	....	11	4	1	5	4	....	....	....	....
2010-11	San Jose	NHL	17	1	3	4	8	0	0	0	11	9.1	–2	0	0.0	12:28	....	....	....	....	....	....	....	....	....
	Carolina	NHL	17	1	4	5	2	1	0	1	23	4.3	7	0	0.0	18:04	....	....	....	....	....	....	....	....	....
2011-12	Carolina	NHL	44	2	2	4	35	0	0	0	36	5.6	–15	1	100.0	10:35	....	....	....	....	....	....	....	....	....
	Charlotte	AHL	4	0	3	3	0	....	....	....	....	....	....	....	....	....	....	....	....	....	....	....	....	....	....
2012-13	Chicago Wolves	AHL	53	2	8	10	40	....	....	....	....	....	....	....	....	....	....	....	....	....	....	....	....	....	....
	Worcester Sharks	AHL	13	2	4	6	7	....	....	....	....	....	....	....	....	....	....	....	....	....	....	....	....	....	....
	Vancouver	NHL	2	0	0	0	0	0	0	0	2	0.0	–2	0	0.0	17:00	....	....	....	....	....	....	....	....	....
	NHL Totals		116	4	12	16	63	1	0	1	100	4.0		1	100.0	12:50	....	....	....	....	....	....	....	....	....

Traded to **Carolina** by **San Jose** for future considerations, February 18, 2011. • Missed majority of 2010-11 due to upper-body injury and as a healthy reserve. Signed as a free agent by **Vancouver**, July 5, 2012. • Re-assigned to **Worcester** (AHL) by **Vancouver** (Chicago-AHL), March 22, 2013.

JOUDREY, Andrew

(JOO-dree, AN-droo)

Center. Shoots left. 5'10", 185 lbs. Born, Halifax, N.S., July 15, 1984. Washington's 5th choice, 249th overall, in 2003 Entry Draft.

Season	Club	League	GP	G	A	Pts	PIM	PP	SH	GW	S	%	+/-	TF	F%	Min	GP	G	A	Pts	PIM	PP	SH	GW	Min
2000-01	Dartmouth	NSMHL	82	51	70	121	....	....	....	....	....	....	....	....	....	....	....	....	....	....	....	....	....	....	....
2001-02	Notre Dame	SJHL	57	24	38	62	14	....	....	....	....	....	....	....	....	....	....	....	....	....	....	....	....	....	....
2002-03	Notre Dame	SJHL	53	27	51	78	16	....	....	....	....	....	....	....	....	....	....	....	....	....	....	....	....	....	....
2003-04	U. of Wisconsin	WCHA	42	7	15	22	2	....	....	....	....	....	....	....	....	....	....	....	....	....	....	....	....	....	....
2004-05	U. of Wisconsin	WCHA	41	7	17	24	18	....	....	....	....	....	....	....	....	....	....	....	....	....	....	....	....	....	....
2005-06	U. of Wisconsin	WCHA	37	8	10	18	14	....	....	....	....	....	....	....	....	....	....	....	....	....	....	....	....	....	....
2006-07	U. of Wisconsin	WCHA	40	9	20	29	18	....	....	....	....	....	....	....	....	....	....	....	....	....	....	....	....	....	....
	Hershey Bears	AHL	5	2	1	3	0	....	....	....	....	....	....	....	....	....	10	0	2	2	0	....	....	....	....
2007-08	Hershey Bears	AHL	61	11	14	25	22	....	....	....	....	....	....	....	....	....	5	0	1	1	0	....	....	....	....
2008-09	Hershey Bears	AHL	69	7	20	27	22	....	....	....	....	....	....	....	....	....	22	1	3	4	6	....	....	....	....
2009-10	Hershey Bears	AHL	78	15	19	34	11	....	....	....	....	....	....	....	....	....	21	1	2	3	4	....	....	....	....
2010-11	Hershey Bears	AHL	66	7	7	14	20	....	....	....	....	....	....	....	....	....	6	0	1	1	0	....	....	....	....
2011-12	Columbus	NHL	1	0	0	0	0	0	0	0	1	0.0	0	1	100.0	9:16	....	....	....	....	....	....	....	....	....
	Springfield	AHL	73	14	11	25	18	....	....	....	....	....	....	....	....	....	....	....	....	....	....	....	....	....	....
2012-13	Springfield	AHL	73	9	13	22	26	....	....	....	....	....	....	....	....	....	6	1	2	3	2	....	....	....	....
	NHL Totals		1	0	0	0	0	0	0	0	1	0.0		1	100.0	9:16	....	....	....	....	....	....	....	....	....

Signed as a free agent by **Columbus**, July 1, 2011.

JOVANOVSKI, Ed

(joh-van-OHV-skee, EHD) **FLA**

Defense. Shoots left. 6'3", 220 lbs. Born, Windsor, Ont., June 26, 1976. Florida's 1st choice, 1st overall, in 1994 Entry Draft.

Season	Club	League	GP	G	A	Pts	PIM	PP	SH	GW	S	%	+/-	TF	F%	Min	GP	G	A	Pts	PIM	PP	SH	GW	Min
1991-92	Windsor	Minor-ON	50	25	40	65	88	....	....	....	....	....	....	....	....	....	....	....	....	....	....	....	....	....	....
1992-93	Windsor Bulldogs	ON-Jr.B	48	7	46	53	88	....	....	....	....	....	....	....	....	....	....	....	....	....	....	....	....	....	....
1993-94	Windsor Spitfires	OHL	62	15	36	51	221	....	....	....	....	....	....	....	....	....	4	0	0	0	15	....	....	....	....
1994-95	Windsor Spitfires	OHL	50	23	42	65	198	....	....	....	....	....	....	....	....	....	9	2	7	9	39	....	....	....	....
1995-96	Florida	NHL	70	10	11	21	137	2	0	2	116	8.6	–3	....	....	....	22	1	8	9	52	0	0	0	....
1996-97	Florida	NHL	61	7	16	23	172	3	0	1	80	8.8	–1	....	....	....	5	0	0	0	4	0	0	0	....
1997-98	Florida	NHL	81	9	14	23	158	2	1	3	142	6.3	–12	....	....	....	....	....	....	....	....	....	....	....	....
1998-99	Florida	NHL	41	3	13	16	82	1	0	1	68	4.4	–4	0	0.0	22:35	....	....	....	....	....	....	....	....	....
	Vancouver	NHL	31	2	9	11	44	0	0	0	41	4.9	–5	0	0.0	21:16	....	....	....	....	....	....	....	....	....
99-2000	Vancouver	NHL	75	5	21	26	54	1	0	1	109	4.6	–3	0	0.0	24:03	....	....	....	....	....	....	....	....	....
2000-01	Vancouver	NHL	79	12	35	47	102	4	0	2	193	6.2	–1	0	0.0	24:57	4	1	1	2	0	0	0	0	25:54
2001-02	Vancouver	NHL	82	17	31	48	101	7	1	3	202	8.4	–7	0	0.0	25:11	6	1	4	5	8	1	0	0	25:48
	Canada	Olympics	6	0	3	3	4	....	....	....	....	....	....	....	....	....	....	....	....	....	....	....	....	....	....
2002-03	Vancouver	NHL	67	6	40	46	113	2	0	1	145	4.1	19	0	0.0	24:15	14	7	1	8	22	4	1	2	23:40
2003-04	Vancouver	NHL	56	7	16	23	64	2	0	1	143	4.9	2	0	0.0	23:11	7	0	4	4	6	0	0	0	26:36
2004-05			DID NOT PLAY																						
2005-06	Vancouver	NHL	44	8	25	33	58	6	0	2	87	9.2	–8	0	0.0	24:26	....	....	....	....	....	....	....	....	....
	Canada	Olympics	DID NOT PLAY – INJURED																						
2006-07	Phoenix	NHL	54	11	18	29	63	6	0	1	135	8.1	–6	0	0.0	23:09	....	....	....	....	....	....	....	....	....
2007-08	Phoenix	NHL	80	12	39	51	73	8	0	2	240	5.0	–13	0	0.0	22:33	....	....	....	....	....	....	....	....	....
2008-09	Phoenix	NHL	82	9	27	36	106	6	0	3	194	4.6	–15	1	0.0	22:10	....	....	....	....	....	....	....	....	....
2009-10	Phoenix	NHL	66	10	24	34	55	5	0	2	117	8.5	–12	1	0.0	21:38	7	1	0	1	4	0	0	0	21:13
2010-11	Phoenix	NHL	50	5	9	14	39	1	0	1	73	6.8	4	0	0.0	20:29	4	0	1	1	2	0	0	0	15:24
2011-12	Florida	NHL	66	3	10	13	31	1	0	0	58	5.2	–11	0	0.0	16:42	7	0	0	0	4	0	0	0	17:42
2012-13	Florida	NHL	6	0	1	1	0	0	0	0	6	0.0	–4	0	0.0	15:40	....	....	....	....	....	....	....	....	....
	NHL Totals		1091	136	359	495	1452	57	2	26	2149	6.3		2	0.0	22:41	76	11	19	30	102	5	1	2	22:39

OHL All-Rookie Team (1994) • OHL Second All-Star Team (1994) • OHL First All-Star Team (1995) • NHL All-Rookie Team (1996)

Played in NHL All-Star Game (2001, 2002, 2003, 2007, 2008)

Traded to **Vancouver** by **Florida** with Dave Gagner, Mike Brown, Kevin Weekes and Florida's 1st round choice (Nathan Smith) in 2000 Entry Draft for Pavel Bure, Bret Hedican, Brad Ference and Vancouver's 3rd round choice (Robert Fried) in 2000 Entry Draft, January 17, 1999. Signed as a free agent by **Phoenix**, July 1, 2006. Signed as a free agent by **Florida**, July 1, 2011. • Missed majority of 2012-13 due to knee injury at Tampa Bay, January 29, 2013.

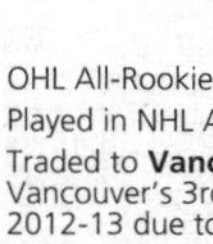

JUNLAND, Jonas

(YUHN-land, YOH-nuhs) **ST.L.**

Defense. Shoots left. 6'2", 200 lbs. Born, Linkoping, Sweden, November 15, 1987. St. Louis' 4th choice, 64th overall, in 2006 Entry Draft.

Season	Club	League	GP	G	A	Pts	PIM	PP	SH	GW	S	%	+/-	TF	F%	Min	GP	G	A	Pts	PIM	PP	SH	GW	Min
2002-03	Linkoping U18	Swe-U18	7	0	0	0	6	....	....	....	....	....	....	....	....	....	....	....	....	....	....	....	....	....	....
2003-04	Linkoping U18	Swe-U18	4	0	0	0	4	....	....	....	....	....	....	....	....	....	....	....	....	....	....	....	....	....	....
	Linkopings HC Jr.	Swe-Jr.	19	1	0	1	12	....	....	....	....	....	....	....	....	....	....	....	....	....	....	....	....	....	....
2004-05	Linkoping U18	Swe-U18	11	6	5	11	35	....	....	....	....	....	....	....	....	....	....	....	....	....	....	....	....	....	....
	Linkopings HC Jr.	Swe-Jr.	32	3	5	8	96	....	....	....	....	....	....	....	....	....	....	....	....	....	....	....	....	....	....
2005-06	Linkopings HC Jr.	Swe-Jr.	32	17	23	40	44	....	....	....	....	....	....	....	....	....	....	....	....	....	....	....	....	....	....
	Linkoping U18	Swe-U18	1	5	0	5	2	....	....	....	....	....	....	....	....	....	....	....	....	....	....	....	....	....	....
	Linkopings HC	Sweden	4	0	0	0	0	....	....	....	....	....	....	....	....	....	....	....	....	....	....	....	....	....	....
2006-07	Linkopings HC Jr.	Swe-Jr.	9	6	7	13	26	....	....	....	....	....	....	....	....	....	....	....	....	....	....	....	....	....	....
	IK Oskarshamn	Sweden-2	4	0	3	3	4	....	....	....	....	....	....	....	....	....	....	....	....	....	....	....	....	....	....
	Linkopings HC	Sweden	41	1	4	5	22	....	....	....	....	....	....	....	....	....	15	0	5	5	20	....	....	....	....
2007-08	Linkopings HC	Sweden	52	3	17	20	42	....	....	....	....	....	....	....	....	....	16	4	3	7	18	....	....	....	....
2008-09	St. Louis	NHL	1	0	0	0	2	0	0	0	0	0.0	0	0	0.0	12:28	....	....	....	....	....	....	....	....	....
	Peoria Rivermen	AHL	70	13	18	31	52	....	....	....	....	....	....	....	....	....	5	0	1	1	6	....	....	....	....
2009-10	St. Louis	NHL	3	0	2	2	0	0	0	0	7	0.0	–3	0	0.0	17:11	....	....	....	....	....	....	....	....	....
	Peoria Rivermen	AHL	74	14	30	44	49	....	....	....	....	....	....	....	....	....	....	....	....	....	....	....	....	....	....
2010-11	Farjestad	Sweden	41	5	17	22	18	....	....	....	....	....	....	....	....	....	14	3	3	6	12	....	....	....	....
2011-12	Barys Astana	KHL	46	4	11	15	30	....	....	....	....	....	....	....	....	....	7	1	1	2	6	....	....	....	....

Season	Club	League	GP	G	A	Pts	PIM	PP	SH	GW	S	%	+/-	TF	F%	Min	Playoffs GP	G	A	Pts	PIM	PP	SH	GW	Min
			Regular Season														Playoffs								
2012-13	Barys Astana	KHL	3	0	0	0	10																		
	Pelicans Lahti	Finland	6	1	1	2	6																		
	NHL Totals		**4**	**0**	**2**	**2**	**2**	**0**	**0**	**0**	**7**	**0.0**		**0**	**0.0**	**16:00**									

Signed as a free agent by **Farjestad** (Sweden), May 1, 2010. Signed as a free agent by **Astana** (KHL), April 27, 2011. Signed as a free agent by **Lahti** (Finland), October 4, 2012.

JURCINA, Milan

(YEWR-chee-nah, MEE-lan)

Defense. Shoots right. 6'4", 253 lbs. Born, Liptovsky Mikulas, Czech., June 7, 1983. Boston's 7th choice, 241st overall, in 2001 Entry Draft.

Season	Club	League	GP	G	A	Pts	PIM	PP	SH	GW	S	%	+/-	TF	F%	Min	Playoffs GP	G	A	Pts	PIM	PP	SH	GW	Min
99-2000	L. Mikulas Jr.	Slovak-Jr.	STATISTICS NOT AVAILABLE																						
2000-01	Halifax	QMJHL	68	0	5	5	56										6	0	2	2	12				
2001-02	Halifax	QMJHL	61	4	16	20	58										13	5	3	8	10				
2002-03	Halifax	QMJHL	51	15	13	28	102										25	6	6	12	40				
2003-04	Providence Bruins	AHL	73	5	12	17	52										2	0	1	1	2				
2004-05	Providence Bruins	AHL	79	6	17	23	92										17	1	3	4	30				
2005-06	**Boston**	**NHL**	**51**	**6**	**5**	**11**	**54**	**2**	**0**	**0**	**64**	**9.4**	**3**	**1**	**0.0**	**16:28**									
	Providence Bruins	AHL	7	0	3	3	8																		
	Slovakia	Olympics	6	0	1	1	8																		
2006-07	**Boston**	**NHL**	**40**	**2**	**1**	**3**	**20**	**0**	**0**	**1**	**29**	**6.9**	**–5**	**0**	**0.0**	**10:42**									
	Washington	**NHL**	**30**	**2**	**7**	**9**	**24**	**0**	**0**	**0**	**42**	**4.8**	**5**	**0**	**0.0**	**23:09**									
2007-08	**Washington**	**NHL**	**75**	**1**	**8**	**9**	**30**	**1**	**0**	**0**	**58**	**1.7**	**4**	**0**	**0.0**	**16:38**	**7**	**0**	**0**	**0**	**6**	**0**	**0**	**0**	**16:26**
2008-09	**Washington**	**NHL**	**79**	**3**	**11**	**14**	**68**	**0**	**0**	**1**	**95**	**3.2**	**1**	**0**	**0.0**	**16:09**	**14**	**2**	**0**	**2**	**12**	**0**	**1**	**0**	**16:46**
2009-10	**Washington**	**NHL**	**27**	**0**	**4**	**4**	**14**	**0**	**0**	**0**	**32**	**0.0**	**0**	**0**	**0.0**	**17:26**									
	Columbus	**NHL**	**17**	**1**	**2**	**3**	**10**	**0**	**0**	**1**	**17**	**5.9**	**2**	**0**	**0.0**	**18:02**									
	Slovakia	Olympics	7	0	0	0	2																		
2010-11	**NY Islanders**	**NHL**	**46**	**4**	**13**	**17**	**30**	**1**	**1**	**0**	**76**	**5.3**	**–4**	**1**	**0.0**	**18:04**									
2011-12	**NY Islanders**	**NHL**	**65**	**3**	**8**	**11**	**30**	**2**	**0**	**0**	**127**	**2.4**	**–34**	**0**	**0.0**	**18:47**									
2012-13	Pirati Chomutov	CzRep	22	0	3	3	20																		
	Lukko Rauma	Finland	14	5	2	7	26										13	1	6	7	20				
	NHL Totals		**430**	**22**	**59**	**81**	**280**	**6**	**1**	**3**	**540**	**4.1**		**2**	**0.0**	**17:01**	**21**	**2**	**0**	**2**	**18**	**0**	**1**	**0**	**16:40**

Traded to **Washington** by **Boston** for Washington's 4th round choice (later traded to Calgary - Calgary selected TJ Brodie) in 2008 Entry Draft, February 1, 2007. Traded to **Columbus** by **Washington** with Chris Clark for Jason Chimera, December 28, 2009. Traded to **Washington** by **Columbus** for future considerations, March 3, 2010. Signed as a free agent by **NY Islanders**, July 2, 2010. Signed as a free agent by **Chomutov** (CzRep), October 5, 2012. Signed as a free agent by **Rauma** (Finland), January 31, 2013.

KABERLE, Tomas

(KA-buhr-lay, TAW-mas)

Defense. Shoots left. 6'1", 214 lbs. Born, Rakovnik, Czech., March 2, 1978. Toronto's 13th choice, 204th overall, in 1996 Entry Draft.

Season	Club	League	GP	G	A	Pts	PIM	PP	SH	GW	S	%	+/-	TF	F%	Min	Playoffs GP	G	A	Pts	PIM	PP	SH	GW	Min
1994-95	HC Kladno Jr.	CzRep-Jr.	37	7	10	17																			
	HC Kladno	CzRep	4	0	1	1	0																		
1995-96	Kladno Jr.	CzRep-Jr.	23	6	13	19																			
	HC Poldi Kladno	CzRep	23	0	1	1	2										2	0	0	0	0				
1996-97	HC Poldi Kladno	CzRep	49	0	5	5	26										3	0	0	0	0				
1997-98	Kladno	CzRep	47	4	19	23	12																		
	St. John's	AHL	2	0	0	0	0																		
1998-99	**Toronto**	**NHL**	**57**	**4**	**18**	**22**	**12**	**0**	**0**	**2**	**71**	**5.6**	**3**	**0**	**0.0**	**18:42**	**14**	**0**	**3**	**3**	**2**	**0**	**0**	**0**	**17:10**
99-2000	**Toronto**	**NHL**	**82**	**7**	**33**	**40**	**24**	**2**	**0**	**0**	**82**	**8.5**	**3**	**0**	**0.0**	**22:55**	**12**	**1**	**4**	**5**	**0**	**0**	**0**	**1**	**23:01**
2000-01	**Toronto**	**NHL**	**82**	**6**	**39**	**45**	**24**	**0**	**0**	**1**	**96**	**6.3**	**10**	**2**	**0.0**	**22:41**	**11**	**1**	**3**	**4**	**0**	**0**	**0**	**1**	**21:33**
2001-02	Kladno	CzRep	9	1	7	8	4																		
	Toronto	**NHL**	**69**	**10**	**29**	**39**	**2**	**5**	**0**	**3**	**85**	**11.8**	**5**	**2**	**100.0**	**25:00**	**20**	**2**	**8**	**10**	**16**	**0**	**0**	**0**	**28:40**
	Czech Republic	Olympics	4	0	1	1	2																		
2002-03	**Toronto**	**NHL**	**82**	**11**	**36**	**47**	**30**	**4**	**1**	**2**	**119**	**9.2**	**20**	**3**	**66.7**	**24:50**	**7**	**2**	**1**	**3**	**0**	**1**	**0**	**1**	**30:04**
2003-04	**Toronto**	**NHL**	**71**	**3**	**28**	**31**	**18**	**0**	**0**	**1**	**88**	**3.4**	**16**	**2**	**0.0**	**23:12**	**13**	**0**	**3**	**3**	**6**	**0**	**0**	**0**	**20:16**
2004-05	HC Rabat Kladno	CzRep	49	8	31	39	38										7	1	0	1	0				
2005-06	**Toronto**	**NHL**	**82**	**9**	**58**	**67**	**46**	**6**	**0**	**2**	**163**	**5.5**	**–1**	**0**	**0.0**	**28:10**									
	Czech Republic	Olympics	8	2	2	4	2																		
2006-07	**Toronto**	**NHL**	**74**	**11**	**47**	**58**	**20**	**2**	**0**	**1**	**128**	**8.6**	**3**	**0**	**0.0**	**25:52**									
2007-08	**Toronto**	**NHL**	**82**	**8**	**45**	**53**	**22**	**6**	**0**	**1**	**155**	**5.2**	**–8**	**2**	**50.0**	**24:52**									
2008-09	**Toronto**	**NHL**	**57**	**4**	**27**	**31**	**8**	**3**	**0**	**1**	**93**	**4.3**	**–8**	**0**	**0.0**	**23:28**									
2009-10	**Toronto**	**NHL**	**82**	**7**	**42**	**49**	**24**	**3**	**0**	**1**	**158**	**4.4**	**–16**	**0**	**0.0**	**22:21**									
	Czech Republic	Olympics	5	1	2	3	0																		
2010-11	**Toronto**	**NHL**	**58**	**3**	**35**	**38**	**16**	**0**	**0**	**1**	**99**	**3.0**	**–2**	**0**	**0.0**	**22:28**									
	♦ **Boston**	**NHL**	**24**	**1**	**8**	**9**	**2**	**0**	**0**	**0**	**31**	**3.2**	**6**	**0**	**0.0**	**21:15**	**25**	**0**	**11**	**11**	**4**	**0**	**0**	**0**	**16:01**
2011-12	**Carolina**	**NHL**	**29**	**0**	**9**	**9**	**2**	**0**	**0**	**0**	**38**	**0.0**	**–12**	**0**	**0.0**	**19:15**									
	Montreal	**NHL**	**43**	**3**	**19**	**22**	**10**	**1**	**0**	**0**	**49**	**6.1**	**–6**	**0**	**0.0**	**16:41**									
2012-13	Rytiri Kladno	CzRep	10	2	4	6	2																		
	Montreal	**NHL**	**10**	**0**	**3**	**3**	**0**	**0**	**0**	**0**	**11**	**0.0**	**4**	**0**	**0.0**	**13:33**									
	NHL Totals		**984**	**87**	**476**	**563**	**260**	**32**	**1**	**16**	**1466**	**5.9**		**11**	**45.5**	**23:15**	**102**	**6**	**33**	**39**	**28**	**1**	**0**	**3**	**21:35**

Played in NHL All-Star Game (2002, 2007, 2008, 2009)

Signed as a restricted free agent by **Kladno** (CzRep) with **Toronto** retaining NHL rights, September 29, 2001. Signed as a free agent by **Kladno** (CzRep), September 17, 2004. Traded to **Boston** by **Toronto** for Joe Colborne, Boston's 1st round choice (later traded to Anaheim – Anaheim selected Rickard Rakell) in 2011 Entry Draft and Boston's 2nd round choice (later traded to Colorado – later traded to Washington – later traded to Dallas – Dallas selected Mike Winther) in 2012 Entry Draft, February 18, 2011. Signed as a free agent by **Carolina**, July 5, 2011. Traded to **Montreal** by **Carolina** for Jaroslav Spacek, December 9, 2011. Signed as a free agent by **Kladno** (CzRep), September 21, 2012. • Missed majority of 2012-13 as a healthy reserve.

KADRI, Nazem

(KAH-dree, NA-zihm) **TOR**

Center. Shoots left. 6', 188 lbs. Born, London, Ont., October 6, 1990. Toronto's 1st choice, 7th overall, in 2009 Entry Draft.

Season	Club	League	GP	G	A	Pts	PIM	PP	SH	GW	S	%	+/-	TF	F%	Min	Playoffs GP	G	A	Pts	PIM	PP	SH	GW	Min
2005-06	Lon. Jr. Knights	Minor-ON	62	49	43	92	82																		
2006-07	Kitchener Rangers	OHL	62	7	15	22	30										9	0	2	2	4				
2007-08	Kitchener Rangers	OHL	68	25	40	65	57										20	9	17	26	26				
2008-09	London Knights	OHL	56	25	53	78	31										14	9	12	21	22				
2009-10	London Knights	OHL	56	35	58	93	105										12	9	18	27	26				
	Toronto	**NHL**	**1**	**0**	**0**	**0**	**0**	**0**	**0**	**0**	**0**	**0.0**	**–1**	**13**	**15.4**	**17:26**									
2010-11	**Toronto**	**NHL**	**29**	**3**	**9**	**12**	**8**	**0**	**0**	**0**	**51**	**5.9**	**–3**	**121**	**40.5**	**15:47**									
	Toronto Marlies	AHL	44	17	24	41	62																		
2011-12	**Toronto**	**NHL**	**21**	**5**	**2**	**7**	**8**	**1**	**0**	**1**	**28**	**17.9**	**2**	**15**	**26.7**	**14:10**									
	Toronto Marlies	AHL	48	18	22	40	39										11	3	7	10	6				
2012-13	Toronto Marlies	AHL	27	8	18	26	26																		
	Toronto	**NHL**	**48**	**18**	**26**	**44**	**23**	**5**	**0**	**1**	**107**	**16.8**	**15**	**565**	**44.3**	**16:03**	**7**	**1**	**3**	**4**	**10**	**0**	**0**	**0**	**13:35**
	NHL Totals		**99**	**26**	**37**	**63**	**39**	**6**	**0**	**2**	**186**	**14.0**		**714**	**42.7**	**15:35**	**7**	**1**	**3**	**4**	**10**	**0**	**0**	**0**	**13:35**

OHL Second All-Star Team (2010)

KALETA, Patrick

(ka-LEH-tuh, PAT-rihk) **BUF**

Right wing. Shoots right. 6'1", 206 lbs. Born, Buffalo, NY, June 8, 1986. Buffalo's 5th choice, 176th overall, in 2004 Entry Draft.

Season	Club	League	GP	G	A	Pts	PIM	PP	SH	GW	S	%	+/-	TF	F%	Min	Playoffs GP	G	A	Pts	PIM	PP	SH	GW	Min
2002-03	Peterborough	OHL	67	7	9	16	67										7	0	0	0	6				
2003-04	Peterborough	OHL	67	14	14	28	124																		
2004-05	Peterborough	OHL	62	24	28	52	146										14	3	3	6	30				
2005-06	Peterborough	OHL	68	16	35	51	121										19	8	10	18	43				
2006-07	**Buffalo**	**NHL**	**7**	**0**	**2**	**2**	**21**	**0**	**0**	**0**	**6**	**0.0**	**3**	**0**	**0.0**	**6:49**									
	Rochester	AHL	58	5	10	15	133										5	0	0	0	12				
2007-08	**Buffalo**	**NHL**	**40**	**3**	**2**	**5**	**41**	**0**	**0**	**0**	**26**	**11.5**	**1**	**6**	**16.7**	**6:19**									
	Rochester	AHL	29	1	3	4	109																		
2008-09	**Buffalo**	**NHL**	**51**	**4**	**5**	**9**	**89**	**0**	**0**	**0**	**35**	**11.4**	**1**	**5**	**20.0**	**8:55**									
2009-10	**Buffalo**	**NHL**	**55**	**10**	**5**	**15**	**89**	**0**	**2**	**4**	**64**	**15.6**	**2**	**2**	**0.0**	**10:09**	**6**	**1**	**1**	**2**	**22**	**0**	**0**	**0**	**10:04**
2010-11	**Buffalo**	**NHL**	**51**	**4**	**5**	**9**	**78**	**0**	**1**	**0**	**65**	**6.2**	**–4**	**12**	**41.7**	**10:11**	**6**	**1**	**2**	**3**	**6**	**0**	**0**	**1**	**10:58**
2011-12	**Buffalo**	**NHL**	**63**	**5**	**5**	**10**	**116**	**0**	**0**	**1**	**69**	**7.2**	**–5**	**19**	**52.6**	**13:09**									
2012-13	**Buffalo**	**NHL**	**34**	**1**	**0**	**1**	**67**	**0**	**0**	**0**	**34**	**2.9**	**–4**	**11**	**45.5**	**10:48**									
	NHL Totals		**301**	**27**	**24**	**51**	**501**	**0**	**3**	**5**	**299**	**9.0**		**55**	**40.0**	**10:04**	**12**	**2**	**3**	**5**	**28**	**0**	**0**	**1**	**10:31**

KAMPFER, Steven

(KAMP-fuhr, STEE-vehn) **MIN**

Defense. Shoots right. 5'11", 197 lbs. Born, Ann Arbor, MI, September 24, 1988. Anaheim's 5th choice, 93rd overall, in 2007 Entry Draft.

			Regular Season														Playoffs								
Season	Club	League	GP	G	A	Pts	PIM	PP	SH	GW	S	%	+/-	TF	F%	Min	GP	G	A	Pts	PIM	PP	SH	GW	Min
2004-05	Sioux City	USHL	47	6	13	19	91	....	....	....	....	....	....	....	....	....	13	2	5	7	12	....	....	....	....
2005-06	Sioux City	USHL	56	6	10	16	99	....	....	....	....	....	....	....	....	....	....	....	....	....	....	....	....	....	....
2006-07	U. of Michigan	CCHA	35	1	3	4	24	....	....	....	....	....	....	....	....	....	....	....	....	....	....	....	....	....	....
2007-08	U. of Michigan	CCHA	42	2	15	17	36	....	....	....	....	....	....	....	....	....	....	....	....	....	....	....	....	....	....
2008-09	U. of Michigan	CCHA	25	1	12	13	24	....	....	....	....	....	....	....	....	....	....	....	....	....	....	....	....	....	....
2009-10	U. of Michigan	CCHA	45	3	23	26	50	....	....	....	....	....	....	....	....	....	....	....	....	....	....	....	....	....	....
	Providence Bruins	AHL	6	1	2	3	4	....	....	....	....	....	....	....	....	....	....	....	....	....	....	....	....	....	....
2010-11	**Boston**	**NHL**	**38**	**5**	**5**	**10**	**12**	**0**	**0**	**1**	**57**	**8.8**	**9**	**0**	**0.0**	**17:44**	....	....	....	....	....	....	....	....	....
	Providence Bruins	AHL	22	3	13	16	12	....	....	....	....	....	....	....	....	....	....	....	....	....	....	....	....	....	....
2011-12	**Boston**	**NHL**	**10**	**0**	**2**	**2**	**4**	**0**	**0**	**0**	**8**	**0.0**	**6**	**0**	**0.0**	**10:30**	....	....	....	....	....	....	....	....	....
	Providence Bruins	AHL	12	1	3	4	8	....	....	....	....	....	....	....	....	....	....	....	....	....	....	....	....	....	....
	Minnesota	**NHL**	**13**	**2**	**1**	**3**	**2**	**0**	**0**	**0**	**12**	**16.7**	**-7**	**0**	**0.0**	**18:17**	....	....	....	....	....	....	....	....	....
	Houston Aeros	AHL	12	1	3	4	8	....	....	....	....	....	....	....	....	....	4	0	0	0	2	....	....	....	....
2012-13	Houston Aeros	AHL	55	4	17	21	28	....	....	....	....	....	....	....	....	....	5	1	1	2	9	....	....	....	....
	NHL Totals		**61**	**7**	**8**	**15**	**18**	**0**	**0**	**1**	**77**	**9.1**		**0**	**0.0**	**16:40**	....	....	....	....	....	....	....	....	....

Traded to **Boston** by **Anaheim** for Boston's 4th round choice (later traded to Carolina - Carolina selected Justin Shugg) in 2010 Entry Draft, March 2, 2010. Traded to **Minnesota** by **Boston** for Greg Zanon, February 27, 2012.

KANE, Evander

(KAYN, ee-VAN-duhr) **WPG**

Left wing. Shoots left. 6'2", 195 lbs. Born, Vancouver, B.C., August 2, 1991. Atlanta's 1st choice, 4th overall, in 2009 Entry Draft.

Season	Club	League	GP	G	A	Pts	PIM	PP	SH	GW	S	%	+/-	TF	F%	Min	GP	G	A	Pts	PIM	PP	SH	GW	Min
2006-07	Greater Van.	BCMML	30	22	32	54	150	....	....	....	....	....	....	....	....	....	....	....	....	....	....	....	....	....	....
	Vancouver Giants	WHL	8	1	0	1	11	....	....	....	....	....	....	....	....	....	5	0	0	0	0	....	....	....	....
2007-08	Vancouver Giants	WHL	65	24	17	41	66	....	....	....	....	....	....	....	....	....	10	1	2	3	8	....	....	....	....
2008-09	Vancouver Giants	WHL	61	48	48	96	89	....	....	....	....	....	....	....	....	....	17	7	8	15	45	....	....	....	....
2009-10	**Atlanta**	**NHL**	**66**	**14**	**12**	**26**	**62**	**0**	**1**	**3**	**127**	**11.0**	**2**	**26**	**53.9**	**14:00**	....	....	....	....	....	....	....	....	....
2010-11	**Atlanta**	**NHL**	**73**	**19**	**24**	**43**	**68**	**4**	**0**	**2**	**234**	**8.1**	**-12**	**64**	**40.6**	**17:52**	....	....	....	....	....	....	....	....	....
2011-12	**Winnipeg**	**NHL**	**74**	**30**	**27**	**57**	**53**	**6**	**0**	**4**	**287**	**10.5**	**11**	**44**	**34.1**	**17:31**	....	....	....	....	....	....	....	....	....
2012-13	Dynamo Minsk	KHL	12	1	1	2	47	....	....	....	....	....	....	....	....	....	....	....	....	....	....	....	....	....	....
	Winnipeg	**NHL**	**48**	**17**	**16**	**33**	**80**	**2**	**0**	**4**	**190**	**8.9**	**-3**	**33**	**39.4**	**20:27**	....	....	....	....	....	....	....	....	....
	NHL Totals		**261**	**80**	**79**	**159**	**263**	**12**	**1**	**13**	**838**	**9.5**		**167**	**40.7**	**17:16**	....	....	....	....	....	....	....	....	....

WHL West First All-Star Team (2009)

• Transferred to **Winnipeg** after **Atlanta** franchise relocated, June 21, 2011. Signed as a free agent by **Minsk** (KHL), September 28, 2012.

KANE, Patrick

(KAYN, PAT-rihk) **CHI**

Right wing. Shoots left. 5'11", 181 lbs. Born, Buffalo, NY, November 19, 1988. Chicago's 1st choice, 1st overall, in 2007 Entry Draft.

Season	Club	League	GP	G	A	Pts	PIM	PP	SH	GW	S	%	+/-	TF	F%	Min	GP	G	A	Pts	PIM	PP	SH	GW	Min
2003-04	Det. Honeybaked	MWEHL	70	83	77	160	....	....	....	....	....	....	....	....	....	....	....	....	....	....	....	....	....	....	....
2004-05	USNTDP	U-17	23	16	17	33	8	....	....	....	....	....	....	....	....	....	....	....	....	....	....	....	....	....	....
	USNTDP	NAHL	40	16	21	37	8	....	....	....	....	....	....	....	....	....	9	7	8	15	2	....	....	....	....
2005-06	USNTDP	U-18	43	35	33	68	10	....	....	....	....	....	....	....	....	....	....	....	....	....	....	....	....	....	....
	USNTDP	NAHL	15	17	17	34	12	....	....	....	....	....	....	....	....	....	....	....	....	....	....	....	....	....	....
2006-07	London Knights	OHL	58	62	83	*145	52	....	....	....	....	....	....	....	....	....	16	10	21	*31	16	....	....	....	....
2007-08	**Chicago**	**NHL**	**82**	**21**	**51**	**72**	**52**	**7**	**0**	**4**	**191**	**11.0**	**-5**	**26**	**61.5**	**18:22**	....	....	....	....	....	....	....	....	....
2008-09	**Chicago**	**NHL**	**80**	**25**	**45**	**70**	**42**	**13**	**0**	**4**	**254**	**9.8**	**-2**	**31**	**41.9**	**18:40**	**16**	**9**	**5**	**14**	**12**	**2**	**0**	**0**	**16:36**
2009-10♦	**Chicago**	**NHL**	**82**	**30**	**58**	**88**	**20**	**9**	**0**	**6**	**261**	**11.5**	**16**	**22**	**40.9**	**19:12**	**22**	**10**	**18**	**28**	**6**	**1**	**1**	**1**	**18:55**
	United States	Olympics	6	3	2	5	2	....	....	....	....	....	....	....	....	....	....	....	....	....	....	....	....	....	....
2010-11	**Chicago**	**NHL**	**73**	**27**	**46**	**73**	**28**	**5**	**0**	**2**	**216**	**12.5**	**7**	**14**	**14.3**	**19:17**	**7**	**1**	**5**	**6**	**2**	**1**	**0**	**0**	**21:50**
2011-12	**Chicago**	**NHL**	**82**	**23**	**43**	**66**	**40**	**4**	**0**	**5**	**253**	**9.1**	**7**	**569**	**42.2**	**20:12**	**6**	**0**	**4**	**4**	**10**	**0**	**0**	**0**	**21:58**
2012-13	EHC Biel-Bienne	Swiss	20	13	10	23	6	....	....	....	....	....	....	....	....	....	....	....	....	....	....	....	....	....	....
	♦ Chicago	**NHL**	**47**	**23**	**32**	**55**	**8**	**8**	**0**	**3**	**138**	**16.7**	**11**	**10**	**20.0**	**20:03**	**23**	**9**	**10**	**19**	**8**	**0**	**0**	**2**	**20:56**
	NHL Totals		**446**	**149**	**275**	**424**	**190**	**46**	**0**	**24**	**1313**	**11.3**		**672**	**42.0**	**19:14**	**74**	**29**	**42**	**71**	**38**	**4**	**1**	**3**	**19:34**

OHL All-Rookie Team (2007) • OHL First All-Star Team (2007) • OHL Rookie of the Year (2007) • Canadian Major Junior First All-Star Team (2007) • Canadian Major Junior Rookie of the Year (2007) • NHL All-Rookie Team (2008) • Calder Memorial Trophy (2008) • NHL First All-Star Team (2010) • Conn Smythe Trophy (2013)

Played in NHL All-Star Game (2009, 2011, 2012)

Signed as a free agent by **Biel-Bienne** (Swiss), October 23, 2012.

KARLSSON, Erik

(KAHRL-suhn, AIR-ihk) **OTT**

Defense. Shoots right. 6', 180 lbs. Born, Landsbro, Sweden, May 31, 1990. Ottawa's 1st choice, 15th overall, in 2008 Entry Draft.

Season	Club	League	GP	G	A	Pts	PIM	PP	SH	GW	S	%	+/-	TF	F%	Min	GP	G	A	Pts	PIM	PP	SH	GW	Min
2006-07	Sodertalje SK U18	Swe-U18	2	0	1	1	33	....	....	....	....	....	....	....	....	....	....	....	....	....	....	....	....	....	....
	Sodertalje SK Jr.	Swe-Jr.	10	2	8	10	8	....	....	....	....	....	....	....	....	....	....	....	....	....	....	....	....	....	....
2007-08	Frolunda U18	Swe-U18	3	1	2	3	2	....	....	....	....	....	....	....	....	....	2	0	1	1	10	....	....	....	....
	Frolunda Jr.	Swe-Jr.	38	13	24	37	68	....	....	....	....	....	....	....	....	....	5	1	0	1	4	....	....	....	....
	Frolunda	Sweden	7	1	0	1	0	....	....	....	....	....	....	....	....	....	6	0	0	0	0	....	....	....	....
2008-09	Frolunda Jr.	Swe-Jr.	1	0	2	2	2	....	....	....	....	....	....	....	....	....	....	....	....	....	....	....	....	....	....
	Boras HC	Sweden-2	7	0	1	1	14	....	....	....	....	....	....	....	....	....	....	....	....	....	....	....	....	....	....
	Frolunda	Sweden	45	5	5	10	10	....	....	....	....	....	....	....	....	....	11	1	2	3	24	....	....	....	....
2009-10	**Ottawa**	**NHL**	**60**	**5**	**21**	**26**	**24**	**1**	**0**	**0**	**112**	**4.5**	**-5**	**0**	**0.0**	**20:07**	**6**	**1**	**5**	**6**	**4**	**1**	**0**	**0**	**25:52**
	Binghamton	AHL	12	0	11	11	22	....	....	....	....	....	....	....	....	....	....	....	....	....	....	....	....	....	....
2010-11	**Ottawa**	**NHL**	**75**	**13**	**32**	**45**	**50**	**4**	**0**	**4**	**182**	**7.1**	**-30**	**0**	**0.0**	**23:31**	....	....	....	....	....	....	....	....	....
2011-12	**Ottawa**	**NHL**	**81**	**19**	**59**	**78**	**42**	**3**	**0**	**5**	**261**	**7.3**	**16**	**1**	**0.0**	**25:19**	**7**	**1**	**0**	**1**	**4**	**1**	**0**	**0**	**25:22**
2012-13	Jokerit Helsinki	Finland	30	9	25	34	24	....	....	....	....	....	....	....	....	....	....	....	....	....	....	....	....	....	....
	Ottawa	**NHL**	**17**	**6**	**8**	**14**	**8**	**2**	**1**	**2**	**79**	**7.6**	**8**	**0**	**0.0**	**27:09**	**10**	**1**	**7**	**8**	**6**	**0**	**0**	**0**	**26:44**
	NHL Totals		**233**	**43**	**120**	**163**	**124**	**10**	**1**	**11**	**634**	**6.8**		**1**	**0.0**	**23:32**	**23**	**3**	**12**	**15**	**14**	**2**	**0**	**0**	**26:05**

NHL First All-Star Team (2012) • James Norris Memorial Trophy (2012)

Played in NHL All-Star Game (2011, 2012)

Signed as a free agent by **Jokerit Helsinki** (Finland), September 26, 2012. • Missed majority of 2012-13 due to knee injury at Pittsburgh, February 13, 2013.

KASSIAN, Matt

(KAS-ee-uhn, MAT) **OTT**

Left wing. Shoots left. 6'5", 247 lbs. Born, Edmonton, Alta., October 28, 1986. Minnesota's 2nd choice, 57th overall, in 2005 Entry Draft.

Season	Club	League	GP	G	A	Pts	PIM	PP	SH	GW	S	%	+/-	TF	F%	Min	GP	G	A	Pts	PIM	PP	SH	GW	Min
2002-03	Sherwood Park	AJHL	33	5	7	12	38	....	....	....	....	....	....	....	....	....	....	....	....	....	....	....	....	....	....
2003-04	Vancouver Giants	WHL	37	1	0	1	42	....	....	....	....	....	....	....	....	....	3	0	0	0	4	....	....	....	....
2004-05	Vancouver Giants	WHL	41	0	3	3	89	....	....	....	....	....	....	....	....	....	....	....	....	....	....	....	....	....	....
	Kamloops Blazers	WHL	28	3	0	3	83	....	....	....	....	....	....	....	....	....	6	1	2	3	14	....	....	....	....
2005-06	Kamloops Blazers	WHL	67	5	6	11	147	....	....	....	....	....	....	....	....	....	....	....	....	....	....	....	....	....	....
2006-07	Kamloops Blazers	WHL	72	8	10	18	162	....	....	....	....	....	....	....	....	....	4	0	1	1	0	....	....	....	....
2007-08	Houston Aeros	AHL	19	0	0	0	48	....	....	....	....	....	....	....	....	....	....	....	....	....	....	....	....	....	....
	Texas Wildcatters	ECHL	47	6	4	10	90	....	....	....	....	....	....	....	....	....	....	....	....	....	....	....	....	....	....
2008-09	Houston Aeros	AHL	56	1	2	3	130	....	....	....	....	....	....	....	....	....	4	0	0	0	10	....	....	....	....
2009-10	Houston Aeros	AHL	59	2	4	6	149	....	....	....	....	....	....	....	....	....	....	....	....	....	....	....	....	....	....
2010-11	**Minnesota**	**NHL**	**4**	**0**	**0**	**0**	**12**	**0**	**0**	**0**	**1**	**0.0**	**-1**	**0**	**0.0**	**5:29**	....	....	....	....	....	....	....	....	....
	Houston Aeros	AHL	60	4	4	8	132	....	....	....	....	....	....	....	....	....	8	0	0	0	2	....	....	....	....
2011-12	**Minnesota**	**NHL**	**24**	**2**	**0**	**2**	**55**	**0**	**0**	**0**	**13**	**15.4**	**-2**	**0**	**0.0**	**5:33**	....	....	....	....	....	....	....	....	....
	Houston Aeros	AHL	26	2	2	4	34	....	....	....	....	....	....	....	....	....	....	....	....	....	....	....	....	....	....
2012-13	Houston Aeros	AHL	9	1	0	1	12	....	....	....	....	....	....	....	....	....	....	....	....	....	....	....	....	....	....
	Ottawa	**NHL**	**15**	**1**	**0**	**1**	**47**	**0**	**0**	**0**	**6**	**16.7**	**0**	**0**	**0.0**	**6:23**	**5**	**0**	**2**	**2**	**17**	**0**	**0**	**0**	**8:51**
	NHL Totals		**43**	**3**	**0**	**3**	**114**	**0**	**0**	**0**	**20**	**15.0**		**0**	**0.0**	**5:50**	**5**	**0**	**2**	**2**	**17**	**0**	**0**	**0**	**8:51**

Traded to **Ottawa** by **Minnesota** for Ottawa's 6th round choice in 2014 Entry Draft, March 12, 2013. • Missed majority of 2012-13 as a healthy reserve.

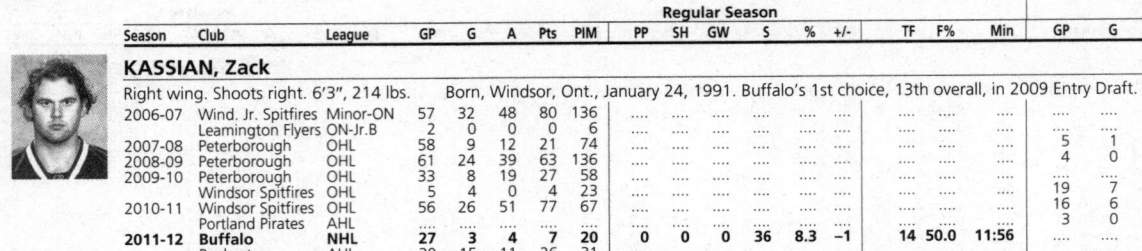

KASSIAN, Zack
(KA-see-uhn, ZAK) **VAN**

Right wing. Shoots right. 6'3", 214 lbs. Born, Windsor, Ont., January 24, 1991. Buffalo's 1st choice, 13th overall, in 2009 Entry Draft.

			Regular Season														Playoffs								
Season	Club	League	GP	G	A	Pts	PIM	PP	SH	GW	S	%	+/-	TF	F%	Min	GP	G	A	Pts	PIM	PP	SH	GW	Min
2006-07	Wind. Jr. Spitfires	Minor-ON	57	32	48	80	136	....	....	....	....	....	....	....	....	....	....	....	....	....	....	....	....	....	....
	Leamington Flyers	ON-Jr.B	2	0	0	0	6	....	....	....	....	....	....	....	....	....	....	....	....	....	....	....	....	....	....
2007-08	Peterborough	OHL	58	9	12	21	74	....	....	....	....	....	....	....	....	....	5	1	0	1	2	....	....	....	....
2008-09	Peterborough	OHL	61	24	39	63	136	....	....	....	....	....	....	....	....	....	4	0	2	2	8	....	....	....	....
2009-10	Peterborough	OHL	33	8	19	27	58	....	....	....	....	....	....	....	....	....	....	....	....	....	....	....	....	....	....
	Windsor Spitfires	OHL	5	4	0	4	23	....	....	....	....	....	....	....	....	....	19	7	9	16	38	....	....	....	....
2010-11	Windsor Spitfires	OHL	56	26	51	77	67	....	....	....	....	....	....	....	....	....	16	6	10	16	37	....	....	....	....
	Portland Pirates	AHL	....	....	....	....	....	....	....	....	....	....	....	....	....	....	3	0	0	0	2	....	....	....	....
2011-12	**Buffalo**	**NHL**	**27**	**3**	**4**	**7**	**20**	**0**	**0**	**0**	**36**	**8.3**	**–1**	**14**	**50.0**	**11:56**	....	....	....	....	....	....	....	....	....
	Rochester	AHL	30	15	11	26	31	....	....	....	....	....	....	....	....	....	....	....	....	....	....	....	....	....	....
	Vancouver	**NHL**	**17**	**1**	**2**	**3**	**31**	**0**	**0**	**0**	**18**	**5.6**	**–1**	**9**	**44.4**	**10:17**	**4**	**0**	**0**	**0**	**2**	**0**	**0**	**0**	**4:51**
2012-13	Chicago Wolves	AHL	29	8	13	21	61	....	....	....	....	....	....	....	....	....	....	....	....	....	....	....	....	....	....
	Vancouver	**NHL**	**39**	**7**	**4**	**11**	**51**	**2**	**0**	**1**	**49**	**14.3**	**–7**	**14**	**42.9**	**13:29**	**4**	**0**	**0**	**0**	**4**	**0**	**0**	**0**	**12:05**
	NHL Totals		**83**	**11**	**10**	**21**	**102**	**2**	**0**	**1**	**103**	**10.7**		**37**	**45.9**	**12:19**	**8**	**0**	**0**	**0**	**6**	**0**	**0**	**0**	**8:28**

Traded to **Vancouver** by **Buffalo** for Cody Hodgson, February 27, 2012.

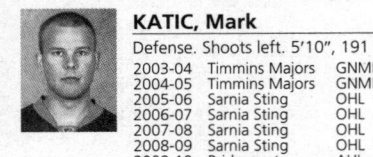

KATIC, Mark
(KA-tihk, MAHRK) **NYI**

Defense. Shoots left. 5'10", 191 lbs. Born, Porcupine, Ont., May 9, 1989. NY Islanders' 1st choice, 62nd overall, in 2007 Entry Draft.

Season	Club	League	GP	G	A	Pts	PIM	PP	SH	GW	S	%	+/-	TF	F%	Min	GP	G	A	Pts	PIM	PP	SH	GW	Min
2003-04	Timmins Majors	GNMHL	40	12	20	32	35	....	....	....	....	....	....	....	....	....	....	....	....	....	....	....	....	....	....
2004-05	Timmins Majors	GNMHL	35	11	21	32	74	....	....	....	....	....	....	....	....	....	....	....	....	....	....	....	....	....	....
2005-06	Sarnia Sting	OHL	51	5	29	34	33	....	....	....	....	....	....	....	....	....	....	....	....	....	....	....	....	....	....
2006-07	Sarnia Sting	OHL	68	5	35	40	31	....	....	....	....	....	....	....	....	....	4	1	3	4	8	....	....	....	....
2007-08	Sarnia Sting	OHL	45	5	26	31	28	....	....	....	....	....	....	....	....	....	6	0	3	3	8	....	....	....	....
2008-09	Sarnia Sting	OHL	63	13	41	54	45	....	....	....	....	....	....	....	....	....	4	1	0	1	6	....	....	....	....
2009-10	Bridgeport	AHL	48	3	11	14	16	....	....	....	....	....	....	....	....	....	....	....	....	....	....	....	....	....	....
2010-11	**NY Islanders**	**NHL**	**11**	**0**	**1**	**1**	**4**	**0**	**0**	**0**	**8**	**0.0**	**–9**	**0**	**0.0**	**16:26**	....	....	....	....	....	....	....	....	....
	Bridgeport	AHL	63	4	26	30	37	....	....	....	....	....	....	....	....	....	....	....	....	....	....	....	....	....	....
2011-12	Bridgeport	AHL	14	0	4	4	6	....	....	....	....	....	....	....	....	....	1	0	0	0	0	....	....	....	....
2012-13	Eisbaren Berlin	Germany	47	6	13	19	22	....	....	....	....	....	....	....	....	....	13	1	0	1	0	....	....	....	....
	NHL Totals		**11**	**0**	**1**	**1**	**4**	**0**	**0**	**0**	**8**	**0.0**		**0**	**0.0**	**16:26**	....	....	....	....	....	....	....	....	....

OHL All-Rookie Team (2006)

• Missed majority of 2011-12 due to pre-season shoulder injury. Signed as a free agent by **Berlin** (Germany), July 4, 2012.

KEARNS, Bracken
(KUHNRZ, BRAK-en) **S.J.**

Center. Shoots right. 6', 195 lbs. Born, Vancouver, B.C., May 12, 1981.

Season	Club	League	GP	G	A	Pts	PIM	PP	SH	GW	S	%	+/-	TF	F%	Min	GP	G	A	Pts	PIM	PP	SH	GW	Min
2001-02	U. of Calgary	CWUAA	26	0	8	8	2	....	....	....	....	....	....	....	....	....	....	....	....	....	....	....	....	....	....
2002-03	U. of Calgary	CWUAA	29	8	9	17	14	....	....	....	....	....	....	....	....	....	....	....	....	....	....	....	....	....	....
2003-04	U. of Calgary	CWUAA	38	11	12	23	22	....	....	....	....	....	....	....	....	....	....	....	....	....	....	....	....	....	....
2004-05	U. of Calgary	CWUAA	43	12	23	35	18	....	....	....	....	....	....	....	....	....	....	....	....	....	....	....	....	....	....
2005-06	Cleveland Barons	AHL	1	0	1	1	0	....	....	....	....	....	....	....	....	....	....	....	....	....	....	....	....	....	....
	Toledo Storm	ECHL	71	33	36	69	66	....	....	....	....	....	....	....	....	....	13	7	6	13	6	....	....	....	....
2006-07	Milwaukee	AHL	79	11	15	26	59	....	....	....	....	....	....	....	....	....	4	0	0	0	8	....	....	....	....
2007-08	Norfolk Admirals	AHL	53	9	16	25	40	....	....	....	....	....	....	....	....	....	....	....	....	....	....	....	....	....	....
	Reading Royals	ECHL	17	5	13	18	17	....	....	....	....	....	....	....	....	....	....	....	....	....	....	....	....	....	....
2008-09	Norfolk Admirals	AHL	53	12	10	22	63	....	....	....	....	....	....	....	....	....	....	....	....	....	....	....	....	....	....
2009-10	Rockford IceHogs	AHL	80	15	36	51	99	....	....	....	....	....	....	....	....	....	4	0	2	2	2	....	....	....	....
2010-11	San Antonio	AHL	72	20	23	43	104	....	....	....	....	....	....	....	....	....	....	....	....	....	....	....	....	....	....
2011-12	**Florida**	**NHL**	**5**	**0**	**0**	**0**	**10**	**0**	**0**	**0**	**0**	**0.0**	**0**	**2**	**50.0**	**7:14**	....	....	....	....	....	....	....	....	....
	San Antonio	AHL	69	22	30	52	58	....	....	....	....	....	....	....	....	....	10	2	5	7	4	....	....	....	....
2012-13	Worcester Sharks	AHL	66	21	25	46	73	....	....	....	....	....	....	....	....	....	....	....	....	....	....	....	....	....	....
	San Jose	**NHL**	**1**	**0**	**0**	**0**	**0**	**0**	**0**	**0**	**0**	**0.0**	**0**	**0**	**0.0**	**12:04**	**7**	**0**	**0**	**0**	**2**	**0**	**0**	**0**	**7:37**
	NHL Totals		**6**	**0**	**0**	**0**	**10**	**0**	**0**	**0**	**0**	**0.0**		**2**	**50.0**	**8:02**	**7**	**0**	**0**	**0**	**2**	**0**	**0**	**0**	**7:37**

Signed as a free agent by **Phoenix**, July 27, 2010. Signed as a free agent by **Florida**, July 14, 2011. Signed as a free agent by **San Jose**, July 2, 2012.

KEITH, Duncan
(KEETH, DUHN-kuhn) **CHI**

Defense. Shoots left. 6'1", 200 lbs. Born, Winnipeg, Man., July 16, 1983. Chicago's 2nd choice, 54th overall, in 2002 Entry Draft.

Season	Club	League	GP	G	A	Pts	PIM	PP	SH	GW	S	%	+/-	TF	F%	Min	GP	G	A	Pts	PIM	PP	SH	GW	Min
1998-99	Penticton	Minor-BC	44	51	57	108	45	....	....	....	....	....	....	....	....	....	....	....	....	....	....	....	....	....	....
99-2000	Penticton	BCHL	59	9	27	36	37	....	....	....	....	....	....	....	....	....	....	....	....	....	....	....	....	....	....
2000-01	Penticton	BCHL	60	18	64	82	61	....	....	....	....	....	....	....	....	....	9	4	6	10	18	....	....	....	....
2001-02	Michigan State	CCHA	41	3	12	15	18	....	....	....	....	....	....	....	....	....	....	....	....	....	....	....	....	....	....
2002-03	Michigan State	CCHA	15	3	6	9	8	....	....	....	....	....	....	....	....	....	....	....	....	....	....	....	....	....	....
	Kelowna Rockets	WHL	37	11	35	46	60	....	....	....	....	....	....	....	....	....	19	3	11	14	12	....	....	....	....
2003-04	Norfolk Admirals	AHL	75	7	18	25	44	....	....	....	....	....	....	....	....	....	8	1	1	2	6	....	....	....	....
2004-05	Norfolk Admirals	AHL	79	9	17	26	78	....	....	....	....	....	....	....	....	....	6	0	0	0	14	....	....	....	....
2005-06	**Chicago**	**NHL**	**81**	**9**	**12**	**21**	**79**	**1**	**1**	**0**	**134**	**6.7**	**–11**	**0**	**0.0**	**23:26**	....	....	....	....	....	....	....	....	....
2006-07	**Chicago**	**NHL**	**82**	**2**	**29**	**31**	**76**	**0**	**0**	**0**	**122**	**1.6**	**0**	**0**	**0.0**	**23:36**	....	....	....	....	....	....	....	....	....
2007-08	**Chicago**	**NHL**	**82**	**12**	**20**	**32**	**56**	**1**	**1**	**0**	**148**	**8.1**	**30**	**0**	**0.0**	**25:34**	....	....	....	....	....	....	....	....	....
2008-09	**Chicago**	**NHL**	**77**	**8**	**36**	**44**	**60**	**2**	**1**	**1**	**173**	**4.6**	**33**	**0**	**0.0**	**25:34**	**17**	**0**	**6**	**6**	**10**	**0**	**0**	**0**	**24:39**
2009-10 ♦	**Chicago**	**NHL**	**82**	**14**	**55**	**69**	**51**	**3**	**1**	**1**	**213**	**6.6**	**21**	**0**	**0.0**	**26:36**	**22**	**2**	**15**	**17**	**10**	**0**	**0**	**0**	**28:11**
	Canada	Olympics	7	0	6	6	2	....	....	....	....	....	....	....	....	....	....	....	....	....	....	....	....	....	....
2010-11	**Chicago**	**NHL**	**82**	**7**	**38**	**45**	**22**	**3**	**1**	**1**	**173**	**4.0**	**–1**	**0**	**0.0**	**26:53**	**7**	**4**	**2**	**6**	**6**	**1**	**0**	**1**	**26:55**
2011-12	**Chicago**	**NHL**	**74**	**4**	**36**	**40**	**42**	**1**	**0**	**1**	**162**	**2.5**	**15**	**0**	**0.0**	**26:54**	**6**	**0**	**1**	**1**	**2**	**0**	**0**	**0**	**30:16**
2012-13 ♦	**Chicago**	**NHL**	**47**	**3**	**24**	**27**	**31**	**2**	**0**	**0**	**91**	**3.3**	**16**	**0**	**0.0**	**24:07**	**22**	**2**	**11**	**13**	**18**	**0**	**0**	**0**	**27:37**
	NHL Totals		**607**	**59**	**250**	**309**	**417**	**13**	**5**	**4**	**1216**	**4.9**		**0**	**0.0**	**25:23**	**74**	**8**	**35**	**43**	**46**	**1**	**0**	**1**	**27:15**

NHL First All-Star Team (2010) • James Norris Memorial Trophy (2010)

Played in NHL All-Star Game (2008, 2011)

• Left **Michigan State University** (CCHA) and signed as a free agent by **Kelowna** (WHL), December 27, 2002.

KELLER, Ryan
(KEHL-uhr, RIGH-uhn)

Center. Shoots right. 5'10", 196 lbs. Born, Saskatoon, Sask., January 6, 1984.

Season	Club	League	GP	G	A	Pts	PIM	PP	SH	GW	S	%	+/-	TF	F%	Min	GP	G	A	Pts	PIM	PP	SH	GW	Min
2001-02	Saskatoon Blades	WHL	52	18	23	41	58	....	....	....	....	....	....	....	....	....	7	1	2	3	14	....	....	....	....
2002-03	Saskatoon Blades	WHL	66	38	41	79	101	....	....	....	....	....	....	....	....	....	6	7	1	8	8	....	....	....	....
2003-04	Saskatoon Blades	WHL	72	24	20	44	59	....	....	....	....	....	....	....	....	....	....	....	....	....	....	....	....	....	....
2004-05	Saskatoon Blades	WHL	67	40	33	73	63	....	....	....	....	....	....	....	....	....	4	1	1	2	9	....	....	....	....
2005-06	Grand Rapids	AHL	10	1	0	1	14	....	....	....	....	....	....	....	....	....	13	0	0	0	0	....	....	....	....
	Muskegon Fury	UHL	65	41	40	81	79	....	....	....	....	....	....	....	....	....	3	2	2	4	0	....	....	....	....
2006-07	Grand Rapids	AHL	38	9	8	17	26	....	....	....	....	....	....	....	....	....	....	....	....	....	....	....	....	....	....
	Syracuse Crunch	AHL	22	5	9	14	14	....	....	....	....	....	....	....	....	....	....	....	....	....	....	....	....	....	....
2007-08	Blues Espoo	Finland	47	22	22	44	24	....	....	....	....	....	....	....	....	....	17	3	6	9	22	....	....	....	....
2008-09	Blues Espoo	Finland	54	21	34	55	38	....	....	....	....	....	....	....	....	....	14	*9	7	16	4	....	....	....	....
2009-10	**Ottawa**	**NHL**	**6**	**0**	**0**	**0**	**0**	**0**	**0**	**0**	**5**	**0.0**	**–1**	**0**	**0.0**	**6:13**	....	....	....	....	....	....	....	....	....
	Binghamton	AHL	72	34	34	68	48	....	....	....	....	....	....	....	....	....	....	....	....	....	....	....	....	....	....
2010-11	Binghamton	AHL	71	32	19	51	38	....	....	....	....	....	....	....	....	....	23	10	*15	25	8	....	....	....	....
2011-12	Oklahoma City	AHL	71	21	28	49	38	....	....	....	....	....	....	....	....	....	14	5	5	10	14	....	....	....	....
2012-13	Geneve	Swiss	46	12	13	25	4	....	....	....	....	....	....	....	....	....	6	0	3	3	2	....	....	....	....
	NHL Totals		**6**	**0**	**0**	**0**	**0**	**0**	**0**	**0**	**5**	**0.0**		**0**	**0.0**	**6:13**	....	....	....	....	....	....	....	....	....

Signed as a free agent by **Ottawa**, June 1, 2009. Signed as a free agent by **Edmonton**, July 4, 2011. Signed as a free agent by **Geneve** (Swiss), July 12. 2012.

KELLY, Chris

(KEHL-lee, KRIHS) **BOS**

Center/Left wing. Shoots left. 6', 198 lbs. Born, Toronto, Ont., November 11, 1980. Ottawa's 4th choice, 94th overall, in 1999 Entry Draft.

			Regular Season														Playoffs								
Season	Club	League	GP	G	A	Pts	PIM	PP	SH	GW	S	%	+/-	TF	F%	Min	GP	G	A	Pts	PIM	PP	SH	GW	Min
1995-96	Toronto Marlies	MTHL	42	25	45	70	25	....	....	....	....	....	....	....	....	....	....	....	....	....	....	....	....	....	....
1996-97	Vaughan Vipers	ON-Jr.A	5	0	0	0	5	....	....	....	....	....	....	....	....	....	....	....	....	....	....	....	....	....	....
	Aurora Tigers	ON-Jr.A	49	14	20	34	11	....	....	....	....	....	....	....	....	....	....	....	....	....	....	....	....	....	....
1997-98	London Knights	OHL	54	15	14	29	4	....	....	....	....	....	....	....	....	....	16	4	5	9	12	....	....	....	....
1998-99	London Knights	OHL	68	36	41	77	60	....	....	....	....	....	....	....	....	....	25	9	17	26	22	....	....	....	....
99-2000	London Knights	OHL	63	29	43	72	57	....	....	....	....	....	....	....	....	....	....	....	....	....	....	....	....	....	....
2000-01	London Knights	OHL	31	21	34	55	46	....	....	....	....	....	....	....	....	....	....	....	....	....	....	....	....	....	....
	Sudbury Wolves	OHL	19	5	16	21	17	....	....	....	....	....	....	....	....	....	12	11	5	16	14	....	....	....	....
2001-02	Grand Rapids	AHL	31	3	3	6	20	....	....	....	....	....	....	....	....	....	5	1	1	2	5	....	....	....	....
	Muskegon Fury	UHL	4	1	2	3	0	....	....	....	....	....	....	....	....	....	....	....	....	....	....	....	....	....	....
2002-03	Binghamton	AHL	77	17	14	31	73	....	....	....	....	....	....	....	....	....	14	2	3	5	8	....	....	....	....
2003-04	**Ottawa**	**NHL**	**4**	**0**	**0**	**0**	**0**	**0**	**0**	**0**	**4**	**0.0**	**–2**	**5**	**40.0**	**9:29**	....	....	....	....	....	....	....	....	....
	Binghamton	AHL	54	15	19	34	40	....	....	....	....	....	....	....	....	....	2	0	0	0	4	....	....	....	....
2004-05	Binghamton	AHL	77	24	36	60	57	....	....	....	....	....	....	....	....	....	6	1	2	3	11	....	....	....	....
2005-06	**Ottawa**	**NHL**	**82**	**10**	**20**	**30**	**76**	**1**	**0**	**2**	**112**	**8.9**	**21**	**808**	**45.8**	**12:20**	**10**	**0**	**0**	**0**	**2**	**0**	**0**	**0**	**11:49**
2006-07	**Ottawa**	**NHL**	**82**	**15**	**23**	**38**	**40**	**1**	**2**	**0**	**131**	**11.5**	**28**	**564**	**49.8**	**15:18**	**20**	**3**	**4**	**7**	**4**	**0**	**0**	**0**	**15:28**
2007-08	**Ottawa**	**NHL**	**75**	**11**	**19**	**30**	**30**	**0**	**1**	**1**	**124**	**8.9**	**3**	**162**	**53.1**	**16:36**	....	....	....	....	....	....	....	....	....
2008-09	**Ottawa**	**NHL**	**82**	**12**	**11**	**23**	**38**	**0**	**1**	**1**	**118**	**10.2**	**–10**	**494**	**47.4**	**15:36**	....	....	....	....	....	....	....	....	....
2009-10	**Ottawa**	**NHL**	**81**	**15**	**17**	**32**	**38**	**0**	**0**	**3**	**112**	**13.4**	**–7**	**894**	**45.6**	**14:58**	**6**	**1**	**5**	**6**	**2**	**1**	**0**	**0**	**18:46**
2010-11	**Ottawa**	**NHL**	**57**	**12**	**11**	**23**	**27**	**0**	**1**	**2**	**89**	**13.5**	**–12**	**726**	**50.1**	**15:39**	....	....	....	....	....	....	....	....	....
	♦ Boston	**NHL**	**24**	**2**	**3**	**5**	**6**	**0**	**0**	**0**	**24**	**8.3**	**–1**	**190**	**53.7**	**14:52**	**25**	**5**	**8**	**13**	**6**	**0**	**0**	**0**	**15:28**
2011-12	**Boston**	**NHL**	**82**	**20**	**19**	**39**	**41**	**1**	**2**	**6**	**122**	**16.4**	**33**	**809**	**51.8**	**14:44**	**7**	**1**	**2**	**3**	**4**	**0**	**0**	**1**	**16:05**
2012-13	Martigny	Swiss-2	8	4	5	9	8	....	....	....	....	....	....	....	....	....	....	....	....	....	....	....	....	....	....
	Boston	**NHL**	**34**	**3**	**6**	**9**	**16**	**1**	**0**	**0**	**40**	**7.5**	**–8**	**373**	**57.9**	**14:58**	**22**	**2**	**1**	**3**	**19**	**0**	**0**	**0**	**15:40**
	NHL Totals		**603**	**100**	**129**	**229**	**312**	**4**	**7**	**15**	**876**	**11.4**		**5025**	**49.4**	**14:56**	**90**	**12**	**20**	**32**	**37**	**1**	**0**	**1**	**15:23**

Traded to **Boston** by **Ottawa** for Boston's 2nd round choice (Shane Prince) in 2011 Entry Draft, February 15, 2011. Signed as a free agent by **Martigny** (Swiss-2), October 31, 2012.

KENNEDY, Tim

(KEH-nuh-dee, TIHM) **PHX**

Left wing. Shoots left. 5'11", 180 lbs. Born, Buffalo, NY, April 30, 1986. Washington's 6th choice, 181st overall, in 2005 Entry Draft.

Season	Club	League	GP	G	A	Pts	PIM	PP	SH	GW	S	%	+/-	TF	F%	Min	GP	G	A	Pts	PIM	PP	SH	GW	Min
2003-04	Sioux City	USHL	56	9	10	19	42	....	....	....	....	....	....	....	....	....	7	2	2	4	6	....	....	....	....
2004-05	Sioux City	USHL	54	30	31	61	112	....	....	....	....	....	....	....	....	....	13	*6	*11	*17	18	....	....	....	....
2005-06	Michigan State	CCHA	29	4	15	19	31	....	....	....	....	....	....	....	....	....	....	....	....	....	....	....	....	....	....
2006-07	Michigan State	CCHA	42	18	25	43	49	....	....	....	....	....	....	....	....	....	....	....	....	....	....	....	....	....	....
2007-08	Michigan State	CCHA	42	20	23	43	50	....	....	....	....	....	....	....	....	....	....	....	....	....	....	....	....	....	....
2008-09	**Buffalo**	**NHL**	**1**	**0**	**0**	**0**	**0**	**0**	**0**	**0**	**1**	**0.0**	**0**	**1**	**0.0**	**11:04**	....	....	....	....	....	....	....	....	....
	Portland Pirates	AHL	73	18	49	67	51	....	....	....	....	....	....	....	....	....	5	0	1	1	2	....	....	....	....
2009-10	**Buffalo**	**NHL**	**78**	**10**	**16**	**26**	**50**	**1**	**0**	**3**	**98**	**10.2**	**–3**	**397**	**33.5**	**12:57**	**6**	**1**	**2**	**3**	**4**	**0**	**0**	**0**	**14:25**
2010-11	Connecticut	AHL	53	12	30	42	44	....	....	....	....	....	....	....	....	....	....	....	....	....	....	....	....	....	....
	Florida	**NHL**	**6**	**0**	**1**	**1**	**0**	**0**	**0**	**0**	**2**	**0.0**	**0**	**30**	**40.0**	**10:23**	....	....	....	....	....	....	....	....	....
	Rochester	AHL	14	0	7	7	8	....	....	....	....	....	....	....	....	....	....	....	....	....	....	....	....	....	....
2011-12	**Florida**	**NHL**	**27**	**1**	**1**	**2**	**4**	**0**	**0**	**1**	**22**	**4.5**	**–11**	**141**	**45.4**	**11:08**	....	....	....	....	....	....	....	....	....
	San Antonio	AHL	18	3	6	9	18	....	....	....	....	....	....	....	....	....	....	....	....	....	....	....	....	....	....
	Worcester Sharks	AHL	35	10	21	31	26	....	....	....	....	....	....	....	....	....	....	....	....	....	....	....	....	....	....
2012-13	Worcester Sharks	AHL	37	13	24	37	14	....	....	....	....	....	....	....	....	....	....	....	....	....	....	....	....	....	....
	San Jose	**NHL**	**13**	**2**	**0**	**2**	**2**	**0**	**0**	**1**	**24**	**8.3**	**–3**	**10**	**30.0**	**13:35**	**3**	**0**	**0**	**0**	**2**	**0**	**0**	**0**	**8:45**
	NHL Totals		**125**	**13**	**18**	**31**	**56**	**1**	**0**	**5**	**147**	**8.8**		**579**	**36.6**	**12:29**	**9**	**1**	**2**	**3**	**6**	**0**	**0**	**0**	**12:32**

USHL Second All-Star Team (2005) • NCAA Championship All-Tournament Team (2007) • CCHA Second All-Star Team (2008) • AHL All-Rookie Team (2009)

Traded to **Buffalo** by **Washington** for Buffalo's 6th round choice (Mathieu Perreault) in 2006 Entry Draft, July 30, 2005. Signed as a free agent by **NY Rangers**, August 30, 2010. Traded to **Florida** by **NY Rangers** with NY Rangers' 3rd round choice (Logan Shaw) in 2011 Entry Draft for Bryan McCabe, February 26, 2011. Traded to **San Jose** by **Florida** for Sean Sullivan, January 26, 2012.

KENNEDY, Tyler

(KEH-nuh-dee, TIGH-luhr) **S.J.**

Center. Shoots right. 5'11", 185 lbs. Born, Sault Ste. Marie, Ont., July 15, 1986. Pittsburgh's 6th choice, 99th overall, in 2004 Entry Draft.

Season	Club	League	GP	G	A	Pts	PIM	PP	SH	GW	S	%	+/-	TF	F%	Min	GP	G	A	Pts	PIM	PP	SH	GW	Min
2002-03	Sault Ste. Marie	OHL	61	5	10	15	28	....	....	....	....	....	....	....	....	....	4	0	0	0	0	....	....	....	....
2003-04	Sault Ste. Marie	OHL	63	16	26	42	28	....	....	....	....	....	....	....	....	....	....	....	....	....	....	....	....	....	....
2004-05	Sault Ste. Marie	OHL	61	21	36	57	37	....	....	....	....	....	....	....	....	....	4	1	3	4	4	....	....	....	....
2005-06	Sault Ste. Marie	OHL	64	22	48	70	60	....	....	....	....	....	....	....	....	....	4	1	2	3	2	....	....	....	....
2006-07	Wilkes-Barre	AHL	40	12	25	37	20	....	....	....	....	....	....	....	....	....	....	....	....	....	....	....	....	....	....
2007-08	**Pittsburgh**	**NHL**	**55**	**10**	**9**	**19**	**35**	**1**	**0**	**4**	**104**	**9.6**	**2**	**8**	**25.0**	**12:13**	**20**	**0**	**4**	**4**	**13**	**0**	**0**	**0**	**10:18**
	Wilkes-Barre	AHL	10	5	4	9	10	....	....	....	....	....	....	....	....	....	....	....	....	....	....	....	....	....	....
2008-09 ♦	**Pittsburgh**	**NHL**	**67**	**15**	**20**	**35**	**30**	**0**	**0**	**3**	**171**	**8.8**	**15**	**78**	**53.9**	**13:46**	**24**	**5**	**4**	**9**	**4**	**0**	**0**	**3**	**13:40**
2009-10	**Pittsburgh**	**NHL**	**64**	**13**	**12**	**25**	**31**	**1**	**0**	**4**	**175**	**7.4**	**10**	**64**	**42.2**	**12:35**	**10**	**0**	**0**	**0**	**2**	**0**	**0**	**0**	**11:57**
2010-11	**Pittsburgh**	**NHL**	**80**	**21**	**24**	**45**	**37**	**7**	**0**	**2**	**234**	**9.0**	**1**	**60**	**45.0**	**14:32**	**7**	**2**	**1**	**3**	**2**	**1**	**0**	**1**	**17:32**
2011-12	**Pittsburgh**	**NHL**	**60**	**11**	**22**	**33**	**29**	**0**	**0**	**1**	**195**	**5.6**	**10**	**89**	**47.2**	**14:22**	**6**	**3**	**3**	**6**	**2**	**0**	**0**	**1**	**14:22**
2012-13	**Pittsburgh**	**NHL**	**46**	**6**	**5**	**11**	**19**	**1**	**0**	**1**	**100**	**6.0**	**–6**	**29**	**44.8**	**12:28**	**9**	**2**	**3**	**5**	**2**	**0**	**0**	**1**	**12:33**
	NHL Totals		**372**	**76**	**92**	**168**	**181**	**10**	**0**	**15**	**979**	**7.8**		**328**	**46.6**	**13:26**	**76**	**12**	**15**	**27**	**25**	**1**	**0**	**6**	**12:50**

Traded to **San Jose** by **Pittsburgh** for San Jose's 2nd round choice (later traded to Columbus – Columbus selected Dillon Heatherington) in 2013 Entry Draft, June 30, 2013.

KESLER, Ryan

(KEHZ-luhr, RIGH-uhn) **VAN**

Center. Shoots right. 6'2", 202 lbs. Born, Livonia, MI, August 31, 1984. Vancouver's 1st choice, 23rd overall, in 2003 Entry Draft.

Season	Club	League	GP	G	A	Pts	PIM	PP	SH	GW	S	%	+/-	TF	F%	Min	GP	G	A	Pts	PIM	PP	SH	GW	Min
99-2000	Det. Honeybaked	MWEHL	72	44	73	117	....	....	....	....	....	....	....	....	....	....	....	....	....	....	....	....	....	....	....
2000-01	USNTDP	U-18	26	8	20	28	24	....	....	....	....	....	....	....	....	....	....	....	....	....	....	....	....	....	....
	USNTDP	NAHL	56	7	21	28	40	....	....	....	....	....	....	....	....	....	....	....	....	....	....	....	....	....	....
2001-02	USNTDP	U-18	46	11	33	44	23	....	....	....	....	....	....	....	....	....	....	....	....	....	....	....	....	....	....
	USNTDP	USHL	13	5	5	10	10	....	....	....	....	....	....	....	....	....	....	....	....	....	....	....	....	....	....
	USNTDP	NAHL	10	5	6	11	4	....	....	....	....	....	....	....	....	....	....	....	....	....	....	....	....	....	....
2002-03	Ohio State	CCHA	40	11	20	31	44	....	....	....	....	....	....	....	....	....	....	....	....	....	....	....	....	....	....
2003-04	**Vancouver**	**NHL**	**28**	**2**	**3**	**5**	**16**	**0**	**0**	**0**	**23**	**8.7**	**–2**	**194**	**40.2**	**10:42**	....	....	....	....	....	....	....	....	....
	Manitoba Moose	AHL	33	3	8	11	29	....	....	....	....	....	....	....	....	....	....	....	....	....	....	....	....	....	....
2004-05	Manitoba Moose	AHL	78	30	27	57	105	....	....	....	....	....	....	....	....	....	14	4	5	9	8	....	....	....	....
2005-06	**Vancouver**	**NHL**	**82**	**10**	**13**	**23**	**79**	**1**	**0**	**2**	**119**	**8.4**	**1**	**984**	**46.8**	**14:03**	....	....	....	....	....	....	....	....	....
2006-07	**Vancouver**	**NHL**	**48**	**6**	**10**	**16**	**40**	**0**	**0**	**0**	**88**	**6.8**	**1**	**690**	**46.1**	**16:26**	**1**	**0**	**0**	**0**	**0**	**0**	**0**	**0**	**27:51**
2007-08	**Vancouver**	**NHL**	**80**	**21**	**16**	**37**	**79**	**4**	**2**	**2**	**177**	**11.9**	**1**	**1358**	**53.0**	**19:03**	....	....	....	....	....	....	....	....	....
2008-09	**Vancouver**	**NHL**	**82**	**26**	**33**	**59**	**61**	**10**	**2**	**2**	**179**	**14.5**	**8**	**976**	**54.0**	**19:28**	**10**	**2**	**2**	**4**	**14**	**1**	**0**	**0**	**20:29**
2009-10	**Vancouver**	**NHL**	**82**	**25**	**50**	**75**	**104**	**12**	**1**	**5**	**214**	**11.7**	**1**	**1401**	**55.1**	**19:38**	**12**	**1**	**9**	**10**	**4**	**0**	**0**	**0**	**21:19**
	United States	Olympics	6	2	0	2	2	....	....	....	....	....	....	....	....	....	....	....	....	....	....	....	....	....	....
2010-11	**Vancouver**	**NHL**	**82**	**41**	**32**	**73**	**66**	**15**	**3**	**7**	**260**	**15.8**	**24**	**1496**	**57.4**	**20:30**	**25**	**7**	**12**	**19**	**47**	**4**	**0**	**2**	**22:34**
2011-12	**Vancouver**	**NHL**	**77**	**22**	**27**	**49**	**56**	**8**	**1**	**1**	**222**	**9.9**	**11**	**1351**	**53.6**	**20:06**	**5**	**0**	**3**	**3**	**6**	**0**	**0**	**0**	**22:04**
2012-13	**Vancouver**	**NHL**	**17**	**4**	**9**	**13**	**12**	**2**	**0**	**1**	**36**	**11.1**	**–5**	**303**	**57.4**	**18:57**	**4**	**2**	**0**	**2**	**0**	**1**	**0**	**0**	**23:06**
	NHL Totals		**578**	**157**	**193**	**350**	**513**	**52**	**9**	**20**	**1318**	**11.9**		**8753**	**52.9**	**18:12**	**57**	**12**	**26**	**38**	**71**	**6**	**0**	**2**	**22:02**

Frank J. Selke Trophy (2011)

Played in NHL All-Star Game (2011)

• Missed majority of 2012-13 due to recurring shoulder injury and foot injuriy vs. Dallas, February 15, 2013..

KESSEL, Phil

(KEH-suhl, FIHL) **TOR**

Right wing. Shoots right. 6', 202 lbs. Born, Madison, WI, October 2, 1987. Boston's 1st choice, 5th overall, in 2006 Entry Draft.

Season	Club	League	GP	G	A	Pts	PIM	PP	SH	GW	S	%	+/-	TF	F%	Min	GP	G	A	Pts	PIM	PP	SH	GW	Min
2003-04	USNTDP	U-17	32	31	18	49	8	....	....	....	....	....	....	....	....	....	....	....	....	....	....	....	....	....	....
	USNTDP	NAHL	30	21	12	33	18	....	....	....	....	....	....	....	....	....	....	....	....	....	....	....	....	....	....
2004-05	USNTDP	U-18	31	41	32	73	16	....	....	....	....	....	....	....	....	....	....	....	....	....	....	....	....	....	....
	USNTDP	NAHL	14	11	14	25	21	....	....	....	....	....	....	....	....	....	....	....	....	....	....	....	....	....	....
2005-06	U. of Minnesota	WCHA	39	18	33	51	28	....	....	....	....	....	....	....	....	....	....	....	....	....	....	....	....	....	....
2006-07	**Boston**	**NHL**	**70**	**11**	**18**	**29**	**12**	**1**	**0**	**0**	**170**	**6.5**	**–12**	**373**	**40.8**	**14:04**	....	....	....	....	....	....	....	....	....
	Providence Bruins	AHL	2	1	0	1	2	....	....	....	....	....	....	....	....	....	....	....	....	....	....	....	....	....	....
2007-08	**Boston**	**NHL**	**82**	**19**	**18**	**37**	**28**	**5**	**0**	**3**	**213**	**8.9**	**–6**	**326**	**42.3**	**15:14**	**4**	**3**	**1**	**4**	**2**	**1**	**0**	**0**	**14:31**

			Regular Season														Playoffs								
Season	Club	League	GP	G	A	Pts	PIM	PP	SH	GW	S	%	+/-	TF	F%	Min	GP	G	A	Pts	PIM	PP	SH	GW	Min
2008-09	**Boston**	**NHL**	**70**	**36**	**24**	**60**	**16**	**8**	**0**	**6**	**232**	**15.5**	**23**	**87**	**48.3**	**16:34**	**11**	**6**	**5**	**11**	**4**	**0**	**0**	**0**	**15:55**
2009-10	**Toronto**	**NHL**	**70**	**30**	**25**	**55**	**21**	**8**	**0**	**5**	**297**	**10.1**	**–8**	**122**	**48.4**	**19:33**	....	....	....	....	....	....	....	....	....
	United States	Olympics	6	1	1	2	0	....	....	....	....	....	....	....	....	....	....	....	....	....	....	....	....	....	....
2010-11	**Toronto**	**NHL**	**82**	**32**	**32**	**64**	**24**	**12**	**1**	**6**	**325**	**9.8**	**–20**	**59**	**40.7**	**19:39**	....	....	....	....	....	....	....	....	....
2011-12	**Toronto**	**NHL**	**82**	**37**	**45**	**82**	**20**	**10**	**0**	**6**	**295**	**12.5**	**–10**	**28**	**32.1**	**20:03**	....	....	....	....	....	....	....	....	....
2012-13	**Toronto**	**NHL**	**48**	**20**	**32**	**52**	**18**	**6**	**0**	**4**	**161**	**12.4**	**–3**	**8**	**62.5**	**19:49**	**7**	**4**	**2**	**6**	**2**	**1**	**0**	**2**	**18:29**
	NHL Totals		**504**	**185**	**194**	**379**	**139**	**50**	**1**	**30**	**1693**	**10.9**		**1003**	**42.8**	**17:47**	**22**	**13**	**8**	**21**	**8**	**2**	**0**	**2**	**16:29**

WCHA All-Rookie Team (2006) • WCHA Rookie of the Year (2006) • Bill Masterton Memorial Trophy (2007)

Played in NHL All-Star Game (2011, 2012)

Traded to **Toronto** by **Boston** for Toronto's 1st (Tyler Seguin) and 2nd (Jared Knight) round choices in 2010 Entry Draft and Toronto's 1st round choice (Dougie Hamilton) in 2011 Entry Draft, September 18, 2009.

KILLORN, Alex (KIHL-ohrn, al-EHX) T.B.

Center. Shoots left. 6'1", 202 lbs. Born, Halifax, N.S., September 14, 1989. Tampa Bay's 3rd choice, 77th overall, in 2007 Entry Draft.

Season	Club	League	GP	G	A	Pts	PIM	PP	SH	GW	S	%	+/-	TF	F%	Min	GP	G	A	Pts	PIM	PP	SH	GW	Min
2005-06	Lac St-Louis Lions	QAAA	43	18	34	52	94	....	....	....	....	....	....	....	....	....	10	9	6	15	8	....	....	....	....
2006-07	Deerfield	High-MA	25	18	14	32	....	....	....	....	....	....	....	....	....	....	....	....	....	....	....	....	....	....	....
2007-08	Deerfield	High-MA	24	28	27	55	....	....	....	....	....	....	....	....	....	....	....	....	....	....	....	....	....	....	....
2008-09	Harvard Crimson	ECAC	30	6	8	14	46	....	....	....	....	....	....	....	....	....	....	....	....	....	....	....	....	....	....
2009-10	Harvard Crimson	ECAC	32	9	11	20	26	....	....	....	....	....	....	....	....	....	....	....	....	....	....	....	....	....	....
2010-11	Harvard Crimson	ECAC	34	15	14	29	36	....	....	....	....	....	....	....	....	....	....	....	....	....	....	....	....	....	....
2011-12	Harvard Crimson	ECAC	34	23	23	46	47	....	....	....	....	....	....	....	....	....	....	....	....	....	....	....	....	....	....
	Norfolk Admirals	AHL	10	2	4	6	2	....	....	....	....	....	....	....	....	....	17	3	9	12	8	....	....	....	....
2012-13	Syracuse Crunch	AHL	44	16	22	38	32	....	....	....	....	....	....	....	....	....	....	....	....	....	....	....	....	....	....
	Tampa Bay	**NHL**	**38**	**7**	**12**	**19**	**14**	**1**	**0**	**2**	**82**	**8.5**	**–6**	**28**	**39.3**	**16:49**	....	....	....	....	....	....	....	....	....
	NHL Totals		**38**	**7**	**12**	**19**	**14**	**1**	**0**	**2**	**82**	**8.5**		**28**	**39.3**	**16:49**	....	....	....	....	....	....	....	....	....

NCAA East First All-American Team (2012)

KINDL, Jakub (KEEHN-duhl, YA-kuhb) DET

Defense. Shoots left. 6'3", 216 lbs. Born, Sumperk, Czech., February 10, 1987. Detroit's 1st choice, 19th overall, in 2005 Entry Draft.

Season	Club	League	GP	G	A	Pts	PIM	PP	SH	GW	S	%	+/-	TF	F%	Min	GP	G	A	Pts	PIM	PP	SH	GW	Min
2002-03	HC Pardubice U17	CzR-U17	3	0	3	3	10	....	....	....	....	....	....	....	....	....	....	....	....	....	....	....	....	....	....
	HC Pardubice Jr.	CzRep-Jr.	27	0	3	3	46	....	....	....	....	....	....	....	....	....	....	....	....	....	....	....	....	....	....
	Pardubice	CzRep	1	0	0	0	0	....	....	....	....	....	....	....	....	....	....	....	....	....	....	....	....	....	....
2003-04	HC Pardubice U17	CzR-U17	2	0	1	1	6	....	....	....	....	....	....	....	....	....	....	....	....	....	....	....	....	....	....
	HC Pardubice Jr.	CzRep-Jr.	48	4	14	18	108	....	....	....	....	....	....	....	....	....	....	....	....	....	....	....	....	....	....
	Hr. Kralove	CzRep-2	1	0	0	0	0	....	....	....	....	....	....	....	....	....	1	0	0	0	0	....	....	....	....
2004-05	Kitchener Rangers	OHL	62	3	11	14	92	....	....	....	....	....	....	....	....	....	12	0	0	0	22	....	....	....	....
2005-06	Kitchener Rangers	OHL	60	12	46	58	112	....	....	....	....	....	....	....	....	....	5	1	0	1	10	....	....	....	....
	Grand Rapids	AHL	3	0	1	1	2	....	....	....	....	....	....	....	....	....	....	....	....	....	....	....	....	....	....
2006-07	Kitchener Rangers	OHL	54	11	44	55	142	....	....	....	....	....	....	....	....	....	9	2	9	11	8	....	....	....	....
	Grand Rapids	AHL	....	....	....	....	....	....	....	....	....	....	....	....	....	....	7	0	2	2	0	....	....	....	....
2007-08	Grand Rapids	AHL	75	3	14	17	82	....	....	....	....	....	....	....	....	....	....	....	....	....	....	....	....	....	....
2008-09	Grand Rapids	AHL	78	6	27	33	76	....	....	....	....	....	....	....	....	....	10	2	1	3	2	....	....	....	....
2009-10	**Detroit**	**NHL**	**3**	**0**	**0**	**0**	**0**	**0**	**0**	**0**	**1**	**0.0**	**–2**	**0**	**0.0**	**10:50**	....	....	....	....	....	....	....	....	....
	Grand Rapids	AHL	73	3	30	33	59	....	....	....	....	....	....	....	....	....	....	....	....	....	....	....	....	....	....
2010-11	**Detroit**	**NHL**	**48**	**2**	**2**	**4**	**36**	**0**	**0**	**0**	**62**	**3.2**	**–6**	**0**	**0.0**	**13:37**	....	....	....	....	....	....	....	....	....
	Grand Rapids	AHL	8	1	4	5	6	....	....	....	....	....	....	....	....	....	....	....	....	....	....	....	....	....	....
2011-12	**Detroit**	**NHL**	**55**	**1**	**12**	**13**	**25**	**0**	**0**	**0**	**69**	**1.4**	**7**	**0**	**0.0**	**14:03**	....	....	....	....	....	....	....	....	....
2012-13	Pardubice	CzRep	27	1	10	11	26	....	....	....	....	....	....	....	....	....	....	....	....	....	....	....	....	....	....
	Detroit	**NHL**	**41**	**4**	**9**	**13**	**28**	**1**	**0**	**2**	**76**	**5.3**	**15**	**0**	**0.0**	**18:33**	**14**	**1**	**4**	**5**	**10**	**1**	**0**	**1**	**17:44**
	NHL Totals		**147**	**7**	**23**	**30**	**89**	**1**	**0**	**2**	**208**	**3.4**		**0**	**0.0**	**15:06**	**14**	**1**	**4**	**5**	**10**	**1**	**0**	**1**	**17:44**

OHL Second All-Star Team (2007)

Signed as a free agent by **Pardubice** (CzRep), September 23, 2012.

KING, D.J. (KIHNG, DEE-JAY)

Center. Shoots left. 6'3", 230 lbs. Born, Meadow Lake, Sask., January 27, 1984. St. Louis' 6th choice, 190th overall, in 2002 Entry Draft.

Season	Club	League	GP	G	A	Pts	PIM	PP	SH	GW	S	%	+/-	TF	F%	Min	GP	G	A	Pts	PIM	PP	SH	GW	Min
2000-01	Beardy's	SMHL	52	30	28	58	120	....	....	....	....	....	....	....	....	....	....	....	....	....	....	....	....	....	....
2001-02	Lethbridge	WHL	65	10	14	24	104	....	....	....	....	....	....	....	....	....	4	1	0	1	2	....	....	....	....
2002-03	Lethbridge	WHL	55	15	17	32	139	....	....	....	....	....	....	....	....	....	....	....	....	....	....	....	....	....	....
2003-04	Lethbridge	WHL	35	8	15	23	102	....	....	....	....	....	....	....	....	....	....	....	....	....	....	....	....	....	....
	Kelowna Rockets	WHL	28	5	2	7	80	....	....	....	....	....	....	....	....	....	17	1	6	7	16	....	....	....	....
2004-05	Worcester IceCats	AHL	74	6	8	14	178	....	....	....	....	....	....	....	....	....	....	....	....	....	....	....	....	....	....
2005-06	Peoria Rivermen	AHL	67	5	6	11	160	....	....	....	....	....	....	....	....	....	2	0	0	0	2	....	....	....	....
	Alaska Aces	ECHL	5	0	4	4	4	....	....	....	....	....	....	....	....	....	....	....	....	....	....	....	....	....	....
2006-07	**St. Louis**	**NHL**	**27**	**1**	**1**	**2**	**52**	**0**	**0**	**0**	**12**	**8.3**	**–3**	**2**	**50.0**	**5:31**	....	....	....	....	....	....	....	....	....
	Peoria Rivermen	AHL	38	5	4	9	102	....	....	....	....	....	....	....	....	....	....	....	....	....	....	....	....	....	....
2007-08	**St. Louis**	**NHL**	**61**	**3**	**3**	**6**	**100**	**0**	**0**	**1**	**36**	**8.3**	**–4**	**7**	**28.6**	**5:36**	....	....	....	....	....	....	....	....	....
2008-09	**St. Louis**	**NHL**	**1**	**0**	**1**	**1**	**0**	**0**	**0**	**0**	**0**	**0.0**	**0**	**0**	**0.0**	**8:20**	....	....	....	....	....	....	....	....	....
2009-10	**St. Louis**	**NHL**	**12**	**0**	**0**	**0**	**33**	**0**	**0**	**0**	**5**	**0.0**	**–4**	**0**	**0.0**	**4:30**	....	....	....	....	....	....	....	....	....
	Peoria Rivermen	AHL	10	0	1	1	13	....	....	....	....	....	....	....	....	....	....	....	....	....	....	....	....	....	....
2010-11	**Washington**	**NHL**	**16**	**0**	**2**	**2**	**30**	**0**	**0**	**0**	**6**	**0.0**	**–3**	**0**	**0.0**	**5:41**	....	....	....	....	....	....	....	....	....
2011-12	**Washington**	**NHL**	**1**	**0**	**0**	**0**	**0**	**0**	**0**	**0**	**1**	**0.0**	**0**	**0**	**0.0**	**6:58**	....	....	....	....	....	....	....	....	....
	Hershey Bears	AHL	29	0	4	4	13	....	....	....	....	....	....	....	....	....	4	1	0	1	0	....	....	....	....
2012-13	Ontario Reign	ECHL	19	5	3	8	22	....	....	....	....	....	....	....	....	....	10	1	2	3	8	....	....	....	....
	NHL Totals		**118**	**4**	**7**	**11**	**215**	**0**	**0**	**1**	**60**	**6.7**		**9**	**33.3**	**5:31**	....	....	....	....	....	....	....	....	....

• Missed majority of 2008-09 due to shoulder injury vs. Dallas, October 16, 2008. • Missed majority of 2009-10 due to hand injury and as a healthy reserve. Traded to **Washigton** by **St. Louis** for Stefan Della Rovere, July 28, 2010. • Missed majority of 2010-11 and 2011-12 as a healthy reserve. Signed as a free agent by **Ontario** (ECHL), February 20, 2013.

KING, Dwight (KIHNG, DWIGHT) L.A.

Left wing. Shoots left. 6'4", 232 lbs. Born, Meadow Lake, Sask., July 5, 1989. Los Angeles' 6th choice, 109th overall, in 2007 Entry Draft.

Season	Club	League	GP	G	A	Pts	PIM	PP	SH	GW	S	%	+/-	TF	F%	Min	GP	G	A	Pts	PIM	PP	SH	GW	Min
2004-05	Beardy's	SMHL	44	26	30	56	16	....	....	....	....	....	....	....	....	....	3	0	1	1	4	....	....	....	....
	Lethbridge	WHL	7	0	0	0	2	....	....	....	....	....	....	....	....	....	4	0	0	0	2	....	....	....	....
2005-06	Lethbridge	WHL	68	8	8	16	22	....	....	....	....	....	....	....	....	....	6	0	0	0	6	....	....	....	....
2006-07	Lethbridge	WHL	62	12	32	44	39	....	....	....	....	....	....	....	....	....	....	....	....	....	....	....	....	....	....
2007-08	Lethbridge	WHL	72	34	35	69	56	....	....	....	....	....	....	....	....	....	19	8	6	14	12	....	....	....	....
2008-09	Lethbridge	WHL	64	25	35	60	51	....	....	....	....	....	....	....	....	....	11	1	7	8	2	....	....	....	....
2009-10	Manchester	AHL	52	10	16	26	42	....	....	....	....	....	....	....	....	....	16	2	7	9	4	....	....	....	....
	Ontario Reign	ECHL	20	4	5	9	9	....	....	....	....	....	....	....	....	....	....	....	....	....	....	....	....	....	....
2010-11	**Los Angeles**	**NHL**	**6**	**0**	**0**	**0**	**2**	**0**	**0**	**0**	**3**	**0.0**	**–2**	**0**	**0.0**	**11:43**	....	....	....	....	....	....	....	....	....
	Manchester	AHL	72	24	28	52	58	....	....	....	....	....	....	....	....	....	7	2	3	5	2	....	....	....	....
2011-12 ♦	**Los Angeles**	**NHL**	**27**	**5**	**9**	**14**	**10**	**0**	**0**	**1**	**42**	**11.9**	**3**	**3**	**66.7**	**14:38**	**20**	**5**	**3**	**8**	**13**	**0**	**0**	**2**	**12:54**
	Manchester	AHL	50	11	18	29	20	....	....	....	....	....	....	....	....	....	....	....	....	....	....	....	....	....	....
2012-13	Manchester	AHL	28	5	12	17	13	....	....	....	....	....	....	....	....	....	....	....	....	....	....	....	....	....	....
	Los Angeles	**NHL**	**47**	**4**	**6**	**10**	**11**	**0**	**0**	**0**	**60**	**6.7**	**–3**	**6**	**33.3**	**12:45**	**18**	**2**	**3**	**5**	**2**	**0**	**1**	**0**	**14:47**
	NHL Totals		**80**	**9**	**15**	**24**	**23**	**0**	**0**	**1**	**105**	**8.6**		**9**	**44.4**	**13:19**	**38**	**7**	**6**	**13**	**15**	**0**	**1**	**2**	**13:47**

KLEIN, Kevin (KLIGHN, KEH-vihn) NSH

Defense. Shoots right. 6'1", 204 lbs. Born, Kitchener, Ont., December 13, 1984. Nashville's 3rd choice, 37th overall, in 2003 Entry Draft.

Season	Club	League	GP	G	A	Pts	PIM	PP	SH	GW	S	%	+/-	TF	F%	Min	GP	G	A	Pts	PIM	PP	SH	GW	Min
99-2000	Kitchener Midgets	Minor-ON	54	12	29	41	40	....	....	....	....	....	....	....	....	....	....	....	....	....	....	....	....	....	....
2000-01	St. Michael's	OHL	58	3	16	19	21	....	....	....	....	....	....	....	....	....	18	0	5	5	17	....	....	....	....
2001-02	St. Michael's	OHL	68	5	22	27	35	....	....	....	....	....	....	....	....	....	15	2	7	9	12	....	....	....	....
2002-03	St. Michael's	OHL	67	11	33	44	88	....	....	....	....	....	....	....	....	....	17	1	9	10	8	....	....	....	....
2003-04	St. Michael's	OHL	5	0	1	1	2	....	....	....	....	....	....	....	....	....	....	....	....	....	....	....	....	....	....
	Guelph Storm	OHL	46	6	23	29	40	....	....	....	....	....	....	....	....	....	22	10	11	21	12	....	....	....	....
2004-05	Milwaukee	AHL	65	4	12	16	22	....	....	....	....	....	....	....	....	....	7	0	0	0	11	....	....	....	....
	Rockford IceHogs	UHL	3	2	1	3	0	....	....	....	....	....	....	....	....	....	....	....	....	....	....	....	....	....	....

			Regular Season														Playoffs								
Season	Club	League	GP	G	A	Pts	PIM	PP	SH	GW	S	%	+/-	TF	F%	Min	GP	G	A	Pts	PIM	PP	SH	GW	Min
2005-06	Nashville	NHL	2	0	0	0	0	0	0	0	0	0.0	-1	0	0.0	13:40	....	....	....	....	....	....	....	....	....
	Milwaukee	AHL	76	10	33	43	31	....	....	....	....	....	....	....	....	....	21	3	7	10	31	....	....	....	....
2006-07	Nashville	NHL	3	1	0	1	0	0	0	0	2	50.0	3	0	0.0	16:37	....	....	....	....	....	....	....	....	....
	Milwaukee	AHL	70	5	15	20	67	....	....	....	....	....	....	....	....	....	4	1	0	1	0	....	....	....	....
2007-08	Nashville	NHL	13	0	2	2	6	0	0	0	14	0.0	-3	0	0.0	14:24	....	....	....	....	....	....	....	....	....
	Milwaukee	AHL	9	0	3	3	2	....	....	....	....	....	....	....	....	....	....	....	....	....	....	....	....	....	....
2008-09	Nashville	NHL	63	4	8	12	19	1	0	0	41	9.8	-2	0	0.0	12:40	....	....	....	....	....	....	....	....	....
2009-10	Nashville	NHL	81	1	10	11	27	0	0	0	67	1.5	-13	0	0.0	19:55	6	0	2	2	4	0	0	0	17:43
2010-11	Nashville	NHL	81	2	16	18	24	0	0	0	99	2.0	9	0	0.0	20:48	12	1	2	3	6	0	0	0	20:14
2011-12	Nashville	NHL	66	4	17	21	4	0	0	2	91	4.4	-8	0	0.0	19:56	10	2	2	4	2	0	0	1	19:31
2012-13	Herlev Eagles	Denmark	8	1	2	3	29	....	....	....	....	....	....	....	....	....	....	....	....	....	....	....	....	....	....
	Nashville	NHL	47	3	11	14	9	0	0	0	54	5.6	-1	0	0.0	20:25	....	....	....	....	....	....	....	....	....
	NHL Totals		**356**	**15**	**64**	**79**	**89**	**1**	**0**	**2**	**368**	**4.1**		**0**	**0.0**	**18:38**	**28**	**3**	**6**	**9**	**12**	**0**	**0**	**1**	**19:26**

Signed as a free agent by **Herlev** (Denmark), November 14, 2012..

KLESLA, Rostislav

(KLEHS-luh, RAHS-tih-slav) **PHX**

Defense. Shoots left. 6'3", 223 lbs. Born, Novy Jicin, Czech., March 21, 1982. Columbus' 1st choice, 4th overall, in 2000 Entry Draft.

Season	Club	League	GP	G	A	Pts	PIM	PP	SH	GW	S	%	+/-	TF	F%	Min	GP	G	A	Pts	PIM	PP	SH	GW	Min
1997-98	HC Opava Jr.	CzRep-Jr.	38	11	18	29	87	....	....	....	....	....	....	....	....	....	8	2	2	4	0	....	....	....	....
1998-99	Sioux City	USHL	54	4	12	16	100	....	....	....	....	....	....	....	....	....	5	2	0	2	2	....	....	....	....
99-2000	Brampton	OHL	67	16	29	45	174	....	....	....	....	....	....	....	....	....	6	1	1	2	21	....	....	....	....
2000-01	Columbus	NHL	8	2	0	2	6	0	0	0	10	20.0	-1	0	0.0	18:25	....	....	....	....	....	....	....	....	....
	Brampton	OHL	45	18	36	54	59	....	....	....	....	....	....	....	....	....	9	2	9	11	26	....	....	....	....
2001-02	Columbus	NHL	75	8	8	16	74	1	0	0	102	7.8	-6	0	0.0	18:52	....	....	....	....	....	....	....	....	....
2002-03	Columbus	NHL	72	2	14	16	71	0	0	0	89	2.2	-22	0	0.0	18:45	....	....	....	....	....	....	....	....	....
2003-04	Columbus	NHL	47	2	11	13	27	0	0	1	74	2.7	-16	0	0.0	18:19	....	....	....	....	....	....	....	....	....
2004-05	HC Vsetin	CzRep	41	7	17	24	136	....	....	....	....	....	....	....	....	....	....	....	....	....	....	....	....	....	....
	HPK Hameenlinna	Finland	9	1	2	3	12	....	....	....	....	....	....	....	....	....	10	0	2	2	12	....	....	....	....
2005-06	Columbus	NHL	51	6	13	19	75	2	0	1	84	7.1	-4	2	100.0	21:27	....	....	....	....	....	....	....	....	....
2006-07	Columbus	NHL	75	9	13	22	105	2	0	0	159	5.7	-13	0	0.0	22:54	....	....	....	....	....	....	....	....	....
2007-08	Columbus	NHL	82	6	12	18	60	3	0	1	130	4.6	7	5	80.0	23:13	....	....	....	....	....	....	....	....	....
2008-09	Columbus	NHL	34	1	8	9	38	0	0	0	30	3.3	2	1	0.0	20:59	4	0	1	1	0	0	0	0	21:22
2009-10	Columbus	NHL	26	2	6	8	26	0	0	1	24	8.3	-7	0	0.0	20:07	....	....	....	....	....	....	....	....	....
2010-11	Columbus	NHL	45	3	7	10	26	0	0	0	45	6.7	10	1	100.0	19:19	....	....	....	....	....	....	....	....	....
	Phoenix	NHL	16	1	0	1	12	0	0	0	22	4.5	-6	0	0.0	18:24	4	0	0	0	7	0	0	0	17:43
2011-12	Phoenix	NHL	65	3	10	13	54	0	0	0	87	3.4	13	2	50.0	19:22	15	2	6	8	4	0	0	0	18:36
2012-13	HC Ocelari Trinec	CzRep	18	0	1	1	30	....	....	....	....	....	....	....	....	....	....	....	....	....	....	....	....	....	....
	Phoenix	NHL	38	2	6	8	22	0	0	0	44	4.5	0	0	0.0	17:38	....	....	....	....	....	....	....	....	....
	NHL Totals		**634**	**47**	**108**	**155**	**596**	**8**	**0**	**4**	**900**	**5.2**		**11**	**72.7**	**20:13**	**23**	**2**	**7**	**9**	**11**	**0**	**0**	**0**	**18:56**

OHL All-Rookie Team (2000) • Canadian Major Junior All-Rookie Team (2000) • OHL First All-Star Team (2001) • NHL All-Rookie Team (2002)

Signed as a free agent by **Vsetin** (CzRep), September 17, 2004. Signed as a free agent by **Hameenlinna** (Finland), January 29, 2005. • Missed majority of 2008-09 due to various injuries. • Missed majority of 2009-10 due to groin injury vs. St. Louis, November 30, 2009. Traded to **Phoenix** by **Columbus** with Dane Byers for Scottie Upshall and Sami Lepisto, February 28, 2011. Signed as a free agent by **Trinec** (CzRep), September 21, 2012.

KLINGBERG, Carl

(KLIHNG-buhrg, KAHRL) **WPG**

Left wing. Shoots right. 6'3", 205 lbs. Born, Goteborg, Sweden, January 28, 1991. Atlanta's 2nd choice, 34th overall, in 2009 Entry Draft.

Season	Club	League	GP	G	A	Pts	PIM	PP	SH	GW	S	%	+/-	TF	F%	Min	GP	G	A	Pts	PIM	PP	SH	GW	Min
2006-07	Frolunda U18	Swe-U18	7	3	1	4	0	....	....	....	....	....	....	....	....	....	....	....	....	....	....	....	....	....	....
	Frolunda Jr.	Swe-Jr.	2	0	0	0	0	....	....	....	....	....	....	....	....	....	....	....	....	....	....	....	....	....	....
2007-08	Frolunda U18	Swe-U18	31	19	24	43	22	....	....	....	....	....	....	....	....	....	5	2	1	3	8	....	....	....	....
2008-09	Frolunda U18	Swe-U18	3	4	1	5	0	....	....	....	....	....	....	....	....	....	5	2	2	4	2	....	....	....	....
	Frolunda Jr.	Swe-Jr.	35	13	13	26	34	....	....	....	....	....	....	....	....	....	2	0	0	0	4	....	....	....	....
	Boras HC	Sweden-2	8	4	2	6	2	....	....	....	....	....	....	....	....	....	....	....	....	....	....	....	....	....	....
	Frolunda	Sweden	10	2	1	3	0	....	....	....	....	....	....	....	....	....	....	....	....	....	....	....	....	....	....
2009-10	Frolunda	Sweden	42	6	7	13	16	....	....	....	....	....	....	....	....	....	7	0	0	0	2	....	....	....	....
	Boras HC	Sweden-2	4	0	5	5	2	....	....	....	....	....	....	....	....	....	....	....	....	....	....	....	....	....	....
2010-11	Frolunda	Sweden	38	2	1	3	12	....	....	....	....	....	....	....	....	....	....	....	....	....	....	....	....	....	....
	Timra IK	Sweden	11	3	2	5	2	....	....	....	....	....	....	....	....	....	....	....	....	....	....	....	....	....	....
	Atlanta	NHL	1	0	0	0	0	0	0	0	0	0.0	0	0	0.0	10:22	....	....	....	....	....	....	....	....	....
	Chicago Wolves	AHL	8	1	0	1	6	....	....	....	....	....	....	....	....	....	....	....	....	....	....	....	....	....	....
2011-12	Winnipeg	NHL	6	0	0	0	4	0	0	0	7	0.0	-1	0	0.0	5:30	....	....	....	....	....	....	....	....	....
	St. John's IceCaps	AHL	66	15	22	37	39	....	....	....	....	....	....	....	....	....	12	1	1	2	0	....	....	....	....
2012-13	St. John's IceCaps	AHL	66	11	12	23	40	....	....	....	....	....	....	....	....	....	....	....	....	....	....	....	....	....	....
	NHL Totals		**7**	**0**	**0**	**0**	**4**	**0**	**0**	**0**	**7**	**0.0**		**0**	**0.0**	**6:12**	....	....	....	....	....	....	....	....	....

• Transferred to **Winnipeg** after **Atlanta** franchise relocated, June 21, 2011.

KLINKHAMMER, Rob

(KLIHNK-ham-uhr, RAWB) **PHX**

Left wing. Shoots left. 6'3", 214 lbs. Born, Lethbridge, Alta., August 12, 1986.

Season	Club	League	GP	G	A	Pts	PIM	PP	SH	GW	S	%	+/-	TF	F%	Min	GP	G	A	Pts	PIM	PP	SH	GW	Min
2003-04	Lethbridge	AMHL	29	20	22	42	8	....	....	....	....	....	....	....	....	....	....	....	....	....	....	....	....	....	....
	Lethbridge	WHL	25	2	3	5	12	....	....	....	....	....	....	....	....	....	....	....	....	....	....	....	....	....	....
2004-05	Lethbridge	WHL	72	14	12	26	81	....	....	....	....	....	....	....	....	....	5	0	1	1	4	....	....	....	....
2005-06	Lethbridge	WHL	35	5	7	12	15	....	....	....	....	....	....	....	....	....	....	....	....	....	....	....	....	....	....
	Seattle	WHL	32	3	5	8	37	....	....	....	....	....	....	....	....	....	7	0	1	1	6	....	....	....	....
2006-07	Seattle	WHL	1	0	0	0	9	....	....	....	....	....	....	....	....	....	....	....	....	....	....	....	....	....	....
	Portland	WHL	37	23	19	42	70	....	....	....	....	....	....	....	....	....	....	....	....	....	....	....	....	....	....
	Brandon	WHL	28	10	21	31	29	....	....	....	....	....	....	....	....	....	11	4	4	8	22	....	....	....	....
2007-08	Norfolk Admirals	AHL	66	12	12	24	41	....	....	....	....	....	....	....	....	....	....	....	....	....	....	....	....	....	....
2008-09	Rockford IceHogs	AHL	76	15	18	33	32	....	....	....	....	....	....	....	....	....	4	0	1	1	0	....	....	....	....
2009-10	Rockford IceHogs	AHL	72	10	13	23	38	....	....	....	....	....	....	....	....	....	4	1	1	2	7	....	....	....	....
2010-11	Chicago	NHL	1	0	0	0	0	0	0	0	1	0.0	1	0	0.0	11:36	....	....	....	....	....	....	....	....	....
	Rockford IceHogs	AHL	76	17	29	46	63	....	....	....	....	....	....	....	....	....	....	....	....	....	....	....	....	....	....
2011-12	Rockford IceHogs	AHL	18	2	4	6	6	....	....	....	....	....	....	....	....	....	....	....	....	....	....	....	....	....	....
	Ottawa	NHL	15	0	2	2	2	0	0	0	26	0.0	0	3	66.7	11:27	....	....	....	....	....	....	....	....	....
	Binghamton	AHL	35	12	23	35	30	....	....	....	....	....	....	....	....	....	....	....	....	....	....	....	....	....	....
2012-13	Portland Pirates	AHL	53	14	30	44	36	....	....	....	....	....	....	....	....	....	....	....	....	....	....	....	....	....	....
	Phoenix	NHL	22	5	6	11	10	1	0	1	34	14.7	7	2	100.0	12:14	....	....	....	....	....	....	....	....	....
	NHL Totals		**38**	**5**	**8**	**13**	**12**	**1**	**0**	**1**	**61**	**8.2**		**5**	**80.0**	**11:54**	....	....	....	....	....	....	....	....	....

Signed as a free agent by **Tampa Bay**, July 24, 2007. Signed as a free agent by **Chicago**, June 8, 2009. Traded to **Ottawa** by **Chicago** for Ottawa's 7th round choice (later traded to Calgary – Calgary selected John Gilmour) in 2013 Entry Draft, December 2, 2011. Signed as a free agent by **Phoenix**, July 3, 2012.

KNUBLE, Mike

(kuh-NOO-buhl, MIGHK)

Right wing. Shoots right. 6'3", 229 lbs. Born, Toronto, Ont., July 4, 1972. Detroit's 4th choice, 76th overall, in 1991 Entry Draft.

Season	Club	League	GP	G	A	Pts	PIM	PP	SH	GW	S	%	+/-	TF	F%	Min	GP	G	A	Pts	PIM	PP	SH	GW	Min
1988-89	East Kentwood	High-MI	28	52	37	89	60	....	....	....	....	....	....	....	....	....	....	....	....	....	....	....	....	....	....
1989-90	East Kentwood	High-MI	29	63	40	103	40	....	....	....	....	....	....	....	....	....	....	....	....	....	....	....	....	....	....
1990-91	Kalamazoo	NAHL	36	18	24	42	30	....	....	....	....	....	....	....	....	....	....	....	....	....	....	....	....	....	....
1991-92	U. of Michigan	CCHA	43	7	8	15	48	....	....	....	....	....	....	....	....	....	....	....	....	....	....	....	....	....	....
1992-93	U. of Michigan	CCHA	39	26	16	42	57	....	....	....	....	....	....	....	....	....	....	....	....	....	....	....	....	....	....
1993-94	U. of Michigan	CCHA	41	32	26	58	71	....	....	....	....	....	....	....	....	....	....	....	....	....	....	....	....	....	....
1994-95	U. of Michigan	CCHA	34	*38	22	60	62	....	....	....	....	....	....	....	....	....	....	....	....	....	....	....	....	....	....
	Adirondack	AHL	....	....	....	....	....	....	....	....	....	....	....	....	....	....	3	0	0	0	0	....	....	....	....
1995-96	Adirondack	AHL	80	22	23	45	59	....	....	....	....	....	....	....	....	....	3	1	0	1	0	....	....	....	....
1996-97	Detroit	NHL	9	1	0	1	0	0	0	0	10	10.0	-1	....	....	....	....	....	....	....	....	....	....	....	....
	Adirondack	AHL	68	28	35	63	54	....	....	....	....	....	....	....	....	....	....	....	....	....	....	....	....	....	....
1997-98♦	Detroit	NHL	53	7	6	13	16	0	0	0	54	13.0	2	....	....	....	3	0	1	1	0	0	0	0	....
1998-99	NY Rangers	NHL	82	15	20	35	26	3	0	1	113	13.3	-7	1	100.0	14:52	....	....	....	....	....	....	....	....	....
99-2000	NY Rangers	NHL	59	9	5	14	18	1	0	1	50	18.0	-5	9	55.6	10:39	....	....	....	....	....	....	....	....	....
	Boston	NHL	14	3	3	6	8	1	0	1	28	10.7	-2	3	0.0	19:29	....	....	....	....	....	....	....	....	....
2000-01	Boston	NHL	82	7	13	20	37	0	1	1	92	7.6	0	115	31.3	10:34	....	....	....	....	....	....	....	....	....
2001-02	Boston	NHL	54	8	6	14	42	0	0	2	77	10.4	9	27	44.4	9:45	2	0	0	0	0	0	0	0	3:30

			Regular Season														Playoffs								
Season	Club	League	GP	G	A	Pts	PIM	PP	SH	GW	S	%	+/-	TF	F%	Min	GP	G	A	Pts	PIM	PP	SH	GW	Min
2002-03	**Boston**	**NHL**	**75**	**30**	**29**	**59**	**45**	**9**	**0**	**4**	**185**	**16.2**	**18**	**34**	**44.1**	**17:24**	**5**	**0**	**2**	**2**	**2**	**0**	**0**	**0**	**17:35**
2003-04	**Boston**	**NHL**	**82**	**21**	**25**	**46**	**32**	**4**	**0**	**3**	**192**	**10.9**	**19**	**54**	**31.5**	**18:47**	**7**	**2**	**0**	**2**	**0**	**1**	**0**	**0**	**19:45**
2004-05	Linkopings HC	Sweden	49	*26	13	39	40	....	....	....	....	....	....	....	....	....	6	0	1	1	2	....	....	....	....
2005-06	**Philadelphia**	**NHL**	**82**	**34**	**31**	**65**	**80**	**13**	**2**	**6**	**217**	**15.7**	**25**	**161**	**32.3**	**20:21**	**6**	**1**	**3**	**4**	**8**	**0**	**0**	**0**	**19:17**
	United States	Olympics	6	1	1	2	4	....	....	....	....	....	....	....	....	....	....	....	....	....	....	....	....	....	....
2006-07	**Philadelphia**	**NHL**	**64**	**24**	**30**	**54**	**56**	**10**	**0**	**1**	**160**	**15.0**	**2**	**62**	**37.1**	**19:38**	....	....	....	....	....	....	....	....	....
2007-08	**Philadelphia**	**NHL**	**82**	**29**	**26**	**55**	**72**	**15**	**1**	**3**	**177**	**16.4**	**–3**	**25**	**40.0**	**18:55**	**12**	**3**	**4**	**7**	**6**	**0**	**0**	**1**	**18:34**
2008-09	**Philadelphia**	**NHL**	**82**	**27**	**20**	**47**	**62**	**11**	**0**	**6**	**173**	**15.6**	**5**	**51**	**35.3**	**18:10**	**6**	**2**	**1**	**3**	**2**	**0**	**0**	**0**	**18:26**
2009-10	**Washington**	**NHL**	**69**	**29**	**24**	**53**	**59**	**6**	**0**	**5**	**151**	**19.2**	**23**	**6**	**0.0**	**16:53**	**7**	**2**	**4**	**6**	**6**	**0**	**1**	**0**	**17:50**
2010-11	**Washington**	**NHL**	**79**	**24**	**16**	**40**	**36**	**7**	**1**	**1**	**203**	**11.8**	**10**	**33**	**30.3**	**17:53**	**6**	**2**	**0**	**2**	**8**	**1**	**0**	**0**	**21:10**
2011-12	**Washington**	**NHL**	**72**	**6**	**12**	**18**	**32**	**0**	**0**	**0**	**91**	**6.6**	**–15**	**27**	**51.9**	**13:57**	**11**	**2**	**1**	**3**	**6**	**0**	**0**	**0**	**9:08**
2012-13	Grand Rapids	AHL	1	0	1	1	0	....	....	....	....	....	....	....	....	....	....	....	....	....	....	....	....	....	....
	Philadelphia	**NHL**	**28**	**4**	**4**	**8**	**20**	**1**	**0**	**1**	**31**	**12.9**	**–4**	**7**	**57.1**	**12:55**	....	....	....	....	....	....	....	....	....
	NHL Totals		**1068**	**278**	**270**	**548**	**641**	**81**	**5**	**36**	**2004**	**13.9**		**615**	**35.3**	**16:10**	**65**	**14**	**16**	**30**	**38**	**2**	**1**	**1**	**16:41**

CCHA Second All-Star Team (1994, 1995) • NCAA West Second All-American Team (1995)

Traded to **NY Rangers** by **Detroit** for NY Rangers' 2nd round choice (Tomas Kopecky) in 2000 Entry Draft, October 1, 1998. Traded to **Boston** by **NY Rangers** for Rob DiMaio, March 10, 2000. Signed as a free agent by **Philadelphia**, July 3, 2004. Signed as a free agent by **Linkopings** (Sweden), August 2, 2004. Signed as a free agent by **Washington**, July 1, 2009. Signed to a PTO (professional try-out) contract by **Grand Rapids** (AHL), January 18, 2013. Signed as a free agent by **Philadelphia**, January 25, 2013.

KOBASEW, Chuck

(KOH-buh-soo, CHUHK)

Right wing. Shoots right. 6', 192 lbs. Born, Vancouver, B.C., April 17, 1982. Calgary's 1st choice, 14th overall, in 2001 Entry Draft.

			Regular Season														Playoffs								
Season	Club	League	GP	G	A	Pts	PIM	PP	SH	GW	S	%	+/-	TF	F%	Min	GP	G	A	Pts	PIM	PP	SH	GW	Min
1997-98	Osoyoos Heat	KIJHL	6	2	2	4	2	....	....	....	....	....	....	....	....	....	....	....	....	....	....	....	....	....	....
1998-99	Osoyoos Heat	KIJHL	23	25	24	49	....	....	....	....	....	....	....	....	....	....	....	....	....	....	....	....	....	....	....
	Penticton	BCHL	30	11	17	28	18	....	....	....	....	....	....	....	....	....	....	....	....	....	....	....	....	....	....
99-2000	Penticton	BCHL	58	*54	52	106	83	....	....	....	....	....	....	....	....	....	....	....	....	....	....	....	....	....	....
2000-01	Boston College	H-East	43	27	22	49	38	....	....	....	....	....	....	....	....	....	....	....	....	....	....	....	....	....	....
2001-02	Kelowna Rockets	WHL	55	41	21	62	114	....	....	....	....	....	....	....	....	....	15	10	5	15	22	....	....	....	....
2002-03	**Calgary**	**NHL**	**23**	**4**	**2**	**6**	**8**	**1**	**0**	**1**	**29**	**13.8**	**–3**	**5**	**0.0**	**11:48**	....	....	....	....	....	....	....	....	....
	Saint John Flames	AHL	48	21	12	33	61	....	....	....	....	....	....	....	....	....	....	....	....	....	....	....	....	....	....
2003-04	**Calgary**	**NHL**	**70**	**6**	**11**	**17**	**51**	**3**	**0**	**0**	**78**	**7.7**	**–12**	**91**	**42.9**	**10:22**	**26**	**0**	**1**	**1**	**24**	**0**	**0**	**0**	**9:02**
2004-05	Lowell	AHL	79	38	37	75	110	....	....	....	....	....	....	....	....	....	11	6	3	9	27	....	....	....	....
2005-06	**Calgary**	**NHL**	**77**	**20**	**11**	**31**	**64**	**10**	**0**	**4**	**143**	**14.0**	**–10**	**47**	**25.5**	**12:16**	**7**	**1**	**0**	**1**	**0**	**0**	**0**	**1**	**12:29**
2006-07	**Calgary**	**NHL**	**40**	**4**	**13**	**17**	**37**	**1**	**0**	**1**	**69**	**5.8**	**7**	**26**	**30.8**	**13:13**	....	....	....	....	....	....	....	....	....
	Boston	**NHL**	**10**	**1**	**1**	**2**	**25**	**1**	**0**	**0**	**24**	**4.2**	**–6**	**6**	**16.7**	**18:51**	....	....	....	....	....	....	....	....	....
2007-08	**Boston**	**NHL**	**73**	**22**	**17**	**39**	**29**	**6**	**3**	**3**	**147**	**15.0**	**6**	**70**	**40.0**	**17:41**	....	....	....	....	....	....	....	....	....
2008-09	**Boston**	**NHL**	**68**	**21**	**21**	**42**	**56**	**6**	**0**	**3**	**129**	**16.3**	**5**	**26**	**23.1**	**14:41**	**11**	**3**	**3**	**6**	**14**	**0**	**0**	**1**	**16:09**
2009-10	**Boston**	**NHL**	**7**	**0**	**1**	**1**	**2**	**0**	**0**	**0**	**13**	**0.0**	**–2**	**0**	**0.0**	**14:22**	....	....	....	....	....	....	....	....	....
	Minnesota	**NHL**	**42**	**9**	**5**	**14**	**16**	**2**	**0**	**2**	**58**	**15.5**	**–9**	**8**	**25.0**	**13:50**	....	....	....	....	....	....	....	....	....
2010-11	**Minnesota**	**NHL**	**63**	**9**	**7**	**16**	**19**	**0**	**0**	**1**	**74**	**12.2**	**–6**	**13**	**46.2**	**11:50**	....	....	....	....	....	....	....	....	....
2011-12	**Colorado**	**NHL**	**58**	**7**	**7**	**14**	**51**	**0**	**1**	**2**	**65**	**10.8**	**–10**	**22**	**31.8**	**11:51**	....	....	....	....	....	....	....	....	....
2012-13	**Colorado**	**NHL**	**37**	**5**	**4**	**9**	**21**	**0**	**0**	**1**	**43**	**11.6**	**6**	**49**	**36.7**	**11:16**	....	....	....	....	....	....	....	....	....
	NHL Totals		**568**	**108**	**100**	**208**	**379**	**30**	**4**	**18**	**872**	**12.4**		**363**	**35.0**	**13:10**	**44**	**4**	**4**	**8**	**38**	**0**	**0**	**2**	**11:21**

Hockey East Second All-Star Team (2001) • Hockey East Rookie of the Year (2001) • NCAA Championship All-Tournament Team (2001) • NCAA Championship Tournament MVP (2001) • AHL First All-Star Team (2005)

• Left **Boston College** (Hockey East) and signed with **Kelowna** (WHL), August 13, 2001. Traded to **Boston** by **Calgary** with Andrew Ference for Brad Stuart, Wayne Primeau and Washington's 4th round choice (previously acquired, Calgary selected T.J. Brodie) in 2008 Entry Draft, February 10, 2007. Traded to **Minnesota** by **Boston** for Craig Weller, Alexander Fallstrom and Minnesota's 2nd round choice (Alexander Khokhlachev) in 2011 Entry Draft, October 18, 2009. Signed as a free agent by **Colorado**, July 1, 2011.

KOIVU, Mikko

(KOI-voo, MEE-koh) **MIN**

Center. Shoots left. 6'3", 217 lbs. Born, Turku, Finland, March 12, 1983. Minnesota's 1st choice, 6th overall, in 2001 Entry Draft.

			Regular Season														Playoffs								
Season	Club	League	GP	G	A	Pts	PIM	PP	SH	GW	S	%	+/-	TF	F%	Min	GP	G	A	Pts	PIM	PP	SH	GW	Min
99-2000	TPS Turku U18	Fin-U18	11	4	9	13	18	....	....	....	....	....	....	....	....	....	....	....	....	....	....	....	....	....	....
	TPS Turku Jr.	Fin-Jr.	30	4	8	12	22	....	....	....	....	....	....	....	....	....	13	1	4	5	8	....	....	....	....
2000-01	TPS Turku U18	Fin-U18	....	....	....	....	....	....	....	....	....	....	....	....	....	....	7	2	10	12	2	....	....	....	....
	TPS Turku Jr.	Fin-Jr.	26	9	36	45	26	....	....	....	....	....	....	....	....	....	3	1	1	2	6	....	....	....	....
	TPS Turku	Finland	21	0	1	1	2	....	....	....	....	....	....	....	....	....	....	....	....	....	....	....	....	....	....
2001-02	TPS Turku Jr.	Fin-Jr.	2	0	1	1	12	....	....	....	....	....	....	....	....	....	....	....	....	....	....	....	....	....	....
	TPS Turku	Finland	48	4	3	7	34	....	....	....	....	....	....	....	....	....	8	0	3	3	4	....	....	....	....
2002-03	TPS Turku	Finland	37	7	13	20	20	....	....	....	....	....	....	....	....	....	7	2	2	4	6	....	....	....	....
2003-04	TPS Turku	Finland	45	6	24	30	36	....	....	....	....	....	....	....	....	....	13	1	7	8	8	....	....	....	....
2004-05	Houston Aeros	AHL	67	20	28	48	47	....	....	....	....	....	....	....	....	....	5	1	0	1	2	....	....	....	....
2005-06	**Minnesota**	**NHL**	**64**	**6**	**15**	**21**	**40**	**3**	**0**	**0**	**96**	**6.3**	**–9**	**724**	**47.4**	**13:17**	....	....	....	....	....	....	....	....	....
	Finland	Olympics	8	0	0	0	6	....	....	....	....	....	....	....	....	....	....	....	....	....	....	....	....	....	....
2006-07	**Minnesota**	**NHL**	**82**	**20**	**34**	**54**	**58**	**9**	**2**	**2**	**162**	**12.3**	**6**	**1165**	**50.9**	**17:29**	**5**	**1**	**0**	**1**	**4**	**0**	**0**	**0**	**17:43**
2007-08	**Minnesota**	**NHL**	**57**	**11**	**31**	**42**	**42**	**2**	**0**	**2**	**144**	**7.6**	**13**	**1032**	**52.5**	**20:53**	**6**	**4**	**1**	**5**	**4**	**0**	**1**	**0**	**21:56**
2008-09	**Minnesota**	**NHL**	**79**	**20**	**47**	**67**	**66**	**5**	**4**	**3**	**236**	**8.5**	**2**	**1625**	**52.7**	**21:29**	....	....	....	....	....	....	....	....	....
2009-10	**Minnesota**	**NHL**	**80**	**22**	**49**	**71**	**50**	**8**	**1**	**2**	**246**	**8.9**	**–2**	**1518**	**56.9**	**20:45**	....	....	....	....	....	....	....	....	....
	Finland	Olympics	6	0	4	4	2	....	....	....	....	....	....	....	....	....	....	....	....	....	....	....	....	....	....
2010-11	**Minnesota**	**NHL**	**71**	**17**	**45**	**62**	**50**	**7**	**1**	**3**	**191**	**8.9**	**4**	**1293**	**52.8**	**19:29**	....	....	....	....	....	....	....	....	....
2011-12	**Minnesota**	**NHL**	**55**	**12**	**32**	**44**	**28**	**2**	**1**	**2**	**129**	**9.3**	**10**	**1123**	**52.3**	**21:21**	....	....	....	....	....	....	....	....	....
2012-13	TPS Turku	Finland	10	5	5	10	16	....	....	....	....	....	....	....	....	....	....	....	....	....	....	....	....	....	....
	Minnesota	**NHL**	**48**	**11**	**26**	**37**	**26**	**0**	**0**	**3**	**127**	**8.7**	**2**	**971**	**54.0**	**21:06**	**5**	**0**	**0**	**0**	**8**	**0**	**0**	**0**	**20:30**
	NHL Totals		**536**	**119**	**279**	**398**	**360**	**36**	**9**	**17**	**1331**	**8.9**		**9451**	**52.8**	**19:24**	**16**	**5**	**1**	**6**	**16**	**0**	**1**	**0**	**20:10**

Signed as a free agent by **TPS Turku** (Finland), October 22, 2012.

KOIVU, Saku

(KOI-voo, SA-koo) **ANA**

Center. Shoots left. 5'10", 182 lbs. Born, Turku, Finland, November 23, 1974. Montreal's 1st choice, 21st overall, in 1993 Entry Draft.

			Regular Season														Playoffs								
Season	Club	League	GP	G	A	Pts	PIM	PP	SH	GW	S	%	+/-	TF	F%	Min	GP	G	A	Pts	PIM	PP	SH	GW	Min
1990-91	TPS Turku U18	Fin-U18	24	20	28	48	26	....	....	....	....	....	....	....	....	....	....	....	....	....	....	....	....	....	....
	TPS Turku Jr.	Fin-Jr.	13	3	7	10	6	....	....	....	....	....	....	....	....	....	....	....	....	....	....	....	....	....	....
1991-92	TPS Turku U18	Fin-U18	12	3	7	10	6	....	....	....	....	....	....	....	....	....	....	....	....	....	....	....	....	....	....
	TPS Turku Jr.	Fin-Jr.	34	25	28	53	57	....	....	....	....	....	....	....	....	....	8	5	9	14	6	....	....	....	....
1992-93	TPS Turku	Finland	46	3	7	10	28	....	....	....	....	....	....	....	....	....	11	3	2	5	2	....	....	....	....
1993-94	TPS Turku	Finland	47	23	30	53	42	....	....	....	....	....	....	....	....	....	11	4	8	12	16	....	....	....	....
	Finland	Olympics	8	4	3	7	12	....	....	....	....	....	....	....	....	....	....	....	....	....	....	....	....	....	....
1994-95	TPS Turku	Finland	45	27	47	74	73	....	....	....	....	....	....	....	....	....	13	7	10	17	16	....	....	....	....
1995-96	**Montreal**	**NHL**	**82**	**20**	**25**	**45**	**40**	**8**	**3**	**2**	**136**	**14.7**	**–7**	....	....	....	**6**	**3**	**1**	**4**	**8**	**0**	**0**	**0**	....
1996-97	**Montreal**	**NHL**	**50**	**17**	**39**	**56**	**38**	**5**	**0**	**3**	**135**	**12.6**	**7**	....	....	....	**5**	**1**	**3**	**4**	**10**	**0**	**0**	**0**	....
1997-98	**Montreal**	**NHL**	**69**	**14**	**43**	**57**	**48**	**2**	**2**	**3**	**145**	**9.7**	**8**	....	....	....	**6**	**2**	**3**	**5**	**2**	**1**	**0**	**0**	....
	Finland	Olympics	6	2	8	10	4	....	....	....	....	....	....	....	....	....	....	....	....	....	....	....	....	....	....
1998-99	**Montreal**	**NHL**	**65**	**14**	**30**	**44**	**38**	**4**	**2**	**0**	**145**	**9.7**	**–7**	**1427**	**52.6**	**20:02**	....	....	....	....	....	....	....	....	....
99-2000	**Montreal**	**NHL**	**24**	**3**	**18**	**21**	**14**	**1**	**0**	**0**	**53**	**5.7**	**7**	**495**	**52.9**	**19:13**	....	....	....	....	....	....	....	....	....
2000-01	**Montreal**	**NHL**	**54**	**17**	**30**	**47**	**40**	**7**	**0**	**3**	**113**	**15.0**	**2**	**1092**	**47.6**	**21:23**	....	....	....	....	....	....	....	....	....
2001-02	**Montreal**	**NHL**	**3**	**0**	**2**	**2**	**0**	**0**	**0**	**0**	**2**	**0.0**	**0**	**13**	**61.5**	**13:57**	**12**	**4**	**6**	**10**	**4**	**1**	**0**	**1**	**15:54**
2002-03	**Montreal**	**NHL**	**82**	**21**	**50**	**71**	**72**	**5**	**1**	**5**	**147**	**14.3**	**5**	**1566**	**49.6**	**19:14**	....	....	....	....	....	....	....	....	....
2003-04	**Montreal**	**NHL**	**68**	**14**	**41**	**55**	**52**	**5**	**0**	**3**	**112**	**12.5**	**–5**	**1194**	**53.9**	**19:18**	**11**	**3**	**8**	**11**	**10**	**2**	**0**	**0**	**20:34**
2004-05	TPS Turku	Finland	20	8	8	16	28	....	....	....	....	....	....	....	....	....	6	3	2	5	30	....	....	....	....
2005-06	**Montreal**	**NHL**	**72**	**17**	**45**	**62**	**70**	**5**	**0**	**4**	**138**	**12.3**	**1**	**1412**	**53.8**	**18:31**	**3**	**0**	**2**	**2**	**2**	**0**	**0**	**0**	**14:24**
	Finland	Olympics	8	3	*8	*11	12	....	....	....	....	....	....	....	....	....	....	....	....	....	....	....	....	....	....
2006-07	**Montreal**	**NHL**	**81**	**22**	**53**	**75**	**74**	**11**	**1**	**4**	**154**	**14.3**	**–21**	**1453**	**54.9**	**18:07**	....	....	....	....	....	....	....	....	....
2007-08	**Montreal**	**NHL**	**77**	**16**	**40**	**56**	**93**	**8**	**0**	**3**	**150**	**10.7**	**–4**	**1341**	**52.3**	**18:07**	**7**	**3**	**6**	**9**	**4**	**2**	**0**	**0**	**19:33**
2008-09	**Montreal**	**NHL**	**65**	**16**	**34**	**50**	**44**	**5**	**0**	**5**	**123**	**13.0**	**4**	**1122**	**54.1**	**17:03**	**4**	**0**	**3**	**3**	**2**	**0**	**0**	**0**	**17:45**
2009-10	**Anaheim**	**NHL**	**71**	**19**	**33**	**52**	**36**	**5**	**1**	**6**	**124**	**15.3**	**14**	**1110**	**51.4**	**18:35**	....	....	....	....	....	....	....	....	....
	Finland	Olympics	6	0	2	2	6	....	....	....	....	....	....	....	....	....	....	....	....	....	....	....	....	....	....
2010-11	**Anaheim**	**NHL**	**75**	**15**	**30**	**45**	**36**	**4**	**0**	**3**	**104**	**14.4**	**–8**	**1339**	**52.8**	**19:08**	**6**	**1**	**6**	**7**	**6**	**0**	**0**	**0**	**18:19**

			Regular Season														Playoffs								
Season	Club	League	GP	G	A	Pts	PIM	PP	SH	GW	S	%	+/-	TF	F%	Min	GP	G	A	Pts	PIM	PP	SH	GW	Min
2011-12	Anaheim	NHL	74	11	27	38	50	0	0	1	107	10.3	7	1233	52.4	18:08	....	....	....	....	....	....	....	....	....
2012-13	Anaheim	NHL	47	8	19	27	18	4	0	0	55	14.5	4	851	51.4	17:36	7	1	2	3	6	1	0	0	17:53
	NHL Totals		1059	244	559	803	763	79	10	45	1943	12.6		15648	52.3	18:44	67	18	40	58	54	7	0	1	18:04

Bill Masterton Memorial Trophy (2002) • Olympic All-Star Team (2006) • King Clancy Memorial Trophy (2007)

Played in NHL All-Star Game (1998)

• Missed majority of 1999-2000 due to shoulder injury vs. NY Rangers, October 30, 1999. • Missed majority of 2001-02 due to non-Hodgkin 's lymphoma, September 6, 2001. Signed as a free agent by **Turku** (Finland), October 21, 2004. Signed as a free agent by **Anaheim**, July 8, 2009.

KOLANOS, Krys

(koh-LA-nohs, KRIHS)

Center. Shoots right. 6'3", 206 lbs. Born, Calgary, Alta., July 27, 1981. Phoenix's 1st choice, 19th overall, in 2000 Entry Draft.

1996-97	Calgary Flames	AAHA	24	24	35	59	....	....	....	....	....	....	....	....	....	....	....	....	....	....	....	....	....	....	....
1997-98	Calgary Buffaloes	AMHL	34	34	43	77	29	....	....	....	....	....	....	....	....	....	....	....	....	....	....	....	....	....	....
1998-99	Calgary Royals	AJHL	58	43	67	110	98	....	....	....	....	....	....	....	....	....	....	....	....	....	....	....	....	....	....
99-2000	Boston College	H-East	42	16	16	32	48	....	....	....	....	....	....	....	....	....	....	....	....	....	....	....	....	....	....
2000-01	Boston College	H-East	41	25	25	50	54	....	....	....	....	....	....	....	....	....	....	....	....	....	....	....	....	....	....
2001-02	Phoenix	NHL	57	11	11	22	48	0	0	5	81	13.6	6	703	46.4	13:05	2	0	0	0	6	0	0	0	11:12
2002-03	Phoenix	NHL	2	0	0	0	0	0	0	0	8	0.0	0	16	31.3	14:06	....	....	....	....	....	....	....	....	....
2003-04	Phoenix	NHL	41	4	6	10	24	1	0	1	61	6.6	–9	283	43.8	13:31	....	....	....	....	....	....	....	....	....
	Springfield	AHL	32	10	11	21	38	....	....	....	....	....	....	....	....	....	....	....	....	....	....	....	....	....	....
2004-05	Blues Espoo	Finland	15	7	9	16	40	....	....	....	....	....	....	....	....	....	....	....	....	....	....	....	....	....	....
	Krefeld Pinguine	Germany	7	3	2	5	16	....	....	....	....	....	....	....	....	....	....	....	....	....	....	....	....	....	....
2005-06	Phoenix	NHL	9	2	1	3	2	1	0	0	15	13.3	2	75	53.3	11:30	....	....	....	....	....	....	....	....	....
	San Antonio	AHL	3	0	1	1	0	....	....	....	....	....	....	....	....	....	....	....	....	....	....	....	....	....	....
	Edmonton	NHL	6	0	0	0	2	0	0	0	7	0.0	–1	32	50.0	7:39	....	....	....	....	....	....	....	....	....
	Lowell	AHL	19	10	11	21	40	....	....	....	....	....	....	....	....	....	....	....	....	....	....	....	....	....	....
	Wilkes-Barre	AHL	18	10	8	18	19	....	....	....	....	....	....	....	....	....	11	2	0	2	16	....	....	....	....
2006-07	Grand Rapids	AHL	17	6	6	12	8	....	....	....	....	....	....	....	....	....	....	....	....	....	....	....	....	....	....
	Langnau	Swiss	14	2	9	11	48	....	....	....	....	....	....	....	....	....	....	....	....	....	....	....	....	....	....
	EV Zug	Swiss	....	....	....	....	....	....	....	....	....	....	....	....	....	....	8	6	0	6	8	....	....	....	....
2007-08	Quad City Flames	AHL	65	30	33	63	84	....	....	....	....	....	....	....	....	....	....	....	....	....	....	....	....	....	....
2008-09	Minnesota	NHL	21	3	3	6	16	1	0	0	30	10.0	3	115	51.3	10:36	....	....	....	....	....	....	....	....	....
	Houston Aeros	AHL	45	31	20	51	42	....	....	....	....	....	....	....	....	....	18	6	8	14	18	....	....	....	....
2009-10	Adirondack	AHL	27	9	6	15	22	....	....	....	....	....	....	....	....	....	....	....	....	....	....	....	....	....	....
2010-11			DID NOT PLAY – INJURED																						
2011-12	Abbotsford Heat	AHL	47	30	31	61	47	....	....	....	....	....	....	....	....	....	7	5	5	10	6	....	....	....	....
	Calgary	NHL	13	0	1	1	2	0	0	0	29	0.0	–1	30	56.7	9:51	....	....	....	....	....	....	....	....	....
2012-13	Abbotsford Heat	AHL	53	18	22	40	63	....	....	....	....	....	....	....	....	....	....	....	....	....	....	....	....	....	....
	NHL Totals		149	20	22	42	94	3	0	6	231	8.7		1254	46.8	12:16	2	0	0	0	6	0	0	0	11:12

Hockey East All-Rookie Team (2000) • Hockey East Second All-Star Team (2001) • NCAA East Second All-American Team (2001) • NCAA Championship All-Tournament Team (2001)

• Missed majority of 2002-03 due to head injury vs. Pittsburgh, March 20, 2002. Signed as a free agent by **Espoo** (Finland), October 25, 2004. Signed as a free agent by **Krefeld** (Germany), February 16, 2005. Claimed on waivers by **Edmonton** from **Phoenix**, November 11, 2005. Claimed on waivers by **Phoenix** from **Edmonton**, December 19, 2005. Traded to **Carolina** by **Phoenix** for Pavel Brendl, December 28, 2005. Traded to **Pittsburgh** by **Carolina** with Niklas Nordgren and Carolina's 2nd round choice (later traded to San Jose, later traded to Philadelphia - Philadelphia selected Kevin Marshall) in 2007 Entry Draft for Mark Recchi, March 9, 2006. Signed as a free agent by **Detroit**, July 15, 2006. Signed as a free agent by **Minnesota**, July 11, 2008. Signed as a free agent by **Philadelphia**, July 23, 2009. • Missed majority of 2009-10 and all of 2010-11 due to hip injury at Norfolk, January 16, 2010 and resulting surgery, February 16, 2010. Signed to PTO (professional tryout) contract by **Abbotsford** (AHL), October 11, 2011. Signed as a free agent by **Abbotsford** (AHL), November 12, 2011. Signed as a free agent by **Calgary**, February 1, 2012.

KOLARIK, Chad

(koh-LAHR-ihk, CHAD)

Center. Shoots right. 5'11", 185 lbs. Born, Abington, PA, January 26, 1986. Phoenix's 7th choice, 199th overall, in 2004 Entry Draft.

2002-03	USNTDP	U-17	21	14	10	24	4	....	....	....	....	....	....	....	....	....	....	....	....	....	....	....	....	....	....
	USNTDP	NAHL	44	16	22	38	43	....	....	....	....	....	....	....	....	....	....	....	....	....	....	....	....	....	....
2003-04	USNTDP	U-18	45	18	20	38	16	....	....	....	....	....	....	....	....	....	....	....	....	....	....	....	....	....	....
	USNTDP	NAHL	10	3	4	7	4	....	....	....	....	....	....	....	....	....	....	....	....	....	....	....	....	....	....
2004-05	U. of Michigan	CCHA	42	18	17	35	53	....	....	....	....	....	....	....	....	....	....	....	....	....	....	....	....	....	....
2005-06	U. of Michigan	CCHA	41	12	26	38	30	....	....	....	....	....	....	....	....	....	....	....	....	....	....	....	....	....	....
2006-07	U. of Michigan	CCHA	41	18	27	45	24	....	....	....	....	....	....	....	....	....	....	....	....	....	....	....	....	....	....
2007-08	U. of Michigan	CCHA	39	30	26	56	24	....	....	....	....	....	....	....	....	....	....	....	....	....	....	....	....	....	....
	San Antonio	AHL	....	....	....	....	....	....	....	....	....	....	....	....	....	....	7	4	2	6	0	....	....	....	....
2008-09	San Antonio	AHL	76	20	30	50	47	....	....	....	....	....	....	....	....	....	....	....	....	....	....	....	....	....	....
2009-10	San Antonio	AHL	59	17	18	35	41	....	....	....	....	....	....	....	....	....	....	....	....	....	....	....	....	....	....
	Columbus	NHL	2	0	0	0	0	0	0	0	2	0.0	–1	0	0.0	6:29	....	....	....	....	....	....	....	....	....
	Syracuse Crunch	AHL	17	9	6	15	14	....	....	....	....	....	....	....	....	....	....	....	....	....	....	....	....	....	....
2010-11	Springfield	AHL	13	4	6	10	18	....	....	....	....	....	....	....	....	....	....	....	....	....	....	....	....	....	....
	NY Rangers	NHL	4	0	1	1	2	0	0	0	4	0.0	–1	0	0.0	9:08	....	....	....	....	....	....	....	....	....
	Connecticut	AHL	36	17	14	31	36	....	....	....	....	....	....	....	....	....	3	3	2	5	0	....	....	....	....
2011-12			DID NOT PLAY – INJURED																						
2012-13	Connecticut	AHL	41	16	19	35	38	....	....	....	....	....	....	....	....	....	....	....	....	....	....	....	....	....	....
	Wilkes-Barre	AHL	35	15	18	33	17	....	....	....	....	....	....	....	....	....	15	5	6	11	17	....	....	....	....
	NHL Totals		6	0	1	1	2	0	0	0	6	0.0		0	0.0	8:15	....	....	....	....	....	....	....	....	....

CCHA First All-Star Team (2008) • NCAA West Second All-American Team (2008)

Traded to **Columbus** by **Phoenix** for Alexandre Picard, March 3, 2010. Traded to **NY Rangers** by **Columbus** for Dane Byers, November 11, 2010. • Missed 2011-12 due to knee injury at NY Rangers training camp, September 20, 2011. Traded to **Pittsburgh** by **NY Rangers** for Benn Ferriero, January 24, 2013. Signed as a free agent by **Linkopings** (Sweden), June 28, 2013.

KOMAROV, Leo

(koh-mah-RAWV, L'YAY-oh) **TOR**

Center. Shoots left. 5'11", 198 lbs. Born, Narva, USSR, January 23, 1987. Toronto's 7th choice, 180th overall, in 2006 Entry Draft.

2003-04	Sport Vaasa U18	Fin-U18	30	9	15	24	8	....	....	....	....	....	....	....	....	....	....	....	....	....	....	....	....	....	....
2004-05	Assat Pori U18	Fin-U18	9	4	5	9	62	....	....	....	....	....	....	....	....	....	....	....	....	....	....	....	....	....	....
	Assat Pori Jr.	Fin-Jr.	38	8	6	13	59	....	....	....	....	....	....	....	....	....	2	0	0	0	2	....	....	....	....
2005-06	Suomi U20	Finland-2	5	0	3	3	4	....	....	....	....	....	....	....	....	....	....	....	....	....	....	....	....	....	....
	Assat Pori Jr.	Fin-Jr.	10	5	6	11	59	....	....	....	....	....	....	....	....	....	2	2	1	3	10	....	....	....	....
	Assat Pori	Finland	44	3	3	6	106	....	....	....	....	....	....	....	....	....	14	1	3	4	22	....	....	....	....
2006-07	Suomi U20	Finland-2	1	1	0	1	0	....	....	....	....	....	....	....	....	....	....	....	....	....	....	....	....	....	....
	Pelicans Lahti	Finland	49	3	9	12	108	....	....	....	....	....	....	....	....	....	6	1	0	1	6	....	....	....	....
2007-08	Pelicans Lahti Jr.	Fin-Jr.	2	0	3	3	0	....	....	....	....	....	....	....	....	....	....	....	....	....	....	....	....	....	....
	Pelicans Lahti	Finland	53	4	10	14	76	....	....	....	....	....	....	....	....	....	6	1	1	2	8	....	....	....	....
2008-09	Pelicans Lahti	Finland	56	8	16	24	144	....	....	....	....	....	....	....	....	....	10	0	1	1	16	....	....	....	....
2009-10	Dynamo Moscow	KHL	47	5	11	16	44	....	....	....	....	....	....	....	....	....	4	0	1	1	16	....	....	....	....
2010-11	Dynamo Moscow	KHL	52	14	12	26	70	....	....	....	....	....	....	....	....	....	6	4	2	6	2	....	....	....	....
2011-12	Dynamo Moscow	KHL	46	11	13	24	58	....	....	....	....	....	....	....	....	....	20	5	2	7	49	....	....	....	....
2012-13	Toronto Marlies	AHL	14	6	3	9	22	....	....	....	....	....	....	....	....	....	....	....	....	....	....	....	....	....	....
	Dynamo Moscow	KHL	13	2	8	10	42	....	....	....	....	....	....	....	....	....	....	....	....	....	....	....	....	....	....
	Toronto	NHL	42	4	5	9	18	0	0	3	51	7.8	–1	57	50.9	13:56	7	0	0	0	17	0	0	0	9:13
	NHL Totals		42	4	5	9	18	0	0	3	51	7.8		57	50.9	13:56	7	0	0	0	17	0	0	0	9:13

Signed as a free agent by **Dynamo Moscow** (KHL), November 16, 2012.

KOMISAREK, Mike

(koh-mih-SAIR-ehk, MIGHK) **CAR**

Defense. Shoots right. 6'4", 235 lbs. Born, West Islip, NY, January 19, 1982. Montreal's 1st choice, 7th overall, in 2001 Entry Draft.

1998-99	N.E. Jr. Coyotes	EJHL	53	17	24	51	....	....	....	....	....	....	....	....	....	....	....	....	....	....	....	....	....	....	....
99-2000	USNTDP	U-18	6	0	0	0	12	....	....	....	....	....	....	....	....	....	....	....	....	....	....	....	....	....	....
	USNTDP	USHL	51	5	8	13	124	....	....	....	....	....	....	....	....	....	....	....	....	....	....	....	....	....	....
	USNTDP	NAHL	1	0	0	0	16	....	....	....	....	....	....	....	....	....	....	....	....	....	....	....	....	....	....
2000-01	U. of Michigan	CCHA	41	4	12	16	77	....	....	....	....	....	....	....	....	....	....	....	....	....	....	....	....	....	....
2001-02	U. of Michigan	CCHA	40	11	19	30	70	....	....	....	....	....	....	....	....	....	....	....	....	....	....	....	....	....	....
2002-03	Montreal	NHL	21	0	1	1	28	0	0	0	26	0.0	–6	0	0.0	16:42	....	....	....	....	....	....	....	....	....
	Hamilton	AHL	56	5	25	30	79	....	....	....	....	....	....	....	....	....	23	1	5	6	60	....	....	....	....
2003-04	Montreal	NHL	46	0	4	4	34	0	0	0	40	0.0	4	0	0.0	12:00	7	0	0	0	8	0	0	0	14:09
	Hamilton	AHL	18	2	7	9	47	....	....	....	....	....	....	....	....	....	....	....	....	....	....	....	....	....	....

Season	Club	League	GP	G	A	Pts	PIM	PP	SH	GW	S	%	+/-	TF	F%	Min	GP	G	A	Pts	PIM	PP	SH	GW	Min
			Regular Season														Playoffs								
2004-05	Hamilton	AHL	20	1	4	5	49	....	....	....	....	....	....	....	....	....	4	0	1	1	8	....	....	....	....
2005-06	Montreal	NHL	71	2	4	6	116	0	0	0	66	3.0	-1	0	0.0	14:40	6	0	0	0	10	0	0	0	18:35
2006-07	Montreal	NHL	82	4	15	19	96	0	2	1	78	5.1	7	0	0.0	19:16	....	....	....	....	....	....	....	....	....
2007-08	Montreal	NHL	75	4	13	17	101	0	0	1	75	5.3	9	1	0.0	21:09	12	1	2	3	18	0	0	1	20:02
2008-09	Montreal	NHL	66	2	9	11	121	0	0	0	56	3.6	0	0	0.0	20:37	4	0	0	0	20	0	0	0	19:00
2009-10	Toronto	NHL	34	0	4	4	40	0	0	0	35	0.0	-9	0	0.0	19:56	....	....	....	....	....	....	....	....	....
2010-11	Toronto	NHL	75	1	9	10	86	0	0	0	48	2.1	-8	0	0.0	13:38	....	....	....	....	....	....	....	....	....
2011-12	Toronto	NHL	45	1	4	5	41	0	0	0	34	2.9	-13	0	0.0	16:39	....	....	....	....	....	....	....	....	....
2012-13	Toronto	NHL	4	0	0	0	2	0	0	0	1	0.0	2	0	0.0	15:21	....	....	....	....	....	....	....	....	....
	Toronto Marlies	AHL	7	0	0	0	10	....	....	....	....	....	....	....	....	....	6	0	1	1	9	....	....	....	....
	NHL Totals		519	14	63	77	665	0	2	2	459	3.1		1	0.0	17:18	29	1	2	3	56	0	0	1	18:10

CCHA First All-Star Team (2002) • NCAA West First All-American Team (2002) • AHL All-Rookie Team (2003)

Played in NHL All-Star Game (2009)

Signed as a free agent by **Toronto**, July 1, 2009. • Missed majority of 2009-10 due to shoulder injury vs. Calgary, January 2, 2010 and resulting surgery. • Missed majorty of 2012-13 as a healthy reserve. Signed as a free agent by **Carolina**, July 5, 2013.

KONAN, Matthew (KOH-nan, MATH-yew) PHI

Defense. Shoots right. 6'4", 186 lbs. Born, Tustin, CA, September 3, 1991.

Season	Club	League	GP	G	A	Pts	PIM	PP	SH	GW	S	%	+/-	TF	F%	Min	GP	G	A	Pts	PIM	PP	SH	GW	Min
2007-08	Medicine Hat	WHL	42	0	4	4	21	....	....	....	....	....	....	....	....	....	3	0	0	0	0	....	....	....	....
2008-09	Medicine Hat	WHL	61	1	11	12	53	....	....	....	....	....	....	....	....	....	11	0	1	1	10	....	....	....	....
2009-10	Medicine Hat	WHL	65	5	15	20	117	....	....	....	....	....	....	....	....	....	12	1	4	5	10	....	....	....	....
2010-11	Medicine Hat	WHL	61	4	13	17	69	....	....	....	....	....	....	....	....	....	15	0	6	6	15	....	....	....	....
2011-12	Medicine Hat	WHL	72	9	45	54	73	....	....	....	....	....	....	....	....	....	8	2	3	5	14	....	....	....	....
2012-13	Adirondack	AHL	45	2	4	6	54	....	....	....	....	....	....	....	....	....	....	....	....	....	....	....	....	....	....
	Trenton Titans	ECHL	5	0	1	1	2	....	....	....	....	....	....	....	....	....	....	....	....	....	....	....	....	....	....
	Philadelphia	NHL	2	0	0	0	0	0	0	0	4	0.0	0	0	0.0	15:56	....	....	....	....	....	....	....	....	....
	NHL Totals		2	0	0	0	0	0	0	0	4	0.0		0	0.0	15:56	....	....	....	....	....	....	....	....	....

Signed as a free agent by **Philadelphia**, April 2, 2012.

KONOPKA, Zenon (kuh-NOHP-kah, ZEH-nohn) MIN

Center. Shoots left. 6', 209 lbs. Born, Niagara on the Lake, Ont., January 2, 1981.

Season	Club	League	GP	G	A	Pts	PIM	PP	SH	GW	S	%	+/-	TF	F%	Min	GP	G	A	Pts	PIM	PP	SH	GW	Min
1998-99	Ottawa 67's	OHL	56	7	8	15	62	....	....	....	....	....	....	....	....	....	7	0	0	0	2	....	....	....	....
99-2000	Ottawa 67's	OHL	59	8	11	19	107	....	....	....	....	....	....	....	....	....	11	1	2	3	8	....	....	....	....
2000-01	Ottawa 67's	OHL	66	20	45	65	120	....	....	....	....	....	....	....	....	....	20	7	13	20	47	....	....	....	....
2001-02	Ottawa 67's	OHL	61	18	68	86	100	....	....	....	....	....	....	....	....	....	13	8	6	14	49	....	....	....	....
2002-03	Wilkes-Barre	AHL	4	0	1	1	9	....	....	....	....	....	....	....	....	....	....	....	....	....	....	....	....	....	....
	Wheeling Nailers	ECHL	68	22	48	70	231	....	....	....	....	....	....	....	....	....	....	....	....	....	....	....	....	....	....
2003-04	Utah Grizzlies	AHL	43	7	4	11	198	....	....	....	....	....	....	....	....	....	....	....	....	....	....	....	....	....	....
	Idaho Steelheads	ECHL	23	6	22	28	82	....	....	....	....	....	....	....	....	....	17	9	8	17	30	....	....	....	....
2004-05	Cincinnati	AHL	75	17	29	46	212	....	....	....	....	....	....	....	....	....	12	3	3	6	26	....	....	....	....
2005-06	Anaheim	NHL	23	4	3	7	48	2	0	0	18	22.2	-4	142	53.5	7:19	....	....	....	....	....	....	....	....	....
	Portland Pirates	AHL	34	18	26	44	57	....	....	....	....	....	....	....	....	....	19	11	18	29	46	....	....	....	....
2006-07	Lada Togliatti	Russia	4	0	0	0	8	....	....	....	....	....	....	....	....	....	....	....	....	....	....	....	....	....	....
	Columbus	NHL	6	0	0	0	20	0	0	0	2	0.0	-2	22	63.6	5:00	....	....	....	....	....	....	....	....	....
	Portland Pirates	AHL	42	11	24	35	97	....	....	....	....	....	....	....	....	....	....	....	....	....	....	....	....	....	....
	Syracuse Crunch	AHL	20	9	11	20	70	....	....	....	....	....	....	....	....	....	....	....	....	....	....	....	....	....	....
2007-08	Columbus	NHL	3	0	0	0	15	0	0	0	4	0.0	0	21	52.4	7:54	....	....	....	....	....	....	....	....	....
	Syracuse Crunch	AHL	62	24	31	55	194	....	....	....	....	....	....	....	....	....	13	3	7	10	42	....	....	....	....
2008-09	Tampa Bay	NHL	7	0	1	1	29	0	0	0	6	0.0	-1	25	68.0	7:01	....	....	....	....	....	....	....	....	....
	Norfolk Admirals	AHL	70	17	40	57	186	....	....	....	....	....	....	....	....	....	....	....	....	....	....	....	....	....	....
2009-10	Tampa Bay	NHL	74	2	3	5	*265	0	0	1	41	4.9	-11	462	62.3	8:08	....	....	....	....	....	....	....	....	....
2010-11	NY Islanders	NHL	82	2	7	9	*307	0	0	0	56	3.6	-14	1075	57.7	10:11	....	....	....	....	....	....	....	....	....
2011-12	Ottawa	NHL	55	3	2	5	193	1	0	1	34	8.8	-4	394	58.9	7:51	6	0	2	2	2	0	0	0	11:17
2012-13	Minnesota	NHL	37	0	0	0	117	0	0	0	18	0.0	-4	267	60.7	8:26	2	0	0	0	0	0	0	0	9:52
	NHL Totals		287	11	16	27	994	3	0	2	179	6.1		2408	59.0	8:33	8	0	2	2	2	0	0	0	10:56

ECHL All-Rookie Team (2003)

Signed as a free agent by **Utah** (AHL), September 10, 2003. Signed as a free agent by **Anaheim**, September 1, 2004. Signed as a free agent by **Togliatti** (Russia), July 26, 2006. Traded to **Columbus** by **Anaheim** with Curtis Glencross and Anaheim's 7th round choice (Trent Vogelhuber) in 2007 Entry Draft for Mark Hartigan, Joe Motzko and Columbus' 4th round choice (Sebastian Stefaniszin) in 2007 Entry Draft, January 26, 2007. Signed as a free agent by **Tampa Bay**, July 10, 2008. Signed as a free agent by **NY Islanders**, July 2, 2010. Signed as a free agent by **Ottawa**, July 5, 2011. Signed as a free agent by **Minnesota**, July 1, 2012.

KOPECKY, Tomas (koh-PEHTS-kee, TAW-mahsh) FLA

Center. Shoots left. 6'3", 203 lbs. Born, Ilava, Czech., February 5, 1982. Detroit's 2nd choice, 38th overall, in 2000 Entry Draft.

Season	Club	League	GP	G	A	Pts	PIM	PP	SH	GW	S	%	+/-	TF	F%	Min	GP	G	A	Pts	PIM	PP	SH	GW	Min
1997-98	Dukla Trencin Jr.	Slovak-Jr.	41	19	22	41	....	....	....	....	....	....	....	....	....	....	....	....	....	....	....	....	....	....	....
1998-99	Dukla Trencin Jr.	Slovak-Jr.	44	13	16	29	18	....	....	....	....	....	....	....	....	....	....	....	....	....	....	....	....	....	....
99-2000	Dukla Trencin Jr.	Slovak-Jr.	14	8	9	17	36	....	....	....	....	....	....	....	....	....	....	....	....	....	....	....	....	....	....
	Dukla Trencin	Slovakia	52	3	4	7	24	....	....	....	....	....	....	....	....	....	5	0	0	0	0	....	....	....	....
2000-01	Lethbridge	WHL	49	22	28	50	52	....	....	....	....	....	....	....	....	....	5	1	1	2	6	....	....	....	....
	Cincinnati	AHL	1	0	0	0	0	....	....	....	....	....	....	....	....	....	....	....	....	....	....	....	....	....	....
2001-02	Lethbridge	WHL	60	34	42	76	94	....	....	....	....	....	....	....	....	....	4	2	1	3	15	....	....	....	....
	Cincinnati	AHL	2	1	1	2	6	....	....	....	....	....	....	....	....	....	2	0	0	0	0	....	....	....	....
2002-03	Grand Rapids	AHL	70	17	21	38	32	....	....	....	....	....	....	....	....	....	14	0	0	0	6	....	....	....	....
2003-04	Grand Rapids	AHL	48	6	6	12	28	....	....	....	....	....	....	....	....	....	1	0	0	0	2	....	....	....	....
2004-05	Grand Rapids	AHL	48	8	8	16	35	....	....	....	....	....	....	....	....	....	....	....	....	....	....	....	....	....	....
2005-06	Detroit	NHL	1	0	0	0	2	0	0	0	1	0.0	1	0	0.0	9:41	....	....	....	....	....	....	....	....	....
	Grand Rapids	AHL	77	32	37	69	108	....	....	....	....	....	....	....	....	....	16	3	4	7	25	....	....	....	....
2006-07	Detroit	NHL	26	1	0	1	22	0	0	0	27	3.7	-2	5	40.0	7:15	4	0	0	0	6	0	0	0	3:38
2007-08 ♦	Detroit	NHL	77	5	7	12	43	0	0	1	87	5.7	2	109	40.4	9:37	....	....	....	....	....	....	....	....	....
2008-09	Detroit	NHL	79	6	13	19	46	1	1	2	110	5.5	-7	79	45.6	10:25	8	0	1	1	7	0	0	0	9:32
2009-10 ♦	Chicago	NHL	74	10	11	21	28	1	0	2	95	10.5	0	118	44.1	9:29	17	4	2	6	8	1	0	1	13:35
	Slovakia	Olympics	7	1	0	1	2	....	....	....	....	....	....	....	....	....	....	....	....	....	....	....	....	....	....
2010-11	Chicago	NHL	81	15	27	42	60	3	0	2	178	8.4	-13	284	42.3	15:19	1	0	0	0	0	0	0	0	2:22
2011-12	Florida	NHL	80	10	22	32	32	2	0	2	143	7.0	-8	266	52.6	17:16	7	1	0	1	4	0	1	0	15:23
2012-13	Dukla Trencin	Slovakia	5	2	2	4	0	....	....	....	....	....	....	....	....	....	....	....	....	....	....	....	....	....	....
	Florida	NHL	47	15	12	27	28	4	1	0	92	16.3	-8	86	48.8	17:41	....	....	....	....	....	....	....	....	....
	NHL Totals		465	62	92	154	261	11	2	9	733	8.5		947	46.0	12:43	37	5	3	8	25	1	1	1	11:40

• Missed majority of 2006-07 due to broken collarbone vs. Chicago, December 14, 2006. Signed as a free agent by **Chicago**, July 1, 2009. Traded to **Florida** by **Chicago** for Florida's 7th round choice (later traded to Buffalo – Buffalo selected Judd Peterson) in 2012 Entry Draft June 27, 2011. Signed as a free agent by **Trencin** (Slovokia), October 13, 2012.

KOPITAR, Anze (KOH-pih-tahr, AHN-zheh) L.A.

Center. Shoots left. 6'3", 225 lbs. Born, Jesenice, Yugoslavia, August 24, 1987. Los Angeles' 1st choice, 11th overall, in 2005 Entry Draft.

Season	Club	League	GP	G	A	Pts	PIM	PP	SH	GW	S	%	+/-	TF	F%	Min	GP	G	A	Pts	PIM	PP	SH	GW	Min
2002-03	Jesenice U18	Sloven-U18	14	38	38	76	10	....	....	....	....	....	....	....	....	....	....	....	....	....	....	....	....	....	....
	Jesenice Jr.	Sloven-Jr.	20	15	12	27	8	....	....	....	....	....	....	....	....	....	....	....	....	....	....	....	....	....	....
	Kranjska Gora	Slovenia	11	4	4	8	4	....	....	....	....	....	....	....	....	....	....	....	....	....	....	....	....	....	....
2003-04	Jesenice Jr.	Sloven-Jr.	25	32	28	60	16	....	....	....	....	....	....	....	....	....	....	....	....	....	....	....	....	....	....
	Kranjska Gora	Slovenia	21	14	11	25	10	....	....	....	....	....	....	....	....	....	4	1	1	2	0	....	....	....	....
2004-05	Sodertalje SK U18	Swe-U18	1	1	2	3	0	....	....	....	....	....	....	....	....	....	1	0	0	0	2	....	....	....	....
	Sodertalje SK Jr.	Swe-Jr.	30	28	21	49	26	....	....	....	....	....	....	....	....	....	2	1	1	2	0	....	....	....	....
	Sodertalje SK	Sweden	5	0	0	0	0	....	....	....	....	....	....	....	....	....	10	0	0	0	0	....	....	....	....
	Slovenia	Oly-Q	3	1	1	2	2	....	....	....	....	....	....	....	....	....	....	....	....	....	....	....	....	....	....
2005-06	Sodertalje SK	Sweden	47	8	12	20	28	....	....	....	....	....	....	....	....	....	....	....	....	....	....	....	....	....	....
	Sodertalje SK	Sweden-Q	10	7	4	11	6	....	....	....	....	....	....	....	....	....	....	....	....	....	....	....	....	....	....
2006-07	Los Angeles	NHL	72	20	41	61	24	7	2	1	193	10.4	-12	1204	46.1	20:32	....	....	....	....	....	....	....	....	....
2007-08	Los Angeles	NHL	82	32	45	77	22	12	2	3	201	15.9	-15	1150	49.2	20:41	....	....	....	....	....	....	....	....	....
2008-09	Los Angeles	NHL	82	27	39	66	32	7	1	3	234	11.5	-17	1355	49.5	20:27	....	....	....	....	....	....	....	....	....
2009-10	Los Angeles	NHL	82	34	47	81	16	14	1	2	259	13.1	6	1211	49.7	21:47	6	2	3	5	2	1	0	1	21:13
2010-11	Los Angeles	NHL	75	25	48	73	20	6	1	6	233	10.7	25	1160	49.9	21:35	....	....	....	....	....	....	....	....	....

			Regular Season														Playoffs								
Season	Club	League	GP	G	A	Pts	PIM	PP	SH	GW	S	%	+/-	TF	F%	Min	GP	G	A	Pts	PIM	PP	SH	GW	Min
2011-12 ♦	**Los Angeles**	**NHL**	**82**	**25**	**51**	**76**	**20**	**8**	**2**	**2**	**230**	**10.9**	**12**	**1418**	**53.8**	**21:20**	**20**	***8**	***12**	***20**	**9**	**0**	***2**	**1**	**22:03**
2012-13	Mora IK	Sweden-2	31	10	24	34	14	....	....	....	....	....	....	....	....	....	....	....	....	....	....	....	....	....	....
	Los Angeles	**NHL**	**47**	**10**	**32**	**42**	**16**	**0**	**0**	**1**	**98**	**10.2**	**14**	**888**	**53.3**	**20:29**	**18**	**3**	**6**	**9**	**12**	**1**	**0**	**1**	**21:15**
	NHL Totals		**522**	**173**	**303**	**476**	**150**	**54**	**9**	**18**	**1448**	**11.9**		**8386**	**50.2**	**21:01**	**44**	**13**	**21**	**34**	**23**	**2**	**2**	**3**	**21:37**

Played in NHL All-Star Game (2008, 2011)
Signed as a free agent by **Mora** (Sweden-2), September 19, 2012.

KORPIKOSKI, Lauri

(kohr-pih-KAWS-kee, LOW-ree) **PHX**

Left wing. Shoots left. 6'1", 205 lbs. Born, Turku, Finland, July 28, 1986. NY Rangers' 2nd choice, 19th overall, in 2004 Entry Draft.

Season	Club	League	GP	G	A	Pts	PIM	PP	SH	GW	S	%	+/-	TF	F%	Min	GP	G	A	Pts	PIM	PP	SH	GW	Min
2002-03	TPS Turku U18	Fin-U18	21	7	4	11	10	....	....	....	....	....	....	....	....	....	....	....	....	....	....	....	....	....	....
2003-04	TPS Turku U18	Fin-U18	....	....	....	....	....	....	....	....	....	....	....	....	....	....	4	5	3	8	16	....	....	....	....
	TPS Turku Jr.	Fin-Jr.	36	12	8	20	20	....	....	....	....	....	....	....	....	....	4	0	2	2	4	....	....	....	....
2004-05	TPS Turku Jr.	Fin-Jr.	3	3	0	3	0	....	....	....	....	....	....	....	....	....	....	....	....	....	....	....	....	....	....
	TPS Turku	Finland	41	0	6	6	12	....	....	....	....	....	....	....	....	....	6	1	0	1	0	....	....	....	....
2005-06	TPS Turku Jr.	Fin-Jr.	1	1	0	1	2	....	....	....	....	....	....	....	....	....	....	....	....	....	....	....	....	....	....
	Suomi U20	Finland-2	3	1	3	4	0	....	....	....	....	....	....	....	....	....	....	....	....	....	....	....	....	....	....
	TPS Turku	Finland	51	3	4	7	16	....	....	....	....	....	....	....	....	....	2	0	1	1	0	....	....	....	....
	Hartford	AHL	5	2	1	3	0	....	....	....	....	....	....	....	....	....	11	1	0	1	2	....	....	....	....
2006-07	Hartford	AHL	78	11	27	38	23	....	....	....	....	....	....	....	....	....	7	0	0	0	0	....	....	....	....
2007-08	Hartford	AHL	79	23	27	50	71	....	....	....	....	....	....	....	....	....	5	1	1	2	0	....	....	....	....
	NY Rangers	**NHL**	....	....	....	....	....	....	....	....	....	....	....	....	....	....	**1**	**1**	**0**	**1**	**0**	**0**	**0**	**0**	**7:14**
2008-09	**NY Rangers**	**NHL**	**68**	**6**	**8**	**14**	**14**	**0**	**0**	**1**	**63**	**9.5**	**–10**	**220**	**40.0**	**10:55**	**7**	**0**	**2**	**2**	**0**	**0**	**0**	**0**	**13:10**
	Hartford	AHL	4	4	2	6	0	....	....	....	....	....	....	....	....	....	....	....	....	....	....	....	....	....	....
2009-10	**Phoenix**	**NHL**	**71**	**5**	**6**	**11**	**16**	**0**	**0**	**1**	**68**	**7.4**	**–10**	**49**	**28.6**	**12:18**	**7**	**1**	**0**	**1**	**2**	**0**	**1**	**0**	**16:16**
2010-11	**Phoenix**	**NHL**	**79**	**19**	**21**	**40**	**20**	**0**	**2**	**4**	**103**	**18.4**	**17**	**244**	**43.9**	**15:32**	**4**	**0**	**1**	**1**	**2**	**0**	**0**	**0**	**16:33**
2011-12	**Phoenix**	**NHL**	**82**	**17**	**20**	**37**	**14**	**0**	**3**	**3**	**146**	**11.6**	**3**	**87**	**26.4**	**17:08**	**11**	**0**	**0**	**0**	**2**	**0**	**0**	**0**	**18:16**
2012-13	TPS Turku	Finland	11	6	11	17	10	....	....	....	....	....	....	....	....	....	....	....	....	....	....	....	....	....	....
	Phoenix	**NHL**	**36**	**6**	**5**	**11**	**12**	**1**	**0**	**0**	**83**	**7.2**	**–3**	**16**	**37.5**	**17:07**	....	....	....	....	....	....	....	....	....
	NHL Totals		**336**	**53**	**60**	**113**	**76**	**1**	**5**	**9**	**463**	**11.4**		**616**	**38.6**	**14:29**	**30**	**2**	**3**	**5**	**6**	**0**	**1**	**0**	**16:01**

Traded to **Phoenix** by **NY Rangers** for Enver Lisin, July 13, 2009. Signed as a free agent by **TPS Turku** (Finland), October 2, 2012.

KOSTITSYN, Andrei

(kaws-TIHT-sihn, AWN-dray)

Left wing. Shoots left. 6', 214 lbs. Born, Novopolotsk, Belarus, February 3, 1985. Montreal's 1st choice, 10th overall, in 2003 Entry Draft.

Season	Club	League	GP	G	A	Pts	PIM	PP	SH	GW	S	%	+/-	TF	F%	Min	GP	G	A	Pts	PIM	PP	SH	GW	Min
99-2000	Belarus	WJ18-A	6	0	0	0	4	....	....	....	....	....	....	....	....	....	....	....	....	....	....	....	....	....	....
2000-01	Novopolotsk	Belarus	1	2	1	3	2	....	....	....	....	....	....	....	....	....	....	....	....	....	....	....	....	....	....
	Novopolotsk	EEHL	5	1	0	1	0	....	....	....	....	....	....	....	....	....	....	....	....	....	....	....	....	....	....
	Yunost Minsk	Belarus	3	1	4	5	8	....	....	....	....	....	....	....	....	....	....	....	....	....	....	....	....	....	....
	HC Vitebsk	Belarus	17	17	6	23	42	....	....	....	....	....	....	....	....	....	....	....	....	....	....	....	....	....	....
	Belarus	WJ18-B	5	7	7	*14	8	....	....	....	....	....	....	....	....	....	....	....	....	....	....	....	....	....	....
2001-02	Novopolotsk	Belarus	17	9	6	15	28	....	....	....	....	....	....	....	....	....	....	....	....	....	....	....	....	....	....
	Novopolotsk	EEHL	29	9	8	17	16	....	....	....	....	....	....	....	....	....	....	....	....	....	....	....	....	....	....
	Yunost Minsk	Belarus	6	2	0	2	8	....	....	....	....	....	....	....	....	....	....	....	....	....	....	....	....	....	....
	Belarus	WJC-A	6	3	0	3	0	....	....	....	....	....	....	....	....	....	....	....	....	....	....	....	....	....	....
2002-03	CSKA Moscow	Russia	6	0	0	0	2	....	....	....	....	....	....	....	....	....	....	....	....	....	....	....	....	....	....
	Voskresensk	Russia-2	2	1	1	2	0	....	....	....	....	....	....	....	....	....	....	....	....	....	....	....	....	....	....
	Yunost Minsk	Belarus	4	6	4	10	43	....	....	....	....	....	....	....	....	....	....	....	....	....	....	....	....	....	....
	CSKA Moscow 2	Russia-3	3	2	2	4	25	....	....	....	....	....	....	....	....	....	....	....	....	....	....	....	....	....	....
	Belarus	WC-A	2	1	0	1	2	....	....	....	....	....	....	....	....	....	....	....	....	....	....	....	....	....	....
2003-04	CSKA Moscow 2	Russia-3	STATISTICS NOT AVAILABLE																						
	CSKA Moscow	Russia	12	0	1	1	2	....	....	....	....	....	....	....	....	....	....	....	....	....	....	....	....	....	....
	Yunost Minsk	Belarus	STATISTICS NOT AVAILABLE																						
2004-05	Hamilton	AHL	66	12	11	23	24	....	....	....	....	....	....	....	....	....	3	0	0	0	0	....	....	....	....
2005-06	**Montreal**	**NHL**	**12**	**2**	**1**	**3**	**2**	**0**	**0**	**0**	**9**	**22.2**	**1**	**1**	**0.0**	**7:32**	....	....	....	....	....	....	....	....	....
	Hamilton	AHL	64	18	29	47	76	....	....	....	....	....	....	....	....	....	....	....	....	....	....	....	....	....	....
2006-07	**Montreal**	**NHL**	**22**	**1**	**10**	**11**	**6**	**0**	**0**	**0**	**38**	**2.6**	**3**	**1**	**0.0**	**13:17**	....	....	....	....	....	....	....	....	....
	Hamilton	AHL	50	21	31	52	50	....	....	....	....	....	....	....	....	....	....	....	....	....	....	....	....	....	....
2007-08	**Montreal**	**NHL**	**78**	**26**	**27**	**53**	**29**	**12**	**0**	**5**	**156**	**16.7**	**15**	**6**	**66.7**	**15:41**	**12**	**5**	**3**	**8**	**2**	**1**	**0**	**1**	**16:01**
2008-09	**Montreal**	**NHL**	**74**	**23**	**18**	**41**	**50**	**6**	**0**	**2**	**169**	**13.6**	**–7**	**6**	**50.0**	**15:35**	**4**	**1**	**0**	**1**	**2**	**0**	**0**	**0**	**14:15**
2009-10	**Montreal**	**NHL**	**59**	**15**	**18**	**33**	**32**	**6**	**0**	**2**	**136**	**11.0**	**1**	**6**	**16.7**	**15:59**	**19**	**3**	**5**	**8**	**12**	**1**	**0**	**0**	**14:15**
2010-11	**Montreal**	**NHL**	**81**	**20**	**25**	**45**	**36**	**5**	**0**	**6**	**196**	**10.2**	**3**	**2**	**0.0**	**15:53**	**6**	**2**	**0**	**2**	**6**	**0**	**0**	**0**	**18:19**
2011-12	**Montreal**	**NHL**	**53**	**12**	**12**	**24**	**16**	**3**	**0**	**3**	**93**	**12.9**	**–8**	**16**	**18.8**	**15:11**	....	....	....	....	....	....	....	....	....
	Nashville	**NHL**	**19**	**4**	**8**	**12**	**10**	**2**	**0**	**2**	**29**	**13.8**	**7**	**1**	**0.0**	**14:56**	**8**	**3**	**1**	**4**	**2**	**0**	**0**	**0**	**15:30**
2012-13	Chelyabinsk	KHL	44	13	8	21	82	....	....	....	....	....	....	....	....	....	23	3	7	10	10	....	....	....	....
	NHL Totals		**398**	**103**	**119**	**222**	**181**	**34**	**0**	**20**	**826**	**12.5**		**39**	**28.2**	**15:16**	**49**	**14**	**9**	**23**	**24**	**2**	**0**	**1**	**15:23**

Traded to **Nashville** by **Montreal** for Nashville's 2nd round choice (Jacob De Rose) in 2013 Entry Draft and Montreal's 5th round choice (previously acquired, later traded to Los Angeles – Los Angeles selected Patrik Bartosak) in 2013 Entry Draft, February 27, 2012. Signed as a free agent by **Chelyabinsk** (KHL), September 14, 2012.

KOSTITSYN, Sergei

(kaws-TIHT-sihn, SAIR-gay)

Left wing. Shoots left. 6', 196 lbs. Born, Novopolotsk, Belarus, March 20, 1987. Montreal's 6th choice, 200th overall, in 2005 Entry Draft.

Season	Club	League	GP	G	A	Pts	PIM	PP	SH	GW	S	%	+/-	TF	F%	Min	GP	G	A	Pts	PIM	PP	SH	GW	Min
2003-04	HK Gomel	EEHL	6	0	1	1	0	....	....	....	....	....	....	....	....	....	....	....	....	....	....	....	....	....	....
	HK Gomel 2	EEHL-B	6	7	2	9	14	....	....	....	....	....	....	....	....	....	....	....	....	....	....	....	....	....	....
	Yunior Minsk	EEHL-B	STATISTICS NOT AVAILABLE																						
	Yunior Minsk	Belarus	3	0	0	0	0	....	....	....	....	....	....	....	....	....	....	....	....	....	....	....	....	....	....
	HK Gomel	Belarus	22	5	4	9	4	....	....	....	....	....	....	....	....	....	11	1	2	3	8	....	....	....	....
2004-05	HK Gomel	BelOpen	40	4	10	14	24	....	....	....	....	....	....	....	....	....	4	2	0	2	12	....	....	....	....
	Belarus	WJ18-B	4	1	5	6	4	....	....	....	....	....	....	....	....	....	....	....	....	....	....	....	....	....	....
2005-06	London Knights	OHL	63	26	52	78	78	....	....	....	....	....	....	....	....	....	19	13	24	37	*44	....	....	....	....
2006-07	London Knights	OHL	59	40	*91	131	76	....	....	....	....	....	....	....	....	....	16	9	12	21	39	....	....	....	....
2007-08	**Montreal**	**NHL**	**52**	**9**	**18**	**27**	**51**	**3**	**1**	**0**	**49**	**18.4**	**9**	**23**	**34.8**	**14:21**	**12**	**3**	**5**	**8**	**14**	**0**	**0**	**0**	**15:09**
	Hamilton	AHL	22	6	16	22	18	....	....	....	....	....	....	....	....	....	....	....	....	....	....	....	....	....	....
2008-09	**Montreal**	**NHL**	**56**	**8**	**15**	**23**	**64**	**5**	**0**	**1**	**74**	**10.8**	**–3**	**9**	**33.3**	**14:08**	**1**	**0**	**0**	**0**	**2**	**0**	**0**	**0**	**12:10**
	Hamilton	AHL	16	5	8	13	18	....	....	....	....	....	....	....	....	....	....	....	....	....	....	....	....	....	....
2009-10	**Montreal**	**NHL**	**47**	**7**	**11**	**18**	**8**	**0**	**0**	**2**	**59**	**11.9**	**4**	**7**	**14.3**	**14:10**	**5**	**0**	**0**	**0**	**0**	**0**	**0**	**0**	**7:59**
	Hamilton	AHL	16	4	9	13	2	....	....	....	....	....	....	....	....	....	....	....	....	....	....	....	....	....	....
	Belarus	Olympics	4	2	3	5	0	....	....	....	....	....	....	....	....	....	....	....	....	....	....	....	....	....	....
2010-11	**Nashville**	**NHL**	**77**	**23**	**27**	**50**	**20**	**4**	**1**	**2**	**93**	**24.7**	**10**	**6**	**16.7**	**15:11**	**12**	**0**	**5**	**5**	**2**	**0**	**0**	**0**	**18:21**
2011-12	**Nashville**	**NHL**	**75**	**17**	**26**	**43**	**34**	**1**	**1**	**3**	**97**	**17.5**	**8**	**6**	**0.0**	**16:28**	**10**	**1**	**1**	**2**	**4**	**0**	**0**	**1**	**15:44**
2012-13	Omsk	KHL	27	9	19	28	42	....	....	....	....	....	....	....	....	....	....	....	....	....	....	....	....	....	....
	Nashville	**NHL**	**46**	**3**	**12**	**15**	**11**	**1**	**0**	**0**	**42**	**7.1**	**–5**	**4**	**75.0**	**16:43**	....	....	....	....	....	....	....	....	....
	NHL Totals		**353**	**67**	**109**	**176**	**188**	**14**	**3**	**8**	**414**	**16.2**		**55**	**29.1**	**15:14**	**40**	**4**	**11**	**15**	**22**	**0**	**0**	**1**	**15:17**

OHL All-Rookie Team (2006)
Traded to **Nashville** by **Montreal** with future considerations for Dan Ellis, Dustin Boyd and future considerations, June 29, 2010. Signed as a free agent by **Omsk** (KHL), October 7, 2012.

KOSTKA, Mike

(KOHST-kuh, MIGHK) **CHI**

Defense. Shoots right. 6'1", 200 lbs. Born, Etobicoke, Ont., November 28, 1985.

Season	Club	League	GP	G	A	Pts	PIM	PP	SH	GW	S	%	+/-	TF	F%	Min	GP	G	A	Pts	PIM	PP	SH	GW	Min
2001-02	Ajax Axemen	ON-Jr.A	19	1	4	5	8	....	....	....	....	....	....	....	....	....	....	....	....	....	....	....	....	....	....
2002-03	Ajax Axemen	ON-Jr.A	39	4	11	15	32	....	....	....	....	....	....	....	....	....	....	....	....	....	....	....	....	....	....
2003-04	Aurora Tigers	ON-Jr.A	42	9	27	36	4	....	....	....	....	....	....	....	....	....	....	....	....	....	....	....	....	....	....
2004-05	Massachusetts	H-East	32	1	5	6	14	....	....	....	....	....	....	....	....	....	....	....	....	....	....	....	....	....	....
2005-06	Massachusetts	H-East	36	2	6	8	20	....	....	....	....	....	....	....	....	....	....	....	....	....	....	....	....	....	....
2006-07	Massachusetts	H-East	39	3	15	18	20	....	....	....	....	....	....	....	....	....	....	....	....	....	....	....	....	....	....
2007-08	Massachusetts	H-East	36	9	12	21	20	....	....	....	....	....	....	....	....	....	....	....	....	....	....	....	....	....	....
	Rochester	AHL	1	0	0	0	2	....	....	....	....	....	....	....	....	....	....	....	....	....	....	....	....	....	....
2008-09	Portland Pirates	AHL	80	4	26	30	33	....	....	....	....	....	....	....	....	....	4	1	0	1	6	....	....	....	....
2009-10	Portland Pirates	AHL	76	2	25	27	37	....	....	....	....	....	....	....	....	....	4	0	0	0	0	....	....	....	....
2010-11	Rochester	AHL	80	16	38	54	46	....	....	....	....	....	....	....	....	....	....	....	....	....	....	....	....	....	....

			Regular Season														Playoffs								
Season	Club	League	GP	G	A	Pts	PIM	PP	SH	GW	S	%	+/-	TF	F%	Min	GP	G	A	Pts	PIM	PP	SH	GW	Min
2011-12	San Antonio	AHL	18	2	4	6	14	....	....	....	....	....	....	....	....	....	....	....	....	....	....	....	....	....	....
	Norfolk Admirals	AHL	52	7	25	32	43	....	....	....	....	....	....	....	....	....	18	6	6	12	8	....	....	....	....
2012-13	Toronto Marlies	AHL	34	6	28	34	38	....	....	....	....	....	....	....	....	....	....	....	....	....	....	....	....	....	....
	Toronto	NHL	35	0	8	8	27	0	0	0	49	0.0	–7	0	0.0	22:05	1	0	0	0	0	0	0	0	22:22
	NHL Totals		35	0	8	8	27	0	0	0	49	0.0		0	0.0	22:05	1	0	0	0	0	0	0	0	22:22

Hockey East Second All-Star Team (2008)

Signed as a free agent by **Buffalo**, March 25, 2008. Signed as a free agent by **Rochester** (AHL), August 25, 2010. Traded to **Tampa Bay** by **Florida** with Evan Oberg for James Wright and Mike Vernace, December 2, 2011. Signed as a free agent by **Toronto**, July 1, 2012. Signed as a free agent by **Chicago**, July 19, 2013.

KOSTOPOULOS, Tom

(kaw-STAWP-oh-lihs, TAWM)

Right wing. Shoots right. 6', 197 lbs. Born, Mississauga, Ont., January 24, 1979. Pittsburgh's 9th choice, 204th overall, in 1999 Entry Draft.

Season	Club	League	GP	G	A	Pts	PIM	PP	SH	GW	S	%	+/-	TF	F%	Min	GP	G	A	Pts	PIM	PP	SH	GW	Min
1995-96	Brampton	ON-Jr.A	24	9	9	18	28	....	....	....	....	....	....	....	....	....	....	....	....	....	....	....	....	....	....
1996-97	London Knights	OHL	64	13	12	25	67	....	....	....	....	....	....	....	....	....	....	....	....	....	....	....	....	....	....
1997-98	London Knights	OHL	66	24	26	50	108	....	....	....	....	....	....	....	....	....	16	6	4	10	26	....	....	....	....
1998-99	London Knights	OHL	66	27	60	87	114	....	....	....	....	....	....	....	....	....	25	19	16	35	32	....	....	....	....
99-2000	Wilkes-Barre	AHL	76	26	32	58	121	....	....	....	....	....	....	....	....	....	....	....	....	....	....	....	....	....	....
2000-01	Wilkes-Barre	AHL	80	16	36	52	120	....	....	....	....	....	....	....	....	....	21	3	9	12	6	....	....	....	....
2001-02	Pittsburgh	NHL	11	1	2	3	9	0	0	0	8	12.5	–1	0	0.0	12:03	....	....	....	....	....	....	....	....	....
	Wilkes-Barre	AHL	70	27	26	53	112	....	....	....	....	....	....	....	....	....	....	....	....	....	....	....	....	....	....
2002-03	Pittsburgh	NHL	8	0	1	1	0	0	0	0	6	0.0	–4	2	0.0	4:33	....	....	....	....	....	....	....	....	....
	Wilkes-Barre	AHL	71	21	42	63	131	....	....	....	....	....	....	....	....	....	6	1	2	3	7	....	....	....	....
2003-04	Pittsburgh	NHL	60	9	13	22	67	2	1	1	101	8.9	–14	10	30.0	14:26	....	....	....	....	....	....	....	....	....
	Wilkes-Barre	AHL	21	7	13	20	43	....	....	....	....	....	....	....	....	....	24	7	16	23	32	....	....	....	....
2004-05	Manchester	AHL	64	25	46	71	99	....	....	....	....	....	....	....	....	....	6	0	7	7	10	....	....	....	....
2005-06	Los Angeles	NHL	76	8	14	22	100	0	0	1	74	10.8	–8	30	36.7	12:56	....	....	....	....	....	....	....	....	....
2006-07	Los Angeles	NHL	76	7	15	22	73	0	0	0	90	7.8	–2	62	29.0	11:34	....	....	....	....	....	....	....	....	....
2007-08	Montreal	NHL	67	7	6	13	113	0	3	1	98	7.1	–3	28	28.6	11:16	12	3	1	4	6	0	0	1	13:35
2008-09	Montreal	NHL	78	8	14	22	106	0	1	0	121	6.6	–1	16	31.3	14:09	4	0	1	1	4	0	0	0	14:01
2009-10	Carolina	NHL	82	8	13	21	106	0	2	0	103	7.8	4	21	47.6	12:31	....	....	....	....	....	....	....	....	....
2010-11	Carolina	NHL	17	1	3	4	30	0	0	0	13	7.7	–1	14	28.6	11:17	....	....	....	....	....	....	....	....	....
	Calgary	NHL	59	7	7	14	44	2	0	0	66	10.6	–3	53	26.4	12:38	....	....	....	....	....	....	....	....	....
2011-12	Calgary	NHL	81	4	8	12	57	1	1	1	91	4.4	–15	84	29.8	12:19	....	....	....	....	....	....	....	....	....
2012-13	Wilkes-Barre	AHL	17	3	4	7	43	....	....	....	....	....	....	....	....	....	....	....	....	....	....	....	....	....	....
	New Jersey	NHL	15	1	0	1	18	0	0	0	13	7.7	0	5	60.0	9:06	....	....	....	....	....	....	....	....	....
	NHL Totals		630	61	96	157	723	5	8	4	784	7.8		325	31.1	12:28	16	3	2	5	10	0	0	1	13:41

Signed as a free agent by **Manchester** (AHL), July 12, 2004. Signed as a free agent by **Los Angeles**, August 1, 2005. Signed as a free agent by **Montreal**, July 4, 2007. Signed as a free agent by **Carolina**, July 14, 2009. Traded to **Calgary** by **Carolina** with Anton Babchuk for Ian White and Brett Sutter, November 17, 2010. Signed as a free Agent by **Wilkes-Barre** (AHL), January 23, 2013. Signed as a free agent by **Pittsburgh**, March 5, 2013. Claimed on waivers by **New Jersey** from **Pittsburgh**, March 6, 2013.

KOVALCHUK, Ilya

(koh-vuhl-CHUHK, IHL-yah)

Left wing. Shoots right. 6'3", 230 lbs. Born, Tver, USSR, April 15, 1983. Atlanta's 1st choice, 1st overall, in 2001 Entry Draft.

Season	Club	League	GP	G	A	Pts	PIM	PP	SH	GW	S	%	+/-	TF	F%	Min	GP	G	A	Pts	PIM	PP	SH	GW	Min
99-2000	Spartak Moscow	Russia-2	49	12	5	17	75	....	....	....	....	....	....	....	....	....	....	....	....	....	....	....	....	....	....
	Spartak 2	Russia-3	2	2	1	3	14	....	....	....	....	....	....	....	....	....	....	....	....	....	....	....	....	....	....
2000-01	Spartak Moscow	Russia-2	40	28	18	46	78	....	....	....	....	....	....	....	....	....	12	14	4	18	38	....	....	....	....
2001-02	Atlanta	NHL	65	29	22	51	28	7	0	4	184	15.8	–19	6	16.7	18:32	....	....	....	....	....	....	....	....	....
	Russia	Olympics	6	1	2	3	14	....	....	....	....	....	....	....	....	....	....	....	....	....	....	....	....	....	....
2002-03	Atlanta	NHL	81	38	29	67	57	9	0	3	257	14.8	–24	15	40.0	19:27	....	....	....	....	....	....	....	....	....
2003-04	Atlanta	NHL	81	*41	46	87	63	16	1	6	341	12.0	–10	28	32.1	23:41	....	....	....	....	....	....	....	....	....
2004-05	Ak Bars Kazan	Russia	53	19	23	42	72	....	....	....	....	....	....	....	....	....	4	0	1	1	0	....	....	....	....
2005-06	Atlanta	NHL	78	52	46	98	68	*27	0	7	323	16.1	–6	47	40.4	22:23	....	....	....	....	....	....	....	....	....
	Russia	Olympics	8	4	1	5	31	....	....	....	....	....	....	....	....	....	....	....	....	....	....	....	....	....	....
2006-07	Atlanta	NHL	82	42	34	76	66	18	0	7	336	12.5	–2	66	39.4	21:32	4	1	1	2	19	0	0	0	18:42
2007-08	Atlanta	NHL	79	52	35	87	52	16	2	4	283	18.4	–12	32	43.8	21:30	....	....	....	....	....	....	....	....	....
2008-09	Atlanta	NHL	79	43	48	91	50	12	0	6	275	15.6	–12	14	35.7	21:48	....	....	....	....	....	....	....	....	....
2009-10	Atlanta	NHL	49	31	27	58	45	10	0	3	179	17.3	1	23	21.7	22:14	....	....	....	....	....	....	....	....	....
	New Jersey	NHL	27	10	17	27	8	2	0	1	111	9.0	9	7	28.6	21:40	5	2	4	6	6	1	0	0	23:38
	Russia	Olympics	4	1	2	3	0	....	....	....	....	....	....	....	....	....	....	....	....	....	....	....	....	....	....
2010-11	New Jersey	NHL	81	31	29	60	28	9	0	9	245	12.7	–26	31	29.0	22:34	....	....	....	....	....	....	....	....	....
2011-12	New Jersey	NHL	77	37	46	83	33	10	3	5	310	11.9	–9	37	35.1	24:26	23	*8	11	19	6	*5	0	0	22:44
2012-13	St. Petersburg	KHL	36	18	24	42	12	....	....	....	....	....	....	....	....	....	....	....	....	....	....	....	....	....	....
	New Jersey	NHL	37	11	20	31	18	2	4	5	123	8.9	–6	22	31.8	24:44	....	....	....	....	....	....	....	....	....
	NHL Totals		816	417	399	816	516	138	10	60	2967	14.1		328	35.4	21:58	32	11	16	27	31	6	0	0	22:22

NHL All-Rookie Team (2002) • NHL Second All-Star Team (2004) • Maurice "Rocket" Richard Trophy (2004) (tied with Jarome Iginla and Rick Nash) • NHL First All-Star Team (2012)

Played in NHL All-Star Game (2004, 2008, 2009)

Signed as a free agent by **Kazan** (Russia) August 22, 2004. Traded to **New Jersey** by **Atlanta** with Anssi Salmela and Atlanta's 2nd round choice (Jonathon Merrill) in 2010 Entry Draft for Johnny Oduya, Niclas Bergfors, Patrice Cormier and New Jersey's 1st (later traded to Chicago - Chicago selected Kevin Hayes) and 2nd (later traded to Chicago - Chicago selected Justin Holl) round choices in 2010 Entry Draft, February 4, 2010. Signed as a free agent by **St. Petersburg** (KHL), September 15, 2012. • Officially announced his retirement from the NHL, July 11, 2013. Signed as a free agent by **St. Petersburg** (KHL), July 15, 2013.

KOVALEV, Alex

(koh-VAH-lehv, AL-ehx)

Right wing. Shoots left. 6'2", 222 lbs. Born, Togliatti, USSR, February 24, 1973. NY Rangers' 1st choice, 15th overall, in 1991 Entry Draft.

Season	Club	League	GP	G	A	Pts	PIM	PP	SH	GW	S	%	+/-	TF	F%	Min	GP	G	A	Pts	PIM	PP	SH	GW	Min
1989-90	Dynamo Moscow	USSR	1	0	0	0	0	....	....	....	....	....	....	....	....	....	....	....	....	....	....	....	....	....	....
1990-91	Dyn'o Moscow 2	USSR-3	21	16	....	....	....	....	....	....	....	....	....	....	....	....	....	....	....	....	....	....	....	....	....
	Dynamo Moscow	USSR	18	1	2	3	4	....	....	....	....	....	....	....	....	....	....	....	....	....	....	....	....	....	....
	Dynamo Moscow	Super-S	1	0	0	0	0	....	....	....	....	....	....	....	....	....	....	....	....	....	....	....	....	....	....
1991-92	Dynamo Moscow	CIS	33	16	9	25	20	....	....	....	....	....	....	....	....	....	....	....	....	....	....	....	....	....	....
	Dyn'o Moscow 2	CIS-3	4	5	0	5	12	....	....	....	....	....	....	....	....	....	....	....	....	....	....	....	....	....	....
	Russia	Olympics	8	1	2	3	14	....	....	....	....	....	....	....	....	....	....	....	....	....	....	....	....	....	....
1992-93	NY Rangers	NHL	65	20	18	38	79	3	0	3	134	14.9	–10	....	....	....	....	....	....	....	....	....	....	....	....
	Binghamton	AHL	13	13	11	24	35	....	....	....	....	....	....	....	....	....	9	3	5	8	14	....	....	....	....
1993-94 ♦	NY Rangers	NHL	76	23	33	56	154	7	0	3	184	12.5	18	....	....	....	23	9	12	21	18	5	0	2	....
1994-95	Lada Togliatti	CIS	12	8	8	16	49	....	....	....	....	....	....	....	....	....	....	....	....	....	....	....	....	....	....
	NY Rangers	NHL	48	13	15	28	30	1	1	1	103	12.6	–6	....	....	....	10	4	7	11	10	0	0	0	....
1995-96	NY Rangers	NHL	81	24	34	58	98	8	1	7	206	11.7	5	....	....	....	11	3	4	7	14	0	0	1	....
1996-97	NY Rangers	NHL	45	13	22	35	42	1	0	0	110	11.8	11	....	....	....	....	....	....	....	....	....	....	....	....
1997-98	NY Rangers	NHL	73	23	30	53	44	8	0	3	173	13.3	–22	....	....	....	....	....	....	....	....	....	....	....	....
1998-99	NY Rangers	NHL	14	3	4	7	12	1	0	1	35	8.6	–6	18	44.4	19:53	....	....	....	....	....	....	....	....	....
	Pittsburgh	NHL	63	20	26	46	37	5	1	4	156	12.8	8	226	43.4	20:30	10	5	7	12	14	0	0	1	20:24
99-2000	Pittsburgh	NHL	82	26	40	66	94	9	2	4	254	10.2	–3	306	47.4	22:53	11	1	5	6	10	0	0	0	26:35
2000-01	Pittsburgh	NHL	79	44	51	95	96	12	2	9	307	14.3	12	255	40.0	23:35	18	5	5	10	16	1	0	0	20:57
2001-02	Pittsburgh	NHL	67	32	44	76	80	8	1	3	266	12.0	2	179	45.3	24:03	....	....	....	....	....	....	....	....	....
	Russia	Olympics	6	3	1	4	4	....	....	....	....	....	....	....	....	....	....	....	....	....	....	....	....	....	....
2002-03	Pittsburgh	NHL	54	27	37	64	50	8	0	1	212	12.7	–11	19	31.6	24:03	....	....	....	....	....	....	....	....	....
	NY Rangers	NHL	24	10	3	13	20	3	0	2	59	16.9	2	19	42.1	20:09	....	....	....	....	....	....	....	....	....
2003-04	NY Rangers	NHL	66	13	29	42	54	3	0	0	178	7.3	–5	29	48.3	19:37	....	....	....	....	....	....	....	....	....
	Montreal	NHL	12	1	2	3	12	0	0	1	29	3.4	–4	2	50.0	15:36	11	6	4	10	8	1	0	1	20:11
2004-05	Ak Bars Kazan	Russia	35	10	12	22	80	....	....	....	....	....	....	....	....	....	4	0	0	0	8	....	....	....	....
2005-06	Montreal	NHL	69	23	42	65	76	9	0	5	206	11.2	–1	47	48.9	19:28	6	4	3	7	4	1	0	0	19:21
	Russia	Olympics	8	4	2	6	4	....	....	....	....	....	....	....	....	....	....	....	....	....	....	....	....	....	....
2006-07	Montreal	NHL	73	18	29	47	78	8	0	5	197	9.1	–19	162	46.3	18:15	....	....	....	....	....	....	....	....	....
2007-08	Montreal	NHL	82	35	49	84	70	17	0	5	230	15.2	18	58	55.2	19:33	12	5	6	11	8	2	1	1	21:41
2008-09	Montreal	NHL	78	26	39	65	74	11	1	4	209	12.4	–5	50	32.0	19:26	4	2	1	3	2	0	0	0	19:54
2009-10	Ottawa	NHL	77	18	31	49	54	4	0	5	165	10.9	–8	3	33.3	18:10	....	....	....	....	....	....	....	....	....
2010-11	Ottawa	NHL	54	14	13	27	28	6	0	3	123	11.4	–9	6	33.3	16:16	....	....	....	....	....	....	....	....	....
	Pittsburgh	NHL	20	2	5	7	16	0	0	0	28	7.1	3	4	25.0	17:10	7	1	1	2	10	0	0	1	16:02

Season	Club	League	GP	G	A	Pts	PIM	PP	SH	GW	S	%	+/-	TF	F%	Min	GP	G	A	Pts	PIM	PP	SH	GW	Min
			Regular Season														Playoffs								
2011-12	Mytischi	KHL	22	1	5	6	16																		
2012-13	Florida	NHL	14	2	3	5	6	1	0	1	21	9.5	−1	3	33.3	15:37									
	NHL Totals		1316	430	599	1029	1304	133	9	70	3585	12.0		1386	44.3	20:17	123	45	55	100	114	10	1	7	21:03

NHL Second All-Star Team (2008)

Played in NHL All-Star Game (2001, 2003, 2009)

Traded to **Pittsburgh** by **NY Rangers** with Harry York for Petr Nedved, Chris Tamer and Sean Pronger, November 25, 1998. Traded to **NY Rangers** by **Pittsburgh** with Mike Wilson, Janne Laukkanen and Dan LaCouture for Joel Bouchard, Richard Lintner, Rico Fata and Mikael Samuelsson, February 10, 2003. Traded to **Montreal** by **NY Rangers** for Jozef Balej and Montreal's 2nd round choice (Bruce Graham) in 2004 Entry Draft, March 2, 2004. Signed as a free agent by **Kazan** (Russia), November 3, 2004. Signed as a free agent by **Ottawa**, July 6, 2009. Traded to **Pittsburgh** by **Ottawa** for Pittsburgh's 7th round choice (Ryan Dzingel) in 2011 Entry Draft, February 24, 2011. Signed as a free agent by **Mytischi** (KHL), July 29, 2011. Signed as a free agent by **Florida**, January 18, 2013. • Officially announced his retirement, March 21, 2013. Signed as a free agent by **Visp** (Swiss), June 10, 2013.

KREIDER, Chris
(KRIGH-duhr, KRIHS) **NYR**

Center. Shoots left. 6'3", 226 lbs. Born, Boxford, MA, April 30, 1991. NY Rangers' 1st choice, 19th overall, in 2009 Entry Draft.

Season	Club	League	GP	G	A	Pts	PIM	PP	SH	GW	S	%	+/-	TF	F%	Min	GP	G	A	Pts	PIM	PP	SH	GW	Min
2005-06	Masconomet	High-MA	19	5	10	15																			
2006-07	Masconomet	High-MA	20	28	13	41																			
2007-08	Andover	High-MA	24	26	15	41																			
2008-09	Andover	High-MA	26	33	23	56	10																		
	Valley Jr. Warriors	Minor-MA	5	4	2	6																			
2009-10	Boston College	H-East	38	15	8	23	26																		
2010-11	Boston College	H-East	32	11	13	24	37																		
2011-12	Boston College	H-East	44	23	22	45	66																		
	NY Rangers	NHL															18	5	2	7	6	2	0	2	13:09
2012-13	Connecticut	AHL	48	12	11	23	73																		
	NY Rangers	NHL	23	2	1	3	6	0	0	0	19	10.5	−1	1	0.0	10:07	8	1	1	2	0	0	0	1	9:42
	NHL Totals		23	2	1	3	6	0	0	0	19	10.5		1	0.0	10:07	26	6	3	9	6	2	0	3	12:05

Hockey East All-Rookie Team (2010) • Hockey East Second All-Star Team (2012)

KREJCI, David
(KRAY-chee, DAY-vihd) **BOS**

Center. Shoots right. 6', 188 lbs. Born, Sternberk, Czech., April 28, 1986. Boston's 1st choice, 63rd overall, in 2004 Entry Draft.

Season	Club	League	GP	G	A	Pts	PIM	PP	SH	GW	S	%	+/-	TF	F%	Min	GP	G	A	Pts	PIM	PP	SH	GW	Min
2000-01	HC Olomouc U17	CzR-U17	26	2	6	8	4										3	1	1	2	0				
2001-02	HC Trinec U17	CzR-U17	48	32	27	59	30										6	2	4	6	2				
2002-03	HC Trinec U17	CzR-U17	22	12	24	36	42																		
	HC Trinec Jr.	CzRep-Jr.	12	4	5	9	2										12	5	5	10	8				
2003-04	HC Kladno Jr.	CzRep-Jr.	50	23	37	60	37										7	3	6	9	4				
2004-05	Gatineau	QMJHL	62	22	41	63	31										10	2	7	9	10				
2005-06	Gatineau	QMJHL	55	27	54	81	54										17	10	22	32	24				
2006-07	Boston	NHL	6	0	0	0	2	0	0	0	2	0.0	−3	14	28.6	4:24									
	Providence Bruins	AHL	69	31	43	74	47										13	3	13	16	22				
2007-08	Boston	NHL	56	6	21	27	20	1	1	0	73	8.2	−3	635	48.2	14:55	7	1	4	5	2	1	0	0	19:09
	Providence Bruins	AHL	25	7	21	28	19																		
2008-09	Boston	NHL	82	22	51	73	26	5	2	6	146	15.1	*37	1048	50.3	16:52	11	2	6	8	2	0	0	1	17:18
2009-10	Boston	NHL	79	17	35	52	26	6	0	3	156	10.9	8	1104	50.7	18:15	9	4	4	8	2	2	0	0	19:06
	Czech Republic	Olympics	5	2	1	3	6																		
2010-11 ♦	Boston	NHL	75	13	49	62	28	1	0	2	157	8.3	23	1149	48.7	18:51	25	*12	11	*23	10	2	0	4	20:07
2011-12	Boston	NHL	79	23	39	62	36	2	0	2	145	15.9	−5	1045	52.1	18:25	7	1	2	3	4	1	0	0	21:29
2012-13	Pardubice	CzRep	24	16	11	27	22																		
	Boston	NHL	47	10	23	33	20	0	0	5	93	10.8	1	654	55.2	18:30	22	9	*17	*26	14	1	0	2	22:15
	NHL Totals		424	91	218	309	158	15	3	18	772	11.8		5649	50.7	17:31	81	29	44	73	34	7	0	7	20:14

Signed as a free agent by **Pardubice** (CzRep), October 3, 2012.

KRONWALL, Niklas
(KRAWN-wahl, NIHK-luhs) **DET**

Defense. Shoots left. 6', 190 lbs. Born, Stockholm, Sweden, January 12, 1981. Detroit's 1st choice, 29th overall, in 2000 Entry Draft.

Season	Club	League	GP	G	A	Pts	PIM	PP	SH	GW	S	%	+/-	TF	F%	Min	GP	G	A	Pts	PIM	PP	SH	GW	Min
1996-97	Djurgarden Jr.	Swe-Jr.	1	0	0	0	0																		
1997-98	Djurgarden Jr.	Swe-Jr.	27	4	3	7	71										2	0	0	0	2				
1998-99	Huddinge IK	Sweden-2	14	0	1	1	10																		
	Huddinge IK Jr.	Swe-Jr.	2	0	0	0	6																		
99-2000	Djurgarden	Sweden	37	1	4	5	16										8	0	0	0	8				
2000-01	Djurgarden	Sweden	31	1	9	10	32										15	0	1	1	8				
2001-02	Djurgarden	Sweden	48	5	7	12	34										5	0	0	0	0				
2002-03	Djurgarden	Sweden	50	5	13	18	46										12	3	2	5	18				
2003-04	Detroit	NHL	20	1	4	5	16	0	0	1	18	5.6	5	0	0.0	13:51									
	Grand Rapids	AHL	25	2	11	13	20																		
2004-05	Grand Rapids	AHL	76	13	40	53	53																		
2005-06	Detroit	NHL	27	1	8	9	28	1	0	0	28	3.6	11	0	0.0	20:31	6	0	3	3	2	0	0	0	22:43
	Grand Rapids	AHL	1	0	0	0	0																		
	Sweden	Olympics	2	1	1	2	8																		
2006-07	Detroit	NHL	68	1	21	22	54	1	0	0	104	1.0	0	0	0.0	20:39									
2007-08 ♦	Detroit	NHL	65	7	28	35	44	0	0	0	108	6.5	25	0	0.0	21:06	22	0	15	15	18	0	0	0	23:20
2008-09	Detroit	NHL	80	6	45	51	50	4	0	1	121	5.0	2	1	100.0	22:54	23	2	7	9	33	2	0	0	23:24
2009-10	Detroit	NHL	48	7	15	22	32	3	0	0	68	10.3	5	0	0.0	21:55	12	0	5	5	12	0	0	0	23:15
	Sweden	Olympics	4	0	0	0	2																		
2010-11	Detroit	NHL	77	11	26	37	36	5	0	3	131	8.4	5	0	0.0	22:52	11	2	4	6	4	1	0	0	23:04
2011-12	Detroit	NHL	82	15	21	36	38	7	0	4	141	10.6	−2	0	0.0	22:52	5	0	2	2	4	0	0	0	22:32
2012-13	Detroit	NHL	48	5	24	29	44	2	0	2	67	7.5	−5	0	0.0	24:22	14	0	2	2	4	0	0	0	25:21
	NHL Totals		515	54	192	246	342	23	0	11	786	6.9		1	100.0	21:56	93	4	38	42	77	3	0	0	23:32

AHL First All-Star Team (2005) • Eddie Shore Award (AHL – Outstanding Defenseman) (2005)

• Missed majority of 2005-06 due to knee injury in pre-season game vs. Colorado, September 27, 2005..

KRUG, Torey
(KROOG, TOHR-ee) **BOS**

Defense. Shoots left. 5'9", 180 lbs. Born, Livonia, MI, April 12, 1991.

Season	Club	League	GP	G	A	Pts	PIM	PP	SH	GW	S	%	+/-	TF	F%	Min	GP	G	A	Pts	PIM	PP	SH	GW	Min
2008-09	Indiana Ice	USHL	59	10	37	47	50										13	1	6	7	13				
2009-10	Michigan State	CCHA	38	3	18	21	67																		
2010-11	Michigan State	CCHA	38	11	17	28	59																		
2011-12	Michigan State	CCHA	38	12	22	34	51																		
	Boston	NHL	2	0	1	1	0	0	0	0	3	0.0	0	0	0.0	17:08									
2012-13	Providence Bruins	AHL	63	13	32	45	37										7	0	3	3	2				
	Boston	NHL	1	0	1	1	0	0	0	0	0	0.0	−1	0	0.0	15:47	15	4	2	6	0	3	0	0	15:49
	NHL Totals		3	0	2	2	0	0	0	0	3	0.0		0	0.0	16:41	15	4	2	6	0	3	0	0	15:49

CCHA All-Rookie Team (2010) • CCHA First All-Star Team (2011, 2012) • CCHA Player of the Year (2012) • NCAA West First All-American Team (2012)

Signed as a free agent by **Boston**, March 25, 2012.

KRUGER, Marcus
(KROO-guhr, MAHR-kuhs) **CHI**

Center. Shoots left. 6', 181 lbs. Born, Stockholm, Sweden, May 27, 1990. Chicago's 5th choice, 149th overall, in 2009 Entry Draft.

Season	Club	League	GP	G	A	Pts	PIM	PP	SH	GW	S	%	+/-	TF	F%	Min	GP	G	A	Pts	PIM	PP	SH	GW	Min
2006-07	Djurgarden U18	Swe-U18	23	5	14	19	10										3	2	1	3	2				
2007-08	Djurgarden U18	Swe-U18	22	11	20	31	22										7	3	8	11	6				
	Djurgarden Jr.	Swe-Jr.	22	3	13	16	16										7	5	3	8	0				
2008-09	Djurgarden Jr.	Swe-Jr.	34	9	30	39	24										6	1	5	6	2				
	Djurgarden	Sweden	15	2	2	4	2																		
2009-10	Djurgarden	Sweden	38	11	20	31	14										16	3	7	10	6				
2010-11	Djurgarden	Sweden	52	6	29	35	52										3	0	1	1	0				
	Chicago	NHL	7	0	0	0	4	0	0	0	7	0.0	−4	39	35.9	11:58	5	0	1	1	0	0	0	0	11:51
2011-12	Chicago	NHL	71	9	17	26	22	0	0	1	89	10.1	11	619	45.9	15:24	6	0	0	0	0	0	0	0	17:48

Season	Club	League	GP	G	A	Pts	PIM	PP	SH	GW	S	%	+/-	TF	F%	Min	GP	G	A	Pts	PIM	PP	SH	GW	Min
			Regular Season														Playoffs								
2012-13	Rockford IceHogs	AHL	34	8	14	22	24	....	....	....	....	....	....	....	....	....	....	....	....	....	....	....	....	....	....
	♦ **Chicago**	**NHL**	**47**	**4**	**9**	**13**	**24**	**0**	**0**	**2**	**50**	**8.0**	**3**	**493**	**46.3**	**14:10**	**23**	**3**	**2**	**5**	**2**	**0**	**0**	**1**	**13:48**
	NHL Totals		**125**	**13**	**26**	**39**	**50**	**0**	**0**	**3**	**146**	**8.9**		**1151**	**45.7**	**14:45**	**34**	**3**	**3**	**6**	**2**	**0**	**0**	**1**	**14:13**

KUBA, Filip

(KOO-bah, FIHL-ihp)

Defense. Shoots left. 6'4", 225 lbs. Born, Ostrava, Czech., December 29, 1976. Florida's 8th choice, 192nd overall, in 1995 Entry Draft.

Season	Club	League	GP	G	A	Pts	PIM	PP	SH	GW	S	%	+/-	TF	F%	Min	GP	G	A	Pts	PIM	PP	SH	GW	Min
1994-95	HC Vitkovice Jr.	CzRep-Jr.	35	10	15	25	....	....	....	....	....	....	....	....	....	....	....	....	....	....	....	....	....	....	....
	HC Vitkovice	CzRep	....	....	....	....	....	....	....	....	....	....	....	....	....	....	4	0	0	0	2	....	....	....	....
1995-96	HC Vitkovice	CzRep	19	0	1	1	....	....	....	....	....	....	....	....	....	....	....	....	....	....	....	....	....	....	....
1996-97	Carolina	AHL	51	0	12	12	38	....	....	....	....	....	....	....	....	....	....	....	....	....	....	....	....	....	....
1997-98	New Haven	AHL	77	4	13	17	58	....	....	....	....	....	....	....	....	....	3	1	1	2	0	....	....	....	....
1998-99	**Florida**	**NHL**	**5**	**0**	**1**	**1**	**0**	**0**	**0**	**0**	**5**	**0.0**	**2**	**0**	**0.0**	**22:29**	....	....	....	....	....	....	....	....	....
	Kentucky	AHL	45	2	8	10	33	....	....	....	....	....	....	....	....	....	10	0	1	1	4	....	....	....	....
99-2000	**Florida**	**NHL**	**13**	**1**	**5**	**6**	**2**	**1**	**0**	**1**	**16**	**6.3**	**–3**	**0**	**0.0**	**13:52**	....	....	....	....	....	....	....	....	....
	Houston Aeros	IHL	27	3	6	9	13	....	....	....	....	....	....	....	....	....	11	1	2	3	4	....	....	....	....
2000-01	**Minnesota**	**NHL**	**75**	**9**	**21**	**30**	**28**	**4**	**0**	**4**	**141**	**6.4**	**–6**	**1**	**0.0**	**24:16**	....	....	....	....	....	....	....	....	....
2001-02	**Minnesota**	**NHL**	**62**	**5**	**19**	**24**	**32**	**3**	**0**	**1**	**101**	**5.0**	**–6**	**0**	**0.0**	**25:30**	....	....	....	....	....	....	....	....	....
2002-03	**Minnesota**	**NHL**	**78**	**8**	**21**	**29**	**29**	**4**	**2**	**1**	**129**	**6.2**	**0**	**1**	**0.0**	**23:56**	**18**	**3**	**5**	**8**	**24**	**3**	**0**	**0**	**26:46**
2003-04	**Minnesota**	**NHL**	**77**	**5**	**19**	**24**	**28**	**2**	**1**	**2**	**114**	**4.4**	**–7**	**2**	**0.0**	**24:06**	....	....	....	....	....	....	....	....	....
2004-05			DID NOT PLAY																						
2005-06	**Minnesota**	**NHL**	**65**	**6**	**19**	**25**	**44**	**1**	**1**	**1**	**69**	**8.7**	**0**	**2**	**0.0**	**21:46**	....	....	....	....	....	....	....	....	....
	Czech Republic	Olympics	8	1	0	1	0	....	....	....	....	....	....	....	....	....	....	....	....	....	....	....	....	....	....
2006-07	**Tampa Bay**	**NHL**	**81**	**15**	**22**	**37**	**36**	**5**	**1**	**2**	**106**	**14.2**	**–9**	**0**	**0.0**	**20:12**	**6**	**1**	**4**	**5**	**4**	**0**	**1**	**0**	**20:47**
2007-08	**Tampa Bay**	**NHL**	**75**	**6**	**25**	**31**	**40**	**2**	**0**	**0**	**113**	**5.3**	**–8**	**2**	**0.0**	**24:57**	....	....	....	....	....	....	....	....	....
2008-09	**Ottawa**	**NHL**	**71**	**3**	**37**	**40**	**28**	**2**	**0**	**0**	**111**	**2.7**	**4**	**0**	**0.0**	**23:17**	....	....	....	....	....	....	....	....	....
2009-10	**Ottawa**	**NHL**	**53**	**3**	**25**	**28**	**28**	**2**	**0**	**0**	**90**	**3.3**	**–5**	**1**	**0.0**	**22:51**	....	....	....	....	....	....	....	....	....
	Czech Republic	Olympics	5	0	1	1	0	....	....	....	....	....	....	....	....	....	....	....	....	....	....	....	....	....	....
2010-11	**Ottawa**	**NHL**	**64**	**2**	**14**	**16**	**16**	**0**	**0**	**1**	**76**	**2.6**	**–26**	**0**	**0.0**	**20:44**	....	....	....	....	....	....	....	....	....
2011-12	**Ottawa**	**NHL**	**73**	**6**	**26**	**32**	**26**	**3**	**0**	**2**	**78**	**7.7**	**26**	**0**	**0.0**	**23:37**	**7**	**0**	**2**	**2**	**10**	**0**	**0**	**0**	**23:26**
2012-13	Vitkovice	CzRep	11	0	4	4	10	....	....	....	....	....	....	....	....	....	....	....	....	....	....	....	....	....	....
	Florida	**NHL**	**44**	**1**	**9**	**10**	**24**	**0**	**0**	**0**	**50**	**2.0**	**–18**	**0**	**0.0**	**21:13**	....	....	....	....	....	....	....	....	....
	NHL Totals		**836**	**70**	**263**	**333**	**361**	**29**	**5**	**15**	**1199**	**5.8**		**9**	**0.0**	**22:57**	**31**	**4**	**11**	**15**	**38**	**3**	**1**	**0**	**24:51**

Played in NHL All-Star Game (2004)

Traded to **Calgary** by **Florida** for Rocky Thompson, March 16, 2000. Claimed by **Minnesota** from **Calgary** in Expansion Draft, June 23, 2000. Signed as a free agent by **Tampa Bay**, July 1, 2006. Traded to **Ottawa** by **Tampa Bay** with Alexandre Picard and San Jose's 1st round choice (previously acquired, later traded to NY Islanders, later traded to Columbus, later traded to Anaheim – Anaheim selected Kyle Palmieri) in 2009 Entry Draft for Andrej Meszaros, August 29, 2008. Signed as a free agent by **Florida**, July 1. 2012. Signed as a free agent by **Vitkovice** (CzRep), November 9, 2012.

KUBALIK, Tomas

(koo-BAHL-ihk, TAW-mahsh)

Right wing. Shoots right. 6'3", 209 lbs. Born, Plzen, Czech., May 1, 1990. Columbus' 6th choice, 135th overall, in 2008 Entry Draft.

Season	Club	League	GP	G	A	Pts	PIM	PP	SH	GW	S	%	+/-	TF	F%	Min	GP	G	A	Pts	PIM	PP	SH	GW	Min
2003-04	HC Plzen U17	CzR-U17	4	0	0	0	0	....	....	....	....	....	....	....	....	....	....	....	....	....	....	....	....	....	....
2004-05	HC Plzen U17	CzR-U17	37	4	1	5	18	....	....	....	....	....	....	....	....	....	....	....	....	....	....	....	....	....	....
2005-06	HC Plzen U17	CzR-U17	35	26	21	47	91	....	....	....	....	....	....	....	....	....	6	1	5	6	16	....	....	....	....
	HC Plzen Jr.	CzRep-Jr.	5	1	2	3	6	....	....	....	....	....	....	....	....	....	....	....	....	....	....	....	....	....	....
2006-07	HC Plzen U17	CzR-U17	2	4	1	5	6	....	....	....	....	....	....	....	....	....	8	5	5	10	30	....	....	....	....
	HC Plzen Jr.	CzRep-Jr.	34	23	15	38	76	....	....	....	....	....	....	....	....	....	3	1	2	3	24	....	....	....	....
	Plzen	CzRep	23	1	0	1	18	....	....	....	....	....	....	....	....	....	....	....	....	....	....	....	....	....	....
2007-08	HC Plzen Jr.	CzRep-Jr.	22	8	13	21	50	....	....	....	....	....	....	....	....	....	5	1	3	4	22	....	....	....	....
	Beroun	CzRep-2	7	0	0	0	2	....	....	....	....	....	....	....	....	....	....	....	....	....	....	....	....	....	....
	Plzen	CzRep	20	2	1	3	8	....	....	....	....	....	....	....	....	....	1	0	0	0	0	....	....	....	....
2008-09	HC Plzen Jr.	CzRep-Jr.	4	1	2	3	10	....	....	....	....	....	....	....	....	....	....	....	....	....	....	....	....	....	....
	Plzen	CzRep	32	1	1	2	64	....	....	....	....	....	....	....	....	....	17	1	0	1	8	....	....	....	....
2009-10	Victoriaville Tigres	QMJHL	58	33	42	75	95	....	....	....	....	....	....	....	....	....	16	4	10	14	8	....	....	....	....
2010-11	**Columbus**	**NHL**	**4**	**0**	**2**	**2**	**0**	**0**	**0**	**0**	**5**	**0.0**	**–3**	**1**	**100.0**	**14:45**	....	....	....	....	....	....	....	....	....
	Springfield	AHL	76	24	29	53	43	....	....	....	....	....	....	....	....	....	....	....	....	....	....	....	....	....	....
2011-12	**Columbus**	**NHL**	**8**	**1**	**1**	**2**	**6**	**0**	**0**	**0**	**8**	**12.5**	**–3**	**0**	**0.0**	**13:18**	....	....	....	....	....	....	....	....	....
	Springfield	AHL	50	11	12	23	42	....	....	....	....	....	....	....	....	....	....	....	....	....	....	....	....	....	....
2012-13	Springfield	AHL	54	14	6	20	50	....	....	....	....	....	....	....	....	....	....	....	....	....	....	....	....	....	....
	St. John's IceCaps	AHL	10	0	3	3	10	....	....	....	....	....	....	....	....	....	....	....	....	....	....	....	....	....	....
	NHL Totals		**12**	**1**	**3**	**4**	**6**	**0**	**0**	**0**	**13**	**7.7**		**1**	**100.0**	**13:47**	....	....	....	....	....	....	....	....	....

Traded to **Winnipeg** by **Columbus** for Spencer Machacek, March 10, 2013. Signed as a free agent by **Lev Praha** (KHL), June 7, 2013.

KULDA , Arturs

(KOOL-da, AHR-tuhrs)

Defense. Shoots left. 6'2", 215 lbs. Born, Riga, Latvia, July 25, 1988. Atlanta's 7th choice, 200th overall, in 2006 Entry Draft.

Season	Club	League	GP	G	A	Pts	PIM	PP	SH	GW	S	%	+/-	TF	F%	Min	GP	G	A	Pts	PIM	PP	SH	GW	Min
2003-04	Prizma/Riga 86	Latvia	11	0	0	0	8	....	....	....	....	....	....	....	....	....	2	0	0	0	0				
2004-05	CSKA Moscow 2	Russia-3	STATISTICS NOT AVAILABLE																						
2005-06	CSKA Moscow 2	Russia-3	44	5	12	17		....	....	....	....	....	....	....	....	....	....	....	....	....	....	....	....	....	....
2006-07	Peterborough	OHL	58	2	9	11	83	....	....	....	....	....	....	....	....	....	....	....	....	....	....	....	....	....	....
2007-08	Peterborough	OHL	55	7	27	34	87	....	....	....	....	....	....	....	....	....	5	1	3	4	6	....	....	....	....
	Chicago Wolves	AHL	5	0	1	1	10	....	....	....	....	....	....	....	....	....	22	1	5	6	32	....	....	....	....
2008-09	Chicago Wolves	AHL	57	1	14	15	59	....	....	....	....	....	....	....	....	....	....	....	....	....	....	....	....	....	....
2009-10	**Atlanta**	**NHL**	**4**	**0**	**2**	**2**	**2**	**0**	**0**	**0**	**5**	**0.0**	**2**	**0**	**0.0**	**11:59**	....	....	....	....	....	....	....	....	....
	Chicago Wolves	AHL	66	6	19	25	46	....	....	....	....	....	....	....	....	....	14	1	4	5	8	....	....	....	....
2010-11	**Atlanta**	**NHL**	**2**	**0**	**0**	**0**	**2**	**0**	**0**	**0**	**3**	**0.0**	**–2**	**0**	**0.0**	**11:06**	....	....	....	....	....	....	....	....	....
	Chicago Wolves	AHL	69	5	12	17	73	....	....	....	....	....	....	....	....	....	....	....	....	....	....	....	....	....	....
2011-12	**Winnipeg**	**NHL**	**9**	**0**	**0**	**0**	**4**	**0**	**0**	**0**	**8**	**0.0**	**3**	**0**	**0.0**	**10:52**	....	....	....	....	....	....	....	....	....
	St. John's IceCaps	AHL	63	6	14	20	62	....	....	....	....	....	....	....	....	....	13	0	1	1	8	....	....	....	....
2012-13	Sibir Novosibirsk	KHL	50	9	6	15	55	....	....	....	....	....	....	....	....	....	7	0	1	1	0	....	....	....	....
	NHL Totals		**15**	**0**	**2**	**2**	**8**	**0**	**0**	**0**	**16**	**0.0**		**0**	**0.0**	**11:12**	....	....	....	....	....	....	....	....	....

• Transferred to **Winnipeg** after **Atlanta** franchise relocated, June 21, 2011. Signed as a free agent by **Novosibirsk** (KHL), July 15, 2012.

KULEMIN, Nikolai

(KOOL-ay-mihn, NIH-koh-ligh) **TOR**

Left wing. Shoots left. 6'1", 225 lbs. Born, Magnitogorsk, USSR, July 14, 1986. Toronto's 2nd choice, 44th overall, in 2006 Entry Draft.

Season	Club	League	GP	G	A	Pts	PIM	PP	SH	GW	S	%	+/-	TF	F%	Min	GP	G	A	Pts	PIM	PP	SH	GW	Min
2003-04	Magnitogorsk 2	Russia-3	43	8	18	26	91	....	....	....	....	....	....	....	....	....	....	....	....	....	....	....	....	....	....
2004-05	Magnitogorsk 2	Russia-3	43	9	13	22	44	....	....	....	....	....	....	....	....	....	....	....	....	....	....	....	....	....	....
2005-06	Magnitogorsk 2	Russia-3	4	3	1	4	6	....	....	....	....	....	....	....	....	....	....	....	....	....	....	....	....	....	....
	Magnitogorsk	Russia	31	5	7	12	8	....	....	....	....	....	....	....	....	....	11	2	4	6	6	....	....	....	....
2006-07	Magnitogorsk	Russia	54	27	12	39	42	....	....	....	....	....	....	....	....	....	15	10	1	11	10	....	....	....	....
2007-08	Magnitogorsk	Russia	57	21	12	33	63	....	....	....	....	....	....	....	....	....	11	2	2	4	29	....	....	....	....
2008-09	**Toronto**	**NHL**	**73**	**15**	**16**	**31**	**18**	**2**	**0**	**1**	**129**	**11.6**	**–8**	**66**	**53.0**	**13:48**	....	....	....	....	....	....	....	....	....
	Toronto Marlies	AHL	5	0	0	0	0	....	....	....	....	....	....	....	....	....	....	....	....	....	....	....	....	....	....
2009-10	**Toronto**	**NHL**	**78**	**16**	**20**	**36**	**16**	**0**	**1**	**3**	**145**	**11.0**	**0**	**66**	**40.9**	**16:22**	....	....	....	....	....	....	....	....	....
2010-11	**Toronto**	**NHL**	**82**	**30**	**27**	**57**	**26**	**5**	**1**	**5**	**173**	**17.3**	**7**	**111**	**54.1**	**17:19**	....	....	....	....	....	....	....	....	....
2011-12	**Toronto**	**NHL**	**70**	**7**	**21**	**28**	**6**	**1**	**0**	**1**	**107**	**6.5**	**2**	**78**	**41.0**	**15:13**	....	....	....	....	....	....	....	....	....
2012-13	Magnitogorsk	KHL	36	14	24	38	26	....	....	....	....	....	....	....	....	....	....	....	....	....	....	....	....	....	....
	Toronto	**NHL**	**48**	**7**	**16**	**23**	**22**	**0**	**0**	**0**	**72**	**9.7**	**–5**	**20**	**50.0**	**16:44**	**7**	**0**	**1**	**1**	**0**	**0**	**0**	**0**	**18:11**
	NHL Totals		**351**	**75**	**100**	**175**	**88**	**8**	**2**	**10**	**626**	**12.0**		**341**	**48.1**	**15:53**	**7**	**0**	**1**	**1**	**0**	**0**	**0**	**0**	**18:11**

Signed as a free agent by **Magnitogorsk** (KHL), September 15, 2012.

KULIKOV, Dmitry

(kool-YIH-kawf, dih-MEE-tree) **FLA**

Defense. Shoots left. 6'1", 205 lbs. Born, Lipetsk, USSR, October 29, 1990. Florida's 1st choice, 14th overall, in 2009 Entry Draft.

Season	Club	League	GP	G	A	Pts	PIM	PP	SH	GW	S	%	+/-	TF	F%	Min	GP	G	A	Pts	PIM	PP	SH	GW	Min
2007-08	Yaroslavl 2	Russia-3	STATISTICS NOT AVAILABLE																						
2008-09	Drummondville	QMJHL	57	12	50	62	46	....	....	....	....	....	....	....	....	....	19	2	18	20	16	....	....	....	....
2009-10	**Florida**	**NHL**	**68**	**3**	**13**	**16**	**32**	**1**	**0**	**0**	**87**	**3.4**	**–5**	**0**	**0.0**	**17:56**	....	....	....	....	....	....	....	....	....
2010-11	**Florida**	**NHL**	**72**	**6**	**20**	**26**	**45**	**1**	**0**	**1**	**83**	**7.2**	**–5**	**0**	**0.0**	**19:57**	....	....	....	....	....	....	....	....	....
2011-12	**Florida**	**NHL**	**58**	**4**	**24**	**28**	**36**	**2**	**0**	**1**	**104**	**3.8**	**–5**	**0**	**0.0**	**21:51**	**7**	**0**	**1**	**1**	**4**	**0**	**0**	**0**	**21:16**

								Regular Season									Playoffs								
Season	Club	League	GP	G	A	Pts	PIM	PP	SH	GW	S	%	+/-	TF	F%	Min	GP	G	A	Pts	PIM	PP	SH	GW	Min
2012-13	Yaroslavl	KHL	22	3	4	7	28	....	....	....	....	....	....	....	....	....	....	....	....	....	....	....	....	....	....
	Florida	**NHL**	**34**	**3**	**7**	**10**	**22**	**2**	**0**	**2**	**52**	**5.8**	**–5**	**0**	**0.0**	**20:59**	....	....	....	....	....	....	....	....	....
	NHL Totals		**232**	**16**	**64**	**80**	**135**	**6**	**0**	**4**	**326**	**4.9**		**0**	**0.0**	**19:59**	**7**	**0**	**1**	**1**	**4**	**0**	**0**	**0**	**21:16**

QMJHL All-Rookie Team (2009) • QMJHL First All-Star Team (2009) • QMJHL Rookie of the Year (2009) • Canadian Major Junior Second All-Star Team (2009) • Canadian Major Junior All-Rookie Team (2009)

Signed as a free agent by **Yaroslavl** (KHL), September 25, 2012.

KUNDRATEK, Tomas

(kuhn-DRAT-ehk, TAW-mahsh) **WSH**

Defense. Shoots right. 6'2", 195 lbs. Born, Prerov, Czech., December 26, 1989. NY Rangers' 4th choice, 90th overall, in 2008 Entry Draft.

Season	Club	League	GP	G	A	Pts	PIM	PP	SH	GW	S	%	+/-	TF	F%	Min	GP	G	A	Pts	PIM	PP	SH	GW	Min
2003-04	HC Prerov U17	CzR-U17	6	0	0	0	0	....	....	....	....	....	....	....	....	....	....	....	....	....	....	....	....	....	....
2004-05	HC Prerov U17	CzR-U17	38	2	7	9	26	....	....	....	....	....	....	....	....	....	4	0	1	1	4	....	....	....	....
2005-06	HC Trinec U17	CzR-U17	39	5	13	18	96	....	....	....	....	....	....	....	....	....	2	0	1	1	10	....	....	....	....
	HC Trinec Jr.	CzRep-Jr.	12	1	1	2	16	....	....	....	....	....	....	....	....	....	7	1	1	2	4	....	....	....	....
2006-07	HC Trinec Jr.	CzRep-Jr.	33	4	13	17	93	....	....	....	....	....	....	....	....	....	3	1	1	2	10	....	....	....	....
	HC Ocelari Trinec	CzRep	22	0	1	1	4	....	....	....	....	....	....	....	....	....	4	0	0	0	6	....	....	....	....
2007-08	HC Trinec Jr.	CzRep-Jr.	14	3	6	9	28	....	....	....	....	....	....	....	....	....	....	....	....	....	....	....	....	....	....
	Prostejov	CzRep-2	15	1	0	1	10	....	....	....	....	....	....	....	....	....	....	....	....	....	....	....	....	....	....
	HC Havirov	CzRep-2	2	0	0	0	2	....	....	....	....	....	....	....	....	....	....	....	....	....	....	....	....	....	....
	HC Ocelari Trinec	CzRep	14	0	1	1	10	....	....	....	....	....	....	....	....	....	7	0	2	2	8	....	....	....	....
2008-09	Medicine Hat	WHL	51	4	19	23	63	....	....	....	....	....	....	....	....	....	11	0	6	6	12	....	....	....	....
	Hartford	AHL	....	....	....	....	....	....	....	....	....	....	....	....	....	....	1	0	0	0	0	....	....	....	....
2009-10	Medicine Hat	WHL	65	2	33	35	62	....	....	....	....	....	....	....	....	....	12	1	5	6	23	....	....	....	....
2010-11	Connecticut	AHL	70	2	10	12	42	....	....	....	....	....	....	....	....	....	6	0	2	2	2	....	....	....	....
2011-12	Connecticut	AHL	7	0	2	2	2	....	....	....	....	....	....	....	....	....	....	....	....	....	....	....	....	....	....
	Washington	**NHL**	**5**	**0**	**0**	**0**	**2**	**0**	**0**	**0**	**2**	**0.0**	**0**	**0**	**0.0**	**9:45**	....	....	....	....	....	....	....	....	....
	Hershey Bears	AHL	55	12	11	23	34	....	....	....	....	....	....	....	....	....	4	0	4	4	4	....	....	....	....
2012-13	Hershey Bears	AHL	49	16	15	31	26	....	....	....	....	....	....	....	....	....	5	0	1	1	2	....	....	....	....
	Washington	**NHL**	**25**	**1**	**6**	**7**	**8**	**0**	**0**	**0**	**23**	**4.3**	**–5**	**0**	**0.0**	**16:09**	....	....	....	....	....	....	....	....	....
	NHL Totals		**30**	**1**	**6**	**7**	**10**	**0**	**0**	**0**	**25**	**4.0**		**0**	**0.0**	**15:05**	....	....	....	....	....	....	....	....	....

Traded to **Washington** by **NY Rangers** for Francois Bouchard, November 8, 2011.

KUNITZ, Chris

(KOO-nihtz, KRIHS) **PIT**

Left wing. Shoots left. 6', 193 lbs. Born, Regina, Sask., September 26, 1979.

Season	Club	League	GP	G	A	Pts	PIM	PP	SH	GW	S	%	+/-	TF	F%	Min	GP	G	A	Pts	PIM	PP	SH	GW	Min
1996-97	Yorkton Mallers	SMHL	64	38	38	76	233	....	....	....	....	....	....	....	....	....	....	....	....	....	....	....	....	....	....
1997-98	Melville	SJHL	STATISTICS NOT AVAILABLE					....	....	....	....	....	....	....	....	....	....	....	....	....	....	....	....	....	....
1998-99	Melville	SJHL	63	57	32	89	222	....	....	....	....	....	....	....	....	....	....	....	....	....	....	....	....	....	....
99-2000	Ferris State	CCHA	38	20	9	29	70	....	....	....	....	....	....	....	....	....	....	....	....	....	....	....	....	....	....
2000-01	Ferris State	CCHA	37	16	13	29	81	....	....	....	....	....	....	....	....	....	....	....	....	....	....	....	....	....	....
2001-02	Ferris State	CCHA	35	*28	10	38	68	....	....	....	....	....	....	....	....	....	....	....	....	....	....	....	....	....	....
2002-03	Ferris State	CCHA	42	*35	*44	*79	56	....	....	....	....	....	....	....	....	....	....	....	....	....	....	....	....	....	....
2003-04	**Anaheim**	**NHL**	**21**	**0**	**6**	**6**	**12**	**0**	**0**	**0**	**31**	**0.0**	**1**	**7**	**14.3**	**9:07**	....	....	....	....	....	....	....	....	....
	Cincinnati	AHL	59	19	25	44	101	....	....	....	....	....	....	....	....	....	9	3	2	5	24	....	....	....	....
2004-05	Cincinnati	AHL	54	22	17	39	71	....	....	....	....	....	....	....	....	....	12	1	7	8	20	....	....	....	....
2005-06	**Atlanta**	**NHL**	**2**	**0**	**0**	**0**	**2**	**0**	**0**	**0**	**0**	**0.0**	**–3**	**0**	**0.0**	**5:43**	....	....	....	....	....	....	....	....	....
	Anaheim	**NHL**	**67**	**19**	**22**	**41**	**69**	**5**	**1**	**2**	**149**	**12.8**	**19**	**15**	**46.7**	**14:08**	**16**	**3**	**5**	**8**	**8**	**0**	**0**	**0**	**12:30**
	Portland Pirates	AHL	5	0	4	4	12	....	....	....	....	....	....	....	....	....	....	....	....	....	....	....	....	....	....
2006-07♦	**Anaheim**	**NHL**	**81**	**25**	**35**	**60**	**81**	**11**	**0**	**5**	**180**	**13.9**	**23**	**13**	**30.8**	**17:03**	**13**	**1**	**5**	**6**	**19**	**0**	**0**	**0**	**17:47**
2007-08	**Anaheim**	**NHL**	**82**	**21**	**29**	**50**	**80**	**7**	**1**	**6**	**196**	**10.7**	**8**	**49**	**32.7**	**16:54**	**6**	**0**	**2**	**2**	**8**	**0**	**0**	**0**	**18:30**
2008-09	**Anaheim**	**NHL**	**62**	**16**	**19**	**35**	**55**	**3**	**0**	**2**	**139**	**11.5**	**9**	**22**	**45.5**	**16:29**	....	....	....	....	....	....	....	....	....
	♦ **Pittsburgh**	**NHL**	**20**	**7**	**11**	**18**	**16**	**3**	**0**	**1**	**39**	**17.9**	**3**	**5**	**60.0**	**16:17**	**24**	**1**	**13**	**14**	**19**	**0**	**0**	**0**	**16:55**
2009-10	**Pittsburgh**	**NHL**	**50**	**13**	**19**	**32**	**39**	**2**	**1**	**0**	**131**	**9.9**	**3**	**15**	**40.0**	**16:26**	**13**	**4**	**7**	**11**	**8**	**1**	**0**	**0**	**17:26**
2010-11	**Pittsburgh**	**NHL**	**66**	**23**	**25**	**48**	**47**	**7**	**1**	**2**	**133**	**17.3**	**18**	**8**	**50.0**	**18:17**	**6**	**1**	**0**	**1**	**6**	**0**	**0**	**0**	**17:22**
2011-12	**Pittsburgh**	**NHL**	**82**	**26**	**35**	**61**	**49**	**6**	**0**	**3**	**230**	**11.3**	**16**	**38**	**52.6**	**18:19**	**6**	**2**	**4**	**6**	**8**	**2**	**0**	**0**	**19:03**
2012-13	**Pittsburgh**	**NHL**	**48**	**22**	**30**	**52**	**39**	**9**	**0**	**5**	**113**	**19.5**	**30**	**9**	**44.4**	**18:01**	**15**	**5**	**5**	**10**	**6**	**3**	**0**	**1**	**18:19**
	NHL Totals		**581**	**172**	**231**	**403**	**489**	**53**	**4**	**26**	**1341**	**12.8**		**181**	**41.4**	**16:38**	**99**	**17**	**41**	**58**	**82**	**6**	**0**	**1**	**16:51**

CCHA First All-Star Team (2002, 2003) • CCHA Player of the Year (2003) • NCAA West First All-American Team (2003) • NHL First All-Star Team (2013)

Signed as a free agent by **Anaheim**, April 1, 2003. Claimed on waivers by **Atlanta** from **Anaheim**, October 4, 2005. Claimed on waivers by **Anaheim** from **Atlanta**, October 18, 2005. Traded to **Pittsburgh** by **Anaheim** with Eric Tangradi for Ryan Whitney, February 26, 2009.

KYTNAR, Milan

(KIHT-nahr, MEE-lan)

Center. Shoots left. 6', 190 lbs. Born, Topolcany, Czech., May 19, 1989. Edmonton's 5th choice, 127th overall, in 2007 Entry Draft.

Season	Club	League	GP	G	A	Pts	PIM	PP	SH	GW	S	%	+/-	TF	F%	Min	GP	G	A	Pts	PIM	PP	SH	GW	Min
2003-04	Topolcany U18	Svk-U18	42	17	22	39	90	....	....	....	....	....	....	....	....	....	....	....	....	....	....	....	....	....	....
2004-05	Topolcany U18	Svk-U18	53	36	65	101	105	....	....	....	....	....	....	....	....	....	....	....	....	....	....	....	....	....	....
	Topolcany Jr.	Slovak-Jr.	10	2	2	4	8	....	....	....	....	....	....	....	....	....	....	....	....	....	....	....	....	....	....
2005-06	HK Trnava U18	Svk-U18	30	18	23	41	106	....	....	....	....	....	....	....	....	....	....	....	....	....	....	....	....	....	....
	HK Trnava Jr.	Slovak-Jr.	12	1	2	3	20	....	....	....	....	....	....	....	....	....	....	....	....	....	....	....	....	....	....
	Topolcany U18	Svk-U18	8	4	4	8	4	....	....	....	....	....	....	....	....	....	....	....	....	....	....	....	....	....	....
	Topolcany Jr.	Slovak-Jr.	6	6	4	10	8	....	....	....	....	....	....	....	....	....	....	....	....	....	....	....	....	....	....
2006-07	Topolcany U18	Svk-U18	53	37	54	91	84	....	....	....	....	....	....	....	....	....	....	....	....	....	....	....	....	....	....
	HC Topolcany	Slovak-2	22	4	7	11	53	....	....	....	....	....	....	....	....	....	5	1	1	2	4	....	....	....	....
2007-08	Kelowna Rockets	WHL	62	9	13	22	66	....	....	....	....	....	....	....	....	....	7	0	0	0	4	....	....	....	....
2008-09	Saskatoon Blades	WHL	65	27	37	64	89	....	....	....	....	....	....	....	....	....	7	3	1	4	14	....	....	....	....
2009-10	Saskatoon Blades	WHL	3	0	1	1	2	....	....	....	....	....	....	....	....	....	....	....	....	....	....	....	....	....	....
	Vancouver Giants	WHL	42	14	25	39	40	....	....	....	....	....	....	....	....	....	16	3	12	15	23	....	....	....	....
2010-11	Oklahoma City	AHL	78	13	16	29	35	....	....	....	....	....	....	....	....	....	1	0	0	0	0	....	....	....	....
2011-12	**Edmonton**	**NHL**	**1**	**0**	**0**	**0**	**0**	**0**	**0**	**0**	**1**	**0.0**	**0**	**1**	**0.0**	**5:31**	....	....	....	....	....	....	....	....	....
	Oklahoma City	AHL	13	1	2	3	4	....	....	....	....	....	....	....	....	....	....	....	....	....	....	....	....	....	....
	Stockton Thunder	ECHL	17	7	5	12	14	....	....	....	....	....	....	....	....	....	....	....	....	....	....	....	....	....	....
	HPK Hameenlinna	Finland	16	0	3	3	12	....	....	....	....	....	....	....	....	....	....	....	....	....	....	....	....	....	....
2012-13	Bratislava	KHL	44	5	5	10	34	....	....	....	....	....	....	....	....	....	3	1	0	1	8	....	....	....	....
	NHL Totals		**1**	**0**	**0**	**0**	**0**	**0**	**0**	**0**	**1**	**0.0**		**1**	**0.0**	**5:31**	....	....	....	....	....	....	....	....	....

Signed as a free agent by **Hameenlinna** (Finland), February 1, 2012. Signed as a free agent by **Bratislava** (KHL), May 23, 2012.

LAAKSO, Teemu

(LAK-soh, TEE-moo) **NSH**

Defense. Shoots right. 6'1", 210 lbs. Born, Tuusula, Finland, August 27, 1987. Nashville's 2nd choice, 78th overall, in 2005 Entry Draft.

Season	Club	League	GP	G	A	Pts	PIM	PP	SH	GW	S	%	+/-	TF	F%	Min	GP	G	A	Pts	PIM	PP	SH	GW	Min
2002-03	KJT U18	Fin-U18	18	2	5	7	24	....	....	....	....	....	....	....	....	....	....	....	....	....	....	....	....	....	....
2003-04	HIFK Helsinki Jr.	Fin-Jr.	41	3	6	9	20	....	....	....	....	....	....	....	....	....	3	0	1	1	0	....	....	....	....
2004-05	HIFK Helsinki U18	Fin-U18	....	....	....	....	....	....	....	....	....	....	....	....	....	....	1	0	0	0	0	....	....	....	....
	HIFK Helsinki Jr.	Fin-Jr.	20	5	4	9	18	....	....	....	....	....	....	....	....	....	....	....	....	....	....	....	....	....	....
	HIFK Helsinki	Finland	15	0	2	2	2	....	....	....	....	....	....	....	....	....	....	....	....	....	....	....	....	....	....
2005-06	HIFK Helsinki Jr.	Fin-Jr.	6	1	2	3	32	....	....	....	....	....	....	....	....	....	....	....	....	....	....	....	....	....	....
	Suomi U20	Finland-2	6	2	0	2	10	....	....	....	....	....	....	....	....	....	....	....	....	....	....	....	....	....	....
	HIFK Helsinki	Finland	47	2	1	3	20	....	....	....	....	....	....	....	....	....	8	1	0	1	0	....	....	....	....
2006-07	Suomi U20	Finland-2	2	0	1	1	4	....	....	....	....	....	....	....	....	....	....	....	....	....	....	....	....	....	....
	HIFK Helsinki	Finland	50	3	6	9	70	....	....	....	....	....	....	....	....	....	5	0	1	1	0	....	....	....	....
2007-08	HIFK Helsinki	Finland	53	3	7	10	40	....	....	....	....	....	....	....	....	....	7	0	0	0	2	....	....	....	....
2008-09	Milwaukee	AHL	42	2	7	9	50	....	....	....	....	....	....	....	....	....	....	....	....	....	....	....	....	....	....
2009-10	**Nashville**	**NHL**	**7**	**0**	**0**	**0**	**2**	**0**	**0**	**0**	**5**	**0.0**	**–2**	**0**	**0.0**	**10:48**	....	....	....	....	....	....	....	....	....
	Milwaukee	AHL	46	4	9	13	42	....	....	....	....	....	....	....	....	....	7	1	2	3	4	....	....	....	....
2010-11	**Nashville**	**NHL**	**1**	**0**	**0**	**0**	**0**	**0**	**0**	**0**	**0**	**0.0**	**0**	**0**	**0.0**	**2:43**	....	....	....	....	....	....	....	....	....
	Milwaukee	AHL	74	8	22	30	46	....	....	....	....	....	....	....	....	....	8	1	1	2	0	....	....	....	....
2011-12	**Nashville**	**NHL**	**9**	**0**	**0**	**0**	**8**	**0**	**0**	**0**	**4**	**0.0**	**–1**	**0**	**0.0**	**11:35**	....	....	....	....	....	....	....	....	....
	Milwaukee	AHL	55	3	17	20	74	....	....	....	....	....	....	....	....	....	3	0	2	2	2	....	....	....	....
2012-13	Cherepovets	KHL	49	4	5	9	28	....	....	....	....	....	....	....	....	....	10	0	2	2	22	....	....	....	....
	NHL Totals		**17**	**0**	**0**	**0**	**10**	**0**	**0**	**0**	**9**	**0.0**		**0**	**0.0**	**10:45**	....	....	....	....	....	....	....	....	....

Signed as a free agent by **Cherepovets** (KHL), June 3, 2012.

LABRIE, Pierre-Cedric

(la-BREE, pee-AIR-SEH-DRIHK) **T.B.**

Left wing. Shoots right. 6'3", 234 lbs. Born, Baie Comeau, Que., December 6, 1986.

			Regular Season														Playoffs								
Season	Club	League	GP	G	A	Pts	PIM	PP	SH	GW	S	%	+/-	TF	F%	Min	GP	G	A	Pts	PIM	PP	SH	GW	Min
2003-04	Coaticook	QJHL	46	13	12	25	96	....	....	....	....	....	....	....	....	....	....	....	....	....	....	....	....	....	....
	Quebec Remparts	QMJHL	1	0	0	0	0	....	....	....	....	....	....	....	....	....	....	....	....	....	....	....	....	....	....
2004-05	Coaticook	QJHL	15	3	4	7	59	....	....	....	....	....	....	....	....	....	....	....	....	....	....	....	....	....	....
2005-06	Restigouche	MJrHL	54	43	43	86	153	....	....	....	....	....	....	....	....	....	4	3	2	5	16	....	....	....	....
	Baie-Comeau	QMJHL	....	....	....	....	....	....	....	....	....	....	....	....	....	....	4	2	2	4	6	....	....	....	....
2006-07	Baie-Comeau	QMJHL	68	35	28	63	113	....	....	....	....	....	....	....	....	....	11	8	6	14	35	....	....	....	....
2007-08	Manitoba Moose	AHL	67	7	11	18	108	....	....	....	....	....	....	....	....	....	3	0	0	0	2	....	....	....	....
2008-09	Manitoba Moose	AHL	63	6	9	15	79	....	....	....	....	....	....	....	....	....	14	0	1	1	37	....	....	....	....
2009-10	Manitoba Moose	AHL	45	5	1	6	69	....	....	....	....	....	....	....	....	....	....	....	....	....	....	....	....	....	....
	Peoria Rivermen	AHL	16	0	1	1	16	....	....	....	....	....	....	....	....	....	....	....	....	....	....	....	....	....	....
2010-11	Norfolk Admirals	AHL	64	7	19	26	148	....	....	....	....	....	....	....	....	....	6	0	1	1	4	....	....	....	....
2011-12	Norfolk Admirals	AHL	56	14	21	35	107	....	....	....	....	....	....	....	....	....	18	5	4	9	34	....	....	....	....
	Tampa Bay	**NHL**	**14**	**0**	**2**	**2**	**15**	**0**	**0**	**0**	**5**	**0.0**	**–2**	**5**	**60.0**	**5:54**	....	....	....	....	....	....	....	....	....
2012-13	Syracuse Crunch	AHL	39	11	7	18	83	....	....	....	....	....	....	....	....	....	....	....	....	....	....	....	....	....	....
	Tampa Bay	**NHL**	**19**	**2**	**1**	**3**	**30**	**0**	**0**	**0**	**16**	**12.5**	**2**	**4**	**50.0**	**8:33**	....	....	....	....	....	....	....	....	....
	NHL Totals		**33**	**2**	**3**	**5**	**45**	**0**	**0**	**0**	**21**	**9.5**		**9**	**55.6**	**7:26**	....	....	....	....	....	....	....	....	....

Signed as a free agent by **Vancouver**, July 3, 2007. Traded to **St. Louis** by **Vancouver** for Yan Stastny, March 3, 2010. Signed as a free agent by **Norfolk** (AHL), December 8, 2010. Signed as a free agent by **Tampa Bay**, December 29, 2011.

LADD, Andrew

(LAD, AN-droo) **WPG**

Left wing. Shoots left. 6'3", 205 lbs. Born, Maple Ridge, B.C., December 12, 1985. Carolina's 1st choice, 4th overall, in 2004 Entry Draft.

			Regular Season														Playoffs								
Season	Club	League	GP	G	A	Pts	PIM	PP	SH	GW	S	%	+/-	TF	F%	Min	GP	G	A	Pts	PIM	PP	SH	GW	Min
2000-01	Port Coquitlam	Minor-BC	50	50	41	91	80	....	....	....	....	....	....	....	....	....	....	....	....	....	....	....	....	....	....
	Okanagan Chiefs	Minor-BC	6	4	8	12	10	....	....	....	....	....	....	....	....	....	....	....	....	....	....	....	....	....	....
2001-02	Port Coquitlam	Minor-BC	50	50	41	91	49	....	....	....	....	....	....	....	....	....	....	....	....	....	....	....	....	....	....
	Vancouver Giants	WHL	1	0	0	0	0	....	....	....	....	....	....	....	....	....	....	....	....	....	....	....	....	....	....
2002-03	Coquitlam	BCHL	58	15	40	55	61	....	....	....	....	....	....	....	....	....	....	....	....	....	....	....	....	....	....
2003-04	Calgary Hitmen	WHL	71	30	45	75	119	....	....	....	....	....	....	....	....	....	7	1	6	7	10	....	....	....	....
2004-05	Calgary Hitmen	WHL	65	19	26	45	167	....	....	....	....	....	....	....	....	....	12	7	4	11	18	....	....	....	....
2005-06♦	**Carolina**	**NHL**	**29**	**6**	**5**	**11**	**4**	**3**	**0**	**0**	**43**	**14.0**	**0**	**0**	**0.0**	**11:10**	**17**	**2**	**3**	**5**	**4**	**0**	**0**	**1**	**9:27**
	Lowell	AHL	25	11	8	19	28	....	....	....	....	....	....	....	....	....	....	....	....	....	....	....	....	....	....
2006-07	**Carolina**	**NHL**	**65**	**11**	**10**	**21**	**46**	**2**	**0**	**3**	**109**	**10.1**	**1**	**1**	**0.0**	**11:12**	....	....	....	....	....	....	....	....	....
2007-08	**Carolina**	**NHL**	**43**	**9**	**9**	**18**	**31**	**0**	**0**	**1**	**76**	**11.8**	**9**	**5**	**60.0**	**11:45**	....	....	....	....	....	....	....	....	....
	Albany River Rats	AHL	2	1	0	1	4	....	....	....	....	....	....	....	....	....	....	....	....	....	....	....	....	....	....
	Chicago	**NHL**	**20**	**5**	**7**	**12**	**4**	**1**	**0**	**0**	**55**	**9.1**	**4**	**3**	**33.3**	**14:58**	....	....	....	....	....	....	....	....	....
2008-09	**Chicago**	**NHL**	**82**	**15**	**34**	**49**	**28**	**0**	**0**	**2**	**195**	**7.7**	**26**	**42**	**23.8**	**14:24**	**17**	**3**	**1**	**4**	**12**	**0**	**0**	**1**	**12:55**
2009-10♦	**Chicago**	**NHL**	**82**	**17**	**21**	**38**	**67**	**0**	**0**	**1**	**148**	**11.5**	**2**	**12**	**41.7**	**13:42**	**19**	**3**	**3**	**6**	**12**	**0**	**0**	**0**	**12:48**
2010-11	**Atlanta**	**NHL**	**81**	**29**	**30**	**59**	**39**	**9**	**2**	**2**	**195**	**14.9**	**–10**	**44**	**34.1**	**20:04**	....	....	....	....	....	....	....	....	....
2011-12	**Winnipeg**	**NHL**	**82**	**28**	**22**	**50**	**64**	**4**	**0**	**6**	**265**	**10.6**	**–8**	**59**	**54.2**	**19:34**	....	....	....	....	....	....	....	....	....
2012-13	**Winnipeg**	**NHL**	**48**	**18**	**28**	**46**	**22**	**3**	**0**	**4**	**121**	**14.9**	**10**	**54**	**53.7**	**19:41**	....	....	....	....	....	....	....	....	....
	NHL Totals		**532**	**138**	**166**	**304**	**305**	**22**	**2**	**19**	**1207**	**11.4**		**220**	**43.2**	**15:40**	**53**	**8**	**7**	**15**	**28**	**0**	**0**	**2**	**11:46**

Traded to **Chicago** by **Carolina** for Tuomo Ruutu, February 26, 2008. Traded to **Atlanta** by **Chicago** for Ivan Vishnevskiy and Winnipeg/Atlanta's 2nd round choice (Adam Clendening) in 2011 Entry Draft, July 1, 2010. • Transferred to **Winnipeg** after **Atlanta** franchise relocated, June 21, 2011.

LAICH, Brooks

(LIGHK, BRUKS) **WSH**

Center. Shoots left. 6'2", 210 lbs. Born, Wawota, Sask., June 23, 1983. Ottawa's 7th choice, 193rd overall, in 2001 Entry Draft.

			Regular Season														Playoffs								
Season	Club	League	GP	G	A	Pts	PIM	PP	SH	GW	S	%	+/-	TF	F%	Min	GP	G	A	Pts	PIM	PP	SH	GW	Min
99-2000	Tisdale Trojans	SMHL	57	51	52	103	....	....	....	....	....	....	....	....	....	....	....	....	....	....	....	....	....	....	....
2000-01	Moose Jaw	WHL	71	9	21	30	28	....	....	....	....	....	....	....	....	....	4	0	0	0	5	....	....	....	....
2001-02	Moose Jaw	WHL	28	6	14	20	12	....	....	....	....	....	....	....	....	....	....	....	....	....	....	....	....	....	....
	Seattle	WHL	47	22	36	58	42	....	....	....	....	....	....	....	....	....	11	5	3	8	11	....	....	....	....
2002-03	Seattle	WHL	60	41	53	94	65	....	....	....	....	....	....	....	....	....	15	5	14	19	24	....	....	....	....
2003-04	**Ottawa**	**NHL**	**1**	**0**	**0**	**0**	**2**	**0**	**0**	**0**	**1**	**0.0**	**0**	**7**	**42.9**	**9:34**	....	....	....	....	....	....	....	....	....
	Binghamton	AHL	44	15	18	33	16	....	....	....	....	....	....	....	....	....	....	....	....	....	....	....	....	....	....
	Washington	**NHL**	**4**	**0**	**1**	**1**	**0**	**0**	**0**	**0**	**2**	**0.0**	**–1**	**49**	**51.0**	**10:50**	....	....	....	....	....	....	....	....	....
	Portland Pirates	AHL	22	1	3	4	12	....	....	....	....	....	....	....	....	....	6	0	0	0	0	....	....	....	....
2004-05	Portland Pirates	AHL	68	16	10	26	33	....	....	....	....	....	....	....	....	....	....	....	....	....	....	....	....	....	....
2005-06	**Washington**	**NHL**	**73**	**7**	**14**	**21**	**26**	**1**	**0**	**1**	**118**	**5.9**	**–9**	**666**	**49.7**	**11:13**	....	....	....	....	....	....	....	....	....
	Hershey Bears	AHL	10	7	6	13	8	....	....	....	....	....	....	....	....	....	21	8	7	15	29	....	....	....	....
2006-07	**Washington**	**NHL**	**73**	**8**	**10**	**18**	**29**	**2**	**3**	**0**	**119**	**6.7**	**–2**	**563**	**51.9**	**13:36**	....	....	....	....	....	....	....	....	....
2007-08	**Washington**	**NHL**	**82**	**21**	**16**	**37**	**35**	**8**	**2**	**4**	**122**	**17.2**	**–3**	**596**	**47.2**	**14:03**	**7**	**1**	**5**	**6**	**4**	**0**	**0**	**0**	**18:37**
2008-09	**Washington**	**NHL**	**82**	**23**	**30**	**53**	**31**	**9**	**1**	**3**	**185**	**12.4**	**–1**	**511**	**51.1**	**17:17**	**14**	**3**	**4**	**7**	**10**	**2**	**0**	**0**	**17:27**
2009-10	**Washington**	**NHL**	**78**	**25**	**34**	**59**	**34**	**12**	**1**	**4**	**222**	**11.3**	**16**	**337**	**45.1**	**18:17**	**7**	**2**	**1**	**3**	**4**	**0**	**0**	**1**	**19:57**
2010-11	**Washington**	**NHL**	**82**	**16**	**32**	**48**	**46**	**4**	**1**	**3**	**207**	**7.7**	**14**	**524**	**51.3**	**18:25**	**9**	**1**	**6**	**7**	**2**	**0**	**0**	**0**	**21:54**
2011-12	**Washington**	**NHL**	**82**	**16**	**25**	**41**	**34**	**5**	**1**	**5**	**191**	**8.4**	**–8**	**1394**	**47.6**	**18:30**	**14**	**2**	**5**	**7**	**6**	**0**	**0**	**0**	**20:13**
2012-13	Kloten Flyers	Swiss	19	6	12	18	28	....	....	....	....	....	....	....	....	....	....	....	....	....	....	....	....	....	....
	Washington	**NHL**	**9**	**1**	**3**	**4**	**6**	**0**	**0**	**0**	**10**	**10.0**	**2**	**81**	**50.6**	**16:32**	....	....	....	....	....	....	....	....	....
	NHL Totals		**566**	**117**	**165**	**282**	**243**	**41**	**9**	**20**	**1177**	**9.9**		**4728**	**49.0**	**15:58**	**51**	**9**	**21**	**30**	**26**	**2**	**0**	**1**	**19:30**

WHL West First All-Star Team (2003)

Traded to **Washington** by **Ottawa** with Ottawa's 2nd round choice (later traded to Colorado - Colorado selected Chris Durand) in 2005 Entry Draft for Peter Bondra, February 18, 2004. Signed as a free agent by **Kloten** (Swiss), September 28, 2012. • Missed majority of 2012-13 due to recurring groin injury and lower-body injury vs. NY Islanders, April 4, 2013.

LAING, Quintin

(LANG, QUIHN-tihn) **CGY**

Left wing. Shoots left. 6'3", 183 lbs. Born, Rosetown, Sask., June 8, 1979. Detroit's 3rd choice, 102nd overall, in 1997 Entry Draft.

			Regular Season														Playoffs								
Season	Club	League	GP	G	A	Pts	PIM	PP	SH	GW	S	%	+/-	TF	F%	Min	GP	G	A	Pts	PIM	PP	SH	GW	Min
1993-94	Delisle Contacts	SAHA	30	25	50	75	25	....	....	....	....	....	....	....	....	....	....	....	....	....	....	....	....	....	....
1994-95	Delisle Contacts	SAHA	30	30	45	75	15	....	....	....	....	....	....	....	....	....	....	....	....	....	....	....	....	....	....
1995-96	Sask. Contacts	SMHL	44	18	12	30	20	....	....	....	....	....	....	....	....	....	....	....	....	....	....	....	....	....	....
1996-97	Kelowna Rockets	WHL	63	13	24	37	54	....	....	....	....	....	....	....	....	....	1	0	0	0	0	....	....	....	....
1997-98	Kelowna Rockets	WHL	59	11	24	35	47	....	....	....	....	....	....	....	....	....	7	0	1	1	8	....	....	....	....
1998-99	Kelowna Rockets	WHL	70	11	10	21	107	....	....	....	....	....	....	....	....	....	6	3	0	3	0	....	....	....	....
99-2000	Kelowna Rockets	WHL	68	22	30	52	61	....	....	....	....	....	....	....	....	....	5	1	1	2	8	....	....	....	....
2000-01	Norfolk Admirals	AHL	10	0	1	1	10	....	....	....	....	....	....	....	....	....	....	....	....	....	....	....	....	....	....
	Jackson Bandits	ECHL	60	13	24	37	39	....	....	....	....	....	....	....	....	....	5	0	0	0	0	....	....	....	....
2001-02	Jackson Bandits	ECHL	16	4	6	10	12	....	....	....	....	....	....	....	....	....	....	....	....	....	....	....	....	....	....
	Norfolk Admirals	AHL	61	6	15	21	32	....	....	....	....	....	....	....	....	....	4	0	0	0	2	....	....	....	....
2002-03	Norfolk Admirals	AHL	69	5	12	17	33	....	....	....	....	....	....	....	....	....	8	2	2	4	0	....	....	....	....
2003-04	**Chicago**	**NHL**	**3**	**0**	**1**	**1**	**0**	**0**	**0**	**0**	**3**	**0.0**	**1**	**0**	**0.0**	**11:57**	....	....	....	....	....	....	....	....	....
	Norfolk Admirals	AHL	78	12	10	22	74	....	....	....	....	....	....	....	....	....	8	5	1	6	4	....	....	....	....
2004-05	Norfolk Admirals	AHL	66	10	13	23	54	....	....	....	....	....	....	....	....	....	4	0	0	0	0	....	....	....	....
2005-06	Norfolk Admirals	AHL	73	14	31	45	70	....	....	....	....	....	....	....	....	....	4	0	0	0	0	....	....	....	....
2006-07	Hershey Bears	AHL	75	15	28	43	44	....	....	....	....	....	....	....	....	....	19	2	5	7	21	....	....	....	....
2007-08	**Washington**	**NHL**	**39**	**1**	**5**	**6**	**10**	**0**	**0**	**1**	**48**	**2.1**	**4**	**6**	**33.3**	**11:33**	....	....	....	....	....	....	....	....	....
	Hershey Bears	AHL	20	2	6	8	28	....	....	....	....	....	....	....	....	....	....	....	....	....	....	....	....	....	....
2008-09	**Washington**	**NHL**	**1**	**0**	**0**	**0**	**0**	**0**	**0**	**0**	**2**	**0.0**	**1**	**0**	**0.0**	**10:19**	....	....	....	....	....	....	....	....	....
	Hershey Bears	AHL	55	9	16	25	21	....	....	....	....	....	....	....	....	....	9	2	2	4	0	....	....	....	....
2009-10	**Washington**	**NHL**	**36**	**2**	**2**	**4**	**21**	**0**	**0**	**0**	**38**	**5.3**	**2**	**7**	**57.1**	**9:38**	....	....	....	....	....	....	....	....	....
	Hershey Bears	AHL	2	0	0	0	0	....	....	....	....	....	....	....	....	....	....	....	....	....	....	....	....	....	....
2010-11	Abbotsford Heat	AHL	59	7	19	26	40	....	....	....	....	....	....	....	....	....	....	....	....	....	....	....	....	....	....
	Victoria	ECHL	4	0	1	1	0	....	....	....	....	....	....	....	....	....	....	....	....	....	....	....	....	....	....
2011-12	Abbotsford Heat	AHL	58	11	11	22	31	....	....	....	....	....	....	....	....	....	1	0	0	0	0	....	....	....	....
2012-13	Abbotsford Heat	AHL	63	6	10	16	45	....	....	....	....	....	....	....	....	....	....	....	....	....	....	....	....	....	....
	NHL Totals		**79**	**3**	**8**	**11**	**31**	**0**	**0**	**1**	**91**	**3.3**		**13**	**46.2**	**10:41**	....	....	....	....	....	....	....	....	....

Signed as a free agent by **Chicago**, June 4, 2003. Signed as a free agent by **Washington**, July 18, 2006. • Missed majority of 2009-10 due to broken jaw at NY Rangers, November 17, 2009 and as a healthy reserve. Signed to a PTO (professional tryout) contract by **Abbotsford** (AHL), November 10, 2010. Signed as a free agent by **Calgary**, July 1, 2011.

LALONDE, Shawn

(la-LAWND, SHAWN) **CHI**

Defense. Shoots right. 6'1", 204 lbs. Born, Ottawa, Ont., March 10, 1990. Chicago's 2nd choice, 68th overall, in 2008 Entry Draft.

Season	Club	League	GP	G	A	Pts	PIM	PP	SH	GW	S	%	+/-	TF	F%	Min	Playoffs GP	G	A	Pts	PIM	PP	SH	GW	Min
2005-06	Cumberland	Minor-ON	60	18	36	54	98	....	....	....	....	....	....	....	....	....	....	....	....	....	....	....	....	....	....
2006-07	Belleville Bulls	OHL	58	6	20	26	71	....	....	....	....	....	....	....	....	....	13	1	1	2	6	....	....	....	....
2007-08	Belleville Bulls	OHL	66	9	22	31	67	....	....	....	....	....	....	....	....	....	21	2	7	9	25	....	....	....	....
2008-09	Belleville Bulls	OHL	66	19	34	53	73	....	....	....	....	....	....	....	....	....	17	3	9	12	36	....	....	....	....
2009-10	Belleville Bulls	OHL	58	13	43	56	87	....	....	....	....	....	....	....	....	....	....	....	....	....	....	....	....	....	....
	Rockford IceHogs	AHL	8	1	1	2	11	....	....	....	....	....	....	....	....	....	3	0	0	0	2	....	....	....	....
2010-11	Rockford IceHogs	AHL	73	5	27	32	76	....	....	....	....	....	....	....	....	....	....	....	....	....	....	....	....	....	....
2011-12	Rockford IceHogs	AHL	64	2	11	13	100	....	....	....	....	....	....	....	....	....	....	....	....	....	....	....	....	....	....
2012-13	Rockford IceHogs	AHL	59	5	18	23	91	....	....	....	....	....	....	....	....	....	....	....	....	....	....	....	....	....	....
	Chicago	**NHL**	**1**	**0**	**0**	**0**	**0**	**0**	**0**	**0**	**0**	**0.0**	**1**	**0**	**0.0**	**14:47**	....	....	....	....	....	....	....	....	....
	NHL Totals		**1**	**0**	**0**	**0**	**0**	**0**	**0**	**0**	**0**	**0.0**		**0**	**0.0**	**14:47**	....	....	....	....	....	....	....	....	....

Signed as a free agent by **Berlin** (Germany), July 24, 2013.

LANDER, Anton

(LAN-duhr, AN-tawn) **EDM**

Center. Shoots left. 6', 194 lbs. Born, Sundsvall, Sweden, April 24, 1991. Edmonton's 2nd choice, 40th overall, in 2009 Entry Draft.

Season	Club	League	GP	G	A	Pts	PIM	PP	SH	GW	S	%	+/-	TF	F%	Min	Playoffs GP	G	A	Pts	PIM	PP	SH	GW	Min
2005-06	Timra IK U18	Swe-U18	14	1	6	7	14	....	....	....	....	....	....	....	....	....	....	....	....	....	....	....	....	....	....
2006-07	Timra IK U18	Swe-U18	12	6	10	16	14	....	....	....	....	....	....	....	....	....	2	1	2	3	0	....	....	....	....
	Timra IK Jr.	Swe-Jr.	10	2	1	3	10	....	....	....	....	....	....	....	....	....	....	....	....	....	....	....	....	....	....
2007-08	Timra IK U18	Swe-U18	4	6	4	10	8	....	....	....	....	....	....	....	....	....	....	....	....	....	....	....	....	....	....
	Timra IK Jr.	Swe-Jr.	18	5	14	19	39	....	....	....	....	....	....	....	....	....	....	....	....	....	....	....	....	....	....
	Timra IK	Sweden	32	1	2	3	4	....	....	....	....	....	....	....	....	....	10	0	0	0	0	....	....	....	....
2008-09	Timra IK Jr.	Swe-Jr.	8	5	1	6	8	....	....	....	....	....	....	....	....	....	....	....	....	....	....	....	....	....	....
	Timra IK	Sweden	47	4	6	10	12	....	....	....	....	....	....	....	....	....	7	0	0	0	4	....	....	....	....
2009-10	Timra IK	Sweden	49	7	9	16	14	....	....	....	....	....	....	....	....	....	5	0	2	2	2	....	....	....	....
2010-11	Timra IK	Sweden	49	11	15	26	38	....	....	....	....	....	....	....	....	....	....	....	....	....	....	....	....	....	....
	Timra IK Jr.	Swe-Jr.	....	....	....	....	....	....	....	....	....	....	....	....	....	....	2	1	2	3	0	....	....	....	....
2011-12	**Edmonton**	**NHL**	**56**	**2**	**4**	**6**	**12**	**0**	**1**	**0**	**54**	**3.7**	**–8**	**344**	**43.3**	**10:37**	....	....	....	....	....	....	....	....	....
	Oklahoma City	AHL	14	1	4	5	10	....	....	....	....	....	....	....	....	....	14	2	2	4	4	....	....	....	....
2012-13	Oklahoma City	AHL	47	9	11	20	22	....	....	....	....	....	....	....	....	....	8	5	3	8	4	....	....	....	....
	Edmonton	**NHL**	**11**	**0**	**1**	**1**	**2**	**0**	**0**	**0**	**11**	**0.0**	**–4**	**55**	**49.1**	**11:02**	....	....	....	....	....	....	....	....	....
	NHL Totals		**67**	**2**	**5**	**7**	**14**	**0**	**1**	**0**	**65**	**3.1**		**399**	**44.1**	**10:41**	....	....	....	....	....	....	....	....	....

LANDESKOG, Gabriel

(LAND-ehs-kawg, GAY-bree-ehl) **COL**

Left wing. Shoots left. 6'1", 204 lbs. Born, Stockholm, Sweden, November 23, 1992. Colorado's 1st choice, 2nd overall, in 2011 Entry Draft.

Season	Club	League	GP	G	A	Pts	PIM	PP	SH	GW	S	%	+/-	TF	F%	Min	Playoffs GP	G	A	Pts	PIM	PP	SH	GW	Min
2007-08	Djurgarden U18	Swe-U18	23	12	10	22	4	....	....	....	....	....	....	....	....	....	2	0	0	0	0	....	....	....	....
	Djurgarden Jr.	Swe-Jr.	1	0	0	0	0	....	....	....	....	....	....	....	....	....	....	....	....	....	....	....	....	....	....
2008-09	Djurgarden U18	Swe-U18	8	5	7	12	41	....	....	....	....	....	....	....	....	....	2	0	0	0	0	....	....	....	....
	Djurgarden Jr.	Swe-Jr.	31	7	14	21	63	....	....	....	....	....	....	....	....	....	6	1	0	1	8	....	....	....	....
	Djurgarden	Sweden	3	0	1	1	2	....	....	....	....	....	....	....	....	....	....	....	....	....	....	....	....	....	....
2009-10	Kitchener Rangers	OHL	61	24	22	46	51	....	....	....	....	....	....	....	....	....	20	8	15	23	18	....	....	....	....
2010-11	Kitchener Rangers	OHL	53	36	30	66	61	....	....	....	....	....	....	....	....	....	7	6	4	10	4	....	....	....	....
2011-12	**Colorado**	**NHL**	**82**	**22**	**30**	**52**	**51**	**6**	**0**	**5**	**270**	**8.1**	**20**	**36**	**22.2**	**18:37**	....	....	....	....	....	....	....	....	....
2012-13	Djurgarden	Sweden-2	17	6	8	14	32	....	....	....	....	....	....	....	....	....	....	....	....	....	....	....	....	....	....
	Colorado	**NHL**	**36**	**9**	**8**	**17**	**22**	**0**	**3**	**1**	**109**	**8.3**	**–4**	**18**	**33.3**	**19:20**	....	....	....	....	....	....	....	....	....
	NHL Totals		**118**	**31**	**38**	**69**	**73**	**6**	**3**	**6**	**379**	**8.2**		**54**	**25.9**	**18:50**	....	....	....	....	....	....	....	....	....

OHL All-Rookie Team (2010) • NHL All-Rookie Team (2012) • Calder Memorial Trophy (2012)

Signed as a free agent by **Djurgarden** (Sweden-2), October 3, 2012.

LANGENBRUNNER, Jamie

(lan-gehn-BRUH-nuhr, JAY-mee)

Right wing. Shoots right. 6'1", 205 lbs. Born, Cloquet, MN, July 24, 1975. Dallas' 2nd choice, 35th overall, in 1993 Entry Draft.

Season	Club	League	GP	G	A	Pts	PIM	PP	SH	GW	S	%	+/-	TF	F%	Min	Playoffs GP	G	A	Pts	PIM	PP	SH	GW	Min
1990-91	Cloquet	High-MN	20	6	16	22	8	....	....	....	....	....	....	....	....	....	....	....	....	....	....	....	....	....	....
1991-92	Cloquet	High-MN	23	16	23	39	24	....	....	....	....	....	....	....	....	....	....	....	....	....	....	....	....	....	....
1992-93	Cloquet	High-MN	27	27	62	89	18	....	....	....	....	....	....	....	....	....	....	....	....	....	....	....	....	....	....
1993-94	Peterborough	OHL	62	33	58	91	53	....	....	....	....	....	....	....	....	....	7	4	6	10	2	....	....	....	....
1994-95	Peterborough	OHL	62	42	57	99	84	....	....	....	....	....	....	....	....	....	11	8	14	22	12	....	....	....	....
	Dallas	**NHL**	**2**	**0**	**0**	**0**	**2**	**0**	**0**	**0**	**1**	**0.0**	**0**	....	....	....	....	....	....	....	....	....	....	....	....
	Kalamazoo Wings	IHL	....	....	....	....	....	....	....	....	....	....	....	....	....	....	11	1	3	4	2	....	....	....	....
1995-96	**Dallas**	**NHL**	**12**	**2**	**2**	**4**	**6**	**1**	**0**	**0**	**15**	**13.3**	**–2**	....	....	....	....	....	....	....	....	....	....	....	....
	Michigan	IHL	59	25	40	65	129	....	....	....	....	....	....	....	....	....	10	3	10	13	8	....	....	....	....
1996-97	**Dallas**	**NHL**	**76**	**13**	**26**	**39**	**51**	**3**	**0**	**3**	**112**	**11.6**	**–2**	....	....	....	**5**	**1**	**1**	**2**	**14**	**0**	**0**	**1**	....
1997-98	**Dallas**	**NHL**	**81**	**23**	**29**	**52**	**61**	**8**	**0**	**6**	**159**	**14.5**	**9**	....	....	....	**16**	**1**	**4**	**5**	**14**	**0**	**0**	**1**	....
	United States	Olympics	3	0	0	0	4	....	....	....	....	....	....	....	....	....	....	....	....	....	....	....	....	....	....
1998-99 ♦	**Dallas**	**NHL**	**75**	**12**	**33**	**45**	**62**	**4**	**0**	**1**	**145**	**8.3**	**10**	**217**	**46.1**	**15:51**	**23**	**10**	**7**	**17**	**16**	***4**	**0**	**3**	**17:43**
99-2000	**Dallas**	**NHL**	**65**	**18**	**21**	**39**	**68**	**4**	**2**	**6**	**153**	**11.8**	**16**	**40**	**50.0**	**17:33**	**15**	**1**	**7**	**8**	**18**	**1**	**0**	**0**	**15:28**
2000-01	**Dallas**	**NHL**	**53**	**12**	**18**	**30**	**57**	**3**	**2**	**4**	**104**	**11.5**	**4**	**316**	**45.3**	**16:30**	**10**	**2**	**2**	**4**	**6**	**0**	**0**	**1**	**19:26**
2001-02	**Dallas**	**NHL**	**68**	**10**	**16**	**26**	**54**	**0**	**1**	**2**	**132**	**7.6**	**–11**	**120**	**45.0**	**15:45**	....	....	....	....	....	....	....	....	....
	New Jersey	**NHL**	**14**	**3**	**3**	**6**	**23**	**0**	**0**	**2**	**31**	**9.7**	**2**	**2**	**50.0**	**15:27**	**5**	**0**	**1**	**1**	**8**	**0**	**0**	**0**	**14:57**
2002-03 ♦	**New Jersey**	**NHL**	**78**	**22**	**33**	**55**	**65**	**5**	**1**	**5**	**197**	**11.2**	**17**	**72**	**47.2**	**17:48**	**24**	***11**	**7**	***18**	**16**	**1**	**0**	***4**	**17:34**
2003-04	**New Jersey**	**NHL**	**53**	**10**	**16**	**26**	**43**	**1**	**2**	**2**	**130**	**7.7**	**9**	**31**	**51.6**	**16:01**	**5**	**0**	**2**	**2**	**2**	**0**	**0**	**0**	**15:04**
2004-05	ERC Ingolstadt	Germany	11	2	2	4	22	....	....	....	....	....	....	....	....	....	11	1	6	7	6	....	....	....	....
2005-06	**New Jersey**	**NHL**	**80**	**19**	**34**	**53**	**74**	**8**	**1**	**1**	**243**	**7.8**	**–1**	**41**	**43.9**	**18:36**	**9**	**3**	**10**	**13**	**16**	**1**	**0**	**1**	**19:46**
2006-07	**New Jersey**	**NHL**	**82**	**23**	**37**	**60**	**64**	**12**	**0**	**7**	**243**	**9.5**	**–9**	**23**	**34.8**	**18:33**	**11**	**2**	**6**	**8**	**7**	**1**	**0**	**1**	**19:16**
2007-08	**New Jersey**	**NHL**	**64**	**13**	**28**	**41**	**30**	**5**	**1**	**2**	**152**	**8.6**	**–1**	**18**	**55.6**	**18:18**	**5**	**0**	**4**	**4**	**4**	**0**	**0**	**0**	**18:30**
2008-09	**New Jersey**	**NHL**	**81**	**29**	**40**	**69**	**56**	**6**	**3**	**7**	**229**	**12.7**	**25**	**25**	**40.0**	**18:06**	**4**	**2**	**1**	**3**	**2**	**0**	**0**	**0**	**16:13**
2009-10	**New Jersey**	**NHL**	**81**	**19**	**42**	**61**	**44**	**6**	**2**	**4**	**228**	**8.3**	**6**	**60**	**48.3**	**19:33**	**5**	**0**	**1**	**1**	**4**	**0**	**0**	**0**	**18:38**
	United States	Olympics	6	1	3	4	0	....	....	....	....	....	....	....	....	....	....	....	....	....	....	....	....	....	....
2010-11	**New Jersey**	**NHL**	**31**	**4**	**10**	**14**	**16**	**0**	**0**	**2**	**76**	**5.3**	**–15**	**10**	**10.0**	**18:33**	....	....	....	....	....	....	....	....	....
	Dallas	**NHL**	**39**	**5**	**13**	**18**	**29**	**1**	**0**	**1**	**77**	**6.5**	**–3**	**18**	**55.6**	**16:33**	....	....	....	....	....	....	....	....	....
2011-12	**St. Louis**	**NHL**	**70**	**6**	**18**	**24**	**32**	**0**	**0**	**3**	**127**	**4.7**	**7**	**27**	**37.0**	**14:37**	**9**	**1**	**0**	**1**	**11**	**0**	**0**	**0**	**9:33**
2012-13	**St. Louis**	**NHL**	**4**	**0**	**1**	**1**	**0**	**0**	**0**	**0**	**5**	**0.0**	**1**	**4**	**0.0**	**9:47**	....	....	....	....	....	....	....	....	....
	NHL Totals		**1109**	**243**	**420**	**663**	**837**	**67**	**15**	**58**	**2559**	**9.5**		**1024**	**45.3**	**17:19**	**146**	**34**	**53**	**87**	**138**	**8**	**0**	**12**	**17:03**

Traded to **New Jersey** by **Dallas** with Joe Nieuwendyk for Jason Arnott, Randy McKay and New Jersey's 1st round choice (later traded to Columbus, later traded to Buffalo – Buffalo selected Daniel Paille) in 2002 Entry Draft, March 19, 2002. Signed as a free agent by **Ingolstadt** (Germany), January 24, 2005. Traded to **Dallas** by **New Jersey** for Dallas's 3rd round choice (Blake Coleman) in 2011 Entry Draft and future considerations, January 6, 2011. Signed as a free agent by **St. Louis**, July 6, 2011. • Missed majority of 2012-13 due to hip surgery, February 9, 2013.

LAPIERRE, Maxim

(la-PEE-air, max-EEM) **ST.L.**

Center. Shoots right. 6'2", 207 lbs. Born, St. Leonard, Que., March 29, 1985. Montreal's 3rd choice, 61st overall, in 2003 Entry Draft.

Season	Club	League	GP	G	A	Pts	PIM	PP	SH	GW	S	%	+/-	TF	F%	Min	Playoffs GP	G	A	Pts	PIM	PP	SH	GW	Min
2001-02	Cap-d-Madeleine	QAAA	42	14	27	41	44	....	....	....	....	....	....	....	....	....	10	3	5	8	16	....	....	....	....
	Montreal Rocket	QMJHL	9	2	0	2	2	....	....	....	....	....	....	....	....	....	....	....	....	....	....	....	....	....	....
2002-03	Montreal Rocket	QMJHL	72	22	21	43	55	....	....	....	....	....	....	....	....	....	7	1	3	4	6	....	....	....	....
2003-04	P.E.I. Rocket	QMJHL	67	25	36	61	138	....	....	....	....	....	....	....	....	....	11	7	2	9	14	....	....	....	....
2004-05	P.E.I. Rocket	QMJHL	69	25	27	52	139	....	....	....	....	....	....	....	....	....	....	....	....	....	....	....	....	....	....
2005-06	**Montreal**	**NHL**	**1**	**0**	**0**	**0**	**0**	**0**	**0**	**0**	**0**	**0.0**	**–1**	**2**	**50.0**	**3:04**	....	....	....	....	....	....	....	....	....
	Hamilton	AHL	73	13	23	36	214	....	....	....	....	....	....	....	....	....	....	....	....	....	....	....	....	....	....
2006-07	**Montreal**	**NHL**	**46**	**6**	**6**	**12**	**24**	**0**	**1**	**2**	**82**	**7.3**	**–7**	**425**	**45.2**	**11:25**	....	....	....	....	....	....	....	....	....
	Hamilton	AHL	37	11	13	24	59	....	....	....	....	....	....	....	....	....	22	6	6	12	41	....	....	....	....
2007-08	**Montreal**	**NHL**	**53**	**7**	**11**	**18**	**60**	**0**	**0**	**0**	**68**	**10.3**	**5**	**527**	**49.2**	**13:10**	**12**	**0**	**3**	**3**	**6**	**0**	**0**	**0**	**11:38**
	Hamilton	AHL	19	7	7	14	63	....	....	....	....	....	....	....	....	....	....	....	....	....	....	....	....	....	....
2008-09	**Montreal**	**NHL**	**79**	**15**	**13**	**28**	**76**	**1**	**2**	**2**	**165**	**9.1**	**9**	**987**	**53.2**	**14:48**	**4**	**0**	**0**	**0**	**26**	**0**	**0**	**0**	**14:56**
2009-10	**Montreal**	**NHL**	**76**	**7**	**7**	**14**	**61**	**0**	**0**	**1**	**101**	**6.9**	**–14**	**425**	**48.9**	**12:16**	**19**	**3**	**1**	**4**	**20**	**0**	**0**	**1**	**12:20**
2010-11	**Montreal**	**NHL**	**38**	**5**	**3**	**8**	**63**	**0**	**0**	**0**	**78**	**6.4**	**–7**	**50**	**58.0**	**11:42**	....	....	....	....	....	....	....	....	....
	Anaheim	**NHL**	**21**	**0**	**3**	**3**	**9**	**0**	**0**	**0**	**28**	**0.0**	**–6**	**133**	**53.4**	**11:35**	....	....	....	....	....	....	....	....	....
	Vancouver	**NHL**	**19**	**1**	**0**	**1**	**8**	**0**	**0**	**0**	**23**	**4.3**	**–1**	**157**	**46.5**	**11:32**	**25**	**3**	**2**	**5**	***66**	**0**	**0**	**1**	**13:34**

			Regular Season														Playoffs								
Season	Club	League	GP	G	A	Pts	PIM	PP	SH	GW	S	%	+/-	TF	F%	Min	GP	G	A	Pts	PIM	PP	SH	GW	Min
2011-12	**Vancouver**	**NHL**	**82**	**9**	**10**	**19**	**130**	**0**	**0**	**0**	**103**	**8.7**	**–3**	**482**	**52.1**	**11:14**	**5**	**0**	**1**	**1**	**16**	**0**	**0**	**0**	**10:20**
2012-13	**Vancouver**	**NHL**	**48**	**4**	**6**	**10**	**45**	**0**	**0**	**1**	**54**	**7.4**	**–6**	**542**	**50.6**	**12:36**	**4**	**0**	**0**	**0**	**6**	**0**	**0**	**0**	**9:30**
	NHL Totals		**463**	**54**	**59**	**113**	**476**	**1**	**3**	**6**	**702**	**7.7**		**3730**	**50.5**	**12:26**	**69**	**6**	**7**	**13**	**140**	**0**	**0**	**2**	**12:30**

Traded to **Anaheim** by **Montreal** for Brett Festerling and Anaheim's 5th round choice (later traded back to Anaheim – Anaheim selected Brian Cooper) in 2012 Entry Draft, December 31, 2010. Traded to **Vancouver** by **Anaheim** with MacGregor Sharp for Joel Perrault and Vancouver's 3rd round choice (Frederik Andersen) in 2012 Entry Draft, February 28, 2011. Signed as a free agent by **St. Louis**, July 5, 2013.

LaROSE, Chad

(lah-ROHZ, CHAD)

Right wing. Shoots right. 5'10", 181 lbs. Born, Fraser, MI, March 27, 1982.

Season	Club	League	GP	G	A	Pts	PIM	PP	SH	GW	S	%	+/-	TF	F%	Min	GP	G	A	Pts	PIM	PP	SH	GW	Min
99-2000	Sioux Falls	USHL	54	29	26	55	28	....	....	....	....	....	....	....	....	....	3	0	1	1	0	....	....	....	....
2000-01	Sioux Falls	USHL	24	11	22	33	50	....	....	....	....	....	....	....	....	....	....	....	....	....	....	....	....	....	....
	Plymouth Whalers	OHL	32	18	7	25	24	....	....	....	....	....	....	....	....	....	19	10	10	20	22	....	....	....	....
2001-02	Plymouth Whalers	OHL	53	32	27	59	40	....	....	....	....	....	....	....	....	....	6	3	4	7	16	....	....	....	....
2002-03	Plymouth Whalers	OHL	67	61	56	117	52	....	....	....	....	....	....	....	....	....	15	9	8	17	25	....	....	....	....
2003-04	Lowell	AHL	36	7	9	16	29	....	....	....	....	....	....	....	....	....	....	....	....	....	....	....	....	....	....
	Florida Everblades	ECHL	41	16	19	35	16	....	....	....	....	....	....	....	....	....	14	3	4	7	20	....	....	....	....
2004-05	Lowell	AHL	66	20	22	42	32	....	....	....	....	....	....	....	....	....	11	3	5	8	10	....	....	....	....
2005-06 ♦	**Carolina**	**NHL**	**49**	**1**	**12**	**13**	**35**	**0**	**0**	**1**	**62**	**1.6**	**7**	**5**	**40.0**	**10:35**	**21**	**0**	**1**	**1**	**10**	**0**	**0**	**0**	**8:58**
	Lowell	AHL	23	14	11	25	10	....	....	....	....	....	....	....	....	....	....	....	....	....	....	....	....	....	....
2006-07	**Carolina**	**NHL**	**80**	**6**	**12**	**18**	**10**	**0**	**2**	**0**	**94**	**6.4**	**–2**	**50**	**30.0**	**10:13**	....	....	....	....	....	....	....	....	....
2007-08	**Carolina**	**NHL**	**58**	**11**	**12**	**23**	**46**	**0**	**1**	**2**	**117**	**9.4**	**6**	**19**	**31.6**	**14:03**	....	....	....	....	....	....	....	....	....
2008-09	**Carolina**	**NHL**	**81**	**19**	**12**	**31**	**35**	**0**	**2**	**4**	**171**	**11.1**	**6**	**18**	**27.8**	**15:08**	**18**	**4**	**7**	**11**	**16**	**0**	**0**	**0**	**17:48**
2009-10	**Carolina**	**NHL**	**56**	**11**	**17**	**28**	**24**	**0**	**1**	**0**	**138**	**8.0**	**–2**	**12**	**16.7**	**15:42**	....	....	....	....	....	....	....	....	....
2010-11	**Carolina**	**NHL**	**82**	**16**	**15**	**31**	**59**	**2**	**1**	**0**	**176**	**9.1**	**–21**	**33**	**33.3**	**16:01**	....	....	....	....	....	....	....	....	....
2011-12	**Carolina**	**NHL**	**67**	**19**	**13**	**32**	**48**	**3**	**1**	**5**	**199**	**9.5**	**–15**	**43**	**41.9**	**16:46**	....	....	....	....	....	....	....	....	....
2012-13	**Carolina**	**NHL**	**35**	**2**	**2**	**4**	**29**	**0**	**0**	**0**	**65**	**3.1**	**–8**	**22**	**40.9**	**12:51**	....	....	....	....	....	....	....	....	....
	NHL Totals		**508**	**85**	**95**	**180**	**286**	**5**	**8**	**12**	**1022**	**8.3**		**202**	**33.7**	**14:03**	**39**	**4**	**8**	**12**	**26**	**0**	**0**	**0**	**13:02**

OHL Second All-Star Team (2003)

Signed as a free agent by **Carolina**, August 6, 2003.

LARSEN, Philip

(LAHR-suhn, FIHL-ihp) **EDM**

Defense. Shoots right. 6', 190 lbs. Born, Esbjerg, Denmark, December 7, 1989. Dallas' 3rd choice, 149th overall, in 2008 Entry Draft.

Season	Club	League	GP	G	A	Pts	PIM	PP	SH	GW	S	%	+/-	TF	F%	Min	GP	G	A	Pts	PIM	PP	SH	GW	Min
2004-05	Esbjerg IK Jr.	Den-Jr.	10	1	0	1	2	....	....	....	....	....	....	....	....	....	....	....	....	....	....	....	....	....	....
2005-06	Rogle Jr.	Swe-Jr.	32	1	4	5	24	....	....	....	....	....	....	....	....	....	....	....	....	....	....	....	....	....	....
	Rogle	Sweden-2	13	0	0	0	0	....	....	....	....	....	....	....	....	....	....	....	....	....	....	....	....	....	....
2006-07	Frolunda U18	Swe-U18	3	1	2	3	2	....	....	....	....	....	....	....	....	....	4	2	1	3	8	....	....	....	....
	Frolunda Jr.	Swe-Jr.	37	3	15	18	50	....	....	....	....	....	....	....	....	....	8	0	1	1	6	....	....	....	....
	Frolunda	Sweden	5	0	0	0	0	....	....	....	....	....	....	....	....	....	....	....	....	....	....	....	....	....	....
2007-08	Frolunda Jr.	Swe-Jr.	8	1	4	5	12	....	....	....	....	....	....	....	....	....	7	0	4	4	6	....	....	....	....
	Boras HC	Sweden-2	24	5	5	10	32	....	....	....	....	....	....	....	....	....	....	....	....	....	....	....	....	....	....
	Frolunda	Sweden	16	0	0	0	2	....	....	....	....	....	....	....	....	....	....	....	....	....	....	....	....	....	....
2008-09	Frolunda Jr.	Swe-Jr.	1	1	0	1	0	....	....	....	....	....	....	....	....	....	....	....	....	....	....	....	....	....	....
	Frolunda	Sweden	53	2	15	17	18	....	....	....	....	....	....	....	....	....	11	2	1	3	4	....	....	....	....
2009-10	Frolunda	Sweden	42	1	9	10	20	....	....	....	....	....	....	....	....	....	7	0	0	0	4	....	....	....	....
	Dallas	**NHL**	**2**	**0**	**1**	**1**	**0**	**0**	**0**	**0**	**1**	**0.0**	**1**	**0**	**0.0**	**12:27**	....	....	....	....	....	....	....	....	....
2010-11	**Dallas**	**NHL**	**6**	**0**	**2**	**2**	**0**	**0**	**0**	**0**	**11**	**0.0**	**1**	**0**	**0.0**	**13:26**	....	....	....	....	....	....	....	....	....
	Texas Stars	AHL	54	4	18	22	12	....	....	....	....	....	....	....	....	....	6	2	3	5	4	....	....	....	....
2011-12	**Dallas**	**NHL**	**55**	**3**	**8**	**11**	**16**	**1**	**0**	**0**	**69**	**4.3**	**11**	**0**	**0.0**	**17:57**	....	....	....	....	....	....	....	....	....
	Texas Stars	AHL	12	1	9	10	6	....	....	....	....	....	....	....	....	....	....	....	....	....	....	....	....	....	....
2012-13	Lukko Rauma	Finland	27	5	10	15	24	....	....	....	....	....	....	....	....	....	....	....	....	....	....	....	....	....	....
	Dallas	**NHL**	**32**	**2**	**3**	**5**	**18**	**1**	**0**	**0**	**30**	**6.7**	**–10**	**0**	**0.0**	**14:53**	....	....	....	....	....	....	....	....	....
	NHL Totals		**95**	**5**	**14**	**19**	**34**	**2**	**0**	**0**	**111**	**4.5**		**0**	**0.0**	**16:31**	....	....	....	....	....	....	....	....	....

• Assigned to **Frolunda** (Sweden) by **Dallas**, September 20. 2009. Signed as a free agent by **Rauma** (Finland), September 27, 2012. Traded to **Edmonton** by **Dallas** with Dallas' 7th round choice in 2016 Entry Draft for Shawn Horcoff, July 5, 2013.

LARSSON, Adam

(LAHR-suhn, A-duhm) **N.J.**

Defense. Shoots right. 6'3", 205 lbs. Born, Skelleftea, Sweden, November 12, 1992. New Jersey's 1st choice, 4th overall, in 2011 Entry Draft.

Season	Club	League	GP	G	A	Pts	PIM	PP	SH	GW	S	%	+/-	TF	F%	Min	GP	G	A	Pts	PIM	PP	SH	GW	Min
2007-08	Skelleftea U18	Swe-U18	24	5	15	20	30	....	....	....	....	....	....	....	....	....	....	....	....	....	....	....	....	....	....
	Skelleftea Jr.	Swe-Jr.	3	0	5	5	6	....	....	....	....	....	....	....	....	....	....	....	....	....	....	....	....	....	....
2008-09	Skelleftea AIK U18	Swe-U18	7	3	8	11	6	....	....	....	....	....	....	....	....	....	8	0	6	6	6	....	....	....	....
	Skelleftea AIK Jr.	Swe-Jr.	26	2	7	9	28	....	....	....	....	....	....	....	....	....	5	0	4	4	2	....	....	....	....
	Skelleftea AIK	Sweden	1	0	0	0	0	....	....	....	....	....	....	....	....	....	....	....	....	....	....	....	....	....	....
2009-10	Skelleftea AIK Jr.	Swe-Jr.	1	1	0	1	2	....	....	....	....	....	....	....	....	....	....	....	....	....	....	....	....	....	....
	Skelleftea AIK	Sweden	49	4	13	17	18	....	....	....	....	....	....	....	....	....	11	0	1	1	31	....	....	....	....
2010-11	Skelleftea AIK	Sweden	37	1	8	9	41	....	....	....	....	....	....	....	....	....	17	0	4	4	12	....	....	....	....
2011-12	**New Jersey**	**NHL**	**65**	**2**	**16**	**18**	**20**	**0**	**0**	**0**	**68**	**2.9**	**–7**	**0**	**0.0**	**20:37**	**5**	**1**	**0**	**1**	**4**	**0**	**0**	**0**	**16:25**
2012-13	Albany Devils	AHL	33	4	15	19	24	....	....	....	....	....	....	....	....	....	....	....	....	....	....	....	....	....	....
	New Jersey	**NHL**	**37**	**0**	**6**	**6**	**12**	**0**	**0**	**0**	**30**	**0.0**	**4**	**0**	**0.0**	**18:06**	....	....	....	....	....	....	....	....	....
	NHL Totals		**102**	**2**	**22**	**24**	**32**	**0**	**0**	**0**	**98**	**2.0**		**0**	**0.0**	**19:42**	**5**	**1**	**0**	**1**	**4**	**0**	**0**	**0**	**16:25**

LARSSON, Johan

(LAHR-suhn, YOH-han) **BUF**

Left wing. Shoots left. 5'10", 200 lbs. Born, Lau, Sweden, July 25, 1992. Minnesota's 3rd choice, 56th overall, in 2010 Entry Draft.

Season	Club	League	GP	G	A	Pts	PIM	PP	SH	GW	S	%	+/-	TF	F%	Min	GP	G	A	Pts	PIM	PP	SH	GW	Min
2005-06	Sudrets	Sweden-4	2	0	2	2	2	....	....	....	....	....	....	....	....	....	....	....	....	....	....	....	....	....	....
2006-07	Sudrets	Sweden-4	29	13	7	20	40	....	....	....	....	....	....	....	....	....	....	....	....	....	....	....	....	....	....
2007-08	Sudrets	Sweden-4	25	11	11	22	71	....	....	....	....	....	....	....	....	....	....	....	....	....	....	....	....	....	....
2008-09	Brynas U18	Swe-U18	11	6	4	10	76	....	....	....	....	....	....	....	....	....	3	0	3	3	2	....	....	....	....
	Brynas IF Gavle Jr.	Swe-Jr.	33	4	5	9	55	....	....	....	....	....	....	....	....	....	5	0	0	0	2	....	....	....	....
2009-10	Brynas U18	Swe-U18	4	1	1	2	2	....	....	....	....	....	....	....	....	....	4	4	4	8	6	....	....	....	....
	Brynas IF Gavle Jr.	Swe-Jr.	40	15	19	34	80	....	....	....	....	....	....	....	....	....	5	1	1	2	2	....	....	....	....
2010-11	Brynas IF Gavle	Sweden	43	4	4	8	18	....	....	....	....	....	....	....	....	....	5	0	2	2	4	....	....	....	....
	Brynas IF Gavle Jr.	Swe-Jr.	10	6	9	15	8	....	....	....	....	....	....	....	....	....	1	0	0	0	0	....	....	....	....
2011-12	Brynas IF Gavle	Sweden	49	12	24	36	34	....	....	....	....	....	....	....	....	....	16	2	7	9	16	....	....	....	....
2012-13	Houston Aeros	AHL	62	15	22	37	38	....	....	....	....	....	....	....	....	....	....	....	....	....	....	....	....	....	....
	Minnesota	**NHL**	**1**	**0**	**0**	**0**	**0**	**0**	**0**	**0**	**2**	**0.0**	**0**	**0**	**0.0**	**14:02**	....	....	....	....	....	....	....	....	....
	Rochester	AHL	7	1	3	4	2	....	....	....	....	....	....	....	....	....	3	0	3	3	6	....	....	....	....
	NHL Totals		**1**	**0**	**0**	**0**	**0**	**0**	**0**	**0**	**2**	**0.0**		**0**	**0.0**	**14:02**	....	....	....	....	....	....	....	....	....

Traded to **Buffalo** by **Minnesota** with Matt Hackett, Minnesota's 1st round choice (Nikita Zadorov) in 2013 Entry Draft and Minnesota's 2nd round choice in 2014 Entry Draft for Jason Pominville and Buffalo's 4th round choice in 2014 Entry Draft, April 3, 2013.

LASHOFF, Brian

(LASH-awf, BRIGH-uhn) **DET**

Defense. Shoots left. 6'3", 212 lbs. Born, Albany, NY, July 16, 1990.

Season	Club	League	GP	G	A	Pts	PIM	PP	SH	GW	S	%	+/-	TF	F%	Min	GP	G	A	Pts	PIM	PP	SH	GW	Min
2006-07	Barrie Colts	OHL	47	2	10	12	20	....	....	....	....	....	....	....	....	....	5	0	1	1	2	....	....	....	....
2007-08	Barrie Colts	OHL	50	5	15	20	44	....	....	....	....	....	....	....	....	....	8	0	1	1	4	....	....	....	....
2008-09	Barrie Colts	OHL	25	1	12	13	19	....	....	....	....	....	....	....	....	....	....	....	....	....	....	....	....	....	....
	Kingston	OHL	35	6	13	19	32	....	....	....	....	....	....	....	....	....	....	....	....	....	....	....	....	....	....
	Grand Rapids	AHL	6	1	4	5	0	....	....	....	....	....	....	....	....	....	8	1	4	5	2	....	....	....	....
2009-10	Kingston	OHL	58	6	21	27	71	....	....	....	....	....	....	....	....	....	7	0	0	0	12	....	....	....	....
	Grand Rapids	AHL	6	0	2	2	2	....	....	....	....	....	....	....	....	....	....	....	....	....	....	....	....	....	....
2010-11	Grand Rapids	AHL	37	0	3	3	25	....	....	....	....	....	....	....	....	....	....	....	....	....	....	....	....	....	....
	Toledo Walleye	ECHL	3	0	1	1	0	....	....	....	....	....	....	....	....	....	....	....	....	....	....	....	....	....	....
2011-12	Grand Rapids	AHL	76	8	11	19	41	....	....	....	....	....	....	....	....	....	....	....	....	....	....	....	....	....	....
2012-13	Grand Rapids	AHL	37	2	4	6	23	....	....	....	....	....	....	....	....	....	18	0	1	1	10	....	....	....	....
	Detroit	**NHL**	**31**	**1**	**4**	**5**	**15**	**0**	**0**	**0**	**26**	**3.8**	**–10**	**0**	**0.0**	**17:47**	**3**	**0**	**0**	**0**	**0**	**0**	**0**	**0**	**18:00**
	NHL Totals		**31**	**1**	**4**	**5**	**15**	**0**	**0**	**0**	**26**	**3.8**		**0**	**0.0**	**17:47**	**3**	**0**	**0**	**0**	**0**	**0**	**0**	**0**	**18:00**

Signed as a free agent by **Detroit**, October 1, 2008.

			Regular Season														Playoffs								
Season	Club	League	GP	G	A	Pts	PIM	PP	SH	GW	S	%	+/-	TF	F%	Min	GP	G	A	Pts	PIM	PP	SH	GW	Min

LASHOFF, Matt

(LASH-awf, MAT)

Defense. Shoots left. 6'2", 204 lbs. Born, East Greenbush, NY, September 29, 1986. Boston's 1st choice, 22nd overall, in 2005 Entry Draft.

Season	Club	League	GP	G	A	Pts	PIM	PP	SH	GW	S	%	+/-	TF	F%	Min	GP	G	A	Pts	PIM	PP	SH	GW	Min
2002-03	USNTDP	U-17	16	1	3	4	14																		
	USNTDP	NAHL	46	2	5	7	53																		
2003-04	Kitchener Rangers	OHL	62	5	19	24	94										5	0	1	1	0				
2004-05	Kitchener Rangers	OHL	44	4	18	22	44										13	0	3	3	18				
2005-06	Kitchener Rangers	OHL	56	7	40	47	146										5	1	1	2	12				
	Providence Bruins	AHL	7	1	1	2	6										6	0	0	0	6				
2006-07	**Boston**	**NHL**	**12**	**0**	**2**	**2**	**12**	**0**	**0**	**0**	**8**	**0.0**	**–6**	**0**	**0.0**	**14:55**									
	Providence Bruins	AHL	64	11	26	37	60																		
2007-08	**Boston**	**NHL**	**18**	**1**	**4**	**5**	**0**	**1**	**0**	**0**	**11**	**9.1**	**–2**	**0**	**0.0**	**13:35**									
	Providence Bruins	AHL	60	9	27	36	79										9	0	4	4	6				
2008-09	**Boston**	**NHL**	**16**	**0**	**1**	**1**	**10**	**0**	**0**	**0**	**6**	**0.0**	**1**	**0**	**0.0**	**13:07**									
	Providence Bruins	AHL	33	5	16	21	36																		
	Tampa Bay	**NHL**	**12**	**0**	**7**	**7**	**10**	**0**	**0**	**0**	**19**	**0.0**	**–7**	**0**	**0.0**	**23:46**									
	Norfolk Admirals	AHL	2	0	0	0	2																		
2009-10	**Tampa Bay**	**NHL**	**5**	**0**	**0**	**0**	**21**	**0**	**0**	**0**	**2**	**0.0**	**–2**	**0**	**0.0**	**8:53**									
	Norfolk Admirals	AHL	68	8	16	24	105																		
2010-11	**Toronto**	**NHL**	**11**	**0**	**1**	**1**	**6**	**0**	**0**	**0**	**8**	**0.0**	**1**	**0**	**0.0**	**13:50**									
	Toronto Marlies	AHL	69	7	21	28	137																		
2011-12	Toronto Marlies	AHL	9	1	4	5	12										8	0	4	4	8				
2012-13	ZSC Lions Zurich	Swiss	49	1	9	10	43										12	0	1	1	14				
	NHL Totals		**74**	**1**	**15**	**16**	**59**	**1**	**0**	**0**	**54**	**1.9**		**0**	**0.0**	**15:04**									

AHL All-Rookie Team (2007)

Traded to **Tampa Bay** by **Boston** with Martins Karsums for Mark Recchi and Tampa Bay's 2nd round choice (later traded to Florida – Florida selected Alexander Petrovic) in 2010 Entry Draft, March 4, 2009. Traded to **Toronto** by **Tampa Bay** for Alex Berry and Stefano Giliati, August 27, 2010. • Missed majority of 2011-12 due to knee injury at Lake Erie (AHL), October 30. 2011. Signed as a free agent by **Zurich** (Swiss), August 3, 2012.

LATENDRESSE, Guillaume

(lah-TEHN-drehs, GEE-OHM)

Left wing. Shoots left. 6'2", 230 lbs. Born, Ste-Catherine, Que., May 24, 1987. Montreal's 2nd choice, 45th overall, in 2005 Entry Draft.

Season	Club	League	GP	G	A	Pts	PIM	PP	SH	GW	S	%	+/-	TF	F%	Min	GP	G	A	Pts	PIM	PP	SH	GW	Min
2003-04	Drummondville	QMJHL	53	24	25	49	66																		
2004-05	Drummondville	QMJHL	65	29	49	78	76										6	6	4	10	7				
2005-06	Drummondville	QMJHL	51	43	40	83	105										5	3	2	5	8				
2006-07	**Montreal**	**NHL**	**80**	**16**	**13**	**29**	**47**	**5**	**0**	**3**	**121**	**13.2**	**–20**	**16**	**12.5**	**12:36**									
2007-08	**Montreal**	**NHL**	**73**	**16**	**11**	**27**	**41**	**2**	**0**	**3**	**116**	**13.8**	**–2**	**8**	**25.0**	**12:15**	**8**	**0**	**1**	**1**	**19**	**0**	**0**	**0**	**10:43**
2008-09	**Montreal**	**NHL**	**56**	**14**	**12**	**26**	**45**	**1**	**0**	**2**	**117**	**12.0**	**4**	**2**	**50.0**	**13:37**	**4**	**0**	**0**	**0**	**12**	**0**	**0**	**0**	**11:44**
2009-10	**Montreal**	**NHL**	**23**	**2**	**1**	**3**	**4**	**0**	**0**	**0**	**27**	**7.4**	**–4**	**0**	**0.0**	**11:21**									
	Minnesota	**NHL**	**55**	**25**	**12**	**37**	**12**	**7**	**0**	**4**	**133**	**18.8**	**1**	**9**	**11.1**	**16:28**									
2010-11	**Minnesota**	**NHL**	**11**	**3**	**3**	**6**	**8**	**1**	**0**	**1**	**18**	**16.7**	**2**	**6**	**0.0**	**12:43**									
2011-12	**Minnesota**	**NHL**	**16**	**5**	**4**	**9**	**20**	**1**	**0**	**1**	**36**	**13.9**	**6**	**4**	**50.0**	**15:11**									
2012-13	**Ottawa**	**NHL**	**27**	**6**	**4**	**10**	**8**	**1**	**0**	**0**	**53**	**11.3**	**–2**	**4**	**0.0**	**14:48**	**3**	**1**	**1**	**2**	**6**	**0**	**0**	**0**	**13:55**
	NHL Totals		**341**	**87**	**60**	**147**	**185**	**18**	**0**	**14**	**621**	**14.0**		**49**	**16.3**	**13:32**	**15**	**1**	**2**	**3**	**37**	**0**	**0**	**0**	**11:38**

QMJHL All-Rookie Team (2004)

Traded to **Minnesota** by **Montreal** for Benoit Pouliot, November 23, 2009. • Missed majority of 2010-11 due to groin injury vs. Los Angeles, October 25, 2010. • Missed majority of 2011-12 due to head injury at San Jose, November 10, 2011. Signed as a free agent by **Ottawa**, July 1. 2012.

LAUGHTON, Scott

(LAW-tuhn, SKAWT) **PHI**

Center. Shoots left. 6'1", 190 lbs. Born, Oakville, Ont., May 30, 1994. Philadelphia's 1st choice, 20th overall, in 2012 Entry Draft.

Season	Club	League	GP	G	A	Pts	PIM	PP	SH	GW	S	%	+/-	TF	F%	Min	GP	G	A	Pts	PIM	PP	SH	GW	Min
2009-10	Tor. Marlboros	GTHL	76	55	40	95	109																		
	St. Michael's	ON-Jr.A	2	0	0	0	4																		
2010-11	Oshawa Generals	OHL	63	12	11	23	58										10	1	1	2	11				
2011-12	Oshawa Generals	OHL	64	21	32	53	101										6	2	3	5	17				
2012-13	Oshawa Generals	OHL	49	23	33	56	72										7	7	6	13	11				
	Philadelphia	**NHL**	**5**	**0**	**0**	**0**	**0**	**0**	**0**	**0**	**10**	**0.0**	**0**	**43**	**44.2**	**11:31**									
	Adirondack	AHL	6	1	2	3	0																		
	NHL Totals		**5**	**0**	**0**	**0**	**0**	**0**	**0**	**0**	**10**	**0.0**		**43**	**44.2**	**11:31**									

LAURIDSEN, Oliver

(LAWR-ihd-suhn, AW-lih-vuhr) **PHI**

Defense. Shoots left. 6'6", 220 lbs. Born, Gentofte, Denmark, March 24, 1989. Philadelphia's 6th choice, 196th overall, in 2009 Entry Draft.

Season	Club	League	GP	G	A	Pts	PIM	PP	SH	GW	S	%	+/-	TF	F%	Min	GP	G	A	Pts	PIM	PP	SH	GW	Min
2004-05	IC Gentofte Jr.	Den-Jr.	24	4	12	16	22																		
	IC Gentofte	Den-2	8	0	1	1	0																		
2005-06	Rogle Jr.	Swe-Jr.	28	1	1	2	32																		
2006-07	Linkopings HC Jr.	Swe-Jr.	34	0	2	2	95										5	0	0	0	8				
2007-08	Linkoping U18	Swe-U18	2	1	3	4	0																		
	Tranas AIF	Sweden-3	1	0	0	0	0																		
	Linkopings HC Jr.	Swe-Jr.	35	5	6	11	159										1	0	1	1	0				
2008-09	St. Cloud State	WCHA	28	0	1	1	38																		
2009-10	St. Cloud State	WCHA	43	6	6	12	54																		
2010-11	St. Cloud State	WCHA	37	1	8	9	51																		
	Adirondack	AHL	2	0	0	0	30																		
2011-12	Adirondack	AHL	65	3	4	7	85																		
2012-13	Adirondack	AHL	59	1	5	6	77																		
	Philadelphia	**NHL**	**15**	**2**	**1**	**3**	**34**	**0**	**0**	**2**	**14**	**14.3**	**0**	**0**	**0.0**	**15:08**									
	NHL Totals		**15**	**2**	**1**	**3**	**34**	**0**	**0**	**2**	**14**	**14.3**		**0**	**0.0**	**15:08**									

LEACH, Jay

(LEECH, JAY)

Defense. Shoots left. 6'5", 220 lbs. Born, Syracuse, NY, September 2, 1979. Phoenix's 5th choice, 115th overall, in 1998 Entry Draft.

Season	Club	League	GP	G	A	Pts	PIM	PP	SH	GW	S	%	+/-	TF	F%	Min	GP	G	A	Pts	PIM	PP	SH	GW	Min
1995-96	Capital District	Exhib.	53	3	8	11	33																		
1996-97	Capital District	Exhib.	57	8	50	58	140																		
1997-98	Providence	H-East	32	0	8	8	29																		
1998-99	Providence	H-East	33	1	8	9	42																		
99-2000	Providence	H-East	37	1	9	10	101																		
2000-01	Providence	H-East	40	4	21	25	104																		
2001-02	Mississippi	ECHL	70	3	13	16	116										10	1	1	2	8				
2002-03	Springfield	AHL	9	0	0	0	0																		
	Augusta Lynx	ECHL	65	8	11	19	162																		
2003-04	Providence Bruins	AHL	3	0	0	0	4																		
	Long Beach	ECHL	3	0	1	1	4																		
	Bridgeport	AHL	23	0	1	1	33										7	0	1	1	10				
	Trenton Titans	ECHL	31	2	11	13	45																		
2004-05	Providence Bruins	AHL	62	4	5	9	92										17	0	0	0	28				
	Trenton Titans	ECHL	11	0	2	2	17																		
2005-06	**Boston**	**NHL**	**2**	**0**	**0**	**0**	**7**	**0**	**0**	**0**	**0**	**0.0**	**1**	**0**	**0.0**	**6:20**									
	Providence Bruins	AHL	71	5	11	16	100										6	0	1	1	15				
2006-07	Providence Bruins	AHL	73	2	5	7	128										13	0	4	4	13				
2007-08	**Tampa Bay**	**NHL**	**2**	**0**	**0**	**0**	**0**	**0**	**0**	**0**	**0**	**0.0**	**–1**	**0**	**0.0**	**4:37**									
	Norfolk Admirals	AHL	55	3	8	11	54																		
	Portland Pirates	AHL	20	3	6	9	30										18	1	0	1	7				
2008-09	**New Jersey**	**NHL**	**24**	**0**	**1**	**1**	**21**	**0**	**0**	**0**	**5**	**0.0**	**0**	**0**	**0.0**	**14:50**									
	Lowell Devils	AHL	24	2	4	6	29																		
2009-10	Lowell Devils	AHL	12	0	3	3	10																		
	Montreal	**NHL**	**7**	**0**	**0**	**0**	**5**	**0**	**0**	**0**	**4**	**0.0**	**0**	**0**	**0.0**	**13:02**									
	San Jose	**NHL**	**28**	**1**	**1**	**2**	**20**	**0**	**0**	**0**	**26**	**3.8**	**3**	**0**	**0.0**	**15:11**									
2010-11	Worcester Sharks	AHL	50	1	4	5	45																		
	New Jersey	**NHL**	**7**	**0**	**0**	**0**	**7**	**0**	**0**	**0**	**2**	**0.0**	**0**	**0**	**0.0**	**14:15**									
	Albany Devils	AHL	16	1	3	4	8																		

			Regular Season														Playoffs								
Season	Club	League	GP	G	A	Pts	PIM	PP	SH	GW	S	%	+/-	TF	F%	Min	GP	G	A	Pts	PIM	PP	SH	GW	Min
2011-12	Albany Devils	AHL	21	0	2	2	12																		
2012-13	Albany Devils	AHL	60	4	10	14	63																		
	NHL Totals		**70**	**1**	**2**	**3**	**60**	**0**	**0**	**0**	**37**	**2.7**		**0**	**0.0**	**14:12**									

Signed as a free agent by **Boston**, September 26, 2003. Signed as a free agent by **Tampa Bay**, July 3, 2007. Traded to **Anaheim** by **Tampa Bay** for Brandon Segal and Anaheim's 7th round choice (David Carle) in 2008 Entry Draft, February 26, 2008. Signed as a free agent by **New Jersey**, July 17, 2008. Claimed on waivers by **Montreal** from **New Jersey**, November 6, 2009. Claimed on waivers by **San Jose** from **Montreal**, December 1, 2009. Traded to **New Jersey** by **San Jose** with Steven Zalewski for Michael Swift and Patrick Davis, February 9, 2011. • Missed majority of 2011-12 due to recurring lower-body injury.

LEBDA, Brett

(LEHB-dah, BREHT)

Defense. Shoots left. 5'9", 195 lbs. Born, Buffalo Grove, IL, January 15, 1982.

Season	Club	League	GP	G	A	Pts	PIM	PP	SH	GW	S	%	+/-	TF	F%	Min	GP	G	A	Pts	PIM	PP	SH	GW	Min
1998-99	USNTDP	U-17	11	1	7	8	4																		
	USNTDP	USHL	3	0	0	0	0																		
	USNTDP	NAHL	52	11	17	28	56																		
99-2000	USNTDP	U-18	4	0	0	0	6																		
	USNTDP	USHL	22	6	7	13	28																		
2000-01	U. of Notre Dame	CCHA	39	7	19	26	109																		
2001-02	U. of Notre Dame	CCHA	34	6	8	14	54																		
2002-03	U. of Notre Dame	CCHA	40	7	14	21	48																		
2003-04	U. of Notre Dame	CCHA	39	6	18	24	42																		
	Grand Rapids	AHL	6	0	1	1	0										4	0	0	0	2				
2004-05	Grand Rapids	AHL	80	2	10	12	34																		
2005-06	**Detroit**	**NHL**	**46**	**3**	**9**	**12**	**20**	**1**	**0**	**1**	**50**	**6.0**	**9**	**2**	**0.0**	**12:38**	**6**	**0**	**0**	**0**	**4**	**0**	**0**	**0**	**13:09**
	Grand Rapids	AHL	25	4	14	18	42										11	1	4	5	8				
2006-07	**Detroit**	**NHL**	**74**	**5**	**13**	**18**	**61**	**1**	**0**	**2**	**107**	**4.7**	**16**	**0**	**0.0**	**14:54**	**12**	**0**	**2**	**2**	**8**	**0**	**0**	**0**	**16:23**
2007-08 ♦	**Detroit**	**NHL**	**78**	**3**	**11**	**14**	**48**	**0**	**0**	**1**	**110**	**2.7**	**–1**	**1**	**0.0**	**16:29**	**19**	**0**	**2**	**2**	**6**	**0**	**0**	**0**	**12:33**
2008-09	**Detroit**	**NHL**	**65**	**6**	**10**	**16**	**48**	**0**	**0**	**1**	**69**	**8.7**	**9**	**1**	**100.0**	**13:39**	**23**	**0**	**6**	**6**	**22**	**0**	**0**	**0**	**13:21**
2009-10	**Detroit**	**NHL**	**63**	**1**	**7**	**8**	**24**	**0**	**0**	**0**	**61**	**1.6**	**–2**	**0**	**0.0**	**14:59**	**2**	**0**	**0**	**0**	**0**	**0**	**0**	**0**	**5:56**
2010-11	**Toronto**	**NHL**	**41**	**1**	**3**	**4**	**14**	**0**	**0**	**0**	**34**	**2.9**	**–14**	**2**	**0.0**	**13:20**									
2011-12	Springfield	AHL	26	1	9	10	18																		
	Columbus	**NHL**	**30**	**1**	**3**	**4**	**14**	**0**	**0**	**0**	**36**	**2.8**	**–1**	**0**	**0.0**	**16:29**									
2012-13	Rockford IceHogs	AHL	27	0	11	11	18																		
	Binghamton	AHL	32	3	15	18	23										3	0	0	0	12				
	NHL Totals		**397**	**20**	**56**	**76**	**229**	**2**	**0**	**5**	**467**	**4.3**		**6**	**16.7**	**14:43**	**62**	**0**	**10**	**10**	**40**	**0**	**0**	**0**	**13:26**

CCHA All-Rookie Team (2001) • CCHA Second All-Star Team (2004)

Signed as a free agent by **Detroit**, April 3, 2004. Signed as a free agent by **Toronto**, July 7, 2010. Traded to **Nashville** by **Toronto** with Robert Slaney and Toronto's 4th round choice (later traded to St. Louis – St. Louis selected Zachary Pochiro) in 2013 Entry Draft for Matthew Lombardi and Cody Franson, July 3, 2011. Signed as a free agent by **Springfield** (AHL), November 7, 2011. Signed as a free agent by **Columbus**, January 19, 2012. Signed as a free agent by **Rockford** (AHL), September 21, 2012. Signed as a free agent by **Binghamton** (AHL), February 5, 2013.

LeBLANC, Drew

(luh-BLAWNK, DROO) **CHI**

Center. Shoots right. 6', 195 lbs. Born, Hermantown, MN, June 29, 1989.

Season	Club	League	GP	G	A	Pts	PIM	PP	SH	GW	S	%	+/-	TF	F%	Min	GP	G	A	Pts	PIM	PP	SH	GW	Min
2004-05	Hermantown	High-MN				26																			
2005-06	Hermantown	High-MN				83																			
2006-07	Hermantown	High-MN				90																			
	Chicago Steel	USHL	14	0	5	5	20										5	0	2	2	4				
2007-08	Chicago Steel	USHL	58	19	35	54	36										7	3	1	4	4				
2008-09	St. Cloud State	WCHA	38	8	7	15	18																		
2009-10	St. Cloud State	WCHA	43	6	25	31	10																		
2010-11	St. Cloud State	WCHA	38	13	26	39	18																		
2011-12	St. Cloud State	WCHA	10	2	10	12	4																		
2012-13	St. Cloud State	WCHA	42	13	*37	50	14																		
	Chicago	**NHL**	**2**	**0**	**0**	**0**	**0**	**0**	**0**	**0**	**3**	**0.0**	**–3**	**18**	**50.0**	**13:20**									
	NHL Totals		**2**	**0**	**0**	**0**	**0**	**0**	**0**	**0**	**3**	**0.0**		**18**	**50.0**	**13:20**									

WCHA First All-Star Team (2013) • WCHA Player of the Year (2013) • NCAA West First All-American Team (2013) • Hobey Baker Memorial Award (Top U.S. Collegiate Player) (2013)

• Missed majority of 2011-12 due to leg injury vs. U. of Wisconsin (WCHA), November 5, 2011. Signed as a free agent by **Chicago**, April 12, 2013.

LEBLANC, Louis

(luh-BLAWNK, LOU-ee) **MTL**

Center. Shoots right. 6', 183 lbs. Born, Pointe-Claire, Que., January 26, 1991. Montreal's 1st choice, 18th overall, in 2009 Entry Draft.

Season	Club	League	GP	G	A	Pts	PIM	PP	SH	GW	S	%	+/-	TF	F%	Min	GP	G	A	Pts	PIM	PP	SH	GW	Min
2006-07	Lac St-Louis Lions	QAAA	40	31	18	49	72										22	14	7	21	10				
2007-08	Lac St-Louis Lions	QAAA	43	54	37	91	152										14	8	14	22	76				
2008-09	Omaha Lancers	USHL	60	28	31	59	78										3	2	1	3	2				
2009-10	Harvard Crimson	ECAC	31	11	12	23	50																		
2010-11	Montreal	QMJHL	51	26	32	58	100										10	6	3	9	16				
2011-12	**Montreal**	**NHL**	**42**	**5**	**5**	**10**	**28**	**0**	**0**	**0**	**58**	**8.6**	**3**	**64**	**43.8**	**11:12**									
	Hamilton	AHL	31	11	11	22	30																		
2012-13	Hamilton	AHL	62	10	8	18	53																		
	NHL Totals		**42**	**5**	**5**	**10**	**28**	**0**	**0**	**0**	**58**	**8.6**		**64**	**43.8**	**11:12**									

USHL All-Rookie Team (2009) • USHL Rookie of the Year (2009) • ECAC All-Rookie Team (2010)

LECAVALIER, Vincent

(luh-KAV-uhl-YAY, VIHN-sihnt) **PHI**

Center. Shoots left. 6'4", 208 lbs. Born, Ile Bizard, Que., April 21, 1980. Tampa Bay's 1st choice, 1st overall, in 1998 Entry Draft.

Season	Club	League	GP	G	A	Pts	PIM	PP	SH	GW	S	%	+/-	TF	F%	Min	GP	G	A	Pts	PIM	PP	SH	GW	Min
1995-96	Notre Dame	SMHL	22	52	52	104																			
1996-97	Rimouski Oceanic	QMJHL	64	42	60	102	36										4	4	3	7	2				
1997-98	Rimouski Oceanic	QMJHL	58	44	71	115	117										18	*15	*26	*41	46				
1998-99	**Tampa Bay**	**NHL**	**82**	**13**	**15**	**28**	**23**	**2**	**0**	**2**	**125**	**10.4**	**–19**	**953**	**40.3**	**13:40**									
99-2000	**Tampa Bay**	**NHL**	**80**	**25**	**42**	**67**	**43**	**6**	**0**	**3**	**166**	**15.1**	**–25**	**1288**	**44.4**	**19:18**									
2000-01	**Tampa Bay**	**NHL**	**68**	**23**	**28**	**51**	**66**	**7**	**0**	**3**	**165**	**13.9**	**–26**	**1278**	**44.9**	**19:57**									
2001-02	**Tampa Bay**	**NHL**	**76**	**20**	**17**	**37**	**61**	**5**	**0**	**3**	**164**	**12.2**	**–18**	**931**	**41.5**	**17:09**									
2002-03	**Tampa Bay**	**NHL**	**80**	**33**	**45**	**78**	**39**	**11**	**2**	**3**	**274**	**12.0**	**0**	**1200**	**43.9**	**19:33**	**11**	**3**	**3**	**6**	**22**	**1**	**0**	**1**	**22:36**
2003-04 ♦	**Tampa Bay**	**NHL**	**81**	**32**	**34**	**66**	**52**	**5**	**2**	**6**	**242**	**13.2**	**24**	**1119**	**41.4**	**18:04**	**23**	**9**	**7**	**16**	**25**	**2**	**0**	**0**	**19:39**
2004-05	Ak Bars Kazan	Russia	30	7	9	16	78										4	1	0	1	6				
2005-06	**Tampa Bay**	**NHL**	**80**	**35**	**40**	**75**	**90**	**13**	**2**	**7**	**309**	**11.3**	**0**	**1366**	**51.2**	**20:08**	**5**	**1**	**3**	**4**	**7**	**1**	**0**	**0**	**22:17**
	Canada	Olympics	6	0	3	3	16																		
2006-07	**Tampa Bay**	**NHL**	**82**	***52**	**56**	**108**	**44**	**16**	**5**	**7**	**339**	**15.3**	**2**	**1653**	**46.6**	**22:36**	**6**	**5**	**2**	**7**	**10**	**1**	**0**	**1**	**26:29**
2007-08	**Tampa Bay**	**NHL**	**81**	**40**	**52**	**92**	**89**	**10**	**1**	**7**	**318**	**12.6**	**–17**	**1671**	**48.8**	**22:57**									
2008-09	**Tampa Bay**	**NHL**	**77**	**29**	**38**	**67**	**54**	**10**	**1**	**6**	**291**	**10.0**	**–9**	**1395**	**50.9**	**20:15**									
2009-10	**Tampa Bay**	**NHL**	**82**	**24**	**46**	**70**	**63**	**5**	**0**	**3**	**295**	**8.1**	**–16**	**1449**	**53.2**	**19:47**									
2010-11	**Tampa Bay**	**NHL**	**65**	**25**	**29**	**54**	**43**	**12**	**0**	**5**	**210**	**11.9**	**–5**	**1161**	**50.9**	**18:27**	**18**	**6**	**13**	**19**	**16**	**3**	**0**	**3**	**19:51**
2011-12	**Tampa Bay**	**NHL**	**64**	**22**	**27**	**49**	**50**	**5**	**0**	**5**	**182**	**12.1**	**–2**	**1162**	**47.9**	**18:56**									
2012-13	**Tampa Bay**	**NHL**	**39**	**10**	**22**	**32**	**29**	**5**	**0**	**0**	**86**	**11.6**	**–5**	**742**	**54.5**	**17:53**									
	NHL Totals		**1037**	**383**	**491**	**874**	**746**	**112**	**13**	**60**	**3166**	**12.1**		**17368**	**47.3**	**19:15**	**63**	**24**	**28**	**52**	**80**	**8**	**0**	**5**	**21:05**

QMJHL All-Rookie Team (1997) • QMJHL Offensive Rookie of the Year (1997) • Canadian Major Junior Rookie of the Year (1997) • QMJHL First All-Star Team (1998) • Canadian Major Junior First All-Star Team (1998) • NHL Second All-Star Team (2007) • Maurice "Rocket" Richard Trophy (2007) • King Clancy Memorial Trophy (2008) • NHL Foundation Player Award (2008)

Played in NHL All-Star Game (2003, 2007, 2008, 2009)

Signed as a free agent by **Kazan** (Russia), November 4, 2004. Signed as a free agent by **Philadelphia**, July 6, 2013.

LEDDY, Nick

(LEH-dee, NIHK) **CHI**

Defense. Shoots left. 6', 191 lbs. Born, Eden Prairie, MN, March 20, 1991. Minnesota's 1st choice, 16th overall, in 2009 Entry Draft.

Season	Club	League	GP	G	A	Pts	PIM	PP	SH	GW	S	%	+/-	TF	F%	Min	GP	G	A	Pts	PIM	PP	SH	GW	Min
2006-07	Eden Prairie	High-MN	28	2	16	18	10																		
2007-08	Eden Prairie	High-MN	27	6	22	28	14																		
	USNTDP	U-18	4	0	2	2																			
2008-09	Eden Prairie	High-MN	31	12	33	45	26																		
	Team Southwest	UMHSEL	24	9	11	20																			
2009-10	U. of Minnesota	WCHA	30	3	8	11	4																		

Season	Club	League	GP	G	A	Pts	PIM	PP	SH	GW	S	%	+/-	TF	F%	Min	GP	G	A	Pts	PIM	PP	SH	GW	Min
			Regular Season														Playoffs								
2010-11	**Chicago**	**NHL**	**46**	**4**	**3**	**7**	**4**	**0**	**0**	**0**	**37**	**10.8**	**-3**	**0**	**0.0**	**14:19**	**7**	**0**	**0**	**0**	**0**	**0**	**0**	**0**	**14:36**
	Rockford IceHogs	AHL	22	2	8	10	2	....	....	....	....	....	....	....	....	....	....	....	....	....	....	....	....	....	....
2011-12	**Chicago**	**NHL**	**82**	**3**	**34**	**37**	**10**	**0**	**0**	**0**	**94**	**3.2**	**-12**	**0**	**0.0**	**22:05**	**6**	**1**	**2**	**3**	**0**	**0**	**0**	**0**	**20:02**
2012-13	Rockford IceHogs	AHL	31	3	13	16	12	....	....	....	....	....	....	....	....	....	....	....	....	....	....	....	....	....	....
	♦ Chicago	**NHL**	**48**	**6**	**12**	**18**	**10**	**2**	**0**	**2**	**65**	**9.2**	**15**	**0**	**0.0**	**17:25**	**23**	**0**	**2**	**2**	**4**	**0**	**0**	**0**	**14:21**
	NHL Totals		**176**	**13**	**49**	**62**	**24**	**2**	**0**	**2**	**196**	**6.6**		**0**	**0.0**	**18:47**	**36**	**1**	**4**	**5**	**4**	**0**	**0**	**0**	**15:20**

Traded to **Chicago** by **Minnesota** with Kim Johnsson for Cam Barker, February 12, 2010.

LEE, Anders

(LEE, AN-duhrz) **NYI**

Center. Shoots left. 6'2", 225 lbs. Born, Edina, MN, July 3, 1990. NY Islanders' 7th choice, 152nd overall, in 2009 Entry Draft.

Season	Club	League	GP	G	A	Pts	PIM	PP	SH	GW	S	%	+/-	TF	F%	Min	GP	G	A	Pts	PIM	PP	SH	GW	Min
2006-07	Saint Thomas	High-MN	31	24	17	41	....	....	....	....	....	....	....	....	....	....	....	....	....	....	....	....	....	....	....
2007-08	Edina Hornets	High-MN	31	32	22	54	....	....	....	....	....	....	....	....	....	....	....	....	....	....	....	....	....	....	....
2008-09	Edina Hornets	High-MN	31	25	59	84	30	....	....	....	....	....	....	....	....	....	....	....	....	....	....	....	....	....	....
	Team Southwest	UMHSEL	18	12	17	29	....	....	....	....	....	....	....	....	....	....	....	....	....	....	....	....	....	....	....
2009-10	Green Bay	USHL	59	35	31	66	54	....	....	....	....	....	....	....	....	....	12	*10	*12	*22	13	....	....	....	....
2010-11	U. of Notre Dame	CCHA	44	24	20	44	16	....	....	....	....	....	....	....	....	....	....	....	....	....	....	....	....	....	....
2011-12	U. of Notre Dame	CCHA	40	17	17	34	24	....	....	....	....	....	....	....	....	....	....	....	....	....	....	....	....	....	....
2012-13	U. of Notre Dame	CCHA	41	*20	18	38	37	....	....	....	....	....	....	....	....	....	....	....	....	....	....	....	....	....	....
	NY Islanders	**NHL**	**2**	**1**	**1**	**2**	**0**	**0**	**0**	**0**	**2**	**50.0**	**-3**	**2**	**0.0**	**8:12**	....	....	....	....	....	....	....	....	....
	NHL Totals		**2**	**1**	**1**	**2**	**0**	**0**	**0**	**0**	**2**	**50.0**		**2**	**0.0**	**8:12**	....	....	....	....	....	....	....	....	....

USHL All-Rookie Team (2010) • USHL First All-Star Team (2010) • USHL Rookie of the Year (2010) • CCHA All-Rookie Team (2011) • CCHA Second All-Star Team (2011) • CCHA First All-Star Team (2013) • NCAA West Second All-American Team (2013)

LEE, Brian

(LEE, BRIGH-uhn) **T.B.**

Defense. Shoots right. 6'3", 200 lbs. Born, Moorhead, MN, March 26, 1987. Ottawa's 1st choice, 9th overall, in 2005 Entry Draft.

Season	Club	League	GP	G	A	Pts	PIM	PP	SH	GW	S	%	+/-	TF	F%	Min	GP	G	A	Pts	PIM	PP	SH	GW	Min
2003-04	Moorhead Spuds	High-MN	29	10	38	48	....	....	....	....	....	....	....	....	....	....	....	....	....	....	....	....	....	....	....
2004-05	Moorhead Spuds	High-MN	25	12	26	38	....	....	....	....	....	....	....	....	....	....	....	....	....	....	....	....	....	....	....
	Lincoln Stars	USHL	12	0	3	3	4	....	....	....	....	....	....	....	....	....	4	2	3	5	2	....	....	....	....
2005-06	North Dakota	WCHA	44	4	23	27	44	....	....	....	....	....	....	....	....	....	....	....	....	....	....	....	....	....	....
2006-07	North Dakota	WCHA	38	2	24	26	69	....	....	....	....	....	....	....	....	....	....	....	....	....	....	....	....	....	....
2007-08	**Ottawa**	**NHL**	**6**	**0**	**1**	**1**	**4**	**0**	**0**	**0**	**6**	**0.0**	**1**	**0**	**0.0**	**16:49**	**4**	**0**	**0**	**0**	**2**	**0**	**0**	**0**	**14:31**
	Binghamton	AHL	55	3	22	25	51	....	....	....	....	....	....	....	....	....	....	....	....	....	....	....	....	....	....
2008-09	**Ottawa**	**NHL**	**53**	**2**	**11**	**13**	**33**	**1**	**0**	**1**	**51**	**3.9**	**-2**	**0**	**0.0**	**18:53**	....	....	....	....	....	....	....	....	....
	Binghamton	AHL	27	2	10	12	41	....	....	....	....	....	....	....	....	....	....	....	....	....	....	....	....	....	....
2009-10	**Ottawa**	**NHL**	**23**	**2**	**1**	**3**	**12**	**0**	**0**	**0**	**22**	**9.1**	**-5**	**0**	**0.0**	**15:33**	....	....	....	....	....	....	....	....	....
	Binghamton	AHL	41	3	12	15	52	....	....	....	....	....	....	....	....	....	....	....	....	....	....	....	....	....	....
2010-11	**Ottawa**	**NHL**	**50**	**0**	**3**	**3**	**24**	**0**	**0**	**0**	**35**	**0.0**	**-10**	**0**	**0.0**	**17:17**	....	....	....	....	....	....	....	....	....
2011-12	**Ottawa**	**NHL**	**35**	**1**	**7**	**8**	**27**	**0**	**0**	**0**	**15**	**6.7**	**-2**	**0**	**0.0**	**14:39**	....	....	....	....	....	....	....	....	....
	Tampa Bay	**NHL**	**20**	**0**	**8**	**8**	**8**	**0**	**0**	**0**	**17**	**0.0**	**-6**	**0**	**0.0**	**17:05**	....	....	....	....	....	....	....	....	....
2012-13	**Tampa Bay**	**NHL**	**22**	**0**	**0**	**0**	**16**	**0**	**0**	**0**	**13**	**0.0**	**-13**	**0**	**0.0**	**13:55**	....	....	....	....	....	....	....	....	....
	Syracuse Crunch	AHL	11	0	1	1	25	....	....	....	....	....	....	....	....	....	7	0	0	0	0	....	....	....	....
	NHL Totals		**209**	**5**	**31**	**36**	**124**	**1**	**0**	**1**	**159**	**3.1**		**0**	**0.0**	**16:40**	**4**	**0**	**0**	**0**	**2**	**0**	**0**	**0**	**14:31**

WCHA All-Rookie Team (2006)

Traded to **Tampa Bay** by **Ottawa** for Matt Gilroy, February 27, 2012.

LEGWAND, David

(LEHG-wawnd, DAY-vihd) **NSH**

Center. Shoots left. 6'2", 204 lbs. Born, Detroit, MI, August 17, 1980. Nashville's 1st choice, 2nd overall, in 1998 Entry Draft.

Season	Club	League	GP	G	A	Pts	PIM	PP	SH	GW	S	%	+/-	TF	F%	Min	GP	G	A	Pts	PIM	PP	SH	GW	Min
1996-97	Det. Compuware	MNHL	44	21	41	62	58	....	....	....	....	....	....	....	....	....	....	....	....	....	....	....	....	....	....
1997-98	Plymouth Whalers	OHL	59	54	51	105	56	....	....	....	....	....	....	....	....	....	15	8	12	20	24	....	....	....	....
1998-99	Plymouth Whalers	OHL	55	31	49	80	65	....	....	....	....	....	....	....	....	....	11	3	8	11	8	....	....	....	....
	Nashville	**NHL**	**1**	**0**	**0**	**0**	**0**	**0**	**0**	**0**	**2**	**0.0**	**0**	**9**	**55.6**	**12:50**	....	....	....	....	....	....	....	....	....
99-2000	**Nashville**	**NHL**	**71**	**13**	**15**	**28**	**30**	**4**	**0**	**2**	**111**	**11.7**	**-6**	**637**	**41.6**	**14:43**	....	....	....	....	....	....	....	....	....
2000-01	**Nashville**	**NHL**	**81**	**13**	**28**	**41**	**38**	**3**	**0**	**3**	**172**	**7.6**	**1**	**888**	**40.3**	**15:14**	....	....	....	....	....	....	....	....	....
2001-02	**Nashville**	**NHL**	**63**	**11**	**19**	**30**	**54**	**1**	**1**	**1**	**121**	**9.1**	**1**	**843**	**40.5**	**16:25**	....	....	....	....	....	....	....	....	....
2002-03	**Nashville**	**NHL**	**64**	**17**	**31**	**48**	**34**	**3**	**1**	**4**	**167**	**10.2**	**-2**	**1095**	**46.6**	**19:14**	....	....	....	....	....	....	....	....	....
2003-04	**Nashville**	**NHL**	**82**	**18**	**29**	**47**	**46**	**5**	**1**	**5**	**165**	**10.9**	**9**	**1109**	**45.1**	**17:17**	**6**	**1**	**0**	**1**	**8**	**0**	**1**	**0**	**15:41**
2004-05	EHC Basel	Swiss-2	3	6	2	8	2	....	....	....	....	....	....	....	....	....	19	16	23	39	20	....	....	....	....
2005-06	**Nashville**	**NHL**	**44**	**7**	**19**	**26**	**34**	**0**	**0**	**5**	**109**	**6.4**	**3**	**580**	**44.7**	**16:50**	**5**	**0**	**1**	**1**	**8**	**0**	**0**	**0**	**17:21**
	Milwaukee	AHL	3	0	0	0	0	....	....	....	....	....	....	....	....	....	....	....	....	....	....	....	....	....	....
2006-07	**Nashville**	**NHL**	**78**	**27**	**36**	**63**	**44**	**3**	**1**	**7**	**153**	**17.6**	**23**	**1108**	**45.3**	**18:22**	**5**	**0**	**3**	**3**	**2**	**0**	**0**	**0**	**22:23**
2007-08	**Nashville**	**NHL**	**65**	**15**	**29**	**44**	**38**	**4**	**0**	**1**	**144**	**10.4**	**-4**	**700**	**43.6**	**18:01**	**3**	**1**	**0**	**1**	**2**	**0**	**0**	**0**	**18:15**
2008-09	**Nashville**	**NHL**	**73**	**20**	**22**	**42**	**32**	**1**	**3**	**1**	**175**	**11.4**	**-3**	**1023**	**49.8**	**19:27**	....	....	....	....	....	....	....	....	....
2009-10	**Nashville**	**NHL**	**82**	**11**	**27**	**38**	**24**	**0**	**1**	**3**	**151**	**7.3**	**-5**	**1124**	**47.9**	**18:42**	**6**	**2**	**5**	**7**	**8**	**0**	**0**	**1**	**19:16**
2010-11	**Nashville**	**NHL**	**64**	**17**	**24**	**41**	**24**	**0**	**2**	**3**	**130**	**13.1**	**13**	**837**	**47.2**	**18:48**	**12**	**6**	**3**	**9**	**8**	**1**	***2**	**0**	**22:06**
2011-12	**Nashville**	**NHL**	**78**	**19**	**34**	**53**	**26**	**5**	**0**	**2**	**140**	**13.6**	**3**	**1109**	**46.2**	**18:31**	**10**	**3**	**3**	**6**	**10**	**1**	**0**	**2**	**18:40**
2012-13	**Nashville**	**NHL**	**48**	**12**	**13**	**25**	**20**	**2**	**0**	**2**	**78**	**15.4**	**-6**	**721**	**50.2**	**18:26**	....	....	....	....	....	....	....	....	....
	NHL Totals		**894**	**200**	**326**	**526**	**444**	**31**	**10**	**39**	**1818**	**11.0**		**11783**	**45.5**	**17:41**	**47**	**13**	**15**	**28**	**46**	**2**	**3**	**3**	**19:28**

OHL All-Rookie Team (1998) • OHL First All-Star Team (1998) • OHL Rookie of the Year (1998) • OHL MVP (1998) • Canadian Major Junior Rookie of the Year (1998)

Signed as a free agent by **Basel** (Swiss-2), January 27, 2005.

LEHTONEN, Mikko

(LEH-tuh-nehn, MEE-koh) **MIN**

Right wing. Shoots right. 6'3", 196 lbs. Born, Espoo, Finland, April 1, 1987. Boston's 3rd choice, 83rd overall, in 2005 Entry Draft.

Season	Club	League	GP	G	A	Pts	PIM	PP	SH	GW	S	%	+/-	TF	F%	Min	GP	G	A	Pts	PIM	PP	SH	GW	Min
2002-03	Blues Espoo U18	Fin-U18	11	1	3	4	2	....	....	....	....	....	....	....	....	....	1	0	0	0	0	....	....	....	....
2003-04	Blues Espoo U18	Fin-U18	20	8	7	15	22	....	....	....	....	....	....	....	....	....	....	....	....	....	....	....	....	....	....
	Blues Espoo Jr.	Fin-Jr.	19	3	0	3	0	....	....	....	....	....	....	....	....	....	5	0	0	0	0	....	....	....	....
2004-05	Blues Espoo U18	Fin-U18	2	0	2	2	0	....	....	....	....	....	....	....	....	....	....	....	....	....	....	....	....	....	....
	Blues Espoo Jr.	Fin-Jr.	37	6	9	15	38	....	....	....	....	....	....	....	....	....	6	3	1	4	0	....	....	....	....
	Blues Espoo	Finland	1	0	0	0	0	....	....	....	....	....	....	....	....	....	....	....	....	....	....	....	....	....	....
2005-06	Blues Espoo Jr.	Fin-Jr.	15	3	4	7	12	....	....	....	....	....	....	....	....	....	10	5	2	7	6	....	....	....	....
	Suomi U20	Finland-2	3	1	0	1	2	....	....	....	....	....	....	....	....	....	....	....	....	....	....	....	....	....	....
	Blues Espoo	Finland	25	4	0	4	0	....	....	....	....	....	....	....	....	....	....	....	....	....	....	....	....	....	....
2006-07	Suomi U20	Finland-2	3	0	3	3	0	....	....	....	....	....	....	....	....	....	....	....	....	....	....	....	....	....	....
	Blues Espoo	Finland	39	6	9	15	24	....	....	....	....	....	....	....	....	....	9	1	1	2	4	....	....	....	....
2007-08	Blues Espoo	Finland	42	8	12	20	12	....	....	....	....	....	....	....	....	....	17	1	8	9	4	....	....	....	....
2008-09	**Boston**	**NHL**	**1**	**0**	**0**	**0**	**0**	**0**	**0**	**0**	**1**	**0.0**	**0**	**0**	**0.0**	**16:14**	....	....	....	....	....	....	....	....	....
	Providence Bruins	AHL	72	28	25	53	39	....	....	....	....	....	....	....	....	....	14	2	5	7	4	....	....	....	....
2009-10	**Boston**	**NHL**	**1**	**0**	**0**	**0**	**0**	**0**	**0**	**0**	**1**	**0.0**	**-1**	**0**	**0.0**	**7:08**	....	....	....	....	....	....	....	....	....
	Providence Bruins	AHL	78	23	27	50	58	....	....	....	....	....	....	....	....	....	....	....	....	....	....	....	....	....	....
2010-11	Skelleftea AIK	Sweden	55	*30	28	58	34	....	....	....	....	....	....	....	....	....	18	4	7	11	16	....	....	....	....
2011-12	Cherepovets	KHL	48	11	10	21	24	....	....	....	....	....	....	....	....	....	6	0	0	0	0	....	....	....	....
2012-13	Cherepovets	KHL	23	3	6	9	8	....	....	....	....	....	....	....	....	....	....	....	....	....	....	....	....	....	....
	ZSC Lions Zurich	Swiss	6	1	3	4	2	....	....	....	....	....	....	....	....	....	11	4	3	7	4	....	....	....	....
	NHL Totals		**2**	**0**	**0**	**0**	**0**	**0**	**0**	**0**	**2**	**0.0**		**0**	**0.0**	**11:41**	....	....	....	....	....	....	....	....	....

Signed as a free agent by **Skelleftea** (Sweden), August 17, 2010. Traded to **Minnesota** by **Boston** with Jeff Penner for Anton Khudobin, February 28, 2011. Signed as a free agent by **Cherepovets** (KHL), May 4, 2011. Signed as a free agent by **Zurich** (Swiss), February 1, 2013. Signed as a free agent by **Bern** (Swiss), June 26, 2013.

LEINO, Ville

(LAY-noh, VIHL-ee) **BUF**

Left wing. Shoots left. 6'1", 190 lbs. Born, Savonlinna, Finland, October 6, 1983.

Season	Club	League	GP	G	A	Pts	PIM	PP	SH	GW	S	%	+/-	TF	F%	Min	GP	G	A	Pts	PIM	PP	SH	GW	Min
2002-03	Ilves Tampere Jr.	Fin-Jr.	26	14	21	35	24	....	....	....	....	....	....	....	....	....	....	....	....	....	....	....	....	....	....
	Ilves Tampere	Finland	23	1	1	2	0	....	....	....	....	....	....	....	....	....	....	....	....	....	....	....	....	....	....
2003-04	Ilves Tampere Jr.	Fin-Jr.	5	4	6	10	6	....	....	....	....	....	....	....	....	....	....	....	....	....	....	....	....	....	....
	Ilves Tampere	Finland	54	9	15	24	26	....	....	....	....	....	....	....	....	....	7	1	1	2	4	....	....	....	....
2004-05	Ilves Tampere	Finland	56	8	11	19	32	....	....	....	....	....	....	....	....	....	7	1	0	1	2	....	....	....	....
2005-06	HPK Hameenlinna	Finland	56	12	31	43	65	....	....	....	....	....	....	....	....	....	13	3	*9	12	4	....	....	....	....
2006-07	HPK Hameenlinna	Finland	50	11	29	40	73	....	....	....	....	....	....	....	....	....	8	1	9	10	31	....	....	....	....

			Regular Season														Playoffs								
Season	Club	League	GP	G	A	Pts	PIM	PP	SH	GW	S	%	+/-	TF	F%	Min	GP	G	A	Pts	PIM	PP	SH	GW	Min
2007-08	Jokerit Helsinki	Finland	55	28	*49	77	18	....	....	....	....	....	....	....	....	....	14	8	11	19	8	....	....	....	....
2008-09	**Detroit**	**NHL**	13	5	4	9	6	0	0	1	17	29.4	5	12	58.3	12:42	7	0	2	2	0	0	0	0	8:44
	Grand Rapids	AHL	57	15	31	46	18	....	....	....	....	....	....	....	....	....	10	3	10	13	10	....	....	....	....
2009-10	**Detroit**	**NHL**	42	4	3	7	6	1	0	1	54	7.4	–10	5	20.0	13:13	....	....	....	....	....	....	....	....	....
	Philadelphia	**NHL**	13	2	2	4	4	0	0	1	23	8.7	2	9	55.6	12:40	19	7	14	21	6	0	0	2	16:16
2010-11	**Philadelphia**	**NHL**	81	19	34	53	22	5	0	2	117	16.2	14	136	57.4	16:01	11	3	2	5	0	1	0	1	16:46
2011-12	**Buffalo**	**NHL**	71	8	17	25	16	1	0	1	78	10.3	–2	230	41.3	15:55	....	....	....	....	....	....	....	....	....
2012-13	**Buffalo**	**NHL**	8	2	4	6	6	1	0	0	11	18.2	0	10	40.0	15:48	....	....	....	....	....	....	....	....	....
	NHL Totals		**228**	**40**	**64**	**104**	**60**	**8**	**0**	**6**	**300**	**13.3**		**402**	**47.3**	**15:05**	**37**	**10**	**18**	**28**	**6**	**1**	**0**	**3**	**15:00**

Signed as a free agent by **Detroit**, May 10, 2008. Traded to **Philadelpia** by **Detroit** for Ole-Kristian Tollefsen and Philadelphia's 5th round choice (Mattias Backman) in 2011 Entry Draft, February 6, 2010. Signed as a free agent by **Buffalo**, July 1, 2011. • Missed majority of 2012-13 due to hip and upper-body injuries.

LEOPOLD, Jordan

(LEE-oh-pohld, JOHR-dahn) **ST.L.**

Defense. Shoots left. 6'1", 206 lbs. Born, Golden Valley, MN, August 3, 1980. Anaheim's 1st choice, 44th overall, in 1999 Entry Draft.

Season	Club	League	GP	G	A	Pts	PIM	PP	SH	GW	S	%	+/-	TF	F%	Min	GP	G	A	Pts	PIM	PP	SH	GW	Min
1995-96	Armstrong	High-MN	19	11	14	25	30	....	....	....	....	....	....	....	....	....	....	....	....	....	....	....	....	....	....
1996-97	Armstrong	High-MN	30	24	36	60	....	....	....	....	....	....	....	....	....	....	....	....	....	....	....	....	....	....	....
1997-98	USNTDP	U-18	25	7	3	10	2	....	....	....	....	....	....	....	....	....	....	....	....	....	....	....	....	....	....
	USNTDP	USHL	19	2	4	6	6	....	....	....	....	....	....	....	....	....	....	....	....	....	....	....	....	....	....
	USNTDP	NAHL	16	2	5	7	8	....	....	....	....	....	....	....	....	....	....	....	....	....	....	....	....	....	....
1998-99	U. of Minnesota	WCHA	39	7	16	23	20	....	....	....	....	....	....	....	....	....	....	....	....	....	....	....	....	....	....
99-2000	U. of Minnesota	WCHA	39	6	18	24	20	....	....	....	....	....	....	....	....	....	....	....	....	....	....	....	....	....	....
2000-01	U. of Minnesota	WCHA	42	12	37	49	38	....	....	....	....	....	....	....	....	....	....	....	....	....	....	....	....	....	....
2001-02	U. of Minnesota	WCHA	44	20	28	48	28	....	....	....	....	....	....	....	....	....	....	....	....	....	....	....	....	....	....
2002-03	**Calgary**	**NHL**	58	4	10	14	12	3	0	0	78	5.1	–15	0	0.0	20:36	....	....	....	....	....	....	....	....	....
	Saint John Flames	AHL	3	1	2	3	0	....	....	....	....	....	....	....	....	....	....	....	....	....	....	....	....	....	....
2003-04	**Calgary**	**NHL**	82	9	24	33	24	6	0	1	138	6.5	8	0	0.0	22:14	26	0	10	10	6	0	0	0	25:41
2004-05			DID NOT PLAY																						
2005-06	**Calgary**	**NHL**	74	2	18	20	68	2	0	1	87	2.3	6	0	0.0	22:20	7	0	1	1	4	0	0	0	19:13
	United States	Olympics	6	1	0	1	4	....	....	....	....	....	....	....	....	....	....	....	....	....	....	....	....	....	....
2006-07	**Colorado**	**NHL**	15	2	3	5	14	1	1	0	19	10.5	–4	0	0.0	19:47	....	....	....	....	....	....	....	....	....
2007-08	**Colorado**	**NHL**	43	5	8	13	20	2	0	1	35	14.3	5	0	0.0	15:59	7	0	3	3	0	0	0	0	17:00
2008-09	**Colorado**	**NHL**	64	6	14	20	18	1	0	1	82	7.3	–10	0	0.0	18:10	....	....	....	....	....	....	....	....	....
	Calgary	**NHL**	19	1	3	4	6	0	0	0	25	4.0	–5	0	0.0	20:58	6	0	1	1	8	0	0	0	23:10
2009-10	**Florida**	**NHL**	61	7	11	18	22	1	0	1	69	10.1	–7	0	0.0	22:25	....	....	....	....	....	....	....	....	....
	Pittsburgh	**NHL**	20	4	4	8	6	0	0	2	26	15.4	5	0	0.0	20:27	8	0	0	0	2	0	0	0	16:31
2010-11	**Buffalo**	**NHL**	71	13	22	35	36	5	0	1	134	9.7	–11	0	0.0	23:20	5	0	1	1	4	0	0	0	20:57
2011-12	**Buffalo**	**NHL**	79	10	14	24	28	1	0	0	110	9.1	4	0	0.0	22:22	....	....	....	....	....	....	....	....	....
2012-13	**Buffalo**	**NHL**	24	2	6	8	14	0	0	0	38	5.3	–6	0	0.0	21:08	....	....	....	....	....	....	....	....	....
	St. Louis	**NHL**	15	0	2	2	0	0	0	0	22	0.0	–2	0	0.0	18:22	6	0	0	0	0	0	0	0	16:33
	NHL Totals		**625**	**65**	**139**	**204**	**268**	**22**	**1**	**8**	**863**	**7.5**		**0**	**0.0**	**21:07**	**65**	**0**	**16**	**16**	**24**	**0**	**0**	**0**	**21:29**

WCHA All-Rookie Team (1999) • WCHA Second All-Star Team (2000) • WCHA First All-Star Team (2001, 2002) • NCAA West First All-American Team (2001) • Hobey Baker Memorial Award (Top U.S. Collegiate Player) (2002)

Traded to **Calgary** by **Anaheim** for Andrei Nazarov and Calgary's 2nd round choice (later traded to Phoenix, later traded back to Calgary – Calgary selected Andrei Taratukhin) in 2001 Entry Draft, September 26, 2000. Traded to **Colorado** by **Calgary** with Calgary's 2nd round choice (Codey Burki) in 2006 Entry Draft and Calgary's 2nd round choice (Trevor Cann) in 2007 Entry Draft for Alex Tanguay, June 24, 2006. • Missed majority of 2006-07 due to off-season hernia surgery, groin injury and wrist injury vs. Calgary, February 15, 2007. Traded to **Calgary** by **Colorado** for Ryan Wilson, Lawrence Nycholat and Montreal's 2nd round choice (previously acquired, Colorado selected Stefan Elliott) in 2009 Entry Draft, March 4, 2009. Traded to **Florida** by **Calgary** with Phoenix's 3rd round choice (previously acquired, Florida selected Josh Birkholz) in 2009 Entry Draft for Jay Bouwmeester, June 27, 2009. Traded to **Pittsburgh** by **Florida** for Pittsburgh's 2nd round choice (Connor Brickley) in 2010 Entry Draft, March 1, 2010. Signed as a free agent by **Buffalo**, July 1, 2010. Traded to **St. Louis** by **Buffalo** for St. Louis' 2nd (Justin Bailey) and 5th (Anthony Florentino) round choices in 2013 Entry Draft, March 30, 2013.

LEPISTO, Sami

(LEH-pihs-toh, SA-mee) **CHI**

Defense. Shoots left. 6', 193 lbs. Born, Espoo, Finland, October 17, 1984. Washington's 6th choice, 66th overall, in 2004 Entry Draft.

Season	Club	League	GP	G	A	Pts	PIM	PP	SH	GW	S	%	+/-	TF	F%	Min	GP	G	A	Pts	PIM	PP	SH	GW	Min
2001-02	Jokerit U18	Fin-U18	20	8	14	22	36	....	....	....	....	....	....	....	....	....	8	4	8	12	12	....	....	....	....
	Jokerit Helsinki Jr.	Fin-Jr.	14	0	5	5	2	....	....	....	....	....	....	....	....	....	....	....	....	....	....	....	....	....	....
2002-03	Jokerit Helsinki Jr.	Fin-Jr.	36	5	14	19	34	....	....	....	....	....	....	....	....	....	11	1	5	6	8	....	....	....	....
2003-04	Suomi U20	Finland-2	1	0	0	0	0	....	....	....	....	....	....	....	....	....	....	....	....	....	....	....	....	....	....
	Jokerit Helsinki	Finland	53	3	4	7	20	....	....	....	....	....	....	....	....	....	8	0	1	1	4	....	....	....	....
2004-05	Jokerit Helsinki	Finland	55	7	18	25	44	....	....	....	....	....	....	....	....	....	12	1	7	8	12	....	....	....	....
2005-06	Jokerit Helsinki	Finland	56	8	21	29	68	....	....	....	....	....	....	....	....	....	....	....	....	....	....	....	....	....	....
2006-07	Jokerit Helsinki	Finland	26	1	9	10	32	....	....	....	....	....	....	....	....	....	10	2	2	4	4	....	....	....	....
2007-08	**Washington**	**NHL**	7	0	1	1	12	0	0	0	8	0.0	–1	0	0.0	13:17	....	....	....	....	....	....	....	....	....
	Hershey Bears	AHL	55	4	41	45	51	....	....	....	....	....	....	....	....	....	5	0	1	1	4	....	....	....	....
2008-09	**Washington**	**NHL**	7	0	4	4	6	0	0	0	7	0.0	–3	0	0.0	19:36	....	....	....	....	....	....	....	....	....
	Hershey Bears	AHL	70	4	38	42	80	....	....	....	....	....	....	....	....	....	....	....	....	....	....	....	....	....	....
2009-10	**Phoenix**	**NHL**	66	1	10	11	60	0	0	1	68	1.5	14	1	100.0	18:14	7	1	0	1	6	0	0	0	15:50
	Finland	Olympics	6	0	1	1	6	....	....	....	....	....	....	....	....	....	....	....	....	....	....	....	....	....	....
2010-11	**Phoenix**	**NHL**	51	4	7	11	37	0	0	0	31	12.9	7	1	100.0	16:38	....	....	....	....	....	....	....	....	....
	Columbus	**NHL**	19	0	5	5	18	0	0	0	25	0.0	3	0	0.0	20:01	....	....	....	....	....	....	....	....	....
2011-12	**Chicago**	**NHL**	26	1	2	3	4	0	0	0	19	5.3	3	0	0.0	10:34	3	0	0	0	0	0	0	0	6:40
2012-13	Yaroslavl	KHL	26	0	3	3	30	....	....	....	....	....	....	....	....	....	....	....	....	....	....	....	....	....	....
	HC Lev Praha	KHL	11	0	5	5	20	....	....	....	....	....	....	....	....	....	3	0	0	0	2	....	....	....	....
	NHL Totals		**176**	**6**	**29**	**35**	**137**	**0**	**0**	**1**	**158**	**3.8**		**2**	**100.0**	**16:41**	**10**	**1**	**0**	**1**	**6**	**0**	**0**	**0**	**13:05**

Traded to **Phoenix** by **Washington** for Phoenix's 5th round choice (Caleb Herbert) in 2010 Entry Draft, June 27, 2009. Traded to **Columbus** by **Phoenix** with Scottie Upshall for Rostislav Klesla and Dane Byers, February 28, 2011. Signed as a free agent by **Chicago**, July 15, 2011. • Missed majority of 2011-12 due to leg injury and as a healthy reserve. Signed as a free agent by **Yaroslavl** (KHL), June 4, 2012. Signed as a free agent by **Lev Praha** (KHL), January 13, 2013.

LETANG, Kris

(leh-TANG, KRIHS) **PIT**

Defense. Shoots right. 6', 201 lbs. Born, Montreal, Que., April 24, 1987. Pittsburgh's 3rd choice, 62nd overall, in 2005 Entry Draft.

Season	Club	League	GP	G	A	Pts	PIM	PP	SH	GW	S	%	+/-	TF	F%	Min	GP	G	A	Pts	PIM	PP	SH	GW	Min
2002-03	Antoine-Girouard	QAAA	42	2	10	12	34	....	....	....	....	....	....	....	....	....	....	....	....	....	....	....	....	....	....
2003-04	Antoine-Girouard	QAAA	39	12	41	53	94	....	....	....	....	....	....	....	....	....	13	7	9	16	38	....	....	....	....
2004-05	Val-d'Or Foreurs	QMJHL	70	13	19	32	79	....	....	....	....	....	....	....	....	....	....	....	....	....	....	....	....	....	....
2005-06	Val-d'Or Foreurs	QMJHL	60	25	43	68	156	....	....	....	....	....	....	....	....	....	5	1	5	6	20	....	....	....	....
2006-07	**Pittsburgh**	**NHL**	7	2	0	2	4	2	0	0	8	25.0	–3	0	0.0	11:33	....	....	....	....	....	....	....	....	....
	Val-d'Or Foreurs	QMJHL	40	14	38	52	74	....	....	....	....	....	....	....	....	....	19	12	19	31	48	....	....	....	....
	Wilkes-Barre	AHL	....	....	....	....	....	....	....	....	....	....	....	....	....	....	1	0	1	1	2	....	....	....	....
2007-08	**Pittsburgh**	**NHL**	63	6	11	17	23	1	0	3	68	8.8	–1	0	0.0	18:10	16	0	2	2	12	0	0	0	17:07
	Wilkes-Barre	AHL	10	1	6	7	4	....	....	....	....	....	....	....	....	....	....	....	....	....	....	....	....	....	....
2008-09 ♦	**Pittsburgh**	**NHL**	74	10	23	33	24	4	1	3	138	7.2	–7	1	0.0	21:09	23	4	9	13	26	2	0	1	19:18
2009-10	**Pittsburgh**	**NHL**	73	3	24	27	51	0	0	0	174	1.7	1	0	0.0	21:34	13	5	2	7	6	4	0	1	23:15
2010-11	**Pittsburgh**	**NHL**	82	8	42	50	101	4	0	2	236	3.4	15	1	100.0	24:02	7	0	4	4	10	0	0	0	26:32
2011-12	**Pittsburgh**	**NHL**	51	10	32	42	34	4	1	3	142	7.0	21	0	0.0	24:50	6	1	4	5	21	1	0	0	23:01
2012-13	**Pittsburgh**	**NHL**	35	5	33	38	8	1	0	1	95	5.3	16	0	0.0	25:38	15	3	13	16	8	2	0	1	27:38
	NHL Totals		**385**	**44**	**165**	**209**	**245**	**16**	**2**	**12**	**861**	**5.1**		**2**	**50.0**	**22:04**	**80**	**13**	**34**	**47**	**83**	**9**	**0**	**3**	**21:59**

QMJHL All-Rookie Team (2005) • Canadian Major Junior All-Rookie Team (2005) • QMJHL First All-Star Team (2006, 2007) • Canadian Major Junior Second All-Star Team (2006. 2007) • NHL Second All-Star Team (2013)

Played in NHL All-Star Game (2011, 2012)

LETESTU, Mark

(luh-TEHS- too, MAHRK) **CBJ**

Center. Shoots right. 5'11", 195 lbs. Born, Elk Point, Alta., February 4, 1985.

Season	Club	League	GP	G	A	Pts	PIM	PP	SH	GW	S	%	+/-	TF	F%	Min	GP	G	A	Pts	PIM	PP	SH	GW	Min
2003-04	Bonnyville	AJHL	58	22	27	49	24	....	....	....	....	....	....	....	....	....	....	....	....	....	....	....	....	....	....
2004-05	Bonnyville	AJHL	63	39	47	86	32	....	....	....	....	....	....	....	....	....	....	....	....	....	....	....	....	....	....
2005-06	Bonnyville	AJHL	58	50	55	105	59	....	....	....	....	....	....	....	....	....	....	....	....	....	....	....	....	....	....
2006-07	Western Mich.	CCHA	37	24	22	46	14	....	....	....	....	....	....	....	....	....	....	....	....	....	....	....	....	....	....
2007-08	Wilkes-Barre	AHL	52	6	12	18	28	....	....	....	....	....	....	....	....	....	13	0	3	3	0	....	....	....	....
	Wheeling Nailers	ECHL	6	1	2	3	4	....	....	....	....	....	....	....	....	....	....	....	....	....	....	....	....	....	....
2008-09	Wilkes-Barre	AHL	73	24	37	61	6	....	....	....	....	....	....	....	....	....	12	2	8	10	4	....	....	....	....

			Regular Season														Playoffs								
Season	Club	League	GP	G	A	Pts	PIM	PP	SH	GW	S	%	+/-	TF	F%	Min	GP	G	A	Pts	PIM	PP	SH	GW	Min
2009-10	**Pittsburgh**	**NHL**	**10**	**1**	**0**	**1**	**2**	**0**	**0**	**0**	**9**	**11.1**	**–2**	**74**	**55.4**	**9:38**	**4**	**0**	**1**	**1**	**0**	**0**	**0**	**0**	**9:39**
	Wilkes-Barre	AHL	63	21	34	55	21	....	....	....	....	....	....	....	....	....	4	0	3	3	0	....	....	....	....
2010-11	**Pittsburgh**	**NHL**	**64**	**14**	**13**	**27**	**13**	**4**	**0**	**3**	**128**	**10.9**	**4**	**734**	**55.5**	**14:15**	**7**	**0**	**1**	**1**	**0**	**0**	**0**	**0**	**15:29**
2011-12	**Pittsburgh**	**NHL**	**11**	**0**	**1**	**1**	**2**	**0**	**0**	**0**	**9**	**0.0**	**–6**	**132**	**55.3**	**12:50**	....	....	....	....	....	....	....	....	....
	Columbus	**NHL**	**51**	**11**	**13**	**24**	**6**	**4**	**0**	**0**	**105**	**10.5**	**–3**	**590**	**51.2**	**16:15**	....	....	....	....	....	....	....	....	....
2012-13	Almtuna	Sweden-2	7	4	0	4	2	....	....	....	....	....	....	....	....	....	....	....	....	....	....	....	....	....	....
	Columbus	**NHL**	**46**	**13**	**14**	**27**	**10**	**3**	**2**	**2**	**92**	**14.1**	**7**	**487**	**50.1**	**16:31**	....	....	....	....	....	....	....	....	....
	NHL Totals		**182**	**39**	**41**	**80**	**33**	**11**	**2**	**5**	**343**	**11.4**		**2017**	**52.9**	**15:03**	**11**	**0**	**2**	**2**	**0**	**0**	**0**	**0**	**13:22**

Signed as a free agent by **Pittsburgh**, March 22, 2007. Traded to **Columbus** by **Pittsburgh** for Columbus's 4th round choice (Matia Marcantuoni) in 2012 Entry Draft, November 8, 2011. Signed as a free agent by **Almtuna** (Sweden-2), December 3, 2012.

LETOURNEAU-LEBLOND, Pierre-Luc

(leh-TOOR-noh-leh-BLAWN)

Left wing. Shoots left. 6'2", 210 lbs. Born, Levis, Que., June 4, 1985. New Jersey's 4th choice, 216th overall, in 2004 Entry Draft.

Season	Club	League	GP	G	A	Pts	PIM	PP	SH	GW	S	%	+/-	TF	F%	Min	GP	G	A	Pts	PIM	PP	SH	GW	Min
2003-04	Baie-Comeau	QMJHL	62	2	3	5	198	....	....	....	....	....	....	....	....	....	4	0	0	0	6	....	....	....	....
2004-05	Baie-Comeau	QMJHL	67	1	6	7	229	....	....	....	....	....	....	....	....	....	6	0	1	1	10	....	....	....	....
2005-06	Albany River Rats	AHL	27	1	1	2	130	....	....	....	....	....	....	....	....	....	....	....	....	....	....	....	....	....	....
	Adirondack	UHL	31	3	6	9	165	....	....	....	....	....	....	....	....	....	6	0	1	1	29	....	....	....	....
2006-07	Trenton Titans	ECHL	52	4	9	13	183	....	....	....	....	....	....	....	....	....	4	0	0	0	15	....	....	....	....
2007-08	Lowell Devils	AHL	36	3	3	6	98	....	....	....	....	....	....	....	....	....	....	....	....	....	....	....	....	....	....
	Trenton Devils	ECHL	6	0	1	1	46	....	....	....	....	....	....	....	....	....	....	....	....	....	....	....	....	....	....
2008-09	**New Jersey**	**NHL**	**8**	**0**	**1**	**1**	**22**	**0**	**0**	**0**	**3**	**0.0**	**3**	**0**	**0.0**	**4:51**	....	....	....	....	....	....	....	....	....
	Lowell Devils	AHL	60	5	5	10	216	....	....	....	....	....	....	....	....	....	....	....	....	....	....	....	....	....	....
2009-10	**New Jersey**	**NHL**	**27**	**0**	**2**	**2**	**48**	**0**	**0**	**0**	**9**	**0.0**	**–4**	**2**	**50.0**	**5:31**	**5**	**0**	**0**	**0**	**10**	**0**	**0**	**0**	**4:34**
	Lowell Devils	AHL	5	0	2	2	18	....	....	....	....	....	....	....	....	....	....	....	....	....	....	....	....	....	....
2010-11	**New Jersey**	**NHL**	**2**	**0**	**0**	**0**	**21**	**0**	**0**	**0**	**0**	**0.0**	**–2**	**0**	**0.0**	**3:28**	....	....	....	....	....	....	....	....	....
	Albany Devils	AHL	64	8	5	13	*334	....	....	....	....	....	....	....	....	....	....	....	....	....	....	....	....	....	....
2011-12	**Calgary**	**NHL**	**3**	**0**	**0**	**0**	**10**	**0**	**0**	**0**	**3**	**0.0**	**1**	**0**	**0.0**	**4:51**	....	....	....	....	....	....	....	....	....
	Abbotsford Heat	AHL	50	1	5	6	167	....	....	....	....	....	....	....	....	....	5	0	0	0	18	....	....	....	....
2012-13	Norfolk Admirals	AHL	33	3	5	8	98	....	....	....	....	....	....	....	....	....	....	....	....	....	....	....	....	....	....
	NHL Totals		**40**	**0**	**3**	**3**	**101**	**0**	**0**	**0**	**15**	**0.0**		**2**	**50.0**	**5:14**	**5**	**0**	**0**	**0**	**10**	**0**	**0**	**0**	**4:34**

• Missed majority of 2009-10 due to upper-body injury and as a healthy reserve. Traded to **Calgary** by **New Jersey** for Calgary's 5th round choice (Graham Black) in 2012 Entry Draft, July 12, 2011. Signed as a free agent by **Anaheim**, January 15, 2013.

LEWIS, Trevor

(LOO-ihs, TREH-vuhr) **L.A.**

Center. Shoots right. 6'1", 199 lbs. Born, Salt Lake City, UT, January 8, 1987. Los Angeles' 2nd choice, 17th overall, in 2006 Entry Draft.

Season	Club	League	GP	G	A	Pts	PIM	PP	SH	GW	S	%	+/-	TF	F%	Min	GP	G	A	Pts	PIM	PP	SH	GW	Min
2004-05	Des Moines	USHL	52	10	12	22	70	....	....	....	....	....	....	....	....	....	....	....	....	....	....	....	....	....	....
2005-06	Des Moines	USHL	56	35	40	75	69	....	....	....	....	....	....	....	....	....	11	3	*13	*16	16	....	....	....	....
2006-07	Owen Sound	OHL	62	29	44	73	51	....	....	....	....	....	....	....	....	....	4	1	2	3	0	....	....	....	....
	Manchester	AHL	8	4	2	6	2	....	....	....	....	....	....	....	....	....	2	0	0	0	0	....	....	....	....
2007-08	Manchester	AHL	76	12	16	28	43	....	....	....	....	....	....	....	....	....	4	0	0	0	2	....	....	....	....
2008-09	**Los Angeles**	**NHL**	**6**	**1**	**2**	**3**	**0**	**0**	**0**	**0**	**10**	**10.0**	**0**	**4**	**25.0**	**11:36**	....	....	....	....	....	....	....	....	....
	Manchester	AHL	75	20	31	51	30	....	....	....	....	....	....	....	....	....	....	....	....	....	....	....	....	....	....
2009-10	**Los Angeles**	**NHL**	**5**	**0**	**0**	**0**	**0**	**0**	**0**	**0**	**4**	**0.0**	**–3**	**5**	**0.0**	**9:08**	....	....	....	....	....	....	....	....	....
	Manchester	AHL	23	5	2	7	6	....	....	....	....	....	....	....	....	....	16	5	4	9	10	....	....	....	....
2010-11	**Los Angeles**	**NHL**	**72**	**3**	**10**	**13**	**6**	**0**	**0**	**2**	**105**	**2.9**	**–11**	**385**	**39.2**	**11:29**	**6**	**1**	**3**	**4**	**2**	**1**	**0**	**0**	**16:39**
2011-12♦	**Los Angeles**	**NHL**	**72**	**3**	**4**	**7**	**26**	**0**	**0**	**1**	**103**	**2.9**	**–3**	**199**	**43.7**	**13:14**	**20**	**3**	**6**	**9**	**2**	**1**	**0**	**0**	**14:54**
2012-13	Utah Grizzlies	ECHL	6	3	6	9	4	....	....	....	....	....	....	....	....	....	....	....	....	....	....	....	....	....	....
	Los Angeles	**NHL**	**48**	**5**	**9**	**14**	**19**	**0**	**1**	**2**	**92**	**5.4**	**5**	**64**	**48.4**	**15:12**	**18**	**1**	**2**	**3**	**2**	**1**	**0**	**1**	**16:25**
	NHL Totals		**203**	**12**	**25**	**37**	**51**	**0**	**1**	**5**	**314**	**3.8**		**657**	**41.1**	**12:56**	**44**	**5**	**11**	**16**	**6**	**3**	**0**	**1**	**15:46**

USHL Player of the Year (2006)

• Missed majority of 2009-10 due to upper-body injury and as a healthy reserve.

LIFFITON, David

(LIH-fih-tuhn, DAY-vihd)

Defense. Shoots left. 6'2", 210 lbs. Born, Windsor, Ont., October 18, 1984. Colorado's 1st choice, 63rd overall, in 2003 Entry Draft.

Season	Club	League	GP	G	A	Pts	PIM	PP	SH	GW	S	%	+/-	TF	F%	Min	GP	G	A	Pts	PIM	PP	SH	GW	Min
2000-01	Aylmer Aces	ON-Jr.B	51	1	9	10	51	....	....	....	....	....	....	....	....	....	....	....	....	....	....	....	....	....	....
2001-02	Plymouth Whalers	OHL	62	3	9	12	65	....	....	....	....	....	....	....	....	....	6	0	0	0	0	....	....	....	....
2002-03	Plymouth Whalers	OHL	64	5	11	16	139	....	....	....	....	....	....	....	....	....	18	1	3	4	29	....	....	....	....
2003-04	Plymouth Whalers	OHL	44	2	9	11	85	....	....	....	....	....	....	....	....	....	9	0	0	0	12	....	....	....	....
2004-05	Hartford	AHL	33	0	1	1	74	....	....	....	....	....	....	....	....	....	....	....	....	....	....	....	....	....	....
	Charlotte	ECHL	16	0	2	2	18	....	....	....	....	....	....	....	....	....	15	1	4	5	27	....	....	....	....
2005-06	**NY Rangers**	**NHL**	**1**	**0**	**0**	**0**	**2**	**0**	**0**	**0**	**0**	**0.0**	**0**	**0**	**0.0**	**8:42**	....	....	....	....	....	....	....	....	....
	Hartford	AHL	50	2	7	9	158	....	....	....	....	....	....	....	....	....	12	0	0	0	13	....	....	....	....
2006-07	**NY Rangers**	**NHL**	**2**	**0**	**0**	**0**	**7**	**0**	**0**	**0**	**2**	**0.0**	**1**	**0**	**0.0**	**11:31**	....	....	....	....	....	....	....	....	....
	Hartford	AHL	72	2	11	13	189	....	....	....	....	....	....	....	....	....	7	1	1	2	18	....	....	....	....
2007-08	Hartford	AHL	21	0	2	2	52	....	....	....	....	....	....	....	....	....	....	....	....	....	....	....	....	....	....
2008-09	Esbjerg	Denmark	25	3	6	9	84	....	....	....	....	....	....	....	....	....	4	0	0	0	4	....	....	....	....
2009-10	Syracuse Crunch	AHL	72	5	15	20	118	....	....	....	....	....	....	....	....	....	....	....	....	....	....	....	....	....	....
2010-11	**Colorado**	**NHL**	**4**	**1**	**0**	**1**	**17**	**0**	**0**	**0**	**2**	**50.0**	**3**	**0**	**0.0**	**7:28**	....	....	....	....	....	....	....	....	....
	Lake Erie	AHL	18	1	3	4	57	....	....	....	....	....	....	....	....	....	....	....	....	....	....	....	....	....	....
2011-12	Lake Erie	AHL	65	3	5	8	149	....	....	....	....	....	....	....	....	....	....	....	....	....	....	....	....	....	....
2012-13	HC Milano	Italy	44	6	4	10	84	....	....	....	....	....	....	....	....	....	6	0	2	2	12	....	....	....	....
	NHL Totals		**7**	**1**	**0**	**1**	**26**	**0**	**0**	**0**	**4**	**25.0**		**0**	**0.0**	**8:48**	....	....	....	....	....	....	....	....	....

Traded to **NY Rangers** by **Colorado** with Chris McAllister and Florida's 2nd round choice (previously acquired, later traded back to Florida – Florida selected David Shantz) in 2004 Entry Draft for Matthew Barnaby and NY Rangers' 3rd round choice (Denis Parshin) in 2004 Entry Draft, March 8, 2004. • Missed majority of 2007-08 due to post-concussion syndrome. Signed as a free agent by **New Jersey**, September 29, 2009. Signed as a free agent by **Colorado**, July 2, 2010. • Missed majority of 2010-11 due to upper-body injury vs. Houston (AHL), December 12, 2010. Signed as a free agent by **Milano** (Italy), September 11, 2012.

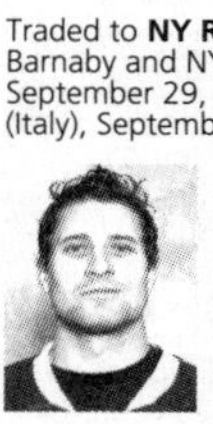

LILES, John-Michael

(LIGH-uhls, JAWN-MIGHK-uhl) **TOR**

Defense. Shoots left. 5'10", 185 lbs. Born, Indianapolis, IN, November 25, 1980. Colorado's 8th choice, 159th overall, in 2000 Entry Draft.

Season	Club	League	GP	G	A	Pts	PIM	PP	SH	GW	S	%	+/-	TF	F%	Min	GP	G	A	Pts	PIM	PP	SH	GW	Min
1997-98	USNTDP	U-17	15	0	6	6	4	....	....	....	....	....	....	....	....	....	....	....	....	....	....	....	....	....	....
	USNTDP	USHL	5	0	1	1	0	....	....	....	....	....	....	....	....	....	....	....	....	....	....	....	....	....	....
	USNTDP	NAHL	42	4	7	11	40	....	....	....	....	....	....	....	....	....	5	2	0	2	0	....	....	....	....
1998-99	USNTDP	USHL	46	4	14	18	47	....	....	....	....	....	....	....	....	....	....	....	....	....	....	....	....	....	....
	USNTDP	NAHL	13	2	5	7	6	....	....	....	....	....	....	....	....	....	....	....	....	....	....	....	....	....	....
99-2000	Michigan State	CCHA	40	8	20	28	26	....	....	....	....	....	....	....	....	....	....	....	....	....	....	....	....	....	....
2000-01	Michigan State	CCHA	42	7	18	25	28	....	....	....	....	....	....	....	....	....	....	....	....	....	....	....	....	....	....
2001-02	Michigan State	CCHA	41	13	22	35	18	....	....	....	....	....	....	....	....	....	....	....	....	....	....	....	....	....	....
2002-03	Michigan State	CCHA	39	16	34	50	46	....	....	....	....	....	....	....	....	....	....	....	....	....	....	....	....	....	....
	Hershey Bears	AHL	5	0	1	1	4	....	....	....	....	....	....	....	....	....	5	0	0	0	2	....	....	....	....
2003-04	**Colorado**	**NHL**	**79**	**10**	**24**	**34**	**28**	**2**	**0**	**1**	**115**	**8.7**	**7**	**0**	**0.0**	**16:14**	**11**	**0**	**1**	**1**	**4**	**0**	**0**	**0**	**16:41**
2004-05	Iserlohn Roosters	Germany	17	5	6	11	24	....	....	....	....	....	....	....	....	....	....	....	....	....	....	....	....	....	....
2005-06	**Colorado**	**NHL**	**82**	**14**	**35**	**49**	**44**	**6**	**0**	**1**	**154**	**9.1**	**5**	**1**	**100.0**	**18:31**	**9**	**1**	**2**	**3**	**6**	**1**	**0**	**0**	**17:35**
	United States	Olympics	6	0	2	2	2	....	....	....	....	....	....	....	....	....	....	....	....	....	....	....	....	....	....
2006-07	**Colorado**	**NHL**	**71**	**14**	**30**	**44**	**24**	**8**	**0**	**3**	**128**	**10.9**	**0**	**0**	**0.0**	**17:46**	....	....	....	....	....	....	....	....	....
2007-08	**Colorado**	**NHL**	**81**	**6**	**26**	**32**	**26**	**5**	**0**	**1**	**163**	**3.7**	**2**	**0**	**0.0**	**19:40**	**10**	**2**	**3**	**5**	**2**	**1**	**0**	**0**	**19:08**
2008-09	**Colorado**	**NHL**	**75**	**12**	**27**	**39**	**31**	**6**	**0**	**1**	**146**	**8.2**	**–19**	**0**	**0.0**	**21:33**	....	....	....	....	....	....	....	....	....
2009-10	**Colorado**	**NHL**	**59**	**6**	**25**	**31**	**30**	**3**	**0**	**2**	**96**	**6.3**	**–2**	**0**	**0.0**	**18:28**	**6**	**1**	**1**	**2**	**4**	**1**	**0**	**0**	**19:01**
2010-11	**Colorado**	**NHL**	**76**	**6**	**40**	**46**	**35**	**3**	**0**	**0**	**163**	**3.7**	**–9**	**0**	**0.0**	**22:01**	....	....	....	....	....	....	....	....	....
2011-12	**Toronto**	**NHL**	**66**	**7**	**20**	**27**	**20**	**4**	**0**	**0**	**106**	**6.6**	**–14**	**0**	**0.0**	**21:21**	....	....	....	....	....	....	....	....	....
2012-13	**Toronto**	**NHL**	**32**	**2**	**9**	**11**	**4**	**0**	**0**	**0**	**47**	**4.3**	**–1**	**1**	**0.0**	**18:46**	**4**	**0**	**0**	**0**	**2**	**0**	**0**	**0**	**15:25**
	NHL Totals		**621**	**77**	**236**	**313**	**242**	**37**	**0**	**9**	**1118**	**6.9**		**2**	**50.0**	**19:24**	**40**	**4**	**7**	**11**	**18**	**3**	**0**	**0**	**17:43**

CCHA Second All-Star Team (2001) • CCHA First All-Star Team (2002, 2003) • NCAA West Second All-American Team (2002) • NCAA West First All-American Team (2003) • NHL All-Rookie Team (2004)

Signed as a free agent by **Iserlohn** (Germany), December 29, 2004. Traded to **Toronto** by **Colorado** for Boston's 2nd round choice (previously acquired, later traded to Washington, later traded to Dallas – Dallas selected Mike Winther) in 2012 Entry Draft, June 24, 2011.

LILJA, Andreas

(LIHL-yuh, awn-DRAY-uhs)

Defense. Shoots left. 6'3", 220 lbs. Born, Helsingborg, Sweden, July 13, 1975. Los Angeles' 2nd choice, 54th overall, in 2000 Entry Draft.

			Regular Season														Playoffs								
Season	Club	League	GP	G	A	Pts	PIM	PP	SH	GW	S	%	+/-	TF	F%	Min	GP	G	A	Pts	PIM	PP	SH	GW	Min
1993-94	Malmo IF Jr.	Swe-Jr.	14	3	7	10	38																		
1994-95	Malmo IF Jr.	Swe-Jr.	30	7	13	20	82																		
	Malmo IF	Sweden	4	0	0	0	2																		
1995-96	Malmo IF Jr.	Swe-Jr.	3	0	1	1	6																		
	Malmo IF	Sweden	40	1	5	6	63										5	0	1	1	2				
1996-97	Malmo	Sweden	47	1	0	1	22										4	0	0	0	10				
1997-98	Malmo	Sweden	10	0	0	0	0																		
	Mora IK	Sweden-2	13	1	4	5	30										4	1	0	1	14				
1998-99	Malmo	Sweden	41	0	3	3	44										1	0	0	0	4				
99-2000	Malmo	Sweden	49	8	11	19	88										6	0	0	0	8				
2000-01	**Los Angeles**	**NHL**	**2**	**0**	**0**	**0**	**4**	**0**	**0**	**0**	**1**	**0.0**	**–2**	**0**	**0.0**	**12:22**	**1**	**0**	**0**	**0**	**0**	**0**	**0**	**0**	**6:56**
	Lowell	AHL	61	7	29	36	149										4	0	6	6	6				
2001-02	**Los Angeles**	**NHL**	**26**	**1**	**4**	**5**	**22**	**1**	**0**	**0**	**12**	**8.3**	**3**	**0**	**0.0**	**11:27**	**5**	**0**	**0**	**0**	**6**	**0**	**0**	**0**	**10:26**
	Manchester	AHL	4	0	1	1	4																		
2002-03	**Los Angeles**	**NHL**	**17**	**0**	**3**	**3**	**14**	**0**	**0**	**0**	**13**	**0.0**	**5**	**0**	**0.0**	**20:04**									
	Florida	**NHL**	**56**	**4**	**8**	**12**	**56**	**0**	**0**	**0**	**59**	**6.8**	**8**	**0**	**0.0**	**19:11**									
2003-04	**Florida**	**NHL**	**79**	**3**	**4**	**7**	**90**	**0**	**0**	**0**	**79**	**3.8**	**–8**	**1**	**0.0**	**19:34**									
2004-05	Mora IK	Sweden	44	3	8	11	67																		
	HC Ambri-Piotta	Swiss															5	0	2	2	6				
2005-06	**Detroit**	**NHL**	**82**	**2**	**13**	**15**	**98**	**0**	**0**	**1**	**78**	**2.6**	**18**	**1**	**0.0**	**19:01**	**6**	**0**	**1**	**1**	**6**	**0**	**0**	**0**	**19:21**
2006-07	**Detroit**	**NHL**	**57**	**0**	**5**	**5**	**54**	**0**	**0**	**0**	**37**	**0.0**	**6**	**1**	**0.0**	**15:25**	**18**	**1**	**0**	**1**	**10**	**0**	**0**	**0**	**19:02**
2007-08 ♦	**Detroit**	**NHL**	**79**	**2**	**10**	**12**	**93**	**0**	**0**	**2**	**72**	**2.8**	**–2**	**1**	**0.0**	**18:14**	**12**	**0**	**1**	**1**	**16**	**0**	**0**	**0**	**14:05**
2008-09	**Detroit**	**NHL**	**60**	**2**	**11**	**13**	**66**	**0**	**0**	**0**	**60**	**3.3**	**13**	**1**	**0.0**	**17:00**									
2009-10	**Detroit**	**NHL**	**20**	**1**	**1**	**2**	**4**	**0**	**0**	**0**	**19**	**5.3**	**–2**	**0**	**0.0**	**14:08**	**11**	**0**	**0**	**0**	**14**	**0**	**0**	**0**	**11:00**
	Grand Rapids	AHL	4	0	0	0	6																		
2010-11	**Anaheim**	**NHL**	**52**	**1**	**6**	**7**	**28**	**0**	**0**	**0**	**31**	**3.2**	**–15**	**0**	**0.0**	**17:26**	**3**	**0**	**0**	**0**	**0**	**0**	**0**	**0**	**11:02**
2011-12	**Philadelphia**	**NHL**	**46**	**0**	**6**	**6**	**34**	**0**	**0**	**0**	**35**	**0.0**	**9**	**0**	**0.0**	**13:41**	**10**	**0**	**0**	**0**	**6**	**0**	**0**	**0**	**13:58**
	Adirondack	AHL	1	0	0	0	0																		
2012-13	Adirondack	AHL	33	1	7	8	44																		
	Philadelphia	**NHL**	**4**	**0**	**0**	**0**	**0**	**0**	**0**	**0**	**2**	**0.0**	**–1**	**0**	**0.0**	**16:47**									
	NHL Totals		**580**	**16**	**71**	**87**	**563**	**1**	**0**	**3**	**498**	**3.2**		**5**	**0.0**	**17:21**	**66**	**1**	**2**	**3**	**58**	**0**	**0**	**0**	**14:52**

• Missed majority of 2001-02 as a healthy reserve. Traded to **Florida** by **Los Angeles** with Jaroslav Bednar for Dmitry Yushkevich and Florida's 5th round choice (previously acquired, Los Angeles selected Brady Murray) in 2003 Entry Draft, November 26, 2002. Signed as a free agent by **Nashville**, July 26, 2004. Signed as a free agent by **Mora** (Sweden), September 15, 2004. Signed as a free agent by **Ambri-Piotta** (Swiss), February 25, 2005. Signed as a free agent by **Detroit**, August 24, 2005. • Missed remainder of 2008-09 and majority of 2009-10 due to head injury at Nashville, February 28, 2009. Signed as a free agent by **Anaheim**, October 11, 2010. Signed as a free agent by **Philadelphia**, July 1, 2011.

LINDSTROM, Joakim

(LIHND-struhm, YOH-ah-kihm)

Center. Shoots left. 6', 187 lbs. Born, Skelleftea, Sweden, December 5, 1983. Columbus' 2nd choice, 41st overall, in 2002 Entry Draft.

Season	Club	League	GP	G	A	Pts	PIM	PP	SH	GW	S	%	+/-	TF	F%	Min	GP	G	A	Pts	PIM	PP	SH	GW	Min
99-2000	MoDo U18	Swe-U18	17	6	*14	20	32																		
	Malmo Jr.	Swe-Jr.	10	4	4	8	2																		
2000-01	Malmo Jr.	Swe-Jr.	12	7	14	21	46										4	2	3	5	24				
	MoDo	Sweden	10	2	3	5	2										7	0	1	1	0				
2001-02	Malmo Jr.	Swe-Jr.	10	9	6	15	67																		
	IF Troja-Ljungby	Sweden-2	3	0	0	0	12																		
	MODO	Sweden	42	4	3	7	20										14	3	5	8	8				
2002-03	MODO	Sweden	29	4	2	6	14										6	1	1	2	2				
	Malmo Jr.	Swe-Jr.	2	5	1	6	8																		
	Ornskoldsviks SK	Sweden-2	2	1	1	2	4																		
2003-04	MODO	Sweden	15	0	2	2	0																		
	Sundsvall	Sweden-2	2	0	5	5	0																		
2004-05	MODO Jr.	Swe-Jr.	2	4	1	5	0																		
	MODO	Sweden	37	2	3	5	24																		
	Syracuse Crunch	AHL	13	4	4	8	0																		
2005-06	**Columbus**	**NHL**	**3**	**0**	**0**	**0**	**0**	**0**	**0**	**0**	**4**	**0.0**	**0**	**0**	**0.0**	**5:11**									
	Syracuse Crunch	AHL	64	14	29	43	52										6	1	1	2	0				
2006-07	**Columbus**	**NHL**	**9**	**1**	**0**	**1**	**4**	**0**	**0**	**0**	**9**	**11.1**	**–3**	**0**	**0.0**	**8:28**									
	Syracuse Crunch	AHL	50	22	26	48	34																		
2007-08	**Columbus**	**NHL**	**25**	**3**	**4**	**7**	**14**	**2**	**0**	**1**	**25**	**12.0**	**0**	**7**	**28.6**	**9:26**									
	Syracuse Crunch	AHL	49	25	35	60	68										13	4	3	7	6				
2008-09	Iowa Chops	AHL	21	7	14	21	33																		
	Phoenix	**NHL**	**44**	**9**	**11**	**20**	**28**	**3**	**0**	**2**	**77**	**11.7**	**–6**	**14**	**35.7**	**14:52**									
2009-10	Nizhny Novgorod	KHL	55	10	20	30	62																		
2010-11	Skelleftea AIK	Sweden	54	28	32	*60	134										18	4	7	11	16				
2011-12	**Colorado**	**NHL**	**16**	**2**	**3**	**5**	**0**	**1**	**0**	**0**	**22**	**9.1**	**–9**	**5**	**40.0**	**13:55**									
	Skelleftea AIK	Sweden	21	7	13	20	45										19	5	12	17	22				
2012-13	Skelleftea AIK	Sweden	53	18	36	54	56										13	4	7	11	4				
	NHL Totals		**97**	**15**	**18**	**33**	**46**	**6**	**0**	**3**	**137**	**10.9**		**26**	**34.6**	**12:25**									

Traded to **Anaheim** by **Columbus** for Anaheim's 4th round choice (Mathieu Corbeil-Theriault) in 2010 Entry Draft, July 14, 2008. Claimed on waivers by **Chicago** from **Anaheim**, October 3, 2008. Claimed on waivers by **Anaheim** from **Chicago**, October 7, 2008. Traded to **Phoenix** by **Anaheim** for Logan Stephenson, December 3, 2008. Signed as a free agent by **Novgorod** (KHL). June 30, 2009. Signed as a free agent by **Skelleftea** (Sweden), May 18, 2010. Signed as a free agent by **Colorado**, June 16, 2011. Signed as a free agent by **Skelleftea** (Sweden), December 2, 2011.

LITTLE, Bryan

(LIH-tuhl, BRIGH-uhn) **WPG**

Right wing. Shoots right. 5'11", 185 lbs. Born, Edmonton, Alta., November 12, 1987. Atlanta's 1st choice, 12th overall, in 2006 Entry Draft.

Season	Club	League	GP	G	A	Pts	PIM	PP	SH	GW	S	%	+/-	TF	F%	Min	GP	G	A	Pts	PIM	PP	SH	GW	Min
2003-04	Barrie Colts	OHL	64	34	24	58	18										12	5	5	10	7				
2004-05	Barrie Colts	OHL	62	36	32	68	34										4	5	1	6	2				
2005-06	Barrie Colts	OHL	64	42	67	109	99										14	8	15	23	19				
2006-07	Barrie Colts	OHL	57	41	66	107	77										8	4	5	9	8				
	Chicago Wolves	AHL															2	0	0	0	0				
2007-08	**Atlanta**	**NHL**	**48**	**6**	**10**	**16**	**18**	**2**	**0**	**1**	**76**	**7.9**	**–2**	**505**	**45.2**	**15:37**									
	Chicago Wolves	AHL	34	9	16	25	10										24	8	5	13	10				
2008-09	**Atlanta**	**NHL**	**79**	**31**	**20**	**51**	**24**	**12**	**0**	**4**	**172**	**18.0**	**–5**	**214**	**43.5**	**16:55**									
2009-10	**Atlanta**	**NHL**	**79**	**13**	**21**	**34**	**20**	**3**	**0**	**1**	**165**	**7.9**	**–6**	**154**	**44.2**	**15:45**									
2010-11	**Atlanta**	**NHL**	**76**	**18**	**30**	**48**	**33**	**2**	**2**	**1**	**158**	**11.4**	**11**	**1331**	**46.3**	**18:27**									
2011-12	**Winnipeg**	**NHL**	**74**	**24**	**22**	**46**	**26**	**6**	**0**	**6**	**162**	**14.8**	**–11**	**1479**	**49.6**	**20:13**									
2012-13	**Winnipeg**	**NHL**	**48**	**7**	**25**	**32**	**4**	**2**	**0**	**2**	**84**	**8.3**	**8**	**842**	**51.2**	**19:48**									
	NHL Totals		**404**	**99**	**128**	**227**	**125**	**27**	**2**	**15**	**817**	**12.1**		**4525**	**47.9**	**17:46**									

OHL Second All-Star Team (2007)

• Transferred to **Winnipeg** after **Atlanta** franchise relocated, June 21, 2011.

LOCKE, Corey

(LAWK, KOH-ree)

Center. Shoots left. 5'9", 185 lbs. Born, Toronto, Ont., May 8, 1984. Montreal's 5th choice, 113th overall, in 2003 Entry Draft.

Season	Club	League	GP	G	A	Pts	PIM	PP	SH	GW	S	%	+/-	TF	F%	Min	GP	G	A	Pts	PIM	PP	SH	GW	Min
2000-01	Newmarket	ON-Jr.A	49	34	51	85	16										16	10	12	22	14				
2001-02	Ottawa 67's	OHL	55	18	25	43	18										13	6	7	13	10				
2002-03	Ottawa 67's	OHL	66	*63	*88	*151	83										23	*19	19	*38	30				
2003-04	Ottawa 67's	OHL	65	*51	67	*118	82										7	7	3	10	10				
2004-05	Hamilton	AHL	78	16	27	43	20										4	0	0	0	2				
2005-06	Hamilton	AHL	77	19	40	59	67																		
2006-07	Hamilton	AHL	80	20	35	55	54										22	*10	12	22	10				
2007-08	**Montreal**	**NHL**	**1**	**0**	**0**	**0**	**0**	**0**	**0**	**0**	**1**	**0.0**	**–1**	**5**	**40.0**	**5:59**									
	Hamilton	AHL	78	30	42	72	50																		
2008-09	Houston Aeros	AHL	77	25	54	79	60										20	12	11	23	32				
2009-10	**NY Rangers**	**NHL**	**3**	**0**	**0**	**0**	**0**	**0**	**0**	**0**	**2**	**0.0**	**1**	**7**	**14.3**	**6:18**									
	Hartford	AHL	76	31	54	85	44																		
2010-11	**Ottawa**	**NHL**	**5**	**0**	**1**	**1**	**0**	**0**	**0**	**0**	**6**	**0.0**	**–1**	**32**	**21.9**	**9:10**									
	Binghamton	AHL	69	21	*65	*86	42										16	3	12	15	12				
2011-12	Binghamton	AHL	38	10	31	41	22																		

			Regular Season														Playoffs								
Season	Club	League	GP	G	A	Pts	PIM	PP	SH	GW	S	%	+/-	TF	F%	Min	GP	G	A	Pts	PIM	PP	SH	GW	Min
2012-13	TPS Turku	Finland	37	5	12	17	22																		
	Eisbaren Berlin	Germany	16	1	6	7	10										13	2	6	8	4				
	NHL Totals		9	0	1	1	0	0	0	0	9	0.0		44	22.7	7:52									

OHL First All-Star Team (2003, 2004) • OHL Player of the Year (2003, 2004) • Canadian Major Junior First All-Star Team (2003, 2004) • Canadian Major Junior Player of the Year (2003) • AHL Second All-Star Team (2010) • AHL First All-Star Team (2011) • John B. Sollenberger Trophy (AHL – Leading Scorer) (2011) • Les Cunningham Award (AHL – MVP) (2011)

Traded to **Minnesota** by **Montreal** for Shawn Belle, July 11, 2008. Signed as a free agent by **NY Rangers**, July 3, 2009. Signed as a free agent by **Ottawa**, July 7, 2010. Signed as a free agent by **TPS Turku** (Finland), June 26, 2012. Signed as a free agent by **Berlin** (Germany), January 11, 2013. Signed as a free agent by **Chicago** (AHL), July 30, 2013.

LOKTIONOV, Andrei

(lawk-too-OH-nawf, ahn-DRAY) **N.J.**

Center. Shoots left. 5'10", 180 lbs. Born, Voskresensk, USSR, May 30, 1990. Los Angeles' 7th choice, 123rd overall, in 2008 Entry Draft.

Season	Club	League	GP	G	A	Pts	PIM	PP	SH	GW	S	%	+/-	TF	F%	Min	GP	G	A	Pts	PIM	PP	SH	GW	Min
2005-06	Spartak 2	Russia-3	4	1	1	2	2																		
2006-07	Yaroslavl 2	Russia-3	31	7	21	28	26																		
2007-08	Yaroslavl 2	Russia-3	STATISTICS NOT AVAILABLE																						
	Yaroslavl	Russia	5	0	1	1	0										1	0	0	0	0				
2008-09	Windsor Spitfires	OHL	51	24	42	66	16										20	11	22	33	2				
2009-10	Los Angeles	NHL	1	0	0	0	0	0	0	0	1	0.0	0	8	12.5	11:52									
	Manchester	AHL	29	9	15	24	12										16	1	8	9	2				
2010-11	Los Angeles	NHL	19	4	3	7	2	0	0	2	26	15.4	2	55	41.8	14:46									
	Manchester	AHL	34	8	23	31	6																		
2011-12	Los Angeles	NHL	39	3	4	7	2	1	0	0	60	5.0	–4	149	43.0	12:32	2	0	0	0	0	0	0	0	4:09
	Manchester	AHL	32	5	15	20	10																		
2012-13	Manchester	AHL	37	7	15	22	6																		
	Albany Devils	AHL	3	0	0	0	0																		
	New Jersey	NHL	28	8	4	12	4	1	0	0	47	17.0	–2	206	38.8	14:15									
	NHL Totals		87	15	11	26	8	2	0	2	134	11.2		418	40.2	13:34	2	0	0	0	0	0	0	0	4:09

• Missed majority of 2009-10 due to shoulder injury at Edmonton, November 26, 2009. Traded to **New Jersey** by **Los Angeles** for New Jersey's 5th round choice (later traded to Florida, later traded to Buffalo – Buffalo selected Gustav Possler) in 2013 Entry Draft, February 6, 2013.

LOMBARDI, Matthew

(lawm-BAHR-dee, MA-thew)

Center. Shoots left. 5'11", 195 lbs. Born, Montreal, Que., March 18, 1982. Calgary's 3rd choice, 90th overall, in 2002 Entry Draft.

Season	Club	League	GP	G	A	Pts	PIM	PP	SH	GW	S	%	+/-	TF	F%	Min	GP	G	A	Pts	PIM	PP	SH	GW	Min
1997-98	Gatineau	QAAA	42	10	13	23											13	4	7	11					
1998-99	Victoriaville Tigres	QMJHL	47	6	10	16	8										5	0	0	0	0				
99-2000	Victoriaville Tigres	QMJHL	65	18	26	44	28										6	0	0	0	6				
2000-01	Victoriaville Tigres	QMJHL	72	28	39	67	66										13	12	6	18	10				
2001-02	Victoriaville Tigres	QMJHL	66	57	73	130	70										22	*17	18	35	18				
2002-03	Saint John Flames	AHL	76	25	21	46	41																		
2003-04	Calgary	NHL	79	16	13	29	32	3	2	4	130	12.3	4	992	47.9	14:26	13	1	5	6	4	0	0	1	14:46
2004-05	Lowell	AHL	9	3	1	4	9										11	0	3	3	16				
2005-06	Calgary	NHL	55	6	20	26	48	1	2	2	72	8.3	–1	499	52.9	14:09	7	0	2	2	2	0	0	0	15:51
	Omaha	AHL	1	1	1	2	0																		
2006-07	Calgary	NHL	81	20	26	46	48	5	4	5	176	11.4	10	965	49.1	16:22	6	1	1	2	0	1	0	0	15:19
2007-08	Calgary	NHL	82	14	22	36	67	2	2	4	181	7.7	–6	955	47.6	17:19	7	0	0	0	4	0	0	0	17:14
2008-09	Calgary	NHL	50	9	21	30	30	0	1	2	119	7.6	11	459	53.4	16:27									
	Phoenix	NHL	19	5	11	16	14	1	0	0	58	8.6	2	384	50.3	20:54									
2009-10	Phoenix	NHL	78	19	34	53	36	4	0	2	174	10.9	8	910	49.7	17:56	7	1	5	6	2	0	0	0	17:36
2010-11	Nashville	NHL	2	0	0	0	0	0	0	0	6	0.0	–1	29	55.2	14:50									
2011-12	Toronto	NHL	62	8	10	18	10	0	1	2	101	7.9	–19	306	49.4	13:34									
2012-13	Phoenix	NHL	21	4	4	8	4	1	0	1	39	10.3	0	180	43.9	14:08									
	Anaheim	NHL	7	0	0	0	4	0	0	0	5	0.0	–2	56	46.4	13:26									
	NHL Totals		536	101	161	262	293	17	12	22	1061	9.5		5735	49.3	15:56	40	3	13	16	12	1	0	1	15:58

• Re-entered NHL Entry Draft. Originally Edmonton's 7th choice, 215th overall, in 2000 Entry Draft.

Memorial Cup All-Star Team (2002) • Ed Chynoweth Trophy (Memorial Cup - Leading Scorer) (2002)

Traded to **Phoenix** by **Calgary** with Brandon Prust and Calgary's 1st round choice (Brandon Gormley) in 2010 Entry Draft for Olli Jokinen and Phoenix's 3rd round choice (later traded to Florida – Florida selected Josh Birkholz) in 2009 Entry Draft, March 4, 2009. Signed as a free agent by **Nashville**, July 2, 2010. • Missed majority of 2010-11 due to head injury at Chicago, October 13, 2010. Traded to **Toronto** by **Nashville** with Cody Franson for Robert Slaney, Brett Lebda and Toronto's 4th round choice (later traded to St. Louis – St. Louis selected Zachary Pochiro) in 2013 Entry Draft, July 3, 2011. Traded to **Phoenix** by **Toronto** for Phoenix's 4th round choice in 2014 Entry Draft, January 16, 2013. Traded to **Anaheim** by **Phoenix** for Brandon McMillan, April 3, 2013.

LOVEJOY, Ben

(LUHV-joi, BEHN) **ANA**

Defense. Shoots right. 6'2", 215 lbs. Born, Concord, NH, February 20, 1984.

Season	Club	League	GP	G	A	Pts	PIM	PP	SH	GW	S	%	+/-	TF	F%	Min	GP	G	A	Pts	PIM	PP	SH	GW	Min
2002-03	Boston College	H-East	22	0	6	6	6																		
2003-04	Dartmouth	ECAC	DID NOT PLAY – TRANSFERRED COLLEGES																						
2004-05	Dartmouth	ECAC	32	2	11	13	28																		
2005-06	Dartmouth	ECAC	32	2	16	18	24																		
2006-07	Dartmouth	ECAC	32	7	16	23	28																		
	Norfolk Admirals	AHL	5	0	0	0	6																		
2007-08	Wilkes-Barre	AHL	72	2	18	20	63										23	2	8	10	18				
2008-09	Pittsburgh	NHL	2	0	0	0	0	0	0	0	1	0.0	0	0	0.0	11:53									
	Wilkes-Barre	AHL	76	7	24	31	84										12	1	1	2	14				
2009-10	Pittsburgh	NHL	12	0	3	3	2	0	0	0	14	0.0	8	0	0.0	16:37									
	Wilkes-Barre	AHL	65	9	20	29	92										2	0	2	2	2				
2010-11	Pittsburgh	NHL	47	3	14	17	48	0	0	0	60	5.0	11	0	0.0	15:00	7	0	2	2	4	0	0	0	10:54
2011-12	Pittsburgh	NHL	34	1	4	5	13	0	0	0	48	2.1	3	0	0.0	13:15	2	0	0	0	0	0	0	0	10:33
2012-13	Pittsburgh	NHL	3	0	0	0	0	0	0	0	7	0.0	–2	0	0.0	13:36									
	Anaheim	NHL	32	0	10	10	29	0	0	0	51	0.0	6	0	0.0	18:13	7	0	2	2	0	0	0	0	21:05
	NHL Totals		130	4	31	35	92	0	0	0	181	2.2		0	0.0	15:24	16	0	4	4	4	0	0	0	15:19

AHL Second All-Star Team (2009)

Signed as a free agent by **Wilkes-Barre** (AHL), June 14, 2007. Signed as a free agent by **Pittsburgh**, July 7, 2008. • Missed majority of 2011-12 due to broken wrist, knee surgery and as a healthy reserve. Traded to **Anaheim** by **Pittsburgh** for Anaheim's 5th round choice in 2014 Entry Draft, February 6, 2013.

LUCIC, Milan

(LOO-cheech, MEE-lahn) **BOS**

Left wing. Shoots left. 6'4", 220 lbs. Born, Vancouver, B.C., June 7, 1988. Boston's 3rd choice, 50th overall, in 2006 Entry Draft.

Season	Club	League	GP	G	A	Pts	PIM	PP	SH	GW	S	%	+/-	TF	F%	Min	GP	G	A	Pts	PIM	PP	SH	GW	Min
2004-05	Coquitlam	BCHL	50	9	14	23	100																		
	Vancouver Giants	WHL	1	0	0	0	2										2	0	0	0	0				
2005-06	Vancouver Giants	WHL	62	9	10	19	149										18	3	4	7	23				
2006-07	Vancouver Giants	WHL	70	30	38	68	147										22	7	12	19	26				
2007-08	Boston	NHL	77	8	19	27	89	1	0	4	88	9.1	–2	8	50.0	12:07	7	2	0	2	4	0	0	0	16:24
2008-09	Boston	NHL	72	17	25	42	136	2	0	3	97	17.5	17	10	60.0	14:57	10	3	6	9	43	0	0	0	15:14
2009-10	Boston	NHL	50	9	11	20	44	0	0	2	72	12.5	–7	14	21.4	14:21	13	5	4	9	19	2	0	1	16:27
2010-11 ♦	Boston	NHL	79	30	32	62	121	5	0	7	173	17.3	28	54	38.9	16:35	25	5	7	12	63	1	0	0	17:54
2011-12	Boston	NHL	81	26	35	61	135	7	0	1	149	17.4	7	30	46.7	17:02	7	0	3	3	8	0	0	0	20:17
2012-13	Boston	NHL	46	7	20	27	75	0	0	0	79	8.9	8	35	48.6	16:55	22	7	12	19	14	0	0	0	20:57
	NHL Totals		405	97	142	239	600	15	0	17	658	14.7		151	43.0	15:18	84	22	32	54	151	3	0	1	18:14

Memorial Cup All-Star Team (2007) • Stafford Smythe Memorial Trophy (Memorial Cup - MVP) (2007)

LUNDIN, Mike

(LUHN-dihn, MIGHK)

Defense. Shoots left. 6'2", 191 lbs. Born, Burnsville, MN, September 24, 1984. Tampa Bay's 3rd choice, 102nd overall, in 2004 Entry Draft.

Season	Club	League	GP	G	A	Pts	PIM	PP	SH	GW	S	%	+/-	TF	F%	Min	GP	G	A	Pts	PIM	PP	SH	GW	Min
2002-03	Apple Valley	High-MN	27	8	20	27																			
2003-04	U. of Maine	H-East	44	3	16	19	34																		
2004-05	U. of Maine	H-East	40	1	13	14	2																		
2005-06	U. of Maine	H-East	36	3	13	16	4																		
2006-07	U. of Maine	H-East	40	6	14	20	2																		
2007-08	Tampa Bay	NHL	81	0	6	6	16	0	0	0	33	0.0	3	0	0.0	13:48									
2008-09	Tampa Bay	NHL	25	0	2	2	4	0	0	0	8	0.0	–4	1	0.0	16:39									
	Norfolk Admirals	AHL	51	4	25	29	18																		

Season	Club	League	Regular Season GP	G	A	Pts	PIM	PP	SH	GW	S	%	+/-	TF	F%	Min	Playoffs GP	G	A	Pts	PIM	PP	SH	GW	Min
2009-10	Tampa Bay	NHL	49	3	10	13	18	0	0	0	42	7.1	–4	0	0.0	21:57	....	....	....	....	....	....	....	....	....
	Norfolk Admirals	AHL	27	2	14	16	4	....	....	....	....	....	....	....	....	....	....	....	....	....	....	....	....	....	....
2010-11	Tampa Bay	NHL	69	1	11	12	12	0	0	0	55	1.8	–3	0	0.0	20:24	18	0	2	2	2	0	0	0	14:40
2011-12	Minnesota	NHL	17	0	2	2	4	0	0	0	9	0.0	–1	0	0.0	20:12	....	....	....	....	....	....	....	....	....
	Houston Aeros	AHL	2	0	0	0	0	....	....	....	....	....	....	....	....	....	....	....	....	....	....	....	....	....	....
2012-13	Almtuna	Sweden-2	7	0	4	4	2	....	....	....	....	....	....	....	....	....	....	....	....	....	....	....	....	....	....
	Ottawa	NHL	11	0	1	1	0	0	0	0	13	0.0	–2	0	0.0	15:30	....	....	....	....	....	....	....	....	....
	NHL Totals		252	4	32	36	54	0	0	0	160	2.5		1	0.0	17:59	18	0	2	2	2	0	0	0	14:41

Hockey East Second All-Star Team (2007)

Signed as a free agent by **Minnesota**, July 9, 2011. • Missed majority of 2011-12 due to back and lower-body injuries, and as a healthy reserve. Signed as a free agent by **Ottawa**, July 1, 2012. Signed as a free agent by **Almtuna** (Sweden-2), November 23, 2012. • Missed majority of 2012-13 due to head and finger injuries, and as a healthy reserve. Signed as a free agent by **Astana** (KHL), June 11, 2013.

LUNDMARK, Jamie

(LUHND-mahrk, JAY-mee)

Center. Shoots right. 6', 197 lbs. Born, Edmonton, Alta., January 16, 1981. NY Rangers' 2nd choice, 9th overall, in 1999 Entry Draft.

Season	Club	League	GP	G	A	Pts	PIM	PP	SH	GW	S	%	+/-	TF	F%	Min	GP	G	A	Pts	PIM	PP	SH	GW	Min
1996-97	St. Albert Saints	AJHL	35	10	9	19	8	....	....	....	....	....	....	....	....	....	....	....	....	....	....	....	....	....	....
1997-98	St. Albert Saints	AJHL	57	33	58	91	171	....	....	....	....	....	....	....	....	....	19	13	18	31	5	....	....	....	....
1998-99	Moose Jaw	WHL	70	40	51	91	123	....	....	....	....	....	....	....	....	....	11	5	4	9	24	....	....	....	....
99-2000	Moose Jaw	WHL	37	21	27	48	33	....	....	....	....	....	....	....	....	....	....	....	....	....	....	....	....	....	....
2000-01	Seattle	WHL	52	35	42	77	49	....	....	....	....	....	....	....	....	....	9	4	4	8	16	....	....	....	....
2001-02	Hartford	AHL	79	27	32	59	56	....	....	....	....	....	....	....	....	....	10	3	4	7	16	....	....	....	....
2002-03	NY Rangers	NHL	55	8	11	19	16	0	0	0	78	10.3	–3	62	43.6	12:04	....	....	....	....	....	....	....	....	....
	Hartford	AHL	22	9	9	18	18	....	....	....	....	....	....	....	....	....	2	0	0	0	0	....	....	....	....
2003-04	NY Rangers	NHL	56	2	8	10	33	0	0	1	68	2.9	–8	379	40.4	12:46	....	....	....	....	....	....	....	....	....
2004-05	HC Forst Bolzano	Italy	14	9	9	18	22	....	....	....	....	....	....	....	....	....	....	....	....	....	....	....	....	....	....
	Hartford	AHL	64	14	27	41	146	....	....	....	....	....	....	....	....	....	6	2	4	6	8	....	....	....	....
2005-06	NY Rangers	NHL	3	1	0	1	6	0	0	0	1	100.0	–2	2	0.0	9:49	....	....	....	....	....	....	....	....	....
	Phoenix	NHL	38	5	13	18	36	1	0	0	61	8.2	–1	366	58.7	12:37	....	....	....	....	....	....	....	....	....
	San Antonio	AHL	4	1	2	3	2	....	....	....	....	....	....	....	....	....	....	....	....	....	....	....	....	....	....
	Calgary	NHL	12	4	6	10	20	1	0	1	16	25.0	2	103	53.4	12:32	4	0	1	1	7	0	0	0	9:44
2006-07	Calgary	NHL	39	0	4	4	31	0	0	0	28	0.0	–4	233	55.4	8:37	....	....	....	....	....	....	....	....	....
	Los Angeles	NHL	29	7	2	9	25	0	0	0	53	13.2	–8	410	47.6	16:03	....	....	....	....	....	....	....	....	....
2007-08	Dynamo Moscow	Russia	17	2	1	3	31	....	....	....	....	....	....	....	....	....	....	....	....	....	....	....	....	....	....
	Lake Erie	AHL	51	13	20	33	71	....	....	....	....	....	....	....	....	....	....	....	....	....	....	....	....	....	....
2008-09	Calgary	NHL	27	8	8	16	17	0	0	0	50	16.0	2	120	51.7	13:59	2	0	0	0	0	0	0	0	7:06
	Quad City Flames	AHL	54	15	37	52	31	....	....	....	....	....	....	....	....	....	....	....	....	....	....	....	....	....	....
2009-10	Calgary	NHL	21	4	5	9	4	1	0	1	36	11.1	–6	62	48.4	15:22	....	....	....	....	....	....	....	....	....
	Abbotsford Heat	AHL	32	9	12	21	64	....	....	....	....	....	....	....	....	....	....	....	....	....	....	....	....	....	....
	Toronto	NHL	15	1	2	3	16	0	0	0	16	6.3	–1	30	50.0	11:34	....	....	....	....	....	....	....	....	....
2010-11	Milwaukee	AHL	34	6	12	18	22	....	....	....	....	....	....	....	....	....	....	....	....	....	....	....	....	....	....
	Timra IK	Sweden	18	3	7	10	12	....	....	....	....	....	....	....	....	....	....	....	....	....	....	....	....	....	....
2011-12	Dynamo Riga	KHL	47	8	8	16	52	....	....	....	....	....	....	....	....	....	7	0	1	1	6	....	....	....	....
2012-13	Klagenfurter AC	Austria	51	29	29	58	34	....	....	....	....	....	....	....	....	....	13	5	9	8	....	....	....	....	....
	NHL Totals		295	40	59	99	204	3	0	3	407	9.8		1767	49.9	12:35	6	0	1	1	7	0	0	0	8:51

WHL All-Rookie Team (1999) • WHL East Second All-Star Team (1999) • WHL West First All-Star Team (2001)

Signed as a free agent by **Bolzano** (Italy), September 21, 2004. Signed as a free agent by **Hartford** (AHL), November 16, 2004. Traded to **Phoenix** by **NY Rangers** for Jeff Taffe, October 18, 2005. Traded to **Calgary** by **Phoenix** for Calgary's 4th round choice (later traded to NY Islanders - NY Islanders selected Doug Rogers) in 2006 Entry Draft, March 9, 2006. Traded to **Los Angeles** by **Calgary** with Calgary's 4th round choice (Dwight King) in 2007 Entry Draft and Calgary's 2nd round choice (later traded back to Calgary - Calgary selected Mitch Wahl) in 2008 Entry Draft for Craig Conroy, January 29, 2007. Signed as a free agent by **Dynamo Moscow** (Russia), July 27, 2007. Signed as a free agent by **Lake Erie** (AHL), December 8, 2007. Signed as a free agent by **Calgary**, July 16, 2008. Claimed on waivers by **Toronto** from **Calgary**, February 16, 2010. Signed as a free agent by **Nashville**, July 16, 2010. Signed as a free agent by **Timra** (Sweden), January 10. 2011. Signed as a free agent by **Riga** (KHL), August 22, 2011. Signed as a free agent by **Klagenfurt** (Austria), May 22, 2012.

LUPUL, Joffrey

(LOO-puhl, JAWF-ree) **TOR**

Left wing. Shoots right. 6'1", 206 lbs. Born, Fort Saskatchewan, Alta., September 23, 1983. Anaheim's 1st choice, 7th overall, in 2002 Entry Draft.

Season	Club	League	GP	G	A	Pts	PIM	PP	SH	GW	S	%	+/-	TF	F%	Min	GP	G	A	Pts	PIM	PP	SH	GW	Min
1998-99	Ft. Saskatchewan	Minor-AB	36	40	50	90	40	....	....	....	....	....	....	....	....	....	....	....	....	....	....	....	....	....	....
99-2000	Ft. Saskatchewan	AMHL	34	43	30	*73	47	....	....	....	....	....	....	....	....	....	4	0	1	1	2	....	....	....	....
2000-01	Medicine Hat	WHL	69	30	26	56	39	....	....	....	....	....	....	....	....	....	22	3	6	9	2	....	....	....	....
2001-02	Medicine Hat	WHL	72	*56	50	106	95	....	....	....	....	....	....	....	....	....	....	....	....	....	....	....	....	....	....
2002-03	Medicine Hat	WHL	50	41	37	78	82	....	....	....	....	....	....	....	....	....	11	4	11	15	20	....	....	....	....
2003-04	Anaheim	NHL	75	13	21	34	28	4	0	2	137	9.5	–6	11	9.1	13:37	....	....	....	....	....	....	....	....	....
	Cincinnati	AHL	3	3	2	5	2	....	....	....	....	....	....	....	....	....	....	....	....	....	....	....	....	....	....
2004-05	Cincinnati	AHL	65	30	26	56	58	....	....	....	....	....	....	....	....	....	12	3	9	12	27	....	....	....	....
2005-06	Anaheim	NHL	81	28	25	53	48	12	2	2	296	9.5	–13	101	37.6	16:38	16	9	2	11	31	1	0	1	16:43
2006-07	Edmonton	NHL	81	16	12	28	45	5	0	1	172	9.3	–29	14	35.7	15:36	....	....	....	....	....	....	....	....	....
2007-08	Philadelphia	NHL	56	20	26	46	35	7	0	3	176	11.4	2	4	75.0	18:13	17	4	6	10	2	2	0	1	16:13
2008-09	Philadelphia	NHL	79	25	25	50	58	6	0	4	194	12.9	1	21	47.6	15:41	6	1	1	2	2	0	0	0	17:07
2009-10	Anaheim	NHL	23	10	4	14	18	0	0	0	66	15.2	3	5	20.0	15:58	....	....	....	....	....	....	....	....	....
2010-11	Anaheim	NHL	26	5	8	13	14	2	0	1	54	9.3	–4	14	50.0	13:13	....	....	....	....	....	....	....	....	....
	Syracuse Crunch	AHL	3	1	3	4	0	....	....	....	....	....	....	....	....	....	....	....	....	....	....	....	....	....	....
	Toronto	NHL	28	9	9	18	19	2	0	1	75	12.0	–7	18	27.8	17:51	....	....	....	....	....	....	....	....	....
2011-12	Toronto	NHL	66	25	42	67	48	8	0	3	191	13.1	1	58	36.2	18:37	....	....	....	....	....	....	....	....	....
2012-13	Avtomobilist	KHL	9	1	3	4	4	....	....	....	....	....	....	....	....	....	....	....	....	....	....	....	....	....	....
	Toronto	NHL	16	11	7	18	12	3	0	3	42	26.2	8	8	37.5	16:07	7	3	1	4	4	1	0	0	18:59
	NHL Totals		531	162	179	341	325	49	2	20	1403	11.5		254	37.0	16:10	46	17	10	27	39	4	0	2	16:56

WHL East First All-Star Team (2002) • Canadian Major Junior First All-Star Team (2002)

Played in NHL All-Star Game (2012)

Traded to **Edmonton** by **Anaheim** with Ladislav Smid, Anaheim's 1st round choice (later traded to Phoenix - Phoenix selected Nick Ross) in 2007 Entry Draft and Anaheim's 1st (Jordan Eberle) and 2nd (later traded to NY Islanders - NY Islanders selected Travis Hamonic) round choices in 2008 Entry Draft for Chris Pronger, July 3, 2006. Traded to **Philadelphia** by **Edmonton** with Jason Smith for Joni Pitkanen, Geoff Sanderson and Philadelphia's 3rd round choice (Cameron Abney) in 2009 Entry Draft, July 1, 2007. Traded to **Anaheim** by **Philadelphia** with Luca Sbisa, Philadelphia's 1st round choice in 2009 (later traded to Columbus - Columbus selected John Moore) and 2010 (Emerson Etem) Entry Drafts and future considerations for Chris Pronger and Ryan Dingle, June 26, 2009. • Missed majority of 2009-10 due to back injury, December 16, 2009. Traded to **Toronto** by **Anaheim** with Jake Gardiner and Anaheim's 4th round choice (later traded to San Jose – San Jose selected Fredrik Bergvik) in 2013 Entry Draft for Francois Beauchemin, February 9, 2011. Signed as a free agent by **Avtomobilist Yekaterinburg** (KHL), October 30, 2012. • Missed majority of 2012-13 due to arm injury at Pittsburgh, January 23, 2013 and head injury vs. Philadelphia. April 4, 2013.

LYDMAN, Toni

(LEWD-man, TOH-nee)

Defense. Shoots left. 6'1", 208 lbs. Born, Lahti, Finland, September 25, 1977. Calgary's 5th choice, 89th overall, in 1996 Entry Draft.

Season	Club	League	GP	G	A	Pts	PIM	PP	SH	GW	S	%	+/-	TF	F%	Min	GP	G	A	Pts	PIM	PP	SH	GW	Min
1993-94	K-Reipas U18	Fin-U18	9	3	1	4	4	....	....	....	....	....	....	....	....	....	....	....	....	....	....	....	....	....	....
	K-Reipas Jr.	Fin-Jr.	1	0	0	0	0	....	....	....	....	....	....	....	....	....	....	....	....	....	....	....	....	....	....
1994-95	K-Reipas U18	Fin-U18	9	7	4	11	12	....	....	....	....	....	....	....	....	....	....	....	....	....	....	....	....	....	....
	K-Reipas Jr.	Fin-Jr.	26	6	4	10	10	....	....	....	....	....	....	....	....	....	....	....	....	....	....	....	....	....	....
1995-96	Reipas Lahti Jr.	Fin-Jr.	9	2	2	4	6	....	....	....	....	....	....	....	....	....	....	....	....	....	....	....	....	....	....
	Reipas Lahti	Finland-2	39	5	2	7	30	....	....	....	....	....	....	....	....	....	3	0	1	1	0	....	....	....	....
1996-97	Tappara Tampere	Finland	49	1	2	3	65	....	....	....	....	....	....	....	....	....	3	0	0	0	6	....	....	....	....
1997-98	Tappara Tampere	Finland	48	4	10	14	48	....	....	....	....	....	....	....	....	....	4	0	2	2	0	....	....	....	....
1998-99	HIFK Helsinki	Finland	42	4	7	11	36	....	....	....	....	....	....	....	....	....	11	0	3	3	2	....	....	....	....
	HIFK Helsinki	EuroHL	6	0	2	2	29	....	....	....	....	....	....	....	....	....	4	1	....	....	....	....	....	....	....
99-2000	HIFK Helsinki	Finland	46	4	18	22	36	....	....	....	....	....	....	....	....	....	9	0	4	4	6	....	....	....	....
2000-01	Calgary	NHL	62	3	16	19	30	1	0	0	80	3.8	–7	0	0.0	20:36	....	....	....	....	....	....	....	....	....
2001-02	Calgary	NHL	79	6	22	28	52	1	0	0	126	4.8	–8	0	0.0	21:10	....	....	....	....	....	....	....	....	....
2002-03	Calgary	NHL	81	6	20	26	28	3	0	0	143	4.2	–7	0	0.0	25:47	....	....	....	....	....	....	....	....	....
2003-04	Calgary	NHL	67	4	16	20	30	2	0	1	93	4.3	6	0	0.0	21:13	6	0	1	1	2	0	0	0	14:30
2004-05	HIFK Helsinki	Finland	8	1	2	3	2	....	....	....	....	....	....	....	....	....	5	0	3	3	0	....	....	....	....
2005-06	Buffalo	NHL	75	1	16	17	82	0	0	0	68	1.5	9	0	0.0	21:38	18	1	4	5	18	0	0	0	23:03
	Finland	Olympics	8	1	0	1	10	....	....	....	....	....	....	....	....	....	....	....	....	....	....	....	....	....	....
2006-07	Buffalo	NHL	67	2	17	19	55	0	0	1	44	4.5	10	0	0.0	20:36	16	2	2	4	14	0	0	0	23:41
2007-08	Buffalo	NHL	82	4	22	26	74	3	0	0	86	4.7	1	1	0.0	21:40	....	....	....	....	....	....	....	....	....
2008-09	Buffalo	NHL	80	3	20	23	70	0	0	0	99	3.0	0	0	0.0	21:47	....	....	....	....	....	....	....	....	....
2009-10	Buffalo	NHL	67	4	16	20	30	0	0	1	77	5.2	10	0	0.0	18:52	6	0	1	1	6	0	0	0	26:15
	Finland	Olympics	6	0	0	0	2	....	....	....	....	....	....	....	....	....	....	....	....	....	....	....	....	....	....

			Regular Season														Playoffs								
Season	Club	League	GP	G	A	Pts	PIM	PP	SH	GW	S	%	+/-	TF	F%	Min	GP	G	A	Pts	PIM	PP	SH	GW	Min
2010-11	**Anaheim**	**NHL**	**78**	**3**	**22**	**25**	**42**	**0**	**0**	**0**	**99**	**3.0**	**32**	**0**	**0.0**	**22:10**	**6**	**0**	**0**	**0**	**2**	**0**	**0**	**0**	**20:09**
2011-12	**Anaheim**	**NHL**	**74**	**0**	**13**	**13**	**46**	**0**	**0**	**0**	**46**	**0.0**	**0**	**0**	**0.0**	**18:54**									
2012-13	**Anaheim**	**NHL**	**35**	**0**	**6**	**6**	**12**	**0**	**0**	**0**	**28**	**0.0**	**–1**	**0**	**0.0**	**19:23**	**3**	**0**	**0**	**0**	**0**	**0**	**0**	**0**	**15:08**
	NHL Totals		**847**	**36**	**206**	**242**	**551**	**10**	**0**	**3**	**989**	**3.6**		**1**	**0.0**	**21:19**	**55**	**3**	**8**	**11**	**42**	**0**	**0**	**0**	**21:54**

Signed as a free agent by **HIFK Helsinki** (Finland), January 31, 2005. Traded to **Buffalo** by **Calgary** for Buffalo's 3rd round choice (John Armstrong) in 2006 Entry Draft, August 25, 2005. Signed as a free agent by **Anaheim**, July 1, 2010.

MacARTHUR, Clarke

(muh-KAR-thuhr, KLAHRK) **OTT**

Left wing. Shoots left. 6', 191 lbs. Born, Lloydminster, Alta., April 6, 1985. Buffalo's 3rd choice, 74th overall, in 2003 Entry Draft.

Season	Club	League	GP	G	A	Pts	PIM	PP	SH	GW	S	%	+/-	TF	F%	Min	GP	G	A	Pts	PIM	PP	SH	GW	Min
99-2000	Lloydminster	CABHL	24	19	45	64	51										5	9	6	15	4				
2000-01	Strathcona	AMBHL	38	36	63	99	44										8	6	2	8	10				
2001-02	Drayton Valley	AJHL	61	22	40	62	33										16	5	8	13	34				
2002-03	Medicine Hat	WHL	70	23	52	75	104										11	3	6	9	8				
2003-04	Medicine Hat	WHL	62	35	40	75	93										20	8	10	18	16				
2004-05	Medicine Hat	WHL	58	30	44	74	100										13	3	8	11	18				
	Rochester	AHL															3	0	1	1	0				
2005-06	Rochester	AHL	69	21	32	53	71																		
2006-07	**Buffalo**	**NHL**	**19**	**3**	**4**	**7**	**4**	**0**	**0**	**0**	**16**	**18.8**	**4**	**50**	**46.0**	**8:54**									
	Rochester	AHL	51	21	42	63	57										6	2	4	6	4				
2007-08	**Buffalo**	**NHL**	**37**	**8**	**7**	**15**	**20**	**0**	**0**	**1**	**51**	**15.7**	**3**	**14**	**28.6**	**14:34**									
	Rochester	AHL	43	14	28	42	26																		
2008-09	**Buffalo**	**NHL**	**71**	**17**	**14**	**31**	**56**	**5**	**0**	**0**	**108**	**15.7**	**–4**	**218**	**34.9**	**13:50**									
2009-10	**Buffalo**	**NHL**	**60**	**13**	**13**	**26**	**47**	**3**	**0**	**3**	**99**	**13.1**	**–14**	**143**	**43.4**	**14:22**									
	Atlanta	**NHL**	**21**	**3**	**6**	**9**	**2**	**1**	**1**	**0**	**30**	**10.0**	**–2**	**10**	**50.0**	**15:37**									
2010-11	**Toronto**	**NHL**	**82**	**21**	**41**	**62**	**37**	**6**	**0**	**3**	**154**	**13.6**	**–3**	**16**	**56.3**	**17:07**									
2011-12	**Toronto**	**NHL**	**73**	**20**	**23**	**43**	**37**	**3**	**0**	**4**	**148**	**13.5**	**3**	**11**	**45.5**	**15:51**									
2012-13	Crimmitschau	German-2	9	4	7	11	16																		
	Toronto	**NHL**	**40**	**8**	**12**	**20**	**26**	**2**	**0**	**1**	**62**	**12.9**	**3**	**6**	**83.3**	**14:55**	**5**	**2**	**1**	**3**	**2**	**0**	**0**	**1**	**12:21**
	NHL Totals		**403**	**93**	**120**	**213**	**229**	**20**	**1**	**12**	**668**	**13.9**		**468**	**40.4**	**14:59**	**5**	**2**	**1**	**3**	**2**	**0**	**0**	**1**	**12:21**

Memorial Cup All-Star Team (2004) • WHL East First All-Star Team (2005)

Traded to **Atlanta** by **Buffalo** for Atlanta's 3rd (Jerome Gauthier-Leduc) and 4th (Steven Shipley) round choices in 2010 Entry Draft, March 3, 2010. Signed as a free agent by **Toronto**, August 28, 2010. Signed as a free agent by **Crimmitschau** (German-2), October 23, 2012. Signed as a free agent by **Ottawa**, July 5, 2013.

MacDERMID, Lane

(MAK-duhr-mihd, LAYN) **DAL**

Left wing. Shoots left. 6'3", 205 lbs. Born, Hartford, CT, August 25, 1989. Boston's 3rd choice, 112th overall, in 2009 Entry Draft.

Season	Club	League	GP	G	A	Pts	PIM	PP	SH	GW	S	%	+/-	TF	F%	Min	GP	G	A	Pts	PIM	PP	SH	GW	Min
2005-06	Owen Sound	ON-Jr.B	48	1	7	8																			
2006-07	Owen Sound	OHL	57	2	5	7	115										4	1	0	1	2				
2007-08	Owen Sound	OHL	66	13	11	24	190																		
2008-09	Owen Sound	OHL	26	8	6	14	85																		
	Windsor Spitfires	OHL	38	7	14	21	112										20	4	5	9	38				
2009-10	Providence Bruins	AHL	65	2	3	5	155																		
2010-11	Providence Bruins	AHL	78	7	12	19	158																		
2011-12	**Boston**	**NHL**	**5**	**0**	**0**	**0**	**5**	**0**	**0**	**0**	**6**	**0.0**	**–2**	**0**	**0.0**	**8:54**									
	Providence Bruins	AHL	69	4	12	16	121																		
2012-13	Providence Bruins	AHL	37	4	2	6	82																		
	Boston	**NHL**	**3**	**0**	**0**	**0**	**10**	**0**	**0**	**0**	**1**	**0.0**	**0**	**0**	**0.0**	**3:34**									
	Dallas	**NHL**	**6**	**2**	**0**	**2**	**9**	**0**	**0**	**0**	**3**	**66.7**	**1**	**0**	**0.0**	**5:06**									
	NHL Totals		**14**	**2**	**0**	**2**	**24**	**0**	**0**	**0**	**10**	**20.0**		**0**	**0.0**	**6:08**									

Traded to **Dallas** by **Boston** with Cody Payne and Boston's 1st round choice (Jason Dickinson) in 2013 Entry Draft for Jaromir Jagr, April 2, 2013.

MacDONALD, Andrew

(MAK-DAWN-uhld, AN-droo) **NYI**

Defense. Shoots left. 6', 185 lbs. Born, Judique, N.S., September 7, 1986. NY Islanders' 10th choice, 160th overall, in 2006 Entry Draft.

Season	Club	League	GP	G	A	Pts	PIM	PP	SH	GW	S	%	+/-	TF	F%	Min	GP	G	A	Pts	PIM	PP	SH	GW	Min
2003-04	Truro Bearcats	MJrHL	50	8	20	28	43										10	0	0	0					
2004-05	Truro Bearcats	MJrHL	56	11	22	33	60										17	6	7	13					
2005-06	Moncton Wildcats	QMJHL	68	6	40	46	62										21	2	11	13	10				
2006-07	Moncton Wildcats	QMJHL	65	14	44	58	81										7	1	5	6	4				
	Bridgeport	AHL	3	0	0	0	0																		
2007-08	Bridgeport	AHL	21	2	3	5	10																		
	Utah Grizzlies	ECHL	37	1	11	12	39										15	3	9	12	12				
2008-09	**NY Islanders**	**NHL**	**3**	**0**	**0**	**0**	**2**	**0**	**0**	**0**	**1**	**0.0**	**2**	**0**	**0.0**	**10:10**									
	Bridgeport	AHL	69	9	24	33	46										5	1	1	2	4				
2009-10	**NY Islanders**	**NHL**	**46**	**1**	**6**	**7**	**20**	**0**	**0**	**0**	**43**	**2.3**	**4**	**1**	**0.0**	**20:05**									
	Bridgeport	AHL	21	2	6	8	29										5	3	1	4	10				
2010-11	**NY Islanders**	**NHL**	**60**	**4**	**23**	**27**	**37**	**1**	**0**	**1**	**72**	**5.6**	**9**	**0**	**0.0**	**23:25**									
2011-12	**NY Islanders**	**NHL**	**75**	**5**	**14**	**19**	**26**	**1**	**0**	**0**	**71**	**7.0**	**–5**	**0**	**0.0**	**23:22**									
2012-13	Karlovy Vary	CzRep	21	1	4	5	10																		
	HC Banik Sokolov	CzRep-3	1	0	0	0	0																		
	NY Islanders	**NHL**	**48**	**3**	**9**	**12**	**20**	**1**	**0**	**1**	**45**	**6.7**	**–2**	**0**	**0.0**	**23:31**	**4**	**0**	**0**	**0**	**4**	**0**	**0**	**0**	**23:26**
	NHL Totals		**232**	**13**	**52**	**65**	**105**	**3**	**0**	**2**	**232**	**5.6**		**1**	**0.0**	**22:36**	**4**	**0**	**0**	**0**	**4**	**0**	**0**	**0**	**23:26**

QMJHL First All-Star Team (2007)

Signed as a free agent by **Karlovy Vary** (CzRep), October 9, 2012. • Loaned to **Banik Sokolov** (CzRep-3) by **Karlovy Vary** (CzRep).

MACENAUER, Maxime

(MAY-sehn-owr, mahx-EEM)

Center. Shoots left. 6', 205 lbs. Born, Laval, Que., January 4, 1989. Anaheim's 3rd choice, 63rd overall, in 2007 Entry Draft.

Season	Club	League	GP	G	A	Pts	PIM	PP	SH	GW	S	%	+/-	TF	F%	Min	GP	G	A	Pts	PIM	PP	SH	GW	Min
2004-05	Ecole Montpetit	QAAA	37	17	22	39	56										3	0	0	0	0				
2005-06	Rimouski Oceanic	QMJHL	41	8	14	22	30																		
2006-07	Rouyn-Noranda	QMJHL	14	1	3	4	10																		
2007-08	Rouyn-Noranda	QMJHL	67	23	37	60	53										17	6	10	16	8				
2008-09	Rouyn-Noranda	QMJHL	35	15	9	24	34																		
	Shawinigan	QMJHL	19	7	9	16	18										21	5	9	14	20				
2009-10	Bakersfield	ECHL	45	5	16	21	49										6	1	0	1	0				
2010-11	Syracuse Crunch	AHL	79	13	19	32	65																		
2011-12	**Anaheim**	**NHL**	**29**	**1**	**3**	**4**	**18**	**0**	**0**	**1**	**14**	**7.1**	**–4**	**227**	**49.8**	**10:49**									
	Syracuse Crunch	AHL	13	4	2	6	2																		
	St. John's IceCaps	AHL	9	0	1	1	2										10	1	0	1	0				
2012-13	St. John's IceCaps	AHL	68	11	11	22	57																		
	NHL Totals		**29**	**1**	**3**	**4**	**18**	**0**	**0**	**1**	**14**	**7.1**		**227**	**49.8**	**10:49**									

Traded to **Winnipeg** by **Anaheim** for Riley Holzapfel, February 13, 2012.

MACHACEK, Spencer

(muh-HA-chehk, SPEHN-suhr) **CBJ**

Right wing. Shoots right. 6'1", 200 lbs. Born, Lethbridge, Alta., October 14, 1988. Atlanta's 1st choice, 67th overall, in 2007 Entry Draft.

Season	Club	League	GP	G	A	Pts	PIM	PP	SH	GW	S	%	+/-	TF	F%	Min	GP	G	A	Pts	PIM	PP	SH	GW	Min
2004-05	Brooks Bandits	AJHL	59	16	20	36	41										10	2	2	4	8				
2005-06	Vancouver Giants	WHL	70	23	22	45	53										18	6	8	14	8				
2006-07	Vancouver Giants	WHL	63	21	24	45	32										22	9	11	20	14				
2007-08	Vancouver Giants	WHL	70	33	45	78	69										10	5	2	7	6				
2008-09	**Atlanta**	**NHL**	**2**	**0**	**0**	**0**	**0**	**0**	**0**	**0**	**1**	**0.0**	**0**	**0**	**0.0**	**8:12**									
	Chicago Wolves	AHL	77	23	25	48	23																		
2009-10	Chicago Wolves	AHL	79	20	29	49	68										13	7	4	11	8				
2010-11	**Atlanta**	**NHL**	**10**	**0**	**0**	**0**	**0**	**0**	**0**	**0**	**7**	**0.0**	**–2**	**0**	**0.0**	**7:41**									
	Chicago Wolves	AHL	67	21	32	53	45																		
2011-12	**Winnipeg**	**NHL**	**13**	**2**	**7**	**9**	**7**	**0**	**0**	**0**	**12**	**16.7**	**8**	**1**	**100.0**	**7:30**									
	St. John's IceCaps	AHL	61	18	32	50	48										11	0	7	7	12				

			Regular Season														Playoffs								
Season	Club	League	GP	G	A	Pts	PIM	PP	SH	GW	S	%	+/-	TF	F%	Min	GP	G	A	Pts	PIM	PP	SH	GW	Min
2012-13	St. John's IceCaps	AHL	57	11	14	25	45	....	....	....	....	....	....	....	....	....	....	....	....	....	....	....	....	....	....
	Springfield	AHL	18	5	9	14	13	....	....	....	....	....	....	....	....	....	6	0	1	1	0	....	....	....	....
	NHL Totals		**25**	**2**	**7**	**9**	**7**	**0**	**0**	**0**	**20**	**10.0**		**1**	**100.0**	**7:38**	....	....	....	....	....	....	....	....	....

• Transferred to **Winnipeg** after **Atlanta** franchise relocated, June 21, 2011. Traded to **Columbus** by **Winnipeg** for Tomas Kubalik, March 10, 2013.

MacINTYRE, Steve

(MAK-ihn-tighr, STEEV) **PIT**

Left wing. Shoots left. 6'5", 250 lbs. Born, Brock, Sask., August 8, 1980.

Season	Club	League	GP	G	A	Pts	PIM	PP	SH	GW	S	%	+/-	TF	F%	Min	GP	G	A	Pts	PIM	PP	SH	GW	Min
2002-03	St. Jean Mission	QSPHL	10	1	1	2	68	....	....	....	....	....	....	....	....	....	....	....	....	....	....	....	....	....	....
	Muskegon Fury	UHL	54	2	1	3	279	....	....	....	....	....	....	....	....	....	5	0	0	0	24	....	....	....	....
2003-04	Hartford	AHL	3	0	0	0	0	....	....	....	....	....	....	....	....	....	....	....	....	....	....	....	....	....	....
	Charlotte	ECHL	61	1	4	5	217	....	....	....	....	....	....	....	....	....	....	....	....	....	....	....	....	....	....
	Jacksonville	WHA2	6	0	2	2	18	....	....	....	....	....	....	....	....	....	5	0	1	1	17	....	....	....	....
2004-05	Hartford	AHL	27	1	1	2	207	....	....	....	....	....	....	....	....	....	....	....	....	....	....	....	....	....	....
	Charlotte	ECHL	46	1	4	5	214	....	....	....	....	....	....	....	....	....	11	0	4	4	17	....	....	....	....
2005-06	Charlotte	ECHL	61	3	2	5	238	....	....	....	....	....	....	....	....	....	1	0	0	0	4	....	....	....	....
2006-07	Quad City	UHL	46	2	1	3	168	....	....	....	....	....	....	....	....	....	5	0	0	0	6	....	....	....	....
2007-08	Providence Bruins	AHL	62	2	3	5	213	....	....	....	....	....	....	....	....	....	5	0	0	0	9	....	....	....	....
2008-09	**Edmonton**	**NHL**	**22**	**2**	**0**	**2**	**40**	**0**	**0**	**1**	**6**	**33.3**	**–2**	**0**	**0.0**	**3:55**	....	....	....	....	....	....	....	....	....
2009-10	**Edmonton**	**NHL**	**4**	**0**	**0**	**0**	**7**	**0**	**0**	**0**	**0**	**0.0**	**0**	**0**	**0.0**	**1:35**	....	....	....	....	....	....	....	....	....
	Florida	**NHL**	**18**	**0**	**1**	**1**	**17**	**0**	**0**	**0**	**3**	**0.0**	**–3**	**0**	**0.0**	**3:10**	....	....	....	....	....	....	....	....	....
	Rochester	AHL	34	0	2	2	86	....	....	....	....	....	....	....	....	....	6	0	0	0	23	....	....	....	....
2010-11	**Edmonton**	**NHL**	**34**	**0**	**1**	**1**	**93**	**0**	**0**	**0**	**6**	**0.0**	**–1**	**0**	**0.0**	**3:32**	....	....	....	....	....	....	....	....	....
2011-12	**Pittsburgh**	**NHL**	**12**	**0**	**0**	**0**	**6**	**0**	**0**	**0**	**0**	**0.0**	**0**	**0**	**0.0**	**3:11**	....	....	....	....	....	....	....	....	....
	Wilkes-Barre	AHL	24	1	0	1	59	....	....	....	....	....	....	....	....	....	....	....	....	....	....	....	....	....	....
2012-13	Wilkes-Barre	AHL	29	0	0	0	70	....	....	....	....	....	....	....	....	....	....	....	....	....	....	....	....	....	....
	Pittsburgh	**NHL**	**1**	**0**	**0**	**0**	**12**	**0**	**0**	**0**	**0**	**0.0**	**0**	**0**	**0.0**	**4:31**	....	....	....	....	....	....	....	....	....
	NHL Totals		**91**	**2**	**2**	**4**	**175**	**0**	**0**	**1**	**15**	**13.3**		**0**	**0.0**	**3:26**	....	....	....	....	....	....	....	....	....

Signed as a free agent by **NY Rangers**, August 15, 2005. Signed as a free agent by **Quad City** (UHL), August 24, 2006. Signed as a free agent by **Florida**, July 3, 2008. Claimed on waivers by **Edmonton** from **Florida**, September 30, 2008. • Missed majority of 2008-09 due to facial injury and as a healthy reserve. Claimed on waivers by **Florida** from **Edmonton**, November 10, 2009. Signed as a free agent by **Edmonton**, July 2, 2010. • Missed majority of 2010-11 as a healthy reserve. Signed as a free agent by **Pittsburgh**, July 12, 2011. • Missed majority of 2011-12 and 2012-13 as a healthy reserve.

MacKENZIE, Derek

(muh-KEHN-zee, DAIR-ihk) **CBJ**

Center. Shoots left. 5'11", 180 lbs. Born, Sudbury, Ont., June 11, 1981. Atlanta's 6th choice, 128th overall, in 1999 Entry Draft.

Season	Club	League	GP	G	A	Pts	PIM	PP	SH	GW	S	%	+/-	TF	F%	Min	GP	G	A	Pts	PIM	PP	SH	GW	Min
1996-97	Rayside-Balfour	NOJHA	40	23	32	55	40	....	....	....	....	....	....	....	....	....	....	....	....	....	....	....	....	....	....
1997-98	Sudbury Wolves	OHL	59	9	11	20	26	....	....	....	....	....	....	....	....	....	....	....	....	....	....	....	....	....	....
1998-99	Sudbury Wolves	OHL	68	22	65	87	74	....	....	....	....	....	....	....	....	....	4	2	4	6	2	....	....	....	....
99-2000	Sudbury Wolves	OHL	68	24	33	57	110	....	....	....	....	....	....	....	....	....	12	5	9	14	16	....	....	....	....
2000-01	Sudbury Wolves	OHL	62	40	49	89	89	....	....	....	....	....	....	....	....	....	12	6	8	14	16	....	....	....	....
2001-02	**Atlanta**	**NHL**	**1**	**0**	**0**	**0**	**2**	**0**	**0**	**0**	**1**	**0.0**	**–1**	**16**	**56.3**	**13:51**	....	....	....	....	....	....	....	....	....
	Chicago Wolves	AHL	68	13	12	25	80	....	....	....	....	....	....	....	....	....	25	4	2	6	20	....	....	....	....
2002-03	Chicago Wolves	AHL	80	14	18	32	97	....	....	....	....	....	....	....	....	....	9	0	0	0	4	....	....	....	....
2003-04	**Atlanta**	**NHL**	**12**	**0**	**1**	**1**	**10**	**0**	**0**	**0**	**7**	**0.0**	**0**	**63**	**46.0**	**6:38**	....	....	....	....	....	....	....	....	....
	Chicago Wolves	AHL	63	19	16	35	67	....	....	....	....	....	....	....	....	....	10	7	1	8	13	....	....	....	....
2004-05	Chicago Wolves	AHL	78	13	20	33	87	....	....	....	....	....	....	....	....	....	18	5	6	11	33	....	....	....	....
2005-06	**Atlanta**	**NHL**	**11**	**0**	**1**	**1**	**8**	**0**	**0**	**0**	**11**	**0.0**	**0**	**59**	**55.9**	**6:33**	....	....	....	....	....	....	....	....	....
	Chicago Wolves	AHL	36	10	12	22	48	....	....	....	....	....	....	....	....	....	....	....	....	....	....	....	....	....	....
2006-07	**Atlanta**	**NHL**	**4**	**0**	**0**	**0**	**0**	**0**	**0**	**0**	**3**	**0.0**	**1**	**16**	**56.3**	**5:00**	....	....	....	....	....	....	....	....	....
	Chicago Wolves	AHL	52	14	23	37	62	....	....	....	....	....	....	....	....	....	....	....	....	....	....	....	....	....	....
2007-08	**Columbus**	**NHL**	**17**	**2**	**0**	**2**	**8**	**0**	**0**	**0**	**19**	**10.5**	**–2**	**73**	**34.3**	**7:47**	....	....	....	....	....	....	....	....	....
	Syracuse Crunch	AHL	62	25	24	49	46	....	....	....	....	....	....	....	....	....	13	6	8	14	22	....	....	....	....
2008-09	**Columbus**	**NHL**	**1**	**0**	**0**	**0**	**2**	**0**	**0**	**0**	**1**	**0.0**	**–1**	**4**	**50.0**	**7:15**	....	....	....	....	....	....	....	....	....
	Syracuse Crunch	AHL	64	22	30	52	50	....	....	....	....	....	....	....	....	....	....	....	....	....	....	....	....	....	....
2009-10	**Columbus**	**NHL**	**18**	**1**	**3**	**4**	**0**	**0**	**0**	**0**	**14**	**7.1**	**3**	**104**	**54.8**	**8:42**	....	....	....	....	....	....	....	....	....
	Syracuse Crunch	AHL	47	17	30	47	30	....	....	....	....	....	....	....	....	....	....	....	....	....	....	....	....	....	....
2010-11	**Columbus**	**NHL**	**63**	**9**	**14**	**23**	**22**	**0**	**1**	**1**	**76**	**11.8**	**14**	**473**	**52.0**	**10:51**	....	....	....	....	....	....	....	....	....
2011-12	**Columbus**	**NHL**	**66**	**7**	**7**	**14**	**40**	**1**	**2**	**2**	**61**	**11.5**	**4**	**429**	**54.6**	**10:30**	....	....	....	....	....	....	....	....	....
2012-13	**Columbus**	**NHL**	**43**	**3**	**5**	**8**	**36**	**0**	**0**	**0**	**33**	**9.1**	**1**	**323**	**59.4**	**10:20**	....	....	....	....	....	....	....	....	....
	NHL Totals		**236**	**22**	**31**	**53**	**128**	**1**	**3**	**3**	**226**	**9.7**		**1560**	**53.6**	**9:45**	....	....	....	....	....	....	....	....	....

Signed as a free agent by **Columbus**, July 11, 2007.

MALHOTRA, Manny

(mal-HOH-truh, MAN-ee)

Center. Shoots left. 6'2", 220 lbs. Born, Mississauga, Ont., May 18, 1980. NY Rangers' 1st choice, 7th overall, in 1998 Entry Draft.

Season	Club	League	GP	G	A	Pts	PIM	PP	SH	GW	S	%	+/-	TF	F%	Min	GP	G	A	Pts	PIM	PP	SH	GW	Min
1995-96	Mississauga Reps	MTHL	54	27	44	71	62	....	....	....	....	....	....	....	....	....	....	....	....	....	....	....	....	....	....
1996-97	Guelph Storm	OHL	61	16	28	44	26	....	....	....	....	....	....	....	....	....	18	7	7	14	11	....	....	....	....
1997-98	Guelph Storm	OHL	57	16	35	51	29	....	....	....	....	....	....	....	....	....	12	7	6	13	8	....	....	....	....
1998-99	**NY Rangers**	**NHL**	**73**	**8**	**8**	**16**	**13**	**1**	**0**	**2**	**61**	**13.1**	**–2**	**588**	**43.9**	**8:36**	....	....	....	....	....	....	....	....	....
99-2000	**NY Rangers**	**NHL**	**27**	**0**	**0**	**0**	**4**	**0**	**0**	**0**	**18**	**0.0**	**–6**	**132**	**44.7**	**6:42**	....	....	....	....	....	....	....	....	....
	Guelph Storm	OHL	5	2	2	4	4	....	....	....	....	....	....	....	....	....	6	0	2	2	4	....	....	....	....
	Hartford	AHL	12	1	5	6	2	....	....	....	....	....	....	....	....	....	23	1	2	3	10	....	....	....	....
2000-01	**NY Rangers**	**NHL**	**50**	**4**	**8**	**12**	**31**	**0**	**0**	**2**	**46**	**8.7**	**–10**	**248**	**44.4**	**9:03**	....	....	....	....	....	....	....	....	....
	Hartford	AHL	28	5	6	11	69	....	....	....	....	....	....	....	....	....	5	0	0	0	0	....	....	....	....
2001-02	**NY Rangers**	**NHL**	**56**	**7**	**6**	**13**	**42**	**0**	**1**	**1**	**41**	**17.1**	**–1**	**310**	**42.9**	**10:14**	....	....	....	....	....	....	....	....	....
	Dallas	**NHL**	**16**	**1**	**0**	**1**	**5**	**0**	**0**	**0**	**19**	**5.3**	**–3**	**121**	**48.8**	**10:37**	....	....	....	....	....	....	....	....	....
2002-03	**Dallas**	**NHL**	**59**	**3**	**7**	**10**	**42**	**0**	**0**	**1**	**62**	**4.8**	**–2**	**447**	**47.0**	**9:22**	**5**	**1**	**0**	**1**	**0**	**0**	**0**	**0**	**8:13**
2003-04	**Dallas**	**NHL**	**9**	**0**	**0**	**0**	**4**	**0**	**0**	**0**	**4**	**0.0**	**–2**	**13**	**61.5**	**7:48**	....	....	....	....	....	....	....	....	....
	Columbus	**NHL**	**56**	**12**	**13**	**25**	**24**	**1**	**0**	**2**	**103**	**11.7**	**–5**	**840**	**53.8**	**14:47**	....	....	....	....	....	....	....	....	....
2004-05	Ljubljana	Slovenia	13	6	7	13	20	....	....	....	....	....	....	....	....	....	....	....	....	....	....	....	....	....	....
	Ljubljana	Interliga	13	7	7	14	16	....	....	....	....	....	....	....	....	....	....	....	....	....	....	....	....	....	....
	HV 71 Jonkoping	Sweden	20	5	2	7	16	....	....	....	....	....	....	....	....	....	....	....	....	....	....	....	....	....	....
2005-06	**Columbus**	**NHL**	**58**	**10**	**21**	**31**	**41**	**1**	**1**	**0**	**102**	**9.8**	**1**	**827**	**56.4**	**16:21**	....	....	....	....	....	....	....	....	....
2006-07	**Columbus**	**NHL**	**82**	**9**	**16**	**25**	**76**	**2**	**0**	**3**	**109**	**8.3**	**–8**	**1127**	**55.1**	**14:48**	....	....	....	....	....	....	....	....	....
2007-08	**Columbus**	**NHL**	**71**	**11**	**18**	**29**	**34**	**2**	**0**	**2**	**112**	**9.8**	**–3**	**1158**	**59.0**	**16:28**	....	....	....	....	....	....	....	....	....
2008-09	**Columbus**	**NHL**	**77**	**11**	**24**	**35**	**28**	**0**	**0**	**3**	**116**	**9.5**	**9**	**1380**	**58.0**	**18:01**	**4**	**0**	**0**	**0**	**0**	**0**	**0**	**0**	**17:54**
2009-10	**San Jose**	**NHL**	**71**	**14**	**19**	**33**	**41**	**2**	**0**	**4**	**111**	**12.6**	**17**	**664**	**62.5**	**15:37**	**15**	**1**	**0**	**1**	**0**	**1**	**0**	**0**	**16:55**
2010-11	**Vancouver**	**NHL**	**72**	**11**	**19**	**30**	**22**	**3**	**1**	**2**	**111**	**9.9**	**9**	**1261**	**61.7**	**16:10**	**6**	**0**	**0**	**0**	**0**	**0**	**0**	**0**	**11:50**
2011-12	**Vancouver**	**NHL**	**78**	**7**	**11**	**18**	**14**	**0**	**0**	**2**	**60**	**11.7**	**–11**	**916**	**58.5**	**12:21**	**5**	**0**	**0**	**0**	**0**	**0**	**0**	**0**	**9:41**
2012-13	**Vancouver**	**NHL**	**9**	**0**	**0**	**0**	**0**	**0**	**0**	**0**	**2**	**0.0**	**–3**	**98**	**65.3**	**11:08**	....	....	....	....	....	....	....	....	....
	NHL Totals		**864**	**108**	**170**	**278**	**421**	**12**	**3**	**24**	**1077**	**10.0**		**10130**	**55.8**	**13:19**	**35**	**2**	**0**	**2**	**0**	**1**	**0**	**0**	**13:53**

Memorial Cup All-Star Team (1998) • George Parsons Trophy (Memorial Cup - Most Sportsmanlike Player) (1998)

Traded to **Dallas** by **NY Rangers** with Barrett Heisten for Martin Rucinsky and Roman Lyashenko, March 12, 2002. Claimed on waivers by **Columbus** from **Dallas**, November 21, 2003. Signed as a free agent by **Ljubljana** (Slovenia), October 8, 2004. Signed as a free agent by **Jonkoping** (Sweden), December 20, 2004. Signed as a free agent by **San Jose**, September 23, 2009. Signed as a free agent by **Vancouver**, July 1, 2010. • Missed majority of 2012-13 due to recurring eye injury,

MALKIN, Evgeni

(MAHL-kihn, ehv-GEH-nee) **PIT**

Center. Shoots left. 6'3", 195 lbs. Born, Magnitogorsk, USSR, July 31, 1986. Pittsburgh's 1st choice, 2nd overall, in 2004 Entry Draft.

Season	Club	League	GP	G	A	Pts	PIM	PP	SH	GW	S	%	+/-	TF	F%	Min	GP	G	A	Pts	PIM	PP	SH	GW	Min
2002-03	Magnitogorsk 2	Russia-3	STATISTICS NOT AVAILABLE																						
2003-04	Magnitogorsk 2	Russia-3	2	1	0	1	8	....	....	....	....	....	....	....	....	....	....	....	....	....	....	....	....	....	....
	Magnitogorsk	Russia	34	3	9	12	12	....	....	....	....	....	....	....	....	....	....	....	....	....	....	....	....	....	....
2004-05	Magnitogorsk 2	Russia-3	2	1	1	2	2	....	....	....	....	....	....	....	....	....	....	....	....	....	....	....	....	....	....
	Magnitogorsk	Russia	52	12	20	32	24	....	....	....	....	....	....	....	....	....	5	0	4	4	0	....	....	....	....
2005-06	Magnitogorsk	Russia	46	21	26	47	46	....	....	....	....	....	....	....	....	....	11	5	10	15	41	....	....	....	....
	Russia	Olympics	7	2	4	6	31	....	....	....	....	....	....	....	....	....	....	....	....	....	....	....	....	....	....
2006-07	**Pittsburgh**	**NHL**	**78**	**33**	**52**	**85**	**80**	**16**	**0**	**6**	**242**	**13.6**	**2**	**728**	**43.3**	**19:10**	**5**	**0**	**4**	**4**	**8**	**0**	**0**	**0**	**19:34**
2007-08	**Pittsburgh**	**NHL**	**82**	**47**	**59**	**106**	**78**	**17**	**0**	**5**	**272**	**17.3**	**16**	**890**	**39.3**	**21:19**	**20**	**10**	**12**	**22**	**24**	**5**	**1**	**3**	**20:48**
2008-09♦	**Pittsburgh**	**NHL**	**82**	**35**	***78**	***113**	**80**	**14**	**2**	**4**	**290**	**12.1**	**17**	**668**	**42.4**	**22:31**	**24**	**14**	***22**	***36**	**51**	***7**	**0**	***3**	**20:57**
2009-10	**Pittsburgh**	**NHL**	**67**	**28**	**49**	**77**	**100**	**13**	**2**	**7**	**268**	**10.4**	**–6**	**498**	**40.0**	**20:51**	**13**	**5**	**6**	**11**	**6**	**4**	**0**	**1**	**21:54**
	Russia	Olympics	4	3	3	6	0	....	....	....	....	....	....	....	....	....	....	....	....	....	....	....	....	....	....

Season	Club	League	GP	G	A	Pts	PIM	PP	SH	GW	S	%	+/-	TF	F%	Min	GP	G	A	Pts	PIM	PP	SH	GW	Min
								Regular Season									Playoffs								
2010-11	**Pittsburgh**	**NHL**	**43**	**15**	**22**	**37**	**18**	**5**	**0**	**3**	**182**	**8.2**	**-4**	**200**	**38.5**	**19:49**									
2011-12	**Pittsburgh**	**NHL**	**75**	**50**	**59**	***109**	**70**	**12**	**0**	**9**	**339**	**14.7**	**18**	**1210**	**47.5**	**21:01**	**6**	**3**	**5**	**8**	**6**	**1**	**0**	**0**	**22:15**
2012-13	Magnitogorsk	KHL	37	23	42	65	58																		
	Pittsburgh	**NHL**	**31**	**9**	**24**	**33**	**36**	**4**	**0**	**3**	**99**	**9.1**	**5**	**413**	**47.2**	**19:42**	**15**	**4**	**12**	**16**	**26**	**0**	**0**	**1**	**20:29**
	NHL Totals		**458**	**217**	**343**	**560**	**462**	**81**	**4**	**37**	**1692**	**12.8**		**4607**	**43.3**	**20:48**	**83**	**36**	**61**	**97**	**121**	**17**	**1**	**8**	**20:59**

NHL All-Rookie Team (2007) • Calder Memorial Trophy (2007) • NHL First All-Star Team (2008, 2009, 2012) • Art Ross Trophy (2009, 2012) • Conn Smythe Trophy (2009) • Ted Lindsay Award (2012) • Hart Memorial Trophy (2012)

Played in NHL All-Star Game (2008, 2009, 2012)

Signed as a free agent by **Magnitogorsk** (KHL), September 16, 2012.

MALONE, Brad (ma-LOHN, BRAD) COL

Center/Left wing. Shoots left. 6'2", 207 lbs. Born, Miramichi, N.B., May 20, 1989. Colorado's 5th choice, 105th overall, in 2007 Entry Draft.

Season	Club	League	GP	G	A	Pts	PIM	PP	SH	GW	S	%	+/-	TF	F%	Min	GP	G	A	Pts	PIM	PP	SH	GW	Min
2005-06	Cushing	High-MA	STATISTICS NOT AVAILABLE																						
2006-07	Sioux Falls	USHL	57	14	19	33	134										8	3	1	4	24				
2007-08	North Dakota	WCHA	34	1	2	3	44																		
2008-09	North Dakota	WCHA	41	5	12	17	75																		
2009-10	North Dakota	WCHA	43	11	14	25	*102																		
2010-11	North Dakota	WCHA	43	16	24	40	*108																		
	Lake Erie	AHL															3	0	1	1	2				
2011-12	**Colorado**	**NHL**	**9**	**0**	**2**	**2**	**0**	**0**	**0**	**0**	**6**	**0.0**	**1**	**8**	**12.5**	**10:03**									
	Lake Erie	AHL	67	11	25	36	89																		
2012-13	Lake Erie	AHL	63	10	14	24	99																		
	Colorado	**NHL**	**13**	**1**	**1**	**2**	**16**	**0**	**0**	**0**	**10**	**10.0**	**-7**	**46**	**47.8**	**8:47**									
	NHL Totals		**22**	**1**	**3**	**4**	**16**	**0**	**0**	**0**	**16**	**6.3**		**54**	**42.6**	**9:18**									

MALONE, Ryan (ma-LOHN, RIGH-uhn) T.B.

Left wing. Shoots left. 6'4", 224 lbs. Born, Pittsburgh, PA, December 1, 1979. Pittsburgh's 5th choice, 115th overall, in 1999 Entry Draft.

Season	Club	League	GP	G	A	Pts	PIM	PP	SH	GW	S	%	+/-	TF	F%	Min	GP	G	A	Pts	PIM	PP	SH	GW	Min
1997-98	Shat.-St. Mary's	High-MN	50	41	44	85	69																		
1998-99	Omaha Lancers	USHL	51	14	22	36	81										12	2	4	6	23				
99-2000	St. Cloud State	WCHA	38	9	21	30	68																		
2000-01	St. Cloud State	WCHA	36	7	18	25	52																		
2001-02	St. Cloud State	WCHA	41	24	25	49	76																		
2002-03	St. Cloud State	WCHA	27	16	20	36	85																		
	Wilkes-Barre	AHL	3	0	1	1	2																		
2003-04	**Pittsburgh**	**NHL**	**81**	**22**	**21**	**43**	**64**	**5**	**3**	**4**	**139**	**15.8**	**-23**	**230**	**27.4**	**18:54**									
2004-05	Blues Espoo	Finland	9	2	1	3	36																		
	SV Renon	Italy	10	6	2	8	20										6	4	4	8	36				
	HC Ambri-Piotta	Swiss															1	0	0	0	2				
2005-06	**Pittsburgh**	**NHL**	**77**	**22**	**22**	**44**	**63**	**10**	**5**	**1**	**153**	**14.4**	**-22**	**728**	**39.6**	**18:06**									
2006-07	**Pittsburgh**	**NHL**	**64**	**16**	**15**	**31**	**71**	**1**	**1**	**0**	**125**	**12.8**	**4**	**109**	**44.0**	**16:15**	**5**	**0**	**0**	**0**	**0**	**0**	**0**	**0**	**13:48**
2007-08	**Pittsburgh**	**NHL**	**77**	**27**	**24**	**51**	**103**	**11**	**2**	**6**	**159**	**17.0**	**14**	**38**	**31.6**	**19:05**	**20**	**6**	**10**	**16**	**25**	**3**	**0**	**2**	**18:43**
2008-09	**Tampa Bay**	**NHL**	**70**	**26**	**19**	**45**	**98**	**7**	**0**	**3**	**124**	**21.0**	**4**	**47**	**29.8**	**17:45**									
2009-10	**Tampa Bay**	**NHL**	**69**	**21**	**26**	**47**	**68**	**7**	**0**	**7**	**172**	**12.2**	**-8**	**97**	**39.2**	**18:46**									
	United States	Olympics	6	3	2	5	6																		
2010-11	**Tampa Bay**	**NHL**	**54**	**14**	**24**	**38**	**51**	**9**	**0**	**1**	**149**	**9.4**	**-3**	**143**	**39.2**	**16:02**	**18**	**3**	**3**	**6**	**24**	**1**	**0**	**1**	**15:35**
2011-12	**Tampa Bay**	**NHL**	**68**	**20**	**28**	**48**	**82**	**5**	**1**	**2**	**144**	**13.9**	**-11**	**79**	**36.7**	**17:41**									
2012-13	**Tampa Bay**	**NHL**	**24**	**6**	**2**	**8**	**22**	**2**	**0**	**1**	**37**	**16.2**	**-3**	**23**	**39.1**	**15:44**									
	NHL Totals		**584**	**174**	**181**	**355**	**622**	**57**	**12**	**25**	**1202**	**14.5**		**1494**	**37.3**	**17:50**	**43**	**9**	**13**	**22**	**49**	**4**	**0**	**3**	**16:50**

NHL All-Rookie Team (2004)

Signed as a free agent by **Espoo** (Finland), September 29, 2004. Signed as a free agent by **Renon** (Italy), January 3, 2005. Signed as a free agent by **Ambri-Piotta** (Swiss), February 25, 2005. Traded to **Tampa Bay** by **Pittsburgh** with Gary Roberts for Tampa Bay's 3rd round choice (Ben Hanowski) in 2009 Entry Draft, June 28, 2008. • Missed half of 2012-13 due to lower-body and shoulder injuries.

MANCARI, Mark (man-KAIR-ee, MAHRK) ST.L.

Right wing. Shoots right. 6'3", 225 lbs. Born, London, Ont., July 11, 1985. Buffalo's 6th choice, 207th overall, in 2004 Entry Draft.

Season	Club	League	GP	G	A	Pts	PIM	PP	SH	GW	S	%	+/-	TF	F%	Min	GP	G	A	Pts	PIM	PP	SH	GW	Min
2001-02	Ottawa 67's	OHL	34	3	3	6	10										2	0	1	1	0				
2002-03	Ottawa 67's	OHL	61	8	11	19	20										11	2	1	3	2				
2003-04	Ottawa 67's	OHL	67	29	36	65	56										7	5	3	8	11				
2004-05	Ottawa 67's	OHL	64	36	32	68	86										21	*14	10	24	24				
2005-06	Rochester	AHL	71	18	24	42	80																		
2006-07	**Buffalo**	**NHL**	**3**	**0**	**1**	**1**	**2**	**0**	**0**	**0**	**1**	**0.0**	**-1**	**0**	**0.0**	**6:12**									
	Rochester	AHL	64	23	34	57	49										6	1	5	6	6				
2007-08	Rochester	AHL	80	21	36	57	78																		
2008-09	**Buffalo**	**NHL**	**7**	**1**	**1**	**2**	**4**	**0**	**0**	**0**	**21**	**4.8**	**-4**	**7**	**57.1**	**13:16**									
	Portland Pirates	AHL	73	29	38	67	61										5	1	2	3	2				
2009-10	**Buffalo**	**NHL**	**6**	**1**	**1**	**2**	**4**	**0**	**0**	**0**	**19**	**5.3**	**3**	**3**	**0.0**	**14:04**									
	Portland Pirates	AHL	74	28	46	74	55										4	1	1	2	2				
2010-11	**Buffalo**	**NHL**	**20**	**1**	**7**	**8**	**12**	**1**	**0**	**0**	**43**	**2.3**	**-1**	**6**	**50.0**	**12:19**	**1**	**0**	**0**	**0**	**0**	**0**	**0**	**0**	**9:50**
	Portland Pirates	AHL	56	32	32	64	57										9	6	6	12	0				
2011-12	**Vancouver**	**NHL**	**6**	**0**	**0**	**0**	**0**	**0**	**0**	**0**	**5**	**0.0**	**0**	**2**	**0.0**	**8:19**									
	Chicago Wolves	AHL	69	30	28	58	40										5	0	7	7	6				
2012-13	Rochester	AHL	76	22	39	61	68										3	0	2	2	12				
	NHL Totals		**42**	**3**	**10**	**13**	**22**	**1**	**0**	**0**	**89**	**3.4**		**18**	**38.9**	**11:43**	**1**	**0**	**0**	**0**	**0**	**0**	**0**	**0**	**9:50**

AHL First All-Star Team (2011)

Signed as a free agent by **Vancouver**, July 1, 2011. Signed as a free agent by **Buffalo**, July 6, 2012. Signed as a free agent by **St. Louis**, July 5, 2013.

MANNING, Brandon (MAN-nihng, BRAN-duhn) PHI

Defense. Shoots left. 6'1", 195 lbs. Born, Prince George, B.C., June 4, 1990.

Season	Club	League	GP	G	A	Pts	PIM	PP	SH	GW	S	%	+/-	TF	F%	Min	GP	G	A	Pts	PIM	PP	SH	GW	Min
2007-08	Prince George	BCHL	58	7	19	26	107										4	0	3	3	6				
	Chilliwack Bruins	WHL	6	0	0	0	8										4	0	0	0	4				
2008-09	Chilliwack Bruins	WHL	72	11	18	29	140																		
2009-10	Chilliwack Bruins	WHL	69	13	41	54	138										6	0	6	6	10				
2010-11	Chilliwack Bruins	WHL	53	21	32	53	129										5	1	0	1	8				
2011-12	**Philadelphia**	**NHL**	**4**	**0**	**0**	**0**	**0**	**0**	**0**	**0**	**6**	**0.0**	**1**	**0**	**0.0**	**13:44**									
	Adirondack	AHL	46	6	13	19	81																		
2012-13	Adirondack	AHL	65	6	15	21	135																		
	Philadelphia	**NHL**	**6**	**0**	**2**	**2**	**0**	**0**	**0**	**0**	**5**	**0.0**	**4**	**0**	**0.0**	**14:48**									
	NHL Totals		**10**	**0**	**2**	**2**	**0**	**0**	**0**	**0**	**11**	**0.0**		**0**	**0.0**	**14:22**									

Signed as a free agent by **Philadelphia**, November 23, 2010.

MARCHAND, Brad (mahr-SHAND, BRAD) BOS

Left wing. Shoots left. 5'9", 183 lbs. Born, Halifax, N.S., May 11, 1988. Boston's 4th choice, 71st overall, in 2006 Entry Draft.

Season	Club	League	GP	G	A	Pts	PIM	PP	SH	GW	S	%	+/-	TF	F%	Min	GP	G	A	Pts	PIM	PP	SH	GW	Min
2003-04	Dartmouth	NSMHL	60	47	47	94	104																		
2004-05	Moncton Wildcats	QMJHL	61	9	20	29	52										11	1	0	1	7				
2005-06	Moncton Wildcats	QMJHL	68	29	37	66	83										20	5	14	19	34				
2006-07	Val-d'Or Foreurs	QMJHL	57	33	47	80	108										20	*16	*24	*40	36				
2007-08	Val-d'Or Foreurs	QMJHL	33	21	23	44	36																		
	Halifax	QMJHL	26	10	19	29	40										14	3	16	19	18				
2008-09	Providence Bruins	AHL	79	18	41	59	67										16	7	8	15	26				
2009-10	**Boston**	**NHL**	**20**	**0**	**1**	**1**	**20**	**0**	**0**	**0**	**32**	**0.0**	**-3**	**11**	**27.3**	**11:58**									
	Providence Bruins	AHL	34	13	19	32	51																		
2010-11 ♦	**Boston**	**NHL**	**77**	**21**	**20**	**41**	**51**	**2**	**5**	**2**	**149**	**14.1**	**25**	**25**	**32.0**	**13:59**	**25**	**11**	**8**	**19**	**40**	**0**	**1**	**1**	**16:46**
2011-12	**Boston**	**NHL**	**76**	**28**	**27**	**55**	**87**	**5**	**1**	**3**	**167**	**16.8**	**31**	**9**	**55.6**	**17:37**	**7**	**1**	**1**	**2**	**2**	**0**	**0**	**0**	**18:04**
2012-13	**Boston**	**NHL**	**45**	**18**	**18**	**36**	**27**	**4**	**2**	**5**	**91**	**19.8**	**23**	**12**	**50.0**	**16:58**	**22**	**4**	**9**	**13**	**21**	**0**	**0**	**1**	**19:35**
	NHL Totals		**218**	**67**	**66**	**133**	**185**	**11**	**8**	**10**	**439**	**15.3**		**57**	**38.6**	**15:41**	**54**	**16**	**18**	**34**	**63**	**0**	**1**	**2**	**18:05**

			Regular Season														Playoffs								
Season	Club	League	GP	G	A	Pts	PIM	PP	SH	GW	S	%	+/-	TF	F%	Min	GP	G	A	Pts	PIM	PP	SH	GW	Min

MARKOV, Andrei (MAHR-kahf, AHN-dray) MTL

Defense. Shoots left. 6', 207 lbs. Born, Voskresensk, USSR, December 20, 1978. Montreal's 6th choice, 162nd overall, in 1998 Entry Draft.

Season	Club	League	GP	G	A	Pts	PIM	PP	SH	GW	S	%	+/-	TF	F%	Min	GP	G	A	Pts	PIM	PP	SH	GW	Min
1995-96	Voskresensk	CIS	38	0	0	0	14	....	....	....	....	....	....	....	....	....	....	....	....	....	....	....	....	....	....
1996-97	Voskresensk	Russia	43	8	4	12	32	....	....	....	....	....	....	....	....	....	2	1	1	2	0	....	....	....	....
1997-98	Voskresensk	Russia	43	10	5	15	83	....	....	....	....	....	....	....	....	....	....	....	....	....	....	....	....	....	....
1998-99	Dynamo Moscow	Russia	38	10	11	21	32	....	....	....	....	....	....	....	....	....	16	3	6	9	6	....	....	....	....
	Dynamo Moscow	EuroHL	12	7	5	12	12	....	....	....	....	....	....	....	....	....	6	2	2	4	4	....	....	....	....
99-2000	Dynamo Moscow	Russia	29	11	12	23	28	....	....	....	....	....	....	....	....	....	17	4	3	7	8	....	....	....	....
2000-01	**Montreal**	**NHL**	**63**	**6**	**17**	**23**	**18**	**2**	**0**	**0**	**82**	**7.3**	**–6**	**2**	**50.0**	**16:53**	....	....	....	....	....	....	....	....	....
	Quebec Citadelles	AHL	14	0	5	5	4	....	....	....	....	....	....	....	....	....	7	1	1	2	2	....	....	....	....
2001-02	**Montreal**	**NHL**	**56**	**5**	**19**	**24**	**24**	**2**	**0**	**1**	**73**	**6.8**	**–1**	**0**	**0.0**	**17:15**	**12**	**1**	**3**	**4**	**8**	**0**	**0**	**1**	**15:53**
	Quebec Citadelles	AHL	12	4	6	10	7	....	....	....	....	....	....	....	....	....	....	....	....	....	....	....	....	....	....
2002-03	**Montreal**	**NHL**	**79**	**13**	**24**	**37**	**34**	**3**	**0**	**2**	**159**	**8.2**	**13**	**1**	**0.0**	**23:17**	....	....	....	....	....	....	....	....	....
2003-04	**Montreal**	**NHL**	**69**	**6**	**22**	**28**	**20**	**2**	**0**	**0**	**105**	**5.7**	**–2**	**2**	**50.0**	**21:29**	**11**	**1**	**4**	**5**	**8**	**0**	**0**	**1**	**22:52**
2004-05	Dynamo Moscow	Russia	42	7	16	23	76	....	....	....	....	....	....	....	....	....	10	2	0	2	22	....	....	....	....
2005-06	**Montreal**	**NHL**	**67**	**10**	**36**	**46**	**74**	**6**	**1**	**1**	**88**	**11.4**	**13**	**1**	**0.0**	**23:33**	**6**	**0**	**1**	**1**	**4**	**0**	**0**	**0**	**25:29**
	Russia	Olympics	8	1	2	3	6	....	....	....	....	....	....	....	....	....	....	....	....	....	....	....	....	....	....
2006-07	**Montreal**	**NHL**	**77**	**6**	**43**	**49**	**56**	**5**	**0**	**2**	**128**	**4.7**	**2**	**1**	**0.0**	**24:29**	....	....	....	....	....	....	....	....	....
2007-08	**Montreal**	**NHL**	**82**	**16**	**42**	**58**	**63**	**10**	**1**	**2**	**145**	**11.0**	**1**	**0**	**0.0**	**24:58**	**12**	**1**	**3**	**4**	**8**	**0**	**0**	**0**	**24:54**
2008-09	**Montreal**	**NHL**	**78**	**12**	**52**	**64**	**36**	**7**	**0**	**3**	**165**	**7.3**	**–2**	**0**	**0.0**	**24:38**	....	....	....	....	....	....	....	....	....
2009-10	**Montreal**	**NHL**	**45**	**6**	**28**	**34**	**32**	**4**	**0**	**1**	**85**	**7.1**	**11**	**0**	**0.0**	**23:48**	**8**	**0**	**4**	**4**	**0**	**0**	**0**	**0**	**23:47**
	Russia	Olympics	4	0	2	2	0	....	....	....	....	....	....	....	....	....	....	....	....	....	....	....	....	....	....
2010-11	**Montreal**	**NHL**	**7**	**1**	**2**	**3**	**4**	**0**	**0**	**1**	**20**	**5.0**	**2**	**0**	**0.0**	**22:55**	....	....	....	....	....	....	....	....	....
2011-12	**Montreal**	**NHL**	**13**	**0**	**3**	**3**	**4**	**0**	**0**	**0**	**17**	**0.0**	**–4**	**0**	**0.0**	**18:00**	....	....	....	....	....	....	....	....	....
2012-13	Vityaz Chekhov	KHL	21	1	7	8	16	....	....	....	....	....	....	....	....	....	....	....	....	....	....	....	....	....	....
	Montreal	**NHL**	**48**	**10**	**20**	**30**	**14**	**8**	**0**	**4**	**79**	**12.7**	**–9**	**0**	**0.0**	**24:08**	**5**	**0**	**1**	**1**	**0**	**0**	**0**	**0**	**23:54**
	NHL Totals		**684**	**91**	**308**	**399**	**379**	**49**	**2**	**17**	**1146**	**7.9**		**7**	**28.6**	**22:31**	**54**	**3**	**16**	**19**	**28**	**0**	**0**	**2**	**22:17**

Played in NHL All-Star Game (2008, 2009)

Signed as a free agent by **Dynamo Moscow** (Russia), June 19, 2004. • Missed majority of 2010-11 and 2011-12 due to knee injury vs. Carolina, November 13, 2010. Signed as a free agent by **Chekhov** (KHL), October 3, 2012.

MARLEAU, Patrick (mahr-LOH, PAT-rihk) S.J.

Center. Shoots left. 6'2", 220 lbs. Born, Aneroid, Sask., September 15, 1979. San Jose's 1st choice, 2nd overall, in 1997 Entry Draft.

Season	Club	League	GP	G	A	Pts	PIM	PP	SH	GW	S	%	+/-	TF	F%	Min	GP	G	A	Pts	PIM	PP	SH	GW	Min
1993-94	Swift Current	SMHL	53	72	95	167	....	....	....	....	....	....	....	....	....	....	....	....	....	....	....	....	....	....	....
1994-95	Swift Current	SMHL	31	30	22	52	18	....	....	....	....	....	....	....	....	....	....	....	....	....	....	....	....	....	....
1995-96	Seattle	WHL	72	32	42	74	22	....	....	....	....	....	....	....	....	....	5	3	4	7	4	....	....	....	....
1996-97	Seattle	WHL	71	51	74	125	37	....	....	....	....	....	....	....	....	....	15	7	16	23	12	....	....	....	....
1997-98	**San Jose**	**NHL**	**74**	**13**	**19**	**32**	**14**	**1**	**0**	**2**	**90**	**14.4**	**5**	....	....	....	**5**	**0**	**1**	**1**	**0**	**0**	**0**	**0**	....
1998-99	**San Jose**	**NHL**	**81**	**21**	**24**	**45**	**24**	**4**	**0**	**4**	**134**	**15.7**	**10**	**1121**	**43.4**	**15:11**	**6**	**2**	**1**	**3**	**4**	**2**	**0**	**0**	**11:08**
99-2000	**San Jose**	**NHL**	**81**	**17**	**23**	**40**	**36**	**3**	**0**	**3**	**161**	**10.6**	**–9**	**851**	**42.0**	**14:11**	**5**	**1**	**1**	**2**	**2**	**1**	**0**	**0**	**11:51**
2000-01	**San Jose**	**NHL**	**81**	**25**	**27**	**52**	**22**	**5**	**0**	**6**	**146**	**17.1**	**7**	**1088**	**44.8**	**16:17**	**6**	**2**	**0**	**2**	**4**	**0**	**0**	**0**	**14:50**
2001-02	**San Jose**	**NHL**	**79**	**21**	**23**	**44**	**40**	**3**	**0**	**5**	**121**	**17.4**	**9**	**897**	**47.3**	**14:04**	**12**	**6**	**5**	**11**	**6**	**1**	**0**	**3**	**15:50**
2002-03	**San Jose**	**NHL**	**82**	**28**	**29**	**57**	**33**	**8**	**1**	**3**	**172**	**16.3**	**–10**	**1403**	**47.3**	**18:31**	....	....	....	....	....	....	....	....	....
2003-04	**San Jose**	**NHL**	**80**	**28**	**29**	**57**	**24**	**9**	**0**	**5**	**220**	**12.7**	**–5**	**1014**	**41.6**	**18:12**	**17**	**8**	**4**	**12**	**6**	**4**	**1**	**2**	**19:16**
2004-05			DID NOT PLAY																						
2005-06	**San Jose**	**NHL**	**82**	**34**	**52**	**86**	**26**	**20**	**1**	**4**	**260**	**13.1**	**–12**	**1216**	**46.8**	**19:56**	**11**	**9**	**5**	**14**	**8**	**4**	**0**	**2**	**21:07**
2006-07	**San Jose**	**NHL**	**77**	**32**	**46**	**78**	**33**	**14**	**0**	**9**	**180**	**17.8**	**9**	**693**	**50.5**	**18:34**	**11**	**3**	**3**	**6**	**2**	**1**	**0**	**1**	**18:59**
2007-08	**San Jose**	**NHL**	**78**	**19**	**29**	**48**	**33**	**7**	**0**	**2**	**185**	**10.3**	**–19**	**605**	**52.4**	**18:14**	**13**	**4**	**4**	**8**	**2**	**0**	***2**	**0**	**23:04**
2008-09	**San Jose**	**NHL**	**76**	**38**	**33**	**71**	**18**	**11**	**5**	**10**	**251**	**15.1**	**16**	**591**	**52.5**	**21:21**	**6**	**2**	**1**	**3**	**8**	**1**	**0**	**2**	**20:29**
2009-10	**San Jose**	**NHL**	**82**	**44**	**39**	**83**	**22**	**12**	**4**	**6**	**274**	**16.1**	**21**	**615**	**51.4**	**21:13**	**14**	**8**	**5**	**13**	**8**	**3**	**1**	**2**	**22:07**
	Canada	Olympics	7	2	3	5	0	....	....	....	....	....	....	....	....	....	....	....	....	....	....	....	....	....	....
2010-11	**San Jose**	**NHL**	**82**	**37**	**36**	**73**	**16**	**11**	**2**	**9**	**279**	**13.3**	**–3**	**549**	**52.5**	**20:47**	**18**	**7**	**6**	**13**	**9**	**3**	**0**	**1**	**22:21**
2011-12	**San Jose**	**NHL**	**82**	**30**	**34**	**64**	**26**	**10**	**0**	**8**	**251**	**12.0**	**10**	**467**	**52.0**	**20:29**	**5**	**0**	**0**	**0**	**4**	**0**	**0**	**0**	**20:21**
2012-13	**San Jose**	**NHL**	**48**	**17**	**14**	**31**	**24**	**6**	**1**	**3**	**150**	**11.3**	**–2**	**150**	**47.3**	**19:07**	**11**	**5**	**3**	**8**	**2**	**1**	**0**	**1**	**21:18**
	NHL Totals		**1165**	**404**	**457**	**861**	**391**	**124**	**14**	**79**	**2874**	**14.1**		**11260**	**47.1**	**18:16**	**140**	**57**	**39**	**96**	**65**	**21**	**4**	**14**	**19:35**

WHL West First All-Star Team (1997)
Played in NHL All-Star Game (2004, 2007, 2009)

MAROON, Patrick (ma-ROON, PAT-rihk) ANA

Left wing. Shoots left. 6'3", 229 lbs. Born, St Louis, MO, April 23, 1988. Philadelphia's 6th choice, 161st overall, in 2007 Entry Draft.

Season	Club	League	GP	G	A	Pts	PIM	PP	SH	GW	S	%	+/-	TF	F%	Min	GP	G	A	Pts	PIM	PP	SH	GW	Min
2005-06	Texarkana Bandits	NAHL	57	23	37	60	61	....	....	....	....	....	....	....	....	....	8	3	1	4	22	....	....	....	....
2006-07	St. Louis Bandits	NAHL	57	40	55	*95	152	....	....	....	....	....	....	....	....	....	12	*10	*13	*23	12	....	....	....	....
2007-08	London Knights	OHL	64	35	55	90	57	....	....	....	....	....	....	....	....	....	5	0	1	1	10	....	....	....	....
	Philadelphia	AHL	1	0	0	0	0	....	....	....	....	....	....	....	....	....	....	....	....	....	....	....	....	....	....
2008-09	Philadelphia	AHL	80	23	31	54	62	....	....	....	....	....	....	....	....	....	4	1	2	3	13	....	....	....	....
2009-10	Adirondack	AHL	67	11	33	44	125	....	....	....	....	....	....	....	....	....	....	....	....	....	....	....	....	....	....
2010-11	Adirondack	AHL	9	5	3	8	30	....	....	....	....	....	....	....	....	....	....	....	....	....	....	....	....	....	....
	Syracuse Crunch	AHL	57	21	27	48	68	....	....	....	....	....	....	....	....	....	....	....	....	....	....	....	....	....	....
2011-12	**Anaheim**	**NHL**	**2**	**0**	**0**	**0**	**2**	**0**	**0**	**0**	**1**	**0.0**	**0**	**0**	**0.0**	**12:33**	....	....	....	....	....	....	....	....	....
	Syracuse Crunch	AHL	75	32	42	74	120	....	....	....	....	....	....	....	....	....	4	0	0	0	4	....	....	....	....
2012-13	Norfolk Admirals	AHL	64	26	24	50	139	....	....	....	....	....	....	....	....	....	....	....	....	....	....	....	....	....	....
	Anaheim	**NHL**	**13**	**2**	**1**	**3**	**10**	**0**	**0**	**0**	**21**	**9.5**	**–1**	**14**	**28.6**	**9:47**	....	....	....	....	....	....	....	....	....
	NHL Totals		**15**	**2**	**1**	**3**	**12**	**0**	**0**	**0**	**22**	**9.1**		**14**	**28.6**	**10:09**	....	....	....	....	....	....	....	....	....

Traded to **Anaheim** by **Philadelphia** with David Laliberte for Danny Syvret and Rob Bordson, November 21, 2010.

MARSHALL, Kevin (MAR-shuhl, KEH-vihn) TOR

Defense. Shoots left. 6'1", 201 lbs. Born, Boucherville, Que., March 10, 1989. Philadelphia's 2nd choice, 41st overall, in 2007 Entry Draft.

Season	Club	League	GP	G	A	Pts	PIM	PP	SH	GW	S	%	+/-	TF	F%	Min	GP	G	A	Pts	PIM	PP	SH	GW	Min
2004-05	C.C. Lemoyne	QAAA	39	2	9	11	88	....	....	....	....	....	....	....	....	....	5	0	1	1	16	....	....	....	....
2005-06	Lewiston	QMJHL	60	1	10	11	112	....	....	....	....	....	....	....	....	....	6	0	1	1	14	....	....	....	....
2006-07	Lewiston	QMJHL	70	5	27	32	141	....	....	....	....	....	....	....	....	....	17	0	7	7	38	....	....	....	....
2007-08	Lewiston	QMJHL	66	11	24	35	143	....	....	....	....	....	....	....	....	....	6	1	1	2	12	....	....	....	....
2008-09	Quebec Remparts	QMJHL	61	9	29	38	125	....	....	....	....	....	....	....	....	....	17	1	10	11	32	....	....	....	....
2009-10	Adirondack	AHL	75	2	7	9	80	....	....	....	....	....	....	....	....	....	....	....	....	....	....	....	....	....	....
2010-11	Adirondack	AHL	78	3	11	14	120	....	....	....	....	....	....	....	....	....	....	....	....	....	....	....	....	....	....
2011-12	**Philadelphia**	**NHL**	**10**	**0**	**0**	**0**	**8**	**0**	**0**	**0**	**6**	**0.0**	**–1**	**0**	**0.0**	**8:46**	....	....	....	....	....	....	....	....	....
	Adirondack	AHL	32	2	3	5	55	....	....	....	....	....	....	....	....	....	....	....	....	....	....	....	....	....	....
	Hershey Bears	AHL	31	0	1	1	61	....	....	....	....	....	....	....	....	....	5	0	2	2	10	....	....	....	....
2012-13	Hershey Bears	AHL	52	1	4	5	77	....	....	....	....	....	....	....	....	....	....	....	....	....	....	....	....	....	....
	Toronto Marlies	AHL	15	1	5	6	10	....	....	....	....	....	....	....	....	....	9	0	2	2	12	....	....	....	....
	NHL Totals		**10**	**0**	**0**	**0**	**8**	**0**	**0**	**0**	**6**	**0.0**		**0**	**0.0**	**8:46**	....	....	....	....	....	....	....	....	....

QMJHL Second All-Star Team (2008)

Traded to **Washington** by **Philadelphia** for Matthew Ford, February 2, 2012. Traded to **Toronto** by **Washington** for Nicolas Deschamps, March 14, 2013.

MARTIN, Matt (MAHR-tihn, MAT) NYI

Left wing. Shoots left. 6'3", 206 lbs. Born, Windsor, Ont., May 8, 1989. NY Islanders' 11th choice, 148th overall, in 2008 Entry Draft.

Season	Club	League	GP	G	A	Pts	PIM	PP	SH	GW	S	%	+/-	TF	F%	Min	GP	G	A	Pts	PIM	PP	SH	GW	Min
2005-06	Blenheim Blast	ON-Jr.C	40	11	12	23	102	....	....	....	....	....	....	....	....	....	....	....	....	....	....	....	....	....	....
2006-07	Sarnia Blast	ON-Jr.B	9	2	5	7	16	....	....	....	....	....	....	....	....	....	....	....	....	....	....	....	....	....	....
	Sarnia Sting	OHL	39	3	3	6	52	....	....	....	....	....	....	....	....	....	4	0	0	0	0	....	....	....	....
2007-08	Sarnia Sting	OHL	66	25	13	38	155	....	....	....	....	....	....	....	....	....	9	3	3	6	16	....	....	....	....
2008-09	Sarnia Sting	OHL	61	35	30	65	142	....	....	....	....	....	....	....	....	....	5	3	0	3	10	....	....	....	....
2009-10	**NY Islanders**	**NHL**	**5**	**0**	**2**	**2**	**26**	**0**	**0**	**0**	**10**	**0.0**	**–1**	**0**	**0.0**	**13:14**	....	....	....	....	....	....	....	....	....
	Bridgeport	AHL	76	12	19	31	113	....	....	....	....	....	....	....	....	....	5	1	2	3	4	....	....	....	....
2010-11	**NY Islanders**	**NHL**	**68**	**5**	**9**	**14**	**147**	**0**	**0**	**1**	**60**	**8.3**	**–13**	**27**	**37.0**	**10:57**	....	....	....	....	....	....	....	....	....
	Bridgeport	AHL	7	1	2	3	11	....	....	....	....	....	....	....	....	....	....	....	....	....	....	....	....	....	....

Season	Club	League	GP	G	A	Pts	PIM	PP	SH	GW	S	%	+/-	TF	F%	Min	GP	G	A	Pts	PIM	PP	SH	GW	Min
			Regular Season														Playoffs								
2011-12	NY Islanders	NHL	80	7	7	14	121	0	0	1	130	5.4	−17	23	43.5	12:09	....	....	....	....	....	....	....	....	....
2012-13	NY Islanders	NHL	48	4	7	11	63	1	0	1	67	6.0	−2	18	33.3	11:54	6	1	0	1	14	0	0	0	12:10
	NHL Totals		201	16	25	41	357	1	0	3	267	6.0		68	38.2	11:43	6	1	0	1	14	0	0	0	12:10

MARTIN, Paul

(MAHR-tihn, PAWL) **PIT**

Defense. Shoots left. 6'1", 200 lbs. Born, Minneapolis, MN, March 5, 1981. New Jersey's 5th choice, 62nd overall, in 2000 Entry Draft.

Season	Club	League	GP	G	A	Pts	PIM	PP	SH	GW	S	%	+/-	TF	F%	Min	GP	G	A	Pts	PIM	PP	SH	GW	Min
1998-99	Elk River Elks	High-MN	24	9	11	20	....	....	....	....	....	....	....	....	....	....	....	....	....	....	....	....	....	....	....
99-2000	Elk River Elks	High-MN	24	15	35	50	26	....	....	....	....	....	....	....	....	....	....	....	....	....	....	....	....	....	....
2000-01	U. of Minnesota	WCHA	38	3	17	20	8	....	....	....	....	....	....	....	....	....	....	....	....	....	....	....	....	....	....
2001-02	U. of Minnesota	WCHA	44	8	30	38	22	....	....	....	....	....	....	....	....	....	....	....	....	....	....	....	....	....	....
2002-03	U. of Minnesota	WCHA	45	9	30	39	32	....	....	....	....	....	....	....	....	....	....	....	....	....	....	....	....	....	....
2003-04	New Jersey	NHL	70	6	18	24	4	2	0	2	82	7.3	12	0	0.0	20:08	5	1	1	2	4	1	0	0	23:40
2004-05	Fribourg	Swiss	11	3	4	7	2	....	....	....	....	....	....	....	....	....	....	....	....	....	....	....	....	....	....
2005-06	New Jersey	NHL	80	5	32	37	32	3	0	0	97	5.2	1	0	0.0	23:37	9	0	3	3	4	0	0	0	24:17
2006-07	New Jersey	NHL	82	3	23	26	18	1	0	0	84	3.6	−9	0	0.0	25:13	11	0	4	4	6	0	0	0	25:09
2007-08	New Jersey	NHL	73	5	27	32	22	2	0	2	93	5.4	20	0	0.0	23:53	5	1	2	3	2	1	0	0	25:35
2008-09	New Jersey	NHL	73	5	28	33	36	2	0	1	107	4.7	21	0	0.0	24:22	7	0	4	4	2	0	0	0	26:20
2009-10	New Jersey	NHL	22	2	9	11	2	1	0	0	21	9.5	10	0	0.0	22:30	5	0	0	0	0	0	0	0	22:24
2010-11	Pittsburgh	NHL	77	3	21	24	16	2	0	1	104	2.9	9	0	0.0	23:22	7	0	2	2	2	0	0	0	24:42
2011-12	Pittsburgh	NHL	73	2	25	27	18	0	0	0	93	2.2	9	0	0.0	23:00	3	1	0	1	0	0	0	0	22:08
2012-13	Pittsburgh	NHL	34	6	17	23	16	2	0	1	38	15.8	14	0	0.0	25:20	15	2	9	11	4	1	0	0	26:38
	NHL Totals		584	37	200	237	164	15	0	7	719	5.1		0	0.0	23:30	67	5	25	30	24	3	0	0	25:01

Minnesota High School Player of the Year (1999) • WCHA All-Rookie Team (2001) • WCHA Second All-Star Team (2002, 2003) • NCAA West Second All-American Team (2003) • NCAA Championship All-Tournament Team (2003)

Signed as a free agent by **Fribourg** (Swiss), November 4, 2004. • Missed majority of 2009-10 due to arm injury at Pittsburgh, October 24, 2009. Signed as a free agent by **Pittsburgh**, July 1, 2010.

MARTINEK, Radek

(MAHR-tee-nihk, RA-dehk)

Defense. Shoots right. 6', 206 lbs. Born, Havlicko Brod, Czech., August 31, 1976. NY Islanders' 12th choice, 228th overall, in 1999 Entry Draft.

Season	Club	League	GP	G	A	Pts	PIM	PP	SH	GW	S	%	+/-	TF	F%	Min	GP	G	A	Pts	PIM	PP	SH	GW	Min
1996-97	C. Budejovice	CzRep	52	3	5	8	40	....	....	....	....	....	....	....	....	....	5	0	1	1	2	....	....	....	....
	C. Budejovice	EuroHL	6	0	0	0	0	....	....	....	....	....	....	....	....	....	2	0	0	0	0	....	....	....	....
1997-98	C. Budejovice	CzRep	42	2	7	9	36	....	....	....	....	....	....	....	....	....	....	....	....	....	....	....	....	....	....
1998-99	C. Budejovice	CzRep	52	12	13	25	50	....	....	....	....	....	....	....	....	....	3	0	2	2	....	....	....	....	....
99-2000	C. Budejovice	CzRep	45	5	18	23	24	....	....	....	....	....	....	....	....	....	3	0	0	0	6	....	....	....	....
2000-01	C. Budejovice	CzRep	44	8	10	18	45	....	....	....	....	....	....	....	....	....	....	....	....	....	....	....	....	....	....
2001-02	NY Islanders	NHL	23	1	4	5	16	0	0	1	25	4.0	5	0	0.0	21:07	....	....	....	....	....	....	....	....	....
2002-03	NY Islanders	NHL	66	2	11	13	26	0	0	1	67	3.0	15	0	0.0	17:15	4	0	0	0	4	0	0	0	10:16
	Bridgeport	AHL	3	0	3	3	2	....	....	....	....	....	....	....	....	....	....	....	....	....	....	....	....	....	....
2003-04	NY Islanders	NHL	47	4	3	7	43	0	0	1	48	8.3	−9	0	0.0	13:03	5	0	1	1	0	0	0	0	12:12
2004-05	C. Budejovice	CzRep-2	30	12	18	30	80	....	....	....	....	....	....	....	....	....	12	2	3	5	6	....	....	....	....
2005-06	NY Islanders	NHL	74	1	16	17	32	0	0	0	79	1.3	−9	1	0.0	18:16	....	....	....	....	....	....	....	....	....
2006-07	NY Islanders	NHL	43	2	15	17	40	0	0	0	44	4.5	19	1	100.0	19:54	....	....	....	....	....	....	....	....	....
2007-08	NY Islanders	NHL	69	0	15	15	40	0	0	0	98	0.0	−9	0	0.0	22:52	....	....	....	....	....	....	....	....	....
2008-09	NY Islanders	NHL	51	6	4	10	28	1	0	1	54	11.1	−16	0	0.0	21:34	....	....	....	....	....	....	....	....	....
2009-10	NY Islanders	NHL	16	2	1	3	12	0	1	0	24	8.3	−1	0	0.0	22:48	....	....	....	....	....	....	....	....	....
2010-11	NY Islanders	NHL	64	3	13	16	35	1	0	0	97	3.1	−5	0	0.0	20:51	....	....	....	....	....	....	....	....	....
2011-12	Columbus	NHL	7	1	0	1	0	0	0	0	10	10.0	−3	0	0.0	19:26	....	....	....	....	....	....	....	....	....
2012-13	C. Budejovice	CzRep	4	0	2	2	0	....	....	....	....	....	....	....	....	....	....	....	....	....	....	....	....	....	....
	NY Islanders	NHL	13	3	0	3	4	0	0	1	12	25.0	−2	0	0.0	16:09	2	0	0	0	2	0	0	0	18:06
	NHL Totals		473	25	82	107	276	2	1	5	558	4.5		2	50.0	19:23	11	0	1	1	6	0	0	0	12:34

• Missed majority of 2001-02 due to knee injury vs. NY Rangers, November 11, 2001. Signed as a free agent by **Ceske Budejovice** (CzRep-2), September 17, 2004. • Missed majority of 2009-10 due to knee injury at New Jersey, November 7, 2009. Signed as a free agent by **Columbus**, July 6, 2011. • Missed majority of 2011-12 due to head injury at Detroit, October 21, 2011. Signed as a free agent by **Ceske Budejovice** (CzRep), September 19, 2012. • Missed majority of 2012-13 due to recurring groin injury and as a healthy reserve.

MARTINEZ, Alec

(mar-TEE-nehz, AL-ehk) **L.A.**

Defense. Shoots left. 6'1", 206 lbs. Born, Rochester Hills, MI, July 26, 1987. Los Angeles' 5th choice, 95th overall, in 2007 Entry Draft.

Season	Club	League	GP	G	A	Pts	PIM	PP	SH	GW	S	%	+/-	TF	F%	Min	GP	G	A	Pts	PIM	PP	SH	GW	Min
2004-05	Cedar Rapids	USHL	58	10	11	21	30	....	....	....	....	....	....	....	....	....	11	1	2	3	8	....	....	....	....
2005-06	Miami U.	CCHA	39	3	8	11	31	....	....	....	....	....	....	....	....	....	....	....	....	....	....	....	....	....	....
2006-07	Miami U.	CCHA	42	9	15	24	40	....	....	....	....	....	....	....	....	....	....	....	....	....	....	....	....	....	....
2007-08	Miami U.	CCHA	42	9	23	32	42	....	....	....	....	....	....	....	....	....	....	....	....	....	....	....	....	....	....
2008-09	Manchester	AHL	72	8	15	23	42	....	....	....	....	....	....	....	....	....	....	....	....	....	....	....	....	....	....
2009-10	Los Angeles	NHL	4	0	0	0	2	0	0	0	6	0.0	−2	0	0.0	15:25	....	....	....	....	....	....	....	....	....
	Manchester	AHL	55	7	23	30	26	....	....	....	....	....	....	....	....	....	16	0	3	3	10	....	....	....	....
2010-11	Los Angeles	NHL	60	5	11	16	18	1	0	0	74	6.8	11	0	0.0	15:17	6	0	1	1	2	0	0	0	13:29
	Manchester	AHL	20	5	11	16	14	....	....	....	....	....	....	....	....	....	....	....	....	....	....	....	....	....	....
2011-12◆	Los Angeles	NHL	51	6	6	12	8	3	0	0	78	7.7	−1	1	0.0	14:43	20	1	2	3	8	0	0	1	14:28
2012-13	TPS Turku	Finland	11	1	1	2	8	....	....	....	....	....	....	....	....	....	....	....	....	....	....	....	....	....	....
	Allen Americans	CHL	3	1	1	2	0	....	....	....	....	....	....	....	....	....	....	....	....	....	....	....	....	....	....
	Los Angeles	NHL	27	1	4	5	10	0	0	0	30	3.3	−2	0	0.0	16:01	7	0	2	2	8	0	0	0	13:14
	NHL Totals		142	12	21	33	38	4	0	0	188	6.4		1	0.0	15:13	33	1	5	6	18	0	0	1	14:02

CCHA First All-Star Team (2008) • NCAA West Second All-American Team (2008)

Signed as a free agent by **TPS Turku** (Finland), October 5, 2012. Signed as a free agent by **Allen** (CHL), December 31, 2012.

MASHINTER, Brandon

(ma-SHIHN-tuhr, BRAN-duhn) **NYR**

Center. Shoots left. 6'4", 220 lbs. Born, Bradford, Ont., September 20, 1988.

Season	Club	League	GP	G	A	Pts	PIM	PP	SH	GW	S	%	+/-	TF	F%	Min	GP	G	A	Pts	PIM	PP	SH	GW	Min
2004-05	Tor. T-Birds	ON-Jr.A	49	3	6	9	19	....	....	....	....	....	....	....	....	....	....	....	....	....	....	....	....	....	....
	Sarnia Sting	OHL	8	0	0	0	9	....	....	....	....	....	....	....	....	....	....	....	....	....	....	....	....	....	....
2005-06	Sarnia Sting	OHL	65	6	1	7	65	....	....	....	....	....	....	....	....	....	....	....	....	....	....	....	....	....	....
2006-07	Sarnia Sting	OHL	55	7	8	15	49	....	....	....	....	....	....	....	....	....	4	0	2	2	0	....	....	....	....
2007-08	Kitchener Rangers	OHL	62	10	10	20	84	....	....	....	....	....	....	....	....	....	20	2	2	4	16	....	....	....	....
2008-09	Kitchener Rangers	OHL	21	14	12	26	24	....	....	....	....	....	....	....	....	....	....	....	....	....	....	....	....	....	....
	Belleville Bulls	OHL	31	20	12	32	32	....	....	....	....	....	....	....	....	....	17	8	3	11	13	....	....	....	....
2009-10	Worcester Sharks	AHL	79	22	15	37	117	....	....	....	....	....	....	....	....	....	11	1	5	6	6	....	....	....	....
2010-11	San Jose	NHL	13	0	0	0	17	0	0	0	5	0.0	−2	0	0.0	6:23	....	....	....	....	....	....	....	....	....
	Worcester Sharks	AHL	62	14	19	33	96	....	....	....	....	....	....	....	....	....	....	....	....	....	....	....	....	....	....
2011-12	Worcester Sharks	AHL	65	16	17	33	67	....	....	....	....	....	....	....	....	....	....	....	....	....	....	....	....	....	....
2012-13	Worcester Sharks	AHL	30	2	3	5	44	....	....	....	....	....	....	....	....	....	....	....	....	....	....	....	....	....	....
	NY Rangers	NHL	4	0	0	0	0	0	0	0	2	0.0	−2	1	100.0	5:55	....	....	....	....	....	....	....	....	....
	Connecticut	AHL	35	10	9	19	52	....	....	....	....	....	....	....	....	....	....	....	....	....	....	....	....	....	....
	NHL Totals		17	0	0	0	17	0	0	0	7	0.0		1	100.0	6:16	....	....	....	....	....	....	....	....	....

Signed as a free agent by **San Jose**, March 3, 2009. Traded to **NY Rangers** by **San Jose** for Tommy Grant and future considerations, January 16, 2013.

MATSUMOTO, Jon

(mat-suh-MOH-toh, JAWN) **FLA**

Center. Shoots left. 6', 184 lbs. Born, Ottawa, Ont., October 13, 1986. Philadelphia's 5th choice, 79th overall, in 2006 Entry Draft.

Season	Club	League	GP	G	A	Pts	PIM	PP	SH	GW	S	%	+/-	TF	F%	Min	GP	G	A	Pts	PIM	PP	SH	GW	Min
2002-03	Cumberland	ON-Jr.A	8	2	3	5	2	....	....	....	....	....	....	....	....	....	10	4	7	11	2	....	....	....	....
2003-04	Cumberland	ON-Jr.A	51	31	32	63	26	....	....	....	....	....	....	....	....	....	7	5	5	10	6	....	....	....	....
2004-05	Bowling Green	CCHA	36	18	14	32	22	....	....	....	....	....	....	....	....	....	....	....	....	....	....	....	....	....	....
2005-06	Bowling Green	CCHA	36	20	28	48	43	....	....	....	....	....	....	....	....	....	....	....	....	....	....	....	....	....	....
2006-07	Bowling Green	CCHA	38	11	22	33	70	....	....	....	....	....	....	....	....	....	....	....	....	....	....	....	....	....	....
	Philadelphia	AHL	16	2	2	4	10	....	....	....	....	....	....	....	....	....	....	....	....	....	....	....	....	....	....
2007-08	Philadelphia	AHL	77	20	24	44	52	....	....	....	....	....	....	....	....	....	12	2	2	4	10	....	....	....	....
2008-09	Philadelphia	AHL	78	29	34	63	77	....	....	....	....	....	....	....	....	....	4	1	2	3	4	....	....	....	....
2009-10	Adirondack	AHL	80	30	32	62	50	....	....	....	....	....	....	....	....	....	....	....	....	....	....	....	....	....	....
2010-11	Carolina	NHL	13	2	0	2	4	0	0	0	11	18.2	−4	83	36.1	7:04	....	....	....	....	....	....	....	....	....
	Charlotte	AHL	65	20	28	48	36	....	....	....	....	....	....	....	....	....	15	3	5	8	12	....	....	....	....

			Regular Season														Playoffs								
Season	Club	League	GP	G	A	Pts	PIM	PP	SH	GW	S	%	+/-	TF	F%	Min	GP	G	A	Pts	PIM	PP	SH	GW	Min
2011-12	Charlotte	AHL	41	13	21	34	22	....	....	....	....	....	....	....	....	....	....	....	....	....	....	....	....	....	....
	Florida	**NHL**	**1**	**0**	**0**	**0**	**0**	0	0	0	0	0.0	0	1	100.0	5:04	....	....	....	....	....	....	....	....	....
	San Antonio	AHL	35	10	16	26	28	....	....	....	....	....	....	....	....	....	10	4	9	13	8	....	....	....	....
2012-13	Worcester Sharks	AHL	60	14	18	32	30	....	....	....	....	....	....	....	....	....	....	....	....	....	....	....	....	....	....
	Chicago Wolves	AHL	5	1	0	1	0	....	....	....	....	....	....	....	....	....	....	....	....	....	....	....	....	....	....
	NHL Totals		**14**	**2**	**0**	**2**	**4**	**0**	**0**	**0**	**11**	**18.2**		**84**	**36.9**	**6:56**	....	....	....	....	....	....	....	....	....

Traded to **Carolina** by **Philadelphia** for Washington's 7th round choice (previously acquired, Philadelphia selected Ricard Blidstrand) in 2010 Entry Draft, June 25, 2010. Traded to **Florida** by **Carolina** with Mattias Lindstrom for A.J. Jenks and Evgeny Dadonov, January 18, 2012. Signed as a free agent by **San Jose**, July 12, 2012. • Loaned to **Chicago** (AHL) by **San Jose** (Worcester-AHL), April 8, 2013. Signed as a free agent by **Florida**, July 8, 2013.

MATTEAU, Stefan

(mah-TOH, steh-FAN) **N.J.**

Left wing. Shoots left. 6'3", 215 lbs. Born, Chicago, IL, February 23, 1994. New Jersey's 1st choice, 29th overall, in 2012 Entry Draft.

Season	Club	League	GP	G	A	Pts	PIM	PP	SH	GW	S	%	+/-	TF	F%	Min	GP	G	A	Pts	PIM	PP	SH	GW	Min
2009-10	Notre Dame	SMHL	40	15	22	37	67	....	....	....	....	....	....	....	....	....	13	4	8	12	6	....	....	....	....
2010-11	USNTDP	USHL	28	4	5	9	47	....	....	....	....	....	....	....	....	....	2	0	0	0	2	....	....	....	....
	USNTDP	U-17	17	3	6	9	18	....	....	....	....	....	....	....	....	....	....	....	....	....	....	....	....	....	....
2011-12	USNTDP	USHL	18	6	4	10	93	....	....	....	....	....	....	....	....	....	....	....	....	....	....	....	....	....	....
	USNTDP	U-18	28	9	13	22	73	....	....	....	....	....	....	....	....	....	....	....	....	....	....	....	....	....	....
2012-13	Blainville-Bois.	QMJHL	35	18	10	28	70	....	....	....	....	....	....	....	....	....	11	3	6	9	16	....	....	....	....
	New Jersey	**NHL**	**17**	**1**	**2**	**3**	**6**	**0**	**0**	**0**	**22**	**4.5**	**–1**	**4**	**0.0**	**9:11**	....	....	....	....	....	....	....	....	....
	NHL Totals		**17**	**1**	**2**	**3**	**6**	**0**	**0**	**0**	**22**	**4.5**		**4**	**0.0**	**9:11**	....	....	....	....	....	....	....	....	....

MATTHIAS, Shawn

(muh-TIGH-uhs, SHAWN) **FLA**

Center. Shoots left. 6'4", 220 lbs. Born, Mississauga, Ont., February 19, 1988. Detroit's 2nd choice, 47th overall, in 2006 Entry Draft.

Season	Club	League	GP	G	A	Pts	PIM	PP	SH	GW	S	%	+/-	TF	F%	Min	GP	G	A	Pts	PIM	PP	SH	GW	Min
2004-05	Belleville Bulls	OHL	37	1	1	2	15	....	....	....	....	....	....	....	....	....	3	0	0	0	0	....	....	....	....
2005-06	Belleville Bulls	OHL	67	13	21	34	42	....	....	....	....	....	....	....	....	....	6	3	0	3	2	....	....	....	....
2006-07	Belleville Bulls	OHL	64	38	35	73	61	....	....	....	....	....	....	....	....	....	15	13	5	18	10	....	....	....	....
2007-08	**Florida**	**NHL**	**4**	**2**	**0**	**2**	**2**	**1**	**0**	**0**	**5**	**40.0**	**–2**	**38**	**44.7**	**13:08**	....	....	....	....	....	....	....	....	....
	Belleville Bulls	OHL	53	32	47	79	50	....	....	....	....	....	....	....	....	....	1	1	0	1	0	....	....	....	....
2008-09	**Florida**	**NHL**	**16**	**0**	**2**	**2**	**2**	**0**	**0**	**0**	**11**	**0.0**	**–3**	**91**	**50.6**	**9:10**	....	....	....	....	....	....	....	....	....
	Rochester	AHL	61	10	10	20	16	....	....	....	....	....	....	....	....	....	....	....	....	....	....	....	....	....	....
2009-10	**Florida**	**NHL**	**55**	**7**	**9**	**16**	**10**	**0**	**0**	**2**	**67**	**10.4**	**–3**	**313**	**38.0**	**10:48**	....	....	....	....	....	....	....	....	....
	Rochester	AHL	27	6	7	13	12	....	....	....	....	....	....	....	....	....	7	2	5	7	7	....	....	....	....
2010-11	**Florida**	**NHL**	**51**	**6**	**10**	**16**	**16**	**0**	**0**	**0**	**90**	**6.7**	**0**	**370**	**50.8**	**11:50**	....	....	....	....	....	....	....	....	....
2011-12	**Florida**	**NHL**	**79**	**10**	**14**	**24**	**49**	**1**	**0**	**1**	**133**	**7.5**	**–2**	**597**	**49.4**	**13:49**	**7**	**0**	**1**	**1**	**6**	**0**	**0**	**0**	**11:08**
2012-13	**Florida**	**NHL**	**48**	**14**	**7**	**21**	**16**	**2**	**1**	**1**	**106**	**13.2**	**–8**	**347**	**44.1**	**15:11**	....	....	....	....	....	....	....	....	....
	NHL Totals		**253**	**39**	**42**	**81**	**95**	**4**	**1**	**4**	**412**	**9.5**		**1756**	**46.6**	**12:43**	**7**	**0**	**1**	**1**	**6**	**0**	**0**	**0**	**11:08**

Traded to **Florida** by **Detroit** with Detroit's 2nd round choice (later traded to Nashville - Nashville selected Nick Spaling) in 2007 Entry Draft for Todd Bertuzzi, February 27, 2007. Signed as a free agent by **Linz** (Austria), December 3, 2012.

MAULDIN, Greg

(MAWL-dihn, GREHG)

Center. Shoots right. 5'11", 195 lbs. Born, Boston, MA, June 10, 1982. Columbus' 10th choice, 199th overall, in 2002 Entry Draft.

Season	Club	League	GP	G	A	Pts	PIM	PP	SH	GW	S	%	+/-	TF	F%	Min	GP	G	A	Pts	PIM	PP	SH	GW	Min
99-2000	Bos. Jr. Bruins	EJHL	58	45	42	87	14	....	....	....	....	....	....	....	....	....	....	....	....	....	....	....	....	....	....
2000-01	Bos. Jr. Bruins	EJHL	53	48	58	106	73	....	....	....	....	....	....	....	....	....	....	....	....	....	....	....	....	....	....
2001-02	Massachusetts	H-East	33	12	12	24	10	....	....	....	....	....	....	....	....	....	....	....	....	....	....	....	....	....	....
2002-03	Massachusetts	H-East	36	21	20	41	26	....	....	....	....	....	....	....	....	....	....	....	....	....	....	....	....	....	....
2003-04	Massachusetts	H-East	29	15	14	29	15	....	....	....	....	....	....	....	....	....	....	....	....	....	....	....	....	....	....
	Columbus	**NHL**	**6**	**0**	**0**	**0**	**4**	**0**	**0**	**0**	**6**	**0.0**	**–2**	**0**	**0.0**	**8:47**	....	....	....	....	....	....	....	....	....
	Syracuse Crunch	AHL	2	0	0	0	0	....	....	....	....	....	....	....	....	....	1	0	0	0	0	....	....	....	....
2004-05	Syracuse Crunch	AHL	66	7	20	27	49	....	....	....	....	....	....	....	....	....	....	....	....	....	....	....	....	....	....
2005-06	Syracuse Crunch	AHL	56	12	17	29	53	....	....	....	....	....	....	....	....	....	....	....	....	....	....	....	....	....	....
	Houston Aeros	AHL	11	1	3	4	0	....	....	....	....	....	....	....	....	....	8	1	1	2	2	....	....	....	....
2006-07	Bloomington	UHL	2	0	0	0	2	....	....	....	....	....	....	....	....	....	....	....	....	....	....	....	....	....	....
	Huddinge IK	Sweden-2	6	1	2	3	0	....	....	....	....	....	....	....	....	....	....	....	....	....	....	....	....	....	....
	IK Oskarshamn	Sweden-2	26	5	8	13	31	....	....	....	....	....	....	....	....	....	....	....	....	....	....	....	....	....	....
2007-08	Binghamton	AHL	71	15	18	33	37	....	....	....	....	....	....	....	....	....	....	....	....	....	....	....	....	....	....
2008-09	Binghamton	AHL	80	24	27	51	41	....	....	....	....	....	....	....	....	....	....	....	....	....	....	....	....	....	....
2009-10	**NY Islanders**	**NHL**	**1**	**0**	**0**	**0**	**0**	**0**	**0**	**0**	**2**	**0.0**	**–1**	**11**	**72.7**	**10:02**	....	....	....	....	....	....	....	....	....
	Bridgeport	AHL	77	25	29	54	35	....	....	....	....	....	....	....	....	....	5	1	2	3	0	....	....	....	....
2010-11	**Colorado**	**NHL**	**29**	**5**	**5**	**10**	**8**	**0**	**2**	**1**	**46**	**10.9**	**5**	**7**	**28.6**	**10:33**	....	....	....	....	....	....	....	....	....
	Lake Erie	AHL	43	18	17	35	20	....	....	....	....	....	....	....	....	....	7	0	2	2	2	....	....	....	....
2011-12	Lake Erie	AHL	59	16	18	34	17	....	....	....	....	....	....	....	....	....	....	....	....	....	....	....	....	....	....
2012-13	Fribourg	Swiss	39	13	8	21	8	....	....	....	....	....	....	....	....	....	18	2	2	4	4	....	....	....	....
	NHL Totals		**36**	**5**	**5**	**10**	**12**	**0**	**2**	**1**	**54**	**9.3**		**18**	**55.6**	**10:14**	....	....	....	....	....	....	....	....	....

EJHL First All-Star Team (2000, 2001) • EJHL MVP (2000)

Signed as a free agent by **Oskarshamn** (Sweden-2), October 23, 2006. Signed as a free agent by **Binghamton** (AHL), August 9, 2007. Signed as a free agent by **Ottawa**, July 7, 2008. Signed as a free agent by **NY Islanders**, July 6, 2009. Signed as a free agent by **Colorado**, July 2, 2010. Signed as a free agent by **Fribourg-Gotteren** (Swiss), July 28, 2012.

MAXWELL, Ben

(MAX-wehl, BEHN)

Center. Shoots left. 6'1", 195 lbs. Born, North Vancouver, B.C., March 30, 1988. Montreal's 2nd choice, 49th overall, in 2006 Entry Draft.

Season	Club	League	GP	G	A	Pts	PIM	PP	SH	GW	S	%	+/-	TF	F%	Min	GP	G	A	Pts	PIM	PP	SH	GW	Min
2003-04	North Delta Flyers	PIJHL	40	17	28	45	46	....	....	....	....	....	....	....	....	....	5	3	6	9	0	....	....	....	....
	Surrey Eagles	BCHL	2	0	0	0	0	....	....	....	....	....	....	....	....	....	....	....	....	....	....	....	....	....	....
	Kootenay Ice	WHL	3	0	1	1	2	....	....	....	....	....	....	....	....	....	1	0	0	0	0	....	....	....	....
2004-05	Kootenay Ice	WHL	68	8	10	18	37	....	....	....	....	....	....	....	....	....	16	0	1	1	6	....	....	....	....
2005-06	Kootenay Ice	WHL	69	28	32	60	52	....	....	....	....	....	....	....	....	....	6	3	5	8	0	....	....	....	....
2006-07	Kootenay Ice	WHL	39	19	34	53	42	....	....	....	....	....	....	....	....	....	7	1	4	5	21	....	....	....	....
2007-08	Kootenay Ice	WHL	31	9	18	27	26	....	....	....	....	....	....	....	....	....	10	6	3	9	14	....	....	....	....
2008-09	**Montreal**	**NHL**	**7**	**0**	**0**	**0**	**2**	**0**	**0**	**0**	**2**	**0.0**	**–1**	**53**	**37.7**	**9:55**	....	....	....	....	....	....	....	....	....
	Hamilton	AHL	73	22	36	58	58	....	....	....	....	....	....	....	....	....	6	3	1	4	4	....	....	....	....
2009-10	**Montreal**	**NHL**	**13**	**0**	**0**	**0**	**6**	**0**	**0**	**0**	**6**	**0.0**	**–2**	**16**	**50.0**	**8:47**	**1**	**0**	**0**	**0**	**0**	**0**	**0**	**0**	**1:03**
	Hamilton	AHL	57	16	28	44	22	....	....	....	....	....	....	....	....	....	1	0	0	0	0	....	....	....	....
2010-11	Hamilton	AHL	47	11	29	40	32	....	....	....	....	....	....	....	....	....	....	....	....	....	....	....	....	....	....
	Atlanta	**NHL**	**12**	**1**	**1**	**2**	**9**	**0**	**0**	**0**	**13**	**7.7**	**–7**	**36**	**44.4**	**12:00**	....	....	....	....	....	....	....	....	....
	Chicago Wolves	AHL	2	0	1	1	0	....	....	....	....	....	....	....	....	....	....	....	....	....	....	....	....	....	....
2011-12	**Winnipeg**	**NHL**	**9**	**1**	**4**	**5**	**0**	**0**	**0**	**0**	**4**	**33.3**	**3**	**25**	**82.7**	**6:03**	....	....	....	....	....	....	....	....	....
	Anaheim	**NHL**	**6**	**0**	**1**	**1**	**2**	**0**	**0**	**0**	**6**	**0.0**	**1**	**34**	**47.1**	**7:45**	....	....	....	....	....	....	....	....	....
	St. John's IceCaps	AHL	43	8	17	25	35	....	....	....	....	....	....	....	....	....	15	3	4	7	4	....	....	....	....
2012-13	St. John's IceCaps	AHL	74	11	29	40	52	....	....	....	....	....	....	....	....	....	....	....	....	....	....	....	....	....	....
	NHL Totals		**47**	**2**	**6**	**8**	**19**	**0**	**0**	**0**	**31**	**6.5**		**164**	**49.4**	**9:07**	**1**	**0**	**0**	**0**	**0**	**0**	**0**	**0**	**1:03**

Traded to **Atlanta** by **Montreal** with Montreal's 4th round choice (later traded back to Montreal - Montreal selected Olivier Archambault) in 2011 Entry Draft for Brent Sopel and Nigel Dawes, February 24, 2011. • Transferred to **Winnipeg** after **Atlanta** franchise relocated, June 21, 2011. Claimed on waivers by **Anaheim** from **Winnipeg**, November 10, 2011. Claimed on waivers by **Winnipeg** from **Anaheim**, December 6, 2011. Signed as a free agent by **Karpat** (Finland), August 12, 2013.

MAYERS, Jamal

(MAI-uhrz, JUH-MAHL)

Right wing. Shoots right. 6'1", 222 lbs. Born, Toronto, Ont., October 24, 1974. St. Louis' 3rd choice, 89th overall, in 1993 Entry Draft.

Season	Club	League	GP	G	A	Pts	PIM	PP	SH	GW	S	%	+/-	TF	F%	Min	GP	G	A	Pts	PIM	PP	SH	GW	Min
1990-91	Markham	ON-Jr.B	44	12	24	36	78	....	....	....	....	....	....	....	....	....	....	....	....	....	....	....	....	....	....
1991-92	Thornhill	ON-Jr.A	56	38	69	107	36	....	....	....	....	....	....	....	....	....	....	....	....	....	....	....	....	....	....
1992-93	Western Mich.	CCHA	38	8	17	25	26	....	....	....	....	....	....	....	....	....	....	....	....	....	....	....	....	....	....
1993-94	Western Mich.	CCHA	40	17	32	49	40	....	....	....	....	....	....	....	....	....	....	....	....	....	....	....	....	....	....
1994-95	Western Mich.	CCHA	39	13	32	45	40	....	....	....	....	....	....	....	....	....	....	....	....	....	....	....	....	....	....
1995-96	Western Mich.	CCHA	38	17	22	39	75	....	....	....	....	....	....	....	....	....	....	....	....	....	....	....	....	....	....
1996-97	**St. Louis**	**NHL**	**6**	**0**	**1**	**1**	**2**	**0**	**0**	**0**	**7**	**0.0**	**–3**	....	....	....	....	....	....	....	....	....	....	....	....
	Worcester IceCats	AHL	62	12	14	26	104	....	....	....	....	....	....	....	....	....	5	4	5	9	4	....	....	....	....
1997-98	Worcester IceCats	AHL	61	19	24	43	117	....	....	....	....	....	....	....	....	....	11	3	4	7	10	....	....	....	....
1998-99	**St. Louis**	**NHL**	**34**	**4**	**5**	**9**	**40**	**0**	**0**	**0**	**48**	**8.3**	**–3**	**2**	**50.0**	**8:08**	**11**	**0**	**1**	**1**	**8**	**0**	**0**	**0**	**8:34**
	Worcester IceCats	AHL	20	9	7	16	34	....	....	....	....	....	....	....	....	....	....	....	....	....	....	....	....	....	....
99-2000	**St. Louis**	**NHL**	**79**	**7**	**10**	**17**	**90**	**0**	**0**	**0**	**99**	**7.1**	**0**	**77**	**52.0**	**9:46**	**7**	**0**	**4**	**4**	**2**	**0**	**0**	**0**	**10:42**

			Regular Season														Playoffs								
Season	Club	League	GP	G	A	Pts	PIM	PP	SH	GW	S	%	+/-	TF	F%	Min	GP	G	A	Pts	PIM	PP	SH	GW	Min
2000-01	**St. Louis**	**NHL**	**77**	**8**	**13**	**21**	**117**	**0**	**0**	**0**	**132**	**6.1**	**-3**	**273**	**51.3**	**11:04**	**15**	**2**	**3**	**5**	**8**	**0**	**0**	**0**	**11:28**
2001-02	**St. Louis**	**NHL**	**77**	**9**	**8**	**17**	**99**	**0**	**1**	**0**	**105**	**8.6**	**9**	**761**	**52.6**	**11:36**	**10**	**3**	**0**	**3**	**2**	**0**	**0**	**2**	**11:14**
2002-03	**St. Louis**	**NHL**	**15**	**2**	**5**	**7**	**8**	**0**	**0**	**0**	**26**	**7.7**	**1**	**111**	**51.4**	**14:21**	....	....	....	....	....	....	....	....	....
2003-04	**St. Louis**	**NHL**	**80**	**6**	**5**	**11**	**91**	**0**	**1**	**3**	**130**	**4.6**	**-19**	**681**	**48.6**	**13:01**	**5**	**0**	**0**	**0**	**0**	**0**	**0**	**0**	**12:55**
2004-05	Hammarby	Sweden-2	19	9	13	22	36	....	....	....	....	....	....	....	....	....	....	....	....	....	....	....	....	....	....
	Missouri	UHL	13	5	2	7	68	....	....	....	....	....	....	....	....	....	....	....	....	....	....	....	....	....	....
2005-06	**St. Louis**	**NHL**	**67**	**15**	**11**	**26**	**129**	**0**	**2**	**1**	**111**	**13.5**	**-22**	**363**	**48.5**	**15:07**	....	....	....	....	....	....	....	....	....
2006-07	**St. Louis**	**NHL**	**80**	**8**	**14**	**22**	**89**	**0**	**2**	**0**	**129**	**6.2**	**-19**	**432**	**57.4**	**14:37**	....	....	....	....	....	....	....	....	....
2007-08	**St. Louis**	**NHL**	**80**	**12**	**15**	**27**	**91**	**0**	**1**	**3**	**153**	**7.8**	**-19**	**683**	**56.2**	**15:56**	....	....	....	....	....	....	....	....	....
2008-09	**Toronto**	**NHL**	**71**	**7**	**9**	**16**	**82**	**0**	**0**	**1**	**72**	**9.7**	**-7**	**429**	**57.3**	**10:33**	....	....	....	....	....	....	....	....	....
2009-10	**Toronto**	**NHL**	**44**	**2**	**6**	**8**	**78**	**0**	**0**	**0**	**47**	**4.3**	**-5**	**264**	**56.8**	**8:55**	....	....	....	....	....	....	....	....	....
	Calgary	**NHL**	**27**	**1**	**5**	**6**	**53**	**0**	**0**	**1**	**28**	**3.6**	**2**	**115**	**55.7**	**9:11**	....	....	....	....	....	....	....	....	....
2010-11	**San Jose**	**NHL**	**78**	**3**	**11**	**14**	**124**	**0**	**0**	**0**	**62**	**4.8**	**3**	**98**	**54.1**	**8:53**	**12**	**0**	**0**	**0**	**12**	**0**	**0**	**0**	**5:37**
2011-12	**Chicago**	**NHL**	**81**	**6**	**9**	**15**	**91**	**0**	**0**	**1**	**70**	**8.6**	**-4**	**558**	**56.1**	**9:48**	**3**	**0**	**0**	**0**	**0**	**0**	**0**	**0**	**8:45**
2012-13♦	**Chicago**	**NHL**	**19**	**0**	**2**	**2**	**16**	**0**	**0**	**0**	**10**	**0.0**	**2**	**78**	**53.9**	**6:58**	....	....	....	....	....	....	....	....	....
	NHL Totals		**915**	**90**	**129**	**219**	**1200**	**0**	**7**	**10**	**1229**	**7.3**		**4925**	**53.7**	**11:34**	**63**	**5**	**8**	**13**	**32**	**0**	**0**	**2**	**9:43**

• Missed majority of 2002-03 due to knee injury vs. Calgary, November 16, 2002. Signed as a free agent by **Hammarby** (Sweden-2), November 16, 2004. Signed as a free agent by **Missouri** (UHL), March 11, 2005. Traded to **Toronto** by **St. Louis** for Florida's 3rd round choice (previously acquired, St. Louis selected James Livingston) in 2008 Entry Draft, June 19, 2008. Traded to **Calgary** by **Toronto** with Matt Stajan, Niklas Hagman and Ian White for Dion Phaneuf, Fredrik Sjostrom and Keith Aulie, January 31, 2010. Signed as a free agent by **San Jose**, August 4, 2010. Signed as a free agent by **Chicago**, July 1, 2011. • Missed majority of 2012-13 as a healthy reserve.

MAYOROV, Maksim

(may-YOHR-ahv, mahx-EEM)

Left wing. Shoots left. 6'2", 202 lbs. Born, Andizhan, USSR, March 26, 1989. Columbus' 5th choice, 94th overall, in 2007 Entry Draft.

Season	Club	League	GP	G	A	Pts	PIM	PP	SH	GW	S	%	+/-	TF	F%	Min	GP	G	A	Pts	PIM	PP	SH	GW	Min
2005-06	Ak Bars Kazan 2	Russia-3	STATISTICS NOT AVAILABLE																						
2006-07	Leninogorsk	Russia-2	28	6	4	10	6	....	....	....	....	....	....	....	....	....	....	....	....	....	....	....	....	....	....
	Almetjevsk	Russia-2	6	1	1	2	0	....	....	....	....	....	....	....	....	....	4	0	0	0	2	....	....	....	....
2007-08	Ak Bars Kazan	Russia	11	1	0	1	16	....	....	....	....	....	....	....	....	....	....	....	....	....	....	....	....	....	....
2008-09	**Columbus**	**NHL**	**3**	**0**	**0**	**0**	**0**	**0**	**0**	**0**	**1**	**0.0**	**0**	**0**	**0.0**	**5:44**	....	....	....	....	....	....	....	....	....
	Syracuse Crunch	AHL	71	17	14	31	30	....	....	....	....	....	....	....	....	....	....	....	....	....	....	....	....	....	....
2009-10	**Columbus**	**NHL**	**4**	**0**	**0**	**0**	**0**	**0**	**0**	**0**	**4**	**0.0**	**-1**	**0**	**0.0**	**7:40**	....	....	....	....	....	....	....	....	....
	Syracuse Crunch	AHL	74	17	15	32	24	....	....	....	....	....	....	....	....	....	....	....	....	....	....	....	....	....	....
2010-11	**Columbus**	**NHL**	**5**	**1**	**0**	**1**	**0**	**0**	**0**	**0**	**3**	**33.3**	**0**	**0**	**0.0**	**8:42**	....	....	....	....	....	....	....	....	....
	Springfield	AHL	69	19	14	33	16	....	....	....	....	....	....	....	....	....	....	....	....	....	....	....	....	....	....
2011-12	**Columbus**	**NHL**	**10**	**1**	**1**	**2**	**2**	**0**	**0**	**0**	**9**	**11.1**	**-3**	**0**	**0.0**	**10:40**	....	....	....	....	....	....	....	....	....
	Springfield	AHL	46	10	13	23	10	....	....	....	....	....	....	....	....	....	....	....	....	....	....	....	....	....	....
2012-13	Mytischi	KHL	40	16	6	22	14	....	....	....	....	....	....	....	....	....	5	0	1	1	0	....	....	....	....
	NHL Totals		**22**	**2**	**1**	**3**	**2**	**0**	**0**	**0**	**17**	**11.8**		**0**	**0.0**	**9:00**	....	....	....	....	....	....	....	....	....

Signed as a free agent by **Mytischi** (KHL), September 24, 2012.

McARDLE, Kenndal

(muh-KAHR-duhl, KEHN-dahl)

Left wing. Shoots left. 5'11", 190 lbs. Born, Toronto, Ont., January 4, 1987. Florida's 1st choice, 20th overall, in 2005 Entry Draft.

Season	Club	League	GP	G	A	Pts	PIM	PP	SH	GW	S	%	+/-	TF	F%	Min	GP	G	A	Pts	PIM	PP	SH	GW	Min
2002-03	Burnaby W.C.	Minor-BC	30	1	9	10	131	....	....	....	....	....	....	....	....	....	....	....	....	....	....	....	....	....	....
	Moose Jaw	WHL	2	0	0	0	0	....	....	....	....	....	....	....	....	....	....	....	....	....	....	....	....	....	....
2003-04	Moose Jaw	WHL	54	8	8	16	57	....	....	....	....	....	....	....	....	....	10	3	2	5	6	....	....	....	....
2004-05	Moose Jaw	WHL	70	37	37	74	122	....	....	....	....	....	....	....	....	....	5	1	0	1	16	....	....	....	....
2005-06	Moose Jaw	WHL	72	28	43	71	135	....	....	....	....	....	....	....	....	....	22	6	10	16	43	....	....	....	....
2006-07	Moose Jaw	WHL	26	10	10	20	75	....	....	....	....	....	....	....	....	....	....	....	....	....	....	....	....	....	....
	Vancouver Giants	WHL	37	9	13	22	54	....	....	....	....	....	....	....	....	....	22	*11	9	20	49	....	....	....	....
2007-08	Rochester	AHL	36	5	5	10	31	....	....	....	....	....	....	....	....	....	....	....	....	....	....	....	....	....	....
	Florida Everblades	ECHL	6	3	1	4	26	....	....	....	....	....	....	....	....	....	3	0	0	0	2	....	....	....	....
2008-09	**Florida**	**NHL**	**3**	**0**	**0**	**0**	**2**	**0**	**0**	**0**	**1**	**0.0**	**-1**	**0**	**0.0**	**7:30**	....	....	....	....	....	....	....	....	....
	Rochester	AHL	58	12	12	24	79	....	....	....	....	....	....	....	....	....	....	....	....	....	....	....	....	....	....
2009-10	**Florida**	**NHL**	**19**	**1**	**2**	**3**	**29**	**0**	**0**	**0**	**10**	**10.0**	**-4**	**0**	**0.0**	**8:54**	....	....	....	....	....	....	....	....	....
	Rochester	AHL	18	3	5	8	63	....	....	....	....	....	....	....	....	....	....	....	....	....	....	....	....	....	....
2010-11	**Florida**	**NHL**	**11**	**0**	**0**	**0**	**16**	**0**	**0**	**0**	**6**	**0.0**	**-3**	**3**	**33.3**	**9:57**	....	....	....	....	....	....	....	....	....
	Rochester	AHL	54	14	12	26	106	....	....	....	....	....	....	....	....	....	....	....	....	....	....	....	....	....	....
2011-12	**Winnipeg**	**NHL**	**9**	**0**	**0**	**0**	**4**	**0**	**0**	**0**	**3**	**0.0**	**-3**	**0**	**0.0**	**6:07**	....	....	....	....	....	....	....	....	....
	St. John's IceCaps	AHL	35	7	5	12	64	....	....	....	....	....	....	....	....	....	....	....	....	....	....	....	....	....	....
	Portland Pirates	AHL	19	3	3	6	34	....	....	....	....	....	....	....	....	....	....	....	....	....	....	....	....	....	....
2012-13	Greenville	ECHL	31	7	15	22	65	....	....	....	....	....	....	....	....	....	....	....	....	....	....	....	....	....	....
	Rockford IceHogs	AHL	30	3	2	5	55	....	....	....	....	....	....	....	....	....	....	....	....	....	....	....	....	....	....
	NHL Totals		**42**	**1**	**2**	**3**	**51**	**0**	**0**	**0**	**20**	**5.0**		**3**	**33.3**	**8:28**	....	....	....	....	....	....	....	....	....

• Missed majority of 2009-10 due to shoulder injury at Nashville, November 28, 2010. Traded to **Winnipeg** by **Florida** for Angelo Esposito, July 9, 2011. Signed as a free agent by **Vasteras** (Sweden), May 13, 2013. • Loaned to **Rockford** (AHL) by **Greenville** (ECHL), January 16, 2013.

McBAIN, Jamie

(muhk-BAYN, JAY-mee) **BUF**

Defense. Shoots right. 6'2", 200 lbs. Born, Edina, MN, February 25, 1988. Carolina's 1st choice, 63rd overall, in 2006 Entry Draft.

Season	Club	League	GP	G	A	Pts	PIM	PP	SH	GW	S	%	+/-	TF	F%	Min	GP	G	A	Pts	PIM	PP	SH	GW	Min
2003-04	Shat.-St. Mary's	High-MN	73	6	27	33	....	....	....	....	....	....	....	....	....	....	....	....	....	....	....	....	....	....	....
2004-05	USNTDP	U-17	14	1	6	7	16	....	....	....	....	....	....	....	....	....	....	....	....	....	....	....	....	....	....
	USNTDP	NAHL	38	2	7	9	22	....	....	....	....	....	....	....	....	....	10	0	3	3	4	....	....	....	....
2005-06	USNTDP	U-18	41	9	16	25	35	....	....	....	....	....	....	....	....	....	....	....	....	....	....	....	....	....	....
	USNTDP	NAHL	14	0	5	5	6	....	....	....	....	....	....	....	....	....	....	....	....	....	....	....	....	....	....
2006-07	U. of Wisconsin	WCHA	36	3	15	18	36	....	....	....	....	....	....	....	....	....	....	....	....	....	....	....	....	....	....
2007-08	U. of Wisconsin	WCHA	35	5	19	24	18	....	....	....	....	....	....	....	....	....	....	....	....	....	....	....	....	....	....
2008-09	U. of Wisconsin	WCHA	40	7	30	37	30	....	....	....	....	....	....	....	....	....	....	....	....	....	....	....	....	....	....
	Albany River Rats	AHL	10	1	1	2	2	....	....	....	....	....	....	....	....	....	....	....	....	....	....	....	....	....	....
2009-10	**Carolina**	**NHL**	**14**	**3**	**7**	**10**	**0**	**1**	**0**	**1**	**29**	**10.3**	**6**	**0**	**0.0**	**25:47**	....	....	....	....	....	....	....	....	....
	Albany River Rats	AHL	68	7	33	40	10	....	....	....	....	....	....	....	....	....	8	4	2	6	8	....	....	....	....
2010-11	**Carolina**	**NHL**	**76**	**7**	**23**	**30**	**32**	**1**	**0**	**2**	**95**	**7.4**	**-8**	**0**	**0.0**	**19:06**	....	....	....	....	....	....	....	....	....
2011-12	**Carolina**	**NHL**	**76**	**8**	**19**	**27**	**4**	**5**	**0**	**1**	**127**	**6.3**	**-7**	**0**	**0.0**	**19:48**	....	....	....	....	....	....	....	....	....
2012-13	Pelicans Lahti	Finland	7	0	1	1	6	....	....	....	....	....	....	....	....	....	....	....	....	....	....	....	....	....	....
	Carolina	**NHL**	**40**	**1**	**7**	**8**	**12**	**0**	**0**	**0**	**46**	**2.2**	**0**	**0**	**0.0**	**18:25**	....	....	....	....	....	....	....	....	....
	NHL Totals		**206**	**19**	**56**	**75**	**48**	**7**	**0**	**4**	**297**	**6.4**		**0**	**0.0**	**19:41**	....	....	....	....	....	....	....	....	....

WCHA All-Rookie Team (2007) • WCHA First All-Star Team (2009) • WCHA Player of the Year (2009) • NCAA West First All-American Team (2009)

Signed as a free agent by **Lahti** (Finland), November 2, 2012. Traded to **Buffalo** by **Carolina** with Carolina's 2nd round choice (J.T. Compher) in 2013 Entry Draft for Andrej Sekera, June 30, 2013.

McCARTHY, John

(muh-KAHR-thee, JAWN) **S.J.**

Left wing. Shoots left. 6'1", 190 lbs. Born, Boston, MA, August 9, 1986. San Jose's 5th choice, 202nd overall, in 2006 Entry Draft.

Season	Club	League	GP	G	A	Pts	PIM	PP	SH	GW	S	%	+/-	TF	F%	Min	GP	G	A	Pts	PIM	PP	SH	GW	Min
2004-05	Des Moines	USHL	60	8	10	18	32	....	....	....	....	....	....	....	....	....	....	....	....	....	....	....	....	....	....
2005-06	Boston University	H-East	32	2	2	4	12	....	....	....	....	....	....	....	....	....	....	....	....	....	....	....	....	....	....
2006-07	Boston University	H-East	39	2	3	5	18	....	....	....	....	....	....	....	....	....	....	....	....	....	....	....	....	....	....
2007-08	Boston University	H-East	38	4	3	7	24	....	....	....	....	....	....	....	....	....	....	....	....	....	....	....	....	....	....
2008-09	Boston University	H-East	45	6	23	29	24	....	....	....	....	....	....	....	....	....	....	....	....	....	....	....	....	....	....
2009-10	**San Jose**	**NHL**	**4**	**0**	**0**	**0**	**0**	**0**	**0**	**0**	**3**	**0.0**	**-3**	**0**	**0.0**	**9:08**	....	....	....	....	....	....	....	....	....
	Worcester Sharks	AHL	74	15	27	42	39	....	....	....	....	....	....	....	....	....	11	2	3	5	10	....	....	....	....
2010-11	**San Jose**	**NHL**	**37**	**2**	**2**	**4**	**8**	**0**	**0**	**0**	**41**	**4.9**	**-8**	**36**	**36.1**	**8:45**	....	....	....	....	....	....	....	....	....
	Worcester Sharks	AHL	25	7	5	12	13	....	....	....	....	....	....	....	....	....	....	....	....	....	....	....	....	....	....
2011-12	**San Jose**	**NHL**	**10**	**0**	**0**	**0**	**10**	**0**	**0**	**0**	**14**	**0.0**	**-2**	**43**	**41.9**	**9:26**	....	....	....	....	....	....	....	....	....
	Worcester Sharks	AHL	65	20	27	47	41	....	....	....	....	....	....	....	....	....	....	....	....	....	....	....	....	....	....
2012-13	Worcester Sharks	AHL	65	9	16	25	12	....	....	....	....	....	....	....	....	....	....	....	....	....	....	....	....	....	....
	NHL Totals		**51**	**2**	**2**	**4**	**18**	**0**	**0**	**0**	**58**	**3.4**		**79**	**39.2**	**8:55**	....	....	....	....	....	....	....	....	....

McCLEMENT, Jay

(muh-KLEHM-ehnt, JAY) **TOR**

Center. Shoots left. 6'1", 205 lbs. Born, Kingston, Ont., March 2, 1983. St. Louis' 1st choice, 57th overall, in 2001 Entry Draft.

Season	Club	League	Regular Season GP	G	A	Pts	PIM	PP	SH	GW	S	%	+/-	TF	F%	Min	Playoffs GP	G	A	Pts	PIM	PP	SH	GW	Min
1997-98	Kingston	ON-Jr.A	48	3	8	11	15																		
1998-99	Kingston	ON-Jr.A	51	25	28	53	34																		
99-2000	Brampton	OHL	63	13	16	29	34										6	0	4	4	8				
2000-01	Brampton	OHL	66	30	19	49	61										9	4	2	6	10				
2001-02	Brampton	OHL	61	26	29	55	43																		
2002-03	Brampton	OHL	45	22	27	49	37										11	3	4	7	11				
	Worcester IceCats	AHL															1	0	0	0	0				
2003-04	Worcester IceCats	AHL	69	12	13	25	20										10	0	3	3	0				
2004-05	Worcester IceCats	AHL	79	17	34	51	45																		
2005-06	St. Louis	NHL	67	6	21	27	30	1	0	2	76	7.9	-23	691	46.9	13:56									
	Peoria Rivermen	AHL	11	4	5	9	4										4	0	2	2	2				
2006-07	St. Louis	NHL	81	8	28	36	55	0	0	0	104	7.7	3	839	52.7	13:53									
2007-08	St. Louis	NHL	81	9	13	22	26	0	0	2	110	8.2	-17	700	52.3	13:55									
2008-09	St. Louis	NHL	82	12	14	26	29	0	3	3	137	8.8	-10	1451	52.1	16:36	4	0	0	0	4	0	0	0	16:28
2009-10	St. Louis	NHL	82	11	18	29	22	0	0	3	109	10.1	0	1412	49.7	16:44									
2010-11	St. Louis	NHL	56	6	10	16	18	1	0	1	89	6.7	-13	831	51.4	17:08									
	Colorado	NHL	24	1	3	4	12	0	0	0	38	2.6	-8	321	52.3	15:39									
2011-12	Colorado	NHL	80	10	7	17	31	0	1	1	95	10.5	-8	873	51.3	13:45									
2012-13	Toronto	NHL	48	8	9	17	11	0	0	0	48	16.7	0	393	51.7	15:15	7	0	0	0	0	0	0	0	14:44
	NHL Totals		601	71	123	194	234	2	4	12	806	8.8		7511	51.1	15:07	11	0	0	0	4	0	0	0	15:22

Traded to **Colorado** by **St. Louis** with Erik Johnson and St. Louis's 1st round choice (Duncan Siemens) in 2011 Entry Draft for Kevin Shattenkirk, Chris Stewart and Colorado's 2nd round choice (Ty Rattie) in 2011 Entry Draft, February 19, 2011. Signed as a free agent by **Toronto**, July 1, 2012.

McCORMICK, Cody

(muh-KOHR-mihk, KOH-dee) **BUF**

Center/Right wing. Shoots right. 6'3", 221 lbs. Born, London, Ont., April 18, 1983. Colorado's 5th choice, 144th overall, in 2001 Entry Draft.

Season	Club	League	Regular Season GP	G	A	Pts	PIM	PP	SH	GW	S	%	+/-	TF	F%	Min	Playoffs GP	G	A	Pts	PIM	PP	SH	GW	Min
1998-99	Elgin-Middlesex	MHAO	58	22	40	62	81																		
99-2000	Belleville Bulls	OHL	45	3	4	7	42										9	1	0	1	10				
2000-01	Belleville Bulls	OHL	66	7	16	23	135										10	1	1	2	23				
2001-02	Belleville Bulls	OHL	63	10	17	27	118										11	2	4	6	24				
2002-03	Belleville Bulls	OHL	61	36	33	69	166										7	4	7	11	11				
2003-04	Colorado	NHL	44	2	3	5	73	0	0	1	33	6.1	-4	110	32.7	8:07									
	Hershey Bears	AHL	32	3	6	9	60																		
2004-05	Hershey Bears	AHL	40	5	6	11	68																		
2005-06	Colorado	NHL	45	4	4	8	29	0	0	1	43	9.3	1	16	25.0	7:42									
	Lowell	AHL	13	1	6	7	34																		
2006-07	Colorado	NHL	6	0	1	1	6	0	0	0	6	0.0	1	3	33.3	6:44									
	Albany River Rats	AHL	42	8	8	16	64										5	1	0	1	4				
2007-08	Colorado	NHL	40	2	2	4	50	0	0	1	45	4.4	5	17	35.3	10:58	4	0	1	1	7	0	0	0	11:53
	Lake Erie	AHL	13	2	4	6	16																		
2008-09	Colorado	NHL	55	1	11	12	92	0	0	0	66	1.5	-5	107	35.5	9:36									
2009-10	Portland Pirates	AHL	66	17	12	29	168										3	0	0	0	9				
	Buffalo	NHL															3	0	2	2	14	0	0	0	10:41
2010-11	Buffalo	NHL	81	8	12	20	142	0	0	1	104	7.7	2	316	41.8	10:57	7	1	0	1	2	0	0	0	8:11
2011-12	Buffalo	NHL	50	1	3	4	56	0	0	0	43	2.3	-7	17	47.1	7:50									
2012-13	Buffalo	NHL	8	0	0	0	10	0	0	0	6	0.0	-2	25	48.0	6:27									
	Rochester	AHL	25	6	5	11	42										3	1	0	1	26				
	NHL Totals		329	18	36	54	458	0	0	4	346	5.2		611	38.8	9:15	14	1	3	4	23	0	0	0	9:47

OHL First All-Star Team (2003)

Signed as a free agent by **Buffalo**, August 1, 2009. • Missed majority of 2012-13 due to recurring upper-body and head injuries.

McDONAGH, Ryan

(muhk-DUHN-uh, RIGH-uhn) **NYR**

Defense. Shoots left. 6'1", 213 lbs. Born, St.Paul, MN, June 13, 1989. Montreal's 1st choice, 12th overall, in 2007 Entry Draft.

Season	Club	League	Regular Season GP	G	A	Pts	PIM	PP	SH	GW	S	%	+/-	TF	F%	Min	Playoffs GP	G	A	Pts	PIM	PP	SH	GW	Min
2004-05	Cretin-Derham	High-MN	28	12	18	30																			
2005-06	Cretin-Derham	High-MN	25	12	33	45																			
2006-07	Cretin-Derham	High-MN	26	14	26	40																			
2007-08	U. of Wisconsin	WCHA	40	5	7	12	42																		
2008-09	U. of Wisconsin	WCHA	36	5	11	16	59																		
2009-10	U. of Wisconsin	WCHA	43	4	14	18	73																		
2010-11	NY Rangers	NHL	40	1	8	9	14	0	0	1	27	3.7	16	0	0.0	18:44	5	0	0	0	4	0	0	0	22:49
	Connecticut	AHL	38	1	7	8	12																		
2011-12	NY Rangers	NHL	82	7	25	32	44	0	0	1	123	5.7	25	2	50.0	24:44	20	0	4	4	11	0	0	0	26:49
2012-13	Barys Astana	KHL	10	0	3	3	6																		
	NY Rangers	NHL	47	4	15	19	22	0	0	1	83	4.8	13	1	0.0	24:21	12	1	3	4	6	0	0	0	25:53
	NHL Totals		169	12	48	60	80	0	0	3	233	5.2		3	33.3	23:13	37	1	7	8	21	0	0	0	25:58

WCHA All-Rookie Team (2008) • WCHA Second All-Star Team (2010)

Traded to **NY Rangers** by **Montreal** with Chris Higgins and Pavel Valentenko for Scott Gomez, Tom Pyatt and Michael Busto, June 30, 2009. Signed as a free agent by **Astana** (KHL), October 9, 2012.

McDONALD, Andy

(muhk-DAWN-uhld, AN-dee)

Left wing/Center. Shoots left. 5'10", 175 lbs. Born, Strathroy, Ont., August 25, 1977.

Season	Club	League	Regular Season GP	G	A	Pts	PIM	PP	SH	GW	S	%	+/-	TF	F%	Min	Playoffs GP	G	A	Pts	PIM	PP	SH	GW	Min
1993-94	Strathroy Blades	ON-Jr.B	7	2	2	4	0																		
1994-95	Strathroy Rockets	ON-Jr.B	50	32	41	73	24																		
1995-96	Strathroy Rockets	ON-Jr.B	52	31	56	87	103																		
1996-97	Colgate	ECAC	33	9	10	19	16																		
1997-98	Colgate	ECAC	35	13	19	32	26																		
1998-99	Colgate	ECAC	35	20	26	46	42																		
99-2000	Colgate	ECAC	34	25	*33	*58	49																		
2000-01	Anaheim	NHL	16	1	0	1	6	0	0	0	21	4.8	0	139	48.9	11:11									
	Cincinnati	AHL	46	15	25	40	21										3	0	1	1	2				
2001-02	Anaheim	NHL	53	7	21	28	10	2	0	3	79	8.9	2	818	53.7	15:59									
	Cincinnati	AHL	21	7	25	32	6																		
2002-03	Anaheim	NHL	46	10	11	21	14	3	0	1	92	10.9	-1	604	56.0	18:31									
2003-04	Anaheim	NHL	79	9	21	30	24	2	1	1	162	5.6	-13	282	54.3	16:34									
2004-05	ERC Ingolstadt	Germany	36	13	17	30	26										10	5	2	7	35				
2005-06	Anaheim	NHL	82	34	51	85	32	13	0	7	229	14.8	24	1095	56.3	16:48	16	2	7	9	10	2	0	0	16:33
2006-07♦	Anaheim	NHL	82	27	51	78	46	8	0	3	252	10.7	16	908	55.4	17:35	21	10	4	14	10	5	0	0	18:37
2007-08	Anaheim	NHL	33	4	12	16	30	0	0	0	79	5.1	-4	392	55.4	16:41									
	St. Louis	NHL	49	14	22	36	32	3	0	1	103	13.6	-17	556	55.8	18:40									
2008-09	St. Louis	NHL	46	15	29	44	24	6	1	1	128	11.7	-13	367	58.0	19:05	4	1	3	4	0	0	0	0	23:35
2009-10	St. Louis	NHL	79	24	33	57	18	6	0	3	191	12.6	-9	447	53.9	18:08									
2010-11	St. Louis	NHL	58	20	30	50	26	5	1	3	180	11.1	18	349	59.3	20:02									
2011-12	St. Louis	NHL	25	10	12	22	2	3	0	2	64	15.6	4	116	56.9	18:32	9	5	5	10	8	2	0	1	20:22
2012-13	St. Louis	NHL	37	7	14	21	16	1	0	2	86	8.1	-2	198	48.0	17:15	6	0	0	0	0	0	0	0	17:32
	NHL Totals		685	182	307	489	280	52	3	27	1666	10.9		6271	55.3	17:35	56	18	19	37	28	9	0	1	18:33

ECAC Second All-Star Team (1999) • ECAC First All-Star Team (2000) • ECAC Player of the Year (2000) • NCAA East First All-American Team (2000)

Played in NHL All-Star Game (2007)

Signed as a free agent by **Anaheim**, April 3, 2000. Signed as a free agent by **Ingolstadt** (Germany), September 17, 2004. Traded to **St. Louis** by **Anaheim** for Doug Weight, Michal Birner and St. Louis' 7th round choice (later traded to Los Angeles, later traded back to St. Louis - St. Louis selected Paul Karpowich) in 2008 Entry Draft, December 14, 2007. • Missed majority of 2011-12 due to head injury at Dallas, October 13, 2011. • Officially announced his retirement, June 6, 2013.

McDONALD, Colin (muhk-DAWN-uhld, KAW-lihn) NYI

Right wing. Shoots right. 6'1", 210 lbs. Born, New Haven, CT, September 30, 1984. Edmonton's 2nd choice, 51st overall, in 2003 Entry Draft.

			Regular Season														Playoffs								
Season	Club	League	GP	G	A	Pts	PIM	PP	SH	GW	S	%	+/-	TF	F%	Min	GP	G	A	Pts	PIM	PP	SH	GW	Min
2001-02	N.E. Jr. Coyotes	EJHL	39	16	20	36	50																		
2002-03	N.E. Jr. Coyotes	EJHL	44	28	40	*68	59																		
2003-04	Providence	H-East	37	10	6	16	47																		
2004-05	Providence	H-East	26	11	5	16	14																		
2005-06	Providence	H-East	36	9	19	28	29																		
2006-07	Providence	H-East	36	13	4	17	30																		
2007-08	Springfield	AHL	73	12	11	23	46																		
2008-09	Springfield	AHL	77	10	12	22	65																		
	Stockton Thunder	ECHL	3	0	2	2	0																		
2009-10	**Edmonton**	**NHL**	**2**	**1**	**0**	**1**	**0**	**0**	**0**	**0**	**3**	**33.3**	**1**	**0**	**0.0**	**6:42**									
	Springfield	AHL	76	12	11	23	38																		
2010-11	Oklahoma City	AHL	80	*42	16	58	63										6	1	1	2	6				
2011-12	**Pittsburgh**	**NHL**	**5**	**0**	**0**	**0**	**0**	**0**	**0**	**0**	**6**	**0.0**	**0**	**0**	**0.0**	**8:28**									
	Wilkes-Barre	AHL	68	14	35	49	41										12	6	7	13	2				
2012-13	Bridgeport	AHL	35	6	21	27	32																		
	NY Islanders	**NHL**	**45**	**7**	**10**	**17**	**32**	**1**	**0**	**0**	**82**	**8.5**	**-1**	**8**	**50.0**	**11:22**	**6**	**2**	**1**	**3**	**2**	**0**	**0**	**0**	**11:57**
	NHL Totals		**52**	**8**	**10**	**18**	**32**	**1**	**0**	**0**	**91**	**8.8**		**8**	**50.0**	**10:55**	**6**	**2**	**1**	**3**	**2**	**0**	**0**	**0**	**11:57**

Hockey East All-Rookie Team (2004) • Willie Marshall Award (AHL – Top Goal-scorer) (2011)

Signed as a free agent by **Oklahoma City** (AHL). July 9, 2010. Signed as a free agent by **Pittsburgh**, July 1, 2011. Signed as a free agent by **NY Islanders**, July 2, 2012.

McGINN, Jamie (muh-GIHN, JAY-mee) COL

Left wing. Shoots left. 6'1", 210 lbs. Born, Fergus, Ont., August 5, 1988. San Jose's 2nd choice, 36th overall, in 2006 Entry Draft.

Season	Club	League	GP	G	A	Pts	PIM	PP	SH	GW	S	%	+/-	TF	F%	Min	GP	G	A	Pts	PIM	PP	SH	GW	Min
2003-04	Tor. Jr. Canadiens	GTHL	31			48											18	14	18	32					
2004-05	Ottawa 67's	OHL	59	10	12	22	35										18	4	7	11	0				
2005-06	Ottawa 67's	OHL	65	26	31	57	113										6	2	2	4	4				
2006-07	Ottawa 67's	OHL	68	46	43	89	49										5	5	1	6	2				
	Worcester Sharks	AHL	4	1	1	2	4										6	0	0	0	8				
2007-08	Ottawa 67's	OHL	51	29	29	58	54										4	2	2	4	4				
	Worcester Sharks	AHL	8	0	2	2	0																		
2008-09	**San Jose**	**NHL**	**35**	**4**	**2**	**6**	**2**	**1**	**0**	**1**	**27**	**14.8**	**-6**	**7**	**85.7**	**8:55**									
	Worcester Sharks	AHL	47	19	11	30	52										6	4	0	4	19				
2009-10	**San Jose**	**NHL**	**59**	**10**	**3**	**13**	**38**	**0**	**0**	**2**	**76**	**13.2**	**-3**	**16**	**43.8**	**10:00**	**15**	**0**	**0**	**0**	**8**	**0**	**0**	**0**	**7:45**
	Worcester Sharks	AHL	27	7	14	21	15																		
2010-11	**San Jose**	**NHL**	**49**	**1**	**5**	**6**	**33**	**0**	**0**	**0**	**63**	**1.6**	**-6**	**11**	**72.7**	**11:35**	**7**	**0**	**1**	**1**	**30**	**0**	**0**	**0**	**6:33**
	Worcester Sharks	AHL	30	9	11	20	27																		
2011-12	**San Jose**	**NHL**	**61**	**12**	**12**	**24**	**26**	**3**	**0**	**0**	**104**	**11.5**	**1**	**3**	**66.7**	**12:33**									
	Colorado	**NHL**	**17**	**8**	**5**	**13**	**11**	**3**	**0**	**2**	**55**	**14.5**	**-4**	**4**	**100.0**	**16:40**									
2012-13	**Colorado**	**NHL**	**47**	**11**	**11**	**22**	**26**	**3**	**0**	**2**	**128**	**8.6**	**-13**	**6**	**50.0**	**17:17**									
	NHL Totals		**268**	**46**	**38**	**84**	**136**	**10**	**0**	**7**	**453**	**10.2**		**47**	**63.8**	**12:26**	**22**	**0**	**1**	**1**	**38**	**0**	**0**	**0**	**7:22**

Traded to **Colorado** by **San Jose** with Michael Sgarbossa and Mike Connolly for T.J. Galiardi, Daniel Winnik and Anaheim's 7th round choice (previously acquired, San Jose selected Emil Galimov) in 2013 Entry Draft, February 27, 2012.

McGINN, Tye (muhk-GIHN, TIGH) PHI

Left wing. Shoots left. 6'2", 205 lbs. Born, Fergus, Ont., July 29, 1990. Philadelphia's 2nd choice, 119th overall, in 2010 Entry Draft.

Season	Club	League	GP	G	A	Pts	PIM	PP	SH	GW	S	%	+/-	TF	F%	Min	GP	G	A	Pts	PIM	PP	SH	GW	Min
2006-07	Waterloo Wolves	Minor-ON	62	41	55	96	42																		
2007-08	Ottawa 67's	OHL	59	3	8	11	25										4	0	0	0	2				
2008-09	Listowel Cyclones	ON-Jr.B	14	10	18	28	10																		
	Gatineau	QMJHL	48	8	22	30	25										10	7	6	13	19				
2009-10	Gatineau	QMJHL	50	27	35	62	50										10	2	5	7	12				
2010-11	Gatineau	QMJHL	42	31	33	64	39										14	5	8	13	17				
2011-12	Adirondack	AHL	63	12	6	18	45																		
2012-13	Adirondack	AHL	46	14	12	26	54																		
	Philadelphia	**NHL**	**18**	**3**	**2**	**5**	**19**	**0**	**0**	**1**	**33**	**9.1**	**0**	**0**	**0.0**	**12:43**									
	NHL Totals		**18**	**3**	**2**	**5**	**19**	**0**	**0**	**1**	**33**	**9.1**		**0**	**0.0**	**12:43**									

McGRATTAN, Brian (muh-GRA-tuhn, BRIGH-uhn) CGY

Right wing. Shoots right. 6'4", 235 lbs. Born, Hamilton, Ont., September 2, 1981. Los Angeles' 5th choice, 104th overall, in 1999 Entry Draft.

Season	Club	League	GP	G	A	Pts	PIM	PP	SH	GW	S	%	+/-	TF	F%	Min	GP	G	A	Pts	PIM	PP	SH	GW	Min
1997-98	Guelph Fire	ON-Jr.B	15	4	3	7	94																		
	Guelph Storm	OHL	25	3	2	5	11																		
1998-99	Guelph Storm	OHL	6	1	3	4	15																		
	Sudbury Wolves	OHL	53	7	10	17	153										4	0	0	0	8				
99-2000	Sudbury Wolves	OHL	25	2	8	10	79																		
	Mississauga	OHL	42	9	13	22	166																		
2000-01	Mississauga	OHL	31	20	9	29	83																		
2001-02	Mississauga	OHL	7	2	3	5	16																		
	Owen Sound	OHL	2	0	0	0	0																		
	Oshawa Generals	OHL	25	10	5	15	72																		
	Sault Ste. Marie	OHL	26	8	7	15	71										6	2	0	2	20				
2002-03	Binghamton	AHL	59	9	10	19	173										1	0	0	0	0				
2003-04	Binghamton	AHL	66	9	11	20	327										1	0	0	0	0				
2004-05	Binghamton	AHL	71	7	1	8	*551										6	0	2	2	28				
2005-06	**Ottawa**	**NHL**	**60**	**2**	**3**	**5**	**141**	**0**	**0**	**0**	**36**	**5.6**	**0**	**0**	**0.0**	**4:14**									
2006-07	**Ottawa**	**NHL**	**45**	**0**	**2**	**2**	**100**	**0**	**0**	**0**	**22**	**0.0**	**-1**	**1**	**100.0**	**3:51**									
2007-08	**Ottawa**	**NHL**	**38**	**0**	**3**	**3**	**46**	**0**	**0**	**0**	**11**	**0.0**	**0**	**0**	**0.0**	**2:52**									
2008-09	**Phoenix**	**NHL**	**5**	**0**	**0**	**0**	**22**	**0**	**0**	**0**	**2**	**0.0**	**-2**	**0**	**0.0**	**5:31**									
	San Antonio	AHL	1	0	0	0	2																		
2009-10	**Calgary**	**NHL**	**34**	**1**	**3**	**4**	**86**	**0**	**0**	**0**	**19**	**5.3**	**3**	**0**	**0.0**	**3:26**									
2010-11	Providence Bruins	AHL	39	4	1	5	97																		
	Syracuse Crunch	AHL	20	6	4	10	56																		
2011-12	**Nashville**	**NHL**	**30**	**0**	**2**	**2**	**61**	**0**	**0**	**0**	**10**	**0.0**	**-1**	**0**	**0.0**	**5:19**									
2012-13	**Nashville**	**NHL**	**2**	**0**	**0**	**0**	**0**	**0**	**0**	**0**	**0**	**0.0**	**0**	**0**	**0.0**	**6:17**									
	Milwaukee	AHL	6	0	0	0	4																		
	Calgary	**NHL**	**19**	**3**	**0**	**3**	**49**	**0**	**0**	**1**	**18**	**16.7**	**-4**	**1**	**0.0**	**7:11**									
	NHL Totals		**233**	**6**	**13**	**19**	**505**	**0**	**0**	**1**	**118**	**5.1**		**2**	**50.0**	**4:15**									

• Missed majority of 2000-01 due to knee injury vs. Kingston (OHL), January 1, 2001. Signed as a free agent by **Ottawa**, June 2, 2002. • Missed majority of 2007-08 as a healthy reserve. Traded to **Phoenix** by **Ottawa** for Boston's 5th round choice (previously acquired, Ottawa selected Jeff Costello) in 2009 Entry Draft, June 25, 2008. Signed as a free agent by **Calgary**, July 11, 2009. • Missed majority of 2009-10 as a healthy reserve. Signed as a free agent by **Boston**, October 11, 2010. Traded to **Anaheim** by **Boston** with Sean Zimmerman for David Laliberte and Stefan Chaput, February 27, 2011. Claimed on waivers by **Nashville** from **Anaheim**, October 11, 2011. • Missed majority of 2011-12 due to upper-body injury vs. St. Louis, February 4, 2012 and as a healthy reserve. Traded to **Calgary** by **Nashville** for Joe Piskula, February 28, 2013.

McINTYRE, David (MAK-ihn-tigh-uhr, DAY-vihd)

Center. Shoots left. 5'11", 194 lbs. Born, Oakville, Ont., February 4, 1987. Dallas' 4th choice, 138th overall, in 2006 Entry Draft.

Season	Club	League	GP	G	A	Pts	PIM	PP	SH	GW	S	%	+/-	TF	F%	Min	GP	G	A	Pts	PIM	PP	SH	GW	Min
2004-05	Newmarket	ON-Jr.A	46	17	14	31	33										16	8	7	15	20				
2005-06	Newmarket	ON-Jr.A	46	42	50	92	143										11	4	8	12	42				
2006-07	Colgate	ECAC	40	9	8	17	75																		
2007-08	Colgate	ECAC	39	15	17	32	38																		
2008-09	Colgate	ECAC	37	21	22	43	54																		
2009-10	Colgate	ECAC	35	11	28	39	60																		
	Lowell Devils	AHL	12	3	2	5	8										5	1	1	2	0				
2010-11	Albany Devils	AHL	78	12	18	30	51																		

			Regular Season														Playoffs								
Season	Club	League	GP	G	A	Pts	PIM	PP	SH	GW	S	%	+/-	TF	F%	Min	GP	G	A	Pts	PIM	PP	SH	GW	Min
2011-12	**Minnesota**	**NHL**	**7**	**1**	**1**	**2**	**2**	**0**	**0**	**0**	**6**	**16.7**	**–1**	**7**	**28.6**	**10:55**	....	....	....	....	....	....	....	....	....
	Houston Aeros	AHL	63	16	17	33	73	....	....	....	....	....	....	....	....	....	4	0	0	0	6	....	....	....	....
2012-13	Houston Aeros	AHL	68	15	18	33	45	....	....	....	....	....	....	....	....	....	5	2	1	3	0	....	....	....	....
	NHL Totals		**7**	**1**	**1**	**2**	**2**	**0**	**0**	**0**	**6**	**16.7**		**7**	**28.6**	**10:55**	....	....	....	....	....	....	....	....	....

ECAC First All-Star Team (2009) • NCAA East First All-American Team (2009) • ECAC Second All-Star Team (2010)

Traded to **Anaheim** by **Dallas** with Dallas' 6th round choice (Andreas Dahlstrom) in 2010 Entry Draft for Brian Sutherby, December 14, 2008. Traded to **New Jersey** by **Anaheim** for Sheldon Brookbank, February 3, 2009. Traded to **Minnesota** by **New Jersey** for Maxim Noreau, June 16, 2011. Signed as a free agent by **Grand Rapids** (AHL), July 25, 2013.

McIVER, Nathan

(muh-KEE-vuhr, NAY-thuhn)

Defense. Shoots left. 6'2", 205 lbs. Born, Summerside, P.E.I., January 6, 1985. Vancouver's 9th choice, 254th overall, in 2003 Entry Draft.

Season	Club	League	GP	G	A	Pts	PIM	PP	SH	GW	S	%	+/-	TF	F%	Min	GP	G	A	Pts	PIM	PP	SH	GW	Min
2001-02	Summerside	MJrHL	47	4	4	8	91	....	....	....	....	....	....	....	....	....	5	0	0	0	9	....	....	....	....
2002-03	St. Michael's	OHL	68	5	10	15	121	....	....	....	....	....	....	....	....	....	19	0	4	4	41	....	....	....	....
2003-04	St. Michael's	OHL	57	4	11	15	183	....	....	....	....	....	....	....	....	....	16	0	1	1	22	....	....	....	....
2004-05	St. Michael's	OHL	67	4	22	26	160	....	....	....	....	....	....	....	....	....	3	0	1	1	13	....	....	....	....
2005-06	Manitoba Moose	AHL	66	1	6	7	155	....	....	....	....	....	....	....	....	....	12	0	0	0	28	....	....	....	....
2006-07	**Vancouver**	**NHL**	**1**	**0**	**0**	**0**	**7**	**0**	**0**	**0**	**0**	**0.0**	**–3**	**0**	**0.0**	**11:20**	....	....	....	....	....	....	....	....	....
	Manitoba Moose	AHL	63	1	2	3	139	....	....	....	....	....	....	....	....	....	2	0	0	0	0	....	....	....	....
2007-08	**Vancouver**	**NHL**	**17**	**0**	**0**	**0**	**52**	**0**	**0**	**0**	**9**	**0.0**	**–8**	**0**	**0.0**	**10:28**	....	....	....	....	....	....	....	....	....
	Manitoba Moose	AHL	43	3	3	6	108	....	....	....	....	....	....	....	....	....	6	0	1	1	11	....	....	....	....
2008-09	**Anaheim**	**NHL**	**18**	**0**	**1**	**1**	**36**	**0**	**0**	**0**	**5**	**0.0**	**2**	**0**	**0.0**	**9:24**	....	....	....	....	....	....	....	....	....
	Manitoba Moose	AHL	28	0	2	2	59	....	....	....	....	....	....	....	....	....	10	0	0	0	10	....	....	....	....
2009-10	Manitoba Moose	AHL	44	1	4	5	109	....	....	....	....	....	....	....	....	....	....	....	....	....	....	....	....	....	....
2010-11	Providence Bruins	AHL	60	0	3	3	176	....	....	....	....	....	....	....	....	....	....	....	....	....	....	....	....	....	....
2011-12	Providence Bruins	AHL	41	1	0	1	68	....	....	....	....	....	....	....	....	....	....	....	....	....	....	....	....	....	....
2012-13	Bridgeport	AHL	62	1	4	5	287	....	....	....	....	....	....	....	....	....	....	....	....	....	....	....	....	....	....
	NHL Totals		**36**	**0**	**1**	**1**	**95**	**0**	**0**	**0**	**14**	**0.0**		**0**	**0.0**	**9:57**	....	....	....	....	....	....	....	....	....

Claimed on waivers by **Anaheim** from **Vancouver**, October 4, 2008. Traded to **Vancouver** by **Anaheim** for Mike Brown, February 4, 2009. Signed as a free agent by **Boston**, July 5, 2010. Signed as a free agent by **NY Islanders**, July 25, 2012.

McLAREN, Frazer

(muh-KLAIR-uhn, FRAY-zuhr) **TOR**

Left wing. Shoots left. 6'5", 230 lbs. Born, Winnipeg, Man., October 29, 1987. San Jose's 8th choice, 203rd overall, in 2007 Entry Draft.

Season	Club	League	GP	G	A	Pts	PIM	PP	SH	GW	S	%	+/-	TF	F%	Min	GP	G	A	Pts	PIM	PP	SH	GW	Min
2002-03	Kelvin	High-MB	56	27	24	51	136	....	....	....	....	....	....	....	....	....	....	....	....	....	....	....	....	....	....
2003-04	Portland	WHL	50	0	3	3	44	....	....	....	....	....	....	....	....	....	1	0	0	0	0	....	....	....	....
2004-05	Portland	WHL	71	6	5	11	124	....	....	....	....	....	....	....	....	....	7	0	0	0	10	....	....	....	....
2005-06	Portland	WHL	70	12	6	18	194	....	....	....	....	....	....	....	....	....	12	0	2	2	27	....	....	....	....
2006-07	Portland	WHL	61	19	12	31	186	....	....	....	....	....	....	....	....	....	....	....	....	....	....	....	....	....	....
2007-08	Portland	WHL	18	4	3	7	45	....	....	....	....	....	....	....	....	....	....	....	....	....	....	....	....	....	....
	Moose Jaw	WHL	48	15	18	33	119	....	....	....	....	....	....	....	....	....	6	1	1	2	8	....	....	....	....
	Worcester Sharks	AHL	4	0	1	1	17	....	....	....	....	....	....	....	....	....	....	....	....	....	....	....	....	....	....
2008-09	Worcester Sharks	AHL	75	7	1	8	181	....	....	....	....	....	....	....	....	....	12	1	4	5	*50	....	....	....	....
2009-10	**San Jose**	**NHL**	**23**	**1**	**5**	**6**	**54**	**0**	**0**	**0**	**13**	**7.7**	**6**	**0**	**0.0**	**6:02**	....	....	....	....	....	....	....	....	....
	Worcester Sharks	AHL	52	4	11	15	148	....	....	....	....	....	....	....	....	....	11	0	0	0	37	....	....	....	....
2010-11	**San Jose**	**NHL**	**9**	**0**	**0**	**0**	**22**	**0**	**0**	**0**	**1**	**0.0**	**–1**	**0**	**0.0**	**4:15**	....	....	....	....	....	....	....	....	....
	Worcester Sharks	AHL	40	2	2	4	71	....	....	....	....	....	....	....	....	....	....	....	....	....	....	....	....	....	....
2011-12	**San Jose**	**NHL**	**7**	**0**	**0**	**0**	**9**	**0**	**0**	**0**	**2**	**0.0**	**0**	**0**	**0.0**	**4:53**	....	....	....	....	....	....	....	....	....
	Worcester Sharks	AHL	20	0	1	1	73	....	....	....	....	....	....	....	....	....	....	....	....	....	....	....	....	....	....
2012-13	Worcester Sharks	AHL	26	0	1	1	87	....	....	....	....	....	....	....	....	....	....	....	....	....	....	....	....	....	....
	San Jose	**NHL**	**1**	**0**	**0**	**0**	**0**	**0**	**0**	**0**	**0**	**0.0**	**0**	**0**	**0.0**	**6:54**	....	....	....	....	....	....	....	....	....
	Toronto	**NHL**	**35**	**3**	**2**	**5**	**102**	**0**	**0**	**2**	**20**	**15.0**	**0**	**11**	**36.4**	**5:09**	**1**	**0**	**0**	**0**	**2**	**0**	**0**	**0**	**7:46**
	NHL Totals		**75**	**4**	**7**	**11**	**187**	**0**	**0**	**2**	**36**	**11.1**		**11**	**36.4**	**5:19**	**1**	**0**	**0**	**0**	**2**	**0**	**0**	**0**	**7:46**

• Missed majority of 2011-12 recovering from off-season hip surgery and as a healthy reserve. Claimed on waivers by **Toronto** from **San Jose**, January 29, 2013.

McLEAN, Brett

(muh-KLAYN, BREHT) **CHI**

Center. Shoots left. 5'11", 185 lbs. Born, Comox, B.C., August 14, 1978. Dallas' 9th choice, 242nd overall, in 1997 Entry Draft.

Season	Club	League	GP	G	A	Pts	PIM	PP	SH	GW	S	%	+/-	TF	F%	Min	GP	G	A	Pts	PIM	PP	SH	GW	Min
1993-94	Notre Dame	SMBHL	71	109	124	233	70	....	....	....	....	....	....	....	....	....	....	....	....	....	....	....	....	....	....
1994-95	Tacoma Rockets	WHL	67	11	23	34	33	....	....	....	....	....	....	....	....	....	4	0	1	1	0	....	....	....	....
1995-96	Kelowna Rockets	WHL	71	37	42	79	60	....	....	....	....	....	....	....	....	....	6	2	2	4	6	....	....	....	....
1996-97	Kelowna Rockets	WHL	72	44	60	104	89	....	....	....	....	....	....	....	....	....	6	4	2	6	12	....	....	....	....
1997-98	Kelowna Rockets	WHL	54	42	45	87	91	....	....	....	....	....	....	....	....	....	7	4	5	9	17	....	....	....	....
1998-99	Kelowna Rockets	WHL	44	32	38	70	46	....	....	....	....	....	....	....	....	....	....	....	....	....	....	....	....	....	....
	Brandon	WHL	21	15	16	31	20	....	....	....	....	....	....	....	....	....	5	1	6	7	8	....	....	....	....
	Cincinnati	AHL	7	0	3	3	6	....	....	....	....	....	....	....	....	....	....	....	....	....	....	....	....	....	....
99-2000	Johnstown Chiefs	ECHL	8	4	7	11	6	....	....	....	....	....	....	....	....	....	....	....	....	....	....	....	....	....	....
	Saint John Flames	AHL	72	15	23	38	115	....	....	....	....	....	....	....	....	....	3	0	1	1	2	....	....	....	....
2000-01	Cleveland	IHL	74	20	24	44	54	....	....	....	....	....	....	....	....	....	4	0	0	0	18	....	....	....	....
2001-02	Houston Aeros	AHL	78	24	21	45	71	....	....	....	....	....	....	....	....	....	14	1	6	7	12	....	....	....	....
2002-03	**Chicago**	**NHL**	**2**	**0**	**0**	**0**	**0**	**0**	**0**	**0**	**1**	**0.0**	**–1**	**19**	**26.3**	**10:47**	....	....	....	....	....	....	....	....	....
	Norfolk Admirals	AHL	77	23	38	61	60	....	....	....	....	....	....	....	....	....	9	2	6	8	9	....	....	....	....
2003-04	**Chicago**	**NHL**	**76**	**11**	**20**	**31**	**54**	**5**	**1**	**0**	**125**	**8.8**	**–11**	**1135**	**51.1**	**17:33**	....	....	....	....	....	....	....	....	....
	Norfolk Admirals	AHL	4	3	3	6	6	....	....	....	....	....	....	....	....	....	....	....	....	....	....	....	....	....	....
2004-05	Malmo	Sweden	38	7	6	13	102	....	....	....	....	....	....	....	....	....	....	....	....	....	....	....	....	....	....
	Malmo	Sweden-Q	9	1	1	2	16	....	....	....	....	....	....	....	....	....	....	....	....	....	....	....	....	....	....
2005-06	**Colorado**	**NHL**	**82**	**9**	**31**	**40**	**51**	**1**	**0**	**0**	**115**	**7.8**	**–7**	**770**	**50.7**	**12:12**	**8**	**0**	**1**	**1**	**4**	**0**	**0**	**0**	**10:40**
2006-07	**Colorado**	**NHL**	**78**	**15**	**20**	**35**	**36**	**0**	**0**	**3**	**134**	**11.2**	**8**	**413**	**50.1**	**13:38**	....	....	....	....	....	....	....	....	....
2007-08	**Florida**	**NHL**	**67**	**14**	**23**	**37**	**34**	**3**	**1**	**1**	**140**	**10.0**	**–5**	**624**	**47.4**	**16:14**	....	....	....	....	....	....	....	....	....
2008-09	**Florida**	**NHL**	**80**	**7**	**12**	**19**	**29**	**0**	**0**	**2**	**114**	**6.1**	**–12**	**456**	**43.2**	**12:26**	....	....	....	....	....	....	....	....	....
2009-10	SC Bern	Swiss	34	13	20	33	24	....	....	....	....	....	....	....	....	....	15	5	7	12	8	....	....	....	....
2010-11	SC Bern	Swiss	50	10	17	27	22	....	....	....	....	....	....	....	....	....	6	3	0	3	6	....	....	....	....
2011-12	Rockford IceHogs	AHL	36	7	14	21	20	....	....	....	....	....	....	....	....	....	....	....	....	....	....	....	....	....	....
	HC Lugano	Swiss	10	5	1	6	4	....	....	....	....	....	....	....	....	....	6	0	3	3	4	....	....	....	....
2012-13	HC Lugano	Swiss	50	13	24	37	44	....	....	....	....	....	....	....	....	....	7	1	7	8	6	....	....	....	....
	NHL Totals		**385**	**56**	**106**	**162**	**204**	**9**	**2**	**6**	**629**	**8.9**		**3417**	**49.0**	**14:17**	**8**	**0**	**1**	**1**	**4**	**0**	**0**	**0**	**10:40**

WHL West Second All-Star Team (1998)

Signed as a free agent by **Calgary**, September 1, 1999. Signed as a free agent by **Minnesota**, July 13, 2000. Signed as a free agent by **Chicago**, July 23, 2002. Signed as a free agent by **Colorado**, July 22, 2004. Signed as a free agent by **Malmo** (Sweden), September 24, 2004. Signed as a free agent by **Florida**, July 1, 2007. Signed as a free agent by **Bern** (Swiss), October 10, 2009. Signed as a free agent by **Chicago**, July 1, 2011. Signed as a free agent by **Lugano** (Swiss), January 18, 2012.

McLEOD, Cody

(muh-KLOWD, KOH-dee) **COL**

Left wing. Shoots left. 6'2", 210 lbs. Born, Binscarth, Man., June 26, 1984.

Season	Club	League	GP	G	A	Pts	PIM	PP	SH	GW	S	%	+/-	TF	F%	Min	GP	G	A	Pts	PIM	PP	SH	GW	Min
2001-02	Portland	WHL	47	10	3	13	86	....	....	....	....	....	....	....	....	....	5	0	0	0	0	....	....	....	....
2002-03	Portland	WHL	71	15	18	33	153	....	....	....	....	....	....	....	....	....	7	1	1	2	13	....	....	....	....
2003-04	Portland	WHL	69	13	18	31	227	....	....	....	....	....	....	....	....	....	5	2	2	4	6	....	....	....	....
2004-05	Portland	WHL	70	31	29	60	195	....	....	....	....	....	....	....	....	....	7	0	3	3	8	....	....	....	....
	Adirondack	UHL	1	0	0	0	0	....	....	....	....	....	....	....	....	....	5	0	0	0	11	....	....	....	....
2005-06	Lowell	AHL	33	4	5	9	87	....	....	....	....	....	....	....	....	....	....	....	....	....	....	....	....	....	....
	San Diego Gulls	ECHL	16	4	5	9	48	....	....	....	....	....	....	....	....	....	2	2	1	3	14	....	....	....	....
2006-07	Albany River Rats	AHL	73	11	8	19	180	....	....	....	....	....	....	....	....	....	5	0	0	0	4	....	....	....	....
2007-08	**Colorado**	**NHL**	**49**	**4**	**5**	**9**	**120**	**0**	**0**	**0**	**60**	**6.7**	**–6**	**3**	**0.0**	**10:07**	**10**	**1**	**1**	**2**	**26**	**0**	**0**	**0**	**12:23**
	Lake Erie	AHL	27	6	7	13	101	....	....	....	....	....	....	....	....	....	....	....	....	....	....	....	....	....	....
2008-09	**Colorado**	**NHL**	**79**	**15**	**5**	**20**	**162**	**0**	**0**	**3**	**118**	**12.7**	**–11**	**5**	**40.0**	**11:35**	....	....	....	....	....	....	....	....	....
2009-10	**Colorado**	**NHL**	**74**	**7**	**11**	**18**	**138**	**0**	**0**	**1**	**117**	**6.0**	**–13**	**13**	**30.8**	**12:56**	**6**	**0**	**0**	**0**	**5**	**0**	**0**	**0**	**11:03**
2010-11	**Colorado**	**NHL**	**71**	**5**	**3**	**8**	**189**	**2**	**0**	**0**	**73**	**6.8**	**–7**	**8**	**37.5**	**9:47**	....	....	....	....	....	....	....	....	....
2011-12	**Colorado**	**NHL**	**75**	**6**	**5**	**11**	**164**	**0**	**0**	**0**	**62**	**9.7**	**0**	**3**	**66.7**	**7:12**	....	....	....	....	....	....	....	....	....
2012-13	**Colorado**	**NHL**	**48**	**8**	**4**	**12**	**83**	**0**	**0**	**0**	**79**	**10.1**	**4**	**17**	**41.2**	**13:05**	....	....	....	....	....	....	....	....	....
	NHL Totals		**396**	**45**	**33**	**78**	**856**	**2**	**0**	**4**	**509**	**8.8**		**49**	**36.7**	**10:41**	**16**	**1**	**1**	**2**	**31**	**0**	**0**	**0**	**11:53**

Signed as a free agent by **Colorado**, July 6, 2006.

McMILLAN, Brandon

(muhk-MIHL-uhn, BRAN-duhn) **PHX**

Left wing. Shoots left. 5'11", 190 lbs. Born, Richmond, B.C., March 22, 1990. Anaheim's 7th choice, 85th overall, in 2008 Entry Draft.

Season	Club	League	GP	G	A	Pts	PIM	PP	SH	GW	S	%	+/-	TF	F%	Min	Playoffs GP	G	A	Pts	PIM	PP	SH	GW	Min
2006-07	Kelowna Rockets	WHL	55	2	10	12	27	....	....	....	....	....	....	....	....	....	....	....	....	....	....	....	....	....	....
2007-08	Kelowna Rockets	WHL	71	15	26	41	56	....	....	....	....	....	....	....	....	....	7	0	0	0	6	....	....	....	....
2008-09	Kelowna Rockets	WHL	70	14	35	49	75	....	....	....	....	....	....	....	....	....	22	0	5	5	20	....	....	....	....
2009-10	Kelowna Rockets	WHL	55	25	42	67	63	....	....	....	....	....	....	....	....	....	12	5	10	15	14	....	....	....	....
2010-11	**Anaheim**	**NHL**	**60**	**11**	**10**	**21**	**18**	**2**	**2**	**2**	**77**	**14.3**	**–5**	**293**	**38.9**	**14:04**	**6**	**1**	**1**	**2**	**0**	**0**	**0**	**0**	**13:08**
	Syracuse Crunch	AHL	16	4	2	6	10	....	....	....	....	....	....	....	....	....	....	....	....	....	....	....	....	....	....
2011-12	**Anaheim**	**NHL**	**25**	**0**	**4**	**4**	**20**	**0**	**0**	**0**	**26**	**0.0**	**–10**	**67**	**34.3**	**11:13**	....	....	....	....	....	....	....	....	....
	Syracuse Crunch	AHL	55	12	18	30	36	....	....	....	....	....	....	....	....	....	4	1	1	2	4	....	....	....	....
2012-13	Norfolk Admirals	AHL	41	8	5	13	42	....	....	....	....	....	....	....	....	....	....	....	....	....	....	....	....	....	....
	Anaheim	**NHL**	**6**	**0**	**1**	**1**	**2**	**0**	**0**	**0**	**2**	**0.0**	**–1**	**26**	**46.2**	**8:45**	....	....	....	....	....	....	....	....	....
	Portland Pirates	AHL	2	0	0	0	2	....	....	....	....	....	....	....	....	....	3	0	0	0	6	....	....	....	....
	NHL Totals		**91**	**11**	**15**	**26**	**40**	**2**	**2**	**2**	**105**	**10.5**		**386**	**38.6**	**12:56**	**6**	**1**	**1**	**2**	**0**	**0**	**0**	**0**	**13:09**

Traded to **Phoenix** by **Anaheim** for Matthew Lombardi, April 3, 2013.

McMILLAN, Carson

(muhk-MIHL-lihn, KAHR-suhn) **MIN**

Right wing. Shoots right. 6'1", 197 lbs. Born, Brandon, Man., September 10, 1988. Minnesota's 5th choice, 200th overall, in 2007 Entry Draft.

Season	Club	League	GP	G	A	Pts	PIM	PP	SH	GW	S	%	+/-	TF	F%	Min	Playoffs GP	G	A	Pts	PIM	PP	SH	GW	Min
2003-04	Crocus Plains	High-MB	STATISTICS NOT AVAILABLE																						
	Brandon	MMHL	4	0	0	0	0	....	....	....	....	....	....	....	....	....	....	....	....	....	....	....	....	....	....
2004-05	Brandon	MMHL	40	17	19	36	34	....	....	....	....	....	....	....	....	....	5	3	4	7	8	....	....	....	....
	Winkler Flyers	MJHL	4	1	1	2	2	....	....	....	....	....	....	....	....	....	....	....	....	....	....	....	....	....	....
2005-06	Calgary Hitmen	WHL	59	3	2	5	42	....	....	....	....	....	....	....	....	....	13	0	0	0	2	....	....	....	....
2006-07	Calgary Hitmen	WHL	72	7	15	22	76	....	....	....	....	....	....	....	....	....	18	2	0	2	17	....	....	....	....
2007-08	Calgary Hitmen	WHL	72	16	26	42	87	....	....	....	....	....	....	....	....	....	16	1	0	1	22	....	....	....	....
2008-09	Calgary Hitmen	WHL	68	31	41	72	93	....	....	....	....	....	....	....	....	....	18	3	8	11	18	....	....	....	....
2009-10	Houston Aeros	AHL	56	4	4	8	70	....	....	....	....	....	....	....	....	....	....	....	....	....	....	....	....	....	....
2010-11	**Minnesota**	**NHL**	**4**	**1**	**1**	**2**	**0**	**0**	**0**	**0**	**5**	**20.0**	**1**	**23**	**39.1**	**9:20**	....	....	....	....	....	....	....	....	....
	Houston Aeros	AHL	78	12	10	22	80	....	....	....	....	....	....	....	....	....	21	3	2	5	14	....	....	....	....
2011-12	**Minnesota**	**NHL**	**11**	**1**	**2**	**3**	**11**	**0**	**0**	**1**	**8**	**12.5**	**1**	**14**	**35.7**	**11:04**	....	....	....	....	....	....	....	....	....
	Houston Aeros	AHL	51	4	8	12	43	....	....	....	....	....	....	....	....	....	4	0	2	2	2	....	....	....	....
2012-13	Houston Aeros	AHL	64	9	9	18	31	....	....	....	....	....	....	....	....	....	4	0	0	0	2	....	....	....	....
	NHL Totals		**15**	**2**	**3**	**5**	**11**	**0**	**0**	**1**	**13**	**15.4**		**37**	**37.8**	**10:36**	....	....	....	....	....	....	....	....	....

McNABB, Brayden

(muhk-NAB, BRAY-duhn) **BUF**

Defense. Shoots left. 6'4", 204 lbs. Born, Saskatoon, Sask., January 21, 1991. Buffalo's 2nd choice, 66th overall, in 2009 Entry Draft.

Season	Club	League	GP	G	A	Pts	PIM	PP	SH	GW	S	%	+/-	TF	F%	Min	Playoffs GP	G	A	Pts	PIM	PP	SH	GW	Min
2006-07	Notre Dame	SMHL	41	5	13	18	72	....	....	....	....	....	....	....	....	....	....	....	....	....	....	....	....	....	....
	Kootenay Ice	WHL	3	0	0	0	0	....	....	....	....	....	....	....	....	....	....	....	....	....	....	....	....	....	....
2007-08	Kootenay Ice	WHL	65	2	9	11	63	....	....	....	....	....	....	....	....	....	10	0	1	1	10	....	....	....	....
2008-09	Kootenay Ice	WHL	67	10	26	36	140	....	....	....	....	....	....	....	....	....	4	0	5	5	2	....	....	....	....
2009-10	Kootenay Ice	WHL	64	17	40	57	121	....	....	....	....	....	....	....	....	....	6	0	4	4	18	....	....	....	....
2010-11	Kootenay Ice	WHL	59	21	51	72	95	....	....	....	....	....	....	....	....	....	19	3	*24	27	37	....	....	....	....
2011-12	**Buffalo**	**NHL**	**25**	**1**	**7**	**8**	**15**	**1**	**0**	**0**	**23**	**4.3**	**–1**	**0**	**0.0**	**17:50**	....	....	....	....	....	....	....	....	....
	Rochester	AHL	45	5	25	30	31	....	....	....	....	....	....	....	....	....	3	0	1	1	0	....	....	....	....
2012-13	Rochester	AHL	62	5	31	36	50	....	....	....	....	....	....	....	....	....	....	....	....	....	....	....	....	....	....
	NHL Totals		**25**	**1**	**7**	**8**	**15**	**1**	**0**	**0**	**23**	**4.3**		**0**	**0.0**	**17:50**	....	....	....	....	....	....	....	....	....

WHL East First All-Star Team (2010, 2011)

McQUAID, Adam

(muh-KWAYD, A-duhm) **BOS**

Defense. Shoots right. 6'5", 209 lbs. Born, Charlottetown, P.E.I., October 12, 1986. Columbus' 2nd choice, 55th overall, in 2005 Entry Draft.

Season	Club	League	GP	G	A	Pts	PIM	PP	SH	GW	S	%	+/-	TF	F%	Min	Playoffs GP	G	A	Pts	PIM	PP	SH	GW	Min
2003-04	Sudbury Wolves	OHL	47	3	6	9	25	....	....	....	....	....	....	....	....	....	7	0	1	1	2	....	....	....	....
2004-05	Sudbury Wolves	OHL	66	3	16	19	98	....	....	....	....	....	....	....	....	....	8	0	2	2	10	....	....	....	....
2005-06	Sudbury Wolves	OHL	68	3	14	17	107	....	....	....	....	....	....	....	....	....	10	0	1	1	16	....	....	....	....
2006-07	Sudbury Wolves	OHL	65	9	22	31	110	....	....	....	....	....	....	....	....	....	21	1	5	6	24	....	....	....	....
2007-08	Providence Bruins	AHL	68	1	8	9	73	....	....	....	....	....	....	....	....	....	10	0	0	0	9	....	....	....	....
2008-09	Providence Bruins	AHL	78	4	11	15	141	....	....	....	....	....	....	....	....	....	16	0	3	3	26	....	....	....	....
2009-10	**Boston**	**NHL**	**19**	**1**	**0**	**1**	**21**	**0**	**0**	**1**	**10**	**10.0**	**–5**	**0**	**0.0**	**10:44**	**9**	**0**	**0**	**0**	**6**	**0**	**0**	**0**	**10:12**
	Providence Bruins	AHL	32	3	7	10	66	....	....	....	....	....	....	....	....	....	....	....	....	....	....	....	....	....	....
2010-11♦	**Boston**	**NHL**	**67**	**3**	**12**	**15**	**96**	**0**	**0**	**0**	**46**	**6.5**	**30**	**0**	**0.0**	**14:52**	**23**	**0**	**4**	**4**	**14**	**0**	**0**	**0**	**13:01**
2011-12	**Boston**	**NHL**	**72**	**2**	**8**	**10**	**99**	**0**	**0**	**0**	**63**	**3.2**	**16**	**0**	**0.0**	**14:57**	....	....	....	....	....	....	....	....	....
2012-13	**Boston**	**NHL**	**32**	**1**	**3**	**4**	**60**	**0**	**0**	**0**	**26**	**3.8**	**0**	**0**	**0.0**	**14:18**	**22**	**2**	**2**	**4**	**10**	**0**	**0**	**1**	**14:47**
	NHL Totals		**190**	**7**	**23**	**30**	**276**	**0**	**0**	**1**	**145**	**4.8**		**0**	**0.0**	**14:23**	**54**	**2**	**6**	**8**	**30**	**0**	**0**	**1**	**13:16**

Traded to **Boston** by **Columbus** for Boston's 5th round choice (later traded to Dallas – Dallas selected Jamie Benn) in 2007 Entry Draft, May 16, 2007.

McRAE, Philip

(muh-KRAY, FIHL-ihp) **ST.L.**

Center. Shoots left. 6'2", 200 lbs. Born, Minneapolis, MN, March 15, 1990. St. Louis' 2nd choice, 33rd overall, in 2008 Entry Draft.

Season	Club	League	GP	G	A	Pts	PIM	PP	SH	GW	S	%	+/-	TF	F%	Min	Playoffs GP	G	A	Pts	PIM	PP	SH	GW	Min
2005-06	USNTDP	U-17	15	1	1	2	0	....	....	....	....	....	....	....	....	....	....	....	....	....	....	....	....	....	....
	USNTDP	NAHL	33	8	8	16	9	....	....	....	....	....	....	....	....	....	10	1	2	3	2	....	....	....	....
2006-07	London Knights	OHL	63	2	8	10	27	....	....	....	....	....	....	....	....	....	16	0	0	0	6	....	....	....	....
2007-08	London Knights	OHL	66	18	28	46	61	....	....	....	....	....	....	....	....	....	4	0	0	0	7	....	....	....	....
2008-09	London Knights	OHL	59	29	31	60	54	....	....	....	....	....	....	....	....	....	14	5	5	10	12	....	....	....	....
2009-10	London Knights	OHL	33	11	26	37	43	....	....	....	....	....	....	....	....	....	....	....	....	....	....	....	....	....	....
	Plymouth Whalers	OHL	19	5	9	14	21	....	....	....	....	....	....	....	....	....	9	6	9	15	11	....	....	....	....
2010-11	**St. Louis**	**NHL**	**15**	**1**	**2**	**3**	**2**	**0**	**0**	**0**	**13**	**7.7**	**–10**	**64**	**53.1**	**9:02**	....	....	....	....	....	....	....	....	....
	Peoria Rivermen	AHL	46	12	14	26	23	....	....	....	....	....	....	....	....	....	....	....	....	....	....	....	....	....	....
2011-12	Peoria Rivermen	AHL	71	23	16	39	26	....	....	....	....	....	....	....	....	....	....	....	....	....	....	....	....	....	....
2012-13	Peoria Rivermen	AHL	45	7	11	18	19	....	....	....	....	....	....	....	....	....	....	....	....	....	....	....	....	....	....
	NHL Totals		**15**	**1**	**2**	**3**	**2**	**0**	**0**	**0**	**13**	**7.7**		**64**	**53.1**	**9:02**	....	....	....	....	....	....	....	....	....

MEECH, Derek

(MEECH, DAIR-ihk)

Defense. Shoots left. 5'11", 205 lbs. Born, Winnipeg, Man., April 21, 1984. Detroit's 7th choice, 229th overall, in 2002 Entry Draft.

Season	Club	League	GP	G	A	Pts	PIM	PP	SH	GW	S	%	+/-	TF	F%	Min	Playoffs GP	G	A	Pts	PIM	PP	SH	GW	Min
99-2000	Wpg. Warriors	MMMHL	36	15	40	55	24	....	....	....	....	....	....	....	....	....	....	....	....	....	....	....	....	....	....
	Red Deer Rebels	WHL	5	1	0	1	2	....	....	....	....	....	....	....	....	....	....	....	....	....	....	....	....	....	....
2000-01	Red Deer Rebels	WHL	60	2	7	9	40	....	....	....	....	....	....	....	....	....	22	0	0	0	9	....	....	....	....
2001-02	Red Deer Rebels	WHL	71	8	19	27	33	....	....	....	....	....	....	....	....	....	13	1	1	2	6	....	....	....	....
2002-03	Red Deer Rebels	WHL	65	6	16	22	53	....	....	....	....	....	....	....	....	....	12	1	1	2	12	....	....	....	....
2003-04	Red Deer Rebels	WHL	62	10	28	38	40	....	....	....	....	....	....	....	....	....	19	4	7	11	10	....	....	....	....
2004-05	Grand Rapids	AHL	78	6	8	14	40	....	....	....	....	....	....	....	....	....	....	....	....	....	....	....	....	....	....
2005-06	Grand Rapids	AHL	79	4	16	20	85	....	....	....	....	....	....	....	....	....	16	0	2	2	4	....	....	....	....
2006-07	**Detroit**	**NHL**	**4**	**0**	**0**	**0**	**2**	**0**	**0**	**0**	**3**	**0.0**	**1**	**0**	**0.0**	**5:47**	....	....	....	....	....	....	....	....	....
	Grand Rapids	AHL	67	6	23	29	40	....	....	....	....	....	....	....	....	....	7	0	1	1	4	....	....	....	....
2007-08	**Detroit**	**NHL**	**32**	**0**	**3**	**3**	**6**	**0**	**0**	**0**	**44**	**0.0**	**–5**	**0**	**0.0**	**12:08**	....	....	....	....	....	....	....	....	....
	Grand Rapids	AHL	6	1	1	2	0	....	....	....	....	....	....	....	....	....	....	....	....	....	....	....	....	....	....
2008-09	**Detroit**	**NHL**	**41**	**2**	**5**	**7**	**12**	**0**	**0**	**0**	**44**	**4.5**	**–12**	**2**	**0.0**	**10:03**	**2**	**0**	**0**	**0**	**0**	**0**	**0**	**0**	**4:04**
2009-10	**Detroit**	**NHL**	**49**	**2**	**4**	**6**	**19**	**1**	**0**	**2**	**57**	**3.5**	**–12**	**0**	**0.0**	**11:55**	....	....	....	....	....	....	....	....	....
2010-11	Grand Rapids	AHL	74	10	27	37	81	....	....	....	....	....	....	....	....	....	....	....	....	....	....	....	....	....	....
2011-12	**Winnipeg**	**NHL**	**2**	**0**	**0**	**0**	**4**	**0**	**0**	**0**	**2**	**0.0**	**1**	**0**	**0.0**	**11:27**	....	....	....	....	....	....	....	....	....
	St. John's IceCaps	AHL	6	0	2	2	0	....	....	....	....	....	....	....	....	....	15	4	5	9	2	....	....	....	....
2012-13	St. John's IceCaps	AHL	46	3	20	23	38	....	....	....	....	....	....	....	....	....	....	....	....	....	....	....	....	....	....
	Winnipeg	**NHL**	**16**	**0**	**1**	**1**	**2**	**0**	**0**	**0**	**5**	**0.0**	**0**	**0**	**0.0**	**14:42**	....	....	....	....	....	....	....	....	....
	NHL Totals		**144**	**4**	**13**	**17**	**45**	**1**	**0**	**2**	**155**	**2.6**		**2**	**0.0**	**11:34**	**2**	**0**	**0**	**0**	**0**	**0**	**0**	**0**	**4:04**

WHL East Second All-Star Team (2004)

• Missed majority of 2007-08 as a healthy reserve. Signed as a free agent by **Winnipeg**, July 2, 2011. • Missed majority of 2011-12 due to lower-body injury.and as a healthy reserve.

MERCIER, Justin
(MUHR-see-uhr, JUHS-tihn)

Forward. Shoots left. 5'11", 190 lbs. Born, Erie, PA, June 25, 1987. Colorado's 8th choice, 168th overall, in 2005 Entry Draft.

Season	Club	League	GP	G	A	Pts	PIM	PP	SH	GW	S	%	+/-	TF	F%	Min	GP	G	A	Pts	PIM	PP	SH	GW	Min
			Regular Season														Playoffs								
2003-04	St. Louis	USHL	60	12	9	21	49	....	....	....	....	....	....	....	....	....	....	....	....	....	....	....	....	....	....
2004-05	USNTDP	U-18	26	1	7	8	31	....	....	....	....	....	....	....	....	....	....	....	....	....	....	....	....	....	....
	USNTDP	NAHL	16	4	3	7	33	....	....	....	....	....	....	....	....	....	....	....	....	....	....	....	....	....	....
2005-06	Miami U.	CCHA	35	3	7	10	32	....	....	....	....	....	....	....	....	....	....	....	....	....	....	....	....	....	....
2006-07	Miami U.	CCHA	40	10	15	25	59	....	....	....	....	....	....	....	....	....	....	....	....	....	....	....	....	....	....
2007-08	Miami U.	CCHA	42	25	15	40	42	....	....	....	....	....	....	....	....	....	....	....	....	....	....	....	....	....	....
2008-09	Miami U.	CCHA	40	14	15	29	58	....	....	....	....	....	....	....	....	....	....	....	....	....	....	....	....	....	....
2009-10	**Colorado**	**NHL**	**9**	**1**	**1**	**2**	**0**	**0**	**0**	**0**	**5**	**20.0**	**2**	**1**	**100.0**	**7:11**	....	....	....	....	....	....	....	....	....
	Lake Erie	AHL	64	13	10	23	54	....	....	....	....	....	....	....	....	....	....	....	....	....	....	....	....	....	....
2010-11	Lake Erie	AHL	80	12	16	28	66	....	....	....	....	....	....	....	....	....	7	3	2	5	2	....	....	....	....
2011-12	Lake Erie	AHL	76	14	11	25	79	....	....	....	....	....	....	....	....	....	....	....	....	....	....	....	....	....	....
2012-13	Wolfsburg	Germany	35	2	3	5	49	....	....	....	....	....	....	....	....	....	12	2	2	4	8	....	....	....	....
	NHL Totals		**9**	**1**	**1**	**2**	**0**	**0**	**0**	**0**	**5**	**20.0**		**1**	**100.0**	**7:11**	....	....	....	....	....	....	....	....	....

Signed as a free agent by **Wolfsburg** (Germany), October 29, 2012.

MESZAROS, Andrej
(MEHT-zahr-ohsh, AWN-dray) **PHI**

Defense. Shoots left. 6'2", 223 lbs. Born, Povazska Bystrica, Czech., October 13, 1985. Ottawa's 1st choice, 23rd overall, in 2004 Entry Draft.

Season	Club	League	GP	G	A	Pts	PIM	PP	SH	GW	S	%	+/-	TF	F%	Min	GP	G	A	Pts	PIM	PP	SH	GW	Min
2002-03	Dukla Trencin Jr.	Slovak-Jr.	33	6	10	16	12	....	....	....	....	....	....	....	....	....	....	....	....	....	....	....	....	....	....
	Dukla Trencin	Slovakia	23	0	1	1	4	....	....	....	....	....	....	....	....	....	....	....	....	....	....	....	....	....	....
2003-04	Dukla Trencin	Slovakia	44	3	3	6	8	....	....	....	....	....	....	....	....	....	14	3	1	4	2	....	....	....	....
	Dukla Trencin Jr.	Slovak-Jr.	5	2	2	4	0	....	....	....	....	....	....	....	....	....	....	....	....	....	....	....	....	....	....
2004-05	Vancouver Giants	WHL	59	11	30	41	94	....	....	....	....	....	....	....	....	....	6	1	3	4	14	....	....	....	....
2005-06	**Ottawa**	**NHL**	**82**	**10**	**29**	**39**	**61**	**5**	**0**	**2**	**137**	**7.3**	**34**	**1**	**0.0**	**18:11**	**10**	**1**	**0**	**1**	**18**	**0**	**0**	**0**	**17:50**
	Slovakia	Olympics	6	0	2	2	4	....	....	....	....	....	....	....	....	....	....	....	....	....	....	....	....	....	....
2006-07	**Ottawa**	**NHL**	**82**	**7**	**28**	**35**	**102**	**0**	**0**	**1**	**147**	**4.8**	**–15**	**0**	**0.0**	**21:41**	**20**	**1**	**6**	**7**	**12**	**0**	**0**	**0**	**20:29**
2007-08	**Ottawa**	**NHL**	**82**	**9**	**27**	**36**	**50**	**6**	**1**	**1**	**160**	**5.6**	**5**	**1**	**0.0**	**21:02**	**4**	**0**	**1**	**1**	**6**	**0**	**0**	**0**	**18:59**
2008-09	**Tampa Bay**	**NHL**	**52**	**2**	**14**	**16**	**36**	**1**	**0**	**1**	**87**	**2.3**	**–4**	**1**	**0.0**	**24:11**	....	....	....	....	....	....	....	....	....
2009-10	**Tampa Bay**	**NHL**	**81**	**6**	**11**	**17**	**50**	**2**	**0**	**1**	**145**	**4.1**	**–14**	**0**	**0.0**	**20:11**	....	....	....	....	....	....	....	....	....
	Slovakia	Olympics	7	0	0	0	4	....	....	....	....	....	....	....	....	....	....	....	....	....	....	....	....	....	....
2010-11	**Philadelphia**	**NHL**	**81**	**8**	**24**	**32**	**42**	**3**	**0**	**2**	**144**	**5.6**	**30**	**0**	**0.0**	**21:07**	**11**	**2**	**4**	**6**	**8**	**0**	**0**	**0**	**26:01**
2011-12	**Philadelphia**	**NHL**	**62**	**7**	**18**	**25**	**38**	**2**	**0**	**2**	**114**	**6.1**	**6**	**0**	**0.0**	**20:40**	**1**	**0**	**0**	**0**	**0**	**0**	**0**	**0**	**19:26**
2012-13	**Philadelphia**	**NHL**	**11**	**0**	**2**	**2**	**2**	**0**	**0**	**0**	**18**	**0.0**	**–9**	**0**	**0.0**	**18:28**	....	....	....	....	....	....	....	....	....
	NHL Totals		**533**	**49**	**153**	**202**	**381**	**19**	**1**	**10**	**952**	**5.1**		**3**	**0.0**	**20:47**	**46**	**4**	**11**	**15**	**44**	**0**	**0**	**0**	**21:05**

WHL West Second All-Star Team (2005) • NHL All-Rookie Team (2006)

Traded to **Tampa Bay** by **Ottawa** for Filip Kuba, Alexandre Picard and San Jose's 1st round choice (previously acquired, later traded to NY Islanders, later traded to Columbus, later traded to Anaheim – Anaheim selected Kyle Palmieri) in 2009 Entry Draft, August 29, 2008. Traded to **Philadelphia** by **Tampa Bay** for Philadelphia's 2nd round choice (Nikita Kucharev) in 2011 Entry Draft, July 1, 2010. • Missed majority of 2012-13 due to shoulder injury vs. NY Rangers, January 24, 2013.

METHOT, Marc
(meh-THAWT, MAHRK) **OTT**

Defense. Shoots left. 6'3", 227 lbs. Born, Ottawa, Ont., June 21, 1985. Columbus' 7th choice, 168th overall, in 2003 Entry Draft.

Season	Club	League	GP	G	A	Pts	PIM	PP	SH	GW	S	%	+/-	TF	F%	Min	GP	G	A	Pts	PIM	PP	SH	GW	Min
2001-02	Kanata Valley	ON-Jr.A	50	3	10	13	22	....	....	....	....	....	....	....	....	....	11	0	1	1	24	....	....	....	....
2002-03	London Knights	OHL	68	2	13	15	46	....	....	....	....	....	....	....	....	....	14	2	4	6	6	....	....	....	....
2003-04	London Knights	OHL	63	2	9	11	66	....	....	....	....	....	....	....	....	....	15	0	3	3	18	....	....	....	....
2004-05	London Knights	OHL	67	4	12	16	88	....	....	....	....	....	....	....	....	....	18	2	1	3	32	....	....	....	....
2005-06	Syracuse Crunch	AHL	70	2	11	13	75	....	....	....	....	....	....	....	....	....	5	0	0	0	8	....	....	....	....
2006-07	**Columbus**	**NHL**	**20**	**0**	**4**	**4**	**12**	**0**	**0**	**0**	**11**	**0.0**	**5**	**0**	**0.0**	**14:38**	....	....	....	....	....	....	....	....	....
	Syracuse Crunch	AHL	59	1	15	16	58	....	....	....	....	....	....	....	....	....	....	....	....	....	....	....	....	....	....
2007-08	**Columbus**	**NHL**	**9**	**0**	**0**	**0**	**8**	**0**	**0**	**0**	**9**	**0.0**	**–1**	**0**	**0.0**	**14:14**	....	....	....	....	....	....	....	....	....
	Syracuse Crunch	AHL	66	7	6	13	130	....	....	....	....	....	....	....	....	....	13	0	6	6	14	....	....	....	....
2008-09	**Columbus**	**NHL**	**66**	**4**	**13**	**17**	**55**	**0**	**0**	**0**	**58**	**6.9**	**7**	**0**	**0.0**	**17:57**	**4**	**0**	**0**	**0**	**2**	**0**	**0**	**0**	**16:15**
2009-10	**Columbus**	**NHL**	**60**	**2**	**6**	**8**	**51**	**0**	**0**	**0**	**42**	**4.8**	**–8**	**0**	**0.0**	**19:31**	....	....	....	....	....	....	....	....	....
2010-11	**Columbus**	**NHL**	**74**	**0**	**15**	**15**	**58**	**0**	**0**	**0**	**58**	**0.0**	**2**	**0**	**0.0**	**19:53**	....	....	....	....	....	....	....	....	....
2011-12	**Columbus**	**NHL**	**46**	**1**	**6**	**7**	**24**	**0**	**0**	**0**	**42**	**2.4**	**–11**	**0**	**0.0**	**20:03**	....	....	....	....	....	....	....	....	....
2012-13	**Ottawa**	**NHL**	**47**	**2**	**9**	**11**	**31**	**0**	**0**	**0**	**53**	**3.8**	**2**	**0**	**0.0**	**22:14**	**10**	**1**	**4**	**5**	**6**	**0**	**0**	**1**	**22:44**
	NHL Totals		**322**	**9**	**53**	**62**	**239**	**0**	**0**	**0**	**273**	**3.3**		**0**	**0.0**	**19:18**	**14**	**1**	**4**	**5**	**8**	**0**	**0**	**1**	**20:53**

Traded to **Ottawa** by **Columbus** for Nick Foligno, July 1, 2012.

MEYER, Stefan
(MAY-uhr, STEH-fan)

Left wing. Shoots left. 6'2", 200 lbs. Born, Medicine Hat, Alta., July 20, 1985. Florida's 4th choice, 55th overall, in 2003 Entry Draft.

Season	Club	League	GP	G	A	Pts	PIM	PP	SH	GW	S	%	+/-	TF	F%	Min	GP	G	A	Pts	PIM	PP	SH	GW	Min
2000-01	Notre Dame	SBHL	50	36	52	88	71	....	....	....	....	....	....	....	....	....	....	....	....	....	....	....	....	....	....
	Medicine Hat	WHL	4	1	1	2	0	....	....	....	....	....	....	....	....	....	....	....	....	....	....	....	....	....	....
2001-02	Medicine Hat	WHL	67	18	22	40	48	....	....	....	....	....	....	....	....	....	....	....	....	....	....	....	....	....	....
2002-03	Medicine Hat	WHL	70	36	16	52	90	....	....	....	....	....	....	....	....	....	11	3	3	6	14	....	....	....	....
2003-04	Medicine Hat	WHL	72	34	41	75	69	....	....	....	....	....	....	....	....	....	19	7	10	17	27	....	....	....	....
2004-05	Medicine Hat	WHL	69	34	43	77	104	....	....	....	....	....	....	....	....	....	13	2	4	6	8	....	....	....	....
2005-06	Rochester	AHL	68	12	16	28	139	....	....	....	....	....	....	....	....	....	....	....	....	....	....	....	....	....	....
2006-07	Rochester	AHL	63	13	9	22	90	....	....	....	....	....	....	....	....	....	6	0	2	2	8	....	....	....	....
2007-08	**Florida**	**NHL**	**4**	**0**	**0**	**0**	**0**	**0**	**0**	**0**	**0**	**0.0**	**–1**	**6**	**50.0**	**2:26**	....	....	....	....	....	....	....	....	....
	Rochester	AHL	70	21	19	40	77	....	....	....	....	....	....	....	....	....	....	....	....	....	....	....	....	....	....
2008-09	Rochester	AHL	65	18	22	40	57	....	....	....	....	....	....	....	....	....	....	....	....	....	....	....	....	....	....
2009-10	San Antonio	AHL	67	10	8	18	86	....	....	....	....	....	....	....	....	....	....	....	....	....	....	....	....	....	....
2010-11	**Calgary**	**NHL**	**16**	**0**	**2**	**2**	**17**	**0**	**0**	**0**	**12**	**0.0**	**0**	**17**	**41.2**	**7:45**	....	....	....	....	....	....	....	....	....
	Abbotsford Heat	AHL	42	12	5	17	50	....	....	....	....	....	....	....	....	....	....	....	....	....	....	....	....	....	....
2011-12	Abbotsford Heat	AHL	6	0	0	0	0	....	....	....	....	....	....	....	....	....	....	....	....	....	....	....	....	....	....
	Farjestad	Sweden	25	1	6	7	40	....	....	....	....	....	....	....	....	....	9	2	0	2	2	....	....	....	....
2012-13	Schwenningen	German-2	39	12	10	22	14	....	....	....	....	....	....	....	....	....	9	1	1	2	12	....	....	....	....
	NHL Totals		**20**	**0**	**2**	**2**	**17**	**0**	**0**	**0**	**12**	**0.0**		**23**	**43.5**	**6:41**	....	....	....	....	....	....	....	....	....

Traded to **Phoenix** by **Florida** for Steve Reinprecht, June 19, 2009. Signed as a free agent by **Calgary**, July 20, 2010. • Re-assigned to **Farjestad** (Sweden) by **Calgary**, December 5, 2011. Signed as a free agent by **Schwenningen** (German-2), August 10, 2012.

MICHALEK, Milan
(mih-KHAL-ihk, MEE-lan) **OTT**

Right wing. Shoots left. 6'2", 225 lbs. Born, Jindrichuv Hradec, Czech., December 7, 1984. San Jose's 1st choice, 6th overall, in 2003 Entry Draft.

Season	Club	League	GP	G	A	Pts	PIM	PP	SH	GW	S	%	+/-	TF	F%	Min	GP	G	A	Pts	PIM	PP	SH	GW	Min
99-2000	C. Budejovice Jr.	CzRep-Jr.	48	16	26	42	42	....	....	....	....	....	....	....	....	....	6	3	1	4	4	....	....	....	....
2000-01	C. Budejovice Jr.	CzRep-Jr.	30	10	13	23	30	....	....	....	....	....	....	....	....	....	4	1	3	4	2	....	....	....	....
	C. Budejovice	CzRep	5	0	0	0	0	....	....	....	....	....	....	....	....	....	....	....	....	....	....	....	....	....	....
2001-02	C. Budejovice	CzRep	47	6	11	17	12	....	....	....	....	....	....	....	....	....	....	....	....	....	....	....	....	....	....
	C. Budejovice Jr.	CzRep-Jr.	5	3	2	5	4	....	....	....	....	....	....	....	....	....	7	5	4	9	14	....	....	....	....
2002-03	C. Budejovice	CzRep	46	3	5	8	14	....	....	....	....	....	....	....	....	....	4	1	0	1	2	....	....	....	....
	Kladno	CzRep-2	....	....	....	....	....	....	....	....	....	....	....	....	....	....	6	2	2	4	16	....	....	....	....
2003-04	**San Jose**	**NHL**	**2**	**1**	**0**	**1**	**4**	**0**	**0**	**0**	**1**	**100.0**	**1**	**0**	**0.0**	**9:05**	....	....	....	....	....	....	....	....	....
	Cleveland Barons	AHL	7	2	2	4	4	....	....	....	....	....	....	....	....	....	....	....	....	....	....	....	....	....	....
2004-05			DID NOT PLAY																						
2005-06	**San Jose**	**NHL**	**81**	**17**	**18**	**35**	**45**	**4**	**0**	**2**	**159**	**10.7**	**1**	**4**	**0.0**	**15:46**	**9**	**1**	**4**	**5**	**8**	**1**	**0**	**0**	**15:11**
2006-07	**San Jose**	**NHL**	**78**	**26**	**40**	**66**	**36**	**11**	**0**	**9**	**191**	**13.6**	**17**	**11**	**18.2**	**16:46**	**11**	**4**	**2**	**6**	**4**	**0**	**0**	**1**	**18:50**
2007-08	**San Jose**	**NHL**	**79**	**24**	**31**	**55**	**47**	**5**	**1**	**8**	**233**	**10.3**	**19**	**10**	**60.0**	**18:05**	**13**	**4**	**0**	**4**	**4**	**1**	**0**	**1**	**17:34**
2008-09	**San Jose**	**NHL**	**77**	**23**	**34**	**57**	**52**	**6**	**0**	**6**	**179**	**12.8**	**11**	**30**	**46.7**	**18:27**	**6**	**1**	**0**	**1**	**2**	**1**	**0**	**0**	**19:22**
2009-10	**Ottawa**	**NHL**	**66**	**22**	**12**	**34**	**18**	**8**	**2**	**3**	**163**	**13.5**	**–12**	**8**	**50.0**	**18:15**	**1**	**0**	**0**	**0**	**0**	**0**	**0**	**0**	**12:08**
	Czech Republic	Olympics	5	2	0	2	0	....	....	....	....	....	....	....	....	....	....	....	....	....	....	....	....	....	....
2010-11	**Ottawa**	**NHL**	**66**	**18**	**15**	**33**	**49**	**1**	**4**	**0**	**167**	**10.8**	**–12**	**13**	**30.8**	**18:04**	....	....	....	....	....	....	....	....	....
2011-12	**Ottawa**	**NHL**	**77**	**35**	**25**	**60**	**32**	**10**	**1**	**3**	**212**	**16.5**	**4**	**6**	**16.7**	**19:33**	**7**	**1**	**1**	**2**	**4**	**0**	**0**	**0**	**21:54**

			Regular Season														Playoffs								
Season	Club	League	GP	G	A	Pts	PIM	PP	SH	GW	S	%	+/-	TF	F%	Min	GP	G	A	Pts	PIM	PP	SH	GW	Min
2012-13	C. Budejovice	CzRep	21	13	11	24	26	....	....	....	....	....	....	....	....	....	....	....	....	....	....	....	....	....	....
	Ottawa	**NHL**	**23**	**4**	**10**	**14**	**17**	**0**	**0**	**0**	**58**	**6.9**	**8**	**4**	**50.0**	**18:11**	**10**	**3**	**2**	**5**	**2**	**0**	**1**	**0**	**17:51**
	NHL Totals		**549**	**170**	**185**	**355**	**300**	**45**	**8**	**31**	**1363**	**12.5**		**86**	**38.4**	**17:48**	**57**	**14**	**9**	**23**	**24**	**3**	**1**	**2**	**18:06**

Played in NHL All-Star Game (2012)

• Missed majority of 2003-04 due to knee injury vs. Calgary, October 11, 2003. Traded to **Ottawa** by **San Jose** with Jonathan Cheechoo and San Jose's 2nd round choice (later traded to NY Islanders, later traded to Chicago - Chicago selected Kent Simpson) in 2010 Entry Draft for Dany Heatley and Ottawa's 5th round choice (Isaac MacLeod) in 2010 Entry Draft, September 12, 2009. Signed as a free agent by **Ceske Budejovice** (CzRep), October 28, 2012.

MICHALEK, Zbynek

(mih-KHAL-ihk, z'BIGH-nehk) **PHX**

Defense. Shoots right. 6'2", 210 lbs. Born, Jindrichuv Hradec, Czech., December 23, 1982.

99-2000	Karlovy Vary Jr.	CzRep-Jr.	40	2	10	12	20	....	....	....	....	....	....	....	....	....	....	....	....	....	....	....	....	....	....
2000-01	Shawinigan	QMJHL	69	10	29	39	52	....	....	....	....	....	....	....	....	....	3	0	0	0	0	....	....	....	....
2001-02	Shawinigan	QMJHL	68	16	35	51	54	....	....	....	....	....	....	....	....	....	12	8	9	17	17	....	....	....	....
2002-03	Houston Aeros	AHL	62	4	10	14	26	....	....	....	....	....	....	....	....	....	23	1	1	2	6	....	....	....	....
2003-04	**Minnesota**	**NHL**	**22**	**1**	**1**	**2**	**4**	**0**	**0**	**0**	**17**	**5.9**	**-7**	**0**	**0.0**	**14:13**	....	....	....	....	....	....	....	....	....
	Houston Aeros	AHL	55	5	16	21	32	....	....	....	....	....	....	....	....	....	2	1	0	1	0	....	....	....	....
2004-05	Houston Aeros	AHL	76	7	17	24	48	....	....	....	....	....	....	....	....	....	5	1	2	3	4	....	....	....	....
2005-06	**Phoenix**	**NHL**	**82**	**9**	**15**	**24**	**62**	**5**	**0**	**2**	**105**	**8.6**	**4**	**0**	**0.0**	**22:50**	....	....	....	....	....	....	....	....	....
2006-07	**Phoenix**	**NHL**	**82**	**4**	**24**	**28**	**34**	**3**	**0**	**0**	**144**	**2.8**	**-20**	**1**	**100.0**	**23:40**	....	....	....	....	....	....	....	....	....
2007-08	**Phoenix**	**NHL**	**75**	**4**	**13**	**17**	**34**	**0**	**0**	**2**	**92**	**4.3**	**9**	**0**	**0.0**	**21:36**	....	....	....	....	....	....	....	....	....
2008-09	**Phoenix**	**NHL**	**82**	**6**	**21**	**27**	**28**	**0**	**0**	**0**	**106**	**5.7**	**-13**	**0**	**0.0**	**22:43**	....	....	....	....	....	....	....	....	....
2009-10	**Phoenix**	**NHL**	**72**	**3**	**14**	**17**	**30**	**2**	**0**	**1**	**104**	**2.9**	**5**	**0**	**0.0**	**22:39**	**7**	**0**	**2**	**2**	**2**	**0**	**0**	**0**	**20:28**
	Czech Republic	Olympics	5	0	0	0	2	....	....	....	....	....	....	....	....	....	....	....	....	....	....	....	....	....	....
2010-11	**Pittsburgh**	**NHL**	**73**	**5**	**14**	**19**	**30**	**1**	**0**	**2**	**104**	**4.8**	**0**	**0**	**0.0**	**21:50**	**7**	**0**	**1**	**1**	**0**	**0**	**0**	**0**	**27:20**
2011-12	**Pittsburgh**	**NHL**	**62**	**2**	**11**	**13**	**24**	**0**	**0**	**0**	**77**	**2.6**	**0**	**0**	**0.0**	**21:39**	**6**	**0**	**1**	**1**	**0**	**0**	**0**	**0**	**21:08**
2012-13	**Phoenix**	**NHL**	**34**	**0**	**2**	**2**	**14**	**0**	**0**	**0**	**42**	**0.0**	**4**	**0**	**0.0**	**21:18**	....	....	....	....	....	....	....	....	....
	NHL Totals		**584**	**34**	**115**	**149**	**260**	**11**	**0**	**7**	**791**	**4.3**		**1**	**100.0**	**22:05**	**20**	**0**	**4**	**4**	**2**	**0**	**0**	**0**	**23:04**

Signed as a free agent by **Minnesota**, September 29, 2001. Traded to **Phoenix** by **Minnesota** for Erik Westrum and Dustin Wood, August 26, 2005. Signed as a free agent by **Pittsburgh**, July 1, 2010. Traded to **Phoenix** by **Pittsburgh** for Harrison Ruopp, Marc Cheverie and Philadelphia's 3rd round choice (previously acquired, Pittsburgh selected Oskar Sundqvist) in 2012 Entry Draft, June 22, 2012.

MIELE, Andy

(MEE-lee, AN-dee) **PHX**

Left wing. Shoots left. 5'9", 175 lbs. Born, Grosse Pointe Woods, MI, April 15, 1988.

2005-06	Cedar Rapids	USHL	52	10	17	27	41	....	....	....	....	....	....	....	....	....	8	0	4	4	4	....	....	....	....
2006-07	Cedar Rapids	USHL	13	7	8	15	15	....	....	....	....	....	....	....	....	....	....	....	....	....	....	....	....	....	....
	Chicago Steel	USHL	45	13	29	42	70	....	....	....	....	....	....	....	....	....	4	2	4	6	14	....	....	....	....
2007-08	Chicago Steel	USHL	29	30	11	41	78	....	....	....	....	....	....	....	....	....	....	....	....	....	....	....	....	....	....
	Miami U.	CCHA	18	6	8	14	4	....	....	....	....	....	....	....	....	....	....	....	....	....	....	....	....	....	....
2008-09	Miami U.	CCHA	41	15	16	31	34	....	....	....	....	....	....	....	....	....	....	....	....	....	....	....	....	....	....
2009-10	Miami U.	CCHA	43	15	29	44	61	....	....	....	....	....	....	....	....	....	....	....	....	....	....	....	....	....	....
2010-11	Miami U.	CCHA	39	24	*47	*71	35	....	....	....	....	....	....	....	....	....	....	....	....	....	....	....	....	....	....
2011-12	**Phoenix**	**NHL**	**7**	**0**	**0**	**0**	**6**	**0**	**0**	**0**	**4**	**0.0**	**-3**	**28**	**25.0**	**8:56**	....	....	....	....	....	....	....	....	....
	Portland Pirates	AHL	69	16	38	54	43	....	....	....	....	....	....	....	....	....	....	....	....	....	....	....	....	....	....
2012-13	Portland Pirates	AHL	70	19	34	53	72	....	....	....	....	....	....	....	....	....	3	1	2	3	15	....	....	....	....
	Phoenix	**NHL**	**1**	**0**	**0**	**0**	**0**	**0**	**0**	**0**	**0**	**0.0**	**1**	**3**	**66.7**	**9:02**	....	....	....	....	....	....	....	....	....
	NHL Totals		**8**	**0**	**0**	**0**	**6**	**0**	**0**	**0**	**4**	**0.0**		**31**	**29.0**	**8:57**	....	....	....	....	....	....	....	....	....

CCHA Second All-Star Team (2010) • CCHA First All-Star Team (2011) • CCHA Player of the Year (2011) • NCAA West First All-American Team (2011) • Hobey Baker Memorial Award (Top U.S. Collegiate Player) (2011)

Signed as a free agent by **Phoenix**, April 2, 2011.

MIETTINEN, Antti

(mih-EHT-tih-nehn, AN-tee)

Right wing. Shoots right. 6', 190 lbs. Born, Hameenlinna, Finland, July 3, 1980. Dallas' 10th choice, 224th overall, in 2000 Entry Draft.

1996-97	HPK U18	Fin-U18	36	24	29	53	34	....	....	....	....	....	....	....	....	....	....	....	....	....	....	....	....	....	....
1997-98	HPK U18	Fin-U18	34	13	28	41	63	....	....	....	....	....	....	....	....	....	....	....	....	....	....	....	....	....	....
	HPK Jr.	Fin-Jr.	8	1	0	1	2	....	....	....	....	....	....	....	....	....	....	....	....	....	....	....	....	....	....
1998-99	HPK Jr.	Fin-Jr.	35	17	22	39	28	....	....	....	....	....	....	....	....	....	3	2	3	5	2	....	....	....	....
	FPS Forssa	Finland-2	4	3	1	4	6	....	....	....	....	....	....	....	....	....	....	....	....	....	....	....	....	....	....
	HPK Hameenlinna	Finland	13	0	0	0	2	....	....	....	....	....	....	....	....	....	4	0	0	0	0	....	....	....	....
99-2000	HPK Jr.	Fin-Jr.	31	24	53	77	28	....	....	....	....	....	....	....	....	....	2	1	6	7	2	....	....	....	....
	HPK Hameenlinna	Finland	39	2	1	3	8	....	....	....	....	....	....	....	....	....	7	1	0	1	0	....	....	....	....
2000-01	HPK Jr.	Fin-Jr.	4	3	10	13	2	....	....	....	....	....	....	....	....	....	....	....	....	....	....	....	....	....	....
	HPK Hameenlinna	Finland	55	13	11	24	20	....	....	....	....	....	....	....	....	....	....	....	....	....	....	....	....	....	....
2001-02	HPK Hameenlinna	Finland	56	19	37	56	50	....	....	....	....	....	....	....	....	....	8	2	4	6	8	....	....	....	....
2002-03	HPK Hameenlinna	Finland	53	25	25	50	54	....	....	....	....	....	....	....	....	....	10	1	7	8	29	....	....	....	....
2003-04	**Dallas**	**NHL**	**16**	**1**	**0**	**1**	**0**	**0**	**0**	**1**	**17**	**5.9**	**-9**	**1**	**0.0**	**9:51**	....	....	....	....	....	....	....	....	....
	Utah Grizzlies	AHL	48	7	23	30	20	....	....	....	....	....	....	....	....	....	....	....	....	....	....	....	....	....	....
2004-05	Hamilton	AHL	35	8	20	28	21	....	....	....	....	....	....	....	....	....	4	1	1	2	6	....	....	....	....
2005-06	**Dallas**	**NHL**	**79**	**11**	**20**	**31**	**46**	**4**	**0**	**1**	**107**	**10.3**	**0**	**1**	**100.0**	**12:06**	**5**	**0**	**1**	**1**	**8**	**0**	**0**	**0**	**12:10**
2006-07	**Dallas**	**NHL**	**74**	**11**	**14**	**25**	**38**	**6**	**0**	**1**	**141**	**7.8**	**-5**	**11**	**18.2**	**14:20**	**4**	**1**	**1**	**2**	**2**	**0**	**0**	**0**	**12:16**
2007-08	**Dallas**	**NHL**	**69**	**15**	**19**	**34**	**34**	**5**	**0**	**3**	**136**	**11.0**	**4**	**23**	**60.9**	**13:59**	**15**	**1**	**1**	**2**	**0**	**0**	**0**	**0**	**9:33**
2008-09	**Minnesota**	**NHL**	**82**	**15**	**29**	**44**	**32**	**4**	**2**	**3**	**186**	**8.1**	**-1**	**60**	**46.7**	**18:17**	....	....	....	....	....	....	....	....	....
2009-10	**Minnesota**	**NHL**	**79**	**20**	**22**	**42**	**44**	**5**	**0**	**4**	**175**	**11.4**	**-2**	**83**	**42.2**	**18:03**	....	....	....	....	....	....	....	....	....
	Finland	Olympics	6	1	0	1	0	....	....	....	....	....	....	....	....	....	....	....	....	....	....	....	....	....	....
2010-11	**Minnesota**	**NHL**	**73**	**16**	**19**	**35**	**38**	**8**	**0**	**4**	**168**	**9.5**	**-3**	**100**	**36.0**	**17:02**	....	....	....	....	....	....	....	....	....
2011-12	Ak Bars Kazan	KHL	20	2	6	8	8	....	....	....	....	....	....	....	....	....	....	....	....	....	....	....	....	....	....
	Winnipeg	**NHL**	**45**	**5**	**8**	**13**	**0**	**1**	**0**	**0**	**58**	**8.6**	**-5**	**21**	**42.9**	**11:42**	....	....	....	....	....	....	....	....	....
2012-13	HPK Hameenlinna	Finland	15	4	4	8	10	....	....	....	....	....	....	....	....	....	....	....	....	....	....	....	....	....	....
	Winnipeg	**NHL**	**22**	**3**	**2**	**5**	**2**	**0**	**0**	**2**	**26**	**11.5**	**-3**	**4**	**0.0**	**12:39**	....	....	....	....	....	....	....	....	....
	NHL Totals		**539**	**97**	**133**	**230**	**234**	**33**	**2**	**19**	**1014**	**9.6**		**304**	**41.1**	**15:03**	**24**	**2**	**3**	**5**	**10**	**0**	**0**	**0**	**10:33**

Signed as a free agent by **Minnesota**, July 3, 2008. Signed as a free agent by **Kazan** (KHL), August 21, 2011. Signed as a free agent by **Tampa Bay**, December 12, 2011. Claimed on waivers by **Winnipeg** from **Tampa Bay** December 12. 2011. Signed as a free agent by **Hameenlinna** (Finland), November 4, 2012. Signed as a free agent by **Fribourg** (Swiss), July 22, 2013.

MIKKELSON, Brendan

(MIGHK-ehl-sohn, BREHN-duhn) **PIT**

Defense. Shoots left. 6'3", 210 lbs. Born, Regina, Sask., June 22, 1987. Anaheim's 2nd choice, 31st overall, in 2005 Entry Draft.

2003-04	Portland	WHL	65	3	12	15	43	....	....	....	....	....	....	....	....	....	5	1	0	1	0	....	....	....	....
2004-05	Portland	WHL	70	5	10	15	60	....	....	....	....	....	....	....	....	....	7	1	2	3	0	....	....	....	....
2005-06	Portland	WHL	3	1	1	2	4	....	....	....	....	....	....	....	....	....	....	....	....	....	....	....	....	....	....
	Vancouver Giants	WHL	19	1	8	9	37	....	....	....	....	....	....	....	....	....	....	....	....	....	....	....	....	....	....
2006-07	Vancouver Giants	WHL	69	6	23	29	60	....	....	....	....	....	....	....	....	....	21	3	7	10	10	....	....	....	....
2007-08	Portland Pirates	AHL	66	6	10	16	50	....	....	....	....	....	....	....	....	....	14	2	6	8	2	....	....	....	....
2008-09	**Anaheim**	**NHL**	**34**	**0**	**2**	**2**	**17**	**0**	**0**	**0**	**19**	**0.0**	**0**	**0**	**0.0**	**13:56**	....	....	....	....	....	....	....	....	....
	Iowa Chops	AHL	31	2	8	10	18	....	....	....	....	....	....	....	....	....	....	....	....	....	....	....	....	....	....
2009-10	**Anaheim**	**NHL**	**28**	**0**	**2**	**2**	**14**	**0**	**0**	**0**	**21**	**0.0**	**-5**	**0**	**0.0**	**15:00**	....	....	....	....	....	....	....	....	....
	Toronto Marlies	AHL	49	7	15	22	43	....	....	....	....	....	....	....	....	....	....	....	....	....	....	....	....	....	....
2010-11	**Anaheim**	**NHL**	**5**	**0**	**1**	**1**	**7**	**0**	**0**	**0**	**4**	**0.0**	**-1**	**0**	**0.0**	**19:24**	....	....	....	....	....	....	....	....	....
	Calgary	**NHL**	**19**	**0**	**1**	**1**	**2**	**0**	**0**	**0**	**10**	**0.0**	**-5**	**0**	**0.0**	**12:52**	....	....	....	....	....	....	....	....	....
	Abbotsford Heat	AHL	4	0	1	1	4	....	....	....	....	....	....	....	....	....	....	....	....	....	....	....	....	....	....
2011-12	**Tampa Bay**	**NHL**	**41**	**1**	**2**	**3**	**13**	**0**	**0**	**0**	**45**	**2.2**	**-4**	**0**	**0.0**	**14:24**	....	....	....	....	....	....	....	....	....
	Abbotsford Heat	AHL	33	3	12	15	29	....	....	....	....	....	....	....	....	....	....	....	....	....	....	....	....	....	....
2012-13	VIK Vasteras HK	Sweden-2	17	3	4	7	20	....	....	....	....	....	....	....	....	....	....	....	....	....	....	....	....	....	....
	Tampa Bay	**NHL**	**4**	**0**	**1**	**1**	**6**	**0**	**0**	**0**	**0**	**0.0**	**1**	**0**	**0.0**	**9:46**	....	....	....	....	....	....	....	....	....
	Syracuse Crunch	AHL	13	0	2	2	6	....	....	....	....	....	....	....	....	....	13	2	0	2	2	....	....	....	....
	NHL Totals		**131**	**1**	**9**	**10**	**59**	**0**	**0**	**0**	**99**	**1.0**		**0**	**0.0**	**14:14**	....	....	....	....	....	....	....	....	....

Memorial Cup All-Star Team (2007)

• Missed majority of 2005-06 due to shoulder and knee injuries. Claimed on waivers by **Calgary** from **Anaheim**, October 19, 2010. Traded to **Tampa Bay** by **Calgary** for Blair Jones, January 6, 2012. Signed as a free agent by **Vasteras** (Sweden-2), October 30, 2012. Signed as a free agent by **Pittsburgh**, July 20, 2013.

MILLER, Drew
(MIH-luhr, DROO) **DET**

Left wing. Shoots left. 6'2", 178 lbs. Born, Dover, NJ, February 17, 1984. Anaheim's 6th choice, 186th overall, in 2003 Entry Draft.

Season	Club	League	GP	G	A	Pts	PIM	PP	SH	GW	S	%	+/-	TF	F%	Min	GP	G	A	Pts	PIM	PP	SH	GW	Min
			Regular Season														Playoffs								
2000-01	Capital Centre	NAHL	37	4	3	7	22	....	....	....	....	....	....	....	....	....	....	....	....	....	....	....	....	....	....
2001-02	Capital Centre	NAHL	54	18	16	34	56	....	....	....	....	....	....	....	....	....	....	....	....	....	....	....	....	....	....
2002-03	Capital Centre	NAHL	11	10	9	19	....	....	....	....	....	....	....	....	....	....	....	....	....	....	....	....	....	....	....
	River City Lancers	USHL	49	14	11	25	22	....	....	....	....	....	....	....	....	....	11	5	4	9	6	....	....	....	....
2003-04	Michigan State	CCHA	41	4	6	10	39	....	....	....	....	....	....	....	....	....	....	....	....	....	....	....	....	....	....
2004-05	Michigan State	CCHA	40	17	16	33	20	....	....	....	....	....	....	....	....	....	....	....	....	....	....	....	....	....	....
2005-06	Michigan State	CCHA	44	18	25	43	30	....	....	....	....	....	....	....	....	....	....	....	....	....	....	....	....	....	....
	Portland Pirates	AHL	....	....	....	....	....	....	....	....	....	....	....	....	....	....	1	0	0	0	0	....	....	....	....
2006-07	Portland Pirates	AHL	79	16	20	36	51	....	....	....	....	....	....	....	....	....	....	....	....	....	....	....	....	....	....
	♦ Anaheim	**NHL**	....	....	....	....	....	....	....	....	....	....	....	....	....	....	**3**	**0**	**0**	**0**	**2**	**0**	**0**	**0**	**7:00**
2007-08	**Anaheim**	**NHL**	**26**	**2**	**3**	**5**	**6**	**0**	**0**	**0**	**30**	**6.7**	**–1**	**9**	**33.3**	**11:11**	....	....	....	....	....	....	....	....	....
	Portland Pirates	AHL	31	16	20	36	12	....	....	....	....	....	....	....	....	....	16	1	7	8	12	....	....	....	....
2008-09	**Anaheim**	**NHL**	**27**	**4**	**6**	**10**	**17**	**0**	**0**	**0**	**45**	**8.9**	**0**	**14**	**21.4**	**12:59**	**13**	**2**	**1**	**3**	**2**	**0**	**0**	**1**	**16:09**
	Iowa Chops	AHL	53	23	15	38	10	....	....	....	....	....	....	....	....	....	....	....	....	....	....	....	....	....	....
2009-10	**Tampa Bay**	**NHL**	**14**	**0**	**0**	**0**	**2**	**0**	**0**	**0**	**10**	**0.0**	**–3**	**2**	**0.0**	**12:14**	....	....	....	....	....	....	....	....	....
	Detroit	**NHL**	**66**	**10**	**9**	**19**	**10**	**1**	**1**	**3**	**93**	**10.8**	**5**	**41**	**34.2**	**12:42**	**12**	**1**	**1**	**2**	**4**	**0**	**0**	**0**	**12:35**
2010-11	**Detroit**	**NHL**	**67**	**10**	**8**	**18**	**13**	**0**	**1**	**2**	**85**	**11.8**	**–2**	**17**	**23.5**	**11:45**	**9**	**1**	**1**	**2**	**4**	**0**	**0**	**0**	**10:17**
2011-12	**Detroit**	**NHL**	**80**	**14**	**11**	**25**	**20**	**0**	**0**	**4**	**131**	**10.7**	**6**	**25**	**20.0**	**12:52**	**5**	**0**	**1**	**1**	**2**	**0**	**0**	**0**	**11:32**
2012-13	Braehead Clan	Britain	23	15	15	30	7	....	....	....	....	....	....	....	....	....	....	....	....	....	....	....	....	....	....
	Detroit	**NHL**	**44**	**4**	**4**	**8**	**2**	**1**	**0**	**2**	**54**	**7.4**	**–8**	**4**	**25.0**	**13:49**	**6**	**1**	**1**	**2**	**2**	**0**	**0**	**1**	**13:13**
	NHL Totals		**324**	**44**	**41**	**85**	**70**	**2**	**2**	**11**	**448**	**9.8**		**112**	**26.8**	**12:35**	**48**	**5**	**5**	**10**	**16**	**0**	**0**	**2**	**12:44**

Traded to **Tampa Bay** by **Anaheim** with Anaheim's 3rd round choice (Adam Janosik) in 2010 Entry Draft for Evgeny Artyukhin, August 13, 2009. Claimed on waivers by **Detroit** from **Tampa Bay**, November 11, 2009. Signed as a free agent by **Braehead** (Britain), October 8, 2012.

MILLER, J.T.
(MIHL-luhr, JAY-TEE) **NYR**

Center. Shoots left. 6'1", 200 lbs. Born, East Palestine, OH, March 14, 1993. NY Rangers' 1st choice, 15th overall, in 2011 Entry Draft.

Season	Club	League	GP	G	A	Pts	PIM	PP	SH	GW	S	%	+/-	TF	F%	Min	GP	G	A	Pts	PIM	PP	SH	GW	Min
2008-09	Pit. Hornets	T1EHL	45	21	21	42	76	....	....	....	....	....	....	....	....	....	....	....	....	....	....	....	....	....	....
2009-10	USNTDP	USHL	29	5	7	12	32	....	....	....	....	....	....	....	....	....	....	....	....	....	....	....	....	....	....
	USNTDP	U-17	17	10	9	19	47	....	....	....	....	....	....	....	....	....	....	....	....	....	....	....	....	....	....
	USNTDP	U-18	1	0	0	0	0	....	....	....	....	....	....	....	....	....	....	....	....	....	....	....	....	....	....
2010-11	USNTDP	USHL	21	3	12	15	48	....	....	....	....	....	....	....	....	....	....	....	....	....	....	....	....	....	....
	USNTDP	U-18	35	12	23	35	38	....	....	....	....	....	....	....	....	....	....	....	....	....	....	....	....	....	....
2011-12	Plymouth Whalers	OHL	61	25	37	62	61	....	....	....	....	....	....	....	....	....	13	2	8	10	18	....	....	....	....
	Connecticut	AHL	....	....	....	....	....	....	....	....	....	....	....	....	....	....	8	0	1	1	2	....	....	....	....
2012-13	Connecticut	AHL	42	8	15	23	29	....	....	....	....	....	....	....	....	....	....	....	....	....	....	....	....	....	....
	NY Rangers	**NHL**	**26**	**2**	**2**	**4**	**8**	**1**	**0**	**0**	**43**	**4.7**	**–7**	**118**	**53.4**	**13:31**	....	....	....	....	....	....	....	....	....
	NHL Totals		**26**	**2**	**2**	**4**	**8**	**1**	**0**	**0**	**43**	**4.7**		**118**	**53.4**	**13:31**	....	....	....	....	....	....	....	....	....

MILLS, Brad
(MIHLS, BRAD)

Right wing. Shoots right. 6', 195 lbs. Born, Terrace, B.C., May 3, 1983.

Season	Club	League	GP	G	A	Pts	PIM	PP	SH	GW	S	%	+/-	TF	F%	Min	GP	G	A	Pts	PIM	PP	SH	GW	Min
2002-03	Fort McMurray	AJHL	62	20	47	67	73	....	....	....	....	....	....	....	....	....	....	....	....	....	....	....	....	....	....
2003-04	Yale	ECAC	27	4	7	11	18	....	....	....	....	....	....	....	....	....	....	....	....	....	....	....	....	....	....
2004-05	Yale	ECAC	27	12	14	26	30	....	....	....	....	....	....	....	....	....	....	....	....	....	....	....	....	....	....
2005-06	Yale	ECAC	22	8	8	16	65	....	....	....	....	....	....	....	....	....	....	....	....	....	....	....	....	....	....
2006-07	Yale	ECAC	20	2	6	8	39	....	....	....	....	....	....	....	....	....	....	....	....	....	....	....	....	....	....
	Lowell Devils	AHL	8	0	1	1	4	....	....	....	....	....	....	....	....	....	....	....	....	....	....	....	....	....	....
2007-08	Lowell Devils	AHL	16	1	2	3	44	....	....	....	....	....	....	....	....	....	....	....	....	....	....	....	....	....	....
	Trenton Devils	ECHL	26	9	7	16	67	....	....	....	....	....	....	....	....	....	....	....	....	....	....	....	....	....	....
2008-09	Lowell Devils	AHL	75	5	16	21	108	....	....	....	....	....	....	....	....	....	....	....	....	....	....	....	....	....	....
2009-10	Lowell Devils	AHL	51	12	7	19	67	....	....	....	....	....	....	....	....	....	2	1	2	3	4	....	....	....	....
2010-11	**New Jersey**	**NHL**	**4**	**1**	**0**	**1**	**5**	**0**	**0**	**0**	**6**	**16.7**	**1**	**17**	**41.2**	**8:16**	....	....	....	....	....	....	....	....	....
	Albany Devils	AHL	53	15	9	24	102	....	....	....	....	....	....	....	....	....	....	....	....	....	....	....	....	....	....
2011-12	**New Jersey**	**NHL**	**27**	**0**	**1**	**1**	**32**	**0**	**0**	**0**	**18**	**0.0**	**–10**	**126**	**61.1**	**7:11**	....	....	....	....	....	....	....	....	....
	Albany Devils	AHL	49	6	16	22	90	....	....	....	....	....	....	....	....	....	....	....	....	....	....	....	....	....	....
2012-13	Utah Grizzlies	ECHL	27	15	20	35	116	....	....	....	....	....	....	....	....	....	....	....	....	....	....	....	....	....	....
	Rockford IceHogs	AHL	33	7	9	16	60	....	....	....	....	....	....	....	....	....	....	....	....	....	....	....	....	....	....
	NHL Totals		**31**	**1**	**1**	**2**	**37**	**0**	**0**	**0**	**24**	**4.2**		**143**	**58.7**	**7:19**									

Signed as a free agent by **Lowell** (AHL), March 16, 2007. Signed as a free agent by **New Jersey**, June 1, 2009. Signed as a free agent by **Utah** (ECHL), October 3, 2012. • Loaned to **Rockford** (AHL) by **Utah** (ECHL), January 14, 2013.

MINARD, Chris
(mih-NAHRD, KRIHS)

Center. Shoots left. 6'1", 205 lbs. Born, Thompson, Man., November 18, 1981.

Season	Club	League	GP	G	A	Pts	PIM	PP	SH	GW	S	%	+/-	TF	F%	Min	GP	G	A	Pts	PIM	PP	SH	GW	Min
1997-98	Owen Sound	OHL	9	0	1	1	1	....	....	....	....	....	....	....	....	....	1	0	0	0	2	....	....	....	....
1998-99	Owen Sound	OHL	43	6	9	15	18	....	....	....	....	....	....	....	....	....	....	....	....	....	....	....	....	....	....
99-2000	Owen Sound	OHL	38	12	14	26	39	....	....	....	....	....	....	....	....	....	....	....	....	....	....	....	....	....	....
	St. Michael's	OHL	28	5	14	19	6	....	....	....	....	....	....	....	....	....	....	....	....	....	....	....	....	....	....
2000-01	St. Michael's	OHL	40	11	8	19	28	....	....	....	....	....	....	....	....	....	....	....	....	....	....	....	....	....	....
	Oshawa Generals	OHL	28	12	12	24	18	....	....	....	....	....	....	....	....	....	....	....	....	....	....	....	....	....	....
2001-02	Oshawa Generals	OHL	67	36	35	71	20	....	....	....	....	....	....	....	....	....	5	2	3	5	6	....	....	....	....
2002-03	Pensacola	ECHL	72	15	17	32	71	....	....	....	....	....	....	....	....	....	4	0	0	0	6	....	....	....	....
2003-04	San Angelo Saints	CHL	64	39	36	75	51	....	....	....	....	....	....	....	....	....	5	1	1	2	2	....	....	....	....
2004-05	Alaska Aces	ECHL	69	*49	29	78	54	....	....	....	....	....	....	....	....	....	15	4	4	8	12	....	....	....	....
	Milwaukee	AHL	1	0	0	0	0	....	....	....	....	....	....	....	....	....	....	....	....	....	....	....	....	....	....
2005-06	Albany River Rats	AHL	37	7	12	19	26	....	....	....	....	....	....	....	....	....	....	....	....	....	....	....	....	....	....
	Alaska Aces	ECHL	33	26	16	42	38	....	....	....	....	....	....	....	....	....	22	*14	5	19	*54	....	....	....	....
2006-07	Lowell Devils	AHL	65	32	17	49	30	....	....	....	....	....	....	....	....	....	....	....	....	....	....	....	....	....	....
2007-08	**Pittsburgh**	**NHL**	**15**	**1**	**1**	**2**	**10**	**0**	**0**	**0**	**9**	**11.1**	**–1**	**0**	**0.0**	**3:53**	....	....	....	....	....	....	....	....	....
	Wilkes-Barre	AHL	56	25	17	42	33	....	....	....	....	....	....	....	....	....	23	11	6	17	10	....	....	....	....
2008-09	**Pittsburgh**	**NHL**	**20**	**1**	**2**	**3**	**4**	**0**	**0**	**1**	**33**	**3.0**	**0**	**2**	**100.0**	**9:25**	....	....	....	....	....	....	....	....	....
	Wilkes-Barre	AHL	54	34	23	57	38	....	....	....	....	....	....	....	....	....	12	6	3	9	12	....	....	....	....
2009-10	**Edmonton**	**NHL**	**5**	**0**	**1**	**1**	**0**	**0**	**0**	**0**	**4**	**0.0**	**–3**	**0**	**0.0**	**9:44**	....	....	....	....	....	....	....	....	....
	Springfield	AHL	40	22	16	38	18	....	....	....	....	....	....	....	....	....	....	....	....	....	....	....	....	....	....
2010-11	Grand Rapids	AHL	79	18	17	35	45	....	....	....	....	....	....	....	....	....	....	....	....	....	....	....	....	....	....
2011-12	Grand Rapids	AHL	39	21	11	32	25	....	....	....	....	....	....	....	....	....	....	....	....	....	....	....	....	....	....
2012-13	Kolner Haie	Germany	52	23	15	38	32	....	....	....	....	....	....	....	....	....	12	3	1	4	18	....	....	....	....
	NHL Totals		**40**	**2**	**4**	**6**	**14**	**0**	**0**	**1**	**46**	**4.3**		**2**	**100.0**	**7:23**	....	....	....	....	....	....	....	....	....

Fred T. Hunt Memorial Award (AHL – Sportsmanship) (2012)

Signed as a free agent by **Albany** (AHL), August 16, 2005. Signed as a free agent by **Pittsburgh**, July 12, 2007. Signed as a free agent by **Edmonton**, July 13, 2009. Signed as a free agent by **Detroit**, July 6, 2010. Signed as a free agent by **Koln** (Germany), July 18, 2012.

MINK, Graham
(MIHNK, GRAY-uhm)

Right wing. Shoots right. 6'2", 225 lbs. Born, Stowe, VT, May 21, 1979.

Season	Club	League	GP	G	A	Pts	PIM	PP	SH	GW	S	%	+/-	TF	F%	Min	GP	G	A	Pts	PIM	PP	SH	GW	Min
1997-98	NMH School	High-MA	25	17	25	42	....	....	....	....	....	....	....	....	....	....	....	....	....	....	....	....	....	....	....
1998-99	U. of Vermont	ECAC	27	4	2	6	34	....	....	....	....	....	....	....	....	....	....	....	....	....	....	....	....	....	....
99-2000	U. of Vermont	ECAC	17	7	4	11	14	....	....	....	....	....	....	....	....	....	....	....	....	....	....	....	....	....	....
2000-01	U. of Vermont	ECAC	32	17	12	29	52	....	....	....	....	....	....	....	....	....	....	....	....	....	....	....	....	....	....
2001-02	Richmond	ECHL	29	8	9	17	78	....	....	....	....	....	....	....	....	....	....	....	....	....	....	....	....	....	....
	Portland Pirates	AHL	56	17	17	34	50	....	....	....	....	....	....	....	....	....	....	....	....	....	....	....	....	....	....
2002-03	Portland Pirates	AHL	71	22	15	37	115	....	....	....	....	....	....	....	....	....	....	....	....	....	....	....	....	....	....
2003-04	**Washington**	**NHL**	**2**	**0**	**0**	**0**	**2**	**0**	**0**	**0**	**0**	**0.0**	**–1**	**1**	**0.0**	**5:32**	....	....	....	....	....	....	....	....	....
	Portland Pirates	AHL	68	18	19	37	74	....	....	....	....	....	....	....	....	....	3	0	1	1	4	....	....	....	....
2004-05	Portland Pirates	AHL	63	18	21	39	86	....	....	....	....	....	....	....	....	....	....	....	....	....	....	....	....	....	....

			Regular Season														Playoffs								
Season	Club	League	GP	G	A	Pts	PIM	PP	SH	GW	S	%	+/-	TF	F%	Min	GP	G	A	Pts	PIM	PP	SH	GW	Min
2005-06	**Washington**	**NHL**	**3**	**0**	**0**	**0**	**0**	**0**	**0**	**0**	**1**	**0.0**	**0**	**0**	**0.0**	**5:32**	....	....	....	....	....	....	....	....	....
	Hershey Bears	AHL	43	21	19	40	50	....	....	....	....	....	....	....	....	....	21	8	13	21	29	....	....	....	....
2006-07	Worcester Sharks	AHL	61	31	32	63	52	....	....	....	....	....	....	....	....	....	6	1	5	6	8	....	....	....	....
2007-08	Worcester Sharks	AHL	71	24	31	55	67	....	....	....	....	....	....	....	....	....	....	....	....	....	....	....	....	....	....
2008-09	**Washington**	**NHL**	**2**	**0**	**0**	**0**	**0**	**0**	**0**	**0**	**4**	**0.0**	**0**	**0**	**0.0**	**8:03**	....	....	....	....	....	....	....	....	....
	Hershey Bears	AHL	68	32	27	59	101	....	....	....	....	....	....	....	....	....	22	7	8	15	16	....	....	....	....
2009-10	Rochester	AHL	67	20	17	37	86	....	....	....	....	....	....	....	....	....	6	3	2	5	23	....	....	....	....
2010-11	Peoria Rivermen	AHL	70	24	26	50	122	....	....	....	....	....	....	....	....	....	4	0	0	0	10	....	....	....	....
2011-12	Hershey Bears	AHL	48	16	26	42	55	....	....	....	....	....	....	....	....	....	5	0	1	1	4	....	....	....	....
2012-13	Providence Bruins	AHL	33	10	8	18	8	....	....	....	....	....	....	....	....	....	7	3	0	3	14	....	....	....	....
	NHL Totals		**7**	**0**	**0**	**0**	**2**	**0**	**0**	**0**	**5**	**0.0**		**1**	**0.0**	**6:15**	....	....	....	....	....	....	....	....	....

Signed as a free agent by **Portland** (AHL), September 30, 2001. Signed as a free agent by **Washington**, April 9, 2002. Signed as a free agent by **San Jose**, July 14, 2006. Signed as a free agent by **Washington**, July 2, 2008. Signed as a free agent by **Florida**, July 10, 2009. Traded to **St. Louis** by **Florida** for T.J. Fast, August 3, 2010. Signed as a free agent by **Providence** (AHL), Janueyary 12, 2013. Signed as a free agent by **Dornbirner** (Austria), August 10, 2013.

MITCHELL, John

(MIH-chuhl, JAWN) **COL**

Center. Shoots left. 6'1", 204 lbs. Born, Oakville, Ont., January 22, 1985. Toronto's 4th choice, 158th overall, in 2003 Entry Draft.

2000-01	Waterloo Siskens	ON-Jr.A	47	15	29	44	33	....	....	....	....	....	....	....	....	....	....	....	....	....	....	....	....	....	....
2001-02	Plymouth Whalers	OHL	62	9	9	18	23	....	....	....	....	....	....	....	....	....	6	1	0	1	4	....	....	....	....
2002-03	Plymouth Whalers	OHL	68	18	37	55	31	....	....	....	....	....	....	....	....	....	18	2	10	12	8	....	....	....	....
2003-04	Plymouth Whalers	OHL	65	28	54	82	45	....	....	....	....	....	....	....	....	....	9	6	6	12	6	....	....	....	....
2004-05	Plymouth Whalers	OHL	63	25	50	75	59	....	....	....	....	....	....	....	....	....	4	1	1	2	0	....	....	....	....
	St. John's	AHL	2	0	0	0	0	....	....	....	....	....	....	....	....	....	....	....	....	....	....	....	....	....	....
2005-06	Toronto Marlies	AHL	51	5	12	17	22	....	....	....	....	....	....	....	....	....	2	0	0	0	0	....	....	....	....
2006-07	Toronto Marlies	AHL	73	16	20	36	46	....	....	....	....	....	....	....	....	....	....	....	....	....	....	....	....	....	....
2007-08	Toronto Marlies	AHL	79	20	31	51	56	....	....	....	....	....	....	....	....	....	19	8	4	12	12	....	....	....	....
2008-09	**Toronto**	**NHL**	**76**	**12**	**17**	**29**	**33**	**2**	**0**	**0**	**98**	**12.2**	**–16**	**669**	**48.7**	**13:48**	....	....	....	....	....	....	....	....	....
2009-10	**Toronto**	**NHL**	**60**	**6**	**17**	**23**	**31**	**1**	**0**	**1**	**90**	**6.7**	**–7**	**477**	**51.2**	**15:49**	....	....	....	....	....	....	....	....	....
2010-11	**Toronto**	**NHL**	**23**	**2**	**1**	**3**	**12**	**1**	**0**	**1**	**28**	**7.1**	**–7**	**149**	**55.7**	**12:31**	....	....	....	....	....	....	....	....	....
	Toronto Marlies	AHL	10	1	4	5	2	....	....	....	....	....	....	....	....	....	....	....	....	....	....	....	....	....	....
	Connecticut	AHL	14	7	5	12	10	....	....	....	....	....	....	....	....	....	6	3	3	6	0	....	....	....	....
2011-12	**NY Rangers**	**NHL**	**63**	**5**	**11**	**16**	**8**	**0**	**0**	**0**	**64**	**7.8**	**10**	**199**	**51.8**	**10:10**	**18**	**0**	**1**	**1**	**2**	**0**	**0**	**0**	**7:05**
	Connecticut	AHL	17	7	7	14	20	....	....	....	....	....	....	....	....	....	....	....	....	....	....	....	....	....	....
2012-13	**Colorado**	**NHL**	**47**	**10**	**10**	**20**	**18**	**1**	**0**	**1**	**72**	**13.9**	**5**	**344**	**49.7**	**16:45**	....	....	....	....	....	....	....	....	....
	NHL Totals		**269**	**35**	**56**	**91**	**102**	**5**	**0**	**3**	**352**	**9.9**		**1838**	**50.4**	**13:48**	**18**	**0**	**1**	**1**	**2**	**0**	**0**	**0**	**7:05**

Traded to **NY Rangers** by **Toronto** for NY Rangers' 7th round choice (Viktor Loov) in 2012 Entry Draft, February 28, 2011. Signed as a free agent by **Colorado**, July 1, 2012.

MITCHELL, Torrey

(MIH-chuhl, TOH-ree) **MIN**

Center. Shoots right. 5'11", 190 lbs. Born, Montreal, Que., January 30, 1985. San Jose's 3rd choice, 126th overall, in 2004 Entry Draft.

2002-03	Hotchkiss School	High-CT	26	19	30	49	33	....	....	....	....	....	....	....	....	....	....	....	....	....	....	....	....	....	....
2003-04	Hotchkiss School	High-CT	25	25	37	62	42	....	....	....	....	....	....	....	....	....	....	....	....	....	....	....	....	....	....
2004-05	U. of Vermont	ECAC	38	11	19	30	74	....	....	....	....	....	....	....	....	....	....	....	....	....	....	....	....	....	....
2005-06	U. of Vermont	H-East	38	12	28	40	34	....	....	....	....	....	....	....	....	....	....	....	....	....	....	....	....	....	....
2006-07	U. of Vermont	H-East	39	12	23	35	46	....	....	....	....	....	....	....	....	....	....	....	....	....	....	....	....	....	....
	Worcester Sharks	AHL	11	2	5	7	27	....	....	....	....	....	....	....	....	....	6	1	1	2	15	....	....	....	....
2007-08	**San Jose**	**NHL**	**82**	**10**	**10**	**20**	**50**	**1**	**2**	**0**	**110**	**9.1**	**–3**	**692**	**49.4**	**14:19**	**13**	**1**	**2**	**3**	**10**	**1**	**0**	**0**	**14:00**
2008-09	Worcester Sharks	AHL	2	1	0	1	0	....	....	....	....	....	....	....	....	....	....	....	....	....	....	....	....	....	....
	San Jose	**NHL**	....	....	....	....	....	....	....	....	....	....	....	....	....	....	**4**	**0**	**0**	**0**	**2**	**0**	**0**	**0**	**9:38**
2009-10	**San Jose**	**NHL**	**56**	**2**	**9**	**11**	**27**	**0**	**0**	**0**	**59**	**3.4**	**6**	**205**	**43.4**	**11:26**	**15**	**0**	**2**	**2**	**2**	**0**	**0**	**0**	**13:05**
	Worcester Sharks	AHL	5	1	2	3	10	....	....	....	....	....	....	....	....	....	....	....	....	....	....	....	....	....	....
2010-11	**San Jose**	**NHL**	**66**	**9**	**14**	**23**	**46**	**0**	**0**	**1**	**116**	**7.8**	**10**	**203**	**48.8**	**13:21**	**18**	**1**	**4**	**5**	**10**	**0**	**0**	**0**	**15:02**
2011-12	**San Jose**	**NHL**	**76**	**9**	**10**	**19**	**29**	**0**	**0**	**0**	**100**	**9.0**	**–6**	**83**	**43.4**	**12:26**	**5**	**0**	**1**	**1**	**6**	**0**	**0**	**0**	**13:02**
2012-13	San Francisco	ECHL	2	1	0	1	0	....	....	....	....	....	....	....	....	....	....	....	....	....	....	....	....	....	....
	Minnesota	**NHL**	**45**	**4**	**4**	**8**	**21**	**0**	**0**	**1**	**39**	**10.3**	**–8**	**42**	**50.0**	**10:30**	**5**	**1**	**0**	**1**	**0**	**0**	**0**	**0**	**11:24**
	NHL Totals		**325**	**34**	**47**	**81**	**173**	**1**	**2**	**2**	**424**	**8.0**		**1225**	**47.9**	**12:39**	**60**	**3**	**9**	**12**	**30**	**1**	**0**	**0**	**13:30**

ECAC All-Rookie Team (2005)

• Missed majority of 2008-09 due to leg injury in training camp, September 18, 2008. Signed as a free agent by **Minnesota**, July 1, 2012.

MITCHELL, Willie

(MIH-chuhl, WIH-lee) **L.A.**

Defense. Shoots left. 6'3", 212 lbs. Born, Port McNeill, B.C., April 23, 1977. New Jersey's 12th choice, 199th overall, in 1996 Entry Draft.

1993-94	Notre Dame	SMHL	31	4	11	15	81	....	....	....	....	....	....	....	....	....	....	....	....	....	....	....	....	....	....
1994-95	Kelowna Spartans	BCHL	42	3	8	11	71	....	....	....	....	....	....	....	....	....	....	....	....	....	....	....	....	....	....
1995-96	Melfort Mustangs	SJHL	19	2	6	8	....	....	....	....	....	....	....	....	....	....	14	0	2	2	12	....	....	....	....
1996-97	Melfort Mustangs	SJHL	64	14	42	56	227	....	....	....	....	....	....	....	....	....	4	0	1	1	23	....	....	....	....
1997-98	Clarkson Knights	ECAC	34	9	17	26	105	....	....	....	....	....	....	....	....	....	....	....	....	....	....	....	....	....	....
1998-99	Clarkson Knights	ECAC	34	10	19	29	40	....	....	....	....	....	....	....	....	....	....	....	....	....	....	....	....	....	....
	Albany River Rats	AHL	6	1	3	4	29	....	....	....	....	....	....	....	....	....	....	....	....	....	....	....	....	....	....
99-2000	**New Jersey**	**NHL**	**2**	**0**	**0**	**0**	**0**	**0**	**0**	**0**	**2**	**0.0**	**1**	**0**	**0.0**	**16:04**	....	....	....	....	....	....	....	....	....
	Albany River Rats	AHL	63	5	14	19	71	....	....	....	....	....	....	....	....	....	5	1	2	3	4	....	....	....	....
2000-01	**New Jersey**	**NHL**	**16**	**0**	**2**	**2**	**29**	**0**	**0**	**0**	**14**	**0.0**	**0**	**0**	**0.0**	**14:52**	....	....	....	....	....	....	....	....	....
	Albany River Rats	AHL	41	3	13	16	94	....	....	....	....	....	....	....	....	....	....	....	....	....	....	....	....	....	....
	Minnesota	**NHL**	**17**	**1**	**7**	**8**	**11**	**0**	**0**	**0**	**16**	**6.3**	**4**	**0**	**0.0**	**20:49**	....	....	....	....	....	....	....	....	....
2001-02	**Minnesota**	**NHL**	**68**	**3**	**10**	**13**	**68**	**0**	**0**	**1**	**67**	**4.5**	**–16**	**0**	**0.0**	**21:25**	....	....	....	....	....	....	....	....	....
2002-03	**Minnesota**	**NHL**	**69**	**2**	**12**	**14**	**84**	**0**	**1**	**1**	**67**	**3.0**	**13**	**0**	**0.0**	**21:28**	**18**	**1**	**3**	**4**	**14**	**0**	**0**	**0**	**24:48**
2003-04	**Minnesota**	**NHL**	**70**	**1**	**13**	**14**	**83**	**0**	**0**	**0**	**58**	**1.7**	**12**	**2**	**50.0**	**22:36**	....	....	....	....	....	....	....	....	....
2004-05			Did not play																						
2005-06	**Minnesota**	**NHL**	**64**	**2**	**6**	**8**	**87**	**0**	**0**	**0**	**48**	**4.2**	**15**	**0**	**0.0**	**20:52**	....	....	....	....	....	....	....	....	....
	Dallas	**NHL**	**16**	**0**	**2**	**2**	**26**	**0**	**0**	**0**	**10**	**0.0**	**4**	**0**	**0.0**	**20:46**	**5**	**0**	**0**	**0**	**2**	**0**	**0**	**0**	**23:21**
2006-07	**Vancouver**	**NHL**	**62**	**1**	**10**	**11**	**45**	**0**	**0**	**0**	**54**	**1.9**	**1**	**0**	**0.0**	**22:13**	**12**	**0**	**1**	**1**	**12**	**0**	**0**	**0**	**27:14**
2007-08	**Vancouver**	**NHL**	**72**	**2**	**10**	**12**	**81**	**0**	**0**	**1**	**65**	**3.1**	**6**	**0**	**0.0**	**23:12**	....	....	....	....	....	....	....	....	....
2008-09	**Vancouver**	**NHL**	**82**	**3**	**20**	**23**	**59**	**0**	**0**	**1**	**88**	**3.4**	**29**	**1**	**0.0**	**22:55**	**10**	**0**	**2**	**2**	**22**	**0**	**0**	**0**	**24:13**
2009-10	**Vancouver**	**NHL**	**48**	**4**	**8**	**12**	**48**	**0**	**0**	**1**	**47**	**8.5**	**13**	**0**	**0.0**	**22:37**	....	....	....	....	....	....	....	....	....
2010-11	**Los Angeles**	**NHL**	**57**	**5**	**5**	**10**	**21**	**0**	**1**	**1**	**59**	**8.5**	**4**	**0**	**0.0**	**21:49**	**6**	**1**	**1**	**2**	**4**	**0**	**0**	**0**	**24:17**
2011-12 ♦	**Los Angeles**	**NHL**	**76**	**5**	**19**	**24**	**44**	**0**	**0**	**2**	**104**	**4.8**	**20**	**1**	**0.0**	**22:14**	**20**	**1**	**2**	**3**	**16**	**1**	**0**	**0**	**25:19**
2012-13	**Los Angeles**	**NHL**	Did not play – injured																						
	NHL Totals		**719**	**29**	**124**	**153**	**686**	**0**	**2**	**8**	**699**	**4.1**		**4**	**25.0**	**21:55**	**71**	**3**	**9**	**12**	**70**	**1**	**0**	**0**	**25:08**

SJHL First All-Star Team (1997) • SJHL Top Defenseman Award (1997) • ECAC Second All-Star Team (1998) • ECAC Rookie of the Year (1998) (co-winner - Erik Cole) • ECAC First All-Star Team (1999) • NCAA East Second All-American Team (1999)

Traded to **Minnesota** by **New Jersey** for Sean O'Donnell, March 4, 2001. Traded to **Dallas** by **Minnesota** with Minnesota's 2nd round choice (Nico Saccheti) in 2007 Entry Draft for Martin Skoula and Shawn Belle, March 9, 2006. Signed as a free agent by **Vancouver**, July 1, 2006. Signed as a free agent by **Los Angeles**, August 25, 2010. • Missed 2012-13 due to recurring knee injury and resulting surgery, January 18, 2013.

MOEN, Travis

(MOH-ehn, TRA-vihs) **MTL**

Left wing. Shoots left. 6'2", 215 lbs. Born, Stewart Valley, Sask., April 6, 1982. Calgary's 6th choice, 155th overall, in 2000 Entry Draft.

1998-99	Swift Current	SMHL	Statistics not available																						
	Kelowna Rockets	WHL	4	0	0	0	0	....	....	....	....	....	....	....	....	....	....	....	....	....	....	....	....	....	....
99-2000	Kelowna Rockets	WHL	66	9	6	15	96	....	....	....	....	....	....	....	....	....	5	1	1	2	2	....	....	....	....
2000-01	Kelowna Rockets	WHL	40	8	8	16	106	....	....	....	....	....	....	....	....	....	....	....	....	....	....	....	....	....	....
2001-02	Kelowna Rockets	WHL	71	10	17	27	197	....	....	....	....	....	....	....	....	....	13	1	0	1	28	....	....	....	....
2002-03	Norfolk Admirals	AHL	42	1	2	3	62	....	....	....	....	....	....	....	....	....	9	0	0	0	20	....	....	....	....
2003-04	**Chicago**	**NHL**	**82**	**4**	**2**	**6**	**142**	**0**	**0**	**2**	**51**	**7.8**	**–17**	**19**	**15.8**	**10:57**	....	....	....	....	....	....	....	....	....
2004-05	Norfolk Admirals	AHL	79	8	12	20	187	....	....	....	....	....	....	....	....	....	6	0	1	1	6	....	....	....	....
2005-06	**Anaheim**	**NHL**	**39**	**4**	**1**	**5**	**72**	**0**	**0**	**0**	**28**	**14.3**	**–3**	**8**	**12.5**	**11:03**	**9**	**1**	**0**	**1**	**10**	**0**	**0**	**0**	**8:25**
2006-07 ♦	**Anaheim**	**NHL**	**82**	**11**	**10**	**21**	**101**	**0**	**0**	**0**	**124**	**8.9**	**–4**	**10**	**30.0**	**14:48**	**21**	**7**	**5**	**12**	**22**	**0**	**0**	**3**	**17:19**
2007-08	**Anaheim**	**NHL**	**77**	**3**	**5**	**8**	**81**	**0**	**1**	**1**	**98**	**3.1**	**–10**	**25**	**32.0**	**15:50**	**6**	**1**	**1**	**2**	**2**	**0**	**0**	**0**	**14:09**
2008-09	**Anaheim**	**NHL**	**63**	**4**	**7**	**11**	**77**	**0**	**2**	**1**	**77**	**5.2**	**–17**	**7**	**28.6**	**14:53**	....	....	....	....	....	....	....	....	....
	San Jose	**NHL**	**19**	**3**	**2**	**5**	**14**	**0**	**1**	**1**	**24**	**12.5**	**–1**	**11**	**18.2**	**15:21**	**6**	**0**	**0**	**0**	**2**	**0**	**0**	**0**	**12:54**

			Regular Season														Playoffs								
Season	Club	League	GP	G	A	Pts	PIM	PP	SH	GW	S	%	+/-	TF	F%	Min	GP	G	A	Pts	PIM	PP	SH	GW	Min
2009-10	Montreal	NHL	81	8	11	19	57	1	2	0	107	7.5	–2	12	25.0	15:00	19	2	1	3	4	0	1	1	13:15
2010-11	Montreal	NHL	79	6	10	16	96	0	1	0	99	6.1	–4	22	36.4	13:11	7	0	1	1	2	0	0	0	16:33
2011-12	Montreal	NHL	48	9	7	16	41	0	1	0	45	20.0	–3	12	41.7	15:43	....	....	....	....	....	....	....	....	....
2012-13	Montreal	NHL	45	2	4	6	32	0	0	0	32	6.3	–4	10	40.0	11:39	5	0	0	0	17	0	0	0	12:53
	NHL Totals		615	54	59	113	713	1	8	5	685	7.9		136	28.7	13:52	73	11	8	19	59	0	1	4	14:09

Signed as a free agent by **Chicago**, October 21, 2002. Traded to **Anaheim** by **Chicago** for Michael Holmqvist, July 30, 2005. • Missed majority of 2005-06 due to knee and shoulder injuries and as a healthy reserve. Traded to **San Jose** by **Anaheim** with Kent Huskins for Timo Pielmeier, Nick Bonino and San Jose's 4th round choice (Andrew O'Brien) in 2012 Entry Draft, March 4, 2009. Signed as a free agent by **Montreal**, July 10, 2009.

MOLLER, Oscar

(MOH-luhr, AH-skuhr) **L.A.**

Center. Shoots right. 5'10", 189 lbs. Born, Stockholm, Sweden, January 22, 1989. Los Angeles' 2nd choice, 52nd overall, in 2007 Entry Draft.

Season	Club	League	GP	G	A	Pts	PIM	PP	SH	GW	S	%	+/-	TF	F%	Min	GP	G	A	Pts	PIM	PP	SH	GW	Min
2003-04	Spanga U18	Swe-U18	32	28	12	40	68	....	....	....	....	....	....	....	....	....	....	....	....	....	....	....	....	....	....
2004-05	Spanga U18	Swe-U18	24	28	16	44	52	....	....	....	....	....	....	....	....	....	....	....	....	....	....	....	....	....	....
	Spanga Jr.	Swe-Jr.	4	6	1	7	6	....	....	....	....	....	....	....	....	....	....	....	....	....	....	....	....	....	....
	Spanga	Sweden-4	6	6	4	10	0	....	....	....	....	....	....	....	....	....	....	....	....	....	....	....	....	....	....
2005-06	Djurgarden U18	Swe-U18	8	8	5	13	6	....	....	....	....	....	....	....	....	....	2	1	0	1	0	....	....	....	....
	Djurgarden Jr.	Swe-Jr.	25	8	5	13	41	....	....	....	....	....	....	....	....	....	4	2	0	2	0	....	....	....	....
2006-07	Chilliwack Bruins	WHL	68	32	37	69	50	....	....	....	....	....	....	....	....	....	5	0	3	3	6	....	....	....	....
2007-08	Chilliwack Bruins	WHL	63	39	43	82	42	....	....	....	....	....	....	....	....	....	4	2	1	3	4	....	....	....	....
	Manchester	AHL	....	....	....	....	....	....	....	....	....	....	....	....	....	....	2	0	1	1	0	....	....	....	....
2008-09	**Los Angeles**	**NHL**	**40**	**7**	**8**	**15**	**16**	**5**	**0**	**0**	**81**	**8.6**	**–3**	**86**	**43.0**	**13:22**	....	....	....	....	....	....	....	....	....
	Manchester	AHL	8	2	3	5	6	....	....	....	....	....	....	....	....	....	....	....	....	....	....	....	....	....	....
2009-10	**Los Angeles**	**NHL**	**34**	**4**	**3**	**7**	**4**	**1**	**0**	**0**	**42**	**9.5**	**–6**	**104**	**30.8**	**8:35**	....	....	....	....	....	....	....	....	....
	Manchester	AHL	43	15	18	33	20	....	....	....	....	....	....	....	....	....	16	2	5	7	0	....	....	....	....
2010-11	**Los Angeles**	**NHL**	**13**	**1**	**3**	**4**	**2**	**0**	**0**	**0**	**27**	**3.7**	**–1**	**5**	**80.0**	**14:36**	**1**	**0**	**0**	**0**	**0**	**0**	**0**	**0**	**10:37**
	Manchester	AHL	59	23	27	50	34	....	....	....	....	....	....	....	....	....	....	....	....	....	....	....	....	....	....
2011-12	Skelleftea AIK	Sweden	54	14	17	31	6	....	....	....	....	....	....	....	....	....	19	7	8	15	8	....	....	....	....
2012-13	Skelleftea AIK	Sweden	28	18	8	26	2	....	....	....	....	....	....	....	....	....	13	5	5	10	2	....	....	....	....
	NHL Totals		**87**	**12**	**14**	**26**	**22**	**6**	**0**	**0**	**150**	**8.0**		**195**	**37.4**	**11:41**	**1**	**0**	**0**	**0**	**0**	**0**	**0**	**0**	**10:37**

WHL West First All-Star Team (2008)

Signed as a free agent by **Skelleftea** (Sweden), May 17, 2011.

MONTADOR, Steve

(MAWN-tuh-dohr, STEEV)

Defense. Shoots right. 6', 210 lbs. Born, Vancouver, B.C., December 21, 1979.

Season	Club	League	GP	G	A	Pts	PIM	PP	SH	GW	S	%	+/-	TF	F%	Min	GP	G	A	Pts	PIM	PP	SH	GW	Min
1995-96	St. Mike's B's	ON-Jr.A	46	3	16	19	145	....	....	....	....	....	....	....	....	....	7	1	2	3	10	....	....	....	....
1996-97	North Bay	OHL	63	7	28	35	129	....	....	....	....	....	....	....	....	....	....	....	....	....	....	....	....	....	....
1997-98	North Bay	OHL	37	5	16	21	54	....	....	....	....	....	....	....	....	....	....	....	....	....	....	....	....	....	....
	Erie Otters	OHL	26	3	17	20	35	....	....	....	....	....	....	....	....	....	7	1	1	2	9	....	....	....	....
1998-99	Erie Otters	OHL	61	9	33	42	114	....	....	....	....	....	....	....	....	....	5	0	2	2	4	....	....	....	....
99-2000	Peterborough	OHL	64	14	42	56	97	....	....	....	....	....	....	....	....	....	5	0	2	2	4	....	....	....	....
	Saint John Flames	AHL	....	....	....	....	....	....	....	....	....	....	....	....	....	....	2	0	0	0	0	....	....	....	....
2000-01	Saint John Flames	AHL	58	1	6	7	95	....	....	....	....	....	....	....	....	....	19	0	8	8	13	....	....	....	....
2001-02	**Calgary**	**NHL**	**11**	**1**	**2**	**3**	**26**	**0**	**0**	**0**	**10**	**10.0**	**–2**	**0**	**0.0**	**12:12**	....	....	....	....	....	....	....	....	....
	Saint John Flames	AHL	67	9	16	25	107	....	....	....	....	....	....	....	....	....	....	....	....	....	....	....	....	....	....
2002-03	**Calgary**	**NHL**	**50**	**1**	**1**	**2**	**114**	**0**	**0**	**0**	**64**	**1.6**	**–9**	**0**	**0.0**	**15:11**	....	....	....	....	....	....	....	....	....
	Saint John Flames	AHL	11	1	7	8	20	....	....	....	....	....	....	....	....	....	....	....	....	....	....	....	....	....	....
2003-04	**Calgary**	**NHL**	**26**	**1**	**2**	**3**	**50**	**0**	**0**	**1**	**31**	**3.2**	**–1**	**1**	**0.0**	**11:46**	**20**	**1**	**2**	**3**	**6**	**0**	**0**	**1**	**17:43**
2004-05	HC Mulhouse	France	15	1	7	8	69	....	....	....	....	....	....	....	....	....	....	....	....	....	....	....	....	....	....
2005-06	**Calgary**	**NHL**	**7**	**1**	**0**	**1**	**11**	**0**	**0**	**0**	**13**	**7.7**	**0**	**0**	**0.0**	**11:49**	....	....	....	....	....	....	....	....	....
	Florida	**NHL**	**51**	**1**	**5**	**6**	**68**	**0**	**0**	**0**	**42**	**2.4**	**4**	**0**	**0.0**	**14:04**	....	....	....	....	....	....	....	....	....
2006-07	**Florida**	**NHL**	**72**	**1**	**8**	**9**	**119**	**0**	**0**	**0**	**88**	**1.1**	**1**	**0**	**0.0**	**13:08**	....	....	....	....	....	....	....	....	....
2007-08	**Florida**	**NHL**	**73**	**8**	**15**	**23**	**73**	**2**	**0**	**0**	**96**	**8.3**	**1**	**0**	**0.0**	**11:39**	....	....	....	....	....	....	....	....	....
2008-09	**Anaheim**	**NHL**	**65**	**4**	**16**	**20**	**125**	**0**	**0**	**0**	**100**	**4.0**	**14**	**0**	**0.0**	**16:12**	....	....	....	....	....	....	....	....	....
	Boston	**NHL**	**13**	**0**	**1**	**1**	**18**	**0**	**0**	**0**	**17**	**0.0**	**3**	**1**	**0.0**	**15:55**	**11**	**1**	**2**	**3**	**18**	**0**	**0**	**0**	**19:33**
2009-10	**Buffalo**	**NHL**	**78**	**5**	**18**	**23**	**75**	**0**	**0**	**2**	**134**	**3.7**	**0**	**1**	**0.0**	**17:06**	**6**	**1**	**0**	**1**	**4**	**0**	**0**	**0**	**23:54**
2010-11	**Buffalo**	**NHL**	**73**	**5**	**21**	**26**	**83**	**0**	**0**	**0**	**118**	**4.2**	**16**	**1**	**0.0**	**19:43**	**6**	**0**	**1**	**1**	**8**	**0**	**0**	**0**	**15:45**
2011-12	**Chicago**	**NHL**	**52**	**5**	**9**	**14**	**45**	**2**	**0**	**1**	**57**	**8.8**	**4**	**0**	**0.0**	**14:46**	....	....	....	....	....	....	....	....	....
2012-13	Rockford IceHogs	AHL	14	2	3	5	13	....	....	....	....	....	....	....	....	....	....	....	....	....	....	....	....	....	....
	NHL Totals		**571**	**33**	**98**	**131**	**807**	**4**	**0**	**4**	**770**	**4.3**		**4**	**0.0**	**15:03**	**43**	**3**	**5**	**8**	**36**	**0**	**0**	**1**	**18:47**

Signed as a free agent by **Calgary**, April 10, 2000. • Missed majority of 2003-04 as a healthy reserve. Signed as a free agent by **Mulhouse** (France), September 17, 2004. Traded to **Florida** by **Calgary** with Dustin Johner for Kristian Huselius, December 2, 2005. Signed as a free agent by **Anaheim**, July 11, 2008. Traded to **Boston** by **Anaheim** for Petteri Nokelainen, March 4, 2009. Signed as a free agent by **Buffalo**, July 1, 2009. Traded to **Chicago** by **Buffalo** for Florida's 7th round choice (previously acquired, Buffalo selected Judd Petersen) in 2012 Entry Draft, June 29, 2011. • Missed majority of 2012-13 due to head injury vs. Nashville, March 31, 2012. Signed as a free agent by **Zagreb** (KHL), August 11, 2013.

MOORE, Dominic

(MOOR, DOHM-ihn-ihk) **NYR**

Center. Shoots left. 6', 192 lbs. Born, Sarnia, Ont., August 3, 1980. NY Rangers' 2nd choice, 95th overall, in 2000 Entry Draft.

Season	Club	League	GP	G	A	Pts	PIM	PP	SH	GW	S	%	+/-	TF	F%	Min	GP	G	A	Pts	PIM	PP	SH	GW	Min
1996-97	Thornhill Rattlers	ON-Jr.A	29	4	6	10	48	....	....	....	....	....	....	....	....	....	1	0	1	1	0	....	....	....	....
1997-98	Aurora Tigers	ON-Jr.A	51	10	15	25	16	....	....	....	....	....	....	....	....	....	....	....	....	....	....	....	....	....	....
1998-99	Aurora Tigers	ON-Jr.A	51	34	53	87	70	....	....	....	....	....	....	....	....	....	....	....	....	....	....	....	....	....	....
99-2000	Harvard Crimson	ECAC	30	12	12	24	28	....	....	....	....	....	....	....	....	....	....	....	....	....	....	....	....	....	....
2000-01	Harvard Crimson	ECAC	32	15	28	43	40	....	....	....	....	....	....	....	....	....	....	....	....	....	....	....	....	....	....
2001-02	Harvard Crimson	ECAC	32	13	16	29	37	....	....	....	....	....	....	....	....	....	....	....	....	....	....	....	....	....	....
2002-03	Harvard Crimson	ECAC	34	*24	27	*51	30	....	....	....	....	....	....	....	....	....	....	....	....	....	....	....	....	....	....
2003-04	**NY Rangers**	**NHL**	**5**	**0**	**3**	**3**	**0**	**0**	**0**	**0**	**3**	**0.0**	**0**	**36**	**30.6**	**9:18**	....	....	....	....	....	....	....	....	....
	Hartford	AHL	70	14	25	39	60	....	....	....	....	....	....	....	....	....	16	3	3	6	8	....	....	....	....
2004-05	Hartford	AHL	78	19	31	50	78	....	....	....	....	....	....	....	....	....	6	1	1	2	4	....	....	....	....
2005-06	**NY Rangers**	**NHL**	**82**	**9**	**9**	**18**	**28**	**2**	**0**	**1**	**139**	**6.5**	**4**	**814**	**46.3**	**12:28**	**4**	**0**	**0**	**0**	**2**	**0**	**0**	**0**	**11:21**
2006-07	**Pittsburgh**	**NHL**	**59**	**6**	**9**	**15**	**46**	**0**	**0**	**0**	**100**	**6.0**	**1**	**678**	**51.6**	**13:04**	....	....	....	....	....	....	....	....	....
	Minnesota	**NHL**	**10**	**2**	**0**	**2**	**10**	**0**	**0**	**1**	**11**	**18.2**	**3**	**66**	**62.1**	**10:12**	....	....	....	....	....	....	....	....	....
2007-08	**Minnesota**	**NHL**	**30**	**1**	**2**	**3**	**10**	**0**	**0**	**0**	**28**	**3.6**	**–11**	**311**	**52.4**	**11:57**	....	....	....	....	....	....	....	....	....
	Toronto	**NHL**	**38**	**4**	**10**	**14**	**14**	**1**	**0**	**0**	**72**	**5.6**	**7**	**393**	**50.6**	**14:21**	....	....	....	....	....	....	....	....	....
2008-09	**Toronto**	**NHL**	**63**	**12**	**29**	**41**	**69**	**4**	**1**	**1**	**132**	**9.1**	**–1**	**1007**	**54.8**	**17:18**	....	....	....	....	....	....	....	....	....
	Buffalo	**NHL**	**18**	**1**	**3**	**4**	**23**	**0**	**0**	**0**	**33**	**3.0**	**–1**	**237**	**51.1**	**15:12**	....	....	....	....	....	....	....	....	....
2009-10	**Florida**	**NHL**	**48**	**8**	**9**	**17**	**35**	**2**	**1**	**0**	**81**	**9.9**	**–7**	**462**	**55.8**	**14:55**	....	....	....	....	....	....	....	....	....
	Montreal	**NHL**	**21**	**2**	**9**	**11**	**8**	**0**	**1**	**0**	**38**	**5.3**	**4**	**201**	**53.2**	**14:40**	**19**	**4**	**1**	**5**	**6**	**0**	**0**	**1**	**14:34**
2010-11	**Tampa Bay**	**NHL**	**77**	**18**	**14**	**32**	**52**	**6**	**0**	**3**	**175**	**10.3**	**–12**	**892**	**53.3**	**15:36**	**18**	**3**	**8**	**11**	**18**	**1**	**0**	**0**	**17:46**
2011-12	**Tampa Bay**	**NHL**	**56**	**4**	**15**	**19**	**48**	**0**	**1**	**1**	**74**	**5.4**	**–10**	**573**	**55.7**	**16:17**	....	....	....	....	....	....	....	....	....
	San Jose	**NHL**	**23**	**0**	**6**	**6**	**6**	**0**	**0**	**0**	**29**	**0.0**	**–8**	**189**	**52.9**	**13:43**	**3**	**0**	**0**	**0**	**5**	**0**	**0**	**0**	**15:08**
2012-13		DID NOT PLAY																							
	NHL Totals		**530**	**67**	**118**	**185**	**349**	**15**	**4**	**7**	**915**	**7.3**		**5859**	**52.4**	**14:27**	**44**	**7**	**9**	**16**	**31**	**1**	**0**	**1**	**15:37**

ECAC All-Rookie Team (2000) • ECAC Second All-Star Team (2001) • ECAC First All-Star Team (2003) • NCAA East First All-American Team (2003)

Traded to **Nashville** by **NY Rangers** for Adam Hall, July 19, 2006. Traded to **Pittsburgh** by **Nashville** with Libor Pivko for Pittsburgh's 3rd round choice (Ryan Thang) in 2007 Entry Draft, July 19, 2006. Traded to **Minnesota** by **Pittsburgh** for Minnesota's 3rd round choice (Casey Pierro-Zabotel) in 2007 Entry Draft, February 27, 2007. Claimed on waivers by **Toronto** from **Minnesota**, January 11, 2008. Traded to **Buffalo** by **Toronto** for Carolina's 2nd round choice (previously acquired, Toronto selected Jesse Blacker) in 2009 Entry Draft, March 4, 2009. Signed as a free agent by **Florida**, October 5, 2009. Traded to **Montreal** by **Florida** for Montreal's 2nd round choice (later traded to San Jose – San Jose selected Matthew Nieto) in 2011 Entry Draft, February 11, 2010. Signed as a free agent by **Tampa Bay**, July 30, 2010. Traded to **San Jose** by **Tampa Bay** with Tampa Bay's 7th round choice (later traded to Chicago – Chicago selected Brandon Whitney) in 2012 Entry Draft for Minnesota's 2nd round choice (previously acquired, later traded to Nashville – Nashville selected Pontius Aberg) in 2012 Entry Draft, February 16, 2012. Signed as a free agent by **NY Rangers**, July 5, 2013. • Missed 2012-13 due to personal reasons.

MOORE, John

(MOOR, JAWN) **NYR**

Defense. Shoots left. 6'3", 202 lbs. Born, Winnetka, IL, November 19, 1990. Columbus' 1st choice, 21st overall, in 2009 Entry Draft.

Season	Club	League	GP	G	A	Pts	PIM	PP	SH	GW	S	%	+/-	TF	F%	Min	GP	G	A	Pts	PIM	PP	SH	GW	Min
2006-07	Chicago Mission	MWEHL	31	1	12	13	26	....	....	....	....	....	....	....	....	....	....	....	....	....	....	....	....	....	....
	Chicago Mission	Exhib.	30	13	37	50	14	....	....	....	....	....	....	....	....	....	....	....	....	....	....	....	....	....	....
2007-08	Chicago Steel	USHL	56	4	11	15	26	....	....	....	....	....	....	....	....	....	7	0	2	2	2	....	....	....	....
2008-09	Chicago Steel	USHL	57	14	25	39	50	....	....	....	....	....	....	....	....	....	....	....	....	....	....	....	....	....	....
2009-10	Kitchener Rangers	OHL	61	10	37	47	53	....	....	....	....	....	....	....	....	....	20	4	12	16	2	....	....	....	....

			Regular Season														Playoffs								
Season	Club	League	GP	G	A	Pts	PIM	PP	SH	GW	S	%	+/-	TF	F%	Min	GP	G	A	Pts	PIM	PP	SH	GW	Min
2010-11	**Columbus**	**NHL**	**2**	**0**	**0**	**0**	**0**	**0**	**0**	**0**	**0**	**0.0**	**0**	**0**	**0.0**	**11:28**									
	Springfield	AHL	73	5	19	24	23																		
2011-12	**Columbus**	**NHL**	**67**	**2**	**5**	**7**	**8**	**0**	**0**	**0**	**64**	**3.1**	**-23**	**0**	**0.0**	**15:49**									
	Springfield	AHL	5	1	1	2	2																		
2012-13	Springfield	AHL	24	3	6	9	10																		
	Columbus	**NHL**	**17**	**0**	**1**	**1**	**2**	**0**	**0**	**0**	**14**	**0.0**	**-5**	**0**	**0.0**	**14:31**									
	NY Rangers	**NHL**	**13**	**1**	**5**	**6**	**5**	**0**	**0**	**0**	**15**	**6.7**	**9**	**0**	**0.0**	**11:46**	**12**	**0**	**1**	**1**	**2**	**0**	**0**	**0**	**17:08**
	NHL Totals		**99**	**3**	**11**	**14**	**15**	**0**	**0**	**0**	**93**	**3.2**		**0**	**0.0**	**14:59**	**12**	**0**	**1**	**1**	**2**	**0**	**0**	**0**	**17:08**

USHL First All-Star Team (2009) • USHL Defenseman of the Year (2009)

Traded to **NY Rangers** by **Columbus** with Derek Dorsett, Derick Brassard and Columbus' 6th round choice in 2014 Entry Draft for Marian Gaborik, Blake Parlett and Steven Delisle, April 3, 2013.

MOORE, Mike

(MOOR, MIGHK) **BOS**

Defense. Shoots left. 6'1", 210 lbs. Born, Calgary, Alta., December 12, 1984.

Season	Club	League	GP	G	A	Pts	PIM	PP	SH	GW	S	%	+/-	TF	F%	Min	GP	G	A	Pts	PIM	PP	SH	GW	Min
2002-03	South Surrey	BCHL	55	3	10	13	187																		
2003-04	Surrey Eagles	BCHL	52	6	21	27	148										10	0	2	2	6				
2004-05	Princeton	ECAC	25	3	7	10	22																		
2005-06	Princeton	ECAC	30	0	4	4	42																		
2006-07	Princeton	ECAC	32	4	10	14	50																		
2007-08	Princeton	ECAC	34	7	17	24	40																		
	Worcester Sharks	AHL	3	0	0	0	16																		
2008-09	Worcester Sharks	AHL	76	5	13	18	132										12	0	1	1	17				
2009-10	Worcester Sharks	AHL	64	3	19	22	82										11	0	0	0	14				
2010-11	**San Jose**	**NHL**	**6**	**1**	**0**	**1**	**7**	**0**	**0**	**0**	**5**	**20.0**	**-1**	**0**	**0.0**	**10:07**									
	Worcester Sharks	AHL	49	2	10	12	50																		
2011-12	Worcester Sharks	AHL	61	4	16	20	85																		
2012-13	Milwaukee	AHL	50	5	11	16	42										4	1	0	1	2				
	NHL Totals		**6**	**1**	**0**	**1**	**7**	**0**	**0**	**0**	**5**	**20.0**		**0**	**0.0**	**10:07**									

ECAC First All-Star Team (2008) • NCAA East First All-American Team (2008)

Signed as a free agent by **San Jose**, April 8, 2008. Signed as a free agent by **Nashville**, July 3, 2012. Signed as a free agent by **Boston**, July 5, 2013.

MORIN, Jeremy

(moh-REHN, JAIR-eh-mee) **CHI**

Left wing. Shoots right. 6'1", 192 lbs. Born, Auburn, NY, April 16, 1991. Atlanta's 3rd choice, 45th overall, in 2009 Entry Draft.

Season	Club	League	GP	G	A	Pts	PIM	PP	SH	GW	S	%	+/-	TF	F%	Min	GP	G	A	Pts	PIM	PP	SH	GW	Min
2006-07	Rochester	EJHL	45	26	28	54	80																		
2007-08	USNTDP	NAHL	30	17	17	34	26																		
	USNTDP	U-17	7	11	1	12	4																		
	USNTDP	U-18	28	20	14	34	36																		
2008-09	USNTDP	NAHL	14	12	15	27	28																		
	USNTDP	U-18	41	21	11	32	79																		
2009-10	Kitchener Rangers	OHL	58	47	36	83	76										20	12	9	21	32				
2010-11	**Chicago**	**NHL**	**9**	**2**	**1**	**3**	**9**	**0**	**0**	**0**	**13**	**15.4**	**2**	**0**	**0.0**	**12:06**									
	Rockford IceHogs	AHL	22	8	4	12	34																		
2011-12	**Chicago**	**NHL**	**3**	**0**	**0**	**0**	**0**	**0**	**0**	**0**	**2**	**0.0**	**-1**	**0**	**0.0**	**8:52**									
	Rockford IceHogs	AHL	69	18	22	40	121																		
2012-13	Rockford IceHogs	AHL	67	30	28	58	86																		
	Chicago	**NHL**	**3**	**1**	**1**	**2**	**0**	**0**	**0**	**0**	**7**	**14.3**	**1**	**4**	**0.0**	**13:01**									
	NHL Totals		**15**	**3**	**2**	**5**	**9**	**0**	**0**	**0**	**22**	**13.6**		**4**	**0.0**	**11:38**									

OHL Second All-Star Team (2010)

Traded to **Chicago** by **Atlanta** with Marty Reasoner, Joey Crabb and New Jersey's 1st (previously acquired, Chicago selected Kevin Hayes) and 2nd (previously acquired, Chicago selected Justin Holl) round choices in 2010 Entry Draft for Dustin Byfuglien, Brent Sopel, Ben Eager and Akim Aliu, June 24, 2010. • Missed majority of 2010-11 due to upper-body injury.

MORIN, Travis

(moh-REHN, TRA-vihs) **DAL**

Center. Shoots left. 6'1", 195 lbs. Born, Minneapolis, MN, January 9, 1984. Washington's 13th choice, 263rd overall, in 2004 Entry Draft.

Season	Club	League	GP	G	A	Pts	PIM	PP	SH	GW	S	%	+/-	TF	F%	Min	GP	G	A	Pts	PIM	PP	SH	GW	Min
2001-02	Chicago Steel	USHL	20	5	8	13											4	0	0	0	2				
2002-03	Chicago Steel	USHL	60	21	26	47	46																		
2003-04	Minnesota State	WCHA	38	9	12	21	14																		
2004-05	Minnesota State	WCHA	36	12	19	31	20																		
2005-06	Minnesota State	WCHA	39	20	22	42	16																		
2006-07	Minnesota State	WCHA	38	17	22	39	34																		
	South Carolina	ECHL	8	2	1	3	0																		
2007-08	Hershey Bears	AHL	4	0	0	0	0																		
	South Carolina	ECHL	68	34	50	84	30										20	*10	7	17	18				
2008-09	Hershey Bears	AHL	1	0	1	1	0																		
	South Carolina	ECHL	71	26	*62	88	46										19	4	*18	22	12				
2009-10	Texas Stars	AHL	80	21	31	52	30										24	4	12	16	6				
2010-11	**Dallas**	**NHL**	**3**	**0**	**0**	**0**	**0**	**0**	**0**	**0**	**2**	**0.0**	**0**	**14**	**57.1**	**8:52**									
	Texas Stars	AHL	64	21	24	45	30										6	3	4	7	0				
2011-12	Texas Stars	AHL	76	13	53	66	46																		
2012-13	Texas Stars	AHL	59	12	32	44	14										7	0	3	3	4				
	NHL Totals		**3**	**0**	**0**	**0**	**0**	**0**	**0**	**0**	**2**	**0.0**		**14**	**57.1**	**8:52**									

WCHA Second All-Star Team (2007) • ECHL First All-Star Team (2009)

Signed as a free agent by **Texas** (AHL), October 21, 2009. Signed as a free agent by **Dallas**, July 12, 2010.

MORMINA, Joey

(mohr-MEE-nah, JOH-ee)

Defense. Shoots left. 6'6", 220 lbs. Born, Montreal, Que., June 29, 1982. Philadelphia's 6th choice, 193rd overall, in 2002 Entry Draft.

Season	Club	League	GP	G	A	Pts	PIM	PP	SH	GW	S	%	+/-	TF	F%	Min	GP	G	A	Pts	PIM	PP	SH	GW	Min
2000-01	Holderness	High-NH	29	15	15	30																			
2001-02	Colgate	ECAC	34	2	13	15	28																		
2002-03	Colgate	ECAC	40	4	9	13	52																		
2003-04	Colgate	ECAC	28	2	10	12	26																		
2004-05	Colgate	ECAC	39	8	8	16	50																		
2005-06	Manchester	AHL	61	0	13	13	70										7	0	0	0	4				
2006-07	Manchester	AHL	62	2	9	11	108										1	0	0	0	2				
2007-08	**Carolina**	**NHL**	**1**	**0**	**0**	**0**	**0**	**0**	**0**	**0**	**1**	**0.0**	**0**	**0**	**0.0**	**7:45**									
	Albany River Rats	AHL	77	4	9	13	96										7	0	0	0	4				
2008-09	Wilkes-Barre	AHL	70	2	9	11	71										12	0	0	0	12				
2009-10	Adirondack	AHL	77	5	18	23	102																		
2010-11	Wilkes-Barre	AHL	50	2	9	11	44										12	0	0	0	16				
2011-12	Wilkes-Barre	AHL	59	6	15	21	70										12	1	1	2	10				
2012-13	Wilkes-Barre	AHL	54	3	7	10	60										15	1	7	8	36				
	NHL Totals		**1**	**0**	**0**	**0**	**0**	**0**	**0**	**0**	**1**	**0.0**		**0**	**0.0**	**7:45**									

Signed as a free agent by **Los Angeles**, August 24, 2005. Signed as a free agent by **Carolina**, July 2, 2007. Signed as a free agent by **Pittsburgh**, July 10, 2008. Signed as a free agent by **Philadelphia**, July 23, 2009. Signed to a PTO (professional tryout) contract by **Wilkes-Barre** (AHL), October 11, 2010. Signed as a free agent by **Wilkes-Barre** (AHL), December 8, 2010. Signed as a free agent by **Syracuse** (AHL), July 3, 2013.

MORRIS, Derek

(MOH-rihs, DAIR-ihk) **PHX**

Defense. Shoots right. 6', 200 lbs. Born, Edmonton, Alta., August 24, 1978. Calgary's 1st choice, 13th overall, in 1996 Entry Draft.

Season	Club	League	GP	G	A	Pts	PIM	PP	SH	GW	S	%	+/-	TF	F%	Min	GP	G	A	Pts	PIM	PP	SH	GW	Min
1994-95	Red Deer Vipers	AMHL	31	6	35	41	74																		
1995-96	Regina Pats	WHL	67	8	44	52	70										11	1	7	8	26				
1996-97	Regina Pats	WHL	67	18	57	75	147										5	0	3	3	9				
	Saint John Flames	AHL	7	0	3	3	7										5	0	3	3	7				
1997-98	**Calgary**	**NHL**	**82**	**9**	**20**	**29**	**88**	**5**	**1**	**1**	**120**	**7.5**	**1**												
1998-99	**Calgary**	**NHL**	**71**	**7**	**27**	**34**	**73**	**3**	**0**	**2**	**150**	**4.7**	**4**	**0**	**0.0**	**20:44**									
99-2000	**Calgary**	**NHL**	**78**	**9**	**29**	**38**	**80**	**3**	**0**	**2**	**193**	**4.7**	**2**	**0**	**0.0**	**24:51**									
2000-01	**Calgary**	**NHL**	**51**	**5**	**23**	**28**	**56**	**3**	**1**	**4**	**142**	**3.5**	**-15**	**0**	**0.0**	**25:51**									
	Saint John Flames	AHL	3	1	2	3	2																		

			Regular Season														Playoffs								
Season	Club	League	GP	G	A	Pts	PIM	PP	SH	GW	S	%	+/-	TF	F%	Min	GP	G	A	Pts	PIM	PP	SH	GW	Min
2001-02	**Calgary**	**NHL**	**61**	**4**	**30**	**34**	**88**	**2**	**0**	**1**	**166**	**2.4**	**–4**	**1**	**100.0**	**24:40**	....	....	....	....	....	....	....	....	....
2002-03	**Colorado**	**NHL**	**75**	**11**	**37**	**48**	**68**	**9**	**0**	**7**	**191**	**5.8**	**16**	**0**	**0.0**	**23:49**	**7**	**0**	**3**	**3**	**6**	**0**	**0**	**0**	**22:44**
2003-04	**Colorado**	**NHL**	**69**	**6**	**22**	**28**	**47**	**2**	**0**	**1**	**139**	**4.3**	**4**	**0**	**0.0**	**20:53**	....	....	....	....	....	....	....	....	....
	Phoenix	**NHL**	**14**	**0**	**4**	**4**	**2**	**0**	**0**	**0**	**28**	**0.0**	**–5**	**0**	**0.0**	**25:02**	....	....	....	....	....	....	....	....	....
2004-05			DID NOT PLAY																						
2005-06	**Phoenix**	**NHL**	**53**	**6**	**21**	**27**	**54**	**4**	**1**	**2**	**91**	**6.6**	**–7**	**1**	**0.0**	**20:52**	....	....	....	....	....	....	....	....	....
2006-07	**Phoenix**	**NHL**	**82**	**6**	**19**	**25**	**115**	**2**	**0**	**1**	**129**	**4.7**	**–18**	**1**	**100.0**	**20:29**	....	....	....	....	....	....	....	....	....
2007-08	**Phoenix**	**NHL**	**82**	**8**	**17**	**25**	**83**	**2**	**0**	**0**	**135**	**5.9**	**8**	**1**	**0.0**	**21:43**	....	....	....	....	....	....	....	....	....
2008-09	**Phoenix**	**NHL**	**57**	**5**	**7**	**12**	**24**	**0**	**1**	**0**	**89**	**5.6**	**–13**	**0**	**0.0**	**21:16**	....	....	....	....	....	....	....	....	....
	NY Rangers	**NHL**	**18**	**0**	**8**	**8**	**16**	**0**	**0**	**0**	**31**	**0.0**	**3**	**0**	**0.0**	**19:41**	**7**	**0**	**2**	**2**	**0**	**0**	**0**	**0**	**16:24**
2009-10	**Boston**	**NHL**	**58**	**3**	**22**	**25**	**26**	**2**	**0**	**0**	**95**	**3.2**	**–2**	**1**	**0.0**	**22:00**	....	....	....	....	....	....	....	....	....
	Phoenix	**NHL**	**18**	**1**	**3**	**4**	**11**	**0**	**0**	**0**	**25**	**4.0**	**4**	**0**	**0.0**	**19:39**	**7**	**1**	**3**	**4**	**11**	**1**	**0**	**1**	**19:35**
2010-11	**Phoenix**	**NHL**	**77**	**5**	**11**	**16**	**58**	**1**	**0**	**1**	**83**	**6.0**	**–2**	**3**	**66.7**	**21:04**	....	....	....	....	....	....	....	....	....
2011-12	**Phoenix**	**NHL**	**59**	**2**	**9**	**11**	**38**	**0**	**0**	**0**	**72**	**2.8**	**–12**	**0**	**0.0**	**18:59**	**16**	**2**	**4**	**6**	**24**	**0**	**0**	**0**	**22:49**
2012-13	**Phoenix**	**NHL**	**39**	**0**	**11**	**11**	**36**	**0**	**0**	**0**	**68**	**0.0**	**–6**	**0**	**0.0**	**21:24**	....	....	....	....	....	....	....	....	....
	NHL Totals		**1044**	**87**	**320**	**407**	**963**	**38**	**4**	**22**	**1947**	**4.5**		**8**	**50.0**	**21:59**	**37**	**3**	**12**	**15**	**41**	**1**	**0**	**1**	**20:59**

WHL East First All-Star Team (1997) • NHL All-Rookie Team (1998)

Traded to **Colorado** by **Calgary** with Jeff Shantz and Dean McAmmond for Chris Drury and Stephane Yelle, October 1, 2002. Traded to **Phoenix** by **Colorado** with Keith Ballard for Ossi Vaananen, Chris Gratton and Phoenix's 2nd round choice (Paul Stastny) in 2005 Entry Draft, March 9, 2004. Traded to **NY Rangers** by **Phoenix** for Dmitri Kalinin, Nigel Dawes and Petr Prucha, March 4, 2009. Signed as a free agent by **Boston**, July 25, 2009. Traded to **Phoenix** by **Boston** for Phoenix's 3rd round choice (Anthony Camera) in 2011 Entry Draft, March 3, 2010.

MORRISONN, Shaone

(MOHR-ih-suhn, SHAWN)

Defense. Shoots left. 6'4", 210 lbs. Born, Vancouver, B.C., December 23, 1982. Boston's 1st choice, 19th overall, in 2001 Entry Draft.

Season	Club	League	GP	G	A	Pts	PIM	PP	SH	GW	S	%	+/-	TF	F%	Min	GP	G	A	Pts	PIM	PP	SH	GW	Min
1997-98	Vancouver T-Birds	Minor-BC	45	16	44	60	75	....	....	....	....	....	....	....	....	....	....	....	....	....	....	....	....	....	....
1998-99	South Surrey	BCHL	19	0	2	2	13	....	....	....	....	....	....	....	....	....	....	....	....	....	....	....	....	....	....
99-2000	Kamloops Blazers	WHL	57	1	6	7	80	....	....	....	....	....	....	....	....	....	4	0	0	0	6	....	....	....	....
2000-01	Kamloops Blazers	WHL	61	13	25	38	132	....	....	....	....	....	....	....	....	....	4	0	0	0	6	....	....	....	....
2001-02	Kamloops Blazers	WHL	61	11	26	37	106	....	....	....	....	....	....	....	....	....	4	0	2	2	2	....	....	....	....
2002-03	**Boston**	**NHL**	**11**	**0**	**0**	**0**	**8**	**0**	**0**	**0**	**4**	**0.0**	**0**	**0**	**0.0**	**8:57**	....	....	....	....	....	....	....	....	....
	Providence Bruins	AHL	60	5	16	21	103	....	....	....	....	....	....	....	....	....	4	0	0	0	6	....	....	....	....
2003-04	**Boston**	**NHL**	**30**	**1**	**7**	**8**	**10**	**0**	**0**	**0**	**13**	**7.7**	**10**	**0**	**0.0**	**18:11**	....	....	....	....	....	....	....	....	....
	Providence Bruins	AHL	18	0	2	2	16	....	....	....	....	....	....	....	....	....	....	....	....	....	....	....	....	....	....
	Washington	**NHL**	**3**	**0**	**0**	**0**	**0**	**0**	**0**	**0**	**1**	**0.0**	**0**	**0**	**0.0**	**18:52**	....	....	....	....	....	....	....	....	....
	Portland Pirates	AHL	13	1	4	5	10	....	....	....	....	....	....	....	....	....	7	0	1	1	4	....	....	....	....
2004-05	Portland Pirates	AHL	71	4	14	18	63	....	....	....	....	....	....	....	....	....	....	....	....	....	....	....	....	....	....
2005-06	**Washington**	**NHL**	**80**	**1**	**13**	**14**	**91**	**0**	**0**	**0**	**56**	**1.8**	**7**	**4**	**0.0**	**20:44**	....	....	....	....	....	....	....	....	....
2006-07	**Washington**	**NHL**	**78**	**3**	**10**	**13**	**106**	**0**	**0**	**0**	**46**	**6.5**	**3**	**2**	**0.0**	**20:57**	....	....	....	....	....	....	....	....	....
2007-08	**Washington**	**NHL**	**76**	**1**	**9**	**10**	**63**	**0**	**0**	**1**	**47**	**2.1**	**4**	**1**	**100.0**	**20:16**	**7**	**0**	**1**	**1**	**6**	**0**	**0**	**0**	**21:18**
2008-09	**Washington**	**NHL**	**72**	**3**	**10**	**13**	**77**	**0**	**0**	**1**	**50**	**6.0**	**4**	**0**	**0.0**	**17:59**	**14**	**0**	**1**	**1**	**8**	**0**	**0**	**0**	**18:03**
2009-10	**Washington**	**NHL**	**68**	**1**	**11**	**12**	**68**	**0**	**0**	**1**	**32**	**3.1**	**8**	**0**	**0.0**	**17:34**	**5**	**0**	**0**	**0**	**2**	**0**	**0**	**0**	**15:54**
2010-11	**Buffalo**	**NHL**	**62**	**1**	**4**	**5**	**32**	**0**	**0**	**1**	**44**	**2.3**	**–2**	**0**	**0.0**	**16:10**	**1**	**0**	**0**	**0**	**2**	**0**	**0**	**0**	**13:22**
2011-12	Rochester	AHL	65	4	11	15	44	....	....	....	....	....	....	....	....	....	1	0	0	0	0	....	....	....	....
2012-13	Spartak Moscow	KHL	46	1	3	4	26	....	....	....	....	....	....	....	....	....	....	....	....	....	....	....	....	....	....
	CSKA Moscow	KHL	2	1	1	2	0	....	....	....	....	....	....	....	....	....	7	0	2	2	0	....	....	....	....
	NHL Totals		**480**	**11**	**64**	**75**	**455**	**0**	**0**	**4**	**293**	**3.8**		**7**	**14.3**	**18:48**	**27**	**0**	**2**	**2**	**18**	**0**	**0**	**0**	**18:19**

Traded to **Washington** by **Boston** with Boston's 1st (Jeff Schultz) and 2nd (Michail Yunkov) round choices in 2004 Entry Draft for Sergei Gonchar, March 3, 2004. Signed as a free agent by **Buffalo**, August 2, 2010. Signed as a free agent by **Spartak Moscow** (KHL), June 13, 2012. Signed as a free agent by **CSKA Moscow** (KHL), January 31, 2013.

MORROW, Brenden

(MOHR-roh, BREHN-duhn)

Left wing. Shoots left. 6', 205 lbs. Born, Carlyle, Sask., January 16, 1979. Dallas' 1st choice, 25th overall, in 1997 Entry Draft.

Season	Club	League	GP	G	A	Pts	PIM	PP	SH	GW	S	%	+/-	TF	F%	Min	GP	G	A	Pts	PIM	PP	SH	GW	Min
1994-95	Estevan	SMBHL	60	117	72	189	45	....	....	....	....	....	....	....	....	....	....	....	....	....	....	....	....	....	....
1995-96	Portland	WHL	65	13	12	25	61	....	....	....	....	....	....	....	....	....	7	0	0	0	8	....	....	....	....
1996-97	Portland	WHL	71	39	49	88	149	....	....	....	....	....	....	....	....	....	6	2	1	3	4	....	....	....	....
1997-98	Portland	WHL	68	34	52	86	184	....	....	....	....	....	....	....	....	....	16	10	8	18	65	....	....	....	....
1998-99	Portland	WHL	61	41	44	85	248	....	....	....	....	....	....	....	....	....	4	0	4	4	18	....	....	....	....
99-2000	**Dallas**	**NHL**	**64**	**14**	**19**	**33**	**81**	**3**	**0**	**3**	**113**	**12.4**	**8**	**25**	**48.0**	**15:51**	**21**	**2**	**4**	**6**	**22**	**1**	**0**	**0**	**15:04**
	Michigan	IHL	9	2	0	2	18	....	....	....	....	....	....	....	....	....	....	....	....	....	....	....	....	....	....
2000-01	**Dallas**	**NHL**	**82**	**20**	**24**	**44**	**128**	**7**	**0**	**6**	**121**	**16.5**	**18**	**22**	**45.5**	**15:29**	**10**	**0**	**3**	**3**	**12**	**0**	**0**	**0**	**17:00**
2001-02	**Dallas**	**NHL**	**72**	**17**	**18**	**35**	**109**	**4**	**0**	**3**	**102**	**16.7**	**12**	**39**	**41.0**	**16:52**	....	....	....	....	....	....	....	....	....
2002-03	**Dallas**	**NHL**	**71**	**21**	**22**	**43**	**134**	**2**	**3**	**4**	**105**	**20.0**	**20**	**29**	**27.6**	**15:43**	**12**	**3**	**5**	**8**	**16**	**2**	**0**	**0**	**21:03**
2003-04	**Dallas**	**NHL**	**81**	**25**	**24**	**49**	**121**	**9**	**0**	**3**	**132**	**18.9**	**10**	**38**	**47.4**	**19:24**	**5**	**0**	**1**	**1**	**4**	**0**	**0**	**0**	**21:29**
2004-05	Oklahoma City	CHL	19	8	14	22	31	....	....	....	....	....	....	....	....	....	....	....	....	....	....	....	....	....	....
2005-06	**Dallas**	**NHL**	**81**	**23**	**42**	**65**	**183**	**8**	**1**	**4**	**146**	**15.8**	**30**	**32**	**37.5**	**19:15**	**5**	**1**	**5**	**6**	**6**	**0**	**0**	**0**	**21:57**
2006-07	**Dallas**	**NHL**	**40**	**16**	**15**	**31**	**33**	**8**	**0**	**3**	**101**	**15.8**	**–2**	**51**	**39.2**	**18:16**	**7**	**2**	**1**	**3**	**18**	**2**	**0**	**1**	**21:54**
2007-08	**Dallas**	**NHL**	**82**	**32**	**42**	**74**	**105**	**12**	**2**	**7**	**207**	**15.5**	**23**	**41**	**39.0**	**20:00**	**18**	**9**	**6**	**15**	**22**	**4**	**0**	**2**	**23:17**
2008-09	**Dallas**	**NHL**	**18**	**5**	**10**	**15**	**49**	**2**	**0**	**0**	**52**	**9.6**	**–4**	**9**	**33.3**	**21:21**	....	....	....	....	....	....	....	....	....
2009-10	**Dallas**	**NHL**	**76**	**20**	**26**	**46**	**69**	**9**	**1**	**2**	**155**	**12.9**	**–3**	**31**	**29.0**	**19:10**	....	....	....	....	....	....	....	....	....
	Canada	Olympics	7	2	1	3	2	....	....	....	....	....	....	....	....	....	....	....	....	....	....	....	....	....	....
2010-11	**Dallas**	**NHL**	**82**	**33**	**23**	**56**	**76**	**9**	**1**	**5**	**209**	**15.8**	**–3**	**11**	**9.1**	**19:14**	....	....	....	....	....	....	....	....	....
2011-12	**Dallas**	**NHL**	**57**	**11**	**15**	**26**	**97**	**5**	**0**	**2**	**88**	**12.5**	**1**	**27**	**40.7**	**17:02**	....	....	....	....	....	....	....	....	....
2012-13	**Dallas**	**NHL**	**29**	**6**	**5**	**11**	**18**	**1**	**0**	**1**	**31**	**19.4**	**–8**	**23**	**56.5**	**14:55**	....	....	....	....	....	....	....	....	....
	Pittsburgh	**NHL**	**15**	**6**	**8**	**14**	**19**	**1**	**0**	**1**	**24**	**25.0**	**5**	**1**	**0.0**	**14:44**	**14**	**2**	**2**	**4**	**8**	**0**	**0**	**1**	**13:47**
	NHL Totals		**850**	**249**	**293**	**542**	**1222**	**80**	**8**	**44**	**1586**	**15.7**		**379**	**39.3**	**17:50**	**92**	**19**	**27**	**46**	**108**	**9**	**0**	**4**	**18:43**

WHL West First All-Star Team (1999)

Signed as a free agent by **Oklahoma City** (CHL), October 19, 2004. • Missed majority of 2006-07 due to groin (November 22, 2006 vs. Nashville) and wrist (December 26, 2006 at Chicago) injuries. • Missed majority of 2008-09 due to knee injury vs. Chicago, November 20, 2008. Traded to **Pittsburgh** by **Dallas** with Minnesota's 3rd round choice (previously acquired, Pittsburgh selected Jake Guentzel) in 2013 Entry Draft for Joe Morrow and Pittsburgh's 5th round choice (Matej Paulovic) in 2013 Entry Draft, March 24, 2013.

MOSS, Dave

(MAWS, DAYV) **PHX**

Left wing. Shoots right. 6'4", 210 lbs. Born, Livonia, MI, December 28, 1981. Calgary's 9th choice, 220th overall, in 2001 Entry Draft.

Season	Club	League	GP	G	A	Pts	PIM	PP	SH	GW	S	%	+/-	TF	F%	Min	GP	G	A	Pts	PIM	PP	SH	GW	Min
99-2000	Catholic Central	High-MI	28	18	20	28	20	....	....	....	....	....	....	....	....	....	....	....	....	....	....	....	....	....	....
2000-01	St. Louis Jr. Blues	CSJHL	9	2	2	4	2	....	....	....	....	....	....	....	....	....	....	....	....	....	....	....	....	....	....
	Cedar Rapids	USHL	51	20	18	38	14	....	....	....	....	....	....	....	....	....	4	0	1	1	2	....	....	....	....
2001-02	U. of Michigan	CCHA	43	4	9	13	10	....	....	....	....	....	....	....	....	....	....	....	....	....	....	....	....	....	....
2002-03	U. of Michigan	CCHA	43	14	17	31	37	....	....	....	....	....	....	....	....	....	....	....	....	....	....	....	....	....	....
2003-04	U. of Michigan	CCHA	38	8	12	20	18	....	....	....	....	....	....	....	....	....	....	....	....	....	....	....	....	....	....
2004-05	U. of Michigan	CCHA	38	10	20	30	26	....	....	....	....	....	....	....	....	....	....	....	....	....	....	....	....	....	....
2005-06	Omaha	AHL	63	21	27	48	28	....	....	....	....	....	....	....	....	....	....	....	....	....	....	....	....	....	....
2006-07	**Calgary**	**NHL**	**41**	**10**	**8**	**18**	**12**	**3**	**0**	**1**	**70**	**14.3**	**5**	**11**	**36.4**	**11:13**	**6**	**0**	**1**	**1**	**0**	**0**	**0**	**0**	**10:30**
	Omaha	AHL	28	9	12	21	22	....	....	....	....	....	....	....	....	....	....	....	....	....	....	....	....	....	....
2007-08	**Calgary**	**NHL**	**41**	**4**	**7**	**11**	**10**	**0**	**0**	**0**	**60**	**6.7**	**–4**	**17**	**41.2**	**12:24**	**5**	**1**	**1**	**2**	**4**	**0**	**0**	**0**	**10:20**
2008-09	**Calgary**	**NHL**	**81**	**20**	**19**	**39**	**22**	**8**	**0**	**4**	**194**	**10.3**	**–5**	**46**	**50.0**	**13:36**	**6**	**3**	**0**	**3**	**0**	**0**	**0**	**1**	**12:50**
2009-10	**Calgary**	**NHL**	**64**	**8**	**9**	**17**	**20**	**3**	**0**	**2**	**133**	**6.0**	**–9**	**43**	**34.9**	**13:43**	....	....	....	....	....	....	....	....	....
2010-11	**Calgary**	**NHL**	**58**	**17**	**13**	**30**	**18**	**5**	**0**	**3**	**127**	**13.4**	**9**	**364**	**43.1**	**13:41**	....	....	....	....	....	....	....	....	....
2011-12	**Calgary**	**NHL**	**32**	**2**	**7**	**9**	**12**	**0**	**0**	**0**	**82**	**2.4**	**–3**	**220**	**42.3**	**14:01**	....	....	....	....	....	....	....	....	....
2012-13	**Phoenix**	**NHL**	**45**	**5**	**15**	**20**	**21**	**1**	**1**	**0**	**82**	**6.1**	**3**	**31**	**29.0**	**15:33**	....	....	....	....	....	....	....	....	....
	NHL Totals		**362**	**66**	**78**	**144**	**115**	**20**	**1**	**10**	**748**	**8.8**		**732**	**42.1**	**13:30**	**17**	**4**	**2**	**6**	**4**	**0**	**0**	**1**	**11:16**

Signed as a free agent by **Phoenix**, July 1. 2012. • Missed majority of 2011-12 due to ankle injury and resulting surgery.

MOTTAU, Mike

(MAW-tuh, MIGHK) **FLA**

Defense. Shoots left. 6', 190 lbs. Born, Quincy, MA, March 19, 1978. NY Rangers' 10th choice, 182nd overall, in 1997 Entry Draft.

Season	Club	League	GP	G	A	Pts	PIM	PP	SH	GW	S	%	+/-	TF	F%	Min	GP	G	A	Pts	PIM	PP	SH	GW	Min
1994-95	Thayer Academy	High-MA	29	7	19	26	....	....	....	....	....	....	....	....	....	....	....	....	....	....	....	....	....	....	....
1995-96	Thayer Academy	High-MA	31	6	20	26	14	....	....	....	....	....	....	....	....	....	....	....	....	....	....	....	....	....	....
1996-97	Boston College	H-East	38	5	18	23	77	....	....	....	....	....	....	....	....	....	....	....	....	....	....	....	....	....	....
1997-98	Boston College	H-East	40	13	36	49	50	....	....	....	....	....	....	....	....	....	....	....	....	....	....	....	....	....	....
1998-99	Boston College	H-East	43	3	39	42	44	....	....	....	....	....	....	....	....	....	....	....	....	....	....	....	....	....	....
99-2000	Boston College	H-East	42	6	37	43	61	....	....	....	....	....	....	....	....	....	....	....	....	....	....	....	....	....	....

			Regular Season														Playoffs								
Season	Club	League	GP	G	A	Pts	PIM	PP	SH	GW	S	%	+/-	TF	F%	Min	GP	G	A	Pts	PIM	PP	SH	GW	Min
2000-01	**NY Rangers**	**NHL**	**18**	**0**	**3**	**3**	**13**	**0**	**0**	**0**	**17**	**0.0**	**–6**	**0**	**0.0**	**15:18**	....	....	....	....	....	....	....	....	....
	Hartford	AHL	61	10	33	43	45	....	....	....	....	....	....	....	....	....	5	0	1	1	19	....	....	....	....
2001-02	**NY Rangers**	**NHL**	**1**	**0**	**0**	**0**	**0**	**0**	**0**	**0**	**0**	**0.0**	**0**	**0**	**0.0**	**6:20**	....	....	....	....	....	....	....	....	....
	Hartford	AHL	80	9	42	51	56	....	....	....	....	....	....	....	....	....	10	0	5	5	4	....	....	....	....
2002-03	Hartford	AHL	29	1	18	19	24	....	....	....	....	....	....	....	....	....	....	....	....	....	....	....	....	....	....
	Calgary	**NHL**	**4**	**0**	**0**	**0**	**0**	**0**	**0**	**0**	**0**	**0.0**	**–1**	**0**	**0.0**	**9:50**	....	....	....	....	....	....	....	....	....
	Saint John Flames	AHL	32	5	12	17	14	....	....	....	....	....	....	....	....	....	....	....	....	....	....	....	....	....	....
2003-04	Cincinnati	AHL	69	9	22	31	79	....	....	....	....	....	....	....	....	....	9	1	2	3	8	....	....	....	....
2004-05	Worcester IceCats	AHL	73	4	31	35	23	....	....	....	....	....	....	....	....	....	....	....	....	....	....	....	....	....	....
2005-06	Peoria Rivermen	AHL	76	8	48	56	81	....	....	....	....	....	....	....	....	....	4	0	1	1	6	....	....	....	....
2006-07	Lowell Devils	AHL	43	1	26	27	33	....	....	....	....	....	....	....	....	....	....	....	....	....	....	....	....	....	....
2007-08	**New Jersey**	**NHL**	**76**	**4**	**13**	**17**	**48**	**1**	**0**	**1**	**68**	**5.9**	**–11**	**0**	**0.0**	**20:39**	**5**	**1**	**0**	**1**	**0**	**0**	**0**	**0**	**21:24**
2008-09	**New Jersey**	**NHL**	**80**	**1**	**14**	**15**	**35**	**0**	**0**	**0**	**71**	**1.4**	**24**	**0**	**0.0**	**17:47**	**7**	**1**	**1**	**2**	**0**	**0**	**0**	**0**	**17:59**
2009-10	**New Jersey**	**NHL**	**79**	**2**	**16**	**18**	**41**	**0**	**0**	**0**	**74**	**2.7**	**4**	**0**	**0.0**	**22:16**	**5**	**0**	**1**	**1**	**0**	**0**	**0**	**0**	**17:57**
2010-11	**NY Islanders**	**NHL**	**20**	**0**	**3**	**3**	**8**	**0**	**0**	**0**	**21**	**0.0**	**–12**	**0**	**0.0**	**20:20**	....	....	....	....	....	....	....	....	....
2011-12	**NY Islanders**	**NHL**	**29**	**0**	**2**	**2**	**15**	**0**	**0**	**0**	**19**	**0.0**	**–10**	**0**	**0.0**	**14:11**	....	....	....	....	....	....	....	....	....
	Boston	**NHL**	**6**	**0**	**0**	**0**	**0**	**0**	**0**	**0**	**3**	**0.0**	**–1**	**0**	**0.0**	**13:36**	**2**	**0**	**0**	**0**	**0**	**0**	**0**	**0**	**10:15**
2012-13	San Antonio	AHL	16	0	7	7	6	....	....	....	....	....	....	....	....	....	....	....	....	....	....	....	....	....	....
	Toronto Marlies	AHL	18	0	7	7	8	....	....	....	....	....	....	....	....	....	7	0	1	1	4	....	....	....	....
	NHL Totals		**313**	**7**	**51**	**58**	**160**	**1**	**0**	**1**	**273**	**2.6**		**0**	**0.0**	**19:05**	**19**	**2**	**2**	**4**	**0**	**0**	**0**	**0**	**18:04**

Hockey East First All-Star Team (1998, 2000) • NCAA East Second All-American Team (1998) • NCAA Championship All-Tournament Team (1998, 2000) • Hockey East Second All-Star Team (1999) • NCAA East First All-American Team (1999, 2000) • Hockey East Player of the Year (2000) (co-winner - Ty Conklin) • Hobey Baker Memorial Award (Top U.S. Collegiate Player) (2000) • AHL All-Rookie Team (2001)

Traded to **Calgary** by **NY Rangers** for Calgary's 6th round choice (Ivan Dornic) in 2003 Entry Draft and future considerations, January 22, 2003. Signed as a free agent by **Anaheim**, July 25, 2003. Signed as a free agent by **Worcester** (AHL), September 30, 2004. Signed as a free agent by **New Jersey**, July 17, 2006. Signed as a free agent by **NY Islanders**, September 28, 2010. • Missed majority of 2010-11 due to hip injury. Traded to **Boston** by **NY Islanders** with Brian Rolston for Marc Cantin and Yannick Riendeau, February 27, 2012. • Missed majority of 2011-12 due to head injury and as a healthy reserve. Signed as a free agent by **San Antonio** (AHL), December 8, 2012. Signed as a free agent by **Toronto**, January 13, 2013. Signed as a free agent by **Florida**, July 5, 2013.

MOULSON, Matt

(MOHL-suhn, MAT) **NYI**

Left wing. Shoots left. 6', 205 lbs. Born, North York, Ont., November 1, 1983. Pittsburgh's 11th choice, 263rd overall, in 2003 Entry Draft.

Season	Club	League	GP	G	A	Pts	PIM	PP	SH	GW	S	%	+/-	TF	F%	Min	GP	G	A	Pts	PIM	PP	SH	GW	Min
2001-02	Guelph	ON-Jr.B	42	56	46	102	80	....	....	....	....	....	....	....	....	....	....	....	....	....	....	....	....	....	....
2002-03	Cornell Big Red	ECAC	33	13	10	23	22	....	....	....	....	....	....	....	....	....	....	....	....	....	....	....	....	....	....
2003-04	Cornell Big Red	ECAC	32	18	17	35	37	....	....	....	....	....	....	....	....	....	....	....	....	....	....	....	....	....	....
2004-05	Cornell Big Red	ECAC	34	22	20	42	33	....	....	....	....	....	....	....	....	....	....	....	....	....	....	....	....	....	....
2005-06	Cornell Big Red	ECAC	35	18	20	38	14	....	....	....	....	....	....	....	....	....	....	....	....	....	....	....	....	....	....
2006-07	Manchester	AHL	77	25	32	57	23	....	....	....	....	....	....	....	....	....	16	2	3	5	8	....	....	....	....
2007-08	**Los Angeles**	**NHL**	**22**	**5**	**4**	**9**	**4**	**0**	**0**	**0**	**35**	**14.3**	**2**	**4**	**25.0**	**12:05**	....	....	....	....	....	....	....	....	....
	Manchester	AHL	57	28	28	56	29	....	....	....	....	....	....	....	....	....	4	2	0	2	4	....	....	....	....
2008-09	**Los Angeles**	**NHL**	**7**	**1**	**0**	**1**	**2**	**0**	**0**	**1**	**6**	**16.7**	**–4**	**0**	**0.0**	**14:30**	....	....	....	....	....	....	....	....	....
	Manchester	AHL	54	21	26	47	35	....	....	....	....	....	....	....	....	....	....	....	....	....	....	....	....	....	....
2009-10	**NY Islanders**	**NHL**	**82**	**30**	**18**	**48**	**16**	**8**	**0**	**5**	**208**	**14.4**	**–1**	**4**	**75.0**	**16:38**	....	....	....	....	....	....	....	....	....
2010-11	**NY Islanders**	**NHL**	**82**	**31**	**22**	**53**	**24**	**9**	**0**	**3**	**237**	**13.1**	**–10**	**9**	**55.6**	**18:52**	....	....	....	....	....	....	....	....	....
2011-12	**NY Islanders**	**NHL**	**82**	**36**	**33**	**69**	**6**	**14**	**0**	**5**	**219**	**16.4**	**1**	**4**	**50.0**	**19:18**	....	....	....	....	....	....	....	....	....
2012-13	**NY Islanders**	**NHL**	**47**	**15**	**29**	**44**	**4**	**8**	**0**	**0**	**154**	**9.7**	**–3**	**1**	**100.0**	**19:09**	**6**	**2**	**1**	**3**	**10**	**1**	**0**	**0**	**17:23**
	NHL Totals		**322**	**118**	**106**	**224**	**56**	**39**	**0**	**14**	**859**	**13.7**		**22**	**54.5**	**17:54**	**6**	**2**	**1**	**3**	**10**	**1**	**0**	**0**	**17:23**

ECAC First All-Star Team (2005) • NCAA East Second All-American Team (2005) • ECAC Second All-Star Team (2006)

Signed as a free agent by **Los Angeles**, September 1, 2006. Signed as a free agent by **NY Islanders**, July 6, 2009.

MUELLER, Chris

(MEW-luhr, KRIHS) **DAL**

Center. Shoots right. 5'11", 203 lbs. Born, West Seneca, NY, March 6, 1986.

Season	Club	League	GP	G	A	Pts	PIM	PP	SH	GW	S	%	+/-	TF	F%	Min	GP	G	A	Pts	PIM	PP	SH	GW	Min
2004-05	Michigan State	CCHA	41	2	16	18	32	....	....	....	....	....	....	....	....	....	....	....	....	....	....	....	....	....	....
2005-06	Michigan State	CCHA	41	11	16	27	47	....	....	....	....	....	....	....	....	....	....	....	....	....	....	....	....	....	....
2006-07	Michigan State	CCHA	42	16	16	32	30	....	....	....	....	....	....	....	....	....	....	....	....	....	....	....	....	....	....
2007-08	Michigan State	CCHA	42	13	14	27	32	....	....	....	....	....	....	....	....	....	....	....	....	....	....	....	....	....	....
	Grand Rapids	AHL	2	0	0	0	0	....	....	....	....	....	....	....	....	....	....	....	....	....	....	....	....	....	....
2008-09	Lake Erie	AHL	59	5	11	16	23	....	....	....	....	....	....	....	....	....	....	....	....	....	....	....	....	....	....
	Johnstown Chiefs	ECHL	3	3	3	6	2	....	....	....	....	....	....	....	....	....	....	....	....	....	....	....	....	....	....
2009-10	Milwaukee	AHL	67	13	14	27	37	....	....	....	....	....	....	....	....	....	7	3	2	5	4	....	....	....	....
	Cincinnati	ECHL	5	4	1	5	0	....	....	....	....	....	....	....	....	....	....	....	....	....	....	....	....	....	....
2010-11	Milwaukee	AHL	67	24	26	50	34	....	....	....	....	....	....	....	....	....	13	4	7	11	13	....	....	....	....
	Nashville	**NHL**	**15**	**0**	**3**	**3**	**2**	**0**	**0**	**0**	**7**	**0.0**	**0**	**89**	**48.3**	**8:38**	....	....	....	....	....	....	....	....	....
2011-12	**Nashville**	**NHL**	**4**	**0**	**0**	**0**	**0**	**0**	**0**	**0**	**4**	**0.0**	**–1**	**27**	**55.6**	**9:09**	....	....	....	....	....	....	....	....	....
	Milwaukee	AHL	73	32	28	60	30	....	....	....	....	....	....	....	....	....	3	1	0	1	0	....	....	....	....
2012-13	Milwaukee	AHL	55	18	18	36	35	....	....	....	....	....	....	....	....	....	2	0	0	0	2	....	....	....	....
	Nashville	**NHL**	**18**	**2**	**3**	**5**	**6**	**0**	**0**	**1**	**22**	**9.1**	**–4**	**185**	**49.7**	**10:42**	....	....	....	....	....	....	....	....	....
	NHL Totals		**37**	**2**	**6**	**8**	**8**	**0**	**0**	**1**	**33**	**6.1**		**301**	**49.8**	**9:42**	....	....	....	....	....	....	....	....	....

Signed to an ATO (amateur tryout) contract by **Grand Rapids** (AHL), April 9, 2008. Signed as a free agent by **Lake Erie** (AHL), October 8, 2008. Signed as a free agent by **Milwaukee** (AHL), October 13, 2009. Signed as a free agent by **Nashville**, December 27, 2010. Signed as a free agent by **Dallas**, July 8, 2013.

MUELLER, Peter

(MEW-luhr, PEE-tuhr)

Center. Shoots right. 6'2", 204 lbs. Born, Bloomington, MN, April 14, 1988. Phoenix's 1st choice, 8th overall, in 2006 Entry Draft.

Season	Club	League	GP	G	A	Pts	PIM	PP	SH	GW	S	%	+/-	TF	F%	Min	GP	G	A	Pts	PIM	PP	SH	GW	Min
2003-04	USNTDP	U-17	17	4	9	13	25	....	....	....	....	....	....	....	....	....	....	....	....	....	....	....	....	....	....
	USNTDP	NAHL	43	10	16	26	26	....	....	....	....	....	....	....	....	....	7	3	2	5	4	....	....	....	....
2004-05	USNTDP	U-18	43	27	27	64	75	....	....	....	....	....	....	....	....	....	....	....	....	....	....	....	....	....	....
	USNTDP	NAHL	14	11	13	24	16	....	....	....	....	....	....	....	....	....	....	....	....	....	....	....	....	....	....
2005-06	Everett Silvertips	WHL	52	26	32	58	44	....	....	....	....	....	....	....	....	....	15	7	6	13	10	....	....	....	....
2006-07	Everett Silvertips	WHL	51	21	57	78	45	....	....	....	....	....	....	....	....	....	12	7	9	16	12	....	....	....	....
2007-08	**Phoenix**	**NHL**	**81**	**22**	**32**	**54**	**32**	**7**	**0**	**3**	**201**	**10.9**	**–13**	**251**	**41.8**	**17:16**	....	....	....	....	....	....	....	....	....
2008-09	**Phoenix**	**NHL**	**72**	**13**	**23**	**36**	**24**	**5**	**0**	**4**	**138**	**9.4**	**–7**	**92**	**44.6**	**16:05**	....	....	....	....	....	....	....	....	....
2009-10	**Phoenix**	**NHL**	**54**	**4**	**13**	**17**	**8**	**1**	**0**	**1**	**89**	**4.5**	**–5**	**42**	**42.9**	**12:55**	....	....	....	....	....	....	....	....	....
	Colorado	**NHL**	**15**	**9**	**11**	**20**	**8**	**3**	**0**	**1**	**35**	**25.7**	**4**	**2**	**0.0**	**17:50**	....	....	....	....	....	....	....	....	....
2010-11			DID NOT PLAY – INJURED																						
2011-12	**Colorado**	**NHL**	**32**	**7**	**9**	**16**	**8**	**1**	**0**	**1**	**82**	**8.5**	**–3**	**10**	**60.0**	**14:39**	....	....	....	....	....	....	....	....	....
2012-13	**Florida**	**NHL**	**43**	**8**	**9**	**17**	**18**	**2**	**0**	**0**	**131**	**6.1**	**–11**	**104**	**44.2**	**16:16**	....	....	....	....	....	....	....	....	....
	NHL Totals		**297**	**63**	**97**	**160**	**98**	**19**	**0**	**10**	**676**	**9.3**		**501**	**43.1**	**15:47**	....	....	....	....	....	....	....	....	....

WHL Rookie ot the Year (2006) • WHL West First All-Star Team (2007) • Canadian Major Junior Second All-Star Team (2007)

Traded to **Colorado** by **Phoenix** with Kevin Porter for Wojtek Wolski, March 3, 2010. • Missed 2010-11 and majority of 2011-12 due to head injury vs. San Jose, April 14, 2010. Signed as a free agent by **Florida**, July 12, 2012.

MURPHY, Ryan

(MUHR-fee, RIGH-uhn) **CAR**

Defense. Shoots right. 5'11", 185 lbs. Born, Aurora, Ont., March 31, 1993. Carolina's 1st choice, 12th overall, in 2011 Entry Draft.

Season	Club	League	GP	G	A	Pts	PIM	PP	SH	GW	S	%	+/-	TF	F%	Min	GP	G	A	Pts	PIM	PP	SH	GW	Min
2008-09	York Simcoe	Minor-ON	73	30	65	95	52	....	....	....	....	....	....	....	....	....	....	....	....	....	....	....	....	....	....
	Villanova Knights	ON-Jr.A	4	4	2	6	0	....	....	....	....	....	....	....	....	....	....	....	....	....	....	....	....	....	....
2009-10	Kitchener Rangers	OHL	62	6	33	39	22	....	....	....	....	....	....	....	....	....	20	5	12	17	16	....	....	....	....
2010-11	Kitchener Rangers	OHL	63	26	53	79	36	....	....	....	....	....	....	....	....	....	7	2	9	11	8	....	....	....	....
2011-12	Kitchener Rangers	OHL	49	11	43	54	30	....	....	....	....	....	....	....	....	....	16	2	20	22	12	....	....	....	....
2012-13	Kitchener Rangers	OHL	54	10	38	48	34	....	....	....	....	....	....	....	....	....	10	3	4	7	8	....	....	....	....
	Carolina	**NHL**	**4**	**0**	**0**	**0**	**2**	**0**	**0**	**0**	**7**	**0.0**	**–4**	**0**	**0.0**	**21:04**	....	....	....	....	....	....	....	....	....
	Charlotte	AHL	3	0	2	2	0	....	....	....	....	....	....	....	....	....	5	0	2	2	2	....	....	....	....
	NHL Totals		**4**	**0**	**0**	**0**	**2**	**0**	**0**	**0**	**7**	**0.0**		**0**	**0.0**	**21:04**	....	....	....	....	....	....	....	....	....

OHL All-Rookie Team (2010) • OHL First All-Star Team (2011) • OHL Second All-Star Team (2012, 2013)

MURRAY, Andrew

(MUHR-ree, AN-droo)

Center. Shoots left. 6'2", 210 lbs. Born, Selkirk, Man., November 6, 1981. Columbus' 11th choice, 242nd overall, in 2001 Entry Draft.

			Regular Season														Playoffs								
Season	Club	League	GP	G	A	Pts	PIM	PP	SH	GW	S	%	+/-	TF	F%	Min	GP	G	A	Pts	PIM	PP	SH	GW	Min
99-2000	Selkirk Steelers	MJHL	63	29	48	77																			
2000-01	Selkirk Steelers	MJHL	64	46	56	102	72										5	3	0	3	6				
2001-02	Bemidji State	CHA	35	15	15	30	22																		
2002-03	Bemidji State	CHA	36	9	18	27	38																		
2003-04	Bemidji State	CHA	25	6	14	20	41																		
2004-05	Bemidji State	CHA	32	16	22	38	30																		
2005-06	Syracuse Crunch	AHL	77	13	16	29	73										6	0	1	1	17				
2006-07	Syracuse Crunch	AHL	72	10	12	22	62																		
2007-08	**Columbus**	**NHL**	**39**	**6**	**4**	**10**	**12**	**0**	**0**	**0**	**45**	**13.3**	**0**	**32**	**46.9**	**11:42**									
	Syracuse Crunch	AHL	34	13	2	15	15																		
2008-09	**Columbus**	**NHL**	**67**	**8**	**3**	**11**	**10**	**1**	**0**	**3**	**89**	**9.0**	**-6**	**85**	**45.9**	**11:16**									
2009-10	**Columbus**	**NHL**	**46**	**5**	**2**	**7**	**6**	**0**	**0**	**0**	**73**	**6.8**	**-6**	**118**	**41.5**	**10:22**									
2010-11	**Columbus**	**NHL**	**29**	**4**	**4**	**8**	**4**	**0**	**0**	**1**	**48**	**8.3**	**2**	**41**	**46.3**	**11:23**									
2011-12	**San Jose**	**NHL**	**39**	**1**	**3**	**4**	**4**	**0**	**0**	**0**	**33**	**3.0**	**3**	**15**	**33.3**	**7:42**									
	Worcester Sharks	AHL	10	2	1	3	0																		
2012-13	Peoria Rivermen	AHL	51	14	17	31	18																		
	St. Louis	**NHL**	**1**	**0**	**0**	**0**	**0**	**0**	**0**	**0**	**2**	**0.0**	**0**	**0**	**0.0**	**7:49**									
	NHL Totals		**221**	**24**	**16**	**40**	**36**	**1**	**0**	**4**	**290**	**8.3**		**291**	**43.6**	**10:32**									

CHA All-Rookie Team (2002)

• Missed majority of 2010-11 due to lower-body injury. Signed as a free agent by **San Jose**, July 19, 2011. Traded to **Detroit** by **San Jose** with San Jose's 7th round choice in 2014 Entry Draft for Brad Stuart, June 10, 2012. Signed as a free agent by **St. Louis**, July 6, 2012. Signed as a free agent by **Zagreb** (KHL), July 29, 2013.

MURRAY, Douglas

(MUHR-ree, DUHG-luhs)

Defense. Shoots left. 6'3", 245 lbs. Born, Bromma, Sweden, March 12, 1980. San Jose's 6th choice, 241st overall, in 1999 Entry Draft.

			Regular Season														Playoffs								
Season	Club	League	GP	G	A	Pts	PIM	PP	SH	GW	S	%	+/-	TF	F%	Min	GP	G	A	Pts	PIM	PP	SH	GW	Min
1998-99	NY Apple Core	EJHL	60	17	47	64	62																		
99-2000	Cornell Big Red	ECAC	32	3	6	9	38																		
2000-01	Cornell Big Red	ECAC	25	5	13	18	39																		
2001-02	Cornell Big Red	ECAC	35	11	21	32	67																		
2002-03	Cornell Big Red	ECAC	35	5	20	25	30																		
2003-04	Cleveland Barons	AHL	72	10	12	22	75										9	3	0	3	37				
2004-05	Cleveland Barons	AHL	54	6	17	23	56																		
2005-06	**San Jose**	**NHL**	**34**	**0**	**1**	**1**	**27**	**0**	**0**	**0**	**21**	**0.0**	**3**	**0**	**0.0**	**13:53**									
	Cleveland Barons	AHL	20	1	7	8	37																		
2006-07	**San Jose**	**NHL**	**35**	**0**	**3**	**3**	**31**	**0**	**0**	**0**	**18**	**0.0**	**0**	**0**	**0.0**	**10:46**									
	Worcester Sharks	AHL	5	2	1	3	8																		
2007-08	**San Jose**	**NHL**	**66**	**1**	**9**	**10**	**98**	**0**	**0**	**0**	**48**	**2.1**	**20**	**2**	**50.0**	**17:28**	**13**	**1**	**1**	**2**	**2**	**0**	**0**	**0**	**18:09**
2008-09	**San Jose**	**NHL**	**75**	**0**	**7**	**7**	**38**	**0**	**0**	**0**	**56**	**0.0**	**6**	**0**	**0.0**	**16:39**	**6**	**0**	**0**	**0**	**9**	**0**	**0**	**0**	**16:51**
2009-10	**San Jose**	**NHL**	**79**	**4**	**13**	**17**	**66**	**1**	**0**	**1**	**85**	**4.7**	**3**	**0**	**0.0**	**20:20**	**15**	**1**	**6**	**7**	**8**	**0**	**0**	**0**	**20:21**
	Sweden	Olympics	4	0	0	0	0																		
2010-11	**San Jose**	**NHL**	**73**	**1**	**13**	**14**	**44**	**0**	**0**	**0**	**102**	**1.0**	**5**	**0**	**0.0**	**19:37**	**18**	**0**	**1**	**1**	**8**	**0**	**0**	**0**	**19:30**
2011-12	**San Jose**	**NHL**	**60**	**0**	**4**	**4**	**31**	**0**	**0**	**0**	**71**	**0.0**	**3**	**0**	**0.0**	**18:23**	**5**	**0**	**0**	**0**	**19**	**0**	**0**	**0**	**16:14**
2012-13	Djurgarden	Sweden-2	14	1	2	3	36																		
	San Jose	**NHL**	**29**	**0**	**3**	**3**	**26**	**0**	**0**	**0**	**13**	**0.0**	**-8**	**0**	**0.0**	**17:09**									
	Pittsburgh	**NHL**	**14**	**1**	**2**	**3**	**9**	**0**	**0**	**0**	**14**	**7.1**	**-1**	**0**	**0.0**	**18:30**	**15**	**2**	**1**	**3**	**32**	**0**	**0**	**0**	**15:19**
	NHL Totals		**465**	**7**	**55**	**62**	**370**	**1**	**0**	**1**	**428**	**1.6**		**2**	**50.0**	**17:31**	**72**	**4**	**9**	**13**	**78**	**0**	**0**	**0**	**18:07**

ECAC First All-Star Team (2002, 2003) • NCAA East First All-American Team (2003)

• Missed majority of 2006-07 due to respiratory infection. Signed as a free agent by **Djurgarden** (Sweden-2), September 23, 2012. Traded to **Pittsburgh** by **San Jose** for Pittsburgh's 2nd round choice (later traded to Detroit – Detroit selected Tyler Bertuzzi) in 2013 Entry Draft and Pittsburgh's 2nd round choice in 2014 Entry Draft, March 25, 2013.

MURSAK , Jan

(MUHR-sak, YAHN)

Left wing. Shoots right. 5'11", 190 lbs. Born, Maribor, Yugoslavia, January 20, 1988. Detroit's 5th choice, 182nd overall, in 2006 Entry Draft.

			Regular Season														Playoffs								
Season	Club	League	GP	G	A	Pts	PIM	PP	SH	GW	S	%	+/-	TF	F%	Min	GP	G	A	Pts	PIM	PP	SH	GW	Min
2002-03	HK Maribor U18	Sloven-U18	13	27	18	45	14																		
2003-04	HK Maribor U18	Sloven-U18	22	27	17	44	14																		
	HK Maribor Jr.	Sloven-Jr.	19	8	8	16	37																		
	HK Maribor	Slovenia	14	3	3	6	16																		
2004-05	HK Maribor Jr.	Sloven-Jr.	19	17	16	33	39																		
	HK Maribor	Slovenia	24	16	29	45	10																		
2005-06	C. Budejovice Jr.	CzRep-Jr.	43	15	15	30	32										5	0	2	2	2				
2006-07	Saginaw Spirit	OHL	62	27	53	80	50										6	1	2	3	10				
	Grand Rapids	AHL															7	0	2	2	2				
2007-08	Saginaw Spirit	OHL	26	6	20	26	15																		
	Belleville Bulls	OHL	31	11	27	38	8										21	9	15	24	10				
2008-09	Grand Rapids	AHL	51	2	7	9	25										6	0	1	1	0				
2009-10	Grand Rapids	AHL	79	24	18	42	46																		
2010-11	**Detroit**	**NHL**	**19**	**1**	**0**	**1**	**4**	**0**	**0**	**0**	**20**	**5.0**	**-3**	**6**	**50.0**	**8:12**									
	Grand Rapids	AHL	54	13	22	35	35																		
2011-12	**Detroit**	**NHL**	**25**	**1**	**2**	**3**	**0**	**0**	**0**	**0**	**22**	**4.5**	**2**	**3**	**33.3**	**7:33**									
	Grand Rapids	AHL	6	0	1	1	2																		
2012-13	Ljubljana	Austria	30	19	29	48	9																		
	Detroit	**NHL**	**2**	**0**	**0**	**0**	**4**	**0**	**0**	**0**	**0**	**0.0**	**0**	**2**	**50.0**	**5:39**									
	Grand Rapids	AHL	23	4	12	16	12										23	11	6	17	26				
	NHL Totals		**46**	**2**	**2**	**4**	**8**	**0**	**0**	**0**	**42**	**4.8**		**11**	**45.5**	**7:44**									

Signed asa a free agent by **Ljubljana** (Austria), September 24, 2012. Signed as a free agent by **Khabarovsk** (KHL), May 7, 2013.

MUZZIN, Jake

(MUH-zihn, JAYK) **L.A.**

Defense. Shoots left. 6'3", 215 lbs. Born, Woodstock, Ont., February 21, 1989. Pittsburgh's 7th choice, 141st overall, in 2007 Entry Draft.

			Regular Season														Playoffs								
Season	Club	League	GP	G	A	Pts	PIM	PP	SH	GW	S	%	+/-	TF	F%	Min	GP	G	A	Pts	PIM	PP	SH	GW	Min
2004-05	Brantford 99ers	Minor-ON	57	20	23	43	78																		
2005-06	Sault Ste. Marie	OHL	DID NOT PLAY – INJURED																						
2006-07	Soo Thunderbirds	NOJHL	4	0	3	3	2																		
	Sault Ste. Marie	OHL	37	1	3	4	10										13	0	4	4	6				
2007-08	Sault Ste. Marie	OHL	67	6	12	18	53										10	1	3	4	4				
2008-09	Sault Ste. Marie	OHL	62	6	23	29	57																		
2009-10	Sault Ste. Marie	OHL	64	15	52	67	76										5	0	1	1	2				
	Manchester	AHL	1	0	1	1	0										13	1	3	4	6				
2010-11	**Los Angeles**	**NHL**	**11**	**0**	**1**	**1**	**0**	**0**	**0**	**0**	**8**	**0.0**	**-2**	**0**	**0.0**	**13:43**									
	Manchester	AHL	45	3	15	18	39										7	3	1	4	2				
2011-12	Manchester	AHL	71	7	24	31	40										3	0	1	1	2				
2012-13	Manchester	AHL	29	2	9	11	24																		
	Los Angeles	**NHL**	**45**	**7**	**9**	**16**	**35**	**3**	**0**	**1**	**77**	**9.1**	**16**	**0**	**0.0**	**17:54**	**17**	**0**	**3**	**3**	**6**	**0**	**0**	**0**	**15:50**
	NHL Totals		**56**	**7**	**10**	**17**	**35**	**3**	**0**	**1**	**85**	**8.2**		**0**	**0.0**	**17:04**	**17**	**0**	**3**	**3**	**6**	**0**	**0**	**0**	**15:50**

OHL First All-Star Team (2010) • Canadian Major Junior First All-Star Team (2010)

• Missed 2005-06 due to off-season back surgery. Signed as a free agent by **Los Angeles**, January 4, 2010.

MYERS, Tyler

(MIGH-uhrz, TIGH-luhr) **BUF**

Defense. Shoots right. 6'8", 227 lbs. Born, Houston, TX, February 1, 1990. Buffalo's 1st choice, 12th overall, in 2008 Entry Draft.

			Regular Season														Playoffs								
Season	Club	League	GP	G	A	Pts	PIM	PP	SH	GW	S	%	+/-	TF	F%	Min	GP	G	A	Pts	PIM	PP	SH	GW	Min
2005-06	Notre Dame	SMHL	34	4	6	10	78																		
	Kelowna Rockets	WHL	9	0	1	1	2										8	1	0	1	2				
2006-07	Kelowna Rockets	WHL	59	2	13	15	78																		
2007-08	Kelowna Rockets	WHL	65	6	13	19	97										7	1	2	3	12				
2008-09	Kelowna Rockets	WHL	58	9	33	42	105										22	5	15	20	29				
2009-10	**Buffalo**	**NHL**	**82**	**11**	**37**	**48**	**32**	**3**	**0**	**1**	**104**	**10.6**	**13**	**0**	**0.0**	**23:44**	**6**	**1**	**0**	**1**	**4**	**0**	**0**	**0**	**25:54**
2010-11	**Buffalo**	**NHL**	**80**	**10**	**27**	**37**	**40**	**3**	**0**	**5**	**122**	**8.2**	**0**	**0**	**0.0**	**22:27**	**7**	**1**	**5**	**6**	**16**	**0**	**0**	**0**	**23:52**
2011-12	**Buffalo**	**NHL**	**55**	**8**	**15**	**23**	**33**	**3**	**0**	**1**	**84**	**9.5**	**5**	**0**	**0.0**	**22:29**									

Season	Club	League	GP	G	A	Pts	PIM	PP	SH	GW	S	%	+/-	TF	F%	Min	GP	G	A	Pts	PIM	PP	SH	GW	Min
			Regular Season														Playoffs								
2012-13	Klagenfurter AC	Austria	17	3	7	10	37	....	....	....	....	....	....	....	....	....	....	....	....	....	....	....	....	....	....
	Buffalo	**NHL**	**39**	**3**	**5**	**8**	**32**	**1**	**0**	**2**	**48**	**6.3**	**−8**	**0**	**0.0**	**21:19**	....	....	....	....	....	....	....	....	....
	NHL Totals		**256**	**32**	**84**	**116**	**137**	**10**	**0**	**9**	**358**	**8.9**		**0**	**0.0**	**22:42**	**13**	**2**	**5**	**7**	**20**	**0**	**0**	**0**	**24:48**

WHL West Second All-Star Team (2009) • NHL All-Rookie Team (2010) • Calder Memorial Trophy (2010)

Signed as a free agent by **Klagenfurt** (Austria), October 15, 2012.

NASH, Brendon

(NASH, BREHN-duhn)

Defense. Shoots left. 6'3", 214 lbs. Born, Kamloops, B.C., March 31, 1987.

Season	Club	League	GP	G	A	Pts	PIM	PP	SH	GW	S	%	+/-	TF	F%	Min	GP	G	A	Pts	PIM	PP	SH	GW	Min
2005-06	Salmon Arm	BCHL	53	9	33	42	80	....	....	....	....	....	....	....	....	....	....	....	....	....	....	....	....	....	....
2006-07	Cornell Big Red	ECAC	29	2	12	14	38	....	....	....	....	....	....	....	....	....	....	....	....	....	....	....	....	....	....
2007-08	Cornell Big Red	ECAC	24	2	14	16	49	....	....	....	....	....	....	....	....	....	....	....	....	....	....	....	....	....	....
2008-09	Cornell Big Red	ECAC	34	2	16	18	38	....	....	....	....	....	....	....	....	....	....	....	....	....	....	....	....	....	....
2009-10	Cornell Big Red	ECAC	33	2	17	19	48	....	....	....	....	....	....	....	....	....	....	....	....	....	....	....	....	....	....
2010-11	**Montreal**	**NHL**	**2**	**0**	**0**	**0**	**0**	**0**	**0**	**0**	**2**	**0.0**	**−1**	**0**	**0.0**	**10:12**	....	....	....	....	....	....	....	....	....
	Hamilton	AHL	75	5	25	30	58	....	....	....	....	....	....	....	....	....	19	0	4	4	14	....	....	....	....
2011-12			DID NOT PLAY – INJURED																						
2012-13	Hamilton	AHL	26	1	7	8	39	....	....	....	....	....	....	....	....	....	....	....	....	....	....	....	....	....	....
	San Antonio	AHL	27	5	6	11	16	....	....	....	....	....	....	....	....	....	....	....	....	....	....	....	....	....	....
	Charlotte	AHL	1	0	0	0	0	....	....	....	....	....	....	....	....	....	....	....	....	....	....	....	....	....	....
	NHL Totals		**2**	**0**	**0**	**0**	**0**	**0**	**0**	**0**	**2**	**0.0**		**0**	**0.0**	**10:12**	....	....	....	....	....	....	....	....	....

ECAC Second All-Star Team (2009) • ECAC First All-Star Team (2010) • NCAA East First All-American Team (2010)

Signed as a free agent by **Montreal**, March 30, 2010. • Missed 2011-12 due to shoulder injury in training camp. Traded to **Florida** by **Montreal** for Jason DeSantis, January 14, 2013. • Loaned to **Charlotte** (AHL) by **Florida** (San Antonio-AHL), April 11, 2013.

NASH, Rick

(NASH, RIHK) **NYR**

Left wing. Shoots left. 6'4", 212 lbs. Born, Brampton, Ont., June 16, 1984. Columbus' 1st choice, 1st overall, in 2002 Entry Draft.

Season	Club	League	GP	G	A	Pts	PIM	PP	SH	GW	S	%	+/-	TF	F%	Min	GP	G	A	Pts	PIM	PP	SH	GW	Min
99-2000	Tor. Marlboros	GTHL	34	61	54	115	34	....	....	....	....	....	....	....	....	....	....	....	....	....	....	....	....	....	....
2000-01	London Knights	OHL	58	31	35	66	56	....	....	....	....	....	....	....	....	....	4	3	3	6	8	....	....	....	....
2001-02	London Knights	OHL	54	32	40	72	88	....	....	....	....	....	....	....	....	....	12	10	9	19	21	....	....	....	....
2002-03	**Columbus**	**NHL**	**74**	**17**	**22**	**39**	**78**	**6**	**0**	**2**	**154**	**11.0**	**−27**	**14**	**35.7**	**13:57**	....	....	....	....	....	....	....	....	....
2003-04	**Columbus**	**NHL**	**80**	***41**	**16**	**57**	**87**	***19**	**0**	**7**	**269**	**15.2**	**−35**	**21**	**28.6**	**17:38**	....	....	....	....	....	....	....	....	....
2004-05	HC Davos	Swiss	44	26	20	46	83	....	....	....	....	....	....	....	....	....	15	9	2	11	26	....	....	....	....
2005-06	**Columbus**	**NHL**	**54**	**31**	**23**	**54**	**51**	**11**	**0**	**4**	**170**	**18.2**	**5**	**38**	**50.0**	**18:16**	....	....	....	....	....	....	....	....	....
	Canada	Olympics	6	0	1	1	10	....	....	....	....	....	....	....	....	....	....	....	....	....	....	....	....	....	....
2006-07	**Columbus**	**NHL**	**75**	**27**	**30**	**57**	**73**	**9**	**1**	**5**	**228**	**11.8**	**−8**	**143**	**42.7**	**19:12**	....	....	....	....	....	....	....	....	....
2007-08	**Columbus**	**NHL**	**80**	**38**	**31**	**69**	**95**	**10**	**4**	**6**	**329**	**11.6**	**2**	**44**	**31.8**	**20:29**	....	....	....	....	....	....	....	....	....
2008-09	**Columbus**	**NHL**	**78**	**40**	**39**	**79**	**52**	**6**	**5**	**5**	**263**	**15.2**	**11**	**18**	**27.8**	**21:10**	**4**	**1**	**2**	**3**	**2**	**0**	**0**	**0**	**20:52**
2009-10	**Columbus**	**NHL**	**76**	**33**	**34**	**67**	**58**	**10**	**2**	**6**	**254**	**13.0**	**−2**	**22**	**50.0**	**20:56**	....	....	....	....	....	....	....	....	....
	Canada	Olympics	7	2	3	5	0	....	....	....	....	....	....	....	....	....	....	....	....	....	....	....	....	....	....
2010-11	**Columbus**	**NHL**	**75**	**32**	**34**	**66**	**34**	**6**	**0**	**7**	**305**	**10.5**	**2**	**24**	**29.2**	**18:56**	....	....	....	....	....	....	....	....	....
2011-12	**Columbus**	**NHL**	**82**	**30**	**29**	**59**	**40**	**6**	**2**	**2**	**306**	**9.8**	**−19**	**19**	**31.6**	**19:05**	....	....	....	....	....	....	....	....	....
2012-13	HC Davos	Swiss	17	12	6	18	8	....	....	....	....	....	....	....	....	....	....	....	....	....	....	....	....	....	....
	NY Rangers	**NHL**	**44**	**21**	**21**	**42**	**26**	**3**	**1**	**3**	**176**	**11.9**	**16**	**12**	**41.7**	**19:58**	**12**	**1**	**4**	**5**	**0**	**0**	**0**	**0**	**20:28**
	NHL Totals		**718**	**310**	**279**	**589**	**594**	**86**	**15**	**47**	**2454**	**12.6**		**355**	**39.2**	**18:58**	**16**	**2**	**6**	**8**	**2**	**0**	**0**	**0**	**20:34**

OHL All-Rookie Team (2001) • OHL Rookie of the Year (2001) • CHL All-Rookie Team (2001) • NHL All-Rookie Team (2003) • Maurice "Rocket" Richard Trophy (2004) (tied with Jarome Iginla and Ilya Kovalchuk) • NHL Foundation Player Award (2009)

Played in NHL All-Star Game (2004, 2007, 2008, 2009, 2011)

Signed as a free agent by **Davos** (Swiss), August 3, 2004. Traded to **NY Rangers** by **Columbus** with Steven Delisle and Columbus' 3rd round choice (Pavel Buchnevich) in 2013 Entry Draft for Brandon Dubinsky, Artem Anisimov, Tim Erixon and NY Rangers' 1st round choice (Kerby Rychel) in 2013 Entry Draft, July 23, 2012. Signed as a free agent by **Davos** (Swiss), September 18, 2012.

NASH, Riley

(NASH, RIGH-lee) **CAR**

Center. Shoots right. 6'1", 200 lbs. Born, Consort, Alta., May 9, 1989. Edmonton's 3rd choice, 21st overall, in 2007 Entry Draft.

Season	Club	League	GP	G	A	Pts	PIM	PP	SH	GW	S	%	+/-	TF	F%	Min	GP	G	A	Pts	PIM	PP	SH	GW	Min
2005-06	Thompson Blazers	BCMML	31	29	31	60	100	....	....	....	....	....	....	....	....	....	....	....	....	....	....	....	....	....	....
	Salmon Arm	BCHL	1	0	0	0	0	....	....	....	....	....	....	....	....	....	5	1	2	3	0	....	....	....	....
2006-07	Salmon Arm	BCHL	55	38	46	84	87	....	....	....	....	....	....	....	....	....	11	4	7	11	31	....	....	....	....
2007-08	Cornell Big Red	ECAC	36	12	20	32	28	....	....	....	....	....	....	....	....	....	....	....	....	....	....	....	....	....	....
2008-09	Cornell Big Red	ECAC	36	13	22	35	34	....	....	....	....	....	....	....	....	....	....	....	....	....	....	....	....	....	....
2009-10	Cornell Big Red	ECAC	30	12	23	35	39	....	....	....	....	....	....	....	....	....	....	....	....	....	....	....	....	....	....
2010-11	Charlotte	AHL	79	14	18	32	26	....	....	....	....	....	....	....	....	....	16	1	3	4	16	....	....	....	....
2011-12	**Carolina**	**NHL**	**5**	**0**	**1**	**1**	**2**	**0**	**0**	**0**	**2**	**0.0**	**1**	**35**	**31.4**	**10:34**	....	....	....	....	....	....	....	....	....
	Charlotte	AHL	58	8	12	20	26	....	....	....	....	....	....	....	....	....	....	....	....	....	....	....	....	....	....
2012-13	Charlotte	AHL	51	13	24	37	20	....	....	....	....	....	....	....	....	....	5	1	2	3	0	....	....	....	....
	Carolina	**NHL**	**32**	**4**	**5**	**9**	**8**	**0**	**0**	**0**	**36**	**11.1**	**−4**	**289**	**44.3**	**12:48**	....	....	....	....	....	....	....	....	....
	NHL Totals		**37**	**4**	**6**	**10**	**10**	**0**	**0**	**0**	**38**	**10.5**		**324**	**42.9**	**12:30**	....	....	....	....	....	....	....	....	....

ECAC All-Rookie Team (2008) • ECAC Rookie of the Year (2008) • ECAC First All-Star Team (2009)

Traded to **Carolina** by **Edmonton** for Ottawa's 2nd round choice (previously acquired, Edmonton selected Martin Marincin) in 2010 Entry Draft, June 25, 2010.

NEAL, James

(NEEL, JAYMS) **PIT**

Left wing. Shoots left. 6'2", 208 lbs. Born, Whitby, Ont., September 3, 1987. Dallas' 2nd choice, 33rd overall, in 2005 Entry Draft.

Season	Club	League	GP	G	A	Pts	PIM	PP	SH	GW	S	%	+/-	TF	F%	Min	GP	G	A	Pts	PIM	PP	SH	GW	Min
2003-04	Bowmanville	ON-Jr.A	43	28	27	55	....	....	....	....	....	....	....	....	....	....	....	....	....	....	....	....	....	....	....
	Plymouth Whalers	OHL	9	2	4	6	0	....	....	....	....	....	....	....	....	....	....	....	....	....	....	....	....	....	....
2004-05	Plymouth Whalers	OHL	67	18	26	44	32	....	....	....	....	....	....	....	....	....	4	1	1	2	6	....	....	....	....
2005-06	Plymouth Whalers	OHL	66	21	37	58	109	....	....	....	....	....	....	....	....	....	13	9	7	16	33	....	....	....	....
2006-07	Plymouth Whalers	OHL	45	27	38	65	94	....	....	....	....	....	....	....	....	....	20	13	12	25	54	....	....	....	....
2007-08	Iowa Stars	AHL	62	18	19	37	63	....	....	....	....	....	....	....	....	....	....	....	....	....	....	....	....	....	....
2008-09	**Dallas**	**NHL**	**77**	**24**	**13**	**37**	**51**	**9**	**0**	**2**	**171**	**14.0**	**−11**	**31**	**35.5**	**15:52**	....	....	....	....	....	....	....	....	....
	Manitoba Moose	AHL	5	4	1	5	2	....	....	....	....	....	....	....	....	....	....	....	....	....	....	....	....	....	....
2009-10	**Dallas**	**NHL**	**78**	**27**	**28**	**55**	**64**	**2**	**1**	**4**	**200**	**13.5**	**−5**	**60**	**31.7**	**18:12**	....	....	....	....	....	....	....	....	....
2010-11	**Dallas**	**NHL**	**59**	**21**	**18**	**39**	**60**	**5**	**0**	**3**	**160**	**13.1**	**8**	**17**	**41.2**	**17:42**	....	....	....	....	....	....	....	....	....
	Pittsburgh	**NHL**	**20**	**1**	**5**	**6**	**6**	**0**	**0**	**0**	**52**	**1.9**	**−1**	**6**	**16.7**	**16:54**	**7**	**1**	**1**	**2**	**6**	**0**	**0**	**1**	**17:25**
2011-12	**Pittsburgh**	**NHL**	**80**	**40**	**41**	**81**	**87**	***18**	**0**	**4**	**329**	**12.2**	**6**	**15**	**26.7**	**19:08**	**5**	**2**	**4**	**6**	**12**	**1**	**0**	**0**	**19:50**
2012-13	**Pittsburgh**	**NHL**	**40**	**21**	**15**	**36**	**26**	**9**	**0**	**6**	**136**	**15.4**	**5**	**6**	**16.7**	**17:28**	**13**	**6**	**4**	**10**	**8**	**2**	**0**	**1**	**17:43**
	NHL Totals		**354**	**134**	**120**	**254**	**294**	**43**	**1**	**19**	**1048**	**12.8**		**135**	**31.9**	**17:40**	**25**	**9**	**9**	**18**	**26**	**3**	**0**	**2**	**18:03**

OHL First All-Star Team (2007) • Canadian Major Junior Second All-Star Team (2007) • NHL First All-Star Team (2012)

Played in NHL All-Star Game (2012)

Traded to **Pittsburgh** by **Dallas** with Matt Niskanen for Alex Goligoski, February 21, 2011.

NEGRIN, John

(NEH-grihn, JAWN)

Defense. Shoots left. 6'2", 195 lbs. Born, West Vancouver, B.C., March 25, 1989. Calgary's 2nd choice, 70th overall, in 2007 Entry Draft.

Season	Club	League	GP	G	A	Pts	PIM	PP	SH	GW	S	%	+/-	TF	F%	Min	GP	G	A	Pts	PIM	PP	SH	GW	Min
2004-05	North Delta Flyers	PIJHL	45	3	12	15	53	....	....	....	....	....	....	....	....	....	....	....	....	....	....	....	....	....	....
	Kootenay Ice	WHL	2	0	0	0	0	....	....	....	....	....	....	....	....	....	....	....	....	....	....	....	....	....	....
2005-06	Kootenay Ice	WHL	55	3	7	10	48	....	....	....	....	....	....	....	....	....	6	0	0	0	6	....	....	....	....
2006-07	Kootenay Ice	WHL	44	1	15	16	57	....	....	....	....	....	....	....	....	....	7	0	2	2	8	....	....	....	....
2007-08	Kootenay Ice	WHL	71	1	41	42	68	....	....	....	....	....	....	....	....	....	10	1	1	2	8	....	....	....	....
2008-09	Kootenay Ice	WHL	38	5	26	31	27	....	....	....	....	....	....	....	....	....	....	....	....	....	....	....	....	....	....
	Swift Current	WHL	25	3	15	18	22	....	....	....	....	....	....	....	....	....	7	2	4	6	8	....	....	....	....
	Calgary	**NHL**	**3**	**0**	**1**	**1**	**2**	**0**	**0**	**0**	**3**	**0.0**	**−2**	**0**	**0.0**	**9:59**	....	....	....	....	....	....	....	....	....
2009-10	Abbotsford Heat	AHL	45	5	10	15	28	....	....	....	....	....	....	....	....	....	....	....	....	....	....	....	....	....	....
2010-11	Abbotsford Heat	AHL	24	0	6	6	24	....	....	....	....	....	....	....	....	....	....	....	....	....	....	....	....	....	....
2011-12	Abbotsford Heat	AHL	26	0	1	1	12	....	....	....	....	....	....	....	....	....	....	....	....	....	....	....	....	....	....
	Utah Grizzlies	ECHL	9	1	5	6	10	....	....	....	....	....	....	....	....	....	....	....	....	....	....	....	....	....	....
	St. John's IceCaps	AHL	14	0	3	3	6	....	....	....	....	....	....	....	....	....	....	....	....	....	....	....	....	....	....

			Regular Season														Playoffs								
Season	Club	League	GP	G	A	Pts	PIM	PP	SH	GW	S	%	+/-	TF	F%	Min	GP	G	A	Pts	PIM	PP	SH	GW	Min
2012-13	Kalamazoo Wings	ECHL	44	2	7	9	37	....	....	....	....	....	....	....	....	....	....	....	....	....	....	....	....	....	....
	Chicago Wolves	AHL	1	0	1	1	0	....	....	....	....	....	....	....	....	....	....	....	....	....	....	....	....	....	....
	Lake Erie	AHL	17	2	2	4	19	....	....	....	....	....	....	....	....	....	....	....	....	....	....	....	....	....	....
	NHL Totals		**3**	**0**	**1**	**1**	**2**	**0**	**0**	**0**	**3**	**0.0**		**0**	**0.0**	**9:59**	....	....	....	....	....	....	....	....	....

WHL East Second All-Star Team (2009)

Traded to **Winnipeg** by **Calgary** for Akim Aliu, January 29. 2012. Signed as a free agent by **Chicago** (AHL), August 20, 2012. Re-assigned to **Kalamazoo** (ECHL) by **Chicago** (AHL), January 18, 2013. • Loaned to **Lake Erie** (AHL) by **Chicago** (AHL), February 27, 2013.

NEIL, Chris

(NEEL, KRIHS) **OTT**

Right wing. Shoots right. 6'1", 215 lbs. Born, Markdale, Ont., June 18, 1979. Ottawa's 7th choice, 161st overall, in 1998 Entry Draft.

Season	Club	League	GP	G	A	Pts	PIM	PP	SH	GW	S	%	+/-	TF	F%	Min	GP	G	A	Pts	PIM	PP	SH	GW	Min
1995-96	Orangeville	ON-Jr.B	43	15	15	30	50	....	....	....	....	....	....	....	....	....	....	....	....	....	....	....	....	....	....
1996-97	North Bay	OHL	65	13	16	29	150	....	....	....	....	....	....	....	....	....	....	....	....	....	....	....	....	....	....
1997-98	North Bay	OHL	59	26	29	55	231	....	....	....	....	....	....	....	....	....	....	....	....	....	....	....	....	....	....
1998-99	North Bay	OHL	66	26	46	72	215	....	....	....	....	....	....	....	....	....	4	1	0	1	15	....	....	....	....
99-2000	Mobile Mysticks	ECHL	4	0	2	2	39	....	....	....	....	....	....	....	....	....	....	....	....	....	....	....	....	....	....
	Grand Rapids	IHL	51	9	10	19	301	....	....	....	....	....	....	....	....	....	8	0	2	2	24	....	....	....	....
2000-01	Grand Rapids	IHL	78	15	21	36	354	....	....	....	....	....	....	....	....	....	10	2	2	4	22	....	....	....	....
2001-02	**Ottawa**	**NHL**	**72**	**10**	**7**	**17**	**231**	**1**	**0**	**0**	**56**	**17.9**	**5**	**0**	**0.0**	**8:22**	**12**	**0**	**0**	**0**	**12**	**0**	**0**	**0**	**7:12**
2002-03	**Ottawa**	**NHL**	**68**	**6**	**4**	**10**	**147**	**0**	**0**	**0**	**62**	**9.7**	**8**	**5**	**60.0**	**7:40**	**15**	**1**	**0**	**1**	**24**	**0**	**0**	**0**	**7:57**
2003-04	**Ottawa**	**NHL**	**82**	**8**	**8**	**16**	**194**	**0**	**0**	**1**	**76**	**10.5**	**13**	**14**	**42.9**	**8:51**	**7**	**0**	**1**	**1**	**19**	**0**	**0**	**0**	**6:45**
2004-05	Binghamton	AHL	22	4	6	10	132	....	....	....	....	....	....	....	....	....	6	1	1	2	26	....	....	....	....
2005-06	**Ottawa**	**NHL**	**79**	**16**	**17**	**33**	**204**	**8**	**0**	**0**	**126**	**12.7**	**9**	**9**	**22.2**	**12:18**	**10**	**1**	**0**	**1**	**14**	**0**	**0**	**0**	**6:58**
2006-07	**Ottawa**	**NHL**	**82**	**12**	**16**	**28**	**177**	**3**	**0**	**3**	**139**	**8.6**	**6**	**13**	**38.5**	**13:08**	**20**	**2**	**2**	**4**	**20**	**0**	**0**	**0**	**10:40**
2007-08	**Ottawa**	**NHL**	**68**	**6**	**14**	**20**	**199**	**0**	**0**	**1**	**78**	**7.7**	**–3**	**0**	**0.0**	**12:46**	**4**	**0**	**1**	**1**	**22**	**0**	**0**	**0**	**11:17**
2008-09	**Ottawa**	**NHL**	**60**	**3**	**7**	**10**	**146**	**0**	**0**	**0**	**59**	**5.1**	**–13**	**6**	**16.7**	**10:58**	....	....	....	....	....	....	....	....	....
2009-10	**Ottawa**	**NHL**	**68**	**10**	**12**	**22**	**175**	**1**	**0**	**2**	**100**	**10.0**	**–1**	**4**	**50.0**	**11:59**	**6**	**3**	**1**	**4**	**20**	**0**	**0**	**0**	**14:11**
2010-11	**Ottawa**	**NHL**	**80**	**6**	**10**	**16**	**210**	**0**	**0**	**2**	**105**	**5.7**	**–14**	**6**	**50.0**	**12:46**	....	....	....	....	....	....	....	....	....
2011-12	**Ottawa**	**NHL**	**72**	**13**	**15**	**28**	**178**	**2**	**0**	**0**	**127**	**10.2**	**–10**	**2**	**0.0**	**12:48**	**7**	**2**	**1**	**3**	**22**	**1**	**0**	**1**	**13:35**
2012-13	**Ottawa**	**NHL**	**48**	**4**	**8**	**12**	**144**	**0**	**0**	**3**	**87**	**4.6**	**0**	**6**	**50.0**	**13:52**	**10**	**0**	**4**	**4**	***39**	**0**	**0**	**0**	**12:42**
	NHL Totals		**779**	**94**	**118**	**212**	**2005**	**15**	**0**	**12**	**1015**	**9.3**		**65**	**38.5**	**11:21**	**91**	**9**	**10**	**19**	**192**	**1**	**0**	**1**	**9:46**

Signed as a free agent by **Binghamton** (AHL), March 2, 2005.

NELSON, Brock

(NEHL-suhn, BRAWK) **NYI**

Center. Shoots left. 6'3", 196 lbs. Born, Warroad, MN, October 15, 1991. NY Islanders' 2nd choice, 30th overall, in 2010 Entry Draft.

Season	Club	League	GP	G	A	Pts	PIM	PP	SH	GW	S	%	+/-	TF	F%	Min	GP	G	A	Pts	PIM	PP	SH	GW	Min
2007-08	Warroad Warriors	High-MN	31	14	9	23	....	....	....	....	....	....	....	....	....	....	....	....	....	....	....	....	....	....	....
2008-09	Warroad Warriors	High-MN	31	45	36	81	....	....	....	....	....	....	....	....	....	....	....	....	....	....	....	....	....	....	....
2009-10	Team Great Plains	UMHSEL	24	5	10	15	....	....	....	....	....	....	....	....	....	....	....	....	....	....	....	....	....	....	....
	Warroad Warriors	High-MN	25	39	34	73	38	....	....	....	....	....	....	....	....	....	6	14	8	22	8	....	....	....	....
2010-11	North Dakota	WCHA	42	8	13	21	27	....	....	....	....	....	....	....	....	....	....	....	....	....	....	....	....	....	....
2011-12	North Dakota	WCHA	42	28	19	47	4	....	....	....	....	....	....	....	....	....	....	....	....	....	....	....	....	....	....
	Bridgeport	AHL	4	0	0	0	0	....	....	....	....	....	....	....	....	....	2	0	0	0	0	....	....	....	....
2012-13	Bridgeport	AHL	66	25	27	52	34	....	....	....	....	....	....	....	....	....	....	....	....	....	....	....	....	....	....
	NY Islanders	**NHL**	....	....	....	....	....	....	....	....	....	....	....	....	....	....	**1**	**0**	**0**	**0**	**0**	**0**	**0**	**0**	**7:44**
	NHL Totals		....	....	....	....	....	....	....	....	....	....	....	....	....	....	**1**	**0**	**0**	**0**	**0**	**0**	**0**	**0**	**7:44**

NEMISZ, Greg

(NEH-mihtz, GREHG) **CGY**

Center. Shoots right. 6'3", 197 lbs. Born, Courtice, Ont., June 5, 1990. Calgary's 1st choice, 25th overall, in 2008 Entry Draft.

Season	Club	League	GP	G	A	Pts	PIM	PP	SH	GW	S	%	+/-	TF	F%	Min	GP	G	A	Pts	PIM	PP	SH	GW	Min
2005-06	Clarington Toros	Minor-ON	32	29	24	53	24	....	....	....	....	....	....	....	....	....	....	....	....	....	....	....	....	....	....
2006-07	Windsor Spitfires	OHL	62	11	23	34	23	....	....	....	....	....	....	....	....	....	....	....	....	....	....	....	....	....	....
2007-08	Windsor Spitfires	OHL	68	34	33	67	52	....	....	....	....	....	....	....	....	....	5	2	1	3	8	....	....	....	....
2008-09	Windsor Spitfires	OHL	65	36	41	77	48	....	....	....	....	....	....	....	....	....	20	8	12	20	22	....	....	....	....
2009-10	Windsor Spitfires	OHL	51	34	36	70	50	....	....	....	....	....	....	....	....	....	15	2	10	12	12	....	....	....	....
2010-11	**Calgary**	**NHL**	**6**	**0**	**1**	**1**	**0**	**0**	**0**	**0**	**5**	**0.0**	**–1**	**3**	**33.3**	**5:06**	....	....	....	....	....	....	....	....	....
	Abbotsford Heat	AHL	68	14	19	33	28	....	....	....	....	....	....	....	....	....	....	....	....	....	....	....	....	....	....
2011-12	**Calgary**	**NHL**	**9**	**0**	**0**	**0**	**0**	**0**	**0**	**0**	**2**	**0.0**	**1**	**48**	**39.6**	**7:43**	....	....	....	....	....	....	....	....	....
	Abbotsford Heat	AHL	51	13	16	29	29	....	....	....	....	....	....	....	....	....	8	2	4	6	4	....	....	....	....
2012-13	Abbotsford Heat	AHL	55	3	7	10	34	....	....	....	....	....	....	....	....	....	....	....	....	....	....	....	....	....	....
	NHL Totals		**15**	**0**	**1**	**1**	**0**	**0**	**0**	**0**	**7**	**0.0**		**51**	**39.2**	**6:40**	....	....	....	....	....	....	....	....	....

OHL Second All-Star Team (2009)

NESS, Aaron

(NEHS, AIR-uhn) **NYI**

Defense. Shoots left. 5'10", 182 lbs. Born, Roseau, MN, May 18, 1990. NY Islanders' 3rd choice, 40th overall, in 2008 Entry Draft.

Season	Club	League	GP	G	A	Pts	PIM	PP	SH	GW	S	%	+/-	TF	F%	Min	GP	G	A	Pts	PIM	PP	SH	GW	Min
2005-06	Roseau Rams	High-MN	30	3	18	21	8	....	....	....	....	....	....	....	....	....	....	....	....	....	....	....	....	....	....
2006-07	Roseau Rams	High-MN	31	13	38	51	12	....	....	....	....	....	....	....	....	....	....	....	....	....	....	....	....	....	....
	Team Great Plains	UMWEHL	11	0	8	8	....	....	....	....	....	....	....	....	....	....	....	....	....	....	....	....	....	....	....
2007-08	Roseau Rams	High-MN	31	28	44	72	16	....	....	....	....	....	....	....	....	....	....	....	....	....	....	....	....	....	....
	Team Great Plains	UMWEHL	11	2	11	13	....	....	....	....	....	....	....	....	....	....	....	....	....	....	....	....	....	....	....
2008-09	U. of Minnesota	WCHA	37	2	15	17	16	....	....	....	....	....	....	....	....	....	....	....	....	....	....	....	....	....	....
2009-10	U. of Minnesota	WCHA	39	2	10	12	24	....	....	....	....	....	....	....	....	....	....	....	....	....	....	....	....	....	....
2010-11	U. of Minnesota	WCHA	35	2	12	14	41	....	....	....	....	....	....	....	....	....	....	....	....	....	....	....	....	....	....
	Bridgeport	AHL	13	1	3	4	4	....	....	....	....	....	....	....	....	....	....	....	....	....	....	....	....	....	....
2011-12	**NY Islanders**	**NHL**	**9**	**0**	**0**	**0**	**2**	**0**	**0**	**0**	**6**	**0.0**	**0**	**0**	**0.0**	**16:56**	....	....	....	....	....	....	....	....	....
	Bridgeport	AHL	69	5	22	27	36	....	....	....	....	....	....	....	....	....	3	0	0	0	4	....	....	....	....
2012-13	Bridgeport	AHL	76	3	24	27	30	....	....	....	....	....	....	....	....	....	....	....	....	....	....	....	....	....	....
	NHL Totals		**9**	**0**	**0**	**0**	**2**	**0**	**0**	**0**	**6**	**0.0**		**0**	**0.0**	**16:56**	....	....	....	....	....	....	....	....	....

NEWBURY, Kris

(new-BUHR-ee, KRIHS) **PHI**

Center. Shoots left. 5'11", 205 lbs. Born, Brampton, Ont., February 19, 1982. San Jose's 4th choice, 139th overall, in 2002 Entry Draft.

Season	Club	League	GP	G	A	Pts	PIM	PP	SH	GW	S	%	+/-	TF	F%	Min	GP	G	A	Pts	PIM	PP	SH	GW	Min
1996-97	Brampton	ON-Jr.A	28	9	4	13	36	....	....	....	....	....	....	....	....	....	....	....	....	....	....	....	....	....	....
1997-98	Brampton	ON-Jr.A	46	11	21	32	161	....	....	....	....	....	....	....	....	....	....	....	....	....	....	....	....	....	....
1998-99	Belleville Bulls	OHL	51	6	8	14	89	....	....	....	....	....	....	....	....	....	....	....	....	....	....	....	....	....	....
99-2000	Belleville Bulls	OHL	34	6	18	24	72	....	....	....	....	....	....	....	....	....	....	....	....	....	....	....	....	....	....
	Sarnia Sting	OHL	27	6	8	14	44	....	....	....	....	....	....	....	....	....	7	0	3	3	16	....	....	....	....
2000-01	Sarnia Sting	OHL	64	28	30	58	126	....	....	....	....	....	....	....	....	....	4	1	3	4	20	....	....	....	....
2001-02	Sarnia Sting	OHL	66	42	62	104	141	....	....	....	....	....	....	....	....	....	5	1	3	4	15	....	....	....	....
2002-03	Sarnia Sting	OHL	64	34	58	92	149	....	....	....	....	....	....	....	....	....	6	4	4	8	16	....	....	....	....
2003-04	St. John's	AHL	72	5	15	20	153	....	....	....	....	....	....	....	....	....	....	....	....	....	....	....	....	....	....
2004-05	St. John's	AHL	55	4	9	13	103	....	....	....	....	....	....	....	....	....	5	0	0	0	36	....	....	....	....
	Pensacola	ECHL	6	2	4	6	20	....	....	....	....	....	....	....	....	....	....	....	....	....	....	....	....	....	....
2005-06	Toronto Marlies	AHL	74	22	37	59	215	....	....	....	....	....	....	....	....	....	5	0	1	1	12	....	....	....	....
2006-07	**Toronto**	**NHL**	**15**	**2**	**2**	**4**	**26**	**0**	**0**	**0**	**30**	**6.7**	**4**	**20**	**45.0**	**7:42**	....	....	....	....	....	....	....	....	....
	Toronto Marlies	AHL	37	12	24	36	87	....	....	....	....	....	....	....	....	....	....	....	....	....	....	....	....	....	....
2007-08	**Toronto**	**NHL**	**28**	**1**	**1**	**2**	**32**	**0**	**0**	**0**	**14**	**7.1**	**–7**	**55**	**40.0**	**4:22**	....	....	....	....	....	....	....	....	....
	Toronto Marlies	AHL	54	16	27	43	101	....	....	....	....	....	....	....	....	....	19	4	9	13	*73	....	....	....	....
2008-09	**Toronto**	**NHL**	**1**	**0**	**0**	**0**	**2**	**0**	**0**	**0**	**0**	**0.0**	**0**	**3**	**33.3**	**4:55**	....	....	....	....	....	....	....	....	....
	Toronto Marlies	AHL	33	6	23	29	72	....	....	....	....	....	....	....	....	....	....	....	....	....	....	....	....	....	....
2009-10	**Detroit**	**NHL**	**4**	**1**	**0**	**1**	**4**	**0**	**0**	**0**	**3**	**33.3**	**1**	**18**	**38.9**	**8:41**	....	....	....	....	....	....	....	....	....
	Grand Rapids	AHL	52	11	22	33	144	....	....	....	....	....	....	....	....	....	....	....	....	....	....	....	....	....	....
	Hartford	AHL	18	4	14	18	61	....	....	....	....	....	....	....	....	....	....	....	....	....	....	....	....	....	....
2010-11	**NY Rangers**	**NHL**	**11**	**0**	**1**	**1**	**35**	**0**	**0**	**0**	**6**	**0.0**	**–1**	**56**	**60.7**	**7:38**	....	....	....	....	....	....	....	....	....
	Connecticut	AHL	69	17	44	61	139	....	....	....	....	....	....	....	....	....	6	2	2	4	2	....	....	....	....
2011-12	**NY Rangers**	**NHL**	**7**	**0**	**0**	**0**	**24**	**0**	**0**	**0**	**2**	**0.0**	**–1**	**17**	**35.3**	**5:53**	....	....	....	....	....	....	....	....	....
	Connecticut	AHL	65	25	39	64	130	....	....	....	....	....	....	....	....	....	9	1	3	4	20	....	....	....	....

			Regular Season														Playoffs								
Season	Club	League	GP	G	A	Pts	PIM	PP	SH	GW	S	%	+/-	TF	F%	Min	GP	G	A	Pts	PIM	PP	SH	GW	Min
2012-13	Connecticut	AHL	70	20	42	62	127	....	....	....	....	....	....	....	....	....	....	....	....	....	....	....	....	....	....
	NY Rangers	**NHL**	**6**	**0**	**1**	**1**	**9**	**0**	**0**	**0**	**4**	**0.0**	**1**	**32**	**50.0**	**7:53**	**3**	**0**	**0**	**0**	**2**	**0**	**0**	**0**	**6:10**
	NHL Totals		**72**	**4**	**5**	**9**	**132**	**0**	**0**	**0**	**59**	**6.8**		**201**	**47.3**	**6:15**	**3**	**0**	**0**	**0**	**2**	**0**	**0**	**0**	**6:10**

OHL Second All-Star Team (2002)

Signed as a free agent by **St. John's** (AHL), October 2, 2003. Signed as a free agent by **Toronto**, July 17, 2006. Signed as a free agent by **Detroit**, July 7, 2009. Traded to **NY Rangers** by **Detroit** for Jordan Owens, March 3, 2010. Traded to **Philadelphia** by **NY Rangers** Danny Syvret, July 1, 2013.

NICHOL, Scott

(NIH-KOHL, SKAWT)

Center. Shoots right. 5'8", 179 lbs. Born, Edmonton, Alta., December 31, 1974. Buffalo's 9th choice, 272nd overall, in 1993 Entry Draft.

Season	Club	League	GP	G	A	Pts	PIM	PP	SH	GW	S	%	+/-	TF	F%	Min	GP	G	A	Pts	PIM	PP	SH	GW	Min
1991-92	Calgary Flames	AMHL	23	26	16	42	132	....	....	....	....	....	....	....	....	....	....	....	....	....	....	....	....	....	....
1992-93	Portland	WHL	67	31	33	64	146	....	....	....	....	....	....	....	....	....	16	8	8	16	41	....	....	....	....
1993-94	Portland	WHL	65	40	53	93	144	....	....	....	....	....	....	....	....	....	10	3	8	11	16	....	....	....	....
1994-95	Rochester	AHL	71	11	16	27	136	....	....	....	....	....	....	....	....	....	5	0	3	3	14	....	....	....	....
1995-96	**Buffalo**	**NHL**	**2**	**0**	**0**	**0**	**10**	**0**	**0**	**0**	**4**	**0.0**	**0**	....	....	....	....	....	....	....	....	....	....	....	....
	Rochester	AHL	62	14	18	32	170	....	....	....	....	....	....	....	....	....	19	7	6	13	36	....	....	....	....
1996-97	Rochester	AHL	68	22	21	43	133	....	....	....	....	....	....	....	....	....	10	2	1	3	26	....	....	....	....
1997-98	**Buffalo**	**NHL**	**3**	**0**	**0**	**0**	**4**	**0**	**0**	**0**	**5**	**0.0**	**0**	....	....	....	....	....	....	....	....	....	....	....	....
	Rochester	AHL	35	13	7	20	113	....	....	....	....	....	....	....	....	....	17	0	6	6	18	....	....	....	....
1998-99	Rochester	AHL	52	13	20	33	120	....	....	....	....	....	....	....	....	....	....	....	....	....	....	....	....	....	....
99-2000	Rochester	AHL	37	7	11	18	141	....	....	....	....	....	....	....	....	....	12	0	3	3	10	....	....	....	....
2000-01	Detroit Vipers	IHL	67	7	24	31	198	....	....	....	....	....	....	....	....	....	11	1	1	2	12	....	....	....	....
2001-02	**Calgary**	**NHL**	**60**	**8**	**9**	**17**	**107**	**2**	**1**	**0**	**49**	**16.3**	**–9**	**458**	**53.1**	**12:41**	....	....	....	....	....	....	....	....	....
2002-03	**Calgary**	**NHL**	**68**	**5**	**5**	**10**	**149**	**0**	**1**	**0**	**66**	**7.6**	**–7**	**357**	**58.3**	**10:47**	....	....	....	....	....	....	....	....	....
2003-04	**Chicago**	**NHL**	**75**	**7**	**11**	**18**	**145**	**0**	**0**	**1**	**112**	**6.3**	**–16**	**1178**	**57.4**	**15:46**	....	....	....	....	....	....	....	....	....
2004-05	London Racers	Britain	16	7	12	19	86	....	....	....	....	....	....	....	....	....	....	....	....	....	....	....	....	....	....
2005-06	**Nashville**	**NHL**	**34**	**3**	**3**	**6**	**79**	**0**	**1**	**0**	**32**	**9.4**	**3**	**242**	**58.3**	**10:30**	**3**	**0**	**0**	**0**	**2**	**0**	**0**	**0**	**7:45**
	Milwaukee	AHL	6	3	5	8	18	....	....	....	....	....	....	....	....	....	....	....	....	....	....	....	....	....	....
2006-07	**Nashville**	**NHL**	**59**	**7**	**6**	**13**	**79**	**1**	**1**	**2**	**58**	**12.1**	**7**	**623**	**58.0**	**12:32**	**5**	**0**	**0**	**0**	**17**	**0**	**0**	**0**	**10:22**
2007-08	**Nashville**	**NHL**	**73**	**10**	**8**	**18**	**72**	**0**	**2**	**1**	**101**	**9.9**	**12**	**738**	**59.8**	**13:16**	**2**	**0**	**0**	**0**	**0**	**0**	**0**	**0**	**7:31**
2008-09	**Nashville**	**NHL**	**43**	**4**	**6**	**10**	**41**	**0**	**0**	**0**	**42**	**9.5**	**0**	**359**	**54.6**	**11:04**	....	....	....	....	....	....	....	....	....
2009-10	**San Jose**	**NHL**	**79**	**4**	**15**	**19**	**72**	**0**	**1**	**0**	**93**	**4.3**	**0**	**832**	**60.6**	**13:04**	**15**	**1**	**1**	**2**	**17**	**0**	**0**	**0**	**8:54**
2010-11	**San Jose**	**NHL**	**56**	**4**	**3**	**7**	**50**	**0**	**0**	**0**	**61**	**6.6**	**–3**	**485**	**59.4**	**9:45**	**15**	**0**	**0**	**0**	**26**	**0**	**0**	**0**	**6:22**
2011-12	**St. Louis**	**NHL**	**80**	**3**	**5**	**8**	**83**	**0**	**0**	**0**	**67**	**4.5**	**–5**	**450**	**57.6**	**9:19**	**9**	**0**	**1**	**1**	**14**	**0**	**0**	**0**	**11:29**
2012-13	**St. Louis**	**NHL**	**30**	**1**	**0**	**1**	**25**	**0**	**0**	**1**	**13**	**7.7**	**–2**	**218**	**60.6**	**9:47**	....	....	....	....	....	....	....	....	....
	NHL Totals		**662**	**56**	**71**	**127**	**916**	**3**	**7**	**5**	**703**	**8.0**		**5940**	**58.1**	**11:55**	**49**	**1**	**2**	**3**	**76**	**0**	**0**	**0**	**8:37**

• Missed majority of 1999-2000 due to knee injury vs. Saint John (AHL), February 16, 2000. Signed as a free agent by **Calgary**, July 1, 2001. Signed as a free agent by **Chicago**, July 1, 2003. Signed as a free agent by **London** (Britain), October 26, 2004. Signed as a free agent by **Nashville**, August 6, 2005. Signed as a free agent by **San Jose**, July 15, 2009. Signed as a free agent by **St. Louis**, July 5, 2011.

NIEDERREITER, Nino

(nee-duhr-RIGH-tuhr, NEE-noh) **MIN**

Right wing. Shoots left. 6'2", 208 lbs. Born, Chur, Switzerland, September 8, 1992. NY Islanders' 1st choice, 5th overall, in 2010 Entry Draft.

Season	Club	League	GP	G	A	Pts	PIM	PP	SH	GW	S	%	+/-	TF	F%	Min	GP	G	A	Pts	PIM	PP	SH	GW	Min
2006-07	HC Davos U18	Swiss-U18	32	43	19	62	38	....	....	....	....	....	....	....	....	....	....	....	....	....	....	....	....	....	....
	HC Davos Jr.	Swiss-Jr.	....	....	....	....	....	....	....	....	....	....	....	....	....	....	1	0	0	0	4	....	....	....	....
2007-08	HC Davos U18	Swiss-U18	32	39	26	65	62	....	....	....	....	....	....	....	....	....	5	6	3	9	4	....	....	....	....
	HC Davos Jr.	Swiss-Jr.	8	7	3	10	4	....	....	....	....	....	....	....	....	....	3	0	1	1	8	....	....	....	....
2008-09	HC Davos U18	Swiss-U18	6	6	6	12	6	....	....	....	....	....	....	....	....	....	....	....	....	....	....	....	....	....	....
	HC Davos Jr.	Swiss-Jr.	30	20	14	34	44	....	....	....	....	....	....	....	....	....	8	5	6	11	12	....	....	....	....
	HC Davos	Swiss	....	....	....	....	....	....	....	....	....	....	....	....	....	....	3	0	1	1	0	....	....	....	....
2009-10	Portland	WHL	65	36	24	60	68	....	....	....	....	....	....	....	....	....	13	8	8	16	16	....	....	....	....
2010-11	**NY Islanders**	**NHL**	**9**	**1**	**1**	**2**	**8**	**0**	**0**	**0**	**12**	**8.3**	**–1**	**0**	**0.0**	**13:36**	....	....	....	....	....	....	....	....	....
	Portland	WHL	55	41	29	70	67	....	....	....	....	....	....	....	....	....	21	9	18	27	30	....	....	....	....
2011-12	**NY Islanders**	**NHL**	**55**	**1**	**0**	**1**	**12**	**0**	**0**	**0**	**74**	**1.4**	**–29**	**2**	**0.0**	**10:07**	....	....	....	....	....	....	....	....	....
	Bridgeport	AHL	6	3	1	4	4	....	....	....	....	....	....	....	....	....	....	....	....	....	....	....	....	....	....
2012-13	Bridgeport	AHL	74	28	22	50	38	....	....	....	....	....	....	....	....	....	....	....	....	....	....	....	....	....	....
	NHL Totals		**64**	**2**	**1**	**3**	**20**	**0**	**0**	**0**	**86**	**2.3**		**2**	**0.0**	**10:36**	....	....	....	....	....	....	....	....	....

WHL West Second All-Star Team (2010)

Traded to **Minnesota** by **NY Islanders** for Cal Clutterbuck and New Jersey's 3rd round choice (previously acquired, Minnesota selected Eamon McAdam) in 2013 Entry Draft, June 30, 2013.

NIELSEN, Frans

(NEEL-sehn, FRAHNZ) **NYI**

Center. Shoots left. 6'1", 180 lbs. Born, Herning, Denmark, April 24, 1984. NY Islanders' 2nd choice, 87th overall, in 2002 Entry Draft.

Season	Club	League	GP	G	A	Pts	PIM	PP	SH	GW	S	%	+/-	TF	F%	Min	GP	G	A	Pts	PIM	PP	SH	GW	Min
99-2000	Herning IK Jr.	Den-Jr.	36	18	16	34	6	....	....	....	....	....	....	....	....	....	....	....	....	....	....	....	....	....	....
	Denmark	WJ18-B	5	3	4	7	0	....	....	....	....	....	....	....	....	....	....	....	....	....	....	....	....	....	....
2000-01	Herning IK	Denmark	38	18	19	37	6	....	....	....	....	....	....	....	....	....	....	....	....	....	....	....	....	....	....
	Denmark	WJ18-B	3	2	1	3	0	....	....	....	....	....	....	....	....	....	....	....	....	....	....	....	....	....	....
2001-02	Malmo	Sweden	20	0	1	1	0	....	....	....	....	....	....	....	....	....	....	....	....	....	....	....	....	....	....
	Malmo Jr.	Swe-Jr.	29	15	27	42	8	....	....	....	....	....	....	....	....	....	7	3	7	10	2	....	....	....	....
2002-03	Malmo	Sweden	47	3	6	9	10	....	....	....	....	....	....	....	....	....	....	....	....	....	....	....	....	....	....
	Malmo Jr.	Swe-Jr.	2	1	3	4	0	....	....	....	....	....	....	....	....	....	....	....	....	....	....	....	....	....	....
	Denmark	WJC-B	5	3	7	10	0	....	....	....	....	....	....	....	....	....	....	....	....	....	....	....	....	....	....
	Denmark	WC-A	6	0	0	0	4	....	....	....	....	....	....	....	....	....	....	....	....	....	....	....	....	....	....
2003-04	Malmo	Sweden	50	9	7	16	28	....	....	....	....	....	....	....	....	....	....	....	....	....	....	....	....	....	....
	Malmo	Sweden-Q	10	3	5	8	2	....	....	....	....	....	....	....	....	....	....	....	....	....	....	....	....	....	....
2004-05	Malmo	Sweden	49	8	7	15	6	....	....	....	....	....	....	....	....	....	....	....	....	....	....	....	....	....	....
	Malmo	Sweden-Q	10	7	2	9	0	....	....	....	....	....	....	....	....	....	....	....	....	....	....	....	....	....	....
	Denmark	Oly-Q	3	2	3	5	0	....	....	....	....	....	....	....	....	....	....	....	....	....	....	....	....	....	....
2005-06	Timra IK	Sweden	50	5	13	18	22	....	....	....	....	....	....	....	....	....	....	....	....	....	....	....	....	....	....
2006-07	**NY Islanders**	**NHL**	**15**	**1**	**1**	**2**	**0**	**0**	**0**	**1**	**16**	**6.3**	**–2**	**53**	**45.3**	**5:13**	....	....	....	....	....	....	....	....	....
	Bridgeport	AHL	54	20	24	44	10	....	....	....	....	....	....	....	....	....	....	....	....	....	....	....	....	....	....
2007-08	**NY Islanders**	**NHL**	**16**	**2**	**1**	**3**	**0**	**0**	**0**	**0**	**17**	**11.8**	**1**	**111**	**48.7**	**8:42**	....	....	....	....	....	....	....	....	....
	Bridgeport	AHL	48	10	28	38	18	....	....	....	....	....	....	....	....	....	....	....	....	....	....	....	....	....	....
2008-09	**NY Islanders**	**NHL**	**59**	**9**	**24**	**33**	**18**	**3**	**1**	**2**	**101**	**8.9**	**–4**	**758**	**47.2**	**16:32**	....	....	....	....	....	....	....	....	....
2009-10	**NY Islanders**	**NHL**	**76**	**12**	**26**	**38**	**6**	**0**	**1**	**1**	**136**	**8.8**	**4**	**1165**	**50.0**	**17:13**	....	....	....	....	....	....	....	....	....
2010-11	**NY Islanders**	**NHL**	**71**	**13**	**31**	**44**	**38**	**0**	***7**	**1**	**156**	**8.3**	**13**	**965**	**46.2**	**17:46**	....	....	....	....	....	....	....	....	....
2011-12	**NY Islanders**	**NHL**	**82**	**17**	**30**	**47**	**6**	**5**	**0**	**1**	**133**	**12.8**	**–3**	**1156**	**45.2**	**17:27**	....	....	....	....	....	....	....	....	....
2012-13	Lukko Rauma	Finland	27	4	20	24	10	....	....	....	....	....	....	....	....	....	....	....	....	....	....	....	....	....	....
	NY Islanders	**NHL**	**48**	**6**	**23**	**29**	**12**	**2**	**1**	**1**	**93**	**6.5**	**–3**	**558**	**48.0**	**18:01**	**6**	**0**	**2**	**2**	**0**	**0**	**0**	**0**	**18:00**
	NHL Totals		**367**	**60**	**136**	**196**	**80**	**10**	**10**	**7**	**652**	**9.2**		**4766**	**47.3**	**16:31**	**6**	**0**	**2**	**2**	**0**	**0**	**0**	**0**	**18:00**

Signed as a free agent by **Rauma** (Finland), September 26, 2012.

NIKITIN, Nikita

(nih-KEE-tihn, nih-KEE-tuh) **CBJ**

Defense. Shoots left. 6'3", 217 lbs. Born, Omsk, USSR, June 16, 1986. St. Louis' 5th choice, 136th overall, in 2004 Entry Draft.

Season	Club	League	GP	G	A	Pts	PIM	PP	SH	GW	S	%	+/-	TF	F%	Min	GP	G	A	Pts	PIM	PP	SH	GW	Min
2002-03	Omsk 2	Russia-3	34	3	7	10	4	....	....	....	....	....	....	....	....	....	....	....	....	....	....	....	....	....	....
2003-04	Omsk 2	Russia-3	34	3	8	11	22	....	....	....	....	....	....	....	....	....	....	....	....	....	....	....	....	....	....
2004-05	Avangard Omsk	Russia	12	0	0	0	2	....	....	....	....	....	....	....	....	....	3	0	0	0	0	....	....	....	....
	Omsk 2	Russia-3	31	3	8	11	20	....	....	....	....	....	....	....	....	....	....	....	....	....	....	....	....	....	....
2005-06	Avangard Omsk	Russia	43	1	2	3	22	....	....	....	....	....	....	....	....	....	13	1	2	3	6	....	....	....	....
	Omsk 2	Russia-3	1	0	0	0	0	....	....	....	....	....	....	....	....	....	....	....	....	....	....	....	....	....	....
2006-07	Avangard Omsk	Russia	54	1	15	16	99	....	....	....	....	....	....	....	....	....	9	0	4	4	35	....	....	....	....
2007-08	Avangard Omsk	Russia	57	3	11	14	48	....	....	....	....	....	....	....	....	....	4	0	1	1	2	....	....	....	....
2008-09	Omsk	KHL	53	4	11	15	28	....	....	....	....	....	....	....	....	....	9	1	2	3	8	....	....	....	....
2009-10	Omsk	KHL	43	4	9	13	14	....	....	....	....	....	....	....	....	....	3	0	0	0	0	....	....	....	....
2010-11	**St. Louis**	**NHL**	**41**	**1**	**8**	**9**	**10**	**0**	**0**	**0**	**46**	**2.2**	**1**	**0**	**0.0**	**16:24**	....	....	....	....	....	....	....	....	....
	Peoria Rivermen	AHL	22	3	11	14	12	....	....	....	....	....	....	....	....	....	....	....	....	....	....	....	....	....	....
2011-12	**St. Louis**	**NHL**	**7**	**0**	**0**	**0**	**4**	**0**	**0**	**0**	**10**	**0.0**	**–5**	**0**	**0.0**	**20:15**	....	....	....	....	....	....	....	....	....
	Columbus	**NHL**	**54**	**7**	**25**	**32**	**14**	**3**	**0**	**3**	**93**	**7.5**	**–5**	**0**	**0.0**	**23:35**	....	....	....	....	....	....	....	....	....

			Regular Season														Playoffs								
Season	Club	League	GP	G	A	Pts	PIM	PP	SH	GW	S	%	+/-	TF	F%	Min	GP	G	A	Pts	PIM	PP	SH	GW	Min
2012-13	Omsk	KHL	33	2	12	14	8	....	....	....	....	....	....	....	....	....	....	....	....	....	....	....	....	....	....
	Columbus	**NHL**	**38**	**3**	**6**	**9**	**17**	**1**	**0**	**0**	**60**	**5.0**	**2**	**0**	**0.0**	**21:12**	....	....	....	....	....	....	....	....	....
	NHL Totals		**140**	**11**	**39**	**50**	**45**	**4**	**0**	**3**	**209**	**5.3**		**0**	**0.0**	**20:40**	....	....	....	....	....	....	....	....	....

Traded to **Columbus** by **St. Louis** for Kris Russell, November 11, 2011. Signed as a free agent by **Omsk** (KHL), September 24, 2012.

NISKANEN, Matt

(NIHS-kah-nehn, MAT) **PIT**

Defense. Shoots right. 6', 209 lbs. Born, Virginia, MN, December 6, 1986. Dallas' 1st choice, 28th overall, in 2005 Entry Draft.

2003-04	Virginia	High-MN	....	24	37	61	....	....	....	....	....	....	....	....	....	....	....	....	....	....	....	....	....	....	....
2004-05	Virginia	High-MN	29	27	38	65	34	....	....	....	....	....	....	....	....	....	....	....	....	....	....	....	....	....	....
2005-06	U. Minn-Duluth	WCHA	38	1	13	14	40	....	....	....	....	....	....	....	....	....	....	....	....	....	....	....	....	....	....
2006-07	U. Minn-Duluth	WCHA	39	9	22	31	42	....	....	....	....	....	....	....	....	....	....	....	....	....	....	....	....	....	....
	Iowa Stars	AHL	13	0	3	3	6	....	....	....	....	....	....	....	....	....	12	2	5	7	10	....	....	....	....
2007-08	**Dallas**	**NHL**	**78**	**7**	**19**	**26**	**36**	**2**	**0**	**0**	**99**	**7.1**	**22**	**0**	**0.0**	**20:30**	**16**	**0**	**3**	**3**	**10**	**0**	**0**	**0**	**16:23**
2008-09	**Dallas**	**NHL**	**80**	**6**	**29**	**35**	**52**	**2**	**0**	**0**	**111**	**5.4**	**–11**	**0**	**0.0**	**19:58**	....	....	....	....	....	....	....	....	....
2009-10	**Dallas**	**NHL**	**74**	**3**	**12**	**15**	**18**	**0**	**0**	**2**	**110**	**2.7**	**–15**	**0**	**0.0**	**18:16**	....	....	....	....	....	....	....	....	....
2010-11	**Dallas**	**NHL**	**45**	**0**	**6**	**6**	**30**	**0**	**0**	**0**	**51**	**0.0**	**–1**	**0**	**0.0**	**15:44**	....	....	....	....	....	....	....	....	....
	Pittsburgh	**NHL**	**18**	**1**	**3**	**4**	**20**	**0**	**0**	**0**	**26**	**3.8**	**–2**	**0**	**0.0**	**18:31**	**7**	**0**	**1**	**1**	**0**	**0**	**0**	**0**	**12:58**
2011-12	**Pittsburgh**	**NHL**	**75**	**4**	**17**	**21**	**47**	**3**	**0**	**0**	**118**	**3.4**	**9**	**0**	**0.0**	**17:56**	**4**	**1**	**2**	**3**	**6**	**1**	**0**	**0**	**18:31**
2012-13	**Pittsburgh**	**NHL**	**40**	**4**	**10**	**14**	**12**	**0**	**0**	**2**	**67**	**6.0**	**4**	**0**	**0.0**	**20:21**	**15**	**0**	**2**	**2**	**11**	**0**	**0**	**0**	**18:55**
	NHL Totals		**410**	**25**	**96**	**121**	**215**	**7**	**0**	**4**	**582**	**4.3**		**0**	**0.0**	**18:54**	**42**	**1**	**8**	**9**	**27**	**1**	**0**	**0**	**16:55**

WCHA First All-Star Team (2007)

Traded to **Pittsburgh** by **Dallas** with James Neal for Alex Goligoski, February 21, 2011.

NODL, Andreas

(NOHD'L, awn-DRAY-uhs)

Right wing. Shoots left. 6'1", 196 lbs. Born, Vienna, Austria, February 28, 1987. Philadelphia's 2nd choice, 39th overall, in 2006 Entry Draft.

2001-02	Wien Jr.	Austria-Jr.	1	0	0	0	0	....	....	....	....	....	....	....	....	....	....	....	....	....	....	....	....	....	....
2002-03	Wien Jr.	Austria-Jr.	STATISTICS NOT AVAILABLE																						
	Austria	WJ18-B	5	2	2	4	4	....	....	....	....	....	....	....	....	....	....	....	....	....	....	....	....	....	....
2003-04	Wien Jr.	Austria-Jr.	15	11	10	21	47	....	....	....	....	....	....	....	....	....	....	....	....	....	....	....	....	....	....
	Vienna Capitals	Austria	25	15	22	37	26	....	....	....	....	....	....	....	....	....	....	....	....	....	....	....	....	....	....
	Austria	WJ18-B	5	2	3	5	26	....	....	....	....	....	....	....	....	....	....	....	....	....	....	....	....	....	....
2004-05	Sioux Falls	USHL	44	7	9	16	24	....	....	....	....	....	....	....	....	....	....	....	....	....	....	....	....	....	....
2005-06	Sioux Falls	USHL	58	29	30	59	16	....	....	....	....	....	....	....	....	....	14	6	9	15	6	....	....	....	....
2006-07	St. Cloud State	WCHA	40	18	28	46	32	....	....	....	....	....	....	....	....	....	....	....	....	....	....	....	....	....	....
2007-08	St. Cloud State	WCHA	40	18	26	44	22	....	....	....	....	....	....	....	....	....	....	....	....	....	....	....	....	....	....
	Philadelphia	AHL	3	1	0	1	0	....	....	....	....	....	....	....	....	....	10	1	0	1	2	....	....	....	....
2008-09	**Philadelphia**	**NHL**	**38**	**1**	**3**	**4**	**2**	**0**	**0**	**0**	**33**	**3.0**	**–15**	**0**	**0.0**	**11:09**	....	....	....	....	....	....	....	....	....
	Philadelphia	AHL	39	6	14	20	20	....	....	....	....	....	....	....	....	....	4	0	1	1	2	....	....	....	....
2009-10	**Philadelphia**	**NHL**	**10**	**0**	**1**	**1**	**0**	**0**	**0**	**0**	**2**	**0.0**	**–2**	**0**	**0.0**	**8:55**	**10**	**0**	**0**	**0**	**0**	**0**	**0**	**0**	**8:28**
	Adirondack	AHL	65	14	20	34	24	....	....	....	....	....	....	....	....	....	....	....	....	....	....	....	....	....	....
2010-11	**Philadelphia**	**NHL**	**67**	**11**	**11**	**22**	**16**	**1**	**1**	**2**	**100**	**11.0**	**14**	**19**	**57.9**	**13:16**	**2**	**0**	**0**	**0**	**0**	**0**	**0**	**0**	**7:25**
2011-12	**Philadelphia**	**NHL**	**12**	**0**	**1**	**1**	**2**	**0**	**0**	**0**	**6**	**0.0**	**–1**	**6**	**33.3**	**10:18**	....	....	....	....	....	....	....	....	....
	Carolina	**NHL**	**48**	**3**	**4**	**7**	**6**	**0**	**0**	**0**	**60**	**5.0**	**–4**	**2**	**50.0**	**12:04**	....	....	....	....	....	....	....	....	....
2012-13	Innsbruck	Austria	17	4	11	15	26	....	....	....	....	....	....	....	....	....	....	....	....	....	....	....	....	....	....
	Carolina	**NHL**	**8**	**0**	**1**	**1**	**2**	**0**	**0**	**0**	**6**	**0.0**	**–1**	**3**	**33.3**	**8:28**	....	....	....	....	....	....	....	....	....
	Charlotte	AHL	6	1	4	5	0	....	....	....	....	....	....	....	....	....	....	....	....	....	....	....	....	....	....
	NHL Totals		**183**	**15**	**21**	**36**	**28**	**1**	**1**	**2**	**207**	**7.2**		**30**	**50.0**	**11:52**	**12**	**0**	**0**	**0**	**0**	**0**	**0**	**0**	**8:17**

USHL First All-Star Team (2006) • WCHA All-Rookie Team (2007) • WCHA Rookie of the Year (2007) • NCAA Rookie of the Year (2007) • WCHA Second All-Star Team (2008)

Claimed on waivers by **Carolina** from **Philadelphia**, November 29, 2011. Signed as a free agent by **Innsbruck** (Austria), October 2, 2012.

NOKELAINEN, Petteri

(noh-kuh-LAY-nehn, PEH-tuh-ree)

Center. Shoots right. 6'1", 202 lbs. Born, Imatra, Finland, January 16, 1986. NY Islanders' 1st choice, 16th overall, in 2004 Entry Draft.

2001-02	SaiPa U18	Fin-U18	6	2	1	3	14	....	....	....	....	....	....	....	....	....	....	....	....	....	....	....	....	....	....
2002-03	SaiPa U18	Fin-U18	10	3	8	11	18	....	....	....	....	....	....	....	....	....	....	....	....	....	....	....	....	....	....
	SaiPa Jr.	Fin-Jr.	28	7	4	11	28	....	....	....	....	....	....	....	....	....	3	1	0	1	4	....	....	....	....
	SaiPa	Finland	2	1	0	1	2	....	....	....	....	....	....	....	....	....	....	....	....	....	....	....	....	....	....
2003-04	Suomi U20	Finland-2	3	0	1	1	0	....	....	....	....	....	....	....	....	....	....	....	....	....	....	....	....	....	....
	SaiPa Jr.	Fin-Jr.	10	5	3	8	4	....	....	....	....	....	....	....	....	....	4	0	1	1	0	....	....	....	....
	SaiPa	Finland	40	4	4	8	16	....	....	....	....	....	....	....	....	....	....	....	....	....	....	....	....	....	....
2004-05	SaiPa	Finland	52	15	5	20	34	....	....	....	....	....	....	....	....	....	....	....	....	....	....	....	....	....	....
2005-06	**NY Islanders**	**NHL**	**15**	**1**	**1**	**2**	**4**	**0**	**0**	**1**	**13**	**7.7**	**–1**	**82**	**48.8**	**7:47**	....	....	....	....	....	....	....	....	....
2006-07	Bridgeport	AHL	60	6	10	16	51	....	....	....	....	....	....	....	....	....	....	....	....	....	....	....	....	....	....
2007-08	**Boston**	**NHL**	**57**	**7**	**3**	**10**	**19**	**0**	**0**	**1**	**40**	**17.5**	**0**	**288**	**52.8**	**8:16**	**7**	**0**	**2**	**2**	**4**	**0**	**0**	**0**	**12:38**
	Providence Bruins	AHL	8	3	5	8	4	....	....	....	....	....	....	....	....	....	6	4	1	5	0	....	....	....	....
2008-09	**Boston**	**NHL**	**33**	**0**	**3**	**3**	**10**	**0**	**0**	**0**	**30**	**0.0**	**–1**	**87**	**62.1**	**9:40**	....	....	....	....	....	....	....	....	....
	Anaheim	**NHL**	**17**	**4**	**2**	**6**	**6**	**0**	**1**	**0**	**26**	**15.4**	**3**	**205**	**49.8**	**14:20**	**9**	**0**	**0**	**0**	**2**	**0**	**0**	**0**	**8:42**
2009-10	**Anaheim**	**NHL**	**50**	**4**	**7**	**11**	**21**	**0**	**0**	**0**	**70**	**5.7**	**–7**	**354**	**43.5**	**12:56**	....	....	....	....	....	....	....	....	....
	Phoenix	**NHL**	**17**	**1**	**1**	**2**	**6**	**0**	**0**	**0**	**18**	**5.6**	**–2**	**90**	**51.1**	**10:24**	**5**	**0**	**0**	**0**	**2**	**0**	**0**	**0**	**8:22**
2010-11	Jokerit Helsinki	Finland	46	11	16	27	116	....	....	....	....	....	....	....	....	....	7	2	0	2	12	....	....	....	....
2011-12	**Phoenix**	**NHL**	**5**	**0**	**1**	**1**	**0**	**0**	**0**	**0**	**3**	**0.0**	**–1**	**31**	**58.1**	**10:58**	....	....	....	....	....	....	....	....	....
	Montreal	**NHL**	**51**	**3**	**3**	**6**	**37**	**0**	**0**	**1**	**34**	**8.8**	**–5**	**278**	**52.9**	**8:35**	....	....	....	....	....	....	....	....	....
2012-13	Hamilton	AHL	17	2	2	4	21	....	....	....	....	....	....	....	....	....	....	....	....	....	....	....	....	....	....
	NHL Totals		**245**	**20**	**21**	**41**	**103**	**0**	**1**	**3**	**234**	**8.5**		**1415**	**50.4**	**10:04**	**21**	**0**	**2**	**2**	**8**	**0**	**0**	**0**	**9:56**

• Missed majority of 2005-06 due to knee injury vs. Pittsburgh, November 3, 2005. Traded to **Boston** by **NY Islanders** for Ben Walter and Boston's 2nd round choice (later traded to Columbus – Columbus selected Kevin Lynch) in 2009 Entry Draft, September 11, 2007. Traded to **Anaheim** by **Boston** for Steve Montador, March 4, 2009. Traded to **Phoenix** by **Anaheim** for Phoenix's 6th round choice (later traded to Ottawa – Ottawa selected Max McCormick) in 2011 Entry Draft, March 3, 2010. Signed as a free agent by **Jokerit Helsinki** (Finland), August 28, 2010. Traded to **Montreal** by **Phoenix** with Garrett Stafford for Brock Trotter and Montreal's 7th round choice (Marek Langhamer) in 2012 Entry Draft, October 23, 2011. • Missed majority of 2012-13 due to recurring back injury and as a healthy reserve.

NOLAN, Jordan

(NOH-luhn, JOHR-dahn) **L.A.**

Center. Shoots left. 6'3", 225 lbs. Born, St. Catharines, Ont., June 23, 1989. Los Angeles' 9th choice, 186th overall, in 2009 Entry Draft.

2005-06	Erie Otters	OHL	33	3	4	7	20	....	....	....	....	....	....	....	....	....	....	....	....	....	....	....	....	....	....
2006-07	Windsor Spitfires	OHL	60	11	16	27	100	....	....	....	....	....	....	....	....	....	....	....	....	....	....	....	....	....	....
2007-08	Windsor Spitfires	OHL	62	13	14	27	69	....	....	....	....	....	....	....	....	....	5	3	0	3	2	....	....	....	....
2008-09	Sault Ste. Marie	OHL	64	16	27	43	158	....	....	....	....	....	....	....	....	....	....	....	....	....	....	....	....	....	....
2009-10	Sault Ste. Marie	OHL	49	23	25	48	88	....	....	....	....	....	....	....	....	....	5	1	1	2	4	....	....	....	....
	Ontario Reign	ECHL	3	1	1	2	4	....	....	....	....	....	....	....	....	....	....	....	....	....	....	....	....	....	....
2010-11	Manchester	AHL	75	5	12	17	115	....	....	....	....	....	....	....	....	....	7	0	2	2	4	....	....	....	....
2011-12 ♦	**Los Angeles**	**NHL**	**26**	**2**	**2**	**4**	**28**	**0**	**0**	**1**	**19**	**10.5**	**2**	**1**	**100.0**	**9:21**	**20**	**1**	**1**	**2**	**21**	**0**	**0**	**0**	**7:17**
	Manchester	AHL	40	9	13	22	119	....	....	....	....	....	....	....	....	....	....	....	....	....	....	....	....	....	....
2012-13	Manchester	AHL	21	2	4	6	21	....	....	....	....	....	....	....	....	....	....	....	....	....	....	....	....	....	....
	Los Angeles	**NHL**	**44**	**2**	**4**	**6**	**46**	**0**	**0**	**0**	**23**	**8.7**	**–5**	**8**	**0.0**	**8:28**	**7**	**0**	**0**	**0**	**4**	**0**	**0**	**0**	**8:53**
	NHL Totals		**70**	**4**	**6**	**10**	**74**	**0**	**0**	**1**	**42**	**9.5**		**9**	**11.1**	**8:48**	**27**	**1**	**1**	**2**	**25**	**0**	**0**	**0**	**7:42**

NOREAU, Maxim

(NOHR-oh, max-EEM) **N.J.**

Defense. Shoots right. 6', 195 lbs. Born, Montreal, Que., May 14, 1987.

2004-05	Victoriaville Tigres	QMJHL	65	5	8	13	47	....	....	....	....	....	....	....	....	....	7	0	0	0	8	....	....	....	....
2005-06	Victoriaville Tigres	QMJHL	69	22	43	65	116	....	....	....	....	....	....	....	....	....	5	2	4	6	7	....	....	....	....
2006-07	Victoriaville Tigres	QMJHL	69	17	53	70	106	....	....	....	....	....	....	....	....	....	6	2	1	3	8	....	....	....	....
2007-08	Houston Aeros	AHL	50	8	8	16	48	....	....	....	....	....	....	....	....	....	5	0	0	0	4	....	....	....	....
	Texas Wildcatters	ECHL	2	0	3	3	0	....	....	....	....	....	....	....	....	....	....	....	....	....	....	....	....	....	....
2008-09	Houston Aeros	AHL	77	14	25	39	49	....	....	....	....	....	....	....	....	....	20	4	7	11	2	....	....	....	....
2009-10	**Minnesota**	**NHL**	**1**	**0**	**0**	**0**	**0**	**0**	**0**	**0**	**0**	**0.0**	**0**	**0**	**0.0**	**7:01**	....	....	....	....	....	....	....	....	....
	Houston Aeros	AHL	76	18	34	52	60	....	....	....	....	....	....	....	....	....	....	....	....	....	....	....	....	....	....

			Regular Season														Playoffs								
Season	Club	League	GP	G	A	Pts	PIM	PP	SH	GW	S	%	+/-	TF	F%	Min	GP	G	A	Pts	PIM	PP	SH	GW	Min
2010-11	**Minnesota**	**NHL**	**5**	**0**	**0**	**0**	**0**	**0**	**0**	**0**	**8**	**0.0**	**-1**	**0**	**0.0**	**14:17**	....	....	....	....	....	....	....	....	....
	Houston Aeros	AHL	76	10	44	54	58	....	....	....	....	....	....	....	....	....	24	2	10	12	23	....	....	....	....
2011-12	HC Ambri-Piotta	Swiss	44	7	23	30	22	....	....	....	....	....	....	....	....	....	13	1	8	9	8	....	....	....	....
2012-13	HC Ambri-Piotta	Swiss	45	10	25	35	38	....	....	....	....	....	....	....	....	....	5	1	3	4	2	....	....	....	....
	NHL Totals		**6**	**0**	**0**	**0**	**0**	**0**	**0**	**0**	**8**	**0.0**		**0**	**0.0**	**13:04**	....	....	....	....	....	....	....	....	....

AHL Second All-Star Team (2010) • AHL First All-Star Team (2011)

Signed as a free agent by **Minnesota**, May 22, 2008. Traded to **New Jersey** by **Minnesota** for David McIntyre, June 16, 2011. Signed as a free agent by **Ambri-Piotta** (Swiss), July 31, 2011.

NUGENT-HOPKINS, Ryan

(NOO-jehnt-HAWP-kihnz, RIGH-uhn) **EDM**

Center. Shoots left. 6'1", 175 lbs. Born, Burnaby, B.C., April 12, 1993. Edmonton's 1st choice, 1st overall, in 2011 Entry Draft.

Season	Club	League	GP	G	A	Pts	PIM	PP	SH	GW	S	%	+/-	TF	F%	Min	GP	G	A	Pts	PIM	PP	SH	GW	Min
2006-07	Burnaby W.C.	Minor-BC	65	43	43	86	34	....	....	....	....	....	....	....	....	....	....	....	....	....	....	....	....	....	....
2007-08	Burnaby W.C.	Minor-BC	66	119	95	214	84	....	....	....	....	....	....	....	....	....	....	....	....	....	....	....	....	....	....
2008-09	Van. NW Giants	BCMML	36	*40	*47	*87	78	....	....	....	....	....	....	....	....	....	5	*5	*5	*10	4	....	....	....	....
	Red Deer Rebels	WHL	5	2	4	6	0	....	....	....	....	....	....	....	....	....	....	....	....	....	....	....	....	....	....
2009-10	Red Deer Rebels	WHL	67	24	41	65	28	....	....	....	....	....	....	....	....	....	4	0	2	2	0	....	....	....	....
2010-11	Red Deer Rebels	WHL	69	31	*75	106	51	....	....	....	....	....	....	....	....	....	9	4	7	11	6	....	....	....	....
2011-12	**Edmonton**	**NHL**	**62**	**18**	**34**	**52**	**16**	**3**	**0**	**2**	**134**	**13.4**	**-2**	**605**	**37.5**	**17:36**	....	....	....	....	....	....	....	....	....
2012-13	Oklahoma City	AHL	19	8	12	20	6	....	....	....	....	....	....	....	....	....	....	....	....	....	....	....	....	....	....
	Edmonton	**NHL**	**40**	**4**	**20**	**24**	**8**	**2**	**0**	**0**	**78**	**5.1**	**3**	**551**	**41.0**	**18:52**	....	....	....	....	....	....	....	....	....
	NHL Totals		**102**	**22**	**54**	**76**	**24**	**5**	**0**	**2**	**212**	**10.4**		**1156**	**39.2**	**18:06**	....	....	....	....	....	....	....	....	....

WHL Rookie of the Year (2010) • Canadian Major Junior All-Rookie Team (2010) • WHL East First All-Star Team (2011) • NHL All-Rookie Team (2012)

NYQUIST, Gustav

(NEW-kwihst, GUHS-tav) **DET**

Right wing. Shoots left. 5'10", 185 lbs. Born, Halmstad, Sweden, September 1, 1989. Detroit's 3rd choice, 121st overall, in 2008 Entry Draft.

Season	Club	League	GP	G	A	Pts	PIM	PP	SH	GW	S	%	+/-	TF	F%	Min	GP	G	A	Pts	PIM	PP	SH	GW	Min
2005-06	Malmo U18	Swe-U18	14	9	3	12	10	....	....	....	....	....	....	....	....	....	6	1	3	4	0	....	....	....	....
2006-07	Malmo Jr.	Swe-Jr.	42	21	23	44	57	....	....	....	....	....	....	....	....	....	4	2	2	4	6	....	....	....	....
2007-08	Malmo Jr.	Swe-Jr.	24	11	20	31	20	....	....	....	....	....	....	....	....	....	7	5	5	10	6	....	....	....	....
2008-09	U. of Maine	H-East	38	13	19	32	28	....	....	....	....	....	....	....	....	....	....	....	....	....	....	....	....	....	....
2009-10	U. of Maine	H-East	39	19	*42	*61	20	....	....	....	....	....	....	....	....	....	....	....	....	....	....	....	....	....	....
2010-11	U. of Maine	H-East	36	18	*33	51	20	....	....	....	....	....	....	....	....	....	....	....	....	....	....	....	....	....	....
	Grand Rapids	AHL	8	1	3	4	2	....	....	....	....	....	....	....	....	....	....	....	....	....	....	....	....	....	....
2011-12	**Detroit**	**NHL**	**18**	**1**	**6**	**7**	**2**	**0**	**0**	**0**	**19**	**5.3**	**2**	**0**	**0.0**	**10:36**	**4**	**0**	**0**	**0**	**0**	**0**	**0**	**0**	**8:52**
	Grand Rapids	AHL	56	22	36	58	18	....	....	....	....	....	....	....	....	....	....	....	....	....	....	....	....	....	....
2012-13	Grand Rapids	AHL	58	23	37	60	34	....	....	....	....	....	....	....	....	....	10	2	5	7	19	....	....	....	....
	Detroit	**NHL**	**22**	**3**	**3**	**6**	**6**	**0**	**0**	**0**	**46**	**6.5**	**0**	**4**	**25.0**	**13:02**	**14**	**2**	**3**	**5**	**2**	**1**	**0**	**1**	**12:36**
	NHL Totals		**40**	**4**	**9**	**13**	**8**	**0**	**0**	**0**	**65**	**6.2**		**4**	**25.0**	**11:56**	**18**	**2**	**3**	**5**	**2**	**1**	**0**	**1**	**11:46**

Hockey East All-Rookie Team (2009) • Hockey East First All-Star Team (2010, 2011) • NCAA East First All-American Team (2010) • NCAA East Second All-American Team (2011) • AHL All-Rookie Team (2012) • AHL First All-Star Team (2013)

NYSTROM, Eric

(NIGH-stuhm, AIR-ihk) **NSH**

Left wing. Shoots left. 6'1", 193 lbs. Born, Syosset, NY, February 14, 1983. Calgary's 1st choice, 10th overall, in 2002 Entry Draft.

Season	Club	League	GP	G	A	Pts	PIM	PP	SH	GW	S	%	+/-	TF	F%	Min	GP	G	A	Pts	PIM	PP	SH	GW	Min
99-2000	USNTDP	NAHL	55	7	16	23	57	....	....	....	....	....	....	....	....	....	3	0	0	0	0	....	....	....	....
2000-01	USNTDP	U-18	43	10	12	22	52	....	....	....	....	....	....	....	....	....	....	....	....	....	....	....	....	....	....
	USNTDP	USHL	23	5	5	10	50	....	....	....	....	....	....	....	....	....	....	....	....	....	....	....	....	....	....
2001-02	U. of Michigan	CCHA	40	18	13	31	42	....	....	....	....	....	....	....	....	....	....	....	....	....	....	....	....	....	....
2002-03	U. of Michigan	CCHA	39	15	11	26	24	....	....	....	....	....	....	....	....	....	....	....	....	....	....	....	....	....	....
2003-04	U. of Michigan	CCHA	43	10	12	22	50	....	....	....	....	....	....	....	....	....	....	....	....	....	....	....	....	....	....
2004-05	U. of Michigan	CCHA	38	13	19	32	33	....	....	....	....	....	....	....	....	....	....	....	....	....	....	....	....	....	....
2005-06	**Calgary**	**NHL**	**2**	**0**	**0**	**0**	**0**	**0**	**0**	**0**	**0**	**0.0**	**-1**	**5**	**60.0**	**12:01**	....	....	....	....	....	....	....	....	....
	Omaha	AHL	78	15	18	33	37	....	....	....	....	....	....	....	....	....	....	....	....	....	....	....	....	....	....
2006-07	Omaha	AHL	12	2	0	2	0	....	....	....	....	....	....	....	....	....	5	0	0	0	2	....	....	....	....
2007-08	**Calgary**	**NHL**	**44**	**3**	**7**	**10**	**48**	**0**	**0**	**0**	**42**	**7.1**	**-5**	**14**	**50.0**	**11:30**	**7**	**0**	**0**	**0**	**2**	**0**	**0**	**0**	**7:39**
	Quad City Flames	AHL	18	4	3	7	15	....	....	....	....	....	....	....	....	....	....	....	....	....	....	....	....	....	....
2008-09	**Calgary**	**NHL**	**76**	**5**	**5**	**10**	**89**	**0**	**1**	**3**	**83**	**6.0**	**-7**	**29**	**37.9**	**9:16**	**6**	**2**	**2**	**4**	**0**	**0**	**0**	**1**	**10:57**
2009-10	**Calgary**	**NHL**	**82**	**11**	**8**	**19**	**54**	**0**	**0**	**2**	**91**	**12.1**	**0**	**279**	**45.5**	**13:11**	....	....	....	....	....	....	....	....	....
2010-11	**Minnesota**	**NHL**	**82**	**4**	**8**	**12**	**30**	**1**	**0**	**0**	**83**	**4.8**	**-16**	**131**	**34.4**	**13:19**	....	....	....	....	....	....	....	....	....
2011-12	Houston Aeros	AHL	1	0	0	0	0	....	....	....	....	....	....	....	....	....	....	....	....	....	....	....	....	....	....
	Dallas	**NHL**	**74**	**16**	**5**	**21**	**24**	**0**	**0**	**1**	**102**	**15.7**	**-10**	**29**	**48.3**	**13:45**	....	....	....	....	....	....	....	....	....
2012-13	Stavanger Oilers	Norway	6	4	10	14	6	....	....	....	....	....	....	....	....	....	....	....	....	....	....	....	....	....	....
	Dallas	**NHL**	**48**	**7**	**4**	**11**	**61**	**0**	**1**	**3**	**49**	**14.3**	**-3**	**26**	**57.7**	**14:21**	....	....	....	....	....	....	....	....	....
	NHL Totals		**408**	**46**	**37**	**83**	**306**	**1**	**2**	**9**	**450**	**10.2**		**513**	**43.3**	**12:32**	**13**	**2**	**2**	**4**	**2**	**0**	**0**	**1**	**9:10**

CCHA All-Rookie Team (2002)

• Missed majority of 2006-07 due to pre-season shoulder injury. Signed as a free agent by **Minnesota**, July 1, 2010. Traded to **Dallas** by **Minnesota** for future considerations, October 12, 2011. Signed as a free agent by **Stavanger** (Norway), November 30, 2012. Signed as a free agent by **Nashville**, July 5, 2013.

OBERG, Evan

(OH-buhrg, EH-vuhn)

Defense. Shoots left. 6', 165 lbs. Born, Forestburg, Alta., February 16, 1988.

Season	Club	League	GP	G	A	Pts	PIM	PP	SH	GW	S	%	+/-	TF	F%	Min	GP	G	A	Pts	PIM	PP	SH	GW	Min
2005-06	Camrose Kodiaks	AJHL	44	4	9	13	56	....	....	....	....	....	....	....	....	....	14	1	1	2	14	....	....	....	....
2006-07	Camrose Kodiaks	AJHL	52	9	14	23	86	....	....	....	....	....	....	....	....	....	16	3	11	14	24	....	....	....	....
2007-08	U. Minn-Duluth	WCHA	24	1	2	3	10	....	....	....	....	....	....	....	....	....	....	....	....	....	....	....	....	....	....
2008-09	U. Minn-Duluth	WCHA	43	7	20	27	50	....	....	....	....	....	....	....	....	....	....	....	....	....	....	....	....	....	....
2009-10	**Vancouver**	**NHL**	**2**	**0**	**0**	**0**	**0**	**0**	**0**	**0**	**0**	**0.0**	**0**	**0**	**0.0**	**6:17**	....	....	....	....	....	....	....	....	....
	Manitoba Moose	AHL	70	3	23	26	64	....	....	....	....	....	....	....	....	....	5	1	1	2	4	....	....	....	....
2010-11	**Vancouver**	**NHL**	**2**	**0**	**0**	**0**	**0**	**0**	**0**	**0**	**1**	**0.0**	**0**	**0**	**0.0**	**9:50**	....	....	....	....	....	....	....	....	....
	Manitoba Moose	AHL	38	6	5	11	28	....	....	....	....	....	....	....	....	....	....	....	....	....	....	....	....	....	....
	Rochester	AHL	5	1	1	2	0	....	....	....	....	....	....	....	....	....	....	....	....	....	....	....	....	....	....
2011-12	San Antonio	AHL	12	0	2	2	14	....	....	....	....	....	....	....	....	....	....	....	....	....	....	....	....	....	....
	Tampa Bay	**NHL**	**3**	**0**	**0**	**0**	**0**	**0**	**0**	**0**	**3**	**0.0**	**2**	**0**	**0.0**	**9:50**	....	....	....	....	....	....	....	....	....
	Norfolk Admirals	AHL	42	7	16	23	32	....	....	....	....	....	....	....	....	....	18	2	8	10	14	....	....	....	....
2012-13	Syracuse Crunch	AHL	56	0	9	9	20	....	....	....	....	....	....	....	....	....	4	0	0	0	6	....	....	....	....
	NHL Totals		**7**	**0**	**0**	**0**	**0**	**0**	**0**	**0**	**4**	**0.0**		**0**	**0.0**	**8:49**	....	....	....	....	....	....	....	....	....

Signed as a free agent by **Vancouver**, April 10, 2009. Traded to **Florida** by **Vancouver** with Vancouver's 3rd round choice (later traded back to Vancouver – Vancouver selected Cole Cassels) in 2013 Entry Draft for Chris Higgins, February 28, 2011. Traded to **Tampa Bay** by **Florida** with Mike Kostka for James Wright and Mike Vernace, December 2, 2011.

O'BRIEN, Jim

(oh-BRIGH-uhn, JIHM) **OTT**

Center. Shoots right. 6'2", 200 lbs. Born, Maplewood, MN, January 29, 1989. Ottawa's 1st choice, 29th overall, in 2007 Entry Draft.

Season	Club	League	GP	G	A	Pts	PIM	PP	SH	GW	S	%	+/-	TF	F%	Min	GP	G	A	Pts	PIM	PP	SH	GW	Min
2003-04	Det. Caesars	MWEHL	68	19	24	43	72	....	....	....	....	....	....	....	....	....	....	....	....	....	....	....	....	....	....
2004-05	USNTDP	U-17	13	6	6	12	10	....	....	....	....	....	....	....	....	....	....	....	....	....	....	....	....	....	....
	USNTDP	NAHL	40	10	12	22	41	....	....	....	....	....	....	....	....	....	1	0	0	0	0	....	....	....	....
2005-06	USNTDP	U-18	38	11	14	25	62	....	....	....	....	....	....	....	....	....	....	....	....	....	....	....	....	....	....
	USNTDP	NAHL	13	6	10	16	14	....	....	....	....	....	....	....	....	....	....	....	....	....	....	....	....	....	....
2006-07	U. of Minnesota	WCHA	43	7	8	15	51	....	....	....	....	....	....	....	....	....	....	....	....	....	....	....	....	....	....
2007-08	Seattle	WHL	70	21	34	55	66	....	....	....	....	....	....	....	....	....	12	2	6	8	14	....	....	....	....
2008-09	Seattle	WHL	63	27	35	62	55	....	....	....	....	....	....	....	....	....	5	1	0	1	10	....	....	....	....
	Binghamton	AHL	6	0	1	1	0	....	....	....	....	....	....	....	....	....	....	....	....	....	....	....	....	....	....
2009-10	Binghamton	AHL	76	8	9	17	49	....	....	....	....	....	....	....	....	....	....	....	....	....	....	....	....	....	....
2010-11	**Ottawa**	**NHL**	**6**	**0**	**0**	**0**	**2**	**0**	**0**	**0**	**11**	**0.0**	**-3**	**16**	**50.0**	**9:40**	....	....	....	....	....	....	....	....	....
	Binghamton	AHL	74	24	32	56	67	....	....	....	....	....	....	....	....	....	23	3	4	7	12	....	....	....	....
2011-12	**Ottawa**	**NHL**	**28**	**3**	**3**	**6**	**4**	**0**	**0**	**1**	**37**	**8.1**	**6**	**256**	**47.3**	**11:45**	**7**	**0**	**1**	**1**	**0**	**0**	**0**	**0**	**8:38**
	Binghamton	AHL	27	7	7	14	10	....	....	....	....	....	....	....	....	....	....	....	....	....	....	....	....	....	....
2012-13	**Ottawa**	**NHL**	**29**	**5**	**1**	**6**	**8**	**1**	**0**	**0**	**38**	**13.2**	**-2**	**219**	**45.7**	**11:25**	....	....	....	....	....	....	....	....	....
	NHL Totals		**63**	**8**	**4**	**12**	**14**	**1**	**0**	**1**	**86**	**9.3**		**491**	**46.6**	**11:24**	**7**	**0**	**1**	**1**	**0**	**0**	**0**	**0**	**8:38**

O'BRIEN, Shane

(oh-BRIGH-uhn, SHAYN) **CGY**

Defense. Shoots left. 6'3", 230 lbs. Born, Port Hope, Ont., August 9, 1983. Anaheim's 8th choice, 250th overall, in 2003 Entry Draft.

Season	Club	League	GP	G	A	Pts	PIM	PP	SH	GW	S	%	+/-	TF	F%	Min	GP	G	A	Pts	PIM	PP	SH	GW	Min
			Regular Season														Playoffs								
99-2000	Port Hope	ON-Jr.A	47	6	27	33	110	....	....	....	....	....	....	....	....	....	....	....	....	....	....	....	....	....	....
2000-01	Kingston	OHL	61	2	12	14	89	....	....	....	....	....	....	....	....	....	4	0	1	1	6	....	....	....	....
2001-02	Kingston	OHL	67	10	23	33	132	....	....	....	....	....	....	....	....	....	1	0	0	0	2	....	....	....	....
2002-03	Kingston	OHL	28	8	15	23	100	....	....	....	....	....	....	....	....	....	....	....	....	....	....	....	....	....	....
	St. Michael's	OHL	34	8	11	19	108	....	....	....	....	....	....	....	....	....	19	4	10	14	*79	....	....	....	....
2003-04	Cincinnati	AHL	60	2	8	10	163	....	....	....	....	....	....	....	....	....	9	0	2	2	20	....	....	....	....
2004-05	Cincinnati	AHL	77	5	20	25	319	....	....	....	....	....	....	....	....	....	12	1	3	4	57	....	....	....	....
2005-06	Portland Pirates	AHL	77	8	33	41	287	....	....	....	....	....	....	....	....	....	19	6	16	22	*81	....	....	....	....
2006-07	**Anaheim**	**NHL**	**62**	**2**	**12**	**14**	**140**	**1**	**0**	**2**	**55**	**3.6**	**5**	**0**	**0.0**	**14:04**	....	....	....	....	....	....	....	....	....
	Tampa Bay	**NHL**	**18**	**0**	**2**	**2**	**36**	**0**	**0**	**0**	**17**	**0.0**	**–8**	**0**	**0.0**	**18:08**	**6**	**0**	**0**	**0**	**12**	**0**	**0**	**0**	**17:12**
2007-08	**Tampa Bay**	**NHL**	**77**	**4**	**17**	**21**	**154**	**0**	**0**	**1**	**69**	**5.8**	**–2**	**0**	**0.0**	**21:13**	....	....	....	....	....	....	....	....	....
2008-09	**Tampa Bay**	**NHL**	**1**	**0**	**0**	**0**	**0**	**0**	**0**	**0**	**0**	**0.0**	**–1**	**0**	**0.0**	**14:04**	....	....	....	....	....	....	....	....	....
	Vancouver	**NHL**	**76**	**0**	**10**	**10**	**196**	**0**	**0**	**0**	**39**	**0.0**	**6**	**0**	**0.0**	**14:56**	**10**	**1**	**1**	**2**	**24**	**0**	**0**	**0**	**12:06**
2009-10	**Vancouver**	**NHL**	**65**	**2**	**6**	**8**	**79**	**0**	**0**	**0**	**37**	**5.4**	**15**	**0**	**0.0**	**17:01**	**12**	**1**	**2**	**3**	**25**	**0**	**0**	**0**	**17:44**
2010-11	**Nashville**	**NHL**	**80**	**2**	**7**	**9**	**83**	**0**	**0**	**0**	**50**	**4.0**	**1**	**0**	**0.0**	**17:07**	**12**	**0**	**0**	**0**	**18**	**0**	**0**	**0**	**16:47**
2011-12	**Colorado**	**NHL**	**76**	**3**	**17**	**20**	**105**	**1**	**0**	**0**	**114**	**2.6**	**2**	**0**	**0.0**	**19:13**	....	....	....	....	....	....	....	....	....
2012-13	**Colorado**	**NHL**	**28**	**0**	**4**	**4**	**60**	**0**	**0**	**0**	**28**	**0.0**	**0**	**0**	**0.0**	**15:30**	....	....	....	....	....	....	....	....	....
	NHL Totals		**483**	**13**	**75**	**88**	**853**	**2**	**0**	**3**	**409**	**3.2**		**0**	**0.0**	**17:17**	**40**	**2**	**3**	**5**	**79**	**0**	**0**	**0**	**15:58**

Traded to **Tampa Bay** by **Anaheim** with Colorado's 3rd round choice (previously acquired, Tampa Bay selected Luca Cunti) in 2007 Entry Draft for Gerald Coleman and Tampa Bay's 1st round choice (later traded to Minnesota - Minnesota selected Colton Gillies) in 2007 Entry Draft, February 24, 2007. Traded to **Vancouver** by **Tampa Bay** with Michel Ouellet for Lukas Krajicek and Juraj Simek, October 6, 2008. Traded to **Nashville** by **Vancouver** with Dan Gendur for Ryan Parent and Jonas Andersson, October 5, 2010. Signed as a free agent by **Colorado**, July 13, 2011. Traded to **Calgary** by **Colorado** with David Jones for Alex Tanguay and Cory Sarich. June 27, 2013.

O'BYRNE, Ryan

(oh-BUHRN, RIGH-uhn)

Defense. Shoots right. 6'5", 234 lbs. Born, Victoria, B.C., July 19, 1984. Montreal's 4th choice, 79th overall, in 2003 Entry Draft.

Season	Club	League	GP	G	A	Pts	PIM	PP	SH	GW	S	%	+/-	TF	F%	Min	GP	G	A	Pts	PIM	PP	SH	GW	Min
2001-02	Victoria Salsa	BCHL	52	2	9	11	91	....	....	....	....	....	....	....	....	....	....	....	....	....	....	....	....	....	....
2002-03	Victoria Salsa	BCHL	32	3	6	9	94	....	....	....	....	....	....	....	....	....	....	....	....	....	....	....	....	....	....
	Nanaimo Clippers	BCHL	9	2	4	6	24	....	....	....	....	....	....	....	....	....	....	....	....	....	....	....	....	....	....
2003-04	Cornell Big Red	ECAC	31	0	2	2	71	....	....	....	....	....	....	....	....	....	....	....	....	....	....	....	....	....	....
2004-05	Cornell Big Red	ECAC	33	3	7	10	68	....	....	....	....	....	....	....	....	....	....	....	....	....	....	....	....	....	....
2005-06	Cornell Big Red	ECAC	28	7	6	13	69	....	....	....	....	....	....	....	....	....	....	....	....	....	....	....	....	....	....
2006-07	Hamilton	AHL	80	0	12	12	129	....	....	....	....	....	....	....	....	....	22	2	5	7	32	....	....	....	....
2007-08	**Montreal**	**NHL**	**33**	**1**	**6**	**7**	**45**	**0**	**0**	**0**	**10**	**10.0**	**7**	**0**	**0.0**	**13:24**	**4**	**0**	**0**	**0**	**0**	**0**	**0**	**0**	**10:46**
	Hamilton	AHL	20	2	6	8	49	....	....	....	....	....	....	....	....	....	....	....	....	....	....	....	....	....	....
2008-09	**Montreal**	**NHL**	**37**	**0**	**5**	**5**	**58**	**0**	**0**	**0**	**14**	**0.0**	**–7**	**0**	**0.0**	**15:06**	**2**	**0**	**0**	**0**	**2**	**0**	**0**	**0**	**13:04**
	Hamilton	AHL	18	1	5	6	35	....	....	....	....	....	....	....	....	....	....	....	....	....	....	....	....	....	....
2009-10	**Montreal**	**NHL**	**55**	**1**	**3**	**4**	**74**	**0**	**0**	**1**	**27**	**3.7**	**–3**	**0**	**0.0**	**15:16**	**13**	**0**	**0**	**0**	**10**	**0**	**0**	**0**	**12:43**
2010-11	**Montreal**	**NHL**	**3**	**0**	**0**	**0**	**4**	**0**	**0**	**0**	**3**	**0.0**	**0**	**0**	**0.0**	**14:55**	....	....	....	....	....	....	....	....	....
	Colorado	**NHL**	**64**	**0**	**10**	**10**	**71**	**0**	**0**	**0**	**42**	**0.0**	**–7**	**0**	**0.0**	**20:24**	....	....	....	....	....	....	....	....	....
2011-12	**Colorado**	**NHL**	**74**	**1**	**6**	**7**	**57**	**0**	**0**	**0**	**42**	**2.4**	**–5**	**0**	**0.0**	**18:51**	....	....	....	....	....	....	....	....	....
2012-13	Florida Everblades	ECHL	16	2	9	11	10	....	....	....	....	....	....	....	....	....	....	....	....	....	....	....	....	....	....
	Colorado	**NHL**	**34**	**1**	**3**	**4**	**54**	**0**	**0**	**0**	**21**	**4.8**	**–8**	**0**	**0.0**	**18:51**	....	....	....	....	....	....	....	....	....
	Toronto	**NHL**	**8**	**1**	**1**	**2**	**6**	**0**	**0**	**0**	**5**	**20.0**	**4**	**0**	**0.0**	**17:11**	**6**	**0**	**0**	**0**	**4**	**0**	**0**	**0**	**15:14**
	NHL Totals		**308**	**5**	**34**	**39**	**369**	**0**	**0**	**1**	**164**	**3.0**		**0**	**0.0**	**17:25**	**25**	**0**	**0**	**0**	**16**	**0**	**0**	**0**	**13:02**

Traded to **Colorado** by **Montreal** for Michael Bournival, November 11, 2010. Signed as a free agent by **Florida** (ECHL), November 30, 2012. Traded to **Toronto** by **Colorado** for a 4th round choice in 2014 Entry Draft, April 3, 2013.

ODUYA, Johnny

(oh-DOO-yuh, JAW-nee) **CHI**

Defense. Shoots left. 6', 190 lbs. Born, Stockholm, Sweden, October 1, 1981. Washington's 6th choice, 221st overall, in 2001 Entry Draft.

Season	Club	League	GP	G	A	Pts	PIM	PP	SH	GW	S	%	+/-	TF	F%	Min	GP	G	A	Pts	PIM	PP	SH	GW	Min
1996-97	Hammarby Jr.	Swe-Jr.	13	0	0	0	....	....	....	....	....	....	....	....	....	....	....	....	....	....	....	....	....	....	....
1997-98	Hammarby Jr.	Swe-Jr.	26	3	11	14	70	....	....	....	....	....	....	....	....	....	....	....	....	....	....	....	....	....	....
1998-99	Hammarby Jr.	Swe-Jr.	38	14	31	45	45	....	....	....	....	....	....	....	....	....	....	....	....	....	....	....	....	....	....
99-2000	Hammarby Jr.	Swe-Jr.	32	3	18	21	48	....	....	....	....	....	....	....	....	....	6	1	2	3	4	....	....	....	....
	Hammarby	Sweden-2	1	0	0	0	0	....	....	....	....	....	....	....	....	....	1	0	0	0	0	....	....	....	....
2000-01	Moncton Wildcats	QMJHL	44	11	38	49	147	....	....	....	....	....	....	....	....	....	....	....	....	....	....	....	....	....	....
	Victoriaville Tigres	QMJHL	24	3	16	19	112	....	....	....	....	....	....	....	....	....	13	4	9	13	10	....	....	....	....
2001-02	Hammarby	Sweden-2	46	11	14	25	66	....	....	....	....	....	....	....	....	....	2	1	0	1	4	....	....	....	....
2002-03	Hammarby	Sweden-2	48	15	25	40	200	....	....	....	....	....	....	....	....	....	....	....	....	....	....	....	....	....	....
2003-04	Djurgarden	Sweden	42	4	4	8	*173	....	....	....	....	....	....	....	....	....	4	0	0	0	6	....	....	....	....
2004-05	Djurgarden	Sweden	49	2	4	6	139	....	....	....	....	....	....	....	....	....	12	0	2	2	39	....	....	....	....
2005-06	Frolunda	Sweden	47	8	11	19	95	....	....	....	....	....	....	....	....	....	17	1	2	3	16	....	....	....	....
2006-07	**New Jersey**	**NHL**	**76**	**2**	**9**	**11**	**61**	**0**	**0**	**0**	**55**	**3.6**	**–5**	**0**	**0.0**	**18:31**	**6**	**0**	**1**	**1**	**6**	**0**	**0**	**0**	**12:59**
2007-08	**New Jersey**	**NHL**	**75**	**6**	**20**	**26**	**46**	**2**	**0**	**0**	**63**	**9.5**	**27**	**0**	**0.0**	**19:02**	**5**	**0**	**1**	**1**	**6**	**0**	**0**	**0**	**20:40**
2008-09	**New Jersey**	**NHL**	**82**	**7**	**22**	**29**	**30**	**1**	**1**	**4**	**108**	**6.5**	**21**	**0**	**0.0**	**20:52**	**7**	**0**	**0**	**0**	**2**	**0**	**0**	**0**	**20:19**
2009-10	**New Jersey**	**NHL**	**40**	**2**	**2**	**4**	**18**	**0**	**0**	**0**	**44**	**4.5**	**2**	**0**	**0.0**	**21:11**	....	....	....	....	....	....	....	....	....
	Atlanta	**NHL**	**27**	**1**	**8**	**9**	**12**	**0**	**0**	**0**	**24**	**4.2**	**6**	**0**	**0.0**	**21:22**	....	....	....	....	....	....	....	....	....
	Sweden	Olympics	4	0	0	0	12	....	....	....	....	....	....	....	....	....	....	....	....	....	....	....	....	....	....
2010-11	**Atlanta**	**NHL**	**82**	**2**	**15**	**17**	**22**	**0**	**0**	**0**	**90**	**2.2**	**–15**	**0**	**0.0**	**20:43**	....	....	....	....	....	....	....	....	....
2011-12	**Winnipeg**	**NHL**	**63**	**2**	**11**	**13**	**33**	**0**	**0**	**1**	**52**	**3.8**	**–9**	**0**	**0.0**	**19:20**	....	....	....	....	....	....	....	....	....
	Chicago	**NHL**	**18**	**1**	**4**	**5**	**0**	**0**	**0**	**0**	**30**	**3.3**	**3**	**0**	**0.0**	**24:25**	**6**	**0**	**3**	**3**	**0**	**0**	**0**	**0**	**23:14**
2012-13	Flying Farangs	Thailand	STATISTICS NOT AVAILABLE																						
	♦ **Chicago**	**NHL**	**48**	**3**	**9**	**12**	**10**	**0**	**0**	**0**	**52**	**5.8**	**12**	**0**	**0.0**	**20:31**	**23**	**3**	**5**	**8**	**16**	**0**	**0**	**1**	**22:45**
	NHL Totals		**511**	**26**	**100**	**126**	**232**	**3**	**1**	**5**	**518**	**5.0**		**0**	**0.0**	**20:11**	**47**	**3**	**10**	**13**	**30**	**0**	**0**	**1**	**20:59**

Signed as a free agent by **New Jersey**, July 24, 2006. Traded to **Atlanta** by **New Jersey** with Niclas Bergfors, Patrice Cormier and New Jersey's 1st (later traded to Chicago - Chicago selected Kevin Hayes) and 2nd (later traded to Chicago - Chicago selected Justin Holl) round choices in 2010 Entry Draft for Ilya Kovalchuk, Anssi Salmela and Atlanta's 2nd round choice (Jonathon Merrill) in 2010 Entry Draft, February 4, 2010. • Transferred to **Winnipeg** after **Atlanta** franchise relocated, June 21, 2011. Signed as a free agent by **Flying Farangs Bangkok** (Thailand), October, 2012. Traded to **Chicago** by **Winnipeg** for Chicago's 2nd (later traded to Washington – Washington selected Zachary Sanford) and 3rd (J.C. Lipon) round choices in 2013 Entry Draft, February 27, 2012.

OHLUND, Mattias

(OH-luhnd, mat-TEE-uhs) **T.B.**

Defense. Shoots left. 6'4", 233 lbs. Born, Pitea, Sweden, September 9, 1976. Vancouver's 1st choice, 13th overall, in 1994 Entry Draft.

Season	Club	League	GP	G	A	Pts	PIM	PP	SH	GW	S	%	+/-	TF	F%	Min	GP	G	A	Pts	PIM	PP	SH	GW	Min
1992-93	Pitea HC	Sweden-2	22	0	6	6	16	....	....	....	....	....	....	....	....	....	....	....	....	....	....	....	....	....	....
1993-94	Pitea HC	Sweden-2	28	7	10	17	66	....	....	....	....	....	....	....	....	....	....	....	....	....	....	....	....	....	....
1994-95	Lulea HF	Sweden	34	6	10	16	34	....	....	....	....	....	....	....	....	....	9	4	0	4	16	....	....	....	....
1995-96	Lulea HF	Sweden	38	4	10	14	26	....	....	....	....	....	....	....	....	....	13	1	3	4	47	....	....	....	....
1996-97	Lulea HF	Sweden	47	7	9	16	38	....	....	....	....	....	....	....	....	....	10	1	2	3	8	....	....	....	....
	Lulea HF	EuroHL	6	0	3	3	0	....	....	....	....	....	....	....	....	....	....	....	....	....	....	....	....	....	....
1997-98	**Vancouver**	**NHL**	**77**	**7**	**23**	**30**	**76**	**1**	**0**	**0**	**172**	**4.1**	**3**	....	....	....	....	....	....	....	....	....	....	....	....
	Sweden	Olympics	4	0	1	1	4	....	....	....	....	....	....	....	....	....	....	....	....	....	....	....	....	....	....
1998-99	**Vancouver**	**NHL**	**74**	**9**	**26**	**35**	**83**	**2**	**1**	**1**	**129**	**7.0**	**–19**	**0**	**0.0**	**26:04**	....	....	....	....	....	....	....	....	....
99-2000	**Vancouver**	**NHL**	**42**	**4**	**16**	**20**	**24**	**2**	**1**	**1**	**63**	**6.3**	**6**	**0**	**0.0**	**27:41**	....	....	....	....	....	....	....	....	....
2000-01	**Vancouver**	**NHL**	**65**	**8**	**20**	**28**	**46**	**1**	**1**	**4**	**136**	**5.9**	**–16**	**0**	**0.0**	**25:00**	**4**	**1**	**3**	**4**	**6**	**1**	**0**	**0**	**26:32**
2001-02	**Vancouver**	**NHL**	**81**	**10**	**26**	**36**	**56**	**4**	**1**	**3**	**193**	**5.2**	**16**	**0**	**0.0**	**25:17**	**6**	**1**	**1**	**2**	**6**	**0**	**0**	**0**	**28:48**
	Sweden	Olympics	4	0	2	2	2	....	....	....	....	....	....	....	....	....	....	....	....	....	....	....	....	....	....
2002-03	**Vancouver**	**NHL**	**59**	**2**	**27**	**29**	**42**	**0**	**0**	**0**	**100**	**2.0**	**1**	**0**	**0.0**	**25:23**	**13**	**3**	**4**	**7**	**12**	**0**	**0**	**0**	**24:01**
2003-04	**Vancouver**	**NHL**	**82**	**14**	**20**	**34**	**73**	**5**	**0**	**3**	**129**	**10.9**	**14**	**0**	**0.0**	**25:47**	**7**	**1**	**4**	**5**	**13**	**0**	**0**	**1**	**27:25**
2004-05	Lulea HF	Sweden	2	1	0	1	4	....	....	....	....	....	....	....	....	....	....	....	....	....	....	....	....	....	....
2005-06	**Vancouver**	**NHL**	**78**	**13**	**20**	**33**	**92**	**8**	**1**	**2**	**183**	**7.1**	**–6**	**1**	**0.0**	**25:40**	....	....	....	....	....	....	....	....	....
	Sweden	Olympics	6	0	2	2	2	....	....	....	....	....	....	....	....	....	....	....	....	....	....	....	....	....	....
2006-07	**Vancouver**	**NHL**	**77**	**11**	**20**	**31**	**80**	**6**	**0**	**2**	**170**	**6.5**	**–3**	**1**	**0.0**	**24:47**	**12**	**2**	**5**	**7**	**12**	**1**	**0**	**0**	**28:18**
2007-08	**Vancouver**	**NHL**	**53**	**9**	**15**	**24**	**79**	**4**	**0**	**2**	**128**	**7.0**	**–1**	**0**	**0.0**	**23:46**	....	....	....	....	....	....	....	....	....
2008-09	**Vancouver**	**NHL**	**82**	**6**	**19**	**25**	**105**	**3**	**0**	**1**	**131**	**4.6**	**14**	**0**	**0.0**	**21:34**	**10**	**1**	**2**	**3**	**6**	**1**	**0**	**0**	**23:54**
2009-10	**Tampa Bay**	**NHL**	**67**	**0**	**13**	**13**	**59**	**0**	**0**	**0**	**71**	**0.0**	**–8**	**0**	**0.0**	**22:49**	....	....	....	....	....	....	....	....	....
	Sweden	Olympics	4	1	0	1	2	....	....	....	....	....	....	....	....	....	....	....	....	....	....	....	....	....	....
2010-11	**Tampa Bay**	**NHL**	**72**	**0**	**5**	**5**	**70**	**0**	**0**	**0**	**39**	**0.0**	**–7**	**0**	**0.0**	**18:43**	**18**	**1**	**2**	**3**	**8**	**0**	**1**	**0**	**20:12**

Season	Club	League	GP	G	A	Pts	PIM	PP	SH	GW	S	%	+/-	TF	F%	Min	GP	G	A	Pts	PIM	PP	SH	GW	Min
			Regular Season														Playoffs								
2011-12	**Tampa Bay**	**NHL**	DID NOT PLAY – INJURED																						
2012-13	**Tampa Bay**	**NHL**	DID NOT PLAY – INJURED																						
	NHL Totals		**909**	**93**	**250**	**343**	**885**	**36**	**5**	**19**	**1644**	**5.7**		**2**	**0.0**	**24:16**	**70**	**10**	**21**	**31**	**63**	**3**	**1**	**1**	**24:39**

NHL All-Rookie Team (1998)
Played in NHL All-Star Game (1999)
Signed as a free agent by **Lulea** (Sweden), December 21, 2004. Signed as a free agent by **Tampa Bay**, July 1, 2009. • Missed 2011-12 and 2012-13 due to knee surgery.

OKPOSO, Kyle
(OH-poh-soh, KIGHL) **NYI**

Right wing. Shoots right. 6', 212 lbs. Born, St. Paul, MN, April 16, 1988. NY Islanders' 1st choice, 7th overall, in 2006 Entry Draft.

Season	Club	League	GP	G	A	Pts	PIM	PP	SH	GW	S	%	+/-	TF	F%	Min	GP	G	A	Pts	PIM	PP	SH	GW	Min
2004-05	Shat.-St. Mary's	High-MN	65	47	45	92	72																		
2005-06	Des Moines	USHL	50	27	31	58	56										11	5	11	*16	8				
2006-07	U. of Minnesota	WCHA	40	19	21	40	34																		
2007-08	U. of Minnesota	WCHA	18	7	4	11	6																		
	NY Islanders	**NHL**	**9**	**2**	**3**	**5**	**2**	**1**	**0**	**1**	**15**	**13.3**	**3**	**0**	**0.0**	**16:28**									
	Bridgeport	AHL	35	9	19	28	12																		
2008-09	**NY Islanders**	**NHL**	**65**	**18**	**21**	**39**	**36**	**9**	**0**	**3**	**165**	**10.9**	**–6**	**15**	**33.3**	**18:01**									
	Bridgeport	AHL															2	1	0	1	2				
2009-10	**NY Islanders**	**NHL**	**80**	**19**	**33**	**52**	**34**	**4**	**0**	**4**	**249**	**7.6**	**–22**	**69**	**47.8**	**20:32**									
2010-11	**NY Islanders**	**NHL**	**38**	**5**	**15**	**20**	**40**	**0**	**0**	**2**	**72**	**6.9**	**3**	**87**	**41.4**	**16:35**									
2011-12	**NY Islanders**	**NHL**	**79**	**24**	**21**	**45**	**46**	**3**	**0**	**2**	**152**	**15.8**	**–15**	**142**	**47.9**	**17:04**									
2012-13	**NY Islanders**	**NHL**	**48**	**4**	**20**	**24**	**38**	**0**	**0**	**0**	**101**	**4.0**	**–2**	**186**	**55.9**	**16:57**	**6**	**3**	**1**	**4**	**5**	**0**	**1**	**1**	**19:13**
	NHL Totals		**319**	**72**	**113**	**185**	**196**	**17**	**0**	**12**	**754**	**9.5**		**499**	**49.3**	**18:02**	**6**	**3**	**1**	**4**	**5**	**0**	**1**	**1**	**19:13**

USHL All-Rookie Team (2006) • USHL First All-Star Team (2006) • USHL Rookie of the Year (2006) • WCHA All-Rookie Team (2007) • WCHA Second All-Star Team (2007)
• Missed majority of 2010-11 due to shoulder injury in training camp and resulting surgery.

OLEKSIAK, Jamie
(oh-LEHK-see-ak, JAY-mih) **DAL**

Defense. Shoots left. 6'7", 252 lbs. Born, Toronto, Ont., December 21, 1992. Dallas' 1st choice, 14th overall, in 2011 Entry Draft.

Season	Club	League	GP	G	A	Pts	PIM	PP	SH	GW	S	%	+/-	TF	F%	Min	GP	G	A	Pts	PIM	PP	SH	GW	Min
2007-08	Tor. Young Nats	GTHL	51	1	10	11	46																		
2008-09	Little Caesars	T1EHL	30	3	7	10	31																		
	Chicago Steel	USHL	29	0	4	4	47																		
2009-10	Chicago Steel	USHL	29	0	10	10	43																		
	Sioux Falls	USHL	24	2	2	4	32										3	0	1	1	2				
2010-11	Northeastern	H-East	38	4	9	13	57																		
2011-12	Saginaw Spirit	OHL	31	6	5	11	24																		
	Niagara Ice Dogs	OHL	28	6	15	21	23										20	0	4	4	6				
2012-13	Texas Stars	AHL	59	6	27	33	29										9	0	1	1	6				
	Dallas	**NHL**	**16**	**0**	**2**	**2**	**14**	**0**	**0**	**0**	**11**	**0.0**	**–5**	**0**	**0.0**	**14:50**									
	NHL Totals		**16**	**0**	**2**	**2**	**14**	**0**	**0**	**0**	**11**	**0.0**		**0**	**0.0**	**14:50**									

OLEKSY, Steven
(oh-LEHK-see, STEE-vehn) **WSH**

Defense. Shoots right. 6', 190 lbs. Born, Chesterfield, MI, February 4, 1986.

Season	Club	League	GP	G	A	Pts	PIM	PP	SH	GW	S	%	+/-	TF	F%	Min	GP	G	A	Pts	PIM	PP	SH	GW	Min
2005-06	Traverse City	NAHL	57	11	19	30	140																		
2006-07	Lake Superior	CCHA	39	2	2	4	24																		
2007-08	Lake Superior	CCHA	36	1	6	7	36																		
2008-09	Lake Superior	CCHA	38	0	9	9	50																		
	Las Vegas	ECHL	2	0	0	0	0																		
2009-10	Toledo Walleye	ECHL	3	0	0	0	2																		
	Port Huron	IHL	28	1	1	2	35																		
	Idaho Steelheads	ECHL	33	1	8	9	72										8	0	0	0	25				
2010-11	Idaho Steelheads	ECHL	55	7	14	21	134																		
	Lake Erie	AHL	17	0	4	4	39										3	0	1	1	2				
2011-12	Idaho Steelheads	ECHL	14	1	7	8	47																		
	Bridgeport	AHL	50	1	14	15	98										3	0	0	0	2				
2012-13	Hershey Bears	AHL	55	2	12	14	151																		
	Washington	**NHL**	**28**	**1**	**8**	**9**	**33**	**0**	**0**	**0**	**25**	**4.0**	**9**	**0**	**0.0**	**17:16**	**7**	**0**	**1**	**1**	**4**	**0**	**0**	**0**	**15:09**
	NHL Totals		**28**	**1**	**8**	**9**	**33**	**0**	**0**	**0**	**25**	**4.0**		**0**	**0.0**	**17:16**	**7**	**0**	**1**	**1**	**4**	**0**	**0**	**0**	**15:09**

Signed as a free agent by **Hershey** (AHL), July 2, 2012. Signed as a free agent by **Washington**, March 4, 2013.

OLESZ, Rostislav
(OH-lehsh, RAHS-tih-slav) **N.J.**

Left wing. Shoots left. 6'2", 215 lbs. Born, Bilovec, Czech., October 10, 1985. Florida's 1st choice, 7th overall, in 2004 Entry Draft.

Season	Club	League	GP	G	A	Pts	PIM	PP	SH	GW	S	%	+/-	TF	F%	Min	GP	G	A	Pts	PIM	PP	SH	GW	Min
2000-01	HC Vitkovice Jr.	CzRep-Jr.	15	10	3	13	14																		
	HC Vitkovice	CzRep	3	0	1	1	0																		
2001-02	HC Vitkovice	CzRep	11	1	2	3	0																		
	HC Vitkovice Jr.	CzRep-Jr.	34	19	20	39	81										2	0	0	0	2				
2002-03	HC Vitkovice Jr.	CzRep-Jr.	7	1	1	2	12																		
	HC Vitkovice	CzRep	40	6	3	9	41										5	0	0	0	2				
	HC Slezan Opava	CzRep-2	1	0	0	0	0																		
2003-04	HC Vitkovice Jr.	CzRep-Jr.	3	2	0	2	0																		
	HC Vitkovice	CzRep	35	1	11	12	10										6	2	1	3	4				
	HC Dukla Jihlava	CzRep-2	2	1	0	1	0										1	0	0	0	0				
2004-05	HC Sparta Praha	CzRep	47	6	7	13	12										5	0	2	2	0				
	Sparta Jr.	CzRep-Jr.															1	0	1	1	0				
2005-06	**Florida**	**NHL**	**59**	**8**	**13**	**21**	**24**	**0**	**1**	**3**	**105**	**7.6**	**–4**	**10**	**30.0**	**14:52**									
	Czech Republic	Olympics	8	0	0	0	2																		
2006-07	**Florida**	**NHL**	**75**	**11**	**19**	**30**	**28**	**2**	**0**	**2**	**164**	**6.7**	**2**	**12**	**58.3**	**15:30**									
	Rochester	AHL	4	1	2	3	4																		
2007-08	**Florida**	**NHL**	**56**	**14**	**12**	**26**	**16**	**5**	**0**	**2**	**139**	**10.1**	**3**	**10**	**70.0**	**17:04**									
2008-09	**Florida**	**NHL**	**37**	**4**	**5**	**9**	**8**	**0**	**0**	**0**	**69**	**5.8**	**–5**	**5**	**20.0**	**13:12**									
2009-10	**Florida**	**NHL**	**78**	**14**	**15**	**29**	**28**	**3**	**0**	**3**	**178**	**7.9**	**–4**	**9**	**22.2**	**15:24**									
2010-11	**Florida**	**NHL**	**44**	**6**	**11**	**17**	**8**	**1**	**0**	**1**	**71**	**8.5**	**–1**	**10**	**20.0**	**13:53**									
2011-12	**Chicago**	**NHL**	**6**	**0**	**0**	**0**	**6**	**0**	**0**	**0**	**6**	**0.0**	**–1**	**2**	**0.0**	**9:06**									
	Rockford IceHogs	AHL	50	17	24	41	32																		
2012-13	Rockford IceHogs	AHL	14	7	12	19	4																		
	NHL Totals		**355**	**57**	**75**	**132**	**118**	**11**	**1**	**11**	**732**	**7.8**		**58**	**37.9**	**15:04**									

• Missed majority of 2008-09 due to groin injury and resulting sports hernia surgery. Traded to **Chicago** by **Florida** for Brian Campbell, June 25, 2011. • Missed majority of 2012-13 due to knee surgery, January 19, 2013. Signed as a free agent by **New Jersey**, July 5, 2013.

OLSEN, Dylan
(OHL-suhn, DIH-luhn) **CHI**

Defense. Shoots left. 6'2", 214 lbs. Born, Salt Lake City, UT, January 3, 1991. Chicago's 1st choice, 28th overall, in 2009 Entry Draft.

Season	Club	League	GP	G	A	Pts	PIM	PP	SH	GW	S	%	+/-	TF	F%	Min	GP	G	A	Pts	PIM	PP	SH	GW	Min
2006-07	Calgary Blazers	SAMHL	53	19	41	60	119																		
	Camrose Kodiaks	AJHL	2	1	0	1	0																		
2007-08	Camrose Kodiaks	AJHL	49	8	16	24	45										16	1	5	6	6				
2008-09	Camrose Kodiaks	AJHL	53	10	19	29	123										10	1	6	7	12				
2009-10	U. Minn-Duluth	WCHA	36	1	10	11	49																		
2010-11	U. Minn-Duluth	WCHA	17	1	12	13	8																		
	Rockford IceHogs	AHL	42	0	4	4	10																		
2011-12	**Chicago**	**NHL**	**28**	**0**	**1**	**1**	**6**	**0**	**0**	**0**	**16**	**0.0**	**–5**	**0**	**0.0**	**13:02**	**1**	**0**	**0**	**0**	**0**	**0**	**0**	**0**	**4:56**
	Rockford IceHogs	AHL	44	4	3	7	44																		
2012-13	Rockford IceHogs	AHL	50	2	9	11	27																		
	NHL Totals		**28**	**0**	**1**	**1**	**6**	**0**	**0**	**0**	**16**	**0.0**		**0**	**0.0**	**13:02**	**1**	**0**	**0**	**0**	**0**	**0**	**0**	**0**	**4:56**

OLVER, Mark

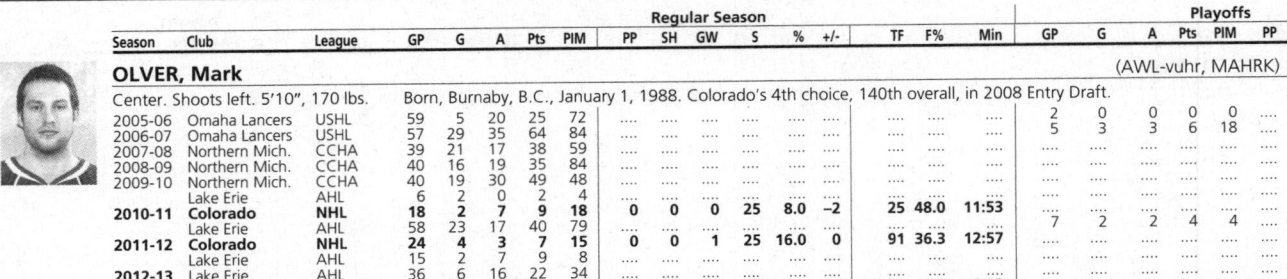

(AWL-vuhr, MAHRK) **COL**

Center. Shoots left. 5'10", 170 lbs. Born, Burnaby, B.C., January 1, 1988. Colorado's 4th choice, 140th overall, in 2008 Entry Draft.

			Regular Season														Playoffs								
Season	Club	League	GP	G	A	Pts	PIM	PP	SH	GW	S	%	+/-	TF	F%	Min	GP	G	A	Pts	PIM	PP	SH	GW	Min
2005-06	Omaha Lancers	USHL	59	5	20	25	72	....	....	....	....	....	....	....	....	....	2	0	0	0	0	....	....	....	....
2006-07	Omaha Lancers	USHL	57	29	35	64	84	....	....	....	....	....	....	....	....	....	5	3	3	6	18	....	....	....	....
2007-08	Northern Mich.	CCHA	39	21	17	38	59	....	....	....	....	....	....	....	....	....	....	....	....	....	....	....	....	....	....
2008-09	Northern Mich.	CCHA	40	16	19	35	84	....	....	....	....	....	....	....	....	....	....	....	....	....	....	....	....	....	....
2009-10	Northern Mich.	CCHA	40	19	30	49	48	....	....	....	....	....	....	....	....	....	....	....	....	....	....	....	....	....	....
	Lake Erie	AHL	6	2	0	2	4	....	....	....	....	....	....	....	....	....	....	....	....	....	....	....	....	....	....
2010-11	**Colorado**	**NHL**	**18**	**2**	**7**	**9**	**18**	**0**	**0**	**0**	**25**	**8.0**	**–2**	**25**	**48.0**	**11:53**	....	....	....	....	....	....	....	....	....
	Lake Erie	AHL	58	23	17	40	79	....	....	....	....	....	....	....	....	....	7	2	2	4	4	....	....	....	....
2011-12	**Colorado**	**NHL**	**24**	**4**	**3**	**7**	**15**	**0**	**0**	**1**	**25**	**16.0**	**0**	**91**	**36.3**	**12:57**	....	....	....	....	....	....	....	....	....
	Lake Erie	AHL	15	2	7	9	8	....	....	....	....	....	....	....	....	....	....	....	....	....	....	....	....	....	....
2012-13	Lake Erie	AHL	36	6	16	22	34	....	....	....	....	....	....	....	....	....	....	....	....	....	....	....	....	....	....
	Colorado	**NHL**	**32**	**4**	**2**	**6**	**6**	**0**	**0**	**0**	**33**	**12.1**	**–5**	**142**	**41.6**	**9:03**	....	....	....	....	....	....	....	....	....
	NHL Totals		**74**	**10**	**12**	**22**	**39**	**0**	**0**	**1**	**83**	**12.0**		**258**	**40.3**	**11:00**	....	....	....	....	....	....	....	....	....

CCHA All-Rookie Team (2008) • CCHA First All-Star Team (2010) • NCAA West First All-American Team (2010)

OMARK, Linus

(OH-mahrk, LIH-nuhs) **EDM**

Left wing. Shoots left. 5'10", 180 lbs. Born, Overtornea, Sweden, February 5, 1987. Edmonton's 4th choice, 97th overall, in 2007 Entry Draft.

Season	Club	League	GP	G	A	Pts	PIM	PP	SH	GW	S	%	+/-	TF	F%	Min	GP	G	A	Pts	PIM	PP	SH	GW	Min
2003-04	Lulea HF U18	Swe-U18	14	14	8	22	18	....	....	....	....	....	....	....	....	....	7	3	4	7	0	....	....	....	....
	Lulea HF Jr.	Swe-Jr.	1	0	0	0	0	....	....	....	....	....	....	....	....	....	....	....	....	....	....	....	....	....	....
2004-05	Lulea HF U18	Swe-U18	1	2	0	2	0	....	....	....	....	....	....	....	....	....	....	....	....	....	....	....	....	....	....
	Lulea HF Jr.	Swe-Jr.	32	8	9	17	44	....	....	....	....	....	....	....	....	....	7	4	2	6	2	....	....	....	....
2005-06	Lulea HF Jr.	Swe-Jr.	32	22	21	43	56	....	....	....	....	....	....	....	....	....	5	1	2	3	28	....	....	....	....
	Lulea HF	Sweden	19	0	1	1	10	....	....	....	....	....	....	....	....	....	3	0	0	0	0	....	....	....	....
2006-07	Lulea HF	Sweden	50	8	9	17	32	....	....	....	....	....	....	....	....	....	4	1	0	1	2	....	....	....	....
2007-08	Lulea HF	Sweden	55	11	21	32	46	....	....	....	....	....	....	....	....	....	....	....	....	....	....	....	....	....	....
2008-09	Lulea HF	Sweden	53	23	32	55	66	....	....	....	....	....	....	....	....	....	5	0	5	5	4	....	....	....	....
2009-10	Dynamo Moscow	KHL	56	20	16	36	34	....	....	....	....	....	....	....	....	....	4	0	0	0	4	....	....	....	....
2010-11	**Edmonton**	**NHL**	**51**	**5**	**22**	**27**	**26**	**1**	**0**	**0**	**76**	**6.6**	**–16**	**8**	**37.5**	**15:21**	....	....	....	....	....	....	....	....	....
	Oklahoma City	AHL	28	14	17	31	32	....	....	....	....	....	....	....	....	....	6	1	2	3	4	....	....	....	....
2011-12	**Edmonton**	**NHL**	**14**	**3**	**0**	**3**	**8**	**0**	**0**	**0**	**24**	**12.5**	**–5**	**7**	**28.6**	**13:27**	....	....	....	....	....	....	....	....	....
	Oklahoma City	AHL	18	6	10	16	8	....	....	....	....	....	....	....	....	....	....	....	....	....	....	....	....	....	....
2012-13	EV Zug	Swiss	48	17	52	69	40	....	....	....	....	....	....	....	....	....	12	2	4	6	12	....	....	....	....
	NHL Totals		**65**	**8**	**22**	**30**	**34**	**1**	**0**	**0**	**100**	**8.0**		**15**	**33.3**	**14:57**	....	....	....	....	....	....	....	....	....

• Missed majority of 2011-12 due to leg injury at Rockford (AHL), November 16, 2011 and as a healthy reserve. Signed as a free agent by **Zug** (Swiss), August 29, 2012.

O'MARRA, Ryan

(oh-MAHR-ah, RIGH-uhn)

Center. Shoots right. 6'2", 220 lbs. Born, Tokyo, Japan, June 9, 1987. NY Islanders' 1st choice, 15th overall, in 2005 Entry Draft.

Season	Club	League	GP	G	A	Pts	PIM	PP	SH	GW	S	%	+/-	TF	F%	Min	GP	G	A	Pts	PIM	PP	SH	GW	Min
2002-03	Miss. Senators	GTHL	76	51	60	111	83	....	....	....	....	....	....	....	....	....	....	....	....	....	....	....	....	....	....
	Georgetown	ON-Jr.A	3	0	2	2	0	....	....	....	....	....	....	....	....	....	....	....	....	....	....	....	....	....	....
	Streetsville Derbys	ON-Jr.A	6	0	1	1	2	....	....	....	....	....	....	....	....	....	....	....	....	....	....	....	....	....	....
2003-04	Erie Otters	OHL	63	16	16	32	33	....	....	....	....	....	....	....	....	....	9	5	5	10	6	....	....	....	....
2004-05	Erie Otters	OHL	64	25	38	63	60	....	....	....	....	....	....	....	....	....	6	4	1	5	0	....	....	....	....
2005-06	Erie Otters	OHL	61	27	50	77	134	....	....	....	....	....	....	....	....	....	....	....	....	....	....	....	....	....	....
	Bridgeport	AHL	8	4	1	5	4	....	....	....	....	....	....	....	....	....	3	0	1	1	2	....	....	....	....
2006-07	Erie Otters	OHL	13	8	6	14	26	....	....	....	....	....	....	....	....	....	....	....	....	....	....	....	....	....	....
	Saginaw Spirit	OHL	33	18	19	37	48	....	....	....	....	....	....	....	....	....	3	2	1	3	4	....	....	....	....
2007-08	Springfield	AHL	31	2	7	9	31	....	....	....	....	....	....	....	....	....	....	....	....	....	....	....	....	....	....
	Stockton Thunder	ECHL	24	11	9	20	45	....	....	....	....	....	....	....	....	....	6	2	7	9	10	....	....	....	....
2008-09	Springfield	AHL	62	1	9	10	49	....	....	....	....	....	....	....	....	....	....	....	....	....	....	....	....	....	....
2009-10	**Edmonton**	**NHL**	**3**	**0**	**1**	**1**	**0**	**0**	**0**	**0**	**2**	**0.0**	**0**	**12**	**58.3**	**6:37**	....	....	....	....	....	....	....	....	....
	Springfield	AHL	74	12	6	18	59	....	....	....	....	....	....	....	....	....	....	....	....	....	....	....	....	....	....
2010-11	**Edmonton**	**NHL**	**21**	**1**	**4**	**5**	**13**	**0**	**0**	**0**	**13**	**7.7**	**–2**	**178**	**42.1**	**11:01**	....	....	....	....	....	....	....	....	....
	Oklahoma City	AHL	53	2	20	22	49	....	....	....	....	....	....	....	....	....	6	0	2	2	0	....	....	....	....
2011-12	**Edmonton**	**NHL**	**7**	**0**	**1**	**1**	**4**	**0**	**0**	**0**	**3**	**0.0**	**0**	**57**	**56.1**	**9:36**	....	....	....	....	....	....	....	....	....
	Oklahoma City	AHL	40	8	9	17	58	....	....	....	....	....	....	....	....	....	....	....	....	....	....	....	....	....	....
	Anaheim	**NHL**	**2**	**0**	**0**	**0**	**0**	**0**	**0**	**0**	**4**	**0.0**	**–1**	**8**	**50.0**	**8:10**	....	....	....	....	....	....	....	....	....
	Syracuse Crunch	AHL	18	1	2	3	29	....	....	....	....	....	....	....	....	....	4	0	2	2	0	....	....	....	....
2012-13	Pelicans Lahti	Finland	8	0	1	1	8	....	....	....	....	....	....	....	....	....	....	....	....	....	....	....	....	....	....
	HC Fassa	Italy	9	6	7	13	12	....	....	....	....	....	....	....	....	....	....	....	....	....	....	....	....	....	....
	Valerengen	Norway	9	2	6	8	16	....	....	....	....	....	....	....	....	....	15	7	6	13	60	....	....	....	....
	NHL Totals		**33**	**1**	**6**	**7**	**17**	**0**	**0**	**0**	**22**	**4.5**		**255**	**46.3**	**10:09**	....	....	....	....	....	....	....	....	....

Traded to **Edmonton** by **NY Islanders** with Robert Nilsson and NY Islanders' 1st round choice (Alex Plante) in 2007 Entry Draft for Ryan Smyth, February 27, 2007. Traded to **Anaheim** by **Edmonton** for Bryan Rodney, February 16, 2012. Signed as a free agent by **Lahti** (Finland), July 27, 2012.

O'REILLY, Cal

(oh-RIGH-lee, KAL)

Center. Shoots left. 6', 188 lbs. Born, Toronto, Ont., September 30, 1986. Nashville's 4th choice, 150th overall, in 2005 Entry Draft.

Season	Club	League	GP	G	A	Pts	PIM	PP	SH	GW	S	%	+/-	TF	F%	Min	GP	G	A	Pts	PIM	PP	SH	GW	Min
2002-03	St. Mary's Lincolns	ON-Jr.B	46	11	19	30	2	....	....	....	....	....	....	....	....	....	....	....	....	....	....	....	....	....	....
2003-04	Windsor Spitfires	OHL	61	3	18	21	2	....	....	....	....	....	....	....	....	....	3	0	1	1	0	....	....	....	....
2004-05	Windsor Spitfires	OHL	68	24	50	74	16	....	....	....	....	....	....	....	....	....	11	4	5	9	4	....	....	....	....
2005-06	Windsor Spitfires	OHL	68	18	81	99	8	....	....	....	....	....	....	....	....	....	7	3	8	11	0	....	....	....	....
	Milwaukee	AHL	2	0	0	0	0	....	....	....	....	....	....	....	....	....	10	0	1	1	0	....	....	....	....
2006-07	Milwaukee	AHL	78	18	47	65	20	....	....	....	....	....	....	....	....	....	4	1	2	3	0	....	....	....	....
2007-08	Milwaukee	AHL	80	16	63	79	22	....	....	....	....	....	....	....	....	....	6	1	2	3	0	....	....	....	....
2008-09	**Nashville**	**NHL**	**11**	**3**	**2**	**5**	**2**	**0**	**0**	**0**	**6**	**50.0**	**2**	**88**	**39.8**	**12:36**	....	....	....	....	....	....	....	....	....
	Milwaukee	AHL	67	13	56	69	20	....	....	....	....	....	....	....	....	....	11	2	6	8	0	....	....	....	....
2009-10	**Nashville**	**NHL**	**31**	**2**	**9**	**11**	**4**	**1**	**0**	**0**	**23**	**8.7**	**1**	**281**	**47.3**	**13:38**	....	....	....	....	....	....	....	....	....
	Milwaukee	AHL	35	9	31	40	8	....	....	....	....	....	....	....	....	....	....	....	....	....	....	....	....	....	....
2010-11	**Nashville**	**NHL**	**38**	**6**	**12**	**18**	**2**	**1**	**0**	**1**	**44**	**13.6**	**4**	**497**	**46.5**	**16:54**	....	....	....	....	....	....	....	....	....
2011-12	**Nashville**	**NHL**	**5**	**0**	**1**	**1**	**2**	**0**	**0**	**0**	**1**	**0.0**	**–2**	**44**	**45.5**	**14:06**	....	....	....	....	....	....	....	....	....
	Phoenix	**NHL**	**22**	**2**	**3**	**5**	**2**	**1**	**0**	**0**	**13**	**15.4**	**–5**	**170**	**44.7**	**12:37**	....	....	....	....	....	....	....	....	....
	Portland Pirates	AHL	5	1	1	2	0	....	....	....	....	....	....	....	....	....	....	....	....	....	....	....	....	....	....
	Pittsburgh	**NHL**	**6**	**0**	**1**	**1**	**0**	**0**	**0**	**0**	**3**	**0.0**	**–4**	**54**	**44.4**	**12:11**	....	....	....	....	....	....	....	....	....
	Wilkes-Barre	AHL	21	0	10	10	8	....	....	....	....	....	....	....	....	....	12	5	4	9	0	....	....	....	....
2012-13	Magnitogorsk	KHL	32	3	16	19	30	....	....	....	....	....	....	....	....	....	7	2	2	4	2	....	....	....	....
	NHL Totals		**113**	**13**	**28**	**41**	**12**	**3**	**0**	**1**	**90**	**14.4**		**1134**	**45.8**	**14:23**	....	....	....	....	....	....	....	....	....

• Missed majority of 2010-11 due to leg injury. Traded to **Phoenix** by **Nashville** for Phoenix's 4th round choice (Mikko Vainonen) in 2012 Entry Draft, October 28, 2011. Claimed on waivers by **Pittsburgh** from **Phoenix**, February 1, 2012. Signed as a free agent by **Magnitogorsk** (KHL), July 18, 2012.

O'REILLY, Ryan

(oh-RIGH-lee, RIGH-uhn) **COL**

Center. Shoots left. 6', 200 lbs. Born, Clinton, Ont., February 7, 1991. Colorado's 2nd choice, 33rd overall, in 2009 Entry Draft.

Season	Club	League	GP	G	A	Pts	PIM	PP	SH	GW	S	%	+/-	TF	F%	Min	GP	G	A	Pts	PIM	PP	SH	GW	Min
2006-07	Tor. Jr. Canadiens	GTHL	50	31	43	74	....	....	....	....	....	....	....	....	....	....	....	....	....	....	....	....	....	....	....
	Tor. Canadiens	ON-Jr.A	1	1	0	1	0	....	....	....	....	....	....	....	....	....	....	....	....	....	....	....	....	....	....
2007-08	Erie Otters	OHL	61	19	33	52	14	....	....	....	....	....	....	....	....	....	....	....	....	....	....	....	....	....	....
2008-09	Erie Otters	OHL	68	16	50	66	26	....	....	....	....	....	....	....	....	....	5	0	5	5	2	....	....	....	....
2009-10	**Colorado**	**NHL**	**81**	**8**	**18**	**26**	**18**	**0**	**2**	**2**	**135**	**5.9**	**4**	**1014**	**47.8**	**16:46**	**6**	**1**	**0**	**1**	**2**	**0**	**0**	**1**	**17:05**
2010-11	**Colorado**	**NHL**	**74**	**13**	**13**	**26**	**16**	**2**	**1**	**0**	**119**	**10.9**	**–7**	**1025**	**51.8**	**16:03**	....	....	....	....	....	....	....	....	....
2011-12	**Colorado**	**NHL**	**81**	**18**	**37**	**55**	**12**	**4**	**0**	**3**	**189**	**9.5**	**–1**	**1443**	**52.8**	**19:32**	....	....	....	....	....	....	....	....	....
2012-13	Magnitogorsk	KHL	12	5	5	10	2	....	....	....	....	....	....	....	....	....	....	....	....	....	....	....	....	....	....
	Colorado	**NHL**	**29**	**6**	**14**	**20**	**4**	**3**	**0**	**0**	**66**	**9.1**	**–3**	**456**	**52.9**	**18:30**	....	....	....	....	....	....	....	....	....
	NHL Totals		**265**	**45**	**82**	**127**	**50**	**9**	**3**	**5**	**509**	**8.8**		**3938**	**51.3**	**17:36**	**6**	**1**	**0**	**1**	**2**	**0**	**0**	**1**	**17:05**

Signed as a free agent by **Magnitogorsk** (KHL), December 7, 2012.

Season	Club	League	GP	G	A	Pts	PIM	PP	SH	GW	S	%	+/-	TF	F%	Min	Playoffs GP	G	A	Pts	PIM	PP	SH	GW	Min

(Regular Season: GP through Min; Playoffs: GP through Min)

ORLOV, Dmitry (ohr-LAWF, dih-MEE-tree) **WSH**

Defense. Shoots left. 6', 210 lbs. Born, Novokuznetsk, USSR, July 23, 1991. Washington's 2nd choice, 55th overall, in 2009 Entry Draft.

Season	Club	League	GP	G	A	Pts	PIM	PP	SH	GW	S	%	+/-	TF	F%	Min	GP	G	A	Pts	PIM	PP	SH	GW	Min
2007-08	Novokuznetsk	Russia	6	0	0	0	0																		
2008-09	Novokuznetsk 2	Russia-3	STATISTICS NOT AVAILABLE																						
	Novokuznetsk	KHL	16	1	0	1	4																		
2009-10	Novokuznetsk	KHL	41	4	3	7	49																		
	Novokuznetsk Jr.	Russia-Jr.	7	7	6	13	6										17	9	10	19	26				
2010-11	Novokuznetsk	KHL	45	2	11	13	43																		
	Novokuznetsk Jr.	Russia-Jr.	1	0	0	0	0																		
	Hershey Bears	AHL	19	2	7	9	12										6	0	1	1	4				
2011-12	**Washington**	**NHL**	**60**	**3**	**16**	**19**	**18**	**0**	**0**	**1**	**51**	**5.9**	**1**	**1**	**0.0**	**16:52**									
	Hershey Bears	AHL	15	4	5	9	12																		
2012-13	Hershey Bears	AHL	31	3	14	17	20										4	1	2	3	4				
	Washington	**NHL**	**5**	**0**	**1**	**1**	**0**	**0**	**0**	**0**	**1**	**0.0**	**5**	**0**	**0.0**	**14:57**									
	NHL Totals		**65**	**3**	**17**	**20**	**18**	**0**	**0**	**1**	**52**	**5.8**		**1**	**0.0**	**16:44**									

ORPIK, Brooks (OHR-pihk, BRUKS) **PIT**

Defense. Shoots left. 6'2", 219 lbs. Born, San Francisco, CA, September 26, 1980. Pittsburgh's 1st choice, 18th overall, in 2000 Entry Draft.

Season	Club	League	GP	G	A	Pts	PIM	PP	SH	GW	S	%	+/-	TF	F%	Min	GP	G	A	Pts	PIM	PP	SH	GW	Min
1996-97	Thayer Academy	High-MA	20	4	1	5																			
1997-98	Thayer Academy	High-MA	22	0	7	7																			
1998-99	Boston College	H-East	41	1	10	11	*96																		
99-2000	Boston College	H-East	38	1	9	10	102																		
2000-01	Boston College	H-East	40	0	20	20	*124																		
2001-02	Wilkes-Barre	AHL	78	2	18	20	99																		
2002-03	**Pittsburgh**	**NHL**	**6**	**0**	**0**	**0**	**2**	**0**	**0**	**0**	**2**	**0.0**	**–5**	**0**	**0.0**	**18:19**									
	Wilkes-Barre	AHL	71	4	14	18	105										6	0	0	0	14				
2003-04	**Pittsburgh**	**NHL**	**79**	**1**	**9**	**10**	**127**	**0**	**0**	**0**	**56**	**1.8**	**–36**	**0**	**0.0**	**18:25**									
	Wilkes-Barre	AHL	3	0	0	0	2										24	0	4	4	53				
2005-06	**Pittsburgh**	**NHL**	**64**	**2**	**7**	**9**	**124**	**0**	**0**	**0**	**32**	**6.3**	**–3**	**0**	**0.0**	**18:50**									
2006-07	**Pittsburgh**	**NHL**	**70**	**0**	**6**	**6**	**82**	**0**	**0**	**0**	**59**	**0.0**	**4**	**0**	**0.0**	**16:37**	**5**	**0**	**0**	**0**	**8**	**0**	**0**	**0**	**15:43**
2007-08	**Pittsburgh**	**NHL**	**78**	**1**	**10**	**11**	**57**	**0**	**0**	**0**	**50**	**2.0**	**11**	**0**	**0.0**	**16:58**	**20**	**0**	**2**	**2**	**18**	**0**	**0**	**0**	**20:47**
2008-09♦	**Pittsburgh**	**NHL**	**79**	**2**	**17**	**19**	**73**	**1**	**0**	**0**	**39**	**5.1**	**10**	**0**	**0.0**	**20:20**	**24**	**0**	**4**	**4**	**22**	**0**	**0**	**0**	**20:04**
2009-10	**Pittsburgh**	**NHL**	**73**	**2**	**23**	**25**	**64**	**0**	**0**	**0**	**61**	**3.3**	**6**	**0**	**0.0**	**20:06**	**13**	**0**	**2**	**2**	**12**	**0**	**0**	**0**	**21:40**
	United States	Olympics	6	0	0	0	0																		
2010-11	**Pittsburgh**	**NHL**	**63**	**1**	**12**	**13**	**66**	**0**	**0**	**0**	**56**	**1.8**	**12**	**1**	**100.0**	**20:53**	**7**	**0**	**3**	**3**	**14**	**0**	**0**	**0**	**24:11**
2011-12	**Pittsburgh**	**NHL**	**73**	**2**	**16**	**18**	**61**	**0**	**0**	**0**	**44**	**4.5**	**19**	**0**	**0.0**	**22:33**	**6**	**0**	**0**	**0**	**4**	**0**	**0**	**0**	**22:17**
2012-13	**Pittsburgh**	**NHL**	**46**	**0**	**8**	**8**	**32**	**0**	**0**	**0**	**32**	**0.0**	**17**	**0**	**0.0**	**22:17**	**12**	**1**	**1**	**2**	**10**	**0**	**0**	**1**	**25:08**
	NHL Totals		**631**	**11**	**108**	**119**	**688**	**1**	**0**	**0**	**431**	**2.6**		**1**	**100.0**	**19:31**	**87**	**1**	**12**	**13**	**88**	**0**	**0**	**1**	**21:24**

ORR, Colton (OHR, KOHL-tuhn) **TOR**

Right wing. Shoots right. 6'3", 222 lbs. Born, Winnipeg, Man., March 3, 1982.

Season	Club	League	GP	G	A	Pts	PIM	PP	SH	GW	S	%	+/-	TF	F%	Min	GP	G	A	Pts	PIM	PP	SH	GW	Min
1998-99	St. Boniface	MJHL	STATISTICS NOT AVAILABLE																						
	Swift Current	WHL	2	0	0	0	0																		
99-2000	Swift Current	WHL	61	3	2	5	130										12	1	0	1	25				
2000-01	Swift Current	WHL	19	0	4	4	67																		
	Kamloops Blazers	WHL	41	8	1	9	179										3	0	0	0	20				
2001-02	Kamloops Blazers	WHL	1	0	0	0	7										2	0	0	0	2				
2002-03	Kamloops Blazers	WHL	3	2	0	2	17																		
	Regina Pats	WHL	37	6	2	8	170										3	0	0	0	19				
	Providence Bruins	AHL	1	0	0	0	7																		
2003-04	**Boston**	**NHL**	**1**	**0**	**0**	**0**	**0**	**0**	**0**	**0**	**0**	**0.0**	**–1**	**0**	**0.0**	**2:13**									
	Providence Bruins	AHL	64	1	4	5	257										2	0	0	0	9				
2004-05	Providence Bruins	AHL	61	1	6	7	279										17	1	0	1	44				
2005-06	**Boston**	**NHL**	**20**	**0**	**0**	**0**	**27**	**0**	**0**	**0**	**1**	**0.0**	**0**	**0**	**0.0**	**1:49**									
	NY Rangers	**NHL**	**15**	**0**	**1**	**1**	**44**	**0**	**0**	**0**	**0**	**0.0**	**1**	**0**	**0.0**	**4:19**	**1**	**0**	**0**	**0**	**2**	**0**	**0**	**0**	**4:17**
2006-07	**NY Rangers**	**NHL**	**53**	**2**	**1**	**3**	**126**	**0**	**0**	**1**	**23**	**8.7**	**–2**	**0**	**0.0**	**5:20**	**4**	**0**	**0**	**0**	**12**	**0**	**0**	**0**	**4:57**
2007-08	**NY Rangers**	**NHL**	**74**	**1**	**1**	**2**	**159**	**0**	**0**	**1**	**24**	**4.2**	**–13**	**2**	**50.0**	**7:49**	**2**	**0**	**0**	**0**	**0**	**0**	**0**	**0**	**4:26**
2008-09	**NY Rangers**	**NHL**	**82**	**1**	**4**	**5**	**193**	**0**	**0**	**0**	**40**	**2.5**	**–15**	**16**	**25.0**	**6:29**	**5**	**0**	**0**	**0**	**16**	**0**	**0**	**0**	**3:50**
2009-10	**Toronto**	**NHL**	**82**	**4**	**2**	**6**	**239**	**0**	**0**	**1**	**43**	**9.3**	**–4**	**2**	**50.0**	**6:52**									
2010-11	**Toronto**	**NHL**	**46**	**2**	**0**	**2**	**128**	**0**	**0**	**1**	**14**	**14.3**	**–1**	**1**	**0.0**	**5:04**									
2011-12	**Toronto**	**NHL**	**5**	**1**	**0**	**1**	**5**	**0**	**0**	**0**	**3**	**33.3**	**1**	**1**	**0.0**	**4:29**									
	Toronto Marlies	AHL	26	1	0	1	46										8	0	0	0	9				
2012-13	**Toronto**	**NHL**	**44**	**1**	**3**	**4**	***155**	**0**	**0**	**0**	**13**	**7.7**	**4**	**1**	**0.0**	**6:23**	**7**	**0**	**0**	**0**	**18**	**0**	**0**	**0**	**6:31**
	NHL Totals		**422**	**12**	**12**	**24**	**1076**	**0**	**0**	**4**	**161**	**7.5**		**23**	**26.1**	**6:09**	**19**	**0**	**0**	**0**	**48**	**0**	**0**	**0**	**5:09**

Signed as a free agent by **Boston**, September 19, 2001. • Missed majority of 2001-02 due to wrist injury vs. Red Deer (WHL), October 20, 2001. Claimed on waivers by **NY Rangers** from **Boston**, November 29, 2005. Signed as a free agent by **Toronto**, July 1, 2009. • Missed majority of 2011-12 as a healthy reserve.

ORTMEYER, Jed (OHRT-migh-uhr, JEHD)

Center. Shoots right. 6', 200 lbs. Born, Omaha, NE, September 3, 1978.

Season	Club	League	GP	G	A	Pts	PIM	PP	SH	GW	S	%	+/-	TF	F%	Min	GP	G	A	Pts	PIM	PP	SH	GW	Min
1997-98	Omaha Lancers	USHL	54	23	25	48	52										14	3	4	7	31				
1998-99	Omaha Lancers	USHL	52	23	36	59	81										12	5	6	11	16				
99-2000	U. of Michigan	CCHA	41	8	16	24	40																		
2000-01	U. of Michigan	CCHA	27	10	11	21	52																		
2001-02	U. of Michigan	CCHA	41	15	23	38	40																		
2002-03	U. of Michigan	CCHA	36	18	16	34	48																		
2003-04	**NY Rangers**	**NHL**	**58**	**2**	**4**	**6**	**16**	**0**	**0**	**0**	**48**	**4.2**	**–10**	**16**	**31.3**	**9:52**									
	Hartford	AHL	13	2	8	10	4										16	5	2	7	6				
2004-05	Hartford	AHL	61	7	20	27	63										6	0	1	1	4				
2005-06	**NY Rangers**	**NHL**	**78**	**5**	**2**	**7**	**38**	**0**	**0**	**1**	**90**	**5.6**	**2**	**21**	**23.8**	**11:06**	**4**	**1**	**0**	**1**	**4**	**0**	**0**	**0**	**11:40**
2006-07	**NY Rangers**	**NHL**	**41**	**2**	**9**	**11**	**22**	**0**	**1**	**0**	**67**	**3.0**	**7**	**8**	**12.5**	**12:35**	**9**	**0**	**0**	**0**	**2**	**0**	**0**	**0**	**9:37**
	Hartford	AHL	8	1	3	4	6																		
2007-08	**Nashville**	**NHL**	**51**	**4**	**4**	**8**	**32**	**0**	**1**	**0**	**68**	**5.9**	**–8**	**12**	**50.0**	**12:27**									
2008-09	**Nashville**	**NHL**	**2**	**0**	**0**	**0**	**0**	**0**	**0**	**0**	**4**	**0.0**	**0**	**0**	**0.0**	**11:01**									
	Milwaukee	AHL	55	10	13	23	51										11	1	6	7	8				
2009-10	**San Jose**	**NHL**	**76**	**8**	**11**	**19**	**37**	**0**	**0**	**1**	**131**	**6.1**	**4**	**18**	**27.8**	**11:31**	**4**	**0**	**1**	**1**	**0**	**0**	**0**	**0**	**6:59**
2010-11	San Antonio	AHL	20	2	1	3	16																		
	Houston Aeros	AHL	40	6	10	16	29										24	6	7	13	4				
	Minnesota	**NHL**	**4**	**0**	**0**	**0**	**2**	**0**	**0**	**0**	**5**	**0.0**	**–1**	**0**	**0.0**	**9:24**									
2011-12	**Minnesota**	**NHL**	**35**	**1**	**1**	**2**	**14**	**0**	**0**	**1**	**41**	**2.4**	**–8**	**9**	**44.4**	**9:43**									
	Houston Aeros	AHL	34	8	10	18	32																		
2012-13	San Antonio	AHL	32	6	9	15	16																		
	NHL Totals		**345**	**22**	**31**	**53**	**161**	**0**	**2**	**3**	**454**	**4.8**		**84**	**31.0**	**11:12**	**17**	**1**	**1**	**2**	**6**	**0**	**0**	**0**	**9:29**

Signed as a free agent by **NY Rangers**, May 10, 2003. Signed as a free agent by **Nashville**, July 2, 2007. Signed as a free agent by **San Jose**, July 16, 2009. Signed to a PTO (professional tryout) contract by **San Antonio** (AHL), October 29, 2010. Signed to a PTO (professional tryout) contract by **Houston** (AHL), January 1, 2011. Signed as a free agent by **Minnesota**, January 4, 2011. Signed as a free agent by **San Antonio** (AHL), January 31, 2013.

OSALA, Oskar (OH-sa-la, AWZ-kuhr) **CAR**

Left wing. Shoots left. 6'4", 219 lbs. Born, Vaasa, Finland, December 26, 1987. Washington's 6th choice, 97th overall, in 2006 Entry Draft.

Season	Club	League	GP	G	A	Pts	PIM	PP	SH	GW	S	%	+/-	TF	F%	Min	GP	G	A	Pts	PIM	PP	SH	GW	Min
2003-04	Sport Vaasa U18	Fin-U18	25	19	18	37	32																		
	Sport Vaasa Jr.	Fin-Jr.	2	0	0	0	4																		
	Sport Vaasa	Finland-2	5	0	0	0	0																		
2004-05	Sport Vaasa U18	Fin-U18	4	4	2	6	16																		
	Sport Vaasa Jr.	Fin-Jr.	19	13	14	27	28										2	0	0	0	2				
	Sport Vaasa	Finland-2	21	1	4	5	6										7	0	0	0	6				
2005-06	Mississauga	OHL	68	17	26	43	86																		
2006-07	Mississauga	OHL	54	22	22	44	81										5	2	2	4	0				
	Suomi U20	Finland-2	2	1	0	1	0																		

Season	Club	League	GP	G	A	Pts	PIM	PP	SH	GW	S	%	+/-	TF	F%	Min	GP	G	A	Pts	PIM	PP	SH	GW	Min
			Regular Season														Playoffs								
2007-08	Blues Espoo	Finland	53	18	17	35	62	....	....	....	....	....	....	....	....	....	17	7	3	10	8	....	....	....	....
2008-09	**Washington**	**NHL**	**2**	**0**	**0**	**0**	**0**	**0**	**0**	**0**	**1**	**0.0**	**–1**	**0**	**0.0**	**8:44**	....	....	....	....	....	....	....	....	....
	Hershey Bears	AHL	75	23	14	37	47	....	....	....	....	....	....	....	....	....	22	6	4	10	17	....	....	....	....
2009-10	**Carolina**	**NHL**	**1**	**0**	**0**	**0**	**0**	**0**	**0**	**0**	**1**	**0.0**	**0**	**0**	**0.0**	**6:46**	....	....	....	....	....	....	....	....	....
	Hershey Bears	AHL	53	15	14	29	57	....	....	....	....	....	....	....	....	....	....	....	....	....	....	....	....	....	....
	Albany River Rats	AHL	16	9	3	12	11	....	....	....	....	....	....	....	....	....	8	2	1	3	2	....	....	....	....
2010-11	Charlotte	AHL	59	13	29	42	55	....	....	....	....	....	....	....	....	....	15	3	2	5	29	....	....	....	....
2011-12	Nizhnekamsk	KHL	41	12	7	19	44	....	....	....	....	....	....	....	....	....	....	....	....	....	....	....	....	....	....
2012-13	Nizhnekamsk	KHL	44	15	11	26	54	....	....	....	....	....	....	....	....	....	4	0	1	1	17	....	....	....	....
	NHL Totals		**3**	**0**	**0**	**0**	**0**	**0**	**0**	**0**	**2**	**0.0**		**0**	**0.0**	**8:04**	....	....	....	....	....	....	....	....	....

Signed as a free agent by **Espoo** (Finland), July 23, 2007. Traded to **Carolina** by **Washington** with Brian Pothier and Washington's 2nd round choice (later traded to NY Rangers, later traded to Calgary – Calgary selected Tyler Wotherspoon) in 2011 Entry Draft for Joe Corvo, March 3, 2010. Signed as a free agent by **Nizhnekamsk** (KHL), May 25, 2011.

OSHIE, T.J.

(OH-shee, TEE-JAY) **ST.L.**

Center. Shoots right. 5'11", 189 lbs. Born, Mt. Vernon, WA, December 23, 1986. St. Louis' 1st choice, 24th overall, in 2005 Entry Draft.

Season	Club	League	GP	G	A	Pts	PIM	PP	SH	GW	S	%	+/-	TF	F%	Min	GP	G	A	Pts	PIM	PP	SH	GW	Min
2004-05	Warroad Warriors	High-MN	31	37	62	99	22	....	....	....	....	....	....	....	....	....	....	....	....	....	....	....	....	....	....
	Sioux Falls	USHL	11	3	2	5	6	....	....	....	....	....	....	....	....	....	....	....	....	....	....	....	....	....	....
2005-06	North Dakota	WCHA	44	24	21	45	33	....	....	....	....	....	....	....	....	....	....	....	....	....	....	....	....	....	....
2006-07	North Dakota	WCHA	43	17	*35	52	30	....	....	....	....	....	....	....	....	....	....	....	....	....	....	....	....	....	....
2007-08	North Dakota	WCHA	42	18	27	45	57	....	....	....	....	....	....	....	....	....	....	....	....	....	....	....	....	....	....
2008-09	**St. Louis**	**NHL**	**57**	**14**	**25**	**39**	**30**	**6**	**1**	**1**	**101**	**13.9**	**16**	**109**	**43.1**	**16:35**	**4**	**0**	**0**	**0**	**2**	**0**	**0**	**0**	**19:01**
2009-10	**St. Louis**	**NHL**	**76**	**18**	**30**	**48**	**36**	**1**	**1**	**3**	**158**	**11.4**	**–1**	**153**	**41.8**	**18:19**	....	....	....	....	....	....	....	....	....
2010-11	**St. Louis**	**NHL**	**49**	**12**	**22**	**34**	**15**	**3**	**1**	**3**	**103**	**11.7**	**10**	**227**	**44.1**	**19:11**	....	....	....	....	....	....	....	....	....
2011-12	**St. Louis**	**NHL**	**80**	**19**	**35**	**54**	**50**	**3**	**1**	**3**	**188**	**10.1**	**15**	**53**	**45.3**	**19:32**	**9**	**0**	**3**	**3**	**6**	**0**	**0**	**0**	**18:49**
2012-13	**St. Louis**	**NHL**	**30**	**7**	**13**	**20**	**15**	**2**	**1**	**1**	**65**	**10.8**	**–5**	**13**	**38.5**	**19:06**	**6**	**2**	**0**	**2**	**2**	**1**	**0**	**0**	**18:31**
	NHL Totals		**292**	**70**	**125**	**195**	**146**	**15**	**5**	**11**	**615**	**11.4**		**555**	**43.2**	**18:32**	**19**	**2**	**3**	**5**	**10**	**1**	**0**	**0**	**18:46**

WCHA All-Rookie Team (2006) • WCHA First All-Star Team (2008) • NCAA West First All-American Team (2008)

OTT, Steve

(AWT, STEEV) **BUF**

Center. Shoots left. 6', 190 lbs. Born, Summerside, P.E.I., August 19, 1982. Dallas' 1st choice, 25th overall, in 2000 Entry Draft.

Season	Club	League	GP	G	A	Pts	PIM	PP	SH	GW	S	%	+/-	TF	F%	Min	GP	G	A	Pts	PIM	PP	SH	GW	Min
1998-99	Leamington Flyers	ON-Jr.B	48	14	30	44	110	....	....	....	....	....	....	....	....	....	....	....	....	....	....	....	....	....	....
99-2000	Windsor Spitfires	OHL	66	23	39	62	131	....	....	....	....	....	....	....	....	....	12	3	5	8	21	....	....	....	....
2000-01	Windsor Spitfires	OHL	55	50	37	87	164	....	....	....	....	....	....	....	....	....	9	3	8	11	27	....	....	....	....
2001-02	Windsor Spitfires	OHL	53	43	45	88	178	....	....	....	....	....	....	....	....	....	14	6	10	16	49	....	....	....	....
2002-03	**Dallas**	**NHL**	**26**	**3**	**4**	**7**	**31**	**0**	**0**	**0**	**25**	**12.0**	**6**	**4**	**50.0**	**8:46**	**1**	**0**	**0**	**0**	**0**	**0**	**0**	**0**	**6:57**
	Utah Grizzlies	AHL	40	9	11	20	98	....	....	....	....	....	....	....	....	....	....	....	....	....	....	....	....	....	....
2003-04	**Dallas**	**NHL**	**73**	**2**	**10**	**12**	**152**	**0**	**0**	**1**	**74**	**2.7**	**–2**	**59**	**49.2**	**10:14**	**4**	**1**	**0**	**1**	**0**	**0**	**0**	**1**	**6:55**
2004-05	Hamilton	AHL	67	18	21	39	279	....	....	....	....	....	....	....	....	....	4	0	0	0	20	....	....	....	....
2005-06	**Dallas**	**NHL**	**82**	**5**	**17**	**22**	**178**	**0**	**0**	**1**	**89**	**5.6**	**1**	**535**	**49.2**	**11:54**	**5**	**0**	**1**	**1**	**2**	**0**	**0**	**0**	**7:41**
2006-07	**Dallas**	**NHL**	**19**	**0**	**4**	**4**	**35**	**0**	**0**	**0**	**17**	**0.0**	**–4**	**39**	**59.0**	**9:11**	**6**	**0**	**0**	**0**	**8**	**0**	**0**	**0**	**6:43**
	Iowa Stars	AHL	3	0	0	0	8	....	....	....	....	....	....	....	....	....	....	....	....	....	....	....	....	....	....
2007-08	**Dallas**	**NHL**	**73**	**11**	**11**	**22**	**147**	**0**	**1**	**2**	**89**	**12.4**	**2**	**311**	**58.8**	**14:28**	**18**	**2**	**1**	**3**	**22**	**1**	**0**	**1**	**13:46**
2008-09	**Dallas**	**NHL**	**64**	**19**	**27**	**46**	**135**	**5**	**0**	**0**	**132**	**14.4**	**3**	**172**	**46.5**	**17:35**	....	....	....	....	....	....	....	....	....
2009-10	**Dallas**	**NHL**	**73**	**22**	**14**	**36**	**153**	**8**	**1**	**2**	**146**	**15.1**	**–14**	**352**	**56.8**	**16:28**	....	....	....	....	....	....	....	....	....
2010-11	**Dallas**	**NHL**	**82**	**12**	**20**	**32**	**183**	**3**	**2**	**4**	**120**	**10.0**	**–9**	**1138**	**56.6**	**17:09**	....	....	....	....	....	....	....	....	....
2011-12	**Dallas**	**NHL**	**74**	**11**	**28**	**39**	**156**	**4**	**0**	**2**	**108**	**10.2**	**5**	**1011**	**55.5**	**18:21**	....	....	....	....	....	....	....	....	....
2012-13	**Buffalo**	**NHL**	**48**	**9**	**15**	**24**	**93**	**2**	**0**	**3**	**73**	**12.3**	**3**	**535**	**55.7**	**18:33**	....	....	....	....	....	....	....	....	....
	NHL Totals		**614**	**94**	**150**	**244**	**1263**	**22**	**4**	**15**	**873**	**10.8**		**4156**	**54.9**	**14:55**	**34**	**3**	**2**	**5**	**32**	**1**	**0**	**2**	**10:37**

Canadian Major Junior Second All-Star Team (2001) • OHL Second All-Star Team (2002)

• Missed majority of 2006-07 due to ankle injury vs. Los Angeles, October 28, 2006. Traded to **Buffalo** by **Dallas** with Adam Pardy for Derek Roy, July 2, 2012.

OVECHKIN, Alex

(oh-VEHCH-kihn, AL-ehx) **WSH**

Left wing. Shoots right. 6'3", 230 lbs. Born, Moscow, USSR, September 17, 1985. Washington's 1st choice, 1st overall, in 2004 Entry Draft.

Season	Club	League	GP	G	A	Pts	PIM	PP	SH	GW	S	%	+/-	TF	F%	Min	GP	G	A	Pts	PIM	PP	SH	GW	Min
2001-02	Dyn'o Moscow 2	Russia-3	19	18	8	26	20	....	....	....	....	....	....	....	....	....	....	....	....	....	....	....	....	....	....
	Dynamo Moscow	Russia	22	2	2	4	4	....	....	....	....	....	....	....	....	....	3	0	0	0	0	....	....	....	....
2002-03	Dynamo Moscow	Russia	40	8	7	15	28	....	....	....	....	....	....	....	....	....	5	0	0	0	2	....	....	....	....
2003-04	Dynamo Moscow	Russia	53	13	11	24	40	....	....	....	....	....	....	....	....	....	3	0	0	0	2	....	....	....	....
2004-05	Dynamo Moscow	Russia	37	13	13	26	32	....	....	....	....	....	....	....	....	....	10	2	4	6	31	....	....	....	....
2005-06	**Washington**	**NHL**	**81**	**52**	**54**	**106**	**52**	**21**	**3**	**5**	**425**	**12.2**	**2**	**16**	**12.5**	**21:37**	....	....	....	....	....	....	....	....	....
	Russia	Olympics	8	5	0	5	8	....	....	....	....	....	....	....	....	....	....	....	....	....	....	....	....	....	....
2006-07	**Washington**	**NHL**	**82**	**46**	**46**	**92**	**52**	**16**	**0**	**8**	**392**	**11.7**	**–19**	**17**	**47.1**	**21:23**	....	....	....	....	....	....	....	....	....
2007-08	**Washington**	**NHL**	**82**	***65**	**47**	***112**	**40**	***22**	**0**	***11**	**446**	**14.6**	**28**	**18**	**38.9**	**23:06**	**7**	**4**	**5**	**9**	**0**	**1**	**0**	**2**	**24:03**
2008-09	**Washington**	**NHL**	**79**	***56**	**54**	**110**	**72**	**19**	**1**	**10**	**528**	**10.6**	**8**	**32**	**25.0**	**23:00**	**14**	**11**	**10**	**21**	**8**	**3**	**0**	**1**	**23:21**
2009-10	**Washington**	**NHL**	**72**	**50**	**59**	**109**	**89**	**13**	**0**	**7**	**368**	**13.6**	**45**	**22**	**45.5**	**21:48**	**7**	**5**	**5**	**10**	**0**	**1**	**0**	**0**	**23:06**
	Russia	Olympics	4	2	2	4	2	....	....	....	....	....	....	....	....	....	....	....	....	....	....	....	....	....	....
2010-11	**Washington**	**NHL**	**79**	**32**	**53**	**85**	**41**	**7**	**0**	***11**	**367**	**8.7**	**24**	**18**	**33.3**	**21:22**	**9**	**5**	**5**	**10**	**10**	**1**	**0**	**1**	**23:30**
2011-12	**Washington**	**NHL**	**78**	**38**	**27**	**65**	**26**	**13**	**0**	**3**	**303**	**12.5**	**–8**	**15**	**40.0**	**19:48**	**14**	**5**	**4**	**9**	**8**	**2**	**0**	**1**	**19:51**
2012-13	Dynamo Moscow	KHL	31	19	21	40	14	....	....	....	....	....	....	....	....	....	....	....	....	....	....	....	....	....	....
	Washington	**NHL**	**48**	***32**	**24**	**56**	**36**	**16**	**0**	**4**	**220**	**14.5**	**2**	**1**	**0.0**	**20:53**	**7**	**1**	**1**	**2**	**4**	**1**	**0**	**0**	**20:44**
	NHL Totals		**601**	**371**	**364**	**735**	**408**	**127**	**4**	**59**	**3049**	**12.2**		**139**	**33.8**	**21:40**	**58**	**31**	**30**	**61**	**30**	**9**	**0**	**5**	**22:16**

Olympic All-Star Team (2006) • NHL All-Rookie Team (2006) • NHL First All-Star Team (2006, 2007, 2008, 2009, 2010, 2013) • Calder Memorial Trophy (2006) • Maurice "Rocket" Richard Trophy (2008, 2009, 2013) • Art Ross Trophy (2008) • Lester B. Pearson Award (2008, 2009) • Hart Memorial Trophy (2008, 2009, 2013) • Ted Lindsay Award (2010) • NHL Second All-Star Team (2011, 2013)

Played in NHL All-Star Game (2007, 2008, 2009, 2011)

Signed as a free agent by **Dynamo Moscow** (KHL), September 19, 2012. • In 2012-13 Ovechkin was voted to the NHL First All-Star Team as a Right wing and voted to the NHL Second All-Star Team as a Left wing.

OYSTRICK, Nathan

(OI-strihk, NAY-thuhn)

Defense. Shoots left. 6', 210 lbs. Born, Regina, Sask., December 17, 1982. Atlanta's 7th choice, 198th overall, in 2002 Entry Draft.

Season	Club	League	GP	G	A	Pts	PIM	PP	SH	GW	S	%	+/-	TF	F%	Min	GP	G	A	Pts	PIM	PP	SH	GW	Min
99-2000	Reg. Pat Cdns.	SMHL	43	6	22	28	214	....	....	....	....	....	....	....	....	....	....	....	....	....	....	....	....	....	....
2000-01	South Surrey	BCHL	STATISTICS NOT AVAILABLE																						
2001-02	South Surrey	BCHL	50	15	42	57	142	....	....	....	....	....	....	....	....	....	....	....	....	....	....	....	....	....	....
2002-03	Northern Mich.	CCHA	34	2	10	12	26	....	....	....	....	....	....	....	....	....	....	....	....	....	....	....	....	....	....
2003-04	Northern Mich.	CCHA	39	8	20	28	98	....	....	....	....	....	....	....	....	....	....	....	....	....	....	....	....	....	....
2004-05	Northern Mich.	CCHA	40	7	13	20	87	....	....	....	....	....	....	....	....	....	....	....	....	....	....	....	....	....	....
2005-06	Northern Mich.	CCHA	38	9	20	29	58	....	....	....	....	....	....	....	....	....	....	....	....	....	....	....	....	....	....
	Chicago Wolves	AHL	2	0	1	1	4	....	....	....	....	....	....	....	....	....	....	....	....	....	....	....	....	....	....
2006-07	Chicago Wolves	AHL	80	15	32	47	105	....	....	....	....	....	....	....	....	....	15	0	6	6	16	....	....	....	....
2007-08	Chicago Wolves	AHL	80	15	28	43	112	....	....	....	....	....	....	....	....	....	24	3	8	11	35	....	....	....	....
2008-09	**Atlanta**	**NHL**	**53**	**4**	**8**	**12**	**50**	**0**	**0**	**0**	**43**	**9.3**	**–2**	**0**	**0.0**	**15:45**	....	....	....	....	....	....	....	....	....
2009-10	**Anaheim**	**NHL**	**3**	**0**	**0**	**0**	**2**	**0**	**0**	**0**	**1**	**0.0**	**–1**	**0**	**0.0**	**10:35**	....	....	....	....	....	....	....	....	....
	Chicago Wolves	AHL	43	7	16	23	96	....	....	....	....	....	....	....	....	....	14	2	8	10	8	....	....	....	....
2010-11	**St. Louis**	**NHL**	**9**	**1**	**2**	**3**	**9**	**1**	**0**	**0**	**11**	**9.1**	**1**	**0**	**0.0**	**12:10**	....	....	....	....	....	....	....	....	....
	Peoria Rivermen	AHL	61	15	30	45	125	....	....	....	....	....	....	....	....	....	4	1	1	2	7	....	....	....	....
2011-12	Portland Pirates	AHL	60	11	32	43	107	....	....	....	....	....	....	....	....	....	....	....	....	....	....	....	....	....	....
2012-13	HC Lev Praha	KHL	43	3	6	9	42	....	....	....	....	....	....	....	....	....	4	0	3	3	2	....	....	....	....
	NHL Totals		**65**	**5**	**10**	**15**	**61**	**1**	**0**	**0**	**55**	**9.1**		**0**	**0.0**	**15:01**									

CCHA Second All-Star Team (2004) • CCHA First All-Star Team (2005, 2006) • NCAA West Second All-American Team (2006) • AHL All-Rookie Team (2007) • AHL Second All-Star Team (2007)

Traded to **Anaheim** by **Atlanta** with future considerations for Evgeny Artyukhin, March 1, 2010. Signed as a free agent by **St. Louis**, July 12, 2010. Signed as a free agent by **Phoenix**, July 6, 2011. Signed as a free agent by **Lev Praha** (KHL), June 2, 2012.

PAAJARVI, Magnus

(pe-ya-YAR-vee, MAG-nuhs) **ST.L.**

Left wing. Shoots left. 6'3", 200 lbs. Born, Norrkoping, Sweden, April 12, 1991. Edmonton's 1st choice, 10th overall, in 2009 Entry Draft.

			Regular Season														Playoffs								
Season	Club	League	GP	G	A	Pts	PIM	PP	SH	GW	S	%	+/-	TF	F%	Min	GP	G	A	Pts	PIM	PP	SH	GW	Min
2005-06	Malmo U18	Swe-U18	13	2	3	5	4	....	....	....	....	....	....	....	....	....	1	0	0	0	0	....	....	....	....
	Malmo Jr.	Swe-Jr.	2	0	0	0	0	....	....	....	....	....	....	....	....	....	....	....	....	....	....	....	....	....	....
2006-07	Malmo U18	Swe-U18	3	3	3	6	0	....	....	....	....	....	....	....	....	....	....	....	....	....	....	....	....	....	....
	Malmo Jr.	Swe-Jr.	20	4	2	6	6	....	....	....	....	....	....	....	....	....	4	0	1	1	0	....	....	....	....
2007-08	Timra IK U18	Swe-U18	5	1	6	7	4	....	....	....	....	....	....	....	....	....	....	....	....	....	....	....	....	....	....
	Timra IK Jr.	Swe-Jr.	18	7	15	22	6	....	....	....	....	....	....	....	....	....	....	....	....	....	....	....	....	....	....
	Timra IK	Sweden	35	1	2	3	2	....	....	....	....	....	....	....	....	....	11	0	0	0	2	....	....	....	....
2008-09	Timra IK Jr.	Swe-Jr.	1	0	0	0	0	....	....	....	....	....	....	....	....	....	....	....	....	....	....	....	....	....	....
	Timra IK	Sweden	50	7	10	17	4	....	....	....	....	....	....	....	....	....	7	1	0	1	0	....	....	....	....
2009-10	Timra IK	Sweden	49	12	17	29	6	....	....	....	....	....	....	....	....	....	5	0	1	1	2	....	....	....	....
2010-11	**Edmonton**	**NHL**	**80**	**15**	**19**	**34**	**16**	**3**	**0**	**0**	**180**	**8.3**	**–13**	**5**	**20.0**	**15:23**	....	....	....	....	....	....	....	....	....
2011-12	**Edmonton**	**NHL**	**41**	**2**	**6**	**8**	**4**	**0**	**0**	**0**	**79**	**2.5**	**–7**	**7**	**28.6**	**13:11**	....	....	....	....	....	....	....	....	....
	Oklahoma City	AHL	34	7	18	25	4	....	....	....	....	....	....	....	....	....	14	2	9	11	2	....	....	....	....
2012-13	Oklahoma City	AHL	38	4	16	20	10	....	....	....	....	....	....	....	....	....	....	....	....	....	....	....	....	....	....
	Edmonton	**NHL**	**42**	**9**	**7**	**16**	**14**	**2**	**1**	**2**	**75**	**12.0**	**–1**	**12**	**33.3**	**14:08**	....	....	....	....	....	....	....	....	....
	NHL Totals		**163**	**26**	**32**	**58**	**34**	**5**	**1**	**2**	**334**	**7.8**		**24**	**29.2**	**14:30**	....	....	....	....	....	....	....	....	....

Traded to **St. Louis** by **Edmonton** with a 2nd round choice in 2014 Entry Draft for David Perron, July 10, 2014.

PACIORETTY, Max

(pahk-OHR-eht-tee, MAX) **MTL**

Left wing. Shoots left. 6'2", 210 lbs. Born, New Canaan, CT, November 20, 1988. Montreal's 2nd choice, 22nd overall, in 2007 Entry Draft.

Season	Club	League	GP	G	A	Pts	PIM	PP	SH	GW	S	%	+/-	TF	F%	Min	GP	G	A	Pts	PIM	PP	SH	GW	Min
2004-05	Taft Rhinos	High-CT	23	5	14	19	....	....	....	....	....	....	....	....	....	....	....	....	....	....	....	....	....	....	....
2005-06	Taft Rhinos	High-CT	26	7	26	33	....	....	....	....	....	....	....	....	....	....	....	....	....	....	....	....	....	....	....
2006-07	Sioux City	USHL	60	21	42	63	119	....	....	....	....	....	....	....	....	....	7	4	6	10	10	....	....	....	....
2007-08	U. of Michigan	CCHA	37	15	24	39	59	....	....	....	....	....	....	....	....	....	....	....	....	....	....	....	....	....	....
2008-09	**Montreal**	**NHL**	**34**	**3**	**8**	**11**	**27**	**1**	**0**	**0**	**57**	**5.3**	**–3**	**2**	**50.0**	**12:37**	....	....	....	....	....	....	....	....	....
	Hamilton	AHL	37	6	23	29	43	....	....	....	....	....	....	....	....	....	....	....	....	....	....	....	....	....	....
2009-10	**Montreal**	**NHL**	**52**	**3**	**11**	**14**	**20**	**0**	**0**	**0**	**74**	**4.1**	**–5**	**7**	**14.3**	**12:43**	....	....	....	....	....	....	....	....	....
	Hamilton	AHL	18	2	9	11	10	....	....	....	....	....	....	....	....	....	5	1	0	1	2	....	....	....	....
2010-11	**Montreal**	**NHL**	**37**	**14**	**10**	**24**	**39**	**7**	**0**	**2**	**112**	**12.5**	**–1**	**1**	**0.0**	**15:54**	....	....	....	....	....	....	....	....	....
	Hamilton	AHL	27	17	15	32	20	....	....	....	....	....	....	....	....	....	....	....	....	....	....	....	....	....	....
2011-12	**Montreal**	**NHL**	**79**	**33**	**32**	**65**	**56**	**4**	**0**	**5**	**286**	**11.5**	**2**	**5**	**20.0**	**18:16**	....	....	....	....	....	....	....	....	....
2012-13	HC Ambri-Piotta	Swiss	5	1	0	1	4	....	....	....	....	....	....	....	....	....	....	....	....	....	....	....	....	....	....
	Montreal	**NHL**	**44**	**15**	**24**	**39**	**28**	**4**	**0**	**0**	**163**	**9.2**	**8**	**7**	**28.6**	**16:31**	**4**	**0**	**0**	**0**	**4**	**0**	**0**	**0**	**17:16**
	NHL Totals		**246**	**68**	**85**	**153**	**170**	**16**	**0**	**7**	**692**	**9.8**		**22**	**22.7**	**15:38**	**4**	**0**	**0**	**0**	**4**	**0**	**0**	**0**	**17:16**

USHL All-Rookie Team (2007) • USHL Rookie of the Year (2007) • CCHA All-Rookie Team (2008) • CCHA Rookie of the Year (2008) • Bill Masterton Memorial Trophy (2012)

Signed as a free agent by **Ambri-Piotta** (Swiss), September 24, 2012.

PAETSCH, Nathan

(PASH, NAY-thuhn)

Defense. Shoots left. 6', 195 lbs. Born, Humboldt, Sask., March 30, 1983. Buffalo's 8th choice, 202nd overall, in 2003 Entry Draft.

Season	Club	League	GP	G	A	Pts	PIM	PP	SH	GW	S	%	+/-	TF	F%	Min	GP	G	A	Pts	PIM	PP	SH	GW	Min
1998-99	Tisdale Trojans	SMHL	74	20	55	75	120	....	....	....	....	....	....	....	....	....	....	....	....	....	....	....	....	....	....
	Moose Jaw	WHL	2	0	0	0	0	....	....	....	....	....	....	....	....	....	1	0	0	0	0	....	....	....	....
99-2000	Moose Jaw	WHL	68	9	35	44	49	....	....	....	....	....	....	....	....	....	4	0	1	1	0	....	....	....	....
2000-01	Moose Jaw	WHL	70	8	54	62	118	....	....	....	....	....	....	....	....	....	4	1	2	3	6	....	....	....	....
2001-02	Moose Jaw	WHL	59	16	36	52	86	....	....	....	....	....	....	....	....	....	12	0	4	4	16	....	....	....	....
2002-03	Moose Jaw	WHL	59	15	39	54	81	....	....	....	....	....	....	....	....	....	13	3	10	13	6	....	....	....	....
2003-04	Rochester	AHL	54	5	5	10	49	....	....	....	....	....	....	....	....	....	16	1	1	2	28	....	....	....	....
2004-05	Rochester	AHL	80	4	19	23	150	....	....	....	....	....	....	....	....	....	9	1	1	2	16	....	....	....	....
2005-06	**Buffalo**	**NHL**	**1**	**0**	**1**	**1**	**0**	**0**	**0**	**0**	**0**	**0.0**	**–1**	**0**	**0.0**	**15:38**	**1**	**0**	**0**	**0**	**0**	**0**	**0**	**0**	**12:06**
	Rochester	AHL	72	11	39	50	90	....	....	....	....	....	....	....	....	....	....	....	....	....	....	....	....	....	....
2006-07	**Buffalo**	**NHL**	**63**	**2**	**22**	**24**	**50**	**0**	**0**	**0**	**62**	**3.2**	**10**	**0**	**0.0**	**15:15**	....	....	....	....	....	....	....	....	....
2007-08	**Buffalo**	**NHL**	**59**	**2**	**7**	**9**	**27**	**0**	**0**	**0**	**49**	**4.1**	**3**	**0**	**0.0**	**13:38**	....	....	....	....	....	....	....	....	....
2008-09	**Buffalo**	**NHL**	**23**	**2**	**4**	**6**	**25**	**0**	**0**	**0**	**21**	**9.5**	**3**	**0**	**0.0**	**12:11**	....	....	....	....	....	....	....	....	....
2009-10	**Buffalo**	**NHL**	**11**	**1**	**1**	**2**	**6**	**0**	**0**	**0**	**9**	**11.1**	**2**	**0**	**0.0**	**9:39**	....	....	....	....	....	....	....	....	....
	Columbus	**NHL**	**10**	**0**	**0**	**0**	**6**	**0**	**0**	**0**	**8**	**0.0**	**–5**	**0**	**0.0**	**11:14**	....	....	....	....	....	....	....	....	....
2010-11	Rochester	AHL	9	1	2	3	2	....	....	....	....	....	....	....	....	....	....	....	....	....	....	....	....	....	....
	Syracuse Crunch	AHL	34	8	9	17	12	....	....	....	....	....	....	....	....	....	....	....	....	....	....	....	....	....	....
2011-12	Wolfsburg	Germany	52	7	18	25	46	....	....	....	....	....	....	....	....	....	2	0	0	0	0	....	....	....	....
2012-13	Grand Rapids	AHL	70	4	27	31	32	....	....	....	....	....	....	....	....	....	24	0	11	11	21	....	....	....	....
	NHL Totals		**167**	**7**	**35**	**42**	**114**	**0**	**0**	**0**	**149**	**4.7**		**0**	**0.0**	**13:39**	**1**	**0**	**0**	**0**	**0**	**0**	**0**	**0**	**12:06**

• Re-entered NHL Entry Draft. Originally Washington's 1st choice, 58th overall, in 2001 Entry Draft.

WHL East Second All-Star Team (2003)

• Missed majority of 2008-09 as a healthy reserve. Traded to **Columbus** by **Buffalo** with Vancouver's 2nd round choice (previously acquired, Columbus selected Petr Straka) in 2010 Entry Draft for Raffi Torres, March 3, 2010. • Missed majority of 2009-10 as a healthy reserve. Signed as a free agent by **Florida**, July 7, 2010. Traded to **Vancouver** by **Florida** for Sean Zimmerman, October 7, 2010. • Re-assigned to **Syracuse** (AHL) by **Vancouver**, November 1, 2010. Signed as a free agent by **Wolfsburg** (Germany), June 22, 2011. Signed as a free agent by **Grand Rapids** (AHL), July 9, 2012.

PAGEAU, Jean-Gabriel

(pah-ZHOH, ZHAWN-ga-BREE-ehl) **OTT**

Center. Shoots right. 5'9", 172 lbs. Born, Ottawa, Ont., November 11, 1992. Ottawa's 5th choice, 96th overall, in 2011 Entry Draft.

Season	Club	League	GP	G	A	Pts	PIM	PP	SH	GW	S	%	+/-	TF	F%	Min	GP	G	A	Pts	PIM	PP	SH	GW	Min
2008-09	Gatineau	QAAA	37	15	16	31	6	....	....	....	....	....	....	....	....	....	....	....	....	....	....	....	....	....	....
2009-10	Gatineau	QMJHL	62	16	15	31	20	....	....	....	....	....	....	....	....	....	4	1	0	1	0	....	....	....	....
2010-11	Gatineau	QMJHL	67	32	47	79	22	....	....	....	....	....	....	....	....	....	24	13	16	29	20	....	....	....	....
2011-12	Gatineau	QMJHL	23	23	16	39	12	....	....	....	....	....	....	....	....	....	....	....	....	....	....	....	....	....	....
	Chicoutimi	QMJHL	23	9	17	26	13	....	....	....	....	....	....	....	....	....	16	4	10	14	6	....	....	....	....
2012-13	Binghamton	AHL	69	7	22	29	33	....	....	....	....	....	....	....	....	....	....	....	....	....	....	....	....	....	....
	Ottawa	**NHL**	**9**	**2**	**2**	**4**	**0**	**0**	**0**	**2**	**14**	**14.3**	**3**	**82**	**48.8**	**11:30**	**10**	**4**	**2**	**6**	**8**	**1**	**0**	**1**	**12:52**
	NHL Totals		**9**	**2**	**2**	**4**	**0**	**0**	**0**	**2**	**14**	**14.3**		**82**	**48.8**	**11:30**	**10**	**4**	**2**	**6**	**8**	**1**	**0**	**1**	**12:52**

PAHLSSON, Samuel

(PAWL-suhn, SAM-yoo-ehl)

Center. Shoots left. 6', 202 lbs. Born, Ange, Sweden, December 17, 1977. Colorado's 10th choice, 176th overall, in 1996 Entry Draft.

Season	Club	League	GP	G	A	Pts	PIM	PP	SH	GW	S	%	+/-	TF	F%	Min	GP	G	A	Pts	PIM	PP	SH	GW	Min
1992-93	Ange IK	Sweden-4	9	0	0	0	0	....	....	....	....	....	....	....	....	....	....	....	....	....	....	....	....	....	....
1993-94	Ange IK	Sweden-4	STATISTICS NOT AVAILABLE																						
1994-95	MoDo	Sweden	1	0	0	0	0																		
1995-96	MoDo Jr.	Swe-Jr.	30	10	11	21	26	....	....	....	....	....	....	....	....	....	....	....	....	....	....	....	....	....	....
	MoDo	Sweden	36	1	3	4	8	....	....	....	....	....	....	....	....	....	4	0	0	0	0	....	....	....	....
1996-97	MoDo	Sweden	49	8	9	17	83	....	....	....	....	....	....	....	....	....	....	....	....	....	....	....	....	....	....
	MoDo Jr.	Swe-Jr.	5	2	6	8	2	....	....	....	....	....	....	....	....	....	....	....	....	....	....	....	....	....	....
1997-98	MoDo	Sweden	23	6	11	17	24	....	....	....	....	....	....	....	....	....	9	3	0	3	6	....	....	....	....
1998-99	MoDo	Sweden	50	17	17	34	44	....	....	....	....	....	....	....	....	....	13	3	3	6	10	....	....	....	....
99-2000	MoDo	Sweden	47	16	11	27	67	....	....	....	....	....	....	....	....	....	13	3	3	6	8	....	....	....	....
	MoDo	EuroHL	4	1	0	1	0	....	....	....	....	....	....	....	....	....	3	1	1	2	2	....	....	....	....
2000-01	**Boston**	**NHL**	**17**	**1**	**1**	**2**	**6**	**0**	**0**	**0**	**13**	**7.7**	**–5**	**239**	**40.2**	**14:19**	....	....	....	....	....	....	....	....	....
	Anaheim	**NHL**	**59**	**3**	**4**	**7**	**14**	**1**	**1**	**1**	**46**	**6.5**	**–9**	**867**	**45.1**	**14:14**	....	....	....	....	....	....	....	....	....
2001-02	**Anaheim**	**NHL**	**80**	**6**	**14**	**20**	**26**	**1**	**1**	**0**	**99**	**6.1**	**–16**	**1201**	**49.8**	**16:24**	....	....	....	....	....	....	....	....	....
2002-03	**Anaheim**	**NHL**	**34**	**4**	**11**	**15**	**18**	**0**	**1**	**2**	**28**	**14.3**	**10**	**118**	**52.5**	**13:20**	**21**	**2**	**4**	**6**	**12**	**0**	**0**	**0**	**16:41**
	Cincinnati	AHL	13	1	7	8	24	....	....	....	....	....	....	....	....	....	....	....	....	....	....	....	....	....	....
2003-04	**Anaheim**	**NHL**	**82**	**8**	**14**	**22**	**52**	**1**	**0**	**2**	**134**	**6.0**	**–2**	**908**	**55.3**	**16:51**	....	....	....	....	....	....	....	....	....
2004-05	Frolunda	Sweden	48	6	18	24	56	....	....	....	....	....	....	....	....	....	14	4	7	11	24	....	....	....	....
2005-06	**Anaheim**	**NHL**	**82**	**11**	**10**	**21**	**34**	**0**	**3**	**1**	**116**	**9.5**	**–1**	**1517**	**52.8**	**16:30**	**16**	**2**	**3**	**5**	**18**	**0**	**0**	**2**	**17:06**
	Sweden	Olympics	8	2	2	4	8	....	....	....	....	....	....	....	....	....	....	....	....	....	....	....	....	....	....
2006-07 ♦	**Anaheim**	**NHL**	**82**	**8**	**18**	**26**	**42**	**0**	**0**	**1**	**111**	**7.2**	**–4**	**1523**	**52.7**	**17:22**	**21**	**3**	**9**	**12**	**20**	**0**	**0**	**2**	**19:25**
2007-08	**Anaheim**	**NHL**	**56**	**6**	**9**	**15**	**34**	**0**	**3**	**3**	**94**	**6.4**	**–2**	**1066**	**55.0**	**18:46**	**6**	**0**	**0**	**0**	**0**	**0**	**0**	**0**	**18:18**
2008-09	**Anaheim**	**NHL**	**52**	**5**	**10**	**15**	**32**	**1**	**0**	**1**	**74**	**6.8**	**–16**	**1064**	**53.5**	**18:31**	....	....	....	....	....	....	....	....	....
	Chicago	**NHL**	**13**	**2**	**1**	**3**	**2**	**0**	**0**	**1**	**14**	**14.3**	**–1**	**173**	**53.8**	**17:25**	**17**	**2**	**3**	**5**	**4**	**1**	**0**	**0**	**16:38**
2009-10	**Columbus**	**NHL**	**79**	**3**	**13**	**16**	**32**	**0**	**0**	**0**	**93**	**3.2**	**–9**	**1273**	**52.9**	**16:17**	....	....	....	....	....	....	....	....	....
	Sweden	Olympics	3	0	1	1	2	....	....	....	....	....	....	....	....	....	....	....	....	....	....	....	....	....	....

Season	Club	League	GP	G	A	Pts	PIM	PP	SH	GW	S	%	+/-	TF	F%	Min	Playoffs GP	G	A	Pts	PIM	PP	SH	GW	Min
			Regular Season																						
2010-11	**Columbus**	**NHL**	**82**	**7**	**13**	**20**	**30**	**0**	**1**	**1**	**108**	**6.5**	**-13**	**1298**	**52.0**	**15:20**									
2011-12	**Columbus**	**NHL**	**61**	**2**	**9**	**11**	**22**	**0**	**1**	**0**	**63**	**3.2**	**-6**	**839**	**51.1**	**15:02**									
	Vancouver	**NHL**	**19**	**2**	**4**	**6**	**12**	**0**	**0**	**1**	**30**	**6.7**	**4**	**187**	**59.4**	**13:56**	**5**	**1**	**0**	**1**	**4**	**0**	**0**	**0**	**14:00**
2012-13	MODO	Sweden	23	0	4	4	8										5	0	0	0	12				
	NHL Totals		**798**	**68**	**131**	**199**	**356**	**4**	**11**	**14**	**1023**	**6.6**		**12273**	**52.0**	**16:15**	**86**	**10**	**19**	**29**	**58**	**1**	**0**	**4**	**17:23**

Traded to **Boston** by **Colorado** with Brian Rolston, Martin Grenier and New Jersey's 1st round choice (previously acquired, Boston selected Martin Samuelsson) in 2000 Entry Draft for Raymond Bourque and Dave Andreychuk, March 6, 2000. Traded to **Anaheim** by **Boston** for Patrick Traverse and Andrei Nazarov, November 18, 2000. Signed as a free agent by **Frolunda** (Sweden), September 15, 2004. Traded to **Chicago** by **Anaheim** with Logan Stephenson and future considerations for James Wisniewski and Petri Kontiola, March 4, 2009. Signed as a free agent by **Columbus**, July 1, 2009. Traded to **Vancouver** by **Columbus** for Taylor Ellington, NY Islanders' 4th round choice (previously acquired, Columbus selected Josh Anderson) in 2012 Entry Draft and Vancouver's 4th round choice (later traded to Philadelphia – Philadelphia selected Taylor Leier) in 2012 Entry Draft, February 27, 2012. Signed as a free agent by **MODO** (Sweden), June 18, 2012.

PAILLE, Daniel
(PIGH-yay, DAN-yehl) **BOS**

Left wing. Shoots left. 6', 200 lbs. Born, Welland, Ont., April 15, 1984. Buffalo's 2nd choice, 20th overall, in 2002 Entry Draft.

Season	Club	League	GP	G	A	Pts	PIM	PP	SH	GW	S	%	+/-	TF	F%	Min	Playoffs GP	G	A	Pts	PIM	PP	SH	GW	Min
99-2000	Welland Cougars	ON-Jr.B	42	14	17	31	19										16	16	16	32					
2000-01	Guelph Storm	OHL	64	22	31	53	57										4	2	0	2	2				
2001-02	Guelph Storm	OHL	62	27	30	57	54										9	5	2	7	9				
2002-03	Guelph Storm	OHL	54	30	27	57	28										11	8	6	14	6				
2003-04	Guelph Storm	OHL	59	37	43	80	63										22	9	9	18	14				
2004-05	Rochester	AHL	79	14	15	29	54										9	2	2	4	6				
2005-06	**Buffalo**	**NHL**	**14**	**1**	**2**	**3**	**2**	**0**	**0**	**0**	**15**	**6.7**	**5**	**4**	**25.0**	**10:24**									
	Rochester	AHL	45	14	13	27	29																		
2006-07	**Buffalo**	**NHL**	**29**	**3**	**8**	**11**	**18**	**0**	**0**	**0**	**45**	**6.7**	**5**	**6**	**33.3**	**12:47**	**1**	**0**	**0**	**0**	**0**	**0**	**0**	**0**	**4:52**
	Rochester	AHL	29	7	14	21	12																		
2007-08	**Buffalo**	**NHL**	**77**	**19**	**16**	**35**	**14**	**0**	**3**	**2**	**110**	**17.3**	**9**	**41**	**36.6**	**13:16**									
2008-09	**Buffalo**	**NHL**	**73**	**12**	**15**	**27**	**20**	**0**	**0**	**2**	**80**	**15.0**	**0**	**17**	**17.7**	**11:54**									
2009-10	**Buffalo**	**NHL**	**2**	**0**	**1**	**1**	**0**	**0**	**0**	**0**	**2**	**0.0**	**1**	**0**	**0.0**	**10:22**									
	Boston	**NHL**	**74**	**10**	**9**	**19**	**12**	**0**	**1**	**0**	**118**	**8.5**	**-4**	**13**	**30.8**	**13:49**	**13**	**0**	**2**	**2**	**2**	**0**	**0**	**0**	**16:01**
2010-11 ♦	**Boston**	**NHL**	**43**	**6**	**7**	**13**	**28**	**0**	**1**	**0**	**48**	**12.5**	**3**	**0**	**0.0**	**11:18**	**25**	**3**	**3**	**6**	**4**	**0**	**1**	**0**	**8:43**
2011-12	**Boston**	**NHL**	**69**	**9**	**6**	**15**	**15**	**0**	**2**	**1**	**86**	**10.5**	**-5**	**7**	**28.6**	**11:30**	**7**	**1**	**0**	**1**	**2**	**0**	**0**	**0**	**9:39**
2012-13	Ilves Tampere	Finland	9	2	4	6	6																		
	Boston	**NHL**	**46**	**10**	**7**	**17**	**8**	**0**	**2**	**1**	**70**	**14.3**	**3**	**10**	**20.0**	**12:41**	**22**	**4**	**5**	**9**	**0**	**0**	**1**	**3**	**12:32**
	NHL Totals		**427**	**70**	**71**	**141**	**117**	**0**	**9**	**6**	**574**	**12.2**		**98**	**29.6**	**12:26**	**68**	**8**	**10**	**18**	**8**	**0**	**2**	**3**	**11:23**

Traded to **Boston** by **Buffalo** for Boston's 3rd round choice (Kevin Sundher) in 2010 Entry Draft, October 20, 2009. Signed as a free agent by **Ilves Tampere** (Finland), December 2, 2012.

PALAT, Ondrej
(PAL-at, AWN-dray) **T.B.**

Left wing. Shoots left. 6', 180 lbs. Born, Frydek-Mistek, Czech., March 28, 1991. Tampa Bay's 6th choice, 208th overall, in 2011 Entry Draft.

Season	Club	League	GP	G	A	Pts	PIM	PP	SH	GW	S	%	+/-	TF	F%	Min	Playoffs GP	G	A	Pts	PIM	PP	SH	GW	Min
2005-06	HC Vitkovice U17	CzR-U17	22	2	7	9	4										1	0	0	0	0				
2006-07	HC Vitkovice U17	CzR-U17	33	32	24	56	18										9	3	6	9	4				
	HC Vitkovice Jr.	CzRep-Jr.	13	5	2	7	12										3	0	0	0	0				
2007-08	HC Vitkovice U17	CzR-U17	4	2	3	5	0										2	1	1	2	2				
	HC Vitkovice Jr.	CzRep-Jr.	42	19	18	37	28										2	1	0	1	2				
2008-09	HC Vitkovice Jr.	CzRep-Jr.	42	23	33	56	14										10	8	6	14	12				
2009-10	Drummondville	QMJHL	59	17	23	40	24										7	1	1	2	0				
2010-11	Drummondville	QMJHL	61	39	57	96	24										10	4	7	11	6				
2011-12	Norfolk Admirals	AHL	61	9	21	30	10										18	4	5	9	6				
2012-13	Syracuse Crunch	AHL	56	13	39	52	35										18	7	*19	*26	12				
	Tampa Bay	**NHL**	**14**	**2**	**2**	**4**	**0**	**0**	**0**	**1**	**16**	**12.5**	**5**	**6**	**0.0**	**11:44**									
	NHL Totals		**14**	**2**	**2**	**4**	**0**	**0**	**0**	**1**	**16**	**12.5**		**6**	**0.0**	**11:44**									

PALMER, Jarod
(PAHL-muhr, JAIR-uhd)

Right wing. Shoots right. 6'1", 200 lbs. Born, Fridley, MN, February 10, 1986.

Season	Club	League	GP	G	A	Pts	PIM	PP	SH	GW	S	%	+/-	TF	F%	Min	Playoffs GP	G	A	Pts	PIM	PP	SH	GW	Min
2002-03	USNTDP	NAHL	33	3	7	10	39																		
2003-04	USNTDP	NAHL	10	3	1	4	22																		
2004-05	Tri-City Storm	USHL	52	15	26	41	67										9	1	0	1	14				
2005-06	Tri-City Storm	USHL	58	15	37	52	91										5	1	1	2	9				
2006-07	Miami U.	CCHA	42	11	19	30	26																		
2007-08	Miami U.	CCHA	42	10	25	35	32																		
2008-09	Miami U.	CCHA	41	8	19	27	34																		
2009-10	Miami U.	CCHA	44	18	27	45	40																		
2010-11	Houston Aeros	AHL	65	9	19	28	64										24	3	2	5	7				
2011-12	**Minnesota**	**NHL**	**6**	**1**	**0**	**1**	**4**	**0**	**0**	**0**	**14**	**7.1**	**-2**	**2**	**50.0**	**13:20**									
	Houston Aeros	AHL	35	5	6	11	27																		
2012-13	Houston Aeros	AHL	17	2	6	8	26																		
	NHL Totals		**6**	**1**	**0**	**1**	**4**	**0**	**0**	**0**	**14**	**7.1**		**2**	**50.0**	**13:20**									

CCHA First All-Star Team (2010)

Signed as a free agent by **Minnesota**, April 26, 2010. • Missed majority of 2012-13 due to upper-body injury vs. Texas (AHL), December 26, 2012.

PALMIERI, Kyle
(pawl-mee-AIR-ee, KIGHL) **ANA**

Right wing. Shoots right. 5'11", 196 lbs. Born, Smithtown, NY, February 1, 1991. Anaheim's 2nd choice, 26th overall, in 2009 Entry Draft.

Season	Club	League	GP	G	A	Pts	PIM	PP	SH	GW	S	%	+/-	TF	F%	Min	Playoffs GP	G	A	Pts	PIM	PP	SH	GW	Min
2007-08	USNTDP	NAHL	32	15	10	25	43																		
	USNTDP	U-17	7	5	0	5	8																		
	USNTDP	U-18	27	9	9	18	20																		
2008-09	USNTDP	NAHL	5	1	1	2	2																		
	USNTDP	U-18	28	14	14	28	49																		
2009-10	U. of Notre Dame	CCHA	33	9	8	17	36																		
2010-11	**Anaheim**	**NHL**	**10**	**1**	**0**	**1**	**0**	**0**	**0**	**0**	**10**	**10.0**	**-1**	**0**	**0.0**	**8:41**	**1**	**0**	**0**	**0**	**0**	**0**	**0**	**0**	**10:07**
	Syracuse Crunch	AHL	62	29	22	51	56																		
2011-12	**Anaheim**	**NHL**	**18**	**4**	**3**	**7**	**6**	**0**	**0**	**0**	**34**	**11.8**	**3**	**2**	**100.0**	**11:31**									
	Syracuse Crunch	AHL	51	33	25	58	53										4	1	1	2	0				
2012-13	Norfolk Admirals	AHL	33	13	12	25	54																		
	Anaheim	**NHL**	**42**	**10**	**11**	**21**	**9**	**2**	**0**	**5**	**92**	**10.9**	**2**	**12**	**8.3**	**12:20**	**7**	**3**	**2**	**5**	**4**	**0**	**0**	**0**	**10:34**
	NHL Totals		**70**	**15**	**14**	**29**	**15**	**2**	**0**	**5**	**136**	**11.0**		**14**	**21.4**	**11:36**	**8**	**3**	**2**	**5**	**4**	**0**	**0**	**0**	**10:31**

AHL First All-Star Team (2012)

PALMIERI, Nick
(pawl-mee-AIR-ee, NIHK)

Right wing. Shoots right. 6'3", 220 lbs. Born, Utica, NY, July 12, 1989. New Jersey's 2nd choice, 79th overall, in 2007 Entry Draft.

Season	Club	League	GP	G	A	Pts	PIM	PP	SH	GW	S	%	+/-	TF	F%	Min	Playoffs GP	G	A	Pts	PIM	PP	SH	GW	Min
2004-05	Northwood	High-NY	STATISTICS NOT AVAILABLE																						
2005-06	Erie Otters	OHL	68	13	10	23	79																		
2006-07	Erie Otters	OHL	56	24	21	45	99																		
2007-08	Erie Otters	OHL	50	28	18	46	122																		
	Lowell Devils	AHL	9	1	0	1	4																		
2008-09	Erie Otters	OHL	18	7	5	12	41																		
	Belleville Bulls	OHL	43	20	9	29	75										17	14	3	17	27				
2009-10	**New Jersey**	**NHL**	**6**	**0**	**1**	**1**	**0**	**0**	**0**	**0**	**10**	**0.0**	**0**	**2**	**50.0**	**11:45**									
	Lowell Devils	AHL	69	21	15	36	36										5	1	3	4	2				
2010-11	**New Jersey**	**NHL**	**43**	**9**	**8**	**17**	**6**	**1**	**0**	**2**	**66**	**13.6**	**9**	**2**	**100.0**	**14:20**									
	Albany Devils	AHL	26	6	5	11	28																		
2011-12	**New Jersey**	**NHL**	**29**	**4**	**3**	**7**	**12**	**0**	**0**	**0**	**42**	**9.5**	**-7**	**10**	**20.0**	**10:38**									
	Albany Devils	AHL	25	5	6	11	24																		
	Minnesota	**NHL**	**9**	**0**	**0**	**0**	**2**	**0**	**0**	**0**	**13**	**0.0**	**-3**	**1**	**0.0**	**10:24**									
	Houston Aeros	AHL	13	3	3	6	8										4	0	1	1	18				

			Regular Season														Playoffs								
Season	Club	League	GP	G	A	Pts	PIM	PP	SH	GW	S	%	+/-	TF	F%	Min	GP	G	A	Pts	PIM	PP	SH	GW	Min
2012-13	Houston Aeros	AHL	40	10	11	21	35																		
	Connecticut	AHL	30	3	6	9	19																		
	NHL Totals		**87**	**13**	**12**	**25**	**20**	**1**	**0**	**2**	**131**	**9.9**		**15**	**33.3**	**12:31**									

Traded to **Minnesota** by **New Jersey** with Kurtis Foster, Stephane Veilleux, Washington's 2nd round choice (previously acquired, Minnesota selected Raphael Bussieres) in 2012 Entry Draft and New Jersey's 3rd round choice (later traded to NY Islanders – NY Islanders selected Eamon McAdam) in 2013 Entry Draft for Marek Zidlicky, February 24, 2012. Traded to **NY Rangers** by **Minnesota** with Darroll Powe for Mke Rupp, February 4, 2013.

PALUSHAJ, Aaron

(puh-LOO-shigh, AIR-ruhn) **CAR**

Right wing. Shoots right. 6', 188 lbs. Born, Livonia, MI, September 7, 1989. St. Louis' 5th choice, 44th overall, in 2007 Entry Draft.

Season	Club	League	GP	G	A	Pts	PIM	PP	SH	GW	S	%	+/-	TF	F%	Min	GP	G	A	Pts	PIM	PP	SH	GW	Min
2005-06	Des Moines	USHL	58	10	23	33	53										11	2	4	6	15				
2006-07	Des Moines	USHL	56	22	45	67	62										8	6	5	11	6				
2007-08	U. of Michigan	CCHA	43	10	*34	44	22																		
2008-09	U. of Michigan	CCHA	39	13	*37	*50	26																		
	Peoria Rivermen	AHL	4	2	0	2	4										4	0	1	1	2				
2009-10	Peoria Rivermen	AHL	44	5	17	22	22																		
	Hamilton	AHL	18	3	7	10	8										19	2	10	12	28				
2010-11	**Montreal**	**NHL**	**3**	**0**	**0**	**0**	**2**	**0**	**0**	**0**	**3**	**0.0**	**1**	**1**	**0.0**	**8:31**									
	Hamilton	AHL	68	22	35	57	42										19	7	12	19	14				
2011-12	**Montreal**	**NHL**	**38**	**1**	**4**	**5**	**8**	**0**	**0**	**0**	**37**	**2.7**	**1**	**4**	**0.0**	**7:34**									
	Hamilton	AHL	35	15	20	35	35																		
2012-13	Hamilton	AHL	21	7	3	10	18																		
	Colorado	**NHL**	**25**	**2**	**7**	**9**	**8**	**0**	**0**	**0**	**29**	**6.9**	**–2**	**8**	**25.0**	**11:19**									
	NHL Totals		**66**	**3**	**11**	**14**	**18**	**0**	**0**	**0**	**69**	**4.3**		**13**	**15.4**	**9:02**									

CCHA First All-Star Team (2009) • NCAA West First All-American Team (2009)

Traded to **Montreal** by **St. Louis** for Matt D'Agostini, March 2, 2010. Claimed on waivers by **Colorado** from **Montreal**, February 5, 2013. Signed as a free agent by **Carolina**, July 11, 2013.

PANDOLFO, Jay

(pan-DAWL-foh, JAY)

Left wing. Shoots left. 6'1", 190 lbs. Born, Winchester, MA, December 27, 1974. New Jersey's 2nd choice, 32nd overall, in 1993 Entry Draft.

Season	Club	League	GP	G	A	Pts	PIM	PP	SH	GW	S	%	+/-	TF	F%	Min	GP	G	A	Pts	PIM	PP	SH	GW	Min
1989-90	Burlington	High-MA	23	33	30	63	18																		
1990-91	Burlington	High-MA	20	19	27	46	10																		
1991-92	Burlington	High-MA	20	35	34	69	14																		
1992-93	Boston University	H-East	37	16	22	38	16																		
1993-94	Boston University	H-East	37	17	25	42	27																		
1994-95	Boston University	H-East	20	7	13	20	6																		
1995-96	Boston University	H-East	39	*38	29	67	6																		
	Albany River Rats	AHL	5	3	1	4	0										3	0	0	0	0				
1996-97	**New Jersey**	**NHL**	**46**	**6**	**8**	**14**	**6**	**0**	**0**	**1**	**61**	**9.8**	**–1**				**6**	**0**	**1**	**1**	**0**	**0**	**0**	**0**	
	Albany River Rats	AHL	12	3	9	12	0																		
1997-98	**New Jersey**	**NHL**	**23**	**1**	**3**	**4**	**4**	**0**	**0**	**0**	**23**	**4.3**	**–4**				**3**	**0**	**2**	**2**	**0**	**0**	**0**	**0**	
	Albany River Rats	AHL	51	18	19	37	24																		
1998-99	**New Jersey**	**NHL**	**70**	**14**	**13**	**27**	**10**	**1**	**1**	**4**	**100**	**14.0**	**3**	**10**	**40.0**	**15:13**	**7**	**1**	**0**	**1**	**0**	**0**	**0**	**0**	**13:19**
99-2000♦	**New Jersey**	**NHL**	**71**	**7**	**8**	**15**	**4**	**0**	**0**	**0**	**86**	**8.1**	**0**	**19**	**47.4**	**13:25**	**23**	**0**	**5**	**5**	**0**	**0**	**0**	**0**	**15:35**
2000-01	**New Jersey**	**NHL**	**63**	**4**	**12**	**16**	**16**	**0**	**0**	**0**	**57**	**7.0**	**3**	**15**	**53.3**	**14:05**	**25**	**1**	**4**	**5**	**4**	**0**	**0**	**0**	**12:38**
2001-02	**New Jersey**	**NHL**	**65**	**4**	**10**	**14**	**15**	**0**	**1**	**0**	**72**	**5.6**	**12**	**12**	**41.7**	**13:59**	**6**	**0**	**0**	**0**	**0**	**0**	**0**	**0**	**16:11**
2002-03♦	**New Jersey**	**NHL**	**68**	**6**	**11**	**17**	**23**	**0**	**1**	**4**	**92**	**6.5**	**12**	**13**	**23.1**	**16:08**	**24**	**6**	**6**	**12**	**2**	**0**	**0**	**1**	**16:34**
2003-04	**New Jersey**	**NHL**	**82**	**13**	**13**	**26**	**14**	**1**	**2**	**4**	**140**	**9.3**	**5**	**25**	**44.0**	**16:00**	**5**	**0**	**0**	**0**	**0**	**0**	**0**	**0**	**13:41**
2004-05	Salzburg	Austria	19	5	7	12	0																		
2005-06	**New Jersey**	**NHL**	**82**	**10**	**10**	**20**	**16**	**0**	**0**	**0**	**116**	**8.6**	**2**	**13**	**30.8**	**18:03**	**9**	**1**	**4**	**5**	**0**	**0**	**1**	**1**	**18:37**
2006-07	**New Jersey**	**NHL**	**82**	**13**	**14**	**27**	**8**	**0**	**1**	**1**	**109**	**11.9**	**–5**	**16**	**6.3**	**18:37**	**11**	**1**	**0**	**1**	**4**	**0**	**0**	**0**	**19:39**
2007-08	**New Jersey**	**NHL**	**54**	**12**	**12**	**24**	**22**	**0**	**0**	**1**	**78**	**15.4**	**10**	**7**	**42.9**	**17:17**	**5**	**0**	**0**	**0**	**2**	**0**	**0**	**0**	**16:15**
2008-09	**New Jersey**	**NHL**	**61**	**5**	**5**	**10**	**10**	**0**	**1**	**1**	**63**	**7.9**	**–12**	**18**	**22.2**	**14:50**	**7**	**1**	**0**	**1**	**0**	**0**	**0**	**0**	**16:35**
2009-10	**New Jersey**	**NHL**	**52**	**4**	**5**	**9**	**6**	**0**	**0**	**3**	**71**	**5.6**	**–10**	**12**	**41.7**	**13:55**									
2010-11	Springfield	AHL	12	2	4	6	4																		
2011-12	**NY Islanders**	**NHL**	**62**	**1**	**2**	**3**	**8**	**0**	**0**	**0**	**44**	**2.3**	**–14**	**136**	**44.9**	**10:55**									
2012-13	**Boston**	**NHL**	**18**	**0**	**0**	**0**	**2**	**0**	**0**	**0**	**11**	**0.0**	**–2**	**5**	**40.0**	**9:04**									
	NHL Totals		**899**	**100**	**126**	**226**	**164**	**2**	**7**	**19**	**1123**	**8.9**		**301**	**39.9**	**15:13**	**131**	**11**	**22**	**33**	**12**	**0**	**1**	**2**	**15:40**

Hockey East First All-Star Team (1996) • Hockey East Player of the Year (1996) • NCAA East First All-American Team (1996)

Signed as a free agent by **Salzburg** (Austria), December 27, 2004. • Signed to a PTO (professional tryout) contract by **Springfield** (AHL), November 22, 2010. Signed as a free agent by **NY Islanders**, October 4, 2011. Signed as a free agent by **Boston**, February 12, 2013. • Missed majority of 2012-13 as a healthy reserve.

PANIK, Richard

(PAH-nihk, RIH-chuhrd) **T.B.**

Right wing. Shoots left. 6'1", 208 lbs. Born, Martin, Czech., February 7, 1991. Tampa Bay's 3rd choice, 52nd overall, in 2009 Entry Draft.

Season	Club	League	GP	G	A	Pts	PIM	PP	SH	GW	S	%	+/-	TF	F%	Min	GP	G	A	Pts	PIM	PP	SH	GW	Min
2005-06	MHC Martin U18	Svk-U18	40	11	13	24	20										4	4	2	6	4				
2006-07	HC Trinec U17	CzR-U17	12	10	6	16	48										3	1	4	5	8				
	HC Trinec Jr.	CzRep-Jr.	27	16	9	25	30										4	1	4	5	6				
2007-08	HC Trinec Jr.	CzRep-Jr.	39	35	27	62	70										8	8	4	12	52				
	HC Ocelari Trinec	CzRep	6	0	0	0	0																		
2008-09	HC Trinec Jr.	CzRep-Jr.	16	10	9	19	36										8	6	1	7	41				
	HC Havirov	CzRep-2	3	2	1	3	0																		
	HC Ocelari Trinec	CzRep	15	1	1	2	4										4	0	0	0	0				
2009-10	Windsor Spitfires	OHL	33	9	9	18	19																		
	Belleville Bulls	OHL	27	12	11	23	36																		
	Norfolk Admirals	AHL	5	0	1	1	0																		
2010-11	Belleville Bulls	OHL	27	14	17	31	33																		
	Guelph Storm	OHL	24	13	12	25	42										6	1	2	3	10				
2011-12	Norfolk Admirals	AHL	64	19	22	41	62										18	5	1	6	23				
2012-13	Syracuse Crunch	AHL	51	22	19	41	81										16	9	5	14	59				
	Tampa Bay	**NHL**	**25**	**5**	**4**	**9**	**4**	**1**	**0**	**1**	**34**	**14.7**	**–2**	**3**	**33.3**	**11:20**									
	NHL Totals		**25**	**5**	**4**	**9**	**4**	**1**	**0**	**1**	**34**	**14.7**		**3**	**33.3**	**11:20**									

PARDY, Adam

(PAHR-dee, A-duhm) **WPG**

Defense. Shoots left. 6'4", 220 lbs. Born, Bonavista, Nfld., March 29, 1984. Calgary's 6th choice, 173rd overall, in 2004 Entry Draft.

Season	Club	League	GP	G	A	Pts	PIM	PP	SH	GW	S	%	+/-	TF	F%	Min	GP	G	A	Pts	PIM	PP	SH	GW	Min
2002-03	Yarmouth	MJrHL	1	0	0	0	2																		
	Antigonish	MJrHL	31	5	16	21	42																		
	Cape Breton	QMJHL	7	0	1	1	2										2	0	0	0	0				
2003-04	Cape Breton	QMJHL	68	4	12	16	137										5	0	1	1	8				
2004-05	Cape Breton	QMJHL	69	12	27	39	163										5	2	2	4	8				
2005-06	Omaha	AHL	24	0	0	0	18																		
	Las Vegas	ECHL	41	1	11	12	55										10	2	1	3	12				
2006-07	Omaha	AHL	70	2	6	8	60										6	1	1	2	0				
2007-08	Quad City Flames	AHL	65	5	13	18	67																		
2008-09	**Calgary**	**NHL**	**60**	**1**	**9**	**10**	**69**	**0**	**0**	**0**	**38**	**2.6**	**3**	**0**	**0.0**	**15:00**	**6**	**0**	**2**	**2**	**5**	**0**	**0**	**0**	**14:51**
2009-10	**Calgary**	**NHL**	**57**	**2**	**7**	**9**	**48**	**0**	**0**	**0**	**40**	**5.0**	**–3**	**0**	**0.0**	**15:51**									
2010-11	**Calgary**	**NHL**	**30**	**1**	**6**	**7**	**24**	**0**	**0**	**0**	**36**	**2.8**	**3**	**0**	**0.0**	**14:41**									
2011-12	**Dallas**	**NHL**	**36**	**0**	**3**	**3**	**16**	**0**	**0**	**0**	**29**	**0.0**	**–5**	**0**	**0.0**	**16:28**									
	Texas Stars	AHL	2	0	4	4	2																		
2012-13	Rochester	AHL	21	2	7	9	22																		
	Buffalo	**NHL**	**17**	**0**	**4**	**4**	**14**	**0**	**0**	**0**	**6**	**0.0**	**4**	**0**	**0.0**	**16:30**									
	NHL Totals		**200**	**4**	**29**	**33**	**171**	**0**	**0**	**0**	**149**	**2.7**		**0**	**0.0**	**15:35**	**6**	**0**	**2**	**2**	**5**	**0**	**0**	**0**	**14:51**

• Missed majority of 2010-11 due to shoulder (October 10, 2010 vs. Los Angeles) and upper-body (February 7, 2011 vs. Chicago) injuries. Signed as a free agent by **Dallas**, July 1, 2011. Traded to **Buffalo** by **Dallas** with Steve Ott for Derek Roy, July 2, 2012. Signed as a free agent by **Winnipeg**, July 6, 2013.

PARENT, Ryan

(PAIR-ehnt, RIGH-uhn)

Defense. Shoots left. 6'3", 198 lbs. Born, Prince Albert, Sask., March 17, 1987. Nashville's 1st choice, 18th overall, in 2005 Entry Draft.

			Regular Season														Playoffs								
Season	Club	League	GP	G	A	Pts	PIM	PP	SH	GW	S	%	+/-	TF	F%	Min	GP	G	A	Pts	PIM	PP	SH	GW	Min
2002-03	Waterloo Siskins	ON-Jr.B	41	2	8	10	35	....	....	....	....	....	....	....	....	....	....	....	....	....	....	....	....	....	....
2003-04	Guelph Storm	OHL	58	1	5	6	18	....	....	....	....	....	....	....	....	....	22	0	0	0	2	....	....	....	....
2004-05	Guelph Storm	OHL	66	2	17	19	36	....	....	....	....	....	....	....	....	....	4	0	1	1	4	....	....	....	....
2005-06	Guelph Storm	OHL	60	4	17	21	122	....	....	....	....	....	....	....	....	....	15	1	4	5	24	....	....	....	....
	Milwaukee	AHL	....	....	....	....	....	....	....	....	....	....	....	....	....	....	10	0	0	0	4	....	....	....	....
2006-07	**Philadelphia**	**NHL**	**1**	**0**	**0**	**0**	**0**	**0**	**0**	**0**	**1**	**0.0**	**0**	**0**	**0.0**	**14:10**	....	....	....	....	....	....	....	....	....
	Philadelphia	AHL	6	1	0	1	4	....	....	....	....	....	....	....	....	....	....	....	....	....	....	....	....	....	....
	Guelph Storm	OHL	43	3	7	10	86	....	....	....	....	....	....	....	....	....	4	0	1	1	14	....	....	....	....
2007-08	**Philadelphia**	**NHL**	**22**	**0**	**0**	**0**	**6**	**0**	**0**	**0**	**9**	**0.0**	**–4**	**0**	**0.0**	**14:59**	**4**	**0**	**1**	**1**	**0**	**0**	**0**	**0**	**16:36**
	Philadelphia	AHL	53	1	7	8	42	....	....	....	....	....	....	....	....	....	....	....	....	....	....	....	....	....	....
2008-09	**Philadelphia**	**NHL**	**31**	**0**	**4**	**4**	**10**	**0**	**0**	**0**	**9**	**0.0**	**3**	**0**	**0.0**	**18:12**	**6**	**0**	**0**	**0**	**6**	**0**	**0**	**0**	**18:52**
	Philadelphia	AHL	15	0	1	1	18	....	....	....	....	....	....	....	....	....	....	....	....	....	....	....	....	....	....
2009-10	**Philadelphia**	**NHL**	**48**	**1**	**2**	**3**	**20**	**0**	**0**	**0**	**27**	**3.7**	**–14**	**0**	**0.0**	**14:46**	**17**	**1**	**0**	**1**	**2**	**0**	**0**	**0**	**7:28**
2010-11	**Vancouver**	**NHL**	**4**	**0**	**0**	**0**	**0**	**0**	**0**	**0**	**3**	**0.0**	**–3**	**0**	**0.0**	**13:54**	....	....	....	....	....	....	....	....	....
	Manitoba Moose	AHL	39	1	1	2	56	....	....	....	....	....	....	....	....	....	....	....	....	....	....	....	....	....	....
2011-12	Chicago Wolves	AHL	22	1	5	6	31	....	....	....	....	....	....	....	....	....	5	0	1	1	10	....	....	....	....
2012-13	Norfolk Admirals	AHL	56	0	5	5	52	....	....	....	....	....	....	....	....	....	....	....	....	....	....	....	....	....	....
	NHL Totals		**106**	**1**	**6**	**7**	**36**	**0**	**0**	**0**	**49**	**2.0**		**0**	**0.0**	**15:47**	**27**	**1**	**1**	**2**	**8**	**0**	**0**	**0**	**11:21**

OHL Second All-Star Team (2006, 2007)

Traded to **Philadelphia** by **Nashville** with Scottie Upshall and Nashville's 1st (later traded back to Nashville - Nashville selected Jonathon Blum) and 3rd (later traded to Washington - Washington selected Phil Desimone) round choices in 2007 Entry Draft for Peter Forsberg, February 15, 2007. Traded to **Nashville** by **Philadelphia** with future considerations for Dan Hamhuis, June 19, 2010. Traded to **Vancouver** by **Nashville** with Jonas Andersson for Shane O'Brien and Dan Gendur, October 5, 2010. • Missed majority of 2011-12 due to various injuries.

PARENTEAU, P.A.

(pair-ehn-TOH, PEE-AY) **COL**

Left wing. Shoots right. 6', 193 lbs. Born, Hull, Que., March 24, 1983. Anaheim's 11th choice, 264th overall, in 2001 Entry Draft.

			Regular Season														Playoffs								
Season	Club	League	GP	G	A	Pts	PIM	PP	SH	GW	S	%	+/-	TF	F%	Min	GP	G	A	Pts	PIM	PP	SH	GW	Min
99-2000	C.C. Lemoyne	QAAA	40	25	40	65	18	....	....	....	....	....	....	....	....	....	16	4	9	13	8	....	....	....	....
2000-01	Moncton Wildcats	QMJHL	45	10	19	29	38	....	....	....	....	....	....	....	....	....	....	....	....	....	....	....	....	....	....
	Chicoutimi	QMJHL	28	10	13	23	14	....	....	....	....	....	....	....	....	....	7	4	7	11	2	....	....	....	....
2001-02	Chicoutimi	QMJHL	68	51	67	118	120	....	....	....	....	....	....	....	....	....	4	3	1	4	10	....	....	....	....
2002-03	Chicoutimi	QMJHL	31	20	35	55	56	....	....	....	....	....	....	....	....	....	....	....	....	....	....	....	....	....	....
	Sherbrooke	QMJHL	28	13	35	48	84	....	....	....	....	....	....	....	....	....	12	8	11	19	6	....	....	....	....
2003-04	Cincinnati	AHL	66	14	16	30	20	....	....	....	....	....	....	....	....	....	7	1	2	3	6	....	....	....	....
2004-05	Cincinnati	AHL	76	17	24	41	58	....	....	....	....	....	....	....	....	....	9	2	0	2	8	....	....	....	....
2005-06	Portland Pirates	AHL	56	22	27	49	42	....	....	....	....	....	....	....	....	....	19	5	17	22	24	....	....	....	....
	Augusta Lynx	ECHL	2	0	1	1	0	....	....	....	....	....	....	....	....	....	....	....	....	....	....	....	....	....	....
2006-07	Portland Pirates	AHL	28	15	13	28	35	....	....	....	....	....	....	....	....	....	....	....	....	....	....	....	....	....	....
	Chicago	**NHL**	**5**	**0**	**1**	**1**	**2**	**0**	**0**	**0**	**7**	**0.0**	**–1**	**2**	**50.0**	**11:05**	....	....	....	....	....	....	....	....	....
	Norfolk Admirals	AHL	40	15	36	51	12	....	....	....	....	....	....	....	....	....	6	2	1	3	2	....	....	....	....
2007-08	Hartford	AHL	75	34	47	81	81	....	....	....	....	....	....	....	....	....	5	3	2	5	13	....	....	....	....
2008-09	Hartford	AHL	74	29	49	78	142	....	....	....	....	....	....	....	....	....	....	....	....	....	....	....	....	....	....
2009-10	**NY Rangers**	**NHL**	**22**	**3**	**5**	**8**	**4**	**1**	**0**	**0**	**38**	**7.9**	**–2**	**12**	**33.3**	**13:42**	....	....	....	....	....	....	....	....	....
	Hartford	AHL	35	20	25	45	63	....	....	....	....	....	....	....	....	....	....	....	....	....	....	....	....	....	....
2010-11	**NY Islanders**	**NHL**	**81**	**20**	**33**	**53**	**46**	**9**	**0**	**2**	**161**	**12.4**	**–8**	**30**	**36.7**	**18:13**	....	....	....	....	....	....	....	....	....
2011-12	**NY Islanders**	**NHL**	**80**	**18**	**49**	**67**	**89**	**6**	**0**	**2**	**167**	**10.8**	**–8**	**26**	**38.5**	**18:39**	....	....	....	....	....	....	....	....	....
2012-13	**Colorado**	**NHL**	**48**	**18**	**25**	**43**	**38**	**6**	**0**	**1**	**105**	**17.1**	**–11**	**13**	**7.7**	**19:09**	....	....	....	....	....	....	....	....	....
	NHL Totals		**236**	**59**	**113**	**172**	**179**	**22**	**0**	**5**	**478**	**12.3**		**83**	**32.5**	**17:59**	....	....	....	....	....	....	....	....	....

AHL Second All-Star Team (2008) • AHL First All-Star Team (2009)

Traded to **Chicago** by **Anaheim** with Bruno St. Jacques for Sebastien Caron, Matt Keith and Chris Durno, December 28, 2006. Traded to **NY Rangers** by **Chicago** for future considerations, October 11, 2007. Signed as a free agent by **NY Islanders**, July 2, 2010. Signed as a free agent by **Colorado**, July 1, 2012.

PARISE, Zach

(pah-REE-say, ZAK) **MIN**

Left wing. Shoots left. 5'11", 195 lbs. Born, Minneapolis, MN, July 28, 1984. New Jersey's 1st choice, 17th overall, in 2003 Entry Draft.

			Regular Season														Playoffs								
Season	Club	League	GP	G	A	Pts	PIM	PP	SH	GW	S	%	+/-	TF	F%	Min	GP	G	A	Pts	PIM	PP	SH	GW	Min
2000-01	Shat.-St. Mary's	High-MN	58	69	93	162	....	....	....	....	....	....	....	....	....	....	....	....	....	....	....	....	....	....	....
2001-02	Shat.-St. Mary's	High-MN	67	77	101	178	58	....	....	....	....	....	....	....	....	....	....	....	....	....	....	....	....	....	....
	USNTDP	U-18	12	7	7	14	6	....	....	....	....	....	....	....	....	....	....	....	....	....	....	....	....	....	....
2002-03	North Dakota	WCHA	39	26	35	61	34	....	....	....	....	....	....	....	....	....	....	....	....	....	....	....	....	....	....
2003-04	North Dakota	WCHA	37	23	32	55	24	....	....	....	....	....	....	....	....	....	....	....	....	....	....	....	....	....	....
2004-05	Albany River Rats	AHL	73	18	40	58	56	....	....	....	....	....	....	....	....	....	....	....	....	....	....	....	....	....	....
2005-06	**New Jersey**	**NHL**	**81**	**14**	**18**	**32**	**28**	**2**	**0**	**5**	**133**	**10.5**	**–1**	**162**	**42.6**	**13:08**	**9**	**1**	**2**	**3**	**2**	**0**	**0**	**0**	**15:03**
2006-07	**New Jersey**	**NHL**	**82**	**31**	**31**	**62**	**30**	**9**	**0**	**7**	**247**	**12.6**	**–3**	**52**	**44.2**	**17:32**	**11**	**7**	**3**	**10**	**8**	**2**	**0**	**1**	**19:08**
2007-08	**New Jersey**	**NHL**	**81**	**32**	**33**	**65**	**25**	**10**	**1**	**8**	**266**	**12.0**	**13**	**104**	**48.1**	**18:04**	**5**	**1**	**4**	**5**	**2**	**1**	**0**	**0**	**18:29**
2008-09	**New Jersey**	**NHL**	**82**	**45**	**49**	**94**	**24**	**14**	**0**	**8**	**364**	**12.4**	**30**	**121**	**44.6**	**18:45**	**7**	**3**	**3**	**6**	**2**	**1**	**0**	**1**	**19:02**
2009-10	**New Jersey**	**NHL**	**81**	**38**	**44**	**82**	**32**	**9**	**1**	**5**	**347**	**11.0**	**24**	**48**	**37.5**	**19:46**	**5**	**1**	**3**	**4**	**0**	**0**	**1**	**0**	**20:44**
	United States	Olympics	6	4	4	8	0	....	....	....	....	....	....	....	....	....	....	....	....	....	....	....	....	....	....
2010-11	**New Jersey**	**NHL**	**13**	**3**	**3**	**6**	**6**	**0**	**0**	**1**	**49**	**6.1**	**–1**	**11**	**36.4**	**19:51**	....	....	....	....	....	....	....	....	....
2011-12	**New Jersey**	**NHL**	**82**	**31**	**38**	**69**	**32**	**7**	**3**	**3**	**293**	**10.6**	**–5**	**63**	**47.6**	**21:29**	**24**	***8**	**7**	**15**	**4**	**3**	**0**	**1**	**20:53**
2012-13	**Minnesota**	**NHL**	**48**	**18**	**20**	**38**	**16**	**7**	**0**	**4**	**182**	**9.9**	**2**	**9**	**33.3**	**20:40**	**5**	**1**	**0**	**1**	**2**	**0**	**0**	**0**	**21:24**
	NHL Totals		**550**	**212**	**236**	**448**	**193**	**58**	**5**	**41**	**1881**	**11.3**		**570**	**44.0**	**18:24**	**66**	**22**	**22**	**44**	**20**	**7**	**1**	**3**	**19:27**

WCHA All-Rookie Team (2003) • WCHA First All-Star Team (2004) • NCAA West First All-American Team (2004) • NHL Second All-Star Team (2009) • Olympic All-Star Team (2010)

Played in NHL All-Star Game (2009)

• Missed majority of 2010-11 due to knee injury at Los Angeles, October 30, 2010. Signed as a free agent by **Minnesota**, July 4, 2012.

PARK, Richard

(PAHRK, RIH-chuhrd)

Right wing. Shoots right. 5'11", 190 lbs. Born, Seoul, South Korea, May 27, 1976. Pittsburgh's 2nd choice, 50th overall, in 1994 Entry Draft.

			Regular Season														Playoffs								
Season	Club	League	GP	G	A	Pts	PIM	PP	SH	GW	S	%	+/-	TF	F%	Min	GP	G	A	Pts	PIM	PP	SH	GW	Min
1991-92	Tor. Young Nats	MTHL	76	49	58	107	91	....	....	....	....	....	....	....	....	....	....	....	....	....	....	....	....	....	....
1992-93	Belleville Bulls	OHL	66	23	38	61	38	....	....	....	....	....	....	....	....	....	5	0	0	0	14	....	....	....	....
1993-94	Belleville Bulls	OHL	59	27	49	76	70	....	....	....	....	....	....	....	....	....	12	3	5	8	18	....	....	....	....
1994-95	Belleville Bulls	OHL	45	28	51	79	35	....	....	....	....	....	....	....	....	....	16	9	18	27	12	....	....	....	....
	Pittsburgh	**NHL**	**1**	**0**	**1**	**1**	**2**	**0**	**0**	**0**	**4**	**0.0**	**1**	....	....	....	**3**	**0**	**0**	**0**	**2**	**0**	**0**	**0**	....
1995-96	Belleville Bulls	OHL	6	7	6	13	2	....	....	....	....	....	....	....	....	....	14	18	12	30	10	....	....	....	....
	Pittsburgh	**NHL**	**56**	**4**	**6**	**10**	**36**	**0**	**1**	**1**	**62**	**6.5**	**3**	....	....	....	**1**	**0**	**0**	**0**	**0**	**0**	**0**	**0**	....
1996-97	**Pittsburgh**	**NHL**	**1**	**0**	**0**	**0**	**0**	**0**	**0**	**0**	**1**	**0.0**	**–1**	....	....	....	....	....	....	....	....	....	....	....	....
	Cleveland	IHL	50	12	15	27	30	....	....	....	....	....	....	....	....	....	....	....	....	....	....	....	....	....	....
	Anaheim	**NHL**	**11**	**1**	**1**	**2**	**10**	**0**	**0**	**0**	**9**	**11.1**	**0**	....	....	....	**11**	**0**	**1**	**1**	**2**	**0**	**0**	**0**	....
1997-98	**Anaheim**	**NHL**	**15**	**0**	**2**	**2**	**8**	**0**	**0**	**0**	**14**	**0.0**	**–3**	....	....	....	....	....	....	....	....	....	....	....	....
	Cincinnati	AHL	56	17	26	43	36	....	....	....	....	....	....	....	....	....	....	....	....	....	....	....	....	....	....
1998-99	**Philadelphia**	**NHL**	**7**	**0**	**0**	**0**	**0**	**0**	**0**	**0**	**5**	**0.0**	**–1**	**15**	**53.3**	**9:21**	....	....	....	....	....	....	....	....	....
	Philadelphia	AHL	75	41	42	83	33	....	....	....	....	....	....	....	....	....	16	9	6	15	4	....	....	....	....
99-2000	Utah Grizzlies	IHL	82	28	32	60	36	....	....	....	....	....	....	....	....	....	5	1	0	1	0	....	....	....	....
2000-01	Cleveland	IHL	75	27	21	48	29	....	....	....	....	....	....	....	....	....	4	0	2	2	4	....	....	....	....
2001-02	**Minnesota**	**NHL**	**63**	**10**	**15**	**25**	**10**	**2**	**1**	**2**	**115**	**8.7**	**–1**	**79**	**41.8**	**16:28**	....	....	....	....	....	....	....	....	....
	Houston Aeros	AHL	13	4	10	14	6	....	....	....	....	....	....	....	....	....	....	....	....	....	....	....	....	....	....
2002-03	**Minnesota**	**NHL**	**81**	**14**	**10**	**24**	**16**	**2**	**2**	**3**	**149**	**9.4**	**–3**	**178**	**48.9**	**16:36**	**18**	**3**	**3**	**6**	**4**	**0**	**0**	**1**	**17:03**
2003-04	**Minnesota**	**NHL**	**73**	**13**	**12**	**25**	**28**	**4**	**0**	**1**	**142**	**9.2**	**0**	**379**	**40.1**	**16:30**	....	....	....	....	....	....	....	....	....
2004-05	Malmo	Sweden	9	1	3	4	4	....	....	....	....	....	....	....	....	....	....	....	....	....	....	....	....	....	....
	Langnau	Swiss	10	3	0	3	8	....	....	....	....	....	....	....	....	....	6	4	1	5	6	....	....	....	....
2005-06	**Vancouver**	**NHL**	**60**	**8**	**10**	**18**	**29**	**0**	**1**	**2**	**97**	**8.2**	**–2**	**26**	**26.9**	**11:00**	....	....	....	....	....	....	....	....	....
2006-07	**NY Islanders**	**NHL**	**82**	**10**	**16**	**26**	**33**	**0**	**2**	**2**	**93**	**10.8**	**4**	**218**	**39.0**	**11:39**	**5**	**0**	**1**	**1**	**2**	**0**	**0**	**0**	**9:16**
2007-08	**NY Islanders**	**NHL**	**82**	**12**	**20**	**32**	**20**	**1**	**4**	**2**	**132**	**9.1**	**–4**	**626**	**50.2**	**15:14**	....	....	....	....	....	....	....	....	....
2008-09	**NY Islanders**	**NHL**	**71**	**14**	**17**	**31**	**34**	**4**	**2**	**1**	**138**	**10.1**	**–13**	**809**	**49.0**	**17:10**	....	....	....	....	....	....	....	....	....
2009-10	**NY Islanders**	**NHL**	**81**	**9**	**22**	**31**	**28**	**0**	**1**	**4**	**146**	**6.2**	**–9**	**1040**	**51.5**	**15:45**	....	....	....	....	....	....	....	....	....
2010-11	Geneve	Swiss	47	15	19	34	16	....	....	....	....	....	....	....	....	....	3	2	1	3	2	....	....	....	....

Season	Club	League	GP	G	A	Pts	PIM	PP	SH	GW	S	%	+/-	TF	F%	Min	GP	G	A	Pts	PIM	PP	SH	GW	Min
			Regular Season														Playoffs								
2011-12	**Pittsburgh**	**NHL**	**54**	**7**	**7**	**14**	**12**	**0**	**1**	**4**	**44**	**15.9**	**–1**	**397**	**55.7**	**10:55**	**2**	**0**	**1**	**1**	**2**	**0**	**0**	**0**	**11:21**
2012-13	HC Ambri-Piotta	Swiss	48	9	22	31	18	....	....	....	....	....	....	....	....	....	5	1	2	3	0	....	....	....	....
	NHL Totals		**738**	**102**	**139**	**241**	**266**	**13**	**15**	**22**	**1151**	**8.9**		**3767**	**48.8**	**14:41**	**40**	**3**	**6**	**9**	**12**	**0**	**0**	**1**	**15:02**

OHL All-Rookie Team (1993) • AHL Second All-Star Team (1999)

Traded to **Anaheim** by **Pittsburgh** for Roman Oksiuta, March 18, 1997. Signed as a free agent by **Philadelphia**, August 24, 1998. Signed as a free agent by **Utah** (IHL), September 22, 1999. Signed as a free agent by **Minnesota**, June 6, 2000. Signed as a free agent by **Malmo** (Sweden), November 8, 2004. Signed as a free agent by **Langnau** (Swiss), January 4, 2005. Signed as a free agent by **Vancouver**, August 8, 2005. Signed as a free agent by **NY Islanders**, October 2, 2006. Signed as a free agent by **Geneve** (Swiss), September 9, 2010. Signed as a free agent by **Pittsburgh**, September 8, 2011. Signed as a free agent by **Ambri-Piotta** (Swiss), August 7, 2012.

PARROS, George
(PAIR-ohs, JOHRJ) **MTL**

Right wing. Shoots right. 6'5", 228 lbs. Born, Washington, PA, December 29, 1979. Los Angeles' 9th choice, 222nd overall, in 1999 Entry Draft.

Season	Club	League	GP	G	A	Pts	PIM	PP	SH	GW	S	%	+/-	TF	F%	Min	GP	G	A	Pts	PIM	PP	SH	GW	Min
1996-97	Delbarton	High-NJ	14	15	8	23	....	....	....	....	....	....	....	....	....	....	....	....	....	....	....	....	....	....	....
1997-98	Delbarton	High-NJ	15	22	17	39	....	....	....	....	....	....	....	....	....	....	....	....	....	....	....	....	....	....	....
1998-99	Chicago Freeze	NAHL	54	30	20	50	126	....	....	....	....	....	....	....	....	....	....	....	....	....	....	....	....	....	....
99-2000	Princeton	ECAC	27	4	2	6	14	....	....	....	....	....	....	....	....	....	....	....	....	....	....	....	....	....	....
2000-01	Princeton	ECAC	31	7	10	17	38	....	....	....	....	....	....	....	....	....	....	....	....	....	....	....	....	....	....
2001-02	Princeton	ECAC	31	9	13	22	36	....	....	....	....	....	....	....	....	....	....	....	....	....	....	....	....	....	....
2002-03	Princeton	ECAC	22	0	7	7	29	....	....	....	....	....	....	....	....	....	....	....	....	....	....	....	....	....	....
	Manchester	AHL	9	0	1	1	7	....	....	....	....	....	....	....	....	....	....	....	....	....	....	....	....	....	....
2003-04	Manchester	AHL	57	3	6	9	126	....	....	....	....	....	....	....	....	....	5	0	0	0	4	....	....	....	....
2004-05	Manchester	AHL	67	14	8	22	247	....	....	....	....	....	....	....	....	....	6	1	1	2	27	....	....	....	....
	Reading Royals	ECHL	3	0	0	0	9	....	....	....	....	....	....	....	....	....	....	....	....	....	....	....	....	....	....
2005-06	**Los Angeles**	**NHL**	**55**	**2**	**3**	**5**	**138**	**0**	**0**	**0**	**23**	**8.7**	**1**	**1**	**0.0**	**4:56**	....	....	....	....	....	....	....	....	....
2006-07	**Colorado**	**NHL**	**2**	**0**	**0**	**0**	**0**	**0**	**0**	**0**	**1**	**0.0**	**–1**	**0**	**0.0**	**3:33**	....	....	....	....	....	....	....	....	....
	♦ Anaheim	**NHL**	**32**	**1**	**0**	**1**	**102**	**0**	**0**	**0**	**18**	**5.6**	**–2**	**0**	**0.0**	**5:09**	**5**	**0**	**0**	**0**	**10**	**0**	**0**	**0**	**3:49**
2007-08	**Anaheim**	**NHL**	**69**	**1**	**4**	**5**	**183**	**0**	**0**	**0**	**30**	**3.3**	**3**	**10**	**30.0**	**5:57**	**1**	**0**	**0**	**0**	**0**	**0**	**0**	**0**	**2:42**
2008-09	**Anaheim**	**NHL**	**74**	**5**	**5**	**10**	**135**	**0**	**0**	**0**	**47**	**10.6**	**8**	**3**	**0.0**	**6:16**	**7**	**0**	**0**	**0**	**9**	**0**	**0**	**0**	**5:33**
2009-10	**Anaheim**	**NHL**	**57**	**4**	**0**	**4**	**136**	**0**	**0**	**0**	**25**	**16.0**	**4**	**7**	**14.3**	**6:00**	....	....	....	....	....	....	....	....	....
2010-11	**Anaheim**	**NHL**	**78**	**3**	**1**	**4**	**171**	**0**	**0**	**1**	**33**	**9.1**	**–4**	**4**	**25.0**	**6:25**	**6**	**0**	**0**	**0**	**16**	**0**	**0**	**0**	**4:06**
2011-12	**Anaheim**	**NHL**	**46**	**1**	**3**	**4**	**85**	**0**	**0**	**0**	**17**	**5.9**	**1**	**0**	**0.0**	**6:23**	....	....	....	....	....	....	....	....	....
2012-13	**Florida**	**NHL**	**39**	**1**	**1**	**2**	**57**	**0**	**0**	**0**	**16**	**6.3**	**–15**	**0**	**0.0**	**6:37**	....	....	....	....	....	....	....	....	....
	NHL Totals		**452**	**18**	**17**	**35**	**1007**	**0**	**0**	**1**	**210**	**8.6**		**25**	**20.0**	**6:00**	**19**	**0**	**0**	**0**	**35**	**0**	**0**	**0**	**4:29**

Claimed on waivers by **Colorado** from **Los Angeles**, October 3, 2006. Traded to **Anaheim** by **Colorado** with Colorado's 3rd round choice (later traded to Tampa Bay - Tampa Bay selected Luca Cunti) in 2007 Entry Draft for Atlanta's 2nd round choice (previously acquired, Colorado selected TJ Galiardi) in 2007 Entry Draft and Anaheim's 3rd round choice (later traded to San Jose - San Jose selected Tyson Sexsmith) in 2007 Entry Draft, November 13, 2006. Signed as a free agent by **Florida**, July 1, 2012. Traded to **Montreal** by **Florida** for Philippe Lefebvre and Florida's 7th round choice (previously acquired) in 2014 Entry Draft, July 5, 2013.

PARSE, Scott
(PARS, SKAWT)

Center. Shoots right. 5'11", 189 lbs. Born, Portage, MI, September 5, 1984. Los Angeles' 5th choice, 174th overall, in 2004 Entry Draft.

Season	Club	League	GP	G	A	Pts	PIM	PP	SH	GW	S	%	+/-	TF	F%	Min	GP	G	A	Pts	PIM	PP	SH	GW	Min
2002-03	Tri-City Storm	USHL	48	21	23	44	32	....	....	....	....	....	....	....	....	....	3	2	1	3	8	....	....	....	....
2003-04	Nebraska-Omaha	CCHA	39	16	19	35	52	....	....	....	....	....	....	....	....	....	....	....	....	....	....	....	....	....	....
2004-05	Nebraska-Omaha	CCHA	39	19	30	49	32	....	....	....	....	....	....	....	....	....	....	....	....	....	....	....	....	....	....
2005-06	Nebraska-Omaha	CCHA	41	20	*41	*61	40	....	....	....	....	....	....	....	....	....	....	....	....	....	....	....	....	....	....
2006-07	Nebraska-Omaha	CCHA	40	24	28	52	36	....	....	....	....	....	....	....	....	....	....	....	....	....	....	....	....	....	....
	Grand Rapids	AHL	10	2	5	7	6	....	....	....	....	....	....	....	....	....	7	1	0	1	8	....	....	....	....
2007-08	Manchester	AHL	14	0	3	3	4	....	....	....	....	....	....	....	....	....	....	....	....	....	....	....	....	....	....
	Reading Royals	ECHL	18	5	11	16	14	....	....	....	....	....	....	....	....	....	....	....	....	....	....	....	....	....	....
2008-09	Manchester	AHL	74	15	24	39	38	....	....	....	....	....	....	....	....	....	....	....	....	....	....	....	....	....	....
2009-10	**Los Angeles**	**NHL**	**59**	**11**	**13**	**24**	**22**	**0**	**0**	**1**	**78**	**14.1**	**13**	**11**	**54.6**	**10:32**	**4**	**0**	**0**	**0**	**0**	**0**	**0**	**0**	**6:38**
	Manchester	AHL	14	4	11	15	21	....	....	....	....	....	....	....	....	....	....	....	....	....	....	....	....	....	....
2010-11	**Los Angeles**	**NHL**	**5**	**1**	**3**	**4**	**0**	**0**	**0**	**0**	**6**	**16.7**	**5**	**0**	**0.0**	**13:47**	**2**	**0**	**0**	**0**	**0**	**0**	**0**	**0**	**8:47**
2011-12♦	**Los Angeles**	**NHL**	**9**	**2**	**0**	**2**	**14**	**1**	**0**	**0**	**9**	**22.2**	**1**	**3**	**33.3**	**11:17**	....	....	....	....	....	....	....	....	....
2012-13	Albany Devils	AHL	15	1	3	4	8	....	....	....	....	....	....	....	....	....	....	....	....	....	....	....	....	....	....
	NHL Totals		**73**	**14**	**16**	**30**	**36**	**1**	**0**	**1**	**93**	**15.1**		**14**	**50.0**	**10:51**	**6**	**0**	**0**	**0**	**0**	**0**	**0**	**0**	**7:21**

USHL All-Rookie Team (2003) • CCHA First All-Star Team (2005, 2007) • CCHA Player of the Year (2006) • NCAA West First All-American Team (2006) • NCAA West Second All-American Team (2007)

• Missed majority of 2010-11 and 2011-12 due to hip injury at San Jose, November 15, 2010, and resulting surgery, December 3, 2011. Signed as a free agent by **Albany** (AHL), September 27, 2012. • Missed majority of 2012-13 due to recurring lower-body injury and as a healthy reserve.

PATERYN, Greg
(PA-tuhr-ihn, GREHG) **MTL**

Defense. Shoots right. 6'2", 222 lbs. Born, Sterling Heights, MI, June 20, 1990. Toronto's 4th choice, 128th overall, in 2008 Entry Draft.

Season	Club	League	GP	G	A	Pts	PIM	PP	SH	GW	S	%	+/-	TF	F%	Min	GP	G	A	Pts	PIM	PP	SH	GW	Min
2004-05	Brother Rice	High-MI	29	2	8	10	42	....	....	....	....	....	....	....	....	....	....	....	....	....	....	....	....	....	....
2005-06	Brother Rice	High-MI	24	0	8	8	34	....	....	....	....	....	....	....	....	....	....	....	....	....	....	....	....	....	....
2006-07	Brother Rice	High-MI	27	9	19	28	44	....	....	....	....	....	....	....	....	....	....	....	....	....	....	....	....	....	....
2007-08	Ohio	USHL	60	3	24	27	145	....	....	....	....	....	....	....	....	....	....	....	....	....	....	....	....	....	....
2008-09	U. of Michigan	CCHA	28	0	5	5	32	....	....	....	....	....	....	....	....	....	....	....	....	....	....	....	....	....	....
2009-10	U. of Michigan	CCHA	33	1	5	6	18	....	....	....	....	....	....	....	....	....	....	....	....	....	....	....	....	....	....
2010-11	U. of Michigan	CCHA	40	3	14	17	28	....	....	....	....	....	....	....	....	....	....	....	....	....	....	....	....	....	....
2011-12	U. of Michigan	CCHA	41	2	13	15	65	....	....	....	....	....	....	....	....	....	....	....	....	....	....	....	....	....	....
2012-13	Hamilton	AHL	39	7	5	12	27	....	....	....	....	....	....	....	....	....	....	....	....	....	....	....	....	....	....
	Montreal	**NHL**	**3**	**0**	**0**	**0**	**0**	**0**	**0**	**0**	**0**	**0.0**	**0**	**0**	**0.0**	**9:36**	....	....	....	....	....	....	....	....	....
	NHL Totals		**3**	**0**	**0**	**0**	**0**	**0**	**0**	**0**	**0**	**0.0**		**0**	**0.0**	**9:36**	....	....	....	....	....	....	....	....	....

Traded to **Montreal** by **Toronto** with Toronto's 2nd round choice (later traded to Chicago, later traded back to Toronto, later traded to Boston - Boston selected Jared Knight) in 2010 Entry Draft for Mikhail Grabovski, July 3, 2008.

PAVELSKI, Joe
(pah-VEHL-skee, JOH) **S.J.**

Center. Shoots right. 5'11", 190 lbs. Born, Plover, WI, July 11, 1984. San Jose's 7th choice, 205th overall, in 2003 Entry Draft.

Season	Club	League	GP	G	A	Pts	PIM	PP	SH	GW	S	%	+/-	TF	F%	Min	GP	G	A	Pts	PIM	PP	SH	GW	Min
2001-02	Stevens Point High	High-WI	STATISTICS NOT AVAILABLE																						
2002-03	Waterloo	USHL	60	36	33	69	32	....	....	....	....	....	....	....	....	....	7	5	7	12	8	....	....	....	....
2003-04	Waterloo	USHL	54	21	31	52	58	....	....	....	....	....	....	....	....	....	12	6	6	12	10	....	....	....	....
2004-05	U. of Wisconsin	WCHA	41	16	29	45	26	....	....	....	....	....	....	....	....	....	....	....	....	....	....	....	....	....	....
2005-06	U. of Wisconsin	WCHA	43	23	33	56	34	....	....	....	....	....	....	....	....	....	....	....	....	....	....	....	....	....	....
2006-07	**San Jose**	**NHL**	**46**	**14**	**14**	**28**	**18**	**5**	**0**	**3**	**111**	**12.6**	**4**	**389**	**48.6**	**15:02**	**6**	**1**	**0**	**1**	**0**	**0**	**0**	**0**	**10:27**
	Worcester Sharks	AHL	16	8	18	26	8	....	....	....	....	....	....	....	....	....	....	....	....	....	....	....	....	....	....
2007-08	**San Jose**	**NHL**	**82**	**19**	**21**	**40**	**28**	**8**	**1**	**4**	**207**	**9.2**	**1**	**501**	**53.5**	**14:07**	**13**	**5**	**4**	**9**	**0**	**2**	**0**	**3**	**22:03**
2008-09	**San Jose**	**NHL**	**80**	**25**	**34**	**59**	**46**	**8**	**3**	**3**	**266**	**9.4**	**5**	**1274**	**56.3**	**18:58**	**6**	**0**	**1**	**1**	**9**	**0**	**0**	**0**	**19:21**
2009-10	**San Jose**	**NHL**	**67**	**25**	**26**	**51**	**26**	**3**	**1**	**5**	**228**	**11.0**	**1**	**821**	**58.1**	**19:29**	**15**	**9**	**8**	**17**	**6**	**5**	**0**	**3**	**21:32**
	United States	Olympics	6	0	3	3	4	....	....	....	....	....	....	....	....	....	....	....	....	....	....	....	....	....	....
2010-11	**San Jose**	**NHL**	**74**	**20**	**46**	**66**	**24**	**11**	**1**	**5**	**282**	**7.1**	**10**	**1020**	**54.3**	**19:39**	**18**	**5**	**5**	**10**	**10**	**1**	**0**	**1**	**21:08**
2011-12	**San Jose**	**NHL**	**82**	**31**	**30**	**61**	**31**	**8**	**1**	**2**	**269**	**11.5**	**18**	**864**	**58.7**	**20:37**	**5**	**0**	**0**	**0**	**5**	**0**	**0**	**0**	**21:00**
2012-13	Dynamo Minsk	KHL	17	7	8	15	10	....	....	....	....	....	....	....	....	....	....	....	....	....	....	....	....	....	....
	San Jose	**NHL**	**48**	**16**	**15**	**31**	**10**	**5**	**0**	**5**	**130**	**12.3**	**2**	**660**	**51.8**	**18:55**	**11**	**4**	**8**	**12**	**0**	**3**	**0**	**0**	**21:13**
	NHL Totals		**479**	**150**	**186**	**336**	**183**	**48**	**7**	**27**	**1493**	**10.0**		**5529**	**55.2**	**18:13**	**74**	**24**	**26**	**50**	**30**	**11**	**0**	**7**	**20:22**

USHL All-Rookie Team (2003) • USHL First All-Star Team (2003) • USHL Rookie of the Year (2003) • WCHA All-Rookie Team (2005) • WCHA Second All-Star Team (2006) • NCAA West Second All-American Team (2006)

Signed as a free agent by **Minsk** (KHL), October 5, 2012.

PEARSON, Tanner
(PEER-suhn, TA-nuhr) **L.A.**

Left wing. Shoots left. 6', 198 lbs. Born, Kitchener, Ont., August 10, 1992. Los Angeles' 1st choice, 30th overall, in 2012 Entry Draft.

Season	Club	League	GP	G	A	Pts	PIM	PP	SH	GW	S	%	+/-	TF	F%	Min	GP	G	A	Pts	PIM	PP	SH	GW	Min
2007-08	Kitchener	Minor-ON	STATISTICS NOT AVAILABLE																						
	Kitchener	ON-Jr.B	1	0	0	0	2	....	....	....	....	....	....	....	....	....	....	....	....	....	....	....	....	....	....
2008-09	Waterloo Siskins	ON-Jr.B	52	15	33	48	28	....	....	....	....	....	....	....	....	....	14	5	4	9	16	....	....	....	....
2009-10	Waterloo Siskins	ON-Jr.B	51	29	41	70	78	....	....	....	....	....	....	....	....	....	11	5	11	16	20	....	....	....	....
2010-11	Barrie Colts	OHL	66	15	27	42	35	....	....	....	....	....	....	....	....	....	....	....	....	....	....	....	....	....	....
2011-12	Barrie Colts	OHL	60	37	54	91	37	....	....	....	....	....	....	....	....	....	....	....	....	....	....	....	....	....	....

			Regular Season														Playoffs								
Season	Club	League	GP	G	A	Pts	PIM	PP	SH	GW	S	%	+/-	TF	F%	Min	GP	G	A	Pts	PIM	PP	SH	GW	Min
2012-13	Manchester	AHL	64	19	28	47	14	....	....	....	....	....	....	....	....	....	4	0	1	1	4	....	....	....	....
	Los Angeles	**NHL**	....	....	....	....	....	....	....	....	....	....	....	....	....	....	**1**	**0**	**0**	**0**	**0**	**0**	**0**	**0**	**5:44**
	NHL Totals		....	....	....	....	....	....	....	....	....	....		....	....	....	**1**	**0**	**0**	**0**	**0**	**0**	**0**	**0**	**5:44**

OHL Second All-Star Team (2012)

PECKHAM, Theo (PEHK-uhm, THEE-oh) CHI

Defense. Shoots left. 6'2", 236 lbs. Born, Richmond Hill, Ont., November 10, 1987. Edmonton's 2nd choice, 75th overall, in 2006 Entry Draft.

Season	Club	League	GP	G	A	Pts	PIM	PP	SH	GW	S	%	+/-	TF	F%	Min	GP	G	A	Pts	PIM	PP	SH	GW	Min
2003-04	North York	ON-Jr.A	29	1	4	5	46	....	....	....	....	....	....	....	....	....	....	....	....	....	....	....	....	....	....
2004-05	Owen Sound	OHL	61	1	9	10	209	....	....	....	....	....	....	....	....	....	8	0	0	0	8	....	....	....	....
2005-06	Owen Sound	OHL	67	6	9	15	236	....	....	....	....	....	....	....	....	....	11	1	6	7	32	....	....	....	....
2006-07	Owen Sound	OHL	53	10	25	35	173	....	....	....	....	....	....	....	....	....	4	0	1	1	0	....	....	....	....
2007-08	**Edmonton**	**NHL**	**1**	**0**	**0**	**0**	**2**	**0**	**0**	**0**	**0**	**0.0**	**0**	**0**	**0.0**	**13:22**	....	....	....	....	....	....	....	....	....
	Springfield	AHL	59	6	7	13	174	....	....	....	....	....	....	....	....	....	....	....	....	....	....	....	....	....	....
2008-09	**Edmonton**	**NHL**	**15**	**0**	**0**	**0**	**59**	**0**	**0**	**0**	**8**	**0.0**	**–1**	**0**	**0.0**	**11:38**	....	....	....	....	....	....	....	....	....
	Springfield	AHL	47	6	13	19	107	....	....	....	....	....	....	....	....	....	....	....	....	....	....	....	....	....	....
2009-10	**Edmonton**	**NHL**	**15**	**0**	**1**	**1**	**43**	**0**	**0**	**0**	**9**	**0.0**	**–8**	**0**	**0.0**	**16:04**	....	....	....	....	....	....	....	....	....
	Springfield	AHL	37	0	6	6	106	....	....	....	....	....	....	....	....	....	....	....	....	....	....	....	....	....	....
2010-11	**Edmonton**	**NHL**	**71**	**3**	**10**	**13**	**198**	**0**	**0**	**0**	**41**	**7.3**	**–5**	**0**	**0.0**	**18:36**	....	....	....	....	....	....	....	....	....
2011-12	**Edmonton**	**NHL**	**54**	**1**	**2**	**3**	**80**	**0**	**0**	**0**	**25**	**4.0**	**0**	**0**	**0.0**	**16:53**	....	....	....	....	....	....	....	....	....
2012-13	San Francisco	ECHL	4	0	0	0	11	....	....	....	....	....	....	....	....	....	....	....	....	....	....	....	....	....	....
	Edmonton	**NHL**	**4**	**0**	**0**	**0**	**6**	**0**	**0**	**0**	**2**	**0.0**	**–1**	**0**	**0.0**	**17:38**	....	....	....	....	....	....	....	....	....
	Oklahoma City	AHL	4	0	1	1	29	....	....	....	....	....	....	....	....	....	....	....	....	....	....	....	....	....	....
	NHL Totals		**160**	**4**	**13**	**17**	**388**	**0**	**0**	**0**	**85**	**4.7**		**0**	**0.0**	**17:04**	....	....	....	....	....	....	....	....	....

Signed as a free agent by **San Francisco** (ECHL), November 5, 2012. • Missed majority of 2012-13 due to recurring hip injury and as a healthy reserve. Signed as a free agent by **Chicago**, July 19, 2013.

PELECH, Matt (PEH-lihk, MAT) S.J.

Right wing. Shoots right. 6'4", 230 lbs. Born, Toronto, Ont., September 4, 1987. Calgary's 1st choice, 26th overall, in 2005 Entry Draft.

Season	Club	League	GP	G	A	Pts	PIM	PP	SH	GW	S	%	+/-	TF	F%	Min	GP	G	A	Pts	PIM	PP	SH	GW	Min
2002-03	Vaughan Kings	GTHL	44	3	13	16	113	....	....	....	....	....	....	....	....	....	....	....	....	....	....	....	....	....	....
2003-04	Sarnia Sting	OHL	62	4	6	10	39	....	....	....	....	....	....	....	....	....	5	0	1	1	12	....	....	....	....
2004-05	Sarnia Sting	OHL	31	1	5	6	74	....	....	....	....	....	....	....	....	....	....	....	....	....	....	....	....	....	....
2005-06	Sarnia Sting	OHL	18	0	2	2	59	....	....	....	....	....	....	....	....	....	....	....	....	....	....	....	....	....	....
	London Knights	OHL	34	1	7	8	80	....	....	....	....	....	....	....	....	....	19	0	0	0	48	....	....	....	....
2006-07	Belleville Bulls	OHL	58	5	30	35	171	....	....	....	....	....	....	....	....	....	12	0	3	3	22	....	....	....	....
2007-08	Quad City Flames	AHL	77	3	6	9	141	....	....	....	....	....	....	....	....	....	....	....	....	....	....	....	....	....	....
2008-09	**Calgary**	**NHL**	**5**	**0**	**3**	**3**	**9**	**0**	**0**	**0**	**4**	**0.0**	**1**	**0**	**0.0**	**13:16**	....	....	....	....	....	....	....	....	....
	Quad City Flames	AHL	59	3	6	9	130	....	....	....	....	....	....	....	....	....	....	....	....	....	....	....	....	....	....
2009-10	Abbotsford Heat	AHL	42	2	8	10	125	....	....	....	....	....	....	....	....	....	13	0	4	4	31	....	....	....	....
2010-11	Abbotsford Heat	AHL	59	3	2	5	198	....	....	....	....	....	....	....	....	....	....	....	....	....	....	....	....	....	....
2011-12	Worcester Sharks	AHL	59	1	7	8	168	....	....	....	....	....	....	....	....	....	....	....	....	....	....	....	....	....	....
2012-13	Worcester Sharks	AHL	58	3	4	7	238	....	....	....	....	....	....	....	....	....	....	....	....	....	....	....	....	....	....
	San Jose	**NHL**	**2**	**0**	**0**	**0**	**7**	**0**	**0**	**0**	**0**	**0.0**	**0**	**0**	**0.0**	**9:03**	....	....	....	....	....	....	....	....	....
	NHL Totals		**7**	**0**	**3**	**3**	**16**	**0**	**0**	**0**	**4**	**0.0**		**0**	**0.0**	**12:04**	....	....	....	....	....	....	....	....	....

Signed as a free agent by **San Jose**, July 6, 2011.

PELLETIER, Pascal (PEHL-tyay, pas-KAL) VAN

Left wing. Shoots right. 5'11", 191 lbs. Born, Labrador City, Nfld., June 16, 1983.

Season	Club	League	GP	G	A	Pts	PIM	PP	SH	GW	S	%	+/-	TF	F%	Min	GP	G	A	Pts	PIM	PP	SH	GW	Min
2000-01	Baie-Comeau	QMJHL	70	15	44	59	176	....	....	....	....	....	....	....	....	....	11	2	11	13	6	....	....	....	....
2001-02	Baie-Comeau	QMJHL	56	12	25	37	115	....	....	....	....	....	....	....	....	....	5	3	4	7	0	....	....	....	....
2002-03	Baie-Comeau	QMJHL	67	46	55	101	113	....	....	....	....	....	....	....	....	....	12	5	7	12	14	....	....	....	....
2003-04	Shawinigan	QMJHL	64	39	52	91	85	....	....	....	....	....	....	....	....	....	11	3	9	12	20	....	....	....	....
2004-05	Louisiana	ECHL	61	10	28	38	75	....	....	....	....	....	....	....	....	....	....	....	....	....	....	....	....	....	....
	Gwinnett	ECHL	6	0	1	1	2	....	....	....	....	....	....	....	....	....	5	0	2	2	2	....	....	....	....
2005-06	Providence Bruins	AHL	53	20	26	46	42	....	....	....	....	....	....	....	....	....	6	2	4	6	23	....	....	....	....
	Gwinnett	ECHL	21	18	12	30	18	....	....	....	....	....	....	....	....	....	....	....	....	....	....	....	....	....	....
2006-07	Providence Bruins	AHL	80	14	35	49	60	....	....	....	....	....	....	....	....	....	13	5	4	9	16	....	....	....	....
2007-08	**Boston**	**NHL**	**6**	**0**	**0**	**0**	**0**	**0**	**0**	**0**	**8**	**0.0**	**–2**	**1**	**100.0**	**11:04**	....	....	....	....	....	....	....	....	....
	Providence Bruins	AHL	73	37	38	75	66	....	....	....	....	....	....	....	....	....	10	6	6	12	4	....	....	....	....
2008-09	**Chicago**	**NHL**	**7**	**0**	**0**	**0**	**0**	**0**	**0**	**0**	**7**	**0.0**	**–4**	**33**	**39.4**	**9:08**	....	....	....	....	....	....	....	....	....
	Rockford IceHogs	AHL	71	29	26	55	45	....	....	....	....	....	....	....	....	....	4	1	0	1	6	....	....	....	....
2009-10	Syracuse Crunch	AHL	25	3	13	16	23	....	....	....	....	....	....	....	....	....	....	....	....	....	....	....	....	....	....
	Peoria Rivermen	AHL	55	14	28	42	41	....	....	....	....	....	....	....	....	....	....	....	....	....	....	....	....	....	....
2010-11	Langnau	Swiss	47	17	21	38	95	....	....	....	....	....	....	....	....	....	4	1	1	2	29	....	....	....	....
2011-12	Langnau	Swiss	43	14	22	36	71	....	....	....	....	....	....	....	....	....	4	2	6	8	2	....	....	....	....
2012-13	Langnau	Swiss	46	19	16	35	76	....	....	....	....	....	....	....	....	....	12	6	2	8	6	....	....	....	....
	Langnau	Swiss-Q	....	....	....	....	....	....	....	....	....	....	....	....	....	....	6	3	6	9	4	....	....	....	....
	NHL Totals		**13**	**0**	**0**	**0**	**0**	**0**	**0**	**0**	**15**	**0.0**		**34**	**41.2**	**10:01**	....	....	....	....	....	....	....	....	....

AHL First All-Star Team (2008)

Signed as a free agent by **Boston**, August 7, 2006. Traded to **Chicago** by **Boston** for Martin St. Pierre, July 24, 2008. Signed as a free agent by **Columbus**, July 6, 2009. Traded to **St. Louis** by **Columbus** for Tomas Kana and Brendan Bell, December 8, 2009. Signed as a free agent by **Langnau** (Swiss), May 20, 2010. Signed as a free agent by **Vancouver**, July 9, 2013.

PELLEY, Rod (PEHL-lee, RAWD) N.J.

Center. Shoots left. 5'11", 200 lbs. Born, Kitimat, B.C., September 1, 1984.

Season	Club	League	GP	G	A	Pts	PIM	PP	SH	GW	S	%	+/-	TF	F%	Min	GP	G	A	Pts	PIM	PP	SH	GW	Min
2002-03	Ohio State	CCHA	43	8	3	11	26	....	....	....	....	....	....	....	....	....	....	....	....	....	....	....	....	....	....
2003-04	Ohio State	CCHA	42	10	12	22	38	....	....	....	....	....	....	....	....	....	....	....	....	....	....	....	....	....	....
2004-05	Ohio State	CCHA	41	22	19	41	54	....	....	....	....	....	....	....	....	....	....	....	....	....	....	....	....	....	....
2005-06	Ohio State	CCHA	39	7	7	14	42	....	....	....	....	....	....	....	....	....	....	....	....	....	....	....	....	....	....
2006-07	**New Jersey**	**NHL**	**9**	**0**	**0**	**0**	**0**	**0**	**0**	**0**	**8**	**0.0**	**–3**	**98**	**40.8**	**11:00**	....	....	....	....	....	....	....	....	....
	Lowell Devils	AHL	65	17	12	29	35	....	....	....	....	....	....	....	....	....	....	....	....	....	....	....	....	....	....
2007-08	**New Jersey**	**NHL**	**58**	**2**	**4**	**6**	**19**	**0**	**0**	**1**	**59**	**3.4**	**–3**	**321**	**46.7**	**9:19**	....	....	....	....	....	....	....	....	....
	Lowell Devils	AHL	11	2	1	3	18	....	....	....	....	....	....	....	....	....	....	....	....	....	....	....	....	....	....
2008-09	Lowell Devils	AHL	75	15	23	38	78	....	....	....	....	....	....	....	....	....	....	....	....	....	....	....	....	....	....
2009-10	**New Jersey**	**NHL**	**63**	**2**	**8**	**10**	**40**	**0**	**0**	**0**	**74**	**2.7**	**–4**	**198**	**49.5**	**7:52**	**3**	**0**	**0**	**0**	**2**	**0**	**0**	**0**	**9:12**
2010-11	**New Jersey**	**NHL**	**74**	**3**	**7**	**10**	**27**	**1**	**0**	**0**	**88**	**3.4**	**–9**	**320**	**52.8**	**11:48**	....	....	....	....	....	....	....	....	....
2011-12	**New Jersey**	**NHL**	**7**	**0**	**0**	**0**	**7**	**0**	**0**	**0**	**3**	**0.0**	**0**	**10**	**30.0**	**6:12**	....	....	....	....	....	....	....	....	....
	Anaheim	**NHL**	**45**	**2**	**1**	**3**	**9**	**0**	**0**	**0**	**41**	**4.9**	**–3**	**244**	**50.0**	**8:00**	....	....	....	....	....	....	....	....	....
2012-13	Norfolk Admirals	AHL	60	3	7	10	34	....	....	....	....	....	....	....	....	....	....	....	....	....	....	....	....	....	....
	NHL Totals		**256**	**9**	**20**	**29**	**102**	**1**	**0**	**1**	**273**	**3.3**		**1191**	**48.9**	**9:25**	**3**	**0**	**0**	**0**	**2**	**0**	**0**	**0**	**9:12**

CCHA Second All-Star Team (2005)

Signed as a free agent by **New Jersey**, July 17, 2006. Traded to **Anaheim** by **New Jersey** with Mark Fraser and New Jersey's 7th round choice (Jaycob Megna) in 2012 Entry Draft for Kurtis Foster and Timo Pielmeier, December 12, 2011. Signed as a free agent by **New Jersey**, July 8, 2013.

PELUSO, Anthony (puh-LOO-soh, AN-toh-nee) WPG

Right wing. Shoots right. 6'3", 235 lbs. Born, North York, Ont., April 18, 1989. St. Louis' 9th choice, 160th overall, in 2007 Entry Draft.

Season	Club	League	GP	G	A	Pts	PIM	PP	SH	GW	S	%	+/-	TF	F%	Min	GP	G	A	Pts	PIM	PP	SH	GW	Min
2004-05	Rich. Hill Stars	Minor-ON	30	22	20	42	80	....	....	....	....	....	....	....	....	....	....	....	....	....	....	....	....	....	....
2005-06	Erie Otters	OHL	68	5	3	8	66	....	....	....	....	....	....	....	....	....	....	....	....	....	....	....	....	....	....
2006-07	Erie Otters	OHL	52	7	3	10	176	....	....	....	....	....	....	....	....	....	....	....	....	....	....	....	....	....	....
2007-08	Erie Otters	OHL	21	3	3	6	41	....	....	....	....	....	....	....	....	....	....	....	....	....	....	....	....	....	....
	Sault Ste. Marie	OHL	42	4	11	15	83	....	....	....	....	....	....	....	....	....	14	2	1	3	12	....	....	....	....
2008-09	Sault Ste. Marie	OHL	36	9	6	15	68	....	....	....	....	....	....	....	....	....	....	....	....	....	....	....	....	....	....
	Brampton	OHL	27	11	11	22	57	....	....	....	....	....	....	....	....	....	21	8	7	15	29	....	....	....	....
2009-10	Peoria Rivermen	AHL	22	1	1	2	57	....	....	....	....	....	....	....	....	....	....	....	....	....	....	....	....	....	....
	Alaska Aces	ECHL	27	4	7	11	48	....	....	....	....	....	....	....	....	....	4	1	0	1	6	....	....	....	....
2010-11	Peoria Rivermen	AHL	62	5	2	7	102	....	....	....	....	....	....	....	....	....	4	1	0	1	0	....	....	....	....
2011-12	Peoria Rivermen	AHL	61	4	5	9	159	....	....	....	....	....	....	....	....	....	....	....	....	....	....	....	....	....	....

			Regular Season														Playoffs								
Season	Club	League	GP	G	A	Pts	PIM	PP	SH	GW	S	%	+/-	TF	F%	Min	GP	G	A	Pts	PIM	PP	SH	GW	Min
2012-13	Peoria Rivermen	AHL	36	5	6	11	58	....	....	....	....	....	....	....	....	....	....	....	....	....	....	....	....	....	....
	Winnipeg	**NHL**	**5**	**0**	**2**	**2**	**14**	**0**	**0**	**0**	**4**	**0.0**	**1**	**0**	**0.0**	**5:00**	....	....	....	....	....	....	....	....	....
	NHL Totals		**5**	**0**	**2**	**2**	**14**	**0**	**0**	**0**	**4**	**0.0**		**0**	**0.0**	**5:00**	....	....	....	....	....	....	....	....	....

Signed as a free agent by **Winnipeg**, July 24, 2013.

PENNER, Dustin

(PEH-nuhr, DUHS-tihn) **ANA**

Left wing. Shoots left. 6'4", 242 lbs. Born, Winkler, Man., September 28, 1982.

Season	Club	League	GP	G	A	Pts	PIM	PP	SH	GW	S	%	+/-	TF	F%	Min	GP	G	A	Pts	PIM	PP	SH	GW	Min
2001-02	MSU - Bottineau	NJCAA	23	20	12	32	30	....	....	....	....	....	....	....	....	....	....	....	....	....	....	....	....	....	....
2002-03	U. of Maine	H-East	DID NOT PLAY – FRESHMAN																						
2003-04	U. of Maine	H-East	43	11	12	23	52	....	....	....	....	....	....	....	....	....	....	....	....	....	....	....	....	....	....
2004-05	Cincinnati	AHL	77	10	18	28	82	....	....	....	....	....	....	....	....	....	9	2	3	5	13	....	....	....	....
2005-06	**Anaheim**	**NHL**	**19**	**4**	**3**	**7**	**14**	**2**	**0**	**1**	**46**	**8.7**	**3**	**1**	**0.0**	**11:58**	**13**	**3**	**6**	**9**	**12**	**0**	**0**	**0**	**13:16**
	Portland Pirates	AHL	57	39	45	84	68	....	....	....	....	....	....	....	....	....	5	4	3	7	0	....	....	....	....
2006-07♦	**Anaheim**	**NHL**	**82**	**29**	**16**	**45**	**58**	**9**	**0**	**5**	**204**	**14.2**	**–2**	**58**	**46.6**	**13:59**	**21**	**3**	**5**	**8**	**2**	**0**	**0**	**2**	**14:05**
2007-08	**Edmonton**	**NHL**	**82**	**23**	**24**	**47**	**45**	**13**	**0**	**4**	**201**	**11.4**	**–12**	**189**	**55.0**	**17:12**	....	....	....	....	....	....	....	....	....
2008-09	**Edmonton**	**NHL**	**78**	**17**	**20**	**37**	**61**	**5**	**0**	**5**	**137**	**12.4**	**7**	**114**	**47.4**	**15:23**	....	....	....	....	....	....	....	....	....
2009-10	**Edmonton**	**NHL**	**82**	**32**	**31**	**63**	**38**	**9**	**0**	**1**	**203**	**15.8**	**6**	**421**	**47.7**	**18:23**	....	....	....	....	....	....	....	....	....
2010-11	**Edmonton**	**NHL**	**62**	**21**	**18**	**39**	**45**	**6**	**1**	**3**	**137**	**15.3**	**–12**	**294**	**43.2**	**18:28**	....	....	....	....	....	....	....	....	....
	Los Angeles	**NHL**	**19**	**2**	**4**	**6**	**2**	**0**	**0**	**0**	**36**	**5.6**	**0**	**12**	**33.3**	**17:01**	**6**	**1**	**1**	**2**	**4**	**0**	**0**	**0**	**14:32**
2011-12♦	**Los Angeles**	**NHL**	**65**	**7**	**10**	**17**	**43**	**1**	**0**	**0**	**119**	**5.9**	**–7**	**32**	**43.8**	**14:19**	**20**	**3**	**8**	**11**	**32**	**0**	**0**	**2**	**13:14**
2012-13	**Los Angeles**	**NHL**	**33**	**2**	**12**	**14**	**18**	**0**	**0**	**0**	**61**	**3.3**	**–2**	**5**	**40.0**	**12:42**	**18**	**3**	**2**	**5**	**8**	**0**	**0**	**1**	**14:32**
	NHL Totals		**522**	**137**	**138**	**275**	**324**	**45**	**1**	**19**	**1144**	**12.0**		**1126**	**47.3**	**15:55**	**78**	**13**	**22**	**35**	**58**	**0**	**0**	**5**	**13:52**

NCAA Championship All-Tournament Team (2004) • AHL Second All-Star Team (2006)

Signed as a free agent by **Anaheim**, May 12, 2004. Signed as a free agent by **Edmonton**, August 2, 2007. Traded to **Los Angeles** by **Edmonton** for Colten Teubert, Los Angeles' 1st round choice (Oscar Klefborn) in 2011 Entry Draft and Los Angeles' 3rd round choice (Daniil Zharkov) in 2012 Entry Draft, February 28, 2011. Signed as a free agent by **Anaheim**, July 16, 2013.

PERREAULT, Mathieu

(pair-OH, MA-tyew) **WSH**

Center. Shoots left. 5'10", 185 lbs. Born, Drummondville, Que., January 5, 1988. Washington's 10th choice, 177th overall, in 2006 Entry Draft.

Season	Club	League	GP	G	A	Pts	PIM	PP	SH	GW	S	%	+/-	TF	F%	Min	GP	G	A	Pts	PIM	PP	SH	GW	Min
2004-05	Magog	QAAA	41	25	47	72	68	....	....	....	....	....	....	....	....	....	9	5	10	15	12	....	....	....	....
2005-06	Acadie-Bathurst	QMJHL	62	18	34	52	42	....	....	....	....	....	....	....	....	....	17	10	11	21	8	....	....	....	....
2006-07	Acadie-Bathurst	QMJHL	67	41	78	119	66	....	....	....	....	....	....	....	....	....	12	6	8	14	8	....	....	....	....
2007-08	Acadie-Bathurst	QMJHL	65	34	*80	*114	61	....	....	....	....	....	....	....	....	....	12	3	19	22	6	....	....	....	....
	Hershey Bears	AHL	....	....	....	....	....	....	....	....	....	....	....	....	....	....	3	0	0	0	0	....	....	....	....
2008-09	Hershey Bears	AHL	77	11	39	50	36	....	....	....	....	....	....	....	....	....	21	2	6	8	8	....	....	....	....
2009-10	**Washington**	**NHL**	**21**	**4**	**5**	**9**	**6**	**1**	**0**	**0**	**27**	**14.8**	**4**	**210**	**45.2**	**11:21**	....	....	....	....	....	....	....	....	....
	Hershey Bears	AHL	56	16	34	50	34	....	....	....	....	....	....	....	....	....	21	7	12	19	18	....	....	....	....
2010-11	**Washington**	**NHL**	**35**	**7**	**7**	**14**	**20**	**1**	**0**	**1**	**41**	**17.1**	**–3**	**305**	**45.6**	**11:53**	....	....	....	....	....	....	....	....	....
	Hershey Bears	AHL	34	11	24	35	38	....	....	....	....	....	....	....	....	....	6	3	3	6	6	....	....	....	....
2011-12	**Washington**	**NHL**	**64**	**16**	**14**	**30**	**24**	**2**	**0**	**4**	**60**	**26.7**	**9**	**451**	**50.8**	**12:02**	**4**	**0**	**0**	**0**	**0**	**0**	**0**	**0**	**10:43**
2012-13	HIFK Helsinki	Finland	7	1	6	7	6	....	....	....	....	....	....	....	....	....	....	....	....	....	....	....	....	....	....
	Washington	**NHL**	**39**	**6**	**11**	**17**	**20**	**2**	**0**	**1**	**47**	**12.8**	**7**	**325**	**51.7**	**11:40**	**7**	**1**	**3**	**4**	**0**	**0**	**0**	**0**	**13:38**
	NHL Totals		**159**	**33**	**37**	**70**	**70**	**6**	**0**	**6**	**175**	**18.9**		**1291**	**48.9**	**11:49**	**11**	**1**	**3**	**4**	**0**	**0**	**0**	**0**	**12:34**

QMJHL First All-Star Team (2007) • QMJHL Player of the Year (2007) • QMJHL Second All-Star Team (2008) • Canadian Major Junior Second All-Star Team (2007, 2008)

Signed as a free agent by **HIFK Helsinki** (Finland), November 24, 2012.

PERRON, David

(peh-RAWN, DAY-vihd) **EDM**

Left wing. Shoots right. 5'11", 196 lbs. Born, Sherbrooke, Que., May 28, 1988. St. Louis' 3rd choice, 26th overall, in 2007 Entry Draft.

Season	Club	League	GP	G	A	Pts	PIM	PP	SH	GW	S	%	+/-	TF	F%	Min	GP	G	A	Pts	PIM	PP	SH	GW	Min
2005-06	St-Jerome	QJHL	51	24	45	69	92	....	....	....	....	....	....	....	....	....	8	4	5	9	8	....	....	....	....
2006-07	Lewiston	QMJHL	70	39	44	83	75	....	....	....	....	....	....	....	....	....	17	12	16	28	22	....	....	....	....
2007-08	**St. Louis**	**NHL**	**62**	**13**	**14**	**27**	**38**	**3**	**0**	**1**	**68**	**19.1**	**16**	**14**	**35.7**	**12:33**	....	....	....	....	....	....	....	....	....
2008-09	**St. Louis**	**NHL**	**81**	**15**	**35**	**50**	**50**	**4**	**0**	**3**	**161**	**9.3**	**13**	**6**	**16.7**	**14:32**	**4**	**1**	**1**	**2**	**4**	**0**	**0**	**0**	**17:12**
2009-10	**St. Louis**	**NHL**	**82**	**20**	**27**	**47**	**60**	**5**	**1**	**2**	**166**	**12.0**	**–10**	**21**	**38.1**	**16:09**	....	....	....	....	....	....	....	....	....
2010-11	**St. Louis**	**NHL**	**10**	**5**	**2**	**7**	**12**	**0**	**0**	**0**	**29**	**17.2**	**7**	**0**	**0.0**	**18:25**	....	....	....	....	....	....	....	....	....
2011-12	**St. Louis**	**NHL**	**57**	**21**	**21**	**42**	**28**	**5**	**1**	**4**	**114**	**18.4**	**19**	**10**	**20.0**	**18:17**	**9**	**1**	**4**	**5**	**10**	**0**	**0**	**1**	**17:06**
2012-13	**St. Louis**	**NHL**	**48**	**10**	**15**	**25**	**44**	**2**	**0**	**2**	**84**	**11.9**	**0**	**22**	**36.4**	**18:00**	**6**	**0**	**2**	**2**	**6**	**0**	**0**	**0**	**17:11**
	NHL Totals		**340**	**84**	**114**	**198**	**232**	**19**	**2**	**12**	**622**	**13.5**		**73**	**32.9**	**15:48**	**19**	**2**	**7**	**9**	**20**	**0**	**0**	**1**	**17:09**

• Missed majority of 2010-11 due to head injury vs. San Jose, November 4, 2010. Traded to **Edmonton** by **St. Louis** for Magnus Paajarvi and a 2nd round choice in 2014 Entry Draft, July 10, 2013.

PERRY, Corey

(PAIR-ee, KOH-ree) **ANA**

Right wing. Shoots right. 6'3", 212 lbs. Born, Peterborough, Ont., May 16, 1985. Anaheim's 2nd choice, 28th overall, in 2003 Entry Draft.

Season	Club	League	GP	G	A	Pts	PIM	PP	SH	GW	S	%	+/-	TF	F%	Min	GP	G	A	Pts	PIM	PP	SH	GW	Min
2000-01	Peterborough	Minor-ON	64	69	46	115	20	....	....	....	....	....	....	....	....	....	3	3	0	3	0	....	....	....	....
2001-02	London Knights	OHL	67	28	31	59	56	....	....	....	....	....	....	....	....	....	12	2	3	5	30	....	....	....	....
2002-03	London Knights	OHL	67	25	53	78	145	....	....	....	....	....	....	....	....	....	14	7	16	23	27	....	....	....	....
2003-04	London Knights	OHL	66	40	*73	113	98	....	....	....	....	....	....	....	....	....	15	7	15	22	20	....	....	....	....
	Cincinnati	AHL	....	....	....	....	....	....	....	....	....	....	....	....	....	....	3	1	1	2	4	....	....	....	....
2004-05	London Knights	OHL	60	*47	*83	*130	117	....	....	....	....	....	....	....	....	....	18	11	*27	*38	46	....	....	....	....
2005-06	**Anaheim**	**NHL**	**56**	**13**	**12**	**25**	**50**	**4**	**0**	**2**	**98**	**13.3**	**1**	**11**	**27.3**	**11:34**	**11**	**0**	**3**	**3**	**16**	**0**	**0**	**0**	**9:33**
	Portland Pirates	AHL	19	16	18	34	32	....	....	....	....	....	....	....	....	....	1	1	0	1	0	....	....	....	....
2006-07♦	**Anaheim**	**NHL**	**82**	**17**	**27**	**44**	**55**	**4**	**0**	**3**	**194**	**8.8**	**12**	**21**	**42.9**	**12:28**	**21**	**6**	**9**	**15**	**37**	**1**	**0**	**1**	**16:30**
2007-08	**Anaheim**	**NHL**	**70**	**29**	**25**	**54**	**108**	**11**	**0**	**4**	**200**	**14.5**	**12**	**16**	**18.8**	**17:57**	**3**	**2**	**1**	**3**	**8**	**0**	**0**	**0**	**14:55**
2008-09	**Anaheim**	**NHL**	**78**	**32**	**40**	**72**	**109**	**10**	**0**	**8**	**283**	**11.3**	**10**	**31**	**29.0**	**18:36**	**13**	**8**	**6**	**14**	**36**	**2**	**0**	**1**	**22:00**
2009-10	**Anaheim**	**NHL**	**82**	**27**	**49**	**76**	**111**	**6**	**1**	**2**	**270**	**10.0**	**0**	**28**	**21.4**	**21:04**	....	....	....	....	....	....	....	....	....
	Canada	Olympics	7	4	1	5	2	....	....	....	....	....	....	....	....	....	....	....	....	....	....	....	....	....	....
2010-11	**Anaheim**	**NHL**	**82**	***50**	**48**	**98**	**104**	**14**	**4**	***11**	**290**	**17.2**	**9**	**22**	**40.9**	**22:19**	**6**	**2**	**6**	**8**	**4**	**1**	**1**	**1**	**25:15**
2011-12	**Anaheim**	**NHL**	**80**	**37**	**23**	**60**	**127**	**14**	**1**	**6**	**277**	**13.4**	**–7**	**48**	**39.6**	**21:23**	....	....	....	....	....	....	....	....	....
2012-13	**Anaheim**	**NHL**	**44**	**15**	**21**	**36**	**72**	**5**	**0**	**5**	**128**	**11.7**	**10**	**29**	**20.7**	**19:04**	**7**	**0**	**2**	**2**	**4**	**0**	**0**	**0**	**20:20**
	NHL Totals		**574**	**220**	**245**	**465**	**736**	**68**	**6**	**41**	**1740**	**12.6**		**206**	**31.1**	**18:16**	**61**	**18**	**27**	**45**	**105**	**4**	**1**	**3**	**17:38**

OHL First All-Star Team (2004, 2005) • Canadian Major Junior Second All-Star Team (2004) • Canadian Major Junior First All-Star Team (2005) • Memorial Cup All-Star Team (2005) • Stafford Smythe Memorial Trophy (Memorial Cup - MVP) (2005) • NHL First All-Star Team (2011) • Maurice "Rocket" Richard Trophy (2011) • Hart Memorial Trophy (2011)

Played in NHL All-Star Game (2008, 2011, 2012)

PESONEN, Harri

(pih-SOH-nihn, HAHR-ree) **N.J.**

Left wing. Shoots left. 6', 200 lbs. Born, Muurame, Finland, August 6, 1988.

Season	Club	League	GP	G	A	Pts	PIM	PP	SH	GW	S	%	+/-	TF	F%	Min	GP	G	A	Pts	PIM	PP	SH	GW	Min
2004-05	JYP Jyvaskyla U18	Fin-U18	19	6	3	9	6	....	....	....	....	....	....	....	....	....	....	....	....	....	....	....	....	....	....
2005-06	JYP Jyvaskyla U18	Fin-U18	33	16	17	33	55	....	....	....	....	....	....	....	....	....	....	....	....	....	....	....	....	....	....
2006-07	JyP Jyvaskyla Jr.	Fin-Jr.	46	11	25	36	14	....	....	....	....	....	....	....	....	....	3	2	0	2	2	....	....	....	....
2007-08	Suomi U20	Finland-2	7	1	2	3	2	....	....	....	....	....	....	....	....	....	....	....	....	....	....	....	....	....	....
	JyP Jyvaskyla Jr.	Fin-Jr.	37	21	24	45	63	....	....	....	....	....	....	....	....	....	9	4	13	17	33	....	....	....	....
	JYP Jyvaskyla	Finland	3	0	0	0	0	....	....	....	....	....	....	....	....	....	....	....	....	....	....	....	....	....	....
2008-09	JYP Jr.	FInland-Jr.	1	0	0	0	2	....	....	....	....	....	....	....	....	....	....	....	....	....	....	....	....	....	....
	D Team Jyvaskyla	Finland-2	10	10	6	16	10	....	....	....	....	....	....	....	....	....	....	....	....	....	....	....	....	....	....
	JYP Jyvaskyla	Finland	47	4	3	7	12	....	....	....	....	....	....	....	....	....	15	4	1	5	8	....	....	....	....
2009-10	JYP Jyvaskyla	Finland	25	4	2	6	35	....	....	....	....	....	....	....	....	....	....	....	....	....	....	....	....	....	....
	D Team Jyvaskyla	Finland-2	18	4	3	7	33	....	....	....	....	....	....	....	....	....	11	1	3	4	8	....	....	....	....
2010-11	D Team Jyvaskyla	Finland-2	2	0	3	3	4	....	....	....	....	....	....	....	....	....	....	....	....	....	....	....	....	....	....
	JYP Jyvaskyla	Finland	54	11	15	26	26	....	....	....	....	....	....	....	....	....	10	4	6	10	6	....	....	....	....
2011-12	JYP Jyvaskyla	Finland	60	21	14	35	52	....	....	....	....	....	....	....	....	....	14	6	5	11	37	....	....	....	....
2012-13	Albany Devils	AHL	64	14	17	31	24	....	....	....	....	....	....	....	....	....	....	....	....	....	....	....	....	....	....
	New Jersey	**NHL**	**4**	**0**	**0**	**0**	**2**	**0**	**0**	**0**	**3**	**0.0**	**–1**	**0**	**0.0**	**9:11**	....	....	....	....	....	....	....	....	....
	NHL Totals		**4**	**0**	**0**	**0**	**2**	**0**	**0**	**0**	**3**	**0.0**		**0**	**0.0**	**9:11**	....	....	....	....	....	....	....	....	....

Signed as a free agent by **New Jersey**, June 15, 2012.

PETERS, Warren

(PEE-tuhrz, WAHR-ihn)

Center. Shoots left. 6', 195 lbs. Born, Saskatoon, Sask., July 10, 1982.

			Regular Season														Playoffs								
Season	Club	League	GP	G	A	Pts	PIM	PP	SH	GW	S	%	+/-	TF	F%	Min	GP	G	A	Pts	PIM	PP	SH	GW	Min
1997-98	Saskatoon Blades	WHL	1	0	0	0	0	....	....	....	....	....	....	....	....	....	....	....	....	....	....	....	....	....	....
1998-99	Saskatoon Blades	WHL	53	8	6	14	111	....	....	....	....	....	....	....	....	....	....	....	....	....	....	....	....	....	....
99-2000	Saskatoon Blades	WHL	70	11	17	28	97	....	....	....	....	....	....	....	....	....	10	1	2	3	13	....	....	....	....
2000-01	Saskatoon Blades	WHL	63	27	14	41	111	....	....	....	....	....	....	....	....	....	....	....	....	....	....	....	....	....	....
2001-02	Saskatoon Blades	WHL	72	34	26	60	115	....	....	....	....	....	....	....	....	....	7	1	4	5	13	....	....	....	....
2002-03	Saskatoon Blades	WHL	71	31	44	75	108	....	....	....	....	....	....	....	....	....	6	1	6	7	6	....	....	....	....
	Portland Pirates	AHL	1	0	0	0	0	....	....	....	....	....	....	....	....	....	....	....	....	....	....	....	....	....	....
2003-04	Utah Grizzlies	AHL	55	4	4	8	63	....	....	....	....	....	....	....	....	....	....	....	....	....	....	....	....	....	....
	Idaho Steelheads	ECHL	21	6	7	13	33	....	....	....	....	....	....	....	....	....	....	....	....	....	....	....	....	....	....
2004-05	Idaho Steelheads	ECHL	69	23	23	46	131	....	....	....	....	....	....	....	....	....	4	0	1	1	12	....	....	....	....
2005-06	Omaha	AHL	77	15	10	25	133	....	....	....	....	....	....	....	....	....	....	....	....	....	....	....	....	....	....
2006-07	Omaha	AHL	79	17	16	33	95	....	....	....	....	....	....	....	....	....	6	2	1	3	4	....	....	....	....
2007-08	Quad City Flames	AHL	75	11	13	24	74	....	....	....	....	....	....	....	....	....	....	....	....	....	....	....	....	....	....
2008-09	**Calgary**	**NHL**	**16**	**1**	**0**	**1**	**12**	**0**	**0**	**0**	**13**	**7.7**	**–2**	**69**	**58.0**	**7:05**	**4**	**0**	**0**	**0**	**0**	**0**	**0**	**0**	**7:03**
	Quad City Flames	AHL	62	11	6	17	51	....	....	....	....	....	....	....	....	....	....	....	....	....	....	....	....	....	....
2009-10	**Dallas**	**NHL**	**11**	**1**	**0**	**1**	**2**	**0**	**0**	**0**	**8**	**12.5**	**1**	**80**	**48.8**	**7:13**	....	....	....	....	....	....	....	....	....
	Texas Stars	AHL	61	20	14	34	52	....	....	....	....	....	....	....	....	....	23	4	4	8	*56	....	....	....	....
2010-11	**Minnesota**	**NHL**	**11**	**1**	**0**	**1**	**4**	**0**	**0**	**0**	**11**	**9.1**	**–2**	**79**	**62.0**	**8:43**	....	....	....	....	....	....	....	....	....
	Houston Aeros	AHL	62	15	17	32	47	....	....	....	....	....	....	....	....	....	24	4	8	12	16	....	....	....	....
2011-12	**Minnesota**	**NHL**	**58**	**1**	**4**	**5**	**54**	**0**	**0**	**0**	**54**	**1.9**	**–15**	**465**	**54.8**	**10:35**	....	....	....	....	....	....	....	....	....
	Houston Aeros	AHL	20	7	4	11	46	....	....	....	....	....	....	....	....	....	....	....	....	....	....	....	....	....	....
2012-13	Wilkes-Barre	AHL	73	11	8	19	76	....	....	....	....	....	....	....	....	....	15	4	1	5	16	....	....	....	....
	NHL Totals		**96**	**4**	**4**	**8**	**72**	**0**	**0**	**0**	**86**	**4.7**		**693**	**55.3**	**9:24**	**4**	**0**	**0**	**0**	**0**	**0**	**0**	**0**	**7:03**

Signed as a free agent by **Calgary**, August 5, 2005. Signed as a free agent by **Dallas**, July 6, 2009. Signed as a free agent by **Minnesota**, July 2, 2010. Signed as a free agent by **Pittsburgh**, July 1, 2012.

PETERSEN, Toby

(PEE-tuhr-suhn, TOH-bee) **DAL**

Center. Shoots left. 5'10", 198 lbs. Born, Minneapolis, MN, October 27, 1978. Pittsburgh's 9th choice, 244th overall, in 1998 Entry Draft.

Season	Club	League	GP	G	A	Pts	PIM	PP	SH	GW	S	%	+/-	TF	F%	Min	GP	G	A	Pts	PIM	PP	SH	GW	Min
1995-96	Jefferson Jaguars	High-MN	25	29	30	59	....	....	....	....	....	....	....	....	....	....	....	....	....	....	....	....	....	....	....
1996-97	Colorado College	WCHA	40	17	21	38	18	....	....	....	....	....	....	....	....	....	....	....	....	....	....	....	....	....	....
1997-98	Colorado College	WCHA	40	16	17	33	34	....	....	....	....	....	....	....	....	....	....	....	....	....	....	....	....	....	....
1998-99	Colorado College	WCHA	21	12	12	24	2	....	....	....	....	....	....	....	....	....	....	....	....	....	....	....	....	....	....
99-2000	Colorado College	WCHA	37	14	19	33	8	....	....	....	....	....	....	....	....	....	....	....	....	....	....	....	....	....	....
2000-01	**Pittsburgh**	**NHL**	**12**	**2**	**6**	**8**	**4**	**0**	**0**	**1**	**25**	**8.0**	**3**	**39**	**35.9**	**13:22**	....	....	....	....	....	....	....	....	....
	Wilkes-Barre	AHL	73	26	41	67	22	....	....	....	....	....	....	....	....	....	21	7	6	13	4	....	....	....	....
2001-02	**Pittsburgh**	**NHL**	**79**	**8**	**10**	**18**	**4**	**1**	**1**	**0**	**116**	**6.9**	**–15**	**338**	**45.6**	**12:16**	....	....	....	....	....	....	....	....	....
2002-03	Wilkes-Barre	AHL	80	31	35	66	24	....	....	....	....	....	....	....	....	....	6	1	3	4	4	....	....	....	....
2003-04	Wilkes-Barre	AHL	62	15	29	44	4	....	....	....	....	....	....	....	....	....	21	2	10	12	12	....	....	....	....
2004-05	Edmonton	AHL	78	14	15	29	21	....	....	....	....	....	....	....	....	....	....	....	....	....	....	....	....	....	....
2005-06	**Edmonton**	**NHL**	....	....	....	....	....	....	....	....	....	....	....	....	....	....	**2**	**1**	**0**	**1**	**0**	**0**	**0**	**0**	**6:23**
	Iowa Stars	AHL	79	26	47	73	48	....	....	....	....	....	....	....	....	....	7	2	4	6	2	....	....	....	....
2006-07	**Edmonton**	**NHL**	**64**	**6**	**9**	**15**	**4**	**0**	**2**	**1**	**92**	**6.5**	**–18**	**214**	**48.1**	**13:40**	....	....	....	....	....	....	....	....	....
	Iowa Stars	AHL	7	2	6	8	0	....	....	....	....	....	....	....	....	....	....	....	....	....	....	....	....	....	....
2007-08	**Dallas**	**NHL**	**8**	**0**	**3**	**3**	**4**	**0**	**0**	**0**	**6**	**0.0**	**0**	**44**	**50.0**	**7:50**	**16**	**0**	**0**	**0**	**2**	**0**	**0**	**0**	**9:45**
	Iowa Stars	AHL	63	21	30	51	24	....	....	....	....	....	....	....	....	....	....	....	....	....	....	....	....	....	....
2008-09	**Dallas**	**NHL**	**57**	**4**	**7**	**11**	**14**	**0**	**0**	**0**	**80**	**5.0**	**1**	**283**	**45.2**	**11:25**	....	....	....	....	....	....	....	....	....
2009-10	**Dallas**	**NHL**	**78**	**9**	**6**	**15**	**6**	**0**	**1**	**0**	**110**	**8.2**	**3**	**171**	**44.4**	**10:55**	....	....	....	....	....	....	....	....	....
2010-11	**Dallas**	**NHL**	**60**	**2**	**4**	**6**	**8**	**0**	**2**	**0**	**58**	**3.4**	**–7**	**120**	**38.3**	**10:02**	....	....	....	....	....	....	....	....	....
	Texas Stars	AHL	1	0	1	1	2	....	....	....	....	....	....	....	....	....	....	....	....	....	....	....	....	....	....
2011-12	**Dallas**	**NHL**	**39**	**2**	**3**	**5**	**6**	**0**	**0**	**0**	**44**	**4.5**	**–7**	**7**	**42.9**	**7:39**	....	....	....	....	....	....	....	....	....
2012-13	Texas Stars	AHL	74	8	16	24	6	....	....	....	....	....	....	....	....	....	9	0	0	0	2	....	....	....	....
	Dallas	**NHL**	**1**	**0**	**0**	**0**	**0**	**0**	**0**	**0**	**0**	**0.0**	**0**	**2**	**50.0**	**6:40**	....	....	....	....	....	....	....	....	....
	NHL Totals		**398**	**33**	**48**	**81**	**50**	**1**	**6**	**2**	**531**	**6.2**		**1218**	**44.9**	**11:15**	**18**	**1**	**0**	**1**	**2**	**0**	**0**	**0**	**9:23**

WCHA All-Rookie Team (1997) • AHL All-Rookie Team (2001)

Signed as a free agent by **Edmonton**, July 30, 2004. Signed as a free agent by **Dallas**, July 6, 2007. • Missed majority of 2011-12 as a healthy reserve.

PETERSSON, Andre

(PEH-tuhr-suhn, AHN-dray) **OTT**

Right wing. Shoots right. 5'9", 172 lbs. Born, Olofstrom, Sweden, September 11, 1990. Ottawa's 4th choice, 109th overall, in 2008 Entry Draft.

Season	Club	League	GP	G	A	Pts	PIM	PP	SH	GW	S	%	+/-	TF	F%	Min	GP	G	A	Pts	PIM	PP	SH	GW	Min
2005-06	Tingsryds AIF U18	Swe-U18	9	5	3	8	0	....	....	....	....	....	....	....	....	....	....	....	....	....	....	....	....	....	....
2006-07	HV 71 U18	Swe-U18	10	14	10	24	6	....	....	....	....	....	....	....	....	....	2	1	2	3	0	....	....	....	....
	HV 71 Jr.	Swe-Jr.	6	1	1	2	8	....	....	....	....	....	....	....	....	....	....	....	....	....	....	....	....	....	....
2007-08	HV 71 U18	Swe-U18	4	4	5	9	4	....	....	....	....	....	....	....	....	....	....	....	....	....	....	....	....	....	....
	HV 71 Jr.	Swe-Jr.	36	16	22	38	34	....	....	....	....	....	....	....	....	....	3	0	0	0	2	....	....	....	....
2008-09	HV 71 Jonkoping	Sweden	10	0	1	1	0	....	....	....	....	....	....	....	....	....	....	....	....	....	....	....	....	....	....
	HV 71 Jr.	Swe-Jr.	36	24	31	55	28	....	....	....	....	....	....	....	....	....	7	7	4	11	8	....	....	....	....
2009-10	HV 71 Jonkoping	Sweden	37	10	5	15	14	....	....	....	....	....	....	....	....	....	6	0	1	1	2	....	....	....	....
	Boras HC	Sweden-2	1	1	0	1	0	....	....	....	....	....	....	....	....	....	....	....	....	....	....	....	....	....	....
2010-11	HV 71 Jonkoping	Sweden	31	8	4	12	18	....	....	....	....	....	....	....	....	....	....	....	....	....	....	....	....	....	....
2011-12	**Ottawa**	**NHL**	**1**	**0**	**0**	**0**	**0**	**0**	**0**	**0**	**0**	**0.0**	**0**	**0**	**0.0**	**5:02**	....	....	....	....	....	....	....	....	....
	Binghamton	AHL	60	23	21	44	20	....	....	....	....	....	....	....	....	....	....	....	....	....	....	....	....	....	....
2012-13	Binghamton	AHL	17	2	3	5	16	....	....	....	....	....	....	....	....	....	....	....	....	....	....	....	....	....	....
	NHL Totals		**1**	**0**	**0**	**0**	**0**	**0**	**0**	**0**	**0**	**0.0**		**0**	**0.0**	**5:02**	....	....	....	....	....	....	....	....	....

• Missed majority of 2012-13 due to hip injury vs. Adirondack (AHL), November 30, 2012 and resulting surgery.

PETIOT, Richard

(PEH-tee-awt, RIH-chuhrd)

Defense. Shoots left. 6'3", 215 lbs. Born, Daysland, Alta., August 20, 1982. Los Angeles' 6th choice, 116th overall, in 2001 Entry Draft.

Season	Club	League	GP	G	A	Pts	PIM	PP	SH	GW	S	%	+/-	TF	F%	Min	GP	G	A	Pts	PIM	PP	SH	GW	Min
2000-01	Camrose Kodiaks	AJHL	55	8	16	24	81	....	....	....	....	....	....	....	....	....	8	2	1	3	8	....	....	....	....
2001-02	Colorado College	WCHA	39	4	6	10	35	....	....	....	....	....	....	....	....	....	....	....	....	....	....	....	....	....	....
2002-03	Colorado College	WCHA	38	1	6	7	86	....	....	....	....	....	....	....	....	....	....	....	....	....	....	....	....	....	....
2003-04	Colorado College	WCHA	39	3	5	8	61	....	....	....	....	....	....	....	....	....	....	....	....	....	....	....	....	....	....
2004-05	Colorado College	WCHA	26	3	5	8	42	....	....	....	....	....	....	....	....	....	....	....	....	....	....	....	....	....	....
2005-06	**Los Angeles**	**NHL**	**2**	**0**	**0**	**0**	**2**	**0**	**0**	**0**	**1**	**0.0**	**–2**	**0**	**0.0**	**4:47**	....	....	....	....	....	....	....	....	....
	Manchester	AHL	63	4	10	14	52	....	....	....	....	....	....	....	....	....	7	1	0	1	6	....	....	....	....
2006-07	Manchester	AHL	13	1	1	2	25	....	....	....	....	....	....	....	....	....	2	0	0	0	2	....	....	....	....
2007-08	Manchester	AHL	40	2	5	7	56	....	....	....	....	....	....	....	....	....	....	....	....	....	....	....	....	....	....
2008-09	Toronto Marlies	AHL	45	3	11	14	59	....	....	....	....	....	....	....	....	....	....	....	....	....	....	....	....	....	....
	Tampa Bay	**NHL**	**11**	**0**	**3**	**3**	**21**	**0**	**0**	**0**	**10**	**0.0**	**5**	**0**	**0.0**	**20:37**	....	....	....	....	....	....	....	....	....
	Norfolk Admirals	AHL	1	0	0	0	0	....	....	....	....	....	....	....	....	....	....	....	....	....	....	....	....	....	....
2009-10	Rockford IceHogs	AHL	80	8	29	37	88	....	....	....	....	....	....	....	....	....	4	0	0	0	4	....	....	....	....
2010-11	**Edmonton**	**NHL**	**2**	**0**	**0**	**0**	**2**	**0**	**0**	**0**	**1**	**0.0**	**1**	**0**	**0.0**	**13:05**	....	....	....	....	....	....	....	....	....
	Oklahoma City	AHL	66	0	15	15	52	....	....	....	....	....	....	....	....	....	6	0	0	0	4	....	....	....	....
2011-12	Norfolk Admirals	AHL	6	0	0	0	7	....	....	....	....	....	....	....	....	....	....	....	....	....	....	....	....	....	....
2012-13	St. John's IceCaps	AHL	24	1	2	3	22	....	....	....	....	....	....	....	....	....	....	....	....	....	....	....	....	....	....
	NHL Totals		**15**	**0**	**3**	**3**	**25**	**0**	**0**	**0**	**12**	**0.0**		**0**	**0.0**	**17:30**	....	....	....	....	....	....	....	....	....

AJHL All-Rookie Team (2001) • AJHL South Second All-Star Team (2001)

• Missed majority of 2006-07 due to knee injury in rookie training camp, October 6, 2006. Signed as a free agent by **Toronto**, July 15, 2008. Traded to **Tampa Bay** by **Toronto** for Olaf Kolzig, Jamie Heward, Andy Rogers and Carolina's 4th round choice (previously acquired – later forfeited) in 2009 Entry Draft, March 4, 2009. Signed as a free agent by **Chicago**, July 9, 2009. Signed as a free agent by **Edmonton**, July 2, 2010. Signed as a free agent by **Tampa Bay**, July 2, 2011. • Missed remainder of 2011-12 and majority of 2012-13 due to knee injury vs. Binghamton (AHL), October 22, 2011 and resulting surgery.

PETRECKI, Nicholas

(peh-TREH-kee, NIH-koh-las) **S.J.**

Defense. Shoots left. 6'3", 230 lbs. Born, Schenectady, NY, July 11, 1989. San Jose's 2nd choice, 28th overall, in 2007 Entry Draft.

Season	Club	League	GP	G	A	Pts	PIM	PP	SH	GW	S	%	+/-	TF	F%	Min	Playoffs GP	G	A	Pts	PIM	PP	SH	GW	Min
2004-05	Capital District	EmJHL	53	5	18	23	159																		
2005-06	Omaha Lancers	USHL	53	0	3	3	110										5	0	0	0	0				
2006-07	Omaha Lancers	USHL	54	11	14	25	177										5	0	0	0	10				
2007-08	Boston College	H-East	42	5	7	12	*102																		
2008-09	Boston College	H-East	35	0	7	7	*161																		
2009-10	Worcester Sharks	AHL	65	2	12	14	106																		
2010-11	Worcester Sharks	AHL	67	3	11	14	129																		
2011-12	Worcester Sharks	AHL	68	1	8	9	107																		
2012-13	Binghamton	AHL	41	1	5	6	135																		
	San Jose	**NHL**	**1**	**0**	**0**	**0**	**0**	**0**	**0**	**0**	**0**	**0.0**	**0**	**0**	**0.0**	**11:58**									
	NHL Totals		**1**	**0**	**0**	**0**	**0**	**0**	**0**	**0**	**0**	**0.0**		**0**	**0.0**	**11:58**									

USHL Second All-Star Team (2007) • Yanick Dupre Memorial Award (AHL – Man of the Year) (2012)

PETRELL, Lennart

(peh-TREHL, LEH-nahrt)

Center. Shoots left. 6'3", 198 lbs. Born, Helsinki, Finland, April 13, 1984. Columbus' 8th choice, 190th overall, in 2004 Entry Draft.

Season	Club	League	GP	G	A	Pts	PIM	PP	SH	GW	S	%	+/-	TF	F%	Min	Playoffs GP	G	A	Pts	PIM	PP	SH	GW	Min
2000-01	K-Kissat Jr.	Fin-Jr.	4	3	2	5	0																		
	K-Kissat	Finland-4	1	0	0	0	0																		
2001-02	HIFK Helsinki U18	Fin-U18	18	10	8	18	12										8	2	0	2	2				
	HIFK Helsinki Jr.	Fin-Jr.	5	0	0	0	0																		
2002-03	HIFK Helsinki Jr.	Fin-Jr.	28	2	2	4	35										7	3	1	4	29				
2003-04	Suomi U20	Finland-2	7	1	0	1	0																		
	HIFK Helsinki Jr.	Fin-Jr.	33	11	17	28	28										10	6	7	13	2				
	HIFK Helsinki	Finland	8	0	0	0	2										1	0	0	0	0				
2004-05	HIFK Helsinki Jr.	Fin-Jr.	12	5	5	10	10										2	0	1	1	0				
	HIFK Helsinki	Finland	35	3	2	5	35										4	0	1	1	2				
2005-06	HIFK Helsinki	Finland	51	12	8	20	88										10	1	2	3	20				
2006-07	HIFK Helsinki	Finland	53	19	11	30	74										5	0	0	0	2				
2007-08	HIFK Helsinki	Finland	48	10	17	27	34										7	1	1	2	2				
2008-09	HIFK Helsinki	Finland	43	7	13	20	85										2	0	0	0	2				
2009-10	HIFK Helsinki	Finland	56	12	12	24	61										6	1	0	1	2				
2010-11	HIFK Helsinki	Finland	56	13	22	35	34										13	7	5	12	8				
2011-12	**Edmonton**	**NHL**	**60**	**4**	**5**	**9**	**45**	**0**	**1**	**0**	**36**	**11.1**	**–10**	**22**	**31.8**	**9:38**									
	Oklahoma City	AHL	9	2	2	4	4																		
2012-13	HIFK Helsinki	Finland	26	11	0	11	12																		
	Edmonton	**NHL**	**35**	**3**	**6**	**9**	**4**	**0**	**1**	**0**	**23**	**13.0**	**–4**	**13**	**23.1**	**11:32**									
	NHL Totals		**95**	**7**	**11**	**18**	**49**	**0**	**2**	**0**	**59**	**11.9**		**35**	**28.6**	**10:20**									

Signed as a free agent by **Edmonton**, June 15, 2011. Signed as a free agent by **HIFK Helsinki** (Finland), September 20, 2012.

PETROVIC, Alex

(peh-TROH-vihch, AL-ehx) **FLA**

Defense. Shoots right. 6'4", 205 lbs. Born, Edmonton, Alta., March 3, 1992. Florida's 5th choice, 36th overall, in 2010 Entry Draft.

Season	Club	League	GP	G	A	Pts	PIM	PP	SH	GW	S	%	+/-	TF	F%	Min	Playoffs GP	G	A	Pts	PIM	PP	SH	GW	Min
2007-08	Edmonton MLAC	AMHL	31	3	8	11	80																		
	Red Deer Rebels	WHL	10	1	0	1	2																		
2008-09	Red Deer Rebels	WHL	66	1	12	13	70																		
2009-10	Red Deer Rebels	WHL	57	8	19	27	87										4	0	0	0	4				
2010-11	Red Deer Rebels	WHL	69	7	50	57	140										9	0	6	6	23				
2011-12	Red Deer Rebels	WHL	68	12	36	48	141																		
	San Antonio	AHL	5	0	1	1	0										9	2	4	6	14				
2012-13	San Antonio	AHL	55	4	13	17	102																		
	Florida	**NHL**	**6**	**0**	**0**	**0**	**25**	**0**	**0**	**0**	**5**	**0.0**	**–8**	**0**	**0.0**	**18:47**									
	NHL Totals		**6**	**0**	**0**	**0**	**25**	**0**	**0**	**0**	**5**	**0.0**		**0**	**0.0**	**18:47**									

WHL East Second All-Star Team (2011) • WHL East First All-Star Team (2012) • WHL Defenseman of the Year (2012)

PETRY, Jeff

(PEH-tree, JEHF) **EDM**

Defense. Shoots right. 6'3", 196 lbs. Born, Ann Arbor, MI, December 9, 1987. Edmonton's 1st choice, 45th overall, in 2006 Entry Draft.

Season	Club	League	GP	G	A	Pts	PIM	PP	SH	GW	S	%	+/-	TF	F%	Min	Playoffs GP	G	A	Pts	PIM	PP	SH	GW	Min
2004-05	St. Mary's Prep	High-MI	23	2	8	10											6	2	5	7					
2005-06	Det. Caesers	MWEHL	33	7	21	28	24																		
	Des Moines	USHL	48	1	14	15	68										11	2	5	7	8				
2006-07	Des Moines	USHL	55	18	27	45	71										8	0	6	6	10				
2007-08	Michigan State	CCHA	42	3	21	24	28																		
2008-09	Michigan State	CCHA	38	2	12	14	32																		
2009-10	Michigan State	CCHA	38	4	25	29	26																		
	Springfield	AHL	8	0	3	3	2																		
2010-11	**Edmonton**	**NHL**	**35**	**1**	**4**	**5**	**10**	**0**	**0**	**0**	**41**	**2.4**	**–12**	**0**	**0.0**	**20:22**									
	Oklahoma City	AHL	41	7	17	24	18										6	0	1	1	4				
2011-12	**Edmonton**	**NHL**	**73**	**2**	**23**	**25**	**26**	**1**	**0**	**0**	**111**	**1.8**	**–7**	**0**	**0.0**	**21:46**									
	Oklahoma City	AHL	2	0	1	1	2																		
2012-13	**Edmonton**	**NHL**	**48**	**3**	**9**	**12**	**29**	**0**	**1**	**0**	**66**	**4.5**	**1**	**1**	**0.0**	**21:55**									
	NHL Totals		**156**	**6**	**36**	**42**	**65**	**1**	**1**	**0**	**218**	**2.8**		**1**	**0.0**	**21:30**									

USHL First All-Star Team (2007) • USHL Defenseman of the Year (2007) • CCHA All-Rookie Team (2008) • CCHA Second All-Star Team (2010) • NCAA West Second All-American Team (2010)

PEVERLEY, Rich

(PEH-vuhr-lee, RIHTCH) **DAL**

Center. Shoots right. 6', 195 lbs. Born, Guelph, Ont., July 8, 1982.

Season	Club	League	GP	G	A	Pts	PIM	PP	SH	GW	S	%	+/-	TF	F%	Min	Playoffs GP	G	A	Pts	PIM	PP	SH	GW	Min
1998-99	Kitchener	ON-Jr.B	STATISTICS NOT AVAILABLE																						
99-2000	Milton Merchants	ON-Jr.A	STATISTICS NOT AVAILABLE																						
2000-01	St. Lawrence	ECAC	29	2	4	6	4																		
2001-02	St. Lawrence	ECAC	34	10	21	31	18																		
2002-03	St. Lawrence	ECAC	34	15	23	38	12																		
2003-04	St. Lawrence	ECAC	41	17	25	42	34																		
2004-05	Portland Pirates	AHL	1	0	0	0	0																		
	South Carolina	ECHL	69	30	28	58	72										4	2	2	4	6				
2005-06	Milwaukee	AHL	65	12	34	46	44										21	2	9	11	18				
	Reading Royals	ECHL	11	4	11	15	4																		
2006-07	Milwaukee	AHL	66	30	38	68	62										4	1	2	3	8				
	Nashville	**NHL**	**13**	**0**	**1**	**1**	**0**	**0**	**0**	**0**	**9**	**0.0**	**–1**	**45**	**48.9**	**7:31**									
2007-08	**Nashville**	**NHL**	**33**	**5**	**5**	**10**	**8**	**0**	**0**	**2**	**43**	**11.6**	**4**	**132**	**46.2**	**10:20**	**6**	**0**	**2**	**2**	**0**	**0**	**0**	**0**	**8:52**
	Milwaukee	AHL	45	14	40	54	50										3	1	0	1	0				
2008-09	**Nashville**	**NHL**	**27**	**2**	**7**	**9**	**15**	**0**	**0**	**0**	**42**	**4.8**	**–3**	**130**	**49.2**	**12:08**									
	Atlanta	**NHL**	**39**	**13**	**22**	**35**	**18**	**2**	**1**	**5**	**75**	**17.3**	**16**	**554**	**52.4**	**18:49**									
2009-10	**Atlanta**	**NHL**	**82**	**22**	**33**	**55**	**36**	**7**	**2**	**7**	**166**	**13.3**	**–14**	**1193**	**54.2**	**18:40**									
2010-11	**Atlanta**	**NHL**	**59**	**14**	**20**	**34**	**35**	**6**	**1**	**2**	**161**	**8.7**	**–16**	**1020**	**55.5**	**19:13**									
	♦ **Boston**	**NHL**	**23**	**4**	**3**	**7**	**2**	**0**	**1**	**1**	**40**	**10.0**	**–1**	**156**	**58.3**	**15:46**	**25**	**4**	**8**	**12**	**17**	**0**	**0**	**2**	**16:11**
2011-12	**Boston**	**NHL**	**57**	**11**	**31**	**42**	**22**	**1**	**0**	**1**	**112**	**9.8**	**20**	**332**	**61.1**	**16:54**	**7**	**3**	**2**	**5**	**4**	**0**	**0**	**0**	**21:12**
2012-13	JYP Jyvaskyla	Finland	29	9	14	23	47																		
	Boston	**NHL**	**47**	**6**	**12**	**18**	**16**	**2**	**0**	**0**	**95**	**6.3**	**–9**	**361**	**58.5**	**15:15**	**21**	**2**	**0**	**2**	**12**	**1**	**0**	**0**	**14:42**
	NHL Totals		**380**	**77**	**134**	**211**	**152**	**18**	**5**	**18**	**743**	**10.4**		**3923**	**54.9**	**16:20**	**59**	**9**	**12**	**21**	**33**	**1**	**0**	**2**	**15:30**

Signed as a free agent by **Nashville**, January 18, 2007. Claimed on waivers by **Atlanta** from **Nashville**, January 10, 2009. Traded to **Boston** by **Atlanta** with Boris Valabik for Blake Wheeler and Mark Stuart, February 18, 2011. Signed as a free agent by **Jyvaskyla** (Finland), September 24, 2012. Traded to **Dallas** by **Boston** with Tyler Seguin and Ryan Button for Loui Eriksson, Joe Morrow, Reilly Smith and Matt Fraser, July 4, 2013.

PHANEUF, Dion
(fah-NUF, DEE-awn) **TOR**

Defense. Shoots left. 6'3", 214 lbs. Born, Edmonton, Alta., April 10, 1985. Calgary's 1st choice, 9th overall, in 2003 Entry Draft.

			Regular Season														Playoffs								
Season	Club	League	GP	G	A	Pts	PIM	PP	SH	GW	S	%	+/-	TF	F%	Min	GP	G	A	Pts	PIM	PP	SH	GW	Min
2000-01	Southgate Lions	AMBHL	35	15	50	65	208	....	....	....	....	....	....	....	....	....	4	3	4	7	15	....	....	....	....
2001-02	Red Deer Rebels	WHL	67	5	12	17	170	....	....	....	....	....	....	....	....	....	21	0	2	2	14	....	....	....	....
2002-03	Red Deer Rebels	WHL	71	16	14	30	185	....	....	....	....	....	....	....	....	....	23	7	7	14	34	....	....	....	....
2003-04	Red Deer Rebels	WHL	62	19	24	43	126	....	....	....	....	....	....	....	....	....	19	2	9	11	30	....	....	....	....
2004-05	Red Deer Rebels	WHL	55	24	32	56	73	....	....	....	....	....	....	....	....	....	7	1	4	5	12	....	....	....	....
2005-06	**Calgary**	**NHL**	**82**	**20**	**29**	**49**	**93**	**16**	**0**	**7**	**242**	**8.3**	**5**	**0**	**0.0**	**21:44**	**7**	**1**	**0**	**1**	**7**	**1**	**0**	**0**	**18:37**
2006-07	**Calgary**	**NHL**	**79**	**17**	**33**	**50**	**98**	**13**	**0**	**4**	**230**	**7.4**	**10**	**0**	**0.0**	**25:40**	**6**	**1**	**0**	**1**	**7**	**1**	**0**	**0**	**26:24**
2007-08	**Calgary**	**NHL**	**82**	**17**	**43**	**60**	**182**	**10**	**1**	**4**	**263**	**6.5**	**12**	**0**	**0.0**	**26:25**	**7**	**3**	**4**	**7**	**4**	**1**	**0**	**0**	**27:07**
2008-09	**Calgary**	**NHL**	**80**	**11**	**36**	**47**	**100**	**4**	**0**	**4**	**277**	**4.0**	**–11**	**0**	**0.0**	**26:32**	**5**	**0**	**3**	**3**	**4**	**0**	**0**	**0**	**24:48**
2009-10	**Calgary**	**NHL**	**55**	**10**	**12**	**22**	**49**	**5**	**0**	**2**	**138**	**7.2**	**3**	**0**	**0.0**	**23:14**	....	....	....	....	....	....	....	....	....
	Toronto	**NHL**	**26**	**2**	**8**	**10**	**34**	**0**	**0**	**1**	**87**	**2.3**	**–2**	**0**	**0.0**	**26:22**	....	....	....	....	....	....	....	....	....
2010-11	**Toronto**	**NHL**	**66**	**8**	**22**	**30**	**88**	**3**	**0**	**1**	**190**	**4.2**	**–2**	**0**	**0.0**	**25:18**	....	....	....	....	....	....	....	....	....
2011-12	**Toronto**	**NHL**	**82**	**12**	**32**	**44**	**92**	**7**	**0**	**1**	**202**	**5.9**	**–10**	**0**	**0.0**	**25:17**	....	....	....	....	....	....	....	....	....
2012-13	**Toronto**	**NHL**	**48**	**9**	**19**	**28**	**65**	**3**	**0**	**1**	**88**	**10.2**	**–4**	**0**	**0.0**	**25:11**	**7**	**1**	**2**	**3**	**6**	**0**	**0**	**0**	**25:22**
	NHL Totals		**600**	**106**	**234**	**340**	**801**	**61**	**1**	**25**	**1717**	**6.2**		**0**	**0.0**	**25:01**	**32**	**6**	**9**	**15**	**28**	**3**	**0**	**0**	**24:23**

WHL East First All-Star Team (2004, 2005) • WHL Defenseman of the Year (2004, 2005) • Canadian Major Junior First All-Star Team (2004, 2005) • NHL All-Rookie Team (2006) • NHL First All-Star Team (2008)

Played in NHL All-Star Game (2007, 2008, 2012)

Traded to **Toronto** by **Calgary** with Fredrik Sjostrom and Keith Aulie for Matt Stajan, Niklas Hagman, Jamal Mayers and Ian White, January 31, 2010.

PHILLIPS, Chris
(FIHL-ihps, KRIHS) **OTT**

Defense. Shoots left. 6'3", 221 lbs. Born, Calgary, Alta., March 9, 1978. Ottawa's 1st choice, 1st overall, in 1996 Entry Draft.

			Regular Season														Playoffs								
Season	Club	League	GP	G	A	Pts	PIM	PP	SH	GW	S	%	+/-	TF	F%	Min	GP	G	A	Pts	PIM	PP	SH	GW	Min
1993-94	Fort McMurray	AJHL	56	6	16	22	72	....	....	....	....	....	....	....	....	....	10	0	3	3	16	....	....	....	....
1994-95	Fort McMurray	AJHL	48	16	32	48	127	....	....	....	....	....	....	....	....	....	11	4	2	6	10	....	....	....	....
1995-96	Prince Albert	WHL	61	10	30	40	97	....	....	....	....	....	....	....	....	....	18	2	12	14	30	....	....	....	....
1996-97	Prince Albert	WHL	32	3	23	26	58	....	....	....	....	....	....	....	....	....	....	....	....	....	....	....	....	....	....
	Lethbridge	WHL	26	4	18	22	28	....	....	....	....	....	....	....	....	....	19	4	*21	25	20	....	....	....	....
1997-98	**Ottawa**	**NHL**	**72**	**5**	**11**	**16**	**38**	**2**	**0**	**2**	**107**	**4.7**	**2**	....	....	....	**11**	**0**	**2**	**2**	**2**	**0**	**0**	**0**	....
1998-99	**Ottawa**	**NHL**	**34**	**3**	**3**	**6**	**32**	**2**	**0**	**0**	**51**	**5.9**	**–5**	**0**	**0.0**	**18:06**	**3**	**0**	**0**	**0**	**0**	**0**	**0**	**0**	**13:50**
99-2000	**Ottawa**	**NHL**	**65**	**5**	**14**	**19**	**39**	**0**	**0**	**1**	**96**	**5.2**	**12**	**0**	**0.0**	**16:50**	**6**	**0**	**1**	**1**	**4**	**0**	**0**	**0**	**18:17**
2000-01	**Ottawa**	**NHL**	**73**	**2**	**12**	**14**	**31**	**2**	**0**	**0**	**77**	**2.6**	**8**	**1**	**0.0**	**21:28**	**1**	**1**	**0**	**1**	**0**	**0**	**0**	**0**	**20:52**
2001-02	**Ottawa**	**NHL**	**63**	**6**	**16**	**22**	**29**	**1**	**0**	**1**	**103**	**5.8**	**5**	**0**	**0.0**	**19:31**	**12**	**0**	**0**	**0**	**12**	**0**	**0**	**0**	**21:44**
2002-03	**Ottawa**	**NHL**	**78**	**3**	**16**	**19**	**71**	**2**	**0**	**1**	**97**	**3.1**	**7**	**0**	**0.0**	**20:13**	**18**	**2**	**4**	**6**	**12**	**0**	**0**	**1**	**21:36**
2003-04	**Ottawa**	**NHL**	**82**	**7**	**16**	**23**	**46**	**0**	**0**	**1**	**93**	**7.5**	**15**	**1**	**100.0**	**20:50**	**7**	**1**	**0**	**1**	**12**	**1**	**0**	**0**	**20:26**
2004-05	Brynas IF Gavle	Sweden	27	5	3	8	45	....	....	....	....	....	....	....	....	....	....	....	....	....	....	....	....	....	....
	Brynas IF Gavle	Sweden-Q	9	1	2	3	2	....	....	....	....	....	....	....	....	....	....	....	....	....	....	....	....	....	....
2005-06	**Ottawa**	**NHL**	**69**	**1**	**18**	**19**	**90**	**0**	**0**	**0**	**79**	**1.3**	**19**	**0**	**0.0**	**20:52**	**9**	**2**	**0**	**2**	**6**	**0**	**0**	**0**	**21:41**
2006-07	**Ottawa**	**NHL**	**82**	**8**	**18**	**26**	**80**	**0**	**1**	**3**	**94**	**8.5**	**36**	**2**	**0.0**	**22:22**	**20**	**0**	**0**	**0**	**24**	**0**	**0**	**0**	**23:11**
2007-08	**Ottawa**	**NHL**	**81**	**5**	**13**	**18**	**56**	**1**	**0**	**1**	**80**	**6.3**	**15**	**1**	**0.0**	**22:29**	**4**	**0**	**0**	**0**	**4**	**0**	**0**	**0**	**22:00**
2008-09	**Ottawa**	**NHL**	**82**	**6**	**16**	**22**	**66**	**0**	**1**	**0**	**88**	**6.8**	**–14**	**0**	**0.0**	**21:52**	....	....	....	....	....	....	....	....	....
2009-10	**Ottawa**	**NHL**	**82**	**8**	**16**	**24**	**45**	**1**	**1**	**2**	**82**	**9.8**	**8**	**0**	**0.0**	**22:21**	**6**	**0**	**0**	**0**	**4**	**0**	**0**	**0**	**24:57**
2010-11	**Ottawa**	**NHL**	**82**	**1**	**8**	**9**	**32**	**0**	**0**	**0**	**81**	**1.2**	**–35**	**0**	**0.0**	**21:31**	....	....	....	....	....	....	....	....	....
2011-12	**Ottawa**	**NHL**	**80**	**5**	**14**	**19**	**16**	**4**	**0**	**1**	**85**	**5.9**	**12**	**0**	**0.0**	**19:07**	**7**	**0**	**1**	**1**	**4**	**0**	**0**	**0**	**21:34**
2012-13	**Ottawa**	**NHL**	**48**	**5**	**9**	**14**	**43**	**1**	**0**	**0**	**89**	**5.6**	**–5**	**0**	**0.0**	**21:03**	**10**	**0**	**1**	**1**	**21**	**0**	**0**	**0**	**21:08**
	NHL Totals		**1073**	**70**	**200**	**270**	**714**	**16**	**3**	**13**	**1302**	**5.4**		**5**	**20.0**	**20:48**	**114**	**6**	**9**	**15**	**105**	**1**	**0**	**1**	**21:35**

WHL Rookie of the Year (1996) • WHL East First All-Star Team (1997) • Canadian Major Junior First All-Star Team (1997) • Memorial Cup All-Star Team (1997)

• Missed majority of 1998-99 due to ankle injury vs. Buffalo, December 30, 1998. Signed as a free agent by **Brynas** (Sweden), November 2, 2004.

PICARD, Alexandre
(pee-KARD, al-ehx-AHN-druh)

Defense. Shoots left. 6'3", 215 lbs. Born, Gatineau, Que., July 5, 1985. Philadelphia's 5th choice, 85th overall, in 2003 Entry Draft.

			Regular Season														Playoffs								
Season	Club	League	GP	G	A	Pts	PIM	PP	SH	GW	S	%	+/-	TF	F%	Min	GP	G	A	Pts	PIM	PP	SH	GW	Min
2000-01	Gatineau	QAAA	42	6	15	21	38	....	....	....	....	....	....	....	....	....	11	0	1	1	8	....	....	....	....
2001-02	Halifax	QMJHL	59	2	12	14	28	....	....	....	....	....	....	....	....	....	13	2	3	5	6	....	....	....	....
2002-03	Halifax	QMJHL	71	4	30	34	64	....	....	....	....	....	....	....	....	....	25	1	5	6	14	....	....	....	....
2003-04	Cape Breton	QMJHL	57	10	26	36	44	....	....	....	....	....	....	....	....	....	5	0	0	0	0	....	....	....	....
2004-05	Halifax	QMJHL	68	15	23	38	46	....	....	....	....	....	....	....	....	....	13	1	5	6	14	....	....	....	....
	Philadelphia	AHL	....	....	....	....	....	....	....	....	....	....	....	....	....	....	2	0	0	0	0	....	....	....	....
2005-06	**Philadelphia**	**NHL**	**6**	**0**	**0**	**0**	**4**	**0**	**0**	**0**	**9**	**0.0**	**–2**	**0**	**0.0**	**9:33**	....	....	....	....	....	....	....	....	....
	Philadelphia	AHL	75	7	26	33	82	....	....	....	....	....	....	....	....	....	....	....	....	....	....	....	....	....	....
2006-07	**Philadelphia**	**NHL**	**62**	**3**	**19**	**22**	**17**	**1**	**0**	**0**	**56**	**5.4**	**–19**	**0**	**0.0**	**18:29**	....	....	....	....	....	....	....	....	....
	Philadelphia	AHL	6	1	2	3	2	....	....	....	....	....	....	....	....	....	....	....	....	....	....	....	....	....	....
2007-08	**Philadelphia**	**NHL**	**4**	**0**	**0**	**0**	**2**	**0**	**0**	**0**	**3**	**0.0**	**–3**	**0**	**0.0**	**13:02**	....	....	....	....	....	....	....	....	....
	Philadelphia	AHL	53	8	30	38	31	....	....	....	....	....	....	....	....	....	....	....	....	....	....	....	....	....	....
	Tampa Bay	**NHL**	**20**	**3**	**3**	**6**	**8**	**1**	**0**	**1**	**21**	**14.3**	**–9**	**0**	**0.0**	**21:54**	....	....	....	....	....	....	....	....	....
	Norfolk Admirals	AHL	1	0	0	0	0	....	....	....	....	....	....	....	....	....	....	....	....	....	....	....	....	....	....
2008-09	**Ottawa**	**NHL**	**47**	**6**	**8**	**14**	**8**	**6**	**0**	**1**	**72**	**8.3**	**–2**	**0**	**0.0**	**18:52**	....	....	....	....	....	....	....	....	....
2009-10	**Ottawa**	**NHL**	**45**	**4**	**11**	**15**	**20**	**1**	**0**	**1**	**64**	**6.3**	**–2**	**0**	**0.0**	**19:03**	....	....	....	....	....	....	....	....	....
	Carolina	**NHL**	**9**	**0**	**0**	**0**	**6**	**0**	**0**	**0**	**7**	**0.0**	**2**	**0**	**0.0**	**15:04**	....	....	....	....	....	....	....	....	....
2010-11	**Montreal**	**NHL**	**43**	**3**	**5**	**8**	**17**	**2**	**0**	**1**	**49**	**6.1**	**0**	**0**	**0.0**	**16:26**	....	....	....	....	....	....	....	....	....
2011-12	**Pittsburgh**	**NHL**	**17**	**0**	**4**	**4**	**4**	**0**	**0**	**0**	**10**	**0.0**	**4**	**0**	**0.0**	**13:09**	....	....	....	....	....	....	....	....	....
	Wilkes-Barre	AHL	43	8	13	21	20	....	....	....	....	....	....	....	....	....	12	0	6	6	6	....	....	....	....
2012-13	HC Lev Praha	KHL	11	1	1	2	4	....	....	....	....	....	....	....	....	....	....	....	....	....	....	....	....	....	....
	NHL Totals		**253**	**19**	**50**	**69**	**86**	**11**	**0**	**4**	**291**	**6.5**		**0**	**0.0**	**17:48**	....	....	....	....	....	....	....	....	....

QMJHL Second All-Star Team (2005) • Jack A. Butterfield Trophy (AHL – Playoff MVP) (2013)

Traded to **Tampa Bay** by **Philadelphia** with Philadelphia's 2nd round choice (Richard Panik) in 2009 Entry Draft for Vaclav Prospal, February 25, 2008. Traded to **Ottawa** by **Tampa Bay** with Filip Kuba and San Jose's 1st round choice (previously acquired, later traded to Columbus, later traded to NY Islanders, later traded to Anahaim - Anaheim selected Kyle Palmieri) in 2009 Entry Draft for Andrej Meszaros, August 29, 2008. Traded to **Carolina** by **Ottawa** with Ottawa's 2nd round choice (later traded to Edmonton - Edmonton selected Martin Marincin) in 2010 Entry Draft for Matt Cullen, February 12, 2010. Signed as a free agent by **Montreal**, July 31, 2010. Signed as a free agent by **Pittsburgh**, July 5, 2011. Signed as a free agent by **Lev Praha** (KHL), July 25, 2012.

PICARD, Alexandre
(pee-KARD, al-ehx-AHN-druh)

Left wing. Shoots left. 6'2", 206 lbs. Born, Les Saules, Que., October 9, 1985. Columbus' 1st choice, 8th overall, in 2004 Entry Draft.

			Regular Season														Playoffs								
Season	Club	League	GP	G	A	Pts	PIM	PP	SH	GW	S	%	+/-	TF	F%	Min	GP	G	A	Pts	PIM	PP	SH	GW	Min
2000-01	St-Francois	QAAA	5	1	1	2	0	....	....	....	....	....	....	....	....	....	....	....	....	....	....	....	....	....	....
2001-02	St-Francois	QAAA	41	21	30	51	48	....	....	....	....	....	....	....	....	....	8	2	7	9	8	....	....	....	....
	Sherbrooke	QMJHL	6	0	3	3	0	....	....	....	....	....	....	....	....	....	....	....	....	....	....	....	....	....	....
2002-03	Sherbrooke	QMJHL	66	14	15	29	41	....	....	....	....	....	....	....	....	....	12	4	0	4	10	....	....	....	....
2003-04	Lewiston	QMJHL	69	39	41	80	88	....	....	....	....	....	....	....	....	....	7	7	4	11	6	....	....	....	....
2004-05	Lewiston	QMJHL	65	40	45	85	160	....	....	....	....	....	....	....	....	....	8	5	2	7	18	....	....	....	....
2005-06	**Columbus**	**NHL**	**17**	**0**	**0**	**0**	**14**	**0**	**0**	**0**	**10**	**0.0**	**–2**	**3**	**33.3**	**9:09**	....	....	....	....	....	....	....	....	....
	Syracuse Crunch	AHL	45	15	15	30	52	....	....	....	....	....	....	....	....	....	6	1	0	1	19	....	....	....	....
2006-07	**Columbus**	**NHL**	**23**	**0**	**1**	**1**	**6**	**0**	**0**	**0**	**20**	**0.0**	**–3**	**0**	**0.0**	**7:49**	....	....	....	....	....	....	....	....	....
	Syracuse Crunch	AHL	48	11	18	29	73	....	....	....	....	....	....	....	....	....	....	....	....	....	....	....	....	....	....
2007-08	**Columbus**	**NHL**	**3**	**0**	**0**	**0**	**2**	**0**	**0**	**0**	**1**	**0.0**	**0**	**0**	**0.0**	**6:46**	....	....	....	....	....	....	....	....	....
	Syracuse Crunch	AHL	50	7	13	20	116	....	....	....	....	....	....	....	....	....	13	2	1	3	14	....	....	....	....
2008-09	**Columbus**	**NHL**	**15**	**0**	**1**	**1**	**26**	**0**	**0**	**0**	**10**	**0.0**	**–1**	**0**	**0.0**	**6:53**	....	....	....	....	....	....	....	....	....
	Syracuse Crunch	AHL	49	22	10	32	107	....	....	....	....	....	....	....	....	....	....	....	....	....	....	....	....	....	....
2009-10	**Columbus**	**NHL**	**9**	**0**	**0**	**0**	**10**	**0**	**0**	**0**	**12**	**0.0**	**–3**	**0**	**0.0**	**7:13**	....	....	....	....	....	....	....	....	....
	Syracuse Crunch	AHL	42	17	18	35	111	....	....	....	....	....	....	....	....	....	....	....	....	....	....	....	....	....	....
	San Antonio	AHL	16	9	6	15	14	....	....	....	....	....	....	....	....	....	....	....	....	....	....	....	....	....	....
2010-11	San Antonio	AHL	59	24	22	46	84	....	....	....	....	....	....	....	....	....	....	....	....	....	....	....	....	....	....
2011-12	Norfolk Admirals	AHL	42	6	19	25	65	....	....	....	....	....	....	....	....	....	18	9	7	16	48	....	....	....	....
2012-13	Geneve	Swiss	32	14	7	21	82	....	....	....	....	....	....	....	....	....	6	2	4	6	4	....	....	....	....
	NHL Totals		**67**	**0**	**2**	**2**	**58**	**0**	**0**	**0**	**53**	**0.0**		**3**	**33.3**	**7:49**	....	....	....	....	....	....	....	....	....

QMJHL Second All-Star Team (2004)

Traded to **Phoenix** by **Columbus** for Chad Kolarik, March 3, 2010. Signed as a free agent by **Tampa Bay**, July 7, 2011. Signed as a free agent by **Geneve** (Swiss), July 17, 2012.

						Regular Season													Playoffs					
Season	Club	League	GP	G	A	Pts	PIM	PP	SH	GW	S	%	+/-	TF	F%	Min	GP	G	A	Pts	PIM	PP	SH	GW	Min

PIETRANGELO, Alex

(puh-TRAN-geh-loh, AL-ehx) **ST.L.**

Defense. Shoots right. 6'3", 201 lbs. Born, King City, Ont., January 18, 1990. St. Louis' 1st choice, 4th overall, in 2008 Entry Draft.

2005-06	Tor. Jr. Canadiens	GTHL	44	13	31	44	33	....	....	....	....	....	....	....	....	....	....	....	....	....	....	....	....	....	....
2006-07	Mississauga	OHL	59	7	45	52	45	....	....	....	....	....	....	....	....	....	4	0	0	0	8	....	....	....	....
2007-08	Niagara Ice Dogs	OHL	60	13	40	53	94	....	....	....	....	....	....	....	....	....	6	5	4	9	4	....	....	....	....
2008-09	Niagara Ice Dogs	OHL	36	8	21	29	32	....	....	....	....	....	....	....	....	....	12	1	5	6	20	....	....	....	....
	St. Louis	**NHL**	**8**	**0**	**1**	**1**	**2**	**0**	**0**	**0**	**7**	**0.0**	**0**	**0**	**0.0**	**16:31**	....	....	....	....	....	....	....	....	....
	Peoria Rivermen	AHL	1	0	0	0	4	....	....	....	....	....	....	....	....	....	7	0	3	3	2	....	....	....	....
2009-10	**St. Louis**	**NHL**	**9**	**1**	**1**	**2**	**6**	**0**	**0**	**0**	**7**	**14.3**	**-9**	**0**	**0.0**	**16:34**	....	....	....	....	....	....	....	....	....
	Barrie Colts	OHL	25	9	20	29	27	....	....	....	....	....	....	....	....	....	17	2	12	14	8	....	....	....	....
2010-11	**St. Louis**	**NHL**	**79**	**11**	**32**	**43**	**19**	**4**	**0**	**1**	**161**	**6.8**	**18**	**0**	**0.0**	**22:00**	....	....	....	....	....	....	....	....	....
2011-12	**St. Louis**	**NHL**	**81**	**12**	**39**	**51**	**36**	**6**	**0**	**6**	**202**	**5.9**	**16**	**0**	**0.0**	**24:44**	**8**	**0**	**5**	**5**	**0**	**0**	**0**	**0**	**25:26**
2012-13	**St. Louis**	**NHL**	**47**	**5**	**19**	**24**	**10**	**2**	**0**	**0**	**93**	**5.4**	**0**	**0**	**0.0**	**25:07**	**6**	**1**	**1**	**2**	**2**	**0**	**0**	**0**	**26:34**
	NHL Totals		**224**	**29**	**92**	**121**	**73**	**12**	**0**	**7**	**470**	**6.2**		**0**	**0.0**	**23:14**	**14**	**1**	**6**	**7**	**2**	**0**	**0**	**0**	**25:55**

NHL Second All-Star Team (2012)

• Missed majority of 2009-10 as a healthy reserve.

PINIZZOTTO, Steve

(pih-nih-ZAW-toh, STEEV) **FLA**

Center. Shoots right. 6'1", 200 lbs. Born, Mississauga, Ont., April 26, 1984.

2001-02	Oakville Blades	ON-Jr.A	34	10	16	26	40	....	....	....	....	....	....	....	....	....	....	....	....	....	....	....	....	....	....
2002-03	Oakville Blades	ON-Jr.A	44	16	24	40	152	....	....	....	....	....	....	....	....	....	2	0	0	0	2	....	....	....	....
2003-04	Oakville Blades	ON-Jr.A	39	17	34	51	177	....	....	....	....	....	....	....	....	....	....	....	....	....	....	....	....	....	....
2004-05	Oakville Blades	ON-Jr.A	48	33	62	95	86	....	....	....	....	....	....	....	....	....	....	....	....	....	....	....	....	....	....
2005-06	RIT Tigers	NCAA	20	7	6	13	32	....	....	....	....	....	....	....	....	....	....	....	....	....	....	....	....	....	....
2006-07	RIT Tigers	AH	34	13	31	44	76	....	....	....	....	....	....	....	....	....	....	....	....	....	....	....	....	....	....
	Hershey Bears	AHL	5	0	0	0	4	....	....	....	....	....	....	....	....	....	....	....	....	....	....	....	....	....	....
2007-08	Hershey Bears	AHL	23	0	4	4	12	....	....	....	....	....	....	....	....	....	5	0	0	0	13	....	....	....	....
	South Carolina	ECHL	40	15	17	32	58	....	....	....	....	....	....	....	....	....	10	1	2	3	34	....	....	....	....
2008-09	Hershey Bears	AHL	45	4	7	11	61	....	....	....	....	....	....	....	....	....	21	3	2	5	28	....	....	....	....
	South Carolina	ECHL	11	4	6	10	19	....	....	....	....	....	....	....	....	....	....	....	....	....	....	....	....	....	....
2009-10	Hershey Bears	AHL	69	13	28	41	124	....	....	....	....	....	....	....	....	....	21	5	3	8	33	....	....	....	....
2010-11	Hershey Bears	AHL	68	17	25	42	178	....	....	....	....	....	....	....	....	....	6	2	2	4	6	....	....	....	....
2011-12			DID NOT PLAY – INJURED																						
2012-13	Chicago Wolves	AHL	24	4	8	12	29	....	....	....	....	....	....	....	....	....	....	....	....	....	....	....	....	....	....
	Vancouver	**NHL**	**12**	**0**	**0**	**0**	**29**	**0**	**0**	**0**	**9**	**0.0**	**-6**	**0**	**0.0**	**10:00**	**1**	**0**	**0**	**0**	**0**	**0**	**0**	**0**	**3:57**
	NHL Totals		**12**	**0**	**0**	**0**	**29**	**0**	**0**	**0**	**9**	**0.0**		**0**	**0.0**	**10:00**	**1**	**0**	**0**	**0**	**0**	**0**	**0**	**0**	**3:57**

Signed as a free agent by **Washington**, March 16, 2007. Signed as a free agent by **Vancouver**, July 3, 2011. • Missed 2011-12 due to shoulder injury in pre-season vs. San Jose, September 25, 2011. • Missed majority of 2012-13 due to recurring groin injury and as a healthy reserve. Signed as a free agent by **Florida**, August 5, 2013.

PIRRI, Brandon

(PIHR-ee, BRAN-duhn) **CHI**

Center. Shoots left. 6', 183 lbs. Born, Toronto, Ont., April 10, 1991. Chicago's 2nd choice, 59th overall, in 2009 Entry Draft.

2006-07	Tor. Young Nats	GTHL	44	54	72	128	18	....	....	....	....	....	....	....	....	....	....	....	....	....	....	....	....	....	....
2007-08	Streetsville Derbys	ON-Jr.A	40	18	32	50	42	....	....	....	....	....	....	....	....	....	....	....	....	....	....	....	....	....	....
2008-09	Streetsville Derbys	ON-Jr.A	18	21	28	49	24	....	....	....	....	....	....	....	....	....	....	....	....	....	....	....	....	....	....
	Georgetown	ON-Jr.A	26	25	20	45	22	....	....	....	....	....	....	....	....	....	14	8	13	21	10	....	....	....	....
2009-10	RPI Engineers	ECAC	39	11	*32	43	67	....	....	....	....	....	....	....	....	....	....	....	....	....	....	....	....	....	....
2010-11	**Chicago**	**NHL**	**1**	**0**	**0**	**0**	**0**	**0**	**0**	**0**	**1**	**0.0**	**-1**	**6**	**33.3**	**8:56**	....	....	....	....	....	....	....	....	....
	Rockford IceHogs	AHL	70	12	31	43	50	....	....	....	....	....	....	....	....	....	....	....	....	....	....	....	....	....	....
2011-12	**Chicago**	**NHL**	**5**	**0**	**2**	**2**	**0**	**0**	**0**	**0**	**5**	**0.0**	**2**	**54**	**48.2**	**13:31**	....	....	....	....	....	....	....	....	....
	Rockford IceHogs	AHL	66	23	33	56	36	....	....	....	....	....	....	....	....	....	....	....	....	....	....	....	....	....	....
2012-13	Rockford IceHogs	AHL	76	22	*53	*75	72	....	....	....	....	....	....	....	....	....	....	....	....	....	....	....	....	....	....
	Chicago	**NHL**	**1**	**0**	**0**	**0**	**0**	**0**	**0**	**0**	**2**	**0.0**	**0**	**14**	**42.9**	**17:55**	....	....	....	....	....	....	....	....	....
	NHL Totals		**7**	**0**	**2**	**2**	**0**	**0**	**0**	**0**	**8**	**0.0**		**74**	**45.9**	**13:29**	....	....	....	....	....	....	....	....	....

ECAC All-Rookie Team (2010) • John P. Sollenberger Trophy (AHL - Top Scorer) (2013)

PISKULA, Joe

(pihs-KOO-luh, JOH) **NSH**

Defense. Shoots left. 6'3", 214 lbs. Born, Antigo, WI, July 5, 1984.

2002-03	Chicago Steel	USHL	13	0	0	0	18	....	....	....	....	....	....	....	....	....	....	....	....	....	....	....	....	....	....
	Des Moines	USHL	32	2	6	8	18	....	....	....	....	....	....	....	....	....	4	0	1	1	4	....	....	....	....
2003-04	Des Moines	USHL	58	2	4	6	68	....	....	....	....	....	....	....	....	....	3	0	1	1	0	....	....	....	....
2004-05	U. of Wisconsin	WCHA	40	0	6	6	24	....	....	....	....	....	....	....	....	....	....	....	....	....	....	....	....	....	....
2005-06	U. of Wisconsin	WCHA	34	2	9	11	22	....	....	....	....	....	....	....	....	....	....	....	....	....	....	....	....	....	....
2006-07	U. of Wisconsin	WCHA	38	1	4	5	34	....	....	....	....	....	....	....	....	....	....	....	....	....	....	....	....	....	....
	Los Angeles	**NHL**	**5**	**0**	**0**	**0**	**6**	**0**	**0**	**0**	**4**	**0.0**	**-3**	**0**	**0.0**	**9:59**	....	....	....	....	....	....	....	....	....
2007-08	Manchester	AHL	55	0	7	7	57	....	....	....	....	....	....	....	....	....	4	0	0	0	4	....	....	....	....
2008-09	Manchester	AHL	67	0	12	12	40	....	....	....	....	....	....	....	....	....	....	....	....	....	....	....	....	....	....
2009-10	Manchester	AHL	72	2	10	12	51	....	....	....	....	....	....	....	....	....	16	2	2	4	12	....	....	....	....
2010-11	Abbotsford Heat	AHL	71	1	11	12	73	....	....	....	....	....	....	....	....	....	....	....	....	....	....	....	....	....	....
2011-12	**Calgary**	**NHL**	**5**	**0**	**0**	**0**	**2**	**0**	**0**	**0**	**2**	**0.0**	**-5**	**0**	**0.0**	**10:54**	....	....	....	....	....	....	....	....	....
	Abbotsford Heat	AHL	59	3	15	18	48	....	....	....	....	....	....	....	....	....	6	0	1	1	0	....	....	....	....
2012-13	Abbotsford Heat	AHL	46	2	8	10	51	....	....	....	....	....	....	....	....	....	....	....	....	....	....	....	....	....	....
	Milwaukee	AHL	23	1	3	4	15	....	....	....	....	....	....	....	....	....	4	0	0	0	0	....	....	....	....
	NHL Totals		**10**	**0**	**0**	**0**	**8**	**0**	**0**	**0**	**6**	**0.0**		**0**	**0.0**	**10:26**	....	....	....	....	....	....	....	....	....

Signed as a free agent by **Los Angeles**, March 21, 2007. Signed as a free agent by **Abbotsford** (AHL), October 6, 2010. Signed as a free agent by **Calgary**, July 1, 2011. Traded to **Nashville** by **Calgary** for Brian McGrattan, February 28, 2013.

PITKANEN, Joni

(PIHT-ka-nuhn, YOH-nee) **CAR**

Defense. Shoots left. 6'3", 220 lbs. Born, Oulu, Finland, September 19, 1983. Philadelphia's 1st choice, 4th overall, in 2002 Entry Draft.

1998-99	Karpat Oulu U18	Fin-U18	30	1	5	6	12	....	....	....	....	....	....	....	....	....	....	....	....	....	....	....	....	....	....
99-2000	Karpat Oulu U18	Fin-U18	36	12	14	26	26	....	....	....	....	....	....	....	....	....	6	1	4	5	2	....	....	....	....
	Karpat Oulu Jr.	Fin-Jr.	2	0	0	0	0	....	....	....	....	....	....	....	....	....	....	....	....	....	....	....	....	....	....
2000-01	Karpat Oulu Jr.	Fin-Jr.	24	6	11	17	77	....	....	....	....	....	....	....	....	....	....	....	....	....	....	....	....	....	....
	Karpat Oulu	Finland	21	0	0	0	10	....	....	....	....	....	....	....	....	....	2	0	0	0	2	....	....	....	....
2001-02	Karpat Oulu Jr.	Fin-Jr.	....	....	....	....	....	....	....	....	....	....	....	....	....	....	1	0	0	0	0	....	....	....	....
	Karpat Oulu	Finland	49	4	15	19	65	....	....	....	....	....	....	....	....	....	4	0	0	0	12	....	....	....	....
2002-03	Karpat Oulu	Finland	35	5	15	20	38	....	....	....	....	....	....	....	....	....	....	....	....	....	....	....	....	....	....
2003-04	**Philadelphia**	**NHL**	**71**	**8**	**19**	**27**	**44**	**5**	**0**	**2**	**133**	**6.0**	**15**	**0**	**0.0**	**16:35**	**15**	**0**	**3**	**3**	**6**	**0**	**0**	**0**	**12:13**
2004-05	Philadelphia	AHL	76	6	35	41	105	....	....	....	....	....	....	....	....	....	21	3	4	7	16	....	....	....	....
2005-06	**Philadelphia**	**NHL**	**58**	**13**	**33**	**46**	**78**	**5**	**0**	**3**	**118**	**11.0**	**22**	**0**	**0.0**	**23:43**	**6**	**0**	**2**	**2**	**2**	**0**	**0**	**0**	**24:12**
	Finland	Olympics	DID NOT PLAY – INJURED																						
2006-07	**Philadelphia**	**NHL**	**77**	**4**	**39**	**43**	**88**	**1**	**0**	**0**	**137**	**2.9**	**-25**	**0**	**0.0**	**24:33**	....	....	....	....	....	....	....	....	....
2007-08	**Edmonton**	**NHL**	**63**	**8**	**18**	**26**	**56**	**1**	**1**	**1**	**101**	**7.9**	**-5**	**0**	**0.0**	**24:07**	....	....	....	....	....	....	....	....	....
2008-09	**Carolina**	**NHL**	**71**	**7**	**26**	**33**	**58**	**2**	**0**	**3**	**147**	**4.8**	**11**	**0**	**0.0**	**24:48**	**18**	**0**	**8**	**8**	**16**	**0**	**0**	**0**	**26:29**
2009-10	**Carolina**	**NHL**	**71**	**6**	**40**	**46**	**72**	**1**	**0**	**1**	**161**	**3.7**	**-11**	**0**	**0.0**	**27:23**	....	....	....	....	....	....	....	....	....
	Finland	Olympics	5	1	2	3	*29	....	....	....	....	....	....	....	....	....	....	....	....	....	....	....	....	....	....
2010-11	**Carolina**	**NHL**	**72**	**5**	**30**	**35**	**60**	**1**	**0**	**1**	**144**	**3.5**	**-2**	**0**	**0.0**	**25:01**	....	....	....	....	....	....	....	....	....
2011-12	**Carolina**	**NHL**	**30**	**5**	**12**	**17**	**16**	**2**	**0**	**2**	**62**	**8.1**	**-15**	**0**	**0.0**	**22:18**	....	....	....	....	....	....	....	....	....
2012-13	**Carolina**	**NHL**	**22**	**1**	**8**	**9**	**12**	**0**	**0**	**0**	**34**	**2.9**	**2**	**0**	**0.0**	**22:49**	....	....	....	....	....	....	....	....	....
	NHL Totals		**535**	**57**	**225**	**282**	**484**	**18**	**1**	**13**	**1037**	**5.5**		**0**	**0.0**	**23:38**	**39**	**0**	**13**	**13**	**24**	**0**	**0**	**0**	**20:39**

NHL All-Rookie Team (2004)

Traded to **Edmonton** by **Philadelphia** with Geoff Sanderson and Philadelphia's 3rd round choice (Cameron Abney) in 2009 Entry Draft for Joffrey Lupul and Jason Smith, July 1, 2007. Traded to **Carolina** by **Edmonton** for Erik Cole, July 1, 2008. • Missed majority of 2011-12 due to head injury at Calgary, December 6, 2011. • Missed majority of 2012-13 due to lower-body and heel injuries.

PLANTE, Alex
(PLAWNT, AL-ehx)

Defense. Shoots right. 6'4", 230 lbs. Born, Brandon, Man., May 9, 1989. Edmonton's 2nd choice, 15th overall, in 2007 Entry Draft.

			Regular Season														Playoffs								
Season	Club	League	GP	G	A	Pts	PIM	PP	SH	GW	S	%	+/-	TF	F%	Min	GP	G	A	Pts	PIM	PP	SH	GW	Min
2004-05	Brandon	MMHL	37	5	21	26	120	....	....	....	....	....	....	....	....	....	....	....	....	....	....	....	....	....	....
	Calgary Hitmen	WHL	8	0	0	0	6	....	....	....	....	....	....	....	....	....	11	0	0	0	17	....	....	....	....
2005-06	Calgary Hitmen	WHL	54	1	3	4	72	....	....	....	....	....	....	....	....	....	13	0	0	0	6	....	....	....	....
2006-07	Calgary Hitmen	WHL	58	8	30	38	81	....	....	....	....	....	....	....	....	....	13	5	6	11	14	....	....	....	....
2007-08	Calgary Hitmen	WHL	36	1	1	2	28	....	....	....	....	....	....	....	....	....	15	0	4	4	10	....	....	....	....
2008-09	Calgary Hitmen	WHL	68	8	37	45	157	....	....	....	....	....	....	....	....	....	18	6	9	15	41	....	....	....	....
2009-10	**Edmonton**	**NHL**	**4**	**0**	**1**	**1**	**2**	**0**	**0**	**0**	**4**	**0.0**	**1**	**0**	**0.0**	**13:36**	....	....	....	....	....	....	....	....	....
	Springfield	AHL	49	2	7	9	122	....	....	....	....	....	....	....	....	....	....	....	....	....	....	....	....	....	....
2010-11	**Edmonton**	**NHL**	**3**	**0**	**0**	**0**	**11**	**0**	**0**	**0**	**5**	**0.0**	**–2**	**0**	**0.0**	**15:03**	....	....	....	....	....	....	....	....	....
	Oklahoma City	AHL	73	2	15	17	138	....	....	....	....	....	....	....	....	....	5	0	0	0	12	....	....	....	....
2011-12	**Edmonton**	**NHL**	**3**	**0**	**1**	**1**	**2**	**0**	**0**	**0**	**0**	**0.0**	**0**	**0**	**0.0**	**10:39**	....	....	....	....	....	....	....	....	....
	Oklahoma City	AHL	41	1	13	14	84	....	....	....	....	....	....	....	....	....	14	0	1	1	26	....	....	....	....
2012-13	Oklahoma City	AHL	49	1	2	3	114	....	....	....	....	....	....	....	....	....	2	0	0	0	2	....	....	....	....
	NHL Totals		**10**	**0**	**2**	**2**	**15**	**0**	**0**	**0**	**9**	**0.0**		**0**	**0.0**	**13:09**	....	....	....	....	....	....	....	....	....

Signed as a free agent by **Dornbirner** (Austria). July 18, 2013.

PLEKANEC, Tomas
(pleh-KA-nehts, TAW-muhs) **MTL**

Left wing. Shoots left. 5'11", 198 lbs. Born, Kladno, Czech., October 31, 1982. Montreal's 4th choice, 71st overall, in 2001 Entry Draft.

			Regular Season														Playoffs								
Season	Club	League	GP	G	A	Pts	PIM	PP	SH	GW	S	%	+/-	TF	F%	Min	GP	G	A	Pts	PIM	PP	SH	GW	Min
1996-97	Kladno U17	CzR-U17	13	1	3	4	....	....	....	....	....	....	....	....	....	....	....	....	....	....	....	....	....	....	....
1997-98	HC Kladno U17	CzR-U17	45	38	26	64	....	....	....	....	....	....	....	....	....	....	....	....	....	....	....	....	....	....	....
1998-99	HC Kladno Jr.	CzRep-Jr.	53	22	20	42	....	....	....	....	....	....	....	....	....	....	....	....	....	....	....	....	....	....	....
99-2000	HC Kladno Jr.	CzRep-Jr.	43	14	16	30	....	....	....	....	....	....	....	....	....	....	....	....	....	....	....	....	....	....	....
	Kralupy	CzRep-3	6	2	2	4	2	....	....	....	....	....	....	....	....	....	....	....	....	....	....	....	....	....	....
	HC CKD Slany	CzRep-3	3	0	1	1	6	....	....	....	....	....	....	....	....	....	....	....	....	....	....	....	....	....	....
2000-01	Kladno	CzRep	47	9	9	18	24	....	....	....	....	....	....	....	....	....	....	....	....	....	....	....	....	....	....
	HC Kladno Jr.	CzRep-Jr.	9	6	4	10	4	....	....	....	....	....	....	....	....	....	....	....	....	....	....	....	....	....	....
2001-02	Kladno	CzRep	48	7	16	23	28	....	....	....	....	....	....	....	....	....	....	....	....	....	....	....	....	....	....
	BK Mlada Boleslav	CzRep-3	6	6	3	9	14	....	....	....	....	....	....	....	....	....	....	....	....	....	....	....	....	....	....
	Kladno	CzRep-Q	5	0	1	1	0	....	....	....	....	....	....	....	....	....	....	....	....	....	....	....	....	....	....
2002-03	Hamilton	AHL	77	19	27	46	74	....	....	....	....	....	....	....	....	....	13	3	2	5	8	....	....	....	....
2003-04	**Montreal**	**NHL**	**2**	**0**	**0**	**0**	**0**	**0**	**0**	**0**	**0**	**0.0**	**0**	**11**	**45.5**	**9:02**	....	....	....	....	....	....	....	....	....
	Hamilton	AHL	74	23	43	66	90	....	....	....	....	....	....	....	....	....	10	2	5	7	6	....	....	....	....
2004-05	Hamilton	AHL	80	29	35	64	68	....	....	....	....	....	....	....	....	....	4	2	4	6	6	....	....	....	....
2005-06	**Montreal**	**NHL**	**67**	**9**	**20**	**29**	**32**	**1**	**0**	**0**	**99**	**9.1**	**4**	**708**	**50.3**	**13:15**	**6**	**0**	**4**	**4**	**6**	**0**	**0**	**0**	**18:00**
	Hamilton	AHL	2	0	0	0	2	....	....	....	....	....	....	....	....	....	....	....	....	....	....	....	....	....	....
2006-07	**Montreal**	**NHL**	**81**	**20**	**27**	**47**	**36**	**5**	**2**	**1**	**150**	**13.3**	**10**	**1159**	**48.3**	**15:59**	....	....	....	....	....	....	....	....	....
2007-08	**Montreal**	**NHL**	**81**	**29**	**40**	**69**	**42**	**12**	**2**	**6**	**186**	**15.6**	**15**	**1381**	**49.5**	**18:05**	**12**	**4**	**5**	**9**	**2**	**2**	**0**	**0**	**18:02**
2008-09	**Montreal**	**NHL**	**80**	**20**	**19**	**39**	**54**	**6**	**3**	**2**	**202**	**9.9**	**–9**	**1351**	**50.6**	**17:15**	**3**	**0**	**0**	**0**	**4**	**0**	**0**	**0**	**13:36**
2009-10	**Montreal**	**NHL**	**82**	**25**	**45**	**70**	**50**	**3**	**1**	**4**	**216**	**11.6**	**5**	**1615**	**49.0**	**19:58**	**19**	**4**	**7**	**11**	**20**	**1**	**0**	**1**	**19:57**
	Czech Republic	Olympics	5	2	1	3	2	....	....	....	....	....	....	....	....	....	....	....	....	....	....	....	....	....	....
2010-11	**Montreal**	**NHL**	**77**	**22**	**35**	**57**	**60**	**3**	**1**	**4**	**227**	**9.7**	**8**	**1577**	**50.0**	**20:15**	**7**	**2**	**3**	**5**	**2**	**0**	**1**	**0**	**23:20**
2011-12	**Montreal**	**NHL**	**81**	**17**	**35**	**52**	**56**	**5**	**3**	**2**	**220**	**7.7**	**–15**	**1678**	**49.1**	**20:45**	....	....	....	....	....	....	....	....	....
2012-13	Rytiri Kladno	CzRep	32	21	25	46	38	....	....	....	....	....	....	....	....	....	....	....	....	....	....	....	....	....	....
	Montreal	**NHL**	**47**	**14**	**19**	**33**	**24**	**4**	**0**	**2**	**133**	**10.5**	**3**	**961**	**50.6**	**19:13**	**5**	**0**	**4**	**4**	**2**	**0**	**0**	**0**	**20:53**
	NHL Totals		**598**	**156**	**240**	**396**	**354**	**39**	**12**	**21**	**1433**	**10.9**		**10441**	**49.6**	**18:06**	**52**	**10**	**23**	**33**	**36**	**3**	**1**	**1**	**19:28**

Signed as a free agent by **Kladno** (CzRep), September 16, 2012.

POCK, Thomas
(POHK, TAW-muhs)

Defense. Shoots left. 6'1", 210 lbs. Born, Klagenfurt, Austria, December 2, 1981.

			Regular Season														Playoffs								
Season	Club	League	GP	G	A	Pts	PIM	PP	SH	GW	S	%	+/-	TF	F%	Min	GP	G	A	Pts	PIM	PP	SH	GW	Min
1998-99	Klagenfurt Jr.	Austria-Jr.	31	0	0	0	2	....	....	....	....	....	....	....	....	....	....	....	....	....	....	....	....	....	....
99-2000	Klagenfurter AC	Austria	15	3	8	11	14	....	....	....	....	....	....	....	....	....	....	....	....	....	....	....	....	....	....
	Klagenfurt	Alpenliga	33	4	11	15	48	....	....	....	....	....	....	....	....	....	....	....	....	....	....	....	....	....	....
2000-01	Massachusetts	H-East	33	6	6	12	59	....	....	....	....	....	....	....	....	....	....	....	....	....	....	....	....	....	....
2001-02	Massachusetts	H-East	23	5	7	12	26	....	....	....	....	....	....	....	....	....	....	....	....	....	....	....	....	....	....
	Austria	Nat-Tm	10	1	2	3	4	....	....	....	....	....	....	....	....	....	....	....	....	....	....	....	....	....	....
	Austria	Olympics	4	0	0	0	2	....	....	....	....	....	....	....	....	....	....	....	....	....	....	....	....	....	....
2002-03	Massachusetts	H-East	37	17	20	37	46	....	....	....	....	....	....	....	....	....	....	....	....	....	....	....	....	....	....
	Austria	WC-A	6	1	0	1	4	....	....	....	....	....	....	....	....	....	....	....	....	....	....	....	....	....	....
2003-04	Massachusetts	H-East	37	16	25	41	48	....	....	....	....	....	....	....	....	....	....	....	....	....	....	....	....	....	....
	NY Rangers	**NHL**	**6**	**2**	**2**	**4**	**0**	**0**	**0**	**0**	**8**	**25.0**	**–4**	**0**	**0.0**	**18:38**	....	....	....	....	....	....	....	....	....
2004-05	Hartford	AHL	50	1	5	6	55	....	....	....	....	....	....	....	....	....	6	0	1	1	8	....	....	....	....
	Charlotte	ECHL	3	0	2	2	2	....	....	....	....	....	....	....	....	....	....	....	....	....	....	....	....	....	....
	Austria	Oly-Q	3	0	1	1	2	....	....	....	....	....	....	....	....	....	....	....	....	....	....	....	....	....	....
2005-06	**NY Rangers**	**NHL**	**8**	**1**	**1**	**2**	**4**	**0**	**0**	**0**	**15**	**6.7**	**–3**	**0**	**0.0**	**15:10**	....	....	....	....	....	....	....	....	....
	Hartford	AHL	67	15	46	61	99	....	....	....	....	....	....	....	....	....	6	0	3	3	15	....	....	....	....
2006-07	**NY Rangers**	**NHL**	**44**	**4**	**4**	**8**	**16**	**0**	**0**	**0**	**76**	**5.3**	**–4**	**0**	**0.0**	**16:14**	**4**	**0**	**3**	**3**	**4**	**0**	**0**	**0**	**13:29**
	Hartford	AHL	4	0	1	1	2	....	....	....	....	....	....	....	....	....	....	....	....	....	....	....	....	....	....
2007-08	**NY Rangers**	**NHL**	**1**	**0**	**0**	**0**	**0**	**0**	**0**	**0**	**2**	**0.0**	**–2**	**0**	**0.0**	**18:53**	....	....	....	....	....	....	....	....	....
	Hartford	AHL	74	7	37	44	63	....	....	....	....	....	....	....	....	....	5	0	0	0	8	....	....	....	....
2008-09	**NY Islanders**	**NHL**	**59**	**1**	**2**	**3**	**35**	**0**	**0**	**0**	**51**	**2.0**	**–17**	**0**	**0.0**	**12:42**	....	....	....	....	....	....	....	....	....
2009-10	Rapperswil	Swiss	49	11	22	33	58	....	....	....	....	....	....	....	....	....	7	2	7	9	8	....	....	....	....
2010-11	Rapperswil	Swiss	47	8	17	25	40	....	....	....	....	....	....	....	....	....	10	2	3	5	4	....	....	....	....
2011-12	MODO	Sweden	55	9	16	25	32	....	....	....	....	....	....	....	....	....	6	0	0	0	6	....	....	....	....
2012-13	Lake Erie	AHL	62	11	22	33	61	....	....	....	....	....	....	....	....	....	....	....	....	....	....	....	....	....	....
	NHL Totals		**118**	**8**	**9**	**17**	**55**	**0**	**0**	**0**	**152**	**5.3**		**0**	**0.0**	**14:32**	**4**	**0**	**3**	**3**	**4**	**0**	**0**	**0**	**13:29**

Hockey East Second All-Star Team (2003) • Hockey East First All-Star Team (2004) • NCAA East First All-American Team (2004) • AHL Second All-Star Team (2006)

Signed as a free agent by **NY Rangers**, March 23, 2004. Claimed on waivers by **NY Islanders** from **NY Rangers**, September 29, 2008. Signed as a free agent by **Rapperswil** (Swiss), May 28, 2009. Signed as a free agent by **MODO** (Sweden), April 28, 2011. Signed as a free agent by **Colorado**, July 13, 2012.

POLAK, Roman
(POH-lahk, ROH-muhn) **ST.L.**

Defense. Shoots right. 6', 236 lbs. Born, Ostrava, Czech., April 28, 1986. St. Louis' 6th choice, 180th overall, in 2004 Entry Draft.

			Regular Season														Playoffs								
Season	Club	League	GP	G	A	Pts	PIM	PP	SH	GW	S	%	+/-	TF	F%	Min	GP	G	A	Pts	PIM	PP	SH	GW	Min
2001-02	HC Ostrava Jr.	CzRep-Jr.	46	4	9	13	84	....	....	....	....	....	....	....	....	....	....	....	....	....	....	....	....	....	....
2002-03	HC Ostrava Jr.	CzRep-Jr.	32	3	12	15	34	....	....	....	....	....	....	....	....	....	....	....	....	....	....	....	....	....	....
2003-04	HC Vitkovice Jr.	CzRep-Jr.	52	4	8	12	48	....	....	....	....	....	....	....	....	....	....	....	....	....	....	....	....	....	....
2004-05	Kootenay Ice	WHL	65	5	18	23	85	....	....	....	....	....	....	....	....	....	9	0	0	0	6	....	....	....	....
2005-06	HC Vitkovice Jr.	CzRep-Jr.	1	0	0	0	4	....	....	....	....	....	....	....	....	....	....	....	....	....	....	....	....	....	....
	Vitkovice	CzRep	37	0	1	1	16	....	....	....	....	....	....	....	....	....	6	0	0	0	6	....	....	....	....
2006-07	**St. Louis**	**NHL**	**19**	**0**	**0**	**0**	**6**	**0**	**0**	**0**	**13**	**0.0**	**–3**	**0**	**0.0**	**13:38**	....	....	....	....	....	....	....	....	....
	Peoria Rivermen	AHL	53	4	8	12	66	....	....	....	....	....	....	....	....	....	....	....	....	....	....	....	....	....	....
2007-08	**St. Louis**	**NHL**	**6**	**0**	**1**	**1**	**0**	**0**	**0**	**0**	**2**	**0.0**	**1**	**0**	**0.0**	**11:32**	....	....	....	....	....	....	....	....	....
	Peoria Rivermen	AHL	34	0	7	7	33	....	....	....	....	....	....	....	....	....	....	....	....	....	....	....	....	....	....
2008-09	**St. Louis**	**NHL**	**69**	**1**	**14**	**15**	**45**	**0**	**0**	**1**	**73**	**1.4**	**–15**	**1**	**0.0**	**21:32**	**4**	**0**	**0**	**0**	**0**	**0**	**0**	**0**	**21:49**
2009-10	**St. Louis**	**NHL**	**78**	**4**	**17**	**21**	**59**	**0**	**0**	**1**	**73**	**5.5**	**7**	**0**	**0.0**	**19:59**	....	....	....	....	....	....	....	....	....
	Czech Republic	Olympics	5	0	0	0	4	....	....	....	....	....	....	....	....	....	....	....	....	....	....	....	....	....	....
2010-11	**St. Louis**	**NHL**	**55**	**3**	**9**	**12**	**33**	**0**	**0**	**1**	**54**	**5.6**	**–4**	**1**	**0.0**	**19:57**	....	....	....	....	....	....	....	....	....
2011-12	**St. Louis**	**NHL**	**77**	**0**	**11**	**11**	**57**	**0**	**0**	**0**	**88**	**0.0**	**6**	**0**	**0.0**	**18:52**	**9**	**0**	**0**	**0**	**19**	**0**	**0**	**0**	**20:41**
2012-13	Vitkovice	CzRep	22	2	6	8	79	....	....	....	....	....	....	....	....	....	....	....	....	....	....	....	....	....	....
	St. Louis	**NHL**	**48**	**1**	**5**	**6**	**48**	**0**	**0**	**1**	**39**	**2.6**	**–2**	**0**	**0.0**	**18:25**	**6**	**0**	**1**	**1**	**2**	**0**	**0**	**0**	**20:09**
	NHL Totals		**352**	**9**	**57**	**66**	**248**	**0**	**0**	**4**	**342**	**2.6**		**2**	**0.0**	**19:20**	**19**	**0**	**1**	**1**	**21**	**0**	**0**	**0**	**20:45**

Signed as a free agent by **Vitkovice** (CzRep), September 20, 2012.

POMINVILLE, Jason (paw-MIHN-vihl, JAY-suhn) MIN

Right wing. Shoots right. 6', 185 lbs. Born, Repentigny, Que., November 30, 1982. Buffalo's 4th choice, 55th overall, in 2001 Entry Draft.

			Regular Season														Playoffs								
Season	Club	League	GP	G	A	Pts	PIM	PP	SH	GW	S	%	+/-	TF	F%	Min	GP	G	A	Pts	PIM	PP	SH	GW	Min
1997-98	Cap-d-Madeleine	QAAA	13	3	7	10																			
1998-99	Cap-d-Madeleine	QAAA	41	18	38	56	16										7	2	7	9	0				
	Shawinigan	QMJHL	2	0	0	0	0																		
99-2000	Shawinigan	QMJHL	60	4	17	21	12										13	2	3	5	0				
2000-01	Shawinigan	QMJHL	71	46	67	113	24										10	6	6	12	0				
2001-02	Shawinigan	QMJHL	66	57	64	121	32										2	0	0	0	0				
2002-03	Rochester	AHL	73	13	21	34	16										3	1	1	2	0				
2003-04	**Buffalo**	**NHL**	**1**	**0**	**0**	**0**	**0**	0	0	0	3	0.0	0	0	0.0	14:22									
	Rochester	AHL	66	34	30	64	30										16	9	10	19	6				
2004-05	Rochester	AHL	78	30	38	68	43																		
2005-06	**Buffalo**	**NHL**	**57**	**18**	**12**	**30**	**22**	10	2	2	124	14.5	–4	5	20.0	14:07	18	5	5	10	8	0	1	1	12:11
	Rochester	AHL	18	19	7	26	11																		
2006-07	**Buffalo**	**NHL**	**82**	**34**	**34**	**68**	**30**	2	2	5	212	16.0	25	14	42.9	17:25	16	4	6	10	0	0	0	0	17:54
2007-08	**Buffalo**	**NHL**	**82**	**27**	**53**	**80**	**20**	2	1	1	232	11.6	16	67	37.3	19:58									
2008-09	**Buffalo**	**NHL**	**82**	**20**	**46**	**66**	**18**	6	1	2	239	8.4	–4	67	37.3	19:46									
2009-10	**Buffalo**	**NHL**	**82**	**24**	**38**	**62**	**22**	8	0	2	252	9.5	13	120	35.0	18:45	6	2	2	4	2	0	0	1	20:17
2010-11	**Buffalo**	**NHL**	**73**	**22**	**30**	**52**	**15**	5	1	2	215	10.2	1	155	43.2	18:09	5	1	3	4	2	0	0	1	15:51
2011-12	**Buffalo**	**NHL**	**82**	**30**	**43**	**73**	**12**	8	2	5	235	12.8	–7	375	47.7	19:41									
2012-13	Adler Mannheim	Germany	7	5	7	12	0																		
	Buffalo	**NHL**	**37**	**10**	**15**	**25**	**8**	1	1	1	94	10.6	1	86	46.5	20:54									
	Minnesota	**NHL**	**10**	**4**	**5**	**9**	**0**	1	0	1	24	16.7	0	19	57.9	17:31	2	0	0	0	0	0	0	0	13:32
	NHL Totals		**588**	**189**	**276**	**465**	**147**	**43**	**10**	**21**	**1630**	**11.6**		**908**	**43.6**	**18:35**	**47**	**12**	**16**	**28**	**12**	**0**	**1**	**3**	**15:37**

QMJHL First All-Star Team (2002)

Played in NHL All-Star Game (2012)

Signed as a free agent by **Mannheim** (Germany), December 4, 2012. Traded to **Minnesota** by **Buffalo** with Buffalo's 4th round choice in 2014 Entry Draft for Johan Larsson, Matt Hackett, Minnesota's 1st round choice (Nikita Zadorov) in 2013 Entry Draft and Minnesota's 2nd round choice in 2014 Entry Draft, April 3, 2013.

PONIKAROVSKY, Alexei (poh-nih-kahr-OHV-skee, al-EHX-ay)

Left wing. Shoots left. 6'4", 225 lbs. Born, Kiev, USSR, April 9, 1980. Toronto's 4th choice, 87th overall, in 1998 Entry Draft.

Season	Club	League	GP	G	A	Pts	PIM	PP	SH	GW	S	%	+/-	TF	F%	Min	GP	G	A	Pts	PIM	PP	SH	GW	Min
1996-97	Dyn'o Moscow 2	Russia-3	60	12	15	27	30																		
	Dyn'o Moscow 2	Russia-3	2	0	0	0	2																		
1997-98	Dynamo Moscow	Russia	24	1	2	3	30																		
1998-99	Krylja Sovetov	Russia	13	2	1	3	2																		
	Dynamo Moscow	Russia															3	0	0	0	2				
99-2000	THK Tver	Russia-2	29	8	14	22	26																		
	Dynamo Moscow	Russia	19	1	0	1	8										1	0	0	0	0				
	Dynamo Moscow	EuroHL	2	0	2	2	0																		
2000-01	**Toronto**	**NHL**	**22**	**1**	**3**	**4**	**14**	0	0	0	21	4.8	–1	7	28.6	8:32									
	St. John's	AHL	49	12	24	36	44										4	0	0	0	4				
2001-02	**Toronto**	**NHL**	**8**	**2**	**0**	**2**	**0**	0	0	1	8	25.0	2	2	50.0	8:03	10	0	0	0	4	0	0	0	8:15
	St. John's	AHL	72	21	27	48	74										5	2	1	3	8				
	Ukraine	Olympics	4	1	1	2	6																		
2002-03	**Toronto**	**NHL**	**13**	**0**	**3**	**3**	**11**	0	0	0	13	0.0	4	4	25.0	10:43									
	St. John's	AHL	63	24	22	46	68																		
2003-04	**Toronto**	**NHL**	**73**	**9**	**19**	**28**	**44**	1	0	2	110	8.2	14	20	30.0	11:36	13	1	3	4	8	0	0	1	14:20
2004-05	Voskresensk	Russia	19	1	5	6	16																		
2005-06	**Toronto**	**NHL**	**81**	**21**	**17**	**38**	**68**	2	4	3	157	13.4	15	13	30.8	14:06									
2006-07	**Toronto**	**NHL**	**71**	**21**	**24**	**45**	**63**	6	0	1	198	10.6	8	4	25.0	17:06									
2007-08	**Toronto**	**NHL**	**66**	**18**	**17**	**35**	**36**	1	0	1	150	12.0	3	4	25.0	15:58									
2008-09	**Toronto**	**NHL**	**82**	**23**	**38**	**61**	**38**	5	0	3	185	12.4	6	11	54.6	15:47									
2009-10	**Toronto**	**NHL**	**61**	**19**	**22**	**41**	**44**	4	0	1	147	12.9	5	37	32.4	16:50									
	Pittsburgh	**NHL**	**16**	**2**	**7**	**9**	**17**	1	0	0	37	5.4	–6	1	0.0	15:05	11	1	4	5	4	0	0	0	13:13
2010-11	**Los Angeles**	**NHL**	**61**	**5**	**10**	**15**	**36**	1	0	1	94	5.3	1	5	20.0	12:36	4	1	0	1	0	0	0	0	10:10
2011-12	**Carolina**	**NHL**	**49**	**7**	**8**	**15**	**26**	4	0	0	98	7.1	–12	8	37.5	14:52									
	New Jersey	**NHL**	**33**	**7**	**11**	**18**	**8**	0	0	2	58	12.1	9	4	25.0	14:34	24	1	8	9	12	0	0	1	14:23
2012-13	Donetsk	KHL	32	5	13	18	16																		
	Winnipeg	**NHL**	**12**	**2**	**0**	**2**	**6**	0	0	1	10	20.0	–2	2	0.0	11:52									
	New Jersey	**NHL**	**30**	**2**	**5**	**7**	**8**	0	0	0	41	4.9	1	5	40.0	13:40									
	NHL Totals		**678**	**139**	**184**	**323**	**419**	**25**	**4**	**16**	**1327**	**10.5**		**127**	**32.3**	**14:22**	**62**	**4**	**15**	**19**	**28**	**0**	**0**	**2**	**12:55**

Signed as a free agent by **Voskresensk** (Russia), November 13, 2004. Traded to **Pittsburgh** by **Toronto** for Martin Skoula and Luca Caputi, March 2, 2010. Signed as a free agent by **Los Angeles**, July 27, 2010. Signed as a free agent by **Carolina**, July 1, 2011. Traded to **New Jersey** by **Carolina** for Joe Sova and New Jersey's 4th round choice (Jaccob Slavin) in 2012 Entry Draft, January 20, 2012. Signed as a free agent by **Winnipeg**, July 1, 2012. Signed as a free agent by **Donetsk** (KHL), September 16, 2012. Traded to **New Jersey** by **Winnipeg** for New Jersey's 7th round choice (Brenden Kichton) in 2013 Entry Draft and a 4th round choice in 2014 Entry Draft, February 13, 2013. Signed as a free agent by **St. Petersburg** (KHL), August 5, 2013.

PORTER, Chris (POHR-tuhr, KRIHS) ST.L.

Center. Shoots left. 6'1", 206 lbs. Born, Toronto, Ont., May 29, 1984. Chicago's 10th choice, 282nd overall, in 2003 Entry Draft.

Season	Club	League	GP	G	A	Pts	PIM	PP	SH	GW	S	%	+/-	TF	F%	Min	GP	G	A	Pts	PIM	PP	SH	GW	Min
2001-02	Shat.-St. Mary's	High-MN	75	10	25	35	32																		
2002-03	Lincoln Stars	USHL	59	13	22	35	74										10	4	3	7	10				
2003-04	North Dakota	WCHA	41	10	15	25	46																		
2004-05	North Dakota	WCHA	45	12	3	15	36																		
2005-06	North Dakota	WCHA	46	7	16	23	40																		
2006-07	North Dakota	WCHA	43	13	17	30	38																		
2007-08	Peoria Rivermen	AHL	80	12	25	37	72																		
2008-09	**St. Louis**	**NHL**	**6**	**1**	**1**	**2**	**0**	0	0	0	7	14.3	–1	3	33.3	10:32									
	Peoria Rivermen	AHL	74	7	16	23	72										7	1	1	2	0				
2009-10	Peoria Rivermen	AHL	80	13	18	31	53																		
2010-11	**St. Louis**	**NHL**	**45**	**3**	**4**	**7**	**16**	0	0	1	55	5.5	–4	22	54.6	10:23									
	Peoria Rivermen	AHL	36	9	11	20	63																		
2011-12	**St. Louis**	**NHL**	**47**	**4**	**3**	**7**	**11**	0	0	1	61	6.6	–1	19	42.1	10:24									
	Peoria Rivermen	AHL	2	0	1	1	2																		
2012-13	Peoria Rivermen	AHL	12	7	3	10	11																		
	St. Louis	**NHL**	**29**	**2**	**6**	**8**	**0**	0	0	2	46	4.3	5	58	43.1	11:38	6	1	0	1	0	0	0	0	9:14
	NHL Totals		**127**	**10**	**14**	**24**	**27**	**0**	**0**	**4**	**169**	**5.9**		**102**	**45.1**	**10:41**	**6**	**1**	**0**	**1**	**0**	**0**	**0**	**0**	**9:14**

Signed as a free agent by **St. Louis**, August 21, 2007.

PORTER, Kevin (POHR-tuhr, KEH-vihn) BUF

Center. Shoots left. 6', 190 lbs. Born, Detroit, MI, March 12, 1986. Phoenix's 5th choice, 119th overall, in 2004 Entry Draft.

Season	Club	League	GP	G	A	Pts	PIM	PP	SH	GW	S	%	+/-	TF	F%	Min	GP	G	A	Pts	PIM	PP	SH	GW	Min
2002-03	USNTDP	U-17	19	9	11	20	8																		
	USNTDP	U-18	13	1	2	3	2																		
	USNTDP	NAHL	40	19	9	28	17																		
2003-04	USNTDP	U-18	44	5	21	26	26																		
	USNTDP	NAHL	11	3	8	11	4																		
2004-05	U. of Michigan	CCHA	39	11	13	24	51																		
2005-06	U. of Michigan	CCHA	39	17	21	38	30																		
2006-07	U. of Michigan	CCHA	41	24	34	58	16																		
2007-08	U. of Michigan	CCHA	43	*33	30	*63	18																		
	San Antonio	AHL															7	0	4	4	0				
2008-09	**Phoenix**	**NHL**	**34**	**5**	**5**	**10**	**4**	1	0	2	39	12.8	–2	95	29.5	13:38									
	San Antonio	AHL	42	13	22	35	14																		
2009-10	**Phoenix**	**NHL**	**4**	**0**	**0**	**0**	**0**	0	0	0	3	0.0	1	15	33.3	7:22									
	San Antonio	AHL	52	15	25	40	31																		
	Colorado	**NHL**	**16**	**2**	**1**	**3**	**0**	0	1	0	18	11.1	–4	27	48.2	13:13	4	0	0	0	0	0	0	0	10:38
	Lake Erie	AHL	4	1	0	1	2																		
2010-11	**Colorado**	**NHL**	**74**	**14**	**11**	**25**	**27**	1	0	3	102	13.7	–11	58	32.8	13:49									
2011-12	**Colorado**	**NHL**	**35**	**4**	**3**	**7**	**17**	0	0	0	32	12.5	–2	46	30.4	9:11									

			Regular Season														Playoffs								
Season	Club	League	GP	G	A	Pts	PIM	PP	SH	GW	S	%	+/-	TF	F%	Min	GP	G	A	Pts	PIM	PP	SH	GW	Min
2012-13	Rochester	AHL	48	15	29	44	38	....	....	....	....	....	....	....	....	....	....	....	....	....	....	....	....	....	....
	Buffalo	**NHL**	**31**	**4**	**5**	**9**	**10**	**0**	**1**	**0**	**37**	**10.8**	**–1**	**271**	**40.2**	**15:14**	....	....	....	....	....	....	....	....	....
	NHL Totals		**194**	**29**	**25**	**54**	**58**	**2**	**2**	**5**	**231**	**12.6**		**512**	**36.7**	**12:59**	**4**	**0**	**0**	**0**	**0**	**0**	**0**	**0**	**10:38**

CCHA Second All-Star Team (2007) • CCHA First All-Star Team (2008) • CCHA Player of the Year (2008) • NCAA West First All-American Team (2008)

Traded to **Colorado** by **Phoenix** with Peter Mueller for Wojtek Wolski, March 3, 2010. Signed as a free agent by **Buffalo**, July 6, 2012. • Missed majority of 2011-12 as a healthy reserve.

POSTMA, Paul

(POHST-muh, PAWL) **WPG**

Defense. Shoots right. 6'3", 195 lbs. Born, Red Deer, Alta., February 22, 1989. Atlanta's 4th choice, 205th overall, in 2007 Entry Draft.

Season	Club	League	GP	G	A	Pts	PIM	PP	SH	GW	S	%	+/-	TF	F%	Min	GP	G	A	Pts	PIM	PP	SH	GW	Min
2004-05	Red Deer	AMHL	36	6	5	11	24	....	....	....	....	....	....	....	....	....	....	....	....	....	....	....	....	....	....
	Swift Current	WHL	4	0	0	0	0	....	....	....	....	....	....	....	....	....	....	....	....	....	....	....	....	....	....
2005-06	Swift Current	WHL	58	2	9	11	6	....	....	....	....	....	....	....	....	....	4	0	0	0	0	....	....	....	....
2006-07	Swift Current	WHL	70	5	19	24	42	....	....	....	....	....	....	....	....	....	6	0	1	1	0	....	....	....	....
2007-08	Swift Current	WHL	2	0	0	0	2	....	....	....	....	....	....	....	....	....	....	....	....	....	....	....	....	....	....
	Calgary Hitmen	WHL	66	14	28	42	30	....	....	....	....	....	....	....	....	....	16	6	4	10	4	....	....	....	....
2008-09	Calgary Hitmen	WHL	70	23	61	84	28	....	....	....	....	....	....	....	....	....	18	5	8	13	10	....	....	....	....
2009-10	Chicago Wolves	AHL	63	15	14	29	24	....	....	....	....	....	....	....	....	....	7	0	2	2	0	....	....	....	....
2010-11	**Atlanta**	**NHL**	**1**	**0**	**0**	**0**	**0**	**0**	**0**	**0**	**1**	**0.0**	**0**	**0**	**0.0**	**9:55**	....	....	....	....	....	....	....	....	....
	Chicago Wolves	AHL	69	12	33	45	20	....	....	....	....	....	....	....	....	....	....	....	....	....	....	....	....	....	....
2011-12	**Winnipeg**	**NHL**	**3**	**0**	**0**	**0**	**0**	**0**	**0**	**0**	**3**	**0.0**	**0**	**0**	**0.0**	**8:31**	....	....	....	....	....	....	....	....	....
	St. John's IceCaps	AHL	56	13	31	44	32	....	....	....	....	....	....	....	....	....	15	1	9	10	14	....	....	....	....
2012-13	St. John's IceCaps	AHL	27	7	11	18	16	....	....	....	....	....	....	....	....	....	....	....	....	....	....	....	....	....	....
	Winnipeg	**NHL**	**34**	**4**	**5**	**9**	**6**	**2**	**0**	**0**	**32**	**12.5**	**–5**	**0**	**0.0**	**15:02**	....	....	....	....	....	....	....	....	....
	NHL Totals		**38**	**4**	**5**	**9**	**6**	**2**	**0**	**0**	**36**	**11.1**		**0**	**0.0**	**14:23**	....	....	....	....	....	....	....	....	....

WHL East First All-Star Team (2009) • Canadian Major Junior Second All-Star Team (2009) • AHL First All-Star Team (2012)

• Transferred to **Winnipeg** after **Atlanta** franchise relocated, June 21, 2011.

POTI, Tom

(POH-tee, TAWM)

Defense. Shoots left. 6'3", 190 lbs. Born, Worcester, MA, March 22, 1977. Edmonton's 4th choice, 59th overall, in 1996 Entry Draft.

Season	Club	League	GP	G	A	Pts	PIM	PP	SH	GW	S	%	+/-	TF	F%	Min	GP	G	A	Pts	PIM	PP	SH	GW	Min
1992-93	St. Peter's Marian	High-MA	55	25	46	71	....	....	....	....	....	....	....	....	....	....	....	....	....	....	....	....	....	....	....
1993-94	Cushing	High-MA	30	10	35	45	....	....	....	....	....	....	....	....	....	....	....	....	....	....	....	....	....	....	....
1994-95	Cushing	High-MA	36	17	54	71	35	....	....	....	....	....	....	....	....	....	....	....	....	....	....	....	....	....	....
	Central-Mass	MBAHL	8	8	10	18	....	....	....	....	....	....	....	....	....	....	....	....	....	....	....	....	....	....	....
1995-96	Cushing	High-MA	29	14	59	73	18	....	....	....	....	....	....	....	....	....	....	....	....	....	....	....	....	....	....
1996-97	Boston University	H-East	38	4	17	21	54	....	....	....	....	....	....	....	....	....	....	....	....	....	....	....	....	....	....
1997-98	Boston University	H-East	38	13	29	42	60	....	....	....	....	....	....	....	....	....	....	....	....	....	....	....	....	....	....
1998-99	**Edmonton**	**NHL**	**73**	**5**	**16**	**21**	**42**	**2**	**0**	**3**	**94**	**5.3**	**10**	**0**	**0.0**	**19:33**	**4**	**0**	**1**	**1**	**2**	**0**	**0**	**0**	**28:02**
99-2000	**Edmonton**	**NHL**	**76**	**9**	**26**	**35**	**65**	**2**	**1**	**1**	**125**	**7.2**	**8**	**0**	**0.0**	**24:10**	**5**	**0**	**1**	**1**	**0**	**0**	**0**	**0**	**23:53**
2000-01	**Edmonton**	**NHL**	**81**	**12**	**20**	**32**	**60**	**6**	**0**	**3**	**161**	**7.5**	**–4**	**0**	**0.0**	**22:44**	**6**	**0**	**2**	**2**	**2**	**0**	**0**	**0**	**20:25**
2001-02	**Edmonton**	**NHL**	**55**	**1**	**16**	**17**	**42**	**1**	**0**	**0**	**100**	**1.0**	**–6**	**0**	**0.0**	**24:32**	....	....	....	....	....	....	....	....	....
	United States	Olympics	6	0	1	1	4	....	....	....	....	....	....	....	....	....	....	....	....	....	....	....	....	....	....
	NY Rangers	**NHL**	**11**	**1**	**7**	**8**	**2**	**1**	**0**	**1**	**9**	**11.1**	**–4**	**0**	**0.0**	**21:45**	....	....	....	....	....	....	....	....	....
2002-03	**NY Rangers**	**NHL**	**80**	**11**	**37**	**48**	**58**	**3**	**0**	**2**	**148**	**7.4**	**–6**	**0**	**0.0**	**24:43**	....	....	....	....	....	....	....	....	....
2003-04	**NY Rangers**	**NHL**	**67**	**10**	**14**	**24**	**47**	**4**	**0**	**5**	**124**	**8.1**	**–1**	**0**	**0.0**	**22:28**	....	....	....	....	....	....	....	....	....
2004-05			DID NOT PLAY																						
2005-06	**NY Rangers**	**NHL**	**73**	**3**	**20**	**23**	**70**	**2**	**0**	**2**	**122**	**2.5**	**16**	**4**	**25.0**	**20:46**	**4**	**0**	**0**	**0**	**2**	**0**	**0**	**0**	**19:39**
2006-07	**NY Islanders**	**NHL**	**78**	**6**	**38**	**44**	**74**	**6**	**0**	**1**	**134**	**4.5**	**–1**	**0**	**0.0**	**25:43**	**5**	**0**	**3**	**3**	**6**	**0**	**0**	**0**	**27:34**
2007-08	**Washington**	**NHL**	**71**	**2**	**27**	**29**	**46**	**0**	**0**	**0**	**99**	**2.0**	**9**	**0**	**0.0**	**23:29**	**7**	**0**	**1**	**1**	**8**	**0**	**0**	**0**	**24:01**
2008-09	**Washington**	**NHL**	**52**	**3**	**10**	**13**	**28**	**0**	**0**	**1**	**48**	**6.3**	**3**	**0**	**0.0**	**21:09**	**14**	**2**	**5**	**7**	**4**	**1**	**0**	**0**	**21:37**
2009-10	**Washington**	**NHL**	**70**	**4**	**20**	**24**	**42**	**2**	**0**	**0**	**69**	**5.8**	**26**	**0**	**0.0**	**21:24**	**6**	**0**	**4**	**4**	**5**	**0**	**0**	**0**	**21:23**
2010-11	**Washington**	**NHL**	**21**	**2**	**5**	**7**	**8**	**0**	**0**	**0**	**20**	**10.0**	**–4**	**0**	**0.0**	**18:22**	....	....	....	....	....	....	....	....	....
2011-12			DID NOT PLAY – INJURED																						
2012-13	Hershey Bears	AHL	2	1	0	1	0	....	....	....	....	....	....	....	....	....	....	....	....	....	....	....	....	....	....
	Washington	**NHL**	**16**	**0**	**2**	**2**	**2**	**0**	**0**	**0**	**8**	**0.0**	**–2**	**0**	**0.0**	**15:13**	....	....	....	....	....	....	....	....	....
	NHL Totals		**824**	**69**	**258**	**327**	**586**	**29**	**1**	**19**	**1261**	**5.5**		**4**	**25.0**	**22:34**	**51**	**2**	**17**	**19**	**29**	**1**	**0**	**0**	**22:56**

NCAA Championship All-Tournament Team (1997) • Hockey East First All-Star Team (1998) • NCAA East First All-American Team (1998) • NHL All-Rookie Team (1999)

Played in NHL All-Star Game (2003)

Traded to **NY Rangers** by **Edmonton** with Rem Murray for Mike York and NY Rangers' 4th round choice (Ivan Koltsov) in 2002 Entry Draft, March 19, 2002. Signed as a free agent by **NY Islanders**, July 8, 2006. Signed as a free agent by **Washington**, July 1, 2007. • Missed majority of 2010-11 and all of 2011-12 due to lower-body injury. • Missed majority of 2012-13 due to upper-body injury vs. Buffalo, March 17, 2013 and as a healthy reserve.

POTTER, Corey

(PAW-tuhr, KOHR-ee) **EDM**

Defense. Shoots right. 6'3", 206 lbs. Born, Lansing, MI, January 5, 1984. NY Rangers' 4th choice, 122nd overall, in 2003 Entry Draft.

Season	Club	League	GP	G	A	Pts	PIM	PP	SH	GW	S	%	+/-	TF	F%	Min	GP	G	A	Pts	PIM	PP	SH	GW	Min
99-2000	Det. Honeybaked	MWEHL	58	10	38	48	....	....	....	....	....	....	....	....	....	....	....	....	....	....	....	....	....	....	....
2000-01	USNTDP	U-17	13	0	0	0	6	....	....	....	....	....	....	....	....	....	....	....	....	....	....	....	....	....	....
	USNTDP	NAHL	53	4	4	8	20	....	....	....	....	....	....	....	....	....	....	....	....	....	....	....	....	....	....
2001-02	USNTDP	U-18	38	4	6	10	49	....	....	....	....	....	....	....	....	....	....	....	....	....	....	....	....	....	....
	USNTDP	USHL	13	2	2	4	12	....	....	....	....	....	....	....	....	....	....	....	....	....	....	....	....	....	....
	USNTDP	NAHL	10	0	3	3	4	....	....	....	....	....	....	....	....	....	....	....	....	....	....	....	....	....	....
2002-03	Michigan State	CCHA	35	4	4	8	30	....	....	....	....	....	....	....	....	....	....	....	....	....	....	....	....	....	....
2003-04	Michigan State	CCHA	38	0	8	8	63	....	....	....	....	....	....	....	....	....	....	....	....	....	....	....	....	....	....
2004-05	Michigan State	CCHA	32	0	6	6	73	....	....	....	....	....	....	....	....	....	....	....	....	....	....	....	....	....	....
2005-06	Michigan State	CCHA	45	4	18	22	117	....	....	....	....	....	....	....	....	....	....	....	....	....	....	....	....	....	....
2006-07	Hartford	AHL	30	2	8	10	21	....	....	....	....	....	....	....	....	....	7	1	4	5	12	....	....	....	....
	Charlotte	ECHL	43	6	13	19	56	....	....	....	....	....	....	....	....	....	....	....	....	....	....	....	....	....	....
2007-08	Hartford	AHL	80	5	27	32	102	....	....	....	....	....	....	....	....	....	5	0	1	1	14	....	....	....	....
2008-09	**NY Rangers**	**NHL**	**5**	**1**	**1**	**2**	**0**	**0**	**0**	**0**	**4**	**25.0**	**–1**	**0**	**0.0**	**13:15**	....	....	....	....	....	....	....	....	....
	Hartford	AHL	67	10	22	32	82	....	....	....	....	....	....	....	....	....	6	1	3	4	23	....	....	....	....
2009-10	**NY Rangers**	**NHL**	**3**	**0**	**0**	**0**	**2**	**0**	**0**	**0**	**2**	**0.0**	**0**	**0**	**0.0**	**12:07**	....	....	....	....	....	....	....	....	....
	Hartford	AHL	69	4	24	28	54	....	....	....	....	....	....	....	....	....	....	....	....	....	....	....	....	....	....
2010-11	**Pittsburgh**	**NHL**	**1**	**0**	**0**	**0**	**0**	**0**	**0**	**0**	**1**	**0.0**	**0**	**0**	**0.0**	**16:43**	....	....	....	....	....	....	....	....	....
	Wilkes-Barre	AHL	75	7	30	37	52	....	....	....	....	....	....	....	....	....	12	2	7	9	10	....	....	....	....
2011-12	**Edmonton**	**NHL**	**62**	**4**	**17**	**21**	**24**	**1**	**0**	**0**	**98**	**4.1**	**–16**	**0**	**0.0**	**19:57**	....	....	....	....	....	....	....	....	....
2012-13	Vienna Capitals	Austria	17	1	3	4	10	....	....	....	....	....	....	....	....	....	....	....	....	....	....	....	....	....	....
	Edmonton	**NHL**	**33**	**3**	**1**	**4**	**6**	**0**	**0**	**0**	**36**	**8.3**	**8**	**0**	**0.0**	**17:27**	....	....	....	....	....	....	....	....	....
	NHL Totals		**104**	**8**	**19**	**27**	**32**	**1**	**0**	**0**	**141**	**5.7**		**0**	**0.0**	**18:35**	....	....	....	....	....	....	....	....	....

Signed as a free agent by **Pittsburgh**, July 16, 2010. Signed as a free agent by **Edmonton**, July 1, 2011. Signed as a free agent by **Vienna** (Austria), October 2, 2012.

POTULNY, Ryan

(poh-TUHL-nee, RIGH-uhn)

Center. Shoots left. 6', 190 lbs. Born, Grand Forks, ND, September 5, 1984. Philadelphia's 6th choice, 87th overall, in 2003 Entry Draft.

Season	Club	League	GP	G	A	Pts	PIM	PP	SH	GW	S	%	+/-	TF	F%	Min	GP	G	A	Pts	PIM	PP	SH	GW	Min
2001-02	Lincoln Stars	USHL	60	23	34	57	65	....	....	....	....	....	....	....	....	....	4	0	1	1	2	....	....	....	....
2002-03	Lincoln Stars	USHL	54	35	*43	*78	18	....	....	....	....	....	....	....	....	....	10	6	*11	*17	8	....	....	....	....
2003-04	U. of Minnesota	WCHA	15	6	8	14	10	....	....	....	....	....	....	....	....	....	....	....	....	....	....	....	....	....	....
2004-05	U. of Minnesota	WCHA	44	24	17	41	20	....	....	....	....	....	....	....	....	....	....	....	....	....	....	....	....	....	....
2005-06	U. of Minnesota	WCHA	41	*38	25	*63	31	....	....	....	....	....	....	....	....	....	....	....	....	....	....	....	....	....	....
	Philadelphia	**NHL**	**2**	**0**	**1**	**1**	**0**	**0**	**0**	**0**	**0**	**0.0**	**1**	**9**	**44.4**	**6:09**	....	....	....	....	....	....	....	....	....
2006-07	**Philadelphia**	**NHL**	**35**	**7**	**5**	**12**	**22**	**0**	**0**	**2**	**56**	**12.5**	**1**	**278**	**43.5**	**11:00**	....	....	....	....	....	....	....	....	....
	Philadelphia	AHL	30	12	14	26	34	....	....	....	....	....	....	....	....	....	....	....	....	....	....	....	....	....	....
2007-08	**Philadelphia**	**NHL**	**7**	**0**	**1**	**1**	**4**	**0**	**0**	**0**	**5**	**0.0**	**0**	**32**	**43.8**	**6:30**	....	....	....	....	....	....	....	....	....
	Philadelphia	AHL	58	21	26	47	51	....	....	....	....	....	....	....	....	....	12	3	5	8	10	....	....	....	....
2008-09	**Edmonton**	**NHL**	**8**	**0**	**3**	**3**	**0**	**0**	**0**	**0**	**9**	**0.0**	**2**	**10**	**10.0**	**10:29**	....	....	....	....	....	....	....	....	....
	Springfield	AHL	70	38	24	62	48	....	....	....	....	....	....	....	....	....	....	....	....	....	....	....	....	....	....
2009-10	**Edmonton**	**NHL**	**64**	**15**	**17**	**32**	**28**	**7**	**1**	**2**	**152**	**9.9**	**–21**	**820**	**47.4**	**16:17**	....	....	....	....	....	....	....	....	....
	Springfield	AHL	14	3	5	8	8	....	....	....	....	....	....	....	....	....	....	....	....	....	....	....	....	....	....

			Regular Season														Playoffs								
Season	Club	League	GP	G	A	Pts	PIM	PP	SH	GW	S	%	+/-	TF	F%	Min	GP	G	A	Pts	PIM	PP	SH	GW	Min
2010-11	Chicago	NHL	3	0	0	0	0	0	0	0	2	0.0	–1	26	38.5	10:07	....	....	....	....	....	....	....	....	....
	Rockford IceHogs	AHL	58	18	23	41	30	....	....	....	....	....	....	....	....	....	....	....	....	....	....	....	....	....	....
	Ottawa	NHL	7	0	0	0	0	0	0	0	5	0.0	0	0	0.0	6:57	....	....	....	....	....	....	....	....	....
	Binghamton	AHL	13	3	5	8	4	....	....	....	....	....	....	....	....	....	23	*14	12	*26	12	....	....	....	....
2011-12	Hershey Bears	AHL	61	33	32	65	32	....	....	....	....	....	....	....	....	....	5	2	2	4	0	....	....	....	....
2012-13	Hershey Bears	AHL	66	19	22	41	30	....	....	....	....	....	....	....	....	....	5	0	2	2	2	....	....	....	....
	NHL Totals		126	22	27	49	54	7	1	4	229	9.6		1175	45.9	13:05	....	....	....	....	....	....	....	....	....

USHL First All-Star Team (2003) • USHL Player of the Year (2003) • WCHA First All-Star Team (2006) • NCAA West First All-American Team (2006)

• Missed majority of 2003-04 due to knee injury vs. North Dakota (WCHA), November 7, 2003. Traded to **Edmonton** by **Philadelphia** for Danny Syvret, June 6, 2008. Signed as a free agent by **Chicago**, September 9, 2010. Traded to **Ottawa** by **Chicago** with Chicago's 2nd round choice (later traded to Detroit – Detroit selected Xavier Ouellet) in 2011 Entry Draft for Chris Campoli and future considerations, February 28, 2011. Signed as a free agent by **Washington**, July 1, 2011. Signed as a free agent by **Omsk** (KHL), May 30, 2013.

POULIOT, Benoit

(POO-lee-oh, BEHN-wah) **NYR**

Left wing. Shoots Left. 6'3", 199 lbs. Born, Alfred, Ont., September 29, 1986. Minnesota's 1st choice, 4th overall, in 2005 Entry Draft.

2002-03	Clarence Beavers	ON-Jr.B	38	13	17	30	86	....	....	....	....	....	....	....	....	....	5	0	2	2	8	....	....	....	....
	Hawkesbury	ON-Jr.A	1	1	0	1	0	....	....	....	....	....	....	....	....	....	....	....	....	....	....	....	....	....	....
2003-04	Hawkesbury	ON-Jr.A	45	21	21	42	85	....	....	....	....	....	....	....	....	....	6	3	7	10	10	....	....	....	....
	Sudbury Wolves	OHL	4	2	2	4	0	....	....	....	....	....	....	....	....	....	4	2	1	3	0	....	....	....	....
2004-05	Sudbury Wolves	OHL	67	29	38	67	102	....	....	....	....	....	....	....	....	....	12	6	8	14	20	....	....	....	....
2005-06	Sudbury Wolves	OHL	51	35	30	65	141	....	....	....	....	....	....	....	....	....	8	8	3	11	16	....	....	....	....
	Houston Aeros	AHL	....	....	....	....	....	....	....	....	....	....	....	....	....	....	2	0	0	0	2	....	....	....	....
2006-07	Minnesota	NHL	3	0	0	0	0	0	0	0	1	0.0	–1	2	0.0	6:58	....	....	....	....	....	....	....	....	....
	Houston Aeros	AHL	67	19	17	36	109	....	....	....	....	....	....	....	....	....	....	....	....	....	....	....	....	....	....
2007-08	Minnesota	NHL	11	2	1	3	0	0	0	0	10	20.0	–1	65	40.0	8:49	1	0	0	0	0	0	0	0	10:16
	Houston Aeros	AHL	46	10	14	24	67	....	....	....	....	....	....	....	....	....	3	0	0	0	2	....	....	....	....
2008-09	Minnesota	NHL	37	5	6	11	18	2	0	1	34	14.7	1	217	42.9	11:51	....	....	....	....	....	....	....	....	....
	Houston Aeros	AHL	30	9	15	24	20	....	....	....	....	....	....	....	....	....	20	1	7	8	28	....	....	....	....
2009-10	Minnesota	NHL	14	2	2	4	12	0	0	0	19	10.5	0	8	50.0	11:56	....	....	....	....	....	....	....	....	....
	Montreal	NHL	39	15	9	24	31	4	0	3	92	16.3	8	3	33.3	16:44	18	0	2	2	6	0	0	0	11:45
	Hamilton	AHL	3	1	2	3	4	....	....	....	....	....	....	....	....	....	....	....	....	....	....	....	....	....	....
2010-11	Montreal	NHL	79	13	17	30	87	1	0	4	129	10.1	2	22	45.5	11:32	3	0	0	0	7	0	0	0	6:12
2011-12	Boston	NHL	74	16	16	32	38	1	0	5	107	15.0	18	18	44.4	12:13	7	1	1	2	6	0	0	0	12:40
2012-13	Tampa Bay	NHL	34	8	12	20	15	0	0	1	60	13.3	8	31	32.3	13:14	....	....	....	....	....	....	....	....	....
	NHL Totals		291	61	63	124	201	8	0	14	452	13.5		366	41.5	12:31	29	1	3	4	19	0	0	0	11:21

OHL All-Rookie Team (2005) • OHL First All-Star Team (2005) • OHL Rookie of the Year (2005) • Canadian Major Junior All-Rookie Team (2005) • Canadian Major Junior Rookie of the Year (2005)

Traded to **Montreal** by **Minnesota** for Guillaume Latendresse, November 23, 2009. Signed as a free agent by **Boston**, July 1, 2011. Traded to **Tampa Bay** by **Boston** for Michel Ouellet and Tampa Bay's 5th round choice (Seth Griffith) in 2012 Entry Draft, June 23, 2012. Signed as a free agent by **NY Rangers**, July 5, 2013.

POULIOT, Marc

(POO-lee-oh, MAHRK)

Center. Shoots right. 6'2", 203 lbs. Born, Quebec, Que., May 22, 1985. Edmonton's 1st choice, 22nd overall, in 2003 Entry Draft.

2000-01	Ste-Foy	QAAA	38	16	39	55	52	....	....	....	....	....	....	....	....	....	16	8	12	20	16	....	....	....	....
2001-02	Rimouski Oceanic	QMJHL	28	9	14	23	32	....	....	....	....	....	....	....	....	....	5	0	0	0	4	....	....	....	....
2002-03	Rimouski Oceanic	QMJHL	65	32	41	73	100	....	....	....	....	....	....	....	....	....	....	....	....	....	....	....	....	....	....
2003-04	Rimouski Oceanic	QMJHL	42	25	33	58	62	....	....	....	....	....	....	....	....	....	9	5	7	12	12	....	....	....	....
2004-05	Rimouski Oceanic	QMJHL	70	45	69	114	83	....	....	....	....	....	....	....	....	....	13	4	15	19	8	....	....	....	....
2005-06	Edmonton	NHL	8	1	0	1	0	0	0	0	5	20.0	1	56	55.4	8:30	....	....	....	....	....	....	....	....	....
	Hamilton	AHL	65	15	30	45	63	....	....	....	....	....	....	....	....	....	....	....	....	....	....	....	....	....	....
2006-07	Edmonton	NHL	46	4	7	11	18	0	0	0	73	5.5	–2	353	48.7	13:03	....	....	....	....	....	....	....	....	....
	Wilkes-Barre	AHL	33	14	17	31	20	....	....	....	....	....	....	....	....	....	11	5	5	10	4	....	....	....	....
2007-08	Edmonton	NHL	24	1	6	7	12	0	0	0	32	3.1	–1	44	47.7	10:20	....	....	....	....	....	....	....	....	....
	Springfield	AHL	55	21	26	47	47	....	....	....	....	....	....	....	....	....	....	....	....	....	....	....	....	....	....
2008-09	Edmonton	NHL	63	8	12	20	23	0	0	2	94	8.5	1	211	48.3	11:30	....	....	....	....	....	....	....	....	....
2009-10	Edmonton	NHL	35	7	7	14	21	1	0	1	60	11.7	–4	235	44.3	12:48	....	....	....	....	....	....	....	....	....
	Springfield	AHL	4	1	5	6	12	....	....	....	....	....	....	....	....	....	....	....	....	....	....	....	....	....	....
2010-11	Tampa Bay	NHL	3	0	0	0	0	0	0	0	2	0.0	–2	13	38.5	10:46	....	....	....	....	....	....	....	....	....
	Norfolk Admirals	AHL	69	25	47	72	53	....	....	....	....	....	....	....	....	....	6	4	3	7	4	....	....	....	....
2011-12	Phoenix	NHL	13	0	4	4	2	0	0	0	19	0.0	–2	88	42.1	11:11	8	1	1	2	2	0	0	0	7:07
	Portland Pirates	AHL	48	12	24	36	63	....	....	....	....	....	....	....	....	....	....	....	....	....	....	....	....	....	....
2012-13	EHC Biel-Bienne	Swiss	48	9	31	40	86	....	....	....	....	....	....	....	....	....	....	....	....	....	....	....	....	....	....
	NHL Totals		192	21	36	57	76	1	0	3	285	7.4		1000	47.2	11:48	8	1	1	2	2	0	0	0	7:07

QMJHL First All-Star Team (2005) • George Parsons Trophy (Memorial Cup - Most Sportsmanlike Player) (2005)

• Missed majority of 2009-10 due to lower-body injury. Signed as a free agent by **Tampa Bay**, July 23, 2010. Traded to **Phoenix** by **Tampa Bay** for Phoenix's 7th round choice (Matthew Peca) in 2011 Entry Draft, June 25, 2011. Signed as a free agent by **Biel-Bienne** (Swiss), June 2, 2012.

POWE, Darroll

(POW, DAIR-ohl) **NYR**

Left wing. Shoots left. 5'11", 212 lbs. Born, Saskatoon, Sask., June 22, 1985.

2001-02	Kanata Valley	ON-Jr.A	48	6	7	13	102	....	....	....	....	....	....	....	....	....	4	2	1	3	....	....	....	....	....
2002-03	Kanata Valley	ON-Jr.A	46	21	20	41	126	....	....	....	....	....	....	....	....	....	4	0	1	1	10	....	....	....	....
2003-04	Princeton	ECAC	29	4	5	9	28	....	....	....	....	....	....	....	....	....	....	....	....	....	....	....	....	....	....
2004-05	Princeton	ECAC	30	5	2	7	41	....	....	....	....	....	....	....	....	....	....	....	....	....	....	....	....	....	....
2005-06	Princeton	ECAC	27	6	10	16	48	....	....	....	....	....	....	....	....	....	....	....	....	....	....	....	....	....	....
2006-07	Princeton	ECAC	34	13	15	28	63	....	....	....	....	....	....	....	....	....	....	....	....	....	....	....	....	....	....
	Philadelphia	AHL	11	2	2	4	20	....	....	....	....	....	....	....	....	....	....	....	....	....	....	....	....	....	....
2007-08	Philadelphia	AHL	76	9	14	23	133	....	....	....	....	....	....	....	....	....	10	1	0	1	6	....	....	....	....
2008-09	Philadelphia	NHL	60	6	5	11	35	0	0	0	72	8.3	–8	263	48.7	10:32	6	1	2	3	7	0	0	0	14:02
	Philadelphia	AHL	8	4	3	7	20	....	....	....	....	....	....	....	....	....	....	....	....	....	....	....	....	....	....
2009-10	Philadelphia	NHL	63	9	6	15	54	0	0	0	103	8.7	0	210	45.2	12:05	23	0	1	1	6	0	0	0	12:33
2010-11	Philadelphia	NHL	81	7	10	17	41	0	2	2	87	8.0	–6	134	49.3	12:17	11	0	1	1	4	0	0	0	12:10
2011-12	Minnesota	NHL	82	6	7	13	57	0	0	1	109	5.5	–20	105	43.8	13:59	....	....	....	....	....	....	....	....	....
2012-13	Minnesota	NHL	8	0	0	0	9	0	0	0	5	0.0	1	4	75.0	10:13	....	....	....	....	....	....	....	....	....
	NY Rangers	NHL	34	0	0	0	18	0	0	0	18	0.0	–2	100	53.0	8:43	3	0	0	0	0	0	0	0	6:25
	NHL Totals		328	28	28	56	214	0	2	3	394	7.1		816	47.9	11:56	43	1	4	5	17	0	0	0	12:14

Signed as a free agent by **Philadelphia**, April 17, 2008. Traded to **Minnesota** by **Philadelphia** for Minnesota's 3rd round choice (later traded to Dallas, later traded to Pittsburgh – Pittsburgh selected Jake Guentzel) in 2013 Entry Draft, June 27, 2011. Traded to **NY Rangers** by **Minnesota** with Nick Palmieri for Mke Rupp, February 4, 2013.

PRONGER, Chris

(PRAWN-guhr, KRIHS) **PHI**

Defense. Shoots left. 6'6", 220 lbs. Born, Dryden, Ont., October 10, 1974. Hartford's 1st choice, 2nd overall, in 1993 Entry Draft.

1990-91	Stratford Cullitons	ON-Jr.B	48	15	37	52	132	....	....	....	....	....	....	....	....	....	....	....	....	....	....	....	....	....	....
1991-92	Peterborough	OHL	63	17	45	62	90	....	....	....	....	....	....	....	....	....	10	1	8	9	28	....	....	....	....
1992-93	Peterborough	OHL	61	15	62	77	108	....	....	....	....	....	....	....	....	....	21	15	25	40	51	....	....	....	....
1993-94	Hartford	NHL	81	5	25	30	113	2	0	0	174	2.9	–3	....	....	....	....	....	....	....	....	....	....	....	....
1994-95	Hartford	NHL	43	5	9	14	54	3	0	1	94	5.3	–12	....	....	....	....	....	....	....	....	....	....	....	....
1995-96	St. Louis	NHL	78	7	18	25	110	3	1	1	138	5.1	–18	....	....	....	13	1	5	6	16	0	0	0	....
1996-97	St. Louis	NHL	79	11	24	35	143	4	0	0	147	7.5	15	....	....	....	6	1	1	2	22	0	0	0	....
1997-98	St. Louis	NHL	81	9	27	36	180	1	0	2	145	6.2	*47	....	....	....	10	1	9	10	26	0	0	0	....
	Canada	Olympics	6	0	0	0	4	....	....	....	....	....	....	....	....	....	....	....	....	....	....	....	....	....	....
1998-99	St. Louis	NHL	67	13	33	46	113	8	0	0	172	7.6	3	0	0.0	30:36	13	1	4	5	28	1	0	0	35:53
99-2000	St. Louis	NHL	79	14	48	62	92	8	0	3	192	7.3	*52	1	0.0	30:14	7	3	4	7	32	2	0	2	30:14
2000-01	St. Louis	NHL	51	8	39	47	75	4	0	0	121	6.6	21	0	0.0	27:45	15	1	7	8	32	0	0	0	33:50
2001-02	St. Louis	NHL	78	7	40	47	120	4	1	3	204	3.4	23	0	0.0	29:28	9	1	7	8	24	0	0	0	27:51
	Canada	Olympics	6	0	1	1	2	....	....	....	....	....	....	....	....	....	....	....	....	....	....	....	....	....	....
2002-03	St. Louis	NHL	5	1	3	4	10	0	0	0	11	9.1	–2	1	0.0	21:39	7	1	3	4	14	0	0	0	24:36
2003-04	St. Louis	NHL	80	14	40	54	88	7	0	3	203	6.9	–1	2	0.0	27:28	5	0	1	1	16	0	0	0	27:54
2004-05			DID NOT PLAY																						
2005-06	Edmonton	NHL	80	12	44	56	74	10	0	3	155	7.7	2	1	0.0	27:59	24	5	16	21	26	3	0	0	30:57
	Canada	Olympics	6	1	2	3	16	....	....	....	....	....	....	....	....	....	....	....	....	....	....	....	....	....	....
2006-07 ♦	Anaheim	NHL	66	13	46	59	69	8	0	2	166	7.8	27	4	25.0	27:06	19	3	12	15	26	1	0	0	30:11

								Regular Season									Playoffs								
Season	Club	League	GP	G	A	Pts	PIM	PP	SH	GW	S	%	+/-	TF	F%	Min	GP	G	A	Pts	PIM	PP	SH	GW	Min
2007-08	Anaheim	NHL	72	12	31	43	128	8	0	4	182	6.6	–1	7	57.1	26:00	6	2	3	5	12	2	0	1	24:14
2008-09	Anaheim	NHL	82	11	37	48	88	4	0	2	196	5.6	0	7	28.6	26:56	13	2	8	10	12	1	0	0	27:13
2009-10	Philadelphia	NHL	82	10	45	55	79	5	0	2	175	5.7	22	0	0.0	25:56	23	4	14	18	*36	3	0	0	29:03
	Canada	Olympics	7	0	5	5	2	....	....	....	....	....	....	....	....	....	....	....	....	....	....	....	....	....	....
2010-11	Philadelphia	NHL	50	4	21	25	44	3	0	1	112	3.6	7	0	0.0	22:30	3	0	1	1	4	0	0	0	13:55
2011-12	Philadelphia	NHL	13	1	11	12	10	1	0	0	23	4.3	1	0	0.0	22:29	....	....	....	....	....	....	....	....	....
2012-13	Philadelphia	NHL	DID NOT PLAY – INJURED																						
	NHL Totals		1167	157	541	698	1590	83	2	27	2610	6.0		23	30.4	27:28	173	26	95	121	326	13	0	3	29:41

OHL All-Rookie Team (1992) • OHL First All-Star Team (1993) • Canadian Major Junior First All-Star Team (1993) • Canadian Major Junior Defenseman of the Year (1993) • NHL All-Rookie Team (1994) • NHL Second All-Star Team (1998, 2004, 2007) • Bud Ice Plus/Minus Award (1998) • NHL First All-Star Team (2000) • Bud Light Plus/Minus Award (2000) • James Norris Memorial Trophy (2000) • Hart Memorial Trophy (2000)

Played in NHL All-Star Game (1999, 2000, 2002, 2004, 2008)

Traded to **St. Louis** by **Hartford** for Brendan Shanahan, July 27, 1995. • Missed majority of 2002-03 due to wrist and knee surgeries, September 10, 2002. Traded to **Edmonton** by **St. Louis** for Eric Brewer, Doug Lynch and Jeff Woywitka, August 2, 2005. Traded to **Anaheim** by **Edmonton** for Joffrey Lupul, Ladislav Smid, Anaheim's 1st round choice (later traded to Phoenix - Phoenix selected Nick Ross) in 2007 Entry Draft and Anaheim's 1st (Jordan Eberle) and 2nd (later traded to NY Islanders - NY Islanders selected Travis Hamonic) round choices in 2008 Entry Draft, July 3, 2006. Traded to **Philadelphia** by **Anaheim** with Ryan Dingle for Joffrey Lupul, Luca Sbisa, Philadelphia's 1st round choices in 2009 (later traded to Columbus - Columbus selected John Moore) and 2010 (Emerson Etem) Entry Drafts and future considerations, June 26, 2009. • Missed majority of 2011-12 and all of 2012-13 due to post-concussion syndrome.

PROSPAL, Vinny

(PRAWS-puhl, vih-NEE)

Center. Shoots left. 6'2", 191 lbs. Born, Ceske Budejovice, Czech., February 17, 1975. Philadelphia's 2nd choice, 71st overall, in 1993 Entry Draft.

Season	Club	League	GP	G	A	Pts	PIM	PP	SH	GW	S	%	+/-	TF	F%	Min	GP	G	A	Pts	PIM	PP	SH	GW	Min
1991-92	C. Budejovice Jr.	Czech-Jr.	36	16	16	32	12	....	....	....	....	....	....	....	....	....	....	....	....	....	....	....	....	....	....
1992-93	C. Budejovice Jr.	Czech-Jr.	32	26	31	57	24	....	....	....	....	....	....	....	....	....	....	....	....	....	....	....	....	....	....
1993-94	Hershey Bears	AHL	55	14	21	35	38	....	....	....	....	....	....	....	....	....	2	0	0	0	2	....	....	....	....
1994-95	Hershey Bears	AHL	69	13	32	45	36	....	....	....	....	....	....	....	....	....	2	1	0	1	4	....	....	....	....
1995-96	Hershey Bears	AHL	68	15	36	51	59	....	....	....	....	....	....	....	....	....	5	2	4	6	2	....	....	....	....
1996-97	Philadelphia	NHL	18	5	10	15	4	0	0	0	35	14.3	3	....	....	....	5	1	3	4	4	0	0	0	....
	Philadelphia	AHL	63	32	63	95	70	....	....	....	....	....	....	....	....	....	....	....	....	....	....	....	....	....	....
1997-98	Philadelphia	NHL	41	5	13	18	17	4	0	0	60	8.3	–10	....	....	....	....	....	....	....	....	....	....	....	....
	Ottawa	NHL	15	1	6	7	4	0	0	0	28	3.6	–1	....	....	....	6	0	0	0	0	0	0	0	....
1998-99	Ottawa	NHL	79	10	26	36	58	2	0	3	114	8.8	8	997	56.2	13:03	4	0	0	0	0	0	0	0	12:37
99-2000	Ottawa	NHL	79	22	33	55	40	5	0	4	204	10.8	–2	1331	49.6	16:26	6	0	4	4	4	0	0	0	17:40
2000-01	Ottawa	NHL	40	1	12	13	12	0	0	0	68	1.5	1	501	50.1	12:57	....	....	....	....	....	....	....	....	....
	Florida	NHL	34	4	12	16	10	1	0	0	68	5.9	–2	487	54.6	16:36	....	....	....	....	....	....	....	....	....
2001-02	Tampa Bay	NHL	81	18	37	55	38	7	0	2	166	10.8	–11	555	52.8	17:31	....	....	....	....	....	....	....	....	....
2002-03	Tampa Bay	NHL	80	22	57	79	53	9	0	4	134	16.4	9	161	51.6	18:39	11	4	2	6	8	2	0	0	21:15
2003-04	Anaheim	NHL	82	19	35	54	54	7	0	4	185	10.3	–9	45	46.7	18:37	....	....	....	....	....	....	....	....	....
2004-05	C. Budejovice	CzRep-2	39	28	60	88	82	....	....	....	....	....	....	....	....	....	16	15	15	30	32	....	....	....	....
2005-06	Tampa Bay	NHL	81	25	55	80	50	10	0	3	236	10.6	–3	267	45.3	19:10	5	0	2	2	0	0	0	0	15:56
	Czech Republic	Olympics	8	4	2	6	2	....	....	....	....	....	....	....	....	....	....	....	....	....	....	....	....	....	....
2006-07	Tampa Bay	NHL	82	14	41	55	36	2	0	1	219	6.4	–24	124	52.4	19:04	6	1	4	5	4	0	0	1	22:19
2007-08	Tampa Bay	NHL	62	29	28	57	39	9	0	4	175	16.6	–7	176	54.6	20:00	....	....	....	....	....	....	....	....	....
	Philadelphia	NHL	18	4	10	14	6	1	0	1	40	10.0	7	86	58.1	17:15	17	3	10	13	6	1	0	0	16:49
2008-09	Tampa Bay	NHL	82	19	26	45	52	7	0	2	194	9.8	–20	202	53.0	17:41	....	....	....	....	....	....	....	....	....
2009-10	NY Rangers	NHL	75	20	38	58	32	6	1	4	180	11.1	8	639	51.2	20:06	....	....	....	....	....	....	....	....	....
2010-11	NY Rangers	NHL	29	9	14	23	8	2	0	0	61	14.8	4	128	53.9	15:20	5	1	0	1	0	0	0	0	19:30
2011-12	Columbus	NHL	82	16	39	55	36	3	0	0	165	9.7	–11	22	40.9	17:53	....	....	....	....	....	....	....	....	....
2012-13	C. Budejovice	CzRep	19	9	14	23	46	....	....	....	....	....	....	....	....	....	....	....	....	....	....	....	....	....	....
	Columbus	NHL	48	12	18	30	32	4	0	2	85	14.1	3	9	44.4	16:32	....	....	....	....	....	....	....	....	....
	NHL Totals		1108	255	510	765	581	79	1	34	2417	10.6		5730	52.0	17:35	65	10	25	35	26	3	0	1	18:17

AHL First All-Star Team (1997)

Traded to **Ottawa** by **Philadelphia** with Pat Falloon and Dallas' 2nd round choice (previously acquired, Ottawa selected Chris Bala) in 1998 Entry Draft for Alexandre Daigle, January 17, 1998. Traded to **Florida** by **Ottawa** for future considerations, January 20, 2001. Traded to **Tampa Bay** by **Florida** for Ryan Johnson and Tampa Bay's 6th round choice (later traded back to Tampa Bay – Tampa Bay selected Doug O'Brien) in 2003 Entry Draft, July 10, 2001. Signed as a free agent by **Anaheim**, July 17, 2003. Traded to **Tampa Bay** by **Anaheim** for Tampa Bay's 2nd round choice (Brendan Mikkelson) in 2005 Entry Draft, August 16, 2004. Signed as a free agent by **Ceske Budejovice** (CzRep-2), September 17, 2004. Traded to **Philadelphia** by **Tampa Bay** for Alexandre Picard and Philadelphia's 2nd round choice (Richard Panik) in 2009 Entry Draft, February 25, 2008. Traded to **Tampa Bay** by **Philadelphia** for Nashville's 7th round choice (previously acquired, Philadelphia selected Joacim Eriksson) in 2008 Entry Draft and future considerations, June 18, 2008. Signed as a free agent by **NY Rangers**, August 17, 2009. • Missed majority of 2010-11 due to knee surgery, October 6, 2010. Signed as a free agent by **Columbus**, July 23. 2011. Signed as a free agent by **Ceske Budejovice** (CzRep), October 28, 2012.

PROSSER, Nate

(PRAW-suhr, NAYT) **MIN**

Defense. Shoots right. 6'2", 207 lbs. Born, Elk River, MN, May 7, 1986.

Season	Club	League	GP	G	A	Pts	PIM	PP	SH	GW	S	%	+/-	TF	F%	Min	GP	G	A	Pts	PIM	PP	SH	GW	Min
2006-07	Colorado College	WCHA	21	0	3	3	8	....	....	....	....	....	....	....	....	....	....	....	....	....	....	....	....	....	....
2007-08	Colorado College	WCHA	39	3	17	20	51	....	....	....	....	....	....	....	....	....	....	....	....	....	....	....	....	....	....
2008-09	Colorado College	WCHA	38	5	8	13	61	....	....	....	....	....	....	....	....	....	....	....	....	....	....	....	....	....	....
2009-10	Minnesota	NHL	3	0	1	1	8	0	0	0	4	0.0	2	0	0.0	19:37	....	....	....	....	....	....	....	....	....
	Colorado College	WCHA	39	4	24	28	58	....	....	....	....	....	....	....	....	....	....	....	....	....	....	....	....	....	....
2010-11	Minnesota	NHL	2	0	0	0	0	0	0	0	1	0.0	0	0	0.0	14:48	....	....	....	....	....	....	....	....	....
	Houston Aeros	AHL	73	8	19	27	31	....	....	....	....	....	....	....	....	....	24	2	2	4	16	....	....	....	....
2011-12	Minnesota	NHL	51	1	11	12	57	0	0	0	32	3.1	–17	0	0.0	19:15	....	....	....	....	....	....	....	....	....
	Houston Aeros	AHL	23	0	4	4	10	....	....	....	....	....	....	....	....	....	2	1	0	1	2	....	....	....	....
2012-13	Minnesota	NHL	17	0	0	0	4	0	0	0	5	0.0	4	0	0.0	11:15	....	....	....	....	....	....	....	....	....
	NHL Totals		73	1	12	13	69	0	0	0	42	2.4		0	0.0	17:17	....	....	....	....	....	....	....	....	....

WCHA Second All-Star Team (2010)

Signed as a free agent by **Minnesota**, March 18, 2010. • Missed majority of 2012-13 as a healthy reserve.

PROUT, Dalton

(PROWT, DAHL-tuhn) **CBJ**

Defense. Shoots right. 6'3", 219 lbs. Born, LaSalle, Ont., March 13, 1990. Columbus' 7th choice, 154th overall, in 2010 Entry Draft.

Season	Club	League	GP	G	A	Pts	PIM	PP	SH	GW	S	%	+/-	TF	F%	Min	GP	G	A	Pts	PIM	PP	SH	GW	Min
2005-06	Wind. Jr. Spitfires	Minor-ON	58	11	19	30	78	....	....	....	....	....	....	....	....	....	....	....	....	....	....	....	....	....	....
2006-07	Sarnia Sting	OHL	49	1	2	3	36	....	....	....	....	....	....	....	....	....	4	0	0	0	0	....	....	....	....
2007-08	Sarnia Sting	OHL	32	0	2	2	43	....	....	....	....	....	....	....	....	....	....	....	....	....	....	....	....	....	....
	Barrie Colts	OHL	25	0	3	3	39	....	....	....	....	....	....	....	....	....	8	0	2	2	16	....	....	....	....
2008-09	Barrie Colts	OHL	65	0	6	6	98	....	....	....	....	....	....	....	....	....	5	0	1	1	10	....	....	....	....
2009-10	Barrie Colts	OHL	63	7	14	21	121	....	....	....	....	....	....	....	....	....	17	1	6	7	20	....	....	....	....
2010-11	Barrie Colts	OHL	23	7	14	21	55	....	....	....	....	....	....	....	....	....	....	....	....	....	....	....	....	....	....
	Saginaw Spirit	OHL	29	2	8	10	44	....	....	....	....	....	....	....	....	....	12	2	0	2	27	....	....	....	....
2011-12	Columbus	NHL	5	0	0	0	0	0	0	0	2	0.0	1	0	0.0	11:48	....	....	....	....	....	....	....	....	....
	Springfield	AHL	62	4	9	13	54	....	....	....	....	....	....	....	....	....	....	....	....	....	....	....	....	....	....
2012-13	Springfield	AHL	40	1	8	9	73	....	....	....	....	....	....	....	....	....	6	0	1	1	14	....	....	....	....
	Columbus	NHL	28	1	6	7	25	0	0	0	16	6.3	15	0	0.0	18:32	....	....	....	....	....	....	....	....	....
	NHL Totals		33	1	6	7	25	0	0	0	18	5.6		0	0.0	17:30	....	....	....	....	....	....	....	....	....

PRUST, Brandon

(PROOST, BRAN-duhn) **MTL**

Left wing. Shoots left. 6'2", 192 lbs. Born, London, Ont., March 16, 1984. Calgary's 2nd choice, 70th overall, in 2004 Entry Draft.

Season	Club	League	GP	G	A	Pts	PIM	PP	SH	GW	S	%	+/-	TF	F%	Min	GP	G	A	Pts	PIM	PP	SH	GW	Min
2001-02	London Nationals	ON-Jr.B	52	17	35	52	38	....	....	....	....	....	....	....	....	....	....	....	....	....	....	....	....	....	....
2002-03	London Knights	OHL	65	12	17	29	94	....	....	....	....	....	....	....	....	....	14	2	1	3	21	....	....	....	....
2003-04	London Knights	OHL	64	19	33	52	269	....	....	....	....	....	....	....	....	....	15	7	13	20	33	....	....	....	....
2004-05	London Knights	OHL	48	10	20	30	174	....	....	....	....	....	....	....	....	....	15	3	5	8	*71	....	....	....	....
2005-06	Omaha	AHL	79	12	14	26	294	....	....	....	....	....	....	....	....	....	....	....	....	....	....	....	....	....	....
2006-07	Calgary	NHL	10	0	0	0	25	0	0	0	1	0.0	1	0	0.0	6:03	....	....	....	....	....	....	....	....	....
	Omaha	AHL	63	17	10	27	211	....	....	....	....	....	....	....	....	....	6	0	3	3	20	....	....	....	....
2007-08	Quad City Flames	AHL	79	10	27	37	248	....	....	....	....	....	....	....	....	....	....	....	....	....	....	....	....	....	....
2008-09	Calgary	NHL	25	1	1	2	79	0	0	1	15	6.7	–4	15	53.3	6:21	....	....	....	....	....	....	....	....	....
	Phoenix	NHL	11	0	1	1	29	0	0	0	8	0.0	–4	16	56.3	9:59	....	....	....	....	....	....	....	....	....
2009-10	Calgary	NHL	43	1	4	5	98	0	0	1	23	4.3	6	29	37.9	6:33	....	....	....	....	....	....	....	....	....
	NY Rangers	NHL	26	4	5	9	65	0	0	2	21	19.0	3	2	100.0	9:20	....	....	....	....	....	....	....	....	....
2010-11	NY Rangers	NHL	82	13	16	29	160	0	5	1	87	14.9	2	9	44.4	13:49	5	0	1	1	4	0	0	0	16:24

			Regular Season														Playoffs								
Season	Club	League	GP	G	A	Pts	PIM	PP	SH	GW	S	%	+/-	TF	F%	Min	GP	G	A	Pts	PIM	PP	SH	GW	Min
2011-12	**NY Rangers**	**NHL**	**82**	**5**	**12**	**17**	**156**	**0**	**2**	**2**	**68**	**7.4**	**–1**	**5**	**60.0**	**11:57**	**19**	**1**	**1**	**2**	**31**	**0**	**0**	**0**	**12:47**
2012-13	**Montreal**	**NHL**	**38**	**5**	**9**	**14**	**110**	**0**	**0**	**1**	**39**	**12.8**	**11**	**55**	**45.5**	**13:38**	**4**	**0**	**1**	**1**	**14**	**0**	**0**	**0**	**15:27**
	NHL Totals		**317**	**29**	**48**	**77**	**722**	**0**	**7**	**8**	**262**	**11.1**		**131**	**47.3**	**10:59**	**28**	**1**	**3**	**4**	**49**	**0**	**0**	**0**	**13:48**

Traded to **Phoenix** by **Calgary** with Matthew Lombardi and Calgary's 1st round choice (Brandon Gormley) in 2010 Entry Draft for Olli Jokinen and Phoenix's 3rd round choice (later traded to Florida – Florida selected Josh Birkholz) in 2009 Entry Draft, March 4, 2009. Traded to **Calgary** by **Phoenix** for Jim Vandermeer, June 27, 2009. Traded to **NY Rangers** by **Calgary** with Olli Jokinen for Chris Higgins and Ales Kotalik, February 2, 2010. Signed as a free agent by **Montreal**, July 1, 2012.

PURCELL, Teddy

(PUHR-sihl, TEH-dee) **T.B.**

Right wing. Shoots right. 6'3", 203 lbs. Born, St. Johns, Nfld., September 8, 1985.

Season	Club	League	GP	G	A	Pts	PIM	PP	SH	GW	S	%	+/-	TF	F%	Min	GP	G	A	Pts	PIM	PP	SH	GW	Min
2003-04	Notre Dame	SJHL	51	21	25	46	8																		
2004-05	Cedar Rapids	USHL	58	20	47	67	22										11	5	9	14	4				
2005-06	Cedar Rapids	USHL	55	19	*52	71	14										8	3	8	11	4				
2006-07	U. of Maine	H-East	40	16	27	43	34																		
2007-08	**Los Angeles**	**NHL**	**10**	**1**	**2**	**3**	**0**	**0**	**0**	**0**	**10**	**10.0**	**2**	**0**	**0.0**	**11:59**									
	Manchester	AHL	67	25	58	83	34										4	0	3	3	0				
2008-09	**Los Angeles**	**NHL**	**40**	**4**	**12**	**16**	**4**	**2**	**0**	**1**	**68**	**5.9**	**–4**	**29**	**17.2**	**13:31**									
	Manchester	AHL	38	16	22	38	12																		
2009-10	**Los Angeles**	**NHL**	**41**	**3**	**3**	**6**	**4**	**1**	**0**	**1**	**55**	**5.5**	**–1**	**3**	**33.3**	**11:22**									
	Tampa Bay	**NHL**	**19**	**3**	**6**	**9**	**6**	**1**	**0**	**0**	**46**	**6.5**	**–8**	**1**	**100.0**	**16:05**									
2010-11	**Tampa Bay**	**NHL**	**81**	**17**	**34**	**51**	**10**	**3**	**0**	**1**	**196**	**8.7**	**5**	**37**	**32.4**	**14:06**	**18**	**6**	**11**	**17**	**2**	**1**	**0**	**1**	**13:42**
2011-12	**Tampa Bay**	**NHL**	**81**	**24**	**41**	**65**	**16**	**8**	**0**	**3**	**152**	**15.8**	**9**	**17**	**17.7**	**16:08**									
2012-13	**Tampa Bay**	**NHL**	**48**	**11**	**25**	**36**	**12**	**3**	**0**	**2**	**94**	**11.7**	**–1**	**6**	**33.3**	**16:45**									
	NHL Totals		**320**	**63**	**123**	**186**	**52**	**18**	**0**	**8**	**621**	**10.1**		**93**	**25.8**	**14:38**	**18**	**6**	**11**	**17**	**2**	**1**	**0**	**1**	**13:42**

AHL All-Rookie Team (2008) • AHL First All-Star Team (2008)

Signed as a free agent by **Los Angeles**, April 27, 2007. Traded to **Tampa Bay** by **Los Angeles** with Florida's 3rd round choice (previously acquired, Tampa Bay selected Brock Beukeboom) in 2010 Entry Draft for Jeff Halpern, March 3, 2010.

PYATT, Taylor

(PIGH-at, TAY-luhr) **NYR**

Left wing. Shoots left. 6'4", 230 lbs. Born, Thunder Bay, Ont., August 19, 1981. NY Islanders' 2nd choice, 8th overall, in 1999 Entry Draft.

Season	Club	League	GP	G	A	Pts	PIM	PP	SH	GW	S	%	+/-	TF	F%	Min	GP	G	A	Pts	PIM	PP	SH	GW	Min
1996-97	Thunder Bay	TBAHA	60	52	61	113	72																		
1997-98	Sudbury Wolves	OHL	58	14	17	31	104										10	3	1	4	8				
1998-99	Sudbury Wolves	OHL	68	37	38	75	95										4	0	4	4	6				
99-2000	Sudbury Wolves	OHL	68	40	49	89	98										12	8	7	15	25				
2000-01	**NY Islanders**	**NHL**	**78**	**4**	**14**	**18**	**39**	**1**	**0**	**2**	**86**	**4.7**	**–17**	**1**	**0.0**	**12:14**									
2001-02	**Buffalo**	**NHL**	**48**	**10**	**10**	**20**	**35**	**0**	**0**	**0**	**61**	**16.4**	**4**	**0**	**0.0**	**13:30**									
	Rochester	AHL	27	6	4	10	36																		
2002-03	**Buffalo**	**NHL**	**78**	**14**	**14**	**28**	**38**	**2**	**0**	**0**	**110**	**12.7**	**–8**	**8**	**25.0**	**14:06**									
2003-04	**Buffalo**	**NHL**	**63**	**8**	**12**	**20**	**25**	**1**	**2**	**4**	**98**	**8.2**	**–7**	**19**	**26.3**	**15:36**									
2004-05	Hammarby	Sweden-2	24	11	9	20	20																		
2005-06	**Buffalo**	**NHL**	**41**	**6**	**6**	**12**	**33**	**0**	**0**	**1**	**62**	**9.7**	**–1**	**11**	**18.2**	**11:14**	**14**	**0**	**5**	**5**	**10**	**0**	**0**	**0**	**11:08**
2006-07	**Vancouver**	**NHL**	**76**	**23**	**14**	**37**	**42**	**9**	**0**	**4**	**150**	**15.3**	**5**	**4**	**0.0**	**13:58**	**12**	**2**	**4**	**6**	**6**	**0**	**0**	**1**	**18:02**
2007-08	**Vancouver**	**NHL**	**79**	**16**	**21**	**37**	**60**	**7**	**0**	**2**	**167**	**9.6**	**9**	**36**	**33.3**	**15:47**									
2008-09	**Vancouver**	**NHL**	**69**	**10**	**9**	**19**	**43**	**0**	**0**	**1**	**99**	**10.1**	**0**	**33**	**48.5**	**14:43**	**4**	**0**	**0**	**0**	**2**	**0**	**0**	**0**	**14:13**
2009-10	**Phoenix**	**NHL**	**74**	**12**	**11**	**23**	**39**	**1**	**0**	**3**	**121**	**9.9**	**13**	**1**	**0.0**	**13:27**	**7**	**1**	**1**	**2**	**2**	**1**	**0**	**0**	**14:22**
2010-11	**Phoenix**	**NHL**	**76**	**18**	**13**	**31**	**27**	**2**	**0**	**6**	**126**	**14.3**	**11**	**20**	**30.0**	**15:30**	**4**	**1**	**0**	**1**	**0**	**0**	**0**	**0**	**14:56**
2011-12	**Phoenix**	**NHL**	**73**	**9**	**10**	**19**	**23**	**0**	**0**	**1**	**111**	**8.1**	**–4**	**11**	**54.6**	**12:19**	**16**	**4**	**2**	**6**	**2**	**1**	**0**	**1**	**15:38**
2012-13	**NY Rangers**	**NHL**	**48**	**6**	**5**	**11**	**6**	**1**	**0**	**0**	**56**	**10.7**	**5**	**10**	**40.0**	**13:06**	**12**	**2**	**2**	**4**	**4**	**0**	**0**	**0**	**13:33**
	NHL Totals		**803**	**136**	**139**	**275**	**410**	**24**	**2**	**24**	**1247**	**10.9**		**154**	**34.4**	**13:55**	**69**	**10**	**14**	**24**	**26**	**2**	**0**	**2**	**14:31**

OHL First All-Star Team (2000)

Traded to **Buffalo** by **NY Islanders** with Tim Connolly for Michael Peca, June 24, 2001. Signed as a free agent by **Hammarby** (Sweden-2), November 16, 2004. • Rights traded to **Vancouver** by **Buffalo** for Vancouver's 4th round choice (later traded to Calgary - Calgary selected Keith Aulie) in 2007 Entry Draft, July 14, 2006. Signed as a free agent by **Phoenix**, September 2, 2009. Signed as a free agent by **NY Rangers**, July 3, 2012.

PYATT, Tom

(PIGH-at, TAWM) **T.B.**

Center. Shoots left. 5'11", 188 lbs. Born, Thunder Bay, Ont., February 14, 1987. NY Rangers' 6th choice, 107th overall, in 2005 Entry Draft.

Season	Club	League	GP	G	A	Pts	PIM	PP	SH	GW	S	%	+/-	TF	F%	Min	GP	G	A	Pts	PIM	PP	SH	GW	Min
2003-04	Saginaw Spirit	OHL	67	9	9	18	21																		
2004-05	Saginaw Spirit	OHL	57	18	30	48	14																		
2005-06	Saginaw Spirit	OHL	58	24	29	53	29										4	1	2	3	4				
2006-07	Saginaw Spirit	OHL	58	43	38	81	18										6	3	5	8	0				
	Hartford	AHL	1	0	0	0	0																		
2007-08	Hartford	AHL	41	4	7	11	6										3	0	0	0	0				
	Charlotte	ECHL	16	6	9	15	8										3	0	0	0	0				
2008-09	Hartford	AHL	73	15	22	37	22										4	0	0	0	2				
2009-10	**Montreal**	**NHL**	**40**	**2**	**3**	**5**	**10**	**0**	**0**	**0**	**48**	**4.2**	**–5**	**50**	**42.0**	**11:04**	**18**	**2**	**2**	**4**	**2**	**0**	**0**	**1**	**13:03**
	Hamilton	AHL	41	13	22	35	8																		
2010-11	**Montreal**	**NHL**	**61**	**2**	**5**	**7**	**9**	**0**	**0**	**0**	**65**	**3.1**	**–1**	**110**	**50.0**	**10:38**	**7**	**0**	**0**	**0**	**0**	**0**	**0**	**0**	**9:54**
2011-12	**Tampa Bay**	**NHL**	**74**	**12**	**7**	**19**	**8**	**1**	**0**	**1**	**95**	**12.6**	**–19**	**281**	**45.6**	**14:48**									
2012-13	**Tampa Bay**	**NHL**	**43**	**8**	**8**	**16**	**12**	**0**	**0**	**1**	**60**	**13.3**	**5**	**290**	**50.0**	**13:35**									
	NHL Totals		**218**	**24**	**23**	**47**	**39**	**1**	**0**	**2**	**268**	**9.0**		**731**	**47.7**	**12:43**	**25**	**2**	**2**	**4**	**2**	**0**	**0**	**1**	**12:10**

Traded to **Montreal** by **NY Rangers** with Scott Gomez and Michael Busto for Chris Higgins, Ryan McDonagh and Pavel Valentenko, June 30, 2009. Signed as a free agent by **Tampa Bay**, July 6, 2011.

PYSYK, Mark

(PEHS-ihk, MAHRK) **BUF**

Defense. Shoots right. 6'1", 195 lbs. Born, Edmonton, Alta., January 11, 1992. Buffalo's 1st choice, 23rd overall, in 2010 Entry Draft.

Season	Club	League	GP	G	A	Pts	PIM	PP	SH	GW	S	%	+/-	TF	F%	Min	GP	G	A	Pts	PIM	PP	SH	GW	Min
2007-08	Sherwood Park	AMHL	34	10	10	20	60										2	1	0	1	16				
	Edmonton	WHL	14	1	2	3	8																		
2008-09	Edmonton	WHL	61	5	15	20	27										4	0	0	0	2				
2009-10	Edmonton	WHL	48	7	17	24	47																		
2010-11	Edmonton	WHL	63	6	34	40	88										4	0	0	0	6				
2011-12	Edmonton	WHL	57	6	32	38	83										20	3	8	11	16				
2012-13	Rochester	AHL	57	4	14	18	20										3	0	0	0	2				
	Buffalo	**NHL**	**19**	**1**	**4**	**5**	**0**	**1**	**0**	**0**	**21**	**4.8**	**–7**	**0**	**0.0**	**16:17**									
	NHL Totals		**19**	**1**	**4**	**5**	**0**	**1**	**0**	**0**	**21**	**4.8**		**0**	**0.0**	**16:17**									

WHL East Second All-Star Team (2012)

QUINCEY, Kyle

(KWIHN-see, KIGHL) **DET**

Defense. Shoots left. 6'2", 207 lbs. Born, Kitchener, Ont., August 12, 1985. Detroit's 2nd choice, 132nd overall, in 2003 Entry Draft.

Season	Club	League	GP	G	A	Pts	PIM	PP	SH	GW	S	%	+/-	TF	F%	Min	GP	G	A	Pts	PIM	PP	SH	GW	Min
2001-02	Mississauga	ON-Jr.A	27	5	14	19	31																		
2002-03	London Knights	OHL	66	6	12	18	77										14	3	4	7	11				
2003-04	London Knights	OHL	3	0	2	2	4																		
	Mississauga	OHL	61	14	23	37	135										24	3	13	16	32				
2004-05	Mississauga	OHL	59	15	31	46	111										5	0	3	3	4				
2005-06	**Detroit**	**NHL**	**1**	**0**	**0**	**0**	**0**	**0**	**0**	**0**	**1**	**0.0**	**0**	**0**	**0.0**	**11:37**									
	Grand Rapids	AHL	70	7	26	33	107										16	0	1	1	27				
2006-07	**Detroit**	**NHL**	**6**	**1**	**0**	**1**	**0**	**0**	**0**	**0**	**7**	**14.3**	**0**	**0**	**0.0**	**11:26**	**13**	**0**	**0**	**0**	**2**	**0**	**0**	**0**	**8:11**
	Grand Rapids	AHL	65	4	18	22	126										2	0	0	0	0				
2007-08	**Detroit**	**NHL**	**6**	**0**	**0**	**0**	**4**	**0**	**0**	**0**	**5**	**0.0**	**–3**	**0**	**0.0**	**13:58**									
	Grand Rapids	AHL	66	5	15	20	149																		
2008-09	**Los Angeles**	**NHL**	**72**	**4**	**34**	**38**	**63**	**2**	**0**	**2**	**150**	**2.7**	**–5**	**0**	**0.0**	**20:59**									
2009-10	**Colorado**	**NHL**	**79**	**6**	**23**	**29**	**76**	**1**	**0**	**0**	**139**	**4.3**	**9**	**1**	**0.0**	**23:37**	**6**	**0**	**0**	**0**	**8**	**0**	**0**	**0**	**22:06**
2010-11	**Colorado**	**NHL**	**21**	**0**	**1**	**1**	**18**	**0**	**0**	**0**	**39**	**0.0**	**–5**	**0**	**0.0**	**19:35**									
2011-12	**Colorado**	**NHL**	**54**	**5**	**18**	**23**	**60**	**3**	**0**	**1**	**131**	**3.8**	**–1**	**1**	**0.0**	**22:21**									
	Detroit	**NHL**	**18**	**2**	**1**	**3**	**29**	**1**	**0**	**0**	**37**	**5.4**	**0**	**0**	**0.0**	**20:22**	**5**	**0**	**2**	**2**	**6**	**0**	**0**	**0**	**16:29**

			Regular Season														Playoffs								
Season	Club	League	GP	G	A	Pts	PIM	PP	SH	GW	S	%	+/-	TF	F%	Min	GP	G	A	Pts	PIM	PP	SH	GW	Min
2012-13	Denver	CHL	12	2	9	11	6																		
	Detroit	**NHL**	**36**	**1**	**2**	**3**	**18**	**0**	**0**	**0**	**36**	**2.8**	**7**	**0**	**0.0**	**19:13**	**14**	**0**	**2**	**2**	**12**	**0**	**0**	**0**	**19:02**
	NHL Totals		**293**	**19**	**79**	**98**	**268**	**7**	**0**	**3**	**545**	**3.5**		**2**	**0.0**	**21:13**	**38**	**0**	**4**	**4**	**28**	**0**	**0**	**0**	**15:28**

OHL Second All-Star Team (2005)

Claimed on waivers by **Los Angeles** from **Detroit**, October 13, 2008. Traded to **Colorado** by **Los Angeles** with Tom Preissing and Los Angeles' 5th round choice (Luke Walker) in 2010 Entry Draft for Ryan Smyth, July 3, 2009. • Missed majority of 2010-11 due to shoulder injury at Atlanta, December 10, 2010. Traded to **Tampa Bay** by **Colorado** for Steve Downie, February 21, 2012. Traded to **Detroit** by **Tampa Bay** for Sebastien Piche and Detroit's 1st round choice (Andrei Vasilevski) in 2012 Entry Draft, February 21, 2012. Signed as a free agent by **Denver** (CHL), October 12, 2012.

RADULOV, Alexander (ra-DEW-lahf, al-EHX-AN-duhr) NSH

Right wing. Shoots left. 6'1", 188 lbs. Born, Nizhny Tagil, USSR, July 5, 1986. Nashville's 1st choice, 15th overall, in 2004 Entry Draft.

2002-03	Dyn'o Moscow 2	Russia-3	STATISTICS NOT AVAILABLE																						
2003-04	Dyn'o Moscow 2	Russia-3	STATISTICS NOT AVAILABLE																						
	THK Tver	Russia-2	42	15	16	31	102																		
	Dynamo Moscow	Russia	1	0	0	0	2																		
2004-05	Quebec Remparts	QMJHL	65	32	43	75	64										13	6	5	11	15				
2005-06	Quebec Remparts	QMJHL	62	61	*91	*152	101										23	21	*34	*55	30				
2006-07	**Nashville**	**NHL**	**64**	**18**	**19**	**37**	**26**	**5**	**0**	**4**	**96**	**18.8**	**19**	**0**	**0.0**	**11:38**	**4**	**3**	**1**	**4**	**19**	**0**	**0**	**0**	**13:10**
	Milwaukee	AHL	11	6	12	18	26																		
2007-08	**Nashville**	**NHL**	**81**	**26**	**32**	**58**	**44**	**4**	**0**	**2**	**183**	**14.2**	**7**	**1**	**0.0**	**16:24**	**6**	**2**	**2**	**4**	**6**	**1**	**0**	**0**	**15:59**
2008-09	Ufa	KHL	52	22	26	48	92										4	0	2	2	4				
2009-10	Ufa	KHL	54	24	39	63	62										16	8	*11	*19	10				
	Russia	Olympics	4	1	1	2	4																		
2010-11	Ufa	KHL	54	20	*60	*80	83										21	3	*15	18	42				
2011-12	Ufa	KHL	50	25	38	63	64										6	0	6	6	2				
	Nashville	**NHL**	**9**	**3**	**4**	**7**	**4**	**0**	**0**	**0**	**21**	**14.3**	**3**	**0**	**0.0**	**19:21**	**8**	**1**	**5**	**6**	**4**	**0**	**0**	**0**	**18:08**
2012-13	CSKA Moscow	KHL	48	22	*46	68	86										9	1	6	7	0				
	NHL Totals		**154**	**47**	**55**	**102**	**74**	**9**	**0**	**6**	**300**	**15.7**		**1**	**0.0**	**14:35**	**18**	**6**	**8**	**14**	**29**	**1**	**0**	**0**	**16:19**

QMJHL All-Rookie Team (2005) • QMJHL First All-Star Team (2006) • QMJHL Player of the Year (2006) • Canadian Major Junior First All-Star Team (2006) • Canadian Major Junior Player of the Year (2006) • Memorial Cup All-Star Team (2006) • Stafford Smythe Memorial Trophy (Memorial Cup - MVP) (2006)

Signed as a free agent by **Ufa** (KHL), July 11, 2008. Signed as a free agent by **CSKA Moscow** (KHL), July 2, 2012.

RAKELL, Rickard (ra-KEHL, REE-kahrd) ANA

Right wing. Shoots right. 6'1", 197 lbs. Born, Sundbyberg, Sweden, May 5, 1993. Anaheim's 1st choice, 30th overall, in 2011 Entry Draft.

2007-08	Spanga Hockey	Sweden-4	24	4	3	7	12																		
2008-09	AIK IF Solna U18	Swe-U18	16	2	3	5	22																		
2009-10	AIK IF Solna U18	Swe-U18	30	25	16	41	18										3	2	2	4	0				
	AIK IF Solna Jr.	Swe-Jr.	8	3	1	4	2										2	1	0	1	0				
2010-11	Plymouth Whalers	OHL	49	20	25	45	12										1	0	0	0	0				
2011-12	Plymouth Whalers	OHL	60	28	34	62	12										13	2	10	12	0				
2012-13	Plymouth Whalers	OHL	40	21	23	44	12										15	6	9	15	10				
	Anaheim	**NHL**	**4**	**0**	**0**	**0**	**0**	**0**	**0**	**0**	**3**	**0.0**	**–2**	**21**	**47.6**	**8:57**									
	NHL Totals		**4**	**0**	**0**	**0**	**0**	**0**	**0**	**0**	**3**	**0.0**		**21**	**47.6**	**8:57**									

RAKHSHANI, Rhett (rahk-SHAH-nee, REHT) NYI

Right wing. Shoots right. 5'10", 182 lbs. Born, Orange, CA, March 6, 1988. NY Islanders' 4th choice, 100th overall, in 2006 Entry Draft.

2003-04	California Wave	Minor-CA	56	54	67	121																			
2004-05	USNTDP	U-17	14	6	5	11	32																		
	USNTDP	NAHL	40	12	15	27	21										9	1	4	5	2				
2005-06	USNTDP	U-18	43	11	12	23	30																		
	USNTDP	NAHL	16	13	13	26	35																		
2006-07	U. of Denver	WCHA	40	10	26	36	38																		
2007-08	U. of Denver	WCHA	37	14	14	28	52																		
2008-09	U. of Denver	WCHA	38	15	22	37	50																		
2009-10	U. of Denver	WCHA	41	21	29	50	40																		
	Bridgeport	AHL	5	0	2	2	2										5	0	0	0	2				
2010-11	**NY Islanders**	**NHL**	**2**	**0**	**0**	**0**	**0**	**0**	**0**	**0**	**2**	**0.0**	**–1**	**0**	**0.0**	**11:42**									
	Bridgeport	AHL	66	24	38	62	32																		
2011-12	**NY Islanders**	**NHL**	**5**	**0**	**0**	**0**	**2**	**0**	**0**	**0**	**3**	**0.0**	**0**	**0**	**0.0**	**12:09**									
	Bridgeport	AHL	49	20	29	49	42										3	1	0	1	0				
2012-13	HV 71 Jonkoping	Sweden	52	14	25	39	46										5	1	4	5	4				
	NHL Totals		**7**	**0**	**0**	**0**	**2**	**0**	**0**	**0**	**5**	**0.0**		**0**	**0.0**	**12:01**									

WCHA First All-Star Team (2010) • NCAA West First All-American Team (2010) • AHL All-Rookie Team (2011)

Signed as a free agent by **Jonkoping** (Sweden), June 19, 2012.

RALLO, Greg (RA-loh, GREHG) FLA

Center. Shoots right. 6', 195 lbs. Born, Gurnee, IL, August 26, 1981.

2002-03	Ferris State	CCHA	41	15	14	29	46																		
2003-04	Ferris State	CCHA	38	7	11	18	42																		
2004-05	Ferris State	CCHA	33	7	15	22	22																		
2005-06	Ferris State	CCHA	40	17	22	39	30																		
	Idaho Steelheads	ECHL	7	2	2	4	2										7	2	1	3	4				
2006-07	Idaho Steelheads	ECHL	37	13	18	31	43										14	8	3	11	12				
	Iowa Stars	AHL	28	3	2	5	25										2	1	0	1	2				
2007-08	Idaho Steelheads	ECHL	39	17	19	36	47																		
	Albany River Rats	AHL	5	0	0	0	0																		
	Rockford IceHogs	AHL	2	0	0	0	0																		
	Manitoba Moose	AHL	13	4	5	9	2										3	0	0	0	9				
2008-09	Manitoba Moose	AHL	55	4	5	9	17										20	2	2	4	9				
2009-10	Texas Stars	AHL	69	19	25	44	25										24	3	7	10	0				
2010-11	Texas Stars	AHL	78	26	28	54	46										6	1	1	2	8				
2011-12	**Florida**	**NHL**	**1**	**0**	**0**	**0**	**0**	**0**	**0**	**0**	**1**	**0.0**	**0**	**0**	**0.0**	**3:31**									
	San Antonio	AHL	72	22	20	42	18										4	0	2	2	0				
2012-13	San Antonio	AHL	66	23	17	40	36																		
	Florida	**NHL**	**10**	**1**	**0**	**1**	**2**	**1**	**0**	**0**	**10**	**10.0**	**–5**	**3**	**33.3**	**9:33**									
	NHL Totals		**11**	**1**	**0**	**1**	**2**	**1**	**0**	**0**	**11**	**9.1**		**3**	**33.3**	**9:00**									

Signed as a free agent by **Florida**, July 2, 2011.

RANGER, Paul (RAIN-juhr, PAWL) TOR

Defense. Shoots left. 6'3", 210 lbs. Born, Whitby, Ont., September 12, 1984. Tampa Bay's 7th choice, 183rd overall, in 2002 Entry Draft.

2000-01	Oshawa Generals	OHL	32	0	1	1	2																		
2001-02	Oshawa Generals	OHL	62	0	9	9	49										5	0	0	0	4				
2002-03	Oshawa Generals	OHL	68	10	28	38	70										13	0	3	3	10				
2003-04	Oshawa Generals	OHL	62	12	31	43	72										7	0	1	1	10				
2004-05	Springfield	AHL	69	3	8	11	46																		
2005-06	**Tampa Bay**	**NHL**	**76**	**1**	**17**	**18**	**58**	**0**	**0**	**1**	**73**	**1.4**	**5**	**0**	**0.0**	**17:07**	**5**	**2**	**4**	**6**	**0**	**1**	**0**	**0**	**21:43**
	Springfield	AHL	1	1	2	3	0																		
2006-07	**Tampa Bay**	**NHL**	**72**	**4**	**24**	**28**	**42**	**0**	**0**	**2**	**90**	**4.4**	**5**	**0**	**0.0**	**20:19**	**6**	**0**	**1**	**1**	**4**	**0**	**0**	**0**	**21:22**
2007-08	**Tampa Bay**	**NHL**	**72**	**10**	**21**	**31**	**56**	**0**	**1**	**0**	**105**	**9.5**	**–13**	**0**	**0.0**	**25:13**									
2008-09	**Tampa Bay**	**NHL**	**42**	**2**	**11**	**13**	**56**	**0**	**0**	**0**	**69**	**2.9**	**–5**	**0**	**0.0**	**24:30**									
2009-10	**Tampa Bay**	**NHL**	**8**	**1**	**1**	**2**	**6**	**0**	**0**	**0**	**11**	**9.1**	**–2**	**0**	**0.0**	**20:19**									

			Regular Season														Playoffs								
Season	Club	League	GP	G	A	Pts	PIM	PP	SH	GW	S	%	+/-	TF	F%	Min	GP	G	A	Pts	PIM	PP	SH	GW	Min
2010-11			Out of Hockey – Retired																						
2011-12			Out of Hockey – Retired																						
2012-13	Toronto Marlies	AHL	51	8	17	25	54										9	2	2	4	14				
	NHL Totals		**270**	**18**	**74**	**92**	**218**	**0**	**1**	**3**	**348**	**5.2**		**0**	**0.0**	**21:23**	**11**	**2**	**5**	**7**	**4**	**1**	**0**	**0**	**21:31**

• Missed majority of 2009-10 and all of 2010-11 and 2011-12 for personal reasons. Signed as a free agent by **Toronto** (AHL), August 21, 2012. Signed as a free agent by **Toronto**, July 24, 2013.

RASK, Joonas

(RASK, YOH-nuhs) **NSH**

Center. Shoots right. 5'10", 176 lbs. Born, Savonlinna, Finland, March 24, 1990. Nashville's 6th choice, 198th overall, in 2010 Entry Draft.

Season	Club	League	GP	G	A	Pts	PIM	PP	SH	GW	S	%	+/-	TF	F%	Min	GP	G	A	Pts	PIM	PP	SH	GW	Min
2005-06	SaPKo Jr.	Fin-Jr.	2	3	1	4	0																		
2006-07	Ilves Tampere U18	Fin-U18	32	17	23	40	46																		
	Ilves Tampere Jr.	Fin-Jr.	1	0	0	0	0																		
2007-08	Ilves Tampere U18	Fin-U18	6	3	9	12	22																		
	Ilves Tampere Jr.	Fin-Jr.	32	11	18	29	34										5	1	3	4	2				
2008-09	Suomi U20	Finland-2	8	0	6	6	0																		
	Ilves Tampere Jr.	Fin-Jr.	25	8	11	19	8																		
	LeKi Lempaala	Finland-2	1	1	2	3	2																		
	Ilves Tampere	Finland	24	1	0	1	8										3	0	1	1	0				
2009-10	Ilves Tampere	Finland	43	10	9	19	32																		
	Suomi U20	Finland-2	1	0	0	0	0																		
	Ilves Tampere Jr.	Fin-Jr.	2	0	0	0	2										4	2	2	4	0				
	Ilves Tampere	Finland-Q															5	3	0	3	0				
2010-11	Ilves Tampere	Finland	60	14	13	27	18										5	1	1	2	2				
2011-12	Ilves Tampere	Finland	32	4	14	18	12																		
	Ilves Tampere	Finland-Q															5	2	2	4	2				
2012-13	Jokerit Helsinki	Finland	52	5	5	10	6										2	0	0	0	0				
	Nashville	**NHL**	**2**	**0**	**1**	**1**	**0**	**0**	**0**	**0**	**0**	**0.0**	**–1**	**0**	**0.0**	**8:01**									
	Milwaukee	AHL	1	1	1	2	0										1	0	0	0	0				
	NHL Totals		**2**	**0**	**1**	**1**	**0**	**0**	**0**	**0**	**0**	**0.0**		**0**	**0.0**	**8:00**									

RAU, Chad

(ROW, CHAD) **MIN**

Center. Shoots right. 5'11", 186 lbs. Born, Eden Prairie, MN, January 18, 1987. Toronto's 6th choice, 228th overall, in 2005 Entry Draft.

Season	Club	League	GP	G	A	Pts	PIM	PP	SH	GW	S	%	+/-	TF	F%	Min	GP	G	A	Pts	PIM	PP	SH	GW	Min
2004-05	Des Moines	USHL	57	31	40	71	32																		
2005-06	Colorado College	WCHA	42	13	17	30	8																		
2006-07	Colorado College	WCHA	39	14	17	31	4																		
2007-08	Colorado College	WCHA	40	*28	14	42	8																		
2008-09	Colorado College	WCHA	38	18	19	37	6																		
2009-10	Houston Aeros	AHL	79	19	19	38	7																		
2010-11	Houston Aeros	AHL	60	13	27	40	12										24	6	3	9	2				
2011-12	**Minnesota**	**NHL**	**9**	**2**	**0**	**2**	**0**	**0**	**0**	**2**	**7**	**28.6**	**–1**	**65**	**53.9**	**10:53**									
	Houston Aeros	AHL	67	14	21	35	2										4	0	0	0	2				
2012-13	Houston Aeros	AHL	60	16	11	27	6										5	1	2	3	0				
	NHL Totals		**9**	**2**	**0**	**2**	**0**	**0**	**0**	**2**	**7**	**28.6**		**65**	**53.8**	**10:53**									

USHL All-Rookie Team (2005) • USHL First All-Star Team (2005) • USHL Rookie of the Year (2005) • WCHA First All-Star Team (2008, 2009) • NCAA West Second All-American Team (2008, 2009)

Signed as a free agent by **Houston** (AHL), October 6, 2009. Signed as a free agent by **Minnesota**, May 17, 2010.

RAYMOND, Mason

(RAY-muhnd, MAY-sohn)

Left wing. Shoots left. 6', 185 lbs. Born, Cochrane, Alta., September 17, 1985. Vancouver's 2nd choice, 51st overall, in 2005 Entry Draft.

Season	Club	League	GP	G	A	Pts	PIM	PP	SH	GW	S	%	+/-	TF	F%	Min	GP	G	A	Pts	PIM	PP	SH	GW	Min
2003-04	Camrose Kodiaks	AJHL		27	35	62																			
2004-05	Camrose Kodiaks	AJHL	55	*41	41	82	80										15	8	*12	20					
2005-06	U. Minn-Duluth	WCHA	40	11	17	28	30																		
2006-07	U. Minn-Duluth	WCHA	39	14	32	46	45																		
	Manitoba Moose	AHL	11	2	2	4	6										13	0	1	1	0				
2007-08	**Vancouver**	**NHL**	**49**	**9**	**12**	**21**	**2**	**1**	**0**	**0**	**80**	**11.3**	**1**	**63**	**38.1**	**12:31**									
	Manitoba Moose	AHL	20	7	10	17	6																		
2008-09	**Vancouver**	**NHL**	**72**	**11**	**12**	**23**	**24**	**4**	**0**	**0**	**145**	**7.6**	**2**	**50**	**34.0**	**13:43**	**10**	**2**	**1**	**3**	**2**	**0**	**0**	**0**	**15:12**
2009-10	**Vancouver**	**NHL**	**82**	**25**	**28**	**53**	**48**	**8**	**0**	**4**	**217**	**11.5**	**0**	**23**	**34.8**	**17:20**	**12**	**3**	**1**	**4**	**6**	**0**	**0**	**1**	**17:36**
2010-11	**Vancouver**	**NHL**	**70**	**15**	**24**	**39**	**10**	**2**	**1**	**5**	**197**	**7.6**	**8**	**65**	**40.0**	**15:48**	**24**	**2**	**6**	**8**	**6**	**0**	**0**	**0**	**17:29**
2011-12	**Vancouver**	**NHL**	**55**	**10**	**10**	**20**	**18**	**1**	**1**	**2**	**125**	**8.0**	**4**	**25**	**28.0**	**15:35**	**5**	**0**	**1**	**1**	**0**	**0**	**0**	**0**	**12:34**
2012-13	Orebro HK	Sweden-2	2	0	1	1	2																		
	Vancouver	**NHL**	**46**	**10**	**12**	**22**	**16**	**4**	**0**	**1**	**79**	**12.7**	**2**	**50**	**34.0**	**15:49**	**4**	**1**	**1**	**2**	**0**	**0**	**0**	**0**	**16:49**
	NHL Totals		**374**	**80**	**98**	**178**	**118**	**20**	**2**	**12**	**843**	**9.5**		**276**	**35.9**	**15:17**	**55**	**8**	**10**	**18**	**14**	**0**	**0**	**1**	**16:36**

AJHL MVP (2005) • WCHA All-Rookie Team (2006) • WCHA First All-Star Team (2007)

Signed as a free agent by **Orebro** (Sweden-2), December 26, 2012.

READ, Matt

(REED, MAT) **PHI**

Right wing. Shoots right. 5'10", 185 lbs. Born, Ilderton, Ont., June 14, 1986.

Season	Club	League	GP	G	A	Pts	PIM	PP	SH	GW	S	%	+/-	TF	F%	Min	GP	G	A	Pts	PIM	PP	SH	GW	Min
2005-06	Milton Icehawks	ON-Jr.A	48	34	34	68	52										11	6	13	19	6				
2006-07	Des Moines	USHL	58	28	34	62	110										8	2	0	2	6				
2007-08	Bemidji State	CHA	36	9	18	27	37																		
2008-09	Bemidji State	CHA	37	15	25	40	50																		
2009-10	Bemidji State	CHA	37	19	22	41	32																		
2010-11	Bemidji State	WCHA	37	22	13	35	34																		
	Adirondack	AHL	11	7	6	13	6																		
2011-12	**Philadelphia**	**NHL**	**79**	**24**	**23**	**47**	**12**	**4**	**2**	**6**	**155**	**15.5**	**13**	**346**	**41.0**	**17:04**	**11**	**3**	**2**	**5**	**4**	**1**	**0**	**1**	**15:14**
2012-13	Sodertalje SK	Sweden-2	20	6	18	24	12																		
	Philadelphia	**NHL**	**42**	**11**	**13**	**24**	**2**	**1**	**0**	**2**	**72**	**15.3**	**1**	**48**	**29.2**	**18:01**									
	NHL Totals		**121**	**35**	**36**	**71**	**14**	**5**	**2**	**8**	**227**	**15.4**		**394**	**39.6**	**17:24**	**11**	**3**	**2**	**5**	**4**	**1**	**0**	**1**	**15:14**

CHA All-Rookie Team (2008) • CHA Rookie of the Year (2008) • CHA First All-Star Team (2009) • NCAA West Second All-American Team (2010)

Signed as a free agent by **Philadelphia**, March 24, 2011. Signed as a free agent by **Sodertalje** (Sweden-2), September 30. 2012.

REASONER, Marty

(REE-suh-nuhr, MAHR-tee)

Center. Shoots left. 6'1", 197 lbs. Born, Honeoye Falls, NY, February 26, 1977. St. Louis' 1st choice, 14th overall, in 1996 Entry Draft.

Season	Club	League	GP	G	A	Pts	PIM	PP	SH	GW	S	%	+/-	TF	F%	Min	GP	G	A	Pts	PIM	PP	SH	GW	Min
1993-94	Deerfield	High-MA	22	27	25	52																			
1994-95	Deerfield	High-MA	26	25	32	57	14																		
1995-96	Boston College	H-East	34	16	29	45	32																		
1996-97	Boston College	H-East	35	20	24	44	31																		
1997-98	Boston College	H-East	42	*33	40	*73	56																		
1998-99	**St. Louis**	**NHL**	**22**	**3**	**7**	**10**	**8**	**1**	**0**	**0**	**33**	**9.1**	**2**	**224**	**53.6**	**13:55**									
	Worcester IceCats	AHL	44	17	22	39	24										4	2	1	3	6				
99-2000	**St. Louis**	**NHL**	**32**	**10**	**14**	**24**	**20**	**3**	**0**	**0**	**51**	**19.6**	**9**	**379**	**49.6**	**15:20**	**7**	**2**	**1**	**3**	**4**	**1**	**0**	**0**	**13:12**
	Worcester IceCats	AHL	44	23	28	51	39																		
2000-01	**St. Louis**	**NHL**	**41**	**4**	**9**	**13**	**14**	**0**	**0**	**0**	**65**	**6.2**	**–5**	**454**	**53.1**	**14:00**	**10**	**3**	**1**	**4**	**0**	**0**	**0**	**1**	**12:21**
	Worcester IceCats	AHL	34	17	18	35	25																		
2001-02	**Edmonton**	**NHL**	**52**	**6**	**5**	**11**	**41**	**3**	**0**	**2**	**66**	**9.1**	**0**	**470**	**55.5**	**11:44**									
2002-03	**Edmonton**	**NHL**	**70**	**11**	**20**	**31**	**28**	**2**	**2**	**0**	**102**	**10.8**	**19**	**968**	**53.5**	**14:50**	**6**	**1**	**0**	**1**	**2**	**1**	**0**	**0**	**14:22**
	Hamilton	AHL	2	0	2	2	2																		
2003-04	**Edmonton**	**NHL**	**17**	**2**	**6**	**8**	**10**	**0**	**0**	**0**	**28**	**7.1**	**5**	**321**	**52.7**	**16:30**									
2004-05	Salzburg	Austria	11	5	4	9	12																		
2005-06	**Edmonton**	**NHL**	**58**	**9**	**17**	**26**	**20**	**5**	**0**	**1**	**63**	**14.3**	**–12**	**524**	**52.5**	**12:45**									
	Boston	**NHL**	**19**	**2**	**6**	**8**	**8**	**1**	**0**	**0**	**39**	**5.1**	**–2**	**227**	**46.7**	**15:09**									
2006-07	**Edmonton**	**NHL**	**72**	**6**	**14**	**20**	**60**	**0**	**0**	**1**	**84**	**7.1**	**–15**	**765**	**54.6**	**13:52**									
2007-08	**Edmonton**	**NHL**	**82**	**11**	**14**	**25**	**50**	**0**	**0**	**0**	**113**	**9.7**	**–17**	**906**	**52.8**	**14:58**									
2008-09	**Atlanta**	**NHL**	**79**	**14**	**16**	**30**	**36**	**0**	**1**	**2**	**131**	**10.7**	**11**	**1141**	**52.9**	**15:19**									
2009-10	**Atlanta**	**NHL**	**80**	**4**	**13**	**17**	**24**	**0**	**0**	**0**	**86**	**4.7**	**–3**	**1006**	**50.9**	**12:30**									
2010-11	**Florida**	**NHL**	**82**	**14**	**18**	**32**	**22**	**0**	**0**	**4**	**124**	**11.3**	**2**	**1284**	**54.5**	**17:10**									

			Regular Season														Playoffs								
Season	Club	League	GP	G	A	Pts	PIM	PP	SH	GW	S	%	+/-	TF	F%	Min	GP	G	A	Pts	PIM	PP	SH	GW	Min
2011-12	**NY Islanders**	**NHL**	**61**	**1**	**5**	**6**	**34**	**0**	**0**	**0**	**69**	**1.4**	**–25**	**572**	**53.0**	**11:37**	....	....	....	....	....	....	....	....	....
2012-13	**NY Islanders**	**NHL**	**31**	**0**	**5**	**5**	**4**	**0**	**0**	**0**	**34**	**0.0**	**–3**	**299**	**52.5**	**11:14**	**1**	**0**	**0**	**0**	**17**	**0**	**0**	**0**	**12:51**
	NHL Totals		**798**	**97**	**169**	**266**	**379**	**15**	**3**	**10**	**1088**	**8.9**		**9540**	**52.9**	**14:04**	**24**	**6**	**2**	**8**	**23**	**2**	**0**	**1**	**13:07**

Hockey East Rookie of the Year (1996) • Hockey East First All-Star Team (1997, 1998) • NCAA East First All-American Team (1998) • NCAA Championship All-Tournament Team (1998)

Traded to **Edmonton** by **St. Louis** with Jochen Hecht and Jan Horacek for Doug Weight and Michel Riesen, July 1, 2001. • Missed majority of 2003-04 due to ankle (November 8, 2003 vs. Toronto) and knee (January 13, 2004 vs. Florida) injuries. Signed as a free agent by **Salzburg** (Austria), January 30, 2005. Traded to **Boston** by **Edmonton** with Yan Stastny and Edmonton's 2nd round choice (Milan Lucic) in 2006 Entry Draft for Sergei Samsonov, March 9, 2006. Signed as a free agent by **Edmonton**, July 4, 2006. Signed as a free agent by **Atlanta**, July 17, 2008. Traded to **Chicago** by **Atlanta** with Joey Crabb, Jeremy Morin and New Jersey's 1st (prevously acquired, Chicago selected Kevin Hayes) and 2nd (previously acquired, Chicago selected Justin Holl) round choices in 2010 Entry Draft for Brent Sopel, Dustin Byfuglien, Ben Eager and Akim Aliu, June 24, 2010. Traded to **Florida** by **Chicago** for Jeff Taffe, July 22, 2010. Signed as a free agent by **NY Islanders**, July 1, 2011.

REAVES, Ryan (REEVZ, RIGH-uhn) ST.L.

Right wing. Shoots right. 6'1", 224 lbs. Born, Winnipeg, Man., January 20, 1987. St. Louis' 4th choice, 156th overall, in 2005 Entry Draft.

Season	Club	League	GP	G	A	Pts	PIM	PP	SH	GW	S	%	+/-	TF	F%	Min	GP	G	A	Pts	PIM	PP	SH	GW	Min
2004-05	Brandon	WHL	64	7	9	16	79	....	....	....	....	....	....	....	....	....	23	2	4	6	43	....	....	....	....
2005-06	Brandon	WHL	68	14	14	28	91	....	....	....	....	....	....	....	....	....	6	0	1	1	8	....	....	....	....
2006-07	Brandon	WHL	69	15	20	35	76	....	....	....	....	....	....	....	....	....	11	1	4	5	19	....	....	....	....
2007-08	Peoria Rivermen	AHL	31	4	3	7	46	....	....	....	....	....	....	....	....	....	....	....	....	....	....	....	....	....	....
	Alaska Aces	ECHL	9	2	0	2	42	....	....	....	....	....	....	....	....	....	2	0	0	0	22	....	....	....	....
2008-09	Peoria Rivermen	AHL	57	8	9	17	130	....	....	....	....	....	....	....	....	....	4	0	0	0	2	....	....	....	....
2009-10	Peoria Rivermen	AHL	76	4	7	11	167	....	....	....	....	....	....	....	....	....	....	....	....	....	....	....	....	....	....
2010-11	**St. Louis**	**NHL**	**28**	**2**	**2**	**4**	**78**	**0**	**0**	**1**	**16**	**12.5**	**–1**	**2**	**0.0**	**6:48**	....	....	....	....	....	....	....	....	....
	Peoria Rivermen	AHL	50	4	6	10	146	....	....	....	....	....	....	....	....	....	....	....	....	....	....	....	....	....	....
2011-12	**St. Louis**	**NHL**	**60**	**3**	**1**	**4**	**124**	**0**	**0**	**1**	**32**	**9.4**	**0**	**2**	**50.0**	**6:32**	**2**	**0**	**0**	**0**	**0**	**0**	**0**	**0**	**7:47**
2012-13	Orlando	ECHL	13	6	3	9	34	....	....	....	....	....	....	....	....	....	....	....	....	....	....	....	....	....	....
	St. Louis	**NHL**	**43**	**4**	**2**	**6**	**79**	**0**	**0**	**1**	**24**	**16.7**	**3**	**3**	**100.0**	**7:27**	**6**	**0**	**0**	**0**	**2**	**0**	**0**	**0**	**7:30**
	NHL Totals		**131**	**9**	**5**	**14**	**281**	**0**	**0**	**3**	**72**	**12.5**		**7**	**57.1**	**6:53**	**8**	**0**	**0**	**0**	**2**	**0**	**0**	**0**	**7:34**

Signed as a free agent by **Orlando** (ECHL), December 8, 2012.

RECHLICZ, Joel (REHK-lihj, JOHL) WSH

Right wing. Shoots right. 6'4", 235 lbs. Born, Brookfield, WI, June 14, 1987.

Season	Club	League	GP	G	A	Pts	PIM	PP	SH	GW	S	%	+/-	TF	F%	Min	GP	G	A	Pts	PIM	PP	SH	GW	Min
2004-05	Santa Fe	NAHL	3	0	1	1	29	....	....	....	....	....	....	....	....	....	....	....	....	....	....	....	....	....	....
2005-06	Des Moines	USHL	2	0	0	0	4	....	....	....	....	....	....	....	....	....	....	....	....	....	....	....	....	....	....
	Indiana Ice	USHL	2	0	0	0	16	....	....	....	....	....	....	....	....	....	....	....	....	....	....	....	....	....	....
	Gatineau	QMJHL	3	0	0	0	17	....	....	....	....	....	....	....	....	....	....	....	....	....	....	....	....	....	....
2006-07	Chicoutimi	QMJHL	55	0	1	1	159	....	....	....	....	....	....	....	....	....	1	0	0	0	2	....	....	....	....
	Chicago Hounds	UHL	2	0	0	0	9	....	....	....	....	....	....	....	....	....	....	....	....	....	....	....	....	....	....
2007-08	Albany River Rats	AHL	25	0	1	1	106	....	....	....	....	....	....	....	....	....	....	....	....	....	....	....	....	....	....
	Kalamazoo Wings	IHL	25	1	0	1	100	....	....	....	....	....	....	....	....	....	....	....	....	....	....	....	....	....	....
2008-09	**NY Islanders**	**NHL**	**17**	**0**	**1**	**1**	**68**	**0**	**0**	**0**	**7**	**0.0**	**–1**	**0**	**0.0**	**4:52**	....	....	....	....	....	....	....	....	....
	Bridgeport	AHL	4	0	0	0	12	....	....	....	....	....	....	....	....	....	....	....	....	....	....	....	....	....	....
	Utah Grizzlies	ECHL	45	0	1	1	110	....	....	....	....	....	....	....	....	....	....	....	....	....	....	....	....	....	....
2009-10	**NY Islanders**	**NHL**	**6**	**0**	**0**	**0**	**27**	**0**	**0**	**0**	**1**	**0.0**	**–2**	**0**	**0.0**	**2:41**	....	....	....	....	....	....	....	....	....
	Bridgeport	AHL	21	0	0	0	128	....	....	....	....	....	....	....	....	....	....	....	....	....	....	....	....	....	....
2010-11	Hershey Bears	AHL	28	1	0	1	132	....	....	....	....	....	....	....	....	....	....	....	....	....	....	....	....	....	....
2011-12	Hershey Bears	AHL	44	1	1	2	267	....	....	....	....	....	....	....	....	....	....	....	....	....	....	....	....	....	....
	Washington	**NHL**	**3**	**0**	**0**	**0**	**10**	**0**	**0**	**0**	**0**	**0.0**	**0**	**0**	**0.0**	**1:59**	....	....	....	....	....	....	....	....	....
2012-13	Portland Pirates	AHL	36	0	0	0	149	....	....	....	....	....	....	....	....	....	....	....	....	....	....	....	....	....	....
	Hershey Bears	AHL	4	0	0	0	5	....	....	....	....	....	....	....	....	....	....	....	....	....	....	....	....	....	....
	NHL Totals		**26**	**0**	**1**	**1**	**105**	**0**	**0**	**0**	**8**	**0.0**		**0**	**0.0**	**4:02**	....	....	....	....	....	....	....	....	....

Signed as a free agent by **NY Islanders**, May 6, 2008. • Missed majority of 2009-10 as a healthy reserve. Signed as a free agent by **Hershey** (AHL), July 29, 2010. Signed as a free agent by **Washington**, January 30, 2012. Signed as a free agent by **Phoenix**, July 11, 2012. Traded to **Washington** by **Phoenix** for Matt Clackson, April 2, 2013.

REDDEN, Wade (REH-duhn, WAYD)

Defense. Shoots left. 6'2", 205 lbs. Born, Lloydminster, Sask., June 12, 1977. NY Islanders' 1st choice, 2nd overall, in 1995 Entry Draft.

Season	Club	League	GP	G	A	Pts	PIM	PP	SH	GW	S	%	+/-	TF	F%	Min	GP	G	A	Pts	PIM	PP	SH	GW	Min
1992-93	Lloydminster	AJHL	34	4	11	15	64	....	....	....	....	....	....	....	....	....	....	....	....	....	....	....	....	....	....
1993-94	Brandon	WHL	63	4	35	39	98	....	....	....	....	....	....	....	....	....	14	2	4	6	10	....	....	....	....
1994-95	Brandon	WHL	64	14	46	60	83	....	....	....	....	....	....	....	....	....	18	5	10	15	8	....	....	....	....
1995-96	Brandon	WHL	51	9	45	54	55	....	....	....	....	....	....	....	....	....	19	5	10	15	19	....	....	....	....
1996-97	**Ottawa**	**NHL**	**82**	**6**	**24**	**30**	**41**	**2**	**0**	**1**	**102**	**5.9**	**1**	....	....	....	**7**	**1**	**3**	**4**	**2**	**0**	**0**	**0**	....
1997-98	**Ottawa**	**NHL**	**80**	**8**	**14**	**22**	**27**	**3**	**0**	**2**	**103**	**7.8**	**17**	....	....	....	**9**	**0**	**2**	**2**	**2**	**0**	**0**	**0**	....
1998-99	**Ottawa**	**NHL**	**72**	**8**	**21**	**29**	**54**	**3**	**0**	**1**	**127**	**6.3**	**7**	**0**	**0.0**	**23:27**	**4**	**1**	**2**	**3**	**2**	**1**	**0**	**0**	**26:39**
99-2000	**Ottawa**	**NHL**	**81**	**10**	**26**	**36**	**49**	**3**	**0**	**2**	**163**	**6.1**	**–1**	**0**	**0.0**	**23:43**	....	....	....	....	....	....	....	....	....
2000-01	**Ottawa**	**NHL**	**78**	**10**	**37**	**47**	**49**	**4**	**0**	**0**	**159**	**6.3**	**22**	**0**	**0.0**	**25:17**	**4**	**0**	**0**	**0**	**0**	**0**	**0**	**0**	**27:29**
2001-02	**Ottawa**	**NHL**	**79**	**9**	**25**	**34**	**48**	**4**	**1**	**1**	**156**	**5.8**	**22**	**1**	**0.0**	**25:06**	**12**	**3**	**2**	**5**	**6**	**1**	**0**	**1**	**27:56**
2002-03	**Ottawa**	**NHL**	**76**	**10**	**35**	**45**	**70**	**4**	**0**	**3**	**154**	**6.5**	**23**	**0**	**0.0**	**25:24**	**18**	**1**	**8**	**9**	**10**	**0**	**0**	**1**	**25:28**
2003-04	**Ottawa**	**NHL**	**81**	**17**	**26**	**43**	**65**	**12**	**0**	**3**	**175**	**9.7**	**21**	**0**	**0.0**	**24:54**	**7**	**1**	**0**	**1**	**2**	**1**	**0**	**0**	**26:47**
2004-05			DID NOT PLAY																						
2005-06	**Ottawa**	**NHL**	**65**	**10**	**40**	**50**	**63**	**8**	**0**	**4**	**153**	**6.5**	***35**	**1**	**100.0**	**23:28**	**9**	**2**	**8**	**10**	**10**	**2**	**0**	**1**	**25:06**
	Canada	Olympics	6	1	0	1	0	....	....	....	....	....	....	....	....	....	....	....	....	....	....	....	....	....	....
2006-07	**Ottawa**	**NHL**	**64**	**7**	**29**	**36**	**50**	**4**	**0**	**3**	**122**	**5.7**	**1**	**0**	**0.0**	**22:54**	**20**	**3**	**7**	**10**	**10**	**3**	**0**	**1**	**23:37**
2007-08	**Ottawa**	**NHL**	**80**	**6**	**32**	**38**	**60**	**4**	**0**	**1**	**136**	**4.4**	**11**	**0**	**0.0**	**22:13**	**4**	**0**	**1**	**1**	**11**	**0**	**0**	**0**	**19:21**
2008-09	**NY Rangers**	**NHL**	**81**	**3**	**23**	**26**	**51**	**2**	**0**	**0**	**161**	**1.9**	**–5**	**0**	**0.0**	**22:20**	**7**	**0**	**2**	**2**	**0**	**0**	**0**	**0**	**23:24**
2009-10	**NY Rangers**	**NHL**	**75**	**2**	**12**	**14**	**27**	**0**	**0**	**0**	**66**	**3.0**	**8**	**1**	**100.0**	**17:31**	....	....	....	....	....	....	....	....	....
2010-11	Connecticut	AHL	70	8	34	42	46	....	....	....	....	....	....	....	....	....	6	0	6	6	0	....	....	....	....
2011-12	Connecticut	AHL	49	4	16	20	26	....	....	....	....	....	....	....	....	....	9	0	1	1	8	....	....	....	....
2012-13	**St. Louis**	**NHL**	**23**	**2**	**3**	**5**	**11**	**0**	**0**	**0**	**23**	**8.7**	**–2**	**0**	**0.0**	**14:59**	....	....	....	....	....	....	....	....	....
	Boston	**NHL**	**6**	**1**	**1**	**2**	**0**	**0**	**0**	**0**	**5**	**20.0**	**0**	**0**	**0.0**	**15:24**	**5**	**1**	**1**	**2**	**0**	**0**	**0**	**0**	**15:49**
	NHL Totals		**1023**	**109**	**348**	**457**	**665**	**53**	**1**	**21**	**1805**	**6.0**		**3**	**66.7**	**23:03**	**106**	**13**	**36**	**49**	**55**	**8**	**0**	**4**	**24:37**

WHL Rookie of the Year (1994) • WHL East Second All-Star Team (1995) • WHL East First All-Star Team (1996) • Memorial Cup All-Star Team (1996)

Played in NHL All-Star Game (2002)

Traded to **Ottawa** by **NY Islanders** with Damian Rhodes for Don Beaupre, Martin Straka and Bryan Berard, January 23, 1996. Signed as a free agent by **NY Rangers**, July 1, 2008. Signed as a free agent by **St. Louis**, January 18, 2013. Traded to **Boston** by **St. Louis** for future considerations, April 3, 2013.

REDMOND, Zach (REHD-muhnd, ZAK) WPG

Defense. Shoots right. 6'2", 197 lbs. Born, Traverse City, MI, July 26, 1988. Atlanta's 7th choice, 184th overall, in 2008 Entry Draft.

Season	Club	League	GP	G	A	Pts	PIM	PP	SH	GW	S	%	+/-	TF	F%	Min	GP	G	A	Pts	PIM	PP	SH	GW	Min
2005-06	Sioux Falls	USHL	48	4	7	11	57	....	....	....	....	....	....	....	....	....	11	1	2	3	4	....	....	....	....
2006-07	Sioux Falls	USHL	60	8	31	39	37	....	....	....	....	....	....	....	....	....	8	3	7	10	8	....	....	....	....
2007-08	Ferris State	CCHA	37	6	13	19	33	....	....	....	....	....	....	....	....	....	....	....	....	....	....	....	....	....	....
2008-09	Ferris State	CCHA	38	3	21	24	48	....	....	....	....	....	....	....	....	....	....	....	....	....	....	....	....	....	....
2009-10	Ferris State	CCHA	40	6	21	27	46	....	....	....	....	....	....	....	....	....	....	....	....	....	....	....	....	....	....
2010-11	Ferris State	CCHA	26	7	13	20	20	....	....	....	....	....	....	....	....	....	....	....	....	....	....	....	....	....	....
	Chicago Wolves	AHL	3	0	0	0	4	....	....	....	....	....	....	....	....	....	....	....	....	....	....	....	....	....	....
2011-12	St. John's IceCaps	AHL	72	8	23	31	33	....	....	....	....	....	....	....	....	....	10	1	2	3	10	....	....	....	....
2012-13	St. John's IceCaps	AHL	38	8	11	19	34	....	....	....	....	....	....	....	....	....	....	....	....	....	....	....	....	....	....
	Winnipeg	**NHL**	**8**	**1**	**3**	**4**	**12**	**0**	**1**	**0**	**13**	**7.7**	**0**	**0**	**0.0**	**19:35**	....	....	....	....	....	....	....	....	....
	NHL Totals		**8**	**1**	**3**	**4**	**12**	**0**	**1**	**0**	**13**	**7.7**		**0**	**0.0**	**19:35**	....	....	....	....	....	....	....	....	....

CCHA Second All-Star Team (2010) • CCHA First All-Star Team (2011) • NCAA West Second All-American Team (2011)

• Transferred to **Winnipeg** after **Atlanta** franchise relocated, June 21, 2011.

REESE, Dylan

(REES, DIH-luhn)

Defense. Shoots right. 6'1", 201 lbs. Born, Pittsburgh, PA, August 29, 1984. NY Rangers' 9th choice, 209th overall, in 2003 Entry Draft.

Season	Club	League	Regular Season GP	G	A	Pts	PIM	PP	SH	GW	S	%	+/-	TF	F%	Min	Playoffs GP	G	A	Pts	PIM	PP	SH	GW	Min
2000-01	Pittsburgh	MWEHL	66	14	42	66																			
2001-02	Pittsburgh Forge	NAHL	48	7	16	23	70										7	0	2	2	4				
2002-03	Pittsburgh Forge	NAHL	56	11	30	41	98										5	2	3	5	6				
2003-04	Harvard Crimson	ECAC	21	1	4	5	18																		
2004-05	Harvard Crimson	ECAC	34	7	12	19	44																		
2005-06	Harvard Crimson	ECAC	33	4	15	19	36																		
2006-07	Harvard Crimson	ECAC	33	9	9	18	26																		
	Hartford	AHL	10	0	4	4	12										2	0	0	0	2				
2007-08	San Antonio	AHL	59	1	6	7	49										3	1	1	2	4				
2008-09	San Antonio	AHL	75	1	27	28	64																		
2009-10	Syracuse Crunch	AHL	51	4	18	22	31																		
	NY Islanders	**NHL**	**19**	**2**	**2**	**4**	**14**	**0**	**0**	**1**	**16**	**12.5**	**4**	**0**	**0.0**	**15:02**									
	Bridgeport	AHL	1	1	1	2	0										5	1	3	4	0				
2010-11	**NY Islanders**	**NHL**	**27**	**0**	**6**	**6**	**15**	**0**	**0**	**0**	**23**	**0.0**	**–12**	**0**	**0.0**	**14:49**									
	Bridgeport	AHL	37	4	14	18	30																		
2011-12	**NY Islanders**	**NHL**	**28**	**1**	**6**	**7**	**11**	**0**	**0**	**0**	**26**	**3.8**	**0**	**0**	**0.0**	**17:05**									
	Bridgeport	AHL	27	2	13	15	12																		
2012-13	Wilkes-Barre	AHL	66	8	17	25	34										5	0	1	1	2				
	Pittsburgh	**NHL**	**3**	**0**	**0**	**0**	**0**	**0**	**0**	**0**	**1**	**0.0**	**0**	**0**	**0.0**	**15:16**									
	NHL Totals		**77**	**3**	**14**	**17**	**40**	**0**	**0**	**1**	**66**	**4.5**		**0**	**0.0**	**15:43**									

ECAC Second All-Star Team (2006, 2007)

Signed as a free agent by **San Antonio** (AHL), September 5, 2007. Signed as a free agent by **Columbus**, September 29, 2009. Traded to **NY Islanders** by **Columbus** for Greg Moore, March 1, 2010. Signed as a free agent by **Pittsburgh**, July 1, 2012. Signed as a free agent by **Khabarovsk** (KHL), June 15, 2013.

REGEHR, Robyn

(reh-GEER, RAW-bihn) **L.A.**

Defense. Shoots left. 6'3", 225 lbs. Born, Recife, Brazil, April 19, 1980. Colorado's 3rd choice, 19th overall, in 1998 Entry Draft.

Season	Club	League	Regular Season GP	G	A	Pts	PIM	PP	SH	GW	S	%	+/-	TF	F%	Min	Playoffs GP	G	A	Pts	PIM	PP	SH	GW	Min
1995-96	Prince Albert	SMHL	59	8	24	32	157																		
1996-97	Kamloops Blazers	WHL	64	4	19	23	67										5	0	1	1	18				
1997-98	Kamloops Blazers	WHL	65	4	10	14	120										5	0	3	3	8				
1998-99	Kamloops Blazers	WHL	54	12	20	32	130										12	1	4	5	21				
99-2000	**Calgary**	**NHL**	**57**	**5**	**7**	**12**	**46**	**2**	**0**	**0**	**64**	**7.8**	**–2**	**0**	**0.0**	**18:24**									
	Saint John Flames	AHL	5	0	0	0	0																		
2000-01	**Calgary**	**NHL**	**71**	**1**	**3**	**4**	**70**	**0**	**0**	**0**	**62**	**1.6**	**–7**	**1**	**0.0**	**19:43**									
2001-02	**Calgary**	**NHL**	**77**	**2**	**6**	**8**	**93**	**0**	**0**	**0**	**82**	**2.4**	**–24**	**0**	**0.0**	**20:54**									
2002-03	**Calgary**	**NHL**	**76**	**0**	**12**	**12**	**87**	**0**	**0**	**0**	**109**	**0.0**	**–9**	**1**	**100.0**	**22:45**									
2003-04	**Calgary**	**NHL**	**82**	**4**	**14**	**18**	**74**	**2**	**0**	**1**	**106**	**3.8**	**14**	**2**	**50.0**	**22:21**	**26**	**2**	**7**	**9**	**20**	**0**	**0**	**0**	**26:27**
2004-05			DID NOT PLAY																						
2005-06	**Calgary**	**NHL**	**68**	**6**	**20**	**26**	**67**	**5**	**0**	**2**	**89**	**6.7**	**6**	**1**	**100.0**	**23:08**	**7**	**1**	**3**	**4**	**6**	**1**	**0**	**0**	**22:22**
	Canada	Olympics	6	0	1	1	2																		
2006-07	**Calgary**	**NHL**	**78**	**2**	**19**	**21**	**75**	**0**	**0**	**0**	**66**	**3.0**	**27**	**1**	**0.0**	**21:55**	**1**	**0**	**0**	**0**	**0**	**0**	**0**	**0**	**11:15**
2007-08	**Calgary**	**NHL**	**82**	**5**	**15**	**20**	**79**	**1**	**1**	**0**	**93**	**5.4**	**11**	**0**	**0.0**	**21:20**	**7**	**0**	**2**	**2**	**2**	**0**	**0**	**0**	**21:50**
2008-09	**Calgary**	**NHL**	**75**	**0**	**8**	**8**	**73**	**0**	**0**	**0**	**79**	**0.0**	**10**	**0**	**0.0**	**21:09**									
2009-10	**Calgary**	**NHL**	**81**	**2**	**15**	**17**	**80**	**0**	**0**	**0**	**78**	**2.6**	**2**	**1**	**0.0**	**21:38**									
2010-11	**Calgary**	**NHL**	**79**	**2**	**15**	**17**	**58**	**1**	**0**	**0**	**72**	**2.8**	**2**	**0**	**0.0**	**21:29**									
2011-12	**Buffalo**	**NHL**	**76**	**1**	**4**	**5**	**56**	**0**	**0**	**0**	**49**	**2.0**	**–12**	**0**	**0.0**	**18:38**									
2012-13	**Buffalo**	**NHL**	**29**	**0**	**2**	**2**	**21**	**0**	**0**	**0**	**15**	**0.0**	**–4**	**0**	**0.0**	**18:39**									
	Los Angeles	**NHL**	**12**	**0**	**2**	**2**	**2**	**0**	**0**	**0**	**12**	**0.0**	**0**	**0**	**0.0**	**21:16**	**18**	**0**	**1**	**1**	**6**	**0**	**0**	**0**	**21:14**
	NHL Totals		**943**	**30**	**142**	**172**	**881**	**11**	**1**	**3**	**976**	**3.1**		**7**	**42.9**	**21:06**	**59**	**3**	**13**	**16**	**34**	**1**	**0**	**0**	**23:34**

WHL West First All-Star Team (1999)

Traded to **Calgary** by **Colorado** with Rene Corbet, Wade Belak and Colorado's 2nd round compensatory choice (Jarret Stoll) in 2000 Entry Draft for Theoren Fleury and Chris Dingman, February 28, 1999. Traded to **Buffalo** by **Calgary** with Ales Kotalik and Calgary's 2nd round choice (Jake McCabe) in 2012 Entry Draft for Chris Butler and Paul Byron, June 25, 2011. Traded to **Los Angeles** by **Buffalo** for Los Angeles' 2nd round choices in 2014 and 2015 Entry Drafts, April 1, 2013.

REGIN, Peter

(REE-gihn, PEE-tuhr) **NYI**

Center. Shoots left. 6'2", 195 lbs. Born, Herning, Denmark, April 16, 1986. Ottawa's 4th choice, 87th overall, in 2004 Entry Draft.

Season	Club	League	Regular Season GP	G	A	Pts	PIM	PP	SH	GW	S	%	+/-	TF	F%	Min	Playoffs GP	G	A	Pts	PIM	PP	SH	GW	Min
2002-03	Herning IK	Denmark	24	0	1	1	4										10	1	3	4	4				
	Denmark	WJC-B	5	2	0	2	0																		
	Denmark	WJ18-B	5	0	2	2	6																		
2003-04	Herning IK	Denmark	33	9	11	20	14																		
	Denmark	WJC-B	5	1	2	3	2																		
	Denmark	WJ18-B	6	5	4	9	0																		
2004-05	Herning Blue Fox	Denmark	36	19	27	46	43										16	5	8	13	2				
	Denmark	Oly-Q	3	1	1	2	2																		
2005-06	Timra IK	Sweden	44	4	7	11	14																		
2006-07	Timra IK	Sweden	51	9	7	16	16										7	2	2	4	2				
2007-08	Timra IK	Sweden	55	12	19	31	36										11	2	7	9	2				
2008-09	**Ottawa**	**NHL**	**11**	**1**	**1**	**2**	**2**	**0**	**0**	**1**	**7**	**14.3**	**0**	**77**	**53.3**	**10:32**									
	Binghamton	AHL	56	18	29	47	36																		
2009-10	**Ottawa**	**NHL**	**75**	**13**	**16**	**29**	**20**	**1**	**0**	**1**	**135**	**9.6**	**10**	**538**	**44.6**	**12:54**	**6**	**3**	**1**	**4**	**6**	**0**	**0**	**0**	**18:06**
2010-11	**Ottawa**	**NHL**	**55**	**3**	**14**	**17**	**12**	**0**	**0**	**1**	**87**	**3.4**	**–4**	**316**	**41.8**	**13:23**									
2011-12	**Ottawa**	**NHL**	**10**	**2**	**2**	**4**	**2**	**0**	**0**	**0**	**15**	**13.3**	**3**	**59**	**49.2**	**14:06**									
2012-13	SC Langenthal	Swiss-2	4	2	3	5	2																		
	Ottawa	**NHL**	**27**	**0**	**3**	**3**	**8**	**0**	**0**	**0**	**37**	**0.0**	**–4**	**210**	**43.8**	**11:31**									
	NHL Totals		**178**	**19**	**36**	**55**	**44**	**1**	**0**	**3**	**281**	**6.8**		**1200**	**44.5**	**12:46**	**6**	**3**	**1**	**4**	**6**	**0**	**0**	**0**	**18:06**

• Missed majority of 2011-12 due to recurring shoulder injury and resulting surgery, January 30, 2012. Signed as a free agent by **Langenthal** (Swiss-2), October 18, 2012. Signed as a free agent by **NY Islanders**, July 5, 2013.

REINHART, Max

(RIGHN-hart, MAX) **CGY**

Center. Shoots left. 6'1", 185 lbs. Born, West Vancouver, B.C., February 4, 1992. Calgary's 1st choice, 64th overall, in 2010 Entry Draft.

Season	Club	League	Regular Season GP	G	A	Pts	PIM	PP	SH	GW	S	%	+/-	TF	F%	Min	Playoffs GP	G	A	Pts	PIM	PP	SH	GW	Min
2008-09	Kootenay Ice	WHL	62	11	16	27	21										4	1	0	1	2				
2009-10	Kootenay Ice	WHL	72	21	30	51	38										6	1	1	2	6				
2010-11	Kootenay Ice	WHL	71	34	45	79	41										19	15	12	27	12				
2011-12	Kootenay Ice	WHL	61	28	50	78	40										3	0	2	2	6				
	Abbotsford Heat	AHL	1	2	0	2	0										4	1	1	2	0				
2012-13	Abbotsford Heat	AHL	67	7	14	21	32																		
	Calgary	**NHL**	**11**	**1**	**2**	**3**	**4**	**0**	**0**	**0**	**26**	**3.8**	**–3**	**91**	**37.4**	**14:25**									
	NHL Totals		**11**	**1**	**2**	**3**	**4**	**0**	**0**	**0**	**26**	**3.8**		**91**	**37.4**	**14:25**									

WHL East Second All-Star Team (2012)

REINPRECHT, Steve

(RIGHN-prehkt, STEEV)

Center. Shoots left. 6', 195 lbs. Born, Edmonton, Alta., May 7, 1976.

Season	Club	League	Regular Season GP	G	A	Pts	PIM	PP	SH	GW	S	%	+/-	TF	F%	Min	Playoffs GP	G	A	Pts	PIM	PP	SH	GW	Min
1993-94	Edmonton SSAC	AMHL	71	48	77	125																			
1994-95	St. Albert Saints	AJHL	56	35	44	79	14																		
1995-96	St. Albert Saints	AJHL	39	24	33	57	16																		
1996-97	U. of Wisconsin	WCHA	38	11	9	20	12																		
1997-98	U. of Wisconsin	WCHA	41	19	24	43	18																		
1998-99	U. of Wisconsin	WCHA	38	16	17	33	14																		
99-2000	U. of Wisconsin	WCHA	37	26	40	*66	14																		
	Los Angeles	**NHL**	**1**	**0**	**0**	**0**	**2**	**0**	**0**	**0**	**0**	**0.0**	**0**	**6**	**50.0**	**6:01**									
2000-01	**Los Angeles**	**NHL**	**59**	**12**	**17**	**29**	**12**	**3**	**2**	**3**	**72**	**16.7**	**11**	**676**	**41.4**	**12:39**									
	♦ Colorado	**NHL**	**21**	**3**	**4**	**7**	**2**	**0**	**0**	**0**	**28**	**10.7**	**–1**	**209**	**51.2**	**15:38**	**22**	**2**	**3**	**5**	**2**	**0**	**0**	**0**	**12:09**
2001-02	**Colorado**	**NHL**	**67**	**19**	**27**	**46**	**18**	**4**	**0**	**3**	**111**	**17.1**	**14**	**413**	**52.1**	**16:32**	**21**	**7**	**5**	**12**	**8**	**0**	**0**	**2**	**16:23**
2002-03	**Colorado**	**NHL**	**77**	**18**	**33**	**51**	**18**	**2**	**1**	**1**	**146**	**12.3**	**–6**	**928**	**46.4**	**17:22**	**7**	**1**	**2**	**3**	**0**	**0**	**0**	**0**	**15:32**

			Regular Season														Playoffs								
Season	Club	League	GP	G	A	Pts	PIM	PP	SH	GW	S	%	+/-	TF	F%	Min	GP	G	A	Pts	PIM	PP	SH	GW	Min
2003-04	Calgary	NHL	44	7	22	29	4	3	0	1	68	10.3	1	120	40.0	17:05									
2004-05	HC Mulhouse	France	22	20	27	47	6										10	7	6	13	2				
2005-06	Calgary	NHL	52	10	19	29	24	5	0	1	72	13.9	10	340	49.4	14:49									
	Phoenix	NHL	28	12	11	23	8	4	1	2	58	20.7	1	526	47.3	19:06									
2006-07	Phoenix	NHL	49	9	24	33	28	2	0	1	71	12.7	–3	537	52.3	15:40									
2007-08	Phoenix	NHL	81	16	30	46	26	5	1	0	105	15.2	–3	1020	50.6	15:42									
2008-09	Phoenix	NHL	73	14	27	41	20	3	0	3	95	14.7	0	886	46.3	15:54									
2009-10	Florida	NHL	82	16	22	38	18	3	0	1	124	12.9	–1	989	47.7	16:05									
2010-11	Florida	NHL	29	4	6	10	6	1	0	1	31	12.9	–2	172	51.7	11:46									
	Adler Mannheim	Germany	18	4	9	13	2										6	1	2	3	2				
2011-12	San Antonio	AHL	5	0	0	0	0																		
	Chicago Wolves	AHL	57	13	30	43	14										4	2	1	3	2				
2012-13	Nurnberg	Germany	33	9	19	28	10										3	2	1	3	0				
	NHL Totals		**663**	**140**	**242**	**382**	**186**	**35**	**5**	**17**	**981**	**14.3**		**6822**	**47.9**	**15:45**	**50**	**10**	**10**	**20**	**10**	**0**	**0**	**2**	**14:24**

WCHA Second All-Star Team (1998) • WCHA First All-Star Team (2000) • WCHA Player of the Year (2000) • NCAA West First All-American Team (2000)

Signed as a free agent by **Los Angeles**, March 31, 2000. Traded to **Colorado** by **Los Angeles** with Rob Blake for Adam Deadmarsh, Aaron Miller, a player to be named later (Jared Aulin, March 22, 2001) and Colorado's 1st round choices in 2001 (Dave Steckel) and 2003 (Brian Boyle) Entry Drafts, February 21, 2001. Traded to **Buffalo** by **Colorado** for Keith Ballard, July 3, 2003. Traded to **Calgary** by **Buffalo** with Rhett Warrener for Chris Drury and Steve Begin, July 3, 2003. Signed as a free agent by **Mulhouse** (France), September 28, 2004. Traded to **Phoenix** by **Calgary** with Philippe Sauve for Brian Boucher and Mike Leclerc, February 2, 2006. Traded to **Florida** by **Phoenix** for Stefan Meyer, June 19, 2009. • Loaned to **Mannheim** (Germany) by **Florida**, January 6, 2011. Traded to **Vancouver** by **Florida** with David Booth and Vancouver's 3rd round choice (previously acquired, Vancouver selected Cole Cassels) in 2013 Entry Draft for Mikael Samuelsson and Marco Sturm, October 22, 2011. Signed as a free agent by **Nurnberg** (Germany), September 26, 2012.

REPIK, Michal

(REH-pihk, MEE-khahl) **FLA**

Right wing. Shoots right. 5'10", 180 lbs. Born, Vlasim, Czech., December 31, 1988. Florida's 2nd choice, 40th overall, in 2007 Entry Draft.

Season	Club	League	GP	G	A	Pts	PIM	PP	SH	GW	S	%	+/-	TF	F%	Min	GP	G	A	Pts	PIM	PP	SH	GW	Min
2002-03	Sparta U17	CzR-U17	18	7	10	17	6										2	0	0	0	0				
2003-04	Sparta U17	CzR-U17	33	25	17	42	42										3	0	0	0	0				
	Sparta Jr.	CzRep-Jr.	23	12	5	17	10																		
2004-05	Sparta U17	CzR-U17	2	2	3	5	6																		
	Sparta Jr.	CzRep-Jr.	45	26	31	57	24										8	2	4	6	10				
2005-06	Vancouver Giants	WHL	69	24	28	52	55										14	3	3	6	19				
2006-07	Vancouver Giants	WHL	56	24	31	55	56										22	10	*16	*26	24				
2007-08	Vancouver Giants	WHL	51	27	34	61	62										10	5	6	11	18				
2008-09	Florida	NHL	5	2	0	2	2	0	0	0	7	28.6	1	1	100.0	7:32									
	Rochester	AHL	75	19	30	49	58																		
2009-10	Florida	NHL	19	3	2	5	6	0	0	0	23	13.0	1	1	100.0	8:35									
	Rochester	AHL	60	22	31	53	57										7	1	1	2	4				
2010-11	Florida	NHL	31	2	6	8	22	0	0	0	54	3.7	–6	7	42.9	12:47									
	Rochester	AHL	53	11	34	45	38																		
2011-12	Florida	NHL	17	2	3	5	6	1	0	0	35	5.7	–3	5	60.0	10:22									
	San Antonio	AHL	55	14	21	35	51										4	1	3	4	6				
2012-13	HC Lev Praha	KHL	47	4	6	10	32										4	1	2	3	8				
	NHL Totals		**72**	**9**	**11**	**20**	**36**	**1**	**0**	**0**	**119**	**7.6**		**14**	**57.1**	**10:44**									

Memorial Cup All-Star Team (2007) • Ed Chynoweth Trophy (Memorial Cup - Leading Scorer) (2007)

Signed as a free agent by **Lev Praha** (KHL), June 20, 2012.

RHEAULT, Jon

(RAY-oh, JAWN) **FLA**

Right wing. Shoots right. 5'11", 200 lbs. Born, Arlington, TX, August 1, 1986. Philadelphia's 8th choice, 145th overall, in 2006 Entry Draft.

Season	Club	League	GP	G	A	Pts	PIM	PP	SH	GW	S	%	+/-	TF	F%	Min	GP	G	A	Pts	PIM	PP	SH	GW	Min
2003-04	N.H. Jr. Monarchs	EJHL		49	46	*95																			
2004-05	Providence	H-East	36	11	8	19	36																		
2005-06	Providence	H-East	35	16	14	30	29																		
2006-07	Providence	H-East	35	12	13	25	38																		
2007-08	Providence	H-East	36	17	14	31	23																		
2008-09	Ontario Reign	ECHL	51	19	22	41	56										7	4	4	8	4				
	Manchester	AHL	24	2	3	5	12																		
2009-10	Ontario Reign	ECHL	30	19	16	35	24																		
	Providence Bruins	AHL	4	0	0	0	4																		
	Manchester	AHL	35	3	3	6	14																		
	Abbotsford Heat	AHL	5	3	2	5	0										13	6	2	8	2				
2010-11	Abbotsford Heat	AHL	79	12	22	34	46																		
2011-12	Abbotsford Heat	AHL	47	16	17	33	29										8	3	1	4	0				
2012-13	San Antonio	AHL	67	20	28	48	40																		
	Florida	NHL	5	0	0	0	0	0	0	0	5	0.0	0	1	0.0	10:34									
	NHL Totals		**5**	**0**	**0**	**0**	**0**	**0**	**0**	**0**	**5**	**0.0**		**1**	**0.0**	**10:34**									

Signed as a free agent by **Ontario** (ECHL), August 29, 2008. Signed to a PTO (professional tryout) contract by **Manchester** (AHL), December 13, 2008. Signed as a free agent by **Ontario** (ECHL), July 21, 2009. Signed to a PTO (professional tryout) contract by **Providence** (AHL), November 13, 2009. Signed to a PTO (professional tryout) contract by **Manchester** (AHL), December 1, 2009. Signed to a PTO (professional tryout) contract by **Abbotsford** (AHL), March 29, 2010. Signed as a free agent by **Abbotsford** (AHL), June 16, 2010. Signed as a free agent by **Calgary**, July 27, 2011. Signed as a free agent by **Florida**, July 1, 2012. Signed as a free agent by **Mannheim** (Germany), July 2, 2013.

RIBEIRO, Mike

(rih-BAIR-roh, MIGHK) **PHX**

Center. Shoots left. 6', 180 lbs. Born, Montreal, Que., February 10, 1980. Montreal's 2nd choice, 45th overall, in 1998 Entry Draft.

Season	Club	League	GP	G	A	Pts	PIM	PP	SH	GW	S	%	+/-	TF	F%	Min	GP	G	A	Pts	PIM	PP	SH	GW	Min
1996-97	Mtl-Bourassa	QAAA	43	32	57	89	48										16	15	23	38	14				
1997-98	Rouyn-Noranda	QMJHL	67	40	*85	125	55										6	3	1	4	0				
1998-99	Rouyn-Noranda	QMJHL	69	*67	*100	*167	137										11	5	11	16	12				
	Fredericton	AHL															5	0	1	1	2				
99-2000	Montreal	NHL	19	1	1	2	2	1	0	0	18	5.6	–6	95	34.7	10:40									
	Quebec Citadelles	AHL	3	0	0	0	2																		
	Rouyn-Noranda	QMJHL	2	1	3	4	0																		
	Quebec Remparts	QMJHL	21	17	28	45	30										11	3	20	23	38				
2000-01	Montreal	NHL	2	0	0	0	2	0	0	0	3	0.0	0	11	18.2	10:38									
	Quebec Citadelles	AHL	74	26	40	66	44										9	1	5	6	23				
2001-02	Montreal	NHL	43	8	10	18	12	3	0	0	48	16.7	–11	141	44.0	13:55									
	Quebec Citadelles	AHL	23	9	14	23	36										3	0	3	3	0				
2002-03	Montreal	NHL	52	5	12	17	6	2	0	0	57	8.8	–3	358	50.3	11:07									
	Hamilton	AHL	3	0	1	1	0																		
2003-04	Montreal	NHL	81	20	45	65	34	7	0	5	103	19.4	15	913	44.8	17:05	11	2	1	3	18	0	0	0	16:31
2004-05	Blues Espoo	Finland	17	8	9	17	4																		
2005-06	Montreal	NHL	79	16	35	51	36	8	0	2	130	12.3	–6	843	44.7	16:35	6	0	2	2	0	0	0	0	18:22
2006-07	Dallas	NHL	81	18	41	59	22	6	0	3	111	16.2	3	678	46.6	14:56	7	0	3	3	4	0	0	0	18:28
2007-08	Dallas	NHL	76	27	56	83	46	7	0	5	107	25.2	21	883	45.0	18:26	18	3	14	17	16	0	0	0	21:45
2008-09	Dallas	NHL	82	22	56	78	52	7	0	1	163	13.5	–4	1240	45.5	20:57									
2009-10	Dallas	NHL	66	19	34	53	38	8	2	0	155	12.3	–5	1102	44.8	19:32									
2010-11	Dallas	NHL	82	19	52	71	28	7	0	4	161	11.8	–4	1213	46.6	19:58									
2011-12	Dallas	NHL	74	18	45	63	66	2	0	5	142	12.7	5	808	42.2	20:03									
2012-13	Washington	NHL	48	13	36	49	53	6	0	1	63	20.6	–4	505	44.8	17:50	7	1	1	2	10	0	0	1	18:33
	NHL Totals		**785**	**186**	**423**	**609**	**397**	**64**	**2**	**26**	**1261**	**14.8**		**8790**	**45.1**	**17:26**	**49**	**6**	**21**	**27**	**48**	**0**	**0**	**1**	**19:14**

QMJHL Second All-Star Team (1998) • QMJHL First All-Star Team (1999) • Canadian Major Junior First All-Star Team (1999)

Played in NHL All-Star Game (2008)

Signed as a free agent by **Espoo** (Finland), January 17, 2005. Traded to **Dallas** by **Montreal** with Montreal's 6th round choice (Matthew Tassone) in 2008 Entry Draft for Janne Niinimaa and Dallas' 5th round choice (Andrew Conboy) in 2007 Entry Draft, September 30, 2006. Traded to **Washington** by **Dallas** for Cody Eakin and Boston's 2nd round choice (previously acquired, Dallas selected Mike Winther) in 2012 Entry Draft, June 22, 2012. Signed as a free agent by **Phoenix**, July 5, 2013.

Season	Club	League	GP	G	A	Pts	PIM	PP	SH	GW	S	%	+/-	TF	F%	Min	GP	G	A	Pts	PIM	PP	SH	GW	Min
			Regular Season														Playoffs								

RICHARDS, Brad

(RIH-chuhrds, BRAD) **NYR**

Center. Shoots left. 6', 196 lbs. Born, Murray Harbour, P.E.I., May 2, 1980. Tampa Bay's 2nd choice, 64th overall, in 1998 Entry Draft.

Season	Club	League	GP	G	A	Pts	PIM	PP	SH	GW	S	%	+/-	TF	F%	Min	GP	G	A	Pts	PIM	PP	SH	GW	Min
1996-97	Notre Dame	SJHL	63	39	48	87	73	....	....	....	....	....	....	....	....	....	....	....	....	....	....	....	....	....	....
1997-98	Rimouski Oceanic	QMJHL	68	33	82	115	44	....	....	....	....	....	....	....	....	....	19	8	24	32	2	....	....	....	....
1998-99	Rimouski Oceanic	QMJHL	59	39	92	131	55	....	....	....	....	....	....	....	....	....	11	9	12	21	6	....	....	....	....
99-2000	Rimouski Oceanic	QMJHL	63	*71	*115	*186	69	....	....	....	....	....	....	....	....	....	12	13	*24	*37	16	....	....	....	....
2000-01	**Tampa Bay**	**NHL**	**82**	**21**	**41**	**62**	**14**	**7**	**0**	**3**	**179**	**11.7**	**-10**	**955**	**41.4**	**16:54**	....	....	....	....	....	....	....	....	....
2001-02	**Tampa Bay**	**NHL**	**82**	**20**	**42**	**62**	**13**	**5**	**0**	**0**	**251**	**8.0**	**-18**	**911**	**41.2**	**19:48**	....	....	....	....	....	....	....	....	....
2002-03	**Tampa Bay**	**NHL**	**80**	**17**	**57**	**74**	**24**	**4**	**0**	**2**	**277**	**6.1**	**3**	**1007**	**47.5**	**19:56**	**11**	**0**	**5**	**5**	**12**	**0**	**0**	**0**	**22:21**
2003-04♦	**Tampa Bay**	**NHL**	**82**	**26**	**53**	**79**	**12**	**5**	**1**	**6**	**244**	**10.7**	**13**	**1167**	**46.7**	**20:26**	**23**	**12**	**14**	***26**	**4**	***7**	**0**	***7**	**23:28**
2004-05	Ak Bars Kazan	Russia	6	2	5	7	16	....	....	....	....	....	....	....	....	....	....	....	....	....	....	....	....	....	....
2005-06	**Tampa Bay**	**NHL**	**82**	**23**	**68**	**91**	**32**	**7**	**4**	**0**	**282**	**8.2**	**0**	**1288**	**50.2**	**22:45**	**5**	**3**	**5**	**8**	**6**	**0**	**0**	**0**	**24:11**
	Canada	Olympics	6	2	2	4	6	....	....	....	....	....	....	....	....	....	....	....	....	....	....	....	....	....	....
2006-07	**Tampa Bay**	**NHL**	**82**	**25**	**45**	**70**	**23**	**12**	**1**	**3**	**272**	**9.2**	**-19**	**1580**	**51.4**	**24:07**	**6**	**3**	**5**	**8**	**6**	**2**	**0**	**0**	**25:39**
2007-08	**Tampa Bay**	**NHL**	**62**	**18**	**33**	**51**	**15**	**9**	**1**	**4**	**228**	**7.9**	**-25**	**944**	**48.1**	**24:17**	....	....	....	....	....	....	....	....	....
	Dallas	**NHL**	**12**	**2**	**9**	**11**	**0**	**0**	**1**	**0**	**21**	**9.5**	**-2**	**130**	**56.2**	**19:15**	**18**	**3**	**12**	**15**	**8**	**0**	**0**	**0**	**21:06**
2008-09	**Dallas**	**NHL**	**56**	**16**	**32**	**48**	**6**	**5**	**0**	**2**	**180**	**8.9**	**-4**	**911**	**50.6**	**20:29**	....	....	....	....	....	....	....	....	....
2009-10	**Dallas**	**NHL**	**80**	**24**	**67**	**91**	**14**	**13**	**0**	**2**	**284**	**8.5**	**-12**	**1140**	**51.5**	**20:52**	....	....	....	....	....	....	....	....	....
2010-11	**Dallas**	**NHL**	**72**	**28**	**49**	**77**	**24**	**7**	**0**	**3**	**272**	**10.3**	**1**	**990**	**50.6**	**21:43**	....	....	....	....	....	....	....	....	....
2011-12	**NY Rangers**	**NHL**	**82**	**25**	**41**	**66**	**22**	**7**	**0**	**9**	**229**	**10.9**	**-1**	**1316**	**51.8**	**20:16**	**20**	**6**	**9**	**15**	**8**	**2**	**0**	**0**	**22:12**
2012-13	**NY Rangers**	**NHL**	**46**	**11**	**23**	**34**	**14**	**3**	**0**	**1**	**110**	**10.0**	**8**	**773**	**50.6**	**18:49**	**10**	**1**	**0**	**1**	**2**	**0**	**0**	**0**	**14:43**
	NHL Totals		**900**	**256**	**560**	**816**	**213**	**84**	**8**	**35**	**2829**	**9.0**		**13112**	**48.8**	**20:51**	**93**	**28**	**50**	**78**	**46**	**11**	**0**	**7**	**21:51**

QMJHL First All-Star Team (2000) • Canadian Major Junior First All-Star Team (2000) • Canadian Major Junior Player of the Year (2000) • Memorial Cup All-Star Team (2000) • Stafford Smythe Memorial Trophy (Memorial Cup - MVP) (2000) • NHL All-Rookie Team (2001) • Lady Byng Memorial Trophy (2004) • Conn Smythe Trophy (2004)

Played in NHL All-Star Game (2011)

Signed as a free agent by **Kazan** (Russia), November 8, 2004. Traded to **Dallas** by **Tampa Bay** with Johan Holmqvist for Jussi Jokinen, Jeff Halpern, Mike Smith and Dallas' 4th round choice (later traded to Minnesota, later traded to Edmonton – Edmonton selected Kyle Bigos) in 2009 Entry Draft, February 26, 2008. Signed as a free agent by **NY Rangers**, July 2, 2011.

RICHARDS, Mike

(RIH-chuhrds, MIGHK) **L.A.**

Center. Shoots left. 5'11", 200 lbs. Born, Kenora, Ont., February 11, 1985. Philadelphia's 2nd choice, 24th overall, in 2003 Entry Draft.

Season	Club	League	GP	G	A	Pts	PIM	PP	SH	GW	S	%	+/-	TF	F%	Min	GP	G	A	Pts	PIM	PP	SH	GW	Min
2000-01	Kenora Stars	NOHA	85	76	73	149	20	....	....	....	....	....	....	....	....	....	....	....	....	....	....	....	....	....	....
2001-02	Kitchener Rangers	OHL	65	20	38	58	52	....	....	....	....	....	....	....	....	....	4	0	1	1	6	....	....	....	....
2002-03	Kitchener Rangers	OHL	67	37	50	87	99	....	....	....	....	....	....	....	....	....	21	9	18	27	24	....	....	....	....
2003-04	Kitchener Rangers	OHL	58	36	53	89	82	....	....	....	....	....	....	....	....	....	1	0	0	0	0	....	....	....	....
2004-05	Kitchener Rangers	OHL	43	22	36	58	75	....	....	....	....	....	....	....	....	....	15	11	17	28	36	....	....	....	....
	Philadelphia	AHL	....	....	....	....	....	....	....	....	....	....	....	....	....	....	14	7	8	15	28	....	....	....	....
2005-06	**Philadelphia**	**NHL**	**79**	**11**	**23**	**34**	**65**	**1**	**3**	**1**	**168**	**6.5**	**6**	**914**	**45.7**	**15:23**	**6**	**0**	**1**	**1**	**0**	**0**	**0**	**0**	**15:41**
2006-07	**Philadelphia**	**NHL**	**59**	**10**	**22**	**32**	**52**	**1**	**4**	**3**	**130**	**7.7**	**-12**	**978**	**47.8**	**17:50**	....	....	....	....	....	....	....	....	....
2007-08	**Philadelphia**	**NHL**	**73**	**28**	**47**	**75**	**76**	**8**	**5**	**6**	**212**	**13.2**	**14**	**1381**	**50.5**	**21:31**	**17**	**7**	**7**	**14**	**10**	**1**	***2**	**0**	**20:55**
2008-09	**Philadelphia**	**NHL**	**79**	**30**	**50**	**80**	**63**	**8**	***7**	**4**	**238**	**12.6**	**22**	**1660**	**49.0**	**21:44**	**6**	**1**	**4**	**5**	**6**	**1**	**0**	**0**	**22:58**
2009-10	**Philadelphia**	**NHL**	**82**	**31**	**31**	**62**	**79**	**13**	**1**	**3**	**237**	**13.1**	**-2**	**1373**	**50.7**	**20:24**	**23**	**7**	**16**	**23**	**18**	**2**	**1**	**1**	**21:45**
	Canada	Olympics	7	2	3	5	0	....	....	....	....	....	....	....	....	....	....	....	....	....	....	....	....	....	....
2010-11	**Philadelphia**	**NHL**	**81**	**23**	**43**	**66**	**62**	**5**	**3**	**4**	**184**	**12.5**	**11**	**1216**	**49.8**	**18:53**	**11**	**1**	**6**	**7**	**15**	**1**	**0**	**0**	**19:19**
2011-12♦	**Los Angeles**	**NHL**	**74**	**18**	**26**	**44**	**71**	**3**	***4**	**1**	**171**	**10.5**	**3**	**1067**	**50.5**	**18:53**	**20**	**4**	**11**	**15**	**17**	**2**	**0**	**1**	**19:31**
2012-13	**Los Angeles**	**NHL**	**48**	**12**	**20**	**32**	**42**	**6**	**0**	**3**	**82**	**14.6**	**-8**	**441**	**49.0**	**16:21**	**15**	**3**	**9**	**12**	**8**	**1**	**0**	**0**	**19:09**
	NHL Totals		**575**	**163**	**262**	**425**	**510**	**45**	**27**	**25**	**1422**	**11.5**		**9030**	**49.3**	**19:02**	**98**	**23**	**54**	**77**	**74**	**8**	**3**	**2**	**20:11**

Memorial Cup All-Star Team (2003) • OHL Second All-Star Team (2005) • Canadian Major Junior Second All-Star Team (2005)

Played in NHL All-Star Game (2008)

Traded to **Los Angeles** by **Philadelphia** with the rights to Rob Bordson for Brayden Schenn, Wayne Simmonds and Los Angeles' 2nd round choice (later traded to Dallas – Dallas selected Devin Shore) in 2012 Entry Draft, June 23, 2011.

RICHARDSON, Brad

(RIH-chuhrd-suhn, BRAD) **VAN**

Center. Shoots left. 5'11", 191 lbs. Born, Belleville, Ont., February 4, 1985. Colorado's 4th choice, 163rd overall, in 2003 Entry Draft.

Season	Club	League	GP	G	A	Pts	PIM	PP	SH	GW	S	%	+/-	TF	F%	Min	GP	G	A	Pts	PIM	PP	SH	GW	Min
2001-02	Owen Sound	OHL	58	12	21	33	20	....	....	....	....	....	....	....	....	....	....	....	....	....	....	....	....	....	....
2002-03	Owen Sound	OHL	67	27	40	67	54	....	....	....	....	....	....	....	....	....	4	1	1	2	10	....	....	....	....
2003-04	Owen Sound	OHL	15	7	9	16	4	....	....	....	....	....	....	....	....	....	....	....	....	....	....	....	....	....	....
2004-05	Owen Sound	OHL	68	41	56	97	60	....	....	....	....	....	....	....	....	....	8	6	4	10	8	....	....	....	....
2005-06	**Colorado**	**NHL**	**41**	**3**	**10**	**13**	**12**	**1**	**0**	**0**	**51**	**5.9**	**0**	**305**	**41.0**	**10:44**	**9**	**1**	**0**	**1**	**6**	**0**	**0**	**0**	**11:41**
	Lowell	AHL	29	4	13	17	20	....	....	....	....	....	....	....	....	....	....	....	....	....	....	....	....	....	....
2006-07	**Colorado**	**NHL**	**73**	**14**	**8**	**22**	**28**	**0**	**3**	**3**	**129**	**10.9**	**4**	**358**	**40.8**	**13:10**	....	....	....	....	....	....	....	....	....
	Albany River Rats	AHL	3	0	1	1	2	....	....	....	....	....	....	....	....	....	....	....	....	....	....	....	....	....	....
2007-08	**Colorado**	**NHL**	**22**	**2**	**3**	**5**	**8**	**0**	**0**	**0**	**32**	**6.3**	**-3**	**60**	**43.3**	**13:29**	....	....	....	....	....	....	....	....	....
	Lake Erie	AHL	38	14	26	40	18	....	....	....	....	....	....	....	....	....	....	....	....	....	....	....	....	....	....
2008-09	**Los Angeles**	**NHL**	**31**	**0**	**5**	**5**	**11**	**0**	**0**	**0**	**37**	**0.0**	**-6**	**95**	**54.7**	**10:48**	....	....	....	....	....	....	....	....	....
	Manchester	AHL	3	1	2	3	0	....	....	....	....	....	....	....	....	....	....	....	....	....	....	....	....	....	....
2009-10	**Los Angeles**	**NHL**	**81**	**11**	**16**	**27**	**37**	**0**	**1**	**4**	**148**	**7.4**	**1**	**391**	**48.1**	**12:51**	**6**	**1**	**1**	**2**	**2**	**0**	**0**	**1**	**14:41**
2010-11	**Los Angeles**	**NHL**	**68**	**7**	**12**	**19**	**47**	**0**	**1**	**1**	**103**	**6.8**	**-13**	**181**	**50.8**	**11:46**	**6**	**2**	**3**	**5**	**2**	**0**	**0**	**0**	**15:37**
2011-12♦	**Los Angeles**	**NHL**	**59**	**5**	**3**	**8**	**30**	**0**	**1**	**0**	**98**	**5.1**	**-6**	**56**	**58.9**	**12:52**	**13**	**1**	**0**	**1**	**4**	**0**	**0**	**0**	**8:35**
2012-13	**Los Angeles**	**NHL**	**16**	**1**	**5**	**6**	**10**	**0**	**0**	**0**	**27**	**3.7**	**2**	**56**	**48.2**	**10:54**	**11**	**0**	**1**	**1**	**0**	**0**	**0**	**0**	**10:46**
	NHL Totals		**391**	**43**	**62**	**105**	**183**	**1**	**6**	**8**	**625**	**6.9**		**1502**	**45.9**	**12:18**	**45**	**5**	**5**	**10**	**14**	**0**	**0**	**1**	**11:29**

Traded to **Los Angeles** by **Colorado** for Detroit's 2nd round choice (previously acquired, Colorado selected Peter Delmas) in 2008 Entry Draft, June 21, 2008. • Missed majority of 2012-13 as a healthy reserve. Signed as a free agent by **Vancouver**, July 5, 2013.

RINALDO, Zac

(rih-NAL-doh, ZAK) **PHI**

Center. Shoots left. 5'11", 185 lbs. Born, Mississauga, Ont., June 15, 1990. Philadelphia's 4th choice, 178th overall, in 2008 Entry Draft.

Season	Club	League	GP	G	A	Pts	PIM	PP	SH	GW	S	%	+/-	TF	F%	Min	GP	G	A	Pts	PIM	PP	SH	GW	Min
2006-07	Hamilton	ON-Jr.A	44	16	16	32	193	....	....	....	....	....	....	....	....	....	16	4	4	8	48	....	....	....	....
	St. Michael's	OHL	6	0	0	0	2	....	....	....	....	....	....	....	....	....	....	....	....	....	....	....	....	....	....
2007-08	St. Michael's	OHL	63	7	7	14	191	....	....	....	....	....	....	....	....	....	4	0	0	0	9	....	....	....	....
2008-09	St. Michael's	OHL	34	6	7	13	*112	....	....	....	....	....	....	....	....	....	....	....	....	....	....	....	....	....	....
	London Knights	OHL	22	4	13	17	*89	....	....	....	....	....	....	....	....	....	8	1	1	2	26	....	....	....	....
2009-10	London Knights	OHL	34	8	7	15	*148	....	....	....	....	....	....	....	....	....	....	....	....	....	....	....	....	....	....
	Barrie Colts	OHL	26	2	8	10	*107	....	....	....	....	....	....	....	....	....	4	2	0	2	11	....	....	....	....
2010-11	Adirondack	AHL	60	3	6	9	331	....	....	....	....	....	....	....	....	....	....	....	....	....	....	....	....	....	....
	Philadelphia	**NHL**	....	....	....	....	....	....	....	....	....	....	....	....	....	....	**2**	**0**	**0**	**0**	**12**	**0**	**0**	**0**	**2:53**
2011-12	**Philadelphia**	**NHL**	**66**	**2**	**7**	**9**	**232**	**0**	**0**	**0**	**54**	**3.7**	**-1**	**9**	**66.7**	**7:29**	**5**	**0**	**0**	**0**	**48**	**0**	**0**	**0**	**5:41**
	Adirondack	AHL	4	1	1	2	11	....	....	....	....	....	....	....	....	....	....	....	....	....	....	....	....	....	....
2012-13	Adirondack	AHL	31	2	3	5	92	....	....	....	....	....	....	....	....	....	....	....	....	....	....	....	....	....	....
	Philadelphia	**NHL**	**32**	**3**	**2**	**5**	**85**	**0**	**0**	**0**	**15**	**20.0**	**-7**	**2**	**50.0**	**8:23**	....	....	....	....	....	....	....	....	....
	NHL Totals		**98**	**5**	**9**	**14**	**317**	**0**	**0**	**0**	**69**	**7.2**		**11**	**63.6**	**7:46**	**7**	**0**	**0**	**0**	**60**	**0**	**0**	**0**	**4:53**

RISSMILLER, Patrick

(RIGHZ-mih-luhr, PAT-rihk)

Left wing. Shoots left. 6'4", 225 lbs. Born, Belmont, MA, October 26, 1978.

Season	Club	League	GP	G	A	Pts	PIM	PP	SH	GW	S	%	+/-	TF	F%	Min	GP	G	A	Pts	PIM	PP	SH	GW	Min
1997-98	The Hill School	High-PA	STATISTICS NOT AVAILABLE																						
1998-99	Holy Cross	MAAC	34	13	28	41	23	....	....	....	....	....	....	....	....	....	....	....	....	....	....	....	....	....	....
99-2000	Holy Cross	MAAC	35	10	17	27	22	....	....	....	....	....	....	....	....	....	....	....	....	....	....	....	....	....	....
2000-01	Holy Cross	MAAC	29	14	15	29	40	....	....	....	....	....	....	....	....	....	....	....	....	....	....	....	....	....	....
2001-02	Holy Cross	MAAC	33	16	*30	*46	31	....	....	....	....	....	....	....	....	....	....	....	....	....	....	....	....	....	....
2002-03	Cleveland Barons	AHL	72	14	26	40	24	....	....	....	....	....	....	....	....	....	....	....	....	....	....	....	....	....	....
	Cincinnati	ECHL	2	2	2	4	0	....	....	....	....	....	....	....	....	....	....	....	....	....	....	....	....	....	....
2003-04	**San Jose**	**NHL**	**4**	**0**	**0**	**0**	**0**	**0**	**0**	**0**	**2**	**0.0**	**0**	**26**	**53.9**	**7:07**	....	....	....	....	....	....	....	....	....
	Cleveland Barons	AHL	75	14	31	45	66	....	....	....	....	....	....	....	....	....	9	0	1	1	8	....	....	....	....
2004-05	Cleveland Barons	AHL	69	21	23	44	50	....	....	....	....	....	....	....	....	....	....	....	....	....	....	....	....	....	....
2005-06	**San Jose**	**NHL**	**18**	**3**	**3**	**6**	**8**	**1**	**0**	**1**	**26**	**11.5**	**1**	**3**	**0.0**	**9:22**	**11**	**2**	**1**	**3**	**6**	**0**	**0**	**0**	**8:06**
	Cleveland Barons	AHL	68	15	37	52	30	....	....	....	....	....	....	....	....	....	....	....	....	....	....	....	....	....	....
2006-07	**San Jose**	**NHL**	**79**	**7**	**15**	**22**	**22**	**1**	**0**	**0**	**100**	**7.0**	**1**	**25**	**36.0**	**12:10**	**11**	**1**	**3**	**4**	**0**	**0**	**0**	**1**	**12:40**

							Regular Season										Playoffs								
Season	Club	League	GP	G	A	Pts	PIM	PP	SH	GW	S	%	+/-	TF	F%	Min	GP	G	A	Pts	PIM	PP	SH	GW	Min
2007-08	**San Jose**	**NHL**	**79**	**8**	**9**	**17**	**30**	**0**	**0**	**2**	**119**	**6.7**	**–8**	**214**	**50.9**	**13:10**	**8**	**0**	**0**	**0**	**4**	**0**	**0**	**0**	**11:25**
2008-09	**NY Rangers**	**NHL**	**2**	**0**	**0**	**0**	**0**	**0**	**0**	**0**	**2**	**0.0**	**–2**	**0**	**0.0**	**9:13**	....	....	....	....	....	....	....	....	....
	Hartford	AHL	64	14	40	54	24	....	....	....	....	....	....	....	....	....	6	0	1	1	6	....	....	....	....
2009-10	Hartford	AHL	6	0	2	2	8	....	....	....	....	....	....	....	....	....	....	....	....	....	....	....	....	....	....
	Grand Rapids	AHL	63	20	25	45	18	....	....	....	....	....	....	....	....	....	....	....	....	....	....	....	....	....	....
2010-11	**Atlanta**	**NHL**	**1**	**0**	**0**	**0**	**0**	**0**	**0**	**0**	**2**	**0.0**	**–1**	**3**	**33.3**	**13:07**	....	....	....	....	....	....	....	....	....
	Chicago Wolves	AHL	6	1	0	1	6	....	....	....	....	....	....	....	....	....	....	....	....	....	....	....	....	....	....
	Lake Erie	AHL	43	11	19	30	10	....	....	....	....	....	....	....	....	....	....	....	....	....	....	....	....	....	....
	Florida	**NHL**	**9**	**0**	**1**	**1**	**0**	**0**	**0**	**0**	**12**	**0.0**	**0**	**1**	**100.0**	**10:04**	....	....	....	....	....	....	....	....	....
	Rochester	AHL	8	2	8	10	6	....	....	....	....	....	....	....	....	....	....	....	....	....	....	....	....	....	....
2011-12	Lake Erie	AHL	49	13	16	29	34	....	....	....	....	....	....	....	....	....	....	....	....	....	....	....	....	....	....
2012-13	Worcester Sharks	AHL	6	0	2	2	2	....	....	....	....	....	....	....	....	....	....	....	....	....	....	....	....	....	....
	Rochester	AHL	25	3	10	13	8	....	....	....	....	....	....	....	....	....	3	0	0	0	4	....	....	....	....
	NHL Totals		**192**	**18**	**28**	**46**	**60**	**2**	**0**	**3**	**263**	**6.8**		**272**	**49.3**	**12:05**	**30**	**3**	**4**	**7**	**10**	**0**	**0**	**1**	**10:40**

MAAC All-Rookie Team (1999) • MAAC First All-Star Team (2002) • MAAC Offensive Player of the Year (2002)

Signed as a free agent by **Cleveland** (AHL), September 23, 2002. Signed as a free agent by **San Jose**, June 30, 2003. Signed as a free agent by **NY Rangers**, July 1, 2008. Traded to **Atlanta** by **NY Rangers** with Donald Brashear for Todd White, August 2, 2010. • Re-assigned to **Lake Erie** (AHL) by **Atlanta**, November 19, 2010. Traded to **Florida** by **Atlanta** with Niclas Bergfors for Radek Dvorak and Carolina's 5th round choice (previously acquired, later traded to San Jose – San Jose selected Sean Kuraly) in 2011 Entry Draft, February 28, 2011. Signed as a free agent by **Colorado**. July 12, 2011. Signed as a free agent by **Worcester** (AHL), January 9, 2013. Signed as a free agent by **Rochester** (AHL), February 2, 2013.

RITOLA, Mattias

(RIH-toh-lah, mat-TEE-uhs)

Right wing. Shoots left. 6', 192 lbs. Born, Borlange, Sweden, March 14, 1987. Detroit's 4th choice, 103rd overall, in 2005 Entry Draft.

2003-04	V.Frolunda U18	Swe-U18	11	4	11	15	35	....	....	....	....	....	....	....	....	....	7	2	7	9	12	....	....	....	....
	V.Frolunda Jr.	Swe-Jr.	24	7	4	11	8	....	....	....	....	....	....	....	....	....	5	0	1	1	0	....	....	....	....
2004-05	Frolunda Jr.	Swe-Jr.	9	2	6	8	6	....	....	....	....	....	....	....	....	....	....	....	....	....	....	....	....	....	....
	Leksands IF U18	Swe-U18	STATISTICS NOT AVAILABLE																						
	Leksands IF Jr.	Swe-Jr.	18	8	10	18	14	....	....	....	....	....	....	....	....	....	5	1	1	2	2	....	....	....	....
2005-06	Leksands IF Jr.	Swe-Jr.	14	4	2	6	16	....	....	....	....	....	....	....	....	....	....	....	....	....	....	....	....	....	....
	Leksands IF	Sweden	30	0	3	3	10	....	....	....	....	....	....	....	....	....	....	....	....	....	....	....	....	....	....
	Leksands IF	Sweden-Q	8	0	0	0	4	....	....	....	....	....	....	....	....	....	....	....	....	....	....	....	....	....	....
2006-07	Leksands IF Jr.	Swe-Jr.	12	5	7	12	16	....	....	....	....	....	....	....	....	....	....	....	....	....	....	....	....	....	....
	Leksands IF	Sweden-2	23	1	4	5	4	....	....	....	....	....	....	....	....	....	....	....	....	....	....	....	....	....	....
	IFK Arboga IK	Sweden-2	3	1	0	1	2	....	....	....	....	....	....	....	....	....	....	....	....	....	....	....	....	....	....
	Borlange HF	Sweden-3	11	4	6	10	14	....	....	....	....	....	....	....	....	....	....	....	....	....	....	....	....	....	....
2007-08	**Detroit**	**NHL**	**2**	**0**	**1**	**1**	**0**	**0**	**0**	**0**	**2**	**0.0**	**0**	**0**	**0.0**	**5:47**	....	....	....	....	....	....	....	....	....
	Grand Rapids	AHL	72	7	15	22	62	....	....	....	....	....	....	....	....	....	....	....	....	....	....	....	....	....	....
2008-09	Grand Rapids	AHL	66	15	27	42	32	....	....	....	....	....	....	....	....	....	8	0	2	2	0	....	....	....	....
2009-10	**Detroit**	**NHL**	**5**	**0**	**0**	**0**	**0**	**0**	**0**	**0**	**9**	**0.0**	**0**	**3**	**0.0**	**11:42**	**1**	**0**	**0**	**0**	**0**	**0**	**0**	**0**	**7:45**
	Grand Rapids	AHL	73	19	23	42	50	....	....	....	....	....	....	....	....	....	....	....	....	....	....	....	....	....	....
2010-11	**Tampa Bay**	**NHL**	**31**	**4**	**4**	**8**	**11**	**0**	**0**	**2**	**42**	**9.5**	**–5**	**44**	**43.2**	**10:04**	**1**	**0**	**0**	**0**	**0**	**0**	**0**	**0**	**2:23**
	Norfolk Admirals	AHL	17	9	18	27	8	....	....	....	....	....	....	....	....	....	4	1	4	5	0	....	....	....	....
2011-12	**Tampa Bay**	**NHL**	**5**	**0**	**0**	**0**	**6**	**0**	**0**	**0**	**14**	**0.0**	**–2**	**3**	**66.7**	**10:50**	....	....	....	....	....	....	....	....	....
	MODO	Sweden	35	7	13	20	30	....	....	....	....	....	....	....	....	....	6	1	1	2	8	....	....	....	....
2012-13	MODO	Sweden	50	11	13	24	12	....	....	....	....	....	....	....	....	....	5	2	1	3	4	....	....	....	....
	NHL Totals		**43**	**4**	**5**	**9**	**17**	**0**	**0**	**2**	**67**	**6.0**		**50**	**42.0**	**10:09**	**2**	**0**	**0**	**0**	**0**	**0**	**0**	**0**	**5:04**

Claimed on waivers by **Tampa Bay** from **Detroit**, October 5, 2010. Signed as a free agent by **MODO** (Sweden), November 10, 2011.

ROBAK, Colby

(ROH-bak, KOHL-bee) **FLA**

Defense. Shoots left. 6'3", 194 lbs. Born, Dauphin, Man., April 24, 1990. Florida's 2nd choice, 46th overall, in 2008 Entry Draft.

2005-06	Parkland Rangers	MMHL	40	14	20	34	14	....	....	....	....	....	....	....	....	....	....	....	....	....	....	....	....	....	....
2006-07	Brandon	WHL	39	2	3	5	12	....	....	....	....	....	....	....	....	....	1	0	0	0	0	....	....	....	....
2007-08	Brandon	WHL	71	6	24	30	25	....	....	....	....	....	....	....	....	....	6	0	2	2	8	....	....	....	....
2008-09	Brandon	WHL	65	13	29	42	41	....	....	....	....	....	....	....	....	....	12	6	8	14	4	....	....	....	....
2009-10	Brandon	WHL	71	16	50	66	9	....	....	....	....	....	....	....	....	....	15	3	9	12	2	....	....	....	....
2010-11	Rochester	AHL	76	7	17	24	22	....	....	....	....	....	....	....	....	....	....	....	....	....	....	....	....	....	....
2011-12	**Florida**	**NHL**	**3**	**0**	**0**	**0**	**0**	**0**	**0**	**0**	**1**	**0.0**	**1**	**0**	**0.0**	**12:34**	....	....	....	....	....	....	....	....	....
	San Antonio	AHL	73	9	30	39	30	....	....	....	....	....	....	....	....	....	8	1	4	5	4	....	....	....	....
2012-13	San Antonio	AHL	63	5	18	23	50	....	....	....	....	....	....	....	....	....	....	....	....	....	....	....	....	....	....
	Florida	**NHL**	**16**	**0**	**1**	**1**	**17**	**0**	**0**	**0**	**15**	**0.0**	**–1**	**0**	**0.0**	**15:11**	....	....	....	....	....	....	....	....	....
	NHL Totals		**19**	**0**	**1**	**1**	**17**	**0**	**0**	**0**	**16**	**0.0**		**0**	**0.0**	**14:46**	....	....	....	....	....	....	....	....	....

WHL East Second All-Star Team (2010)

ROBIDAS, Stephane

(ROH-bih-dah, STEH-fan) **DAL**

Defense. Shoots right. 5'11", 196 lbs. Born, Sherbrooke, Que., March 3, 1977. Montreal's 7th choice, 164th overall, in 1995 Entry Draft.

1992-93	Magog	QAAA	41	3	12	15	16	....	....	....	....	....	....	....	....	....	5	1	1	2	2	....	....	....	....
1993-94	Shawinigan	QMJHL	67	3	19	22	33	....	....	....	....	....	....	....	....	....	1	0	0	0	0	....	....	....	....
1994-95	Shawinigan	QMJHL	71	13	56	69	44	....	....	....	....	....	....	....	....	....	15	7	12	19	4	....	....	....	....
1995-96	Shawinigan	QMJHL	67	23	56	79	53	....	....	....	....	....	....	....	....	....	6	1	5	6	10	....	....	....	....
1996-97	Shawinigan	QMJHL	67	24	51	75	59	....	....	....	....	....	....	....	....	....	7	4	6	10	14	....	....	....	....
1997-98	Fredericton	AHL	79	10	21	31	50	....	....	....	....	....	....	....	....	....	4	0	2	2	0	....	....	....	....
1998-99	Fredericton	AHL	79	8	33	41	59	....	....	....	....	....	....	....	....	....	15	1	5	6	10	....	....	....	....
99-2000	**Montreal**	**NHL**	**1**	**0**	**0**	**0**	**0**	**0**	**0**	**0**	**0**	**0.0**	**0**	**0**	**0.0**	**15:54**	....	....	....	....	....	....	....	....	....
	Quebec Citadelles	AHL	76	14	31	45	36	....	....	....	....	....	....	....	....	....	3	0	1	1	0	....	....	....	....
2000-01	**Montreal**	**NHL**	**65**	**6**	**6**	**12**	**14**	**1**	**0**	**0**	**77**	**7.8**	**0**	**1**	**100.0**	**20:44**	....	....	....	....	....	....	....	....	....
2001-02	**Montreal**	**NHL**	**56**	**1**	**10**	**11**	**14**	**1**	**0**	**0**	**68**	**1.5**	**–25**	**3**	**33.3**	**18:58**	**2**	**0**	**0**	**0**	**4**	**0**	**0**	**0**	**13:07**
2002-03	**Dallas**	**NHL**	**76**	**3**	**7**	**10**	**35**	**0**	**0**	**1**	**47**	**6.4**	**15**	**1**	**100.0**	**12:54**	**12**	**0**	**1**	**1**	**20**	**0**	**0**	**0**	**13:54**
2003-04	**Dallas**	**NHL**	**14**	**1**	**0**	**1**	**8**	**1**	**0**	**0**	**8**	**12.5**	**–2**	**1**	**100.0**	**12:57**	....	....	....	....	....	....	....	....	....
	Chicago	**NHL**	**45**	**2**	**10**	**12**	**33**	**0**	**1**	**1**	**55**	**3.6**	**6**	**0**	**0.0**	**20:56**	....	....	....	....	....	....	....	....	....
2004-05	Frankfurt Lions	Germany	51	15	32	47	64	....	....	....	....	....	....	....	....	....	6	1	2	3	6	....	....	....	....
2005-06	**Dallas**	**NHL**	**75**	**5**	**15**	**20**	**67**	**1**	**1**	**0**	**95**	**5.3**	**15**	**0**	**0.0**	**16:59**	**5**	**0**	**2**	**2**	**4**	**0**	**0**	**0**	**16:42**
2006-07	**Dallas**	**NHL**	**75**	**0**	**17**	**17**	**86**	**0**	**0**	**0**	**106**	**0.0**	**–1**	**0**	**0.0**	**18:04**	**7**	**0**	**1**	**1**	**2**	**0**	**0**	**0**	**19:02**
2007-08	**Dallas**	**NHL**	**82**	**9**	**17**	**26**	**85**	**7**	**0**	**2**	**153**	**5.9**	**0**	**0**	**0.0**	**20:39**	**18**	**3**	**8**	**11**	**12**	**3**	**0**	**0**	**25:31**
2008-09	**Dallas**	**NHL**	**72**	**3**	**23**	**26**	**76**	**1**	**0**	**0**	**158**	**1.9**	**10**	**1**	**100.0**	**24:32**	....	....	....	....	....	....	....	....	....
2009-10	**Dallas**	**NHL**	**82**	**10**	**31**	**41**	**70**	**7**	**0**	**1**	**199**	**5.0**	**–10**	**0**	**0.0**	**24:29**	....	....	....	....	....	....	....	....	....
2010-11	**Dallas**	**NHL**	**81**	**5**	**25**	**30**	**67**	**1**	**0**	**1**	**106**	**4.7**	**–7**	**0**	**0.0**	**24:32**	....	....	....	....	....	....	....	....	....
2011-12	**Dallas**	**NHL**	**75**	**5**	**17**	**22**	**48**	**2**	**0**	**1**	**75**	**6.7**	**–5**	**0**	**0.0**	**22:46**	....	....	....	....	....	....	....	....	....
2012-13	HIFK Helsinki	Finland	15	2	3	5	22	....	....	....	....	....	....	....	....	....	....	....	....	....	....	....	....	....	....
	Dallas	**NHL**	**48**	**1**	**12**	**13**	**56**	**0**	**0**	**0**	**46**	**2.2**	**2**	**0**	**0.0**	**22:14**	....	....	....	....	....	....	....	....	....
	NHL Totals		**847**	**51**	**190**	**241**	**659**	**22**	**2**	**7**	**1193**	**4.3**		**7**	**71.4**	**20:32**	**44**	**3**	**12**	**15**	**42**	**3**	**0**	**0**	**19:45**

QMJHL First All-Star Team (1996, 1997)

Played in NHL All-Star Game (2009)

Claimed by **Atlanta** from **Montreal** in Waiver Draft, October 4, 2002. Traded to **Dallas** by **Atlanta** for future considerations, October 4, 2002. Traded to **Chicago** by **Dallas** with Dallas' 2nd round choice (Jakub Sindel) in 2004 Entry Draft for Jon Klemm and NY Rangers' 4th round choice (previously acquired, Dallas selected Fredrik Naslund) in 2004 Entry Draft, November 17, 2003. Signed as a free agent by **Frankfurt** (Germany), September 17, 2004. Signed as a free agent by **Dallas**, August 6, 2005. Signed as a free agent by **HIFK Helsinki** (Finland), October 8, 2012.

RODNEY, Bryan

(ROHD-nee, BRIGH-uhn) **NSH**

Defense. Shoots right. 6', 204 lbs. Born, London, Ont., April 22, 1984.

2000-01	Ottawa 67's	OHL	65	0	15	15	26	....	....	....	....	....	....	....	....	....	20	1	4	5	20	....	....	....	....
2001-02	Ottawa 67's	OHL	30	3	8	11	14	....	....	....	....	....	....	....	....	....	....	....	....	....	....	....	....	....	....
	Kingston	OHL	18	2	8	10	8	....	....	....	....	....	....	....	....	....	1	0	0	0	0	....	....	....	....
2002-03	Kingston	OHL	67	8	52	60	60	....	....	....	....	....	....	....	....	....	....	....	....	....	....	....	....	....	....
2003-04	Kingston	OHL	67	11	65	76	68	....	....	....	....	....	....	....	....	....	5	1	4	5	8	....	....	....	....
2004-05	London Knights	OHL	64	23	39	62	48	....	....	....	....	....	....	....	....	....	12	5	10	15	20	....	....	....	....
2005-06	Hartford	AHL	8	1	2	3	0	....	....	....	....	....	....	....	....	....	....	....	....	....	....	....	....	....	....
	Charlotte	ECHL	59	4	21	25	47	....	....	....	....	....	....	....	....	....	3	0	1	1	0	....	....	....	....
2006-07	Charlotte	ECHL	31	2	19	21	14	....	....	....	....	....	....	....	....	....	....	....	....	....	....	....	....	....	....
	Columbia Inferno	ECHL	14	2	9	11	12	....	....	....	....	....	....	....	....	....	....	....	....	....	....	....	....	....	....

					Regular Season												Playoffs								
Season	Club	League	GP	G	A	Pts	PIM	PP	SH	GW	S	%	+/-	TF	F%	Min	GP	G	A	Pts	PIM	PP	SH	GW	Min
2007-08	Albany River Rats	AHL	42	4	11	15	22										7	3	3	6	2				
	Columbia Inferno	ECHL	17	2	9	11	10																		
	Elmira Jackals	ECHL	6	5	5	10	2																		
2008-09	**Carolina**	**NHL**	**8**	**0**	**2**	**2**	**2**	**0**	**0**	**0**	**3**	**0.0**	**–3**	**0**	**0.0**	**12:38**									
	Albany River Rats	AHL	58	3	33	36	28																		
2009-10	**Carolina**	**NHL**	**22**	**1**	**10**	**11**	**8**	**0**	**0**	**0**	**24**	**4.2**	**–4**	**0**	**0.0**	**16:44**									
	Albany River Rats	AHL	54	7	28	35	42										8	0	4	4	8				
2010-11	**Carolina**	**NHL**	**3**	**0**	**0**	**0**	**2**	**0**	**0**	**0**	**3**	**0.0**	**0**	**0**	**0.0**	**8:44**									
	Charlotte	AHL	77	9	38	47	38										16	0	4	4	12				
2011-12	Syracuse Crunch	AHL	41	5	15	20	10																		
	Edmonton	**NHL**	**1**	**0**	**0**	**0**	**0**	**0**	**0**	**0**	**0**	**0.0**	**–1**	**0**	**0.0**	**13:17**									
	Oklahoma City	AHL	26	1	9	10	18										14	2	8	10	12				
2012-13	Manchester	AHL	44	4	11	15	10																		
	NHL Totals		**34**	**1**	**12**	**13**	**12**	**0**	**0**	**0**	**30**	**3.3**		**0**	**0.0**	**14:58**									

Signed as a free agent by **Charlotte** (ECHL), October 21, 2005. Signed as a free agent by **Albany** (AHL), December 16, 2007. Signed as a free agent by **Carolina**, May 12, 2008. Signed as a free agent by **Anaheim**, July 5, 2011. Traded to **Edmonton** by **Anaheim** for Ryan O'Marra, February 16, 2012. Signed as a free agent by **Manchester** (AHL), December 3, 2012. Signed as a free agent by **Nashville**, July 29, 2013.

ROME, Aaron

(ROHM, AIR-uhn) **DAL**

Defense. Shoots left. 6'1", 218 lbs. Born, Nesbitt, Man., September 27, 1983. Los Angeles' 4th choice, 104th overall, in 2002 Entry Draft.

1998-99	Sask. Contacts	SMHL	STATISTICS NOT AVAILABLE																						
	Saskatoon Blades	WHL	1	0	0	0	0																		
99-2000	Saskatoon Blades	WHL	47	0	6	6	22										1	0	0	0	0				
2000-01	Saskatoon Blades	WHL	3	0	0	0	2																		
	Kootenay Ice	WHL	53	2	8	10	43										11	1	3	4	6				
2001-02	Kootenay Ice	WHL	33	4	13	17	55																		
	Swift Current	WHL	37	3	11	14	113										10	1	4	5	23				
2002-03	Swift Current	WHL	61	12	44	56	201										4	1	0	1	20				
2003-04	Swift Current	WHL	41	7	26	33	122																		
	Moose Jaw	WHL	28	3	16	19	88										8	0	6	6	17				
2004-05	Cincinnati	AHL	75	2	14	16	130										12	3	3	6	33				
2005-06	Portland Pirates	AHL	64	5	19	24	87										18	1	4	5	33				
2006-07 ♦	**Anaheim**	**NHL**	**1**	**0**	**0**	**0**	**0**	**0**	**0**	**0**	**1**	**0.0**	**–1**	**0**	**0.0**	**14:31**	**1**	**0**	**0**	**0**	**0**	**0**	**0**	**0**	**11:01**
	Portland Pirates	AHL	76	8	17	25	139																		
2007-08	**Columbus**	**NHL**	**17**	**1**	**1**	**2**	**33**	**0**	**0**	**0**	**15**	**6.7**	**–4**	**0**	**0.0**	**18:11**									
	Portland Pirates	AHL	14	2	3	5	31																		
	Syracuse Crunch	AHL	41	3	21	24	126																		
2008-09	**Columbus**	**NHL**	**8**	**0**	**1**	**1**	**0**	**0**	**0**	**0**	**7**	**0.0**	**1**	**0**	**0.0**	**15:28**	**1**	**0**	**1**	**1**	**0**	**0**	**0**	**0**	**15:24**
	Syracuse Crunch	AHL	48	7	21	28	153																		
2009-10	**Vancouver**	**NHL**	**49**	**0**	**4**	**4**	**24**	**0**	**0**	**0**	**49**	**0.0**	**–2**	**0**	**0.0**	**15:11**	**1**	**0**	**0**	**0**	**0**	**0**	**0**	**0**	**9:32**
	Manitoba Moose	AHL	7	6	1	7	15																		
2010-11	**Vancouver**	**NHL**	**56**	**1**	**4**	**5**	**53**	**0**	**0**	**0**	**50**	**2.0**	**1**	**0**	**0.0**	**17:25**	**14**	**1**	**0**	**1**	**37**	**0**	**0**	**0**	**13:01**
2011-12	**Vancouver**	**NHL**	**43**	**4**	**6**	**10**	**46**	**1**	**0**	**1**	**42**	**9.5**	**–4**	**0**	**0.0**	**15:14**	**1**	**0**	**0**	**0**	**0**	**0**	**0**	**0**	**12:42**
2012-13	**Dallas**	**NHL**	**27**	**0**	**5**	**5**	**18**	**0**	**0**	**0**	**15**	**0.0**	**–2**	**0**	**0.0**	**15:20**									
	NHL Totals		**201**	**6**	**21**	**27**	**174**	**1**	**0**	**1**	**179**	**3.4**		**0**	**0.0**	**16:06**	**18**	**1**	**1**	**2**	**37**	**0**	**0**	**0**	**12:50**

WHL East Second All-Star Team (2004)

Signed as a free agent by **Anaheim**, June 7, 2004. Traded to **Columbus** by **Anaheim** with Clay Wilson for Geoff Platt, November 15, 2007. Signed as a free agent by **Vancouver**, July 1, 2009. Signed as a free agent by **Dallas**, July 1, 2012.

ROSEHILL, Jay

(ROHZ-hihl, JAY) **PHI**

Left wing. Shoots left. 6'3", 215 lbs. Born, Olds, Alta., July 16, 1985. Tampa Bay's 6th choice, 227th overall, in 2003 Entry Draft.

2002-03	Olds Grizzlys	AJHL	59	1	4	5	219																		
2003-04	Olds Grizzlys	AJHL	42	4	12	16	172										14	2	2	4					
2004-05	U. Minn-Duluth	WCHA	34	0	5	5	103																		
2005-06	Springfield	AHL	45	1	2	3	68																		
	Johnstown Chiefs	ECHL	5	0	0	0	13										5	0	0	0	4				
2006-07	Springfield	AHL	64	0	6	6	85																		
	Johnstown Chiefs	ECHL	1	0	0	0	2																		
2007-08	Norfolk Admirals	AHL	66	3	4	7	194																		
	Mississippi	ECHL	2	0	0	0	6																		
2008-09	Norfolk Admirals	AHL	57	5	7	12	221																		
	Toronto Marlies	AHL	13	2	1	3	54										6	0	0	0	4				
2009-10	**Toronto**	**NHL**	**15**	**1**	**1**	**2**	**67**	**0**	**0**	**0**	**6**	**16.7**	**–2**	**3**	**33.3**	**6:14**									
	Toronto Marlies	AHL	46	1	2	3	172																		
2010-11	**Toronto**	**NHL**	**26**	**1**	**2**	**3**	**71**	**0**	**0**	**0**	**12**	**8.3**	**–6**	**0**	**0.0**	**5:12**									
	Toronto Marlies	AHL	32	7	6	13	114																		
2011-12	**Toronto**	**NHL**	**31**	**0**	**0**	**0**	**60**	**0**	**0**	**0**	**15**	**0.0**	**–4**	**4**	**25.0**	**5:55**									
	Toronto Marlies	AHL	4	0	0	0	20										13	0	0	0	44				
2012-13	Norfolk Admirals	AHL	33	4	4	8	90																		
	Philadelphia	**NHL**	**11**	**1**	**0**	**1**	**64**	**0**	**0**	**1**	**7**	**14.3**	**–4**	**0**	**0.0**	**6:48**									
	NHL Totals		**83**	**3**	**3**	**6**	**262**	**0**	**0**	**1**	**40**	**7.5**		**7**	**28.6**	**5:52**									

Signed as a free agent by **Toronto**, July 6 2009. • Missed majority of 2011-12 as a healthy reserve. Signed to a PTO (professional tryout) contract by **Norfolk** (AHL), October 3, 2012. Signed as a free agent by **Anaheim**, January 17, 2013. Traded to **Philadelphia** by **Anaheim** for Harry Zolnierczyk, April 1, 2013.

ROUSSEL, Antoine

(roo-SEHL, an-TWAHN) **DAL**

Left wing. Shoots left. 5'11", 192 lbs. Born, Roubaix, France, November 21, 1989.

2006-07	Chicoutimi	QMJHL	56	7	13	20	55										4	0	0	0	14				
2007-08	Chicoutimi	QMJHL	70	13	24	37	121										5	0	4	4	29				
2008-09	Chicoutimi	QMJHL	58	15	20	35	110										4	0	2	2	15				
2009-10	Chicoutimi	QMJHL	68	24	23	47	131										7	4	5	9	10				
2010-11	Providence Bruins	AHL	42	1	7	8	88																		
	Reading Royals	ECHL	5	0	1	1	7										8	0	3	3	14				
2011-12	Chicago Wolves	AHL	61	4	5	9	177										2	0	0	0	6				
2012-13	Texas Stars	AHL	43	8	11	19	107																		
	Dallas	**NHL**	**39**	**7**	**7**	**14**	**85**	**0**	**0**	**0**	**46**	**15.2**	**3**	**55**	**54.6**	**9:24**									
	NHL Totals		**39**	**7**	**7**	**14**	**85**	**0**	**0**	**0**	**46**	**15.2**		**55**	**54.5**	**9:24**									

Signed as a free agent by **Chicago** (AHL), October 2, 2011. Signed as a free agent by **Dallas**, July 2, 2012.

ROY, Derek

(ROI, DAIR-ihk) **ST.L.**

Center. Shoots left. 5'9", 184 lbs. Born, Ottawa, Ont., May 4, 1983. Buffalo's 2nd choice, 32nd overall, in 2001 Entry Draft.

1998-99	Ontario East	Minor-ON	34	61	31	92	42																		
99-2000	Kitchener Rangers	OHL	66	34	53	87	44										5	4	1	5	6				
2000-01	Kitchener Rangers	OHL	65	42	39	81	114																		
2001-02	Kitchener Rangers	OHL	62	43	46	89	92										4	1	2	3	2				
2002-03	Kitchener Rangers	OHL	49	28	50	78	73										21	9	*23	32	14				
2003-04	**Buffalo**	**NHL**	**49**	**9**	**10**	**19**	**12**	**1**	**0**	**4**	**71**	**12.7**	**–8**	**715**	**47.4**	**15:19**									
	Rochester	AHL	26	10	16	26	20										16	6	8	14	18				
2004-05	Rochester	AHL	67	16	45	61	60										9	6	5	11	6				
2005-06	**Buffalo**	**NHL**	**70**	**18**	**28**	**46**	**57**	**5**	**1**	**1**	**151**	**11.9**	**1**	**807**	**48.0**	**17:02**	**18**	**5**	**10**	**15**	**16**	**1**	**1**	**0**	**17:03**
	Rochester	AHL	8	7	13	20	10																		
2006-07	**Buffalo**	**NHL**	**75**	**21**	**42**	**63**	**60**	**6**	**1**	**3**	**130**	**16.2**	**37**	**1129**	**48.5**	**18:28**	**16**	**2**	**5**	**7**	**14**	**0**	**0**	**0**	**18:03**
2007-08	**Buffalo**	**NHL**	**78**	**32**	**49**	**81**	**46**	**6**	**3**	**4**	**218**	**14.7**	**13**	**1393**	**51.2**	**20:58**									
2008-09	**Buffalo**	**NHL**	**82**	**28**	**42**	**70**	**38**	**9**	**1**	**9**	**221**	**12.7**	**–5**	**1469**	**50.7**	**21:12**									
2009-10	**Buffalo**	**NHL**	**80**	**26**	**43**	**69**	**48**	**10**	**1**	**6**	**215**	**12.1**	**9**	**1225**	**50.4**	**19:23**	**6**	**0**	**2**	**2**	**4**	**0**	**0**	**0**	**22:59**
2010-11	**Buffalo**	**NHL**	**35**	**10**	**25**	**35**	**16**	**2**	**0**	**1**	**89**	**11.2**	**–1**	**528**	**46.4**	**19:32**	**1**	**0**	**1**	**1**	**0**	**0**	**0**	**0**	**20:01**
2011-12	**Buffalo**	**NHL**	**80**	**17**	**27**	**44**	**54**	**6**	**1**	**2**	**176**	**9.7**	**–7**	**1329**	**50.6**	**19:19**									

			Regular Season														Playoffs								
Season	Club	League	GP	G	A	Pts	PIM	PP	SH	GW	S	%	+/-	TF	F%	Min	GP	G	A	Pts	PIM	PP	SH	GW	Min
2012-13	Dallas	NHL	30	4	18	22	4	1	0	1	65	6.2	3	520	46.7	18:58	....	....	....	....	....	....	....	....	....
	Vancouver	NHL	12	3	3	6	2	1	0	0	20	15.0	1	127	40.9	17:39	4	0	1	1	2	0	0	0	17:15
	NHL Totals		591	168	287	455	337	47	8	31	1356	12.4		9242	49.4	19:03	45	7	19	26	36	1	1	0	18:17

OHL All-Rookie Team (2000) • OHL Rookie of the Year (2000) • CHL All-Rookie Team (2000) • CHL Plus/Minus Award (2000) • CHL Most Sportsmanlike Player (2000) • Memorial Cup All-Star Team (2003) • Stafford Smythe Memorial Trophy (Memorial Cup - MVP) (2003)

• Missed majority of 2010-11 due to leg injury vs. Florida, December 23, 2010. Traded to **Dallas** by **Buffalo** for Steve Ott and Adam Pardy, July 2, 2012. Traded to **Vancouver** by **Dallas** for Kevin Connauton and Vancouver 2nd round choice (Philippe Desrosiers) in 2013 Entry Draft, April 2, 2013. Signed as a free agent by **St. Louis**, July 6, 2013.

ROY, Mathieu

(WAH, MA-tyew)

Defense. Shoots right. 6'2", 214 lbs. Born, St-Georges, Que., August 10, 1983. Edmonton's 10th choice, 215th overall, in 2003 Entry Draft.

Season	Club	League	GP	G	A	Pts	PIM	PP	SH	GW	S	%	+/-	TF	F%	Min	GP	G	A	Pts	PIM	PP	SH	GW	Min
1998-99	Levis	QAAA	11	4	1	5	16	....	....	....	....	....	....	....	....	....	....	....	....	....	....	....	....	....	....
99-2000	Levis	QAAA	24	3	4	7	88	....	....	....	....	....	....	....	....	....	6	1	1	2	22	....	....	....	....
	Val-d'Or Foreurs	QMJHL	48	1	4	5	66	....	....	....	....	....	....	....	....	....	....	....	....	....	....	....	....	....	....
2000-01	Val-d'Or Foreurs	QMJHL	30	0	7	7	60	....	....	....	....	....	....	....	....	....	17	0	0	0	4	....	....	....	....
2001-02	Val-d'Or Foreurs	QMJHL	53	7	26	33	103	....	....	....	....	....	....	....	....	....	7	0	2	2	19	....	....	....	....
2002-03	Val-d'Or Foreurs	QMJHL	52	11	21	32	164	....	....	....	....	....	....	....	....	....	7	1	0	1	8	....	....	....	....
2003-04	Toronto	AHL	30	0	2	2	46	....	....	....	....	....	....	....	....	....	....	....	....	....	....	....	....	....	....
	Columbus	ECHL	10	1	2	3	13	....	....	....	....	....	....	....	....	....	....	....	....	....	....	....	....	....	....
2004-05	Edmonton	AHL	51	3	22	25	68	....	....	....	....	....	....	....	....	....	....	....	....	....	....	....	....	....	....
2005-06	Edmonton	NHL	1	0	0	0	0	0	0	0	0	0.0	–1	0	0.0	13:00	....	....	....	....	....	....	....	....	....
	Hamilton	AHL	50	3	16	19	82	....	....	....	....	....	....	....	....	....	....	....	....	....	....	....	....	....	....
2006-07	Edmonton	NHL	16	2	0	2	30	0	0	0	18	11.1	–7	0	0.0	14:06	....	....	....	....	....	....	....	....	....
	Hamilton	AHL	31	6	12	18	40	....	....	....	....	....	....	....	....	....	....	....	....	....	....	....	....	....	....
2007-08	Edmonton	NHL	13	0	1	1	27	0	0	0	8	0.0	0	0	0.0	10:23	....	....	....	....	....	....	....	....	....
	Springfield	AHL	20	2	8	10	34	....	....	....	....	....	....	....	....	....	....	....	....	....	....	....	....	....	....
2008-09	Springfield	AHL	59	2	15	17	120	....	....	....	....	....	....	....	....	....	....	....	....	....	....	....	....	....	....
2009-10	Columbus	NHL	31	0	10	10	17	0	0	0	32	0.0	–2	1	100.0	18:19	....	....	....	....	....	....	....	....	....
	Syracuse Crunch	AHL	14	0	4	4	32	....	....	....	....	....	....	....	....	....	....	....	....	....	....	....	....	....	....
	Rochester	AHL	1	0	0	0	0	....	....	....	....	....	....	....	....	....	6	0	0	0	11	....	....	....	....
2010-11	Tampa Bay	NHL	4	0	0	0	2	0	0	0	1	0.0	–2	0	0.0	4:43	....	....	....	....	....	....	....	....	....
	Norfolk Admirals	AHL	45	4	18	22	68	....	....	....	....	....	....	....	....	....	6	0	1	1	4	....	....	....	....
2011-12	Charlotte	AHL	62	6	12	18	57	....	....	....	....	....	....	....	....	....	....	....	....	....	....	....	....	....	....
2012-13	Hamburg Freezers	Germany	51	8	18	26	46	....	....	....	....	....	....	....	....	....	6	0	5	5	8	....	....	....	....
	Tampa Bay	NHL	1	0	0	0	0	0	0	0	0	0.0	–1	0	0.0	14:07	....	....	....	....	....	....	....	....	....
	NHL Totals		66	2	11	13	76	0	0	0	59	3.4		1	100.0	14:46	....	....	....	....	....	....	....	....	....

• Missed majority of 2007-08 due to shoulder injury and as a healthy reserve. Signed as a free agent by **Columbus**, July 14, 2009. Traded to **Florida** by **Columbus** for Matt Rust, March 3, 2010. Signed as a free agent by **Tampa Bay**, July 29, 2010. Signed as a free agent by **Carolina**, September 14, 2011. Signed as a free agent by **Hamburg** (Germany), July 12, 2012. Signed as a free agent by **Tampa Bay**, April 23, 2013.

ROZSIVAL, Michal

(roh-ZIH-vahl, MEE-khahl) **CHI**

Defense. Shoots right. 6'1", 212 lbs. Born, Vlasim, Czech., September 3, 1978. Pittsburgh's 5th choice, 105th overall, in 1996 Entry Draft.

Season	Club	League	GP	G	A	Pts	PIM	PP	SH	GW	S	%	+/-	TF	F%	Min	GP	G	A	Pts	PIM	PP	SH	GW	Min
1994-95	Jihlava Jr.	CzRep-Jr.	31	8	13	21	....	....	....	....	....	....	....	....	....	....	....	....	....	....	....	....	....	....	....
1995-96	HC Dukla Jihlava	CzRep	36	3	4	7	....	....	....	....	....	....	....	....	....	....	....	....	....	....	....	....	....	....	....
1996-97	Swift Current	WHL	63	8	31	39	69	....	....	....	....	....	....	....	....	....	10	0	6	6	15	....	....	....	....
1997-98	Swift Current	WHL	71	14	55	69	122	....	....	....	....	....	....	....	....	....	12	0	5	5	33	....	....	....	....
1998-99	Syracuse Crunch	AHL	49	3	22	25	72	....	....	....	....	....	....	....	....	....	....	....	....	....	....	....	....	....	....
99-2000	Pittsburgh	NHL	75	4	17	21	48	1	0	1	73	5.5	11	1	0.0	19:01	2	0	0	0	4	0	0	0	30:56
2000-01	Pittsburgh	NHL	30	1	4	5	26	0	0	0	17	5.9	3	1	100.0	17:06	....	....	....	....	....	....	....	....	....
	Wilkes-Barre	AHL	29	8	8	16	32	....	....	....	....	....	....	....	....	....	21	3	*19	22	23	....	....	....	....
2001-02	Pittsburgh	NHL	79	9	20	29	47	4	0	4	89	10.1	–6	0	0.0	20:01	....	....	....	....	....	....	....	....	....
2002-03	Pittsburgh	NHL	53	4	6	10	40	1	0	0	61	6.6	–5	0	0.0	20:25	....	....	....	....	....	....	....	....	....
2003-04	Wilkes-Barre	AHL	1	0	0	0	2	....	....	....	....	....	....	....	....	....	....	....	....	....	....	....	....	....	....
2004-05	HC Ocelari Trinec	CzRep	35	1	10	11	40	....	....	....	....	....	....	....	....	....	....	....	....	....	....	....	....	....	....
	Pardubice	CzRep	16	1	3	4	30	....	....	....	....	....	....	....	....	....	16	1	2	3	34	....	....	....	....
2005-06	NY Rangers	NHL	82	5	25	30	90	3	0	3	115	4.3	*35	1	0.0	22:27	4	0	1	1	8	0	0	0	24:31
2006-07	NY Rangers	NHL	80	10	30	40	52	7	0	3	104	9.6	10	3	0.0	23:46	10	3	4	7	10	2	0	1	24:45
2007-08	NY Rangers	NHL	80	13	25	38	80	6	2	0	127	10.2	0	0	0.0	24:33	10	1	5	6	10	0	0	0	25:05
2008-09	NY Rangers	NHL	76	8	22	30	52	3	0	2	120	6.7	–7	0	0.0	22:31	7	0	0	0	4	0	0	0	22:41
2009-10	NY Rangers	NHL	82	3	20	23	78	1	0	1	80	3.8	3	1	100.0	21:26	....	....	....	....	....	....	....	....	....
2010-11	NY Rangers	NHL	32	3	12	15	22	0	0	1	24	12.5	3	0	0.0	22:03	....	....	....	....	....	....	....	....	....
	Phoenix	NHL	33	3	3	6	20	2	0	2	31	9.7	3	0	0.0	19:59	4	0	0	0	2	0	0	0	19:54
2011-12	Phoenix	NHL	54	1	12	13	34	0	0	0	49	2.0	8	0	0.0	19:20	15	0	0	0	2	0	0	0	21:48
2012-13 ♦	Chicago	NHL	27	0	12	12	14	0	0	0	13	0.0	18	2	0.0	18:07	23	0	4	4	16	0	0	0	19:16
	NHL Totals		783	64	208	272	603	28	2	17	903	7.1		9	22.2	21:18	75	4	14	18	56	2	0	1	22:13

WHL East First All-Star Team (1998)

• Missed majority of 2003-04 due to knee injury in training camp, September 18, 2003. Signed as a free agent by **Trinec** (CzRep), September 17, 2004. Signed as a free agent by **Pardubice** (CzRep), January, 2005. Signed as a free agent by **NY Rangers**, August 29, 2005. Traded to **Phoenix** by **NY Rangers** for Wojtek Wolski, January 10, 2011. Signed as a free agent by **Chicago**, September 11, 2012.

RUHWEDEL, Chad

(ROO-WEE-dehl, CHAD) **BUF**

Defense. Shoots right. 5'11", 182 lbs. Born, San Diego, CA, May 7, 1990.

Season	Club	League	GP	G	A	Pts	PIM	PP	SH	GW	S	%	+/-	TF	F%	Min	GP	G	A	Pts	PIM	PP	SH	GW	Min
2008-09	Sioux Falls	USHL	55	0	11	11	30	....	....	....	....	....	....	....	....	....	4	0	1	1	4	....	....	....	....
2009-10	Sioux Falls	USHL	59	5	17	22	55	....	....	....	....	....	....	....	....	....	3	0	1	1	2	....	....	....	....
2010-11	U. Mass-Lowell	H-East	32	2	13	15	10	....	....	....	....	....	....	....	....	....	....	....	....	....	....	....	....	....	....
2011-12	U. Mass-Lowell	H-East	37	6	19	25	26	....	....	....	....	....	....	....	....	....	....	....	....	....	....	....	....	....	....
2012-13	U. Mass-Lowell	H-East	41	7	16	23	20	....	....	....	....	....	....	....	....	....	....	....	....	....	....	....	....	....	....
	Buffalo	NHL	7	0	0	0	0	0	0	0	8	0.0	0	0	0.0	14:12	....	....	....	....	....	....	....	....	....
	NHL Totals		7	0	0	0	0	0	0	0	8	0.0		0	0.0	14:12	....	....	....	....	....	....	....	....	....

Hockey East First All-Star Team (2013) • NCAA East First All-American Team (2013)

Signed as a free agent by **Buffalo**, April 13, 2013.

RUNDBLAD, David

(RUHND-blahd, DAY-vihd) **PHX**

Defense. Shoots right. 6'2", 195 lbs. Born, Lycksele, Sweden, October 8, 1990. St. Louis' 1st choice, 17th overall, in 2009 Entry Draft.

Season	Club	League	GP	G	A	Pts	PIM	PP	SH	GW	S	%	+/-	TF	F%	Min	GP	G	A	Pts	PIM	PP	SH	GW	Min
2004-05	Lycksele SK	Sweden-4	1	0	0	0	0	....	....	....	....	....	....	....	....	....	....	....	....	....	....	....	....	....	....
2005-06	Lycksele SK	Sweden-4	11	5	2	7	2	....	....	....	....	....	....	....	....	....	....	....	....	....	....	....	....	....	....
2006-07	Skelleftea U18	Swe-U18	4	1	1	2	0	....	....	....	....	....	....	....	....	....	....	....	....	....	....	....	....	....	....
	Skelleftea Jr.	Swe-Jr.	14	3	4	7	12	....	....	....	....	....	....	....	....	....	2	0	0	0	2	....	....	....	....
2007-08	Skelleftea U18	Swe-U18	4	3	2	5	29	....	....	....	....	....	....	....	....	....	....	....	....	....	....	....	....	....	....
	Skelleftea Jr.	Swe-Jr.	35	11	15	26	44	....	....	....	....	....	....	....	....	....	2	1	3	4	6	....	....	....	....
	Skelleftea AIK HK	Sweden	6	0	0	0	2	....	....	....	....	....	....	....	....	....	....	....	....	....	....	....	....	....	....
2008-09	Skelleftea AIK Jr.	Swe-Jr.	10	8	7	15	2	....	....	....	....	....	....	....	....	....	....	....	....	....	....	....	....	....	....
	Skelleftea AIK	Sweden	45	0	10	10	8	....	....	....	....	....	....	....	....	....	10	1	1	2	2	....	....	....	....
2009-10	Skelleftea AIK Jr.	Swe-Jr.	3	2	2	4	4	....	....	....	....	....	....	....	....	....	....	....	....	....	....	....	....	....	....
	Skelleftea AIK	Sweden	47	1	12	13	14	....	....	....	....	....	....	....	....	....	12	0	1	1	2	....	....	....	....
2010-11	Skelleftea AIK	Sweden	55	11	*39	50	14	....	....	....	....	....	....	....	....	....	18	3	7	10	20	....	....	....	....
2011-12	Ottawa	NHL	24	1	3	4	6	0	0	0	26	3.8	–11	0	0.0	15:14	....	....	....	....	....	....	....	....	....
	Phoenix	NHL	6	0	3	3	0	0	0	0	8	0.0	–1	0	0.0	14:07	....	....	....	....	....	....	....	....	....
	Portland Pirates	AHL	30	7	9	16	27	....	....	....	....	....	....	....	....	....	....	....	....	....	....	....	....	....	....
2012-13	Portland Pirates	AHL	50	9	30	39	26	....	....	....	....	....	....	....	....	....	3	1	0	1	0	....	....	....	....
	Phoenix	NHL	8	0	1	1	0	0	0	0	9	0.0	–5	0	0.0	13:44	....	....	....	....	....	....	....	....	....
	NHL Totals		38	1	7	8	6	0	0	0	43	2.3		0	0.0	14:44	....	....	....	....	....	....	....	....	....

Traded to **Ottawa** by **St. Louis** for Ottawa's 1st round choice (Vladimir Tarasenko) in 2010 Entry Draft, June 25, 2010. Traded to **Phoenix** by **Ottawa** with Ottawa's 2nd round choice (later traded to Columbus, later traded to Philadelphia – Philadelphia selected Anthony Stolarz) in 2012 Entry Draft for Kyle Turris, December 17, 2011.

RUPP, Mike

(RUHP, MIGHK) **MIN**

Center. Shoots left. 6'5", 243 lbs. Born, Cleveland, OH, January 13, 1980. New Jersey's 7th choice, 76th overall, in 2000 Entry Draft.

			Regular Season														Playoffs								
Season	Club	League	GP	G	A	Pts	PIM	PP	SH	GW	S	%	+/-	TF	F%	Min	GP	G	A	Pts	PIM	PP	SH	GW	Min
1996-97	St. Edward's	High-OH	20	26	24	50	....	....	....	....	....	....	....	....	....	....	....	....	....	....	....	....	....	....	....
1997-98	Windsor Spitfires	OHL	38	9	8	17	60	....	....	....	....	....	....	....	....	....	....	....	....	....	....	....	....	....	....
	Erie Otters	OHL	26	7	3	10	57	....	....	....	....	....	....	....	....	....	7	3	1	4	6	....	....	....	....
1998-99	Erie Otters	OHL	63	22	25	47	102	....	....	....	....	....	....	....	....	....	5	0	2	2	25	....	....	....	....
99-2000	Erie Otters	OHL	58	32	21	53	134	....	....	....	....	....	....	....	....	....	13	5	5	10	22	....	....	....	....
2000-01	Albany River Rats	AHL	71	10	10	20	63	....	....	....	....	....	....	....	....	....	....	....	....	....	....	....	....	....	....
2001-02	Albany River Rats	AHL	78	13	17	30	90	....	....	....	....	....	....	....	....	....	....	....	....	....	....	....	....	....	....
2002-03 ♦	**New Jersey**	**NHL**	**26**	**5**	**3**	**8**	**21**	**2**	**0**	**3**	**34**	**14.7**	**0**	**150**	**44.7**	**11:39**	**4**	**1**	**3**	**4**	**0**	**0**	**0**	**1**	**11:28**
	Albany River Rats	AHL	47	8	11	19	74	....	....	....	....	....	....	....	....	....	....	....	....	....	....	....	....	....	....
2003-04	**New Jersey**	**NHL**	**51**	**6**	**5**	**11**	**41**	**1**	**0**	**1**	**64**	**9.4**	**–1**	**386**	**47.9**	**10:38**	....	....	....	....	....	....	....	....	....
	Phoenix	**NHL**	**6**	**0**	**1**	**1**	**6**	**0**	**0**	**0**	**12**	**0.0**	**–3**	**94**	**57.5**	**16:59**	....	....	....	....	....	....	....	....	....
2004-05	Danbury Trashers	UHL	14	5	5	10	30	....	....	....	....	....	....	....	....	....	11	3	4	7	38	....	....	....	....
2005-06	**Phoenix**	**NHL**	**1**	**0**	**0**	**0**	**0**	**0**	**0**	**0**	**1**	**0.0**	**0**	**1**	**0.0**	**6:30**	....	....	....	....	....	....	....	....	....
	Columbus	**NHL**	**39**	**4**	**2**	**6**	**58**	**0**	**0**	**0**	**38**	**10.5**	**–3**	**264**	**48.1**	**9:04**	....	....	....	....	....	....	....	....	....
	Syracuse Crunch	AHL	3	1	2	3	12	....	....	....	....	....	....	....	....	....	....	....	....	....	....	....	....	....	....
2006-07	**New Jersey**	**NHL**	**76**	**6**	**3**	**9**	**92**	**0**	**0**	**1**	**60**	**10.0**	**–10**	**33**	**45.5**	**6:27**	**9**	**0**	**1**	**1**	**7**	**0**	**0**	**0**	**2:46**
2007-08	**New Jersey**	**NHL**	**64**	**3**	**6**	**9**	**58**	**1**	**0**	**0**	**69**	**4.3**	**–8**	**155**	**48.4**	**8:04**	**5**	**0**	**1**	**1**	**2**	**0**	**0**	**0**	**7:48**
2008-09	**New Jersey**	**NHL**	**72**	**3**	**6**	**9**	**136**	**0**	**0**	**0**	**76**	**3.9**	**–2**	**90**	**51.1**	**8:44**	**7**	**0**	**0**	**0**	**14**	**0**	**0**	**0**	**6:55**
2009-10	**Pittsburgh**	**NHL**	**81**	**13**	**6**	**19**	**120**	**0**	**0**	**1**	**87**	**14.9**	**5**	**143**	**44.1**	**9:03**	**11**	**0**	**0**	**0**	**8**	**0**	**0**	**0**	**7:28**
2010-11	**Pittsburgh**	**NHL**	**81**	**9**	**8**	**17**	**124**	**0**	**0**	**1**	**81**	**11.1**	**–4**	**162**	**50.6**	**10:03**	**7**	**1**	**1**	**2**	**4**	**0**	**0**	**0**	**9:07**
2011-12	**NY Rangers**	**NHL**	**60**	**4**	**1**	**5**	**97**	**0**	**0**	**2**	**31**	**12.9**	**–1**	**34**	**55.9**	**6:39**	**20**	**0**	**0**	**0**	**36**	**0**	**0**	**0**	**6:13**
2012-13	**NY Rangers**	**NHL**	**8**	**0**	**0**	**0**	**12**	**0**	**0**	**0**	**2**	**0.0**	**–3**	**8**	**50.0**	**6:15**	....	....	....	....	....	....	....	....	....
	Minnesota	**NHL**	**32**	**1**	**3**	**4**	**67**	**0**	**0**	**0**	**27**	**3.7**	**1**	**19**	**63.2**	**8:53**	**4**	**0**	**0**	**0**	**12**	**0**	**0**	**0**	**6:38**
	NHL Totals		**597**	**54**	**44**	**98**	**832**	**4**	**0**	**9**	**582**	**9.3**		**1539**	**48.7**	**8:45**	**67**	**2**	**6**	**8**	**83**	**0**	**0**	**1**	**6:48**

• Re-entered NHL Entry Draft. Originally NY Islanders' 1st choice, 9th overall, in 1998 Entry Draft.

Traded to **Phoenix** by **New Jersey** with New Jersey's 2nd round choice (later traded to Edmonton – Edmonton selected Geoff Paukovich) in 2004 Entry Draft for Jan Hrdina, March 5, 2004. Signed as a free agent by **Danbury** (UHL), February 10, 2005. Traded to **Columbus** by **Phoenix** with Cale Hulse and Jason Chimera for Geoff Sanderson and Tim Jackman, October 8, 2005. Signed as a free agent by **New Jersey**, July 10, 2006. Signed as a free agent by **Pittsburgh**, July 1, 2009. Signed as a free agent by **NY Rangers**, July 1, 2011. Traded to **Minnesota** by **NY Rangers** for Darroll Powe and Nick Palmieri, February 4, 2013.

RUSSELL, Kris

(RUH-sehl, KRIHS) **CGY**

Defense. Shoots left. 5'10", 173 lbs. Born, Caroline, Alta., May 2, 1987. Columbus' 3rd choice, 67th overall, in 2005 Entry Draft.

2003-04	Medicine Hat	WHL	55	4	15	19	30	....	....	....	....	....	....	....	....	....	20	3	2	5	4	....	....	....	....
2004-05	Medicine Hat	WHL	72	26	35	61	37	....	....	....	....	....	....	....	....	....	10	2	1	3	4	....	....	....	....
2005-06	Medicine Hat	WHL	55	14	33	47	18	....	....	....	....	....	....	....	....	....	13	4	8	12	11	....	....	....	....
2006-07	Medicine Hat	WHL	59	32	37	69	56	....	....	....	....	....	....	....	....	....	23	4	15	19	24	....	....	....	....
2007-08	**Columbus**	**NHL**	**67**	**2**	**8**	**10**	**14**	**1**	**0**	**1**	**90**	**2.2**	**–12**	**0**	**0.0**	**14:47**	....	....	....	....	....	....	....	....	....
2008-09	**Columbus**	**NHL**	**66**	**2**	**19**	**21**	**28**	**1**	**0**	**1**	**86**	**2.3**	**–10**	**0**	**0.0**	**16:07**	**4**	**1**	**1**	**2**	**2**	**0**	**0**	**0**	**16:40**
	Syracuse Crunch	AHL	14	3	5	8	0	....	....	....	....	....	....	....	....	....	....	....	....	....	....	....	....	....	....
2009-10	**Columbus**	**NHL**	**70**	**7**	**15**	**22**	**32**	**0**	**0**	**1**	**108**	**6.5**	**3**	**0**	**0.0**	**18:35**	....	....	....	....	....	....	....	....	....
2010-11	**Columbus**	**NHL**	**73**	**5**	**18**	**23**	**37**	**1**	**0**	**0**	**88**	**5.7**	**–9**	**0**	**0.0**	**17:31**	....	....	....	....	....	....	....	....	....
2011-12	**Columbus**	**NHL**	**12**	**2**	**1**	**3**	**13**	**0**	**0**	**0**	**20**	**10.0**	**–1**	**0**	**0.0**	**17:34**	....	....	....	....	....	....	....	....	....
	St. Louis	**NHL**	**43**	**4**	**5**	**9**	**12**	**0**	**0**	**1**	**36**	**11.1**	**13**	**0**	**0.0**	**16:51**	**9**	**0**	**3**	**3**	**5**	**0**	**0**	**0**	**19:27**
2012-13	TPS Turku	Finland	15	2	12	14	8	....	....	....	....	....	....	....	....	....	....	....	....	....	....	....	....	....	....
	St. Louis	**NHL**	**33**	**1**	**6**	**7**	**9**	**1**	**0**	**0**	**41**	**2.4**	**6**	**0**	**0.0**	**16:03**	....	....	....	....	....	....	....	....	....
	NHL Totals		**364**	**23**	**72**	**95**	**145**	**4**	**0**	**4**	**469**	**4.9**		**0**	**0.0**	**16:45**	**13**	**1**	**4**	**5**	**7**	**0**	**0**	**0**	**18:36**

WHL East Second All-Star Team (2005) • WHL East First All-Star Team (2006, 2007) • WHL Defenseman of the Year (2006, 2007) • Canadian Major Junior Second All-Star Team (2006) • Canadian Major Junior Sportsman of the Year (2006) • WHL Player of the Year (2007) • Canadian Major Junior First All-Star Team (2007) • Canadian Major Junior Defenseman of the Year (2007)

Traded to **St. Louis** by **Columbus** for Nikita Nikitin, November 11, 2011. Signed as a free agent by **TPS Turku** (Finland), September 26, 2012. Traded to **Calgary** by **St. Louis** for Calgary's 5th round choice in 2014 Entry Draft, July 5, 2013.

RUSSELL, Ryan

(RUH-sehl, RIGH-uhn)

Center. Shoots left. 5'10", 178 lbs. Born, Caroline, Alta., May 2, 1987. NY Rangers' 9th choice, 211th overall, in 2005 Entry Draft.

2003-04	Kootenay Ice	WHL	67	3	9	12	27	....	....	....	....	....	....	....	....	....	4	0	0	0	0	....	....	....	....
2004-05	Kootenay Ice	WHL	66	32	21	53	18	....	....	....	....	....	....	....	....	....	16	6	7	13	12	....	....	....	....
2005-06	Kootenay Ice	WHL	72	33	42	75	30	....	....	....	....	....	....	....	....	....	6	3	5	8	2	....	....	....	....
2006-07	Kootenay Ice	WHL	58	30	46	76	40	....	....	....	....	....	....	....	....	....	7	3	6	9	2	....	....	....	....
2007-08	Hamilton	AHL	25	2	1	3	4	....	....	....	....	....	....	....	....	....	....	....	....	....	....	....	....	....	....
	Cincinnati	ECHL	12	6	4	10	4	....	....	....	....	....	....	....	....	....	15	3	4	7	0	....	....	....	....
2008-09	Hamilton	AHL	79	20	19	39	24	....	....	....	....	....	....	....	....	....	6	1	3	4	2	....	....	....	....
2009-10	Hamilton	AHL	74	19	18	37	8	....	....	....	....	....	....	....	....	....	19	7	5	12	0	....	....	....	....
2010-11	Hamilton	AHL	65	10	11	21	48	....	....	....	....	....	....	....	....	....	20	7	2	9	0	....	....	....	....
2011-12	**Columbus**	**NHL**	**41**	**2**	**0**	**2**	**2**	**0**	**0**	**0**	**39**	**5.1**	**–7**	**5**	**0.0**	**11:41**	....	....	....	....	....	....	....	....	....
	Springfield	AHL	31	9	6	15	15	....	....	....	....	....	....	....	....	....	....	....	....	....	....	....	....	....	....
2012-13	Springfield	AHL	62	10	6	16	16	....	....	....	....	....	....	....	....	....	7	1	3	4	4	....	....	....	....
	NHL Totals		**41**	**2**	**0**	**2**	**2**	**0**	**0**	**0**	**39**	**5.1**		**5**	**0.0**	**11:41**	....	....	....	....	....	....	....	....	....

Traded to **Montreal** by **NY Rangers** for Montreal's 7th round choice (David Skokan) in 2007 Entry Draft, May 31, 2007. Traded to **Columbus** by **Montreal** for Mike Blunden, July 7, 2011.

RUUTU, Tuomo

(ROO-too, TOO-oh-moh) **CAR**

Center/Left wing. Shoots left. 6', 205 lbs. Born, Vantaa, Finland, February 16, 1983. Chicago's 1st choice, 9th overall, in 2001 Entry Draft.

1998-99	HIFK Helsinki U18	Fin-U18	25	9	11	20	88	....	....	....	....	....	....	....	....	....	2	1	1	2	2	....	....	....	....
99-2000	HIFK Helsinki U18	Fin-U18	5	0	3	3	12	....	....	....	....	....	....	....	....	....	3	1	2	3	2	....	....	....	....
	HIFK Helsinki Jr.	Fin-Jr.	35	11	16	27	32	....	....	....	....	....	....	....	....	....	3	0	1	1	4	....	....	....	....
	HIFK Helsinki	Finland	1	0	0	0	2	....	....	....	....	....	....	....	....	....	....	....	....	....	....	....	....	....	....
2000-01	Jokerit Helsinki Jr.	Fin-Jr.	2	1	0	1	0	....	....	....	....	....	....	....	....	....	....	....	....	....	....	....	....	....	....
	Jokerit Helsinki	Finland	47	11	11	22	94	....	....	....	....	....	....	....	....	....	5	0	0	0	4	....	....	....	....
2001-02	Jokerit Helsinki	Finland	51	7	16	23	69	....	....	....	....	....	....	....	....	....	10	0	6	6	29	....	....	....	....
2002-03	HIFK Helsinki	Finland	30	12	15	27	24	....	....	....	....	....	....	....	....	....	....	....	....	....	....	....	....	....	....
2003-04	**Chicago**	**NHL**	**82**	**23**	**21**	**44**	**58**	**10**	**0**	**3**	**174**	**13.2**	**–31**	**317**	**46.4**	**16:24**	....	....	....	....	....	....	....	....	....
2004-05			DID NOT PLAY																						
2005-06	**Chicago**	**NHL**	**15**	**2**	**3**	**5**	**31**	**1**	**0**	**0**	**30**	**6.7**	**–7**	**90**	**46.7**	**14:43**	....	....	....	....	....	....	....	....	....
2006-07	**Chicago**	**NHL**	**71**	**17**	**21**	**38**	**95**	**1**	**0**	**1**	**115**	**14.8**	**4**	**347**	**42.7**	**17:21**	....	....	....	....	....	....	....	....	....
2007-08	**Chicago**	**NHL**	**60**	**6**	**15**	**21**	**75**	**1**	**0**	**1**	**71**	**8.5**	**3**	**49**	**53.1**	**15:35**	....	....	....	....	....	....	....	....	....
	Carolina	**NHL**	**17**	**4**	**7**	**11**	**16**	**3**	**0**	**0**	**29**	**13.8**	**1**	**17**	**11.8**	**17:01**	....	....	....	....	....	....	....	....	....
2008-09	**Carolina**	**NHL**	**79**	**26**	**28**	**54**	**79**	**10**	**0**	**4**	**190**	**13.7**	**0**	**37**	**51.4**	**18:19**	**16**	**1**	**3**	**4**	**8**	**0**	**0**	**0**	**14:16**
2009-10	**Carolina**	**NHL**	**54**	**14**	**21**	**35**	**50**	**5**	**0**	**1**	**122**	**11.5**	**–4**	**47**	**40.4**	**16:23**	....	....	....	....	....	....	....	....	....
	Finland	Olympics	6	1	0	1	2	....	....	....	....	....	....	....	....	....	....	....	....	....	....	....	....	....	....
2010-11	**Carolina**	**NHL**	**82**	**19**	**38**	**57**	**54**	**7**	**0**	**1**	**148**	**12.8**	**1**	**643**	**41.2**	**16:50**	....	....	....	....	....	....	....	....	....
2011-12	**Carolina**	**NHL**	**72**	**18**	**16**	**34**	**50**	**3**	**0**	**2**	**156**	**11.5**	**–3**	**124**	**35.5**	**16:28**	....	....	....	....	....	....	....	....	....
2012-13	**Carolina**	**NHL**	**17**	**4**	**5**	**9**	**8**	**0**	**0**	**0**	**30**	**13.3**	**–6**	**8**	**12.5**	**15:14**	....	....	....	....	....	....	....	....	....
	NHL Totals		**549**	**133**	**175**	**308**	**516**	**41**	**0**	**13**	**1065**	**12.5**		**1679**	**42.5**	**16:43**	**16**	**1**	**3**	**4**	**8**	**0**	**0**	**0**	**14:16**

• Missed majority of 2005-06 due to back (October 15, 2005 at San Jose) and ankle (January 8, 2006 vs. Nashville) injuries. Traded to **Carolina** by **Chicago** for Andrew Ladd, February 26, 2008. • Missed majority of 2012-13 due to hip surgery.

RYAN, Bobby

(RIGH-uhn, BAW-bee) **OTT**

Left wing. Shoots right. 6'2", 200 lbs. Born, Cherry Hill, NJ, March 17, 1987. Anaheim's 1st choice, 2nd overall, in 2005 Entry Draft.

2003-04	Owen Sound	OHL	65	22	17	39	52	....	....	....	....	....	....	....	....	....	7	1	2	3	2	....	....	....	....
2004-05	Owen Sound	OHL	62	37	52	89	51	....	....	....	....	....	....	....	....	....	8	2	7	9	8	....	....	....	....
2005-06	Owen Sound	OHL	59	31	64	95	44	....	....	....	....	....	....	....	....	....	11	5	7	12	14	....	....	....	....
	Portland Pirates	AHL	....	....	....	....	....	....	....	....	....	....	....	....	....	....	19	1	7	8	22	....	....	....	....
2006-07	Owen Sound	OHL	63	43	59	102	63	....	....	....	....	....	....	....	....	....	4	1	1	2	2	....	....	....	....
	Portland Pirates	AHL	8	3	6	9	6	....	....	....	....	....	....	....	....	....	....	....	....	....	....	....	....	....	....
2007-08	**Anaheim**	**NHL**	**23**	**5**	**5**	**10**	**6**	**3**	**0**	**0**	**37**	**13.5**	**–1**	**1**	**100.0**	**11:16**	**2**	**0**	**0**	**0**	**2**	**0**	**0**	**0**	**11:09**
	Portland Pirates	AHL	48	21	28	49	38	....	....	....	....	....	....	....	....	....	16	8	12	20	18	....	....	....	....

			Regular Season														Playoffs								
Season	Club	League	GP	G	A	Pts	PIM	PP	SH	GW	S	%	+/-	TF	F%	Min	GP	G	A	Pts	PIM	PP	SH	GW	Min
2008-09	Anaheim	NHL	64	31	26	57	33	12	0	3	174	17.8	13	13	46.2	15:26	13	5	2	7	0	2	0	1	19:41
	Iowa Chops	AHL	14	9	10	19	19	....	....	....	....	....	....	....	....	....	....	....	....	....	....	....	....	....	....
2009-10	Anaheim	NHL	81	35	29	64	81	11	0	3	258	13.6	9	93	44.1	18:29	....	....	....	....	....	....	....	....	....
	United States	Olympics	6	1	1	2	2	....	....	....	....	....	....	....	....	....	....	....	....	....	....	....	....	....	....
2010-11	Anaheim	NHL	82	34	37	71	61	5	1	5	270	12.6	15	219	39.7	20:11	4	3	1	4	2	0	0	0	20:29
2011-12	Anaheim	NHL	82	31	26	57	53	3	2	3	204	15.2	1	69	29.0	18:21	....	....	....	....	....	....	....	....	....
2012-13	Mora IK	Sweden-2	11	10	3	13	8	....	....	....	....	....	....	....	....	....	....	....	....	....	....	....	....	....	....
	Anaheim	NHL	46	11	19	30	17	2	0	1	101	10.9	3	81	30.9	16:35	7	2	2	4	0	0	0	0	16:17
	NHL Totals		378	147	142	289	251	36	3	15	1044	14.1		476	37.8	17:38	26	10	5	15	4	2	0	1	18:14

OHL First All-Star Team (2005) • AHL All-Rookie Team (2008) • NHL All-Rookie Team (2009)

Signed as a free agent by **Mora** (Sweden-2), November 21, 2012. Traded to **Ottawa** by **Anaheim** for Jakob Silfverberg, Stefan Noesen and Ottawa's 1st round choice in 2014 Entry Draft, July 5, 2013.

RYDER, Michael (RIGH-duhr, MIGH-kuhl) N.J.

Right wing. Shoots right. 6'1", 200 lbs. Born, Bonavista, Nfld., March 31, 1980. Montreal's 9th choice, 216th overall, in 1998 Entry Draft.

Season	Club	League	GP	G	A	Pts	PIM	PP	SH	GW	S	%	+/-	TF	F%	Min	GP	G	A	Pts	PIM	PP	SH	GW	Min
1996-97	Bonavista Saints	NFAHA	23	31	17	48	....	....	....	....	....	....	....	....	....	....	....	....	....	....	....	....	....	....	....
1997-98	Hull Olympiques	QMJHL	69	34	28	62	41	....	....	....	....	....	....	....	....	....	10	4	2	6	4	....	....	....	....
1998-99	Hull Olympiques	QMJHL	69	44	43	87	65	....	....	....	....	....	....	....	....	....	23	*20	16	36	39	....	....	....	....
99-2000	Hull Olympiques	QMJHL	63	50	58	108	50	....	....	....	....	....	....	....	....	....	15	11	17	28	28	....	....	....	....
2000-01	Tallahassee	ECHL	5	4	5	9	6	....	....	....	....	....	....	....	....	....	....	....	....	....	....	....	....	....	....
	Quebec Citadelles	AHL	61	6	9	15	14	....	....	....	....	....	....	....	....	....	....	....	....	....	....	....	....	....	....
2001-02	Mississippi	ECHL	20	14	13	27	2	....	....	....	....	....	....	....	....	....	....	....	....	....	....	....	....	....	....
	Quebec Citadelles	AHL	50	11	17	28	9	....	....	....	....	....	....	....	....	....	3	0	1	1	2	....	....	....	....
2002-03	Hamilton	AHL	69	34	33	67	43	....	....	....	....	....	....	....	....	....	23	11	6	17	8	....	....	....	....
2003-04	Montreal	NHL	81	25	38	63	26	10	0	4	215	11.6	10	25	24.0	16:00	11	1	2	3	4	0	0	0	16:52
2004-05	Leksands IF	Sweden-2	42	34	27	61	32	....	....	....	....	....	....	....	....	....	....	....	....	....	....	....	....	....	....
2005-06	Montreal	NHL	81	30	25	55	40	18	0	6	243	12.3	-5	17	52.9	16:10	6	2	3	5	0	1	0	1	16:09
2006-07	Montreal	NHL	82	30	28	58	60	17	2	3	221	13.6	-25	28	42.9	16:17	....	....	....	....	....	....	....	....	....
2007-08	Montreal	NHL	70	14	17	31	30	1	0	2	134	10.4	-4	19	26.3	13:15	4	0	0	0	2	0	0	0	10:46
2008-09	Boston	NHL	74	27	26	53	26	10	0	7	185	14.6	28	15	46.7	14:55	11	5	8	13	8	1	0	1	15:45
2009-10	Boston	NHL	82	18	15	33	35	7	0	1	191	9.4	3	15	13.3	15:18	13	4	1	5	2	1	0	0	15:47
2010-11 ♦	Boston	NHL	79	18	23	41	26	8	0	6	165	10.9	-1	8	62.5	14:29	25	8	9	17	8	2	0	2	14:34
2011-12	Dallas	NHL	82	35	27	62	46	7	0	6	211	16.6	17	71	47.9	17:23	....	....	....	....	....	....	....	....	....
2012-13	Dallas	NHL	19	6	8	14	8	2	0	2	42	14.3	4	6	33.3	16:22	....	....	....	....	....	....	....	....	....
	Montreal	NHL	27	10	11	21	8	6	0	3	59	16.9	-2	3	33.3	15:49	5	1	1	2	2	0	0	0	14:51
	NHL Totals		677	213	218	431	305	86	2	40	1666	12.8		207	40.1	15:34	75	21	24	45	26	5	0	4	15:14

NHL All-Rookie Team (2004)

Signed as a free agent by **Leksands** (Sweden-2), September 19, 2004. Signed as a free agent by **Boston**, July 1, 2008. Signed as a free agent by **Dallas**, July 1, 2011. Traded to **Montreal** by **Dallas** for Erik Cole and Dallas' 3rd round choice (Connor Crisp) in 2013 Entry Draft, February 26, 2013. Signed as a free agent by **New Jersey**, July 5, 2013.

SAAD, Brandon (SAHD, BRAN-duhn) CHI

Left wing. Shoots left. 6'1", 202 lbs. Born, Pittsburgh, PA, October 27, 1992. Chicago's 4th choice, 43rd overall, in 2011 Entry Draft.

Season	Club	League	GP	G	A	Pts	PIM	PP	SH	GW	S	%	+/-	TF	F%	Min	GP	G	A	Pts	PIM	PP	SH	GW	Min
2007-08	Pittsburgh	MWEHL	26	11	19	30	16	....	....	....	....	....	....	....	....	....	....	....	....	....	....	....	....	....	....
2008-09	Mahoning Valley	NAHL	47	29	18	47	48	....	....	....	....	....	....	....	....	....	7	5	1	6	10	....	....	....	....
	USNTDP	U-17	7	6	5	11	2	....	....	....	....	....	....	....	....	....	....	....	....	....	....	....	....	....	....
2009-10	USNTDP	USHL	24	12	14	26	18	....	....	....	....	....	....	....	....	....	....	....	....	....	....	....	....	....	....
	USNTDP	U-18	39	17	15	32	16	....	....	....	....	....	....	....	....	....	....	....	....	....	....	....	....	....	....
2010-11	Saginaw Spirit	OHL	59	27	28	55	47	....	....	....	....	....	....	....	....	....	12	3	9	12	10	....	....	....	....
2011-12	Saginaw Spirit	OHL	44	34	42	76	38	....	....	....	....	....	....	....	....	....	12	8	9	17	4	....	....	....	....
	Chicago	NHL	2	0	0	0	0	0	0	0	3	0.0	0	0	0.0	14:01	2	0	1	1	0	0	0	0	12:21
2012-13	Rockford IceHogs	AHL	31	8	12	20	10	....	....	....	....	....	....	....	....	....	....	....	....	....	....	....	....	....	....
	♦ Chicago	NHL	46	10	17	27	12	0	1	2	98	10.2	17	46	37.0	16:28	23	1	5	6	4	0	0	0	16:24
	NHL Totals		48	10	17	27	12	0	1	2	101	9.9		46	37.0	16:22	25	1	6	7	4	0	0	0	16:04

OHL First All-Star Team (2012) • NHL All-Rookie Team (2013)

ST. DENIS, Frederic (SAINT-deh-nee, FREHD-uhr-ihk) CBJ

Defense. Shoots left. 5'11", 193 lbs. Born, Greenfield Park, Que., January 23, 1986.

Season	Club	League	GP	G	A	Pts	PIM	PP	SH	GW	S	%	+/-	TF	F%	Min	GP	G	A	Pts	PIM	PP	SH	GW	Min
2001-02	C.C. Lemoyne	QAAA	42	4	6	10	4	....	....	....	....	....	....	....	....	....	....	....	....	....	....	....	....	....	....
2002-03	C.C. Lemoyne	QAAA	31	8	15	23	6	....	....	....	....	....	....	....	....	....	....	....	....	....	....	....	....	....	....
	Drummondville	QMJHL	14	0	0	0	0	....	....	....	....	....	....	....	....	....	....	....	....	....	....	....	....	....	....
2003-04	Drummondville	QMJHL	67	7	10	17	30	....	....	....	....	....	....	....	....	....	5	0	1	1	2	....	....	....	....
2004-05	Drummondville	QMJHL	70	11	22	33	36	....	....	....	....	....	....	....	....	....	6	2	3	5	0	....	....	....	....
2005-06	Drummondville	QMJHL	69	17	50	67	74	....	....	....	....	....	....	....	....	....	....	....	....	....	....	....	....	....	....
2006-07	Drummondville	QMJHL	65	9	29	38	59	....	....	....	....	....	....	....	....	....	12	1	7	8	8	....	....	....	....
2007-08	U. Quebec T-R	OUAA	28	4	14	18	4	....	....	....	....	....	....	....	....	....	....	....	....	....	....	....	....	....	....
2008-09	Hamilton	AHL	7	1	1	2	6	....	....	....	....	....	....	....	....	....	....	....	....	....	....	....	....	....	....
	Cincinnati	ECHL	41	1	22	23	22	....	....	....	....	....	....	....	....	....	15	0	5	5	14	....	....	....	....
2009-10	Hamilton	AHL	59	3	14	17	38	....	....	....	....	....	....	....	....	....	19	0	1	1	20	....	....	....	....
2010-11	Hamilton	AHL	76	5	18	23	34	....	....	....	....	....	....	....	....	....	20	1	9	10	12	....	....	....	....
2011-12	Montreal	NHL	17	1	2	3	10	0	0	0	11	9.1	3	0	0.0	14:31	....	....	....	....	....	....	....	....	....
	Hamilton	AHL	58	3	25	28	18	....	....	....	....	....	....	....	....	....	....	....	....	....	....	....	....	....	....
2012-13	Hamilton	AHL	63	7	11	18	24	....	....	....	....	....	....	....	....	....	....	....	....	....	....	....	....	....	....
	NHL Totals		17	1	2	3	10	0	0	0	11	9.1		0	0.0	14:31	....	....	....	....	....	....	....	....	....

QMJHL Second All-Star Team (2006)

Signed as a free agent by **Hamilton** (AHL), September 27, 2008. Signed as a free agent by **Montreal**. July 1, 2010. Signed as a free agent by **Columbus**, July 7, 2013.

ST. LOUIS, Martin (SAINT loo-EE, mahr-TEHN) T.B.

Right wing. Shoots left. 5'8", 180 lbs. Born, Laval, Que., June 18, 1975.

Season	Club	League	GP	G	A	Pts	PIM	PP	SH	GW	S	%	+/-	TF	F%	Min	GP	G	A	Pts	PIM	PP	SH	GW	Min
1991-92	Laval-Laurentides	QAAA	42	29	*74	*103	38	....	....	....	....	....	....	....	....	....	12	7	15	22	16	....	....	....	....
1992-93	Hawkesbury	ON-Jr.A	31	37	50	87	70	....	....	....	....	....	....	....	....	....	....	....	....	....	....	....	....	....	....
1993-94	U. of Vermont	ECAC	33	15	36	51	24	....	....	....	....	....	....	....	....	....	....	....	....	....	....	....	....	....	....
1994-95	U. of Vermont	ECAC	35	23	48	71	36	....	....	....	....	....	....	....	....	....	....	....	....	....	....	....	....	....	....
1995-96	U. of Vermont	ECAC	35	29	56	85	38	....	....	....	....	....	....	....	....	....	....	....	....	....	....	....	....	....	....
1996-97	U. of Vermont	ECAC	36	24	*36	60	65	....	....	....	....	....	....	....	....	....	....	....	....	....	....	....	....	....	....
1997-98	Cleveland	IHL	56	16	34	50	24	....	....	....	....	....	....	....	....	....	....	....	....	....	....	....	....	....	....
	Saint John Flames	AHL	25	15	11	26	20	....	....	....	....	....	....	....	....	....	20	5	15	20	16	....	....	....	....
1998-99	Calgary	NHL	13	1	1	2	10	0	0	0	14	7.1	-2	0	0.0	8:15	....	....	....	....	....	....	....	....	....
	Saint John Flames	AHL	53	28	34	62	30	....	....	....	....	....	....	....	....	....	7	4	4	8	2	....	....	....	....
99-2000	Calgary	NHL	56	3	15	18	22	0	0	1	73	4.1	-5	3	0.0	14:41	....	....	....	....	....	....	....	....	....
	Saint John Flames	AHL	17	15	11	26	14	....	....	....	....	....	....	....	....	....	....	....	....	....	....	....	....	....	....
2000-01	Tampa Bay	NHL	78	18	22	40	12	3	3	4	141	12.8	-4	48	41.7	15:14	....	....	....	....	....	....	....	....	....
2001-02	Tampa Bay	NHL	53	16	19	35	20	6	1	2	105	15.2	4	33	39.4	18:41	....	....	....	....	....	....	....	....	....
2002-03	Tampa Bay	NHL	82	33	37	70	32	12	3	5	201	16.4	10	37	37.8	19:43	11	7	5	12	0	1	*2	3	22:21
2003-04 ♦	Tampa Bay	NHL	82	38	*56	*94	24	8	*8	7	212	17.9	*35	24	33.3	20:35	23	9	*15	24	14	3	1	3	22:52
2004-05	Lausanne HC	Swiss	23	9	16	25	16	....	....	....	....	....	....	....	....	....	....	....	....	....	....	....	....	....	....
2005-06	Tampa Bay	NHL	80	31	30	61	38	9	3	7	221	14.0	-3	13	23.1	20:59	5	4	0	4	2	1	0	1	22:53
	Canada	Olympics	6	2	1	3	0	....	....	....	....	....	....	....	....	....	....	....	....	....	....	....	....	....	....
2006-07	Tampa Bay	NHL	82	43	59	102	28	14	5	7	273	15.8	7	20	35.0	24:09	6	3	5	8	8	1	0	0	28:07
2007-08	Tampa Bay	NHL	82	25	58	83	26	10	2	5	241	10.4	-23	12	25.0	24:17	....	....	....	....	....	....	....	....	....
2008-09	Tampa Bay	NHL	82	30	50	80	14	7	2	3	262	11.5	4	30	46.7	21:17	....	....	....	....	....	....	....	....	....
2009-10	Tampa Bay	NHL	82	29	65	94	12	7	1	7	242	12.0	-8	157	45.2	21:49	....	....	....	....	....	....	....	....	....
2010-11	Tampa Bay	NHL	82	31	68	99	12	4	0	7	254	12.2	0	131	38.2	20:59	18	10	10	20	4	4	0	1	21:11

			Regular Season														Playoffs								
Season	Club	League	GP	G	A	Pts	PIM	PP	SH	GW	S	%	+/-	TF	F%	Min	GP	G	A	Pts	PIM	PP	SH	GW	Min
2011-12	Tampa Bay	NHL	77	25	49	74	16	4	0	3	185	13.5	–3	41	43.9	22:38	....	....	....	....	....	....	....	....	....
2012-13	Tampa Bay	NHL	48	17	*43	*60	14	3	0	2	112	15.2	0	28	42.9	21:59	....	....	....	....	....	....	....	....	....
	NHL Totals		979	340	572	912	280	87	28	60	2536	13.4		577	40.4	20:33	63	33	35	68	28	10	3	8	22:48

ECAC First All-Star Team (1995, 1996, 1997) • ECAC Player of the Year (1995) • NCAA East First All-American Team (1995, 1996, 1997) • NCAA Championship All-Tournament Team (1996) • NHL First All-Star Team (2004) • Art Ross Trophy (2004, 2013) • Lester B. Pearson Award (2004) • Hart Memorial Trophy (2004) • NHL Second All-Star Team (2007, 2010, 2011, 2013) • Lady Byng Memorial Trophy (2010, 2011, 2013)

Played in NHL All-Star Game (2003, 2004, 2007, 2008, 2009, 2011)

Signed as a free agent by **Calgary**, February 19, 1998. Signed as a free agent by **Tampa Bay**, July 31, 2000. Signed as a free agent by **Lausanne** (Swiss), November 4, 2004.

ST. PIERRE, Martin

(SAINT PEE-aihr, mahr-TEHN) **MTL**

Center. Shoots left. 5'9", 187 lbs. Born, Ottawa, Ont., August 11, 1983.

Season	Club	League	GP	G	A	Pts	PIM	PP	SH	GW	S	%	+/-	TF	F%	Min	GP	G	A	Pts	PIM	PP	SH	GW	Min
2000-01	Guelph Storm	OHL	68	20	49	69	40	....	....	....	....	....	....	....	....	....	4	0	0	0	4	....	....	....	....
2001-02	Guelph Storm	OHL	66	32	53	85	68	....	....	....	....	....	....	....	....	....	9	3	9	12	12	....	....	....	....
2002-03	Guelph Storm	OHL	55	11	45	56	74	....	....	....	....	....	....	....	....	....	11	5	11	16	4	....	....	....	....
2003-04	Guelph Storm	OHL	68	45	65	110	95	....	....	....	....	....	....	....	....	....	22	8	*27	*35	20	....	....	....	....
2004-05	Greenville	ECHL	45	14	39	53	55	....	....	....	....	....	....	....	....	....	7	2	5	7	6	....	....	....	....
	Edmonton	AHL	18	4	3	7	8	....	....	....	....	....	....	....	....	....	....	....	....	....	....	....	....	....	....
2005-06	Chicago	NHL	2	0	0	0	0	0	0	0	1	0.0	–1	15	33.3	12:02	....	....	....	....	....	....	....	....	....
	Norfolk Admirals	AHL	77	23	50	73	98	....	....	....	....	....	....	....	....	....	4	0	3	3	2	....	....	....	....
2006-07	Chicago	NHL	14	1	3	4	8	1	0	0	13	7.7	–3	129	48.1	12:29	....	....	....	....	....	....	....	....	....
	Norfolk Admirals	AHL	65	27	72	99	100	....	....	....	....	....	....	....	....	....	6	0	1	1	6	....	....	....	....
2007-08	Mytischi	Russia	14	1	6	7	16	....	....	....	....	....	....	....	....	....	....	....	....	....	....	....	....	....	....
	Chicago	NHL	5	0	0	0	0	0	0	0	2	0.0	–3	59	55.9	15:17	....	....	....	....	....	....	....	....	....
	Rockford IceHogs	AHL	69	21	67	88	80	....	....	....	....	....	....	....	....	....	12	2	12	14	12	....	....	....	....
2008-09	Boston	NHL	14	2	2	4	4	0	1	1	15	13.3	–1	101	42.6	11:24	....	....	....	....	....	....	....	....	....
	Providence Bruins	AHL	61	15	51	66	58	....	....	....	....	....	....	....	....	....	16	5	11	16	26	....	....	....	....
2009-10	Ottawa	NHL	3	0	0	0	0	0	0	0	0	0.0	–2	20	45.0	9:37	....	....	....	....	....	....	....	....	....
	Binghamton	AHL	77	24	48	72	50	....	....	....	....	....	....	....	....	....	....	....	....	....	....	....	....	....	....
2010-11	Nizhnekamsk	KHL	8	1	1	2	8	....	....	....	....	....	....	....	....	....	....	....	....	....	....	....	....	....	....
	Karpat Oulu	Finland	27	8	6	14	6	....	....	....	....	....	....	....	....	....	....	....	....	....	....	....	....	....	....
	Salzburg	Austria	11	3	9	12	18	....	....	....	....	....	....	....	....	....	....	....	....	....	....	....	....	....	....
2011-12	Springfield	AHL	73	11	53	64	56	....	....	....	....	....	....	....	....	....	....	....	....	....	....	....	....	....	....
2012-13	Rockford IceHogs	AHL	76	26	33	59	59	....	....	....	....	....	....	....	....	....	....	....	....	....	....	....	....	....	....
	NHL Totals		38	3	5	8	12	1	1	1	31	9.7		324	46.9	12:12	....	....	....	....	....	....	....	....	....

AHL All-Rookie Team (2006) • AHL First All-Star Team (2007) • AHL Second All-Star Team (2008)

Signed as a free agent by **Chicago**, November 3, 2005. Signed as a free agent by **Mytischi** (Russia), June 22, 2007. Traded to **Boston** by **Chicago** for Pascal Pelletier, July 24, 2008. Signed as a free agent by **Ottawa**, July 1, 2009. Signed as a free agent by **Nizhnekamsk** (KHL), June 6, 2010. Signed as a free agent by **Oulu** (Finland), October 19, 2010. Signed as a free agent by **Salzburg** (Austria), January 22, 2011. Signed as a free agent by **Columbus**, July 11, 2011. Signed as a free agent by **Rockford** (AHL), July 3, 2012. Signed as a free agent by **Montreal**, July 6, 2013.

SALO, Sami

(SA-loh, SA-mee) **T.B.**

Defense. Shoots right. 6'3", 215 lbs. Born, Turku, Finland, September 2, 1974. Ottawa's 7th choice, 239th overall, in 1996 Entry Draft.

Season	Club	League	GP	G	A	Pts	PIM	PP	SH	GW	S	%	+/-	TF	F%	Min	GP	G	A	Pts	PIM	PP	SH	GW	Min
1991-92	Kiekko-67 Jr.	Fin-Jr.	23	4	5	9	26	....	....	....	....	....	....	....	....	....	....	....	....	....	....	....	....	....	....
1992-93	Kiekko-67 Jr.	Fin-Jr.	21	9	4	13	4	....	....	....	....	....	....	....	....	....	....	....	....	....	....	....	....	....	....
1993-94	TPS Turku Jr.	Fin-Jr.	36	7	13	20	16	....	....	....	....	....	....	....	....	....	7	0	1	1	10	....	....	....	....
1994-95	TPS Turku Jr.	Fin-Jr.	14	1	3	4	6	....	....	....	....	....	....	....	....	....	....	....	....	....	....	....	....	....	....
	Kiekko-67 Turku	Finland-2	19	4	2	6	4	....	....	....	....	....	....	....	....	....	....	....	....	....	....	....	....	....	....
	TPS Turku	Finland	7	1	2	3	6	....	....	....	....	....	....	....	....	....	1	0	0	0	0	....	....	....	....
1995-96	TPS Turku	Finland	47	7	14	21	32	....	....	....	....	....	....	....	....	....	11	1	3	4	8	....	....	....	....
1996-97	TPS Turku	Finland	48	9	6	15	10	....	....	....	....	....	....	....	....	....	10	2	3	5	4	....	....	....	....
	TPS Turku	EuroHL	6	0	2	2	6	....	....	....	....	....	....	....	....	....	2	0	0	0	2	....	....	....	....
1997-98	Jokerit Helsinki	Finland	35	3	5	8	24	....	....	....	....	....	....	....	....	....	8	0	1	1	2	....	....	....	....
	Jokerit Helsinki	EuroHL	6	1	1	2	2	....	....	....	....	....	....	....	....	....	....	....	....	....	....	....	....	....	....
1998-99	Ottawa	NHL	61	7	12	19	24	2	0	1	106	6.6	20	0	0.0	19:42	4	0	0	0	0	0	0	0	21:32
	Detroit Vipers	IHL	5	0	2	2	0	....	....	....	....	....	....	....	....	....	....	....	....	....	....	....	....	....	....
99-2000	Ottawa	NHL	37	6	8	14	2	3	0	1	85	7.1	6	0	0.0	20:18	6	1	1	2	0	1	0	0	24:11
2000-01	Ottawa	NHL	31	2	16	18	10	1	0	0	61	3.3	9	0	0.0	19:44	4	0	0	0	0	0	0	0	22:30
2001-02	Ottawa	NHL	66	4	14	18	14	1	1	2	122	3.3	1	0	0.0	19:52	12	2	1	3	4	0	0	0	20:23
	Finland	Olympics	4	0	0	0	0	....	....	....	....	....	....	....	....	....	....	....	....	....	....	....	....	....	....
2002-03	Vancouver	NHL	79	9	21	30	10	4	0	1	126	7.1	9	0	0.0	20:08	12	1	3	4	0	0	0	0	20:52
2003-04	Vancouver	NHL	74	7	19	26	22	5	0	2	143	4.9	8	1	100.0	22:14	7	1	2	3	2	1	0	0	22:59
2004-05	Frolunda	Sweden	41	6	8	14	18	....	....	....	....	....	....	....	....	....	14	1	6	7	2	....	....	....	....
2005-06	Vancouver	NHL	59	10	23	33	38	9	0	2	140	7.1	9	0	0.0	24:30	....	....	....	....	....	....	....	....	....
	Finland	Olympics	6	1	3	4	0	....	....	....	....	....	....	....	....	....	....	....	....	....	....	....	....	....	....
2006-07	Vancouver	NHL	67	14	23	37	26	5	0	6	143	9.8	21	0	0.0	21:27	10	0	1	1	4	0	0	0	25:53
2007-08	Vancouver	NHL	63	8	17	25	38	6	0	1	122	6.6	8	0	0.0	23:39	....	....	....	....	....	....	....	....	....
2008-09	Vancouver	NHL	60	5	20	25	26	5	0	2	110	4.5	5	0	0.0	20:11	7	3	4	7	2	2	0	2	18:36
2009-10	Vancouver	NHL	68	9	19	28	18	6	0	3	119	7.6	14	0	0.0	20:41	12	1	5	6	2	1	0	0	20:40
	Finland	Olympics	6	1	1	2	4	....	....	....	....	....	....	....	....	....	....	....	....	....	....	....	....	....	....
2010-11	Vancouver	NHL	27	3	4	7	14	1	0	0	39	7.7	–3	0	0.0	20:21	21	3	2	5	2	3	0	1	19:13
	Manitoba Moose	AHL	3	2	0	2	2	....	....	....	....	....	....	....	....	....	....	....	....	....	....	....	....	....	....
2011-12	Vancouver	NHL	69	9	16	25	10	7	0	3	136	6.6	7	0	0.0	20:27	5	0	0	0	2	0	0	0	18:49
2012-13	Tampa Bay	NHL	46	2	15	17	16	1	0	0	48	4.2	5	0	0.0	20:59	....	....	....	....	....	....	....	....	....
	NHL Totals		807	95	227	322	268	56	1	24	1500	6.3		1	100.0	21:06	100	12	19	31	18	8	0	3	21:07

NHL All-Rookie Team (1999)

• Missed majority of 1999-2000 due to wrist injury vs. Philadelphia, November 28, 1999. • Missed majority of 2000-01 due to shoulder injury vs. Atlanta, December 14, 2000. Traded to **Vancouver** by **Ottawa** for Peter Schaefer, September 21, 2002. Signed as a free agent by **Frolunda** (Sweden), September 24, 2004. • Missed majority of 2010-11 due to torn achilles tendon during off-season training, July 22, 2010. Signed as a free agent by **Tampa Bay**, July 1, 2012.

SALVADOR, Bryce

(SAL-vuh-dohr, BRIGHS) **N.J.**

Defense. Shoots left. 6'3", 215 lbs. Born, Brandon, Man., February 11, 1976. Tampa Bay's 6th choice, 138th overall, in 1994 Entry Draft.

Season	Club	League	GP	G	A	Pts	PIM	PP	SH	GW	S	%	+/-	TF	F%	Min	GP	G	A	Pts	PIM	PP	SH	GW	Min
1991-92	Brandon	MAHA	52	6	23	29	38	....	....	....	....	....	....	....	....	....	....	....	....	....	....	....	....	....	....
1992-93	Lethbridge	WHL	64	1	4	5	29	....	....	....	....	....	....	....	....	....	4	0	0	0	0	....	....	....	....
1993-94	Lethbridge	WHL	61	4	14	18	36	....	....	....	....	....	....	....	....	....	9	0	1	1	2	....	....	....	....
1994-95	Lethbridge	WHL	67	1	9	10	88	....	....	....	....	....	....	....	....	....	....	....	....	....	....	....	....	....	....
1995-96	Lethbridge	WHL	56	4	12	16	75	....	....	....	....	....	....	....	....	....	3	0	1	1	2	....	....	....	....
1996-97	Lethbridge	WHL	63	8	32	40	81	....	....	....	....	....	....	....	....	....	19	0	7	7	14	....	....	....	....
1997-98	Worcester IceCats	AHL	46	2	8	10	74	....	....	....	....	....	....	....	....	....	11	0	1	1	45	....	....	....	....
1998-99	Worcester IceCats	AHL	69	5	13	18	129	....	....	....	....	....	....	....	....	....	4	0	1	1	2	....	....	....	....
99-2000	Worcester IceCats	AHL	55	0	13	13	53	....	....	....	....	....	....	....	....	....	9	0	1	1	2	....	....	....	....
2000-01	St. Louis	NHL	75	2	8	10	69	0	0	1	60	3.3	–4	1	0.0	16:38	14	2	0	2	18	0	0	1	14:41
2001-02	St. Louis	NHL	66	5	7	12	78	1	0	2	37	13.5	3	0	0.0	16:55	10	0	1	1	4	0	0	0	12:34
2002-03	St. Louis	NHL	71	2	8	10	95	1	0	0	73	2.7	7	0	0.0	18:57	7	0	0	0	2	0	0	0	17:17
2003-04	St. Louis	NHL	69	3	5	8	47	0	0	1	60	5.0	–4	0	0.0	17:29	5	0	0	0	2	0	0	0	14:31
	Worcester IceCats	AHL	2	0	1	1	0	....	....	....	....	....	....	....	....	....	....	....	....	....	....	....	....	....	....
2004-05	Missouri	UHL	7	0	0	0	16	....	....	....	....	....	....	....	....	....	3	0	0	0	0	....	....	....	....
2005-06	St. Louis	NHL	46	1	4	5	26	0	0	0	23	4.3	–24	1	0.0	19:48	....	....	....	....	....	....	....	....	....
2006-07	St. Louis	NHL	64	2	5	7	55	0	0	0	40	5.0	–5	0	0.0	19:44	....	....	....	....	....	....	....	....	....
2007-08	St. Louis	NHL	56	1	10	11	43	0	0	1	29	3.4	12	1	0.0	19:38	....	....	....	....	....	....	....	....	....
	New Jersey	NHL	8	0	0	0	11	0	0	0	0	0.0	0	0	0.0	20:54	5	1	0	1	2	0	0	0	17:55
2008-09	New Jersey	NHL	76	3	13	16	78	0	0	2	68	4.4	–1	1	100.0	19:29	4	0	0	0	4	0	0	0	15:29
2009-10	New Jersey	NHL	79	4	10	14	57	0	0	2	47	8.5	8	0	0.0	18:52	5	0	0	0	6	0	0	0	16:04
2010-11			DID NOT PLAY – INJURED																						
2011-12	New Jersey	NHL	82	0	9	9	66	0	0	0	52	0.0	18	0	0.0	20:13	24	4	10	14	26	0	1	1	22:25
2012-13	New Jersey	NHL	39	0	2	2	22	0	0	0	29	0.0	–12	0	0.0	21:20	....	....	....	....	....	....	....	....	....
	NHL Totals		731	23	81	104	647	2	0	9	518	4.4		4	25.0	18:54	74	7	11	18	64	0	1	2	17:30

Signed as a free agent by **St. Louis**, December 16, 1996. Signed as a free agent by **Missouri** (UHL), March 11, 2005. Traded to **New Jersey** by **St. Louis** for Cam Janssen, February 26, 2008. • Missed 2010-11 due to head injury in pre-season vs. Philadelphia, September 28, 2010.

SAMSON, Jerome

(SAM-sohn, jeh-ROHM) **WPG**

Right wing. Shoots right. 6', 195 lbs. Born, Greenfield Park, Que., September 4, 1987.

			Regular Season														Playoffs								
Season	Club	League	GP	G	A	Pts	PIM	PP	SH	GW	S	%	+/-	TF	F%	Min	GP	G	A	Pts	PIM	PP	SH	GW	Min
2004-05	Moncton Wildcats	QMJHL	63	6	11	17	22	....	....	....	....	....	....	....	....	....	12	1	4	5	8	....	....	....	....
2005-06	Moncton Wildcats	QMJHL	62	20	32	52	46	....	....	....	....	....	....	....	....	....	21	6	12	18	15	....	....	....	....
2006-07	Moncton Wildcats	QMJHL	38	19	33	52	20	....	....	....	....	....	....	....	....	....	....	....	....	....	....	....	....	....	....
	Val-d'Or Foreurs	QMJHL	33	25	22	47	16	....	....	....	....	....	....	....	....	....	20	14	12	26	10	....	....	....	....
2007-08	Albany River Rats	AHL	65	21	18	39	38	....	....	....	....	....	....	....	....	....	7	1	1	2	2	....	....	....	....
2008-09	Albany River Rats	AHL	70	22	32	54	56	....	....	....	....	....	....	....	....	....	....	....	....	....	....	....	....	....	....
2009-10	**Carolina**	**NHL**	**7**	**0**	**2**	**2**	**10**	**0**	**0**	**0**	**17**	**0.0**	**–1**	**1**	**0.0**	**8:27**	....	....	....	....	....	....	....	....	....
	Albany River Rats	AHL	74	37	41	78	66	....	....	....	....	....	....	....	....	....	8	6	3	9	8	....	....	....	....
2010-11	**Carolina**	**NHL**	**23**	**0**	**2**	**2**	**0**	**0**	**0**	**0**	**28**	**0.0**	**0**	**3**	**66.7**	**6:51**	....	....	....	....	....	....	....	....	....
	Charlotte	AHL	53	26	28	54	44	....	....	....	....	....	....	....	....	....	....	....	....	....	....	....	....	....	....
2011-12	**Carolina**	**NHL**	**16**	**2**	**3**	**5**	**8**	**1**	**0**	**0**	**31**	**6.5**	**–3**	**0**	**0.0**	**12:17**	....	....	....	....	....	....	....	....	....
	Charlotte	AHL	57	20	17	37	26	....	....	....	....	....	....	....	....	....	....	....	....	....	....	....	....	....	....
2012-13	Charlotte	AHL	37	7	11	18	27	....	....	....	....	....	....	....	....	....	....	....	....	....	....	....	....	....	....
	NHL Totals		**46**	**2**	**7**	**9**	**18**	**1**	**0**	**0**	**76**	**2.6**		**4**	**50.0**	**8:59**	....	....	....	....	....	....	....	....	....

AHL First All-Star Team (2010)

Signed as a free agent by **Carolina**, July 2, 2007. Signed as a free agent by **Winnipeg**, July 6, 2013.

SAMUELSSON, Mikael

(SAM-yuhl-suhn, MIH-kigh-ehl) **DET**

Right wing. Shoots right. 6'2", 218 lbs. Born, Mariefred, Sweden, December 23, 1976. San Jose's 7th choice, 145th overall, in 1998 Entry Draft.

			Regular Season														Playoffs								
Season	Club	League	GP	G	A	Pts	PIM	PP	SH	GW	S	%	+/-	TF	F%	Min	GP	G	A	Pts	PIM	PP	SH	GW	Min
1994-95	Sodertalje SK Jr.	Swe-Jr.	30	8	6	14	12	....	....	....	....	....	....	....	....	....	....	....	....	....	....	....	....	....	....
1995-96	Sodertalje SK Jr.	Swe-Jr.	22	13	12	25	20	....	....	....	....	....	....	....	....	....	....	....	....	....	....	....	....	....	....
	Sodertalje SK	Sweden-2	18	5	1	6	0	....	....	....	....	....	....	....	....	....	4	0	0	0	0	....	....	....	....
1996-97	Sodertalje SK Jr.	Swe-Jr.	2	2	1	3	....	....	....	....	....	....	....	....	....	....	....	....	....	....	....	....	....	....	....
	Sodertalje SK	Sweden	29	3	2	5	10	....	....	....	....	....	....	....	....	....	10	0	0	0	4	....	....	....	....
1997-98	Nykoping	Sweden-2	10	5	1	6	14	....	....	....	....	....	....	....	....	....	....	....	....	....	....	....	....	....	....
	Sodertalje SK	Sweden	41	11	9	20	66	....	....	....	....	....	....	....	....	....	....	....	....	....	....	....	....	....	....
1998-99	Sodertalje SK	Sweden-2	18	13	10	23	26	....	....	....	....	....	....	....	....	....	10	2	2	4	12	....	....	....	....
	V.Frolunda	Sweden	27	0	5	5	10	....	....	....	....	....	....	....	....	....	....	....	....	....	....	....	....	....	....
99-2000	Brynas IF Gavle	Sweden	40	4	3	7	76	....	....	....	....	....	....	....	....	....	11	7	2	9	6	....	....	....	....
	Brynas IF Gavle	EuroHL	4	0	2	2	4	....	....	....	....	....	....	....	....	....	....	....	....	....	....	....	....	....	....
2000-01	**San Jose**	**NHL**	**4**	**0**	**0**	**0**	**0**	**0**	**0**	**0**	**3**	**0.0**	**0**	**0**	**0.0**	**4:41**	....	....	....	....	....	....	....	....	....
	Kentucky	AHL	66	32	46	78	58	....	....	....	....	....	....	....	....	....	3	1	0	1	0	....	....	....	....
2001-02	**NY Rangers**	**NHL**	**67**	**6**	**10**	**16**	**23**	**1**	**2**	**1**	**94**	**6.4**	**10**	**5**	**40.0**	**11:52**	....	....	....	....	....	....	....	....	....
	Hartford	AHL	8	3	6	9	12	....	....	....	....	....	....	....	....	....	....	....	....	....	....	....	....	....	....
2002-03	**NY Rangers**	**NHL**	**58**	**8**	**14**	**22**	**32**	**1**	**1**	**2**	**118**	**6.8**	**0**	**35**	**42.9**	**15:32**	....	....	....	....	....	....	....	....	....
	Pittsburgh	**NHL**	**22**	**2**	**0**	**2**	**8**	**1**	**0**	**0**	**36**	**5.6**	**–21**	**8**	**75.0**	**14:04**	....	....	....	....	....	....	....	....	....
2003-04	**Florida**	**NHL**	**37**	**3**	**6**	**9**	**35**	**0**	**0**	**1**	**50**	**6.0**	**0**	**28**	**28.6**	**12:15**	....	....	....	....	....	....	....	....	....
2004-05	Geneve	Swiss	12	2	4	6	14	....	....	....	....	....	....	....	....	....	....	....	....	....	....	....	....	....	....
	Sodertalje SK	Sweden	29	7	13	20	45	....	....	....	....	....	....	....	....	....	10	3	3	6	24	....	....	....	....
2005-06	Rapperswil	Swiss	1	0	0	0	0	....	....	....	....	....	....	....	....	....	....	....	....	....	....	....	....	....	....
	Detroit	**NHL**	**71**	**23**	**22**	**45**	**42**	**7**	**0**	**3**	**187**	**12.3**	**27**	**11**	**27.3**	**13:31**	**6**	**0**	**1**	**1**	**6**	**0**	**0**	**0**	**15:33**
	Sweden	Olympics	8	1	3	4	2	....	....	....	....	....	....	....	....	....	....	....	....	....	....	....	....	....	....
2006-07	**Detroit**	**NHL**	**53**	**14**	**20**	**34**	**28**	**6**	**0**	**2**	**189**	**7.4**	**1**	**3**	**66.7**	**15:09**	**18**	**3**	**8**	**11**	**14**	**1**	**0**	**1**	**15:27**
2007-08 ♦	**Detroit**	**NHL**	**73**	**11**	**29**	**40**	**26**	**3**	**0**	**1**	**249**	**4.4**	**21**	**14**	**42.9**	**16:16**	**22**	**5**	**8**	**13**	**8**	**0**	**0**	**1**	**15:56**
2008-09	**Detroit**	**NHL**	**81**	**19**	**21**	**40**	**50**	**7**	**0**	**1**	**257**	**7.4**	**0**	**8**	**25.0**	**15:22**	**23**	**5**	**5**	**10**	**6**	**0**	**0**	**2**	**15:08**
2009-10	**Vancouver**	**NHL**	**74**	**30**	**23**	**53**	**64**	**7**	**0**	**4**	**219**	**13.7**	**10**	**31**	**35.5**	**17:10**	**12**	**8**	**7**	**15**	**16**	**3**	**0**	**1**	**17:58**
2010-11	**Vancouver**	**NHL**	**75**	**18**	**32**	**50**	**36**	**5**	**0**	**2**	**215**	**8.4**	**8**	**28**	**32.1**	**16:38**	**11**	**1**	**2**	**3**	**8**	**0**	**0**	**1**	**16:26**
2011-12	**Vancouver**	**NHL**	**6**	**1**	**2**	**3**	**6**	**1**	**0**	**0**	**13**	**7.7**	**–1**	**0**	**0.0**	**15:53**	....	....	....	....	....	....	....	....	....
	Florida	**NHL**	**48**	**13**	**15**	**28**	**14**	**6**	**0**	**1**	**125**	**10.4**	**2**	**33**	**36.4**	**15:57**	**7**	**0**	**5**	**5**	**2**	**0**	**0**	**0**	**16:06**
2012-13	**Detroit**	**NHL**	**4**	**0**	**1**	**1**	**0**	**0**	**0**	**0**	**4**	**0.0**	**–3**	**0**	**0.0**	**12:52**	**5**	**1**	**1**	**2**	**2**	**0**	**0**	**0**	**13:05**
	NHL Totals		**673**	**148**	**195**	**343**	**364**	**45**	**3**	**18**	**1759**	**8.4**		**204**	**37.3**	**15:01**	**104**	**23**	**37**	**60**	**62**	**4**	**0**	**6**	**15:49**

Traded to **NY Rangers** by **San Jose** with Christian Gosselin for Adam Graves and future considerations, June 24, 2001. Traded to **Pittsburgh** by **NY Rangers** with Joel Bouchard, Richard Lintner and Rico Fata for Mike Wilson, Alex Kovalev, Janne Laukkanen and Dan LaCouture, February 10, 2003. Traded to **Florida** by **Pittsburgh** with Pittsburgh's 1st round choice (Nathan Horton) and 2nd round compensatory choice (Stefan Meyer) in 2003 Entry Draft for Florida's 1st (Marc-Andre Fleury) and 3rd (Daniel Carcillo) round choices in 2003 Entry Draft, June 21, 2003. • Missed majority of 2003-04 due to jaw (November 21, 2003 vs. Washington) and hand (January 21, 2004 vs. Columbus) injuries. Signed as a free agent by **Geneve** (Swiss), September 8, 2004. Signed as a free agent by **Sodertalje** (Sweden), October 26, 2004. Signed as a free agent by **Detroit**, September 17, 2005. Signed as a free agent by **Vancouver**, July 3, 2009. Traded to **Florida** by **Vancouver** with Marco Sturm for David Booth, Steve Reinprecht and Vancouver's 3rd round choice (previously acquired, Vancouver selected Cole Cassels) in 2013 Entry Draft, October 22, 2011. Signed as a free agent by **Detroit**, July 1, 2012. • Missed majority of 2012-13 due to various injuries.

SANGUINETTI, Bobby

(san-GIH-neh-tee, BAW-bee)

Defense. Shoots right. 6'3", 190 lbs. Born, Trenton, NJ, February 29, 1988. NY Rangers' 1st choice, 21st overall, in 2006 Entry Draft.

			Regular Season														Playoffs								
Season	Club	League	GP	G	A	Pts	PIM	PP	SH	GW	S	%	+/-	TF	F%	Min	GP	G	A	Pts	PIM	PP	SH	GW	Min
2003-04	Lawrenceville	High-NJ	26	4	17	21	....	....	....	....	....	....	....	....	....	....	....	....	....	....	....	....	....	....	....
2004-05	Owen Sound	OHL	67	4	20	24	12	....	....	....	....	....	....	....	....	....	5	0	2	2	0	....	....	....	....
2005-06	Owen Sound	OHL	68	14	51	65	44	....	....	....	....	....	....	....	....	....	11	5	10	15	4	....	....	....	....
2006-07	Owen Sound	OHL	67	23	30	53	48	....	....	....	....	....	....	....	....	....	4	3	3	6	2	....	....	....	....
	Hartford	AHL	5	0	3	3	2	....	....	....	....	....	....	....	....	....	7	0	1	1	2	....	....	....	....
2007-08	Brampton	OHL	61	29	41	70	38	....	....	....	....	....	....	....	....	....	5	1	3	4	10	....	....	....	....
	Hartford	AHL	6	0	1	1	2	....	....	....	....	....	....	....	....	....	5	0	0	0	2	....	....	....	....
2008-09	Hartford	AHL	78	6	36	42	42	....	....	....	....	....	....	....	....	....	6	1	4	5	6	....	....	....	....
2009-10	**NY Rangers**	**NHL**	**5**	**0**	**0**	**0**	**4**	**0**	**0**	**0**	**5**	**0.0**	**0**	**0**	**0.0**	**11:32**	....	....	....	....	....	....	....	....	....
	Hartford	AHL	61	9	29	38	22	....	....	....	....	....	....	....	....	....	....	....	....	....	....	....	....	....	....
2010-11	Charlotte	AHL	31	3	12	15	6	....	....	....	....	....	....	....	....	....	10	0	2	2	6	....	....	....	....
2011-12	**Carolina**	**NHL**	**3**	**0**	**0**	**0**	**0**	**0**	**0**	**0**	**5**	**0.0**	**0**	**0**	**0.0**	**11:56**	....	....	....	....	....	....	....	....	....
	Charlotte	AHL	60	10	40	50	20	....	....	....	....	....	....	....	....	....	....	....	....	....	....	....	....	....	....
2012-13	Charlotte	AHL	36	6	15	21	16	....	....	....	....	....	....	....	....	....	....	....	....	....	....	....	....	....	....
	Carolina	**NHL**	**37**	**2**	**4**	**6**	**4**	**0**	**0**	**1**	**48**	**4.2**	**–6**	**1**	**0.0**	**14:45**	....	....	....	....	....	....	....	....	....
	NHL Totals		**45**	**2**	**4**	**6**	**8**	**0**	**0**	**1**	**58**	**3.4**		**1**	**0.0**	**14:12**	....	....	....	....	....	....	....	....	....

OHL Second All-Star Team (2008)

Traded to **Carolina** by **NY Rangers** for Carolina's 6th round choice (Jesper Fasth) in 2010 Entry Draft and Washington's 2nd round choice (previously acquired, later traded to Calgary – Calgary selected Tyler Wotherspoon) in 2011 Entry Draft, June 25, 2010. • Missed majority of 2010-11 due to hip injury vs. Adirondack (AHL), November 19, 2010. Signed as a free agent by **Mytischi** (KHL), July 11, 2013.

SANTORELLI, Mike

(san-toh-REHL-ee, MIGHK) **VAN**

Center. Shoots right. 6', 189 lbs. Born, Vancouver, B.C., December 14, 1985. Nashville's 6th choice, 178th overall, in 2004 Entry Draft.

			Regular Season														Playoffs								
Season	Club	League	GP	G	A	Pts	PIM	PP	SH	GW	S	%	+/-	TF	F%	Min	GP	G	A	Pts	PIM	PP	SH	GW	Min
2003-04	Vernon Vipers	BCHL	60	43	53	96	26	....	....	....	....	....	....	....	....	....	5	0	2	2	0	....	....	....	....
2004-05	Northern Mich.	CCHA	40	16	14	30	22	....	....	....	....	....	....	....	....	....	....	....	....	....	....	....	....	....	....
2005-06	Northern Mich.	CCHA	40	15	18	33	24	....	....	....	....	....	....	....	....	....	....	....	....	....	....	....	....	....	....
2006-07	Northern Mich.	CCHA	41	*30	17	47	28	....	....	....	....	....	....	....	....	....	....	....	....	....	....	....	....	....	....
2007-08	Milwaukee	AHL	80	21	21	42	60	....	....	....	....	....	....	....	....	....	6	0	0	0	2	....	....	....	....
2008-09	**Nashville**	**NHL**	**7**	**0**	**0**	**0**	**2**	**0**	**0**	**0**	**11**	**0.0**	**–5**	**47**	**44.7**	**12:15**	....	....	....	....	....	....	....	....	....
	Milwaukee	AHL	70	27	43	70	36	....	....	....	....	....	....	....	....	....	11	6	5	11	6	....	....	....	....
2009-10	**Nashville**	**NHL**	**25**	**2**	**1**	**3**	**8**	**0**	**0**	**0**	**36**	**5.6**	**–8**	**105**	**45.7**	**10:57**	....	....	....	....	....	....	....	....	....
	Milwaukee	AHL	57	26	33	59	20	....	....	....	....	....	....	....	....	....	7	3	4	7	2	....	....	....	....
2010-11	**Florida**	**NHL**	**82**	**20**	**21**	**41**	**20**	**5**	**1**	**1**	**193**	**10.4**	**–17**	**1032**	**50.2**	**16:41**	....	....	....	....	....	....	....	....	....
2011-12	**Florida**	**NHL**	**60**	**9**	**2**	**11**	**18**	**2**	**0**	**1**	**117**	**7.7**	**–10**	**389**	**45.2**	**12:24**	....	....	....	....	....	....	....	....	....
2012-13	Tingsryds AIF	Sweden-2	4	0	1	1	0	....	....	....	....	....	....	....	....	....	....	....	....	....	....	....	....	....	....
	Florida	**NHL**	**24**	**2**	**1**	**3**	**2**	**0**	**0**	**0**	**21**	**9.5**	**–7**	**52**	**57.7**	**11:06**	....	....	....	....	....	....	....	....	....
	San Antonio	AHL	7	2	3	5	0	....	....	....	....	....	....	....	....	....	....	....	....	....	....	....	....	....	....
	Winnipeg	**NHL**	**10**	**0**	**1**	**1**	**0**	**0**	**0**	**0**	**14**	**0.0**	**–5**	**42**	**61.9**	**13:43**	....	....	....	....	....	....	....	....	....
	NHL Totals		**208**	**33**	**26**	**59**	**50**	**7**	**1**	**2**	**392**	**8.4**		**1667**	**49.1**	**13:49**	....	....	....	....	....	....	....	....	....

CCHA All-Rookie Team (2005) • CCHA First All-Star Team (2007) • NCAA West Second All-American Team (2007)

Traded to **Florida** by **Nashville** for Florida's 4th round choice (Josh Shalla) in 2011 Entry Draft, August 5, 2010. Signed as a free agent by **Tingsryds** (Sweden-2), October 15, 2012. Claimed on waivers by **Winnipeg** from **Florida**, April 3, 2013. Signed as a free agent by **Vancouver**, July 6, 2013.

SARICH, Cory
(SAHR-ihch, KOH-ree) **COL**

Defense. Shoots right. 6'4", 207 lbs. Born, Saskatoon, Sask., August 16, 1978. Buffalo's 2nd choice, 27th overall, in 1996 Entry Draft.

			Regular Season														Playoffs								
Season	Club	League	GP	G	A	Pts	PIM	PP	SH	GW	S	%	+/-	TF	F%	Min	GP	G	A	Pts	PIM	PP	SH	GW	Min
1994-95	Sask. Contacts	SMHL	31	5	22	27	99	....	....	....	....	....	....	....	....	....	....	....	....	....	....	....	....	....	....
	Saskatoon Blades	WHL	6	0	0	0	4	....	....	....	....	....	....	....	....	....	3	0	1	1	0	....	....	....	....
1995-96	Saskatoon Blades	WHL	59	5	18	23	54	....	....	....	....	....	....	....	....	....	3	0	0	0	4	....	....	....	....
1996-97	Saskatoon Blades	WHL	58	6	27	33	133	....	....	....	....	....	....	....	....	....	....	....	....	....	....	....	....	....	....
1997-98	Saskatoon Blades	WHL	33	5	24	29	90	....	....	....	....	....	....	....	....	....	....	....	....	....	....	....	....	....	....
	Seattle	WHL	13	3	16	19	47	....	....	....	....	....	....	....	....	....	....	....	....	....	....	....	....	....	....
1998-99	**Buffalo**	**NHL**	**4**	**0**	**0**	**0**	**0**	**0**	**0**	**0**	**2**	**0.0**	**3**	**0**	**0.0**	**13:11**	....	....	....	....	....	....	....	....	....
	Rochester	AHL	77	3	26	29	82	....	....	....	....	....	....	....	....	....	20	2	4	6	14	....	....	....	....
99-2000	**Buffalo**	**NHL**	**42**	**0**	**4**	**4**	**35**	**0**	**0**	**0**	**49**	**0.0**	**2**	**0**	**0.0**	**17:42**	....	....	....	....	....	....	....	....	....
	Rochester	AHL	15	0	6	6	44	....	....	....	....	....	....	....	....	....	....	....	....	....	....	....	....	....	....
	Tampa Bay	**NHL**	**17**	**0**	**2**	**2**	**42**	**0**	**0**	**0**	**20**	**0.0**	**-8**	**0**	**0.0**	**20:42**	....	....	....	....	....	....	....	....	....
2000-01	**Tampa Bay**	**NHL**	**73**	**1**	**8**	**9**	**106**	**0**	**0**	**1**	**66**	**1.5**	**-25**	**3**	**0.0**	**18:44**	....	....	....	....	....	....	....	....	....
	Detroit Vipers	IHL	3	0	2	2	2	....	....	....	....	....	....	....	....	....	....	....	....	....	....	....	....	....	....
2001-02	**Tampa Bay**	**NHL**	**72**	**0**	**11**	**11**	**105**	**0**	**0**	**0**	**55**	**0.0**	**-4**	**2**	**50.0**	**16:06**	....	....	....	....	....	....	....	....	....
	Springfield	AHL	2	0	0	0	0	....	....	....	....	....	....	....	....	....	....	....	....	....	....	....	....	....	....
2002-03	**Tampa Bay**	**NHL**	**82**	**5**	**9**	**14**	**63**	**0**	**0**	**2**	**79**	**6.3**	**-3**	**3**	**0.0**	**19:36**	**11**	**0**	**2**	**2**	**6**	**0**	**0**	**0**	**21:18**
2003-04 ♦	**Tampa Bay**	**NHL**	**82**	**3**	**16**	**19**	**89**	**0**	**1**	**1**	**93**	**3.2**	**5**	**1**	**0.0**	**18:31**	**23**	**0**	**2**	**2**	**25**	**0**	**0**	**0**	**19:11**
2004-05			DID NOT PLAY																						
2005-06	**Tampa Bay**	**NHL**	**82**	**1**	**14**	**15**	**79**	**0**	**0**	**0**	**88**	**1.1**	**-2**	**0**	**0.0**	**18:34**	**5**	**0**	**1**	**1**	**4**	**0**	**0**	**0**	**15:46**
2006-07	**Tampa Bay**	**NHL**	**82**	**0**	**15**	**15**	**70**	**0**	**0**	**0**	**64**	**0.0**	**-6**	**1**	**0.0**	**18:07**	**6**	**0**	**0**	**0**	**2**	**0**	**0**	**0**	**16:37**
2007-08	**Calgary**	**NHL**	**80**	**2**	**5**	**7**	**135**	**0**	**0**	**0**	**57**	**3.5**	**2**	**0**	**0.0**	**18:49**	**7**	**0**	**1**	**1**	**4**	**0**	**0**	**0**	**19:35**
2008-09	**Calgary**	**NHL**	**76**	**2**	**18**	**20**	**112**	**0**	**0**	**0**	**57**	**3.5**	**12**	**0**	**0.0**	**17:53**	**5**	**0**	**1**	**1**	**4**	**0**	**0**	**0**	**18:44**
2009-10	**Calgary**	**NHL**	**57**	**1**	**5**	**6**	**58**	**0**	**0**	**1**	**46**	**2.2**	**4**	**0**	**0.0**	**15:57**	....	....	....	....	....	....	....	....	....
2010-11	**Calgary**	**NHL**	**76**	**4**	**13**	**17**	**75**	**0**	**0**	**1**	**75**	**5.3**	**11**	**1**	**0.0**	**17:53**	....	....	....	....	....	....	....	....	....
2011-12	**Calgary**	**NHL**	**62**	**1**	**6**	**7**	**66**	**0**	**0**	**0**	**36**	**2.8**	**1**	**0**	**0.0**	**16:07**	....	....	....	....	....	....	....	....	....
2012-13	**Calgary**	**NHL**	**28**	**0**	**2**	**2**	**16**	**0**	**0**	**0**	**14**	**0.0**	**-8**	**0**	**0.0**	**14:52**	....	....	....	....	....	....	....	....	....
	NHL Totals		**915**	**20**	**128**	**148**	**1051**	**0**	**1**	**6**	**801**	**2.5**		**11**	**9.1**	**17:52**	**57**	**0**	**7**	**7**	**45**	**0**	**0**	**0**	**19:02**

WHL West Second All-Star Team (1998) • AHL All-Rookie Team (1999)

Traded to **Tampa Bay** by **Buffalo** with Wayne Primeau, Brian Holzinger and Buffalo's 3rd round choice (Alexander Kharitonov) in 2000 Entry Draft for Chris Gratton and Tampa Bay's 2nd round choice (Derek Roy) in 2001 Entry Draft, March 9, 2000. Signed as a free agent by **Calgary**, July 1, 2007. Traded to **Colorado** by **Calgary** with Alex Tanguay for David Jones and Shane O'Brien, June 27, 2013.

SAUER, Michael
(SAW-uhr, MIGH-kuhl)

Defense. Shoots right. 6'3", 213 lbs. Born, St. Cloud, MN, August 7, 1987. NY Rangers' 2nd choice, 40th overall, in 2005 Entry Draft.

			Regular Season														Playoffs								
Season	Club	League	GP	G	A	Pts	PIM	PP	SH	GW	S	%	+/-	TF	F%	Min	GP	G	A	Pts	PIM	PP	SH	GW	Min
2003-04	St. Cloud Tech	High-MN	18	12	16	28	34	....	....	....	....	....	....	....	....	....	....	....	....	....	....	....	....	....	....
2004-05	Portland	WHL	32	2	11	13	10	....	....	....	....	....	....	....	....	....	....	....	....	....	....	....	....	....	....
2005-06	Portland	WHL	59	8	23	31	68	....	....	....	....	....	....	....	....	....	12	4	2	6	8	....	....	....	....
2006-07	Portland	WHL	33	4	8	12	46	....	....	....	....	....	....	....	....	....	....	....	....	....	....	....	....	....	....
	Medicine Hat	WHL	32	1	10	11	29	....	....	....	....	....	....	....	....	....	23	1	5	6	34	....	....	....	....
2007-08	Hartford	AHL	71	4	7	11	80	....	....	....	....	....	....	....	....	....	2	0	0	0	0	....	....	....	....
2008-09	**NY Rangers**	**NHL**	**3**	**0**	**0**	**0**	**0**	**0**	**0**	**0**	**2**	**0.0**	**-1**	**0**	**0.0**	**9:21**	....	....	....	....	....	....	....	....	....
	Hartford	AHL	64	6	17	23	35	....	....	....	....	....	....	....	....	....	6	0	0	0	10	....	....	....	....
2009-10	Hartford	AHL	42	3	9	12	45	....	....	....	....	....	....	....	....	....	....	....	....	....	....	....	....	....	....
2010-11	**NY Rangers**	**NHL**	**76**	**3**	**12**	**15**	**75**	**1**	**0**	**2**	**54**	**5.6**	**20**	**0**	**0.0**	**17:31**	**5**	**0**	**1**	**1**	**0**	**0**	**0**	**0**	**23:16**
2011-12	**NY Rangers**	**NHL**	**19**	**1**	**2**	**3**	**21**	**0**	**0**	**0**	**14**	**7.1**	**9**	**0**	**0.0**	**18:44**	....	....	....	....	....	....	....	....	....
2012-13	**NY Rangers**	**NHL**	DID NOT PLAY – INJURED																						
	NHL Totals		**98**	**4**	**14**	**18**	**96**	**1**	**0**	**2**	**70**	**5.7**		**0**	**0.0**	**17:30**	**5**	**0**	**1**	**1**	**0**	**0**	**0**	**0**	**23:16**

• Missed majority of 2004-05 due to hip injury. • Missed remainder of 2011-12 and all of 2012-13 due to head injury vs. Toronto, December 5, 2011.

SAUVE, Max
(soh-VAY, max)

Center. Shoots left. 6', 185 lbs. Born, Tours, France, January 30, 1990. Boston's 2nd choice, 47th overall, in 2008 Entry Draft.

			Regular Season														Playoffs								
Season	Club	League	GP	G	A	Pts	PIM	PP	SH	GW	S	%	+/-	TF	F%	Min	GP	G	A	Pts	PIM	PP	SH	GW	Min
2005-06	Laval-Laurentides	QAAA	41	16	30	46	54	....	....	....	....	....	....	....	....	....	5	1	3	4	2	....	....	....	....
2006-07	Quebec Remparts	QMJHL	60	10	6	16	24	....	....	....	....	....	....	....	....	....	2	0	0	0	2	....	....	....	....
2007-08	Quebec Remparts	QMJHL	38	12	20	32	22	....	....	....	....	....	....	....	....	....	....	....	....	....	....	....	....	....	....
	Val-d'Or Foreurs	QMJHL	32	14	19	33	8	....	....	....	....	....	....	....	....	....	4	2	3	5	2	....	....	....	....
2008-09	Val-d'Or Foreurs	QMJHL	64	27	49	76	43	....	....	....	....	....	....	....	....	....	....	....	....	....	....	....	....	....	....
2009-10	Val-d'Or Foreurs	QMJHL	25	13	22	35	26	....	....	....	....	....	....	....	....	....	6	5	2	7	2	....	....	....	....
	Providence Bruins	AHL	6	2	0	2	2	....	....	....	....	....	....	....	....	....	....	....	....	....	....	....	....	....	....
2010-11	Providence Bruins	AHL	61	21	17	38	36	....	....	....	....	....	....	....	....	....	....	....	....	....	....	....	....	....	....
2011-12	**Boston**	**NHL**	**1**	**0**	**0**	**0**	**0**	**0**	**0**	**0**	**0**	**0.0**	**0**	**0**	**0.0**	**3:43**	....	....	....	....	....	....	....	....	....
	Providence Bruins	AHL	39	11	15	26	40	....	....	....	....	....	....	....	....	....	....	....	....	....	....	....	....	....	....
2012-13	Providence Bruins	AHL	52	10	13	23	4	....	....	....	....	....	....	....	....	....	....	....	....	....	....	....	....	....	....
	Rockford IceHogs	AHL	8	1	2	3	4	....	....	....	....	....	....	....	....	....	....	....	....	....	....	....	....	....	....
	NHL Totals		**1**	**0**	**0**	**0**	**0**	**0**	**0**	**0**	**0**	**0.0**		**0**	**0.0**	**3:43**	....	....	....	....	....	....	....	....	....

• Missed majority of 2011-12 due to head injury vs. Manchester (AHL), December 9, 2011. Traded to **Chicago** by **Boston** for Rob Flick, April 3, 2013.

SAUVE, Yann
(soh-VAY, YAHN) **VAN**

Defense. Shoots left. 6'3", 213 lbs. Born, Montreal, Que., February 18, 1990. Vancouver's 2nd choice, 41st overall, in 2008 Entry Draft.

			Regular Season														Playoffs								
Season	Club	League	GP	G	A	Pts	PIM	PP	SH	GW	S	%	+/-	TF	F%	Min	GP	G	A	Pts	PIM	PP	SH	GW	Min
2005-06	Chateauguay	QAAA	42	14	15	29	63	....	....	....	....	....	....	....	....	....	19	2	12	14	44	....	....	....	....
2006-07	Saint John	QMJHL	60	2	13	15	75	....	....	....	....	....	....	....	....	....	....	....	....	....	....	....	....	....	....
2007-08	Saint John	QMJHL	69	6	15	21	92	....	....	....	....	....	....	....	....	....	14	1	2	3	23	....	....	....	....
2008-09	Saint John	QMJHL	61	5	25	30	64	....	....	....	....	....	....	....	....	....	4	0	2	2	8	....	....	....	....
2009-10	Saint John	QMJHL	61	7	29	36	65	....	....	....	....	....	....	....	....	....	21	5	10	15	36	....	....	....	....
2010-11	**Vancouver**	**NHL**	**5**	**0**	**0**	**0**	**0**	**0**	**0**	**0**	**6**	**0.0**	**-2**	**0**	**0.0**	**13:00**	....	....	....	....	....	....	....	....	....
	Manitoba Moose	AHL	39	3	11	14	24	....	....	....	....	....	....	....	....	....	13	0	1	1	4	....	....	....	....
	Victoria	ECHL	8	0	2	2	4	....	....	....	....	....	....	....	....	....	....	....	....	....	....	....	....	....	....
2011-12	Chicago Wolves	AHL	73	3	6	9	78	....	....	....	....	....	....	....	....	....	3	0	1	1	2	....	....	....	....
2012-13	Chicago Wolves	AHL	17	0	2	2	10	....	....	....	....	....	....	....	....	....	....	....	....	....	....	....	....	....	....
	Kalamazoo Wings	ECHL	32	10	9	19	40	....	....	....	....	....	....	....	....	....	....	....	....	....	....	....	....	....	....
	NHL Totals		**5**	**0**	**0**	**0**	**0**	**0**	**0**	**0**	**6**	**0.0**		**0**	**0.0**	**13:00**	....	....	....	....	....	....	....	....	....

SAVARD, David
(suh-VAHRD, DAY-vihd) **CBJ**

Defense. Shoots right. 6'2", 219 lbs. Born, St. Hyacinthe, Que., October 22, 1990. Columbus' 3rd choice, 94th overall, in 2009 Entry Draft.

			Regular Season														Playoffs								
Season	Club	League	GP	G	A	Pts	PIM	PP	SH	GW	S	%	+/-	TF	F%	Min	GP	G	A	Pts	PIM	PP	SH	GW	Min
2006-07	Sem. St-Francois	QAAA	44	10	16	26	52	....	....	....	....	....	....	....	....	....	18	1	12	13	10	....	....	....	....
2007-08	Baie-Comeau	QMJHL	35	1	6	7	22	....	....	....	....	....	....	....	....	....	....	....	....	....	....	....	....	....	....
	Moncton Wildcats	QMJHL	32	0	5	5	18	....	....	....	....	....	....	....	....	....	....	....	....	....	....	....	....	....	....
2008-09	Moncton Wildcats	QMJHL	68	9	35	44	33	....	....	....	....	....	....	....	....	....	10	5	5	10	10	....	....	....	....
2009-10	Moncton Wildcats	QMJHL	64	13	*64	77	36	....	....	....	....	....	....	....	....	....	21	1	14	15	8	....	....	....	....
2010-11	Springfield	AHL	72	11	32	43	18	....	....	....	....	....	....	....	....	....	....	....	....	....	....	....	....	....	....
2011-12	**Columbus**	**NHL**	**31**	**2**	**8**	**10**	**16**	**1**	**0**	**0**	**34**	**5.9**	**0**	**0**	**0.0**	**16:34**	....	....	....	....	....	....	....	....	....
	Springfield	AHL	44	4	18	22	72	....	....	....	....	....	....	....	....	....	....	....	....	....	....	....	....	....	....
2012-13	Springfield	AHL	60	5	26	31	40	....	....	....	....	....	....	....	....	....	8	2	3	5	8	....	....	....	....
	Columbus	**NHL**	**4**	**0**	**0**	**0**	**0**	**0**	**0**	**0**	**1**	**0.0**	**-3**	**0**	**0.0**	**13:12**	....	....	....	....	....	....	....	....	....
	NHL Totals		**35**	**2**	**8**	**10**	**16**	**1**	**0**	**0**	**35**	**5.7**		**0**	**0.0**	**16:11**	....	....	....	....	....	....	....	....	....

QMJHL First All-Star Team (2010) • Canadian Major Junior First All-Star Team (2010) • Canadian Major Junior Defenseman of the Year (2010)

SAVARD, Marc

(suh-VAHRD, MAHRK) **BOS**

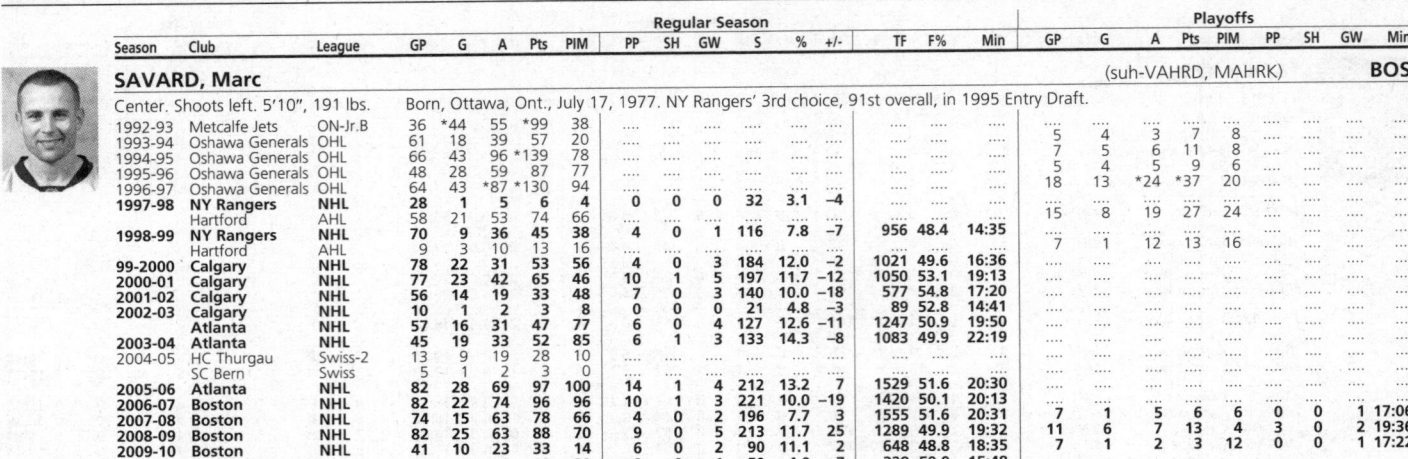

Center. Shoots left. 5'10", 191 lbs. Born, Ottawa, Ont., July 17, 1977. NY Rangers' 3rd choice, 91st overall, in 1995 Entry Draft.

			Regular Season														Playoffs								
Season	Club	League	GP	G	A	Pts	PIM	PP	SH	GW	S	%	+/-	TF	F%	Min	GP	G	A	Pts	PIM	PP	SH	GW	Min
1992-93	Metcalfe Jets	ON-Jr.B	36	*44	55	*99	38	....	....	....	....	....	....	....	....	....	....	....	....	....	....	....	....	....	....
1993-94	Oshawa Generals	OHL	61	18	39	57	20	....	....	....	....	....	....	....	....	....	5	4	3	7	8	....	....	....	....
1994-95	Oshawa Generals	OHL	66	43	96	*139	78	....	....	....	....	....	....	....	....	....	7	5	6	11	8	....	....	....	....
1995-96	Oshawa Generals	OHL	48	28	59	87	77	....	....	....	....	....	....	....	....	....	5	4	5	9	6	....	....	....	....
1996-97	Oshawa Generals	OHL	64	43	*87	*130	94	....	....	....	....	....	....	....	....	....	18	13	*24	*37	20	....	....	....	....
1997-98	**NY Rangers**	**NHL**	**28**	**1**	**5**	**6**	**4**	**0**	**0**	**0**	**32**	**3.1**	**–4**	....	....	....	....	....	....	....	....	....	....	....	....
	Hartford	AHL	58	21	53	74	66	....	....	....	....	....	....	....	....	....	15	8	19	27	24	....	....	....	....
1998-99	**NY Rangers**	**NHL**	**70**	**9**	**36**	**45**	**38**	**4**	**0**	**1**	**116**	**7.8**	**–7**	**956**	**48.4**	**14:35**	....	....	....	....	....	....	....	....	....
	Hartford	AHL	9	3	10	13	16	....	....	....	....	....	....	....	....	....	7	1	12	13	16	....	....	....	....
99-2000	**Calgary**	**NHL**	**78**	**22**	**31**	**53**	**56**	**4**	**0**	**3**	**184**	**12.0**	**–2**	**1021**	**49.6**	**16:36**	....	....	....	....	....	....	....	....	....
2000-01	**Calgary**	**NHL**	**77**	**23**	**42**	**65**	**46**	**10**	**1**	**5**	**197**	**11.7**	**–12**	**1050**	**53.1**	**19:13**	....	....	....	....	....	....	....	....	....
2001-02	**Calgary**	**NHL**	**56**	**14**	**19**	**33**	**48**	**7**	**0**	**3**	**140**	**10.0**	**–18**	**577**	**54.8**	**17:20**	....	....	....	....	....	....	....	....	....
2002-03	**Calgary**	**NHL**	**10**	**1**	**2**	**3**	**8**	**0**	**0**	**0**	**21**	**4.8**	**–3**	**89**	**52.8**	**14:41**	....	....	....	....	....	....	....	....	....
	Atlanta	**NHL**	**57**	**16**	**31**	**47**	**77**	**6**	**0**	**4**	**127**	**12.6**	**–11**	**1247**	**50.9**	**19:50**	....	....	....	....	....	....	....	....	....
2003-04	**Atlanta**	**NHL**	**45**	**19**	**33**	**52**	**85**	**6**	**1**	**3**	**133**	**14.3**	**–8**	**1083**	**49.9**	**22:19**	....	....	....	....	....	....	....	....	....
2004-05	HC Thurgau	Swiss-2	13	9	19	28	10	....	....	....	....	....	....	....	....	....	....	....	....	....	....	....	....	....	....
	SC Bern	Swiss	5	1	2	3	0	....	....	....	....	....	....	....	....	....	....	....	....	....	....	....	....	....	....
2005-06	**Atlanta**	**NHL**	**82**	**28**	**69**	**97**	**100**	**14**	**1**	**4**	**212**	**13.2**	**7**	**1529**	**51.6**	**20:30**	....	....	....	....	....	....	....	....	....
2006-07	**Boston**	**NHL**	**82**	**22**	**74**	**96**	**96**	**10**	**1**	**3**	**221**	**10.0**	**–19**	**1420**	**50.1**	**20:13**	....	....	....	....	....	....	....	....	....
2007-08	**Boston**	**NHL**	**74**	**15**	**63**	**78**	**66**	**4**	**0**	**2**	**196**	**7.7**	**3**	**1555**	**51.6**	**20:31**	**7**	**1**	**5**	**6**	**6**	**0**	**0**	**1**	**17:06**
2008-09	**Boston**	**NHL**	**82**	**25**	**63**	**88**	**70**	**9**	**0**	**5**	**213**	**11.7**	**25**	**1289**	**49.9**	**19:32**	**11**	**6**	**7**	**13**	**4**	**3**	**0**	**2**	**19:36**
2009-10	**Boston**	**NHL**	**41**	**10**	**23**	**33**	**14**	**6**	**0**	**2**	**90**	**11.1**	**2**	**648**	**48.8**	**18:35**	**7**	**1**	**2**	**3**	**12**	**0**	**0**	**1**	**17:22**
2010-11 ♦	**Boston**	**NHL**	**25**	**2**	**8**	**10**	**29**	**0**	**0**	**1**	**50**	**4.0**	**–7**	**328**	**50.9**	**15:48**	....	....	....	....	....	....	....	....	....
2011-12	**Boston**	**NHL**	DID NOT PLAY – INJURED																						
2012-13	**Boston**	**NHL**	DID NOT PLAY – INJURED																						
	NHL Totals		**807**	**207**	**499**	**706**	**737**	**80**	**4**	**36**	**1932**	**10.7**		**12792**	**50.8**	**18:49**	**25**	**8**	**14**	**22**	**22**	**3**	**0**	**4**	**18:16**

OHL Second All-Star Team (1995) • AHL All-Rookie Team (1998)

Played in NHL All-Star Game (2008, 2009)

Traded to **Calgary** by **NY Rangers** with NY Rangers 1st round choice (Oleg Saprykin) in 1999 Entry Draft for the rights to Jan Hlavac and Calgary's 1st (Jamie Lundmark) and 3rd (later traded back to Calgary – Calgary selected Craig Andersson) round choices in 1999 Entry Draft, June 26, 1999. Traded to **Atlanta** by **Calgary** for Ruslan Zainullin, November 15, 2002. Signed as a free agent by **Thurgau** (Swiss-2), October 11, 2004. Signed as a free agent by **Bern** (Swiss), November 23, 2004. Signed as a free agent by **Boston**, July 1, 2006. • Missed majority of 2010-11 and all of 2011-12 and 2012-13 due to head injuries at Pittsburgh, March 7, 2010, and at Colorado, January 22, 2011.

SAWADA, Raymond

(suh-WAW-duh, RAY-muhnd)

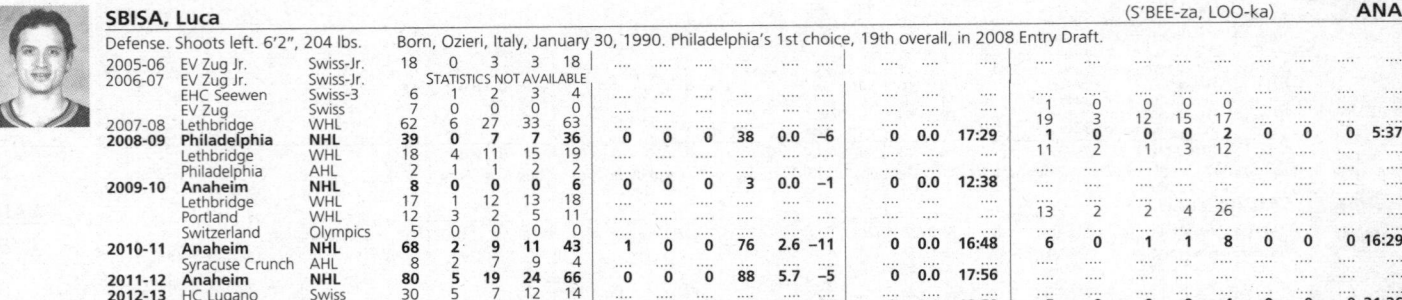

Right wing. Shoots right. 6'2", 207 lbs. Born, Richmond, B.C., February 19, 1985. Dallas' 3rd choice, 52nd overall, in 2004 Entry Draft.

			Regular Season														Playoffs								
Season	Club	League	GP	G	A	Pts	PIM	PP	SH	GW	S	%	+/-	TF	F%	Min	GP	G	A	Pts	PIM	PP	SH	GW	Min
2002-03	Richmond	PIJHL	36	7	17	24	155	....	....	....	....	....	....	....	....	....	....	....	....	....	....	....	....	....	....
2003-04	Nanaimo Clippers	BCHL	54	20	32	52	93	....	....	....	....	....	....	....	....	....	25	6	16	22	22	....	....	....	....
2004-05	Cornell Big Red	ECAC	35	4	5	9	48	....	....	....	....	....	....	....	....	....	....	....	....	....	....	....	....	....	....
2005-06	Cornell Big Red	ECAC	35	7	13	20	20	....	....	....	....	....	....	....	....	....	....	....	....	....	....	....	....	....	....
2006-07	Cornell Big Red	ECAC	31	10	11	21	29	....	....	....	....	....	....	....	....	....	....	....	....	....	....	....	....	....	....
2007-08	Cornell Big Red	ECAC	36	10	16	26	34	....	....	....	....	....	....	....	....	....	....	....	....	....	....	....	....	....	....
	Iowa Stars	AHL	10	2	7	9	14	....	....	....	....	....	....	....	....	....	....	....	....	....	....	....	....	....	....
2008-09	**Dallas**	**NHL**	**5**	**1**	**0**	**1**	**0**	**0**	**0**	**0**	**2**	**50.0**	**–1**	**0**	**0.0**	**8:42**	....	....	....	....	....	....	....	....	....
	Manitoba Moose	AHL	52	6	15	21	31	....	....	....	....	....	....	....	....	....	22	4	4	8	4	....	....	....	....
2009-10	**Dallas**	**NHL**	**5**	**0**	**0**	**0**	**0**	**0**	**0**	**0**	**2**	**0.0**	**1**	**0**	**0.0**	**8:09**	....	....	....	....	....	....	....	....	....
	Texas Stars	AHL	60	8	11	19	92	....	....	....	....	....	....	....	....	....	24	3	5	8	20	....	....	....	....
2010-11	**Dallas**	**NHL**	**1**	**0**	**0**	**0**	**0**	**0**	**0**	**0**	**1**	**0.0**	**–1**	**0**	**0.0**	**5:50**	....	....	....	....	....	....	....	....	....
	Texas Stars	AHL	57	11	18	29	91	....	....	....	....	....	....	....	....	....	6	1	5	6	2	....	....	....	....
2011-12	Texas Stars	AHL	26	6	10	16	19	....	....	....	....	....	....	....	....	....	....	....	....	....	....	....	....	....	....
	St. John's IceCaps	AHL	17	1	2	3	14	....	....	....	....	....	....	....	....	....	15	3	3	6	10	....	....	....	....
2012-13	St. John's IceCaps	AHL	65	13	16	29	88	....	....	....	....	....	....	....	....	....	....	....	....	....	....	....	....	....	....
	NHL Totals		**11**	**1**	**0**	**1**	**0**	**0**	**0**	**0**	**5**	**20.0**		**0**	**0.0**	**8:11**	....	....	....	....	....	....	....	....	....

Signed as a free agent by **St. John's** (AHL), August 9, 2012.

SBISA, Luca

(S'BEE-za, LOO-ka) **ANA**

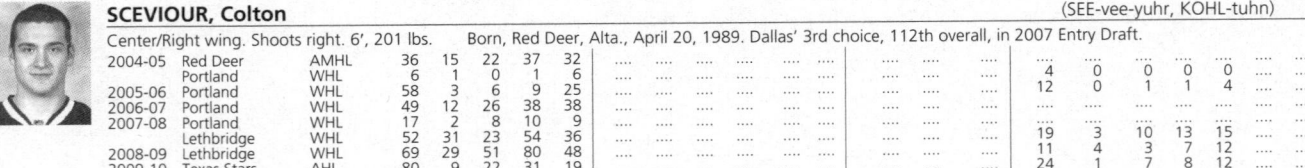

Defense. Shoots left. 6'2", 204 lbs. Born, Ozieri, Italy, January 30, 1990. Philadelphia's 1st choice, 19th overall, in 2008 Entry Draft.

			Regular Season														Playoffs								
Season	Club	League	GP	G	A	Pts	PIM	PP	SH	GW	S	%	+/-	TF	F%	Min	GP	G	A	Pts	PIM	PP	SH	GW	Min
2005-06	EV Zug Jr.	Swiss-Jr.	18	0	3	3	18	....	....	....	....	....	....	....	....	....	....	....	....	....	....	....	....	....	....
2006-07	EV Zug Jr.	Swiss-Jr.	STATISTICS NOT AVAILABLE																						
	EHC Seewen	Swiss-3	6	1	2	3	4	....	....	....	....	....	....	....	....	....	....	....	....	....	....	....	....	....	....
	EV Zug	Swiss	7	0	0	0	0	....	....	....	....	....	....	....	....	....	1	0	0	0	0	....	....	....	....
2007-08	Lethbridge	WHL	62	6	27	33	63	....	....	....	....	....	....	....	....	....	19	3	12	15	17	....	....	....	....
2008-09	**Philadelphia**	**NHL**	**39**	**0**	**7**	**7**	**36**	**0**	**0**	**0**	**38**	**0.0**	**–6**	**0**	**0.0**	**17:29**	**1**	**0**	**0**	**0**	**2**	**0**	**0**	**0**	**5:37**
	Lethbridge	WHL	18	4	11	15	19	....	....	....	....	....	....	....	....	....	11	2	1	3	12	....	....	....	....
	Philadelphia	AHL	2	1	1	2	2	....	....	....	....	....	....	....	....	....	....	....	....	....	....	....	....	....	....
2009-10	**Anaheim**	**NHL**	**8**	**0**	**0**	**0**	**6**	**0**	**0**	**0**	**3**	**0.0**	**–1**	**0**	**0.0**	**12:38**	....	....	....	....	....	....	....	....	....
	Lethbridge	WHL	17	1	12	13	18	....	....	....	....	....	....	....	....	....	....	....	....	....	....	....	....	....	....
	Portland	WHL	12	3	2	5	11	....	....	....	....	....	....	....	....	....	13	2	2	4	26	....	....	....	....
	Switzerland	Olympics	5	0	0	0	0	....	....	....	....	....	....	....	....	....	....	....	....	....	....	....	....	....	....
2010-11	**Anaheim**	**NHL**	**68**	**2**	**9**	**11**	**43**	**1**	**0**	**0**	**76**	**2.6**	**–11**	**0**	**0.0**	**16:48**	**6**	**0**	**1**	**1**	**8**	**0**	**0**	**0**	**16:29**
	Syracuse Crunch	AHL	8	2	7	9	4	....	....	....	....	....	....	....	....	....	....	....	....	....	....	....	....	....	....
2011-12	**Anaheim**	**NHL**	**80**	**5**	**19**	**24**	**66**	**0**	**0**	**0**	**88**	**5.7**	**–5**	**0**	**0.0**	**17:56**	....	....	....	....	....	....	....	....	....
2012-13	HC Lugano	Swiss	30	5	7	12	14	....	....	....	....	....	....	....	....	....	....	....	....	....	....	....	....	....	....
	Anaheim	**NHL**	**41**	**1**	**7**	**8**	**23**	**0**	**0**	**1**	**39**	**2.6**	**0**	**0**	**0.0**	**19:50**	**5**	**0**	**0**	**0**	**4**	**0**	**0**	**0**	**21:26**
	NHL Totals		**236**	**8**	**42**	**50**	**174**	**1**	**0**	**1**	**244**	**3.3**		**0**	**0.0**	**17:41**	**12**	**0**	**1**	**1**	**14**	**0**	**0**	**0**	**17:39**

Traded to **Anaheim** by **Philadelphia** with Joffrey Lupul, Philadelphia's 1st round choices in 2009 (later traded to Columbus - Columbus selected John Moore) and 2010 (Emerson Etem) Entry Drafts and future considerations for Chris Pronger and Ryan Dingle, June 26, 2009. Signed as a free agent by **Lugano** (Swiss), September 19, 2012.

SCANDELLA, Marco

(skan-DEHL-a, MAHR-koh) **MIN**

Defense. Shoots left. 6'3", 210 lbs. Born, Montreal, Que., February 23, 1990. Minnesota's 2nd choice, 55th overall, in 2008 Entry Draft.

			Regular Season														Playoffs								
Season	Club	League	GP	G	A	Pts	PIM	PP	SH	GW	S	%	+/-	TF	F%	Min	GP	G	A	Pts	PIM	PP	SH	GW	Min
2005-06	Ecole Montpetit	QAAA	42	3	4	7	40	....	....	....	....	....	....	....	....	....	3	0	0	0	2	....	....	....	....
2006-07	Mtl. Predateurs	QAAA	42	7	13	20	66	....	....	....	....	....	....	....	....	....	3	0	1	1	10	....	....	....	....
2007-08	Val-d'Or Foreurs	QMJHL	65	4	10	14	35	....	....	....	....	....	....	....	....	....	4	0	1	1	4	....	....	....	....
2008-09	Val-d'Or Foreurs	QMJHL	58	10	27	37	64	....	....	....	....	....	....	....	....	....	....	....	....	....	....	....	....	....	....
	Houston Aeros	AHL	2	0	0	0	0	....	....	....	....	....	....	....	....	....	6	0	0	0	2	....	....	....	....
2009-10	Val-d'Or Foreurs	QMJHL	31	9	22	31	41	....	....	....	....	....	....	....	....	....	6	2	4	6	4	....	....	....	....
	Houston Aeros	AHL	7	0	1	1	7	....	....	....	....	....	....	....	....	....	....	....	....	....	....	....	....	....	....
2010-11	**Minnesota**	**NHL**	**20**	**0**	**2**	**2**	**2**	**0**	**0**	**0**	**13**	**0.0**	**–9**	**0**	**0.0**	**14:58**	....	....	....	....	....	....	....	....	....
	Houston Aeros	AHL	33	3	16	19	17	....	....	....	....	....	....	....	....	....	20	2	6	8	8	....	....	....	....
2011-12	**Minnesota**	**NHL**	**63**	**3**	**9**	**12**	**19**	**1**	**0**	**1**	**77**	**3.9**	**–22**	**0**	**0.0**	**21:47**	....	....	....	....	....	....	....	....	....
	Houston Aeros	AHL	9	2	3	5	4	....	....	....	....	....	....	....	....	....	....	....	....	....	....	....	....	....	....
2012-13	Houston Aeros	AHL	45	2	15	17	23	....	....	....	....	....	....	....	....	....	2	1	0	1	2	....	....	....	....
	Minnesota	**NHL**	**6**	**1**	**0**	**1**	**4**	**0**	**0**	**0**	**7**	**14.3**	**–1**	**0**	**0.0**	**14:26**	**5**	**1**	**1**	**2**	**0**	**0**	**0**	**0**	**18:01**
	NHL Totals		**89**	**4**	**11**	**15**	**25**	**1**	**0**	**1**	**97**	**4.1**		**0**	**0.0**	**19:45**	**5**	**1**	**1**	**2**	**0**	**0**	**0**	**0**	**18:01**

SCEVIOUR, Colton

(SEE-vee-yuhr, KOHL-tuhn) **DAL**

Center/Right wing. Shoots right. 6', 201 lbs. Born, Red Deer, Alta., April 20, 1989. Dallas' 3rd choice, 112th overall, in 2007 Entry Draft.

			Regular Season														Playoffs								
Season	Club	League	GP	G	A	Pts	PIM	PP	SH	GW	S	%	+/-	TF	F%	Min	GP	G	A	Pts	PIM	PP	SH	GW	Min
2004-05	Red Deer	AMHL	36	15	22	37	32	....	....	....	....	....	....	....	....	....	....	....	....	....	....	....	....	....	....
	Portland	WHL	6	1	0	1	6	....	....	....	....	....	....	....	....	....	4	0	0	0	0	....	....	....	....
2005-06	Portland	WHL	58	3	6	9	25	....	....	....	....	....	....	....	....	....	12	0	1	1	4	....	....	....	....
2006-07	Portland	WHL	49	12	26	38	38	....	....	....	....	....	....	....	....	....	....	....	....	....	....	....	....	....	....
2007-08	Portland	WHL	17	2	8	10	9	....	....	....	....	....	....	....	....	....	....	....	....	....	....	....	....	....	....
	Lethbridge	WHL	52	31	23	54	36	....	....	....	....	....	....	....	....	....	19	3	10	13	15	....	....	....	....
2008-09	Lethbridge	WHL	69	29	51	80	48	....	....	....	....	....	....	....	....	....	11	4	3	7	12	....	....	....	....
2009-10	Texas Stars	AHL	80	9	22	31	19	....	....	....	....	....	....	....	....	....	24	1	7	8	12	....	....	....	....

Season	Club	League	GP	G	A	Pts	PIM	PP	SH	GW	S	%	+/-	TF	F%	Min	GP	G	A	Pts	PIM	PP	SH	GW	Min
			Regular Season														Playoffs								
2010-11	**Dallas**	**NHL**	**1**	**0**	**0**	**0**	**0**	**0**	**0**	**0**	**0**	**0.0**	**–1**	**0**	**0.0**	**5:09**	....	....	....	....	....	....	....	....	....
	Texas Stars	AHL	77	16	25	41	17	....	....	....	....	....	....	....	....	....	6	1	0	1	0	....	....	....	....
2011-12	Texas Stars	AHL	75	21	32	53	25	....	....	....	....	....	....	....	....	....	....	....	....	....	....	....	....	....	....
2012-13	Texas Stars	AHL	62	21	31	52	20	....	....	....	....	....	....	....	....	....	9	1	3	4	4	....	....	....	....
	Dallas	**NHL**	**1**	**0**	**1**	**1**	**0**	**0**	**0**	**0**	**0**	**0.0**	**–1**	**3**	**33.3**	**4:51**	....	....	....	....	....	....	....	....	....
	NHL Totals		**2**	**0**	**1**	**1**	**0**	**0**	**0**	**0**	**0**	**0.0**		**3**	**33.3**	**5:00**	....	....	....	....	....	....	....	....	....

SCHEIFELE, Mark

(SHIHF-lee, MAHRK) **WPG**

Center. Shoots right. 6'2", 192 lbs. Born, Kitchener, Ont., March 15, 1993. Winnipeg's 1st choice, 7th overall, in 2011 Entry Draft.

2008-09	Kit. Jr. Rangers	Minor-ON	31	20	19	39	16	....	....	....	....	....	....	....	....	....	....	....	....	....	....	....	....	....	....
	Kit. Jr. Rangers	Exhib.	18	20	20	40	14	....	....	....	....	....	....	....	....	....	....	....	....	....	....	....	....	....	....
2009-10	Kitchener	ON-Jr.B	51	18	37	55	20	....	....	....	....	....	....	....	....	....	5	0	3	3	6	....	....	....	....
2010-11	Barrie Colts	OHL	66	22	53	75	35	....	....	....	....	....	....	....	....	....	....	....	....	....	....	....	....	....	....
2011-12	**Winnipeg**	**NHL**	**7**	**1**	**0**	**1**	**0**	**1**	**0**	**0**	**5**	**20.0**	**0**	**51**	**35.3**	**10:57**	....	....	....	....	....	....	....	....	....
	Barrie Colts	OHL	47	23	40	63	36	....	....	....	....	....	....	....	....	....	13	5	7	12	12	....	....	....	....
	St. John's IceCaps	AHL	....	....	....	....	....	....	....	....	....	....	....	....	....	....	10	0	1	1	2	....	....	....	....
2012-13	Barrie Colts	OHL	45	39	40	79	30	....	....	....	....	....	....	....	....	....	21	15	*26	*41	14	....	....	....	....
	Winnipeg	**NHL**	**4**	**0**	**0**	**0**	**0**	**0**	**0**	**0**	**6**	**0.0**	**0**	**14**	**71.4**	**11:32**	....	....	....	....	....	....	....	....	....
	NHL Totals		**11**	**1**	**0**	**1**	**0**	**1**	**0**	**0**	**11**	**9.1**		**65**	**43.1**	**11:09**	....	....	....	....	....	....	....	....	....

SCHENN, Brayden

(SHEHN, BRAY-duhn) **PHI**

Center. Shoots left. 6'1", 190 lbs. Born, Saskatoon, Sask., August 22, 1991. Los Angeles' 1st choice, 5th overall, in 2009 Entry Draft.

2006-07	Sask. Contacts	SMHL	41	27	43	70	63	....	....	....	....	....	....	....	....	....	....	....	....	....	....	....	....	....	....
2007-08	Brandon	WHL	66	28	43	71	48	....	....	....	....	....	....	....	....	....	6	2	1	3	14	....	....	....	....
2008-09	Brandon	WHL	70	32	56	88	82	....	....	....	....	....	....	....	....	....	12	8	10	18	12	....	....	....	....
2009-10	Brandon	WHL	59	34	65	99	55	....	....	....	....	....	....	....	....	....	15	8	11	19	2	....	....	....	....
	Los Angeles	**NHL**	**1**	**0**	**0**	**0**	**0**	**0**	**0**	**0**	**0**	**0.0**	**–1**	**14**	**28.6**	**12:31**	....	....	....	....	....	....	....	....	....
2010-11	**Los Angeles**	**NHL**	**8**	**0**	**2**	**2**	**0**	**0**	**0**	**0**	**11**	**0.0**	**–1**	**51**	**33.3**	**11:15**	....	....	....	....	....	....	....	....	....
	Brandon	WHL	2	1	3	4	2	....	....	....	....	....	....	....	....	....	....	....	....	....	....	....	....	....	....
	Saskatoon Blades	WHL	27	21	32	53	23	....	....	....	....	....	....	....	....	....	10	6	5	11	14	....	....	....	....
	Manchester	AHL	7	3	4	7	4	....	....	....	....	....	....	....	....	....	5	1	3	4	0	....	....	....	....
2011-12	**Philadelphia**	**NHL**	**54**	**12**	**6**	**18**	**34**	**4**	**0**	**3**	**97**	**12.4**	**–7**	**436**	**46.1**	**14:07**	**11**	**3**	**6**	**9**	**8**	**2**	**0**	**0**	**14:16**
	Adirondack	AHL	7	6	6	12	4	....	....	....	....	....	....	....	....	....	....	....	....	....	....	....	....	....	....
2012-13	Adirondack	AHL	33	13	20	33	15	....	....	....	....	....	....	....	....	....	....	....	....	....	....	....	....	....	....
	Philadelphia	**NHL**	**47**	**8**	**18**	**26**	**24**	**2**	**0**	**0**	**79**	**10.1**	**–8**	**453**	**45.5**	**15:32**	....	....	....	....	....	....	....	....	....
	NHL Totals		**110**	**20**	**26**	**46**	**58**	**6**	**0**	**3**	**187**	**10.7**		**954**	**44.9**	**14:30**	**11**	**3**	**6**	**9**	**8**	**2**	**0**	**0**	**14:16**

WHL Rookie of the Year (2008) • Canadian Major Junior All-Rookie Team (2008) • WHL East Second All-Star Team (2009, 2011) • WHL East First All-Star Team (2010)

Traded to **Philadelphia** by **Los Angeles** with Wayne Simmonds and Los Angeles' 2nd round choice (Devin Shore) in 2012 Entry Draft for Mike Richards and the righjts to Rob Bordson, June 23, 2011.

SCHENN, Luke

(SHEHN, LEWK) **PHI**

Defense. Shoots right. 6'2", 229 lbs. Born, Saskatoon, Sask., November 2, 1989. Toronto's 1st choice, 5th overall, in 2008 Entry Draft.

2004-05	Sask. Contacts	SMHL	41	5	22	27	69	....	....	....	....	....	....	....	....	....	....	....	....	....	....	....	....	....	....
2005-06	Kelowna Rockets	WHL	60	3	8	11	86	....	....	....	....	....	....	....	....	....	12	0	0	0	14	....	....	....	....
2006-07	Kelowna Rockets	WHL	72	2	27	29	139	....	....	....	....	....	....	....	....	....	....	....	....	....	....	....	....	....	....
2007-08	Kelowna Rockets	WHL	57	7	21	28	100	....	....	....	....	....	....	....	....	....	7	2	2	4	6	....	....	....	....
2008-09	**Toronto**	**NHL**	**70**	**2**	**12**	**14**	**71**	**1**	**0**	**0**	**102**	**2.0**	**–12**	**0**	**0.0**	**21:32**	....	....	....	....	....	....	....	....	....
2009-10	**Toronto**	**NHL**	**79**	**5**	**12**	**17**	**50**	**0**	**0**	**1**	**101**	**5.0**	**2**	**0**	**0.0**	**16:53**	....	....	....	....	....	....	....	....	....
2010-11	**Toronto**	**NHL**	**82**	**5**	**17**	**22**	**34**	**0**	**0**	**0**	**128**	**3.9**	**–7**	**0**	**0.0**	**22:22**	....	....	....	....	....	....	....	....	....
2011-12	**Toronto**	**NHL**	**79**	**2**	**20**	**22**	**62**	**0**	**0**	**0**	**81**	**2.5**	**–6**	**0**	**0.0**	**16:02**	....	....	....	....	....	....	....	....	....
2012-13	**Philadelphia**	**NHL**	**47**	**3**	**8**	**11**	**34**	**0**	**0**	**0**	**81**	**3.7**	**3**	**0**	**0.0**	**21:52**	....	....	....	....	....	....	....	....	....
	NHL Totals		**357**	**17**	**69**	**86**	**251**	**1**	**0**	**1**	**493**	**3.4**		**0**	**0.0**	**19:31**	....	....	....	....	....	....	....	....	....

WHL West Second All-Star Team (2008) • NHL All-Rookie Team (2009)

Traded to **Philadelphia** by **Toronto** for James van Riemsdyk, June 23, 2012.

SCHILLING, Cameron

(SHIHL-ihng, KAM-r'uhn) **WSH**

Defense. Shoots left. 6'2", 197 lbs. Born, Carmel, IN, October 7, 1988.

2007-08	Indiana Ice	USHL	55	2	8	10	91	....	....	....	....	....	....	....	....	....	4	0	0	0	2	....	....	....	....
2008-09	Miami U.	CCHA	25	0	7	7	43	....	....	....	....	....	....	....	....	....	....	....	....	....	....	....	....	....	....
2009-10	Miami U.	CCHA	42	4	15	19	58	....	....	....	....	....	....	....	....	....	....	....	....	....	....	....	....	....	....
2010-11	Miami U.	CCHA	38	3	14	17	34	....	....	....	....	....	....	....	....	....	....	....	....	....	....	....	....	....	....
2011-12	Miami U.	CCHA	39	1	13	14	20	....	....	....	....	....	....	....	....	....	....	....	....	....	....	....	....	....	....
	Hershey Bears	AHL	7	0	0	0	14	....	....	....	....	....	....	....	....	....	4	2	0	2	4	....	....	....	....
2012-13	Hershey Bears	AHL	70	7	9	16	61	....	....	....	....	....	....	....	....	....	5	0	1	1	4	....	....	....	....
	Washington	**NHL**	**1**	**0**	**0**	**0**	**0**	**0**	**0**	**0**	**0**	**0.0**	**–1**	**0**	**0.0**	**11:58**	....	....	....	....	....	....	....	....	....
	NHL Totals		**1**	**0**	**0**	**0**	**0**	**0**	**0**	**0**	**0**	**0.0**		**0**	**0.0**	**11:58**	....	....	....	....	....	....	....	....	....

Signed as a free agent by **Washington**, March 27, 2012.

SCHLEMKO, David

(SHLEHM-koh, DAY-vihd) **PHX**

Defense. Shoots left. 6'1", 190 lbs. Born, Edmonton, Alta., May 7, 1987.

2004-05	Medicine Hat	WHL	65	5	24	29	23	....	....	....	....	....	....	....	....	....	13	0	3	3	10	....	....	....	....
2005-06	Medicine Hat	WHL	69	9	35	44	44	....	....	....	....	....	....	....	....	....	13	2	5	7	15	....	....	....	....
2006-07	Medicine Hat	WHL	64	8	50	58	78	....	....	....	....	....	....	....	....	....	23	3	13	16	12	....	....	....	....
2007-08	San Antonio	AHL	1	0	0	0	4	....	....	....	....	....	....	....	....	....	....	....	....	....	....	....	....	....	....
	Arizona Sundogs	CHL	58	10	29	39	24	....	....	....	....	....	....	....	....	....	14	3	5	8	6	....	....	....	....
2008-09	**Phoenix**	**NHL**	**3**	**0**	**1**	**1**	**0**	**0**	**0**	**0**	**3**	**0.0**	**–2**	**0**	**0.0**	**19:16**	....	....	....	....	....	....	....	....	....
	San Antonio	AHL	68	7	22	29	20	....	....	....	....	....	....	....	....	....	....	....	....	....	....	....	....	....	....
2009-10	**Phoenix**	**NHL**	**17**	**1**	**4**	**5**	**8**	**0**	**0**	**0**	**19**	**5.3**	**1**	**0**	**0.0**	**17:49**	....	....	....	....	....	....	....	....	....
	San Antonio	AHL	55	5	26	31	30	....	....	....	....	....	....	....	....	....	....	....	....	....	....	....	....	....	....
2010-11	**Phoenix**	**NHL**	**43**	**4**	**10**	**14**	**24**	**0**	**0**	**0**	**47**	**8.5**	**8**	**0**	**0.0**	**16:02**	**4**	**1**	**0**	**1**	**4**	**1**	**0**	**0**	**15:54**
	San Antonio	AHL	3	0	0	0	2	....	....	....	....	....	....	....	....	....	....	....	....	....	....	....	....	....	....
2011-12	**Phoenix**	**NHL**	**46**	**1**	**10**	**11**	**10**	**0**	**0**	**0**	**58**	**1.7**	**7**	**0**	**0.0**	**18:21**	**5**	**0**	**0**	**0**	**0**	**0**	**0**	**0**	**16:13**
2012-13	Arizona Sundogs	CHL	14	3	7	10	4	....	....	....	....	....	....	....	....	....	....	....	....	....	....	....	....	....	....
	Phoenix	**NHL**	**30**	**1**	**5**	**6**	**12**	**0**	**0**	**0**	**35**	**2.9**	**8**	**0**	**0.0**	**17:13**	....	....	....	....	....	....	....	....	....
	NHL Totals		**139**	**7**	**30**	**37**	**54**	**0**	**0**	**0**	**162**	**4.3**		**0**	**0.0**	**17:21**	**9**	**1**	**0**	**1**	**4**	**1**	**0**	**0**	**16:05**

WHL East Second All-Star Team (2007)

Signed as a free agent by **Phoenix**, July 19, 2007. Signed as a free agent by **Arizona** (CHL), October 2, 2012.

SCHROEDER, Jordan

(SHRAY-duhr, JOHR-dahn) **VAN**

Center. Shoots right. 5'8", 175 lbs. Born, Prior Lake, MN, September 29, 1990. Vancouver's 1st choice, 22nd overall, in 2009 Entry Draft.

2005-06	Saint Thomas	High-MN	31	27	35	62	....	....	....	....	....	....	....	....	....	....	....	....	....	....	....	....	....	....	....
	Team Southeast	UMHSEL	....	7	14	21	....	....	....	....	....	....	....	....	....	....	....	....	....	....	....	....	....	....	....
2006-07	USNTDP	NAHL	31	12	11	23	10	....	....	....	....	....	....	....	....	....	....	....	....	....	....	....	....	....	....
	USNTDP	U-17	8	2	8	10	2	....	....	....	....	....	....	....	....	....	....	....	....	....	....	....	....	....	....
	USNTDP	U-18	17	6	13	19	4	....	....	....	....	....	....	....	....	....	....	....	....	....	....	....	....	....	....
2007-08	USNTDP	NAHL	14	1	8	9	4	....	....	....	....	....	....	....	....	....	....	....	....	....	....	....	....	....	....
	USNTDP	U-18	41	21	23	44	12	....	....	....	....	....	....	....	....	....	....	....	....	....	....	....	....	....	....
2008-09	U. of Minnesota	WCHA	35	13	32	45	29	....	....	....	....	....	....	....	....	....	....	....	....	....	....	....	....	....	....
2009-10	U. of Minnesota	WCHA	37	9	19	28	14	....	....	....	....	....	....	....	....	....	....	....	....	....	....	....	....	....	....
	Manitoba Moose	AHL	11	4	5	9	0	....	....	....	....	....	....	....	....	....	6	3	3	6	4	....	....	....	....
2010-11	Manitoba Moose	AHL	61	10	18	28	10	....	....	....	....	....	....	....	....	....	14	1	5	6	2	....	....	....	....
2011-12	Chicago Wolves	AHL	76	21	23	44	18	....	....	....	....	....	....	....	....	....	5	1	1	2	0	....	....	....	....

			Regular Season														Playoffs								
Season	Club	League	GP	G	A	Pts	PIM	PP	SH	GW	S	%	+/-	TF	F%	Min	GP	G	A	Pts	PIM	PP	SH	GW	Min
2012-13	Chicago Wolves	AHL	42	12	21	33	14	....	....	....	....	....	....	....	....	....	....	....	....	....	....	....	....	....	....
	Vancouver	NHL	31	3	6	9	4	1	0	2	28	10.7	0	321	43.6	13:43	....	....	....	....	....	....	....	....	....
	NHL Totals		31	3	6	9	4	1	0	2	28	10.7		321	43.6	13:43	....	....	....	....	....	....	....	....	....

WCHA All-Rookie Team (2009) • WCHA Second All-Star Team (2009) • WCHA Rookie of the Year (2009)

SCHULTZ, Jeff
(SHUHLTZ, JEHF) **L.A.**

Defense. Shoots left. 6'6", 230 lbs. Born, Calgary, Alta., February 25, 1986. Washington's 2nd choice, 27th overall, in 2004 Entry Draft.

2000-01	Calgary Hawks	CBHL	27	7	8	15	20	....	....	....	....	....	....	....	....	....	....	....	....	....	....	....	....	....	....
2001-02	Calgary Rangers	CBHL	27	5	18	23	42	....	....	....	....	....	....	....	....	....	....	....	....	....	....	....	....	....	....
2002-03	Calgary Hitmen	WHL	50	2	1	3	4	....	....	....	....	....	....	....	....	....	4	0	0	0	0	....	....	....	....
2003-04	Calgary Hitmen	WHL	72	11	24	35	33	....	....	....	....	....	....	....	....	....	7	1	1	2	0	....	....	....	....
2004-05	Calgary Hitmen	WHL	72	2	27	29	31	....	....	....	....	....	....	....	....	....	12	2	1	3	6	....	....	....	....
2005-06	Calgary Hitmen	WHL	68	7	33	40	36	....	....	....	....	....	....	....	....	....	13	4	6	10	6	....	....	....	....
	Hershey Bears	AHL	....	....	....	....	....	....	....	....	....	....	....	....	....	....	7	1	3	4	4	....	....	....	....
2006-07	Washington	NHL	38	0	3	3	16	0	0	0	22	0.0	5	0	0.0	18:13	....	....	....	....	....	....	....	....	....
	Hershey Bears	AHL	44	2	10	12	39	....	....	....	....	....	....	....	....	....	19	0	1	1	18	....	....	....	....
2007-08	Washington	NHL	72	5	13	18	28	0	0	0	36	13.9	12	1	100.0	18:05	2	0	0	0	2	0	0	0	10:25
	Hershey Bears	AHL	1	0	0	0	0	....	....	....	....	....	....	....	....	....	....	....	....	....	....	....	....	....	....
2008-09	Washington	NHL	64	1	11	12	21	0	1	0	40	2.5	13	0	0.0	19:46	1	0	0	0	0	0	0	0	12:26
2009-10	Washington	NHL	73	3	20	23	32	0	0	0	43	7.0	50	0	0.0	19:52	7	0	1	1	4	0	0	0	19:43
2010-11	Washington	NHL	72	1	9	10	12	0	0	1	34	2.9	6	0	0.0	19:47	9	0	0	0	6	0	0	0	20:45
2011-12	Washington	NHL	54	1	5	6	12	0	0	0	22	4.5	–2	0	0.0	15:18	10	0	0	0	2	0	0	0	15:35
2012-13	Washington	NHL	26	0	3	3	12	0	0	0	12	0.0	–6	0	0.0	14:15	....	....	....	....	....	....	....	....	....
	NHL Totals		399	11	64	75	133	0	1	1	209	5.3		1	100.0	18:22	29	0	1	1	14	0	0	0	17:43

WHL East Second All-Star Team (2006)
• Missed majority of 2012-13 as a healthy reserve. Signed as a free agent by **Los Angeles**, July 5, 2013.

SCHULTZ, Justin
(SHUHLTZ, JUHS-tihn) **EDM**

Defense. Shoots right. 6'2", 185 lbs. Born, Kelowna, B.C., July 6, 1990. Anaheim's 4th choice, 43rd overall, in 2008 Entry Draft.

2006-07	Westside Warriors	Minor-BC	....	29	29	58	29	....	....	....	....	....	....	....	....	....	....	....	....	....	....	....	....	....	....
2007-08	Westside Warriors	BCHL	57	9	31	40	28	....	....	....	....	....	....	....	....	....	11	3	5	8	4	....	....	....	....
2008-09	Westside Warriors	BCHL	49	15	35	50	29	....	....	....	....	....	....	....	....	....	6	1	2	3	2	....	....	....	....
2009-10	U. of Wisconsin	WCHA	43	6	16	22	12	....	....	....	....	....	....	....	....	....	....	....	....	....	....	....	....	....	....
2010-11	U. of Wisconsin	WCHA	41	18	29	47	28	....	....	....	....	....	....	....	....	....	....	....	....	....	....	....	....	....	....
2011-12	U. of Wisconsin	WCHA	37	16	28	44	12	....	....	....	....	....	....	....	....	....	....	....	....	....	....	....	....	....	....
2012-13	Oklahoma City	AHL	34	18	30	48	6	....	....	....	....	....	....	....	....	....	....	....	....	....	....	....	....	....	....
	Edmonton	NHL	48	8	19	27	8	4	0	3	85	9.4	–17	1	0.0	21:27	....	....	....	....	....	....	....	....	....
	NHL Totals		48	8	19	27	8	4	0	3	85	9.4		1	0.0	21:27	....	....	....	....	....	....	....	....	....

WCHA All-Rookie Team (2010) • WCHA First All-Star Team (2011, 2012) • NCAA West First All-American Team (2011, 2012) • AHL All-Rookie Team (2013) • AHL First All-Star Team (2013) • Eddie Shore Award (AHL - Outstanding Defenseman) (2013) • NHL All-Rookie Team (2013)
Signed as a free agent by **Edmonton**, July 1, 2012.

SCHULTZ, Nick
(SHUHLTZ, NIHK) **EDM**

Defense. Shoots left. 6'1", 200 lbs. Born, Strasbourg, Sask., August 25, 1982. Minnesota's 2nd choice, 33rd overall, in 2000 Entry Draft.

1997-98	Yorkton Mallers	SMHL	59	10	30	40	74	....	....	....	....	....	....	....	....	....	....	....	....	....	....	....	....	....	....
1998-99	Prince Albert	WHL	58	5	18	23	37	....	....	....	....	....	....	....	....	....	14	0	7	7	0	....	....	....	....
99-2000	Prince Albert	WHL	72	11	33	44	38	....	....	....	....	....	....	....	....	....	6	0	3	3	2	....	....	....	....
2000-01	Prince Albert	WHL	59	17	30	47	120	....	....	....	....	....	....	....	....	....	....	....	....	....	....	....	....	....	....
	Cleveland	IHL	4	1	1	2	2	....	....	....	....	....	....	....	....	....	3	0	1	1	0	....	....	....	....
2001-02	Minnesota	NHL	52	4	6	10	14	1	0	1	47	8.5	0	0	0.0	16:08	....	....	....	....	....	....	....	....	....
	Houston Aeros	AHL	....	....	....	....	....	....	....	....	....	....	....	....	....	....	14	1	5	6	2	....	....	....	....
2002-03	Minnesota	NHL	75	3	7	10	23	0	0	1	70	4.3	11	0	0.0	18:28	18	0	1	1	10	0	0	0	19:39
2003-04	Minnesota	NHL	79	6	10	16	16	1	0	0	72	8.3	12	0	0.0	20:19	....	....	....	....	....	....	....	....	....
2004-05	Kassel Huskies	Germany	46	7	15	22	26	....	....	....	....	....	....	....	....	....	7	0	4	4	6	....	....	....	....
2005-06	Minnesota	NHL	79	2	12	14	43	0	0	0	45	4.4	2	0	0.0	17:58	....	....	....	....	....	....	....	....	....
2006-07	Minnesota	NHL	82	2	10	12	42	0	0	1	69	2.9	0	0	0.0	20:13	5	0	1	1	0	0	0	0	18:06
2007-08	Minnesota	NHL	81	2	13	15	42	0	0	0	52	3.8	9	0	0.0	20:10	1	0	0	0	0	0	0	0	16:11
2008-09	Minnesota	NHL	79	2	9	11	31	0	0	0	48	4.2	–4	1	0.0	20:33	....	....	....	....	....	....	....	....	....
2009-10	Minnesota	NHL	80	1	19	20	43	1	0	0	83	1.2	–8	0	0.0	20:58	....	....	....	....	....	....	....	....	....
2010-11	Minnesota	NHL	74	3	14	17	38	0	0	0	46	6.5	–4	1	100.0	20:13	....	....	....	....	....	....	....	....	....
2011-12	Minnesota	NHL	62	1	2	3	30	1	0	0	38	2.6	–10	0	0.0	19:36	....	....	....	....	....	....	....	....	....
	Edmonton	NHL	20	0	4	4	10	0	0	0	13	0.0	–2	0	0.0	20:04	....	....	....	....	....	....	....	....	....
2012-13	Edmonton	NHL	48	1	8	9	24	0	0	0	33	3.0	–13	2	0.0	18:38	....	....	....	....	....	....	....	....	....
	NHL Totals		811	27	114	141	356	4	0	3	616	4.4		4	25.0	19:32	24	0	2	2	10	0	0	0	19:11

Signed as a free agent by **Kassel** (Germany), September 24, 2004. Traded to **Edmonton** by **Minnesota** for Tom Gilbert, February 27, 2012.

SCHWARTZ, Jaden
(SHWOHRTZ, JAY-duhn) **ST.L.**

Center. Shoots left. 5'10", 190 lbs. Born, Melfort, Sask., June 25, 1992. St. Louis' 1st choice, 14th overall, in 2010 Entry Draft.

2008-09	Notre Dame	SJHL	46	34	42	76	15	....	....	....	....	....	....	....	....	....	....	....	....	....	....	....	....	....	....
2009-10	Tri-City Storm	USHL	60	33	50	*83	18	....	....	....	....	....	....	....	....	....	3	3	0	3	0	....	....	....	....
2010-11	Colorado College	WCHA	30	17	30	47	22	....	....	....	....	....	....	....	....	....	....	....	....	....	....	....	....	....	....
2011-12	Colorado College	WCHA	30	15	26	41	18	....	....	....	....	....	....	....	....	....	....	....	....	....	....	....	....	....	....
	St. Louis	NHL	7	2	1	3	0	1	0	1	6	33.3	1	2	50.0	11:41	....	....	....	....	....	....	....	....	....
2012-13	Peoria Rivermen	AHL	33	9	10	19	14	....	....	....	....	....	....	....	....	....	....	....	....	....	....	....	....	....	....
	St. Louis	NHL	45	7	6	13	4	0	0	1	50	14.0	–4	27	55.6	12:28	6	0	1	1	2	0	0	0	16:06
	NHL Totals		52	9	7	16	4	1	0	2	56	16.1		29	55.2	12:22	6	0	1	1	2	0	0	0	16:06

USHL First All-Star Team (2010) • WCHA All-Rookie Team (2011) • WCHA Second All-Star Team (2012) • NCAA West First All-American Team (2012)

SCOTT, John
(SKAWT, JAWN) **BUF**

Left wing. Shoots left. 6'8", 270 lbs. Born, St. Catharines, Ont., September 26, 1982.

2002-03	Michigan Tech	WCHA	31	1	3	4	64	....	....	....	....	....	....	....	....	....	....	....	....	....	....	....	....	....	....
2003-04	Michigan Tech	WCHA	35	1	3	4	100	....	....	....	....	....	....	....	....	....	....	....	....	....	....	....	....	....	....
2004-05	Michigan Tech	WCHA	36	2	4	6	101	....	....	....	....	....	....	....	....	....	....	....	....	....	....	....	....	....	....
2005-06	Michigan Tech	WCHA	24	3	2	5	87	....	....	....	....	....	....	....	....	....	....	....	....	....	....	....	....	....	....
2006-07	Houston Aeros	AHL	65	1	5	6	107	....	....	....	....	....	....	....	....	....	....	....	....	....	....	....	....	....	....
2007-08	Houston Aeros	AHL	64	3	0	3	184	....	....	....	....	....	....	....	....	....	5	0	0	0	13	....	....	....	....
2008-09	Minnesota	NHL	20	0	1	1	21	0	0	0	6	0.0	–1	0	0.0	9:14	....	....	....	....	....	....	....	....	....
	Houston Aeros	AHL	44	2	2	4	111	....	....	....	....	....	....	....	....	....	....	....	....	....	....	....	....	....	....
2009-10	Minnesota	NHL	51	1	1	2	90	0	0	0	22	4.5	–3	0	0.0	8:36	....	....	....	....	....	....	....	....	....
2010-11	Chicago	NHL	40	0	1	1	72	0	0	0	15	0.0	0	3	0.0	6:15	4	0	0	0	22	0	0	0	6:37
2011-12	Chicago	NHL	29	0	1	1	48	0	0	0	8	0.0	0	0	0.0	6:56	....	....	....	....	....	....	....	....	....
	NY Rangers	NHL	6	0	0	0	5	0	0	0	1	0.0	–1	0	0.0	5:33	....	....	....	....	....	....	....	....	....
2012-13	Buffalo	NHL	34	0	0	0	69	0	0	0	15	0.0	–1	0	0.0	5:27	....	....	....	....	....	....	....	....	....
	NHL Totals		180	1	4	5	305	0	0	0	67	1.5		3	0.0	7:11	4	0	0	0	22	0	0	0	6:38

Signed as a free agent by **Houston** (AHL), September 26, 2006. Signed as a free agent by **Minnesota**, December 31, 2006. Signed as a free agent by **Chicago**, July 2, 2010. • Missed majority of 2010-11 and 2011-12 as a healthy reserve. Traded to **NY Rangers** by **Chicago** for NY Rangers' 5th round choice (Travis Brown) in 2012 Entry Draft, February 27, 2012. Signed as a free agent by **Buffalo**, July 1, 2012.

SCUDERI, Rob

(SKUD-uh-ree, RAWB) **PIT**

Defense. Shoots left. 6'1", 219 lbs. Born, Syosset, NY, December 30, 1978. Pittsburgh's 5th choice, 134th overall, in 1998 Entry Draft.

			Regular Season													Playoffs								
Season	Club	League	GP	G	A	Pts	PIM	PP	SH	GW	S	%	+/-	TF	F%	Min	GP	G	A	Pts	PIM	PP	SH	GW	Min
1995-96	NY Apple Core	MtJHL	76	18	60	78	....	....	....	....	....	....	....	....	....	....	....	....	....	....	....	....	....	....	....
1996-97	NY Apple Core	MtJHL	82	42	70	112	64	....	....	....	....	....	....	....	....	....	....	....	....	....	....	....	....	....	....
1997-98	Boston College	H-East	42	0	24	24	12	....	....	....	....	....	....	....	....	....	....	....	....	....	....	....	....	....	....
1998-99	Boston College	H-East	41	2	8	10	20	....	....	....	....	....	....	....	....	....	....	....	....	....	....	....	....	....	....
99-2000	Boston College	H-East	42	1	12	13	22	....	....	....	....	....	....	....	....	....	....	....	....	....	....	....	....	....	....
2000-01	Boston College	H-East	43	4	19	23	42	....	....	....	....	....	....	....	....	....	....	....	....	....	....	....	....	....	....
2001-02	Wilkes-Barre	AHL	75	1	22	23	66	....	....	....	....	....	....	....	....	....	....	....	....	....	....	....	....	....	....
2002-03	Wilkes-Barre	AHL	74	4	17	21	44	....	....	....	....	....	....	....	....	....	6	0	1	1	4	....	....	....	....
2003-04	Pittsburgh	NHL	13	1	2	3	4	0	0	0	4	25.0	2	0	0.0	20:06	....	....	....	....	....	....	....	....	....
	Wilkes-Barre	AHL	64	1	15	16	54	....	....	....	....	....	....	....	....	....	24	0	3	3	14	....	....	....	....
2004-05	Wilkes-Barre	AHL	79	2	18	20	34	....	....	....	....	....	....	....	....	....	11	2	1	3	2	....	....	....	....
2005-06	Pittsburgh	NHL	57	0	4	4	36	0	0	0	28	0.0	–18	0	0.0	20:15	....	....	....	....	....	....	....	....	....
	Wilkes-Barre	AHL	13	0	8	8	8	....	....	....	....	....	....	....	....	....	....	....	....	....	....	....	....	....	....
2006-07	Pittsburgh	NHL	78	1	10	11	28	0	0	0	31	3.2	3	0	0.0	18:49	5	0	0	0	2	0	0	0	17:14
2007-08	Pittsburgh	NHL	71	0	5	5	26	0	0	0	28	0.0	3	0	0.0	18:45	20	0	3	3	2	0	0	0	19:02
2008-09♦	Pittsburgh	NHL	81	1	15	16	18	0	0	0	51	2.0	23	0	0.0	19:10	24	1	4	5	6	0	0	0	20:30
2009-10	Los Angeles	NHL	73	0	11	11	21	0	0	0	38	0.0	16	0	0.0	19:16	6	0	0	0	6	0	0	0	20:40
2010-11	Los Angeles	NHL	82	2	13	15	16	0	0	1	46	4.3	1	0	0.0	20:17	6	0	2	2	0	0	0	0	20:49
2011-12♦	Los Angeles	NHL	82	1	8	9	16	0	0	0	63	1.6	–7	0	0.0	20:37	20	0	1	1	4	0	0	0	21:44
2012-13	Los Angeles	NHL	48	1	11	12	4	0	0	0	33	3.0	–6	1	0.0	21:47	18	0	3	3	0	0	0	0	23:18
	NHL Totals		585	7	79	86	169	0	0	1	322	2.2		1	0.0	19:47	99	1	13	14	20	0	0	0	20:50

NCAA Championship All-Tournament Team (2001)

Signed as a free agent by **Los Angeles** July 2, 2009. Signed as a free agent by **Pittsburgh**, July 5, 2013.

SEABROOK, Brent

(SEE-bruk, BREHNT) **CHI**

Defense. Shoots right. 6'3", 221 lbs. Born, Richmond, B.C., April 20, 1985. Chicago's 1st choice, 14th overall, in 2003 Entry Draft.

			Regular Season													Playoffs								
Season	Club	League	GP	G	A	Pts	PIM	PP	SH	GW	S	%	+/-	TF	F%	Min	GP	G	A	Pts	PIM	PP	SH	GW	Min
2000-01	Delta Ice Hawks	PIJHL	54	16	26	42	55	....	....	....	....	....	....	....	....	....	....	....	....	....	....	....	....	....	....
	Lethbridge	WHL	4	0	0	0	0	....	....	....	....	....	....	....	....	....	....	....	....	....	....	....	....	....	....
2001-02	Lethbridge	WHL	67	6	33	39	70	....	....	....	....	....	....	....	....	....	4	1	1	2	2	....	....	....	....
2002-03	Lethbridge	WHL	69	9	33	42	113	....	....	....	....	....	....	....	....	....	....	....	....	....	....	....	....	....	....
2003-04	Lethbridge	WHL	61	12	29	41	107	....	....	....	....	....	....	....	....	....	....	....	....	....	....	....	....	....	....
2004-05	Lethbridge	WHL	63	12	42	54	107	....	....	....	....	....	....	....	....	....	5	1	2	3	10	....	....	....	....
	Norfolk Admirals	AHL	3	0	0	0	2	....	....	....	....	....	....	....	....	....	6	0	1	1	6	....	....	....	....
2005-06	Chicago	NHL	69	5	27	32	60	1	0	2	114	4.4	5	0	0.0	20:02	....	....	....	....	....	....	....	....	....
2006-07	Chicago	NHL	81	4	20	24	104	0	0	0	144	2.8	–6	2	50.0	20:46	....	....	....	....	....	....	....	....	....
2007-08	Chicago	NHL	82	9	23	32	90	4	0	2	152	5.9	13	1	0.0	21:30	....	....	....	....	....	....	....	....	....
2008-09	Chicago	NHL	82	8	18	26	62	3	1	1	132	6.1	23	0	0.0	23:19	17	1	11	12	14	1	0	0	26:00
2009-10♦	Chicago	NHL	78	4	26	30	59	0	0	2	129	3.1	20	0	0.0	23:13	22	4	7	11	14	1	0	0	24:11
	Canada	Olympics	7	0	1	1	2	....	....	....	....	....	....	....	....	....	....	....	....	....	....	....	....	....	....
2010-11	Chicago	NHL	82	9	39	48	47	5	0	1	135	6.7	0	0	0.0	24:23	5	0	1	1	6	0	0	0	22:57
2011-12	Chicago	NHL	78	9	25	34	22	2	0	3	156	5.8	21	0	0.0	24:43	6	1	2	3	0	0	0	0	30:01
2012-13♦	Chicago	NHL	47	8	12	20	23	3	0	1	65	12.3	12	0	0.0	22:00	23	3	1	4	4	0	0	2	23:05
	NHL Totals		599	56	190	246	467	18	1	12	1027	5.5		3	33.3	22:34	73	9	22	31	38	2	0	2	24:39

WHL East Second All-Star Team (2005)

SEDIN, Daniel

(suh-DEEN, DAN-yehl) **VAN**

Left wing. Shoots left. 6'1", 187 lbs. Born, Ornskoldsvik, Sweden, September 26, 1980. Vancouver's 1st choice, 2nd overall, in 1999 Entry Draft.

			Regular Season													Playoffs								
Season	Club	League	GP	G	A	Pts	PIM	PP	SH	GW	S	%	+/-	TF	F%	Min	GP	G	A	Pts	PIM	PP	SH	GW	Min
1997-98	Malmo Jr.	Swe-Jr.	4	3	3	6	4	....	....	....	....	....	....	....	....	....	....	....	....	....	....	....	....	....	....
	MoDo Jr.	Swe-Jr.	26	26	14	40	....	....	....	....	....	....	....	....	....	....	....	....	....	....	....	....	....	....	....
	MoDo	Sweden	45	4	8	12	26	....	....	....	....	....	....	....	....	....	9	0	0	0	2	....	....	....	....
1998-99	MoDo	Sweden	50	21	21	42	20	....	....	....	....	....	....	....	....	....	13	4	8	12	14	....	....	....	....
99-2000	MoDo	Sweden	50	19	26	45	28	....	....	....	....	....	....	....	....	....	13	*8	6	14	18	....	....	....	....
	MoDo	EuroHL	4	3	3	6	0	....	....	....	....	....	....	....	....	....	2	0	0	0	0	....	....	....	....
2000-01	Vancouver	NHL	75	20	14	34	24	10	0	3	127	15.7	–3	10	60.0	13:00	4	1	2	3	0	0	0	0	16:15
2001-02	Vancouver	NHL	79	9	23	32	32	4	0	2	117	7.7	1	18	33.3	12:22	6	0	1	1	0	0	0	0	10:44
2002-03	Vancouver	NHL	79	14	17	31	34	4	0	2	134	10.4	8	24	45.8	12:26	14	1	5	6	8	1	0	1	12:23
2003-04	Vancouver	NHL	82	18	36	54	18	1	0	3	153	11.8	18	71	47.9	13:33	7	1	2	3	0	1	0	0	16:03
2004-05	MODO	Sweden	49	13	20	33	40	....	....	....	....	....	....	....	....	....	6	0	3	3	6	....	....	....	....
2005-06	Vancouver	NHL	82	22	49	71	34	11	0	4	204	10.8	7	49	42.9	16:40	....	....	....	....	....	....	....	....	....
	Sweden	Olympics	8	1	3	4	2	....	....	....	....	....	....	....	....	....	....	....	....	....	....	....	....	....	....
2006-07	Vancouver	NHL	81	36	48	84	36	16	0	8	236	15.3	19	44	22.7	18:04	12	2	3	5	4	0	0	0	21:31
2007-08	Vancouver	NHL	82	29	45	74	50	12	0	7	247	11.7	6	38	44.7	19:03	....	....	....	....	....	....	....	....	....
2008-09	Vancouver	NHL	82	31	51	82	36	9	0	7	285	10.9	24	35	40.0	18:48	10	4	6	10	8	2	0	0	18:37
2009-10	Vancouver	NHL	63	29	56	85	28	8	0	8	225	12.9	36	33	33.3	19:08	12	5	9	14	12	1	0	2	19:46
	Sweden	Olympics	4	1	2	3	0	....	....	....	....	....	....	....	....	....	....	....	....	....	....	....	....	....	....
2010-11	Vancouver	NHL	82	41	63	*104	32	*18	0	10	266	15.4	30	17	23.5	18:33	25	9	11	20	32	*5	0	2	20:12
2011-12	Vancouver	NHL	72	30	37	67	40	10	0	6	229	13.1	14	19	31.6	18:49	2	0	2	2	0	0	0	0	20:07
2012-13	Vancouver	NHL	47	12	28	40	18	3	0	3	138	8.7	12	7	42.9	19:01	4	0	3	3	14	0	0	0	20:43
	NHL Totals		906	291	467	758	382	106	0	63	2361	12.3		365	39.2	16:30	96	23	44	67	78	10	0	5	17:58

NHL Second All-Star Team (2010) • NHL First All-Star Team (2011) • Art Ross Trophy (2011) • Ted Lindsay Award (2011)

Played in NHL All-Star Game (2011, 2012)

Signed as a free agent by **MODO** (Sweden), September 18, 2004.

SEDIN, Henrik

(suh-DEEN, HEHN-rihk) **VAN**

Center. Shoots left. 6'2", 188 lbs. Born, Ornskoldsvik, Sweden, September 26, 1980. Vancouver's 2nd choice, 3rd overall, in 1999 Entry Draft.

			Regular Season													Playoffs								
Season	Club	League	GP	G	A	Pts	PIM	PP	SH	GW	S	%	+/-	TF	F%	Min	GP	G	A	Pts	PIM	PP	SH	GW	Min
1997-98	Malmo Jr.	Swe-Jr.	8	4	7	11	6	....	....	....	....	....	....	....	....	....	....	....	....	....	....	....	....	....	....
	MoDo Jr.	Swe-Jr.	26	14	22	36	....	....	....	....	....	....	....	....	....	....	....	....	....	....	....	....	....	....	....
	MoDo	Sweden	39	1	4	5	8	....	....	....	....	....	....	....	....	....	7	0	0	0	0	....	....	....	....
1998-99	MoDo	Sweden	49	12	22	34	32	....	....	....	....	....	....	....	....	....	13	2	8	10	6	....	....	....	....
99-2000	MoDo	Sweden	50	9	38	47	22	....	....	....	....	....	....	....	....	....	13	5	9	14	2	....	....	....	....
2000-01	Vancouver	NHL	82	9	20	29	38	2	0	1	98	9.2	–2	1020	44.1	13:31	4	0	4	4	0	0	0	0	16:31
2001-02	Vancouver	NHL	82	16	20	36	36	3	0	1	78	20.5	9	785	47.4	12:48	6	3	0	3	0	0	0	1	11:55
2002-03	Vancouver	NHL	78	8	31	39	38	4	1	1	81	9.9	9	995	48.2	13:58	14	3	2	5	8	1	0	0	13:01
2003-04	Vancouver	NHL	76	11	31	42	32	2	0	2	99	11.1	23	961	50.0	14:02	7	2	2	4	2	2	0	0	16:02
2004-05	MODO	Sweden	44	14	22	36	50	....	....	....	....	....	....	....	....	....	6	1	3	4	6	....	....	....	....
2005-06	Vancouver	NHL	82	18	57	75	56	5	1	0	113	15.9	11	1238	50.7	16:54	....	....	....	....	....	....	....	....	....
	Sweden	Olympics	8	3	1	4	2	....	....	....	....	....	....	....	....	....	....	....	....	....	....	....	....	....	....
2006-07	Vancouver	NHL	82	10	71	81	66	1	0	2	134	7.5	19	1220	52.5	18:26	12	2	2	4	14	1	0	1	22:12
2007-08	Vancouver	NHL	82	15	61	76	56	4	1	2	141	10.6	6	1369	47.0	19:31	....	....	....	....	....	....	....	....	....
2008-09	Vancouver	NHL	82	22	60	82	48	4	0	8	143	15.4	22	1364	49.6	19:31	10	4	6	10	2	1	0	0	20:07
2009-10	Vancouver	NHL	82	29	*83	*112	48	4	2	5	166	17.5	35	1527	49.5	19:41	12	3	11	14	6	0	0	1	20:38
	Sweden	Olympics	4	0	2	2	2	....	....	....	....	....	....	....	....	....	....	....	....	....	....	....	....	....	....
2010-11	Vancouver	NHL	82	19	*75	94	40	8	0	4	157	12.1	26	1387	52.0	19:16	25	3	*19	22	16	2	0	1	20:56
2011-12	Vancouver	NHL	82	14	*67	81	52	8	0	6	113	12.4	23	1302	50.1	19:05	5	2	3	5	4	2	0	0	21:21
2012-13	Vancouver	NHL	48	11	34	45	24	1	1	1	70	15.7	19	891	49.4	19:21	4	0	3	3	4	0	0	0	20:45
	NHL Totals		940	182	610	792	534	46	6	33	1393	13.1		14059	49.4	17:08	99	22	52	74	56	9	0	4	18:48

NHL First All-Star Team (2010, 2011) • Art Ross Trophy (2010) • Hart Memorial Trophy (2010)

Played in NHL All-Star Game (2008, 2011, 2012)

Signed as a free agent by **MODO** (Sweden), September 18, 2004.

SEGAL, Brandon

(SEE-guhl, BRAN-duhn)

Right wing. Shoots right. 6'2", 215 lbs. Born, Richmond, B.C., July 12, 1983. Nashville's 2nd choice, 102nd overall, in 2002 Entry Draft.

			Regular Season														Playoffs								
Season	Club	League	GP	G	A	Pts	PIM	PP	SH	GW	S	%	+/-	TF	F%	Min	GP	G	A	Pts	PIM	PP	SH	GW	Min
99-2000	Calgary Hitmen	WHL	44	2	6	8	76	....	....	....	....	....	....	....	....	....	13	1	1	2	13	....	....	....	....
	Delta Ice Hawks	PIJHL	....	....	....	....	....	....	....	....	....	....	....	....	....	....	3	0	1	1	2	....	....	....	....
2000-01	Calgary Hitmen	WHL	72	16	11	27	103	....	....	....	....	....	....	....	....	....	12	1	1	2	17	....	....	....	....
2001-02	Calgary Hitmen	WHL	71	43	40	83	122	....	....	....	....	....	....	....	....	....	7	1	4	5	16	....	....	....	....
2002-03	Calgary Hitmen	WHL	71	31	27	58	104	....	....	....	....	....	....	....	....	....	5	2	2	4	4	....	....	....	....
2003-04	Calgary Hitmen	WHL	28	18	12	30	29	....	....	....	....	....	....	....	....	....	....	....	....	....	....	....	....	....	....
	Milwaukee	AHL	44	11	10	21	54	....	....	....	....	....	....	....	....	....	13	2	1	3	21	....	....	....	....
2004-05	Milwaukee	AHL	59	7	8	15	45	....	....	....	....	....	....	....	....	....	3	1	0	1	11	....	....	....	....
	Rockford IceHogs	UHL	10	5	4	9	27	....	....	....	....	....	....	....	....	....	11	11	5	16	10	....	....	....	....
2005-06	Milwaukee	AHL	79	18	15	33	126	....	....	....	....	....	....	....	....	....	21	1	2	3	16	....	....	....	....
2006-07	Milwaukee	AHL	77	20	9	29	84	....	....	....	....	....	....	....	....	....	4	1	0	1	2	....	....	....	....
2007-08	Portland Pirates	AHL	54	5	9	14	46	....	....	....	....	....	....	....	....	....	....	....	....	....	....	....	....	....	....
	Norfolk Admirals	AHL	22	7	6	13	25	....	....	....	....	....	....	....	....	....	....	....	....	....	....	....	....	....	....
2008-09	**Tampa Bay**	**NHL**	**2**	**0**	**0**	**0**	**0**	**0**	**0**	**0**	**2**	**0.0**	**0**	**0**	**0.0**	**13:48**	....	....	....	....	....	....	....	....	....
	Norfolk Admirals	AHL	69	26	26	52	95	....	....	....	....	....	....	....	....	....	....	....	....	....	....	....	....	....	....
2009-10	**Los Angeles**	**NHL**	**25**	**1**	**1**	**2**	**20**	**0**	**0**	**0**	**24**	**4.2**	**0**	**3**	**0.0**	**6:47**	....	....	....	....	....	....	....	....	....
	Manchester	AHL	21	6	8	14	34	....	....	....	....	....	....	....	....	....	....	....	....	....	....	....	....	....	....
	Dallas	**NHL**	**19**	**5**	**5**	**10**	**18**	**0**	**0**	**2**	**31**	**16.1**	**3**	**0**	**0.0**	**11:20**	....	....	....	....	....	....	....	....	....
2010-11	**Dallas**	**NHL**	**46**	**5**	**5**	**10**	**41**	**0**	**0**	**1**	**40**	**12.5**	**0**	**4**	**50.0**	**8:17**	....	....	....	....	....	....	....	....	....
	Texas Stars	AHL	30	7	10	17	38	....	....	....	....	....	....	....	....	....	....	....	....	....	....	....	....	....	....
2011-12	Rockford IceHogs	AHL	53	13	12	25	63	....	....	....	....	....	....	....	....	....	....	....	....	....	....	....	....	....	....
	Tampa Bay	**NHL**	**10**	**0**	**0**	**0**	**4**	**0**	**0**	**0**	**8**	**0.0**	**–2**	**4**	**25.0**	**6:35**	....	....	....	....	....	....	....	....	....
	Norfolk Admirals	AHL	8	5	6	11	6	....	....	....	....	....	....	....	....	....	18	5	4	9	17	....	....	....	....
2012-13	Connecticut	AHL	73	24	20	44	82	....	....	....	....	....	....	....	....	....	....	....	....	....	....	....	....	....	....
	NY Rangers	**NHL**	**1**	**0**	**0**	**0**	**2**	**0**	**0**	**0**	**0**	**0.0**	**0**	**0**	**0.0**	**5:21**	....	....	....	....	....	....	....	....	....
	NHL Totals		**103**	**11**	**11**	**22**	**85**	**0**	**0**	**3**	**105**	**10.5**		**11**	**27.3**	**8:24**	....	....	....	....	....	....	....	....	....

Traded to **Anaheim** by **Nashville** for future considerations, June 25, 2007. Traded to **Tampa Bay** by **Anaheim** with Anaheim's 7th round choice (David Carle) in 2008 Entry Draft for Jay Leach, February 26, 2008. Signed as a free agent by **Los Angeles**, July 13, 2009. Claimed on waivers by **Dallas** from **Los Angeles**, February 11, 2010. Signed as a free agent by **Chicago**, September 1, 2011. Traded to **Tampa Bay** by **Chicago** for future considerations, February 21, 2012. Signed as a free agent by **NY Rangers**, July 11, 2012.

SEGUIN, Tyler

(SAY-gihn, TIGH-luhr) **DAL**

Center. Shoots right. 6'1", 182 lbs. Born, Brampton, Ont., January 31, 1992. Boston's 1st choice, 2nd overall, in 2010 Entry Draft.

			Regular Season														Playoffs								
Season	Club	League	GP	G	A	Pts	PIM	PP	SH	GW	S	%	+/-	TF	F%	Min	GP	G	A	Pts	PIM	PP	SH	GW	Min
2007-08	Tor. Young Nats	GTHL	51	39	47	86	56	....	....	....	....	....	....	....	....	....	....	....	....	....	....	....	....	....	....
2008-09	Plymouth Whalers	OHL	61	21	46	67	28	....	....	....	....	....	....	....	....	....	11	5	11	16	8	....	....	....	....
2009-10	Plymouth Whalers	OHL	63	48	58	*106	54	....	....	....	....	....	....	....	....	....	9	5	5	10	8	....	....	....	....
2010-11 ♦	**Boston**	**NHL**	**74**	**11**	**11**	**22**	**18**	**1**	**0**	**0**	**131**	**8.4**	**–4**	**303**	**49.5**	**12:13**	**13**	**3**	**4**	**7**	**2**	**0**	**0**	**0**	**10:35**
2011-12	**Boston**	**NHL**	**81**	**29**	**38**	**67**	**30**	**5**	**0**	**7**	**242**	**12.0**	**34**	**106**	**43.4**	**16:56**	**7**	**2**	**1**	**3**	**0**	**0**	**0**	**1**	**18:14**
2012-13	EHC Biel-Bienne	Swiss	29	25	15	40	24	....	....	....	....	....	....	....	....	....	....	....	....	....	....	....	....	....	....
	Boston	**NHL**	**48**	**16**	**16**	**32**	**16**	**4**	**0**	**2**	**161**	**9.9**	**23**	**45**	**48.9**	**17:01**	**22**	**1**	**7**	**8**	**4**	**0**	**0**	**0**	**16:03**
	NHL Totals		**203**	**56**	**65**	**121**	**64**	**10**	**0**	**9**	**534**	**10.5**		**454**	**48.0**	**15:14**	**42**	**6**	**12**	**18**	**6**	**0**	**0**	**1**	**14:43**

OHL First All-Star Team (2010) • OHL Player of the Year (2010) • Canadian Major Junior First All-Star Team (2010)

Played in NHL All-Star Game (2012)

Signed as a free agent by **Biel-Bienne** (Swiss), September 20, 2012. Traded to **Dallas** by **Boston** with Rich Peverley and Ryan Button for Loui Eriksson, Joe Morrow, Reilly Smith and Matt Fraser, July 4, 2013.

SEIDENBERG, Dennis

(SIGH-dehn-buhrg, DEH-nihs) **BOS**

Defense. Shoots left. 6'1", 210 lbs. Born, Schwenningen, West Germany, July 18, 1981. Philadelphia's 6th choice, 172nd overall, in 2001 Entry Draft.

			Regular Season														Playoffs								
Season	Club	League	GP	G	A	Pts	PIM	PP	SH	GW	S	%	+/-	TF	F%	Min	GP	G	A	Pts	PIM	PP	SH	GW	Min
99-2000	Mannheim Jr.	Ger-Jr.	52	12	28	40	28	....	....	....	....	....	....	....	....	....	....	....	....	....	....	....	....	....	....
	Adler Mannheim	Germany	3	0	0	0	0	....	....	....	....	....	....	....	....	....	....	....	....	....	....	....	....	....	....
2000-01	Mannheim Jr.	Ger-Jr.	9	3	8	11	20	....	....	....	....	....	....	....	....	....	....	....	....	....	....	....	....	....	....
	Adler Mannheim	Germany	55	2	5	7	6	....	....	....	....	....	....	....	....	....	12	0	1	1	10	....	....	....	....
2001-02	Adler Mannheim	Germany	55	7	13	20	56	....	....	....	....	....	....	....	....	....	8	0	0	0	2	....	....	....	....
2002-03	**Philadelphia**	**NHL**	**58**	**4**	**9**	**13**	**20**	**1**	**0**	**0**	**123**	**3.3**	**8**	**1**	**0.0**	**16:50**	....	....	....	....	....	....	....	....	....
	Philadelphia	AHL	19	5	6	11	17	....	....	....	....	....	....	....	....	....	....	....	....	....	....	....	....	....	....
2003-04	**Philadelphia**	**NHL**	**5**	**0**	**0**	**0**	**2**	**0**	**0**	**0**	**14**	**0.0**	**–4**	**0**	**0.0**	**17:20**	**3**	**0**	**0**	**0**	**0**	**0**	**0**	**0**	**7:36**
	Philadelphia	AHL	33	7	12	19	31	....	....	....	....	....	....	....	....	....	9	2	2	4	4	....	....	....	....
2004-05	Philadelphia	AHL	79	13	28	41	47	....	....	....	....	....	....	....	....	....	18	2	8	10	19	....	....	....	....
2005-06	**Philadelphia**	**NHL**	**29**	**2**	**5**	**7**	**4**	**1**	**0**	**0**	**34**	**5.9**	**–4**	**1**	**0.0**	**14:22**	....	....	....	....	....	....	....	....	....
	Phoenix	**NHL**	**34**	**1**	**10**	**11**	**14**	**1**	**0**	**0**	**49**	**2.0**	**–9**	**0**	**0.0**	**19:13**	....	....	....	....	....	....	....	....	....
	Germany	Olympics	5	0	0	0	6	....	....	....	....	....	....	....	....	....	....	....	....	....	....	....	....	....	....
2006-07	**Phoenix**	**NHL**	**32**	**1**	**1**	**2**	**16**	**0**	**0**	**0**	**36**	**2.8**	**–4**	**0**	**0.0**	**14:43**	....	....	....	....	....	....	....	....	....
	Carolina	**NHL**	**20**	**1**	**5**	**6**	**2**	**0**	**0**	**0**	**47**	**2.1**	**–12**	**0**	**0.0**	**18:29**	....	....	....	....	....	....	....	....	....
2007-08	**Carolina**	**NHL**	**47**	**0**	**15**	**15**	**18**	**0**	**0**	**0**	**80**	**0.0**	**6**	**1**	**100.0**	**18:50**	....	....	....	....	....	....	....	....	....
2008-09	**Carolina**	**NHL**	**70**	**5**	**25**	**30**	**37**	**2**	**0**	**1**	**129**	**3.9**	**–9**	**0**	**0.0**	**22:20**	**16**	**1**	**5**	**6**	**16**	**0**	**0**	**0**	**22:25**
2009-10	**Florida**	**NHL**	**62**	**2**	**21**	**23**	**33**	**1**	**0**	**0**	**116**	**1.7**	**–3**	**1**	**0.0**	**22:55**	....	....	....	....	....	....	....	....	....
	Boston	**NHL**	**17**	**2**	**7**	**9**	**6**	**1**	**0**	**1**	**37**	**5.4**	**9**	**0**	**0.0**	**22:57**	....	....	....	....	....	....	....	....	....
	Germany	Olympics	4	1	0	1	2	....	....	....	....	....	....	....	....	....	....	....	....	....	....	....	....	....	....
2010-11 ♦	**Boston**	**NHL**	**81**	**7**	**25**	**32**	**41**	**1**	**0**	**2**	**166**	**4.2**	**3**	**0**	**0.0**	**23:33**	**25**	**1**	**10**	**11**	**31**	**0**	**0**	**0**	**27:37**
2011-12	**Boston**	**NHL**	**80**	**5**	**18**	**23**	**39**	**0**	**0**	**2**	**174**	**2.9**	**15**	**0**	**0.0**	**24:02**	**7**	**1**	**2**	**3**	**2**	**0**	**0**	**0**	**26:43**
2012-13	Adler Mannheim	Germany	26	2	18	20	20	....	....	....	....	....	....	....	....	....	....	....	....	....	....	....	....	....	....
	Boston	**NHL**	**46**	**4**	**13**	**17**	**10**	**0**	**0**	**2**	**83**	**4.8**	**18**	**0**	**0.0**	**23:48**	**18**	**0**	**1**	**1**	**4**	**0**	**0**	**0**	**25:59**
	NHL Totals		**581**	**34**	**154**	**188**	**242**	**8**	**0**	**8**	**1088**	**3.1**		**4**	**25.0**	**20:56**	**69**	**3**	**18**	**21**	**53**	**0**	**0**	**0**	**25:02**

• Missed majority of 2003-04 due to leg injury vs. Edmonton, January 10, 2004. Traded to **Phoenix** by **Philadelphia** with Philadelphia's 4th round choice (later traded to NY Islanders - NY Islanders selected Tomas Marcinko) in 2006 Entry Draft for Petr Nedved and Phoenix's 4th round choice (Joonas Lehtivuori) in 2006 Entry Draft, January 20, 2006. Traded to **Carolina** by **Phoenix** for Kevyn Adams, January 8, 2007. Signed as a free agent by **Florida**, September 14, 2009. Traded to **Boston** by **Florida** with Matt Bartkowski for Byron Bitz, Craig Weller and Tampa Bay's 2nd round choice (previously acquired, Florida selected Alexander Petrovic) in 2010 Entry Draft, March 3, 2010. Signed as a free agent by **Mannheim** (Germany), September 21, 2012.

SEKERA, Andrej

(seh-KAIR-ah, AWN-dray) **CAR**

Defense. Shoots left. 6', 201 lbs. Born, Bojnice, Czech., June 8, 1986. Buffalo's 3rd choice, 71st overall, in 2004 Entry Draft.

			Regular Season														Playoffs								
Season	Club	League	GP	G	A	Pts	PIM	PP	SH	GW	S	%	+/-	TF	F%	Min	GP	G	A	Pts	PIM	PP	SH	GW	Min
2001-02	Dukla Trencin Jr.	Slovak-Jr.	52	5	10	15	10	....	....	....	....	....	....	....	....	....	....	....	....	....	....	....	....	....	....
2002-03	Dukla Trencin Jr.	Slovak-Jr.	48	9	15	24	20	....	....	....	....	....	....	....	....	....	....	....	....	....	....	....	....	....	....
2003-04	Dukla Trencin Jr.	Slovak-Jr.	42	5	12	17	40	....	....	....	....	....	....	....	....	....	2	0	1	1	4	....	....	....	....
	Dukla Trencin	Slovakia	3	0	0	0	2	....	....	....	....	....	....	....	....	....	....	....	....	....	....	....	....	....	....
	Dukla Trencin U18	Svk-U18	5	0	0	0	0	....	....	....	....	....	....	....	....	....	....	....	....	....	....	....	....	....	....
2004-05	Owen Sound	OHL	51	7	21	28	18	....	....	....	....	....	....	....	....	....	6	0	4	4	4	....	....	....	....
2005-06	Owen Sound	OHL	51	21	34	55	54	....	....	....	....	....	....	....	....	....	11	5	8	13	9	....	....	....	....
2006-07	**Buffalo**	**NHL**	**2**	**0**	**0**	**0**	**2**	**0**	**0**	**0**	**0**	**0.0**	**1**	**0**	**0.0**	**7:31**	....	....	....	....	....	....	....	....	....
	Rochester	AHL	54	3	16	19	28	....	....	....	....	....	....	....	....	....	....	....	....	....	....	....	....	....	....
2007-08	**Buffalo**	**NHL**	**37**	**2**	**6**	**8**	**16**	**0**	**0**	**1**	**28**	**7.1**	**5**	**0**	**0.0**	**19:37**	....	....	....	....	....	....	....	....	....
	Rochester	AHL	40	2	15	17	22	....	....	....	....	....	....	....	....	....	....	....	....	....	....	....	....	....	....
2008-09	**Buffalo**	**NHL**	**69**	**3**	**16**	**19**	**22**	**1**	**0**	**1**	**84**	**3.6**	**–11**	**1**	**0.0**	**20:42**	....	....	....	....	....	....	....	....	....
2009-10	**Buffalo**	**NHL**	**49**	**4**	**7**	**11**	**6**	**0**	**0**	**0**	**59**	**6.8**	**–1**	**1**	**0.0**	**17:27**	**6**	**0**	**0**	**0**	**7**	**0**	**0**	**0**	**13:55**
	Slovakia	Olympics	7	1	0	1	0	....	....	....	....	....	....	....	....	....	....	....	....	....	....	....	....	....	....
2010-11	**Buffalo**	**NHL**	**76**	**3**	**26**	**29**	**34**	**0**	**0**	**0**	**88**	**3.4**	**11**	**0**	**0.0**	**21:06**	**2**	**1**	**0**	**1**	**4**	**0**	**0**	**0**	**16:18**
2011-12	**Buffalo**	**NHL**	**69**	**3**	**10**	**13**	**18**	**1**	**0**	**0**	**88**	**3.4**	**3**	**1**	**0.0**	**19:36**	....	....	....	....	....	....	....	....	....
2012-13	Bratislava	KHL	25	3	9	12	8	....	....	....	....	....	....	....	....	....	....	....	....	....	....	....	....	....	....
	Buffalo	**NHL**	**37**	**2**	**10**	**12**	**4**	**0**	**0**	**0**	**33**	**6.1**	**–2**	**0**	**0.0**	**21:12**	....	....	....	....	....	....	....	....	....
	NHL Totals		**339**	**17**	**75**	**92**	**102**	**2**	**0**	**2**	**380**	**4.5**		**3**	**0.0**	**19:57**	**8**	**1**	**0**	**1**	**11**	**0**	**0**	**0**	**14:31**

OHL All-Rookie Team (2005) • OHL First All-Star Team (2006)

Signed as a free agent by **Bratislava** (KHL), September 27, 2012. Traded to **Carolina** by **Buffalo** for Jamie McBain and Carolina's 2nd round choice (J.T. Compher) in 2013 Entry Draft, June 30, 2013.

SELANNE, Teemu

(seh-LAH-nee, TEE-moo) **ANA**

Right wing. Shoots right. 6', 200 lbs. Born, Helsinki, Finland, July 3, 1970. Winnipeg's 1st choice, 10th overall, in 1988 Entry Draft.

			Regular Season														Playoffs								
Season	Club	League	GP	G	A	Pts	PIM	PP	SH	GW	S	%	+/-	TF	F%	Min	GP	G	A	Pts	PIM	PP	SH	GW	Min
1986-87	Jokerit U18	Fin-U18	....	....	....	....	....	....	....	....	....	....	....	....	....	....	7	10	3	13	2	....	....	....	....
	Jokerit Helsinki Jr.	Fin-Jr.	33	10	12	22	8	....	....	....	....	....	....	....	....	....	....	....	....	....	....	....	....	....	....
1987-88	Jokerit Helsinki Jr.	Fin-Jr.	33	43	23	66	18	....	....	....	....	....	....	....	....	....	5	4	3	7	2	....	....	....	....
	Jokerit Helsinki	Finland-2	5	1	1	2	0	....	....	....	....	....	....	....	....	....	....	....	....	....	....	....	....	....	....
1988-89	PvUK Lahti Jr.	Fin-Jr.	3	3	1	4	2	....	....	....	....	....	....	....	....	....	....	....	....	....	....	....	....	....	....
	Jokerit Helsinki Jr.	Fin-Jr.	3	8	8	16	4	....	....	....	....	....	....	....	....	....	....	....	....	....	....	....	....	....	....
	Jokerit Helsinki	Finland-2	35	36	33	69	14	....	....	....	....	....	....	....	....	....	5	7	3	10	4	....	....	....	....
1989-90	Jokerit Helsinki	Finland	11	4	8	12	0	....	....	....	....	....	....	....	....	....	....	....	....	....	....	....	....	....	....
1990-91	Jokerit Helsinki Jr.	Fin-Jr.	4	3	2	5	10	....	....	....	....	....	....	....	....	....	....	....	....	....	....	....	....	....	....
	Jokerit Helsinki	Finland	42	33	25	58	12	....	....	....	....	....	....	....	....	....	....	....	....	....	....	....	....	....	....
1991-92	Jokerit Helsinki	Finland	44	39	23	62	20	....	....	....	....	....	....	....	....	....	10	10	7	17	18	....	....	....	....
	Finland	Olympics	8	7	4	11	6	....	....	....	....	....	....	....	....	....	....	....	....	....	....	....	....	....	....
1992-93	**Winnipeg**	**NHL**	**84**	***76**	**56**	**132**	**45**	**24**	**0**	**7**	**387**	**19.6**	**8**	....	....	....	**6**	**4**	**2**	**6**	**2**	**2**	**0**	**2**	....
1993-94	**Winnipeg**	**NHL**	**51**	**25**	**29**	**54**	**22**	**11**	**0**	**2**	**191**	**13.1**	**–23**	....	....	....	....	....	....	....	....	....	....	....	....
1994-95	Jokerit Helsinki	Finland	20	7	12	19	6	....	....	....	....	....	....	....	....	....	....	....	....	....	....	....	....	....	....
	Winnipeg	**NHL**	**45**	**22**	**26**	**48**	**2**	**8**	**2**	**1**	**167**	**13.2**	**1**	....	....	....	....	....	....	....	....	....	....	....	....
1995-96	**Winnipeg**	**NHL**	**51**	**24**	**48**	**72**	**18**	**6**	**1**	**4**	**163**	**14.7**	**3**	....	....	....	....	....	....	....	....	....	....	....	....
	Anaheim	**NHL**	**28**	**16**	**20**	**36**	**4**	**3**	**0**	**1**	**104**	**15.4**	**2**	....	....	....	....	....	....	....	....	....	....	....	....
1996-97	**Anaheim**	**NHL**	**78**	**51**	**58**	**109**	**34**	**11**	**1**	**8**	**273**	**18.7**	**28**	....	....	....	**11**	**7**	**3**	**10**	**4**	**3**	**0**	**1**	....
1997-98	**Anaheim**	**NHL**	**73**	***52**	**34**	**86**	**30**	**10**	**1**	**10**	**268**	**19.4**	**12**	....	....	....	....	....	....	....	....	....	....	....	....
	Finland	Olympics	5	4	6	10	8	....	....	....	....	....	....	....	....	....	....	....	....	....	....	....	....	....	....
1998-99	**Anaheim**	**NHL**	**75**	***47**	**60**	**107**	**30**	***25**	**0**	**7**	**281**	**16.7**	**18**	**5**	**20.0**	**22:47**	**4**	**2**	**2**	**4**	**2**	**1**	**0**	**0**	**22:23**
99-2000	**Anaheim**	**NHL**	**79**	**33**	**52**	**85**	**12**	**8**	**0**	**6**	**236**	**14.0**	**6**	**13**	**23.1**	**22:44**	....	....	....	....	....	....	....	....	....
2000-01	**Anaheim**	**NHL**	**61**	**26**	**33**	**59**	**36**	**10**	**0**	**5**	**202**	**12.9**	**–8**	**4**	**50.0**	**21:51**	....	....	....	....	....	....	....	....	....
	San Jose	**NHL**	**12**	**7**	**6**	**13**	**0**	**2**	**0**	**2**	**31**	**22.6**	**1**	**4**	**75.0**	**18:14**	**6**	**0**	**2**	**2**	**2**	**0**	**0**	**0**	**17:13**
2001-02	**San Jose**	**NHL**	**82**	**29**	**25**	**54**	**40**	**9**	**1**	**8**	**202**	**14.4**	**–11**	**12**	**25.0**	**16:58**	**12**	**5**	**3**	**8**	**2**	**2**	**0**	**1**	**16:51**
	Finland	Olympics	4	3	0	3	2	....	....	....	....	....	....	....	....	....	....	....	....	....	....	....	....	....	....
2002-03	**San Jose**	**NHL**	**82**	**28**	**36**	**64**	**30**	**7**	**0**	**5**	**253**	**11.1**	**–6**	**107**	**42.1**	**19:14**	....	....	....	....	....	....	....	....	....
2003-04	**Colorado**	**NHL**	**78**	**16**	**16**	**32**	**32**	**6**	**1**	**4**	**182**	**8.8**	**2**	**80**	**43.8**	**16:10**	**10**	**0**	**3**	**3**	**2**	**0**	**0**	**0**	**12:53**
2004-05			DID NOT PLAY																						
2005-06	**Anaheim**	**NHL**	**80**	**40**	**50**	**90**	**44**	**18**	**0**	**5**	**267**	**15.0**	**28**	**209**	**41.6**	**17:48**	**16**	**6**	**8**	**14**	**6**	**1**	**0**	**2**	**17:56**
	Finland	Olympics	8	*6	5	*11	4	....	....	....	....	....	....	....	....	....	....	....	....	....	....	....	....	....	....
2006-07 ◆	**Anaheim**	**NHL**	**82**	**48**	**46**	**94**	**82**	***25**	**0**	***10**	**257**	**18.7**	**26**	**351**	**50.7**	**17:42**	**21**	**5**	**10**	**15**	**10**	**0**	**0**	**2**	**19:08**
2007-08	**Anaheim**	**NHL**	**26**	**12**	**11**	**23**	**8**	**7**	**0**	**2**	**87**	**13.8**	**5**	**67**	**50.8**	**18:07**	**6**	**2**	**2**	**4**	**6**	**2**	**0**	**1**	**19:35**
2008-09	**Anaheim**	**NHL**	**65**	**27**	**27**	**54**	**36**	**16**	**0**	**5**	**186**	**14.5**	**–3**	**224**	**49.1**	**16:29**	**13**	**4**	**2**	**6**	**4**	**2**	**0**	**1**	**15:08**
2009-10	**Anaheim**	**NHL**	**54**	**27**	**21**	**48**	**16**	**14**	**0**	**5**	**173**	**15.6**	**3**	**131**	**47.3**	**17:19**	....	....	....	....	....	....	....	....	....
	Finland	Olympics	6	0	2	2	0	....	....	....	....	....	....	....	....	....	....	....	....	....	....	....	....	....	....
2010-11	**Anaheim**	**NHL**	**73**	**31**	**49**	**80**	**49**	**16**	**0**	**5**	**213**	**14.6**	**6**	**218**	**44.5**	**17:56**	**6**	**6**	**1**	**7**	**12**	**4**	**0**	**0**	**18:58**
2011-12	**Anaheim**	**NHL**	**82**	**26**	**40**	**66**	**50**	**12**	**0**	**4**	**210**	**12.4**	**–1**	**300**	**48.3**	**17:53**	....	....	....	....	....	....	....	....	....
2012-13	**Anaheim**	**NHL**	**46**	**12**	**12**	**24**	**28**	**3**	**0**	**1**	**96**	**12.5**	**–10**	**168**	**50.6**	**15:42**	**7**	**1**	**2**	**3**	**6**	**1**	**0**	**1**	**14:00**
	NHL Totals		**1387**	**675**	**755**	**1430**	**648**	**251**	**7**	**107**	**4429**	**15.2**		**1893**	**47.0**	**18:34**	**118**	**42**	**40**	**82**	**58**	**18**	**0**	**11**	**17:13**

NHL All-Rookie Team (1993) • NHL First All-Star Team (1993, 1997) • Calder Memorial Trophy (1993) • NHL Second All-Star Team (1998, 1999) • Maurice "Rocket" Richard Trophy (1999) • Olympic All-Star Team (2006) • Best Forward - Olympics (2006) • Bill Masterton Memorial Trophy (2006)

Played in NHL All-Star Game (1993, 1994, 1996, 1997, 1998, 1999, 2000, 2002, 2003, 2007)

• Missed majority of 1989-90 due to leg injury vs. JyP HT Jyvaskyla (Finland), October 19, 1989. Traded to **Anaheim** by **Winnipeg** with Marc Chouinard and Winnipeg's 4th round choice (later traded to Toronto, later traded to Montreal – Montreal selected Kim Staal) in 1996 Entry Draft for Chad Kilger, Oleg Tverdovsky and Anaheim's 3rd round choice (Per-Anton Lundstrom) in 1996 Entry Draft, February 7, 1996. Traded to **San Jose** by **Anaheim** for Jeff Friesen, Steve Shields and San Jose's 2nd round choice (later traded to Dallas – Dallas selected Vojtech Polak) in 2003 Entry Draft, March 5, 2001. Signed as a free agent by **Colorado**, July 3, 2003. Signed as a free agent by **Anaheim**, August 22, 2005. • Missed majority of 2007-08 contemplating retirement.

SELLECK, Eric

(SEHL-ehk, AIR-ihk) **FLA**

Left wing. Shoots left. 6'2", 208 lbs. Born, Spencerville, Ont., October 20, 1987.

Season	Club	League	GP	G	A	Pts	PIM	PP	SH	GW	S	%	+/-	TF	F%	Min	GP	G	A	Pts	PIM	PP	SH	GW	Min
2006-07	Pembroke	ON-Jr.A	53	23	24	47	137	....	....	....	....	....	....	....	....	....	15	4	8	12	29	....	....	....	....
2007-08	Pembroke	ON-Jr.A	49	43	38	81	120	....	....	....	....	....	....	....	....	....	14	8	21	29	28	....	....	....	....
2008-09	Oswego State	NCAA-3	26	13	13	26	45	....	....	....	....	....	....	....	....	....	....	....	....	....	....	....	....	....	....
2009-10	Oswego State	NCAA-3	28	21	33	54	48	....	....	....	....	....	....	....	....	....	....	....	....	....	....	....	....	....	....
2010-11	Rochester	AHL	67	5	11	16	214	....	....	....	....	....	....	....	....	....	....	....	....	....	....	....	....	....	....
2011-12	San Antonio	AHL	71	5	4	9	204	....	....	....	....	....	....	....	....	....	9	0	0	0	4	....	....	....	....
2012-13	San Antonio	AHL	60	5	11	16	181	....	....	....	....	....	....	....	....	....	....	....	....	....	....	....	....	....	....
	Florida	**NHL**	**2**	**0**	**1**	**1**	**17**	**0**	**0**	**0**	**2**	**0.0**	**2**	**0**	**0.0**	**7:55**	....	....	....	....	....	....	....	....	....
	NHL Totals		**2**	**0**	**1**	**1**	**17**	**0**	**0**	**0**	**2**	**0.0**		**0**	**0.0**	**7:55**	....	....	....	....	....	....	....	....	....

SUNYAC (NCAA-3) Rookie of the Year (2009) • SUNYAC (NCAA-3) Player of the Year (2010) • NCAA-3 East All-American Team (2010)

Signed as a free agent by **Florida**, April 21, 2010.

SEMIN, Alexander

(SEH-min, al-EHX-AN-duhr) **CAR**

Left wing. Shoots right. 6'2", 209 lbs. Born, Krasnoyarsk, USSR, March 3, 1984. Washington's 2nd choice, 13th overall, in 2002 Entry Draft.

Season	Club	League	GP	G	A	Pts	PIM	PP	SH	GW	S	%	+/-	TF	F%	Min	GP	G	A	Pts	PIM	PP	SH	GW	Min
2001-02	Chelyabinsk	Russia-2	46	13	8	21	52	....	....	....	....	....	....	....	....	....	2	2	0	2	0	....	....	....	....
2002-03	Lada Togliatti	Russia	47	10	7	17	36	....	....	....	....	....	....	....	....	....	10	*5	3	8	10	....	....	....	....
2003-04	**Washington**	**NHL**	**52**	**10**	**12**	**22**	**36**	**4**	**0**	**2**	**92**	**10.9**	**–2**	**6**	**50.0**	**12:37**	....	....	....	....	....	....	....	....	....
	Portland Pirates	AHL	4	3	1	4	6	....	....	....	....	....	....	....	....	....	7	4	7	11	19	....	....	....	....
2004-05	Lada Togliatti	Russia	50	19	11	30	56	....	....	....	....	....	....	....	....	....	10	1	1	2	0	....	....	....	....
2005-06	Lada Togliatti	Russia	16	5	4	9	52	....	....	....	....	....	....	....	....	....	....	....	....	....	....	....	....	....	....
	Mytischi	Russia	26	3	7	10	24	....	....	....	....	....	....	....	....	....	8	3	2	5	6	....	....	....	....
2006-07	**Washington**	**NHL**	**77**	**38**	**35**	**73**	**90**	**17**	**0**	**6**	**243**	**15.6**	**–7**	**44**	**27.3**	**18:24**	....	....	....	....	....	....	....	....	....
2007-08	**Washington**	**NHL**	**63**	**26**	**16**	**42**	**54**	**10**	**0**	**2**	**185**	**14.1**	**–18**	**11**	**36.4**	**16:55**	**7**	**3**	**5**	**8**	**8**	**2**	**0**	**1**	**19:45**
2008-09	**Washington**	**NHL**	**62**	**34**	**45**	**79**	**77**	**8**	**0**	**8**	**223**	**15.2**	**25**	**24**	**50.0**	**19:14**	**14**	**5**	**9**	**14**	**16**	**1**	**0**	**1**	**19:58**
2009-10	**Washington**	**NHL**	**73**	**40**	**44**	**84**	**66**	**8**	**2**	**5**	**278**	**14.4**	**36**	**16**	**37.5**	**19:07**	**7**	**0**	**2**	**2**	**4**	**0**	**0**	**0**	**19:21**
	Russia	Olympics	4	0	2	2	4	....	....	....	....	....	....	....	....	....	....	....	....	....	....	....	....	....	....
2010-11	**Washington**	**NHL**	**65**	**28**	**26**	**54**	**71**	**6**	**1**	**4**	**196**	**14.3**	**22**	**13**	**30.8**	**18:04**	**9**	**4**	**2**	**6**	**8**	**0**	**0**	**1**	**18:36**
2011-12	**Washington**	**NHL**	**77**	**21**	**33**	**54**	**56**	**2**	**0**	**1**	**183**	**11.5**	**9**	**11**	**9.1**	**16:47**	**14**	**3**	**1**	**4**	**10**	**2**	**0**	**1**	**17:28**
2012-13	Sokol Krasnoyarsk	Russia-2	4	2	2	4	8	....	....	....	....	....	....	....	....	....	....	....	....	....	....	....	....	....	....
	Nizhny Novgorod	KHL	20	7	10	17	10	....	....	....	....	....	....	....	....	....	....	....	....	....	....	....	....	....	....
	Carolina	**NHL**	**44**	**13**	**31**	**44**	**46**	**4**	**0**	**1**	**150**	**8.7**	**14**	**21**	**23.8**	**20:57**	....	....	....	....	....	....	....	....	....
	NHL Totals		**513**	**210**	**242**	**452**	**496**	**59**	**3**	**29**	**1550**	**13.5**		**146**	**32.2**	**17:46**	**51**	**15**	**19**	**34**	**46**	**5**	**0**	**4**	**18:56**

Signed as a free agent by **Togliatti** (Russia), September 25, 2004. • Suspended by **Washington** for failing to report to **Portland** (AHL), September 28, 2004. Signed as a free agent by **Mytischi** (Russia), November 22, 2005. Signed as a free agent by **Carolina**, July 26, 2012. Signed as a free agent by **Krasnoyarsk** (Russia-2), September 25, 2012. Signed as a free agent by **Nizhny Novgorod** (KHL), October 12, 2012.

SESTITO, Tim

(sehs-TEE-toh, TIHM) **N.J.**

Center. Shoots left. 5'11", 200 lbs. Born, Rome, NY, August 28, 1984.

Season	Club	League	GP	G	A	Pts	PIM	PP	SH	GW	S	%	+/-	TF	F%	Min	GP	G	A	Pts	PIM	PP	SH	GW	Min
2001-02	Plymouth Whalers	OHL	51	10	11	21	40	....	....	....	....	....	....	....	....	....	6	0	0	0	0	....	....	....	....
2002-03	Plymouth Whalers	OHL	61	11	7	18	49	....	....	....	....	....	....	....	....	....	18	2	3	5	4	....	....	....	....
2003-04	Plymouth Whalers	OHL	57	10	20	30	68	....	....	....	....	....	....	....	....	....	9	4	1	5	14	....	....	....	....
2004-05	Plymouth Whalers	OHL	67	14	18	32	93	....	....	....	....	....	....	....	....	....	4	0	0	0	14	....	....	....	....
	Bridgeport	AHL	9	2	1	3	12	....	....	....	....	....	....	....	....	....	....	....	....	....	....	....	....	....	....
2005-06	Greenville	ECHL	72	21	23	44	127	....	....	....	....	....	....	....	....	....	6	2	2	4	24	....	....	....	....
2006-07	Wilkes-Barre	AHL	4	0	0	0	6	....	....	....	....	....	....	....	....	....	....	....	....	....	....	....	....	....	....
	Stockton Thunder	ECHL	66	13	13	26	132	....	....	....	....	....	....	....	....	....	6	2	1	3	6	....	....	....	....
2007-08	Springfield	AHL	77	7	10	17	175	....	....	....	....	....	....	....	....	....	....	....	....	....	....	....	....	....	....
2008-09	**Edmonton**	**NHL**	**1**	**0**	**0**	**0**	**0**	**0**	**0**	**0**	**1**	**0.0**	**0**	**2**	**50.0**	**5:53**	....	....	....	....	....	....	....	....	....
	Springfield	AHL	51	5	3	8	77	....	....	....	....	....	....	....	....	....	....	....	....	....	....	....	....	....	....
2009-10	**New Jersey**	**NHL**	**9**	**0**	**1**	**1**	**2**	**0**	**0**	**0**	**7**	**0.0**	**–2**	**64**	**53.1**	**12:16**	....	....	....	....	....	....	....	....	....
	Lowell Devils	AHL	66	18	17	35	38	....	....	....	....	....	....	....	....	....	5	0	0	0	8	....	....	....	....
2010-11	**New Jersey**	**NHL**	**36**	**0**	**2**	**2**	**9**	**0**	**0**	**0**	**22**	**0.0**	**–5**	**253**	**45.9**	**10:49**	....	....	....	....	....	....	....	....	....
	Albany Devils	AHL	23	5	8	13	28	....	....	....	....	....	....	....	....	....	....	....	....	....	....	....	....	....	....

			Regular Season														Playoffs								
Season	Club	League	GP	G	A	Pts	PIM	PP	SH	GW	S	%	+/-	TF	F%	Min	GP	G	A	Pts	PIM	PP	SH	GW	Min
2011-12	**New Jersey**	**NHL**	**18**	**0**	**0**	**0**	**7**	**0**	**0**	**0**	**6**	**0.0**	**–5**	**75**	**41.3**	**8:15**	**1**	**0**	**0**	**0**	**0**	**0**	**0**	**0**	**6:51**
	Albany Devils	AHL	45	9	10	19	127	....	....	....	....	....	....	....	....	....	....	....	....	....	....	....	....	....	....
2012-13	Albany Devils	AHL	67	7	16	23	106	....	....	....	....	....	....	....	....	....	....	....	....	....	....	....	....	....	....
	New Jersey	**NHL**	**6**	**0**	**0**	**0**	**2**	**0**	**0**	**0**	**4**	**0.0**	**1**	**26**	**53.9**	**7:52**	....	....	....	....	....	....	....	....	....
	NHL Totals		**70**	**0**	**3**	**3**	**20**	**0**	**0**	**0**	**40**	**0.0**		**420**	**46.7**	**10:01**	**1**	**0**	**0**	**0**	**0**	**0**	**0**	**0**	**6:51**

Signed as a free agent by **Edmonton**, August 28, 2006. Traded to **New Jersey** by **Edmonton** for future considerations, July 9, 2009.

SESTITO, Tom (sehs-TEE-toh, TAWM) VAN

Left wing. Shoots left. 6'5", 228 lbs. Born, Rome, NY, September 28, 1987. Columbus' 3rd choice, 85th overall, in 2006 Entry Draft.

Season	Club	League	GP	G	A	Pts	PIM	PP	SH	GW	S	%	+/-	TF	F%	Min	GP	G	A	Pts	PIM	PP	SH	GW	Min
2003-04	Syracuse Jr. Stars	EmJHL	31	13	16	29	137	....	....	....	....	....	....	....	....	....	6	5	6	11	32	....	....	....	....
2004-05	Plymouth Whalers	OHL	35	1	3	4	88	....	....	....	....	....	....	....	....	....	....	....	....	....	....	....	....	....	....
2005-06	Plymouth Whalers	OHL	57	10	10	20	176	....	....	....	....	....	....	....	....	....	13	5	2	7	29	....	....	....	....
2006-07	Plymouth Whalers	OHL	60	42	22	64	135	....	....	....	....	....	....	....	....	....	19	11	6	17	57	....	....	....	....
2007-08	**Columbus**	**NHL**	**1**	**0**	**0**	**0**	**17**	**0**	**0**	**0**	**0**	**0.0**	**0**	**0**	**0.0**	**4:36**	....	....	....	....	....	....	....	....	....
	Syracuse Crunch	AHL	66	7	16	23	202	....	....	....	....	....	....	....	....	....	9	3	0	3	57	....	....	....	....
2008-09	Syracuse Crunch	AHL	52	8	12	20	168	....	....	....	....	....	....	....	....	....	....	....	....	....	....	....	....	....	....
2009-10	**Columbus**	**NHL**	**3**	**0**	**0**	**0**	**7**	**0**	**0**	**0**	**0**	**0.0**	**0**	**0**	**0.0**	**5:34**	....	....	....	....	....	....	....	....	....
	Syracuse Crunch	AHL	36	10	7	17	138	....	....	....	....	....	....	....	....	....	....	....	....	....	....	....	....	....	....
2010-11	**Columbus**	**NHL**	**9**	**2**	**2**	**4**	**40**	**1**	**0**	**0**	**7**	**28.6**	**–4**	**1**	**100.0**	**9:32**	....	....	....	....	....	....	....	....	....
	Springfield	AHL	46	11	21	32	192	....	....	....	....	....	....	....	....	....	....	....	....	....	....	....	....	....	....
	Adirondack	AHL	11	2	1	3	45	....	....	....	....	....	....	....	....	....	....	....	....	....	....	....	....	....	....
2011-12	**Philadelphia**	**NHL**	**14**	**0**	**1**	**1**	**83**	**0**	**0**	**0**	**4**	**0.0**	**–3**	**4**	**50.0**	**6:54**	....	....	....	....	....	....	....	....	....
	Adirondack	AHL	34	9	8	17	120	....	....	....	....	....	....	....	....	....	....	....	....	....	....	....	....	....	....
2012-13	Sheffield Steelers	Britain	17	8	11	19	69	....	....	....	....	....	....	....	....	....	....	....	....	....	....	....	....	....	....
	Philadelphia	**NHL**	**7**	**2**	**0**	**2**	**12**	**0**	**0**	**1**	**3**	**66.7**	**1**	**1**	**100.0**	**5:46**	....	....	....	....	....	....	....	....	....
	Adirondack	AHL	1	0	0	0	2	....	....	....	....	....	....	....	....	....	....	....	....	....	....	....	....	....	....
	Vancouver	**NHL**	**23**	**1**	**0**	**1**	**53**	**0**	**0**	**0**	**11**	**9.1**	**–3**	**1**	**0.0**	**6:38**	**1**	**0**	**0**	**0**	**2**	**0**	**0**	**0**	**5:51**
	NHL Totals		**57**	**5**	**3**	**8**	**212**	**1**	**0**	**1**	**25**	**20.0**		**7**	**57.1**	**6:57**	**1**	**0**	**0**	**0**	**2**	**0**	**0**	**0**	**5:51**

Traded to **Philadelphia** by **Columbus** for Michael Chaput and Greg Moore, February 28, 2011. Signed as a free agent by **Sheffield** (Britain), October 8, 2012. Claimed on waivers by **Vancouver** from **Philadelphia**, March 1, 2013.

SETOGUCHI, Devin (SEHT-oh-GOO-chee, DEH-vihn) WPG

Right wing. Shoots right. 6'2", 205 lbs. Born, Taber, Alta., January 1, 1987. San Jose's 1st choice, 8th overall, in 2005 Entry Draft.

Season	Club	League	GP	G	A	Pts	PIM	PP	SH	GW	S	%	+/-	TF	F%	Min	GP	G	A	Pts	PIM	PP	SH	GW	Min
2003-04	Saskatoon Blades	WHL	66	13	18	31	53	....	....	....	....	....	....	....	....	....	....	....	....	....	....	....	....	....	....
2004-05	Saskatoon Blades	WHL	69	33	31	64	34	....	....	....	....	....	....	....	....	....	4	0	1	1	0	....	....	....	....
2005-06	Saskatoon Blades	WHL	65	36	47	83	69	....	....	....	....	....	....	....	....	....	10	8	4	12	8	....	....	....	....
2006-07	Prince George	WHL	55	36	29	65	55	....	....	....	....	....	....	....	....	....	15	*11	10	21	24	....	....	....	....
2007-08	**San Jose**	**NHL**	**44**	**11**	**6**	**17**	**8**	**3**	**0**	**2**	**105**	**10.5**	**6**	**17**	**64.7**	**14:15**	**9**	**1**	**1**	**2**	**2**	**0**	**0**	**0**	**10:25**
	Worcester Sharks	AHL	23	8	11	19	25	....	....	....	....	....	....	....	....	....	....	....	....	....	....	....	....	....	....
2008-09	**San Jose**	**NHL**	**81**	**31**	**34**	**65**	**25**	**11**	**0**	**3**	**246**	**12.6**	**16**	**21**	**28.6**	**16:13**	**6**	**1**	**2**	**3**	**2**	**0**	**0**	**0**	**16:21**
2009-10	**San Jose**	**NHL**	**70**	**20**	**16**	**36**	**19**	**8**	**0**	**4**	**165**	**12.1**	**0**	**10**	**30.0**	**15:18**	**15**	**5**	**4**	**9**	**6**	**1**	**0**	**1**	**18:25**
2010-11	**San Jose**	**NHL**	**72**	**22**	**19**	**41**	**37**	**4**	**0**	**5**	**199**	**11.1**	**–2**	**11**	**45.5**	**15:12**	**18**	**7**	**3**	**10**	**12**	**3**	**0**	**2**	**17:26**
2011-12	**Minnesota**	**NHL**	**69**	**19**	**17**	**36**	**28**	**7**	**0**	**2**	**174**	**10.9**	**–17**	**11**	**27.3**	**17:36**	....	....	....	....	....	....	....	....	....
2012-13	Ontario Reign	ECHL	10	4	9	13	2	....	....	....	....	....	....	....	....	....	....	....	....	....	....	....	....	....	....
	Minnesota	**NHL**	**48**	**13**	**14**	**27**	**20**	**5**	**0**	**3**	**97**	**13.4**	**5**	**17**	**41.2**	**14:26**	**5**	**1**	**0**	**1**	**0**	**0**	**0**	**0**	**16:04**
	NHL Totals		**384**	**116**	**106**	**222**	**137**	**38**	**0**	**19**	**986**	**11.8**		**87**	**40.2**	**15:40**	**53**	**15**	**10**	**25**	**22**	**4**	**0**	**3**	**16:16**

WHL East Second All-Star Team (2006)

Traded to **Minnesota** by **San Jose** with Charlie Coyle and San Jose's 1st round choice (Zack Phillips) in 2011 Entry Draft for Brent Burns and Minnesota's 2nd round choice (later traded to Tampa Bay – later traded to Nashville – Nashville selected Pontius Aberg) in 2012 Entry Draft, June 24, 2011. Signed as a free agent by **Ontario** (ECHL), October 30, 2012. Traded to **Winnipeg** by **Minnesota** for Winnipeg's 4th round choice in 2014 Entry Draft, July 5, 2013.

SEXTON, Dan (SEHKS-tuhn, DAN) T.B.

Right wing. Shoots right. 5'9", 180 lbs. Born, Apple Valley, MN, April 29, 1987.

Season	Club	League	GP	G	A	Pts	PIM	PP	SH	GW	S	%	+/-	TF	F%	Min	GP	G	A	Pts	PIM	PP	SH	GW	Min
2005-06	Wichita Falls	NAHL	58	22	37	59	16	....	....	....	....	....	....	....	....	....	5	2	1	3	0	....	....	....	....
2006-07	Sioux Falls	USHL	58	14	10	24	20	....	....	....	....	....	....	....	....	....	8	*8	1	9	0	....	....	....	....
2007-08	Bowling Green	CCHA	38	7	14	21	42	....	....	....	....	....	....	....	....	....	....	....	....	....	....	....	....	....	....
2008-09	Bowling Green	CCHA	38	17	22	39	20	....	....	....	....	....	....	....	....	....	....	....	....	....	....	....	....	....	....
2009-10	**Anaheim**	**NHL**	**41**	**9**	**10**	**19**	**16**	**2**	**0**	**0**	**93**	**9.7**	**–3**	**1**	**0.0**	**13:30**	....	....	....	....	....	....	....	....	....
	Manitoba Moose	AHL	13	5	7	12	2	....	....	....	....	....	....	....	....	....	6	2	3	5	2	....	....	....	....
	Bakersfield	ECHL	18	13	13	26	14	....	....	....	....	....	....	....	....	....	....	....	....	....	....	....	....	....	....
2010-11	**Anaheim**	**NHL**	**47**	**4**	**9**	**13**	**4**	**1**	**0**	**0**	**78**	**5.1**	**–6**	**4**	**25.0**	**11:35**	**1**	**0**	**0**	**0**	**2**	**0**	**0**	**0**	**8:47**
	Syracuse Crunch	AHL	17	9	8	17	4	....	....	....	....	....	....	....	....	....	....	....	....	....	....	....	....	....	....
2011-12	Syracuse Crunch	AHL	71	13	30	43	22	....	....	....	....	....	....	....	....	....	4	1	2	3	0	....	....	....	....
2012-13	Norfolk Admirals	AHL	27	5	11	16	6	....	....	....	....	....	....	....	....	....	....	....	....	....	....	....	....	....	....
	Syracuse Crunch	AHL	16	4	8	12	8	....	....	....	....	....	....	....	....	....	18	6	6	12	6	....	....	....	....
	NHL Totals		**88**	**13**	**19**	**32**	**20**	**3**	**0**	**0**	**171**	**7.6**		**5**	**20.0**	**12:29**	**1**	**0**	**0**	**0**	**2**	**0**	**0**	**0**	**8:47**

Signed as a free agent by **Anaheim**, April 7, 2009. Traded to **Tampa Bay** by **Anaheim** for Kyle Wilson, March 11, 2013. Signed as a free agent by **TPS Turku** (Finland), July 9, 2013.

SGARBOSSA, Michael (s'gahr-BOH-suh, MIGH-kuhl) COL

Center. Shoots left. 5'11", 175 lbs. Born, Campbellville, Ont., July 25, 1992.

Season	Club	League	GP	G	A	Pts	PIM	PP	SH	GW	S	%	+/-	TF	F%	Min	GP	G	A	Pts	PIM	PP	SH	GW	Min
2008-09	Barrie Colts	OHL	67	10	33	43	43	....	....	....	....	....	....	....	....	....	5	3	3	6	10	....	....	....	....
2009-10	Barrie Colts	OHL	19	7	13	20	14	....	....	....	....	....	....	....	....	....	....	....	....	....	....	....	....	....	....
	Saginaw Spirit	OHL	48	13	19	32	49	....	....	....	....	....	....	....	....	....	6	0	2	2	4	....	....	....	....
2010-11	Saginaw Spirit	OHL	26	7	13	20	24	....	....	....	....	....	....	....	....	....	....	....	....	....	....	....	....	....	....
	Sudbury Wolves	OHL	37	29	33	62	53	....	....	....	....	....	....	....	....	....	8	5	9	14	16	....	....	....	....
2011-12	Sudbury Wolves	OHL	66	47	55	*102	68	....	....	....	....	....	....	....	....	....	4	2	1	3	6	....	....	....	....
2012-13	Lake Erie	AHL	57	19	25	44	71	....	....	....	....	....	....	....	....	....	....	....	....	....	....	....	....	....	....
	Colorado	**NHL**	**6**	**0**	**0**	**0**	**4**	**0**	**0**	**0**	**6**	**0.0**	**–3**	**25**	**36.0**	**10:22**	....	....	....	....	....	....	....	....	....
	NHL Totals		**6**	**0**	**0**	**0**	**4**	**0**	**0**	**0**	**6**	**0.0**		**25**	**36.0**	**10:22**	....	....	....	....	....	....	....	....	....

OHL First All-Star Team (2012)

Signed as a free agent by **San Jose**, September 20, 2010. Traded to **Colorado** by **San Jose** with Jamie McGinn and Mike Connolly for T.J. Galiardi, Daniel Winnik and Anaheim's 7th round choice (previously acquired, San Jose selected Emil Galimov) in 2013 Entry Draft, February 27, 2012.

SHANNON, Ryan (SHA-nuhn, RIGH-uhn)

Center. Shoots right. 5'9", 175 lbs. Born, Darien, CT, March 2, 1983.

Season	Club	League	GP	G	A	Pts	PIM	PP	SH	GW	S	%	+/-	TF	F%	Min	GP	G	A	Pts	PIM	PP	SH	GW	Min
2001-02	Boston College	H-East	38	8	17	25	12	....	....	....	....	....	....	....	....	....	....	....	....	....	....	....	....	....	....
2002-03	Boston College	H-East	36	14	24	38	4	....	....	....	....	....	....	....	....	....	....	....	....	....	....	....	....	....	....
2003-04	Boston College	H-East	42	15	27	42	22	....	....	....	....	....	....	....	....	....	....	....	....	....	....	....	....	....	....
2004-05	Boston College	H-East	38	14	31	45	22	....	....	....	....	....	....	....	....	....	....	....	....	....	....	....	....	....	....
	Cincinnati	AHL	4	1	0	1	2	....	....	....	....	....	....	....	....	....	....	....	....	....	....	....	....	....	....
2005-06	Portland Pirates	AHL	71	27	59	86	44	....	....	....	....	....	....	....	....	....	19	11	11	22	8	....	....	....	....
2006-07 ♦	**Anaheim**	**NHL**	**53**	**2**	**9**	**11**	**10**	**0**	**0**	**0**	**77**	**2.6**	**–2**	**25**	**52.0**	**10:39**	**11**	**0**	**0**	**0**	**6**	**0**	**0**	**0**	**4:04**
	Portland Pirates	AHL	14	2	7	9	12	....	....	....	....	....	....	....	....	....	....	....	....	....	....	....	....	....	....
2007-08	**Vancouver**	**NHL**	**27**	**5**	**8**	**13**	**24**	**4**	**0**	**0**	**34**	**14.7**	**–1**	**82**	**39.0**	**12:53**	....	....	....	....	....	....	....	....	....
	Manitoba Moose	AHL	13	1	7	8	10	....	....	....	....	....	....	....	....	....	....	....	....	....	....	....	....	....	....
2008-09	**Ottawa**	**NHL**	**35**	**8**	**12**	**20**	**2**	**3**	**0**	**1**	**61**	**13.1**	**–1**	**6**	**33.3**	**15:04**	....	....	....	....	....	....	....	....	....
	Binghamton	AHL	36	10	25	35	16	....	....	....	....	....	....	....	....	....	....	....	....	....	....	....	....	....	....
2009-10	**Ottawa**	**NHL**	**66**	**5**	**11**	**16**	**20**	**1**	**0**	**1**	**109**	**4.6**	**–12**	**51**	**37.3**	**12:40**	**2**	**0**	**0**	**0**	**0**	**0**	**0**	**0**	**6:13**
2010-11	**Ottawa**	**NHL**	**79**	**11**	**16**	**27**	**24**	**5**	**1**	**1**	**118**	**9.3**	**3**	**207**	**42.0**	**12:56**	....	....	....	....	....	....	....	....	....

			Regular Season														Playoffs								
Season	Club	League	GP	G	A	Pts	PIM	PP	SH	GW	S	%	+/-	TF	F%	Min	GP	G	A	Pts	PIM	PP	SH	GW	Min
2011-12	Tampa Bay	NHL	45	4	8	12	10	1	0	0	46	8.7	–11	40	55.0	12:02	....	....	....	....	....	....	....	....	....
2012-13	ZSC Lions Zurich	Swiss	42	12	22	34	26	....	....	....	....	....	....	....	....	....	12	2	5	7	2	....	....	....	....
	NHL Totals		305	35	64	99	90	14	1	3	445	7.9		411	42.6	12:35	13	0	0	0	6	0	0	0	4:24

Hockey East First All-Star Team (2004) • NCAA East Second All-American Team (2004) • AHL All-Rookie Team (2006)

Signed as a free agent by **Anaheim**, November 28, 2005. Traded to **Vancouver** by **Anaheim** for Jason King and future considerations, June 23, 2007. Traded to **Ottawa** by **Vancouver** for Lawrence Nycholat, September 2, 2008. Signed as a free agent by **Tampa Bay**, July 7, 2011. Signed as a free agent by **Zurich** (Swiss), May 22, 2012.

SHARP, Patrick (SHAHRP, PAT-rihk) CHI

Left wing. Shoots right. 6'1", 199 lbs. Born, Winnipeg, Man., December 27, 1981. Philadelphia's 2nd choice, 95th overall, in 2001 Entry Draft.

Season	Club	League	GP	G	A	Pts	PIM	PP	SH	GW	S	%	+/-	TF	F%	Min	GP	G	A	Pts	PIM	PP	SH	GW	Min
1997-98	Kanata Valley	ON-Jr.A	54	11	23	34	22	....	....	....	....	....	....	....	....	....	7	0	5	5	0	....	....	....	....
1998-99	Thunder Bay	USHL	55	19	24	43	48	....	....	....	....	....	....	....	....	....	3	1	1	2	0	....	....	....	....
99-2000	Thunder Bay	USHL	56	20	35	55	41	....	....	....	....	....	....	....	....	....	....	....	....	....	....	....	....	....	....
2000-01	U. of Vermont	ECAC	34	12	15	27	36	....	....	....	....	....	....	....	....	....	....	....	....	....	....	....	....	....	....
2001-02	U. of Vermont	ECAC	31	13	13	26	50	....	....	....	....	....	....	....	....	....	....	....	....	....	....	....	....	....	....
2002-03	**Philadelphia**	**NHL**	**3**	**0**	**0**	**0**	**2**	**0**	**0**	**0**	**3**	**0.0**	**0**	**7**	**42.9**	**5:59**	....	....	....	....	....	....	....	....	....
	Philadelphia	AHL	53	14	19	33	39	....	....	....	....	....	....	....	....	....	....	....	....	....	....	....	....	....	....
2003-04	**Philadelphia**	**NHL**	**41**	**5**	**2**	**7**	**55**	**0**	**0**	**1**	**44**	**11.4**	**–3**	**272**	**46.7**	**9:56**	**12**	**1**	**0**	**1**	**2**	**0**	**0**	**0**	**6:12**
	Philadelphia	AHL	35	15	14	29	45	....	....	....	....	....	....	....	....	....	1	2	0	2	0	....	....	....	....
2004-05	Philadelphia	AHL	75	23	29	52	80	....	....	....	....	....	....	....	....	....	21	8	13	*21	20	....	....	....	....
2005-06	**Philadelphia**	**NHL**	**22**	**5**	**3**	**8**	**10**	**1**	**0**	**3**	**33**	**15.2**	**4**	**38**	**52.6**	**7:43**	....	....	....	....	....	....	....	....	....
	Chicago	**NHL**	**50**	**9**	**14**	**23**	**36**	**0**	**1**	**2**	**111**	**8.1**	**1**	**664**	**48.0**	**16:19**	....	....	....	....	....	....	....	....	....
2006-07	**Chicago**	**NHL**	**80**	**20**	**15**	**35**	**74**	**5**	**3**	**1**	**160**	**12.5**	**–15**	**1008**	**46.5**	**17:04**	....	....	....	....	....	....	....	....	....
2007-08	**Chicago**	**NHL**	**80**	**36**	**26**	**62**	**55**	**9**	***7**	**7**	**209**	**17.2**	**23**	**594**	**51.4**	**18:47**	....	....	....	....	....	....	....	....	....
2008-09	**Chicago**	**NHL**	**61**	**26**	**18**	**44**	**41**	**9**	**0**	**4**	**184**	**14.1**	**6**	**566**	**45.8**	**17:57**	**17**	**7**	**4**	**11**	**6**	**3**	**0**	**2**	**16:17**
2009-10 ♦	**Chicago**	**NHL**	**82**	**25**	**41**	**66**	**28**	**4**	**2**	**4**	**266**	**9.4**	**24**	**466**	**51.7**	**18:07**	**22**	**11**	**11**	**22**	**16**	**3**	**1**	**1**	**17:52**
2010-11	**Chicago**	**NHL**	**74**	**34**	**37**	**71**	**38**	**12**	**2**	**6**	**268**	**12.7**	**–1**	**508**	**48.0**	**19:25**	**7**	**3**	**2**	**5**	**2**	**3**	**0**	**0**	**18:55**
2011-12	**Chicago**	**NHL**	**74**	**33**	**36**	**69**	**38**	**7**	**1**	**8**	**282**	**11.7**	**28**	**291**	**47.8**	**19:54**	**6**	**1**	**0**	**1**	**4**	**0**	**0**	**0**	**20:18**
2012-13 ♦	**Chicago**	**NHL**	**28**	**6**	**14**	**20**	**14**	**1**	**0**	**1**	**88**	**6.8**	**8**	**62**	**64.5**	**18:50**	**23**	***10**	**6**	**16**	**8**	**2**	**0**	**2**	**18:15**
	NHL Totals		**595**	**199**	**206**	**405**	**391**	**48**	**16**	**37**	**1648**	**12.1**		**4476**	**48.4**	**17:18**	**87**	**33**	**23**	**56**	**38**	**11**	**1**	**5**	**16:18**

Traded to **Chicago** by **Philadelphia** with Eric Meloche for Matt Ellison and Chicago's 3rd round choice (later traded to Montreal - Montreal selected Ryan White) in 2006 Entry Draft, December 5, 2005.
Played in NHL All-Star Game (2011)

SHATTENKIRK, Kevin (SHAH-tehn-kuhrk, KEH-vihn) ST.L.

Defense. Shoots right. 5'11", 207 lbs. Born, New Rochelle, NY, January 29, 1989. Colorado's 1st choice, 14th overall, in 2007 Entry Draft.

Season	Club	League	GP	G	A	Pts	PIM	PP	SH	GW	S	%	+/-	TF	F%	Min	GP	G	A	Pts	PIM	PP	SH	GW	Min
2004-05	Brunswick Bruins	High-CT	22	10	18	28	....	....	....	....	....	....	....	....	....	....	....	....	....	....	....	....	....	....	....
2005-06	USNTDP	U-17	13	4	4	8	4	....	....	....	....	....	....	....	....	....	....	....	....	....	....	....	....	....	....
	USNTDP	NAHL	28	6	9	15	17	....	....	....	....	....	....	....	....	....	12	3	7	10	10	....	....	....	....
2006-07	USNTDP	U-18	43	8	19	27	36	....	....	....	....	....	....	....	....	....	....	....	....	....	....	....	....	....	....
	USNTDP	NAHL	14	5	8	13	26	....	....	....	....	....	....	....	....	....	....	....	....	....	....	....	....	....	....
2007-08	Boston University	H-East	40	4	17	21	38	....	....	....	....	....	....	....	....	....	....	....	....	....	....	....	....	....	....
2008-09	Boston University	H-East	43	7	21	28	40	....	....	....	....	....	....	....	....	....	....	....	....	....	....	....	....	....	....
2009-10	Boston University	H-East	38	7	22	29	38	....	....	....	....	....	....	....	....	....	....	....	....	....	....	....	....	....	....
	Lake Erie	AHL	3	0	2	2	0	....	....	....	....	....	....	....	....	....	....	....	....	....	....	....	....	....	....
2010-11	**Colorado**	**NHL**	**46**	**7**	**19**	**26**	**20**	**2**	**0**	**1**	**67**	**10.4**	**–11**	**0**	**0.0**	**19:50**	....	....	....	....	....	....	....	....	....
	Lake Erie	AHL	10	0	0	0	10	....	....	....	....	....	....	....	....	....	....	....	....	....	....	....	....	....	....
	St. Louis	**NHL**	**26**	**2**	**15**	**17**	**16**	**1**	**0**	**1**	**41**	**4.9**	**7**	**0**	**0.0**	**19:51**	....	....	....	....	....	....	....	....	....
2011-12	**St. Louis**	**NHL**	**81**	**9**	**34**	**43**	**60**	**5**	**0**	**2**	**178**	**5.1**	**20**	**4**	**25.0**	**21:36**	**9**	**1**	**1**	**2**	**6**	**0**	**0**	**0**	**21:26**
2012-13	TPS Turku	Finland	12	2	4	6	22	....	....	....	....	....	....	....	....	....	....	....	....	....	....	....	....	....	....
	St. Louis	**NHL**	**48**	**5**	**18**	**23**	**20**	**2**	**0**	**0**	**84**	**6.0**	**2**	**0**	**0.0**	**21:18**	**6**	**0**	**2**	**2**	**6**	**0**	**0**	**0**	**18:38**
	NHL Totals		**201**	**23**	**86**	**109**	**116**	**10**	**0**	**4**	**370**	**6.2**		**4**	**25.0**	**20:54**	**15**	**1**	**3**	**4**	**12**	**0**	**0**	**0**	**20:19**

Hockey East All-Rookie Team (2008) • Hockey East Second All-Star Team (2009) • NCAA East Second All-American Team (2009)

Traded to **St. Louis** by **Colorado** with Chris Stewart and Colorado's 2nd round choice (Ty Rattie) in 2011 Entry Draft for Erik Johnson, Jay McClement and St. Louis's 1st round choice (Duncan Siemens) in 2011 Entry Draft, February 19, 2011. Signed as a free agent by **TPS Turku** (Finland), November 24, 2012.

SHAW, Andrew (SHAW, AN-droo) CHI

Center. Shoots right. 5'10", 180 lbs. Born, Belleville, Ont., July 20, 1991. Chicago's 8th choice, 139th overall, in 2011 Entry Draft.

Season	Club	League	GP	G	A	Pts	PIM	PP	SH	GW	S	%	+/-	TF	F%	Min	GP	G	A	Pts	PIM	PP	SH	GW	Min
2006-07	Quinte Red Devils	Minor-ON	32	24	27	51	88	....	....	....	....	....	....	....	....	....	3	1	2	3	....	....	....	....	....
	Quinte Red Devils	Exhib.	18	14	18	32	....	....	....	....	....	....	....	....	....	....	....	....	....	....	....	....	....	....	....
2007-08	Quinte Red Devils	Minor-ON	STATISTICS NOT AVAILABLE																						
2008-09	Niagara Ice Dogs	OHL	56	8	9	17	97	....	....	....	....	....	....	....	....	....	12	2	1	3	22	....	....	....	....
2009-10	Niagara Ice Dogs	OHL	68	11	25	36	129	....	....	....	....	....	....	....	....	....	5	0	0	0	4	....	....	....	....
2010-11	Owen Sound	OHL	66	22	32	54	135	....	....	....	....	....	....	....	....	....	20	10	7	17	*53	....	....	....	....
2011-12	**Chicago**	**NHL**	**37**	**12**	**11**	**23**	**50**	**0**	**0**	**2**	**74**	**16.2**	**–1**	**88**	**46.6**	**15:12**	**3**	**0**	**0**	**0**	**15**	**0**	**0**	**0**	**13:55**
	Rockford IceHogs	AHL	38	12	11	23	99	....	....	....	....	....	....	....	....	....	....	....	....	....	....	....	....	....	....
2012-13	Rockford IceHogs	AHL	28	8	6	14	84	....	....	....	....	....	....	....	....	....	....	....	....	....	....	....	....	....	....
	♦ **Chicago**	**NHL**	**48**	**9**	**6**	**15**	**38**	**2**	**0**	**2**	**64**	**14.1**	**6**	**457**	**44.0**	**15:03**	**23**	**5**	**4**	**9**	**35**	**1**	**0**	**2**	**14:49**
	NHL Totals		**85**	**21**	**17**	**38**	**88**	**2**	**0**	**4**	**138**	**15.2**		**545**	**44.4**	**15:07**	**26**	**5**	**4**	**9**	**50**	**1**	**0**	**2**	**14:43**

Memorial Cup All-Star Team (2011) • Ed Chynoweth Trophy (Memorial Cup – Leading Scorer) (2011)

SHEAHAN, Riley (SHEE-huhn, RIGH-lee) DET

Center. Shoots left. 6'2", 212 lbs. Born, St. Catharines, Ont., December 7, 1991. Detroit's 1st choice, 21st overall, in 2010 Entry Draft.

Season	Club	League	GP	G	A	Pts	PIM	PP	SH	GW	S	%	+/-	TF	F%	Min	GP	G	A	Pts	PIM	PP	SH	GW	Min
2007-08	St. Catharines	ON-Jr.B	45	22	39	61	39	....	....	....	....	....	....	....	....	....	16	5	10	15	14	....	....	....	....
2008-09	St. Catharines	ON-Jr.B	40	27	46	73	55	....	....	....	....	....	....	....	....	....	11	8	5	13	30	....	....	....	....
2009-10	U. of Notre Dame	CCHA	37	6	11	17	22	....	....	....	....	....	....	....	....	....	....	....	....	....	....	....	....	....	....
2010-11	U. of Notre Dame	CCHA	40	5	17	22	28	....	....	....	....	....	....	....	....	....	....	....	....	....	....	....	....	....	....
2011-12	U. of Notre Dame	CCHA	37	9	16	25	24	....	....	....	....	....	....	....	....	....	....	....	....	....	....	....	....	....	....
	Detroit	**NHL**	**1**	**0**	**0**	**0**	**4**	**0**	**0**	**0**	**3**	**0.0**	**0**	**0**	**0.0**	**6:03**	....	....	....	....	....	....	....	....	....
	Grand Rapids	AHL	7	1	1	2	0	....	....	....	....	....	....	....	....	....	....	....	....	....	....	....	....	....	....
2012-13	Grand Rapids	AHL	72	16	20	36	33	....	....	....	....	....	....	....	....	....	24	3	13	16	10	....	....	....	....
	Detroit	**NHL**	**1**	**0**	**0**	**0**	**0**	**0**	**0**	**0**	**1**	**0.0**	**0**	**1**	**0.0**	**6:47**	....	....	....	....	....	....	....	....	....
	NHL Totals		**2**	**0**	**0**	**0**	**4**	**0**	**0**	**0**	**4**	**0.0**		**1**	**0.0**	**6:25**	....	....	....	....	....	....	....	....	....

SHELLEY, Jody (SHEH-lee, JOH-dee)

Left wing. Shoots left. 6'3", 230 lbs. Born, Thompson, Man., February 7, 1976.

Season	Club	League	GP	G	A	Pts	PIM	PP	SH	GW	S	%	+/-	TF	F%	Min	GP	G	A	Pts	PIM	PP	SH	GW	Min
1994-95	Halifax	QMJHL	72	10	12	22	194	....	....	....	....	....	....	....	....	....	7	0	1	1	12	....	....	....	....
1995-96	Halifax	QMJHL	50	13	19	32	319	....	....	....	....	....	....	....	....	....	6	0	2	2	36	....	....	....	....
1996-97	Halifax	QMJHL	59	25	19	44	*420	....	....	....	....	....	....	....	....	....	17	6	6	12	*125	....	....	....	....
1997-98	Dalhousie	AUAA	19	6	11	17	145	....	....	....	....	....	....	....	....	....	....	....	....	....	....	....	....	....	....
	Saint John Flames	AHL	18	1	1	2	50	....	....	....	....	....	....	....	....	....	....	....	....	....	....	....	....	....	....
1998-99	Saint John Flames	AHL	8	0	0	0	46	....	....	....	....	....	....	....	....	....	....	....	....	....	....	....	....	....	....
	Johnstown Chiefs	ECHL	52	12	17	29	325	....	....	....	....	....	....	....	....	....	....	....	....	....	....	....	....	....	....
99-2000	Johnstown Chiefs	ECHL	36	9	17	26	256	....	....	....	....	....	....	....	....	....	....	....	....	....	....	....	....	....	....
	Saint John Flames	AHL	22	1	4	5	93	....	....	....	....	....	....	....	....	....	3	0	0	0	2	....	....	....	....
2000-01	Syracuse Crunch	AHL	69	1	7	8	*357	....	....	....	....	....	....	....	....	....	5	0	0	0	21	....	....	....	....
	Columbus	**NHL**	**1**	**0**	**0**	**0**	**10**	**0**	**0**	**0**	**0**	**0.0**	**0**	**0**	**0.0**	**1:33**	....	....	....	....	....	....	....	....	....
2001-02	**Columbus**	**NHL**	**52**	**3**	**3**	**6**	**206**	**0**	**0**	**0**	**35**	**8.6**	**1**	**0**	**0.0**	**6:32**	....	....	....	....	....	....	....	....	....
	Syracuse Crunch	AHL	22	3	5	8	165	....	....	....	....	....	....	....	....	....	....	....	....	....	....	....	....	....	....
2002-03	**Columbus**	**NHL**	**68**	**1**	**4**	**5**	***249**	**0**	**0**	**0**	**39**	**2.6**	**–5**	**1**	**0.0**	**6:08**	....	....	....	....	....	....	....	....	....
2003-04	**Columbus**	**NHL**	**76**	**3**	**3**	**6**	**228**	**1**	**0**	**0**	**62**	**4.8**	**–10**	**3**	**0.0**	**7:14**	....	....	....	....	....	....	....	....	....
2004-05	JYP Jyvaskyla	Finland	11	0	1	1	20	....	....	....	....	....	....	....	....	....	3	0	0	0	25	....	....	....	....
2005-06	**Columbus**	**NHL**	**80**	**3**	**7**	**10**	**163**	**0**	**0**	**1**	**39**	**7.7**	**–4**	**7**	**14.3**	**5:58**	....	....	....	....	....	....	....	....	....
2006-07	**Columbus**	**NHL**	**72**	**1**	**1**	**2**	**125**	**0**	**0**	**0**	**32**	**3.1**	**–6**	**2**	**0.0**	**4:52**	....	....	....	....	....	....	....	....	....
2007-08	**Columbus**	**NHL**	**31**	**0**	**0**	**0**	**44**	**0**	**0**	**0**	**10**	**0.0**	**–2**	**1**	**0.0**	**4:20**	....	....	....	....	....	....	....	....	....
	San Jose	**NHL**	**31**	**1**	**6**	**7**	**91**	**0**	**0**	**0**	**31**	**3.2**	**–2**	**1**	**0.0**	**7:24**	**6**	**0**	**0**	**0**	**2**	**0**	**0**	**0**	**3:16**
2008-09	**San Jose**	**NHL**	**70**	**2**	**2**	**4**	**116**	**0**	**0**	**1**	**44**	**4.5**	**–6**	**7**	**42.9**	**6:11**	**1**	**0**	**0**	**0**	**0**	**0**	**0**	**0**	**2:02**

			Regular Season														Playoffs								
Season	Club	League	GP	G	A	Pts	PIM	PP	SH	GW	S	%	+/-	TF	F%	Min	GP	G	A	Pts	PIM	PP	SH	GW	Min
2009-10	**San Jose**	**NHL**	**36**	**0**	**3**	**3**	**78**	**0**	**0**	**0**	**20**	**0.0**	**1**	**5**	**40.0**	**6:34**									
	NY Rangers	**NHL**	**21**	**2**	**4**	**6**	**37**	**0**	**0**	**0**	**29**	**6.9**	**4**	**1**	**0.0**	**7:07**									
2010-11	**Philadelphia**	**NHL**	**58**	**2**	**2**	**4**	**127**	**0**	**0**	**0**	**31**	**6.5**	**0**	**4**	**50.0**	**6:11**	**2**	**0**	**0**	**0**	**2**	**0**	**0**	**0**	**3:58**
2011-12	**Philadelphia**	**NHL**	**30**	**0**	**1**	**1**	**64**	**0**	**0**	**0**	**19**	**0.0**	**–6**	**2**	**0.0**	**5:39**									
2012-13	**Philadelphia**	**NHL**	**1**	**0**	**0**	**0**	**0**	**0**	**0**	**0**	**0**	**0.0**	**0**	**0**	**0.0**	**7:58**									
	NHL Totals		**627**	**18**	**36**	**54**	**1538**	**1**	**0**	**2**	**391**	**4.6**		**34**	**23.5**	**6:09**	**9**	**0**	**0**	**0**	**4**	**0**	**0**	**0**	**3:17**

Signed as a free agent by **Calgary**, September 1, 1998. Signed as a free agent by **Syracuse** (AHL), September 15, 2000. Signed as a free agent by **Columbus**, January 31, 2001. Signed as a free agent by **Jyvaskyla** (Finland), January 17, 2005. Traded to **San Jose** by **Columbus** for San Jose's 6th round choice (later traded to Atlanta, later traded to Chicago – Chicago selected David Pacan) in 2009 Entry Draft, January 29, 2008. Traded to **NY Rangers** by **San Jose** for NY Rangers' 6th round choice (Daniil Sobchenko) in 2011 Entry Draft, February 12, 2010. Signed as a free agent by **Philadelphia**, July 1, 2010. • Missed majority of 2012-13 due to hip injury. • Officially announced his retirement, August 9, 2013.

SHEPPARD, James
(sheh-PUHRD, JAYMZ) **S.J.**

Center. Shoots left. 6'1", 215 lbs. Born, Halifax, N.S., April 25, 1988. Minnesota's 1st choice, 9th overall, in 2006 Entry Draft.

Season	Club	League	GP	G	A	Pts	PIM	PP	SH	GW	S	%	+/-	TF	F%	Min	GP	G	A	Pts	PIM	PP	SH	GW	Min
2003-04	Dartmouth	NSMHL	61	38	54	92	46																		
2004-05	Cape Breton	QMJHL	65	14	31	45	40										5	1	3	4	2				
2005-06	Cape Breton	QMJHL	66	30	54	84	78										9	2	5	7	12				
2006-07	Cape Breton	QMJHL	56	33	63	96	62										16	8	12	20	14				
2007-08	**Minnesota**	**NHL**	**78**	**4**	**15**	**19**	**29**	**0**	**0**	**1**	**57**	**7.0**	**0**	**655**	**41.5**	**10:37**	**6**	**0**	**1**	**1**	**4**	**0**	**0**	**0**	**10:37**
2008-09	**Minnesota**	**NHL**	**82**	**5**	**19**	**24**	**41**	**0**	**0**	**1**	**88**	**5.7**	**–14**	**870**	**41.5**	**15:11**									
2009-10	**Minnesota**	**NHL**	**64**	**2**	**4**	**6**	**38**	**0**	**0**	**0**	**64**	**3.1**	**–14**	**343**	**45.2**	**11:59**									
2010-11			DID NOT PLAY – INJURED																						
2011-12	Worcester Sharks	AHL	4	0	0	0	2																		
2012-13	Worcester Sharks	AHL	34	8	15	23	52																		
	San Jose	**NHL**	**32**	**1**	**3**	**4**	**12**	**0**	**0**	**1**	**40**	**2.5**	**–9**	**6**	**33.3**	**11:45**	**11**	**0**	**0**	**0**	**4**	**0**	**0**	**0**	**10:28**
	NHL Totals		**256**	**12**	**41**	**53**	**120**	**0**	**0**	**3**	**249**	**4.8**		**1874**	**42.2**	**12:34**	**17**	**0**	**1**	**1**	**8**	**0**	**0**	**0**	**10:31**

QMJHL Second All-Star Team (2007)

• Missed 2010-11 and majority of 2011-12 due to off-season knee injury, September 4. 2010. Traded to **San Jose** by **Minnesota** for San Jose's 3rd round choice (Kurtis Gabriel) in 2013 Entry Draft, August 7, 2011.

SHIROKOV, Sergei
(sheer-OH-kawv, SAIR-gay) **FLA**

Right wing. Shoots right. 5'10", 195 lbs. Born, Ozery, USSR, March 10, 1986. Vancouver's 3rd choice, 163rd overall, in 2006 Entry Draft.

Season	Club	League	GP	G	A	Pts	PIM	PP	SH	GW	S	%	+/-	TF	F%	Min	GP	G	A	Pts	PIM	PP	SH	GW	Min
2001-02	HK CSKA 2	Russia-3	18	2	3	5	0																		
2002-03	CSKA Moscow 2	Russia-3	2	0	0	0	0																		
2003-04	CSKA Moscow 2	Russia-3	66	39	41	80	66																		
2004-05	CSKA Moscow 2	Russia-3	25	16	13	29	47																		
	CSKA Moscow	Russia	8	0	0	0	0																		
	CSKA Moscow	Russia	8	0	0	0	0																		
2005-06	CSKA Moscow	Russia	39	7	7	14	26										4	0	0	0	0				
2006-07	CSKA Moscow	Russia	52	16	19	35	36										12	4	6	10	4				
2007-08	CSKA Moscow	Russia	57	12	21	33	28										6	0	3	3	4				
2008-09	CSKA Moscow	KHL	56	17	23	40	36										8	1	3	4	4				
2009-10	**Vancouver**	**NHL**	**6**	**0**	**0**	**0**	**2**	**0**	**0**	**0**	**4**	**0.0**	**–4**	**2**	**50.0**	**12:50**									
	Manitoba Moose	AHL	76	22	23	45	32										6	0	2	2	4				
2010-11	**Vancouver**	**NHL**	**2**	**1**	**0**	**1**	**0**	**0**	**0**	**0**	**6**	**16.7**	**1**	**0**	**0.0**	**10:18**									
	Manitoba Moose	AHL	76	22	36	58	51										14	7	3	10	4				
2011-12	CSKA Moscow	KHL	53	18	29	47	26										5	1	0	1	2				
2012-13	CSKA Moscow	KHL	33	5	8	13	22										9	1	2	3	12				
	NHL Totals		**8**	**1**	**0**	**1**	**2**	**0**	**0**	**0**	**10**	**10.0**		**2**	**50.0**	**12:12**									

Signed as a free agent by **CSKA Moscow** (KHL), July 1, 2011. Traded to **Florida** by **Vancouver** for Mike Duco, July 8, 2011.

SHORE, Drew
(SHOHR, DROO) **FLA**

Center. Shoots right. 6'2", 195 lbs. Born, Denver, CO, January 29, 1991. Florida's 2nd choice, 44th overall, in 2009 Entry Draft.

Season	Club	League	GP	G	A	Pts	PIM	PP	SH	GW	S	%	+/-	TF	F%	Min	GP	G	A	Pts	PIM	PP	SH	GW	Min
2006-07	Det. Honeybaked	MWEHL	31	9	25	34	20																		
	Det. Honeybaked	Exhib.	34	17	23	40	....																		
2007-08	USNTDP	NAHL	35	9	16	25	12										3	0	1	1	0				
	USNTDP	U-17	16	4	8	12	6																		
2008-09	USNTDP	NAHL	15	7	7	14	16																		
	USNTDP	U-18	47	10	25	35	30																		
2009-10	U. of Denver	WCHA	41	5	14	19	18																		
2010-11	U. of Denver	WCHA	40	23	23	46	38																		
2011-12	U. of Denver	WCHA	42	22	31	53	45																		
	San Antonio	AHL	8	1	2	3	4										9	2	0	2	2				
2012-13	San Antonio	AHL	41	10	20	30	18																		
	Florida	**NHL**	**43**	**3**	**10**	**13**	**14**	**1**	**1**	**1**	**96**	**3.1**	**–10**	**443**	**47.9**	**15:48**									
	NHL Totals		**43**	**3**	**10**	**13**	**14**	**1**	**1**	**1**	**96**	**3.1**		**443**	**47.9**	**15:48**									

WCHA Second All-Star Team (2011, 2012)

SILFVERBERG, Jakob
(SIHL-vuhr-buhrg, YA-kuhb) **ANA**

Left wing. Shoots right. 6'2", 195 lbs. Born, Gavle, Sweden, October 13, 1990. Ottawa's 2nd choice, 39th overall, in 2009 Entry Draft.

Season	Club	League	GP	G	A	Pts	PIM	PP	SH	GW	S	%	+/-	TF	F%	Min	GP	G	A	Pts	PIM	PP	SH	GW	Min
2005-06	Brynas U18	Swe-U18	8	0	0	0	0																		
2006-07	Brynas U18	Swe-U18	14	3	8	11	6										3	0	0	0	0				
	Brynas IF Gavle Jr.	Swe-Jr.	6	1	3	4	0																		
2007-08	Brynas U18	Swe-U18	5	5	3	8	2										5	3	4	7	2				
	Brynas IF Gavle Jr.	Swe-Jr.	30	8	12	20	8										7	3	0	3	2				
2008-09	Brynas IF Gavle Jr.	Swe-Jr.	30	14	24	38	6																		
	Brynas IF Gavle	Sweden	16	3	1	4	2										4	0	0	0	2				
2009-10	Brynas IF Gavle Jr.	Swe-Jr.	1	1	1	2	0										3	3	2	5	0				
	Brynas IF Gavle	Sweden	48	8	8	16	4										5	1	1	2	2				
2010-11	Brynas IF Gavle	Sweden	53	18	16	34	16										5	0	4	4	2				
2011-12	Brynas IF Gavle	Sweden	49	24	30	54	10										17	13	7	20	4				
	Ottawa	**NHL**															**2**	**0**	**0**	**0**	**2**	**0**	**0**	**0**	**9:11**
2012-13	Binghamton	AHL	34	13	16	29	2																		
	Ottawa	**NHL**	**48**	**10**	**9**	**19**	**12**	**2**	**1**	**2**	**134**	**7.5**	**9**	**13**	**38.5**	**16:14**	**10**	**2**	**2**	**4**	**2**	**1**	**0**	**0**	**16:39**
	NHL Totals		**48**	**10**	**9**	**19**	**12**	**2**	**1**	**2**	**134**	**7.5**		**13**	**38.5**	**16:14**	**12**	**2**	**2**	**4**	**4**	**1**	**0**	**0**	**15:24**

Traded to **Anaheim** by **Ottawa** wirh Stefan Noesen and Ottawa's 1st round choice in 2014 Entry Draft for Bobby Ryan, July 5, 2013.

SIM, Jon
(SIHM, JAWN)

Left wing. Shoots left. 5'10", 195 lbs. Born, New Glasgow, N.S., September 29, 1977. Dallas' 2nd choice, 70th overall, in 1996 Entry Draft.

Season	Club	League	GP	G	A	Pts	PIM	PP	SH	GW	S	%	+/-	TF	F%	Min	GP	G	A	Pts	PIM	PP	SH	GW	Min
1994-95	Laval Titan	QMJHL	9	0	1	1	6																		
	Sarnia Sting	OHL	25	9	12	21	19										4	3	2	5	2				
1995-96	Sarnia Sting	OHL	63	56	46	102	130										10	8	7	15	26				
1996-97	Sarnia Sting	OHL	64	*56	39	95	109										12	9	5	14	32				
1997-98	Sarnia Sting	OHL	59	44	50	94	95										5	1	4	5	14				
1998-99 ♦	**Dallas**	**NHL**	**7**	**1**	**0**	**1**	**12**	**0**	**0**	**0**	**8**	**12.5**	**1**	**6**	**50.0**	**11:26**	**4**	**0**	**0**	**0**	**0**	**0**	**0**	**0**	**6:27**
	Michigan	IHL	68	24	27	51	91										5	3	1	4	18				
99-2000	**Dallas**	**NHL**	**25**	**5**	**3**	**8**	**10**	**2**	**0**	**1**	**44**	**11.4**	**4**	**4**	**75.0**	**10:51**	**7**	**1**	**0**	**1**	**6**	**0**	**0**	**0**	**11:11**
	Michigan	IHL	35	14	16	30	65																		
2000-01	**Dallas**	**NHL**	**15**	**0**	**3**	**3**	**6**	**0**	**0**	**0**	**18**	**0.0**	**–2**	**1**	**100.0**	**8:47**									
	Utah Grizzlies	IHL	39	16	13	29	44																		
2001-02	**Dallas**	**NHL**	**26**	**3**	**0**	**3**	**10**	**1**	**0**	**0**	**43**	**7.0**	**–3**	**3**	**0.0**	**9:30**									
	Utah Grizzlies	AHL	31	21	6	27	63																		
2002-03	**Dallas**	**NHL**	**4**	**0**	**0**	**0**	**0**	**0**	**0**	**0**	**7**	**0.0**	**–1**	**2**	**50.0**	**9:10**									
	Utah Grizzlies	AHL	42	16	31	47	85																		
	Nashville	**NHL**	**4**	**1**	**0**	**1**	**0**	**0**	**0**	**0**	**3**	**33.3**	**0**	**14**	**35.7**	**9:18**									
	Los Angeles	**NHL**	**14**	**0**	**2**	**2**	**19**	**0**	**0**	**0**	**29**	**0.0**	**–3**	**3**	**33.3**	**12:05**									

			Regular Season														Playoffs								
Season	Club	League	GP	G	A	Pts	PIM	PP	SH	GW	S	%	+/-	TF	F%	Min	GP	G	A	Pts	PIM	PP	SH	GW	Min
2003-04	**Los Angeles**	**NHL**	**48**	**6**	**7**	**13**	**27**	**0**	**0**	**1**	**73**	**8.2**	**0**	**19**	**31.6**	**10:01**	....	....	....	....	....	....	....	....	....
	Pittsburgh	**NHL**	**15**	**2**	**3**	**5**	**6**	**0**	**0**	**1**	**27**	**7.4**	**–4**	**0**	**0.0**	**13:39**	....	....	....	....	....	....	....	....	....
2004-05	Utah Grizzlies	AHL	10	2	2	4	12	....	....	....	....	....	....	....	....	....	....	....	....	....	....	....	....	....	....
	Philadelphia	AHL	63	35	26	61	66	....	....	....	....	....	....	....	....	....	21	*10	7	17	44	....	....	....	....
2005-06	**Philadelphia**	**NHL**	**39**	**7**	**7**	**14**	**28**	**4**	**0**	**2**	**80**	**8.8**	**–6**	**1**	**0.0**	**10:59**	....	....	....	....	....	....	....	....	....
	Florida	**NHL**	**33**	**10**	**8**	**18**	**26**	**4**	**0**	**3**	**92**	**10.9**	**–1**	**0**	**0.0**	**12:28**	....	....	....	....	....	....	....	....	....
2006-07	**Atlanta**	**NHL**	**77**	**17**	**12**	**29**	**60**	**2**	**0**	**1**	**141**	**12.1**	**–1**	**9**	**22.2**	**11:45**	**4**	**0**	**0**	**0**	**0**	**0**	**0**	**0**	**5:29**
2007-08	**NY Islanders**	**NHL**	**2**	**0**	**1**	**1**	**2**	**0**	**0**	**0**	**8**	**0.0**	**–1**	**0**	**0.0**	**14:19**	....	....	....	....	....	....	....	....	....
2008-09	**NY Islanders**	**NHL**	**49**	**9**	**6**	**15**	**42**	**3**	**0**	**0**	**90**	**10.0**	**–12**	**6**	**16.7**	**12:10**	....	....	....	....	....	....	....	....	....
	Bridgeport	AHL	18	13	10	23	12	....	....	....	....	....	....	....	....	....	5	2	3	5	10	....	....	....	....
2009-10	**NY Islanders**	**NHL**	**77**	**13**	**9**	**22**	**44**	**1**	**0**	**0**	**128**	**10.2**	**–4**	**18**	**50.0**	**11:39**	....	....	....	....	....	....	....	....	....
2010-11	**NY Islanders**	**NHL**	**34**	**1**	**3**	**4**	**22**	**0**	**0**	**0**	**38**	**2.6**	**–10**	**11**	**45.5**	**11:24**	....	....	....	....	....	....	....	....	....
	Bridgeport	AHL	8	7	2	9	6	....	....	....	....	....	....	....	....	....	....	....	....	....	....	....	....	....	....
	Fribourg	Swiss	7	1	0	1	2	....	....	....	....	....	....	....	....	....	3	0	0	0	12	....	....	....	....
2011-12	Pardubice	CzRep	20	2	4	6	22	....	....	....	....	....	....	....	....	....	....	....	....	....	....	....	....	....	....
	HC Slavia Praha	CzRep	8	1	1	2	12	....	....	....	....	....	....	....	....	....	....	....	....	....	....	....	....	....	....
	Eisbaren Berlin	Germany	14	2	4	6	27	....	....	....	....	....	....	....	....	....	13	0	0	0	33	....	....	....	....
2012-13	San Antonio	AHL	22	6	7	13	14	....	....	....	....	....	....	....	....	....	....	....	....	....	....	....	....	....	....
	Adirondack	AHL	34	6	13	19	22	....	....	....	....	....	....	....	....	....	....	....	....	....	....	....	....	....	....
	NHL Totals		**469**	**75**	**64**	**139**	**314**	**17**	**0**	**9**	**829**	**9.0**		**97**	**38.1**	**11:20**	**15**	**1**	**0**	**1**	**6**	**0**	**0**	**0**	**8:24**

OHL Second All-Star Team (1998)

Traded to **Nashville** by **Dallas** for Bubba Berenzweig and future considerations, February 17, 2003. Claimed on waivers by **Los Angeles** from **Nashville**, March 8, 2003. Claimed on waivers by **Pittsburgh** from **Los Angeles**, March 4, 2004. Signed as a free agent by **Phoenix**, September 2, 2004. • Loaned to **Philadelphia** (AHL) by **Phoenix** (Utah – AHL) for the loan of Peter White, November 14, 2004. Signed as a free agent by **Philadelphia**, August 2, 2005. Traded to **Florida** by **Philadelphia** for Florida's 6th round choice (Patrick Maroon) in 2007 Entry Draft, January 23, 2006. Signed as a free agent by **Atlanta**, July 14, 2006. Signed as a free agent by **NY Islanders**, July 1, 2007. Signed as a free agent by **Fribourg** (Swiss), January 16, 2011. Signed as a free agent by **Pardubice** (CzRep), August 13, 2011. • Loaned to **Slavia Praha** (CzRep) by **Pardubice** (CzRep), November 18, 2011. Signed as a free agent by **Berlin** (Germany), January 18, 2012. Signed as a free agent by **San Antonio** (AHL), December 8, 2012. Signed as a free agent by **Adirondack** (AHL), January 31, 2013.

SIMMONDS, Wayne

(SIH-muhnds, WAYN) **PHI**

Right wing. Shoots right. 6'2", 183 lbs. Born, Scarborough, Ont., August 26, 1988. Los Angeles' 3rd choice, 61st overall, in 2007 Entry Draft.

Season	Club	League	GP	G	A	Pts	PIM	PP	SH	GW	S	%	+/-	TF	F%	Min	GP	G	A	Pts	PIM	PP	SH	GW	Min
2004-05	Tor. Jr. Canadiens	GTHL	67	32	40	72	97	....	....	....	....	....	....	....	....	....	....	....	....	....	....	....	....	....	....
2005-06	Brockville Braves	ON-Jr.A	49	24	19	43	127	....	....	....	....	....	....	....	....	....	7	4	2	6	12	....	....	....	....
2006-07	Owen Sound	OHL	66	23	26	49	112	....	....	....	....	....	....	....	....	....	4	1	1	2	4	....	....	....	....
2007-08	Owen Sound	OHL	29	17	22	39	43	....	....	....	....	....	....	....	....	....	....	....	....	....	....	....	....	....	....
	Sault Ste. Marie	OHL	31	16	20	36	68	....	....	....	....	....	....	....	....	....	14	5	9	14	22	....	....	....	....
2008-09	**Los Angeles**	**NHL**	**82**	**9**	**14**	**23**	**73**	**2**	**0**	**2**	**127**	**7.1**	**–8**	**25**	**36.0**	**13:50**	....	....	....	....	....	....	....	....	....
2009-10	**Los Angeles**	**NHL**	**78**	**16**	**24**	**40**	**116**	**0**	**0**	**2**	**127**	**12.6**	**22**	**10**	**30.0**	**14:29**	**6**	**2**	**1**	**3**	**9**	**0**	**0**	**0**	**14:21**
2010-11	**Los Angeles**	**NHL**	**80**	**14**	**16**	**30**	**75**	**1**	**0**	**3**	**117**	**12.0**	**–2**	**19**	**36.8**	**13:27**	**6**	**1**	**2**	**3**	**20**	**0**	**0**	**0**	**14:44**
2011-12	**Philadelphia**	**NHL**	**82**	**28**	**21**	**49**	**114**	**11**	**0**	**4**	**197**	**14.2**	**–1**	**17**	**41.2**	**15:55**	**11**	**1**	**5**	**6**	**38**	**1**	**0**	**0**	**14:52**
2012-13	Crimmitschau	German-2	9	4	10	14	35	....	....	....	....	....	....	....	....	....	....	....	....	....	....	....	....	....	....
	Liberec	CzRep	6	4	2	6	16	....	....	....	....	....	....	....	....	....	....	....	....	....	....	....	....	....	....
	Philadelphia	**NHL**	**45**	**15**	**17**	**32**	**82**	**6**	**0**	**4**	**110**	**13.6**	**–7**	**3**	**66.7**	**15:38**	....	....	....	....	....	....	....	....	....
	NHL Totals		**367**	**82**	**92**	**174**	**460**	**20**	**0**	**15**	**678**	**12.1**		**74**	**37.8**	**14:34**	**23**	**4**	**8**	**12**	**67**	**1**	**0**	**0**	**14:42**

Traded to **Philadelphia** by **Los Angeles** with Brayden Schenn and Los Angeles' 2nd round choice (later traded to Dallas – Dallas selected Devin Shore) in 2012 Entry Draft for Mike Richards and the rights to Rob Bordson, June 23, 2011. Signed as a free agent by **Crimmitschau** (German-2), September 24, 2012. Signed as a free agent by **Liberec** (CzRep), October 23, 2012.

SKILLE, Jack

(SKIH-lee, JAK) **CBJ**

Right wing. Shoots right. 6'1", 219 lbs. Born, Madison, WI, May 19, 1987. Chicago's 1st choice, 7th overall, in 2005 Entry Draft.

Season	Club	League	GP	G	A	Pts	PIM	PP	SH	GW	S	%	+/-	TF	F%	Min	GP	G	A	Pts	PIM	PP	SH	GW	Min
2003-04	USNTDP	U-17	33	14	10	24	30	....	....	....	....	....	....	....	....	....	....	....	....	....	....	....	....	....	....
	USNTDP	NAHL	28	11	9	20	31	....	....	....	....	....	....	....	....	....	....	....	....	....	....	....	....	....	....
2004-05	USNTDP	U-18	26	9	11	20	36	....	....	....	....	....	....	....	....	....	....	....	....	....	....	....	....	....	....
	USNTDP	NAHL	16	6	11	17	20	....	....	....	....	....	....	....	....	....	....	....	....	....	....	....	....	....	....
2005-06	U. of Wisconsin	WCHA	41	13	8	21	37	....	....	....	....	....	....	....	....	....	....	....	....	....	....	....	....	....	....
2006-07	U. of Wisconsin	WCHA	26	8	10	18	12	....	....	....	....	....	....	....	....	....	....	....	....	....	....	....	....	....	....
	Norfolk Admirals	AHL	9	4	4	8	0	....	....	....	....	....	....	....	....	....	3	0	0	0	2	....	....	....	....
2007-08	**Chicago**	**NHL**	**16**	**3**	**2**	**5**	**0**	**0**	**0**	**0**	**23**	**13.0**	**1**	**4**	**50.0**	**11:59**	....	....	....	....	....	....	....	....	....
	Rockford IceHogs	AHL	59	16	18	34	44	....	....	....	....	....	....	....	....	....	12	2	1	3	6	....	....	....	....
2008-09	**Chicago**	**NHL**	**8**	**1**	**0**	**1**	**5**	**0**	**0**	**0**	**14**	**7.1**	**–3**	**0**	**0.0**	**9:26**	....	....	....	....	....	....	....	....	....
	Rockford IceHogs	AHL	58	20	25	45	56	....	....	....	....	....	....	....	....	....	....	....	....	....	....	....	....	....	....
2009-10	**Chicago**	**NHL**	**6**	**1**	**1**	**2**	**0**	**0**	**0**	**0**	**9**	**11.1**	**–3**	**0**	**0.0**	**7:40**	....	....	....	....	....	....	....	....	....
	Rockford IceHogs	AHL	63	23	26	49	50	....	....	....	....	....	....	....	....	....	4	0	0	0	0	....	....	....	....
2010-11	**Chicago**	**NHL**	**49**	**7**	**10**	**17**	**25**	**1**	**0**	**1**	**121**	**5.8**	**3**	**4**	**50.0**	**10:44**	....	....	....	....	....	....	....	....	....
	Florida	**NHL**	**13**	**1**	**1**	**2**	**4**	**0**	**0**	**0**	**33**	**3.0**	**–12**	**6**	**16.7**	**16:25**	....	....	....	....	....	....	....	....	....
2011-12	**Florida**	**NHL**	**46**	**4**	**6**	**10**	**28**	**0**	**1**	**1**	**76**	**5.3**	**–9**	**16**	**50.0**	**11:58**	....	....	....	....	....	....	....	....	....
2012-13	Rosenborg Elite	Norway	9	6	6	12	20	....	....	....	....	....	....	....	....	....	....	....	....	....	....	....	....	....	....
	Florida	**NHL**	**40**	**3**	**9**	**12**	**11**	**0**	**0**	**0**	**69**	**4.3**	**–9**	**16**	**50.0**	**13:19**	....	....	....	....	....	....	....	....	....
	NHL Totals		**178**	**20**	**29**	**49**	**73**	**1**	**1**	**2**	**345**	**5.8**		**46**	**45.7**	**12:00**	....	....	....	....	....	....	....	....	....

Traded to **Florida** by **Chicago** with Hugh Jessiman and David Pacan for Michael Frolik and Alexander Salak, February 9, 2011. Signed as a free agent by **Rosenborg** (Norway), October 11, 2012. Signed as a free agent by **Columbus**, July 7, 2013.

SKINNER, Jeff

(SKIH-nuhr, JEHF) **CAR**

Center. Shoots left. 5'11", 200 lbs. Born, Markham, Ont., May 16, 1992. Carolina's 1st choice, 7th overall, in 2010 Entry Draft.

Season	Club	League	GP	G	A	Pts	PIM	PP	SH	GW	S	%	+/-	TF	F%	Min	GP	G	A	Pts	PIM	PP	SH	GW	Min
2007-08	Tor. Young Nats	GTHL	56	65	44	109	163	....	....	....	....	....	....	....	....	....	....	....	....	....	....	....	....	....	....
2008-09	Kitchener Rangers	OHL	63	27	24	51	34	....	....	....	....	....	....	....	....	....	....	....	....	....	....	....	....	....	....
2009-10	Kitchener Rangers	OHL	64	50	40	90	72	....	....	....	....	....	....	....	....	....	20	*20	13	33	14	....	....	....	....
2010-11	**Carolina**	**NHL**	**82**	**31**	**32**	**63**	**46**	**6**	**0**	**2**	**215**	**14.4**	**3**	**157**	**36.9**	**16:44**	....	....	....	....	....	....	....	....	....
2011-12	**Carolina**	**NHL**	**64**	**20**	**24**	**44**	**56**	**4**	**0**	**5**	**210**	**9.5**	**–8**	**159**	**42.1**	**18:37**	....	....	....	....	....	....	....	....	....
2012-13	**Carolina**	**NHL**	**42**	**13**	**11**	**24**	**26**	**5**	**0**	**0**	**159**	**8.2**	**–21**	**44**	**47.7**	**18:28**	....	....	....	....	....	....	....	....	....
	NHL Totals		**188**	**64**	**67**	**131**	**128**	**15**	**0**	**7**	**584**	**11.0**		**360**	**40.6**	**17:46**	....	....	....	....	....	....	....	....	....

NHL All-Rookie Team (2011) • Calder Memorial Trophy (2011)
Played in NHL All-Star Game (2011)

SLATER, Jim

(SLAY-tuhr, JIHM) **WPG**

Center. Shoots left. 6', 200 lbs. Born, Lapeer, MI, December 9, 1982. Atlanta's 2nd choice, 30th overall, in 2002 Entry Draft.

Season	Club	League	GP	G	A	Pts	PIM	PP	SH	GW	S	%	+/-	TF	F%	Min	GP	G	A	Pts	PIM	PP	SH	GW	Min
1998-99	USNTDP	U-18	3	0	1	1	0	....	....	....	....	....	....	....	....	....	....	....	....	....	....	....	....	....	....
	Cleveland Barons	NAHL	50	13	20	33	58	....	....	....	....	....	....	....	....	....	2	0	0	0	2	....	....	....	....
99-2000	Cleveland Barons	NAHL	56	35	50	85	129	....	....	....	....	....	....	....	....	....	3	1	3	4	4	....	....	....	....
2000-01	Cleveland Barons	NAHL	48	27	37	64	122	....	....	....	....	....	....	....	....	....	6	6	6	12	6	....	....	....	....
2001-02	Michigan State	CCHA	37	11	21	32	50	....	....	....	....	....	....	....	....	....	....	....	....	....	....	....	....	....	....
2002-03	Michigan State	CCHA	37	18	26	44	26	....	....	....	....	....	....	....	....	....	....	....	....	....	....	....	....	....	....
2003-04	Michigan State	CCHA	42	19	29	*48	38	....	....	....	....	....	....	....	....	....	....	....	....	....	....	....	....	....	....
2004-05	Michigan State	CCHA	41	16	32	48	30	....	....	....	....	....	....	....	....	....	....	....	....	....	....	....	....	....	....
2005-06	**Atlanta**	**NHL**	**71**	**10**	**10**	**20**	**46**	**1**	**0**	**0**	**108**	**9.3**	**1**	**287**	**56.5**	**10:06**	....	....	....	....	....	....	....	....	....
	Chicago Wolves	AHL	4	0	2	2	2	....	....	....	....	....	....	....	....	....	....	....	....	....	....	....	....	....	....
2006-07	**Atlanta**	**NHL**	**74**	**5**	**14**	**19**	**62**	**0**	**0**	**2**	**90**	**5.6**	**8**	**373**	**54.4**	**10:14**	**4**	**0**	**0**	**0**	**2**	**0**	**0**	**0**	**5:10**
2007-08	**Atlanta**	**NHL**	**69**	**8**	**5**	**13**	**41**	**0**	**2**	**0**	**95**	**8.4**	**–10**	**367**	**52.0**	**10:24**	....	....	....	....	....	....	....	....	....
	Chicago Wolves	AHL	3	0	0	0	0	....	....	....	....	....	....	....	....	....	....	....	....	....	....	....	....	....	....
2008-09	**Atlanta**	**NHL**	**60**	**8**	**10**	**18**	**52**	**0**	**2**	**0**	**94**	**8.5**	**0**	**462**	**53.0**	**11:15**	....	....	....	....	....	....	....	....	....
2009-10	**Atlanta**	**NHL**	**61**	**11**	**7**	**18**	**60**	**1**	**0**	**2**	**107**	**10.3**	**1**	**431**	**58.9**	**12:12**	....	....	....	....	....	....	....	....	....
2010-11	**Atlanta**	**NHL**	**36**	**5**	**7**	**12**	**19**	**0**	**0**	**1**	**53**	**9.4**	**4**	**301**	**61.5**	**10:35**	....	....	....	....	....	....	....	....	....
2011-12	**Winnipeg**	**NHL**	**78**	**13**	**8**	**21**	**42**	**0**	**1**	**1**	**118**	**11.0**	**–9**	**1165**	**54.4**	**14:46**	....	....	....	....	....	....	....	....	....
2012-13	**Winnipeg**	**NHL**	**26**	**1**	**1**	**2**	**19**	**0**	**0**	**0**	**22**	**4.5**	**–3**	**267**	**54.3**	**10:27**	....	....	....	....	....	....	....	....	....
	NHL Totals		**475**	**61**	**62**	**123**	**341**	**2**	**5**	**6**	**687**	**8.9**		**3653**	**55.3**	**11:24**	**4**	**0**	**0**	**0**	**2**	**0**	**0**	**0**	**5:10**

CCHA All-Rookie Team (2002) • CCHA First All-Star Team (2003, 2004) • NCAA West Second All-American Team (2004)

• Missed majority of 2010-11 due to head injury at New Jersey, December 31, 2010. • Transferred to **Winnipeg** after **Atlanta** franchise relocated, June 21, 2011.

SLOAN, Tyler

(SLOHN, TIGH-luhr)

Defense. Shoots left. 6'3", 205 lbs. Born, Calgary, Alta., March 15, 1981.

			Regular Season														Playoffs								
Season	Club	League	GP	G	A	Pts	PIM	PP	SH	GW	S	%	+/-	TF	F%	Min	GP	G	A	Pts	PIM	PP	SH	GW	Min
1997-98	Calgary Buffaloes	AMHL	36	2	11	13	24	....	....	....	....	....	....	....	....	....	10	0	4	4	2	....	....	....	....
1998-99	Calgary Royals	AJHL	STATISTICS NOT AVAILABLE																						
99-2000	Calgary Royals	AJHL	45	5	26	31	80	....	....	....	....	....	....	....	....	....	....	....	....	....	....	....	....	....	....
2000-01	Kamloops Blazers	WHL	70	5	28	33	146	....	....	....	....	....	....	....	....	....	4	0	0	0	4	....	....	....	....
2001-02	Kamloops Blazers	WHL	70	3	29	32	89	....	....	....	....	....	....	....	....	....	4	0	0	0	15	....	....	....	....
	Syracuse Crunch	AHL	2	0	0	0	5	....	....	....	....	....	....	....	....	....	....	....	....	....	....	....	....	....	....
2002-03	Syracuse Crunch	AHL	39	2	1	3	46	....	....	....	....	....	....	....	....	....	....	....	....	....	....	....	....	....	....
	Dayton Bombers	ECHL	14	1	2	3	22	....	....	....	....	....	....	....	....	....	....	....	....	....	....	....	....	....	....
2003-04	Syracuse Crunch	AHL	69	2	4	6	50	....	....	....	....	....	....	....	....	....	7	0	0	0	8	....	....	....	....
2004-05	Syracuse Crunch	AHL	14	0	2	2	18	....	....	....	....	....	....	....	....	....	....	....	....	....	....	....	....	....	....
	Dayton Bombers	ECHL	43	6	11	17	84	....	....	....	....	....	....	....	....	....	....	....	....	....	....	....	....	....	....
2005-06	Las Vegas	ECHL	48	4	16	20	71	....	....	....	....	....	....	....	....	....	13	0	4	4	27	....	....	....	....
	Manitoba Moose	AHL	4	0	0	0	0	....	....	....	....	....	....	....	....	....	....	....	....	....	....	....	....	....	....
	Hershey Bears	AHL	....	....	....	....	....	....	....	....	....	....	....	....	....	....	2	0	1	1	2	....	....	....	....
2006-07	Hershey Bears	AHL	68	2	9	11	104	....	....	....	....	....	....	....	....	....	17	0	7	7	30	....	....	....	....
2007-08	Hershey Bears	AHL	56	1	7	8	90	....	....	....	....	....	....	....	....	....	5	0	0	0	8	....	....	....	....
2008-09	**Washington**	**NHL**	**26**	**1**	**4**	**5**	**14**	**0**	**0**	**0**	**8**	**12.5**	**4**	**0**	**0.0**	**16:39**	**2**	**0**	**1**	**1**	**0**	**0**	**0**	**0**	**18:24**
	Hershey Bears	AHL	46	2	10	12	61	....	....	....	....	....	....	....	....	....	16	0	5	5	14	....	....	....	....
2009-10	**Washington**	**NHL**	**40**	**2**	**4**	**6**	**22**	**0**	**0**	**0**	**34**	**5.9**	**–1**	**3**	**66.7**	**14:15**	**2**	**0**	**0**	**0**	**0**	**0**	**0**	**0**	**13:06**
	Hershey Bears	AHL	2	0	1	1	0	....	....	....	....	....	....	....	....	....	....	....	....	....	....	....	....	....	....
2010-11	**Washington**	**NHL**	**33**	**1**	**5**	**6**	**14**	**0**	**0**	**0**	**12**	**8.3**	**–6**	**0**	**0.0**	**12:30**	....	....	....	....	....	....	....	....	....
	Hershey Bears	AHL	6	0	2	2	6	....	....	....	....	....	....	....	....	....	....	....	....	....	....	....	....	....	....
2011-12	Milwaukee	AHL	62	1	9	10	58	....	....	....	....	....	....	....	....	....	3	0	0	0	0	....	....	....	....
2012-13	Texas Stars	AHL	42	3	6	9	55	....	....	....	....	....	....	....	....	....	1	0	0	0	0	....	....	....	....
	NHL Totals		**99**	**4**	**13**	**17**	**50**	**0**	**0**	**0**	**54**	**7.4**		**3**	**66.7**	**14:18**	**4**	**0**	**1**	**1**	**0**	**0**	**0**	**0**	**15:45**

Signed as a free agent by **Columbus**, September 24, 2000. Signed as a free agent by **Hershey** (AHL), August 15, 2007. Signed as a free agent by **Washington**, July 2, 2008. • Missed majority of 2010-11 due to recurring hip injury and as a healthy reserve. Signed as a free agent by **Nashville**, July 29, 2011. Signed as a free agent by **Dallas**, July 6, 2012.

SMID, Ladislav

(SHMIHD, LA-dih-slahv) **EDM**

Defense. Shoots left. 6'3", 210 lbs. Born, Frydlant V Cechach, Czech., February 1, 1986. Anaheim's 1st choice, 9th overall, in 2004 Entry Draft.

2001-02	HC Liberec Jr.	CzRep-Jr.	43	6	10	16	87	....	....	....	....	....	....	....	....	....	....	....	....	....	....	....	....	....	....
2002-03	HC Liberec Jr.	CzRep-Jr.	32	1	14	15	12	....	....	....	....	....	....	....	....	....	8	2	1	3	31	....	....	....	....
	Liberec	CzRep	4	0	0	0	0	....	....	....	....	....	....	....	....	....	....	....	....	....	....	....	....	....	....
2003-04	HC Liberec Jr.	CzRep-Jr.	14	4	10	14	38	....	....	....	....	....	....	....	....	....	2	1	0	1	6	....	....	....	....
	Liberec	CzRep	45	1	1	2	51	....	....	....	....	....	....	....	....	....	....	....	....	....	....	....	....	....	....
	Beroun	CzRep-2	....	....	....	....	....	....	....	....	....	....	....	....	....	....	3	1	1	2	4	....	....	....	....
2004-05	HC Liberec Jr.	CzRep-Jr.	3	0	1	1	4	....	....	....	....	....	....	....	....	....	....	....	....	....	....	....	....	....	....
	Liberec	CzRep	39	1	3	4	14	....	....	....	....	....	....	....	....	....	12	0	0	0	6	....	....	....	....
2005-06	Portland Pirates	AHL	71	3	25	28	48	....	....	....	....	....	....	....	....	....	16	0	1	1	16	....	....	....	....
2006-07	**Edmonton**	**NHL**	**77**	**3**	**7**	**10**	**37**	**0**	**0**	**0**	**53**	**5.7**	**–16**	**0**	**0.0**	**19:14**	....	....	....	....	....	....	....	....	....
2007-08	**Edmonton**	**NHL**	**65**	**0**	**4**	**4**	**58**	**0**	**0**	**0**	**45**	**0.0**	**–15**	**0**	**0.0**	**17:52**	....	....	....	....	....	....	....	....	....
	Springfield	AHL	8	1	4	5	15	....	....	....	....	....	....	....	....	....	....	....	....	....	....	....	....	....	....
2008-09	**Edmonton**	**NHL**	**60**	**0**	**11**	**11**	**57**	**0**	**0**	**0**	**33**	**0.0**	**–6**	**0**	**0.0**	**14:57**	....	....	....	....	....	....	....	....	....
2009-10	**Edmonton**	**NHL**	**51**	**1**	**8**	**9**	**39**	**0**	**0**	**0**	**36**	**2.8**	**5**	**0**	**0.0**	**19:11**	....	....	....	....	....	....	....	....	....
2010-11	**Edmonton**	**NHL**	**78**	**0**	**10**	**10**	**85**	**0**	**0**	**0**	**48**	**0.0**	**–10**	**0**	**0.0**	**20:17**	....	....	....	....	....	....	....	....	....
2011-12	**Edmonton**	**NHL**	**78**	**5**	**10**	**15**	**44**	**0**	**0**	**0**	**47**	**10.6**	**4**	**0**	**0.0**	**20:54**	....	....	....	....	....	....	....	....	....
2012-13	Liberec	CzRep	22	2	12	14	22	....	....	....	....	....	....	....	....	....	....	....	....	....	....	....	....	....	....
	Edmonton	**NHL**	**48**	**1**	**3**	**4**	**55**	**0**	**0**	**0**	**30**	**3.3**	**–1**	**0**	**0.0**	**20:19**	....	....	....	....	....	....	....	....	....
	NHL Totals		**457**	**10**	**53**	**63**	**375**	**0**	**0**	**0**	**292**	**3.4**		**0**	**0.0**	**19:03**	....	....	....	....	....	....	....	....	....

Traded to **Edmonton** by **Anaheim** with Joffrey Lupul, Anaheim's 1st round choice (later traded to Phoenix - Phoenix selected Nick Ross) in 2007 Entry Draft and Anaheim's 1st (Jordan Eberle) and 2nd (later traded to NY Islanders - NY Islanders selected Travis Hamonic) round choices in 2008 Entry Draft for Chris Pronger, July 3, 2006. Signed as a free agent by **Liberec** (CzRep), September 21, 2012.

SMITH, Ben

(SMIHTH, BEHN) **CHI**

Right wing. Shoots right. 5'11", 207 lbs. Born, Winston-Salem, NC, July 11, 1988. Chicago's 5th choice, 169th overall, in 2008 Entry Draft.

2006-07	Boston College	H-East	42	10	8	18	10	....	....	....	....	....	....	....	....	....	....	....	....	....	....	....	....	....	....
2007-08	Boston College	H-East	44	25	25	50	12	....	....	....	....	....	....	....	....	....	....	....	....	....	....	....	....	....	....
2008-09	Boston College	H-East	37	6	11	17	6	....	....	....	....	....	....	....	....	....	....	....	....	....	....	....	....	....	....
2009-10	Boston College	H-East	42	16	21	37	8	....	....	....	....	....	....	....	....	....	....	....	....	....	....	....	....	....	....
	Rockford IceHogs	AHL	....	....	....	....	....	....	....	....	....	....	....	....	....	....	3	1	0	1	0	....	....	....	....
2010-11	**Chicago**	**NHL**	**6**	**1**	**0**	**1**	**0**	**0**	**0**	**0**	**6**	**16.7**	**1**	**8**	**75.0**	**13:47**	**7**	**3**	**0**	**3**	**0**	**0**	**0**	**1**	**14:50**
	Rockford IceHogs	AHL	63	19	12	31	16	....	....	....	....	....	....	....	....	....	....	....	....	....	....	....	....	....	....
2011-12	**Chicago**	**NHL**	**13**	**2**	**0**	**2**	**0**	**0**	**0**	**0**	**18**	**11.1**	**–5**	**14**	**50.0**	**9:49**	....	....	....	....	....	....	....	....	....
	Rockford IceHogs	AHL	38	15	16	31	10	....	....	....	....	....	....	....	....	....	....	....	....	....	....	....	....	....	....
2012-13	Rockford IceHogs	AHL	54	27	20	47	13	....	....	....	....	....	....	....	....	....	....	....	....	....	....	....	....	....	....
	♦ Chicago	**NHL**	**1**	**1**	**0**	**1**	**0**	**0**	**0**	**0**	**1**	**100.0**	**1**	**2**	**0.0**	**18:21**	**1**	**0**	**0**	**0**	**0**	**0**	**0**	**0**	**10:23**
	NHL Totals		**20**	**4**	**0**	**4**	**0**	**0**	**0**	**0**	**25**	**16.0**		**24**	**54.2**	**11:26**	**8**	**3**	**0**	**3**	**0**	**0**	**0**	**1**	**14:17**

NCAA Championship All-Tournament Team (2008, 2010) • NCAA Championship Tournament MVP (2010)

SMITH, Brendan

(SMIHTH, BREHN-duhn) **DET**

Defense. Shoots left. 6'1", 198 lbs. Born, Toronto, Ont., February 8, 1989. Detroit's 1st choice, 27th overall, in 2007 Entry Draft.

2004-05	Tor. Marlboros	GTHL	66	22	63	85	120	....	....	....	....	....	....	....	....	....	....	....	....	....	....	....	....	....	....
2005-06	St. Michael's	ON-Jr.A	39	5	21	26	55	....	....	....	....	....	....	....	....	....	17	1	5	6	44	....	....	....	....
2006-07	St. Michael's	ON-Jr.A	39	12	24	36	90	....	....	....	....	....	....	....	....	....	16	6	14	20	30	....	....	....	....
2007-08	U. of Wisconsin	WCHA	22	2	10	12	26	....	....	....	....	....	....	....	....	....	....	....	....	....	....	....	....	....	....
2008-09	U. of Wisconsin	WCHA	31	9	14	23	75	....	....	....	....	....	....	....	....	....	....	....	....	....	....	....	....	....	....
2009-10	U. of Wisconsin	WCHA	42	15	37	52	76	....	....	....	....	....	....	....	....	....	....	....	....	....	....	....	....	....	....
2010-11	Grand Rapids	AHL	63	12	20	32	124	....	....	....	....	....	....	....	....	....	....	....	....	....	....	....	....	....	....
2011-12	**Detroit**	**NHL**	**14**	**1**	**6**	**7**	**13**	**0**	**0**	**0**	**13**	**7.7**	**3**	**0**	**0.0**	**15:38**	....	....	....	....	....	....	....	....	....
	Grand Rapids	AHL	57	10	24	34	90	....	....	....	....	....	....	....	....	....	....	....	....	....	....	....	....	....	....
2012-13	Grand Rapids	AHL	32	5	15	20	49	....	....	....	....	....	....	....	....	....	....	....	....	....	....	....	....	....	....
	Detroit	**NHL**	**34**	**0**	**8**	**8**	**36**	**0**	**0**	**0**	**33**	**0.0**	**1**	**0**	**0.0**	**18:24**	**14**	**2**	**3**	**5**	**10**	**0**	**0**	**1**	**19:08**
	NHL Totals		**48**	**1**	**14**	**15**	**49**	**0**	**0**	**0**	**46**	**2.2**		**0**	**0.0**	**17:36**	**14**	**2**	**3**	**5**	**10**	**0**	**0**	**1**	**19:08**

WCHA First All-Star Team (2010) • NCAA West First All-American Team (2010) • NCAA Championship All-Tournament Team (2010) • AHL All-Rookie Team (2011)

SMITH, Craig

(SMIHTH, KRAYG) **NSH**

Center. Shoots right. 6'1", 199 lbs. Born, Madison, WI, September 5, 1989. Nashville's 6th choice, 98th overall, in 2009 Entry Draft.

2004-05	Madison Lancers	High-WI	20	16	24	40	....	....	....	....	....	....	....	....	....	....	....	....	....	....	....	....	....	....	....
2005-06	Madison Lancers	High-WI	20	35	26	61	....	....	....	....	....	....	....	....	....	....	....	....	....	....	....	....	....	....	....
2006-07	Waterloo	USHL	45	8	10	18	28	....	....	....	....	....	....	....	....	....	4	0	1	1	8	....	....	....	....
2007-08	Waterloo	USHL	58	13	10	23	90	....	....	....	....	....	....	....	....	....	11	2	3	5	8	....	....	....	....
2008-09	Waterloo	USHL	54	28	48	76	108	....	....	....	....	....	....	....	....	....	3	1	3	4	26	....	....	....	....
2009-10	U. of Wisconsin	WCHA	41	8	25	33	72	....	....	....	....	....	....	....	....	....	....	....	....	....	....	....	....	....	....
2010-11	U. of Wisconsin	WCHA	41	19	24	43	87	....	....	....	....	....	....	....	....	....	....	....	....	....	....	....	....	....	....
2011-12	**Nashville**	**NHL**	**72**	**14**	**22**	**36**	**30**	**6**	**0**	**1**	**172**	**8.1**	**–9**	**393**	**44.0**	**14:11**	**2**	**0**	**1**	**1**	**0**	**0**	**0**	**0**	**8:25**
2012-13	KalPa Kuopio	Finland	8	4	4	8	20	....	....	....	....	....	....	....	....	....	....	....	....	....	....	....	....	....	....
	Nashville	**NHL**	**44**	**4**	**8**	**12**	**20**	**2**	**0**	**0**	**83**	**4.8**	**–11**	**200**	**39.5**	**13:51**	....	....	....	....	....	....	....	....	....
	Milwaukee	AHL	4	1	4	5	0	....	....	....	....	....	....	....	....	....	....	....	....	....	....	....	....	....	....
	NHL Totals		**116**	**18**	**30**	**48**	**50**	**8**	**0**	**1**	**255**	**7.1**		**593**	**42.5**	**14:04**	**2**	**0**	**1**	**1**	**0**	**0**	**0**	**0**	**8:25**

USHL First All-Star Team (2009) • WCHA All-Rookie Team (2010)

Signed as a free agent by **Kuopio** (Finland), October 2, 2012.

SMITH, Derek
(SMIHTH, DAIR-ihk) **CGY**

Defense. Shoots left. 6'1", 197 lbs. Born, Belleville, Ont., October 13, 1984.

			Regular Season														Playoffs								
Season	Club	League	GP	G	A	Pts	PIM	PP	SH	GW	S	%	+/-	TF	F%	Min	GP	G	A	Pts	PIM	PP	SH	GW	Min
2000-01	Wellington Dukes	ON-Jr.A	12	1	1	2	4	....	....	....	....	....	....	....	....	....	....	....	....	....	....	....	....	....	....
2001-02	Wellington Dukes	ON-Jr.A	46	5	15	20	26	....	....	....	....	....	....	....	....	....	....	....	....	....	....	....	....	....	....
2002-03	Wellington Dukes	ON-Jr.A	21	6	10	16	26	....	....	....	....	....	....	....	....	....	....	....	....	....	....	....	....	....	....
2003-04	Wellington Dukes	ON-Jr.A	44	8	26	34	34	....	....	....	....	....	....	....	....	....	....	....	....	....	....	....	....	....	....
2004-05	Lake Superior	CCHA	38	1	4	5	28	....	....	....	....	....	....	....	....	....	....	....	....	....	....	....	....	....	....
2005-06	Lake Superior	CCHA	36	2	8	10	18	....	....	....	....	....	....	....	....	....	....	....	....	....	....	....	....	....	....
2006-07	Lake Superior	CCHA	43	10	20	30	10	....	....	....	....	....	....	....	....	....	....	....	....	....	....	....	....	....	....
2007-08	Binghamton	AHL	52	2	11	13	18	....	....	....	....	....	....	....	....	....	....	....	....	....	....	....	....	....	....
	Elmira Jackals	ECHL	1	0	1	1	0	....	....	....	....	....	....	....	....	....	....	....	....	....	....	....	....	....	....
2008-09	Binghamton	AHL	75	7	17	24	49	....	....	....	....	....	....	....	....	....	....	....	....	....	....	....	....	....	....
2009-10	**Ottawa**	**NHL**	**2**	**0**	**0**	**0**	**0**	**0**	**0**	**0**	**4**	**0.0**	**–4**	**0**	**0.0**	**12:20**	....	....	....	....	....	....	....	....	....
	Binghamton	AHL	74	14	37	51	24	....	....	....	....	....	....	....	....	....	....	....	....	....	....	....	....	....	....
2010-11	**Ottawa**	**NHL**	**9**	**0**	**1**	**1**	**0**	**0**	**0**	**0**	**13**	**0.0**	**3**	**0**	**0.0**	**15:19**	....	....	....	....	....	....	....	....	....
	Binghamton	AHL	71	10	44	54	21	....	....	....	....	....	....	....	....	....	6	1	1	2	6	....	....	....	....
2011-12	**Calgary**	**NHL**	**47**	**2**	**9**	**11**	**12**	**0**	**0**	**1**	**44**	**4.5**	**–1**	**0**	**0.0**	**15:56**	....	....	....	....	....	....	....	....	....
2012-13	**Calgary**	**NHL**	**22**	**0**	**1**	**1**	**10**	**0**	**0**	**0**	**18**	**0.0**	**–5**	**0**	**0.0**	**12:15**	....	....	....	....	....	....	....	....	....
	NHL Totals		**80**	**2**	**11**	**13**	**22**	**0**	**0**	**1**	**79**	**2.5**		**0**	**0.0**	**14:46**	....	....	....	....	....	....	....	....	....

Signed as a free agent by **Ottawa**, April 12, 2007. Signed as a free agent by **Calgary**, July 13, 2011. • Missed majority of 2012-13 due to upper-body injury and as a healthy reserve.

SMITH, Reilly
(SMIHTH, RIGH-lee) **BOS**

Right wing. Shoots left. 6', 185 lbs. Born, Toronto, Ont., April 1, 1991. Dallas' 3rd choice, 69th overall, in 2009 Entry Draft.

Season	Club	League	GP	G	A	Pts	PIM	PP	SH	GW	S	%	+/-	TF	F%	Min	GP	G	A	Pts	PIM	PP	SH	GW	Min
2007-08	Tor. Young Nats	GTHL	70	80	77	157	56	....	....	....	....	....	....	....	....	....	....	....	....	....	....	....	....	....	....
	St. Michael's	ON-Jr.A	13	2	7	9	22	....	....	....	....	....	....	....	....	....	1	0	0	0	2	....	....	....	....
2008-09	St. Michael's	ON-Jr.A	49	27	48	75	44	....	....	....	....	....	....	....	....	....	6	9	6	15	10	....	....	....	....
2009-10	Miami U.	CCHA	44	8	12	20	24	....	....	....	....	....	....	....	....	....	....	....	....	....	....	....	....	....	....
2010-11	Miami U.	CCHA	38	28	26	54	18	....	....	....	....	....	....	....	....	....	....	....	....	....	....	....	....	....	....
2011-12	Miami U.	CCHA	39	30	18	48	22	....	....	....	....	....	....	....	....	....	....	....	....	....	....	....	....	....	....
	Dallas	**NHL**	**3**	**0**	**0**	**0**	**2**	**0**	**0**	**0**	**2**	**0.0**	**–3**	**1**	**100.0**	**8:24**	....	....	....	....	....	....	....	....	....
2012-13	Texas Stars	AHL	45	14	21	35	20	....	....	....	....	....	....	....	....	....	7	0	4	4	0	....	....	....	....
	Dallas	**NHL**	**37**	**3**	**6**	**9**	**8**	**0**	**0**	**0**	**34**	**8.8**	**0**	**4**	**75.0**	**10:55**	....	....	....	....	....	....	....	....	....
	NHL Totals		**40**	**3**	**6**	**9**	**10**	**0**	**0**	**0**	**36**	**8.3**		**5**	**80.0**	**10:44**	....	....	....	....	....	....	....	....	....

CCHA First All-Star Team (2011, 2012) • NCAA West First All-American Team (2012)

Traded to **Boston** by **Dallas** with Loui Eriksson, Joe Morrow and Matt Fraser for Tyler Seguin, Rich Peverley and Ryan Button, July 4, 2013.

SMITH, Trevor
(SMIHTH, TREH-vuhr) **TOR**

Center. Shoots left. 6'1", 195 lbs. Born, Ottawa, Ont., February 8, 1985.

Season	Club	League	GP	G	A	Pts	PIM	PP	SH	GW	S	%	+/-	TF	F%	Min	GP	G	A	Pts	PIM	PP	SH	GW	Min
2003-04	Quesnel	BCHL	44	28	19	47	50	....	....	....	....	....	....	....	....	....	....	....	....	....	....	....	....	....	....
2004-05	Omaha Lancers	USHL	60	29	39	68	78	....	....	....	....	....	....	....	....	....	5	3	1	4	2	....	....	....	....
2005-06	New Hampshire	H-East	39	10	10	20	34	....	....	....	....	....	....	....	....	....	....	....	....	....	....	....	....	....	....
2006-07	New Hampshire	H-East	39	21	22	43	39	....	....	....	....	....	....	....	....	....	....	....	....	....	....	....	....	....	....
	Bridgeport	AHL	8	1	2	3	2	....	....	....	....	....	....	....	....	....	....	....	....	....	....	....	....	....	....
2007-08	Bridgeport	AHL	53	20	17	37	16	....	....	....	....	....	....	....	....	....	....	....	....	....	....	....	....	....	....
	Utah Grizzlies	ECHL	22	11	14	25	28	....	....	....	....	....	....	....	....	....	....	....	....	....	....	....	....	....	....
2008-09	**NY Islanders**	**NHL**	**7**	**1**	**0**	**1**	**0**	**0**	**0**	**0**	**7**	**14.3**	**–3**	**9**	**66.7**	**11:48**	....	....	....	....	....	....	....	....	....
	Bridgeport	AHL	76	30	32	62	40	....	....	....	....	....	....	....	....	....	5	1	3	4	0	....	....	....	....
2009-10	Bridgeport	AHL	77	21	26	47	73	....	....	....	....	....	....	....	....	....	5	1	2	3	2	....	....	....	....
2010-11	Syracuse Crunch	AHL	35	12	15	27	16	....	....	....	....	....	....	....	....	....	....	....	....	....	....	....	....	....	....
	Springfield	AHL	33	8	8	16	10	....	....	....	....	....	....	....	....	....	....	....	....	....	....	....	....	....	....
2011-12	**Tampa Bay**	**NHL**	**16**	**2**	**3**	**5**	**4**	**0**	**0**	**0**	**17**	**11.8**	**2**	**83**	**41.0**	**12:28**	....	....	....	....	....	....	....	....	....
	Norfolk Admirals	AHL	64	26	43	69	70	....	....	....	....	....	....	....	....	....	18	5	11	16	20	....	....	....	....
2012-13	Wilkes-Barre	AHL	75	23	31	54	64	....	....	....	....	....	....	....	....	....	15	5	8	13	9	....	....	....	....
	Pittsburgh	**NHL**	**1**	**0**	**0**	**0**	**0**	**0**	**0**	**0**	**0**	**0.0**	**0**	**0**	**0.0**	**10:24**	....	....	....	....	....	....	....	....	....
	NHL Totals		**24**	**3**	**3**	**6**	**4**	**0**	**0**	**0**	**24**	**12.5**		**92**	**43.5**	**12:11**	....	....	....	....	....	....	....	....	....

NCAA East Second All-American Team (2007)

Signed as a free agent by **NY Islanders**, April 2, 2007. Signed as a free agent by **Anaheim**, July 2, 2010. Traded to **Columbus** by **Anaheim** for Nate Guenin, January 4, 2011. Signed as a free agent by **Tampa Bay**, July 5, 2011. Signed as a free agent by **Pittsburgh**, July 1, 2012. Signed as a free agent by **Toronto**, July 5, 2013.

SMITH, Zack
(SMIHTH, ZAK) **OTT**

Center. Shoots left. 6'2", 212 lbs. Born, Medicine Hat, Alta., April 5, 1988. Ottawa's 3rd choice, 79th overall, in 2008 Entry Draft.

Season	Club	League	GP	G	A	Pts	PIM	PP	SH	GW	S	%	+/-	TF	F%	Min	GP	G	A	Pts	PIM	PP	SH	GW	Min
2004-05	Swift Current	SMHL	43	15	27	42	83	....	....	....	....	....	....	....	....	....	....	....	....	....	....	....	....	....	....
	Swift Current	WHL	14	1	1	2	0	....	....	....	....	....	....	....	....	....	....	....	....	....	....	....	....	....	....
2005-06	Swift Current	WHL	64	2	5	7	78	....	....	....	....	....	....	....	....	....	3	0	0	0	9	....	....	....	....
2006-07	Swift Current	WHL	71	16	15	31	130	....	....	....	....	....	....	....	....	....	6	0	2	2	11	....	....	....	....
2007-08	Swift Current	WHL	72	22	47	69	136	....	....	....	....	....	....	....	....	....	12	5	5	10	29	....	....	....	....
	Manitoba Moose	AHL	....	....	....	....	....	....	....	....	....	....	....	....	....	....	6	0	1	1	0	....	....	....	....
2008-09	**Ottawa**	**NHL**	**1**	**0**	**0**	**0**	**0**	**0**	**0**	**0**	**0**	**0.0**	**0**	**1**	**0.0**	**7:01**	....	....	....	....	....	....	....	....	....
	Binghamton	AHL	79	24	24	48	132	....	....	....	....	....	....	....	....	....	....	....	....	....	....	....	....	....	....
2009-10	**Ottawa**	**NHL**	**15**	**2**	**1**	**3**	**14**	**0**	**1**	**0**	**11**	**18.2**	**1**	**61**	**47.5**	**9:03**	**6**	**0**	**0**	**0**	**5**	**0**	**0**	**0**	**7:25**
	Binghamton	AHL	68	14	27	41	100	....	....	....	....	....	....	....	....	....	....	....	....	....	....	....	....	....	....
2010-11	**Ottawa**	**NHL**	**55**	**4**	**5**	**9**	**120**	**0**	**0**	**0**	**78**	**5.1**	**–11**	**388**	**53.9**	**12:36**	....	....	....	....	....	....	....	....	....
	Binghamton	AHL	22	7	5	12	32	....	....	....	....	....	....	....	....	....	23	8	12	20	36	....	....	....	....
2011-12	**Ottawa**	**NHL**	**81**	**14**	**12**	**26**	**98**	**1**	**2**	**3**	**134**	**10.4**	**4**	**990**	**48.9**	**14:04**	**7**	**0**	**1**	**1**	**10**	**0**	**0**	**0**	**13:22**
2012-13	Frederikshavn	Denmark	7	4	6	10	18	....	....	....	....	....	....	....	....	....	....	....	....	....	....	....	....	....	....
	Ottawa	**NHL**	**48**	**4**	**11**	**15**	**56**	**0**	**0**	**0**	**94**	**4.3**	**–9**	**731**	**51.9**	**15:09**	**10**	**1**	**1**	**2**	**31**	**0**	**0**	**0**	**13:17**
	NHL Totals		**200**	**24**	**29**	**53**	**288**	**1**	**3**	**3**	**317**	**7.6**		**2171**	**50.7**	**13:31**	**23**	**1**	**2**	**3**	**46**	**0**	**0**	**0**	**11:47**

Signed as a free agent by **Frederikshavn** (Denmark), November 26, 2012.

SMITH-PELLY, Devante
(SMITH-PEH-lee, deh-VAHN-tay) **ANA**

Right wing. Shoots right. 6', 225 lbs. Born, Scarborough, Ont., June 14, 1992. Anaheim's 3rd choice, 42nd overall, in 2010 Entry Draft.

Season	Club	League	GP	G	A	Pts	PIM	PP	SH	GW	S	%	+/-	TF	F%	Min	GP	G	A	Pts	PIM	PP	SH	GW	Min
2007-08	Tor. Jr. Canadiens	GTHL	85	38	39	77	159	....	....	....	....	....	....	....	....	....	....	....	....	....	....	....	....	....	....
2008-09	St. Michael's	OHL	57	13	12	25	24	....	....	....	....	....	....	....	....	....	11	2	3	5	4	....	....	....	....
2009-10	St. Michael's	OHL	60	29	33	62	35	....	....	....	....	....	....	....	....	....	16	8	6	14	20	....	....	....	....
2010-11	St. Michael's	OHL	67	36	30	66	50	....	....	....	....	....	....	....	....	....	20	*15	6	21	16	....	....	....	....
2011-12	**Anaheim**	**NHL**	**49**	**7**	**6**	**13**	**16**	**1**	**1**	**1**	**66**	**10.6**	**–7**	**21**	**28.6**	**12:03**	....	....	....	....	....	....	....	....	....
	Syracuse Crunch	AHL	4	0	1	1	2	....	....	....	....	....	....	....	....	....	....	....	....	....	....	....	....	....	....
2012-13	Norfolk Admirals	AHL	65	14	18	32	65	....	....	....	....	....	....	....	....	....	....	....	....	....	....	....	....	....	....
	Anaheim	**NHL**	**7**	**0**	**0**	**0**	**0**	**0**	**0**	**0**	**5**	**0.0**	**–4**	**0**	**0.0**	**9:00**	....	....	....	....	....	....	....	....	....
	NHL Totals		**56**	**7**	**6**	**13**	**16**	**1**	**1**	**1**	**71**	**9.9**		**21**	**28.6**	**11:40**	....	....	....	....	....	....	....	....	....

Memorial Cup All-Star Team (2011)

SMITHSON, Jerred
(SMIHTH-suhn, JEHR-rehd)

Center. Shoots right. 6'3", 209 lbs. Born, Vernon, B.C., February 4, 1979.

Season	Club	League	GP	G	A	Pts	PIM	PP	SH	GW	S	%	+/-	TF	F%	Min	GP	G	A	Pts	PIM	PP	SH	GW	Min
1994-95	Vernon	Minor-BC	64	39	46	85	120	....	....	....	....	....	....	....	....	....	....	....	....	....	....	....	....	....	....
1995-96	Calgary Hitmen	WHL	60	4	2	6	16	....	....	....	....	....	....	....	....	....	....	....	....	....	....	....	....	....	....
1996-97	Calgary Hitmen	WHL	65	3	6	9	49	....	....	....	....	....	....	....	....	....	....	....	....	....	....	....	....	....	....
1997-98	Calgary Hitmen	WHL	65	12	9	21	65	....	....	....	....	....	....	....	....	....	18	0	2	2	25	....	....	....	....
1998-99	Calgary Hitmen	WHL	63	14	22	36	108	....	....	....	....	....	....	....	....	....	21	3	7	10	17	....	....	....	....
99-2000	Calgary Hitmen	WHL	66	14	25	39	111	....	....	....	....	....	....	....	....	....	10	1	1	2	16	....	....	....	....
2000-01	Lowell	AHL	24	1	1	2	10	....	....	....	....	....	....	....	....	....	4	0	0	0	2	....	....	....	....
	Trenton Titans	ECHL	3	0	1	1	2	....	....	....	....	....	....	....	....	....	....	....	....	....	....	....	....	....	....
2001-02	Manchester	AHL	78	5	13	18	45	....	....	....	....	....	....	....	....	....	5	0	1	1	4	....	....	....	....

Season	Club	League	GP	G	A	Pts	PIM	PP	SH	GW	S	%	+/-	TF	F%	Min	GP	G	A	Pts	PIM	PP	SH	GW	Min
			Regular Season														Playoffs								
2002-03	Los Angeles	NHL	22	0	2	2	21	0	0	0	9	0.0	–5	175	48.0	8:50									
	Manchester	AHL	38	4	21	25	60										3	0	0	0	4				
2003-04	Los Angeles	NHL	8	0	1	1	4	0	0	0	2	0.0	0	86	64.0	10:39									
	Manchester	AHL	66	7	13	20	51										6	0	1	1	10				
2004-05	Milwaukee	AHL	80	11	11	22	92										5	0	0	0	4				
2005-06	Nashville	NHL	66	5	9	14	54	0	0	1	50	10.0	9	613	54.3	11:50	3	0	0	0	4	0	0	0	9:26
	Milwaukee	AHL	8	0	0	0	12																		
2006-07	Nashville	NHL	64	5	7	12	42	1	1	2	47	10.6	–8	420	56.4	11:03	5	0	0	0	17	0	0	0	11:30
2007-08	Nashville	NHL	81	7	9	16	50	0	2	2	61	11.5	–9	572	52.1	12:05	6	0	0	0	2	0	0	0	11:52
2008-09	Nashville	NHL	82	4	9	13	49	0	0	0	74	5.4	–6	722	52.6	13:51									
2009-10	Nashville	NHL	69	9	4	13	54	0	2	1	54	16.7	–4	548	54.9	13:58	6	1	0	1	6	0	0	0	15:36
2010-11	Nashville	NHL	82	5	8	13	34	0	0	0	73	6.8	–6	1006	57.5	14:51	11	1	1	2	8	0	0	1	14:09
2011-12	Nashville	NHL	53	1	4	5	30	0	0	0	25	4.0	–6	513	55.6	11:56									
	Florida	NHL	16	0	1	1	4	0	0	0	12	0.0	1	132	58.3	11:00	5	0	1	1	2	0	0	0	11:04
2012-13	Florida	NHL	35	2	3	5	10	0	0	0	22	9.1	–4	363	54.8	10:22									
	Edmonton	NHL	10	1	0	1	2	0	0	0	7	14.3	0	115	57.4	11:43									
	NHL Totals		588	39	57	96	354	1	5	6	436	8.9		5265	54.9	12:30	36	2	2	4	39	0	0	1	12:49

Signed as a free agent by **Los Angeles**, February 18, 2000. Signed as a free agent by **Nashville**, July 22, 2004. Traded to **Florida** by **Nashville** for Dallas' 6th round choice (previously acquired, Nashville selected Simon Fernholm) in 2012 Entry Draft, February 24, 2012. Traded to **Edmonton** by **Florida** for Edmonton's 4th round choice (Matt Buckles) in 2013 Entry Draft, April 3, 2013.

SMYTH, Ryan (SMIHTH, RIGH-uhn) EDM

Left wing. Shoots left. 6'1", 192 lbs. Born, Banff, Alta., February 21, 1976. Edmonton's 2nd choice, 6th overall, in 1994 Entry Draft.

Season	Club	League	GP	G	A	Pts	PIM	PP	SH	GW	S	%	+/-	TF	F%	Min	GP	G	A	Pts	PIM	PP	SH	GW	Min
1990-91	Banff Blazers	Minor-AB	25	100	50	150																			
	Lethbridge	AMHL	34	8	21	29																			
1991-92	Caronport	SMHL	35	55	61	116	98																		
	Moose Jaw	WHL	2	0	0	0	0																		
1992-93	Moose Jaw	WHL	64	19	14	33	59																		
1993-94	Moose Jaw	WHL	72	50	55	105	88																		
1994-95	Moose Jaw	WHL	50	41	45	86	66										10	6	9	15	22				
	Edmonton	NHL	3	0	0	0	0	0	0	0	2	0.0	–1												
1995-96	Edmonton	NHL	48	2	9	11	28	1	0	0	65	3.1	–10												
	Cape Breton	AHL	9	6	5	11	4																		
1996-97	Edmonton	NHL	82	39	22	61	76	*20	0	4	265	14.7	–7				12	5	5	10	12	1	0	2	
1997-98	Edmonton	NHL	65	20	13	33	44	10	0	2	205	9.8	–24				12	1	3	4	16	1	0	0	
1998-99	Edmonton	NHL	71	13	18	31	62	6	0	2	161	8.1	0	5	20.0	14:26	3	3	0	3	0	2	0	0	24:35
99-2000	Edmonton	NHL	82	28	26	54	58	11	0	4	238	11.8	–2	24	54.2	19:12	5	1	0	1	6	0	1	0	19:18
2000-01	Edmonton	NHL	82	31	39	70	58	11	0	6	245	12.7	10	17	35.3	19:58	6	3	4	7	4	0	0	0	24:46
2001-02	Edmonton	NHL	61	15	35	50	48	7	1	5	150	10.0	7	12	41.7	19:27									
	Canada	Olympics	6	0	1	1	0																		
2002-03	Edmonton	NHL	66	27	34	61	67	10	0	3	199	13.6	5	42	42.9	19:21	6	2	0	2	16	0	1	0	17:39
2003-04	Edmonton	NHL	82	23	36	59	70	8	2	6	245	9.4	11	484	47.1	19:39									
2004-05			Did Not Play																						
2005-06	Edmonton	NHL	75	36	30	66	58	19	2	3	230	15.7	–5	159	47.8	20:13	24	7	9	16	22	4	0	1	21:27
	Canada	Olympics	6	0	1	1	4																		
2006-07	Edmonton	NHL	53	31	22	53	38	14	1	5	161	19.3	2	63	47.6	20:09									
	NY Islanders	NHL	18	5	10	15	14	1	0	0	49	10.2	0	9	22.2	22:26	5	1	3	4	4	0	0	0	22:42
2007-08	Colorado	NHL	55	14	23	37	50	2	0	3	168	8.3	–4	33	39.4	19:37	8	2	3	5	2	1	0	1	17:29
2008-09	Colorado	NHL	77	26	33	59	62	10	1	3	257	10.1	–15	174	51.2	20:17									
2009-10	Los Angeles	NHL	67	22	31	53	42	11	0	3	206	10.7	8	62	50.0	19:41	6	1	1	2	6	0	0	0	18:39
2010-11	Los Angeles	NHL	82	23	24	47	35	9	0	2	195	11.8	–1	132	43.2	18:02	6	2	3	5	0	0	0	0	18:20
2011-12	Edmonton	NHL	82	19	27	46	82	4	0	4	194	9.8	–5	150	44.0	19:05									
2012-13	Edmonton	NHL	47	2	11	13	40	0	1	0	69	2.9	–5	202	43.1	15:22									
	NHL Totals		1198	376	443	819	932	154	8	55	3304	11.4		1568	46.0	19:01	93	28	31	59	88	9	2	4	20:30

WHL East Second All-Star Team (1995)

Played in NHL All-Star Game (2007)

Traded to **NY Islanders** by **Edmonton** for Ryan O'Marra, Robert Nilsson and NY Islanders' 1st round choice (Alex Plante) in 2007 Entry Draft, February 27, 2007. Signed as a free agent by **Colorado**, July 1, 2007. Traded to **Los Angeles** by **Colorado** for Kyle Quincey, Tom Preissing and Los Angeles' 5th round choice (Luke Walker) in 2010 Entry Draft, July 3, 2009. Traded to **Edmonton** by **Los Angeles** for Colin Fraser and Edmonton's 7th round choice (later traded to Dallas – Dallas selected Dmitri Sinitsyn) in 2012 Entry Draft, June 26, 2011.

SNEEP, Carl (SNEEP, KAHRL)

Defense. Shoots right. 6'4", 210 lbs. Born, St. Louis Park, MN, November 5, 1987. Pittsburgh's 2nd choice, 32nd overall, in 2006 Entry Draft.

Season	Club	League	GP	G	A	Pts	PIM	PP	SH	GW	S	%	+/-	TF	F%	Min	GP	G	A	Pts	PIM	PP	SH	GW	Min
2004-05	Brainerd	High-MN	26	20	21	41	25																		
2005-06	Brainerd	High-MN	26	14	23	37	34																		
	Lincoln Stars	USHL	13	1	3	4	9										9	0	1	1	6				
2006-07	Boston College	H-East	38	1	9	10	8																		
2007-08	Boston College	H-East	44	3	12	15	15																		
2008-09	Boston College	H-East	33	2	9	11	26																		
2009-10	Boston College	H-East	42	11	17	28	26																		
2010-11	Wilkes-Barre	AHL	61	4	13	17	39										2	0	0	0	0				
2011-12	Pittsburgh	NHL	1	0	1	1	0	0	0	0	0	0.0	1	0	0.0	16:19									
	Wilkes-Barre	AHL	40	0	10	10	26																		
2012-13	Wilkes-Barre	AHL	1	0	0	0	0																		
	Wheeling Nailers	ECHL	29	3	12	15	22																		
	Texas Stars	AHL	25	2	4	6	10																		
	Peoria Rivermen	AHL	6	0	0	0	2																		
	NHL Totals		1	0	1	1	0	0	0	0	0	0.0		0	0.0	16:19									

Traded to **Dallas** by **Pittsburgh** for future considerations, January 24, 2013. • Loaned to **Peoria** (AHL) by **Dallas** (Texas-AHL), April 9, 2013.

SOBOTKA, Vladimir (suh-BOHT-kah, vla-DIH-meer) ST.L.

Center. Shoots left. 5'10", 197 lbs. Born, Trebic, Czech., July 2, 1987. Boston's 5th choice, 106th overall, in 2005 Entry Draft.

Season	Club	League	GP	G	A	Pts	PIM	PP	SH	GW	S	%	+/-	TF	F%	Min	GP	G	A	Pts	PIM	PP	SH	GW	Min
2002-03	Slavia U17	CzR-U17	46	16	24	40	48										8	1	1	2	29				
2003-04	Slavia U17	CzR-U17	35	24	41	65	109										7	7	12	19	8				
	Slavia Jr.	CzRep-Jr.	18	6	6	12	16																		
	HC Slavia Praha	CzRep	1	0	0	0	0																		
2004-05	Slavia Jr.	CzRep-Jr.	27	12	21	33	93																		
	HC Slavia Praha	CzRep	18	0	1	1	8																		
	Havl. Brod	CzRep-3	7	3	0	3	31										7	1	5	6	0				
2005-06	Slavia Jr.	CzRep-Jr.	8	10	4	14	42																		
	HC Slavia Praha	CzRep	33	1	9	10	28										11	2	3	5	10				
2006-07	HC Slavia Praha	CzRep	33	7	6	13	38																		
2007-08	Boston	NHL	48	1	6	7	24	0	0	1	40	2.5	1	247	48.6	8:50	6	2	0	2	0	0	0	0	8:37
	Providence Bruins	AHL	18	10	10	20	37										6	0	4	4	0				
2008-09	Boston	NHL	25	1	4	5	10	0	0	0	19	5.3	–10	52	57.7	10:33									
	Providence Bruins	AHL	44	20	24	44	83										14	2	11	13	43				
2009-10	Boston	NHL	61	4	6	10	30	0	0	0	67	6.0	–7	361	54.3	11:06	13	0	2	2	15	0	0	0	13:20
	Providence Bruins	AHL	6	4	6	10	4																		
2010-11	St. Louis	NHL	65	7	22	29	69	1	1	0	75	9.3	–4	419	51.6	16:11									
2011-12	St. Louis	NHL	73	5	15	20	42	0	1	1	117	4.3	12	501	56.1	15:51	9	1	1	2	15	0	0	1	13:09
2012-13	HC Slavia Praha	CzRep	27	10	15	25	8																		
	St. Louis	NHL	48	8	11	19	35	1	0	2	69	11.6	–4	506	56.5	15:27	6	0	3	3	0	0	0	0	16:37
	NHL Totals		320	26	64	90	210	2	2	4	387	6.7		2086	54.1	13:29	34	3	6	9	30	0	0	1	13:02

Traded to **St. Louis** by **Boston** for David Warsofsky, June 26, 2010. Signed as a free agent by **Slavia Praha** (CzRep), September 15, 2012.

SODERBERG, Carl

(SOH-dehr-buhrg, KAHRL) **BOS**

Center. Shoots left. 6'3", 198 lbs. Born, Malmo, Sweden, October 12, 1985. St. Louis' 2nd choice, 49th overall, in 2004 Entry Draft.

			Regular Season														Playoffs								
Season	Club	League	GP	G	A	Pts	PIM	PP	SH	GW	S	%	+/-	TF	F%	Min	GP	G	A	Pts	PIM	PP	SH	GW	Min
2000-01	Skane	Exhib.	8	1	2	3	2																		
	Malmo U18	Swe-U18	3	1	1	2	0																		
2001-02	Malmo U18	Swe-U18	13	9	20	29	18																		
	Malmo Jr.	Swe-Jr.	4	0	2	2	2										7	0	2	2	4				
2002-03	Malmo U18	Swe-U18	4	6	3	9	25																		
	Malmo Jr.	Swe-Jr.	28	17	18	35	22										6	2	4	6	8				
2003-04	Malmo U18	Swe-U18	27	23	25	48	30										6	1	2	3	10				
	Malmo	Sweden	24	1	1	2	8																		
	Malmo	Sweden-Q	8	1	1	2	4																		
2004-05	Morrums GoIS IK	Sweden-2	14	5	6	11	8																		
	Malmo Jr.	Swe-Jr.	12	13	6	19	43										3	2	1	3	12				
	Malmo	Sweden	38	0	5	5	8																		
	Malmo	Sweden-Q	7	0	0	0	0																		
2005-06	Malmo	Sweden-2	49	20	27	47	47																		
2006-07	Malmo	Sweden	31	12	18	30	14																		
2007-08	Malmo	Sweden-2	42	22	36	58	18																		
2008-09	Malmo	Sweden-2	45	18	41	59	26																		
2009-10	Malmo	Sweden-2	51	20	31	51	53										5	0	1	1	0				
2010-11	Malmo	Sweden-2	52	12	34	46	18																		
2011-12	Linkopings HC	Sweden	42	14	21	35	20																		
2012-13	Linkopings HC	Sweden	54	*31	29	60	48										6	1	1	2	27				
	Boston	**NHL**	**6**	**0**	**2**	**2**	**6**	**0**	**0**	**0**	**6**	**0.0**	**–2**	**13**	**53.9**	**14:44**	**2**	**0**	**0**	**0**	**0**	**0**	**0**	**0**	**12:15**
	NHL Totals		**6**	**0**	**2**	**2**	**6**	**0**	**0**	**0**	**6**	**0.0**		**13**	**53.8**	**14:44**	**2**	**0**	**0**	**0**	**0**	**0**	**0**	**0**	**12:15**

Traded to **Boston** by **St. Louis** for Hannu Toivonen, July 23, 2007.

SOPEL, Brent

(SOH-puhl, BREHNT)

Defense. Shoots right. 6'2", 205 lbs. Born, Calgary, Alta., January 7, 1977. Vancouver's 6th choice, 144th overall, in 1995 Entry Draft.

			Regular Season														Playoffs								
Season	Club	League	GP	G	A	Pts	PIM	PP	SH	GW	S	%	+/-	TF	F%	Min	GP	G	A	Pts	PIM	PP	SH	GW	Min
1992-93	Sask. Legion	SMHL	36	7	17	24	95																		
1993-94	Saskatoon Blazers	SMHL	34	9	30	39	180																		
	Saskatoon Blades	WHL	11	2	2	4	2																		
1994-95	Saskatoon Blades	WHL	22	1	10	11	31																		
	Swift Current	WHL	41	4	19	23	50										3	0	3	3	0				
1995-96	Swift Current	WHL	71	13	48	61	87										6	1	2	3	4				
	Syracuse Crunch	AHL	1	0	0	0	0																		
1996-97	Swift Current	WHL	62	15	41	56	109										10	5	11	16	32				
	Syracuse Crunch	AHL	2	0	0	0	0										3	0	0	0	0				
1997-98	Syracuse Crunch	AHL	76	10	33	43	70										5	0	7	7	12				
1998-99	**Vancouver**	**NHL**	**5**	**1**	**0**	**1**	**4**	**1**	**0**	**0**	**5**	**20.0**	**–1**	**0**	**0.0**	**11:58**									
	Syracuse Crunch	AHL	53	10	21	31	59																		
99-2000	**Vancouver**	**NHL**	**18**	**2**	**4**	**6**	**12**	**0**	**0**	**1**	**11**	**18.2**	**9**	**0**	**0.0**	**10:31**									
	Syracuse Crunch	AHL	50	6	25	31	67										4	0	2	2	8				
2000-01	**Vancouver**	**NHL**	**52**	**4**	**10**	**14**	**10**	**0**	**0**	**1**	**57**	**7.0**	**4**	**0**	**0.0**	**16:01**	**4**	**0**	**0**	**0**	**2**	**0**	**0**	**0**	**19:05**
	Kansas City	IHL	4	0	1	1	0																		
2001-02	**Vancouver**	**NHL**	**66**	**8**	**17**	**25**	**44**	**1**	**0**	**3**	**116**	**6.9**	**21**	**0**	**0.0**	**19:01**	**6**	**0**	**2**	**2**	**2**	**0**	**0**	**0**	**24:45**
2002-03	**Vancouver**	**NHL**	**81**	**7**	**30**	**37**	**23**	**6**	**0**	**1**	**167**	**4.2**	**–15**	**0**	**0.0**	**21:42**	**14**	**2**	**6**	**8**	**4**	**1**	**0**	**1**	**22:33**
2003-04	**Vancouver**	**NHL**	**80**	**10**	**32**	**42**	**36**	**6**	**0**	**2**	**173**	**5.8**	**11**	**0**	**0.0**	**21:56**	**7**	**0**	**1**	**1**	**0**	**0**	**0**	**0**	**23:55**
2004-05			DID NOT PLAY																						
2005-06	**NY Islanders**	**NHL**	**57**	**2**	**25**	**27**	**64**	**2**	**0**	**0**	**121**	**1.7**	**–9**	**0**	**0.0**	**23:35**									
	Los Angeles	**NHL**	**11**	**0**	**1**	**1**	**6**	**0**	**0**	**0**	**12**	**0.0**	**–4**	**0**	**0.0**	**22:02**									
2006-07	**Los Angeles**	**NHL**	**44**	**4**	**19**	**23**	**14**	**2**	**0**	**2**	**104**	**3.8**	**2**	**3**	**33.3**	**21:06**									
	Vancouver	**NHL**	**20**	**1**	**4**	**5**	**10**	**0**	**0**	**0**	**27**	**3.7**	**0**	**0**	**0.0**	**18:25**	**11**	**0**	**0**	**0**	**2**	**0**	**0**	**0**	**19:44**
2007-08	**Chicago**	**NHL**	**58**	**1**	**19**	**20**	**28**	**0**	**0**	**0**	**56**	**1.8**	**9**	**0**	**0.0**	**20:18**									
2008-09	**Chicago**	**NHL**	**23**	**1**	**1**	**2**	**8**	**0**	**0**	**1**	**15**	**6.7**	**–4**	**0**	**0.0**	**13:49**									
2009-10 ♦	**Chicago**	**NHL**	**73**	**1**	**7**	**8**	**34**	**0**	**0**	**0**	**48**	**2.1**	**3**	**0**	**0.0**	**14:52**	**22**	**1**	**5**	**6**	**8**	**0**	**0**	**0**	**18:30**
2010-11	**Atlanta**	**NHL**	**59**	**2**	**5**	**7**	**16**	**0**	**0**	**0**	**40**	**5.0**	**7**	**0**	**0.0**	**16:26**									
	Montreal	**NHL**	**12**	**0**	**0**	**0**	**0**	**0**	**0**	**0**	**4**	**0.0**	**–1**	**0**	**0.0**	**15:54**	**7**	**1**	**0**	**1**	**2**	**0**	**0**	**0**	**14:51**
2011-12	Novokuznetsk	KHL	47	2	6	8	33																		
2012-13	Novokuznetsk	KHL	47	4	6	10	12																		
	Ufa	KHL	4	0	2	2	0										14	4	1	5	6				
	NHL Totals		**659**	**44**	**174**	**218**	**309**	**18**	**0**	**11**	**956**	**4.6**		**3**	**33.3**	**18:56**	**71**	**4**	**14**	**18**	**20**	**1**	**0**	**1**	**20:14**

Traded to **NY Islanders** by **Vancouver** for NY Islanders' 2nd round choice (later traded to Anaheim - Anaheim selected Bryce Swan) in 2006 Entry Draft, August 3, 2005. Traded to **Los Angeles** by **NY Islanders** with Mark Parrish for Denis Grebeshkov and Jeff Tambellini, March 8, 2006. Traded to **Vancouver** by **Los Angeles** for Anaheim's 2nd round choice (previously acquired, Los Angeles selected Wayne Simmonds) in 2007 Entry Draft and and Vancouver's 4th round choice (later traded to Buffalo - Buffalo selected Justin Jokinen) in 2008 Entry Draft, February 26, 2007. Signed as a free agent by **Chicago**, October 3, 2007. • Missed majority of 2008-09 due to recurring elbow injury. Traded to **Atlanta** by **Chicago** with Dustin Byfuglien, Ben Eager and Akim Aliu for Marty Reasoner, Joey Crabb, Jeremy Morin and New Jersey's 1st (previously acquired, Chicago selected Kevin Hayes) and 2nd (previously acquired, Chicago selected Justin Holl) round choices in 2010 Entry Draft, June 24, 2010. Traded to **Montreal** by **Atlanta** with Nigel Dawes for Ben Maxwell and Montreal's 4th round choice (later traded back to Montreal - Montreal selected Olivier Archambault) in 2011 Entry Draft, February 24, 2011. Signed as a free agent by **Novokuznetsk** (KHL), July 29, 2011. Signed as a free agent by **Ufa** (KHL), January 31, 2013.

SOURAY, Sheldon

(SOO-ray, SHEHL-duhn) **ANA**

Defense. Shoots left. 6'4", 237 lbs. Born, Elk Point, Alta., July 13, 1976. New Jersey's 3rd choice, 71st overall, in 1994 Entry Draft.

			Regular Season														Playoffs								
Season	Club	League	GP	G	A	Pts	PIM	PP	SH	GW	S	%	+/-	TF	F%	Min	GP	G	A	Pts	PIM	PP	SH	GW	Min
1990-91	Bonnyville Sabres	AAHA	30	15	20	35	100																		
1991-92	Quesnel	Minor-BC	20	5	15	20	200																		
	Alberta Cycle	AMHL	11	0	5	5	67																		
1992-93	Ft. Saskatchewan	AJHL	35	0	12	12	125																		
	Tri-City	WHL	2	0	0	0	0																		
1993-94	Tri-City	WHL	42	3	6	9	122																		
1994-95	Tri-City	WHL	40	2	24	26	140																		
	Prince George	WHL	11	2	3	5	23																		
	Albany River Rats	AHL	7	0	2	2	8																		
1995-96	Prince George	WHL	32	9	18	27	91																		
	Kelowna Rockets	WHL	27	7	20	27	94										6	0	5	5	2				
	Albany River Rats	AHL	6	0	2	2	12										4	0	1	1	4				
1996-97	Albany River Rats	AHL	70	2	11	13	160										16	2	3	5	47				
1997-98	**New Jersey**	**NHL**	**60**	**3**	**7**	**10**	**85**	**0**	**0**	**1**	**74**	**4.1**	**18**				**3**	**0**	**1**	**1**	**2**	**0**	**0**	**0**	
	Albany River Rats	AHL	6	0	0	0	8																		
1998-99	**New Jersey**	**NHL**	**70**	**1**	**7**	**8**	**110**	**0**	**0**	**0**	**101**	**1.0**	**5**	**0**	**0.0**	**14:56**	**2**	**0**	**1**	**1**	**0**	**0**	**0**	**0**	**12:57**
99-2000	**New Jersey**	**NHL**	**52**	**0**	**8**	**8**	**70**	**0**	**0**	**0**	**74**	**0.0**	**–6**	**0**	**0.0**	**17:12**									
	Montreal	**NHL**	**19**	**3**	**0**	**3**	**44**	**0**	**0**	**0**	**39**	**7.7**	**7**	**0**	**0.0**	**19:18**									
2000-01	**Montreal**	**NHL**	**52**	**3**	**8**	**11**	**95**	**0**	**0**	**2**	**103**	**2.9**	**–11**	**0**	**0.0**	**20:36**									
2001-02	**Montreal**	**NHL**	**34**	**3**	**5**	**8**	**62**	**1**	**0**	**0**	**56**	**5.4**	**–5**	**1**	**100.0**	**18:11**	**12**	**0**	**1**	**1**	**16**	**0**	**0**	**0**	**19:01**
2002-03	**Montreal**	**NHL**	DID NOT PLAY – INJURED																						
2003-04	**Montreal**	**NHL**	**63**	**15**	**20**	**35**	**104**	**6**	**1**	**3**	**186**	**8.1**	**4**	**0**	**0.0**	**23:26**	**11**	**0**	**2**	**2**	**39**	**0**	**0**	**0**	**23:55**
2004-05	Farjestad	Sweden	39	9	8	17	117										15	1	6	7	77				
2005-06	**Montreal**	**NHL**	**75**	**12**	**27**	**39**	**116**	**7**	**1**	**0**	**202**	**5.9**	**–11**	**0**	**0.0**	**22:15**	**6**	**3**	**2**	**5**	**8**	**2**	**0**	**0**	**18:47**
2006-07	**Montreal**	**NHL**	**81**	**26**	**38**	**64**	**135**	**19**	**1**	**6**	**224**	**11.6**	**–28**	**2**	**100.0**	**23:11**									
2007-08	**Edmonton**	**NHL**	**26**	**3**	**7**	**10**	**36**	**2**	**0**	**1**	**71**	**4.2**	**–7**	**0**	**0.0**	**24:21**									
2008-09	**Edmonton**	**NHL**	**81**	**23**	**30**	**53**	**98**	**12**	**1**	**5**	**268**	**8.6**	**1**	**0**	**0.0**	**24:51**									
2009-10	**Edmonton**	**NHL**	**37**	**4**	**9**	**13**	**65**	**0**	**0**	**0**	**113**	**3.5**	**–19**	**0**	**0.0**	**22:37**									
2010-11	Hershey Bears	AHL	40	4	15	19	85										6	1	1	2	16				

Season	Club	League	GP	G	A	Pts	PIM	PP	SH	GW	S	%	+/-	TF	F%	Min	GP	G	A	Pts	PIM	PP	SH	GW	Min
			Regular Season														Playoffs								
2011-12	**Dallas**	**NHL**	64	6	15	21	73	2	1	1	179	3.4	11	0	0.0	20:28	....	....	....	....	....	....	....	....	....
2012-13	**Anaheim**	**NHL**	44	7	10	17	52	2	0	3	80	8.8	19	1	100.0	20:56	6	0	1	1	4	0	0	0	19:31
	NHL Totals		758	109	191	300	1145	51	5	22	1770	6.2		4	100.0	21:06	40	3	8	11	69	2	0	0	20:11

WHL West Second All-Star Team (1996)

Played in NHL All-Star Game (2004, 2007, 2009)

Traded to **Montreal** by **New Jersey** with Josh DeWolf and New Jersey's 2nd round choice (later traded to Washington, later traded to Tampa Bay – Tampa Bay selected Andreas Holmqvist) in 2001 Entry Draft for Vladimir Malakhov, March 1, 2000. • Missed remainder of 2001-02, and 2002-03 due to wrist injury vs. Tampa Bay, November 17, 2001. Signed as a free agent by **Farjestad** (Sweden), September 22, 2004. Signed as a free agent by **Edmonton**, July 12, 2007. • Missed majority of 2007-08 due to shoulder injury at Vancouver, October 13, 2007, February 8, 2008. • Missed majority of 2009-10 due to head (October 8, 2009 vs. Calgary) and hand (January 30, 2010 at Calgary) injuries. • Loaned to **Hershey** (AHL) by **Edmonton**, October 6, 2010. Signed as a free agent by **Dallas**, July 1, 2011. Signed as a free agent by **Anaheim**, July 1, 2012.

SPALING, Nick (SPAHL-ihng, NIHK) NSH

Center. Shoots left. 6'1", 198 lbs. Born, Palmerston, Ont., September 19, 1988. Nashville's 3rd choice, 58th overall, in 2007 Entry Draft.

Season	Club	League	GP	G	A	Pts	PIM	PP	SH	GW	S	%	+/-	TF	F%	Min	GP	G	A	Pts	PIM	PP	SH	GW	Min
2004-05	Listowel Cyclones	ON-Jr.B	61	25	27	52	58	....	....	....	....	....	....	....	....	....	....	....	....	....	....	....	....	....	....
2005-06	Kitchener Rangers	OHL	62	10	15	25	22	....	....	....	....	....	....	....	....	....	5	0	3	3	0	....	....	....	....
2006-07	Kitchener Rangers	OHL	61	23	36	59	41	....	....	....	....	....	....	....	....	....	9	2	3	5	4	....	....	....	....
2007-08	Kitchener Rangers	OHL	56	38	34	72	18	....	....	....	....	....	....	....	....	....	20	14	16	30	9	....	....	....	....
2008-09	Milwaukee	AHL	79	12	23	35	28	....	....	....	....	....	....	....	....	....	11	0	3	3	8	....	....	....	....
2009-10	**Nashville**	**NHL**	28	0	3	3	0	0	0	0	26	0.0	3	95	41.1	11:03	6	0	0	0	0	0	0	0	8:24
	Milwaukee	AHL	48	7	10	17	21	....	....	....	....	....	....	....	....	....	....	....	....	....	....	....	....	....	....
2010-11	**Nashville**	**NHL**	74	8	6	14	20	1	0	2	75	10.7	−10	497	50.9	13:56	12	2	4	6	0	0	0	1	15:19
	Milwaukee	AHL	4	1	1	2	2	....	....	....	....	....	....	....	....	....	....	....	....	....	....	....	....	....	....
2011-12	**Nashville**	**NHL**	77	10	12	22	18	0	0	3	107	9.3	−7	894	50.1	15:43	10	0	3	3	0	0	0	0	15:49
2012-13	**Nashville**	**NHL**	47	9	4	13	18	1	0	2	57	15.8	−10	482	46.3	15:52	....	....	....	....	....	....	....	....	....
	NHL Totals		226	27	25	52	56	2	0	7	265	10.2		1968	48.9	14:35	28	2	7	9	0	0	0	1	14:01

SPEZZA, Jason (SPEHT-zuh, JAY-suhn) OTT

Center. Shoots right. 6'3", 216 lbs. Born, Mississauga, Ont., June 13, 1983. Ottawa's 1st choice, 2nd overall, in 2001 Entry Draft.

Season	Club	League	GP	G	A	Pts	PIM	PP	SH	GW	S	%	+/-	TF	F%	Min	GP	G	A	Pts	PIM	PP	SH	GW	Min
1997-98	Toronto Marlies	MTHL	54	53	61	114	42	....	....	....	....	....	....	....	....	....	....	....	....	....	....	....	....	....	....
1998-99	Brampton	OHL	67	22	49	71	18	....	....	....	....	....	....	....	....	....	....	....	....	....	....	....	....	....	....
99-2000	Mississauga	OHL	52	24	37	61	33	....	....	....	....	....	....	....	....	....	....	....	....	....	....	....	....	....	....
2000-01	Mississauga	OHL	15	7	23	30	11	....	....	....	....	....	....	....	....	....	....	....	....	....	....	....	....	....	....
	Windsor Spitfires	OHL	41	36	50	86	32	....	....	....	....	....	....	....	....	....	9	4	5	9	10	....	....	....	....
2001-02	Windsor Spitfires	OHL	27	19	26	45	16	....	....	....	....	....	....	....	....	....	....	....	....	....	....	....	....	....	....
	Belleville Bulls	OHL	26	23	37	60	26	....	....	....	....	....	....	....	....	....	11	5	6	11	18	....	....	....	....
	Grand Rapids	AHL	....	....	....	....	....	....	....	....	....	....	....	....	....	....	3	1	0	1	2	....	....	....	....
2002-03	**Ottawa**	**NHL**	33	7	14	21	8	3	0	0	65	10.8	−3	330	45.8	12:40	3	1	1	2	0	1	0	0	11:34
	Binghamton	AHL	43	22	32	54	71	....	....	....	....	....	....	....	....	....	2	1	2	3	4	....	....	....	....
2003-04	**Ottawa**	**NHL**	78	22	33	55	71	5	0	3	142	15.5	22	956	47.7	14:38	3	0	0	0	2	0	0	0	9:44
2004-05	Binghamton	AHL	80	32	*85	*117	50	....	....	....	....	....	....	....	....	....	6	1	3	4	6	....	....	....	....
2005-06	**Ottawa**	**NHL**	68	19	71	90	33	7	0	5	156	12.2	23	1220	52.6	19:00	10	5	9	14	2	3	0	1	17:59
2006-07	**Ottawa**	**NHL**	67	34	53	87	45	13	1	5	162	21.0	19	1261	53.0	19:17	20	7	*15	*22	10	3	0	0	20:58
2007-08	**Ottawa**	**NHL**	76	34	58	92	66	11	0	6	210	16.2	26	1445	50.5	20:40	4	0	1	1	0	0	0	0	19:45
2008-09	**Ottawa**	**NHL**	82	32	41	73	79	13	1	3	246	13.0	−14	1477	53.3	19:41	....	....	....	....	....	....	....	....	....
2009-10	**Ottawa**	**NHL**	60	23	34	57	20	11	0	5	165	13.9	0	1018	50.5	19:04	6	1	6	7	4	1	0	0	22:46
2010-11	**Ottawa**	**NHL**	62	21	36	57	28	7	0	2	188	11.2	−7	1210	56.3	20:12	....	....	....	....	....	....	....	....	....
2011-12	**Ottawa**	**NHL**	80	34	50	84	36	10	0	2	232	14.7	11	1700	53.5	19:55	7	3	2	5	8	0	0	1	20:59
2012-13	Rapperswil	Swiss	28	9	21	30	12	....	....	....	....	....	....	....	....	....	....	....	....	....	....	....	....	....	....
	Ottawa	**NHL**	5	2	3	5	2	1	0	0	12	16.7	3	119	57.1	19:11	3	0	1	1	0	0	0	0	18:27
	NHL Totals		611	228	393	621	388	81	2	31	1578	14.4		10736	52.2	18:41	56	17	35	52	26	8	0	2	19:18

OHL All-Rookie Team (1999) • AHL All-Rookie Team (2003) • AHL First All-Star Team (2005) • John P. Sollenberger Trophy (AHL - Top Scorer) (2005) • Les Cunningham Award (AHL – MVP) (2005)

Played in NHL All-Star Game (2008, 2012)

Signed as a free agent by **Rapperswil** (Swiss), September 19, 2012.

SPOONER, Ryan (SPOO-nuhr, RIGH-uhn) BOS

Center. Shoots left. 5'10", 180 lbs. Born, Ottawa, Ont., January 30, 1992. Boston's 3rd choice, 45th overall, in 2010 Entry Draft.

Season	Club	League	GP	G	A	Pts	PIM	PP	SH	GW	S	%	+/-	TF	F%	Min	GP	G	A	Pts	PIM	PP	SH	GW	Min
2007-08	Ott. Jr. Senators	Minor-ON	53	52	45	97	16	....	....	....	....	....	....	....	....	....	....	....	....	....	....	....	....	....	....
2008-09	Peterborough	OHL	62	30	28	58	8	....	....	....	....	....	....	....	....	....	4	0	1	1	0	....	....	....	....
2009-10	Peterborough	OHL	47	19	35	54	12	....	....	....	....	....	....	....	....	....	3	0	1	1	2	....	....	....	....
2010-11	Peterborough	OHL	14	10	9	19	2	....	....	....	....	....	....	....	....	....	....	....	....	....	....	....	....	....	....
	Kingston	OHL	50	25	37	62	6	....	....	....	....	....	....	....	....	....	5	4	2	6	2	....	....	....	....
	Providence Bruins	AHL	3	2	1	3	0	....	....	....	....	....	....	....	....	....	....	....	....	....	....	....	....	....	....
2011-12	Kingston	OHL	27	14	18	32	8	....	....	....	....	....	....	....	....	....	....	....	....	....	....	....	....	....	....
	Sarnia Sting	OHL	30	15	19	34	8	....	....	....	....	....	....	....	....	....	6	1	2	3	8	....	....	....	....
	Providence Bruins	AHL	5	1	3	4	0	....	....	....	....	....	....	....	....	....	....	....	....	....	....	....	....	....	....
2012-13	Providence Bruins	AHL	59	17	40	57	14	....	....	....	....	....	....	....	....	....	12	2	3	5	4	....	....	....	....
	Boston	**NHL**	4	0	0	0	0	0	0	0	4	0.0	0	24	45.8	9:07	....	....	....	....	....	....	....	....	....
	NHL Totals		4	0	0	0	0	0	0	0	4	0.0		24	45.8	9:07	....	....	....	....	....	....	....	....	....

AHL All-Rookie Team (2013)

SPURGEON, Jared (SPUHR-juhn, JAIR-uhd) MIN

Defense. Shoots right. 5'9", 185 lbs. Born, Edmonton, Alta., November 29, 1989. NY Islanders' 12th choice, 156th overall, in 2008 Entry Draft.

Season	Club	League	GP	G	A	Pts	PIM	PP	SH	GW	S	%	+/-	TF	F%	Min	GP	G	A	Pts	PIM	PP	SH	GW	Min
2004-05	K of C Pats	AMHL	26	9	21	30	16	....	....	....	....	....	....	....	....	....	....	....	....	....	....	....	....	....	....
2005-06	Spokane Chiefs	WHL	46	3	9	12	28	....	....	....	....	....	....	....	....	....	....	....	....	....	....	....	....	....	....
2006-07	Spokane Chiefs	WHL	38	4	15	19	16	....	....	....	....	....	....	....	....	....	....	....	....	....	....	....	....	....	....
2007-08	Spokane Chiefs	WHL	69	12	31	43	19	....	....	....	....	....	....	....	....	....	21	0	5	5	16	....	....	....	....
2008-09	Spokane Chiefs	WHL	59	10	35	45	37	....	....	....	....	....	....	....	....	....	12	2	3	5	10	....	....	....	....
2009-10	Spokane Chiefs	WHL	54	8	43	51	18	....	....	....	....	....	....	....	....	....	7	0	4	4	2	....	....	....	....
2010-11	**Minnesota**	**NHL**	53	4	8	12	2	2	0	1	38	10.5	−1	0	0.0	15:04	....	....	....	....	....	....	....	....	....
	Houston Aeros	AHL	23	2	7	9	10	....	....	....	....	....	....	....	....	....	23	1	10	11	10	....	....	....	....
2011-12	**Minnesota**	**NHL**	70	3	20	23	6	2	0	1	92	3.3	−4	0	0.0	21:36	....	....	....	....	....	....	....	....	....
2012-13	Langnau	Swiss	12	3	4	7	6	....	....	....	....	....	....	....	....	....	....	....	....	....	....	....	....	....	....
	Minnesota	**NHL**	39	5	10	15	4	4	0	2	67	7.5	1	0	0.0	21:33	5	0	0	0	2	0	0	0	21:15
	NHL Totals		162	12	38	50	12	8	0	4	197	6.1		0	0.0	19:27	5	0	0	0	2	0	0	0	21:15

Signed as a free agent by **Minnesota**, September 23, 2010. Signed as a free agent by **Langnau** (Swiss), September 21, 2012.

STAAL, Eric (STAHL, AIR-ihk) CAR

Center. Shoots left. 6'4", 205 lbs. Born, Thunder Bay, Ont., October 29, 1984. Carolina's 1st choice, 2nd overall, in 2003 Entry Draft.

Season	Club	League	GP	G	A	Pts	PIM	PP	SH	GW	S	%	+/-	TF	F%	Min	GP	G	A	Pts	PIM	PP	SH	GW	Min
99-2000	Thunder Bay	Exhib.	7	4	8	12	0	....	....	....	....	....	....	....	....	....	....	....	....	....	....	....	....	....	....
2000-01	Peterborough	OHL	63	19	30	49	23	....	....	....	....	....	....	....	....	....	7	2	5	7	4	....	....	....	....
2001-02	Peterborough	OHL	56	23	39	62	40	....	....	....	....	....	....	....	....	....	6	3	6	9	10	....	....	....	....
2002-03	Peterborough	OHL	66	39	59	98	36	....	....	....	....	....	....	....	....	....	7	9	5	14	6	....	....	....	....
2003-04	**Carolina**	**NHL**	81	11	20	31	40	2	1	3	164	6.7	−6	669	43.1	16:40	....	....	....	....	....	....	....	....	....
2004-05	Lowell	AHL	77	26	51	77	88	....	....	....	....	....	....	....	....	....	11	2	8	10	12	....	....	....	....
2005-06♦	**Carolina**	**NHL**	82	45	55	100	81	19	4	4	279	16.1	−8	1309	42.6	19:39	25	9	*19	*28	8	*7	0	1	19:48
2006-07	**Carolina**	**NHL**	82	30	40	70	68	12	1	1	288	10.4	−6	1238	45.2	20:08	....	....	....	....	....	....	....	....	....
2007-08	**Carolina**	**NHL**	82	38	44	82	50	14	0	7	310	12.3	−2	1708	44.9	21:38	....	....	....	....	....	....	....	....	....
2008-09	**Carolina**	**NHL**	82	40	35	75	50	14	1	8	372	10.8	15	1586	45.3	21:03	18	10	5	15	4	3	0	1	21:31
2009-10	**Carolina**	**NHL**	70	29	41	70	68	13	0	5	277	10.5	4	1162	41.8	20:43	....	....	....	....	....	....	....	....	....
	Canada	Olympics	7	1	5	6	6	....	....	....	....	....	....	....	....	....	....	....	....	....	....	....	....	....	....
2010-11	**Carolina**	**NHL**	81	33	43	76	72	12	3	8	296	11.1	−10	1751	48.0	21:56	....	....	....	....	....	....	....	....	....

			Regular Season														Playoffs								
Season	Club	League	GP	G	A	Pts	PIM	PP	SH	GW	S	%	+/-	TF	F%	Min	GP	G	A	Pts	PIM	PP	SH	GW	Min
2011-12	Carolina	NHL	82	24	46	70	48	7	3	3	262	9.2	–20	1681	52.5	21:33	....	....	....	....	....	....	....	....	....
2012-13	Carolina	NHL	48	18	35	53	54	3	1	4	152	11.8	5	1014	52.0	21:00	....	....	....	....	....	....	....	....	....
	NHL Totals		690	268	359	627	531	96	14	43	2400	11.2		12118	46.4	20:27	43	19	24	43	12	10	0	2	20:31

OHL Second All-Star Team (2003) • Canadian Major Junior First All-Star Team (2003) • NHL Second All-Star Team (2006)
Played in NHL All-Star Game (2007, 2008, 2009, 2011)

STAAL, Jared

(STAWL, JAIR-uhd) **CAR**

Right wing. Shoots right. 6'4", 210 lbs. Born, Thunder Bay, Ont., August 21, 1990. Phoenix's 3rd choice, 49th overall, in 2008 Entry Draft.

Season	Club	League	GP	G	A	Pts	PIM	PP	SH	GW	S	%	+/-	TF	F%	Min	GP	G	A	Pts	PIM	PP	SH	GW	Min
2005-06	Thunder Bay	Minor-ON	64	24	25	49	72	....	....	....	....	....	....	....	....	....	....	....	....	....	....	....	....	....	....
2006-07	Sudbury Wolves	OHL	63	2	1	3	18	....	....	....	....	....	....	....	....	....	21	1	0	1	2	....	....	....	....
2007-08	Sudbury Wolves	OHL	60	21	28	49	44	....	....	....	....	....	....	....	....	....	....	....	....	....	....	....	....	....	....
2008-09	Sudbury Wolves	OHL	67	19	33	52	38	....	....	....	....	....	....	....	....	....	6	0	1	1	2	....	....	....	....
	San Antonio	AHL	5	0	0	0	0	....	....	....	....	....	....	....	....	....	....	....	....	....	....	....	....	....	....
2009-10	Sudbury Wolves	OHL	59	12	37	49	57	....	....	....	....	....	....	....	....	....	3	0	0	0	4	....	....	....	....
	San Antonio	AHL	5	0	1	1	2	....	....	....	....	....	....	....	....	....	....	....	....	....	....	....	....	....	....
2010-11	Charlotte	AHL	13	1	1	2	2	....	....	....	....	....	....	....	....	....	....	....	....	....	....	....	....	....	....
	Florida Everblades	ECHL	33	6	5	11	6	....	....	....	....	....	....	....	....	....	....	....	....	....	....	....	....	....	....
2011-12	Charlotte	AHL	37	3	3	6	18	....	....	....	....	....	....	....	....	....	....	....	....	....	....	....	....	....	....
	Providence Bruins	AHL	7	0	2	2	2	....	....	....	....	....	....	....	....	....	....	....	....	....	....	....	....	....	....
2012-13	Charlotte	AHL	52	4	3	7	25	....	....	....	....	....	....	....	....	....	3	0	0	0	0	....	....	....	....
	Carolina	NHL	2	0	0	0	2	0	0	0	3	0.0	–2	0	0.0	13:23	....	....	....	....	....	....	....	....	....
	NHL Totals		2	0	0	0	2	0	0	0	3	0.0		0	0.0	13:23	....	....	....	....	....	....	....	....	....

Traded to **Carolina** by **Phoenix** for Nashville's 5th round choice (previously acquired, Phoenix selected Louis Domingue) in 2010 Entry Draft, May 13, 2010.

STAAL, Jordan

(STAHL, JOHR-dahn) **CAR**

Center. Shoots left. 6'4", 220 lbs. Born, Thunder Bay, Ont., September 10, 1988. Pittsburgh's 1st choice, 2nd overall, in 2006 Entry Draft.

Season	Club	League	GP	G	A	Pts	PIM	PP	SH	GW	S	%	+/-	TF	F%	Min	GP	G	A	Pts	PIM	PP	SH	GW	Min
2004-05	Peterborough	OHL	66	9	19	28	29	....	....	....	....	....	....	....	....	....	14	5	5	10	16	....	....	....	....
2005-06	Peterborough	OHL	68	28	40	68	69	....	....	....	....	....	....	....	....	....	19	10	6	16	16	....	....	....	....
2006-07	Pittsburgh	NHL	81	29	13	42	24	4	*7	4	131	22.1	16	383	37.1	14:56	5	3	0	3	2	0	0	0	16:00
2007-08	Pittsburgh	NHL	82	12	16	28	55	3	0	4	183	6.6	–5	1202	42.2	18:16	20	6	1	7	14	1	0	1	18:16
2008-09 ♦	Pittsburgh	NHL	82	22	27	49	37	2	1	3	166	13.3	5	1206	47.0	19:51	24	4	5	9	8	0	1	0	19:13
2009-10	Pittsburgh	NHL	82	21	28	49	57	1	2	1	195	10.8	19	1324	48.3	19:24	11	3	2	5	6	2	0	0	18:14
2010-11	Pittsburgh	NHL	42	11	19	30	24	3	0	4	91	12.1	7	801	46.9	21:21	7	1	2	3	2	0	0	0	21:28
2011-12	Pittsburgh	NHL	62	25	25	50	34	5	3	0	149	16.8	11	1158	51.0	20:03	6	6	3	9	2	1	0	1	19:49
2012-13	Carolina	NHL	48	10	21	31	32	1	0	1	114	8.8	–18	914	50.1	20:06	....	....	....	....	....	....	....	....	....
	NHL Totals		479	130	149	279	263	19	13	17	1029	12.6		6988	46.9	18:51	73	23	13	36	34	4	1	2	18:51

NHL All-Rookie Team (2007)
Traded to **Carolina** by **Pittsburgh** for Brandon Sutter, Brian Dumoulin and Carolina's 1st round choice (Derrick Pouliot) in 2012 Entry Draft, June 22, 2012.

STAAL, Marc

(STAHL, MAHRK) **NYR**

Defense. Shoots left. 6'4", 207 lbs. Born, Thunder Bay, Ont., January 13, 1987. NY Rangers' 1st choice, 12th overall, in 2005 Entry Draft.

Season	Club	League	GP	G	A	Pts	PIM	PP	SH	GW	S	%	+/-	TF	F%	Min	GP	G	A	Pts	PIM	PP	SH	GW	Min
2003-04	Sudbury Wolves	OHL	61	1	13	14	34	....	....	....	....	....	....	....	....	....	7	1	2	3	2	....	....	....	....
2004-05	Sudbury Wolves	OHL	65	6	20	26	53	....	....	....	....	....	....	....	....	....	12	0	4	4	15	....	....	....	....
2005-06	Sudbury Wolves	OHL	57	11	38	49	60	....	....	....	....	....	....	....	....	....	10	0	8	8	8	....	....	....	....
	Hartford	AHL	....	....	....	....	....	....	....	....	....	....	....	....	....	....	12	0	2	2	8	....	....	....	....
2006-07	Sudbury Wolves	OHL	53	5	29	34	68	....	....	....	....	....	....	....	....	....	21	5	15	20	22	....	....	....	....
2007-08	NY Rangers	NHL	80	2	8	10	42	0	0	0	78	2.6	2	0	0.0	18:48	10	1	2	3	8	0	0	1	22:21
2008-09	NY Rangers	NHL	82	3	12	15	64	0	0	1	96	3.1	–7	0	0.0	21:08	7	1	0	1	0	0	0	0	21:33
2009-10	NY Rangers	NHL	82	8	19	27	44	0	0	2	78	10.3	11	0	0.0	23:08	....	....	....	....	....	....	....	....	....
2010-11	NY Rangers	NHL	77	7	22	29	50	4	2	2	116	6.0	8	0	0.0	25:44	5	0	1	1	0	0	0	0	28:01
2011-12	NY Rangers	NHL	46	2	3	5	16	1	0	0	61	3.3	–7	0	0.0	19:54	20	3	3	6	12	2	0	1	25:18
2012-13	NY Rangers	NHL	21	2	9	11	14	1	0	0	20	10.0	4	0	0.0	24:27	1	0	0	0	0	0	0	0	17:17
	NHL Totals		388	24	73	97	230	6	2	5	449	5.3		0	0.0	22:01	43	5	6	11	20	2	0	2	24:08

OHL First All-Star Team (2006, 2007) • Canadian Major Junior First All-Star Team (2006, 2007)
Played in NHL All-Star Game (2011)
• Missed majority of 2012-13 due to eye injury vs. Philadelphia, March 5, 2013.

STAFFORD, Drew

(STA-fuhrd, DROO) **BUF**

Right wing. Shoots right. 6'2", 214 lbs. Born, Milwaukee, WI, October 30, 1985. Buffalo's 1st choice, 13th overall, in 2004 Entry Draft.

Season	Club	League	GP	G	A	Pts	PIM	PP	SH	GW	S	%	+/-	TF	F%	Min	GP	G	A	Pts	PIM	PP	SH	GW	Min
2001-02	Shat.-St. Mary's	High-MN	45	35	53	88	30	....	....	....	....	....	....	....	....	....	....	....	....	....	....	....	....	....	....
2002-03	Shat.-St. Mary's	High-MN	65	49	67	116	....	....	....	....	....	....	....	....	....	....	....	....	....	....	....	....	....	....	....
2003-04	North Dakota	WCHA	36	11	21	32	30	....	....	....	....	....	....	....	....	....	....	....	....	....	....	....	....	....	....
2004-05	North Dakota	WCHA	42	13	25	38	34	....	....	....	....	....	....	....	....	....	....	....	....	....	....	....	....	....	....
2005-06	North Dakota	WCHA	42	24	24	48	63	....	....	....	....	....	....	....	....	....	....	....	....	....	....	....	....	....	....
2006-07	Buffalo	NHL	41	13	14	27	33	3	0	3	67	19.4	5	13	46.2	13:08	10	2	2	4	4	0	0	0	11:52
	Rochester	AHL	34	22	22	44	30	....	....	....	....	....	....	....	....	....	....	....	....	....	....	....	....	....	....
2007-08	Buffalo	NHL	64	16	22	38	51	1	0	5	103	15.5	3	21	38.1	13:32	....	....	....	....	....	....	....	....	....
2008-09	Buffalo	NHL	79	20	25	45	29	9	0	0	183	10.9	3	20	20.0	15:38	....	....	....	....	....	....	....	....	....
2009-10	Buffalo	NHL	71	14	20	34	35	5	0	1	181	7.7	4	86	47.7	14:28	3	0	0	0	0	0	0	0	14:06
2010-11	Buffalo	NHL	62	31	21	52	34	11	0	4	179	17.3	13	56	30.4	16:32	7	1	2	3	2	1	0	0	20:01
2011-12	Buffalo	NHL	80	20	30	50	46	3	1	4	226	8.8	5	86	52.3	17:39	....	....	....	....	....	....	....	....	....
2012-13	Buffalo	NHL	46	6	12	18	21	0	0	0	121	5.0	–16	84	44.1	17:01	....	....	....	....	....	....	....	....	....
	NHL Totals		443	120	144	264	249	32	1	17	1060	11.3		366	43.2	15:33	20	3	4	7	6	1	0	0	15:03

STAFFORD, Garrett

(STA-fuhrd, GAIR-reht)

Defense. Shoots right. 6'1", 207 lbs. Born, Los Angeles, CA, January 28, 1980.

Season	Club	League	GP	G	A	Pts	PIM	PP	SH	GW	S	%	+/-	TF	F%	Min	GP	G	A	Pts	PIM	PP	SH	GW	Min
1996-97	Des Moines	USHL	37	1	10	11	40	....	....	....	....	....	....	....	....	....	5	0	0	0	0	....	....	....	....
1997-98	Des Moines	USHL	53	6	17	23	89	....	....	....	....	....	....	....	....	....	12	1	3	4	42	....	....	....	....
1998-99	Des Moines	USHL	56	8	33	41	54	....	....	....	....	....	....	....	....	....	13	2	2	4	18	....	....	....	....
99-2000	New Hampshire	H-East	38	3	9	12	28	....	....	....	....	....	....	....	....	....	....	....	....	....	....	....	....	....	....
2000-01	New Hampshire	H-East	37	5	21	26	44	....	....	....	....	....	....	....	....	....	....	....	....	....	....	....	....	....	....
2001-02	New Hampshire	H-East	36	5	22	27	42	....	....	....	....	....	....	....	....	....	....	....	....	....	....	....	....	....	....
2002-03	New Hampshire	H-East	23	1	15	16	24	....	....	....	....	....	....	....	....	....	....	....	....	....	....	....	....	....	....
2003-04	Cleveland Barons	AHL	73	12	34	46	71	....	....	....	....	....	....	....	....	....	6	0	0	0	6	....	....	....	....
2004-05	Cleveland Barons	AHL	68	6	18	24	55	....	....	....	....	....	....	....	....	....	....	....	....	....	....	....	....	....	....
2005-06	Cleveland Barons	AHL	80	11	28	39	86	....	....	....	....	....	....	....	....	....	....	....	....	....	....	....	....	....	....
2006-07	Worcester Sharks	AHL	77	11	30	41	58	....	....	....	....	....	....	....	....	....	6	0	3	3	2	....	....	....	....
2007-08	Detroit	NHL	2	0	0	0	0	0	0	0	1	0.0	0	0	0.0	6:45	....	....	....	....	....	....	....	....	....
	Grand Rapids	AHL	69	11	33	44	36	....	....	....	....	....	....	....	....	....	....	....	....	....	....	....	....	....	....
2008-09	Dallas	NHL	3	0	2	2	0	0	0	0	5	0.0	0	0	0.0	18:00	....	....	....	....	....	....	....	....	....
	Grand Rapids	AHL	70	11	34	45	50	....	....	....	....	....	....	....	....	....	10	0	5	5	4	....	....	....	....
2009-10	Texas Stars	AHL	60	7	25	32	22	....	....	....	....	....	....	....	....	....	21	4	6	10	10	....	....	....	....
2010-11	Phoenix	NHL	2	0	0	0	0	0	0	0	2	0.0	0	0	0.0	12:24	....	....	....	....	....	....	....	....	....
	San Antonio	AHL	65	14	32	46	74	....	....	....	....	....	....	....	....	....	....	....	....	....	....	....	....	....	....
2011-12	Portland Pirates	AHL	6	1	3	4	6	....	....	....	....	....	....	....	....	....	....	....	....	....	....	....	....	....	....
	Hamilton	AHL	42	8	16	24	14	....	....	....	....	....	....	....	....	....	....	....	....	....	....	....	....	....	....
2012-13	Hershey Bears	AHL	48	1	20	21	36	....	....	....	....	....	....	....	....	....	....	....	....	....	....	....	....	....	....
	Oklahoma City	AHL	8	0	2	2	0	....	....	....	....	....	....	....	....	....	17	2	2	4	10	....	....	....	....
	NHL Totals		7	0	2	2	0	0	0	0	8	0.0		0	0.0	13:11	....	....	....	....	....	....	....	....	....

Hockey East Second All-Star Team (2002) • AHL All-Rookie Team (2004) • AHL Second All-Star Team (2004)

Signed as a free agent by **Cleveland** (AHL), October 10, 2003. Signed as a free agent by **San Jose**, December 9, 2003. Signed as a free agent by **Detroit**, July 16, 2007. Signed as a free agent by **Dallas**, July 3, 2008. Signed as a free agent by **Phoenix**, July 3, 2010. Traded to **Montreal** by **Phoenix** with Petteri Nokelainen for Brock Trotter and Montreal's 7th round choice (Marek Langhamer) in 2012 Entry Draft, October 23, 2011. Signed as a free agent by **Washington**, July 2, 2012. Traded to **Edmonton** by **Washington** for Dane Byers, April 2, 2013. Signed as a free agent by **Farjestad** (Sweden), June 12, 2013.

STAJAN, Matt
(STAY-juhn, MAT) **CGY**

Center. Shoots left. 6'1", 192 lbs. Born, Mississauga, Ont., December 19, 1983. Toronto's 2nd choice, 57th overall, in 2002 Entry Draft.

			Regular Season														Playoffs								
Season	Club	League	GP	G	A	Pts	PIM	PP	SH	GW	S	%	+/-	TF	F%	Min	GP	G	A	Pts	PIM	PP	SH	GW	Min
99-2000	Miss. Senators	GTHL	STATISTICS NOT AVAILABLE																						
2000-01	Belleville Bulls	OHL	57	9	18	27	27	....	....	....	....	....	....	....	....	....	7	1	6	7	5	....	....	....	....
2001-02	Belleville Bulls	OHL	68	33	52	85	50	....	....	....	....	....	....	....	....	....	11	3	8	11	14	....	....	....	....
2002-03	Belleville Bulls	OHL	57	34	60	94	75	....	....	....	....	....	....	....	....	....	7	5	8	13	16	....	....	....	....
	St. John's	AHL	1	0	1	1	0	....	....	....	....	....	....	....	....	....	....	....	....	....	....	....	....	....	....
	Toronto	**NHL**	**1**	**1**	**0**	**1**	**0**	**0**	**0**	**0**	**1**	**100.0**	**1**	**12**	**33.3**	**11:00**	....	....	....	....	....	....	....	....	....
2003-04	**Toronto**	**NHL**	**69**	**14**	**13**	**27**	**22**	**0**	**0**	**0**	**63**	**22.2**	**7**	**450**	**38.9**	**11:00**	**3**	**0**	**0**	**0**	**2**	**0**	**0**	**0**	**11:13**
2004-05	St. John's	AHL	80	23	43	66	43	....	....	....	....	....	....	....	....	....	5	2	2	4	6	....	....	....	....
2005-06	**Toronto**	**NHL**	**80**	**15**	**12**	**27**	**50**	**3**	**4**	**5**	**83**	**18.1**	**5**	**373**	**44.5**	**11:38**	....	....	....	....	....	....	....	....	....
2006-07	**Toronto**	**NHL**	**82**	**10**	**29**	**39**	**44**	**1**	**1**	**1**	**132**	**7.6**	**3**	**985**	**46.1**	**16:09**	....	....	....	....	....	....	....	....	....
2007-08	**Toronto**	**NHL**	**82**	**16**	**17**	**33**	**47**	**2**	**1**	**3**	**127**	**12.6**	**-11**	**1293**	**47.6**	**18:54**	....	....	....	....	....	....	....	....	....
2008-09	**Toronto**	**NHL**	**76**	**15**	**40**	**55**	**54**	**5**	**1**	**1**	**114**	**13.2**	**-4**	**1177**	**51.4**	**16:56**	....	....	....	....	....	....	....	....	....
2009-10	**Toronto**	**NHL**	**55**	**16**	**25**	**41**	**30**	**7**	**0**	**2**	**99**	**16.2**	**-3**	**926**	**51.6**	**18:47**	....	....	....	....	....	....	....	....	....
	Calgary	**NHL**	**27**	**3**	**13**	**16**	**2**	**0**	**0**	**2**	**33**	**9.1**	**-3**	**408**	**52.0**	**19:11**	....	....	....	....	....	....	....	....	....
2010-11	**Calgary**	**NHL**	**76**	**6**	**25**	**31**	**32**	**0**	**1**	**0**	**81**	**7.4**	**1**	**845**	**51.6**	**14:14**	....	....	....	....	....	....	....	....	....
2011-12	**Calgary**	**NHL**	**61**	**8**	**10**	**18**	**29**	**0**	**0**	**1**	**77**	**10.4**	**-3**	**639**	**51.8**	**13:01**	....	....	....	....	....	....	....	....	....
2012-13	**Calgary**	**NHL**	**43**	**5**	**18**	**23**	**26**	**0**	**0**	**1**	**44**	**11.4**	**7**	**770**	**46.2**	**17:10**	....	....	....	....	....	....	....	....	....
	NHL Totals		**652**	**109**	**202**	**311**	**336**	**18**	**8**	**16**	**854**	**12.8**		**7878**	**48.6**	**15:23**	**3**	**0**	**0**	**0**	**2**	**0**	**0**	**0**	**11:13**

• Scored a goal in his first NHL game (April 5, 2003 vs. Ottawa).

Traded to **Calgary** by **Toronto** with Niklas Hagman, Jamal Mayers and Ian White for Dion Phaneuf, Fredrik Sjostrom and Keith Aulie, January 31, 2010.

STALBERG, Viktor
(STAHL-buhrg, VIHK-tohr) **NSH**

Left wing. Shoots left. 6'3", 209 lbs. Born, Stockholm, Sweden, January 17, 1986. Toronto's 5th choice, 161st overall, in 2006 Entry Draft.

			Regular Season														Playoffs								
Season	Club	League	GP	G	A	Pts	PIM	PP	SH	GW	S	%	+/-	TF	F%	Min	GP	G	A	Pts	PIM	PP	SH	GW	Min
2003-04	Molndal U18	Swe-U18	13	14	13	27	....	....	....	....	....	....	....	....	....	....	....	....	....	....	....	....	....	....	....
	Molndal Jr.	Swe-Jr.	18	25	10	35	....	....	....	....	....	....	....	....	....	....	....	....	....	....	....	....	....	....	....
	Molndal	Sweden-4	....	11	9	20	....	....	....	....	....	....	....	....	....	....	....	....	....	....	....	....	....	....	....
2004-05	Molndal Jr.	Swe-Jr.	11	16	7	23	....	....	....	....	....	....	....	....	....	....	....	....	....	....	....	....	....	....	....
	Molndal	Sweden-3	29	6	9	15	54	....	....	....	....	....	....	....	....	....	....	....	....	....	....	....	....	....	....
2005-06	Frolunda Jr.	Swe-Jr.	41	27	26	53	89	....	....	....	....	....	....	....	....	....	7	6	5	11	6	....	....	....	....
2006-07	U. of Vermont	H-East	39	7	8	15	53	....	....	....	....	....	....	....	....	....	....	....	....	....	....	....	....	....	....
2007-08	U. of Vermont	H-East	39	10	13	23	34	....	....	....	....	....	....	....	....	....	....	....	....	....	....	....	....	....	....
2008-09	U. of Vermont	H-East	39	24	22	46	32	....	....	....	....	....	....	....	....	....	....	....	....	....	....	....	....	....	....
	Toronto Marlies	AHL	....	....	....	....	....	....	....	....	....	....	....	....	....	....	2	0	1	1	0	....	....	....	....
2009-10	**Toronto**	**NHL**	**40**	**9**	**5**	**14**	**30**	**0**	**0**	**0**	**117**	**7.7**	**-13**	**9**	**33.3**	**14:37**	....	....	....	....	....	....	....	....	....
	Toronto Marlies	AHL	39	12	21	33	36	....	....	....	....	....	....	....	....	....	....	....	....	....	....	....	....	....	....
2010-11	**Chicago**	**NHL**	**77**	**12**	**12**	**24**	**43**	**0**	**0**	**3**	**135**	**8.9**	**2**	**9**	**55.6**	**10:42**	**7**	**1**	**0**	**1**	**5**	**0**	**0**	**0**	**12:17**
2011-12	**Chicago**	**NHL**	**79**	**22**	**21**	**43**	**34**	**0**	**0**	**6**	**215**	**10.2**	**6**	**11**	**45.5**	**14:04**	**6**	**0**	**2**	**2**	**8**	**0**	**0**	**0**	**14:54**
2012-13	Frolunda	Sweden	11	7	5	12	10	....	....	....	....	....	....	....	....	....	....	....	....	....	....	....	....	....	....
	Mytischi	KHL	14	3	7	10	4	....	....	....	....	....	....	....	....	....	....	....	....	....	....	....	....	....	....
	♦ **Chicago**	**NHL**	**47**	**9**	**14**	**23**	**25**	**0**	**0**	**1**	**113**	**8.0**	**16**	**1**	**0.0**	**14:07**	**19**	**0**	**3**	**3**	**6**	**0**	**0**	**0**	**10:35**
	NHL Totals		**243**	**52**	**52**	**104**	**132**	**0**	**0**	**10**	**580**	**9.0**		**30**	**43.3**	**13:06**	**32**	**1**	**5**	**6**	**19**	**0**	**0**	**0**	**11:46**

Hockey East First All-Star Team (2009) • NCAA East First All-American Team (2009)

Traded to **Chicago** by **Toronto** with Chris Didomenico and Phillipe Paradis for Kris Versteeg and Bill Sweatt, June 30, 2010. Signed as a free agent by **Frolunda** (Sweden), October 11, 2012. Signed as a free agent by **Mytischi** (KHL), November 20, 2012. Signed as a free agent by **Nashville**, July 5, 2013.

STAMKOS, Steven
(STAM-kohs, STEE-vehn) **T.B.**

Center. Shoots right. 6'1", 191 lbs. Born, Markham, Ont., February 7, 1990. Tampa Bay's 1st choice, 1st overall, in 2008 Entry Draft.

			Regular Season														Playoffs								
Season	Club	League	GP	G	A	Pts	PIM	PP	SH	GW	S	%	+/-	TF	F%	Min	GP	G	A	Pts	PIM	PP	SH	GW	Min
2005-06	Markham Waxers	Minor-ON	66	105	92	197	87	....	....	....	....	....	....	....	....	....	....	....	....	....	....	....	....	....	....
2006-07	Sarnia Sting	OHL	63	42	50	92	56	....	....	....	....	....	....	....	....	....	4	3	3	6	0	....	....	....	....
2007-08	Sarnia Sting	OHL	61	58	47	105	88	....	....	....	....	....	....	....	....	....	9	11	0	11	20	....	....	....	....
2008-09	**Tampa Bay**	**NHL**	**79**	**23**	**23**	**46**	**39**	**9**	**0**	**1**	**181**	**12.7**	**-13**	**557**	**45.4**	**14:56**	....	....	....	....	....	....	....	....	....
2009-10	**Tampa Bay**	**NHL**	**82**	***51**	**44**	**95**	**38**	**24**	**1**	**5**	**297**	**17.2**	**-2**	**1004**	**47.9**	**20:33**	....	....	....	....	....	....	....	....	....
2010-11	**Tampa Bay**	**NHL**	**82**	**45**	**46**	**91**	**74**	**17**	**0**	**8**	**272**	**16.5**	**3**	**927**	**46.5**	**20:12**	**18**	**6**	**7**	**13**	**6**	**3**	**0**	**1**	**19:43**
2011-12	**Tampa Bay**	**NHL**	**82**	***60**	**37**	**97**	**66**	**12**	**0**	***12**	**303**	**19.8**	**7**	**1227**	**45.5**	**22:01**	....	....	....	....	....	....	....	....	....
2012-13	**Tampa Bay**	**NHL**	**48**	**29**	**28**	**57**	**32**	**10**	**0**	**2**	**157**	**18.5**	**-4**	**819**	**49.6**	**22:01**	....	....	....	....	....	....	....	....	....
	NHL Totals		**373**	**208**	**178**	**386**	**249**	**72**	**1**	**28**	**1210**	**17.2**		**4534**	**47.0**	**19:48**	**18**	**6**	**7**	**13**	**6**	**3**	**0**	**1**	**19:44**

OHL Second All-Star Team (2008) • Canadian Major Junior First All-Star Team (2008) • Maurice "Rocket" Richard Trophy (2010) (tied with Sidney Crosby) • NHL Second All-Star Team (2011, 2012) • Maurice "Rocket" Richard Trophy (2012)

Played in NHL All-Star Game (2011, 2012)

STANTON, Ryan
(STAN-tuhn, RIGH-uhn) **CHI**

Defense. Shoots left. 6'2", 196 lbs. Born, St. Albert, Alta., July 20, 1989.

			Regular Season														Playoffs								
Season	Club	League	GP	G	A	Pts	PIM	PP	SH	GW	S	%	+/-	TF	F%	Min	GP	G	A	Pts	PIM	PP	SH	GW	Min
2004-05	St. Albert	Minor-AB	32	4	10	14	77	....	....	....	....	....	....	....	....	....	....	....	....	....	....	....	....	....	....
	St. Albert Raiders	AMHL	8	0	0	0	2	....	....	....	....	....	....	....	....	....	....	....	....	....	....	....	....	....	....
2005-06	St. Albert Raiders	AMHL	35	3	15	18	64	....	....	....	....	....	....	....	....	....	....	....	....	....	....	....	....	....	....
	Moose Jaw	WHL	2	0	0	0	2	....	....	....	....	....	....	....	....	....	....	....	....	....	....	....	....	....	....
2006-07	Moose Jaw	WHL	54	0	8	8	75	....	....	....	....	....	....	....	....	....	....	....	....	....	....	....	....	....	....
2007-08	Moose Jaw	WHL	58	4	16	20	68	....	....	....	....	....	....	....	....	....	6	0	0	0	2	....	....	....	....
2008-09	Moose Jaw	WHL	69	5	29	34	111	....	....	....	....	....	....	....	....	....	....	....	....	....	....	....	....	....	....
2009-10	Moose Jaw	WHL	59	10	30	40	81	....	....	....	....	....	....	....	....	....	7	0	6	6	4	....	....	....	....
	Rockford IceHogs	AHL	2	0	1	1	0	....	....	....	....	....	....	....	....	....	2	0	0	0	0	....	....	....	....
2010-11	Rockford IceHogs	AHL	73	3	14	17	76	....	....	....	....	....	....	....	....	....	....	....	....	....	....	....	....	....	....
2011-12	Rockford IceHogs	AHL	76	3	14	17	130	....	....	....	....	....	....	....	....	....	....	....	....	....	....	....	....	....	....
2012-13	Rockford IceHogs	AHL	73	3	22	25	126	....	....	....	....	....	....	....	....	....	....	....	....	....	....	....	....	....	....
	Chicago	**NHL**	**1**	**0**	**0**	**0**	**2**	**0**	**0**	**0**	**1**	**0.0**	**1**	**0**	**0.0**	**17:05**	....	....	....	....	....	....	....	....	....
	NHL Totals		**1**	**0**	**0**	**0**	**2**	**0**	**0**	**0**	**1**	**0.0**		**0**	**0.0**	**17:05**	....	....	....	....	....	....	....	....	....

Signed as a free agent by **Chicago**, March 12, 2010.

STAPLETON, Tim
(STAY-puhl-TOHN, TIHM)

Center. Shoots right. 5'9", 180 lbs. Born, La Grange, IL, July 9, 1982.

			Regular Season														Playoffs								
Season	Club	League	GP	G	A	Pts	PIM	PP	SH	GW	S	%	+/-	TF	F%	Min	GP	G	A	Pts	PIM	PP	SH	GW	Min
2000-01	Green Bay	USHL	52	7	15	22	8	....	....	....	....	....	....	....	....	....	4	1	2	3	4	....	....	....	....
2001-02	Green Bay	USHL	61	24	36	60	10	....	....	....	....	....	....	....	....	....	7	4	7	11	0	....	....	....	....
2002-03	U. Minn-Duluth	WCHA	42	14	28	42	6	....	....	....	....	....	....	....	....	....	....	....	....	....	....	....	....	....	....
2003-04	U. Minn-Duluth	WCHA	43	16	25	41	18	....	....	....	....	....	....	....	....	....	....	....	....	....	....	....	....	....	....
2004-05	U. Minn-Duluth	WCHA	38	19	20	39	6	....	....	....	....	....	....	....	....	....	....	....	....	....	....	....	....	....	....
2005-06	U. Minn-Duluth	WCHA	39	14	16	30	4	....	....	....	....	....	....	....	....	....	....	....	....	....	....	....	....	....	....
	Portland Pirates	AHL	9	0	5	5	4	....	....	....	....	....	....	....	....	....	4	0	0	0	2	....	....	....	....
2006-07	Jokerit Helsinki	Finland	56	19	29	48	24	....	....	....	....	....	....	....	....	....	10	6	4	10	8	....	....	....	....
2007-08	Jokerit Helsinki	Finland	55	29	33	62	36	....	....	....	....	....	....	....	....	....	14	*9	8	17	8	....	....	....	....
2008-09	**Toronto**	**NHL**	**4**	**1**	**0**	**1**	**0**	**0**	**0**	**0**	**9**	**11.1**	**-3**	**5**	**20.0**	**15:06**	....	....	....	....	....	....	....	....	....
	Toronto Marlies	AHL	70	28	51	79	26	....	....	....	....	....	....	....	....	....	6	2	0	2	2	....	....	....	....
2009-10	**Atlanta**	**NHL**	**6**	**2**	**0**	**2**	**2**	**1**	**0**	**0**	**6**	**33.3**	**1**	**36**	**61.1**	**11:53**	....	....	....	....	....	....	....	....	....
	Chicago Wolves	AHL	73	30	29	59	18	....	....	....	....	....	....	....	....	....	14	4	9	13	12	....	....	....	....
2010-11	San Antonio	AHL	20	8	7	15	2	....	....	....	....	....	....	....	....	....	....	....	....	....	....	....	....	....	....
	Atlanta	**NHL**	**45**	**5**	**2**	**7**	**12**	**1**	**0**	**1**	**44**	**11.4**	**-10**	**225**	**48.4**	**11:07**	....	....	....	....	....	....	....	....	....
	Chicago Wolves	AHL	4	1	3	4	2	....	....	....	....	....	....	....	....	....	....	....	....	....	....	....	....	....	....
2011-12	**Winnipeg**	**NHL**	**63**	**11**	**16**	**27**	**10**	**4**	**0**	**3**	**74**	**14.9**	**-2**	**216**	**44.9**	**10:09**	....	....	....	....	....	....	....	....	....
2012-13	Dynamo Minsk	KHL	52	24	16	40	30	....	....	....	....	....	....	....	....	....	6	2	3	5	0	....	....	....	....
	NHL Totals		**118**	**19**	**18**	**37**	**24**	**6**	**0**	**4**	**133**	**14.3**		**482**	**47.5**	**10:46**	....	....	....	....	....	....	....	....	....

Signed as a free agent by **Toronto**, June 6, 2008. Traded to **Atlanta** by **Toronto** with Pavel Kubina for Garnet Exelby and Colin Stuart, July 1, 2009. Signed to a PTO (professional tryout) contract by **San Antonio** (AHL), September 28, 2010. Signed as a free agent by **Atlanta**, November 30, 2010. • Transferred to **Winnipeg** after **Atlanta** franchise relocated, June 21, 2011. Signed as a free agent by **Minsk** (KHL), July 10, 2012.

STASTNY, Paul

(STAS-nee, PAWL) **COL**

Center. Shoots left. 6', 208 lbs. Born, Quebec City, Que., December 27, 1985. Colorado's 2nd choice, 44th overall, in 2005 Entry Draft.

			Regular Season															Playoffs								
Season	Club	League	GP	G	A	Pts	PIM	PP	SH	GW	S	%	+/-	TF	F%	Min	GP	G	A	Pts	PIM	PP	SH	GW	Min
2002-03	River City Lancers	USHL	57	10	20	30	39	....	....	....	....	....	....	....	....	....	8	0	1	1	2	....	....	....	....
2003-04	River City Lancers	USHL	56	30	*47	77	46	....	....	....	....	....	....	....	....	....	3	1	2	3	0	....	....	....	....
2004-05	U. of Denver	WCHA	42	17	28	45	30	....	....	....	....	....	....	....	....	....	....	....	....	....	....	....	....	....	....
2005-06	U. of Denver	WCHA	39	19	34	53	79	....	....	....	....	....	....	....	....	....	....	....	....	....	....	....	....	....	....
2006-07	**Colorado**	**NHL**	**82**	**28**	**50**	**78**	**42**	**11**	**0**	**6**	**185**	**15.1**	**4**	**1226**	**48.5**	**18:10**	....	....	....	....	....	....	....	....	....
2007-08	**Colorado**	**NHL**	**66**	**24**	**47**	**71**	**24**	**3**	**0**	**4**	**138**	**17.4**	**22**	**1101**	**51.0**	**21:05**	**9**	**2**	**1**	**3**	**6**	**0**	**0**	**1**	**19:56**
2008-09	**Colorado**	**NHL**	**45**	**11**	**25**	**36**	**22**	**7**	**0**	**2**	**118**	**9.3**	**–9**	**850**	**51.8**	**21:14**	....	....	....	....	....	....	....	....	....
2009-10	**Colorado**	**NHL**	**81**	**20**	**59**	**79**	**50**	**9**	**0**	**2**	**199**	**10.1**	**2**	**1703**	**50.0**	**21:24**	**6**	**1**	**4**	**5**	**4**	**1**	**0**	**0**	**20:23**
	United States	Olympics	6	1	2	3	0	....	....	....	....	....	....	....	....	....	....	....	....	....	....	....	....	....	....
2010-11	**Colorado**	**NHL**	**74**	**22**	**35**	**57**	**56**	**4**	**1**	**3**	**181**	**12.2**	**–7**	**1524**	**53.2**	**19:44**	....	....	....	....	....	....	....	....	....
2011-12	**Colorado**	**NHL**	**79**	**21**	**32**	**53**	**34**	**7**	**0**	**2**	**190**	**11.1**	**–8**	**1424**	**55.4**	**18:50**	....	....	....	....	....	....	....	....	....
2012-13	EHC Munchen	Germany	13	7	11	18	20	....	....	....	....	....	....	....	....	....	....	....	....	....	....	....	....	....	....
	Colorado	**NHL**	**40**	**9**	**15**	**24**	**14**	**2**	**0**	**1**	**87**	**10.3**	**–7**	**781**	**52.4**	**19:21**	....	....	....	....	....	....	....	....	....
	NHL Totals		**467**	**135**	**263**	**398**	**242**	**43**	**1**	**20**	**1098**	**12.3**		**8609**	**51.7**	**19:54**	**15**	**3**	**5**	**8**	**10**	**1**	**0**	**1**	**20:06**

WCHA All-Rookie Team (2005) • WCHA Rookie of the Year (2005) • NCAA Championship All-Tournament Team (2005) • WCHA First All-Star Team (2006) • NCAA West Second All-American Team (2006) • NHL All-Rookie Team (2007)

Played in NHL All-Star Game (2011)

Signed as a free agent by **Munchen** (Germany), November 16, 2012.

STAUBITZ, Brad

(STAW-bihtz, BRAD) **ANA**

Right wing. Shoots right. 6'1", 215 lbs. Born, Bright's Grove, Ont., July 28, 1984.

Season	Club	League	GP	G	A	Pts	PIM	PP	SH	GW	S	%	+/-	TF	F%	Min	GP	G	A	Pts	PIM	PP	SH	GW	Min
2001-02	Sault Ste. Marie	OHL	45	0	3	3	46	....	....	....	....	....	....	....	....	....	3	0	0	0	2	....	....	....	....
2002-03	Sault Ste. Marie	OHL	55	2	6	8	116	....	....	....	....	....	....	....	....	....	4	0	0	0	7	....	....	....	....
2003-04	Sault Ste. Marie	OHL	66	6	18	24	140	....	....	....	....	....	....	....	....	....	....	....	....	....	....	....	....	....	....
2004-05	Sault Ste. Marie	OHL	40	2	11	13	101	....	....	....	....	....	....	....	....	....	....	....	....	....	....	....	....	....	....
	Ottawa 67's	OHL	30	5	8	13	80	....	....	....	....	....	....	....	....	....	21	4	16	20	70	....	....	....	....
2005-06	Cleveland Barons	AHL	71	0	6	6	245	....	....	....	....	....	....	....	....	....	....	....	....	....	....	....	....	....	....
2006-07	Worcester Sharks	AHL	51	1	4	5	137	....	....	....	....	....	....	....	....	....	5	0	0	0	13	....	....	....	....
2007-08	Worcester Sharks	AHL	73	6	14	20	195	....	....	....	....	....	....	....	....	....	....	....	....	....	....	....	....	....	....
2008-09	**San Jose**	**NHL**	**35**	**1**	**2**	**3**	**76**	**0**	**0**	**1**	**22**	**4.5**	**0**	**2**	**0.0**	**6:13**	....	....	....	....	....	....	....	....	....
	Worcester Sharks	AHL	38	0	5	5	130	....	....	....	....	....	....	....	....	....	10	0	2	2	15	....	....	....	....
2009-10	**San Jose**	**NHL**	**47**	**3**	**3**	**6**	**110**	**0**	**0**	**1**	**24**	**12.5**	**0**	**4**	**0.0**	**6:13**	....	....	....	....	....	....	....	....	....
2010-11	**Minnesota**	**NHL**	**71**	**4**	**5**	**9**	**173**	**0**	**0**	**1**	**29**	**13.8**	**–5**	**4**	**0.0**	**6:31**	....	....	....	....	....	....	....	....	....
2011-12	**Minnesota**	**NHL**	**43**	**0**	**0**	**0**	**73**	**0**	**0**	**0**	**17**	**0.0**	**–7**	**5**	**60.0**	**6:30**	....	....	....	....	....	....	....	....	....
	Montreal	**NHL**	**19**	**1**	**0**	**1**	**48**	**0**	**0**	**0**	**10**	**10.0**	**2**	**1**	**0.0**	**6:34**	....	....	....	....	....	....	....	....	....
	Houston Aeros	AHL	4	0	0	0	9	....	....	....	....	....	....	....	....	....	....	....	....	....	....	....	....	....	....
2012-13	**Anaheim**	**NHL**	**15**	**1**	**1**	**2**	**41**	**0**	**0**	**1**	**5**	**20.0**	**0**	**0**	**0.0**	**6:13**	....	....	....	....	....	....	....	....	....
	NHL Totals		**230**	**10**	**11**	**21**	**521**	**0**	**0**	**4**	**107**	**9.3**		**16**	**18.8**	**6:23**	....	....	....	....	....	....	....	....	....

Signed as a free agent by **San Jose**, September 19, 2005. Traded to **Minnesota** by **San Jose** for Minnesota's 5th round choice (Freddie Hamilton) in 2010 Entry Draft, June 21, 2010. Claimed on waivers by **Montreal** from **Minnesota**, February 27, 2012. Signed as a free agent by **Anaheim**, July 1, 2012. • Missed majority of 2012-13 as a healthy reserve.

STECKEL, David

(STEH-kuhl, DAY-vihd)

Center. Shoots left. 6'6", 215 lbs. Born, Milwaukee, WI, March 15, 1982. Los Angeles' 2nd choice, 30th overall, in 2001 Entry Draft.

Season	Club	League	GP	G	A	Pts	PIM	PP	SH	GW	S	%	+/-	TF	F%	Min	GP	G	A	Pts	PIM	PP	SH	GW	Min
1998-99	USNTDP	USHL	2	0	0	0	2	....	....	....	....	....	....	....	....	....	....	....	....	....	....	....	....	....	....
	USNTDP	NAHL	51	3	14	17	18	....	....	....	....	....	....	....	....	....	....	....	....	....	....	....	....	....	....
99-2000	USNTDP	U-18	6	2	5	7	14	....	....	....	....	....	....	....	....	....	....	....	....	....	....	....	....	....	....
	USNTDP	USHL	52	13	13	26	94	....	....	....	....	....	....	....	....	....	....	....	....	....	....	....	....	....	....
2000-01	Ohio State	CCHA	33	17	18	35	80	....	....	....	....	....	....	....	....	....	....	....	....	....	....	....	....	....	....
2001-02	Ohio State	CCHA	36	6	16	22	75	....	....	....	....	....	....	....	....	....	....	....	....	....	....	....	....	....	....
2002-03	Ohio State	CCHA	36	10	8	18	50	....	....	....	....	....	....	....	....	....	....	....	....	....	....	....	....	....	....
2003-04	Ohio State	CCHA	41	17	13	30	44	....	....	....	....	....	....	....	....	....	....	....	....	....	....	....	....	....	....
2004-05	Manchester	AHL	63	10	7	17	26	....	....	....	....	....	....	....	....	....	6	1	1	2	4	....	....	....	....
2005-06	**Washington**	**NHL**	**7**	**0**	**0**	**0**	**0**	**0**	**0**	**0**	**6**	**0.0**	**1**	**48**	**35.4**	**7:39**	....	....	....	....	....	....	....	....	....
	Hershey Bears	AHL	74	14	20	34	58	....	....	....	....	....	....	....	....	....	21	10	5	15	20	....	....	....	....
2006-07	**Washington**	**NHL**	**5**	**0**	**0**	**0**	**2**	**0**	**0**	**0**	**4**	**0.0**	**–2**	**43**	**65.1**	**12:26**	....	....	....	....	....	....	....	....	....
	Hershey Bears	AHL	71	30	31	61	46	....	....	....	....	....	....	....	....	....	19	6	9	15	16	....	....	....	....
2007-08	**Washington**	**NHL**	**67**	**5**	**7**	**12**	**34**	**0**	**0**	**1**	**66**	**7.6**	**1**	**900**	**56.3**	**13:34**	**7**	**1**	**1**	**2**	**4**	**0**	**0**	**0**	**14:23**
2008-09	**Washington**	**NHL**	**76**	**8**	**11**	**19**	**34**	**0**	**2**	**1**	**103**	**7.8**	**2**	**886**	**57.9**	**13:49**	**14**	**3**	**2**	**5**	**4**	**0**	**0**	**1**	**16:03**
2009-10	**Washington**	**NHL**	**79**	**5**	**11**	**16**	**19**	**1**	**0**	**1**	**90**	**5.6**	**4**	**1076**	**59.2**	**12:24**	**3**	**0**	**0**	**0**	**0**	**0**	**0**	**0**	**10:28**
2010-11	**Washington**	**NHL**	**57**	**5**	**6**	**11**	**24**	**0**	**1**	**1**	**61**	**8.2**	**–3**	**670**	**63.7**	**11:34**	....	....	....	....	....	....	....	....	....
	New Jersey	**NHL**	**18**	**1**	**0**	**1**	**2**	**0**	**0**	**0**	**18**	**5.6**	**–3**	**150**	**56.0**	**12:50**	....	....	....	....	....	....	....	....	....
2011-12	**Toronto**	**NHL**	**76**	**8**	**5**	**13**	**10**	**1**	**2**	**0**	**79**	**10.1**	**–14**	**1108**	**58.0**	**12:50**	....	....	....	....	....	....	....	....	....
2012-13	**Toronto**	**NHL**	**13**	**0**	**1**	**1**	**0**	**0**	**0**	**0**	**4**	**0.0**	**–2**	**81**	**46.9**	**7:04**	....	....	....	....	....	....	....	....	....
	Anaheim	**NHL**	**21**	**1**	**5**	**6**	**4**	**0**	**0**	**0**	**19**	**5.3**	**2**	**240**	**57.1**	**10:37**	**7**	**1**	**1**	**2**	**0**	**0**	**0**	**0**	**9:46**
	NHL Totals		**419**	**33**	**46**	**79**	**129**	**2**	**5**	**4**	**450**	**7.3**		**5202**	**58.3**	**12:30**	**31**	**5**	**4**	**9**	**8**	**0**	**0**	**1**	**13:43**

CCHA All-Rookie Team (2001)

Signed as a free agent by **Washington**, August 25, 2005. Traded to **New Jersey** by **Washington** with Washington's 2nd round choice (later traded to Minnesota – Minnesota selected Raphael Bussieres) in 2012 Entry Draft for Jason Arnott, February 28, 2011. Traded to **Toronto** by **New Jersey** for Toronto's 4th round choice (Ben Thomson) in 2012 Entry Draft, October 4, 2011. Traded to **Anaheim** by **Toronto** for Ryan Lasch and Anaheim's 7th round choice in 2014 Entry Draft, March 15, 2013.

STEEN, Alex

(STEEN, AL-ehx) **ST.L.**

Center. Shoots left. 5'11", 212 lbs. Born, Winnipeg, Man., March 1, 1984. Toronto's 1st choice, 24th overall, in 2002 Entry Draft.

Season	Club	League	GP	G	A	Pts	PIM	PP	SH	GW	S	%	+/-	TF	F%	Min	GP	G	A	Pts	PIM	PP	SH	GW	Min
99-2000	V.Frolunda Jr.	Swe-Jr.	8	5	7	12	0	....	....	....	....	....	....	....	....	....	....	....	....	....	....	....	....	....	....
	V.Frolunda U18	Swe-U18	14	3	5	8	16	....	....	....	....	....	....	....	....	....	....	....	....	....	....	....	....	....	....
2000-01	V.Frolunda Jr.	Swe-Jr.	23	11	12	23	15	....	....	....	....	....	....	....	....	....	3	1	0	1	2	....	....	....	....
	V.Frolunda U18	Swe-U18	6	3	3	6	9	....	....	....	....	....	....	....	....	....	....	....	....	....	....	....	....	....	....
2001-02	V.Frolunda Jr.	Swe-Jr.	23	21	17	38	47	....	....	....	....	....	....	....	....	....	2	1	1	2	2	....	....	....	....
	V.Frolunda	Sweden	26	0	3	3	14	....	....	....	....	....	....	....	....	....	10	1	2	3	0	....	....	....	....
2002-03	V.Frolunda	Sweden	45	5	10	15	18	....	....	....	....	....	....	....	....	....	16	2	3	5	4	....	....	....	....
	V.Frolunda Jr.	Swe-Jr.	2	0	2	2	0	....	....	....	....	....	....	....	....	....	....	....	....	....	....	....	....	....	....
2003-04	V.Frolunda	Sweden	48	10	14	24	50	....	....	....	....	....	....	....	....	....	10	4	6	10	14	....	....	....	....
2004-05	MODO	Sweden	50	9	8	17	26	....	....	....	....	....	....	....	....	....	6	1	0	1	4	....	....	....	....
2005-06	**Toronto**	**NHL**	**75**	**18**	**27**	**45**	**42**	**9**	**1**	**3**	**176**	**10.2**	**–9**	**29**	**24.1**	**17:37**	....	....	....	....	....	....	....	....	....
2006-07	**Toronto**	**NHL**	**82**	**15**	**20**	**35**	**26**	**4**	**0**	**5**	**192**	**7.8**	**5**	**44**	**34.1**	**15:42**	....	....	....	....	....	....	....	....	....
2007-08	**Toronto**	**NHL**	**76**	**15**	**27**	**42**	**32**	**2**	**1**	**2**	**169**	**8.9**	**0**	**179**	**33.0**	**18:05**	....	....	....	....	....	....	....	....	....
2008-09	**Toronto**	**NHL**	**20**	**2**	**2**	**4**	**6**	**1**	**0**	**0**	**31**	**6.5**	**–4**	**82**	**52.4**	**15:38**	....	....	....	....	....	....	....	....	....
	St. Louis	**NHL**	**61**	**6**	**18**	**24**	**24**	**2**	**1**	**0**	**117**	**5.1**	**–6**	**154**	**41.6**	**16:34**	**4**	**0**	**1**	**1**	**0**	**0**	**0**	**0**	**17:47**
2009-10	**St. Louis**	**NHL**	**68**	**24**	**23**	**47**	**30**	**7**	**2**	**4**	**189**	**12.7**	**6**	**73**	**41.1**	**16:17**	....	....	....	....	....	....	....	....	....
2010-11	**St. Louis**	**NHL**	**72**	**20**	**31**	**51**	**26**	**1**	**2**	**5**	**218**	**9.2**	**–3**	**106**	**38.7**	**19:33**	....	....	....	....	....	....	....	....	....
2011-12	**St. Louis**	**NHL**	**43**	**15**	**13**	**28**	**28**	**3**	**0**	**3**	**134**	**11.2**	**24**	**95**	**55.8**	**19:08**	**9**	**1**	**2**	**3**	**6**	**1**	**0**	**1**	**20:54**
2012-13	MODO	Sweden	20	8	15	23	28	....	....	....	....	....	....	....	....	....	....	....	....	....	....	....	....	....	....
	St. Louis	**NHL**	**40**	**8**	**19**	**27**	**14**	**3**	**0**	**3**	**129**	**6.2**	**5**	**204**	**46.1**	**19:00**	**6**	**3**	**0**	**3**	**6**	**1**	**1**	**1**	**20:56**
	NHL Totals		**537**	**123**	**180**	**303**	**228**	**32**	**7**	**25**	**1355**	**9.1**		**966**	**42.0**	**17:31**	**19**	**4**	**3**	**7**	**12**	**2**	**1**	**2**	**20:15**

Traded to **St. Louis** by **Toronto** with Carlo Colaiacovo for Lee Stempniak, November 24, 2008. Signed as a free agent by **MODO** (Sweden), September 25, 2012.

STEMPNIAK, Lee

(STEHMP-nee-ak, LEE) **CGY**

Right wing. Shoots right. 5'11", 196 lbs. Born, Buffalo, NY, February 4, 1983. St. Louis' 7th choice, 148th overall, in 2003 Entry Draft.

Season	Club	League	GP	G	A	Pts	PIM	PP	SH	GW	S	%	+/-	TF	F%	Min	GP	G	A	Pts	PIM	PP	SH	GW	Min
2000-01	Buffalo Lightning	ON-Jr.A	48	34	51	86	36	....	....	....	....	....	....	....	....	....	....	....	....	....	....	....	....	....	....
2001-02	Dartmouth	ECAC	32	12	9	21	8	....	....	....	....	....	....	....	....	....	....	....	....	....	....	....	....	....	....
2002-03	Dartmouth	ECAC	34	21	28	49	32	....	....	....	....	....	....	....	....	....	....	....	....	....	....	....	....	....	....
2003-04	Dartmouth	ECAC	34	16	22	38	42	....	....	....	....	....	....	....	....	....	....	....	....	....	....	....	....	....	....
2004-05	Dartmouth	ECAC	35	14	*29	43	34	....	....	....	....	....	....	....	....	....	....	....	....	....	....	....	....	....	....

										Regular Season										Playoffs					
Season	Club	League	GP	G	A	Pts	PIM	PP	SH	GW	S	%	+/-	TF	F%	Min	GP	G	A	Pts	PIM	PP	SH	GW	Min
2005-06	**St. Louis**	**NHL**	**57**	**14**	**13**	**27**	**22**	**5**	**0**	**2**	**100**	**14.0**	**–10**	**7**	**42.9**	**14:22**	....	....	....	....	....	....	....	....	....
	Peoria Rivermen	AHL	26	8	7	15	32	....	....	....	....	....	....	....	....	....	3	0	3	3	2	....	....	....	....
2006-07	**St. Louis**	**NHL**	**82**	**27**	**25**	**52**	**33**	**8**	**0**	**4**	**166**	**16.3**	**–2**	**7**	**14.3**	**14:43**	....	....	....	....	....	....	....	....	....
2007-08	**St. Louis**	**NHL**	**80**	**13**	**25**	**38**	**40**	**3**	**0**	**2**	**162**	**8.0**	**0**	**11**	**36.4**	**15:53**	....	....	....	....	....	....	....	....	....
2008-09	**St. Louis**	**NHL**	**14**	**3**	**10**	**13**	**2**	**0**	**0**	**1**	**43**	**7.0**	**–3**	**1**	**0.0**	**19:28**	....	....	....	....	....	....	....	....	....
	Toronto	**NHL**	**61**	**11**	**20**	**31**	**31**	**3**	**0**	**0**	**128**	**8.6**	**–9**	**12**	**33.3**	**15:52**	....	....	....	....	....	....	....	....	....
2009-10	**Toronto**	**NHL**	**62**	**14**	**16**	**30**	**18**	**5**	**1**	**1**	**164**	**8.5**	**–10**	**25**	**36.0**	**17:53**	....	....	....	....	....	....	....	....	....
	Phoenix	**NHL**	**18**	**14**	**4**	**18**	**8**	**4**	**0**	**1**	**48**	**29.2**	**10**	**14**	**57.1**	**15:22**	**7**	**0**	**2**	**2**	**0**	**0**	**0**	**0**	**14:28**
2010-11	**Phoenix**	**NHL**	**82**	**19**	**19**	**38**	**19**	**2**	**0**	**0**	**199**	**9.5**	**4**	**45**	**40.0**	**15:15**	**4**	**0**	**0**	**0**	**0**	**0**	**0**	**0**	**12:13**
2011-12	**Calgary**	**NHL**	**61**	**14**	**14**	**28**	**16**	**2**	**0**	**2**	**130**	**10.8**	**–2**	**26**	**26.9**	**16:14**	....	....	....	....	....	....	....	....	....
2012-13	**Calgary**	**NHL**	**47**	**9**	**23**	**32**	**12**	**4**	**0**	**2**	**113**	**8.0**	**2**	**23**	**13.0**	**17:54**	....	....	....	....	....	....	....	....	....
	NHL Totals		**564**	**138**	**169**	**307**	**201**	**36**	**1**	**15**	**1253**	**11.0**		**171**	**33.3**	**15:58**	**11**	**0**	**2**	**2**	**0**	**0**	**0**	**0**	**13:39**

ECAC All-Rookie Team (2002) • ECAC First All-Star Team (2004, 2005) • NCAA East First All-American Team (2004) • NCAA East Second All-American Team (2005)

Traded to **Toronto** by **St. Louis** for Alex Steen and Carlo Colaiacovo, November 24, 2008. Traded to **Phoenix** by **Toronto** for Matt Jones and Phoenix's 4th (later traded to Washington – Washington selected Philipp Grubauer) and 7th (later traded to Edmonton – Edmonton selected Kellen Jones) round choices in 2010 Entry Draft, March 3, 2010. Traded to **Calgary** by **Phoenix** for Daymond Langkow, August 29, 2011.

STEPAN, Derek

(STEH-pan, DAIR-ihk) **NYR**

Center. Shoots right. 6', 196 lbs. Born, Hastings, MN, June 18, 1990. NY Rangers' 2nd choice, 51st overall, in 2008 Entry Draft.

2006-07	Shat.-St. Mary's	High-MN	63	38	32	70	22	....	....	....	....	....	....	....	....	....	....	....	....	....	....	....	....	....	....
2007-08	Shat.-St. Mary's	High-MN	60	44	67	111	22	....	....	....	....	....	....	....	....	....	....	....	....	....	....	....	....	....	....
2008-09	U. of Wisconsin	WCHA	40	9	24	33	6	....	....	....	....	....	....	....	....	....	....	....	....	....	....	....	....	....	....
2009-10	U. of Wisconsin	WCHA	41	12	*42	*54	8	....	....	....	....	....	....	....	....	....	....	....	....	....	....	....	....	....	....
2010-11	**NY Rangers**	**NHL**	**82**	**21**	**24**	**45**	**20**	**3**	**0**	**3**	**166**	**12.7**	**8**	**719**	**38.5**	**16:27**	**5**	**0**	**0**	**0**	**2**	**0**	**0**	**0**	**20:29**
2011-12	**NY Rangers**	**NHL**	**82**	**17**	**34**	**51**	**22**	**4**	**0**	**4**	**169**	**10.1**	**14**	**867**	**44.5**	**18:57**	**20**	**1**	**8**	**9**	**4**	**1**	**0**	**0**	**19:07**
2012-13	KalPa Kuopio	Finland	12	2	2	4	0	....	....	....	....	....	....	....	....	....	....	....	....	....	....	....	....	....	....
	NY Rangers	**NHL**	**48**	**18**	**26**	**44**	**12**	**4**	**1**	**6**	**108**	**16.7**	**25**	**977**	**45.9**	**20:55**	**12**	**4**	**1**	**5**	**2**	**0**	**0**	**2**	**22:30**
	NHL Totals		**212**	**56**	**84**	**140**	**54**	**11**	**1**	**13**	**443**	**12.6**		**2563**	**43.3**	**18:26**	**37**	**5**	**9**	**14**	**8**	**1**	**0**	**2**	**20:24**

Signed as a free agent by **Kuopio** (Finland), November 11, 2012.

STERLING, Brett

(STUHR-lihng, BREHT)

Left wing. Shoots left. 5'7", 175 lbs. Born, Los Angeles, CA, April 24, 1984. Atlanta's 5th choice, 145th overall, in 2003 Entry Draft.

99-2000	L.A. Jr. Kings	SCAHA	35	45	25	70	....	....	....	....	....	....	....	....	....	....	....	....	....	....	....	....	....	....	....
2000-01	USNTDP	U-17	13	....	....	....	....	....	....	....	....	....	....	....	....	....	....	....	....	....	....	....	....	....	....
	USNTDP	NAHL	47	29	15	44	72	....	....	....	....	....	....	....	....	....	....	....	....	....	....	....	....	....	....
2001-02	USNTDP	U-18	31	21	15	36	18	....	....	....	....	....	....	....	....	....	....	....	....	....	....	....	....	....	....
	USNTDP	USHL	10	6	3	9	8	....	....	....	....	....	....	....	....	....	....	....	....	....	....	....	....	....	....
	USNTDP	NAHL	9	2	1	3	10	....	....	....	....	....	....	....	....	....	....	....	....	....	....	....	....	....	....
2002-03	Colorado College	WCHA	36	27	11	38	30	....	....	....	....	....	....	....	....	....	....	....	....	....	....	....	....	....	....
2003-04	Colorado College	WCHA	30	16	12	28	40	....	....	....	....	....	....	....	....	....	....	....	....	....	....	....	....	....	....
2004-05	Colorado College	WCHA	43	*34	29	63	74	....	....	....	....	....	....	....	....	....	....	....	....	....	....	....	....	....	....
2005-06	Colorado College	WCHA	42	31	24	55	66	....	....	....	....	....	....	....	....	....	....	....	....	....	....	....	....	....	....
2006-07	Chicago Wolves	AHL	77	*55	42	97	96	....	....	....	....	....	....	....	....	....	15	7	5	12	24	....	....	....	....
2007-08	**Atlanta**	**NHL**	**13**	**1**	**2**	**3**	**14**	**0**	**0**	**0**	**14**	**7.1**	**–2**	**3**	**66.7**	**12:24**	....	....	....	....	....	....	....	....	....
	Chicago Wolves	AHL	70	38	33	71	116	....	....	....	....	....	....	....	....	....	16	4	5	9	18	....	....	....	....
2008-09	**Atlanta**	**NHL**	**6**	**1**	**0**	**1**	**2**	**0**	**0**	**0**	**11**	**9.1**	**–3**	**0**	**0.0**	**13:53**	....	....	....	....	....	....	....	....	....
	Chicago Wolves	AHL	52	16	23	39	84	....	....	....	....	....	....	....	....	....	....	....	....	....	....	....	....	....	....
2009-10	Chicago Wolves	AHL	55	34	22	56	38	....	....	....	....	....	....	....	....	....	9	4	6	10	4	....	....	....	....
2010-11	**Pittsburgh**	**NHL**	**7**	**3**	**2**	**5**	**16**	**1**	**0**	**0**	**14**	**21.4**	**1**	**3**	**66.7**	**15:07**	....	....	....	....	....	....	....	....	....
	Wilkes-Barre	AHL	65	27	26	53	88	....	....	....	....	....	....	....	....	....	12	2	4	6	10	....	....	....	....
2011-12	**St. Louis**	**NHL**	**4**	**0**	**0**	**0**	**0**	**0**	**0**	**0**	**5**	**0.0**	**–1**	**4**	**75.0**	**7:34**	....	....	....	....	....	....	....	....	....
	Peoria Rivermen	AHL	54	22	26	48	74	....	....	....	....	....	....	....	....	....	....	....	....	....	....	....	....	....	....
2012-13	Chicago Wolves	AHL	48	24	21	45	50	....	....	....	....	....	....	....	....	....	....	....	....	....	....	....	....	....	....
	NHL Totals		**30**	**5**	**4**	**9**	**32**	**1**	**0**	**0**	**44**	**11.4**		**10**	**70.0**	**12:41**	....	....	....	....	....	....	....	....	....

WCHA All-Rookie Team (2003) • WCHA First All-Star Team (2005, 2006) • NCAA West First All-American Team (2005, 2006) • AHL All-Rookie Team (2007) • AHL First All-Star Team (2007) • Dudley "Red" Garrett Memorial Award (AHL - Rookie of the Year) (2007) • Willie Marshall Award (AHL - Top Goal-scorer) (2007) • AHL Second All-Star Team (2008)

Traded to **San Jose** by **Atlanta** with Mike Vernace and Atlanta's 7th round choice (Lee Moffie) in 2010 Entry Draft for future considerations, June 23, 2010. Signed as a free agent by **Pittsburgh**, July 3, 2010. Signed as a free agent by **St. Louis**, July 4, 2011. Signed as a free agent by **Jonkoping** (Sweden), May 8, 2013.

STEWART, Anthony

(STEW-ahrt, AN-thu-nee)

Right wing. Shoots right. 6'3", 230 lbs. Born, LaSalle, Que., January 5, 1985. Florida's 2nd choice, 25th overall, in 2003 Entry Draft.

2000-01	North York	MTHL	34	30	70	100	....	....	....	....	....	....	....	....	....	....	....	....	....	....	....	....	....	....	....
	St. Mike's B's	ON-Jr.A	5	0	2	2	0	....	....	....	....	....	....	....	....	....	....	....	....	....	....	....	....	....	....
2001-02	Kingston	OHL	65	19	24	43	12	....	....	....	....	....	....	....	....	....	1	0	0	0	0	....	....	....	....
2002-03	Kingston	OHL	68	32	38	70	47	....	....	....	....	....	....	....	....	....	....	....	....	....	....	....	....	....	....
2003-04	Kingston	OHL	53	35	23	58	76	....	....	....	....	....	....	....	....	....	5	3	4	7	7	....	....	....	....
2004-05	Kingston	OHL	62	32	35	67	70	....	....	....	....	....	....	....	....	....	....	....	....	....	....	....	....	....	....
	San Antonio	AHL	10	1	2	3	14	....	....	....	....	....	....	....	....	....	....	....	....	....	....	....	....	....	....
2005-06	**Florida**	**NHL**	**10**	**2**	**1**	**3**	**2**	**1**	**0**	**0**	**16**	**12.5**	**2**	**1**	**0.0**	**7:13**	....	....	....	....	....	....	....	....	....
	Rochester	AHL	4	2	3	5	0	....	....	....	....	....	....	....	....	....	....	....	....	....	....	....	....	....	....
2006-07	**Florida**	**NHL**	**10**	**0**	**1**	**1**	**2**	**0**	**0**	**0**	**8**	**0.0**	**1**	**0**	**0.0**	**6:51**	....	....	....	....	....	....	....	....	....
	Rochester	AHL	62	13	14	27	64	....	....	....	....	....	....	....	....	....	6	2	0	2	2	....	....	....	....
2007-08	**Florida**	**NHL**	**26**	**0**	**1**	**1**	**0**	**0**	**0**	**0**	**21**	**0.0**	**–1**	**0**	**0.0**	**6:08**	....	....	....	....	....	....	....	....	....
	Rochester	AHL	54	13	18	31	61	....	....	....	....	....	....	....	....	....	....	....	....	....	....	....	....	....	....
2008-09	**Florida**	**NHL**	**59**	**2**	**5**	**7**	**34**	**0**	**0**	**0**	**56**	**3.6**	**–6**	**3**	**33.3**	**7:39**	....	....	....	....	....	....	....	....	....
2009-10	Chicago Wolves	AHL	77	12	19	31	67	....	....	....	....	....	....	....	....	....	13	9	3	12	6	....	....	....	....
2010-11	**Atlanta**	**NHL**	**80**	**14**	**25**	**39**	**55**	**5**	**0**	**2**	**141**	**9.9**	**–10**	**18**	**38.9**	**14:58**	....	....	....	....	....	....	....	....	....
2011-12	**Carolina**	**NHL**	**77**	**9**	**11**	**20**	**30**	**0**	**0**	**1**	**64**	**14.1**	**–2**	**17**	**17.7**	**8:07**	....	....	....	....	....	....	....	....	....
2012-13	Nottingham	Britain	19	6	5	11	14	....	....	....	....	....	....	....	....	....	....	....	....	....	....	....	....	....	....
	Manchester	AHL	30	4	3	7	31	....	....	....	....	....	....	....	....	....	4	1	0	1	0	....	....	....	....
	NHL Totals		**262**	**27**	**44**	**71**	**123**	**6**	**0**	**3**	**306**	**8.8**		**39**	**28.2**	**9:50**	....	....	....	....	....	....	....	....	....

• Missed remainder of 2005-06 due to wrist injury vs. Carolina, November 11, 2005. Signed as a free agent by **Atlanta**, July 13, 2009. Signed as a free agent by **Carolina**, July 2, 2011. Signed as a free agent by **Nottingham** (Britain), September 24, 2012. Traded to **Los Angeles** by **Carolina** with Carolina's 4th round choice (later traded to Edmonton – Edmonton selected Kyle Platzer) in 2013 Entry Draft for Kevin Westgarth, January 13, 2013.

STEWART, Chris

(STEW-ahrt, KRIHS) **ST.L.**

Right wing. Shoots right. 6'2", 231 lbs. Born, Toronto, Ont., October 30, 1987. Colorado's 1st choice, 18th overall, in 2006 Entry Draft.

2004-05	Kingston	OHL	64	18	12	30	45	....	....	....	....	....	....	....	....	....	....	....	....	....	....	....	....	....	....
2005-06	Kingston	OHL	62	37	50	87	118	....	....	....	....	....	....	....	....	....	6	2	0	2	13	....	....	....	....
2006-07	Kingston	OHL	61	36	46	82	108	....	....	....	....	....	....	....	....	....	5	4	2	6	6	....	....	....	....
	Albany River Rats	AHL	5	1	2	3	2	....	....	....	....	....	....	....	....	....	1	0	0	0	0	....	....	....	....
2007-08	Lake Erie	AHL	77	25	19	44	93	....	....	....	....	....	....	....	....	....	....	....	....	....	....	....	....	....	....
2008-09	**Colorado**	**NHL**	**53**	**11**	**8**	**19**	**54**	**1**	**1**	**1**	**98**	**11.2**	**–18**	**21**	**33.3**	**12:20**	....	....	....	....	....	....	....	....	....
	Lake Erie	AHL	19	5	6	11	23	....	....	....	....	....	....	....	....	....	....	....	....	....	....	....	....	....	....
2009-10	**Colorado**	**NHL**	**77**	**28**	**36**	**64**	**73**	**3**	**0**	**5**	**221**	**12.7**	**4**	**8**	**37.5**	**16:42**	**6**	**3**	**0**	**3**	**4**	**0**	**0**	**1**	**18:00**
	Lake Erie	AHL	2	0	0	0	2	....	....	....	....	....	....	....	....	....	....	....	....	....	....	....	....	....	....
2010-11	**Colorado**	**NHL**	**36**	**13**	**17**	**30**	**38**	**5**	**0**	**3**	**95**	**13.7**	**–10**	**6**	**33.3**	**16:56**	....	....	....	....	....	....	....	....	....
	St. Louis	**NHL**	**26**	**15**	**8**	**23**	**15**	**7**	**0**	**2**	**67**	**22.4**	**4**	**26**	**42.3**	**18:16**	....	....	....	....	....	....	....	....	....
2011-12	**St. Louis**	**NHL**	**79**	**15**	**15**	**30**	**109**	**2**	**0**	**1**	**166**	**9.0**	**1**	**13**	**23.1**	**15:26**	**7**	**2**	**0**	**2**	**12**	**0**	**0**	**0**	**10:47**
2012-13	Crimmitschau	German-2	15	6	14	20	24	....	....	....	....	....	....	....	....	....	....	....	....	....	....	....	....	....	....
	Liberec	CzRep	5	0	1	1	2	....	....	....	....	....	....	....	....	....	....	....	....	....	....	....	....	....	....
	St. Louis	**NHL**	**48**	**18**	**18**	**36**	**40**	**6**	**0**	**3**	**97**	**18.6**	**0**	**27**	**29.6**	**15:49**	**6**	**0**	**1**	**1**	**0**	**0**	**0**	**0**	**16:32**
	NHL Totals		**319**	**100**	**102**	**202**	**329**	**24**	**1**	**15**	**744**	**13.4**		**101**	**33.7**	**15:41**	**19**	**5**	**1**	**6**	**16**	**0**	**0**	**1**	**14:53**

Traded to **St. Louis** by **Colorado** with Kevin Shattenkirk and Colorado's 2nd round choice (Ty Rattie) in 2011 Entry Draft for Erik Johnson, Jay McClement and St. Louis's 1st round choice (Duncan Siemens) in 2011 Entry Draft, February 19, 2011. Signed as a free agent by **Crimmitschau** (German-2), September 24, 2012. Signed as a free agent by **Liberec** (CzRep), October 23, 2012.

Season	Club	League	Regular Season GP	G	A	Pts	PIM	PP	SH	GW	S	%	+/-	TF	F%	Min	Playoffs GP	G	A	Pts	PIM	PP	SH	GW	Min

STOA, Ryan

(STOH-ah, RIGH-uhn) **WSH**

Center. Shoots left. 6'3", 200 lbs. Born, Bloomington, MN, April 13, 1987. Colorado's 1st choice, 34th overall, in 2005 Entry Draft.

Season	Club	League	GP	G	A	Pts	PIM	PP	SH	GW	S	%	+/-	TF	F%	Min	GP	G	A	Pts	PIM	PP	SH	GW	Min
2003-04	USNTDP	U-17	18	9	8	17	....	....	....	....	....	....	....	....	....	....	....	....	....	....	....	....	....	....	....
	USNTDP	NAHL	42	10	12	22	26	....	....	....	....	....	....	....	....	....	7	7	1	8	2	....	....	....	....
2004-05	USNTDP	U-18	23	4	11	15	16	....	....	....	....	....	....	....	....	....	....	....	....	....	....	....	....	....	....
	USNTDP	NAHL	15	10	13	23	20	....	....	....	....	....	....	....	....	....	....	....	....	....	....	....	....	....	....
2005-06	U. of Minnesota	WCHA	41	10	15	25	43	....	....	....	....	....	....	....	....	....	....	....	....	....	....	....	....	....	....
2006-07	U. of Minnesota	WCHA	41	12	12	24	44	....	....	....	....	....	....	....	....	....	....	....	....	....	....	....	....	....	....
2007-08	U. of Minnesota	WCHA	2	1	1	2	2	....	....	....	....	....	....	....	....	....	....	....	....	....	....	....	....	....	....
2008-09	U. of Minnesota	WCHA	36	24	22	46	76	....	....	....	....	....	....	....	....	....	....	....	....	....	....	....	....	....	....
2009-10	**Colorado**	**NHL**	**12**	**2**	**1**	**3**	**0**	**0**	**0**	**0**	**26**	**7.7**	**–3**	**0**	**0.0**	**11:04**	**1**	**0**	**0**	**0**	**2**	**0**	**0**	**0**	**8:45**
	Lake Erie	AHL	54	23	17	40	42	....	....	....	....	....	....	....	....	....	....	....	....	....	....	....	....	....	....
2010-11	**Colorado**	**NHL**	**25**	**2**	**2**	**4**	**20**	**0**	**0**	**1**	**45**	**4.4**	**–4**	**5**	**40.0**	**13:21**	....	....	....	....	....	....	....	....	....
	Lake Erie	AHL	48	16	17	33	55	....	....	....	....	....	....	....	....	....	7	1	0	1	4	....	....	....	....
2011-12	Lake Erie	AHL	75	16	20	36	65	....	....	....	....	....	....	....	....	....	....	....	....	....	....	....	....	....	....
2012-13	Hershey Bears	AHL	46	11	8	19	43	....	....	....	....	....	....	....	....	....	4	1	0	1	0	....	....	....	....
	NHL Totals		**37**	**4**	**3**	**7**	**20**	**0**	**0**	**1**	**71**	**5.6**		**5**	**40.0**	**12:36**	**1**	**0**	**0**	**0**	**2**	**0**	**0**	**0**	**8:45**

WCHA First All-Star Team (2009) • NCAA West First All-American Team (2009)

• Missed remainder of 2007-08 due to knee injury vs. University of Michigan (CCHA), October 13, 2007. Signed as a free agent by **Washington**, July 7, 2012.

STOLL, Jarret

(STOHL, JAIR-iht) **L.A.**

Center. Shoots right. 6'1", 212 lbs. Born, Melville, Sask., June 24, 1982. Edmonton's 3rd choice, 36th overall, in 2002 Entry Draft.

Season	Club	League	GP	G	A	Pts	PIM	PP	SH	GW	S	%	+/-	TF	F%	Min	GP	G	A	Pts	PIM	PP	SH	GW	Min
1997-98	Saskatoon Blazers	SMHL	44	45	44	*89	78	....	....	....	....	....	....	....	....	....	....	....	....	....	....	....	....	....	....
	Edmonton Ice	WHL	8	2	3	5	4	....	....	....	....	....	....	....	....	....	....	....	....	....	....	....	....	....	....
1998-99	Kootenay Ice	WHL	57	13	21	34	38	....	....	....	....	....	....	....	....	....	4	0	0	0	2	....	....	....	....
99-2000	Kootenay Ice	WHL	71	37	38	75	64	....	....	....	....	....	....	....	....	....	20	7	9	16	24	....	....	....	....
2000-01	Kootenay Ice	WHL	62	40	66	106	105	....	....	....	....	....	....	....	....	....	11	5	9	14	22	....	....	....	....
2001-02	Kootenay Ice	WHL	47	32	34	66	64	....	....	....	....	....	....	....	....	....	22	6	14	20	35	....	....	....	....
2002-03	**Edmonton**	**NHL**	**4**	**0**	**1**	**1**	**0**	**0**	**0**	**0**	**5**	**0.0**	**–3**	**30**	**63.3**	**7:44**	....	....	....	....	....	....	....	....	....
	Hamilton	AHL	76	21	33	54	86	....	....	....	....	....	....	....	....	....	23	5	8	13	25	....	....	....	....
2003-04	**Edmonton**	**NHL**	**68**	**10**	**11**	**21**	**42**	**1**	**1**	**2**	**107**	**9.3**	**8**	**1019**	**54.1**	**13:54**	....	....	....	....	....	....	....	....	....
2004-05	Edmonton	AHL	66	21	17	38	92	....	....	....	....	....	....	....	....	....	....	....	....	....	....	....	....	....	....
2005-06	**Edmonton**	**NHL**	**82**	**22**	**46**	**68**	**74**	**11**	**1**	**4**	**243**	**9.1**	**4**	**1348**	**56.8**	**18:23**	**24**	**4**	**6**	**10**	**24**	**2**	**0**	**1**	**17:06**
2006-07	**Edmonton**	**NHL**	**51**	**13**	**26**	**39**	**48**	**6**	**1**	**2**	**115**	**11.3**	**2**	**901**	**55.6**	**18:12**	....	....	....	....	....	....	....	....	....
2007-08	**Edmonton**	**NHL**	**81**	**14**	**22**	**36**	**74**	**8**	**3**	**1**	**187**	**7.5**	**–23**	**1229**	**55.1**	**17:56**	....	....	....	....	....	....	....	....	....
2008-09	**Los Angeles**	**NHL**	**74**	**18**	**23**	**41**	**68**	**10**	**0**	**1**	**155**	**11.6**	**–7**	**1047**	**57.2**	**17:05**	....	....	....	....	....	....	....	....	....
2009-10	**Los Angeles**	**NHL**	**73**	**16**	**31**	**47**	**40**	**4**	**0**	**4**	**164**	**9.8**	**13**	**1105**	**56.0**	**17:25**	**6**	**1**	**0**	**1**	**4**	**1**	**0**	**0**	**15:51**
2010-11	**Los Angeles**	**NHL**	**82**	**20**	**23**	**43**	**42**	**4**	**1**	**5**	**187**	**10.7**	**–6**	**1310**	**57.5**	**17:10**	**5**	**0**	**3**	**3**	**0**	**0**	**0**	**0**	**18:44**
2011-12 ♦	**Los Angeles**	**NHL**	**78**	**6**	**15**	**21**	**60**	**1**	**0**	**0**	**133**	**4.5**	**2**	**1204**	**55.0**	**16:41**	**20**	**2**	**3**	**5**	**18**	**1**	**0**	**2**	**17:06**
2012-13	**Los Angeles**	**NHL**	**48**	**7**	**11**	**18**	**28**	**1**	**1**	**3**	**73**	**9.6**	**1**	**746**	**56.0**	**16:31**	**12**	**0**	**1**	**1**	**4**	**0**	**0**	**0**	**16:01**
	NHL Totals		**641**	**126**	**209**	**335**	**476**	**46**	**8**	**22**	**1369**	**9.2**		**9939**	**56.0**	**17:00**	**67**	**7**	**13**	**20**	**50**	**4**	**0**	**3**	**16:55**

• Re-entered NHL Entry Draft. Originally Calgary's 3rd choice, 46th overall, in 2000 Entry Draft.

WHL East First All-Star Team (2001) • Canadian Major Junior First All-Star Team (2001) • WHL West First All-Star Team (2002)

Traded to **Los Angeles** by **Edmonton** with Matt Greene for Lubomir Visnovsky, June 29, 2008.

STONE, Mark

(STOHN, MAHRK) **OTT**

Right wing. Shoots right. 6'2", 211 lbs. Born, Winnipeg, Man., May 13, 1992. Ottawa's 3rd choice, 178th overall, in 2010 Entry Draft.

Season	Club	League	GP	G	A	Pts	PIM	PP	SH	GW	S	%	+/-	TF	F%	Min	GP	G	A	Pts	PIM	PP	SH	GW	Min
2007-08	Wpg. Thrashers	MMHL	40	22	31	53	28	....	....	....	....	....	....	....	....	....	9	7	7	14	2	....	....	....	....
2008-09	Brandon	WHL	56	17	22	39	27	....	....	....	....	....	....	....	....	....	12	1	3	4	4	....	....	....	....
2009-10	Brandon	WHL	39	11	17	28	25	....	....	....	....	....	....	....	....	....	15	1	3	4	4	....	....	....	....
2010-11	Brandon	WHL	71	37	69	106	28	....	....	....	....	....	....	....	....	....	6	1	9	10	4	....	....	....	....
2011-12	Brandon	WHL	66	41	*82	123	22	....	....	....	....	....	....	....	....	....	8	2	4	6	6	....	....	....	....
	Ottawa	**NHL**	....	....	....	....	....	....	....	....	....	....	....	....	....	....	**1**	**0**	**1**	**1**	**0**	**0**	**0**	**0**	**8:43**
2012-13	Binghamton	AHL	54	15	23	38	14	....	....	....	....	....	....	....	....	....	3	1	2	3	0	....	....	....	....
	Ottawa	**NHL**	**4**	**0**	**0**	**0**	**2**	**0**	**0**	**0**	**3**	**0.0**	**–1**	**1**	**100.0**	**10:00**	**1**	**0**	**0**	**0**	**0**	**0**	**0**	**0**	**11:23**
	NHL Totals		**4**	**0**	**0**	**0**	**2**	**0**	**0**	**0**	**3**	**0.0**		**1**	**100.0**	**10:00**	**2**	**0**	**1**	**1**	**0**	**0**	**0**	**0**	**10:03**

WHL East First All-Star Team (2011, 2012) • Canadian Major Junior Sportsman of the Year (2012)

STONE, Michael

(STOHN, MIGH-kuhl) **PHX**

Defense. Shoots right. 6'3", 210 lbs. Born, Winnipeg, Man., June 7, 1990. Phoenix's 4th choice, 69th overall, in 2008 Entry Draft.

Season	Club	League	GP	G	A	Pts	PIM	PP	SH	GW	S	%	+/-	TF	F%	Min	GP	G	A	Pts	PIM	PP	SH	GW	Min
2005-06	Wpg. Thrashers	MMHL	40	14	18	32	14	....	....	....	....	....	....	....	....	....	....	....	....	....	....	....	....	....	....
2006-07	Calgary Hitmen	WHL	55	2	18	20	32	....	....	....	....	....	....	....	....	....	17	0	3	3	14	....	....	....	....
2007-08	Calgary Hitmen	WHL	71	10	25	35	28	....	....	....	....	....	....	....	....	....	14	3	4	7	10	....	....	....	....
2008-09	Calgary Hitmen	WHL	69	19	42	61	87	....	....	....	....	....	....	....	....	....	18	2	11	13	16	....	....	....	....
2009-10	Calgary Hitmen	WHL	69	21	44	65	91	....	....	....	....	....	....	....	....	....	23	5	15	20	26	....	....	....	....
2010-11	San Antonio	AHL	70	2	11	13	27	....	....	....	....	....	....	....	....	....	....	....	....	....	....	....	....	....	....
2011-12	**Phoenix**	**NHL**	**13**	**1**	**2**	**3**	**2**	**0**	**0**	**0**	**13**	**7.7**	**7**	**0**	**0.0**	**13:53**	**2**	**0**	**0**	**0**	**0**	**0**	**0**	**0**	**11:19**
	Portland Pirates	AHL	51	9	13	22	24	....	....	....	....	....	....	....	....	....	....	....	....	....	....	....	....	....	....
2012-13	Portland Pirates	AHL	36	6	22	28	20	....	....	....	....	....	....	....	....	....	1	0	1	1	4	....	....	....	....
	Phoenix	**NHL**	**40**	**5**	**4**	**9**	**16**	**1**	**0**	**0**	**50**	**10.0**	**2**	**0**	**0.0**	**16:41**	....	....	....	....	....	....	....	....	....
	NHL Totals		**53**	**6**	**6**	**12**	**18**	**1**	**0**	**0**	**63**	**9.5**		**0**	**0.0**	**16:00**	**2**	**0**	**0**	**0**	**0**	**0**	**0**	**0**	**11:19**

WHL East Second All-Star Team (2009) • WHL East First All-Star Team (2010)

STONER, Clayton

(STOH-nuhr, KLAY-tuhn) **MIN**

Defense. Shoots left. 6'4", 213 lbs. Born, Port McNeill, B.C., February 19, 1985. Minnesota's 4th choice, 79th overall, in 2004 Entry Draft.

Season	Club	League	GP	G	A	Pts	PIM	PP	SH	GW	S	%	+/-	TF	F%	Min	GP	G	A	Pts	PIM	PP	SH	GW	Min
2000-01	Campbell River	VIJHL	47	4	16	20	57	....	....	....	....	....	....	....	....	....	....	....	....	....	....	....	....	....	....
2001-02	Campbell River	VIJHL	42	12	35	47	199	....	....	....	....	....	....	....	....	....	....	....	....	....	....	....	....	....	....
2002-03	Tri-City	WHL	58	4	12	16	85	....	....	....	....	....	....	....	....	....	....	....	....	....	....	....	....	....	....
2003-04	Tri-City	WHL	71	7	24	31	109	....	....	....	....	....	....	....	....	....	11	1	1	2	8	....	....	....	....
2004-05	Tri-City	WHL	60	12	34	46	81	....	....	....	....	....	....	....	....	....	4	0	3	3	2	....	....	....	....
2005-06	Houston Aeros	AHL	73	6	18	24	92	....	....	....	....	....	....	....	....	....	3	1	1	2	7	....	....	....	....
2006-07	Houston Aeros	AHL	65	1	6	7	104	....	....	....	....	....	....	....	....	....	....	....	....	....	....	....	....	....	....
2007-08	Houston Aeros	AHL	56	3	12	15	78	....	....	....	....	....	....	....	....	....	....	....	....	....	....	....	....	....	....
2008-09	Houston Aeros	AHL	63	2	22	24	81	....	....	....	....	....	....	....	....	....	20	1	4	5	27	....	....	....	....
2009-10	**Minnesota**	**NHL**	**8**	**0**	**2**	**2**	**12**	**0**	**0**	**0**	**5**	**0.0**	**1**	**0**	**0.0**	**13:19**	....	....	....	....	....	....	....	....	....
	Houston Aeros	AHL	26	3	7	10	52	....	....	....	....	....	....	....	....	....	....	....	....	....	....	....	....	....	....
2010-11	**Minnesota**	**NHL**	**57**	**2**	**7**	**9**	**96**	**0**	**0**	**1**	**40**	**5.0**	**5**	**0**	**0.0**	**16:52**	....	....	....	....	....	....	....	....	....
2011-12	**Minnesota**	**NHL**	**51**	**1**	**4**	**5**	**62**	**0**	**0**	**0**	**47**	**2.1**	**3**	**0**	**0.0**	**17:36**	....	....	....	....	....	....	....	....	....
2012-13	B. Bystrica	Slovakia	8	1	4	5	16	....	....	....	....	....	....	....	....	....	....	....	....	....	....	....	....	....	....
	Minnesota	**NHL**	**48**	**0**	**10**	**10**	**42**	**0**	**0**	**0**	**40**	**0.0**	**0**	**0**	**0.0**	**18:13**	**1**	**0**	**1**	**1**	**0**	**0**	**0**	**0**	**8:18**
	NHL Totals		**164**	**3**	**23**	**26**	**212**	**0**	**0**	**1**	**132**	**2.3**		**0**	**0.0**	**17:19**	**1**	**0**	**1**	**1**	**0**	**0**	**0**	**0**	**8:18**

WHL West Second All-Star Team (2005)

• Missed majority of 2009-10 due to groin injury. Signed as a free agent by **Banska Bystrica** (Slovakia), November 29, 2012.

STORTINI, Zack

(stohr-TEE-nee, ZAK) **ANA**

Right wing. Shoots right. 6'4", 215 lbs. Born, Elliot Lake, Ont., September 11, 1985. Edmonton's 5th choice, 94th overall, in 2003 Entry Draft.

Season	Club	League	GP	G	A	Pts	PIM	PP	SH	GW	S	%	+/-	TF	F%	Min	GP	G	A	Pts	PIM	PP	SH	GW	Min
2000-01	Newmarket	ON-Jr.A	34	3	10	13	68	....	....	....	....	....	....	....	....	....	....	....	....	....	....	....	....	....	....
2001-02	Sudbury Wolves	OHL	65	8	6	14	187	....	....	....	....	....	....	....	....	....	5	1	0	1	24	....	....	....	....
2002-03	Sudbury Wolves	OHL	62	13	16	29	222	....	....	....	....	....	....	....	....	....	....	....	....	....	....	....	....	....	....
2003-04	Sudbury Wolves	OHL	62	21	16	37	151	....	....	....	....	....	....	....	....	....	7	1	1	2	14	....	....	....	....
	Toronto	AHL	2	0	0	0	7	....	....	....	....	....	....	....	....	....	3	0	0	0	4	....	....	....	....
2004-05	Sudbury Wolves	OHL	58	13	27	40	186	....	....	....	....	....	....	....	....	....	12	2	5	7	27	....	....	....	....

			Regular Season														Playoffs								
Season	Club	League	GP	G	A	Pts	PIM	PP	SH	GW	S	%	+/-	TF	F%	Min	GP	G	A	Pts	PIM	PP	SH	GW	Min
2005-06	Iowa Stars	AHL	27	2	1	3	108	....	....	....	....	....	....	....	....	....	....	....	....	....	....	....	....	....	....
	Milwaukee	AHL	37	0	7	7	153	....	....	....	....	....	....	....	....	....	17	2	0	2	19	....	....	....	....
2006-07	**Edmonton**	**NHL**	**29**	**1**	**0**	**1**	**105**	**0**	**0**	**0**	**17**	**5.9**	**-7**	**3**	**100.0**	**7:09**	....	....	....	....	....	....	....	....	....
	Hamilton	AHL	47	9	6	15	195	....	....	....	....	....	....	....	....	....	22	3	0	3	*56	....	....	....	....
2007-08	**Edmonton**	**NHL**	**66**	**3**	**9**	**12**	**201**	**0**	**0**	**0**	**38**	**7.9**	**3**	**7**	**42.9**	**8:10**	....	....	....	....	....	....	....	....	....
	Springfield	AHL	4	3	2	5	21	....	....	....	....	....	....	....	....	....	....	....	....	....	....	....	....	....	....
2008-09	**Edmonton**	**NHL**	**52**	**6**	**5**	**11**	**181**	**0**	**0**	**0**	**23**	**26.1**	**-3**	**11**	**63.6**	**7:17**	....	....	....	....	....	....	....	....	....
2009-10	**Edmonton**	**NHL**	**77**	**4**	**9**	**13**	**155**	**1**	**0**	**1**	**46**	**8.7**	**3**	**183**	**47.5**	**9:17**	....	....	....	....	....	....	....	....	....
2010-11	**Edmonton**	**NHL**	**32**	**0**	**4**	**4**	**76**	**0**	**0**	**0**	**16**	**0.0**	**-2**	**33**	**42.4**	**7:06**	....	....	....	....	....	....	....	....	....
	Oklahoma City	AHL	29	1	2	3	53	....	....	....	....	....	....	....	....	....	5	1	0	1	6	....	....	....	....
2011-12	**Nashville**	**NHL**	**1**	**0**	**0**	**0**	**7**	**0**	**0**	**0**	**1**	**0.0**	**0**	**0**	**0.0**	**4:53**	....	....	....	....	....	....	....	....	....
	Milwaukee	AHL	74	9	6	15	146	....	....	....	....	....	....	....	....	....	3	0	1	1	2	....	....	....	....
2012-13	Hamilton	AHL	73	2	4	6	241	....	....	....	....	....	....	....	....	....	....	....	....	....	....	....	....	....	....
	NHL Totals		**257**	**14**	**27**	**41**	**725**	**1**	**0**	**1**	**141**	**9.9**		**237**	**48.1**	**8:04**	....	....	....	....	....	....	....	....	....

Signed as a free agent by **Nashville**, July 5, 2011. Signed as a free agent by **Hamilton** (AHL), September 21, 2012. Signed as a free agent by **Anaheim**, July 8, 2013.

STRACHAN, Tyson

(STRAWN, TIGH-suhn) **WSH**

Defense. Shoots right. 6'3", 215 lbs. Born, Melfort, Sask., October 30, 1984. Carolina's 6th choice, 137th overall, in 2003 Entry Draft.

Season	Club	League	GP	G	A	Pts	PIM	PP	SH	GW	S	%	+/-	TF	F%	Min	GP	G	A	Pts	PIM	PP	SH	GW	Min
2001-02	Tisdale Trojans	SMHL	42	5	18	23	70	....	....	....	....	....	....	....	....	....	....	....	....	....	....	....	....	....	....
	Melville	SJHL	2	0	0	0	0	....	....	....	....	....	....	....	....	....	....	....	....	....	....	....	....	....	....
2002-03	Vernon Vipers	BCHL	56	6	22	28	99	....	....	....	....	....	....	....	....	....	....	....	....	....	....	....	....	....	....
2003-04	Ohio State	CCHA	30	2	5	7	8	....	....	....	....	....	....	....	....	....	....	....	....	....	....	....	....	....	....
2004-05	Ohio State	CCHA	31	1	4	5	32	....	....	....	....	....	....	....	....	....	....	....	....	....	....	....	....	....	....
2005-06	Ohio State	CCHA	23	3	2	5	37	....	....	....	....	....	....	....	....	....	....	....	....	....	....	....	....	....	....
2006-07	Ohio State	CCHA	35	7	11	18	55	....	....	....	....	....	....	....	....	....	....	....	....	....	....	....	....	....	....
	Albany River Rats	AHL	1	0	0	0	0	....	....	....	....	....	....	....	....	....	....	....	....	....	....	....	....	....	....
2007-08	Peoria Rivermen	AHL	34	1	2	3	61	....	....	....	....	....	....	....	....	....	....	....	....	....	....	....	....	....	....
	Las Vegas	ECHL	25	2	7	9	68	....	....	....	....	....	....	....	....	....	16	0	4	4	12	....	....	....	....
2008-09	**St. Louis**	**NHL**	**30**	**0**	**3**	**3**	**39**	**0**	**0**	**0**	**21**	**0.0**	**8**	**0**	**0.0**	**13:26**	....	....	....	....	....	....	....	....	....
	Peoria Rivermen	AHL	29	2	3	5	67	....	....	....	....	....	....	....	....	....	3	0	0	0	11	....	....	....	....
2009-10	**St. Louis**	**NHL**	**8**	**0**	**2**	**2**	**4**	**0**	**0**	**0**	**7**	**0.0**	**3**	**0**	**0.0**	**14:02**	....	....	....	....	....	....	....	....	....
	Peoria Rivermen	AHL	65	5	21	26	75	....	....	....	....	....	....	....	....	....	....	....	....	....	....	....	....	....	....
2010-11	**St. Louis**	**NHL**	**29**	**0**	**1**	**1**	**39**	**0**	**0**	**0**	**28**	**0.0**	**-10**	**0**	**0.0**	**12:08**	....	....	....	....	....	....	....	....	....
	Peoria Rivermen	AHL	13	0	8	8	4	....	....	....	....	....	....	....	....	....	1	0	0	0	2	....	....	....	....
2011-12	**Florida**	**NHL**	**15**	**1**	**2**	**3**	**5**	**0**	**0**	**0**	**14**	**7.1**	**1**	**0**	**0.0**	**14:21**	**2**	**0**	**1**	**1**	**0**	**0**	**0**	**0**	**13:30**
	San Antonio	AHL	50	3	14	17	41	....	....	....	....	....	....	....	....	....	7	1	3	4	0	....	....	....	....
2012-13	San Antonio	AHL	24	1	8	9	22	....	....	....	....	....	....	....	....	....	....	....	....	....	....	....	....	....	....
	Florida	**NHL**	**38**	**0**	**4**	**4**	**40**	**0**	**0**	**0**	**42**	**0.0**	**-13**	**0**	**0.0**	**18:58**	....	....	....	....	....	....	....	....	....
	NHL Totals		**120**	**1**	**12**	**13**	**127**	**0**	**0**	**0**	**112**	**0.9**		**0**	**0.0**	**15:02**	**2**	**0**	**1**	**1**	**0**	**0**	**0**	**0**	**13:30**

Signed as a free agent by **St. Louis**, October 9, 2008. Signed as a free agent by **Florida**, July 12, 2011. Signed as a free agent by **Washington**, July 8, 2013.

STRAIT, Brian

(STRAYT, BRIGH-uhn) **NYI**

Defense. Shoots left. 6'1", 200 lbs. Born, Boston, MA, January 4, 1988. Pittsburgh's 3rd choice, 65th overall, in 2006 Entry Draft.

Season	Club	League	GP	G	A	Pts	PIM	PP	SH	GW	S	%	+/-	TF	F%	Min	GP	G	A	Pts	PIM	PP	SH	GW	Min
2003-04	NMH School	High-MA	30	5	15	20	....	....	....	....	....	....	....	....	....	....	....	....	....	....	....	....	....	....	....
2004-05	USNTDP	U-17	18	1	5	6	8	....	....	....	....	....	....	....	....	....	....	....	....	....	....	....	....	....	....
	USNTDP	NAHL	42	4	8	12	42	....	....	....	....	....	....	....	....	....	10	0	2	2	2	....	....	....	....
2005-06	USNTDP	U-18	40	2	7	9	31	....	....	....	....	....	....	....	....	....	....	....	....	....	....	....	....	....	....
	USNTDP	NAHL	15	0	5	5	41	....	....	....	....	....	....	....	....	....	....	....	....	....	....	....	....	....	....
2006-07	Boston University	H-East	36	3	3	6	47	....	....	....	....	....	....	....	....	....	....	....	....	....	....	....	....	....	....
2007-08	Boston University	H-East	37	0	10	10	20	....	....	....	....	....	....	....	....	....	....	....	....	....	....	....	....	....	....
2008-09	Boston University	H-East	38	2	5	7	67	....	....	....	....	....	....	....	....	....	....	....	....	....	....	....	....	....	....
2009-10	Wilkes-Barre	AHL	78	2	12	14	73	....	....	....	....	....	....	....	....	....	4	0	1	1	0	....	....	....	....
2010-11	**Pittsburgh**	**NHL**	**3**	**0**	**0**	**0**	**0**	**0**	**0**	**0**	**0**	**0.0**	**-1**	**0**	**0.0**	**13:32**	....	....	....	....	....	....	....	....	....
	Wilkes-Barre	AHL	75	2	8	10	49	....	....	....	....	....	....	....	....	....	12	1	3	4	10	....	....	....	....
2011-12	**Pittsburgh**	**NHL**	**9**	**0**	**1**	**1**	**4**	**0**	**0**	**0**	**4**	**0.0**	**-2**	**0**	**0.0**	**12:53**	**3**	**0**	**0**	**0**	**0**	**0**	**0**	**0**	**9:35**
	Wilkes-Barre	AHL	41	4	12	16	26	....	....	....	....	....	....	....	....	....	2	0	1	1	0	....	....	....	....
2012-13	Wilkes-Barre	AHL	26	0	0	0	34	....	....	....	....	....	....	....	....	....	....	....	....	....	....	....	....	....	....
	NY Islanders	**NHL**	**19**	**0**	**4**	**4**	**10**	**0**	**0**	**0**	**13**	**0.0**	**4**	**0**	**0.0**	**17:09**	**6**	**1**	**0**	**1**	**12**	**0**	**0**	**0**	**20:35**
	NHL Totals		**31**	**0**	**5**	**5**	**14**	**0**	**0**	**0**	**17**	**0.0**		**0**	**0.0**	**15:34**	**9**	**1**	**0**	**1**	**12**	**0**	**0**	**0**	**16:55**

Claimed on waivers by **NY Islanders** from **Pittsburgh**, January 18, 2013. • Missed majority of 2012-13 due to ankle injury vs. Philadelphia, February 18, 2013.

STRALMAN, Anton

(STROHL-muhn, AN-tawn) **NYR**

Defense. Shoots right. 5'11", 190 lbs. Born, Tibro, Sweden, August 1, 1986. Toronto's 5th choice, 216th overall, in 2005 Entry Draft.

Season	Club	League	GP	G	A	Pts	PIM	PP	SH	GW	S	%	+/-	TF	F%	Min	GP	G	A	Pts	PIM	PP	SH	GW	Min
2002-03	Skovde IK Jr.	Swe-Jr.	46	20	9	29	38	....	....	....	....	....	....	....	....	....	....	....	....	....	....	....	....	....	....
2003-04	Skovde IK	Sweden-3	27	4	8	12	18	....	....	....	....	....	....	....	....	....	....	....	....	....	....	....	....	....	....
2004-05	Skovde IK	Sweden-2	50	10	11	21	40	....	....	....	....	....	....	....	....	....	....	....	....	....	....	....	....	....	....
2005-06	Timra IK	Sweden	45	1	4	5	28	....	....	....	....	....	....	....	....	....	....	....	....	....	....	....	....	....	....
	Timra IK Jr.	Swe-Jr.	....	....	....	....	....	....	....	....	....	....	....	....	....	....	3	0	0	0	4	....	....	....	....
2006-07	Timra IK	Sweden	53	10	11	21	34	....	....	....	....	....	....	....	....	....	7	1	3	4	10	....	....	....	....
2007-08	**Toronto**	**NHL**	**50**	**3**	**6**	**9**	**18**	**0**	**0**	**0**	**40**	**7.5**	**-10**	**0**	**0.0**	**12:49**	....	....	....	....	....	....	....	....	....
	Toronto Marlies	AHL	21	0	11	11	22	....	....	....	....	....	....	....	....	....	....	....	....	....	....	....	....	....	....
2008-09	**Toronto**	**NHL**	**38**	**1**	**12**	**13**	**20**	**0**	**0**	**1**	**43**	**2.3**	**-2**	**1**	**100.0**	**15:34**	....	....	....	....	....	....	....	....	....
	Toronto Marlies	AHL	36	7	9	16	24	....	....	....	....	....	....	....	....	....	6	1	2	3	0	....	....	....	....
2009-10	**Columbus**	**NHL**	**73**	**6**	**28**	**34**	**37**	**4**	**0**	**0**	**121**	**5.0**	**-17**	**0**	**0.0**	**20:29**	....	....	....	....	....	....	....	....	....
2010-11	**Columbus**	**NHL**	**51**	**1**	**17**	**18**	**22**	**1**	**0**	**1**	**80**	**1.3**	**-11**	**0**	**0.0**	**19:44**	....	....	....	....	....	....	....	....	....
2011-12	**NY Rangers**	**NHL**	**53**	**2**	**16**	**18**	**20**	**0**	**0**	**0**	**55**	**3.6**	**9**	**0**	**0.0**	**17:06**	**20**	**3**	**3**	**6**	**4**	**2**	**0**	**0**	**16:56**
2012-13	**NY Rangers**	**NHL**	**48**	**4**	**3**	**7**	**16**	**0**	**0**	**0**	**66**	**6.1**	**14**	**1**	**0.0**	**18:03**	**10**	**0**	**0**	**0**	**0**	**0**	**0**	**0**	**21:06**
	NHL Totals		**313**	**17**	**82**	**99**	**133**	**5**	**0**	**2**	**405**	**4.2**		**2**	**50.0**	**17:36**	**30**	**3**	**3**	**6**	**4**	**2**	**0**	**0**	**18:19**

Traded to **Calgary** by **Toronto** with Colin Stuart and Toronto's 7th round choice (Matt DeBlouw) in 2012 Entry Draft for Wayne Primeau and Calgary's 2nd round choice (later traded to Chicago – Chicago selected Brandon Saad) in 2011 Entry Draft, July 27, 2009. Traded to **Columbus** by **Calgary** for Columbus' 3rd round choice (Max Reinhart) in 2010 Entry Draft, September 29, 2009. Signed as a free agent by **NY Rangers**, November 5, 2011.

STREET, Ben

(STREET, BEHN) **CGY**

Center. Shoots left. 5'11", 185 lbs. Born, Coquitlam, B.C., February 13, 1987.

Season	Club	League	GP	G	A	Pts	PIM	PP	SH	GW	S	%	+/-	TF	F%	Min	GP	G	A	Pts	PIM	PP	SH	GW	Min
2003-04	Salmon Arm	BCHL	54	13	21	34	14	....	....	....	....	....	....	....	....	....	13	1	9	10	0	....	....	....	....
2004-05	Salmon Arm	BCHL	56	29	39	68	21	....	....	....	....	....	....	....	....	....	11	7	8	15	0	....	....	....	....
2005-06	U. of Minnesota	WCHA	43	10	5	15	0	....	....	....	....	....	....	....	....	....	....	....	....	....	....	....	....	....	....
2006-07	U. of Wisconsin	WCHA	41	10	7	17	16	....	....	....	....	....	....	....	....	....	....	....	....	....	....	....	....	....	....
2007-08	U. of Wisconsin	WCHA	40	13	17	30	36	....	....	....	....	....	....	....	....	....	....	....	....	....	....	....	....	....	....
2008-09	U. of Wisconsin	WCHA	4	1	0	1	8	....	....	....	....	....	....	....	....	....	....	....	....	....	....	....	....	....	....
2009-10	U. of Wisconsin	WCHA	43	14	16	30	30	....	....	....	....	....	....	....	....	....	....	....	....	....	....	....	....	....	....
2010-11	Wilkes-Barre	AHL	36	12	11	23	8	....	....	....	....	....	....	....	....	....	8	0	1	1	0	....	....	....	....
	Wheeling Nailers	ECHL	38	24	27	51	10	....	....	....	....	....	....	....	....	....	....	....	....	....	....	....	....	....	....
2011-12	Wilkes-Barre	AHL	71	27	30	57	24	....	....	....	....	....	....	....	....	....	12	1	2	3	2	....	....	....	....
2012-13	Abbotsford Heat	AHL	69	15	22	37	22	....	....	....	....	....	....	....	....	....	....	....	....	....	....	....	....	....	....
	Calgary	**NHL**	**6**	**0**	**1**	**1**	**0**	**0**	**0**	**0**	**13**	**0.0**	**-1**	**51**	**47.1**	**13:37**	....	....	....	....	....	....	....	....	....
	NHL Totals		**6**	**0**	**1**	**1**	**0**	**0**	**0**	**0**	**13**	**0.0**		**51**	**47.1**	**13:37**	....	....	....	....	....	....	....	....	....

Signed as a free agent by **Calgary**, July 2, 2012.

Season	Club	League	Regular Season GP	G	A	Pts	PIM	PP	SH	GW	S	%	+/-	TF	F%	Min	Playoffs GP	G	A	Pts	PIM	PP	SH	GW	Min

STREIT, Mark

(STRIGHT, MAHRK) **PHI**

Defense. Shoots left. 5'11", 191 lbs. Born, Bern, Switz., December 11, 1977. Montreal's 8th choice, 262nd overall, in 2004 Entry Draft.

1995-96	Fribourg	Swiss	34	2	2	4	6	....	....	....	....	....	....	....	....	....	4	0	0	0	2	....	....	....	....
1996-97	HC Davos	Swiss	46	2	9	11	18	....	....	....	....	....	....	....	....	....	6	0	0	0	0	....	....	....	....
1997-98	HC Ambri-Piotta	Swiss	2	0	0	0	0	....	....	....	....	....	....	....	....	....	....	....	....	....	....	....	....	....	....
	HC Davos	Swiss	38	4	10	14	14	....	....	....	....	....	....	....	....	....	18	1	5	6	20	....	....	....	....
1998-99	HC Davos	Swiss	44	7	18	25	42	....	....	....	....	....	....	....	....	....	6	3	3	6	8	....	....	....	....
99-2000	Springfield	AHL	43	3	12	15	18	....	....	....	....	....	....	....	....	....	5	0	0	0	2	....	....	....	....
	Utah Grizzlies	IHL	1	0	1	1	2	....	....	....	....	....	....	....	....	....	....	....	....	....	....	....	....	....	....
	Tallahassee	ECHL	14	0	5	5	16	....	....	....	....	....	....	....	....	....	....	....	....	....	....	....	....	....	....
2000-01	ZSC Lions Zurich	Swiss	44	5	11	16	48	....	....	....	....	....	....	....	....	....	16	2	5	7	37	....	....	....	....
2001-02	ZSC Lions Zurich	Swiss	28	6	17	23	36	....	....	....	....	....	....	....	....	....	16	0	6	6	14	....	....	....	....
	Switzerland	Olympics	4	1	1	2	0	....	....	....	....	....	....	....	....	....	....	....	....	....	....	....	....	....	....
2002-03	ZSC Lions Zurich	Swiss	37	4	19	23	62	....	....	....	....	....	....	....	....	....	12	1	7	8	2	....	....	....	....
2003-04	ZSC Lions Zurich	Swiss	48	12	24	36	78	....	....	....	....	....	....	....	....	....	13	5	2	7	14	....	....	....	....
2004-05	ZSC Lions Zurich	Swiss	44	14	29	43	46	....	....	....	....	....	....	....	....	....	15	4	11	15	20	....	....	....	....
2005-06	**Montreal**	**NHL**	**48**	**2**	**9**	**11**	**28**	**2**	**0**	**0**	**52**	**3.8**	**–6**	**1**	**0.0**	**14:36**	**1**	**0**	**0**	**0**	**0**	**0**	**0**	**0**	**3:29**
	Switzerland	Olympics	6	2	1	3	6	....	....	....	....	....	....	....	....	....	....	....	....	....	....	....	....	....	....
2006-07	**Montreal**	**NHL**	**76**	**10**	**26**	**36**	**14**	**2**	**1**	**1**	**102**	**9.8**	**–5**	**12**	**33.3**	**14:01**	....	....	....	....	....	....	....	....	....
2007-08	**Montreal**	**NHL**	**81**	**13**	**49**	**62**	**28**	**7**	**0**	**3**	**165**	**7.9**	**–6**	**1**	**0.0**	**17:31**	**11**	**1**	**3**	**4**	**8**	**0**	**0**	**0**	**14:48**
2008-09	**NY Islanders**	**NHL**	**74**	**16**	**40**	**56**	**62**	**10**	**1**	**1**	**150**	**10.7**	**5**	**0**	**0.0**	**25:13**	....	....	....	....	....	....	....	....	....
2009-10	**NY Islanders**	**NHL**	**82**	**11**	**38**	**49**	**48**	**9**	**0**	**2**	**187**	**5.9**	**0**	**1**	**0.0**	**25:42**	....	....	....	....	....	....	....	....	....
	Switzerland	Olympics	5	0	3	3	0	....	....	....	....	....	....	....	....	....	....	....	....	....	....	....	....	....	....
2010-11			DID NOT PLAY – INJURED					....	....	....	....	....	....	....	....	....	....	....	....	....	....	....	....	....	....
2011-12	**NY Islanders**	**NHL**	**82**	**7**	**40**	**47**	**46**	**3**	**0**	**1**	**149**	**4.7**	**–27**	**1**	**0.0**	**23:23**	....	....	....	....	....	....	....	....	....
2012-13	SC Bern	Swiss	32	7	19	26	30	....	....	....	....	....	....	....	....	....	....	....	....	....	....	....	....	....	....
	NY Islanders	**NHL**	**48**	**6**	**21**	**27**	**22**	**3**	**0**	**1**	**83**	**7.2**	**–14**	**0**	**0.0**	**23:21**	**6**	**2**	**3**	**5**	**4**	**1**	**0**	**0**	**20:18**
	NHL Totals		**491**	**65**	**223**	**288**	**248**	**36**	**2**	**9**	**888**	**7.3**		**16**	**25.0**	**20:46**	**18**	**3**	**6**	**9**	**12**	**1**	**0**	**0**	**16:00**

Played in NHL All-Star Game (2009)

Signed as a free agent by **NY Islanders**, July 1, 2008. • Missed 2010-11 due to shoulder injury in training camp, September 25, 2010. Signed as a free agent by **Bern** (Swiss), September 15, 2012. Traded to **Philadelphia** by **NY Islanders** for Shane Harper and Philadelphia's 4th round choice in 2014 Entry Draft, June 12, 2013.

STUART, Brad

(STEW-ahrt, BRAD) **S.J.**

Defense. Shoots left. 6'2", 215 lbs. Born, Rocky Mountain House, Alta., November 6, 1979. San Jose's 1st choice, 3rd overall, in 1998 Entry Draft.

1995-96	Red Deer	AMHL	35	12	25	37	83	....	....	....	....	....	....	....	....	....	....	....	....	....	....	....	....	....	....
	Regina Pats	WHL	3	0	0	0	0	....	....	....	....	....	....	....	....	....	....	....	....	....	....	....	....	....	....
1996-97	Regina Pats	WHL	57	7	36	43	49	....	....	....	....	....	....	....	....	....	5	0	4	4	14	....	....	....	....
1997-98	Regina Pats	WHL	72	20	45	65	82	....	....	....	....	....	....	....	....	....	9	3	4	7	10	....	....	....	....
1998-99	Regina Pats	WHL	29	10	19	29	43	....	....	....	....	....	....	....	....	....	....	....	....	....	....	....	....	....	....
	Calgary Hitmen	WHL	30	11	22	33	26	....	....	....	....	....	....	....	....	....	21	8	15	23	59	....	....	....	....
99-2000	**San Jose**	**NHL**	**82**	**10**	**26**	**36**	**32**	**5**	**1**	**3**	**133**	**7.5**	**3**	**0**	**0.0**	**20:24**	**12**	**1**	**0**	**1**	**6**	**1**	**0**	**0**	**16:30**
2000-01	**San Jose**	**NHL**	**77**	**5**	**18**	**23**	**56**	**1**	**0**	**2**	**119**	**4.2**	**10**	**0**	**0.0**	**20:06**	**5**	**1**	**0**	**1**	**0**	**0**	**0**	**0**	**20:19**
2001-02	**San Jose**	**NHL**	**82**	**6**	**23**	**29**	**39**	**2**	**0**	**2**	**96**	**6.3**	**13**	**0**	**0.0**	**21:41**	**12**	**0**	**3**	**3**	**8**	**0**	**0**	**0**	**19:42**
2002-03	**San Jose**	**NHL**	**36**	**4**	**10**	**14**	**46**	**2**	**0**	**1**	**63**	**6.3**	**–6**	**0**	**0.0**	**20:53**	....	....	....	....	....	....	....	....	....
2003-04	**San Jose**	**NHL**	**77**	**9**	**30**	**39**	**34**	**5**	**0**	**0**	**129**	**7.0**	**9**	**0**	**0.0**	**22:09**	**17**	**1**	**5**	**6**	**13**	**0**	**0**	**0**	**23:23**
2004-05			DID NOT PLAY																						
2005-06	**San Jose**	**NHL**	**23**	**2**	**10**	**12**	**14**	**1**	**0**	**0**	**41**	**4.9**	**–2**	**0**	**0.0**	**23:15**	....	....	....	....	....	....	....	....	....
	Boston	**NHL**	**55**	**10**	**21**	**31**	**38**	**6**	**0**	**2**	**122**	**8.2**	**–6**	**0**	**0.0**	**25:40**	....	....	....	....	....	....	....	....	....
2006-07	**Boston**	**NHL**	**48**	**7**	**10**	**17**	**26**	**1**	**0**	**2**	**74**	**9.5**	**–22**	**0**	**0.0**	**22:55**	....	....	....	....	....	....	....	....	....
	Calgary	**NHL**	**27**	**0**	**5**	**5**	**18**	**0**	**0**	**0**	**35**	**0.0**	**12**	**0**	**0.0**	**22:48**	**6**	**0**	**1**	**1**	**6**	**0**	**0**	**0**	**25:16**
2007-08	**Los Angeles**	**NHL**	**63**	**5**	**16**	**21**	**67**	**2**	**0**	**1**	**111**	**4.5**	**–16**	**4**	**0.0**	**21:13**	....	....	....	....	....	....	....	....	....
	♦ Detroit	**NHL**	**9**	**1**	**1**	**2**	**2**	**0**	**0**	**0**	**21**	**4.8**	**6**	**0**	**0.0**	**20:46**	**21**	**1**	**6**	**7**	**14**	**0**	**0**	**1**	**21:40**
2008-09	**Detroit**	**NHL**	**67**	**2**	**13**	**15**	**26**	**1**	**0**	**0**	**105**	**1.9**	**–3**	**0**	**0.0**	**20:13**	**23**	**3**	**6**	**9**	**12**	**1**	**0**	**0**	**24:09**
2009-10	**Detroit**	**NHL**	**82**	**4**	**16**	**20**	**22**	**1**	**0**	**2**	**153**	**2.6**	**–12**	**2**	**50.0**	**23:10**	**12**	**2**	**4**	**6**	**8**	**0**	**0**	**0**	**22:04**
2010-11	**Detroit**	**NHL**	**67**	**3**	**17**	**20**	**40**	**1**	**0**	**1**	**81**	**3.7**	**4**	**0**	**0.0**	**21:32**	**11**	**0**	**2**	**2**	**8**	**0**	**0**	**0**	**21:33**
2011-12	**Detroit**	**NHL**	**81**	**6**	**15**	**21**	**29**	**1**	**1**	**2**	**96**	**6.3**	**16**	**0**	**0.0**	**21:03**	**5**	**0**	**1**	**1**	**0**	**0**	**0**	**0**	**19:22**
2012-13	**San Jose**	**NHL**	**48**	**0**	**6**	**6**	**25**	**0**	**0**	**0**	**39**	**0.0**	**4**	**0**	**0.0**	**20:27**	**11**	**1**	**2**	**3**	**2**	**0**	**0**	**0**	**19:09**
	NHL Totals		**924**	**74**	**237**	**311**	**514**	**29**	**2**	**18**	**1418**	**5.2**		**6**	**16.7**	**21:40**	**135**	**10**	**30**	**40**	**77**	**2**	**0**	**1**	**21:31**

WHL East Second All-Star Team (1998) • WHL East First All-Star Team (1999) • Canadian Major Junior First All-Star Team (1999) • Canadian Major Junior Defenseman of the Year (1999) • NHL All-Rookie Team (2000)

• Missed majority of 2002-03 due to ankle (January 4, 2003 vs. Los Angeles) and head (February 21, 2003 vs. Columbus) injuries. Traded to **Boston** by **San Jose** with Marco Sturm and Wayne Primeau for Joe Thornton, November 30, 2005. Traded to **Calgary** by **Boston** with Wayne Primeau and Washington's 4th round choice (previously acquired, Calgary selected T.J. Brodie) in 2008 Entry Draft for Andrew Ference and Chuck Kobasew, February 10, 2007. Signed as a free agent by **Los Angeles**, July 3, 2007. Traded to **Detroit** by **Los Angeles** for Detroit's 2nd round choice (later traded to Colorado – Colorado selected Peter Delmas) in 2008 Entry Draft and Detroit's 4th round choice (later traded to Atlanta – Atlanta selected Ben Chiarot) in 2009 Entry Draft, February 26, 2008. Traded to **San Jose** by **Detroit** for Andrew Murray and San Jose's 7th round choice in 2014 Entry Draft, June 10, 2012.

STUART, Colin

(STEW-ahrt, KAW-lihn) **VAN**

Left wing. Shoots left. 6'2", 205 lbs. Born, Rochester, MN, July 8, 1982. Atlanta's 5th choice, 135th overall, in 2001 Entry Draft.

1998-99	Roch. Lourdes	High-MN	23	22	32	54	....	....	....	....	....	....	....	....	....	....	....	....	....	....	....	....	....	....	....
99-2000	Lincoln Stars	USHL	53	18	19	37	38	....	....	....	....	....	....	....	....	....	9	1	3	4	2	....	....	....	....
2000-01	Colorado College	WCHA	41	2	7	9	26	....	....	....	....	....	....	....	....	....	....	....	....	....	....	....	....	....	....
2001-02	Colorado College	WCHA	43	13	9	22	34	....	....	....	....	....	....	....	....	....	....	....	....	....	....	....	....	....	....
2002-03	Colorado College	WCHA	42	13	11	24	56	....	....	....	....	....	....	....	....	....	....	....	....	....	....	....	....	....	....
2003-04	Colorado College	WCHA	30	10	12	22	38	....	....	....	....	....	....	....	....	....	....	....	....	....	....	....	....	....	....
2004-05	Chicago Wolves	AHL	39	3	2	5	12	....	....	....	....	....	....	....	....	....	....	....	....	....	....	....	....	....	....
	Gwinnett	ECHL	5	1	3	4	4	....	....	....	....	....	....	....	....	....	....	....	....	....	....	....	....	....	....
2005-06	Chicago Wolves	AHL	78	13	14	27	65	....	....	....	....	....	....	....	....	....	....	....	....	....	....	....	....	....	....
2006-07	Chicago Wolves	AHL	67	18	11	29	75	....	....	....	....	....	....	....	....	....	15	2	5	7	10	....	....	....	....
2007-08	**Atlanta**	**NHL**	**18**	**3**	**2**	**5**	**6**	**0**	**1**	**1**	**19**	**15.8**	**2**	**7**	**57.1**	**12:20**	....	....	....	....	....	....	....	....	....
	Chicago Wolves	AHL	58	8	8	16	45	....	....	....	....	....	....	....	....	....	24	3	3	6	18	....	....	....	....
2008-09	**Atlanta**	**NHL**	**33**	**5**	**3**	**8**	**18**	**0**	**3**	**0**	**54**	**9.3**	**3**	**12**	**41.7**	**12:29**	....	....	....	....	....	....	....	....	....
	Chicago Wolves	AHL	42	9	6	15	38	....	....	....	....	....	....	....	....	....	....	....	....	....	....	....	....	....	....
2009-10	Abbotsford Heat	AHL	67	17	19	36	36	....	....	....	....	....	....	....	....	....	3	0	0	0	6	....	....	....	....
2010-11	**Buffalo**	**NHL**	**3**	**0**	**0**	**0**	**2**	**0**	**0**	**0**	**5**	**0.0**	**1**	**2**	**50.0**	**13:09**	....	....	....	....	....	....	....	....	....
	Portland Pirates	AHL	72	16	28	44	53	....	....	....	....	....	....	....	....	....	12	3	4	7	8	....	....	....	....
2011-12	**Buffalo**	**NHL**	**2**	**0**	**0**	**0**	**0**	**0**	**0**	**0**	**0**	**0.0**	**–3**	**0**	**0.0**	**6:12**	....	....	....	....	....	....	....	....	....
	Rochester	AHL	51	13	19	32	32	....	....	....	....	....	....	....	....	....	3	0	0	0	4	....	....	....	....
2012-13	Iserlohn Roosters	Germany	45	9	12	21	35	....	....	....	....	....	....	....	....	....	....	....	....	....	....	....	....	....	....
	NHL Totals		**56**	**8**	**5**	**13**	**26**	**0**	**4**	**1**	**78**	**10.3**		**21**	**47.6**	**12:15**	....	....	....	....	....	....	....	....	....

Traded to **Toronto** by **Atlanta** with Garnet Exelby for Pavel Kubina and Tim Stapleton, July 1, 2009. Traded to **Calgary** by **Toronto** with Anton Stralman and Toronto's 7th round choice (Matt DeBlouw) in 2012 Entry Draft for Wayne Primeau and Calgary's 2nd round choice (later traded to Chicago – Chicago selected Brandon Saad) in 2011 Entry Draft, July 27, 2009. Signed as a free agent by **Buffalo**, August 26, 2010. Signed as a free agent by **Iserlohn** (Germany), September 18, 2012. Signed as a free agent by **Vancouver**, July 25, 2013.

STUART, Mark

(STEW-uhrt, MAHRK) **WPG**

Defense. Shoots left. 6'2", 213 lbs. Born, Rochester, MN, April 27, 1984. Boston's 1st choice, 21st overall, in 2003 Entry Draft.

99-2000	Roch. Lourdes	High-MN	28	19	22	41	....	....	....	....	....	....	....	....	....	....	....	....	....	....	....	....	....	....	....
2000-01	USNTDP	U-17	12	1	5	6	6	....	....	....	....	....	....	....	....	....	....	....	....	....	....	....	....	....	....
	USNTDP	NAHL	52	2	11	13	114	....	....	....	....	....	....	....	....	....	....	....	....	....	....	....	....	....	....
2001-02	USNTDP	U-18	40	9	9	18	....	....	....	....	....	....	....	....	....	....	....	....	....	....	....	....	....	....	....
	USNTDP	USHL	12	0	1	1	25	....	....	....	....	....	....	....	....	....	....	....	....	....	....	....	....	....	....
	USNTDP	NAHL	9	0	1	1	18	....	....	....	....	....	....	....	....	....	....	....	....	....	....	....	....	....	....
2002-03	Colorado College	WCHA	38	3	17	20	81	....	....	....	....	....	....	....	....	....	....	....	....	....	....	....	....	....	....
2003-04	Colorado College	WCHA	37	4	11	15	100	....	....	....	....	....	....	....	....	....	....	....	....	....	....	....	....	....	....
2004-05	Colorado College	WCHA	43	5	14	19	94	....	....	....	....	....	....	....	....	....	....	....	....	....	....	....	....	....	....
2005-06	**Boston**	**NHL**	**17**	**1**	**1**	**2**	**10**	**0**	**0**	**0**	**9**	**11.1**	**–1**	**0**	**0.0**	**17:46**	....	....	....	....	....	....	....	....	....
	Providence Bruins	AHL	60	4	3	7	76	....	....	....	....	....	....	....	....	....	6	0	0	0	25	....	....	....	....
2006-07	**Boston**	**NHL**	**15**	**0**	**1**	**1**	**14**	**0**	**0**	**0**	**4**	**0.0**	**7**	**0**	**0.0**	**10:23**	....	....	....	....	....	....	....	....	....
	Providence Bruins	AHL	49	4	16	20	62	....	....	....	....	....	....	....	....	....	3	0	1	1	9	....	....	....	....

			Regular Season														Playoffs								
Season	Club	League	GP	G	A	Pts	PIM	PP	SH	GW	S	%	+/-	TF	F%	Min	GP	G	A	Pts	PIM	PP	SH	GW	Min
2007-08	Boston	NHL	82	4	4	8	81	0	0	1	60	6.7	2	0	0.0	15:22	7	0	1	1	8	0	0	0	16:00
2008-09	Boston	NHL	82	5	12	17	76	0	0	1	61	8.2	20	0	0.0	15:25	11	0	1	1	7	0	0	0	17:57
2009-10	Boston	NHL	56	2	5	7	80	0	0	0	53	3.8	1	0	0.0	17:01	4	0	0	0	6	0	0	0	14:39
2010-11	Boston	NHL	31	1	4	5	23	0	0	1	20	5.0	8	1	100.0	16:15	....	....	....	....	....	....	....	....	....
	Atlanta	NHL	23	1	0	1	24	0	0	0	21	4.8	–8	0	0.0	14:51	....	....	....	....	....	....	....	....	....
2011-12	Winnipeg	NHL	80	3	11	14	98	0	1	1	60	5.0	–4	0	0.0	17:12	....	....	....	....	....	....	....	....	....
2012-13	Florida Everblades	ECHL	9	2	1	3	12	....	....	....	....	....	....	....	....	....	....	....	....	....	....	....	....	....	....
	Winnipeg	NHL	42	2	2	4	53	0	0	0	40	5.0	5	0	0.0	16:42	....	....	....	....	....	....	....	....	....
	NHL Totals		428	19	40	59	459	0	1	4	328	5.8		1	100.0	16:02	22	0	2	2	21	0	0	0	16:44

WCHA All-Rookie Team (2003) • WCHA Second All-Star Team (2005) • NCAA West First All-American Team (2005)

Traded to **Atlanta** by **Boston** with Blake Wheeler for Rich Peverley and Boris Valabik, February 18, 2011. • Transferred to **Winnipeg** after **Atlanta** franchise relocated, June 21, 2011. Signed as a free agent by **Florida** (ECHL), December 11, 2012.

STURM, Marco

(STUHRM, MAHR-koh)

Left wing. Shoots left. 6', 196 lbs. Born, Dingolfing, West Germany, September 8, 1978. San Jose's 2nd choice, 21st overall, in 1996 Entry Draft.

Season	Club	League	GP	G	A	Pts	PIM	PP	SH	GW	S	%	+/-	TF	F%	Min	GP	G	A	Pts	PIM	PP	SH	GW	Min
1995-96	EV Landshut	Germany	47	12	20	32	50	....	....	....	....	....	....	....	....	....	11	1	3	4	18	....	....	....	....
1996-97	EV Landshut	Germany	46	16	27	43	40	....	....	....	....	....	....	....	....	....	7	1	4	5	6	....	....	....	....
1997-98	San Jose	NHL	74	10	20	30	40	2	0	3	118	8.5	–2	....	....	....	2	0	0	0	0	0	0	0	....
	Germany	Olympics	2	0	0	0	0	....	....	....	....	....	....	....	....	....	....	....	....	....	....	....	....	....	....
1998-99	San Jose	NHL	78	16	22	38	52	3	2	3	140	11.4	7	576	45.0	15:23	6	2	2	4	4	0	0	1	14:16
99-2000	San Jose	NHL	74	12	15	27	22	2	4	3	120	10.0	4	183	45.4	14:07	12	1	3	4	6	0	0	0	13:00
2000-01	San Jose	NHL	81	14	18	32	28	2	3	5	153	9.2	9	517	40.2	16:06	6	0	2	2	0	0	0	0	18:18
2001-02	San Jose	NHL	77	21	20	41	32	4	3	5	174	12.1	23	105	47.6	15:39	12	3	2	5	2	0	0	0	15:33
	Germany	Olympics	5	0	1	1	0	....	....	....	....	....	....	....	....	....	....	....	....	....	....	....	....	....	....
2002-03	San Jose	NHL	82	28	20	48	16	6	0	2	208	13.5	9	83	48.2	16:31	....	....	....	....	....	....	....	....	....
2003-04	San Jose	NHL	64	21	20	41	36	10	2	6	158	13.3	0	7	42.9	16:25	....	....	....	....	....	....	....	....	....
2004-05	ERC Ingolstadt	Germany	45	22	16	38	56	....	....	....	....	....	....	....	....	....	11	3	4	7	12	....	....	....	....
2005-06	San Jose	NHL	23	6	10	16	16	3	0	0	48	12.5	–8	9	44.4	17:28	....	....	....	....	....	....	....	....	....
	Boston	NHL	51	23	20	43	32	5	0	6	132	17.4	14	3	33.3	18:44	....	....	....	....	....	....	....	....	....
2006-07	Boston	NHL	76	27	17	44	46	10	2	1	224	12.1	–24	13	61.5	18:36	....	....	....	....	....	....	....	....	....
2007-08	Boston	NHL	80	27	29	56	40	10	1	5	229	11.8	11	34	29.4	18:00	7	2	2	4	6	0	1	1	18:20
2008-09	Boston	NHL	19	7	6	13	8	4	0	0	45	15.6	9	4	75.0	16:01	....	....	....	....	....	....	....	....	....
2009-10	Boston	NHL	76	22	15	37	30	4	1	2	203	10.8	14	11	18.2	16:46	7	0	0	0	4	0	0	0	14:15
	Germany	Olympics	4	0	1	1	0	....	....	....	....	....	....	....	....	....	....	....	....	....	....	....	....	....	....
2010-11	Los Angeles	NHL	17	4	5	9	17	1	0	0	27	14.8	6	1	100.0	14:28	....	....	....	....	....	....	....	....	....
	Washington	NHL	18	1	6	7	6	0	0	1	30	3.3	0	14	35.7	14:01	9	1	2	3	4	1	0	0	14:38
2011-12	Vancouver	NHL	6	0	0	0	2	0	0	0	3	0.0	–5	2	100.0	13:53	....	....	....	....	....	....	....	....	....
	Florida	NHL	42	3	2	5	23	0	0	1	62	4.8	–8	11	63.6	12:05	7	0	0	0	4	0	0	0	11:33
2012-13	Kolner Haie	Germany	5	0	0	0	6	....	....	....	....	....	....	....	....	....	12	6	3	9	18	....	....	....	....
	NHL Totals		938	242	245	487	446	66	18	43	2074	11.7		1573	43.6	16:15	68	9	13	22	30	1	1	2	14:49

Played in NHL All-Star Game (1999)

Signed as a free agent by **Ingolstadt** (Germany), August 8, 2004. Traded to **Boston** by **San Jose** with Brad Stuart and Wayne Primeau for Joe Thornton, November 30, 2005. • Missed majority of 2008-09 due to knee injury vs. Toronto, December 18, 2008. Traded to **Los Angeles** by **Boston** for future considerations, December 11, 2010. Claimed on waivers by **Washington** from **Los Angeles**, February 26, 2011. • Missed majority of 2010-11 due to knee injury in playoffs vs. Philadelphia, May 1, 2010. Signed as a free agent by **Vancouver**, July 1, 2011. Traded to **Florida** by **Vancouver** with Mikael Samuelsson for David Booth, Steve Reinprecht and Vancouver's 3rd round choice (previously acquired, Vancouver selected Cole Cassels) in 2013 Entry Draft, October 22, 2011. Signed as a free agent by **Koln** (Germany), February 3, 2013.

SUBBAN, P.K.

(soo-BAN, PEE-KAY) **MTL**

Defense. Shoots right. 6', 206 lbs. Born, Toronto, Ont., May 13, 1989. Montreal's 3rd choice, 43rd overall, in 2007 Entry Draft.

Season	Club	League	GP	G	A	Pts	PIM	PP	SH	GW	S	%	+/-	TF	F%	Min	GP	G	A	Pts	PIM	PP	SH	GW	Min
2004-05	Markham	GTHL	67	15	28	43	179	....	....	....	....	....	....	....	....	....	....	....	....	....	....	....	....	....	....
2005-06	Belleville Bulls	OHL	52	5	7	12	70	....	....	....	....	....	....	....	....	....	3	0	0	0	2	....	....	....	....
2006-07	Belleville Bulls	OHL	68	15	41	56	89	....	....	....	....	....	....	....	....	....	15	5	8	13	26	....	....	....	....
2007-08	Belleville Bulls	OHL	58	8	38	46	100	....	....	....	....	....	....	....	....	....	21	8	15	23	28	....	....	....	....
2008-09	Belleville Bulls	OHL	56	14	62	76	94	....	....	....	....	....	....	....	....	....	17	3	12	15	22	....	....	....	....
2009-10	Montreal	NHL	2	0	2	2	2	0	0	0	4	0.0	1	0	0.0	20:06	14	1	7	8	6	0	0	0	20:44
	Hamilton	AHL	77	18	35	53	82	....	....	....	....	....	....	....	....	....	7	3	7	10	6	....	....	....	....
2010-11	Montreal	NHL	77	14	24	38	124	9	0	3	197	7.1	–8	0	0.0	22:16	7	2	2	4	2	2	0	0	28:33
2011-12	Montreal	NHL	81	7	29	36	119	5	0	0	205	3.4	9	0	0.0	24:18	....	....	....	....	....	....	....	....	....
2012-13	Montreal	NHL	42	11	27	38	57	7	0	0	126	8.7	12	0	0.0	23:15	5	2	2	4	31	1	0	0	23:56
	NHL Totals		202	32	82	114	302	21	0	3	532	6.0		0	0.0	23:16	26	5	11	16	39	3	0	0	23:27

OHL First All-Star Team (2009) • AHL All-Rookie Team (2010) • AHL First All-Star Team (2010) • NHL All-Rookie Team (2011) • NHL First All-Star Team (2013) • James Norris Memorial Trophy (2013)

SULLIVAN, Steve

(SUHL-ih-vuhn, STEEV)

Right wing. Shoots right. 5'9", 165 lbs. Born, Timmins, Ont., July 6, 1974. New Jersey's 10th choice, 233rd overall, in 1994 Entry Draft.

Season	Club	League	GP	G	A	Pts	PIM	PP	SH	GW	S	%	+/-	TF	F%	Min	GP	G	A	Pts	PIM	PP	SH	GW	Min
1991-92	Timmins	NOJHA	47	66	55	121	141	....	....	....	....	....	....	....	....	....	....	....	....	....	....	....	....	....	....
1992-93	Sault Ste. Marie	OHL	62	36	27	63	44	....	....	....	....	....	....	....	....	....	16	3	8	11	18	....	....	....	....
1993-94	Sault Ste. Marie	OHL	63	51	62	113	82	....	....	....	....	....	....	....	....	....	14	9	16	25	22	....	....	....	....
1994-95	Albany River Rats	AHL	75	31	50	81	124	....	....	....	....	....	....	....	....	....	14	4	7	11	10	....	....	....	....
1995-96	New Jersey	NHL	16	5	4	9	8	2	0	1	23	21.7	3	....	....	....	....	....	....	....	....	....	....	....	....
	Albany River Rats	AHL	53	33	42	75	127	....	....	....	....	....	....	....	....	....	4	3	0	3	6	....	....	....	....
1996-97	New Jersey	NHL	33	8	14	22	14	2	0	2	63	12.7	9	....	....	....	....	....	....	....	....	....	....	....	....
	Albany River Rats	AHL	15	8	7	15	16	....	....	....	....	....	....	....	....	....	....	....	....	....	....	....	....	....	....
	Toronto	NHL	21	5	11	16	23	1	0	1	45	11.1	5	....	....	....	....	....	....	....	....	....	....	....	....
1997-98	Toronto	NHL	63	10	18	28	40	1	0	1	112	8.9	–8	....	....	....	....	....	....	....	....	....	....	....	....
1998-99	Toronto	NHL	63	20	20	40	28	4	0	5	110	18.2	12	685	44.4	14:12	13	3	3	6	14	2	0	0	16:20
99-2000	Toronto	NHL	7	0	1	1	4	0	0	0	11	0.0	–1	47	48.9	11:52	....	....	....	....	....	....	....	....	....
	Chicago	NHL	73	22	42	64	52	2	1	6	169	13.0	20	692	48.0	18:05	....	....	....	....	....	....	....	....	....
2000-01	Chicago	NHL	81	34	41	75	54	6	*8	3	204	16.7	3	649	42.4	20:32	....	....	....	....	....	....	....	....	....
2001-02	Chicago	NHL	78	21	39	60	67	3	0	8	155	13.5	23	758	48.9	19:10	5	1	0	1	2	0	0	0	18:04
2002-03	Chicago	NHL	82	26	35	61	42	4	2	3	190	13.7	15	382	46.1	19:15	....	....	....	....	....	....	....	....	....
2003-04	Chicago	NHL	56	15	28	43	36	4	2	4	140	10.7	–7	103	44.7	21:19	....	....	....	....	....	....	....	....	....
	Nashville	NHL	24	9	21	30	12	7	0	0	78	11.5	8	124	43.6	20:02	6	1	1	2	6	0	0	1	18:58
2004-05			DID NOT PLAY																						
2005-06	Nashville	NHL	69	31	37	68	50	13	4	5	192	16.1	2	42	52.4	19:06	5	0	2	2	0	0	0	0	17:02
2006-07	Nashville	NHL	57	22	38	60	20	6	3	4	122	18.0	16	39	38.5	19:25	....	....	....	....	....	....	....	....	....
2007-08	Nashville	NHL	DID NOT PLAY – INJURED																						
2008-09	Nashville	NHL	41	11	21	32	30	3	0	2	83	13.3	2	4	0.0	18:29	....	....	....	....	....	....	....	....	....
2009-10	Nashville	NHL	82	17	34	51	35	5	0	4	152	11.2	2	10	10.0	17:55	6	0	3	3	2	0	0	0	17:59
2010-11	Nashville	NHL	44	10	12	22	28	3	0	1	79	12.7	4	13	38.5	16:02	9	2	1	3	2	0	0	1	9:23
2011-12	Pittsburgh	NHL	79	17	31	48	20	5	0	1	140	12.1	–3	9	44.4	15:22	6	2	4	6	4	2	0	0	14:58
2012-13	Phoenix	NHL	33	5	7	12	20	2	0	0	48	10.4	–8	1	0.0	14:22	....	....	....	....	....	....	....	....	....
	New Jersey	NHL	9	2	3	5	4	2	0	1	13	15.4	–4	5	60.0	15:16	....	....	....	....	....	....	....	....	....
	NHL Totals		1011	290	457	747	587	75	20	52	2129	13.6		3563	45.8	18:06	50	9	14	23	30	4	0	2	15:40

AHL First All-Star Team (1996) • Bill Masterton Memorial Trophy (2009)

Traded to **Toronto** by **New Jersey** with Jason Smith and the rights to Alyn McCauley for Doug Gilmour, Dave Ellett and New Jersey's 3rd round choice (previously acquired, New Jersey selected Andre Lakos) in 1999 Entry Draft, February 25, 1997. Claimed on waivers by **Chicago** from **Toronto**, October 23, 1999. Traded to **Nashville** by **Chicago** for Nashville's 2nd round choice in 2004 (Ryan Garlock) and 2005 (Michael Blunden) Entry Drafts, February 16, 2004. • Missed remainder of 2006-07, all of 2007-08 and start of 2008-09 due to back injury vs. Montreal, February 22, 2006. Signed as a free agent by **Pittsburgh**, July 1, 2011. Signed as a free agent by **Phoenix**, July 4, 2012. Traded to **New Jersey** by **Phoenix** for New Jersey's 7th round choice in 2014 Entry Draft, April 3, 2013.

SULZER, Alexander

(ZUHLT-suhr, al-EHX-AN-duhr) **BUF**

Defense. Shoots left. 6'1", 204 lbs. Born, Kaufbeuren, West Germany, May 30, 1984. Nashville's 7th choice, 92nd overall, in 2003 Entry Draft.

Season	Club	League	GP	G	A	Pts	PIM	PP	SH	GW	S	%	+/-	TF	F%	Min	GP	G	A	Pts	PIM	PP	SH	GW	Min
2000-01	ESV Kaufbeuren	German-3	38	3	6	9	20	....	....	....	....	....	....	....	....	....	....	....	....	....	....	....	....	....	....
	Kaufbeuren Jr.	Ger-Jr.	1	0	2	2	2	....	....	....	....	....	....	....	....	....	....	....	....	....	....	....	....	....	....
2001-02	ESV Kaufbeuren	German-3	19	1	9	10	14	....	....	....	....	....	....	....	....	....	....	....	....	....	....	....	....	....	....
	Kaufbeuren Jr.	Ger-Jr.	1	0	0	0	4	....	....	....	....	....	....	....	....	....	....	....	....	....	....	....	....	....	....
2002-03	ESV Kaufbeuren	German-2	26	5	3	8	38	....	....	....	....	....	....	....	....	....	1	0	1	1	4	....	....	....	....
	Hamburg Freezers	Germany	18	0	1	1	18	....	....	....	....	....	....	....	....	....	5	0	0	0	12	....	....	....	....

			Regular Season														Playoffs								
Season	Club	League	GP	G	A	Pts	PIM	PP	SH	GW	S	%	+/-	TF	F%	Min	GP	G	A	Pts	PIM	PP	SH	GW	Min
2003-04	Dusseldorf	Germany	46	4	1	5	56	....	....	....	....	....	....	....	....	....	4	0	0	0	8	....	....	....	....
2004-05	Dusseldorf	Germany	42	5	6	11	68	....	....	....	....	....	....	....	....	....	....	....	....	....	....	....	....	....	....
	EV Duisburg	German-2	....	....	....	....	....	....	....	....	....	....	....	....	....	....	7	0	3	3	6	....	....	....	....
2005-06	Dusseldorf	Germany	48	3	15	18	82	....	....	....	....	....	....	....	....	....	13	3	6	9	22	....	....	....	....
	Germany	Olympics	5	0	1	1	2	....	....	....	....	....	....	....	....	....	....	....	....	....	....	....	....	....	....
2006-07	Dusseldorf	Germany	44	4	11	15	82	....	....	....	....	....	....	....	....	....	9	2	1	3	20	....	....	....	....
2007-08	Milwaukee	AHL	61	7	25	32	47	....	....	....	....	....	....	....	....	....	....	....	....	....	....	....	....	....	....
2008-09	Nashville	NHL	2	0	0	0	0	0	0	0	0	0.0	0	0	0.0	6:34	....	....	....	....	....	....	....	....	....
	Milwaukee	AHL	48	8	26	34	36	....	....	....	....	....	....	....	....	....	....	....	....	....	....	....	....	....	....
2009-10	Nashville	NHL	20	0	2	2	4	0	0	0	15	0.0	4	0	0.0	13:23	....	....	....	....	....	....	....	....	....
	Milwaukee	AHL	36	7	23	30	8	....	....	....	....	....	....	....	....	....	7	1	5	6	2	....	....	....	....
	Germany	Olympics	4	0	0	0	4	....	....	....	....	....	....	....	....	....	....	....	....	....	....	....	....	....	....
2010-11	Nashville	NHL	31	1	3	4	14	0	0	0	30	3.3	–5	1	100.0	17:42	....	....	....	....	....	....	....	....	....
	Florida	NHL	9	0	1	1	0	0	0	0	7	0.0	–3	0	0.0	17:00	....	....	....	....	....	....	....	....	....
2011-12	Vancouver	NHL	12	0	1	1	2	0	0	0	11	0.0	6	0	0.0	15:59	....	....	....	....	....	....	....	....	....
	Buffalo	NHL	15	3	5	8	6	0	0	0	22	13.6	2	0	0.0	19:18	....	....	....	....	....	....	....	....	....
2012-13	ERC Ingolstadt	Germany	21	2	14	16	8	....	....	....	....	....	....	....	....	....	....	....	....	....	....	....	....	....	....
	Buffalo	NHL	17	3	1	4	10	0	0	1	15	20.0	3	0	0.0	16:31	....	....	....	....	....	....	....	....	....
	NHL Totals		106	7	13	20	36	0	0	1	100	7.0		1	100.0	16:28	....	....	....	....	....	....	....	....	....

Traded to **Florida** by **Nashville** for future considerations, February 25, 2011. • Missed majority of 2010-11 as a healthy reserve. Signed as a free agent by **Vancouver**, July 7, 2011. Traded to **Buffalo** by **Vancouver** for Marc-Andre Gragnani, February 27, 2012. Signed as a free agent by **Ingolstadt** (Germany), October 17, 2012.

SUMMERS, Chris

(SUHM-mehrs, KRIHS) **PHX**

Defense. Shoots left. 6'2", 209 lbs. Born, Ann Arbor, MI, February 5, 1988. Phoenix's 2nd choice, 29th overall, in 2006 Entry Draft.

Season	Club	League	GP	G	A	Pts	PIM	PP	SH	GW	S	%	+/-	TF	F%	Min	GP	G	A	Pts	PIM	PP	SH	GW	Min
2004-05	USNTDP	U-17	13	2	2	4	10	....	....	....	....	....	....	....	....	....	....	....	....	....	....	....	....	....	....
	USNTDP	NAHL	31	2	5	7	20	....	....	....	....	....	....	....	....	....	7	1	0	1	0	....	....	....	....
2005-06	USNTDP	U-18	42	4	9	13	67	....	....	....	....	....	....	....	....	....	....	....	....	....	....	....	....	....	....
	USNTDP	NAHL	17	2	2	4	20	....	....	....	....	....	....	....	....	....	....	....	....	....	....	....	....	....	....
2006-07	U. of Michigan	CCHA	41	6	8	14	58	....	....	....	....	....	....	....	....	....	....	....	....	....	....	....	....	....	....
2007-08	U. of Michigan	CCHA	41	2	11	13	65	....	....	....	....	....	....	....	....	....	....	....	....	....	....	....	....	....	....
2008-09	U. of Michigan	CCHA	41	4	13	17	40	....	....	....	....	....	....	....	....	....	....	....	....	....	....	....	....	....	....
2009-10	U. of Michigan	CCHA	40	4	12	16	28	....	....	....	....	....	....	....	....	....	....	....	....	....	....	....	....	....	....
	San Antonio	AHL	6	1	0	1	0	....	....	....	....	....	....	....	....	....	....	....	....	....	....	....	....	....	....
2010-11	Phoenix	NHL	2	0	0	0	4	0	0	0	0	0.0	–3	0	0.0	13:52	....	....	....	....	....	....	....	....	....
	San Antonio	AHL	75	1	9	10	54	....	....	....	....	....	....	....	....	....	....	....	....	....	....	....	....	....	....
2011-12	Phoenix	NHL	21	0	3	3	11	0	0	0	10	0.0	–4	0	0.0	12:27	....	....	....	....	....	....	....	....	....
	Portland Pirates	AHL	28	0	2	2	37	....	....	....	....	....	....	....	....	....	....	....	....	....	....	....	....	....	....
2012-13	Portland Pirates	AHL	60	2	10	12	53	....	....	....	....	....	....	....	....	....	3	0	0	0	0	....	....	....	....
	Phoenix	NHL	6	0	0	0	9	0	0	0	5	0.0	–3	0	0.0	12:39	....	....	....	....	....	....	....	....	....
	NHL Totals		29	0	3	3	24	0	0	0	15	0.0		0	0.0	12:35	....	....	....	....	....	....	....	....	....

SUSTR, Andrej

(SHOO-stuhr, an-DRAY) **T.B.**

Defense. Shoots right. 6'8", 225 lbs. Born, Plzen, Czech., November 29, 1990.

Season	Club	League	GP	G	A	Pts	PIM	PP	SH	GW	S	%	+/-	TF	F%	Min	GP	G	A	Pts	PIM	PP	SH	GW	Min
2006-07	Jihlava U17	CzR-U17	37	5	15	20	56	....	....	....	....	....	....	....	....	....	....	....	....	....	....	....	....	....	....
	Jihlava Jr.	CzRep-Jr.	5	0	0	0	4	....	....	....	....	....	....	....	....	....	....	....	....	....	....	....	....	....	....
2007-08	HC Plzen Jr.	CzRep-Jr.	41	2	8	10	44	....	....	....	....	....	....	....	....	....	5	1	0	1	4	....	....	....	....
2008-09	HC Plzen Jr.	CzRep-Jr.	13	1	4	5	14	....	....	....	....	....	....	....	....	....	....	....	....	....	....	....	....	....	....
	HC Rokycany	CzRep-3	2	0	0	0	2	....	....	....	....	....	....	....	....	....	....	....	....	....	....	....	....	....	....
	Kenai River	NAHL	36	1	7	8	58	....	....	....	....	....	....	....	....	....	2	0	0	0	2	....	....	....	....
2009-10	Youngstown	USHL	50	1	18	19	95	....	....	....	....	....	....	....	....	....	....	....	....	....	....	....	....	....	....
2010-11	Nebraska-Omaha	WCHA	39	2	7	9	38	....	....	....	....	....	....	....	....	....	....	....	....	....	....	....	....	....	....
2011-12	Nebraska-Omaha	WCHA	33	4	13	17	26	....	....	....	....	....	....	....	....	....	....	....	....	....	....	....	....	....	....
2012-13	Nebraska-Omaha	WCHA	39	9	16	25	53	....	....	....	....	....	....	....	....	....	....	....	....	....	....	....	....	....	....
	Tampa Bay	NHL	2	0	0	0	0	0	0	0	2	0.0	1	0	0.0	10:43	....	....	....	....	....	....	....	....	....
	Syracuse Crunch	AHL	8	2	1	3	8	....	....	....	....	....	....	....	....	....	18	2	5	7	25	....	....	....	....
	NHL Totals		2	0	0	0	0	0	0	0	2	0.0		0	0.0	10:43	....	....	....	....	....	....	....	....	....

Signed as a free agent by **Tampa Bay** March 21, 2013.

SUTER, Ryan

(SOO-tuhr, RIGH-uhn) **MIN**

Defense. Shoots left. 6'1", 198 lbs. Born, Madison, WI, January 21, 1985. Nashville's 1st choice, 7th overall, in 2003 Entry Draft.

Season	Club	League	GP	G	A	Pts	PIM	PP	SH	GW	S	%	+/-	TF	F%	Min	GP	G	A	Pts	PIM	PP	SH	GW	Min
2000-01	Culver Academy	High-IN	26	13	32	45	....	....	....	....	....	....	....	....	....	....	....	....	....	....	....	....	....	....	....
2001-02	USNTDP	U-17	8	2	11	13	21	....	....	....	....	....	....	....	....	....	....	....	....	....	....	....	....	....	....
	USNTDP	U-18	27	4	10	14	6	....	....	....	....	....	....	....	....	....	....	....	....	....	....	....	....	....	....
	USNTDP	NAHL	35	2	10	12	75	....	....	....	....	....	....	....	....	....	....	....	....	....	....	....	....	....	....
2002-03	USNTDP	NAHL	9	2	5	7	12	....	....	....	....	....	....	....	....	....	....	....	....	....	....	....	....	....	....
	USNTDP	U-18	42	7	17	24	124	....	....	....	....	....	....	....	....	....	....	....	....	....	....	....	....	....	....
2003-04	U. of Wisconsin	WCHA	39	3	16	19	93	....	....	....	....	....	....	....	....	....	....	....	....	....	....	....	....	....	....
2004-05	Milwaukee	AHL	63	7	16	23	70	....	....	....	....	....	....	....	....	....	7	1	5	6	16	....	....	....	....
2005-06	Nashville	NHL	71	1	15	16	66	0	0	0	84	1.2	7	0	0.0	17:21	....	....	....	....	....	....	....	....	....
2006-07	Nashville	NHL	82	8	16	24	54	1	0	0	87	9.2	10	0	0.0	20:09	5	1	0	1	8	0	0	0	23:19
2007-08	Nashville	NHL	76	7	24	31	71	1	0	1	138	5.1	3	0	0.0	20:35	6	1	1	2	4	0	0	0	21:12
2008-09	Nashville	NHL	82	7	38	45	73	3	0	3	143	4.9	–16	0	0.0	24:16	....	....	....	....	....	....	....	....	....
2009-10	Nashville	NHL	82	4	33	37	48	2	0	1	125	3.2	4	1	0.0	23:59	6	0	0	0	0	0	0	0	24:09
	United States	Olympics	6	0	4	4	2	....	....	....	....	....	....	....	....	....	....	....	....	....	....	....	....	....	....
2010-11	Nashville	NHL	70	4	35	39	54	1	0	1	115	3.5	20	1	0.0	25:12	12	1	5	6	6	0	0	0	28:51
2011-12	Nashville	NHL	79	7	39	46	30	3	1	1	134	5.2	15	1	0.0	26:30	10	1	3	4	4	1	0	0	28:50
2012-13	Minnesota	NHL	48	4	28	32	24	3	0	1	91	4.4	2	0	0.0	27:17	5	0	0	0	4	0	0	0	31:37
	NHL Totals		590	42	228	270	420	14	1	8	917	4.6		3	0.0	23:00	44	4	9	13	26	1	0	0	26:51

WCHA All-Rookie Team (2004) • NHL First All-Star Team (2013)

Played in NHL All-Star Game (2012)

Signed as a free agent by **Minnesota**, July 4, 2012.

SUTHERBY, Brian

(SUH-thur-bee, BRIGH-uhn)

Center. Shoots left. 6'2", 208 lbs. Born, Edmonton, Alta., March 1, 1982. Washington's 1st choice, 26th overall, in 2000 Entry Draft.

Season	Club	League	GP	G	A	Pts	PIM	PP	SH	GW	S	%	+/-	TF	F%	Min	GP	G	A	Pts	PIM	PP	SH	GW	Min
1997-98	CAC Cement	AMHL	36	36	23	59	60	....	....	....	....	....	....	....	....	....	....	....	....	....	....	....	....	....	....
1998-99	Moose Jaw	WHL	66	9	12	21	47	....	....	....	....	....	....	....	....	....	11	0	1	1	0	....	....	....	....
99-2000	Moose Jaw	WHL	47	18	17	35	102	....	....	....	....	....	....	....	....	....	4	1	1	2	12	....	....	....	....
2000-01	Moose Jaw	WHL	59	34	43	77	138	....	....	....	....	....	....	....	....	....	4	2	1	3	10	....	....	....	....
2001-02	Washington	NHL	7	0	0	0	2	0	0	0	3	0.0	–3	39	35.9	7:17	....	....	....	....	....	....	....	....	....
	Moose Jaw	WHL	36	18	27	45	75	....	....	....	....	....	....	....	....	....	12	7	5	12	33	....	....	....	....
2002-03	Washington	NHL	72	2	9	11	93	0	0	0	38	5.3	7	288	43.8	9:44	5	0	0	0	10	0	0	0	4:10
	Portland Pirates	AHL	5	0	5	5	11	....	....	....	....	....	....	....	....	....	....	....	....	....	....	....	....	....	....
2003-04	Washington	NHL	30	2	0	2	28	0	0	0	24	8.3	–5	116	41.4	10:15	....	....	....	....	....	....	....	....	....
	Portland Pirates	AHL	6	2	4	6	16	....	....	....	....	....	....	....	....	....	....	....	....	....	....	....	....	....	....
2004-05	Portland Pirates	AHL	53	10	19	29	115	....	....	....	....	....	....	....	....	....	....	....	....	....	....	....	....	....	....
2005-06	Washington	NHL	76	14	16	30	73	0	2	0	85	16.5	–17	904	48.7	13:44	....	....	....	....	....	....	....	....	....
2006-07	Washington	NHL	69	7	10	17	78	1	0	0	87	8.0	–9	762	50.1	13:41	....	....	....	....	....	....	....	....	....
2007-08	Washington	NHL	5	1	0	1	7	0	0	0	3	33.3	–2	23	52.2	6:49	....	....	....	....	....	....	....	....	....
	Anaheim	NHL	45	0	1	1	57	0	0	0	46	0.0	–2	255	45.5	8:47	5	0	0	0	2	0	0	0	5:29
2008-09	Anaheim	NHL	17	3	3	6	19	0	0	0	17	17.6	6	45	48.9	7:12	....	....	....	....	....	....	....	....	....
	Dallas	NHL	42	5	4	9	52	0	1	0	50	10.0	–5	219	41.1	12:25	....	....	....	....	....	....	....	....	....
2009-10	Dallas	NHL	46	5	4	9	66	0	0	0	49	10.2	8	41	43.9	8:37	....	....	....	....	....	....	....	....	....
2010-11	Dallas	NHL	51	2	2	4	58	0	0	0	32	6.3	–10	32	59.4	7:25	....	....	....	....	....	....	....	....	....

			Regular Season														Playoffs								
Season	Club	League	GP	G	A	Pts	PIM	PP	SH	GW	S	%	+/-	TF	F%	Min	GP	G	A	Pts	PIM	PP	SH	GW	Min
2011-12	San Antonio	AHL	15	1	3	4	18	....	....	....	....	....	....	....	....	....	....	....	....	....	....	....	....	....	....
2012-13	Lake Erie	AHL	25	1	1	2	35	....	....	....	....	....	....	....	....	....	....	....	....	....	....	....	....	....	....
	NHL Totals		**460**	**41**	**49**	**90**	**533**	**1**	**3**	**0**	**434**	**9.4**		**2724**	**47.2**	**10:39**	**10**	**0**	**0**	**0**	**12**	**0**	**0**	**0**	**4:49**

• Missed majority of 2003-04 due to groin injury vs. St. Louis, October 18, 2003. Traded to **Anaheim** by **Washington** for Anaheim's 2nd round choice (later traded to Montreal, later traded to Atlanta – Atlanta selected Jeremy Morin) in 2009 Entry Draft, November 19, 2007. Traded to **Dallas** by **Anaheim** for David McIntyre and Dallas' 6th round choice (Andreas Dahlstrom) in 2010 Entry Draft, December 14, 2008. • Missed majority of 2011-12 due to off-season back surgery. Signed as a free agent by **Lake Erie** (AHL), January 4, 2013.

SUTTER, Brandon

(SUH-tuhr, BRAN-duhn) **PIT**

Center/Right wing. Shoots right. 6'3", 183 lbs. Born, Huntington, NY, February 14, 1989. Carolina's 1st choice, 11th overall, in 2007 Entry Draft.

Season	Club	League	GP	G	A	Pts	PIM	PP	SH	GW	S	%	+/-	TF	F%	Min	GP	G	A	Pts	PIM	PP	SH	GW	Min
2003-04	Red Deer Chiefs	AMBHL	35	25	34	59	28	....	....	....	....	....	....	....	....	....	11	5	4	9	....	....	....	....	....
2004-05	Red Deer	AMHL	34	4	16	20	28	....	....	....	....	....	....	....	....	....	....	....	....	....	....	....	....	....	....
	Red Deer Rebels	WHL	7	0	2	2	8	....	....	....	....	....	....	....	....	....	7	1	4	5	2	....	....	....	....
2005-06	Red Deer Rebels	WHL	68	22	24	46	36	....	....	....	....	....	....	....	....	....	....	....	....	....	....	....	....	....	....
2006-07	Red Deer Rebels	WHL	71	20	37	57	54	....	....	....	....	....	....	....	....	....	7	0	3	3	14	....	....	....	....
2007-08	Red Deer Rebels	WHL	59	26	23	49	38	....	....	....	....	....	....	....	....	....	....	....	....	....	....	....	....	....	....
	Albany River Rats	AHL	7	1	1	2	2	....	....	....	....	....	....	....	....	....	7	0	2	2	4	....	....	....	....
2008-09	**Carolina**	**NHL**	**50**	**1**	**5**	**6**	**16**	**0**	**0**	**0**	**57**	**1.8**	**–1**	**332**	**38.6**	**8:50**	....	....	....	....	....	....	....	....	....
	Albany River Rats	AHL	22	4	8	12	6	....	....	....	....	....	....	....	....	....	....	....	....	....	....	....	....	....	....
2009-10	**Carolina**	**NHL**	**72**	**21**	**19**	**40**	**2**	**5**	**0**	**3**	**168**	**12.5**	**–1**	**997**	**49.1**	**16:33**	....	....	....	....	....	....	....	....	....
	Albany River Rats	AHL	7	1	3	4	2	....	....	....	....	....	....	....	....	....	....	....	....	....	....	....	....	....	....
2010-11	**Carolina**	**NHL**	**82**	**14**	**15**	**29**	**25**	**1**	**0**	**3**	**145**	**9.7**	**13**	**1349**	**44.3**	**16:51**	....	....	....	....	....	....	....	....	....
2011-12	**Carolina**	**NHL**	**82**	**17**	**15**	**32**	**21**	**2**	**3**	**0**	**171**	**9.9**	**–3**	**1295**	**50.5**	**17:24**	....	....	....	....	....	....	....	....	....
2012-13	**Pittsburgh**	**NHL**	**48**	**11**	**8**	**19**	**4**	**3**	**0**	**5**	**82**	**13.4**	**3**	**761**	**50.2**	**16:24**	**15**	**2**	**1**	**3**	**0**	**0**	**0**	**0**	**16:18**
	NHL Totals		**334**	**64**	**62**	**126**	**68**	**11**	**3**	**11**	**623**	**10.3**		**4734**	**47.5**	**15:39**	**15**	**2**	**1**	**3**	**0**	**0**	**0**	**0**	**16:18**

Traded to **Pittsburgh** by **Carolina** with Brian Dumoulin and Carolina's 1st round choice (Derrick Pouliot) in 2012 Entry Draft for Jordan Staal, June 22, 2012.

SUTTER, Brett

(SUH-tuhr, BREHT) **CAR**

Left wing. Shoots left. 6', 200 lbs. Born, Viking, Alta., June 2, 1987. Calgary's 7th choice, 179th overall, in 2005 Entry Draft.

Season	Club	League	GP	G	A	Pts	PIM	PP	SH	GW	S	%	+/-	TF	F%	Min	GP	G	A	Pts	PIM	PP	SH	GW	Min
2003-04	Kootenay Ice	WHL	44	5	7	12	26	....	....	....	....	....	....	....	....	....	4	0	0	0	4	....	....	....	....
2004-05	Kootenay Ice	WHL	70	8	11	19	70	....	....	....	....	....	....	....	....	....	16	1	2	3	16	....	....	....	....
2005-06	Kootenay Ice	WHL	16	8	7	15	21	....	....	....	....	....	....	....	....	....	....	....	....	....	....	....	....	....	....
	Red Deer Rebels	WHL	57	9	26	35	80	....	....	....	....	....	....	....	....	....	....	....	....	....	....	....	....	....	....
2006-07	Red Deer Rebels	WHL	67	28	29	57	77	....	....	....	....	....	....	....	....	....	7	3	4	7	11	....	....	....	....
2007-08	Quad City Flames	AHL	75	4	6	10	63	....	....	....	....	....	....	....	....	....	....	....	....	....	....	....	....	....	....
2008-09	**Calgary**	**NHL**	**4**	**1**	**0**	**1**	**2**	**0**	**0**	**0**	**6**	**16.7**	**–2**	**1**	**0.0**	**8:04**	....	....	....	....	....	....	....	....	....
	Quad City Flames	AHL	71	10	15	25	50	....	....	....	....	....	....	....	....	....	....	....	....	....	....	....	....	....	....
2009-10	**Calgary**	**NHL**	**10**	**0**	**0**	**0**	**5**	**0**	**0**	**0**	**9**	**0.0**	**–1**	**5**	**20.0**	**9:40**	....	....	....	....	....	....	....	....	....
	Abbotsford Heat	AHL	66	9	15	24	69	....	....	....	....	....	....	....	....	....	13	4	7	11	20	....	....	....	....
2010-11	**Calgary**	**NHL**	**4**	**0**	**1**	**1**	**5**	**0**	**0**	**0**	**3**	**0.0**	**–1**	**23**	**52.2**	**10:07**	....	....	....	....	....	....	....	....	....
	Charlotte	AHL	60	9	12	21	84	....	....	....	....	....	....	....	....	....	16	4	10	14	15	....	....	....	....
	Carolina	**NHL**	**1**	**0**	**0**	**0**	**0**	**0**	**0**	**0**	**0**	**0.0**	**0**	**3**	**33.3**	**4:09**	....	....	....	....	....	....	....	....	....
2011-12	**Carolina**	**NHL**	**15**	**0**	**3**	**3**	**11**	**0**	**0**	**0**	**11**	**0.0**	**–1**	**21**	**66.7**	**7:34**	....	....	....	....	....	....	....	....	....
	Charlotte	AHL	63	13	16	29	58	....	....	....	....	....	....	....	....	....	....	....	....	....	....	....	....	....	....
2012-13	Charlotte	AHL	70	19	29	48	62	....	....	....	....	....	....	....	....	....	5	0	0	0	0	....	....	....	....
	Carolina	**NHL**	**3**	**0**	**0**	**0**	**4**	**0**	**0**	**0**	**2**	**0.0**	**–1**	**14**	**57.1**	**8:21**	....	....	....	....	....	....	....	....	....
	NHL Totals		**37**	**1**	**4**	**5**	**27**	**0**	**0**	**0**	**31**	**3.2**		**67**	**53.7**	**8:26**	....	....	....	....	....	....	....	....	....

Traded to **Carolina** by **Calgary** with Ian White for Anton Babchuk and Tom Kostopoulos, November 17, 2010.

SWEATT, Bill

(SWEHT, BIHL)

Left wing. Shoots left. 6', 190 lbs. Born, Elburn, IL, September 21, 1988. Chicago's 2nd choice, 38th overall, in 2007 Entry Draft.

Season	Club	League	GP	G	A	Pts	PIM	PP	SH	GW	S	%	+/-	TF	F%	Min	GP	G	A	Pts	PIM	PP	SH	GW	Min
2003-04	Team Illinois	MWEHL	74	33	37	70	....	....	....	....	....	....	....	....	....	....	....	....	....	....	....	....	....	....	....
2004-05	USNTDP	U-17	11	5	10	15	54	....	....	....	....	....	....	....	....	....	....	....	....	....	....	....	....	....	....
	USNTDP	NAHL	41	7	9	16	12	....	....	....	....	....	....	....	....	....	10	4	3	7	6	....	....	....	....
2005-06	USNTDP	U-18	42	19	11	30	24	....	....	....	....	....	....	....	....	....	....	....	....	....	....	....	....	....	....
	USNTDP	NAHL	17	10	15	25	4	....	....	....	....	....	....	....	....	....	....	....	....	....	....	....	....	....	....
2006-07	Colorado College	WCHA	30	9	17	26	18	....	....	....	....	....	....	....	....	....	....	....	....	....	....	....	....	....	....
2007-08	Colorado College	WCHA	37	10	17	27	38	....	....	....	....	....	....	....	....	....	....	....	....	....	....	....	....	....	....
2008-09	Colorado College	WCHA	37	12	11	23	28	....	....	....	....	....	....	....	....	....	....	....	....	....	....	....	....	....	....
2009-10	Colorado College	WCHA	39	15	18	33	18	....	....	....	....	....	....	....	....	....	....	....	....	....	....	....	....	....	....
2010-11	Manitoba Moose	AHL	80	19	27	46	28	....	....	....	....	....	....	....	....	....	14	1	5	6	2	....	....	....	....
2011-12	**Vancouver**	**NHL**	**2**	**0**	**0**	**0**	**0**	**0**	**0**	**0**	**2**	**0.0**	**0**	**0**	**0.0**	**5:21**	....	....	....	....	....	....	....	....	....
	Chicago Wolves	AHL	71	16	18	34	24	....	....	....	....	....	....	....	....	....	5	1	1	2	0	....	....	....	....
2012-13	Chicago Wolves	AHL	66	15	21	36	12	....	....	....	....	....	....	....	....	....	....	....	....	....	....	....	....	....	....
	Vancouver	**NHL**	**1**	**0**	**0**	**0**	**0**	**0**	**0**	**0**	**0**	**0.0**	**–1**	**0**	**0.0**	**12:24**	....	....	....	....	....	....	....	....	....
	NHL Totals		**3**	**0**	**0**	**0**	**0**	**0**	**0**	**0**	**2**	**0.0**		**0**	**0.0**	**7:42**	....	....	....	....	....	....	....	....	....

Traded to **Toronto** by **Chicago** with Kris Versteeg for Viktor Stalberg, Chris Didomenico and Phillipe Paradis, June 30, 2010. Signed as a free agent by **Vancouver**, August 19, 2010. Signed as a free agent by **Gavle**, July 11, 2013.

SYVRET, Danny

(SIHV-reht, DA-nee) **NYR**

Defense. Shoots left. 5'11", 203 lbs. Born, Millgrove, Ont., June 13, 1985. Edmonton's 3rd choice, 81st overall, in 2005 Entry Draft.

Season	Club	League	GP	G	A	Pts	PIM	PP	SH	GW	S	%	+/-	TF	F%	Min	GP	G	A	Pts	PIM	PP	SH	GW	Min
2001-02	Cambridge	ON-Jr.B	43	6	41	47	23	....	....	....	....	....	....	....	....	....	....	....	....	....	....	....	....	....	....
	London Knights	OHL	1	0	0	0	0	....	....	....	....	....	....	....	....	....	....	....	....	....	....	....	....	....	....
2002-03	London Knights	OHL	68	8	14	22	31	....	....	....	....	....	....	....	....	....	14	1	6	7	11	....	....	....	....
2003-04	London Knights	OHL	68	3	28	31	32	....	....	....	....	....	....	....	....	....	15	1	6	7	4	....	....	....	....
2004-05	London Knights	OHL	62	23	46	69	33	....	....	....	....	....	....	....	....	....	18	5	15	20	4	....	....	....	....
2005-06	**Edmonton**	**NHL**	**10**	**0**	**0**	**0**	**6**	**0**	**0**	**0**	**8**	**0.0**	**–1**	**0**	**0.0**	**12:19**	....	....	....	....	....	....	....	....	....
	Hamilton	AHL	62	0	20	20	38	....	....	....	....	....	....	....	....	....	....	....	....	....	....	....	....	....	....
2006-07	**Edmonton**	**NHL**	**16**	**0**	**1**	**1**	**6**	**0**	**0**	**0**	**15**	**0.0**	**–10**	**0**	**0.0**	**18:28**	....	....	....	....	....	....	....	....	....
	Grand Rapids	AHL	57	4	16	20	16	....	....	....	....	....	....	....	....	....	....	....	....	....	....	....	....	....	....
2007-08	Springfield	AHL	36	1	7	8	14	....	....	....	....	....	....	....	....	....	....	....	....	....	....	....	....	....	....
	Hershey Bears	AHL	27	1	11	12	29	....	....	....	....	....	....	....	....	....	5	0	0	0	0	....	....	....	....
2008-09	**Philadelphia**	**NHL**	**2**	**0**	**0**	**0**	**0**	**0**	**0**	**0**	**0**	**0.0**	**–1**	**0**	**0.0**	**9:26**	....	....	....	....	....	....	....	....	....
	Philadelphia	AHL	76	12	45	57	44	....	....	....	....	....	....	....	....	....	4	0	1	1	0	....	....	....	....
2009-10	**Philadelphia**	**NHL**	**21**	**2**	**2**	**4**	**12**	**0**	**0**	**0**	**14**	**14.3**	**1**	**0**	**0.0**	**12:29**	....	....	....	....	....	....	....	....	....
	Adirondack	AHL	15	5	8	13	6	....	....	....	....	....	....	....	....	....	....	....	....	....	....	....	....	....	....
2010-11	**Anaheim**	**NHL**	**6**	**1**	**1**	**2**	**4**	**0**	**0**	**0**	**8**	**12.5**	**–3**	**0**	**0.0**	**16:27**	....	....	....	....	....	....	....	....	....
	Syracuse Crunch	AHL	8	0	4	4	11	....	....	....	....	....	....	....	....	....	....	....	....	....	....	....	....	....	....
	Philadelphia	**NHL**	**4**	**0**	**0**	**0**	**2**	**0**	**0**	**0**	**3**	**0.0**	**0**	**0**	**0.0**	**12:58**	**10**	**0**	**0**	**0**	**0**	**0**	**0**	**0**	**6:49**
	Adirondack	AHL	51	10	26	36	27	....	....	....	....	....	....	....	....	....	....	....	....	....	....	....	....	....	....
2011-12	Peoria Rivermen	AHL	75	7	35	42	24	....	....	....	....	....	....	....	....	....	....	....	....	....	....	....	....	....	....
2012-13	Adirondack	AHL	76	6	34	40	34	....	....	....	....	....	....	....	....	....	....	....	....	....	....	....	....	....	....
	NHL Totals		**59**	**3**	**4**	**7**	**30**	**0**	**0**	**0**	**48**	**6.3**		**0**	**0.0**	**14:24**	**10**	**0**	**0**	**0**	**0**	**0**	**0**	**0**	**6:49**

OHL First All-Star Team (2005) • Canadian Major Junior Defenseman of the Year (2005) • Canadian Major Junior First All-Star Team (2005) • Memorial Cup All-Star Team.. (2005) • AHL First All-Star Team (2009)

Traded to **Philadelphia** by **Edmonton** for Ryan Potulny, June 6, 2008. • Missed majority of 2009-10 due to upper-body injury and as a healthy reserve. Signed as a free agent by **Anaheim**, July 21, 2010. Traded to **Philadelphia** by **Anaheim** with Rob Bordson for Patrick Maroon and David Laliberte, November 21, 2010. Signed as a free agent by **St. Louis**, August 8, 2011. Signed as a free agent by **Philadelphia**, July 3, 2012. Traded to **NY Rangers** by **Philadelphia** for Kris Newbury, July 1, 2013.

Season	Club	League	Regular Season														Playoffs								
			GP	G	A	Pts	PIM	PP	SH	GW	S	%	+/-	TF	F%	Min	GP	G	A	Pts	PIM	PP	SH	GW	Min

SZCZECHURA, Paul

(sha-HUR-uh, PAWL)

Right wing. Shoots right. 5'10", 186 lbs. Born, Brantford, Ont., November 30, 1985.

Season	Club	League	GP	G	A	Pts	PIM	PP	SH	GW	S	%	+/-	TF	F%	Min	GP	G	A	Pts	PIM	PP	SH	GW	Min
2003-04	Western Mich.	CCHA	39	9	11	20	12	....	....	....	....	....	....	....	....	....	....	....	....	....	....	....	....	....	....
2004-05	Western Mich.	CCHA	37	6	23	29	22	....	....	....	....	....	....	....	....	....	....	....	....	....	....	....	....	....	....
2005-06	Western Mich.	CCHA	40	10	26	36	47	....	....	....	....	....	....	....	....	....	....	....	....	....	....	....	....	....	....
2006-07	Western Mich.	CCHA	37	19	26	45	26	....	....	....	....	....	....	....	....	....	....	....	....	....	....	....	....	....	....
	Iowa Stars	AHL	14	3	4	7	19	....	....	....	....	....	....	....	....	....	10	3	1	4	8	....	....	....	....
2007-08	Iowa Stars	AHL	29	2	3	5	15	....	....	....	....	....	....	....	....	....	....	....	....	....	....	....	....	....	....
	Norfolk Admirals	AHL	24	14	12	26	16	....	....	....	....	....	....	....	....	....	....	....	....	....	....	....	....	....	....
2008-09	**Tampa Bay**	**NHL**	**31**	**4**	**5**	**9**	**12**	**1**	**0**	**0**	**51**	**7.8**	**–1**	**232**	**40.5**	**13:33**	....	....	....	....	....	....	....	....	....
	Norfolk Admirals	AHL	33	13	16	29	26	....	....	....	....	....	....	....	....	....	....	....	....	....	....	....	....	....	....
2009-10	**Tampa Bay**	**NHL**	**52**	**5**	**2**	**7**	**18**	**1**	**0**	**1**	**83**	**6.0**	**–15**	**403**	**46.2**	**13:05**	....	....	....	....	....	....	....	....	....
	Norfolk Admirals	AHL	35	8	21	29	24	....	....	....	....	....	....	....	....	....	....	....	....	....	....	....	....	....	....
2010-11	Norfolk Admirals	AHL	79	21	30	51	43	....	....	....	....	....	....	....	....	....	3	1	0	1	4	....	....	....	....
2011-12	**Buffalo**	**NHL**	**9**	**1**	**3**	**4**	**4**	**0**	**0**	**0**	**11**	**9.1**	**0**	**67**	**41.8**	**11:26**	....	....	....	....	....	....	....	....	....
	Rochester	AHL	57	21	25	46	26	....	....	....	....	....	....	....	....	....	3	0	1	1	0	....	....	....	....
2012-13	HC Lev Praha	KHL	3	0	0	0	2	....	....	....	....	....	....	....	....	....	....	....	....	....	....	....	....	....	....
	Dynamo Riga	KHL	43	8	20	28	18	....	....	....	....	....	....	....	....	....	13	5	7	12	18	....	....	....	....
	NHL Totals		**92**	**10**	**10**	**20**	**34**	**2**	**0**	**1**	**145**	**6.9**		**702**	**43.9**	**13:05**	....	....	....	....	....	....	....	....	....

Signed as a free agent by **Tampa Bay**, April 24, 2008. Signed as a free agent by **Buffalo**, August 9, 2011. Signed as a free agent by **Lev Praha** (KHL), May 24, 2012. Signed as a free agent by **Riga** (KHL), September 26, 2012.

TAFFE, Jeff

(TAYF, JEHF)

Center. Shoots left. 6'3", 207 lbs. Born, Hastings, MN, February 19, 1981. St. Louis' 1st choice, 30th overall, in 2000 Entry Draft.

Season	Club	League	GP	G	A	Pts	PIM	PP	SH	GW	S	%	+/-	TF	F%	Min	GP	G	A	Pts	PIM	PP	SH	GW	Min
1996-97	Hastings Raiders	High-MN	25	21	37	58	....	....	....	....	....	....	....	....	....	....	....	....	....	....	....	....	....	....	....
1997-98	Hastings Raiders	High-MN	28	37	29	66	....	....	....	....	....	....	....	....	....	....	....	....	....	....	....	....	....	....	....
1998-99	Hastings Raiders	High-MN	28	39	51	90	....	....	....	....	....	....	....	....	....	....	....	....	....	....	....	....	....	....	....
	Rochester	USHL	17	12	9	21	26	....	....	....	....	....	....	....	....	....	....	....	....	....	....	....	....	....	....
99-2000	U. of Minnesota	WCHA	39	10	10	20	22	....	....	....	....	....	....	....	....	....	....	....	....	....	....	....	....	....	....
2000-01	U. of Minnesota	WCHA	38	12	23	35	56	....	....	....	....	....	....	....	....	....	....	....	....	....	....	....	....	....	....
2001-02	U. of Minnesota	WCHA	43	34	24	58	86	....	....	....	....	....	....	....	....	....	....	....	....	....	....	....	....	....	....
2002-03	**Phoenix**	**NHL**	**20**	**3**	**1**	**4**	**4**	**1**	**0**	**1**	**18**	**16.7**	**–4**	**113**	**29.2**	**11:34**	....	....	....	....	....	....	....	....	....
	Springfield	AHL	57	23	26	49	44	....	....	....	....	....	....	....	....	....	5	0	3	3	8	....	....	....	....
2003-04	**Phoenix**	**NHL**	**59**	**8**	**10**	**18**	**20**	**5**	**0**	**0**	**67**	**11.9**	**–8**	**219**	**43.4**	**11:02**	....	....	....	....	....	....	....	....	....
	Springfield	AHL	15	10	6	16	19	....	....	....	....	....	....	....	....	....	....	....	....	....	....	....	....	....	....
2004-05	Utah Grizzlies	AHL	27	9	10	19	35	....	....	....	....	....	....	....	....	....	....	....	....	....	....	....	....	....	....
2005-06	**NY Rangers**	**NHL**	**2**	**0**	**0**	**0**	**0**	**0**	**0**	**0**	**1**	**0.0**	**0**	**0**	**0.0**	**3:49**	....	....	....	....	....	....	....	....	....
	Hartford	AHL	36	6	16	22	34	....	....	....	....	....	....	....	....	....	....	....	....	....	....	....	....	....	....
	Phoenix	**NHL**	**2**	**0**	**0**	**0**	**0**	**0**	**0**	**0**	**2**	**0.0**	**0**	**1**	**100.0**	**9:06**	....	....	....	....	....	....	....	....	....
	San Antonio	AHL	33	5	6	11	29	....	....	....	....	....	....	....	....	....	....	....	....	....	....	....	....	....	....
2006-07	**Phoenix**	**NHL**	**17**	**4**	**2**	**6**	**2**	**1**	**0**	**0**	**34**	**11.8**	**–7**	**64**	**39.1**	**14:12**	....	....	....	....	....	....	....	....	....
	San Antonio	AHL	59	20	20	40	22	....	....	....	....	....	....	....	....	....	....	....	....	....	....	....	....	....	....
2007-08	**Pittsburgh**	**NHL**	**45**	**5**	**7**	**12**	**8**	**1**	**0**	**1**	**56**	**8.9**	**2**	**152**	**48.7**	**9:35**	....	....	....	....	....	....	....	....	....
	Wilkes-Barre	AHL	27	11	10	21	22	....	....	....	....	....	....	....	....	....	....	....	....	....	....	....	....	....	....
2008-09	**Pittsburgh**	**NHL**	**8**	**0**	**2**	**2**	**2**	**0**	**0**	**0**	**5**	**0.0**	**–4**	**40**	**52.5**	**8:30**	....	....	....	....	....	....	....	....	....
	Wilkes-Barre	AHL	74	25	50	75	65	....	....	....	....	....	....	....	....	....	12	5	6	11	22	....	....	....	....
2009-10	**Florida**	**NHL**	**21**	**1**	**1**	**2**	**4**	**0**	**0**	**0**	**18**	**5.6**	**–1**	**74**	**44.6**	**8:25**	....	....	....	....	....	....	....	....	....
	Rochester	AHL	61	28	28	56	47	....	....	....	....	....	....	....	....	....	7	1	6	7	9	....	....	....	....
2010-11	**Chicago**	**NHL**	**1**	**0**	**0**	**0**	**0**	**0**	**0**	**0**	**0**	**0.0**	**0**	**5**	**40.0**	**4:05**	....	....	....	....	....	....	....	....	....
	Rockford IceHogs	AHL	74	30	37	67	22	....	....	....	....	....	....	....	....	....	....	....	....	....	....	....	....	....	....
2011-12	**Minnesota**	**NHL**	**5**	**0**	**2**	**2**	**0**	**0**	**0**	**0**	**7**	**0.0**	**2**	**6**	**16.7**	**12:55**	....	....	....	....	....	....	....	....	....
	Houston Aeros	AHL	70	18	35	53	16	....	....	....	....	....	....	....	....	....	4	0	0	0	0	....	....	....	....
2012-13	Hershey Bears	AHL	73	18	*53	71	27	....	....	....	....	....	....	....	....	....	5	0	4	4	2	....	....	....	....
	NHL Totals		**180**	**21**	**25**	**46**	**40**	**8**	**0**	**2**	**208**	**10.1**		**674**	**42.3**	**10:31**	....	....	....	....	....	....	....	....	....

• Rights traded to **Phoenix** by **St. Louis** with Michal Handzus, Ladislav Nagy and St. Louis' 1st round choice (Ben Eager) in 2002 Entry Draft for Keith Tkachuk, March 13, 2001. Traded to **NY Rangers** by **Phoenix** for Jamie Lundmark, October 18, 2005. Traded to **Phoenix** by **NY Rangers** for Martin Sonnenberg, January 24, 2006. Signed as a free agent by **Pittsburgh**, July 13, 2007. Signed as a free agent by **Florida**, July 6, 2009. Traded to **Chicago** by **Florida** for Marty Reasoner, July 22, 2010. Signed as a free agent by **Minnesota**, July 5, 2011. Signed as a free agent by **Hershey** (AHL), July 2, 2012. Signed as a free agent by **Linkoping** (Sweden), May 17, 2013.

TALBOT, Maxime

(TAL-buht, max-EEM) **PHI**

Center. Shoots left. 5'11", 190 lbs. Born, Lemoyne, Que., February 11, 1984. Pittsburgh's 9th choice, 234th overall, in 2002 Entry Draft.

Season	Club	League	GP	G	A	Pts	PIM	PP	SH	GW	S	%	+/-	TF	F%	Min	GP	G	A	Pts	PIM	PP	SH	GW	Min
99-2000	Antoine-Girouard	QAAA	42	19	21	40	32	....	....	....	....	....	....	....	....	....	7	3	6	9	0	....	....	....	....
2000-01	Rouyn-Noranda	QMJHL	40	9	15	24	78	....	....	....	....	....	....	....	....	....	....	....	....	....	....	....	....	....	....
	Hull Olympiques	QMJHL	24	6	7	13	60	....	....	....	....	....	....	....	....	....	5	1	0	1	2	....	....	....	....
2001-02	Hull Olympiques	QMJHL	65	24	36	60	174	....	....	....	....	....	....	....	....	....	12	4	6	10	51	....	....	....	....
2002-03	Hull Olympiques	QMJHL	69	46	58	104	130	....	....	....	....	....	....	....	....	....	20	14	*30	*44	33	....	....	....	....
2003-04	Gatineau	QMJHL	51	25	73	98	41	....	....	....	....	....	....	....	....	....	15	*11	*16	*27	0	....	....	....	....
2004-05	Wilkes-Barre	AHL	75	7	12	19	62	....	....	....	....	....	....	....	....	....	11	0	1	1	22	....	....	....	....
2005-06	**Pittsburgh**	**NHL**	**48**	**5**	**3**	**8**	**59**	**0**	**2**	**1**	**45**	**11.1**	**–12**	**473**	**42.9**	**10:58**	....	....	....	....	....	....	....	....	....
	Wilkes-Barre	AHL	42	12	20	32	80	....	....	....	....	....	....	....	....	....	11	3	6	9	16	....	....	....	....
2006-07	**Pittsburgh**	**NHL**	**75**	**13**	**11**	**24**	**53**	**0**	**4**	**4**	**88**	**14.8**	**–2**	**903**	**44.4**	**13:54**	**5**	**0**	**1**	**1**	**7**	**0**	**0**	**0**	**15:51**
	Wilkes-Barre	AHL	5	4	0	4	2	....	....	....	....	....	....	....	....	....	....	....	....	....	....	....	....	....	....
2007-08	**Pittsburgh**	**NHL**	**63**	**12**	**14**	**26**	**53**	**0**	**2**	**1**	**80**	**15.0**	**8**	**513**	**45.0**	**15:28**	**17**	**3**	**6**	**9**	**36**	**0**	**0**	**1**	**14:27**
2008-09 ♦	**Pittsburgh**	**NHL**	**75**	**12**	**10**	**22**	**63**	**0**	**2**	**1**	**102**	**11.8**	**–9**	**542**	**51.1**	**14:08**	**24**	**8**	**5**	**13**	**19**	**0**	**0**	**2**	**15:14**
2009-10	**Pittsburgh**	**NHL**	**45**	**2**	**5**	**7**	**30**	**0**	**0**	**0**	**49**	**4.1**	**–9**	**165**	**41.2**	**12:13**	**13**	**2**	**4**	**6**	**11**	**0**	**1**	**1**	**14:15**
2010-11	**Pittsburgh**	**NHL**	**82**	**8**	**13**	**21**	**66**	**0**	**2**	**2**	**117**	**6.8**	**–3**	**874**	**48.6**	**15:04**	**7**	**1**	**3**	**4**	**14**	**0**	**0**	**0**	**16:53**
2011-12	**Philadelphia**	**NHL**	**81**	**19**	**15**	**34**	**59**	**1**	**2**	**2**	**115**	**16.5**	**5**	**640**	**44.4**	**16:00**	**11**	**4**	**2**	**6**	**10**	**1**	***2**	**0**	**17:02**
2012-13	Ilves Tampere	Finland	12	3	3	6	34	....	....	....	....	....	....	....	....	....	....	....	....	....	....	....	....	....	....
	Philadelphia	**NHL**	**35**	**5**	**5**	**10**	**23**	**0**	**1**	**0**	**41**	**12.2**	**2**	**192**	**47.9**	**15:26**	....	....	....	....	....	....	....	....	....
	NHL Totals		**504**	**76**	**76**	**152**	**406**	**1**	**15**	**11**	**637**	**11.9**		**4302**	**46.0**	**14:20**	**77**	**18**	**21**	**39**	**97**	**1**	**3**	**4**	**15:20**

QMJHL Second All-Star Team (2003, 2004)

Signed as a free agent by **Philadelphia**, July 1, 2011. Signed as a free agent by **Ilves Tampere** (Finland), November 7, 2012.

TALLINDER, Henrik

(tah-LIHN-duhr, HEHN-rihk) **BUF**

Defense. Shoots left. 6'4", 215 lbs. Born, Stockholm, Sweden, January 10, 1979. Buffalo's 2nd choice, 48th overall, in 1997 Entry Draft.

Season	Club	League	GP	G	A	Pts	PIM	PP	SH	GW	S	%	+/-	TF	F%	Min	GP	G	A	Pts	PIM	PP	SH	GW	Min
1996-97	AIK Solna Jr.	Swe-Jr.	40	4	13	17	55	....	....	....	....	....	....	....	....	....	....	....	....	....	....	....	....	....	....
	AIK Solna	Sweden	1	0	0	0	0	....	....	....	....	....	....	....	....	....	....	....	....	....	....	....	....	....	....
1997-98	AIK Solna	Sweden	34	0	0	0	26	....	....	....	....	....	....	....	....	....	....	....	....	....	....	....	....	....	....
1998-99	AIK Solna	Sweden	36	0	0	0	30	....	....	....	....	....	....	....	....	....	....	....	....	....	....	....	....	....	....
99-2000	AIK Solna	Sweden	50	0	2	2	59	....	....	....	....	....	....	....	....	....	....	....	....	....	....	....	....	....	....
2000-01	TPS Turku	Finland	56	5	9	14	62	....	....	....	....	....	....	....	....	....	10	2	1	3	8	....	....	....	....
2001-02	**Buffalo**	**NHL**	**2**	**0**	**0**	**0**	**0**	**0**	**0**	**0**	**4**	**0.0**	**–1**	**0**	**0.0**	**18:10**	....	....	....	....	....	....	....	....	....
	Rochester	AHL	73	6	14	20	26	....	....	....	....	....	....	....	....	....	2	0	0	0	0	....	....	....	....
2002-03	**Buffalo**	**NHL**	**46**	**3**	**10**	**13**	**28**	**1**	**0**	**0**	**37**	**8.1**	**–3**	**0**	**0.0**	**19:53**	....	....	....	....	....	....	....	....	....
2003-04	**Buffalo**	**NHL**	**72**	**1**	**9**	**10**	**26**	**0**	**0**	**0**	**63**	**1.6**	**5**	**1**	**0.0**	**18:23**	....	....	....	....	....	....	....	....	....
2004-05	Linkopings HC	Sweden	44	6	10	16	63	....	....	....	....	....	....	....	....	....	....	....	....	....	....	....	....	....	....
	SC Bern	Swiss	....	....	....	....	....	....	....	....	....	....	....	....	....	....	10	1	1	2	4	....	....	....	....
2005-06	**Buffalo**	**NHL**	**82**	**6**	**15**	**21**	**74**	**0**	**1**	**1**	**79**	**7.6**	**10**	**0**	**0.0**	**20:21**	**14**	**2**	**6**	**8**	**16**	**0**	**0**	**0**	**22:16**
2006-07	**Buffalo**	**NHL**	**47**	**4**	**10**	**14**	**34**	**0**	**0**	**0**	**34**	**11.8**	**19**	**1**	**0.0**	**21:07**	**16**	**0**	**2**	**2**	**10**	**0**	**0**	**0**	**23:40**
2007-08	**Buffalo**	**NHL**	**71**	**1**	**17**	**18**	**48**	**0**	**0**	**0**	**70**	**1.4**	**5**	**0**	**0.0**	**21:02**	....	....	....	....	....	....	....	....	....
2008-09	**Buffalo**	**NHL**	**66**	**1**	**11**	**12**	**36**	**0**	**0**	**1**	**35**	**2.9**	**–2**	**0**	**0.0**	**18:26**	....	....	....	....	....	....	....	....	....
2009-10	**Buffalo**	**NHL**	**82**	**4**	**16**	**20**	**32**	**0**	**0**	**0**	**53**	**7.5**	**13**	**0**	**0.0**	**20:37**	**6**	**0**	**2**	**2**	**2**	**0**	**0**	**0**	**22:41**
	Sweden	Olympics	4	0	0	0	4	....	....	....	....	....	....	....	....	....	....	....	....	....	....	....	....	....	....
2010-11	**New Jersey**	**NHL**	**82**	**5**	**11**	**16**	**40**	**0**	**1**	**2**	**102**	**4.9**	**–6**	**0**	**0.0**	**22:32**	....	....	....	....	....	....	....	....	....

			Regular Season														Playoffs								
Season	Club	League	GP	G	A	Pts	PIM	PP	SH	GW	S	%	+/-	TF	F%	Min	GP	G	A	Pts	PIM	PP	SH	GW	Min
2011-12	New Jersey	NHL	39	0	6	6	16	0	0	0	43	0.0	–11	0	0.0	21:19	3	0	0	0	0	0	0	0	19:16
2012-13	New Jersey	NHL	25	1	3	4	10	0	0	0	22	4.5	0	0	0.0	17:34	....	....	....	....	....	....	....	....	....
	NHL Totals		614	26	108	134	344	1	2	4	542	4.8		2	0.0	20:17	39	2	10	12	28	0	0	0	22:40

Signed as a free agent by **Linkopings** (Sweden), September 9, 2004. Signed as a free agent by **Bern** (Swiss), February 22, 2005. Signed as a free agent by **New Jersey**, July 1, 2010. • Missed majority of 2011-12 due to leg injury vs. Winnipeg, January 17, 2012. Traded to **Buffalo** by **New Jersey** for Riley Boychuk, July 7, 2013.

TANEV, Chris

(TA-nehv, KRIHS) **VAN**

Defense. Shoots right. 6'2", 185 lbs. Born, Toronto, Ont., December 20, 1989.

Season	Club	League	GP	G	A	Pts	PIM	PP	SH	GW	S	%	+/-	TF	F%	Min	GP	G	A	Pts	PIM	PP	SH	GW	Min
2006-07	Durham Fury	ON-Jr.A	40	0	9	9	8	....	....	....	....	....	....	....	....	....	4	0	3	3	6	....	....	....	....
2007-08	Durham Fury	ON-Jr.A	19	1	6	7	12	....	....	....	....	....	....	....	....	....	....	....	....	....	....	....	....	....	....
	Stouffville Spirit	ON-Jr.A	4	0	0	0	0	....	....	....	....	....	....	....	....	....	....	....	....	....	....	....	....	....	....
	Markham Waxers	ON-Jr.A	26	1	9	10	12	....	....	....	....	....	....	....	....	....	23	1	2	3	4	....	....	....	....
2008-09	Markham Waxers	ON-Jr.A	50	4	37	41	33	....	....	....	....	....	....	....	....	....	14	1	5	6	8	....	....	....	....
2009-10	RIT Tigers	AH	41	10	18	28	4	....	....	....	....	....	....	....	....	....	....	....	....	....	....	....	....	....	....
2010-11	**Vancouver**	**NHL**	29	0	1	1	0	0	0	0	15	0.0	0	0	0.0	13:47	5	0	0	0	0	0	0	0	14:40
	Manitoba Moose	AHL	39	1	8	9	16	....	....	....	....	....	....	....	....	....	14	1	2	3	4	....	....	....	....
2011-12	**Vancouver**	**NHL**	25	0	2	2	2	0	0	0	15	0.0	10	0	0.0	16:43	5	0	0	0	0	0	0	0	15:11
	Chicago Wolves	AHL	34	0	14	14	6	....	....	....	....	....	....	....	....	....	....	....	....	....	....	....	....	....	....
2012-13	Chicago Wolves	AHL	29	2	10	12	6	....	....	....	....	....	....	....	....	....	....	....	....	....	....	....	....	....	....
	Vancouver	**NHL**	38	2	5	7	10	0	0	1	20	10.0	4	0	0.0	17:17	....	....	....	....	....	....	....	....	....
	NHL Totals		92	2	8	10	12	0	0	1	50	4.0		0	0.0	16:02	10	0	0	0	0	0	0	0	14:55

Signed as a free agent by **Vancouver**, May 31, 2010.

TANGRADI, Eric

(tan-GRAY-dee, AIR-ihk) **WPG**

Center. Shoots left. 6'4", 221 lbs. Born, Philadelphia, PA, February 10, 1989. Anaheim's 2nd choice, 42nd overall, in 2007 Entry Draft.

Season	Club	League	GP	G	A	Pts	PIM	PP	SH	GW	S	%	+/-	TF	F%	Min	GP	G	A	Pts	PIM	PP	SH	GW	Min
2005-06	Wyoming Prep	High-PA	38	21	23	44	120	....	....	....	....	....	....	....	....	....	....	....	....	....	....	....	....	....	....
2006-07	Belleville Bulls	OHL	65	5	15	20	32	....	....	....	....	....	....	....	....	....	15	8	9	17	14	....	....	....	....
2007-08	Belleville Bulls	OHL	56	24	36	60	41	....	....	....	....	....	....	....	....	....	21	7	11	18	20	....	....	....	....
2008-09	Belleville Bulls	OHL	55	38	50	88	61	....	....	....	....	....	....	....	....	....	16	8	13	21	12	....	....	....	....
2009-10	**Pittsburgh**	**NHL**	1	0	0	0	0	0	0	0	3	0.0	0	0	0.0	13:49	....	....	....	....	....	....	....	....	....
	Wilkes-Barre	AHL	65	17	22	39	31	....	....	....	....	....	....	....	....	....	4	1	1	2	6	....	....	....	....
2010-11	**Pittsburgh**	**NHL**	15	1	2	3	10	0	0	0	18	5.6	–4	3	33.3	11:12	1	0	0	0	0	0	0	0	15:12
	Wilkes-Barre	AHL	42	18	15	33	86	....	....	....	....	....	....	....	....	....	....	....	....	....	....	....	....	....	....
2011-12	**Pittsburgh**	**NHL**	24	0	2	2	16	0	0	0	20	0.0	–4	2	0.0	8:56	2	0	1	1	0	0	0	0	8:07
	Wilkes-Barre	AHL	37	15	16	31	40	....	....	....	....	....	....	....	....	....	10	4	5	9	14	....	....	....	....
2012-13	Wilkes-Barre	AHL	34	10	8	18	57	....	....	....	....	....	....	....	....	....	....	....	....	....	....	....	....	....	....
	Pittsburgh	**NHL**	5	0	0	0	0	0	0	0	4	0.0	2	0	0.0	8:32	....	....	....	....	....	....	....	....	....
	Winnipeg	**NHL**	36	1	3	4	22	0	0	0	44	2.3	–4	2	0.0	10:18	....	....	....	....	....	....	....	....	....
	NHL Totals		81	2	7	9	48	0	0	0	89	2.2		7	14.3	10:00	3	0	1	1	0	0	0	0	10:29

Traded to **Pittsburgh** by **Anaheim** with Chris Kunitz for Ryan Whitney, February 26, 2009. Traded to **Winnipeg** by **Pittsburgh** for Winnipeg's 6th round choice (Dane Birks) in 2013 Entry Draft, February 13, 2013.

TANGUAY, Alex

(TAHNG-ay, AL-ehx) **COL**

Left wing. Shoots left. 6'1", 194 lbs. Born, Ste-Justine, Que., November 21, 1979. Colorado's 1st choice, 12th overall, in 1998 Entry Draft.

Season	Club	League	GP	G	A	Pts	PIM	PP	SH	GW	S	%	+/-	TF	F%	Min	GP	G	A	Pts	PIM	PP	SH	GW	Min
1994-95	Cap-d-Madeleine	QAAA	1	0	1	1	0	....	....	....	....	....	....	....	....	....	....	....	....	....	....	....	....	....	....
1995-96	Cap-d-Madeleine	QAAA	44	29	34	63	64	....	....	....	....	....	....	....	....	....	5	2	4	6	14	....	....	....	....
1996-97	Halifax	QMJHL	70	27	41	68	50	....	....	....	....	....	....	....	....	....	12	4	8	12	8	....	....	....	....
1997-98	Halifax	QMJHL	51	47	38	85	32	....	....	....	....	....	....	....	....	....	5	7	6	13	4	....	....	....	....
1998-99	Halifax	QMJHL	31	27	34	61	30	....	....	....	....	....	....	....	....	....	5	1	2	3	2	....	....	....	....
	Hershey Bears	AHL	5	1	2	3	2	....	....	....	....	....	....	....	....	....	5	0	2	2	0	....	....	....	....
99-2000	**Colorado**	**NHL**	76	17	34	51	22	5	0	3	74	23.0	6	11	45.5	15:38	17	2	1	3	2	1	0	1	10:49
2000-01 ♦	**Colorado**	**NHL**	82	27	50	77	37	7	1	3	135	20.0	35	30	43.3	17:51	23	6	15	21	8	1	0	2	19:18
2001-02	**Colorado**	**NHL**	70	13	35	48	36	7	0	2	90	14.4	8	37	40.5	18:20	19	5	8	13	0	3	0	0	17:25
2002-03	**Colorado**	**NHL**	82	26	41	67	36	3	0	5	142	18.3	34	123	39.0	17:48	7	1	2	3	4	0	0	1	19:06
2003-04	**Colorado**	**NHL**	69	25	54	79	42	7	0	5	117	21.4	30	71	40.9	18:21	8	2	2	4	2	1	0	1	15:46
2004-05	HC Lugano	Swiss	6	3	3	6	4	....	....	....	....	....	....	....	....	....	....	....	....	....	....	....	....	....	....
2005-06	**Colorado**	**NHL**	71	29	49	78	46	8	0	4	125	23.2	8	20	30.0	18:22	9	2	4	6	12	0	0	1	18:20
2006-07	**Calgary**	**NHL**	81	22	59	81	44	5	0	0	107	20.6	12	24	25.0	17:40	6	1	3	4	8	1	0	0	17:56
2007-08	**Calgary**	**NHL**	78	18	40	58	48	3	2	3	121	14.9	11	20	35.0	18:46	7	0	4	4	4	0	0	0	18:15
2008-09	**Montreal**	**NHL**	50	16	25	41	34	5	0	3	76	21.1	13	9	33.3	16:05	2	0	1	1	2	0	0	0	15:29
2009-10	**Tampa Bay**	**NHL**	80	10	27	37	32	3	0	2	91	11.0	–2	25	44.0	15:47	....	....	....	....	....	....	....	....	....
2010-11	**Calgary**	**NHL**	79	22	47	69	24	3	0	2	120	18.3	0	107	39.3	19:46	....	....	....	....	....	....	....	....	....
2011-12	**Calgary**	**NHL**	64	13	36	49	28	1	1	3	84	15.5	7	67	37.3	19:03	....	....	....	....	....	....	....	....	....
2012-13	**Calgary**	**NHL**	40	11	16	27	22	2	1	1	44	25.0	–13	173	39.3	19:22	....	....	....	....	....	....	....	....	....
	NHL Totals		922	249	513	762	451	59	5	36	1326	18.8		717	38.8	17:53	98	19	40	59	42	7	0	6	16:50

QMJHL All-Rookie Team (1997)
Played in NHL All-Star Game (2004)

Signed as a free agent by **Lugano** (Swiss), October 7, 2004. Traded to **Calgary** by **Colorado** for Jordan Leopold, Calgary's 2nd round choice (Codey Burki) in 2006 Entry Draft and Calgary's 2nd round choice (Trevor Cann) in 2007 Entry Draft, June 24, 2006. Traded to **Montreal** by **Calgary** with Calgary's 5th round choice (Maxim Trunev) in 2008 Entry Draft for Montreal's 1st round choice (Greg Nemisz) in 2008 Entry Draft and Montreal's 2nd round choice (later traded to Colorado – Colorado selected Stefan Elliott) in 2009 Entry Draft, June 20, 2008. Signed as a free agent by **Tampa Bay**, September 1, 2009. Signed as a free agent by **Calgary**, July 1, 2010. Traded to **Colorado** by **Calgary** with Cory Sarich for David Jones and Shane O'Brien, June 27, 2013.

TAORMINA, Matt

(tah'ohr-MEE-nah, MAT) **T.B.**

Defense. Shoots left. 5'10", 182 lbs. Born, Warren, MI, October 20, 1986.

Season	Club	League	GP	G	A	Pts	PIM	PP	SH	GW	S	%	+/-	TF	F%	Min	GP	G	A	Pts	PIM	PP	SH	GW	Min
2004-05	Texarkana Bandits	NAHL	52	14	30	44	44	....	....	....	....	....	....	....	....	....	9	3	3	6	6	....	....	....	....
2005-06	Providence	H-East	36	1	10	11	16	....	....	....	....	....	....	....	....	....	....	....	....	....	....	....	....	....	....
2006-07	Providence	H-East	35	5	2	7	6	....	....	....	....	....	....	....	....	....	....	....	....	....	....	....	....	....	....
2007-08	Providence	H-East	36	9	18	27	12	....	....	....	....	....	....	....	....	....	....	....	....	....	....	....	....	....	....
2008-09	Providence	H-East	34	5	15	20	16	....	....	....	....	....	....	....	....	....	....	....	....	....	....	....	....	....	....
	Binghamton	AHL	11	2	3	5	4	....	....	....	....	....	....	....	....	....	....	....	....	....	....	....	....	....	....
2009-10	Lowell Devils	AHL	75	10	40	50	45	....	....	....	....	....	....	....	....	....	5	1	3	4	4	....	....	....	....
2010-11	**New Jersey**	**NHL**	17	3	2	5	2	1	0	0	38	7.9	–2	0	0.0	20:40	....	....	....	....	....	....	....	....	....
2011-12	**New Jersey**	**NHL**	30	1	6	7	4	0	0	0	33	3.0	6	0	0.0	16:32	....	....	....	....	....	....	....	....	....
	Albany Devils	AHL	33	6	10	16	12	....	....	....	....	....	....	....	....	....	....	....	....	....	....	....	....	....	....
2012-13	Syracuse Crunch	AHL	55	4	20	24	21	....	....	....	....	....	....	....	....	....	18	2	10	12	4	....	....	....	....
	Tampa Bay	**NHL**	2	0	0	0	0	0	0	0	0	0.0	–1	0	0.0	16:39	....	....	....	....	....	....	....	....	....
	NHL Totals		49	4	8	12	6	1	0	0	71	5.6		0	0.0	17:58	....	....	....	....	....	....	....	....	....

Signed as a free agent by **Binghamton** (AHL), March 10, 2009. Signed as a free agent by **Lowell** (AHL), August 14, 2009. Signed as a free agent by **New Jersey**, February 26, 2010. • Missed majority of 2010-11 due to ankle injury at Boston, November 15, 2010. Signed as a free agent by **Tampa Bay**, July 6, 2012.

TARASENKO, Vladimir

(ta-rah-SEHN-koh, vla-DIH-meer) **ST.L.**

Right wing. Shoots left. 6', 219 lbs. Born, Yaroslavl, USSR, December 13, 1991. St. Louis' 2nd choice, 16th overall, in 2010 Entry Draft.

Season	Club	League	GP	G	A	Pts	PIM	PP	SH	GW	S	%	+/-	TF	F%	Min	GP	G	A	Pts	PIM	PP	SH	GW	Min
2007-08	Sibir Novosibirsk 2	Russia-3	17	6	4	10	2	....	....	....	....	....	....	....	....	....	....	....	....	....	....	....	....	....	....
2008-09	Sibir Novosibirsk 2	Russia-3	STATISTICS NOT AVAILABLE																						
	Sibir Novosibirsk	KHL	38	7	3	10	2	....	....	....	....	....	....	....	....	....	....	....	....	....	....	....	....	....	....
2009-10	Novosibirsk Jr.	Russia-Jr.	1	1	0	1	0	....	....	....	....	....	....	....	....	....	....	....	....	....	....	....	....	....	....
	Sibir Novosibirsk	KHL	42	13	11	24	18	....	....	....	....	....	....	....	....	....	....	....	....	....	....	....	....	....	....
2010-11	Sibir Novosibirsk	KHL	42	9	10	19	8	....	....	....	....	....	....	....	....	....	3	0	0	0	0	....	....	....	....
	Novosibirsk Jr.	Russia-Jr.	3	2	2	4	2	....	....	....	....	....	....	....	....	....	....	....	....	....	....	....	....	....	....
2011-12	Sibir Novosibirsk	KHL	39	18	20	38	15	....	....	....	....	....	....	....	....	....	....	....	....	....	....	....	....	....	....
	St. Petersburg	KHL	15	5	4	9	0	....	....	....	....	....	....	....	....	....	15	10	6	16	6	....	....	....	....

Season	Club	League	GP	G	A	Pts	PIM	PP	SH	GW	S	%	+/-	TF	F%	Min	GP	G	A	Pts	PIM	PP	SH	GW	Min
			Regular Season														Playoffs								
2012-13	St. Petersburg	KHL	31	14	18	32	8	....	....	....	....	....	....	....	....	....	....	....	....	....	....	....	....	....	....
	St. Louis	NHL	38	8	11	19	10	3	0	1	75	10.7	1	1	100.0	13:25	1	0	0	0	0	0	0	0	5:51
	NHL Totals		38	8	11	19	10	3	0	1	75	10.7		1	100.0	13:25	1	0	0	0	0	0	0	0	5:51

Signed as a free agent by **St. Petersburg** (KHL), September 24, 2012.

TARDIF, Jamie
(tahr-DIHF, JAY-mee) **BUF**

Right wing. Shoots right. 6', 205 lbs. Born, Welland, Ont., January 23, 1985. Calgary's 4th choice, 112th overall, in 2003 Entry Draft.

2001-02	Peterborough	OHL	64	22	22	44	30	....	....	....	....	....	....	....	....	....	6	0	1	1	2	....	....	....	....
2002-03	Peterborough	OHL	68	31	29	60	32	....	....	....	....	....	....	....	....	....	7	3	4	7	0	....	....	....	....
2003-04	Peterborough	OHL	64	25	28	53	56	....	....	....	....	....	....	....	....	....	....	....	....	....	....	....	....	....	....
2004-05	Peterborough	OHL	66	37	27	64	84	....	....	....	....	....	....	....	....	....	14	8	3	11	14	....	....	....	....
2005-06	Peterborough	OHL	62	40	29	69	108	....	....	....	....	....	....	....	....	....	19	6	6	12	18	....	....	....	....
2006-07	Toledo Storm	ECHL	34	10	20	30	37	....	....	....	....	....	....	....	....	....	....	....	....	....	....	....	....	....	....
	Manitoba Moose	AHL	1	0	0	0	0	....	....	....	....	....	....	....	....	....	....	....	....	....	....	....	....	....	....
	Iowa Stars	AHL	2	0	0	0	0	....	....	....	....	....	....	....	....	....	....	....	....	....	....	....	....	....	....
	Grand Rapids	AHL	27	9	6	15	18	....	....	....	....	....	....	....	....	....	2	0	0	0	0	....	....	....	....
2007-08	Grand Rapids	AHL	80	17	17	34	90	....	....	....	....	....	....	....	....	....	....	....	....	....	....	....	....	....	....
2008-09	Grand Rapids	AHL	55	9	9	18	43	....	....	....	....	....	....	....	....	....	10	2	0	2	8	....	....	....	....
2009-10	Grand Rapids	AHL	77	16	17	33	90	....	....	....	....	....	....	....	....	....	....	....	....	....	....	....	....	....	....
2010-11	Grand Rapids	AHL	77	27	27	54	81	....	....	....	....	....	....	....	....	....	....	....	....	....	....	....	....	....	....
2011-12	Providence Bruins	AHL	57	15	15	30	28	....	....	....	....	....	....	....	....	....	....	....	....	....	....	....	....	....	....
2012-13	Providence Bruins	AHL	62	30	15	45	48	....	....	....	....	....	....	....	....	....	12	7	4	11	10	....	....	....	....
	Boston	NHL	2	0	0	0	0	0	0	0	1	0.0	0	0	0.0	4:56	....	....	....	....	....	....	....	....	....
	NHL Totals		2	0	0	0	0	0	0	0	1	0.0		0	0.0	4:56	....	....	....	....	....	....	....	....	....

Signed as a free agent by **Toledo** (ECHL), October 5, 2006. Signed to PTO (professional tryout) contract by **Manitoba** (AHL), December 2, 2006. • Loaned to **Iowa** (AHL) by **Toledo** (ECHL), December 29, 2006. Signed as a free agent by **Grand Rapids** (AHL), February 2, 2007. Signed as a free agent by **Detroit** July 26, 2007. Signed as a free agent by **Boston**, July 5, 2011. Signed as a free agent by **Buffalo**, August 6, 2013.

TARNASKY, Nick
(tahr-NAS-kee, NIHK) **MTL**

Center. Shoots left. 6'2", 224 lbs. Born, Rocky Mtn. House, Alta., November 25, 1984. Tampa Bay's 11th choice, 287th overall, in 2003 Entry Draft.

99-2000	Leduc Oil Kings	AMBHL	36	21	11	32	59	....	....	....	....	....	....	....	....	....	....	....	....	....	....	....	....	....	....
2000-01	Leduc Oil Kings	AMHL	35	39	29	68	95	....	....	....	....	....	....	....	....	....	....	....	....	....	....	....	....	....	....
2001-02	Drayton Valley	AJHL	20	7	4	11	10	....	....	....	....	....	....	....	....	....	....	....	....	....	....	....	....	....	....
	Vancouver Giants	WHL	10	1	0	1	5	....	....	....	....	....	....	....	....	....	....	....	....	....	....	....	....	....	....
2002-03	Kelowna Rockets	WHL	39	4	12	16	39	....	....	....	....	....	....	....	....	....	....	....	....	....	....	....	....	....	....
	Lethbridge	WHL	30	5	8	13	45	....	....	....	....	....	....	....	....	....	....	....	....	....	....	....	....	....	....
2003-04	Lethbridge	WHL	71	26	23	49	108	....	....	....	....	....	....	....	....	....	....	....	....	....	....	....	....	....	....
2004-05	Springfield	AHL	80	7	10	17	176	....	....	....	....	....	....	....	....	....	....	....	....	....	....	....	....	....	....
2005-06	Tampa Bay	NHL	12	0	1	1	4	0	0	0	9	0.0	-3	15	40.0	4:40	....	....	....	....	....	....	....	....	....
	Springfield	AHL	68	14	9	23	100	....	....	....	....	....	....	....	....	....	....	....	....	....	....	....	....	....	....
2006-07	Tampa Bay	NHL	77	5	4	9	80	0	0	1	41	12.2	-6	13	30.8	6:30	6	0	0	0	10	0	0	0	6:13
2007-08	Tampa Bay	NHL	80	6	4	10	78	1	0	1	91	6.6	-15	9	44.4	8:15	....	....	....	....	....	....	....	....	....
2008-09	Nashville	NHL	11	0	1	1	17	0	0	0	6	0.0	1	0	0.0	5:38	....	....	....	....	....	....	....	....	....
	Florida	NHL	34	1	5	6	33	0	0	0	32	3.1	-2	1	0.0	7:52	....	....	....	....	....	....	....	....	....
2009-10	Florida	NHL	31	1	2	3	85	0	0	0	19	5.3	-5	0	0.0	6:49	....	....	....	....	....	....	....	....	....
	Rochester	AHL	5	3	0	3	7	....	....	....	....	....	....	....	....	....	....	....	....	....	....	....	....	....	....
2010-11	Florida Everblades	ECHL	3	1	2	3	0	....	....	....	....	....	....	....	....	....	....	....	....	....	....	....	....	....	....
	Springfield	AHL	66	7	13	20	150	....	....	....	....	....	....	....	....	....	....	....	....	....	....	....	....	....	....
2011-12	Vityaz Chekhov	KHL	36	5	7	12	173	....	....	....	....	....	....	....	....	....	....	....	....	....	....	....	....	....	....
2012-13	Rochester	AHL	74	16	10	26	138	....	....	....	....	....	....	....	....	....	3	1	0	1	4	....	....	....	....
	NHL Totals		245	13	17	30	297	1	0	2	198	6.6		38	36.8	7:10	6	0	0	0	10	0	0	0	6:13

Traded to **Nashville** by **Tampa Bay** for Nashville's 6th round choice (Jaroslav Janus) in 2009 Entry Draft, September 29, 2008. Traded to **Florida** by **Nashville** for Wade Belak, November 27, 2008. • Missed majority of 2009-10 due to eye injury in pre-season at Ottawa, September 16, 2009. Signed as a free agent by **Florida** (ECHL), November 5, 2010. Signed to a PTO (professional tryout) contract by **Springfield** (AHL), November 11, 2010. Signed as a free agent by **Chekhov** (KHL), July 3, 2011. Signed as a free agent by **Buffalo**, July 17, 2012. Signed as a free agent by **Montreal**, July 6, 2013.

TATAR, Tomas
(TAH-tahr, TAW-mahsh) **DET**

Center. Shoots left. 5'10", 186 lbs. Born, Ilava, Czech., December 1, 1990. Detroit's 2nd choice, 60th overall, in 2009 Entry Draft.

2004-05	Dubnica U18	Svk-U18	1	0	0	0	0	....	....	....	....	....	....	....	....	....	....	....	....	....	....	....	....	....	....
2005-06	Dubnica U18	Svk-U18	43	11	15	26	18	....	....	....	....	....	....	....	....	....	....	....	....	....	....	....	....	....	....
2006-07	Dubnica Jr.	Slovak-Jr.	6	3	0	3	2	....	....	....	....	....	....	....	....	....	....	....	....	....	....	....	....	....	....
	Dukla Trencin U18	Svk-U18	48	33	44	77	42	....	....	....	....	....	....	....	....	....	....	....	....	....	....	....	....	....	....
2007-08	Dukla Trencin U18	Svk-U18	4	9	4	13	0	....	....	....	....	....	....	....	....	....	....	....	....	....	....	....	....	....	....
	Dukla Trencin Jr.	Slovak-Jr.	42	41	35	76	32	....	....	....	....	....	....	....	....	....	....	....	....	....	....	....	....	....	....
2008-09	HC 07 Detva	Slovak-2	1	1	1	2	2	....	....	....	....	....	....	....	....	....	....	....	....	....	....	....	....	....	....
	HKm Zvolen	Slovakia	48	7	8	15	20	....	....	....	....	....	....	....	....	....	13	5	3	8	4	....	....	....	....
2009-10	Grand Rapids	AHL	58	16	16	32	12	....	....	....	....	....	....	....	....	....	....	....	....	....	....	....	....	....	....
2010-11	Detroit	NHL	9	1	0	1	0	0	0	0	6	16.7	0	0	0.0	9:36	....	....	....	....	....	....	....	....	....
	Grand Rapids	AHL	70	24	33	57	45	....	....	....	....	....	....	....	....	....	....	....	....	....	....	....	....	....	....
2011-12	Grand Rapids	AHL	76	24	34	58	45	....	....	....	....	....	....	....	....	....	....	....	....	....	....	....	....	....	....
2012-13	SHK 37 Piestany	Slovakia	8	5	5	10	6	....	....	....	....	....	....	....	....	....	....	....	....	....	....	....	....	....	....
	Grand Rapids	AHL	61	23	26	49	50	....	....	....	....	....	....	....	....	....	24	*16	5	21	23	....	....	....	....
	Detroit	NHL	18	4	3	7	4	1	0	0	32	12.5	2	1	100.0	11:22	....	....	....	....	....	....	....	....	....
	NHL Totals		27	5	3	8	4	1	0	0	38	13.2		1	100.0	10:47	....	....	....	....	....	....	....	....	....

Jack A. Butterfield Trophy (AHL - Playoff MVP) (2013)

Signed as a free agent by **Piestany** (Slovakia), September 20, 2012.

TAVARES, John
(tah-VAHR-ehs, JAWN) **NYI**

Center. Shoots left. 6', 199 lbs. Born, Mississauga, Ont., September 20, 1990. NY Islanders' 1st choice, 1st overall, in 2009 Entry Draft.

2004-05	Tor. Marlboros	GTHL	72	91	67	158	....	....	....	....	....	....	....	....	....	....	....	....	....	....	....	....	....	....	....
	Milton Icehawks	ON-Jr.A	20	13	15	28	10	....	....	....	....	....	....	....	....	....	....	....	....	....	....	....	....	....	....
2005-06	Oshawa Generals	OHL	65	45	32	77	72	....	....	....	....	....	....	....	....	....	....	....	....	....	....	....	....	....	....
2006-07	Oshawa Generals	OHL	67	*72	62	134	60	....	....	....	....	....	....	....	....	....	9	7	12	19	6	....	....	....	....
2007-08	Oshawa Generals	OHL	59	40	78	118	69	....	....	....	....	....	....	....	....	....	15	3	13	16	20	....	....	....	....
2008-09	Oshawa Generals	OHL	32	*26	28	*54	32	....	....	....	....	....	....	....	....	....	....	....	....	....	....	....	....	....	....
	London Knights	OHL	24	*32	18	*50	22	....	....	....	....	....	....	....	....	....	14	10	11	21	8	....	....	....	....
2009-10	NY Islanders	NHL	82	24	30	54	22	11	0	2	186	12.9	-15	1129	47.5	18:00	....	....	....	....	....	....	....	....	....
2010-11	NY Islanders	NHL	79	29	38	67	53	9	0	4	243	11.9	-16	1319	52.5	19:15	....	....	....	....	....	....	....	....	....
2011-12	NY Islanders	NHL	82	31	50	81	26	7	0	8	286	10.8	-6	1586	51.3	20:34	....	....	....	....	....	....	....	....	....
2012-13	SC Bern	Swiss	28	17	25	42	28	....	....	....	....	....	....	....	....	....	....	....	....	....	....	....	....	....	....
	NY Islanders	NHL	48	28	19	47	18	9	0	5	162	17.3	-2	930	49.4	20:46	6	3	2	5	4	0	0	1	20:34
	NHL Totals		291	112	137	249	119	36	0	19	877	12.8		4964	50.4	19:31	6	3	2	5	4	0	0	1	20:34

OHL All-Rookie Team (2006) • Canadian Major Junior Rookie of the Year (2006) • OHL First All-Star Team (2007) • Canadian Major Junior First All-Star Team (2007, 2009) • Canadian Major Junior Player of the Year (2007) • OHL Second All-Star Team (2009) • NHL All-Rookie Team (2010)

Played in NHL All-Star Game (2012)

Signed as a free agent by **Bern** (Swiss), September 28, 2012.

TEDENBY, Mattias
(TEH-dehn-bew, muh-TIGH-uhs) **N.J.**

Left wing. Shoots left. 5'9", 175 lbs. Born, Vetlanda, Sweden, February 21, 1990. New Jersey's 1st choice, 24th overall, in 2008 Entry Draft.

2005-06	HV 71 U18	Swe-U18	13	8	7	15	24	....	....	....	....	....	....	....	....	....	5	1	0	1	10	....	....	....	....
2006-07	HV 71 U18	Swe-U18	2	4	0	4	2	....	....	....	....	....	....	....	....	....	5	7	2	9	14	....	....	....	....
	HV 71 Jr.	Swe-Jr.	27	10	10	20	43	....	....	....	....	....	....	....	....	....	4	3	1	4	2	....	....	....	....
2007-08	HV 71 U18	Swe-U18	1	1	0	1	0	....	....	....	....	....	....	....	....	....	....	....	....	....	....	....	....	....	....
	HV 71 Jr.	Swe-Jr.	25	14	16	30	14	....	....	....	....	....	....	....	....	....	2	0	0	0	0	....	....	....	....
	HV 71 Jonkoping	Sweden	23	3	3	6	6	....	....	....	....	....	....	....	....	....	5	0	0	0	0	....	....	....	....

Season	Club	League	GP	G	A	Pts	PIM	PP	SH	GW	S	%	+/-	TF	F%	Min	GP	G	A	Pts	PIM	PP	SH	GW	Min
			Regular Season														Playoffs								
2008-09	IK Oskarshamn	Sweden-2	13	2	9	11	6	....	....	....	....	....	....	....	....	....	....	....	....	....	....	....	....	....	....
	HV 71 Jonkoping	Sweden	32	3	1	4	6	....	....	....	....	....	....	....	....	....	18	6	3	9	6	....	....	....	....
2009-10	HV 71 Jonkoping	Sweden	44	12	7	19	30	....	....	....	....	....	....	....	....	....	16	2	3	5	6	....	....	....	....
2010-11	**New Jersey**	**NHL**	58	8	14	22	14	2	0	2	87	9.2	3	0	0.0	12:33	....	....	....	....	....	....	....	....	....
	Albany Devils	AHL	12	3	2	5	6	....	....	....	....	....	....	....	....	....	....	....	....	....	....	....	....	....	....
2011-12	**New Jersey**	**NHL**	43	1	5	6	16	0	0	0	46	2.2	–15	3	33.3	10:45	....	....	....	....	....	....	....	....	....
	Albany Devils	AHL	35	6	14	20	22	....	....	....	....	....	....	....	....	....	....	....	....	....	....	....	....	....	....
2012-13	Albany Devils	AHL	37	10	9	19	12	....	....	....	....	....	....	....	....	....	....	....	....	....	....	....	....	....	....
	New Jersey	**NHL**	4	0	1	1	2	0	0	0	2	0.0	0	0	0.0	9:00	....	....	....	....	....	....	....	....	....
	NHL Totals		105	9	20	29	32	2	0	2	135	6.7		3	33.3	11:40	....	....	....	....	....	....	....	....	....

TENNYSON, Matt

(TEHN-ihs-suhn, MAT) **S.J.**

Defense. Shoots right. 6'2", 205 lbs. Born, Pleasanton, CA, April 23, 1990.

Season	Club	League	GP	G	A	Pts	PIM	PP	SH	GW	S	%	+/-	TF	F%	Min	GP	G	A	Pts	PIM	PP	SH	GW	Min
2007-08	Texas Tornado	NAHL	58	4	10	14	80	....	....	....	....	....	....	....	....	....	....	....	....	....	....	....	....	....	....
2008-09	Cedar Rapids	USHL	57	4	6	10	51	....	....	....	....	....	....	....	....	....	5	0	0	0	2	....	....	....	....
2009-10	Western Mich.	CCHA	34	2	7	9	30	....	....	....	....	....	....	....	....	....	....	....	....	....	....	....	....	....	....
2010-11	Western Mich.	CCHA	42	9	12	21	38	....	....	....	....	....	....	....	....	....	....	....	....	....	....	....	....	....	....
2011-12	Western Mich.	CCHA	41	11	13	24	28	....	....	....	....	....	....	....	....	....	....	....	....	....	....	....	....	....	....
	Worcester Sharks	AHL	7	1	1	2	0	....	....	....	....	....	....	....	....	....	....	....	....	....	....	....	....	....	....
2012-13	Worcester Sharks	AHL	60	5	22	27	44	....	....	....	....	....	....	....	....	....	....	....	....	....	....	....	....	....	....
	San Jose	**NHL**	4	0	2	2	2	0	0	0	8	0.0	2	0	0.0	15:43	....	....	....	....	....	....	....	....	....
	NHL Totals		4	0	2	2	2	0	0	0	8	0.0		0	0.0	15:43	....	....	....	....	....	....	....	....	....

CCHA Second All-Star Team (2012)

Signed as a free agent by **San Jose**, March 29, 2012.

TERRY, Chris

(TAIR-ee, KRIHS) **CAR**

Left wing. Shoots left. 5'10", 195 lbs. Born, Brampton, Ont., April 7, 1989. Carolina's 4th choice, 132nd overall, in 2007 Entry Draft.

Season	Club	League	GP	G	A	Pts	PIM	PP	SH	GW	S	%	+/-	TF	F%	Min	GP	G	A	Pts	PIM	PP	SH	GW	Min
2003-04	Markham	GTHL	66	39	50	89	....	....	....	....	....	....	....	....	....	....	....	....	....	....	....	....	....	....	....
2004-05	Markham	GTHL	60	42	53	95	113	....	....	....	....	....	....	....	....	....	9	0	9	9	14	....	....	....	....
2005-06	Plymouth Whalers	OHL	64	9	19	28	72	....	....	....	....	....	....	....	....	....	11	3	2	5	4	....	....	....	....
2006-07	Plymouth Whalers	OHL	68	22	44	66	98	....	....	....	....	....	....	....	....	....	20	8	10	18	21	....	....	....	....
2007-08	Plymouth Whalers	OHL	68	44	57	101	107	....	....	....	....	....	....	....	....	....	4	4	3	7	6	....	....	....	....
	Albany River Rats	AHL	1	0	0	0	0	....	....	....	....	....	....	....	....	....	....	....	....	....	....	....	....	....	....
2008-09	Plymouth Whalers	OHL	53	39	55	94	75	....	....	....	....	....	....	....	....	....	11	7	9	16	18	....	....	....	....
2009-10	Albany River Rats	AHL	80	17	30	47	47	....	....	....	....	....	....	....	....	....	8	2	4	6	0	....	....	....	....
2010-11	Charlotte	AHL	80	34	30	64	52	....	....	....	....	....	....	....	....	....	16	6	3	9	14	....	....	....	....
2011-12	Charlotte	AHL	74	16	43	59	67	....	....	....	....	....	....	....	....	....	....	....	....	....	....	....	....	....	....
2012-13	Charlotte	AHL	70	25	35	60	40	....	....	....	....	....	....	....	....	....	5	2	2	4	8	....	....	....	....
	Carolina	**NHL**	3	1	0	1	0	0	0	1	1	100.0	0	1	100.0	9:36	....	....	....	....	....	....	....	....	....
	NHL Totals		3	1	0	1	0	0	0	1	1	100.0		1	100.0	9:36	....	....	....	....	....	....	....	....	....

TEUBERT, Colten

(TEW-buhrt, KOHL-tuhn)

Defense. Shoots right. 6'4", 195 lbs. Born, White Rock, B.C., March 8, 1990. Los Angeles' 2nd choice, 13th overall, in 2008 Entry Draft.

Season	Club	League	GP	G	A	Pts	PIM	PP	SH	GW	S	%	+/-	TF	F%	Min	GP	G	A	Pts	PIM	PP	SH	GW	Min
2005-06	South West	Minor-BC	29	8	12	20	122	....	....	....	....	....	....	....	....	....	....	....	....	....	....	....	....	....	....
	Regina Pats	WHL	14	0	2	2	16	....	....	....	....	....	....	....	....	....	6	0	1	1	4	....	....	....	....
2006-07	Regina Pats	WHL	63	3	8	11	91	....	....	....	....	....	....	....	....	....	10	0	1	1	13	....	....	....	....
2007-08	Regina Pats	WHL	66	7	16	23	135	....	....	....	....	....	....	....	....	....	6	1	4	5	6	....	....	....	....
2008-09	Regina Pats	WHL	60	12	25	37	136	....	....	....	....	....	....	....	....	....	....	....	....	....	....	....	....	....	....
	Ontario Reign	ECHL	8	0	1	1	10	....	....	....	....	....	....	....	....	....	6	0	1	1	19	....	....	....	....
2009-10	Regina Pats	WHL	60	10	30	40	115	....	....	....	....	....	....	....	....	....	....	....	....	....	....	....	....	....	....
	Ontario Reign	ECHL	10	1	2	3	10	....	....	....	....	....	....	....	....	....	....	....	....	....	....	....	....	....	....
2010-11	Manchester	AHL	39	2	8	10	57	....	....	....	....	....	....	....	....	....	....	....	....	....	....	....	....	....	....
	Oklahoma City	AHL	20	2	5	7	26	....	....	....	....	....	....	....	....	....	2	0	0	0	0	....	....	....	....
2011-12	**Edmonton**	**NHL**	24	0	1	1	25	0	0	0	13	0.0	–5	0	0.0	12:39	....	....	....	....	....	....	....	....	....
	Oklahoma City	AHL	46	2	8	10	60	....	....	....	....	....	....	....	....	....	4	0	0	0	2	....	....	....	....
2012-13	Oklahoma City	AHL	62	4	6	10	113	....	....	....	....	....	....	....	....	....	1	0	0	0	4	....	....	....	....
	NHL Totals		24	0	1	1	25	0	0	0	13	0.0		0	0.0	12:39	....	....	....	....	....	....	....	....	....

Traded to **Edmonton** by **Los Angeles** with Los Angeles' 1st round choice (Oscar Klefborn) in 2011 Entry Draft and Los Angeles' 3rd round choice (Daniil Zharkov) in 2012 Entry Draft for Dustin Penner, February 28, 2011.

THANG, Ryan

(THAYNG, RIGH-uhn) **NSH**

Left wing. Shoots right. 6', 194 lbs. Born, Chicago, IL, May 11, 1987. Nashville's 4th choice, 81st overall, in 2007 Entry Draft.

Season	Club	League	GP	G	A	Pts	PIM	PP	SH	GW	S	%	+/-	TF	F%	Min	GP	G	A	Pts	PIM	PP	SH	GW	Min
2004-05	Sioux Falls	USHL	58	9	22	31	45	....	....	....	....	....	....	....	....	....	....	....	....	....	....	....	....	....	....
2005-06	Sioux Falls	USHL	32	8	14	22	52	....	....	....	....	....	....	....	....	....	....	....	....	....	....	....	....	....	....
	Omaha Lancers	USHL	25	15	15	30	26	....	....	....	....	....	....	....	....	....	5	2	1	3	2	....	....	....	....
2006-07	U. of Notre Dame	CCHA	42	20	21	41	22	....	....	....	....	....	....	....	....	....	....	....	....	....	....	....	....	....	....
2007-08	U. of Notre Dame	CCHA	47	18	14	32	48	....	....	....	....	....	....	....	....	....	....	....	....	....	....	....	....	....	....
2008-09	U. of Notre Dame	CCHA	33	10	9	19	36	....	....	....	....	....	....	....	....	....	....	....	....	....	....	....	....	....	....
2009-10	U. of Notre Dame	CCHA	37	9	14	23	55	....	....	....	....	....	....	....	....	....	....	....	....	....	....	....	....	....	....
	Milwaukee	AHL	12	3	3	6	4	....	....	....	....	....	....	....	....	....	7	1	3	4	2	....	....	....	....
2010-11	Milwaukee	AHL	78	14	27	41	32	....	....	....	....	....	....	....	....	....	13	5	8	13	10	....	....	....	....
2011-12	**Nashville**	**NHL**	1	0	0	0	0	0	0	0	0	0.0	0	0	0.0	8:32	....	....	....	....	....	....	....	....	....
	Milwaukee	AHL	75	18	20	38	44	....	....	....	....	....	....	....	....	....	3	0	0	0	2	....	....	....	....
2012-13	Augsburg	Germany	50	14	15	29	34	....	....	....	....	....	....	....	....	....	2	0	0	0	2	....	....	....	....
	NHL Totals		1	0	0	0	0	0	0	0	0	0.0		0	0.0	8:32	....	....	....	....	....	....	....	....	....

CCHA All-Rookie Team (2007)

Signed as a free agent by **Augsburg** (Germany). June 15, 2012. Signed as a free agent by **Mora** (Sweden-2). June 20, 2013.

THOMAS, Bill

(TAW-mas, BIHL)

Right wing. Shoots right. 6'1", 185 lbs. Born, Pittsburgh, PA, June 20, 1983.

Season	Club	League	GP	G	A	Pts	PIM	PP	SH	GW	S	%	+/-	TF	F%	Min	GP	G	A	Pts	PIM	PP	SH	GW	Min
2002-03	Tri-City Storm	USHL	60	29	21	50	20	....	....	....	....	....	....	....	....	....	3	0	3	3	4	....	....	....	....
2003-04	Tri-City Storm	USHL	60	31	38	69	30	....	....	....	....	....	....	....	....	....	11	*9	7	*16	4	....	....	....	....
2004-05	Nebraska-Omaha	CCHA	39	19	26	45	12	....	....	....	....	....	....	....	....	....	....	....	....	....	....	....	....	....	....
2005-06	Nebraska-Omaha	CCHA	41	*27	23	50	43	....	....	....	....	....	....	....	....	....	....	....	....	....	....	....	....	....	....
	Phoenix	**NHL**	9	1	2	3	8	1	0	0	15	6.7	–2	2	50.0	13:30	....	....	....	....	....	....	....	....	....
2006-07	**Phoenix**	**NHL**	24	8	6	14	2	4	0	1	60	13.3	–6	0	0.0	13:29	....	....	....	....	....	....	....	....	....
	San Antonio	AHL	47	13	20	33	20	....	....	....	....	....	....	....	....	....	....	....	....	....	....	....	....	....	....
2007-08	**Phoenix**	**NHL**	7	0	0	0	0	0	0	0	9	0.0	–2	0	0.0	13:08	....	....	....	....	....	....	....	....	....
	San Antonio	AHL	75	24	28	52	40	....	....	....	....	....	....	....	....	....	7	1	2	3	0	....	....	....	....
2008-09	**Pittsburgh**	**NHL**	16	2	1	3	2	0	1	0	17	11.8	–4	101	51.5	9:31	....	....	....	....	....	....	....	....	....
	Wilkes-Barre	AHL	39	8	10	18	24	....	....	....	....	....	....	....	....	....	12	1	4	5	12	....	....	....	....
2009-10	Springfield	AHL	33	5	12	17	14	....	....	....	....	....	....	....	....	....	....	....	....	....	....	....	....	....	....
	HC Lugano	Swiss	6	2	1	3	2	....	....	....	....	....	....	....	....	....	2	0	0	0	0	....	....	....	....
2010-11	**Florida**	**NHL**	24	4	3	7	6	0	0	2	33	12.1	1	22	59.1	8:30	....	....	....	....	....	....	....	....	....
	Rochester	AHL	53	16	20	36	12	....	....	....	....	....	....	....	....	....	....	....	....	....	....	....	....	....	....
2011-12	**Florida**	**NHL**	7	1	0	1	0	0	0	0	9	11.1	0	3	0.0	8:44	....	....	....	....	....	....	....	....	....
	San Antonio	AHL	65	27	25	52	18	....	....	....	....	....	....	....	....	....	10	5	5	10	0	....	....	....	....
2012-13	Lake Erie	AHL	76	22	21	43	33	....	....	....	....	....	....	....	....	....	....	....	....	....	....	....	....	....	....
	NHL Totals		87	16	12	28	18	5	1	3	143	11.2		128	51.6	10:59	....	....	....	....	....	....	....	....	....

CCHA All-Rookie Team (2005) • CCHA Rookie of the Year (2005) • CCHA Second All-Star Team (2005) • CCHA First All-Star Team (2006)

Signed as a free agent by **Phoenix**. March 27, 2006. Signed as a free agent by **Pittsburgh**. July 15, 2008. Signed to a PTO (professional tryout) contract by **Springfield** (AHL), November 3, 2009. Signed as a free agent by **Lugano** (Swiss), January 12, 2010. Signed as a free agent by **Florida**, July 2, 2010. Signed as a free agent by **Colorado**, July 13, 2012. Signed as a free agent by **Zagreb** (KHL), June 14, 2013.

THOMAS, Christian

(TAW-mas, KRIHS-ch'yehn) **MTL**

Right wing. Shoots right. 5'9", 174 lbs. Born, Toronto, Ont., May 26, 1992. NY Rangers' 2nd choice, 40th overall, in 2010 Entry Draft.

			Regular Season														Playoffs								
Season	Club	League	GP	G	A	Pts	PIM	PP	SH	GW	S	%	+/-	TF	F%	Min	GP	G	A	Pts	PIM	PP	SH	GW	Min
2007-08	Tor. Marlboros	GTHL	52	32	34	66	36	....	....	....	....	....	....	....	....	....	....	....	....	....	....	....	....	....	....
2008-09	London Knights	OHL	32	4	7	11	4	....	....	....	....	....	....	....	....	....	....	....	....	....	....	....	....	....	....
	Oshawa Generals	OHL	27	4	10	14	10	....	....	....	....	....	....	....	....	....	....	....	....	....	....	....	....	....	....
2009-10	Oshawa Generals	OHL	64	41	25	66	27	....	....	....	....	....	....	....	....	....	....	....	....	....	....	....	....	....	....
2010-11	Oshawa Generals	OHL	66	54	45	99	38	....	....	....	....	....	....	....	....	....	10	9	10	19	4	....	....	....	....
2011-12	Oshawa Generals	OHL	55	34	33	67	12	....	....	....	....	....	....	....	....	....	6	2	2	4	0	....	....	....	....
	Connecticut	AHL	5	1	1	2	0	....	....	....	....	....	....	....	....	....	6	0	0	0	0	....	....	....	....
2012-13	Connecticut	AHL	73	19	16	35	15	....	....	....	....	....	....	....	....	....	....	....	....	....	....	....	....	....	....
	NY Rangers	**NHL**	**1**	**0**	**0**	**0**	**0**	**0**	**0**	**0**	**2**	**0.0**	**0**	**0**	**0.0**	**12:46**	....	....	....	....	....	....	....	....	....
	NHL Totals		**1**	**0**	**0**	**0**	**0**	**0**	**0**	**0**	**2**	**0.0**		**0**	**0.0**	**12:46**	....	....	....	....	....	....	....	....	....

Traded to **Montreal** by **NY Rangers** for Danny Kristo, July 2, 2013.

THOMPSON, Nate

(TAWM-suhn, NAYT) **T.B.**

Center. Shoots left. 6', 212 lbs. Born, Anchorage, AK, October 5, 1984. Boston's 8th choice, 183rd overall, in 2003 Entry Draft.

			Regular Season														Playoffs								
Season	Club	League	GP	G	A	Pts	PIM	PP	SH	GW	S	%	+/-	TF	F%	Min	GP	G	A	Pts	PIM	PP	SH	GW	Min
2001-02	Seattle	WHL	69	13	26	39	42	....	....	....	....	....	....	....	....	....	11	1	3	4	13	....	....	....	....
2002-03	Seattle	WHL	61	10	24	34	48	....	....	....	....	....	....	....	....	....	15	5	4	9	6	....	....	....	....
2003-04	Seattle	WHL	65	13	23	36	24	....	....	....	....	....	....	....	....	....	....	....	....	....	....	....	....	....	....
2004-05	Seattle	WHL	58	19	15	34	39	....	....	....	....	....	....	....	....	....	12	1	2	3	2	....	....	....	....
	Providence Bruins	AHL	....	....	....	....	....	....	....	....	....	....	....	....	....	....	11	0	1	1	6	....	....	....	....
2005-06	Providence Bruins	AHL	74	8	10	18	58	....	....	....	....	....	....	....	....	....	3	0	0	0	10	....	....	....	....
2006-07	**Boston**	**NHL**	**4**	**0**	**0**	**0**	**0**	**0**	**0**	**0**	**5**	**0.0**	**0**	**10**	**40.0**	**4:46**	....	....	....	....	....	....	....	....	....
	Providence Bruins	AHL	67	8	15	23	74	....	....	....	....	....	....	....	....	....	13	0	2	2	9	....	....	....	....
2007-08	Providence Bruins	AHL	75	19	20	39	83	....	....	....	....	....	....	....	....	....	10	2	3	5	4	....	....	....	....
2008-09	**NY Islanders**	**NHL**	**43**	**2**	**2**	**4**	**49**	**0**	**1**	**0**	**56**	**3.6**	**–11**	**429**	**50.4**	**12:05**	....	....	....	....	....	....	....	....	....
2009-10	**NY Islanders**	**NHL**	**39**	**1**	**5**	**6**	**39**	**0**	**0**	**0**	**48**	**2.1**	**–14**	**210**	**49.5**	**12:56**	....	....	....	....	....	....	....	....	....
	Tampa Bay	**NHL**	**32**	**1**	**3**	**4**	**17**	**0**	**0**	**0**	**44**	**2.3**	**–3**	**385**	**56.9**	**13:58**	....	....	....	....	....	....	....	....	....
2010-11	**Tampa Bay**	**NHL**	**79**	**10**	**15**	**25**	**29**	**0**	**1**	**2**	**123**	**8.1**	**–6**	**664**	**54.2**	**15:05**	**18**	**1**	**3**	**4**	**4**	**0**	**0**	**0**	**15:37**
2011-12	**Tampa Bay**	**NHL**	**68**	**9**	**6**	**15**	**21**	**0**	**0**	**1**	**85**	**10.6**	**–23**	**592**	**49.5**	**14:49**	....	....	....	....	....	....	....	....	....
2012-13	Alaska Aces	ECHL	24	7	14	21	23	....	....	....	....	....	....	....	....	....	....	....	....	....	....	....	....	....	....
	Tampa Bay	**NHL**	**45**	**7**	**8**	**15**	**17**	**0**	**0**	**0**	**58**	**12.1**	**–2**	**605**	**51.2**	**14:20**	....	....	....	....	....	....	....	....	....
	NHL Totals		**310**	**30**	**39**	**69**	**172**	**0**	**2**	**3**	**419**	**7.2**		**2895**	**52.0**	**13:59**	**18**	**1**	**3**	**4**	**4**	**0**	**0**	**0**	**15:38**

Claimed on waivers by **NY Islanders** from **Boston**, October 8, 2008. Claimed on waivers by **Tampa Bay** from **NY Islanders**, January 21, 2010. Signed to a PTO (professional tryout) contract by **Alaska** (ECHL), September 28, 2012.

THORBURN, Chris

(THOHR-buhrn, KRIHS) **WPG**

Right wing. Shoots right. 6'3", 230 lbs. Born, Sault Ste. Marie, Ont., June 3, 1983. Buffalo's 3rd choice, 50th overall, in 2001 Entry Draft.

			Regular Season														Playoffs								
Season	Club	League	GP	G	A	Pts	PIM	PP	SH	GW	S	%	+/-	TF	F%	Min	GP	G	A	Pts	PIM	PP	SH	GW	Min
1998-99	Elliot Lake Vikings	NOJHA	40	21	12	33	28	....	....	....	....	....	....	....	....	....	....	....	....	....	....	....	....	....	....
99-2000	North Bay	OHL	56	12	8	20	33	....	....	....	....	....	....	....	....	....	6	0	2	2	0	....	....	....	....
2000-01	North Bay	OHL	66	22	32	54	64	....	....	....	....	....	....	....	....	....	4	0	1	1	9	....	....	....	....
2001-02	North Bay	OHL	67	15	43	58	112	....	....	....	....	....	....	....	....	....	5	1	2	3	8	....	....	....	....
2002-03	Saginaw Spirit	OHL	37	19	19	38	68	....	....	....	....	....	....	....	....	....	....	....	....	....	....	....	....	....	....
	Plymouth Whalers	OHL	27	11	22	33	56	....	....	....	....	....	....	....	....	....	18	11	9	20	10	....	....	....	....
2003-04	Rochester	AHL	58	6	16	22	77	....	....	....	....	....	....	....	....	....	16	3	2	5	18	....	....	....	....
2004-05	Rochester	AHL	73	12	17	29	185	....	....	....	....	....	....	....	....	....	4	0	1	1	2	....	....	....	....
2005-06	**Buffalo**	**NHL**	**2**	**0**	**1**	**1**	**7**	**0**	**0**	**0**	**1**	**0.0**	**–1**	**1**	**0.0**	**6:52**	....	....	....	....	....	....	....	....	....
	Rochester	AHL	77	23	27	50	134	....	....	....	....	....	....	....	....	....	....	....	....	....	....	....	....	....	....
2006-07	**Pittsburgh**	**NHL**	**39**	**3**	**2**	**5**	**69**	**0**	**0**	**1**	**40**	**7.5**	**1**	**8**	**25.0**	**7:54**	....	....	....	....	....	....	....	....	....
	Wilkes-Barre	AHL	3	0	1	1	2	....	....	....	....	....	....	....	....	....	....	....	....	....	....	....	....	....	....
2007-08	**Atlanta**	**NHL**	**73**	**5**	**13**	**18**	**92**	**0**	**0**	**1**	**72**	**6.9**	**–4**	**20**	**60.0**	**8:56**	....	....	....	....	....	....	....	....	....
2008-09	**Atlanta**	**NHL**	**82**	**7**	**8**	**15**	**104**	**0**	**0**	**1**	**85**	**8.2**	**–10**	**37**	**40.5**	**9:35**	....	....	....	....	....	....	....	....	....
2009-10	**Atlanta**	**NHL**	**76**	**4**	**9**	**13**	**89**	**0**	**3**	**0**	**63**	**6.3**	**6**	**29**	**55.2**	**9:59**	....	....	....	....	....	....	....	....	....
2010-11	**Atlanta**	**NHL**	**82**	**9**	**10**	**19**	**77**	**2**	**0**	**0**	**114**	**7.9**	**–4**	**251**	**49.8**	**13:48**	....	....	....	....	....	....	....	....	....
2011-12	**Winnipeg**	**NHL**	**72**	**4**	**7**	**11**	**83**	**0**	**0**	**0**	**69**	**5.8**	**–6**	**67**	**58.2**	**10:11**	....	....	....	....	....	....	....	....	....
2012-13	**Winnipeg**	**NHL**	**42**	**2**	**2**	**4**	**70**	**0**	**0**	**0**	**13**	**15.4**	**–5**	**46**	**43.5**	**6:19**	....	....	....	....	....	....	....	....	....
	NHL Totals		**468**	**34**	**52**	**86**	**591**	**2**	**3**	**3**	**457**	**7.4**		**459**	**49.9**	**9:56**	....	....	....	....	....	....	....	....	....

Claimed on waivers by **Pittsburgh** from **Buffalo**, October 3, 2006. Traded to **Atlanta** by **Pittsburgh** for NY Rangers' 3rd round choice (previously acquired, Pittsburgh selected Robert Bortuzzo) in 2007 Entry Draft, June 22, 2007. • Transferred to **Winnipeg** after **Atlanta** franchise relocated, June 21, 2011.

THORNTON, Joe

(THOHRN-tuhn, JOH) **S.J.**

Center. Shoots left. 6'4", 220 lbs. Born, London, Ont., July 2, 1979. Boston's 1st choice, 1st overall, in 1997 Entry Draft.

			Regular Season														Playoffs								
Season	Club	League	GP	G	A	Pts	PIM	PP	SH	GW	S	%	+/-	TF	F%	Min	GP	G	A	Pts	PIM	PP	SH	GW	Min
1993-94	Elgin-Mid. Chiefs	Minor-ON	67	*83	*85	*168	45	....	....	....	....	....	....	....	....	....	....	....	....	....	....	....	....	....	....
	St. Thomas Stars	ON-Jr.B	6	2	6	8	2	....	....	....	....	....	....	....	....	....	....	....	....	....	....	....	....	....	....
1994-95	St. Thomas Stars	ON-Jr.B	50	40	64	104	53	....	....	....	....	....	....	....	....	....	....	....	....	....	....	....	....	....	....
1995-96	Sault Ste. Marie	OHL	66	30	46	76	53	....	....	....	....	....	....	....	....	....	4	1	1	2	11	....	....	....	....
1996-97	Sault Ste. Marie	OHL	59	41	81	122	123	....	....	....	....	....	....	....	....	....	11	11	8	19	24	....	....	....	....
1997-98	**Boston**	**NHL**	**55**	**3**	**4**	**7**	**19**	**0**	**0**	**1**	**33**	**9.1**	**–6**	....	....	....	**6**	**0**	**0**	**0**	**9**	**0**	**0**	**0**	....
1998-99	**Boston**	**NHL**	**81**	**16**	**25**	**41**	**69**	**7**	**0**	**1**	**128**	**12.5**	**3**	**1073**	**48.7**	**15:21**	**11**	**3**	**6**	**9**	**4**	**2**	**0**	**2**	**19:52**
99-2000	**Boston**	**NHL**	**81**	**23**	**37**	**60**	**82**	**5**	**0**	**3**	**171**	**13.5**	**–5**	**1861**	**49.5**	**21:18**	....	....	....	....	....	....	....	....	....
2000-01	**Boston**	**NHL**	**72**	**37**	**34**	**71**	**107**	**19**	**1**	**5**	**181**	**20.4**	**–4**	**1651**	**52.1**	**21:45**	....	....	....	....	....	....	....	....	....
2001-02	**Boston**	**NHL**	**66**	**22**	**46**	**68**	**127**	**6**	**0**	**5**	**152**	**14.5**	**7**	**1341**	**49.1**	**19:59**	**6**	**2**	**4**	**6**	**10**	**0**	**0**	**0**	**21:09**
2002-03	**Boston**	**NHL**	**77**	**36**	**65**	**101**	**109**	**12**	**2**	**4**	**196**	**18.4**	**12**	**1766**	**49.5**	**22:33**	**5**	**1**	**2**	**3**	**4**	**1**	**0**	**0**	**20:13**
2003-04	**Boston**	**NHL**	**77**	**23**	**50**	**73**	**98**	**4**	**0**	**6**	**187**	**12.3**	**18**	**1671**	**56.3**	**21:38**	**7**	**0**	**0**	**0**	**14**	**0**	**0**	**0**	**21:30**
2004-05	HC Davos	Swiss	40	10	44	54	80	....	....	....	....	....	....	....	....	....	14	4	*20	*24	29	....	....		....
2005-06	**Boston**	**NHL**	**23**	**9**	***24**	***33**	**6**	**3**	**0**	**2**	**60**	**15.0**	**0**	**511**	**52.3**	**21:33**	....	....	....	....	....	....	....	....	....
	San Jose	**NHL**	**58**	**20**	***72**	***92**	**55**	**8**	**0**	**4**	**135**	**14.8**	**31**	**1287**	**50.9**	**21:15**	**11**	**2**	**7**	**9**	**12**	**1**	**0**	**1**	**25:09**
	Canada	Olympics	6	1	2	3	0	....	....	....	....	....	....	....	....	....	....	....	....	....	....	....	....	....	....
2006-07	**San Jose**	**NHL**	**82**	**22**	***92**	**114**	**44**	**10**	**0**	**5**	**213**	**10.3**	**24**	**1522**	**51.1**	**20:19**	**11**	**1**	**10**	**11**	**10**	**0**	**0**	**0**	**22:00**
2007-08	**San Jose**	**NHL**	**82**	**29**	***67**	**96**	**59**	**11**	**0**	**5**	**178**	**16.3**	**18**	**1485**	**52.9**	**21:24**	**13**	**2**	**8**	**10**	**2**	**1**	**0**	**1**	**24:42**
2008-09	**San Jose**	**NHL**	**82**	**25**	**61**	**86**	**56**	**11**	**0**	**3**	**139**	**18.0**	**16**	**1295**	**55.4**	**19:28**	**6**	**1**	**4**	**5**	**5**	**1**	**0**	**0**	**19:14**
2009-10	**San Jose**	**NHL**	**79**	**20**	**69**	**89**	**54**	**4**	**1**	**2**	**141**	**14.2**	**17**	**1228**	**53.9**	**19:51**	**15**	**3**	**9**	**12**	**18**	**1**	**0**	**1**	**21:20**
	Canada	Olympics	7	1	1	2	0	....	....	....	....	....	....	....	....	....	....	....	....	....	....	....	....	....	....
2010-11	**San Jose**	**NHL**	**80**	**21**	**49**	**70**	**47**	**9**	**2**	**3**	**149**	**14.1**	**4**	**1240**	**54.4**	**19:52**	**18**	**3**	**14**	**17**	**16**	**0**	**0**	**2**	**22:15**
2011-12	**San Jose**	**NHL**	**82**	**18**	**59**	**77**	**31**	**4**	**0**	**2**	**156**	**11.5**	**17**	**993**	**56.1**	**20:28**	**5**	**2**	**3**	**5**	**2**	**0**	**0**	**0**	**21:54**
2012-13	HC Davos	Swiss	33	12	24	36	43	....	....	....	....	....	....	....	....	....	....	....	....	....	....	....	....	....	....
	San Jose	**NHL**	**48**	**7**	**33**	**40**	**26**	**2**	**0**	**1**	**85**	**8.2**	**6**	**701**	**58.5**	**18:23**	**11**	**2**	**8**	**10**	**2**	**1**	**0**	**0**	**20:17**
	NHL Totals		**1125**	**331**	**787**	**1118**	**989**	**115**	**6**	**52**	**2304**	**14.4**		**19625**	**52.4**	**20:18**	**125**	**22**	**75**	**97**	**108**	**8**	**0**	**7**	**21:54**

OHL All-Rookie Team (1996) • OHL Rookie of the Year (1996) • Canadian Major Junior Rookie of the Year (1996) • OHL Second All-Star Team (1997) • NHL Second All-Star Team (2003, 2008) • NHL First All-Star Team (2006) • Art Ross Trophy (2006) • Hart Memorial Trophy (2006)

Played in NHL All-Star Game (2002, 2003, 2004, 2007, 2008, 2009)

Signed as a free agent by **Davos** (Swiss), July 8, 2004. Traded to **San Jose** by **Boston** for Brad Stuart, Marco Sturm and Wayne Primeau, November 30, 2005. Signed as a free agent by **Davos** (Swiss), September 16, 2012.

THORNTON, Shawn

(THOHRN-tuhn, SHAWN) **BOS**

Right wing. Shoots right. 6'2", 217 lbs. Born, Oshawa, Ont., July 23, 1977. Toronto's 6th choice, 190th overall, in 1997 Entry Draft.

			Regular Season														Playoffs								
Season	Club	League	GP	G	A	Pts	PIM	PP	SH	GW	S	%	+/-	TF	F%	Min	GP	G	A	Pts	PIM	PP	SH	GW	Min
1995-96	Peterborough	OHL	63	4	10	14	192	....	....	....	....	....	....	....	....	....	24	3	0	3	25	....	....	....	....
1996-97	Peterborough	OHL	61	19	10	29	204	....	....	....	....	....	....	....	....	....	11	2	4	6	20	....	....	....	....
1997-98	St. John's	AHL	59	0	3	3	225	....	....	....	....	....	....	....	....	....	....	....	....	....	....	....	....	....	....
1998-99	St. John's	AHL	78	8	11	19	354	....	....	....	....	....	....	....	....	....	5	0	0	0	9	....	....	....	....
99-2000	St. John's	AHL	60	4	12	16	316	....	....	....	....	....	....	....	....	....	....	....	....	....	....	....	....	....	....
2000-01	St. John's	AHL	79	5	12	17	320	....	....	....	....	....	....	....	....	....	3	1	2	3	2	....	....	....	....
2001-02	Norfolk Admirals	AHL	70	8	14	22	281	....	....	....	....	....	....	....	....	....	4	0	0	0	4	....	....	....	....
2002-03	**Chicago**	**NHL**	**13**	**1**	**1**	**2**	**31**	**0**	**0**	**0**	**15**	**6.7**	**–4**	**3**	**66.7**	**8:30**	....	....	....	....	....	....	....	....	....
	Norfolk Admirals	AHL	50	11	2	13	213	....	....	....	....	....	....	....	....	....	9	0	2	2	28	....	....	....	....

			Regular Season														Playoffs								
Season	Club	League	GP	G	A	Pts	PIM	PP	SH	GW	S	%	+/-	TF	F%	Min	GP	G	A	Pts	PIM	PP	SH	GW	Min
2003-04	**Chicago**	**NHL**	**8**	**1**	**0**	**1**	**23**	**0**	**0**	**0**	**14**	**7.1**	**2**	**19**	**42.1**	**11:14**	....	....	....	....	....	....	....	....	....
	Norfolk Admirals	AHL	64	6	11	17	259	....	....	....	....	....	....	....	....	....	8	1	1	2	6	....	....	....	....
2004-05	Norfolk Admirals	AHL	71	5	9	14	253	....	....	....	....	....	....	....	....	....	6	0	0	0	8	....	....	....	....
2005-06	**Chicago**	**NHL**	**10**	**0**	**0**	**0**	**16**	**0**	**0**	**0**	**16**	**0.0**	**–5**	**17**	**58.8**	**7:18**	....	....	....	....	....	....	....	....	....
	Norfolk Admirals	AHL	59	10	22	32	192	....	....	....	....	....	....	....	....	....	4	0	0	0	35	....	....	....	....
2006-07 ♦	**Anaheim**	**NHL**	**48**	**2**	**7**	**9**	**88**	**0**	**0**	**0**	**60**	**3.3**	**3**	**8**	**25.0**	**8:26**	**15**	**0**	**0**	**0**	**19**	**0**	**0**	**0**	**3:58**
	Portland Pirates	AHL	15	4	4	8	55	....	....	....	....	....	....	....	....	....	....	....	....	....	....	....	....	....	....
2007-08	**Boston**	**NHL**	**58**	**4**	**3**	**7**	**74**	**0**	**0**	**1**	**65**	**6.2**	**–1**	**7**	**28.6**	**7:24**	**7**	**0**	**0**	**0**	**6**	**0**	**0**	**0**	**8:04**
2008-09	**Boston**	**NHL**	**79**	**6**	**5**	**11**	**123**	**0**	**0**	**2**	**136**	**4.4**	**–2**	**5**	**20.0**	**10:02**	**10**	**1**	**0**	**1**	**6**	**0**	**0**	**0**	**9:07**
2009-10	**Boston**	**NHL**	**74**	**1**	**9**	**10**	**141**	**0**	**0**	**0**	**119**	**0.8**	**–9**	**23**	**47.8**	**9:03**	**12**	**0**	**0**	**0**	**4**	**0**	**0**	**0**	**7:08**
2010-11 ♦	**Boston**	**NHL**	**79**	**10**	**10**	**20**	**122**	**0**	**0**	**2**	**151**	**6.6**	**8**	**31**	**54.8**	**10:05**	**18**	**0**	**1**	**1**	**24**	**0**	**0**	**0**	**6:57**
2011-12	**Boston**	**NHL**	**81**	**5**	**8**	**13**	**154**	**0**	**1**	**0**	**114**	**4.4**	**–7**	**38**	**42.1**	**9:11**	**5**	**0**	**0**	**0**	**0**	**0**	**0**	**0**	**7:30**
2012-13	**Boston**	**NHL**	**45**	**3**	**4**	**7**	**60**	**0**	**0**	**0**	**55**	**5.5**	**1**	**17**	**41.2**	**8:06**	**22**	**0**	**4**	**4**	**18**	**0**	**0**	**0**	**7:21**
	NHL Totals		**495**	**33**	**47**	**80**	**832**	**0**	**1**	**5**	**745**	**4.4**		**168**	**45.2**	**9:02**	**89**	**1**	**5**	**6**	**77**	**0**	**0**	**0**	**6:56**

Traded to **Chicago** by **Toronto** for Marty Wilford, September 30, 2001. Signed as a free agent by **Anaheim**, July 14, 2006. Signed as a free agent by **Boston**, July 1, 2007.

THURESSON, Andreas

(THUR-eh-suhn, an-DRAY-uhs)

Center. Shoots right. 6'1", 212 lbs. Born, Kristianstad, Sweden, November 18, 1987. Nashville's 7th choice, 144th overall, in 2007 Entry Draft.

2003-04	Malmo Jr.	Swe-Jr.	19	2	2	4	16	....	....	....	....	....	....	....	....	....	8	0	0	0	6	....	....	....	....
	Tyringe SoSS	Sweden-3	12	0	1	1	0	....	....	....	....	....	....	....	....	....	....	....	....	....	....	....	....	....	....
	Malmo U18	Swe-U18	3	0	0	0	4	....	....	....	....	....	....	....	....	....	....	....	....	....	....	....	....	....	....
2004-05	Malmo U18	Swe-U18	3	1	1	2	4	....	....	....	....	....	....	....	....	....	....	....	....	....	....	....	....	....	....
	Malmo Jr.	Swe-Jr.	30	4	4	8	28	....	....	....	....	....	....	....	....	....	3	2	1	3	2	....	....	....	....
2005-06	Malmo U18	Swe-U18	2	1	0	1	4	....	....	....	....	....	....	....	....	....	....	....	....	....	....	....	....	....	....
	Malmo Jr.	Swe-Jr.	38	15	18	33	71	....	....	....	....	....	....	....	....	....	....	....	....	....	....	....	....	....	....
	Malmo	Sweden-2	20	0	2	2	10	....	....	....	....	....	....	....	....	....	....	....	....	....	....	....	....	....	....
2006-07	Malmo	Sweden	48	10	5	15	26	....	....	....	....	....	....	....	....	....	....	....	....	....	....	....	....	....	....
	Malmo	Sweden-Q	10	2	2	4	2	....	....	....	....	....	....	....	....	....	....	....	....	....	....	....	....	....	....
2007-08	Milwaukee	AHL	77	11	7	18	37	....	....	....	....	....	....	....	....	....	6	0	0	0	4	....	....	....	....
2008-09	Milwaukee	AHL	74	14	15	29	32	....	....	....	....	....	....	....	....	....	11	3	1	4	4	....	....	....	....
2009-10	**Nashville**	**NHL**	**22**	**1**	**2**	**3**	**4**	**0**	**0**	**0**	**30**	**3.3**	**–5**	**10**	**30.0**	**9:59**	....	....	....	....	....	....	....	....	....
	Milwaukee	AHL	50	14	19	33	24	....	....	....	....	....	....	....	....	....	7	2	7	9	16	....	....	....	....
2010-11	**Nashville**	**NHL**	**3**	**0**	**0**	**0**	**2**	**0**	**0**	**0**	**2**	**0.0**	**–1**	**2**	**0.0**	**10:09**	....	....	....	....	....	....	....	....	....
	Milwaukee	AHL	76	14	24	38	41	....	....	....	....	....	....	....	....	....	13	3	3	6	10	....	....	....	....
2011-12	Connecticut	AHL	73	13	8	21	40	....	....	....	....	....	....	....	....	....	9	1	2	3	0	....	....	....	....
2012-13	Brynas IF Gavle	Sweden	48	11	8	19	50	....	....	....	....	....	....	....	....	....	4	0	1	1	12	....	....	....	....
	NHL Totals		**25**	**1**	**2**	**3**	**6**	**0**	**0**	**0**	**32**	**3.1**		**12**	**25.0**	**10:00**	....	....	....	....	....	....	....	....	....

Traded to **NY Rangers** by **Nashville** for Brodie Dupont, July 2, 2011. Signed as a free agent by **Gavle** (Sweden), May 18, 2012.

TIKHONOV, Viktor

(TIHK-uh-nawf, VIHK-tohr) **PHX**

Right wing. Shoots right. 6'2", 187 lbs. Born, Riga, Latvia, May 12, 1988. Phoenix's 2nd choice, 28th overall, in 2008 Entry Draft.

2004-05	CSKA Moscow 2	Russia-3	STATISTICS NOT AVAILABLE																						
2005-06	CSKA Moscow 2	Russia-3	STATISTICS NOT AVAILABLE																						
	HK Dmitrov	Russia-2	36	6	8	14	10	....	....	....	....	....	....	....	....	....	....	....	....	....	....	....	....	....	....
2006-07	Cherepovets 2	Russia-3	STATISTICS NOT AVAILABLE																						
	Cherepovets	Russia	4	0	0	0	0	....	....	....	....	....	....	....	....	....	....	....	....	....	....	....	....	....	....
2007-08	Cherepovets	Russia	43	7	5	12	43	....	....	....	....	....	....	....	....	....	8	0	1	1	4	....	....	....	....
2008-09	**Phoenix**	**NHL**	**61**	**8**	**8**	**16**	**20**	**1**	**0**	**1**	**71**	**11.3**	**–3**	**60**	**38.3**	**12:08**	....	....	....	....	....	....	....	....	....
	San Antonio	AHL	4	2	1	3	0	....	....	....	....	....	....	....	....	....	....	....	....	....	....	....	....	....	....
2009-10	San Antonio	AHL	18	2	6	8	12	....	....	....	....	....	....	....	....	....	....	....	....	....	....	....	....	....	....
	Cherepovets	KHL	25	14	1	15	12	....	....	....	....	....	....	....	....	....	....	....	....	....	....	....	....	....	....
2010-11	San Antonio	AHL	60	10	23	33	26	....	....	....	....	....	....	....	....	....	....	....	....	....	....	....	....	....	....
2011-12	St. Petersburg	KHL	42	17	13	30	18	....	....	....	....	....	....	....	....	....	10	4	2	6	4	....	....	....	....
2012-13	St. Petersburg	KHL	39	12	15	27	16	....	....	....	....	....	....	....	....	....	15	*10	8	18	20	....	....	....	....
	NHL Totals		**61**	**8**	**8**	**16**	**20**	**1**	**0**	**1**	**71**	**11.3**		**60**	**38.3**	**12:08**	....	....	....	....	....	....	....	....	....

• Loaned to **Cherepovets** (KHL) by **Phoenix** (San Antonio-AHL), November 28, 2009. Signed as a free agent by **St. Petersburg** (KHL), October 11, 2011.

TIMMINS, Scott

(TIHM-mihnz, SKAWT) **FLA**

Center. Shoots left. 5'11", 191 lbs. Born, Hamilton, Ont., September 11, 1989. Florida's 7th choice, 165th overall, in 2009 Entry Draft.

2005-06	Burlington	ON-Jr.A	31	8	4	12	8	....	....	....	....	....	....	....	....	....	4	1	1	2	0	....	....	....	....
2006-07	Kitchener Rangers	OHL	42	2	5	7	8	....	....	....	....	....	....	....	....	....	....	....	....	....	....	....	....	....	....
2007-08	Kitchener Rangers	OHL	62	17	12	29	46	....	....	....	....	....	....	....	....	....	20	3	5	8	10	....	....	....	....
2008-09	Kitchener Rangers	OHL	38	25	24	49	28	....	....	....	....	....	....	....	....	....	....	....	....	....	....	....	....	....	....
	Windsor Spitfires	OHL	28	10	14	24	33	....	....	....	....	....	....	....	....	....	20	6	10	16	26	....	....	....	....
2009-10	Windsor Spitfires	OHL	56	30	24	54	47	....	....	....	....	....	....	....	....	....	19	11	11	22	18	....	....	....	....
2010-11	**Florida**	**NHL**	**19**	**1**	**0**	**1**	**8**	**0**	**0**	**0**	**13**	**7.7**	**–8**	**130**	**46.9**	**10:49**	....	....	....	....	....	....	....	....	....
	Rochester	AHL	45	10	12	22	18	....	....	....	....	....	....	....	....	....	....	....	....	....	....	....	....	....	....
2011-12	San Antonio	AHL	70	11	16	27	34	....	....	....	....	....	....	....	....	....	10	1	0	1	8	....	....	....	....
2012-13	San Antonio	AHL	65	11	13	24	58	....	....	....	....	....	....	....	....	....	....	....	....	....	....	....	....	....	....
	Florida	**NHL**	**5**	**0**	**0**	**0**	**4**	**0**	**0**	**0**	**6**	**0.0**	**–2**	**31**	**48.4**	**10:35**	....	....	....	....	....	....	....	....	....
	NHL Totals		**24**	**1**	**0**	**1**	**12**	**0**	**0**	**0**	**19**	**5.3**		**161**	**47.2**	**10:46**	....	....	....	....	....	....	....	....	....

TIMONEN, Kimmo

(TEEM-oh-nehn, KEE-moh) **PHI**

Defense. Shoots left. 5'10", 194 lbs. Born, Kuopio, Finland, March 18, 1975. Los Angeles' 11th choice, 250th overall, in 1993 Entry Draft.

1990-91	KalPa Kuopio Jr.	Fin-Jr.	4	0	1	1	2	....	....	....	....	....	....	....	....	....	....	....	....	....	....	....	....	....	....
1991-92	KalPa Kuopio Jr.	Fin-Jr.	32	7	10	17	4	....	....	....	....	....	....	....	....	....	....	....	....	....	....	....	....	....	....
	KalPa Kuopio	Finland	5	0	0	0	0	....	....	....	....	....	....	....	....	....	....	....	....	....	....	....	....	....	....
1992-93	KalPa Kuopio U18	Fin-U18	3	0	5	5	0	....	....	....	....	....	....	....	....	....	....	....	....	....	....	....	....	....	....
	KalPa Kuopio Jr.	Fin-Jr.	16	9	15	24	10	....	....	....	....	....	....	....	....	....	....	....	....	....	....	....	....	....	....
	KalPa Kuopio	Finland	33	0	2	2	4	....	....	....	....	....	....	....	....	....	....	....	....	....	....	....	....	....	....
1993-94	KalPa Kuopio Jr.	Fin-Jr.	5	4	7	11	0	....	....	....	....	....	....	....	....	....	....	....	....	....	....	....	....	....	....
	KalPa Kuopio	Finland	46	6	7	13	55	....	....	....	....	....	....	....	....	....	....	....	....	....	....	....	....	....	....
1994-95	TPS Turku Jr.	Fin-Jr.	1	0	0	0	0	....	....	....	....	....	....	....	....	....	....	....	....	....	....	....	....	....	....
	TPS Turku	Finland	45	3	4	7	10	....	....	....	....	....	....	....	....	....	13	0	1	1	6	....	....	....	....
1995-96	TPS Turku	Finland	48	3	21	24	22	....	....	....	....	....	....	....	....	....	9	1	2	3	12	....	....	....	....
1996-97	TPS Turku	Finland	50	10	14	24	18	....	....	....	....	....	....	....	....	....	12	2	7	9	6	....	....	....	....
	TPS Turku	EuroHL	6	1	0	1	27	....	....	....	....	....	....	....	....	....	4	0	1	1	0	....	....	....	....
1997-98	HIFK Helsinki	Finland	45	10	15	25	24	....	....	....	....	....	....	....	....	....	9	3	4	7	8	....	....	....	....
	Finland	Olympics	6	0	1	1	2	....	....	....	....	....	....	....	....	....	....	....	....	....	....	....	....	....	....
1998-99	**Nashville**	**NHL**	**50**	**4**	**8**	**12**	**30**	**1**	**0**	**0**	**75**	**5.3**	**–4**	**0**	**0.0**	**19:04**	....	....	....	....	....	....	....	....	....
	Milwaukee	IHL	29	2	13	15	22	....	....	....	....	....	....	....	....	....	....	....	....	....	....	....	....	....	....
99-2000	**Nashville**	**NHL**	**51**	**8**	**25**	**33**	**26**	**2**	**1**	**2**	**97**	**8.2**	**–5**	**0**	**0.0**	**21:06**	....	....	....	....	....	....	....	....	....
2000-01	**Nashville**	**NHL**	**82**	**12**	**13**	**25**	**50**	**6**	**0**	**3**	**151**	**7.9**	**–6**	**2**	**50.0**	**23:11**	....	....	....	....	....	....	....	....	....
2001-02	**Nashville**	**NHL**	**82**	**13**	**29**	**42**	**28**	**9**	**0**	**1**	**154**	**8.4**	**2**	**0**	**0.0**	**24:12**	....	....	....	....	....	....	....	....	....
	Finland	Olympics	4	0	1	1	2	....	....	....	....	....	....	....	....	....	....	....	....	....	....	....	....	....	....
2002-03	**Nashville**	**NHL**	**72**	**6**	**34**	**40**	**46**	**4**	**0**	**0**	**144**	**4.2**	**–3**	**0**	**0.0**	**22:25**	....	....	....	....	....	....	....	....	....
2003-04	**Nashville**	**NHL**	**77**	**12**	**32**	**44**	**52**	**8**	**0**	**1**	**180**	**6.7**	**–7**	**1**	**0.0**	**23:52**	**6**	**0**	**0**	**0**	**10**	**0**	**0**	**0**	**24:16**
2004-05	HC Lugano	Swiss	3	0	1	1	0	....	....	....	....	....	....	....	....	....	....	....	....	....	....	....	....	....	....
	Brynas IF Gavle	Sweden	10	5	3	8	8	....	....	....	....	....	....	....	....	....	....	....	....	....	....	....	....	....	....
	KalPa Kuopio	Finland-2	12	4	13	17	6	....	....	....	....	....	....	....	....	....	8	3	7	10	4	....	....	....	....
2005-06	**Nashville**	**NHL**	**79**	**11**	**39**	**50**	**74**	**8**	**0**	**1**	**156**	**7.1**	**–3**	**5**	**80.0**	**22:26**	**5**	**1**	**3**	**4**	**4**	**0**	**1**	**0**	**24:42**
	Finland	Olympics	8	1	4	5	2	....	....	....	....	....	....	....	....	....	....	....	....	....	....	....	....	....	....
2006-07	**Nashville**	**NHL**	**80**	**13**	**42**	**55**	**42**	**8**	**0**	**2**	**121**	**10.7**	**20**	**1**	**0.0**	**21:51**	**5**	**0**	**2**	**2**	**4**	**0**	**0**	**0**	**24:33**
2007-08	**Philadelphia**	**NHL**	**80**	**8**	**36**	**44**	**50**	**3**	**1**	**1**	**125**	**6.4**	**0**	**0**	**0.0**	**23:35**	**13**	**0**	**6**	**6**	**8**	**0**	**0**	**0**	**24:41**
2008-09	**Philadelphia**	**NHL**	**77**	**3**	**40**	**43**	**54**	**2**	**0**	**0**	**104**	**2.9**	**19**	**2**	**0.0**	**24:31**	**6**	**0**	**1**	**1**	**12**	**0**	**0**	**0**	**26:21**
2009-10	**Philadelphia**	**NHL**	**82**	**6**	**33**	**39**	**50**	**1**	**2**	**1**	**121**	**5.0**	**–2**	**0**	**0.0**	**22:53**	**23**	**1**	**10**	**11**	**20**	**0**	**0**	**0**	**26:38**
	Finland	Olympics	6	2	2	4	2	....	....	....	....	....	....	....	....	....	....	....	....	....	....	....	....	....	....
2010-11	**Philadelphia**	**NHL**	**82**	**6**	**31**	**37**	**36**	**1**	**2**	**0**	**147**	**4.1**	**11**	**1**	**0.0**	**22:28**	**11**	**1**	**5**	**6**	**14**	**0**	**0**	**0**	**24:53**

			Regular Season														Playoffs								
Season	Club	League	GP	G	A	Pts	PIM	PP	SH	GW	S	%	+/-	TF	F%	Min	GP	G	A	Pts	PIM	PP	SH	GW	Min
2011-12	Philadelphia	NHL	76	4	39	43	46	4	0	0	130	3.1	8	1	100.0	21:14	11	1	3	4	23	1	0	0	20:11
2012-13	Philadelphia	NHL	45	5	24	29	36	3	0	1	78	6.4	3	0	0.0	21:46	....	....	....	....	....	....	....	....	....
	NHL Totals		1015	111	425	536	620	60	6	13	1783	6.2		13	46.2	22:38	80	4	30	34	95	1	1	0	24:44

Olympic All-Star Team (2006)

Played in NHL All-Star Game (2004, 2007, 2008, 2012)

Traded to **Nashville** by **Los Angeles** with Jan Vopat for future considerations, June 26, 1998. Signed as a free agent by **Lugano** (Swiss), October 31, 2004. Signed as a free agent by **Gavle** (Sweden), November 8, 2004. Signed as a free agent by **Kuopio** (Finland-2), January 3, 2005. Traded to **Philadelphia** by **Nashville** with Scott Hartnell for Nashville's 1st round choice (previously acquired, Nashville selected Jonathon Blum) in 2007 Entry Draft, June 18, 2007.

TINORDI, Jarred

(tih-NOHR-dee, JAIR-uhd) **MTL**

Defense. Shoots left. 6'6", 227 lbs. Born, Burnsville, MN, February 20, 1992. Montreal's 1st choice, 22nd overall, in 2010 Entry Draft.

2008-09	USNTDP	NAHL	42	2	13	15	53	....	....	....	....	....	....	....	....	....	9	1	0	1	6	....	....	....	....
	USNTDP	U-17	16	3	1	4	12	....	....	....	....	....	....	....	....	....	....	....	....	....	....	....	....	....	....
	USNTDP	U-18	1	0	1	1	0	....	....	....	....	....	....	....	....	....	....	....	....	....	....	....	....	....	....
2009-10	USNTDP	USHL	26	4	5	9	68	....	....	....	....	....	....	....	....	....	....	....	....	....	....	....	....	....	....
	USNTDP	U-18	39	2	6	8	37	....	....	....	....	....	....	....	....	....	....	....	....	....	....	....	....	....	....
2010-11	London Knights	OHL	63	1	13	14	140	....	....	....	....	....	....	....	....	....	6	0	0	0	17	....	....	....	....
2011-12	London Knights	OHL	48	2	14	16	63	....	....	....	....	....	....	....	....	....	19	3	5	8	27	....	....	....	....
2012-13	Hamilton	AHL	67	2	11	13	71	....	....	....	....	....	....	....	....	....	....	....	....	....	....	....	....	....	....
	Montreal	**NHL**	**8**	**0**	**2**	**2**	**2**	**0**	**0**	**0**	**5**	**0.0**	**5**	**0**	**0.0**	**11:43**	**5**	**0**	**1**	**1**	**15**	**0**	**0**	**0**	**13:05**
	NHL Totals		**8**	**0**	**2**	**2**	**2**	**0**	**0**	**0**	**5**	**0.0**		**0**	**0.0**	**11:43**	**5**	**0**	**1**	**1**	**15**	**0**	**0**	**0**	**13:05**

Memorial Cup All-Star Team (2012)

TLUSTY, Jiri

(T'LOO-stee, YIH-ree) **CAR**

Center. Shoots left. 6', 209 lbs. Born, Slany, Czech., March 16, 1988. Toronto's 1st choice, 13th overall, in 2006 Entry Draft.

2002-03	HC Kladno U17	CzR-U17	48	28	17	45	22	....	....	....	....	....	....	....	....	....	10	5	4	9	12	....	....	....	....
2003-04	HC Kladno U17	CzR-U17	1	0	0	0	2	....	....	....	....	....	....	....	....	....	1	0	0	0	2	....	....	....	....
	HC Kladno Jr.	CzRep-Jr.	51	10	3	13	12	....	....	....	....	....	....	....	....	....	1	0	0	0	0	....	....	....	....
2004-05	HC Kladno Jr.	CzRep-Jr.	42	15	12	27	54	....	....	....	....	....	....	....	....	....	10	2	2	4	8	....	....	....	....
2005-06	HC Kladno Jr.	CzRep-Jr.	6	4	2	6	2	....	....	....	....	....	....	....	....	....	6	7	6	13	6	....	....	....	....
	HC Rabat Kladno	CzRep	44	7	3	10	51	....	....	....	....	....	....	....	....	....	....	....	....	....	....	....	....	....	....
2006-07	Sault Ste. Marie	OHL	37	13	21	34	28	....	....	....	....	....	....	....	....	....	13	9	8	17	14	....	....	....	....
	Toronto Marlies	AHL	6	3	1	4	4	....	....	....	....	....	....	....	....	....	....	....	....	....	....	....	....	....	....
2007-08	**Toronto**	**NHL**	**58**	**10**	**6**	**16**	**14**	**2**	**0**	**2**	**69**	**14.5**	**–12**	**2**	**50.0**	**10:55**	....	....	....	....	....	....	....	....	....
	Toronto Marlies	AHL	14	7	11	18	8	....	....	....	....	....	....	....	....	....	19	2	8	10	8	....	....	....	....
2008-09	**Toronto**	**NHL**	**14**	**0**	**4**	**4**	**0**	**0**	**0**	**0**	**22**	**0.0**	**0**	**3**	**33.3**	**12:42**	....	....	....	....	....	....	....	....	....
	Toronto Marlies	AHL	66	25	41	66	26	....	....	....	....	....	....	....	....	....	6	1	2	3	2	....	....	....	....
2009-10	**Toronto**	**NHL**	**2**	**0**	**0**	**0**	**0**	**0**	**0**	**0**	**2**	**0.0**	**–2**	**0**	**0.0**	**12:13**	....	....	....	....	....	....	....	....	....
	Toronto Marlies	AHL	19	8	7	15	4	....	....	....	....	....	....	....	....	....	....	....	....	....	....	....	....	....	....
	Carolina	**NHL**	**18**	**1**	**5**	**6**	**6**	**0**	**0**	**0**	**15**	**6.7**	**2**	**2**	**100.0**	**12:36**	....	....	....	....	....	....	....	....	....
	Albany River Rats	AHL	20	6	9	15	10	....	....	....	....	....	....	....	....	....	5	0	1	1	0	....	....	....	....
2010-11	**Carolina**	**NHL**	**57**	**6**	**6**	**12**	**14**	**0**	**0**	**0**	**53**	**11.3**	**1**	**15**	**13.3**	**9:52**	....	....	....	....	....	....	....	....	....
	Charlotte	AHL	5	1	1	2	4	....	....	....	....	....	....	....	....	....	....	....	....	....	....	....	....	....	....
2011-12	**Carolina**	**NHL**	**79**	**17**	**19**	**36**	**26**	**2**	**0**	**1**	**136**	**12.5**	**1**	**11**	**27.3**	**14:54**	....	....	....	....	....	....	....	....	....
2012-13	Rytiri Kladno	CzRep	24	12	11	23	12	....	....	....	....	....	....	....	....	....	....	....	....	....	....	....	....	....	....
	Carolina	**NHL**	**48**	**23**	**15**	**38**	**18**	**4**	**0**	**3**	**117**	**19.7**	**15**	**18**	**16.7**	**18:15**	....	....	....	....	....	....	....	....	....
	NHL Totals		**276**	**57**	**55**	**112**	**78**	**8**	**0**	**6**	**414**	**13.8**		**51**	**23.5**	**13:20**	....	....	....	....	....	....	....	....	....

Traded to **Carolina** by **Toronto** for Philippe Paradis, December 3, 2009. Signed as a free agent by **Kladno** (CzRep), September 17, 2012.

TOEWS, Jonathan

(TAYVZ, JAWN-ah-thuhn) **CHI**

Center. Shoots left. 6'2", 208 lbs. Born, Winnipeg, Man., April 29, 1988. Chicago's 1st choice, 3rd overall, in 2006 Entry Draft.

2004-05	Shat.-St. Mary's	High-MN	64	48	62	110	38	....	....	....	....	....	....	....	....	....	....	....	....	....	....	....	....	....	....
2005-06	North Dakota	WCHA	42	22	17	39	22	....	....	....	....	....	....	....	....	....	....	....	....	....	....	....	....	....	....
2006-07	North Dakota	WCHA	34	18	28	46	10	....	....	....	....	....	....	....	....	....	....	....	....	....	....	....	....	....	....
2007-08	**Chicago**	**NHL**	**64**	**24**	**30**	**54**	**44**	**7**	**0**	**4**	**144**	**16.7**	**11**	**956**	**53.2**	**18:40**	....	....	....	....	....	....	....	....	....
2008-09	**Chicago**	**NHL**	**82**	**34**	**35**	**69**	**51**	**12**	**0**	**7**	**195**	**17.4**	**12**	**1287**	**54.7**	**18:38**	**17**	**7**	**6**	**13**	**26**	**5**	**0**	**2**	**16:14**
2009-10♦	**Chicago**	**NHL**	**76**	**25**	**43**	**68**	**47**	**9**	**1**	**3**	**202**	**12.4**	**22**	**1397**	**57.3**	**20:00**	**22**	**7**	***22**	**29**	**4**	**5**	**0**	**3**	**20:58**
	Canada	Olympics	7	1	*7	8	2	....	....	....	....	....	....	....	....	....	....	....	....	....	....	....	....	....	....
2010-11	**Chicago**	**NHL**	**80**	**32**	**44**	**76**	**26**	**10**	**1**	**8**	**233**	**13.7**	**25**	**1653**	**56.7**	**20:46**	**7**	**1**	**3**	**4**	**2**	**0**	**1**	**0**	**22:31**
2011-12	**Chicago**	**NHL**	**59**	**29**	**28**	**57**	**28**	**5**	**1**	**4**	**185**	**15.7**	**17**	**1137**	**59.4**	**20:51**	**6**	**2**	**2**	**4**	**6**	**0**	**0**	**1**	**22:17**
2012-13♦	**Chicago**	**NHL**	**47**	**23**	**25**	**48**	**27**	**2**	**2**	**5**	**143**	**16.1**	**28**	**933**	**59.9**	**19:21**	**23**	**3**	**11**	**14**	**18**	**1**	**0**	**0**	**21:33**
	NHL Totals		**408**	**167**	**205**	**372**	**223**	**45**	**5**	**31**	**1102**	**15.2**		**7363**	**56.8**	**19:43**	**75**	**20**	**44**	**64**	**56**	**11**	**1**	**6**	**20:19**

WCHA Second All-Star Team (2007) • NCAA West First All-American Team (2007) • NHL All-Rookie Team (2008) • Olympic All-Star Team (2010) • Olympics – Best Forward (2010) • Conn Smythe Trophy (2010) • Frank J. Selke Trophy (2013) • NHL Second All-Star Team (2013)

Played in NHL All-Star Game (2009, 2011)

TOFFOLI, Tyler

(TAW-foh-lee, TIGH-luhr) **L.A.**

Center. Shoots right. 6'1", 187 lbs. Born, Scarborough, Ont., April 24, 1992. Los Angeles' 2nd choice, 47th overall, in 2010 Entry Draft.

2007-08	Tor. Jr. Canadiens	GTHL	83	68	106	174	72																		
2008-09	Ottawa 67's	OHL	54	17	29	46	16	....	....	....	....	....	....	....	....	....	7	2	6	8	4	....	....	....	....
2009-10	Ottawa 67's	OHL	65	37	42	79	54	....	....	....	....	....	....	....	....	....	12	7	6	13	10	....	....	....	....
2010-11	Ottawa 67's	OHL	68	*57	51	*108	33	....	....	....	....	....	....	....	....	....	4	3	5	8	4	....	....	....	....
	Manchester	AHL	1	1	0	1	0	....	....	....	....	....	....	....	....	....	5	1	0	1	6	....	....	....	....
2011-12	Ottawa 67's	OHL	65	*52	48	100	22	....	....	....	....	....	....	....	....	....	18	11	7	18	21	....	....	....	....
2012-13	Manchester	AHL	58	28	23	51	18	....	....	....	....	....	....	....	....	....	....	....	....	....	....	....	....	....	....
	Los Angeles	**NHL**	**10**	**2**	**3**	**5**	**2**	**1**	**0**	**0**	**20**	**10.0**	**3**	**0**	**0.0**	**11:59**	**12**	**2**	**4**	**6**	**0**	**1**	**0**	**0**	**10:46**
	NHL Totals		**10**	**2**	**3**	**5**	**2**	**1**	**0**	**0**	**20**	**10.0**		**0**	**0.0**	**11:59**	**12**	**2**	**4**	**6**	**0**	**1**	**0**	**0**	**10:46**

OHL First All-Star Team (2011, 2012) • AHL All-Rookie Team (2013) • Dudley "Red" Garrett Memorial Trophy (AHL - Top Rookie) (2013)

TOOTOO, Jordin

(TOO-TOO, JOHR-dahn) **DET**

Right wing. Shoots right. 5'9", 199 lbs. Born, Churchill, Man., February 2, 1983. Nashville's 6th choice, 98th overall, in 2001 Entry Draft.

1997-98	Spruce Grove	AMBHL	STATISTICS NOT AVAILABLE																						
1998-99	OCN Blizzard	MJHL	47	16	21	37	251	....	....	....	....	....	....	....	....	....	....	....	....	....	....	....	....	....	....
99-2000	Brandon	WHL	45	6	10	16	214	....	....	....	....	....	....	....	....	....	....	....	....	....	....	....	....	....	....
2000-01	Brandon	WHL	60	20	28	48	172	....	....	....	....	....	....	....	....	....	6	2	4	6	18	....	....	....	....
2001-02	Brandon	WHL	64	32	39	71	272	....	....	....	....	....	....	....	....	....	16	4	3	7	*58	....	....	....	....
2002-03	Brandon	WHL	51	35	39	74	216	....	....	....	....	....	....	....	....	....	17	6	3	9	49	....	....	....	....
2003-04	**Nashville**	**NHL**	**70**	**4**	**4**	**8**	**137**	**2**	**0**	**0**	**92**	**4.3**	**–6**	**18**	**55.6**	**8:29**	**5**	**0**	**0**	**0**	**4**	**0**	**0**	**0**	**5:09**
2004-05	Milwaukee	AHL	59	10	12	22	266	....	....	....	....	....	....	....	....	....	6	0	0	0	41	....	....	....	....
2005-06	**Nashville**	**NHL**	**34**	**4**	**6**	**10**	**55**	**0**	**0**	**0**	**61**	**6.6**	**9**	**17**	**70.6**	**9:15**	**3**	**0**	**0**	**0**	**0**	**0**	**0**	**0**	**4:04**
	Milwaukee	AHL	41	13	14	27	133	....	....	....	....	....	....	....	....	....	15	9	2	11	35	....	....	....	....
2006-07	**Nashville**	**NHL**	**65**	**3**	**6**	**9**	**116**	**0**	**0**	**0**	**77**	**3.9**	**–11**	**12**	**33.3**	**8:24**	**4**	**0**	**1**	**1**	**21**	**0**	**0**	**0**	**9:32**
2007-08	**Nashville**	**NHL**	**63**	**11**	**7**	**18**	**100**	**0**	**0**	**1**	**98**	**11.2**	**–8**	**4**	**50.0**	**9:54**	**6**	**2**	**0**	**2**	**4**	**0**	**0**	**0**	**12:31**
2008-09	**Nashville**	**NHL**	**72**	**4**	**12**	**16**	**124**	**0**	**0**	**1**	**138**	**2.9**	**–15**	**16**	**56.3**	**12:05**	....	....	....	....	....	....	....	....	....
2009-10	**Nashville**	**NHL**	**51**	**6**	**10**	**16**	**40**	**0**	**0**	**1**	**101**	**5.9**	**2**	**8**	**25.0**	**10:50**	**6**	**0**	**1**	**1**	**2**	**0**	**0**	**0**	**7:58**
2010-11	**Nashville**	**NHL**	**54**	**8**	**10**	**18**	**61**	**0**	**0**	**1**	**85**	**9.4**	**8**	**3**	**66.7**	**11:53**	**12**	**1**	**5**	**6**	**28**	**0**	**0**	**0**	**13:26**
2011-12	**Nashville**	**NHL**	**77**	**6**	**24**	**30**	**92**	**1**	**0**	**1**	**136**	**4.4**	**–5**	**12**	**33.3**	**13:09**	**3**	**0**	**0**	**0**	**4**	**0**	**0**	**0**	**7:46**
2012-13	**Detroit**	**NHL**	**42**	**3**	**5**	**8**	**78**	**0**	**0**	**1**	**45**	**6.7**	**0**	**0**	**0.0**	**9:05**	**1**	**0**	**0**	**0**	**2**	**0**	**0**	**0**	**6:24**
	NHL Totals		**528**	**49**	**84**	**133**	**803**	**3**	**0**	**6**	**833**	**5.9**		**90**	**50.0**	**10:29**	**40**	**3**	**7**	**10**	**65**	**0**	**0**	**0**	**9:45**

WHL East First All-Star Team (2003)

Signed as a free agent by **Detroit**, July 1, 2012.

TORRES, Raffi

(TOHR-ehz, RA-fee) **S.J.**

Left wing. Shoots left. 6', 215 lbs. Born, Toronto, Ont., October 8, 1981. NY Islanders' 2nd choice, 5th overall, in 2000 Entry Draft.

			Regular Season														Playoffs								
Season	Club	League	GP	G	A	Pts	PIM	PP	SH	GW	S	%	+/-	TF	F%	Min	GP	G	A	Pts	PIM	PP	SH	GW	Min
1997-98	Thornhill Rattlers	ON-Jr.A	46	17	16	33	90	....	....	....	....	....	....	....	....	....	....	....	....	....	....	....	....	....	....
1998-99	Brampton	OHL	62	35	27	62	32	....	....	....	....	....	....	....	....	....	....	....	....	....	....	....	....	....	....
99-2000	Brampton	OHL	68	43	48	91	40	....	....	....	....	....	....	....	....	....	6	5	2	7	23	....	....	....	....
2000-01	Brampton	OHL	55	33	37	70	76	....	....	....	....	....	....	....	....	....	8	7	4	11	19	....	....	....	....
2001-02	**NY Islanders**	**NHL**	**14**	**0**	**1**	**1**	**6**	**0**	**0**	**0**	**9**	**0.0**	**2**	**0**	**0.0**	**7:35**	....	....	....	....	....	....	....	....	....
	Bridgeport	AHL	59	20	10	30	45	....	....	....	....	....	....	....	....	....	20	8	9	17	26	....	....	....	....
2002-03	**NY Islanders**	**NHL**	**17**	**0**	**5**	**5**	**10**	**0**	**0**	**0**	**12**	**0.0**	**0**	**4**	**25.0**	**7:40**	....	....	....	....	....	....	....	....	....
	Bridgeport	AHL	49	17	15	32	54	....	....	....	....	....	....	....	....	....	....	....	....	....	....	....	....	....	....
	Hamilton	AHL	11	1	7	8	14	....	....	....	....	....	....	....	....	....	23	6	1	7	29	....	....	....	....
2003-04	**Edmonton**	**NHL**	**80**	**20**	**14**	**34**	**65**	**5**	**0**	**3**	**136**	**14.7**	**12**	**21**	**28.6**	**12:38**	....	....	....	....	....	....	....	....	....
2004-05	Edmonton	AHL	67	21	25	46	165	....	....	....	....	....	....	....	....	....	....	....	....	....	....	....	....	....	....
2005-06	**Edmonton**	**NHL**	**82**	**27**	**14**	**41**	**50**	**6**	**0**	**3**	**164**	**16.5**	**4**	**60**	**41.7**	**13:24**	**22**	**4**	**7**	**11**	**16**	**1**	**0**	**1**	**13:15**
2006-07	**Edmonton**	**NHL**	**82**	**15**	**19**	**34**	**88**	**1**	**0**	**0**	**154**	**9.7**	**–7**	**50**	**44.0**	**14:19**	....	....	....	....	....	....	....	....	....
2007-08	**Edmonton**	**NHL**	**32**	**5**	**6**	**11**	**36**	**1**	**0**	**2**	**87**	**5.7**	**–4**	**20**	**65.0**	**17:01**	....	....	....	....	....	....	....	....	....
2008-09	**Columbus**	**NHL**	**51**	**12**	**8**	**20**	**23**	**2**	**0**	**6**	**74**	**16.2**	**–4**	**19**	**57.9**	**12:06**	**4**	**0**	**2**	**2**	**2**	**0**	**0**	**0**	**12:04**
2009-10	**Columbus**	**NHL**	**60**	**19**	**12**	**31**	**32**	**7**	**0**	**3**	**99**	**19.2**	**–8**	**47**	**36.2**	**13:34**	....	....	....	....	....	....	....	....	....
	Buffalo	**NHL**	**14**	**0**	**5**	**5**	**2**	**0**	**0**	**0**	**21**	**0.0**	**–3**	**3**	**33.3**	**13:21**	**4**	**0**	**2**	**2**	**12**	**0**	**0**	**0**	**12:55**
2010-11	**Vancouver**	**NHL**	**80**	**14**	**15**	**29**	**78**	**3**	**0**	**4**	**115**	**12.2**	**4**	**32**	**31.3**	**12:29**	**23**	**3**	**4**	**7**	**28**	**0**	**0**	**1**	**11:51**
2011-12	**Phoenix**	**NHL**	**79**	**15**	**11**	**26**	**83**	**1**	**0**	**1**	**99**	**15.2**	**2**	**15**	**46.7**	**11:22**	**3**	**1**	**1**	**2**	**2**	**0**	**0**	**0**	**19:16**
2012-13	**Phoenix**	**NHL**	**28**	**5**	**7**	**12**	**13**	**0**	**0**	**0**	**40**	**12.5**	**–1**	**6**	**66.7**	**13:00**	....	....	....	....	....	....	....	....	....
	San Jose	**NHL**	**11**	**2**	**4**	**6**	**4**	**1**	**0**	**0**	**20**	**10.0**	**1**	**7**	**28.6**	**13:57**	**5**	**1**	**0**	**1**	**2**	**0**	**0**	**1**	**17:42**
	NHL Totals		**630**	**134**	**121**	**255**	**490**	**27**	**0**	**22**	**1030**	**13.0**		**284**	**41.9**	**12:51**	**61**	**9**	**16**	**25**	**62**	**1**	**0**	**3**	**13:17**

OHL All-Rookie Team (1999) • OHL Second All-Star Team (2000, 2001)

Traded to **Edmonton** by **NY Islanders** with Brad Isbister for Janne Niinimaa and Washington's 2nd round choice (previously acquired, NY Islanders selected Evgeni Tunik) in 2003 Entry Draft, March 11, 2003. • Missed majority of 2007-08 due to knee injury vs. Detroit, December 15, 2007. Traded to **Columbus** by **Edmonton** for Gilbert Brule, July 1, 2008. Traded to **Buffalo** by **Columbus** for Nathan Paetsch and Vancouver's 2nd round choice (previously acquired, Columbus selected Petr Straka) in 2010 Entry Draft, March 3, 2010. Signed as a free agent by **Vancouver**, August 25, 2010. Signed as a free agent by **Phoenix**, July 1, 2011. Traded to **San Jose** by **Phoenix** for Florida's 3rd round choice (previously acquired, later traded to Phoenix – Phoenix selected Pavel Laplante) in 2013 Entry Draft, April 3, 2013.

TROPP, Corey

(TROHP, KOHR-ee) **BUF**

Right wing. Shoots right. 6', 183 lbs. Born, Grosse Pointe, MI, July 25, 1989. Buffalo's 3rd choice, 89th overall, in 2007 Entry Draft.

			Regular Season														Playoffs								
Season	Club	League	GP	G	A	Pts	PIM	PP	SH	GW	S	%	+/-	TF	F%	Min	GP	G	A	Pts	PIM	PP	SH	GW	Min
2005-06	Sioux Falls	USHL	46	7	8	15	21	....	....	....	....	....	....	....	....	....	14	2	3	5	8	....	....	....	....
2006-07	Sioux Falls	USHL	54	26	36	62	76	....	....	....	....	....	....	....	....	....	8	4	9	*13	0	....	....	....	....
2007-08	Michigan State	CCHA	42	6	11	17	16	....	....	....	....	....	....	....	....	....	....	....	....	....	....	....	....	....	....
2008-09	Michigan State	CCHA	21	3	8	11	45	....	....	....	....	....	....	....	....	....	....	....	....	....	....	....	....	....	....
2009-10	Michigan State	CCHA	37	20	22	42	50	....	....	....	....	....	....	....	....	....	....	....	....	....	....	....	....	....	....
2010-11	Portland Pirates	AHL	76	10	30	40	113	....	....	....	....	....	....	....	....	....	12	2	5	7	12	....	....	....	....
2011-12	**Buffalo**	**NHL**	**34**	**3**	**5**	**8**	**20**	**0**	**0**	**1**	**32**	**9.4**	**0**	**5**	**0.0**	**10:05**	....	....	....	....	....	....	....	....	....
	Rochester	AHL	27	9	13	22	46	....	....	....	....	....	....	....	....	....	3	0	0	0	8	....	....	....	....
2012-13	Rochester	AHL	6	2	2	4	7	....	....	....	....	....	....	....	....	....	....	....	....	....	....	....	....	....	....
	NHL Totals		**34**	**3**	**5**	**8**	**20**	**0**	**0**	**1**	**32**	**9.4**		**5**	**0.0**	**10:05**	....	....	....	....	....	....	....	....	....

CCHA Second All-Star Team (2010)

TURNBULL, Travis

(TUHRN-buhl, TRA-vihs)

Center. Shoots right. 6', 197 lbs. Born, Chesterfield, MO, July 7, 1986.

			Regular Season														Playoffs								
Season	Club	League	GP	G	A	Pts	PIM	PP	SH	GW	S	%	+/-	TF	F%	Min	GP	G	A	Pts	PIM	PP	SH	GW	Min
2003-04	Sioux City	USHL	56	7	12	19	73	....	....	....	....	....	....	....	....	....	7	0	0	0	9	....	....	....	....
2004-05	Sioux City	USHL	44	17	21	38	103	....	....	....	....	....	....	....	....	....	13	4	2	6	61	....	....	....	....
2005-06	U. of Michigan	CCHA	41	9	9	18	67	....	....	....	....	....	....	....	....	....	....	....	....	....	....	....	....	....	....
2006-07	U. of Michigan	CCHA	41	8	9	17	54	....	....	....	....	....	....	....	....	....	....	....	....	....	....	....	....	....	....
2007-08	U. of Michigan	CCHA	43	15	12	27	48	....	....	....	....	....	....	....	....	....	....	....	....	....	....	....	....	....	....
2008-09	U. of Michigan	CCHA	41	8	20	28	74	....	....	....	....	....	....	....	....	....	....	....	....	....	....	....	....	....	....
	Portland Pirates	AHL	3	0	0	0	5	....	....	....	....	....	....	....	....	....	5	0	0	0	4	....	....	....	....
2009-10	Portland Pirates	AHL	57	9	9	18	98	....	....	....	....	....	....	....	....	....	4	0	0	0	2	....	....	....	....
2010-11	Portland Pirates	AHL	20	5	4	9	28	....	....	....	....	....	....	....	....	....	10	1	1	2	2	....	....	....	....
2011-12	**Buffalo**	**NHL**	**3**	**1**	**0**	**1**	**5**	**0**	**0**	**0**	**3**	**33.3**	**0**	**10**	**50.0**	**4:55**	....	....	....	....	....	....	....	....	....
	Rochester	AHL	63	12	15	27	117	....	....	....	....	....	....	....	....	....	3	0	0	0	4	....	....	....	....
2012-13	Dusseldorf	Germany	50	12	34	46	88	....	....	....	....	....	....	....	....	....	....	....	....	....	....	....	....	....	....
	NHL Totals		**3**	**1**	**0**	**1**	**5**	**0**	**0**	**0**	**3**	**33.3**		**10**	**50.0**	**4:55**	....	....	....	....	....	....	....	....	....

Signed as a free agent by **Buffalo**, April 6, 2009. Signed as a free agent by **Dusseldorf** (Germany), August 1, 2012.

TURRIS, Kyle

(TUH-rihs, KIGHL) **OTT**

Center. Shoots right. 6'1", 195 lbs. Born, New Westminster, B.C., August 14, 1989. Phoenix's 1st choice, 3rd overall, in 2007 Entry Draft.

			Regular Season														Playoffs								
Season	Club	League	GP	G	A	Pts	PIM	PP	SH	GW	S	%	+/-	TF	F%	Min	GP	G	A	Pts	PIM	PP	SH	GW	Min
2004-05	Grandview	Minor-BC	30	13	20	33	....	....	....	....	....	....	....	....	....	....	12	3	6	9	....	....	....	....	....
2005-06	Burnaby Express	BCHL	57	36	36	72	32	....	....	....	....	....	....	....	....	....	20	10	13	23	6	....	....	....	....
2006-07	Burnaby Express	BCHL	53	66	55	121	83	....	....	....	....	....	....	....	....	....	14	12	14	26	16	....	....	....	....
2007-08	U. of Wisconsin	WCHA	36	11	24	35	38	....	....	....	....	....	....	....	....	....	....	....	....	....	....	....	....	....	....
	Phoenix	**NHL**	**3**	**0**	**1**	**1**	**2**	**0**	**0**	**0**	**11**	**0.0**	**–5**	**42**	**40.5**	**19:45**	....	....	....	....	....	....	....	....	....
2008-09	**Phoenix**	**NHL**	**63**	**8**	**12**	**20**	**21**	**3**	**0**	**3**	**91**	**8.8**	**–15**	**567**	**42.9**	**12:55**	....	....	....	....	....	....	....	....	....
	San Antonio	AHL	8	4	3	7	6	....	....	....	....	....	....	....	....	....	....	....	....	....	....	....	....	....	....
2009-10	San Antonio	AHL	76	24	39	63	60	....	....	....	....	....	....	....	....	....	....	....	....	....	....	....	....	....	....
2010-11	**Phoenix**	**NHL**	**65**	**11**	**14**	**25**	**16**	**0**	**0**	**1**	**116**	**9.5**	**0**	**540**	**50.0**	**11:16**	**4**	**1**	**2**	**3**	**2**	**0**	**0**	**0**	**13:49**
	San Antonio	AHL	2	0	1	1	2	....	....	....	....	....	....	....	....	....	....	....	....	....	....	....	....	....	....
2011-12	**Phoenix**	**NHL**	**6**	**0**	**0**	**0**	**4**	**0**	**0**	**0**	**9**	**0.0**	**–2**	**51**	**41.2**	**12:45**	....	....	....	....	....	....	....	....	....
	Ottawa	**NHL**	**49**	**12**	**17**	**29**	**27**	**1**	**0**	**2**	**133**	**9.0**	**12**	**672**	**47.2**	**17:21**	**7**	**1**	**2**	**3**	**2**	**0**	**0**	**1**	**16:37**
2012-13	Karpat Oulu	Finland	21	7	12	19	24	....	....	....	....	....	....	....	....	....	....	....	....	....	....	....	....	....	....
	Ottawa	**NHL**	**48**	**12**	**17**	**29**	**24**	**3**	**0**	**2**	**118**	**10.2**	**6**	**920**	**49.0**	**19:38**	**10**	**6**	**3**	**9**	**13**	**1**	**1**	**1**	**19:58**
	NHL Totals		**234**	**43**	**61**	**104**	**94**	**7**	**0**	**8**	**478**	**9.0**		**2792**	**47.2**	**14:51**	**21**	**8**	**7**	**15**	**17**	**1**	**1**	**2**	**17:41**

WCHA All-Rookie Team (2008)

Traded to **Ottawa** by **Phoenix** for David Rundblad and Ottawa's 2nd round choice (later traded to Columbus, later traded to Philadelphia – Philadelphia selected Anthony Stolarz) in 2012 Entry Draft, December 17, 2011. Signed as a free agent by **Oulu** (Finland), October 6, 2012.

TYRELL, Dana

(TIH-rehl, DAY-nuh) **T.B.**

Center/Right wing. Shoots left. 5'11", 192 lbs. Born, Airdrie, Alta., April 23, 1989. Tampa Bay's 1st choice, 47th overall, in 2007 Entry Draft.

			Regular Season														Playoffs								
Season	Club	League	GP	G	A	Pts	PIM	PP	SH	GW	S	%	+/-	TF	F%	Min	GP	G	A	Pts	PIM	PP	SH	GW	Min
2003-04	Airdrie Xtreme	AMBHL	35	21	47	68	28	....	....	....	....	....	....	....	....	....	7	6	4	10	....	....	....	....	....
2004-05	UFA Bisons	AMHL	34	16	23	39	32	....	....	....	....	....	....	....	....	....	16	8	9	*17	....	....	....	....	....
	Prince George	WHL	1	0	0	0	2	....	....	....	....	....	....	....	....	....	....	....	....	....	....	....	....	....	....
2005-06	Prince George	WHL	69	7	11	18	44	....	....	....	....	....	....	....	....	....	5	0	0	0	2	....	....	....	....
2006-07	Prince George	WHL	72	30	26	56	51	....	....	....	....	....	....	....	....	....	15	1	6	7	4	....	....	....	....
2007-08	Prince George	WHL	68	25	40	65	47	....	....	....	....	....	....	....	....	....	....	....	....	....	....	....	....	....	....
	Norfolk Admirals	AHL	11	1	5	6	6	....	....	....	....	....	....	....	....	....	....	....	....	....	....	....	....	....	....
2008-09	Prince George	WHL	30	19	21	40	27	....	....	....	....	....	....	....	....	....	....	....	....	....	....	....	....	....	....
2009-10	Norfolk Admirals	AHL	74	9	27	36	22	....	....	....	....	....	....	....	....	....	....	....	....	....	....	....	....	....	....
2010-11	**Tampa Bay**	**NHL**	**78**	**6**	**9**	**15**	**12**	**0**	**0**	**1**	**73**	**8.2**	**–5**	**11**	**45.5**	**12:03**	**7**	**0**	**0**	**0**	**2**	**0**	**0**	**0**	**7:24**
2011-12	**Tampa Bay**	**NHL**	**26**	**0**	**5**	**5**	**6**	**0**	**0**	**0**	**23**	**0.0**	**–5**	**3**	**0.0**	**10:31**	....	....	....	....	....	....	....	....	....
	Norfolk Admirals	AHL	18	4	5	9	8	....	....	....	....	....	....	....	....	....	....	....	....	....	....	....	....	....	....
2012-13	B. Bystrica	Slovakia	4	0	3	3	2	....	....	....	....	....	....	....	....	....	....	....	....	....	....	....	....	....	....
	Tampa Bay	**NHL**	**21**	**1**	**3**	**4**	**4**	**0**	**0**	**0**	**19**	**5.3**	**–3**	**15**	**33.3**	**10:21**	....	....	....	....	....	....	....	....	....
	Syracuse Crunch	AHL	15	5	3	8	11	....	....	....	....	....	....	....	....	....	....	....	....	....	....	....	....	....	....
	NHL Totals		**125**	**7**	**17**	**24**	**22**	**0**	**0**	**1**	**115**	**6.1**		**29**	**34.5**	**11:27**	**7**	**0**	**0**	**0**	**2**	**0**	**0**	**0**	**7:25**

Signed as a free agent by **Banska Bystrica** (Slovakia), December 4, 2012.

TYUTIN, Fedor

(T'YOO-tihn, FEH-duhr) **CBJ**

Defense. Shoots left. 6'2", 216 lbs. Born, Izhevsk, USSR, July 19, 1983. NY Rangers' 2nd choice, 40th overall, in 2001 Entry Draft.

			Regular Season														Playoffs								
Season	Club	League	GP	G	A	Pts	PIM	PP	SH	GW	S	%	+/-	TF	F%	Min	GP	G	A	Pts	PIM	PP	SH	GW	Min
1998-99	Magnitogorsk 2	Russia-4	7	0	1	1	2																		
99-2000	Izhstal Izhevsk 2	Russia-3	38	11	8	19	68																		
	Izhstal Izhevsk	Russia-2	10	0	1	1	12																		
2000-01	St. Petersburg	Russia	34	2	4	6	20																		
2001-02	Guelph Storm	OHL	53	19	40	59	54										9	2	8	10	8				
2002-03	St. Petersburg	Russia	10	1	1	2	16																		
	Ak Bars Kazan	Russia	10	0	0	0	8										5	0	0	0	4				
2003-04	**NY Rangers**	**NHL**	**25**	**2**	**5**	**7**	**14**	**0**	**1**	**0**	**33**	**6.1**	**–4**	**1**	**0.0**	**20:08**									
	Hartford	AHL	43	5	9	14	50										16	0	5	5	18				
2004-05	Hartford	AHL	13	2	1	3	10																		
	St. Petersburg	Russia	35	5	3	8	24																		
2005-06	**NY Rangers**	**NHL**	**77**	**6**	**19**	**25**	**58**	**4**	**0**	**2**	**102**	**5.9**	**1**	**1**	**0.0**	**20:33**	**4**	**0**	**1**	**1**	**0**	**0**	**0**	**0**	**17:50**
	Russia	Olympics	8	0	1	1	4																		
2006-07	**NY Rangers**	**NHL**	**66**	**2**	**12**	**14**	**44**	**1**	**1**	**0**	**75**	**2.7**	**–8**	**1**	**0.0**	**20:02**	**10**	**0**	**5**	**5**	**8**	**0**	**0**	**0**	**19:30**
2007-08	**NY Rangers**	**NHL**	**82**	**5**	**15**	**20**	**43**	**1**	**0**	**0**	**131**	**3.8**	**5**	**0**	**0.0**	**20:27**	**10**	**0**	**3**	**3**	**4**	**0**	**0**	**0**	**19:52**
2008-09	**Columbus**	**NHL**	**82**	**9**	**25**	**34**	**81**	**5**	**1**	**0**	**167**	**5.4**	**1**	**1**	**100.0**	**23:31**	**4**	**0**	**0**	**0**	**0**	**0**	**0**	**0**	**23:16**
2009-10	**Columbus**	**NHL**	**80**	**6**	**26**	**32**	**49**	**3**	**0**	**2**	**149**	**4.0**	**–7**	**3**	**33.3**	**23:31**									
	Russia	Olympics	4	0	2	2	2																		
2010-11	**Columbus**	**NHL**	**80**	**7**	**20**	**27**	**32**	**1**	**0**	**0**	**128**	**5.5**	**–12**	**2**	**50.0**	**22:42**									
2011-12	**Columbus**	**NHL**	**66**	**5**	**21**	**26**	**49**	**1**	**0**	**0**	**124**	**4.0**	**–21**	**0**	**0.0**	**24:09**									
2012-13	Mytischi	KHL	17	1	2	3	8																		
	Columbus	**NHL**	**48**	**4**	**18**	**22**	**28**	**0**	**0**	**1**	**56**	**7.1**	**9**	**1**	**100.0**	**24:06**									
	NHL Totals		**606**	**46**	**161**	**207**	**398**	**16**	**3**	**5**	**965**	**4.8**		**10**	**40.0**	**22:13**	**28**	**0**	**9**	**9**	**12**	**0**	**0**	**0**	**19:56**

Signed as a free agent by **St. Petersburg** (Russia), November 11, 2004. Traded to **Columbus** by **NY Rangers** with Christian Backman for Nikolai Zherdev and Dan Fritsche, July 2, 2008. Signed as a free agent by **Mytischi** (KHL), November 12, 2012.

ULLSTROM, David

(UHL-struhm, DAY-vihd) **NYI**

Center. Shoots left. 6'2", 195 lbs. Born, Jonkoping, Sweden, April 22, 1989. NY Islanders' 9th choice, 102nd overall, in 2008 Entry Draft.

Season	Club	League	GP	G	A	Pts	PIM	PP	SH	GW	S	%	+/-	TF	F%	Min	GP	G	A	Pts	PIM	PP	SH	GW	Min
2005-06	HV 71 U18	Swe-U18	13	5	8	13	14										5	4	1	5	14				
	HV 71 Jr.	Swe-Jr.	1	0	0	0	0																		
2006-07	HV 71 U18	Swe-U18	1	0	0	0	2										5	2	6	8	10				
	HV 71 Jr.	Swe-Jr.	39	16	14	30	30										4	0	2	2	0				
2007-08	HV 71 Jr.	Swe-Jr.	40	27	27	54	86										3	2	2	4	0				
	HV 71 Jonkoping	Sweden	7	0	0	0	0																		
2008-09	HV 71 Jr.	Swe-Jr.	2	0	0	0	0																		
	Boras HC	Sweden-2	15	9	7	16	22																		
	HV 71 Jonkoping	Sweden	19	1	3	4	6										14	1	0	1	4				
2009-10	HV 71 Jonkoping	Sweden	47	5	11	16	27										16	2	0	2	0				
	HV 71 Jr.	Swe-Jr.	1	1	0	1	2																		
2010-11	Bridgeport	AHL	67	17	24	41	36																		
2011-12	**NY Islanders**	**NHL**	**29**	**4**	**4**	**8**	**6**	**1**	**0**	**1**	**40**	**10.0**	**–2**	**10**	**60.0**	**10:59**									
	Bridgeport	AHL	40	24	6	30	22										3	1	1	2	4				
2012-13	Bridgeport	AHL	33	9	17	26	14																		
	NY Islanders	**NHL**	**20**	**2**	**3**	**5**	**6**	**0**	**0**	**1**	**28**	**7.1**	**–2**	**18**	**55.6**	**9:30**	**3**	**0**	**1**	**1**	**0**	**0**	**0**	**0**	**7:03**
	NHL Totals		**49**	**6**	**7**	**13**	**12**	**1**	**0**	**2**	**68**	**8.8**		**28**	**57.1**	**10:22**	**3**	**0**	**1**	**1**	**0**	**0**	**0**	**0**	**7:03**

Signed as a free agent by **Yaroslavl** (KHL), June 19, 2013.

UMBERGER, R.J.

(UHM-buhr-guhr, AHR-JAY) **CBJ**

Center. Shoots left. 6'2", 220 lbs. Born, Pittsburgh, PA, May 3, 1982. Vancouver's 1st choice, 16th overall, in 2001 Entry Draft.

Season	Club	League	GP	G	A	Pts	PIM	PP	SH	GW	S	%	+/-	TF	F%	Min	GP	G	A	Pts	PIM	PP	SH	GW	Min
1997-98	Plum Mustangs	High-PA	26	*60	*56	*116																			
1998-99	USNTDP	USHL	5	2	2	4	0																		
	USNTDP	NAHL	50	21	21	42	32																		
99-2000	USNTDP	U-18	6	1	0	1	2																		
	USNTDP	USHL	57	33	35	68	20																		
2000-01	Ohio State	CCHA	32	14	23	37	18																		
2001-02	Ohio State	CCHA	37	18	21	39	31																		
2002-03	Ohio State	CCHA	43	26	27	53	16																		
2003-04			DID NOT PLAY																						
2004-05	Philadelphia	AHL	80	21	44	65	36										21	3	7	10	12				
2005-06	**Philadelphia**	**NHL**	**73**	**20**	**18**	**38**	**18**	**5**	**0**	**2**	**138**	**14.5**	**9**	**163**	**50.3**	**13:14**	**5**	**1**	**0**	**1**	**2**	**0**	**0**	**0**	**11:15**
	Philadelphia	AHL	8	3	7	10	8																		
2006-07	**Philadelphia**	**NHL**	**81**	**16**	**12**	**28**	**41**	**2**	**2**	**1**	**134**	**11.9**	**–32**	**535**	**44.5**	**14:32**									
2007-08	**Philadelphia**	**NHL**	**74**	**13**	**37**	**50**	**19**	**4**	**0**	**3**	**173**	**7.5**	**0**	**117**	**38.5**	**17:52**	**17**	**10**	**5**	**15**	**10**	**1**	**0**	**2**	**16:51**
2008-09	**Columbus**	**NHL**	**82**	**26**	**20**	**46**	**53**	**9**	**0**	**2**	**234**	**11.1**	**–10**	**841**	**48.0**	**18:46**	**4**	**3**	**0**	**3**	**0**	**2**	**0**	**0**	**16:22**
2009-10	**Columbus**	**NHL**	**82**	**23**	**32**	**55**	**40**	**8**	**1**	**4**	**221**	**10.4**	**–16**	**704**	**52.8**	**19:10**									
2010-11	**Columbus**	**NHL**	**82**	**25**	**32**	**57**	**38**	**8**	**3**	**3**	**220**	**11.4**	**3**	**220**	**50.5**	**19:13**									
2011-12	**Columbus**	**NHL**	**77**	**20**	**20**	**40**	**27**	**5**	**0**	**3**	**200**	**10.0**	**–10**	**306**	**49.0**	**18:11**									
2012-13	**Columbus**	**NHL**	**48**	**8**	**10**	**18**	**16**	**2**	**0**	**0**	**96**	**8.3**	**3**	**108**	**50.0**	**18:29**									
	NHL Totals		**599**	**151**	**181**	**332**	**252**	**43**	**6**	**18**	**1416**	**10.7**		**2994**	**48.6**	**17:26**	**26**	**14**	**5**	**19**	**12**	**3**	**0**	**2**	**15:42**

CCHA All-Rookie Team (2001) • CCHA Rookie of the Year (2001) • CCHA First All-Star Team (2003) • NCAA West Second All-American Team (2003)

• Missed 2003-04 due to contract dispute. Traded to **NY Rangers** by **Vancouver** with Martin Grenier for Martin Rucinsky, March 9, 2004. Signed as a free agent by **Philadelphia**, June 16, 2004. Traded to **Columbus** by **Philadelphia** with Philadelphia's 4th round choice (Drew Olson) in 2008 Entry Draft for Colorado's 1st round choice (previously acquired, Philadelphia selected Luca Sbisa) in 2008 Entry Draft and Columbus's 3rd round choice (Marc-Andre Bourdon) in 2008 Entry Draft, June 20, 2008.

UPSHALL, Scottie

(UHP-shuhl, SKAW-tee) **FLA**

Left wing. Shoots left. 6', 200 lbs. Born, Fort McMurray, Alta., October 7, 1983. Nashville's 1st choice, 6th overall, in 2002 Entry Draft.

Season	Club	League	GP	G	A	Pts	PIM	PP	SH	GW	S	%	+/-	TF	F%	Min	GP	G	A	Pts	PIM	PP	SH	GW	Min
1998-99	Fort McMurray	AMHL	28	62	40	102	100																		
99-2000	Fort McMurray	AJHL	52	26	26	52	65																		
2000-01	Kamloops Blazers	WHL	70	42	45	87	111										4	0	2	2	10				
2001-02	Kamloops Blazers	WHL	61	32	51	83	139										4	1	2	3	21				
2002-03	**Nashville**	**NHL**	**8**	**1**	**0**	**1**	**0**	**0**	**0**	**0**	**6**	**16.7**	**2**	**2**	**0.0**	**8:42**									
	Kamloops Blazers	WHL	42	25	31	56	111										6	0	2	2	34				
	Milwaukee	AHL	2	1	0	1	2										6	0	0	0	2				
2003-04	**Nashville**	**NHL**	**7**	**0**	**1**	**1**	**0**	**0**	**0**	**0**	**6**	**0.0**	**–2**	**8**	**37.5**	**9:11**									
	Milwaukee	AHL	31	13	11	24	42										8	3	0	3	4				
2004-05	Milwaukee	AHL	62	19	27	46	108										5	2	2	4	8				
2005-06	**Nashville**	**NHL**	**48**	**8**	**16**	**24**	**34**	**1**	**0**	**2**	**72**	**11.1**	**14**	**11**	**45.5**	**10:26**	**2**	**0**	**0**	**0**	**0**	**0**	**0**	**0**	**11:57**
	Milwaukee	AHL	23	17	16	33	44										14	6	10	16	20				
2006-07	**Nashville**	**NHL**	**14**	**2**	**1**	**3**	**18**	**0**	**0**	**2**	**27**	**7.4**	**–1**	**0**	**0.0**	**10:28**									
	Milwaukee	AHL	5	0	1	1	6																		
	Philadelphia	**NHL**	**18**	**6**	**7**	**13**	**8**	**1**	**1**	**2**	**60**	**10.0**	**4**	**18**	**44.4**	**18:05**									
2007-08	**Philadelphia**	**NHL**	**61**	**14**	**16**	**30**	**74**	**3**	**0**	**1**	**128**	**10.9**	**2**	**7**	**28.6**	**13:20**	**17**	**3**	**4**	**7**	***44**	**1**	**0**	**1**	**13:57**
2008-09	**Philadelphia**	**NHL**	**55**	**7**	**14**	**21**	**63**	**2**	**0**	**0**	**126**	**5.6**	**5**	**10**	**10.0**	**13:13**									
	Phoenix	**NHL**	**19**	**8**	**5**	**13**	**26**	**3**	**0**	**1**	**66**	**12.1**	**2**	**9**	**44.4**	**18:35**									
2009-10	**Phoenix**	**NHL**	**49**	**18**	**14**	**32**	**50**	**2**	**0**	**4**	**119**	**15.1**	**5**	**17**	**41.2**	**15:03**									
2010-11	**Phoenix**	**NHL**	**61**	**16**	**11**	**27**	**42**	**2**	**0**	**2**	**144**	**11.1**	**5**	**19**	**21.1**	**13:27**									
	Columbus	**NHL**	**21**	**6**	**1**	**7**	**10**	**0**	**0**	**0**	**47**	**12.8**	**–12**	**6**	**66.7**	**15:46**									
2011-12	**Florida**	**NHL**	**26**	**2**	**3**	**5**	**29**	**1**	**0**	**1**	**53**	**3.8**	**–3**	**6**	**50.0**	**12:43**	**7**	**1**	**2**	**3**	**4**	**0**	**0**	**0**	**13:22**
2012-13	**Florida**	**NHL**	**27**	**4**	**1**	**5**	**25**	**1**	**0**	**1**	**54**	**7.4**	**–8**	**14**	**64.3**	**13:30**									
	NHL Totals		**414**	**92**	**90**	**182**	**379**	**16**	**1**	**16**	**908**	**10.1**		**127**	**39.4**	**13:29**	**26**	**4**	**6**	**10**	**48**	**1**	**0**	**1**	**13:38**

WHL All-Rookie Team (2001) • WHL Rookie of the Year (2001) • CHL All-Rookie Team (2001) • Canadian Major Junior Rookie of the Year (2001) • WHL West Second All-Star Team (2002)

• Missed majority of 2003-04 due to knee injury vs. Phoenix, December 22, 2003. Traded to **Philadelphia** by **Nashville** with Ryan Parent and Nashville's 1st (later traded back to Nashville – Nashville selected Jonathon Blum) and 3rd (later traded to Washington – Washington selected Phil Desimone) round choices in 2007 Entry Draft for Peter Forsberg, February 15, 2007. Traded to **Phoenix** by **Philadelphia** with Philadelphia's 2nd round choice (Lucas Lessio) in 2011 Entry Draft for Daniel Carcillo, March 4, 2009. Traded to **Columbus** by **Phoenix** with Sami Lepisto for Rostislav Klesla and Dane Byers, February 28, 2011. Signed as a free agent by **Florida**, July 1, 2011.

URBOM, Alexander (OOR-bohm, al-ehx-AN-duhr) N.J.

Defense. Shoots left. 6'5", 215 lbs. Born, Stockholm, Sweden, December 20, 1990. New Jersey's 3rd choice, 73rd overall, in 2009 Entry Draft.

Season	Club	League	Regular Season GP	G	A	Pts	PIM	PP	SH	GW	S	%	+/-	TF	F%	Min	Playoffs GP	G	A	Pts	PIM	PP	SH	GW	Min
2005-06	Djurgarden U18	Swe-U18	2	0	0	0	0	....	....	....	....	....	....	....	....	....	....	....	....	....	....	....	....	....	....
2006-07	Djurgarden U18	Swe-U18	31	6	11	17	36	....	....	....	....	....	....	....	....	....	3	0	1	1	2	....	....	....	....
2007-08	Djurgarden U18	Swe-U18	7	2	6	8	6	....	....	....	....	....	....	....	....	....	5	1	0	1	2	....	....	....	....
	Djurgarden Jr.	Swe-Jr.	39	3	8	11	54	....	....	....	....	....	....	....	....	....	7	0	1	1	2	....	....	....	....
2008-09	Djurgarden Jr.	Swe-Jr.	16	5	6	11	45	....	....	....	....	....	....	....	....	....	....	....	....	....	....	....	....	....	....
	Djurgarden	Sweden	28	0	0	0	2	....	....	....	....	....	....	....	....	....	....	....	....	....	....	....	....	....	....
	Djurgarden U18	Swe-U18	....	....	....	....	....	....	....	....	....	....	....	....	....	....	5	1	0	1	2	....	....	....	....
2009-10	Brandon	WHL	66	12	21	33	87	....	....	....	....	....	....	....	....	....	15	4	3	7	17	....	....	....	....
2010-11	**New Jersey**	**NHL**	**8**	**1**	**0**	**1**	**0**	**0**	**0**	**1**	**5**	**20.0**	**–2**	**0**	**0.0**	**12:35**	....	....	....	....	....	....	....	....	....
	Albany Devils	AHL	72	2	21	23	64	....	....	....	....	....	....	....	....	....	....	....	....	....	....	....	....	....	....
2011-12	**New Jersey**	**NHL**	**5**	**1**	**0**	**1**	**9**	**0**	**0**	**0**	**3**	**33.3**	**1**	**0**	**0.0**	**13:36**	....	....	....	....	....	....	....	....	....
	Albany Devils	AHL	50	2	10	12	33	....	....	....	....	....	....	....	....	....	....	....	....	....	....	....	....	....	....
2012-13	Albany Devils	AHL	68	0	8	8	64	....	....	....	....	....	....	....	....	....	....	....	....	....	....	....	....	....	....
	New Jersey	**NHL**	**1**	**0**	**0**	**0**	**0**	**0**	**0**	**0**	**0**	**0.0**	**–1**	**0**	**0.0**	**14:11**	....	....	....	....	....	....	....	....	....
	NHL Totals		**14**	**2**	**0**	**2**	**9**	**0**	**0**	**1**	**8**	**25.0**		**0**	**0.0**	**13:03**	....	....	....	....	....	....	....	....	....

VALABIK, Boris (vuh-LA-bihk, BOHR-ihs)

Defense. Shoots left. 6'7", 245 lbs. Born, Nitra, Czech., February 14, 1986. Atlanta's 1st choice, 10th overall, in 2004 Entry Draft.

Season	Club	League	Regular Season GP	G	A	Pts	PIM	PP	SH	GW	S	%	+/-	TF	F%	Min	Playoffs GP	G	A	Pts	PIM	PP	SH	GW	Min
2002-03	HKM Nitra Jr.	Slovak-Jr.	46	2	12	14	145	....	....	....	....	....	....	....	....	....	....	....	....	....	....	....	....	....	....
2003-04	Kitchener Rangers	OHL	68	3	13	16	278	....	....	....	....	....	....	....	....	....	5	0	0	0	8	....	....	....	....
2004-05	Kitchener Rangers	OHL	43	0	4	4	231	....	....	....	....	....	....	....	....	....	15	0	0	0	56	....	....	....	....
2005-06	Kitchener Rangers	OHL	52	1	9	10	216	....	....	....	....	....	....	....	....	....	5	0	2	2	14	....	....	....	....
2006-07	Chicago Wolves	AHL	50	2	7	9	184	....	....	....	....	....	....	....	....	....	8	0	1	1	37	....	....	....	....
2007-08	**Atlanta**	**NHL**	**7**	**0**	**0**	**0**	**42**	**0**	**0**	**0**	**5**	**0.0**	**–2**	**0**	**0.0**	**16:42**	....	....	....	....	....	....	....	....	....
	Chicago Wolves	AHL	58	1	7	8	229	....	....	....	....	....	....	....	....	....	24	3	1	4	71	....	....	....	....
2008-09	**Atlanta**	**NHL**	**50**	**0**	**5**	**5**	**132**	**0**	**0**	**0**	**16**	**0.0**	**–14**	**0**	**0.0**	**15:15**	....	....	....	....	....	....	....	....	....
	Chicago Wolves	AHL	11	1	2	3	21	....	....	....	....	....	....	....	....	....	....	....	....	....	....	....	....	....	....
2009-10	**Atlanta**	**NHL**	**23**	**0**	**2**	**2**	**36**	**0**	**0**	**0**	**22**	**0.0**	**2**	**0**	**0.0**	**13:14**	....	....	....	....	....	....	....	....	....
	Chicago Wolves	AHL	6	0	0	0	10	....	....	....	....	....	....	....	....	....	....	....	....	....	....	....	....	....	....
2010-11	Chicago Wolves	AHL	49	0	9	9	165	....	....	....	....	....	....	....	....	....	....	....	....	....	....	....	....	....	....
	Providence Bruins	AHL	10	0	2	2	24	....	....	....	....	....	....	....	....	....	....	....	....	....	....	....	....	....	....
2011-12	Wilkes-Barre	AHL	3	0	0	0	7	....	....	....	....	....	....	....	....	....	....	....	....	....	....	....	....	....	....
2012-13	HC Kometa Brno	CzRep	29	1	2	3	106	....	....	....	....	....	....	....	....	....	....	....	....	....	....	....	....	....	....
	Portland Pirates	AHL	24	2	4	6	92	....	....	....	....	....	....	....	....	....	1	0	0	0	17	....	....	....	....
	NHL Totals		**80**	**0**	**7**	**7**	**210**	**0**	**0**	**0**	**43**	**0.0**		**0**	**0.0**	**14:47**	....	....	....	....	....	....	....	....	....

OHL All-Rookie Team (2004) • Canadian Major Junior All-Rookie Team (2004)

• Missed majority of 2009-10 due to ankle injury in practice, October 5, 2009 and knee injury at Washington, February 5, 2010. Traded to **Boston** by **Atlanta** with Rich Peverley for Blake Wheeler and Mark Stuart, February 18, 2011. Signed as a free agent by **Pittsburgh**, July 3, 2011. • Missed majority of 2011-12 due to knee injury in Pittsburgh practice, October 3, 2011. Signed as a free agent by **Brno** (CzRep), August 14, 2012.

VAN DER GULIK, David (VAN DUHR-GOO-lihk, DAY-vihd) COL

Right wing. Shoots left. 5'10", 173 lbs. Born, Abbotsford, B.C., April 20, 1983. Calgary's 10th choice, 206th overall, in 2002 Entry Draft.

Season	Club	League	Regular Season GP	G	A	Pts	PIM	PP	SH	GW	S	%	+/-	TF	F%	Min	Playoffs GP	G	A	Pts	PIM	PP	SH	GW	Min
99-2000	Chilliwack Chiefs	BCHL	41	35	46	81	....	....	....	....	....	....	....	....	....	....	....	....	....	....	....	....	....	....	....
2000-01	Chilliwack Chiefs	BCHL	60	42	38	80	....	....	....	....	....	....	....	....	....	....	....	....	....	....	....	....	....	....	....
2001-02	Chilliwack Chiefs	BCHL	56	38	62	100	90	....	....	....	....	....	....	....	....	....	13	8	11	19	....	....	....	....	....
2002-03	Boston University	H-East	40	10	10	20	56	....	....	....	....	....	....	....	....	....	....	....	....	....	....	....	....	....	....
2003-04	Boston University	H-East	35	13	7	20	74	....	....	....	....	....	....	....	....	....	....	....	....	....	....	....	....	....	....
2004-05	Boston University	H-East	41	18	13	31	48	....	....	....	....	....	....	....	....	....	....	....	....	....	....	....	....	....	....
2005-06	Boston University	H-East	25	11	11	22	26	....	....	....	....	....	....	....	....	....	....	....	....	....	....	....	....	....	....
2006-07	Omaha	AHL	80	16	27	43	69	....	....	....	....	....	....	....	....	....	6	0	2	2	4	....	....	....	....
2007-08	Quad City Flames	AHL	80	19	23	42	62	....	....	....	....	....	....	....	....	....	....	....	....	....	....	....	....	....	....
2008-09	**Calgary**	**NHL**	**6**	**0**	**2**	**2**	**0**	**0**	**0**	**0**	**11**	**0.0**	**–1**	**1**	**0.0**	**8:29**	....	....	....	....	....	....	....	....	....
	Quad City Flames	AHL	73	17	19	36	58	....	....	....	....	....	....	....	....	....	....	....	....	....	....	....	....	....	....
2009-10	Abbotsford Heat	AHL	64	16	24	40	58	....	....	....	....	....	....	....	....	....	13	4	2	6	10	....	....	....	....
2010-11	**Colorado**	**NHL**	**6**	**1**	**2**	**3**	**2**	**0**	**0**	**0**	**12**	**8.3**	**4**	**1**	**0.0**	**6:45**	....	....	....	....	....	....	....	....	....
	Lake Erie	AHL	48	15	21	36	36	....	....	....	....	....	....	....	....	....	7	2	2	4	8	....	....	....	....
2011-12	**Colorado**	**NHL**	**25**	**1**	**5**	**6**	**2**	**0**	**0**	**0**	**20**	**5.0**	**3**	**38**	**29.0**	**8:12**	....	....	....	....	....	....	....	....	....
	Lake Erie	AHL	40	12	16	28	36	....	....	....	....	....	....	....	....	....	....	....	....	....	....	....	....	....	....
2012-13	Lake Erie	AHL	60	18	17	35	58	....	....	....	....	....	....	....	....	....	....	....	....	....	....	....	....	....	....
	Colorado	**NHL**	**9**	**0**	**2**	**2**	**6**	**0**	**0**	**0**	**10**	**0.0**	**2**	**8**	**50.0**	**9:26**	....	....	....	....	....	....	....	....	....
	NHL Totals		**46**	**2**	**11**	**13**	**10**	**0**	**0**	**0**	**53**	**3.8**		**48**	**31.3**	**8:18**	....	....	....	....	....	....	....	....	....

Hockey East All-Rookie Team (2003)

Signed as a free agent by **Colorado**, July 2, 2010.

van RIEMSDYK, James (VAN REEMZ-dighk, JAYMZ) TOR

Left wing. Shoots left. 6'3", 200 lbs. Born, Middletown, NJ, May 4, 1989. Philadelphia's 1st choice, 2nd overall, in 2007 Entry Draft.

Season	Club	League	Regular Season GP	G	A	Pts	PIM	PP	SH	GW	S	%	+/-	TF	F%	Min	Playoffs GP	G	A	Pts	PIM	PP	SH	GW	Min
2004-05	Christian Bros.	High-NJ	30	36	24	60	....	....	....	....	....	....	....	....	....	....	....	....	....	....	....	....	....	....	....
2005-06	USNTDP	U-17	11	7	5	12	18	....	....	....	....	....	....	....	....	....	....	....	....	....	....	....	....	....	....
	USNTDP	U-18	14	1	3	4	6	....	....	....	....	....	....	....	....	....	....	....	....	....	....	....	....	....	....
	USNTDP	NAHL	37	18	11	29	26	....	....	....	....	....	....	....	....	....	7	1	0	1	8	....	....	....	....
2006-07	USNTDP	U-18	39	25	28	53	48	....	....	....	....	....	....	....	....	....	....	....	....	....	....	....	....	....	....
	USNTDP	NAHL	12	13	12	25	37	....	....	....	....	....	....	....	....	....	....	....	....	....	....	....	....	....	....
2007-08	New Hampshire	H-East	31	11	23	34	36	....	....	....	....	....	....	....	....	....	....	....	....	....	....	....	....	....	....
2008-09	New Hampshire	H-East	36	17	23	40	47	....	....	....	....	....	....	....	....	....	....	....	....	....	....	....	....	....	....
	Philadelphia	AHL	7	1	1	2	2	....	....	....	....	....	....	....	....	....	4	0	0	0	2	....	....	....	....
2009-10	**Philadelphia**	**NHL**	**78**	**15**	**20**	**35**	**30**	**4**	**0**	**6**	**173**	**8.7**	**–1**	**2**	**0.0**	**12:58**	**21**	**3**	**3**	**6**	**4**	**0**	**0**	**1**	**11:54**
2010-11	**Philadelphia**	**NHL**	**75**	**21**	**19**	**40**	**35**	**3**	**0**	**4**	**173**	**12.1**	**15**	**3**	**0.0**	**14:32**	**11**	**7**	**0**	**7**	**4**	**2**	**0**	**1**	**19:23**
2011-12	**Philadelphia**	**NHL**	**43**	**11**	**13**	**24**	**24**	**2**	**0**	**1**	**121**	**9.1**	**–1**	**5**	**40.0**	**15:10**	**7**	**1**	**1**	**2**	**4**	**0**	**0**	**0**	**13:45**
2012-13	**Toronto**	**NHL**	**48**	**18**	**14**	**32**	**26**	**5**	**0**	**3**	**140**	**12.9**	**–7**	**43**	**55.8**	**19:12**	**7**	**2**	**5**	**7**	**4**	**1**	**0**	**0**	**19:41**
	NHL Totals		**244**	**65**	**66**	**131**	**115**	**14**	**0**	**14**	**607**	**10.7**		**53**	**49.1**	**15:04**	**46**	**13**	**9**	**22**	**16**	**3**	**0**	**1**	**15:09**

Hockey East All-Rookie Team (2008) • Hockey East Second All-Star Team (2009)

Traded to **Toronto** by **Philadelphia** for Luke Schenn, June 23, 2012.

VANDERMEER, Jim (VAN-duhr-meer, JIHM)

Defense. Shoots left. 6'1", 210 lbs. Born, Caroline, Alta., February 21, 1980.

Season	Club	League	Regular Season GP	G	A	Pts	PIM	PP	SH	GW	S	%	+/-	TF	F%	Min	Playoffs GP	G	A	Pts	PIM	PP	SH	GW	Min
1997-98	Red Deer	AMHL	26	4	8	12	51	....	....	....	....	....	....	....	....	....	....	....	....	....	....	....	....	....	....
	Red Deer Rebels	WHL	35	0	3	3	55	....	....	....	....	....	....	....	....	....	2	0	0	0	0	....	....	....	....
1998-99	Red Deer Rebels	WHL	70	5	23	28	258	....	....	....	....	....	....	....	....	....	9	0	1	1	24	....	....	....	....
99-2000	Red Deer Rebels	WHL	71	8	30	38	221	....	....	....	....	....	....	....	....	....	4	0	1	1	16	....	....	....	....
2000-01	Red Deer Rebels	WHL	72	21	44	65	180	....	....	....	....	....	....	....	....	....	22	3	13	16	43	....	....	....	....
2001-02	Philadelphia	AHL	74	1	13	14	88	....	....	....	....	....	....	....	....	....	5	0	2	2	14	....	....	....	....
2002-03	**Philadelphia**	**NHL**	**24**	**2**	**1**	**3**	**27**	**0**	**0**	**0**	**22**	**9.1**	**9**	**0**	**0.0**	**13:42**	**8**	**0**	**1**	**1**	**9**	**0**	**0**	**0**	**12:42**
	Philadelphia	AHL	48	4	8	12	122	....	....	....	....	....	....	....	....	....	....	....	....	....	....	....	....	....	....
2003-04	**Philadelphia**	**NHL**	**23**	**3**	**2**	**5**	**25**	**0**	**0**	**1**	**24**	**12.5**	**–5**	**0**	**0.0**	**15:47**	....	....	....	....	....	....	....	....	....
	Philadelphia	AHL	26	1	6	7	120	....	....	....	....	....	....	....	....	....	....	....	....	....	....	....	....	....	....
	Chicago	**NHL**	**23**	**2**	**10**	**12**	**58**	**1**	**1**	**0**	**37**	**5.4**	**–6**	**1**	**100.0**	**22:03**	....	....	....	....	....	....	....	....	....
2004-05	Norfolk Admirals	AHL	52	3	10	13	164	....	....	....	....	....	....	....	....	....	....	....	....	....	....	....	....	....	....
2005-06	**Chicago**	**NHL**	**76**	**6**	**18**	**24**	**116**	**2**	**0**	**1**	**93**	**6.5**	**–2**	**1**	**100.0**	**21:47**	....	....	....	....	....	....	....	....	....
2006-07	**Chicago**	**NHL**	**46**	**1**	**6**	**7**	**53**	**1**	**0**	**0**	**50**	**2.0**	**–3**	**0**	**0.0**	**17:50**	....	....	....	....	....	....	....	....	....
2007-08	**Chicago**	**NHL**	**26**	**2**	**7**	**9**	**44**	**1**	**0**	**0**	**23**	**8.7**	**3**	**0**	**0.0**	**19:37**	....	....	....	....	....	....	....	....	....
	Philadelphia	**NHL**	**28**	**1**	**5**	**6**	**27**	**1**	**0**	**0**	**26**	**3.8**	**–1**	**0**	**0.0**	**19:34**	....	....	....	....	....	....	....	....	....
	Calgary	**NHL**	**21**	**0**	**2**	**2**	**39**	**0**	**0**	**0**	**23**	**0.0**	**4**	**0**	**0.0**	**19:44**	**7**	**0**	**0**	**0**	**4**	**0**	**0**	**0**	**16:18**
2008-09	**Calgary**	**NHL**	**45**	**1**	**6**	**7**	**108**	**0**	**0**	**0**	**31**	**3.2**	**1**	**0**	**0.0**	**16:01**	**6**	**0**	**1**	**1**	**4**	**0**	**0**	**0**	**16:33**
2009-10	**Phoenix**	**NHL**	**62**	**4**	**8**	**12**	**60**	**0**	**0**	**1**	**64**	**6.3**	**3**	**0**	**0.0**	**17:41**	....	....	....	....	....	....	....	....	....

Season	Club	League	GP	G	A	Pts	PIM	PP	SH	GW	S	%	+/-	TF	F%	Min	GP	G	A	Pts	PIM	PP	SH	GW	Min
			Regular Season														Playoffs								
2010-11	**Edmonton**	**NHL**	**62**	**2**	**12**	**14**	**74**	**0**	**0**	**0**	**57**	**3.5**	**–15**	**0**	**0.0**	**18:12**	....	....	....	....	....	....	....	....	....
2011-12	**San Jose**	**NHL**	**25**	**1**	**3**	**4**	**33**	**0**	**0**	**0**	**19**	**5.3**	**3**	**0**	**0.0**	**10:25**	....	....	....	....	....	....	....	....	....
2012-13	Chicago Wolves	AHL	34	5	5	10	66	....	....	....	....	....	....	....	....	....	....	....	....	....	....	....	....	....	....
	NHL Totals		**461**	**25**	**80**	**105**	**664**	**5**	**1**	**3**	**469**	**5.3**			**2100.0**	**18:07**	**21**	**0**	**2**	**2**	**17**	**0**	**0**	**0**	**15:00**

WHL East First All-Star Team (2001) • Canadian Major Junior Humanitarian Player of the Year (2001)

Signed as a free agent by **Philadelphia**, December 21, 2000. Traded to **Chicago** by **Philadelphia** with the rights to Colin Fraser and Los Angeles' 2nd round choice (previously acquired, Chicago selected Bryan Bickell) in 2004 Entry Draft for Alex Zhamnov and Washington's 4th round choice (previously acquired, Philadelphia selected R.J. Anderson) in 2004 Entry Draft, February 19, 2004. Traded to **Philadelphia** by **Chicago** for Ben Eager, December 18, 2007. Traded to **Calgary** by **Philadelphia** for Calgary's 3rd round choice (Adam Morrison) in 2009 Entry Draft, February 20, 2008. Traded to **Phoenix** by **Calgary** for Brandon Prust, June 27. 2009. Traded to **Edmonton** by **Phoenix** for Patrick O'Sullivan, June 30, 2010. Signed as a free agent by **San Jose**, July 1, 2011. Signed as a free agent by **Vancouver**, January 14, 2013.

VANDEVELDE, Chris

(VAN-deh VEHLD, KRIHS)

Center. Shoots left. 6'2", 190 lbs. Born, Moorhead, MN, March 15, 1987. Edmonton's 5th choice, 97th overall, in 2005 Entry Draft.

Season	Club	League	GP	G	A	Pts	PIM	PP	SH	GW	S	%	+/-	TF	F%	Min	GP	G	A	Pts	PIM	PP	SH	GW	Min
2003-04	Moorhead Spuds	High-MN	29	19	24	43	....	....	....	....	....	....	....	....	....	....	....	....	....	....	....	....	....	....	....
2004-05	Moorhead Spuds	High-MN	30	35	32	67	28	....	....	....	....	....	....	....	....	....	....	....	....	....	....	....	....	....	....
	Lincoln Stars	USHL	7	1	4	5	0	....	....	....	....	....	....	....	....	....	4	0	2	2	0	....	....	....	....
2005-06	Lincoln Stars	USHL	56	16	20	36	70	....	....	....	....	....	....	....	....	....	9	1	3	4	10	....	....	....	....
2006-07	North Dakota	WCHA	38	3	6	9	37	....	....	....	....	....	....	....	....	....	....	....	....	....	....	....	....	....	....
2007-08	North Dakota	WCHA	43	15	17	32	38	....	....	....	....	....	....	....	....	....	....	....	....	....	....	....	....	....	....
2008-09	North Dakota	WCHA	43	18	17	35	69	....	....	....	....	....	....	....	....	....	....	....	....	....	....	....	....	....	....
2009-10	North Dakota	WCHA	42	16	25	41	22	....	....	....	....	....	....	....	....	....	....	....	....	....	....	....	....	....	....
2010-11	**Edmonton**	**NHL**	**12**	**0**	**2**	**2**	**12**	**0**	**0**	**0**	**16**	**0.0**	**–6**	**159**	**52.8**	**17:17**	....	....	....	....	....	....	....	....	....
	Oklahoma City	AHL	67	12	4	16	45	....	....	....	....	....	....	....	....	....	6	1	0	1	6	....	....	....	....
2011-12	**Edmonton**	**NHL**	**5**	**1**	**0**	**1**	**2**	**0**	**0**	**0**	**1**	**100.0**	**2**	**40**	**45.0**	**9:52**	....	....	....	....	....	....	....	....	....
	Oklahoma City	AHL	68	7	16	23	33	....	....	....	....	....	....	....	....	....	14	6	0	6	10	....	....	....	....
2012-13	Oklahoma City	AHL	57	7	13	20	27	....	....	....	....	....	....	....	....	....	17	2	2	4	10	....	....	....	....
	Edmonton	**NHL**	**11**	**0**	**0**	**0**	**4**	**0**	**0**	**0**	**7**	**0.0**	**–3**	**44**	**47.7**	**7:03**	....	....	....	....	....	....	....	....	....
	NHL Totals		**28**	**1**	**2**	**3**	**18**	**0**	**0**	**0**	**24**	**4.2**		**243**	**50.6**	**11:56**	....	....	....	....	....	....	....	....	....

VANEK, Thomas

(VAN-ehk, TAW-muhs) **BUF**

Left wing. Shoots right. 6'2", 205 lbs. Born, Vienna, Austria, January 19, 1984. Buffalo's 1st choice, 5th overall, in 2003 Entry Draft.

Season	Club	League	GP	G	A	Pts	PIM	PP	SH	GW	S	%	+/-	TF	F%	Min	GP	G	A	Pts	PIM	PP	SH	GW	Min
99-2000	Sioux Falls	USHL	35	15	18	33	12	....	....	....	....	....	....	....	....	....	3	0	1	1	0	....	....	....	....
2000-01	Sioux Falls	USHL	20	19	10	29	15	....	....	....	....	....	....	....	....	....	8	5	4	9	2	....	....	....	....
2001-02	Sioux Falls	USHL	53	46	45	91	54	....	....	....	....	....	....	....	....	....	3	0	0	0	9	....	....	....	....
2002-03	U. of Minnesota	WCHA	45	31	31	62	60	....	....	....	....	....	....	....	....	....	....	....	....	....	....	....	....	....	....
	Austria	WJC-B	5	9	4	13	10	....	....	....	....	....	....	....	....	....	....	....	....	....	....	....	....	....	....
2003-04	U. of Minnesota	WCHA	38	26	25	51	72	....	....	....	....	....	....	....	....	....	....	....	....	....	....	....	....	....	....
2004-05	Rochester	AHL	74	42	26	68	62	....	....	....	....	....	....	....	....	....	5	2	3	5	10	....	....	....	....
	Austria	Oly-Q	3	1	0	1	0	....	....	....	....	....	....	....	....	....	....	....	....	....	....	....	....	....	....
2005-06	**Buffalo**	**NHL**	**81**	**25**	**23**	**48**	**72**	**11**	**0**	**4**	**204**	**12.3**	**–11**	**23**	**21.7**	**14:44**	**10**	**2**	**0**	**2**	**6**	**2**	**0**	**0**	**10:45**
2006-07	**Buffalo**	**NHL**	**82**	**43**	**41**	**84**	**40**	**15**	**0**	**5**	**237**	**18.1**	***47**	**39**	**28.2**	**16:47**	**16**	**6**	**4**	**10**	**10**	**1**	**0**	**2**	**16:27**
2007-08	**Buffalo**	**NHL**	**82**	**36**	**28**	**64**	**64**	**19**	**0**	**9**	**240**	**15.0**	**–5**	**13**	**46.2**	**16:51**	....	....	....	....	....	....	....	....	....
2008-09	**Buffalo**	**NHL**	**73**	**40**	**24**	**64**	**44**	***20**	**2**	**5**	**211**	**19.0**	**–1**	**6**	**16.7**	**17:12**	....	....	....	....	....	....	....	....	....
2009-10	**Buffalo**	**NHL**	**71**	**28**	**25**	**53**	**42**	**10**	**0**	**6**	**182**	**15.4**	**9**	**9**	**22.2**	**16:46**	**3**	**2**	**1**	**3**	**2**	**0**	**0**	**0**	**13:38**
2010-11	**Buffalo**	**NHL**	**80**	**32**	**41**	**73**	**24**	**11**	**0**	**5**	**238**	**13.4**	**2**	**26**	**30.8**	**17:21**	**7**	**5**	**0**	**5**	**0**	**4**	**0**	**0**	**17:10**
2011-12	**Buffalo**	**NHL**	**78**	**26**	**35**	**61**	**52**	**10**	**0**	**5**	**204**	**12.7**	**–6**	**6**	**50.0**	**16:56**	....	....	....	....	....	....	....	....	....
2012-13	Graz 99ers	Austria	11	5	10	15	4	....	....	....	....	....	....	....	....	....	....	....	....	....	....	....	....	....	....
	Buffalo	**NHL**	**38**	**20**	**21**	**41**	**20**	**9**	**1**	**2**	**119**	**16.8**	**–1**	**12**	**66.7**	**18:24**	....	....	....	....	....	....	....	....	....
	NHL Totals		**585**	**250**	**238**	**488**	**358**	**105**	**3**	**41**	**1635**	**15.3**		**134**	**32.8**	**16:46**	**36**	**15**	**5**	**20**	**18**	**7**	**0**	**2**	**14:46**

USHL First All-Star Team (2002) • USHL MVP (2002) • WCHA All-Rookie Team (2003) • WCHA Second All-Star Team (2003, 2004) • WCHA Rookie of the Year (2003) • NCAA Championship All-Tournament Team (2003) • NCAA Championship Tournament MVP (2003) • NCAA West Second All-American Team (2004) • AHL All-Rookie Team (2005) • NHL Second All-Star Team (2007)

Played in NHL All-Star Game (2009)

Signed as a free agent by **Graz** (Austria), October 1, 2012.

VATANEN, Sami

(VAH-ta-nehn, SA-mee) **ANA**

Defense. Shoots right. 5'10", 180 lbs. Born, Jyvaskyla, Finland, June 3, 1991. Anaheim's 5th choice, 106th overall, in 2009 Entry Draft.

Season	Club	League	GP	G	A	Pts	PIM	PP	SH	GW	S	%	+/-	TF	F%	Min	GP	G	A	Pts	PIM	PP	SH	GW	Min
2006-07	JyP Jyvaskyla U18	Fin-U18	....	....	....	....	....	....	....	....	....	....	....	....	....	....	7	1	0	1	2	....	....	....	....
2007-08	JyP Jyvaskyla U18	Fin-U18	35	9	29	38	30	....	....	....	....	....	....	....	....	....	1	0	0	0	0	....	....	....	....
	JyP Jyvaskyla Jr.	Fin-Jr.	....	....	....	....	....	....	....	....	....	....	....	....	....	....	2	0	0	0	0	....	....	....	....
2008-09	JyP Jyvaskyla U18	Fin-U18	2	0	0	0	0	....	....	....	....	....	....	....	....	....	1	1	1	2	14	....	....	....	....
	Suomi U20	Finland-2	2	0	0	0	2	....	....	....	....	....	....	....	....	....	....	....	....	....	....	....	....	....	....
	D Team Jyvaskyla	Finland-2	5	1	1	2	8	....	....	....	....	....	....	....	....	....	....	....	....	....	....	....	....	....	....
	JyP Jyvaskyla Jr.	Fin-Jr.	20	3	7	10	22	....	....	....	....	....	....	....	....	....	....	....	....	....	....	....	....	....	....
2009-10	Suomi U20	Finland-2	1	0	0	0	2	....	....	....	....	....	....	....	....	....	....	....	....	....	....	....	....	....	....
	JYP Jyvaskyla	Finland	55	7	23	30	44	....	....	....	....	....	....	....	....	....	14	3	4	7	6	....	....	....	....
2010-11	Suomi U20	Finland-2	1	0	0	0	0	....	....	....	....	....	....	....	....	....	....	....	....	....	....	....	....	....	....
	JYP Jyvaskyla	Finland	52	11	20	31	30	....	....	....	....	....	....	....	....	....	3	1	1	2	0	....	....	....	....
2011-12	JYP Jyvaskyla	Finland	49	14	28	42	40	....	....	....	....	....	....	....	....	....	4	2	0	2	4	....	....	....	....
2012-13	Norfolk Admirals	AHL	62	9	36	45	44	....	....	....	....	....	....	....	....	....	....	....	....	....	....	....	....	....	....
	Anaheim	**NHL**	**8**	**2**	**0**	**2**	**0**	**1**	**0**	**0**	**6**	**33.3**	**3**	**0**	**0.0**	**15:49**	....	....	....	....	....	....	....	....	....
	NHL Totals		**8**	**2**	**0**	**2**	**0**	**1**	**0**	**0**	**6**	**33.3**		**0**	**0.0**	**15:49**	....	....	....	....	....	....	....	....	....

AHL All-Rookie Team (2013) • AHL First All-Star Team (2013)

VEILLEUX, Stephane

(VAY-yew, STEH-fan) **MIN**

Left wing. Shoots left. 6'1", 200 lbs. Born, Beauceville, Que., November 16, 1981. Minnesota's 4th choice, 93rd overall, in 2001 Entry Draft.

Season	Club	League	GP	G	A	Pts	PIM	PP	SH	GW	S	%	+/-	TF	F%	Min	GP	G	A	Pts	PIM	PP	SH	GW	Min
1997-98	Beauce-Amiante	QAAA	21	20	17	37	....	....	....	....	....	....	....	....	....	....	....	....	....	....	....	....	....	....	....
	Levis-Lauzon	QAAA	14	3	5	8	....	....	....	....	....	....	....	....	....	....	1	0	0	0	0	....	....	....	....
1998-99	Victoriaville Tigres	QMJHL	65	6	13	19	35	....	....	....	....	....	....	....	....	....	6	1	3	4	2	....	....	....	....
99-2000	Victoriaville Tigres	QMJHL	22	1	4	5	17	....	....	....	....	....	....	....	....	....	....	....	....	....	....	....	....	....	....
	Val-d'Or Foreurs	QMJHL	50	14	28	42	100	....	....	....	....	....	....	....	....	....	....	....	....	....	....	....	....	....	....
2000-01	Val-d'Or Foreurs	QMJHL	68	48	67	115	90	....	....	....	....	....	....	....	....	....	21	15	18	33	42	....	....	....	....
2001-02	Houston Aeros	AHL	77	13	22	35	113	....	....	....	....	....	....	....	....	....	14	2	4	6	20	....	....	....	....
2002-03	**Minnesota**	**NHL**	**38**	**3**	**2**	**5**	**23**	**1**	**0**	**0**	**52**	**5.8**	**–6**	**13**	**7.7**	**12:08**	....	....	....	....	....	....	....	....	....
	Houston Aeros	AHL	29	8	4	12	43	....	....	....	....	....	....	....	....	....	23	7	11	18	12	....	....	....	....
2003-04	**Minnesota**	**NHL**	**19**	**2**	**8**	**10**	**20**	**1**	**1**	**1**	**37**	**5.4**	**0**	**10**	**40.0**	**14:20**	....	....	....	....	....	....	....	....	....
	Houston Aeros	AHL	64	13	25	38	66	....	....	....	....	....	....	....	....	....	2	1	1	2	2	....	....	....	....
2004-05	Houston Aeros	AHL	59	15	24	39	35	....	....	....	....	....	....	....	....	....	....	....	....	....	....	....	....	....	....
2005-06	**Minnesota**	**NHL**	**71**	**7**	**9**	**16**	**63**	**0**	**0**	**1**	**87**	**8.0**	**–13**	**33**	**33.3**	**12:58**	....	....	....	....	....	....	....	....	....
2006-07	**Minnesota**	**NHL**	**75**	**7**	**11**	**18**	**47**	**0**	**0**	**1**	**84**	**8.3**	**3**	**32**	**21.9**	**12:17**	**5**	**0**	**0**	**0**	**4**	**0**	**0**	**0**	**12:40**
2007-08	**Minnesota**	**NHL**	**77**	**11**	**7**	**18**	**61**	**0**	**0**	**0**	**136**	**8.1**	**–13**	**45**	**37.8**	**14:32**	**6**	**0**	**0**	**0**	**27**	**0**	**0**	**0**	**15:43**
2008-09	**Minnesota**	**NHL**	**81**	**13**	**10**	**23**	**40**	**0**	**1**	**1**	**146**	**8.9**	**–17**	**22**	**27.3**	**15:48**	....	....	....	....	....	....	....	....	....
2009-10	**Tampa Bay**	**NHL**	**77**	**3**	**6**	**9**	**48**	**0**	**0**	**0**	**94**	**3.2**	**–14**	**25**	**40.0**	**12:17**	....	....	....	....	....	....	....	....	....
2010-11	Blues Espoo	Finland	25	1	6	7	18	....	....	....	....	....	....	....	....	....	....	....	....	....	....	....	....	....	....
	HC Ambri-Piotta	Swiss	7	0	0	0	4	....	....	....	....	....	....	....	....	....	11	0	1	1	31	....	....	....	....
2011-12	**New Jersey**	**NHL**	**1**	**0**	**0**	**0**	**0**	**0**	**0**	**0**	**0**	**0.0**	**0**	**0**	**0.0**	**4:34**	....	....	....	....	....	....	....	....	....
	Albany Devils	AHL	40	11	11	22	53	....	....	....	....	....	....	....	....	....	....	....	....	....	....	....	....	....	....
	Minnesota	**NHL**	**21**	**0**	**2**	**2**	**15**	**0**	**0**	**0**	**16**	**0.0**	**–2**	**10**	**30.0**	**10:04**	....	....	....	....	....	....	....	....	....
2012-13	Houston Aeros	AHL	33	3	5	8	45	....	....	....	....	....	....	....	....	....	3	0	2	2	6	....	....	....	....
	Minnesota	**NHL**	....	....	....	....	....	....	....	....	....	....	....	....	....	....	**2**	**0**	**0**	**0**	**0**	**0**	**0**	**0**	**7:32**
	NHL Totals		**460**	**46**	**55**	**101**	**317**	**2**	**2**	**4**	**652**	**7.1**		**190**	**31.1**	**13:20**	**13**	**0**	**0**	**0**	**31**	**0**	**0**	**0**	**13:17**

Signed as a free agent by **Tampa Bay**, July 7, 2009. Signed as a free agent by **Espoo** (Finland), October 15, 2010. Signed as a free agent by **Ambri-Piotta** (Swiss), January 23, 2011. Signed as a free agent by **New Jersey**, July 30, 2011. Traded to **Minnesota** by **New Jersey** with Kurtis Foster, Nick Palmieri, Washington's 2nd round choice (previously acquired, Minnesota selected Raphael Bussieres) in 2012 Entry Draft and New Jersey's 3rd round choice (later traded to NY Islanders – NY Islanders selected Eamon McAdam) in 2013 Entry Draft for Marek Zidlicky, February 24, 2012.

VERMETTE, Antoine
(vuhr-MEHT, AN-twuhn) **PHX**

Center. Shoots left. 6'1", 198 lbs. Born, St-Agapit, Que., July 20, 1982. Ottawa's 3rd choice, 55th overall, in 2000 Entry Draft.

			Regular Season														Playoffs								
Season	Club	League	GP	G	A	Pts	PIM	PP	SH	GW	S	%	+/-	TF	F%	Min	GP	G	A	Pts	PIM	PP	SH	GW	Min
1997-98	Quebec Select	QAHA	19	11	20	31	36	....	....	....	....	....	....	....	....	....	....	....	....	....	....	....	....	....	....
	Levis-Lauzon	QAAA	8	1	1	2	4	....	....	....	....	....	....	....	....	....	1	0	0	0	0	....	....	....	....
1998-99	Quebec Remparts	QMJHL	57	9	17	26	32	....	....	....	....	....	....	....	....	....	13	0	0	0	2	....	....	....	....
99-2000	Victoriaville Tigres	QMJHL	71	30	41	71	87	....	....	....	....	....	....	....	....	....	6	0	1	1	6	....	....	....	....
2000-01	Victoriaville Tigres	QMJHL	71	57	62	119	102	....	....	....	....	....	....	....	....	....	9	4	6	10	14	....	....	....	....
2001-02	Victoriaville Tigres	QMJHL	4	0	2	2	6	....	....	....	....	....	....	....	....	....	22	10	16	26	10	....	....	....	....
2002-03	Binghamton	AHL	80	34	28	62	57	....	....	....	....	....	....	....	....	....	14	2	9	11	10	....	....	....	....
2003-04	**Ottawa**	**NHL**	**57**	**7**	**7**	**14**	**16**	**0**	**1**	**0**	**63**	**11.1**	**5**	**100**	**44.0**	**11:59**	**4**	**0**	**1**	**1**	**4**	**0**	**0**	**0**	**11:35**
	Binghamton	AHL	3	0	0	0	6	....	....	....	....	....	....	....	....	....	....	....	....	....	....	....	....	....	....
2004-05	Binghamton	AHL	78	28	45	73	36	....	....	....	....	....	....	....	....	....	6	1	4	5	10	....	....	....	....
2005-06	**Ottawa**	**NHL**	**82**	**21**	**12**	**33**	**44**	**1**	**6**	**4**	**123**	**17.1**	**17**	**537**	**57.9**	**12:35**	**10**	**2**	**0**	**2**	**4**	**0**	**0**	**1**	**15:00**
2006-07	**Ottawa**	**NHL**	**77**	**19**	**20**	**39**	**52**	**2**	**3**	**2**	**151**	**12.6**	**–2**	**834**	**53.0**	**15:42**	**20**	**2**	**3**	**5**	**6**	**0**	**0**	**0**	**16:20**
2007-08	**Ottawa**	**NHL**	**81**	**24**	**29**	**53**	**51**	**4**	**3**	**3**	**175**	**13.7**	**3**	**1217**	**56.7**	**17:35**	**4**	**0**	**0**	**0**	**4**	**0**	**0**	**0**	**20:33**
2008-09	**Ottawa**	**NHL**	**62**	**9**	**19**	**28**	**42**	**2**	**0**	**0**	**141**	**6.4**	**–12**	**771**	**58.4**	**18:03**	....	....	....	....	....	....	....	....	....
	Columbus	**NHL**	**17**	**7**	**6**	**13**	**8**	**1**	**1**	**1**	**33**	**21.2**	**5**	**341**	**56.3**	**19:29**	**4**	**0**	**0**	**0**	**10**	**0**	**0**	**0**	**16:47**
2009-10	**Columbus**	**NHL**	**82**	**27**	**38**	**65**	**32**	**6**	**2**	**1**	**156**	**17.3**	**2**	**1573**	**54.2**	**20:09**	....	....	....	....	....	....	....	....	....
2010-11	**Columbus**	**NHL**	**82**	**19**	**28**	**47**	**60**	**3**	**1**	**3**	**183**	**10.4**	**0**	**1540**	**55.6**	**18:49**	....	....	....	....	....	....	....	....	....
2011-12	**Columbus**	**NHL**	**60**	**8**	**19**	**27**	**12**	**2**	**1**	**3**	**106**	**7.5**	**–17**	**804**	**56.3**	**17:14**	....	....	....	....	....	....	....	....	....
	Phoenix	**NHL**	**22**	**3**	**7**	**10**	**16**	**2**	**0**	**1**	**43**	**7.0**	**4**	**336**	**57.1**	**17:07**	**16**	**5**	**5**	**10**	**24**	**3**	**0**	**0**	**18:04**
2012-13	**Phoenix**	**NHL**	**48**	**13**	**8**	**21**	**36**	**3**	**0**	**3**	**91**	**14.3**	**–3**	**839**	**57.5**	**18:15**	....	....	....	....	....	....	....	....	....
	NHL Totals		**670**	**157**	**193**	**350**	**369**	**26**	**18**	**21**	**1265**	**12.4**		**8892**	**55.8**	**16:50**	**58**	**9**	**9**	**18**	**52**	**3**	**0**	**1**	**16:34**

AHL All-Rookie Team (2003)

• Missed majority of 2001-02 due to neck injury in Team Canada Jr. Selection Camp, June 3, 2001. Traded to **Columbus** by **Ottawa** for Pascal Leclaire and Columbus' 2nd round choice (Robin Lehner) in 2009 Entry Draft, March 4, 2009. Traded to **Phoenix** by **Columbus** for Curtis McElhinney, Ottawa's 2nd round choice (previously acquired, later traded to Philadelphia – Philadelphia selected Anthony Stolarz) in 2012 Entry Draft and Phoenix's 4th round choice (later traded to Philadelphia, later traded to Los Angeles – Los Angeles selected Justin Auger) in 2013 Entry Draft, February 22, 2012.

VERNACE, Mike
(vuhr-NAYS, MIGHK)

Defense. Shoots left. 6', 216 lbs. Born, Toronto, Ont., May 26, 1986. San Jose's 6th choice, 201st overall, in 2004 Entry Draft.

			Regular Season														Playoffs								
Season	Club	League	GP	G	A	Pts	PIM	PP	SH	GW	S	%	+/-	TF	F%	Min	GP	G	A	Pts	PIM	PP	SH	GW	Min
2003-04	Bramalea Blues	ON-Jr.A	33	3	12	15	16	....	....	....	....	....	....	....	....	....	....	....	....	....	....	....	....	....	....
	Brampton	OHL	2	1	1	2	0	....	....	....	....	....	....	....	....	....	11	2	3	5	8	....	....	....	....
2004-05	Brampton	OHL	68	12	38	50	42	....	....	....	....	....	....	....	....	....	6	2	2	4	0	....	....	....	....
2005-06	Brampton	OHL	68	10	62	72	54	....	....	....	....	....	....	....	....	....	11	1	5	6	6	....	....	....	....
2006-07	Albany River Rats	AHL	30	1	11	12	35	....	....	....	....	....	....	....	....	....	....	....	....	....	....	....	....	....	....
	Arizona Sundogs	CHL	24	3	11	14	20	....	....	....	....	....	....	....	....	....	....	....	....	....	....	....	....	....	....
2007-08	Lake Erie	AHL	79	3	26	29	59	....	....	....	....	....	....	....	....	....	....	....	....	....	....	....	....	....	....
2008-09	**Colorado**	**NHL**	**12**	**0**	**0**	**0**	**8**	**0**	**0**	**0**	**9**	**0.0**	**–5**	**0**	**0.0**	**19:39**	....	....	....	....	....	....	....	....	....
	Lake Erie	AHL	65	3	14	17	52	....	....	....	....	....	....	....	....	....	....	....	....	....	....	....	....	....	....
2009-10	Chicago Wolves	AHL	47	2	10	12	29	....	....	....	....	....	....	....	....	....	....	....	....	....	....	....	....	....	....
	Hamilton	AHL	15	0	1	1	23	....	....	....	....	....	....	....	....	....	18	0	4	4	8	....	....	....	....
2010-11	**Tampa Bay**	**NHL**	**10**	**0**	**1**	**1**	**2**	**0**	**0**	**0**	**6**	**0.0**	**–2**	**0**	**0.0**	**8:42**	....	....	....	....	....	....	....	....	....
	Norfolk Admirals	AHL	68	7	21	28	60	....	....	....	....	....	....	....	....	....	6	0	2	2	8	....	....	....	....
2011-12	Norfolk Admirals	AHL	22	2	10	12	23	....	....	....	....	....	....	....	....	....	....	....	....	....	....	....	....	....	....
	San Antonio	AHL	22	0	4	4	7	....	....	....	....	....	....	....	....	....	....	....	....	....	....	....	....	....	....
	Connecticut	AHL	21	1	1	2	20	....	....	....	....	....	....	....	....	....	9	0	2	2	0	....	....	....	....
2012-13	Connecticut	AHL	69	8	27	35	51	....	....	....	....	....	....	....	....	....	....	....	....	....	....	....	....	....	....
	NHL Totals		**22**	**0**	**1**	**1**	**10**	**0**	**0**	**0**	**15**	**0.0**		**0**	**0.0**	**14:41**	....	....	....	....	....	....	....	....	....

OHL All-Rookie Team (2005)

Traded to **Colorado** by **San Jose** for Colorado's 6th round choice (Patrick Zackrisson) in 2007 Entry Draft, June 1, 2006. Signed as a free agent by **Atlanta**, July 30, 2009. Traded to **San Jose** by **Atlanta** with Brett Sterling and Atlanta's 7th round choice (Lee Moffie) in 2010 Entry Draft for future considerations, June 23, 2010. Signed as a free agent by **Tampa Bay**, July 29, 2010. Traded to **Florida** by **Tampa Bay** with James Wright for Mike Kostka and Evan Oberg, December 2, 2011. Traded to **NY Rangers** by **Florida** with Florida's 3rd round choice (later traded to San Jose, later traded to Phoenix – Phoenix selected Pavel Laplante) in 2013 Entry Draft for Wojtek Wolski, February 25, 2012.

VERSTEEG, Kris
(vuhr-STEEG, KRIHS) **FLA**

Right wing. Shoots right. 5'11", 183 lbs. Born, Lethbridge, Alta., May 13, 1986. Boston's 4th choice, 134th overall, in 2004 Entry Draft.

			Regular Season														Playoffs								
Season	Club	League	GP	G	A	Pts	PIM	PP	SH	GW	S	%	+/-	TF	F%	Min	GP	G	A	Pts	PIM	PP	SH	GW	Min
2002-03	Lethbridge	WHL	57	8	10	18	32	....	....	....	....	....	....	....	....	....	....	....	....	....	....	....	....	....	....
2003-04	Lethbridge	WHL	68	16	33	49	85	....	....	....	....	....	....	....	....	....	....	....	....	....	....	....	....	....	....
2004-05	Lethbridge	WHL	68	22	30	52	68	....	....	....	....	....	....	....	....	....	5	0	1	1	4	....	....	....	....
2005-06	Kamloops Blazers	WHL	14	6	6	12	24	....	....	....	....	....	....	....	....	....	....	....	....	....	....	....	....	....	....
	Red Deer Rebels	WHL	57	10	26	36	103	....	....	....	....	....	....	....	....	....	....	....	....	....	....	....	....	....	....
	Providence Bruins	AHL	13	2	4	6	13	....	....	....	....	....	....	....	....	....	3	0	0	0	6	....	....	....	....
2006-07	Providence Bruins	AHL	43	22	27	49	19	....	....	....	....	....	....	....	....	....	....	....	....	....	....	....	....	....	....
	Norfolk Admirals	AHL	27	4	19	23	20	....	....	....	....	....	....	....	....	....	2	0	0	0	2	....	....	....	....
2007-08	**Chicago**	**NHL**	**13**	**2**	**2**	**4**	**6**	**0**	**0**	**0**	**21**	**9.5**	**–1**	**3**	**66.7**	**15:52**	....	....	....	....	....	....	....	....	....
	Rockford IceHogs	AHL	56	18	31	49	174	....	....	....	....	....	....	....	....	....	12	6	5	11	6	....	....	....	....
2008-09	**Chicago**	**NHL**	**78**	**22**	**31**	**53**	**55**	**6**	**4**	**3**	**139**	**15.8**	**15**	**266**	**46.6**	**17:02**	**17**	**4**	**8**	**12**	**22**	**3**	**0**	**0**	**16:14**
2009-10 ♦	**Chicago**	**NHL**	**79**	**20**	**24**	**44**	**35**	**4**	**3**	**4**	**184**	**10.9**	**8**	**183**	**42.1**	**15:44**	**22**	**6**	**8**	**14**	**14**	**0**	**0**	**2**	**17:13**
2010-11	**Toronto**	**NHL**	**53**	**14**	**21**	**35**	**29**	**5**	**0**	**0**	**128**	**10.9**	**–13**	**77**	**52.0**	**18:56**	....	....	....	....	....	....	....	....	....
	Philadelphia	**NHL**	**27**	**7**	**4**	**11**	**24**	**1**	**1**	**0**	**52**	**13.5**	**4**	**53**	**43.4**	**15:22**	**11**	**1**	**5**	**6**	**12**	**0**	**0**	**0**	**15:00**
2011-12	**Florida**	**NHL**	**71**	**23**	**31**	**54**	**49**	**8**	**1**	**5**	**181**	**12.7**	**4**	**65**	**32.3**	**19:55**	**7**	**3**	**2**	**5**	**8**	**2**	**0**	**1**	**20:34**
2012-13	**Florida**	**NHL**	**10**	**2**	**2**	**4**	**8**	**0**	**0**	**0**	**20**	**10.0**	**–8**	**5**	**0.0**	**16:53**	....	....	....	....	....	....	....	....	....
	NHL Totals		**331**	**90**	**115**	**205**	**206**	**24**	**9**	**12**	**725**	**12.4**		**652**	**44.0**	**17:27**	**57**	**14**	**23**	**37**	**56**	**5**	**0**	**3**	**16:54**

NHL All-Rookie Team (2009)

Traded to **Chicago** by **Boston** with future considerations for Brandon Bochenski, February 3, 2007. Traded to **Toronto** by **Chicago** with Bill Sweatt for Viktor Stalberg, Chris Didomenico and Phillipe Paradis, June 30, 2010. Traded to **Philadelphia** by **Toronto** for Philadelphia's 1st (Stuart Percy) and 3rd (Josh Leivo) round choices in 2011 Entry Draft, February 14, 2011. Traded to **Florida** by **Philadelphia** for Florida's 2nd round choice (later traded to Tampa Bay – Tampa Bay selected Brian Hart) in 2012 Entry Draft and San Jose's 3rd round choice (previously acquired, Philadelphia selected Shayne Gostibehere) in 2012 Entry Draft, July 1, 2011. • Missed majority of 2012-13 due to recurring chest injury, knee injury vs. Tampa Bay, March 12, 2013 and resulting surgery.

VINCOUR, Tomas
(VIHN-tsoh-oor, TAW-mahsh) **COL**

Center. Shoots right. 6'2", 199 lbs. Born, Brno, Czech., November 19, 1990. Dallas' 4th choice, 129th overall, in 2009 Entry Draft.

			Regular Season														Playoffs								
Season	Club	League	GP	G	A	Pts	PIM	PP	SH	GW	S	%	+/-	TF	F%	Min	GP	G	A	Pts	PIM	PP	SH	GW	Min
2004-05	Brno U17	CzR-U17	42	23	13	36	36	....	....	....	....	....	....	....	....	....	....	....	....	....	....	....	....	....	....
2005-06	Brno U17	CzR-U17	21	13	14	27	77	....	....	....	....	....	....	....	....	....	....	....	....	....	....	....	....	....	....
	Brno Jr.	CzRep-Jr.	28	8	10	18	61	....	....	....	....	....	....	....	....	....	....	....	....	....	....	....	....	....	....
	Brno	CzRep-2	1	0	0	0	0	....	....	....	....	....	....	....	....	....	....	....	....	....	....	....	....	....	....
2006-07	Brno U17	CzR-U17	1	0	0	0	0	....	....	....	....	....	....	....	....	....	2	0	2	2	0	....	....	....	....
	Brno Jr.	CzRep-Jr.	41	15	24	39	58	....	....	....	....	....	....	....	....	....	....	....	....	....	....	....	....	....	....
	Brno	CzRep-2	4	0	1	1	0	....	....	....	....	....	....	....	....	....	....	....	....	....	....	....	....	....	....
2007-08	Edmonton	WHL	65	16	23	39	36	....	....	....	....	....	....	....	....	....	....	....	....	....	....	....	....	....	....
2008-09	Edmonton	WHL	49	17	19	36	23	....	....	....	....	....	....	....	....	....	....	....	....	....	....	....	....	....	....
2009-10	Edmonton	WHL	33	17	9	26	31	....	....	....	....	....	....	....	....	....	....	....	....	....	....	....	....	....	....
	Vancouver Giants	WHL	24	12	10	22	17	....	....	....	....	....	....	....	....	....	15	7	6	13	8	....	....	....	....
2010-11	**Dallas**	**NHL**	**24**	**1**	**1**	**2**	**4**	**0**	**0**	**0**	**26**	**3.8**	**–5**	**4**	**75.0**	**9:26**	....	....	....	....	....	....	....	....	....
	Texas Stars	AHL	44	5	7	12	10	....	....	....	....	....	....	....	....	....	6	0	1	1	4	....	....	....	....
2011-12	**Dallas**	**NHL**	**47**	**4**	**6**	**10**	**2**	**0**	**0**	**1**	**65**	**6.2**	**–2**	**9**	**11.1**	**10:20**	....	....	....	....	....	....	....	....	....
	Texas Stars	AHL	22	12	4	16	8	....	....	....	....	....	....	....	....	....	....	....	....	....	....	....	....	....	....
2012-13	Texas Stars	AHL	47	13	15	28	20	....	....	....	....	....	....	....	....	....	....	....	....	....	....	....	....	....	....
	Dallas	**NHL**	**15**	**2**	**1**	**3**	**2**	**0**	**0**	**0**	**11**	**18.2**	**0**	**5**	**0.0**	**8:50**	....	....	....	....	....	....	....	....	....
	Lake Erie	AHL	6	5	6	11	2	....	....	....	....	....	....	....	....	....	....	....	....	....	....	....	....	....	....
	Colorado	**NHL**	**2**	**0**	**1**	**1**	**2**	**0**	**0**	**0**	**1**	**0.0**	**–1**	**0**	**0.0**	**9:04**	....	....	....	....	....	....	....	....	....
	NHL Totals		**88**	**7**	**9**	**16**	**10**	**0**	**0**	**1**	**103**	**6.8**		**18**	**22.2**	**9:48**	....	....	....	....	....	....	....	....	....

Traded to **Colorado** by **Dallas** for Cameron Gaunce, April 2, 2013. Signed as a free agent by **Kazan** (KHL), June 18, 2013.

VISNOVSKY, Lubomir
(vihsh-NAWV-skee, LOO-boh-mihr) **NYI**

Defense. Shoots left. 5'10", 197 lbs. Born, Topolcany, Czech., August 11, 1976. Los Angeles' 4th choice, 118th overall, in 2000 Entry Draft.

			Regular Season														Playoffs								
Season	Club	League	GP	G	A	Pts	PIM	PP	SH	GW	S	%	+/-	TF	F%	Min	GP	G	A	Pts	PIM	PP	SH	GW	Min
1994-95	Bratislava	Slovakia	36	11	12	23	10	....	....	....	....	....	....	....	....	....	9	1	3	4	2	....	....	....	....
1995-96	Bratislava	Slovakia	35	8	6	14	22	....	....	....	....	....	....	....	....	....	13	1	5	6	2	....	....	....	....
1996-97	Bratislava	Slovakia	44	11	12	23	....	....	....	....	....	....	....	....	....	....	2	0	1	1	....	....	....	....	....
	Bratislava	EuroHL	6	3	1	4	2	....	....	....	....	....	....	....	....	....	2	0	0	0	6	....	....	....	....
1997-98	Bratislava	Slovakia	36	7	9	16	16	....	....	....	....	....	....	....	....	....	11	2	4	6	8	....	....	....	....
	Bratislava	EuroHL	6	1	0	1	4	....	....	....	....	....	....	....	....	....	....	....	....	....	....	....	....	....	....
	Slovakia	Olympics	3	0	0	0	2	....	....	....	....	....	....	....	....	....	....	....	....	....	....	....	....	....	....
1998-99	Bratislava	Slovakia	40	9	10	19	31	....	....	....	....	....	....	....	....	....	10	5	5	10	0	....	....	....	....
	Bratislava	EuroHL	6	0	3	3	4	....	....	....	....	....	....	....	....	....	....	....	....	....	....	....	....	....	....
99-2000	Bratislava	Slovakia	52	21	24	45	38	....	....	....	....	....	....	....	....	....	8	5	3	8	16	....	....	....	....
2000-01	**Los Angeles**	**NHL**	**81**	**7**	**32**	**39**	**36**	**3**	**0**	**3**	**105**	**6.7**	**16**	**0**	**0.0**	**16:58**	**8**	**0**	**0**	**0**	**0**	**0**	**0**	**0**	**13:57**
2001-02	**Los Angeles**	**NHL**	**72**	**4**	**17**	**21**	**14**	**1**	**0**	**2**	**95**	**4.2**	**–5**	**0**	**0.0**	**16:15**	**4**	**0**	**1**	**1**	**0**	**0**	**0**	**0**	**8:22**
	Slovakia	Olympics	3	1	2	3	0	....	....	....	....	....	....	....	....	....	....	....	....	....	....	....	....	....	....
2002-03	**Los Angeles**	**NHL**	**57**	**8**	**16**	**24**	**28**	**1**	**0**	**1**	**85**	**9.4**	**2**	**0**	**0.0**	**19:20**	....	....	....	....	....	....	....	....	....
2003-04	**Los Angeles**	**NHL**	**58**	**8**	**21**	**29**	**26**	**5**	**0**	**0**	**114**	**7.0**	**8**	**0**	**0.0**	**24:02**	....	....	....	....	....	....	....	....	....
2004-05	Bratislava	Slovakia	43	13	25	38	40	....	....	....	....	....	....	....	....	....	14	2	10	12	10	....	....	....	....
2005-06	**Los Angeles**	**NHL**	**80**	**17**	**50**	**67**	**50**	**10**	**0**	**3**	**152**	**11.2**	**7**	**1**	**100.0**	**23:16**	....	....	....	....	....	....	....	....	....
	Slovakia	Olympics	6	1	1	2	0	....	....	....	....	....	....	....	....	....	....	....	....	....	....	....	....	....	....
2006-07	**Los Angeles**	**NHL**	**69**	**18**	**40**	**58**	**26**	**8**	**0**	**0**	**159**	**11.3**	**1**	**6**	**33.3**	**24:27**	....	....	....	....	....	....	....	....	....
2007-08	**Los Angeles**	**NHL**	**82**	**8**	**33**	**41**	**34**	**3**	**0**	**1**	**153**	**5.2**	**–18**	**8**	**12.5**	**23:00**	....	....	....	....	....	....	....	....	....
2008-09	**Edmonton**	**NHL**	**50**	**8**	**23**	**31**	**30**	**5**	**0**	**1**	**86**	**9.3**	**6**	**0**	**0.0**	**23:01**	....	....	....	....	....	....	....	....	....
2009-10	**Edmonton**	**NHL**	**57**	**10**	**22**	**32**	**16**	**4**	**0**	**1**	**78**	**12.8**	**–4**	**0**	**0.0**	**20:45**	....	....	....	....	....	....	....	....	....
	Slovakia	Olympics	7	2	1	3	0	....	....	....	....	....	....	....	....	....	....	....	....	....	....	....	....	....	....
	Anaheim	**NHL**	**16**	**5**	**8**	**13**	**4**	**1**	**0**	**1**	**53**	**9.4**	**–6**	**0**	**0.0**	**26:00**	....	....	....	....	....	....	....	....	....
2010-11	**Anaheim**	**NHL**	**81**	**18**	**50**	**68**	**24**	**5**	**0**	**4**	**152**	**11.8**	**18**	**0**	**0.0**	**24:18**	**6**	**0**	**3**	**3**	**2**	**0**	**0**	**0**	**21:21**
2011-12	**Anaheim**	**NHL**	**68**	**6**	**21**	**27**	**47**	**1**	**0**	**1**	**112**	**5.4**	**7**	**1**	**100.0**	**20:47**	....	....	....	....	....	....	....	....	....
2012-13	Bratislava	KHL	32	6	10	16	22	....	....	....	....	....	....	....	....	....	....	....	....	....	....	....	....	....	....
	NY Islanders	**NHL**	**35**	**3**	**11**	**14**	**20**	**1**	**0**	**0**	**69**	**4.3**	**12**	**0**	**0.0**	**22:48**	**6**	**0**	**2**	**2**	**2**	**0**	**0**	**0**	**22:51**
	NHL Totals		**806**	**120**	**344**	**464**	**355**	**48**	**0**	**18**	**1413**	**8.5**		**16**	**31.3**	**21:36**	**24**	**0**	**6**	**6**	**4**	**0**	**0**	**0**	**17:06**

NHL All-Rookie Team (2001) • NHL Second All-Star Team (2011)

Played in NHL All-Star Game (2007)

Signed as a free agent by **Bratislava** (Slovakia), September 27, 2004. Traded to **Edmonton** by **Los Angeles** for Jarret Stoll and Matt Greene, June 29, 2008. Traded to **Anaheim** by **Edmonton** for Ryan Whitney and Anaheim's 6th round choice (Brandon Davidson) in 2010 Entry Draft, March 3, 2010. Traded to **NY Islanders** by **Anaheim** for NY Islanders' 2nd round choice (Nick Sorensen) in 2013 Entry Draft, June 22, 2012. Signed as a free agent by **Bratislava** (KHL), September 15, 2012.

VITALE, Joe
(vih-TA-lee, JOH) **PIT**

Center. Shoots right. 5'11", 205 lbs. Born, St. Louis, MO, August 20, 1985. Pittsburgh's 7th choice, 195th overall, in 2005 Entry Draft.

			Regular Season														Playoffs								
Season	Club	League	GP	G	A	Pts	PIM	PP	SH	GW	S	%	+/-	TF	F%	Min	GP	G	A	Pts	PIM	PP	SH	GW	Min
2003-04	St. Louis Jr. Blues	CSJHL	43	21	29	50	42	....	....	....	....	....	....	....	....	....	....	....	....	....	....	....	....	....	....
2004-05	Sioux Falls	USHL	53	11	20	31	62	....	....	....	....	....	....	....	....	....	....	....	....	....	....	....	....	....	....
2005-06	Northeastern	H-East	31	8	8	16	71	....	....	....	....	....	....	....	....	....	....	....	....	....	....	....	....	....	....
2006-07	Northeastern	H-East	35	7	9	16	54	....	....	....	....	....	....	....	....	....	....	....	....	....	....	....	....	....	....
2007-08	Northeastern	H-East	37	12	23	35	75	....	....	....	....	....	....	....	....	....	....	....	....	....	....	....	....	....	....
2008-09	Northeastern	H-East	40	7	20	27	68	....	....	....	....	....	....	....	....	....	....	....	....	....	....	....	....	....	....
	Wilkes-Barre	AHL	5	2	2	4	2	....	....	....	....	....	....	....	....	....	12	0	0	0	12	....	....	....	....
2009-10	Wilkes-Barre	AHL	74	6	26	32	70	....	....	....	....	....	....	....	....	....	4	0	2	2	0	....	....	....	....
2010-11	**Pittsburgh**	**NHL**	**9**	**1**	**1**	**2**	**13**	**0**	**0**	**0**	**13**	**7.7**	**–1**	**64**	**56.3**	**10:34**	....	....	....	....	....	....	....	....	....
	Wilkes-Barre	AHL	60	9	21	30	64	....	....	....	....	....	....	....	....	....	11	3	3	6	18	....	....	....	....
2011-12	**Pittsburgh**	**NHL**	**68**	**4**	**10**	**14**	**56**	**0**	**0**	**1**	**70**	**5.7**	**–5**	**723**	**55.7**	**11:11**	**4**	**0**	**0**	**0**	**12**	**0**	**0**	**0**	**6:09**
2012-13	**Pittsburgh**	**NHL**	**33**	**2**	**3**	**5**	**17**	**0**	**0**	**1**	**26**	**7.7**	**–7**	**257**	**61.1**	**9:31**	**6**	**0**	**1**	**1**	**6**	**0**	**0**	**0**	**9:53**
	NHL Totals		**110**	**7**	**14**	**21**	**86**	**0**	**0**	**2**	**109**	**6.4**		**1044**	**57.1**	**10:38**	**10**	**0**	**1**	**1**	**18**	**0**	**0**	**0**	**8:24**

Hockey East Second All-Star Team (2008)

VLASIC, Marc-Edouard
(vih-LASH-ihc, MAHRK-EHD-wahrd) **S.J.**

Defense. Shoots left. 6'1", 205 lbs. Born, Montreal, Que., March 30, 1987. San Jose's 2nd choice, 35th overall, in 2005 Entry Draft.

			Regular Season														Playoffs								
Season	Club	League	GP	G	A	Pts	PIM	PP	SH	GW	S	%	+/-	TF	F%	Min	GP	G	A	Pts	PIM	PP	SH	GW	Min
2003-04	Quebec Remparts	QMJHL	41	1	9	10	4	....	....	....	....	....	....	....	....	....	5	0	1	1	0	....	....	....	....
2004-05	Quebec Remparts	QMJHL	70	5	25	30	33	....	....	....	....	....	....	....	....	....	13	2	7	9	2	....	....	....	....
2005-06	Quebec Remparts	QMJHL	66	16	57	73	57	....	....	....	....	....	....	....	....	....	23	5	24	29	10	....	....	....	....
2006-07	**San Jose**	**NHL**	**81**	**3**	**23**	**26**	**18**	**2**	**0**	**0**	**66**	**4.5**	**13**	**0**	**0.0**	**22:12**	**11**	**0**	**1**	**1**	**2**	**0**	**0**	**0**	**22:52**
2007-08	**San Jose**	**NHL**	**82**	**2**	**12**	**14**	**24**	**1**	**0**	**0**	**72**	**2.8**	**–12**	**0**	**0.0**	**21:37**	**13**	**0**	**1**	**1**	**0**	**0**	**0**	**0**	**24:39**
	Worcester Sharks	AHL	1	0	2	2	0	....	....	....	....	....	....	....	....	....	....	....	....	....	....	....	....	....	....
2008-09	**San Jose**	**NHL**	**82**	**6**	**30**	**36**	**42**	**3**	**0**	**1**	**104**	**5.8**	**15**	**0**	**0.0**	**23:54**	**6**	**0**	**1**	**1**	**0**	**0**	**0**	**0**	**20:39**
2009-10	**San Jose**	**NHL**	**64**	**3**	**13**	**16**	**33**	**1**	**0**	**0**	**74**	**4.1**	**21**	**0**	**0.0**	**22:05**	**15**	**0**	**3**	**3**	**4**	**0**	**0**	**0**	**21:53**
2010-11	**San Jose**	**NHL**	**80**	**4**	**14**	**18**	**18**	**0**	**0**	**2**	**116**	**3.4**	**14**	**0**	**0.0**	**20:52**	**18**	**0**	**3**	**3**	**4**	**0**	**0**	**0**	**21:45**
2011-12	**San Jose**	**NHL**	**82**	**4**	**19**	**23**	**40**	**0**	**0**	**1**	**119**	**3.4**	**11**	**0**	**0.0**	**23:09**	**5**	**0**	**0**	**0**	**2**	**0**	**0**	**0**	**20:53**
2012-13	**San Jose**	**NHL**	**48**	**3**	**4**	**7**	**29**	**0**	**0**	**0**	**59**	**5.1**	**5**	**0**	**0.0**	**20:49**	**11**	**1**	**1**	**2**	**6**	**0**	**0**	**0**	**20:40**
	NHL Totals		**519**	**25**	**115**	**140**	**204**	**7**	**0**	**4**	**610**	**4.1**		**0**	**0.0**	**22:11**	**79**	**1**	**10**	**11**	**18**	**0**	**0**	**0**	**22:07**

NHL All-Rookie Team (2007)

VOLCHENKOV, Anton
(vohl-chen-KAHF, AN-tawn) **N.J.**

Defense. Shoots left. 6'1", 225 lbs. Born, Moscow, USSR, February 25, 1982. Ottawa's 1st choice, 21st overall, in 2000 Entry Draft.

			Regular Season														Playoffs								
Season	Club	League	GP	G	A	Pts	PIM	PP	SH	GW	S	%	+/-	TF	F%	Min	GP	G	A	Pts	PIM	PP	SH	GW	Min
99-2000	HK Moscow 2	Russia-3	6	0	1	1	10	....	....	....	....	....	....	....	....	....	....	....	....	....	....	....	....	....	....
	HK Moscow	Russia-2	30	2	9	11	36	....	....	....	....	....	....	....	....	....	....	....	....	....	....	....	....	....	....
2000-01	Krylja Sovetov	Russia-2	34	3	4	7	56	....	....	....	....	....	....	....	....	....	....	....	....	....	....	....	....	....	....
2001-02	Krylja Sovetov 2	Russia-3	1	0	0	0	0	....	....	....	....	....	....	....	....	....	....	....	....	....	....	....	....	....	....
	Krylja Sovetov	Russia	47	4	16	20	50	....	....	....	....	....	....	....	....	....	3	0	0	0	29	....	....	....	....
2002-03	**Ottawa**	**NHL**	**57**	**3**	**13**	**16**	**40**	**0**	**0**	**0**	**75**	**4.0**	**–4**	**0**	**0.0**	**15:30**	**17**	**1**	**1**	**2**	**4**	**0**	**0**	**1**	**13:31**
2003-04	**Ottawa**	**NHL**	**19**	**1**	**2**	**3**	**8**	**0**	**0**	**0**	**15**	**6.7**	**1**	**0**	**0.0**	**13:04**	**5**	**0**	**0**	**0**	**6**	**0**	**0**	**0**	**11:52**
2004-05	Binghamton	AHL	69	10	35	45	62	....	....	....	....	....	....	....	....	....	6	0	3	3	0	....	....	....	....
2005-06	**Ottawa**	**NHL**	**75**	**4**	**13**	**17**	**53**	**0**	**0**	**0**	**82**	**4.9**	**21**	**0**	**0.0**	**18:03**	**9**	**0**	**4**	**4**	**8**	**0**	**0**	**0**	**13:53**
	Russia	Olympics	8	0	0	0	2	....	....	....	....	....	....	....	....	....	....	....	....	....	....	....	....	....	....
2006-07	**Ottawa**	**NHL**	**78**	**1**	**18**	**19**	**67**	**0**	**0**	**0**	**85**	**1.2**	**37**	**0**	**0.0**	**21:17**	**20**	**2**	**4**	**6**	**24**	**0**	**0**	**1**	**23:19**
2007-08	**Ottawa**	**NHL**	**67**	**1**	**14**	**15**	**55**	**0**	**0**	**1**	**71**	**1.4**	**14**	**0**	**0.0**	**20:31**	**4**	**0**	**1**	**1**	**2**	**0**	**0**	**0**	**17:11**
2008-09	**Ottawa**	**NHL**	**68**	**2**	**8**	**10**	**36**	**0**	**0**	**1**	**79**	**2.5**	**–10**	**0**	**0.0**	**20:08**	....	....	....	....	....	....	....	....	....
2009-10	**Ottawa**	**NHL**	**64**	**4**	**10**	**14**	**38**	**0**	**0**	**0**	**69**	**5.8**	**2**	**0**	**0.0**	**20:41**	**6**	**0**	**2**	**2**	**4**	**0**	**0**	**0**	**22:30**
	Russia	Olympics	4	0	1	1	2	....	....	....	....	....	....	....	....	....	....	....	....	....	....	....	....	....	....
2010-11	**New Jersey**	**NHL**	**57**	**0**	**8**	**8**	**36**	**0**	**0**	**0**	**65**	**0.0**	**3**	**0**	**0.0**	**18:06**	....	....	....	....	....	....	....	....	....
2011-12	**New Jersey**	**NHL**	**72**	**2**	**9**	**11**	**34**	**0**	**0**	**1**	**63**	**3.2**	**3**	**0**	**0.0**	**17:59**	**24**	**1**	**1**	**2**	**10**	**0**	**0**	**0**	**16:04**
2012-13	Nizhny Novgorod	KHL	11	0	1	1	16	....	....	....	....	....	....	....	....	....	....	....	....	....	....	....	....	....	....
	New Jersey	**NHL**	**37**	**1**	**4**	**5**	**37**	**0**	**0**	**0**	**38**	**2.6**	**–1**	**0**	**0.0**	**16:03**	....	....	....	....	....	....	....	....	....
	NHL Totals		**594**	**19**	**99**	**118**	**404**	**0**	**0**	**3**	**642**	**3.0**		**0**	**0.0**	**18:45**	**85**	**4**	**13**	**17**	**58**	**0**	**0**	**2**	**17:18**

• Missed majority of 2003-04 due to shoulder injury vs. Boston, December 8, 2003. Signed as a free agent by **New Jersey**, July 1, 2010. Signed as a free agent by **Nizhny Novgorod** (KHL), October 9, 2012.

VOLPATTI, Aaron
(vohl-PA-tee, AIR-uhn) **WSH**

Left wing. Shoots left. 6', 225 lbs. Born, Revelstoke, B.C., May 30, 1985.

			Regular Season														Playoffs								
Season	Club	League	GP	G	A	Pts	PIM	PP	SH	GW	S	%	+/-	TF	F%	Min	GP	G	A	Pts	PIM	PP	SH	GW	Min
2003-04	Vernon Vipers	BCHL	55	1	4	5	134	....	....	....	....	....	....	....	....	....	....	....	....	....	....	....	....	....	....
2004-05	Vernon Vipers	BCHL	57	6	12	18	106	....	....	....	....	....	....	....	....	....	....	....	....	....	....	....	....	....	....
2005-06	Vernon Vipers	BCHL	25	6	8	14	39	....	....	....	....	....	....	....	....	....	....	....	....	....	....	....	....	....	....
2006-07	Brown U.	ECAC	23	5	2	7	39	....	....	....	....	....	....	....	....	....	....	....	....	....	....	....	....	....	....
2007-08	Brown U.	ECAC	31	4	6	10	28	....	....	....	....	....	....	....	....	....	....	....	....	....	....	....	....	....	....
2008-09	Brown U.	ECAC	32	6	6	12	54	....	....	....	....	....	....	....	....	....	....	....	....	....	....	....	....	....	....
2009-10	Brown U.	ECAC	37	17	15	32	*115	....	....	....	....	....	....	....	....	....	....	....	....	....	....	....	....	....	....
	Manitoba Moose	AHL	8	1	1	2	17	....	....	....	....	....	....	....	....	....	5	1	0	1	21	....	....	....	....

			Regular Season														Playoffs								
Season	Club	League	GP	G	A	Pts	PIM	PP	SH	GW	S	%	+/-	TF	F%	Min	GP	G	A	Pts	PIM	PP	SH	GW	Min
2010-11	**Vancouver**	**NHL**	**15**	**1**	**1**	**2**	**16**	**0**	**0**	**0**	**6**	**16.7**	**–1**	**0**	**0.0**	**6:50**	....	....	....	....	....	....	....	....	....
	Manitoba Moose	AHL	53	2	9	11	74	....	....	....	....	....	....	....	....	....	12	1	2	3	36	....	....	....	....
2011-12	**Vancouver**	**NHL**	**23**	**1**	**0**	**1**	**37**	**0**	**0**	**0**	**17**	**5.9**	**–2**	**4**	**100.0**	**8:58**	....	....	....	....	....	....	....	....	....
2012-13	**Vancouver**	**NHL**	**16**	**1**	**0**	**1**	**28**	**0**	**0**	**0**	**11**	**9.1**	**0**	**2**	**0.0**	**7:19**	....	....	....	....	....	....	....	....	....
	Washington	**NHL**	**17**	**0**	**1**	**1**	**7**	**0**	**0**	**0**	**10**	**0.0**	**–2**	**2**	**50.0**	**9:18**	....	....	....	....	....	....	....	....	....
	NHL Totals		**71**	**3**	**2**	**5**	**88**	**0**	**0**	**0**	**44**	**6.8**		**8**	**62.5**	**8:13**	....	....	....	....	....	....	....	....	....

Signed as a free agent by **Vancouver**, March 22, 2010. • Missed majority of 2011-12 due to shoulder injury at Los Angeles, November 10, 2011 and resulting surgery. Claimed on waivers by **Washington**, February 28, 2013.

VORACEK, Jakub

(VOHR-rah-chehk, YA-kuhb) **PHI**

Right wing. Shoots left. 6'2", 214 lbs. Born, Kladno, Czech., August 15, 1989. Columbus' 1st choice, 7th overall, in 2007 Entry Draft.

Season	Club	League	GP	G	A	Pts	PIM	PP	SH	GW	S	%	+/-	TF	F%	Min	GP	G	A	Pts	PIM	PP	SH	GW	Min
2002-03	HC Kladno U17	CzR-U17	2	1	1	2	2	....	....	....	....	....	....	....	....	....	2	1	1	2	0	....	....	....	....
2003-04	HC Kladno U17	CzR-U17	52	30	24	54	26	....	....	....	....	....	....	....	....	....	2	0	0	0	2	....	....	....	....
2004-05	HC Kladno U17	CzR-U17	30	23	39	62	44	....	....	....	....	....	....	....	....	....	7	5	4	9	14	....	....	....	....
	HC Kladno Jr.	CzRep-Jr.	16	5	7	12	6	....	....	....	....	....	....	....	....	....	1	1	0	1	2	....	....	....	....
2005-06	HC Kladno U17	CzR-U17	....	....	....	....	....	....	....	....	....	....	....	....	....	....	2	1	3	4	31	....	....	....	....
	HC Kladno Jr.	CzRep-Jr.	46	21	38	59	54	....	....	....	....	....	....	....	....	....	6	7	4	11	2	....	....	....	....
	HC Rabat Kladno	CzRep	1	0	0	0	0	....	....	....	....	....	....	....	....	....	....	....	....	....	....	....	....	....	....
2006-07	Halifax	QMJHL	59	23	63	86	26	....	....	....	....	....	....	....	....	....	12	7	17	24	6	....	....	....	....
2007-08	Halifax	QMJHL	53	33	68	101	42	....	....	....	....	....	....	....	....	....	15	5	13	18	14	....	....	....	....
2008-09	**Columbus**	**NHL**	**80**	**9**	**29**	**38**	**44**	**0**	**0**	**1**	**101**	**8.9**	**11**	**3**	**0.0**	**12:40**	**4**	**0**	**1**	**1**	**8**	**0**	**0**	**0**	**12:06**
2009-10	**Columbus**	**NHL**	**81**	**16**	**34**	**50**	**26**	**4**	**0**	**1**	**154**	**10.4**	**–7**	**6**	**33.3**	**15:37**	....	....	....	....	....	....	....	....	....
2010-11	**Columbus**	**NHL**	**80**	**14**	**32**	**46**	**26**	**2**	**0**	**2**	**183**	**7.7**	**–3**	**65**	**36.9**	**16:58**	....	....	....	....	....	....	....	....	....
2011-12	**Philadelphia**	**NHL**	**78**	**18**	**31**	**49**	**32**	**0**	**0**	**2**	**190**	**9.5**	**11**	**23**	**30.4**	**16:17**	**11**	**2**	**8**	**10**	**8**	**1**	**0**	**1**	**15:58**
2012-13	HC Lev Praha	KHL	23	7	13	20	22	....	....	....	....	....	....	....	....	....	....	....	....	....	....	....	....	....	....
	Philadelphia	**NHL**	**48**	**22**	**24**	**46**	**35**	**8**	**0**	**3**	**129**	**17.1**	**–7**	**5**	**40.0**	**17:14**	....	....	....	....	....	....	....	....	....
	NHL Totals		**367**	**79**	**150**	**229**	**163**	**14**	**0**	**9**	**757**	**10.4**		**102**	**34.3**	**15:37**	**15**	**2**	**9**	**11**	**16**	**1**	**0**	**1**	**14:56**

QMJHL All-Rookie Team (2007) • QMJHL Rookie of the Year (2007) • QMJHL Second All-Star Team (2008)

Traded to **Philadelphia** by **Columbus** with Columbus's 1st (Sean Couturier) and 3rd (Nick Cousins) round choices in 2011 Entry Draft for Jeff Carter, June 23, 2011. Signed as a free agent by **Lev Praha** (KHL), September 16, 2012.

VOYNOV, Slava

(VOY-nawf, SLA-vuh) **L.A.**

Defense. Shoots right. 6', 190 lbs. Born, Chelyabinsk, USSR, January 15, 1990. Los Angeles' 3rd choice, 32nd overall, in 2008 Entry Draft.

Season	Club	League	GP	G	A	Pts	PIM	PP	SH	GW	S	%	+/-	TF	F%	Min	GP	G	A	Pts	PIM	PP	SH	GW	Min
2005-06	Chelyabinsk 2	Russia-3	2	0	0	0	0	....	....	....	....	....	....	....	....	....	....	....	....	....	....	....	....	....	....
2006-07	Chelyabinsk	Russia	31	0	0	0	12	....	....	....	....	....	....	....	....	....	....	....	....	....	....	....	....	....	....
2007-08	Chelyabinsk 2	Russia-3	2	1	0	1	0	....	....	....	....	....	....	....	....	....	....	....	....	....	....	....	....	....	....
	Chelyabinsk	Russia	36	1	3	4	20	....	....	....	....	....	....	....	....	....	2	0	0	0	0	....	....	....	....
2008-09	Manchester	AHL	61	8	15	23	46	....	....	....	....	....	....	....	....	....	....	....	....	....	....	....	....	....	....
2009-10	Manchester	AHL	79	10	19	29	43	....	....	....	....	....	....	....	....	....	9	1	3	4	0	....	....	....	....
2010-11	Manchester	AHL	76	15	36	51	36	....	....	....	....	....	....	....	....	....	7	2	3	5	6	....	....	....	....
2011-12 ◆	**Los Angeles**	**NHL**	**54**	**8**	**12**	**20**	**12**	**3**	**0**	**2**	**86**	**9.3**	**12**	**0**	**0.0**	**18:32**	**20**	**1**	**2**	**3**	**4**	**0**	**0**	**0**	**19:32**
	Manchester	AHL	15	2	2	4	4	....	....	....	....	....	....	....	....	....	....	....	....	....	....	....	....	....	....
2012-13	Manchester	AHL	35	7	9	16	22	....	....	....	....	....	....	....	....	....	....	....	....	....	....	....	....	....	....
	Los Angeles	**NHL**	**48**	**6**	**19**	**25**	**14**	**1**	**0**	**2**	**79**	**7.6**	**5**	**2**	**100.0**	**22:18**	**18**	**6**	**7**	**13**	**0**	**0**	**0**	**4**	**21:55**
	NHL Totals		**102**	**14**	**31**	**45**	**26**	**4**	**0**	**4**	**165**	**8.5**		**2**	**100.0**	**20:18**	**38**	**7**	**9**	**16**	**4**	**0**	**0**	**4**	**20:40**

AHL Second All-Star Team (2011)

VRBATA, Radim

(vuhr-BA-tuh, RA-dihm) **PHX**

Right wing. Shoots right. 6'1", 194 lbs. Born, Mlada Boleslav, Czech., June 13, 1981. Colorado's 10th choice, 212th overall, in 1999 Entry Draft.

Season	Club	League	GP	G	A	Pts	PIM	PP	SH	GW	S	%	+/-	TF	F%	Min	GP	G	A	Pts	PIM	PP	SH	GW	Min
1997-98	Ml. Boleslav Jr.	CzRep-Jr.	35	42	31	73	4	....	....	....	....	....	....	....	....	....	....	....	....	....	....	....	....	....	....
1998-99	Hull Olympiques	QMJHL	54	22	38	60	16	....	....	....	....	....	....	....	....	....	23	6	13	19	6	....	....	....	....
99-2000	Hull Olympiques	QMJHL	58	29	45	74	26	....	....	....	....	....	....	....	....	....	15	3	9	12	8	....	....	....	....
2000-01	Shawinigan	QMJHL	55	56	64	120	67	....	....	....	....	....	....	....	....	....	10	4	7	11	4	....	....	....	....
	Hershey Bears	AHL	....	....	....	....	....	....	....	....	....	....	....	....	....	....	1	0	1	1	2	....	....	....	....
2001-02	**Colorado**	**NHL**	**52**	**18**	**12**	**30**	**14**	**6**	**0**	**3**	**112**	**16.1**	**7**	**8**	**37.5**	**14:32**	**9**	**0**	**0**	**0**	**0**	**0**	**0**	**0**	**13:05**
	Hershey Bears	AHL	20	8	14	22	8	....	....	....	....	....	....	....	....	....	....	....	....	....	....	....	....	....	....
2002-03	**Colorado**	**NHL**	**66**	**11**	**19**	**30**	**16**	**3**	**0**	**4**	**171**	**6.4**	**0**	**14**	**50.0**	**13:55**	....	....	....	....	....	....	....	....	....
	Carolina	**NHL**	**10**	**5**	**0**	**5**	**2**	**3**	**0**	**0**	**44**	**11.4**	**–7**	**15**	**46.7**	**19:00**	....	....	....	....	....	....	....	....	....
2003-04	**Carolina**	**NHL**	**80**	**12**	**13**	**25**	**24**	**4**	**0**	**2**	**195**	**6.2**	**–10**	**21**	**38.1**	**13:42**	....	....	....	....	....	....	....	....	....
2004-05	Liberec	CzRep	45	18	21	39	91	....	....	....	....	....	....	....	....	....	12	3	2	5	0	....	....	....	....
2005-06	**Carolina**	**NHL**	**16**	**2**	**3**	**5**	**6**	**1**	**0**	**0**	**38**	**5.3**	**0**	**3**	**33.3**	**12:37**	....	....	....	....	....	....	....	....	....
	Chicago	**NHL**	**45**	**13**	**21**	**34**	**16**	**5**	**0**	**0**	**147**	**8.8**	**4**	**6**	**50.0**	**15:43**	....	....	....	....	....	....	....	....	....
2006-07	**Chicago**	**NHL**	**77**	**14**	**27**	**41**	**26**	**5**	**0**	**2**	**215**	**6.5**	**–4**	**12**	**33.3**	**16:53**	....	....	....	....	....	....	....	....	....
2007-08	**Phoenix**	**NHL**	**76**	**27**	**29**	**56**	**14**	**7**	**3**	**5**	**246**	**11.0**	**6**	**19**	**36.8**	**18:12**	....	....	....	....	....	....	....	....	....
2008-09	**Tampa Bay**	**NHL**	**18**	**3**	**3**	**6**	**8**	**1**	**0**	**0**	**41**	**7.3**	**–1**	**3**	**33.3**	**14:13**	....	....	....	....	....	....	....	....	....
	BK Mlada Boleslav	CzRep	11	5	3	8	18	....	....	....	....	....	....	....	....	....	....	....	....	....	....	....	....	....	....
	Liberec	CzRep	7	7	2	9	2	....	....	....	....	....	....	....	....	....	3	0	1	1	2	....	....	....	....
2009-10	**Phoenix**	**NHL**	**82**	**24**	**19**	**43**	**24**	**7**	**0**	**4**	**266**	**9.0**	**6**	**8**	**25.0**	**16:13**	**7**	**2**	**2**	**4**	**4**	**1**	**0**	**1**	**15:42**
2010-11	**Phoenix**	**NHL**	**79**	**19**	**29**	**48**	**20**	**10**	**0**	**2**	**240**	**7.9**	**5**	**7**	**28.6**	**16:22**	**4**	**2**	**3**	**5**	**0**	**1**	**0**	**0**	**19:55**
2011-12	**Phoenix**	**NHL**	**77**	**35**	**27**	**62**	**24**	**9**	**1**	***12**	**232**	**15.1**	**24**	**67**	**40.3**	**18:39**	**16**	**2**	**3**	**5**	**8**	**1**	**0**	**0**	**17:20**
2012-13	BK Mlada Boleslav	CzRep-2	2	1	1	2	0	....	....	....	....	....	....	....	....	....	....	....	....	....	....	....	....	....	....
	Phoenix	**NHL**	**34**	**12**	**16**	**28**	**14**	**2**	**1**	**1**	**106**	**11.3**	**6**	**32**	**31.3**	**18:19**	....	....	....	....	....	....	....	....	....
	NHL Totals		**712**	**195**	**218**	**413**	**208**	**63**	**5**	**35**	**2053**	**9.5**		**215**	**38.1**	**16:08**	**36**	**6**	**8**	**14**	**12**	**3**	**0**	**1**	**16:14**

QMJHL First All-Star Team (2001)

Traded to **Carolina** by **Colorado** for Bates Battaglia, March 11, 2003. Signed as a free agent by **Liberec** (CzRep), September 4, 2004. Traded to **Chicago** by **Carolina** for Chicago's 4th round choice (later traded to St. Louis - St. Louis selected Cade Fairchild) in 2007 Entry Draft, December 29, 2005. Traded to **Phoenix** by **Chicago** for Kevyn Adams, August 11, 2007. Signed as a free agent by **Tampa Bay**, July 1, 2008. • Assigned to **Mlada Boleslav** (CzRep) by **Tampa Bay**, December 9, 2008. • Loaned to **Liberec** (CzRep) by **Mlada Boleslav** (CzRep), January 29, 2009. Traded to **Phoenix** by **Tampa Bay** for Todd Fedoruk and David Hale, July 21, 2009. Signed as a free agent by **Mlada Boleslav** (CzRep-2), November 1, 2012.

WALKER, Matt

(WAW-kuhr, MAT)

Defense. Shoots right. 6'4", 215 lbs. Born, Beaverlodge, Alta., April 7, 1980. St. Louis' 3rd choice, 83rd overall, in 1998 Entry Draft.

Season	Club	League	GP	G	A	Pts	PIM	PP	SH	GW	S	%	+/-	TF	F%	Min	GP	G	A	Pts	PIM	PP	SH	GW	Min
1996-97	Grand Prairie	AAHA	68	22	62	74	186	....	....	....	....	....	....	....	....	....	....	....	....	....	....	....	....	....	....
1997-98	Portland	WHL	64	2	13	15	124	....	....	....	....	....	....	....	....	....	16	0	0	0	21	....	....	....	....
1998-99	Portland	WHL	64	1	10	11	151	....	....	....	....	....	....	....	....	....	4	0	1	1	6	....	....	....	....
99-2000	Portland	WHL	38	2	7	9	97	....	....	....	....	....	....	....	....	....	....	....	....	....	....	....	....	....	....
	Kootenay Ice	WHL	31	4	19	23	53	....	....	....	....	....	....	....	....	....	21	5	13	18	24	....	....	....	....
2000-01	Worcester IceCats	AHL	61	4	8	12	131	....	....	....	....	....	....	....	....	....	11	0	0	0	6	....	....	....	....
	Peoria Rivermen	ECHL	8	1	0	1	70	....	....	....	....	....	....	....	....	....	....	....	....	....	....	....	....	....	....
2001-02	Worcester IceCats	AHL	49	2	11	13	164	....	....	....	....	....	....	....	....	....	3	0	0	0	8	....	....	....	....
2002-03	**St. Louis**	**NHL**	**16**	**0**	**1**	**1**	**38**	**0**	**0**	**0**	**13**	**0.0**	**0**	**1**	**100.0**	**11:09**	....	....	....	....	....	....	....	....	....
	Worcester IceCats	AHL	40	1	8	9	58	....	....	....	....	....	....	....	....	....	....	....	....	....	....	....	....	....	....
2003-04	**St. Louis**	**NHL**	**14**	**0**	**1**	**1**	**25**	**0**	**0**	**0**	**8**	**0.0**	**0**	**0**	**0.0**	**11:23**	**4**	**0**	**0**	**0**	**0**	**0**	**0**	**0**	**9:43**
	Worcester IceCats	AHL	4	0	1	1	7	....	....	....	....	....	....	....	....	....	....	....	....	....	....	....	....	....	....
2004-05	Worcester IceCats	AHL	20	2	4	6	44	....	....	....	....	....	....	....	....	....	....	....	....	....	....	....	....	....	....
2005-06	**St. Louis**	**NHL**	**54**	**0**	**2**	**2**	**79**	**0**	**0**	**0**	**59**	**0.0**	**–7**	**0**	**0.0**	**14:15**	....	....	....	....	....	....	....	....	....
2006-07	**St. Louis**	**NHL**	**48**	**0**	**5**	**5**	**72**	**0**	**0**	**0**	**34**	**0.0**	**7**	**0**	**0.0**	**15:15**	....	....	....	....	....	....	....	....	....
	Peoria Rivermen	AHL	2	0	1	1	0	....	....	....	....	....	....	....	....	....	....	....	....	....	....	....	....	....	....
2007-08	**St. Louis**	**NHL**	**43**	**1**	**1**	**2**	**61**	**0**	**0**	**0**	**47**	**2.1**	**–3**	**0**	**0.0**	**15:54**	....	....	....	....	....	....	....	....	....
2008-09	**Chicago**	**NHL**	**65**	**1**	**13**	**14**	**79**	**0**	**0**	**0**	**83**	**1.2**	**7**	**0**	**0.0**	**16:38**	**17**	**0**	**2**	**2**	**14**	**0**	**0**	**0**	**15:21**
2009-10	**Tampa Bay**	**NHL**	**66**	**2**	**3**	**5**	**90**	**0**	**0**	**0**	**54**	**3.7**	**–11**	**0**	**0.0**	**16:09**	....	....	....	....	....	....	....	....	....
2010-11	**Philadelphia**	**NHL**	**4**	**0**	**0**	**0**	**4**	**0**	**0**	**0**	**3**	**0.0**	**0**	**0**	**0.0**	**11:38**	....	....	....	....	....	....	....	....	....
	Adirondack	AHL	11	0	2	2	8	....	....	....	....	....	....	....	....	....	....	....	....	....	....	....	....	....	....
2011-12	**Philadelphia**	**NHL**	**4**	**0**	**0**	**0**	**16**	**0**	**0**	**0**	**2**	**0.0**	**–2**	**0**	**0.0**	**10:58**	....	....	....	....	....	....	....	....	....
	Adirondack	AHL	33	1	4	5	41	....	....	....	....	....	....	....	....	....	....	....	....	....	....	....	....	....	....

			Regular Season														Playoffs								
Season	Club	League	GP	G	A	Pts	PIM	PP	SH	GW	S	%	+/-	TF	F%	Min	GP	G	A	Pts	PIM	PP	SH	GW	Min
2012-13	**Philadelphia**	**NHL**	DID NOT PLAY – INJURED																						
	NHL Totals		**314**	**4**	**26**	**30**	**464**	**0**	**0**	**0**	**303**	**1.3**		**11**	**100.0**	**15:10**	**21**	**0**	**2**	**2**	**14**	**0**	**0**	**0**	**14:17**

• Missed majority of 2003-04 due to groin injury in training camp, September 23, 2003. Signed as a free agent by **Chicago**, July 7, 2008. Signed as a free agent by **Tampa Bay**, July 1, 2009. Traded to **Philadelphia** by **Tampa Bay** with Tampa Bay's 4th round choice (Marcel Noebels) in 2011 Entry Draft for Simon Gagne, July 19, 2010. • Missed majority of 2010-11 due to pre-season hip injury. • Missed 2012-13 due to recurring back and hip injuries.

WALLACE, Tim

(WAHL-uhs, TIHM)

Right wing. Shoots right. 6'1", 207 lbs. Born, Anchorage, AK, August 6, 1984.

2000-01	USNTDP	NAHL	56	8	11	19	45	....	....	....	....	....	....	....	....	....	....	....	....	....	....	....	....	....	....
2001-02	USNTDP	USHL	11	1	5	6	10	....	....	....	....	....	....	....	....	....	....	....	....	....	....	....	....	....	....
	USNTDP	NAHL	10	3	2	5	6	....	....	....	....	....	....	....	....	....	....	....	....	....	....	....	....	....	....
2002-03	U. of Notre Dame	CCHA	40	6	5	11	28	....	....	....	....	....	....	....	....	....	....	....	....	....	....	....	....	....	....
2003-04	U. of Notre Dame	CCHA	39	3	8	11	10	....	....	....	....	....	....	....	....	....	....	....	....	....	....	....	....	....	....
2004-05	U. of Notre Dame	CCHA	38	5	9	14	20	....	....	....	....	....	....	....	....	....	....	....	....	....	....	....	....	....	....
2005-06	U. of Notre Dame	CCHA	36	11	12	23	28	....	....	....	....	....	....	....	....	....	....	....	....	....	....	....	....	....	....
2006-07	Wilkes-Barre	AHL	32	5	9	14	39	....	....	....	....	....	....	....	....	....	11	1	1	2	2	....	....	....	....
	Wheeling Nailers	ECHL	19	6	11	17	23	....	....	....	....	....	....	....	....	....	....	....	....	....	....	....	....	....	....
2007-08	Wilkes-Barre	AHL	74	12	14	26	82	....	....	....	....	....	....	....	....	....	23	2	6	8	21	....	....	....	....
2008-09	**Pittsburgh**	**NHL**	**16**	**0**	**2**	**2**	**7**	**0**	**0**	**0**	**17**	**0.0**	**2**	**3**	**66.7**	**8:07**	....	....	....	....	....	....	....	....	....
	Wilkes-Barre	AHL	58	11	8	19	51	....	....	....	....	....	....	....	....	....	7	0	2	2	2	....	....	....	....
2009-10	**Pittsburgh**	**NHL**	**1**	**0**	**0**	**0**	**0**	**0**	**0**	**0**	**0**	**0.0**	**0**	**0**	**0.0**	**5:50**	....	....	....	....	....	....	....	....	....
	Wilkes-Barre	AHL	78	27	14	41	61	....	....	....	....	....	....	....	....	....	4	0	0	0	2	....	....	....	....
2010-11	**Pittsburgh**	**NHL**	**7**	**0**	**0**	**0**	**5**	**0**	**0**	**0**	**1**	**0.0**	**–3**	**3**	**100.0**	**8:03**	....	....	....	....	....	....	....	....	....
	Wilkes-Barre	AHL	62	20	17	37	61	....	....	....	....	....	....	....	....	....	10	1	4	5	6	....	....	....	....
2011-12	**NY Islanders**	**NHL**	**31**	**0**	**1**	**1**	**6**	**0**	**0**	**0**	**16**	**0.0**	**–7**	**9**	**44.4**	**8:40**	....	....	....	....	....	....	....	....	....
	Bridgeport	AHL	24	9	11	20	13	....	....	....	....	....	....	....	....	....	....	....	....	....	....	....	....	....	....
	Tampa Bay	**NHL**	**18**	**3**	**5**	**8**	**10**	**0**	**0**	**1**	**10**	**30.0**	**4**	**11**	**36.4**	**8:28**	....	....	....	....	....	....	....	....	....
2012-13	Charlotte	AHL	47	9	13	22	44	....	....	....	....	....	....	....	....	....	3	1	1	2	0	....	....	....	....
	Carolina	**NHL**	**28**	**1**	**1**	**2**	**17**	**0**	**0**	**0**	**20**	**5.0**	**–9**	**30**	**30.0**	**10:02**	....	....	....	....	....	....	....	....	....
	NHL Totals		**101**	**4**	**9**	**13**	**45**	**0**	**0**	**1**	**64**	**6.3**		**56**	**39.3**	**8:51**	....	....	....	....	....	....	....	....	....

Signed as a free agent by **Pittsburgh**, May 29, 2007. Signed as a free agent by **NY Islanders**, July 21, 2011. Claimed on waivers by **Tampa Bay** from **NY Islanders**, February 23, 2012. Signed as a free agent by **Carolina**, July 19, 2012.

WALTER, Ben

(WAHL-tuhr, BEHN)

Center. Shoots left. 6', 185 lbs. Born, Beaconsfield, Que., May 11, 1984. Boston's 5th choice, 160th overall, in 2004 Entry Draft.

2000-01	Langley Hornets	BCHL	50	8	22	30	19	....	....	....	....	....	....	....	....	....	....	....	....	....	....	....	....	....	....
2001-02	Langley Hornets	BCHL	50	29	47	76	29	....	....	....	....	....	....	....	....	....	....	....	....	....	....	....	....	....	....
2002-03	U. Mass-Lowell	H-East	35	5	12	17	12	....	....	....	....	....	....	....	....	....	....	....	....	....	....	....	....	....	....
2003-04	U. Mass-Lowell	H-East	36	18	16	34	18	....	....	....	....	....	....	....	....	....	....	....	....	....	....	....	....	....	....
2004-05	U. Mass-Lowell	H-East	36	*26	13	39	28	....	....	....	....	....	....	....	....	....	....	....	....	....	....	....	....	....	....
2005-06	**Boston**	**NHL**	**6**	**0**	**0**	**0**	**4**	**0**	**0**	**0**	**6**	**0.0**	**2**	**32**	**53.1**	**11:49**	....	....	....	....	....	....	....	....	....
	Providence Bruins	AHL	62	16	24	40	33	....	....	....	....	....	....	....	....	....	3	2	0	2	2	....	....	....	....
2006-07	**Boston**	**NHL**	**4**	**0**	**0**	**0**	**0**	**0**	**0**	**0**	**0**	**0.0**	**0**	**24**	**41.7**	**6:11**	....	....	....	....	....	....	....	....	....
	Providence Bruins	AHL	73	24	43	67	58	....	....	....	....	....	....	....	....	....	13	4	4	8	6	....	....	....	....
2007-08	**NY Islanders**	**NHL**	**8**	**1**	**0**	**1**	**0**	**1**	**0**	**0**	**6**	**16.7**	**–1**	**33**	**30.3**	**6:05**	....	....	....	....	....	....	....	....	....
	Bridgeport	AHL	68	20	46	66	31	....	....	....	....	....	....	....	....	....	....	....	....	....	....	....	....	....	....
2008-09	**NY Islanders**	**NHL**	**4**	**0**	**0**	**0**	**0**	**0**	**0**	**0**	**2**	**0.0**	**–2**	**43**	**41.9**	**10:58**	....	....	....	....	....	....	....	....	....
	Bridgeport	AHL	65	20	30	50	10	....	....	....	....	....	....	....	....	....	5	1	4	5	2	....	....	....	....
2009-10	**New Jersey**	**NHL**	**2**	**0**	**0**	**0**	**2**	**0**	**0**	**0**	**0**	**0.0**	**0**	**6**	**33.3**	**5:48**	....	....	....	....	....	....	....	....	....
	Lowell Devils	AHL	78	22	36	58	26	....	....	....	....	....	....	....	....	....	5	1	1	2	2	....	....	....	....
2010-11	Lake Erie	AHL	77	23	47	70	24	....	....	....	....	....	....	....	....	....	7	3	2	5	4	....	....	....	....
2011-12	Abbotsford Heat	AHL	75	19	40	59	30	....	....	....	....	....	....	....	....	....	8	1	7	8	2	....	....	....	....
2012-13	Abbotsford Heat	AHL	68	15	34	49	18	....	....	....	....	....	....	....	....	....	....	....	....	....	....	....	....	....	....
	NHL Totals		**24**	**1**	**0**	**1**	**6**	**1**	**0**	**0**	**14**	**7.1**		**138**	**41.3**	**8:19**	....	....	....	....	....	....	....	....	....

Hockey East Second All-Star Team (2005)

Traded to **NY Islanders** by **Boston** with Boston's 2nd round choice (later traded to Columbus – Columbus selected Kevin Lynch) in 2009 Entry Draft for Petteri Nokelainen, September 11, 2007. Traded to **New Jersey** by **NY Islanders** with future considerations for Tony Romano, June 30, 2009. Signed as a free agent by **Colorado**, July 7, 2010. Signed as a free agent by **Calgary**, July 2, 2011. Signed as a free agent by **Orebro** (Sweden), May 24, 2013.

WANDELL, Tom

(VAHN-dehl, TAWM)

Center. Shoots left. 6'1", 200 lbs. Born, Sodertalje, Sweden, January 29, 1987. Dallas' 5th choice, 146th overall, in 2005 Entry Draft.

2002-03	Sodertalje SK U18	Swe-U18	13	8	7	15	6	....	....	....	....	....	....	....	....	....	....	....	....	....	....	....	....	....	....
2003-04	Sodertalje SK U18	Swe-U18	6	5	7	12	6	....	....	....	....	....	....	....	....	....	2	0	0	0	0	....	....	....	....
	Sodertalje SK Jr.	Swe-Jr.	33	7	15	22	14	....	....	....	....	....	....	....	....	....	2	0	0	0	0	....	....	....	....
2004-05	Sodertalje SK Jr.	Swe-Jr.	5	1	2	3	4	....	....	....	....	....	....	....	....	....	....	....	....	....	....	....	....	....	....
2005-06	Sodertalje SK Jr.	Swe-Jr.	41	19	20	39	45	....	....	....	....	....	....	....	....	....	4	1	0	1	2	....	....	....	....
	Sodertalje SK	Sweden	6	0	0	0	0	....	....	....	....	....	....	....	....	....	....	....	....	....	....	....	....	....	....
	Sodertalje SK	Sweden-Q	1	1	0	1	0	....	....	....	....	....	....	....	....	....	....	....	....	....	....	....	....	....	....
2006-07	Assat Pori Jr.	Fin-Jr.	4	1	1	2	0	....	....	....	....	....	....	....	....	....	....	....	....	....	....	....	....	....	....
	Assat Pori	Finland	50	6	6	12	20	....	....	....	....	....	....	....	....	....	....	....	....	....	....	....	....	....	....
2007-08	Iowa Stars	AHL	53	10	9	19	16	....	....	....	....	....	....	....	....	....	....	....	....	....	....	....	....	....	....
	Idaho Steelheads	ECHL	3	3	0	3	2	....	....	....	....	....	....	....	....	....	....	....	....	....	....	....	....	....	....
2008-09	Timra IK	Sweden	51	15	26	41	26	....	....	....	....	....	....	....	....	....	7	0	4	4	0	....	....	....	....
	Dallas	**NHL**	**14**	**1**	**2**	**3**	**4**	**0**	**0**	**0**	**23**	**4.3**	**–1**	**113**	**51.3**	**11:09**	....	....	....	....	....	....	....	....	....
2009-10	**Dallas**	**NHL**	**50**	**5**	**10**	**15**	**14**	**0**	**0**	**3**	**85**	**5.9**	**2**	**486**	**44.0**	**13:52**	....	....	....	....	....	....	....	....	....
2010-11	**Dallas**	**NHL**	**75**	**7**	**2**	**9**	**14**	**0**	**0**	**1**	**94**	**7.4**	**–5**	**435**	**43.7**	**11:45**	....	....	....	....	....	....	....	....	....
2011-12	**Dallas**	**NHL**	**72**	**6**	**9**	**15**	**16**	**0**	**0**	**0**	**103**	**5.8**	**–5**	**324**	**43.5**	**9:44**	....	....	....	....	....	....	....	....	....
2012-13	Cherepovets	KHL	26	2	7	9	18	....	....	....	....	....	....	....	....	....	....	....	....	....	....	....	....	....	....
	Dallas	**NHL**	**18**	**1**	**0**	**1**	**4**	**0**	**0**	**1**	**14**	**7.1**	**0**	**111**	**41.4**	**8:27**	....	....	....	....	....	....	....	....	....
	Texas Stars	AHL	11	0	4	4	4	....	....	....	....	....	....	....	....	....	....	....	....	....	....	....	....	....	....
	NHL Totals		**229**	**20**	**23**	**43**	**52**	**0**	**0**	**5**	**319**	**6.3**		**1469**	**44.2**	**11:17**	....	....	....	....	....	....	....	....	....

• Assigned to **Timra** (Sweden) by **Dallas**, July 24, 2008 . Signed as a free agent by **Cherepovets** (KHL), October 3, 2012. Signed as a free agent by **Spartak Moscow** (KHL), May 3, 2013.

WARD, Joel

(WOHRD, JOHL) **WSH**

Right wing. Shoots right. 6'1", 226 lbs. Born, Toronto, Ont., December 2, 1980.

1997-98	Owen Sound	OHL	47	8	4	12	14	....	....	....	....	....	....	....	....	....	11	1	1	2	5	....	....	....	....
1998-99	Owen Sound	OHL	58	19	16	35	23	....	....	....	....	....	....	....	....	....	16	2	4	6	0	....	....	....	....
99-2000	Owen Sound	OHL	63	23	20	43	51	....	....	....	....	....	....	....	....	....	....	....	....	....	....	....	....	....	....
2000-01	Owen Sound	OHL	67	26	36	62	45	....	....	....	....	....	....	....	....	....	5	2	4	6	4	....	....	....	....
	Long Beach	WCHL	....	....	....	....	....	....	....	....	....	....	....	....	....	....	8	0	0	0	0	....	....	....	....
2001-02	U. of P.E.I.	CIS	22	13	14	27	16	....	....	....	....	....	....	....	....	....	....	....	....	....	....	....	....	....	....
2002-03	U. of P.E.I.	CIS	19	11	15	26	24	....	....	....	....	....	....	....	....	....	....	....	....	....	....	....	....	....	....
2003-04	U. of P.E.I.	CIS	27	14	24	38	42	....	....	....	....	....	....	....	....	....	....	....	....	....	....	....	....	....	....
2004-05	U. of P.E.I.	CIS	28	16	28	44	42	....	....	....	....	....	....	....	....	....	....	....	....	....	....	....	....	....	....
2005-06	Houston Aeros	AHL	66	8	14	22	34	....	....	....	....	....	....	....	....	....	8	4	2	6	4	....	....	....	....
2006-07	**Minnesota**	**NHL**	**11**	**0**	**1**	**1**	**0**	**0**	**0**	**0**	**12**	**0.0**	**0**	**1**	**0.0**	**7:42**	....	....	....	....	....	....	....	....	....
	Houston Aeros	AHL	64	9	14	23	45	....	....	....	....	....	....	....	....	....	....	....	....	....	....	....	....	....	....
2007-08	Houston Aeros	AHL	79	21	20	41	47	....	....	....	....	....	....	....	....	....	4	0	2	2	0	....	....	....	....
2008-09	**Nashville**	**NHL**	**79**	**17**	**18**	**35**	**29**	**3**	**2**	**2**	**133**	**12.8**	**1**	**46**	**43.5**	**16:01**	....	....	....	....	....	....	....	....	....
2009-10	**Nashville**	**NHL**	**71**	**13**	**21**	**34**	**18**	**3**	**1**	**1**	**134**	**9.7**	**–5**	**81**	**38.3**	**17:33**	**6**	**2**	**2**	**4**	**2**	**0**	**1**	**0**	**19:54**
2010-11	**Nashville**	**NHL**	**80**	**10**	**19**	**29**	**42**	**5**	**0**	**4**	**157**	**6.4**	**–1**	**168**	**48.8**	**17:04**	**12**	**7**	**6**	**13**	**6**	**2**	**0**	**1**	**20:25**

			Regular Season														Playoffs								
Season	Club	League	GP	G	A	Pts	PIM	PP	SH	GW	S	%	+/-	TF	F%	Min	GP	G	A	Pts	PIM	PP	SH	GW	Min
2011-12	**Washington**	**NHL**	**73**	**6**	**12**	**18**	**20**	**0**	**0**	**0**	**79**	**7.6**	**12**	**52**	**55.8**	**12:26**	**14**	**1**	**4**	**5**	**6**	**0**	**0**	**1**	**10:57**
2012-13	**Washington**	**NHL**	**39**	**8**	**12**	**20**	**12**	**1**	**1**	**1**	**52**	**15.4**	**7**	**65**	**58.5**	**15:08**	**7**	**1**	**3**	**4**	**6**	**1**	**0**	**0**	**13:11**
	NHL Totals		**353**	**54**	**83**	**137**	**121**	**12**	**4**	**8**	**567**	**9.5**		**413**	**48.4**	**15:28**	**39**	**11**	**15**	**26**	**20**	**3**	**1**	**2**	**15:38**

Signed as a free agent by **Houston** (AHL), December 4, 2005. Signed as a free agent by **Minnesota**, September 27, 2006. Signed as a free agent by **Nashville**, July 14, 2008. Signed as a free agent by **Washington**, July 1, 2011.

WATHIER, Francis

(waw-TEE-ay, FRAN-sihs) **DAL**

Left wing. Shoots left. 6'4", 218 lbs. Born, St Isidore, Ont., December 7, 1984. Dallas' 8th choice, 185th overall, in 2003 Entry Draft.

Season	Club	League	GP	G	A	Pts	PIM	PP	SH	GW	S	%	+/-	TF	F%	Min	GP	G	A	Pts	PIM	PP	SH	GW	Min
2001-02	Hull Olympiques	QMJHL	63	1	3	4	68	....	....	....	....	....	....	....	....	....	12	1	2	3	30	....	....	....	....
2002-03	Hull Olympiques	QMJHL	72	9	18	27	143	....	....	....	....	....	....	....	....	....	20	1	6	7	20	....	....	....	....
2003-04	Gatineau	QMJHL	51	9	16	25	127	....	....	....	....	....	....	....	....	....	15	0	2	2	23	....	....	....	....
2004-05	Gatineau	QMJHL	67	15	20	35	96	....	....	....	....	....	....	....	....	....	10	0	2	2	8	....	....	....	....
2005-06	Iowa Stars	AHL	11	0	1	1	26	....	....	....	....	....	....	....	....	....	....	....	....	....	....	....	....	....	....
2006-07	Iowa Stars	AHL	57	14	3	17	78	....	....	....	....	....	....	....	....	....	12	0	4	4	25	....	....	....	....
	Idaho Steelheads	ECHL	17	4	9	13	31	....	....	....	....	....	....	....	....	....	7	1	1	2	4	....	....	....	....
2007-08	Iowa Stars	AHL	19	2	3	5	17	....	....	....	....	....	....	....	....	....	....	....	....	....	....	....	....	....	....
2008-09	Iowa Chops	AHL	77	6	10	16	127	....	....	....	....	....	....	....	....	....	....	....	....	....	....	....	....	....	....
2009-10	**Dallas**	**NHL**	**5**	**0**	**0**	**0**	**5**	**0**	**0**	**0**	**4**	**0.0**	**0**	**1**	**100.0**	**5:18**	....	....	....	....	....	....	....	....	....
	Texas Stars	AHL	76	19	21	40	101	....	....	....	....	....	....	....	....	....	24	2	6	8	18	....	....	....	....
2010-11	**Dallas**	**NHL**	**3**	**0**	**0**	**0**	**0**	**0**	**0**	**0**	**0**	**0.0**	**–2**	**0**	**0.0**	**3:55**	....	....	....	....	....	....	....	....	....
	Texas Stars	AHL	68	19	16	35	78	....	....	....	....	....	....	....	....	....	6	0	0	0	4	....	....	....	....
2011-12	**Dallas**	**NHL**	**1**	**0**	**0**	**0**	**0**	**0**	**0**	**0**	**0**	**0.0**	**0**	**0**	**0.0**	**5:25**	....	....	....	....	....	....	....	....	....
	Texas Stars	AHL	75	18	24	42	94	....	....	....	....	....	....	....	....	....	....	....	....	....	....	....	....	....	....
2012-13	Texas Stars	AHL	61	4	16	20	77	....	....	....	....	....	....	....	....	....	9	1	0	1	4	....	....	....	....
	Dallas	**NHL**	**1**	**0**	**0**	**0**	**0**	**0**	**0**	**0**	**0**	**0.0**	**0**	**2**	**0.0**	**5:40**	....	....	....	....	....	....	....	....	....
	NHL Totals		**10**	**0**	**0**	**0**	**5**	**0**	**0**	**0**	**4**	**0.0**		**3**	**33.3**	**4:56**	....	....	....	....	....	....	....	....	....

• Missed majority of 2005-06 and 2007-08 due to shoulder injuries.

WATKINS, Matt

(WAHT-kihns, MAT) **WSH**

Right wing. Shoots left. 5'10", 181 lbs. Born, Aylesbury, Sask., November 22, 1986. Dallas' 6th choice, 160th overall, in 2005 Entry Draft.

Season	Club	League	GP	G	A	Pts	PIM	PP	SH	GW	S	%	+/-	TF	F%	Min	GP	G	A	Pts	PIM	PP	SH	GW	Min
2003-04	Tisdale Trojans	SMHL	44	34	37	71	52	....	....	....	....	....	....	....	....	....	....	....	....	....	....	....	....	....	....
2004-05	Vernon Vipers	BCHL	60	36	38	74	53	....	....	....	....	....	....	....	....	....	14	4	6	10	6	....	....	....	....
2005-06	North Dakota	WCHA	46	5	4	9	45	....	....	....	....	....	....	....	....	....	....	....	....	....	....	....	....	....	....
2006-07	North Dakota	WCHA	38	6	11	17	31	....	....	....	....	....	....	....	....	....	....	....	....	....	....	....	....	....	....
2007-08	North Dakota	WCHA	43	8	10	18	34	....	....	....	....	....	....	....	....	....	....	....	....	....	....	....	....	....	....
2008-09	North Dakota	WCHA	41	7	7	14	40	....	....	....	....	....	....	....	....	....	....	....	....	....	....	....	....	....	....
2009-10	San Antonio	AHL	51	12	10	22	17	....	....	....	....	....	....	....	....	....	....	....	....	....	....	....	....	....	....
	Las Vegas	ECHL	14	4	7	11	12	....	....	....	....	....	....	....	....	....	....	....	....	....	....	....	....	....	....
2010-11	San Antonio	AHL	64	15	20	35	45	....	....	....	....	....	....	....	....	....	....	....	....	....	....	....	....	....	....
2011-12	**Phoenix**	**NHL**	**1**	**0**	**0**	**0**	**0**	**0**	**0**	**0**	**0**	**0.0**	**–1**	**5**	**0.0**	**6:37**	....	....	....	....	....	....	....	....	....
	Portland Pirates	AHL	70	11	25	36	48	....	....	....	....	....	....	....	....	....	....	....	....	....	....	....	....	....	....
2012-13	Bridgeport	AHL	68	11	19	30	43	....	....	....	....	....	....	....	....	....	....	....	....	....	....	....	....	....	....
	NHL Totals		**1**	**0**	**0**	**0**	**0**	**0**	**0**	**0**	**0**	**0.0**		**5**	**0.0**	**6:37**	....	....	....	....	....	....	....	....	....

Signed as a free agent by **Phoenix**, September 30, 2009. Signed as a free agent by **NY Islanders**, July 1, 2012. Signed as a free agent by **Washington**, July 8, 2013.

WATSON, Austin

(WAWT-suhn, AW-stuhn) **NSH**

Left wing. Shoots right. 6'3", 201 lbs. Born, Ann Arbor, MI, January 13, 1992. Nashville's 1st choice, 18th overall, in 2010 Entry Draft.

Season	Club	League	GP	G	A	Pts	PIM	PP	SH	GW	S	%	+/-	TF	F%	Min	GP	G	A	Pts	PIM	PP	SH	GW	Min
2007-08	Det. Compuware	Minor-MI	....	45	104	149		....	....	....	....	....	....	....	....	....	....	....	....	....	....	....	....	....	....
2008-09	Windsor Spitfires	OHL	63	10	19	29	41	....	....	....	....	....	....	....	....	....	20	0	3	3	15	....	....	....	....
2009-10	Windsor Spitfires	OHL	42	11	23	34	14	....	....	....	....	....	....	....	....	....	....	....	....	....	....	....	....	....	....
	Peterborough	OHL	10	9	11	20	8	....	....	....	....	....	....	....	....	....	4	2	0	2	2	....	....	....	....
2010-11	Peterborough	OHL	68	34	34	68	54	....	....	....	....	....	....	....	....	....	....	....	....	....	....	....	....	....	....
	Milwaukee	AHL	5	0	0	0	0	....	....	....	....	....	....	....	....	....	3	0	0	0	0	....	....	....	....
2011-12	Peterborough	OHL	32	14	19	33	33	....	....	....	....	....	....	....	....	....	....	....	....	....	....	....	....	....	....
	London Knights	OHL	29	11	24	35	14	....	....	....	....	....	....	....	....	....	19	10	7	17	10	....	....	....	....
2012-13	Milwaukee	AHL	72	20	17	37	22	....	....	....	....	....	....	....	....	....	4	1	0	1	0	....	....	....	....
	Nashville	**NHL**	**6**	**1**	**0**	**1**	**0**	**0**	**0**	**0**	**4**	**25.0**	**–2**	**44**	**43.2**	**12:42**	....	....	....	....	....	....	....	....	....
	NHL Totals		**6**	**1**	**0**	**1**	**0**	**0**	**0**	**0**	**4**	**25.0**		**44**	**43.2**	**12:42**	....	....	....	....	....	....	....	....	....

Memorial Cup All-Star Team (2012)

WEAVER, Mike

(WEE-vuhr, MIGHK) **FLA**

Defense. Shoots right. 5'10", 180 lbs. Born, Bramalea, Ont., May 2, 1978.

Season	Club	League	GP	G	A	Pts	PIM	PP	SH	GW	S	%	+/-	TF	F%	Min	GP	G	A	Pts	PIM	PP	SH	GW	Min
1995-96	Bramalea Blues	ON-Jr.A	48	10	39	49	103	....	....	....	....	....	....	....	....	....	....	....	....	....	....	....	....	....	....
1996-97	Michigan State	CCHA	39	0	7	7	46	....	....	....	....	....	....	....	....	....	....	....	....	....	....	....	....	....	....
1997-98	Michigan State	CCHA	44	4	22	26	68	....	....	....	....	....	....	....	....	....	....	....	....	....	....	....	....	....	....
1998-99	Michigan State	CCHA	42	1	6	7	54	....	....	....	....	....	....	....	....	....	....	....	....	....	....	....	....	....	....
99-2000	Michigan State	CCHA	26	0	7	7	20	....	....	....	....	....	....	....	....	....	....	....	....	....	....	....	....	....	....
2000-01	Orlando	IHL	68	0	8	8	34	....	....	....	....	....	....	....	....	....	16	0	2	2	8	....	....	....	....
2001-02	**Atlanta**	**NHL**	**16**	**0**	**1**	**1**	**10**	**0**	**0**	**0**	**9**	**0.0**	**0**	**0**	**0.0**	**13:54**	....	....	....	....	....	....	....	....	....
	Chicago Wolves	AHL	58	2	8	10	67	....	....	....	....	....	....	....	....	....	25	1	3	4	21	....	....	....	....
2002-03	**Atlanta**	**NHL**	**40**	**0**	**5**	**5**	**20**	**0**	**0**	**0**	**21**	**0.0**	**–5**	**0**	**0.0**	**18:38**	....	....	....	....	....	....	....	....	....
	Chicago Wolves	AHL	33	2	2	4	32	....	....	....	....	....	....	....	....	....	9	0	3	3	4	....	....	....	....
2003-04	**Atlanta**	**NHL**	**1**	**0**	**0**	**0**	**0**	**0**	**0**	**0**	**0**	**0.0**	**–1**	**0**	**0.0**	**8:28**	....	....	....	....	....	....	....	....	....
	Chicago Wolves	AHL	78	3	14	17	89	....	....	....	....	....	....	....	....	....	9	2	2	4	20	....	....	....	....
2004-05	Manchester	AHL	79	1	22	23	61	....	....	....	....	....	....	....	....	....	6	0	1	1	0	....	....	....	....
2005-06	**Los Angeles**	**NHL**	**53**	**0**	**9**	**9**	**14**	**0**	**0**	**0**	**21**	**0.0**	**–3**	**0**	**0.0**	**15:03**	....	....	....	....	....	....	....	....	....
2006-07	**Los Angeles**	**NHL**	**39**	**3**	**6**	**9**	**16**	**1**	**0**	**1**	**22**	**13.6**	**–4**	**3**	**66.7**	**15:20**	....	....	....	....	....	....	....	....	....
	Manchester	AHL	7	1	3	4	2	....	....	....	....	....	....	....	....	....	....	....	....	....	....	....	....	....	....
2007-08	**Vancouver**	**NHL**	**55**	**0**	**1**	**1**	**33**	**0**	**0**	**0**	**33**	**0.0**	**1**	**1**	**0.0**	**14:02**	....	....	....	....	....	....	....	....	....
2008-09	**St. Louis**	**NHL**	**58**	**0**	**7**	**7**	**12**	**0**	**0**	**0**	**36**	**0.0**	**–3**	**0**	**0.0**	**17:16**	**4**	**0**	**0**	**0**	**0**	**0**	**0**	**0**	**17:02**
2009-10	**St. Louis**	**NHL**	**77**	**1**	**9**	**10**	**29**	**0**	**0**	**0**	**33**	**3.0**	**10**	**2**	**50.0**	**16:58**	....	....	....	....	....	....	....	....	....
2010-11	**Florida**	**NHL**	**82**	**2**	**11**	**13**	**34**	**0**	**0**	**1**	**53**	**3.8**	**1**	**0**	**0.0**	**20:48**	....	....	....	....	....	....	....	....	....
2011-12	**Florida**	**NHL**	**82**	**0**	**16**	**16**	**14**	**0**	**0**	**0**	**51**	**0.0**	**–2**	**0**	**0.0**	**20:20**	**7**	**1**	**0**	**1**	**0**	**0**	**0**	**0**	**22:21**
2012-13	**Florida**	**NHL**	**27**	**1**	**8**	**9**	**8**	**0**	**0**	**0**	**21**	**4.8**	**–3**	**0**	**0.0**	**20:08**	....	....	....	....	....	....	....	....	....
	NHL Totals		**530**	**7**	**73**	**80**	**190**	**1**	**0**	**2**	**300**	**2.3**		**6**	**50.0**	**17:40**	**11**	**1**	**0**	**1**	**0**	**0**	**0**	**0**	**20:25**

OPJHL Defenseman of the Year (1996) • CCHA All-Tournament Team (1997) • CCHA First All-Star Team (1999, 2000) • CCHA Best Defensive Defenseman Award (1999, 2000) • NCAA West Second All-American Team (1999, 2000)

Signed as a free agent by **Atlanta**, June 15, 2000. Signed as a free agent by **Los Angeles**, July 16, 2004. Signed as a free agent by **Pittsburgh**, August 8, 2007. Claimed on waivers by **Vancouver** from **Pittsburgh**, October 2, 2007. Signed as a free agent by **St. Louis**, July 10, 2008. Signed as a free agent by **Florida**, August 3, 2010.

WEBER, Mike

(WEH-buhr, MIGHK) **BUF**

Defense. Shoots left. 6'2", 211 lbs. Born, Pittsburgh, PA, December 16, 1987. Buffalo's 3rd choice, 57th overall, in 2006 Entry Draft.

Season	Club	League	GP	G	A	Pts	PIM	PP	SH	GW	S	%	+/-	TF	F%	Min	GP	G	A	Pts	PIM	PP	SH	GW	Min
2002-03	Jr. Penguins	EmJHL	28	4	11	15	109	....	....	....	....	....	....	....	....	....	3	0	0	0	20	....	....	....	....
2003-04	Windsor Spitfires	OHL	65	0	2	2	49	....	....	....	....	....	....	....	....	....	....	....	....	....	....	....	....	....	....
2004-05	Windsor Spitfires	OHL	68	2	6	8	132	....	....	....	....	....	....	....	....	....	11	0	1	1	18	....	....	....	....
2005-06	Windsor Spitfires	OHL	68	5	21	26	181	....	....	....	....	....	....	....	....	....	7	0	0	0	12	....	....	....	....
2006-07	Windsor Spitfires	OHL	30	3	16	19	86	....	....	....	....	....	....	....	....	....	....	....	....	....	....	....	....	....	....
	Barrie Colts	OHL	30	3	12	15	86	....	....	....	....	....	....	....	....	....	7	0	6	6	10	....	....	....	....
2007-08	**Buffalo**	**NHL**	**16**	**0**	**3**	**3**	**14**	**0**	**0**	**0**	**12**	**0.0**	**12**	**0**	**0.0**	**16:41**	....	....	....	....	....	....	....	....	....
	Rochester	AHL	59	1	13	14	178	....	....	....	....	....	....	....	....	....	....	....	....	....	....	....	....	....	....
2008-09	**Buffalo**	**NHL**	**7**	**0**	**0**	**0**	**19**	**0**	**0**	**0**	**2**	**0.0**	**–3**	**0**	**0.0**	**14:10**	....	....	....	....	....	....	....	....	....
	Portland Pirates	AHL	42	1	7	8	94	....	....	....	....	....	....	....	....	....	....	....	....	....	....	....	....	....	....
2009-10	Portland Pirates	AHL	80	5	16	21	153	....	....	....	....	....	....	....	....	....	4	1	0	1	14	....	....	....	....
2010-11	**Buffalo**	**NHL**	**58**	**4**	**13**	**17**	**69**	**0**	**0**	**0**	**53**	**7.5**	**13**	**0**	**0.0**	**16:54**	**7**	**0**	**1**	**1**	**6**	**0**	**0**	**0**	**15:51**
2011-12	**Buffalo**	**NHL**	**51**	**1**	**4**	**5**	**64**	**0**	**0**	**0**	**51**	**2.0**	**–19**	**0**	**0.0**	**18:35**	....	....	....	....	....	....	....	....	....

			Regular Season														Playoffs								
Season	Club	League	GP	G	A	Pts	PIM	PP	SH	GW	S	%	+/-	TF	F%	Min	GP	G	A	Pts	PIM	PP	SH	GW	Min
2012-13	Lorenskog IK	Norway	5	1	5	6	10	....	....	....	....	....	....	....	....	....	....	....	....	....	....	....	....	....	....
	Buffalo	**NHL**	**42**	**1**	**6**	**7**	**70**	**0**	**0**	**0**	**25**	**4.0**	**3**	**0**	**0.0**	**18:22**	....	....	....	....	....	....	....	....	....
	NHL Totals		**174**	**6**	**26**	**32**	**236**	**0**	**0**	**0**	**143**	**4.2**		**0**	**0.0**	**17:37**	**7**	**0**	**1**	**1**	**6**	**0**	**0**	**0**	**15:51**

Signed as a free agent by **Lorenskog** (Norway), November 15, 2012.

WEBER, Shea

(WEH-buhr, SHAY) **NSH**

Defense. Shoots right. 6'4", 234 lbs. Born, Sicamous, B.C., August 14, 1985. Nashville's 4th choice, 49th overall, in 2003 Entry Draft.

Season	Club	League	GP	G	A	Pts	PIM	PP	SH	GW	S	%	+/-	TF	F%	Min	GP	G	A	Pts	PIM	PP	SH	GW	Min
2001-02	Sicamous Eagles	KIJHL	47	9	33	42	87	....	....	....	....	....	....	....	....	....	....	....	....	....	....	....	....	....	....
	Kelowna Rockets	WHL	5	0	0	0	0	....	....	....	....	....	....	....	....	....	....	....	....	....	....	....	....	....	....
2002-03	Kelowna Rockets	WHL	70	2	16	18	167	....	....	....	....	....	....	....	....	....	19	1	4	5	26	....	....	....	....
2003-04	Kelowna Rockets	WHL	60	12	20	32	126	....	....	....	....	....	....	....	....	....	17	3	14	17	16	....	....	....	....
2004-05	Kelowna Rockets	WHL	55	12	29	41	95	....	....	....	....	....	....	....	....	....	18	9	8	17	25	....	....	....	....
2005-06	**Nashville**	**NHL**	**28**	**2**	**8**	**10**	**42**	**2**	**0**	**1**	**46**	**4.3**	**8**	**0**	**0.0**	**17:00**	**4**	**2**	**0**	**2**	**8**	**1**	**0**	**0**	**14:12**
	Milwaukee	AHL	46	12	15	27	49	....	....	....	....	....	....	....	....	....	14	6	5	11	16	....	....	....	....
2006-07	**Nashville**	**NHL**	**79**	**17**	**23**	**40**	**60**	**6**	**0**	**2**	**152**	**11.2**	**13**	**0**	**0.0**	**19:23**	**5**	**0**	**3**	**3**	**2**	**0**	**0**	**0**	**21:41**
2007-08	**Nashville**	**NHL**	**54**	**6**	**14**	**20**	**49**	**5**	**0**	**2**	**152**	**3.9**	**–6**	**0**	**0.0**	**19:30**	**6**	**1**	**3**	**4**	**6**	**0**	**0**	**0**	**19:30**
2008-09	**Nashville**	**NHL**	**81**	**23**	**30**	**53**	**80**	**10**	**1**	**4**	**251**	**9.2**	**1**	**0**	**0.0**	**23:58**	....	....	....	....	....	....	....	....	....
2009-10	**Nashville**	**NHL**	**78**	**16**	**27**	**43**	**36**	**7**	**0**	**3**	**222**	**7.2**	**0**	**0**	**0.0**	**23:10**	**6**	**2**	**1**	**3**	**4**	**0**	**0**	**0**	**24:27**
	Canada	Olympics	7	2	4	6	2	....	....	....	....	....	....	....	....	....	....	....	....	....	....	....	....	....	....
2010-11	**Nashville**	**NHL**	**82**	**16**	**32**	**48**	**56**	**6**	**1**	**3**	**254**	**6.3**	**7**	**0**	**0.0**	**25:19**	**12**	**3**	**2**	**5**	**8**	**2**	**0**	**0**	**27:58**
2011-12	**Nashville**	**NHL**	**78**	**19**	**30**	**49**	**46**	**10**	**2**	**1**	**230**	**8.3**	**21**	**0**	**0.0**	**26:10**	**10**	**2**	**1**	**3**	**9**	**1**	**0**	**0**	**28:27**
2012-13	**Nashville**	**NHL**	**48**	**9**	**19**	**28**	**48**	**3**	**0**	**1**	**124**	**7.3**	**–2**	**0**	**0.0**	**25:55**	....	....	....	....	....	....	....	....	....
	NHL Totals		**528**	**108**	**183**	**291**	**417**	**49**	**4**	**17**	**1431**	**7.5**		**0**	**0.0**	**23:03**	**43**	**10**	**10**	**20**	**37**	**4**	**0**	**0**	**24:24**

WHL West Second All-Star Team (2004) • Memorial Cup All-Star Team (2004) • WHL West First All-Star Team (2005) • Canadian Major Junior Second All-Star Team (2005) • Olympic All-Star Team (2010) • NHL First All-Star Team (2011, 2012)

Played in NHL All-Star Game (2009, 2011, 2012)

WEBER, Yannick

(WEH-buhr, YAH-nihk) **VAN**

Defense. Shoots right. 5'11", 199 lbs. Born, Morges, Switz., September 23, 1988. Montreal's 5th choice, 73rd overall, in 2007 Entry Draft.

Season	Club	League	GP	G	A	Pts	PIM	PP	SH	GW	S	%	+/-	TF	F%	Min	GP	G	A	Pts	PIM	PP	SH	GW	Min
2003-04	SC Bern Jr.	Swiss-Jr.	32	2	3	5	39	....	....	....	....	....	....	....	....	....	8	2	0	2	8	....	....	....	....
2004-05	SC Bern Jr.	Swiss-Jr.	37	5	4	9	62	....	....	....	....	....	....	....	....	....	5	0	0	0	22	....	....	....	....
2005-06	SC Bern Future Jr.	Swiss-Jr.	17	1	6	7	46	....	....	....	....	....	....	....	....	....	....	....	....	....	....	....	....	....	....
	SC Langenthal	Swiss-2	28	3	0	3	8	....	....	....	....	....	....	....	....	....	....	....	....	....	....	....	....	....	....
2006-07	SC Bern Future Jr.	Swiss-Jr.	1	0	0	0	2	....	....	....	....	....	....	....	....	....	....	....	....	....	....	....	....	....	....
	Kitchener Rangers	OHL	51	13	28	41	42	....	....	....	....	....	....	....	....	....	9	3	6	9	8	....	....	....	....
2007-08	Kitchener Rangers	OHL	59	20	35	55	79	....	....	....	....	....	....	....	....	....	17	4	13	17	24	....	....	....	....
2008-09	**Montreal**	**NHL**	**3**	**0**	**1**	**1**	**2**	**0**	**0**	**0**	**6**	**0.0**	**–1**	**0**	**0.0**	**15:06**	**3**	**1**	**1**	**2**	**0**	**0**	**0**	**0**	**13:36**
	Hamilton	AHL	68	16	28	44	42	....	....	....	....	....	....	....	....	....	2	0	1	1	10	....	....	....	....
2009-10	**Montreal**	**NHL**	**5**	**0**	**0**	**0**	**4**	**0**	**0**	**0**	**2**	**0.0**	**–5**	**0**	**0.0**	**13:53**	....	....	....	....	....	....	....	....	....
	Hamilton	AHL	65	7	25	32	58	....	....	....	....	....	....	....	....	....	3	0	0	0	2	....	....	....	....
	Switzerland	Olympics	5	0	0	0	6	....	....	....	....	....	....	....	....	....	....	....	....	....	....	....	....	....	....
2010-11	**Montreal**	**NHL**	**41**	**1**	**10**	**11**	**14**	**0**	**0**	**0**	**63**	**1.6**	**0**	**0**	**0.0**	**16:34**	**3**	**2**	**0**	**2**	**0**	**1**	**0**	**0**	**8:46**
	Hamilton	AHL	15	8	4	12	10	....	....	....	....	....	....	....	....	....	....	....	....	....	....	....	....	....	....
2011-12	**Montreal**	**NHL**	**60**	**4**	**14**	**18**	**30**	**4**	**0**	**0**	**88**	**4.5**	**–7**	**0**	**0.0**	**15:37**	....	....	....	....	....	....	....	....	....
2012-13	Geneve	Swiss	32	5	16	21	40	....	....	....	....	....	....	....	....	....	....	....	....	....	....	....	....	....	....
	Montreal	**NHL**	**6**	**0**	**2**	**2**	**2**	**0**	**0**	**0**	**3**	**0.0**	**–1**	**0**	**0.0**	**13:45**	....	....	....	....	....	....	....	....	....
	NHL Totals		**115**	**5**	**27**	**32**	**52**	**4**	**0**	**0**	**162**	**3.1**		**0**	**0.0**	**15:46**	**6**	**3**	**1**	**4**	**0**	**1**	**0**	**0**	**11:11**

OHL Second All-Star Team (2008) • AHL All-Rookie Team (2009)

Signed as a free agent by **Geneve** (Swiss), September 18, 2012. Signed as a free agent by **Vancouver**, July 5, 2013.

WEISE, Dale

(WEES, DAYL) **VAN**

Right wing. Shoots right. 6'2", 210 lbs. Born, Winnipeg, Man., August 5, 1988. NY Rangers' 5th choice, 111th overall, in 2008 Entry Draft.

Season	Club	League	GP	G	A	Pts	PIM	PP	SH	GW	S	%	+/-	TF	F%	Min	GP	G	A	Pts	PIM	PP	SH	GW	Min
2005-06	Swift Current	WHL	53	4	14	18	57	....	....	....	....	....	....	....	....	....	4	0	0	0	2	....	....	....	....
2006-07	Swift Current	WHL	67	18	25	43	94	....	....	....	....	....	....	....	....	....	6	0	1	1	8	....	....	....	....
2007-08	Swift Current	WHL	53	29	22	51	84	....	....	....	....	....	....	....	....	....	12	7	6	13	20	....	....	....	....
2008-09	Hartford	AHL	74	11	12	23	64	....	....	....	....	....	....	....	....	....	6	3	1	4	2	....	....	....	....
2009-10	Hartford	AHL	73	28	22	50	114	....	....	....	....	....	....	....	....	....	....	....	....	....	....	....	....	....	....
2010-11	**NY Rangers**	**NHL**	**10**	**0**	**0**	**0**	**19**	**0**	**0**	**0**	**9**	**0.0**	**–1**	**0**	**0.0**	**6:30**	....	....	....	....	....	....	....	....	....
	Connecticut	AHL	47	18	20	38	73	....	....	....	....	....	....	....	....	....	5	2	1	3	8	....	....	....	....
2011-12	**Vancouver**	**NHL**	**68**	**4**	**4**	**8**	**81**	**0**	**0**	**0**	**48**	**8.3**	**–1**	**4**	**0.0**	**8:10**	**2**	**0**	**0**	**0**	**0**	**0**	**0**	**0**	**4:16**
2012-13	Trappers Tilburg	Nether.	19	22	26	48	79	....	....	....	....	....	....	....	....	....	....	....	....	....	....	....	....	....	....
	Vancouver	**NHL**	**40**	**3**	**3**	**6**	**43**	**0**	**0**	**2**	**35**	**8.6**	**–7**	**8**	**12.5**	**9:33**	**4**	**0**	**0**	**0**	**4**	**0**	**0**	**0**	**5:38**
	NHL Totals		**118**	**7**	**7**	**14**	**143**	**0**	**0**	**2**	**92**	**7.6**		**12**	**8.3**	**8:30**	**6**	**0**	**0**	**0**	**4**	**0**	**0**	**0**	**5:10**

Claimed on waivers by **Vancouver** from **NY Rangers**, October 4, 2011. Signed as a free agent by **Tilburg** (Netherlands), October 10, 2012.

WEISS, Stephen

(WIGHS, STEE-vehn) **DET**

Center. Shoots left. 5'11", 190 lbs. Born, Toronto, Ont., April 3, 1983. Florida's 1st choice, 4th overall, in 2001 Entry Draft.

Season	Club	League	GP	G	A	Pts	PIM	PP	SH	GW	S	%	+/-	TF	F%	Min	GP	G	A	Pts	PIM	PP	SH	GW	Min
1997-98	Tor. Young Nats	MTHL	48	51	58	109	....	....	....	....	....	....	....	....	....	....	....	....	....	....	....	....	....	....	....
1998-99	North York	ON-Jr.A	35	15	22	37	10	....	....	....	....	....	....	....	....	....	....	....	....	....	....	....	....	....	....
99-2000	Plymouth Whalers	OHL	64	24	42	66	35	....	....	....	....	....	....	....	....	....	23	8	18	26	18	....	....	....	....
2000-01	Plymouth Whalers	OHL	62	40	47	87	45	....	....	....	....	....	....	....	....	....	18	7	16	23	10	....	....	....	....
2001-02	**Florida**	**NHL**	**7**	**1**	**1**	**2**	**0**	**1**	**0**	**0**	**15**	**6.7**	**0**	**107**	**52.3**	**16:14**	....	....	....	....	....	....	....	....	....
	Plymouth Whalers	OHL	46	25	45	70	69	....	....	....	....	....	....	....	....	....	6	2	7	9	13	....	....	....	....
2002-03	**Florida**	**NHL**	**77**	**6**	**15**	**21**	**17**	**0**	**0**	**2**	**87**	**6.9**	**–13**	**1065**	**46.3**	**14:17**	....	....	....	....	....	....	....	....	....
2003-04	**Florida**	**NHL**	**50**	**12**	**17**	**29**	**10**	**3**	**0**	**2**	**82**	**14.6**	**–10**	**799**	**44.9**	**17:42**	....	....	....	....	....	....	....	....	....
	San Antonio	AHL	10	6	3	9	14	....	....	....	....	....	....	....	....	....	....	....	....	....	....	....	....	....	....
2004-05	San Antonio	AHL	62	15	23	38	38	....	....	....	....	....	....	....	....	....	....	....	....	....	....	....	....	....	....
	Chicago Wolves	AHL	18	7	9	16	12	....	....	....	....	....	....	....	....	....	18	2	7	9	17	....	....	....	....
2005-06	**Florida**	**NHL**	**41**	**9**	**12**	**21**	**22**	**5**	**0**	**1**	**74**	**12.2**	**–2**	**514**	**49.6**	**15:15**	....	....	....	....	....	....	....	....	....
2006-07	**Florida**	**NHL**	**74**	**20**	**28**	**48**	**28**	**10**	**0**	**1**	**176**	**11.4**	**–1**	**1182**	**45.9**	**17:07**	....	....	....	....	....	....	....	....	....
2007-08	**Florida**	**NHL**	**74**	**13**	**29**	**42**	**40**	**4**	**0**	**4**	**132**	**9.8**	**14**	**1198**	**51.2**	**17:35**	....	....	....	....	....	....	....	....	....
2008-09	**Florida**	**NHL**	**78**	**14**	**47**	**61**	**22**	**4**	**1**	**4**	**154**	**9.1**	**19**	**1277**	**50.9**	**17:48**	....	....	....	....	....	....	....	....	....
2009-10	**Florida**	**NHL**	**80**	**28**	**32**	**60**	**40**	**12**	**0**	**2**	**180**	**15.6**	**–7**	**1551**	**52.4**	**20:00**	....	....	....	....	....	....	....	....	....
2010-11	**Florida**	**NHL**	**76**	**21**	**28**	**49**	**49**	**3**	**2**	**1**	**172**	**12.2**	**–9**	**1279**	**53.9**	**20:06**	....	....	....	....	....	....	....	....	....
2011-12	**Florida**	**NHL**	**80**	**20**	**37**	**57**	**60**	**5**	**1**	**6**	**149**	**13.4**	**5**	**1469**	**53.2**	**20:31**	**7**	**3**	**2**	**5**	**6**	**3**	**0**	**0**	**21:06**
2012-13	**Florida**	**NHL**	**17**	**1**	**3**	**4**	**25**	**1**	**0**	**0**	**19**	**5.3**	**–13**	**276**	**51.1**	**18:28**	....	....	....	....	....	....	....	....	....
	NHL Totals		**654**	**145**	**249**	**394**	**313**	**48**	**4**	**23**	**1240**	**11.7**		**10717**	**50.3**	**17:59**	**7**	**3**	**2**	**5**	**6**	**3**	**0**	**0**	**21:06**

OHL All-Rookie Team (2000)

• Loaned to **Chicago** (AHL) by **San Antonio** (AHL) for cash, March 8, 2005. • Missed majority of 2012-13 due to recurring wrist injury. Signed as a free agent by **Detroit**, July 5, 2013.

WELLMAN, Casey

(WEHL-man, KAY-see) **WSH**

Center. Shoots right. 6', 173 lbs. Born, Brentwood, CA, October 18, 1987.

Season	Club	League	GP	G	A	Pts	PIM	PP	SH	GW	S	%	+/-	TF	F%	Min	GP	G	A	Pts	PIM	PP	SH	GW	Min
2006-07	Cedar Rapids	USHL	50	6	13	19	30	....	....	....	....	....	....	....	....	....	6	1	2	3	0	....	....	....	....
2007-08	Cedar Rapids	USHL	59	22	23	45	30	....	....	....	....	....	....	....	....	....	3	1	1	2	4	....	....	....	....
2008-09	Massachusetts	H-East	39	11	22	33	32	....	....	....	....	....	....	....	....	....	....	....	....	....	....	....	....	....	....
2009-10	Massachusetts	H-East	36	23	22	45	38	....	....	....	....	....	....	....	....	....	....	....	....	....	....	....	....	....	....
	Minnesota	**NHL**	**12**	**1**	**3**	**4**	**0**	**0**	**0**	**0**	**18**	**5.6**	**–2**	**32**	**53.1**	**12:03**	....	....	....	....	....	....	....	....	....
2010-11	**Minnesota**	**NHL**	**15**	**1**	**1**	**2**	**4**	**0**	**0**	**1**	**20**	**5.0**	**–1**	**16**	**50.0**	**10:39**	....	....	....	....	....	....	....	....	....
	Houston Aeros	AHL	42	14	21	35	14	....	....	....	....	....	....	....	....	....	24	6	5	11	6	....	....	....	....
2011-12	**Minnesota**	**NHL**	**14**	**2**	**5**	**7**	**0**	**0**	**0**	**1**	**25**	**8.0**	**–4**	**9**	**66.7**	**12:44**	....	....	....	....	....	....	....	....	....
	Houston Aeros	AHL	26	14	11	25	21	....	....	....	....	....	....	....	....	....	....	....	....	....	....	....	....	....	....
	Connecticut	AHL	31	9	13	22	10	....	....	....	....	....	....	....	....	....	9	4	5	9	10	....	....	....	....

			Regular Season														Playoffs								
Season	Club	League	GP	G	A	Pts	PIM	PP	SH	GW	S	%	+/-	TF	F%	Min	GP	G	A	Pts	PIM	PP	SH	GW	Min
2012-13	San Antonio	AHL	37	7	16	23	14	....	....	....	....	....	....	....	....	....	....	....	....	....	....	....	....	....	....
	Hershey Bears	AHL	33	9	21	30	4	....	....	....	....	....	....	....	....	....	5	3	0	3	2	....	....	....	....
	NHL Totals		**41**	**4**	**9**	**13**	**4**	**0**	**0**	**2**	**63**	**6.3**		**57**	**54.4**	**11:46**	....	....	....	....	....	....	....	....	....

Hockey East All-Rookie Team (2009)

Signed as a free agent by **Minnesota**, March 16, 2010. Traded to **NY Rangers** by **Minnesota** for Erik Christensen and NY Rangers' 7th round choice (Alexandre Belanger) in 2013 Entry Draft, February 3, 2012. Traded to **Florida** by **NY Rangers** for Florida's 5th round choice in 2014 Entry Draft, July 20, 2012. Traded to **Washington** by **Florida** for Zach Hamill, January 31, 2013.

WELLWOOD, Eric (WEHL-wud, AIR-ihk) PHI

Left wing. Shoots left. 5'11", 180 lbs. Born, Windsor, Ont., March 6, 1990. Philadelphia's 5th choice, 172nd overall, in 2009 Entry Draft.

2006-07	Tecumseh Chiefs	ON-Jr.B	34	10	10	20	33	....	....	....	....	....	....	....	....	....	....	....	....	....	....	....	....	....	....
	Windsor Spitfires	OHL	23	2	5	7	0	....	....	....	....	....	....	....	....	....	....	....	....	....	....	....	....	....	....
2007-08	Windsor Spitfires	OHL	68	9	7	16	12	....	....	....	....	....	....	....	....	....	5	0	0	0	2	....	....	....	....
2008-09	Windsor Spitfires	OHL	61	16	18	34	12	....	....	....	....	....	....	....	....	....	20	10	11	21	12	....	....	....	....
2009-10	Windsor Spitfires	OHL	65	31	37	68	36	....	....	....	....	....	....	....	....	....	19	4	6	10	6	....	....	....	....
2010-11	**Philadelphia**	**NHL**	**3**	**0**	**1**	**1**	**2**	**0**	**0**	**0**	**8**	**0.0**	**1**	**0**	**0.0**	**13:25**	....	....	....	....	....	....	....	....	....
	Adirondack	AHL	73	16	12	28	24	....	....	....	....	....	....	....	....	....	....	....	....	....	....	....	....	....	....
2011-12	**Philadelphia**	**NHL**	**24**	**5**	**4**	**9**	**2**	**0**	**0**	**1**	**36**	**13.9**	**12**	**35**	**51.4**	**10:57**	**11**	**0**	**0**	**0**	**2**	**0**	**0**	**0**	**11:42**
	Adirondack	AHL	33	9	12	21	8	....	....	....	....	....	....	....	....	....	....	....	....	....	....	....	....	....	....
2012-13	Adirondack	AHL	58	9	8	17	10	....	....	....	....	....	....	....	....	....	....	....	....	....	....	....	....	....	....
	Philadelphia	**NHL**	**4**	**0**	**0**	**0**	**0**	**0**	**0**	**0**	**2**	**0.0**	**0**	**6**	**0.0**	**9:25**	....	....	....	....	....	....	....	....	....
	NHL Totals		**31**	**5**	**5**	**10**	**4**	**0**	**0**	**1**	**46**	**10.9**		**41**	**43.9**	**11:00**	**11**	**0**	**0**	**0**	**2**	**0**	**0**	**0**	**11:42**

WELLWOOD, Kyle (WEHL-wud, KIGHL)

Center. Shoots right. 5'10", 181 lbs. Born, Windsor, Ont., May 16, 1983. Toronto's 6th choice, 134th overall, in 2001 Entry Draft.

1998-99	Tecumseh	ON-Jr.B	51	22	41	63	12	....	....	....	....	....	....	....	....	....	....	....	....	....	....	....	....	....	....
99-2000	Belleville Bulls	OHL	65	14	37	51	14	....	....	....	....	....	....	....	....	....	16	3	7	10	6	....	....	....	....
2000-01	Belleville Bulls	OHL	68	35	*83	*118	24	....	....	....	....	....	....	....	....	....	10	3	16	19	4	....	....	....	....
2001-02	Belleville Bulls	OHL	28	16	24	40	4	....	....	....	....	....	....	....	....	....	....	....	....	....	....	....	....	....	....
	Windsor Spitfires	OHL	26	14	21	35	0	....	....	....	....	....	....	....	....	....	16	12	12	24	0	....	....	....	....
2002-03	Windsor Spitfires	OHL	57	41	59	100	0	....	....	....	....	....	....	....	....	....	7	5	9	14	0	....	....	....	....
2003-04	**Toronto**	**NHL**	**1**	**0**	**0**	**0**	**0**	**0**	**0**	**0**	**1**	**0.0**	**–1**	**13**	**30.8**	**7:56**	....	....	....	....	....	....	....	....	....
	St. John's	AHL	76	20	35	55	6	....	....	....	....	....	....	....	....	....	....	....	....	....	....	....	....	....	....
2004-05	St. John's	AHL	80	38	49	87	20	....	....	....	....	....	....	....	....	....	5	2	2	4	2	....	....	....	....
2005-06	**Toronto**	**NHL**	**81**	**11**	**34**	**45**	**14**	**3**	**0**	**0**	**117**	**9.4**	**0**	**593**	**56.3**	**12:47**	....	....	....	....	....	....	....	....	....
2006-07	**Toronto**	**NHL**	**48**	**12**	**30**	**42**	**0**	**7**	**0**	**2**	**99**	**12.1**	**3**	**291**	**56.4**	**16:38**	....	....	....	....	....	....	....	....	....
2007-08	**Toronto**	**NHL**	**59**	**8**	**13**	**21**	**0**	**5**	**0**	**1**	**57**	**14.0**	**–12**	**325**	**54.8**	**12:39**	....	....	....	....	....	....	....	....	....
2008-09	**Vancouver**	**NHL**	**74**	**18**	**9**	**27**	**4**	**10**	**0**	**3**	**94**	**19.1**	**2**	**621**	**57.5**	**13:48**	**10**	**1**	**5**	**6**	**0**	**0**	**0**	**0**	**15:05**
2009-10	**Vancouver**	**NHL**	**75**	**14**	**11**	**25**	**12**	**3**	**0**	**2**	**98**	**14.3**	**6**	**725**	**53.8**	**13:52**	**12**	**2**	**5**	**7**	**0**	**1**	**0**	**0**	**15:44**
2010-11	Mytischi	KHL	25	5	3	8	2	....	....	....	....	....	....	....	....	....	....	....	....	....	....	....	....	....	....
	San Jose	**NHL**	**35**	**5**	**8**	**13**	**0**	**0**	**0**	**0**	**50**	**10.0**	**10**	**132**	**49.2**	**13:41**	**18**	**1**	**6**	**7**	**0**	**0**	**0**	**0**	**13:49**
2011-12	**Winnipeg**	**NHL**	**77**	**18**	**29**	**47**	**4**	**4**	**0**	**1**	**93**	**19.4**	**3**	**250**	**54.0**	**14:57**	....	....	....	....	....	....	....	....	....
2012-13	**Winnipeg**	**NHL**	**39**	**6**	**9**	**15**	**2**	**0**	**0**	**2**	**37**	**16.2**	**0**	**78**	**55.1**	**12:59**	....	....	....	....	....	....	....	....	....
	NHL Totals		**489**	**92**	**143**	**235**	**36**	**32**	**0**	**11**	**646**	**14.2**		**3028**	**55.2**	**13:53**	**40**	**4**	**16**	**20**	**0**	**1**	**0**	**0**	**14:43**

OHL First All-Star Team (2001) • Canadian Major Junior Sportsman of the Year (2003)

Claimed on waivers by **Vancouver** from **Toronto**, June 25, 2008. Signed as a free agent by **Mytischi** (KHL), October 4, 2010. Signed as a free agent by **St. Louis**, January 17, 2011. Claimed on waivers by **San Jose** from **St. Louis**, January 18, 2011. Signed as a free agent by **Winnipeg**, September 9, 2011.

WELSH, Jeremy (WELSH, JAIR-ih-mee) CAR

Center. Shoots left. 6'3", 210 lbs. Born, Bayfield, Ont., April 30, 1988.

2007-08	Oakville Blades	ON-Jr.A	48	17	35	52	26	....	....	....	....	....	....	....	....	....	21	6	14	20	8	....	....	....	....
2008-09	Oakville Blades	ON-Jr.A	49	36	47	83	38	....	....	....	....	....	....	....	....	....	28	17	17	34	4	....	....	....	....
2009-10	Union College	ECAC	39	10	9	19	45	....	....	....	....	....	....	....	....	....	....	....	....	....	....	....	....	....	....
2010-11	Union College	ECAC	40	16	21	37	34	....	....	....	....	....	....	....	....	....	....	....	....	....	....	....	....	....	....
2011-12	Union College	ECAC	40	27	17	44	47	....	....	....	....	....	....	....	....	....	....	....	....	....	....	....	....	....	....
	Carolina	**NHL**	**1**	**0**	**0**	**0**	**4**	**0**	**0**	**0**	**2**	**0.0**	**0**	**13**	**30.8**	**16:32**	....	....	....	....	....	....	....	....	....
2012-13	Charlotte	AHL	69	14	12	26	16	....	....	....	....	....	....	....	....	....	5	0	3	3	2	....	....	....	....
	Carolina	**NHL**	**5**	**0**	**1**	**1**	**0**	**0**	**0**	**0**	**4**	**0.0**	**1**	**20**	**75.0**	**5:51**	....	....	....	....	....	....	....	....	....
	NHL Totals		**6**	**0**	**1**	**1**	**4**	**0**	**0**	**0**	**6**	**0.0**		**33**	**57.6**	**7:38**	....	....	....	....	....	....	....	....	....

ECAC Second All-Star Team (2012)

Signed as a free agent by **Carolina**, April 5, 2012.

WESTGARTH, Kevin (WEHST-garth, KEH-vihn) CAR

Right wing. Shoots right. 6'4", 234 lbs. Born, Amherstburg, Ont., February 7, 1984.

2003-04	Princeton	ECAC	25	3	3	6	48	....	....	....	....	....	....	....	....	....	....	....	....	....	....	....	....	....	....
2004-05	Princeton	ECAC	29	4	3	7	36	....	....	....	....	....	....	....	....	....	....	....	....	....	....	....	....	....	....
2005-06	Princeton	ECAC	29	10	13	23	36	....	....	....	....	....	....	....	....	....	....	....	....	....	....	....	....	....	....
2006-07	Princeton	ECAC	33	8	16	24	40	....	....	....	....	....	....	....	....	....	....	....	....	....	....	....	....	....	....
	Manchester	AHL	14	1	2	3	44	....	....	....	....	....	....	....	....	....	....	....	....	....	....	....	....	....	....
2007-08	Manchester	AHL	69	6	6	12	191	....	....	....	....	....	....	....	....	....	4	0	0	0	6	....	....	....	....
2008-09	**Los Angeles**	**NHL**	**9**	**0**	**0**	**0**	**9**	**0**	**0**	**0**	**1**	**0.0**	**1**	**1**	**0.0**	**5:02**	....	....	....	....	....	....	....	....	....
	Manchester	AHL	65	4	6	10	165	....	....	....	....	....	....	....	....	....	....	....	....	....	....	....	....	....	....
2009-10	Manchester	AHL	76	11	14	25	180	....	....	....	....	....	....	....	....	....	6	1	0	1	10	....	....	....	....
2010-11	**Los Angeles**	**NHL**	**56**	**0**	**3**	**3**	**105**	**0**	**0**	**0**	**20**	**0.0**	**–6**	**4**	**50.0**	**5:26**	**6**	**0**	**2**	**2**	**14**	**0**	**0**	**0**	**6:15**
2011-12♦	**Los Angeles**	**NHL**	**25**	**1**	**1**	**2**	**39**	**0**	**0**	**0**	**13**	**7.7**	**–3**	**1**	**0.0**	**5:16**	....	....	....	....	....	....	....	....	....
2012-13	**Carolina**	**NHL**	**31**	**2**	**2**	**4**	**45**	**0**	**0**	**0**	**16**	**12.5**	**1**	**3**	**0.0**	**5:43**	....	....	....	....	....	....	....	....	....
	NHL Totals		**121**	**3**	**6**	**9**	**198**	**0**	**0**	**0**	**50**	**6.0**		**9**	**22.2**	**5:27**	**6**	**0**	**2**	**2**	**14**	**0**	**0**	**0**	**6:15**

Signed as a free agent by **Los Angeles**, March 16, 2007. Traded to **Carolina** by **Los Angeles** for Anthony Stewart and Carolina's 4th round choice (later traded to Edmonton – Edmonton selected Jackson Houck) in 2013 Entry Draft, January 13, 2013.

WHEELER, Blake (WEE-luhr, BLAYK) WPG

Right wing. Shoots right. 6'5", 205 lbs. Born, Robbinsdale, MN, August 31, 1986. Phoenix's 1st choice, 5th overall, in 2004 Entry Draft.

2002-03	Breck Mustangs	High-MN	26	15	27	42	....	....	....	....	....	....	....	....	....	....	....	....	....	....	....	....	....	....	....
2003-04	Team Northwest	UMEHL	24	5	6	11	....	....	....	....	....	....	....	....	....	....	....	....	....	....	....	....	....	....	....
	Breck Mustangs	High-MN	27	39	50	89	34	....	....	....	....	....	....	....	....	....	3	6	5	11	0	....	....	....	....
2004-05	Green Bay	USHL	58	19	28	47	43	....	....	....	....	....	....	....	....	....	....	....	....	....	....	....	....	....	....
2005-06	U. of Minnesota	WCHA	39	9	14	23	41	....	....	....	....	....	....	....	....	....	....	....	....	....	....	....	....	....	....
2006-07	U. of Minnesota	WCHA	44	18	20	38	42	....	....	....	....	....	....	....	....	....	....	....	....	....	....	....	....	....	....
2007-08	U. of Minnesota	WCHA	44	15	20	35	72	....	....	....	....	....	....	....	....	....	....	....	....	....	....	....	....	....	....
2008-09	**Boston**	**NHL**	**81**	**21**	**24**	**45**	**46**	**3**	**2**	**3**	**150**	**14.0**	**36**	**34**	**38.2**	**13:41**	**8**	**0**	**0**	**0**	**0**	**0**	**0**	**0**	**12:08**
2009-10	**Boston**	**NHL**	**82**	**18**	**20**	**38**	**53**	**3**	**1**	**2**	**159**	**11.3**	**–4**	**27**	**48.2**	**15:47**	**13**	**1**	**5**	**6**	**6**	**0**	**0**	**0**	**14:14**
2010-11	**Boston**	**NHL**	**58**	**11**	**16**	**27**	**32**	**0**	**0**	**2**	**101**	**10.9**	**8**	**136**	**38.2**	**15:12**	....	....	....	....	....	....	....	....	....
	Atlanta	**NHL**	**23**	**7**	**10**	**17**	**14**	**0**	**0**	**0**	**78**	**9.0**	**2**	**12**	**0.0**	**18:53**	....	....	....	....	....	....	....	....	....
2011-12	**Winnipeg**	**NHL**	**80**	**17**	**47**	**64**	**55**	**6**	**0**	**3**	**208**	**8.2**	**3**	**10**	**40.0**	**19:05**	....	....	....	....	....	....	....	....	....
2012-13	EHC Munchen	Germany	15	6	14	20	51	....	....	....	....	....	....	....	....	....	....	....	....	....	....	....	....	....	....
	Winnipeg	**NHL**	**48**	**19**	**22**	**41**	**28**	**2**	**0**	**2**	**129**	**14.7**	**–3**	**18**	**22.2**	**18:48**	....	....	....	....	....	....	....	....	....
	NHL Totals		**372**	**93**	**139**	**232**	**228**	**14**	**3**	**12**	**825**	**11.3**		**237**	**36.3**	**16:32**	**21**	**1**	**5**	**6**	**6**	**0**	**0**	**0**	**13:26**

USHL All-Rookie Team (2005)

Signed as a free agent by **Boston**, July 1, 2008. Traded to **Atlanta** by **Boston** with Mark Stuart for Rich Peverley and Boris Valabik, February 18, 2011. • Transferred to **Winnipeg** after **Atlanta** franchise relocated, June 21, 2011. Signed as a free agent by **Munchen** (Germany), October 28, 2012.

WHITE, Ian

(WIGHT, EE-an)

Defense. Shoots right. 5'10", 191 lbs. Born, Steinbach, Man., June 4, 1984. Toronto's 6th choice, 191st overall, in 2002 Entry Draft.

Season	Club	League	Regular Season GP	G	A	Pts	PIM	PP	SH	GW	S	%	+/-	TF	F%	Min	Playoffs GP	G	A	Pts	PIM	PP	SH	GW	Min
99-2000	Eastman Selects	MAHA	32	29	33	62	36	....	....	....	....	....	....	....	....	....	....	....	....	....	....	....	....	....	....
2000-01	Swift Current	WHL	69	12	31	43	24	....	....	....	....	....	....	....	....	....	....	....	....	....	....	....	....	....	....
2001-02	Swift Current	WHL	70	32	47	79	40	....	....	....	....	....	....	....	....	....	12	4	5	9	12	....	....	....	....
2002-03	Swift Current	WHL	64	24	44	68	44	....	....	....	....	....	....	....	....	....	4	0	4	4	0	....	....	....	....
2003-04	Swift Current	WHL	43	9	23	32	32	....	....	....	....	....	....	....	....	....	5	1	3	4	8	....	....	....	....
	St. John's	AHL	8	0	4	4	2	....	....	....	....	....	....	....	....	....	....	....	....	....	....	....	....	....	....
2004-05	St. John's	AHL	78	4	22	26	54	....	....	....	....	....	....	....	....	....	5	0	2	2	2	....	....	....	....
2005-06	**Toronto**	**NHL**	**12**	**1**	**5**	**6**	**10**	**0**	**0**	**0**	**21**	**4.8**	**2**	**0**	**0.0**	**19:07**	....	....	....	....	....	....	....	....	....
	Toronto Marlies	AHL	59	8	30	38	42	....	....	....	....	....	....	....	....	....	5	1	4	5	4	....	....	....	....
2006-07	**Toronto**	**NHL**	**76**	**3**	**23**	**26**	**40**	**1**	**0**	**1**	**138**	**2.2**	**8**	**0**	**0.0**	**18:32**	....	....	....	....	....	....	....	....	....
2007-08	**Toronto**	**NHL**	**81**	**5**	**16**	**21**	**44**	**0**	**0**	**2**	**116**	**4.3**	**–9**	**0**	**0.0**	**18:48**	....	....	....	....	....	....	....	....	....
2008-09	**Toronto**	**NHL**	**71**	**10**	**16**	**26**	**57**	**2**	**0**	**2**	**158**	**6.3**	**6**	**0**	**0.0**	**22:51**	....	....	....	....	....	....	....	....	....
2009-10	**Toronto**	**NHL**	**56**	**9**	**17**	**26**	**39**	**2**	**0**	**1**	**130**	**6.9**	**1**	**0**	**0.0**	**23:47**	....	....	....	....	....	....	....	....	....
	Calgary	**NHL**	**27**	**4**	**8**	**12**	**12**	**1**	**0**	**0**	**43**	**9.3**	**7**	**0**	**0.0**	**20:43**	....	....	....	....	....	....	....	....	....
2010-11	**Calgary**	**NHL**	**16**	**2**	**4**	**6**	**6**	**1**	**0**	**0**	**34**	**5.9**	**–10**	**0**	**0.0**	**21:44**	....	....	....	....	....	....	....	....	....
	Carolina	**NHL**	**39**	**0**	**10**	**10**	**12**	**0**	**0**	**0**	**53**	**0.0**	**4**	**0**	**0.0**	**19:19**	....	....	....	....	....	....	....	....	....
	San Jose	**NHL**	**23**	**2**	**8**	**10**	**8**	**0**	**0**	**0**	**51**	**3.9**	**9**	**0**	**0.0**	**19:56**	**17**	**1**	**8**	**9**	**8**	**1**	**0**	**0**	**20:04**
2011-12	**Detroit**	**NHL**	**77**	**7**	**25**	**32**	**22**	**0**	**0**	**0**	**196**	**3.6**	**23**	**0**	**0.0**	**22:59**	**5**	**1**	**0**	**1**	**0**	**0**	**0**	**0**	**18:34**
2012-13	**Detroit**	**NHL**	**25**	**2**	**2**	**4**	**4**	**0**	**0**	**0**	**27**	**7.4**	**5**	**1**	**100.0**	**19:35**	....	....	....	....	....	....	....	....	....
	NHL Totals		**503**	**45**	**134**	**179**	**254**	**7**	**0**	**6**	**967**	**4.7**		**1**	**100.0**	**20:52**	**22**	**2**	**8**	**10**	**8**	**1**	**0**	**0**	**19:44**

WHL East Second All-Star Team (2002) • WHL East First All-Star Team (2003) • Canadian Major Junior Second All-Star Team (2003)

Traded to **Calgary** by **Toronto** with Matt Stajan, Niklas Hagman and Jamal Mayers for Dion Phaneuf, Fredrik Sjostrom and Keith Aulie, January 31, 2010. Traded to **Carolina** by **Calgary** with Brett Sutter for Anton Babchuk and Tom Kostopoulos, November 17, 2010. Traded to **San Jose** by **Carolina** for San Jose's 2nd round choice (Brock McGinn) in 2012 Entry Draft, February 18, 2011. Signed as a free agent by **Detroit**, July 2, 2011.

WHITE, Ryan

(WIGHT, RIGH-uhn) **MTL**

Center. Shoots right. 6', 199 lbs. Born, Brandon, Man., March 17, 1988. Montreal's 4th choice, 66th overall, in 2006 Entry Draft.

Season	Club	League	Regular Season GP	G	A	Pts	PIM	PP	SH	GW	S	%	+/-	TF	F%	Min	Playoffs GP	G	A	Pts	PIM	PP	SH	GW	Min
2003-04	Brandon	MMHL	39	21	41	62	90	....	....	....	....	....	....	....	....	....	11	7	7	14	22	....	....	....	....
2004-05	Calgary Hitmen	WHL	63	9	14	23	95	....	....	....	....	....	....	....	....	....	12	2	1	3	26	....	....	....	....
2005-06	Calgary Hitmen	WHL	72	20	33	53	121	....	....	....	....	....	....	....	....	....	13	3	4	7	18	....	....	....	....
2006-07	Calgary Hitmen	WHL	72	34	55	89	97	....	....	....	....	....	....	....	....	....	18	6	8	14	36	....	....	....	....
2007-08	Calgary Hitmen	WHL	68	28	44	72	98	....	....	....	....	....	....	....	....	....	16	6	11	17	8	....	....	....	....
2008-09	Hamilton	AHL	80	11	18	29	68	....	....	....	....	....	....	....	....	....	6	3	1	4	9	....	....	....	....
2009-10	**Montreal**	**NHL**	**16**	**0**	**2**	**2**	**16**	**0**	**0**	**0**	**5**	**0.0**	**–6**	**10**	**70.0**	**11:09**	....	....	....	....	....	....	....	....	....
	Hamilton	AHL	62	17	17	34	173	....	....	....	....	....	....	....	....	....	19	4	5	9	47	....	....	....	....
2010-11	**Montreal**	**NHL**	**27**	**2**	**3**	**5**	**38**	**0**	**0**	**0**	**30**	**6.7**	**5**	**32**	**40.6**	**8:55**	**7**	**0**	**0**	**0**	**2**	**0**	**0**	**0**	**6:35**
	Hamilton	AHL	33	3	9	12	77	....	....	....	....	....	....	....	....	....	13	2	6	8	37	....	....	....	....
2011-12	**Montreal**	**NHL**	**20**	**0**	**3**	**3**	**61**	**0**	**0**	**0**	**12**	**0.0**	**–7**	**59**	**49.2**	**14:31**	....	....	....	....	....	....	....	....	....
	Hamilton	AHL	4	4	1	5	26	....	....	....	....	....	....	....	....	....	....	....	....	....	....	....	....	....	....
2012-13	**Montreal**	**NHL**	**26**	**1**	**0**	**1**	**67**	**0**	**0**	**0**	**16**	**6.3**	**1**	**167**	**54.5**	**9:25**	**3**	**1**	**0**	**1**	**23**	**0**	**0**	**0**	**9:06**
	NHL Totals		**89**	**3**	**8**	**11**	**182**	**0**	**0**	**0**	**63**	**4.8**		**268**	**52.2**	**10:43**	**10**	**1**	**0**	**1**	**25**	**0**	**0**	**0**	**7:20**

WHL East First All-Star Team (2007) • WHL East Second All-Star Team (2008)

• Missed majority of 2011-12 due to sports hernia injury in training camp.

WHITFIELD, Trent

(WHIHT-feeld, TREHNT)

Center. Shoots left. 5'11", 209 lbs. Born, Estevan, Sask., June 17, 1977. Boston's 5th choice, 100th overall, in 1996 Entry Draft.

Season	Club	League	Regular Season GP	G	A	Pts	PIM	PP	SH	GW	S	%	+/-	TF	F%	Min	Playoffs GP	G	A	Pts	PIM	PP	SH	GW	Min
1993-94	Saskatoon Blazers	SMHL	36	26	22	48	42	....	....	....	....	....	....	....	....	....	....	....	....	....	....	....	....	....	....
	Spokane Chiefs	WHL	5	1	1	2	0	....	....	....	....	....	....	....	....	....	....	....	....	....	....	....	....	....	....
1994-95	Spokane Chiefs	WHL	48	8	17	25	26	....	....	....	....	....	....	....	....	....	11	7	6	13	5	....	....	....	....
1995-96	Spokane Chiefs	WHL	72	33	51	84	75	....	....	....	....	....	....	....	....	....	18	8	10	18	10	....	....	....	....
1996-97	Spokane Chiefs	WHL	58	34	42	76	74	....	....	....	....	....	....	....	....	....	9	5	7	12	10	....	....	....	....
1997-98	Spokane Chiefs	WHL	65	38	44	82	97	....	....	....	....	....	....	....	....	....	18	9	10	19	15	....	....	....	....
1998-99	Portland Pirates	AHL	50	10	8	18	20	....	....	....	....	....	....	....	....	....	....	....	....	....	....	....	....	....	....
	Hampton Roads	ECHL	19	13	12	25	12	....	....	....	....	....	....	....	....	....	4	2	0	2	14	....	....	....	....
99-2000	Portland Pirates	AHL	79	18	35	53	52	....	....	....	....	....	....	....	....	....	3	1	1	2	2	....	....	....	....
	Washington	**NHL**	....	....	....	....	....	....	....	....	....	....	....	....	....	....	**3**	**0**	**0**	**0**	**0**	**0**	**0**	**0**	**5:47**
2000-01	**Washington**	**NHL**	**61**	**2**	**4**	**6**	**35**	**0**	**0**	**0**	**47**	**4.3**	**3**	**520**	**51.9**	**9:39**	**5**	**0**	**0**	**0**	**2**	**0**	**0**	**0**	**7:07**
	Portland Pirates	AHL	19	9	11	20	27	....	....	....	....	....	....	....	....	....	....	....	....	....	....	....	....	....	....
2001-02	**Washington**	**NHL**	**24**	**0**	**1**	**1**	**28**	**0**	**0**	**0**	**15**	**0.0**	**–3**	**189**	**54.0**	**7:06**	....	....	....	....	....	....	....	....	....
	Portland Pirates	AHL	10	4	4	8	8	....	....	....	....	....	....	....	....	....	....	....	....	....	....	....	....	....	....
	NY Rangers	**NHL**	**1**	**0**	**0**	**0**	**0**	**0**	**0**	**0**	**0**	**0.0**	**1**	**18**	**50.0**	**12:44**	....	....	....	....	....	....	....	....	....
	Portland Pirates	AHL	24	10	16	26	16	....	....	....	....	....	....	....	....	....	....	....	....	....	....	....	....	....	....
2002-03	**Washington**	**NHL**	**14**	**1**	**1**	**2**	**6**	**0**	**0**	**1**	**4**	**25.0**	**1**	**124**	**57.3**	**8:30**	**6**	**0**	**0**	**0**	**10**	**0**	**0**	**0**	**11:01**
	Portland Pirates	AHL	64	27	34	61	42	....	....	....	....	....	....	....	....	....	....	....	....	....	....	....	....	....	....
2003-04	**Washington**	**NHL**	**44**	**6**	**5**	**11**	**14**	**0**	**1**	**2**	**38**	**15.8**	**–2**	**598**	**55.4**	**12:48**	....	....	....	....	....	....	....	....	....
	Portland Pirates	AHL	24	8	7	15	22	....	....	....	....	....	....	....	....	....	....	....	....	....	....	....	....	....	....
2004-05	Portland Pirates	AHL	67	17	38	55	75	....	....	....	....	....	....	....	....	....	....	....	....	....	....	....	....	....	....
2005-06	**St. Louis**	**NHL**	**30**	**2**	**5**	**7**	**14**	**1**	**0**	**0**	**41**	**4.9**	**–3**	**330**	**54.6**	**11:56**	....	....	....	....	....	....	....	....	....
	Peoria Rivermen	AHL	41	19	34	53	18	....	....	....	....	....	....	....	....	....	....	....	....	....	....	....	....	....	....
2006-07	Peoria Rivermen	AHL	79	33	45	78	70	....	....	....	....	....	....	....	....	....	....	....	....	....	....	....	....	....	....
2007-08	Peoria Rivermen	AHL	80	22	30	52	51	....	....	....	....	....	....	....	....	....	....	....	....	....	....	....	....	....	....
2008-09	**St. Louis**	**NHL**	**3**	**0**	**1**	**1**	**0**	**0**	**0**	**0**	**4**	**0.0**	**2**	**26**	**73.1**	**11:03**	....	....	....	....	....	....	....	....	....
	Peoria Rivermen	AHL	69	20	30	50	37	....	....	....	....	....	....	....	....	....	7	2	1	3	0	....	....	....	....
2009-10	**Boston**	**NHL**	**16**	**0**	**1**	**1**	**7**	**0**	**0**	**0**	**15**	**0.0**	**–2**	**178**	**57.9**	**11:03**	**4**	**0**	**0**	**0**	**0**	**0**	**0**	**0**	**8:32**
	Providence Bruins	AHL	52	17	26	43	22	....	....	....	....	....	....	....	....	....	....	....	....	....	....	....	....	....	....
2010-11	Providence Bruins	AHL	45	18	18	36	42	....	....	....	....	....	....	....	....	....	....	....	....	....	....	....	....	....	....
2011-12	**Boston**	**NHL**	**1**	**0**	**0**	**0**	**0**	**0**	**0**	**0**	**1**	**0.0**	**0**	**0**	**0.0**	**13:59**	....	....	....	....	....	....	....	....	....
	Providence Bruins	AHL	50	9	7	16	32	....	....	....	....	....	....	....	....	....	....	....	....	....	....	....	....	....	....
2012-13	Providence Bruins	AHL	48	6	6	12	20	....	....	....	....	....	....	....	....	....	11	0	2	2	14	....	....	....	....
	NHL Totals		**194**	**11**	**18**	**29**	**104**	**1**	**1**	**3**	**165**	**6.7**		**1983**	**54.7**	**10:30**	**18**	**0**	**0**	**0**	**12**	**0**	**0**	**0**	**8:31**

WHL West First All-Star Team (1997) • WHL West Second All-Star Team (1998)

Signed as a free agent by **Washington**, September 1, 1998. Claimed on waivers by **NY Rangers** from **Washington**, January 16, 2002. Claimed on waivers by **Washington** from **NY Rangers**, February 1, 2002. Signed as a free agent by **St. Louis**, August 2, 2005. Signed as a free agent by **Boston**, July 13, 2009.

WHITMORE, Derek

(WHIHT-mohr, DAIR-ihk)

Left wing. Shoots left. 5'11", 185 lbs. Born, Rochester, NY, December 17, 1984.

Season	Club	League	Regular Season GP	G	A	Pts	PIM	PP	SH	GW	S	%	+/-	TF	F%	Min	Playoffs GP	G	A	Pts	PIM	PP	SH	GW	Min
2002-03	Waterloo	USHL	58	15	13	28	51	....	....	....	....	....	....	....	....	....	6	1	0	1	0	....	....	....	....
2003-04	Waterloo	USHL	10	2	0	2	6	....	....	....	....	....	....	....	....	....	....	....	....	....	....	....	....	....	....
	Lincoln Stars	USHL	45	19	23	42	22	....	....	....	....	....	....	....	....	....	....	....	....	....	....	....	....	....	....
2004-05	Bowling Green	CCHA	33	11	6	17	14	....	....	....	....	....	....	....	....	....	....	....	....	....	....	....	....	....	....
2005-06	Bowling Green	CCHA	34	13	6	19	17	....	....	....	....	....	....	....	....	....	....	....	....	....	....	....	....	....	....
2006-07	Bowling Green	CCHA	38	19	10	29	20	....	....	....	....	....	....	....	....	....	....	....	....	....	....	....	....	....	....
2007-08	Bowling Green	CCHA	38	27	10	37	33	....	....	....	....	....	....	....	....	....	....	....	....	....	....	....	....	....	....
	Rochester	AHL	8	1	0	1	2	....	....	....	....	....	....	....	....	....	....	....	....	....	....	....	....	....	....
2008-09	Portland Pirates	AHL	77	11	11	22	17	....	....	....	....	....	....	....	....	....	5	1	1	2	2	....	....	....	....
2009-10	Portland Pirates	AHL	78	18	16	34	24	....	....	....	....	....	....	....	....	....	4	2	1	3	0	....	....	....	....
2010-11	Portland Pirates	AHL	80	27	20	47	20	....	....	....	....	....	....	....	....	....	12	4	4	8	4	....	....	....	....
2011-12	**Buffalo**	**NHL**	**2**	**0**	**0**	**0**	**0**	**0**	**0**	**0**	**2**	**0.0**	**0**	**0**	**0.0**	**12:31**	....	....	....	....	....	....	....	....	....
	Rochester	AHL	75	28	16	44	25	....	....	....	....	....	....	....	....	....	3	0	0	0	0	....	....	....	....
2012-13	Augsburg	Germany	26	9	14	23	40	....	....	....	....	....	....	....	....	....	2	1	0	1	0	....	....	....	....
	St. John's IceCaps	AHL	7	1	3	4	2	....	....	....	....	....	....	....	....	....	....	....	....	....	....	....	....	....	....
	NHL Totals		**2**	**0**	**0**	**0**	**0**	**0**	**0**	**0**	**2**	**0.0**		**0**	**0.0**	**12:31**	....	....	....	....	....	....	....	....	....

CCHA Second All-Star Team (2008)

Signed as a free agent by **Buffalo**, March 26, 2008. Signed as a free agent by **St. John's** (AHL), September 21, 2012. Signed as a free agent by **Augsburg** (Germany), November 28, 2012.

WHITNEY, Ray

(WHIHT-nee, RAY) **DAL**

Left wing. Shoots right. 5'10", 180 lbs. Born, Fort Saskatchewan, Alta., May 8, 1972. San Jose's 2nd choice, 23rd overall, in 1991 Entry Draft.

			Regular Season														Playoffs								
Season	Club	League	GP	G	A	Pts	PIM	PP	SH	GW	S	%	+/-	TF	F%	Min	GP	G	A	Pts	PIM	PP	SH	GW	Min
1987-88	Ft. Saskatchewan	AMHL	71	80	155	235	119	....	....	....	....	....	....	....	....	....	....	....	....	....	....	....	....	....	....
1988-89	Spokane Chiefs	WHL	71	17	33	50	16	....	....	....	....	....	....	....	....	....	....	....	....	....	....	....	....	....	....
1989-90	Spokane Chiefs	WHL	71	57	56	113	50	....	....	....	....	....	....	....	....	....	6	3	4	7	6	....	....	....	....
1990-91	Spokane Chiefs	WHL	72	67	118	*185	36	....	....	....	....	....	....	....	....	....	15	13	18	*31	12	....	....	....	....
1991-92	Kolner EC	Germany	10	3	6	9	4	....	....	....	....	....	....	....	....	....	....	....	....	....	....	....	....	....	....
	Canada	Nat-Tm	5	1	0	1	6	....	....	....	....	....	....	....	....	....	....	....	....	....	....	....	....	....	....
	San Jose	NHL	2	0	3	3	0	0	0	0	4	0.0	–1	....	....	....	....	....	....	....	....	....	....	....	....
	San Diego Gulls	IHL	63	36	54	90	12	....	....	....	....	....	....	....	....	....	4	0	0	0	0	....	....	....	....
1992-93	San Jose	NHL	26	4	6	10	4	1	0	0	24	16.7	–14	....	....	....	....	....	....	....	....	....	....	....	....
	Kansas City	IHL	46	20	33	53	14	....	....	....	....	....	....	....	....	....	12	5	7	12	2	....	....	....	....
1993-94	San Jose	NHL	61	14	26	40	14	1	0	0	82	17.1	2	....	....	....	14	0	4	4	8	0	0	0	....
1994-95	San Jose	NHL	39	13	12	25	14	4	0	1	67	19.4	–7	....	....	....	11	4	4	8	2	0	0	1	....
1995-96	San Jose	NHL	60	17	24	41	16	4	2	2	106	16.0	–23	....	....	....	....	....	....	....	....	....	....	....	....
1996-97	San Jose	NHL	12	0	2	2	4	0	0	0	24	0.0	–6	....	....	....	....	....	....	....	....	....	....	....	....
	Kentucky	AHL	9	1	7	8	2	....	....	....	....	....	....	....	....	....	....	....	....	....	....	....	....	....	....
	Utah Grizzlies	IHL	43	13	35	48	34	....	....	....	....	....	....	....	....	....	7	3	1	4	6	....	....	....	....
1997-98	Edmonton	NHL	9	1	3	4	0	0	0	0	19	5.3	–1	....	....	....	....	....	....	....	....	....	....	....	....
	Florida	NHL	68	32	29	61	28	12	0	2	156	20.5	10	....	....	....	....	....	....	....	....	....	....	....	....
1998-99	Florida	NHL	81	26	38	64	18	7	0	6	193	13.5	–3	144	43.8	18:20	....	....	....	....	....	....	....	....	....
99-2000	Florida	NHL	81	29	42	71	35	5	0	3	198	14.6	16	198	49.0	18:41	4	1	0	1	4	0	0	0	18:13
2000-01	Florida	NHL	43	10	21	31	28	5	0	0	117	8.5	–16	38	39.5	17:41	....	....	....	....	....	....	....	....	....
	Columbus	NHL	3	0	3	3	2	0	0	0	3	0.0	–1	19	36.8	20:17	....	....	....	....	....	....	....	....	....
2001-02	Columbus	NHL	67	21	40	61	12	6	0	3	210	10.0	–22	21	47.6	20:13	....	....	....	....	....	....	....	....	....
2002-03	Columbus	NHL	81	24	52	76	22	8	2	2	235	10.2	–26	29	44.8	21:00	....	....	....	....	....	....	....	....	....
2003-04	Detroit	NHL	67	14	29	43	22	3	1	4	119	11.8	7	18	38.9	16:24	12	1	3	4	4	0	0	1	11:56
2004-05			DID NOT PLAY																						
2005-06 ♦	Carolina	NHL	63	17	38	55	42	12	0	2	147	11.6	0	13	38.5	17:11	24	9	6	15	14	5	0	1	14:07
2006-07	Carolina	NHL	81	32	51	83	46	6	0	6	215	14.9	–5	7	28.6	18:42	....	....	....	....	....	....	....	....	....
2007-08	Carolina	NHL	66	25	36	61	30	6	0	4	204	12.3	–6	5	60.0	18:56	....	....	....	....	....	....	....	....	....
2008-09	Carolina	NHL	82	24	53	77	32	7	0	2	219	11.0	2	4	50.0	18:25	18	3	8	11	4	0	0	1	18:36
2009-10	Carolina	NHL	80	21	37	58	26	7	0	5	171	12.3	–6	9	33.3	19:09	....	....	....	....	....	....	....	....	....
2010-11	Phoenix	NHL	75	17	40	57	24	3	0	1	156	10.9	0	100	45.0	16:57	4	1	2	3	2	1	0	0	19:24
2011-12	Phoenix	NHL	82	24	53	77	28	8	0	1	185	13.0	26	15	26.7	18:39	16	2	5	7	10	0	0	1	19:08
2012-13	Dallas	NHL	32	11	18	29	4	4	0	1	62	17.7	1	51	31.4	19:24	....	....	....	....	....	....	....	....	....
	NHL Totals		1261	376	656	1032	451	109	5	45	2916	12.9		671	43.5	18:35	103	21	32	53	48	6	0	5	16:19

WHL West First All-Star Team (1991) • WHL Player of the Year (1991) • Memorial Cup All-Star Team (1991) • George Parsons Trophy (Memorial Cup - Most Sportsmanlike Player) (1991) • NHL Second All-Star Team (2012)

Played in NHL All-Star Game (2000, 2003)

Signed as a free agent by **Edmonton**, October 1, 1997. Claimed on waivers by **Florida** from **Edmonton**, November 6, 1997. Traded to **Columbus** by **Florida** with future considerations for Kevyn Adams and Columbus's 4th round choice (Michael Woodford) in 2001 Entry Draft, March 13, 2001. Signed as a free agent by **Detroit**, July 30, 2003. Signed as a free agent by **Carolina**, August 7, 2005. Signed as a free agent by **Phoenix**, July 1, 2010. Signed as a free agent by **Dallas**, July 1, 2012.

WHITNEY, Ryan

(WHIHT-nee, RIGH-uhn)

Defense. Shoots left. 6'3", 206 lbs. Born, Boston, MA, February 19, 1983. Pittsburgh's 1st choice, 5th overall, in 2002 Entry Draft.

			Regular Season														Playoffs								
Season	Club	League	GP	G	A	Pts	PIM	PP	SH	GW	S	%	+/-	TF	F%	Min	GP	G	A	Pts	PIM	PP	SH	GW	Min
99-2000	Thayer Academy	High-MA	22	5	33	38	....	....	....	....	....	....	....	....	....	....	....	....	....	....	....	....	....	....	....
2000-01	USNTDP	U-18	40	7	23	30	64	....	....	....	....	....	....	....	....	....	....	....	....	....	....	....	....	....	....
	USNTDP	USHL	20	2	8	10	22	....	....	....	....	....	....	....	....	....	....	....	....	....	....	....	....	....	....
2001-02	Boston University	H-East	35	4	17	21	46	....	....	....	....	....	....	....	....	....	....	....	....	....	....	....	....	....	....
2002-03	Boston University	H-East	34	3	10	13	48	....	....	....	....	....	....	....	....	....	....	....	....	....	....	....	....	....	....
2003-04	Boston University	H-East	38	9	16	25	56	....	....	....	....	....	....	....	....	....	....	....	....	....	....	....	....	....	....
	Wilkes-Barre	AHL	....	....	....	....	....	....	....	....	....	....	....	....	....	....	20	1	9	10	6	....	....	....	....
2004-05	Wilkes-Barre	AHL	80	6	35	41	101	....	....	....	....	....	....	....	....	....	11	2	7	9	12	....	....	....	....
2005-06	Pittsburgh	NHL	68	6	32	38	85	2	0	1	113	5.3	–7	1	0.0	23:50	....	....	....	....	....	....	....	....	....
	Wilkes-Barre	AHL	9	5	9	14	6	....	....	....	....	....	....	....	....	....	11	1	4	5	8	....	....	....	....
2006-07	Pittsburgh	NHL	81	14	45	59	77	9	0	2	129	10.9	9	5	20.0	23:56	5	1	1	2	6	1	0	0	22:51
2007-08	Pittsburgh	NHL	76	12	28	40	45	7	1	1	119	10.1	–2	0	0.0	22:27	20	1	5	6	25	1	0	0	20:46
2008-09	Pittsburgh	NHL	28	2	11	13	16	1	0	0	42	4.8	–15	0	0.0	24:34	....	....	....	....	....	....	....	....	....
	Wilkes-Barre	AHL	1	0	1	1	2	....	....	....	....	....	....	....	....	....	....	....	....	....	....	....	....	....	....
	Anaheim	NHL	20	0	10	10	12	0	0	0	29	0.0	1	0	0.0	22:53	13	1	5	6	9	1	0	0	21:34
2009-10	Anaheim	NHL	62	4	24	28	48	3	0	0	107	3.7	–6	1	0.0	24:34	....	....	....	....	....	....	....	....	....
	United States	Olympics	6	0	0	0	0	....	....	....	....	....	....	....	....	....	....	....	....	....	....	....	....	....	....
	Edmonton	NHL	19	3	8	11	22	0	0	1	44	6.8	7	0	0.0	25:23	....	....	....	....	....	....	....	....	....
2010-11	Edmonton	NHL	35	2	25	27	33	0	0	0	43	4.7	13	0	0.0	25:20	....	....	....	....	....	....	....	....	....
2011-12	Edmonton	NHL	51	3	17	20	16	2	0	0	41	7.3	–16	0	0.0	20:58	....	....	....	....	....	....	....	....	....
2012-13	Edmonton	NHL	34	4	9	13	23	0	0	0	30	13.3	–7	0	0.0	18:29	....	....	....	....	....	....	....	....	....
	NHL Totals		474	50	209	259	377	24	1	5	697	7.2		7	14.3	23:12	38	3	11	14	40	3	0	0	21:19

Hockey East All-Rookie Team (2002)

Traded to **Anaheim** by **Pittsburgh** for Chris Kunitz and Eric Tangradi, February 26, 2009. Traded to **Edmonton** by **Anaheim** with Anaheim's 6th round choice (Brandon Davidson) in 2010 Entry Draft for Lubomir Visnovsky, March 3, 2010. • Missed majority of 2010-11 due to ankle injury vs. Buffalo, December 28, 2010.

WIDEMAN, Dennis

(WIGHD-muhn, DEH-nihs) **CGY**

Defense. Shoots right. 6', 200 lbs. Born, Kitchener, Ont., March 20, 1983. Buffalo's 9th choice, 241st overall, in 2002 Entry Draft.

			Regular Season														Playoffs								
Season	Club	League	GP	G	A	Pts	PIM	PP	SH	GW	S	%	+/-	TF	F%	Min	GP	G	A	Pts	PIM	PP	SH	GW	Min
1998-99	Elmira	ON-Jr.B	47	18	30	48	142	....	....	....	....	....	....	....	....	....	....	....	....	....	....	....	....	....	....
99-2000	Sudbury Wolves	OHL	63	10	26	36	64	....	....	....	....	....	....	....	....	....	12	1	2	3	22	....	....	....	....
2000-01	Sudbury Wolves	OHL	25	7	11	18	37	....	....	....	....	....	....	....	....	....	....	....	....	....	....	....	....	....	....
	London Knights	OHL	24	8	8	16	38	....	....	....	....	....	....	....	....	....	5	0	4	4	6	....	....	....	....
2001-02	London Knights	OHL	65	27	42	69	141	....	....	....	....	....	....	....	....	....	12	4	9	13	26	....	....	....	....
2002-03	London Knights	OHL	55	20	27	47	83	....	....	....	....	....	....	....	....	....	14	6	6	12	10	....	....	....	....
2003-04	London Knights	OHL	60	24	41	65	85	....	....	....	....	....	....	....	....	....	15	7	10	17	17	....	....	....	....
2004-05	Worcester IceCats	AHL	79	13	30	43	65	....	....	....	....	....	....	....	....	....	....	....	....	....	....	....	....	....	....
2005-06	St. Louis	NHL	67	8	16	24	83	5	1	1	150	5.3	–31	1	0.0	21:41	....	....	....	....	....	....	....	....	....
	Peoria Rivermen	AHL	12	2	4	6	31	....	....	....	....	....	....	....	....	....	....	....	....	....	....	....	....	....	....
2006-07	St. Louis	NHL	55	5	17	22	44	4	0	1	94	5.3	–7	0	0.0	20:12	....	....	....	....	....	....	....	....	....
	Boston	NHL	20	1	2	3	27	0	0	0	28	3.6	–3	1	0.0	17:20	....	....	....	....	....	....	....	....	....
2007-08	Boston	NHL	81	13	23	36	70	9	0	1	171	7.6	11	0	0.0	25:09	6	0	3	3	0	0	0	0	24:21
2008-09	Boston	NHL	79	13	37	50	34	6	1	2	169	7.7	32	0	0.0	24:39	11	0	7	7	4	0	0	0	24:42
2009-10	Boston	NHL	76	6	24	30	34	2	0	2	146	4.1	–14	0	0.0	23:33	13	1	11	12	4	0	0	0	26:02
2010-11	Florida	NHL	61	9	24	33	33	8	0	1	135	6.7	–26	1	100.0	23:58	....	....	....	....	....	....	....	....	....
	Washington	NHL	14	1	6	7	6	1	0	0	25	4.0	7	0	0.0	24:05	....	....	....	....	....	....	....	....	....
2011-12	Washington	NHL	82	11	35	46	46	4	0	3	175	6.3	–8	0	0.0	23:54	14	0	3	3	2	0	0	0	20:44
2012-13	Calgary	NHL	46	6	16	22	12	4	0	1	94	6.4	–9	1	0.0	25:01	....	....	....	....	....	....	....	....	....
	NHL Totals		581	73	200	273	389	43	2	12	1187	6.1		4	25.0	23:24	44	1	24	25	10	0	0	0	23:47

OHL First All-Star Team (2004) • Canadian Major Junior Second All-Star Team (2004)

Played in NHL All-Star Game (2012)

Signed as a free agent by **St. Louis**, June 30, 2004. Traded to **Boston** by **St. Louis** for Brad Boyes, February 27, 2007. Traded to **Florida** by **Boston** with Boston's 1st round choice (later traded to Los Angeles – Los Angeles selected Derek Forbert) in 2010 Entry Draft and Boston's 3rd round choice (Kyle Rau) in 2011 Entry Draft for Nathan Horton and Gregory Campbell, June 22, 2010. Traded to **Washington** by **Florida** for Jake Hauswirth and Washington's 3rd round choice (Jonathan Racine) in 2011 Entry Draft, February 28, 2011. Traded to **Calgary** by **Washington** for Jordan Henry and Calgary's 5th round choice (later traded to Winnipeg – Winnipeg selected Tucker Poolman) in 2013 Entry Draft, June 27, 2012.

WIERCIOCH, Patrick

(WEER-kawsh, PAT-rihk) **OTT**

Defense. Shoots left. 6'4", 200 lbs. Born, Burnaby, B.C., September 12, 1990. Ottawa's 2nd choice, 42nd overall, in 2008 Entry Draft.

Season	Club	League	Regular Season GP	G	A	Pts	PIM	PP	SH	GW	S	%	+/-	TF	F%	Min	Playoffs GP	G	A	Pts	PIM	PP	SH	GW	Min
2006-07	Burnaby Express	BCHL	42	9	16	25	46	....	....	....	....	....	....	....	....	....	14	3	4	7	10	....	....	....	....
2007-08	Omaha Lancers	USHL	40	3	18	21	24	....	....	....	....	....	....	....	....	....	14	2	9	11	22	....	....	....	....
2008-09	U. of Denver	WCHA	36	12	23	35	26	....	....	....	....	....	....	....	....	....	....	....	....	....	....	....	....	....	....
2009-10	U. of Denver	WCHA	39	6	21	27	34	....	....	....	....	....	....	....	....	....	....	....	....	....	....	....	....	....	....
2010-11	**Ottawa**	**NHL**	**8**	**0**	**2**	**2**	**4**	**0**	**0**	**0**	**3**	**0.0**	**0**	**0**	**0.0**	**13:54**	....	....	....	....	....	....	....	....	....
	Binghamton	AHL	67	4	14	18	25	....	....	....	....	....	....	....	....	....	15	0	1	1	0	....	....	....	....
2011-12	Binghamton	AHL	57	4	16	20	34	....	....	....	....	....	....	....	....	....	....	....	....	....	....	....	....	....	....
2012-13	Binghamton	AHL	32	10	9	19	22	....	....	....	....	....	....	....	....	....	....	....	....	....	....	....	....	....	....
	Ottawa	**NHL**	**42**	**5**	**14**	**19**	**39**	**3**	**0**	**0**	**81**	**6.2**	**9**	**0**	**0.0**	**15:42**	**1**	**0**	**0**	**0**	**0**	**0**	**0**	**0**	**1:47**
	NHL Totals		**50**	**5**	**16**	**21**	**43**	**3**	**0**	**0**	**84**	**6.0**		**0**	**0.0**	**15:24**	**1**	**0**	**0**	**0**	**0**	**0**	**0**	**0**	**1:47**

WCHA All-Rookie Team (2009) • WCHA Second All-Star Team (2009) • WCHA First All-Star Team (2010) • NCAA West First All-American Team (2010)

WILLIAMS, Jason

(WIHL-yuhms, JAY-suhn)

Center. Shoots right. 5'11", 192 lbs. Born, London, Ont., August 11, 1980.

Season	Club	League	Regular Season GP	G	A	Pts	PIM	PP	SH	GW	S	%	+/-	TF	F%	Min	Playoffs GP	G	A	Pts	PIM	PP	SH	GW	Min
1995-96	Mount Brydges	ON-Jr.D	36	31	28	59	18	....	....	....	....	....	....	....	....	....	....	....	....	....	....	....	....	....	....
1996-97	Peterborough	OHL	60	4	8	12	8	....	....	....	....	....	....	....	....	....	10	1	0	1	2	....	....	....	....
1997-98	Peterborough	OHL	55	8	27	35	31	....	....	....	....	....	....	....	....	....	4	0	1	1	2	....	....	....	....
1998-99	Peterborough	OHL	68	26	48	74	42	....	....	....	....	....	....	....	....	....	5	1	2	3	2	....	....	....	....
99-2000	Peterborough	OHL	66	36	37	75	64	....	....	....	....	....	....	....	....	....	5	2	1	3	2	....	....	....	....
2000-01	**Detroit**	**NHL**	**5**	**0**	**3**	**3**	**2**	**0**	**0**	**0**	**7**	**0.0**	**1**	**56**	**39.3**	**12:24**	**2**	**0**	**0**	**0**	**0**	**0**	**0**	**0**	**11:45**
	Cincinnati	AHL	76	24	45	69	48	....	....	....	....	....	....	....	....	....	1	0	0	0	2	....	....	....	....
2001-02 ♦	**Detroit**	**NHL**	**25**	**8**	**2**	**10**	**4**	**4**	**0**	**0**	**32**	**25.0**	**2**	**208**	**47.6**	**10:50**	**9**	**0**	**0**	**0**	**2**	**0**	**0**	**0**	**6:12**
	Cincinnati	AHL	52	23	27	50	27	....	....	....	....	....	....	....	....	....	3	0	1	1	6	....	....	....	....
2002-03	**Detroit**	**NHL**	**16**	**3**	**3**	**6**	**2**	**1**	**0**	**0**	**20**	**15.0**	**3**	**78**	**51.3**	**10:43**	....	....	....	....	....	....	....	....	....
	Grand Rapids	AHL	45	23	22	45	18	....	....	....	....	....	....	....	....	....	15	1	7	8	16	....	....	....	....
2003-04	**Detroit**	**NHL**	**49**	**6**	**7**	**13**	**15**	**0**	**0**	**0**	**44**	**13.6**	**1**	**315**	**49.2**	**9:27**	**3**	**0**	**0**	**0**	**2**	**0**	**0**	**0**	**6:11**
2004-05	Assat Pori	Finland	43	26	17	43	52	....	....	....	....	....	....	....	....	....	2	1	1	2	4	....	....	....	....
2005-06	**Detroit**	**NHL**	**80**	**21**	**37**	**58**	**26**	**6**	**0**	**4**	**177**	**11.9**	**4**	**29**	**55.2**	**14:55**	**6**	**1**	**1**	**2**	**6**	**0**	**0**	**0**	**18:10**
2006-07	**Detroit**	**NHL**	**58**	**11**	**15**	**26**	**24**	**3**	**0**	**2**	**111**	**9.9**	**7**	**11**	**45.5**	**14:26**	....	....	....	....	....	....	....	....	....
	Chicago	**NHL**	**20**	**4**	**2**	**6**	**20**	**2**	**1**	**0**	**38**	**10.5**	**–6**	**193**	**42.5**	**18:17**	....	....	....	....	....	....	....	....	....
2007-08	**Chicago**	**NHL**	**43**	**13**	**23**	**36**	**22**	**6**	**0**	**4**	**101**	**12.9**	**–2**	**15**	**60.0**	**16:35**	....	....	....	....	....	....	....	....	....
2008-09	**Atlanta**	**NHL**	**41**	**7**	**11**	**18**	**8**	**4**	**0**	**2**	**79**	**8.9**	**–9**	**381**	**49.1**	**16:05**	....	....	....	....	....	....	....	....	....
	Columbus	**NHL**	**39**	**12**	**17**	**29**	**16**	**3**	**0**	**2**	**74**	**16.2**	**5**	**237**	**40.9**	**15:38**	**4**	**0**	**1**	**1**	**2**	**0**	**0**	**0**	**14:12**
2009-10	**Detroit**	**NHL**	**44**	**6**	**9**	**15**	**8**	**3**	**0**	**1**	**96**	**6.3**	**–7**	**60**	**50.0**	**13:32**	**3**	**0**	**0**	**0**	**0**	**0**	**0**	**0**	**8:12**
2010-11	Connecticut	AHL	17	4	5	9	10	....	....	....	....	....	....	....	....	....	....	....	....	....	....	....	....	....	....
	Dallas	**NHL**	**27**	**2**	**3**	**5**	**6**	**0**	**0**	**1**	**18**	**11.1**	**–2**	**44**	**40.9**	**8:07**	....	....	....	....	....	....	....	....	....
2011-12	**Pittsburgh**	**NHL**	**8**	**1**	**1**	**2**	**4**	**0**	**0**	**0**	**4**	**25.0**	**1**	**1**	**0.0**	**10:34**	....	....	....	....	....	....	....	....	....
	Wilkes-Barre	AHL	59	13	29	42	32	....	....	....	....	....	....	....	....	....	12	3	10	13	2	....	....	....	....
2012-13	HC Ambri-Piotta	Swiss	47	*26	20	46	16	....	....	....	....	....	....	....	....	....	3	0	2	2	0	....	....	....	....
	NHL Totals		**455**	**94**	**133**	**227**	**157**	**32**	**1**	**16**	**801**	**11.7**		**1628**	**46.7**	**13:43**	**27**	**1**	**2**	**3**	**12**	**0**	**0**	**0**	**10:40**

Signed as a free agent by **Detroit**, September 18, 2000. Signed as a free agent by **Pori** (Finland), October 18, 2004. Traded to **Chicago** by **Detroit** for Kyle Calder, February 26, 2007. Signed as a free agent by **Atlanta**, July 14, 2008. Traded to **Columbus** by **Atlanta** for Clay Wilson and San Jose's 6th round choice (previously acquired, later traded to Chicago – Chicago selected David Pacan) in 2009 Entry Draft, January 14, 2009. Signed as a free agent by **Detroit**, August 4, 2009. Signed to a PTO (professional tryout) contract by **Connecticut** (AHL), December 26, 2010. Signed as a free agent by **Dallas**, February 12, 2011. Signed as a free agent by **Pittsburgh**, July 26, 2011. Signed as a free agent by **Ambri-Piotta** (Swiss), May 29, 2012.

WILLIAMS, Justin

(WIHL-yuhms, JUHS-tihn) **L.A.**

Right wing. Shoots right. 6'1", 188 lbs. Born, Cobourg, Ont., October 4, 1981. Philadelphia's 1st choice, 28th overall, in 2000 Entry Draft.

Season	Club	League	Regular Season GP	G	A	Pts	PIM	PP	SH	GW	S	%	+/-	TF	F%	Min	Playoffs GP	G	A	Pts	PIM	PP	SH	GW	Min
1997-98	Colborne Colts	ON-Jr.C	36	32	35	67	26	....	....	....	....	....	....	....	....	....	....	....	....	....	....	....	....	....	....
	Cobourg Cougars	ON-Jr.A	17	0	3	3	5	....	....	....	....	....	....	....	....	....	....	....	....	....	....	....	....	....	....
1998-99	Plymouth Whalers	OHL	47	4	8	12	28	....	....	....	....	....	....	....	....	....	7	1	2	3	0	....	....	....	....
99-2000	Plymouth Whalers	OHL	68	37	46	83	46	....	....	....	....	....	....	....	....	....	23	*14	16	*30	10	....	....	....	....
2000-01	**Philadelphia**	**NHL**	**63**	**12**	**13**	**25**	**22**	**0**	**0**	**0**	**99**	**12.1**	**6**	**13**	**53.9**	**12:31**	....	....	....	....	....	....	....	....	....
2001-02	**Philadelphia**	**NHL**	**75**	**17**	**23**	**40**	**32**	**0**	**0**	**1**	**162**	**10.5**	**11**	**16**	**25.0**	**14:27**	**5**	**0**	**0**	**0**	**4**	**0**	**0**	**0**	**16:42**
2002-03	**Philadelphia**	**NHL**	**41**	**8**	**16**	**24**	**22**	**0**	**0**	**2**	**105**	**7.6**	**15**	**16**	**50.0**	**15:57**	**12**	**1**	**5**	**6**	**8**	**0**	**0**	**1**	**14:11**
2003-04	**Philadelphia**	**NHL**	**47**	**6**	**20**	**26**	**32**	**3**	**0**	**1**	**107**	**5.6**	**10**	**38**	**31.6**	**15:30**	....	....	....	....	....	....	....	....	....
	Carolina	**NHL**	**32**	**5**	**13**	**18**	**32**	**1**	**0**	**0**	**96**	**5.2**	**2**	**25**	**36.0**	**18:52**	....	....	....	....	....	....	....	....	....
2004-05	Lulea HF	Sweden	49	14	18	32	61	....	....	....	....	....	....	....	....	....	4	0	1	1	29	....	....	....	....
2005-06 ♦	**Carolina**	**NHL**	**82**	**31**	**45**	**76**	**60**	**8**	**4**	**4**	**255**	**12.2**	**1**	**17**	**29.4**	**21:08**	**25**	**7**	**11**	**18**	**34**	**0**	**1**	**1**	**21:36**
2006-07	**Carolina**	**NHL**	**82**	**33**	**34**	**67**	**73**	**12**	**2**	**8**	**258**	**12.8**	**–11**	**24**	**37.5**	**20:51**	....	....	....	....	....	....	....	....	....
2007-08	**Carolina**	**NHL**	**37**	**9**	**21**	**30**	**43**	**2**	**0**	**0**	**106**	**8.5**	**2**	**13**	**38.5**	**19:18**	....	....	....	....	....	....	....	....	....
2008-09	**Carolina**	**NHL**	**32**	**3**	**7**	**10**	**9**	**2**	**0**	**0**	**80**	**3.8**	**–9**	**20**	**30.0**	**15:08**	....	....	....	....	....	....	....	....	....
	Los Angeles	**NHL**	**12**	**1**	**3**	**4**	**8**	**1**	**0**	**0**	**28**	**3.6**	**1**	**2**	**50.0**	**17:51**	....	....	....	....	....	....	....	....	....
2009-10	**Los Angeles**	**NHL**	**49**	**10**	**19**	**29**	**39**	**1**	**0**	**1**	**140**	**7.1**	**3**	**11**	**36.4**	**16:23**	**3**	**0**	**1**	**1**	**2**	**0**	**0**	**0**	**11:24**
2010-11	**Los Angeles**	**NHL**	**73**	**22**	**35**	**57**	**59**	**5**	**0**	**3**	**213**	**10.3**	**14**	**14**	**50.0**	**17:15**	**6**	**3**	**1**	**4**	**2**	**1**	**0**	**0**	**16:44**
2011-12 ♦	**Los Angeles**	**NHL**	**82**	**22**	**37**	**59**	**44**	**9**	**0**	**2**	**241**	**9.1**	**10**	**25**	**44.0**	**17:09**	**20**	**4**	**11**	**15**	**12**	**1**	**0**	**0**	**18:24**
2012-13	**Los Angeles**	**NHL**	**48**	**11**	**22**	**33**	**22**	**1**	**0**	**3**	**142**	**7.7**	**15**	**6**	**33.3**	**16:59**	**18**	**6**	**3**	**9**	**8**	**1**	**0**	**2**	**18:36**
	NHL Totals		**755**	**190**	**308**	**498**	**497**	**45**	**6**	**25**	**2032**	**9.4**		**240**	**37.5**	**17:13**	**89**	**21**	**32**	**53**	**70**	**3**	**1**	**4**	**18:20**

Played in NHL All-Star Game (2007)

• Missed majority of 2002-03 due to shoulder (November 15, 2002 vs. Carolina) and knee (January 18, 2003 vs. Tampa Bay) injuries. Traded to **Carolina** by **Philadelphia** for Danny Markov, January 20, 2004. Signed as a free agent by **Lulea** (Sweden), September 21, 2004. • Missed majority of 2007-08 due to knee injury at Florida, December 20, 2007. Traded to **Los Angeles** by **Carolina** for Patrick O'Sullivan and Calgary's 2nd round choice (previously acquired, Carolina selected Brian Dumoulin) in 2009 Entry Draft, March 4. 2009.

WILSON, Clay

(WIHL-suhn, KLAY)

Defense. Shoots left. 6', 195 lbs. Born, Sturgeon Lake, MN, April 5, 1983.

Season	Club	League	Regular Season GP	G	A	Pts	PIM	PP	SH	GW	S	%	+/-	TF	F%	Min	Playoffs GP	G	A	Pts	PIM	PP	SH	GW	Min
2001-02	Michigan Tech	WCHA	38	4	8	12	18	....	....	....	....	....	....	....	....	....	....	....	....	....	....	....	....	....	....
2002-03	Michigan Tech	WCHA	38	8	17	25	37	....	....	....	....	....	....	....	....	....	....	....	....	....	....	....	....	....	....
2003-04	Michigan Tech	WCHA	37	2	11	13	22	....	....	....	....	....	....	....	....	....	....	....	....	....	....	....	....	....	....
2004-05	Michigan Tech	WCHA	35	3	4	7	42	....	....	....	....	....	....	....	....	....	....	....	....	....	....	....	....	....	....
	Muskegon Fury	UHL	14	3	3	6	2	....	....	....	....	....	....	....	....	....	17	0	2	2	8	....	....	....	....
2005-06	Muskegon Fury	UHL	13	3	9	12	9	....	....	....	....	....	....	....	....	....	....	....	....	....	....	....	....	....	....
	Grand Rapids	AHL	60	10	27	37	40	....	....	....	....	....	....	....	....	....	16	0	3	3	8	....	....	....	....
2006-07	Portland Pirates	AHL	79	9	34	43	52	....	....	....	....	....	....	....	....	....	....	....	....	....	....	....	....	....	....
2007-08	Portland Pirates	AHL	14	3	5	8	6	....	....	....	....	....	....	....	....	....	....	....	....	....	....	....	....	....	....
	Columbus	**NHL**	**7**	**1**	**1**	**2**	**2**	**0**	**0**	**0**	**12**	**8.3**	**3**	**0**	**0.0**	**16:55**	....	....	....	....	....	....	....	....	....
	Syracuse Crunch	AHL	57	11	28	39	29	....	....	....	....	....	....	....	....	....	13	2	5	7	4	....	....	....	....
2008-09	**Columbus**	**NHL**	**5**	**0**	**1**	**1**	**0**	**0**	**0**	**0**	**9**	**0.0**	**–2**	**0**	**0.0**	**9:26**	....	....	....	....	....	....	....	....	....
	Syracuse Crunch	AHL	33	8	12	20	6	....	....	....	....	....	....	....	....	....	....	....	....	....	....	....	....	....	....
	Atlanta	**NHL**	**2**	**0**	**0**	**0**	**0**	**0**	**0**	**0**	**4**	**0.0**	**–1**	**0**	**0.0**	**15:55**	....	....	....	....	....	....	....	....	....
	Chicago Wolves	AHL	37	6	18	24	10	....	....	....	....	....	....	....	....	....	....	....	....	....	....	....	....	....	....
2009-10	**Florida**	**NHL**	**2**	**0**	**0**	**0**	**0**	**0**	**0**	**0**	**0**	**0.0**	**–5**	**0**	**0.0**	**11:07**	....	....	....	....	....	....	....	....	....
	Rochester	AHL	75	14	46	60	58	....	....	....	....	....	....	....	....	....	7	2	0	2	22	....	....	....	....
2010-11	**Florida**	**NHL**	**15**	**3**	**2**	**5**	**6**	**0**	**0**	**0**	**22**	**13.6**	**4**	**0**	**0.0**	**14:51**	....	....	....	....	....	....	....	....	....
	Rochester	AHL	66	12	36	48	24	....	....	....	....	....	....	....	....	....	....	....	....	....	....	....	....	....	....
2011-12	**Calgary**	**NHL**	**5**	**0**	**0**	**0**	**4**	**0**	**0**	**0**	**7**	**0.0**	**0**	**0**	**0.0**	**13:15**	....	....	....	....	....	....	....	....	....
	Abbotsford Heat	AHL	66	16	27	43	41	....	....	....	....	....	....	....	....	....	8	2	4	6	12	....	....	....	....
2012-13	Donetsk	KHL	51	8	12	20	26	....	....	....	....	....	....	....	....	....	4	1	1	2	2	....	....	....	....
	NHL Totals		**36**	**4**	**4**	**8**	**12**	**0**	**0**	**0**	**54**	**7.4**		**0**	**0.0**	**14:08**	....	....	....	....	....	....	....	....	....

AHL Second All-Star Team (2010, 2012)

Signed as a free agent by **Anaheim**, July 11, 2006. Traded to **Columbus** by **Anaheim** with Aaron Rome for Geoff Platt, November 15, 2007. Traded to **Atlanta** by **Columbus** with San Jose's 6th round choice (previously acquired, later traded to Chicago – Chicago selected David Pacan) in 2009 Entry Draft for Jason Williams, January 14, 2009. Signed as a free agent by **Florida**, July 2, 2009. Signed as a free agent by **Calgary**, July 2, 2011. Signed as a free agent by **Donetsk** (KHL), August 3, 2012.

			Regular Season														Playoffs								
Season	Club	League	GP	G	A	Pts	PIM	PP	SH	GW	S	%	+/-	TF	F%	Min	GP	G	A	Pts	PIM	PP	SH	GW	Min

WILSON, Colin (WIHL-suhn, KAW-lihn) NSH

Center. Shoots left. 6'1", 212 lbs. Born, Greenwich, CT, October 20, 1989. Nashville's 1st choice, 7th overall, in 2008 Entry Draft.

Season	Club	League	GP	G	A	Pts	PIM	PP	SH	GW	S	%	+/-	TF	F%	Min	GP	G	A	Pts	PIM	PP	SH	GW	Min
2005-06	USNTDP	U-17	15	9	7	16	2	....	....	....	....	....	....	....	....	....	....	....	....	....	....	....	....	....	....
	USNTDP	U-18	16	2	4	6	8	....	....	....	....	....	....	....	....	....	....	....	....	....	....	....	....	....	....
	USNTDP	NAHL	34	10	11	21	10	....	....	....	....	....	....	....	....	....	2	0	0	0	2	....	....	....	....
2006-07	USNTDP	U-18	41	19	31	50	32	....	....	....	....	....	....	....	....	....	....	....	....	....	....	....	....	....	....
	USNTDP	NAHL	15	11	13	24	21	....	....	....	....	....	....	....	....	....	....	....	....	....	....	....	....	....	....
2007-08	Boston University	H-East	37	12	23	35	22	....	....	....	....	....	....	....	....	....	....	....	....	....	....	....	....	....	....
2008-09	Boston University	H-East	43	17	*38	*55	52	....	....	....	....	....	....	....	....	....	....	....	....	....	....	....	....	....	....
2009-10	**Nashville**	**NHL**	**35**	**8**	**7**	**15**	**7**	**1**	**0**	**3**	**58**	**13.8**	**-2**	**124**	**50.0**	**15:10**	**6**	**0**	**1**	**1**	**0**	**0**	**0**	**0**	**13:43**
	Milwaukee	AHL	40	13	21	34	19	....	....	....	....	....	....	....	....	....	....	....	....	....	....	....	....	....	....
2010-11	**Nashville**	**NHL**	**82**	**16**	**18**	**34**	**17**	**2**	**0**	**2**	**101**	**15.8**	**9**	**228**	**47.4**	**13:18**	**3**	**0**	**0**	**0**	**0**	**0**	**0**	**0**	**11:37**
2011-12	**Nashville**	**NHL**	**68**	**15**	**20**	**35**	**21**	**5**	**0**	**5**	**114**	**13.2**	**5**	**77**	**50.7**	**16:08**	**4**	**1**	**0**	**1**	**0**	**0**	**0**	**0**	**13:25**
2012-13	**Nashville**	**NHL**	**25**	**7**	**12**	**19**	**4**	**2**	**0**	**1**	**26**	**26.9**	**1**	**21**	**38.1**	**16:34**	....	....	....	....	....	....	....	....	....
	NHL Totals		**210**	**46**	**57**	**103**	**49**	**10**	**0**	**11**	**299**	**15.4**		**450**	**48.2**	**14:55**	**13**	**1**	**1**	**2**	**0**	**0**	**0**	**0**	**13:08**

Hockey East All-Rookie Team (2008) • Hockey East Rookie of the Year (2008) • Hockey East First All-Star Team (2009) • NCAA East First All-American Team (2009) • NCAA Championship All-Tournament Team (2009)

WILSON, Kyle (WIHL-suhn, KIGHL)

Center. Shoots right. 6', 201 lbs. Born, Oakville, Ont., December 15, 1984. Minnesota's 12th choice, 272nd overall, in 2004 Entry Draft.

Season	Club	League	GP	G	A	Pts	PIM	PP	SH	GW	S	%	+/-	TF	F%	Min	GP	G	A	Pts	PIM	PP	SH	GW	Min
2000-01	Strathroy Rockets	ON-Jr.B	33	12	17	29	15	....	....	....	....	....	....	....	....	....	5	2	2	4	2	....	....	....	....
2001-02	Strathroy Rockets	ON-Jr.B	53	42	25	67	16	....	....	....	....	....	....	....	....	....	....	....	....	....	....	....	....	....	....
2002-03	Colgate	ECAC	33	4	2	6	15	....	....	....	....	....	....	....	....	....	....	....	....	....	....	....	....	....	....
2003-04	Colgate	ECAC	37	14	17	31	23	....	....	....	....	....	....	....	....	....	....	....	....	....	....	....	....	....	....
2004-05	Colgate	ECAC	30	5	18	23	12	....	....	....	....	....	....	....	....	....	....	....	....	....	....	....	....	....	....
2005-06	Colgate	ECAC	39	*23	18	41	22	....	....	....	....	....	....	....	....	....	....	....	....	....	....	....	....	....	....
2006-07	San Antonio	AHL	7	1	0	1	2	....	....	....	....	....	....	....	....	....	....	....	....	....	....	....	....	....	....
	South Carolina	ECHL	5	3	2	5	4	....	....	....	....	....	....	....	....	....	....	....	....	....	....	....	....	....	....
	Hershey Bears	AHL	54	24	30	54	26	....	....	....	....	....	....	....	....	....	19	7	9	16	8	....	....	....	....
2007-08	Hershey Bears	AHL	80	30	31	61	26	....	....	....	....	....	....	....	....	....	5	0	3	3	2	....	....	....	....
2008-09	Hershey Bears	AHL	80	28	30	58	31	....	....	....	....	....	....	....	....	....	22	3	7	10	2	....	....	....	....
2009-10	**Washington**	**NHL**	**2**	**0**	**2**	**2**	**0**	**0**	**0**	**0**	**1**	**0.0**	**1**	**13**	**30.8**	**9:42**	....	....	....	....	....	....	....	....	....
	Hershey Bears	AHL	77	24	29	53	23	....	....	....	....	....	....	....	....	....	21	6	6	12	4	....	....	....	....
2010-11	**Columbus**	**NHL**	**32**	**4**	**7**	**11**	**12**	**0**	**0**	**0**	**38**	**10.5**	**-3**	**133**	**47.4**	**10:38**	....	....	....	....	....	....	....	....	....
	Springfield	AHL	23	12	12	24	2	....	....	....	....	....	....	....	....	....	....	....	....	....	....	....	....	....	....
2011-12	**Nashville**	**NHL**	**5**	**0**	**0**	**0**	**0**	**0**	**0**	**0**	**2**	**0.0**	**-1**	**1**	**0.0**	**8:09**	....	....	....	....	....	....	....	....	....
	Milwaukee	AHL	68	22	32	54	25	....	....	....	....	....	....	....	....	....	3	1	2	3	2	....	....	....	....
2012-13	Syracuse Crunch	AHL	22	5	0	5	6	....	....	....	....	....	....	....	....	....	....	....	....	....	....	....	....	....	....
	Norfolk Admirals	AHL	16	3	6	9	2	....	....	....	....	....	....	....	....	....	....	....	....	....	....	....	....	....	....
	NHL Totals		**39**	**4**	**9**	**13**	**12**	**0**	**0**	**0**	**41**	**9.8**		**147**	**45.6**	**10:16**	....	....	....	....	....	....	....	....	....

ECAC Second All-Star Team (2006)

Signed as a free agent by **San Antonio** (AHL), October 6, 2006. Signed as a free agent by **Washington**, July 5, 2007. Signed as a free agent by **Columbus**, July 2, 2010. Signed as a free agent by **Nashville**, July 5, 2011. Traded to **Tampa Bay** by **Nashville** with Anders Lindback and Nashville's 7th round choice (Nikita Gusev) in 2012 Entry Draft for Sebastian Caron, Minnesota's 2nd round choice (previously acquired, Nashville selected Pontus Aberg) in 2012 Entry Draft, Philadelphia's 2nd round choice (previously acquired, Nashville selected Colton Sissons) in 2012 Entry Draft and Tampa Bay's 3rd round choice (Jonathan-Ismael Diaby) in 2013 Entry Draft, June 15, 2012. Traded to **Anaheim** by **Tampa Bay** for Dan Sexton. March 11, 2013. Signed as a free agent by **Riga** (KHL), June 12, 2013.

WILSON, Ryan (WIHL-suhn, RIGH-uhn) COL

Defense. Shoots left. 6'1", 207 lbs. Born, Windsor, Ont., February 3, 1987.

Season	Club	League	GP	G	A	Pts	PIM	PP	SH	GW	S	%	+/-	TF	F%	Min	GP	G	A	Pts	PIM	PP	SH	GW	Min
2003-04	St. Michael's	OHL	58	3	22	25	88	....	....	....	....	....	....	....	....	....	18	3	7	10	16	....	....	....	....
2004-05	St. Michael's	OHL	68	13	24	37	149	....	....	....	....	....	....	....	....	....	10	4	5	9	12	....	....	....	....
2005-06	St. Michael's	OHL	64	12	49	61	145	....	....	....	....	....	....	....	....	....	4	1	3	4	12	....	....	....	....
2006-07	Sarnia Sting	OHL	68	17	58	75	136	....	....	....	....	....	....	....	....	....	4	1	3	4	14	....	....	....	....
2007-08	Sarnia Sting	OHL	58	7	64	71	84	....	....	....	....	....	....	....	....	....	9	0	7	7	19	....	....	....	....
2008-09	Quad City Flames	AHL	60	4	16	20	56	....	....	....	....	....	....	....	....	....	....	....	....	....	....	....	....	....	....
	Lake Erie	AHL	8	0	2	2	25	....	....	....	....	....	....	....	....	....	....	....	....	....	....	....	....	....	....
2009-10	**Colorado**	**NHL**	**61**	**3**	**18**	**21**	**36**	**0**	**0**	**0**	**46**	**6.5**	**13**	**0**	**0.0**	**16:16**	**4**	**0**	**1**	**1**	**0**	**0**	**0**	**0**	**14:39**
	Lake Erie	AHL	3	0	0	0	17	....	....	....	....	....	....	....	....	....	....	....	....	....	....	....	....	....	....
2010-11	**Colorado**	**NHL**	**67**	**3**	**13**	**16**	**68**	**1**	**0**	**0**	**62**	**4.8**	**-8**	**0**	**0.0**	**19:48**	....	....	....	....	....	....	....	....	....
2011-12	**Colorado**	**NHL**	**59**	**1**	**20**	**21**	**33**	**0**	**0**	**0**	**63**	**1.6**	**11**	**1**	**0.0**	**18:44**	....	....	....	....	....	....	....	....	....
2012-13	**Colorado**	**NHL**	**12**	**0**	**3**	**3**	**8**	**0**	**0**	**0**	**23**	**0.0**	**4**	**0**	**0.0**	**18:30**	....	....	....	....	....	....	....	....	....
	NHL Totals		**199**	**7**	**54**	**61**	**145**	**1**	**0**	**0**	**194**	**3.6**		**1**	**0.0**	**18:20**	**4**	**0**	**1**	**1**	**0**	**0**	**0**	**0**	**14:39**

Signed as a free agent by **Calgary**, July 1, 2008. Traded to **Colorado** by **Calgary** with Lawrence Nycholat and Montreal's 2nd round choice (previously acquired, Colorado selected Stefan Elliott) in 2009 Entry Draft for Jordan Leopold, March 4, 2009. • Missed majority of 2012-13 due to ankle injury vs. Edmonton, February 2, 2013..

WILSON, Tom (WIHL-suhn, TAWM) WSH

Right wing. Shoots right. 6'4", 205 lbs. Born, Toronto, Ont., March 29, 1994. Washington's 2nd choice, 16th overall, in 2012 Entry Draft.

Season	Club	League	GP	G	A	Pts	PIM	PP	SH	GW	S	%	+/-	TF	F%	Min	GP	G	A	Pts	PIM	PP	SH	GW	Min
2009-10	Tor. Jr. Canadiens	GTHL	73	44	61	105	140	....	....	....	....	....	....	....	....	....	....	....	....	....	....	....	....	....	....
2010-11	Plymouth Whalers	OHL	28	3	3	6	71	....	....	....	....	....	....	....	....	....	....	....	....	....	....	....	....	....	....
2011-12	Plymouth Whalers	OHL	49	9	18	27	141	....	....	....	....	....	....	....	....	....	13	7	6	13	39	....	....	....	....
2012-13	Plymouth Whalers	OHL	48	23	35	58	104	....	....	....	....	....	....	....	....	....	12	9	8	17	41	....	....	....	....
	Hershey Bears	AHL	....	....	....	....	....	....	....	....	....	....	....	....	....	....	3	1	0	1	6	....	....	....	....
	Washington	**NHL**	....	....	....	....	....	....	....	....	....	....	....	....	....	....	**3**	**0**	**0**	**0**	**0**	**0**	**0**	**0**	**6:53**
	NHL Totals		....	....	....	....	....	....	....	....	....	....	....	....	....	....	**3**	**0**	**0**	**0**	**0**	**0**	**0**	**0**	**6:53**

WINCHESTER, Brad (WIHN-chehs-tuhr, BRAD) CHI

Center/Left wing. Shoots left. 6'5", 230 lbs. Born, Madison, WI, March 1, 1981. Edmonton's 2nd choice, 35th overall, in 2000 Entry Draft.

Season	Club	League	GP	G	A	Pts	PIM	PP	SH	GW	S	%	+/-	TF	F%	Min	GP	G	A	Pts	PIM	PP	SH	GW	Min
1997-98	USNTDP	U-17	24	8	5	13	64	....	....	....	....	....	....	....	....	....	....	....	....	....	....	....	....	....	....
	USNTDP	USHL	5	2	1	3	6	....	....	....	....	....	....	....	....	....	....	....	....	....	....	....	....	....	....
	USNTDP	NAHL	40	11	17	28	84	....	....	....	....	....	....	....	....	....	5	1	0	1	8	....	....	....	....
1998-99	USNTDP	U-18	6	0	3	3	6	....	....	....	....	....	....	....	....	....	....	....	....	....	....	....	....	....	....
	USNTDP	USHL	48	14	23	37	103	....	....	....	....	....	....	....	....	....	....	....	....	....	....	....	....	....	....
99-2000	U. of Wisconsin	WCHA	33	9	9	18	48	....	....	....	....	....	....	....	....	....	....	....	....	....	....	....	....	....	....
2000-01	U. of Wisconsin	WCHA	41	7	9	16	71	....	....	....	....	....	....	....	....	....	....	....	....	....	....	....	....	....	....
2001-02	U. of Wisconsin	WCHA	38	14	20	34	38	....	....	....	....	....	....	....	....	....	....	....	....	....	....	....	....	....	....
2002-03	U. of Wisconsin	WCHA	38	10	6	16	58	....	....	....	....	....	....	....	....	....	....	....	....	....	....	....	....	....	....
2003-04	Toronto	AHL	65	13	6	19	85	....	....	....	....	....	....	....	....	....	3	0	0	0	2	....	....	....	....
2004-05	Edmonton	AHL	76	22	18	40	143	....	....	....	....	....	....	....	....	....	....	....	....	....	....	....	....	....	....
2005-06	**Edmonton**	**NHL**	**19**	**0**	**1**	**1**	**21**	**0**	**0**	**0**	**19**	**0.0**	**-2**	**2**	**100.0**	**6:05**	**10**	**1**	**2**	**3**	**4**	**0**	**0**	**1**	**9:14**
	Hamilton	AHL	40	26	14	40	118	....	....	....	....	....	....	....	....	....	....	....	....	....	....	....	....	....	....
2006-07	**Edmonton**	**NHL**	**59**	**4**	**5**	**9**	**86**	**0**	**0**	**0**	**66**	**6.1**	**-10**	**3**	**33.3**	**8:04**	....	....	....	....	....	....	....	....	....
2007-08	**Dallas**	**NHL**	**41**	**1**	**2**	**3**	**46**	**0**	**0**	**0**	**36**	**2.8**	**-9**	**2**	**0.0**	**7:34**	**6**	**0**	**0**	**0**	**8**	**0**	**0**	**0**	**6:50**
	Iowa Stars	AHL	1	0	0	0	2	....	....	....	....	....	....	....	....	....	....	....	....	....	....	....	....	....	....
2008-09	**St. Louis**	**NHL**	**64**	**13**	**8**	**21**	**89**	**5**	**0**	**3**	**82**	**15.9**	**-1**	**20**	**45.0**	**12:10**	**4**	**0**	**0**	**0**	**10**	**0**	**0**	**0**	**11:42**
	Peoria Rivermen	AHL	13	4	2	6	46	....	....	....	....	....	....	....	....	....	....	....	....	....	....	....	....	....	....
2009-10	**St. Louis**	**NHL**	**64**	**3**	**5**	**8**	**108**	**1**	**0**	**0**	**69**	**4.3**	**3**	**12**	**25.0**	**9:04**	....	....	....	....	....	....	....	....	....
2010-11	**St. Louis**	**NHL**	**57**	**9**	**5**	**14**	**86**	**3**	**0**	**1**	**67**	**13.4**	**-9**	**7**	**28.6**	**10:29**	....	....	....	....	....	....	....	....	....
	Anaheim	**NHL**	**19**	**1**	**1**	**2**	**28**	**0**	**0**	**0**	**23**	**4.3**	**-9**	**1**	**0.0**	**10:28**	**3**	**0**	**0**	**0**	**4**	**0**	**0**	**0**	**5:24**
2011-12	**San Jose**	**NHL**	**67**	**6**	**4**	**10**	**88**	**0**	**0**	**0**	**72**	**8.3**	**-5**	**33**	**60.6**	**7:48**	**1**	**0**	**0**	**0**	**0**	**0**	**0**	**0**	**6:41**
2012-13	Milwaukee	AHL	37	9	18	27	66	....	....	....	....	....	....	....	....	....	2	0	1	1	2	....	....	....	....
	NHL Totals		**390**	**37**	**31**	**68**	**552**	**9**	**0**	**4**	**434**	**8.5**		**80**	**46.3**	**9:11**	**24**	**1**	**2**	**3**	**26**	**0**	**0**	**1**	**8:27**

Signed as a free agent by **Dallas**, July 6, 2007. Signed as a free agent by **St. Louis**, July 16, 2008. Traded to **Anaheim** by **St. Louis** for Anaheim's 3rd round choice (Mackenzie MacEachern) in 2012 Entry Draft, February 28, 2011. Signed as a free agent by **San Jose**, October 3, 2011. Signed to a PTO (professional tryout) contract by **Milwaukee** (AHL), January 22, 2013. Signed as a free agent by **Chicago**, August 2, 2013.

WINCHESTER, Jesse

(WIHN-chehs-tuhr, JEH-see) **FLA**

Center. Shoots right. 6'1", 206 lbs. Born, Long Sault, Ont., October 4, 1983.

Season	Club	League	GP	G	A	Pts	PIM	PP	SH	GW	S	%	+/-	TF	F%	Min	GP	G	A	Pts	PIM	PP	SH	GW	Min
2004-05	Colgate	ECAC	28	2	2	4	22	....	....	....	....	....	....	....	....	....	....	....	....	....	....	....	....	....	....
2005-06	Colgate	ECAC	37	14	22	36	31	....	....	....	....	....	....	....	....	....	....	....	....	....	....	....	....	....	....
2006-07	Colgate	ECAC	37	16	21	37	52	....	....	....	....	....	....	....	....	....	....	....	....	....	....	....	....	....	....
2007-08	Colgate	ECAC	40	8	*29	37	51	....	....	....	....	....	....	....	....	....	....	....	....	....	....	....	....	....	....
	Ottawa	**NHL**	**1**	**0**	**0**	**0**	**2**	**0**	**0**	**0**	**1**	**0.0**	**0**	**0**	**0.0**	**14:00**	....	....	....	....	....	....	....	....	....
2008-09	**Ottawa**	**NHL**	**76**	**3**	**15**	**18**	**33**	**0**	**0**	**1**	**115**	**2.6**	**0**	**199**	**56.8**	**10:35**	....	....	....	....	....	....	....	....	....
2009-10	**Ottawa**	**NHL**	**52**	**2**	**11**	**13**	**22**	**0**	**1**	**0**	**77**	**2.6**	**–1**	**377**	**55.4**	**10:01**	**6**	**0**	**0**	**0**	**0**	**0**	**0**	**0**	**9:38**
	Binghamton	AHL	4	2	2	4	0	....	....	....	....	....	....	....	....	....	....	....	....	....	....	....	....	....	....
2010-11	**Ottawa**	**NHL**	**72**	**4**	**9**	**13**	**42**	**0**	**0**	**0**	**118**	**3.4**	**–9**	**545**	**55.6**	**10:50**	....	....	....	....	....	....	....	....	....
2011-12	**Ottawa**	**NHL**	**32**	**2**	**6**	**8**	**22**	**0**	**1**	**0**	**52**	**3.8**	**2**	**235**	**53.6**	**10:38**	**4**	**0**	**0**	**0**	**0**	**0**	**0**	**0**	**10:53**
2012-13	TuTo Turku	Finland-2	11	3	7	10	58	....	....	....	....	....	....	....	....	....	....	....	....	....	....	....	....	....	....
	Jokerit Helsinki	Finland	5	0	3	3	2	....	....	....	....	....	....	....	....	....	....	....	....	....	....	....	....	....	....
	NHL Totals		**233**	**11**	**41**	**52**	**121**	**0**	**2**	**1**	**363**	**3.0**		**1356**	**55.4**	**10:34**	**10**	**0**	**0**	**0**	**0**	**0**	**0**	**0**	**10:08**

Signed as a free agent by **Ottawa**, March 24, 2008. • Missed majority of 2011-12 due to upper-body injury vs. Buffalo, December 20. 2011. Signed as a free agent by **TuTo Turku** (Finland-2), November 13, 2012. Signed as a free agent by **Jokerit Helsinki** (Finland), January 27, 2013. Signed as a free agent by **Florida**, July 5, 2013.

WINGELS, Tommy

(WIHN-guhls, TAW-mee) **S.J.**

Center. Shoots right. 6', 200 lbs. Born, Evanston, IL, April 12, 1988. San Jose's 5th choice, 177th overall, in 2008 Entry Draft.

Season	Club	League	GP	G	A	Pts	PIM	PP	SH	GW	S	%	+/-	TF	F%	Min	GP	G	A	Pts	PIM	PP	SH	GW	Min
2006-07	Cedar Rapids	USHL	47	10	18	28	52	....	....	....	....	....	....	....	....	....	6	3	0	3	6	....	....	....	....
2007-08	Miami U.	CCHA	42	15	14	29	22	....	....	....	....	....	....	....	....	....	....	....	....	....	....	....	....	....	....
2008-09	Miami U.	CCHA	41	11	17	28	66	....	....	....	....	....	....	....	....	....	....	....	....	....	....	....	....	....	....
2009-10	Miami U.	CCHA	44	17	25	42	49	....	....	....	....	....	....	....	....	....	....	....	....	....	....	....	....	....	....
2010-11	**San Jose**	**NHL**	**5**	**0**	**0**	**0**	**0**	**0**	**0**	**0**	**1**	**0.0**	**–1**	**3**	**33.3**	**5:07**	....	....	....	....	....	....	....	....	....
	Worcester Sharks	AHL	69	17	16	33	69	....	....	....	....	....	....	....	....	....	....	....	....	....	....	....	....	....	....
2011-12	**San Jose**	**NHL**	**33**	**3**	**6**	**9**	**18**	**0**	**0**	**0**	**71**	**4.2**	**–1**	**17**	**41.2**	**13:45**	**5**	**0**	**1**	**1**	**7**	**0**	**0**	**0**	**10:30**
	Worcester Sharks	AHL	29	13	8	21	28	....	....	....	....	....	....	....	....	....	....	....	....	....	....	....	....	....	....
2012-13	KooKoo Kouvola	Finland-2	18	8	14	22	33	....	....	....	....	....	....	....	....	....	....	....	....	....	....	....	....	....	....
	San Jose	**NHL**	**42**	**5**	**8**	**13**	**26**	**0**	**1**	**0**	**69**	**7.2**	**–9**	**16**	**25.0**	**14:14**	**11**	**0**	**2**	**2**	**6**	**0**	**0**	**0**	**13:53**
	NHL Totals		**80**	**8**	**14**	**22**	**44**	**0**	**1**	**0**	**141**	**5.7**		**36**	**33.3**	**13:28**	**16**	**0**	**3**	**3**	**13**	**0**	**0**	**0**	**12:50**

NCAA Championship All-Tournament Team (2009) • CCHA Second All-Star Team (2010)

Signed as a free agent by **Kouvola** (Finland-2), October 4, 2012.

WINNIK, Daniel

(WIHN-ihk, DAN-yehl) **ANA**

Center/Left wing. Shoots left. 6'2", 213 lbs. Born, Toronto, Ont., March 6, 1985. Phoenix's 10th choice, 265th overall, in 2004 Entry Draft.

Season	Club	League	GP	G	A	Pts	PIM	PP	SH	GW	S	%	+/-	TF	F%	Min	GP	G	A	Pts	PIM	PP	SH	GW	Min
2002-03	Wexford Raiders	ON-Jr.A	47	20	33	53	70	....	....	....	....	....	....	....	....	....	18	11	11	22	24	....	....	....	....
2003-04	New Hampshire	H-East	38	4	10	14	12	....	....	....	....	....	....	....	....	....	....	....	....	....	....	....	....	....	....
2004-05	New Hampshire	H-East	42	18	22	40	26	....	....	....	....	....	....	....	....	....	....	....	....	....	....	....	....	....	....
2005-06	New Hampshire	H-East	39	15	26	41	44	....	....	....	....	....	....	....	....	....	....	....	....	....	....	....	....	....	....
	San Antonio	AHL	7	1	1	2	8	....	....	....	....	....	....	....	....	....	....	....	....	....	....	....	....	....	....
2006-07	San Antonio	AHL	66	9	12	21	34	....	....	....	....	....	....	....	....	....	....	....	....	....	....	....	....	....	....
	Phoenix	ECHL	5	0	6	6	9	....	....	....	....	....	....	....	....	....	....	....	....	....	....	....	....	....	....
2007-08	**Phoenix**	**NHL**	**79**	**11**	**15**	**26**	**25**	**0**	**0**	**1**	**122**	**9.0**	**–3**	**154**	**42.2**	**14:06**	....	....	....	....	....	....	....	....	....
2008-09	**Phoenix**	**NHL**	**49**	**3**	**4**	**7**	**63**	**0**	**0**	**0**	**66**	**4.5**	**1**	**138**	**37.0**	**13:04**	....	....	....	....	....	....	....	....	....
	San Antonio	AHL	5	0	0	0	4	....	....	....	....	....	....	....	....	....	....	....	....	....	....	....	....	....	....
2009-10	**Phoenix**	**NHL**	**74**	**4**	**15**	**19**	**12**	**0**	**0**	**1**	**83**	**4.8**	**1**	**110**	**45.5**	**13:09**	**7**	**0**	**0**	**0**	**0**	**0**	**0**	**0**	**12:45**
2010-11	**Colorado**	**NHL**	**80**	**11**	**15**	**26**	**35**	**2**	**2**	**1**	**167**	**6.6**	**–2**	**69**	**36.2**	**16:33**	....	....	....	....	....	....	....	....	....
2011-12	**Colorado**	**NHL**	**63**	**5**	**13**	**18**	**42**	**0**	**1**	**0**	**155**	**3.2**	**–11**	**47**	**46.8**	**17:42**	....	....	....	....	....	....	....	....	....
	San Jose	**NHL**	**21**	**3**	**2**	**5**	**10**	**0**	**0**	**1**	**29**	**10.3**	**0**	**19**	**57.9**	**13:40**	**5**	**0**	**1**	**1**	**6**	**0**	**0**	**0**	**12:25**
2012-13	**Anaheim**	**NHL**	**48**	**6**	**13**	**19**	**16**	**0**	**0**	**1**	**95**	**6.3**	**13**	**53**	**30.2**	**16:50**	**7**	**0**	**1**	**1**	**7**	**0**	**0**	**0**	**15:04**
	NHL Totals		**414**	**43**	**77**	**120**	**203**	**2**	**3**	**5**	**717**	**6.0**		**590**	**40.7**	**15:07**	**19**	**0**	**2**	**2**	**13**	**0**	**0**	**0**	**13:31**

Hockey East Second All-Star Team (2006)

Traded to **Colorado** by **Phoenix** for Colorado's 4th round choice (Rhett Holland) in 2012 Entry Draft, June 28, 2010. Traded to **San Jose** by **Colorado** with T.J. Galiardi and Anaheim's 7th round choice (previously acquired, San Jose selected Emil Galimov) in 2013 Entry Draft for Jamie McGinn, Michael Sgarbossa and Mike Connolly, February 27, 2012. Signed as a free agent by **Anaheim**, July 20, 2012.

WISHART, Ty

(wih-SHAHRT, TIGH)

Defense. Shoots left. 6'4", 225 lbs. Born, Belleville, Ont., May 19, 1988. San Jose's 1st choice, 16th overall, in 2006 Entry Draft.

Season	Club	League	GP	G	A	Pts	PIM	PP	SH	GW	S	%	+/-	TF	F%	Min	GP	G	A	Pts	PIM	PP	SH	GW	Min
2003-04	Comox Valley	Minor-BC	47	26	27	53	48	....	....	....	....	....	....	....	....	....	....	....	....	....	....	....	....	....	....
2004-05	Prince George	WHL	58	1	7	8	41	....	....	....	....	....	....	....	....	....	....	....	....	....	....	....	....	....	....
2005-06	Prince George	WHL	70	5	32	37	68	....	....	....	....	....	....	....	....	....	5	0	0	0	4	....	....	....	....
2006-07	Prince George	WHL	62	11	38	49	59	....	....	....	....	....	....	....	....	....	15	3	8	11	6	....	....	....	....
2007-08	Prince George	WHL	40	12	28	40	34	....	....	....	....	....	....	....	....	....	....	....	....	....	....	....	....	....	....
	Moose Jaw	WHL	32	4	23	27	18	....	....	....	....	....	....	....	....	....	6	1	3	4	2	....	....	....	....
	Worcester Sharks	AHL	5	0	0	0	0	....	....	....	....	....	....	....	....	....	....	....	....	....	....	....	....	....	....
2008-09	**Tampa Bay**	**NHL**	**5**	**0**	**1**	**1**	**0**	**0**	**0**	**0**	**2**	**0.0**	**0**	**0**	**0.0**	**10:07**	....	....	....	....	....	....	....	....	....
	Norfolk Admirals	AHL	61	1	6	7	25	....	....	....	....	....	....	....	....	....	....	....	....	....	....	....	....	....	....
2009-10	Norfolk Admirals	AHL	76	9	23	32	44	....	....	....	....	....	....	....	....	....	....	....	....	....	....	....	....	....	....
2010-11	Norfolk Admirals	AHL	31	4	14	18	33	....	....	....	....	....	....	....	....	....	....	....	....	....	....	....	....	....	....
	NY Islanders	**NHL**	**20**	**1**	**4**	**5**	**10**	**1**	**0**	**0**	**23**	**4.3**	**5**	**0**	**0.0**	**16:49**	....	....	....	....	....	....	....	....	....
	Bridgeport	AHL	20	0	9	9	8	....	....	....	....	....	....	....	....	....	....	....	....	....	....	....	....	....	....
2011-12	**NY Islanders**	**NHL**	**1**	**0**	**0**	**0**	**0**	**0**	**0**	**0**	**0**	**0.0**	**0**	**0**	**0.0**	**17:16**	....	....	....	....	....	....	....	....	....
	Bridgeport	AHL	71	5	14	19	32	....	....	....	....	....	....	....	....	....	3	0	0	0	2	....	....	....	....
2012-13	Bridgeport	AHL	62	7	17	24	32	....	....	....	....	....	....	....	....	....	....	....	....	....	....	....	....	....	....
	NHL Totals		**26**	**1**	**5**	**6**	**10**	**1**	**0**	**0**	**25**	**4.0**		**0**	**0.0**	**15:33**	....	....	....	....	....	....	....	....	....

WHL West Second All-Star Team (2007) • WHL East Second All-Star Team (2008)

Traded to **Tampa Bay** by **San Jose** with Matt Carle, San Jose's 1st round choice (later traded to Ottawa, later traded to NY Islanders, later traded to Columbus, later traded to Anahaim - Anaheim selected Kyle Palmieri) in 2009 Entry Draft and San Jose's 4th round choice (James Mullin) in 2010 Entry Draft for Dan Boyle and Brad Lukowich, July 4, 2008. Traded to **NY Islanders** by **Tampa Bay** for Dwayne Roloson, January 2, 2011.

WISNIEWSKI, James

(wihz-NOO-skee, JAYMZ) **CBJ**

Defense. Shoots right. 6', 208 lbs. Born, Canton, MI, February 21, 1984. Chicago's 5th choice, 156th overall, in 2002 Entry Draft.

Season	Club	League	GP	G	A	Pts	PIM	PP	SH	GW	S	%	+/-	TF	F%	Min	GP	G	A	Pts	PIM	PP	SH	GW	Min
99-2000	Det. Compuware	NAHL	50	5	11	16	67	....	....	....	....	....	....	....	....	....	5	0	3	3	4	....	....	....	....
2000-01	Plymouth Whalers	OHL	53	6	23	29	72	....	....	....	....	....	....	....	....	....	19	3	10	13	34	....	....	....	....
2001-02	Plymouth Whalers	OHL	62	11	25	36	100	....	....	....	....	....	....	....	....	....	6	1	2	3	6	....	....	....	....
2002-03	Plymouth Whalers	OHL	52	18	34	52	60	....	....	....	....	....	....	....	....	....	18	2	10	12	14	....	....	....	....
2003-04	Plymouth Whalers	OHL	50	17	53	70	63	....	....	....	....	....	....	....	....	....	9	3	7	10	8	....	....	....	....
2004-05	Norfolk Admirals	AHL	66	7	18	25	110	....	....	....	....	....	....	....	....	....	5	1	3	4	2	....	....	....	....
2005-06	**Chicago**	**NHL**	**19**	**2**	**5**	**7**	**36**	**0**	**0**	**0**	**25**	**8.0**	**0**	**1**	**0.0**	**15:52**	....	....	....	....	....	....	....	....	....
	Norfolk Admirals	AHL	61	7	28	35	67	....	....	....	....	....	....	....	....	....	4	1	2	3	6	....	....	....	....
2006-07	**Chicago**	**NHL**	**50**	**2**	**8**	**10**	**39**	**0**	**0**	**0**	**55**	**3.6**	**3**	**1**	**0.0**	**19:00**	....	....	....	....	....	....	....	....	....
	Norfolk Admirals	AHL	10	0	6	6	8	....	....	....	....	....	....	....	....	....	....	....	....	....	....	....	....	....	....
2007-08	**Chicago**	**NHL**	**68**	**7**	**19**	**26**	**103**	**1**	**1**	**0**	**82**	**8.5**	**12**	**0**	**0.0**	**17:00**	....	....	....	....	....	....	....	....	....
2008-09	**Chicago**	**NHL**	**31**	**2**	**11**	**13**	**14**	**1**	**0**	**0**	**70**	**2.9**	**6**	**0**	**0.0**	**19:15**	....	....	....	....	....	....	....	....	....
	Rockford IceHogs	AHL	2	3	1	4	0	....	....	....	....	....	....	....	....	....	....	....	....	....	....	....	....	....	....
	Anaheim	**NHL**	**17**	**1**	**10**	**11**	**16**	**0**	**0**	**0**	**19**	**5.3**	**3**	**0**	**0.0**	**20:57**	**12**	**1**	**2**	**3**	**10**	**0**	**0**	**0**	**20:22**
2009-10	**Anaheim**	**NHL**	**69**	**3**	**27**	**30**	**56**	**2**	**0**	**0**	**146**	**2.1**	**–5**	**0**	**0.0**	**24:21**	....	....	....	....	....	....	....	....	....
2010-11	**NY Islanders**	**NHL**	**32**	**3**	**18**	**21**	**18**	**3**	**0**	**0**	**71**	**4.2**	**–18**	**0**	**0.0**	**23:15**	....	....	....	....	....	....	....	....	....
	Montreal	**NHL**	**43**	**7**	**23**	**30**	**20**	**4**	**0**	**2**	**87**	**8.0**	**4**	**0**	**0.0**	**22:43**	**6**	**0**	**2**	**2**	**7**	**0**	**0**	**0**	**22:23**

			Regular Season														Playoffs								
Season	Club	League	GP	G	A	Pts	PIM	PP	SH	GW	S	%	+/-	TF	F%	Min	GP	G	A	Pts	PIM	PP	SH	GW	Min
2011-12	**Columbus**	**NHL**	**48**	**6**	**21**	**27**	**37**	**2**	**0**	**2**	**99**	**6.1**	**–13**	**1**	**0.0**	**24:48**	....	....	....	....	....	....	....	....	....
2012-13	**Columbus**	**NHL**	**30**	**5**	**9**	**14**	**15**	**4**	**0**	**0**	**62**	**8.1**	**–1**	**0**	**0.0**	**22:50**	....	....	....	....	....	....	....	....	....
	NHL Totals		**407**	**38**	**151**	**189**	**354**	**17**	**1**	**4**	**716**	**5.3**		**3**	**0.0**	**21:13**	**18**	**1**	**4**	**5**	**17**	**0**	**0**	**0**	**21:02**

OHL First All-Star Team (2004) • OHL Defenseman of the Year (2004) • Canadian Major Junior First All-Star Team (2004) • Canadian Major Junior Defenseman of the Year (2004)

Traded to **Anaheim** by **Chicago** with Petri Kontiola for Samuel Pahlsson, Logan Stephenson and future considerations, March 4, 2009. Traded to **NY Islanders** by **Anaheim** for NY Islanders' 3rd round choice (Joseph Cramarossa) in 2011 Entry Draft, July 30, 2010. Traded to **Montreal** by **NY Islanders** for Montreal's 2nd round compensatory choice (Johan Sundstrom) in 2011 Entry Draft, December 28, 2010. Traded to **Columbus** by **Montreal** for Columbus's 5th round choice (Charles Hudson) in 2012 Entry Draft, June 29, 2011.

WOLSKI, Wojtek

(VOHL-skee, VOI-tehk)

Left wing. Shoots left. 6'3", 215 lbs. Born, Zabrze, Poland, February 24, 1986. Colorado's 1st choice, 21st overall, in 2004 Entry Draft.

2001-02	St. Mike's B's	ON-Jr.A	33	16	33	49	40	....	....	....	....	....	....	....	....	....	....	....	....	....	....	....	....	....	....
2002-03	Brampton	OHL	64	25	32	57	26	....	....	....	....	....	....	....	....	....	11	5	0	5	6	....	....	....	....
2003-04	Brampton	OHL	66	29	41	70	30	....	....	....	....	....	....	....	....	....	12	5	3	8	8	....	....	....	....
2004-05	Brampton	OHL	67	29	44	73	41	....	....	....	....	....	....	....	....	....	6	2	5	7	6	....	....	....	....
2005-06	**Colorado**	**NHL**	**9**	**2**	**4**	**6**	**4**	**2**	**0**	**0**	**9**	**22.2**	**–5**	**4**	**0.0**	**9:44**	**8**	**1**	**3**	**4**	**2**	**0**	**0**	**0**	**12:06**
	Brampton	OHL	56	47	81	128	46	....	....	....	....	....	....	....	....	....	11	7	11	18	4	....	....	....	....
2006-07	**Colorado**	**NHL**	**76**	**22**	**28**	**50**	**14**	**7**	**0**	**2**	**165**	**13.3**	**2**	**3**	**100.0**	**15:31**	....	....	....	....	....	....	....	....	....
2007-08	**Colorado**	**NHL**	**77**	**18**	**30**	**48**	**14**	**4**	**0**	**6**	**158**	**11.4**	**10**	**48**	**50.0**	**15:56**	**7**	**2**	**3**	**5**	**2**	**1**	**0**	**1**	**13:15**
2008-09	**Colorado**	**NHL**	**78**	**14**	**28**	**42**	**28**	**2**	**1**	**3**	**169**	**8.3**	**–13**	**515**	**48.2**	**18:23**	....	....	....	....	....	....	....	....	....
2009-10	**Colorado**	**NHL**	**62**	**17**	**30**	**47**	**21**	**2**	**0**	**4**	**156**	**10.9**	**15**	**23**	**47.8**	**18:57**	....	....	....	....	....	....	....	....	....
	Phoenix	**NHL**	**18**	**6**	**12**	**18**	**6**	**0**	**0**	**1**	**39**	**15.4**	**6**	**13**	**38.5**	**18:01**	**7**	**4**	**1**	**5**	**0**	**1**	**0**	**0**	**17:25**
2010-11	**Phoenix**	**NHL**	**36**	**6**	**10**	**16**	**10**	**0**	**0**	**0**	**57**	**10.5**	**–6**	**24**	**58.3**	**14:41**	....	....	....	....	....	....	....	....	....
	NY Rangers	**NHL**	**37**	**6**	**13**	**19**	**8**	**1**	**0**	**1**	**78**	**7.7**	**12**	**7**	**14.3**	**14:29**	**5**	**1**	**2**	**3**	**0**	**0**	**0**	**0**	**12:16**
2011-12	**NY Rangers**	**NHL**	**9**	**0**	**3**	**3**	**2**	**0**	**0**	**0**	**11**	**0.0**	**–2**	**1**	**100.0**	**11:20**	....	....	....	....	....	....	....	....	....
	Connecticut	AHL	6	3	2	5	0	....	....	....	....	....	....	....	....	....	....	....	....	....	....	....	....	....	....
	Florida	**NHL**	**22**	**4**	**5**	**9**	**0**	**0**	**0**	**0**	**39**	**10.3**	**–3**	**9**	**44.4**	**14:45**	**2**	**0**	**0**	**0**	**4**	**0**	**0**	**0**	**10:25**
2012-13	Ciarko Sanok	Poland	9	3	8	11	37	....	....	....	....	....	....	....	....	....	....	....	....	....	....	....	....	....	....
	Washington	**NHL**	**27**	**4**	**5**	**9**	**6**	**0**	**0**	**2**	**49**	**8.2**	**1**	**5**	**20.0**	**13:21**	....	....	....	....	....	....	....	....	....
	NHL Totals		**451**	**99**	**168**	**267**	**113**	**18**	**1**	**19**	**930**	**10.6**		**652**	**47.9**	**16:08**	**29**	**8**	**9**	**17**	**8**	**2**	**0**	**1**	**13:34**

OHL First All-Star Team (2004) • OHL Second All-Star Team (2006)

Traded to **Phoenix** by **Colorado** for Peter Mueller and Kevin Porter, March 3, 2010. Traded to **NY Rangers** by **Phoenix** for Michael Rozsival, January 10. 2011. Traded to **Florida** by **NY Rangers** for Mike Vernace and Florida's 3rd round choice (later traded to San Jose, later traded to Phoenix – Phoenix selected Pavel Laplante) in 2013 Entry Draft, February 25, 2012. Signed as a free agent by **Washington**, July 11, 2012. Signed as a free agent by **Sanok** (Poland), October 6, 2012. Signed as a free agent by **Nizhny Novgorod** (KHL), May 20, 2013.

WOYWITKA, Jeff

(WOI-wiht-ka, JEHF)

Defense. Shoots left. 6'3", 227 lbs. Born, Vermilion, Alta., September 1, 1983. Philadelphia's 1st choice, 27th overall, in 2001 Entry Draft.

1998-99	Wainwright	AAHA	26	7	15	22	60	....	....	....	....	....	....	....	....	....	....	....	....	....	....	....	....	....	....
99-2000	Red Deer Rebels	WHL	67	4	12	16	40	....	....	....	....	....	....	....	....	....	4	0	3	3	2	....	....	....	....
2000-01	Red Deer Rebels	WHL	72	7	28	35	113	....	....	....	....	....	....	....	....	....	22	2	8	10	25	....	....	....	....
2001-02	Red Deer Rebels	WHL	72	14	23	37	109	....	....	....	....	....	....	....	....	....	23	2	10	12	22	....	....	....	....
2002-03	Red Deer Rebels	WHL	57	16	36	52	65	....	....	....	....	....	....	....	....	....	23	1	9	10	25	....	....	....	....
2003-04	Philadelphia	AHL	29	0	6	6	51	....	....	....	....	....	....	....	....	....	....	....	....	....	....	....	....	....	....
	Toronto	AHL	53	4	18	22	41	....	....	....	....	....	....	....	....	....	3	0	0	0	2	....	....	....	....
2004-05	Edmonton	AHL	80	6	20	26	84	....	....	....	....	....	....	....	....	....	....	....	....	....	....	....	....	....	....
2005-06	**St. Louis**	**NHL**	**26**	**0**	**2**	**2**	**25**	**0**	**0**	**0**	**23**	**0.0**	**–12**	**0**	**0.0**	**10:38**	....	....	....	....	....	....	....	....	....
	Peoria Rivermen	AHL	53	1	14	15	58	....	....	....	....	....	....	....	....	....	4	0	0	0	4	....	....	....	....
2006-07	**St. Louis**	**NHL**	**34**	**1**	**6**	**7**	**12**	**0**	**0**	**0**	**28**	**3.6**	**4**	**0**	**0.0**	**14:45**	....	....	....	....	....	....	....	....	....
	Peoria Rivermen	AHL	41	0	18	18	20	....	....	....	....	....	....	....	....	....	....	....	....	....	....	....	....	....	....
2007-08	**St. Louis**	**NHL**	**27**	**2**	**6**	**8**	**12**	**0**	**0**	**0**	**25**	**8.0**	**2**	**0**	**0.0**	**16:04**	....	....	....	....	....	....	....	....	....
	Peoria Rivermen	AHL	52	10	20	30	35	....	....	....	....	....	....	....	....	....	....	....	....	....	....	....	....	....	....
2008-09	**St. Louis**	**NHL**	**65**	**3**	**15**	**18**	**57**	**2**	**0**	**1**	**71**	**4.2**	**8**	**0**	**0.0**	**18:29**	**4**	**0**	**0**	**0**	**0**	**0**	**0**	**0**	**18:48**
	Peoria Rivermen	AHL	7	0	7	7	2	....	....	....	....	....	....	....	....	....	....	....	....	....	....	....	....	....	....
2009-10	**Dallas**	**NHL**	**36**	**0**	**3**	**3**	**11**	**0**	**0**	**0**	**44**	**0.0**	**–6**	**0**	**0.0**	**14:06**	....	....	....	....	....	....	....	....	....
2010-11	**Dallas**	**NHL**	**63**	**2**	**9**	**11**	**24**	**1**	**0**	**0**	**72**	**2.8**	**5**	**0**	**0.0**	**17:57**	....	....	....	....	....	....	....	....	....
2011-12	**NY Rangers**	**NHL**	**27**	**1**	**5**	**6**	**8**	**0**	**0**	**0**	**13**	**7.7**	**2**	**0**	**0.0**	**10:25**	....	....	....	....	....	....	....	....	....
	Connecticut	AHL	6	0	3	3	6	....	....	....	....	....	....	....	....	....	....	....	....	....	....	....	....	....	....
2012-13	Peoria Rivermen	AHL	34	1	10	11	22	....	....	....	....	....	....	....	....	....	....	....	....	....	....	....	....	....	....
	NHL Totals		**278**	**9**	**46**	**55**	**149**	**3**	**0**	**1**	**276**	**3.3**		**0**	**0.0**	**15:35**	**4**	**0**	**0**	**0**	**0**	**0**	**0**	**0**	**18:48**

WHL East Second All-Star Team (2002) • WHL East First All-Star Team (2003)

Traded to **Edmonton** by **Philadelphia** with Philadelphia's 1st round choice (Rob Schremp) in 2004 Entry Draft and Philadelphia's 3rd round choice (Danny Syvret) in 2005 Entry Draft for Mike Comrie, December 16, 2003. Traded to **St. Louis** by **Edmonton** with Eric Brewer and Doug Lynch for Chris Pronger, August 2, 2005. Signed as a free agent by **Dallas**, July 7, 2009. • Missed majority of 2009-10 as a healthy reserve. Signed as a free agent by **Montreal**, August 15, 2011. Claimed on waivers by **NY Rangers** from **Montreal**, October 6, 2011. Signed as a free agent by **St. Louis**, July 2, 2012.

WRIGHT, James

(RIGHT, JAYMZ) **WPG**

Center. Shoots left. 6'4", 200 lbs. Born, Saskatoon, Sask., March 24, 1990. Tampa Bay's 2nd choice, 117th overall, in 2008 Entry Draft.

2005-06	Sask. Contacts	SMHL	41	13	19	32	43	....	....	....	....	....	....	....	....	....	....	....	....	....	....	....	....	....	....
	Vancouver Giants	WHL	2	0	0	0	2	....	....	....	....	....	....	....	....	....	....	....	....	....	....	....	....	....	....
2006-07	Vancouver Giants	WHL	48	5	7	12	31	....	....	....	....	....	....	....	....	....	14	3	1	4	0	....	....	....	....
2007-08	Vancouver Giants	WHL	60	13	23	36	21	....	....	....	....	....	....	....	....	....	6	1	0	1	2	....	....	....	....
2008-09	Vancouver Giants	WHL	71	21	26	47	54	....	....	....	....	....	....	....	....	....	17	3	7	10	13	....	....	....	....
2009-10	**Tampa Bay**	**NHL**	**48**	**2**	**3**	**5**	**18**	**0**	**0**	**0**	**25**	**8.0**	**–9**	**169**	**45.6**	**11:39**	....	....	....	....	....	....	....	....	....
	Vancouver Giants	WHL	21	6	13	19	17	....	....	....	....	....	....	....	....	....	16	7	9	16	4	....	....	....	....
2010-11	**Tampa Bay**	**NHL**	**1**	**0**	**0**	**0**	**0**	**0**	**0**	**0**	**0**	**0.0**	**–2**	**2**	**0.0**	**4:36**	....	....	....	....	....	....	....	....	....
	Norfolk Admirals	AHL	80	16	31	47	64	....	....	....	....	....	....	....	....	....	6	1	0	1	8	....	....	....	....
2011-12	Norfolk Admirals	AHL	22	1	4	5	6	....	....	....	....	....	....	....	....	....	....	....	....	....	....	....	....	....	....
	San Antonio	AHL	54	11	17	28	23	....	....	....	....	....	....	....	....	....	10	3	4	7	2	....	....	....	....
2012-13	San Antonio	AHL	40	5	12	17	31	....	....	....	....	....	....	....	....	....	....	....	....	....	....	....	....	....	....
	Winnipeg	**NHL**	**38**	**2**	**3**	**5**	**31**	**0**	**0**	**0**	**32**	**6.3**	**–5**	**46**	**47.8**	**11:36**	....	....	....	....	....	....	....	....	....
	NHL Totals		**87**	**4**	**6**	**10**	**49**	**0**	**0**	**0**	**57**	**7.0**		**217**	**45.6**	**11:33**	....	....	....	....	....	....	....	....	....

Traded to **Florida** by **Tampa Bay** with Mike Vernace for Mike Kostka and Evan Oberg, December 2, 2011. Claimed on waivers by **Winnipeg** from **Florida**, January 18, 2013.

WYMAN, J.T.

(WIGH-muhn, JAY-tea) **COL**

Right wing. Shoots right. 6'2", 199 lbs. Born, Edina, MN, February 27, 1986. Montreal's 3rd choice, 100th overall, in 2004 Entry Draft.

2001-02	Blake Bears	High-MN	26	7	5	12	....	....	....	....	....	....	....	....	....	....	....	....	....	....	....	....	....	....	....
2002-03	Blake Bears	High-MN	28	17	23	40	12	....	....	....	....	....	....	....	....	....	....	....	....	....	....	....	....	....	....
2003-04	Blake Bears	High-MN	27	31	24	55	4	....	....	....	....	....	....	....	....	....	....	....	....	....	....	....	....	....	....
	Team Southwest	UMEHL	24	8	8	16	....	....	....	....	....	....	....	....	....	....	....	....	....	....	....	....	....	....	....
2004-05	Dartmouth	ECAC	33	5	6	11	4	....	....	....	....	....	....	....	....	....	....	....	....	....	....	....	....	....	....
2005-06	Dartmouth	ECAC	28	8	12	20	6	....	....	....	....	....	....	....	....	....	....	....	....	....	....	....	....	....	....
2006-07	Dartmouth	ECAC	33	13	11	24	20	....	....	....	....	....	....	....	....	....	....	....	....	....	....	....	....	....	....
2007-08	Dartmouth	ECAC	29	15	15	30	18	....	....	....	....	....	....	....	....	....	....	....	....	....	....	....	....	....	....
	Hamilton	AHL	8	0	1	1	5	....	....	....	....	....	....	....	....	....	....	....	....	....	....	....	....	....	....
2008-09	Hamilton	AHL	52	6	5	11	8	....	....	....	....	....	....	....	....	....	6	0	1	1	2	....	....	....	....
	Cincinnati	ECHL	15	0	8	8	4	....	....	....	....	....	....	....	....	....	....	....	....	....	....	....	....	....	....
2009-10	**Montreal**	**NHL**	**3**	**0**	**0**	**0**	**0**	**0**	**0**	**0**	**0**	**0.0**	**–2**	**1**	**0.0**	**4:23**	....	....	....	....	....	....	....	....	....
	Hamilton	AHL	76	17	20	37	12	....	....	....	....	....	....	....	....	....	19	1	3	4	2	....	....	....	....
2010-11	Hamilton	AHL	80	18	18	36	36	....	....	....	....	....	....	....	....	....	20	3	5	8	8	....	....	....	....
2011-12	**Tampa Bay**	**NHL**	**40**	**2**	**9**	**11**	**8**	**0**	**0**	**1**	**31**	**6.5**	**1**	**57**	**38.6**	**10:33**	....	....	....	....	....	....	....	....	....
	Norfolk Admirals	AHL	29	6	6	12	6	....	....	....	....	....	....	....	....	....	....	....	....	....	....	....	....	....	....
2012-13	Syracuse Crunch	AHL	76	13	25	38	34	....	....	....	....	....	....	....	....	....	18	3	4	7	11	....	....	....	....
	Tampa Bay	**NHL**	**1**	**0**	**0**	**0**	**0**	**0**	**0**	**0**	**0**	**0.0**	**–1**	**11**	**63.6**	**13:31**	....	....	....	....	....	....	....	....	....
	NHL Totals		**44**	**2**	**9**	**11**	**8**	**0**	**0**	**1**	**31**	**6.5**		**69**	**42.0**	**10:12**	....	....	....	....	....	....	....	....	....

Signed as a free agent by **Tampa Bay**, July 1, 2011. Signed as a free agent by **Colorado**, July 6, 2013.

YAKUPOV, Nail

(YA-kuh-pawv, NAY-uhl) **EDM**

Right wing. Shoots left. 5'11", 185 lbs. Born, Nizhnekamsk, Russia, October 6, 1993. Edmonton's 1st choice, 1st overall, in 2012 Entry Draft.

			Regular Season														Playoffs								
Season	Club	League	GP	G	A	Pts	PIM	PP	SH	GW	S	%	+/-	TF	F%	Min	GP	G	A	Pts	PIM	PP	SH	GW	Min
2009-10	Nizhnekamsk Jr.	Russia-Jr.	14	4	2	6	26	....	....	....	....	....	....	....	....	....	....	....	....	....	....	....	....	....	....
2010-11	Sarnia Sting	OHL	65	49	52	101	71	....	....	....	....	....	....	....	....	....	....	....	....	....	....	....	....	....	....
2011-12	Sarnia Sting	OHL	42	31	38	69	30	....	....	....	....	....	....	....	....	....	6	2	3	5	4	....	....	....	....
2012-13	Nizhnekamsk	KHL	22	9	9	18	33	....	....	....	....	....	....	....	....	....	....	....	....	....	....	....	....	....	....
	Edmonton	NHL	48	17	14	31	24	6	0	2	81	21.0	-4	6	0.0	14:34	....	....	....	....	....	....	....	....	....
	NHL Totals		48	17	14	31	24	6	0	2	81	21.0		6	0.0	14:34	....	....	....	....	....	....	....	....	....

OHL All-Rookie Team (2011) • OHL Rookie of the Year (2011) • Canadian Major Junior Rookie of the Year (2011) • Canadian Major Junior Top Prospect of the Year (2012)
Signed as a free agent by **Nizhnekamsk** (KHL), September 20, 2012.

YANDLE, Keith

(Yan-duhl, KEETH) **PHX**

Defense. Shoots left. 6'1", 190 lbs. Born, Boston, MA, September 9, 1986. Phoenix's 3rd choice, 105th overall, in 2005 Entry Draft.

2004-05	Cushing	High-MA	34	14	40	54	52	....	....	....	....	....	....	....	....	....	....	....	....	....	....	....	....	....	....
2005-06	Moncton Wildcats	QMJHL	66	25	59	84	109	....	....	....	....	....	....	....	....	....	21	6	14	20	36	....	....	....	....
2006-07	Phoenix	NHL	7	0	2	2	8	0	0	0	10	0.0	0	0	0.0	20:10	....	....	....	....	....	....	....	....	....
	San Antonio	AHL	69	6	27	33	97	....	....	....	....	....	....	....	....	....	....	....	....	....	....	....	....	....	....
2007-08	Phoenix	NHL	43	5	7	12	14	4	0	0	72	6.9	-12	0	0.0	14:04	....	....	....	....	....	....	....	....	....
	San Antonio	AHL	30	1	14	15	80	....	....	....	....	....	....	....	....	....	5	0	0	0	8	....	....	....	....
2008-09	Phoenix	NHL	69	4	26	30	37	1	0	0	118	3.4	-4	0	0.0	16:37	....	....	....	....	....	....	....	....	....
2009-10	Phoenix	NHL	82	12	29	41	45	5	0	2	145	8.3	16	0	0.0	20:14	7	2	3	5	4	1	0	0	17:12
2010-11	Phoenix	NHL	82	11	48	59	68	3	0	0	199	5.5	12	0	0.0	24:23	4	0	5	5	0	0	0	0	25:50
2011-12	Phoenix	NHL	82	11	32	43	51	0	0	2	196	5.6	5	0	0.0	22:20	16	1	8	9	10	0	0	0	21:27
2012-13	Phoenix	NHL	48	10	20	30	54	5	0	3	130	7.7	4	0	0.0	22:15	....	....	....	....	....	....	....	....	....
	NHL Totals		413	53	164	217	277	18	0	7	870	6.1		0	0.0	20:28	27	3	16	19	14	1	0	0	21:00

QMJHL First All-Star Team (2006) • Canadian Major Junior First All-Star Team (2006) • Canadian Major Junior Defenseman of the Year (2006)
Played in NHL All-Star Game (2011, 2012)

YIP, Brandon

(YIHP, BRAN-duhn) **PHX**

Right wing. Shoots right. 6'1", 200 lbs. Born, Vancouver, B.C., April 25, 1985. Colorado's 7th choice, 239th overall, in 2004 Entry Draft.

2003-04	Coquitlam	BCHL	56	31	38	69	87	....	....	....	....	....	....	....	....	....	4	1	2	3	14	....	....	....	....
2004-05	Coquitlam	BCHL	43	20	42	62	92	....	....	....	....	....	....	....	....	....	7	6	1	7	12	....	....	....	....
2005-06	Boston University	H-East	39	9	22	31	59	....	....	....	....	....	....	....	....	....	....	....	....	....	....	....	....	....	....
2006-07	Boston University	H-East	18	5	6	11	29	....	....	....	....	....	....	....	....	....	....	....	....	....	....	....	....	....	....
2007-08	Boston University	H-East	37	11	12	23	28	....	....	....	....	....	....	....	....	....	....	....	....	....	....	....	....	....	....
2008-09	Boston University	H-East	45	20	23	43	118	....	....	....	....	....	....	....	....	....	....	....	....	....	....	....	....	....	....
2009-10	Colorado	NHL	32	11	8	19	22	4	0	2	65	16.9	5	1	0.0	14:41	6	2	2	4	6	0	0	0	17:51
	Lake Erie	AHL	6	2	0	2	4	....	....	....	....	....	....	....	....	....	....	....	....	....	....	....	....	....	....
2010-11	Colorado	NHL	71	12	10	22	54	3	1	1	127	9.4	-22	14	35.7	13:44	....	....	....	....	....	....	....	....	....
2011-12	Colorado	NHL	10	0	0	0	8	0	0	0	12	0.0	1	2	0.0	9:55	....	....	....	....	....	....	....	....	....
	Nashville	NHL	25	3	4	7	20	0	0	0	29	10.3	0	5	40.0	10:59	10	1	1	2	6	0	0	0	8:57
2012-13	Nashville	NHL	34	3	5	8	26	0	0	0	35	8.6	-3	21	38.1	12:02	....	....	....	....	....	....	....	....	....
	NHL Totals		172	29	27	56	130	7	1	3	268	10.8		43	34.9	12:57	16	3	3	6	12	0	0	0	12:17

Hockey East All-Rookie Team (2006) • Hockey East Rookie of the Year (2006)
• Missed majority of 2009-10 due to hand injury in pre-season game at St. Louis, September 18, 2009. Claimed on waivers by **Nashville** from **Colorado**, January 19, 2012. Signed as a free agent by **Phoenix**, July 19, 2013.

YONKMAN, Nolan

(YAWNK-man, NOH-luhn) **ANA**

Defense. Shoots right. 6'6", 253 lbs. Born, Punnichy, Sask., April 1, 1981. Washington's 5th choice, 37th overall, in 1999 Entry Draft.

1996-97	Naicam Vikings	SAHA	64	15	23	38	36	....	....	....	....	....	....	....	....	....	....	....	....	....	....	....	....	....	....
	Kelowna Rockets	WHL	4	0	0	0	0	....	....	....	....	....	....	....	....	....	....	....	....	....	....	....	....	....	....
1997-98	Kelowna Rockets	WHL	65	0	2	2	36	....	....	....	....	....	....	....	....	....	7	0	0	0	2	....	....	....	....
1998-99	Kelowna Rockets	WHL	61	1	6	7	129	....	....	....	....	....	....	....	....	....	6	0	0	0	6	....	....	....	....
99-2000	Kelowna Rockets	WHL	71	5	7	12	153	....	....	....	....	....	....	....	....	....	5	0	0	0	8	....	....	....	....
2000-01	Kelowna Rockets	WHL	7	0	1	1	19	....	....	....	....	....	....	....	....	....	....	....	....	....	....	....	....	....	....
	Brandon	WHL	51	6	10	16	94	....	....	....	....	....	....	....	....	....	6	0	1	1	12	....	....	....	....
2001-02	Washington	NHL	11	1	0	1	4	0	0	0	7	14.3	3	0	0.0	12:44	....	....	....	....	....	....	....	....	....
	Portland Pirates	AHL	59	4	3	7	116	....	....	....	....	....	....	....	....	....	....	....	....	....	....	....	....	....	....
2002-03	Portland Pirates	AHL	24	1	4	5	40	....	....	....	....	....	....	....	....	....	3	0	1	1	2	....	....	....	....
2003-04	Washington	NHL	1	0	0	0	0	0	0	0	0	0.0	0	0	0.0	5:00	....	....	....	....	....	....	....	....	....
	Portland Pirates	AHL	4	0	0	0	11	....	....	....	....	....	....	....	....	....	....	....	....	....	....	....	....	....	....
2004-05	Portland Pirates	AHL	32	0	3	3	68	....	....	....	....	....	....	....	....	....	....	....	....	....	....	....	....	....	....
2005-06	Washington	NHL	38	0	7	7	86	0	0	0	14	0.0	1	0	0.0	8:13	....	....	....	....	....	....	....	....	....
	Hershey Bears	AHL	6	0	0	0	15	....	....	....	....	....	....	....	....	....	....	....	....	....	....	....	....	....	....
2006-07	Milwaukee	AHL	77	3	10	13	113	....	....	....	....	....	....	....	....	....	4	0	0	0	2	....	....	....	....
2007-08	Milwaukee	AHL	69	0	7	7	103	....	....	....	....	....	....	....	....	....	6	0	1	1	18	....	....	....	....
2008-09	Milwaukee	AHL	61	3	7	10	80	....	....	....	....	....	....	....	....	....	11	0	0	0	15	....	....	....	....
2009-10	Milwaukee	AHL	76	2	7	9	170	....	....	....	....	....	....	....	....	....	7	0	1	1	2	....	....	....	....
2010-11	Phoenix	NHL	16	0	1	1	39	0	0	0	8	0.0	5	0	0.0	12:08	....	....	....	....	....	....	....	....	....
	San Antonio	AHL	56	1	4	5	104	....	....	....	....	....	....	....	....	....	....	....	....	....	....	....	....	....	....
2011-12	Florida	NHL	1	0	0	0	0	0	0	0	0	0.0	0	0	0.0	6:19	....	....	....	....	....	....	....	....	....
	San Antonio	AHL	66	2	11	13	102	....	....	....	....	....	....	....	....	....	10	0	2	2	8	....	....	....	....
2012-13	San Antonio	AHL	71	0	7	7	93	....	....	....	....	....	....	....	....	....	....	....	....	....	....	....	....	....	....
	Florida	NHL	7	0	0	0	11	0	0	0	4	0.0	-1	0	0.0	9:46	....	....	....	....	....	....	....	....	....
	NHL Totals		74	1	8	9	140	0	0	0	33	3.0		0	0.0	9:49	....	....	....	....	....	....	....	....	....

• Missed majority of 2002-03 due to abdominal injury in training camp, September 25, 2002. • Missed majority of 2003-04 and 2004-05 due to knee injury vs. Worcester (AHL), October 23, 2003. Signed as a free agent by **Nashville**, July 17, 2006. Signed as a free agent by **Phoenix**, July 3, 2010. Signed as a free agent by **Florida**, July 1, 2011. Signed as a free agent by **Anaheim**, July 9, 2013.

ZAJAC, Travis

(ZAY-jak, TRA-vihs) **N.J.**

Center. Shoots right. 6'3", 205 lbs. Born, Winnipeg, Man., May 13, 1985. New Jersey's 1st choice, 20th overall, in 2004 Entry Draft.

2002-03	Salmon Arm	BCHL	59	16	36	52	27	....	....	....	....	....	....	....	....	....	11	2	4	6	6	....	....	....	....
2003-04	Salmon Arm	BCHL	59	43	69	112	110	....	....	....	....	....	....	....	....	....	14	10	13	23	10	....	....	....	....
2004-05	North Dakota	WCHA	45	20	19	39	16	....	....	....	....	....	....	....	....	....	....	....	....	....	....	....	....	....	....
2005-06	North Dakota	WCHA	46	18	29	47	20	....	....	....	....	....	....	....	....	....	....	....	....	....	....	....	....	....	....
	Albany River Rats	AHL	2	0	1	1	2	....	....	....	....	....	....	....	....	....	....	....	....	....	....	....	....	....	....
2006-07	New Jersey	NHL	80	17	25	42	16	6	0	2	134	12.7	1	904	46.9	16:03	11	1	4	5	4	0	0	0	16:22
2007-08	New Jersey	NHL	82	14	20	34	31	5	0	1	155	9.0	-11	1032	51.2	16:44	5	0	1	1	4	0	0	0	13:35
2008-09	New Jersey	NHL	82	20	42	62	29	5	1	2	185	10.8	33	1287	53.1	18:39	7	1	3	4	6	0	0	1	17:51
2009-10	New Jersey	NHL	82	25	42	67	24	6	0	4	210	11.9	22	1373	52.9	20:13	5	1	1	2	2	0	0	0	21:46
2010-11	New Jersey	NHL	82	13	31	44	24	2	1	1	173	7.5	-6	1278	55.3	19:47	....	....	....	....	....	....	....	....	....
2011-12	New Jersey	NHL	15	2	4	6	4	1	0	1	25	8.0	-3	204	57.8	17:22	24	7	7	14	4	1	0	2	20:29
2012-13	New Jersey	NHL	48	7	13	20	22	1	1	1	82	8.5	-5	881	57.4	19:32	....	....	....	....	....	....	....	....	....
	NHL Totals		471	98	177	275	150	26	3	12	964	10.2		6959	53.1	18:24	52	10	16	26	20	1	0	3	18:43

WCHA All-Rookie Team (2005) • NCAA Championship All-Tournament Team (2005)
• Missed majority of 2011-12 due to leg injury during off-ice workout, August 17, 2011.

ZALEWSKI, Steven

(zuh-LEH-skee, STEE-vehn)

Center. Shoots left. 6', 195 lbs. Born, Utica, NY, August 20, 1986. San Jose's 5th choice, 153rd overall, in 2004 Entry Draft.

			Regular Season														Playoffs								
Season	Club	League	GP	G	A	Pts	PIM	PP	SH	GW	S	%	+/-	TF	F%	Min	GP	G	A	Pts	PIM	PP	SH	GW	Min
2003-04	Northwood	High-NY	40	32	34	66	22	....	....	....	....	....	....	....	....	....	....	....	....	....	....	....	....	....	....
2004-05	Clarkson Knights	ECAC	39	12	7	19	60	....	....	....	....	....	....	....	....	....	....	....	....	....	....	....	....	....	....
2005-06	Clarkson Knights	ECAC	35	9	13	22	50	....	....	....	....	....	....	....	....	....	....	....	....	....	....	....	....	....	....
2006-07	Clarkson Knights	ECAC	39	16	18	34	44	....	....	....	....	....	....	....	....	....	....	....	....	....	....	....	....	....	....
2007-08	Clarkson Knights	ECAC	38	21	12	33	34	....	....	....	....	....	....	....	....	....	....	....	....	....	....	....	....	....	....
	Worcester Sharks	AHL	7	2	4	6	0	....	....	....	....	....	....	....	....	....	....	....	....	....	....	....	....	....	....
2008-09	Worcester Sharks	AHL	75	13	26	39	26	....	....	....	....	....	....	....	....	....	12	0	1	1	6	....	....	....	....
2009-10	**San Jose**	**NHL**	**3**	**0**	**0**	**0**	**0**	**0**	**0**	**0**	**3**	**0.0**	**–2**	**5**	**40.0**	**8:19**	....	....	....	....	....	....	....	....	....
	Worcester Sharks	AHL	78	22	40	62	20	....	....	....	....	....	....	....	....	....	11	1	5	6	4	....	....	....	....
2010-11	Worcester Sharks	AHL	50	4	17	21	14	....	....	....	....	....	....	....	....	....	....	....	....	....	....	....	....	....	....
	Albany Devils	AHL	31	11	12	23	14	....	....	....	....	....	....	....	....	....	....	....	....	....	....	....	....	....	....
2011-12	**New Jersey**	**NHL**	**7**	**0**	**0**	**0**	**0**	**0**	**0**	**0**	**6**	**0.0**	**–2**	**44**	**50.0**	**10:34**	....	....	....	....	....	....	....	....	....
	Albany Devils	AHL	69	19	22	41	48	....	....	....	....	....	....	....	....	....	....	....	....	....	....	....	....	....	....
2012-13	Albany Devils	AHL	73	11	30	41	52	....	....	....	....	....	....	....	....	....	....	....	....	....	....	....	....	....	....
	NHL Totals		**10**	**0**	**0**	**0**	**0**	**0**	**0**	**0**	**9**	**0.0**		**49**	**49.0**	**9:53**	....	....	....	....	....	....	....	....	....

ECAC First All-Star Team (2008)

Traded to **New Jersey** by **San Jose** with Jay Leach for Michael Swift and Patrick Davis, February 9, 2011. Signed as a free agent by **Rauma** (Finland), July 18, 2013.

ZANON, Greg

(ZA-nuhn, GREHG)

Defense. Shoots left. 5'11", 201 lbs. Born, Burnaby, B.C., June 5, 1980. Ottawa's 6th choice, 156th overall, in 2000 Entry Draft.

			Regular Season														Playoffs								
Season	Club	League	GP	G	A	Pts	PIM	PP	SH	GW	S	%	+/-	TF	F%	Min	GP	G	A	Pts	PIM	PP	SH	GW	Min
1995-96	Burnaby Beavers	Minor-BC	49	16	27	43	142	....	....	....	....	....	....	....	....	....	....	....	....	....	....	....	....	....	....
1996-97	Victoria Salsa	BCHL	53	4	13	17	124	....	....	....	....	....	....	....	....	....	....	....	....	....	....	....	....	....	....
1997-98	Victoria Salsa	BCHL	59	11	21	32	108	....	....	....	....	....	....	....	....	....	7	0	2	2	10	....	....	....	....
1998-99	South Surrey	BCHL	59	17	54	71	154	....	....	....	....	....	....	....	....	....	....	....	....	....	....	....	....	....	....
99-2000	Nebraska-Omaha	CCHA	42	3	26	29	56	....	....	....	....	....	....	....	....	....	....	....	....	....	....	....	....	....	....
2000-01	Nebraska-Omaha	CCHA	39	12	16	28	64	....	....	....	....	....	....	....	....	....	....	....	....	....	....	....	....	....	....
2001-02	Nebraska-Omaha	CCHA	41	9	16	25	54	....	....	....	....	....	....	....	....	....	....	....	....	....	....	....	....	....	....
2002-03	Nebraska-Omaha	CCHA	32	6	19	25	44	....	....	....	....	....	....	....	....	....	....	....	....	....	....	....	....	....	....
2003-04	Milwaukee	AHL	62	4	12	16	59	....	....	....	....	....	....	....	....	....	22	2	6	8	31	....	....	....	....
2004-05	Milwaukee	AHL	80	2	17	19	59	....	....	....	....	....	....	....	....	....	7	0	1	1	10	....	....	....	....
2005-06	**Nashville**	**NHL**	**4**	**0**	**2**	**2**	**6**	**0**	**0**	**0**	**3**	**0.0**	**0**	**0**	**0.0**	**17:19**	....	....	....	....	....	....	....	....	....
	Milwaukee	AHL	71	8	27	35	55	....	....	....	....	....	....	....	....	....	21	1	7	8	24	....	....	....	....
2006-07	**Nashville**	**NHL**	**66**	**3**	**5**	**8**	**32**	**0**	**0**	**0**	**43**	**7.0**	**16**	**0**	**0.0**	**17:20**	**5**	**0**	**2**	**2**	**2**	**0**	**0**	**0**	**20:44**
	Milwaukee	AHL	2	0	2	2	0	....	....	....	....	....	....	....	....	....	....	....	....	....	....	....	....	....	....
2007-08	**Nashville**	**NHL**	**78**	**0**	**5**	**5**	**24**	**0**	**0**	**0**	**38**	**0.0**	**–5**	**0**	**0.0**	**18:28**	**6**	**0**	**2**	**2**	**4**	**0**	**0**	**0**	**18:45**
2008-09	**Nashville**	**NHL**	**82**	**4**	**7**	**11**	**38**	**0**	**0**	**1**	**54**	**7.4**	**8**	**0**	**0.0**	**20:51**	....	....	....	....	....	....	....	....	....
2009-10	**Minnesota**	**NHL**	**81**	**2**	**13**	**15**	**36**	**0**	**0**	**0**	**59**	**3.4**	**–10**	**1**	**0.0**	**22:22**	....	....	....	....	....	....	....	....	....
2010-11	**Minnesota**	**NHL**	**82**	**0**	**7**	**7**	**48**	**0**	**0**	**0**	**55**	**0.0**	**–5**	**0**	**0.0**	**21:33**	....	....	....	....	....	....	....	....	....
2011-12	**Minnesota**	**NHL**	**39**	**2**	**4**	**6**	**14**	**0**	**0**	**1**	**27**	**7.4**	**–1**	**0**	**0.0**	**18:37**	....	....	....	....	....	....	....	....	....
	Boston	**NHL**	**17**	**1**	**1**	**2**	**4**	**0**	**0**	**1**	**14**	**7.1**	**4**	**0**	**0.0**	**15:54**	**7**	**0**	**1**	**1**	**0**	**0**	**0**	**0**	**13:43**
2012-13	**Colorado**	**NHL**	**44**	**0**	**6**	**6**	**28**	**0**	**0**	**0**	**40**	**0.0**	**–16**	**0**	**0.0**	**19:20**	....	....	....	....	....	....	....	....	....
	NHL Totals		**493**	**12**	**50**	**62**	**230**	**0**	**0**	**3**	**333**	**3.6**		**1**	**0.0**	**19:51**	**18**	**0**	**5**	**5**	**6**	**0**	**0**	**0**	**17:20**

CCHA First All-Star Team (2001) • NCAA West Second All-American Team (2001, 2002) • CCHA Second All-Star Team (2002)

Signed as a free agent by **Nashville**, July 9, 2004. Signed as a free agent by **Minnesota**, July 1, 2009. Traded to **Boston** by **Minnesota** for Steven Kampfer, February 27, 2012. Signed as a free agent by **Colorado**, July 1, 2012.

ZEILER, John

(ZIGH-luhr, JAWN)

Right wing. Shoots right. 5'11", 204 lbs. Born, Jefferson Hills, PA, November 21, 1982. Phoenix's 7th choice, 132nd overall, in 2002 Entry Draft.

			Regular Season														Playoffs								
Season	Club	League	GP	G	A	Pts	PIM	PP	SH	GW	S	%	+/-	TF	F%	Min	GP	G	A	Pts	PIM	PP	SH	GW	Min
99-2000	Pittsburgh	PAHA	27	17	15	32	94	....	....	....	....	....	....	....	....	....	....	....	....	....	....	....	....	....	....
2000-01	Sioux City	USHL	56	8	20	28	45	....	....	....	....	....	....	....	....	....	2	0	0	0	26	....	....	....	....
2001-02	Sioux City	USHL	60	23	27	50	116	....	....	....	....	....	....	....	....	....	12	2	3	5	25	....	....	....	....
2002-03	St. Lawrence	ECAC	37	10	17	27	28	....	....	....	....	....	....	....	....	....	....	....	....	....	....	....	....	....	....
2003-04	St. Lawrence	ECAC	41	8	*28	36	42	....	....	....	....	....	....	....	....	....	....	....	....	....	....	....	....	....	....
2004-05	St. Lawrence	ECAC	38	9	23	32	42	....	....	....	....	....	....	....	....	....	....	....	....	....	....	....	....	....	....
2005-06	St. Lawrence	ECAC	28	13	15	28	28	....	....	....	....	....	....	....	....	....	....	....	....	....	....	....	....	....	....
	San Antonio	AHL	8	0	1	1	10	....	....	....	....	....	....	....	....	....	....	....	....	....	....	....	....	....	....
	Lubbock	CHL	4	2	0	2	16	....	....	....	....	....	....	....	....	....	....	....	....	....	....	....	....	....	....
2006-07	Manchester	AHL	56	12	16	28	70	....	....	....	....	....	....	....	....	....	16	3	2	5	14	....	....	....	....
	Los Angeles	**NHL**	**23**	**1**	**2**	**3**	**22**	**0**	**0**	**0**	**12**	**8.3**	**–2**	**22**	**40.9**	**8:36**	....	....	....	....	....	....	....	....	....
2007-08	**Los Angeles**	**NHL**	**36**	**0**	**1**	**1**	**23**	**0**	**0**	**0**	**18**	**0.0**	**–6**	**31**	**38.7**	**8:29**	....	....	....	....	....	....	....	....	....
	Manchester	AHL	45	6	5	11	40	....	....	....	....	....	....	....	....	....	4	0	2	2	8	....	....	....	....
2008-09	**Los Angeles**	**NHL**	**27**	**0**	**1**	**1**	**42**	**0**	**0**	**0**	**3**	**0.0**	**–2**	**5**	**60.0**	**6:33**	....	....	....	....	....	....	....	....	....
	Manchester	AHL	2	0	1	1	4	....	....	....	....	....	....	....	....	....	....	....	....	....	....	....	....	....	....
2009-10	Manchester	AHL	65	11	9	20	31	....	....	....	....	....	....	....	....	....	16	4	3	7	4	....	....	....	....
2010-11	**Los Angeles**	**NHL**	**4**	**0**	**0**	**0**	**0**	**0**	**0**	**0**	**1**	**0.0**	**–1**	**10**	**50.0**	**5:36**	....	....	....	....	....	....	....	....	....
	Manchester	AHL	69	9	19	28	86	....	....	....	....	....	....	....	....	....	5	1	1	2	4	....	....	....	....
2011-12	Augsburg	Germany	52	7	21	28	58	....	....	....	....	....	....	....	....	....	2	0	0	0	4	....	....	....	....
2012-13	Augsburg	Germany	52	8	15	23	89	....	....	....	....	....	....	....	....	....	2	0	1	1	2	....	....	....	....
	NHL Totals		**90**	**1**	**4**	**5**	**87**	**0**	**0**	**0**	**34**	**2.9**		**68**	**42.6**	**7:48**	....	....	....	....	....	....	....	....	....

ECAC All-Rookie Team (2003)

Signed as a free agent by **San Antonio** (AHL), March 18, 2006. Signed as a free agent by **Los Angeles**, February 17, 2007. • Missed majority of 2008-09 due to pre-season groin injury and as a healthy reserve. Signed as a free agent by **Augsburg** (Germany), August 9, 2011.

ZETTERBERG, Henrik

(ZEH-tuhr-buhrg, HEHN-rihk) **DET**

Left wing. Shoots left. 5'11", 197 lbs. Born, Njurunda, Sweden, October 9, 1980. Detroit's 4th choice, 210th overall, in 1999 Entry Draft.

			Regular Season														Playoffs								
Season	Club	League	GP	G	A	Pts	PIM	PP	SH	GW	S	%	+/-	TF	F%	Min	GP	G	A	Pts	PIM	PP	SH	GW	Min
1997-98	Timra IK Jr.	Swe-Jr.	18	9	5	14	4	....	....	....	....	....	....	....	....	....	....	....	....	....	....	....	....	....	....
	Timra IK	Sweden-2	16	1	2	3	4	....	....	....	....	....	....	....	....	....	4	0	1	1	0	....	....	....	....
1998-99	Timra IK	Sweden-2	37	15	13	28	2	....	....	....	....	....	....	....	....	....	4	2	1	3	2	....	....	....	....
99-2000	Timra IK	Sweden-2	32	20	14	34	20	....	....	....	....	....	....	....	....	....	10	10	4	14	4	....	....	....	....
2000-01	Timra IK	Sweden	47	15	31	46	24	....	....	....	....	....	....	....	....	....	....	....	....	....	....	....	....	....	....
2001-02	Timra IK	Sweden	48	10	22	32	20	....	....	....	....	....	....	....	....	....	....	....	....	....	....	....	....	....	....
	Sweden	Olympics	4	0	1	1	0	....	....	....	....	....	....	....	....	....	....	....	....	....	....	....	....	....	....
2002-03	**Detroit**	**NHL**	**79**	**22**	**22**	**44**	**8**	**5**	**1**	**4**	**135**	**16.3**	**6**	**401**	**46.1**	**16:19**	**4**	**1**	**0**	**1**	**0**	**0**	**0**	**0**	**18:19**
2003-04	**Detroit**	**NHL**	**61**	**15**	**28**	**43**	**14**	**7**	**1**	**2**	**137**	**10.9**	**15**	**627**	**45.6**	**18:15**	**12**	**2**	**2**	**4**	**4**	**0**	**0**	**0**	**17:17**
2004-05	Timra IK	Sweden	50	19	31	*50	24	....	....	....	....	....	....	....	....	....	7	6	2	8	2	....	....	....	....
2005-06	**Detroit**	**NHL**	**77**	**39**	**46**	**85**	**30**	**17**	**1**	**9**	**270**	**14.4**	**29**	**583**	**50.3**	**18:57**	**6**	**6**	**0**	**6**	**2**	**4**	**0**	**0**	**21:43**
	Sweden	Olympics	8	3	3	6	0	....	....	....	....	....	....	....	....	....	....	....	....	....	....	....	....	....	....
2006-07	**Detroit**	**NHL**	**63**	**33**	**35**	**68**	**36**	**11**	**1**	***10**	**224**	**14.7**	**26**	**888**	**52.5**	**20:50**	**18**	**6**	**8**	**14**	**12**	**3**	**0**	**1**	**22:45**
2007-08 ◆	**Detroit**	**NHL**	**75**	**43**	**49**	**92**	**34**	**16**	**1**	**7**	**358**	**12.0**	**30**	**1210**	**55.0**	**22:04**	**22**	***13**	**14**	***27**	**16**	**4**	***2**	**4**	**22:36**
2008-09	**Detroit**	**NHL**	**77**	**31**	**42**	**73**	**36**	**12**	**2**	**5**	**309**	**10.0**	**13**	**1189**	**53.3**	**19:53**	**23**	**11**	**13**	**24**	**13**	**4**	**0**	**0**	**22:10**
2009-10	**Detroit**	**NHL**	**74**	**23**	**47**	**70**	**26**	**3**	**0**	**6**	**309**	**7.4**	**12**	**1098**	**49.5**	**20:04**	**12**	**7**	**8**	**15**	**6**	**2**	**0**	**2**	**20:25**
	Sweden	Olympics	4	1	0	1	2	....	....	....	....	....	....	....	....	....	....	....	....	....	....	....	....	....	....
2010-11	**Detroit**	**NHL**	**80**	**24**	**56**	**80**	**40**	**10**	**0**	**3**	**306**	**7.8**	**–1**	**984**	**52.4**	**19:35**	**7**	**3**	**5**	**8**	**2**	**1**	**0**	**0**	**21:59**
2011-12	**Detroit**	**NHL**	**82**	**22**	**47**	**69**	**47**	**3**	**0**	**4**	**267**	**8.2**	**14**	**1115**	**49.2**	**19:50**	**5**	**2**	**1**	**3**	**4**	**2**	**0**	**0**	**23:05**
2012-13	EV Zug	Swiss	23	16	16	32	20	....	....	....	....	....	....	....	....	....	....	....	....	....	....	....	....	....	....
	Detroit	**NHL**	**46**	**11**	**37**	**48**	**18**	**4**	**2**	**5**	**173**	**6.4**	**2**	**544**	**48.4**	**20:31**	**14**	**4**	**8**	**12**	**8**	**1**	**0**	**1**	**19:59**
	NHL Totals		**714**	**263**	**409**	**672**	**289**	**88**	**9**	**55**	**2488**	**10.6**		**8639**	**50.9**	**19:35**	**123**	**55**	**59**	**114**	**67**	**21**	**2**	**8**	**21:19**

Swedish Elite League Rookie of the Year (2001) • NHL All-Rookie Team (2003) • NHL Second All-Star Team (2008) • Conn Smythe Trophy (2008) • NHL Foundation Player Award (2013)

Signed as a free agent by **Timra** (Sweden), September 20, 2004. Signed as a free agent by **Zug** (Swiss), October 8, 2012.

ZHARKOV, Vladimir

(zhar-KAWV, vla-DIH-meer) **N.J.**

Right wing. Shoots left. 6'1", 205 lbs. Born, Elektrostal, USSR, January 10, 1988. New Jersey's 4th choice, 77th overall, in 2006 Entry Draft.

			Regular Season														Playoffs								
Season	Club	League	GP	G	A	Pts	PIM	PP	SH	GW	S	%	+/-	TF	F%	Min	GP	G	A	Pts	PIM	PP	SH	GW	Min
2004-05	CSKA Moscow 2	Russia-3	STATISTICS NOT AVAILABLE																						
2005-06	CSKA Moscow	Russia	4	0	1	1	4										1	0	0	0	0				
	CSKA Moscow 2	Russia-3	48	17	22	39	86																		
2006-07	CSKA Moscow	Russia	47	4	1	5	18										12	0	1	1	2				
2007-08	CSKA Moscow	Russia	30	5	2	7	6																		
	CSKA Moscow 2	Russia-3	4	3	4	7	4										12	8	7	15	8				
2008-09	Lowell Devils	AHL	69	11	23	34	26																		
2009-10	**New Jersey**	**NHL**	**40**	**0**	**10**	**10**	**8**	**0**	**0**	**0**	**54**	**0.0**	**2**	**4**	**25.0**	**11:26**									
	Lowell Devils	AHL	23	6	15	21	6																		
2010-11	**New Jersey**	**NHL**	**38**	**2**	**2**	**4**	**2**	**0**	**0**	**0**	**40**	**5.0**	**3**	**6**	**33.3**	**11:20**									
	Albany Devils	AHL	31	8	11	19	19																		
2011-12	**New Jersey**	**NHL**	**4**	**0**	**0**	**0**	**0**	**0**	**0**	**0**	**0**	**0.0**	**–2**	**0**	**0.0**	**4:53**									
	Albany Devils	AHL	62	16	23	39	45																		
2012-13	CSKA Moscow	KHL	47	9	2	11	4										3	0	0	0	0				
	NHL Totals		**82**	**2**	**12**	**14**	**10**	**0**	**0**	**0**	**94**	**2.1**		**10**	**30.0**	**11:04**									

Signed as a free agent by **CSKA Moscow** (KHL), July 3, 2013.

ZIBANEJAD, Mika

(zih-BAN-ih-jad, MEEKA) **OTT**

Center. Shoots right. 6'2", 212 lbs. Born, Huddinge, Sweden, April 18, 1993. Ottawa's 1st choice, 6th overall, in 2011 Entry Draft.

2008-09	AIK IF Solna U18	Swe-U18	11	2	2	4	2																		
2009-10	Djurgarden U18	Swe-U18	28	14	22	36	18										5	5	4	9	4				
	Djurgarden Jr.	Swe-Jr.	14	2	2	4	4																		
2010-11	Djurgarden U18	Swe-U18	2	3	2	5	2																		
	Djurgarden Jr.	Swe-Jr.	27	12	9	21	12										3	1	2	3	0				
	Djurgarden	Sweden	26	5	4	9	2										7	1	1	2	2				
2011-12	**Ottawa**	**NHL**	**9**	**0**	**1**	**1**	**2**	**0**	**0**	**0**	**12**	**0.0**	**–3**	**50**	**44.0**	**12:54**									
	Djurgarden	Sweden	26	5	8	13	4																		
	Djurgarden Jr.	Swe-Jr.	1	0	0	0	2																		
	Djurgarden	Sweden-Q	10	4	2	6	2																		
2012-13	Binghamton	AHL	23	4	7	11	10																		
	Ottawa	**NHL**	**42**	**7**	**13**	**20**	**6**	**3**	**0**	**0**	**90**	**7.8**	**9**	**343**	**46.4**	**13:34**	**10**	**1**	**3**	**4**	**0**	**0**	**0**	**0**	**13:36**
	NHL Totals		**51**	**7**	**14**	**21**	**8**	**3**	**0**	**0**	**102**	**6.9**		**393**	**46.1**	**13:27**	**10**	**1**	**3**	**4**	**0**	**0**	**0**	**0**	**13:36**

• Assigned to **Djurgarden** (Sweden) by **Ottawa**, October 26, 2011.

ZIDLICKY, Marek

(zihd-LIH-kee, MAIR-ehk) **N.J.**

Defense. Shoots right. 5'11", 190 lbs. Born, Most, Czech., February 3, 1977. NY Rangers' 6th choice, 176th overall, in 2001 Entry Draft.

1994-95	HC Kladno	CzRep	30	2	2	4	38										11	1	1	2	10				
1995-96	HC Poldi Kladno	CzRep	37	4	5	9	74										7	1	1	2	8				
1996-97	HC Poldi Kladno	CzRep	49	5	16	21	60										2	0	0	0	0				
1997-98	Kladno	CzRep	51	2	13	15	121																		
1998-99	Kladno	CzRep	50	10	12	22	94																		
99-2000	HIFK Helsinki	Finland	47	4	16	20	66										9	3	2	5	24				
	HIFK Helsinki	EuroHL	4	2	2	4	10										1	0	0	0	0				
2000-01	HIFK Helsinki	Finland	51	12	25	37	146										5	0	1	1	6				
2001-02	HIFK Helsinki	Finland	56	11	29	40	107																		
2002-03	HIFK Helsinki	Finland	54	10	37	47	79										4	0	0	0	4				
2003-04	**Nashville**	**NHL**	**82**	**14**	**39**	**53**	**82**	**9**	**0**	**4**	**143**	**9.8**	**–16**	**0**	**0.0**	**20:02**	**1**	**0**	**0**	**0**	**0**	**0**	**0**	**0**	**2:16**
2004-05	HIFK Helsinki	Finland	49	11	20	31	91										5	0	3	3	14				
2005-06	**Nashville**	**NHL**	**67**	**12**	**37**	**49**	**82**	**10**	**0**	**1**	**113**	**10.6**	**8**	**0**	**0.0**	**20:04**	**2**	**0**	**1**	**1**	**2**	**0**	**0**	**0**	**15:19**
	Czech Republic	Olympics	7	4	1	5	16																		
2006-07	**Nashville**	**NHL**	**79**	**4**	**26**	**30**	**72**	**2**	**0**	**1**	**114**	**3.5**	**8**	**0**	**0.0**	**19:43**	**5**	**0**	**2**	**2**	**4**	**0**	**0**	**0**	**19:19**
2007-08	**Nashville**	**NHL**	**79**	**5**	**38**	**43**	**63**	**4**	**0**	**0**	**122**	**4.1**	**–5**	**0**	**0.0**	**20:50**	**6**	**0**	**3**	**3**	**8**	**0**	**0**	**0**	**19:04**
2008-09	**Minnesota**	**NHL**	**76**	**12**	**30**	**42**	**76**	**10**	**0**	**3**	**147**	**8.2**	**–12**	**0**	**0.0**	**22:07**									
2009-10	**Minnesota**	**NHL**	**78**	**6**	**37**	**43**	**67**	**4**	**0**	**3**	**116**	**5.2**	**–16**	**0**	**0.0**	**24:10**									
	Czech Republic	Olympics	5	0	5	5	2																		
2010-11	**Minnesota**	**NHL**	**46**	**7**	**17**	**24**	**30**	**3**	**0**	**0**	**53**	**13.2**	**–6**	**0**	**0.0**	**21:46**									
2011-12	**Minnesota**	**NHL**	**41**	**0**	**14**	**14**	**24**	**0**	**0**	**0**	**50**	**0.0**	**–6**	**0**	**0.0**	**20:40**									
	New Jersey	**NHL**	**22**	**2**	**6**	**8**	**10**	**2**	**0**	**1**	**20**	**10.0**	**0**	**0**	**0.0**	**22:34**	**24**	**1**	**8**	**9**	**22**	**0**	**0**	**0**	**23:47**
2012-13	Rytiri Kladno	CzRep	25	3	22	25	28																		
	New Jersey	**NHL**	**48**	**4**	**15**	**19**	**38**	**1**	**0**	**0**	**101**	**4.0**	**–12**	**0**	**0.0**	**21:00**									
	NHL Totals		**618**	**66**	**259**	**325**	**544**	**45**	**0**	**13**	**979**	**6.7**		**0**	**0.0**	**21:13**	**38**	**1**	**14**	**15**	**36**	**0**	**0**	**0**	**21:26**

Traded to **Nashville** by **NY Rangers** with Rem Murray and Tomas Kloucek for Mike Dunham, December 12, 2002. Signed as a free agent by **HIFK Helsinki** (Finland), September 17, 2004. Traded to **Minnesota** by **Nashville** for Ryan Jones and Minnesota's 2nd round choice (Charles-Olivier Roussel) in 2009 Entry Draft, July 1, 2008. Traded to **New Jersey** by **Minnesota** for Kurtis Foster, Nick Palmieri, Stephane Veilleux, Washington's 2nd round choice (previously acquired, later traded to Minnesota – Minnesota selected Raphael Bussieres) in 2012 Entry Draft and New Jersey's 3rd round choice (later traded to NY Islanders – NY Islanders selected Eamon McAdam), February 24 2012. Signed as a free agent by **Kladno** (CzRep), September 9, 2012.

ZIGOMANIS, Mike

(zih-goh-MAN-ihs, MIGHK)

Center. Shoots right. 6', 200 lbs. Born, Toronto, Ont., January 17, 1981. Carolina's 2nd choice, 46th overall, in 2001 Entry Draft.

1996-97	Wexford Raiders	MTHL	40	37	48	85	23																		
	Wexford Raiders	ON-Jr.A	8	2	5	7	2																		
1997-98	Kingston	OHL	62	23	51	74	30										12	1	6	7	2				
1998-99	Kingston	OHL	67	29	56	85	36										5	1	7	8	2				
99-2000	Kingston	OHL	59	40	54	94	49										5	0	4	4	0				
2000-01	Kingston	OHL	52	40	37	77	44																		
2001-02	Lowell	AHL	79	18	30	48	24										5	1	1	2	2				
2002-03	**Carolina**	**NHL**	**19**	**2**	**1**	**3**	**0**	**1**	**1**	**0**	**19**	**10.5**	**–4**	**147**	**59.2**	**9:43**									
	Lowell	AHL	38	13	18	31	19																		
2003-04	**Carolina**	**NHL**	**17**	**0**	**3**	**3**	**2**	**0**	**0**	**0**	**13**	**0.0**	**–1**	**108**	**53.7**	**8:37**									
	Lowell	AHL	61	17	35	52	56																		
2004-05	Lowell	AHL	76	29	31	60	71										11	4	7	11	8				
2005-06	**Carolina**	**NHL**	**21**	**1**	**0**	**1**	**4**	**0**	**0**	**0**	**16**	**6.3**	**1**	**72**	**50.0**	**9:25**									
	Lowell	AHL	11	6	7	13	19																		
	St. Louis	**NHL**	**2**	**0**	**0**	**0**	**0**	**0**	**0**	**0**	**1**	**0.0**	**0**	**1**	**100.0**	**7:39**									
	Peoria Rivermen	AHL	28	10	18	28	16										4	2	4	6	6				
2006-07	**Phoenix**	**NHL**	**75**	**14**	**9**	**23**	**46**	**2**	**1**	**0**	**142**	**9.9**	**–8**	**1010**	**56.2**	**14:53**									
2007-08	**Phoenix**	**NHL**	**33**	**2**	**1**	**3**	**6**	**0**	**0**	**0**	**35**	**5.7**	**–7**	**328**	**59.8**	**12:24**									
	San Antonio	AHL	27	10	15	25	14										7	0	5	5	10				
2008-09 •	**Pittsburgh**	**NHL**	**22**	**2**	**4**	**6**	**27**	**0**	**0**	**0**	**23**	**8.7**	**–2**	**251**	**63.0**	**11:26**									
2009-10	Toronto Marlies	AHL	7	0	13	13	0																		
	Djurgarden	Sweden	27	4	7	11	12										5	0	0	0	8				
2010-11	**Toronto**	**NHL**	**8**	**0**	**1**	**1**	**4**	**0**	**0**	**0**	**7**	**0.0**	**0**	**40**	**52.5**	**6:58**									
	Toronto Marlies	AHL	64	14	33	47	66																		
2011-12	Toronto Marlies	AHL	68	19	42	61	52										13	4	2	6	10				
2012-13	Toronto Marlies	AHL	65	7	28	35	42										9	2	7	9	8				
	NHL Totals		**197**	**21**	**19**	**40**	**89**	**3**	**2**	**0**	**256**	**8.2**		**1957**	**57.5**	**12:04**									

• Re-entered NHL Entry Draft. Originally Buffalo's 4th choice, 64th overall, in 1999 Entry Draft.

Yanick Dupre Memorial Award (AHL - Outstanding Humanitarian Contribution) (2013)

Traded to **St. Louis** by **Carolina** with Jesse Boulerice, the rights to Magnus Kahnberg, Carolina's 1st round choice (later traded to New Jersey - New Jersey selected Matthew Corrente) in 2006 Entry Draft, Toronto's 4th round choice (previously acquired, St. Louis selected Reto Berra) in 2006 Entry Draft and Chicago's 4th round choice (previously acquired, St. Louis selected Cade Fairchild) in 2007 Entry Draft for Doug Weight and Erkki Rajamaki, January 30, 2006. Signed as a free agent by **Phoenix**, July 21, 2006. Traded to **Pittsburgh** by **Phoenix** for future considerations, October 9, 2008. • Missed majority of 2008-09 due to shoulder surgery. Signed to a PTO (professional tryout) contract by **Toronto** (AHL), October 19, 2009. Signed as a free agent by **Djurgarden** (Sweden), November 10, 2009. Signed as a free agent by **Toronto**, July 15, 2010. Signed as a free agent by **Toronto** (AHL), July 12, 2011. Signed as a free agent by **Rochester** (AHL), July 10, 2013.

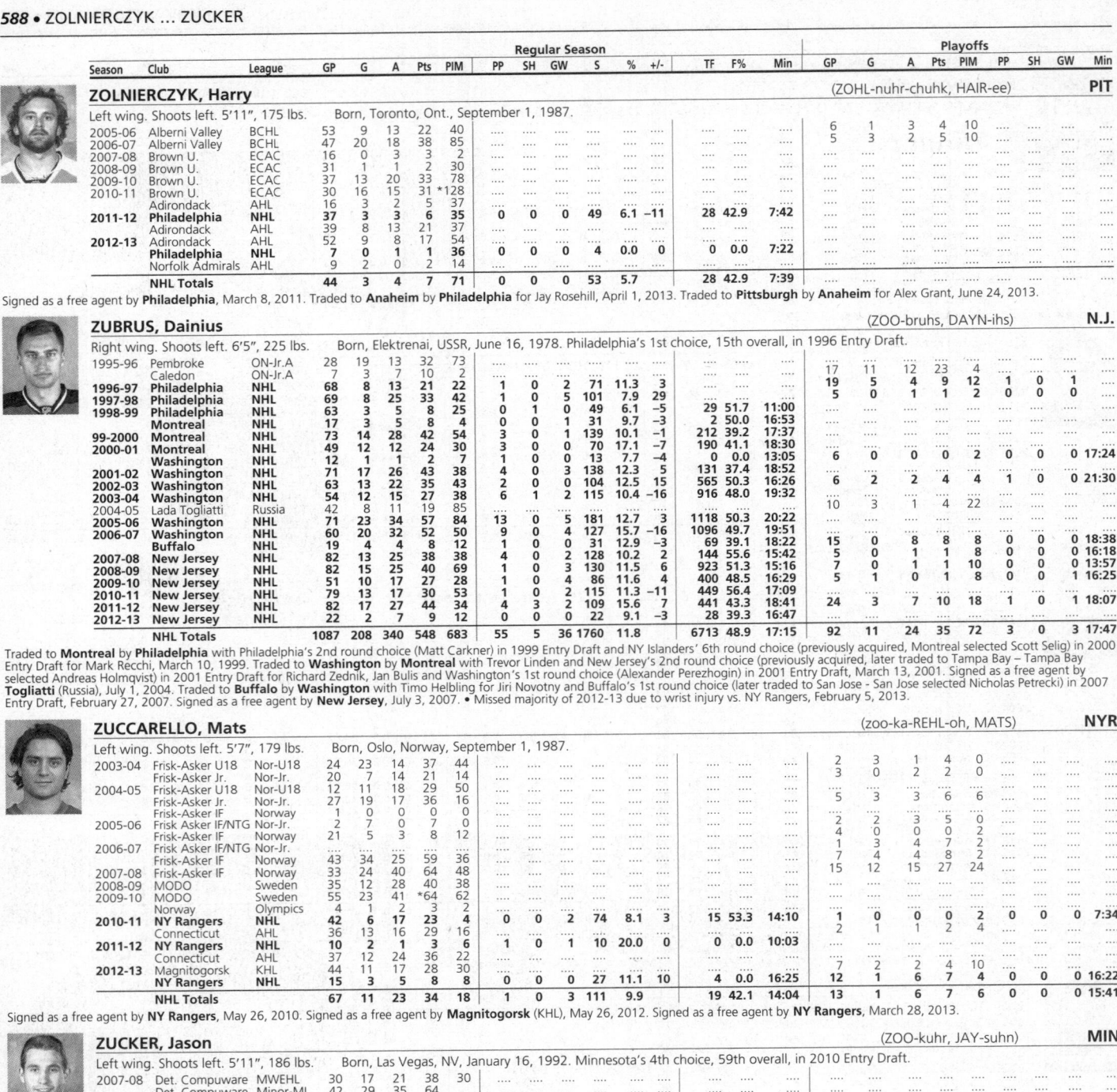

			Regular Season														Playoffs								
Season	Club	League	GP	G	A	Pts	PIM	PP	SH	GW	S	%	+/-	TF	F%	Min	GP	G	A	Pts	PIM	PP	SH	GW	Min

ZOLNIERCZYK, Harry

(ZOHL-nuhr-chuhk, HAIR-ee) **PIT**

Left wing. Shoots left. 5'11", 175 lbs. Born, Toronto, Ont., September 1, 1987.

Season	Club	League	GP	G	A	Pts	PIM	PP	SH	GW	S	%	+/-	TF	F%	Min	GP	G	A	Pts	PIM	PP	SH	GW	Min
2005-06	Alberni Valley	BCHL	53	9	13	22	40	....	....	....	....	....	....	....	....	....	6	1	3	4	10	....	....	....	....
2006-07	Alberni Valley	BCHL	47	20	18	38	85	....	....	....	....	....	....	....	....	....	5	3	2	5	10	....	....	....	....
2007-08	Brown U.	ECAC	16	0	3	3	2	....	....	....	....	....	....	....	....	....	....	....	....	....	....	....	....	....	....
2008-09	Brown U.	ECAC	31	1	1	2	30	....	....	....	....	....	....	....	....	....	....	....	....	....	....	....	....	....	....
2009-10	Brown U.	ECAC	37	13	20	33	78	....	....	....	....	....	....	....	....	....	....	....	....	....	....	....	....	....	....
2010-11	Brown U.	ECAC	30	16	15	31	*128	....	....	....	....	....	....	....	....	....	....	....	....	....	....	....	....	....	....
	Adirondack	AHL	16	3	2	5	37	....	....	....	....	....	....	....	....	....	....	....	....	....	....	....	....	....	....
2011-12	**Philadelphia**	**NHL**	**37**	**3**	**3**	**6**	**35**	**0**	**0**	**0**	**49**	**6.1**	**–11**	**28**	**42.9**	**7:42**	....	....	....	....	....	....	....	....	....
	Adirondack	AHL	39	8	13	21	37	....	....	....	....	....	....	....	....	....	....	....	....	....	....	....	....	....	....
2012-13	Adirondack	AHL	52	9	8	17	54	....	....	....	....	....	....	....	....	....	....	....	....	....	....	....	....	....	....
	Philadelphia	**NHL**	**7**	**0**	**1**	**1**	**36**	**0**	**0**	**0**	**4**	**0.0**	**0**	**0**	**0.0**	**7:22**	....	....	....	....	....	....	....	....	....
	Norfolk Admirals	AHL	9	2	0	2	14	....	....	....	....	....	....	....	....	....	....	....	....	....	....	....	....	....	....
	NHL Totals		**44**	**3**	**4**	**7**	**71**	**0**	**0**	**0**	**53**	**5.7**		**28**	**42.9**	**7:39**	....	....	....	....	....	....	....	....	....

Signed as a free agent by **Philadelphia**, March 8, 2011. Traded to **Anaheim** by **Philadelphia** for Jay Rosehill, April 1, 2013. Traded to **Pittsburgh** by **Anaheim** for Alex Grant, June 24, 2013.

ZUBRUS, Dainius

(ZOO-bruhs, DAYN-ihs) **N.J.**

Right wing. Shoots left. 6'5", 225 lbs. Born, Elektrenai, USSR, June 16, 1978. Philadelphia's 1st choice, 15th overall, in 1996 Entry Draft.

Season	Club	League	GP	G	A	Pts	PIM	PP	SH	GW	S	%	+/-	TF	F%	Min	GP	G	A	Pts	PIM	PP	SH	GW	Min
1995-96	Pembroke	ON-Jr.A	28	19	13	32	73	....	....	....	....	....	....	....	....	....	....	....	....	....	....	....	....	....	....
	Caledon	ON-Jr.A	7	3	7	10	2	....	....	....	....	....	....	....	....	....	17	11	12	23	4	....	....	....	....
1996-97	**Philadelphia**	**NHL**	**68**	**8**	**13**	**21**	**22**	**1**	**0**	**2**	**71**	**11.3**	**3**	....	....	....	**19**	**5**	**4**	**9**	**12**	**1**	**0**	**1**	....
1997-98	**Philadelphia**	**NHL**	**69**	**8**	**25**	**33**	**42**	**1**	**0**	**5**	**101**	**7.9**	**29**	....	....	....	**5**	**0**	**1**	**1**	**2**	**0**	**0**	**0**	....
1998-99	**Philadelphia**	**NHL**	**63**	**3**	**5**	**8**	**25**	**0**	**1**	**0**	**49**	**6.1**	**–5**	**29**	**51.7**	**11:00**	....	....	....	....	....	....	....	....	....
	Montreal	**NHL**	**17**	**3**	**5**	**8**	**4**	**0**	**0**	**1**	**31**	**9.7**	**–3**	**2**	**50.0**	**16:53**	....	....	....	....	....	....	....	....	....
99-2000	**Montreal**	**NHL**	**73**	**14**	**28**	**42**	**54**	**3**	**0**	**1**	**139**	**10.1**	**–1**	**212**	**39.2**	**17:37**	....	....	....	....	....	....	....	....	....
2000-01	**Montreal**	**NHL**	**49**	**12**	**12**	**24**	**30**	**3**	**0**	**0**	**70**	**17.1**	**–7**	**190**	**41.1**	**18:30**	....	....	....	....	....	....	....	....	....
	Washington	**NHL**	**12**	**1**	**1**	**2**	**7**	**1**	**0**	**0**	**13**	**7.7**	**–4**	**0**	**0.0**	**13:05**	**6**	**0**	**0**	**0**	**2**	**0**	**0**	**0**	**17:24**
2001-02	**Washington**	**NHL**	**71**	**17**	**26**	**43**	**38**	**4**	**0**	**3**	**138**	**12.3**	**5**	**131**	**37.4**	**18:52**	....	....	....	....	....	....	....	....	....
2002-03	**Washington**	**NHL**	**63**	**13**	**22**	**35**	**43**	**2**	**0**	**0**	**104**	**12.5**	**15**	**565**	**50.3**	**16:26**	**6**	**2**	**2**	**4**	**4**	**1**	**0**	**0**	**21:30**
2003-04	**Washington**	**NHL**	**54**	**12**	**15**	**27**	**38**	**6**	**1**	**2**	**115**	**10.4**	**–16**	**916**	**48.0**	**19:32**	....	....	....	....	....	....	....	....	....
2004-05	Lada Togliatti	Russia	42	8	11	19	85	....	....	....	....	....	....	....	....	....	10	3	1	4	22	....	....	....	....
2005-06	**Washington**	**NHL**	**71**	**23**	**34**	**57**	**84**	**13**	**0**	**5**	**181**	**12.7**	**3**	**1118**	**50.3**	**20:22**	....	....	....	....	....	....	....	....	....
2006-07	**Washington**	**NHL**	**60**	**20**	**32**	**52**	**50**	**9**	**0**	**4**	**127**	**15.7**	**–16**	**1096**	**49.7**	**19:51**	....	....	....	....	....	....	....	....	....
	Buffalo	**NHL**	**19**	**4**	**4**	**8**	**12**	**1**	**0**	**0**	**31**	**12.9**	**–3**	**69**	**39.1**	**18:22**	**15**	**0**	**8**	**8**	**8**	**0**	**0**	**0**	**18:38**
2007-08	**New Jersey**	**NHL**	**82**	**13**	**25**	**38**	**38**	**4**	**0**	**2**	**128**	**10.2**	**2**	**144**	**55.6**	**15:42**	**5**	**0**	**1**	**1**	**8**	**0**	**0**	**0**	**16:18**
2008-09	**New Jersey**	**NHL**	**82**	**15**	**25**	**40**	**69**	**1**	**0**	**3**	**130**	**11.5**	**6**	**923**	**51.3**	**15:16**	**7**	**0**	**1**	**1**	**10**	**0**	**0**	**0**	**13:57**
2009-10	**New Jersey**	**NHL**	**51**	**10**	**17**	**27**	**28**	**1**	**0**	**4**	**86**	**11.6**	**4**	**400**	**48.5**	**16:29**	**5**	**1**	**0**	**1**	**8**	**0**	**0**	**1**	**16:25**
2010-11	**New Jersey**	**NHL**	**79**	**13**	**17**	**30**	**53**	**1**	**0**	**2**	**115**	**11.3**	**–11**	**449**	**56.4**	**17:09**	....	....	....	....	....	....	....	....	....
2011-12	**New Jersey**	**NHL**	**82**	**17**	**27**	**44**	**34**	**4**	**3**	**2**	**109**	**15.6**	**7**	**441**	**43.3**	**18:41**	**24**	**3**	**7**	**10**	**18**	**1**	**0**	**1**	**18:07**
2012-13	**New Jersey**	**NHL**	**22**	**2**	**7**	**9**	**12**	**0**	**0**	**0**	**22**	**9.1**	**–3**	**28**	**39.3**	**16:47**	....	....	....	....	....	....	....	....	....
	NHL Totals		**1087**	**208**	**340**	**548**	**683**	**55**	**5**	**36**	**1760**	**11.8**		**6713**	**48.9**	**17:15**	**92**	**11**	**24**	**35**	**72**	**3**	**0**	**3**	**17:47**

Traded to **Montreal** by **Philadelphia** with Philadelphia's 2nd round choice (Matt Carkner) in 1999 Entry Draft and NY Islanders' 6th round choice (previously acquired, Montreal selected Scott Selig) in 2000 Entry Draft for Mark Recchi, March 10, 1999. Traded to **Washington** by **Montreal** with Trevor Linden and New Jersey's 2nd round choice (previously acquired, later traded to Tampa Bay – Tampa Bay selected Andreas Holmqvist) in 2001 Entry Draft for Richard Zednik, Jan Bulis and Washington's 1st round choice (Alexander Perezhogin) in 2001 Entry Draft, March 13, 2001. Signed as a free agent by **Togliatti** (Russia), July 1, 2004. Traded to **Buffalo** by **Washington** with Timo Helbling for Jiri Novotny and Buffalo's 1st round choice (later traded to San Jose - San Jose selected Nicholas Petrecki) in 2007 Entry Draft, February 27, 2007. Signed as a free agent by **New Jersey**, July 3, 2007. • Missed majority of 2012-13 due to wrist injury vs. NY Rangers, February 5, 2013.

ZUCCARELLO, Mats

(zoo-ka-REHL-oh, MATS) **NYR**

Left wing. Shoots left. 5'7", 179 lbs. Born, Oslo, Norway, September 1, 1987.

Season	Club	League	GP	G	A	Pts	PIM	PP	SH	GW	S	%	+/-	TF	F%	Min	GP	G	A	Pts	PIM	PP	SH	GW	Min
2003-04	Frisk-Asker U18	Nor-U18	24	23	14	37	44	....	....	....	....	....	....	....	....	....	2	3	1	4	0	....	....	....	....
	Frisk-Asker Jr.	Nor-Jr.	20	7	14	21	14	....	....	....	....	....	....	....	....	....	3	0	2	2	0	....	....	....	....
2004-05	Frisk-Asker U18	Nor-U18	12	11	18	29	50	....	....	....	....	....	....	....	....	....	....	....	....	....	....	....	....	....	....
	Frisk-Asker Jr.	Nor-Jr.	27	19	17	36	16	....	....	....	....	....	....	....	....	....	5	3	3	6	6	....	....	....	....
	Frisk-Asker IF	Norway	1	0	0	0	0	....	....	....	....	....	....	....	....	....	....	....	....	....	....	....	....	....	....
2005-06	Frisk Asker IF/NTG	Nor-Jr.	2	7	0	7	0	....	....	....	....	....	....	....	....	....	2	2	3	5	0	....	....	....	....
	Frisk-Asker IF	Norway	21	5	3	8	12	....	....	....	....	....	....	....	....	....	4	0	0	0	2	....	....	....	....
2006-07	Frisk Asker IF/NTG	Nor-Jr.	....	....	....	....	....	....	....	....	....	....	....	....	....	....	1	3	4	7	2	....	....	....	....
	Frisk-Asker IF	Norway	43	34	25	59	36	....	....	....	....	....	....	....	....	....	7	4	4	8	2	....	....	....	....
2007-08	Frisk-Asker IF	Norway	33	24	40	64	48	....	....	....	....	....	....	....	....	....	15	12	15	27	24	....	....	....	....
2008-09	MODO	Sweden	35	12	28	40	38	....	....	....	....	....	....	....	....	....	....	....	....	....	....	....	....	....	....
2009-10	MODO	Sweden	55	23	41	*64	62	....	....	....	....	....	....	....	....	....	....	....	....	....	....	....	....	....	....
	Norway	Olympics	4	1	2	3	2	....	....	....	....	....	....	....	....	....	....	....	....	....	....	....	....	....	....
2010-11	**NY Rangers**	**NHL**	**42**	**6**	**17**	**23**	**4**	**0**	**0**	**2**	**74**	**8.1**	**3**	**15**	**53.3**	**14:10**	**1**	**0**	**0**	**0**	**2**	**0**	**0**	**0**	**7:34**
	Connecticut	AHL	36	13	16	29	16	....	....	....	....	....	....	....	....	....	2	1	1	2	4	....	....	....	....
2011-12	**NY Rangers**	**NHL**	**10**	**2**	**1**	**3**	**6**	**1**	**0**	**1**	**10**	**20.0**	**0**	**0**	**0.0**	**10:03**	....	....	....	....	....	....	....	....	....
	Connecticut	AHL	37	12	24	36	22	....	....	....	....	....	....	....	....	....	....	....	....	....	....	....	....	....	....
2012-13	Magnitogorsk	KHL	44	11	17	28	30	....	....	....	....	....	....	....	....	....	7	2	2	4	10	....	....	....	....
	NY Rangers	**NHL**	**15**	**3**	**5**	**8**	**8**	**0**	**0**	**0**	**27**	**11.1**	**10**	**4**	**0.0**	**16:25**	**12**	**1**	**6**	**7**	**4**	**0**	**0**	**0**	**16:22**
	NHL Totals		**67**	**11**	**23**	**34**	**18**	**1**	**0**	**3**	**111**	**9.9**		**19**	**42.1**	**14:04**	**13**	**1**	**6**	**7**	**6**	**0**	**0**	**0**	**15:41**

Signed as a free agent by **NY Rangers**, May 26, 2010. Signed as a free agent by **Magnitogorsk** (KHL), May 26, 2012. Signed as a free agent by **NY Rangers**, March 28, 2013.

ZUCKER, Jason

(ZOO-kuhr, JAY-suhn) **MIN**

Left wing. Shoots left. 5'11", 186 lbs. Born, Las Vegas, NV, January 16, 1992. Minnesota's 4th choice, 59th overall, in 2010 Entry Draft.

Season	Club	League	GP	G	A	Pts	PIM	PP	SH	GW	S	%	+/-	TF	F%	Min	GP	G	A	Pts	PIM	PP	SH	GW	Min
2007-08	Det. Compuware	MWEHL	30	17	21	38	30	....	....	....	....	....	....	....	....	....	....	....	....	....	....	....	....	....	....
	Det. Compuware	Minor-MI	42	29	35	64	....	....	....	....	....	....	....	....	....	....	....	....	....	....	....	....	....	....	....
2008-09	USNTDP	NAHL	36	11	4	15	55	....	....	....	....	....	....	....	....	....	....	....	....	....	....	....	....	....	....
	USNTDP	U-17	12	8	6	14	....	....	....	....	....	....	....	....	....	....	....	....	....	....	....	....	....	....	....
	USNTDP	U-18	16	2	6	8	8	....	....	....	....	....	....	....	....	....	....	....	....	....	....	....	....	....	....
2009-10	USNTDP	USHL	22	11	7	18	23	....	....	....	....	....	....	....	....	....	....	....	....	....	....	....	....	....	....
	USNTDP	U-18	38	18	17	35	24	....	....	....	....	....	....	....	....	....	....	....	....	....	....	....	....	....	....
2010-11	U. of Denver	WCHA	40	23	22	45	59	....	....	....	....	....	....	....	....	....	....	....	....	....	....	....	....	....	....
2011-12	U. of Denver	WCHA	38	22	24	46	38	....	....	....	....	....	....	....	....	....	....	....	....	....	....	....	....	....	....
	Minnesota	**NHL**	**6**	**0**	**2**	**2**	**2**	**0**	**0**	**0**	**10**	**0.0**	**–2**	**0**	**0.0**	**11:02**	....	....	....	....	....	....	....	....	....
2012-13	Houston Aeros	AHL	55	24	26	50	43	....	....	....	....	....	....	....	....	....	1	0	0	0	4	....	....	....	....
	Minnesota	**NHL**	**20**	**4**	**1**	**5**	**8**	**0**	**0**	**0**	**34**	**11.8**	**4**	**1**	**0.0**	**11:16**	**5**	**1**	**1**	**2**	**0**	**0**	**0**	**1**	**13:29**
	NHL Totals		**26**	**4**	**3**	**7**	**10**	**0**	**0**	**0**	**44**	**9.1**		**1**	**0.0**	**11:13**	**5**	**1**	**1**	**2**	**0**	**0**	**0**	**1**	**13:29**

WCHA All-Rookie Team (2011) • WCHA Second All-Star Team (2011, 2012) • WCHA Rookie of the Year (2011) • NCAA West Second All-American Team (2012) • AHL All-Rookie Team (2013)

2012-13
NHL Three Stars of the Week/Month Award Winners

Three Stars

Period Ending	First Star	Second Star	Third Star
Jan. 27	Patrick Marleau, S.J.	Corey Crawford, Chi.	Martin St. Louis, T.B.
January	**Craig Anderson, Ott.**	**Patrick Marleau, S.J.**	**Thomas Vanek, Buf.**
Feb. 3	Thomas Vanek, Buf.	Chris Kunitz, Pit.	Roberto Luongo, Van.
Feb. 10	Patrick Kane, Chi.	Jamie Benn, Dal.	Martin Brodeur, N.J.
Feb. 17	John Tavares, NYI	Viktor Fasth, Ana.	Jiri Tlusty, Car.
Feb. 24	Jakub Voracek, Phi.	Steven Stamkos, T.B.	Ben Bishop, Ott.
February	**Steven Stamkos, T.B.**	**Sidney Crosby, Pit.**	**Ray Emery, Chi.**
Mar. 3	Max Pacioretty, Mtl.	Patrice Bergeron, Bos.	Niklas Backstrom, Min.
Mar. 10	Sergei Bobrovsky, CBJ	Sideny Crosby, Pit.	Jeff Carter, L.A.
Mar. 17	Chris Stewart, St.L.	Kyle Turris, Ott.	Sergei Bobrovsky, CBJ
Mar. 24	Alex Ovechkin, Wsh.	Nicklas Backstrom, Min.	Nazem Kadri, Tor.
Mar. 31	Joffrey Lupul, Tor.	Antti Niemi, S.J.	Taylor Hall, Edm.
March	**Sidney Crosby, Pit.**	**P.K. Subban, Mtl.**	**Sergei Bobrovsky, CBJ**
Apr. 7	Alex Ovechkin, Wsh.	Brian Elliott, St.L.	Henrik Lundqvist, NYR
Apr. 14	Sergei Bobrovsky, CBJ	Phil Kessel, Tor.	Richard Bachman, Dal.
Apr. 21	Andrew Ladd, Wpg.	Brad Richards, NYR	Logan Couture, S.J.
Apr. 28	Jimmy Howard, Det.	Henrik Zetterberg, Det.	Nail Yakupov, Edm.
April	**Alex Ovechkin, Wsh.**	**Brian Elliott, St.L.**	**Derek Stepan, NYR**

Rookies of the Month

Month	Player
January	Vladimir Tarasenko, St. Louis
February	Jonathan Huberdeau, Florida
March	Jake Muzzin, Los Angeles
April	Nail Yakupov, Edmonton

Steven Stamkos (top) of the Tampa Bay Lightning had 10 goals and 10 assists for 20 points in 14 games in February to earn First Star of the Month honors. Stamkos scored goals in six straight games (seven goals in all) from February 16 through 26 for the longest streak in the NHL in 2012-13.

Toronto's Joffrey Lupul (right) returned strong after missing six weeks with a broken forearm and earned First Star of the Week for the week ending March 31. Lupul had five goals, including three game winners, and four assists in four games as the Maple Leafs posted a record of 3-0-1.

Brian Elliott of St. Louis (far right) was hot down the stretch with an 11-2-0 record, a 1.28 goals-against average and a .948 save percentage. His strong play helped the Blues secure the fourth playoff seed in the Western Conference. He was named April's Second Star of the Month.

NHL Goaltenders

Jake Allen · Craig Anderson · Niklas Backstrom · Jonathan Bernier · Martin Biron · Ben Bishop · Sergei Bobrovsky · Brian Boucher · Martin Brodeur

Ilya Bryzgalov · Peter Budaj · Scott Clemmensen · Corey Crawford · Yann Danis · Mark Dekanich · Cedrick Desjardins · Jeff Deslauriers · Devan Dubnyk

Brian Elliott · Dan Ellis · Ray Emery · Jhonas Enroth · Viktor Fasth · Marc-Andre Fleury · Mathieu Garon · Jean-Sebastien Giguere · Thomas Greiss

Matt Hackett · Jaroslav Halak · Josh Harding · Johan Hedberg · Jonas Hiller · Braden Holtby · Jimmy Howard · Leland Irving · Chad Johnson

Nikolai Khabibulin · Anton Khudobin · Jason LaBarbera · Robin Lehner · Kari Lehtonen · Anders Lindback · Henrik Lundqvist · Roberto Luongo · Joey MacDonald

Jacob Markstrom · Chris Mason · Steve Mason · Curtis McElhinney · Mike McKenna · Ryan Miller · Al Montoya · Evgeni Nabokov · Michal Neuvirth

Antti Niemi · Cristopher Nilstorp · Ondrej Pavelec · Justin Peters · Kevin Poulin · Carey Price · Jonathan Quick · Tuukka Rask · James Reimer

Pekka Rinne · Cory Schneider · Ben Scrivens · Mike Smith · Jose Theodore · Tim Thomas · Semyon Varlamov · Tomas Vokoun · Cam Ward

2013-14 Goaltender Register

Note: The 2013-14 Goaltender Register lists all active NHL goaltenders, every goaltender drafted in the 2013 Entry Draft, goaltenders on NHL Reserve Lists and other goaltenders.

Trades and roster changes are current as of August 12, 2013.

To calculate a goaltender's goals-against per game average **(Avg)**, divide goals against **(GA)** by minutes played **(Mins)** and multiply this result by **60**.

Abbreviations: GP – games played; **W** – wins; **L** – losses; **O/T** – overtime losses/ties; **Mins** – minutes played; **GA** – goals against; **SO** – shutouts; **Avg** – goals-against-per-game average; ***** – league-leading total ♦ – member of Stanley Cup-winning team.

NHL Player Register begins on page 348.
Prospect Register begins on page 281.
Retired Player Index begins on page 616.
Retired Goaltender Index begins on page 659.
League Abbreviations are listed on page 670.

AITTOKALLIO, Sami (ay-toh-KAHL-ee-oh, SAHM-ee) COL

Goaltender. Catches left. 6'1", 174 lbs. Born, Tampere, Finland, August 6, 1992.
(Colorado's 5th choice, 107th overall, in 2010 Entry Draft).

			Regular Season								Playoffs						
Season	Club	League	GP	W	L	O/T	Mins	GA	SO	Avg	GP	W	L	Mins	GA	SO	Avg
2008-09	Ilves Tampere U18	Fin-U18	5	5	0	0	305	9	1	1.77	....	....	....	....	....	....	....
	Ilves Tampere Jr.	Fin-Jr.	13	7	6	0	731	33	1	2.71	....	....	....	....	....	....	....
2009-10	Ilves Tampere	Finland	1	0	0	0	2	0	0	0.00	....	....	....	....	....	....	....
	LeKi Lempaala	Finland-2	2	1	1	0	124	7	0	3.38	....	....	....	....	....	....	....
	Suomi U20	Finland-2	2	1	1	0	120	8	0	4.00	....	....	....	....	....	....	....
	Ilves Tampere U18	Fin-U18	9	6	3	0	542	19	1	2.10	....	....	....	....	....	....	....
	Ilves Tampere Jr.	Fin-Jr.	23	13	9	0	1257	67	2	3.20	9	6	3	504	19	0	2.26
2010-11	Ilves Tampere	Finland	16	5	8	0	790	36	1	2.73	2	0	2	117	5	0	2.57
	Suomi U20	Finland-2	4	2	2	0	196	14	0	4.28	....	....	....	....	....	....	....
	Ilves Tampere Jr.	Fin-Jr.	6	4	2	0	359	14	1	2.34	3	1	2	174	11	0	3.80
	LeKi Lempaala	Finland-2	6	3	3	0	322	20	0	3.73	....	....	....	....	....	....	....
2011-12	Ilves Tampere	Finland	11	1	6	3	596	28	0	2.82	....	....	....	....	....	....	....
	Ilves Tampere Jr.	Fin-Jr.	6	2	4	0	347	18	0	3.11	....	....	....	....	....	....	....
	LeKi Lempaala	Finland-2	7	1	6	0	416	30	0	4.33	....	....	....	....	....	....	....
2012-13	Lake Erie Monsters	AHL	27	14	12	1	1540	77	1	3.00	....	....	....	....	....	....	....
	Colorado	**NHL**	**1**	**0**	**0**	**0**	**49**	**2**	**0**	**2.45**	....	....	....	....	....	....	....
	NHL Totals		**1**	**0**	**0**	**0**	**49**	**2**	**0**	**2.45**	....	....	....	....	....	....	....

ALLEN, Jake (A-lehn, JAYK) ST.L.

Goaltender. Catches left. 6'2", 195 lbs. Born, Fredericton, N.B., August 7, 1990.
(St. Louis' 3rd choice, 34th overall, in 2008 Entry Draft).

			Regular Season								Playoffs						
Season	Club	League	GP	W	L	O/T	Mins	GA	SO	Avg	GP	W	L	Mins	GA	SO	Avg
2006-07	Fredericton	NBPEI					STATISTICS NOT AVAILABLE										
2007-08	St. John's	QMJHL	30	9	12	0	1507	79	2	3.14	4	2	1	128	8	0	3.74
2008-09	Montreal	QMJHL	53	28	25	0	3023	144	3	2.86	10	4	6	585	35	1	3.59
2009-10	Montreal	QMJHL	23	11	11	0	1241	55	1	2.66	....	....	....	....	....	....	....
	Drummondville	QMJHL	22	18	3	0	1271	37	3	1.75	14	9	5	840	34	1	2.43
2010-11	Peoria Rivermen	AHL	47	25	19	3	2805	118	6	2.52	3	0	3	189	12	0	3.80
2011-12	Peoria Rivermen	AHL	38	13	20	2	2148	105	1	2.93	....	....	....	....	....	....	....
	St. Louis	**NHL**	....	....	....	....	....	....	....	....	**1**	**0**	**0**	**1**	**0**	**0**	**0.00**
2012-13	Peoria Rivermen	AHL	35	13	19	2	2054	99	2	2.89	....	....	....	....	....	....	....
	St. Louis	**NHL**	**15**	**9**	**4**	**0**	**804**	**33**	**1**	**2.46**	....	....	....	....	....	....	....
	NHL Totals		**15**	**9**	**4**	**0**	**804**	**33**	**1**	**2.46**	**1**	**0**	**0**	**1**	**0**	**0**	**0.00**

QMJHL First All-Star Team (2010) • Canadian Major Junior First All-Star Team (2010) • Canadian Major Junior Goaltender of the Year (2010) • NHL All-Rookie Team (2013)

ALTSHULLER, Daniel (awl-SHOO-luhr, DAN-yehl) CAR

Goaltender. Catches left. 6'3", 200 lbs. Born, Ottawa, Ont., July 24, 1994.
(Carolina's 3rd choice, 69th overall, in 2012 Entry Draft).

			Regular Season								Playoffs						
Season	Club	League	GP	W	L	O/T	Mins	GA	SO	Avg	GP	W	L	Mins	GA	SO	Avg
2009-10	Ott. Jr. 67's M.M.	Minor-ON	24	....	....	....	1080	40	3	1.74	....	....	....	....	....	....	....
	Nepean Raiders	ON-Jr.A	1	0	1	0	60	2	0	2.00	....	....	....	....	....	....	....
2010-11	Nepean Raiders	ON-Jr.A	43	19	13	10	2515	135	1	3.22	....	....	....	....	....	....	....
2011-12	Oshawa Generals	OHL	30	11	16	3	1756	104	0	3.55	5	2	2	279	18	0	3.87
2012-13	Oshawa Generals	OHL	58	*36	18	2	3363	147	3	2.62	9	4	5	541	27	0	3.00

OHL All-Rookie Team (2012)

ANDERSEN, Frederik (AHN-duhr-suhn, FREH-duhr-ihk) ANA

Goaltender. Catches left. 6'4", 245 lbs. Born, Herning, Denmark, October 2, 1989.
(Anaheim's 3rd choice, 87th overall, in 2012 Entry Draft).

			Regular Season								Playoffs						
Season	Club	League	GP	W	L	O/T	Mins	GA	SO	Avg	GP	W	L	Mins	GA	SO	Avg
2005-06	Herning IK Jr.	Den-Jr.	29	....	....	....	....	....	....	....	6	....	....	....	....	....	....
	Herning IK II	Den-2	3	....	....	....	....	....	....	....	....	....	....	....	....	....	....
2006-07	Herning IK Jr.	Den-Jr.	27	....	....	....	....	....	....	....	....	....	....	....	....	....	....
	Herning IK II	Den-2	18	....	....	....	....	....	....	....	....	....	....	....	....	....	....
2007-08	Herning IK Jr.	Den-Jr.	17	....	....	....	....	....	....	....	....	....	....	....	....	....	....
	Herning IK II	Den-2	9	....	....	....	....	....	....	....	....	....	....	....	....	....	....
2008-09	Herning IK II	Den-2	1	....	....	....	....	....	....	....	....	....	....	....	....	....	....
	Herning Blue Fox	Denmark	22	....	....	....	1249	51	1	2.45	....	....	....	....	....	....	....
2009-10	Frederikshavn	Denmark	30	....	....	....	1754	64	6	2.19	10	....	....	607	29	0	2.86
2010-11	Frederikshavn	Denmark	35	....	....	....	1953	81	....	2.49	11	....	....	666	26	....	2.34
2011-12	Frolunda	Sweden	39	....	....	....	2335	65	7	1.67	6	....	....	379	17	0	2.69
2012-13	Norfolk Admirals	AHL	47	24	18	1	2685	98	4	2.19	....	....	....	....	....	....	....

• Re-entered NHL Entry Draft. Originally Carolina's 8th choice, 187th overall, in 2010 Entry Draft.

ANDERSON, Brandon (AN-duhr-suhn, BRAN-duhn) WSH

Goaltender. Catches left. 6'1", 170 lbs. Born, Langley, B.C., July 13, 1992.

			Regular Season								Playoffs						
Season	Club	League	GP	W	L	O/T	Mins	GA	SO	Avg	GP	W	L	Mins	GA	SO	Avg
2008-09	Columbia Valley	KIJHL	33	12	18	0	1879	119	0	3.80	....	....	....	....	....	....	....
	Lethbridge	WHL	5	0	1	0	175	12	0	4.11	1	0	1	60	5	0	5.00
2009-10	Lethbridge	WHL	37	12	19	2	2009	117	0	3.49	....	....	....	....	....	....	....
2010-11	Lethbridge	WHL	59	17	26	12	3282	206	0	3.77	....	....	....	....	....	....	....
2011-12	Lethbridge	WHL	6	2	3	1	365	23	0	3.78	....	....	....	....	....	....	....
	Brandon	WHL	31	13	14	2	1562	103	0	3.96	1	0	0	45	2	0	2.66
2012-13	Reading Royals	ECHL	16	8	6	1	906	48	2	3.18	....	....	....	....	....	....	....

Signed as a free agent by **Washington**, September 21, 2010.

ANDERSON, Craig (AN-duhr-suhn, KRAYG) OTT

Goaltender. Catches left. 6'2", 180 lbs. Born, Park Ridge, IL, May 21, 1981.
(Chicago's 4th choice, 73rd overall, in 2001 Entry Draft).

			Regular Season								Playoffs						
Season	Club	League	GP	W	L	O/T	Mins	GA	SO	Avg	GP	W	L	Mins	GA	SO	Avg
1997-98	Chicago Jets	MEHL	50	....	....	....	2991	143	2	2.86	....	....	....	....	....	....	....
1998-99	Chicago Freeze	NAHL	14	11	3	0	840	40	0	2.56	....	....	....	....	....	....	....
	Guelph Storm	OHL	21	12	5	1	1006	52	1	3.10	3	0	2	114	9	0	4.74
99-2000	Guelph Storm	OHL	38	12	17	2	1955	117	0	3.59	3	0	1	110	5	0	2.73
2000-01	Guelph Storm	OHL	59	30	19	9	3555	156	3	2.63	4	0	4	240	17	0	4.25
2001-02	Norfolk Admirals	AHL	28	9	13	4	1568	77	2	2.95	1	0	1	21	1	0	2.83
2002-03	**Chicago**	**NHL**	**6**	**0**	**3**	**2**	**270**	**18**	**0**	**4.00**	....	....	....	....	....	....	....
	Norfolk Admirals	AHL	32	15	11	5	1795	58	4	1.94	5	2	3	345	15	0	2.61
2003-04	**Chicago**	**NHL**	**21**	**6**	**14**	**0**	**1205**	**57**	**1**	**2.84**	....	....	....	....	....	....	....
	Norfolk Admirals	AHL	37	17	20	0	2108	74	3	2.11	5	2	3	327	10	0	1.84
2004-05	Norfolk Admirals	AHL	15	9	4	1	886	27	2	1.83	6	2	4	356	14	0	2.36
2005-06	**Chicago**	**NHL**	**29**	**6**	**12**	**4**	**1554**	**86**	**1**	**3.32**	....	....	....	....	....	....	....
2006-07	**Florida**	**NHL**	**5**	**1**	**1**	**1**	**217**	**8**	**0**	**2.21**	....	....	....	....	....	....	....
	Rochester	AHL	34	23	10	1	2060	88	1	2.56	6	2	4	376	18	0	2.87
2007-08	**Florida**	**NHL**	**17**	**8**	**6**	**1**	**935**	**35**	**2**	**2.25**	....	....	....	....	....	....	....
2008-09	**Florida**	**NHL**	**31**	**15**	**7**	**5**	**1636**	**74**	**3**	**2.71**	....	....	....	....	....	....	....
2009-10	**Colorado**	**NHL**	**71**	**38**	**25**	**7**	**4235**	**186**	**7**	**2.64**	**6**	**2**	**4**	**366**	**16**	**1**	**2.62**
2010-11	**Colorado**	**NHL**	**33**	**13**	**15**	**3**	**1810**	**99**	**0**	**3.28**	....	....	....	....	....	....	....
	Ottawa	**NHL**	**18**	**11**	**5**	**1**	**1055**	**36**	**2**	**2.05**	....	....	....	....	....	....	....
2011-12	**Ottawa**	**NHL**	**63**	**33**	**22**	**6**	**3492**	**165**	**3**	**2.84**	**7**	**3**	**4**	**419**	**14**	**1**	**2.00**
2012-13	**Ottawa**	**NHL**	**24**	**12**	**9**	**2**	**1421**	**40**	**3**	***1.69**	**10**	**5**	**4**	**578**	**29**	**0**	**3.01**
	NHL Totals		**318**	**143**	**119**	**32**	**17830**	**804**	**22**	**2.71**	**23**	**10**	**12**	**1363**	**59**	**2**	**2.60**

• Re-entered NHL Entry Draft. Originally Calgary's 3rd choice, 77th overall, in 1999 Entry Draft.

OHL First All-Star Team (2001)

Claimed on waivers by **Boston** from **Chicago**, January 19, 2006. Claimed on waivers by **St. Louis** from **Boston**, January 31, 2006. Claimed on waivers by **Chicago** from **St. Louis**, February 3, 2006. Traded to **Florida** by **Chicago** for Florida's 6th round choice (later traded to Tampa Bay - Tampa Bay selected Luke Witkowski) in 2008 Entry Draft, June 24, 2006. Signed as a free agent by **Colorado**, July 1, 2009. Traded to **Ottawa** by **Colorado** for Brian Elliott, February 18, 2011.

ANDERSON, J.P. (AN-duhr-suhn, JAY-PEE) S.J.

Goaltender. Catches right. 5'11", 185 lbs. Born, Toronto, Ont., April 27, 1992.

			Regular Season								Playoffs						
Season	Club	League	GP	W	L	O/T	Mins	GA	SO	Avg	GP	W	L	Mins	GA	SO	Avg
2008-09	St. Michael's	OHL	26	12	12	0	1409	69	1	2.94	11	6	5	697	29	0	*2.50
2009-10	St. Michael's	OHL	36	23	10	1	2028	88	1	2.60	10	4	5	519	24	0	2.78
2010-11	St. Michael's	OHL	51	*38	10	1	2897	114	*6	*2.36	*20	*15	5	*1223	43	*4	*2.11
2011-12	St. Michael's	OHL	31	15	11	4	1855	94	0	3.04	....	....	....	....	....	....	....
	Sarnia Sting	OHL	26	12	12	2	1473	74	3	3.01	6	2	3	355	22	0	3.71
2012-13	Sarnia Sting	OHL	53	26	21	5	3031	167	1	3.31	4	0	4	239	24	0	6.02

OHL Second All-Star Team (2011)

Signed as a free agent by **San Jose**, September 20, 2010.

BACHMAN, Richard (BAWK-mahn, RIH-chuhrd) EDM

Goaltender. Catches left. 5'10", 175 lbs. Born, Salt Lake City, UT, July 25, 1987.
(Dallas' 3rd choice, 120th overall, in 2006 Entry Draft).

			Regular Season								Playoffs						
Season	**Club**	**League**	**GP**	**W**	**L**	**O/T**	**Mins**	**GA**	**SO**	**Avg**	**GP**	**W**	**L**	**Mins**	**GA**	**SO**	**Avg**
2004-05	Cushing	High-MA	28	....	....	....	1498	53	3	1.89	....	....	....	....	....	....	....
	Junior Bruins	EmJHL	25	....	....	....	....	....	....	....	....	....	....	....	....	....	....
2005-06	Cushing	High-MA	30	....	....	....	1598	60	4	2.25	....	....	....	....	....	....	....
	Junior Bruins	EmJHL	....	31	1	2	....	....	....	1.69	....	....	....	....	....	....	....
2006-07	Chicago Steel	USHL	7	2	5	0	359	29	0	4.85	....	....	....	....	....	....	....
	Cedar Rapids	USHL	26	14	10	2	1565	78	4	2.99	6	4	1	329	7	*2	*1.28
2007-08	Colorado College	WCHA	35	25	9	1	2103	65	4	1.85	....	....	....	....	....	....	....
2008-09	Colorado College	WCHA	35	14	11	10	2073	91	3	2.63	....	....	....	....	....	....	....
2009-10	Texas Stars	AHL	8	4	4	0	446	16	1	2.15	....	....	....	....	....	....	....
	Idaho Steelheads	ECHL	35	22	7	4	2028	77	*4	*2.28	8	6	2	492	13	1	1.59
2010-11	**Dallas**	**NHL**	**1**	**0**	**0**	**0**	**10**	**0**	**0**	**0.00**	....	....	....	....	....	....	....
	Texas Stars	AHL	55	28	19	5	3191	117	6	2.20	6	2	4	394	15	0	2.29
2011-12	**Dallas**	**NHL**	**18**	**8**	**5**	**1**	**933**	**43**	**1**	**2.77**	....	....	....	....	....	....	....
	Texas Stars	AHL	15	7	6	1	844	44	2	3.13	....	....	....	....	....	....	....
2012-13	Texas Stars	AHL	6	5	1	0	363	14	0	2.31	....	....	....	....	....	....	....
	Dallas	**NHL**	**13**	**6**	**5**	**0**	**609**	**33**	**0**	**3.25**	....	....	....	....	....	....	....
	NHL Totals		**32**	**14**	**10**	**1**	**1552**	**76**	**1**	**2.94**	....	....	....	....	....	....	....

WCHA All-Rookie Team (2008) • WCHA First All-Star Team (2008) • WCHA Rookie of the Year (2008) • WCHA Player of the Year (2008) • NCAA West First All-American Team (2008) • NCAA Rookie of the Year (2008)

Signed as a free agent by **Edmonton**, July 6, 2013.

BACKSTROM, Niklas (BAK-struhm, NIHK-luhs) MIN

Goaltender. Catches left. 6'2", 194 lbs. Born, Helsinki, Finland, February 13, 1978.

			Regular Season								Playoffs						
Season	**Club**	**League**	**GP**	**W**	**L**	**O/T**	**Mins**	**GA**	**SO**	**Avg**	**GP**	**W**	**L**	**Mins**	**GA**	**SO**	**Avg**
1994-95	HIFK Helsinki U18	Fin-U18					STATISTICS NOT AVAILABLE										
1995-96	HIFK Helsinki U18	Fin-U18	12	....	....	....	699	44	....	3.77	4	....	....	203	9	....	2.66
1996-97	HIFK Helsinki Jr.	Fin-Jr.	21	....	....	....	1243	57	....	2.75	....	....	....	....	....	....	....
	PiTa Helsinki	Finland-2	8	....	....	....	390	24	....	3.69	....	....	....	....	....	....	....
	HIFK Helsinki	Finland	2	0	0	0	30	3	0	5.85	....	....	....	....	....	....	....
1997-98	HIFK Helsinki Jr.	Fin-Jr.	14	7	7	0	847	42	....	2.98	....	....	....	....	....	....	....
	Hermes Kokkola	Finland-2	9	4	3	1	468	23	1	2.95	....	....	....	....	....	....	....
1998-99	HIFK Helsinki	Finland	16	9	5	1	923	26	1	*1.69	....	....	....	....	....	....	....
	HIFK Helsinki Jr.	Fin-Jr.	15	7	7	1	898	45	1	3.01	....	....	....	....	....	....	....
99-2000	HIFK Helsinki	Finland	4	0	4	0	155	17	0	6.58	....	....	....	....	....	....	....
	FPS Forssa	Finland-2	22	13	8	1	1320	50	1	2.27	3	1	2	178	8	0	2.69
2000-01	SaiPa	Finland	49	22	24	3	2826	120	2	2.55	....	....	....	....	....	....	....
2001-02	AIK Solna	Sweden	40	....	....	....	2186	111	1	3.05	....	....	....	....	....	....	....
	AIK Solna	Sweden-Q	9	....	....	....	543	20	0	2.21	....	....	....	....	....	....	....
2002-03	Karpat Oulu	Finland	36	16	8	9	2136	77	4	2.16	*15	7	8	*990	33	1	2.00
2003-04	Karpat Oulu	Finland	43	24	8	0	2572	87	7	2.03	*15	*9	6	*927	36	1	2.33
2004-05	Karpat Oulu	Finland	47	27	10	10	2819	102	7	2.17	*12	*10	2	720	15	*3	*1.25
2005-06	Karpat Oulu	Finland	51	*32	9	10	3077	86	*10	*1.68	4	3	1	195	6	0	1.84
	Finland	Olympics					DID NOT PLAY – SPARE GOALTENDER										
2006-07	**Minnesota**	**NHL**	**41**	**23**	**8**	**6**	**2227**	**73**	**5**	***1.97**	**5**	**1**	**4**	**297**	**11**	**0**	**2.22**
2007-08	**Minnesota**	**NHL**	**58**	**33**	**13**	**8**	**3409**	**131**	**4**	**2.31**	**6**	**2**	**4**	**361**	**17**	**0**	**2.83**
2008-09	**Minnesota**	**NHL**	**71**	**37**	**24**	**8**	**4088**	**159**	**8**	**2.33**	....	....	....	....	....	....	....
2009-10	**Minnesota**	**NHL**	**60**	**26**	**23**	**8**	**3489**	**158**	**2**	**2.72**	....	....	....	....	....	....	....
	Finland	Olympics	2	1	0	0	110	2	1	*1.09	....	....	....	....	....	....	....
2010-11	**Minnesota**	**NHL**	**51**	**22**	**23**	**5**	**2978**	**132**	**3**	**2.66**	....	....	....	....	....	....	....
2011-12	**Minnesota**	**NHL**	**46**	**19**	**18**	**7**	**2590**	**105**	**4**	**2.43**	....	....	....	....	....	....	....
2012-13	**Minnesota**	**NHL**	**42**	***24**	**15**	**3**	**2368**	**98**	**2**	**2.48**	....	....	....	....	....	....	....
	NHL Totals		**369**	**184**	**124**	**45**	**21149**	**856**	**28**	**2.43**	**11**	**3**	**8**	**658**	**28**	**0**	**2.55**

MBNA Roger Crozier Saving Grace Award (2007) • William M. Jennings Trophy (2007) (shared with Manny Fernandez)

Played in NHL All-Star Game (2009)

Signed as a free agent by **Minnesota**, June 1, 2006.

BARTOSAK, Patrik (BAHR-toh-shak, PAT-rihk) L.A.

Goaltender. Catches left. 6'1", 181 lbs. Born, Koprivnice, Czech Rep., March 29, 1993.
(Los Angeles' 4th choice, 146th overall, in 2013 Entry Draft).

			Regular Season								Playoffs						
Season	**Club**	**League**	**GP**	**W**	**L**	**O/T**	**Mins**	**GA**	**SO**	**Avg**	**GP**	**W**	**L**	**Mins**	**GA**	**SO**	**Avg**
2007-08	HC Vitkovice U17	CzR-U17	8	....	....	....	484	26	0	3.22	....	....	....	....	....	....	....
2008-09	HC Vitkovice U17	CzR-U17	18	....	....	....	1064	48	1	2.71	4	....	....	229	10	0	2.62
	HC Vitkovice Jr.	CzRep-Jr.	....	....	....	....	....	....	....	....	1	....	....	2	1	0	30.00
2009-10	HC Vitkovice U18	CzR-U18	36	....	....	....	2023	65	3	1.93	2	....	....	130	6	0	2.77
	Frydek-Mistek U18	CzR-U18	7	....	....	....	415	60	0	8.67	....	....	....	....	....	....	....
	HC Vitkovice Jr.	CzRep-Jr.	1	....	....	....	60	1	0	1.00	....	....	....	....	....	....	....
2010-11	HC Vitkovice U18	CzR-U18	13	....	....	....	783	31	1	2.38	4	....	....	243	8	0	1.98
	HC Vitkovice Jr.	CzRep-Jr.	37	....	....	....	2074	95	3	2.75	1	....	....	60	3	0	3.00
2011-12	Red Deer Rebels	WHL	25	14	10	1	1466	67	1	2.74	....	....	....	....	....	....	....
2012-13	Red Deer Rebels	WHL	55	33	14	5	3134	118	5	2.26	9	5	4	548	18	1	1.97

WHL East First All-Star Team (2013) • Canadian Major Junior Goaltender of the Year (2013)

BARULIN, Konstantin (bah-ROO-lihn, KAWN-stan-tihn) ST.L.

Goaltender. Catches left. 6'2", 200 lbs. Born, Karaganda, USSR, September 4, 1984.
(St. Louis' 3rd choice, 84th overall, in 2003 Entry Draft).

			Regular Season								Playoffs						
Season	**Club**	**League**	**GP**	**W**	**L**	**O/T**	**Mins**	**GA**	**SO**	**Avg**	**GP**	**W**	**L**	**Mins**	**GA**	**SO**	**Avg**
2001-02	Gazovik Tyumen	Russia-2	4	....	....	....	190	15	0	4.73	....	....	....	....	....	....	....
2002-03	Gazovik Tyumen	Russia-2	41	....	....	....	2361	67	5	1.70	....	....	....	....	....	....	....
2003-04	Gazovik Tyumen	Russia-2	11	....	....	....	663	24	....	2.17	....	....	....	....	....	....	....
	SKA St. Petersburg	Russia	1	....	....	....	1	0	0	0.00	....	....	....	....	....	....	....
	St. Petersburg 2	Russia-3	11	....	....	....	668	24	1	2.15	....	....	....	....	....	....	....
2004-05	Gazovik Tyumen	Russia-2	30	....	....	....	1773	59	6	2.00	3	....	....	136	9	0	3.97
2005-06	Spartak Moscow	Russia	36	....	....	....	2102	75	2	2.14	2	....	....	104	4	0	2.30
2006-07	Mytischi	Russia	26	....	....	....	1249	45	1	2.16	1	....	....	48	3	0	3.76
2007-08	Mytischi	Russia	11	....	....	....	434	20	0	2.77	....	....	....	....	....	....	....
2008-09	CSKA Moscow	KHL	41	....	....	....	2443	100	2	2.46	2	....	....	100	9	0	5.40
2009-10	CSKA Moscow	KHL	45	....	....	....	2277	80	3	2.11	3	....	....	136	10	0	4.43
2010-11	Mytischi	KHL	28	....	....	....	1505	48	6	*1.91	*22	....	....	*1286	44	2	2.05
2011-12	Mytischi	KHL	45	18	16	0	2652	100	5	2.26	12	6	6	694	27	1	2.33
2012-13	Ak Bars Kazan	KHL	43	23	11	0	2551	83	4	1.95	18	11	7	1234	36	2	1.75

BELANGER, Alexandre (buh-LAWN-zhay, al-ehx-AN-druh) MIN

Goaltender. Catches left. 6'1", 184 lbs. Born, Sherbrooke, Que., August 19, 1995.
(Minnesota's 7th choice, 200th overall, in 2013 Entry Draft).

			Regular Season								Playoffs						
Season	**Club**	**League**	**GP**	**W**	**L**	**O/T**	**Mins**	**GA**	**SO**	**Avg**	**GP**	**W**	**L**	**Mins**	**GA**	**SO**	**Avg**
2010-11	Magog	QAAA	26	14	9	2	1428	80	1	3.36	9	6	3	504	22	1	2.62
2011-12	Magog	QAAA	33	14	15	4	1960	98	0	3.00	8	4	4	462	24	1	3.12
	Rouyn-Noranda	QMJHL	2	0	1	0	113	4	0	2.12	....	....	....	....	....	....	....
2012-13	Rouyn-Noranda	QMJHL	44	24	13	4	2409	139	1	3.46	14	8	5	828	49	0	3.55

BERGVIK, Fredrik (BAIRG-vihk, FREHD-RIHK) S.J.

Goaltender. Catches left. 6'1", 175 lbs. Born, Stockholm, Sweden, February 14, 1995.
(San Jose's 3rd choice, 117th overall, in 2013 Entry Draft).

			Regular Season								Playoffs						
Season	**Club**	**League**	**GP**	**W**	**L**	**O/T**	**Mins**	**GA**	**SO**	**Avg**	**GP**	**W**	**L**	**Mins**	**GA**	**SO**	**Avg**
2010-11	Djurgarden U18	Swe-U18	1	....	....	....	60	1	0	1.00	....	....	....	....	....	....	....
2011-12	Frolunda U18	Swe-U18	21	....	....	....	1259	47	4	2.24	....	....	....	....	....	....	....
2012-13	Frolunda U18	Swe-U18	8	5	2	0	465	20	1	2.58	3	1	1	145	11	0	4.55
	Frolunda Jr.	Swe-Jr.	14	12	1	0	834	18	4	1.29	....	....	....	....	....	....	....

BERNIER, Jonathan (BAIRN-yay, JAWN-ah-thuhn) TOR

Goaltender. Catches left. 6', 185 lbs. Born, Laval, Que., August 7, 1988.
(Los Angeles' 1st choice, 11th overall, in 2006 Entry Draft).

			Regular Season								Playoffs						
Season	**Club**	**League**	**GP**	**W**	**L**	**O/T**	**Mins**	**GA**	**SO**	**Avg**	**GP**	**W**	**L**	**Mins**	**GA**	**SO**	**Avg**
2003-04	Laval Regents	QAAA	27	16	4	0	1329	62	2	2.80	3	1	2	180	5	0	1.70
2004-05	Lewiston	QMJHL	23	7	12	3	1353	67	0	2.97	1	0	0	20	0	0	0.00
2005-06	Lewiston	QMJHL	54	27	26	0	3241	146	2	2.70	6	2	4	359	17	1	2.84
2006-07	Lewiston	QMJHL	37	26	10	0	2186	94	2	2.58	17	*16	1	1025	40	1	2.34
2007-08	**Los Angeles**	**NHL**	**4**	**1**	**3**	**0**	**238**	**16**	**0**	**4.03**	....	....	....	....	....	....	....
	Lewiston	QMJHL	34	18	15	0	2024	92	0	2.73	6	2	4	348	17	0	2.93
	Manchester	AHL	3	1	1	1	184	5	0	1.63	3	0	3	195	9	0	2.76
2008-09	Manchester	AHL	54	23	24	4	3101	124	5	2.40	....	....	....	....	....	....	....
2009-10	**Los Angeles**	**NHL**	**3**	**3**	**0**	**0**	**185**	**4**	**1**	**1.30**	....	....	....	....	....	....	....
	Manchester	AHL	58	30	21	6	3424	116	*9	2.03	16	10	6	996	30	*3	*1.81
2010-11	**Los Angeles**	**NHL**	**25**	**11**	**8**	**3**	**1378**	**57**	**3**	**2.48**	....	....	....	....	....	....	....
2011-12 ♦	**Los Angeles**	**NHL**	**16**	**5**	**6**	**2**	**890**	**35**	**1**	**2.36**	....	....	....	....	....	....	....
2012-13	Heilbronner Falken	German-2	13	6	7	0	793	34	1	2.57	....	....	....	....	....	....	....
	Los Angeles	**NHL**	**14**	**9**	**3**	**1**	**768**	**24**	**1**	**1.88**	**1**	**0**	**0**	**30**	**0**	**0**	**0.00**
	NHL Totals		**62**	**29**	**20**	**6**	**3459**	**136**	**6**	**2.36**	**1**	**0**	**0**	**30**	**0**	**0**	**0.00**

QMJHL Second All-Star Team (2007) • Canadian Major Junior Second All-Star Team (2007) • AHL First All-Star Team (2010) • Aldege "Baz" Bastien Award (AHL – Outstanding Goaltender) (2010)

Signed as a free agent by **Heilbronner** (German-2), October 10, 2012. Traded to **Toronto** by **Los Angeles** for Ben Scrivens, Matt Frattin and Toronto's 2nd round choice in 2014 or 2015 Entry Draft, June 23, 2013.

BERRA, Reto (BAIR-uh, REH-toh) CGY

Goaltender. Catches left. 6'4", 209 lbs. Born, Bulach, Switz., January 3, 1987.
(St. Louis' 6th choice, 106th overall, in 2006 Entry Draft).

			Regular Season								Playoffs						
Season	**Club**	**League**	**GP**	**W**	**L**	**O/T**	**Mins**	**GA**	**SO**	**Avg**	**GP**	**W**	**L**	**Mins**	**GA**	**SO**	**Avg**
2004-05	GCK Zurich Jr.	Swiss-Jr.	22	....	....	....	....	....	....	....	....	....	....	....	....	....	....
	GCK Lions Zurich	Swiss-2	3	....	....	....	180	12	0	4.00	....	....	....	....	....	....	....
	EHC Dubendorf	Swiss-3					STATISTICS NOT AVAILABLE										
2005-06	GCK Zurich Jr.	Swiss-Jr.	23	....	....	....	....	....	....	....	....	....	....	....	....	....	....
	GCK Lions Zurich	Swiss-2	15	....	....	....	835	51	1	3.56	....	....	....	....	....	....	....
	ZSC Lions Zurich	Swiss	2	0	1	0	90	6	0	3.99	....	....	....	....	....	....	....
2006-07	Switzerland U20	Swiss-2	3	0	3	0	179	13	0	4.69	....	....	....	....	....	....	....
	GCK Lions Zurich	Swiss-2	6	4	2	0	359	18	0	3.01	....	....	....	....	....	....	....
	ZSC Lions Zurich	Swiss	2	1	0	0	78	4	0	3.08	4	0	3	188	9	0	2.87
2007-08	HC Davos	Swiss	16	9	7	0	966	44	0	2.73	....	....	....	....	....	....	....
2008-09	EV Zug	Swiss	6	1	5	0	368	17	0	2.77	....	....	....	....	....	....	....
	SCL Tigers Langnau	Swiss	2	1	1	0	120	9	0	4.50	....	....	....	....	....	....	....
	HC Davos	Swiss	8	3	4	0	445	20	0	2.70	4	3	1	216	5	0	1.39
2009-10	EHC Biel-Bienne	Swiss	40	16	20	0	2319	130	3	3.36	10	3	7	582	33	0	3.40
	EHC Biel-Bienne	Swiss-Q	....	....	....	....	....	....	....	....	7	4	3	419	20	0	2.86
2010-11	EHC Biel-Bienne	Swiss	41	17	24	0	2452	122	3	2.99	....	....	....	....	....	....	....
2011-12	EHC Biel-Bienne	Swiss	49	23	26	0	2865	117	7	2.45	5	1	4	302	18	0	3.57
2012-13	EHC Biel-Bienne	Swiss	49	24	25	0	*2973	149	3	3.01	7	3	4	455	24	0	3.17

Traded to **Calgary** by **St. Louis** with Mark Cundari and St. Louis' 1st round choice (Emile Poirier) in 2013 Entry Draft for Jay Bouwmeester, April 1, 2013.

BERUBE, Jean-Francois (beh-ROO-bay, ZHAWN-fran-SWUH) L.A.

Goaltender. Catches left. 6'1", 174 lbs. Born, Repentigny, Que., July 13, 1991.
(Los Angeles' 4th choice, 95th overall, in 2009 Entry Draft).

			Regular Season								Playoffs						
Season	**Club**	**League**	**GP**	**W**	**L**	**O/T**	**Mins**	**GA**	**SO**	**Avg**	**GP**	**W**	**L**	**Mins**	**GA**	**SO**	**Avg**
2007-08	Laurentides	QAAA	10	0	6	1	511	35	0	4.11	....	....	....	....	....	....	....
	Lachute Stars	QueAA					STATISTICS NOT AVAILABLE										
2008-09	Montreal	QMJHL	20	6	9	0	1059	51	1	2.89	1	0	0	20	1	0	3.00
2009-10	Montreal	QMJHL	45	17	23	0	2394	121	1	3.03	7	3	4	449	18	0	2.40
	Manchester	AHL	3	2	1	0	180	11	0	3.67	....	....	....	....	....	....	....
2010-11	Montreal	QMJHL	50	32	7	8	2935	127	3	2.60	10	6	4	623	29	*2	2.79
2011-12	Ontario Reign	ECHL	37	17	13	4	2091	100	4	2.87	4	1	2	206	11	0	3.20
2012-13	Ontario Reign	ECHL	24	15	6	2	1418	53	1	2.24	10	6	4	608	21	1	2.07
	Manchester	AHL	2	0	2	0	97	7	0	4.32	....	....	....	....	....	....	....

BIBEAU, Antoine (Bee-BOH, an-TWAHN) TOR

Goaltender. Catches left. 6'2", 210 lbs. Born, Victoriaville, Que., May 1, 1994.
(Toronto's 4th choice, 172nd overall, in 2013 Entry Draft).

			Regular Season								Playoffs						
Season	**Club**	**League**	**GP**	**W**	**L**	**O/T**	**Mins**	**GA**	**SO**	**Avg**	**GP**	**W**	**L**	**Mins**	**GA**	**SO**	**Avg**
2009-10	Trois-Rivieres	QAAA	22	8	4	3	1023	59	0	3.46	2	0	1	79	4	0	3.05
2010-11	Trois-Rivieres	QAAA	29	16	8	2	1521	83	0	3.27	5	2	3	266	21	0	4.74
	Lewiston	QMJHL	3	2	0	0	144	5	0	2.10	....	....	....	....	....	....	....
2011-12	P.E.I. Rocket	QMJHL	29	7	9	1	1183	88	0	4.46	....	....	....	....	....	....	....
2012-13	P.E.I. Rocket	QMJHL	46	28	11	3	2521	118	*5	2.81	6	2	4	374	21	0	3.37

BINNINGTON, Jordan (BIHN-ihng-tuhn, JOHR-duhn) ST.L.

Goaltender. Catches left. 6'2", 162 lbs. Born, Richmond Hill, Ont., July 11, 1993.
(St. Louis' 4th choice, 88th overall, in 2011 Entry Draft).

			Regular Season								Playoffs						
Season	**Club**	**League**	**GP**	**W**	**L**	**O/T**	**Mins**	**GA**	**SO**	**Avg**	**GP**	**W**	**L**	**Mins**	**GA**	**SO**	**Avg**
2008-09	Vaughan Kings	GTHL	....	34	15	....	....	....	....	2.18	....	....	....	....	....	....	....
	Dixie Beehives	ON-Jr.A	1	0	1	0	59	3	0	3.04	....	....	....	....	....	....	....
2009-10	Owen Sound	OHL	22	6	10	2	1068	78	0	4.38	....	....	....	....	....	....	....
2010-11	Owen Sound	OHL	46	27	12	5	2596	132	1	3.05	7	4	2	355	19	0	3.21
2011-12	Owen Sound	OHL	39	21	17	1	2304	115	1	2.99	2	0	2	120	10	0	5.00
	Peoria Rivermen	AHL	1	0	1	0	60	3	0	3.02	....	....	....	....	....	....	....
2012-13	Owen Sound	OHL	50	32	12	6	3011	109	*7	2.17	12	6	6	705	33	0	2.81

Memorial Cup All-Star Team (2011) • Hap Emms Memorial Trophy (Memorial Cup – Top Goaltender) (2011) • OHL First All-Star Team (2013)

BIRON, Martin (BEE-rawn, MAHR-tihn) NYR

Goaltender. Catches left. 6'2", 186 lbs. Born, Lac-St-Charles, Que., August 15, 1977.
(Buffalo's 2nd choice, 16th overall, in 1995 Entry Draft).

			Regular Season								Playoffs						
Season	**Club**	**League**	**GP**	**W**	**L**	**O/T**	**Mins**	**GA**	**SO**	**Avg**	**GP**	**W**	**L**	**Mins**	**GA**	**SO**	**Avg**
1993-94	Trois-Rivieres	QAAA	23	14	8	1	1412	80	1	3.40	2	1	1	112	7	0	3.73
1994-95	Beauport Harfangs	QMJHL	56	29	16	9	3199	132	3	*2.48	16	8	7	903	37	*4	2.46
1995-96	Beauport Harfangs	QMJHL	55	29	17	7	3207	152	1	2.84	*19	*12	7	1135	64	0	3.38
	Buffalo	**NHL**	**3**	**0**	**2**	**0**	**119**	**10**	**0**	**5.04**	....	....	....	....	....	....	....

1996-97	Beauport Harfangs	QMJHL	18	6	10	1	935	62	1	3.98	....	....	....	....	....	....	....
	Hull Olympiques	QMJHL	16	11	4	1	972	43	2	2.66	6	3	1	326	19	0	3.50
1997-98	South Carolina	ECHL	2	0	1	1	86	3	0	2.09	....	....	....	....	....	....	....
	Rochester	AHL	41	14	18	6	2312	113	*5	2.93	4	1	3	239	16	0	4.01
1998-99	**Buffalo**	**NHL**	**6**	**1**	**2**	**1**	**281**	**10**	**0**	**2.14**	....	....	....	....	....	....	....
	Rochester	AHL	52	36	13	3	3129	108	*6	*2.07	*20	12	8	1167	42	1	*2.16
99-2000	**Buffalo**	**NHL**	**41**	**19**	**18**	**2**	**2229**	**90**	**5**	**2.42**	....	....	....	....	....	....	....
	Rochester	AHL	6	6	0	0	344	12	1	2.09	....	....	....	....	....	....	....
2000-01	**Buffalo**	**NHL**	**18**	**7**	**7**	**1**	**918**	**39**	**2**	**2.55**	....	....	....	....	....	....	....
	Rochester	AHL	4	3	1	0	239	4	1	1.00	....	....	....	....	....	....	....
2001-02	**Buffalo**	**NHL**	**72**	**31**	**28**	**10**	**4085**	**151**	**4**	**2.22**	....	....	....	....	....	....	....
2002-03	**Buffalo**	**NHL**	**54**	**17**	**28**	**6**	**3170**	**135**	**4**	**2.56**	....	....	....	....	....	....	....
2003-04	**Buffalo**	**NHL**	**52**	**26**	**18**	**5**	**2972**	**125**	**2**	**2.52**	....	....	....	....	....	....	....
2004-05								Did not play									
2005-06	**Buffalo**	**NHL**	**35**	**21**	**8**	**3**	**1934**	**93**	**1**	**2.89**	....	....	....	....	....	....	....
2006-07	**Buffalo**	**NHL**	**19**	**12**	**4**	**1**	**1066**	**54**	**0**	**3.04**	....	....	....	....	....	....	....
	Philadelphia	**NHL**	**16**	**6**	**8**	**2**	**935**	**47**	**0**	**3.02**	....	....	....	....	....	....	....
2007-08	**Philadelphia**	**NHL**	**62**	**30**	**20**	**9**	**3539**	**153**	**5**	**2.59**	**17**	**9**	**8**	**1049**	**52**	**1**	**2.97**
2008-09	**Philadelphia**	**NHL**	**55**	**29**	**19**	**5**	**3177**	**146**	**2**	**2.76**	**6**	**2**	**4**	**375**	**16**	**1**	**2.56**
2009-10	**NY Islanders**	**NHL**	**29**	**9**	**14**	**4**	**1634**	**89**	**1**	**3.27**	....	....	....	....	....	....	....
	Bridgeport	AHL	2	1	1	0	124	7	0	3.40	....	....	....	....	....	....	....
2010-11	**NY Rangers**	**NHL**	**17**	**8**	**6**	**0**	**928**	**33**	**0**	**2.13**	....	....	....	....	....	....	....
2011-12	**NY Rangers**	**NHL**	**21**	**12**	**6**	**2**	**1220**	**50**	**2**	**2.46**	....	....	....	....	....	....	....
2012-13	**NY Rangers**	**NHL**	**6**	**2**	**2**	**1**	**336**	**13**	**0**	**2.32**	....	....	....	....	....	....	....
	NHL Totals		**506**	**230**	**190**	**52**	**28543**	**1238**	**28**	**2.60**	**23**	**11**	**12**	**1424**	**68**	**2**	**2.87**

QMJHL All-Rookie Team (1995) • Canadian Major Junior First All-Star Team (1995) • Canadian Major Junior Goaltender of the Year (1995) • AHL First All-Star Team (1999) • Harry "Hap" Holmes Memorial Award (AHL – fewest goals against) (1999) (shared with Tom Draper) • Aldege "Baz" Bastien Memorial Award (AHL – Outstanding Goaltender) (1999)

Traded to **Philadelphia** by **Buffalo** for Philadelphia's 2nd round choice (T.J. Brennan) in 2007 Entry Draft, February 27, 2007. Signed as a free agent by **NY Islanders**, July 22, 2009. Signed as a free agent by **NY Rangers**, July 1, 2010.

BISHOP, Ben (BIH-shuhp, BEHN) T.B.

Goaltender. Catches left. 6'7", 214 lbs. Born, Denver, CO, November 21, 1986.
(St. Louis' 3rd choice, 85th overall, in 2005 Entry Draft).

			Regular Season								Playoffs						
Season	Club	League	GP	W	L	O/T	Mins	GA	SO	Avg	GP	W	L	Mins	GA	SO	Avg
2003-04	St.L. AAA Blues	MAHL	11	8	1	2	660	19	1	1.73	....	....	....	....	....	....	....
	St.L. AAA Blues	Exhib.	26	15	7	4	1480	62	3	2.51	....	....	....	....	....	....	....
2004-05	Texas Tornado	NAHL	45	*35	8	0	2577	83	5	1.93	*11	*9	2	*660	30	0	2.73
2005-06	University of Maine	H-East	31	21	8	2	1788	68	0	2.28	....	....	....	....	....	....	....
2006-07	University of Maine	H-East	34	21	9	2	1907	68	3	2.14	....	....	....	....	....	....	....
2007-08	University of Maine	H-East	34	13	18	3	1972	80	2	2.43	....	....	....	....	....	....	....
	Peoria Rivermen	AHL	5	2	2	1	302	12	0	2.38	....	....	....	....	....	....	....
2008-09	**St. Louis**	**NHL**	**6**	**1**	**1**	**1**	**245**	**12**	**0**	**2.94**	....	....	....	....	....	....	....
	Peoria Rivermen	AHL	33	15	16	1	1898	89	1	2.81	....	....	....	....	....	....	....
2009-10	Peoria Rivermen	AHL	48	23	18	4	2793	129	0	2.77	....	....	....	....	....	....	....
2010-11	**St. Louis**	**NHL**	**7**	**3**	**4**	**0**	**369**	**17**	**1**	**2.76**	....	....	....	....	....	....	....
	Peoria Rivermen	AHL	35	17	14	2	2043	87	2	2.55	1	0	1	59	2	0	2.04
2011-12	Peoria Rivermen	AHL	38	24	14	0	2258	85	*6	2.26	....	....	....	....	....	....	....
	Ottawa	**NHL**	**10**	**3**	**3**	**2**	**532**	**22**	**0**	**2.48**	....	....	....	....	....	....	....
	Binghamton	AHL	3	2	1	0	179	7	0	2.35	....	....	....	....	....	....	....
2012-13	Binghamton	AHL	13	8	3	2	787	34	0	2.59	....	....	....	....	....	....	....
	Ottawa	**NHL**	**13**	**8**	**5**	**0**	**758**	**31**	**1**	**2.45**	....	....	....	....	....	....	....
	Tampa Bay	**NHL**	**9**	**3**	**4**	**1**	**502**	**25**	**1**	**2.99**	....	....	....	....	....	....	....
	NHL Totals		**45**	**18**	**17**	**4**	**2406**	**107**	**3**	**2.67**	....	....	....	....	....	....	....

Hockey East All-Rookie Team (2006) • Hockey East Second All-Star Team (2008) • AHL Second All-Star Team (2012)

Traded to **Ottawa** by **St. Louis** for Ottawa's 2nd round choice (Thomas Vannelli) in 2013 Entry Draft, February 26. 2012. Traded to **Tampa Bay** by **Ottawa** for Cory Conacher and Philadelphia's 4th round choice (previously acquired, Ottawa selected Tobias Lindberg) in 2013 Entry Draft, April 3, 2013.

BOBKOV, Igor (bawb-KAWF, EE-gohr) ANA

Goaltender. Catches left. 6'6", 228 lbs. Born, Surgut, USSR, January 2, 1991.
(Anaheim's 4th choice, 76th overall, in 2009 Entry Draft).

			Regular Season								Playoffs						
Season	Club	League	GP	W	L	O/T	Mins	GA	SO	Avg	GP	W	L	Mins	GA	SO	Avg
2008-09	Magnitogorsk 2	Russia-3	9	....	....	....	....	24	....	....	....	....	....	....	....	....	....
2009-10	Magnitogorsk Jr.	Russia-Jr.	14	....	....	....	665	30	2	2.71	2	....	....	59	3	0	3.05
2010-11	London Knights	OHL	21	4	10	0	1048	72	0	4.12	3	0	0	29	2	0	4.14
	Syracuse Crunch	AHL	2	2	0	0	120	7	0	3.51	....	....	....	....	....	....	....
2011-12	Kingston	OHL	58	17	32	6	3300	200	1	3.64	....	....	....	....	....	....	....
	Syracuse Crunch	AHL	4	2	1	1	246	11	0	2.68	....	....	....	....	....	....	....
2012-13	Norfolk Admirals	AHL	28	11	17	0	1570	82	2	3.13	....	....	....	....	....	....	....

BOBROVSKY, Sergei (bawb-RAWF-skee, SAIR-gay) CBJ

Goaltender. Catches left. 6'2", 190 lbs. Born, Novokuznetsk, USSR, September 20, 1988.

			Regular Season								Playoffs						
Season	Club	League	GP	W	L	O/T	Mins	GA	SO	Avg	GP	W	L	Mins	GA	SO	Avg
2006-07	Novokuznetsk	Russia	8	....	....	....	280	13	0	2.78	....	....	....	....	....	....	....
2007-08	Novokuznetsk	Russia	24	....	....	....	1153	57	1	2.97	....	....	....	....	....	....	....
2008-09	Novokuznetsk	KHL	32	....	....	....	1636	69	1	2.53	....	....	....	....	....	....	....
2009-10	Novokuznetsk	KHL	35	....	....	....	1964	89	1	2.72	....	....	....	....	....	....	....
2010-11	**Philadelphia**	**NHL**	**54**	**28**	**13**	**8**	**3017**	**130**	**0**	**2.59**	**6**	**0**	**2**	**186**	**10**	**0**	**3.23**
2011-12	**Philadelphia**	**NHL**	**29**	**14**	**10**	**2**	**1550**	**78**	**0**	**3.02**	**1**	**0**	**0**	**37**	**5**	**0**	**8.11**
2012-13	SKA St. Petersburg	KHL	24	18	3	0	1420	46	4	1.94	....	....	....	....	....	....	....
	Columbus	**NHL**	**38**	**21**	**11**	**6**	**2219**	**74**	**4**	**2.00**	....	....	....	....	....	....	....
	NHL Totals		**121**	**63**	**34**	**16**	**6786**	**282**	**4**	**2.49**	**7**	**0**	**2**	**223**	**15**	**0**	**4.04**

NHL First All-Star Team (2013) • Vezina Trophy (2013)

Signed as a free agent by **Philadelphia**, May 6, 2010. Traded to **Columbus** by **Philadelphia** for Ottawa's 2nd round choice (previously acquired, Philadelphia selected Anthony Stolarz) in 2012 Entry Draft, Vancouver's 4th round choice (previously acquired, Philadelphia selected Taylor Leier) in 2012 Entry Draft and Phoenix's 4th round choice (previously acquired, later traded to Los Angeles – Los Angeles selected Justin Auger) in 2013 Entry Draft, June 22, 2012. Signed as a free agent by **St. Petersburg** (KHL), September 21, 2012.

BOUCHER, Brian (BOO-shay, BRIGH-uhn)

Goaltender. Catches left. 6'2", 198 lbs. Born, Woonsocket, RI, January 2, 1977.
(Philadelphia's 1st choice, 22nd overall, in 1995 Entry Draft).

			Regular Season								Playoffs						
Season	Club	League	GP	W	L	O/T	Mins	GA	SO	Avg	GP	W	L	Mins	GA	SO	Avg
1993-94	Mount St. Charles	High-RI	15	*14	0	1	*504	*8	*9	*0.57	4	*4	0	*180	*6	*1	*1.20
1994-95	Wexford Raiders	ON-Jr.A	8	....	....	....	425	23	0	3.25	....	....	....	....	....	....	....
	Tri-City Americans	WHL	35	17	11	2	1969	108	1	3.29	13	6	5	795	50	0	3.77
1995-96	Tri-City Americans	WHL	55	33	19	2	3183	181	1	3.41	11	6	5	653	37	*2	3.40
1996-97	Tri-City Americans	WHL	41	10	24	6	2458	149	1	3.64	....	....	....	....	....	....	....
1997-98	Philadelphia	AHL	34	16	12	3	1901	101	0	3.19	2	0	0	30	1	0	1.95
1998-99	Philadelphia	AHL	36	20	8	5	2061	89	2	2.59	16	9	7	947	45	0	2.85
99-2000	**Philadelphia**	**NHL**	**35**	**20**	**10**	**3**	**2038**	**65**	**4**	***1.91**	**18**	**11**	**7**	**1183**	**40**	**1**	**2.03**
	Philadelphia	AHL	1	0	0	1	65	3	0	2.77	....	....	....	....	....	....	....
2000-01	**Philadelphia**	**NHL**	**27**	**8**	**12**	**5**	**1470**	**80**	**1**	**3.27**	**1**	**0**	**0**	**37**	**3**	**0**	**4.86**
2001-02	**Philadelphia**	**NHL**	**41**	**18**	**16**	**4**	**2295**	**92**	**2**	**2.41**	**2**	**0**	**1**	**88**	**2**	**0**	**1.36**
2002-03	**Phoenix**	**NHL**	**45**	**15**	**20**	**8**	**2544**	**128**	**0**	**3.02**	....	....	....	....	....	....	....
2003-04	**Phoenix**	**NHL**	**40**	**10**	**19**	**10**	**2364**	**108**	**5**	**2.74**	....	....	....	....	....	....	....
2004-05	HV 71 Jonkoping	Sweden	4	....	....	....	235	13	0	3.32	....	....	....	....	....	....	....
2005-06	**Phoenix**	**NHL**	**11**	**3**	**6**	**0**	**512**	**33**	**0**	**3.87**	....	....	....	....	....	....	....
	San Antonio	AHL	6	2	3	0	345	8	0	1.39	....	....	....	....	....	....	....
	Calgary	**NHL**	**3**	**1**	**2**	**0**	**182**	**15**	**0**	**4.95**	....	....	....	....	....	....	....
2006-07	**Chicago**	**NHL**	**15**	**1**	**10**	**3**	**827**	**45**	**1**	**3.26**	....	....	....	....	....	....	....
	Columbus	**NHL**	**3**	**1**	**1**	**0**	**142**	**9**	**0**	**3.80**	....	....	....	....	....	....	....
2007-08	Philadelphia	AHL	42	23	16	1	2288	94	4	2.47	....	....	....	....	....	....	....
	San Jose	**NHL**	**5**	**3**	**1**	**1**	**238**	**7**	**1**	**1.76**	**1**	**0**	**0**	**2**	**0**	**0**	**0.00**
2008-09	**San Jose**	**NHL**	**22**	**12**	**6**	**3**	**1291**	**47**	**2**	**2.18**	....	....	....	....	....	....	....
2009-10	**Philadelphia**	**NHL**	**33**	**9**	**18**	**3**	**1742**	**80**	**1**	**2.76**	**12**	**6**	**6**	**656**	**27**	**1**	**2.47**
	Adirondack	AHL	1	1	0	0	60	2	0	2.00	....	....	....	....	....	....	....
2010-11	**Philadelphia**	**NHL**	**34**	**18**	**10**	**4**	**1885**	**76**	**0**	**2.42**	**9**	**4**	**4**	**422**	**22**	**0**	**3.13**
2011-12	**Carolina**	**NHL**	**10**	**1**	**6**	**1**	**546**	**31**	**0**	**3.41**	....	....	....	....	....	....	....
2012-13	Adirondack	AHL	16	6	8	1	911	39	0	2.57	....	....	....	....	....	....	....
	Philadelphia	**NHL**	**4**	**0**	**2**	**0**	**144**	**6**	**0**	**2.50**	....	....	....	....	....	....	....
	NHL Totals		**328**	**120**	**139**	**45**	**18220**	**822**	**17**	**2.71**	**43**	**21**	**18**	**2388**	**94**	**2**	**2.36**

WHL West Second All-Star Team (1996) • WHL West First All-Star Team (1997) • WHL Goaltender of the Year (1997) • NHL All-Rookie Team (2000)

Traded to **Phoenix** by **Philadelphia** with Nashville's 3rd round choice (previously acquired, Phoenix selected Joe Callahan) in 2002 Entry Draft for Michal Handzus and Robert Esche, June 12, 2002. Signed as a free agent by **Jonkoping** (Sweden), October 20, 2004. Traded to **Calgary** by **Phoenix** with Mike Leclerc for Steve Reinprecht and Philippe Sauve, February 2, 2006. Signed as a free agent by **Chicago**, September 24, 2006. Claimed on waivers by **Columbus** from **Chicago**, February 27, 2007. Signed as a free agent by **Philadelphia** (AHL), July 23, 2007. Signed as a free agent by **San Jose**, February 26, 2008. Signed as a free agent by **Philadelphia**, July 1, 2009. Signed as a free agent by **Carolina**, July 1, 2011. Traded to **Philadelphia** by **Carolina** with Mark Alt for Luke Pither, January 13, 2013. Signed as a free agent by **Zug** (Swiss), July 17, 2013.

BRASSARD, Francois (brah-SAHR, frahn-SWUH) OTT

Goaltender. Catches left. 6'1", 167 lbs. Born, Gatineau, Que., January 31, 1994.
(Ottawa's 6th choice, 166th overall, in 2012 Entry Draft).

			Regular Season								Playoffs						
Season	Club	League	GP	W	L	O/T	Mins	GA	SO	Avg	GP	W	L	Mins	GA	SO	Avg
2010-11	Lac St-Louis Lions	QAAA	28	23	3	1	1628	67	2	2.47	15	13	2	911	40	0	2.63
2011-12	Quebec Remparts	QMJHL	37	20	10	3	1953	91	2	2.80	....	....	....	....	....	....	....
2012-13	Quebec Remparts	QMJHL	*58	33	18	4	*3292	150	2	2.73	11	5	6	656	35	1	3.20

BRITTAIN, Sam (brih-TAYN, SAM) FLA

Goaltender. Catches left. 6'3", 215 lbs. Born, Calgary, Alta., May 10, 1992.
(Florida's 8th choice, 92nd overall, in 2010 Entry Draft).

			Regular Season								Playoffs						
Season	Club	League	GP	W	L	O/T	Mins	GA	SO	Avg	GP	W	L	Mins	GA	SO	Avg
2008-09	Calgary Buffaloes	AMHL	26	14	9	3	1542	67	....	2.61	15	11	4	901	45	....	3.00
	Canmore Eagles	AJHL	3	1	2	0	179	9	0	3.02	....	....	....	....	....	....	....
2009-10	Canmore Eagles	AJHL	52	23	19	8	3065	167	2	3.27	9	5	4	559	28	0	3.01
2010-11	U. of Denver	WCHA	33	19	9	5	1998	76	1	2.28	....	....	....	....	....	....	....
2011-12	U. of Denver	WCHA	12	8	4	0	736	29	1	2.36	....	....	....	....	....	....	....
2012-13	U. of Denver	WCHA	13	5	7	0	752	37	0	2.95	....	....	....	....	....	....	....

WCHA All-Rookie Team (2011)

BRODEUR, Anthony (broh-DUHR, AN-thuh-nee) N.J.

Goaltender. Catches left. 5'11", 180 lbs. Born, Paterson, NJ, June 8, 1995.
(New Jersey's 5th choice, 208th overall, in 2013 Entry Draft).

			Regular Season								Playoffs						
Season	Club	League	GP	W	L	O/T	Mins	GA	SO	Avg	GP	W	L	Mins	GA	SO	Avg
2009-10	Shattuck Bantam	High-MN	29	18	6	3	....	....	....	1.70	....	....	....	....	....	....	....
2010-11	Shattuck U16	High-MN	27	25	2	0	1389	59	3	2.18	....	....	....	....	....	....	....
2011-12	Shat.-St. Mary's	High-MN	29	24	3	1	1635	63	4	2.31	....	....	....	....	....	....	....
2012-13	Shattuck St. Mary's	High-MN	28	21	5	2	1548	64	5	2.48	....	....	....	....	....	....	....

BRODEUR, Martin (broh-DUHR, MAHR-tihn) N.J.

Goaltender. Catches left. 6'2", 220 lbs. Born, Montreal, Que., May 6, 1972.
(New Jersey's 1st choice, 20th overall, in 1990 Entry Draft).

			Regular Season								Playoffs						
Season	Club	League	GP	W	L	O/T	Mins	GA	SO	Avg	GP	W	L	Mins	GA	SO	Avg
1988-89	Montreal-Bourassa	QAAA	27	13	12	1	1580	98	0	3.72	3	0	3	210	14	0	3.99
1989-90	St-Hyacinthe Laser	QMJHL	42	23	12	2	2331	156	0	4.02	12	5	7	680	46	0	4.06
1990-91	St-Hyacinthe Laser	QMJHL	52	22	22	4	2946	162	2	3.30	4	0	4	232	16	0	4.14
1991-92	St-Hyacinthe Laser	QMJHL	48	27	14	4	2846	161	2	3.39	5	2	3	317	14	0	2.65
	New Jersey	**NHL**	**4**	**2**	**1**	**0**	**179**	**10**	**0**	**3.35**	**1**	**0**	**1**	**32**	**3**	**0**	**5.63**
1992-93	Utica Devils	AHL	32	14	13	5	1952	131	0	4.03	4	1	3	258	18	0	4.19
1993-94	**New Jersey**	**NHL**	**47**	**27**	**11**	**8**	**2625**	**105**	**3**	**2.40**	**17**	**8**	**9**	**1171**	**38**	**1**	**1.95**
1994-95 ♦	**New Jersey**	**NHL**	**40**	**19**	**11**	**6**	**2184**	**89**	**3**	**2.45**	***20**	***16**	**4**	***1222**	**34**	***3**	***1.67**
1995-96	**New Jersey**	**NHL**	**77**	**34**	**30**	**12**	***4433**	**173**	**6**	**2.34**	....	....	....	....	....	....	....
1996-97	**New Jersey**	**NHL**	**67**	**37**	**14**	**13**	**3838**	**120**	***10**	***1.88**	**10**	**5**	**5**	**659**	**19**	**2**	***1.73**

1997-98	New Jersey	NHL	70	*43	17	8	4128	130	10	1.89	6	2	4	366	12	0	1.97
1998-99	New Jersey	NHL	*70	*39	21	10	*4239	162	4	2.29	7	3	4	425	20	0	2.82
99-2000 ♦	New Jersey	NHL	72	*43	20	8	4312	161	6	2.24	*23	*16	7	*1450	39	2	*1.61
2000-01	New Jersey	NHL	72	*42	17	11	4297	166	9	2.32	*25	15	10	*1505	52	*4	2.07
2001-02	New Jersey	NHL	*73	38	26	9	*4347	156	4	2.15	6	2	4	381	9	1	1.42
	Canada	Olympics	5	*4	0	1	300	9	0	*1.80	....	....	....	....	....	....	....
2002-03 ♦	New Jersey	NHL	73	*41	23	9	4374	147	*9	2.02	*24	*16	8	*1491	41	*7	1.65
2003-04	New Jersey	NHL	*75	*38	26	11	*4555	154	*11	2.03	5	1	4	298	13	0	2.62
2004-05			DID NOT PLAY														
2005-06	New Jersey	NHL	73	*43	23	7	4365	187	5	2.57	9	5	4	533	20	1	2.25
	Canada	Olympics	4	2	2	0	239	8	0	2.01	....	....	....	....	....	....	....
2006-07	New Jersey	NHL	*78	*48	23	7	*4697	171	*12	2.18	11	5	6	688	28	1	2.44
2007-08	New Jersey	NHL	*77	44	27	6	*4635	168	4	2.17	5	1	4	301	16	0	3.19
2008-09	New Jersey	NHL	31	19	9	3	1814	73	5	2.41	7	3	4	427	17	1	2.39
2009-10	New Jersey	NHL	*77	*45	25	6	*4499	168	*9	2.24	5	1	4	299	15	0	3.01
	Canada	Olympics	2	1	1	0	124	6	0	2.90	....	....	....	....	....	....	....
2010-11	New Jersey	NHL	56	23	26	3	3116	127	6	2.45	....	....	....	....	....	....	....
2011-12	New Jersey	NHL	59	31	21	4	3392	136	3	2.41	*24	14	9	*1471	52	1	2.12
2012-13	New Jersey	NHL	29	13	9	7	1757	65	2	2.22	....	....	....	....	....	....	....
	NHL Totals		1220	669	380	148	71786	2668	121	2.23	205	113	91	12719	428	24	2.02

QMJHL All-Rookie Team (1990) • QMJHL Second All-Star Team (1992) • NHL All-Rookie Team (1994) • Calder Memorial Trophy (1994) • NHL Second All-Star Team (1997, 1998, 2006, 2008) • William M. Jennings Trophy (1997) (shared with Mike Dunham) • William M. Jennings Trophy (1998, 2004, 2010) • NHL First All-Star Team (2003, 2004, 2007) • William M. Jennings Trophy (2003) (tied with Roman Cechmanek/Robert Esche) • Vezina Trophy (2003, 2004, 2007, 2008)

Played in NHL All-Star Game (1996, 1997, 1998, 1999, 2000, 2001, 2003, 2004, 2007)

• Scored a goal in playoffs vs. Montreal, April 17, 1997. • Missed majority of 2008-09 due to elbow injury vs. Atlanta, November 1, 2008.

BROSSOIT, Laurent (BRAH-sah, LAWR-ehnt) CGY

Goaltender. Catches left. 6'3", 200 lbs. Born, Port Alberni, B.C., March 23, 1993.
(Calgary's 5th choice, 164th overall, in 2011 Entry Draft).

			Regular Season								Playoffs						
Season	Club	League	GP	W	L	O/T	Mins	GA	SO	Avg	GP	W	L	Mins	GA	SO	Avg
2008-09	Valley West Hawks	BCMML	STATISTICS NOT AVAILABLE														
	Edmonton	WHL	1	0	0	0	37	5	0	8.11	....	....	....	....	....	....	....
2009-10	Cowichan Valley	BCHL	21	10	8	0	999	61	2	3.66	5	1	3	259	17	0	3.93
	Edmonton	WHL	2	0	1	0	86	4	0	2.79	....	....	....	....	....	....	....
2010-11	Edmonton	WHL	34	13	12	2	1664	92	2	3.32	2	0	2	117	7	0	3.59
2011-12	Edmonton	WHL	61	*42	13	5	3574	147	3	2.47	20	*16	4	1204	41	*2	*2.04
2012-13	Edmonton	WHL	49	33	8	6	2854	107	5	2.25	*22	14	8	*1322	40	*5	1.82

WHL East Second All-Star Team (2013)

BRYZGALOV, Ilya (breez-GAH-lahf, IHL-yah)

Goaltender. Catches left. 6'3", 213 lbs. Born, Togliatti, USSR, June 22, 1980.
(Anaheim's 2nd choice, 44th overall, in 2000 Entry Draft).

			Regular Season								Playoffs						
Season	Club	League	GP	W	L	O/T	Mins	GA	SO	Avg	GP	W	L	Mins	GA	SO	Avg
1996-97	Lada Togliatti 2	Russia-3	5	....	....	....	....	....	....	....	....	....	....	....	....	....	....
1997-98	Lada Togliatti 2	Russia-3	8	....	....	....	....	28	....	....	....	....	....	....	....	....	....
1998-99	Lada Togliatti 2	Russia-4	20	....	....	....	....	43	....	....	....	....	....	....	....	....	....
99-2000	Spartak Moscow	Russia-2	10	....	....	....	500	21	....	2.52	....	....	....	....	....	....	....
	Lada Togliatti 2	Russia-3	2	....	....	....	....	5	....	....	....	....	....	....	....	....	....
	Lada Togliatti	Russia	14	....	....	....	796	18	3	1.36	7	....	....	407	10	1	1.47
2000-01	Lada Togliatti	Russia	34	....	....	....	1992	61	8	1.84	5	....	....	249	8	0	1.93
2001-02	Anaheim	NHL	1	0	0	0	32	1	0	1.88	....	....	....	....	....	....	....
	Cincinnati	AHL	45	20	16	4	2399	99	4	2.48	....	....	....	....	....	....	....
	Russia	Olympics	DID NOT PLAY – SPARE GOALTENDER														
2002-03	Cincinnati	AHL	54	12	26	9	3020	142	1	2.82	....	....	....	....	....	....	....
2003-04	Anaheim	NHL	1	1	0	0	60	2	0	2.00	....	....	....	....	....	....	....
	Cincinnati	AHL	*64	27	25	10	*3748	145	6	2.32	9	5	4	536	27	1	3.02
2004-05	Cincinnati	AHL	36	17	13	1	2007	87	4	2.60	7	3	3	314	13	0	2.48
2005-06	Anaheim	NHL	31	13	12	1	1575	66	1	2.51	11	6	4	659	16	*3	*1.46
	Russia	Olympics	1	0	1	0	60	5	0	5.00	....	....	....	....	....	....	....
2006-07 ♦	Anaheim	NHL	27	10	8	6	1509	62	1	2.47	5	3	1	267	10	0	2.25
2007-08	Anaheim	NHL	9	2	3	1	447	19	0	2.55	....	....	....	....	....	....	....
	Phoenix	NHL	55	26	22	5	3167	128	3	2.43	....	....	....	....	....	....	....
2008-09	Phoenix	NHL	65	26	31	6	3760	187	3	2.98	....	....	....	....	....	....	....
2009-10	Phoenix	NHL	69	42	20	6	4084	156	8	2.29	7	3	4	419	24	0	3.44
	Russia	Olympics	2	0	1	0	101	3	0	1.78	....	....	....	....	....	....	....
2010-11	Phoenix	NHL	68	36	20	10	4060	168	7	2.48	4	0	4	234	17	0	4.36
2011-12	Philadelphia	NHL	59	33	16	7	3415	141	6	2.48	11	5	6	642	37	0	3.46
2012-13	CSKA Moscow	KHL	12	6	5	0	647	23	0	2.13	....	....	....	....	....	....	....
	Philadelphia	NHL	40	19	17	3	2298	107	1	2.79	....	....	....	....	....	....	....
	NHL Totals		425	208	149	45	24407	1037	30	2.55	38	17	19	2221	104	3	2.81

NHL Second All-Star Team (2010)

Claimed on waivers by **Phoenix** from **Anaheim**, November 17, 2007. Traded to **Philadelphia** by **Phoenix** for Matt Clackson, Philadelphia's 3rd round choice (later traded to Pittsburgh – Pittsburgh selected Oskar Sundqvist) in 2012 Entry Draft and future considerations, June 7, 2011. Signed as a free agent by **CSKA Moscow** (KHL), September 19, 2012.

BUDAJ, Peter (BOO-digh, PEE-tuhr) MTL

Goaltender. Catches left. 6'1", 195 lbs. Born, Banska Bystrica, Czech., September 18, 1982.
(Colorado's 1st choice, 63rd overall, in 2001 Entry Draft).

			Regular Season								Playoffs						
Season	Club	League	GP	W	L	O/T	Mins	GA	SO	Avg	GP	W	L	Mins	GA	SO	Avg
99-2000	St. Michael's	OHL	34	6	18	1	1676	112	1	4.01	....	....	....	....	....	....	....
2000-01	St. Michael's	OHL	37	17	12	3	1996	95	3	2.86	11	6	4	621	26	1	2.51
2001-02	St. Michael's	OHL	42	26	9	5	2329	89	2	*2.29	12	5	6	621	34	*1	3.29
2002-03	Hershey Bears	AHL	28	10	10	2	1467	65	2	2.66	1	0	0	6	2	0	20.81
2003-04	Hershey Bears	AHL	46	17	20	6	2574	120	3	2.80	....	....	....	....	....	....	....
2004-05	Hershey Bears	AHL	59	29	25	2	3356	148	5	2.65	....	....	....	....	....	....	....
2005-06	Colorado	NHL	34	14	10	6	1803	86	2	2.86	....	....	....	....	....	....	....
	Slovakia	Olympics	3	2	1	0	179	6	0	2.01	....	....	....	....	....	....	....
2006-07	Colorado	NHL	57	31	16	6	3199	143	3	2.68	....	....	....	....	....	....	....
2007-08	Colorado	NHL	35	16	10	4	1912	82	0	2.57	3	0	0	108	6	0	3.33
2008-09	Colorado	NHL	56	20	29	5	3232	154	2	2.86	....	....	....	....	....	....	....
2009-10	Colorado	NHL	15	5	5	2	728	32	1	2.64	1	0	0	9	1	0	6.67
	Slovakia	Olympics	DID NOT PLAY – SPARE GOALTENDER														
2010-11	Colorado	NHL	45	15	21	4	2439	130	1	3.20	....	....	....	....	....	....	....
2011-12	Montreal	NHL	17	5	7	5	1037	44	0	2.55	....	....	....	....	....	....	....
2012-13	Montreal	NHL	13	8	1	1	656	25	1	2.29	2	0	2	63	7	0	6.67
	NHL Totals		272	114	99	33	15006	696	10	2.78	6	0	2	180	14	0	4.67

OHL Second All-Star Team (2002)

Signed as a free agent by **Montreal**, July 1, 2011.

BUNZ, Tyler (BUHNZ, TIGH-luhr) EDM

Goaltender. Catches left. 6'2", 199 lbs. Born, Regina, Sask., February 11, 1992.
(Edmonton's 7th choice, 121st overall, in 2010 Entry Draft).

			Regular Season								Playoffs						
Season	Club	League	GP	W	L	O/T	Mins	GA	SO	Avg	GP	W	L	Mins	GA	SO	Avg
2007-08	St. Albert	AMHL	24	11	9	4	1503	80	....	3.19	4	2	2	240	16	....	4.00
	Medicine Hat	WHL	1	1	0	0	60	3	0	3.00	....	....	....	....	....	....	....
2008-09	Medicine Hat	WHL	22	9	6	1	1007	58	0	3.46	2	0	1	73	6	0	4.93
2009-10	Medicine Hat	WHL	57	31	19	5	3214	156	2	2.91	12	6	6	720	35	0	2.92
2010-11	Medicine Hat	WHL	56	35	13	8	3350	138	3	2.47	10	4	6	566	28	1	2.97
2011-12	Medicine Hat	WHL	61	39	17	5	3616	155	3	2.57	8	4	4	496	23	1	2.78
2012-13	Stockton Thunder	ECHL	37	16	16	4	2130	119	1	3.35	4	1	1	178	9	0	3.03
	Oklahoma City	AHL	1	0	0	0	28	5	0	10.56	....	....	....	....	....	....	....

WHL East Second All-Star Team (2011) • WHL East First All-Star Team (2012) • WHL Goaltender of the Year (2012)

BURKE, Brendan (BUHRK, BREHN-duhn) PHX

Goaltender. Catches left. 6'3", 180 lbs. Born, Scottsdale, AZ, March 11, 1995.
(Phoenix's 5th choice, 163rd overall, in 2013 Entry Draft).

			Regular Season								Playoffs						
Season	Club	League	GP	W	L	O/T	Mins	GA	SO	Avg	GP	W	L	Mins	GA	SO	Avg
2009-10	P.F. Chang's	T1EHL	24	3	14	2	1019	74	0	3.92	....	....	....	....	....	....	....
2010-11	Phx. Jr. Coyotes	T1EHL	23	9	10	3	1211	76	0	3.39	....	....	....	....	....	....	....
2011-12	Portland	WHL	18	7	2	2	754	45	0	3.58	1	0	0	12	1	0	4.85
2012-13	Portland	WHL	33	24	5	1	1876	83	4	2.65	1	0	0	10	2	0	12.52

CAMPBELL, Jack (KAM-behl, JAK) DAL

Goaltender. Catches left. 6'2", 182 lbs. Born, Port Huron, MI, January 9, 1992.
(Dallas' 1st choice, 11th overall, in 2010 Entry Draft).

			Regular Season								Playoffs						
Season	Club	League	GP	W	L	O/T	Mins	GA	SO	Avg	GP	W	L	Mins	GA	SO	Avg
2007-08	Det. Honeybaked	MWEHL	12	8	2	2	630	24	2	2.06	....	....	....	....	....	....	....
	Det. Honeybaked	Minor-MI	25	20	4	1	....	....	....	....	....	....	....	....	....	....	....
2008-09	USNTDP	NAHL	21	14	6	1	1262	53	1	2.52	....	....	....	....	....	....	....
	USNTDP	U-17	7	6	0	1	394	7	3	1.07	....	....	....	....	....	....	....
	USNTDP	U-18	7	7	0	0	421	12	2	1.71	....	....	....	....	....	....	....
2009-10	USNTDP	USHL	11	6	3	1	569	21	1	2.21	....	....	....	....	....	....	....
	USNTDP	U-18	25	16	9	0	1469	54	3	2.21	....	....	....	....	....	....	....
2010-11	Windsor Spitfires	OHL	45	24	14	4	2447	155	0	3.80	18	9	9	1124	70	2	3.74
2011-12	Windsor Spitfires	OHL	12	6	3	2	729	38	1	3.13	....	....	....	....	....	....	....
	Sault Ste. Marie	OHL	34	15	12	5	1945	116	1	3.58	....	....	....	....	....	....	....
	Texas Stars	AHL	12	4	7	0	676	34	1	3.02	....	....	....	....	....	....	....
2012-13	Texas Stars	AHL	40	19	13	3	2108	93	2	2.65	....	....	....	....	....	....	....

CANNATA, Joe (ka-NA-tuh, JOH) VAN

Goaltender. Catches left. 6'1", 200 lbs. Born, Wakefield, MA, January 2, 1990.
(Vancouver's 6th choice, 173rd overall, in 2009 Entry Draft).

			Regular Season								Playoffs						
Season	Club	League	GP	W	L	O/T	Mins	GA	SO	Avg	GP	W	L	Mins	GA	SO	Avg
2007-08	USNTDP	NAHL	5	3	1	1	307	12	0	2.35	....	....	....	....	....	....	....
	USNTDP	U-18	28	13	13	2	1474	64	1	2.61	....	....	....	....	....	....	....
2008-09	Merrimack College	H-East	23	7	11	4	1353	53	2	2.35	....	....	....	....	....	....	....
2009-10	Merrimack College	H-East	24	10	13	1	1362	69	2	3.04	....	....	....	....	....	....	....
2010-11	Merrimack College	H-East	*39	25	10	4	2252	93	1	2.48	....	....	....	....	....	....	....
2011-12	Merrimack College	H-East	36	17	12	7	2179	79	2	2.18	....	....	....	....	....	....	....
	Chicago Wolves	AHL	1	1	0	0	60	2	0	2.00	....	....	....	....	....	....	....
2012-13	Kalamazoo Wings	ECHL	7	3	4	0	419	23	0	3.29	....	....	....	....	....	....	....
	Chicago Wolves	AHL	14	6	6	0	747	33	0	2.65	....	....	....	....	....	....	....

Hockey East First All-Star Team (2012) • NCAA East Second All-American Team (2012)

CARROZZI, Chris (ka-ROH-zee, KRIHS)

Goaltender. Catches left. 6'3", 195 lbs. Born, Ottawa, Ont., March 2, 1990.
(Atlanta's 6th choice, 154th overall, in 2008 Entry Draft).

			Regular Season								Playoffs						
Season	Club	League	GP	W	L	O/T	Mins	GA	SO	Avg	GP	W	L	Mins	GA	SO	Avg
2005-06	Nepean Raiders	Minor-ON	23	....	....	....	....	42	4	1.82	....	....	....	....	....	....	....
2006-07	St. Michael's	OHL	25	6	7	2	1130	81	0	4.30	....	....	....	....	....	....	....
2007-08	St. Michael's	OHL	47	25	18	2	2505	115	*4	2.75	4	0	4	240	18	0	4.50
2008-09	St. Michael's	OHL	47	27	14	3	2715	133	2	2.94	2	0	0	33	3	0	5.52
2009-10	St. Michael's	OHL	37	19	10	5	2089	82	*5	2.36	8	5	2	448	16	1	*2.14
2010-11	Chicago Wolves	AHL	1	0	1	0	65	6	0	5.55	....	....	....	....	....	....	....
	Gwinnett	ECHL	47	16	20	6	2546	137	2	3.23	....	....	....	....	....	....	....
2011-12	St. John's IceCaps	AHL	2	1	1	0	120	7	0	3.50	....	....	....	....	....	....	....
	Colorado Eagles	ECHL	1	0	1	0	60	6	0	6.00	....	....	....	....	....	....	....
	Ontario Reign	ECHL	29	17	6	4	1609	61	3	2.27	2	1	1	100	6	0	3.60
2012-13	Ontario Reign	ECHL	28	19	7	2	1677	77	4	2.75	1	0	0	20	1	0	3.00
	St. John's IceCaps	AHL	3	1	1	0	150	7	0	2.80	....	....	....	....	....	....	....

OHL First All-Star Team (2010)

• Transferred to **Winnipeg** after **Atlanta** franchise relocated, June 21, 2011.

CARRUTH, Mac (kair-UHTH, MAK) CHI

Goaltender. Catches left. 6'2", 180 lbs. Born, Salt Lake City, UT, March 25, 1992.
(Chicago's 10th choice, 191st overall, in 2010 Entry Draft).

			Regular Season								Playoffs						
Season	Club	League	GP	W	L	O/T	Mins	GA	SO	Avg	GP	W	L	Mins	GA	SO	Avg
2008-09	Wenatchee Wild	NAHL	26	18	7	1	1462	74	1	3.04	5	2	2	232	15	0	3.88
2009-10	Wenatchee Wild	NAHL	16	11	4	0	866	35	1	2.42	....	....	....	....	....	....	....
	Portland	WHL	26	14	9	1	1427	81	1	3.41	11	5	4	614	39	0	3.81
2010-11	Portland	WHL	48	31	13	1	2729	140	1	3.08	*21	13	8	*1251	62	1	2.97
2011-12	Portland	WHL	63	*42	17	2	3592	177	2	2.96	*22	15	7	*1328	64	*2	2.89
2012-13	Portland	WHL	39	30	7	2	2275	78	*7	2.06	21	*16	5	1254	34	*5	*1.63

WHL West First All-Star Team (2013)

CLEMMENSEN, Scott (KLEH-mehn-sehn, SKAWT) FLA

Goaltender. Catches left. 6'2", 201 lbs. Born, Des Moines, IA, July 23, 1977.
(New Jersey's 7th choice, 215th overall, in 1997 Entry Draft).

			Regular Season								Playoffs						
Season	**Club**	**League**	**GP**	**W**	**L**	**O/T**	**Mins**	**GA**	**SO**	**Avg**	**GP**	**W**	**L**	**Mins**	**GA**	**SO**	**Avg**
1995-96	Dubuque	USHL	20	10	7	1	1082	62	0	3.44	....	....	....	....	....	....	....
1996-97	Des Moines	USHL	36	22	9	2	2042	111	1	3.26	4	1	2	200	9	1	2.70
1997-98	Boston College	H-East	37	24	9	4	2205	102	*4	2.78	....	....	....	....	....	....	....
1998-99	Boston College	H-East	*42	26	12	4	*2507	120	1	2.87	....	....	....	....	....	....	....
99-2000	Boston College	H-East	29	19	7	0	1610	59	*5	2.20	....	....	....	....	....	....	....
2000-01	Boston College	H-East	*39	*30	7	2	*2312	82	3	2.13	....	....	....	....	....	....	....
2001-02	**New Jersey**	**NHL**	**2**	**0**	**0**	**0**	**20**	**1**	**0**	**3.00**	....	....	....	....	....	....	....
	Albany River Rats	AHL	29	5	19	4	1677	92	0	3.29	....	....	....	....	....	....	....
2002-03	Albany River Rats	AHL	47	12	24	8	2694	119	1	2.65	....	....	....	....	....	....	....
2003-04	**New Jersey**	**NHL**	**4**	**3**	**1**	**0**	**238**	**4**	**2**	**1.01**	....	....	....	....	....	....	....
	Albany River Rats	AHL	22	5	12	4	1309	67	0	3.07	....	....	....	....	....	....	....
2004-05	Albany River Rats	AHL	46	13	25	5	2645	124	2	2.81	....	....	....	....	....	....	....
2005-06	**New Jersey**	**NHL**	**13**	**3**	**4**	**2**	**627**	**35**	**0**	**3.35**	**1**	**0**	**0**	**7**	**0**	**0**	**0.00**
	Albany River Rats	AHL	1	0	1	0	59	5	0	5.05	....	....	....	....	....	....	....
2006-07	**New Jersey**	**NHL**	**6**	**1**	**1**	**2**	**305**	**16**	**0**	**3.15**	....	....	....	....	....	....	....
	Lowell Devils	AHL	1	1	0	0	60	0	1	0.00	....	....	....	....	....	....	....
2007-08	**Toronto**	**NHL**	**3**	**1**	**1**	**0**	**154**	**10**	**0**	**3.90**	....	....	....	....	....	....	....
	Toronto Marlies	AHL	40	23	14	2	2363	96	1	2.44	17	8	9	992	50	0	3.02
2008-09	**New Jersey**	**NHL**	**40**	**25**	**13**	**1**	**2356**	**94**	**2**	**2.39**	....	....	....	....	....	....	....
	Lowell Devils	AHL	12	6	5	1	707	40	0	3.39	....	....	....	....	....	....	....
2009-10	**Florida**	**NHL**	**23**	**9**	**8**	**2**	**1215**	**59**	**1**	**2.91**	....	....	....	....	....	....	....
2010-11	**Florida**	**NHL**	**31**	**8**	**11**	**7**	**1696**	**74**	**1**	**2.62**	....	....	....	....	....	....	....
2011-12	**Florida**	**NHL**	**30**	**14**	**6**	**6**	**1566**	**67**	**1**	**2.57**	**3**	**1**	**2**	**179**	**7**	**0**	**2.35**
	San Antonio	AHL	1	1	0	0	60	1	0	1.00	....	....	....	....	....	....	....
2012-13	**Florida**	**NHL**	**19**	**3**	**7**	**2**	**866**	**53**	**0**	**3.67**	....	....	....	....	....	....	....
	NHL Totals		**171**	**67**	**52**	**22**	**9043**	**413**	**7**	**2.74**	**4**	**1**	**2**	**186**	**7**	**0**	**2.26**

NCAA Championship All-Tournament Team (2001)

Signed as a free agent by **Toronto**, July 6, 2007. Signed as a free agent by **New Jersey**, July 10, 2008. Signed as a free agent by **Florida**, July 1, 2009.

CLERMONT, Maxime (KLAIR-mawnt, max-EEM) N.J.

Goaltender. Catches left. 6'1", 200 lbs. Born, Montreal, Que., December 31, 1991.
(New Jersey's 4th choice, 174th overall, in 2010 Entry Draft).

			Regular Season								Playoffs						
Season	**Club**	**League**	**GP**	**W**	**L**	**O/T**	**Mins**	**GA**	**SO**	**Avg**	**GP**	**W**	**L**	**Mins**	**GA**	**SO**	**Avg**
2006-07	Crabtree Draveurs	QAAA	26	10	11	2	1436	74	1	3.09	3	0	2	95	10	0	6.31
2007-08	Gatineau	QMJHL	29	13	7	0	1285	62	1	2.89	3	0	1	56	3	0	3.20
2008-09	Gatineau	QMJHL	49	25	20	0	2665	143	1	3.22	2	0	0	10	1	0	5.99
2009-10	Gatineau	QMJHL	59	24	31	0	3354	157	4	2.81	11	4	6	635	38	0	3.59
2010-11	Gatineau	QMJHL	48	28	10	5	2659	113	4	2.55	*21	11	10	*1325	49	1	2.22
2011-12	Albany Devils	AHL	2	1	1	0	119	4	0	2.01	....	....	....	....	....	....	....
	Kalamazoo Wings	ECHL	31	13	10	3	1684	96	0	3.42	1	0	0	35	3	0	5.08
2012-13	Elmira Jackals	ECHL	41	20	13	5	2333	126	0	3.24	3	1	2	180	13	0	4.33
	Albany Devils	AHL	1	0	0	1	65	1	0	0.92	....	....	....	....	....	....	....

CLIMIE, Matt (KLIGH-mee, MAT)

Goaltender. Catches left. 6'3", 194 lbs. Born, Leduc, Alta., February 11, 1983.

			Regular Season								Playoffs						
Season	**Club**	**League**	**GP**	**W**	**L**	**O/T**	**Mins**	**GA**	**SO**	**Avg**	**GP**	**W**	**L**	**Mins**	**GA**	**SO**	**Avg**
2002-03	Truro Bearcats	MJrHL					Statistics not available										
2003-04	Truro Bearcats	MJrHL	45	30	10	0	2731	119	0	2.61	....	....	....	....	....	....	....
2004-05	Bemidji State	CHA	21	12	5	1	1167	35	4	*1.80	....	....	....	....	....	....	....
2005-06	Bemidji State	CHA	18	8	7	2	1065	48	1	2.70	....	....	....	....	....	....	....
2006-07	Bemidji State	CHA	29	11	10	5	*1666	84	*2	*3.03	....	....	....	....	....	....	....
2007-08	Bemidji State	CHA	27	14	8	3	1529	55	*5	*2.16	....	....	....	....	....	....	....
	Iowa Stars	AHL	6	1	4	1	346	23	0	....	....	....	....	....	....	....	....
2008-09	**Dallas**	**NHL**	**3**	**2**	**1**	**0**	**185**	**9**	**0**	**2.92**	....	....	....	....	....	....	....
	Idaho Steelheads	ECHL	42	27	12	1	2404	92	4	2.30	4	0	4	199	8	0	2.41
	Houston Aeros	AHL	....	....	....	....	....	....	....	....	5	1	1	191	6	0	1.88
2009-10	**Dallas**	**NHL**	**1**	**0**	**1**	**0**	**60**	**5**	**0**	**5.00**	....	....	....	....	....	....	....
	Texas Stars	AHL	43	21	17	3	2539	104	3	2.46	15	7	6	885	40	0	2.71
2010-11	**Phoenix**	**NHL**	**1**	**0**	**0**	**0**	**32**	**1**	**0**	**1.88**	....	....	....	....	....	....	....
	San Antonio	AHL	55	26	22	3	3040	134	3	2.64	....	....	....	....	....	....	....
2011-12	Chicago Wolves	AHL	32	20	11	0	1810	76	1	2.52	1	0	1	34	4	0	7.15
2012-13	Chicago Wolves	AHL	53	24	25	3	3094	125	6	2.42	....	....	....	....	....	....	....
	NHL Totals		**5**	**2**	**2**	**0**	**277**	**15**	**0**	**3.25**	....	....	....	....	....	....	....

CHA Second All-Star Team (2008)

Signed as a free agent by **Dallas**, March 20, 2008. Signed as a free agent by **Phoenix**, July 3, 2010. Signed as a free agent by **Vancouver**, July 7, 2011.

COMRIE, Eric (KAWM-ree, AIR-ihk) WPG

Goaltender. Catches left. 6'1", 167 lbs. Born, Edmonton, Alta., July 6, 1995.
(Winnipeg's 3rd choice, 59th overall, in 2013 Entry Draft).

			Regular Season								Playoffs						
Season	**Club**	**League**	**GP**	**W**	**L**	**O/T**	**Mins**	**GA**	**SO**	**Avg**	**GP**	**W**	**L**	**Mins**	**GA**	**SO**	**Avg**
2010-11	L.A. Selects	T1EHL	19	16	2	0	966	24	5	1.34	....	....	....	....	....	....	....
	Tri-City Americans	WHL	....	....	....	....	....	....	....	....	1	0	0	20	1	0	3.00
2011-12	Tri-City Americans	WHL	31	19	6	2	1663	74	3	2.67	....	....	....	....	....	....	....
2012-13	Tri-City Americans	WHL	37	20	14	3	2178	95	2	2.62	0	0	0	0	0	0	0.00

CONDON, Mike (KAWN-duhn, MIGHK) MTL

Goaltender. Catches left. 6'2", 209 lbs. Born, Needham, MA, April 27, 1990.

			Regular Season								Playoffs						
Season	**Club**	**League**	**GP**	**W**	**L**	**O/T**	**Mins**	**GA**	**SO**	**Avg**	**GP**	**W**	**L**	**Mins**	**GA**	**SO**	**Avg**
2008-09	Belmont Hill	High-MA	31	....	....	....	....	....	....	2.12	....	....	....	....	....	....	....
2009-10	Princeton	ECAC	4	0	1	0	123	5	0	2.44	....	....	....	....	....	....	....
2010-11	Princeton	ECAC	11	6	4	1	660	31	1	2.82	....	....	....	....	....	....	....
2011-12	Princeton	ECAC	14	4	6	3	832	40	0	2.88	....	....	....	....	....	....	....
2012-13	Princeton	ECAC	24	8	11	4	1354	56	2	2.48	....	....	....	....	....	....	....
	Ontario Reign	ECHL	4	3	1	0	243	6	1	1.48	....	....	....	....	....	....	....
	Houston Aeros	AHL	5	3	0	0	226	9	0	2.39	....	....	....	....	....	....	....

Signed to ATO (amateur tryout) contract by **Ontario** (ECHL), March 20, 2013. Signed to PTO (professional tryout) contract by **Houston** (AHL), April 7, 2013. Signed as a free agent by **Montreal**, May 8, 2013.

COREAU, Jared (KOHR-oh, JAIR-uhd) DET

Goaltender. Catches left. 6'5", 200 lbs. Born, Perth, Ont., November 5, 1991.

			Regular Season								Playoffs						
Season	**Club**	**League**	**GP**	**W**	**L**	**O/T**	**Mins**	**GA**	**SO**	**Avg**	**GP**	**W**	**L**	**Mins**	**GA**	**SO**	**Avg**
2008-09	Peterborough Stars	ON-Jr.A	12	8	1	1	304	23	0	2.16	2	0	0	22	0	0	0.00
2009-10	Lincoln Stars	USHL	38	7	22	4	1988	120	1	3.62	....	....	....	....	....	....	....
2010-11	Northern Mich.	CCHA	15	5	5	2	662	41	0	3.71	....	....	....	....	....	....	....
2011-12	Northern Mich.	CCHA	23	12	7	2	1244	46	1	2.22	....	....	....	....	....	....	....
2012-13	Northern Mich.	CCHA	38	15	19	4	2182	98	1	2.70	....	....	....	....	....	....	....

Signed as a free agent by **Detroit**, April 3, 2013.

COWLEY, Evan (KOW-lee, EH-vuhn) FLA

Goaltender. Catches left. 6'4", 182 lbs. Born, Cranbrook, B.C., July 31, 1995.
(Florida's 3rd choice, 92nd overall, in 2013 Entry Draft).

			Regular Season								Playoffs						
Season	**Club**	**League**	**GP**	**W**	**L**	**O/T**	**Mins**	**GA**	**SO**	**Avg**	**GP**	**W**	**L**	**Mins**	**GA**	**SO**	**Avg**
2010-11	Arvada H.A.	Minor-CO	14	5	7	0	573	39	1	3.27	....	....	....	....	....	....	....
	Ralston Valley	High-CO	....	....	....	....	305	14	2	2.34	....	....	....	....	....	....	....
2011-12	Arvada H.A.	Minor-CO	10	4	2	4	493	21	2	1.92	....	....	....	....	....	....	....
	Ralston Valley	High-CO					Statistics not available										
2012-13	Wichita Falls	NAHL	*50	22	24	4	2897	140	3	2.90	....	....	....	....	....	....	....
	USNTDP	U-18	3	2	1	0	180	7	0	2.33	....	....	....	....	....	....	....

• Signed Letter of Intent to attend **University of Denver** (WCHA) in fall of 2013.

CRAWFORD, Corey (KRAW-fohrd, KOH-ree) CHI

Goaltender. Catches left. 6'2", 208 lbs. Born, Montreal, Que., December 31, 1984.
(Chicago's 2nd choice, 52nd overall, in 2003 Entry Draft).

			Regular Season								Playoffs						
Season	**Club**	**League**	**GP**	**W**	**L**	**O/T**	**Mins**	**GA**	**SO**	**Avg**	**GP**	**W**	**L**	**Mins**	**GA**	**SO**	**Avg**
2000-01	Gatineau Intrepide	QAAA	21	17	3	1	1260	40	2	1.92	....	....	....	....	....	....	....
2001-02	Moncton Wildcats	QMJHL	38	9	20	3	1863	116	1	3.74	....	....	....	....	....	....	....
2002-03	Moncton Wildcats	QMJHL	50	24	17	6	2855	130	2	2.73	6	2	3	303	20	0	3.97
2003-04	Moncton Wildcats	QMJHL	54	*35	15	3	3019	132	2	2.62	*20	*13	6	*1170	42	0	2.15
2004-05	Moncton Wildcats	QMJHL	51	28	16	6	2942	121	*5	2.47	12	6	6	725	33	*1	2.73
2005-06	**Chicago**	**NHL**	**2**	**0**	**0**	**1**	**86**	**5**	**0**	**3.49**	....	....	....	....	....	....	....
	Norfolk Admirals	AHL	48	22	23	1	2734	134	1	2.94	1	0	0	17	1	0	3.49
2006-07	Norfolk Admirals	AHL	60	38	20	2	3467	164	1	2.84	6	2	4	363	20	0	3.31
2007-08	**Chicago**	**NHL**	**5**	**1**	**2**	**0**	**224**	**8**	**1**	**2.14**	....	....	....	....	....	....	....
	Rockford IceHogs	AHL	55	29	19	5	3028	143	3	2.83	12	7	5	741	27	0	2.19
2008-09	Rockford IceHogs	AHL	47	22	20	3	2686	116	2	2.59	2	0	2	117	5	0	2.57
	Chicago	**NHL**	....	....	....	....	....	....	....	....	**1**	**0**	**0**	**16**	**1**	**0**	**3.75**
2009-10	**Chicago**	**NHL**	**1**	**0**	**1**	**0**	**59**	**3**	**0**	**3.05**	....	....	....	....	....	....	....
	Rockford IceHogs	AHL	45	24	16	2	2521	112	1	2.67	4	0	4	216	13	0	3.61
2010-11	**Chicago**	**NHL**	**57**	**33**	**18**	**6**	**3337**	**128**	**4**	**2.30**	**7**	**3**	**4**	**435**	**16**	**1**	**2.21**
2011-12	**Chicago**	**NHL**	**57**	**30**	**17**	**7**	**3218**	**146**	**0**	**2.72**	**6**	**2**	**4**	**396**	**17**	**0**	**2.58**
2012-13 ♦	**Chicago**	**NHL**	**30**	**19**	**5**	**5**	**1761**	**57**	**3**	**1.94**	***23**	***16**	**7**	***1504**	**46**	**1**	***1.84**
	NHL Totals		**152**	**83**	**43**	**19**	**8685**	**347**	**8**	**2.40**	**37**	**21**	**15**	**2351**	**80**	**2**	**2.04**

QMJHL Second All-Star Team (2004, 2005) • NHL All-Rookie Team (2011) • William M. Jennings Trophy (2013) (shared with Ray Emery)

DANIS, Yann (DA-nihs, YAN) PHI

Goaltender. Catches left. 6', 185 lbs. Born, Lafontaine, Que., June 21, 1981.

			Regular Season								Playoffs						
Season	**Club**	**League**	**GP**	**W**	**L**	**O/T**	**Mins**	**GA**	**SO**	**Avg**	**GP**	**W**	**L**	**Mins**	**GA**	**SO**	**Avg**
99-2000	St-Jerome	QJHL					Statistics not available										
	Cornwall Colts	ON-Jr.A	26	15	5	0	1367	71	0	3.12	13	11	2	786	37	0	2.82
2000-01	Brown U.	ECAC	12	2	8	1	667	40	0	3.60	....	....	....	....	....	....	....
2001-02	Brown U.	ECAC	24	11	10	2	1451	45	3	1.86	....	....	....	....	....	....	....
2002-03	Brown U.	ECAC	*34	15	14	5	*2074	80	5	2.31	....	....	....	....	....	....	....
2003-04	Brown U.	ECAC	30	15	11	4	1821	55	*5	*1.81	....	....	....	....	....	....	....
	Hamilton Bulldogs	AHL	2	2	0	0	120	3	1	1.50	1	0	0	12	0	0	0.00
2004-05	Hamilton Bulldogs	AHL	53	28	17	6	3075	120	5	2.34	4	0	4	237	13	0	3.29
2005-06	**Montreal**	**NHL**	**6**	**3**	**2**	**0**	**312**	**14**	**1**	**2.69**	....	....	....	....	....	....	....
	Hamilton Bulldogs	AHL	39	17	17	3	2242	111	0	2.97	....	....	....	....	....	....	....
2006-07	Hamilton Bulldogs	AHL	44	23	14	5	2540	119	1	2.81	1	1	0	54	1	0	1.12
2007-08	Hamilton Bulldogs	AHL	38	11	19	4	2064	113	0	3.28	....	....	....	....	....	....	....
2008-09	**NY Islanders**	**NHL**	**31**	**10**	**17**	**3**	**1760**	**84**	**2**	**2.86**	....	....	....	....	....	....	....
	Bridgeport	AHL	10	7	3	0	611	23	0	2.26	....	....	....	....	....	....	....
2009-10	**New Jersey**	**NHL**	**12**	**3**	**2**	**1**	**467**	**16**	**0**	**2.06**	....	....	....	....	....	....	....
2010-11	Amur Khabarovsk	KHL	31	....	....	....	1652	84	2	3.05	....	....	....	....	....	....	....
2011-12	**Edmonton**	**NHL**	**1**	**0**	**0**	**0**	**32**	**2**	**0**	**3.75**	....	....	....	....	....	....	....
	Oklahoma City	AHL	43	26	14	2	2545	88	5	2.07	14	8	6	842	33	1	2.35
2012-13	Oklahoma City	AHL	47	26	15	6	2775	120	2	2.59	17	10	7	1019	41	1	2.41
	Edmonton	**NHL**	**3**	**1**	**0**	**0**	**110**	**7**	**0**	**3.82**	....	....	....	....	....	....	....
	NHL Totals		**53**	**17**	**21**	**4**	**2681**	**123**	**3**	**2.75**	....	....	....	....	....	....	....

ECAC Second All-Star Team (2002, 2003) • ECAC First All-Star Team (2004) • ECAC Goaltender of the Year (2004) • ECAC Player of the Year (2004) • NCAA East First All-American Team (2004) • AHL First All-Star Team (2012) • Baz Bastien Memorial Trophy (AHL –Top Goaltender) (2012)

Signed as a free agent by **Montreal**, March 19, 2004. Signed as a free agent by **NY Islanders**, July 2, 2008. Signed as a free agent by **New Jersey**, July 10, 2009. Signed as a free agent by **Khabarovsk** (KHL), July 27, 2010. Signed as a free agent by **Edmonton**, July 4, 2011. Signed as a free agent by **Philadelphia**, July 5, 2013.

DANSK, Oscar (DANSK, AWS-kuhr) CBJ

Goaltender. Catches left. 6'3", 187 lbs. Born, Stockholm, Sweden, February 28, 1994.
(Columbus' 2nd choice, 31st overall, in 2012 Entry Draft).

			Regular Season								Playoffs						
Season	**Club**	**League**	**GP**	**W**	**L**	**O/T**	**Mins**	**GA**	**SO**	**Avg**	**GP**	**W**	**L**	**Mins**	**GA**	**SO**	**Avg**
2007-08	Shattuck Bantam	High-MN	39	....	....	....	....	....	....	1.98	....	....	....	....	....	....	....
2008-09	Shattuck Bantam	High-MN	32	....	....	....	....	....	....	1.43	....	....	....	....	....	....	....
2009-10	Shat.-St. Mary's	High-MN	18	13	2	1	....	....	....	1.89	....	....	....	....	....	....	....
2010-11	Brynas U18	Swe-U18	17	....	....	....	1017	30	2	1.77	5	....	....	317	20	0	3.78
	Brynas IF Gavle Jr.	Swe-Jr.	21	....	....	....	1157	52	1	2.70	1	....	....	57	5	0	5.22
2011-12	Brynas U18	Swe-U18	2	....	....	....	121	4	0	1.98	3	....	....	180	3	1	1.00
	Brynas IF Gavle Jr.	Swe-Jr.	28	....	....	....	1511	71	2	2.82	2	....	....	120	7	0	3.49
2012-13	Erie Otters	OHL	43	11	23	6	2393	164	0	4.11	....	....	....	....	....	....	....

DEKANICH, Mark (DEHK-ihn-ihch, MAHRK)

Goaltender. Catches left. 6'2", 192 lbs. Born, N. Vancouver, B.C., May 10, 1986.
(Nashville's 3rd choice, 146th overall, in 2006 Entry Draft).

			Regular Season								Playoffs						
Season	**Club**	**League**	**GP**	**W**	**L**	**O/T**	**Mins**	**GA**	**SO**	**Avg**	**GP**	**W**	**L**	**Mins**	**GA**	**SO**	**Avg**
2003-04	Coquitlam Express	BCHL	30	13	15	1	1647	89	2	3.24	....	....	....	....	....	....	....
2004-05	Colgate	ECAC	5	1	1	0	162	5	0	1.85	....	....	....	....	....	....	....
2005-06	Colgate	ECAC	36	18	11	6	2126	81	4	2.29	....	....	....	....	....	....	....
2006-07	Colgate	ECAC	36	15	17	4	2136	83	1	2.33	....	....	....	....	....	....	....
2007-08	Colgate	ECAC	*41	18	16	6	*2389	86	*6	2.16	....	....	....	....	....	....	....
2008-09	Milwaukee	AHL	30	15	10	2	1663	58	1	2.09	....	....	....	....	....	....	....
2009-10	Milwaukee	AHL	49	27	16	4	2804	109	4	2.33	7	3	4	408	19	1	2.79
	Cincinnati	ECHL	2	2	0	0	125	1	1	0.48	....	....	....	....	....	....	....
2010-11	**Nashville**	**NHL**	**1**	**0**	**0**	**0**	**50**	**3**	**0**	**3.60**	....	....	....	....	....	....	....
	Milwaukee	AHL	43	23	12	5	2500	84	4	2.02	....	....	....	....	....	....	....
2011-12	Springfield Falcons	AHL	5	1	2	1	240	16	0	4.00	....	....	....	....	....	....	....
2012-13	St. John's IceCaps	AHL	35	16	14	1	1914	95	2	2.98	....	....	....	....	....	....	....
	NHL Totals		**1**	**0**	**0**	**0**	**50**	**3**	**0**	**3.60**	....	....	....	....	....	....	....

ECAC First All-Star Team (2006) • ECAC Second All-Star Team (2007)

Signed as a free agent by **Columbus**, July 1, 2011. • Missed majority of 2011-12 due to ankle injury and resulting surgery. Signed as a free agent by **Winnipeg**, July 6, 2012. Signed as a free agent by **Zagreb** (KHL), May 20, 2013.

DELMAS, Peter (DEHL-mas, PEE-tuhr) MTL

Goaltender. Catches left. 6'3", 195 lbs. Born, Alliston, Ont., February 16, 1990.
(Colorado's 2nd choice, 61st overall, in 2008 Entry Draft).

			Regular Season								Playoffs						
Season	Club	League	GP	W	L	O/T	Mins	GA	SO	Avg	GP	W	L	Mins	GA	SO	Avg
2006-07	Lewiston	QMJHL	34	23	10	....	1983	93	3	2.81	....	....	....	....	....	....	....
2007-08	Lewiston	QMJHL	34	17	17	....	1987	94	0	2.84	....	....	....	....	....	....	....
2008-09	Lewiston	QMJHL	38	9	27	....	2090	146	0	4.19	2	0	2	75	15	0	11.96
2009-10	Quebec Remparts	QMJHL	27	15	9	....	1459	76	1	3.15	....	....	....	....	....	....	....
	Halifax	QMJHL	14	5	7	....	771	44	0	3.42	....	....	....	....	....	....	....
2010-11	Halifax	QMJHL	2	0	2	0	117	8	0	4.10	....	....	....	....	....	....	....
	Hamilton Bulldogs	AHL	2	1	0	1	125	4	0	1.92	....	....	....	....	....	....	....
	Wichita Thunder	CHL	5	0	3	1	272	22	0	4.85	....	....	....	....	....	....	....
	Wheeling Nailers	ECHL	24	15	6	2	1417	48	3	2.03	15	8	6	804	42	0	3.13
2011-12	Hamilton Bulldogs	AHL	4	1	2	0	186	7	0	2.26	....	....	....	....	....	....	....
	Wheeling Nailers	ECHL	37	18	14	3	2113	88	3	2.50	....	....	....	....	....	....	....
2012-13	Hamilton Bulldogs	AHL	3	0	2	0	172	10	0	3.49	....	....	....	....	....	....	....
	Wheeling Nailers	ECHL	31	15	12	4	1808	82	3	2.72	....	....	....	....	....	....	....

QMJHL All-Rookie Team (2007) • Canadian Major Junior Rookie All-Star Team (2007)

Signed as a free agent by **Montreal**, July 5, 2011.

DESJARDINS, Cedrick (deh-ZHAHR-dai, SEH-DRIHK) T.B.

Goaltender. Catches left. 6', 192 lbs. Born, Edmundston, N.B., September 30, 1985.

			Regular Season								Playoffs						
Season	Club	League	GP	W	L	O/T	Mins	GA	SO	Avg	GP	W	L	Mins	GA	SO	Avg
2002-03	Coaticook	QJHL	STATISTICS NOT AVAILABLE														
	Rimouski Oceanic	QMJHL	23	1	19	0	1239	109	0	5.28	....	....	....	....	....	....	....
2003-04	Rimouski Oceanic	QMJHL	20	8	11	0	1119	72	0	3.86	1	0	0	14	0	0	0.00
2004-05	Rimouski Oceanic	QMJHL	44	*30	7	4	2439	120	2	2.95	13	*12	1	*767	34	*1	2.66
2005-06	Quebec Remparts	QMJHL	41	28	10	0	2254	111	*5	2.95	*23	14	9	*1413	60	1	2.55
2006-07	Hamilton Bulldogs	AHL	3	0	2	0	142	7	0	2.96	....	....	....	....	....	....	....
	Cincinnati	ECHL	45	24	19	1	2648	112	4	2.54	....	....	....	....	....	....	....
2007-08	Hamilton Bulldogs	AHL	12	4	3	2	572	29	0	3.04	....	....	....	....	....	....	....
	Cincinnati	ECHL	22	16	4	2	1285	41	*5	1.91	16	11	4	947	29	1	*1.83
2008-09	Hamilton Bulldogs	AHL	30	16	12	0	1718	73	4	2.55	....	....	....	....	....	....	....
2009-10	Hamilton Bulldogs	AHL	47	29	9	4	2576	86	6	*2.00	10	6	4	596	26	1	2.62
2010-11	**Tampa Bay**	**NHL**	**2**	**2**	**0**	**0**	**120**	**2**	**0**	**1.00**	....	....	....	....	....	....	....
	Norfolk Admirals	AHL	24	15	6	1	1391	60	1	2.59	....	....	....	....	....	....	....
2011-12	Lake Erie Monsters	AHL	32	16	11	5	1936	68	3	2.11	....	....	....	....	....	....	....
2012-13	Hamilton Bulldogs	AHL	22	7	13	2	1285	63	2	2.94	....	....	....	....	....	....	....
	Tampa Bay	**NHL**	**3**	**0**	**3**	**0**	**160**	**8**	**0**	**3.00**	....	....	....	....	....	....	....
	Syracuse Crunch	AHL	14	8	5	1	851	30	3	2.12	18	13	5	1098	42	3	2.30
	NHL Totals		**5**	**2**	**3**	**0**	**280**	**10**	**0**	**2.14**	....	....	....	....	....	....	....

Memorial Cup All-Star Team (2006) • Hap Emms Memorial Trophy (Memorial Cup - Top Goaltender) (2006) • ECHL All-Rookie-Team (2007) • ECHL Playoff MVP (2009) • AHL Second All-Star Team (2010) • Harry ''Hap'' Holmes Memorial Award (AHL – fewest goals against) (2010) (shared with Curtis Sanford)

Signed as a free agent by **Hamilton** (AHL), July 26, 2006. Signed as a free agent by **Montreal**, July 3, 2008. Traded to **Tampa Bay** by **Montreal** for Karri Ramo, August 16, 2010. Signed as a free agent by **Colorado**. July 8, 2011. Signed as a free agent by **Montreal**, July 1, 2012. Traded to **Tampa Bay** by **Montreal** for Dustin Tokarski, February 14, 2013.

DESLAURIERS, Jeff (duh-LAW-ree-yay, JEHF)

Goaltender. Catches right. 6'4", 203 lbs. Born, St-Jean-Richelieu, Que., May 15, 1984.
(Edmonton's 2nd choice, 31st overall, in 2002 Entry Draft).

			Regular Season								Playoffs						
Season	Club	League	GP	W	L	O/T	Mins	GA	SO	Avg	GP	W	L	Mins	GA	SO	Avg
2000-01	Gatineau Intrepide	QAAA	22	10	9	2	1194	61	2	3.07	2	1	0	125	6	0	2.89
2001-02	Chicoutimi	QMJHL	51	28	20	1	2909	170	1	3.51	4	0	3	197	20	0	6.11
2002-03	Chicoutimi	QMJHL	48	18	24	1	2583	164	0	3.81	4	0	4	240	15	0	3.75
2003-04	Chicoutimi	QMJHL	50	21	20	6	2701	129	1	2.87	18	10	8	956	50	1	3.14
2004-05	Edmonton	AHL	22	6	13	2	1258	62	0	2.96	....	....	....	....	....	....	....
	Greenville Grrrowl	ECHL	11	7	3	1	673	26	1	2.32	....	....	....	....	....	....	....
2005-06	Hamilton Bulldogs	AHL	13	4	7	0	666	35	0	3.15	....	....	....	....	....	....	....
	Greenville Grrrowl	ECHL	6	2	4	0	335	17	0	3.05	....	....	....	....	....	....	....
2006-07	Wilkes-Barre	AHL	40	22	12	3	2231	92	4	2.47	....	....	....	....	....	....	....
2007-08	Springfield Falcons	AHL	57	26	23	5	3045	147	0	2.90	....	....	....	....	....	....	....
2008-09	**Edmonton**	**NHL**	**10**	**4**	**3**	**0**	**540**	**30**	**0**	**3.33**	....	....	....	....	....	....	....
	Springfield Falcons	AHL	5	1	4	0	286	13	0	2.73	....	....	....	....	....	....	....
2009-10	**Edmonton**	**NHL**	**48**	**16**	**28**	**4**	**2798**	**152**	**3**	**3.26**	....	....	....	....	....	....	....
2010-11	Oklahoma City	AHL	35	17	13	4	1945	91	3	2.81	....	....	....	....	....	....	....
2011-12	**Anaheim**	**NHL**	**4**	**3**	**1**	**0**	**241**	**11**	**0**	**2.74**	....	....	....	....	....	....	....
	Syracuse Crunch	AHL	16	6	9	0	864	54	0	3.75	....	....	....	....	....	....	....
2012-13	Norfolk Admirals	AHL	2	1	1	0	120	7	0	3.51	....	....	....	....	....	....	....
	Fort Wayne	ECHL	15	6	8	1	867	47	0	3.25	....	....	....	....	....	....	....
	Houston Aeros	AHL	3	1	1	0	103	2	1	1.17	....	....	....	....	....	....	....
	NHL Totals		**62**	**23**	**32**	**4**	**3579**	**193**	**3**	**3.24**	....	....	....	....	....	....	....

QMJHL All-Rookie Team (2002)

Signed as a free agent by **Anaheim**. July 12, 2011. • Re-assigned to **Fort Wayne** (ECHL) by **Anaheim** (Norfolk-AHL), February 19, 2013. Traded to **Minnesota** by **Anaheim** for future considerations, April 3, 2013.

DESROSIERS, Philippe (duh-ROHZ-ee-yay, fihl-EEP) DAL

Goaltender. Catches left. 6'1", 182 lbs. Born, Saint-Hyacinthe, Que., August 16, 1995.
(Dallas' 4th choice, 54th overall, in 2013 Entry Draft).

			Regular Season								Playoffs						
Season	Club	League	GP	W	L	O/T	Mins	GA	SO	Avg	GP	W	L	Mins	GA	SO	Avg
2010-11	Antoine-Girouard	QAAA	20	10	9	0	1100	65	2	3.54	3	1	2	139	8	0	3.45
2011-12	Antoine-Girouard	QAAA	23	16	4	3	1320	61	1	2.77	11	6	3	673	29	0	2.58
	Rimouski Oceanic	QMJHL	3	1	2	0	155	9	0	3.48	....	....	....	....	....	....	....
2012-13	Rimouski Oceanic	QMJHL	43	22	8	5	2305	118	1	3.07	4	2	2	239	9	0	2.26

DiPIETRO, Rick (dee-pee-EHT-roh, RIHK)

Goaltender. Catches right. 6', 185 lbs. Born, Winthrop, MA, September 19, 1981.
(NY Islanders' 1st choice, 1st overall, in 2000 Entry Draft).

			Regular Season								Playoffs						
Season	Club	League	GP	W	L	O/T	Mins	GA	SO	Avg	GP	W	L	Mins	GA	SO	Avg
1997-98	USNTDP	U-17	10	6	4	0	800	31	0	2.33	....	....	....	....	....	....	....
	USNTDP	USHL	3	0	2	0	117	8	0	4.09	....	....	....	....	....	....	....
	USNTDP	NAHL	30	13	12	0	1602	85	1	3.18	3	2	1	179	7	1	2.35
	St. Sebastian's	High-MA	STATISTICS NOT AVAILABLE														
1998-99	USNTDP	U-18	16	9	5	1	1027	46	....	2.69	....	....	....	....	....	....	....
	USNTDP	USHL	30	22	6	1	1733	67	3	2.32	....	....	....	....	....	....	....
99-2000	Boston University	H-East	29	18	5	5	1790	73	2	2.45	....	....	....	....	....	....	....
2000-01	**NY Islanders**	**NHL**	**20**	**3**	**15**	**1**	**1083**	**63**	**0**	**3.49**	....	....	....	....	....	....	....
	Chicago Wolves	IHL	14	4	5	2	778	44	0	3.39	....	....	....	....	....	....	....
2001-02	Bridgeport	AHL	59	*30	22	7	3472	134	4	2.32	20	12	8	*1270	45	*3	2.13
2002-03	**NY Islanders**	**NHL**	**10**	**2**	**5**	**2**	**585**	**29**	**0**	**2.97**	**1**	**0**	**0**	**15**	**0**	**0**	**0.00**
	Bridgeport	AHL	34	16	10	8	2044	73	3	2.14	5	2	3	299	10	1	2.01
2003-04	**NY Islanders**	**NHL**	**50**	**23**	**18**	**5**	**2844**	**112**	**5**	**2.36**	**5**	**1**	**4**	**303**	**11**	**1**	**2.18**
	Bridgeport	AHL	2	0	2	0	119	3	0	1.51	....	....	....	....	....	....	....
2004-05			DID NOT PLAY														
2005-06	**NY Islanders**	**NHL**	**63**	**30**	**24**	**5**	**3572**	**180**	**1**	**3.02**	....	....	....	....	....	....	....
	United States	Olympics	4	1	3	0	237	9	0	2.28	....	....	....	....	....	....	....
2006-07	**NY Islanders**	**NHL**	**62**	**32**	**19**	**9**	**3627**	**156**	**5**	**2.58**	**4**	**1**	**3**	**236**	**13**	**0**	**3.31**
2007-08	**NY Islanders**	**NHL**	**63**	**26**	**28**	**7**	**3707**	**174**	**3**	**2.82**	....	....	....	....	....	....	....
2008-09	**NY Islanders**	**NHL**	**5**	**1**	**3**	**0**	**256**	**15**	**0**	**3.52**	....	....	....	....	....	....	....
2009-10	**NY Islanders**	**NHL**	**8**	**2**	**5**	**0**	**462**	**20**	**1**	**2.60**	....	....	....	....	....	....	....
	Bridgeport	AHL	4	1	2	0	199	11	0	3.31	....	....	....	....	....	....	....
2010-11	**NY Islanders**	**NHL**	**26**	**8**	**14**	**4**	**1533**	**88**	**1**	**3.44**	....	....	....	....	....	....	....
2011-12	**NY Islanders**	**NHL**	**8**	**3**	**2**	**3**	**354**	**22**	**0**	**3.73**	....	....	....	....	....	....	....
2012-13	Riessersee	German-2	1	0	1	0	59	3	0	3.03	....	....	....	....	....	....	....
	NY Islanders	**NHL**	**3**	**0**	**3**	**0**	**176**	**12**	**0**	**4.09**	....	....	....	....	....	....	....
	Bridgeport	AHL	18	9	9	0	1022	50	1	2.93	....	....	....	....	....	....	....
	NHL Totals		**318**	**130**	**136**	**36**	**18199**	**871**	**16**	**2.87**	**10**	**2**	**7**	**554**	**24**	**1**	**2.60**

Hockey East Second All-Star Team (2000) • Hockey East Rookie of the Year (2000)

Played in NHL All-Star Game (2008)

• Missed majority of 2008-09 and 2009-10 due to arthroscopic knee surgery, October 31, 2008.
• Missed majority of 2011-12 due to groin, hernia and knee injuries. Signed as a free agent by **Riessersee** (German-2), October 10, 2012.

DOMINGUE, Louis (doh-MIHN-gay, LOO-ee) PHX

Goaltender. Catches right. 6'3", 205 lbs. Born, Mont St. Hilaire, Que., March 6, 1992.
(Phoenix's 5th choice, 138th overall, in 2010 Entry Draft).

			Regular Season								Playoffs						
Season	Club	League	GP	W	L	O/T	Mins	GA	SO	Avg	GP	W	L	Mins	GA	SO	Avg
2007-08	Lac St-Louis Lions	QAAA	35	22	9	0	1732	90	2	3.12	13	8	2	761	33	1	2.60
2008-09	Moncton Wildcats	QMJHL	12	5	5	0	621	26	0	2.51	....	....	....	....	....	....	....
2009-10	Moncton Wildcats	QMJHL	22	11	9	0	1196	56	1	2.81	....	....	....	....	....	....	....
	Quebec Remparts	QMJHL	19	9	8	0	1017	43	2	2.54	9	3	5	455	33	0	4.35
2010-11	Quebec Remparts	QMJHL	*57	*37	12	3	3033	134	2	2.65	18	11	6	996	41	1	2.47
2011-12	Quebec Remparts	QMJHL	39	23	8	4	2162	94	4	2.61	11	7	4	679	30	0	2.65
2012-13	Gwinnett	ECHL	34	23	9	2	2051	92	3	2.69	10	6	4	619	23	2	2.23
	Portland Pirates	AHL	2	1	0	0	100	4	0	2.40	....	....	....	....	....	....	....

DRIEDGER, Chris (DREE-guhr, KRIHS) OTT

Goaltender. Catches left. 6'3", 200 lbs. Born, Winnipeg, MB, May 18, 1994.
(Ottawa's 2nd choice, 76th overall, in 2012 Entry Draft).

			Regular Season								Playoffs						
Season	Club	League	GP	W	L	O/T	Mins	GA	SO	Avg	GP	W	L	Mins	GA	SO	Avg
2009-10	Wpg. Monarchs	Minor-MB	12	....	....	....	....	....	....	1.75	....	....	....	....	....	....	....
2010-11	Tri-City Americans	WHL	22	6	6	1	977	57	0	3.50	....	....	....	....	....	....	....
2011-12	Calgary Hitmen	WHL	44	24	12	3	2294	107	3	2.80	2	0	2	82	9	0	6.59
2012-13	Calgary Hitmen	WHL	54	36	14	4	3199	134	2	2.51	17	11	6	1006	40	1	2.39

DUBNYK, Devan (DOOB-nihk, DEH-vuhn) EDM

Goaltender. Catches left. 6'5", 210 lbs. Born, Regina, Sask., May 4, 1986.
(Edmonton's 1st choice, 14th overall, in 2004 Entry Draft).

			Regular Season								Playoffs						
Season	Club	League	GP	W	L	O/T	Mins	GA	SO	Avg	GP	W	L	Mins	GA	SO	Avg
2000-01	Calgary Bruins	CBHL	14	....	....	....	815	39	2	3.10	....	....	....	....	....	....	....
2001-02	Calgary Bruins	CBHL	18	7	9	2	1105	68	1	3.69	....	....	....	....	....	....	....
	Kamloops Blazers	WHL	3	1	1	0	143	13	0	5.44	....	....	....	....	....	....	....
2002-03	Kamloops Blazers	WHL	26	12	8	1	1278	66	2	3.10	....	....	....	....	....	....	....
2003-04	Kamloops Blazers	WHL	44	20	18	5	2532	106	6	2.51	4	1	3	245	12	0	2.94
2004-05	Kamloops Blazers	WHL	*65	23	34	7	3699	166	6	2.69	6	2	4	362	22	0	3.65
2005-06	Kamloops Blazers	WHL	54	27	26	1	3207	136	1	2.54	....	....	....	....	....	....	....
2006-07	Wilkes-Barre	AHL	4	2	1	0	204	10	0	2.94	....	....	....	....	....	....	....
	Stockton Thunder	ECHL	43	24	11	7	2529	108	2	2.56	6	2	4	395	18	0	2.73
2007-08	Springfield Falcons	AHL	33	9	17	0	1772	92	0	3.12	....	....	....	....	....	....	....
2008-09	Springfield Falcons	AHL	*62	18	41	2	*3635	180	3	2.97	....	....	....	....	....	....	....
2009-10	**Edmonton**	**NHL**	**19**	**4**	**10**	**2**	**1075**	**64**	**0**	**3.57**	....	....	....	....	....	....	....
	Springfield Falcons	AHL	33	13	17	2	1985	100	0	3.02	....	....	....	....	....	....	....
2010-11	**Edmonton**	**NHL**	**35**	**12**	**13**	**8**	**2061**	**93**	**2**	**2.71**	....	....	....	....	....	....	....
2011-12	**Edmonton**	**NHL**	**47**	**20**	**20**	**3**	**2653**	**118**	**2**	**2.67**	....	....	....	....	....	....	....
2012-13	**Edmonton**	**NHL**	**38**	**14**	**16**	**6**	**2101**	**90**	**2**	**2.57**	....	....	....	....	....	....	....
	NHL Totals		**139**	**50**	**59**	**19**	**7890**	**365**	**6**	**2.78**	....	....	....	....	....	....	....

Canadian Major Junior Scholastic Player of the Year (2004)

ELLIOTT, Brian (EHL-lee-awt, BRIGH-uhn) ST.L.

Goaltender. Catches left. 6'2", 209 lbs. Born, Newmarket, Ont., April 9, 1985.
(Ottawa's 9th choice, 291st overall, in 2003 Entry Draft).

			Regular Season								Playoffs						
Season	Club	League	GP	W	L	O/T	Mins	GA	SO	Avg	GP	W	L	Mins	GA	SO	Avg
2002-03	Ajax Axemen	ON-Jr.A	39	....	....	....	2097	135	0	3.86	....	....	....	....	....	....	....
2003-04	U. of Wisconsin	WCHA	6	3	3	0	336	12	0	2.14	....	....	....	....	....	....	....
2004-05	U. of Wisconsin	WCHA	9	6	2	1	467	9	3	1.16	....	....	....	....	....	....	....
2005-06	U. of Wisconsin	WCHA	35	*27	5	3	2128	55	*8	*1.55	....	....	....	....	....	....	....
2006-07	U. of Wisconsin	WCHA	36	15	17	2	2053	72	*5	2.10	....	....	....	....	....	....	....
	Binghamton	AHL	8	3	4	0	425	30	0	4.24	....	....	....	....	....	....	....
2007-08	**Ottawa**	**NHL**	**1**	**1**	**0**	**0**	**60**	**1**	**0**	**1.00**	....	....	....	....	....	....	....
	Binghamton	AHL	44	18	19	1	2394	112	2	2.81	....	....	....	....	....	....	....
2008-09	**Ottawa**	**NHL**	**31**	**16**	**8**	**3**	**1667**	**77**	**1**	**2.77**	....	....	....	....	....	....	....
	Binghamton	AHL	30	18	8	1	1691	65	2	2.31	....	....	....	....	....	....	....
2009-10	**Ottawa**	**NHL**	**55**	**29**	**18**	**4**	**3038**	**130**	**5**	**2.57**	**4**	**1**	**2**	**203**	**14**	**0**	**4.14**
2010-11	**Ottawa**	**NHL**	**43**	**13**	**19**	**8**	**2293**	**122**	**3**	**3.19**	....	....	....	....	....	....	....
	Colorado	**NHL**	**12**	**2**	**8**	**1**	**690**	**44**	**0**	**3.83**	....	....	....	....	....	....	....

2011-12	St. Louis	NHL	38	23	10	4	2235	58	9	*1.56	8	3	4	455	18	0	2.37
2012-13	St. Louis	NHL	24	14	8	1	1292	49	3	2.28	6	2	4	378	12	0	1.90
	Peoria Rivermen	AHL	2	1	1	0	119	3	1	1.51	....	....	....	....	....	....	....
	NHL Totals		204	98	71	21	11275	481	21	2.56	18	6	10	1036	44	0	2.55

WCHA Second All-Star Team (2006, 2007) • NCAA West First All-American Team (2006) • NCAA Championship All-Tournament Team (2006) • William M. Jennings Trophy (2012) (shared with Jaroslav Halak)

Played in NHL All-Star Game (2012)

Traded to **Colorado** by **Ottawa** for Craig Anderson, February 18, 2011. Signed as a free agent by **St. Louis**, July 1, 2011.

ELLIS, Dan (EHL-ihs, DAN) DAL

Goaltender. Catches left. 6'1", 191 lbs. Born, Saskatoon, Sask., June 19, 1980.
(Dallas' 2nd choice, 60th overall, in 2000 Entry Draft).

			Regular Season								Playoffs						
Season	Club	League	GP	W	L	O/T	Mins	GA	SO	Avg	GP	W	L	Mins	GA	SO	Avg
1998-99	Newmarket	ON-Jr.A	28	24	3	1	1670	63	3	2.25	....	....	....	....	....	....	....
99-2000	Omaha Lancers	USHL	55	*34	16	4	*3274	123	*11	*2.25	4	1	3	238	10	0	2.52
2000-01	Nebraska-Omaha	CCHA	40	21	14	3	2285	95	2	2.49	....	....	....	....	....	....	....
2001-02	Nebraska-Omaha	CCHA	40	20	15	4	2405	97	3	2.42	....	....	....	....	....	....	....
2002-03	Nebraska-Omaha	CCHA	39	11	21	5	2211	117	3	3.18	....	....	....	....	....	....	....
2003-04	**Dallas**	**NHL**	**1**	**1**	**0**	**0**	**60**	**3**	**0**	**3.00**	....	....	....	....	....	....	....
	Utah Grizzlies	AHL	20	5	14	0	1130	55	2	2.92	....	....	....	....	....	....	....
	Idaho Steelheads	ECHL	23	13	8	1	1334	57	2	2.56	*16	*13	3	*966	30	*3	*1.86
2004-05	Hamilton Bulldogs	AHL	31	10	19	0	1774	82	1	2.77	....	....	....	....	....	....	....
2005-06	Iowa Stars	AHL	34	16	13	1	1857	86	2	2.78	....	....	....	....	....	....	....
2006-07	Iowa Stars	AHL	55	30	21	1	3194	148	4	2.78	12	6	6	679	35	0	3.09
2007-08	**Nashville**	**NHL**	**44**	**23**	**10**	**3**	**2229**	**87**	**6**	**2.34**	**6**	**2**	**4**	**357**	**15**	**0**	**2.52**
2008-09	**Nashville**	**NHL**	**35**	**11**	**19**	**4**	**1965**	**96**	**3**	**2.93**	....	....	....	....	....	....	....
2009-10	**Nashville**	**NHL**	**31**	**15**	**13**	**1**	**1715**	**77**	**1**	**2.69**	....	....	....	....	....	....	....
2010-11	**Tampa Bay**	**NHL**	**31**	**13**	**7**	**6**	**1679**	**82**	**2**	**2.93**	....	....	....	....	....	....	....
	Anaheim	**NHL**	**13**	**8**	**3**	**1**	**729**	**29**	**0**	**2.39**	**1**	**0**	**1**	**41**	**4**	**0**	**5.85**
2011-12	**Anaheim**	**NHL**	**10**	**1**	**5**	**0**	**419**	**19**	**0**	**2.72**	....	....	....	....	....	....	....
2012-13	Charlotte Checkers	AHL	18	8	7	2	1026	42	2	2.46	....	....	....	....	....	....	....
	Carolina	**NHL**	**19**	**6**	**8**	**2**	**997**	**52**	**1**	**3.13**	....	....	....	....	....	....	....
	NHL Totals		**184**	**78**	**65**	**17**	**9793**	**445**	**13**	**2.73**	**7**	**2**	**5**	**398**	**19**	**0**	**2.86**

USHL First All-Star Team (2000) • USHL Goaltender of the Year (2000) • USHL Player of the Year (2000) • CCHA Second All-Star Team (2002) • ECHL Playoff MVP (2004)

Signed as a free agent by **Nashville**, July 5, 2007. Traded to **Montreal** by **Nashville** with Dustin Boyd and future considerations for Sergei Kostitsyn and future considerations, June 29, 2010. Signed as a free agent by **Tampa Bay**, July 1, 2010. Traded to **Anaheim** by **Tampa Bay** for Curtis McElhinney, February 24, 2011. Signed as a free agent by **Charlotte** (ECHL). September 24, 2012. Signed as a free agent by **Carolina**, January 13, 2013. Signed as a free agent by **Dallas**, July 5, 2013.

EMERY, Ray (EH-muhr-ee, RAY) PHI

Goaltender. Catches left. 6'2", 196 lbs. Born, Cayuga, Ont., September 28, 1982.
(Ottawa's 4th choice, 99th overall, in 2001 Entry Draft).

			Regular Season								Playoffs						
Season	Club	League	GP	W	L	O/T	Mins	GA	SO	Avg	GP	W	L	Mins	GA	SO	Avg
1998-99	Dunnville Terriers	ON-Jr.C	22	3	19	0	1320	140	0	6.37	....	....	....	....	....	....	....
99-2000	Welland Cougars	ON-Jr.B	23	13	10	1	1323	62	1	2.68	....	....	....	....	....	....	....
	Sault Ste. Marie	OHL	16	9	3	0	716	36	1	3.02	15	8	7	884	33	*3	2.24
2000-01	Sault Ste. Marie	OHL	52	18	29	2	2938	174	1	3.55	....	....	....	....	....	....	....
2001-02	Sault Ste. Marie	OHL	*59	*33	17	9	*3477	158	4	2.73	6	2	4	360	19	*1	3.17
2002-03	**Ottawa**	**NHL**	**3**	**1**	**0**	**0**	**85**	**2**	**0**	**1.41**	....	....	....	....	....	....	....
	Binghamton	AHL	50	27	17	6	2924	118	*7	2.42	14	8	6	848	40	*2	2.83
2003-04	**Ottawa**	**NHL**	**3**	**2**	**0**	**0**	**126**	**5**	**0**	**2.38**	....	....	....	....	....	....	....
	Binghamton	AHL	53	21	23	7	3109	128	3	2.47	2	0	2	120	6	0	3.01
2004-05	Binghamton	AHL	51	28	18	5	2993	132	0	2.65	6	2	4	409	14	0	2.05
2005-06	**Ottawa**	**NHL**	**39**	**23**	**11**	**4**	**2168**	**102**	**3**	**2.82**	**10**	**5**	**5**	**604**	**29**	**0**	**2.88**
2006-07	**Ottawa**	**NHL**	**58**	**33**	**16**	**6**	**3351**	**138**	**5**	**2.47**	***20**	***13**	**7**	***1249**	**47**	***3**	**2.26**
2007-08	**Ottawa**	**NHL**	**31**	**12**	**13**	**4**	**1689**	**88**	**0**	**3.13**	....	....	....	....	....	....	....
	Binghamton	AHL	2	1	1	0	120	6	0	3.00	....	....	....	....	....	....	....
2008-09	Mytischi	KHL	36	....	....	....	2070	73	2	2.12	7	....	....	419	13	1	1.86
2009-10	**Philadelphia**	**NHL**	**29**	**16**	**11**	**1**	**1684**	**74**	**3**	**2.64**	....	....	....	....	....	....	....
	Adirondack	AHL	1	0	1	0	59	2	0	2.03	....	....	....	....	....	....	....
2010-11	**Anaheim**	**NHL**	**10**	**7**	**2**	**0**	**527**	**20**	**0**	**2.28**	**6**	**2**	**3**	**319**	**17**	**0**	**3.20**
	Syracuse Crunch	AHL	5	4	1	0	303	10	0	1.98	....	....	....	....	....	....	....
2011-12	**Chicago**	**NHL**	**34**	**15**	**9**	**4**	**1774**	**83**	**0**	**2.81**	....	....	....	....	....	....	....
2012-13 ♦	**Chicago**	**NHL**	**21**	**17**	**1**	**0**	**1116**	**36**	**3**	**1.94**	....	....	....	....	....	....	....
	NHL Totals		**228**	**126**	**63**	**19**	**12520**	**548**	**14**	**2.63**	**36**	**20**	**15**	**2172**	**93**	**3**	**2.57**

OHL First All-Star Team (2002) • Canadian Major Junior First All-Star Team (2002) • Canadian Major Junior Goaltender of the Year (2002) • AHL All-Rookie Team (2003) • William M. Jennings Trophy (2013) (shared with Corey Crawford)

Signed as a free agent by **Mytischi** (KHL), July 9, 2008. Signed as a free agent by **Philadelphia** June 10, 2009. Signed as a free agent by **Anaheim**, February 7, 2011. Signed as a free agent by **Chicago**, October 3, 2011. Signed as a free agent by **Philadelphia**, July 5, 2013.

ENGREN, Atte (EHN-grehn, AH-tay) NSH

Goaltender. Catches left. 6'1", 188 lbs. Born, Rauma, Finland, February 19, 1988.
(Nashville's 9th choice, 204th overall, in 2007 Entry Draft).

			Regular Season								Playoffs						
Season	Club	League	GP	W	L	O/T	Mins	GA	SO	Avg	GP	W	L	Mins	GA	SO	Avg
2004-05	Lukko Rauma U18	Fin-U18	10	....	....	....	603	22	0	2.19	....	....	....	....	....	....	....
2005-06	Lukko Rauma U18	Fin-U18	16	....	....	....	966	44	0	2.73	....	....	....	....	....	....	....
	Lukko Rauma Jr.	Fin-Jr.	11	....	....	....	637	30	0	2.83	9	....	....	509	27	0	3.18
2006-07	Lukko Rauma Jr.	Fin-Jr.	38	....	....	....	2277	115	1	3.03	....	....	....	....	....	....	....
	Suomi U20	Finland-2	2	....	....	....	100	7	0	4.20	....	....	....	....	....	....	....
2007-08	Hokki Kajaani	Finland-2	1	0	0	0	15	4	0	15.70	....	....	....	....	....	....	....
	Lukko Rauma	Finland	1	0	1	0	59	3	0	3.04	....	....	....	....	....	....	....
	Lukko Rauma Jr.	Fin-Jr.	31	14	13	0	1791	89	1	2.98	2	2	0	120	3	0	1.50
2008-09	TPS Turku Jr.	Fin-Jr.	4	3	1	0	240	11	0	2.75	....	....	....	....	....	....	....
	Kiekko-Vantaa	Finland-2	5	3	2	0	264	9	0	2.05	....	....	....	....	....	....	....
	TPS Turku	Finland	6	1	4	1	317	17	1	3.22	....	....	....	....	....	....	....
2009-10	TuTo Turku	Finland-2	1	1	0	0	60	1	1	1.00	2	....	....	59	3	0	3.05
	TPS Turku	Finland	35	15	13	1	1778	78	2	2.63	8	7	1	494	15	1	1.82
2010-11	TPS Turku	Finland	51	10	25	13	2914	137	4	2.82	....	....	....	....	....	....	....
	Milwaukee	AHL	4	2	2	0	247	10	0	2.43	....	....	....	....	....	....	....
2011-12	Milwaukee	AHL	23	8	11	3	1200	49	0	2.45	....	....	....	....	....	....	....
2012-13	TPS Turku	Finland	47	10	18	16	2657	117	1	2.64	....	....	....	....	....	....	....

Signed as a free agent by **TPS Turku** (Finland), May 2, 2012.

ENROTH, Jhonas (EHN-rawth, YOH-nuhs) BUF

Goaltender. Catches left. 5'10", 166 lbs. Born, Stockholm, Sweden, June 25, 1988.
(Buffalo's 2nd choice, 46th overall, in 2006 Entry Draft).

			Regular Season								Playoffs						
Season	Club	League	GP	W	L	O/T	Mins	GA	SO	Avg	GP	W	L	Mins	GA	SO	Avg
2003-04	Huddinge IK U18	Swe-U18	6	....	....	....	324	15	0	2.77	....	....	....	....	....	....	....
2004-05	Huddinge IK Jr.	Swe-Jr.	19	....	....	....	1144	49	3	2.57	3	....	....	186	6	1	1.93
	Huddinge IK U18	Swe-U18	2	....	....	....	125	5	0	2.40	....	....	....	....	....	....	....
	Huddinge IK	Sweden-2	2	....	....	....	51	6	0	6.95	....	....	....	....	....	....	....
2005-06	Sodertalje SK Jr.	Swe-Jr.	39	....	....	....	2378	86	1	2.17	4	....	....	243	9	0	2.22
	Sodertalje SK U18	Swe-U18	2	....	....	....	120	5	0	2.50	....	....	....	....	....	....	....
2006-07	Sodertalje SK Jr.	Swe-Jr.	3	....	....	....	180	4	0	1.33	....	....	....	....	....	....	....
	Sodertalje SK	Sweden-2	33	....	....	....	1938	57	3	1.76	....	....	....	....	....	....	....
2007-08	Sodertalje SK Jr.	Swe-Jr.	1	....	....	....	59	4	0	4.05	....	....	....	....	....	....	....
	Sodertalje SK	Sweden	27	....	....	....	1578	56	2	*2.13	....	....	....	....	....	....	....
2008-09	Portland Pirates	AHL	58	26	23	6	3424	157	3	2.75	5	1	4	264	10	1	2.27
2009-10	**Buffalo**	**NHL**	**1**	**0**	**1**	**0**	**58**	**4**	**0**	**4.14**	....	....	....	....	....	....	....
	Portland Pirates	AHL	48	28	18	1	2781	110	5	2.37	....	....	....	....	....	....	....
2010-11	**Buffalo**	**NHL**	**14**	**9**	**2**	**2**	**769**	**35**	**1**	**2.73**	**1**	**0**	**0**	**17**	**1**	**0**	**3.53**
	Portland Pirates	AHL	41	20	17	2	2393	111	0	2.78	4	1	2	217	10	0	2.77
2011-12	**Buffalo**	**NHL**	**26**	**8**	**11**	**4**	**1399**	**63**	**1**	**2.70**	....	....	....	....	....	....	....
2012-13	Huddinge IK	Sweden-3	2	2	0	0	120	5	0	2.50	....	....	....	....	....	....	....
	Almtuna	Sweden-2	14	....	....	....	....	....	....	2.31	....	....	....	....	....	....	....
	Buffalo	**NHL**	**12**	**4**	**4**	**1**	**623**	**27**	**1**	**2.60**	....	....	....	....	....	....	....
	NHL Totals		**53**	**21**	**18**	**7**	**2849**	**129**	**3**	**2.72**	**1**	**0**	**0**	**17**	**1**	**0**	**3.53**

NHL All-Rookie Team (2012)

Signed as a free agent by **Huddinge** (Sweden-3). October 25, 2012. Signed as a free agent by **Almtuna** (Sweden-2), November 5, 2012.

ERIKSSON, Joacim (AIR-ihk-suhn, YOH-a-kihm) VAN

Goaltender. Catches right. 6'1", 189 lbs. Born, Gavle, Sweden, April 9, 1990.
(Philadelphia's 5th choice, 196th overall, in 2008 Entry Draft).

			Regular Season								Playoffs						
Season	Club	League	GP	W	L	O/T	Mins	GA	SO	Avg	GP	W	L	Mins	GA	SO	Avg
2006-07	Valbo AIF Jr.	Swe-Jr.	18	....	....	....	1072	55	....	3.08	....	....	....	....	....	....	....
	Valbo AIF	Sweden-3	1	....	....	....	34	2	0	3.51	....	....	....	....	....	....	....
2007-08	Brynas U18	Swe-U18	9	....	....	....	545	21	2	2.31	5	....	....	296	7	2	1.42
	Brynas IF Gavle Jr.	Swe-Jr.	16	....	....	....	960	53	0	3.31	7	....	....	426	13	1	1.83
	Valbo HC	Sweden-3	2	....	....	....	123	8	0	3.91	....	....	....	....	....	....	....
2008-09	Brynas IF Gavle Jr.	Swe-Jr.	33	....	....	....	1962	65	6	1.99	7	....	....	468	19	0	2.43
2009-10	Leksands IF Jr.	Swe-Jr.	1	....	....	....	60	0	1	0.00	....	....	....	....	....	....	....
	Leksands IF	Sweden-2	48	....	....	....	2877	115	5	2.40	....	....	....	....	....	....	....
2010-11	Skelleftea AIK Jr.	Swe-Jr.	2	....	....	....	119	7	0	3.54	....	....	....	....	....	....	....
	Skelleftea AIK	Sweden	17	....	....	....	939	40	1	2.56	....	....	....	....	....	....	....
2011-12	Skelleftea AIK	Sweden	33	....	....	....	2016	61	3	1.82	19	....	....	1200	44	1	2.20
2012-13	Skelleftea AIK	Sweden	30	21	9	0	1726	48	5	1.67	10	10	0	623	11	3	1.06

Signed as a free agent by **Vancouver**, June 17, 2013.

FASTH, Viktor (FAWST, VIHK-tohr) ANA

Goaltender. Catches left. 6', 186 lbs. Born, Kalix, Sweden, August 8, 1982.

			Regular Season								Playoffs						
Season	Club	League	GP	W	L	O/T	Mins	GA	SO	Avg	GP	W	L	Mins	GA	SO	Avg
2007-08	Vaxjo Lakers HC	Sweden-2	30	....	....	0	4	....	....	2.26	....	....	....	....	....	....	....
2008-09	Vaxjo Lakers HC	Sweden-2	9	....	....	....	....	....	....	3.04	....	....	....	....	....	....	....
2009-10	Vaxjo Lakers HC	Sweden-2	23	....	....	....	....	....	....	2.15	....	....	....	....	....	....	....
2010-11	AIK IF Solna	Sweden	42	....	....	....	2473	93	2	2.26	8	....	....	472	14	1	1.78
2011-12	AIK Solna	Sweden	46	....	....	....	2683	95	5	2.12	12	....	....	752	35	1	2.79
2012-13	Tingsryds AIF	Sweden-2	12	4	7	0	677	19	1	1.68	....	....	....	....	....	....	....
	Norfolk Admirals	AHL	3	1	2	0	183	6	0	1.96	....	....	....	....	....	....	....
	Anaheim	**NHL**	**25**	**15**	**6**	**2**	**1428**	**52**	**4**	**2.18**	....	....	....	....	....	....	....
	NHL Totals		**25**	**15**	**6**	**2**	**1428**	**52**	**4**	**2.18**	....	....	....	....	....	....	....

Signed as a free agent by **Anaheim**, May 21, 2012. Signed as a free agent by **Tingsryds** (Sweden-2), September 21, 2012.

FLEURY, Marc-Andre (fluh-REE, MAHRK-AWN-dray) PIT

Goaltender. Catches left. 6'2", 180 lbs. Born, Sorel, Que., November 28, 1984.
(Pittsburgh's 1st choice, 1st overall, in 2003 Entry Draft).

			Regular Season								Playoffs						
Season	Club	League	GP	W	L	O/T	Mins	GA	SO	Avg	GP	W	L	Mins	GA	SO	Avg
99-2000	C.C. Lemoyne	QAAA	15	4	9	0	780	36	1	2.77	....	....	....	....	....	....	....
2000-01	Cape Breton	QMJHL	35	12	13	2	1705	115	0	4.05	2	0	1	32	4	0	7.50
2001-02	Cape Breton	QMJHL	55	26	14	8	3043	141	2	2.78	16	9	7	1003	55	0	3.29
2002-03	Cape Breton	QMJHL	51	17	24	6	2889	162	2	3.36	4	0	4	228	17	0	4.47
2003-04	**Pittsburgh**	**NHL**	**21**	**4**	**14**	**2**	**1154**	**70**	**1**	**3.64**	....	....	....	....	....	....	....
	Cape Breton	QMJHL	10	8	1	1	606	20	0	1.98	4	1	3	251	13	0	3.10
	Wilkes-Barre	AHL	....	....	....	....	....	....	....	....	2	0	1	92	6	0	3.90
2004-05	Wilkes-Barre	AHL	54	26	19	4	3029	127	5	2.52	4	0	2	151	11	0	4.36
2005-06	**Pittsburgh**	**NHL**	**50**	**13**	**27**	**6**	**2809**	**152**	**1**	**3.25**	....	....	....	....	....	....	....
	Wilkes-Barre	AHL	12	10	2	0	727	19	0	1.57	5	2	3	311	18	0	3.48
2006-07	**Pittsburgh**	**NHL**	**67**	**40**	**16**	**9**	**3905**	**184**	**5**	**2.83**	**5**	**1**	**4**	**287**	**18**	**0**	**3.76**
2007-08	**Pittsburgh**	**NHL**	**35**	**19**	**10**	**2**	**1857**	**72**	**4**	**2.33**	***20**	***14**	**6**	***1251**	**41**	***3**	**1.97**
	Wilkes-Barre	AHL	5	3	2	0	297	7	0	1.42	....	....	....	....	....	....	....
2008-09 ♦	**Pittsburgh**	**NHL**	**62**	**35**	**18**	**7**	**3641**	**162**	**4**	**2.67**	***24**	***16**	**8**	***1447**	**63**	**0**	**2.61**
2009-10	**Pittsburgh**	**NHL**	**67**	**37**	**21**	**6**	**3798**	**168**	**1**	**2.65**	**13**	**7**	**6**	**798**	**37**	**1**	**2.78**
	Canada	Olympics	DID NOT PLAY – SPARE GOALTENDER														
2010-11	**Pittsburgh**	**NHL**	**65**	**36**	**20**	**5**	**3695**	**143**	**3**	**2.32**	**7**	**3**	**4**	**405**	**17**	**1**	**2.52**
2011-12	**Pittsburgh**	**NHL**	**67**	**42**	**17**	**4**	**3896**	**153**	**3**	**2.36**	**6**	**2**	**4**	**337**	**26**	**0**	**4.63**
2012-13	**Pittsburgh**	**NHL**	**33**	**23**	**8**	**0**	**1858**	**74**	**1**	**2.39**	**5**	**2**	**2**	**290**	**17**	**1**	**3.52**
	NHL Totals		**467**	**249**	**151**	**41**	**26613**	**1178**	**23**	**2.66**	**80**	**45**	**34**	**4815**	**219**	**6**	**2.73**

QMJHL Second All-Star Team (2003)

Played in NHL All-Star Game (2011)

FORSBERG, Anton (FOHRZ-buhrg, AN-tawn) CBJ

Goaltender. Catches left. 6'3", 183 lbs. Born, Harnosand, Sweden, November 27, 1992.
(Columbus' 6th choice, 188th overall, in 2011 Entry Draft).

			Regular Season								Playoffs						
Season	Club	League	GP	W	L	O/T	Mins	GA	SO	Avg	GP	W	L	Mins	GA	SO	Avg
2007-08	Harnosand Jr.	Swe-Jr.	9	....	....	....	....	....	....	....	....	....	....	....	....	....	....
	Harnosand	Sweden-3	1	....	....	....	20	2	0	6.00	....	....	....	....	....	....	....
2008-09	MODO U18	Swe-U18	12	....	....	....	619	34	0	3.29	5	....	....	225	11	1	2.93
2009-10	MODO U18	Swe-U18	9	....	....	....	538	26	0	2.90	2	....	....	120	5	0	2.50
	MODO Jr.	Swe-Jr.	21	....	....	....	1183	73	1	3.70	3	....	....	177	7	0	2.37
2010-11	MODO Jr.	Swe-Jr.	33	....	....	....	1942	94	3	2.90	6	....	....	358	17	0	2.85
	AIK Harnosand	Sweden-3	1	....	....	....	59	5	0	5.11	....	....	....	....	....	....	....
2011-12	MODO	Sweden	14	....	....	....	609	32	0	3.15	....	....	....	....	....	....	....
	MODO Jr.	Swe-Jr.	14	....	....	....	847	31	2	2.19	4	....	....	248	14	0	3.39
2012-13	Sodertalje SK	Sweden-2	41	26	14	0	2432	90	3	2.22	....	....	....	....	....	....	....

FRAZEE, Jeff (FRAY-zee, JEHF)

Goaltender. Catches left. 6', 195 lbs. Born, Edina, MN, May 13, 1987.
(New Jersey's 2nd choice, 38th overall, in 2005 Entry Draft).

			Regular Season								Playoffs						
Season	Club	League	GP	W	L	O/T	Mins	GA	SO	Avg	GP	W	L	Mins	GA	SO	Avg
2001-02	Holy Angels	High-MN	6	6	0	0	....	....	....	....	....	....	....	....	....	....	....
2002-03	Holy Angels	High-MN	16	14	1	1	....	....	....	....	....	....	....	....	....	....	....
2003-04	USNTDP	U-17	16	9	3	0	781	31	....	2.38	....	....	....	....	....	....	....
	USNTDP	NAHL	25	14	8	3	1463	71	3	2.91	....	....	....	....	....	....	....
2004-05	USNTDP	U-18	24	....	....	....	1309	59	3	2.71	....	....	....	....	....	....	....
	USNTDP	NAHL	9	8	1	0	500	18	1	2.16	....	....	....	....	....	....	....
2005-06	U. of Minnesota	WCHA	12	6	3	2	660	26	2	2.36	....	....	....	....	....	....	....
2006-07	U. of Minnesota	WCHA	20	14	3	1	1148	45	1	2.35	....	....	....	....	....	....	....
2007-08	U. of Minnesota	WCHA	14	6	7	0	798	39	1	2.93	....	....	....	....	....	....	....
	Lowell Devils	AHL	1	0	1	0	40	3	0	4.50	....	....	....	....	....	....	....
2008-09	Lowell Devils	AHL	58	28	22	6	3407	149	4	2.62	....	....	....	....	....	....	....
	Trenton Devils	ECHL	5	2	2	0	272	12	0	2.65	4	2	2	271	10	0	2.22
2009-10	Lowell Devils	AHL	31	14	16	0	1778	83	1	2.80	....	....	....	....	....	....	....
2010-11	Albany Devils	AHL	33	11	15	3	1842	89	2	2.90	....	....	....	....	....	....	....
2011-12	Albany Devils	AHL	36	12	19	2	2042	91	2	2.67	....	....	....	....	....	....	....
2012-13	Albany Devils	AHL	28	8	14	5	1654	71	1	2.58	....	....	....	....	....	....	....
	New Jersey	**NHL**	**1**	**0**	**0**	**0**	**19**	**0**	**0**	**0.00**	....	....	....	....	....	....	....
	NHL Totals		**1**	**0**	**0**	**0**	**19**	**0**	**0**	**0.00**	....	....	....	....	....	....	....

FUCALE, Zachary (fuh-KAL-ee, za-KAH-ree) MTL

Goaltender. Catches left. 6'1", 177 lbs. Born, Rosemere, Que., May 28, 1995.
(Montreal's 3rd choice, 36th overall, in 2013 Entry Draft).

			Regular Season								Playoffs						
Season	Club	League	GP	W	L	O/T	Mins	GA	SO	Avg	GP	W	L	Mins	GA	SO	Avg
2010-11	Saint-Eustache	QAAA	28	15	5	3	1513	78	3	3.09	10	7	3	664	40	0	3.61
2011-12	Halifax	QMJHL	58	32	18	6	3249	171	2	3.16	17	10	7	1022	49	0	2.88
2012-13	Halifax	QMJHL	55	*45	5	3	3162	124	2	2.35	17	*16	1	*1042	35	*3	*2.02

QMJHL First All-Star Team (2013)

GARON, Mathieu (gah-ROHN, MA-tyew)

Goaltender. Catches right. 6'1", 206 lbs. Born, Chandler, Que., January 9, 1978.
(Montreal's 2nd choice, 44th overall, in 1996 Entry Draft).

			Regular Season								Playoffs						
Season	Club	League	GP	W	L	O/T	Mins	GA	SO	Avg	GP	W	L	Mins	GA	SO	Avg
1993-94	Jonquiere Elites	QAAA	17	0	13	0	834	88	0	6.33	....	....	....	....	....	....	....
1994-95	Jonquiere Elites	QAAA	27	13	13	1	1554	94	0	3.63	9	6	2	467	26	0	3.34
1995-96	Victoriaville Tigres	QMJHL	51	18	27	0	2716	189	1	4.17	12	7	4	676	38	1	3.37
1996-97	Victoriaville Tigres	QMJHL	53	29	18	3	3026	148	*6	2.93	6	2	4	330	23	0	4.18
1997-98	Victoriaville Tigres	QMJHL	47	27	18	2	2802	125	5	2.68	6	2	4	345	22	0	3.82
1998-99	Fredericton	AHL	40	14	22	2	2222	114	3	3.08	6	1	1	208	12	0	3.47
99-2000	Quebec Citadelles	AHL	53	17	28	3	2884	149	2	3.10	1	0	0	20	3	0	8.82
2000-01	**Montreal**	**NHL**	**11**	**4**	**5**	**1**	**589**	**24**	**2**	**2.44**	....	....	....	....	....	....	....
	Quebec Citadelles	AHL	31	16	13	1	1768	86	1	2.92	8	4	4	459	22	1	2.88
2001-02	**Montreal**	**NHL**	**5**	**1**	**4**	**0**	**261**	**19**	**0**	**4.37**	....	....	....	....	....	....	....
	Quebec Citadelles	AHL	50	21	15	12	2988	136	2	2.73	3	0	3	198	12	0	3.63
2002-03	**Montreal**	**NHL**	**8**	**3**	**5**	**0**	**482**	**16**	**2**	**1.99**	....	....	....	....	....	....	....
	Hamilton Bulldogs	AHL	20	15	2	2	1150	34	4	1.77	....	....	....	....	....	....	....
2003-04	**Montreal**	**NHL**	**19**	**8**	**6**	**2**	**1003**	**38**	**0**	**2.27**	**1**	**0**	**0**	**12**	**0**	**0**	**0.00**
2004-05	Manchester	AHL	52	32	14	4	2969	105	8	2.12	6	2	4	285	17	0	3.58
2005-06	**Los Angeles**	**NHL**	**63**	**31**	**26**	**3**	**3446**	**185**	**4**	**3.22**	....	....	....	....	....	....	....
2006-07	**Los Angeles**	**NHL**	**32**	**13**	**10**	**6**	**1779**	**79**	**2**	**2.66**	....	....	....	....	....	....	....
2007-08	**Edmonton**	**NHL**	**47**	**26**	**18**	**1**	**2658**	**118**	**4**	**2.66**	....	....	....	....	....	....	....
2008-09	**Edmonton**	**NHL**	**15**	**6**	**8**	**0**	**815**	**43**	**0**	**3.17**	....	....	....	....	....	....	....
	◆ **Pittsburgh**	**NHL**	**4**	**2**	**1**	**0**	**206**	**10**	**0**	**2.91**	**1**	**0**	**0**	**24**	**0**	**0**	**0.00**
2009-10	**Columbus**	**NHL**	**35**	**12**	**9**	**6**	**1771**	**83**	**2**	**2.81**	....	....	....	....	....	....	....
2010-11	**Columbus**	**NHL**	**36**	**10**	**14**	**6**	**1938**	**88**	**3**	**2.72**	....	....	....	....	....	....	....
2011-12	**Tampa Bay**	**NHL**	**48**	**23**	**16**	**4**	**2484**	**118**	**1**	**2.85**	....	....	....	....	....	....	....
2012-13	**Tampa Bay**	**NHL**	**18**	**5**	**9**	**2**	**910**	**44**	**0**	**2.90**	....	....	....	....	....	....	....
	NHL Totals		**341**	**144**	**131**	**31**	**18342**	**865**	**20**	**2.83**	**2**	**0**	**0**	**36**	**0**	**0**	**0.00**

QMJHL All-Rookie Team (1996) • QMJHL Defensive Rookie of the Year (1996) • QMJHL First All-Star Team (1998) • Canadian Major Junior First All-Star Team (1998) • Canadian Major Junior Goaltender of the Year (1998)

Traded to **Los Angeles** by **Montreal** with San Jose's 3rd round choice (previously acquired, Los Angeles selected Paul Baier) in 2004 Entry Draft for Radek Bonk and Cristobal Huet, June 26, 2004. Signed as a free agent by **Edmonton**, July 3, 2007. Traded to **Pittsburgh** by **Edmonton** for Dany Sabourin, Ryan Stone and Pittsburgh's 4th round choice (Tobias Rieder) in 2011 Entry Draft, January 17, 2009. Signed as a free agent by **Columbus**, July 1, 2009. Signed as a free agent by **Tampa Bay**, July 1, 2011.

GAYDUCHENKO, Sergei (gay-doo-CHEHN-koh, SAIR-gay) FLA

Goaltender. Catches left. 6'5", 222 lbs. Born, Kiev, USSR, June 6, 1989.
(Florida's 8th choice, 202nd overall, in 2007 Entry Draft).

			Regular Season								Playoffs						
Season	Club	League	GP	W	L	O/T	Mins	GA	SO	Avg	GP	W	L	Mins	GA	SO	Avg
2006-07	Yaroslavl 2	Russia-3	23	....	....	....	1180	57	3	2.90	....	....	....	....	....	....	....
2007-08	Novokuznetsk 2	Russia-3	2	....	....	....	....	5	....	....	....	....	....	....	....	....	....
	Novokuznetsk	Russia	11	....	....	....	533	27	0	3.04	....	....	....	....	....	....	....
2008-09	Yaroslavl 2	Russia-3					STATISTICS NOT AVAILABLE										
	Yaroslavl	KHL	3	....	....	....	185	6	0	1.95	....	....	....	....	....	....	....
2009-10	Yaroslavl	KHL	20	....	....	....	1091	44	0	2.42	....	....	....	....	....	....	....
2010-11	CSKA Moscow	KHL	23	....	....	....	1201	58	1	2.90	....	....	....	....	....	....	....
	CSKA Jr.	Russia-Jr.	7	....	....	....	332	21	1	3.80	15	....	....	872	28	2	1.93
2011-12	CSKA Moscow	KHL	13	2	6	0	623	30	0	2.86	2	0	0	105	7	0	4.01
2012-13	Sibir Novosibirsk	KHL	19	6	9	0	975	39	1	2.40	1	0	0	20	2	0	6.00

GIBSON, Christopher (GIHB-suhn, KRIHS-tuh-fuhr) TOR

Goaltender. Catches left. 6'1", 195 lbs. Born, Karkkila, Finland, December 27, 1992.
(Los Angeles' 1st choice, 49th overall, in 2011 Entry Draft).

			Regular Season								Playoffs						
Season	Club	League	GP	W	L	O/T	Mins	GA	SO	Avg	GP	W	L	Mins	GA	SO	Avg
2008-09	Notre Dame	SMHL	18	16	1	0	1049	46	1	2.63	6	6	0	360	11	1	1.83
2009-10	Chicoutimi	QMJHL	29	8	19	0	1592	93	2	3.50	4	2	1	230	13	0	3.39
2010-11	Chicoutimi	QMJHL	37	14	15	8	2235	90	4	2.42	4	0	4	219	19	0	5.20
2011-12	Chicoutimi	QMJHL	48	27	17	4	2809	139	3	2.97	18	9	9	1116	58	*1	3.12
2012-13	Chicoutimi	QMJHL	41	17	18	4	2279	117	4	3.08	6	2	4	356	23	0	3.87

QMJHL First All-Star Team (2011)

Signed as a free agent by **Toronto**, July 21, 2013.

GIBSON, John (GIHB-suhn, JAWN) ANA

Goaltender. Catches left. 6'3", 212 lbs. Born, Pittsburgh, PA, July 14, 1993.
(Anaheim's 2nd choice, 39th overall, in 2011 Entry Draft).

			Regular Season								Playoffs						
Season	Club	League	GP	W	L	O/T	Mins	GA	SO	Avg	GP	W	L	Mins	GA	SO	Avg
2009-10	USNTDP	USHL	18	7	9	0	1023	63	0	3.69	....	....	....	....	....	....	....
	USNTDP	U-17	6	3	1	1	335	16	0	2.87	....	....	....	....	....	....	....
	USNTDP	U-18	2	2	0	0	120	4	0	2.00	....	....	....	....	....	....	....
2010-11	USNTDP	USHL	17	9	4	3	983	39	1	2.38	....	....	....	....	....	....	....
	USNTDP	U-18	23	15	7	0	1255	56	0	2.68	....	....	....	....	....	....	....
2011-12	Kitchener Rangers	OHL	32	21	10	0	1897	87	1	2.75	16	8	7	898	40	1	2.67
2012-13	Kitchener Rangers	OHL	27	17	9	1	1615	65	1	2.41	10	5	5	609	22	1	2.17
	Norfolk Admirals	AHL	1	0	0	0	40	3	0	4.50	....	....	....	....	....	....	....

OHL Second All-Star Team (2013)

GIGUERE, Jean-Sebastien (zhih-GAIR, ZHAWN-suh-BAS-t'yehn) COL

Goaltender. Catches left. 6'1", 202 lbs. Born, Montreal, Que., May 16, 1977.
(Hartford's 1st choice, 13th overall, in 1995 Entry Draft).

			Regular Season								Playoffs						
Season	Club	League	GP	W	L	O/T	Mins	GA	SO	Avg	GP	W	L	Mins	GA	SO	Avg
1992-93	Laval-Laurentides	QAAA	25	12	11	2	1498	76	0	3.02	11	6	5	654	38	0	3.49
1993-94	Verdun	QMJHL	26	13	7	2	1288	69	1	3.21	1	0	0	29	2	0	4.14
1994-95	Halifax	QMJHL	47	14	27	5	2762	181	2	3.93	7	3	4	418	17	1	*2.44
1995-96	Halifax	QMJHL	55	26	23	2	3236	185	1	3.43	6	1	5	357	24	0	4.04
1996-97	**Hartford**	**NHL**	**8**	**1**	**4**	**0**	**394**	**24**	**0**	**3.65**	....	....	....	....	....	....	....
	Halifax	QMJHL	50	28	19	3	3009	169	2	3.37	16	9	7	954	58	0	3.65
1997-98	Saint John Flames	AHL	31	16	10	3	1758	72	2	2.46	10	5	3	536	27	0	3.02
1998-99	**Calgary**	**NHL**	**15**	**6**	**7**	**1**	**860**	**46**	**0**	**3.21**	....	....	....	....	....	....	....
	Saint John Flames	AHL	39	18	16	3	2145	123	3	3.44	7	3	2	304	21	0	4.14
99-2000	**Calgary**	**NHL**	**7**	**1**	**3**	**1**	**330**	**15**	**0**	**2.73**	....	....	....	....	....	....	....
	Saint John Flames	AHL	41	17	17	3	2243	114	0	3.05	3	0	3	178	9	0	3.03
2000-01	**Anaheim**	**NHL**	**34**	**11**	**17**	**5**	**2031**	**87**	**4**	**2.57**	....	....	....	....	....	....	....
	Cincinnati	AHL	23	12	7	2	1306	53	0	2.43	....	....	....	....	....	....	....
2001-02	**Anaheim**	**NHL**	**53**	**20**	**25**	**6**	**3127**	**111**	**4**	**2.13**	....	....	....	....	....	....	....
2002-03	**Anaheim**	**NHL**	**65**	**34**	**22**	**6**	**3775**	**145**	**8**	**2.30**	**21**	**15**	**6**	**1407**	**38**	**5**	***1.62**
2003-04	**Anaheim**	**NHL**	**55**	**17**	**31**	**6**	**3210**	**140**	**3**	**2.62**	....	....	....	....	....	....	....
2004-05	Hamburg Freezers	Germany	6	....	....	....	301	12	0	2.39	2	....	....	100	7	0	4.20
2005-06	**Anaheim**	**NHL**	**60**	**30**	**15**	**11**	**3381**	**150**	**2**	**2.66**	**6**	**3**	**3**	**318**	**18**	**0**	**3.40**
2006-07 ◆	**Anaheim**	**NHL**	**56**	**36**	**10**	**8**	**3245**	**122**	**4**	**2.26**	**18**	***13**	**4**	**1067**	**35**	**1**	**1.97**
2007-08	**Anaheim**	**NHL**	**58**	**35**	**17**	**6**	**3310**	**117**	**4**	**2.12**	**6**	**2**	**4**	**358**	**19**	**0**	**3.18**
2008-09	**Anaheim**	**NHL**	**46**	**19**	**18**	**6**	**2458**	**127**	**2**	**3.10**	**1**	**0**	**0**	**17**	**0**	**0**	**0.00**
2009-10	**Anaheim**	**NHL**	**20**	**4**	**8**	**5**	**1108**	**58**	**1**	**3.14**	....	....	....	....	....	....	....
	Toronto	**NHL**	**15**	**6**	**7**	**2**	**915**	**38**	**2**	**2.49**	....	....	....	....	....	....	....
2010-11	**Toronto**	**NHL**	**33**	**11**	**11**	**4**	**1633**	**78**	**0**	**2.87**	....	....	....	....	....	....	....
2011-12	**Colorado**	**NHL**	**32**	**15**	**11**	**3**	**1820**	**69**	**2**	**2.27**	....	....	....	....	....	....	....
2012-13	**Colorado**	**NHL**	**18**	**5**	**4**	**4**	**908**	**43**	**0**	**2.84**	....	....	....	....	....	....	....
	NHL Totals		**575**	**251**	**210**	**74**	**32505**	**1370**	**36**	**2.53**	**52**	**33**	**17**	**3167**	**110**	**6**	**2.08**

QMJHL Second All-Star Team (1997) • AHL All-Rookie Team (1998) • Harry "Hap" Holmes Memorial Award (AHL – fewest goals against) (1998) (shared with Tyler Moss) • Conn Smythe Trophy (2003)

Played in NHL All-Star Game (2009)

• Transferred to **Carolina** after **Hartford** franchise relocated, June 25, 1997. Traded to **Calgary** by **Carolina** with Andrew Cassels for Gary Roberts and Trevor Kidd, August 25, 1997. Traded to **Anaheim** by **Calgary** for Anaheim's 2nd round choice (later traded to Washington – Washington selected Matt Pettinger) in 2000 Entry Draft, June 10, 2000. Signed as a free agent by **Hamburg** (Germany), January 31, 2005. Traded to **Toronto** by **Anaheim** for Vesa Toskala and Jason Blake, January 31, 2010. Signed as a free agent by **Colorado**, July 1, 2011.

GILLIES, Jon (GIHL-eez, JAWN) CGY

Goaltender. Catches left. 6'5", 216 lbs. Born, Concord, NH, January 22, 1994.
(Calgary's 3rd choice, 75th overall, in 2012 Entry Draft).

			Regular Season								Playoffs						
Season	Club	League	GP	W	L	O/T	Mins	GA	SO	Avg	GP	W	L	Mins	GA	SO	Avg
2009-10	Salisbury School	High-CT	8	....	....	....	313	....	1	1.99	....	....	....	....	....	....	....
	Neponset Valley	Minor-MA					STATISTICS NOT AVAILABLE										
2010-11	Indiana Ice	USHL	25	15	6	2	1447	68	3	2.82	2	0	1	82	3	0	2.20
2011-12	Indiana Ice	USHL	53	31	11	9	2967	137	3	2.77	6	3	3	359	17	0	2.84
2012-13	Providence College	H-East	35	17	12	6	2105	73	5	2.08	....	....	....	....	....	....	....

Hockey East All-Rookie Team (2013) • Hockey East First All-Star Team (2013) • Hockey East Rookie of the Year (2013) • NCAA East Second All-American Team (2013)

GOTHBERG, Zane (GAWTH-buhrg, ZAYN) BOS

Goaltender. Catches left. 6'2", 200 lbs. Born, Grand Forks, ND, August 20, 1992.
(Boston's 6th choice, 165th overall, in 2010 Entry Draft).

			Regular Season								Playoffs						
Season	Club	League	GP	W	L	O/T	Mins	GA	SO	Avg	GP	W	L	Mins	GA	SO	Avg
2007-08	Thief River Falls	High-MN	....	14	12	0	....	....	....	2.15	....	....	....	....	....	....	....
2008-09	Thief River Falls	High-MN	27	20	5	2	1354	....	4	1.49	....	....	....	....	....	....	....
2009-10	Team Great Plains	UMHSEL	5	0	4	0	250	32	0	7.68	....	....	....	....	....	....	....
	Thief River Falls	High-MN	28	18	8	1	1434	51	3	1.84	....	....	....	....	....	....	....
2010-11	Fargo Force	USHL	23	14	8	0	1318	49	2	2.23	1	0	1	55	3	0	3.25
2011-12	Fargo Force	USHL	46	26	16	4	2758	102	*7	2.22	6	3	3	370	11	0	1.78
2012-13	North Dakota	WCHA	17	9	4	3	1001	41	0	2.46	....	....	....	....	....	....	....

USHL First All-Star Team (2012)

GREISS, Thomas (GRIGHS, TAW-muhs) PHX

Goaltender. Catches left. 6'1", 215 lbs. Born, Straubing, West Germany, January 29, 1986.
(San Jose's 2nd choice, 94th overall, in 2004 Entry Draft).

			Regular Season								Playoffs						
Season	Club	League	GP	W	L	O/T	Mins	GA	SO	Avg	GP	W	L	Mins	GA	SO	Avg
2001-02	EV Fussen Jr.	Ger-Jr.					STATISTICS NOT AVAILABLE										
2002-03	Koln Jr.	Ger-Jr.	25	....	....	....	1613	58	0	2.16	3	1	2	180	8	1	2.67
2003-04	Koln Jr.	Ger-Jr.	24	....	....	....	1286	56	....	2.61	....	....	....	....	....	....	....
	Kolner Haie	Germany	1	....	....	....	20	4	0	12.00	....	....	....	....	....	....	....
2004-05	Kolner Haie	Germany	8	....	....	....	459	16	0	2.09	....	....	....	....	....	....	....
	Regensburg	German-2	1	....	....	....	60	2	0	2.00	2	....	....	56	2	0	2.14
2005-06	Kolner Haie	Germany	27	....	....	....	1560	64	1	2.46	9	....	....	533	27	*1	3.04
	Germany	Olympics	1	0	1	0	60	5	0	5.00	....	....	....	....	....	....	....
2006-07	Worcester Sharks	AHL	43	26	15	2	2555	111	0	2.61	3	0	3	172	12	0	4.18
	Fresno Falcons	ECHL	3	1	2	0	180	7	0	2.34	....	....	....	....	....	....	....
2007-08	**San Jose**	**NHL**	**3**	**0**	**1**	**1**	**129**	**7**	**0**	**3.26**	....	....	....	....	....	....	....
	Worcester Sharks	AHL	41	18	21	2	2424	125	0	3.09	....	....	....	....	....	....	....
2008-09	Worcester Sharks	AHL	57	30	24	2	3346	138	1	2.47	12	6	6	742	30	2	2.43
2009-10	**San Jose**	**NHL**	**16**	**7**	**4**	**1**	**782**	**35**	**0**	**2.69**	**1**	**0**	**0**	**40**	**2**	**0**	**3.00**
	Germany	Olympics	3	0	3	0	179	15	0	5.03	....	....	....	....	....	....	....
2010-11	Brynas IF Gavle	Sweden	32	....	....	....	1850	90	2	2.92	5	....	....	317	18	0	3.40
2011-12	**San Jose**	**NHL**	**19**	**9**	**7**	**1**	**1043**	**40**	**0**	**2.30**	....	....	....	....	....	....	....
2012-13	Hannover Scorp.	Germany	9	3	6	0	535	31	0	3.47	....	....	....	....	....	....	....
	San Jose	**NHL**	**6**	**1**	**4**	**0**	**308**	**13**	**1**	**2.53**	....	....	....	....	....	....	....
	Worcester Sharks	AHL	1	0	1	0	60	5	0	5.04	....	....	....	....	....	....	....
	NHL Totals		**44**	**17**	**16**	**3**	**2262**	**95**	**1**	**2.52**	**1**	**0**	**0**	**40**	**2**	**0**	**3.00**

• Assigned to **Gavle** (Sweden) by **San Jose**, October 21, 2010. Signed as a free agent by **Hannover** (Germany), November 20, 2012. Signed as a free agent by **Phoenix**, July 5, 2013.

GROSENICK, Troy (GOHS-nihk, TROI) S.J.

Goaltender. Catches left. 6'1", 190 lbs. Born, Brookfield, WI, August 27, 1989.

			Regular Season								Playoffs						
Season	Club	League	GP	W	L	O/T	Mins	GA	SO	Avg	GP	W	L	Mins	GA	SO	Avg
2010-11	Union College	ECAC	3	0	0	1	85	3	0	2.12	....	....	....	....	....	....	....
2011-12	Union College	ECAC	34	22	6	3	1922	53	5	1.65	....	....	....	....	....	....	....
2012-13	Union College	ECAC	34	17	10	5	1929	68	2	2.12	....	....	....	....	....	....	....

ECAC First All-Star Team (2012) • NCAA East First All-American Team (2012)

Signed as a free agent by **San Jose**, April 8, 2013.

GRUBAUER, Philipp (groo-BAHW-uhr, FIHL-ihp) WSH

Goaltender. Catches left. 6'1", 186 lbs. Born, Rosenheim, Germany, November 25, 1991.
(Washington's 3rd choice, 112th overall, in 2010 Entry Draft).

			Regular Season								Playoffs						
Season	Club	League	GP	W	L	O/T	Mins	GA	SO	Avg	GP	W	L	Mins	GA	SO	Avg
2006-07	Rosenheim Jr.	Ger-Jr.	6	....	....	....	354	49	....	8.32	3	....	....	180	12	....	4.00
2007-08	Rosenheim Jr.	Ger-Jr.	23	....	....	....	1288	71	....	3.31	3	....	....	181	8	....	2.65
	Rosenheim	German-3	5	....	....	....	307	14	1	2.74	7	....	....	420	12	....	1.71
2008-09	Belleville Bulls	OHL	17	7	8	0	947	62	1	3.93	1	0	0	56	4	0	4.26
2009-10	Belleville Bulls	OHL	31	10	14	5	1717	90	5	3.14	....	....	....	....	....	....	....
	Windsor Spitfires	OHL	19	13	1	2	1011	40	2	2.37	18	*16	2	1094	49	0	2.69
2010-11	Kingston	OHL	38	22	13	3	2239	135	2	3.62	....	....	....	....	....	....	....
2011-12	South Carolina	ECHL	43	23	13	5	2536	94	1	2.22	....	....	....	....	....	....	....
2012-13	Reading Royals	ECHL	26	19	5	1	1542	59	0	2.30	....	....	....	....	....	....	....
	Hershey Bears	AHL	28	15	9	2	1624	61	2	2.25	5	2	3	301	19	0	3.79
	Washington	**NHL**	**2**	**0**	**1**	**0**	**84**	**5**	**0**	**3.57**	....	....	....	....	....	....	....
	NHL Totals		**2**	**0**	**1**	**0**	**84**	**5**	**0**	**3.57**	....	....	....	....	....	....	....

GRUMET-MORRIS, Dov (groo-MAY-MAW-rihs, DAWV) FLA

Goaltender. Catches left. 6'2", 205 lbs. Born, Evanston, IL, February 28, 1982.
(Philadelphia's 4th choice, 161st overall, in 2002 Entry Draft).

			Regular Season								Playoffs						
Season	Club	League	GP	W	L	O/T	Mins	GA	SO	Avg	GP	W	L	Mins	GA	SO	Avg
2000-01	Danville Wings	NAHL	27	19	5	2	1547	57	3	2.21	5	2	2	300	17	0	3.40
2001-02	Harvard Crimson	ECAC	21	10	8	1	1226	58	1	2.84	....	....	....	....	....	....	....
2002-03	Harvard Crimson	ECAC	29	18	9	2	1741	69	1	2.38	....	....	....	....	....	....	....
2003-04	Harvard Crimson	ECAC	33	16	14	3	1933	76	3	2.36	....	....	....	....	....	....	....
2004-05	Harvard Crimson	ECAC	31	19	9	3	1911	52	6	1.63	....	....	....	....	....	....	....
2005-06	San Antonio	AHL	1	0	1	0	60	7	0	7.04	....	....	....	....	....	....	....
	Laredo Bucks	CHL	25	18	5	2	1477	50	3	*2.03	10	*8	2	644	21	*1	1.96
2006-07	Portland Pirates	AHL	11	1	6	3	594	30	1	3.03	....	....	....	....	....	....	....
	Hamilton Bulldogs	AHL	2	1	0	1	125	2	1	0.96	....	....	....	....	....	....	....
	Manitoba Moose	AHL	4	2	1	1	245	5	2	1.23	....	....	....	....	....	....	....
	Cincinnati	ECHL	22	11	8	3	1341	62	0	2.78	....	....	....	....	....	....	....
2007-08	Milwaukee	AHL	9	4	4	0	511	23	0	2.70	1	0	0	20	0	0	0.00
	Cincinnati	ECHL	26	20	3	1	1496	59	0	2.37	....	....	....	....	....	....	....
2008-09	EC Graz	Austria	44	....	....	....	....	....	....	2.71	4	....	....	....	....	....	3.02
2009-10	HK Acroni Jesenice	Austria	39	....	....	....	....	....	....	3.40	....	....	....	....	....	....	....
	HK Acroni Jesenice	Slovenia	3	....	....	....	....	....	....	0.36	6	....	....	....	....	....	2.89
2010-11	Greenville	ECHL	24	15	8	1	1446	56	3	2.32	....	....	....	....	....	....	....
	Connecticut Whale	AHL	22	13	5	1	1219	43	1	2.12	6	2	3	329	17	0	3.10
2011-12	San Antonio	AHL	34	19	13	1	1958	76	3	2.33	2	0	2	118	4	0	2.03
2012-13	Lorenskog IK	Norway	14	....	....	....	....	2.21	....	....	....	....	....	....	....	....	....
	San Antonio	AHL	43	12	22	5	2311	125	2	3.24	....	....	....	....	....	....	....

ECAC Second All-Star Team (2005) • NCAA East Second All-American Team (2005)

Signed as a free agent by **Nashville**, July 2, 2007. Signed as a free agent by **Graz** (Austria), July 16, 2008. Signed as a free agent by **Jesenice** (Austria), October 8. 2009. Signed as a free agent by **Greenville** (ECHL), September 11, 2010. • Loaned to **Conneticut** (AHL) by **Greenville** (ECHL), February 4, 2011. Signed as a free agent by **Lorenskog** (Norway), September 3, 2011. Signed as a free agent by **San Antonio** (AHL), November 21, 2011. Signed as a free agent by **Florida**, July 1, 2012.

GUDLEVSKIS, Kristers (guhd-LEHV-skihz, KRIHS-tuhrs) T.B.

Goaltender. Catches left. 6'3", 205 lbs. Born, Aizkraukle, Latvia, July 31, 1992.
(Tampa Bay's 3rd choice, 124th overall, in 2013 Entry Draft).

			Regular Season								Playoffs						
Season	Club	League	GP	W	L	O/T	Mins	GA	SO	Avg	GP	W	L	Mins	GA	SO	Avg
2009-10	HK Ogre	Latvia	9	....	....	....	....	....	....	6.12	....	....	....	....	....	....	....
	Ozolnieki-Juniors	Belarus-2	31	....	....	....	....	157	....	....	....	....	....	....	....	....	....
2010-11	HK Riga Jr.	Russia-Jr.	49	....	....	....	2760	101	7	2.20	3	....	....	188	13	0	4.16
2011-12	HK Riga Jr.	Russia-Jr.	40	....	....	....	2285	91	1	2.39	4	....	....	257	15	0	3.50
2012-13	Dynamo Riga	KHL	2	1	1	0	82	3	0	2.18	....	....	....	....	....	....	....
	HK Riga Jr.	Russia-Jr.	56	....	....	....	3190	111	3	2.09	3	....	....	154	19	0	7.42
	Juniors Riga Jr.	Russia-Jr. B	2	....	....	....	120	6	0	3.00	....	....	....	....	....	....	....
	HK Juniors Riga Jr.	Latvia	....	....	....	....	....	....	....	....	1	....	....	59	1	0	1.02

GUSTAFSSON, Johan (GUHS-tahf-suhn, YOH-han) MIN

Goaltender. Catches left. 6'2", 202 lbs. Born, Koping, Sweden, February 28, 1992.
(Minnesota's 5th choice, 159th overall, in 2010 Entry Draft).

			Regular Season								Playoffs						
Season	Club	League	GP	W	L	O/T	Mins	GA	SO	Avg	GP	W	L	Mins	GA	SO	Avg
2006-07	IFK Arboga IK	Sweden-2	4	....	....	....	201	22	0	6.55	....	....	....	....	....	....	....
2007-08	Kopings HC	Sweden-4					STATISTICS NOT AVAILABLE										
2008-09	Farjestad U18	Swe-U18	27	....	....	....	1581	47	5	1.78	4	....	....	228	14	0	3.68
2009-10	Farjestad U18	Swe-U18	10	....	....	....	600	34	1	3.40	7	....	....	417	22	0	3.16
	Farjestad	Sweden	3	....	....	....	136	9	0	3.96	....	....	....	....	....	....	....
	Skare BK	Sweden-3	26	....	....	....	1553	74	2	2.86	....	....	....	....	....	....	....
2010-11	VIK Vasteras HK Jr.	Swe-Jr.	7	....	....	....	424	20	1	2.83	....	....	....	....	....	....	....
	VIK Vasteras HK	Sweden-2	28	....	....	....	1632	64	2	2.35	....	....	....	....	....	....	....
2011-12	Lulea HF	Sweden	29	....	....	....	1754	51	6	1.74	3	....	....	179	10	0	3.36
2012-13	Lulea HF	Sweden	33	20	13	0	2016	57	4	1.70	15	8	7	946	32	0	2.03

GUSTAVSSON, Jonas (GUHS-tahv-suhn, YOH-nuhs) DET

Goaltender. Catches left. 6'3", 192 lbs. Born, Danderyd, Sweden, October 24, 1984.

			Regular Season								Playoffs						
Season	Club	League	GP	W	L	O/T	Mins	GA	SO	Avg	GP	W	L	Mins	GA	SO	Avg
2000-01	AIK Solna U18	Swe-U18	12	....	....	....	667	42	1	3.78	....	....	....	....	....	....	....
2001-02	AIK Solna U18	Swe-U18	8	....	....	....	439	13	2	1.78	4	....	....	239	12	0	3.01
2002-03	AIK Solna Jr.	Swe-Jr.	21	....	....	....	1261	69	0	3.28	4	....	....	198	9	0	2.72
2003-04	AIK Solna Jr.	Swe-Jr.	9	....	....	....	505	24	0	2.85	....	....	....	....	....	....	....
	AIK Solna	Sweden-2	1	....	....	....	20	1	0	2.95	....	....	....	....	....	....	....
2004-05	AIK Solna Jr.	Swe-Jr.	10	....	....	....	557	32	0	3.45	....	....	....	....	....	....	....
	AIK Solna	Sweden-3	22	....	....	....	1270	32	4	1.51	....	....	....	....	....	....	....
2005-06	AIK Solna Jr.	Swe-Jr.	5	....	....	....	258	14	0	3.26	....	....	....	....	....	....	....
	AIK Solna	Sweden-2	6	....	....	....	351	14	0	2.39	....	....	....	....	....	....	....
2006-07	AIK IF Solna	Sweden-2	23	....	....	....	1269	59	2	2.79	....	....	....	....	....	....	....
2007-08	Skare BK	Sweden-3	6	....	....	....	368	16	0	2.61	....	....	....	....	....	....	....
	Farjestad	Sweden	20	....	....	....	1102	44	2	2.40	10	....	....	517	31	0	3.60
2008-09	Farjestad	Sweden	42	....	....	....	2475	81	3	*1.96	13	....	....	819	14	*5	*1.03
2009-10	**Toronto**	**NHL**	**42**	**16**	**15**	**9**	**2340**	**112**	**1**	**2.87**	....	....	....	....	....	....	....
	Sweden	Olympics	1	1	0	0	60	2	0	2.00	....	....	....	....	....	....	....
2010-11	**Toronto**	**NHL**	**23**	**6**	**13**	**2**	**1242**	**68**	**0**	**3.29**	....	....	....	....	....	....	....
	Toronto Marlies	AHL	5	3	1	1	263	5	0	1.14	....	....	....	....	....	....	....
2011-12	**Toronto**	**NHL**	**42**	**17**	**17**	**4**	**2301**	**112**	**4**	**2.92**	....	....	....	....	....	....	....
2012-13	**Detroit**	**NHL**	**7**	**2**	**2**	**1**	**349**	**17**	**0**	**2.92**	....	....	....	....	....	....	....
	Grand Rapids	AHL	1	1	0	0	60	1	0	1.00	....	....	....	....	....	....	....
	NHL Totals		**114**	**41**	**47**	**16**	**6232**	**309**	**5**	**2.97**	....	....	....	....	....	....	....

Signed as a free agent by **Toronto**, July 7, 2009. • Rights traded to **Winnipeg** by **Toronto** for future considerations, June 23, 2012. Signed as a free agent by **Detroit**, July 1, 2012.

HACKETT, Matt (HA-keht, MA-thew) BUF

Goaltender. Catches left. 6'2", 173 lbs. Born, London, Ont., March 7, 1990.
(Minnesota's 2nd choice, 77th overall, in 2009 Entry Draft).

			Regular Season								Playoffs						
Season	Club	League	GP	W	L	O/T	Mins	GA	SO	Avg	GP	W	L	Mins	GA	SO	Avg
2006-07	London Jr. Knights	Minor-ON	38	28	7	3	....	52	20	1.39	6	5	1	....	12	2	2.00
	St. Catharines	ON-Jr.B	16	7	7	0	902	63	0	4.19	....	....	....	....	....	....	....
	Windsor Spitfires	OHL	7	0	7	0	429	36	0	5.04	....	....	....	....	....	....	....
2007-08	Windsor Spitfires	OHL	4	1	1	0	130	10	0	4.61	....	....	....	....	....	....	....
	Plymouth Whalers	OHL	18	6	9	1	978	56	0	3.44	1	0	0	16	0	0	0.00
2008-09	Plymouth Whalers	OHL	55	34	15	3	3036	154	2	3.04	11	6	5	638	32	*1	3.01
2009-10	Plymouth Whalers	OHL	56	33	18	3	3165	138	4	2.62	8	3	4	429	24	0	3.36
2010-11	Houston Aeros	AHL	45	23	16	4	2552	101	2	2.37	*24	*14	10	*1465	61	1	2.50
2011-12	**Minnesota**	**NHL**	**12**	**3**	**6**	**0**	**556**	**22**	**0**	**2.37**	....	....	....	....	....	....	....
	Houston Aeros	AHL	44	20	17	6	2546	101	1	2.38	2	0	2	61	6	0	5.93
2012-13	Houston Aeros	AHL	43	19	20	3	2574	114	0	2.66	....	....	....	....	....	....	....
	Minnesota	**NHL**	**1**	**0**	**1**	**0**	**59**	**5**	**0**	**5.08**	....	....	....	....	....	....	....
	Rochester	AHL	3	3	0	0	185	5	0	1.62	1	0	1	58	2	0	2.08
	NHL Totals		**13**	**3**	**7**	**0**	**615**	**27**	**0**	**2.63**	....	....	....	....	....	....	....

OHL Second All-Star Team (2010)

Traded to **Buffalo** by **Minnesota** with Johan Larsson, Minnesota's 1st round choice (Nikita Zadorov) in 2013 Entry Draft and Minnesota's 2nd round choice in 2014 Entry Draft for Jason Pominville and Buffalo's 4th round choice in 2014 Entry Draft, April 3, 2013.

HALAK, Jaroslav (HA-lak, YAHR-roh-slav) ST.L.

Goaltender. Catches left. 5'10", 186 lbs. Born, Bratislava, Czech., May 13, 1985.
(Montreal's 11th choice, 271st overall, in 2003 Entry Draft).

			Regular Season								Playoffs						
Season	Club	League	GP	W	L	O/T	Mins	GA	SO	Avg	GP	W	L	Mins	GA	SO	Avg
2001-02	Bratislava Jr.	Slovak-Jr.	22	....	....	....	1257	41	0	1.96	6	6	0	353	7	2	1.19
2002-03	Bratislava Jr.	Slovak-Jr.	20	13	3	3	1200	41	1	2.02	....	....	....	....	....	....	....
2003-04	Bratislava Jr.	Slovak-Jr.	29	....	....	....	1694	51	....	1.81	....	....	....	....	....	....	....
	HK 91 Senica	Slovak-2	21	....	....	....	1240	54	....	2.61	....	....	....	....	....	....	....
	Bratislava	Slovakia	12	....	....	....	650	18	0	1.66	1	....	....	45	6	0	8.00
2004-05	Lewiston	QMJHL	47	24	17	4	2697	125	4	2.78	8	4	4	460	27	0	3.52
2005-06	Hamilton Bulldogs	AHL	13	7	6	0	786	30	3	2.29	....	....	....	....	....	....	....
	Long Beach	ECHL	20	11	4	2	1026	35	2	2.05	4	2	2	252	13	0	3.10
2006-07	**Montreal**	**NHL**	**16**	**10**	**6**	**0**	**912**	**44**	**2**	**2.89**	....	....	....	....	....	....	....
	Hamilton Bulldogs	AHL	28	16	11	0	1618	54	6	*2.00	....	....	....	....	....	....	....
2007-08	**Montreal**	**NHL**	**6**	**2**	**1**	**1**	**285**	**10**	**1**	**2.11**	**2**	**0**	**1**	**77**	**3**	**0**	**2.34**
	Hamilton Bulldogs	AHL	28	15	10	2	1630	57	2	2.10	....	....	....	....	....	....	....
2008-09	**Montreal**	**NHL**	**34**	**18**	**14**	**1**	**1931**	**92**	**1**	**2.86**	**1**	**0**	**0**	**20**	**0**	**0**	**0.00**
2009-10	**Montreal**	**NHL**	**45**	**26**	**13**	**5**	**2630**	**105**	**5**	**2.40**	**18**	**9**	**9**	**1013**	**43**	**0**	**2.55**
	Slovakia	Olympics	7	3	4	0	423	17	1	2.41	....	....	....	....	....	....	....
2010-11	**St. Louis**	**NHL**	**57**	**27**	**21**	**7**	**3294**	**136**	**7**	**2.48**	....	....	....	....	....	....	....
2011-12	**St. Louis**	**NHL**	**46**	**26**	**12**	**7**	**2747**	**90**	**6**	**1.97**	**2**	**1**	**1**	**104**	**3**	**0**	**1.73**
2012-13	Weiswasser	German-2	1	1	0	0	65	1	0	0.92	....	....	....	....	....	....	....
	St. Louis	**NHL**	**16**	**6**	**5**	**1**	**813**	**29**	**3**	**2.14**	....	....	....	....	....	....	....
	NHL Totals		**220**	**115**	**72**	**22**	**12612**	**506**	**25**	**2.41**	**23**	**10**	**11**	**1214**	**49**	**0**	**2.42**

AHL All-Rookie Team (2007) • William M. Jennings Trophy (2012) (shared with Brian Elliott)

Traded to **St. Louis** by **Montreal** for Lars Eller and Ian Schultz, June 17, 2010. Signed as a free agent by **Weiswasser** (German-2), November 21, 2012.

HAMMOND, Andrew (HAM-uhnd, AN-droo) OTT

Goaltender. Catches left. 6'1", 196 lbs. Born, Surrey, B.C., February 11, 1988.

			Regular Season								Playoffs						
Season	Club	League	GP	W	L	O/T	Mins	GA	SO	Avg	GP	W	L	Mins	GA	SO	Avg
2006-07	Alberni Valley	BCHL	1	0	1	0	34	4	0	7.03	....	....	....	....	....	....	....
2007-08	Vernon Vipers	BCHL	41	21	17	1	2106	112	3	3.19	....	....	....	....	....	....	....
2008-09	Vernon Vipers	BCHL	43	27	12	1	2479	95	5	2.30	....	....	....	....	....	....	....
2009-10	Bowling Green	CCHA	19	0	12	2	837	60	0	4.30	....	....	....	....	....	....	....
2010-11	Bowling Green	CCHA	27	6	17	3	1528	68	2	2.67	....	....	....	....	....	....	....
2011-12	Bowling Green	CCHA	44	14	24	5	2615	119	2	2.73	....	....	....	....	....	....	....
2012-13	Bowling Green	CCHA	29	10	15	3	1625	67	3	2.47	....	....	....	....	....	....	....

Signed as a free agent by **Ottawa**, March 20, 2013.

HARDING, Josh (HAHR-dihng, JAWSH) MIN

Goaltender. Catches right. 6'2", 202 lbs. Born, Regina, Sask., June 18, 1984.
(Minnesota's 2nd choice, 38th overall, in 2002 Entry Draft).

			Regular Season								Playoffs						
Season	Club	League	GP	W	L	O/T	Mins	GA	SO	Avg	GP	W	L	Mins	GA	SO	Avg
2000-01	Reg. Pat Cdns.	SMHL	36	17	13	0	2106	96	2	2.75	3	1	2	170	11	0	3.88
2001-02	Regina Pats	WHL	42	27	13	1	2389	95	*4	2.39	6	2	4	326	16	0	2.95
2002-03	Regina Pats	WHL	57	18	25	13	*3384	155	3	2.75	5	1	4	320	13	0	2.44
2003-04	Regina Pats	WHL	28	12	14	2	1664	67	2	2.42							
	Brandon	WHL	27	13	11	3	1612	65	5	2.42	11	5	6	660	36	0	3.27
2004-05	Houston Aeros	AHL	42	21	16	3	2388	80	4	2.01	2	0	2	119	8	0	4.03
2005-06	**Minnesota**	**NHL**	**3**	**2**	**1**	**0**	**185**	**8**	**1**	**2.59**							
	Houston Aeros	AHL	38	29	8	0	2215	99	2	2.68	8	4	4	476	30	0	3.79
2006-07	**Minnesota**	**NHL**	**7**	**3**	**2**	**1**	**361**	**7**	**1**	**1.16**							
	Houston Aeros	AHL	38	17	16	4	2270	94	1	2.48							
2007-08	**Minnesota**	**NHL**	**29**	**11**	**15**	**2**	**1571**	**77**	**1**	**2.94**	**1**	**0**	**0**	**20**	**0**	**0**	**0.00**
2008-09	**Minnesota**	**NHL**	**19**	**3**	**9**	**1**	**870**	**32**	**0**	**2.21**							
2009-10	**Minnesota**	**NHL**	**25**	**9**	**12**	**0**	**1300**	**66**	**1**	**3.05**							
2010-11	**Minnesota**	**NHL**	DID NOT PLAY – INJURED														
2011-12	**Minnesota**	**NHL**	**34**	**13**	**12**	**4**	**1855**	**81**	**2**	**2.62**							
2012-13	**Minnesota**	**NHL**	**5**	**1**	**1**	**0**	**185**	**10**	**1**	**3.24**	**5**	**1**	**4**	**245**	**12**	**0**	**2.94**
	Houston Aeros	AHL	2	1	1	0	100	5	0	3.00							
	NHL Totals		**122**	**42**	**52**	**8**	**6327**	**281**	**7**	**2.66**	**6**	**1**	**4**	**265**	**12**	**0**	**2.72**

WHL East Second All-Star Team (2002) • WHL East First All-Star Team (2003) • WHL Goaltender of the Year (2003) • WHL Player of the Year (2003) • Canadian Major Junior Second All-Star Team (2003) • Bill Masterton Memorial Trophy (2013)

• Missed 2010-11 due to knee injury at St. Louis, September 24, 2010. • Missed majority of 2012-13 season after being diagnosed with multiple sclerosis, February 12, 2013.

HARTZELL, Eric (HART-zehl, AIR-ihk) PIT

Goaltender. Catches left. 6'4", 205 lbs. Born, White Bear Lake, MN, May 28, 1989.

			Regular Season								Playoffs						
Season	Club	League	GP	W	L	O/T	Mins	GA	SO	Avg	GP	W	L	Mins	GA	SO	Avg
2006-07	Sioux Falls	USHL	1	0	1	0	60	5	0	5.00							
2007-08	Sioux Falls	USHL	32	19	9	2	1835	84	5	2.75							
2008-09	Sioux Falls	USHL	46	20	22	2	2599	142	2	3.28							
2009-10	Quinnipiac	ECAC	6	4	2	0	299	13	1	2.61							
2010-11	Quinnipiac	ECAC	28	12	7	6	1570	58	3	2.22							
2011-12	Quinnipiac	ECAC	30	12	11	6	1748	64	1	2.20							
2012-13	Quinnipiac	ECAC	*42	*30	7	2	*2522	66	*5	*1.57							

Signed as a free agent by **Pittsburgh**, April 16, 2013.

HEDBERG, Johan (HEHD-buhrg, YOH-han)

Goaltender. Catches left. 6', 190 lbs. Born, Stockholm, Sweden, May 5, 1973.
(Philadelphia's 8th choice, 218th overall, in 1994 Entry Draft).

			Regular Season								Playoffs						
Season	Club	League	GP	W	L	O/T	Mins	GA	SO	Avg	GP	W	L	Mins	GA	SO	Avg
1992-93	Leksands IF	Sweden	10				600	24		2.40							
1993-94	Leksands IF	Sweden	17				1020	48		2.82							
1994-95	Leksands IF	Sweden	17				986	58		3.53							
1995-96	Leksands IF	Sweden	34				2013	95		2.83	4			240	13		3.25
1996-97	Leksands IF	Sweden	38				2260	95	3	2.52	8			581	18	1	1.86
1997-98	Detroit Vipers	IHL	16	7	2	2	726	32	1	2.64							
	Baton Rouge	ECHL	2	1	1	0	100	7	0	4.20							
	Manitoba Moose	IHL	14	8	4	1	745	32	1	2.58	2	0	2	105	6	0	3.40
	Sweden	Olympics	DID NOT PLAY – SPARE GOALTENDER														
1998-99	Leksands IF	Sweden	*48				*2940	140	0	2.86	4			255	15	0	3.53
99-2000	Kentucky	AHL	33	18	9	5	1973	88	3	2.68	5	3	2	311	10	1	1.93
2000-01	Manitoba Moose	IHL	46	23	13	7	2697	115	1	2.56							
	Pittsburgh	**NHL**	**9**	**7**	**1**	**1**	**545**	**24**	**0**	**2.64**	**18**	**9**	**9**	**1123**	**43**	**2**	**2.30**
2001-02	**Pittsburgh**	**NHL**	**66**	**25**	**34**	**7**	**3877**	**178**	**6**	**2.75**							
	Sweden	Olympics	1	1	0	0	60	1	0	1.00							
2002-03	**Pittsburgh**	**NHL**	**41**	**14**	**22**	**4**	**2410**	**126**	**1**	**3.14**							
2003-04	**Vancouver**	**NHL**	**21**	**8**	**6**	**2**	**1098**	**46**	**3**	**2.51**	**2**	**1**	**1**	**98**	**4**	**0**	**2.45**
	Manitoba Moose	AHL	2	0	2	0	125	9	0	4.32							
2004-05	Leksands IF	Sweden-2	21				1274	45	1	2.12							
2005-06	**Dallas**	**NHL**	**19**	**12**	**4**	**1**	**1079**	**48**	**0**	**2.67**							
2006-07	**Atlanta**	**NHL**	**21**	**9**	**4**	**2**	**1057**	**51**	**0**	**2.89**	**2**	**0**	**2**	**117**	**5**	**0**	**2.56**
2007-08	**Atlanta**	**NHL**	**36**	**14**	**15**	**3**	**1927**	**111**	**1**	**3.46**							
2008-09	**Atlanta**	**NHL**	**33**	**13**	**12**	**3**	**1717**	**100**	**0**	**3.49**							
2009-10	**Atlanta**	**NHL**	**47**	**21**	**16**	**6**	**2632**	**115**	**3**	**2.62**							
2010-11	**New Jersey**	**NHL**	**34**	**15**	**12**	**2**	**1717**	**68**	**3**	**2.38**							
2011-12	**New Jersey**	**NHL**	**27**	**17**	**7**	**2**	**1591**	**59**	**4**	**2.23**	**1**	**0**	**1**	**36**	**1**	**0**	**1.67**
2012-13	**New Jersey**	**NHL**	**19**	**6**	**10**	**3**	**1108**	**51**	**1**	**2.76**							
	NHL Totals		**373**	**161**	**143**	**36**	**20758**	**977**	**22**	**2.82**	**23**	**10**	**13**	**1374**	**53**	**2**	**2.31**

• Rights traded to **San Jose** by **Philadelphia** for San Jose's 7th round choice (Pavel Kasparik) in 1999 Entry Draft, August 6, 1998. Traded to **Pittsburgh** by **San Jose** with Bobby Dollas for Jeff Norton, March 12, 2001. Traded to **Vancouver** by **Pittsburgh** for Vancouver's 2nd round choice (Alex Goligoski) in 2004 Entry Draft, August 25, 2003. Signed as a free agent by **Leksands** (Sweden-2), August 1, 2004. Signed as a free agent by **Dallas**, August 5, 2005. Signed as a free agent by **Atlanta**, July 1, 2006. Signed as a free agent by **New Jersey**, July 1, 2010.

HEETER, Cal (HEE-tuhr, KAL) PHI

Goaltender. Catches left. 6'4", 195 lbs. Born, St. Louis, MO, November 2, 1988.

			Regular Season								Playoffs						
Season	Club	League	GP	W	L	O/T	Mins	GA	SO	Avg	GP	W	L	Mins	GA	SO	Avg
2006-07	Wichita Falls	NAHL	31	13	13	3	1828	96	1	3.15							
2007-08	St. Louis Bandits	NAHL	34	25	6	1	1972	80	2	2.43							
2008-09	Ohio State	CCHA	5	2	1	0	200	11	0	3.29							
2009-10	Ohio State	CCHA	20	9	6	2	1108	59	1	3.19							
2010-11	Ohio State	CCHA	32	15	18	4	2191	84	2	2.30							
2011-12	Ohio State	CCHA	32	13	11	5	1760	72	2	2.45							
2012-13	Adirondack	AHL	32	12	16	3	1811	88	0	2.92							
	Trenton Titans	ECHL	8	3	3	0	453	24	0	3.18							

Signed as a free agent by **Philadelphia**, March 6, 2012.

HELENIUS, Riku (heh-lehn-NEE-uhs, REE-koo) T.B.

Goaltender. Catches left. 6'2", 201 lbs. Born, Palkane, Finland, March 1, 1988.
(Tampa Bay's 1st choice, 15th overall, in 2006 Entry Draft).

			Regular Season								Playoffs						
Season	Club	League	GP	W	L	O/T	Mins	GA	SO	Avg	GP	W	L	Mins	GA	SO	Avg
2004-05	Ilves Tampere U18	Fin-U18	16				903	30	3	1.99	5			295	15	0	3.05
	Ilves Tampere Jr.	Fin-Jr.	2				86	4	0	2.77							
2005-06	Suomi U20	Finland-2	1				60	3	0	3.00							
	Ilves Tampere U18	Fin-U18	2				120	2	0	1.00	5			300	13	0	2.60
	Ilves Tampere Jr.	Fin-Jr.	26				1565	70	4	2.68	2			135	7	0	3.11
2006-07	Ilves Tampere Jr.	Fin-Jr.	2	2	0	0	120	4	0	2.00							
2007-08	Seattle	WHL	41	22	12	6	2358	95	3	2.42	9	4	5	534	24	0	2.70
2008-09	**Tampa Bay**	**NHL**	**1**	**0**	**0**	**0**	**7**	**0**	**0**	**0.00**							
	Norfolk Admirals	AHL	25	9	15	0	1388	63	1	2.72							
	Augusta Lynx	ECHL	8	3	4	1	463	34	0	4.41							
	Mississippi	ECHL	3	1	1	1	184	7	0	2.28							
	Elmira Jackals	ECHL									2	0	1	87	10	0	6.91
2009-10	Norfolk Admirals	AHL	12	5	7	0	719	33	0	2.75							
	Sodertalje SK	Sweden	9				545	22	0	2.42							
	Sodertalje SK	Sweden-Q	9				548	25	1	2.74							
2010-11	Sodertalje SK	Sweden	18				911	46	0	3.03							
	Sodertalje SK	Sweden-Q	5				198	7	0	2.23							
2011-12	JYP Jyvaskyla	Finland	33	17	9	5	1908	52	7	1.64	13	11	2	833	24	0	1.73
2012-13	Syracuse Crunch	AHL	32	17	14	0	1772	76	4	2.57							
	NHL Totals		**1**	**0**	**0**	**0**	**7**	**0**	**0**	**0.00**							

• Re-assigned to **Sodertalje** (Sweden) by **Tampa Bay** (Norfolk-AHL), January 24, 2010.

HELLBERG, Magnus (HEHL-buhrg, MAG-nuhs) NSH

Goaltender. Catches left. 6'6", 195 lbs. Born, Uppsala, Sweden, April 4, 1991.
(Nashville's 1st choice, 38th overall, in 2011 Entry Draft).

			Regular Season								Playoffs						
Season	Club	League	GP	W	L	O/T	Mins	GA	SO	Avg	GP	W	L	Mins	GA	SO	Avg
2007-08	Arlanda U18	Swe-U18	11														
	Arlanda Jr.	Swe-Jr.	1							8.00							
2008-09	Arlanda U18	Swe-U18	33				1979	103	2	3.12							
	Wings HC Arlanda	Sweden-3	2				119	7	0	3.52							
2009-10	Almtuna Jr.	Swe-Jr.	22				1339	44	2	1.97							
	IF Vallentuna BK	Sweden-3	1				24	3	0	7.57							
2010-11	IFK Kumla IK	Sweden-3	3				179	6	0	2.01							
	Almtuna	Sweden-2	31				1790	61	5	2.04	5			277	15	0	3.24
2011-12	Frolunda	Sweden	17				1016	44	2	2.60							
	Frolunda Jr.	Swe-Jr.	2				120	8	0	4.00							
	Orebro HK	Sweden-2	3				180	10	0	3.33							
2012-13	Milwaukee	AHL	39	22	13	0	2107	75	6	2.14	4	1	3	248	7	1	1.69
	Cincinnati	ECHL	2	1	1	0	119	5	0	2.52							

HELLEBUYCK, Connor (hehl-ee-BUHK, KAW-nuhr) WPG

Goaltender. Catches left. 6'4", 200 lbs. Born, Commerence, MI, May 19, 1993.
(Winnipeg's 4th choice, 130th overall, in 2012 Entry Draft).

			Regular Season								Playoffs						
Season	Club	League	GP	W	L	O/T	Mins	GA	SO	Avg	GP	W	L	Mins	GA	SO	Avg
2010-11	Walled Lake	High-MI	STATISTICS NOT AVAILABLE														
	Team Michigan	Exhib.	STATISTICS NOT AVAILABLE														
2011-12	Odessa Jackalopes	NAHL	*53	26	21	5	*3085	128	3	2.49	4	1	3	243	14	0	3.46
2012-13	U. Mass-Lowell	H-East	24	20	3	0	1397	32	*6	*1.37							

NAHL Rookie of the Year (2012) • NAHL Goaltender of the Year (2012) • Hockey East All-Rookie Team (2013) • Hockey East Second All-Star Team (2013)

HILLER, Jonas (HIHL-uhr, YOH-nuhs) ANA

Goaltender. Catches right. 6'2", 194 lbs. Born, Felben Wellhausen, Switz., February 12, 1982.

			Regular Season								Playoffs						
Season	Club	League	GP	W	L	O/T	Mins	GA	SO	Avg	GP	W	L	Mins	GA	SO	Avg
2000-01	HC Davos	Swiss	1	0	0	0	9	0	0	0.00							
2001-02	HC Davos	Swiss	DID NOT PLAY														
2002-03	HC Davos	Swiss	DID NOT PLAY														
2003-04	Lausanne HC	Swiss	21				1161	64	1	3.31							
	Chaux-de-Fonds	Swiss-2	1	0	1	0	60	4	0	4.00							
	Lausanne HC	Swiss-Q									4	4	0	251	7	0	1.67
2004-05	HC Davos	Swiss	43	26	12	4	2519	95	*8	2.26	*15	12	3	*932	34	0	*2.19
2005-06	HC Davos	Swiss	*44	23	16	5	*2676	110	3	2.47	15	9	6	900	45	1	3.00
2006-07	HC Davos	Swiss	*44	*28	16	0	*2656	115	3	2.60	*19	*12	7	*1138	39	3	2.05
2007-08	**Anaheim**	**NHL**	**23**	**10**	**7**	**1**	**1223**	**42**	**0**	**2.06**							
	Portland Pirates	AHL	6	3	2	1	370	13	0	2.11							
2008-09	**Anaheim**	**NHL**	**46**	**23**	**15**	**1**	**2486**	**99**	**4**	**2.39**	**13**	**7**	**6**	**807**	**30**	***2**	**2.23**
2009-10	**Anaheim**	**NHL**	**59**	**30**	**23**	**4**	**3338**	**152**	**2**	**2.73**							
	Switzerland	Olympics	5	2	3	0	356	13	0	2.47							
2010-11	**Anaheim**	**NHL**	**49**	**26**	**16**	**3**	**2672**	**114**	**5**	**2.56**							
2011-12	**Anaheim**	**NHL**	***73**	**29**	**30**	**12**	***4253**	**182**	**4**	**2.57**							
2012-13	**Anaheim**	**NHL**	**26**	**15**	**6**	**4**	**1498**	**59**	**1**	**2.36**	**7**	**3**	**4**	**439**	**18**	**1**	**2.46**
	NHL Totals		**276**	**133**	**97**	**25**	**15470**	**648**	**16**	**2.51**	**20**	**10**	**10**	**1246**	**48**	**3**	**2.31**

Signed as a free agent by **Anaheim**, May 25, 2007.
Played in NHL All-Star Game (2011)

HOGBERG, Marcus (HOHG-buhrg, MAHR-kuhs) OTT

Goaltender. Catches left. 6'5", 209 lbs. Born, Orebro, Sweden, November 25, 1994.
(Ottawa's 2nd choice, 78th overall, in 2013 Entry Draft).

			Regular Season								Playoffs						
Season	Club	League	GP	W	L	O/T	Mins	GA	SO	Avg	GP	W	L	Mins	GA	SO	Avg
2010-11	Linkopings HC U18	Swe-U18	27				1631	53	4	1.95	5			305	13	0	2.55
	Linkopings HC Jr.	Swe-Jr.	4				163	12	0	4.42							
2011-12	Linkopings HC U18	Swe-U18	3				179	9	0	3.01	1			60	2	0	2.00
	Linkopings HC Jr.	Swe-Jr.	35				2055	85	4	2.48	6			366	10	2	1.64
2012-13	Linkopings HC Jr.	Swe-Jr.	23	13	9	0	1369	55	2	2.41							
	Linkopings HC	Sweden	3	1	1	0	140	6	0	2.57							

HOLTBY, Braden (HOHLT-bee, BRAY-duhn) WSH

Goaltender. Catches left. 6'2", 203 lbs. Born, Lloydminster, Sask., September 16, 1989.
(Washington's 5th choice, 93rd overall, in 2008 Entry Draft).

			Regular Season								Playoffs						
Season	Club	League	GP	W	L	O/T	Mins	GA	SO	Avg	GP	W	L	Mins	GA	SO	Avg
2005-06	Saskatoon Blazers	SMHL	STATISTICS NOT AVAILABLE														
	Saskatoon Blades	WHL	1	0	1	0	59	4	0	4.07							
2006-07	Saskatoon Blades	WHL	51	17	29	3	2725	146	0	3.21							
2007-08	Saskatoon Blades	WHL	*64	25	29	8	3632	172	1	2.84							
2008-09	Saskatoon Blades	WHL	*61	40	16	4	*3571	156	6	2.62	7	3	4	414	16	0	2.32
2009-10	Hershey Bears	AHL	37	25	8	2	2146	83	2	2.32	3	2	1	200	12	0	3.60
	South Carolina	ECHL	12	7	2	3	712	35	0	2.95							
2010-11	**Washington**	**NHL**	**14**	**10**	**2**	**2**	**736**	**22**	**2**	**1.79**							
	Hershey Bears	AHL	30	17	10	2	1785	68	5	2.29	6	2	4	359	18	0	3.01
2011-12	**Washington**	**NHL**	**7**	**4**	**2**	**1**	**361**	**15**	**1**	**2.49**	**14**	**7**	**7**	**922**	**30**	**0**	**1.95**
	Hershey Bears	AHL	40	20	15	2	2322	101	3	2.61							
2012-13	Hershey Bears	AHL	25	12	12	1	1458	52	4	2.14							
	Washington	**NHL**	**36**	**23**	**12**	**1**	**2089**	**90**	**4**	**2.58**	**7**	**3**	**4**	**433**	**16**	**1**	**2.22**
	NHL Totals		**57**	**37**	**16**	**4**	**3186**	**127**	**7**	**2.39**	**21**	**10**	**11**	**1355**	**46**	**1**	**2.04**

WHL East First All-Star Team (2009)

HONZIK, David (HAWN-zihk, DAY-vihd) VAN

Goaltender. Catches left. 6'3", 206 lbs. Born, Milevsko, Czech Rep., August 9, 1993.
(Vancouver's 2nd choice, 71st overall, in 2011 Entry Draft).

			Regular Season								Playoffs						
Season	Club	League	GP	W	L	O/T	Mins	GA	SO	Avg	GP	W	L	Mins	GA	SO	Avg
2008-09	Karlovy Vary U17	CzR-U17	32	....	....	....	1762	78	1	2.66	2	....	....	129	10	0	4.65
2009-10	Karlovy Vary U18	CzR-U18	38	....	....	....	2174	95	2	2.62	3	....	....	190	8	0	2.53
	Karlovy Vary Jr.	CzRep-Jr.	1	....	....	....	60	1	0	1.00	....	....	....	....	....	....	....
2010-11	Victoriaville Tigres	QMJHL	36	17	12	1	1781	105	1	3.54	9	5	4	548	30	0	3.28
2011-12	Victoriaville Tigres	QMJHL	43	22	14	2	2271	132	3	3.49	3	0	2	113	10	0	5.33
2012-13	Cape Breton	QMJHL	32	4	23	1	1528	112	1	4.40	....	....	....	....	....	....	....

HOUSER, Michael (HOW-zuhr, MIGH-kuhl) FLA

Goaltender. Catches left. 6'2", 190 lbs. Born, Wexford, PA, September 13, 1992.

			Regular Season								Playoffs						
Season	Club	League	GP	W	L	O/T	Mins	GA	SO	Avg	GP	W	L	Mins	GA	SO	Avg
2008-09	Des Moines	USHL	32	5	18	0	1523	102	0	4.02	....	....	....	....	....	....	....
2009-10	London Knights	OHL	25	17	4	1	1450	75	0	3.10	3	0	0	53	7	0	7.92
2010-11	London Knights	OHL	54	30	19	5	3088	171	1	3.32	6	2	4	332	15	0	2.71
2011-12	London Knights	OHL	62	*46	15	1	*3698	152	6	2.47	19	*16	3	1173	44	1	2.25
2012-13	Cincinnati	ECHL	29	17	10	2	1694	72	2	2.55	17	9	8	1154	43	1	2.24

OHL All-Rookie Team (2010) • Canadian Major Junior All-Rookie Team (2010) • OHL First All-Star Team (2012) • Canadian Major Junior Goaltender of the Year (2012) • Memorial Cup All-Star Team (2012)

Signed as a free agent by **Florida**, July 12, 2012.

HOWARD, Jimmy (HOW-uhrd, JIHM-ee) DET

Goaltender. Catches left. 6', 218 lbs. Born, Syracuse, NY, March 26, 1984.
(Detroit's 1st choice, 64th overall, in 2003 Entry Draft).

			Regular Season								Playoffs						
Season	Club	League	GP	W	L	O/T	Mins	GA	SO	Avg	GP	W	L	Mins	GA	SO	Avg
2000-01	Kanata Valley	ON-Jr.A	25	10	10	2	1350	83	1	3.69	....	....	....	....	....	....	....
2001-02	USNTDP	U-18	19	15	4	1	1170	37	4	1.90	....	....	....	....	....	....	....
	USNTDP	USHL	8	4	3	0	425	14	0	1.98	....	....	....	....	....	....	....
	USNTDP	NAHL	8	3	4	0	381	25	0	3.93	....	....	....	....	....	....	....
2002-03	University of Maine	H-East	21	14	6	0	1151	47	3	2.45	....	....	....	....	....	....	....
2003-04	University of Maine	H-East	23	14	4	3	1364	27	*6	*1.19	....	....	....	....	....	....	....
2004-05	University of Maine	H-East	*39	*19	13	7	*2310	74	*6	1.92	....	....	....	....	....	....	....
2005-06	**Detroit**	**NHL**	**4**	**1**	**2**	**0**	**201**	**10**	**0**	**2.99**	....	....	....	....	....	....	....
	Grand Rapids	AHL	38	27	6	2	2140	92	2	2.58	13	5	7	763	44	0	3.46
2006-07	Grand Rapids	AHL	49	21	21	3	2776	125	6	2.70	7	3	4	434	14	0	*1.93
2007-08	**Detroit**	**NHL**	**4**	**0**	**2**	**0**	**197**	**7**	**0**	**2.13**	....	....	....	....	....	....	....
	Grand Rapids	AHL	54	21	28	2	3097	146	2	2.83	....	....	....	....	....	....	....
2008-09	**Detroit**	**NHL**	**1**	**0**	**1**	**0**	**59**	**4**	**0**	**4.07**	....	....	....	....	....	....	....
	Grand Rapids	AHL	45	21	18	4	2644	112	4	2.54	10	4	6	598	24	0	2.41
2009-10	**Detroit**	**NHL**	**63**	**37**	**15**	**10**	**3740**	**141**	**3**	**2.26**	**12**	**5**	**7**	**720**	**33**	**1**	**2.75**
2010-11	**Detroit**	**NHL**	**63**	**37**	**17**	**5**	**3615**	**168**	**2**	**2.79**	**11**	**7**	**4**	**673**	**28**	**0**	**2.50**
2011-12	**Detroit**	**NHL**	**57**	**35**	**17**	**4**	**3360**	**119**	**6**	**2.13**	**5**	**1**	**4**	**295**	**13**	**0**	**2.64**
2012-13	**Detroit**	**NHL**	**42**	**21**	**13**	**7**	**2446**	**87**	***5**	**2.13**	**14**	**7**	**7**	**859**	**35**	**1**	**2.44**
	NHL Totals		**234**	**131**	**67**	**26**	**13618**	**536**	**16**	**2.36**	**42**	**20**	**22**	**2547**	**109**	**2**	**2.57**

Hockey East All-Rookie Team (2003) • Hockey East Rookie of the Year (2003) • Hockey East First All-Star Team (2004) • NCAA East Second All-American Team (2004) • AHL All-Rookie Team (2006) • NHL All-Rookie Team (2010)

Played in NHL All-Star Game (2012)

HUTCHINSON, Michael (HUH-chihn-suhn, MIGH-kuhl) WPG

Goaltender. Catches right. 6'3", 192 lbs. Born, Barrie, Ont., March 2, 1990.
(Boston's 3rd choice, 77th overall, in 2008 Entry Draft).

			Regular Season								Playoffs						
Season	Club	League	GP	W	L	O/T	Mins	GA	SO	Avg	GP	W	L	Mins	GA	SO	Avg
2005-06	Markham Majors	GTHL	34	....	....	....	1530	69	9	2.02	....	....	....	....	....	....	....
2006-07	Orangeville	ON-Jr.A	8	1	4	0	289	24	0	4.99	....	....	....	....	....	....	....
	Barrie Colts	OHL	14	8	3	0	768	27	0	2.11	1	1	0	45	1	0	1.33
2007-08	Barrie Colts	OHL	32	12	15	4	1826	92	1	3.02	8	4	4	500	22	1	2.64
2008-09	Barrie Colts	OHL	38	15	20	1	2146	108	5	3.02	3	0	2	112	10	0	5.37
2009-10	London Knights	OHL	46	32	12	2	2667	127	3	2.86	12	7	5	686	47	0	4.11
2010-11	Providence Bruins	AHL	28	13	10	1	1476	77	1	3.13	....	....	....	....	....	....	....
	Reading Royals	ECHL	18	9	5	4	1049	50	1	2.86	....	....	....	....	....	....	....
2011-12	Providence Bruins	AHL	29	13	14	1	1680	66	3	2.36	....	....	....	....	....	....	....
	Reading Royals	ECHL	2	1	1	0	120	7	0	3.50	....	....	....	....	....	....	....
2012-13	Providence Bruins	AHL	30	13	13	3	1749	67	3	2.30	2	0	0	49	1	0	1.22

Signed as a free agent by **Winnipeg**, July 19, 2013.

HUTTON, Carter (HUH-tuhn, KAR-tuhr) NSH

Goaltender. Catches left. 6'1", 195 lbs. Born, Thunder Bay, Ont., December 19, 1985.

			Regular Season								Playoffs						
Season	Club	League	GP	W	L	O/T	Mins	GA	SO	Avg	GP	W	L	Mins	GA	SO	Avg
2005-06	F-Wm. North Stars	SIJHL	36	33	1	0	2053	63	10	1.84	15	12	3	928	36	2	2.33
2006-07	U. Mass-Lowell	H-East	19	3	10	5	1097	52	1	2.84	....	....	....	....	....	....	....
2007-08	U. Mass-Lowell	H-East	20	7	11	2	1187	49	2	2.48	....	....	....	....	....	....	....
2008-09	U. Mass-Lowell	H-East	19	9	8	1	1106	38	*3	2.06	....	....	....	....	....	....	....
2009-10	U. Mass-Lowell	H-East	27	13	12	2	1614	55	*4	*2.04	....	....	....	....	....	....	....
	Adirondack	AHL	4	1	2	1	244	11	0	2.71	....	....	....	....	....	....	....
2010-11	Worcester Sharks	AHL	22	11	7	2	1174	59	2	3.01	....	....	....	....	....	....	....
2011-12	Toledo Walleye	ECHL	14	7	7	0	819	43	0	3.15	....	....	....	....	....	....	....
	Rockford IceHogs	AHL	43	22	13	4	2372	93	3	2.35	....	....	....	....	....	....	....
2012-13	Rockford IceHogs	AHL	51	26	22	1	2908	132	2	2.72	....	....	....	....	....	....	....
	Chicago	**NHL**	**1**	**0**	**1**	**0**	**59**	**3**	**0**	**3.05**	....	....	....	....	....	....	....
	NHL Totals		**1**	**0**	**1**	**0**	**59**	**3**	**0**	**3.05**	....	....	....	....	....	....	....

Hockey East Second All-Star Team (2010)

Signed to an ATO (amateur tryout) contract by **Adirondack** (AHL), March 20, 2010. Signed as a free agent by **San Jose**, June 1, 2010. Signed as a free agent by **Chicago**, February 24, 2012. Signed as a free agent by **Nashville**, July 5, 2013.

IRVING, Leland (UHR-vihng, LEE-land)

Goaltender. Catches left. 6', 175 lbs. Born, Barrhead, Alta., April 11, 1988.
(Calgary's 1st choice, 26th overall, in 2006 Entry Draft).

			Regular Season								Playoffs						
Season	Club	League	GP	W	L	O/T	Mins	GA	SO	Avg	GP	W	L	Mins	GA	SO	Avg
2002-03	Spruce Grove	AMBHL	....	11	11	4	1559	94	....	3.62	....	....	....	....	....	....	....
2003-04	Spruce Grove	RAMHL	19	....	....	....	1017	44	1	2.60	....	....	....	....	....	....	....
	Everett Silvertips	WHL	1	0	0	0	8	0	0	0.00	....	....	....	....	....	....	....
2004-05	Everett Silvertips	WHL	23	9	7	1	1132	35	2	1.86	....	....	....	....	....	....	....
2005-06	Everett Silvertips	WHL	*67	37	22	4	*3791	121	4	1.91	12	8	4	747	21	3	1.69
2006-07	Everett Silvertips	WHL	48	34	9	3	2802	87	*11	1.86	12	6	5	639	30	0	2.82
2007-08	Everett Silvertips	WHL	56	27	24	3	3258	133	4	2.45	3	0	3	139	10	0	4.30
2008-09	Quad City Flames	AHL	47	24	18	2	2658	99	1	2.23	....	....	....	....	....	....	....
2009-10	Abbotsford Heat	AHL	35	14	17	2	1850	85	1	2.76	1	0	1	14	3	0	12.97
	Victoria	ECHL	8	2	4	2	490	25	0	3.06	....	....	....	....	....	....	....
2010-11	Abbotsford Heat	AHL	*61	30	24	2	*3437	132	*8	2.30	....	....	....	....	....	....	....
2011-12	**Calgary**	**NHL**	**7**	**1**	**3**	**3**	**394**	**21**	**0**	**3.20**	....	....	....	....	....	....	....
	Abbotsford Heat	AHL	39	22	13	2	2177	97	3	2.67	1	0	1	60	4	0	4.02
2012-13	Abbotsford Heat	AHL	12	3	7	2	599	34	0	3.40	....	....	....	....	....	....	....
	Calgary	**NHL**	**6**	**2**	**1**	**1**	**270**	**15**	**0**	**3.33**	....	....	....	....	....	....	....
	NHL Totals		**13**	**3**	**4**	**4**	**664**	**36**	**0**	**3.25**	....	....	....	....	....	....	....

WHL West Second All-Star Team (2006, 2007)

JANUS, Jaroslav (YA-nuhs, YAHR-roh-slav) T.B.

Goaltender. Catches left. 6', 191 lbs. Born, Presov, Czech., September 21, 1989.
(Tampa Bay's 6th choice, 162nd overall, in 2009 Entry Draft).

			Regular Season								Playoffs						
Season	Club	League	GP	W	L	O/T	Mins	GA	SO	Avg	GP	W	L	Mins	GA	SO	Avg
2003-04	Presov U18	Svk-U18	14	....	....	....	....	....	....	....	....	....	....	....	....	....	....
2004-05	PHK Presov U18	Svk-U18	34	....	....	....	1743	53	3	1.82	....	....	....	....	....	....	....
	PHK Presov Jr.	Slovak-Jr.	1	....	....	....	60	7	0	7.00	1	....	....	23	1	0	2.61
2005-06	Bratislava U18	Svk-U18	37	....	....	....	1913	92	2	2.89	8	....	....	486	19	0	2.34
	Bratislava Jr.	Slovak-Jr.	13	....	....	....	609	25	0	2.46	....	....	....	....	....	....	....
2006-07	Bratislava U18	Svk-U18	35	....	....	....	2010	84	1	2.51	....	....	....	....	....	....	....
	Bratislava Jr.	Slovak-Jr.	24	....	....	....	1355	49	4	2.17	1	....	....	33	4	0	7.28
2007-08	Erie Otters	OHL	48	13	29	3	2740	201	0	4.40	....	....	....	....	....	....	....
2008-09	Erie Otters	OHL	49	25	20	4	2818	152	3	3.24	5	1	4	285	20	*1	4.21
2009-10	Erie Otters	OHL	13	7	4	2	770	36	0	2.81	....	....	....	....	....	....	....
	Norfolk Admirals	AHL	13	7	6	0	783	27	1	2.07	....	....	....	....	....	....	....
2010-11	Norfolk Admirals	AHL	9	2	5	1	478	29	0	3.64	....	....	....	....	....	....	....
	Florida Everblades	ECHL	27	12	13	0	1491	76	0	3.06	....	....	....	....	....	....	....
2011-12	Norfolk Admirals	AHL	34	23	8	2	1986	78	1	2.36	4	3	1	249	7	1	1.69
2012-13	Bratislava	KHL	47	18	16	0	2879	104	5	2.17	2	0	2	119	8	0	4.03

Signed as a free agent by **Bratislava** (KHL), August 22, 2012.

JARRY, Tristan (JAIR-ee, TRIH-STAN) PIT

Goaltender. Catches left. 6'1", 183 lbs. Born, Surrey, B.C., April 29, 1995.
(Pittsburgh's 1st choice, 44th overall, in 2013 Entry Draft).

			Regular Season								Playoffs						
Season	Club	League	GP	W	L	O/T	Mins	GA	SO	Avg	GP	W	L	Mins	GA	SO	Avg
2009-10	North Delta	Minor-BC	26	....	....	....	....	....	....	1.65	....	....	....	....	....	....	....
2010-11	Greater Van.	BCMML	20	....	....	....	....	....	....	2.31	6	....	....	....	....	....	....
2011-12	Edmonton	WHL	14	8	2	1	718	35	0	2.93	....	....	....	....	....	....	....
2012-13	Edmonton	WHL	27	18	7	0	1495	40	6	*1.61	1	0	0	27	0	0	0.00

JOHNSON, Chad (JAWN-suhn, CHAD) BOS

Goaltender. Catches left. 6'3", 205 lbs. Born, Calgary, Alta., June 10, 1986.
(Pittsburgh's 4th choice, 125th overall, in 2006 Entry Draft).

			Regular Season								Playoffs						
Season	Club	League	GP	W	L	O/T	Mins	GA	SO	Avg	GP	W	L	Mins	GA	SO	Avg
2002-03	Calgary Buffaloes	AMHL	....	8	8	2	1145	62	....	3.25	1	0	1	60	3	0	3.00
2003-04	Brooks Bandits	AJHL	31	6	20	3	1782	117	0	3.94	....	....	....	....	....	....	....
2004-05	Brooks Bandits	AJHL	43	25	16	2	2505	109	2	2.61	119	4	5	493	....	....	....
2005-06	Alaska	CCHA	18	6	7	4	985	42	0	2.56	....	....	....	....	....	....	....
2006-07	Alaska	CCHA	19	5	6	2	1002	52	1	3.11	....	....	....	....	....	....	....
2007-08	Alaska	CCHA	7	0	6	0	357	20	0	3.36	....	....	....	....	....	....	....
2008-09	Alaska	CCHA	35	14	16	5	2062	57	6	*1.66	....	....	....	....	....	....	....
2009-10	**NY Rangers**	**NHL**	**5**	**1**	**2**	**1**	**281**	**11**	**0**	**2.35**	....	....	....	....	....	....	....
	Hartford Wolf Pack	AHL	47	24	18	2	2649	112	3	2.54	....	....	....	....	....	....	....
2010-11	**NY Rangers**	**NHL**	**1**	**0**	**0**	**0**	**20**	**2**	**0**	**6.00**	....	....	....	....	....	....	....
	Connecticut Whale	AHL	40	16	19	3	2271	103	2	2.72	....	....	....	....	....	....	....
2011-12	Connecticut Whale	AHL	49	22	18	6	2775	115	1	2.49	....	....	....	....	....	....	....
2012-13	Portland Pirates	AHL	34	16	15	1	1938	97	2	3.00	3	0	3	204	12	0	3.53
	Phoenix	**NHL**	**4**	**2**	**0**	**2**	**247**	**5**	**1**	**1.21**	....	....	....	....	....	....	....
	NHL Totals		**10**	**3**	**2**	**3**	**548**	**18**	**1**	**1.97**	....	....	....	....	....	....	....

AJHL South Division First All-Star Team (2005) • CCHA First All-Star Team (2009) • CCHA Rookie of the Year (2009) • NCAA West Second All-American Team (2009)

Traded to **NY Rangers** by **Pittsburgh** for Pittsburgh's 5th round choice (previously acquired, Pittsburgh selected Andy Bathgate) in 2009 Entry Draft, June 27, 2009. Signed as a free agent by **Phoenix**, July 1. 2012. Signed as a free agent by **Boston**, July 5, 2013.

JONES, Martin (JOHNZ, MAR-tihn) L.A.

Goaltender. Catches left. 6'4", 189 lbs. Born, North Vancouver, B.C., January 10, 1990.

			Regular Season								Playoffs						
Season	Club	League	GP	W	L	O/T	Mins	GA	SO	Avg	GP	W	L	Mins	GA	SO	Avg
2006-07	Calgary Hitmen	WHL	18	9	4	3	1029	52	0	3.03	....	....	....	....	....	....	....
2007-08	Calgary Hitmen	WHL	27	18	8	1	1529	54	1	2.12	5	2	1	250	12	0	2.88
2008-09	Calgary Hitmen	WHL	55	*45	5	4	3295	114	*7	2.08	18	14	4	1095	34	2	1.86
2009-10	Calgary Hitmen	WHL	48	36	11	1	2851	105	*8	*2.21	*23	*16	7	*1401	55	*2	*2.36
2010-11	Manchester	AHL	39	23	12	1	2187	82	4	2.25	4	2	1	213	9	0	2.54
	Ontario Reign	ECHL	1	1	0	0	64	4	0	3.76	....	....	....	....	....	....	....
2011-12	Manchester	AHL	41	18	17	2	2166	94	1	2.60	3	1	1	155	6	0	2.33
2012-13	Manchester	AHL	56	27	25	4	3347	141	5	2.53	4	1	3	277	10	0	2.16

WHL East Second All-Star Team (2009) • WHL East First All-Star Team (2010) • WHL Goaltender of the Year (2010) • Canadian Major Junior Second All-Star Team (2010) • Memorial Cup All-Star Team (2010) • Hap Emms Memorial Trophy (Memorial Cup – Top Goaltender) (2010)

Signed as a free agent by **Los Angeles**, October 2, 2008.

JUVONEN, Janne (YOO-voh-nehn, YAH-neh) NSH

Goaltender. Catches left. 6', 170 lbs. Born, Kiihtelysvaara, Finland, October 3, 1994.
(Nashville's 10th choice, 203rd overall, in 2013 Entry Draft).

			Regular Season								Playoffs						
Season	Club	League	GP	W	L	O/T	Mins	GA	SO	Avg	GP	W	L	Mins	GA	SO	Avg
2009-10	Jokipojat U18	Fin-U18	19	....	....	....	....	....	....	3.91	....	....	....	....	....	....	....
	Jokipojat Jr.	Fin-Jr.	1	....	....	....	60	3	0	3.02	....	....	....	....	....	....	....
2010-11	Jokipojat U18	Fin-U18	4	....	....	....	240	4	1	1.00	....	....	....	....	....	....	....
	Jokipojat Jr.	Fin-Jr.	27	....	....	....	1575	91	1	3.46	....	....	....	....	....	....	....
2011-12	Pelicans Lahti U18	Fin-U18	15	6	9	0	902	35	3	2.33	....	....	....	....	....	....	....
	Pelicans Lahti Jr.	Fin-Jr.	20	11	9	0	1215	58	1	2.86	....	....	....	....	....	....	....
	Pelicans Lahti	Finland	2	1	1	0	90	4	0	2.66	2	0	2	99	4	0	2.43
2012-13	Pelicans Lahti Jr.	Fin-Jr.	11	....	....	....	646	32	1	2.97	....	....	....	....	....	....	....
	Pelicans Lahti	Finland	4	1	3	0	188	11	0	3.51	....	....	....	....	....	....	....
	Peliitat Heinola	Finland-2	17	....	....	....	961	51	1	3.18	....	....	....	....	....	....	....

KARLSSON, Henrik (KARL-suhn, HEHN-rihk)

Goaltender. Catches left. 6'6", 209 lbs. Born, Stockholm, Sweden, November 27, 1983.

			Regular Season								Playoffs						
Season	Club	League	GP	W	L	O/T	Mins	GA	SO	Avg	GP	W	L	Mins	GA	SO	Avg
2000-01	Hammarby U18	Swe-U18	2	....	....	....	120	7	0	3.50	....	....	....	....	....	....	....
	Hammarby Jr.	Swe-Jr.	13	....	....	....	706	56	0	4.76	....	....	....	....	....	....	....
2001-02	Hammarby Jr.	Swe-Jr.	23	....	....	....	1356	97	1	4.29	....	....	....	....	....	....	....
2002-03	Botkyrka	Sweden-3	....	....	....	....	....	....	....	2.58	....	....	....	....	....	....	....
2003-04	Botkyrka	Sweden-3	21	....	....	....	....	....	....	2.49	6	....	....	236	15	0	3.82
2004-05	Olofstroms IK	Sweden-3	1	....	....	....	60	0	1	0.00	....	....	....	....	....	....	....
	IK Oskarshamn	Sweden-2	11	....	....	....	613	25	1	2.45	2	....	....	109	7	0	3.87
2005-06	IK Oskarshamn	Sweden-2	1	....	....	....	40	3	0	4.54	....	....	....	....	....	....	....
2006-07	Hammarby Jr.	Swe-Jr.	1	....	....	....	59	2	0	2.04	....	....	....	....	....	....	....
	Hammarby	Sweden-2	35	....	....	....	1893	111	1	3.52	....	....	....	....	....	....	....
2007-08	Hammarby	Sweden-2	29	....	....	....	1692	109	1	3.86	....	....	....	....	....	....	....
	Malmo	Sweden-2	3	....	....	....	180	8	0	2.67	....	....	....	....	....	....	....
2008-09	Malmo	Sweden-2	32	....	....	....	1888	77	4	2.45	....	....	....	....	....	....	....
	Sodertalje SK	Sweden	7	....	....	....	410	17	0	2.49	....	....	....	....	....	....	....
	Sodertalje SK	Sweden-Q	8	....	....	....	483	16	0	1.99	....	....	....	....	....	....	....
2009-10	Farjestad	Sweden	34	....	....	....	1934	79	3	2.45	....	....	....	....	....	....	....
2010-11	**Calgary**	**NHL**	**17**	**4**	**5**	**6**	**838**	**36**	**0**	**2.58**	....	....	....	....	....	....	....
2011-12	**Calgary**	**NHL**	**9**	**1**	**4**	**2**	**454**	**24**	**0**	**3.17**	....	....	....	....	....	....	....
	Abbotsford Heat	AHL	4	2	2	0	239	9	0	2.26	....	....	....	....	....	....	....
2012-13	Rockford IceHogs	AHL	18	11	5	0	1007	48	0	2.86	....	....	....	....	....	....	....
	NHL Totals		**26**	**5**	**9**	**8**	**1292**	**60**	**0**	**2.79**	....	....	....	....	....	....	....

Signed as a free agent by **Malmo** (Sweden), January 31, 2008. Signed as a free agent by **Sodertalje** (Sweden), January 30, 2009. Signed as a free agent by **San Jose**, August 12, 2009. • Loaned to **Farjestad** (Sweden) by **San Jose**, August 13, 2009. Traded to **Calgary** by **San Jose** for Calgary's 6th round choice (Konrad Abeltshauser) in 2010 Entry Draft, June 25, 2010. Traded to **Chicago** by **Calgary** for Ottawa's 7th round choice (previously acquired, Calgary selected John Gilmour) in 2013 Entry Draft, January 21, 2013. Signed as a free agent by **Skelleftea** (Sweden), June 25, 2013.

KASDORF, Jason (KAZ-dawrf, JAY-suhn) WPG

Goaltender. Catches left. 6'4", 195 lbs. Born, Winnipeg, Man., May 18, 1992.
(Winnipeg's 6th choice, 157th overall, in 2011 Entry Draft).

			Regular Season								Playoffs						
Season	Club	League	GP	W	L	O/T	Mins	GA	SO	Avg	GP	W	L	Mins	GA	SO	Avg
2008-09	Wpg. Thrashers	MMHL	44	....	....	....	1032	36	4	2.09	....	....	....	....	....	....	....
2009-10	Portage Terriers	MJHL	....	19	10	5	2094	89	2	2.55	....	....	....	....	....	....	....
2010-11	Portage Terriers	MJHL	34	24	10	0	2018	85	2	2.53	16	10	5	930	34	2	2.19
2011-12	Des Moines	USHL	33	10	16	5	1750	100	3	3.43	....	....	....	....	....	....	....
2012-13	RPI Engineers	ECAC	23	14	5	2	1330	36	3	1.62	....	....	....	....	....	....	....

ECAC All-Rookie Team (2013) • ECAC Second All-Star Team (2013)

KHABIBULIN, Nikolai (khah-bee-BOO-lihn, NIH-koh-ligh) CHI

Goaltender. Catches left. 6'1", 208 lbs. Born, Sverdlovsk, USSR, January 13, 1973.
(Winnipeg's 8th choice, 204th overall, in 1992 Entry Draft).

			Regular Season								Playoffs						
Season	Club	League	GP	W	L	O/T	Mins	GA	SO	Avg	GP	W	L	Mins	GA	SO	Avg
1988-89	Sverdlovsk	USSR	1	....	....	....	3	0	0	0.00	....	....	....	....	....	....	....
1989-90	Luch Sverdlovsk	USSR-2					STATISTICS NOT AVAILABLE										
1990-91	Nizhny Tagil	USSR-3	10	....	....	....	....	....	....	....	....	....	....	....	....	....	....
	Sverdlovsk	USSR-Q	2	....	....	....	....	7	....	....	....	....	....	....	....	....	....
1991-92	CSKA Moscow 2	CIS-3	11	....	....	....	....	....	....	....	....	....	....	....	....	....	....
	CSKA Moscow	CIS	2	....	....	....	34	2	0	3.53	....	....	....	....	....	....	....
	Russia	Olympics					DID NOT PLAY – SPARE GOALTENDER										
1992-93	CSKA Moscow	CIS	13	....	....	....	491	27	....	3.29	....	....	....	....	....	....	....
	Serov	CIS-2	18	....	....	....	....	....	....	....	....	....	....	....	....	....	....
1993-94	CSKA Moscow	CIS	46	....	....	....	2625	116	....	2.65	....	....	....	....	....	....	....
	Russian Penguins	IHL	12	2	7	2	639	47	0	4.41	....	....	....	....	....	....	....
1994-95	Springfield Indians	AHL	23	9	9	3	1240	80	0	3.87	....	....	....	....	....	....	....
	Winnipeg	**NHL**	**26**	**8**	**9**	**4**	**1339**	**76**	**0**	**3.41**	....	....	....	....	....	....	....
1995-96	**Winnipeg**	**NHL**	**53**	**26**	**20**	**3**	**2914**	**152**	**2**	**3.13**	**6**	**2**	**4**	**359**	**19**	**0**	**3.18**
1996-97	**Phoenix**	**NHL**	**72**	**30**	**33**	**6**	**4091**	**193**	**7**	**2.83**	**7**	**3**	**4**	**426**	**15**	**1**	**2.11**
1997-98	**Phoenix**	**NHL**	**70**	**30**	**28**	**10**	**4026**	**184**	**4**	**2.74**	**4**	**2**	**1**	**185**	**13**	**0**	**4.22**
1998-99	**Phoenix**	**NHL**	**63**	**32**	**23**	**7**	**3657**	**130**	**8**	**2.13**	**7**	**3**	**4**	**449**	**18**	**0**	**2.41**
99-2000	Long Beach	IHL	33	21	11	1	1936	59	5	*1.83	5	2	3	321	15	0	2.81
2000-01	**Tampa Bay**	**NHL**	**2**	**1**	**1**	**0**	**123**	**6**	**0**	**2.93**	....	....	....	....	....	....	....
2001-02	**Tampa Bay**	**NHL**	**70**	**24**	**32**	**10**	**3896**	**153**	**7**	**2.36**	....	....	....	....	....	....	....
	Russia	Olympics	6	3	2	1	*359	14	*1	2.34	....	....	....	....	....	....	....
2002-03	**Tampa Bay**	**NHL**	**65**	**30**	**22**	**11**	**3787**	**156**	**4**	**2.47**	**10**	**5**	**5**	**644**	**26**	**0**	**2.42**
2003-04 ◆	**Tampa Bay**	**NHL**	**55**	**28**	**19**	**7**	**3274**	**127**	**3**	**2.33**	**23**	***16**	**7**	**1401**	**40**	***5**	**1.71**
2004-05	Ak Bars Kazan	Russia	24	....	....	....	1457	40	5	1.65	2	....	....	118	6	0	3.04
2005-06	**Chicago**	**NHL**	**50**	**17**	**26**	**6**	**2815**	**157**	**0**	**3.35**	....	....	....	....	....	....	....
	Russia	Olympics					DID NOT PLAY – INJURED										
2006-07	**Chicago**	**NHL**	**60**	**25**	**26**	**5**	**3425**	**163**	**1**	**2.86**	....	....	....	....	....	....	....
2007-08	**Chicago**	**NHL**	**50**	**23**	**20**	**6**	**2892**	**127**	**2**	**2.63**	....	....	....	....	....	....	....
2008-09	**Chicago**	**NHL**	**42**	**25**	**8**	**7**	**2467**	**96**	**3**	**2.33**	**15**	**8**	**6**	**881**	**43**	**0**	**2.93**
2009-10	**Edmonton**	**NHL**	**18**	**7**	**9**	**2**	**1089**	**55**	**0**	**3.03**	....	....	....	....	....	....	....
2010-11	**Edmonton**	**NHL**	**47**	**10**	**32**	**4**	**2701**	**153**	**2**	**3.40**	....	....	....	....	....	....	....
2011-12	**Edmonton**	**NHL**	**40**	**12**	**20**	**7**	**2261**	**100**	**2**	**2.65**	....	....	....	....	....	....	....
2012-13	**Edmonton**	**NHL**	**12**	**4**	**6**	**1**	**684**	**29**	**1**	**2.54**	....	....	....	....	....	....	....
	NHL Totals		**795**	**332**	**334**	**96**	**45441**	**2057**	**46**	**2.72**	**72**	**39**	**31**	**4345**	**174**	**6**	**2.40**

James Gatschene Memorial Trophy (IHL – MVP) (2000) (co-winner - Frederic Chabot)

Played in NHL All-Star Game (1998, 1999, 2002, 2003)

• Transferred to **Phoenix** after **Winnipeg** franchise relocated, July 1, 1996. • Missed 1999-2000 NHL season and majority of 2000-01 after failing to come to contract terms with **Phoenix**. Signed as a free agent by **Long Beach** (IHL) with **Phoenix** retaining NHL rights, January 14, 2000. Traded to **Tampa Bay** by **Phoenix** with Stan Neckar for Mike Johnson, Paul Mara, Ruslan Zainullin and NY Islanders' 2nd round choice (previously acquired, Phoenix selected Matthew Spiller) in 2001 Entry Draft, March 5, 2001. Signed as a free agent by **Kazan** (Russia), November 8, 2004. Signed as a free agent by **Chicago**, August 5, 2005. Signed as a free agent by **Edmonton**, July 1, 2009. Signed as a free agent by **Chicago**, July 5, 2013.

KHUDOBIN, Anton (hoo-DOH-bihn, AN-tawn) CAR

Goaltender. Catches left. 5'11", 203 lbs. Born, Ust-Kamenogorsk, USSR, May 7, 1986.
(Minnesota's 11th choice, 206th overall, in 2004 Entry Draft).

			Regular Season								Playoffs						
Season	Club	League	GP	W	L	O/T	Mins	GA	SO	Avg	GP	W	L	Mins	GA	SO	Avg
2003-04	Magnitogorsk 2	Russia-3	38	....	....	....	....	80	....	....	....	....	....	....	....	....	....
2004-05	Magnitogorsk	Russia	4	....	....	....	133	0	1	0.00	....	....	....	....	....	....	....
	Magnitogorsk 2	Russia-3	27	....	....	....	....	52	....	....	....	....	....	....	....	....	....
2005-06	Saskatoon Blades	WHL	44	23	13	3	2362	114	4	2.90	10	4	6	685	32	0	2.80
2006-07	Magnitogorsk	Russia	16	....	....	....	618	28	0	2.72	3	....	....	26	1	0	2.30
2007-08	Houston Aeros	AHL	12	2	2	1	482	16	1	1.99	....	....	....	....	....	....	....
	Texas Wildcatters	ECHL	27	20	1	4	1549	51	3	*1.98	9	5	4	547	20	1	2.19
2008-09	Houston Aeros	AHL	10	3	6	1	512	26	0	3.04	17	8	8	890	40	2	2.70
	Florida Everblades	ECHL	33	18	10	1	1706	77	4	2.71	....	....	....	....	....	....	....
2009-10	**Minnesota**	**NHL**	**2**	**2**	**0**	**0**	**69**	**1**	**0**	**0.87**	....	....	....	....	....	....	....
	Houston Aeros	AHL	40	14	19	4	2247	91	4	2.43	....	....	....	....	....	....	....
2010-11	**Minnesota**	**NHL**	**4**	**2**	**1**	**0**	**189**	**5**	**1**	**1.59**	....	....	....	....	....	....	....
	Houston Aeros	AHL	34	19	12	1	1883	81	1	2.58	....	....	....	....	....	....	....
	Providence Bruins	AHL	16	9	4	1	901	36	1	2.40	....	....	....	....	....	....	....
2011-12	**Boston**	**NHL**	**1**	**1**	**0**	**0**	**60**	**1**	**0**	**1.00**	....	....	....	....	....	....	....
	Providence Bruins	AHL	44	21	19	3	2597	113	2	2.61	....	....	....	....	....	....	....
2012-13	Mytischi	KHL	26	6	14	0	1500	74	1	2.96	....	....	....	....	....	....	....
	Boston	**NHL**	**14**	**9**	**4**	**1**	**803**	**31**	**1**	**2.32**	....	....	....	....	....	....	....
	NHL Totals		**21**	**14**	**5**	**1**	**1121**	**38**	**2**	**2.03**	....	....	....	....	....	....	....

ECHL First All-Star Team (2008) • ECHL Goaltender of the Year (2008)

Traded to **Boston** by **Minnesota** for Jeff Penner and Mikko Lehtonen, February 28, 2011. Signed as a free agent by **Mytischi** (KHL), September 21, 2012. Signed as a free agent by **Carolina**, July 5, 2013.

KILLEEN, Patrick (kih-LEEN, PAT-rihk)

Goaltender. Catches left. 6'4", 194 lbs. Born, Almonte, Ont., April 15, 1990.
(Pittsburgh's 3rd choice, 180th overall, in 2008 Entry Draft).

			Regular Season								Playoffs						
Season	Club	League	GP	W	L	O/T	Mins	GA	SO	Avg	GP	W	L	Mins	GA	SO	Avg
2005-06	Ott. Valley Titans	Minor-ON	36	....	....	....	1620	74	6	2.05	....	....	....	....	....	....	....
2006-07	Ottawa Jr. Sens	ON-Jr.A	7	5	1	0	376	20	0	3.19	....	....	....	....	....	....	....
	Brampton Battalion	OHL	8	1	3	0	304	29	0	5.72	....	....	....	....	....	....	....
2007-08	Brampton Battalion	OHL	34	20	9	2	1959	90	1	2.76	....	....	....	....	....	....	....
2008-09	Brampton Battalion	OHL	34	19	11	2	1916	91	2	2.85	2	0	0	26	4	0	9.27
2009-10	Brampton Battalion	OHL	*63	23	25	13	*3693	149	*5	2.42	11	4	7	664	38	0	3.43
2010-11	Wilkes-Barre	AHL	2	0	0	0	19	2	0	6.38	....	....	....	....	....	....	....
	Wheeling Nailers	ECHL	40	19	16	2	2233	107	3	2.87	5	1	2	247	11	0	2.68
2011-12	Wilkes-Barre	AHL	5	2	2	0	266	13	0	2.93	....	....	....	....	....	....	....
	Wheeling Nailers	ECHL	36	19	12	4	2116	95	2	2.69	4	1	3	238	14	0	3.54
2012-13	Wheeling Nailers	ECHL	13	3	5	4	758	41	0	3.25	....	....	....	....	....	....	....
	Orlando	ECHL	22	7	8	3	1155	68	1	3.53	....	....	....	....	....	....	....

• Re-assigned to **Orlando** (ECHL) by **Pittsburgh** (Wheeling-ECHL), January 25, 2013. Traded to **Columbus** by **Pittsburgh** for future considerations, April 3, 2013.

KINKAID, Keith (kihn-KAID, KEETH) N.J.

Goaltender. Catches left. 6'2", 190 lbs. Born, Farmingville, NY, July 4, 1989.

			Regular Season								Playoffs						
Season	Club	League	GP	W	L	O/T	Mins	GA	SO	Avg	GP	W	L	Mins	GA	SO	Avg
2007-08	Des Moines	USHL	15	4	9	2	844	48	0	3.41	....	....	....	....	....	....	....
2008-09	St. Louis Bandits	NAHL	40	*30	5	4	2393	71	*7	*1.78	*12	*10	2	*728	14	*3	*1.15
2009-10	Union College	ECAC	25	12	8	3	1478	61	1	2.48	....	....	....	....	....	....	....
2010-11	Union College	ECAC	*38	25	10	3	*2266	75	3	1.99	....	....	....	....	....	....	....
2011-12	Albany Devils	AHL	42	17	20	3	2347	115	3	2.94	....	....	....	....	....	....	....
2012-13	Albany Devils	AHL	45	21	17	6	2644	120	2	2.72	....	....	....	....	....	....	....
	New Jersey	**NHL**	**1**	**0**	**0**	**0**	**26**	**1**	**0**	**2.31**	....	....	....	....	....	....	....
	NHL Totals		**1**	**0**	**0**	**0**	**26**	**1**	**0**	**2.31**	....	....	....	....	....	....	....

ECAC All-Rookie Team (2010) • ECAC First All-Star Team (2011) • NCAA East First All-American Team (2011)

Signed as a free agent by **New Jersey**, April 18, 2011.

KIPRUSOFF, Miikka (KIHP-roo-sawf, MEE-kah)

Goaltender. Catches left. 6'1", 185 lbs. Born, Turku, Finland, October 26, 1976.
(San Jose's 5th choice, 116th overall, in 1995 Entry Draft).

			Regular Season								Playoffs						
Season	Club	League	GP	W	L	O/T	Mins	GA	SO	Avg	GP	W	L	Mins	GA	SO	Avg
1993-94	TPS Turku Jr.	Fin-Jr.	35	20	9	5	2101	100	0	2.85	6	3	3	369	26	0	4.23
1994-95	TPS Turku Jr.	Fin-Jr.	31	13	14	4	1896	92	2	2.91	....	....	....	....	....	....	....
	Kiekko-67 Turku	Finland-2	1	0	1	0	60	6	0	6.00	....	....	....	....	....	....	....
	TPS Turku	Finland	4	3	1	0	240	12	0	3.00	2	2	0	120	7	0	3.50
1995-96	TPS Turku Jr.	Fin-Jr.	3	1	2	0	180	9	0	3.00	....	....	....	....	....	....	....
	Kiekko-67 Turku	Finland-2	5	5	0	0	300	7	1	1.40	....	....	....	....	....	....	....
	TPS Turku	Finland	12	5	3	1	550	38	0	4.14	3	0	1	113	4	0	2.12
1996-97	AIK Solna	Sweden	42	....	....	....	2440	93	3	2.29	7	....	....	420	22	0	3.14
1997-98	AIK Solna	Sweden	43	....	....	....	2517	111	1	2.65	....	....	....	....	....	....	....
	AIK Solna	Sweden-Q	9	....	....	....	540	15	2	1.67	....	....	....	....	....	....	....
1998-99	TPS Turku	Finland	39	26	6	6	2259	70	4	1.86	10	9	1	580	15	3	1.55
99-2000	Kentucky	AHL	47	23	19	4	2759	114	3	2.48	5	1	3	239	13	0	3.27
2000-01	**San Jose**	**NHL**	**5**	**2**	**1**	**0**	**154**	**5**	**0**	**1.95**	**3**	**1**	**1**	**149**	**5**	**0**	**2.01**
	Kentucky	AHL	36	19	9	6	2038	76	2	2.24	....	....	....	....	....	....	....
2001-02	**San Jose**	**NHL**	**20**	**7**	**6**	**3**	**1037**	**43**	**2**	**2.49**	**1**	**0**	**0**	**8**	**0**	**0**	**0.00**
	Cleveland Barons	AHL	4	4	0	0	242	7	0	1.73	....	....	....	....	....	....	....
2002-03	**San Jose**	**NHL**	**22**	**5**	**14**	**0**	**1199**	**65**	**1**	**3.25**	....	....	....	....	....	....	....
2003-04	**Calgary**	**NHL**	**38**	**24**	**10**	**4**	**2301**	**65**	**4**	***1.69**	***26**	**15**	**11**	***1655**	**51**	***5**	**1.85**
2004-05	Timra IK	Sweden	46	....	....	....	2719	97	5	2.14	6	....	....	356	13	0	2.19
2005-06	**Calgary**	**NHL**	**74**	**42**	**20**	**11**	***4380**	**151**	***10**	***2.07**	**7**	**3**	**4**	**428**	**16**	**0**	**2.24**
	Finland	Olympics					DID NOT PLAY – INJURED										
2006-07	**Calgary**	**NHL**	**74**	**40**	**24**	**9**	**4419**	**181**	**7**	**2.46**	**6**	**2**	**4**	**384**	**18**	**0**	**2.81**
2007-08	**Calgary**	**NHL**	**76**	**39**	**26**	**10**	**4398**	**197**	**2**	**2.69**	**7**	**2**	**4**	**336**	**18**	**1**	**3.21**
2008-09	**Calgary**	**NHL**	***76**	***45**	**24**	**5**	***4418**	**209**	**4**	**2.84**	**6**	**2**	**4**	**324**	**19**	**0**	**3.52**
2009-10	**Calgary**	**NHL**	**73**	**35**	**28**	**10**	**4235**	**163**	**4**	**2.31**	....	....	....	....	....	....	....
	Finland	Olympics	5	3	2	0	250	11	1	2.64	....	....	....	....	....	....	....
2010-11	**Calgary**	**NHL**	**71**	**37**	**24**	**6**	**4156**	**182**	**6**	**2.63**	....	....	....	....	....	....	....
2011-12	**Calgary**	**NHL**	**70**	**35**	**22**	**11**	**4128**	**162**	**4**	**2.35**	....	....	....	....	....	....	....
2012-13	**Calgary**	**NHL**	**24**	**8**	**14**	**2**	**1344**	**77**	**0**	**3.44**	....	....	....	....	....	....	....
	NHL Totals		**623**	**319**	**213**	**71**	**36169**	**1500**	**44**	**2.49**	**56**	**25**	**28**	**3284**	**127**	**6**	**2.32**

NHL First All-Star Team (2006) • William M. Jennings Trophy (2006) • Vezina Trophy (2006)

Played in NHL All-Star Game (2007)

Traded to **Calgary** by **San Jose** for Calgary's 2nd round choice (Marc-Edouard Vlasic) in 2005 Entry Draft, November 16, 2003. Signed as a free agent by **Timra** (Sweden), September 20, 2004.

KIVIAHO, Henri (kih-vee-A-hoh, HEHN-ree) DAL

Goaltender. Catches left. 6'1", 167 lbs. Born, Lappeenranta, Finland, February 26, 1994.
(Dallas' 8th choice, 144th overall, in 2012 Entry Draft).

			Regular Season								Playoffs						
Season	Club	League	GP	W	L	O/T	Mins	GA	SO	Avg	GP	W	L	Mins	GA	SO	Avg
2009-10	SaiPa U18	Fin-U18	9	1	5	0	464	59	0	7.64	....	....	....	....	....	....	....
2010-11	SaiPa U18	Fin-U18	8	1	5	0	417	30	0	4.31	....	....	....	....	....	....	....
	SaiPa Jr.	Fin-Jr.	11	4	4	0	503	33	0	3.93	....	....	....	....	....	....	....
2011-12	KalPa Kuopio Jr.	Fin-Jr.	28	16	11	0	1638	76	2	2.78	9	3	6	535	36	0	4.04
2012-13	KalPa Kuopio Jr.	Fin-Jr.	31	....	....	....	1846	82	4	2.66	3	....	....	179	8	0	2.68

KNAPP, Connor (NAP, KAW-nuhr) BUF

Goaltender. Catches left. 6'6", 225 lbs. Born, New York, NY, May 1, 1990.
(Buffalo's 5th choice, 164th overall, in 2009 Entry Draft).

			Regular Season								Playoffs						
Season	Club	League	GP	W	L	O/T	Mins	GA	SO	Avg	GP	W	L	Mins	GA	SO	Avg
2005-06	Buffalo Saints	Minor-NY	26	....	....	....	1326	64	5	2.46	....	....	....	....	....	....	....
2006-07	Junior Bruins	EmJHL	23	*22	1	0	1340	37	3	*1.66	5	5	0	290	6	*2	*1.24
2007-08	Bos. Jr. Bruins	EJHL	25	14	7	2	1259	44	3	2.10	....	....	....	....	....	....	....
	Junior Bruins	EmJHL	1	1	0	0	45	2	0	2.67	....	....	....	....	....	....	....
2008-09	Miami U.	CCHA	23	13	5	3	1350	47	2	2.09	....	....	....	....	....	....	....
2009-10	Miami U.	CCHA	20	10	4	4	1127	37	4	1.97	....	....	....	....	....	....	....
2010-11	Miami U.	CCHA	17	8	5	4	976	33	2	2.03	....	....	....	....	....	....	....
2011-12	Miami U.	CCHA	24	15	8	0	1349	38	5	1.69	....	....	....	....	....	....	....
2012-13	Rochester	AHL	7	1	6	0	413	23	0	3.34	....	....	....	....	....	....	....
	Greenville	ECHL	12	5	7	0	728	37	0	3.05	4	1	3	221	10	0	2.71

EmJHL Goaltender of the Year (2007) • CCHA All-Rookie Team (2009)

KORPISALO, Joonas (kohr-pih-SAL-loh, YOH-nuhs) CBJ

Goaltender. Catches left. 6'2", 172 lbs. Born, Pori, Finland, April 28, 1994.
(Columbus' 3rd choice, 62nd overall, in 2012 Entry Draft).

			Regular Season								Playoffs						
Season	Club	League	GP	W	L	O/T	Mins	GA	SO	Avg	GP	W	L	Mins	GA	SO	Avg
2010-11	Jokerit U18	Fin-U18	20	16	4	0	1200	53	0	2.65	8	5	3	460	22	0	2.87
2011-12	Jokerit Helsinki Jr.	Fin-Jr.	38	28	11	0	2295	78	4	2.04	4	3	1	270	8	1	1.77
2012-13	Jokerit Helsinki Jr.	Fin-Jr.	13	....	....	....	787	35	1	2.67	....	....	....	....	....	....	....
	Kiekko-Vantaa	Finland-2	18	....	....	....	997	45	0	2.71	....	....	....	....	....	....	....
	Jokerit Helsinki	Finland	1	0	0	0	15	0	0	0.00	....	....	....	....	....	....	....

KOSHECHKIN, Vasily (KOH-shech-kihn, va-SEE-lee) T.B.

Goaltender. Catches left. 6'6", 210 lbs. Born, Togliatti, USSR, March 27, 1983.
(Tampa Bay's 9th choice, 233rd overall, in 2002 Entry Draft).

			Regular Season								Playoffs						
Season	Club	League	GP	W	L	O/T	Mins	GA	SO	Avg	GP	W	L	Mins	GA	SO	Avg
1998-99	Lada Togliatti 2	Russia-4	8	....	....	....	....	8	....	....	....	....	....	....	....	....	....
99-2000	Lada Togliatti 2	Russia-3	18	....	....	....	....	20	....	....	....	....	....	....	....	....	....
2000-01	Lada Togliatti 2	Russia-3					Statistics not available										
2001-02	Lada Togliatti 2	Russia-3					Statistics not available										
2002-03	Lada Togliatti 2	Russia-3					Statistics not available										
	Kirovo-Chepetsk	Russia-2	10	....	....	....	613	14	3	1.37	....	....	....	....	....	....	....
	Almetjevsk	Russia-2	14	....	....	....	675	29	1	2.58	....	....	....	....	....	....	....
2003-04	Lada Togliatti 2	Russia-3	13	....	....	....	....	19	1	....	3	....	....	....	....	....	....
	Lada Togliatti	Russia	8	....	....	....	247	10	0	2.43	1	....	....	40	3	0	4.50
2004-05	Lada Togliatti	Russia	4	....	....	....	121	5	0	2.47	....	....	....	....	....	....	....
2005-06	Lada Togliatti	Russia	41	....	....	....	2375	63	9	1.59	8	....	....	474	20	1	2.53
2006-07	Lada Togliatti	Russia	42	....	....	....	2430	82	5	2.02	3	....	....	179	13	0	4.35
2007-08	Ak Bars Kazan	Russia	19	....	....	....	990	45	0	2.73	....	....	....	....	....	....	....
2008-09	Lada Togliatti	KHL	43	....	....	....	2404	67	8	1.67	5	....	....	280	9	1	1.93
2009-10	Lada Togliatti	KHL	*23	....	....	....	1304	46	*2	2.12	....	....	....	....	....	....	....
	Magnitogorsk	KHL	*26	....	....	....	1536	47	*6	1.84	9	....	....	535	18	1	2.02
2010-11	Cherepovets	KHL	32	....	....	....	1809	88	2	2.92	6	....	....	327	12	0	2.20
2011-12	Cherepovets	KHL	34	12	11	0	1795	71	6	2.37	6	2	4	365	8	1	1.32
2012-13	Cherepovets	KHL	*51	22	20	0	*3102	110	*8	2.13	10	4	6	653	28	0	2.57

KOSKINEN, Mikko (KAWS-kih-nehn, MEE-koh) NYI

Goaltender. Catches left. 6'6", 205 lbs. Born, Vantaa, Finland, July 18, 1988.
(NY Islanders' 3rd choice, 31st overall, in 2009 Entry Draft).

			Regular Season								Playoffs						
Season	Club	League	GP	W	L	O/T	Mins	GA	SO	Avg	GP	W	L	Mins	GA	SO	Avg
2004-05	Blues-T U18	Fin-U18	21	....	....	....	1138	67	0	3.53	....	....	....	....	....	....	....
2005-06	Blues Espoo U18	Fin-U18	3	....	....	....	142	12	0	5.07	....	....	....	....	....	....	....
2006-07	Kiekko-Vantaa Jr.	Fin-Jr.	27	16	8	0	1567	62	3	2.37	....	....	....	....	....	....	....
2007-08	Blues Espoo Jr.	Fin-Jr.	20	12	4	0	1176	45	2	2.30	2	0	2	81	7	0	5.18
	Blues Espoo	Finland	1	1	0	0	60	0	1	0.00	....	....	....	....	....	....	....
2008-09	Blues Espoo Jr.	Fin-Jr.	9	9	0	0	545	15	2	1.65	....	....	....	....	....	....	....
	Blues Espoo	Finland	33	17	9	7	1921	61	1	1.91	14	6	8	856	37	0	2.59
2009-10	Bridgeport	AHL	2	1	1	0	123	5	0	2.45	3	1	1	147	7	0	2.85
	Utah Grizzlies	ECHL	6	6	0	0	360	15	0	2.50	4	2	1	172	10	0	3.49
2010-11	**NY Islanders**	**NHL**	**4**	**2**	**1**	**0**	**208**	**15**	**0**	**4.33**	....	....	....	....	....	....	....
	Bridgeport	AHL	36	12	21	1	2063	120	0	3.49	....	....	....	....	....	....	....
2011-12	Bridgeport	AHL	3	0	2	0	149	7	0	2.82	....	....	....	....	....	....	....
	KalPa Kuopio	Finland	25	13	5	4	1382	53	5	2.30	6	3	2	323	12	2	2.23
2012-13	KalPa Kuopio	Finland	49	21	15	13	2953	101	7	2.05	5	1	4	295	10	1	2.03
	NHL Totals		**4**	**2**	**1**	**0**	**208**	**15**	**0**	**4.33**	....	....	....	....	....	....	....

Signed as a free agent by **Kuopio** (Finland), November 12, 2011.

KOSTENKO, Sergey (kawz-TEHN-koh, sair-GAY) WSH

Goaltender. Catches left. 5'11", 187 lbs. Born, Novokuznetsk, Russia, September 17, 1992.
(Washington's 10th choice, 203rd overall, in 2012 Entry Draft).

			Regular Season								Playoffs						
Season	Club	League	GP	W	L	O/T	Mins	GA	SO	Avg	GP	W	L	Mins	GA	SO	Avg
2009-10	Novokuznetsk Jr.	Russia-Jr.	19	6	9	0	950	54	1	3.41	....	....	....	....	....	....	....
2010-11	Novokuznetsk Jr.	Russia-Jr.	28	6	18	0	1551	75	0	2.90	....	....	....	....	....	....	....
2011-12	Novokuznetsk Jr.	Russia-Jr.	40	15	11	0	1995	99	4	2.98	7	3	3	427	15	1	2.11
2012-13	Reading Royals	ECHL	6	2	1	2	314	21	0	4.01	....	....	....	....	....	....	....
	Ontario Reign	ECHL	3	2	1	0	179	9	0	3.02	....	....	....	....	....	....	....

• Loaned to **Ontario** (ECHL) by **Washington** (Reading-ECHL), February 22, 2013.

KUEMPER, Darcy (KEHM-puhr, DAHR-see) MIN

Goaltender. Catches left. 6'5", 205 lbs. Born, Saskatoon, Sask., May 5, 1990.
(Minnesota's 5th choice, 161st overall, in 2009 Entry Draft).

			Regular Season								Playoffs						
Season	Club	League	GP	W	L	O/T	Mins	GA	SO	Avg	GP	W	L	Mins	GA	SO	Avg
2006-07	Sask. Contacts	SMHL	25	8	14	3	1489	87	1	3.51	4	1	3	200	19	0	5.70
	Spokane Chiefs	WHL	....	....	....	....	....	....	....	....	1	0	0	0	0	0	0.00
2007-08	Saskatoon Blazers	SMHL	26	15	7	4	1578	62	1	2.36	13	7	6	781	34	1	2.61
2008-09	Red Deer Rebels	WHL	55	21	25	8	3167	156	3	2.96	....	....	....	....	....	....	....
2009-10	Red Deer Rebels	WHL	61	28	23	4	3234	147	3	2.73	2	0	2	61	6	0	5.90
	Houston Aeros	AHL	4	2	1	0	199	8	0	2.41	....	....	....	....	....	....	....
2010-11	Red Deer Rebels	WHL	62	*45	12	5	3685	114	*13	*1.86	7	4	3	403	19	0	2.83
2011-12	Houston Aeros	AHL	19	6	6	4	1070	42	1	2.36	....	....	....	....	....	....	....
	Ontario Reign	ECHL	8	7	1	0	484	14	0	1.74	....	....	....	....	....	....	....
2012-13	Houston Aeros	AHL	21	13	8	0	1210	38	4	1.88	2	1	1	119	3	1	1.51
	Orlando	ECHL	3	0	2	1	184	8	0	2.61	....	....	....	....	....	....	....
	Minnesota	**NHL**	**6**	**1**	**2**	**0**	**288**	**10**	**0**	**2.08**	**2**	**0**	**0**	**73**	**4**	**0**	**3.29**
	NHL Totals		**6**	**1**	**2**	**0**	**288**	**10**	**0**	**2.08**	**2**	**0**	**0**	**73**	**4**	**0**	**3.29**

WHL East Second All-Star Team (2010) • WHL East First All-Star Team (2011) • Canadian Major Junior Goaltender of the Year (2011)

LaBARBERA, Jason (luh-BAHR-buhr-ah, JAY-suhn) EDM

Goaltender. Catches left. 6'3", 234 lbs. Born, Burnaby, B.C., January 18, 1980.
(NY Rangers' 3rd choice, 66th overall, in 1998 Entry Draft).

			Regular Season								Playoffs						
Season	Club	League	GP	W	L	O/T	Mins	GA	SO	Avg	GP	W	L	Mins	GA	SO	Avg
1995-96	Prince George	Minor-BC	31	....	....	....	1860	83	0	2.68	....	....	....	....	....	....	....
1996-97	Tri-City Americans	WHL	2	1	0	0	63	4	0	3.81	....	....	....	....	....	....	....
	Portland	WHL	9	5	1	1	443	18	0	2.44	....	....	....	....	....	....	....
1997-98	Portland	WHL	23	18	4	0	1305	72	1	3.31	....	....	....	....	....	....	....
1998-99	Portland	WHL	51	18	23	9	2991	170	4	3.41	4	0	4	252	19	0	4.52
99-2000	Portland	WHL	34	8	24	2	2005	123	1	3.68	....	....	....	....	....	....	....
	Spokane Chiefs	WHL	21	12	6	2	1146	50	0	2.62	9	6	1	435	18	1	2.48
2000-01	**NY Rangers**	**NHL**	**1**	**0**	**0**	**0**	**10**	**0**	**0**	**0.00**	....	....	....	....	....	....	....
	Hartford Wolf Pack	AHL	4	1	1	0	156	12	0	4.61	....	....	....	....	....	....	....
	Charlotte Checkers	ECHL	35	18	10	7	2100	112	1	3.20	2	1	1	143	5	0	2.09
2001-02	Hartford Wolf Pack	AHL	20	7	11	1	1058	55	0	3.12	....	....	....	....	....	....	....
	Charlotte Checkers	ECHL	13	9	3	1	744	29	0	2.34	4	2	2	212	12	0	3.39
2002-03	Hartford Wolf Pack	AHL	46	18	17	6	2452	105	2	2.57	2	0	2	117	6	0	3.07
2003-04	**NY Rangers**	**NHL**	**4**	**1**	**2**	**0**	**198**	**16**	**0**	**4.85**	....	....	....	....	....	....	....
	Hartford Wolf Pack	AHL	59	34	9	9	3393	90	*13	1.59	16	11	5	1043	30	*3	*1.73
2004-05	Hartford Wolf Pack	AHL	53	31	16	2	2937	90	6	1.84	4	1	3	238	9	0	2.27
2005-06	**Los Angeles**	**NHL**	**29**	**11**	**9**	**2**	**1433**	**69**	**1**	**2.89**	....	....	....	....	....	....	....
	Manchester	AHL	3	1	1	1	185	10	0	3.25	....	....	....	....	....	....	....
2006-07	Manchester	AHL	*62	*39	20	1	*3619	133	*7	2.21	13	6	7	824	38	1	2.77
2007-08	**Los Angeles**	**NHL**	**45**	**17**	**23**	**2**	**2421**	**121**	**1**	**3.00**	....	....	....	....	....	....	....
2008-09	**Los Angeles**	**NHL**	**19**	**5**	**8**	**4**	**995**	**47**	**2**	**2.83**	....	....	....	....	....	....	....
	Vancouver	**NHL**	**9**	**3**	**2**	**2**	**451**	**20**	**0**	**2.66**	....	....	....	....	....	....	....
2009-10	**Phoenix**	**NHL**	**17**	**8**	**5**	**1**	**928**	**33**	**0**	**2.13**	....	....	....	....	....	....	....
2010-11	**Phoenix**	**NHL**	**17**	**7**	**6**	**3**	**883**	**48**	**2**	**3.26**	....	....	....	....	....	....	....
2011-12	**Phoenix**	**NHL**	**19**	**3**	**9**	**3**	**1015**	**43**	**0**	**2.54**	....	....	....	....	....	....	....
2012-13	**Phoenix**	**NHL**	**15**	**4**	**6**	**2**	**726**	**32**	**0**	**2.64**	....	....	....	....	....	....	....
	NHL Totals		**175**	**59**	**70**	**19**	**9060**	**429**	**6**	**2.84**	....	....	....	....	....	....	....

AHL First All-Star Team (2004, 2007) • Aldege "Baz" Bastien Memorial Award (AHL - Outstanding Goaltender) (2004, 2007) • Les Cunningham Award (AHL - MVP) (2004) • Harry "Hap" Holmes Memorial Trophy (AHL - fewest goals against) (2005) (shared with Steve Valiquette) • Harry "Hap" Holmes Memorial Trophy (AHL - fewest goals against) (2007)

Signed as a free agent by **Los Angeles**, August 2, 2005. Traded to **Vancouver** by **Los Angeles** for Vancouver's 7th round choice (later traded to Atlanta – Atlanta selected Jordan Samuels-Thomas) in 2009 Entry Draft, December 30, 2008. Signed as a free agent by **Phoenix**, July 1, 2009. Signed as a free agent by **Edmonton**, July 5, 2013.

LACK, Eddie (LAK, EH-dee) VAN

Goaltender. Catches left. 6'4", 187 lbs. Born, Norrtalje, Sweden, January 5, 1988.

			Regular Season								Playoffs						
Season	Club	League	GP	W	L	O/T	Mins	GA	SO	Avg	GP	W	L	Mins	GA	SO	Avg
2004-05	Djurgarden U18	Swe-U18	9	....	....	....	527	21	1	2.39	3	....	....	140	6	0	2.57
	Djurgarden Jr.	Swe-Jr.	1	....	....	....	60	6	0	6.00	....	....	....	....	....	....	....
2005-06	Djurgarden Jr.	Swe-Jr.	23	....	....	....	1400	49	3	2.10	....	....	....	....	....	....	....
2006-07	Leksands IF Jr.	Swe-Jr.	30	....	....	....	1782	85	0	2.86	....	....	....	....	....	....	....
	Leksands IF	Sweden-2	3	....	....	....	137	7	0	3.06	....	....	....	....	....	....	....
2007-08	Leksands IF Jr.	Swe-Jr.	18	....	....	....	1077	47	4	2.62	3	....	....	179	8	0	2.68
	Leksands IF	Sweden-2	26	....	....	....	1530	50	4	1.96	....	....	....	....	....	....	....
2008-09	Leksands IF Jr.	Swe-Jr.	2	....	....	....	120	4	1	2.00	....	....	....	....	....	....	....
	Leksands IF	Sweden-2	38	....	....	....	2260	78	4	2.07	....	....	....	....	....	....	....
2009-10	Brynas IF Gavle Jr.	Swe-Jr.	6	....	....	....	359	21	0	....	....	....	....	....	....	....	....
	Brynas IF Gavle	Sweden	14	....	....	....	809	36	0	2.67	2	....	....	79	2	0	1.53
2010-11	Manitoba Moose	AHL	53	28	21	4	3135	118	5	2.26	12	6	5	752	25	2	1.99
2011-12	Chicago Wolves	AHL	46	21	20	3	2703	104	4	2.31	5	2	2	304	11	0	2.17
2012-13	Chicago Wolves	AHL	13	7	4	1	760	38	1	3.00	....	....	....	....	....	....	....

AHL All-Rookie Team (2011)

Signed as a free agent by **Vancouver**, April 6, 2010.

LAGACE, Maxime (luh-ga-SEE, max-EEM) DAL

Goaltender. Catches left. 6'1", 176 lbs. Born, St-Augustin, Que., January 12, 1993.

			Regular Season								Playoffs						
Season	Club	League	GP	W	L	O/T	Mins	GA	SO	Avg	GP	W	L	Mins	GA	SO	Avg
2008-09	Quebec Typhons	Minor-QU					Statistics not available										
	St-Francois Blizzard	QAAA	8	1	1	2	346	27	0	4.68	....	....	....	....	....	....	....
2009-10	St-Francois Blizzard	QAAA	22	18	3	1	1256	39	1	1.86	1	1	0	60	5	0	5.00
2010-11	P.E.I. Rocket	QMJHL	18	8	4	0	870	52	1	3.59	....	....	....	....	....	....	....
2011-12	P.E.I. Rocket	QMJHL	56	12	34	5	2912	219	1	4.51	....	....	....	....	....	....	....
2012-13	P.E.I. Rocket	QMJHL	33	13	12	1	1571	106	1	4.05	1	0	0	27	1	0	2.19

Signed as a free agent by **Dallas**, July 23, 2012.

LANGHAMER, Marek (lang-HAHM-uhr, MAHR-ehk) PHX

Goaltender. Catches left. 6'2", 185 lbs. Born, Pisek, Czech Rep., July 22, 1994.
(Phoenix's 7th choice, 184th overall, in 2012 Entry Draft).

			Regular Season								Playoffs						
Season	Club	League	GP	W	L	O/T	Mins	GA	SO	Avg	GP	W	L	Mins	GA	SO	Avg
2008-09	HC Pardubice U17	CzR-U17	29	....	....	....	1433	87	0	3.64	6	....	....	352	12	0	2.05
2009-10	HC Pardubice U18	CzR-U18	35	....	....	....	2031	83	4	2.45	6	....	....	327	14	1	2.57
	HC Pardubice Jr.	CzRep-Jr.	2	....	....	....	30	0	0	0.00	....	....	....	....	....	....	....
2010-11	HC Pardubice U18	CzR-U18	17	....	....	....	1028	43	1	2.51	5	....	....	320	12	0	2.25
	HC Pardubice Jr.	CzRep-Jr.	37	....	....	....	2162	113	3	3.14	....	....	....	....	....	....	....
	HC Chrudim	CzRep-2	4	....	....	....	172	5	0	1.74	....	....	....	....	....	....	....
2011-12	HC Pardubice Jr.	CzRep-Jr.	33	....	....	....	1916	105	0	3.29	....	....	....	....	....	....	....
2012-13	Medicine Hat	WHL	30	15	12	1	1450	83	2	3.44	1	0	0	38	5	0	7.83

LAWSON, Nathan
(LAW-suhn, NAY-thuhn) **OTT**

Goaltender. Catches left. 6'2", 203 lbs. Born, Calgary, Alta., September 29, 1983.

			Regular Season								Playoffs						
Season	Club	League	GP	W	L	O/T	Mins	GA	SO	Avg	GP	W	L	Mins	GA	SO	Avg
2004-05	Alaska Anchorage	WCHA	27	7	15	3	1482	82	1	3.32	....	....	....	....	....	....	....
2005-06	Alaska Anchorage	WCHA	21	4	11	3	1063	61	1	3.44	....	....	....	....	....	....	....
2006-07	Alaska Anchorage	WCHA	27	10	15	2	1523	77	0	3.03	....	....	....	....	....	....	....
2007-08	Phoenix	ECHL	5	3	2	0	279	14	1	3.01	....	....	....	....	....	....	....
	Utah Grizzlies	ECHL	24	14	7	1	1390	67	1	2.89	10	5	4	543	26	2	2.87
2008-09	Bridgeport	AHL	31	19	9	2	1723	62	2	2.16	2	0	2	123	8	0	3.89
	Utah Grizzlies	ECHL	3	2	0	0	158	6	0	2.28	....	....	....	....	....	....	....
2009-10	Bridgeport	AHL	36	16	16	3	2121	89	1	2.52	1	0	0	46	2	0	2.63
2010-11	**NY Islanders**	**NHL**	**10**	**1**	**4**	**2**	**384**	**26**	**0**	**4.06**	....	....	....	....	....	....	....
	Bridgeport	AHL	16	6	5	4	953	46	0	2.90	....	....	....	....	....	....	....
2011-12	Hamilton Bulldogs	AHL	44	19	17	4	2402	103	5	2.57	....	....	....	....	....	....	....
2012-13	Binghamton	AHL	23	12	6	2	1258	46	2	2.19	3	0	3	165	8	0	2.60
	Elmira Jackals	ECHL	1	1	0	0	60	2	0	2.00	....	....	....	....	....	....	....
	NHL Totals		**10**	**1**	**4**	**2**	**384**	**26**	**0**	**4.06**	....	....	....	....	....	....	....

AHL All-Rookie Team (2009)

Signed as a free agent by **NY Islanders**, March 2, 2008. Signed as a free agent by **Montreal**, July 5, 2011. Signed as a free agent by **Ottawa**, July 16, 2012.

LEE, Mike
(LEE, MIGHK) **PHX**

Goaltender. Catches left. 6'1", 190 lbs. Born, Fargo, ND, October 5, 1990.
(Phoenix's 3rd choice, 91st overall, in 2009 Entry Draft).

			Regular Season								Playoffs						
Season	Club	League	GP	W	L	O/T	Mins	GA	SO	Avg	GP	W	L	Mins	GA	SO	Avg
2006-07	Roseau Rams	High-MN	12	12	0	0	612	9	6	0.75	....	....	....	....	....	....	....
2007-08	Roseau Rams	High-MN	29	27	2	0	1482	32	12	1.10	1	0	0	16	0	0	0.00
2008-09	Fargo Force	USHL	48	26	15	4	2745	110	3	2.40	10	7	3	546	24	*1	2.64
2009-10	St. Cloud State	WCHA	26	12	9	3	1477	69	2	2.80	....	....	....	....	....	....	....
2010-11	St. Cloud State	WCHA	32	12	14	4	1879	86	1	2.75	....	....	....	....	....	....	....
2011-12	St. Cloud State	WCHA	16	8	6	2	969	36	1	2.23	....	....	....	....	....	....	....
2012-13	Portland Pirates	AHL	16	9	6	0	837	38	0	2.72	....	....	....	....	....	....	....
	Gwinnett	ECHL	28	14	12	1	1580	62	2	2.35	....	....	....	....	....	....	....

USHL All-Rookie Team (2009) • USHL Goaltender of the Year (2009)

LEGGIO, David
(LEH-JEE-oh, DAY-vihd) **WSH**

Goaltender. Catches left. 6', 180 lbs. Born, Buffalo, NY, July 31, 1984.

			Regular Season								Playoffs						
Season	Club	League	GP	W	L	O/T	Mins	GA	SO	Avg	GP	W	L	Mins	GA	SO	Avg
2003-04	Capital District	EJHL	42	25	10	6	....	....	4	2.80	....	....	....	....	....	....	....
2004-05	Clarkson Knights	ECAC	5	2	1	0	182	9	0	2.97	....	....	....	....	....	....	....
2005-06	Clarkson Knights	ECAC	23	11	9	3	1446	62	1	2.57	....	....	....	....	....	....	....
2006-07	Clarkson Knights	ECAC	37	24	7	5	2167	78	2	2.16	....	....	....	....	....	....	....
2007-08	Clarkson Knights	ECAC	38	22	12	4	2211	81	5	2.20	....	....	....	....	....	....	....
	Binghamton	AHL	1	0	1	0	30	2	0	4.06	....	....	....	....	....	....	....
2008-09	Albany River Rats	AHL	1	0	1	0	60	7	0	7.00	....	....	....	....	....	....	....
	Florida Everblades	ECHL	39	27	7	3	2284	86	4	2.26	11	6	5	734	30	0	2.45
2009-10	TPS Turku	Finland	30	12	13	3	1598	78	1	2.93	7	5	2	419	11	1	1.57
2010-11	Portland Pirates	AHL	36	22	12	0	1993	93	3	2.80	9	5	4	510	27	0	3.18
2011-12	Rochester	AHL	54	28	24	2	3243	142	2	2.63	3	0	3	175	11	0	3.76
2012-13	Rochester	AHL	*64	*38	24	1	*3800	162	4	2.56	2	0	2	125	8	0	3.84

ECAC Second All-Star Team (2008)

Signed as a free agent by **TPS Turku** (Finland), June 4, 2009. Signed as a free agent by **Buffalo**, November 12, 2010. Signed as a free agent by **Washington**, July 8, 2013.

LEHNER, Robin
(LEH-nuhr, RAW-bihn) **OTT**

Goaltender. Catches left. 6'4", 210 lbs. Born, Goteborg, Sweden, July 24, 1991.
(Ottawa's 3rd choice, 46th overall, in 2009 Entry Draft).

			Regular Season								Playoffs						
Season	Club	League	GP	W	L	O/T	Mins	GA	SO	Avg	GP	W	L	Mins	GA	SO	Avg
2007-08	Frolunda U18	Swe-U18	19	....	....	....	1147	34	6	1.78	4	....	....	243	15	0	3.70
2008-09	Frolunda U18	Swe-U18	2	....	....	....	117	5	0	2.56	7	....	....	438	19	0	2.60
	Frolunda Jr.	Swe-Jr.	22	....	....	....	1318	67	1	3.05	1	....	....	58	3	0	3.08
2009-10	Sault Ste. Marie	OHL	47	27	13	3	2574	120	*5	2.80	5	1	4	279	20	0	4.30
	Binghamton	AHL	2	2	0	0	120	6	0	3.00	....	....	....	....	....	....	....
2010-11	**Ottawa**	**NHL**	**8**	**1**	**4**	**0**	**341**	**20**	**0**	**3.52**	....	....	....	....	....	....	....
	Binghamton	AHL	22	10	8	2	1246	56	3	2.70	19	*14	4	1112	39	*3	2.10
2011-12	**Ottawa**	**NHL**	**5**	**3**	**2**	**0**	**299**	**10**	**1**	**2.01**	....	....	....	....	....	....	....
	Binghamton	AHL	40	13	22	1	2192	119	2	3.26	....	....	....	....	....	....	....
2012-13	Binghamton	AHL	31	18	10	2	1841	65	3	2.12	....	....	....	....	....	....	....
	Ottawa	**NHL**	**12**	**5**	**3**	**4**	**735**	**27**	**0**	**2.20**	**2**	**0**	**1**	**49**	**2**	**0**	**2.45**
	NHL Totals		**25**	**9**	**9**	**4**	**1375**	**57**	**1**	**2.49**	**2**	**0**	**1**	**49**	**2**	**0**	**2.45**

Jack A. Butterfield Trophy (AHL – Playoff MVP) (2011)

LEHTONEN, Kari
(LEH-tuh-nehn, KAH-ree) **DAL**

Goaltender. Catches left. 6'4", 217 lbs. Born, Helsinki, Finland, November 16, 1983.
(Atlanta's 1st choice, 2nd overall, in 2002 Entry Draft).

			Regular Season								Playoffs						
Season	Club	League	GP	W	L	O/T	Mins	GA	SO	Avg	GP	W	L	Mins	GA	SO	Avg
1998-99	Jokerit U18	Fin-U18	2	....	....	....	....	....	....	....	4	2	2	240	7	0	1.75
99-2000	Jokerit Helsinki Jr.	Fin-Jr.	33	21	9	3	1974	86	2	2.61	12	9	3	758	14	4	1.11
2000-01	Jokerit U18	Fin-U18	....	....	....	....	....	....	....	....	6	....	....	....	....	....	....
	Jokerit Helsinki Jr.	Fin-Jr.	31	20	9	1	1799	71	3	2.37	1	0	1	54	4	0	4.44
	Jokerit Helsinki	Finland	4	3	1	0	189	6	0	1.90	....	....	....	....	....	....	....
2001-02	Jokerit Helsinki Jr.	Fin-Jr.	6	5	1	0	360	11	1	1.83	....	....	....	....	....	....	....
	Jokerit Helsinki	Finland	23	13	5	2	1242	37	4	1.79	11	8	2	623	18	3	1.73
2002-03	Jokerit Helsinki	Finland	45	23	14	6	2634	87	5	1.98	10	6	4	626	17	2	1.63
2003-04	**Atlanta**	**NHL**	**4**	**4**	**0**	**0**	**240**	**5**	**1**	**1.25**	....	....	....	....	....	....	....
	Chicago Wolves	AHL	39	20	14	2	2192	88	3	2.41	10	6	4	663	23	1	2.08
2004-05	Chicago Wolves	AHL	57	38	17	2	3378	128	5	2.27	16	10	6	983	28	2	*1.71
2005-06	**Atlanta**	**NHL**	**38**	**20**	**15**	**0**	**2166**	**106**	**2**	**2.94**	....	....	....	....	....	....	....
	Finland	Olympics					DID NOT PLAY – INJURED										
2006-07	**Atlanta**	**NHL**	**68**	**34**	**24**	**9**	**3934**	**183**	**4**	**2.79**	**2**	**0**	**2**	**118**	**11**	**0**	**5.59**
2007-08	**Atlanta**	**NHL**	**48**	**17**	**22**	**5**	**2707**	**131**	**4**	**2.90**	....	....	....	....	....	....	....
	Chicago Wolves	AHL	2	2	0	0	124	4	0	1.93	....	....	....	....	....	....	....
2008-09	**Atlanta**	**NHL**	**46**	**19**	**22**	**3**	**2624**	**134**	**3**	**3.06**	....	....	....	....	....	....	....
2009-10	**Dallas**	**NHL**	**12**	**6**	**4**	**0**	**663**	**31**	**0**	**2.81**	....	....	....	....	....	....	....
	Chicago Wolves	AHL	4	1	1	2	247	11	0	2.67	....	....	....	....	....	....	....
2010-11	**Dallas**	**NHL**	**69**	**34**	**24**	**11**	**4119**	**175**	**3**	**2.55**	....	....	....	....	....	....	....
2011-12	**Dallas**	**NHL**	**59**	**32**	**22**	**4**	**3497**	**136**	**4**	**2.33**	....	....	....	....	....	....	....
2012-13	**Dallas**	**NHL**	**36**	**15**	**14**	**3**	**1986**	**88**	**1**	**2.66**	....	....	....	....	....	....	....
	NHL Totals		**380**	**181**	**147**	**35**	**21936**	**989**	**22**	**2.71**	**2**	**0**	**2**	**118**	**11**	**0**	**5.59**

AHL Second All-Star Team (2005)

• Missed majority of 2009-10 due to off-season back surgery. Traded to **Dallas** by **Atlanta** for Ivan Vishnevskiy and Dallas' 4th round choice (Ivan Telegin) in 2010 Entry Draft, February 9, 2010.

LEIGHTON, Michael
(LAY-tohn, MIGH-kuhl)

Goaltender. Catches left. 6'3", 186 lbs. Born, Petrolia, Ont., May 19, 1981.
(Chicago's 5th choice, 165th overall, in 1999 Entry Draft).

			Regular Season								Playoffs						
Season	Club	League	GP	W	L	O/T	Mins	GA	SO	Avg	GP	W	L	Mins	GA	SO	Avg
1997-98	Petrolia Jets	ON-Jr.B	30	....	....	....	1583	87	2	3.30	....	....	....	....	....	....	....
1998-99	Windsor Spitfires	OHL	28	4	15	9	1390	112	0	4.83	3	0	1	81	10	0	7.43
99-2000	Windsor Spitfires	OHL	42	17	17	2	2272	118	1	3.12	12	5	6	617	32	0	3.11
2000-01	Windsor Spitfires	OHL	54	32	13	5	3035	138	2	2.73	9	4	5	519	27	1	3.12
2001-02	Norfolk Admirals	AHL	52	27	16	8	3114	111	6	2.14	4	1	2	238	8	0	2.02
2002-03	**Chicago**	**NHL**	**8**	**2**	**3**	**2**	**447**	**21**	**1**	**2.82**	....	....	....	....	....	....	....
	Norfolk Admirals	AHL	36	18	13	5	2184	91	4	2.50	4	3	1	240	7	1	1.75
2003-04	**Chicago**	**NHL**	**34**	**6**	**18**	**8**	**1988**	**99**	**2**	**2.99**	....	....	....	....	....	....	....
	Norfolk Admirals	AHL	18	10	7	1	1081	33	1	1.83	4	2	1	212	2	2	0.57
2004-05	Norfolk Admirals	AHL	41	20	16	3	2319	78	7	2.02	....	....	....	....	....	....	....
2005-06	Rochester	AHL	40	15	22	1	2318	124	2	3.21	....	....	....	....	....	....	....
2006-07	Portland Pirates	AHL	16	8	6	1	962	37	2	2.31	....	....	....	....	....	....	....
	Nashville	**NHL**	**1**	**0**	**0**	**0**	**20**	**2**	**0**	**6.00**	....	....	....	....	....	....	....
	Philadelphia	**NHL**	**4**	**2**	**2**	**0**	**195**	**12**	**0**	**3.69**	....	....	....	....	....	....	....
	Philadelphia	AHL	5	2	0	2	270	7	0	1.56	....	....	....	....	....	....	....
2007-08	**Carolina**	**NHL**	**3**	**1**	**1**	**0**	**158**	**7**	**0**	**2.66**	....	....	....	....	....	....	....
	Albany River Rats	AHL	58	28	25	4	3451	121	*7	2.10	7	3	4	510	10	*2	*1.18
2008-09	**Carolina**	**NHL**	**19**	**6**	**7**	**2**	**1029**	**50**	**0**	**2.92**	....	....	....	....	....	....	....
2009-10	**Carolina**	**NHL**	**7**	**1**	**4**	**0**	**350**	**25**	**0**	**4.29**	....	....	....	....	....	....	....
	Philadelphia	**NHL**	**27**	**16**	**5**	**2**	**1449**	**60**	**1**	**2.48**	**14**	**8**	**3**	**757**	**31**	***3**	***2.46**
2010-11	**Philadelphia**	**NHL**	**1**	**1**	**0**	**0**	**60**	**4**	**0**	**4.00**	**2**	**0**	**1**	**70**	**4**	**0**	**3.43**
	Adirondack	AHL	30	14	12	3	1783	66	5	2.22	....	....	....	....	....	....	....
2011-12	Adirondack	AHL	*56	28	26	1	3237	139	2	2.58	....	....	....	....	....	....	....
2012-13	**Philadelphia**	**NHL**	**1**	**0**	**1**	**0**	**59**	**5**	**0**	**5.08**	....	....	....	....	....	....	....
	Adirondack	AHL	2	1	1	0	119	4	0	2.02	....	....	....	....	....	....	....
	NHL Totals		**105**	**35**	**41**	**14**	**5755**	**285**	**4**	**2.97**	**16**	**8**	**4**	**827**	**35**	**3**	**2.54**

AHL All-Rookie Team (2002) • AHL First All-Star Team (2008) • Aldege "Baz" Bastien Memorial Award (AHL – Outstanding Goaltender) (2008)

Traded to **Buffalo** by **Chicago** for Milan Bartovic, October 4, 2005. Signed as a free agent by **Anaheim**, July 13, 2006. Claimed on waivers by **Nashville** from **Anaheim**, November 27, 2006. Claimed on waivers by **Philadelphia** from **Nashville**, January 11, 2007. Claimed on waivers by **Montreal** from **Philadelphia**, February 27, 2007. Traded to **Carolina** by **Montreal** for Carolina's 7th round choice (Scott Kishel) in 2007 Entry Draft, June 23, 2007. Claimed on waivers by **Philadelphia** from **Carolina**, December 15, 2009. Traded to **Columbus** by **Philadelphia** with Philadelphia's 3rd round choice in 2015 Entry Draft for Steve Mason, April 3, 2013.

LIEUWEN, Nathan
(l'YEW-uhn, NAY-thun) **BUF**

Goaltender. Catches left. 6'5", 190 lbs. Born, Abbotsford, B.C., August 8, 1991.
(Buffalo's 5th choice, 167th overall, in 2011 Entry Draft).

			Regular Season								Playoffs						
Season	Club	League	GP	W	L	O/T	Mins	GA	SO	Avg	GP	W	L	Mins	GA	SO	Avg
2007-08	Westside Warriors	BCHL	13	9	2	0	710	23	0	1.94	3	0	2	139	10	0	4.32
	Kootenay Ice	WHL	3	1	1	0	184	10	0	3.26	....	....	....	....	....	....	....
2008-09	Kootenay Ice	WHL	37	14	12	2	1915	94	3	2.95	....	....	....	....	....	....	....
2009-10	Kootenay Ice	WHL	26	10	10	0	1244	64	0	3.09	3	0	1	125	4	0	1.92
2010-11	Kootenay Ice	WHL	55	33	16	4	3098	144	3	2.79	19	*16	3	1178	44	*3	*2.24
2011-12	Kootenay Ice	WHL	57	27	20	8	3340	139	3	2.50	4	0	4	238	14	0	3.53
2012-13	Greenville	ECHL	27	14	10	2	1598	78	1	2.93	....	....	....	....	....	....	....
	Rochester	AHL	4	1	2	0	204	9	1	2.65	....	....	....	....	....	....	....

WHL East Second All-Star Team (2012)

• Re-assigned to **Greenville** (ECHL) by **Buffalo**, October 10, 2013.

LINDBACK, Anders
(LIHND-bak, AN-duhrs) **T.B.**

Goaltender. Catches left. 6'6", 210 lbs. Born, Gavle, Sweden, May 3, 1988.
(Nashville's 7th choice, 207th overall, in 2008 Entry Draft).

			Regular Season								Playoffs						
Season	Club	League	GP	W	L	O/T	Mins	GA	SO	Avg	GP	W	L	Mins	GA	SO	Avg
2003-04	Brynas U18	Swe-U18	3	....	....	....	178	13	0	4.38	....	....	....	....	....	....	....
2004-05	Brynas U18	Swe-U18	49	....	....	....	2940	108	7	2.20	....	....	....	....	....	....	....
2005-06	Brynas U18	Swe-U18	11	....	....	....	666	36	2	3.24	....	....	....	....	....	....	....
	Brynas IF Gavle Jr.	Swe-Jr.	5	....	....	....	257	7	2	1.64	....	....	....	....	....	....	....
2006-07	Brynas IF Gavle Jr.	Swe-Jr.	36	....	....	....	2143	81	5	2.27	3	....	....	180	6	0	2.00
2007-08	Almtuna	Sweden-2	18	....	....	....	1034	53	0	3.07	....	....	....	....	....	....	....
2008-09	Brynas IF Gavle Jr.	Swe-Jr.	3	....	....	....	179	7	0	2.35	....	....	....	....	....	....	....
	Brynas IF Gavle	Sweden	24	....	....	....	1332	57	1	2.57	3	....	....	177	7	0	2.37
2009-10	Timra IK	Sweden	42	....	....	....	2537	104	3	2.46	5	....	....	306	15	0	2.94
2010-11	**Nashville**	**NHL**	**22**	**11**	**5**	**2**	**1131**	**49**	**2**	**2.60**	**1**	**0**	**0**	**13**	**0**	**0**	**0.00**
	Milwaukee	AHL	4	2	2	0	241	11	0	2.73	....	....	....	....	....	....	....
2011-12	**Nashville**	**NHL**	**16**	**5**	**8**	**0**	**792**	**32**	**0**	**2.42**	....	....	....	....	....	....	....
	Milwaukee	AHL	2	1	1	0	119	7	0	3.53	....	....	....	....	....	....	....
2012-13	Ilves Tampere	Finland	13	3	6	4	797	31	3	2.33	....	....	....	....	....	....	....
	Tampa Bay	**NHL**	**24**	**10**	**10**	**1**	**1304**	**63**	**0**	**2.90**	....	....	....	....	....	....	....
	NHL Totals		**62**	**26**	**23**	**3**	**3227**	**144**	**2**	**2.68**	**1**	**0**	**0**	**13**	**0**	**0**	**0.00**

Traded to **Tampa Bay** by **Nashville** with Kyle Wilson and Nashville's 7th round choice (Nikita Gusev) in 2012 Entry Draft for Sebastian Caron, Minnesota's 2nd round choice (previously acquired, Nashville selected Pontus Aberg) in 2012 Entry Draft, Philadelphia's 2nd round choice (previously acquired, Nashville selected Colton Sissons) in 2012 Entry Draft and Tampa Bay's 3rd round choice (Jonathan-Ismael Diaby) in 2013 Entry Draft, June 15, 2012. Signed as a free agent by **Ilves Tampere** (Finland), October 27, 2012.

LUNDQVIST, Henrik
(LUHND-kvihst, HEHN-rihk) **NYR**

Goaltender. Catches left. 6'1", 188 lbs. Born, Are, Sweden, March 2, 1982.
(NY Rangers' 7th choice, 205th overall, in 2000 Entry Draft).

			Regular Season								Playoffs						
Season	Club	League	GP	W	L	O/T	Mins	GA	SO	Avg	GP	W	L	Mins	GA	SO	Avg
1998-99	V.Frolunda Jr.	Swe-Jr.	35	....	....	....	2100	95	0	2.73	....	....	....	....	....	....	....
99-2000	V.Frolunda Jr.	Swe-Jr.	30	....	....	....	1726	73	0	2.54	5	4	1	300	7	2	1.40
2000-01	V.Frolunda U18	Swe-U18	2	....	....	....	120	5	0	2.50	3	2	1	182	5	0	1.62
	V.Frolunda Jr.	Swe-Jr.	19	....	....	....	1140	50	2	2.64	....	....	....	....	....	....	....
	IF Molndal Hockey	Sweden-2	7	....	....	....	420	29	0	4.22	....	....	....	....	....	....	....
	V.Frolunda	Sweden	4	....	....	....	190	11	0	3.47	....	....	....	....	....	....	....
2001-02	V.Frolunda	Sweden	20	....	....	....	1152	52	2	2.71	8	8	0	489	18	*2	2.21
	V.Frolunda Jr.	Swe-Jr.	1	1	0	0	60	4	0	4.00	....	....	....	....	....	....	....
2002-03	V.Frolunda	Sweden	28	....	....	....	1650	40	*6	*1.45	12	....	....	739	26	*2	2.11
	V.Frolunda Jr.	Swe-Jr.	1	1	0	0	60	4	0	4.00	....	....	....	....	....	....	....
2003-04	V.Frolunda	Sweden	*48	....	....	....	*2897	105	7	2.17	10	....	....	610	20	0	1.97
2004-05	Frolunda	Sweden	44	*33	8	3	2642	79	*6	*1.79	*14	*12	2	854	15	*6	*1.05
2005-06	**NY Rangers**	**NHL**	**53**	**30**	**12**	**9**	**3112**	**116**	**2**	**2.24**	**3**	**0**	**3**	**177**	**13**	**0**	**4.41**
	Sweden	Olympics	6	5	1	0	360	14	0	2.33	....	....	....	....	....	....	....
2006-07	**NY Rangers**	**NHL**	**70**	**37**	**22**	**8**	**4109**	**160**	**5**	**2.34**	**10**	**6**	**4**	**637**	**22**	**1**	**2.07**
2007-08	**NY Rangers**	**NHL**	**72**	**37**	**24**	**10**	**4305**	**160**	***10**	**2.23**	**10**	**5**	**5**	**608**	**26**	**1**	**2.57**
2008-09	**NY Rangers**	**NHL**	**70**	**38**	**25**	**7**	**4153**	**168**	**3**	**2.43**	**7**	**3**	**4**	**380**	**19**	**1**	**3.00**
2009-10	**NY Rangers**	**NHL**	**73**	**35**	**27**	**10**	**4204**	**167**	**4**	**2.38**	....	....	....	....	....	....	....
	Sweden	Olympics	3	2	1	0	179	4	*2	1.34	....	....	....	....	....	....	....
2010-11	**NY Rangers**	**NHL**	**68**	**36**	**27**	**5**	**4007**	**152**	***11**	**2.28**	**5**	**1**	**4**	**346**	**13**	**0**	**2.25**
2011-12	**NY Rangers**	**NHL**	**62**	**39**	**18**	**5**	**3754**	**123**	**8**	**1.97**	**20**	**10**	**10**	**1251**	**38**	***3**	**1.82**
2012-13	**NY Rangers**	**NHL**	**43**	***24**	**16**	**3**	**2575**	**88**	**2**	**2.05**	**12**	**5**	**7**	**756**	**27**	**2**	**2.14**
	NHL Totals		**511**	**276**	**171**	**57**	**30219**	**1134**	**45**	**2.25**	**67**	**30**	**37**	**4155**	**158**	**8**	**2.28**

NHL All-Rookie Team (2006) • NHL First All-Star Team (2012) • Vezina Trophy (2012) • NHL Second All-Star Team (2013)

Played in NHL All-Star Game (2009, 2011, 2012)

LUNDSTROM, Niklas (LOOND-struhm, NIHK-luhs) ST.L.

Goaltender. Catches left. 6'2", 187 lbs. Born, Varmdo, Sweden, January 10, 1993.
(St. Louis' 6th choice, 132nd overall, in 2011 Entry Draft).

			Regular Season								Playoffs						
Season	Club	League	GP	W	L	O/T	Mins	GA	SO	Avg	GP	W	L	Mins	GA	SO	Avg
2008-09	AIK IF Solna U18	Swe-U18	8	....	....	....	465	18	0	2.32	....	....	....	....	....	....	....
2009-10	AIK IF Solna U18	Swe-U18	16	....	....	....	963	39	3	2.43	2	....	....	117	3	0	1.54
	AIK IF Solna Jr.	Swe-Jr.	17	....	....	....	939	46	3	2.94	3	....	....	190	7	0	2.22
	AIK IF Solna	Sweden-2	1	....	....	....	34	1	0	1.79	....	....	....	....	....	....	....
2010-11	AIK IF Solna U18	Swe-U18	1	....	....	....	60	3	0	3.00	6	....	....	388	16	0	2.47
	AIK IF Solna Jr.	Swe-Jr.	22	....	....	....	1260	64	1	3.05	....	....	....	....	....	....	....
	AIK IF Solna	Sweden	1	....	....	....	47	5	0	6.34	....	....	....	....	....	....	....
	Lindlovens IF	Sweden-3	2	....	....	....	128	5	0	2.35	....	....	....	....	....	....	....
2011-12	AIK Solna	Sweden	2	....	....	....	120	3	0	1.50	....	....	....	....	....	....	....
	IK Oskarshamn	Sweden-2	3	....	....	....	185	7	0	2.27	....	....	....	....	....	....	....
	AIK Solna Jr.	Swe-Jr.	31	....	....	....	1737	73	1	2.52	3	....	....	187	8	0	2.57
2012-13	AIK Solna	Sweden	14	3	9	0	754	39	0	3.10	....	....	....	....	....	....	....
	AIK Solna Jr.	Swe-Jr.	11	9	1	0	603	15	0	1.49	3	1	2	177	7	0	2.37

LUONGO, Roberto (loo-WAHN-goh, roh-BUHR-toh) VAN

Goaltender. Catches left. 6'3", 217 lbs. Born, Montreal, Que., April 4, 1979.
(NY Islanders' 1st choice, 4th overall, in 1997 Entry Draft).

			Regular Season								Playoffs						
Season	Club	League	GP	W	L	O/T	Mins	GA	SO	Avg	GP	W	L	Mins	GA	SO	Avg
1994-95	Montreal-Bourassa	QAAA	25	10	14	0	1465	94	0	3.85	....	....	....	....	....	....	....
1995-96	Val-d'Or Foreurs	QMJHL	23	6	11	4	1201	74	0	3.70	3	0	1	68	5	0	4.41
1996-97	Val-d'Or Foreurs	QMJHL	60	32	21	2	3305	171	2	3.10	13	8	5	777	44	0	3.40
1997-98	Val-d'Or Foreurs	QMJHL	54	27	20	5	3046	157	*7	3.09	*17	*14	3	*1020	37	*2	*2.18
1998-99	Val-d'Or Foreurs	QMJHL	21	6	10	2	1177	77	1	3.93	....	....	....	....	....	....	....
	Acadie-Bathurst	QMJHL	22	14	7	1	1341	74	0	3.31	*23	*16	6	*1400	64	0	2.74
99-2000	**NY Islanders**	**NHL**	**24**	**7**	**14**	**1**	**1292**	**70**	**1**	**3.25**	....	....	....	....	....	....	....
	Lowell	AHL	26	10	12	4	1517	74	1	2.93	6	3	3	359	18	0	3.01
2000-01	**Florida**	**NHL**	**47**	**12**	**24**	**7**	**2628**	**107**	**5**	**2.44**	....	....	....	....	....	....	....
	Louisville Panthers	AHL	3	1	2	0	178	10	0	3.38	....	....	....	....	....	....	....
2001-02	**Florida**	**NHL**	**58**	**16**	**33**	**4**	**3030**	**140**	**4**	**2.77**	....	....	....	....	....	....	....
2002-03	**Florida**	**NHL**	**65**	**20**	**34**	**7**	**3627**	**164**	**6**	**2.71**	....	....	....	....	....	....	....
2003-04	**Florida**	**NHL**	**72**	**25**	**33**	**14**	**4252**	**172**	**7**	**2.43**	....	....	....	....	....	....	....
2004-05							DID NOT PLAY										
2005-06	**Florida**	**NHL**	***75**	**35**	**30**	**9**	**4305**	**213**	**4**	**2.97**	....	....	....	....	....	....	....
	Canada	Olympics	2	1	1	0	119	3	0	1.51	....	....	....	....	....	....	....
2006-07	**Vancouver**	**NHL**	**76**	**47**	**22**	**6**	**4490**	**171**	**5**	**2.29**	**12**	**5**	**7**	**847**	**25**	**0**	**1.77**
2007-08	**Vancouver**	**NHL**	**73**	**35**	**29**	**9**	**4233**	**168**	**6**	**2.38**	....	....	....	....	....	....	....
2008-09	**Vancouver**	**NHL**	**54**	**33**	**13**	**7**	**3181**	**124**	**9**	**2.34**	**10**	**6**	**4**	**618**	**26**	**1**	**2.52**
2009-10	**Vancouver**	**NHL**	**68**	**40**	**22**	**4**	**3899**	**167**	**4**	**2.57**	**12**	**6**	**6**	**707**	**38**	**0**	**3.22**
	Canada	Olympics	5	5	0	0	308	9	1	1.76	....	....	....	....	....	....	....
2010-11	**Vancouver**	**NHL**	**60**	***38**	**15**	**7**	**3590**	**126**	**4**	**2.11**	***25**	**15**	**10**	**1427**	**61**	***4**	**2.56**
2011-12	**Vancouver**	**NHL**	**55**	**31**	**14**	**8**	**3162**	**127**	**5**	**2.41**	**2**	**0**	**2**	**117**	**7**	**0**	**3.59**
2012-13	**Vancouver**	**NHL**	**20**	**9**	**6**	**3**	**1197**	**51**	**2**	**2.56**	**3**	**0**	**2**	**140**	**6**	**0**	**2.57**
	NHL Totals		**747**	**348**	**289**	**86**	**42886**	**1800**	**62**	**2.52**	**64**	**32**	**31**	**3856**	**163**	**5**	**2.54**

NHL Second All-Star Team (2004, 2007) • William M. Jennings Trophy (2011) (shared with Cory Schneider)

Played in NHL All-Star Game (2004, 2007, 2009)

Traded to **Florida** by **NY Islanders** with Olli Jokinen for Mark Parrish and Oleg Kvasha, June 24, 2000. Traded to **Vancouver** by **Florida** with Lukas Krajicek and Florida's 6th round choice (Sergei Shirokov) in 2006 Entry Draft for Todd Bertuzzi, Bryan Allen and Alex Auld, June 23, 2006.

MacDONALD, Joey (MAK-DAWN-uhld, JOH-ee) CGY

Goaltender. Catches left. 6', 197 lbs. Born, Pictou, N.S., February 7, 1980.

			Regular Season								Playoffs						
Season	Club	League	GP	W	L	O/T	Mins	GA	SO	Avg	GP	W	L	Mins	GA	SO	Avg
1997-98	Halifax	QMJHL	17	3	12	0	816	54	0	3.97	3	1	2	140	15	0	6.43
1998-99	Peterborough	OHL	47	22	15	2	2483	123	3	2.97	3	0	2	145	13	0	5.38
99-2000	Peterborough	OHL	48	20	15	6	2641	125	2	2.84	5	1	4	280	16	1	3.43
2000-01	Peterborough	OHL	57	25	21	7	3284	161	1	2.94	7	3	4	426	18	0	2.54
2001-02	Toledo Storm	ECHL	38	12	15	7	2084	100	1	2.88	....	....	....	....	....	....	....
	Cincinnati	AHL	....	....	....	....	....	....	....	....	1	0	1	84	3	0	2.14
2002-03	Grand Rapids	AHL	25	14	6	0	1337	49	3	2.20	1	0	0	8	1	0	7.95
2003-04	Grand Rapids	AHL	39	22	12	3	2249	74	6	1.97	1	0	1	40	4	0	6.04
2004-05	Grand Rapids	AHL	*66	34	29	2	*3755	143	5	2.29	....	....	....	....	....	....	....
2005-06	Grand Rapids	AHL	32	17	9	2	1745	91	2	3.13	....	....	....	....	....	....	....
	Toledo Storm	ECHL	1	1	0	0	60	1	0	1.00	....	....	....	....	....	....	....
2006-07	**Detroit**	**NHL**	**8**	**1**	**5**	**1**	**468**	**27**	**0**	**3.46**	....	....	....	....	....	....	....
	Grand Rapids	AHL	2	1	1	0	123	6	0	2.93	....	....	....	....	....	....	....
	Boston	**NHL**	**7**	**2**	**2**	**1**	**358**	**16**	**0**	**2.68**	....	....	....	....	....	....	....
2007-08	**NY Islanders**	**NHL**	**2**	**0**	**1**	**1**	**120**	**6**	**0**	**3.00**	....	....	....	....	....	....	....
	Bridgeport	AHL	38	16	19	2	2266	109	2	2.89	....	....	....	....	....	....	....
2008-09	**NY Islanders**	**NHL**	**49**	**14**	**26**	**6**	**2792**	**157**	**1**	**3.37**	....	....	....	....	....	....	....
2009-10	**Toronto**	**NHL**	**6**	**1**	**4**	**0**	**319**	**17**	**0**	**3.20**	....	....	....	....	....	....	....
	Toronto Marlies	AHL	36	14	19	3	2112	112	2	3.18	....	....	....	....	....	....	....
2010-11	**Detroit**	**NHL**	**15**	**5**	**5**	**3**	**721**	**31**	**1**	**2.58**	....	....	....	....	....	....	....
	Grand Rapids	AHL	20	10	9	1	1164	54	1	2.78	....	....	....	....	....	....	....
2011-12	**Detroit**	**NHL**	**14**	**8**	**5**	**1**	**806**	**29**	**0**	**2.16**	....	....	....	....	....	....	....
	Grand Rapids	AHL	26	11	11	3	1412	62	3	2.63	....	....	....	....	....	....	....
2012-13	**Calgary**	**NHL**	**21**	**8**	**9**	**1**	**1148**	**55**	**0**	**2.87**	....	....	....	....	....	....	....
	NHL Totals		**122**	**39**	**57**	**14**	**6732**	**338**	**2**	**3.01**	....	....	....	....	....	....	....

Harry "Hap" Holmes Memorial Award (AHL – fewest goals against) (2003) (shared with Marc Lamothe)

Signed as a free agent by **Detroit**, December 21, 2001. Claimed on waivers by **Boston** from **Detroit**, February 24, 2007. Signed as a free agent by **NY Islanders**, July 7, 2007. Signed as a free agent by **Toronto**, August 10, 2009. Traded to **Anaheim** by **Toronto** for Anaheim's 7th round choice (Max Everson) in 2011 Entry Draft, March 3, 2010. Signed as a free agent by **Detroit**, July 6, 2010. Claimed on waivers by **Calgary** from **Detroit**, February 11, 2013.

MacINTYRE, Drew (MAK-ihn-tighr, DROO) TOR

Goaltender. Catches left. 6'1", 190 lbs. Born, Charlottetown, P.E.I., June 24, 1983.
(Detroit's 2nd choice, 121st overall, in 2001 Entry Draft).

			Regular Season								Playoffs						
Season	Club	League	GP	W	L	O/T	Mins	GA	SO	Avg	GP	W	L	Mins	GA	SO	Avg
1998-99	Trenton Sting	ON-Jr.A	20	....	....	....	1173	71	2	3.63	....	....	....	....	....	....	....
99-2000	Sherbrooke	QMJHL	24	10	7	2	1254	67	0	3.21	....	....	....	....	....	....	....
2000-01	Sherbrooke	QMJHL	48	17	22	3	2552	139	4	3.27	4	0	4	238	19	0	4.78
2001-02	Sherbrooke	QMJHL	55	15	34	3	3028	201	1	3.98	....	....	....	....	....	....	....
2002-03	Sherbrooke	QMJHL	*61	31	24	5	*3515	161	2	2.75	12	5	7	767	52	0	4.07
2003-04	Toledo Storm	ECHL	11	6	4	0	574	25	0	2.61	....	....	....	....	....	....	....
2004-05	Grand Rapids	AHL	24	7	8	0	1049	47	1	2.69	....	....	....	....	....	....	....
	Toledo Storm	ECHL	2	0	1	0	87	6	0	4.12	....	....	....	....	....	....	....
2005-06	Grand Rapids	AHL	13	8	4	0	681	33	0	2.91	5	3	1	260	7	0	1.62
	Toledo Storm	ECHL	33	24	7	2	1981	68	2	*2.06	6	5	1	360	12	0	2.00
2006-07	Manitoba Moose	AHL	41	24	12	2	2290	83	3	2.17	11	4	6	633	21	1	1.99
2007-08	**Vancouver**	**NHL**	**2**	**0**	**1**	**0**	**61**	**3**	**0**	**2.95**	....	....	....	....	....	....	....
	Manitoba Moose	AHL	46	25	18	2	2736	106	2	2.32	1	1	0	31	2	0	3.93
2008-09	Milwaukee	AHL	55	*34	15	4	3180	122	4	2.30	11	7	4	655	18	1	*1.65
2009-10	Chicago Wolves	AHL	41	20	17	2	2246	95	3	2.54	5	1	2	228	11	1	2.90
2010-11	Chicago Wolves	AHL	20	12	5	1	1135	55	0	2.91	....	....	....	....	....	....	....
	Hamilton Bulldogs	AHL	21	12	6	2	1241	39	1	1.89	20	11	9	1289	42	1	1.95
2011-12	**Buffalo**	**NHL**	**2**	**0**	**0**	**0**	**43**	**1**	**0**	**1.40**	....	....	....	....	....	....	....
	Rochester	AHL	23	8	12	2	1375	73	1	3.19	....	....	....	....	....	....	....
2012-13	HC Lev Praha	KHL	2	0	1	0	123	6	0	2.92	....	....	....	....	....	....	....
	Reading Royals	ECHL	10	6	3	1	589	19	0	1.93	....	....	....	....	....	....	....
	Toronto Marlies	AHL	21	13	5	3	1243	38	0	1.83	9	5	4	527	25	1	2.85
	NHL Totals		**4**	**0**	**1**	**0**	**104**	**4**	**0**	**2.31**	....	....	....	....	....	....	....

AHL Second All-Star Team (2008, 2009)

• Missed majority of 2003-04 due to thigh injury in practice, December 27, 2003. Traded to **Vancouver** by **Detroit** for future considerations, September 12, 2006. Signed as a free agent by **Nashville**, July 1, 2008. Signed as a free agent by **Atlanta**, July 6, 2009. Traded to **Montreal** by **Atlanta** for Brett Festerling, February 28, 2011. Signed as a free agent by **Buffalo**, July 7, 2011. Signed as a free agent by **Lev Praha** (KHL), June 3, 2012. Signed as a free agent by **Reading** (ECHL), January 3, 2013. Signed to a PTO (professional tryout) contract by **Toronto** (AHL), February 13, 2013. Signed as a free agent by **Toronto**, April 2, 2013.

MADSEN, Merrick (MAD-sehn, MAIR-ihk) PHI

Goaltender. Catches left. 6'5", 177 lbs. Born, Preston, ID, August 22, 1995.
(Philadelphia's 5th choice, 162nd overall, in 2013 Entry Draft).

			Regular Season								Playoffs						
Season	Club	League	GP	W	L	O/T	Mins	GA	SO	Avg	GP	W	L	Mins	GA	SO	Avg
2011-12	Proctor Academy	High-NH	20	....	....	....	748	....	....	4.00	....	....	....	....	....	....	....
2012-13	Proctor Academy	High-NH	26	10	13	3	1171	82	1	3.19	....	....	....	....	....	....	....

• Signed Letter of Intent to attend **Harvard University** (ECAC) in fall of 2014.

MAGUIRE, Sean (muh-GWIGH-uhr, SHAWN) PIT

Goaltender. Catches left. 6'2", 202 lbs. Born, Edmonton, Alta., February 2, 1993.
(Pittsburgh's 7th choice, 113th overall, in 2012 Entry Draft).

			Regular Season								Playoffs						
Season	Club	League	GP	W	L	O/T	Mins	GA	SO	Avg	GP	W	L	Mins	GA	SO	Avg
2009-10	North Island	BCMML	20	....	....	....	....	....	....	....	1	....	....	....	....	....	....
2010-11	Powell River Kings	BCHL	15	10	3	0	841	35	2	2.50	2	0	0	44	1	0	1.36
2011-12	Powell River Kings	BCHL	31	17	12	1	1774	69	3	2.33	15	7	6	808	28	2	2.08
2012-13	Boston University	H-East	21	13	8	0	1230	52	4	2.54	....	....	....	....	....	....	....

MAKAROV, Andrey (mah-KAH-rahv, an-DRAY) BUF

Goaltender. Catches left. 6'1", 185 lbs. Born, Kazan, Russia, April 20, 1993.

			Regular Season								Playoffs						
Season	Club	League	GP	W	L	O/T	Mins	GA	SO	Avg	GP	W	L	Mins	GA	SO	Avg
2008-09	Lada Togliatti 2	Russia-3	9	....	....	....	....	....	....	3.27	....	....	....	....	....	....	....
2009-10	Ladja Togliatti Jr.	Russia-Jr.	22	....	....	....	1114	....	....	4.04	....	....	....	....	....	....	....
2010-11	Lewiston	QMJHL	27	11	12	2	1390	78	2	3.37	3	....	....	....	....	....	....
2011-12	Saskatoon Blades	WHL	54	29	21	2	3107	156	2	3.01	4	0	4	249	17	0	4.10
2012-13	Saskatoon Blades	WHL	61	*37	17	5	3487	152	7	2.62	4	0	4	196	12	0	3.66

Hap Emms Memorial Trophy (Memorial Cup Tournament – Top Goaltender) (2013)

Signed as a free agent by **Buffalo**, September 14, 2012.

MANNINO, Peter (ma-NEE-noh, PE-tuhr)

Goaltender. Catches right. 6'1", 195 lbs. Born, Farmington Hills, MI, February 17, 1984.

			Regular Season								Playoffs						
Season	Club	League	GP	W	L	O/T	Mins	GA	SO	Avg	GP	W	L	Mins	GA	SO	Avg
2001-02	Pittsburgh Forge	NAHL	11	....	....	....	....	....	....	....	....	....	....	....	....	....	....
2002-03	Pittsburgh Forge	NAHL	45	....	....	....	....	....	....	....	....	....	....	....	....	....	....
2003-04	Tri-City Storm	USHL	38	26	7	0	1988	70	5	*2.11	7	4	1	334	12	*1	2.15
2004-05	U. of Denver	WCHA	21	16	4	1	1224	46	*5	2.25	....	....	....	....	....	....	....
2005-06	U. of Denver	WCHA	22	12	8	1	1241	56	1	2.71	....	....	....	....	....	....	....
2006-07	U. of Denver	WCHA	18	8	6	2	1021	39	3	2.29	....	....	....	....	....	....	....
2007-08	U. of Denver	WCHA	40	25	14	1	2302	87	*6	2.27	....	....	....	....	....	....	....
2008-09	**NY Islanders**	**NHL**	**3**	**1**	**1**	**0**	**133**	**10**	**0**	**4.51**	....	....	....	....	....	....	....
	Bridgeport	AHL	34	17	12	2	1959	96	1	2.94	3	1	2	189	10	0	3.18
	Utah Grizzlies	ECHL	9	4	3	2	549	25	0	2.73	....	....	....	....	....	....	....
2009-10	Chicago Wolves	AHL	38	26	5	1	2026	79	2	2.34	12	6	5	653	34	2	3.12
2010-11	**Atlanta**	**NHL**	**2**	**0**	**0**	**0**	**73**	**5**	**0**	**4.11**	....	....	....	....	....	....	....
	Chicago Wolves	AHL	42	16	17	4	2232	116	0	3.12	....	....	....	....	....	....	....
2011-12	**Winnipeg**	**NHL**	**1**	**0**	**0**	**0**	**20**	**0**	**0**	**0.00**	....	....	....	....	....	....	....
	St. John's IceCaps	AHL	10	4	5	0	585	27	1	2.77	....	....	....	....	....	....	....
	Chicago Express	ECHL	22	10	8	4	1334	70	1	3.15	....	....	....	....	....	....	....
	Portland Pirates	AHL	15	8	6	1	854	49	0	3.44	....	....	....	....	....	....	....
2012-13	Manchester	AHL	20	10	7	0	1069	44	0	2.47	....	....	....	....	....	....	....
	NHL Totals		**6**	**1**	**1**	**0**	**226**	**15**	**0**	**3.98**	....	....	....	....	....	....	....

Signed as a free agent by **NY Islanders**, July 3, 2008. Signed as a free agent by **Atlanta**, July 6, 2009. • Transferred to **Winnipeg** after **Atlanta** franchise relocated, June 21, 2011.

MARKSTROM, Jacob (MAHRK-struhm, JAY-kawb) FLA

Goaltender. Catches left. 6'3", 178 lbs. Born, Gavle, Sweden, January 31, 1990.
(Florida's 1st choice, 31st overall, in 2008 Entry Draft).

			Regular Season								Playoffs						
Season	**Club**	**League**	**GP**	**W**	**L**	**O/T**	**Mins**	**GA**	**SO**	**Avg**	**GP**	**W**	**L**	**Mins**	**GA**	**SO**	**Avg**
2006-07	Brynas U18	Swe-U18	13	....	....	....	789	27	0	2.05	3	....	....	193	6	1	1.86
	Brynas IF Gavle Jr.	Swe-Jr.	1	....	....	....	65	3	0	2.77	1	....	....	25	4	0	9.76
2007-08	Brynas U18	Swe-U18	1	....	....	....	60	3	0	3.00	....	....	....	....	....	....	....
	Brynas IF Gavle Jr.	Swe-Jr.	22	....	....	....	1320	44	2	2.00	....	....	....	....	....	....	....
	Brynas IF Gavle	Sweden	7	....	....	....	423	22	0	3.12	....	....	....	....	....	....	....
	Brynas IF Gavle	Sweden-Q	9	....	....	....	505	15	2	1.78	....	....	....	....	....	....	....
2008-09	Brynas IF Gavle	Sweden	35	....	....	....	1992	79	3	2.38	1	....	....	59	2	0	2.02
2009-10	Brynas IF Gavle	Sweden	43	....	....	....	2542	85	*5	*2.01	4	....	....	224	12	0	3.21
	Brynas IF Gavle Jr.	Swe-Jr.	....	....	....	....	....	....	....	....	2	....	....	119	6	0	3.03
2010-11	**Florida**	**NHL**	**1**	**0**	**1**	**0**	**40**	**2**	**0**	**3.00**	....	....	....	....	....	....	....
	Rochester	AHL	37	16	20	1	2174	108	1	2.98	....	....	....	....	....	....	....
2011-12	**Florida**	**NHL**	**7**	**2**	**4**	**1**	**383**	**17**	**0**	**2.66**	....	....	....	....	....	....	....
	San Antonio	AHL	32	17	12	1	1839	71	1	2.32	8	4	4	546	26	0	2.85
2012-13	San Antonio	AHL	33	16	15	2	1972	87	3	2.65	....	....	....	....	....	....	....
	Florida	**NHL**	**23**	**8**	**14**	**1**	**1266**	**68**	**0**	**3.22**	....	....	....	....	....	....	....
	NHL Totals		**31**	**10**	**19**	**2**	**1689**	**87**	**0**	**3.09**	....	....	....	....	....	....	....

MARTIN, Spencer (MAHR-tihn, SPEHN-suhr) COL

Goaltender. Catches left. 6'2", 198 lbs. Born, Oakville, Ont., June 8, 1995.
(Colorado's 3rd choice, 63rd overall, in 2013 Entry Draft).

			Regular Season								Playoffs						
Season	**Club**	**League**	**GP**	**W**	**L**	**O/T**	**Mins**	**GA**	**SO**	**Avg**	**GP**	**W**	**L**	**Mins**	**GA**	**SO**	**Avg**
2010-11	Tor. Jr. Canadiens	GTHL	50	....	....	....	2250	115	5	2.27	....	....	....	....	....	....	....
2011-12	St. Michael's	OHL	15	2	7	1	753	50	0	3.98	....	....	....	....	....	....	....
2012-13	Mississauga	OHL	46	17	21	4	2504	126	0	3.02	2	0	1	90	9	0	6.01

MASON, Chris (MAY-sohn, KRIHS)

Goaltender. Catches left. 6', 198 lbs. Born, Red Deer, Alta., April 20, 1976.
(New Jersey's 7th choice, 122nd overall, in 1995 Entry Draft).

			Regular Season								Playoffs						
Season	**Club**	**League**	**GP**	**W**	**L**	**O/T**	**Mins**	**GA**	**SO**	**Avg**	**GP**	**W**	**L**	**Mins**	**GA**	**SO**	**Avg**
1992-93	Red Deer	AMHL	20	....	....	....	1280	76	0	3.35	....	....	....	....	....	....	....
1993-94	Victoria Cougars	WHL	5	1	4	0	237	27	0	6.84	....	....	....	....	....	....	....
1994-95	Prince George	WHL	44	8	30	1	2288	192	1	5.03	....	....	....	....	....	....	....
1995-96	Prince George	WHL	59	16	37	1	3289	236	1	4.31	....	....	....	....	....	....	....
1996-97	Prince George	WHL	50	19	24	4	2851	172	2	3.62	15	9	6	938	44	*1	2.81
1997-98	Cincinnati	AHL	47	13	19	7	2368	136	0	3.45	....	....	....	....	....	....	....
1998-99	**Nashville**	**NHL**	**3**	**0**	**0**	**0**	**69**	**6**	**0**	**5.22**	....	....	....	....	....	....	....
	Milwaukee	IHL	34	15	12	6	1901	92	1	2.90	....	....	....	....	....	....	....
99-2000	Milwaukee	IHL	53	20	21	8	2952	137	2	2.78	3	1	2	252	11	0	2.62
2000-01	**Nashville**	**NHL**	**1**	**0**	**1**	**0**	**59**	**2**	**0**	**2.03**	....	....	....	....	....	....	....
	Milwaukee	IHL	37	17	14	5	2226	87	5	2.35	4	1	3	239	12	0	3.02
2001-02	Milwaukee	AHL	48	17	21	7	2755	116	2	2.53	....	....	....	....	....	....	....
2002-03	San Antonio	AHL	50	25	18	6	2914	122	1	2.51	3	0	3	195	9	0	2.77
2003-04	**Nashville**	**NHL**	**17**	**4**	**4**	**1**	**744**	**27**	**1**	**2.18**	....	....	....	....	....	....	....
	Milwaukee	AHL	1	1	0	0	60	2	0	2.00	....	....	....	....	....	....	....
2004-05	Valerengen IF Oslo	Norway	20	....	....	....	1204	36	1	1.79	11	....	....	657	22	1	2.01
2005-06	**Nashville**	**NHL**	**23**	**12**	**5**	**1**	**1227**	**52**	**2**	**2.54**	**5**	**1**	**4**	**296**	**17**	**0**	**3.45**
2006-07	**Nashville**	**NHL**	**40**	**24**	**11**	**4**	**2342**	**93**	**5**	**2.38**	....	....	....	....	....	....	....
2007-08	**Nashville**	**NHL**	**51**	**18**	**22**	**6**	**2692**	**130**	**4**	**2.90**	....	....	....	....	....	....	....
2008-09	**St. Louis**	**NHL**	**57**	**27**	**21**	**7**	**3215**	**129**	**6**	**2.41**	**4**	**0**	**4**	**256**	**10**	**0**	**2.34**
2009-10	**St. Louis**	**NHL**	**61**	**30**	**22**	**8**	**3512**	**148**	**2**	**2.53**	....	....	....	....	....	....	....
2010-11	**Atlanta**	**NHL**	**33**	**13**	**13**	**3**	**1682**	**95**	**1**	**3.39**	....	....	....	....	....	....	....
2011-12	**Winnipeg**	**NHL**	**20**	**8**	**7**	**1**	**995**	**43**	**2**	**2.59**	....	....	....	....	....	....	....
2012-13	**Nashville**	**NHL**	**11**	**1**	**7**	**1**	**467**	**29**	**0**	**3.73**	....	....	....	....	....	....	....
	NHL Totals		**317**	**137**	**113**	**32**	**17004**	**754**	**23**	**2.66**	**9**	**1**	**8**	**552**	**27**	**0**	**2.93**

Signed as a free agent by **Anaheim**, June 27, 1997. Traded to **Nashville** by **Anaheim** with Marc Moro for Dominic Roussel, October 5, 1998. Signed as a free agent by **Florida**, August 20, 2002. Claimed by **Nashville** from **Florida** in Waiver Draft, October 3, 2003. Signed as a free agent by **Oslo** (Norway), November 30, 2004. Traded to **St. Louis** by **Nashville** for NY Rangers' 4th round choice (previously acquired, later traded back to NY Rangers – NY Rangers selected Dale Weise) in 2008 Entry Draft, June 20, 2008. Signed as a free agent by **Atlanta**, July 1, 2010. • Transferred to **Winnipeg** after **Atlanta** franchise relocated, June 21, 2011. Signed as a free agent by **Nashville**, July 1, 2012.

MASON, Steve (MAY-sohn, STEEV) PHI

Goaltender. Catches right. 6'4", 217 lbs. Born, Oakville, Ont., May 29, 1988.
(Columbus' 2nd choice, 69th overall, in 2006 Entry Draft).

			Regular Season								Playoffs						
Season	**Club**	**League**	**GP**	**W**	**L**	**O/T**	**Mins**	**GA**	**SO**	**Avg**	**GP**	**W**	**L**	**Mins**	**GA**	**SO**	**Avg**
2003-04	Oakville Rangers	Minor-ON	27	....	....	....	1209	41	5	1.58	....	....	....	....	....	....	....
2004-05	Grimsby	ON-Jr.C	45	....	....	....	2800	....	6	1.75	....	....	....	....	....	....	....
2005-06	Petrolia Jets	ON-Jr.B	9	6	3	0	522	22	1	2.53	5	3	2	348	9	0	1.55
	London Knights	OHL	12	5	3	0	497	22	0	2.66	4	0	1	150	7	0	2.80
2006-07	London Knights	OHL	*62	*45	13	4	*3733	199	2	3.20	16	9	7	931	54	0	3.48
2007-08	London Knights	OHL	26	19	4	3	1569	73	2	2.79	....	....	....	....	....	....	....
	Kitchener Rangers	OHL	16	13	3	0	961	33	1	2.06	5	5	0	313	10	1	1.92
2008-09	**Columbus**	**NHL**	**61**	**33**	**20**	**7**	**3664**	**140**	***10**	**2.29**	**4**	**0**	**4**	**239**	**17**	**0**	**4.27**
	Syracuse Crunch	AHL	3	2	1	0	184	5	0	1.63	....	....	....	....	....	....	....
2009-10	**Columbus**	**NHL**	**58**	**20**	**26**	**9**	**3201**	**163**	**5**	**3.06**	....	....	....	....	....	....	....
2010-11	**Columbus**	**NHL**	**54**	**24**	**21**	**7**	**3027**	**153**	**3**	**3.03**	....	....	....	....	....	....	....
2011-12	**Columbus**	**NHL**	**46**	**16**	**26**	**3**	**2534**	**143**	**1**	**3.39**	....	....	....	....	....	....	....
2012-13	**Columbus**	**NHL**	**13**	**3**	**6**	**1**	**712**	**35**	**0**	**2.95**	....	....	....	....	....	....	....
	Philadelphia	**NHL**	**7**	**4**	**2**	**0**	**378**	**12**	**0**	**1.90**	....	....	....	....	....	....	....
	NHL Totals		**239**	**100**	**101**	**27**	**13516**	**646**	**19**	**2.87**	**4**	**0**	**4**	**239**	**17**	**0**	**4.27**

OHL First All-Star Team (2007) • OHL Second All-Star Team (2008) • NHL All-Rookie Team (2009) • NHL Second All-Star Team (2009) • Calder Memorial Trophy (2009)

Traded to **Philadelphia** by **Columbus** for Michael Leighton and Philadelphia's 3rd round choice in 2015 Entry Draft, April 3, 2013.

MATTSSON, Johan (MAT-suhn, YOH-han) CHI

Goaltender. Catches left. 6'4", 192 lbs. Born, Huddinge, Sweden, April 25, 1992.
(Chicago's 11th choice, 211th overall, in 2011 Entry Draft).

			Regular Season								Playoffs						
Season	**Club**	**League**	**GP**	**W**	**L**	**O/T**	**Mins**	**GA**	**SO**	**Avg**	**GP**	**W**	**L**	**Mins**	**GA**	**SO**	**Avg**
2008-09	Sodertalje SK U18	Swe-U18	23	....	....	....	1291	66	1	3.06	4	....	....	240	17	0	4.25
	Sodertalje SK Jr.	Swe-Jr.	1	....	....	....	60	3	0	3.00	....	....	....	....	....	....	....
	Sodertalje SK	Sweden-Q	1	....	....	....	25	3	0	7.20	....	....	....	....	....	....	....
2009-10	Sodertalje SK U18	Swe-U18	12	....	....	....	720	31	2	2.58	2	....	....	118	8	0	4.08
	Sodertalje SK Jr.	Swe-Jr.	20	....	....	....	1156	72	1	3.74	....	....	....	....	....	....	....
2010-11	Sodertalje SK Jr.	Swe-Jr.	26	....	....	....	1559	68	0	2.62	2	....	....	119	10	0	5.04
2011-12	Sudbury Wolves	OHL	37	23	11	3	2163	114	0	3.16	3	0	3	149	12	0	4.82
2012-13	Tri-City Storm	USHL	33	12	15	3	1799	90	1	3.00	....	....	....	....	....	....	....

MAYER, Robert (MAY-uhr, RAW-buhrt) MTL

Goaltender. Catches left. 6'1", 192 lbs. Born, Havirov, Czech., October 9, 1989.

			Regular Season								Playoffs						
Season	**Club**	**League**	**GP**	**W**	**L**	**O/T**	**Mins**	**GA**	**SO**	**Avg**	**GP**	**W**	**L**	**Mins**	**GA**	**SO**	**Avg**
2005-06	ESV Kaufbeuren	German-2	3	....	....	....	....	....	....	....	....	....	....	....	....	....	....
2006-07	ESV Kaufbeuren	German-2	7	....	....	....	....	....	....	....	....	....	....	....	....	....	....
	Kloten Flyers	Swiss	1	0	0	0	10	1	0	6.00	....	....	....	....	....	....	....
2007-08	Saint John	QMJHL	32	16	11	0	1669	105	2	3.77	2	0	0	65	5	0	4.61
2008-09	Saint John	QMJHL	57	26	28	0	3155	169	2	3.21	4	0	3	204	16	0	4.70
2009-10	Hamilton Bulldogs	AHL	1	0	0	1	65	2	0	1.85	1	0	0	37	3	0	4.83
	Cincinnati	ECHL	31	19	10	1	1750	82	2	2.81	9	6	1	508	13	*3	*1.54
2010-11	Hamilton Bulldogs	AHL	21	9	10	2	1215	62	0	3.06	....	....	....	....	....	....	....
2011-12	Hamilton Bulldogs	AHL	39	14	18	1	2001	98	0	2.94	....	....	....	....	....	....	....
2012-13	Hamilton Bulldogs	AHL	38	16	17	3	2088	102	0	2.93	....	....	....	....	....	....	....

Signed as a free agent by **Montreal**, September 25, 2008.

MAZANEC, Marek (muh-ZAN-ehk, MAHR-ehk) NSH

Goaltender. Catches right. 6'4", 197 lbs. Born, Pisek, Czech., July 18, 1991.
(Nashville's 9th choice, 179th overall, in 2012 Entry Draft).

			Regular Season								Playoffs						
Season	**Club**	**League**	**GP**	**W**	**L**	**O/T**	**Mins**	**GA**	**SO**	**Avg**	**GP**	**W**	**L**	**Mins**	**GA**	**SO**	**Avg**
2004-05	IHC Pisek U17	CzR-U17	1	....	....	....	30	7	0	14.00	....	....	....	....	....	....	....
2006-07	HC Plzen U17	CzR-U17	14	....	....	....	666	32	2	2.88	1	....	....	27	1	0	2.22
2007-08	HC Plzen U17	CzR-U17	41	....	....	....	2457	99	5	2.42	8	....	....	492	15	1	1.83
2008-09	HC Plzen Jr.	CzRep-Jr.	27	....	....	....	1577	68	0	2.59	5	....	....	309	9	0	1.75
2009-10	HC Plzen 1929	CzRep	1	....	....	....	20	3	0	9.00	....	....	....	....	....	....	....
	SHC Klatovy	CzRep-3	3	....	....	....	185	10	0	3.24	....	....	....	....	....	....	....
	HC Plzen Jr.	CzRep-Jr.	43	....	....	....	2560	111	3	2.60	2	....	....	120	7	0	3.50
2010-11	HC Plzen Jr.	CzRep-Jr.	30	....	....	....	1683	59	7	2.10	....	....	....	....	....	....	....
	HC Plzen 1929	CzRep	15	....	....	....	860	40	1	2.79	....	....	....	....	....	....	....
	IHC Komterm Pisek	CzRep-2	9	....	....	....	435	17	1	2.34	....	....	....	....	....	....	....
2011-12	HC Plzen Jr.	CzRep-Jr.	1	....	....	....	60	4	0	4.00	....	....	....	....	....	....	....
	HC Plzen 1929	CzRep	19	....	....	....	973	48	1	2.96	5	....	....	222	8	0	2.16
	SHC Klatovy	CzRep-3	17	....	....	....	1033	65	0	3.78	6	....	....	359	19	1	3.18
2012-13	HC Plzen Jr.	CzRep-Jr.	2	....	....	....	120	5	0	2.50	....	....	....	....	....	....	....
	IHC Pisek	CzRep-2	12	....	....	....	706	50	0	4.25	....	....	....	....	....	....	....
	HC Skoda Plzen	CzRep	21	....	....	....	1255	52	1	2.49	*20	....	....	*1241	44	2	2.13

McADAM, Eamon (muhk-A-duhm, AY-muhn) NYI

Goaltender. Catches left. 6'2", 189 lbs. Born, Doylestown, PA, September 24, 1994.
(NY Islanders' 2nd choice, 70th overall, in 2013 Entry Draft).

			Regular Season								Playoffs						
Season	**Club**	**League**	**GP**	**W**	**L**	**O/T**	**Mins**	**GA**	**SO**	**Avg**	**GP**	**W**	**L**	**Mins**	**GA**	**SO**	**Avg**
2010-11	Austin Bruins	NAHL	9	2	4	2	506	28	0	3.32	....	....	....	....	....	....	....
	Waterloo	USHL	4	2	2	0	190	11	0	3.48	....	....	....	....	....	....	....
2011-12	Waterloo	USHL	23	11	7	0	1149	67	0	3.50	....	....	....	....	....	....	....
2012-13	Waterloo	USHL	31	17	9	3	1806	104	2	3.45	....	....	....	....	....	....	....

• Signed Letter of Intent to attend **Penn State University** (NCAA) in fall of 2013..

McCOLLUM, Thomas (muh-KAW-luhm, TAW-muhs) DET

Goaltender. Catches left. 6'2", 215 lbs. Born, Amherst, NY, December 7, 1989.
(Detroit's 1st choice, 30th overall, in 2008 Entry Draft).

			Regular Season								Playoffs						
Season	**Club**	**League**	**GP**	**W**	**L**	**O/T**	**Mins**	**GA**	**SO**	**Avg**	**GP**	**W**	**L**	**Mins**	**GA**	**SO**	**Avg**
2005-06	Wheatfield Blades	EmJHL	24	2	19	3	1448	109	1	4.52	....	....	....	....	....	....	....
2006-07	Guelph Storm	OHL	55	26	18	10	3158	126	*5	2.39	4	0	4	233	17	0	4.38
2007-08	Guelph Storm	OHL	51	25	17	6	2978	124	*4	2.50	10	5	5	596	19	1	1.91
2008-09	Guelph Storm	OHL	31	17	10	4	1859	69	*3	2.23	....	....	....	....	....	....	....
	Brampton Battalion	OHL	23	17	6	0	1333	43	*4	1.94	*21	13	8	*1284	62	*1	2.90
2009-10	Grand Rapids	AHL	32	10	16	2	1741	101	0	3.48	....	....	....	....	....	....	....
	Toledo Walleye	ECHL	4	2	1	0	188	14	0	4.48	....	....	....	....	....	....	....
2010-11	**Detroit**	**NHL**	**1**	**0**	**0**	**0**	**15**	**3**	**0**	**12.00**	....	....	....	....	....	....	....
	Grand Rapids	AHL	22	6	12	2	1152	64	1	3.33	....	....	....	....	....	....	....
	Toledo Walleye	ECHL	23	11	9	2	1305	60	3	2.76	....	....	....	....	....	....	....
2011-12	Grand Rapids	AHL	28	11	16	0	1580	92	0	3.49	....	....	....	....	....	....	....
	Toledo Walleye	ECHL	15	6	6	2	870	38	0	2.62	....	....	....	....	....	....	....
2012-13	Grand Rapids	AHL	31	18	11	2	1846	81	2	2.63	....	....	....	....	....	....	....
	NHL Totals		**1**	**0**	**0**	**0**	**15**	**3**	**0**	**12.00**	....	....	....	....	....	....	....

OHL Second All-Star Team (2009)

McELHINNEY, Curtis (MAK-IHL-ehn-ee, KUHR-this) CBJ

Goaltender. Catches left. 6'2", 207 lbs. Born, London, Ont., May 23, 1983.
(Calgary's 9th choice, 176th overall, in 2002 Entry Draft).

			Regular Season								Playoffs						
Season	**Club**	**League**	**GP**	**W**	**L**	**O/T**	**Mins**	**GA**	**SO**	**Avg**	**GP**	**W**	**L**	**Mins**	**GA**	**SO**	**Avg**
2000-01	Notre Dame	SJHL	STATISTICS NOT AVAILABLE														
2001-02	Colorado College	WCHA	9	6	0	1	441	15	1	2.04	....	....	....	....	....	....	....
2002-03	Colorado College	WCHA	*37	*25	6	5	*2147	85	*4	2.37	....	....	....	....	....	....	....
2003-04	Colorado College	WCHA	19	10	6	1	1015	41	2	2.42	....	....	....	....	....	....	....
2004-05	Colorado College	WCHA	26	*21	4	1	1550	58	2	2.24	....	....	....	....	....	....	....
2005-06	Omaha	AHL	33	9	14	2	1621	68	3	2.52	....	....	....	....	....	....	....
2006-07	Omaha	AHL	57	35	17	1	3181	113	*7	2.13	5	2	3	311	11	0	2.12
2007-08	**Calgary**	**NHL**	**5**	**0**	**2**	**0**	**150**	**5**	**0**	**2.00**	....	....	....	....	....	....	....
	Quad City Flames	AHL	41	20	18	2	2320	88	3	2.28	....	....	....	....	....	....	....
2008-09	**Calgary**	**NHL**	**14**	**1**	**6**	**1**	**518**	**31**	**0**	**3.59**	**1**	**0**	**0**	**34**	**1**	**0**	**1.76**
2009-10	**Calgary**	**NHL**	**10**	**3**	**4**	**0**	**502**	**27**	**0**	**3.23**	....	....	....	....	....	....	....
	Anaheim	**NHL**	**10**	**5**	**1**	**2**	**521**	**24**	**0**	**2.76**	....	....	....	....	....	....	....
2010-11	**Anaheim**	**NHL**	**21**	**6**	**9**	**1**	**996**	**57**	**2**	**3.43**	....	....	....	....	....	....	....
	Ottawa	**NHL**	**7**	**3**	**4**	**0**	**399**	**17**	**0**	**2.56**	....	....	....	....	....	....	....
2011-12	**Phoenix**	**NHL**	**2**	**1**	**0**	**0**	**72**	**2**	**0**	**1.67**	....	....	....	....	....	....	....
	Portland Pirates	AHL	25	10	13	0	1379	70	0	3.04	....	....	....	....	....	....	....
2012-13	Springfield Falcons	AHL	49	29	16	3	2926	113	*9	2.32	8	3	5	483	25	0	3.10
	NHL Totals		**69**	**19**	**26**	**4**	**3158**	**163**	**2**	**3.10**	**1**	**0**	**0**	**34**	**1**	**0**	**1.76**

WCHA First All-Star Team (2003, 2005) • NCAA West Second All-American Team (2003) • NCAA West First All-American Team (2005) • AHL Second All-Star Team (2007, 2013)

Traded to **Anaheim** by **Calgary** for Vesa Toskala, March 3, 2010. Traded to **Tampa Bay** by **Anaheim** for Dan Ellis, February 24, 2011. Claimed on waivers by **Ottawa** from **Tampa Bay**, February 28, 2011. Signed as a free agent by **Phoenix**, July 4, 2011. Traded to **Columbus** by **Phoenix** with Ottawa's 2nd round choice (previously acquired, later traded to Philadelphia – Philadelphia selected Anthony Stolarz) in 2012 Entry Draft and Phoenix's 4th round choice (later traded to Philadelphia, later traded to Los Angeles – Los Angeles selected Justin Auger) in 2013 Entry Draft for Antoine Vermette, February 22, 2012.

McKENNA, Mike (mih-KEHN-ah, MIGHK) CBJ

Goaltender. Catches right. 6'3", 195 lbs. Born, St. Louis, MO, April 11, 1983.
(Nashville's 4th choice, 172nd overall, in 2002 Entry Draft).

			Regular Season								Playoffs						
Season	Club	League	GP	W	L	O/T	Mins	GA	SO	Avg	GP	W	L	Mins	GA	SO	Avg
2001-02	St. Lawrence	ECAC	20	7	10	1	1121	59	0	3.16	....	....	....	....	....	....	....
2002-03	St. Lawrence	ECAC	15	1	7	2	618	38	0	3.69	....	....	....	....	....	....	....
2003-04	St. Lawrence	ECAC	27	9	10	3	1475	60	3	2.44	....	....	....	....	....	....	....
2004-05	St. Lawrence	ECAC	35	15	17	2	2022	92	3	2.73	....	....	....	....	....	....	....
2005-06	Norfolk Admirals	AHL	7	4	2	1	388	25	0	3.86	....	....	....	....	....	....	....
	Las Vegas	ECHL	25	19	2	1	1383	49	1	2.13	4	1	1	173	9	0	3.12
2006-07	Milwaukee	AHL	1	0	0	0	11	3	0	15.72	....	....	....	....	....	....	....
	Omaha	AHL	2	0	1	0	96	6	0	3.74	....	....	....	....	....	....	....
	Las Vegas	ECHL	38	27	4	7	2258	83	5	*2.21	6	3	3	358	15	0	2.51
2007-08	Portland Pirates	AHL	41	24	13	1	2269	103	3	2.72	6	2	4	320	18	0	3.38
2008-09	**Tampa Bay**	**NHL**	**15**	**4**	**8**	**1**	**776**	**46**	**1**	**3.56**	....	....	....	....	....	....	....
	Norfolk Admirals	AHL	24	11	10	1	1315	65	1	2.97	....	....	....	....	....	....	....
2009-10	Lowell Devils	AHL	50	24	17	6	2891	119	3	2.47	5	1	4	317	17	0	3.22
2010-11	Albany Devils	AHL	39	14	20	2	2062	124	1	3.61	....	....	....	....	....	....	....
	New Jersey	**NHL**	**2**	**0**	**1**	**0**	**118**	**6**	**0**	**3.05**	....	....	....	....	....	....	....
2011-12	Binghamton	AHL	41	14	22	1	2196	109	0	2.98	....	....	....	....	....	....	....
2012-13	Peoria Rivermen	AHL	39	19	18	1	2307	93	4	2.42	....	....	....	....	....	....	....
	NHL Totals		**17**	**4**	**9**	**1**	**894**	**52**	**1**	**3.49**	....	....	....	....	....	....	....

ECHL Second All-Star Team (2007)

Signed as a free agent by **Tampa Bay**, February 3, 2009. Signed as a free agent by **Lowell** (AHL), October 7, 2009. Signed as a free agent by **New Jersey**, February 10, 2010. Signed as a free agent by **Ottawa**, July 8, 2011. Signed as a free agent by **St. Louis**, July 1, 2012. Signed as a free agent by **Columbus**, July 6, 2013.

MICHALEK, Steve (MIGH-KUHL-ehk, STEEV) MIN

Goaltender. Catches left. 6'3", 197 lbs. Born, Hartford, CT, August 6, 1993.
(Minnesota's 5th choice, 161st overall, in 2011 Entry Draft).

			Regular Season								Playoffs						
Season	Club	League	GP	W	L	O/T	Mins	GA	SO	Avg	GP	W	L	Mins	GA	SO	Avg
2009-10	Loomis Chaffee	High-CT	35	....	....	....	1121	106	....	....	....	....	....	....	....	....	....
2010-11	Loomis Chaffee	High-CT	23	2	19	2	1203	91	....	3.95	....	....	....	....	....	....	....
	Boston Little Bruins	Minor-MA					STATISTICS NOT AVAILABLE										
2011-12	Harvard Crimson	ECAC	24	7	7	8	1336	71	0	3.19	....	....	....	....	....	....	....
2012-13	Cedar Rapids	USHL	17	7	6	3	992	51	0	3.09	....	....	....	....	....	....	....

ECAC All-Rookie Team (2012)

MILLAN, Kieran (MIH-luhn, KEER-uhn) COL

Goaltender. Catches left. 6', 190 lbs. Born, Edmonton, Alta., August 31, 1989.
(Colorado's 5th choice, 124th overall, in 2009 Entry Draft).

			Regular Season								Playoffs						
Season	Club	League	GP	W	L	O/T	Mins	GA	SO	Avg	GP	W	L	Mins	GA	SO	Avg
2006-07	Spruce Grove	AJHL	32	20	7	4	1883	82	3	2.61	4	2	2	200	10	1	3.00
2007-08	Spruce Grove	AJHL	43	21	12	8	2391	121	1	3.04	15	8	7	931	34	1	2.19
2008-09	Boston University	H-East	35	29	2	3	2073	67	3	1.94	....	....	....	....	....	....	....
2009-10	Boston University	H-East	32	16	16	0	1869	98	1	3.15	....	....	....	....	....	....	....
2010-11	Boston University	H-East	36	16	10	8	2127	95	1	2.68	....	....	....	....	....	....	....
2011-12	Boston University	H-East	35	20	14	1	2120	92	3	2.60	....	....	....	....	....	....	....
2012-13	Denver Cutthroats	CHL	38	15	15	4	2083	101	2	2.91	4	1	3	201	10	0	2.99
	Lake Erie Monsters	AHL	1	0	1	0	60	4	0	4.00	....	....	....	....	....	....	....

Hockey East All-Rookie Team (2009) • Hockey East Second All-Star Team (2009, 2011) • Hockey East Rookie of the Year (2009) • NCAA Rookie of the Year (2009) • NCAA Championship All-Tournament Team (2009)

MILLER, Ryan (MIH-luhr, RIGH-uhn) BUF

Goaltender. Catches left. 6'2", 175 lbs. Born, East Lansing, MI, July 17, 1980.
(Buffalo's 7th choice, 138th overall, in 1999 Entry Draft).

			Regular Season								Playoffs						
Season	Club	League	GP	W	L	O/T	Mins	GA	SO	Avg	GP	W	L	Mins	GA	SO	Avg
1997-98	Soo Indians	NAHL	37	21	14	0	2113	82	3	2.33	2	0	2	158	7	0	2.66
1998-99	Soo Indians	NAHL	47	31	14	1	2711	104	8	2.30	4	2	2	218	10	1	2.76
99-2000	Michigan State	CCHA	26	16	5	3	1525	39	*8	*1.53	....	....	....	....	....	....	....
2000-01	Michigan State	CCHA	40	*31	5	4	2447	54	*10	*1.32	....	....	....	....	....	....	....
2001-02	Michigan State	CCHA	40	26	9	5	2411	71	*8	*1.77	....	....	....	....	....	....	....
2002-03	**Buffalo**	**NHL**	**15**	**6**	**8**	**1**	**912**	**40**	**1**	**2.63**	....	....	....	....	....	....	....
	Rochester	AHL	47	23	18	5	2817	110	2	2.34	3	1	2	190	13	0	4.11
2003-04	**Buffalo**	**NHL**	**3**	**0**	**3**	**0**	**178**	**15**	**0**	**5.06**	....	....	....	....	....	....	....
	Rochester	AHL	60	27	25	7	3579	132	5	2.21	14	7	7	857	26	2	1.82
2004-05	Rochester	AHL	63	*41	17	4	3741	153	8	2.45	9	5	4	547	24	0	2.63
2005-06	**Buffalo**	**NHL**	**48**	**30**	**14**	**3**	**2862**	**124**	**1**	**2.60**	**18**	**11**	**7**	**1123**	**48**	**1**	**2.56**
	Rochester	AHL	2	1	1	0	120	5	0	2.50	....	....	....	....	....	....	....
2006-07	**Buffalo**	**NHL**	**63**	**40**	**16**	**6**	**3692**	**168**	**2**	**2.73**	**16**	**9**	**7**	**1029**	**38**	**0**	**2.22**
2007-08	**Buffalo**	**NHL**	**76**	**36**	**27**	**10**	**4474**	**197**	**3**	**2.64**	....	....	....	....	....	....	....
2008-09	**Buffalo**	**NHL**	**59**	**34**	**18**	**6**	**3443**	**145**	**5**	**2.53**	....	....	....	....	....	....	....
2009-10	**Buffalo**	**NHL**	**69**	**41**	**18**	**8**	**4047**	**150**	**5**	**2.22**	**6**	**2**	**4**	**384**	**15**	**0**	**2.34**
	United States	Olympics	6	5	1	0	355	8	1	1.35	....	....	....	....	....	....	....
2010-11	**Buffalo**	**NHL**	**66**	**34**	**22**	**8**	**3829**	**165**	**5**	**2.59**	**7**	**3**	**4**	**410**	**20**	**2**	**2.93**
2011-12	**Buffalo**	**NHL**	**61**	**31**	**21**	**7**	**3536**	**150**	**6**	**2.55**	....	....	....	....	....	....	....
2012-13	**Buffalo**	**NHL**	**40**	**17**	**17**	**5**	**2302**	**108**	**0**	**2.81**	....	....	....	....	....	....	....
	NHL Totals		**500**	**269**	**164**	**54**	**29275**	**1262**	**28**	**2.59**	**47**	**25**	**22**	**2946**	**121**	**3**	**2.46**

CCHA Second All-Star Team (2000) • CCHA First All-Star Team (2001, 2002) • CCHA Player of the Year (2001, 2002) • NCAA West First All-American Team (2001, 2002) • Hobey Baker Memorial Award (Top U.S. Collegiate Player) (2001) • AHL First All-Star Team (2005) • Aldege "Baz" Bastien Memorial Award (AHL – Outstanding Goaltender) (2005) • Olympic All-Star Team (2010) • Olympics – Best Goaltender (2010) • Olympics – MVP (2010) • NHL First All-Star Team (2010) • NHL Foundation Player Award (2010) • Vezina Trophy (2010)

Played in NHL All-Star Game (2007)

MISSIAEN, Jason (MIHS-ee-ehn, JAY-suhn) NYR

Goaltender. Catches left. 6'8", 198 lbs. Born, Chatham, Ont., April 25, 1990.
(Montreal's 3rd choice, 116th overall, in 2008 Entry Draft).

			Regular Season								Playoffs						
Season	Club	League	GP	W	L	O/T	Mins	GA	SO	Avg	GP	W	L	Mins	GA	SO	Avg
2004-05	Dresden Jr. Kings	ON-Jr.C	16	11	4	1	919	47	1	3.07	....	....	....	....	....	....	....
2005-06	Dresden Jr. Kings	ON-Jr.C	26	13	8	2	1560	76	1	2.93	....	....	....	....	....	....	....
	Petrolia Jets	ON-Jr.B	1	0	0	0	14	0	0	0.00	1	0	0	2	0	0	0.00
2006-07	Peterborough	OHL	12	1	7	0	559	48	0	5.15	....	....	....	....	....	....	....
2007-08	Peterborough	OHL	22	8	8	1	1134	62	1	3.28	....	....	....	....	....	....	....
2008-09	Peterborough	OHL	38	12	21	2	2221	141	1	3.81	4	0	4	241	17	0	4.23
2009-10	Peterborough	OHL	59	27	29	3	3358	206	1	3.68	4	0	4	238	11	0	2.77
2010-11	Baie-Comeau	QMJHL	53	10	33	8	3026	168	1	3.33	....	....	....	....	....	....	....
2011-12	Greenville	ECHL	40	22	13	3	2371	107	3	2.71	1	0	1	59	4	0	4.07
2012-13	Connecticut Whale	AHL	25	10	8	2	1348	69	2	3.07	....	....	....	....	....	....	....
	Greenville	ECHL	5	4	1	0	305	14	0	2.75	....	....	....	....	....	....	....

Signed as a free agent by **NY Rangers**, March 24, 2011.

MONTOYA, Al (mawn-TOI-uh, AL) WPG

Goaltender. Catches left. 6'2", 203 lbs. Born, Chicago, IL, February 13, 1985.
(NY Rangers' 1st choice, 6th overall, in 2004 Entry Draft).

			Regular Season								Playoffs						
Season	Club	League	GP	W	L	O/T	Mins	GA	SO	Avg	GP	W	L	Mins	GA	SO	Avg
99-2000	Loyola Academy	High-MN	28	12	13	3	1685	56	1	2.01	....	....	....	....	....	....	....
2000-01	Texas Tornado	NAHL	15	10	3	0	780	38	0	2.92	1	1	0	60	2	0	2.00
	United States	Nat-Tm	2	2	0	0	120	4	0	2.00	....	....	....	....	....	....	....
2001-02	USNTDP	U-17	10	5	5	0	570	24	0	2.53	....	....	....	....	....	....	....
	USNTDP	NAHL	24	6	11	4	1344	79	0	3.53	....	....	....	....	....	....	....
2002-03	U. of Michigan	CCHA	*43	*30	10	3	*2547	99	4	2.33	....	....	....	....	....	....	....
2003-04	U. of Michigan	CCHA	*40	*26	12	2	*2340	87	6	2.23	....	....	....	....	....	....	....
2004-05	U. of Michigan	CCHA	*40	*30	7	3	*2359	99	3	2.52	....	....	....	....	....	....	....
2005-06	Hartford Wolf Pack	AHL	40	23	9	1	2094	91	2	2.61	5	2	1	257	8	1	1.87
	Charlotte Checkers	ECHL	2	1	1	0	123	8	0	3.92	....	....	....	....	....	....	....
2006-07	Hartford Wolf Pack	AHL	48	27	17	0	2556	98	6	2.30	7	3	4	391	20	1	3.07
2007-08	Hartford Wolf Pack	AHL	31	16	8	3	1704	72	0	2.54	....	....	....	....	....	....	....
	San Antonio	AHL	14	8	6	0	789	34	1	2.59	1	0	1	59	4	0	4.04
2008-09	**Phoenix**	**NHL**	**5**	**3**	**1**	**0**	**259**	**9**	**1**	**2.08**	....	....	....	....	....	....	....
	San Antonio	AHL	29	7	17	2	1562	84	0	3.23	....	....	....	....	....	....	....
2009-10	San Antonio	AHL	14	4	7	1	771	34	0	2.65	....	....	....	....	....	....	....
2010-11	**NY Islanders**	**NHL**	**20**	**9**	**5**	**5**	**1154**	**46**	**1**	**2.39**	....	....	....	....	....	....	....
	San Antonio	AHL	21	11	8	0	1130	60	0	3.19	....	....	....	....	....	....	....
2011-12	**NY Islanders**	**NHL**	**31**	**9**	**11**	**5**	**1720**	**89**	**0**	**3.10**	....	....	....	....	....	....	....
2012-13	**Winnipeg**	**NHL**	**7**	**3**	**1**	**0**	**351**	**17**	**1**	**2.91**	....	....	....	....	....	....	....
	NHL Totals		**63**	**24**	**18**	**10**	**3484**	**161**	**3**	**2.77**	....	....	....	....	....	....	....

CCHA All-Rookie Team (2003) • NCAA West Second All-American Team (2004)

Traded to **Phoenix** by **NY Rangers** with Marcel Hossa for Josh Gratton, David LeNeveu, Fredrik Sjostrom and Phoenix's 5th round choice (Roman Horak) in 2009 Entry Draft, February 26, 2008. Traded to **NY Islanders** by **Phoenix** for NY Islanders' 6th round choice (Andrew Fritsch) in 2011 Entry Draft, February 9, 2011. Signed as a free agent by **Winnipeg**, July 4, 2012.

MORRISON, Adam (MOHR-ih-suhn, A-duhm) BOS

Goaltender. Catches left. 6'3", 192 lbs. Born, Edmonton, Alta., February 9, 1991.
(Philadelphia's 1st choice, 81st overall, in 2009 Entry Draft).

			Regular Season								Playoffs						
Season	Club	League	GP	W	L	O/T	Mins	GA	SO	Avg	GP	W	L	Mins	GA	SO	Avg
2007-08	Valley West Hawks	BCMML	....	12	6	2	....	....	....	2.92	....	....	....	....	....	....	....
2008-09	Saskatoon Blades	WHL	13	9	1	1	746	31	1	2.49	....	....	....	....	....	....	....
2009-10	Saskatoon Blades	WHL	36	18	13	3	2040	112	1	3.29	....	....	....	....	....	....	....
2010-11	Saskatoon Blades	WHL	30	16	7	3	1601	77	2	2.89	....	....	....	....	....	....	....
2011-12	Saskatoon Blades	WHL	2	1	1	0	120	9	0	4.50	....	....	....	....	....	....	....
	Vancouver Giants	WHL	55	35	16	3	3137	144	1	2.75	6	2	4	363	22	0	3.64
	Providence Bruins	AHL	1	0	1	0	59	4	0	4.09	....	....	....	....	....	....	....
2012-13	South Carolina	ECHL	10	1	6	2	574	39	0	4.07	....	....	....	....	....	....	....
	Utah Grizzlies	ECHL	14	6	6	2	833	48	0	3.46	....	....	....	....	....	....	....

Signed as a free agent by **Boston**, March 15, 2012.

MRAZEK, Petr (M'RAZ-ihk, PEH-tuhr) DET

Goaltender. Catches left. 6'1", 184 lbs. Born, Ostrava, Czech., February 14, 1992.
(Detroit's 5th choice, 141st overall, in 2010 Entry Draft).

			Regular Season								Playoffs						
Season	Club	League	GP	W	L	O/T	Mins	GA	SO	Avg	GP	W	L	Mins	GA	SO	Avg
2006-07	HC Vitkovice U17	CzR-U17	23	....	....	....	1273	51	2	2.40	9	....	....	486	15	1	1.85
2007-08	HC Vitkovice U17	CzR-U17	34	....	....	....	1974	81	4	2.46	3	....	....	179	8	0	2.68
	HC Vitkovice Steel	CzRep	1	....	....	....	24	4	0	10.00	....	....	....	....	....	....	....
2008-09	HC Vitkovice U17	CzR-U17	28	....	....	....	1601	53	5	1.99	4	....	....	193	3	2	0.93
	HC Vitkovice Jr.	CzRep-Jr.	13	....	....	....	795	33	0	2.49	1	....	....	60	1	0	1.00
2009-10	Ottawa 67's	OHL	30	12	9	1	1562	78	2	3.00	8	4	4	451	18	0	2.39
2010-11	Ottawa 67's	OHL	52	33	15	3	3089	146	4	2.84	4	0	3	224	21	0	5.63
2011-12	Ottawa 67's	OHL	50	30	13	6	3016	143	3	2.84	17	9	8	1065	46	0	2.59
2012-13	Grand Rapids	AHL	42	23	16	2	2498	97	1	2.33	*24	*15	9	*1431	55	*4	2.31
	Toledo Walleye	ECHL	3	2	1	0	179	6	0	2.02	....	....	....	....	....	....	....
	Detroit	**NHL**	**2**	**1**	**1**	**0**	**119**	**4**	**0**	**2.02**	....	....	....	....	....	....	....
	NHL Totals		**2**	**1**	**1**	**0**	**119**	**4**	**0**	**2.02**	....	....	....	....	....	....	....

MURPHY, Mike (MUHR-fee, MIGHK) CAR

Goaltender. Catches left. 5'11", 172 lbs. Born, Kingston, Ont., January 15, 1989.
(Carolina's 4th choice, 165th overall, in 2008 Entry Draft).

			Regular Season								Playoffs						
Season	Club	League	GP	W	L	O/T	Mins	GA	SO	Avg	GP	W	L	Mins	GA	SO	Avg
2004-05	Kingston Predators	Minor-ON	25	....	....	....	1120	34	4	1.41	....	....	....	....	....	....	....
2005-06	Kingston	ON-Jr.A	33	16	13	2	....	102	3	3.30	4	0	3	174	19	0	6.55
	Belleville Bulls	OHL	3	1	1	0	93	9	0	5.81	....	....	....	....	....	....	....
2006-07	Belleville Bulls	OHL	18	8	6	2	995	61	0	3.68	....	....	....	....	....	....	....
2007-08	Belleville Bulls	OHL	49	36	7	4	2942	110	3	*2.24	*19	*14	4	*1085	42	1	2.32
2008-09	Belleville Bulls	OHL	54	40	9	4	3169	110	5	*2.08	17	10	7	1007	43	0	2.56
2009-10	Albany River Rats	AHL	20	10	9	0	1109	52	2	2.81	....	....	....	....	....	....	....
2010-11	Charlotte Checkers	AHL	39	21	11	3	2159	91	2	2.53	14	7	7	817	35	1	2.57
2011-12	**Carolina**	**NHL**	**2**	**0**	**1**	**0**	**36**	**0**	**0**	**0.00**	....	....	....	....	....	....	....
	Charlotte Checkers	AHL	37	18	15	2	2039	93	1	2.74	....	....	....	....	....	....	....
2012-13	Spartak Moscow	KHL	7	....	....	....	....	....	....	4.34	....	....	....	....	....	....	....
	Charlotte Checkers	AHL	1	0	1	0	60	5	0	5.04	1	0	0	35	4	0	6.95
	NHL Totals		**2**	**0**	**1**	**0**	**36**	**0**	**0**	**0.00**	....	....	....	....	....	....	....

OHL First All-Star Team (2008, 2009) • Canadian Major Junior Second All-Star Team (2008) • Canadian Major Junior First All-Star Team (2009) • Canadian Major Junior Goaltender of the Year (2009)

Signed as a free agent by **Spartak Moscow** (KHL), June 6, 2012.

MURRAY, Matt (MUHR-ee, MAT) PIT

Goaltender. Catches left. 6'4", 166 lbs. Born, Thunder Bay, Ont., May 25, 1994.
(Pittsburgh's 5th choice, 83rd overall, in 2012 Entry Draft).

			Regular Season								Playoffs						
Season	Club	League	GP	W	L	O/T	Mins	GA	SO	Avg	GP	W	L	Mins	GA	SO	Avg
2009-10	Thunder Bay Kings	Minor-ON	40	32	5	0	1975	75	6	1.71	....	....	....	....	....	....	....
2010-11	Sault Ste. Marie	OHL	28	8	11	3	1377	87	1	3.79	....	....	....	....	....	....	....
2011-12	Sault Ste. Marie	OHL	36	13	19	1	1912	130	0	4.08	....	....	....	....	....	....	....
2012-13	Sault Ste. Marie	OHL	53	26	19	4	2910	178	2	3.67	6	2	4	381	17	1	2.67

NABOKOV, Evgeni (na-BAW-kahv, ehv-GEH-nee) NYI

Goaltender. Catches left. 6', 202 lbs. Born, Ust-Kamenogorsk, USSR, July 25, 1975.
(San Jose's 9th choice, 219th overall, in 1994 Entry Draft).

			Regular Season								Playoffs						
Season	Club	League	GP	W	L	O/T	Mins	GA	SO	Avg	GP	W	L	Mins	GA	SO	Avg
1991-92	Ust-Kamenogorsk	CIS	1	....	....	....	20	1	0	3.00	....	....	....	....	....	....	....
1992-93	Ust-Kam'gorsk 2	CIS-2	19	....	....	....	....	....	....	....	....	....	....	....	....	....	....
	Ust-Kamenogorsk	CIS	4	....	....	....	109	5	0	2.75	....	....	....	....	....	....	....
1993-94	Ust-Kamenogorsk	CIS	11	....	....	....	539	29	....	3.23	....	....	....	....	....	....	....
1994-95	Dynamo Moscow	CIS	24	....	....	....	1326	40	3	1.81	13	....	....	806	30	2	2.23
1995-96	Dynamo Moscow	CIS	39	....	....	....	2008	67	5	2.00	....	....	....	....	....	....	....
1996-97	Dynamo Moscow	Russia	27	....	....	....	1588	56	2	2.11	4	....	....	255	12	0	2.82
	Dynamo Moscow 2	Russia-3	1	....	....	....	....	2	....	....	....	....	....	....	....	....	....
1997-98	Kentucky	AHL	33	10	21	2	1866	122	0	3.92	1	0	0	23	1	0	2.59
1998-99	Kentucky	AHL	43	26	14	1	2429	106	5	2.62	11	6	5	599	30	*2	3.00
99-2000	**San Jose**	**NHL**	**11**	**2**	**2**	**1**	**414**	**15**	**1**	**2.17**	**1**	**0**	**0**	**20**	**0**	**0**	**0.00**
	Kentucky	AHL	2	1	1	0	120	3	1	1.50	....	....	....	....	....	....	....
	Cleveland	IHL	20	12	4	3	1164	52	0	2.68	....	....	....	....	....	....	....
2000-01	**San Jose**	**NHL**	**66**	**32**	**21**	**7**	**3700**	**135**	**6**	**2.19**	**4**	**1**	**3**	**218**	**10**	**1**	**2.75**
2001-02	**San Jose**	**NHL**	**67**	**37**	**24**	**5**	**3901**	**149**	**7**	**2.29**	**12**	**7**	**5**	**712**	**31**	**0**	**2.61**
2002-03	**San Jose**	**NHL**	**55**	**19**	**28**	**8**	**3227**	**146**	**3**	**2.71**	....	....	....	....	....	....	....
2003-04	**San Jose**	**NHL**	**59**	**31**	**19**	**8**	**3456**	**127**	**9**	**2.20**	**17**	**10**	**7**	**1052**	**30**	**3**	**1.71**
2004-05	Magnitogorsk	Russia	14	....	....	....	808	27	3	2.00	5	....	....	307	13	0	2.53
2005-06	**San Jose**	**NHL**	**45**	**16**	**19**	**7**	**2575**	**133**	**1**	**3.10**	**1**	**0**	**0**	**12**	**1**	**0**	**5.00**
	Russia	Olympics	7	4	2	0	359	8	3	1.34	....	....	....	....	....	....	....
2006-07	**San Jose**	**NHL**	**50**	**25**	**16**	**4**	**2778**	**106**	**7**	**2.29**	**11**	**6**	**5**	**701**	**26**	**1**	**2.23**
2007-08	**San Jose**	**NHL**	***77**	***46**	**21**	**8**	**4561**	**163**	**6**	**2.14**	**13**	**6**	**7**	**853**	**31**	**1**	**2.18**
2008-09	**San Jose**	**NHL**	**62**	**41**	**12**	**8**	**3686**	**150**	**7**	**2.44**	**6**	**2**	**4**	**362**	**17**	**0**	**2.82**
2009-10	**San Jose**	**NHL**	**71**	**44**	**16**	**10**	**4194**	**170**	**3**	**2.43**	**15**	**8**	**7**	**890**	**38**	**1**	**2.56**
	Russia	Olympics	3	2	1	0	144	10	0	4.16	....	....	....	....	....	....	....
2010-11	SKA St. Petersburg	KHL	22	....	....	....	1230	62	2	3.02	....	....	....	....	....	....	....
2011-12	**NY Islanders**	**NHL**	**42**	**19**	**18**	**3**	**2378**	**101**	**2**	**2.55**	....	....	....	....	....	....	....
2012-13	**NY Islanders**	**NHL**	**41**	**23**	**11**	**7**	**2475**	**103**	**3**	**2.50**	**6**	**2**	**4**	**324**	**24**	**0**	**4.44**
	NHL Totals		**646**	**335**	**207**	**76**	**37345**	**1498**	**55**	**2.41**	**86**	**42**	**42**	**5144**	**208**	**7**	**2.43**

NHL All-Rookie Team (2001) • Calder Memorial Trophy (2001) • NHL First All-Star Team (2008)

Played in NHL All-Star Game (2001, 2008)

• Scored a goal vs. Vancouver, March 10, 2002. Signed as a free agent by **Magnitogorsk** (Russia), December 2, 2004. Signed as a free agent by **St. Petersburg** (KHL), July 7, 2010. Signed as a free agent by **Detroit**, January 20, 2011. Claimed on waivers by **NY Islanders** from **Detroit**, January 22, 2011. • Suspended by **NY Islanders** for failing to report to team after waiver claim, January 25, 2011.

NEUVIRTH, Michal (NOI-vihrt, MIGHK-ahl) WSH

Goaltender. Catches left. 6'1", 209 lbs. Born, Usti nad Labem, Czech., March 23, 1988.
(Washington's 3rd choice, 34th overall, in 2006 Entry Draft).

			Regular Season								Playoffs						
Season	Club	League	GP	W	L	O/T	Mins	GA	SO	Avg	GP	W	L	Mins	GA	SO	Avg
2003-04	Sparta U17	CzR-U17	55	....	....	....	3137	96	5	1.84	3	....	....	180	13	0	4.33
2004-05	Sparta U17	CzR-U17	20	....	....	....	1178	49	3	2.50	8	....	....	482	17	0	2.12
	Sparta Jr.	CzRep-Jr.	10	....	....	....	501	20	1	2.40	....	....	....	....	....	....	....
2005-06	Sparta Jr.	CzRep-Jr.	42	....	....	....	2516	82	5	1.96	3	....	....	179	9	0	3.02
2006-07	Plymouth Whalers	OHL	41	26	8	4	2223	86	4	*2.32	*18	*14	4	*1080	44	0	*2.44
2007-08	Plymouth Whalers	OHL	10	5	4	1	600	26	0	2.60	....	....	....	....	....	....	....
	Windsor Spitfires	OHL	8	6	1	1	482	17	0	2.12	....	....	....	....	....	....	....
	Oshawa Generals	OHL	15	6	2	6	844	57	0	4.05	9	7	2	507	21	0	2.49
2008-09	**Washington**	**NHL**	**5**	**2**	**1**	**0**	**220**	**11**	**0**	**3.00**	....	....	....	....	....	....	....
	Hershey Bears	AHL	17	9	5	2	1001	45	1	2.70	*22	*16	6	*1346	43	*4	1.92
	South Carolina	ECHL	13	6	7	0	762	29	2	2.28	....	....	....	....	....	....	....
2009-10	**Washington**	**NHL**	**17**	**9**	**4**	**0**	**872**	**40**	**0**	**2.75**	....	....	....	....	....	....	....
	Hershey Bears	AHL	22	15	6	0	1231	46	1	2.24	*18	*14	4	*1133	39	1	2.07
2010-11	**Washington**	**NHL**	**48**	**27**	**12**	**4**	**2689**	**110**	**4**	**2.45**	**9**	**4**	**5**	**590**	**23**	**1**	**2.34**
2011-12	**Washington**	**NHL**	**38**	**13**	**13**	**5**	**2020**	**95**	**3**	**2.82**	....	....	....	....	....	....	....
2012-13	HC Sparta Praha	CzRep	24	....	....	....	1342	55	1	2.46	....	....	....	....	....	....	....
	Washington	**NHL**	**13**	**4**	**5**	**2**	**723**	**33**	**0**	**2.74**	....	....	....	....	....	....	....
	NHL Totals		**121**	**55**	**35**	**11**	**6524**	**289**	**7**	**2.66**	**9**	**4**	**5**	**590**	**23**	**1**	**2.34**

OHL Second All-Star Team (2007) • Jack A. Butterfield Trophy (AHL – Playoff MVP) (2009)

Signed as a free agent by **Sparta Praha** (CzRep), September 20, 2012.

NIEMI, Antti (nee-YEH-mee, AN-tee) S.J.

Goaltender. Catches left. 6'2", 210 lbs. Born, Vantaa, Finland, August 29, 1983.

			Regular Season								Playoffs						
Season	Club	League	GP	W	L	O/T	Mins	GA	SO	Avg	GP	W	L	Mins	GA	SO	Avg
2000-01	Kiekko-Vantaa Jr.	Fin-Jr.	4	....	....	....	....	....	....	6.86	....	....	....	....	....	....	....
2001-02	Kiekko-Vantaa	Finland-2	24	....	....	....	....	....	....	....	3	....	....	....	....	....	....
2002-03	Kiekko-Vantaa	Finland-2	....	....	....	....	364	16	0	2.63	....	....	....	....	....	....	....
2003-04	Kiekko-Vantaa Jr.	Fin-Jr.	19	....	....	....	1095	58	2	3.18	....	....	....	....	....	....	....
	Kiekko-Vantaa	Finland-2	19	....	....	....	1048	47	1	2.52	3	....	....	187	13	0	4.17
2004-05	Kiekko-Vantaa	Finland-2	38	....	....	....	2261	95	1	2.52	3	....	....	187	13	0	4.17
2005-06	Pelicans Lahti	Finland	40	12	17	8	2263	103	3	2.73	....	....	....	....	....	....	....
2006-07	Pelicans Lahti	Finland	48	18	21	7	2780	119	3	2.57	6	2	4	371	9	1	1.46
2007-08	Pelicans Lahti	Finland	49	26	14	6	2778	109	4	2.35	6	2	3	327	21	0	3.85
2008-09	**Chicago**	**NHL**	**3**	**1**	**1**	**1**	**141**	**8**	**0**	**3.40**	....	....	....	....	....	....	....
	Rockford IceHogs	AHL	38	18	14	3	2095	85	2	2.43	2	0	2	115	7	0	3.65
2009-10♦	**Chicago**	**NHL**	**39**	**26**	**7**	**4**	**2190**	**82**	**7**	**2.25**	***22**	***16**	**6**	***1322**	**58**	**2**	**2.63**
2010-11	**San Jose**	**NHL**	**60**	**35**	**18**	**6**	**3524**	**140**	**6**	**2.38**	**18**	**8**	**9**	**1044**	**56**	**0**	**3.22**
2011-12	**San Jose**	**NHL**	**68**	**34**	**22**	**9**	**3936**	**159**	**6**	**2.42**	**5**	**1**	**4**	**318**	**13**	**0**	**2.45**
2012-13	Pelicans Lahti	Finland	10	3	5	2	597	31	0	3.11	....	....	....	....	....	....	....
	San Jose	**NHL**	**43**	***24**	**12**	**6**	***2581**	**93**	**4**	**2.16**	**11**	**7**	**4**	**673**	**21**	**0**	**1.87**
	NHL Totals		**213**	**120**	**60**	**26**	**12372**	**482**	**23**	**2.34**	**56**	**32**	**23**	**3357**	**148**	**2**	**2.65**

Signed as a free agent by **Chicago**, May 5, 2008. Signed as a free agent by **San Jose**, September 2, 2010. Signed as a free agent by **Lahti** (Finland), October 5, 2012.,

NILSSON, Anders (NIHL-suhn, AN-duhrz) NYI

Goaltender. Catches left. 6'5", 227 lbs. Born, Lulea, Sweden, March 19, 1990.
(NY Islanders' 4th choice, 62nd overall, in 2009 Entry Draft).

			Regular Season								Playoffs						
Season	Club	League	GP	W	L	O/T	Mins	GA	SO	Avg	GP	W	L	Mins	GA	SO	Avg
2004-05	Lulea HF Jr.	Swe-Jr.	1	....	....	....	24	4	0	9.90	....	....	....	....	....	....	....
2007-08	Lulea HF U18	Swe-U18	11	....	....	....	625	31	0	2.97	....	....	....	....	....	....	....
	Lulea HF Jr.	Swe-Jr.	16	....	....	....	898	31	2	2.07	1	....	....	60	6	0	6.00
2008-09	Lulea HF Jr.	Swe-Jr.	37	....	....	....	2199	75	4	2.05	6	....	....	357	14	1	2.35
	Lulea HF	Sweden	1	....	....	....	28	0	0	0.00	....	....	....	....	....	....	....
	Kalix Ungdoms HC	Sweden-3	1	....	....	....	59	3	0	3.05	....	....	....	....	....	....	....
2009-10	Lulea HF Jr.	Swe-Jr.	4	....	....	....	244	12	0	2.95	....	....	....	....	....	....	....
	Lulea HF	Sweden	27	....	....	....	1383	61	2	2.65	....	....	....	....	....	....	....
2010-11	Lulea HF	Sweden	31	....	....	....	1876	60	6	*1.92	13	....	....	827	27	0	1.96
2011-12	**NY Islanders**	**NHL**	**4**	**1**	**2**	**0**	**218**	**10**	**1**	**2.75**	....	....	....	....	....	....	....
	Bridgeport	AHL	25	15	8	2	1441	58	1	2.42	....	....	....	....	....	....	....
2012-13	Bridgeport	AHL	21	8	11	0	1208	60	1	2.98	....	....	....	....	....	....	....
	NHL Totals		**4**	**1**	**2**	**0**	**218**	**10**	**1**	**2.75**	....	....	....	....	....	....	....

NILSTORP, Cristopher (NIHL-stohrp, krihs-TOH-fuhr) DAL

Goaltender. Catches right. 6'3", 192 lbs. Born, Burlov, Sweden, February 16, 1984.

			Regular Season								Playoffs						
Season	Club	League	GP	W	L	O/T	Mins	GA	SO	Avg	GP	W	L	Mins	GA	SO	Avg
2002-03	Malmo Jr.	Swe-Jr.	29	....	....	....	1751	....	1	2.88	....	....	....	....	....	....	....
2003-04	Malmo Jr.	Swe-Jr.	22	....	....	....	1261	....	2	....	....	....	....	....	....	....	....
	Malmo	Sweden	5	....	....	....	252	14	0	3.33	....	....	....	....	....	....	....
2004-05	Morrums GoIS IK	Sweden-2	16	....	....	....	885	48	2	3.25	....	....	....	....	....	....	....
	Malmo	Sweden	4	....	....	....	196	10	0	3.06	....	....	....	....	....	....	....
2005-06	Nybro Vikings IF	Sweden-2	9	....	....	....	428	23	0	3.22	....	....	....	....	....	....	....
	Malmo	Sweden-2	29	....	....	....	....	....	....	....	....	....	....	....	....	....	....
2006-07	Rogle	Sweden-2	37	....	....	....	....	....	....	....	....	....	....	....	....	....	....
2007-08	Rogle	Sweden-2	35	....	....	....	....	....	....	....	....	....	....	....	....	....	....
2008-09	Vaxjo Lakers HC	Sweden-2	1	....	....	....	....	3	....	....	....	....	....	....	....	....	....
	Rogle	Sweden	15	....	....	....	782	45	0	3.45	....	....	....	....	....	....	....
2009-10	Rogle	Sweden	33	....	....	....	1949	98	1	3.02	....	....	....	....	....	....	....
2010-11	Farjestad	Sweden	23	....	....	....	1268	46	2	2.18	9	....	....	....	....	....	1.60
2011-12	Farjestad	Sweden	45	....	....	....	2590	88	5	2.04	7	....	....	400	12	1	1.80
2012-13	Texas Stars	AHL	39	19	13	3	2146	85	4	2.38	9	4	5	547	21	1	2.30
	Dallas	**NHL**	**5**	**1**	**3**	**1**	**291**	**15**	**0**	**3.09**	....	....	....	....	....	....	....
	NHL Totals		**5**	**1**	**3**	**1**	**291**	**15**	**0**	**3.09**	....	....	....	....	....	....	....

Signed as a free agent by **Dallas**, June 5, 2012.

OLKINUORA, Juho (ohl-KIHN-oh-rah, YOO-hoh) WPG

Goaltender. Catches left. 6'2", 200 lbs. Born, Helsinki, Finland, November 4, 1990.

			Regular Season								Playoffs						
Season	Club	League	GP	W	L	O/T	Mins	GA	SO	Avg	GP	W	L	Mins	GA	SO	Avg
2010-11	Sioux Falls	USHL	27	14	13	0	1576	73	1	2.78	....	....	....	....	....	....	....
2011-12	U. of Denver	WCHA	22	9	8	3	1236	45	2	2.18	....	....	....	....	....	....	....
2012-13	U. of Denver	WCHA	24	13	6	5	1428	56	3	2.35	....	....	....	....	....	....	....
	St. John's IceCaps	AHL	1	0	1	0	59	3	0	3.03	....	....	....	....	....	....	....

WCHA All-Rookie Team (2012) • WCHA Second All-Star Team (2013) • NCAA West Second All-American Team (2013)

Signed to an ATO (amateur tryout) contract by **St. John's** (AHL), April 7, 2013. Signed as a free agent by **Winnipeg**, April 24, 2013.

OLSON, Collin (OHL-suhn, KAW-lihn) CAR

Goaltender. Catches left. 6'3", 205 lbs. Born, Burnsville, MN, April 4, 1994.
(Carolina's 8th choice, 159th overall, in 2012 Entry Draft).

			Regular Season								Playoffs						
Season	Club	League	GP	W	L	O/T	Mins	GA	SO	Avg	GP	W	L	Mins	GA	SO	Avg
2009-10	Apple Valley	High-MN	9	3	2	0	262	20	0	3.90	....	....	....	....	....	....	....
2010-11	USNTDP	USHL	19	10	8	1	1099	52	3	2.84	1	0	0	20	1	0	3.00
	USNTDP	U-17	10	7	1	0	492	16	0	1.95	....	....	....	....	....	....	....
2011-12	USNTDP	USHL	16	7	6	2	846	36	1	2.55	....	....	....	....	....	....	....
	USNTDP	U-17	1	0	1	0	60	4	0	4.00	....	....	....	....	....	....	....
	USNTDP	U-18	21	12	5	0	1063	40	3	2.26	....	....	....	....	....	....	....
2012-13	Ohio State	CCHA	9	2	3	1	408	21	0	3.09	....	....	....	....	....	....	....

ORTIO, Joni (OHR-tee-oh, YOH-nee) CGY

Goaltender. Catches left. 6'1", 181 lbs. Born, Turku, Finland, April 16, 1991.
(Calgary's 5th choice, 171st overall, in 2009 Entry Draft).

			Regular Season								Playoffs						
Season	Club	League	GP	W	L	O/T	Mins	GA	SO	Avg	GP	W	L	Mins	GA	SO	Avg
2007-08	TuTo Turku U18	Fin-U18	7	1	6	0	392	34	0	5.20	....	....	....	....	....	....	....
	TuTo Turku Jr.	Fin-Jr.	5	1	3	0	302	16	0	3.18	....	....	....	....	....	....	....
2008-09	TPS Turku U18	Fin-U18	1	1	0	0	60	4	0	4.00	....	....	....	....	....	....	....
	TPS Turku Jr.	Fin-Jr.	26	18	8	0	1573	69	1	2.63	12	6	6	716	23	0	1.93
2009-10	Suomi U20	Finland-2	5	3	2	0	312	11	0	2.12	....	....	....	....	....	....	....
	TuTo Turku	Finland-2	9	5	4	0	546	27	0	2.96	....	....	....	....	....	....	....
	TPS Turku Jr.	Fin-Jr.	16	8	6	0	935	45	1	2.89	....	....	....	....	....	....	....
	TPS Turku	Finland	3	1	0	0	108	8	0	4.45	....	....	....	....	....	....	....
2010-11	TPS Turku	Finland	15	2	7	3	730	38	1	3.12	....	....	....	....	....	....	....
	Abbotsford Heat	AHL	1	0	1	0	60	6	0	6.03	....	....	....	....	....	....	....
2011-12	Abbotsford Heat	AHL	9	1	4	0	387	19	0	2.94	....	....	....	....	....	....	....
	TPS Turku	Finland	14	3	6	3	753	33	2	2.63	2	0	1	87	3	0	2.06
2012-13	HIFK Helsinki	Finland	*54	23	20	9	*3120	126	4	2.42	8	3	5	481	20	0	2.49

OUELLETTE, Martin (OO-leht, MAHR-tihn) CBJ

Goaltender. Catches left. 6'2", 173 lbs. Born, Saint-Jerome, Que., December 30, 1991.
(Columbus' 8th choice, 184th overall, in 2010 Entry Draft).

			Regular Season								Playoffs						
Season	Club	League	GP	W	L	O/T	Mins	GA	SO	Avg	GP	W	L	Mins	GA	SO	Avg
2008-09	Kimball Union	High-NH	16	....	....	....	....	....	....	2.93	....	....	....	....	....	....	....
2009-10	Kimball Union	High-NH	29	21	6	2	1461	45	....	1.61	....	....	....	....	....	....	....
2010-11	University of Maine	H-East	9	3	3	2	490	26	1	3.18	....	....	....	....	....	....	....
2011-12	University of Maine	H-East	9	1	3	0	316	18	0	3.42	....	....	....	....	....	....	....
2012-13	University of Maine	H-East	30	9	12	8	1757	71	2	2.42	....	....	....	....	....	....	....

PASQUALE, Eddie (pas-KWAHL-ee, EH-dee) WPG

Goaltender. Catches left. 6'3", 215 lbs. Born, Toronto, Ont., November 20, 1990.
(Atlanta's 4th choice, 117th overall, in 2009 Entry Draft).

			Regular Season								Playoffs						
Season	Club	League	GP	W	L	O/T	Mins	GA	SO	Avg	GP	W	L	Mins	GA	SO	Avg
2005-06	Tor. Red Wings	GTHL	53	....	....	....	2385	98	5	1.84	....	....	....	....	....	....	....
2006-07	Wellington Dukes	ON-Jr.A	18	13	3	2	1091	35	1	1.92	....	....	....	....	....	....	....
	Belleville Bulls	OHL	7	4	1	0	367	19	0	3.11	....	....	....	....	....	....	....
2007-08	Belleville Bulls	OHL	10	4	4	2	558	27	1	2.90	....	....	....	....	....	....	....
	Saginaw Spirit	OHL	13	8	5	0	661	39	0	3.54	2	0	1	97	5	0	3.09
2008-09	Saginaw Spirit	OHL	*61	32	21	6	*3536	178	0	3.02	8	4	4	530	34	0	3.85
2009-10	Saginaw Spirit	OHL	51	27	17	5	2898	153	1	3.17	6	2	4	361	14	0	2.33
2010-11	Chicago Wolves	AHL	24	11	11	1	1372	67	1	2.93	....	....	....	....	....	....	....
	Gwinnett	ECHL	12	7	4	0	715	44	0	3.69	....	....	....	....	....	....	....
2011-12	St. John's IceCaps	AHL	38	23	12	1	2163	87	4	2.41	15	7	8	917	37	0	2.42
2012-13	St. John's IceCaps	AHL	43	15	23	4	2453	114	4	2.79	....	....	....	....	....	....	....

AHL All-Rookie Team (2012)

• Transferred to **Winnipeg** after **Atlanta** franchise relocated, June 21, 2011.

PATERSON, Jake (pa-TUHR-suhn, JAYK) DET

Goaltender. Catches left. 6'1", 176 lbs. Born, Mississauga, Ont., May 3, 1994.
(Detroit's 2nd choice, 80th overall, in 2012 Entry Draft).

			Regular Season								Playoffs						
Season	Club	League	GP	W	L	O/T	Mins	GA	SO	Avg	GP	W	L	Mins	GA	SO	Avg
2009-10	Toronto Marlboros	GTHL	50	38	7	4	2250	70	15	1.41	....	....	....	....	....	....	....
2010-11	Soo Eagles	NOJHL	13	10	1	2	793	39	2	2.95	15	11	4	916	37	3	2.42
	Saginaw Spirit	OHL	5	3	0	2	303	15	0	2.97	....	....	....	....	....	....	....
2011-12	Saginaw Spirit	OHL	42	18	18	3	2265	129	1	3.42	12	6	6	689	35	0	3.05
2012-13	Saginaw Spirit	OHL	50	25	18	5	2893	170	1	3.53	4	0	4	235	21	0	5.36

PATTERSON, Kent (PA-tuhr-suhn, KEHNT) COL

Goaltender. Catches left. 6', 184 lbs. Born, St. Louis Park, MN, September 15, 1989.
(Colorado's 6th choice, 113th overall, in 2007 Entry Draft).

			Regular Season								Playoffs						
Season	Club	League	GP	W	L	O/T	Mins	GA	SO	Avg	GP	W	L	Mins	GA	SO	Avg
2004-05	Blake Bears	High-MN	14	9	4	1	673	27	....	2.05	....	....	....	....	....	....	....
2005-06	Blake Bears	High-MN	25	14	8	2	1249	66	....	2.70	....	....	....	....	....	....	....
2006-07	Cedar Rapids	USHL	29	20	5	3	1710	83	2	2.91	1	0	1	41	6	0	8.78
2007-08	Cedar Rapids	USHL	20	10	6	1	1110	46	1	2.49	....	....	....	....	....	....	....
2008-09	U. of Minnesota	WCHA	7	0	2	1	231	9	0	2.34	....	....	....	....	....	....	....
2009-10	U. of Minnesota	WCHA	8	2	4	1	406	21	0	3.10	....	....	....	....	....	....	....
2010-11	U. of Minnesota	WCHA	30	14	9	6	1724	73	0	2.54	....	....	....	....	....	....	....
2011-12	U. of Minnesota	WCHA	43	28	14	1	2557	99	7	2.32	....	....	....	....	....	....	....
2012-13	Denver Cutthroats	CHL	33	14	10	6	1812	91	1	3.01	....	....	....	....	....	....	....
	Lake Erie Monsters	AHL	5	1	2	1	259	11	1	2.55	....	....	....	....	....	....	....

USHL All-Rookie Team (2007) • WCHA Second All-Star Team (2011) • WCHA First All-Star Team (2012) • NCAA West Second All-American Team (2012)

PAVELEC, Ondrej (pah-vah-LEK, AWN-dray) WPG

Goaltender. Catches left. 6'3", 220 lbs. Born, Kladno, Czech., August 31, 1987.
(Atlanta's 2nd choice, 41st overall, in 2005 Entry Draft).

			Regular Season								Playoffs						
Season	Club	League	GP	W	L	O/T	Mins	GA	SO	Avg	GP	W	L	Mins	GA	SO	Avg
2003-04	HC Kladno U17	CzR-U17	38	....	....	....	2079	77	3	2.22	2	....	....	67	7	0	6.27
2004-05	HC Kladno Jr.	CzRep-Jr.	39	....	....	....	2218	85	7	2.30	10	....	....	587	24	1	2.45
	HK LEV Slany	CzRep-3	1	....	....	....	60	4	0	4.00	....	....	....	....	....	....	....
2005-06	Cape Breton	QMJHL	47	27	18	0	2578	108	3	2.51	9	4	5	507	19	0	*2.25
2006-07	Cape Breton	QMJHL	43	28	11	0	2335	98	1	*2.52	16	11	5	970	37	*2	*2.29
2007-08	**Atlanta**	**NHL**	**7**	**3**	**3**	**0**	**347**	**18**	**0**	**3.11**	....	....	....	....	....	....	....
	Chicago Wolves	AHL	52	33	16	3	3033	140	2	2.77	*24	*16	8	*1438	56	*2	2.34
2008-09	**Atlanta**	**NHL**	**12**	**3**	**7**	**0**	**599**	**36**	**0**	**3.61**	....	....	....	....	....	....	....
	Chicago Wolves	AHL	40	18	20	2	2417	104	3	2.58	....	....	....	....	....	....	....
2009-10	**Atlanta**	**NHL**	**42**	**14**	**18**	**7**	**2317**	**127**	**2**	**3.29**	....	....	....	....	....	....	....
	Czech Republic	Olympics	DID NOT PLAY – SPARE GOALTENDER														
2010-11	**Atlanta**	**NHL**	**58**	**21**	**23**	**9**	**3225**	**147**	**4**	**2.73**	....	....	....	....	....	....	....
	Chicago Wolves	AHL	1	0	1	0	58	3	0	3.10	....	....	....	....	....	....	....
2011-12	**Winnipeg**	**NHL**	**68**	**29**	**28**	**9**	**3932**	**191**	**4**	**2.91**	....	....	....	....	....	....	....
2012-13	Liberec	CzRep	14	....	....	....	772	45	0	3.50	....	....	....	....	....	....	....
	Pelicans Lahti	Finland	6	....	....	....	....	....	....	2.68	....	....	....	....	....	....	....
	Winnipeg	**NHL**	***44**	**21**	**20**	**3**	**2553**	**119**	**0**	**2.80**	....	....	....	....	....	....	....
	NHL Totals		**231**	**91**	**99**	**28**	**12973**	**638**	**10**	**2.95**	....	....	....	....	....	....	....

QMJHL All-Rookie Team (2006) • QMJHL First All-Star Team (2006, 2007) • QMJHL Defensive Rookie of the Year (2006)

• Transferred to **Winnipeg** after **Atlanta** franchise relocated, June 21, 2011. Signed as a free agent by **Liberec** (CzRep), September 21, 2012. Signed as a free agent by **Lahti** (Finland), November 25, 2012.

PEARCE, Jordan (PEERS-JOHR-dahn)

Goaltender. Catches left. 6'1", 195 lbs. Born, Anchorage, AK, October 10, 1986.

			Regular Season								Playoffs						
Season	Club	League	GP	W	L	O/T	Mins	GA	SO	Avg	GP	W	L	Mins	GA	SO	Avg
2004-05	Lincoln Stars	USHL	38	22	10	4	2227	114	0	3.07	2	0	1	69	7	0	6.06
2005-06	U. of Notre Dame	CCHA	9	4	4	0	442	24	1	3.25	....	....	....	....	....	....	....
2006-07	U. of Notre Dame	CCHA	3	2	1	0	180	6	1	2.01	....	....	....	....	....	....	....
2007-08	U. of Notre Dame	CCHA	*43	23	15	4	*2558	87	2	2.04	....	....	....	....	....	....	....
2008-09	U. of Notre Dame	CCHA	*39	*30	6	3	*2326	65	8	1.68	....	....	....	....	....	....	....
	Grand Rapids	AHL	1	0	1	0	59	5	0	5.11	....	....	....	....	....	....	....
2009-10	Grand Rapids	AHL	5	1	2	0	236	15	0	3.82	....	....	....	....	....	....	....
	Toledo Walleye	ECHL	37	15	16	2	2047	124	2	3.63	4	1	3	247	16	0	3.88
2010-11	Grand Rapids	AHL	44	20	15	5	2452	118	1	2.89	....	....	....	....	....	....	....
	Toledo Walleye	ECHL	8	3	4	1	451	31	1	4.13	....	....	....	....	....	....	....
2011-12	Grand Rapids	AHL	19	3	8	1	880	54	1	3.68	....	....	....	....	....	....	....
	Toledo Walleye	ECHL	2	1	1	0	118	8	0	4.05	....	....	....	....	....	....	....
2012-13	Grand Rapids	AHL	4	0	3	0	181	13	0	4.32	....	....	....	....	....	....	....
	Toledo Walleye	ECHL	31	15	11	3	1696	78	2	2.76	4	2	1	215	7	0	1.95

Signed as a free agent by **Detroit**, April 10, 2009.

PECHURSKI, Alexander (puh-CHUHR-skee, al-ehx-AN-duhr) PIT

Goaltender. Catches left. 6', 187 lbs. Born, Magnitogorsk, USSR, June 4, 1990.
(Pittsburgh's 2nd choice, 150th overall, in 2008 Entry Draft).

			Regular Season								Playoffs						
Season	Club	League	GP	W	L	O/T	Mins	GA	SO	Avg	GP	W	L	Mins	GA	SO	Avg
2007-08	Magnitogorsk 2	Russia-3	27	....	....	....	....	62	....	....	....	....	....	....	....	....	....
	Magnitogorsk	Russia	1	....	....	....	1	0	0	0.00	....	....	....	....	....	....	....
2008-09	Magnitogorsk 2	Russia-3	20	....	....	....	....	54	....	....	....	....	....	....	....	....	....
2009-10	Magnitogorsk	KHL	1	....	....	....	30	3	0	6.00	....	....	....	....	....	....	....
	Magnitogorsk Jr.	Russia-Jr.	5	....	....	....	299	14	0	2.81	....	....	....	....	....	....	....
	Pittsburgh	**NHL**	**1**	**0**	**0**	**0**	**36**	**1**	**0**	**1.67**	....	....	....	....	....	....	....
	Tri-City Americans	WHL	27	13	10	1	1403	61	4	2.61	7	1	2	305	15	0	2.95
2010-11	Tri-City Americans	WHL	3	2	0	1	184	11	0	3.60	....	....	....	....	....	....	....
	Mississippi	CHL	37	17	14	2	2030	103	1	3.04	....	....	....	....	....	....	....
2011-12	Magnitogorsk	KHL	5	0	2	0	259	11	0	2.55	....	....	....	....	....	....	....
	Titan Klin	Russia-2	12	....	....	....	....	....	....	2.32	....	....	....	....	....	....	....
2012-13	Yuzhny Ural Orsk	Russia-2	35	....	....	....	....	....	....	1.83	....	....	....	....	....	....	....
	NHL Totals		**1**	**0**	**0**	**0**	**36**	**1**	**0**	**1.67**	....	....	....	....	....	....	....

Signed as a free agent by **Magnitogorsk** (KHL), June 6, 2011. Signed as a free agent by **Klin** (Russia-2), January 19, 2012. Signed as a free agent by **Orsk** (Russia-2), September 20, 2012.

PERHONEN, Samu (PAIR-hoh-nehn, SA-moo)

Goaltender. Catches left. 6'5", 184 lbs. Born, Jamsankoski, Finland, March 7, 1993.
(Edmonton's 4th choice, 62nd overall, in 2011 Entry Draft).

			Regular Season								Playoffs						
Season	Club	League	GP	W	L	O/T	Mins	GA	SO	Avg	GP	W	L	Mins	GA	SO	Avg
2008-09	JyP Jyvaskyla U18	Fin-U18	1	1	0	0	60	0	1	0.00	....	....	....	....	....	....	....
2009-10	JyP Jyvaskyla U18	Fin-U18	13	5	5	0	745	41	1	3.30	....	....	....	....	....	....	....
	JyP Jyvaskyla Jr.	Fin-Jr.	1	0	1	0	26	2	0	4.67	....	....	....	....	....	....	....
2010-11	Suomi U20	Finland-2	1	0	1	0	59	3	0	3.04	....	....	....	....	....	....	....
	JyP Jyvaskyla Jr.	Fin-Jr.	29	16	11	0	1659	75	2	2.71	12	8	4	736	30	2	2.45
2011-12	JyP Jyvaskyla Jr.	Fin-Jr.	5	4	0	0	268	14	0	3.14	....	....	....	....	....	....	....
	JYP-Akatemia	Finland-2	11	3	8	0	630	40	0	3.81	....	....	....	....	....	....	....
2012-13	JyP Jyvaskyla Jr.	Fin-Jr.	3	....	....	....	112	10	0	5.32	....	....	....	....	....	....	....
	JYP-Akatemia	Finland-2	14	....	....	....	784	43	0	3.29	....	....	....	....	....	....	....

PETERS, Justin (PEE-tuhrz, JUHS-tihn) CAR

Goaltender. Catches left. 6'1", 210 lbs. Born, Blyth, Ont., August 30, 1986.
(Carolina's 2nd choice, 38th overall, in 2004 Entry Draft).

			Regular Season								Playoffs						
Season	Club	League	GP	W	L	O/T	Mins	GA	SO	Avg	GP	W	L	Mins	GA	SO	Avg
2001-02	Huron-Perth	Minor-ON	17	11	2	4	810	32	1	1.89	13	9	4	285	30	1	2.31
2002-03	St. Michael's	OHL	23	6	10	1	1052	54	0	3.08	7	1	0	126	4	0	1.90
2003-04	St. Michael's	OHL	53	30	16	6	3149	139	4	2.65	18	10	8	1109	37	4	2.00
2004-05	St. Michael's	OHL	58	23	23	5	3150	146	3	2.78	10	4	4	524	25	0	2.86
2005-06	St. Michael's	OHL	20	10	6	3	1174	75	0	3.83	....	....	....	....	....	....	....
	Plymouth Whalers	OHL	35	19	15	1	2073	95	1	2.75	13	6	7	789	42	0	3.19
2006-07	Albany River Rats	AHL	34	10	18	0	1765	96	1	3.26	....	....	....	....	....	....	....
	Florida Everblades	ECHL	1	0	0	1	65	6	0	5.54	....	....	....	....	....	....	....
2007-08	Albany River Rats	AHL	11	7	3	0	645	29	0	2.70	....	....	....	....	....	....	....
	Florida Everblades	ECHL	31	18	10	2	1846	79	1	2.57	....	....	....	....	....	....	....
2008-09	Albany River Rats	AHL	56	19	30	4	3178	153	4	2.89	....	....	....	....	....	....	....
2009-10	**Carolina**	**NHL**	**9**	**6**	**3**	**0**	**488**	**23**	**0**	**2.83**	....	....	....	....	....	....	....
	Albany River Rats	AHL	47	26	18	2	2763	117	1	2.54	8	4	4	509	29	0	3.42
2010-11	**Carolina**	**NHL**	**12**	**3**	**5**	**1**	**648**	**43**	**0**	**3.98**	....	....	....	....	....	....	....
2011-12	**Carolina**	**NHL**	**7**	**2**	**3**	**2**	**387**	**16**	**1**	**2.48**	....	....	....	....	....	....	....
	Charlotte Checkers	AHL	28	10	13	2	1604	74	1	2.77	....	....	....	....	....	....	....
2012-13	Charlotte Checkers	AHL	37	22	12	1	2072	79	6	2.29	....	....	....	....	....	....	....
	Carolina	**NHL**	**19**	**4**	**11**	**1**	**954**	**55**	**1**	**3.46**	....	....	....	....	....	....	....
	NHL Totals		**47**	**15**	**22**	**4**	**2477**	**137**	**2**	**3.32**	....	....	....	....	....	....	....

PETERSEN, Calvin (PEE-tuhr-suhn, KAL-vihn) BUF

Goaltender. Catches right. 6'2", 183 lbs. Born, Waterloo, IA, October 19, 1994.
(Buffalo's 7th choice, 129th overall, in 2013 Entry Draft).

			Regular Season								Playoffs						
Season	Club	League	GP	W	L	O/T	Mins	GA	SO	Avg	GP	W	L	Mins	GA	SO	Avg
2010-11	Chi. Americans	T1EHL	24	13	6	5	1244	53	4	2.30	....	....	....	....	....	....	....
2011-12	Chi. Americans	HPHL	12	3	6	2	680	35	0	3.09	....	....	....	....	....	....	....
	Topeka	NAHL	2	1	0	1	129	4	0	1.86	....	....	....	....	....	....	....
	Waterloo	USHL	5	3	1	0	265	13	0	2.94	....	....	....	....	....	....	....
2012-13	Waterloo	USHL	35	21	11	1	1937	96	3	2.97	4	2	2	211	15	0	4.26

USHL All-Rookie Team (2013)

• Signed Letter of Intent to attend **University of Notre Dame** (CCHA) in fall of 2013.

PHILLIPS, Jamie (FIHL-ihps, JAY-mee) WPG

Goaltender. Catches left. 6'3", 188 lbs. Born, Caledonia, Ont., March 24, 1993.
(Winnipeg's 6th choice, 190th overall, in 2012 Entry Draft).

			Regular Season								Playoffs						
Season	Club	League	GP	W	L	O/T	Mins	GA	SO	Avg	GP	W	L	Mins	GA	SO	Avg
2008-09	St. Cath. Falcons	Minor-ON	41	....	....	....	1845	57	1	2.61	....	....	....	....	....	....	....
	Brantford	ON-Jr.B	....	....	....	....	....	....	....	....	1	0	1	60	3	0	3.00
2009-10	Welland	ON-Jr.B	6	0	2	0	202	16	0	4.76	....	....	....	....	....	....	....
	Brantford	ON-Jr.B	3	2	0	0	140	7	0	3.00	....	....	....	....	....	....	....
2010-11	Pembroke	ON-Jr.A	33	25	6	1	1857	66	*6	*2.13	2	2	0	12	3	1	1.50
2011-12	Powell River Kings	BCHL	26	16	6	1	....	....	....	2.01	....	....	....	....	....	....	....
	Tor. Canadiens	ON-Jr.A	11	4	4	0	637	33	1	3.11	10	5	5	581	29	0	2.99
2012-13	Michigan Tech	WCHA	9	2	2	0	324	13	1	2.40	....	....	....	....	....	....	....

PICKARD, Calvin (pih-KARD, KAL-vihn) COL

Goaltender. Catches left. 6', 196 lbs. Born, Moncton, N.B., April 15, 1992.
(Colorado's 2nd choice, 49th overall, in 2010 Entry Draft).

			Regular Season								Playoffs						
Season	Club	League	GP	W	L	O/T	Mins	GA	SO	Avg	GP	W	L	Mins	GA	SO	Avg
2007-08	Winnipeg Wild	MMHL	40	....	....	....	....	....	....	1.91	....	....	....	....	....	....	....
2008-09	Seattle	WHL	47	23	16	5	2694	137	3	3.05	5	1	4	297	15	0	3.03
2009-10	Seattle	WHL	*62	16	34	12	*3688	190	3	3.09	....	....	....	....	....	....	....
2010-11	Seattle	WHL	*68	27	33	8	*4013	225	1	3.36	....	....	....	....	....	....	....
2011-12	Seattle	WHL	*64	25	37	2	*3630	217	*5	3.59	....	....	....	....	....	....	....
	Lake Erie Monsters	AHL	2	1	0	0	77	4	0	3.12	....	....	....	....	....	....	....
2012-13	Lake Erie Monsters	AHL	47	20	19	5	2749	113	5	2.47	....	....	....	....	....	....	....

WHL West First All-Star Team (2010) • WHL West Second All-Star Team (2011)

POULIN, Kevin (POO-lihn, KEH-vihn) NYI

Goaltender. Catches left. 6'2", 192 lbs. Born, Montreal, Que., April 12, 1990.
(NY Islanders' 10th choice, 126th overall, in 2008 Entry Draft).

			Regular Season								Playoffs						
Season	Club	League	GP	W	L	O/T	Mins	GA	SO	Avg	GP	W	L	Mins	GA	SO	Avg
2005-06	C.C. Lemoyne	QAAA	27	13	8	2	1440	71	1	2.96	7	4	3	373	16	1	2.57
2006-07	Victoriaville Tigres	QMJHL	24	10	6	0	1220	68	0	3.34	2	0	2	42	5	0	7.20
2007-08	Victoriaville Tigres	QMJHL	52	18	24	0	2734	168	0	3.69	6	2	4	279	27	0	5.80
2008-09	Victoriaville Tigres	QMJHL	39	18	19	0	2273	120	1	3.17	4	0	4	249	18	0	4.34
2009-10	Victoriaville Tigres	QMJHL	54	*35	16	0	3105	136	*7	2.63	16	10	6	971	46	0	2.84
2010-11	**NY Islanders**	**NHL**	**10**	**4**	**2**	**1**	**491**	**20**	**0**	**2.44**	....	....	....	....	....	....	....
	Bridgeport	AHL	15	10	5	0	903	33	2	2.19	....	....	....	....	....	....	....
2011-12	**NY Islanders**	**NHL**	**6**	**2**	**4**	**0**	**296**	**15**	**0**	**3.04**	....	....	....	....	....	....	....
	Bridgeport	AHL	49	26	18	4	2943	137	3	2.79	3	0	3	194	10	0	3.09
2012-13	Bridgeport	AHL	32	15	14	3	1824	98	1	3.22	....	....	....	....	....	....	....
	NY Islanders	**NHL**	**5**	**1**	**3**	**0**	**258**	**13**	**0**	**3.02**	**2**	**0**	**0**	**52**	**1**	**0**	**1.15**
	NHL Totals		**21**	**7**	**9**	**1**	**1045**	**48**	**0**	**2.76**	**2**	**0**	**0**	**52**	**1**	**0**	**1.15**

QMJHL Second All-Star Team (2010)

PRICE, Carey (PRIGHS, KAIR-ee) MTL

Goaltender. Catches left. 6'3", 221 lbs. Born, Anahim Lake, B.C., August 16, 1987.
(Montreal's 1st choice, 5th overall, in 2005 Entry Draft).

			Regular Season								Playoffs						
Season	Club	League	GP	W	L	O/T	Mins	GA	SO	Avg	GP	W	L	Mins	GA	SO	Avg
2002-03	Williams Lake	Minor-BC	18	....	....	....	1050	48	1	2.70	....	....	....	....	....	....	....
	Tri-City Americans	WHL	1	0	0	0	20	2	0	6.00	....	....	....	....	....	....	....
2003-04	Tri-City Americans	WHL	28	8	9	3	1362	54	1	2.38	8	5	3	470	19	0	2.43
2004-05	Tri-City Americans	WHL	63	24	31	8	3712	145	8	2.34	5	1	4	324	12	0	2.22
2005-06	Tri-City Americans	WHL	55	21	25	6	3072	147	3	2.87	5	1	4	302	12	0	2.39
2006-07	Tri-City Americans	WHL	46	30	13	1	2722	111	3	2.45	6	2	4	348	17	0	2.93
	Hamilton Bulldogs	AHL	2	1	1	0	117	3	0	1.53	*22	*15	6	*1314	45	*2	2.06
2007-08	**Montreal**	**NHL**	**41**	**24**	**12**	**3**	**2413**	**103**	**3**	**2.56**	**11**	**5**	**6**	**648**	**30**	**2**	**2.78**
	Hamilton Bulldogs	AHL	10	6	4	0	581	26	1	2.69	....	....	....	....	....	....	....
2008-09	**Montreal**	**NHL**	**52**	**23**	**16**	**10**	**3036**	**143**	**1**	**2.83**	**4**	**0**	**4**	**219**	**15**	**0**	**4.11**
2009-10	**Montreal**	**NHL**	**41**	**13**	**20**	**5**	**2358**	**109**	**0**	**2.77**	**4**	**0**	**1**	**135**	**8**	**0**	**3.56**
2010-11	**Montreal**	**NHL**	**72**	***38**	**28**	**6**	**4206**	**165**	**8**	**2.35**	**7**	**3**	**4**	**455**	**16**	**1**	**2.11**
2011-12	**Montreal**	**NHL**	**65**	**26**	**28**	**11**	**3944**	**160**	**4**	**2.43**	....	....	....	....	....	....	....
2012-13	**Montreal**	**NHL**	**39**	**21**	**13**	**4**	**2249**	**97**	**3**	**2.59**	**4**	**1**	**2**	**239**	**13**	**0**	**3.26**
	NHL Totals		**310**	**145**	**117**	**39**	**18206**	**777**	**19**	**2.56**	**30**	**9**	**17**	**1696**	**82**	**3**	**2.90**

WHL West First All-Star Team (2007) • WHL Goaltender of the Year (2007) • Canadian Major Junior First All-Star Team (2007) • Canadian Major Junior Goaltender of the Year (2007) • Jack A. Butterfield Trophy (AHL - Playoff MVP) (2007) • NHL All-Rookie Team (2008)

Played in NHL All-Star Game (2009, 2011, 2012)

QUICK, Jonathan (KWIHK, JAWN-ah-thuhn) L.A.

Goaltender. Catches left. 6'1", 218 lbs. Born, Milford, CT, January 21, 1986.
(Los Angeles' 4th choice, 72nd overall, in 2005 Entry Draft).

			Regular Season								Playoffs						
Season	Club	League	GP	W	L	O/T	Mins	GA	SO	Avg	GP	W	L	Mins	GA	SO	Avg
2002-03	Avon Old Farms	High-CT	13	8	5	0	780	38	0	2.92	....	....	....	....	....	....	....
2003-04	Avon Old Farms	High-CT	21	20	1	0	1260	26	2	1.71	....	....	....	....	....	....	....
2004-05	Avon Old Farms	High-CT	27	25	2	0	1413	27	9	1.14	....	....	....	....	....	....	....
2005-06	Massachusetts	H-East	17	4	10	1	905	45	0	2.98	....	....	....	....	....	....	....
2006-07	Massachusetts	H-East	37	19	12	5	2224	80	3	2.16	....	....	....	....	....	....	....
2007-08	**Los Angeles**	**NHL**	**3**	**1**	**2**	**0**	**141**	**9**	**0**	**3.83**	....	....	....	....	....	....	....
	Manchester	AHL	19	11	8	0	1085	42	3	2.32	1	0	1	59	1	0	1.02
	Reading Royals	ECHL	38	23	11	3	2257	105	1	2.79	....	....	....	....	....	....	....
2008-09	**Los Angeles**	**NHL**	**44**	**21**	**18**	**2**	**2495**	**103**	**4**	**2.48**	....	....	....	....	....	....	....
	Manchester	AHL	14	6	5	2	827	37	0	2.68	....	....	....	....	....	....	....
2009-10	**Los Angeles**	**NHL**	**72**	**39**	**24**	**7**	**4258**	**180**	**4**	**2.54**	**6**	**2**	**4**	**360**	**21**	**0**	**3.50**
	United States	Olympics	DID NOT PLAY – SPARE GOALTENDER														
2010-11	**Los Angeles**	**NHL**	**61**	**35**	**22**	**3**	**3591**	**134**	**6**	**2.24**	**6**	**2**	**4**	**380**	**20**	**1**	**3.16**
2011-12 ♦	**Los Angeles**	**NHL**	**69**	**35**	**21**	**13**	**4099**	**133**	***10**	**1.95**	**20**	***16**	**4**	**1238**	**29**	***3**	***1.41**
2012-13	**Los Angeles**	**NHL**	**37**	**18**	**13**	**4**	**2134**	**87**	**1**	**2.45**	**18**	**9**	**9**	**1099**	**34**	***3**	**1.86**
	NHL Totals		**286**	**149**	**100**	**29**	**16718**	**646**	**25**	**2.32**	**50**	**29**	**21**	**3077**	**104**	**7**	**2.03**

Hockey East Second All-Star Team (2007) • NCAA East Second All-American Team (2007) • NHL Second All-Star Team (2012) • Conn Smythe Trophy (2012)

Played in NHL All-Star Game (2012)

RAANTA, Antti (RAHN-tah, AN-tee) CHI

Goaltender. Catches left. 6', 182 lbs. Born, Rauma, Finland, May 12, 1989.

			Regular Season								Playoffs						
Season	Club	League	GP	W	L	O/T	Mins	GA	SO	Avg	GP	W	L	Mins	GA	SO	Avg
2007-08	Lukko Rauma Jr.	Fin-Jr.	13	....	....	....	....	....	....	3.23	....	....	....	....	....	....	....
2008-09	Lukko Rauma	Finland	2	....	....	....	....	....	....	2.51	....	....	....	....	....	....	....
2009-10	Lukko Rauma Jr.	Fin-Jr.	15	....	....	....	....	....	....	2.20	4	....	....	....	....	....	1.51
	Lukko Rauma	Finland	15	6	7	1	836	37	2	2.66	....	....	....	....	....	....	....
2010-11	Lukko Rauma	Finland	20	....	....	....	....	....	....	2.37	2	....	....	....	....	....	4.28
2011-12	Assat Pori	Finland	38	....	....	....	....	....	....	2.23	3	....	....	....	....	....	3.07
2012-13	Assat Pori	Finland	45	21	10	11	2595	80	5	*1.85	*16	*12	4	*1039	23	*4	*1.33

Signed as a free agent by **Chicago**, June 3, 2013.

RAMO, Karri (RAH-moh, KAH-ree) CGY

Goaltender. Catches left. 6', 215 lbs. Born, Asikkala, Finland, July 1, 1986.
(Tampa Bay's 7th choice, 191st overall, in 2004 Entry Draft).

			Regular Season								Playoffs						
Season	Club	League	GP	W	L	O/T	Mins	GA	SO	Avg	GP	W	L	Mins	GA	SO	Avg
2002-03	K-Reipas U18	Fin-U18	19	12	3	2	1013	47	0	2.78	4	2	2	182	11	0	3.62
2003-04	Pelicans Lahti U18	Fin-U18	3	3	0	0	180	7	0	2.33	5	2	2	268	10	0	2.24
	Pelicans Lahti Jr.	Fin-Jr.	18	5	9	2	960	53	0	3.31	2	2	0	120	1	1	0.50
	Pelicans Lahti	Finland	3	0	2	0	138	10	0	4.34	....	....	....	....	....	....	....
2004-05	Pelicans Lahti Jr.	Fin-Jr.	21	10	5	6	1269	36	6	1.70	4	1	3	206	16	0	4.66
	Pelicans Lahti	Finland	26	4	12	4	1267	84	1	3.98	....	....	....	....	....	....	....
2005-06	Haukat Jarvenpaa	Finland-2	1	....	....	....	60	5	0	5.00	....	....	....	....	....	....	....
	Suomi U20	Finland-2	3	....	....	....	183	12	0	3.93	....	....	....	....	....	....	....
	HPK Hameenlinna	Finland	24	7	8	7	1359	49	2	2.16	3	2	1	204	5	1	1.46
2006-07	**Tampa Bay**	**NHL**	**2**	**0**	**0**	**0**	**70**	**4**	**0**	**3.43**	....	....	....	....	....	....	....
	Springfield Falcons	AHL	45	15	24	1	2432	127	1	3.13	....	....	....	....	....	....	....
2007-08	**Tampa Bay**	**NHL**	**22**	**7**	**11**	**3**	**1269**	**64**	**0**	**3.03**	....	....	....	....	....	....	....
	Norfolk Admirals	AHL	6	2	4	0	342	19	0	3.33	....	....	....	....	....	....	....
2008-09	**Tampa Bay**	**NHL**	**24**	**4**	**10**	**7**	**1312**	**80**	**0**	**3.66**	....	....	....	....	....	....	....
	Norfolk Admirals	AHL	26	7	14	4	1507	95	0	3.78	....	....	....	....	....	....	....
2009-10	Omsk	KHL	44	....	....	....	2582	91	4	2.11	3	....	....	158	8	0	3.04
2010-11	Omsk	KHL	44	....	....	....	2593	85	5	1.97	14	....	....	891	32	1	2.16
2011-12	Omsk	KHL	45	19	17	0	2667	87	5	1.96	21	14	6	1209	31	3	1.54
2012-13	Omsk	KHL	40	*26	9	0	2401	80	4	2.00	12	5	7	725	24	3	1.99
	NHL Totals		**48**	**11**	**21**	**10**	**2651**	**148**	**0**	**3.35**	....	....	....	....	....	....	....

Signed as a free agent by **Omsk** (KHL), June 23, 2009. Traded to **Montreal** by **Tampa Bay** for Cedrick Desjardins, August 16, 2010. Traded to **Calgary** by **Montreal** with Mike Cammalleri and Montreal's 5th round choice (Ryan Culkin) in 2012 Entry Draft for Rene Bourque, Patrick Holland and Calgary's 2nd round choice (Zachary Fucale) in 2013 Entry Draft, January 12, 2012.

RASK, Tuukka (RASK, TU-kah) BOS

Goaltender. Catches left. 6'3", 185 lbs. Born, Savonlinna, Finland, March 10, 1987.
(Toronto's 1st choice, 21st overall, in 2005 Entry Draft).

			Regular Season								Playoffs						
Season	Club	League	GP	W	L	O/T	Mins	GA	SO	Avg	GP	W	L	Mins	GA	SO	Avg
2003-04	Ilves Tampere U18	Fin-U18	9	4	3	2	533	25	0	2.81	....	....	....	....	....	....	....
	Ilves Tampere Jr.	Fin-Jr.	30	12	10	7	1767	65	2	2.21	3	1	2	178	6	0	2.02
2004-05	Ilves Tampere Jr.	Fin-Jr.	26	17	3	4	1517	47	2	1.86	10	9	1	619	9	6	0.87
	Ilves Tampere	Finland	4	0	1	1	201	15	0	4.46	....	....	....	....	....	....	....
2005-06	Ilves Tampere Jr.	Fin-Jr.	1	....	....	....	60	2	0	2.00	....	....	....	....	....	....	....
	Suomi U20	Finland-2	3	....	....	....	179	6	0	2.01	....	....	....	....	....	....	....
	Ilves Tampere	Finland	30	12	8	7	1724	60	2	2.09	3	0	3	180	7	0	2.33
2006-07	Suomi U20	Finland-2	1	0	1	0	58	4	0	4.14	....	....	....	....	....	....	....
	Ilves Tampere	Finland	49	18	18	10	2872	114	3	2.38	7	2	5	397	20	0	3.02
2007-08	**Boston**	**NHL**	**4**	**2**	**1**	**1**	**184**	**10**	**0**	**3.26**	....	....	....	....	....	....	....
	Providence Bruins	AHL	45	27	13	2	2570	100	1	2.33	10	6	4	605	22	*2	2.18
2008-09	**Boston**	**NHL**	**1**	**1**	**0**	**0**	**60**	**0**	**1**	**0.00**	....	....	....	....	....	....	....
	Providence Bruins	AHL	57	33	20	4	3340	139	4	2.50	16	9	7	977	36	0	2.21
2009-10	**Boston**	**NHL**	**45**	**22**	**12**	**5**	**2562**	**84**	**5**	***1.97**	**13**	**7**	**6**	**829**	**36**	**0**	**2.61**
2010-11 ♦	**Boston**	**NHL**	**29**	**11**	**14**	**2**	**1594**	**71**	**2**	**2.67**	....	....	....	....	....	....	....
2011-12	**Boston**	**NHL**	**23**	**11**	**8**	**3**	**1289**	**44**	**3**	**2.05**	....	....	....	....	....	....	....
2012-13	HC Skoda Plzen	CzRep	17	....	....	....	993	35	1	2.11	....	....	....	....	....	....	....
	Boston	**NHL**	**36**	**19**	**10**	**5**	**2104**	**70**	***5**	**2.00**	**22**	**14**	**8**	**1466**	**46**	***3**	**1.88**
	NHL Totals		**138**	**66**	**45**	**16**	**7793**	**279**	**16**	**2.15**	**35**	**21**	**14**	**2295**	**82**	**3**	**2.14**

Traded to **Boston** by **Toronto** for Andrew Raycroft, June 24, 2006. Signed as a free agent by **Plzen** (CzRep), September 25, 2012.

RAWLINGS, Chris (RAW-lihngz, KRIHS) PHX

Goaltender. Catches left. 6'5", 220 lbs. Born, North Delta, B.C., September 19, 1988.

			Regular Season								Playoffs						
Season	Club	League	GP	W	L	O/T	Mins	GA	SO	Avg	GP	W	L	Mins	GA	SO	Avg
2005-06	Salmon Arm	BCHL	22	13	5	0	1145	47	3	2.46	....	....	....	....	....	....	....
2006-07	Powell River Kings	BCHL	43	24	14	2	2484	174	3	4.20	....	....	....	....	....	....	....
2007-08	Powell River Kings	BCHL	47	20	25	1	2758	153	0	3.33	....	....	....	....	....	....	....
2008-09	Cowichan Valley	BCHL	48	30	15	1	2778	131	2	2.83	....	....	....	....	....	....	....
2009-10	Northeastern	H-East	31	15	14	2	1822	86	3	2.83	....	....	....	....	....	....	....
2010-11	Northeastern	H-East	35	12	13	8	2034	91	5	2.68	....	....	....	....	....	....	....
2011-12	Northeastern	H-East	31	12	14	5	1771	80	1	2.71	....	....	....	....	....	....	....
2012-13	Northeastern	H-East	26	8	14	1	1398	75	1	3.22	....	....	....	....	....	....	....
	Idaho Steelheads	ECHL	2	1	0	0	99	1	1	0.60	....	....	....	....	....	....	....
	Portland Pirates	AHL	1	0	0	0	40	1	0	1.50	....	....	....	....	....	....	....

Signed as a free agent by **Phoenix**, July 19, 2013.

REIMER, James (RIGH-muhr, JAYMZ) TOR

Goaltender. Catches left. 6'2", 208 lbs. Born, Morweena, Man., March 15, 1988.
(Toronto's 3rd choice, 99th overall, in 2006 Entry Draft).

			Regular Season								Playoffs						
Season	Club	League	GP	W	L	O/T	Mins	GA	SO	Avg	GP	W	L	Mins	GA	SO	Avg
2003-04	Interlake Lightning	MMHL	27	....	....	....	....	....	1	2.85	....	....	....	....	....	....	....
2004-05	Interlake Lightning	MMHL	37	....	....	....	....	....	4	2.11	....	....	....	....	....	....	....
2005-06	Red Deer Rebels	WHL	34	7	18	3	1709	80	0	2.81	....	....	....	....	....	....	....
2006-07	Red Deer Rebels	WHL	60	26	23	7	3339	148	3	2.66	7	3	4	417	27	0	3.88
2007-08	Red Deer Rebels	WHL	30	8	15	4	1668	76	1	2.73	....	....	....	....	....	....	....
2008-09	Toronto Marlies	AHL	3	1	2	0	183	10	0	3.28	....	....	....	....	....	....	....
	Reading Royals	ECHL	22	10	7	3	1236	68	0	3.30	....	....	....	....	....	....	....
	South Carolina	ECHL	6	6	0	0	363	8	2	1.32	8	4	3	497	18	1	2.17
2009-10	Toronto Marlies	AHL	26	14	8	2	1520	57	1	2.25	....	....	....	....	....	....	....
2010-11	**Toronto**	**NHL**	**37**	**20**	**10**	**5**	**2080**	**90**	**3**	**2.60**	....	....	....	....	....	....	....
	Toronto Marlies	AHL	15	9	5	1	858	37	3	2.59	....	....	....	....	....	....	....
2011-12	**Toronto**	**NHL**	**34**	**14**	**14**	**4**	**1879**	**97**	**3**	**3.10**	....	....	....	....	....	....	....
2012-13	**Toronto**	**NHL**	**33**	**19**	**8**	**5**	**1856**	**76**	**4**	**2.46**	**7**	**3**	**4**	**438**	**21**	**0**	**2.88**
	NHL Totals		**104**	**53**	**32**	**14**	**5815**	**263**	**10**	**2.71**	**7**	**3**	**4**	**438**	**21**	**0**	**2.88**

ECHL Playoff MVP (2009)

RINNE, Pekka (RIH-neh, PEH-kuh) NSH

Goaltender. Catches left. 6'5", 206 lbs. Born, Kempele, Finland, November 3, 1982.
(Nashville's 10th choice, 258th overall, in 2004 Entry Draft).

			Regular Season								Playoffs						
Season	Club	League	GP	W	L	O/T	Mins	GA	SO	Avg	GP	W	L	Mins	GA	SO	Avg
2000-01	Karpat Oulu Jr.	Fin-Jr.	20	9	4	5	1148	63	0	3.29	....	....	....	....	....	....	....
2001-02	Karpat Oulu Jr.	Fin-Jr.	30	19	7	3	1724	61	3	2.12	3	1	2	184	10	1	3.26
2002-03	Karpat Oulu Jr.	Fin-Jr.	25	14	8	3	1479	48	5	1.95	4	1	3	238	7	0	1.76
	Karpat Oulu	Finland	1	0	1	0	60	7	0	7.00	....	....	....	....	....	....	....
2003-04	Karpat Oulu	Finland	14	5	4	4	824	41	0	2.99	2	1	0	22	0	0	0.00
	Hokki Kajaani	Finland-2	8	5	2	1	463	16	2	2.07	....	....	....	....	....	....	....
2004-05	Karpat Oulu	Finland	10	8	0	1	571	16	0	1.68	....	....	....	....	....	....	....
2005-06	**Nashville**	**NHL**	**2**	**1**	**1**	**0**	**63**	**4**	**0**	**3.81**	....	....	....	....	....	....	....
	Milwaukee	AHL	51	30	18	2	2960	139	2	2.82	14	10	4	734	35	3	2.86
2006-07	Milwaukee	AHL	29	15	7	6	1670	65	3	2.34	4	0	4	247	12	0	2.91
2007-08	**Nashville**	**NHL**	**1**	**0**	**0**	**0**	**29**	**0**	**0**	**0.00**	....	....	....	....	....	....	....
	Milwaukee	AHL	*65	*36	24	3	*3840	158	5	2.47	6	2	4	358	15	1	2.51
2008-09	**Nashville**	**NHL**	**52**	**29**	**15**	**4**	**2999**	**119**	**7**	**2.38**	....	....	....	....	....	....	....
2009-10	**Nashville**	**NHL**	**58**	**32**	**16**	**5**	**3246**	**137**	**7**	**2.53**	**6**	**2**	**4**	**358**	**16**	**0**	**2.68**
2010-11	**Nashville**	**NHL**	**64**	**33**	**22**	**9**	**3789**	**134**	**6**	**2.12**	**12**	**6**	**6**	**748**	**32**	**0**	**2.57**
2011-12	**Nashville**	**NHL**	***73**	***43**	**18**	**8**	**4169**	**166**	**5**	**2.39**	**10**	**5**	**5**	**609**	**21**	**1**	**2.07**
2012-13	Dynamo Minsk	KHL	22	9	11	0	1327	68	1	3.08	....	....	....	....	....	....	....
	Nashville	**NHL**	**43**	**15**	**16**	**8**	**2444**	**99**	***5**	**2.43**	....	....	....	....	....	....	....
	NHL Totals		**293**	**153**	**88**	**34**	**16739**	**659**	**30**	**2.36**	**28**	**13**	**15**	**1715**	**69**	**1**	**2.41**

NHL Second All-Star Team (2011)

Signed as a free agent by **Minsk** (KHL), September 25, 2012.

ROY, Olivier (WAH, oh-LIHV-ee-ay) EDM

Goaltender. Catches left. 6', 180 lbs. Born, Amqui, Que., July 12, 1991.
(Edmonton's 7th choice, 133rd overall, in 2009 Entry Draft).

			Regular Season								Playoffs						
Season	Club	League	GP	W	L	O/T	Mins	GA	SO	Avg	GP	W	L	Mins	GA	SO	Avg
2006-07	Ecole Notre Dame	QAAA	27	15	8	0	1459	65	2	2.67	4	2	1	206	13	0	3.79
2007-08	Cape Breton	QMJHL	47	27	15	0	2428	116	4	2.87	11	5	6	707	30	1	2.55
2008-09	Cape Breton	QMJHL	54	35	13	0	2935	137	3	2.80	11	7	4	740	30	0	2.43
2009-10	Cape Breton	QMJHL	54	32	21	0	3156	138	5	2.62	5	1	4	311	19	0	3.66
	Springfield Falcons	AHL	3	1	1	0	140	6	0	2.57	....	....	....	....	....	....	....
2010-11	Acadie-Bathurst	QMJHL	45	29	13	2	2604	121	2	2.79	3	0	2	106	12	0	6.88
2011-12	Stockton Thunder	ECHL	40	16	18	5	2388	99	4	2.49	8	4	4	488	20	0	2.46
	Oklahoma City	AHL	3	1	0	0	128	5	0	2.34	....	....	....	....	....	....	....
2012-13	Oklahoma City	AHL	22	9	9	1	1190	55	0	2.77	....	....	....	....	....	....	....
	Stockton Thunder	ECHL	9	7	2	0	545	11	1	1.21	*22	12	9	*1261	59	0	2.81

QMJHL All-Rookie Team (2008)

RYNNAS, Jussi (RIH-nuhs, YEW-see)

Goaltender. Catches left. 6'5", 212 lbs. Born, Pori, Finland, May 22, 1987.

			Regular Season								Playoffs						
Season	Club	League	GP	W	L	O/T	Mins	GA	SO	Avg	GP	W	L	Mins	GA	SO	Avg
2006-07	Assat Pori Jr.	Fin-Jr.	23	....	....	....	....	....	....	4.20	....	....	....	....	....	....	....
2007-08	Assat Pori Jr.	Fin-Jr.	27	....	....	....	....	....	....	2.90	....	....	....	....	....	....	....
2008-09	Assat Pori	Finland	DID NOT PLAY – SPARE GOALTENDER														
	Sport Vaasa	Finland-2	1	....	....	....	....	....	....	6.00	....	....	....	....	....	....	....
	Kiekko-Vantaa	Finland-2	7	....	....	....	....	....	....	3.99	....	....	....	....	....	....	....
2009-10	Assat Pori	Finland	31	14	13	1	1717	71	2	2.48	....	....	....	....	....	....	....
2010-11	Toronto Marlies	AHL	30	10	15	3	1660	75	2	2.71	....	....	....	....	....	....	....
2011-12	**Toronto**	**NHL**	**2**	**0**	**1**	**0**	**99**	**7**	**0**	**4.24**	....	....	....	....	....	....	....
	Toronto Marlies	AHL	22	11	9	1	1272	54	3	2.55	....	....	....	....	....	....	....
	Reading Royals	ECHL	14	8	5	1	767	41	1	3.21	....	....	....	....	....	....	....
2012-13	Toronto Marlies	AHL	21	10	9	1	1231	54	3	2.63	....	....	....	....	....	....	....
	Toronto	**NHL**	**1**	**0**	**0**	**0**	**10**	**0**	**0**	**0.00**	....	....	....	....	....	....	....
	NHL Totals		**3**	**0**	**1**	**0**	**109**	**7**	**0**	**3.85**	....	....	....	....	....	....	....

Signed as a free agent by **Toronto**, April 23, 2010. Signed as a free agent by **Oulu** (Finland), July 10, 2013.

SABOURIN, Dany (SA-boo-rihn, DA-nee)

Goaltender. Catches left. 6'4", 204 lbs. Born, Val-d'Or, Que., September 2, 1980.
(Calgary's 5th choice, 108th overall, in 1998 Entry Draft).

			Regular Season								Playoffs						
Season	**Club**	**League**	**GP**	**W**	**L**	**O/T**	**Mins**	**GA**	**SO**	**Avg**	**GP**	**W**	**L**	**Mins**	**GA**	**SO**	**Avg**
1996-97	Amos Forestiers	QAAA	24	6	16	0	1440	107	0	4.48							
1997-98	Sherbrooke	QMJHL	37	15	15	2	1907	128	1	4.03							
1998-99	Sherbrooke	QMJHL	30	8	13	2	1477	102	1	4.14	1	0	1	49	2	0	2.43
	Saint John Flames	AHL									1	0	1	57	4	0	4.19
99-2000	Sherbrooke	QMJHL	55	25	22	5	3067	181	1	3.54	5	1	4	324	18	0	3.33
2000-01	Saint John Flames	AHL	1	1	0	0	40	0	0	0.00							
	Johnstown Chiefs	ECHL	19	4	9	1	903	56	0	3.72	1	0	0	40	2	0	3.00
2001-02	Johnstown Chiefs	ECHL	27	14	10	1	1539	84	0	3.28	3	0	2	137	5	0	2.18
2002-03	Saint John Flames	AHL	41	15	17	4	2220	100	4	2.70							
2003-04	**Calgary**	**NHL**	**4**	**0**	**3**	**0**	**169**	**10**	**0**	**3.55**							
	Lowell	AHL	14	5	7	2	821	39	0	2.85							
	Las Vegas	ECHL	10	6	3	1	613	24	0	2.35	1	0	1	58	2	0	2.07
2004-05	Wilkes-Barre	AHL	20	8	8	2	1029	38	1	2.22							
	Wheeling Nailers	ECHL	27	19	6	1	1579	44	5	*1.67							
2005-06	**Pittsburgh**	**NHL**	**1**	**0**	**1**	**0**	**21**	**4**	**0**	**11.43**							
	Wilkes-Barre	AHL	49	30	14	4	2943	111	4	*2.26	6	2	4	362	13	1	2.15
2006-07	**Vancouver**	**NHL**	**9**	**2**	**4**	**1**	**480**	**21**	**0**	**2.63**	**2**	**0**	**0**	**14**	**1**	**0**	**4.29**
	Manitoba Moose	AHL	2	1	1	0	119	4	1	2.01							
2007-08	**Pittsburgh**	**NHL**	**24**	**10**	**9**	**1**	**1242**	**57**	**2**	**2.75**							
2008-09	**Pittsburgh**	**NHL**	**19**	**6**	**8**	**2**	**989**	**47**	**0**	**2.85**							
	Springfield Falcons	AHL	13	5	6	2	795	42	0	3.17							
2009-10	Providence Bruins	AHL	56	28	27	0	3278	146	3	2.67							
2010-11	Hershey Bears	AHL	23	14	9	0	1299	53	2	2.45							
2011-12	Hershey Bears	AHL	37	18	12	5	2047	94	2	2.76	5	2	3	301	16	0	3.19
2012-13	Hershey Bears	AHL	28	9	13	3	1521	69	0	2.72							
	NHL Totals		**57**	**18**	**25**	**4**	**2901**	**139**	**2**	**2.87**	**2**	**0**	**0**	**14**	**1**	**0**	**4.29**

AHL First All-Star Team (2006) • Aldege "Baz" Bastien Memorial Award (AHL – Outstanding Goaltender) (2006)

Signed as a free agent by **Pittsburgh**, August 10, 2005. Claimed on waivers by **Vancouver** from **Pittsburgh**, October 4, 2006. Signed as a free agent by **Pittsburgh**, July 1, 2007. Traded to **Edmonton** by **Pittsburgh** with Ryan Stone and Pittsburgh's 4th round choice Tobias Rieder) in 2011 Entry Draft for Mathieu Garon, January 17, 2009. Signed as a free agent by **Boston**, July 7, 2009. Signed as a free agent by **Washington**, July 2, 2010. Signed as a free agent by **Graz** (Austria), July 2, 2013.

SALAK, Alexander (SAL-ak, al-EHX-AN-duhr) CHI

Goaltender. Catches left. 6'1", 189 lbs. Born, Strakonice, Czech., January 5, 1987.

			Regular Season								Playoffs						
Season	**Club**	**League**	**GP**	**W**	**L**	**O/T**	**Mins**	**GA**	**SO**	**Avg**	**GP**	**W**	**L**	**Mins**	**GA**	**SO**	**Avg**
2006-07	Jokipojat Joensuu	Finland-2	35							2.81							
2007-08	TPS Turku	Finland	31	7	12	6	1757	76	1	2.59							
2008-09	TPS Turku	Finland	52	20	20	9	2981	119	4	2.40	8	4	4	489	16	0	1.96
2009-10	**Florida**	**NHL**	**2**	**0**	**1**	**0**	**67**	**6**	**0**	**5.37**							
	Rochester	AHL	48	29	14	0	2557	123	1	2.89	2	0	1	69	5	0	4.37
2010-11	Farjestad	Sweden	32				1857	61	*7	1.97	9			562	22	0	2.35
2011-12	Rockford IceHogs	AHL	21	6	10	0	1048	47	0	2.69							
2012-13	Farjestad	Sweden	41	25	15	0	2453	66	7	*1.61	10	5	5	616	24	1	2.34
	NHL Totals		**2**	**0**	**1**	**0**	**67**	**6**	**0**	**5.37**							

Signed as a free agent by **Florida**, May 29, 2009. • Loaned to **Farjestad** (Sweden) by **Florida** (Rochester-AHL), August 8, 2010. Traded to **Chicago** by **Florida** with Michael Frolik for Jack Skille, Hugh Jessiman and David Pacan, February 9, 2011. Signed as a free agent by **Farjestad** (Sweden), June 18, 2012.

SANFORD, Curtis (SAN-fohrd, KUHR-this)

Goaltender. Catches left. 5'11", 187 lbs. Born, Owen Sound, Ont., October 5, 1979.

			Regular Season								Playoffs						
Season	**Club**	**League**	**GP**	**W**	**L**	**O/T**	**Mins**	**GA**	**SO**	**Avg**	**GP**	**W**	**L**	**Mins**	**GA**	**SO**	**Avg**
1994-95	Wiarton Wolves	ON-Jr.C	18				949	98	0	6.20							
1995-96	Collingwood Blues	ON-Jr.A	21				2128	74	0	3.54							
1996-97	Owen Sound	OHL	19	4	8	1	847	77	0	5.45							
	Owen Sound	ON-Jr.B	6				360	28	0	4.68							
1997-98	Owen Sound	OHL	30	13	10	2	1542	114	1	4.44	9	4	4	456	30	1	3.95
1998-99	Owen Sound	OHL	56	30	16	5	2998	191	2	3.82	16	9	7	960	58	0	3.63
99-2000	Owen Sound	OHL	53	18	26	6	3124	198	1	3.80							
	Missouri	UHL	6	3	1	0	237	6	0	1.52							
	Rochester	AHL									1	0	0	14	1	0	4.25
2000-01	Worcester IceCats	AHL	5	3	0	1	237	16	0	4.06							
	Peoria Rivermen	ECHL	27	15	7	4	1511	48	3	*1.91	14	9	4	813	28	*2	2.07
2001-02	Worcester IceCats	AHL	9	5	4	0	537	22	0	2.46							
	Peoria Rivermen	ECHL	24	13	8	2	1418	58	1	2.45							
2002-03	**St. Louis**	**NHL**	**8**	**5**	**1**	**0**	**397**	**13**	**1**	**1.96**							
	Worcester IceCats	AHL	41	18	14	8	2317	93	3	2.41	3	0	3	179	8	0	2.68
2003-04	Worcester IceCats	AHL	43	20	16	3	2367	84	5	2.13	9	4	5	569	24	0	2.53
2004-05	Worcester IceCats	AHL	50	19	25	2	2743	123	2	2.69							
2005-06	**St. Louis**	**NHL**	**34**	**13**	**13**	**5**	**1830**	**81**	**3**	**2.66**							
	Peoria Rivermen	AHL	6	4	2	0	358	11	2	1.84							
2006-07	**St. Louis**	**NHL**	**31**	**8**	**12**	**5**	**1492**	**79**	**0**	**3.18**							
	Peoria Rivermen	AHL	2	1	1	0	119	5	0	2.52							
2007-08	**Vancouver**	**NHL**	**16**	**4**	**3**	**1**	**679**	**32**	**0**	**2.83**							
2008-09	**Vancouver**	**NHL**	**19**	**7**	**8**	**0**	**973**	**42**	**1**	**2.59**							
	Manitoba Moose	AHL	16	7	3	3	865	25	2	1.73	1	0	1	43	1	0	1.40
2009-10	Hamilton Bulldogs	AHL	41	23	11	3	2230	79	4	2.13	9	5	4	565	19	2	2.02
2010-11	Hamilton Bulldogs	AHL	40	22	13	2	2274	73	5	*1.93							
2011-12	**Columbus**	**NHL**	**36**	**10**	**18**	**4**	**1983**	**86**	**1**	**2.60**							
2012-13	Yaroslavl	KHL	24	12	7	0	1385	52	0	2.25	6	2	4	414	14	0	2.03
	NHL Totals		**144**	**47**	**55**	**15**	**7354**	**333**	**6**	**2.72**							

ECHL Second All-Star Team (2001) • Harry "Hap" Holmes Memorial Award (AHL – fewest goals against) (2010) (shared with Cedrick Desjardins) • AHL Second All-Star Team (2011)

Signed as a free agent by **St. Louis**, October 1, 2000. Signed as a free agent by **Vancouver**, July 2, 2007. Signed as a free agent by **Montreal**, July 20, 2009. Signed as a free agent by **Columbus**, July 1, 2011. Signed as a free agent by **Yaroslavl** (KHL), June 4, 2012.

SAROS, Juuse (SA-ruhs, YOO-seh) NSH

Goaltender. Catches left. 5'11", 176 lbs. Born, Forssa, Finland, April 19, 1995.
(Nashville's 4th choice, 99th overall, in 2013 Entry Draft).

			Regular Season								Playoffs						
Season	**Club**	**League**	**GP**	**W**	**L**	**O/T**	**Mins**	**GA**	**SO**	**Avg**	**GP**	**W**	**L**	**Mins**	**GA**	**SO**	**Avg**
2011-12	HPK U18	Fin-U18	14	11	3	0	844	19	2	1.35							
	HPK Jr.	Fin-Jr.	31	20	10	0	1804	76	2	2.53	10	6	4	630	22	0	2.10
2012-13	HPK Jr.	Fin-Jr.	37	24	13	0	2220	69	4	1.86	11	9	2	661	23	0	2.09

SATERI, Harri (SA-teh-ree, HAR-ree) S.J.

Goaltender. Catches left. 6'1", 205 lbs. Born, Toijala, Finland, December 29, 1989.
(San Jose's 3rd choice, 106th overall, in 2008 Entry Draft).

			Regular Season								Playoffs						
Season	**Club**	**League**	**GP**	**W**	**L**	**O/T**	**Mins**	**GA**	**SO**	**Avg**	**GP**	**W**	**L**	**Mins**	**GA**	**SO**	**Avg**
2005-06	HPK U18	Fin-U18	27				1515	66	5	2.61	2			118	10	0	5.08
	HPK Jr.	Fin-Jr.	1				50	3	0	3.60							
2006-07	Tappara U18	Fin-U18	2				119	4	0	2.02							
	Tappara Jr.	Fin-Jr.	23				1346	59	2	2.63	10			614	31	0	3.03
2007-08	Tappara Jr.	Fin-Jr.	34	13	17	0	2048	102	1	2.99	3	0	3	178	8	0	2.70
2008-09	Suomi U20	Finland-2	4	2	2	0	247	12	0	2.91							
2009-10	Tappara Tampere	Finland	49	21	22	4	2836	129	2	2.73	9	4	5	572	27	0	2.83
2010-11	Tappara Tampere	Finland	37	9	19	8	2147	106	2	2.96							
	Worcester Sharks	AHL	7	1	3	1	351	15	0	2.56							
2011-12	Worcester Sharks	AHL	38	15	20	1	2116	101	2	2.86							
2012-13	Worcester Sharks	AHL	39	14	21	3	2201	106	1	2.89							

SCHNEIDER, Cory (SHNIGH-duhr, KOHR-ee) N.J.

Goaltender. Catches left. 6'2", 195 lbs. Born, Marblehead, MA, March 18, 1986.
(Vancouver's 1st choice, 26th overall, in 2004 Entry Draft).

			Regular Season								Playoffs						
Season	**Club**	**League**	**GP**	**W**	**L**	**O/T**	**Mins**	**GA**	**SO**	**Avg**	**GP**	**W**	**L**	**Mins**	**GA**	**SO**	**Avg**
2002-03	Andover	High-MA	23	13	7	2	1385	39	3	1.69							
2003-04	Andover	High-MA	24	17	5	2	1336	32	6	1.42							
	USNTDP	U-18	10	9	1	0	559	15	1	1.61							
	USNTDP	NAHL	2	2	0	0	120	6	0	3.00							
2004-05	Boston College	H-East	18	13	1	4	1102	35	1	1.90							
2005-06	Boston College	H-East	*39	*24	13	2	*2362	83	*8	2.11							
2006-07	Boston College	H-East	*42	*29	12	1	*2517	90	6	2.15							
2007-08	Manitoba Moose	AHL	36	21	12	2	2054	78	3	2.28	6	1	4	375	12	0	1.92
2008-09	**Vancouver**	**NHL**	**8**	**2**	**4**	**1**	**355**	**20**	**0**	**3.38**							
	Manitoba Moose	AHL	40	28	10	1	2324	79	5	*2.04	*22	14	7	1315	47	0	2.15
2009-10	**Vancouver**	**NHL**	**2**	**0**	**1**	**0**	**79**	**5**	**0**	**3.80**							
	Manitoba Moose	AHL	60	35	23	2	*3557	149	4	2.51	6	2	4	366	19	0	3.12
2010-11	**Vancouver**	**NHL**	**25**	**16**	**4**	**2**	**1372**	**51**	**1**	**2.23**	**5**	**0**	**0**	**163**	**7**	**0**	**2.58**
2011-12	**Vancouver**	**NHL**	**33**	**20**	**8**	**1**	**1833**	**60**	**3**	**1.96**	**3**	**1**	**2**	**183**	**4**	**0**	**1.31**
2012-13	HC Ambri-Piotta	Swiss	8	4	4	0	485	26	0	3.22							
	Vancouver	**NHL**	**30**	**17**	**9**	**4**	**1733**	**61**	***5**	**2.11**	**2**	**0**	**2**	**117**	**9**	**0**	**4.62**
	NHL Totals		**98**	**55**	**26**	**8**	**5372**	**197**	**9**	**2.20**	**10**	**1**	**4**	**463**	**20**	**0**	**2.59**

Hockey East All-Rookie Team (2005) (co-winners - Kevin Regan and Peter Vetri) • Hockey East Second All-Star Team (2006) • NCAA East First All-American Team (2006) • AHL First All-Star Team (2009) • Harry "Hap" Holmes Memorial Award (AHL – fewest goals against) (2009) (shared with Karl Goehring) • Aldege "Baz" Bastien Memorial Award (AHL – Outstanding Goaltender) (2009) • William M. Jennings Trophy (2011) (shared with Roberto Luongo)

Signed as a free agent by **Ambri-Piotta** (Swiss), November 28, 2012. Traded to **New Jersey** by **Vancouver** for New Jersey's 1st round choice (Bo Horvat) in 2013 Entry Draft, June 30, 2013.

SCRIVENS, Ben (SKRIH-vehnz, BEHN) L.A.

Goaltender. Catches left. 6'2", 192 lbs. Born, Spruce Grove, Alta., September 11, 1986.

			Regular Season								Playoffs						
Season	**Club**	**League**	**GP**	**W**	**L**	**O/T**	**Mins**	**GA**	**SO**	**Avg**	**GP**	**W**	**L**	**Mins**	**GA**	**SO**	**Avg**
2004-05	Drayton Valley	AJHL	1	0	1	0	59	3	0	3.03							
	Calgary Canucks	AJHL	16	7	3	3	857	43	1	3.01							
2005-06	Spruce Grove	AJHL	45	27	12	2	2469	100	3	2.43	13	9	4	777	37	*2	2.86
2006-07	Cornell Big Red	ECAC	12	3	6	2	574	22	1	2.30							
2007-08	Cornell Big Red	ECAC	35	*19	12	3	1965	66	4	*2.02							
2008-09	Cornell Big Red	ECAC	36	*22	10	4	2153	65	*7	*1.81							
2009-10	Cornell Big Red	ECAC	34	*21	9	4	*2018	63	*7	*1.87							
2010-11	Toronto Marlies	AHL	33	13	12	5	1929	75	2	2.33							
	Reading Royals	ECHL	13	10	3	0	779	29	0	2.23	3	0	1	107	9	0	5.04
2011-12	**Toronto**	**NHL**	**12**	**4**	**5**	**2**	**672**	**35**	**0**	**3.13**							
	Toronto Marlies	AHL	39	22	15	1	2293	78	4	*2.04	*17	11	6	*1030	33	*3	1.92
2012-13	Toronto Marlies	AHL	22	14	7	1	1325	49	2	2.22							
	Toronto	**NHL**	**20**	**7**	**9**	**0**	**1025**	**46**	**2**	**2.69**							
	NHL Totals		**32**	**11**	**14**	**2**	**1697**	**81**	**2**	**2.86**							

ECAC Second All-Star Team (2009) • ECAC First All-Star Team (2010) • NCAA East First All-American Team (2010) • Harry "Hap" Holmes Memorial Award (AHL – fewest goals against) (2012)

Signed as a free agent by **Toronto**, April 28, 2010. Traded to **Los Angeles** by **Toronto** with Matt Frattin and Toronto's 2nd round choice in 2014 or 2015 Entry Draft for Jonathan Bernier, June 23, 2013.

SIMPSON, Kent (SIHMP-suhn, KEHNT) CHI

Goaltender. Catches left. 6'2", 198 lbs. Born, Edmonton, Alta., March 26, 1992.
(Chicago's 4th choice, 58th overall, in 2010 Entry Draft).

			Regular Season								Playoffs						
Season	**Club**	**League**	**GP**	**W**	**L**	**O/T**	**Mins**	**GA**	**SO**	**Avg**	**GP**	**W**	**L**	**Mins**	**GA**	**SO**	**Avg**
2007-08	AMC Bulldogs	Minor-AB	....	4	10	6	1126	93	....	4.96							
	Everett Silvertips	WHL	1	0	0	0	29	1	0	2.07							
2008-09	Everett Silvertips	WHL	27	8	11	4	1451	93	1	3.85							
2009-10	Everett Silvertips	WHL	34	22	9	1	1938	73	1	2.26	5	2	3	298	13	1	2.62
2010-11	Everett Silvertips	WHL	53	21	20	9	3132	145	2	2.78							
2011-12	Rockford IceHogs	AHL	1	0	0	1	63	3	0	2.85							
	Everett Silvertips	WHL	60	20	31	7	3481	193	2	3.33	4	0	4	225	15	0	4.00
2012-13	Toledo Walleye	ECHL	41	20	14	5	2387	94	2	2.36	3	0	3	193	11	0	3.42
	Rockford IceHogs	AHL	2	1	1	0	98	5	0	3.07							

SKAPSKI, Mackenzie (SKAP-skee, muh-KEHN-zee) NYR

Goaltender. Catches left. 6'3", 186 lbs. Born, Abbotsford, B.C., June 15, 1994.
(NY Rangers' 5th choice, 170th overall, in 2013 Entry Draft).

			Regular Season								Playoffs						
Season	**Club**	**League**	**GP**	**W**	**L**	**O/T**	**Mins**	**GA**	**SO**	**Avg**	**GP**	**W**	**L**	**Mins**	**GA**	**SO**	**Avg**
2009-10	Fraser Valley Bruins	BCMML	STATISTICS NOT AVAILABLE														
2010-11	Ridge Meadow	PIJHL	21	6	11	0	987	75	1	4.56	6	3	3	360	17	0	2.83
	Kootenay Ice	WHL	4	3	1	0	247	13	0	3.16							
2011-12	Kootenay Ice	WHL	19	9	6	2	1020	53	0	3.12							
2012-13	Kootenay Ice	WHL	65	34	25	1	3642	169	7	2.78	5	1	4	258	17	0	3.95

SMITH, Jeremy (SMIHTH, JAIR-eh-mee) CBJ

Goaltender. Catches left. 6', 173 lbs. Born, Dearborn, MI, April 13, 1989.
(Nashville's 2nd choice, 54th overall, in 2007 Entry Draft).

Season	Club	League	Regular Season GP	W	L	O/T	Mins	GA	SO	Avg	Playoffs GP	W	L	Mins	GA	SO	Avg
2005-06	Det. Compuware	MWEHL	13	5	6	0	696	31	0	2.67	....	....	....	....	....	....	....
	Det. Compuware	Exhib.	3	2	1	0	178	8	0	2.70	....	....	....	....	....	....	....
	Plymouth Whalers	OHL	5	0	2	0	111	11	0	5.95	....	....	....	....	....	....	....
2006-07	Plymouth Whalers	OHL	34	23	6	1	1901	82	4	2.59	3	2	0	149	8	0	3.22
2007-08	Plymouth Whalers	OHL	40	23	13	4	2431	116	3	2.86	4	0	4	224	29	0	7.77
2008-09	Plymouth Whalers	OHL	17	3	9	2	901	72	0	4.80	....	....	....	....	....	....	....
	Niagara Ice Dogs	OHL	26	12	9	3	1488	79	1	3.19	12	5	7	724	45	*1	3.73
2009-10	Milwaukee	AHL	1	0	0	0	5	0	0	0.00	....	....	....	....	....	....	....
	Cincinnati	ECHL	42	23	15	2	2468	108	2	2.63	*17	9	8	*988	44	1	2.67
2010-11	Milwaukee	AHL	28	16	8	2	1513	57	2	2.26	13	7	6	843	32	0	2.28
	Cincinnati	ECHL	1	0	0	1	65	3	0	2.78	....	....	....	....	....	....	....
2011-12	Milwaukee	AHL	*56	31	19	2	*3284	119	5	2.17	3	0	3	177	11	0	3.73
2012-13	Milwaukee	AHL	43	19	19	3	2471	114	1	2.77	....	....	....	....	....	....	....

ECHL Playoff MVP (2010) (co-winner - Robert Mayer)

Signed as a free agent by **Columbus**, July 5, 2013.

SMITH, Mike (SMIHTH, MIGHK) PHX

Goaltender. Catches left. 6'4", 215 lbs. Born, Kingston, Ont., March 22, 1982.
(Dallas' 5th choice, 161st overall, in 2001 Entry Draft).

Season	Club	League	Regular Season GP	W	L	O/T	Mins	GA	SO	Avg	Playoffs GP	W	L	Mins	GA	SO	Avg
1998-99	Kingston	ON-Jr.A	16	....	....	....	906	53	0	3.51	....	....	....	....	....	....	....
99-2000	Kingston	OHL	15	4	5	0	666	42	0	3.78	....	....	....	....	....	....	....
2000-01	Kingston	OHL	3	0	0	2	136	8	0	3.53	....	....	....	....	....	....	....
	Sudbury Wolves	OHL	43	22	13	7	2571	108	3	2.52	12	7	5	735	26	2	*2.12
2001-02	Sudbury Wolves	OHL	53	19	28	5	3082	157	3	3.06	5	1	4	302	15	0	2.98
2002-03	Utah Grizzlies	AHL	11	5	5	0	614	33	0	3.23	....	....	....	....	....	....	....
	Lexington	ECHL	27	11	10	4	1553	66	1	2.55	2	0	1	93	8	0	5.14
2003-04	Utah Grizzlies	AHL	21	8	11	0	1186	56	2	2.83	....	....	....	....	....	....	....
2004-05	Houston Aeros	AHL	45	19	17	3	2408	97	5	2.42	3	1	2	181	4	0	1.33
2005-06	Iowa Stars	AHL	50	25	19	6	2998	125	3	2.50	7	3	4	417	19	0	2.74
2006-07	**Dallas**	**NHL**	**23**	**12**	**5**	**2**	**1213**	**45**	**3**	**2.23**	....	....	....	....	....	....	....
2007-08	**Dallas**	**NHL**	**21**	**12**	**9**	**0**	**1172**	**48**	**2**	**2.46**	....	....	....	....	....	....	....
	Tampa Bay	**NHL**	**13**	**3**	**10**	**0**	**774**	**36**	**1**	**2.79**	....	....	....	....	....	....	....
2008-09	**Tampa Bay**	**NHL**	**41**	**14**	**18**	**9**	**2471**	**108**	**2**	**2.62**	....	....	....	....	....	....	....
2009-10	**Tampa Bay**	**NHL**	**42**	**13**	**18**	**7**	**2273**	**117**	**2**	**3.09**	....	....	....	....	....	....	....
2010-11	**Tampa Bay**	**NHL**	**22**	**13**	**6**	**1**	**1202**	**58**	**1**	**2.90**	**3**	**1**	**1**	**120**	**2**	**0**	**1.00**
	Norfolk Admirals	AHL	5	1	4	0	296	9	1	1.83	....	....	....	....	....	....	....
2011-12	**Phoenix**	**NHL**	**67**	**38**	**18**	**10**	**3903**	**144**	**8**	**2.21**	**16**	**9**	**7**	**1027**	**34**	***3**	**1.99**
2012-13	**Phoenix**	**NHL**	**34**	**15**	**12**	**5**	**1956**	**84**	***5**	**2.58**	....	....	....	....	....	....	....
	NHL Totals		**263**	**120**	**96**	**34**	**14964**	**640**	**24**	**2.57**	**19**	**10**	**8**	**1147**	**36**	**3**	**1.88**

NHL All-Rookie Team (2007)

Traded to **Tampa Bay** by **Dallas** with Jussi Jokinen, Jeff Halpern and Dallas' 4th round choice (later traded to Minnesota, later traded to Edmonton – Edmonton selected Kyle Bigos) in 2009 Entry Draft for Brad Richards and Johan Holmqvist, February 26, 2008. Signed as a free agent by **Phoenix**, July 1, 2011.

SPARKS, Garret (SPARKS, GAIR-eht) TOR

Goaltender. Catches left. 6'2", 213 lbs. Born, Elmhurst, IL, June 28, 1993.
(Toronto's 8th choice, 190th overall, in 2011 Entry Draft).

Season	Club	League	Regular Season GP	W	L	O/T	Mins	GA	SO	Avg	Playoffs GP	W	L	Mins	GA	SO	Avg
2008-09	Team Illinois	T1EHL	18	9	6	2	854	51	0	3.05	....	....	....	....	....	....	....
2009-10	Chicago Mission	T1EHL	27	19	7	2	1392	51	3	1.98	....	....	....	....	....	....	....
2010-11	Guelph Storm	OHL	19	8	6	1	972	59	0	3.64	....	....	....	....	....	....	....
2011-12	Guelph Storm	OHL	59	27	25	4	3304	171	5	3.11	6	2	4	323	24	0	4.45
2012-13	Guelph Storm	OHL	*60	*36	17	4	*3440	152	*7	2.65	5	1	4	275	14	0	3.05
	Toronto Marlies	AHL	3	2	0	1	189	8	0	2.53	1	0	0	14	1	0	4.23

STAJCER, Scott (STA-chuhr, SKAWT) NYR

Goaltender. Catches left. 6'3", 195 lbs. Born, Cambridge, Ont., June 14, 1991.
(NY Rangers' 5th choice, 140th overall, in 2009 Entry Draft).

Season	Club	League	Regular Season GP	W	L	O/T	Mins	GA	SO	Avg	Playoffs GP	W	L	Mins	GA	SO	Avg
2006-07	Mississauga Rebels	GTHL	39	....	....	....	1755	81	6	2.07	....	....	....	....	....	....	....
2007-08	Owen Sound	ON-Jr.B	32	8	21	2	1862	130	0	3.90	....	....	....	....	....	....	....
	Owen Sound	OHL	6	1	3	1	306	22	0	4.31	....	....	....	....	....	....	....
2008-09	Owen Sound	OHL	35	15	15	5	1969	117	0	3.57	4	0	3	211	20	0	5.70
2009-10	Owen Sound	OHL	55	21	23	6	3042	186	1	3.67	....	....	....	....	....	....	....
2010-11	Owen Sound	OHL	14	10	3	0	782	38	1	2.92	13	8	4	688	32	0	2.79
2011-12	Owen Sound	OHL	28	10	11	6	1680	83	1	2.96	3	1	2	184	12	0	3.91
2012-13	Connecticut Whale	AHL	3	0	2	0	139	10	0	4.32	....	....	....	....	....	....	....
	Greenville	ECHL	23	10	7	6	1396	62	0	2.66	1	0	1	60	5	0	5.00

STALOCK, Alex (STAY-lahk, AL-ehx) S.J.

Goaltender. Catches left. 6', 190 lbs. Born, St. Paul, MN, July 28, 1987.
(San Jose's 3rd choice, 112th overall, in 2005 Entry Draft).

Season	Club	League	Regular Season GP	W	L	O/T	Mins	GA	SO	Avg	Playoffs GP	W	L	Mins	GA	SO	Avg
2003-04	South St. Paul	High-MN	31	23	7	1	....	....	....	2.20	....	....	....	....	....	....	....
2004-05	Cedar Rapids	USHL	32	19	9	3	1801	82	1	2.73	9	7	2	582	14	*1	*1.44
2005-06	Cedar Rapids	USHL	44	*28	13	3	2641	112	4	2.54	8	3	5	472	25	0	3.18
2006-07	U. Minn-Duluth	WCHA	23	5	14	3	1364	76	1	3.34	....	....	....	....	....	....	....
2007-08	U. Minn-Duluth	WCHA	36	13	17	6	2170	85	3	2.35	....	....	....	....	....	....	....
2008-09	U. Minn-Duluth	WCHA	*42	21	13	8	*2534	90	*5	*2.13	....	....	....	....	....	....	....
2009-10	Worcester Sharks	AHL	*61	*39	19	2	3534	155	4	2.63	11	6	5	683	26	0	2.28
2010-11	**San Jose**	**NHL**	**1**	**1**	**0**	**0**	**30**	**0**	**0**	**0.00**	....	....	....	....	....	....	....
	Worcester Sharks	AHL	41	19	17	4	2397	105	0	2.63	....	....	....	....	....	....	....
2011-12	Stockton Thunder	ECHL	6	5	1	0	360	17	0	2.83	....	....	....	....	....	....	....
	Worcester Sharks	AHL	2	1	1	0	119	5	0	2.51	....	....	....	....	....	....	....
	Peoria Rivermen	AHL	3	2	0	0	106	2	1	1.13	....	....	....	....	....	....	....
2012-13	Worcester Sharks	AHL	38	17	16	4	2281	99	2	2.60	....	....	....	....	....	....	....
	San Jose	**NHL**	**2**	**0**	**0**	**1**	**42**	**2**	**0**	**2.86**	....	....	....	....	....	....	....
	NHL Totals		**3**	**1**	**0**	**1**	**72**	**2**	**0**	**1.67**	....	....	....	....	....	....	....

USHL Playoff MVP (2005) • USHL First All-Star Team (2006) • USHL Goaltender of the Year (2006) • WCHA All-Rookie Team (2007) • WCHA First All-Star Team (2009) • NCAA West First All-American Team (2009) • AHL All-Rookie Team (2010)

• Missed remainder of 2010-11 and majority of 2011-12 due to leg injury vs. Manchester (AHL), February 4, 2011. • Re-assigned to **Peoria** (AHL) by **San Jose** (Stockton-ECHL), March 3, 2012.

STOLARZ, Anthony (STOHL-ahrz, AN-thuh-nee) PHI

Goaltender. Catches left. 6'5", 210 lbs. Born, Edison, NJ, January 20, 1994.
(Philadelphia's 2nd choice, 45th overall, in 2012 Entry Draft).

Season	Club	League	Regular Season GP	W	L	O/T	Mins	GA	SO	Avg	Playoffs GP	W	L	Mins	GA	SO	Avg
2010-11	Jersey Hitmen	EmJHL	....	12	4	0	884	47	0	3.19	3	1	2	153	8	0	3.13
2011-12	Corpus Christi	NAHL	50	23	22	4	2939	139	3	2.84	....	....	....	....	....	....	....
2012-13	Nebraska-Omaha	WCHA	8	2	5	0	421	18	1	2.56	....	....	....	....	....	....	....

SUBBAN, Malcolm (soo-BAN, MAL-kuhm) BOS

Goaltender. Catches left. 6'2", 200 lbs. Born, Toronto, Ont., December 21, 1993.
(Boston's 1st choice, 24th overall, in 2012 Entry Draft).

Season	Club	League	Regular Season GP	W	L	O/T	Mins	GA	SO	Avg	Playoffs GP	W	L	Mins	GA	SO	Avg
2009-10	Mississauga Reps	GTHL	14	....	....	....	....	....	....	1.86	7	....	....	....	....	....	2.00
	Tor. Canadiens	ON-Jr.A	2	0	1	0	71	4	0	3.39	....	....	....	....	....	....	....
	Belleville Bulls	OHL	1	0	0	0	13	0	0	0.00	....	....	....	....	....	....	....
2010-11	Belleville Bulls	OHL	32	10	17	2	1785	94	0	3.16	3	0	3	178	6	0	2.02
2011-12	Belleville Bulls	OHL	39	25	14	0	2258	94	3	2.50	6	2	4	369	18	0	2.93
2012-13	Belleville Bulls	OHL	46	29	11	4	2695	96	5	*2.14	17	11	6	1021	34	*3	*2.00

OHL All-Rookie Team (2011)

SVEDBERG, Niklas (SVEHD-buhrg, NIHK-luhs) BOS

Goaltender. Catches left. 6', 176 lbs. Born, Sollentuna, Sweden, September 4, 1989.

Season	Club	League	Regular Season GP	W	L	O/T	Mins	GA	SO	Avg	Playoffs GP	W	L	Mins	GA	SO	Avg
2007-08	MODO	Sweden	1	0	0	0	8	7.11	....	....	....	....	....	....	....	....	....
2008-09	Huddinge IK	Sweden-2	24	....	....	....	....	....	....	....	....	....	....	....	....	....	....
	MODO	Sweden	3	....	....	....	178	16	0	5.41	....	....	....	....	....	....	....
2009-10	MODO	Sweden	21	....	....	....	1261	82	1	2.59	....	....	....	....	....	....	....
2010-11	Brynas IF Gavle	Sweden	21	....	....	....	1261	48	2	2.28	....	....	....	....	....	....	....
2011-12	Brynas IF Gavle	Sweden	29	....	....	....	1726	71	0	2.47	13	....	....	814	23	4	1.70
2012-13	Providence Bruins	AHL	48	37	8	2	2873	104	4	2.17	12	6	6	675	37	0	3.29

AHL All-Rookie Team (2013) • AHL First All-Star Team (2013) • Aldege "Baz" Bastien Memorial Award (AHL – Outstanding Goaltender) (2013)

Signed as a free agent by **Boston**, May 29, 2012.

TALBOT, Cameron (TAL-buht, KAM-ruhn) NYR

Goaltender. Catches left. 6'3", 205 lbs. Born, Caledonia, Ont., June 5, 1987.

Season	Club	League	Regular Season GP	W	L	O/T	Mins	GA	SO	Avg	Playoffs GP	W	L	Mins	GA	SO	Avg
2005-06	Hamilton	ON-Jr.A	35	21	13	1	2046	87	1	2.55	14	8	6	903	52	1	3.46
2006-07	Hamilton	ON-Jr.A	28	19	5	2	1644	57	1	2.08	19	13	6	1243	51	0	2.46
2007-08	AL-Huntsville	CHA	13	1	10	0	583	45	0	4.63	....	....	....	....	....	....	....
2008-09	AL-Huntsville	CHA	24	2	16	3	1320	65	1	2.95	....	....	....	....	....	....	....
2009-10	AL-Huntsville	CHA	*33	12	18	3	*1958	85	1	2.61	....	....	....	....	....	....	....
	Hartford Wolf Pack	AHL	1	0	0	0	19	3	0	9.70	....	....	....	....	....	....	....
2010-11	Connecticut Whale	AHL	22	11	9	2	1308	62	2	2.84	1	0	1	38	2	0	3.13
	Greenville	ECHL	2	1	0	1	122	5	0	2.46	....	....	....	....	....	....	....
2011-12	Connecticut Whale	AHL	33	14	15	1	1865	81	4	2.61	9	5	4	571	20	2	2.10
2012-13	Connecticut Whale	AHL	55	25	28	1	3105	136	2	2.63	....	....	....	....	....	....	....

Signed as a free agent by **NY Rangers**, March 30, 2010.

TARKKI, Iiro (TAHR-kee, EE-roh)

Goaltender. Catches . 6'2", 191 lbs. Born, Rauma, Finland, July 1, 1985.

Season	Club	League	Regular Season GP	W	L	O/T	Mins	GA	SO	Avg	Playoffs GP	W	L	Mins	GA	SO	Avg
2002-03	Lukko Rauma Jr.	Fin-Jr.	20	....	....	....	....	4.15	....	....	....	....	....	....	....	....	....
2003-04	Lukko Rauma Jr.	Fin-Jr.	34	....	....	....	....	....	....	3.74	....	....	....	....	....	....	....
	Suomi U20	Finland-2	1	....	....	....	....	....	....	0.94	....	....	....	....	....	....	....
2004-05	Lukko Rauma	Finland	1	....	....	....	20	0	0	0.00	....	....	....	....	....	....	....
2005-06	Lukko Rauma	Finland	6	....	....	....	....	....	....	....	....	....	....	....	....	....	....
2006-07	SaPKo Savonlinna	Finland-2	21	....	....	....	....	....	....	3.84	....	....	....	....	....	....	....
	SaiPa	Finland	2	....	....	....	120	7	0	3.50	....	....	....	....	....	....	....
2007-08	SaiPa	Finland	40	....	....	....	2330	94	4	2.42	....	....	....	....	....	....	....
2008-09	SaiPa	Finland	48	14	27	6	2753	129	1	2.81	3	....	....	189	8	0	1.80
2009-10	Blues Espoo	Finland	54	22	22	9	3228	131	2	2.44	3	....	....	219	7	0	1.91
2010-11	Blues Espoo	Finland	55	20	20	14	3218	112	5	2.09	18	10	8	1098	40	3	2.19
2011-12	**Anaheim**	**NHL**	**1**	**1**	**0**	**0**	**41**	**3**	**0**	**4.39**	....	....	....	....	....	....	....
	Syracuse Crunch	AHL	50	24	17	4	2788	114	2	2.45	4	1	3	244	15	0	3.68
2012-13	Ufa	KHL	39	20	11	0	2279	90	4	2.37	14	7	7	881	35	2	2.38
	NHL Totals		**1**	**1**	**0**	**0**	**41**	**3**	**0**	**4.39**	....	....	....	....	....	....	....

Signed as a free agent by **Anaheim**, May 6, 2011. Signed as a free agent by **Ufa** (KHL), May 14, 2012.

TAYLOR, Daniel (TAY-luhr, DAN-yehl)

Goaltender. Catches left. 5'11", 179 lbs. Born, Plymouth, England, April 28, 1986.
(Los Angeles' 8th choice, 221st overall, in 2004 Entry Draft).

Season	Club	League	Regular Season GP	W	L	O/T	Mins	GA	SO	Avg	Playoffs GP	W	L	Mins	GA	SO	Avg
2002-03	Cumberland Grads	ON-Jr.A	23	13	3	1	1009	41	1	2.44	6	3	3	432	17	0	2.36
2003-04	Guelph Storm	OHL	26	16	4	3	1462	66	0	2.71	3	1	1	159	9	0	3.40
2004-05	Guelph Storm	OHL	31	13	14	3	1821	80	2	2.64	1	0	1	59	4	0	4.07
2005-06	Kingston	OHL	57	32	15	6	3319	172	3	3.11	....	....	....	....	....	....	....
2006-07	Bakersfield	ECHL	17	7	7	2	969	70	0	4.33	....	....	....	....	....	....	....
	Wheeling Nailers	ECHL	1	0	0	1	62	4	0	3.86	....	....	....	....	....	....	....
	Texas Wildcatters	ECHL	2	0	1	0	74	2	0	1.61	....	....	....	....	....	....	....
2007-08	**Los Angeles**	**NHL**	**1**	**0**	**0**	**0**	**20**	**2**	**0**	**6.00**	....	....	....	....	....	....	....
	Manchester	AHL	23	13	5	2	1275	51	4	2.40	....	....	....	....	....	....	....
	Reading Royals	ECHL	5	3	0	0	182	8	0	2.63	13	7	6	815	38	1	2.80
2008-09	Manchester	AHL	15	7	4	2	744	33	0	2.66	....	....	....	....	....	....	....
2009-10	Syracuse Crunch	AHL	9	2	4	0	397	24	0	3.63	....	....	....	....	....	....	....
	Gwinnett	ECHL	37	18	13	5	2181	126	1	3.47	....	....	....	....	....	....	....
2010-11	Springfield Falcons	AHL	4	2	2	0	230	9	0	2.35	....	....	....	....	....	....	....
	Hamburg Freezers	Germany	28	14	14	....	1679	81	1	2.90	....	....	....	....	....	....	....
2011-12	Springfield Falcons	AHL	10	5	3	0	512	22	0	2.58	....	....	....	....	....	....	....
	Abbotsford Heat	AHL	33	17	10	3	1815	67	5	2.21	7	4	3	426	16	0	2.26
2012-13	Abbotsford Heat	AHL	40	18	10	2	2108	72	3	2.05	....	....	....	....	....	....	....
	Calgary	**NHL**	**2**	**1**	**1**	**0**	**120**	**6**	**0**	**3.00**	....	....	....	....	....	....	....
	NHL Totals		**3**	**1**	**1**	**0**	**140**	**8**	**0**	**3.43**	....	....	....	....	....	....	....

Signed to a PTO (professional tryout) contract by **Springfield** (AHL), October, 2010. Signed as a free agent by **Hamburg** (Germany), November 14, 2010. Signed as a free agent by **Abbotsford** (AHL), December 1, 2011. Signed as a free agent by **Calgary**, February 6, 2013. Signed as a free agent by **Farjestad** (Sweden), May 22, 2013.

THEODORE, Jose (THEE-uh-dohr, joh-SAY)

Goaltender. Catches right. 5'11", 172 lbs. Born, Laval, Que., September 13, 1976.
(Montreal's 2nd choice, 44th overall, in 1994 Entry Draft).

Season	Club	League	Regular Season GP	W	L	O/T	Mins	GA	SO	Avg	Playoffs GP	W	L	Mins	GA	SO	Avg
1990-91	Richelieu	QAHA	42	....	....	....	2520	80	0	1.90	....	....	....	....	....	....	....
1991-92	Richelieu Riverains	QAAA	24	9	13	2	1440	96	0	3.99	5	2	3	295	26	0	5.28
1992-93	St-Jean Lynx	QMJHL	33	12	14	2	1775	111	0	3.75	3	0	3	175	11	0	3.77
1993-94	St-Jean Lynx	QMJHL	57	20	28	6	3230	196	0	3.64	5	1	4	296	18	0	3.65
1994-95	St-Jean Lynx	QMJHL	14	5	8	1	833	67	0	4.83	....	....	....	....	....	....	....
	Hull Olympiques	QMJHL	*43	*27	14	1	*2521	126	5	3.00	*21	*15	6	*1267	59	*1	2.79
	Fredericton	AHL	....	....	....	....	....	....	....	....	1	0	1	60	3	0	3.00
1995-96	**Montreal**	**NHL**	**1**	**0**	**0**	**0**	**9**	**1**	**0**	**6.67**	....	....	....	....	....	....	....
	Hull Olympiques	QMJHL	48	33	11	2	2809	158	0	3.38	5	2	3	300	20	0	4.00
1996-97	**Montreal**	**NHL**	**16**	**5**	**6**	**2**	**821**	**53**	**0**	**3.87**	**2**	**1**	**1**	**168**	**7**	**0**	**2.50**
	Fredericton	AHL	26	12	12	0	1469	87	0	3.55	....	....	....	....	....	....	....
1997-98	Fredericton	AHL	53	20	23	8	3053	145	2	2.85	4	1	3	237	13	0	3.28
	Montreal	**NHL**	....	....	....	....	....	....	....	....	**3**	**0**	**1**	**120**	**1**	**0**	**0.50**

1998-99	Montreal	NHL	18	4	12	0	913	50	1	3.29	....	....	....	....	....	....	....
	Fredericton	AHL	27	12	13	2	1609	77	2	2.87	13	8	5	694	35	1	3.03
99-2000	Montreal	NHL	30	12	13	2	1655	58	5	2.10	....	....	....	....	....	....	....
2000-01	Montreal	NHL	59	20	29	5	3298	141	2	2.57	....	....	....	....	....	....	....
	Quebec Citadelles	AHL	3	3	0	0	180	9	0	3.00	....	....	....	....	....	....	....
2001-02	Montreal	NHL	67	30	24	10	3864	136	7	2.11	12	6	6	686	35	0	3.06
2002-03	Montreal	NHL	57	20	31	6	3419	165	2	2.90	....	....	....	....	....	....	....
2003-04	Montreal	NHL	67	33	28	5	3961	150	6	2.27	11	4	7	678	27	1	2.39
2004-05	Djurgarden	Sweden	17	....	....	....	1024	42	0	2.46	12	....	....	728	27	0	2.23
2005-06	Montreal	NHL	38	17	15	5	2114	122	0	3.46	....	....	....	....	....	....	....
	Colorado	NHL	5	1	3	1	296	15	0	3.04	9	4	5	573	29	0	3.04
2006-07	Colorado	NHL	33	13	15	1	1748	95	0	3.26	....	....	....	....	....	....	....
2007-08	Colorado	NHL	53	28	21	3	3028	123	3	2.44	10	4	6	514	27	0	3.15
	Lake Erie Monsters	AHL	1	0	1	0	60	3	0	3.02	....	....	....	....	....	....	....
2008-09	Washington	NHL	57	32	17	5	3287	157	2	2.87	2	0	1	97	6	0	3.71
2009-10	Washington	NHL	47	30	7	7	2586	121	1	2.81	2	0	1	81	5	0	3.70
2010-11	Minnesota	NHL	32	15	11	3	1793	81	1	2.71	....	....	....	....	....	....	....
2011-12	Florida	NHL	53	22	16	11	3049	125	3	2.46	5	2	2	268	11	1	2.46
2012-13	Florida	NHL	15	4	6	3	766	42	0	3.29	....	....	....	....	....	....	....
	NHL Totals		**648**	**286**	**254**	**69**	**36607**	**1635**	**33**	**2.68**	**56**	**21**	**30**	**3185**	**148**	**2**	**2.79**

QMJHL Second All-Star Team (1995, 1996) • NHL Second All-Star Team (2002) • MBNA Roger Crozier Saving Grace Award (2002) • Vezina Trophy (2002) • Hart Memorial Trophy (2002) • Bill Masterton Memorial Trophy (2010)

Played in NHL All-Star Game (2002, 2004)

• Scored a goal vs. NY Islanders, January 2, 2001. Signed as a free agent by **Djurgarden** (Sweden), December 20, 2004. Traded to **Colorado** by **Montreal** for David Aebischer, March 8, 2006. Signed as a free agent by **Washington**, July 1, 2008. Signed as a free agent by **Minnesota**, October 2, 2010. Signed as a free agent by **Florida**, July 1, 2011.

THIESSEN, Brad (THEE-suhn, BRAD)

Goaltender. Catches left. 6', 180 lbs. Born, Aldergrove, B.C., March 19, 1986.

			Regular Season								Playoffs						
Season	Club	League	GP	W	L	O/T	Mins	GA	SO	Avg	GP	W	L	Mins	GA	SO	Avg
2003-04	Penticton Panthers	BCHL	42	13	17	1	2131	122	2	3.44	....	....	....	....	....	....	....
2004-05	Penticton Vees	BCHL	26	7	18	1	1492	86	1	3.46	....	....	....	....	....	....	....
	Prince George	BCHL	10	5	4	0	561	31	0	3.31	3	1	1	158	9	0	3.42
2005-06	Prince George	BCHL	36	14	17	4	2058	99	5	2.89	....	....	....	....	....	....	....
	Merritt	BCHL	13	8	4	0	754	36	2	2.87	6	3	3	261	16	1	3.68
2006-07	Northeastern	H-East	33	11	17	5	1985	82	4	2.48	....	....	....	....	....	....	....
2007-08	Northeastern	H-East	37	16	17	3	2180	96	2	2.64	....	....	....	....	....	....	....
2008-09	Northeastern	H-East	*41	25	12	4	*2496	88	*3	2.12	....	....	....	....	....	....	....
2009-10	Wilkes-Barre	AHL	30	14	14	1	1763	72	4	2.45	....	....	....	....	....	....	....
	Wheeling Nailers	ECHL	12	8	3	0	674	30	1	2.67	....	....	....	....	....	....	....
2010-11	Wilkes-Barre	AHL	46	*35	8	1	2567	83	7	1.94	12	6	6	720	20	2	*1.67
2011-12	Pittsburgh	NHL	5	3	1	0	258	16	0	3.72	....	....	....	....	....	....	....
	Wilkes-Barre	AHL	41	23	15	2	2321	109	2	2.82	12	6	6	756	27	0	2.14
2012-13	Wilkes-Barre	AHL	32	16	12	2	1793	80	4	2.68	12	6	4	654	15	2	*1.38
	NHL Totals		**5**	**3**	**1**	**0**	**258**	**16**	**0**	**3.72**	....	....	....	....	....	....	....

Hockey East First All-Star Team (2009) • Hockey East Player of the Year (2009) • NCAA East First All-American Team (2009) • AHL First All-Star Team (2011) • Harry ''Hap'' Holmes Memorial Award (AHL – fewest goals against) (2011) (shared with John Curry) • Aldege "Baz" Bastien Award (AHL – Outstanding Goaltender) (2011) • Harry ''Hap'' Holmes Memorial Award (AHL – fewest goals against) (2013) (shared with Jeff Zatkoff)

Signed as a free agent by **Pittsburgh**, April 8, 2009. Signed as a free agent by **HIFK Helsinki** (Finland), July 15, 2013.

THOMAS, Tim (TAW-mas, TIHM)

Goaltender. Catches left. 5'11", 201 lbs. Born, Flint, MI, April 15, 1974.
(Quebec's 11th choice, 217th overall, in 1994 Entry Draft).

			Regular Season								Playoffs						
Season	Club	League	GP	W	L	O/T	Mins	GA	SO	Avg	GP	W	L	Mins	GA	SO	Avg
1992-93	Davison High	High-MI	27	....	....	....	1580	87	....	3.30	....	....	....	....	....	....	....
1993-94	U. of Vermont	ECAC	*33	15	12	6	1864	94	0	3.03	....	....	....	....	....	....	....
1994-95	U. of Vermont	ECAC	34	18	13	2	2010	90	*4	*2.69	....	....	....	....	....	....	....
1995-96	U. of Vermont	ECAC	37	*26	7	4	*2254	88	*3	*2.34	....	....	....	....	....	....	....
1996-97	U. of Vermont	ECAC	36	22	11	3	2158	101	2	2.81	....	....	....	....	....	....	....
1997-98	Birmingham Bulls	ECHL	6	4	1	1	360	13	1	2.17	....	....	....	....	....	....	....
	Houston Aeros	IHL	1	0	1	0	59	4	0	4.01	....	....	....	....	....	....	....
	HIFK Helsinki	Finland	18	13	4	1	1034	28	2	1.62	9	9	0	551	14	3	1.52
1998-99	Hamilton Bulldogs	AHL	15	6	8	0	837	45	0	3.23	....	....	....	....	....	....	....
	HIFK Helsinki	Finland	14	8	3	3	833	31	2	2.23	11	7	4	658	25	0	2.28
99-2000	Detroit Vipers	IHL	36	10	21	3	2020	120	1	3.56	....	....	....	....	....	....	....
2000-01	AIK Solna	Sweden	43	....	....	....	2542	105	3	2.48	5	....	....	299	20	0	4.01
2001-02	Karpat Oulu	Finland	32	15	12	5	1937	79	4	2.44	3	1	2	180	12	0	4.00
2002-03	Boston	NHL	4	3	1	0	220	11	0	3.00	....	....	....	....	....	....	....
	Providence Bruins	AHL	35	18	12	5	2049	98	1	2.87	....	....	....	....	....	....	....
2003-04	Providence Bruins	AHL	43	20	16	6	2544	78	9	1.84	2	0	2	84	10	0	7.13
2004-05	Jokerit Helsinki	Finland	54	34	13	7	3266	86	15	1.58	12	8	4	720	22	0	1.83
2005-06	Boston	NHL	38	12	13	10	2187	101	1	2.77	....	....	....	....	....	....	....
	Providence Bruins	AHL	26	15	11	0	1515	57	1	2.26	....	....	....	....	....	....	....
2006-07	Boston	NHL	66	30	29	4	3619	189	3	3.13	....	....	....	....	....	....	....
2007-08	Boston	NHL	57	28	19	6	3342	136	3	2.44	7	3	4	430	19	0	2.65
2008-09	Boston	NHL	54	36	11	7	3259	114	5	*2.10	11	7	4	680	21	1	*1.85
2009-10	Boston	NHL	43	17	18	8	2442	104	5	2.56	....	....	....	....	....	....	....
	United States	Olympics	1	0	0	0	12	1	0	5.21	....	....	....	....	....	....	....
2010-11 ♦	Boston	NHL	57	35	11	9	3364	112	9	*2.00	*25	*16	9	*1542	51	*4	*1.98
2011-12	Boston	NHL	59	35	19	1	3352	132	5	2.36	7	3	4	448	16	1	2.14
2012-13			DID NOT PLAY – SUSPENDED														
	NHL Totals		**378**	**196**	**121**	**45**	**21785**	**899**	**31**	**2.48**	**50**	**29**	**21**	**3100**	**107**	**6**	**2.07**

ECAC First All-Star Team (1995, 1996) • ECAC Goaltender of the Year (1996) • NCAA East Second All-American Team (1995) • NCAA East First All-American Team (1996) • NHL First All-Star Team (2009, 2011) • William M. Jennings Trophy (2009) (shared with Manny Fernandez) • Vezina Trophy (2009, 2011) • Conn Smythe Trophy (2011)

Played in NHL All-Star Game (2008, 2009, 2011, 2012)

• Rights transferred to **Colorado** after **Quebec** franchise relocated, June 21, 1995. Signed as a free agent by **Edmonton**, June 4, 1998. Signed as free agent by **Solna** (Sweden), July 26, 2000. Signed as a free agent by **Boston**, August 8, 2002. Signed as a free agent by **Jokerit Helsinki** (Finland), May 17, 2004. • Suspended by **Boston** for failing to report to training camp, January 14, 2013. Traded to **NY Islanders** by **Boston** for future considerations, February 7, 2013.

TOKARSKI, Dustin (toh-KAHR-skee, DUHS-tihn) MTL

Goaltender. Catches left. 5'11", 198 lbs. Born, Humboldt, Sask., September 16, 1989.
(Tampa Bay's 3rd choice, 122nd overall, in 2008 Entry Draft).

			Regular Season								Playoffs						
Season	Club	League	GP	W	L	O/T	Mins	GA	SO	Avg	GP	W	L	Mins	GA	SO	Avg
2006-07	Spokane Chiefs	WHL	30	13	11	2	1674	78	2	2.80	6	2	4	364	17	0	2.80
2007-08	Spokane Chiefs	WHL	45	30	10	3	2543	87	6	2.05	*21	*16	5	*1352	31	*3	*1.38
2008-09	Spokane Chiefs	WHL	54	34	18	2	3264	107	*7	*1.97	12	7	5	812	23	1	*1.70
2009-10	Tampa Bay	NHL	2	0	0	0	44	3	0	4.09	....	....	....	....	....	....	....
	Norfolk Admirals	AHL	55	27	25	3	3319	139	4	2.51	....	....	....	....	....	....	....
2010-11	Norfolk Admirals	AHL	46	21	20	4	2691	119	2	2.65	6	2	4	355	13	1	2.19
2011-12	Tampa Bay	NHL	5	1	3	1	244	14	0	3.44	....	....	....	....	....	....	....
	Norfolk Admirals	AHL	45	*32	11	0	2583	96	5	2.23	14	*12	2	866	21	*3	*1.46
2012-13	Syracuse Crunch	AHL	33	18	8	4	1881	77	3	2.46	....	....	....	....	....	....	....
	Hamilton Bulldogs	AHL	15	6	8	0	836	31	3	2.22	....	....	....	....	....	....	....
	NHL Totals		**7**	**1**	**3**	**1**	**288**	**17**	**0**	**3.54**	....	....	....	....	....	....	....

Memorial Cup All-Star Team (2008) • Hap Emms Memorial Trophy (Memorial Cup - Top Goaltender) (2008) • Stafford Smythe Memorial Trophy (Memorial Cup - MVP) (2008) • WHL West Second All-Star Team (2009)

Traded to **Montreal** by **Tampa Bay** for Cedrick Desjardins, February 14, 2013.

TOMKINS, Matt (TAWM-kihnz, MAT) CHI

Goaltender. Catches left. 6'2", 176 lbs. Born, Edmonton, Alta., June 19, 1994.
(Chicago's 8th choice, 199th overall, in 2012 Entry Draft).

			Regular Season								Playoffs						
Season	Club	League	GP	W	L	O/T	Mins	GA	SO	Avg	GP	W	L	Mins	GA	SO	Avg
2008-09	Leduc Oil Kings	AMBHL	....	8	8	3	1093	75	0	4.12	1	0	1	60	5	0	5.00
2009-10	Sherwood Park	Minor-AB	18	8	5	5	1047	47	0	2.69	8	*8	0	490	17	1	2.08
2010-11	Sherwood Park	AMHL	16	6	8	1	1002	64	0	3.83	6	3	3	333	23	0	4.14
2011-12	Sherwood Park	AJHL	33	18	11	2	1898	108	0	3.41	10	4	6	595	35	1	3.53
2012-13	Sherwood Park	AJHL	44	22	14	6	2533	108	4	2.56	10	5	5	607	33	0	3.26

• Signed Letter of Intent to attend **Ohio State University** (CCHA) in fall of 2013.

TREMBLAY, Francois (TRAWM-blay, frahn-SWUH) ST.L.

Goaltender. Catches left. 6'1", 193 lbs. Born, Baie-Comeau, Que., August 29, 1994.
(St. Louis' 6th choice, 146th overall, in 2012 Entry Draft).

			Regular Season								Playoffs						
Season	Club	League	GP	W	L	O/T	Mins	GA	SO	Avg	GP	W	L	Mins	GA	SO	Avg
2009-10	Jonquiere Elites	QAAA	25	12	8	5	1386	72	0	3.12	5	2	3	303	17	0	3.36
2010-11	Val-d'Or Foreurs	QMJHL	26	5	10	4	1261	82	0	3.91	3	0	2	107	11	0	6.20
2011-12	Val-d'Or Foreurs	QMJHL	57	22	28	4	3118	197	2	3.79	4	0	3	209	19	0	5.45
2012-13	Val-d'Or Foreurs	QMJHL	46	22	16	3	2546	145	0	3.42	2	0	0	42	5	0	7.21

TUOHIMAA, Frans (too-OH-hay-ma, FRANZ) EDM

Goaltender. Catches left. 6'2", 178 lbs. Born, Helsinki, Finland, August 19, 1991.
(Edmonton's 9th choice, 182nd overall, in 2011 Entry Draft).

			Regular Season								Playoffs						
Season	Club	League	GP	W	L	O/T	Mins	GA	SO	Avg	GP	W	L	Mins	GA	SO	Avg
2007-08	HIFK Helsinki U18	Fin-U18	22	11	8	0	1251	55	3	2.64	2	0	1	71	13	0	10.98
	HIFK Helsinki Jr.	Fin-Jr.	1	0	0	0	17	3	0	10.71	....	....	....	....	....	....	....
2008-09	HIFK Helsinki U18	Fin-U18	13	12	1	0	780	20	4	1.54	8	7	1	478	14	2	1.76
	HIFK Helsinki Jr.	Fin-Jr.	18	4	13	0	983	65	0	3.97	....	....	....	....	....	....	....
2009-10	Suomi U20	Finland-2	1	0	1	0	60	3	0	3.01	....	....	....	....	....	....	....
	HIFK Helsinki Jr.	Fin-Jr.	20	14	5	0	1144	55	2	2.89	12	7	5	696	31	1	2.67
2010-11	Jokerit Helsinki Jr.	Fin-Jr.	37	24	13	0	2183	78	6	2.14	7	3	4	425	21	0	2.97
2011-12	Jokerit Helsinki	Finland	18	6	6	5	1042	46	2	2.65	....	....	....	....	....	....	....
	Kiekko-Vantaa	Finland-2	16	6	10	0	956	45	2	2.82	4	0	4	237	18	0	4.56
	Jokerit Helsinki Jr.	Fin-Jr.	1	1	0	0	65	1	0	0.93	8	4	4	499	14	1	1.68
2012-13	Jokerit Helsinki	Finland	13	5	2	6	787	30	0	2.29	2	0	1	78	1	0	0.77
	Kiekko-Vantaa	Finland-2	16	....	....	....	971	40	1	2.47	....	....	....	....	....	....	....

ULLMARK, Linus (UHL-mahrk, LIH-nuhs) BUF

Goaltender. Catches left. 6'3", 198 lbs. Born, Lugnvik, Sweden, July 31, 1993.
(Buffalo's 6th choice, 163rd overall, in 2012 Entry Draft).

			Regular Season								Playoffs						
Season	Club	League	GP	W	L	O/T	Mins	GA	SO	Avg	GP	W	L	Mins	GA	SO	Avg
2008-09	Kramfors U18	Swe-U18	14	....	....	....	824	54	0	3.93	....	....	....	....	....	....	....
2009-10	Kramfors U18	Swe-U18	2	....	....	....	120	11	0	5.50	....	....	....	....	....	....	....
	MODO U18	Swe-U18	8	....	....	....	484	26	1	3.22	2	....	....	120	7	0	3.50
2010-11	MODO U18	Swe-U18	24	....	....	....	1387	51	5	2.20	2	....	....	103	6	0	3.49
	MODO Jr.	Swe-Jr.	1	....	....	....	60	2	0	2.00	....	....	....	....	....	....	....
2011-12	MODO Jr.	Swe-Jr.	25	....	....	....	1521	70	1	2.76	5	....	....	242	9	1	2.24
	MODO	Sweden	3	....	....	....	148	8	0	3.24	....	....	....	....	....	....	....
2012-13	MODO Jr.	Swe-Jr.	23	18	5	0	1352	46	2	2.04	5	4	1	....	1	....	1.39
	Mora IK	Sweden-2	6	4	2	0	343	12	0	2.10	....	....	....	....	....	....	....
	MODO	Sweden	6	3	1	0	320	11	0	2.07	2	1	1	123	3	0	1.47

VARLAMOV, Semyon (vahr-LA-mawv, sehm-YAWN) COL

Goaltender. Catches left. 6'2", 209 lbs. Born, Kuybyshev, USSR, April 27, 1988.
(Washington's 2nd choice, 23rd overall, in 2006 Entry Draft).

			Regular Season								Playoffs						
Season	Club	League	GP	W	L	O/T	Mins	GA	SO	Avg	GP	W	L	Mins	GA	SO	Avg
2004-05	Yaroslavl 2	Russia-3	8	....	....	....	369	15	1	2.43	....	....	....	....	....	....	....
2005-06	Yaroslavl 2	Russia-3	33	....	....	....	1782	60	8	2.02	....	....	....	....	....	....	....
2006-07	Yaroslavl 2	Russia-3	2	....	....	....	120	3	0	1.50	....	....	....	....	....	....	....
	Yaroslavl	Russia	33	....	....	....	1936	70	3	2.17	6	....	....	368	18	0	2.94
2007-08	Yaroslavl	Russia	44	....	....	....	2592	106	3	2.45	*16	....	....	*924	25	*5	1.62
2008-09	Washington	NHL	6	4	0	1	329	13	0	2.37	13	7	6	759	32	*2	2.53
	Hershey Bears	AHL	27	19	7	1	1551	62	2	2.40	....	....	....	....	....	....	....
2009-10	Washington	NHL	26	15	4	6	1527	65	2	2.55	6	3	3	349	14	0	2.41
	Hershey Bears	AHL	3	3	0	0	185	6	0	1.95	....	....	....	....	....	....	....
	Russia	Olympics	DID NOT PLAY – SPARE GOALTENDER														
2010-11	Washington	NHL	27	11	9	5	1560	58	2	2.23	....	....	....	....	....	....	....
	Hershey Bears	AHL	3	2	1	0	179	10	0	3.36	....	....	....	....	....	....	....
2011-12	Colorado	NHL	53	26	24	3	3151	136	4	2.59	....	....	....	....	....	....	....
2012-13	Yaroslavl	KHL	16	8	4	0	929	27	3	*1.74	....	....	....	....	....	....	....
	Colorado	NHL	35	11	21	3	1950	98	3	3.02	....	....	....	....	....	....	....
	NHL Totals		**147**	**67**	**58**	**18**	**8517**	**370**	**11**	**2.61**	**19**	**10**	**9**	**1108**	**46**	**2**	**2.49**

Traded to **Colorado** by **Washington** for Colorado's 1st round choice (Filip Forsberg) in 2012 Entry Draft and Boston's 2nd round choice (previously acquired, later traded to Dallas – Dallas selected Mike Winther) in 2012 Entry Draft, July 1, 2011. Signed as a free agent by **Yaroslavl** (KHL), September 27, 2012.

VASILEVSKIY, Andrey (va-sihl-EHV-skee, an-DRAY) T.B.

Goaltender. Catches left. 6'3", 204 lbs. Born, Tyumen, Russia, July 25, 1994.
(Tampa Bay's 2nd choice, 19th overall, in 2012 Entry Draft).

			Regular Season								Playoffs						
Season	Club	League	GP	W	L	O/T	Mins	GA	SO	Avg	GP	W	L	Mins	GA	SO	Avg
2010-11	Tolpar Ufa Jr.	Russia-Jr.	14	8	2	0	730	22	3	1.81	2	1	1	88	3	0	2.05
2011-12	Tolpar Ufa Jr.	Russia-Jr.	27	15	8	0	1477	55	3	2.23	2	0	2	120	5	0	2.50
2012-13	Ufa	KHL	8	4	1	0	298	11	1	2.22	....	....	....	....	....	....	....
	Tolpar Ufa Jr.	Russia-Jr.	27	17	6	0	1613	52	3	1.93	3	0	2	190	9	0	2.85

VISENTIN, Mark (vih-SEHN-tihn, MAHRK) PHX

Goaltender. Catches left. 6'2", 205 lbs. Born, Hamilton, Ont., August 7, 1992.
(Phoenix's 2nd choice, 27th overall, in 2010 Entry Draft).

			Regular Season								Playoffs						
Season	Club	League	GP	W	L	O/T	Mins	GA	SO	Avg	GP	W	L	Mins	GA	SO	Avg
2007-08	Halton Hurricanes	Minor-ON	44	....	....	....	1980	98	3	2.22	....	....	....	....	....	....	....
2008-09	Niagara Ice Dogs	OHL	23	5	11	3	1099	78	2	4.26	....	....	....	....	....	....	....
2009-10	Niagara Ice Dogs	OHL	55	24	26	5	3209	160	7	2.99	5	1	4	305	18	0	3.54
2010-11	Niagara Ice Dogs	OHL	46	30	9	6	2714	114	4	2.52	14	9	5	823	35	1	2.55
2011-12	Niagara Ice Dogs	OHL	42	30	9	2	2407	80	*10	*1.99	*20	13	7	*1217	51	0	2.51
2012-13	Portland Pirates	AHL	30	15	12	1	1669	83	2	2.98	....	....	....	....	....	....	....
	Gwinnett	ECHL	1	1	0	0	60	2	0	2.00	....	....	....	....	....	....	....

OHL First All-Star Team (2011) • OHL Second All-Star Team (2012)

VOKOUN, Tomas (voh-KOON, TAW-mas) PIT

Goaltender. Catches right. 6'1", 210 lbs. Born, Karlovy Vary, Czech., July 2, 1976.
(Montreal's 11th choice, 226th overall, in 1994 Entry Draft).

			Regular Season								Playoffs						
Season	Club	League	GP	W	L	O/T	Mins	GA	SO	Avg	GP	W	L	Mins	GA	SO	Avg
1993-94	HC Kladno	CzRep	1	0	0	0	20	2	0	6.01	....	....	....	....	....	....	....
1994-95	HC Kladno	CzRep	26	....	....	....	1368	70	....	3.07	5	....	....	240	19	....	4.75
1995-96	Wheeling	ECHL	35	20	10	2	1912	117	0	3.67	7	4	3	436	19	0	2.61
	Fredericton	AHL	....	....	....	....	....	....	....	....	1	0	1	59	4	0	4.09
1996-97	**Montreal**	**NHL**	**1**	**0**	**0**	**0**	**20**	**4**	**0**	**12.00**	....	....	....	....	....	....	....
	Fredericton	AHL	47	12	26	7	2645	154	2	3.49	....	....	....	....	....	....	....
1997-98	Fredericton	AHL	31	13	13	2	1735	90	0	3.11	....	....	....	....	....	....	....
1998-99	**Nashville**	**NHL**	**37**	**12**	**18**	**4**	**1954**	**96**	**1**	**2.95**	....	....	....	....	....	....	....
	Milwaukee	IHL	9	3	2	4	539	22	1	2.45	2	0	2	149	8	0	3.22
99-2000	**Nashville**	**NHL**	**33**	**9**	**20**	**1**	**1879**	**87**	**1**	**2.78**	....	....	....	....	....	....	....
	Milwaukee	IHL	7	5	2	0	364	17	0	2.80	....	....	....	....	....	....	....
2000-01	**Nashville**	**NHL**	**37**	**13**	**17**	**5**	**2088**	**85**	**2**	**2.44**	....	....	....	....	....	....	....
2001-02	**Nashville**	**NHL**	**29**	**5**	**14**	**4**	**1471**	**66**	**2**	**2.69**	....	....	....	....	....	....	....
2002-03	**Nashville**	**NHL**	**69**	**25**	**31**	**11**	**3974**	**146**	**3**	**2.20**	....	....	....	....	....	....	....
2003-04	**Nashville**	**NHL**	**73**	**34**	**29**	**10**	**4221**	**178**	**3**	**2.53**	**6**	**2**	**4**	**356**	**12**	**1**	**2.02**
2004-05	Znojmo	CzRep	27	....	....	....	1599	69	3	2.59	....	....	....	....	....	....	....
	HIFK Helsinki	Finland	19	11	4	4	1149	35	2	1.83	4	0	3	205	12	0	3.51
2005-06	**Nashville**	**NHL**	**61**	**36**	**18**	**7**	**3601**	**160**	**4**	**2.67**	....	....	....	....	....	....	....
	Czech Republic	Olympics	7	3	4	0	342	14	1	2.46	....	....	....	....	....	....	....
2006-07	**Nashville**	**NHL**	**44**	**27**	**12**	**4**	**2601**	**104**	**5**	**2.40**	**5**	**1**	**4**	**324**	**16**	**0**	**2.96**
2007-08	**Florida**	**NHL**	**69**	**30**	**29**	**8**	**4031**	**180**	**4**	**2.68**	....	....	....	....	....	....	....
2008-09	**Florida**	**NHL**	**59**	**26**	**23**	**6**	**3324**	**138**	**6**	**2.49**	....	....	....	....	....	....	....
2009-10	**Florida**	**NHL**	**63**	**23**	**28**	**11**	**3695**	**157**	**7**	**2.55**	....	....	....	....	....	....	....
	Czech Republic	Olympics	5	3	2	0	304	9	0	1.78	....	....	....	....	....	....	....
2010-11	**Florida**	**NHL**	**57**	**22**	**28**	**5**	**3224**	**137**	**6**	**2.55**	....	....	....	....	....	....	....
2011-12	**Washington**	**NHL**	**48**	**25**	**17**	**2**	**2583**	**108**	**4**	**2.51**	....	....	....	....	....	....	....
2012-13	**Pittsburgh**	**NHL**	**20**	**13**	**4**	**0**	**1029**	**42**	**3**	**2.45**	**11**	**6**	**5**	**685**	**23**	**1**	**2.01**
	NHL Totals		**700**	**300**	**288**	**78**	**39695**	**1688**	**51**	**2.55**	**22**	**9**	**13**	**1365**	**51**	**2**	**2.24**

Played in NHL All-Star Game (2004, 2008)

Claimed by **Nashville** from **Montreal** in Expansion Draft, June 26, 1998. Signed as a free agent by **Znojmo** (CzRep), September 6, 2004. Signed as a free agent by **HIFK Helsinki** (Finland), December 20, 2004. Traded to **Florida** by **Nashville** for Detroit's 2nd round choice (previously acquired, Nashville selected Nick Spaling) in 2007 Entry Draft and Florida's 1st (later traded to NY Islanders – NY Islanders selected Joshua Bailey) and 2nd (later traded to NY Islanders – NY Islanders selected Aaron Ness) round choices in 2008 Entry Draft, June 22, 2007. Signed as a free agent by **Washington**, July 2, 2011. Traded to **Pittsburgh** by **Washington** for Pittsburgh's 7th round choice (Sergei Kostenko) in 2012 Entry Draft, June 4, 2012.

WARD, Cam (WOHRD, KAM) CAR

Goaltender. Catches left. 6'1", 185 lbs. Born, Saskatoon, Sask., February 29, 1984.
(Carolina's 1st choice, 25th overall, in 2002 Entry Draft).

			Regular Season								Playoffs						
Season	Club	League	GP	W	L	O/T	Mins	GA	SO	Avg	GP	W	L	Mins	GA	SO	Avg
1998-99	Sherwood Park	Minor-AB	24	13	7	4	1403	85	0	3.64	....	....	....	....	....	....	....
99-2000	Sherwood Park	AMHL	20	9	5	1	1194	71	0	3.57	7	4	3	262	22	0	3.57
2000-01	Sherwood Park	AMHL	25	14	6	3	1449	70	0	2.90	....	....	....	....	....	....	....
	Red Deer Rebels	WHL	1	1	0	0	60	0	1	0.00	....	....	....	....	....	....	....
2001-02	Red Deer Rebels	WHL	46	30	11	4	2695	102	1	*2.27	*23	14	9	*1503	52	*2	2.08
2002-03	Red Deer Rebels	WHL	57	*40	13	2	3367	118	5	2.10	*23	14	9	*1407	49	3	2.09
2003-04	Red Deer Rebels	WHL	56	31	16	8	3338	114	4	2.05	19	10	9	1199	37	3	1.85
2004-05	Lowell	AHL	50	27	17	3	2829	94	6	1.99	11	5	6	664	28	2	2.53
2005-06 ♦	**Carolina**	**NHL**	**28**	**14**	**8**	**2**	**1484**	**91**	**0**	**3.68**	***23**	***15**	**8**	***1320**	**47**	**2**	**2.14**
	Lowell	AHL	2	0	2	0	118	5	0	2.54	....	....	....	....	....	....	....
2006-07	**Carolina**	**NHL**	**60**	**30**	**21**	**6**	**3422**	**167**	**2**	**2.93**	....	....	....	....	....	....	....
2007-08	**Carolina**	**NHL**	**69**	**37**	**25**	**5**	**3930**	**180**	**4**	**2.75**	....	....	....	....	....	....	....
2008-09	**Carolina**	**NHL**	**68**	**39**	**23**	**5**	**3928**	**160**	**6**	**2.44**	**18**	**8**	**10**	**1101**	**49**	***2**	**2.67**
2009-10	**Carolina**	**NHL**	**47**	**18**	**23**	**5**	**2651**	**119**	**0**	**2.69**	....	....	....	....	....	....	....
2010-11	**Carolina**	**NHL**	***74**	**37**	**26**	**10**	***4318**	**184**	**4**	**2.56**	....	....	....	....	....	....	....
2011-12	**Carolina**	**NHL**	**68**	**30**	**23**	**13**	**3988**	**182**	**5**	**2.74**	....	....	....	....	....	....	....
2012-13	**Carolina**	**NHL**	**17**	**9**	**6**	**1**	**929**	**44**	**0**	**2.84**	....	....	....	....	....	....	....
	NHL Totals		**431**	**214**	**155**	**47**	**24650**	**1127**	**21**	**2.74**	**41**	**23**	**18**	**2421**	**96**	**4**	**2.38**

WHL East First All-Star Team (2002, 2004) • Canadian Major Junior Second All-Star Team (2002) • WHL East Second All-Star Team (2003) • WHL Goaltender of the Year (2002, 2004) • WHL Player of the Year (2004) • Canadian Major Junior First All-Star Team (2004) • Canadian Major Junior Goaltender of the Year (2004) • AHL All-Rookie Team (2005) • Conn Smythe Trophy (2006)

Played in NHL All-Star Game (2011)

• Scored a goal vs. New Jersey, December 26, 2011.

WEDGEWOOD, Scott (WEHJ-wud, SKAWT) N.J.

Goaltender. Catches left. 6'1", 195 lbs. Born, Etobicoke, Ont., August 14, 1992.
(New Jersey's 2nd choice, 84th overall, in 2010 Entry Draft).

			Regular Season								Playoffs						
Season	Club	League	GP	W	L	O/T	Mins	GA	SO	Avg	GP	W	L	Mins	GA	SO	Avg
2007-08	Miss. Senators	GTHL	29	....	....	....	1305	63	2	2.17	....	....	....	....	....	....	....
2008-09	Plymouth Whalers	OHL	6	0	2	0	158	12	0	4.56	3	0	0	26	2	0	4.62
2009-10	Plymouth Whalers	OHL	18	5	9	0	938	51	2	3.26	4	1	1	116	4	0	2.07
2010-11	Plymouth Whalers	OHL	55	28	18	2	3046	152	2	2.99	10	4	6	606	33	0	3.27
2011-12	Plymouth Whalers	OHL	43	28	10	3	2482	125	3	3.02	13	7	6	781	31	*2	2.38
2012-13	Trenton Titans	ECHL	48	20	22	5	2741	147	1	3.22	....	....	....	....	....	....	....
	Albany Devils	AHL	5	2	2	0	242	14	0	3.47	....	....	....	....	....	....	....

WHITNEY, Brandon (WHIHT-nee, BRAN-duhn) CHI

Goaltender. Catches left. 6'5", 193 lbs. Born, Centreville, N.S., May 11, 1994.
(Chicago's 7th choice, 191st overall, in 2012 Entry Draft).

			Regular Season								Playoffs						
Season	Club	League	GP	W	L	O/T	Mins	GA	SO	Avg	GP	W	L	Mins	GA	SO	Avg
2009-10	Valley Wildcats	NSMHL	26	3	19	1	1332	128	0	6.04	2	0	2	85	14	0	9.85
2010-11	Halifax Titans	NSMHL	8	5	3	0	461	23	0	2.99	8	5	3	479	18	1	2.26
	Victoriaville Tigres	QMJHL	3	0	2	0	27	2	0	4.67	....	....	....	....	....	....	....
2011-12	Victoriaville Tigres	QMJHL	36	22	4	4	1841	84	2	2.74	3	0	2	131	12	0	5.49
2012-13	Victoriaville Tigres	QMJHL	*58	27	20	6	3124	161	4	3.09	9	4	5	534	26	2	2.92

WILCOX, Adam (WIHL-cawx, A-duhm) T.B.

Goaltender. Catches left. 6', 183 lbs. Born, South St. Paul, MN, November 26, 1992.
(Tampa Bay's 4th choice, 178th overall, in 2011 Entry Draft).

			Regular Season								Playoffs						
Season	Club	League	GP	W	L	O/T	Mins	GA	SO	Avg	GP	W	L	Mins	GA	SO	Avg
2009-10	South St. Paul	High-MN	23	11	11	0	1119	73	0	3.33	2	1	1	102	8	0	4.00
2010-11	Green Bay	USHL	24	16	6	1	1420	52	1	2.20	2	1	0	88	1	0	0.68
2011-12	Green Bay	USHL	9	7	2	0	529	20	2	2.27	....	....	....	....	....	....	....
	Tri-City Storm	USHL	34	16	17	1	1896	92	1	2.91	....	....	....	....	....	....	....
2012-13	U. of Minnesota	WCHA	39	*25	8	5	*2331	73	3	*1.88	....	....	....	....	....	....	....

WILLIAMS, Stephon (WIHL-yuhms, STEH-fawn) NYI

Goaltender. Catches left. 6'2", 194 lbs. Born, Fairbanks, AK, April 28, 1993.
(NY Islanders' 4th choice, 106th overall, in 2013 Entry Draft).

			Regular Season								Playoffs						
Season	Club	League	GP	W	L	O/T	Mins	GA	SO	Avg	GP	W	L	Mins	GA	SO	Avg
2010-11	Sioux Falls	USHL	35	20	7	6	2042	88	1	2.59	5	4	1	298	11	0	2.21
2011-12	Sioux Falls	USHL	21	6	9	2	1113	50	1	2.70	....	....	....	....	....	....	....
	Waterloo	USHL	19	10	6	2	1054	49	1	2.79	*15	10	5	*895	34	*1	2.28
2012-13	Minnesota State	WCHA	35	21	12	2	2043	68	*4	2.00	....	....	....	....	....	....	....

YORK, Allen (YOHRK, AL-ihn)

Goaltender. Catches left. 6'3", 188 lbs. Born, Wetaskiwin, Alta., June 17, 1989.
(Columbus' 6th choice, 158th overall, in 2007 Entry Draft).

			Regular Season								Playoffs						
Season	Club	League	GP	W	L	O/T	Mins	GA	SO	Avg	GP	W	L	Mins	GA	SO	Avg
2006-07	Camrose Kodiaks	AJHL	32	23	4	0	1661	60	2	2.17	22	16	6	1391	46	4	1.98
2007-08	Camrose Kodiaks	AJHL	....	24	5	3	2005	75	3	2.24	....	....	....	....	....	....	....
2008-09	RPI Engineers	ECAC	16	5	10	0	913	46	1	3.02	....	....	....	....	....	....	....
2009-10	RPI Engineers	ECAC	33	14	12	4	1935	82	1	2.54	....	....	....	....	....	....	....
2010-11	RPI Engineers	ECAC	34	18	11	4	2051	74	2	2.17	....	....	....	....	....	....	....
	Springfield Falcons	AHL	4	3	1	0	206	7	1	2.04	....	....	....	....	....	....	....
2011-12	**Columbus**	**NHL**	**11**	**3**	**2**	**0**	**417**	**16**	**0**	**2.30**	....	....	....	....	....	....	....
	Springfield Falcons	AHL	5	1	1	0	183	12	0	3.94	....	....	....	....	....	....	....
	Chicago Express	ECHL	11	4	4	2	604	33	0	3.28	....	....	....	....	....	....	....
2012-13	Evansville IceMen	ECHL	5	3	1	1	265	12	0	2.72	....	....	....	....	....	....	....
	Springfield Falcons	AHL	19	13	6	0	1130	45	0	2.39	1	0	0	30	0	0	0.00
	NHL Totals		**11**	**3**	**2**	**0**	**417**	**16**	**0**	**2.30**	....	....	....	....	....	....	....

ECAC Second All-Star Team (2010)

ZATKOFF, Jeff (ZAT-kawf, JEHF) PIT

Goaltender. Catches left. 6'2", 179 lbs. Born, Detroit, MI, June 9, 1987.
(Los Angeles' 4th choice, 74th overall, in 2006 Entry Draft).

			Regular Season								Playoffs						
Season	Club	League	GP	W	L	O/T	Mins	GA	SO	Avg	GP	W	L	Mins	GA	SO	Avg
2004-05	Sioux City	USHL	24	13	6	3	1271	54	1	2.55	2	0	0	68	10	0	8.88
2005-06	Miami U.	CCHA	20	14	5	1	1217	41	3	2.02	....	....	....	....	....	....	....
2006-07	Miami U.	CCHA	26	14	8	3	1542	58	1	2.26	....	....	....	....	....	....	....
2007-08	Miami U.	CCHA	36	27	8	1	2161	62	3	*1.72	....	....	....	....	....	....	....
2008-09	Manchester	AHL	3	1	2	0	182	7	0	2.31	....	....	....	....	....	....	....
	Ontario Reign	ECHL	37	17	15	3	2164	107	1	2.97	7	3	4	418	26	0	3.73
2009-10	Manchester	AHL	22	10	9	0	1170	57	2	2.92	....	....	....	....	....	....	....
2010-11	Manchester	AHL	45	20	17	5	2508	112	3	2.68	5	1	3	253	16	0	3.80
2011-12	Manchester	AHL	44	21	17	1	2432	101	3	2.49	2	0	2	97	7	0	4.34
2012-13	Wilkes-Barre	AHL	49	26	20	0	2799	90	5	*1.93	5	2	3	253	23	0	5.45

CCHA Second All-Star Team (2008) • Harry ''Hap'' Holmes Memorial Award (AHL – fewest goals against) (2013) (shared with Brad Thiessen)

Signed as a free agent by **Pittsburgh**, July 1, 2012.

Late Additions to Player Register

FREE AGENT SIGNINGS

FISTRIC, Mark *(see page 411 for data panel)* **ANA**

Defense — Signed as a free agent by **Anaheim**, August 20, 2013.

NASH, Brendon *(see page 495 for data panel)*

Defense — Signed as a free agent by **Hartford** (AHL), August 20, 2013.

NOKELAINEN, Petteri *(see page 498 for data panel)*

Center — Signed as a free agent by **Gavle** (Sweden), August 16, 2013.

OBERG, Evan *(see page 499 for data panel)*

Defense — Signed as a free agent by **Chicago** (AHL), August 19, 2013.

O'MARRA, Ryan *(see page 502 for data panel)*

Center — Signed as a free agent by **Fassa** (Italy), December 24, 2012.
Signed as a free agent by **Valerengen** (Norway), January 23, 2013.

SEGAL, Brandon *(see page 540 for data panel)* **WSH**

Right wing — Signed as a free agent by **Washington**, August 20, 2013.

TARASOV, DANILL (TAIR-ah-sawv, DAN-ihl) **S.J.**

Right wing. Shoots right. 6'0", 195 lbs. Born, Moscow, USSR, June 20, 1991.

			Regular Season					Playoffs				
Season	**Club**	**League**	**GP**	**G**	**A**	**Pts**	**PIM**	**GP**	**G**	**A**	**Pts**	**PIM**
2010-11	Indiana	USHL	57	37	38	75	46	5	2	4	6	6
2011-12	Indiana	USHL	60	47	41	88	86	6	5	5	10	8
2012-13	Worcester	AHL	43	14	14	28	20	...	...	...	...	...
	San Francisco	ECHL	17	3	11	14	5	...	...	...	...	...

Signed as a free agent by **Worcester** (AHL), June 1, 2012. Signed as a free agent by **San Jose**, April 2, 2013.

2013 LESTER PATRICK TROPHY WINNER

KEVIN ALLEN *(see page 217 for previous winners)*

An annual award "for outstanding service to hockey in the United States." See page 212 for more on the trophy's history and selection criteria.

Kevin Allen has covered hockey for *USA Today* since 1986. He is the president of the Professional Hockey Writers' Association and is the author of several books about the sport including *USA Hockey: The Celebration of a Great Tradition* (1997) and *Star-Spangled Hockey: Celebrating 75 Years of USA Hockey* (2011). He has contributed to numerous publications and wrote about the origins of American hockey for the *Total Hockey Encyclopedia*.

ADDITIONAL STATISTICS

MATTHIAS, Shawn *(see page 480 for data panel)* **FLA**

			Regular Season					Playoffs				
Season	**Club**	**League**	**GP**	**G**	**A**	**Pts**	**PIM**	**GP**	**G**	**A**	**Pts**	**PIM**
2012-13	Linz	Austria	4	1	2	3	0	...	...	...	...	...

Gene Achtymichuk

George Allen

Niklas Andersson

Jason Arnott

Retired NHL Player Index

Abbreviations: Teams/Cities: – **Ana.** – Anaheim; **Atl.** – Atlanta; **Bos.** – Boston; **Bro.** – Brooklyn; **Buf.** – Buffalo; **Cgy.** – Calgary; **Cal.** – California; **Car.** – Carolina; **Chi.** – Chicago; **Cle.** – Cleveland; **Col.** – Colorado; **CBJ** – Columbus; **Dal.** – Dallas; **Det.** – Detroit; **Edm.** – Edmonton; **Fla.** – Florida; **Ham.** – Hamilton; **Hfd.** – Hartford; **K.C.** – Kansas City; **L.A.** – Los Angeles; **Min.** – Minnesota; **Mtl.** – Montreal; **Mtl.M.** – Montreal Maroons; **Mtl.W.** – Montreal Wanderers; **Nsh.** – Nashville; **N.J.** – New Jersey; **NYA** – NY Americans; **NYI** – NY Islanders; **NYR** – New York Rangers; **Oak.** – Oakland; **Ott.** – Ottawa; **Phi.** – Philadelphia; **Phx.** – Phoenix; **Pit.** – Pittsburgh; **Que.** – Quebec; **St.L.** – St. Louis; **S.J.** – San Jose; **T.B.** – Tampa Bay; **Tor.** – Toronto; **Van.** – Vancouver; **Wsh.** – Washington; **Wpg.** – Winnipeg

A – assists; **G** – goals; **GP** – games played; **PIM** – penalties in minutes; **TP** – total points.
• – deceased. Assists not recorded during 1917-18 season ‡ – Remains active in other leagues.

NHL Seasons – A player or goaltender who does not play in a regular season but who does appear in that year's playoffs is credited with an NHL Season in this Index. Total seasons are rounded off to the nearest full season.

			Regular Schedule					Playoffs							
Name	NHL Teams	NHL Seasons	GP	G	A	TP	PIM	GP	G	A	TP	PIM	NHL Cup Wins	First NHL Season	Last NHL Season
A															
Aalto, Antti	Ana.	4	151	11	17	28	52	4	0	0	0	2	....	1997-98	2000-01
Abbott, Reg	Mtl.	1	3	0	0	0	0	....	....	....	....	....	....	1952-53	1952-53
• Abel, Clarence	NYR, Chi.	8	333	19	18	37	359	38	1	1	2	58	2	1926-27	1933-34
Abel, Gerry	Det.	1	1	0	0	0	0	....	....	....	....	....	....	1966-67	1966-67
• Abel, Sid	Det., Chi.	14	612	189	283	472	376	97	28	30	58	79	3	1938-39	1953-54
Abgrall, Dennis	L.A.	1	13	0	2	2	4	....	....	....	....	....	....	1975-76	1975-76
‡ Abid, Ramzi	Phx., Pit., Atl., Nsh.	4	68	14	16	30	78	2	0	0	0	0	....	2002-03	2006-07
Abrahamsson, Thommy	Hfd.	1	32	6	11	17	16	....	....	....	....	....	....	1980-81	1980-81
Achtymichuk, Gene	Mtl., Det.	4	32	3	5	8	2	....	....	....	....	....	....	1951-52	1958-59
Acomb, Doug	Tor.	1	2	0	1	1	0	....	....	....	....	....	....	1969-70	1969-70
Acton, Keith	Mtl., Min., Edm., Phi., Wsh., NYI	15	1023	226	358	584	1172	66	12	21	33	88	1	1979-80	1993-94
• Adam, Douglas	NYR	1	4	0	1	1	0	....	....	....	....	....	....	1949-50	1949-50
Adam, Russ	Tor.	1	8	1	2	3	11	....	....	....	....	....	....	1982-83	1982-83
‡ Adams, Bryan	Atl.	2	11	0	1	1	2	....	....	....	....	....	....	1999-00	2000-01
Adams, Greg	Phi., Hfd., Wsh., Edm., Van., Que., Det.	10	545	84	143	227	1173	43	2	11	13	153	....	1980-81	1989-90
Adams, Greg	N.J., Van., Dal., Phx., Fla.	17	1056	355	388	743	326	81	20	22	42	16	....	1984-85	2000-01
• Adams, Jack	Tor., Ott.	7	173	83	32	115	366	10	2	0	2	13	2	1917-18	1926-27
Adams, John	Mtl.	1	42	6	12	18	11	3	0	0	0	0	....	1940-41	1940-41
Adams, Kevyn	Tor., CBJ, Fla., Car., Phx., Chi.	10	540	59	77	136	317	67	2	2	4	39	1	1997-98	2007-08
• Adams, Stew	Chi., Tor.	4	95	9	26	35	60	11	3	3	6	14	....	1929-30	1932-33
Adduono, Rick	Bos., Atl.	2	4	0	0	0	2	....	....	....	....	....	....	1975-76	1979-80
‡ Afanasenkov, Dmitry	T.B., Phi.	5	227	27	27	54	52	28	1	3	4	8	1	2000-01	2006-07
Affleck, Bruce	St.L., Van., NYI	7	280	14	66	80	86	8	0	0	0	0	....	1974-75	1983-84
‡ Afinogenov, Maxim	Buf., Atl.	10	651	158	237	395	486	49	10	13	23	22	....	1999-00	2009-10
Agnew, Jim	Van., Hfd.	6	81	0	1	1	257	4	0	0	0	6	....	1986-87	1992-93
Ahern, Fred	Cal., Cle., Col.	4	146	31	30	61	130	2	0	1	1	2	....	1974-75	1977-78
• Ahlin, Rudy	Chi.	1	1	0	0	0	0	....	....	....	....	....	....	1937-38	1937-38
Ahola, Peter	L.A., Pit., S.J., Cgy.	3	123	10	17	27	137	6	0	0	0	2	....	1991-92	1993-94
Ahrens, Chris	Min.	6	52	0	3	3	84	1	0	0	0	0	....	1972-73	1977-78
• Ailsby, Lloyd	NYR	1	3	0	0	0	2	....	....	....	....	....	....	1951-52	1951-52
Aitken, Brad	Pit., Edm.	2	14	1	3	4	25	....	....	....	....	....	....	1987-88	1990-91
Aitken, Johnathan	Bos., Chi.	2	44	0	1	1	70	....	....	....	....	....	....	1999-00	2003-04
Aivazoff, Micah	Det., Edm., NYI	3	92	4	6	10	46	....	....	....	....	....	....	1993-94	1995-96
Alatalo, Mika	Phx.	2	152	17	29	46	58	5	0	0	0	2	....	1999-00	2000-01
Albelin, Tommy	Que., N.J., Cgy.	18	952	44	211	255	417	81	7	15	22	22	2	1987-88	2005-06
• Albright, Clint	NYR	1	59	14	5	19	19	....	....	....	....	....	....	1948-49	1948-49
Aldcorn, Gary	Tor., Det., Bos.	5	226	41	56	97	78	6	1	2	3	4	....	1956-57	1960-61
Aldridge, Keith	Dal.	1	4	0	0	0	0	....	....	....	....	....	....	1999-00	1999-00
Alexander, Claire	Tor., Van.	4	155	18	47	65	36	16	2	4	6	4	....	1974-75	1977-78
• Alexandre, Art	Mtl.	2	11	0	2	2	8	4	0	0	0	0	....	1931-32	1932-33
Alexeev, Nikita	T.B., Chi.	3	159	20	17	37	28	11	1	0	1	0	....	2001-02	2006-07
Allan, Jeff	Cle.	1	4	0	0	0	2	....	....	....	....	....	....	1977-78	1977-78
Allen, Bobby	Edm., Bos.	3	51	0	3	3	12	....	....	....	....	....	....	2002-03	2007-08
‡ Allen, Chris	Fla.	2	2	0	0	0	2	....	....	....	....	....	....	1997-98	1998-99
• Allen, George	NYR, Chi., Mtl.	8	339	82	115	197	179	41	9	10	19	32	....	1938-39	1946-47
Allen, Keith	Det.	2	28	0	4	4	8	5	0	0	0	0	1	1953-54	1954-55
Allen, Peter	Pit.	1	8	0	0	0	8	....	....	....	....	....	....	1995-96	1995-96
• Allen, Viv	NYA	1	6	0	1	1	0	....	....	....	....	....	....	1940-41	1940-41
Alley, Steve	Hfd.	2	15	3	3	6	11	3	0	1	1	0	....	1979-80	1980-81
Allison, Dave	Mtl.	1	3	0	0	0	12	....	....	....	....	....	....	1983-84	1983-84
Allison, Jamie	Cgy., Chi., CBJ, Nsh., Fla.	10	372	7	23	30	639	....	....	....	....	....	....	1994-95	2005-06
Allison, Jason	Wsh., Bos., L.A., Tor.	12	552	154	331	485	441	25	7	18	25	14	....	1993-94	2005-06
Allison, Mike	NYR, Tor., L.A.	10	499	102	166	268	630	82	9	17	26	135	....	1980-81	1989-90
Allison, Ray	Hfd., Phi.	7	238	64	93	157	223	12	2	3	5	20	....	1979-80	1986-87
• Allum, Bill	NYR	1	1	0	1	1	0	....	....	....	....	....	....	1940-41	1940-41
• Amadio, Dave	Det., L.A.	3	125	5	11	16	163	16	1	2	3	18	....	1957-58	1968-69
Ambroziak, Peter	Buf.	1	12	0	1	1	0	....	....	....	....	....	....	1994-95	1994-95
Amodeo, Mike	Wpg.	1	19	0	0	0	2	....	....	....	....	....	....	1979-80	1979-80
Amonte, Tony	NYR, Chi., Phx., Phi., Cgy.	16	1174	416	484	900	752	99	22	33	55	56	....	1990-91	2006-07
• Anderson, Bill	Bos.	1	....	....	....	....	....	1	0	0	0	0	....	1942-43	1942-43
Anderson, Dale	Det.	1	13	0	0	0	6	2	0	0	0	0	....	1956-57	1956-57
Anderson, Doug	Mtl.	1	....	....	....	....	....	2	0	0	0	0	....	1952-53	1952-53
Anderson, Earl	Det., Bos.	3	109	19	19	38	22	5	0	1	1	0	....	1974-75	1976-77
Anderson, Glenn	Edm., Tor., NYR, St.L.	16	1129	498	601	1099	1120	225	93	121	214	442	6	1980-81	1995-96
Anderson, Jim	L.A.	1	7	1	2	3	2	....	....	....	....	....	....	1967-68	1967-68
Anderson, John	Tor., Que., Hfd.	12	814	282	349	631	263	37	9	18	27	2	....	1977-78	1988-89
Anderson, Murray	Wsh.	1	40	0	1	1	68	....	....	....	....	....	....	1974-75	1974-75
Anderson, Perry	St.L., N.J., S.J.	10	400	50	59	109	1051	36	2	1	3	161	....	1981-82	1991-92
Anderson, Ron	Det., L.A., St.L., Buf.	5	251	28	30	58	146	5	0	0	0	4	....	1967-68	1971-72
Anderson, Ron	Wsh.	1	28	9	7	16	8	....	....	....	....	....	....	1974-75	1974-75
Anderson, Russ	Pit., Hfd., L.A.	9	519	22	99	121	1086	10	0	3	3	28	....	1976-77	1984-85
Anderson, Shawn	Buf., Que., Wsh., Phi.	8	255	11	51	62	117	19	1	1	2	16	....	1986-87	1994-95
• Anderson, Tom	Det., NYA, Bro.	8	319	62	127	189	180	16	2	7	9	8	....	1934-35	1941-42
Andersson, Erik	Cgy.	1	12	2	1	3	8	....	....	....	....	....	....	1997-98	1997-98
‡ Andersson, Jonas	Nsh., Van.	2	9	0	0	0	2	....	....	....	....	....	....	2001-02	2010-11
Andersson, Kent-Erik	Min., NYR	7	456	72	103	175	78	50	4	11	15	4	....	1977-78	1983-84
Andersson, Mikael	Buf., Hfd., T.B., Phi., NYI	15	761	95	169	264	134	25	2	7	9	10	....	1985-86	1999-00
Andersson, Niklas	Que., NYI, S.J., Nsh., Cgy.	6	164	29	53	82	85	....	....	....	....	....	....	1992-93	2000-01
Andersson, Peter	Wsh., Que.	3	172	10	41	51	81	7	0	2	2	2	....	1983-84	1985-86
Andersson, Peter	NYR, Fla.	2	47	6	13	19	20	....	....	....	....	....	....	1992-93	1993-94
Andrascik, Steve	NYR	1	....	....	....	....	....	1	0	0	0	0	....	1971-72	1971-72
Andrea, Paul	NYR, Pit., Cal., Buf.	4	150	31	49	80	10	....	....	....	....	....	....	1965-66	1970-71
• Andrews, Lloyd	Tor.	4	53	8	5	13	10	2	0	0	0	0	1	1921-22	1924-25
Andreychuk, Dave	Buf., Tor., N.J., Bos., Col., T.B.	23	1639	640	698	1338	1125	162	43	54	97	162	1	1982-83	2005-06
Andrievski, Alexander	Chi.	1	1	0	0	0	0	....	....	....	....	....	....	1992-93	1992-93
Andruff, Ron	Mtl., Col.	5	153	19	36	55	54	2	0	0	0	0	....	1974-75	1978-79
Andrusak, Greg	Pit., Tor.	5	28	0	6	6	16	15	1	0	1	8	....	1993-94	1999-00
Angelstad, Mel	Wsh.	1	2	0	0	0	2	....	....	....	....	....	....	2003-04	2003-04
Angotti, Lou	NYR, Chi., Phi., Pit., St.L.	10	653	103	186	289	228	65	8	8	16	17	....	1964-65	1973-74
Anholt, Darrel	Chi.	1	1	0	0	0	0	....	....	....	....	....	....	1983-84	1983-84
• Anslow, Hub	NYR	1	2	0	0	0	0	....	....	....	....	....	....	1947-48	1947-48
Antonovich, Mike	Min., Hfd., N.J.	5	87	10	15	25	37	....	....	....	....	....	....	1975-76	1983-84
Antoski, Shawn	Van., Phi., Pit., Ana.	8	183	3	5	8	599	36	1	3	4	74	....	1990-91	1997-98
• Apps, Syl	Tor.	10	423	201	231	432	56	69	25	29	54	8	3	1936-37	1947-48
Apps, Syl	NYR, Pit., L.A.	10	727	183	423	606	311	23	5	5	10	23	....	1970-71	1979-80
Arbour, Al	Det., Chi., Tor., St.L.	16	626	12	58	70	617	86	1	8	9	92	4	1953-54	1970-71
• Arbour, Amos	Mtl., Ham., Tor.	6	113	52	20	72	77	....	....	....	....	....	....	1918-19	1923-24
• Arbour, Jack	Det., Tor.	2	47	5	1	6	56	....	....	....	....	....	....	1926-27	1928-29
Arbour, John	Bos., Pit., Van., St.L.	5	106	1	9	10	149	5	0	0	0	0	....	1965-66	1971-72
• Arbour, Ty	Pit., Chi.	5	207	28	28	56	112	11	2	0	2	6	....	1926-27	1930-31
Archambault, Michel	Chi.	1	3	0	0	0	0	....	....	....	....	....	....	1976-77	1976-77

			Regular Schedule					Playoffs							
Name	**NHL Teams**	**NHL Seasons**	**GP**	**G**	**A**	**TP**	**PIM**	**GP**	**G**	**A**	**TP**	**PIM**	**NHL Cup Wins**	**First NHL Season**	**Last NHL Season**
Archibald, Dave	Min., NYR, Ott., NYI	8	323	57	67	124	139	5	0	1	1	0	....	1987-88	1996-97
Archibald, Jim	Min.	3	16	1	2	3	45	....	....	....	....	....	....	1984-85	1986-87
Areshenkoff, Ron	Edm.	1	4	0	0	0	0	....	....	....	....	....	....	1979-80	1979-80
Arkhipov, Denis	Nsh., Chi.	5	352	56	82	138	128	....	....	....	....	....	....	2000-01	2006-07
Armstrong, Bill	Phi.	1	1	0	1	1	0	....	....	....	....	....	....	1990-91	1990-91
• Armstrong, Bob	Bos.	12	542	13	86	99	671	42	1	7	8	28	....	1950-51	1961-62
Armstrong, Chris	Min., Ana.	2	7	0	1	1	0	....	....	....	....	....	....	2000-01	2003-04
Armstrong, Derek	NYI, Ott., NYR, L.A., St.L.	14	477	72	149	221	355	....	....	....	....	....	....	1993-94	2009-10
Armstrong, George	Tor.	21	1187	296	417	713	721	110	26	34	60	52	4	1949-50	1970-71
• Armstrong, Murray	Tor., NYA, Bro., Det.	8	270	67	121	188	72	30	4	6	10	2	....	1937-38	1945-46
• Armstrong, Norm	Tor.	1	7	1	1	2	2	....	....	....	....	....	....	1962-63	1962-63
‡ Armstrong, Riley	S.J.	1	2	0	0	0	2	....	....	....	....	....	....	2008-09	2008-09
Armstrong, Tim	Tor.	1	11	1	0	1	6	....	....	....	....	....	....	1988-89	1988-89
Arnason, Chuck	Mtl., Atl., Pit., K.C., Col., Cle., Min., Wsh.	8	401	109	90	199	122	9	2	4	6	4	....	1971-72	1978-79
‡ Arnason, Tyler	Chi., Ott., Col.	7	487	88	157	245	140	13	2	3	5	2	....	2001-02	2008-09
Arniel, Scott	Wpg., Buf., Bos.	11	730	149	189	338	599	34	3	3	6	39	....	1981-82	1991-92
Arnott, Jason	Edm., N.J., Dal., Nsh., Wsh., St.L.	18	1244	417	521	938	1242	122	32	41	73	76	1	1993-94	2011-12
Arthur, Fred	Hfd., Phi.	3	80	1	8	9	49	4	0	0	0	2	....	1980-81	1982-83
‡ Artyukhin, Evgeny	T.B., Ana., Atl.	3	199	19	30	49	313	5	1	0	1	6	....	2005-06	2009-10
• Arundel, John	Tor.	1	3	0	0	0	9	....	....	....	....	....	....	1949-50	1949-50
Arvedson, Magnus	Ott., Van.	7	434	100	125	225	241	52	3	8	11	34	....	1997-98	2003-04
• Ashbee, Barry	Bos., Phi.	5	284	15	70	85	291	17	0	4	4	22	1	1965-66	1973-74
• Ashby, Don	Tor., Col., Edm.	6	188	40	56	96	40	12	1	0	1	4	....	1975-76	1980-81
Ashton, Brent	Van., Col., N.J., Min., Que., Det., Wpg., Bos., Cgy.	14	998	284	345	629	635	85	24	25	49	70	....	1979-80	1992-93
Ashworth, Frank	Chi.	1	18	5	4	9	2	....	....	....	....	....	....	1946-47	1946-47
• Asmundson, Oscar	NYR, Det., St.L., NYA, Mtl.	5	111	11	23	34	30	9	0	2	2	4	1	1932-33	1937-38
• Astashenko, Kaspars	T.B.	2	23	1	2	3	8	....	....	....	....	....	....	1999-00	2000-01
Astley, Mark	Buf.	3	75	4	19	23	92	2	0	0	0	0	....	1993-94	1995-96
• Atanas, Walt	NYR	1	49	13	8	21	40	....	....	....	....	....	....	1944-45	1944-45
Atcheynum, Blair	Ott., St.L., Nsh., Chi.	5	196	27	33	60	36	23	1	3	4	8	....	1992-93	2000-01
• Atkinson, Steve	Bos., Buf., Wsh.	6	302	60	51	111	104	1	0	0	0	0	....	1968-69	1974-75
Attwell, Bob	Col.	2	22	1	5	6	0	....	....	....	....	....	....	1979-80	1980-81
Attwell, Ron	St.L., NYR	1	22	1	7	8	8	....	....	....	....	....	....	1967-68	1967-68
Aubin, Norm	Tor.	2	69	18	13	31	30	1	0	0	0	0	....	1981-82	1982-83
‡ Aubin, Serge	Col., CBJ, Atl.	7	374	44	64	108	361	22	0	1	1	10	....	1998-99	2005-06
Aubry, Pierre	Que., Det.	5	202	24	26	50	133	20	1	1	2	32	....	1980-81	1984-85
• Aubuchon, Ossie	Bos., NYR	2	50	20	12	32	4	6	1	0	1	0	....	1942-43	1943-44
Audet, Philippe	Det.	1	4	0	0	0	0	....	....	....	....	....	....	1998-99	1998-99
Audette, Donald	Buf., L.A., Atl., Dal., Mtl., Fla.	15	735	260	249	509	584	73	21	27	48	46	....	1989-90	2003-04
• Auge, Les	Col.	1	6	0	3	3	4	....	....	....	....	....	....	1980-81	1980-81
Augusta, Patrik	Tor., Wsh.	2	4	0	0	0	0	....	....	....	....	....	....	1993-94	1998-99
Aulin, Jared	L.A.	1	17	2	2	4	0	....	....	....	....	....	....	2002-03	2002-03
• Aurie, Larry	Det.	12	489	147	129	276	279	24	6	9	15	10	2	1927-28	1938-39
‡ Avery, Sean	Det., L.A., NYR, Dal.	10	580	90	157	247	1533	28	5	10	15	69	....	2001-02	2011-12
Awrey, Don	Bos., St.L., Mtl., Pit., NYR, Col.	16	979	31	158	189	1065	71	0	18	18	150	2	1963-64	1978-79
Axelsson, P.J.	Bos.	11	797	103	184	287	276	54	4	3	7	24	....	1997-98	2008-09
• Ayres, Vern	NYA, Mtl.M., St.L., NYR	6	211	6	11	17	350	....	....	....	....	....	....	1930-31	1935-36

B

			Regular Schedule					Playoffs							
Name	**NHL Teams**	**NHL Seasons**	**GP**	**G**	**A**	**TP**	**PIM**	**GP**	**G**	**A**	**TP**	**PIM**	**NHL Cup Wins**	**First NHL Season**	**Last NHL Season**
Babando, Pete	Bos., Det., Chi., NYR	6	351	86	73	159	194	17	3	3	6	6	1	1947-48	1952-53
Babcock, Bobby	Wsh.	2	2	0	0	0	2	....	....	....	....	....	....	1990-91	1992-93
Babe, Warren	Min.	3	21	2	5	7	23	2	0	0	0	0	....	1987-88	1990-91
‡ Babenko, Yuri	Col.	1	3	0	0	0	0	....	....	....	....	....	....	2000-01	2000-01
Babin, Mitch	St.L.	1	8	0	0	0	0	....	....	....	....	....	....	1975-76	1975-76
Baby, John	Cle., Min.	2	26	2	8	10	26	....	....	....	....	....	....	1977-78	1978-79
Babych, Dave	Wpg., Hfd., Van., Phi., L.A.	19	1195	142	581	723	970	114	21	41	62	113	....	1980-81	1998-99
Babych, Wayne	St.L., Pit., Que., Hfd.	9	519	192	246	438	498	41	7	9	16	24	....	1978-79	1986-87
Baca, Jergus	Hfd.	2	10	0	2	2	14	....	....	....	....	....	....	1990-91	1991-92
‡ Backman, Christian	St.L., NYR, CBJ	6	302	23	56	79	182	13	0	2	2	16	....	2002-03	2008-09
Backman, Mike	NYR	3	18	1	6	7	18	10	2	2	4	2	....	1981-82	1983-84
• Backor, Pete	Tor.	1	36	4	5	9	6	....	....	....	....	....	1	1944-45	1944-45
Backstrom, Ralph	Mtl., L.A., Chi.	17	1032	278	361	639	386	116	27	32	59	68	6	1956-57	1972-73
• Bailey, Ace	Tor.	8	313	111	82	193	472	21	3	4	7	12	1	1926-27	1933-34
• Bailey, Bob	Tor., Det., Chi.	5	150	15	21	36	207	15	0	4	4	22	....	1953-54	1957-58
• Bailey, Garnet	Bos., Det., St.L., Wsh.	10	568	107	171	278	633	15	2	4	6	28	2	1968-69	1977-78
Bailey, Reid	Phi., Tor., Hfd.	4	40	1	3	4	105	16	0	2	2	25	....	1980-81	1983-84
Baillargeon, Joel	Wpg., Que.	3	20	0	2	2	31	....	....	....	....	....	....	1986-87	1988-89
Baird, Ken	Cal.	1	10	0	2	2	15	....	....	....	....	....	....	1971-72	1971-72
Baker, Bill	Mtl., Col., St.L., NYR	3	143	7	25	32	175	6	0	0	0	0	....	1980-81	1982-83
Baker, Jamie	Que., Ott., S.J., Tor.	10	404	71	79	150	271	25	5	4	9	42	....	1989-90	1998-99
Bakovic, Peter	Van.	1	10	2	0	2	48	....	....	....	....	....	....	1987-88	1987-88
Bala, Chris	Ott.	1	6	0	1	1	0	....	....	....	....	....	....	2001-02	2001-02
‡ Balastik, Jaroslav	CBJ	2	74	13	11	24	30	....	....	....	....	....	....	2005-06	2006-07
Balderis, Helmut	Min.	1	26	3	6	9	2	....	....	....	....	....	....	1989-90	1989-90
• Baldwin, Doug	Tor., Det., Chi.	3	24	0	1	1	8	....	....	....	....	....	....	1945-46	1947-48
‡ Balej, Jozef	Mtl., NYR, Van.	2	18	1	5	6	4	....	....	....	....	....	....	2003-04	2005-06
Balfour, Earl	Tor., Chi.	7	288	30	22	52	78	26	0	3	3	4	1	1951-52	1960-61
• Balfour, Murray	Mtl., Chi., Bos.	8	306	67	90	157	393	40	9	10	19	45	1	1956-57	1964-65
Ball, Terry	Phi., Buf.	4	74	7	19	26	26	....	....	....	....	....	....	1967-68	1971-72
Balmochnykh, Maxim	Ana.	1	6	0	1	1	2	....	....	....	....	....	....	1999-00	1999-00
• Balon, Dave	NYR, Mtl., Min., Van.	14	776	192	222	414	607	78	14	21	35	109	2	1959-60	1972-73
Baltimore, Bryon	Edm.	1	2	0	0	0	4	....	....	....	....	....	....	1979-80	1979-80
Baluik, Stan	Bos.	1	7	0	0	0	2	....	....	....	....	....	....	1959-60	1959-60
Bancroft, Steve	Chi., S.J.	2	6	0	1	1	2	....	....	....	....	....	....	1992-93	2001-02
Bandura, Jeff	NYR	1	2	0	1	1	0	....	....	....	....	....	....	1980-81	1980-81
‡ Banham, Frank	Ana., Phx.	4	32	9	2	11	16	....	....	....	....	....	....	1996-97	2002-03
Banks, Darren	Bos.	2	20	2	2	4	73	....	....	....	....	....	....	1992-93	1993-94
Bannister, Drew	T.B., Edm., Ana., NYR	6	164	5	25	30	161	12	0	0	0	30	....	1995-96	2001-02
Barahona, Ralph	Bos.	2	6	2	2	4	0	....	....	....	....	....	....	1990-91	1991-92
‡ Baranka, Ivan	NYR	1	1	0	1	1	0	....	....	....	....	....	....	2007-08	2007-08
• Barbe, Andy	Tor.	1	1	0	0	0	2	....	....	....	....	....	....	1950-51	1950-51
Barber, Bill	Phi.	12	903	420	463	883	623	129	53	55	108	109	2	1972-73	1983-84
Barber, Don	Min., Wpg., Que., S.J.	4	115	25	32	57	64	11	4	4	8	10	....	1988-89	1991-92
• Barilko, Bill	Tor.	5	252	26	36	62	456	47	5	7	12	104	4	1946-47	1950-51
‡ Barinka, Michal	Chi.	2	34	0	2	2	26	....	....	....	....	....	....	2003-04	2005-06
Barkley, Doug	Chi., Det.	6	253	24	80	104	382	30	0	9	9	63	....	1957-58	1965-66
Barlow, Bob	Min.	2	77	16	17	33	10	6	2	2	4	6	....	1969-70	1970-71
Barnaby, Matthew	Buf., Pit., T.B., NYR, Col., Chi., Dal.	14	834	113	187	300	2562	62	7	15	22	170	....	1992-93	2006-07
• Barnes, Blair	L.A.	1	1	0	0	0	0	....	....	....	....	....	....	1982-83	1982-83
Barnes, Norm	Phi., Hfd.	5	156	6	38	44	178	12	0	0	0	8	....	1976-77	1981-82
Barnes, Ryan	Det.	1	2	0	0	0	0	....	....	....	....	....	....	2003-04	2003-04
Barnes, Stu	Wpg., Fla., Pit., Buf., Dal.	16	1136	261	336	597	438	116	30	32	62	24	....	1991-92	2007-08
‡ Barney, Scott	L.A., Atl.	3	27	5	6	11	4	....	....	....	....	....	....	2002-03	2005-06
Baron, Murray	Phi., St.L., Mtl., Phx., Van.	15	988	35	94	129	1309	73	2	8	10	78	....	1989-90	2003-04
Baron, Normand	Mtl., St.L.	2	27	2	0	2	51	3	0	0	0	22	....	1983-84	1985-86
Barr, Dave	Bos., NYR, St.L., Hfd., Det., N.J., Dal.	13	614	128	204	332	520	71	12	10	22	70	....	1981-82	1993-94
Barrault, Doug	Min., Fla.	2	4	0	0	0	2	....	....	....	....	....	....	1992-93	1993-94
Barrett, Fred	Min., L.A.	13	745	25	123	148	671	44	0	2	2	60	....	1970-71	1983-84
Barrett, John	Det., Wsh., Min.	8	488	20	77	97	604	16	2	2	4	50	....	1980-81	1987-88
Barrie, Doug	Pit., Buf., L.A.	3	158	10	42	52	268	....	....	....	....	....	....	1968-69	1971-72
Barrie, Len	Phi., Fla., Pit., L.A.	7	184	19	45	64	290	8	1	0	1	8	....	1989-90	2000-01
Barry, Ed	Bos.	1	19	1	3	4	2	....	....	....	....	....	....	1946-47	1946-47
• Barry, Marty	NYA, Bos., Det., Mtl.	12	509	195	192	387	231	43	15	18	33	34	2	1927-28	1939-40
Barry, Ray	Bos.	1	18	1	2	3	6	....	....	....	....	....	....	1951-52	1951-52
‡ Bartecko, Lubos	St.L., Atl.	5	257	46	65	111	107	12	1	1	2	2	....	1998-99	2002-03
Bartel, Robin	Cgy., Van.	2	41	0	1	1	14	6	0	0	0	16	....	1985-86	1986-87
Bartlett, Jim	Mtl., NYR, Bos.	5	191	34	23	57	273	2	0	0	0	0	....	1954-55	1960-61
• Barton, Cliff	Pit., Phi., NYR	3	85	10	9	19	22	....	....	....	....	....	....	1929-30	1939-40
Bartos, Peter	Min.	1	13	4	2	6	6	....	....	....	....	....	....	2000-01	2000-01
‡ Bartovic, Milan	Buf., Chi.	3	50	3	14	17	26	....	....	....	....	....	....	2002-03	2005-06
Bashkirov, Andrei	Mtl.	3	30	0	3	3	0	....	....	....	....	....	....	1998-99	2000-01
Bassen, Bob	NYI, Chi., St.L., Que., Dal., Cgy.	15	765	88	144	232	1004	93	9	15	24	134	....	1985-86	1999-00
Bast, Ryan	Phi.	1	2	0	1	1	0	....	....	....	....	....	....	1998-99	1998-99

Ossie Aubuchon

Sean Avery

Paul Baxter

Harvey Bennett

Bobby Benson

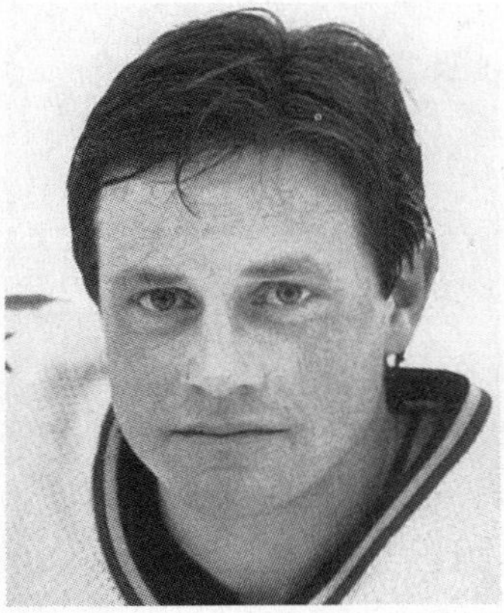

Bo Berglund

Jason Blake

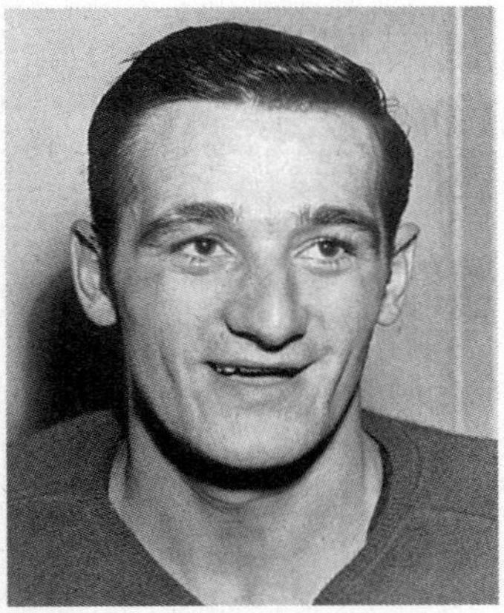

Marcel Bonin

Name	NHL Teams	NHL Seasons	Regular Schedule GP	G	A	TP	PIM	Playoffs GP	G	A	TP	PIM	NHL Cup Wins	First NHL Season	Last NHL Season
Bates, Shawn	Bos., NYI	10	465	72	126	198	266	29	3	4	7	19	....	1997-98	2007-08
Bathe, Frank	Det., Phi.	9	224	3	28	31	542	27	1	3	4	42	....	1974-75	1983-84
Bathgate, Andy	NYR, Tor., Det., Pit.	17	1069	349	624	973	624	54	21	14	35	76	1	1952-53	1970-71
Bathgate, Frank	NYR	1	2	0	0	0	2	....	....	....	....	....	....	1952-53	1952-53
Battaglia, Bates	Car., Col., Wsh., Tor.	9	580	80	118	198	385	42	5	16	21	28	....	1997-98	2007-08
● Batters, Jeff	St.L.	2	16	0	0	0	28	....	....	....	....	....	....	1993-94	1994-95
Batyrshin, Ruslan	L.A.	1	2	0	0	0	6	....	....	....	....	....	....	1995-96	1995-96
● Bauer, Bobby	Bos.	9	327	123	137	260	36	48	11	8	19	6	2	1936-37	1951-52
Baumgartner, Ken	L.A., NYI, Tor., Ana., Bos.	12	696	13	41	54	2244	51	1	2	3	106	....	1987-88	1998-99
Baumgartner, Mike	K.C.	1	17	0	0	0	0	....	....	....	....	....	....	1974-75	1974-75
‡ Baumgartner, Nolan	Wsh., Chi., Van., Pit., Phi., Dal.	10	143	7	40	47	69	4	0	0	0	10	....	1995-96	2009-10
Baun, Bob	Tor., Oak., Det.	17	964	37	187	224	1493	96	3	12	15	171	4	1956-57	1972-73
Bautin, Sergei	Wpg., Det., S.J.	3	132	5	25	30	176	6	0	0	0	2	....	1992-93	1995-96
Bawa, Robin	Wsh., Van., S.J., Ana.	4	61	6	1	7	60	1	0	0	0	0	....	1989-90	1993-94
Baxter, Paul	Que., Pit., Cgy.	8	472	48	121	169	1564	40	0	5	5	162	....	1979-80	1986-87
‡ Bayda, Ryan	Car.	5	179	16	24	40	94	15	2	2	4	18	....	2002-03	2008-09
Beadle, Sandy	Wpg.	1	6	1	0	1	2	....	....	....	....	....	....	1980-81	1980-81
Beaton, Frank	NYR	2	25	1	1	2	43	....	....	....	....	....	....	1978-79	1979-80
● Beattie, Red	Bos., Det., NYA	9	334	62	85	147	137	24	4	2	6	8	....	1930-31	1938-39
Beaudin, Norm	St.L., Min.	2	25	1	2	3	4	....	....	....	....	....	....	1967-68	1970-71
‡ Beaudoin, Eric	Fla.	3	53	3	8	11	41	....	....	....	....	....	....	2001-02	2003-04
Beaudoin, Serge	Atl.	1	3	0	0	0	0	....	....	....	....	....	....	1979-80	1979-80
Beaudoin, Yves	Wsh.	3	11	0	0	0	5	....	....	....	....	....	....	1985-86	1987-88
Beaufait, Mark	S.J.	1	5	1	0	1	0	....	....	....	....	....	....	1992-93	1992-93
Beck, Barry	Col., NYR, L.A.	10	615	104	251	355	1016	51	10	23	33	77	....	1977-78	1989-90
Beckett, Bob	Bos.	4	68	7	6	13	18	....	....	....	....	....	....	1956-57	1963-64
Bedard, James	Chi.	2	22	1	1	2	8	....	....	....	....	....	....	1949-50	1950-51
Beddoes, Clayton	Bos.	2	60	2	8	10	57	....	....	....	....	....	....	1995-96	1996-97
‡ Bednar, Jaroslav	L.A., Fla.	3	102	10	25	35	30	3	0	0	0	0	....	2001-02	2003-04
Bednarski, John	NYR, Edm.	4	100	2	18	20	114	1	0	0	0	17	....	1974-75	1979-80
‡ Beech, Kris	Wsh., Pit., Nsh., CBJ, Van.	7	198	25	42	67	113	....	....	....	....	....	....	2000-01	2007-08
Beers, Bob	Bos., T.B., Edm., NYI	8	258	28	79	107	225	21	1	1	2	22	....	1989-90	1996-97
Beers, Eddy	Cgy., St.L.	5	250	94	116	210	256	41	7	10	17	47	....	1981-82	1985-86
● Behling, Dick	Det.	2	5	1	0	1	2	....	....	....	....	....	....	1940-41	1942-43
● Beisler, Frank	NYA	2	2	0	0	0	0	....	....	....	....	....	....	1936-37	1939-40
Bekar, Derek	St.L., L.A., NYI	3	11	0	0	0	6	....	....	....	....	....	....	1999-00	2003-04
● Belak, Wade	Col., Cgy., Tor., Fla., Nsh.	14	549	8	25	33	1263	22	1	0	1	36	....	1996-97	2010-11
Belanger, Alain	Tor.	1	9	0	1	1	6	....	....	....	....	....	....	1977-78	1977-78
Belanger, Francis	Mtl.	1	10	0	0	0	29	....	....	....	....	....	....	2000-01	2000-01
Belanger, Jesse	Mtl., Fla., Van., Edm., NYI	8	246	59	76	135	56	12	0	3	3	2	1	1991-92	2000-01
Belanger, Ken	Tor., NYI, Bos., L.A.	11	248	11	12	23	695	12	1	0	1	16	....	1994-95	2005-06
● Belanger, Roger	Pit.	1	44	3	5	8	32	....	....	....	....	....	....	1984-85	1984-85
Belisle, Danny	NYR	1	4	2	0	2	0	....	....	....	....	....	....	1960-61	1960-61
Beliveau, Jean	Mtl.	20	1125	507	712	1219	1029	162	79	97	176	211	10	1950-51	1970-71
● Bell, Billy	Mtl.W., Mtl., Ott.	6	66	3	2	5	14	5	0	0	0	0	1	1917-18	1923-24
Bell, Bruce	Que., St.L., NYR, Edm.	5	209	12	64	76	113	34	3	5	8	41	....	1984-85	1989-90
● Bell, Huddy	NYR	1	1	0	1	1	0	....	....	....	....	....	....	1946-47	1946-47
Bell, Joe	NYR	2	62	8	9	17	18	....	....	....	....	....	....	1942-43	1946-47
Belland, Neil	Van., Pit.	6	109	13	32	45	54	21	2	9	11	23	....	1981-82	1986-87
Bellefeuille, Blake	CBJ	2	5	0	1	1	0	....	....	....	....	....	....	2001-02	2002-03
● Bellefeuille, Pete	Tor., Det.	4	92	26	4	30	58	....	....	....	....	....	....	1925-26	1929-30
● Bellemer, Andy	Mtl.M.	1	15	0	0	0	0	....	....	....	....	....	....	1932-33	1932-33
Bellows, Brian	Min., Mtl., T.B., Ana., Wsh.	17	1188	485	537	1022	718	143	51	71	122	143	1	1982-83	1998-99
● Bend, Lin	NYR	1	8	3	1	4	2	....	....	....	....	....	....	1942-43	1942-43
‡ Benda, Jan	Wsh.	1	9	0	3	3	6	....	....	....	....	....	....	1997-98	1997-98
Bennett, Adam	Chi., Edm.	3	69	3	8	11	69	....	....	....	....	....	....	1991-92	1993-94
Bennett, Bill	Bos., Hfd.	2	31	4	7	11	65	....	....	....	....	....	....	1978-79	1979-80
Bennett, Curt	St.L., NYR, Atl.	10	580	152	182	334	347	21	1	1	2	57	....	1970-71	1979-80
Bennett, Frank	Det.	1	7	0	1	1	2	....	....	....	....	....	....	1943-44	1943-44
Bennett, Harvey	Pit., Wsh., Phi., Min., St.L.	5	268	44	46	90	347	4	0	0	0	2	....	1974-75	1978-79
● Bennett, Max	Mtl.	1	1	0	0	0	0	....	....	....	....	....	....	1935-36	1935-36
Bennett, Rick	NYR	3	15	1	1	2	13	....	....	....	....	....	....	1989-90	1991-92
Benning, Brian	St.L., L.A., Phi., Edm., Fla.	11	568	63	233	296	963	48	3	20	23	74	....	1984-85	1994-95
Benning, Jim	Tor., Van.	9	605	52	191	243	461	7	1	1	2	2	....	1981-82	1989-90
● Benoit, Joe	Mtl.	5	185	75	69	144	94	11	6	3	9	11	1	1940-41	1946-47
● Benson, Bill	NYA, Bro.	2	67	11	25	36	35	....	....	....	....	....	....	1940-41	1941-42
● Benson, Bobby	Bos.	1	8	0	1	1	4	....	....	....	....	....	....	1924-25	1924-25
‡ Bentivoglio, Sean	NYI	1	1	0	0	0	2	....	....	....	....	....	....	2008-09	2008-09
● Bentley, Doug	Chi., NYR	13	566	219	324	543	217	23	9	8	17	12	....	1939-40	1953-54
● Bentley, Max	Chi., Tor., NYR	12	646	245	299	544	179	51	18	27	45	14	3	1940-41	1953-54
● Bentley, Reg	Chi.	1	11	1	2	3	2	....	....	....	....	....	....	1942-43	1942-43
Benysek, Ladislav	Edm., Min.	4	161	3	12	15	74	....	....	....	....	....	....	1997-98	2002-03
Beraldo, Paul	Bos.	2	10	0	0	0	4	....	....	....	....	....	....	1987-88	1988-89
Beranek, Josef	Edm., Phi., Van., Pit.	9	531	118	144	262	398	57	5	8	13	24	....	1991-92	2000-01
Berard, Bryan	NYI, Tor., NYR, Bos., Chi., CBJ	10	619	76	247	323	500	20	2	8	10	10	....	1996-97	2007-08
Berehowsky, Drake	Tor., Pit., Edm., Nsh., Van., Phx.	13	549	37	112	149	848	22	1	3	4	30	....	1990-91	2003-04
Berenson, Red	Mtl., NYR, St.L., Det.	17	987	261	397	658	305	85	23	14	37	49	1	1961-62	1977-78
Berenzweig, Bubba	Nsh.	4	37	3	7	10	14	....	....	....	....	....	....	1999-00	2002-03
Berezan, Perry	Cgy., Min., S.J.	9	378	61	75	136	279	31	4	7	11	34	....	1984-85	1992-93
Berezin, Sergei	Tor., Phx., Mtl., Chi., Wsh.	7	502	160	126	286	54	52	13	17	30	6	....	1996-97	2002-03
Berg, Aki	L.A., Tor.	9	606	15	70	85	374	54	1	7	8	47	....	1995-96	2005-06
Berg, Bill	NYI, Tor., NYR, Ott.	10	546	55	67	122	488	61	3	4	7	34	....	1988-89	1998-99
● Bergdinon, Fred	Bos.	1	2	0	0	0	0	....	....	....	....	....	....	1925-26	1925-26
Bergen, Todd	Phi.	1	14	11	5	16	4	17	4	9	13	8	....	1984-85	1984-85
Berger, Mike	Min.	2	30	3	1	4	67	....	....	....	....	....	....	1987-88	1988-89
Bergeron, Michel	Det., NYI, Wsh.	5	229	80	58	138	165	....	....	....	....	....	....	1974-75	1978-79
Bergeron, Yves	Pit.	2	3	0	0	0	0	....	....	....	....	....	....	1974-75	1976-77
Bergevin, Marc	Chi., NYI, Hfd., T.B., Det., St.L., Pit., Van.	20	1191	36	145	181	1090	80	3	6	9	52	....	1984-85	2003-04
‡ Bergfors, Niclas	N.J., Atl., Fla., Nsh.	5	173	35	48	83	20	....	....	....	....	....	....	2007-08	2011-12
Bergkvist, Stefan	Pit.	2	7	0	0	0	9	4	0	0	0	2	....	1995-96	1996-97
Bergland, Tim	Wsh., T.B.	5	182	17	26	43	75	26	2	2	4	22	....	1989-90	1993-94
Bergloff, Bob	Min.	1	2	0	0	0	5	....	....	....	....	....	....	1982-83	1982-83
Berglund, Bo	Que., Min., Phi.	3	130	28	39	67	40	9	2	0	2	6	....	1983-84	1985-86
‡ Berglund, Christian	N.J., Fla.	3	86	11	16	27	42	3	0	0	0	2	....	2001-02	2003-04
● Bergman, Gary	Det., Min., K.C.	12	838	68	299	367	1249	21	0	5	5	20	....	1964-65	1975-76
Bergman, Thommie	Det.	6	246	21	44	65	243	7	0	2	2	2	....	1972-73	1979-80
Bergqvist, Jonas	Cgy.	1	22	2	5	7	10	....	....	....	....	....	....	1989-90	1989-90
● Berlinguette, Louis	Mtl., Mtl.M., Pit.	8	193	45	33	78	129	11	0	5	5	9	....	1917-18	1925-26
Bernier, Serge	Phi., L.A., Que.	7	302	78	119	197	234	5	1	1	2	0	....	1968-69	1980-81
Berry, Bob	Mtl., L.A.	8	541	159	191	350	344	26	2	6	8	6	....	1968-69	1976-77
Berry, Brad	Wpg., Min., Dal.	8	241	4	28	32	323	13	0	1	1	16	....	1985-86	1993-94
Berry, Doug	Col.	2	121	10	33	43	25	....	....	....	....	....	....	1979-80	1980-81
Berry, Fred	Det.	1	3	0	0	0	0	....	....	....	....	....	....	1976-77	1976-77
Berry, Ken	Edm., Van.	4	55	8	10	18	30	....	....	....	....	....	....	1981-82	1988-89
Berry, Rick	Col., Pit., Wsh.	4	197	2	13	15	314	....	....	....	....	....	....	2000-01	2003-04
Berti, Adam	Chi.	1	2	0	0	0	0	....	....	....	....	....	....	2007-08	2007-08
Bertrand, Eric	N.J., Atl., Mtl.	2	15	0	0	0	4	....	....	....	....	....	....	1999-00	2000-01
Berube, Craig	Phi., Tor., Cgy., Wsh., NYI	17	1054	61	98	159	3149	89	3	1	4	211	....	1986-87	2002-03
● Besler, Phil	Bos., Chi., Det.	2	30	1	4	5	18	....	....	....	....	....	....	1935-36	1938-39
● Bessone, Pete	Det.	1	6	0	1	1	6	....	....	....	....	....	....	1937-38	1937-38
Bethel, John	Wpg.	1	17	0	2	2	4	....	....	....	....	....	....	1979-80	1979-80
Betik, Karel	T.B.	1	3	0	2	2	2	....	....	....	....	....	....	1998-99	1998-99
Bets, Maxim	Ana.	1	3	0	0	0	0	....	....	....	....	....	....	1993-94	1993-94
● Bettio, Sam	Bos.	1	44	9	12	21	32	....	....	....	....	....	....	1949-50	1949-50
Betts, Blair	Cgy., NYR, Phi.	9	477	41	37	78	118	62	2	2	4	12	....	2001-02	2010-11
Beukeboom, Jeff	Edm., NYR	14	804	30	129	159	1890	99	3	16	19	197	4	1985-86	1998-99
Beverley, Nick	Bos., Pit., NYR, Min., L.A., Col.	11	502	18	94	112	156	7	0	1	1	0	....	1966-67	1979-80
‡ Bezina, Goran	Phx.	1	3	0	0	0	2	....	....	....	....	....	....	2003-04	2003-04
Bialowas, Dwight	Atl., Min.	4	164	11	46	57	46	....	....	....	....	....	....	1973-74	1976-77
Bialowas, Frank	Tor.	1	3	0	0	0	12	....	....	....	....	....	....	1993-94	1993-94
Bianchin, Wayne	Pit., Edm.	7	276	68	41	109	137	3	0	1	1	6	....	1973-74	1979-80
Bicanek, Radim	Ott., Chi., CBJ	7	122	1	11	12	62	7	0	0	0	8	....	1994-95	2001-02
‡ Bicek, Jiri	N.J.	4	62	6	7	13	29	7	0	0	0	0	1	2000-01	2003-04
Bidner, Todd	Wsh.	1	12	2	1	3	7	....	....	....	....	....	....	1981-82	1981-82
Biggs, Don	Min., Phi.	2	12	2	0	2	8	....	....	....	....	....	....	1984-85	1989-90

Name	NHL Teams	NHL Seasons	Regular Schedule GP	G	A	TP	PIM	Playoffs GP	G	A	TP	PIM	NHL Cup Wins	First NHL Season	Last NHL Season
Bignell, Larry	Pit.	2	20	0	3	3	2	3	0	0	0	2	....	1973-74	1974-75
● Bilodeau, Gilles	Que.	1	9	0	1	1	25	....	....	....	....	....	....	1979-80	1979-80
● Bionda, Jack	Tor., Bos.	4	93	3	9	12	113	11	0	1	1	14	....	1955-56	1958-59
Biron, Mathieu	NYI, T.B., Fla., Wsh.	6	253	12	32	44	177	....	....	....	....	....	....	1999-00	2005-06
Bisaillon, Sebastien	Edm.	1	2	0	0	0	0	....	....	....	....	....	....	2006-07	2006-07
Bishai, Mike	Edm.	1	14	0	2	2	19	....	....	....	....	....	....	2003-04	2003-04
Bissett, Tom	Det.	1	5	0	0	0	0	....	....	....	....	....	....	1990-91	1990-91
Bjugstad, Scott	Min., Pit., L.A.	9	317	76	68	144	144	9	0	1	1	2	....	1983-84	1991-92
Black, James	Hfd., Min., Dal., Buf., Chi., Wsh.	11	352	58	57	115	84	13	2	1	3	4	....	1989-90	2000-01
● Black, Steve	Det., Chi.	2	113	11	20	31	77	13	0	0	0	13	1	1949-50	1950-51
Blackburn, Bob	NYR, Pit.	3	135	8	12	20	105	6	0	0	0	4	....	1968-69	1970-71
Blackburn, Don	Bos., Phi., NYR, NYI, Min.	6	185	23	44	67	87	12	3	0	3	10	....	1962-63	1972-73
● Blade, Hank	Chi.	2	24	2	3	5	2	....	....	....	....	....	....	1946-47	1947-48
Bladon, Tom	Phi., Pit., Edm., Wpg., Det.	9	610	73	197	270	392	86	8	29	37	70	2	1972-73	1980-81
● Blaine, Garry	Mtl.	1	1	0	0	0	0	....	....	....	....	....	....	1954-55	1954-55
● Blair, Andy	Tor., Chi.	9	402	74	86	160	323	38	6	6	12	32	1	1928-29	1936-37
● Blair, Chuck	Tor.	1	1	0	0	0	0	....	....	....	....	....	....	1948-49	1948-49
Blair, Dusty	Tor.	1	2	0	0	0	0	....	....	....	....	....	....	1950-51	1950-51
Blaisdell, Mike	Det., NYR, Pit., Tor.	9	343	70	84	154	166	6	1	2	3	10	....	1980-81	1988-89
● Blake, Bob	Bos.	1	12	0	0	0	0	....	....	....	....	....	....	1935-36	1935-36
Blake, Jason	L.A., NYI, Tor., Ana.	13	871	213	273	486	455	30	6	5	11	19	....	1998-99	2011-12
● Blake, Mickey	Mtl.M., St.L., Tor.	3	10	1	1	2	4	....	....	....	....	....	....	1932-33	1935-36
Blake, Rob	L.A., Col., S.J.	20	1270	240	537	777	1679	146	26	47	73	166	1	1989-90	2009-10
● Blake, Toe	Mtl.M., Mtl.	14	577	235	292	527	272	58	25	37	62	23	3	1934-35	1947-48
Blatny, Zdenek	Atl., Bos.	3	25	3	0	3	8	....	....	....	....	....	....	2002-03	2005-06
● Blight, Rick	Van., L.A.	7	326	96	125	221	170	5	0	5	5	2	....	1975-76	1982-83
● Blinco, Russ	Mtl.M., Chi.	6	268	59	66	125	24	19	3	3	6	4	1	1933-34	1938-39
‡ Bliznak, Mario	Van.	2	6	1	0	1	0	....	....	....	....	....	....	2009-10	2010-11
Block, Ken	Van.	1	1	0	0	0	0	....	....	....	....	....	....	1970-71	1970-71
Bloemberg, Jeff	NYR	4	43	3	6	9	25	7	0	3	3	5	....	1988-89	1991-92
Blomqvist, Timo	Wsh., N.J.	5	243	4	53	57	293	13	0	0	0	24	....	1981-82	1986-87
Blomsten, Arto	Wpg., L.A.	3	25	0	4	4	8	....	....	....	....	....	....	1993-94	1995-96
Bloom, Mike	Wsh., Det.	3	201	30	47	77	215	....	....	....	....	....	....	1974-75	1976-77
Blouin, Sylvain	NYR, Mtl., Min.	6	115	3	4	7	336	....	....	....	....	....	....	1996-97	2002-03
Blum, John	Edm., Bos., Wsh., Det.	8	250	7	34	41	610	20	0	2	2	27	....	1982-83	1989-90
‡ Bochenski, Brandon	Ott., Chi., Bos., Ana., Nsh., T.B.	5	156	28	40	68	54	3	0	0	0	0	....	2005-06	2009-10
Bodak, Bob	Cgy., Hfd.	2	4	0	0	0	29	....	....	....	....	....	....	1987-88	1989-90
Boddy, Gregg	Van.	5	273	23	44	67	263	3	0	0	0	0	....	1971-72	1975-76
Bodger, Doug	Pit., Buf., S.J., N.J., L.A., Van.	16	1071	106	422	528	1007	47	6	18	24	25	....	1984-85	1999-00
● Bodnar, Gus	Tor., Chi., Bos.	12	667	142	254	396	207	32	4	3	7	10	2	1943-44	1954-55
Boehm, Ron	Oak.	1	16	2	1	3	10	....	....	....	....	....	....	1967-68	1967-68
● Boesch, Garth	Tor.	4	197	9	28	37	205	34	2	5	7	18	3	1946-47	1949-50
Boguniecki, Eric	Fla., St.L., Pit., NYI	7	178	34	42	76	105	9	1	3	4	2	....	1999-00	2006-07
Boh, Rick	Min.	1	8	2	1	3	4	....	....	....	....	....	....	1987-88	1987-88
Bohonos, Lonny	Van., Tor.	4	83	19	16	35	22	9	3	6	9	2	....	1995-96	1998-99
Boikov, Alexandre	Nsh.	2	10	0	0	0	15	....	....	....	....	....	....	1999-00	2000-01
● Boileau, Marc	Det.	1	54	5	6	11	8	....	....	....	....	....	....	1961-62	1961-62
Boileau, Patrick	Wsh., Det., Pit.	5	48	5	11	16	26	....	....	....	....	....	....	1996-97	2003-04
● Boileau, Rene	NYA	1	7	0	0	0	0	....	....	....	....	....	....	1925-26	1925-26
Boimistruck, Fred	Tor.	2	83	4	14	18	45	....	....	....	....	....	....	1981-82	1982-83
‡ Bois, Danny	Ott.	1	1	0	0	0	7	....	....	....	....	....	....	2006-07	2006-07
Boisvert, Serge	Tor., Mtl.	5	46	5	7	12	8	23	3	7	10	4	1	1982-83	1987-88
Boivin, Claude	Phi., Ott.	4	132	12	19	31	364	....	....	....	....	....	....	1991-92	1994-95
Boivin, Leo	Tor., Bos., Det., Pit., Min.	19	1150	72	250	322	1192	54	3	10	13	59	....	1951-52	1969-70
Boland, Mike	Phi.	1	2	0	0	0	0	....	....	....	....	....	....	1974-75	1974-75
Boland, Mike	K.C., Buf.	2	23	1	2	3	29	3	1	0	1	2	....	1974-75	1978-79
Boldirev, Ivan	Bos., Cal., Chi., Atl., Van., Det.	16	1052	361	505	866	507	48	13	20	33	14	1	1969-70	1984-85
Bolduc, Danny	Det., Cgy.	3	102	22	19	41	33	1	0	0	0	0	....	1978-79	1983-84
Bolduc, Michel	Que.	2	10	0	0	0	6	....	....	....	....	....	....	1981-82	1982-83
● Boll, Buzz	Tor., NYA, Bro., Bos.	12	437	133	130	263	148	31	7	3	10	13	....	1932-33	1943-44
Bolonchuk, Larry	Van., Wsh.	4	74	3	9	12	97	....	....	....	....	....	....	1972-73	1977-78
● Bolton, Hugh	Tor.	8	235	10	51	61	221	17	0	5	5	14	1	1949-50	1956-57
Bombardir, Brad	N.J., Min., Nsh.	7	356	8	46	54	127	16	0	1	1	2	1	1997-98	2003-04
Bonar, Dan	L.A.	3	170	25	39	64	208	14	3	4	7	22	....	1980-81	1982-83
Bondra, Peter	Wsh., Ott., Atl., Chi.	16	1081	503	389	892	761	80	30	26	56	60	....	1990-91	2006-07
Bonin, Brian	Pit., Min.	2	12	0	0	0	0	3	0	0	0	0	....	1998-99	2000-01
Bonin, Marcel	Det., Bos., Mtl.	9	454	97	175	272	336	50	11	14	25	51	4	1952-53	1961-62
‡ Bonk, Radek	Ott., Mtl., Nsh.	14	969	194	303	497	581	73	12	15	27	42	....	1994-95	2008-09
Bonni, Ryan	Van.	1	3	0	0	0	0	....	....	....	....	....	....	1999-00	1999-00
Bonsignore, Jason	Edm., T.B.	4	79	3	13	16	34	....	....	....	....	....	....	1994-95	1998-99
Bonvie, Dennis	Edm., Chi., Pit., Bos., Ott., Col.	9	92	1	2	3	311	1	0	0	0	0	....	1994-95	2003-04
Boo, Jim	Min.	1	6	0	0	0	22	....	....	....	....	....	....	1977-78	1977-78
● Boogaard, Derek	Min., NYR	6	277	3	13	16	589	10	0	1	1	44	....	2005-06	2010-11
● Boone, Buddy	Bos.	2	34	5	3	8	28	22	2	1	3	25	....	1956-57	1957-58
● Boothman, George	Tor.	2	58	17	19	36	18	5	2	1	3	2	....	1942-43	1943-44
‡ Bootland, Darryl	Det., NYI	3	32	1	2	3	85	....	....	....	....	....	....	2003-04	2007-08
Bordeleau, Christian	Mtl., St.L., Chi.	4	205	38	65	103	82	19	4	7	11	17	1	1968-69	1971-72
Bordeleau, J.P.	Chi.	10	519	97	126	223	143	48	3	6	9	12	....	1969-70	1979-80
Bordeleau, Paulin	Van.	3	183	33	56	89	47	5	2	1	3	0	....	1973-74	1975-76
‡ Bordeleau, Sebastien	Mtl., Nsh., Min., Phx.	7	251	37	61	98	118	5	0	0	0	2	....	1995-96	2001-02
‡ Borer, Casey	Car.	3	16	1	2	3	9	....	....	....	....	....	....	2007-08	2009-10
Borotsik, Jack	St.L.	1	1	0	0	0	0	....	....	....	....	....	....	1974-75	1974-75
Borsato, Luciano	Wpg.	5	203	35	55	90	113	7	1	0	1	4	....	1990-91	1994-95
Borschevsky, Nikolai	Tor., Cgy., Dal.	4	162	49	73	122	44	31	4	9	13	4	....	1992-93	1995-96
Boschman, Laurie	Tor., Edm., Wpg., N.J., Ott.	14	1009	229	348	577	2265	57	8	13	21	140	....	1979-80	1992-93
Bossy, Mike	NYI	10	752	573	553	1126	210	129	85	75	160	38	4	1977-78	1986-87
● Bostrom, Helge	Chi.	4	96	3	3	6	58	13	0	0	0	16	....	1929-30	1932-33
Botell, Mark	Phi.	1	32	4	10	14	31	....	....	....	....	....	....	1981-82	1981-82
Bothwell, Tim	NYR, St.L., Hfd.	11	502	28	93	121	382	49	0	3	3	56	....	1978-79	1988-89
Botterill, Jason	Dal., Atl., Cgy., Buf.	6	88	5	9	14	89	....	....	....	....	....	....	1997-98	2003-04
Botting, Cam	Atl.	1	2	0	1	1	0	....	....	....	....	....	....	1975-76	1975-76
Boucha, Henry	Det., Min., K.C., Col.	6	247	53	49	102	157	....	....	....	....	....	....	1971-72	1976-77
● Bouchard, Butch	Mtl.	15	785	49	144	193	863	113	11	21	32	121	4	1941-42	1955-56
● Bouchard, Dick	NYR	1	1	0	0	0	0	....	....	....	....	....	....	1954-55	1954-55
● Bouchard, Edmond	Mtl., Ham., NYA, Pit.	8	211	19	21	40	117	....	....	....	....	....	....	1921-22	1928-29
Bouchard, Joel	Cgy., Nsh., Dal., Phx., N.J., NYR, Pit., NYI	11	364	22	53	75	264	....	....	....	....	....	....	1994-95	2005-06
Bouchard, Pierre	Mtl., Wsh.	12	595	24	82	106	433	76	3	10	13	56	5	1970-71	1981-82
● Boucher, Billy	Mtl., Bos., NYA	7	213	93	38	131	409	14	3	0	3	17	1	1921-22	1927-28
● Boucher, Bobby	Mtl.	1	11	1	0	1	0	2	0	0	0	0	1	1923-24	1923-24
● Boucher, Clarence	NYA	2	47	2	2	4	133	....	....	....	....	....	....	1926-27	1927-28
● Boucher, Frank	Ott., NYR	14	557	160	263	423	119	55	16	20	36	12	2	1921-22	1943-44
● Boucher, George	Ott., Mtl.M., Chi.	15	449	117	87	204	838	28	5	3	8	88	4	1917-18	1931-32
Boucher, Philippe	Buf., L.A., Dal., Pit.	16	748	94	206	300	702	65	4	10	14	39	1	1992-93	2008-09
‡ Bouck, Tyler	Dal., Phx., Van.	5	91	4	8	12	93	2	0	0	0	0	....	2000-01	2006-07
Boudreau, Bruce	Tor., Chi.	8	141	28	42	70	46	9	2	0	2	0	....	1976-77	1985-86
Boudrias, Andre	Mtl., Min., Chi., St.L., Van.	12	662	151	340	491	216	34	6	10	16	12	....	1963-64	1975-76
Boughner, Barry	Oak., Cal.	2	20	0	0	0	11	....	....	....	....	....	....	1969-70	1970-71
Boughner, Bob	Buf., Nsh., Pit., Cgy., Car., Col.	10	630	15	57	72	1382	65	0	12	12	67	....	1995-96	2005-06
Boulerice, Jesse	Phi., Car., St.L., Edm.	6	172	8	2	10	333	....	....	....	....	....	....	2001-02	2008-09
‡ Boumedienne, Josef	N.J., T.B., Wsh.	3	47	4	12	16	36	....	....	....	....	....	....	2001-02	2003-04
Bourbonnais, Dan	Hfd.	2	59	3	25	28	11	....	....	....	....	....	....	1981-82	1983-84
Bourbonnais, Rick	St.L.	3	71	9	15	24	29	4	0	1	1	0	....	1975-76	1977-78
● Bourcier, Conrad	Mtl.	1	6	0	0	0	0	....	....	....	....	....	....	1935-36	1935-36
● Bourcier, Jean	Mtl.	1	9	0	1	1	0	....	....	....	....	....	....	1935-36	1935-36
● Bourdon, Luc	Van.	2	36	2	0	2	24	....	....	....	....	....	....	2006-07	2007-08
● Bourgeault, Leo	Tor., NYR, Ott., Mtl.	8	307	24	20	44	334	24	1	1	2	18	1	1926-27	1934-35
Bourgeois, Charlie	Cgy., St.L., Hfd.	7	290	16	54	70	788	40	2	3	5	194	....	1981-82	1987-88
Bourne, Bob	NYI, L.A.	14	964	258	324	582	605	139	40	56	96	108	4	1974-75	1987-88
Bourque, Phil	Pit., NYR, Ott.	12	477	88	111	199	516	56	13	12	25	107	2	1983-84	1995-96
Bourque, Raymond	Bos., Col.	22	1612	410	1169	1579	1141	214	41	139	180	171	1	1979-80	2000-01
Boutette, Pat	Tor., Hfd., Pit.	10	756	171	282	453	1354	46	10	14	24	109	....	1975-76	1984-85
Boutilier, Paul	NYI, Bos., Min., NYR, Wpg.	8	288	27	83	110	358	41	1	9	10	45	1	1981-82	1988-89
Bowen, Jason	Phi., Edm.	6	77	2	6	8	109	....	....	....	....	....	....	1992-93	1997-98
Bowler, Bill	CBJ	1	9	0	2	2	8	....	....	....	....	....	....	2000-01	2000-01
Bowman, Kirk	Chi.	3	88	11	17	28	19	7	1	0	1	0	....	1976-77	1978-79

Dick Bouchard

Bobby Boucher

George Boucher

Darren Boyko

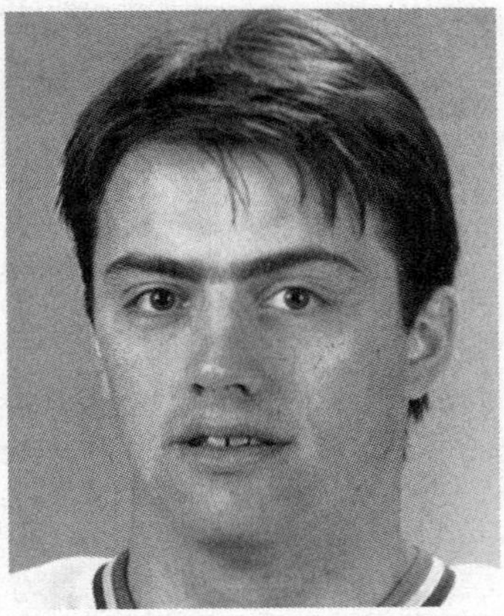
Philippe Bozon

Andy Brickley

Jiri Bubla

Fred Burchell

			Regular Schedule					Playoffs							
Name	NHL Teams	NHL Seasons	GP	G	A	TP	PIM	GP	G	A	TP	PIM	NHL Cup Wins	First NHL Season	Last NHL Season
• Bowman, Ralph	Ott., St.L., Det.	7	274	8	17	25	260	22	2	2	4	6	2	1933-34	1939-40
• Bownass, Jack	Mtl., NYR	4	80	3	8	11	58	....	....	....	....	....	....	1957-58	1961-62
Bowness, Rick	Atl., Det., St.L., Wpg.	7	173	18	37	55	191	5	0	0	0	2	....	1975-76	1981-82
• Boyd, Bill	NYR, NYA	4	138	15	7	22	72	10	0	0	0	4	1	1926-27	1929-30
‡ Boyd, Dustin	Cgy., Nsh., Mtl.	5	220	32	31	63	41	9	1	0	1	0	....	2006-07	2010-11
• Boyd, Irwin	Bos., Det.	4	96	10	10	20	30	5	0	1	1	4	....	1931-32	1943-44
Boyd, Randy	Pit., Chi., NYI, Van.	8	257	20	67	87	328	13	0	2	2	26	....	1981-82	1988-89
Boyer, Wally	Tor., Chi., Oak., Pit.	7	365	54	105	159	163	15	1	3	4	0	....	1965-66	1971-72
Boyer, Zac	Dal.	2	3	0	0	0	0	2	0	0	0	0	....	1994-95	1995-96
Boyko, Darren	Wpg.	1	1	0	0	0	0	....	....	....	....	....	....	1988-89	1988-89
Boynton, Nick	Bos., Phx., Fla., Ana., Chi., Phi.	11	605	34	110	144	862	21	1	5	6	16	1	1999-00	2010-11
Bozek, Steve	L.A., Cgy., St.L., Van., S.J.	11	641	164	167	331	309	58	12	11	23	69	....	1981-82	1991-92
Bozon, Philippe	St.L.	4	144	16	25	41	101	19	2	0	2	31	....	1991-92	1994-95
• Brackenborough, John	Bos.	1	7	0	0	0	0	....	....	....	....	....	....	1925-26	1925-26
Brackenbury, Curt	Que., Edm., St.L.	4	141	9	17	26	226	2	0	0	0	0	....	1979-80	1982-83
• Bradley, Bart	Bos.	1	1	0	0	0	0	....	....	....	....	....	....	1949-50	1949-50
Bradley, Brian	Cgy., Van., Tor., T.B.	13	651	182	321	503	528	13	3	7	10	16	....	1985-86	1997-98
Bradley, Lyle	Cal., Cle.	2	6	1	0	1	2	....	....	....	....	....	....	1973-74	1976-77
Brady, Neil	N.J., Ott., Dal.	5	89	9	22	31	95	....	....	....	....	....	....	1989-90	1993-94
Bragnalo, Rick	Wsh.	4	145	15	35	50	46	....	....	....	....	....	....	1975-76	1978-79
‡ Brandner, Christoph	Min.	1	35	4	5	9	8	....	....	....	....	....	....	2003-04	2003-04
• Branigan, Andy	NYA, Bro.	2	27	1	2	3	31	....	....	....	....	....	....	1940-41	1941-42
Brasar, Per-Olov	Min., Van.	5	348	64	142	206	33	13	1	2	3	0	....	1977-78	1981-82
Brashear, Donald	Mtl., Van., Phi., Wsh., NYR	16	1025	85	120	205	2634	60	3	6	9	121	....	1993-94	2009-10
• Brayshaw, Russ	Chi.	1	43	5	9	14	24	....	....	....	....	....	....	1944-45	1944-45
Breault, Francis	L.A.	3	27	2	4	6	42	....	....	....	....	....	....	1990-91	1992-93
Breitenbach, Ken	Buf.	3	68	1	13	14	49	8	0	1	1	4	....	1975-76	1978-79
‡ Bremberg, Fredrik	Edm.	1	8	0	0	0	2	....	....	....	....	....	....	1998-99	1998-99
‡ Brendl, Pavel	Phi., Car., Phx.	4	78	11	11	22	16	2	0	0	0	0	....	2001-02	2005-06
Brennan, Dan	L.A.	2	8	0	1	1	9	....	....	....	....	....	....	1983-84	1985-86
• Brennan, Doug	NYR	3	123	9	7	16	152	16	1	0	1	21	1	1931-32	1933-34
Brennan, Kip	L.A., Atl., Ana., NYI	5	61	1	1	2	222	....	....	....	....	....	....	2001-02	2007-08
Brennan, Rich	Col., S.J., NYR, L.A., Nsh., Bos.	6	50	2	6	8	33	....	....	....	....	....	....	1996-97	2002-03
• Brennan, Tom	Bos.	2	12	2	2	4	2	....	....	....	....	....	....	1943-44	1944-45
Brenneman, John	Chi., NYR, Tor., Det., Oak.	5	152	21	19	40	46	....	....	....	....	....	1	1964-65	1968-69
• Bretto, Joe	Chi.	1	3	0	0	0	4	....	....	....	....	....	....	1944-45	1944-45
• Brewer, Carl	Tor., Det., St.L.	12	604	25	198	223	1037	72	3	17	20	146	3	1957-58	1979-80
Brickley, Andy	Phi., Pit., N.J., Bos., Wpg.	11	385	82	140	222	81	17	1	4	5	4	....	1982-83	1993-94
• Briden, Archie	Bos., Det., Pit.	2	71	9	5	14	56	....	....	....	....	....	....	1926-27	1929-30
Bridgman, Mel	Phi., Cgy., N.J., Det., Van.	14	977	252	449	701	1625	125	28	39	67	298	....	1975-76	1988-89
• Briere, Michel	Pit.	1	76	12	32	44	20	10	5	3	8	17	....	1969-70	1969-70
Brigley, Travis	Cgy., Col.	3	55	3	6	9	16	....	....	....	....	....	....	1997-98	2003-04
Brimanis, Aris	Phi., NYI, Ana., St.L.	7	113	2	12	14	57	....	....	....	....	....	....	1993-94	2003-04
Brind'Amour, Rod	St.L., Phi., Car.	21	1484	452	732	1184	1100	159	51	60	111	97	1	1988-89	2009-10
Brindley, Doug	Tor.	1	3	0	0	0	0	....	....	....	....	....	....	1970-71	1970-71
‡ Brine, David	Fla.	1	9	0	1	1	4	....	....	....	....	....	....	2007-08	2007-08
• Brink, Milt	Chi.	1	5	0	0	0	0	....	....	....	....	....	....	1936-37	1936-37
Brisebois, Patrice	Mtl., Col.	18	1009	98	322	420	623	98	9	23	32	76	1	1990-91	2008-09
Brisson, Gerry	Mtl.	1	4	0	2	2	4	....	....	....	....	....	....	1962-63	1962-63
Britz, Greg	Tor., Hfd.	3	8	0	0	0	4	....	....	....	....	....	....	1983-84	1986-87
• Broadbent, Punch	Ott., Mtl.M., NYA	11	303	121	51	172	564	23	4	6	10	60	4	1918-19	1928-29
Brochu, Stephane	NYR	1	1	0	0	0	0	....	....	....	....	....	....	1988-89	1988-89
Broden, Connie	Mtl.	3	6	2	1	3	2	7	0	1	1	0	2	1955-56	1957-58
‡ Brookbank, Wade	Nsh., Van., Bos., Car.	5	127	6	3	9	345	....	....	....	....	....	....	2003-04	2008-09
Brooke, Bob	NYR, Min., N.J.	7	447	69	97	166	520	34	9	9	18	59	....	1983-84	1989-90
Brooks, Alex	N.J.	1	19	0	1	1	4	....	....	....	....	....	....	2006-07	2006-07
Brooks, Gord	St.L., Wsh.	3	70	7	18	25	37	....	....	....	....	....	....	1971-72	1974-75
‡ Brophey, Evan	Chi., Col.	2	4	0	0	0	0	....	....	....	....	....	....	2010-11	2011-12
• Brophy, Bernie	Mtl.M., Det.	3	62	4	4	8	25	2	0	0	0	2	1	1925-26	1929-30
Brossart, Willie	Phi., Tor., Wsh.	6	129	1	14	15	88	1	0	0	0	0	....	1970-71	1975-76
Broten, Aaron	Col., N.J., Min., Que., Tor., Wpg.	12	748	186	329	515	441	34	7	18	25	40	....	1980-81	1991-92
Broten, Neal	Min., Dal., N.J., L.A.	17	1099	289	634	923	569	135	35	63	98	77	1	1980-81	1996-97
Broten, Paul	NYR, Dal., St.L.	7	322	46	55	101	264	38	4	6	10	18	....	1989-90	1995-96
Brousseau, Paul	Col., T.B., Fla.	4	26	1	3	4	29	....	....	....	....	....	....	1995-96	2000-01
• Brown, Adam	Det., Chi., Bos.	10	391	104	113	217	378	26	2	4	6	14	1	1941-42	1951-52
Brown, Arnie	Tor., NYR, Det., NYI, Atl.	12	681	44	141	185	738	22	0	6	6	23	....	1961-62	1973-74
Brown, Brad	Mtl., Chi., NYR, Min., Buf.	7	330	2	27	29	747	11	0	0	0	16	....	1996-97	2003-04
Brown, Cam	Van.	1	1	0	0	0	7	....	....	....	....	....	....	1990-91	1990-91
• Brown, Connie	Det.	5	73	15	24	39	12	14	2	3	5	0	1	1938-39	1942-43
Brown, Curtis	Buf., S.J., Chi.	13	736	129	171	300	398	87	14	15	29	58	....	1994-95	2007-08
Brown, Dave	Phi., Edm., S.J.	14	729	45	52	97	1789	80	2	3	5	209	1	1982-83	1995-96
Brown, Doug	N.J., Pit., Det.	15	854	160	214	374	210	109	23	23	46	26	2	1986-87	2000-01
• Brown, Fred	Mtl.M.	1	19	1	0	1	0	9	0	0	0	0	....	1927-28	1927-28
Brown, George	Mtl.	3	79	6	22	28	34	7	0	0	0	2	....	1936-37	1938-39
• Brown, Gerry	Det.	2	23	4	5	9	2	12	2	1	3	4	....	1941-42	1945-46
Brown, Greg	Buf., Pit., Wpg.	4	94	4	14	18	86	6	0	1	1	4	....	1990-91	1994-95
Brown, Harold	NYR	1	13	2	1	3	2	....	....	....	....	....	....	1945-46	1945-46
Brown, Jeff	Que., St.L., Van., Hfd., Car., Tor., Wsh.	13	747	154	430	584	498	87	20	45	65	59	....	1985-86	1997-98
Brown, Jim	L.A.	1	3	0	1	1	5	....	....	....	....	....	....	1982-83	1982-83
Brown, Keith	Chi., Fla.	16	876	68	274	342	916	103	4	32	36	184	....	1979-80	1994-95
Brown, Kevin	L.A., Hfd., Car., Edm.	6	64	7	9	16	28	1	0	0	0	0	....	1994-95	1999-00
Brown, Larry	NYR, Det., Phi., L.A.	9	455	7	53	60	180	35	0	4	4	10	....	1969-70	1977-78
Brown, Mike	Van., Ana., Chi.	4	34	1	2	3	130	....	....	....	....	....	....	2000-01	2005-06
Brown, Rob	Pit., Hfd., Chi., Dal., L.A.	11	543	190	248	438	599	54	12	14	26	45	....	1987-88	1999-00
Brown, Sean	Edm., Bos., N.J., Van.	9	436	14	43	57	907	9	0	0	0	37	....	1996-97	2005-06
• Brown, Stan	NYR, Det.	2	48	8	2	10	18	2	0	0	0	0	....	1926-27	1927-28
Brown, Wayne	Bos.	1	....	....	....	....	....	4	0	0	0	2	....	1953-54	1953-54
• Browne, Cecil	Chi.	1	13	2	0	2	4	....	....	....	....	....	....	1927-28	1927-28
Brownschidle, Jack	St.L., Hfd.	9	494	39	162	201	151	26	0	5	5	18	....	1977-78	1985-86
• Brownschidle, Jeff	Hfd.	2	7	0	1	1	2	....	....	....	....	....	....	1981-82	1982-83
Brubaker, Jeff	Hfd., Mtl., Cgy., Tor., Edm., NYR, Det.	8	178	16	9	25	512	2	0	0	0	27	....	1979-80	1988-89
Bruce, David	Van., St.L., S.J.	8	234	48	39	87	338	3	0	0	0	2	....	1985-86	1993-94
• Bruce, Gordie	Bos.	3	28	4	9	13	13	7	2	3	5	4	....	1940-41	1945-46
• Bruce, Morley	Ott.	4	71	8	3	11	27	3	0	0	0	2	2	1917-18	1921-22
Brule, Steve	N.J., Col.	2	2	0	0	0	0	1	0	0	0	0	1	1999-00	2002-03
Brumwell, Murray	Min., N.J.	7	128	12	31	43	70	2	0	0	0	2	....	1980-81	1987-88
Brunet, Benoit	Mtl., Dal., Ott.	13	539	101	161	262	229	54	5	20	25	32	1	1988-89	2001-02
• Bruneteau, Eddie	Det.	7	180	40	42	82	35	31	7	6	13	0	....	1940-41	1948-49
• Bruneteau, Mud	Det.	11	411	139	138	277	80	77	23	14	37	22	3	1935-36	1945-46
Brunette, Andrew	Wsh., Nsh., Atl., Min., Col., Chi.	16	1110	268	465	733	314	49	17	18	35	14	....	1995-96	2011-12
• Brydge, Bill	Tor., Det., NYA	9	368	26	52	78	506	2	0	0	0	4	....	1926-27	1935-36
Brydges, Paul	Buf.	1	15	2	2	4	6	....	....	....	....	....	....	1986-87	1986-87
• Brydson, Glenn	Mtl.M., St.L., NYR, Chi.	8	299	56	79	135	203	11	0	0	0	8	....	1930-31	1937-38
• Brydson, Gord	Tor.	1	8	2	0	2	8	....	....	....	....	....	....	1929-30	1929-30
‡ Brylin, Sergei	N.J.	13	765	129	179	308	273	109	15	19	34	32	3	1994-95	2007-08
Bubla, Jiri	Van.	5	256	17	101	118	202	6	0	0	0	7	....	1981-82	1985-86
• Buchanan, Al	Tor.	2	4	0	1	1	2	....	....	....	....	....	....	1948-49	1949-50
• Buchanan, Bucky	NYR	1	2	0	0	0	0	....	....	....	....	....	....	1948-49	1948-49
Buchanan, Jeff	Col.	1	6	0	0	0	6	....	....	....	....	....	....	1998-99	1998-99
Buchanan, Mike	Chi.	1	1	0	0	0	0	....	....	....	....	....	....	1951-52	1951-52
Buchanan, Ron	Bos., St.L.	2	5	0	0	0	0	....	....	....	....	....	....	1966-67	1969-70
Buchberger, Kelly	Edm., Atl., L.A., Phx., Pit.	18	1182	105	204	309	2297	97	10	15	25	129	2	1986-87	2003-04
Bucyk, John	Det., Bos.	23	1540	556	813	1369	497	124	41	62	103	42	2	1955-56	1977-78
Bucyk, Randy	Mtl., Cgy.	2	19	4	2	6	8	2	0	0	0	0	....	1985-86	1987-88
• Buhr, Doug	K.C.	1	6	0	2	2	4	....	....	....	....	....	....	1974-75	1974-75
• Bukovich, Tony	Det.	2	17	7	3	10	6	6	0	1	1	0	....	1943-44	1944-45
‡ Bulis, Jan	Wsh., Mtl., Van.	9	552	96	149	245	268	35	3	3	6	14	....	1997-98	2006-07
Bullard, Mike	Pit., Cgy., St.L., Phi., Tor.	11	727	329	345	674	703	40	11	18	29	44	....	1980-81	1991-92
• Buller, Hy	Det., NYR	5	188	22	58	80	215	....	....	....	....	....	....	1943-44	1953-54
Bulley, Ted	Chi., Wsh., Pit.	8	414	101	113	214	704	29	5	5	10	24	....	1976-77	1983-84
Burakovsky, Robert	Ott.	1	23	2	3	5	6	....	....	....	....	....	....	1993-94	1993-94
• Burch, Billy	Ham., NYA, Bos., Chi.	11	390	137	61	198	255	2	0	0	0	0	....	1922-23	1932-33
• Burchell, Fred	Mtl.	2	4	0	0	0	2	....	....	....	....	....	....	1950-51	1953-54
Burdon, Glen	K.C.	1	11	0	2	2	0	....	....	....	....	....	....	1974-75	1974-75
Bure, Pavel	Van., Fla., NYR	12	702	437	342	779	484	64	35	35	70	74	....	1991-92	2002-03
Bure, Valeri	Mtl., Cgy., Fla., St.L., Dal.	10	621	174	226	400	221	22	0	7	7	16	....	1994-95	2003-04

Name	NHL Teams	NHL Seasons	Regular Schedule GP	G	A	TP	PIM	Playoffs GP	G	A	TP	PIM	NHL Cup Wins	First NHL Season	Last NHL Season
Bureau, Marc	Cgy., Min., T.B., Mtl., Phi.	11	567	55	83	138	327	50	5	7	12	46	....	1989-90	1999-00
Burega, Bill	Tor.	1	4	0	1	1	4	....	....	....	....	....	....	1955-56	1955-56
• Burke, Eddie	Bos., NYA	4	106	29	20	49	55	....	....	....	....	....	....	1931-32	1934-35
• Burke, Marty	Mtl., Pit., Ott., Chi.	11	494	19	47	66	560	31	2	4	6	44	2	1927-28	1937-38
• Burmister, Roy	NYA	3	67	4	3	7	2	....	....	....	....	....	....	1929-30	1931-32
Burnett, Garrett	Ana.	1	39	1	2	3	184	....	....	....	....	....	....	2003-04	2003-04
Burnett, Kelly	NYR	1	3	1	0	1	0	....	....	....	....	....	....	1952-53	1952-53
• Burns, Bobby	Chi.	3	20	1	0	1	8	....	....	....	....	....	....	1927-28	1929-30
Burns, Charlie	Det., Bos., Oak., Pit., Min.	11	749	106	198	304	252	31	5	4	9	6	....	1958-59	1972-73
Burns, Gary	NYR	2	11	2	2	4	18	5	0	0	0	2	....	1980-81	1981-82
• Burns, Norm	NYR	1	11	0	4	4	2	....	....	....	....	....	....	1941-42	1941-42
Burns, Robin	Pit., K.C.	5	190	31	38	69	139	....	....	....	....	....	....	1970-71	1975-76
• Burr, Shawn	Det., T.B., S.J.	16	878	181	259	440	1069	91	16	19	35	95	....	1984-85	1999-00
Burridge, Randy	Bos., Wsh., L.A., Buf.	13	706	199	251	450	458	107	18	34	52	103	....	1985-86	1997-98
Burrows, Dave	Pit., Tor.	10	724	29	135	164	373	29	1	5	6	25	....	1971-72	1980-81
• Burry, Bert	Ott.	1	4	0	0	0	0	....	....	....	....	....	....	1932-33	1932-33
Burt, Adam	Hfd., Car., Phi., Atl.	13	737	37	115	152	961	21	0	1	1	8	....	1988-89	2000-01
Burton, Cummy	Det.	3	43	0	2	2	21	3	0	0	0	0	....	1955-56	1958-59
Burton, Nelson	Wsh.	2	8	1	0	1	21	....	....	....	....	....	....	1977-78	1978-79
• Bush, Eddie	Det.	2	26	4	6	10	40	11	1	6	7	23	....	1938-39	1941-42
Buskas, Rod	Pit., Van., L.A., Chi.	11	556	19	63	82	1294	18	0	3	3	45	....	1982-83	1992-93
Busniuk, Mike	Phi.	2	143	3	23	26	297	25	2	5	7	34	....	1979-80	1980-81
Busniuk, Ron	Buf.	2	6	0	3	3	13	....	....	....	....	....	....	1972-73	1973-74
• Buswell, Walt	Det., Mtl.	8	368	10	40	50	164	24	2	1	3	10	....	1932-33	1939-40
Butcher, Garth	Van., St.L., Que., Tor.	14	897	48	158	206	2302	50	6	5	11	122	....	1981-82	1994-95
‡ Butenschon, Sven	Pit., Edm., NYI, Van.	8	140	2	12	14	86	4	0	0	0	0	....	1997-98	2005-06
• Butler, Dick	Chi.	1	7	2	0	2	0	....	....	....	....	....	....	1947-48	1947-48
Butler, Jerry	NYR, St.L., Tor., Van., Wpg.	11	641	99	120	219	515	48	3	3	6	79	....	1972-73	1982-83
Butsayev, Viacheslav	Phi., S.J., Ana., Fla., Ott., T.B.	6	132	17	26	43	133	....	....	....	....	....	....	1992-93	1999-00
Butsayev, Yuri	Det., Atl.	4	99	10	4	14	28	....	....	....	....	....	....	1999-00	2002-03
Butters, Bill	Min.	2	72	1	4	5	77	....	....	....	....	....	....	1977-78	1978-79
• Buttrey, Gord	Chi.	1	10	0	0	0	0	....	....	....	....	....	....	1943-44	1943-44
Buynak, Gord	St.L.	1	4	0	0	0	2	....	....	....	....	....	....	1974-75	1974-75
Buzek, Petr	Dal., Atl., Cgy.	6	157	9	22	31	94	....	....	....	....	....	....	1997-98	2002-03
Byakin, Ilja	Edm., S.J.	2	57	8	25	33	44	....	....	....	....	....	....	1993-94	1994-95
Byce, John	Bos.	3	21	2	3	5	6	8	2	0	2	2	....	1989-90	1991-92
• Byers, Gord	Bos.	1	1	0	1	1	0	....	....	....	....	....	....	1949-50	1949-50
• Byers, Jerry	Min., Atl., NYR	4	43	3	4	7	15	....	....	....	....	....	....	1972-73	1977-78
Byers, Lyndon	Bos., S.J.	10	279	28	43	71	1081	37	2	2	4	96	....	1983-84	1992-93
• Byers, Mike	Tor., Phi., L.A., Buf.	4	166	42	34	76	39	4	0	1	1	0	....	1967-68	1971-72
‡ Bykov, Dmitri	Det.	1	71	2	10	12	43	4	0	0	0	0	....	2002-03	2002-03
Bylsma, Dan	L.A., Ana.	9	429	19	43	62	184	16	0	1	1	2	....	1995-96	2003-04
Byram, Shawn	NYI, Chi.	2	5	0	0	0	14	....	....	....	....	....	....	1990-91	1991-92

C

Name	NHL Teams	NHL Seasons	Regular Schedule GP	G	A	TP	PIM	Playoffs GP	G	A	TP	PIM	NHL Cup Wins	First NHL Season	Last NHL Season
• Caffery, Jack	Tor., Bos.	3	57	3	2	5	22	10	1	0	1	4	....	1954-55	1957-58
Caffery, Terry	Chi., Min.	2	14	0	0	0	0	1	0	0	0	0	....	1969-70	1970-71
• Cahan, Larry	Tor., NYR, Oak., L.A.	13	666	38	92	130	700	29	1	1	2	38	....	1954-55	1970-71
• Cahill, Charles	Bos.	2	32	0	1	1	4	....	....	....	....	....	....	1925-26	1926-27
• Cain, Francis	Mtl.M., Tor.	2	61	4	0	4	35	....	....	....	....	....	....	1924-25	1925-26
• Cain, Herb	Mtl.M., Mtl., Bos.	13	570	206	194	400	178	67	16	13	29	13	2	1933-34	1945-46
Cairns, Don	K.C., Col.	2	9	0	1	1	2	....	....	....	....	....	....	1975-76	1976-77
Cairns, Eric	NYR, NYI, Fla., Pit.	10	457	10	32	42	1182	16	0	0	0	28	....	1996-97	2006-07
‡ Cajanek, Petr	St.L.	4	269	46	107	153	144	7	0	2	2	4	....	2002-03	2006-07
Calder, Eric	Wsh.	2	2	0	0	0	0	....	....	....	....	....	....	1981-82	1982-83
‡ Calder, Kyle	Chi., Phi., Det., L.A., Ana.	10	590	114	180	294	309	18	2	1	3	10	....	1999-00	2009-10
‡ Caldwell, Ryan	NYI, Phx.	2	4	0	0	0	4	....	....	....	....	....	....	2005-06	2007-08
• Calladine, Norm	Bos.	3	63	19	29	48	8	....	....	....	....	....	....	1942-43	1944-45
Callander, Drew	Phi., Van.	4	39	6	2	8	7	....	....	....	....	....	....	1976-77	1979-80
Callander, Jock	Pit., T.B.	5	109	22	29	51	116	22	3	8	11	12	1	1987-88	1992-93
Callighen, Brett	Edm.	3	160	56	89	145	132	14	4	6	10	8	....	1979-80	1981-82
• Callighen, Patsy	NYR	1	36	0	0	0	32	9	0	0	0	0	1	1927-28	1927-28
Caloun, Jan	S.J., CBJ	3	24	8	6	14	2	....	....	....	....	....	....	1995-96	2000-01
Camazzola, James	Chi.	2	3	0	0	0	0	....	....	....	....	....	....	1983-84	1986-87
Camazzola, Tony	Wsh.	1	3	0	0	0	4	....	....	....	....	....	....	1981-82	1981-82
Cameron, Al	Det., Wpg.	6	282	11	44	55	356	7	0	1	1	2	....	1975-76	1980-81
• Cameron, Billy	Mtl., NYA	2	39	0	0	0	2	2	0	0	0	0	1	1923-24	1925-26
Cameron, Craig	Det., St.L., Min., NYI	9	552	87	65	152	196	27	3	1	4	17	....	1966-67	1975-76
Cameron, Dave	Col., N.J.	3	168	25	28	53	238	....	....	....	....	....	....	1981-82	1983-84
• Cameron, Harry	Tor., Ott., Mtl.	6	128	88	51	139	189	11	5	4	9	16	2	1917-18	1922-23
• Cameron, Scotty	NYR	1	35	8	11	19	0	....	....	....	....	....	....	1942-43	1942-43
‡ Campanale, Matt	NYI	1	1	0	0	0	2	....	....	....	....	....	....	2010-11	2010-11
Campbell, Bryan	L.A., Chi.	5	260	35	71	106	74	22	3	4	7	2	....	1967-68	1971-72
Campbell, Colin	Pit., Col., Edm., Van., Det.	11	636	25	103	128	1292	45	4	10	14	181	....	1974-75	1984-85
‡ Campbell, Darcy	CBJ	1	1	0	0	0	0	....	....	....	....	....	....	2006-07	2006-07
• Campbell, Dave	Mtl.	1	2	0	0	0	0	....	....	....	....	....	....	1920-21	1920-21
Campbell, Don	Chi.	1	17	1	3	4	8	....	....	....	....	....	....	1943-44	1943-44
• Campbell, Earl	Ott., NYA	3	76	6	3	9	14	1	0	0	0	6	....	1923-24	1925-26
Campbell, Jim	Ana., St.L., Mtl., Chi., Fla., T.B.	9	285	61	75	136	268	14	8	3	11	18	....	1995-96	2005-06
Campbell, Scott	Wpg., St.L.	3	80	4	21	25	243	....	....	....	....	....	....	1979-80	1981-82
Campbell, Wade	Wpg., Bos.	6	213	9	27	36	305	10	0	0	0	20	....	1982-83	1987-88
• Campeau, Tod	Mtl.	3	42	5	9	14	16	1	0	0	0	0	....	1943-44	1948-49
Campedelli, Dom	Mtl.	1	2	0	0	0	0	....	....	....	....	....	....	1985-86	1985-86
Capuano, Dave	Pit., Van., T.B., S.J.	4	104	17	38	55	56	6	1	1	2	5	....	1989-90	1993-94
Capuano, Jack	Tor., Van., Bos.	3	6	0	0	0	0	....	....	....	....	....	....	1989-90	1991-92
• Carbol, Leo	Chi.	1	6	0	1	1	4	....	....	....	....	....	....	1942-43	1942-43
Carbonneau, Guy	Mtl., St.L., Dal.	19	1318	260	403	663	820	231	38	55	93	161	3	1980-81	1999-00
‡ Card, Mike	Buf.	1	4	0	0	0	0	....	....	....	....	....	....	2006-07	2006-07
Cardin, Claude	St.L.	1	1	0	0	0	0	....	....	....	....	....	....	1967-68	1967-68
Cardwell, Steve	Pit.	3	53	9	11	20	35	4	0	0	0	2	....	1970-71	1972-73
• Carey, George	Que., Ham., Tor.	5	72	21	12	33	20	....	....	....	....	....	....	1919-20	1923-24
Carkner, Terry	NYR, Que., Phi., Det., Fla.	13	858	42	188	230	1588	54	1	9	10	48	....	1986-87	1998-99
Carleton, Wayne	Tor., Bos., Cal.	7	278	55	73	128	172	18	2	4	6	14	1	1965-66	1971-72
Carlin, Brian	L.A.	1	5	1	0	1	0	....	....	....	....	....	....	1971-72	1971-72
Carlson, Jack	Min., St.L.	6	236	30	15	45	417	25	1	2	3	72	....	1978-79	1986-87
Carlson, Kent	Mtl., St.L., Wsh.	5	113	7	11	18	148	8	0	0	0	13	....	1983-84	1988-89
Carlson, Steve	L.A.	1	52	9	12	21	23	4	1	1	2	7	....	1979-80	1979-80
Carlsson, Anders	N.J.	3	104	7	26	33	34	3	1	0	1	2	....	1986-87	1988-89
Carlyle, Randy	Tor., Pit., Wpg.	17	1055	148	499	647	1400	69	9	24	33	120	....	1976-77	1992-93
Carnback, Patrik	Mtl., Ana.	4	154	24	38	62	122	....	....	....	....	....	....	1992-93	1995-96
Carney, Keith	Buf., Chi., Phx., Ana., Van., Min.	16	1018	45	183	228	904	91	3	19	22	67	....	1991-92	2007-08
• Caron, Alain	Oak., Mtl.	2	60	9	13	22	18	....	....	....	....	....	....	1967-68	1968-69
Carpenter, Bob	Wsh., NYR, L.A., Bos., N.J.	18	1178	320	408	728	919	140	21	38	59	136	1	1981-82	1998-99
• Carpenter, Ed	Que., Ham.	2	45	10	5	15	41	....	....	....	....	....	....	1919-20	1920-21
Carr, Gene	St.L., NYR, L.A., Pit., Atl.	8	465	79	136	215	365	35	5	8	13	66	....	1971-72	1978-79
• Carr, Lorne	NYR, NYA, Tor.	13	580	204	222	426	132	53	10	9	19	13	2	1933-34	1945-46
• Carr, Red	Tor.	1	5	0	1	1	2	....	....	....	....	....	....	1943-44	1943-44
Carriere, Larry	Buf., Atl., Van., L.A., Tor.	7	367	16	74	90	462	27	0	3	3	42	....	1972-73	1979-80
• Carrigan, Gene	NYR, Det., St.L.	3	37	2	1	3	13	4	0	0	0	0	....	1930-31	1934-35
Carroll, Billy	NYI, Edm., Det.	7	322	30	54	84	113	71	6	12	18	18	4	1980-81	1986-87
• Carroll, George	Mtl.M., Bos.	1	16	0	0	0	11	....	....	....	....	....	....	1924-25	1924-25
Carroll, Greg	Wsh., Det., Hfd.	2	131	20	34	54	44	....	....	....	....	....	....	1978-79	1979-80
Carruthers, Dwight	Det., Phi.	2	2	0	0	0	0	....	....	....	....	....	....	1965-66	1967-68
• Carse, Bill	NYR, Chi.	4	124	28	43	71	38	13	3	2	5	0	....	1938-39	1941-42
• Carse, Bob	Chi., Mtl.	5	167	32	55	87	52	10	0	2	2	2	....	1939-40	1947-48
• Carson, Bill	Tor., Bos.	4	159	54	24	78	156	11	3	0	3	14	1	1926-27	1929-30
• Carson, Frank	Mtl.M., NYA, Det.	7	248	42	48	90	166	27	0	2	2	9	1	1925-26	1933-34
• Carson, Gerry	Mtl., NYR, Mtl.M.	6	261	12	11	23	205	22	0	0	0	12	1	1928-29	1936-37
Carson, Jimmy	L.A., Edm., Det., Van., Hfd.	10	626	275	286	561	254	55	17	15	32	22	....	1986-87	1995-96
Carson, Lindsay	Phi., Hfd.	7	373	66	80	146	524	49	4	10	14	56	....	1981-82	1987-88
Carter, Anson	Wsh., Bos., Edm., NYR, L.A., Van., CBJ, Car.	10	674	202	219	421	229	24	8	5	13	4	....	1996-97	2006-07
Carter, Billy	Mtl., Bos.	3	16	0	0	0	6	....	....	....	....	....	....	1957-58	1961-62
Carter, John	Bos., S.J.	8	244	40	50	90	201	31	7	5	12	51	....	1985-86	1992-93
Carter, Ron	Edm.	1	2	0	0	0	0	....	....	....	....	....	....	1979-80	1979-80

Shawn Burr

Gerry Carson

Lindsay Carson

John Carter

Murph Chamberlain

Marian Cisar

Kim Clackson

Wally Clune

			Regular Schedule					Playoffs					NHL	First	Last
Name	NHL Teams	NHL Seasons	GP	G	A	TP	PIM	GP	G	A	TP	PIM	Cup Wins	NHL Season	NHL Season
• Carveth, Joe	Det., Bos., Mtl.	11	504	150	189	339	81	69	21	16	37	28	2	1940-41	1950-51
Cashman, Wayne	Bos.	17	1027	277	516	793	1041	145	31	57	88	250	2	1964-65	1982-83
Casselman, Mike	Fla.	1	3	0	0	0	0	....	....	....	....	....	....	1995-96	1995-96
Cassels, Andrew	Mtl., Hfd., Cgy., Van., CBJ, Wsh.	16	1015	204	528	732	410	21	4	7	11	8	....	1989-90	2005-06
Cassidy, Bruce	Chi.	6	36	4	13	17	10	1	0	0	0	0	....	1983-84	1989-90
Cassidy, Tom	Pit.	1	26	3	4	7	15	....	....	....	....	....	....	1977-78	1977-78
Cassolato, Tony	Wsh.	3	23	1	6	7	4	....	....	....	....	....	....	1979-80	1981-82
Caufield, Jay	NYR, Min., Pit.	7	208	5	8	13	759	17	0	0	0	42	2	1986-87	1992-93
Cavallini, Gino	Cgy., St.L., Que.	9	593	114	159	273	507	74	14	19	33	66	....	1984-85	1992-93
Cavallini, Paul	Wsh., St.L., Dal.	10	564	56	177	233	750	69	8	27	35	114	....	1986-87	1995-96
• Cavanagh, Tom	S.J.	2	18	1	2	3	4	....	....	....	....	....	....	2007-08	2008-09
Ceresino, Ray	Tor.	1	12	1	1	2	2	....	....	....	....	....	....	1948-49	1948-49
Cernik, Frantisek	Det.	1	49	5	4	9	13	....	....	....	....	....	....	1984-85	1984-85
Chabot, John	Mtl., Pit., Det.	8	508	84	228	312	85	33	6	20	26	2	....	1983-84	1990-91
• Chad, John	Chi.	3	80	15	22	37	29	10	0	1	1	2	....	1939-40	1945-46
• Chalmers, Chick	NYR	1	1	0	0	0	0	....	....	....	....	....	....	1953-54	1953-54
Chalupa, Milan	Det.	1	14	0	5	5	6	....	....	....	....	....	....	1984-85	1984-85
• Chamberlain, Murph	Tor., Mtl., Bro., Bos.	12	510	100	175	275	769	66	14	17	31	96	2	1937-38	1948-49
Chambers, Shawn	Min., Wsh., T.B., N.J., Dal.	13	625	50	185	235	364	94	7	26	33	72	2	1987-88	1999-00
Champagne, Andre	Tor.	1	2	0	0	0	0	....	....	....	....	....	....	1962-63	1962-63
Chapdelaine, Rene	L.A.	3	32	0	2	2	32	....	....	....	....	....	....	1990-91	1992-93
• Chapman, Art	Bos., NYA	10	438	62	176	238	140	26	1	5	6	9	....	1930-31	1939-40
Chapman, Blair	Pit., St.L.	7	402	106	125	231	158	25	4	6	10	15	....	1976-77	1982-83
Chapman, Brian	Hfd.	1	3	0	0	0	29	....	....	....	....	....	....	1990-91	1990-91
Charbonneau, Jose	Mtl., Van.	4	71	9	13	22	67	11	1	0	1	8	....	1987-88	1994-95
Charbonneau, Stephane	Que.	1	2	0	0	0	0	....	....	....	....	....	....	1991-92	1991-92
Charlebois, Bob	Min.	1	7	1	0	1	0	....	....	....	....	....	....	1967-68	1967-68
Charlesworth, Todd	Pit., NYR	6	93	3	9	12	47	....	....	....	....	....	....	1983-84	1989-90
Charron, Eric	Mtl., T.B., Wsh., Cgy.	8	130	2	7	9	127	6	0	0	0	8	....	1992-93	1999-00
Charron, Guy	Mtl., Det., K.C., Wsh.	12	734	221	309	530	146	....	....	....	....	....	....	1969-70	1980-81
Chartier, Dave	Wpg.	1	1	0	0	0	0	....	....	....	....	....	....	1980-81	1980-81
Chartrand, Brad	L.A.	5	215	25	25	50	122	11	1	1	2	8	....	1999-00	2003-04
Chartraw, Rick	Mtl., L.A., NYR, Edm.	10	420	28	64	92	399	75	7	9	16	80	4	1974-75	1983-84
Chase, Kelly	St.L., Hfd., Tor.	11	458	17	36	53	2017	27	1	1	2	100	....	1989-90	1999-00
Chasse, Denis	St.L., Wsh., Wpg., Ott.	4	132	11	14	25	292	7	1	7	8	23	....	1993-94	1996-97
Chebaturkin, Vladimir	NYI, St.L., Chi.	5	62	2	7	9	52	3	0	0	0	2	....	1997-98	2001-02
• Check, Lude	Det., Chi.	2	27	6	2	8	4	....	....	....	....	....	....	1943-44	1944-45
‡ Cheechoo, Jonathan	S.J., Ott.	7	501	170	135	305	324	59	16	19	35	32	....	2002-03	2009-10
Chelios, Chris	Mtl., Chi., Det., Atl.	26	1651	185	763	948	2891	266	31	113	144	423	3	1983-84	2009-10
• Chernoff, Mike	Min.	1	1	0	0	0	0	....	....	....	....	....	....	1968-69	1968-69
Chernomaz, Rich	Col., N.J., Cgy.	7	51	9	7	16	18	....	....	....	....	....	....	1981-82	1991-92
Cherry, Dick	Bos., Phi.	3	145	12	10	22	45	4	1	0	1	4	....	1956-57	1969-70
Cherry, Don	Bos.	1	....	....	....	....	....	1	0	0	0	0	....	1954-55	1954-55
Chervyakov, Denis	Bos.	1	2	0	0	0	2	....	....	....	....	....	....	1992-93	1992-93
• Chevrefils, Real	Bos., Det.	8	387	104	97	201	185	30	5	4	9	20	....	1951-52	1958-59
• Chiasson, Steve	Det., Cgy., Hfd., Car.	13	751	93	305	398	1107	63	16	19	35	119	....	1986-87	1998-99
Chibirev, Igor	Hfd.	2	45	7	12	19	2	....	....	....	....	....	....	1993-94	1994-95
Chicoine, Dan	Cle., Min.	3	31	1	2	3	12	1	0	0	0	0	....	1977-78	1979-80
Chinnick, Rick	Min.	2	4	0	2	2	0	....	....	....	....	....	....	1973-74	1974-75
Chipperfield, Ron	Edm., Que.	2	83	22	24	46	34	....	....	....	....	....	....	1979-80	1980-81
Chisholm, Art	Bos.	1	3	0	0	0	0	....	....	....	....	....	....	1960-61	1960-61
Chisholm, Colin	Min.	1	1	0	0	0	0	....	....	....	....	....	....	1986-87	1986-87
• Chisholm, Lex	Tor.	2	54	10	8	18	19	3	1	0	1	0	....	1939-40	1940-41
‡ Chistov, Stanislav	Ana., Bos.	3	196	19	42	61	116	21	4	2	6	8	....	2002-03	2006-07
Chorney, Marc	Pit., L.A.	4	210	8	27	35	209	7	0	1	1	2	....	1980-81	1983-84
Chorske, Tom	Mtl., N.J., Ott., NYI, Wsh., Cgy., Pit.	11	596	115	122	237	225	50	5	12	17	10	1	1989-90	1999-00
‡ Chouinard, Eric	Mtl., Phi., Min.	4	90	11	11	22	16	....	....	....	....	....	....	2000-01	2005-06
• Chouinard, Gene	Ott.	1	8	0	0	0	0	....	....	....	....	....	....	1927-28	1927-28
Chouinard, Guy	Atl., Cgy., St.L.	10	578	205	370	575	120	46	9	28	37	12	....	1974-75	1983-84
Chouinard, Marc	Ana., Min., Van.	6	320	37	41	78	123	15	1	0	1	0	....	2000-01	2006-07
Christian, Dave	Wpg., Wsh., Bos., St.L., Chi.	15	1009	340	433	773	284	102	32	25	57	27	....	1979-80	1993-94
Christian, Jeff	N.J., Pit., Phx.	5	18	2	2	4	17	....	....	....	....	....	....	1991-92	1997-98
Christie, Mike	Cal., Cle., Col., Van.	7	412	15	101	116	550	2	0	0	0	0	....	1974-75	1980-81
‡ Christie, Ryan	Dal., Cgy.	2	7	0	0	0	0	....	....	....	....	....	....	1999-00	2001-02
Christoff, Steve	Min., Cgy., L.A.	5	248	77	64	141	108	35	16	12	28	25	....	1979-80	1983-84
Chrystal, Bob	NYR	2	132	11	14	25	112	....	....	....	....	....	....	1953-54	1954-55
Chubarov, Artem	Van.	5	228	25	33	58	40	27	0	4	4	4	....	1999-00	2003-04
Chucko, Kris	Cgy.	1	2	0	0	0	2	....	....	....	....	....	....	2008-09	2008-09
Church, Brad	Wsh.	1	2	0	0	0	0	....	....	....	....	....	....	1997-98	1997-98
• Church, Jack	Tor., Bro., Bos.	5	130	4	19	23	154	25	1	1	2	18	....	1938-39	1945-46
Churla, Shane	Hfd., Cgy., Min., Dal., L.A., NYR	11	488	26	45	71	2301	78	5	7	12	282	....	1986-87	1996-97
Chychrun, Jeff	Phi., L.A., Pit., Edm.	8	262	3	22	25	744	19	0	2	2	65	1	1986-87	1993-94
Chynoweth, Dean	NYI, Bos.	9	241	4	18	22	667	6	0	0	0	26	....	1988-89	1997-98
Chyzowski, Dave	NYI, Chi.	6	126	15	16	31	144	2	0	0	0	0	....	1989-90	1996-97
Ciavaglia, Peter	Buf.	2	5	0	0	0	0	....	....	....	....	....	....	1991-92	1992-93
‡ Cibak, Martin	T.B.	3	154	5	18	23	60	11	0	1	1	0	1	2001-02	2005-06
Ciccarelli, Dino	Min., Wsh., Det., T.B., Fla.	19	1232	608	592	1200	1425	141	73	45	118	211	....	1980-81	1998-99
Ciccone, Enrico	Min., Wsh., T.B., Chi., Car., Van., Mtl.	9	374	10	18	28	1469	13	1	0	1	48	....	1991-92	2000-01
Cichocki, Chris	Det., N.J.	4	68	11	12	23	27	....	....	....	....	....	....	1985-86	1988-89
Ciernik, Ivan	Ott., Wsh.	5	89	12	14	26	32	2	0	1	1	6	....	1997-98	2003-04
Cierny, Jozef	Edm.	1	1	0	0	0	0	....	....	....	....	....	....	1993-94	1993-94
• Ciesla, Hank	Chi., NYR	4	269	26	51	77	87	6	0	2	2	0	....	1955-56	1958-59
Ciger, Zdeno	N.J., Edm., NYR, T.B.	7	352	94	134	228	101	13	2	6	8	4	....	1990-91	2001-02
Cimellaro, Tony	Ott.	1	2	0	0	0	0	....	....	....	....	....	....	1992-93	1992-93
Cimetta, Rob	Bos., Tor.	4	103	16	16	32	66	1	0	0	0	15	....	1988-89	1991-92
Cirella, Joe	Col., N.J., Que., NYR, Fla., Ott.	15	828	64	211	275	1446	38	0	13	13	98	....	1981-82	1995-96
Cirone, Jason	Wpg.	1	3	0	0	0	2	....	....	....	....	....	....	1991-92	1991-92
Cisar, Marian	Nsh.	3	73	13	17	30	57	....	....	....	....	....	....	1999-00	2001-02
Clackson, Kim	Pit., Que.	2	106	0	8	8	370	8	0	0	0	70	....	1979-80	1980-81
• Clancy, King	Ott., Tor.	16	592	136	147	283	914	55	8	8	16	88	3	1921-22	1936-37
Clancy, Terry	Oak., Tor.	4	93	6	6	12	39	....	....	....	....	....	....	1967-68	1972-73
• Clapper, Dit	Bos.	20	833	228	246	474	462	82	13	17	30	50	3	1927-28	1946-47
‡ Clark, Chris	Cgy., Wsh., CBJ	11	607	103	111	214	700	34	4	3	7	38	....	1999-00	2010-11
Clark, Dan	NYR	1	4	0	1	1	6	....	....	....	....	....	....	1978-79	1978-79
Clark, Dean	Edm.	1	1	0	0	0	0	....	....	....	....	....	....	1983-84	1983-84
Clark, Gordie	Bos.	2	8	0	1	1	0	1	0	0	0	0	....	1974-75	1975-76
• Clark, Nobby	Bos.	1	5	0	0	0	0	....	....	....	....	....	....	1927-28	1927-28
Clark, Wendel	Tor., Que., NYI, T.B., Det., Chi.	15	793	330	234	564	1690	95	37	32	69	201	....	1985-86	1999-00
Clarke, Bobby	Phi.	15	1144	358	852	1210	1453	136	42	77	119	152	2	1969-70	1983-84
‡ Clarke, Dale	St.L.	1	3	0	0	0	0	....	....	....	....	....	....	2000-01	2000-01
‡ Clarke, Noah	L.A., N.J.	4	21	3	1	4	4	....	....	....	....	....	....	2003-04	2007-08
Classen, Greg	Nsh.	3	90	7	10	17	48	....	....	....	....	....	....	2000-01	2002-03
• Cleghorn, Odie	Mtl., Pit.	10	181	95	34	129	142	12	7	2	9	5	1	1918-19	1927-28
• Cleghorn, Sprague	Ott., Tor., Mtl., Bos.	10	259	83	55	138	538	21	4	3	7	26	2	1918-19	1927-28
Clement, Bill	Phi., Wsh., Atl., Cgy.	11	719	148	208	356	383	50	5	3	8	26	2	1971-72	1981-82
Cline, Bruce	NYR	1	30	2	3	5	10	....	....	....	....	....	....	1956-57	1956-57
Clippingdale, Steve	L.A., Wsh.	2	19	1	2	3	9	1	0	0	0	0	....	1976-77	1979-80
Cloutier, Real	Que., Buf.	6	317	146	198	344	119	25	7	5	12	20	....	1979-80	1984-85
Cloutier, Rejean	Det.	2	5	0	2	2	2	....	....	....	....	....	....	1979-80	1981-82
Cloutier, Roland	Det., Que.	3	34	8	9	17	2	....	....	....	....	....	....	1977-78	1979-80
Cloutier, Sylvain	Chi.	1	7	0	0	0	0	....	....	....	....	....	....	1998-99	1998-99
• Clune, Wally	Mtl.	1	5	0	0	0	6	....	....	....	....	....	....	1955-56	1955-56
Clymer, Ben	T.B., Wsh.	7	438	52	77	129	367	16	0	2	2	6	1	1999-00	2006-07
Coalter, Gary	Cal., K.C.	2	34	2	4	6	2	....	....	....	....	....	....	1973-74	1974-75
Coates, Steve	Det.	1	5	1	0	1	24	....	....	....	....	....	....	1976-77	1976-77
Cochrane, Glen	Phi., Van., Chi., Edm.	10	411	17	72	89	1556	18	1	1	2	31	....	1978-79	1988-89
Coffey, Paul	Edm., Pit., L.A., Det., Hfd., Phi., Chi., Car., Bos.	21	1409	396	1135	1531	1802	194	59	137	196	264	4	1980-81	2000-01
Coflin, Hugh	Chi.	1	31	0	3	3	33	....	....	....	....	....	....	1950-51	1950-51
Cole, Danton	Wpg., T.B., N.J., NYI, Chi.	7	318	58	60	118	125	1	0	0	0	0	1	1989-90	1995-96
Colley, Kevin	NYI	1	16	0	0	0	52	....	....	....	....	....	....	2005-06	2005-06
Colley, Tom	Min.	1	1	0	0	0	2	....	....	....	....	....	....	1974-75	1974-75
Collings, Norm	Mtl.	1	1	0	1	1	0	....	....	....	....	....	....	1934-35	1934-35
Collins, Bill	Min., Mtl., Det., St.L., NYR, Phi., Wsh.	11	768	157	154	311	415	18	3	5	8	12	....	1967-68	1977-78
Collins, Gary	Tor.	1	....	....	....	....	....	2	0	0	0	0	....	1958-59	1958-59
Collins, Rob	NYI	1	8	1	1	2	0	....	....	....	....	....	....	2005-06	2005-06

			Regular Schedule					Playoffs							
Name	NHL Teams	NHL Seasons	GP	G	A	TP	PIM	GP	G	A	TP	PIM	NHL Cup Wins	First NHL Season	Last NHL Season
‡ Colliton, Jeremy	NYI	5	57	3	3	6	26	....	....	....	....	....	....	2005-06	2010-11
Collyard, Bob	St.L.	1	10	1	3	4	4	....	....	....	....	....	....	1973-74	1973-74
• Colman, Michael	S.J.	1	15	0	1	1	32	....	....	....	....	....	....	1991-92	1991-92
• Colville, Mac	NYR	9	353	71	104	175	130	40	9	10	19	14	1	1935-36	1946-47
• Colville, Neil	NYR	12	464	99	166	265	213	46	7	19	26	32	1	1935-36	1948-49
Colwill, Les	NYR	1	69	7	6	13	16	....	....	....	....	....	....	1958-59	1958-59
Comeau, Rey	Mtl., Atl., Col.	9	564	98	141	239	175	9	2	1	3	8	....	1971-72	1979-80
Comrie, Mike	Edm., Phi., Phx., Ott., NYI, Pit.	10	589	168	197	365	443	32	4	6	10	27	....	2000-01	2010-11
Comrie, Paul	Edm.	1	15	1	2	3	4	....	....	....	....	....	....	1999-00	1999-00
Conacher, Brian	Tor., Det.	5	155	28	28	56	84	12	3	2	5	21	1	1961-62	1971-72
• Conacher, Charlie	Tor., Det., NYA	12	459	225	173	398	523	49	17	18	35	49	1	1929-30	1940-41
Conacher, Jim	Det., Chi., NYR	8	328	85	117	202	91	19	5	2	7	4	....	1945-46	1952-53
• Conacher, Lionel	Pit., NYA, Mtl.M., Chi.	12	498	80	105	185	882	35	2	2	4	34	2	1925-26	1936-37
Conacher, Pat	NYR, Edm., N.J., L.A., Cgy., NYI	13	521	63	76	139	235	67	11	10	21	40	1	1979-80	1995-96
Conacher, Pete	Chi., NYR, Tor.	6	229	47	39	86	57	7	0	0	0	0	....	1951-52	1957-58
• Conacher, Roy	Bos., Det., Chi.	11	490	226	200	426	90	42	15	15	30	14	2	1938-39	1951-52
‡ Conboy, Tim	Car.	3	59	0	6	6	121	3	0	0	0	9	....	2007-08	2009-10
• Conn, Red	NYA	2	96	9	28	37	22	....	....	....	....	....	....	1933-34	1934-35
Conn, Rob	Chi., Buf.	2	30	2	5	7	20	....	....	....	....	....	....	1991-92	1995-96
• Connelly, Bert	NYR, Chi.	3	87	13	15	28	37	14	1	0	1	0	1	1934-35	1937-38
Connelly, Wayne	Mtl., Bos., Min., Det., St.L., Van.	10	543	133	174	307	156	24	11	7	18	4	....	1960-61	1971-72
‡ Connolly, Mike	Col.	1	2	0	0	0	2	....	....	....	....	....	....	2011-12	2011-12
Connor, Cam	Mtl., Edm., NYR	5	89	9	22	31	256	20	5	0	5	6	1	1978-79	1982-83
• Connor, Harry	Bos., NYA, Ott.	4	134	16	5	21	149	10	0	0	0	2	....	1927-28	1930-31
• Connors, Bob	NYA, Det.	3	78	17	10	27	110	2	0	0	0	10	....	1926-27	1929-30
Conroy, Al	Phi.	3	114	9	14	23	156	....	....	....	....	....	....	1991-92	1993-94
Conroy, Craig	Mtl., St.L., Cgy., L.A.	16	1009	182	360	542	603	81	10	20	30	52	....	1994-95	2010-11
Contini, Joe	Col., Min.	3	68	17	21	38	34	2	0	0	0	0	....	1977-78	1980-81
Convery, Brandon	Tor., Van., L.A.	4	72	9	19	28	36	5	0	0	0	2	....	1995-96	1998-99
• Convey, Eddie	NYA	3	36	1	1	2	33	....	....	....	....	....	....	1930-31	1932-33
• Cook, Bill	NYR	11	474	229	138	367	386	46	13	11	24	68	2	1926-27	1936-37
• Cook, Bob	Van., Det., NYI, Min.	4	72	13	9	22	22	....	....	....	....	....	....	1970-71	1974-75
• Cook, Bud	Bos., Ott., St.L.	3	50	5	4	9	22	....	....	....	....	....	....	1931-32	1934-35
• Cook, Bun	NYR, Bos.	11	473	158	144	302	444	46	15	3	18	50	2	1926-27	1936-37
• Cook, Lloyd	Bos.	1	4	1	0	1	0	....	....	....	....	....	....	1924-25	1924-25
• Cook, Tom	Chi., Mtl.M.	9	349	77	98	175	184	24	2	4	6	19	1	1929-30	1937-38
• Cooper, Carson	Bos., Mtl., Det.	8	294	110	57	167	111	7	0	0	0	2	....	1924-25	1931-32
Cooper, David	Tor.	3	30	3	7	10	24	....	....	....	....	....	....	1996-97	2000-01
Cooper, Ed	Col.	2	49	8	7	15	46	....	....	....	....	....	....	1980-81	1981-82
• Cooper, Hal	NYR	1	8	0	0	0	2	....	....	....	....	....	....	1944-45	1944-45
• Cooper, Joe	NYR, Chi.	11	420	30	66	96	442	35	3	5	8	58	....	1935-36	1946-47
• Copp, Bobby	Tor.	2	40	3	9	12	26	....	....	....	....	....	....	1942-43	1950-51
Corazzini, Carl	Bos., Chi.	2	19	2	1	3	2	....	....	....	....	....	....	2003-04	2006-07
• Corbeau, Bert	Mtl., Ham., Tor.	10	258	63	49	112	629	9	2	2	4	38	....	1917-18	1926-27
Corbet, Rene	Que., Col., Cgy., Pit.	8	362	58	74	132	420	53	7	6	13	52	1	1993-94	2000-01
• Corbett, Mike	L.A.	1	....	....	....	....	....	2	0	1	1	2	....	1967-68	1967-68
Corcoran, Norm	Bos., Det., Chi.	4	29	1	3	4	21	4	0	0	0	6	....	1949-50	1955-56
Corkum, Bob	Buf., Ana., Phi., Phx., L.A., N.J., Atl.	12	720	97	103	200	281	62	7	7	14	24	....	1989-90	2001-02
• Cormier, Roger	Mtl.	1	1	0	0	0	0	....	....	....	....	....	....	1925-26	1925-26
Cornforth, Mark	Bos.	1	6	0	0	0	4	....	....	....	....	....	....	1995-96	1995-96
• Corrigan, Chuck	Tor., NYA	2	19	2	2	4	2	....	....	....	....	....	....	1937-38	1940-41
Corrigan, Mike	L.A., Van., Pit.	10	594	152	195	347	698	17	2	3	5	20	....	1967-68	1977-78
Corrinet, Chris	Wsh.	1	8	0	1	1	6	....	....	....	....	....	....	2001-02	2001-02
• Corriveau, Andre	Mtl.	1	3	0	1	1	0	....	....	....	....	....	....	1953-54	1953-54
Corriveau, Yvon	Wsh., Hfd., S.J.	9	280	48	40	88	310	29	5	7	12	50	....	1985-86	1993-94
‡ Corso, Daniel	St.L., Atl.	4	77	14	11	25	20	14	0	1	1	0	....	2000-01	2003-04
Corson, Shayne	Mtl., Edm., St.L., Tor., Dal.	19	1156	273	420	693	2357	140	38	49	87	291	....	1985-86	2003-04
Cory, Ross	Wpg.	2	51	2	10	12	41	....	....	....	....	....	....	1979-80	1980-81
Cossette, Jacques	Pit.	3	64	8	6	14	29	3	0	1	1	4	....	1975-76	1978-79
• Costello, Les	Tor.	3	15	2	3	5	11	6	2	2	4	2	1	1947-48	1949-50
Costello, Murray	Chi., Bos., Det.	4	162	13	19	32	54	5	0	0	0	2	....	1953-54	1956-57
Costello, Rich	Tor.	2	12	2	2	4	2	....	....	....	....	....	....	1983-84	1985-86
• Cotch, Charlie	Ham., Tor.	1	12	1	0	1	0	....	....	....	....	....	....	1924-25	1924-25
Cote, Alain	Que.	10	696	103	190	293	383	67	9	15	24	44	....	1979-80	1988-89
Cote, Alain	Bos., Wsh., Mtl., T.B., Que.	9	119	2	18	20	124	11	0	2	2	26	....	1985-86	1993-94
‡ Cote, Jean-Philippe	Mtl.	1	8	0	0	0	4	....	....	....	....	....	....	2005-06	2005-06
Cote, Patrick	Dal., Nsh., Edm.	6	105	1	2	3	377	....	....	....	....	....	....	1995-96	2000-01
Cote, Ray	Edm.	3	15	0	0	0	4	14	3	2	5	0	....	1982-83	1984-85
Cote, Riley	Phi.	4	156	1	6	7	411	3	0	0	0	0	....	2006-07	2009-10
Cote, Sylvain	Hfd., Wsh., Tor., Chi., Dal.	19	1171	122	313	435	545	102	11	22	33	62	....	1984-85	2002-03
• Cotton, Baldy	Pit., Tor., NYA	12	503	101	103	204	419	43	4	9	13	46	1	1925-26	1936-37
• Coughlin, Jack	Tor., Que., Mtl., Ham.	3	19	2	0	2	3	....	....	....	....	....	1	1917-18	1920-21
Coulis, Tim	Wsh., Min.	4	47	4	5	9	138	3	1	0	1	2	....	1979-80	1985-86
‡ Coulombe, Patrick	Van.	1	7	0	1	1	4	....	....	....	....	....	....	2006-07	2006-07
• Coulson, D'arcy	Phi.	1	28	0	0	0	103	....	....	....	....	....	....	1930-31	1930-31
• Coulter, Art	Chi., NYR	11	465	30	82	112	543	49	4	5	9	61	2	1931-32	1941-42
Coulter, Neal	NYI	3	26	5	5	10	11	....	....	....	....	....	....	1985-86	1987-88
• Coulter, Thomas	Chi.	1	2	0	0	0	0	....	....	....	....	....	....	1933-34	1933-34
Cournoyer, Yvan	Mtl.	16	968	428	435	863	255	147	64	63	127	47	10	1963-64	1978-79
Courteau, Yves	Cgy., Hfd.	3	22	2	5	7	4	1	0	0	0	0	....	1984-85	1986-87
Courtenay, Ed	S.J.	2	44	7	13	20	10	....	....	....	....	....	....	1991-92	1992-93
Courtnall, Geoff	Bos., Edm., Wsh., St.L., Van.	17	1048	367	432	799	1465	156	39	70	109	262	1	1983-84	1999-00
Courtnall, Russ	Tor., Mtl., Min., Dal., Van., NYR, L.A.	16	1029	297	447	744	557	129	39	44	83	83	....	1983-84	1998-99
Courville, Larry	Van.	3	33	1	2	3	16	....	....	....	....	....	....	1995-96	1997-98
• Coutu, Billy	Mtl., Ham., Bos.	10	244	33	21	54	478	19	1	1	2	39	1	1917-18	1926-27
• Couture, Gerry	Det., Mtl., Chi.	10	385	86	70	156	89	45	9	7	16	4	1	1944-45	1953-54
• Couture, Rosie	Chi., Mtl.	8	309	48	56	104	184	23	1	5	6	15	1	1928-29	1935-36
Couturier, Sylvain	L.A.	3	33	4	5	9	4	....	....	....	....	....	....	1988-89	1991-92
‡ Cowan, Jeff	Cgy., Atl., L.A., Van.	8	413	47	34	81	695	10	2	0	2	22	....	1999-00	2007-08
Cowick, Bruce	Phi., Wsh., St.L.	3	70	5	6	11	43	8	0	0	0	9	1	1973-74	1975-76
Cowie, Rob	L.A.	2	78	7	12	19	52	....	....	....	....	....	....	1994-95	1995-96
• Cowley, Bill	St.L., Bos.	13	549	195	353	548	143	64	12	34	46	22	2	1934-35	1946-47
• Cox, Danny	Tor., Ott., Det., NYR	8	319	47	49	96	128	10	0	1	1	6	....	1926-27	1933-34
Coxe, Craig	Van., Cgy., St.L., S.J.	8	235	14	31	45	713	5	1	0	1	18	....	1984-85	1991-92
Craig, Mike	Min., Dal., Tor., S.J.	9	423	71	97	168	550	26	2	2	4	49	....	1990-91	2001-02
Craighead, John	Tor.	1	5	0	0	0	10	....	....	....	....	....	....	1996-97	1996-97
Craigwell, Dale	S.J.	3	98	11	18	29	28	....	....	....	....	....	....	1991-92	1993-94
Crashley, Bart	Det., K.C., L.A.	6	140	7	36	43	50	....	....	....	....	....	....	1965-66	1975-76
Craven, Murray	Det., Phi., Hfd., Van., Chi., S.J.	18	1071	266	493	759	524	118	27	43	70	64	....	1982-83	1999-00
Crawford, Bob	St.L., Hfd., NYR, Wsh.	7	246	71	71	142	72	11	0	1	1	8	....	1979-80	1986-87
Crawford, Bobby	Col., Det.	2	16	1	3	4	6	....	....	....	....	....	....	1980-81	1982-83
• Crawford, Jack	Bos.	13	548	38	140	178	202	66	3	13	16	36	2	1937-38	1949-50
Crawford, Lou	Bos.	2	26	2	1	3	29	1	0	0	0	0	....	1989-90	1991-92
Crawford, Marc	Van.	6	176	19	31	50	229	20	1	2	3	44	....	1981-82	1986-87
• Crawford, Rusty	Ott., Tor.	2	38	10	8	18	117	2	2	1	3	9	1	1917-18	1918-19
Creighton, Adam	Buf., Chi., NYI, T.B., St.L.	14	708	187	216	403	1077	61	11	14	25	137	....	1983-84	1996-97
Creighton, Dave	Bos., Tor., Chi., NYR	12	616	140	174	314	223	51	11	13	24	20	....	1948-49	1959-60
• Creighton, Jimmy	Det.	1	11	1	0	1	2	....	....	....	....	....	....	1930-31	1930-31
Cressman, Dave	Min.	2	85	6	8	14	37	....	....	....	....	....	....	1974-75	1975-76
Cressman, Glen	Mtl.	1	4	0	0	0	2	....	....	....	....	....	....	1956-57	1956-57
Crisp, Terry	Bos., St.L., NYI, Phi.	11	536	67	134	201	135	110	15	28	43	40	2	1965-66	1976-77
Cristofoli, Ed	Mtl.	1	9	0	1	1	4	....	....	....	....	....	....	1989-90	1989-90
• Croghan, Maurice	Mtl.M.	1	16	0	0	0	4	....	....	....	....	....	....	1937-38	1937-38
Crombeen, Mike	Cle., St.L., Hfd.	8	475	55	68	123	218	27	6	2	8	32	....	1977-78	1984-85
Cronin, Shawn	Wsh., Wpg., Phi., S.J.	7	292	3	18	21	877	32	1	0	1	38	....	1988-89	1994-95
Cross, Cory	T.B., Tor., NYR, Edm., Pit., Det.	12	659	34	97	131	684	47	2	4	6	62	....	1993-94	2005-06
• Crossett, Stan	Phi.	1	21	0	0	0	10	....	....	....	....	....	....	1930-31	1930-31
Crossman, Doug	Chi., Phi., L.A., NYI, Hfd., Det., T.B., St.L.	14	914	105	359	464	534	97	12	39	51	105	....	1980-81	1993-94
Croteau, Gary	L.A., Det., Cal., K.C., Col.	12	684	144	175	319	143	11	3	2	5	8	....	1968-69	1979-80
Crowder, Bruce	Bos., Pit.	4	243	47	51	98	156	31	8	4	12	41	....	1981-82	1984-85
Crowder, Keith	Bos., L.A.	10	662	223	271	494	1354	85	14	22	36	218	....	1980-81	1989-90
Crowder, Troy	N.J., Det., L.A., Van.	7	150	9	7	16	433	4	0	0	0	22	....	1987-88	1996-97
Crowe, Phil	L.A., Phi., Ott., Nsh.	6	94	4	5	9	173	3	0	0	0	16	....	1993-94	1999-00
Crowley, Mike	Ana.	3	67	5	15	20	44	....	....	....	....	....	....	1997-98	2000-01
Crowley, Ted	Hfd., Col., NYI	2	34	2	4	6	12	....	....	....	....	....	....	1993-94	1998-99

Wayne Connelly

Rich Costello

Baldy Cotton

Yvan Cournoyer

Mathieu Darche

Joe Day

Lulu Denis

Gerard Desaulniers

				Regular Schedule					Playoffs							
	Name	NHL Teams	NHL Seasons	GP	G	A	TP	PIM	GP	G	A	TP	PIM	NHL Cup Wins	First NHL Season	Last NHL Season
	Crozier, Greg	Pit.	1	1	0	0	0	0	....	....	....	....	....	....	2000-01	2000-01
	Crozier, Joe	Tor.	1	5	0	3	3	2	....	....	....	....	....	....	1959-60	1959-60
•	Crutchfield, Nels	Mtl.	1	41	5	5	10	20	2	0	1	1	22	....	1934-35	1934-35
	Culhane, Jim	Hfd.	1	6	0	1	1	4	....	....	....	....	....	....	1989-90	1989-90
	Cullen, Barry	Tor., Det.	5	219	32	52	84	111	6	0	0	0	2	....	1955-56	1959-60
	Cullen, Brian	Tor., NYR	7	326	56	100	156	92	19	3	0	3	2	....	1954-55	1960-61
	Cullen, David	Phx., Min.	2	19	0	0	0	6	....	....	....	....	....	....	2000-01	2001-02
	Cullen, John	Pit., Hfd., Tor., T.B.	11	621	187	363	550	898	53	12	22	34	58	....	1988-89	1998-99
	Cullen, Ray	NYR, Det., Min., Van.	6	313	92	123	215	120	20	3	10	13	2	....	1965-66	1970-71
‡	Cullimore, Jassen	Van., Mtl., T.B., Chi., Fla.	15	812	26	85	111	704	35	1	3	4	24	1	1994-95	2010-11
	Cummins, Barry	Cal.	1	36	1	2	3	39	....	....	....	....	....	....	1973-74	1973-74
	Cummins, Jim	Det., Phi., T.B., Chi., Phx., Mtl., Ana., NYI, Col.	12	511	24	36	60	1538	37	1	2	3	43	....	1991-92	2003-04
	Cunneyworth, Randy	Buf., Pit., Wpg., Hfd., Chi., Ott.	16	866	189	225	414	1280	45	7	7	14	61	....	1980-81	1998-99
	Cunningham, Bob	NYR	2	4	0	1	1	0	....	....	....	....	....	....	1960-61	1961-62
•	Cunningham, Jim	Phi.	1	1	0	0	0	4	....	....	....	....	....	....	1977-78	1977-78
•	Cunningham, Les	NYA, Chi.	2	60	7	19	26	21	1	0	0	0	0	....	1936-37	1939-40
•	Cupolo, Bill	Bos.	1	47	11	13	24	10	7	1	2	3	0	....	1944-45	1944-45
	Curran, Brian	Bos., NYI, Tor., Buf., Wsh.	10	381	7	33	40	1461	24	0	1	1	122	....	1983-84	1993-94
	Currie, Dan	Edm., L.A.	4	22	2	1	3	4	....	....	....	....	....	....	1990-91	1993-94
	Currie, Glen	Wsh., L.A.	8	326	39	79	118	100	12	1	3	4	4	....	1979-80	1987-88
	Currie, Hugh	Mtl.	1	1	0	0	0	0	....	....	....	....	....	....	1950-51	1950-51
	Currie, Tony	St.L., Van., Hfd.	8	290	92	119	211	83	16	4	12	16	14	....	1977-78	1984-85
•	Curry, Floyd	Mtl.	11	601	105	99	204	147	91	23	17	40	38	4	1947-48	1957-58
	Curtale, Tony	Cgy.	1	2	0	0	0	0	....	....	....	....	....	....	1980-81	1980-81
	Curtis, Paul	Mtl., L.A., St.L.	4	185	3	34	37	161	5	0	0	0	2	....	1969-70	1972-73
	Cushenan, Ian	Chi., Mtl., NYR, Det.	5	129	3	11	14	134	....	....	....	....	....	1	1956-57	1963-64
	Cusson, Jean	Oak.	1	2	0	0	0	0	....	....	....	....	....	....	1967-68	1967-68
‡	Cutta, Jakub	Wsh.	3	8	0	0	0	0	....	....	....	....	....	....	2000-01	2003-04
	Cyr, Denis	Cgy., Chi., St.L.	6	193	41	43	84	36	4	0	0	0	0	....	1980-81	1985-86
•	Cyr, Paul	Buf., NYR, Hfd.	9	470	101	140	241	623	24	4	6	10	31	....	1982-83	1991-92
	Czerkawski, Mariusz	Bos., Edm., NYI, Mtl., Tor.	12	745	215	220	435	274	42	8	7	15	18	....	1993-94	2005-06

D

‡	Dackell, Andreas	Ott., Mtl.	8	613	91	159	250	162	44	5	5	10	10	....	1996-97	2003-04
	Dagenais, Pierre	N.J., Fla., Mtl.	5	142	35	23	58	58	8	0	1	1	6	....	2000-01	2005-06
	Dahl, Kevin	Cgy., Phx., Tor., CBJ	8	188	7	22	29	153	16	0	2	2	12	....	1992-93	2000-01
	Dahlen, Ulf	NYR, Min., Dal., S.J., Chi., Wsh.	14	966	301	354	655	230	85	15	25	40	12	....	1987-88	2002-03
	Dahlin, Kjell	Mtl.	3	166	57	59	116	10	35	6	11	17	6	1	1985-86	1987-88
	Dahlman, Toni	Ott.	2	22	1	1	2	0	....	....	....	....	....	....	2001-02	2002-03
	Dahlquist, Chris	Pit., Min., Cgy., Ott.	11	532	19	71	90	488	39	4	7	11	30	....	1985-86	1995-96
•	Dahlstrom, Cully	Chi.	8	342	88	118	206	58	29	6	8	14	4	1	1937-38	1944-45
	Daigle, Alain	Chi.	6	389	56	50	106	122	17	0	1	1	0	....	1974-75	1979-80
	Daigle, Alexandre	Ott., Phi., T.B., NYR, Pit., Min.	10	616	129	198	327	186	12	0	2	2	2	....	1993-94	2005-06
	Daigneault, J.J.	Van., Phi., Mtl., St.L., Pit., Ana., NYI, Nsh., Phx., Min.	16	899	53	197	250	687	99	5	26	31	100	1	1984-85	2000-01
	Dailey, Bob	Van., Phi.	9	561	94	231	325	814	63	12	34	46	105	....	1973-74	1981-82
•	Daley, Frank	Det.	1	5	0	0	0	0	2	0	0	0	0	....	1928-29	1928-29
	Daley, Pat	Wpg.	2	12	1	0	1	13	....	....	....	....	....	....	1979-80	1980-81
	Dalgarno, Brad	NYI	10	321	49	71	120	332	27	2	4	6	37	....	1985-86	1995-96
‡	Dallman, Kevin	Bos., St.L., L.A.	3	154	8	23	31	45	....	....	....	....	....	....	2005-06	2007-08
	Dallman, Marty	Tor.	2	6	0	1	1	0	....	....	....	....	....	....	1987-88	1988-89
	Dallman, Rod	NYI, Phi.	4	6	1	0	1	26	1	0	1	1	0	....	1987-88	1991-92
•	Dame, Bunny	Mtl.	1	34	2	5	7	4	....	....	....	....	....	....	1941-42	1941-42
•	Damore, Hank	NYR	1	4	1	0	1	2	....	....	....	....	....	....	1943-44	1943-44
	Damphousse, Vincent	Tor., Edm., Mtl., S.J.	18	1378	432	773	1205	1190	140	41	63	104	144	1	1986-87	2003-04
	Dandenault, Mathieu	Det., Mtl.	13	868	68	135	203	516	83	3	8	11	24	3	1995-96	2008-09
	Daneyko, Ken	N.J.	20	1283	36	142	178	2519	175	5	17	22	296	3	1983-84	2002-03
	Daniels, Jeff	Pit., Fla., Hfd., Car., Nsh.	12	425	17	26	43	83	41	3	5	8	2	1	1990-91	2002-03
	Daniels, Kimbi	Phi.	2	27	1	2	3	4	....	....	....	....	....	....	1990-91	1991-92
	Daniels, Scott	Hfd., Phi., N.J.	6	149	8	12	20	667	1	0	0	0	0	....	1992-93	1998-99
‡	Danton, Mike	N.J., St.L.	3	87	9	5	14	182	5	1	0	1	2	....	2000-01	2003-04
	Daoust, Dan	Mtl., Tor.	8	522	87	167	254	544	32	7	5	12	83	....	1982-83	1989-90
	Darby, Craig	Mtl., NYI, Phi., N.J.	9	196	21	35	56	32	....	....	....	....	....	....	1994-95	2003-04
	Darche, Mathieu	CBJ, Nsh., S.J., T.B., Mtl.	9	250	30	42	72	58	18	1	2	3	2	....	2000-01	2011-12
	Dark, Michael	St.L.	2	43	5	6	11	14	....	....	....	....	....	....	1986-87	1987-88
•	Darragh, Harold	Pit., Phi., Bos., Tor.	8	308	68	49	117	50	16	1	3	4	4	1	1925-26	1932-33
•	Darragh, Jack	Ott.	6	121	66	46	112	113	11	3	0	3	9	3	1917-18	1923-24
	David, Richard	Que.	3	31	4	4	8	10	1	0	0	0	0	....	1979-80	1982-83
•	Davidson, Bob	Tor.	12	491	94	160	254	398	79	5	17	22	76	2	1934-35	1945-46
•	Davidson, Gord	NYR	2	51	3	6	9	8	....	....	....	....	....	....	1942-43	1943-44
	Davidson, Matt	CBJ	3	56	5	7	12	28	....	....	....	....	....	....	2000-01	2002-03
‡	Davidsson, Johan	Ana., NYI	2	83	6	9	15	16	1	0	0	0	0	....	1998-99	1999-00
•	Davie, Bob	Bos.	3	41	0	1	1	25	....	....	....	....	....	....	1933-34	1935-36
•	Davies, Buck	NYR	1	....	....	....	....	....	1	0	0	0	0	....	1947-48	1947-48
•	Davis, Bob	Det.	1	3	0	0	0	0	....	....	....	....	....	....	1932-33	1932-33
	Davis, Kim	Pit., Tor.	4	36	5	7	12	51	4	0	0	0	0	....	1977-78	1980-81
•	Davis, Lorne	Mtl., Chi., Det., Bos.	6	95	8	12	20	20	18	3	1	4	10	1	1951-52	1959-60
	Davis, Mal	Det., Buf.	6	100	31	22	53	34	7	1	0	1	0	....	1978-79	1985-86
‡	Davis, Patrick	N.J.	2	9	1	0	1	0	....	....	....	....	....	....	2008-09	2009-10
•	Davison, Murray	Bos.	1	1	0	0	0	0	....	....	....	....	....	....	1965-66	1965-66
	Davydov, Evgeny	Wpg., Fla., Ott.	4	155	40	39	79	120	11	2	2	4	2	....	1991-92	1994-95
	Daw, Jeff	Col.	1	1	0	1	1	0	....	....	....	....	....	....	2001-02	2001-02
	Dawe, Jason	Buf., NYI, Mtl., NYR	8	366	86	90	176	162	22	4	3	7	18	....	1993-94	2001-02
•	Dawes, Bob	Tor., Mtl.	4	32	2	7	9	6	10	0	0	0	2	1	1946-47	1950-51
‡	Dawes, Nigel	NYR, Phx., Cgy., Atl., Mtl.	5	212	39	45	84	43	11	2	2	4	0	....	2006-07	2010-11
•	Day, Hap	Tor., NYA	14	581	86	116	202	601	53	4	7	11	56	1	1924-25	1937-38
	Day, Joe	Hfd., NYI	3	72	1	10	11	87	....	....	....	....	....	....	1991-92	1993-94
	Daze, Eric	Chi.	11	601	226	172	398	176	37	5	7	12	8	....	1994-95	2005-06
	de Vries, Greg	Edm., Nsh., Col., NYR, Ott., Atl.	13	878	48	146	194	780	111	8	14	22	91	1	1995-96	2008-09
	Dea, Billy	NYR, Det., Chi., Pit.	8	397	67	54	121	44	11	2	1	3	6	....	1953-54	1970-71
•	Deacon, Don	Det.	3	30	6	4	10	6	2	2	1	3	0	....	1936-37	1939-40
	Deadmarsh, Adam	Que., Col., L.A.	10	567	184	189	373	819	105	26	40	66	100	1	1994-95	2003-04
	Deadmarsh, Butch	Buf., Atl., K.C.	5	137	12	5	17	155	4	0	0	0	17	....	1970-71	1974-75
	Dean, Barry	Col., Phi.	3	165	25	56	81	146	....	....	....	....	....	....	1976-77	1978-79
	Dean, Kevin	N.J., Atl., Dal., Chi.	7	331	7	48	55	138	16	2	2	4	2	1	1994-95	2000-01
	Debenedet, Nelson	Det., Pit.	2	46	10	4	14	13	....	....	....	....	....	....	1973-74	1974-75
	DeBlois, Lucien	NYR, Col., Wpg., Mtl., Que., Tor.	15	993	249	276	525	814	52	7	6	13	38	1	1977-78	1991-92
	Debol, Dave	Hfd.	2	92	26	26	52	4	3	0	0	0	0	....	1979-80	1980-81
	DeBrusk, Louie	Edm., T.B., Phx., Chi.	11	401	24	17	41	1161	15	2	0	2	10	....	1991-92	2002-03
	DeFauw, Brad	Car.	1	9	3	0	3	2	....	....	....	....	....	....	2002-03	2002-03
	Defazio, Dean	Pit.	1	22	0	2	2	28	....	....	....	....	....	....	1983-84	1983-84
	DeGray, Dale	Cgy., Tor., L.A., Buf.	5	153	18	47	65	195	13	1	3	4	28	....	1985-86	1989-90
•	Delisle, Jonathan	Mtl.	1	1	0	0	0	0	....	....	....	....	....	....	1998-99	1998-99
	Delisle, Xavier	T.B., Mtl.	2	16	3	2	5	6	....	....	....	....	....	....	1998-99	2000-01
•	Delmonte, Armand	Bos.	1	1	0	0	0	0	....	....	....	....	....	....	1945-46	1945-46
‡	Delmore, Andy	Phi., Nsh., Buf., CBJ	7	283	43	58	101	105	20	6	2	8	16	....	1998-99	2005-06
	Delorme, Gilbert	Mtl., St.L., Que., Det., Pit.	9	541	31	92	123	520	56	1	9	10	56	....	1981-82	1989-90
	Delorme, Ron	Col., Van.	9	524	83	83	166	667	25	1	2	3	59	....	1976-77	1984-85
	Delory, Val	NYR	1	1	0	0	0	0	....	....	....	....	....	....	1948-49	1948-49
	Delparte, Guy	Col.	1	48	1	8	9	18	....	....	....	....	....	....	1976-77	1976-77
	Delvecchio, Alex	Det.	24	1549	456	825	1281	383	121	35	69	104	29	3	1950-51	1973-74
•	DeMarco, Ab	Chi., Tor., Bos., NYR	7	209	72	93	165	53	11	3	0	3	2	....	1938-39	1946-47
	DeMarco, Ab	NYR, St.L., Pit., Van., L.A., Bos.	9	344	44	80	124	75	25	1	2	3	17	....	1969-70	1978-79
•	Demers, Tony	Mtl., NYR	6	83	20	22	42	23	2	0	0	0	0	....	1937-38	1943-44
•	Demitra, Pavol	Ott., St.L., L.A., Min., Van.	16	847	304	464	768	284	94	23	36	59	34	....	1993-94	2009-10
	Dempsey, Nathan	Tor., Chi., L.A., Bos.	8	260	21	67	88	120	6	0	2	2	0	....	1996-97	2006-07
	Denis, Jean-Paul	NYR	2	10	0	2	2	2	....	....	....	....	....	....	1946-47	1949-50
	Denis, Lulu	Mtl.	2	3	0	1	1	0	....	....	....	....	....	....	1949-50	1950-51
•	Denneny, Corb	Tor., Ham., Chi.	9	176	103	42	145	148	6	1	0	1	7	2	1917-18	1927-28
•	Denneny, Cy	Ott., Bos.	12	328	248	85	333	301	25	16	2	18	23	5	1917-18	1928-29
	Dennis, Norm	St.L.	4	12	3	0	3	11	5	0	0	0	2	....	1968-69	1971-72
•	Denoird, Gerry	Tor.	1	17	0	1	1	0	....	....	....	....	....	....	1922-23	1922-23
	DePalma, Larry	Min., S.J., Pit.	7	148	21	20	41	408	3	0	0	0	6	....	1985-86	1993-94
	Derlago, Bill	Van., Tor., Bos., Wpg., Que.	9	555	189	227	416	247	13	5	0	5	8	....	1978-79	1986-87

Name	NHL Teams	NHL Seasons	Regular Schedule GP	G	A	TP	PIM	Playoffs GP	G	A	TP	PIM	NHL Cup Wins	First NHL Season	Last NHL Season
• Desaulniers, Gerard	Mtl.	3	8	0	2	2	4	....	....	....	....	....	....	1950-51	1953-54
Descoteaux, Matthieu	Mtl.	1	5	1	1	2	4	....	....	....	....	....	....	2000-01	2000-01
• Desilets, Joffre	Mtl., Chi.	5	192	37	45	82	57	7	1	0	1	7	....	1935-36	1939-40
Desjardins, Eric	Mtl., Phi.	17	1143	136	439	575	757	168	23	57	80	93	1	1988-89	2005-06
Desjardins, Martin	Mtl.	1	8	0	2	2	2	....	....	....	....	....	....	1989-90	1989-90
• Desjardins, Vic	Chi., NYR	2	87	6	15	21	27	16	0	0	0	0	....	1930-31	1931-32
Deslauriers, Jacques	Mtl.	1	2	0	0	0	0	....	....	....	....	....	....	1955-56	1955-56
Deuling, Jarrett	NYI	2	15	0	1	1	11	....	....	....	....	....	....	1995-96	1996-97
Devereaux, Boyd	Edm., Det., Phx., Tor.	11	627	67	112	179	205	27	3	4	7	4	1	1997-98	2008-09
Devine, Kevin	NYI	1	2	0	1	1	8	....	....	....	....	....	....	1982-83	1982-83
• Dewar, Tom	NYR	1	9	0	2	2	4	....	....	....	....	....	....	1943-44	1943-44
• Dewsbury, Al	Det., Chi.	9	347	30	78	108	365	14	1	5	6	16	1	1946-47	1955-56
Deziel, Michel	Buf.	1	....	....	....	....	....	1	0	0	0	0	....	1974-75	1974-75
• Dheere, Marcel	Mtl.	1	11	1	2	3	2	5	0	0	0	6	....	1942-43	1942-43
Diachuk, Edward	Det.	1	12	0	0	0	19	....	....	....	....	....	....	1960-61	1960-61
• Dick, Harry	Chi.	1	12	0	1	1	12	....	....	....	....	....	....	1946-47	1946-47
• Dickens, Ernie	Tor., Chi.	6	278	12	44	56	98	13	0	0	0	4	1	1941-42	1950-51
Dickenson, Herb	NYR	2	48	18	17	35	10	....	....	....	....	....	....	1951-52	1952-53
Diduck, Gerald	NYI, Mtl., Van., Chi., Hfd., Phx., Tor., Dal.	17	932	56	156	212	1612	114	8	16	24	212	....	1984-85	2000-01
Dietrich, Don	Chi., N.J.	2	28	0	7	7	10	....	....	....	....	....	....	1983-84	1985-86
• Dill, Bob	NYR	2	76	15	15	30	135	....	....	....	....	....	....	1943-44	1944-45
• Dillabough, Bob	Det., Bos., Pit., Oak.	9	283	32	54	86	76	17	3	0	3	0	....	1961-62	1969-70
• Dillon, Cecil	NYR, Det.	10	453	167	131	298	105	43	14	9	23	14	1	1930-31	1939-40
Dillon, Gary	Col.	1	13	1	1	2	29	....	....	....	....	....	....	1980-81	1980-81
Dillon, Wayne	NYR, Wpg.	4	229	43	66	109	60	3	0	1	1	0	....	1975-76	1979-80
DiMaio, Rob	NYI, T.B., Phi., Bos., NYR, Car., Dal.	17	894	106	171	277	840	62	7	9	16	40	....	1988-89	2005-06
‡ Dimitrakos, Niko	S.J., Phi.	4	158	24	38	62	95	20	1	8	9	10	....	2002-03	2006-07
Dineen, Bill	Det., Chi.	5	323	51	44	95	122	37	1	1	2	18	2	1953-54	1957-58
• Dineen, Gary	Min.	1	4	0	1	1	0	....	....	....	....	....	....	1968-69	1968-69
Dineen, Gord	NYI, Min., Pit., Ott.	13	528	16	90	106	695	40	1	7	8	68	....	1982-83	1994-95
Dineen, Kevin	Hfd., Phi., Car., Ott., CBJ	19	1188	355	405	760	2229	59	23	18	41	127	....	1984-85	2002-03
Dineen, Peter	L.A., Det.	2	13	0	2	2	13	....	....	....	....	....	....	1986-87	1989-90
Dingman, Chris	Cgy., Col., Car., T.B.	8	385	15	19	34	769	52	2	5	7	100	2	1997-98	2005-06
• Dinsmore, Chuck	Mtl.M.	4	100	6	2	8	50	8	1	0	1	2	1	1924-25	1929-30
Dionne, Gilbert	Mtl., Phi., Fla.	6	223	61	79	140	108	39	10	12	22	34	1	1990-91	1995-96
Dionne, Marcel	Det., L.A., NYR	18	1348	731	1040	1771	600	49	21	24	45	17	....	1971-72	1988-89
DiPenta, Joe	Atl., Ana.	4	174	6	17	23	110	32	0	0	0	17	1	2002-03	2007-08
‡ DiPietro, Paul	Mtl., Tor., L.A.	6	192	31	49	80	96	31	11	10	21	10	1	1991-92	1996-97
Dirk, Robert	St.L., Van., Chi., Ana., Mtl.	9	402	13	29	42	786	39	0	1	1	56	....	1987-88	1995-96
‡ Divisek, Tomas	Phi.	2	5	1	0	1	0	....	....	....	....	....	....	2000-01	2001-02
Djoos, Per	Det., NYR	3	82	2	31	33	58	....	....	....	....	....	....	1990-91	1992-93
Doak, Gary	Det., Bos., Van., NYR	16	789	23	107	130	908	78	2	4	6	121	1	1965-66	1980-81
Dobbin, Brian	Phi., Bos.	5	63	7	8	15	61	2	0	0	0	17	....	1986-87	1991-92
Dobson, Jim	Min., Col., Que.	4	12	0	0	0	6	....	....	....	....	....	....	1979-80	1983-84
‡ Doell, Kevin	Atl.	1	8	0	1	1	4	....	....	....	....	....	....	2007-08	2007-08
• Doherty, Fred	Mtl.	1	1	0	0	0	0	....	....	....	....	....	....	1918-19	1918-19
Doig, Jason	Wpg., Phx., NYR, Wsh.	7	158	6	18	24	285	6	0	1	1	6	....	1995-96	2003-04
Dollas, Bobby	Wpg., Que., Det., Ana., Edm., Pit., Ott., Cgy., S.J.	16	646	42	96	138	467	47	2	1	3	41	....	1983-84	2000-01
Dome, Robert	Pit., Cgy.	3	53	7	7	14	12	....	....	....	....	....	....	1997-98	2002-03
‡ Domenichelli, Hnat	Hfd., Cgy., Atl., Min.	7	267	52	61	113	104	....	....	....	....	....	....	1996-97	2002-03
Domi, Tie	Tor., NYR, Wpg.	16	1020	104	141	245	3515	98	7	12	19	238	....	1989-90	2005-06
Donaldson, Gary	Chi.	1	1	0	0	0	0	....	....	....	....	....	....	1973-74	1973-74
Donatelli, Clark	Min., Bos.	2	35	3	4	7	39	2	0	0	0	0	....	1989-90	1991-92
Donato, Ted	Bos., NYI, Ott., Ana., Dal., St.L., L.A., NYR	13	796	150	197	347	396	58	8	10	18	22	....	1991-92	2003-04
• Donnelly, Babe	Mtl.M.	1	34	0	1	1	14	2	0	0	0	0	....	1926-27	1926-27
Donnelly, Dave	Bos., Chi., Edm.	5	137	15	24	39	150	5	0	0	0	0	....	1983-84	1987-88
Donnelly, Gord	Que., Wpg., Buf., Dal.	12	554	28	41	69	2069	26	0	2	2	61	....	1983-84	1994-95
Donnelly, Mike	NYR, Buf., L.A., Dal., NYI	11	465	114	121	235	255	47	12	12	24	30	....	1986-87	1996-97
Donovan, Shean	S.J., Col., Atl., Pit., Cgy., Bos., Ott.	15	951	112	129	241	705	49	6	6	12	39	....	1994-95	2009-10
Doornbosch, Jamie	NYI	1	1	0	0	0	0	....	....	....	....	....	....	2010-11	2010-11
Dopita, Jiri	Phi., Edm.	2	73	12	21	33	19	....	....	....	....	....	....	2001-02	2002-03
• Doran, John	NYA, Det., Mtl.	5	98	5	10	15	110	3	0	0	0	0	....	1933-34	1939-40
• Doran, Lloyd	Det.	1	24	3	2	5	10	....	....	....	....	....	....	1946-47	1946-47
• Doraty, Ken	Chi., Tor., Det.	5	103	15	26	41	24	15	7	2	9	2	....	1926-27	1937-38
Dore, Andre	NYR, St.L., Que.	7	257	14	81	95	261	23	1	2	3	32	....	1978-79	1984-85
Dore, Daniel	Que.	2	17	2	3	5	59	....	....	....	....	....	....	1989-90	1990-91
Dorey, Jim	Tor., NYR	4	232	25	74	99	553	11	0	2	2	40	....	1968-69	1971-72
Dorion, Dan	N.J.	2	4	1	1	2	2	....	....	....	....	....	....	1985-86	1987-88
Dornhoefer, Gary	Bos., Phi.	14	787	214	328	542	1291	80	17	19	36	203	2	1963-64	1977-78
• Dorohoy, Eddie	Mtl.	1	16	0	0	0	6	....	....	....	....	....	....	1948-49	1948-49
Douglas, Jordy	Hfd., Min., Wpg.	6	268	76	62	138	160	6	0	0	0	4	....	1979-80	1984-85
• Douglas, Kent	Tor., Oak., Det.	7	428	33	115	148	631	19	1	3	4	33	3	1962-63	1968-69
• Douglas, Les	Det.	4	52	6	12	18	8	10	3	2	5	2	1	1940-41	1946-47
Doull, Doug	Bos., Wsh.	2	37	0	1	1	151	....	....	....	....	....	....	2003-04	2005-06
Douris, Peter	Wpg., Bos., Ana., Dal.	11	321	54	67	121	80	27	3	5	8	14	....	1985-86	1997-98
Dowd, Jim	N.J., Van., NYI, Cgy., Edm., Min., Mtl., Chi., Col., Phi.	16	728	71	168	239	390	99	9	17	26	50	1	1991-92	2007-08
Downey, Aaron	Bos., Chi., Dal., St.L., Mtl., Det.	9	243	8	10	18	494	5	0	0	0	8	1	1999-00	2008-09
• Downie, Dave	Tor.	1	11	0	1	1	2	....	....	....	....	....	....	1932-33	1932-33
Doyon, Mario	Chi., Que.	3	28	3	4	7	16	....	....	....	....	....	....	1988-89	1990-91
Drake, Dallas	Det., Wpg., Phx., St.L.	15	1009	177	300	477	885	90	14	19	33	79	1	1992-93	2007-08
• Draper, Bruce	Tor.	1	1	0	0	0	0	....	....	....	....	....	....	1962-63	1962-63
Draper, Kris	Wpg., Det.	20	1157	161	203	364	790	222	24	22	46	160	4	1990-91	2010-11
• Drillon, Gordie	Tor., Mtl.	7	311	155	139	294	56	50	26	15	41	10	1	1936-37	1942-43
Driscoll, Peter	Edm.	2	60	3	8	11	97	3	0	0	0	0	....	1979-80	1980-81
Driver, Bruce	N.J., NYR	15	922	96	390	486	670	108	10	40	50	64	1	1983-84	1997-98
Drolet, Rene	Phi., Det.	2	2	0	0	0	0	....	....	....	....	....	....	1971-72	1974-75
Droppa, Ivan	Chi.	2	19	0	1	1	14	....	....	....	....	....	....	1993-94	1995-96
• Drouillard, Clarence	Det.	1	10	0	1	1	0	....	....	....	....	....	....	1937-38	1937-38
Drouin, Jude	Mtl., Min., NYI, Wpg.	12	666	151	305	456	346	72	27	41	68	33	....	1968-69	1980-81
Drouin, P.C.	Bos.	1	3	0	0	0	0	....	....	....	....	....	....	1996-97	1996-97
• Drouin, Polly	Mtl.	7	160	23	50	73	80	5	0	1	1	5	....	1934-35	1940-41
Druce, John	Wsh., Wpg., L.A., Phi.	10	531	113	126	239	347	53	17	6	23	38	....	1988-89	1997-98
Druken, Harold	Van., Car., Tor.	5	146	27	36	63	36	4	0	1	1	0	....	1999-00	2003-04
Drulia, Stan	T.B.	3	126	15	27	42	52	....	....	....	....	....	....	1992-93	2000-01
• Drummond, Jim	NYR	1	2	0	0	0	0	....	....	....	....	....	....	1944-45	1944-45
Drury, Chris	Col., Cgy., Buf., NYR	12	892	255	360	615	468	135	47	42	89	46	1	1998-99	2010-11
• Drury, Herb	Pit., Phi.	6	213	24	13	37	203	4	1	1	2	0	....	1925-26	1930-31
Drury, Ted	Cgy., Hfd., Ott., Ana., NYI, CBJ	8	414	41	52	93	367	14	1	0	1	4	....	1993-94	2000-01
‡ Dube, Christian	NYR	2	33	1	1	2	4	3	0	0	0	0	....	1996-97	1998-99
Dube, Gilles	Mtl., Det.	2	12	1	2	3	2	2	0	0	0	0	1	1949-50	1953-54
Dube, Norm	K.C.	2	57	8	10	18	54	....	....	....	....	....	....	1974-75	1975-76
Duberman, Justin	Pit.	1	4	0	0	0	0	....	....	....	....	....	....	1993-94	1993-94
Dubinsky, Steve	Chi., Cgy., Nsh., St.L.	10	375	25	45	70	164	10	1	0	1	14	....	1993-94	2002-03
• Duchesne, Gaetan	Wsh., Que., Min., S.J., Fla.	14	1028	179	254	433	617	84	14	13	27	97	....	1981-82	1994-95
Duchesne, Steve	L.A., Phi., Que., St.L., Ott., Det.	16	1113	227	525	752	824	121	16	61	77	96	1	1986-87	2001-02
Dudley, Rick	Buf., Wpg.	6	309	75	99	174	292	25	7	2	9	69	....	1972-73	1980-81
Duerden, Dave	Fla.	1	2	0	0	0	0	....	....	....	....	....	....	1999-00	1999-00
Duff, Dick	Tor., NYR, Mtl., L.A., Buf.	18	1030	283	289	572	743	114	30	49	79	78	6	1954-55	1971-72
Dufour, Luc	Bos., Que., St.L.	3	167	23	21	44	199	18	1	0	1	32	....	1982-83	1984-85
Dufour, Marc	NYR, L.A.	3	14	1	0	1	2	....	....	....	....	....	....	1963-64	1968-69
Dufresne, Donald	Mtl., T.B., L.A., St.L., Edm.	9	268	6	36	42	258	34	1	3	4	47	1	1988-89	1996-97
• Duggan, John	Ott.	1	27	0	0	0	0	2	0	0	0	0	....	1925-26	1925-26
Duggan, Ken	Min.	1	1	0	0	0	0	....	....	....	....	....	....	1987-88	1987-88
Duguay, Ron	NYR, Det., Pit., L.A.	12	864	274	346	620	582	89	31	22	53	118	....	1977-78	1988-89
• Duguid, Lorne	Mtl.M., Det., Bos.	6	135	9	15	24	57	4	1	0	1	6	....	1931-32	1936-37
• Dukowski, Duke	Chi., NYA, NYR	5	200	16	30	46	172	6	0	0	0	6	....	1926-27	1933-34
• Dumart, Woody	Bos.	16	772	211	218	429	99	88	12	15	27	23	2	1935-36	1953-54
‡ Dumont, J.P.	Chi., Buf., Nsh.	12	822	214	309	523	364	51	17	17	34	28	....	1998-99	2010-11
Dunbar, Dale	Van., Bos.	2	2	0	0	0	2	....	....	....	....	....	....	1985-86	1988-89
• Duncan, Art	Det., Tor.	5	156	18	16	34	225	5	0	0	0	4	....	1926-27	1930-31
Duncan, Iain	Wpg.	4	127	34	55	89	149	11	0	3	3	6	....	1986-87	1990-91
Duncanson, Craig	L.A., Wpg., NYR	7	38	5	4	9	61	....	....	....	....	....	....	1985-86	1992-93

Al Dewsbury

Bill Dineen

Marc Dufour

Blake Dunlop

Dallas Eakins

Roland Eriksson

Andre Faust

Sid Finney

			Regular Schedule					Playoffs					NHL	First	Last
Name	NHL Teams	NHL Seasons	GP	G	A	TP	PIM	GP	G	A	TP	PIM	Cup Wins	NHL Season	NHL Season
Dundas, Rocky	Tor.	1	5	0	0	0	14	....	....	....	....	....	....	1989-90	1989-90
● Dunlap, Frank	Tor.	1	15	0	1	1	2	....	....	....	....	....	....	1943-44	1943-44
Dunlop, Blake	Min., Phi., St.L., Det.	11	550	130	274	404	172	40	4	10	14	18	....	1973-74	1983-84
Dunn, Dave	Van., Tor.	3	184	14	41	55	313	10	1	1	2	41	....	1973-74	1975-76
Dunn, Richie	Buf., Cgy., Hfd.	12	483	36	140	176	314	36	3	15	18	24	....	1977-78	1988-89
Dupere, Denis	Tor., Wsh., St.L., K.C., Col.	8	421	80	99	179	66	16	1	0	1	0	....	1970-71	1977-78
Dupont, Andre	NYR, St.L., Phi., Que.	13	800	59	185	244	1986	140	14	18	32	352	2	1970-71	1982-83
‡ Dupont, Brodie	NYR	1	1	0	0	0	0	....	....	....	....	....	....	2010-11	2010-11
Dupont, Jerome	Chi., Tor.	6	214	7	29	36	468	20	0	2	2	56	....	1981-82	1986-87
‡ DuPont, Micki	Cgy., Pit., St.L.	4	23	1	3	4	12	....	....	....	....	....	....	2001-02	2007-08
Dupont, Norm	Mtl., Wpg., Hfd.	5	256	55	85	140	52	13	4	2	6	0	....	1979-80	1983-84
● Dupre, Yanick	Phi.	3	35	2	0	2	16	....	....	....	....	....	....	1991-92	1995-96
● Durbano, Steve	St.L., Pit., K.C., Col.	6	220	13	60	73	1127	5	0	2	2	8	....	1972-73	1978-79
Duris, Vitezslav	Tor.	2	89	3	20	23	62	3	0	1	1	2	....	1980-81	1982-83
‡ Durno, Chris	Col.	2	43	4	4	8	47	1	0	0	0	0	....	2008-09	2009-10
Dusablon, Benoit	NYR	1	3	0	0	0	2	....	....	....	....	....	....	2003-04	2003-04
● Dussault, Norm	Mtl.	4	206	31	62	93	47	7	3	1	4	0	....	1947-48	1950-51
● Dutton, Red	Mtl.M., NYA	10	449	29	67	96	871	18	1	0	1	33	....	1926-27	1935-36
● Dvorak, Miroslav	Phi.	3	193	11	74	85	51	18	0	2	2	6	....	1982-83	1984-85
Dwyer, Gordie	T.B., NYR, Mtl.	5	108	0	5	5	394	....	....	....	....	....	....	1999-00	2003-04
Dwyer, Mike	Col., Cgy.	4	31	2	6	8	25	1	1	0	1	0	....	1978-79	1981-82
● Dyck, Henry	NYR	1	1	0	0	0	0	....	....	....	....	....	....	1943-44	1943-44
● Dye, Babe	Tor., Ham., Chi., NYA	11	271	201	47	248	221	10	2	0	2	11	1	1919-20	1930-31
Dykhuis, Karl	Chi., Phi., T.B., Mtl.	12	644	42	91	133	495	62	8	10	18	50	....	1991-92	2003-04
Dykstra, Steve	Buf., Edm., Pit., Hfd.	5	217	8	32	40	545	1	0	0	0	2	....	1985-86	1989-90
● Dyte, Jack	Chi.	1	27	1	0	1	31	....	....	....	....	....	....	1943-44	1943-44
Dziedzic, Joe	Pit., Phx.	3	130	14	14	28	131	21	1	3	4	23	....	1995-96	1998-99
E															
Eagles, Mike	Que., Chi., Wpg., Wsh.	16	853	74	122	196	928	44	2	6	8	34	....	1982-83	1999-00
Eakin, Bruce	Cgy., Det.	4	13	2	2	4	4	....	....	....	....	....	....	1981-82	1985-86
Eakins, Dallas	Wpg., Fla., St.L., Phx., NYR, Tor., NYI, Cgy.	10	120	0	9	9	208	5	0	0	0	4	....	1992-93	2001-02
‡ Earl, Robbie	Tor., Min.	3	47	6	1	7	6	....	....	....	....	....	....	2007-08	2010-11
Eastwood, Mike	Tor., Wpg., Phx., NYR, St.L., Chi., Pit.	13	783	87	149	236	354	97	8	11	19	64	....	1991-92	2003-04
Eatough, Jeff	Buf.	1	1	0	0	0	0	....	....	....	....	....	....	1981-82	1981-82
Eaves, Mike	Min., Cgy.	8	324	83	143	226	80	43	7	10	17	14	....	1978-79	1985-86
Eaves, Murray	Wpg., Det.	8	57	4	13	17	9	4	0	1	1	2	....	1980-81	1989-90
Ecclestone, Tim	St.L., Det., Tor., Atl.	11	692	126	233	359	344	48	6	11	17	76	....	1967-68	1977-78
Edberg, Rolf	Wsh.	3	184	45	58	103	24	....	....	....	....	....	....	1978-79	1980-81
● Eddolls, Frank	Mtl., NYR	8	317	23	43	66	114	31	0	2	2	10	1	1944-45	1951-52
Edestrand, Darryl	St.L., Phi., Pit., Bos., L.A.	10	455	34	90	124	404	42	3	9	12	57	....	1967-68	1978-79
Edmundson, Garry	Mtl., Tor.	3	43	4	6	10	49	11	0	1	1	8	....	1951-52	1960-61
Edur, Tom	Col., Pit.	2	158	17	70	87	67	....	....	....	....	....	....	1976-77	1977-78
● Egan, Pat	NYA, Bro., Det., Bos., NYR	11	554	77	153	230	776	46	9	4	13	48	....	1939-40	1950-51
Egeland, Allan	T.B.	3	17	0	0	0	16	....	....	....	....	....	....	1995-96	1997-98
Egers, Jack	NYR, St.L., Wsh.	7	284	64	69	133	154	32	5	6	11	32	....	1969-70	1975-76
● Ehman, Gerry	Bos., Det., Tor., Oak., Cal.	9	429	96	118	214	100	41	10	10	20	12	1	1957-58	1970-71
Eisenhut, Neil	Van., Cgy.	2	16	1	3	4	21	....	....	....	....	....	....	1993-94	1994-95
Eklund, Pelle	Phi., Dal.	9	594	120	335	455	109	66	10	36	46	8	....	1985-86	1993-94
Ekman, Nils	T.B., S.J., Pit.	5	264	60	91	151	188	28	2	5	7	16	....	1999-00	2006-07
Eldebrink, Anders	Van., Que.	2	55	3	11	14	29	14	0	0	0	10	....	1981-82	1982-83
Elich, Matt	T.B.	2	16	1	1	2	0	....	....	....	....	....	....	1999-00	2000-01
● Elik, Bo	Det.	1	3	0	0	0	0	....	....	....	....	....	....	1962-63	1962-63
Elik, Todd	L.A., Min., Edm., S.J., St.L., Bos.	8	448	110	219	329	453	52	15	27	42	48	....	1989-90	1996-97
Ellett, Dave	Wpg., Tor., N.J., Bos., St.L.	16	1129	153	415	568	985	116	11	46	57	87	....	1984-85	1999-00
● Elliott, Fred	Ott.	1	43	2	0	2	6	....	....	....	....	....	....	1928-29	1928-29
Ellis, Ron	Tor.	16	1034	332	308	640	207	70	18	8	26	20	1	1963-64	1980-81
‡ Ellison, Matt	Chi., Phi.	3	43	3	11	14	19	....	....	....	....	....	....	2003-04	2006-07
Elomo, Miika	Wsh.	1	2	0	1	1	2	....	....	....	....	....	....	1999-00	1999-00
Eloranta, Kari	Cgy., St.L.	5	267	13	103	116	155	26	1	7	8	19	....	1981-82	1986-87
Eloranta, Mikko	Bos., L.A.	4	264	32	44	76	186	7	1	1	2	2	....	1999-00	2002-03
Elynuik, Pat	Wpg., Wsh., T.B., Ott.	9	506	154	188	342	459	20	6	9	15	25	....	1987-88	1995-96
● Emberg, Eddie	Mtl.	1	....	....	....	....	....	2	1	0	1	0	....	1944-45	1944-45
Emerson, Nelson	St.L., Wpg., Hfd., Car., Chi., Ott., Atl., L.A.	12	771	195	293	488	575	40	7	15	22	33	....	1990-91	2001-02
Emma, David	N.J., Bos., Fla.	5	34	5	6	11	2	....	....	....	....	....	....	1992-93	2000-01
Emmons, Gary	S.J.	1	3	1	0	1	0	....	....	....	....	....	....	1993-94	1993-94
Emmons, John	Ott., T.B., Bos.	3	85	2	4	6	64	....	....	....	....	....	....	1999-00	2001-02
● Emms, Hap	Mtl.M., NYA, Det., Bos.	10	320	36	53	89	311	14	0	0	0	12	....	1926-27	1937-38
Endean, Craig	Wpg.	1	2	0	1	1	0	....	....	....	....	....	....	1986-87	1986-87
Endicott, Shane	Pit.	2	45	1	2	3	47	....	....	....	....	....	....	2001-02	2005-06
Engblom, Brian	Mtl., Wsh., L.A., Buf., Cgy.	11	659	29	177	206	599	48	3	9	12	43	2	1976-77	1986-87
Engele, Jerry	Min.	3	100	2	13	15	162	2	0	1	1	0	....	1975-76	1977-78
English, John	L.A.	1	3	1	3	4	4	1	0	0	0	0	....	1987-88	1987-88
Ennis, Jim	Edm.	1	5	1	0	1	10	....	....	....	....	....	....	1987-88	1987-88
● Erickson, Aut	Bos., Chi., Tor., Oak.	7	226	7	24	31	182	7	0	0	0	2	1	1959-60	1969-70
Erickson, Bryan	Wsh., L.A., Pit., Wpg.	9	351	80	125	205	141	14	3	4	7	7	....	1983-84	1993-94
Erickson, Grant	Bos., Min.	2	6	1	0	1	0	....	....	....	....	....	....	1968-69	1969-70
‡ Eriksson, Anders	Det., Chi., Fla., Tor., CBJ, Cgy., Phx., NYR	13	572	22	154	176	242	36	0	6	6	18	1	1995-96	2009-10
Eriksson, Peter	Edm.	1	20	3	3	6	24	....	....	....	....	....	....	1989-90	1989-90
Eriksson, Roland	Min., Van.	3	193	48	95	143	26	2	1	0	1	0	....	1976-77	1978-79
Eriksson, Thomas	Phi.	5	208	22	76	98	107	19	0	3	3	12	....	1980-81	1985-86
Erixon, Jan	NYR	10	556	57	159	216	167	58	7	7	14	16	....	1983-84	1992-93
Errey, Bob	Pit., Buf., S.J., Det., Dal., NYR	15	895	170	212	382	1005	99	13	16	29	109	2	1983-84	1997-98
Esau, Len	Tor., Que., Cgy., Edm.	4	27	0	10	10	24	....	....	....	....	....	....	1991-92	1994-95
Esposito, Phil	Chi., Bos., NYR	18	1282	717	873	1590	910	130	61	76	137	138	2	1963-64	1980-81
● Evans, Chris	Tor., Buf., St.L., Det., K.C.	5	241	19	42	61	143	12	1	1	2	8	....	1969-70	1974-75
Evans, Daryl	L.A., Wsh., Tor.	6	113	22	30	52	25	11	5	8	13	12	....	1981-82	1986-87
Evans, Doug	St.L., Wpg., Phi.	8	355	48	87	135	502	22	3	4	7	38	....	1985-86	1992-93
● Evans, Jack	NYR, Chi.	14	752	19	80	99	989	56	2	2	4	97	1	1948-49	1962-63
Evans, Kevin	Min., S.J.	2	9	0	1	1	44	....	....	....	....	....	....	1990-91	1991-92
Evans, Paul	Tor.	2	11	1	1	2	21	2	0	0	0	0	....	1976-77	1977-78
Evans, Paul	Phi.	3	103	14	25	39	34	1	0	0	0	0	....	1978-79	1982-83
Evans, Shawn	St.L., NYI	2	9	1	0	1	2	....	....	....	....	....	....	1985-86	1989-90
● Evans, Stewart	Det., Mtl.M., Mtl.	8	367	28	49	77	425	26	0	0	0	20	1	1930-31	1938-39
Evason, Dean	Wsh., Hfd., S.J., Dal., Cgy.	13	803	139	233	372	1002	55	9	20	29	132	....	1983-84	1995-96
Ewen, Todd	St.L., Mtl., Ana., S.J.	11	518	36	40	76	1911	26	0	0	0	87	1	1986-87	1996-97
● Ezinicki, Bill	Tor., Bos., NYR	9	368	79	105	184	713	40	5	8	13	87	3	1944-45	1954-55
F															
‡ Fahey, Brian	Wsh.	1	7	0	1	1	2	....	....	....	....	....	....	2010-11	2010-11
Fahey, Jim	S.J., N.J.	4	92	1	24	25	67	2	0	0	0	0	....	2002-03	2006-07
Fahey, Trevor	NYR	1	1	0	0	0	0	....	....	....	....	....	....	1964-65	1964-65
Fairbairn, Bill	NYR, Min., St.L.	11	658	162	261	423	173	54	13	22	35	42	....	1968-69	1978-79
Fairchild, Kelly	Tor., Dal., Col.	4	34	2	3	5	6	....	....	....	....	....	....	1995-96	2001-02
Falkenberg, Bob	Det.	5	54	1	5	6	26	....	....	....	....	....	....	1966-67	1971-72
Falloon, Pat	S.J., Phi., Ott., Edm., Pit.	9	575	143	179	322	141	66	11	7	18	16	....	1991-92	1999-00
Farkas, Jeff	Tor., Atl.	4	11	0	2	2	6	5	1	0	1	0	....	1999-00	2002-03
● Farrant, Walt	Chi.	1	1	0	0	0	0	....	....	....	....	....	....	1943-44	1943-44
Farrell, Mike	Wsh., Nsh.	3	13	0	0	0	2	....	....	....	....	....	....	2001-02	2003-04
Farrish, Dave	NYR, Que., Tor.	7	430	17	110	127	440	14	0	2	2	24	....	1976-77	1983-84
Fashoway, Gordie	Chi.	1	13	3	2	5	14	....	....	....	....	....	....	1950-51	1950-51
Fast, Brad	Car.	1	1	1	0	1	0	....	....	....	....	....	....	2003-04	2003-04
‡ Fata, Drew	NYI	2	8	1	1	2	9	1	0	0	0	0	....	2006-07	2007-08
‡ Fata, Rico	Cgy., NYR, Pit., Atl., Wsh.	8	230	27	36	63	104	....	....	....	....	....	....	1998-99	2006-07
Faubert, Mario	Pit.	7	231	21	90	111	292	10	2	2	4	6	....	1974-75	1981-82
Faulkner, Alex	Tor., Det.	3	101	15	17	32	15	12	5	0	5	2	....	1961-62	1963-64
Fauss, Ted	Tor.	2	28	0	2	2	15	....	....	....	....	....	....	1986-87	1987-88
Faust, Andre	Phi.	2	47	10	7	17	14	....	....	....	....	....	....	1992-93	1993-94
Feamster, Dave	Chi.	4	169	13	24	37	154	33	3	5	8	61	....	1981-82	1984-85
Featherstone, Glen	St.L., Bos., NYR, Hfd., Cgy.	9	384	19	61	80	939	28	0	2	2	103	....	1988-89	1996-97
Featherstone, Tony	Oak., Cal., Min.	3	130	17	21	38	65	2	0	0	0	0	....	1969-70	1973-74

Name	NHL Teams	NHL Seasons	Regular Schedule					Playoffs					NHL Cup Wins	First NHL Season	Last NHL Season
			GP	G	A	TP	PIM	GP	G	A	TP	PIM			
Federko, Bernie	St.L., Det.	14	1000	369	761	1130	487	91	35	66	101	83	....	1976-77	1989-90
‡ Fedorov, Fedor	Van., NYR	3	18	0	2	2	14	....	....	....	....	....	....	2002-03	2005-06
‡ Fedorov, Sergei	Det., Ana., CBJ, Wsh.	18	1248	483	696	1179	839	183	52	124	176	133	3	1990-91	2008-09
Fedoruk, Todd	Phi., Ana., Dal., Min., Phx., T.B.	9	545	32	65	97	1050	25	1	1	2	54	....	2000-01	2009-10
Fedotov, Anatoli	Wpg., Ana.	2	4	0	2	2	0	....	....	....	....	....	....	1992-93	1993-94
Fedyk, Brent	Det., Phi., Dal., NYR	10	470	97	112	209	308	16	3	2	5	12	....	1987-88	1998-99
Felix, Chris	Wsh.	4	35	1	12	13	10	2	0	1	1	0	....	1987-88	1990-91
Felsner, Brian	Chi.	1	12	1	3	4	12	....	....	....	....	....	....	1997-98	1997-98
Felsner, Denny	St.L.	4	18	1	4	5	6	10	2	3	5	2	....	1991-92	1994-95
Feltrin, Tony	Pit., NYR	4	48	3	3	6	65	....	....	....	....	....	....	1980-81	1985-86
Fenton, Paul	Hfd., NYR, L.A., Wpg., Tor., Cgy., S.J.	8	411	100	83	183	198	17	4	1	5	27	....	1984-85	1991-92
Fenyves, David	Buf., Phi.	9	206	3	32	35	119	11	0	0	0	9	....	1982-83	1990-91
Ference, Brad	Fla., Phx., Cgy.	6	250	4	30	34	565	....	....	....	....	....	....	1999-00	2006-07
Fergus, Tom	Bos., Tor., Van.	12	726	235	346	581	499	65	21	17	38	48	....	1981-82	1992-93
Ferguson, Craig	Mtl., Cgy., Fla.	5	27	1	1	2	6	....	....	....	....	....	....	1993-94	1999-00
Ferguson, George	Tor., Pit., Min.	12	797	160	238	398	431	86	14	23	37	44	....	1972-73	1983-84
• Ferguson, John	Mtl.	8	500	145	158	303	1214	85	20	18	38	260	5	1963-64	1970-71
• Ferguson, Lorne	Bos., Det., Chi.	8	422	82	80	162	193	31	6	3	9	24	....	1949-50	1958-59
Ferguson, Norm	Oak., Cal.	4	279	73	66	139	72	10	1	4	5	7	....	1968-69	1971-72
Ferguson, Scott	Edm., Ana., Min.	7	218	7	14	21	310	11	0	0	0	8	....	1997-98	2005-06
Ferland, Jonathan	Mtl.	1	7	1	0	1	2	....	....	....	....	....	....	2005-06	2005-06
Ferner, Mark	Buf., Wsh., Ana., Det.	6	91	3	10	13	51	....	....	....	....	....	....	1986-87	1994-95
Ferraro, Chris	NYR, Pit., Edm., NYI, Wsh.	6	74	7	9	16	57	....	....	....	....	....	....	1995-96	2001-02
Ferraro, Peter	NYR, Pit., Bos., Wsh.	6	92	9	15	24	58	2	0	0	0	0	....	1995-96	2001-02
Ferraro, Ray	Hfd., NYI, NYR, L.A., Atl., St.L.	18	1258	408	490	898	1288	68	21	22	43	54	....	1984-85	2001-02
Fetisov, Viacheslav	N.J., Det.	9	546	36	192	228	656	116	2	26	28	147	2	1989-90	1997-98
Fibiger, Jesse	S.J.	1	16	0	0	0	2	....	....	....	....	....	....	2002-03	2002-03
Fidler, Mike	Cle., Min., Hfd., Chi.	7	271	84	97	181	124	....	....	....	....	....	....	1976-77	1982-83
• Field, Wilf	NYA, Bro., Mtl., Chi.	6	219	17	25	42	151	2	0	0	0	2	....	1936-37	1944-45
Fielder, Guyle	Chi., Det., Bos.	4	9	0	0	0	2	6	0	0	0	2	....	1950-51	1957-58
Filewich, Jonathan	Pit.	1	5	0	0	0	0	....	....	....	....	....	....	2007-08	2007-08
Filimonov, Dmitri	Ott.	1	30	1	4	5	18	....	....	....	....	....	....	1993-94	1993-94
Fillion, Bob	Mtl.	7	327	42	61	103	84	33	7	4	11	10	2	1943-44	1949-50
• Fillion, Marcel	Bos.	1	1	0	0	0	0	....	....	....	....	....	....	1944-45	1944-45
• Filmore, Tommy	Det., NYA, Bos.	4	117	15	12	27	33	....	....	....	....	....	....	1930-31	1933-34
Finger, Jeff	Col., Tor.	4	199	17	40	57	114	5	0	2	2	4	....	2006-07	2009-10
• Finkbeiner, Lloyd	NYA	1	2	0	0	0	0	....	....	....	....	....	....	1940-41	1940-41
Finley, Jeff	NYI, Phi., Wpg., Phx., NYR, St.L.	15	708	13	70	83	457	52	1	6	7	38	....	1987-88	2003-04
Finn, Steven	Que., T.B., L.A.	12	725	34	78	112	1724	23	0	4	4	39	....	1985-86	1996-97
• Finney, Sid	Chi.	3	59	10	7	17	4	7	0	2	2	0	....	1951-52	1953-54
• Finnigan, Ed	St.L., Bos.	2	15	1	1	2	2	....	....	....	....	....	....	1934-35	1935-36
• Finnigan, Frank	Ott., Tor., St.L.	14	553	115	88	203	407	38	6	9	15	22	2	1923-24	1936-37
Fiorentino, Peter	NYR	1	1	0	0	0	0	....	....	....	....	....	....	1991-92	1991-92
Fischer, Jiri	Det.	6	305	11	49	60	295	38	4	3	7	55	1	1999-00	2005-06
Fischer, Patrick	Phx.	1	27	4	6	10	24	....	....	....	....	....	....	2006-07	2006-07
Fischer, Ron	Buf.	2	18	0	7	7	6	....	....	....	....	....	....	1981-82	1982-83
• Fisher, Alvin	Tor.	1	9	1	0	1	4	....	....	....	....	....	....	1924-25	1924-25
Fisher, Craig	Phi., Wpg., Fla.	4	12	0	0	0	2	....	....	....	....	....	....	1989-90	1996-97
Fisher, Dunc	NYR, Bos., Det.	7	275	45	70	115	104	21	4	4	8	14	....	1947-48	1958-59
• Fisher, Joe	Det.	4	65	8	12	20	13	12	2	1	3	6	1	1939-40	1942-43
Fitchner, Bob	Que.	2	78	12	20	32	59	3	0	0	0	10	....	1979-80	1980-81
Fitzgerald, Rusty	Pit.	2	25	2	2	4	12	5	0	0	0	4	....	1994-95	1995-96
Fitzgerald, Tom	NYI, Fla., Col., Nsh., Chi., Tor., Bos.	17	1097	139	190	329	776	78	7	12	19	90	....	1988-89	2005-06
Fitzpatrick, Rory	Mtl., St.L., Nsh., Buf., Van., Phi.	10	287	10	25	35	201	20	1	5	6	22	....	1995-96	2007-08
Fitzpatrick, Ross	Phi.	4	20	5	2	7	0	....	....	....	....	....	....	1982-83	1985-86
Fitzpatrick, Sandy	NYR, Min.	2	22	3	6	9	8	12	0	0	0	0	....	1964-65	1967-68
• Flaman, Fern	Bos., Tor.	17	910	34	174	208	1370	63	4	8	12	93	1	1944-45	1960-61
Flatley, Pat	NYI, NYR	14	780	170	340	510	686	70	18	15	33	75	....	1983-84	1996-97
Fleming, Gerry	Mtl.	2	11	0	0	0	42	....	....	....	....	....	....	1993-94	1994-95
• Fleming, Reggie	Mtl., Chi., Bos., NYR, Phi., Buf.	12	749	108	132	240	1468	50	3	6	9	106	1	1959-60	1970-71
Flesch, John	Min., Pit., Col.	4	124	18	23	41	117	....	....	....	....	....	....	1974-75	1979-80
Fletcher, Steven	Mtl., Wpg.	2	3	0	0	0	5	1	0	0	0	5	....	1987-88	1988-89
• Flett, Bill	L.A., Phi., Tor., Atl., Edm.	11	689	202	215	417	501	52	7	16	23	42	1	1967-68	1979-80
Fleury, Theoren	Cgy., Col., NYR, Chi.	15	1084	455	633	1088	1840	77	34	45	79	116	1	1988-89	2002-03
Flichel, Todd	Wpg.	3	6	0	1	1	4	....	....	....	....	....	....	1987-88	1989-90
Flinn, Ryan	L.A.	3	31	1	0	1	84	....	....	....	....	....	....	2001-02	2005-06
Flockhart, Rob	Van., Min.	5	55	2	5	7	14	1	1	0	1	2	....	1976-77	1980-81
Flockhart, Ron	Phi., Pit., Mtl., St.L., Bos.	9	453	145	183	328	208	19	4	6	10	14	....	1980-81	1988-89
Floyd, Larry	N.J.	2	12	2	3	5	9	....	....	....	....	....	....	1982-83	1983-84
Focht, Dan	Phx., Pit.	3	82	2	6	8	145	1	0	1	1	0	....	2001-02	2003-04
• Fogarty, Bryan	Que., Pit., Mtl.	6	156	22	52	74	119	....	....	....	....	....	....	1989-90	1994-95
• Fogolin, Lee	Det., Chi.	9	427	10	48	58	575	28	0	2	2	30	1	1947-48	1955-56
Fogolin, Lee	Buf., Edm.	13	924	44	195	239	1318	108	5	19	24	173	2	1974-75	1986-87
Folco, Peter	Van.	1	2	0	0	0	0	....	....	....	....	....	....	1973-74	1973-74
Foley, Gerry	Tor., NYR, L.A.	4	142	9	14	23	99	9	0	1	1	2	....	1954-55	1968-69
Foley, Rick	Chi., Phi., Det.	3	67	11	26	37	180	4	0	1	1	4	....	1970-71	1973-74
Foligno, Mike	Det., Buf., Tor., Fla.	15	1018	355	372	727	2049	57	15	17	32	185	....	1979-80	1993-94
Folk, Bill	Det.	2	12	0	0	0	4	....	....	....	....	....	....	1951-52	1952-53
Fontaine, Len	Det.	2	46	8	11	19	10	....	....	....	....	....	....	1972-73	1973-74
Fontas, Jon	Min.	2	2	0	0	0	0	....	....	....	....	....	....	1979-80	1980-81
Fonteyne, Val	Det., NYR, Pit.	13	820	75	154	229	26	59	3	10	13	8	....	1959-60	1971-72
Fontinato, Lou	NYR, Mtl.	9	535	26	78	104	1247	21	0	2	2	42	....	1954-55	1962-63
Foote, Adam	Que., Col., CBJ	19	1154	66	242	308	1534	170	7	35	42	298	2	1991-92	2010-11
Forbes, Colin	Phi., T.B., Ott., NYR, Wsh.	9	311	33	28	61	213	13	1	0	1	16	....	1996-97	2005-06
Forbes, Dave	Bos., Wsh.	6	363	64	64	128	341	45	1	4	5	13	....	1973-74	1978-79
Forbes, Mike	Bos., Edm.	3	50	1	11	12	41	....	....	....	....	....	....	1977-78	1981-82
Forey, Connie	St.L.	1	4	0	0	0	2	....	....	....	....	....	....	1973-74	1973-74
Forsberg, Peter	Que., Col., Phi., Nsh.	14	708	249	636	885	690	151	64	107	171	163	2	1994-95	2010-11
• Forsey, Jack	Tor.	1	19	7	9	16	10	3	0	1	1	0	....	1942-43	1942-43
• Forslund, Gus	Ott.	1	48	4	9	13	2	....	....	....	....	....	....	1932-33	1932-33
Forslund, Tomas	Cgy.	2	44	5	11	16	12	....	....	....	....	....	....	1991-92	1992-93
Forsyth, Alex	Wsh.	1	1	0	0	0	0	....	....	....	....	....	....	1976-77	1976-77
Fortier, Dave	Tor., NYI, Van.	4	205	8	21	29	335	20	0	2	2	33	....	1972-73	1976-77
Fortier, Marc	Que., Ott., L.A.	6	212	42	60	102	135	....	....	....	....	....	....	1987-88	1992-93
Fortin, Jean-Francois	Wsh.	3	71	1	4	5	42	....	....	....	....	....	....	2001-02	2003-04
Fortin, Ray	St.L.	3	92	2	6	8	33	6	0	0	0	8	....	1967-68	1969-70
‡ Foster, Alex	Tor.	1	3	0	0	0	0	....	....	....	....	....	....	2007-08	2007-08
Foster, Corey	N.J., Phi., Pit., NYI	4	45	5	6	11	24	3	0	0	0	4	....	1988-89	1996-97
Foster, Dwight	Bos., Col., N.J., Det.	10	541	111	163	274	420	35	5	12	17	4	....	1977-78	1986-87
• Foster, Herb	NYR	2	6	1	0	1	5	....	....	....	....	....	....	1940-41	1947-48
• Foster, Yip	NYR, Bos., Det.	4	83	3	2	5	32	....	....	....	....	....	....	1929-30	1934-35
Fotiu, Nick	NYR, Hfd., Cgy., Phi., Edm.	13	646	60	77	137	1362	38	0	4	4	67	....	1976-77	1988-89
• Fowler, Jimmy	Tor.	3	135	18	29	47	39	18	0	3	3	2	....	1936-37	1938-39
Fowler, Tom	Chi.	1	24	0	1	1	18	....	....	....	....	....	....	1946-47	1946-47
Fox, Greg	Atl., Chi., Pit.	8	494	14	92	106	637	44	1	9	10	67	....	1977-78	1984-85
Fox, Jim	L.A.	9	578	186	293	479	143	22	4	8	12	0	....	1980-81	1989-90
Foy, Matt	Min.	3	56	6	7	13	48	1	0	0	0	0	....	2005-06	2007-08
• Foyston, Frank	Det.	2	64	17	7	24	32	....	....	....	....	....	....	1926-27	1927-28
Frampton, Bob	Mtl.	1	2	0	0	0	0	3	0	0	0	0	....	1949-50	1949-50
Franceschetti, Lou	Wsh., Tor., Buf.	10	459	59	81	140	747	44	3	2	5	111	....	1981-82	1991-92
Francis, Bobby	Det.	1	14	2	0	2	0	....	....	....	....	....	....	1982-83	1982-83
Francis, Ron	Hfd., Pit., Car., Tor.	23	1731	549	1249	1798	979	171	46	97	143	95	2	1981-82	2003-04
• Fraser, Archie	NYR	1	3	0	1	1	0	....	....	....	....	....	....	1943-44	1943-44
• Fraser, Charles	Ham.	1	1	0	0	0	0	....	....	....	....	....	....	1923-24	1923-24
Fraser, Curt	Van., Chi., Min.	12	704	193	240	433	1306	65	15	18	33	198	....	1978-79	1989-90
• Fraser, Gord	Chi., Det., Mtl., Pit., Phi.	5	144	24	12	36	224	2	1	0	1	6	....	1926-27	1930-31
• Fraser, Harvey	Chi.	1	21	5	4	9	0	....	....	....	....	....	....	1944-45	1944-45
Fraser, Iain	NYI, Que., Dal., Edm., Wpg., S.J.	5	94	23	23	46	31	4	0	0	0	0	....	1992-93	1996-97
‡ Fraser, Jamie	NYI	1	1	0	0	0	0	....	....	....	....	....	....	2008-09	2008-09
Fraser, Scott	Mtl., Edm., NYR	3	72	16	15	31	24	11	1	1	2	0	....	1995-96	1998-99
Frawley, Dan	Chi., Pit.	6	273	37	40	77	674	1	0	0	0	0	....	1983-84	1988-89
Freadrich, Kyle	T.B.	2	23	0	1	1	75	....	....	....	....	....	....	1999-00	2000-01
• Fredrickson, Frank	Det., Bos., Pit.	5	161	39	34	73	206	10	2	3	5	24	....	1926-27	1930-31
Freer, Mark	Phi., Ott., Cgy.	7	124	16	23	39	61	....	....	....	....	....	....	1986-87	1993-94
• Frew, Irv	Mtl.M., St.L., Mtl.	3	96	2	5	7	146	4	0	0	0	6	....	1933-34	1935-36
Friday, Tim	Det.	1	23	0	3	3	6	....	....	....	....	....	....	1985-86	1985-86

Ross Fitzpatrick

John Flesch

Lee Fogolin Sr.

Curt Fraser

Ron Friest

Armand Gaudreault

Jean Gauthier

Gary Geldart

			Regular Schedule					Playoffs							
Name	NHL Teams	NHL Seasons	GP	G	A	TP	PIM	GP	G	A	TP	PIM	NHL Cup Wins	First NHL Season	Last NHL Season
Fridgen, Dan	Hfd.	2	13	2	3	5	2	....	....	....	....	....	....	1981-82	1982-83
Friedman, Doug	Edm., Nsh.	2	18	0	1	1	34	....	....	....	....	....	....	1997-98	1998-99
Friesen, Jeff	S.J., Ana., N.J., Wsh., Cgy.	12	893	218	298	516	488	84	18	15	33	48	1	1994-95	2006-07
Friest, Ron	Min.	3	64	7	7	14	191	6	1	0	1	7	....	1980-81	1982-83
Frig, Len	Chi., Cal., Cle., St.L.	7	311	13	51	64	479	14	2	1	3	0	....	1972-73	1979-80
‡ Frischmon, Trevor	CBJ	1	3	0	0	0	4	....	....	....	....	....	....	2009-10	2009-10
‡ Fritsch, Jamie	Phi.	1	1	0	0	0	0	....	....	....	....	....	....	2008-09	2008-09
‡ Fritsche, Dan	CBJ, NYR, Min.	5	256	34	42	76	103	....	....	....	....	....	....	2003-04	2008-09
Fritz, Mitch	NYI	1	20	0	0	0	42	....	....	....	....	....	....	2008-09	2008-09
‡ Frogren, Jonas	Tor.	1	41	1	6	7	28	....	....	....	....	....	....	2008-09	2008-09
‡ Frolov, Alex	L.A., NYR	8	579	175	222	397	218	6	1	3	4	0	....	2002-03	2010-11
• Frost, Harry	Bos.	1	4	0	0	0	0	1	0	0	0	0	1	1938-39	1938-39
Frycer, Miroslav	Que., Tor., Det., Edm.	8	415	147	183	330	486	17	3	8	11	16	....	1981-82	1988-89
• Fryday, Bob	Mtl.	2	5	1	0	1	0	....	....	....	....	....	....	1949-50	1951-52
Ftorek, Robbie	Det., Que., NYR	8	334	77	150	227	262	19	9	6	15	28	....	1972-73	1984-85
Fullan, Larry	Wsh.	1	4	1	0	1	0	....	....	....	....	....	....	1974-75	1974-75
Funk, Michael	Buf.	2	9	0	2	2	0	....	....	....	....	....	....	2006-07	2007-08
Fusco, Mark	Hfd.	2	80	3	12	15	42	....	....	....	....	....	....	1983-84	1984-85
Fussey, Owen	Wsh.	1	4	0	1	1	0	....	....	....	....	....	....	2003-04	2003-04

G

Gadsby, Bill	Chi., NYR, Det.	20	1248	130	438	568	1539	67	4	23	27	92	....	1946-47	1965-66
Gaetz, Link	Min., S.J.	3	65	6	8	14	412	....	....	....	....	....	....	1988-89	1991-92
Gage, Jody	Det., Buf.	6	68	14	15	29	26	....	....	....	....	....	....	1980-81	1991-92
• Gagne, Art	Mtl., Bos., Ott., Det.	6	228	67	33	100	257	11	2	1	3	20	....	1926-27	1931-32
Gagne, Paul	Col., N.J., Tor., NYI	8	390	110	101	211	127	....	....	....	....	....	....	1980-81	1989-90
Gagne, Pierre	Bos.	1	2	0	0	0	0	....	....	....	....	....	....	1959-60	1959-60
Gagner, Dave	NYR, Min., Dal., Tor., Cgy., Fla., Van.	15	946	318	401	719	1018	57	22	26	48	64	....	1984-85	1998-99
Gagnon, Germain	Mtl., NYI, Chi., K.C.	5	259	40	101	141	72	19	2	3	5	2	....	1971-72	1975-76
• Gagnon, Johnny	Mtl., Bos., NYA	10	454	120	141	261	295	32	12	12	24	37	1	1930-31	1939-40
Gagnon, Sean	Phx., Ott.	3	12	0	1	1	34	....	....	....	....	....	....	1997-98	2000-01
Gainey, Bob	Mtl.	16	1160	239	262	501	585	182	25	48	73	151	5	1973-74	1988-89
Gainey, Steve	Dal., Phx.	4	33	0	2	2	34	....	....	....	....	....	....	2000-01	2005-06
• Gainor, Dutch	Bos., NYR, Ott., Mtl.M.	7	246	51	56	107	129	22	2	1	3	14	2	1927-28	1934-35
Galanov, Maxim	NYR, Pit., Atl., T.B.	4	122	8	12	20	44	1	0	0	0	0	....	1997-98	2000-01
Galarneau, Michel	Hfd.	3	78	7	10	17	34	....	....	....	....	....	....	1980-81	1982-83
• Galbraith, Percy	Bos., Ott.	8	347	29	31	60	224	31	4	7	11	24	1	1926-27	1933-34
• Gallagher, John	Mtl.M., Det., NYA	7	205	14	19	33	153	24	2	3	5	27	1	1930-31	1938-39
Gallant, Gerard	Det., T.B.	11	615	211	269	480	1674	58	18	21	39	178	....	1984-85	1994-95
Galley, Garry	L.A., Wsh., Bos., Phi., Buf., NYI	17	1149	125	475	600	1218	89	7	23	30	119	....	1984-85	2000-01
Gallimore, Jamie	Min.	1	2	0	0	0	0	....	....	....	....	....	....	1977-78	1977-78
• Gallinger, Don	Bos.	5	222	65	88	153	89	23	5	5	10	19	....	1942-43	1947-48
Gamache, Simon	Atl., Nsh., St.L., Tor.	4	48	6	7	13	18	....	....	....	....	....	....	2002-03	2007-08
Gamble, Dick	Mtl., Chi., Tor.	8	195	41	41	82	66	14	1	2	3	4	1	1950-51	1966-67
Gambucci, Gary	Min.	2	51	2	7	9	9	....	....	....	....	....	....	1971-72	1973-74
Ganchar, Perry	St.L., Mtl., Pit.	4	42	3	7	10	36	7	3	1	4	0	....	1983-84	1988-89
Gans, Dave	L.A.	2	6	0	0	0	2	....	....	....	....	....	....	1982-83	1985-86
Gardiner, Bruce	Ott., T.B., CBJ, N.J.	6	312	34	54	88	263	21	1	4	5	8	....	1996-97	2001-02
• Gardiner, Herb	Mtl., Chi.	3	108	10	9	19	52	9	0	1	1	16	....	1926-27	1928-29
Gardner, Bill	Chi., Hfd.	9	380	73	115	188	68	45	3	8	11	17	....	1980-81	1988-89
• Gardner, Cal	NYR, Tor., Chi., Bos.	12	696	154	238	392	517	61	7	10	17	20	2	1945-46	1956-57
Gardner, Dave	Mtl., St.L., Cal., Cle., Phi.	7	350	75	115	190	41	....	....	....	....	....	....	1972-73	1979-80
Gardner, Paul	Col., Tor., Pit., Wsh., Buf.	10	447	201	201	402	207	16	2	6	8	14	....	1976-77	1985-86
Gare, Danny	Buf., Det., Edm.	13	827	354	331	685	1285	64	25	21	46	195	....	1974-75	1986-87
• Gariepy, Ray	Bos., Tor.	2	36	1	6	7	43	....	....	....	....	....	....	1953-54	1955-56
• Garland, Scott	Tor., L.A.	3	91	13	24	37	115	7	1	2	3	35	....	1975-76	1978-79
Garner, Rob	Pit.	1	1	0	0	0	0	....	....	....	....	....	....	1982-83	1982-83
Garpenlov, Johan	Det., S.J., Fla., Atl.	10	609	114	197	311	276	44	10	9	19	22	....	1990-91	1999-00
• Garrett, Red	NYR	1	23	1	1	2	18	....	....	....	....	....	....	1942-43	1942-43
Gartner, Mike	Wsh., Min., NYR, Tor., Phx.	19	1432	708	627	1335	1159	122	43	50	93	125	....	1979-80	1997-98
• Gassoff, Bob	St.L.	4	245	11	47	58	866	9	0	1	1	16	....	1973-74	1976-77
Gassoff, Brad	Van.	4	122	19	17	36	163	3	0	0	0	0	....	1975-76	1978-79
Gatzos, Steve	Pit.	4	89	15	20	35	83	1	0	0	0	0	....	1981-82	1984-85
Gaudreau, Rob	S.J., Ott.	4	231	51	54	105	69	14	2	0	2	0	....	1992-93	1995-96
• Gaudreault, Armand	Bos.	1	44	15	9	24	27	7	0	2	2	8	....	1944-45	1944-45
• Gaudreault, Leo	Mtl.	3	67	8	4	12	30	....	....	....	....	....	....	1927-28	1932-33
Gaul, Mike	Col., CBJ	2	3	0	0	0	4	....	....	....	....	....	....	1998-99	2000-01
Gaulin, Jean-Marc	Que.	4	26	4	3	7	8	1	0	0	0	0	....	1982-83	1985-86
Gaume, Dallas	Hfd.	1	4	1	1	2	0	....	....	....	....	....	....	1988-89	1988-89
• Gauthier, Art	Mtl.	1	13	0	0	0	0	1	0	0	0	0	....	1926-27	1926-27
Gauthier, Daniel	Chi.	1	5	0	0	0	0	....	....	....	....	....	....	1994-95	1994-95
Gauthier, Denis	Cgy., Phx., Phi., L.A.	10	554	17	60	77	748	12	0	2	2	23	....	1997-98	2008-09
• Gauthier, Fern	NYR, Mtl., Det.	6	229	46	50	96	35	22	5	1	6	7	....	1943-44	1948-49
Gauthier, Gabe	L.A.	2	8	0	0	0	2	....	....	....	....	....	....	2006-07	2007-08
Gauthier, Jean	Mtl., Phi., Bos.	10	166	6	29	35	150	14	1	3	4	22	1	1960-61	1969-70
Gauthier, Luc	Mtl.	1	3	0	0	0	2	....	....	....	....	....	....	1990-91	1990-91
Gauvreau, Jocelyn	Mtl.	1	2	0	0	0	0	....	....	....	....	....	....	1983-84	1983-84
Gavey, Aaron	T.B., Cgy., Dal., Min., Tor., Ana.	9	360	41	50	91	272	19	1	2	3	14	....	1995-96	2005-06
Gavin, Stew	Tor., Hfd., Min.	13	768	130	155	285	584	66	14	20	34	75	....	1980-81	1992-93
Geale, Bob	Pit.	1	1	0	0	0	2	....	....	....	....	....	....	1984-85	1984-85
• Gee, George	Chi., Det.	9	551	135	183	318	345	41	6	13	19	32	1	1945-46	1953-54
Geldart, Gary	Min.	1	4	0	0	0	5	....	....	....	....	....	....	1970-71	1970-71
Gelinas, Martin	Edm., Que., Van., Car., Cgy., Fla., Nsh.	19	1273	309	351	660	820	147	23	33	56	120	1	1988-89	2007-08
Gendron, Jean-Guy	NYR, Bos., Mtl., Phi.	14	863	182	201	383	701	42	7	4	11	47	....	1955-56	1971-72
Gendron, Martin	Wsh., Chi.	3	30	4	2	6	10	....	....	....	....	....	....	1994-95	1997-98
• Geoffrion, Bernie	Mtl., NYR	16	883	393	429	822	689	132	58	60	118	88	6	1950-51	1967-68
‡ Geoffrion, Blake	Nsh., Mtl.	2	55	8	5	13	34	12	0	2	2	4	....	2010-11	2011-12
Geoffrion, Danny	Mtl., Wpg.	3	111	20	32	52	99	2	0	0	0	7	....	1979-80	1981-82
• Geran, Gerry	Mtl.W., Bos.	2	37	5	1	6	6	....	....	....	....	....	....	1917-18	1925-26
• Gerard, Eddie	Ott.	6	128	50	48	98	108	11	4	0	4	17	3	1917-18	1922-23
Germain, Eric	L.A.	1	4	0	1	1	13	1	0	0	0	4	....	1987-88	1987-88
Germyn, Carsen	Cgy.	2	4	0	0	0	0	....	....	....	....	....	....	2005-06	2006-07
Gernander, Ken	NYR	3	12	2	3	5	6	15	0	0	0	0	....	1995-96	2003-04
• Getliffe, Ray	Bos., Mtl.	10	393	136	137	273	250	45	9	10	19	30	2	1935-36	1944-45
Giallonardo, Mario	Col.	2	23	0	3	3	6	....	....	....	....	....	....	1979-80	1980-81
Gibbs, Barry	Bos., Min., Atl., St.L., L.A.	13	797	58	224	282	945	36	4	2	6	67	....	1967-68	1979-80
Gibson, Don	Van.	1	14	0	3	3	20	....	....	....	....	....	....	1990-91	1990-91
Gibson, Doug	Bos., Wsh.	3	63	9	19	28	0	1	0	0	0	0	....	1973-74	1977-78
Gibson, John	L.A., Tor., Wpg.	3	48	0	2	2	120	....	....	....	....	....	....	1980-81	1983-84
• Giesebrecht, Gus	Det.	4	135	27	51	78	13	17	2	3	5	0	....	1938-39	1941-42
Giffin, Lee	Pit.	2	27	1	3	4	9	....	....	....	....	....	....	1986-87	1987-88
Gilbert, Ed	K.C., Pit.	3	166	21	31	52	22	....	....	....	....	....	....	1974-75	1976-77
Gilbert, Greg	NYI, Chi., NYR, St.L.	15	837	150	228	378	576	133	17	33	50	162	3	1981-82	1995-96
Gilbert, Jeannot	Bos.	2	9	0	1	1	4	....	....	....	....	....	....	1962-63	1964-65
Gilbert, Rod	NYR	18	1065	406	615	1021	508	79	34	33	67	43	....	1960-61	1977-78
Gilbertson, Stan	Cal., St.L., Wsh., Pit.	6	428	85	89	174	148	3	1	1	2	2	....	1971-72	1976-77
Gilchrist, Brent	Mtl., Edm., Min., Dal., Det., Nsh.	15	792	135	170	305	400	90	17	14	31	48	1	1988-89	2002-03
Giles, Curt	Min., NYR, St.L.	14	895	43	199	242	733	103	6	16	22	118	....	1979-80	1992-93
Gilhen, Randy	Hfd., Wpg., Pit., L.A., NYR, T.B., Fla.	11	457	55	60	115	314	33	3	2	5	26	1	1982-83	1995-96
Gill, Todd	Tor., S.J., St.L., Det., Phx., Col., Chi.	19	1007	82	272	354	1214	103	7	30	37	193	....	1984-85	2002-03
Gillen, Don	Phi., Hfd.	2	35	2	4	6	22	....	....	....	....	....	....	1979-80	1981-82
• Gillie, Farrand	Det.	1	1	0	0	0	0	....	....	....	....	....	....	1928-29	1928-29
Gillies, Clark	NYI, Buf.	14	958	319	378	697	1023	164	47	47	94	287	4	1974-75	1987-88
Gillis, Jere	Van., NYR, Que., Buf., Phi.	9	386	78	95	173	230	19	4	7	11	9	....	1977-78	1986-87
Gillis, Mike	Col., Bos.	6	246	33	43	76	186	27	2	5	7	10	....	1978-79	1983-84
Gillis, Paul	Que., Chi., Hfd.	11	624	88	154	242	1498	42	3	14	17	156	....	1982-83	1992-93
Gilmour, Doug	St.L., Cgy., Tor., N.J., Chi., Buf., Mtl.	20	1474	450	964	1414	1301	182	60	128	188	235	1	1983-84	2002-03
Gingras, Gaston	Mtl., Tor., St.L.	10	476	61	174	235	161	52	6	18	24	20	1	1979-80	1988-89
Girard, Bob	Cal., Cle., Wsh.	5	305	45	69	114	140	....	....	....	....	....	....	1975-76	1979-80
Girard, Jonathan	Bos.	5	150	10	34	44	46	3	0	1	1	2	....	1998-99	2002-03
Girard, Kenny	Tor.	3	7	0	1	1	2	....	....	....	....	....	....	1956-57	1959-60
‡ Giroux, Alexandre	NYR, Wsh., Edm., CBJ	6	48	6	6	12	26	....	....	....	....	....	....	2005-06	2011-12
• Giroux, Art	Mtl., Bos., Det.	3	54	6	4	10	14	2	0	0	0	0	....	1932-33	1935-36
Giroux, Larry	St.L., K.C., Det., Hfd.	7	274	15	74	89	333	5	0	0	0	4	....	1973-74	1979-80
Giroux, Pierre	L.A.	1	6	1	0	1	17	....	....	....	....	....	....	1982-83	1982-83

			Regular Schedule					Playoffs							
Name	NHL Teams	NHL Seasons	GP	G	A	TP	PIM	GP	G	A	TP	PIM	NHL Cup Wins	First NHL Season	Last NHL Season
‡ Giroux, Raymond	NYI, N.J.	4	38	0	13	13	22	4	0	0	0	0	....	1999-00	2003-04
‡ Giuliano, Jeff	L.A.	2	101	3	10	13	40	....	....	....	....	....	....	2005-06	2007-08
Gladney, Bob	L.A., Pit.	2	14	1	5	6	4	....	....	....	....	....	....	1982-83	1983-84
Gladu, Jean-Paul	Bos.	1	40	6	14	20	2	7	2	2	4	0	....	1944-45	1944-45
Glennie, Brian	Tor., L.A.	10	572	14	100	114	621	32	0	1	1	66	....	1969-70	1978-79
Glennon, Matt	Bos.	1	3	0	0	0	2	....	....	....	....	....	....	1991-92	1991-92
Globke, Rob	Fla.	3	46	1	1	2	8	....	....	....	....	....	....	2005-06	2007-08
Gloeckner, Lorry	Det.	1	13	0	2	2	6	....	....	....	....	....	....	1978-79	1978-79
Gloor, Dan	Van.	1	2	0	0	0	0	....	....	....	....	....	....	1973-74	1973-74
• Glover, Fred	Det., Chi.	5	92	13	11	24	62	8	0	0	0	0	1	1948-49	1952-53
Glover, Howie	Chi., Det., NYR, Mtl.	5	144	29	17	46	101	11	1	2	3	2	....	1958-59	1968-69
‡ Glumac, Mike	St.L.	3	40	7	6	13	38	....	....	....	....	....	....	2005-06	2007-08
Glynn, Brian	Cgy., Min., Edm., Ott., Van., Hfd.	10	431	25	79	104	410	57	6	10	16	40	....	1987-88	1996-97
‡ Goc, Sascha	N.J., T.B.	2	22	0	0	0	4	....	....	....	....	....	....	2000-01	2001-02
Godard, Eric	NYI, Cgy., Pit.	8	335	6	12	18	833	7	0	1	1	6	1	2002-03	2010-11
Godden, Ernie	Tor.	1	5	1	1	2	6	....	....	....	....	....	....	1981-82	1981-82
• Godfrey, Warren	Bos., Det.	16	786	32	125	157	752	52	1	4	5	42	....	1952-53	1967-68
Godin, Eddy	Wsh.	2	27	3	6	9	12	....	....	....	....	....	....	1977-78	1978-79
• Godin, Sam	Ott., Mtl.	3	83	4	3	7	36	....	....	....	....	....	....	1927-28	1933-34
Godynyuk, Alexander	Tor., Cgy., Fla., Hfd.	7	223	10	39	49	224	....	....	....	....	....	....	1990-91	1996-97
• Goegan, Pete	Det., NYR, Min.	11	383	19	67	86	365	33	1	3	4	61	....	1957-58	1967-68
Goertz, Dave	Pit.	1	2	0	0	0	2	....	....	....	....	....	....	1987-88	1987-88
‡ Goertzen, Steven	CBJ, Phx., Car.	4	68	2	2	4	83	....	....	....	....	....	....	2005-06	2009-10
• Goldham, Bob	Tor., Chi., Det.	12	650	28	143	171	400	66	3	14	17	53	5	1941-42	1955-56
Goldmann, Erich	Ott.	1	1	0	0	0	0	....	....	....	....	....	....	1999-00	1999-00
• Goldsworthy, Bill	Bos., Min., NYR	14	771	283	258	541	793	40	18	19	37	30	....	1964-65	1977-78
• Goldsworthy, Leroy	NYR, Det., Chi., Mtl., Bos., NYA	10	336	66	57	123	79	24	1	0	1	4	1	1928-29	1938-39
Goldup, Glenn	Mtl., L.A.	9	291	52	67	119	303	16	4	3	7	22	....	1973-74	1981-82
• Goldup, Hank	Tor., NYR	6	202	63	80	143	97	26	5	1	6	6	1	1939-40	1945-46
Golubovsky, Yan	Det., Fla.	4	56	1	7	8	32	....	....	....	....	....	....	1997-98	2000-01
Goneau, Daniel	NYR	3	53	12	3	15	14	....	....	....	....	....	....	1996-97	1999-00
• Gooden, Bill	NYR	2	53	9	11	20	15	....	....	....	....	....	....	1942-43	1943-44
Goodenough, Larry	Phi., Van.	6	242	22	77	99	179	22	3	15	18	10	1	1974-75	1979-80
• Goodfellow, Ebbie	Det.	14	557	134	190	324	511	45	8	8	16	65	3	1929-30	1942-43
Gordiouk, Viktor	Buf.	2	26	3	8	11	0	....	....	....	....	....	....	1992-93	1994-95
• Gordon, Fred	Det., Bos.	2	81	8	7	15	68	2	0	0	0	0	....	1926-27	1927-28
Gordon, Jack	NYR	3	36	3	10	13	0	9	1	1	2	7	....	1948-49	1950-51
Gordon, Robb	Van.	1	4	0	0	0	2	....	....	....	....	....	....	1998-99	1998-99
‡ Goren, Lee	Bos., Fla., Van.	5	67	5	4	9	44	5	0	0	0	5	....	2000-01	2006-07
Gorence, Tom	Phi., Edm.	6	303	58	53	111	89	37	9	6	15	47	....	1978-79	1983-84
Goring, Butch	L.A., NYI, Bos.	16	1107	375	513	888	102	134	38	50	88	32	4	1969-70	1984-85
Gorman, Dave	Atl.	1	3	0	0	0	0	....	....	....	....	....	....	1979-80	1979-80
• Gorman, Ed	Ott., Tor.	4	111	14	6	20	108	8	0	0	0	2	1	1924-25	1927-28
Gosselin, Benoit	NYR	1	7	0	0	0	33	....	....	....	....	....	....	1977-78	1977-78
Gosselin, David	Nsh.	2	13	2	1	3	11	....	....	....	....	....	....	1999-00	2001-02
Gosselin, Guy	Wpg.	1	5	0	0	0	6	....	....	....	....	....	....	1987-88	1987-88
Gotaas, Steve	Pit., Min.	3	49	6	9	15	53	3	0	1	1	5	....	1987-88	1990-91
• Gottselig, Johnny	Chi.	16	589	176	195	371	203	43	13	13	26	18	2	1928-29	1944-45
Gould, Bobby	Atl., Cgy., Wsh., Bos.	11	697	145	159	304	572	78	15	13	28	58	....	1979-80	1989-90
Gould, John	Buf., Van., Atl.	9	504	131	138	269	113	14	3	2	5	4	....	1971-72	1979-80
Gould, Larry	Van.	1	2	0	0	0	0	....	....	....	....	....	....	1973-74	1973-74
Goulet, Michel	Que., Chi.	15	1089	548	604	1152	825	92	39	39	78	110	....	1979-80	1993-94
• Goupille, Red	Mtl.	8	222	12	28	40	256	8	2	0	2	6	....	1935-36	1942-43
Gove, David	Car.	2	2	0	1	1	0	....	....	....	....	....	....	2005-06	2006-07
Govedaris, Chris	Hfd., Tor.	4	45	4	6	10	24	4	0	0	0	2	....	1989-90	1993-94
Goyer, Gerry	Chi.	1	40	1	2	3	4	3	0	0	0	2	....	1967-68	1967-68
Goyette, Phil	Mtl., NYR, St.L., Buf.	16	941	207	467	674	131	94	17	29	46	26	4	1956-57	1971-72
• Graboski, Tony	Mtl.	3	66	6	10	16	24	3	0	0	0	6	....	1940-41	1942-43
• Gracie, Bob	Tor., Bos., NYA, Mtl.M., Mtl., Chi.	9	379	82	109	191	205	33	4	7	11	4	2	1930-31	1938-39
Gradin, Thomas	Van., Bos.	9	677	209	384	593	298	42	17	25	42	20	....	1978-79	1986-87
Graham, Dirk	Min., Chi.	12	772	219	270	489	917	90	17	27	44	92	....	1983-84	1994-95
• Graham, Leth	Ott., Ham.	6	27	3	0	3	0	1	0	0	0	0	1	1920-21	1925-26
Graham, Pat	Pit., Tor.	3	103	11	17	28	136	4	0	0	0	2	....	1981-82	1983-84
Graham, Rod	Bos.	1	14	2	1	3	7	....	....	....	....	....	....	1974-75	1974-75
• Graham, Ted	Chi., Mtl.M., Det., St.L., Bos., NYA	9	346	14	25	39	300	24	3	1	4	30	....	1927-28	1936-37
Granato, Tony	NYR, L.A., S.J.	13	773	248	244	492	1425	79	16	27	43	141	....	1988-89	2000-01
‡ Grand-Pierre, Jean-Luc	Buf., CBJ, Atl., Wsh.	6	269	7	13	20	311	4	0	0	0	4	....	1998-99	2003-04
Grant, Danny	Mtl., Min., Det., L.A.	13	736	263	273	536	239	43	10	14	24	19	1	1965-66	1978-79
‡ Gratton, Benoit	Wsh., Cgy., Mtl.	6	58	6	10	16	58	....	....	....	....	....	....	1997-98	2003-04
Gratton, Chris	T.B., Phi., Buf., Phx., Col., Fla., CBJ	15	1092	214	354	568	1638	40	8	7	15	82	....	1993-94	2008-09
Gratton, Dan	L.A.	1	7	1	0	1	5	....	....	....	....	....	....	1987-88	1987-88
‡ Gratton, Josh	Phi., Phx.	4	86	3	3	6	294	....	....	....	....	....	....	2005-06	2008-09
Gratton, Norm	NYR, Atl., Buf., Min.	5	201	39	44	83	64	6	0	1	1	2	....	1971-72	1975-76
Gravelle, Leo	Mtl., Det.	5	223	44	34	78	42	17	4	1	5	2	....	1946-47	1950-51
Graves, Adam	Det., Edm., NYR, S.J.	16	1152	329	287	616	1224	125	38	27	65	119	2	1987-88	2002-03
Graves, Hilliard	Cal., Atl., Van., Wpg.	9	556	118	163	281	209	2	0	0	0	0	....	1970-71	1979-80
Graves, Steve	Edm.	3	35	5	4	9	10	....	....	....	....	....	....	1983-84	1987-88
• Gray, Alex	NYR, Tor.	2	50	7	0	7	32	13	1	0	1	0	1	1927-28	1928-29
Gray, Terry	Bos., Mtl., L.A., St.L.	6	147	26	28	54	64	35	5	5	10	22	....	1961-62	1970-71
Green, Mike	Fla., NYR	1	24	1	3	4	4	....	....	....	....	....	....	2003-04	2003-04
• Green, Red	Ham., NYA, Bos., Det.	6	195	59	26	85	290	1	0	0	0	0	1	1923-24	1928-29
Green, Rick	Wsh., Mtl., Det., NYI	15	845	43	220	263	588	100	3	16	19	73	1	1976-77	1991-92
• Green, Shorty	Ham., NYA	4	103	33	20	53	151	....	....	....	....	....	....	1923-24	1926-27
Green, Ted	Bos.	11	620	48	206	254	1029	31	4	8	12	54	1	1960-61	1971-72
Green, Travis	NYI, Ana., Phx., Tor., Bos.	14	970	193	262	455	764	56	10	11	21	60	....	1992-93	2006-07
Greenlaw, Jeff	Wsh., Fla.	6	57	3	6	9	108	2	0	0	0	21	....	1986-87	1993-94
‡ Greentree, Kyle	Phi., Cgy.	2	4	0	0	0	0	....	....	....	....	....	....	2007-08	2008-09
Gregg, Randy	Edm., Van.	10	474	41	152	193	333	137	13	38	51	127	5	1981-82	1991-92
• Greig, Bruce	Cal.	2	9	0	1	1	46	....	....	....	....	....	....	1973-74	1974-75
Greig, Mark	Hfd., Tor., Cgy., Phi.	9	125	13	27	40	90	5	0	1	1	0	....	1990-91	2002-03
Grenier, Lucien	Mtl., L.A.	4	151	14	14	28	18	2	0	0	0	0	....	1968-69	1971-72
Grenier, Martin	Phx., Van., Phi.	4	18	1	0	1	14	....	....	....	....	....	....	2001-02	2006-07
Grenier, Richard	NYI	1	10	1	1	2	2	....	....	....	....	....	....	1972-73	1972-73
Greschner, Ron	NYR	16	982	179	431	610	1226	84	17	32	49	106	....	1974-75	1989-90
Gretzky, Brent	T.B.	2	13	1	3	4	2	....	....	....	....	....	....	1993-94	1994-95
Gretzky, Wayne	Edm., L.A., St.L., NYR	20	1487	894	1963	2857	577	208	122	260	382	66	4	1979-80	1998-99
Grier, Mike	Edm., Wsh., Buf., S.J.	14	1060	162	221	383	510	101	14	14	28	72	....	1996-97	2010-11
Grieve, Brent	NYI, Edm., Chi., L.A.	4	97	20	16	36	87	....	....	....	....	....	....	1993-94	1996-97
• Grigor, George	Chi.	1	2	1	0	1	0	1	0	0	0	0	....	1943-44	1943-44
Grimson, Stu	Cgy., Chi., Ana., Det., Hfd., Car., L.A., Nsh.	14	729	17	22	39	2113	42	1	1	2	120	....	1988-89	2001-02
Grisdale, John	Tor., Van.	6	250	4	39	43	346	10	0	1	1	15	....	1972-73	1978-79
Groleau, Francois	Mtl.	3	8	0	1	1	6	....	....	....	....	....	....	1995-96	1997-98
‡ Gron, Stanislav	N.J.	1	1	0	0	0	0	....	....	....	....	....	....	2000-01	2000-01
Gronman, Tuomas	Chi., Pit.	2	38	1	3	4	38	1	0	0	0	0	....	1996-97	1997-98
• Gronsdahl, Lloyd	Bos.	1	10	1	2	3	0	....	....	....	....	....	....	1941-42	1941-42
Gronstrand, Jari	Min., NYR, Que., NYI	5	185	8	26	34	135	3	0	0	0	4	....	1986-87	1990-91
Grosek, Michal	Wpg., Buf., Chi., NYR, Bos.	11	526	84	137	221	509	45	9	11	20	77	....	1993-94	2003-04
• Gross, Lloyd	Tor., NYA, Bos., Det.	3	52	11	5	16	20	1	0	0	0	0	....	1926-27	1934-35
• Grosso, Don	Det., Chi., Bos.	9	336	87	117	204	90	48	15	14	29	63	1	1938-39	1946-47
• Grosvenor, Len	Ott., NYA, Mtl.	6	149	9	11	20	78	4	0	0	0	2	....	1927-28	1932-33
Groulx, Wayne	Que.	1	1	0	0	0	0	....	....	....	....	....	....	1984-85	1984-85
Gruden, John	Bos., Ott., Wsh.	6	92	1	8	9	46	3	0	1	1	0	....	1993-94	2003-04
Gruen, Danny	Det., Col.	3	49	9	13	22	19	....	....	....	....	....	....	1972-73	1976-77
Gruhl, Scott	L.A., Pit.	3	20	3	3	6	6	....	....	....	....	....	....	1981-82	1987-88
Gryp, Bob	Bos., Wsh.	3	74	11	13	24	33	....	....	....	....	....	....	1973-74	1975-76
Guay, Francois	Buf.	1	1	0	0	0	0	....	....	....	....	....	....	1989-90	1989-90
Guay, Paul	Phi., L.A., Bos., NYI	7	117	11	23	34	92	9	0	1	1	12	....	1983-84	1990-91
Guerard, Daniel	Ott.	1	2	0	0	0	0	....	....	....	....	....	....	1994-95	1994-95
Guerard, Stephane	Que.	2	34	0	0	0	40	....	....	....	....	....	....	1987-88	1989-90
Guerin, Bill	N.J., Edm., Bos., Dal., St.L., S.J., NYI, Pit.	18	1263	429	427	856	1660	140	39	35	74	162	2	1991-92	2009-10
Guevremont, Jocelyn	Van., Buf., NYR	9	571	84	223	307	319	40	4	17	21	18	....	1971-72	1979-80
Guidolin, Aldo	NYR	4	182	9	15	24	117	....	....	....	....	....	....	1952-53	1955-56
• Guidolin, Bep	Bos., Det., Chi.	9	519	107	171	278	606	24	5	7	12	35	....	1942-43	1951-52
Guindon, Bobby	Wpg.	1	6	0	1	1	0	....	....	....	....	....	....	1979-80	1979-80

Don Gibson

Dave Gorman

Norm Gratton

Randy Gregg

Len Grosvenor

Reg Hamilton

Ed Hatoum

Alan Haworth

			Regular Schedule					Playoffs					NHL	First	Last
Name	NHL Teams	NHL Seasons	GP	G	A	TP	PIM	GP	G	A	TP	PIM	Cup Wins	NHL Season	NHL Season
‡ Guite, Ben	Bos., Col., Nsh.	5	175	19	26	45	97	10	1	0	1	14	....	2005-06	2009-10
Guolla, Steve	S.J., T.B., Atl., N.J.	6	205	40	46	86	60	....	....	....	....	....	....	1996-97	2002-03
Guren, Miloslav	Mtl.	2	36	1	3	4	16	....	....	....	....	....	....	1998-99	1999-00
Gusarov, Alexei	Que., Col., NYR, St.L.	11	607	39	128	167	313	68	0	14	14	38	1	1990-91	2000-01
Gusev, Sergey	Dal., T.B.	4	89	4	10	14	34	....	....	....	....	....	....	1997-98	2000-01
Gusmanov, Ravil	Wpg.	1	4	0	0	0	0	....	....	....	....	....	....	1995-96	1995-96
Gustafsson, Bengt-Ake	Wsh.	9	629	196	359	555	196	32	9	19	28	16	....	1979-80	1988-89
Gustafsson, Per	Fla., Tor., Ott.	2	89	8	27	35	38	1	0	0	0	0	....	1996-97	1997-98
Gustavsson, Peter	Col.	1	2	0	0	0	0	....	....	....	....	....	....	1981-82	1981-82
Guy, Kevan	Cgy., Van.	6	156	5	20	25	138	5	0	1	1	23	....	1986-87	1991-92
H															
Haakana, Kari	Edm.	1	13	0	0	0	4	....	....	....	....	....	....	2002-03	2002-03
Haanpaa, Ari	NYI	3	60	6	11	17	37	6	0	0	0	10	....	1985-86	1987-88
Haas, David	Edm., Cgy.	2	7	2	1	3	7	....	....	....	....	....	....	1990-91	1993-94
Habscheid, Marc	Edm., Min., Det., Cgy.	11	345	72	91	163	171	12	1	3	4	13	....	1981-82	1991-92
Hachborn, Len	Phi., L.A.	3	102	20	39	59	29	7	0	3	3	7	....	1983-84	1985-86
Haddon, Lloyd	Det.	1	8	0	0	0	2	1	0	0	0	0	....	1959-60	1959-60
Hadfield, Vic	NYR, Pit.	16	1002	323	389	712	1154	73	27	21	48	117	....	1961-62	1976-77
• Haggarty, Jim	Mtl.	1	5	1	1	2	0	3	2	1	3	0	....	1941-42	1941-42
Haggerty, Sean	Tor., NYI, Nsh.	4	14	1	2	3	4	....	....	....	....	....	....	1995-96	2000-01
• Hagglund, Roger	Que.	1	3	0	0	0	0	....	....	....	....	....	....	1984-85	1984-85
Hagman, Matti	Bos., Edm.	4	237	56	89	145	36	20	5	2	7	6	....	1976-77	1981-82
‡ Hagman, Niklas	Fla., Dal., Tor., Cgy., Ana.	10	770	147	154	301	220	30	4	3	7	28	....	2001-02	2011-12
‡ Hahl, Riku	Col.	3	92	5	8	13	38	34	2	4	6	4	....	2001-02	2003-04
• Haidy, Gord	Det.	1	....	....	....	....	....	1	0	0	0	0	....	1949-50	1949-50
Hajdu, Richard	Buf.	2	5	0	0	0	4	....	....	....	....	....	....	1985-86	1986-87
Hajt, Bill	Buf.	14	854	42	202	244	433	80	2	16	18	70	....	1973-74	1986-87
Hajt, Chris	Edm., Wsh.	2	6	0	0	0	2	....	....	....	....	....	....	2000-01	2003-04
Hakansson, Anders	Min., Pit., L.A.	5	330	52	46	98	141	6	0	0	0	2	....	1981-82	1985-86
• Halderson, Harold	Det., Tor.	1	44	3	2	5	65	....	....	....	....	....	....	1926-27	1926-27
Hale, David	N.J., Cgy., Phx., T.B., Ott.	7	327	4	25	29	242	17	0	2	2	20	....	2003-04	2010-11
Hale, Larry	Phi.	4	196	5	37	42	90	8	0	0	0	12	....	1968-69	1971-72
Haley, Len	Det.	2	30	2	2	4	14	6	1	3	4	6	....	1959-60	1960-61
Halkidis, Bob	Buf., L.A., Tor., Det., T.B., NYI	11	256	8	32	40	825	20	0	1	1	51	....	1984-85	1995-96
Halko, Steven	Car.	6	155	0	15	15	71	4	0	0	0	2	....	1997-98	2002-03
• Hall, Bob	NYA	1	8	0	0	0	0	....	....	....	....	....	....	1925-26	1925-26
Hall, Del	Cal.	3	9	2	0	2	2	....	....	....	....	....	....	1971-72	1973-74
• Hall, Joe	Mtl.	2	37	15	9	24	235	7	0	1	1	38	....	1917-18	1918-19
Hall, Murray	Chi., Det., Min., Van.	9	164	35	48	83	46	6	0	0	0	0	....	1961-62	1971-72
Hall, Taylor	Van., Bos.	5	41	7	9	16	29	....	....	....	....	....	....	1983-84	1987-88
Hall, Wayne	NYR	1	4	0	0	0	0	....	....	....	....	....	....	1960-61	1960-61
Haller, Kevin	Buf., Mtl., Phi., Hfd., Car., Ana., NYI	13	642	41	97	138	907	64	7	16	23	71	1	1989-90	2001-02
• Halliday, Milt	Ott.	3	67	1	0	1	4	6	0	0	0	0	1	1926-27	1928-29
Hallin, Mats	NYI, Min.	5	152	17	14	31	193	15	1	0	1	13	1	1982-83	1986-87
Halverson, Trevor	Wsh.	1	17	0	4	4	28	....	....	....	....	....	....	1998-99	1998-99
Halward, Doug	Bos., L.A., Van., Det., Edm.	14	653	69	224	293	774	47	7	10	17	113	....	1975-76	1988-89
‡ Hamel, Denis	Buf., Ott., Atl., Phi.	7	192	19	12	31	77	....	....	....	....	....	....	1999-00	2006-07
Hamel, Gilles	Buf., Wpg., L.A.	9	519	127	147	274	276	27	4	5	9	10	....	1980-81	1988-89
• Hamel, Herb	Tor.	1	2	0	0	0	4	....	....	....	....	....	....	1930-31	1930-31
Hamel, Jean	St.L., Det., Que., Mtl.	12	699	26	95	121	766	33	0	2	2	44	....	1972-73	1983-84
• Hamill, Red	Bos., Chi.	12	419	128	94	222	160	24	1	2	3	20	1	1937-38	1950-51
Hamilton, Al	NYR, Buf., Edm.	7	257	10	78	88	258	7	0	0	0	2	....	1965-66	1979-80
Hamilton, Chuck	Mtl., St.L.	2	4	0	2	2	2	....	....	....	....	....	....	1961-62	1972-73
• Hamilton, Jack	Tor.	3	102	28	32	60	20	11	2	1	3	0	....	1942-43	1945-46
Hamilton, Jeff	NYI, Chi., Car., Tor.	5	157	32	45	77	44	....	....	....	....	....	....	2003-04	2008-09
Hamilton, Jim	Pit.	8	95	14	18	32	28	6	3	0	3	0	....	1977-78	1984-85
• Hamilton, Reg	Tor., Chi.	12	424	21	87	108	412	64	3	8	11	46	2	1935-36	1946-47
Hammarstrom, Inge	Tor., St.L.	6	427	116	123	239	86	13	2	3	5	4	....	1973-74	1978-79
Hammond, Ken	L.A., Edm., NYR, Tor., Bos., S.J., Van., Ott.	8	193	18	29	47	290	15	0	0	0	24	....	1984-85	1992-93
Hampson, Gord	Cgy.	1	4	0	0	0	5	....	....	....	....	....	....	1982-83	1982-83
Hampson, Ted	Tor., NYR, Det., Oak., Cal., Min.	12	676	108	245	353	94	35	7	10	17	2	....	1959-60	1971-72
Hampton, Rick	Cal., Cle., L.A.	6	337	59	113	172	147	2	0	0	0	0	....	1974-75	1979-80
Hamr, Radek	Ott.	2	11	0	0	0	0	....	....	....	....	....	....	1992-93	1993-94
Hamway, Mark	NYI	3	53	5	13	18	9	1	0	0	0	0	....	1984-85	1986-87
Handy, Ron	NYI, St.L.	2	14	0	3	3	0	....	....	....	....	....	....	1984-85	1987-88
Hangsleben, Al	Hfd., Wsh., L.A.	3	185	21	48	69	396	....	....	....	....	....	....	1979-80	1981-82
Hankinson, Ben	N.J., T.B.	3	43	3	3	6	45	2	1	0	1	4	....	1992-93	1994-95
Hankinson, Casey	Chi., Ana.	3	18	0	1	1	13	....	....	....	....	....	....	2000-01	2003-04
• Hanna, John	NYR, Mtl., Phi.	5	198	6	26	32	206	....	....	....	....	....	....	1958-59	1967-68
Hannan, Dave	Pit., Edm., Tor., Buf., Col., Ott.	16	841	114	191	305	942	63	6	7	13	46	2	1981-82	1996-97
• Hannigan, Gord	Tor.	4	161	29	31	60	117	9	2	0	2	8	....	1952-53	1955-56
• Hannigan, Pat	Tor., NYR, Phi.	5	182	30	39	69	116	11	1	2	3	11	....	1959-60	1968-69
Hannigan, Ray	Tor.	1	3	0	0	0	2	....	....	....	....	....	....	1948-49	1948-49
Hansen, Richie	NYI, St.L.	4	20	2	8	10	4	....	....	....	....	....	....	1976-77	1981-82
Hansen, Tavis	Wpg., Phx.	5	34	2	1	3	16	2	0	0	0	0	....	1994-95	2000-01
Hanson, Dave	Det., Min.	2	33	1	1	2	65	....	....	....	....	....	....	1978-79	1979-80
• Hanson, Emil	Det.	1	7	0	0	0	6	....	....	....	....	....	....	1932-33	1932-33
Hanson, Keith	Cgy.	1	25	0	2	2	77	....	....	....	....	....	....	1983-84	1983-84
• Hanson, Oscar	Chi.	1	8	0	0	0	0	....	....	....	....	....	....	1937-38	1937-38
• Harbaruk, Nick	Pit., St.L.	5	364	45	75	120	273	14	3	1	4	20	....	1969-70	1973-74
Harding, Jeff	Phi.	2	15	0	0	0	47	....	....	....	....	....	....	1988-89	1989-90
Hardy, Joe	Oak., Cal.	2	63	9	14	23	51	4	0	0	0	0	....	1969-70	1970-71
Hardy, Mark	L.A., NYR, Min.	15	915	62	306	368	1293	67	5	16	21	158	....	1979-80	1993-94
Hargreaves, Jim	Van.	2	66	1	7	8	105	....	....	....	....	....	....	1970-71	1972-73
‡ Harju, Johan	T.B.	1	10	1	2	3	2	....	....	....	....	....	....	2010-11	2010-11
Harkins, Brett	Bos., Fla., CBJ	4	78	6	30	36	22	....	....	....	....	....	....	1994-95	2001-02
Harkins, Todd	Cgy., Hfd.	3	48	3	3	6	78	....	....	....	....	....	....	1991-92	1993-94
Harlock, David	Tor., Wsh., NYI, Atl.	8	212	2	14	16	188	....	....	....	....	....	....	1993-94	2001-02
Harlow, Scott	St.L.	1	1	0	1	1	0	....	....	....	....	....	....	1987-88	1987-88
• Harmon, Glen	Mtl.	9	452	50	96	146	334	53	5	10	15	37	2	1942-43	1950-51
• Harms, John	Chi.	2	44	5	5	10	21	4	3	0	3	2	....	1943-44	1944-45
• Harnott, Walter	Bos.	1	6	0	0	0	2	....	....	....	....	....	....	1933-34	1933-34
Harper, Terry	Mtl., L.A., Det., St.L., Col.	19	1066	35	221	256	1362	112	4	13	17	140	5	1962-63	1980-81
Harrer, Tim	Cgy.	1	3	0	0	0	2	....	....	....	....	....	....	1982-83	1982-83
• Harrington, Hago	Bos., Mtl.	3	72	9	3	12	15	4	1	0	1	2	....	1925-26	1932-33
• Harris, Billy	Tor., Det., Oak., Pit.	13	769	126	219	345	205	62	8	10	18	30	3	1955-56	1968-69
Harris, Billy	NYI, L.A., Tor.	12	897	231	327	558	394	71	19	19	38	48	....	1972-73	1983-84
Harris, Duke	Min., Tor.	1	26	1	4	5	4	....	....	....	....	....	....	1967-68	1967-68
• Harris, Henry	Bos.	1	32	2	4	6	20	....	....	....	....	....	....	1930-31	1930-31
Harris, Hugh	Buf.	1	60	12	26	38	17	3	0	0	0	0	....	1972-73	1972-73
Harris, Ron	Det., Oak., Atl., NYR	11	476	20	91	111	474	28	4	3	7	33	....	1962-63	1975-76
• Harris, Smokey	Bos.	1	6	3	1	4	8	....	....	....	....	....	....	1924-25	1924-25
Harris, Ted	Mtl., Min., Det., St.L., Phi.	12	788	30	168	198	1000	100	1	22	23	230	5	1963-64	1974-75
• Harrison, Ed	Bos., NYR	4	194	27	24	51	53	9	1	0	1	2	....	1947-48	1950-51
Harrison, Jim	Bos., Tor., Chi., Edm.	8	324	67	86	153	435	13	1	1	2	43	....	1968-69	1979-80
Hart, Gerry	Det., NYI, Que., St.L.	15	730	29	150	179	1240	78	3	12	15	175	....	1968-69	1982-83
• Hart, Gizzy	Det., Mtl.	3	104	6	8	14	12	8	0	1	1	0	....	1926-27	1932-33
‡ Hartigan, Mark	Atl., CBJ, Ana., Det.	6	102	19	11	30	58	5	0	1	1	4	1	2001-02	2007-08
Hartman, Mike	Buf., Wpg., T.B., NYR	9	397	43	35	78	1388	21	0	0	0	106	1	1986-87	1994-95
Hartsburg, Craig	Min.	10	570	98	315	413	818	61	15	27	42	70	....	1979-80	1988-89
• Harvey, Buster	Min., Atl., K.C., Det.	7	407	90	118	208	131	14	0	2	2	8	....	1970-71	1976-77
• Harvey, Doug	Mtl., NYR, Det., St.L.	20	1113	88	452	540	1216	137	8	64	72	152	6	1947-48	1968-69
Harvey, Hugh	K.C.	2	18	1	1	2	4	....	....	....	....	....	....	1974-75	1975-76
Harvey, Todd	Dal., NYR, S.J., Edm.	11	671	91	132	223	950	68	3	6	9	52	....	1994-95	2005-06
• Hassard, Bob	Tor., Chi.	5	126	9	28	37	22	....	....	....	....	....	1	1949-50	1954-55
Hatcher, Derian	Min., Dal., Det., Phi.	16	1045	80	251	331	1581	133	7	26	33	248	1	1991-92	2007-08
Hatcher, Kevin	Wsh., Dal., Pit., NYR, Car.	17	1157	227	450	677	1392	118	22	37	59	252	....	1984-85	2000-01
Hatoum, Ed	Det., Van.	3	47	3	6	9	25	....	....	....	....	....	....	1968-69	1970-71
Hauer, Brett	Edm., Nsh.	3	37	4	4	8	38	....	....	....	....	....	....	1995-96	2001-02
Havelid, Niclas	Ana., Atl., N.J.	9	628	34	137	171	342	32	0	7	7	4	....	1999-00	2008-09
Hawerchuk, Dale	Wpg., Buf., St.L., Phi.	16	1188	518	891	1409	730	97	30	69	99	67	....	1981-82	1996-97
Hawgood, Greg	Bos., Edm., Phi., Fla., Pit., S.J., Van., Dal.	12	474	60	164	224	426	42	2	8	10	37	....	1987-88	2001-02

Name	NHL Teams	NHL Seasons	Regular Schedule					Playoffs					NHL Cup Wins	First NHL Season	Last NHL Season
			GP	G	A	TP	PIM	GP	G	A	TP	PIM			
Hawkins, Todd	Van., Tor.	3	10	0	0	0	15	....	....	....	....	....	....	1988-89	1991-92
Haworth, Alan	Buf., Wsh., Que.	8	524	189	211	400	425	42	12	16	28	28	....	1980-81	1987-88
Haworth, Gord	NYR	1	2	0	1	1	0	....	....	....	....	....	....	1952-53	1952-53
Hawryliw, Neil	NYI	1	1	0	0	0	0	....	....	....	....	....	....	1981-82	1981-82
Hay, Bill	Chi.	8	506	113	273	386	244	67	15	21	36	62	1	1959-60	1966-67
Hay, Dwayne	Wsh., Fla., T.B., Cgy.	4	79	2	4	6	22	....	....	....	....	....	....	1997-98	2000-01
• Hay, George	Chi., Det.	6	238	74	60	134	84	8	2	3	5	2	....	1926-27	1932-33
Hay, Jim	Det.	3	75	1	5	6	22	9	1	0	1	2	1	1952-53	1954-55
Hayek, Peter	Min.	1	1	0	0	0	0	....	....	....	....	....	....	1981-82	1981-82
Hayes, Chris	Bos.	1	....	....	....	....	....	1	0	0	0	0	....	1971-72	1971-72
• Haynes, Paul	Mtl.M., Bos., Mtl.	11	391	61	134	195	164	24	2	8	10	13	....	1930-31	1940-41
Hayward, Rick	L.A.	1	4	0	0	0	5	....	....	....	....	....	....	1990-91	1990-91
Hazlett, Steve	Van.	1	1	0	0	0	0	....	....	....	....	....	....	1979-80	1979-80
Head, Galen	Det.	1	1	0	0	0	0	....	....	....	....	....	....	1967-68	1967-68
• Headley, Fern	Bos., Mtl.	1	30	1	3	4	10	1	0	0	0	0	....	1924-25	1924-25
Healey, Eric	Bos.	1	2	0	0	0	2	....	....	....	....	....	....	2005-06	2005-06
Healey, Paul	Phi., Tor., NYR, Col.	6	77	6	14	20	44	22	0	2	2	4	....	1996-97	2005-06
Healey, Rich	Det.	1	1	0	0	0	2	....	....	....	....	....	....	1960-61	1960-61
Heaphy, Shawn	Cgy.	1	1	0	0	0	0	....	....	....	....	....	....	1992-93	1992-93
Heaslip, Mark	NYR, L.A.	3	117	10	19	29	110	5	0	0	0	2	....	1976-77	1978-79
Heath, Randy	NYR	2	13	2	4	6	15	....	....	....	....	....	....	1984-85	1985-86
Hebenton, Andy	NYR, Bos.	9	630	189	202	391	83	22	6	5	11	8	....	1955-56	1963-64
Hecl, Radoslav	Buf.	1	14	0	0	0	2	....	....	....	....	....	....	2002-03	2002-03
Hedberg, Anders	NYR	7	465	172	225	397	144	58	22	24	46	31	....	1978-79	1984-85
Hedican, Bret	St.L., Van., Fla., Car., Ana.	17	1039	55	239	294	893	108	4	22	26	108	1	1991-92	2008-09
‡ Hedin, Pierre	Tor.	1	3	0	1	1	0	....	....	....	....	....	....	2003-04	2003-04
‡ Hedstrom, Jonathan	Ana.	2	83	13	14	27	48	3	0	1	1	2	....	2002-03	2005-06
Heerema, Jeff	Car., St.L.	2	32	4	2	6	6	....	....	....	....	....	....	2002-03	2003-04
• Heffernan, Frank	Tor.	1	19	0	1	1	10	....	....	....	....	....	....	1919-20	1919-20
• Heffernan, Gerry	Mtl.	3	83	33	35	68	27	11	3	3	6	8	1	1941-42	1943-44
Heidt, Mike	L.A.	1	6	0	1	1	7	....	....	....	....	....	....	1983-84	1983-84
‡ Heikkinen, Ilkka	NYR	1	7	0	0	0	0	....	....	....	....	....	....	2009-10	2009-10
• Heindl, Bill	Min., NYR	3	18	2	1	3	0	....	....	....	....	....	....	1970-71	1972-73
Heinrich, Lionel	Bos.	1	35	1	1	2	33	....	....	....	....	....	....	1955-56	1955-56
‡ Heins, Shawn	S.J., Pit., Atl.	6	125	4	12	16	154	2	0	0	0	0	....	1998-99	2003-04
Heinze, Steve	Bos., CBJ, Buf., L.A.	12	694	178	158	336	379	69	11	15	26	48	....	1991-92	2002-03
Heiskala, Earl	Phi.	3	127	13	11	24	294	....	....	....	....	....	....	1968-69	1970-71
Heisten, Barrett	NYR	1	10	0	0	0	2	....	....	....	....	....	....	2001-02	2001-02
Helander, Peter	L.A.	1	7	0	1	1	0	....	....	....	....	....	....	1982-83	1982-83
‡ Helbling, Timo	T.B., Wsh.	2	11	0	1	1	8	....	....	....	....	....	....	2005-06	2006-07
Helenius, Sami	Cgy., T.B., Col., Dal., Chi.	6	155	2	4	6	260	1	0	0	0	0	....	1996-97	2002-03
• Heller, Ott	NYR	15	647	55	176	231	465	61	6	8	14	61	2	1931-32	1945-46
• Helman, Harry	Ott.	3	44	1	0	1	7	2	0	0	0	0	1	1922-23	1924-25
Helmer, Bryan	Phx., St.L., Van., Wsh.	7	146	8	18	26	135	6	0	0	0	0	....	1998-99	2008-09
Helminen, Dwight	Car., S.J.	2	27	2	1	3	0	8	1	0	1	4	....	2008-09	2009-10
Helminen, Raimo	NYR, Min., NYI	3	117	13	46	59	16	2	0	0	0	0	....	1985-86	1988-89
‡ Hemingway, Colin	St.L.	1	3	0	0	0	0	....	....	....	....	....	....	2005-06	2005-06
• Hemmerling, Tony	NYA	2	22	3	3	6	4	....	....	....	....	....	....	1935-36	1936-37
Henderson, Archie	Wsh., Min., Hfd.	3	23	3	1	4	92	....	....	....	....	....	....	1980-81	1982-83
Henderson, Jay	Bos.	4	33	1	3	4	37	....	....	....	....	....	....	1998-99	2001-02
Henderson, Matt	Nsh., Chi.	2	6	0	1	1	2	....	....	....	....	....	....	1998-99	2001-02
Henderson, Murray	Bos.	8	405	24	62	86	305	41	2	3	5	23	....	1944-45	1951-52
Henderson, Paul	Det., Tor., Atl.	13	707	236	241	477	304	56	11	14	25	28	....	1962-63	1979-80
Hendrickson, Darby	Tor., NYI, Van., Min., Col.	11	518	65	64	129	370	25	3	3	6	6	....	1993-94	2003-04
Hendrickson, John	Det.	3	5	0	0	0	4	....	....	....	....	....	....	1957-58	1961-62
Henning, Lorne	NYI	9	543	73	111	184	102	81	7	7	14	8	2	1972-73	1980-81
‡ Henry, Alex	Edm., Wsh., Min., Mtl.	4	177	2	9	11	269	....	....	....	....	....	....	2002-03	2008-09
Henry, Burke	Chi.	2	39	2	6	8	33	....	....	....	....	....	....	2002-03	2003-04
• Henry, Camille	NYR, Chi., St.L.	14	727	279	249	528	88	47	6	12	18	7	....	1953-54	1969-70
Henry, Dale	NYI	6	132	13	26	39	263	14	1	0	1	19	....	1984-85	1989-90
‡ Hentunen, Jukka	Cgy., Nsh.	1	38	4	5	9	4	....	....	....	....	....	....	2001-02	2001-02
Hepple, Alan	N.J.	3	3	0	0	0	7	....	....	....	....	....	....	1983-84	1985-86
Herbers, Ian	Edm., T.B., NYI	2	65	0	5	5	79	....	....	....	....	....	....	1993-94	1999-00
• Herbert, Jimmy	Bos., Tor., Det.	6	206	83	31	114	253	9	3	0	3	10	....	1924-25	1929-30
• Herchenratter, Art	Det.	1	10	1	2	3	2	....	....	....	....	....	....	1940-41	1940-41
• Hergerts, Fred	NYA	2	20	2	4	6	2	....	....	....	....	....	....	1934-35	1935-36
• Hergesheimer, Phil	Chi., Bos.	4	125	21	41	62	19	6	0	0	0	2	....	1939-40	1942-43
Hergesheimer, Wally	NYR, Chi.	7	351	114	85	199	106	5	1	0	1	0	....	1951-52	1958-59
• Heron, Red	Tor., Bro., Mtl.	4	106	21	19	40	38	21	2	2	4	6	....	1938-39	1941-42
Heroux, Yves	Que.	1	1	0	0	0	0	....	....	....	....	....	....	1986-87	1986-87
Herperger, Chris	Chi., Ott., Atl.	4	169	18	25	43	75	....	....	....	....	....	....	1999-00	2002-03
Herr, Matt	Wsh., Fla., Bos.	4	58	4	5	9	25	....	....	....	....	....	....	1998-99	2002-03
Herter, Jason	NYI	1	1	0	1	1	0	....	....	....	....	....	....	1995-96	1995-96
Hervey, Matt	Wpg., Bos., T.B.	3	35	0	5	5	97	5	0	0	0	6	....	1988-89	1992-93
‡ Heshka, Shaun	Phx.	1	8	0	2	2	4	....	....	....	....	....	....	2009-10	2009-10
Hess, Bob	St.L., Buf., Hfd.	8	329	27	95	122	178	4	1	1	2	2	....	1974-75	1983-84
Heward, Jamie	Tor., Nsh., NYI, CBJ, Wsh., L.A., T.B.	9	394	38	86	124	221	....	....	....	....	....	....	1995-96	2008-09
• Heximer, Obs	NYR, Bos., NYA	3	84	13	7	20	16	5	0	0	0	2	....	1929-30	1934-35
• Hextall, Bryan	NYR	11	449	187	175	362	227	37	8	9	17	19	1	1936-37	1947-48
Hextall, Bryan	NYR, Pit., Atl., Det., Min.	8	549	99	161	260	738	18	0	4	4	59	....	1962-63	1975-76
Hextall, Dennis	NYR, L.A., Cal., Min., Det., Wsh.	13	681	153	350	503	1398	22	3	3	6	45	....	1967-68	1979-80
• Heyliger, Vic	Chi.	2	33	2	3	5	2	....	....	....	....	....	....	1937-38	1943-44
• Hicke, Bill	Mtl., NYR, Oak., Cal., Pit.	14	729	168	234	402	395	42	3	10	13	41	2	1958-59	1971-72
Hicke, Ernie	Cal., Atl., NYI, Min., L.A.	8	520	132	140	272	407	2	1	0	1	0	....	1970-71	1977-78
Hickey, Greg	NYR	1	1	0	0	0	0	....	....	....	....	....	....	1977-78	1977-78
Hickey, Pat	NYR, Col., Tor., Que., St.L.	10	646	192	212	404	351	55	5	11	16	37	....	1975-76	1984-85
Hicks, Alex	Ana., Pit., S.J., Fla.	5	258	25	54	79	247	15	0	2	2	8	....	1995-96	1999-00
Hicks, Doug	Min., Chi., Edm., Wsh.	9	561	37	131	168	442	18	2	1	3	15	....	1974-75	1982-83
Hicks, Glenn	Det.	2	108	6	12	18	127	....	....	....	....	....	....	1979-80	1980-81
• Hicks, Henry	Mtl.M., Det.	3	96	7	2	9	72	....	....	....	....	....	....	1928-29	1930-31
Hicks, Wayne	Chi., Bos., Mtl., Phi., Pit.	5	115	13	23	36	22	2	0	1	1	2	1	1959-60	1967-68
Hidi, Andre	Wsh.	2	7	2	1	3	9	2	0	0	0	0	....	1983-84	1984-85
Hiemer, Uli	N.J.	3	143	19	54	73	176	....	....	....	....	....	....	1984-85	1986-87
Higgins, Matt	Mtl.	4	57	1	2	3	6	....	....	....	....	....	....	1997-98	2000-01
Higgins, Paul	Tor.	2	25	0	0	0	152	1	0	0	0	0	....	1981-82	1982-83
Higgins, Tim	Chi., N.J., Det.	11	706	154	198	352	719	65	5	8	13	77	....	1978-79	1988-89
Hilbert, Andy	Bos., Chi., Pit., NYI, Min.	8	307	42	62	104	132	10	1	0	1	2	....	2001-02	2009-10
• Hildebrand, Ike	NYR, Chi.	2	41	7	11	18	16	....	....	....	....	....	....	1953-54	1954-55
Hill, Al	Phi.	8	221	40	55	95	227	51	8	11	19	43	....	1976-77	1987-88
Hill, Brian	Hfd.	1	19	1	1	2	4	....	....	....	....	....	....	1979-80	1979-80
• Hill, Mel	Bos., Bro., Tor.	9	324	89	109	198	128	43	12	7	19	18	3	1937-38	1945-46
Hill, Sean	Mtl., Ana., Ott., Car., St.L., Fla., NYI, Min.	17	876	62	236	298	1008	55	5	5	10	42	1	1990-91	2007-08
• Hiller, Dutch	NYR, Det., Bos., Mtl.	9	383	91	113	204	163	48	9	8	17	21	2	1937-38	1945-46
Hiller, Jim	L.A., Det., NYR	2	63	8	12	20	116	2	0	0	0	4	....	1992-93	1993-94
Hillier, Randy	Bos., Pit., NYI, Buf.	11	543	16	110	126	906	28	0	2	2	93	1	1981-82	1991-92
Hillman, Floyd	Bos.	1	6	0	0	0	10	....	....	....	....	....	....	1956-57	1956-57
Hillman, Larry	Det., Bos., Tor., Min., Mtl., Phi., L.A., Buf.	19	790	36	196	232	579	74	2	9	11	30	6	1954-55	1972-73
• Hillman, Wayne	Chi., NYR, Min., Phi.	13	691	18	86	104	534	28	0	3	3	19	1	1960-61	1972-73
Hilworth, John	Det.	3	57	1	1	2	89	....	....	....	....	....	....	1977-78	1979-80
• Himes, Normie	NYA	9	402	106	113	219	127	2	0	0	0	0	....	1926-27	1934-35
Hindmarch, Dave	Cgy.	4	99	21	17	38	25	10	0	0	0	6	....	1980-81	1983-84
Hinote, Dan	Col., St.L.	9	503	38	52	90	383	72	6	9	15	67	1	1999-00	2008-09
Hinse, Andre	Tor.	1	4	0	0	0	0	....	....	....	....	....	....	1967-68	1967-68
Hinton, Dan	Chi.	1	14	0	0	0	16	....	....	....	....	....	....	1976-77	1976-77
Hirsch, Tom	Min.	3	31	1	7	8	30	12	0	0	0	6	....	1983-84	1987-88
• Hirschfeld, Bert	Mtl.	2	33	1	4	5	2	5	1	0	1	0	....	1949-50	1950-51
Hislop, Jamie	Que., Cgy.	5	345	75	103	178	86	28	3	2	5	11	....	1979-80	1983-84
• Hitchman, Lionel	Ott., Bos.	12	417	28	34	62	523	35	2	2	4	73	2	1922-23	1933-34
‡ Hlavac, Jan	NYR, Phi., Van., Car., T.B., Nsh.	6	436	90	134	224	138	11	0	3	3	2	....	1999-00	2007-08
• Hlinka, Ivan	Van.	2	137	42	81	123	28	16	3	10	13	8	....	1981-82	1982-83
‡ Hlinka, Jaroslav	Col.	1	63	8	20	28	16	1	0	0	0	0	....	2007-08	2007-08
Hlushko, Todd	Phi., Cgy., Pit.	6	79	8	13	21	84	3	0	0	0	2	....	1993-94	1998-99
Hnidy, Shane	Ott., Nsh., Atl., Ana., Bos., Min.	10	550	16	55	71	633	40	4	2	6	34	....	2000-01	2010-11
Hocking, Justin	L.A.	1	1	0	0	0	0	....	....	....	....	....	....	1993-94	1993-94

Gord Haworth

Neil Hawryliw

Paul Haynes

Paul Henderson

Bob Hess

Normie Himes

Tomas Holmstrom

Pete Horeck

			Regular Schedule					Playoffs							
Name	NHL Teams	NHL Seasons	GP	G	A	TP	PIM	GP	G	A	TP	PIM	NHL Cup Wins	First NHL Season	Last NHL Season
Hodge, Ken	Chi., Bos., NYR	14	881	328	472	800	779	97	34	47	81	120	2	1964-65	1977-78
Hodge, Ken	Min., Bos., T.B.	4	142	39	48	87	32	15	4	6	10	6	....	1988-89	1992-93
Hodgson, Dan	Tor., Van.	4	114	29	45	74	64	....	....	....	....	....	....	1985-86	1988-89
Hodgson, Rick	Hfd.	1	6	0	0	0	6	1	0	0	0	0	....	1979-80	1979-80
Hodgson, Ted	Bos.	1	4	0	0	0	0	....	....	....	....	....	....	1966-67	1966-67
Hoekstra, Cec	Mtl.	1	4	0	0	0	0	....	....	....	....	....	....	1959-60	1959-60
• Hoekstra, Ed	Phi.	1	70	15	21	36	6	7	0	1	1	0	....	1967-68	1967-68
Hoene, Phil	L.A.	3	37	2	4	6	22	....	....	....	....	....	....	1972-73	1974-75
• Hoffinger, Val	Chi.	2	28	0	1	1	30	....	....	....	....	....	....	1927-28	1928-29
Hoffman, Mike	Hfd.	3	9	1	3	4	2	....	....	....	....	....	....	1982-83	1985-86
Hoffmeyer, Bob	Chi., Phi., N.J.	6	198	14	52	66	325	3	0	1	1	25	....	1977-78	1984-85
Hofford, Jim	Buf., L.A.	3	18	0	0	0	47	....	....	....	....	....	....	1985-86	1988-89
Hogaboam, Bill	Atl., Det., Min.	8	332	80	109	189	100	2	0	0	0	0	....	1972-73	1979-80
Hoganson, Dale	L.A., Mtl., Que.	7	343	13	77	90	186	11	0	3	3	12	....	1969-70	1981-82
Hoglund, Jonas	Cgy., Mtl., Tor.	7	545	117	145	262	112	59	8	11	19	8	....	1996-97	2002-03
Hogue, Benoit	Buf., NYI, Tor., Dal., T.B., Phx., Bos., Wsh.	15	863	222	321	543	877	92	17	16	33	124	1	1987-88	2001-02
Holan, Milos	Phi., Ana.	3	49	5	11	16	42	....	....	....	....	....	....	1993-94	1995-96
Holbrook, Terry	Min.	2	43	3	6	9	4	6	0	0	0	0	....	1972-73	1973-74
‡ Holden, Josh	Van., Car., Tor.	6	60	5	9	14	16	....	....	....	....	....	....	1998-99	2003-04
Holik, Bobby	Hfd., N.J., NYR, Atl.	18	1314	326	421	747	1423	141	20	39	59	120	2	1990-91	2008-09
‡ Holland, Jason	NYI, Buf., L.A.	7	81	4	5	9	36	1	0	0	0	0	....	1996-97	2003-04
Holland, Jerry	NYR	2	37	8	4	12	6	....	....	....	....	....	....	1974-75	1975-76
• Hollett, Flash	Tor., Ott., Bos., Det.	13	562	132	181	313	358	79	8	26	34	38	2	1933-34	1945-46
Hollinger, Terry	St.L.	2	7	0	0	0	2	....	....	....	....	....	....	1993-94	1994-95
• Hollingworth, Gord	Chi., Det.	4	163	4	14	18	201	3	0	0	0	2	....	1954-55	1957-58
Holloway, Bruce	Van.	1	2	0	0	0	0	....	....	....	....	....	....	1984-85	1984-85
‡ Hollweg, Ryan	NYR, Tor., Phx.	5	228	5	9	14	349	14	0	1	1	23	....	2005-06	2010-11
• Holmes, Bill	Mtl., NYA	3	52	6	4	10	35	....	....	....	....	....	....	1925-26	1929-30
Holmes, Chuck	Det.	2	23	1	3	4	10	....	....	....	....	....	....	1958-59	1961-62
• Holmes, Lou	Chi.	2	59	1	4	5	6	2	0	0	0	2	....	1931-32	1932-33
Holmes, Warren	L.A.	3	45	8	18	26	7	....	....	....	....	....	....	1981-82	1983-84
Holmgren, Paul	Phi., Min.	10	527	144	179	323	1684	82	19	32	51	195	....	1975-76	1984-85
‡ Holmqvist, Michael	Ana., Chi.	3	156	18	17	35	72	....	....	....	....	....	....	2003-04	2006-07
‡ Holmstrom, Tomas	Det.	15	1026	243	287	530	769	180	46	51	97	162	4	1996-97	2011-12
• Holota, John	Det.	2	15	2	0	2	0	....	....	....	....	....	....	1942-43	1945-46
Holst, Greg	NYR	3	11	0	0	0	0	....	....	....	....	....	....	1975-76	1977-78
Holt, Gary	Cal., Cle., St.L.	5	101	13	11	24	133	....	....	....	....	....	....	1973-74	1977-78
Holt, Randy	Chi., Cle., Van., L.A., Cgy., Wsh., Phi.	10	395	4	37	41	1438	21	2	3	5	83	....	1974-75	1983-84
• Holway, Albert	Tor., Mtl.M., Pit.	5	112	7	2	9	48	6	0	0	0	0	1	1923-24	1928-29
Holzinger, Brian	Buf., T.B., Pit., CBJ	10	547	93	145	238	339	52	11	18	29	61	....	1994-95	2003-04
Homenuke, Ron	Van.	1	1	0	0	0	0	....	....	....	....	....	....	1972-73	1972-73
Hoover, Ron	Bos., St.L.	3	18	4	0	4	31	8	0	0	0	18	....	1989-90	1991-92
Hopkins, Dean	L.A., Edm., Que.	6	223	23	51	74	306	18	1	5	6	29	....	1979-80	1988-89
Hopkins, Larry	Tor., Wpg.	4	60	13	16	29	26	6	0	0	0	2	....	1977-78	1982-83
Horacek, Tony	Phi., Chi.	5	154	10	19	29	316	2	1	0	1	2	....	1989-90	1994-95
Horava, Miloslav	NYR	3	80	5	17	22	38	2	0	1	1	0	....	1988-89	1990-91
Horbul, Doug	K.C.	1	4	1	0	1	2	....	....	....	....	....	....	1974-75	1974-75
Hordy, Mike	NYI	2	11	0	0	0	7	....	....	....	....	....	....	1978-79	1979-80
• Horeck, Pete	Chi., Det., Bos.	8	426	106	118	224	340	34	6	8	14	43	....	1944-45	1951-52
• Horne, George	Mtl.M., Tor.	3	54	9	3	12	34	4	0	0	0	4	1	1925-26	1928-29
• Horner, Red	Tor.	12	490	42	110	152	1254	71	7	10	17	170	1	1928-29	1939-40
• Hornung, Larry	St.L.	2	48	2	9	11	10	11	0	2	2	2	....	1970-71	1971-72
• Horton, Tim	Tor., NYR, Pit., Buf.	24	1446	115	403	518	1611	126	11	39	50	183	4	1949-50	1973-74
Horvath, Bronco	NYR, Mtl., Bos., Chi., Tor., Min.	9	434	141	185	326	319	36	12	9	21	18	....	1955-56	1967-68
Hospodar, Ed	NYR, Hfd., Phi., Min., Buf.	9	450	17	51	68	1314	44	4	1	5	208	....	1979-80	1987-88
‡ Hossa, Marcel	Mtl., NYR, Phx.	6	237	31	30	61	106	14	2	2	4	10	....	2001-02	2007-08
Hostak, Martin	Phi.	2	55	3	11	14	24	....	....	....	....	....	....	1990-91	1991-92
Hotham, Greg	Tor., Pit.	6	230	15	74	89	139	5	0	3	3	6	....	1979-80	1984-85
Houck, Paul	Min.	3	16	1	2	3	2	....	....	....	....	....	....	1985-86	1987-88
Houda, Doug	Det., Hfd., L.A., Buf., NYI, Ana.	15	561	19	63	82	1104	18	0	3	3	21	....	1985-86	2002-03
Houde, Claude	K.C.	2	59	3	6	9	40	....	....	....	....	....	....	1974-75	1975-76
Houde, Eric	Mtl.	3	30	2	3	5	4	....	....	....	....	....	....	1996-97	1998-99
Hough, Mike	Que., Fla., NYI	14	707	100	156	256	675	44	5	5	10	38	....	1984-85	1998-99
Houlder, Bill	Wsh., Buf., Ana., St.L., T.B., S.J., Nsh.	16	846	59	191	250	412	30	5	6	11	14	....	1987-88	2002-03
Houle, Rejean	Mtl.	11	635	161	247	408	395	90	14	34	48	66	5	1969-70	1982-83
Housley, Phil	Buf., Wpg., St.L., Cgy., N.J., Wsh., Chi., Tor.	21	1495	338	894	1232	822	85	13	43	56	36	....	1982-83	2002-03
Houston, Ken	Atl., Cgy., Wsh., L.A.	9	570	161	167	328	624	35	10	9	19	66	....	1975-76	1983-84
Howard, Jack	Tor.	1	2	0	0	0	0	....	....	....	....	....	....	1936-37	1936-37
Howatt, Garry	NYI, Hfd., N.J.	12	720	112	156	268	1836	87	12	14	26	289	2	1972-73	1983-84
Howe, Gordie	Det., Hfd.	26	1767	801	1049	1850	1685	157	68	92	160	220	4	1946-47	1979-80
Howe, Mark	Hfd., Phi., Det.	16	929	197	545	742	455	101	10	51	61	34	....	1979-80	1994-95
Howe, Marty	Hfd., Bos.	6	197	2	29	31	99	15	1	2	3	9	....	1979-80	1984-85
• Howe, Syd	Ott., Phi., Tor., St.L., Det.	17	698	237	291	528	212	70	17	27	44	10	3	1929-30	1945-46
Howe, Vic	NYR	3	33	3	4	7	10	....	....	....	....	....	....	1950-51	1954-55
Howell, Harry	NYR, Oak., Cal., L.A.	21	1411	94	324	418	1298	38	3	3	6	32	....	1952-53	1972-73
• Howell, Ron	NYR	2	4	0	0	0	0	....	....	....	....	....	....	1954-55	1955-56
Howse, Don	L.A.	1	33	2	5	7	6	2	0	0	0	0	....	1979-80	1979-80
Howson, Scott	NYI	2	18	5	3	8	4	....	....	....	....	....	....	1984-85	1985-86
Hoyda, Dave	Phi., Wpg.	4	132	6	17	23	299	12	0	0	0	17	....	1977-78	1980-81
Hrdina, Jan	Pit., Phx., N.J., CBJ	7	513	101	196	297	341	45	12	14	26	24	....	1998-99	2005-06
Hrdina, Jiri	Cgy., Pit.	5	250	45	85	130	92	46	2	5	7	24	3	1987-88	1991-92
• Hrechkosy, Dave	Cal., St.L.	4	140	42	24	66	41	3	1	0	1	2	....	1973-74	1976-77
Hrkac, Tony	St.L., Que., S.J., Chi., Dal., Edm., NYI, Ana., Atl.	13	758	132	239	371	173	41	7	7	14	12	1	1986-87	2002-03
Hrycuik, Jim	Wsh.	1	21	5	5	10	12	....	....	....	....	....	....	1974-75	1974-75
Hrymnak, Steve	Chi., Det.	2	18	2	1	3	4	2	0	0	0	0	....	1951-52	1952-53
Hrynewich, Tim	Pit.	2	55	6	8	14	82	....	....	....	....	....	....	1982-83	1983-84
Huard, Bill	Bos., Ott., Que., Dal., Edm., L.A.	8	223	16	18	34	594	5	0	0	0	2	....	1992-93	1999-00
• Huard, Rolly	Tor.	1	1	1	0	1	0	....	....	....	....	....	....	1930-31	1930-31
‡ Hubacek, Petr	Phi.	1	6	1	0	1	2	....	....	....	....	....	....	2000-01	2000-01
• Huber, Willie	Det., NYR, Van., Phi.	10	655	104	217	321	950	33	5	5	10	35	....	1978-79	1987-88
Hubick, Greg	Tor., Van.	2	77	6	9	15	10	....	....	....	....	....	....	1975-76	1979-80
Huck, Fran	Mtl., St.L.	3	94	24	30	54	38	11	3	4	7	2	....	1969-70	1972-73
Hucul, Fred	Chi., St.L.	5	164	11	30	41	113	6	1	0	1	10	....	1950-51	1967-68
Huddy, Charlie	Edm., L.A., Buf., St.L.	17	1017	99	354	453	785	183	19	66	85	135	5	1980-81	1996-97
Hudson, Dave	NYI, K.C., Col.	6	409	59	124	183	89	2	1	1	2	0	....	1972-73	1977-78
Hudson, Lex	Pit.	1	2	0	0	0	0	2	0	0	0	0	....	1978-79	1978-79
Hudson, Mike	Chi., Edm., NYR, Pit., Tor., St.L., Phx.	9	416	49	87	136	414	49	4	10	14	64	1	1988-89	1996-97
Hudson, Ron	Det.	2	33	5	2	7	2	....	....	....	....	....	....	1937-38	1939-40
Huffman, Kerry	Phi., Que., Ott.	10	401	37	108	145	361	11	0	0	0	2	....	1986-87	1995-96
Huggins, Al	Mtl.M.	1	20	1	1	2	2	....	....	....	....	....	....	1930-31	1930-31
• Hughes, Albert	NYA	2	60	6	8	14	22	....	....	....	....	....	....	1930-31	1931-32
Hughes, Brent	L.A., Phi., St.L., Det., K.C.	8	435	15	117	132	440	22	1	3	4	53	....	1967-68	1974-75
Hughes, Brent	Wpg., Bos., Buf., NYI	8	357	41	39	80	831	29	4	1	5	53	....	1988-89	1996-97
Hughes, Frank	Cal.	1	5	0	0	0	0	....	....	....	....	....	....	1971-72	1971-72
Hughes, Howie	L.A.	3	168	25	32	57	30	14	2	0	2	2	....	1967-68	1969-70
Hughes, Jack	Col.	2	46	2	5	7	104	....	....	....	....	....	....	1980-81	1981-82
• Hughes, James	Det.	1	40	0	1	1	48	....	....	....	....	....	....	1929-30	1929-30
Hughes, John	Van., Edm., NYR	2	70	2	14	16	211	7	0	1	1	16	....	1979-80	1980-81
Hughes, Pat	Mtl., Pit., Edm., Buf., St.L., Hfd.	10	573	130	128	258	646	71	8	25	33	77	3	1977-78	1986-87
Hughes, Ryan	Bos.	1	3	0	0	0	0	....	....	....	....	....	....	1995-96	1995-96
Hulbig, Joe	Edm., Bos.	5	55	4	4	8	16	6	0	1	1	2	....	1996-97	2000-01
Hull, Bobby	Chi., Wpg., Hfd.	16	1063	610	560	1170	640	119	62	67	129	102	1	1957-58	1979-80
Hull, Brett	Cgy., St.L., Dal., Det., Phx.	20	1269	741	650	1391	458	202	103	87	190	73	2	1985-86	2005-06
Hull, Dennis	Chi., Det.	14	959	303	351	654	261	104	33	34	67	30	....	1964-65	1977-78
Hull, Jody	Hfd., NYR, Ott., Fla., T.B., Phi.	16	831	124	137	261	156	69	4	5	9	14	....	1988-89	2003-04
Hulse, Cale	N.J., Cgy., Nsh., Phx., CBJ	10	619	16	79	95	1000	1	0	0	0	0	....	1995-96	2005-06
‡ Huml, Ivan	Bos.	3	49	6	12	18	36	....	....	....	....	....	....	2001-02	2003-04
• Hunt, Fred	NYA, NYR	2	59	15	14	29	6	....	....	....	....	....	....	1940-41	1944-45
Hunt, Jamie	Wsh.	1	1	0	0	0	0	....	....	....	....	....	....	2006-07	2006-07
Hunter, Dale	Que., Wsh., Col.	19	1407	323	697	1020	3565	186	42	76	118	729	....	1980-81	1998-99
Hunter, Dave	Edm., Pit., Wpg.	10	746	133	190	323	918	105	16	24	40	211	3	1979-80	1988-89
Hunter, Mark	Mtl., St.L., Cgy., Hfd., Wsh.	12	628	213	171	384	1426	79	18	20	38	230	1	1981-82	1992-93
Hunter, Tim	Cgy., Que., Van., S.J.	16	815	62	76	138	3146	132	5	7	12	426	1	1981-82	1996-97

Name	NHL Teams	NHL Seasons	Regular Schedule GP	G	A	TP	PIM	Playoffs GP	G	A	TP	PIM	NHL Cup Wins	First NHL Season	Last NHL Season
Hunter, Trent	NYI, L.A.	10	497	101	135	236	209	14	4	1	5	6	....	2001-02	2011-12
Huras, Larry	NYR	1	2	0	0	0	0	....	....	....	....	....	....	1976-77	1976-77
Hurlburt, Bob	Van.	1	1	0	0	0	2	....	....	....	....	....	....	1974-75	1974-75
Hurlbut, Mike	NYR, Que., Buf.	5	29	1	8	9	20	....	....	....	....	....	....	1992-93	1999-00
Hurley, Paul	Bos.	1	1	0	1	1	0	....	....	....	....	....	....	1968-69	1968-69
Hurst, Ron	Tor.	2	64	9	7	16	70	3	0	2	2	4	....	1955-56	1956-57
Huscroft, Jamie	N.J., Bos., Cgy., T.B., Van., Phx., Wsh.	10	352	5	33	38	1065	21	0	1	1	46	....	1988-89	1999-00
Huselius, Kristian	Fla., Cgy., CBJ	10	662	190	261	451	256	24	3	11	14	18	....	2001-02	2011-12
Huska, Ryan	Chi.	1	1	0	0	0	0	....	....	....	....	....	....	1997-98	1997-98
Hussey, Matt	Pit., Det.	3	21	2	2	4	2	....	....	....	....	....	....	2003-04	2006-07
Huston, Ron	Cal.	2	79	15	31	46	8	....	....	....	....	....	....	1973-74	1974-75
‡ Hutchinson, Andrew	Nsh., Car., T.B., Dal., Pit.	5	140	12	27	39	70	....	....	....	....	....	1	2003-04	2010-11
Hutchinson, Ron	NYR	1	9	0	0	0	0	....	....	....	....	....	....	1960-61	1960-61
Hutchison, Dave	L.A., Tor., Chi., N.J.	10	584	19	97	116	1550	48	2	12	14	149	....	1974-75	1983-84
• Hutton, Bill	Bos., Ott., Phi.	2	64	3	2	5	8	2	0	0	0	0	....	1929-30	1930-31
• Hyland, Harry	Mtl.W., Ott.	1	17	14	2	16	65	....	....	....	....	....	....	1917-18	1917-18
Hynes, Dave	Bos.	2	22	4	0	4	2	....	....	....	....	....	....	1973-74	1974-75
Hynes, Gord	Bos., Phi.	2	52	3	9	12	22	12	1	2	3	6	....	1991-92	1992-93
‡ Hyvonen, Hannes	S.J., CBJ	2	42	4	5	9	22	....	....	....	....	....	....	2001-02	2002-03

I

Name	NHL Teams	NHL Seasons	Regular Schedule GP	G	A	TP	PIM	Playoffs GP	G	A	TP	PIM	NHL Cup Wins	First NHL Season	Last NHL Season
Iafrate, Al	Tor., Wsh., Bos., S.J.	12	799	152	311	463	1301	71	19	16	35	77	....	1984-85	1997-98
‡ Iggulden, Mike	S.J., NYI	2	12	1	4	5	4	....	....	....	....	....	....	2007-08	2008-09
Ignatjev, Victor	Pit.	1	11	0	1	1	6	1	0	0	0	2	....	1998-99	1998-99
Ihnacak, Miroslav	Tor., Det.	3	56	8	9	17	39	1	0	0	0	0	....	1985-86	1988-89
Ihnacak, Peter	Tor.	8	417	102	165	267	175	28	4	10	14	25	....	1982-83	1989-90
Imlach, Brent	Tor.	2	3	0	0	0	0	....	....	....	....	....	....	1965-66	1966-67
‡ Immonen, Jarkko	NYR	2	20	3	5	8	4	....	....	....	....	....	....	2005-06	2006-07
Ingarfield, Earl	NYR, Pit., Oak., Cal.	13	746	179	226	405	239	21	9	8	17	10	....	1958-59	1970-71
Ingarfield, Earl	Atl., Cgy., Det.	2	39	4	4	8	22	2	0	1	1	0	....	1979-80	1980-81
Inglis, Billy	L.A., Buf.	3	36	1	3	4	4	11	1	2	3	4	....	1967-68	1970-71
• Ingoldsby, Jack	Tor.	2	29	5	1	6	15	....	....	....	....	....	....	1942-43	1943-44
• Ingram, Frank	Chi.	3	101	24	16	40	69	11	0	1	1	2	....	1929-30	1931-32
• Ingram, John	Bos.	1	1	0	0	0	0	....	....	....	....	....	....	1924-25	1924-25
• Ingram, Ron	Chi., Det., NYR	4	114	5	15	20	81	2	0	0	0	0	....	1956-57	1964-65
‡ Intranuovo, Ralph	Edm., Tor.	3	22	2	4	6	4	....	....	....	....	....	....	1994-95	1996-97
‡ Irmen, Danny	Min.	1	2	0	0	0	0	....	....	....	....	....	....	2009-10	2009-10
• Irvin, Dick	Chi.	3	94	29	23	52	78	2	2	0	2	4	....	1926-27	1928-29
Irvine, Ted	Bos., L.A., NYR, St.L.	11	724	154	177	331	657	83	16	24	40	115	....	1963-64	1976-77
‡ Irwin, Brayden	Tor.	1	2	0	0	0	2	....	....	....	....	....	....	2009-10	2009-10
Irwin, Ivan	Mtl., NYR	5	155	2	27	29	214	5	0	0	0	8	....	1952-53	1957-58
• Isaksson, Ulf	L.A.	1	50	7	15	22	10	....	....	....	....	....	....	1982-83	1982-83
Isbister, Brad	Phx., NYI, Edm., Bos., NYR, Van.	10	541	106	116	222	615	18	1	2	3	33	....	1997-98	2007-08
Issel, Kim	Edm.	1	4	0	0	0	0	....	....	....	....	....	....	1988-89	1988-89
‡ Ivanans, Raitis	Mtl., L.A., Cgy.	7	282	12	6	18	569	1	0	0	0	0	....	2005-06	2011-12

J

Name	NHL Teams	NHL Seasons	Regular Schedule GP	G	A	TP	PIM	Playoffs GP	G	A	TP	PIM	NHL Cup Wins	First NHL Season	Last NHL Season
Jacina, Greg	Fla.	2	14	0	1	1	6	....	....	....	....	....	....	2005-06	2006-07
‡ Jackman, Ric	Dal., Bos., Tor., Pit., Fla., Ana.	7	231	19	58	77	166	7	1	1	2	2	1	1999-00	2006-07
• Jackson, Art	Tor., Bos., NYA	11	468	123	178	301	144	52	8	12	20	29	2	1934-35	1944-45
• Jackson, Busher	Tor., NYA, Bos.	15	633	241	234	475	437	71	18	12	30	53	1	1929-30	1943-44
Jackson, Dane	Van., Buf., NYI	4	45	12	6	18	58	6	0	0	0	10	....	1993-94	1997-98
Jackson, Don	Min., Edm., NYR	10	311	16	52	68	640	53	4	5	9	147	2	1977-78	1986-87
• Jackson, Harold	Chi., Det.	8	219	17	34	51	208	31	1	2	3	33	2	1936-37	1946-47
Jackson, Jack	Chi.	1	48	2	5	7	38	....	....	....	....	....	....	1946-47	1946-47
Jackson, Jeff	Tor., NYR, Que., Chi.	8	263	38	48	86	313	6	1	1	2	16	....	1984-85	1991-92
Jackson, Jim	Cgy., Buf.	4	112	17	30	47	20	14	3	2	5	6	....	1982-83	1987-88
• Jackson, Lloyd	NYA	1	14	1	1	2	0	....	....	....	....	....	....	1936-37	1936-37
Jackson, Scott	T.B.	1	1	0	0	0	0	....	....	....	....	....	....	2009-10	2009-10
• Jackson, Stan	Tor., Bos., Ott.	5	86	9	6	15	75	....	....	....	....	....	1	1921-22	1926-27
Jackson, Walter	NYA, Bos.	4	84	16	11	27	18	....	....	....	....	....	....	1932-33	1935-36
• Jacobs, Paul	Tor.	1	1	0	0	0	0	....	....	....	....	....	....	1918-19	1918-19
Jacobs, Tim	Cal.	1	46	0	10	10	35	....	....	....	....	....	....	1975-76	1975-76
Jakopin, John	Fla., Pit., S.J.	6	113	1	6	7	145	....	....	....	....	....	....	1997-98	2002-03
Jalo, Risto	Edm.	1	3	0	3	3	0	....	....	....	....	....	....	1985-86	1985-86
Jalonen, Kari	Cgy., Edm.	2	37	9	6	15	4	5	1	0	1	0	....	1982-83	1983-84
‡ James, Connor	L.A., Pit.	3	16	1	0	1	2	....	....	....	....	....	....	2005-06	2008-09
James, Gerry	Tor.	5	149	14	26	40	257	15	1	0	1	8	....	1954-55	1959-60
James, Val	Buf., Tor.	2	11	0	0	0	30	3	0	0	0	0	....	1981-82	1986-87
Jamieson, Jim	NYR	1	1	0	1	1	0	....	....	....	....	....	....	1943-44	1943-44
Jancevski, Dan	Dal., T.B.	3	9	0	0	0	2	....	....	....	....	....	....	2005-06	2008-09
• Jankowski, Lou	Det., Chi.	4	127	19	18	37	15	1	0	0	0	0	....	1950-51	1954-55
Janney, Craig	Bos., St.L., S.J., Wpg., Phx., T.B., NYI	12	760	188	563	751	170	120	24	86	110	53	....	1987-88	1998-99
Janssens, Mark	NYR, Min., Hfd., Ana., NYI, Phx., Chi.	14	711	40	73	113	1422	27	5	1	6	33	....	1987-88	2000-01
Jantunen, Marko	Cgy.	1	3	0	0	0	0	....	....	....	....	....	....	1996-97	1996-97
‡ Jardine, Ryan	Fla.	1	8	0	2	2	2	....	....	....	....	....	....	2001-02	2001-02
Jarrett, Cole	NYI	1	1	0	0	0	0	....	....	....	....	....	....	2005-06	2005-06
Jarrett, Doug	Chi., NYR	13	775	38	182	220	631	99	7	16	23	82	....	1964-65	1976-77
Jarrett, Gary	Tor., Det., Oak., Cal.	7	341	72	92	164	131	11	3	1	4	9	....	1960-61	1971-72
Jarry, Pierre	NYR, Tor., Det., Min.	7	344	88	117	205	142	5	0	1	1	0	....	1971-72	1977-78
Jarvenpaa, Hannu	Wpg.	3	114	11	26	37	83	....	....	....	....	....	....	1986-87	1988-89
‡ Jarventie, Martti	Mtl.	1	1	0	0	0	0	....	....	....	....	....	....	2001-02	2001-02
Jarvi, Iiro	Que.	2	116	18	43	61	58	....	....	....	....	....	....	1988-89	1989-90
Jarvis, Doug	Mtl., Wsh., Hfd.	13	964	139	264	403	263	105	14	27	41	42	4	1975-76	1987-88
• Jarvis, James	Pit., Phi., Tor.	3	112	17	15	32	62	....	....	....	....	....	....	1929-30	1936-37
Jarvis, Wes	Wsh., Min., L.A., Tor.	9	237	31	55	86	98	2	0	0	0	2	....	1979-80	1987-88
‡ Jaspers, Jason	Phx.	3	9	0	1	1	6	....	....	....	....	....	....	2001-02	2003-04
• Javanainen, Arto	Pit.	1	14	4	1	5	2	....	....	....	....	....	....	1984-85	1984-85
Jay, Bob	L.A.	1	3	0	1	1	0	....	....	....	....	....	....	1993-94	1993-94
Jeffrey, Larry	Det., Tor., NYR	8	368	39	62	101	293	38	4	10	14	42	1	1961-62	1968-69
Jelinek, Tomas	Ott.	1	49	7	6	13	52	....	....	....	....	....	....	1992-93	1992-93
Jenkins, Dean	L.A.	1	5	0	0	0	2	....	....	....	....	....	....	1983-84	1983-84
• Jenkins, Roger	Chi., Tor., Mtl., Bos., Mtl.M., NYA	8	325	15	39	54	253	27	1	7	8	12	2	1930-31	1938-39
• Jennings, Bill	Det., Bos.	5	108	32	33	65	45	20	4	4	8	6	....	1940-41	1944-45
Jennings, Grant	Wsh., Hfd., Pit., Tor., Buf.	9	389	14	43	57	804	54	2	1	3	68	2	1987-88	1995-96
Jensen, Chris	NYR, Phi.	6	74	9	12	21	27	....	....	....	....	....	....	1985-86	1991-92
Jensen, David	Min.	3	18	0	2	2	11	....	....	....	....	....	....	1983-84	1985-86
Jensen, David	Hfd., Wsh.	4	69	9	13	22	22	11	0	0	0	2	....	1984-85	1987-88
Jensen, Joe	Car.	1	6	1	0	1	2	....	....	....	....	....	....	2007-08	2007-08
Jensen, Steve	Min., L.A.	7	438	113	107	220	318	12	0	3	3	9	....	1975-76	1981-82
• Jeremiah, Ed	NYA, Bos.	1	15	0	1	1	0	....	....	....	....	....	....	1931-32	1931-32
Jerrard, Paul	Min.	1	5	0	0	0	4	....	....	....	....	....	....	1988-89	1988-89
• Jerwa, Frank	Bos., St.L.	4	81	11	16	27	53	....	....	....	....	....	....	1931-32	1934-35
• Jerwa, Joe	NYR, Bos., NYA	7	234	29	58	87	309	17	2	3	5	16	....	1930-31	1938-39
‡ Jessiman, Hugh	Fla.	1	2	0	0	0	5	....	....	....	....	....	....	2010-11	2010-11
Jillson, Jeff	S.J., Bos., Buf.	4	140	9	32	41	96	8	0	0	0	0	....	2001-02	2005-06
• Jirik, Jaroslav	St.L.	1	3	0	0	0	0	....	....	....	....	....	....	1969-70	1969-70
• Joanette, Rosario	Mtl.	1	2	0	1	1	4	....	....	....	....	....	....	1944-45	1944-45
Jodzio, Rick	Col., Cle.	1	70	2	8	10	71	....	....	....	....	....	....	1977-78	1977-78
Johannesen, Glenn	NYI	1	2	0	0	0	0	....	....	....	....	....	....	1985-86	1985-86
Johannson, John	N.J.	1	5	0	0	0	0	....	....	....	....	....	....	1983-84	1983-84
• Johansen, Bill	Tor.	1	1	0	0	0	0	....	....	....	....	....	....	1949-50	1949-50
Johansen, Trevor	Tor., Col., L.A.	5	286	11	46	57	282	13	0	3	3	21	....	1977-78	1981-82
Johansson, Andreas	NYI, Pit., Ott., T.B., Cgy., NYR, Nsh.	8	377	81	88	169	190	9	0	0	0	0	....	1995-96	2003-04
Johansson, Bjorn	Cle.	2	15	1	1	2	10	....	....	....	....	....	....	1976-77	1977-78
Johansson, Calle	Buf., Wsh., Tor.	17	1109	119	416	535	519	105	12	43	55	44	....	1987-88	2003-04
Johansson, Jonas	Wsh.	1	1	0	0	0	2	....	....	....	....	....	....	2005-06	2005-06
‡ Johansson, Magnus	Chi., Fla.	1	45	0	14	14	18	....	....	....	....	....	....	2007-08	2007-08
Johansson, Mathias	Cgy., Pit.	1	58	5	10	15	16	....	....	....	....	....	....	2002-03	2002-03
Johansson, Roger	Cgy., Chi.	4	161	9	34	43	163	5	0	1	1	2	....	1989-90	1994-95
Johns, Don	NYR, Mtl., Min.	6	153	2	21	23	76	....	....	....	....	....	....	1960-61	1967-68
Johnson, Allan	Mtl., Det.	4	105	21	28	49	30	11	2	2	4	6	....	1956-57	1962-63
Johnson, Brian	Det.	1	3	0	0	0	5	....	....	....	....	....	....	1983-84	1983-84
• Johnson, Ching	NYR, NYA	12	436	38	48	86	808	61	5	2	7	161	2	1926-27	1937-38

Fred Hucul

Al Iafrate

Jim Johnson

Tom Johnson

Ross Johnstone

Brad Jones

Walter Kalbfleisch

Steve Kasper

Name	NHL Teams	NHL Seasons	Regular Schedule GP	G	A	TP	PIM	Playoffs GP	G	A	TP	PIM	NHL Cup Wins	First NHL Season	Last NHL Season
Johnson, Craig	St.L., L.A., Ana., Tor., Wsh.	10	557	75	98	173	260	16	3	2	5	10	....	1994-95	2003-04
● Johnson, Danny	Tor., Van., Det.	3	121	18	19	37	24	....	....	....	....	....	....	1969-70	1971-72
Johnson, Earl	Det.	1	1	0	0	0	0	....	....	....	....	....	1	1953-54	1953-54
Johnson, Greg	Det., Pit., Chi., Nsh.	12	785	145	224	369	345	37	7	6	13	14	....	1993-94	2005-06
Johnson, Jim	NYR, Phi., L.A.	8	302	75	111	186	73	7	0	2	2	2	....	1964-65	1971-72
Johnson, Jim	Pit., Min., Dal., Wsh., Phx.	13	829	29	166	195	1197	51	1	11	12	132	....	1985-86	1997-98
Johnson, Mark	Pit., Min., Hfd., St.L., N.J.	11	669	203	305	508	260	37	16	12	28	10	....	1979-80	1989-90
Johnson, Matt	L.A., Atl., Min.	10	473	23	20	43	1523	16	0	0	0	31	....	1994-95	2003-04
Johnson, Mike	Tor., T.B., Phx., Mtl., St.L.	11	661	129	246	375	315	22	4	3	7	10	....	1996-97	2007-08
Johnson, Norm	Bos., Chi.	3	61	5	20	25	41	14	4	0	4	6	....	1957-58	1959-60
Johnson, Ryan	Fla., T.B., St.L., Van., Chi.	13	701	38	84	122	250	29	1	4	5	12	....	1997-98	2010-11
Johnson, Terry	Que., St.L., Cgy., Tor.	9	285	3	24	27	580	38	0	4	4	118	....	1979-80	1987-88
● Johnson, Tom	Mtl., Bos.	17	978	51	213	264	960	111	8	15	23	109	6	1947-48	1964-65
● Johnson, Virgil	Chi.	3	75	1	11	12	27	19	0	3	3	4	1	1937-38	1944-45
Johnsson, Kim	NYR, Phi., Min., Chi.	10	739	67	217	284	406	43	2	10	12	38	....	1999-00	2009-10
Johnston, Bernie	Hfd.	2	57	12	24	36	16	3	0	1	1	0	....	1979-80	1980-81
● Johnston, George	Chi.	4	58	20	12	32	2	....	....	....	....	....	....	1941-42	1946-47
Johnston, Greg	Bos., Tor.	9	187	26	29	55	124	22	2	1	3	12	....	1983-84	1991-92
Johnston, Jay	Wsh.	2	8	0	0	0	13	....	....	....	....	....	....	1980-81	1981-82
Johnston, Joey	Min., Cal., Chi.	6	331	85	106	191	320	....	....	....	....	....	....	1968-69	1975-76
Johnston, Larry	L.A., Det., K.C., Col.	7	320	9	64	73	580	....	....	....	....	....	....	1967-68	1976-77
Johnston, Marshall	Min., Cal.	7	251	14	52	66	58	6	0	0	0	2	....	1967-68	1973-74
Johnston, Randy	NYI	1	4	0	0	0	4	....	....	....	....	....	....	1979-80	1979-80
Johnstone, Eddie	NYR, Det.	10	426	122	136	258	375	55	13	10	23	83	....	1975-76	1986-87
● Johnstone, Ross	Tor.	2	42	5	4	9	14	3	0	0	0	0	1	1943-44	1944-45
‡ Jokela, Mikko	Van.	1	1	0	0	0	0	....	....	....	....	....	....	2002-03	2002-03
● Joliat, Aurele	Mtl.	16	655	270	190	460	771	45	9	13	22	66	3	1922-23	1937-38
● Joliat, Rene	Mtl.	1	1	0	0	0	0	....	....	....	....	....	....	1924-25	1924-25
Joly, Greg	Wsh., Det.	9	365	21	76	97	250	5	0	0	0	8	....	1974-75	1982-83
Joly, Yvan	Mtl.	3	2	0	0	0	0	1	0	0	0	0	....	1979-80	1982-83
Jomphe, Jean-Francois	Ana., Phx., Mtl.	4	111	10	29	39	102	....	....	....	....	....	....	1995-96	1998-99
Jonathan, Stan	Bos., Pit.	8	411	91	110	201	751	63	8	4	12	137	....	1975-76	1982-83
Jones, Bob	NYR	1	2	0	0	0	0	....	....	....	....	....	....	1968-69	1968-69
Jones, Brad	Wpg., L.A., Phi.	6	148	25	31	56	122	9	1	1	2	2	....	1986-87	1991-92
● Jones, Buck	Det., Tor.	4	50	2	2	4	36	12	0	1	1	18	....	1938-39	1942-43
Jones, Jim	Cal.	1	2	0	0	0	0	....	....	....	....	....	....	1971-72	1971-72
Jones, Jimmy	Tor.	3	148	13	18	31	68	19	1	5	6	11	....	1977-78	1979-80
Jones, Keith	Wsh., Col., Phi.	9	491	117	141	258	765	63	12	12	24	120	....	1992-93	2000-01
Jones, Matt	Phx.	3	106	1	10	11	63	....	....	....	....	....	....	2005-06	2007-08
Jones, Ron	Bos., Pit., Wsh.	5	54	1	4	5	31	....	....	....	....	....	....	1971-72	1975-76
Jones, Ty	Chi., Fla.	2	14	0	0	0	19	....	....	....	....	....	....	1998-99	2003-04
Jonsson, Hans	Pit.	4	242	10	38	48	92	27	0	1	1	14	....	1999-00	2002-03
Jonsson, Jorgen	NYI, Ana.	1	81	12	19	31	16	....	....	....	....	....	....	1999-00	1999-00
Jonsson, Kenny	Tor., NYI	10	686	63	204	267	298	19	1	3	4	6	....	1994-95	2003-04
‡ Jonsson, Lars	Phi.	1	8	0	2	2	6	....	....	....	....	....	....	2006-07	2006-07
Jonsson, Tomas	NYI, Edm.	8	552	85	259	344	482	80	11	26	37	97	2	1981-82	1988-89
Joseph, Chris	Pit., Edm., T.B., Van., Phi., Phx., Atl.	14	510	39	112	151	567	31	3	4	7	24	....	1987-88	2000-01
Joseph, Tony	Wpg.	1	2	1	0	1	0	....	....	....	....	....	....	1988-89	1988-89
Joyal, Eddie	Det., Tor., L.A., Phi.	9	466	128	134	262	103	50	11	8	19	18	....	1962-63	1971-72
Joyce, Bob	Bos., Wsh., Wpg.	6	158	34	49	83	90	46	15	9	24	29	....	1987-88	1992-93
Joyce, Duane	Dal.	1	3	0	0	0	0	....	....	....	....	....	....	1993-94	1993-94
● Juckes, Bing	NYR	2	16	2	1	3	6	....	....	....	....	....	....	1947-48	1949-50
Juhlin, Patrik	Phi.	2	56	7	6	13	23	13	1	0	1	2	....	1994-95	1995-96
Julien, Claude	Que.	2	14	0	1	1	25	....	....	....	....	....	....	1984-85	1985-86
Juneau, Joe	Bos., Wsh., Buf., Ott., Phx., Mtl.	13	828	156	416	572	272	112	25	54	79	69	....	1991-92	2003-04
Junker, Steve	NYI	2	5	0	0	0	0	3	0	1	1	0	....	1992-93	1993-94
Jutila, Timo	Buf.	1	10	1	5	6	13	....	....	....	....	....	....	1984-85	1984-85
● Juzda, Bill	NYR, Tor.	9	398	14	54	68	398	42	0	3	3	46	2	1940-41	1951-52

K

Name	NHL Teams	NHL Seasons	Regular Schedule GP	G	A	TP	PIM	Playoffs GP	G	A	TP	PIM	NHL Cup Wins	First NHL Season	Last NHL Season
Kabel, Bob	NYR	2	48	5	13	18	34	....	....	....	....	....	....	1959-60	1960-61
‡ Kaberle, Frantisek	L.A., Atl., Car.	9	523	29	164	193	218	32	4	10	14	10	1	1999-00	2008-09
Kachowski, Mark	Pit.	3	64	6	5	11	209	....	....	....	....	....	....	1987-88	1989-90
Kachur, Ed	Chi.	2	96	10	14	24	35	....	....	....	....	....	....	1956-57	1957-58
Kaese, Trent	Buf.	1	1	0	0	0	0	....	....	....	....	....	....	1988-89	1988-89
‡ Kaigorodov, Alexei	Ott.	1	6	0	1	1	0	....	....	....	....	....	....	2006-07	2006-07
● Kaiser, Vern	Mtl.	1	50	7	5	12	33	2	0	0	0	0	....	1950-51	1950-51
● Kalbfleisch, Walter	Ott., St.L., NYA, Bos.	4	36	0	4	4	32	5	0	0	0	2	....	1933-34	1936-37
● Kaleta, Alex	Chi., NYR	7	387	92	121	213	190	17	1	6	7	2	....	1941-42	1950-51
‡ Kalinin, Dmitri	Buf., NYR, Phx.	9	539	36	126	162	321	37	2	7	9	20	....	1999-00	2008-09
‡ Kalinski, Jon	Phi.	2	22	1	4	5	0	....	....	....	....	....	....	2008-09	2009-10
‡ Kallio, Tomi	Atl., CBJ, Phi.	3	140	24	31	55	48	....	....	....	....	....	....	2000-01	2002-03
Kallur, Anders	NYI	6	383	101	110	211	149	78	12	23	35	32	4	1979-80	1984-85
‡ Kalus, Petr	Bos., Min.	2	11	4	1	5	6	....	....	....	....	....	....	2006-07	2009-10
Kamensky, Valeri	Que., Col., NYR, Dal., N.J.	11	637	200	301	501	383	66	25	35	60	72	1	1991-92	2001-02
Kaminski, Kevin	Min., Que., Wsh.	7	139	3	10	13	528	8	0	0	0	52	....	1988-89	1996-97
● Kaminsky, Max	Ott., St.L., Bos., Mtl.M.	4	130	22	34	56	38	4	0	0	0	0	....	1933-34	1936-37
Kaminsky, Yan	Wpg., NYI	2	26	3	2	5	4	2	0	0	0	4	....	1993-94	1994-95
● Kampman, Bingo	Tor.	5	189	14	30	44	287	47	1	4	5	38	1	1937-38	1941-42
‡ Kana, Tomas	CBJ	1	6	0	2	2	2	....	....	....	....	....	....	2009-10	2009-10
‡ Kane, Boyd	Phi., Wsh.	5	31	0	3	3	39	....	....	....	....	....	....	2003-04	2009-10
Kane, Francis	Det.	1	2	0	0	0	0	....	....	....	....	....	....	1943-44	1943-44
Kanko, Petr	L.A.	1	10	1	0	1	0	....	....	....	....	....	....	2005-06	2005-06
Kannegiesser, Gord	St.L.	2	23	0	1	1	15	....	....	....	....	....	....	1967-68	1971-72
Kannegiesser, Sheldon	Pit., NYR, L.A., Van.	8	366	14	67	81	292	18	0	2	2	10	....	1970-71	1977-78
‡ Kapanen, Niko	Dal., Atl., Phx.	6	397	36	90	126	160	18	5	4	9	22	....	2001-02	2007-08
Kapanen, Sami	Hfd., Car., Phi.	12	831	189	269	458	175	87	13	22	35	22	....	1995-96	2007-08
Karabin, Ladislav	Pit.	1	9	0	0	0	2	....	....	....	....	....	....	1993-94	1993-94
‡ Karalahti, Jere	L.A., Nsh.	3	149	8	19	27	97	17	0	1	1	20	....	1999-00	2001-02
Karamnov, Vitali	St.L.	3	92	12	20	32	65	2	0	0	0	2	....	1992-93	1994-95
Kariya, Paul	Ana., Col., Nsh., St.L.	15	989	402	587	989	399	46	16	23	39	12	....	1994-95	2009-10
Kariya, Steve	Van.	3	65	9	18	27	32	....	....	....	....	....	....	1999-00	2001-02
Karjalainen, Kyosti	L.A.	1	28	1	8	9	12	3	0	1	1	2	....	1991-92	1991-92
Karlander, Al	Det.	4	212	36	56	92	70	4	0	1	1	0	....	1969-70	1972-73
Karlsson, Andreas	Atl., T.B.	5	264	16	35	51	72	6	0	0	0	0	....	1999-00	2007-08
Karpa, Dave	Que., Ana., Car., NYR	12	557	18	80	98	1374	19	1	1	2	39	....	1991-92	2002-03
Karpov, Valeri	Ana.	3	76	14	15	29	32	....	....	....	....	....	....	1994-95	1996-97
● Karpovtsev, Alexander	NYR, Tor., Chi., NYI, Fla.	12	596	34	154	188	430	74	4	14	18	52	1	1993-94	2005-06
‡ Karsums, Martins	Bos., T.B.	1	24	1	5	6	6	....	....	....	....	....	....	2008-09	2008-09
Kasatonov, Alexei	N.J., Ana., St.L., Bos.	7	383	38	122	160	326	33	4	7	11	40	....	1989-90	1995-96
‡ Kaspar, Lukas	S.J.	2	16	2	2	4	8	....	....	....	....	....	....	2007-08	2008-09
Kasparaitis, Darius	NYI, Pit., Col., NYR	14	863	27	136	163	1379	83	2	10	12	107	....	1992-93	2006-07
Kasper, Steve	Bos., L.A., Phi., T.B.	13	821	177	291	468	554	94	20	28	48	82	....	1980-81	1992-93
Kastelic, Ed	Wsh., Hfd.	7	220	11	10	21	719	8	1	0	1	32	....	1985-86	1991-92
Kaszycki, Mike	NYI, Wsh., Tor.	5	226	42	80	122	108	19	2	6	8	10	....	1977-78	1982-83
Kavanagh, Pat	Van., Phi.	4	14	2	0	2	4	3	0	0	0	2	....	2000-01	2005-06
● Kea, Ed	Atl., St.L.	10	583	30	145	175	508	32	2	4	6	39	....	1973-74	1982-83
Keane, Mike	Mtl., Col., NYR, Dal., St.L., Van.	16	1161	168	302	470	881	220	34	40	74	135	3	1988-89	2003-04
Kearns, Dennis	Van.	10	677	31	290	321	386	11	1	2	3	8	....	1971-72	1980-81
● Keating, Jack	Det.	2	11	3	0	3	4	....	....	....	....	....	....	1938-39	1939-40
● Keating, John	NYA	2	35	5	5	10	17	....	....	....	....	....	....	1931-32	1932-33
Keating, Mike	NYR	1	1	0	0	0	0	....	....	....	....	....	....	1977-78	1977-78
● Keats, Duke	Bos., Det., Chi.	3	82	30	19	49	113	....	....	....	....	....	....	1926-27	1928-29
Keczmer, Dan	Min., Hfd., Cgy., Dal., Nsh.	10	235	8	38	46	212	12	0	1	1	8	....	1990-91	1999-00
Keefe, Sheldon	T.B.	3	125	12	12	24	78	....	....	....	....	....	....	2000-01	2002-03
● Keeling, Butch	Tor., NYR	12	525	157	63	220	331	47	11	11	22	34	1	1926-27	1937-38
Keenan, Larry	Tor., St.L., Buf., Phi.	6	233	38	64	102	28	46	15	16	31	12	....	1961-62	1971-72
Kehoe, Rick	Tor., Pit.	14	906	371	396	767	120	39	4	17	21	4	....	1971-72	1984-85
‡ Keith, Matt	Chi., NYI	4	27	2	3	5	14	....	....	....	....	....	....	2003-04	2007-08
Kekalainen, Jarmo	Bos., Ott.	3	55	5	8	13	28	....	....	....	....	....	....	1989-90	1993-94
Kelleher, Chris	Bos.	1	1	0	0	0	0	....	....	....	....	....	....	2001-02	2001-02
Keller, Ralph	NYR	1	3	1	0	1	6	....	....	....	....	....	....	1962-63	1962-63
Kellgren, Christer	Col.	1	5	0	0	0	0	....	....	....	....	....	....	1981-82	1981-82
Kelly, Bob	Phi., Wsh.	12	837	154	208	362	1454	101	9	14	23	172	2	1970-71	1981-82
Kelly, Bob	St.L., Pit., Chi.	6	425	87	109	196	687	23	6	3	9	40	....	1973-74	1978-79

Name	NHL Teams	NHL Seasons	Regular Schedule GP	G	A	TP	PIM	Playoffs GP	G	A	TP	PIM	NHL Cup Wins	First NHL Season	Last NHL Season
Kelly, Dave	Det.	1	16	2	0	2	4	....	....	....	....	....	....	1976-77	1976-77
Kelly, John Paul	L.A.	7	400	54	70	124	366	18	1	1	2	41	....	1979-80	1985-86
• Kelly, Pep	Tor., Chi., Bro.	8	288	74	53	127	105	38	7	6	13	10	....	1934-35	1941-42
• Kelly, Pete	St.L., Det., NYA, Bro.	7	177	21	38	59	68	19	3	1	4	2	2	1934-35	1941-42
Kelly, Red	Det., Tor.	20	1316	281	542	823	327	164	33	59	92	51	8	1947-48	1966-67
Kelly, Steve	Edm., T.B., N.J., L.A., Min.	9	149	9	12	21	83	25	0	0	0	8	1	1996-97	2007-08
• Kemp, Kevin	Hfd.	1	3	0	0	0	4	....	....	....	....	....	....	1980-81	1980-81
• Kemp, Stan	Tor.	1	1	0	0	0	2	....	....	....	....	....	....	1948-49	1948-49
Kenady, Chris	St.L., NYR	2	7	0	2	2	0	....	....	....	....	....	....	1997-98	1999-00
• Kendall, Bill	Chi., Tor.	5	131	16	10	26	28	6	0	0	0	0	1	1933-34	1937-38
Kennedy, Dean	L.A., NYR, Buf., Wpg., Edm.	12	717	26	110	136	1118	36	1	7	8	59	....	1982-83	1994-95
Kennedy, Forbes	Chi., Det., Bos., Phi., Tor.	11	603	70	108	178	988	12	2	4	6	64	....	1956-57	1968-69
‡ Kennedy, Mike	Dal., Tor., NYI	5	145	16	36	52	112	5	0	0	0	9	....	1994-95	1998-99
Kennedy, Sheldon	Det., Cgy., Bos.	8	310	49	58	107	233	24	6	4	10	20	....	1989-90	1996-97
• Kennedy, Ted	Tor.	14	696	231	329	560	432	78	29	31	60	32	5	1942-43	1956-57
• Kenny, Ernest	NYR, Chi.	2	10	0	0	0	18	....	....	....	....	....	....	1930-31	1934-35
Keon, Dave	Tor., Hfd.	18	1296	396	590	986	117	92	32	36	68	6	4	1960-61	1981-82
Kerch, Alexander	Edm.	1	5	0	0	0	2	....	....	....	....	....	....	1993-94	1993-94
Kerr, Alan	NYI, Det., Wpg.	9	391	72	94	166	826	38	5	4	9	70	....	1984-85	1992-93
Kerr, Reg	Cle., Chi., Edm.	6	263	66	94	160	169	7	1	0	1	7	....	1977-78	1983-84
Kerr, Tim	Phi., NYR, Hfd.	13	655	370	304	674	596	81	40	31	71	58	....	1980-81	1992-93
Kesa, Dan	Van., Dal., Pit., T.B.	4	139	8	22	30	66	13	1	0	1	0	....	1993-94	1999-00
Kessell, Rick	Pit., Cal.	5	135	4	24	28	6	....	....	....	....	....	....	1969-70	1973-74
Ketola, Veli-Pekka	Col.	1	44	9	5	14	4	....	....	....	....	....	....	1981-82	1981-82
Ketter, Kerry	Atl.	1	41	0	2	2	58	....	....	....	....	....	....	1972-73	1972-73
Kharin, Sergei	Wpg.	1	7	2	3	5	2	....	....	....	....	....	....	1990-91	1990-91
Kharitonov, Alexander	T.B., NYI	2	71	7	15	22	12	....	....	....	....	....	....	2000-01	2001-02
Khavanov, Alexander	St.L., Tor.	5	348	27	75	102	233	26	5	5	10	18	....	2000-01	2005-06
Khmylev, Yuri	Buf., St.L.	5	263	64	88	152	133	26	8	6	14	24	....	1992-93	1996-97
Khristich, Dmitri	Wsh., L.A., Bos., Tor.	12	811	259	337	596	422	75	15	25	40	41	....	1990-91	2001-02
Kidd, Ian	Van.	2	20	4	7	11	25	....	....	....	....	....	....	1987-88	1988-89
Kiessling, Udo	Min.	1	1	0	0	0	2	....	....	....	....	....	....	1981-82	1981-82
Kilger, Chad	Ana., Wpg., Phx., Chi., Edm., Mtl., Tor.	12	714	107	111	218	363	36	3	2	5	13	....	1995-96	2007-08
Kilrea, Brian	Det., L.A.	2	26	3	5	8	12	....	....	....	....	....	....	1957-58	1967-68
• Kilrea, Hec	Ott., Det., Tor.	15	633	167	129	296	438	48	8	7	15	18	3	1925-26	1939-40
• Kilrea, Ken	Det.	5	91	16	23	39	8	15	2	2	4	4	....	1938-39	1943-44
• Kilrea, Wally	Ott., Phi., NYA, Mtl.M., Det.	9	329	35	58	93	87	25	2	4	6	6	2	1929-30	1937-38
Kimble, Darin	Que., St.L., Bos., Chi.	7	311	23	20	43	1082	23	0	0	0	52	....	1988-89	1994-95
Kindrachuk, Orest	Phi., Pit., Wsh.	10	508	118	261	379	648	76	20	20	40	53	2	1972-73	1981-82
King, Derek	NYI, Hfd., Tor., St.L.	14	830	261	351	612	417	47	4	17	21	24	....	1986-87	1999-00
King, Frank	Mtl.	1	10	1	0	1	2	....	....	....	....	....	....	1950-51	1950-51
‡ King, Jason	Van., Ana.	3	59	12	11	23	8	1	0	0	0	0	....	2002-03	2007-08
King, Kris	Det., NYR, Wpg., Phx., Tor., Chi.	14	849	66	85	151	2030	67	8	5	13	142	....	1987-88	2000-01
King, Steven	NYR, Ana.	3	67	17	8	25	75	....	....	....	....	....	....	1992-93	1995-96
King, Wayne	Cal.	3	73	5	18	23	34	....	....	....	....	....	....	1973-74	1975-76
Kinnear, Geordie	Atl.	1	4	0	0	0	13	....	....	....	....	....	....	1999-00	1999-00
‡ Kinrade, Geoff	T.B.	1	1	0	0	0	0	....	....	....	....	....	....	2008-09	2008-09
Kinsella, Brian	Wsh.	2	10	0	1	1	0	....	....	....	....	....	....	1975-76	1976-77
• Kinsella, Ray	Ott.	1	14	0	0	0	0	....	....	....	....	....	....	1930-31	1930-31
Kiprusoff, Marko	Mtl., NYI	2	51	0	10	10	12	....	....	....	....	....	....	1995-96	2001-02
• Kirk, Bobby	NYR	1	39	4	8	12	14	....	....	....	....	....	....	1937-38	1937-38
• Kirkpatrick, Bob	NYR	1	49	12	12	24	6	....	....	....	....	....	....	1942-43	1942-43
Kirton, Mark	Tor., Det., Van.	6	266	57	56	113	121	4	1	2	3	7	....	1979-80	1984-85
Kisio, Kelly	Det., NYR, S.J., Cgy.	13	761	229	429	658	768	39	6	15	21	52	....	1982-83	1994-95
• Kitchen, Bill	Mtl., Tor.	4	41	1	4	5	40	3	0	1	1	0	....	1981-82	1984-85
• Kitchen, Hobie	Mtl.M., Det.	2	47	5	4	9	58	....	....	....	....	....	1	1925-26	1926-27
Kitchen, Mike	Col., N.J.	8	474	12	62	74	370	2	0	0	0	2	....	1976-77	1983-84
Kjellberg, Patric	Mtl., Nsh., Ana.	6	394	64	96	160	84	10	0	0	0	0	....	1992-93	2002-03
‡ Klasen, Linus	Nsh.	1	4	0	0	0	0	....	....	....	....	....	....	2010-11	2010-11
Klassen, Ralph	Cal., Cle., Col., St.L.	9	497	52	93	145	120	26	4	2	6	12	....	1975-76	1983-84
Klatt, Trent	Min., Dal., Phi., Van., L.A.	13	782	143	200	343	307	74	16	9	25	20	....	1991-92	2003-04
Klee, Ken	Wsh., Tor., N.J., Col., Atl., Ana., Phx.	14	934	55	140	195	880	51	2	2	4	50	....	1994-95	2008-09
• Klein, Lloyd	Bos., NYA	8	164	30	24	54	68	5	0	0	0	2	1	1928-29	1937-38
Kleinendorst, Scot	NYR, Hfd., Wsh.	8	281	12	46	58	452	26	2	7	9	40	....	1982-83	1989-90
‡ Klementyev, Anton	NYI	1	1	0	0	0	0	....	....	....	....	....	....	2009-10	2009-10
Klemm, Jon	Que., Col., Chi., Dal., L.A.	15	773	42	100	142	436	105	7	7	14	47	2	1991-92	2007-08
‡ Klepis, Jakub	Wsh.	2	66	4	10	14	36	....	....	....	....	....	....	2005-06	2006-07
Klima, Petr	Det., Edm., T.B., L.A., Pit.	13	786	313	260	573	671	95	28	24	52	83	1	1985-86	1998-99
Klimovich, Sergei	Chi.	1	1	0	0	0	2	....	....	....	....	....	....	1996-97	1996-97
• Klingbeil, Ike	Chi.	1	5	1	2	3	2	....	....	....	....	....	....	1936-37	1936-37
‡ Kloucek, Tomas	NYR, Nsh., Atl.	5	141	2	8	10	250	....	....	....	....	....	....	2000-01	2005-06
• Klukay, Joe	Tor., Bos.	11	566	109	127	236	189	71	13	10	23	23	4	1942-43	1955-56
Kluzak, Gord	Bos.	7	299	25	98	123	543	46	6	13	19	129	....	1982-83	1990-91
• Knibbs, Bill	Bos.	1	53	7	10	17	4	....	....	....	....	....	....	1964-65	1964-65
Knipscheer, Fred	Bos., St.L.	3	28	6	3	9	18	16	2	1	3	6	....	1993-94	1995-96
• Knott, Nick	Bro.	1	14	3	1	4	9	....	....	....	....	....	....	1941-42	1941-42
Knox, Paul	Tor.	1	1	0	0	0	0	....	....	....	....	....	....	1954-55	1954-55
Knutsen, Espen	Ana., CBJ	5	207	30	81	111	105	....	....	....	....	....	....	1997-98	2003-04
Koalska, Matt	NYI	1	3	0	0	0	2	....	....	....	....	....	....	2005-06	2005-06
‡ Koci, David	Chi., T.B., St.L., Col.	5	142	3	1	4	461	....	....	....	....	....	....	2006-07	2010-11
Kocur, Joe	Det., NYR, Van.	15	820	80	82	162	2519	118	10	12	22	231	3	1984-85	1998-99
Koehler, Greg	Car.	1	1	0	0	0	0	....	....	....	....	....	....	2000-01	2000-01
‡ Kohn, Dustin	NYI	1	22	0	4	4	4	....	....	....	....	....	....	2009-10	2009-10
‡ Kohn, Ladislav	Cgy., Tor., Ana., Atl., Det.	7	186	14	28	42	125	2	0	0	0	5	....	1995-96	2002-03
‡ Koistinen, Ville	Nsh., Fla.	3	103	8	24	32	40	....	....	....	....	....	....	2007-08	2009-10
Koivisto, Tom	St.L.	1	22	2	4	6	10	....	....	....	....	....	....	2002-03	2002-03
‡ Kolarik, Pavel	Bos.	2	23	0	0	0	10	....	....	....	....	....	....	2000-01	2001-02
Kolesar, Mark	Tor.	2	28	2	2	4	14	3	1	0	1	2	....	1995-96	1996-97
‡ Kolnik, Juraj	NYI, Fla.	6	240	46	49	95	84	....	....	....	....	....	....	2000-01	2006-07
Kolstad, Dean	Min., S.J.	3	40	1	7	8	69	....	....	....	....	....	....	1988-89	1992-93
‡ Koltsov, Konstantin	Pit.	3	144	12	26	38	50	....	....	....	....	....	....	2002-03	2005-06
Komadoski, Neil	L.A., St.L.	8	502	16	76	92	632	23	0	2	2	47	....	1972-73	1979-80
Komarniski, Zenith	Van., CBJ	3	21	1	1	2	10	....	....	....	....	....	....	1999-00	2003-04
Kondratiev, Maxim	Tor., NYR, Ana.	3	40	1	2	3	24	....	....	....	....	....	....	2003-04	2007-08
Konik, George	Pit.	1	52	7	8	15	26	....	....	....	....	....	....	1967-68	1967-68
Konowalchuk, Steve	Wsh., Col.	14	790	171	225	396	703	52	9	12	21	60	....	1991-92	2005-06
Konroyd, Steve	Cgy., NYI, Chi., Hfd., Det., Ott.	15	895	41	195	236	863	97	10	15	25	99	....	1980-81	1994-95
Konstantinov, Vladimir	Det.	6	446	47	128	175	838	82	5	14	19	107	1	1991-92	1996-97
‡ Kontiola, Petri	Chi.	1	12	0	5	5	6	....	....	....	....	....	....	2007-08	2007-08
Kontos, Chris	NYR, Pit., L.A., T.B.	8	230	54	69	123	103	20	11	0	11	12	....	1982-83	1992-93
• Kopak, Russ	Bos.	1	24	7	9	16	0	....	....	....	....	....	....	1943-44	1943-44
Korab, Jerry	Chi., Van., Buf., L.A.	15	975	114	341	455	1629	93	8	18	26	201	....	1970-71	1984-85
Kordic, Dan	Phi.	6	197	4	8	12	584	12	1	0	1	22	....	1991-92	1998-99
• Kordic, John	Mtl., Tor., Wsh., Que.	7	244	17	18	35	997	41	4	3	7	131	1	1985-86	1991-92
Korn, Jim	Det., Tor., Buf., N.J., Cgy.	10	597	66	122	188	1801	16	1	2	3	109	....	1979-80	1989-90
Korney, Mike	Det., NYR	4	77	9	10	19	59	....	....	....	....	....	....	1973-74	1978-79
Korolev, Evgeny	NYI	3	42	1	4	5	20	2	0	0	0	0	....	1999-00	2001-02
• Korolev, Igor	St.L., Wpg., Phx., Tor., Chi.	12	795	119	227	346	330	41	0	8	8	6	....	1992-93	2003-04
Koroll, Cliff	Chi.	11	814	208	254	462	376	85	19	29	48	67	....	1969-70	1979-80
‡ Korolyuk, Alexander	S.J.	6	296	62	80	142	140	34	6	8	14	18	....	1997-98	2003-04
Kortko, Roger	NYI	2	79	7	17	24	28	10	0	3	3	17	....	1984-85	1985-86
Kostynski, Doug	Bos.	2	15	3	1	4	4	....	....	....	....	....	....	1983-84	1984-85
‡ Kotalik, Ales	Buf., Edm., NYR, Cgy.	9	542	136	148	284	348	34	6	9	15	16	....	2001-02	2010-11
Kotanen, Dick	NYR	1	1	0	0	0	0	....	....	....	....	....	....	1950-51	1950-51
Kotsopoulos, Chris	NYR, Hfd., Tor., Det.	10	479	44	109	153	827	31	1	3	4	91	....	1980-81	1989-90
Kovalenko, Andrei	Que., Col., Mtl., Edm., Phi., Car., Bos.	9	620	173	206	379	389	33	5	6	11	20	....	1992-93	2000-01
Kowal, Joe	Buf.	2	22	0	5	5	13	2	0	0	0	0	....	1976-77	1977-78
Kozak, Don	L.A., Van.	7	437	96	86	182	480	29	7	2	9	69	....	1972-73	1978-79
Kozak, Les	Tor.	1	12	1	0	1	2	....	....	....	....	....	....	1961-62	1961-62
‡ Kozlov, Viktor	S.J., Fla., N.J., NYI, Wsh.	14	897	198	339	537	248	35	4	8	12	10	....	1994-95	2008-09
‡ Kozlov, Vyacheslav	Det., Buf., Atl.	18	1182	356	497	853	704	118	42	37	79	82	2	1991-92	2009-10
Kraft, Milan	Pit.	4	207	41	41	82	52	8	0	0	0	2	....	2000-01	2003-04
Kraft, Ryan	S.J.	1	7	0	1	1	0	....	....	....	....	....	....	2002-03	2002-03
• Kraftcheck, Stephen	Bos., NYR, Tor.	4	157	11	18	29	83	6	0	0	0	7	....	1950-51	1958-59
‡ Krajicek, Lukas	Fla., Van., T.B., Phi.	7	328	11	61	72	245	34	0	5	5	20	....	2001-02	2009-10
Krake, Skip	Bos., L.A., Buf.	7	249	23	40	63	182	10	1	0	1	17	....	1963-64	1970-71

Mike Kaszycki

Jarmo Kekalainen

Bill Kendall

Alan Kerr

Roger Kortko

Skip Krake

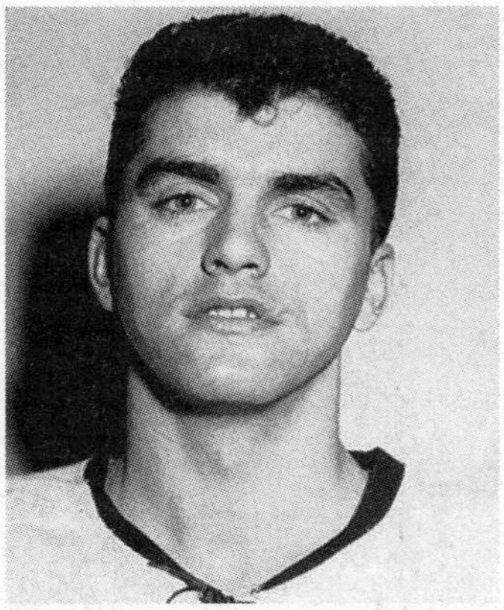

Hec Lalande

Gord Lane

			Regular Schedule					Playoffs					NHL	First	Last
Name	NHL Teams	NHL Seasons	GP	G	A	TP	PIM	GP	G	A	TP	PIM	Cup Wins	NHL Season	NHL Season
Kravchuk, Igor	Chi., Edm., St.L., Ott., Cgy., Fla.	12	699	64	210	274	251	51	6	15	21	18	....	1991-92	2002-03
Kravets, Mikhail	S.J.	2	2	0	0	0	0	....	....	....	....	....	....	1991-92	1992-93
Krentz, Dale	Det.	3	30	5	3	8	9	2	0	0	0	0	....	1986-87	1988-89
‡ Kreps, Kamil	Fla.	4	232	18	42	60	71	....	....	....	....	....	....	2006-07	2009-10
‡ Krestanovich, Jordan	Col.	2	22	0	2	2	6	....	....	....	....	....	....	2001-02	2003-04
‡ Kristek, Jaroslav	Buf.	1	6	0	0	0	4	....	....	....	....	....	....	2002-03	2002-03
Krivokrasov, Sergei	Chi., Nsh., Cgy., Min., Ana.	10	450	86	109	195	288	21	2	0	2	14	....	1992-93	2001-02
‡ Krog, Jason	NYI, Ana., Atl., NYR, Van.	7	202	22	37	59	46	21	3	1	4	4	....	1999-00	2008-09
• Krol, Joe	NYR, Bro.	3	26	10	4	14	8	....	....	....	....	....	....	1936-37	1941-42
Kromm, Richard	Cgy., NYI	9	372	70	103	173	138	36	2	6	8	22	....	1983-84	1992-93
Kron, Robert	Van., Hfd., Car., CBJ	12	771	144	194	338	119	16	3	2	5	2	....	1990-91	2001-02
‡ Kronwall, Staffan	Tor., Wsh., Cgy.	4	66	1	3	4	23	....	....	....	....	....	....	2005-06	2009-10
Krook, Kevin	Col.	1	3	0	0	0	2	....	....	....	....	....	....	1978-79	1978-79
Kroupa, Vlastimil	S.J., N.J.	5	105	4	19	23	66	20	1	2	3	25	....	1993-94	1997-98
Krulicki, Jim	NYR, Det.	1	41	0	3	3	6	....	....	....	....	....	....	1970-71	1970-71
Krupp, Uwe	Buf., NYI, Que., Col., Det., Atl.	15	729	69	212	281	660	81	6	23	29	86	1	1986-87	2002-03
Kruppke, Gord	Det.	3	23	0	0	0	32	....	....	....	....	....	....	1990-91	1993-94
Kruse, Paul	Cgy., NYI, Buf., S.J.	11	423	38	33	71	1074	28	5	2	7	36	....	1990-91	2000-01
Krushelnyski, Mike	Bos., Edm., L.A., Tor., Det.	14	897	241	328	569	699	139	29	43	72	106	3	1981-82	1994-95
• Krutov, Vladimir	Van.	1	61	11	23	34	20	....	....	....	....	....	....	1989-90	1989-90
Krygier, Todd	Hfd., Wsh., Ana.	9	543	100	143	243	533	48	10	7	17	40	....	1989-90	1997-98
Kryskow, Dave	Chi., Wsh., Det., Atl.	4	231	33	56	89	174	12	2	0	2	4	....	1972-73	1975-76
• Kryzanowski, Ed	Bos., Chi.	5	237	15	22	37	65	18	0	1	1	4	....	1948-49	1952-53
‡ Kubina, Pavel	T.B., Tor., Atl., Phi.	14	970	110	276	386	1123	51	3	7	10	110	1	1997-98	2011-12
Kucera, Frantisek	Chi., Hfd., Van., Phi., CBJ, Pit., Wsh.	9	465	24	95	119	251	12	0	1	1	0	....	1990-91	2001-02
‡ Kudashov, Alexei	Tor.	1	25	1	0	1	4	....	....	....	....	....	....	1993-94	1993-94
Kudelski, Bob	L.A., Ott., Fla.	9	442	139	102	241	218	22	4	4	8	4	....	1987-88	1995-96
‡ Kudroc, Kristian	T.B., Fla.	3	26	2	2	4	38	....	....	....	....	....	....	2000-01	2003-04
• Kuhn, Gord	NYA	1	12	1	1	2	4	....	....	....	....	....	....	1932-33	1932-33
‡ Kukkonen, Lasse	Chi., Phi.	4	159	6	16	22	90	14	0	2	2	6	....	2003-04	2008-09
• Kukulowicz, Aggie	NYR	2	4	1	0	1	0	....	....	....	....	....	....	1952-53	1953-54
Kulak, Stu	Van., Edm., NYR, Que., Wpg.	4	90	8	4	12	130	3	0	0	0	2	....	1982-83	1988-89
Kuleshov, Mikhail	Col.	1	3	0	0	0	0	....	....	....	....	....	....	2003-04	2003-04
• Kullman, Arnie	Bos.	2	13	0	1	1	11	....	....	....	....	....	....	1947-48	1949-50
• Kullman, Eddie	NYR	6	343	56	70	126	298	6	1	0	1	2	....	1947-48	1953-54
Kultanen, Jarno	Bos.	3	102	2	11	13	59	....	....	....	....	....	....	2000-01	2002-03
Kumpel, Mark	Que., Det., Wpg.	6	288	38	46	84	113	39	6	4	10	14	....	1984-85	1990-91
• Kuntz, Alan	NYR	2	45	10	12	22	12	6	1	0	1	2	....	1941-42	1945-46
Kuntz, Murray	St.L.	1	7	1	2	3	0	....	....	....	....	....	....	1974-75	1974-75
‡ Kurka, Tomas	Car.	2	17	3	2	5	2	....	....	....	....	....	....	2002-03	2003-04
Kurri, Jari	Edm., L.A., NYR, Ana., Col.	17	1251	601	797	1398	545	200	106	127	233	123	5	1980-81	1997-98
Kurtenbach, Orland	NYR, Bos., Tor., Van.	13	639	119	213	332	628	19	2	4	6	70	....	1960-61	1973-74
Kurtz, Justin	Van.	1	27	3	5	8	14	....	....	....	....	....	....	2001-02	2001-02
Kurvers, Tom	Mtl., Buf., N.J., Tor., Van., NYI, Ana.	11	659	93	328	421	350	57	8	22	30	68	1	1984-85	1994-95
Kuryluk, Merv	Chi.	1	....	....	....	....	....	2	0	0	0	0	....	1961-62	1961-62
Kushner, Dale	NYI, Phi.	3	84	10	13	23	215	....	....	....	....	....	....	1989-90	1991-92
‡ Kutlak, Zdenek	Bos.	3	16	1	2	3	4	....	....	....	....	....	....	2000-01	2003-04
Kuznetsov, Maxim	Det., L.A.	4	136	2	8	10	137	....	....	....	....	....	....	2000-01	2003-04
Kuznik, Greg	Car.	1	1	0	0	0	0	....	....	....	....	....	....	2000-01	2000-01
Kuzyk, Ken	Cle.	2	41	5	9	14	8	....	....	....	....	....	....	1976-77	1977-78
Kvartalnov, Dmitri	Bos.	2	112	42	49	91	26	4	0	0	0	0	....	1992-93	1993-94
‡ Kvasha, Oleg	Fla., NYI, Phx.	7	493	81	136	217	335	21	1	2	3	8	....	1998-99	2005-06
‡ Kwiatkowski, Joel	Ott., Wsh., Fla., Pit., Atl.	7	282	16	29	45	245	6	0	0	0	2	....	2000-01	2007-08
Kwong, Larry	NYR	1	1	0	0	0	0	....	....	....	....	....	....	1947-48	1947-48
• Kyle, Bill	NYR	2	3	0	3	3	0	....	....	....	....	....	....	1949-50	1950-51
• Kyle, Gus	NYR, Bos.	3	203	6	20	26	362	14	1	2	3	34	....	1949-50	1951-52
Kyllonen, Markku	Wpg.	1	9	0	2	2	2	....	....	....	....	....	....	1988-89	1988-89
Kypreos, Nick	Wsh., Hfd., NYR, Tor.	8	442	46	44	90	1210	34	1	3	4	65	1	1989-90	1996-97
Kyte, Jim	Wpg., Pit., Cgy., Ott., S.J.	13	598	17	49	66	1342	42	0	6	6	94	....	1982-83	1995-96

L

Laaksonen, Antti	Bos., Min., Col.	8	483	81	87	168	152	25	1	5	6	6	....	1998-99	2006-07
Labadie, Mike	NYR	1	3	0	0	0	0	....	....	....	....	....	....	1952-53	1952-53
Labatte, Neil	St.L.	2	26	0	2	2	19	....	....	....	....	....	....	1978-79	1981-82
L'Abbe, Moe	Chi.	1	5	0	1	1	0	....	....	....	....	....	....	1972-73	1972-73
Labelle, Marc	Dal.	1	9	0	0	0	46	....	....	....	....	....	....	1996-97	1996-97
• Labine, Leo	Bos., Det.	11	643	128	193	321	730	60	12	11	23	82	....	1951-52	1961-62
Labossiere, Gord	NYR, L.A., Min.	6	215	44	62	106	75	10	2	3	5	28	....	1963-64	1971-72
Labovitch, Max	NYR	1	5	0	0	0	4	....	....	....	....	....	....	1943-44	1943-44
Labraaten, Dan	Det., Cgy.	4	268	71	73	144	47	8	1	0	1	4	....	1978-79	1981-82
Labre, Yvon	Pit., Wsh.	9	371	14	87	101	788	....	....	....	....	....	....	1970-71	1980-81
• Labrie, Guy	Bos., NYR	2	42	4	9	13	16	....	....	....	....	....	....	1943-44	1944-45
Lach, Elmer	Mtl.	14	664	215	408	623	478	76	19	45	64	36	3	1940-41	1953-54
Lachance, Michel	Col.	1	21	0	4	4	22	....	....	....	....	....	....	1978-79	1978-79
Lachance, Scott	NYI, Mtl., Van., CBJ	13	819	31	112	143	567	11	1	2	3	6	....	1991-92	2003-04
Lacombe, Francois	Oak., Buf., Que.	4	78	2	17	19	54	3	1	0	1	0	....	1968-69	1979-80
Lacombe, Normand	Buf., Edm., Phi.	7	319	53	62	115	196	26	5	1	6	49	1	1984-85	1990-91
LaCouture, Dan	Edm., Pit., NYR, Bos., N.J., Car.	9	337	20	25	45	348	6	0	0	0	2	....	1998-99	2008-09
Lacroix, Andre	Phi., Chi., Hfd.	6	325	79	119	198	44	16	2	5	7	0	....	1967-68	1979-80
Lacroix, Daniel	NYR, Bos., Phi., Edm., NYI	7	188	11	7	18	379	16	0	1	1	26	....	1993-94	1999-00
Lacroix, Eric	Tor., L.A., Col., NYR, Ott.	8	472	67	70	137	361	30	1	5	6	25	....	1993-94	2000-01
Lacroix, Pierre	Que., Hfd.	4	274	24	108	132	197	8	0	2	2	10	....	1979-80	1982-83
Ladouceur, Randy	Det., Hfd., Ana.	14	930	30	126	156	1322	40	5	8	13	59	....	1982-83	1995-96
LaFayette, Nathan	St.L., Van., NYR, L.A.	6	187	17	20	37	103	32	2	7	9	8	....	1993-94	1998-99
Laflamme, Christian	Chi., Edm., Mtl., St.L.	8	324	2	45	47	282	9	0	1	1	6	....	1996-97	2003-04
Lafleur, Guy	Mtl., NYR, Que.	17	1126	560	793	1353	399	128	58	76	134	67	5	1971-72	1990-91
• Lafleur, Roland	Mtl.	1	1	0	0	0	0	....	....	....	....	....	....	1924-25	1924-25
LaFontaine, Pat	NYI, Buf., NYR	15	865	468	545	1013	552	69	26	36	62	36	....	1983-84	1997-98
• Laforce, Ernie	Mtl.	1	1	0	0	0	0	....	....	....	....	....	....	1942-43	1942-43
LaForest, Bob	L.A.	1	5	1	0	1	2	....	....	....	....	....	....	1983-84	1983-84
Laforge, Claude	Mtl., Det., Phi.	8	193	24	33	57	82	5	1	2	3	15	....	1957-58	1968-69
Laforge, Marc	Hfd., Edm.	2	14	0	0	0	64	....	....	....	....	....	....	1989-90	1993-94
• Laframboise, Pete	Cal., Wsh., Pit.	4	227	33	55	88	70	9	1	0	1	0	....	1971-72	1974-75
Lafrance, Adie	Mtl.	1	3	0	0	0	2	2	0	0	0	0	....	1933-34	1933-34
• Lafrance, Leo	Mtl., Chi.	2	33	2	0	2	6	....	....	....	....	....	....	1926-27	1927-28
Lafreniere, Jason	Que., NYR, T.B.	5	146	34	53	87	22	15	1	5	6	19	....	1986-87	1993-94
Lafreniere, Roger	Det., St.L.	2	13	0	0	0	4	....	....	....	....	....	....	1962-63	1972-73
Lagace, Jean-Guy	Pit., Buf., K.C.	6	197	9	39	48	251	....	....	....	....	....	....	1968-69	1975-76
Laidlaw, Tom	NYR, L.A.	10	705	25	139	164	717	69	4	17	21	78	....	1980-81	1989-90
Laird, Robbie	Min.	1	1	0	0	0	0	....	....	....	....	....	....	1979-80	1979-80
Lajeunesse, Serge	Det., Phi.	5	103	1	4	5	103	....	....	....	....	....	....	1970-71	1974-75
Lakovic, Sasha	Cgy., N.J.	3	37	0	4	4	118	....	....	....	....	....	....	1996-97	1998-99
• Lalande, Hec	Chi., Det.	4	151	21	39	60	120	....	....	....	....	....	....	1953-54	1957-58
‡ Laliberte, David	Phi.	1	11	2	1	3	6	1	0	0	0	2	....	2009-10	2009-10
Lalonde, Bobby	Van., Atl., Bos., Cgy.	11	641	124	210	334	298	16	4	2	6	6	....	1971-72	1981-82
• Lalonde, Newsy	Mtl., NYA	6	99	125	41	166	183	7	15	4	19	32	....	1917-18	1926-27
Lalonde, Ron	Pit., Wsh.	7	397	45	78	123	106	....	....	....	....	....	....	1972-73	1978-79
Lalor, Mike	Mtl., St.L., Wsh., Wpg., S.J., Dal.	12	687	17	88	105	677	92	5	10	15	167	1	1985-86	1996-97
• Lamb, Joe	Mtl.M., Ott., NYA, Bos., Mtl., St.L., Det.	11	443	108	101	209	601	18	1	1	2	51	....	1927-28	1937-38
Lamb, Mark	Cgy., Det., Edm., Ott., Phi., Mtl.	11	403	46	100	146	291	70	7	19	26	51	1	1985-86	1995-96
Lambert, Dan	Que.	2	29	6	9	15	22	....	....	....	....	....	....	1990-91	1991-92
Lambert, Denny	Ana., Ott., Nsh., Atl.	8	487	27	66	93	1391	17	0	1	1	28	....	1994-95	2001-02
Lambert, Lane	Det., NYR, Que.	6	283	58	66	124	521	17	2	4	6	40	....	1983-84	1988-89
Lambert, Yvon	Mtl., Buf.	10	683	206	273	479	340	90	27	22	49	67	4	1972-73	1981-82
Lamby, Dick	St.L.	3	22	0	5	5	22	....	....	....	....	....	....	1978-79	1980-81
• Lamirande, Jean-Paul	NYR, Mtl.	4	49	5	5	10	26	8	0	0	0	4	....	1946-47	1954-55
Lammens, Hank	Ott.	1	27	1	2	3	22	....	....	....	....	....	....	1993-94	1993-94
• Lamoureux, Leo	Mtl.	6	235	19	79	98	175	28	1	6	7	16	2	1941-42	1946-47
Lamoureux, Mitch	Pit., Phi.	3	73	11	9	20	59	....	....	....	....	....	....	1983-84	1987-88
‡ Lampman, Bryce	NYR	3	10	0	0	0	2	....	....	....	....	....	....	2003-04	2006-07
Lampman, Mike	St.L., Van., Wsh.	4	96	17	20	37	34	....	....	....	....	....	....	1972-73	1976-77
• Lancien, Jack	NYR	4	63	1	5	6	35	6	0	1	1	2	....	1946-47	1950-51
Landon, Larry	Mtl., Tor.	2	9	0	0	0	2	....	....	....	....	....	....	1983-84	1984-85
Landry, Eric	Cgy., Mtl.	4	68	5	9	14	47	....	....	....	....	....	....	1997-98	2001-02
Lane, Gord	Wsh., NYI	10	539	19	94	113	1228	75	3	14	17	214	4	1975-76	1984-85

Name	NHL Teams	NHL Seasons	Regular Schedule					Playoffs					NHL Cup Wins	First NHL Season	Last NHL Season
			GP	G	A	TP	PIM	GP	G	A	TP	PIM			
• Lane, Myles	NYR, Bos.	3	71	4	1	5	41	11	0	0	0	0	1	1928-29	1933-34
Lang, Robert	L.A., Bos., Pit., Wsh., Det., Chi., Mtl., Phx.	16	989	261	442	703	422	91	18	28	46	24	....	1992-93	2009-10
Langdon, Darren	NYR, Car., Van., Mtl., N.J.	11	521	16	23	39	1251	25	1	0	1	20	....	1994-95	2005-06
Langdon, Steve	Bos.	3	7	0	1	1	2	4	0	0	0	0	....	1974-75	1977-78
• Langelle, Pete	Tor.	4	136	22	51	73	11	39	5	9	14	4	1	1938-39	1941-42
Langevin, Chris	Buf.	2	22	3	1	4	22	....	....	....	....	....	....	1983-84	1985-86
Langevin, Dave	NYI, Min., L.A.	8	513	12	107	119	530	87	2	17	19	106	4	1979-80	1986-87
Langfeld, Josh	Ott., S.J., Bos., Det., Nsh.	6	143	9	23	32	60	1	0	0	0	0	....	2001-02	2007-08
Langkow, Daymond	T.B., Phi., Phx., Cgy.	16	1090	270	402	672	547	75	15	29	44	43	....	1995-96	2011-12
Langlais, Alain	Min.	2	25	4	4	8	10	....	....	....	....	....	....	1973-74	1974-75
Langlois, Albert	Mtl., NYR, Det., Bos.	9	497	21	91	112	488	53	1	5	6	50	3	1957-58	1965-66
• Langlois, Charlie	Ham., NYA, Pit., Mtl.	4	151	22	5	27	189	2	0	0	0	0	....	1924-25	1927-28
Langway, Rod	Mtl., Wsh.	15	994	51	278	329	849	104	5	22	27	97	1	1978-79	1992-93
Lank, Jeff	Phi.	1	2	0	0	0	2	....	....	....	....	....	....	1999-00	1999-00
Lanthier, Jean-Marc	Van.	4	105	16	16	32	29	....	....	....	....	....	....	1983-84	1987-88
• Lanyon, Ted	Pit.	1	5	0	0	0	4	....	....	....	....	....	....	1967-68	1967-68
Lanz, Rick	Van., Tor., Chi.	10	569	65	221	286	448	28	3	8	11	35	....	1980-81	1991-92
Laperriere, Daniel	St.L., Ott.	4	48	2	5	7	27	....	....	....	....	....	....	1992-93	1995-96
Laperriere, Ian	St.L., NYR, L.A., Col., Phi.	17	1083	121	215	336	1956	67	3	10	13	102	....	1993-94	2010-11
Laperriere, Jacques	Mtl.	12	691	40	242	282	674	88	9	22	31	101	6	1962-63	1973-74
Laplante, Darryl	Det.	3	35	0	6	6	10	....	....	....	....	....	....	1997-98	1999-00
Lapointe, Claude	Que., Col., Cgy., NYI, Phi.	14	879	127	178	305	721	34	4	7	11	44	....	1990-91	2003-04
Lapointe, Guy	Mtl., St.L., Bos.	16	884	171	451	622	893	123	26	44	70	138	6	1968-69	1983-84
Lapointe, Martin	Det., Bos., Chi., Ott.	16	991	181	200	381	1417	108	19	24	43	202	2	1991-92	2007-08
• Lapointe, Rick	Det., Phi., St.L., Que., L.A.	11	664	44	176	220	831	46	2	7	9	64	....	1975-76	1985-86
Lappin, Peter	Min., S.J.	2	7	0	0	0	2	....	....	....	....	....	....	1989-90	1991-92
Laprade, Edgar	NYR	10	500	108	172	280	42	18	4	9	13	4	....	1945-46	1954-55
• LaPrairie, Benjamin	Chi.	1	7	0	0	0	0	....	....	....	....	....	....	1936-37	1936-37
Laraque, Georges	Edm., Phx., Pit., Mtl.	12	695	53	100	153	1126	57	4	8	12	72	....	1997-98	2009-10
Larionov, Igor	Van., S.J., Det., Fla., N.J.	14	921	169	475	644	474	150	30	67	97	60	3	1989-90	2003-04
Lariviere, Garry	Que., Edm.	4	219	6	57	63	167	14	0	5	5	8	....	1979-80	1982-83
Larman, Drew	Fla., Bos.	3	26	2	1	3	4	....	....	....	....	....	....	2006-07	2009-10
Larmer, Jeff	Col., N.J., Chi.	5	158	37	51	88	57	5	1	0	1	2	....	1981-82	1985-86
Larmer, Steve	Chi., NYR	15	1006	441	571	1012	532	140	56	75	131	89	1	1980-81	1994-95
• Larochelle, Wildor	Mtl., Chi.	12	474	92	74	166	211	34	6	4	10	24	2	1925-26	1936-37
Larocque, Denis	L.A.	1	8	0	1	1	18	....	....	....	....	....	....	1987-88	1987-88
Larocque, Mario	T.B.	1	5	0	0	0	16	....	....	....	....	....	....	1998-99	1998-99
• Larose, Bonner	Bos.	1	6	0	0	0	0	....	....	....	....	....	....	1925-26	1925-26
Larose, Claude	Mtl., Min., St.L.	16	943	226	257	483	887	97	14	18	32	143	5	1962-63	1977-78
Larose, Claude	NYR	2	25	4	7	11	2	2	0	0	0	0	....	1979-80	1981-82
Larose, Cory	NYR	1	7	0	1	1	4	....	....	....	....	....	....	2003-04	2003-04
Larose, Guy	Wpg., Tor., Cgy., Bos.	6	70	10	9	19	63	4	0	0	0	0	....	1988-89	1994-95
Larouche, Pierre	Pit., Mtl., Hfd., NYR	14	812	395	427	822	237	64	20	34	54	16	2	1974-75	1987-88
Larouche, Steve	Ott., NYR, L.A.	2	26	9	9	18	10	....	....	....	....	....	....	1994-95	1995-96
Larsen, Brad	Col., Atl., Ana.	9	294	19	29	48	134	25	1	3	4	13	....	1997-98	2008-09
• Larson, Norm	NYA, Bro., NYR	3	89	25	18	43	12	....	....	....	....	....	....	1940-41	1946-47
Larson, Reed	Det., Bos., Edm., NYI, Min., Buf.	14	904	222	463	685	1391	32	4	7	11	63	....	1976-77	1989-90
Larter, Tyler	Wsh.	1	1	0	0	0	0	....	....	....	....	....	....	1989-90	1989-90
Latal, Jiri	Phi.	3	92	12	36	48	24	....	....	....	....	....	....	1989-90	1991-92
Latos, James	NYR	1	1	0	0	0	0	....	....	....	....	....	....	1988-89	1988-89
Latreille, Phil	NYR	1	4	0	0	0	2	....	....	....	....	....	....	1960-61	1960-61
Latta, David	Que.	4	36	4	8	12	4	....	....	....	....	....	....	1985-86	1990-91
• Lauder, Martin	Bos.	1	3	0	0	0	2	....	....	....	....	....	....	1927-28	1927-28
Lauen, Mike	Wpg.	1	4	0	1	1	0	....	....	....	....	....	....	1983-84	1983-84
Lauer, Brad	NYI, Chi., Ott., Pit.	9	323	44	67	111	218	34	7	5	12	24	....	1986-87	1995-96
Laughlin, Craig	Mtl., Wsh., L.A., Tor.	8	549	136	205	341	364	33	6	6	12	20	....	1981-82	1988-89
Laughton, Mike	Oak., Cal.	4	189	39	48	87	101	11	3	4	7	0	....	1967-68	1970-71
Laukkanen, Janne	Que., Col., Ott., Pit., T.B.	9	407	22	99	121	335	59	7	9	16	46	....	1994-95	2002-03
Laurence, Don	Atl., St.L.	2	79	15	22	37	14	....	....	....	....	....	....	1978-79	1979-80
Laus, Paul	Fla.	9	530	14	58	72	1702	30	2	7	9	74	....	1993-94	2001-02
LaVallee, Kevin	Cgy., L.A., St.L., Pit.	7	366	110	125	235	85	32	5	8	13	21	....	1980-81	1986-87
LaVarre, Mark	Chi.	3	78	9	16	25	58	1	0	0	0	2	....	1985-86	1987-88
Lavender, Brian	St.L., NYI, Det., Cal.	4	184	16	26	42	174	3	0	0	0	2	....	1971-72	1974-75
Lavigne, Eric	L.A.	1	1	0	0	0	0	....	....	....	....	....	....	1994-95	1994-95
• Laviolette, Jack	Mtl.	1	18	2	1	3	6	2	0	0	0	0	....	1917-18	1917-18
Laviolette, Peter	NYR	1	12	0	0	0	6	....	....	....	....	....	....	1988-89	1988-89
Lavoie, Dominic	St.L., Ott., Bos., L.A.	6	38	5	8	13	32	....	....	....	....	....	....	1988-89	1993-94
Law, Kirby	Phi.	3	9	0	1	1	4	....	....	....	....	....	....	2000-01	2003-04
Lawless, Paul	Hfd., Phi., Van., Tor.	7	239	49	77	126	54	3	0	2	2	2	....	1982-83	1989-90
Lawrence, Mark	Dal., NYI	6	142	18	26	44	115	....	....	....	....	....	....	1994-95	2000-01
• Lawson, Danny	Det., Min., Buf.	5	219	28	29	57	61	16	0	1	1	2	....	1967-68	1971-72
Lawton, Brian	Min., NYR, Hfd., Que., Bos., S.J.	9	483	112	154	266	401	11	1	1	2	12	....	1983-84	1992-93
Laxdal, Derek	Tor., NYI	6	67	12	7	19	88	1	0	2	2	2	....	1984-85	1990-91
• Laycoe, Hal	NYR, Mtl., Bos.	11	531	25	77	102	292	40	2	5	7	39	....	1945-46	1955-56
Lazaro, Jeff	Bos., Ott.	3	102	14	23	37	114	28	3	3	6	32	....	1990-91	1992-93
Leach, Jamie	Pit., Hfd., Fla.	5	81	11	9	20	12	....	....	....	....	....	1	1989-90	1993-94
Leach, Larry	Bos.	3	126	13	29	42	91	7	1	1	2	8	....	1958-59	1961-62
Leach, Reggie	Bos., Cal., Phi., Det.	13	934	381	285	666	387	94	47	22	69	22	1	1970-71	1982-83
Leach, Stephen	Wsh., Bos., St.L., Car., Ott., Phx., Pit.	15	702	130	153	283	978	92	15	11	26	87	....	1985-86	1999-00
‡ Leahy, Patrick	Bos., Nsh.	3	50	4	4	8	19	....	....	....	....	....	....	2003-04	2006-07
Leavins, Jim	Det., NYR	2	41	2	12	14	30	....	....	....	....	....	....	1985-86	1986-87
Lebeau, Patrick	Mtl., Cgy., Fla., Pit.	4	15	3	2	5	6	....	....	....	....	....	....	1990-91	1998-99
Lebeau, Stephan	Mtl., Ana.	7	373	118	159	277	105	30	9	7	16	12	1	1988-89	1994-95
LeBlanc, Fern	Det.	3	34	5	6	11	0	....	....	....	....	....	....	1976-77	1978-79
LeBlanc, J.P.	Chi., Det.	5	153	14	30	44	87	2	0	0	0	0	....	1968-69	1978-79
LeBlanc, John	Van., Edm., Wpg.	7	83	26	13	39	28	1	0	0	0	0	....	1986-87	1994-95
LeBoutillier, Peter	Ana.	2	35	2	1	3	176	....	....	....	....	....	....	1996-97	1997-98
LeBrun, Al	NYR	2	6	0	2	2	4	....	....	....	....	....	....	1960-61	1965-66
Lecaine, Bill	Pit.	1	4	0	0	0	0	....	....	....	....	....	....	1968-69	1968-69
• Leclair, Jackie	Mtl.	3	160	20	40	60	56	20	6	1	7	6	1	1954-55	1956-57
LeClair, John	Mtl., Phi., Pit.	16	967	406	413	819	501	154	42	47	89	94	1	1990-91	2006-07
Leclerc, Mike	Ana., Phx., Cgy.	9	341	64	94	158	288	26	2	9	11	14	....	1996-97	2005-06
Leclerc, Rene	Det.	2	87	10	11	21	105	....	....	....	....	....	....	1968-69	1970-71
Lecuyer, Doug	Chi., Wpg., Pit.	4	126	11	31	42	178	7	4	0	4	15	....	1978-79	1982-83
‡ Ledin, Per	Col.	1	3	0	0	0	2	....	....	....	....	....	....	2008-09	2008-09
Ledingham, Walt	Chi., NYI	3	15	0	2	2	4	....	....	....	....	....	....	1972-73	1976-77
• Leduc, Albert	Mtl., Ott., NYR	10	383	57	35	92	614	28	5	6	11	32	2	1925-26	1934-35
LeDuc, Rich	Bos., Que.	4	130	28	38	66	69	5	0	0	0	9	....	1972-73	1980-81
Ledyard, Grant	NYR, L.A., Wsh., Buf., Dal., Van., Bos., Ott., T.B.	18	1028	90	276	366	766	83	6	12	18	96	....	1984-85	2001-02
• Lee, Bobby	Mtl.	1	1	0	0	0	0	....	....	....	....	....	....	1942-43	1942-43
Lee, Edward	Que.	1	2	0	0	0	5	....	....	....	....	....	....	1984-85	1984-85
Lee, Peter	Pit.	6	431	114	131	245	257	19	0	8	8	4	....	1977-78	1982-83
Leeb, Brad	Van., Tor.	3	5	0	0	0	2	....	....	....	....	....	....	1999-00	2003-04
Leeb, Greg	Dal.	1	2	0	0	0	0	....	....	....	....	....	....	2000-01	2000-01
Leeman, Gary	Tor., Cgy., Mtl., Van., St.L.	14	667	199	267	466	531	36	8	16	24	36	1	1982-83	1996-97
Leetch, Brian	NYR, Tor., Bos.	18	1205	247	781	1028	571	95	28	69	97	36	1	1987-88	2005-06
Lefebvre, Guillaume	Phi., Pit., Bos.	4	39	2	4	6	13	....	....	....	....	....	....	2001-02	2009-10
Lefebvre, Patrice	Wsh.	1	3	0	0	0	2	....	....	....	....	....	....	1998-99	1998-99
Lefebvre, Sylvain	Mtl., Tor., Que., Col., NYR	14	945	30	154	184	674	129	4	14	18	101	1	1989-90	2002-03
• Lefley, Bryan	NYI, K.C., Col.	5	228	7	29	36	101	2	0	0	0	0	....	1972-73	1977-78
Lefley, Chuck	Mtl., St.L.	9	407	128	164	292	137	29	5	8	13	10	2	1970-71	1980-81
• Leger, Roger	NYR, Mtl.	5	187	18	53	71	71	20	0	7	7	14	....	1943-44	1949-50
Legge, Barry	Que., Wpg.	3	107	1	11	12	144	....	....	....	....	....	....	1979-80	1981-82
Legge, Randy	NYR	1	12	0	2	2	2	....	....	....	....	....	....	1972-73	1972-73
‡ Lehman, Scott	Atl.	1	1	0	0	0	0	....	....	....	....	....	....	2008-09	2008-09
Lehman, Tommy	Bos., Edm.	3	36	5	5	10	16	....	....	....	....	....	....	1987-88	1989-90
‡ Lehoux, Yanick	Phx.	2	10	2	2	4	6	....	....	....	....	....	....	2005-06	2006-07
Lehtinen, Jere	Dal.	14	875	243	271	514	210	108	27	22	49	12	1	1995-96	2009-10
Lehto, Petteri	Pit.	1	6	0	0	0	4	....	....	....	....	....	....	1984-85	1984-85
Lehtonen, Antero	Wsh.	1	65	9	12	21	14	....	....	....	....	....	....	1979-80	1979-80
‡ Lehtonen, Mikko	Nsh.	1	15	1	2	3	8	....	....	....	....	....	....	2006-07	2006-07
Lehvonen, Henry	K.C.	1	4	0	0	0	0	....	....	....	....	....	....	1974-75	1974-75
Leier, Edward	Chi.	2	16	2	1	3	2	....	....	....	....	....	....	1949-50	1950-51
Leinonen, Mikko	NYR, Wsh.	4	162	31	78	109	71	20	2	11	13	28	....	1981-82	1984-85

Rod Langway

Ian Laperriere

Denis Larocque

Don Laurence

Peter Laviolette

Bobby Leiter

Ken Leiter

Pit Lepine

Name	NHL Teams	NHL Seasons	Regular Schedule					Playoffs					NHL Cup Wins	First NHL Season	Last NHL Season
			GP	G	A	TP	PIM	GP	G	A	TP	PIM			
Leiter, Bobby	Bos., Pit., Atl.	10	447	98	126	224	144	8	3	0	3	2	....	1962-63	1975-76
Leiter, Ken	NYI, Min.	5	143	14	36	50	62	15	0	6	6	8	....	1984-85	1989-90
Lemaire, Jacques	Mtl.	12	853	366	469	835	217	145	61	78	139	63	8	1967-68	1978-79
Lemay, Moe	Van., Edm., Bos., Wpg.	8	317	72	94	166	442	28	6	3	9	55	1	1981-82	1988-89
Lemelin, Roger	K.C., Col.	4	36	1	2	3	27	....	....	....	....	....	....	1974-75	1977-78
Lemieux, Alain	St.L., Que., Pit.	6	119	28	44	72	38	19	4	6	10	0	....	1981-82	1986-87
Lemieux, Bob	Oak.	1	19	0	1	1	12	....	....	....	....	....	....	1967-68	1967-68
Lemieux, Claude	Mtl., N.J., Col., Phx., Dal., S.J.	21	1215	379	407	786	1777	234	80	78	158	529	4	1983-84	2008-09
Lemieux, Jacques	L.A.	3	19	0	4	4	8	1	0	0	0	0	....	1967-68	1969-70
Lemieux, Jean	Atl., Wsh.	5	204	23	63	86	39	3	1	1	2	0	....	1973-74	1977-78
Lemieux, Jocelyn	St.L., Mtl., Chi., Hfd., N.J., Cgy., Phx.	12	598	80	84	164	740	60	5	10	15	88	....	1986-87	1997-98
Lemieux, Mario	Pit.	18	915	690	1033	1723	834	107	76	96	172	87	2	1984-85	2005-06
• Lemieux, Real	Det., L.A., NYR, Buf.	8	456	51	104	155	262	18	2	4	6	10	....	1966-67	1973-74
Lemieux, Rich	Van., K.C., Atl.	5	274	39	82	121	132	2	0	0	0	0	....	1971-72	1975-76
Lenardon, Tim	N.J., Van.	2	15	2	1	3	4	....	....	....	....	....	....	1986-87	1989-90
• Lepine, Hec	Mtl.	1	33	5	2	7	2	....	....	....	....	....	....	1925-26	1925-26
• Lepine, Pit	Mtl.	13	526	143	98	241	392	41	7	5	12	26	2	1925-26	1937-38
Leroux, Francois	Edm., Ott., Pit., Col.	10	249	3	20	23	577	33	1	3	4	34	....	1988-89	1997-98
Leroux, Gaston	Mtl.	1	2	0	0	0	0	....	....	....	....	....	....	1935-36	1935-36
Leroux, Jean-Yves	Chi.	5	220	16	22	38	146	....	....	....	....	....	....	1996-97	2000-01
Leschyshyn, Curtis	Que., Col., Wsh., Hfd., Car., Min., Ott.	16	1033	47	165	212	669	68	2	6	8	34	1	1988-89	2003-04
• Lesieur, Art	Mtl., Chi.	4	100	4	2	6	50	14	0	0	0	4	1	1928-29	1935-36
‡ Lessard, Francis	Atl., Ott.	5	115	1	3	4	346	....	....	....	....	....	....	2001-02	2010-11
Lessard, Junior	Dal., T.B.	3	27	3	1	4	23	....	....	....	....	....	....	2005-06	2007-08
Lessard, Rick	Cgy., S.J.	3	15	0	4	4	18	....	....	....	....	....	....	1988-89	1991-92
Lesuk, Bill	Bos., Phi., L.A., Wsh., Wpg.	8	388	44	63	107	368	9	1	0	1	12	1	1968-69	1979-80
• Leswick, Jack	Chi.	1	37	1	7	8	16	....	....	....	....	....	1	1933-34	1933-34
• Leswick, Pete	NYA, Bos.	2	3	1	0	1	0	....	....	....	....	....	....	1936-37	1944-45
• Leswick, Tony	NYR, Det., Chi.	12	740	165	159	324	900	59	13	10	23	91	3	1945-46	1957-58
‡ Letang, Alan	Dal., Cgy., NYI	3	14	0	0	0	2	....	....	....	....	....	....	1999-00	2002-03
Letowski, Trevor	Phx., Van., CBJ, Car.	9	616	84	117	201	209	17	1	3	4	12	....	1998-99	2007-08
• Levandoski, Joe	NYR	1	8	1	1	2	0	....	....	....	....	....	....	1946-47	1946-47
Leveille, Normand	Bos.	2	75	17	25	42	49	....	....	....	....	....	....	1981-82	1982-83
• Leveque, Guy	L.A.	2	17	2	2	4	21	....	....	....	....	....	....	1992-93	1993-94
Lever, Don	Van., Atl., Cgy., Col., N.J., Buf.	15	1020	313	367	680	593	30	7	10	17	26	....	1972-73	1986-87
Levie, Craig	Wpg., Min., St.L., Van.	6	183	22	53	75	177	16	2	3	5	32	....	1981-82	1986-87
Levins, Scott	Wpg., Fla., Ott., Phx.	5	124	13	20	33	316	....	....	....	....	....	....	1992-93	1997-98
• Levinsky, Alex	Tor., NYR, Chi.	9	367	19	49	68	307	37	2	1	3	26	2	1930-31	1938-39
Levo, Tapio	Col., N.J.	2	107	16	53	69	36	....	....	....	....	....	....	1981-82	1982-83
Lewicki, Danny	Tor., NYR, Chi.	9	461	105	135	240	177	28	0	4	4	8	1	1950-51	1958-59
Lewis, Dale	NYR	1	8	0	0	0	0	....	....	....	....	....	....	1975-76	1975-76
Lewis, Dave	NYI, L.A., N.J., Det.	15	1008	36	187	223	953	91	1	20	21	143	....	1973-74	1987-88
• Lewis, Doug	Mtl.	1	3	0	0	0	0	....	....	....	....	....	....	1946-47	1946-47
‡ Lewis, Grant	Atl.	1	1	0	0	0	0	....	....	....	....	....	....	2008-09	2008-09
• Lewis, Herbie	Det.	11	483	148	161	309	248	38	13	10	23	6	2	1928-29	1938-39
Ley, Rick	Tor., Hfd.	6	310	12	72	84	528	14	0	2	2	20	....	1968-69	1980-81
Liba, Igor	NYR, L.A.	1	37	7	18	25	36	2	0	0	0	2	....	1988-89	1988-89
Libby, Jeff	NYI	1	1	0	0	0	0	....	....	....	....	....	....	1997-98	1997-98
Libett, Nick	Det., Pit.	14	982	237	268	505	472	16	6	2	8	2	....	1967-68	1980-81
Licari, Tony	Det.	1	9	0	1	1	0	....	....	....	....	....	....	1946-47	1946-47
Liddington, Bob	Tor.	1	11	0	1	1	2	....	....	....	....	....	....	1970-71	1970-71
Lidster, Doug	Van., NYR, St.L., Dal.	16	897	75	268	343	679	80	6	15	21	64	1	1983-84	1998-99
‡ Lidstrom, Nicklas	Det.	20	1564	264	878	1142	514	263	54	129	183	76	4	1991-92	2011-12
Lilley, John	Ana.	3	23	3	8	11	13	....	....	....	....	....	....	1993-94	1995-96
Lind, Juha	Dal., Mtl.	3	133	9	13	22	20	15	2	2	4	8	....	1997-98	2000-01
Lindberg, Chris	Cgy., Que.	3	116	17	25	42	47	2	0	1	1	2	....	1991-92	1993-94
Lindbom, Johan	NYR	1	38	1	3	4	28	....	....	....	....	....	....	1997-98	1997-98
Linden, Jamie	Fla.	1	4	0	0	0	17	....	....	....	....	....	....	1994-95	1994-95
Linden, Trevor	Van., NYI, Mtl., Wsh.	19	1382	375	492	867	895	124	34	65	99	104	....	1988-89	2007-08
Lindgren, Lars	Van., Min.	6	394	25	113	138	325	40	5	6	11	20	....	1978-79	1983-84
Lindgren, Mats	Edm., NYI, Van.	8	387	54	74	128	146	24	1	5	6	10	....	1996-97	2003-04
‡ Lindgren, Perttu	Dal.	1	1	0	0	0	0	....	....	....	....	....	....	2009-10	2009-10
Lindholm, Mikael	L.A.	1	18	2	2	4	2	....	....	....	....	....	....	1989-90	1989-90
Lindros, Brett	NYI	2	51	2	5	7	147	....	....	....	....	....	....	1994-95	1995-96
Lindros, Eric	Phi., NYR, Tor., Dal.	14	760	372	493	865	1398	53	24	33	57	122	....	1992-93	2006-07
Lindsay, Bill	Que., Fla., Cgy., S.J., Mtl., Atl.	13	777	83	141	224	922	42	7	8	15	44	....	1991-92	2003-04
Lindsay, Ted	Det., Chi.	17	1068	379	472	851	1808	133	47	49	96	194	4	1944-45	1964-65
Lindstrom, Willy	Wpg., Edm., Pit.	8	582	161	162	323	200	57	14	18	32	24	2	1979-80	1986-87
‡ Ling, David	Mtl., CBJ	5	93	4	4	8	191	....	....	....	....	....	....	1996-97	2003-04
‡ Linglet, Charles	Edm.	1	5	0	0	0	2	....	....	....	....	....	....	2009-10	2009-10
Linseman, Ken	Phi., Edm., Bos., Tor.	14	860	256	551	807	1727	113	43	77	120	325	1	1978-79	1991-92
‡ Lintner, Richard	Nsh., NYR, Pit.	3	112	8	12	20	54	....	....	....	....	....	....	1999-00	2002-03
Lipuma, Chris	T.B., S.J.	5	72	0	9	9	146	....	....	....	....	....	....	1992-93	1996-97
• Liscombe, Carl	Det.	9	373	137	140	277	117	59	22	19	41	20	1	1937-38	1945-46
‡ Lisin, Enver	Phx., NYR	4	135	24	18	42	64	....	....	....	....	....	....	2006-07	2009-10
• Litzenberger, Ed	Mtl., Chi., Det., Tor.	12	618	178	238	416	283	40	5	13	18	34	4	1952-53	1963-64
Loach, Lonnie	Ott., L.A., Ana.	2	56	10	13	23	29	1	0	0	0	0	....	1992-93	1993-94
• Locas, Jacques	Mtl.	2	59	7	8	15	66	....	....	....	....	....	....	1947-48	1948-49
Lochead, Bill	Det., Col., NYR	6	330	69	62	131	180	7	3	0	3	6	....	1974-75	1979-80
• Locking, Norm	Chi.	2	48	2	6	8	26	....	....	....	....	....	....	1934-35	1935-36
Loewen, Darcy	Buf., Ott.	5	135	4	8	12	211	....	....	....	....	....	....	1989-90	1993-94
Lofthouse, Mark	Wsh., Det.	6	181	42	38	80	73	....	....	....	....	....	....	1977-78	1982-83
Logan, Dave	Chi., Van.	6	218	5	29	34	470	12	0	0	0	10	....	1975-76	1980-81
Logan, Robert	Buf., L.A.	3	42	10	5	15	0	....	....	....	....	....	....	1986-87	1988-89
Loiselle, Claude	Det., N.J., Que., Tor., NYI	13	616	92	117	209	1149	41	4	11	15	58	....	1981-82	1993-94
‡ Lojek, Martin	Fla.	2	5	0	1	1	0	....	....	....	....	....	....	2006-07	2007-08
• Lomakin, Andrei	Phi., Fla.	4	215	42	62	104	92	....	....	....	....	....	....	1991-92	1994-95
Loney, Brian	Van.	1	12	2	3	5	6	....	....	....	....	....	....	1995-96	1995-96
Loney, Troy	Pit., Ana., NYI, NYR	12	624	87	110	197	1091	67	8	14	22	97	2	1983-84	1994-95
Long, Barry	L.A., Det., Wpg.	5	280	11	68	79	250	5	0	1	1	18	....	1972-73	1981-82
• Long, Stan	Mtl.	1	....	....	....	....	....	3	0	0	0	0	....	1951-52	1951-52
Lonsberry, Ross	Bos., L.A., Phi., Pit.	15	968	256	310	566	806	100	21	25	46	87	2	1966-67	1980-81
Loob, Hakan	Cgy.	6	450	193	236	429	189	73	26	28	54	16	1	1983-84	1988-89
Loob, Peter	Que.	1	8	1	2	3	0	....	....	....	....	....	....	1984-85	1984-85
Lorentz, Jim	Bos., St.L., NYR, Buf.	10	659	161	238	399	208	54	12	10	22	30	1	1968-69	1977-78
Lorimer, Bob	NYI, Col., N.J.	10	529	22	90	112	431	49	3	10	13	83	2	1976-77	1985-86
• Lorrain, Rod	Mtl.	6	179	28	39	67	30	11	0	3	3	0	....	1935-36	1941-42
• Loughlin, Clem	Det., Chi.	3	101	8	6	14	77	....	....	....	....	....	....	1926-27	1928-29
• Loughlin, Wilf	Tor.	1	14	0	0	0	2	....	....	....	....	....	....	1923-24	1923-24
Lovsin, Ken	Wsh.	1	1	0	0	0	0	....	....	....	....	....	....	1990-91	1990-91
Low, Reed	St.L., Chi.	5	256	3	16	19	725	....	....	....	....	....	....	2000-01	2006-07
Lowdermilk, Dwayne	Wsh.	1	2	0	1	1	2	....	....	....	....	....	....	1980-81	1980-81
Lowe, Darren	Pit.	1	8	1	2	3	0	....	....	....	....	....	....	1983-84	1983-84
Lowe, Kevin	Edm., NYR	19	1254	84	347	431	1498	214	10	48	58	192	6	1979-80	1997-98
Lowe, Odie	NYR	1	4	1	1	2	0	....	....	....	....	....	....	1949-50	1949-50
• Lowe, Ross	Bos., Mtl.	3	77	6	8	14	82	2	0	0	0	0	....	1949-50	1951-52
• Lowrey, Ed	Ott., Ham.	3	27	2	2	4	6	....	....	....	....	....	....	1917-18	1920-21
• Lowrey, Fred	Mtl.M., Pit.	2	53	1	1	2	10	2	0	0	0	6	....	1924-25	1925-26
• Lowrey, Gerry	Tor., Pit., Phi., Chi., Ott.	6	211	48	48	96	148	2	1	0	1	2	....	1927-28	1932-33
Lowry, Dave	Van., St.L., Fla., S.J., Cgy.	19	1084	164	187	351	1191	111	16	20	36	181	....	1985-86	2003-04
Loyns, Lynn	S.J., Cgy.	3	34	3	2	5	21	....	....	....	....	....	....	2002-03	2005-06
Lucas, Danny	Phi.	1	6	1	0	1	0	....	....	....	....	....	....	1978-79	1978-79
Lucas, Dave	Det.	1	1	0	0	0	0	....	....	....	....	....	....	1962-63	1962-63
Luce, Don	NYR, Det., Buf., L.A., Tor.	13	894	225	329	554	364	71	17	22	39	52	....	1969-70	1981-82
Ludvig, Jan	N.J., Buf.	7	314	54	87	141	418	....	....	....	....	....	....	1982-83	1988-89
Ludwig, Craig	Mtl., NYI, Min., Dal.	17	1256	38	184	222	1437	177	4	25	29	244	2	1982-83	1998-99
Ludzik, Steve	Chi., Buf.	9	424	46	93	139	333	44	4	8	12	70	....	1981-82	1989-90
Luhning, Warren	NYI, Dal.	3	29	0	1	1	21	....	....	....	....	....	....	1997-98	1999-00
Lukowich, Bernie	Pit., St.L.	2	79	13	15	28	34	2	0	0	0	0	....	1973-74	1974-75
Lukowich, Brad	Dal., T.B., NYI, N.J., S.J., Van.	13	658	23	90	113	369	71	1	5	6	22	1	1997-98	2010-11
Lukowich, Morris	Wpg., Bos., L.A.	8	582	199	219	418	584	11	0	2	2	24	....	1979-80	1986-87
Luksa, Charlie	Hfd.	1	8	0	1	1	4	....	....	....	....	....	....	1979-80	1979-80
Lumley, Dave	Mtl., Edm., Hfd.	9	437	98	160	258	680	61	6	8	14	131	2	1978-79	1986-87
Lumme, Jyrki	Mtl., Van., Phx., Dal., Tor.	15	985	114	354	468	620	105	9	35	44	52	....	1988-89	2002-03
• Lund, Pentti	Bos., NYR	7	259	44	55	99	40	19	7	5	12	0	....	1946-47	1952-53
Lundberg, Brian	Pit.	1	1	0	0	0	2	....	....	....	....	....	....	1982-83	1982-83

Name	NHL Teams	NHL Seasons	Regular Schedule					Playoffs					NHL Cup Wins	First NHL Season	Last NHL Season
			GP	G	A	TP	PIM	GP	G	A	TP	PIM			
• Lunde, Len	Det., Chi., Min., Van.	8	321	39	83	122	75	20	3	2	5	2	....	1958-59	1970-71
Lundholm, Bengt	Wpg.	5	275	48	95	143	72	14	3	4	7	14	....	1981-82	1985-86
‡ Lundqvist, Joel	Dal.	3	134	7	19	26	56	25	4	5	9	14	....	2006-07	2008-09
Lundrigan, Joe	Tor., Wsh.	2	52	2	8	10	22	....	....	....	....	....	....	1972-73	1974-75
Lundstrom, Tord	Det.	1	11	1	1	2	0	....	....	....	....	....	....	1973-74	1973-74
• Lundy, Pat	Det., Chi.	5	150	37	32	69	31	16	2	2	4	2	....	1945-46	1950-51
‡ Luoma, Mikko	Edm.	1	3	0	1	1	0	....	....	....	....	....	....	2003-04	2003-04
Luongo, Chris	Det., Ott., NYI	5	218	8	23	31	176	....	....	....	....	....	....	1990-91	1995-96
‡ Lupaschuk, Ross	Pit.	1	3	0	0	0	4	....	....	....	....	....	....	2002-03	2002-03
Lupien, Gilles	Mtl., Pit., Hfd.	5	226	5	25	30	416	25	0	0	0	21	2	1977-78	1981-82
• Lupul, Gary	Van.	7	293	70	75	145	243	25	4	7	11	11	....	1979-80	1985-86
• Lyashenko, Roman	Dal., NYR	4	139	14	9	23	55	17	2	1	3	0	....	1999-00	2002-03
Lyle, George	Det., Hfd.	4	99	24	38	62	51	....	....	....	....	....	....	1979-80	1982-83
Lynch, Doug	Edm.	1	2	0	0	0	0	....	....	....	....	....	....	2003-04	2003-04
Lynch, Jack	Pit., Det., Wsh.	7	382	24	106	130	336	....	....	....	....	....	....	1972-73	1978-79
• Lynn, Vic	NYR, Det., Mtl., Tor., Bos., Chi.	11	327	49	76	125	274	47	7	10	17	46	3	1942-43	1953-54
Lyon, Steve	Pit.	1	3	0	0	0	2	....	....	....	....	....	....	1976-77	1976-77
• Lyons, Ron	Bos., Phi.	1	36	2	4	6	27	5	0	0	0	0	....	1930-31	1930-31
Lysak, Brett	Car.	1	2	0	0	0	2	....	....	....	....	....	....	2003-04	2003-04
Lysiak, Tom	Atl., Chi.	13	919	292	551	843	567	76	25	38	63	49	....	1973-74	1985-86

M

Name	NHL Teams	NHL Seasons	Regular Schedule					Playoffs					NHL Cup Wins	First NHL Season	Last NHL Season
			GP	G	A	TP	PIM	GP	G	A	TP	PIM			
MacAdam, Al	Phi., Cal., Cle., Min., Van.	12	864	240	351	591	509	64	20	24	44	21	....	1973-74	1984-85
MacDermid, Paul	Hfd., Wpg., Wsh., Que.	14	690	116	142	258	1303	43	5	11	16	116	....	1981-82	1994-95
MacDonald, Blair	Edm., Van.	4	219	91	100	191	65	11	0	6	6	2	....	1979-80	1982-83
MacDonald, Brett	Van.	1	1	0	0	0	0	....	....	....	....	....	....	1987-88	1987-88
‡ MacDonald, Craig	Car., Fla., Bos., Cgy., Chi., T.B., CBJ	8	233	11	24	35	91	7	0	0	0	2	....	1998-99	2008-09
MacDonald, Doug	Buf.	3	11	1	0	1	2	....	....	....	....	....	....	1992-93	1994-95
MacDonald, Jason	NYR	1	4	0	0	0	19	....	....	....	....	....	....	2003-04	2003-04
MacDonald, Kevin	Ott.	1	1	0	0	0	2	....	....	....	....	....	....	1993-94	1993-94
• MacDonald, Kilby	NYR	4	151	36	34	70	47	15	1	2	3	4	1	1939-40	1944-45
MacDonald, Lowell	Det., L.A., Pit.	13	506	180	210	390	92	30	11	11	22	12	....	1961-62	1977-78
MacDonald, Parker	Tor., NYR, Det., Bos., Min.	14	676	144	179	323	253	75	14	14	28	20	....	1952-53	1968-69
MacDougall, Kim	Min.	1	1	0	0	0	0	....	....	....	....	....	....	1974-75	1974-75
MacEachern, Shane	St.L.	1	1	0	0	0	0	....	....	....	....	....	....	1987-88	1987-88
• Macey, Hub	NYR, Mtl.	3	30	6	9	15	0	8	0	0	0	0	....	1941-42	1946-47
MacGregor, Bruce	Det., NYR	14	893	213	257	470	217	107	19	28	47	44	....	1960-61	1973-74
MacGregor, Randy	Hfd.	1	2	1	1	2	2	....	....	....	....	....	....	1981-82	1981-82
MacGuigan, Garth	NYI	2	5	0	1	1	2	....	....	....	....	....	....	1979-80	1983-84
‡ Macias, Ray	Col.	2	8	0	1	1	2	....	....	....	....	....	....	2008-09	2010-11
MacInnis, Al	Cgy., St.L.	23	1416	340	934	1274	1511	177	39	121	160	255	1	1981-82	2003-04
MacIntosh, Ian	NYR	1	4	0	0	0	4	....	....	....	....	....	....	1952-53	1952-53
MacIver, Don	Wpg.	1	6	0	0	0	2	....	....	....	....	....	....	1979-80	1979-80
Maciver, Norm	NYR, Hfd., Edm., Ott., Pit., Wpg., Phx.	12	500	55	230	285	350	56	3	11	14	32	....	1986-87	1997-98
MacKasey, Blair	Tor.	1	1	0	0	0	2	....	....	....	....	....	....	1976-77	1976-77
• MacKay, Calum	Det., Mtl.	8	237	50	55	105	214	38	5	13	18	20	1	1946-47	1954-55
MacKay, Dave	Chi.	1	29	3	0	3	26	5	0	1	1	2	....	1940-41	1940-41
• MacKay, Mickey	Chi., Pit., Bos.	4	147	44	19	63	79	11	0	0	0	6	1	1926-27	1929-30
• MacKay, Murdo	Mtl.	4	19	0	3	3	0	15	1	2	3	0	....	1945-46	1948-49
MacKell, Fleming	Tor., Bos.	13	665	149	220	369	562	80	22	41	63	75	2	1947-48	1959-60
• MacKell, Jack	Ott.	2	45	4	2	6	59	2	0	0	0	0	2	1919-20	1920-21
‡ MacKenzie, Aaron	Col.	1	5	0	0	0	0	....	....	....	....	....	....	2008-09	2008-09
MacKenzie, Barry	Min.	1	6	0	1	1	6	....	....	....	....	....	....	1968-69	1968-69
• MacKenzie, Bill	Mtl.M., NYR, Mtl., Chi.	6	228	11	10	21	132	21	1	1	2	11	1	1933-34	1939-40
• MacKenzie, Clarence	Chi.	1	36	4	4	8	13	....	....	....	....	....	....	1932-33	1932-33
Mackey, David	Chi., Min., St.L.	6	126	8	12	20	305	3	0	0	0	2	....	1987-88	1993-94
• Mackey, Reg	NYR	1	34	0	0	0	16	1	0	0	0	0	....	1926-27	1926-27
• Mackie, Howie	Det.	2	20	1	0	1	4	8	0	0	0	0	1	1936-37	1937-38
MacKinnon, Paul	Wsh.	5	147	5	23	28	91	....	....	....	....	....	....	1979-80	1983-84
Maclean, Brett	Phx., Wpg.	2	18	2	3	5	4	....	....	....	....	....	....	2010-11	2011-12
MacLean, Don	L.A., Tor., CBJ, Det., Phx.	6	41	8	5	13	6	3	0	0	0	0	....	1997-98	2006-07
MacLean, John	N.J., S.J., NYR, Dal.	18	1194	413	429	842	1328	104	35	48	83	152	1	1983-84	2001-02
MacLean, Paul	St.L., Wpg., Det.	11	719	324	349	673	968	53	21	14	35	110	....	1980-81	1990-91
MacLeish, Rick	Phi., Hfd., Pit., Det.	14	846	349	410	759	434	114	54	53	107	38	2	1970-71	1983-84
MacLellan, Brian	L.A., NYR, Min., Cgy., Det.	10	606	172	241	413	551	47	5	9	14	42	1	1982-83	1991-92
MacLeod, Pat	Min., S.J., Dal.	4	53	5	13	18	14	....	....	....	....	....	....	1990-91	1995-96
MacMillan, Billy	Tor., Atl., NYI	7	446	74	77	151	184	53	6	6	12	40	....	1970-71	1976-77
MacMillan, Bob	NYR, St.L., Atl., Cgy., Col., N.J., Chi.	11	753	228	349	577	260	31	8	11	19	16	....	1974-75	1984-85
MacMillan, Jeff	Dal.	1	4	0	0	0	0	....	....	....	....	....	....	2003-04	2003-04
MacMillan, John	Tor., Det.	5	104	5	10	15	32	12	0	1	1	2	2	1960-61	1964-65
MacNeil, Al	Tor., Mtl., Chi., NYR, Pit.	11	524	17	75	92	617	37	0	4	4	67	....	1955-56	1967-68
MacNeil, Bernie	St.L.	1	4	0	0	0	0	....	....	....	....	....	....	1973-74	1973-74
MacNeil, Ian	Phi.	1	2	0	0	0	0	....	....	....	....	....	....	2002-03	2002-03
Macoun, Jamie	Cgy., Tor., Det.	16	1128	76	282	358	1208	159	10	32	42	169	2	1982-83	1998-99
• MacPherson, Bud	Mtl.	7	259	5	33	38	233	29	0	3	3	21	1	1948-49	1956-57
• MacSweyn, Ralph	Phi.	5	47	0	5	5	10	8	0	0	0	6	....	1967-68	1971-72
MacTavish, Craig	Bos., Edm., NYR, Phi., St.L.	17	1093	213	267	480	891	193	20	38	58	218	4	1979-80	1996-97
MacWilliam, Mike	NYI	1	6	0	0	0	14	....	....	....	....	....	....	1995-96	1995-96
‡ Madden, John	N.J., Chi., Min., Fla.	13	898	165	183	348	219	141	21	22	43	26	3	1998-99	2011-12
Madigan, Connie	St.L.	1	20	0	3	3	25	5	0	0	0	4	....	1972-73	1972-73
Madill, Jeff	N.J.	1	14	4	0	4	46	7	0	2	2	8	....	1990-91	1990-91
Magee, Dean	Min.	1	7	0	0	0	4	....	....	....	....	....	....	1977-78	1977-78
Maggs, Darryl	Chi., Cal., Tor.	3	135	14	19	33	54	4	0	0	0	0	....	1971-72	1979-80
Magnan, Marc	Tor.	1	4	0	1	1	5	....	....	....	....	....	....	1982-83	1982-83
‡ Magnan, Olivier	N.J.	1	18	0	0	0	4	....	....	....	....	....	....	2010-11	2010-11
• Magnuson, Keith	Chi.	11	589	14	125	139	1442	68	3	9	12	164	....	1969-70	1979-80
Maguire, Kevin	Tor., Buf., Phi.	6	260	29	30	59	782	11	0	0	0	86	....	1986-87	1991-92
Mahaffy, John	Mtl., NYR	3	37	11	25	36	4	1	0	1	1	0	....	1942-43	1944-45
Mahovlich, Frank	Tor., Det., Mtl.	18	1181	533	570	1103	1056	137	51	67	118	163	6	1956-57	1973-74
Mahovlich, Pete	Det., Mtl., Pit.	16	884	288	485	773	916	88	30	42	72	134	4	1965-66	1980-81
Mailhot, Jacques	Que.	1	5	0	0	0	33	....	....	....	....	....	....	1988-89	1988-89
• Mailley, Frank	Mtl.	1	1	0	0	0	0	....	....	....	....	....	....	1942-43	1942-43
Mair, Adam	Tor., L.A., Buf., N.J.	12	615	38	76	114	829	35	3	5	8	36	....	1998-99	2010-11
Mair, Jim	Phi., NYI, Van.	5	76	4	15	19	49	3	1	2	3	4	....	1970-71	1974-75
• Majeau, Fern	Mtl.	2	56	22	24	46	43	1	0	0	0	0	1	1943-44	1944-45
‡ Majesky, Ivan	Fla., Atl., Wsh.	3	202	8	23	31	234	....	....	....	....	....	....	2002-03	2005-06
Major, Bruce	Que.	1	4	0	0	0	0	....	....	....	....	....	....	1990-91	1990-91
Major, Mark	Det.	1	2	0	0	0	5	....	....	....	....	....	....	1996-97	1996-97
Makarov, Sergei	Cgy., S.J., Dal.	7	424	134	250	384	317	34	12	11	23	8	....	1989-90	1996-97
Makela, Mikko	NYI, L.A., Buf., Bos.	7	423	118	147	265	139	18	3	8	11	14	....	1985-86	1994-95
Maki, Chico	Chi.	15	841	143	292	435	345	113	17	36	53	43	1	1960-61	1975-76
‡ Maki, Tomi	Cgy.	1	1	0	0	0	0	....	....	....	....	....	....	2006-07	2006-07
• Maki, Wayne	Chi., St.L., Van.	6	246	57	79	136	184	2	1	0	1	2	....	1967-68	1972-73
Makkonen, Kari	Edm.	1	9	2	2	4	0	....	....	....	....	....	....	1979-80	1979-80
Malakhov, Vladimir	NYI, Mtl., N.J., NYR, Phi.	13	712	86	260	346	697	75	8	19	27	64	1	1992-93	2005-06
‡ Malec, Tomas	Car., Ott.	4	46	0	2	2	47	....	....	....	....	....	....	2002-03	2006-07
Maley, David	Mtl., N.J., Edm., S.J., NYI	9	466	43	81	124	1043	46	5	5	10	111	1	1985-86	1993-94
Malgunas, Stewart	Phi., Wpg., Wsh., Cgy.	7	129	1	5	6	144	....	....	....	....	....	....	1993-94	1999-00
‡ Malik, Marek	Hfd., Car., Van., NYR, T.B.	13	691	33	135	168	620	65	2	8	10	64	....	1994-95	2008-09
Malinowski, Merlin	Col., N.J., Hfd.	5	282	54	111	165	121	....	....	....	....	....	....	1978-79	1982-83
Malkoc, Dean	Van., Bos., NYI	4	116	1	3	4	299	....	....	....	....	....	....	1995-96	1998-99
Mallette, Troy	NYR, Edm., N.J., Ott., Bos., T.B.	9	456	51	68	119	1226	15	2	2	4	99	....	1989-90	1997-98
‡ Malmivaara, Olli	N.J.	1	2	0	0	0	0	....	....	....	....	....	....	2007-08	2007-08
• Malone, Cliff	Mtl.	1	3	0	0	0	0	....	....	....	....	....	....	1951-52	1951-52
Malone, Greg	Pit., Hfd., Que.	11	704	191	310	501	661	20	3	5	8	32	....	1976-77	1986-87
• Malone, Joe	Mtl., Que., Ham.	7	126	143	32	175	57	9	6	2	8	6	1	1917-18	1923-24
Maloney, Dan	Chi., L.A., Det., Tor.	11	737	192	259	451	1489	40	4	7	11	35	....	1970-71	1981-82
Maloney, Dave	NYR, Buf.	11	657	71	246	317	1154	49	7	17	24	91	....	1974-75	1984-85
Maloney, Don	NYR, Hfd., NYI	13	765	214	350	564	815	94	22	35	57	101	....	1978-79	1990-91
Maloney, Phil	Bos., Tor., Chi.	5	158	28	43	71	16	6	0	0	0	0	....	1949-50	1959-60
Maltais, Steve	Wsh., Min., T.B., Det., CBJ	6	120	9	18	27	53	1	0	0	0	0	....	1989-90	2000-01
Maltby, Kirk	Edm., Det.	16	1072	128	132	260	867	169	16	15	31	149	4	1993-94	2009-10
Maluta, Ray	Bos.	2	25	2	3	5	6	2	0	0	0	0	....	1975-76	1976-77
• Manastersky, Tom	Mtl.	1	6	0	0	0	11	....	....	....	....	....	....	1950-51	1950-51

Nicklas Lidstrom

Bill MacKenzie

Craig MacTavish

John Madden

Fern Majeau

Tom Manastersky

Brian Marchinko

Gus Marker

			Regular Schedule					Playoffs					NHL	First	Last
Name	NHL Teams	NHL Seasons	GP	G	A	TP	PIM	GP	G	A	TP	PIM	Cup Wins	NHL Season	NHL Season
• Mancuso, Gus	Mtl., NYR	4	42	7	9	16	17	....	....	....	....	....	....	1937-38	1942-43
Manderville, Kent	Tor., Edm., Hfd., Car., Phi., Pit.	12	646	37	67	104	348	67	3	3	6	44	....	1991-92	2002-03
Mandich, Dan	Min.	4	111	5	11	16	303	7	0	0	0	2	....	1982-83	1985-86
Maneluk, Mike	Phi., Chi., NYR, CBJ	3	85	11	10	21	57	....	....	....	....	....	....	1998-99	2000-01
Manery, Kris	Cle., Min., Van., Wpg.	4	250	63	64	127	91	....	....	....	....	....	....	1977-78	1980-81
Manery, Randy	Det., Atl., L.A.	10	582	50	206	256	415	13	0	2	2	12	....	1970-71	1979-80
Manlow, Eric	Bos., NYI	4	37	2	4	6	8	....	....	....	....	....	....	2000-01	2003-04
Mann, Cameron	Bos., Nsh.	5	93	14	10	24	40	1	0	0	0	0	....	1997-98	2002-03
Mann, Jack	NYR	2	9	3	4	7	0	....	....	....	....	....	....	1943-44	1944-45
Mann, Jimmy	Wpg., Que., Pit.	8	293	10	20	30	895	22	0	0	0	89	....	1979-80	1987-88
Mann, Ken	Det.	1	1	0	0	0	0	....	....	....	....	....	....	1975-76	1975-76
• Mann, Norm	Tor.	3	31	0	3	3	4	2	0	0	0	0	....	1935-36	1940-41
• Manners, Rennison	Pit., Phi.	2	37	3	2	5	14	....	....	....	....	....	....	1929-30	1930-31
‡ Manning, Paul	CBJ	1	8	0	0	0	2	....	....	....	....	....	....	2002-03	2002-03
Manno, Bob	Van., Tor., Det.	8	371	41	131	172	274	17	2	4	6	12	....	1976-77	1984-85
Manson, Dave	Chi., Edm., Wpg., Phx., Mtl., Dal., Tor.	16	1103	102	288	390	2792	112	7	24	31	343	....	1986-87	2001-02
• Manson, Ray	Bos., NYR	2	2	0	1	1	0	....	....	....	....	....	....	1947-48	1948-49
• Mantha, Georges	Mtl.	13	488	89	102	191	148	36	6	2	8	24	2	1928-29	1940-41
Mantha, Moe	Wpg., Pit., Edm., Min., Phi.	12	656	81	289	370	501	17	5	10	15	18	....	1980-81	1991-92
• Mantha, Sylvio	Mtl., Bos.	14	542	63	78	141	671	39	5	5	10	64	3	1923-24	1936-37
‡ Mapletoft, Justin	NYI	2	38	3	6	9	8	2	0	0	0	0	....	2002-03	2003-04
Mara, Paul	T.B., Phx., Bos., NYR, Mtl., Ana.	12	734	64	189	253	776	33	3	4	7	50	....	1998-99	2010-11
• Maracle, Bud	NYR	1	11	1	3	4	4	4	0	0	0	0	....	1930-31	1930-31
Marcetta, Milan	Tor., Min.	3	54	7	15	22	10	17	7	7	14	4	1	1966-67	1968-69
• March, Mush	Chi.	17	759	153	230	383	540	45	12	15	27	41	2	1928-29	1944-45
Marchant, Todd	NYR, Edm., CBJ, Ana.	17	1195	186	312	498	774	95	13	21	34	88	1	1993-94	2010-11
Marchinko, Brian	Tor., NYI	4	47	2	6	8	0	....	....	....	....	....	....	1970-71	1973-74
Marchment, Bryan	Wpg., Chi., Hfd., Edm., T.B., S.J., Col., Tor., Cgy.	17	926	40	142	182	2307	83	4	3	7	102	....	1988-89	2005-06
Marcinyshyn, Dave	N.J., Que., NYR	3	16	0	1	1	49	....	....	....	....	....	....	1990-91	1992-93
Marcon, Lou	Det.	3	60	0	4	4	42	....	....	....	....	....	....	1958-59	1962-63
Marcotte, Don	Bos.	15	868	230	254	484	317	132	34	27	61	81	2	1965-66	1981-82
‡ Marha, Josef	Col., Ana., Chi.	6	159	21	32	53	32	....	....	....	....	....	....	1995-96	2000-01
Marini, Hector	NYI, N.J.	5	154	27	46	73	246	10	3	6	9	14	2	1978-79	1983-84
Marinucci, Chris	NYI, L.A.	2	13	1	4	5	2	....	....	....	....	....	....	1994-95	1996-97
• Mario, Frank	Bos.	2	53	9	19	28	24	....	....	....	....	....	....	1941-42	1944-45
• Mariucci, John	Chi.	5	223	11	34	45	308	12	0	3	3	26	....	1940-41	1947-48
‡ Marjamaki, Masi	NYI	1	1	0	0	0	0	....	....	....	....	....	....	2005-06	2005-06
Mark, Gordon	N.J., Edm.	4	85	3	10	13	187	....	....	....	....	....	....	1986-87	1994-95
Markell, John	Wpg., St.L., Min.	4	55	11	10	21	36	....	....	....	....	....	....	1979-80	1984-85
• Marker, Gus	Det., Mtl.M., Tor., Bro.	10	322	64	69	133	133	46	5	7	12	36	1	1932-33	1941-42
Markham, Ray	NYR	1	14	1	1	2	21	7	1	0	1	24	....	1979-80	1979-80
• Markle, Jack	Tor.	1	8	0	1	1	0	....	....	....	....	....	....	1935-36	1935-36
Markov, Danny	Tor., Phx., Car., Phi., Nsh., Det.	9	538	29	118	147	456	81	2	12	14	84	....	1997-98	2006-07
• Marks, Jack	Mtl.W., Tor., Que.	2	7	0	0	0	4	....	....	....	....	....	1	1917-18	1919-20
Marks, John	Chi.	10	657	112	163	275	330	57	5	9	14	60	....	1972-73	1981-82
Markwart, Nevin	Bos., Cgy.	8	309	41	68	109	794	19	1	0	1	33	....	1983-84	1991-92
Marois, Daniel	Tor., NYI, Bos., Dal.	8	350	117	93	210	419	19	3	3	6	28	....	1987-88	1995-96
Marois, Mario	NYR, Van., Que., Wpg., St.L.	15	955	76	357	433	1746	100	4	34	38	182	....	1977-78	1991-92
• Marotte, Gilles	Bos., Chi., L.A., NYR, St.L.	12	808	56	265	321	919	29	3	3	6	26	....	1965-66	1976-77
Marquess, Mark	Bos.	1	27	5	4	9	6	4	0	0	0	0	....	1946-47	1946-47
Marsh, Brad	Atl., Cgy., Phi., Tor., Det., Ott.	15	1086	23	175	198	1241	97	6	18	24	124	....	1978-79	1992-93
Marsh, Gary	Det., Tor.	2	7	1	3	4	4	....	....	....	....	....	....	1967-68	1968-69
Marsh, Peter	Wpg., Chi.	5	278	48	71	119	224	26	1	5	6	33	....	1979-80	1983-84
Marshall, Bert	Det., Oak., Cal., NYR, NYI	14	868	17	181	198	926	72	4	22	26	99	....	1965-66	1978-79
Marshall, Don	Mtl., NYR, Buf., Tor.	19	1176	265	324	589	127	94	8	15	23	14	5	1951-52	1971-72
Marshall, Grant	Dal., CBJ, N.J.	11	700	92	147	239	793	90	6	11	17	95	2	1994-95	2005-06
Marshall, Jason	St.L., Ana., Wsh., Min., S.J.	12	526	16	51	67	1004	43	2	3	5	55	....	1991-92	2005-06
Marshall, Paul	Pit., Tor., Hfd.	4	95	15	18	33	17	1	0	0	0	0	....	1979-80	1982-83
Marshall, Willie	Tor.	4	33	1	5	6	2	....	....	....	....	....	....	1952-53	1958-59
Marson, Mike	Wsh., L.A.	6	196	24	24	48	233	....	....	....	....	....	....	1974-75	1979-80
‡ Martensson, Tony	Ana.	1	6	1	1	2	0	....	....	....	....	....	....	2003-04	2003-04
• Martin, Clare	Bos., Det., Chi., NYR	6	237	12	28	40	78	27	0	2	2	6	1	1941-42	1951-52
Martin, Craig	Wpg., Fla.	2	21	0	1	1	24	....	....	....	....	....	....	1994-95	1996-97
• Martin, Frank	Bos., Chi.	6	282	11	46	57	122	10	0	2	2	2	....	1952-53	1957-58
Martin, Grant	Van., Wsh.	4	44	0	4	4	55	1	1	0	1	2	....	1983-84	1986-87
Martin, Jack	Tor.	1	1	0	0	0	0	....	....	....	....	....	....	1960-61	1960-61
Martin, Matt	Tor.	4	76	0	5	5	71	....	....	....	....	....	....	1993-94	1996-97
• Martin, Pit	Det., Bos., Chi., Van.	17	1101	324	485	809	609	100	27	31	58	56	....	1961-62	1978-79
• Martin, Rick	Buf., L.A.	11	685	384	317	701	477	63	24	29	53	74	....	1971-72	1981-82
• Martin, Ron	NYA	2	94	13	16	29	36	....	....	....	....	....	....	1932-33	1933-34
Martin, Terry	Buf., Que., Tor., Edm., Min.	10	479	104	101	205	202	21	4	2	6	26	....	1975-76	1984-85
Martin, Tom	Tor.	1	3	1	0	1	0	....	....	....	....	....	....	1967-68	1967-68
Martin, Tom	Wpg., Hfd., Min.	6	92	12	11	23	249	4	0	0	0	6	....	1984-85	1989-90
• Martineau, Don	Atl., Min., Det.	4	90	6	10	16	63	....	....	....	....	....	....	1973-74	1976-77
Martini, Darcy	Edm.	1	2	0	0	0	0	....	....	....	....	....	....	1993-94	1993-94
Martins, Steve	Hfd., Car., Ott., T.B., NYI, St.L.	10	267	21	25	46	142	5	0	1	1	0	....	1995-96	2005-06
Martinson, Steve	Det., Mtl., Min.	4	49	2	1	3	244	1	0	0	0	10	....	1987-88	1991-92
Maruk, Dennis	Cal., Cle., Min., Wsh.	14	888	356	522	878	761	34	14	22	36	26	....	1975-76	1988-89
Masnick, Paul	Mtl., Chi., Tor.	6	232	18	41	59	139	33	4	5	9	27	1	1950-51	1957-58
• Mason, Charley	NYR, NYA, Det., Chi.	4	95	7	18	25	44	4	0	1	1	0	....	1934-35	1938-39
• Massecar, George	NYA	3	100	12	11	23	46	....	....	....	....	....	....	1929-30	1931-32
Masters, Jamie	St.L.	3	33	1	13	14	2	2	0	0	0	0	....	1975-76	1978-79
• Masterton, Bill	Min.	1	38	4	8	12	4	....	....	....	....	....	....	1967-68	1967-68
• Mathers, Frank	Tor.	3	23	1	3	4	4	....	....	....	....	....	....	1948-49	1951-52
Mathiasen, Dwight	Pit.	3	33	1	7	8	18	....	....	....	....	....	....	1985-86	1987-88
Mathieson, Jim	Wsh.	1	2	0	0	0	4	....	....	....	....	....	....	1989-90	1989-90
Mathieu, Marquis	Bos.	3	16	0	2	2	14	....	....	....	....	....	....	1998-99	2000-01
Matte, Christian	Col., Min.	5	25	2	3	5	12	....	....	....	....	....	....	1996-97	2000-01
• Matte, Joe	Tor., Ham., Bos., Mtl.	4	68	17	15	32	54	....	....	....	....	....	....	1919-20	1925-26
• Matte, Joe	Det., Chi.	2	24	0	3	3	8	....	....	....	....	....	....	1929-30	1942-43
Matteau, Stephane	Cgy., Chi., NYR, St.L., S.J., Fla.	13	848	144	172	316	742	109	12	22	34	80	1	1990-91	2002-03
Matteucci, Mike	Min.	2	6	0	0	0	4	....	....	....	....	....	....	2000-01	2001-02
Mattiussi, Dick	Pit., Oak., Cal.	4	200	8	31	39	124	8	0	1	1	6	....	1967-68	1970-71
Matvichuk, Richard	Min., Dal., N.J.	14	796	39	139	178	624	123	5	19	24	128	1	1992-93	2006-07
• Matz, Johnny	Mtl.	1	30	2	3	5	0	1	0	0	0	0	....	1924-25	1924-25
Maxner, Wayne	Bos.	2	62	8	9	17	48	....	....	....	....	....	....	1964-65	1965-66
Maxwell, Brad	Min., Que., Tor., Van., NYR	10	612	98	270	368	1292	79	12	49	61	178	....	1977-78	1986-87
Maxwell, Bryan	Min., St.L., Wpg., Pit.	8	331	18	77	95	745	15	1	1	2	86	....	1977-78	1984-85
Maxwell, Kevin	Min., Col., N.J.	3	66	6	15	21	61	16	3	4	7	24	....	1980-81	1983-84
Maxwell, Wally	Tor.	1	2	0	0	0	0	....	....	....	....	....	....	1952-53	1952-53
May, Alan	Bos., Edm., Wsh., Dal., Cgy.	8	393	31	45	76	1348	40	1	2	3	80	....	1987-88	1994-95
May, Brad	Buf., Van., Phx., Col., Ana., Tor., Det.	18	1041	127	161	288	2248	88	4	9	13	112	1	1991-92	2009-10
Mayer, Derek	Ott.	1	17	2	2	4	8	....	....	....	....	....	....	1993-94	1993-94
Mayer, Jim	NYR	1	4	0	0	0	0	....	....	....	....	....	....	1979-80	1979-80
Mayer, Pat	Pit.	1	1	0	0	0	4	....	....	....	....	....	....	1987-88	1987-88
• Mayer, Shep	Tor.	1	12	1	2	3	4	....	....	....	....	....	....	1942-43	1942-43
• Mazur, Eddie	Mtl., Chi.	6	107	8	20	28	120	25	4	5	9	22	1	1950-51	1956-57
Mazur, Jay	Van.	4	47	11	7	18	20	6	0	1	1	8	....	1988-89	1991-92
McAdam, Gary	Buf., Pit., Det., Cgy., Wsh., N.J., Tor.	11	534	96	132	228	243	30	6	5	11	16	....	1975-76	1985-86
• McAdam, Sam	NYR	1	5	0	0	0	0	....	....	....	....	....	....	1930-31	1930-31
McAllister, Chris	Van., Tor., Phi., Col., NYR	7	301	4	17	21	634	9	0	1	1	4	....	1997-98	2003-04
McAlpine, Chris	N.J., St.L., T.B., Atl., Chi., L.A.	8	289	6	24	30	245	28	0	1	1	18	1	1994-95	2002-03
McAmmond, Dean	Chi., Edm., Phi., Cgy., Col., St.L., Ott., NYI, N.J.	17	996	186	262	448	490	46	6	7	13	35	....	1991-92	2009-10
• McAndrew, Hazen	Bro.	1	7	0	1	1	6	....	....	....	....	....	....	1941-42	1941-42
McAneeley, Ted	Cal.	3	158	8	35	43	141	....	....	....	....	....	....	1972-73	1974-75
• McAtee, Jud	Det.	3	46	15	13	28	6	14	2	1	3	0	....	1942-43	1944-45
• McAtee, Norm	Bos.	1	13	0	1	1	0	....	....	....	....	....	....	1946-47	1946-47
• McAvoy, George	Mtl.	1	....	....	....	....	....	4	0	0	0	0	....	1954-55	1954-55
McBain, Andrew	Wpg., Pit., Van., Ott.	11	608	129	172	301	633	24	5	7	12	39	....	1983-84	1993-94
McBain, Jason	Hfd.	2	9	0	0	0	0	....	....	....	....	....	....	1995-96	1996-97
McBain, Mike	T.B.	2	64	0	7	7	22	....	....	....	....	....	....	1997-98	1998-99
McBean, Wayne	L.A., NYI, Wpg.	6	211	10	39	49	168	2	1	1	2	0	....	1987-88	1993-94
• McBride, Cliff	Mtl.M., Tor.	2	2	0	0	0	0	....	....	....	....	....	....	1928-29	1929-30
McBurney, Jim	Chi.	1	1	0	1	1	0	....	....	....	....	....	....	1952-53	1952-53

Name	NHL Teams	NHL Seasons	Regular Schedule					Playoffs					NHL Cup Wins	First NHL Season	Last NHL Season
			GP	G	A	TP	PIM	GP	G	A	TP	PIM			
McCabe, Bryan	NYI, Van., Chi., Tor., Fla., NYR	15	1135	145	383	528	1732	56	10	18	28	84	....	1995-96	2010-11
• McCabe, Stan	Det., Mtl.M.	4	78	9	4	13	49	....	....	....	....	....	....	1929-30	1933-34
• McCaffrey, Bert	Tor., Pit., Mtl.	7	260	43	30	73	202	8	2	1	3	10	1	1924-25	1930-31
McCahill, John	Col.	1	1	0	0	0	0	....	....	....	....	....	....	1977-78	1977-78
• McCaig, Doug	Det., Chi.	7	263	8	21	29	255	7	0	1	1	10	....	1941-42	1950-51
• McCallum, Dunc	NYR, Pit.	5	187	14	35	49	230	10	1	2	3	12	....	1965-66	1970-71
• McCalmon, Eddie	Chi., Phi.	2	39	5	0	5	14	....	....	....	....	....	....	1927-28	1930-31
McCann, Rick	Det.	6	43	1	4	5	6	....	....	....	....	....	....	1967-68	1974-75
McCarthy, Dan	NYR	1	5	4	0	4	4	....	....	....	....	....	....	1980-81	1980-81
McCarthy, Kevin	Phi., Van., Pit.	10	537	67	191	258	527	21	2	3	5	20	....	1977-78	1986-87
McCarthy, Sandy	Cgy., T.B., Phi., Car., NYR, Bos.	11	736	72	76	148	1534	23	0	2	2	61	....	1993-94	2003-04
‡ McCarthy, Steve	Chi., Van., Atl.	8	302	17	38	55	168	....	....	....	....	....	....	1999-00	2007-08
• McCarthy, Thomas	Que., Ham.	2	35	22	7	29	10	....	....	....	....	....	....	1919-20	1920-21
McCarthy, Tom	Det., Bos.	4	60	8	9	17	8	....	....	....	....	....	....	1956-57	1960-61
McCarthy, Tom	Min., Bos.	9	460	178	221	399	330	68	12	26	38	67	....	1979-80	1987-88
• McCartney, Walt	Mtl.	1	2	0	0	0	0	....	....	....	....	....	....	1932-33	1932-33
McCarty, Darren	Det., Cgy.	15	758	127	161	288	1477	174	23	26	49	228	4	1993-94	2008-09
McCaskill, Ted	Min.	1	4	0	2	2	0	....	....	....	....	....	....	1967-68	1967-68
McCauley, Alyn	Tor., S.J., L.A.	9	488	69	97	166	116	52	7	12	19	18	....	1997-98	2006-07
McClanahan, Rob	Buf., Hfd., NYR	5	224	38	63	101	126	34	4	12	16	31	....	1979-80	1983-84
McCleary, Trent	Ott., Bos., Mtl.	4	192	8	15	23	134	....	....	....	....	....	....	1995-96	1999-00
McClelland, Kevin	Pit., Edm., Det., Tor., Wpg.	12	588	68	112	180	1672	98	11	18	29	281	4	1981-82	1993-94
McCord, Bob	Bos., Det., Min., St.L.	7	316	10	58	68	262	14	2	5	7	10	....	1963-64	1972-73
• McCord, Dennis	Van.	1	3	0	0	0	6	....	....	....	....	....	....	1973-74	1973-74
McCormack, John	Tor., Mtl., Chi.	8	311	25	49	74	35	22	1	1	2	0	2	1947-48	1954-55
McCosh, Shawn	L.A., NYR	2	9	1	0	1	6	....	....	....	....	....	....	1991-92	1994-95
McCourt, Dale	Det., Buf., Tor.	7	532	194	284	478	124	21	9	7	16	6	....	1977-78	1983-84
McCreary, Bill	NYR, Det., Mtl., St.L.	8	309	53	62	115	108	48	6	16	22	14	....	1953-54	1970-71
McCreary, Bill	Tor.	1	12	1	0	1	4	....	....	....	....	....	....	1980-81	1980-81
• McCreary, Keith	Mtl., Pit., Atl.	10	532	131	112	243	294	16	0	4	4	6	....	1961-62	1974-75
• McCreedy, John	Tor.	2	64	17	12	29	25	21	4	3	7	16	2	1941-42	1944-45
• McCrimmon, Brad	Bos., Phi., Cgy., Det., Hfd., Phx.	18	1222	81	322	403	1416	116	11	18	29	176	1	1979-80	1996-97
McCrimmon, Jim	St.L.	1	2	0	0	0	0	....	....	....	....	....	....	1974-75	1974-75
• McCulley, Bob	Mtl.	1	1	0	0	0	0	....	....	....	....	....	....	1934-35	1934-35
• McCurry, Duke	Pit.	4	148	21	11	32	119	4	0	2	2	2	....	1925-26	1928-29
McCutcheon, Brian	Det.	3	37	3	1	4	7	....	....	....	....	....	....	1974-75	1976-77
McCutcheon, Darwin	Tor.	1	1	0	0	0	2	....	....	....	....	....	....	1981-82	1981-82
• McDill, Jeff	Chi.	1	1	0	0	0	0	....	....	....	....	....	....	1976-77	1976-77
McDonagh, Bill	NYR	1	4	0	0	0	2	....	....	....	....	....	....	1949-50	1949-50
McDonald, Ab	Mtl., Chi., Bos., Det., Pit., St.L.	15	762	182	248	430	200	84	21	29	50	42	4	1957-58	1971-72
McDonald, Brian	Chi., Buf.	2	12	0	0	0	29	8	0	0	0	2	....	1967-68	1970-71
• McDonald, Bucko	Det., Tor., NYR	11	446	35	88	123	206	50	6	1	7	24	3	1934-35	1944-45
• McDonald, Butch	Det., Chi.	2	66	8	20	28	2	5	0	2	2	10	....	1939-40	1944-45
McDonald, Gerry	Hfd.	2	8	0	0	0	4	....	....	....	....	....	....	1981-82	1983-84
• McDonald, Jack	Mtl.W., Mtl., Que., Tor.	5	69	26	14	40	30	7	1	3	4	3	....	1917-18	1921-22
McDonald, Jack	NYR	1	43	10	9	19	6	....	....	....	....	....	....	1943-44	1943-44
McDonald, Lanny	Tor., Col., Cgy.	16	1111	500	506	1006	899	117	44	40	84	120	1	1973-74	1988-89
McDonald, Robert	NYR	1	1	0	0	0	0	....	....	....	....	....	....	1943-44	1943-44
McDonald, Terry	K.C.	1	8	0	1	1	6	....	....	....	....	....	....	1975-76	1975-76
‡ McDonell, Kent	CBJ	2	32	1	2	3	36	....	....	....	....	....	....	2002-03	2003-04
McDonnell, Joe	Van., Pit.	3	50	2	10	12	34	....	....	....	....	....	....	1981-82	1985-86
• McDonnell, Moylan	Ham.	1	22	1	2	3	2	....	....	....	....	....	....	1920-21	1920-21
McDonough, Al	L.A., Pit., Atl., Det.	5	237	73	88	161	73	8	0	1	1	2	....	1970-71	1977-78
McDonough, Hubie	L.A., NYI, S.J.	5	195	40	26	66	67	5	1	0	1	4	....	1988-89	1992-93
McDougal, Mike	NYR, Hfd.	4	61	8	10	18	43	....	....	....	....	....	....	1978-79	1982-83
McDougall, Bill	Det., Edm., T.B.	3	28	5	5	10	12	1	0	0	0	0	....	1990-91	1993-94
McEachern, Shawn	Pit., L.A., Bos., Ott., Atl.	14	911	256	323	579	506	97	12	25	37	62	1	1991-92	2005-06
McElmury, Jim	Min., K.C., Col.	5	180	14	47	61	49	....	....	....	....	....	....	1972-73	1977-78
McEwen, Mike	NYR, Col., NYI, L.A., Wsh., Det., Hfd.	12	716	108	296	404	460	78	12	36	48	48	3	1976-77	1987-88
• McFadden, Jim	Det., Chi.	8	412	100	126	226	89	49	10	9	19	30	1	1946-47	1953-54
• McFadyen, Don	Chi.	4	179	12	33	45	77	11	2	2	4	5	1	1932-33	1935-36
McFall, Dan	Wpg.	2	9	0	1	1	0	....	....	....	....	....	....	1984-85	1985-86
• McFarlane, Gord	Chi.	1	2	0	0	0	0	....	....	....	....	....	....	1926-27	1926-27
McGeough, Jim	Wsh., Pit.	4	57	7	10	17	32	....	....	....	....	....	....	1981-82	1986-87
• McGibbon, Irv	Mtl.	1	1	0	0	0	2	....	....	....	....	....	....	1942-43	1942-43
McGill, Bob	Tor., Chi., S.J., Det., NYI, Hfd.	13	705	17	55	72	1766	49	0	0	0	88	....	1981-82	1993-94
• McGill, Jack	Mtl.	3	134	27	10	37	71	3	2	0	2	0	....	1934-35	1936-37
• McGill, Jack	Bos.	4	97	23	36	59	42	27	7	4	11	17	....	1941-42	1946-47
McGill, Ryan	Chi., Phi., Edm.	4	151	4	15	19	391	....	....	....	....	....	....	1991-92	1994-95
McGillis, Dan	Edm., Phi., S.J., Bos., N.J.	9	634	56	182	238	570	64	8	14	22	76	....	1996-97	2005-06
McGregor, Sandy	NYR	1	2	0	0	0	2	....	....	....	....	....	....	1963-64	1963-64
• McGuire, Mickey	Pit.	2	36	3	0	3	6	....	....	....	....	....	....	1926-27	1927-28
McHugh, Mike	Min., S.J.	4	20	1	0	1	16	....	....	....	....	....	....	1988-89	1991-92
McIlhargey, Jack	Phi., Van., Hfd.	8	393	11	36	47	1102	27	0	3	3	68	....	1974-75	1981-82
• McInenly, Bert	Det., NYA, Ott., Bos.	6	166	19	15	34	144	4	0	0	0	2	....	1930-31	1935-36
McInnis, Marty	NYI, Cgy., Ana., Bos.	12	796	170	250	420	330	22	3	2	5	4	....	1991-92	2002-03
McIntosh, Bruce	Min.	1	2	0	0	0	0	....	....	....	....	....	....	1972-73	1972-73
McIntosh, Paul	Buf.	2	48	0	2	2	66	2	0	0	0	7	....	1974-75	1975-76
• McIntyre, Jack	Bos., Chi., Det.	11	499	109	102	211	173	29	7	6	13	4	....	1949-50	1959-60
McIntyre, John	Tor., L.A., NYR, Van.	6	351	24	54	78	516	44	0	6	6	54	....	1989-90	1994-95
McIntyre, Larry	Tor.	2	41	0	3	3	26	....	....	....	....	....	....	1969-70	1972-73
McKay, Doug	Det.	1	....	....	....	....	....	1	0	0	0	0	1	1949-50	1949-50
McKay, Randy	Det., N.J., Dal., Mtl.	15	932	162	201	363	1731	123	20	23	43	123	2	1988-89	2002-03
McKay, Ray	Chi., Buf., Cal.	6	140	2	16	18	102	1	0	0	0	0	....	1968-69	1973-74
McKay, Scott	Ana.	1	1	0	0	0	0	....	....	....	....	....	....	1993-94	1993-94
McKechnie, Walt	Min., Cal., Bos., Det., Wsh., Cle., Tor., Col.	16	955	214	392	606	469	15	7	5	12	7	....	1967-68	1982-83
McKee, Jay	Buf., St.L., Pit.	14	802	21	104	125	622	60	3	6	9	66	....	1995-96	2009-10
McKee, Mike	Que.	1	48	3	12	15	41	....	....	....	....	....	....	1993-94	1993-94
McKegney, Ian	Chi.	1	3	0	0	0	2	....	....	....	....	....	....	1976-77	1976-77
McKegney, Tony	Buf., Que., Min., NYR, St.L., Det., Chi.	13	912	320	319	639	517	79	24	23	47	56	....	1978-79	1990-91
McKendry, Alex	NYI, Cgy.	4	46	3	6	9	21	6	2	2	4	0	1	1977-78	1980-81
McKenna, Sean	Buf., L.A., Tor.	9	414	82	80	162	181	15	1	2	3	2	....	1981-82	1989-90
McKenna, Steve	L.A., Min., Pit., NYR	8	373	18	14	32	824	3	0	1	1	8	....	1996-97	2003-04
McKenney, Don	Bos., NYR, Tor., Det., St.L.	13	798	237	345	582	211	58	18	29	47	10	1	1954-55	1967-68
McKenny, Jim	Tor., Min.	14	604	82	247	329	294	37	7	9	16	10	....	1965-66	1978-79
McKenzie, Brian	Pit.	1	6	1	1	2	4	....	....	....	....	....	....	1971-72	1971-72
McKenzie, Jim	Hfd., Dal., Pit., Wpg., Phx., Ana., Wsh., N.J., Nsh.	15	880	48	52	100	1739	51	0	0	0	38	1	1989-90	2003-04
McKenzie, John	Chi., Det., NYR, Bos.	12	691	206	268	474	917	69	15	32	47	133	2	1958-59	1971-72
McKim, Andrew	Bos., Det.	3	38	1	4	5	6	....	....	....	....	....	....	1992-93	1994-95
• McKinnon, Alex	Ham., NYA, Chi.	5	193	19	11	30	237	....	....	....	....	....	....	1924-25	1928-29
• McKinnon, John	Mtl., Pit., Phi.	6	208	28	11	39	224	2	0	0	0	4	....	1925-26	1930-31
McLaren, Kyle	Bos., S.J.	12	719	46	161	207	671	70	1	13	14	78	....	1995-96	2007-08
McLaren, Steve	St.L.	1	6	0	0	0	25	....	....	....	....	....	....	2003-04	2003-04
McLean, Don	Wsh.	1	9	0	0	0	6	....	....	....	....	....	....	1975-76	1975-76
• McLean, Fred	Que., Ham.	2	8	0	0	0	2	....	....	....	....	....	....	1919-20	1920-21
• McLean, Jack	Tor.	3	67	14	24	38	76	13	2	2	4	8	1	1942-43	1944-45
• McLean, Jeff	S.J.	1	6	1	0	1	0	....	....	....	....	....	....	1993-94	1993-94
‡ McLean, Kurtis	NYI	1	4	1	0	1	0	....	....	....	....	....	....	2008-09	2008-09
• McLellan, John	Tor.	1	2	0	0	0	0	....	....	....	....	....	....	1951-52	1951-52
McLellan, Scott	Bos.	1	2	0	0	0	0	....	....	....	....	....	....	1982-83	1982-83
McLellan, Todd	NYI	1	5	1	1	2	0	....	....	....	....	....	....	1987-88	1987-88
• McLenahan, Rollie	Det.	1	9	2	1	3	10	2	0	0	0	0	....	1945-46	1945-46
McLeod, Al	Det.	1	26	2	2	4	24	....	....	....	....	....	....	1973-74	1973-74
McLeod, Jackie	NYR	5	106	14	23	37	12	7	0	0	0	0	....	1949-50	1954-55
McLlwain, Dave	Pit., Wpg., Buf., NYI, Tor., Ott.	10	501	100	107	207	292	20	0	2	2	2	....	1987-88	1996-97
• McMahon, Mike	Mtl., Bos.	3	57	7	18	25	102	13	1	2	3	30	1	1942-43	1945-46
• McMahon, Mike	NYR, Min., Chi., Det., Pit., Buf.	8	224	15	68	83	171	14	3	7	10	4	....	1963-64	1971-72
McManama, Bob	Pit.	3	99	11	25	36	28	8	0	1	1	6	....	1973-74	1975-76
• McManus, Sammy	Mtl.M., Bos.	2	26	0	1	1	8	1	0	0	0	0	1	1934-35	1936-37
McMorrow, Sean	Buf.	1	1	0	0	0	0	....	....	....	....	....	....	2002-03	2002-03
McMurchy, Tom	Chi., Edm.	4	55	8	4	12	65	....	....	....	....	....	....	1983-84	1987-88
• McNab, Max	Det.	4	128	16	19	35	24	25	1	0	1	4	1	1947-48	1950-51
McNab, Peter	Buf., Bos., Van., N.J.	14	954	363	450	813	179	107	40	42	82	20	....	1973-74	1986-87
• McNabney, Sid	Mtl.	1	....	....	....	....	....	5	0	1	1	2	....	1950-51	1950-51

Gary Marsh

Peter Marsh

John McCahill

Doug McCaig

John McCormack

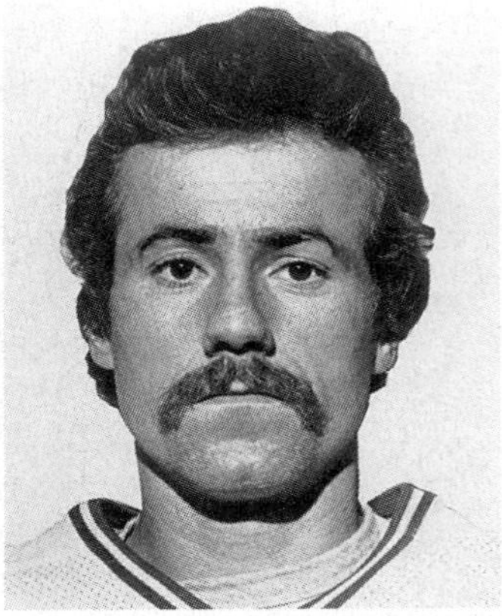

Gerry McDonald

Bob McGill

Jack McIntyre

			Regular Schedule					Playoffs							
Name	NHL Teams	NHL Seasons	GP	G	A	TP	PIM	GP	G	A	TP	PIM	NHL Cup Wins	First NHL Season	Last NHL Season
• McNamara, Howard	Mtl.	1	10	1	0	1	4	....	....	....	....	....	....	1919-20	1919-20
• McNaughton, George	Que.	1	1	0	0	0	0	....	....	....	....	....	....	1919-20	1919-20
• McNeill, Billy	Det.	6	257	21	46	67	142	4	1	1	2	4	....	1956-57	1963-64
McNeill, Grant	Fla.	1	3	0	0	0	5	....	....	....	....	....	....	2003-04	2003-04
McNeill, Mike	Chi., Que.	2	63	5	11	16	18	....	....	....	....	....	....	1990-91	1991-92
McNeill, Stu	Det.	3	10	1	1	2	2	....	....	....	....	....	....	1957-58	1959-60
McPhee, George	NYR, N.J.	7	115	24	25	49	257	29	5	3	8	69	....	1982-83	1988-89
McPhee, Mike	Mtl., Min., Dal.	11	744	200	199	399	661	134	28	27	55	193	1	1983-84	1993-94
McRae, Basil	Que., Tor., Det., Min., T.B., St.L., Chi.	16	576	53	83	136	2457	78	8	4	12	349	....	1981-82	1996-97
McRae, Chris	Tor., Det.	3	21	1	0	1	122	....	....	....	....	....	....	1987-88	1989-90
McRae, Ken	Que., Tor.	7	137	14	21	35	364	6	0	0	0	4	....	1987-88	1993-94
• McReavy, Pat	Bos., Det.	4	55	5	10	15	4	22	3	3	6	9	1	1938-39	1941-42
McReynolds, Brian	Wpg., NYR, L.A.	3	30	1	5	6	8	....	....	....	....	....	....	1989-90	1993-94
McSheffrey, Bryan	Van., Buf.	3	90	13	7	20	44	....	....	....	....	....	....	1972-73	1974-75
McSorley, Marty	Pit., Edm., L.A., NYR, S.J., Bos.	17	961	108	251	359	3381	115	10	19	29	374	2	1983-84	1999-00
McSween, Don	Buf., Ana.	5	47	3	10	13	55	....	....	....	....	....	....	1987-88	1995-96
McTaggart, Jim	Wsh.	2	71	3	10	13	205	....	....	....	....	....	....	1980-81	1981-82
McTavish, Dale	Cgy.	1	9	1	2	3	2	....	....	....	....	....	....	1996-97	1996-97
McTavish, Gord	St.L., Wpg.	2	11	1	3	4	2	....	....	....	....	....	....	1978-79	1979-80
• McVeigh, Charley	Chi., NYA	9	397	84	88	172	138	4	0	0	0	2	....	1926-27	1934-35
• McVicar, Jack	Mtl.M.	2	88	2	4	6	63	6	0	0	0	2	....	1930-31	1931-32
Meagher, Rick	Mtl., Hfd., N.J., St.L.	12	691	144	165	309	383	62	8	7	15	41	....	1979-80	1990-91
Meehan, Gerry	Tor., Phi., Buf., Van., Atl., Wsh.	10	670	180	243	423	111	10	0	1	1	0	....	1968-69	1978-79
Meeke, Brent	Cal., Cle.	5	75	9	22	31	8	....	....	....	....	....	....	1972-73	1976-77
Meeker, Howie	Tor.	8	346	83	102	185	329	42	6	9	15	50	4	1946-47	1953-54
Meeker, Mike	Pit.	1	4	0	0	0	5	....	....	....	....	....	....	1978-79	1978-79
• Meeking, Harry	Tor., Det., Bos.	3	64	18	12	30	66	9	3	0	3	6	....	1917-18	1926-27
Meger, Paul	Mtl.	6	212	39	52	91	118	35	3	8	11	16	1	1949-50	1954-55
Meighan, Ron	Min., Pit.	2	48	3	7	10	18	....	....	....	....	....	....	1981-82	1982-83
Meissner, Barrie	Min.	2	6	0	1	1	4	....	....	....	....	....	....	1967-68	1968-69
• Meissner, Dick	Bos., NYR	5	171	11	15	26	37	....	....	....	....	....	....	1959-60	1964-65
Melametsa, Anssi	Wpg.	1	27	0	3	3	2	....	....	....	....	....	....	1985-86	1985-86
Melanson, Dean	Buf., Wsh.	2	9	0	0	0	8	....	....	....	....	....	....	1994-95	2001-02
Melichar, Josef	Pit., Car., T.B.	7	349	7	42	49	300	5	0	0	0	2	....	2000-01	2008-09
‡ Melin, Bjorn	Ana.	1	3	1	0	1	0	....	....	....	....	....	....	2006-07	2006-07
Melin, Roger	Min.	2	3	0	0	0	0	....	....	....	....	....	....	1980-81	1981-82
Mellanby, Scott	Phi., Edm., Fla., St.L., Atl.	21	1431	364	476	840	2479	136	24	29	53	220	....	1985-86	2006-07
Mellor, Tom	Det.	2	26	2	4	6	25	....	....	....	....	....	....	1973-74	1974-75
• Melnyk, Gerry	Det., Chi., St.L.	6	269	39	77	116	34	53	6	6	12	6	....	1955-56	1967-68
Melnyk, Larry	Bos., Edm., NYR, Van.	10	432	11	63	74	686	66	2	9	11	127	1	1980-81	1989-90
Meloche, Eric	Pit., Phi.	4	74	9	11	20	36	....	....	....	....	....	....	2001-02	2006-07
Melrose, Barry	Wpg., Tor., Det.	6	300	10	23	33	728	7	0	2	2	38	....	1979-80	1985-86
Menard, Hillary	Chi.	1	1	0	0	0	0	....	....	....	....	....	....	1953-54	1953-54
Menard, Howie	Det., L.A., Chi., Oak.	4	151	23	42	65	87	19	3	7	10	36	....	1963-64	1969-70
Mercredi, Vic	Atl.	1	2	0	0	0	0	....	....	....	....	....	....	1974-75	1974-75
Meredith, Greg	Cgy.	2	38	6	4	10	8	5	3	1	4	4	....	1980-81	1982-83
Merkosky, Glenn	Hfd., N.J., Det.	5	66	5	12	17	22	....	....	....	....	....	....	1981-82	1989-90
• Meronek, Bill	Mtl.	2	19	5	8	13	0	1	0	0	0	0	....	1939-40	1942-43
Merrick, Wayne	St.L., Cal., Cle., NYI	12	774	191	265	456	303	102	19	30	49	30	4	1972-73	1983-84
• Merrill, Horace	Ott.	2	8	0	0	0	3	....	....	....	....	....	1	1917-18	1919-20
Mertzig, Jan	NYR	1	23	0	2	2	8	....	....	....	....	....	....	1998-99	1998-99
Messier, Eric	Col., Fla.	8	406	25	50	75	146	72	3	5	8	22	1	1996-97	2003-04
Messier, Joby	NYR	3	25	0	4	4	24	....	....	....	....	....	....	1992-93	1994-95
Messier, Mark	Edm., NYR, Van.	25	1756	694	1193	1887	1910	236	109	186	295	244	6	1979-80	2003-04
Messier, Mitch	Min.	4	20	0	2	2	11	....	....	....	....	....	....	1987-88	1990-91
Messier, Paul	Col.	1	9	0	0	0	4	....	....	....	....	....	....	1978-79	1978-79
Metcalfe, Scott	Edm., Buf.	3	19	1	2	3	18	....	....	....	....	....	....	1987-88	1989-90
‡ Metropolit, Glen	Wsh., T.B., Atl., St.L., Bos., Phi., Mtl.	8	407	57	102	159	148	30	1	4	5	12	....	1999-00	2009-10
• Metz, Don	Tor.	9	172	20	35	55	42	42	7	8	15	12	5	1938-39	1948-49
• Metz, Nick	Tor.	12	518	131	119	250	149	76	19	20	39	31	4	1934-35	1947-48
Meyer, Freddy	Phi., NYI, Phx., Atl.	7	281	20	53	73	155	6	0	1	1	8	....	2003-04	2010-11
‡ Mezei, Branislav	NYI, Fla.	7	240	5	19	24	311	....	....	....	....	....	....	2000-01	2007-08
• Michaluk, Art	Chi.	1	5	0	0	0	0	....	....	....	....	....	....	1947-48	1947-48
Michaluk, John	Chi.	1	1	0	0	0	0	....	....	....	....	....	....	1950-51	1950-51
Michayluk, Dave	Phi., Pit.	3	14	2	6	8	8	7	1	1	2	0	1	1981-82	1991-92
Micheletti, Joe	St.L., Col.	3	158	11	60	71	114	11	1	11	12	10	....	1979-80	1981-82
Micheletti, Pat	Min.	1	12	2	0	2	8	....	....	....	....	....	....	1987-88	1987-88
• Mickey, Larry	Chi., NYR, Tor., Mtl., L.A., Phi., Buf.	11	292	39	53	92	160	9	1	0	1	10	....	1964-65	1974-75
• Mickoski, Nick	NYR, Chi., Det., Bos.	13	703	158	185	343	319	18	1	6	7	6	....	1947-48	1959-60
Middendorf, Max	Que., Edm.	4	13	2	4	6	6	....	....	....	....	....	....	1986-87	1990-91
Middleton, Rick	NYR, Bos.	14	1005	448	540	988	157	114	45	55	100	19	....	1974-75	1987-88
Miehm, Kevin	St.L.	2	22	1	4	5	8	2	0	1	1	0	....	1992-93	1993-94
Migay, Rudy	Tor.	10	418	59	92	151	293	15	1	0	1	20	....	1949-50	1959-60
‡ Mihalik, Vladimir	T.B.	2	15	0	3	3	8	....	....	....	....	....	....	2008-09	2009-10
Mika, Petr	NYI	1	3	0	0	0	0	....	....	....	....	....	....	1999-00	1999-00
‡ Mikhnov, Alexei	Edm.	1	2	0	0	0	0	....	....	....	....	....	....	2006-07	2006-07
Mikita, Stan	Chi.	22	1394	541	926	1467	1270	155	59	91	150	169	1	1958-59	1979-80
Mikkelson, Bill	L.A., NYI, Wsh.	4	147	4	18	22	105	....	....	....	....	....	....	1971-72	1976-77
Mikol, Jim	Tor., NYR	2	34	1	4	5	8	....	....	....	....	....	....	1962-63	1964-65
Mikulchik, Oleg	Wpg., Ana.	3	37	0	3	3	33	....	....	....	....	....	....	1993-94	1995-96
Milbury, Mike	Bos.	12	754	49	189	238	1552	86	4	24	28	219	....	1975-76	1986-87
• Milks, Hib	Pit., Phi., NYR, Ott.	8	317	87	41	128	179	11	0	0	0	2	....	1925-26	1932-33
Millar, Craig	Edm., Nsh., T.B.	5	114	8	14	22	73	....	....	....	....	....	....	1996-97	2000-01
• Millar, Hugh	Det.	1	4	0	0	0	0	1	0	0	0	0	....	1946-47	1946-47
Millar, Mike	Hfd., Wsh., Bos., Tor.	5	78	18	18	36	12	....	....	....	....	....	....	1986-87	1990-91
Millen, Corey	NYR, L.A., N.J., Dal., Cgy.	8	335	90	119	209	236	47	5	7	12	22	....	1989-90	1996-97
Miller, Aaron	Que., Col., L.A., Van.	14	677	25	94	119	422	80	3	9	12	40	....	1993-94	2007-08
• Miller, Bill	Mtl.M., Mtl.	3	95	7	3	10	16	12	0	0	0	0	1	1934-35	1936-37
Miller, Bob	Bos., Col., L.A.	6	404	75	119	194	220	36	4	7	11	27	....	1977-78	1984-85
Miller, Brad	Buf., Ott., Cgy.	6	82	1	5	6	321	....	....	....	....	....	....	1988-89	1993-94
• Miller, Earl	Chi., Tor.	5	109	19	14	33	124	10	1	0	1	6	1	1927-28	1931-32
• Miller, Jack	Chi.	2	17	0	0	0	4	....	....	....	....	....	....	1949-50	1950-51
Miller, Jason	N.J.	3	6	0	0	0	0	....	....	....	....	....	....	1990-91	1992-93
Miller, Jay	Bos., L.A.	7	446	40	44	84	1723	48	2	3	5	243	....	1985-86	1991-92
Miller, Kelly	NYR, Wsh.	15	1057	181	282	463	512	119	20	34	54	65	....	1984-85	1998-99
Miller, Kevin	NYR, Det., Wsh., St.L., S.J., Pit., Chi., NYI, Ott.	13	620	150	185	335	429	61	7	10	17	49	....	1988-89	2003-04
Miller, Kip	Que., Min., S.J., NYI, Chi., Pit., Ana., Wsh.	12	449	74	165	239	105	25	6	11	17	23	....	1990-91	2003-04
Miller, Paul	Col.	1	3	0	3	3	0	....	....	....	....	....	....	1981-82	1981-82
Miller, Perry	Det.	4	217	10	51	61	387	....	....	....	....	....	....	1977-78	1980-81
Miller, Tom	Det., NYI	4	118	16	25	41	34	....	....	....	....	....	....	1970-71	1974-75
Miller, Warren	NYR, Hfd.	4	262	40	50	90	137	6	1	0	1	0	....	1979-80	1982-83
Milley, Norm	Buf., T.B.	4	29	2	4	6	12	....	....	....	....	....	....	2001-02	2005-06
Mills, Craig	Wpg., Chi.	3	31	0	5	5	36	1	0	0	0	0	....	1995-96	1998-99
‡ Milroy, Duncan	Mtl.	1	5	0	1	1	0	....	....	....	....	....	....	2006-07	2006-07
Miner, John	Edm.	1	14	2	3	5	16	....	....	....	....	....	....	1987-88	1987-88
Minor, Gerry	Van.	5	140	11	21	32	173	12	1	3	4	25	....	1979-80	1983-84
Mironov, Boris	Wpg., Edm., Chi., NYR	11	716	76	231	307	891	25	5	11	16	45	....	1993-94	2003-04
Mironov, Dmitri	Tor., Pit., Ana., Det., Wsh.	10	556	54	206	260	568	75	10	26	36	48	1	1991-92	2000-01
Miszuk, John	Det., Chi., Phi., Min.	6	237	7	39	46	232	19	0	3	3	19	....	1963-64	1969-70
Mitchell, Bill	Det.	1	1	0	0	0	0	....	....	....	....	....	....	1963-64	1963-64
• Mitchell, Herb	Bos.	2	44	6	0	6	36	....	....	....	....	....	....	1924-25	1925-26
Mitchell, Jeff	Dal.	1	7	0	0	0	7	....	....	....	....	....	....	1997-98	1997-98
• Mitchell, Red	Chi.	3	83	4	5	9	67	....	....	....	....	....	....	1941-42	1944-45
Mitchell, Roy	Min.	1	3	0	0	0	0	....	....	....	....	....	....	1992-93	1992-93
Modano, Mike	Min., Dal., Det.	22	1499	561	813	1374	930	176	58	88	146	128	1	1988-89	2010-11
Modin, Fredrik	Tor., T.B., CBJ, L.A., Atl., Cgy.	14	898	232	230	462	453	57	14	12	26	42	1	1996-97	2010-11
‡ Modry, Jaroslav	N.J., Ott., L.A., Atl., Dal., Phi.	13	725	49	201	250	510	28	1	5	6	6	....	1993-94	2007-08
• Moe, Bill	NYR	5	261	11	42	53	163	1	0	0	0	0	....	1944-45	1948-49
Moffat, Lyle	Tor., Wpg.	3	97	12	16	28	51	....	....	....	....	....	....	1972-73	1979-80
• Moffat, Ron	Det.	3	37	1	1	2	8	7	0	0	0	0	....	1932-33	1934-35
Moger, Sandy	Bos., L.A.	5	236	41	38	79	212	5	2	2	4	12	....	1994-95	1998-99
Mogilny, Alexander	Buf., Van., N.J., Tor.	16	990	473	559	1032	432	124	39	47	86	58	1	1989-90	2005-06
Moher, Mike	N.J.	1	9	0	1	1	28	....	....	....	....	....	....	1982-83	1982-83
Mohns, Doug	Bos., Chi., Min., Atl., Wsh.	22	1390	248	462	710	1250	94	14	36	50	122	....	1953-54	1974-75

			Regular Schedule					Playoffs							
Name	NHL Teams	NHL Seasons	GP	G	A	TP	PIM	GP	G	A	TP	PIM	NHL Cup Wins	First NHL Season	Last NHL Season
• Mohns, Lloyd	NYR	1	1	0	0	0	0	....	....	....	....	....	....	1943-44	1943-44
‡ Mojzis, Tomas	Van., St.L., Min.	3	17	1	2	3	14	....	....	....	....	....	....	2005-06	2008-09
Mokosak, Carl	Cgy., L.A., Phi., Pit., Bos.	6	83	11	15	26	170	1	0	0	0	0	....	1981-82	1988-89
Mokosak, John	Det.	2	41	0	2	2	96	....	....	....	....	....	....	1988-89	1989-90
Molin, Lars	Van.	3	172	33	65	98	37	19	2	9	11	7	....	1981-82	1983-84
Moller, Mike	Buf., Edm.	7	134	15	28	43	41	3	0	1	1	0	....	1980-81	1986-87
Moller, Randy	Que., NYR, Buf., Fla.	14	815	45	180	225	1692	78	6	16	22	197	....	1981-82	1994-95
Molloy, Mitch	Buf.	1	2	0	0	0	10	....	....	....	....	....	....	1989-90	1989-90
• Molyneaux, Larry	NYR	2	45	0	1	1	20	10	0	0	0	8	....	1937-38	1938-39
Momesso, Sergio	Mtl., St.L., Van., Tor., NYR	13	710	152	193	345	1557	119	18	26	44	311	....	1983-84	1996-97
Monahan, Garry	Mtl., Det., L.A., Tor., Van.	12	748	116	169	285	484	22	3	1	4	13	....	1967-68	1978-79
Monahan, Hartland	Cal., NYR, Wsh., Pit., L.A., St.L.	7	334	61	80	141	163	6	0	0	0	4	....	1973-74	1980-81
• Mondou, Armand	Mtl.	12	386	47	71	118	99	32	3	5	8	12	2	1928-29	1939-40
Mondou, Pierre	Mtl.	9	548	194	262	456	179	69	17	28	45	26	3	1976-77	1984-85
• Mongeau, Michel	St.L., T.B.	4	54	6	19	25	10	2	0	1	1	0	....	1989-90	1992-93
Mongrain, Bob	Buf., L.A.	6	81	13	14	27	14	11	1	2	3	2	....	1979-80	1985-86
Monteith, Hank	Det.	3	77	5	12	17	6	4	0	0	0	0	....	1968-69	1970-71
Montgomery, Jim	St.L., Mtl., Phi., S.J., Dal.	6	122	9	25	34	80	8	1	0	1	2	....	1993-94	2002-03
Moore, Barrie	Buf., Edm., Wsh.	3	39	2	6	8	18	....	....	....	....	....	....	1995-96	1999-00
Moore, Dickie	Mtl., Tor., St.L.	14	719	261	347	608	652	135	46	64	110	122	6	1951-52	1967-68
‡ Moore, Greg	NYR, CBJ	2	10	0	0	0	0	....	....	....	....	....	....	2007-08	2009-10
Moore, Steve	Col.	3	69	5	7	12	41	....	....	....	....	....	....	2001-02	2003-04
• Moran, Amby	Mtl., Chi.	2	35	1	1	2	24	....	....	....	....	....	....	1926-27	1927-28
‡ Moran, Brad	CBJ, Van.	3	8	1	2	3	4	....	....	....	....	....	....	2001-02	2006-07
Moran, Ian	Pit., Bos., Ana.	12	489	21	50	71	321	66	1	7	8	24	....	1994-95	2006-07
Moravec, David	Buf.	1	1	0	0	0	0	....	....	....	....	....	....	1999-00	1999-00
More, Jay	NYR, Min., S.J., Phx., Chi., Nsh.	10	406	18	54	72	702	31	0	6	6	45	....	1988-89	1998-99
‡ Moreau, Ethan	Chi., Edm., CBJ, L.A.	16	928	147	140	287	1110	46	3	6	9	52	....	1995-96	2011-12
• Morenz, Howie	Mtl., Chi., NYR	14	550	271	201	472	546	39	13	9	22	58	3	1923-24	1936-37
Moretto, Angelo	Cle.	1	5	1	2	3	2	....	....	....	....	....	....	1976-77	1976-77
Morgan, Gavin	Dal.	1	6	0	0	0	21	....	....	....	....	....	....	2003-04	2003-04
Morgan, Jason	L.A., Cgy., Nsh., Chi., Min.	5	44	2	5	7	18	....	....	....	....	....	....	1996-97	2006-07
• Morin, Pete	Mtl.	1	31	10	12	22	7	1	0	0	0	0	....	1941-42	1941-42
• Morin, Stephane	Que., Van.	5	90	16	39	55	52	....	....	....	....	....	....	1989-90	1993-94
Morisset, Dave	Fla.	1	4	0	0	0	5	....	....	....	....	....	....	2001-02	2001-02
Morissette, Dave	Mtl.	2	11	0	0	0	57	....	....	....	....	....	....	1998-99	1999-00
Moro, Marc	Ana., Nsh., Tor.	4	30	0	0	0	77	....	....	....	....	....	....	1997-98	2001-02
Morozov, Aleksey	Pit.	7	451	84	135	219	98	39	4	5	9	8	....	1997-98	2003-04
• Morris, Bernie	Bos.	1	6	1	0	1	0	....	....	....	....	....	....	1924-25	1924-25
Morris, Jon	N.J., S.J., Bos.	6	103	16	33	49	47	11	1	7	8	25	....	1988-89	1993-94
• Morris, Moe	Tor., NYR	4	135	13	29	42	58	18	4	2	6	16	1	1943-44	1948-49
Morrison, Brendan	N.J., Van., Ana., Dal., Wsh., Cgy., Chi.	14	934	200	401	601	452	61	9	21	30	40	....	1997-98	2011-12
Morrison, Dave	L.A., Van.	4	39	3	3	6	4	....	....	....	....	....	....	1980-81	1984-85
• Morrison, Don	Det., Chi.	3	112	18	28	46	12	3	0	1	1	0	....	1947-48	1950-51
Morrison, Doug	Bos.	4	23	7	3	10	15	....	....	....	....	....	....	1979-80	1984-85
Morrison, Gary	Phi.	3	43	1	15	16	70	5	0	1	1	2	....	1979-80	1981-82
• Morrison, George	St.L.	2	115	17	21	38	13	3	0	0	0	0	....	1970-71	1971-72
Morrison, Jim	Bos., Tor., Det., NYR, Pit.	12	704	40	160	200	542	36	0	12	12	38	....	1951-52	1970-71
• Morrison, John	NYA	1	18	0	0	0	0	....	....	....	....	....	....	1925-26	1925-26
Morrison, Kevin	Col.	1	41	4	11	15	23	....	....	....	....	....	....	1979-80	1979-80
Morrison, Lew	Phi., Atl., Wsh., Pit.	9	564	39	52	91	107	17	0	0	0	2	....	1969-70	1977-78
Morrison, Mark	NYR	2	10	1	1	2	0	....	....	....	....	....	....	1981-82	1983-84
• Morrison, Rod	Det.	1	34	8	7	15	4	3	0	0	0	0	....	1947-48	1947-48
Morrow, Ken	NYI	10	550	17	88	105	309	127	11	22	33	97	4	1979-80	1988-89
Morrow, Scott	Cgy.	1	4	0	0	0	0	....	....	....	....	....	....	1994-95	1994-95
Morton, Dean	Det.	1	1	1	0	1	2	....	....	....	....	....	....	1989-90	1989-90
Mortson, Gus	Tor., Chi., Det.	13	797	46	152	198	1380	54	5	8	13	68	4	1946-47	1958-59
• Mosdell, Ken	Bro., Mtl., Chi.	16	693	141	168	309	475	80	16	13	29	48	4	1941-42	1958-59
• Mosienko, Bill	Chi.	14	711	258	282	540	121	22	10	4	14	15	....	1941-42	1954-55
‡ Motin, Johan	Edm.	1	1	0	0	0	0	....	....	....	....	....	....	2009-10	2009-10
Mott, Morris	Cal.	3	199	18	32	50	49	....	....	....	....	....	....	1972-73	1974-75
• Motter, Alex	Bos., Det.	8	255	39	64	103	135	41	3	9	12	41	1	1934-35	1942-43
‡ Motzko, Joe	CBJ, Ana., Wsh., Atl.	5	25	4	2	6	0	3	0	0	0	2	1	2003-04	2008-09
Mowers, Mark	Nsh., Det., Bos., Ana.	7	278	18	44	62	70	3	0	0	0	0	....	1998-99	2007-08
Moxey, Jim	Cal., Cle., L.A.	3	127	22	27	49	59	....	....	....	....	....	....	1974-75	1976-77
Mrozik, Rick	Cgy.	1	2	0	0	0	0	....	....	....	....	....	....	2002-03	2002-03
Muckalt, Bill	Van., NYI, Ott., Min.	5	256	40	57	97	204	5	0	0	0	0	....	1998-99	2002-03
‡ Mueller, Marcel	Tor.	1	3	0	0	0	2	....	....	....	....	....	....	2010-11	2010-11
Muir, Bryan	Edm., N.J., Chi., T.B., Col., L.A., Wsh.	11	279	16	37	53	281	29	0	0	0	6	1	1995-96	2006-07
Mulhern, Richard	Atl., L.A., Tor., Wpg.	6	303	27	93	120	217	7	0	3	3	5	....	1975-76	1980-81
Mulhern, Ryan	Wsh.	1	3	0	0	0	0	....	....	....	....	....	....	1997-98	1997-98
Mullen, Brian	Wpg., NYR, S.J., NYI	11	832	260	362	622	414	62	12	18	30	30	....	1982-83	1992-93
Mullen, Joe	St.L., Cgy., Pit., Bos.	17	1062	502	561	1063	241	143	60	46	106	42	3	1979-80	1996-97
Muller, Kirk	N.J., Mtl., NYI, Tor., Fla., Dal.	19	1349	357	602	959	1223	127	33	36	69	153	1	1984-85	2002-03
Muloin, Wayne	Det., Oak., Cal., Min.	3	147	3	21	24	93	11	0	0	0	2	....	1963-64	1970-71
Mulvenna, Glenn	Pit., Phi.	2	2	0	0	0	4	....	....	....	....	....	....	1991-92	1992-93
Mulvey, Grant	Chi., N.J.	10	586	149	135	284	816	42	10	5	15	70	....	1974-75	1983-84
Mulvey, Paul	Wsh., Pit., L.A.	4	225	30	51	81	613	....	....	....	....	....	....	1978-79	1981-82
• Mummery, Harry	Tor., Que., Mtl., Ham.	6	106	33	19	52	226	2	1	1	2	17	....	1917-18	1922-23
Muni, Craig	Tor., Edm., Chi., Buf., Wpg., Pit., Dal.	16	819	28	119	147	775	113	0	17	17	108	3	1981-82	1997-98
• Munro, Dunc	Mtl.M., Mtl.	8	239	28	18	46	172	21	2	2	4	18	1	1924-25	1931-32
• Munro, Gerry	Mtl.M., Tor.	2	34	1	0	1	37	....	....	....	....	....	....	1924-25	1925-26
Murdoch, Bob	Mtl., L.A., Atl., Cgy.	12	757	60	218	278	764	69	4	18	22	92	2	1970-71	1981-82
Murdoch, Bob	Cal., Cle., St.L.	4	260	72	85	157	127	....	....	....	....	....	....	1975-76	1978-79
Murdoch, Don	NYR, Edm., Det.	6	320	121	117	238	155	24	10	8	18	16	....	1976-77	1981-82
• Murdoch, Murray	NYR	11	508	84	108	192	197	55	9	12	21	28	2	1926-27	1936-37
‡ Murley, Matt	Pit., Phx.	3	62	2	7	9	38	....	....	....	....	....	....	2003-04	2007-08
Murphy, Brian	Det.	1	1	0	0	0	0	....	....	....	....	....	....	1974-75	1974-75
‡ Murphy, Cory	Fla., T.B., N.J.	3	91	9	27	36	38	....	....	....	....	....	....	2007-08	2009-10
‡ Murphy, Curtis	Min.	1	1	0	0	0	0	....	....	....	....	....	....	2002-03	2002-03
Murphy, Gord	Phi., Bos., Fla., Atl.	14	862	85	238	323	668	53	3	16	19	35	....	1988-89	2001-02
Murphy, Joe	Det., Edm., Chi., St.L., S.J., Bos., Wsh.	15	779	233	295	528	810	120	34	43	77	185	1	1986-87	2000-01
Murphy, Larry	L.A., Wsh., Min., Pit., Tor., Det.	21	1615	287	929	1216	1084	215	37	115	152	201	4	1980-81	2000-01
Murphy, Mike	St.L., NYR, L.A.	12	831	238	318	556	514	66	13	23	36	54	....	1971-72	1982-83
Murphy, Rob	Van., Ott., L.A.	7	125	9	12	21	152	4	0	0	0	2	....	1987-88	1993-94
Murphy, Ron	NYR, Chi., Det., Bos.	18	889	205	274	479	460	53	7	8	15	26	2	1952-53	1969-70
• Murray, Allan	NYA	7	271	5	9	14	163	14	0	0	0	10	....	1933-34	1939-40
Murray, Bob	Atl., Van.	4	194	6	16	22	98	10	1	1	2	15	....	1973-74	1976-77
Murray, Bob	Chi.	15	1008	132	382	514	873	112	19	37	56	106	....	1975-76	1989-90
‡ Murray, Brady	L.A.	1	4	1	0	1	6	....	....	....	....	....	....	2007-08	2007-08
Murray, Chris	Mtl., Hfd., Car., Ott., Chi., Dal.	6	242	16	18	34	550	15	1	0	1	12	....	1994-95	1999-00
Murray, Garth	NYR, Mtl., Fla., Phx.	5	116	8	2	10	131	6	0	0	0	0	....	2003-04	2008-09
Murray, Glen	Bos., Pit., L.A.	16	1009	337	314	651	679	94	20	22	42	66	....	1991-92	2007-08
Murray, Jim	L.A.	1	30	0	2	2	14	....	....	....	....	....	....	1967-68	1967-68
Murray, Ken	Tor., NYI, Det., K.C.	5	106	1	10	11	135	....	....	....	....	....	....	1969-70	1975-76
• Murray, Leo	Mtl.	1	6	0	0	0	2	....	....	....	....	....	....	1932-33	1932-33
Murray, Marty	Cgy., Phi., Car., L.A.	8	261	31	42	73	41	9	0	1	1	4	....	1995-96	2006-07
Murray, Mike	Phi.	1	1	0	0	0	0	....	....	....	....	....	....	1987-88	1987-88
Murray, Pat	Phi.	2	25	3	1	4	15	....	....	....	....	....	....	1990-91	1991-92
Murray, Randy	Tor.	1	3	0	0	0	2	....	....	....	....	....	....	1969-70	1969-70
Murray, Rem	Edm., NYR, Nsh.	9	560	94	121	215	161	62	5	12	17	18	....	1996-97	2005-06
Murray, Rob	Wsh., Wpg., Phx.	8	107	4	15	19	111	9	0	0	0	18	....	1989-90	1998-99
Murray, Terry	Cal., Phi., Det., Wsh.	8	302	4	76	80	199	18	2	2	4	10	....	1972-73	1981-82
Murray, Troy	Chi., Wpg., Ott., Pit., Col.	15	915	230	354	584	875	113	17	26	43	145	1	1981-82	1995-96
Murzyn, Dana	Hfd., Cgy., Van.	14	838	52	152	204	1571	82	9	10	19	166	1	1985-86	1998-99
Musil, Frantisek	Min., Cgy., Ott., Edm.	15	797	34	106	140	1241	42	2	4	6	47	....	1986-87	2000-01
Myers, Hap	Buf.	1	13	0	0	0	6	....	....	....	....	....	....	1970-71	1970-71
Myhres, Brantt	T.B., Phi., S.J., Nsh., Wsh., Bos.	7	154	6	2	8	687	....	....	....	....	....	....	1994-95	2002-03
• Myles, Vic	NYR	1	45	6	9	15	57	....	....	....	....	....	....	1942-43	1942-43
Myrvold, Anders	Col., Bos., NYI, Det.	4	33	0	5	5	12	....	....	....	....	....	....	1995-96	2003-04

N

Nabokov, Dmitri	Chi., NYI	3	55	11	13	24	28	....	....	....	....	....	....	1997-98	1999-00
Nachbaur, Don	Hfd., Edm., Phi.	8	223	23	46	69	465	11	1	1	2	24	....	1980-81	1989-90
‡ Nagy, Ladislav	St.L., Phx., Dal., L.A.	8	435	115	196	311	358	18	2	2	4	23	....	1999-00	2007-08

Doug McKay

Michael McMahon

Jay Miller

Ethan Moreau

Lou Nanne

Simon Nolet

Hank Nowak

Bob Nystrom

			Regular Schedule					Playoffs					NHL	First	Last
Name	NHL Teams	NHL Seasons	GP	G	A	TP	PIM	GP	G	A	TP	PIM	Cup Wins	NHL Season	NHL Season
Nahrgang, Jim	Det.	3	57	5	12	17	34	....	....	....	....	....	....	1974-75	1976-77
Namestnikov, John	Van., NYI, Nsh.	6	43	0	9	9	24	2	0	0	0	2	....	1993-94	1999-00
Nanne, Lou	Min.	11	635	68	157	225	356	32	4	10	14	8	....	1967-68	1977-78
Nantais, Rich	Min.	3	63	5	4	9	79	....	....	....	....	....	....	1974-75	1976-77
Napier, Mark	Mtl., Min., Edm., Buf.	11	767	235	306	541	157	82	18	24	42	11	2	1978-79	1988-89
Nash, Tyson	St.L., Phx.	7	374	27	37	64	673	23	3	2	5	52	....	1998-99	2005-06
Naslund, Markus	Pit., Van., NYR	15	1117	395	474	869	736	52	14	22	36	56	....	1993-94	2008-09
Naslund, Mats	Mtl., Bos.	9	651	251	383	634	111	102	35	57	92	33	1	1982-83	1994-95
Nasreddine, Alain	Chi., Mtl., NYI, Pit.	5	74	1	4	5	84	....	....	....	....	....	....	1998-99	2007-08
Nattrass, Ralph	Chi.	4	223	18	38	56	308	....	....	....	....	....	....	1946-47	1949-50
Nattress, Ric	Mtl., St.L., Cgy., Tor., Phi.	11	536	29	135	164	377	67	5	10	15	60	1	1982-83	1992-93
Natyshak, Mike	Que.	1	4	0	0	0	0	....	....	....	....	....	....	1987-88	1987-88
Nazarov, Andrei	S.J., T.B., Cgy., Ana., Bos., Phx., Min.	12	571	53	71	124	1409	9	0	0	0	11	....	1993-94	2005-06
Ndur, Rumun	Buf., NYR, Atl.	4	69	2	3	5	137	....	....	....	....	....	....	1996-97	1999-00
Neaton, Pat	Pit.	1	9	1	1	2	12	....	....	....	....	....	....	1993-94	1993-94
Nechayev, Viktor	L.A.	1	3	1	0	1	0	....	....	....	....	....	....	1982-83	1982-83
Neckar, Stan	Ott., NYR, Phx., T.B., Nsh.	10	510	12	41	53	316	29	0	3	3	8	1	1994-95	2003-04
Nedomansky, Vaclav	Det., NYR, St.L.	6	421	122	156	278	88	7	3	5	8	0	....	1977-78	1982-83
‡ Nedorost, Andrej	CBJ	3	28	2	3	5	12	....	....	....	....	....	....	2001-02	2003-04
‡ Nedorost, Vaclav	Col., Fla.	3	99	10	10	20	34	....	....	....	....	....	....	2001-02	2003-04
‡ Nedved, Petr	Van., St.L., NYR, Pit., Edm., Phx., Phi.	15	982	310	407	717	708	71	19	23	42	64	....	1990-91	2006-07
Nedved, Zdenek	Tor.	3	31	4	6	10	14	....	....	....	....	....	....	1994-95	1996-97
Needham, Mike	Pit., Dal.	3	86	9	5	14	16	14	2	0	2	4	1	1991-92	1993-94
Neely, Bob	Tor., Col.	5	283	39	59	98	266	26	5	7	12	15	....	1973-74	1977-78
Neely, Cam	Van., Bos.	13	726	395	299	694	1241	93	57	32	89	168	....	1983-84	1995-96
Neilson, Jim	NYR, Cal., Cle.	16	1023	69	299	368	904	65	1	17	18	61	....	1962-63	1977-78
Nelson, Gordie	Tor.	1	3	0	0	0	11	....	....	....	....	....	....	1969-70	1969-70
Nelson, Jeff	Wsh., Nsh.	3	52	3	8	11	20	3	0	0	0	4	....	1994-95	1998-99
Nelson, Todd	Pit., Wsh.	2	3	1	0	1	2	4	0	0	0	0	....	1991-92	1993-94
Nemchinov, Sergei	NYR, Van., NYI, N.J.	11	761	152	193	345	251	105	11	20	31	24	2	1991-92	2001-02
Nemecek, Jan	L.A.	2	7	1	0	1	4	....	....	....	....	....	....	1998-99	1999-00
Nemeth, Steve	NYR	1	12	2	0	2	2	....	....	....	....	....	....	1987-88	1987-88
Nemirovsky, David	Fla.	4	91	16	22	38	42	3	1	0	1	0	....	1995-96	1998-99
Nesterenko, Eric	Tor., Chi.	21	1219	250	324	574	1273	124	13	24	37	127	1	1951-52	1971-72
Nethery, Lance	NYR, Edm.	2	41	11	14	25	14	14	5	3	8	9	....	1980-81	1981-82
Neufeld, Ray	Hfd., Wpg., Bos.	11	595	157	200	357	816	28	8	6	14	55	....	1979-80	1989-90
• Neville, Mike	Tor., NYA	3	65	5	5	10	14	2	0	0	0	0	....	1924-25	1930-31
Nevin, Bob	Tor., NYR, Min., L.A.	18	1128	307	419	726	211	84	16	18	34	24	2	1957-58	1975-76
Newberry, John	Mtl., Hfd.	4	22	0	4	4	6	2	0	0	0	0	....	1982-83	1985-86
Newell, Rick	Det.	2	6	0	0	0	0	....	....	....	....	....	....	1972-73	1973-74
Newman, Dan	NYR, Mtl., Edm.	4	126	17	24	41	63	3	0	0	0	4	....	1976-77	1979-80
• Newman, John	Det.	1	8	1	1	2	0	....	....	....	....	....	....	1930-31	1930-31
Nicholls, Bernie	L.A., NYR, Edm., N.J., Chi., S.J.	18	1127	475	734	1209	1292	118	42	72	114	164	....	1981-82	1998-99
• Nicholson, Al	Bos.	2	19	0	1	1	4	....	....	....	....	....	....	1955-56	1956-57
• Nicholson, Ed	Det.	1	1	0	0	0	0	....	....	....	....	....	....	1947-48	1947-48
• Nicholson, Hickey	Chi.	1	2	1	0	1	0	....	....	....	....	....	....	1937-38	1937-38
Nicholson, Neil	Oak., NYI	4	39	3	1	4	23	2	0	0	0	0	....	1969-70	1977-78
• Nicholson, Paul	Wsh.	3	62	4	8	12	18	....	....	....	....	....	....	1974-75	1976-77
Nickulas, Eric	Bos., St.L., Chi.	6	118	15	23	38	82	1	0	0	0	2	....	1998-99	2005-06
Nicolson, Graeme	Bos., Col., NYR	3	52	2	7	9	60	....	....	....	....	....	....	1978-79	1982-83
Nieckar, Barry	Hfd., Cgy., Ana.	4	8	0	0	0	21	....	....	....	....	....	....	1992-93	1997-98
‡ Niedermayer, Rob	Fla., Cgy., Ana., N.J., Buf.	17	1153	186	283	469	904	116	18	25	43	111	1	1993-94	2010-11
Niedermayer, Scott	N.J., Ana.	18	1263	172	568	740	784	202	25	73	98	155	4	1991-92	2009-10
Niekamp, Jim	Det.	2	29	0	2	2	37	....	....	....	....	....	....	1970-71	1971-72
Nielsen, Chris	CBJ	2	52	6	8	14	8	....	....	....	....	....	....	2000-01	2001-02
Nielsen, Jeff	NYR, Ana., Min.	5	252	20	27	47	70	4	0	0	0	2	....	1996-97	2000-01
Nielsen, Kirk	Bos.	1	6	0	0	0	0	....	....	....	....	....	....	1997-98	1997-98
‡ Niemi, Antti-Jussi	Ana.	2	29	1	1	2	22	....	....	....	....	....	....	2000-01	2001-02
‡ Nieminen, Ville	Col., Pit., Chi., Cgy., NYR, S.J., St.L.	7	385	48	69	117	333	58	8	12	20	99	1	1999-00	2006-07
Nienhuis, Kraig	Bos.	3	87	20	16	36	39	2	0	0	0	14	....	1985-86	1987-88
Nieuwendyk, Joe	Cgy., Dal., N.J., Tor., Fla.	20	1257	564	562	1126	677	158	66	50	116	91	3	1986-87	2006-07
• Nighbor, Frank	Ott., Tor.	13	349	139	98	237	249	20	4	9	13	13	4	1917-18	1929-30
Nigro, Frank	Tor.	2	68	8	18	26	39	3	0	0	0	2	....	1982-83	1983-84
‡ Niinimaa, Janne	Phi., Edm., NYI, Dal., Mtl.	10	741	54	265	319	733	59	3	21	24	60	....	1996-97	2006-07
Nikolishin, Andrei	Hfd., Wsh., Chi., Col.	10	628	93	187	280	270	43	1	17	18	22	....	1994-95	2003-04
‡ Nikulin, Alexander	Ott., Phx.	2	3	0	0	0	0	....	....	....	....	....	....	2007-08	2008-09
Nikulin, Igor	Ana.	1	....	....	....	....	....	1	0	0	0	0	....	1996-97	1996-97
Nilan, Chris	Mtl., NYR, Bos.	13	688	110	115	225	3043	111	8	9	17	541	1	1979-80	1991-92
Nill, Jim	St.L., Van., Bos., Wpg., Det.	9	524	58	87	145	854	59	10	5	15	203	....	1981-82	1989-90
‡ Nilson, Marcus	Fla., Cgy.	9	521	67	101	168	270	34	4	7	11	14	....	1998-99	2007-08
Nilsson, Kent	Atl., Cgy., Min., Edm.	9	553	264	422	686	116	59	11	41	52	14	1	1979-80	1994-95
‡ Nilsson, Robert	NYI, Edm.	5	252	37	81	118	90	....	....	....	....	....	....	2005-06	2009-10
Nilsson, Ulf	NYR	4	170	57	112	169	85	25	8	14	22	27	....	1978-79	1982-83
‡ Niskala, Janne	T.B.	1	6	1	2	3	6	....	....	....	....	....	....	2008-09	2008-09
Nistico, Lou	Col.	1	3	0	0	0	0	....	....	....	....	....	....	1977-78	1977-78
• Noble, Reg	Tor., Mtl.M., Det.	16	510	168	106	274	916	18	2	2	4	33	3	1917-18	1932-33
Noel, Claude	Wsh.	1	7	0	0	0	0	....	....	....	....	....	....	1979-80	1979-80
Nolan, Brandon	Car.	1	6	0	1	1	0	....	....	....	....	....	....	2007-08	2007-08
Nolan, Owen	Que., Col., S.J., Tor., Phx., Cgy., Min.	18	1200	422	463	885	1793	65	21	19	40	66	....	1990-91	2009-10
• Nolan, Paddy	Tor.	1	2	0	0	0	0	....	....	....	....	....	....	1921-22	1921-22
Nolan, Ted	Det., Pit.	3	78	6	16	22	105	....	....	....	....	....	....	1981-82	1985-86
Nolet, Simon	Phi., K.C., Pit., Col.	10	562	150	182	332	187	34	6	3	9	8	1	1967-68	1976-77
Noonan, Brian	Chi., NYR, St.L., Van., Phx.	12	629	116	159	275	518	71	17	19	36	77	1	1987-88	1998-99
Nordgren, Niklas	Car., Pit.	1	58	4	2	6	34	....	....	....	....	....	....	2005-06	2005-06
Nordmark, Robert	St.L., Van.	4	236	13	70	83	254	7	3	2	5	8	....	1987-88	1990-91
Nordqvist, Jonas	Chi.	1	3	0	2	2	2	....	....	....	....	....	....	2006-07	2006-07
Nordstrom, Peter	Bos.	1	2	0	0	0	0	....	....	....	....	....	....	1998-99	1998-99
Noris, Joe	Pit., St.L., Buf.	3	55	2	5	7	22	....	....	....	....	....	....	1971-72	1973-74
Norris, Dwayne	Que., Ana.	3	20	2	4	6	8	....	....	....	....	....	....	1993-94	1995-96
Norrish, Rod	Min.	2	21	3	3	6	2	....	....	....	....	....	....	1973-74	1974-75
Norstrom, Mattias	NYR, L.A., Dal.	14	903	18	147	165	661	56	2	5	7	54	....	1993-94	2007-08
• Northcott, Baldy	Mtl.M., Chi.	11	446	133	112	245	273	31	8	5	13	14	1	1928-29	1938-39
Norton, Brad	Fla., L.A., Wsh., Ott., Det., S.J.	6	124	3	8	11	287	....	....	....	....	....	....	2001-02	2007-08
Norton, Jeff	NYI, S.J., St.L., Edm., T.B., Fla., Pit., Bos.	15	799	52	332	384	615	65	4	21	25	89	....	1987-88	2001-02
Norwich, Craig	Wpg., St.L., Col.	2	104	17	58	75	60	....	....	....	....	....	....	1979-80	1980-81
Norwood, Lee	Que., Wsh., St.L., Det., N.J., Hfd., Cgy.	12	503	58	153	211	1099	65	6	22	28	171	....	1980-81	1993-94
‡ Novak, Filip	Ott., CBJ	2	17	0	0	0	6	....	....	....	....	....	....	2005-06	2006-07
Novoseltsev, Ivan	Fla., Phx.	5	234	31	44	75	112	....	....	....	....	....	....	1999-00	2003-04
‡ Novotny, Jiri	Buf., Wsh., CBJ	4	189	20	31	51	66	4	0	0	0	0	....	2005-06	2008-09
Novy, Milan	Wsh.	1	73	18	30	48	16	2	0	0	0	0	....	1982-83	1982-83
Nowak, Hank	Pit., Det., Bos.	4	180	26	29	55	161	13	1	0	1	8	....	1973-74	1976-77
‡ Nummelin, Petteri	CBJ, Min.	3	139	9	36	45	34	7	1	2	3	0	....	2000-01	2007-08
Numminen, Teppo	Wpg., Phx., Dal., Buf.	20	1372	117	520	637	513	82	9	14	23	28	....	1988-89	2008-09
Nurminen, Kai	L.A., Min.	2	69	17	11	28	24	....	....	....	....	....	....	1996-97	2000-01
‡ Nycholat, Lawrence	NYR, Wsh., Ott., Van., Col.	4	50	2	7	9	24	....	....	....	....	....	....	2003-04	2008-09
Nykoluk, Mike	Tor.	1	32	3	1	4	20	....	....	....	....	....	....	1956-57	1956-57
‡ Nylander, Michael	Hfd., Cgy., T.B., Chi., Wsh., Bos., NYR	15	920	209	470	679	468	47	12	22	34	14	....	1992-93	2008-09
Nylund, Gary	Tor., Chi., NYI	11	608	32	139	171	1235	24	0	6	6	63	....	1982-83	1992-93
• Nyrop, Bill	Mtl., Min.	4	207	12	51	63	101	35	1	7	8	22	3	1975-76	1981-82
Nystrom, Bob	NYI	14	900	235	278	513	1248	157	39	44	83	236	4	1972-73	1985-86

O

Oates, Adam	Det., St.L., Bos., Wsh., Phi., Ana., Edm.	19	1337	341	1079	1420	415	163	42	114	156	66	....	1985-86	2003-04
• Oatman, Russell	Det., Mtl.M., NYR	3	120	20	9	29	100	15	1	0	1	18	....	1926-27	1928-29
O'Brien, Dennis	Min., Col., Cle., Bos.	10	592	31	91	122	1017	34	1	2	3	101	....	1970-71	1979-80
O'Brien, Doug	T.B.	1	5	0	0	0	2	....	....	....	....	....	....	2005-06	2005-06
• O'Brien, Ellard	Bos.	1	2	0	0	0	0	....	....	....	....	....	....	1955-56	1955-56
‡ Obsut, Jaroslav	St.L., Col.	2	7	0	0	0	2	....	....	....	....	....	....	2000-01	2001-02
O'Callahan, Jack	Chi., N.J.	7	389	27	104	131	541	32	4	11	15	41	....	1982-83	1988-89
O'Connell, Mike	Chi., Bos., Det.	13	860	105	334	439	605	82	8	24	32	64	....	1977-78	1989-90
• O'Connor, Buddy	Mtl., NYR	10	509	140	257	397	34	53	15	21	36	6	2	1941-42	1950-51
O'Connor, Myles	N.J., Ana.	4	43	3	4	7	69	....	....	....	....	....	....	1990-91	1993-94
Oddleifson, Chris	Bos., Van.	9	524	95	191	286	464	14	1	6	7	8	....	1972-73	1980-81

Name	NHL Teams	NHL Seasons	Regular Schedule GP	G	A	TP	PIM	Playoffs GP	G	A	TP	PIM	NHL Cup Wins	First NHL Season	Last NHL Season
Odelein, Lyle	Mtl., N.J., Phx., CBJ, Chi., Dal., Fla., Pit.	16	1056	50	202	252	2316	86	5	13	18	209	1	1989-90	2005-06
Odelein, Selmar	Edm.	3	18	0	2	2	35	....	....	....	....	....	....	1985-86	1988-89
Odgers, Jeff	S.J., Bos., Col., Atl.	12	821	75	70	145	2364	47	2	1	3	73	....	1991-92	2002-03
Odjick, Gino	Van., NYI, Phi., Mtl.	12	605	64	73	137	2567	44	4	1	5	142	....	1990-91	2001-02
O'Donnell, Fred	Bos.	2	115	15	11	26	98	5	0	1	1	5	....	1972-73	1973-74
O'Donnell, Sean	L.A., Min., N.J., Bos., Phx., Ana., Phi., Chi.	17	1224	31	198	229	1809	106	6	13	19	129	1	1994-95	2011-12
• O'Donoghue, Don	Oak., Cal.	3	125	18	17	35	35	3	0	0	0	0	....	1969-70	1971-72
Odrowski, Gerry	Det., Oak., St.L.	6	309	12	19	31	111	30	0	1	1	16	....	1960-61	1971-72
O'Dwyer, Bill	L.A., Bos.	5	120	9	13	22	108	10	0	0	0	2	....	1983-84	1989-90
O'Flaherty, Gerry	Tor., Van., Atl.	8	438	99	95	194	168	7	2	2	4	6	....	1971-72	1978-79
• O'Flaherty, Peanuts	NYA, Bro.	2	21	5	1	6	0	....	....	....	....	....	....	1940-41	1941-42
Ogilvie, Brian	Chi., St.L.	6	90	15	21	36	29	....	....	....	....	....	....	1972-73	1978-79
• O'Grady, George	Mtl.W.	1	4	0	0	0	0	....	....	....	....	....	....	1917-18	1917-18
Ogrodnick, John	Det., Que., NYR	14	928	402	425	827	260	41	18	8	26	6	....	1979-80	1992-93
Ojanen, Janne	N.J.	4	98	21	23	44	28	3	0	2	2	0	....	1988-89	1992-93
Okerlund, Todd	NYI	1	4	0	0	0	2	....	....	....	....	....	....	1987-88	1987-88
Oksiuta, Roman	Edm., Van., Ana., Pit.	4	153	46	41	87	100	10	2	3	5	0	....	1993-94	1996-97
Olausson, Fredrik	Wpg., Edm., Ana., Pit., Det.	16	1022	147	434	581	450	71	6	23	29	28	1	1986-87	2002-03
Olczyk, Ed	Chi., Tor., Wpg., NYR, L.A., Pit.	16	1031	342	452	794	874	57	19	15	34	57	1	1984-85	1999-00
Oliver, David	Edm., NYR, Ott., Phx., Dal.	9	233	49	49	98	84	10	0	0	0	2	....	1994-95	2005-06
• Oliver, Harry	Bos., NYA	11	463	127	85	212	147	35	10	6	16	24	1	1926-27	1936-37
Oliver, Murray	Det., Bos., Tor., Min.	17	1127	274	454	728	320	35	9	16	25	10	....	1957-58	1974-75
Oliwa, Krzysztof	N.J., CBJ, Pit., NYR, Bos., Cgy.	9	410	17	28	45	1447	32	2	0	2	47	1	1996-97	2005-06
Olmstead, Bert	Chi., Mtl., Tor.	14	848	181	421	602	884	115	16	43	59	101	5	1948-49	1961-62
Olsen, Darryl	Cgy.	1	1	0	0	0	0	....	....	....	....	....	....	1991-92	1991-92
Olson, Dennis	Det.	1	4	0	0	0	0	....	....	....	....	....	....	1957-58	1957-58
Olson, Josh	Fla.	1	5	1	0	1	0	....	....	....	....	....	....	2003-04	2003-04
Olsson, Christer	St.L., Ott.	2	56	4	12	16	24	3	0	0	0	0	....	1995-96	1996-97
‡ Olvecky, Peter	Min., Nsh.	2	32	2	5	7	12	....	....	....	....	....	....	2008-09	2009-10
‡ Olvestad, Jimmie	T.B.	2	111	3	14	17	40	....	....	....	....	....	....	2001-02	2002-03
‡ Ondrus, Ben	Tor.	4	52	0	2	2	77	....	....	....	....	....	....	2005-06	2008-09
• O'Neil, Jim	Bos., Mtl.	6	156	6	30	36	109	9	1	1	2	13	....	1933-34	1941-42
O'Neil, Paul	Van., Bos.	2	6	0	0	0	0	....	....	....	....	....	....	1973-74	1975-76
O'Neill, Jeff	Hfd., Car., Tor.	11	821	237	259	496	670	34	9	8	17	37	....	1995-96	2006-07
• O'Neill, Tom	Tor.	2	66	10	12	22	53	4	0	0	0	6	1	1943-44	1944-45
‡ O'Neill, Wes	Col.	2	5	0	0	0	6	....	....	....	....	....	....	2008-09	2009-10
Orban, Bill	Chi., Min.	3	114	8	15	23	67	3	0	0	0	0	....	1967-68	1969-70
O'Ree, Willie	Bos.	2	45	4	10	14	26	....	....	....	....	....	....	1957-58	1960-61
O'Regan, Tom	Pit.	3	61	5	12	17	10	....	....	....	....	....	....	1983-84	1985-86
O'Reilly, Terry	Bos.	14	891	204	402	606	2095	108	25	42	67	335	....	1971-72	1984-85
‡ Oreskovic, Phil	Tor.	1	10	1	1	2	21	....	....	....	....	....	....	2008-09	2008-09
Oreskovich, Victor	Fla., Van.	3	67	2	7	9	41	19	0	0	0	12	....	2009-10	2011-12
Orlando, Gates	Buf.	3	98	18	26	44	51	5	0	4	4	14	....	1984-85	1986-87
• Orlando, Jimmy	Det.	6	199	6	25	31	375	36	0	9	9	105	1	1936-37	1942-43
Orleski, Dave	Mtl.	2	2	0	0	0	0	....	....	....	....	....	....	1980-81	1981-82
Orr, Bobby	Bos., Chi.	12	657	270	645	915	953	74	26	66	92	107	2	1966-67	1978-79
Orszagh, Vladimir	NYI, Nsh., St.L.	7	289	54	65	119	194	6	2	0	2	4	....	1997-98	2005-06
Osborne, Keith	St.L., T.B.	2	16	1	3	4	16	....	....	....	....	....	....	1989-90	1992-93
Osborne, Mark	Det., NYR, Tor., Wpg.	14	919	212	319	531	1152	87	12	16	28	141	....	1981-82	1994-95
Osburn, Randy	Tor., Phi.	2	27	0	2	2	0	....	....	....	....	....	....	1972-73	1974-75
O'Shea, Danny	Min., Chi., St.L.	5	369	64	115	179	265	39	3	7	10	61	....	1968-69	1972-73
• O'Shea, Kevin	Buf., St.L.	3	134	13	18	31	85	12	2	1	3	10	....	1970-71	1972-73
Osiecki, Mark	Cgy., Ott., Wpg., Min.	2	93	3	11	14	43	....	....	....	....	....	....	1991-92	1992-93
O'Sullivan, Chris	Cgy., Van., Ana.	5	62	2	17	19	16	....	....	....	....	....	....	1996-97	2002-03
O'Sullivan, Patrick	L.A., Edm., Car., Min., Phx.	6	334	58	103	161	116	....	....	....	....	....	....	2006-07	2011-12
Otevrel, Jaroslav	S.J.	2	16	3	4	7	2	....	....	....	....	....	....	1992-93	1993-94
Otto, Joel	Cgy., Phi.	14	943	195	313	508	1934	122	27	47	74	207	1	1984-85	1997-98
Ouellet, Michel	Pit., T.B., Van.	4	190	52	64	116	58	5	0	2	2	6	....	2005-06	2008-09
Ouellette, Eddie	Chi.	1	43	3	2	5	11	1	0	0	0	0	....	1935-36	1935-36
Ouellette, Gerry	Bos.	1	34	5	4	9	0	....	....	....	....	....	....	1960-61	1960-61
Owchar, Dennis	Pit., Col.	6	288	30	85	115	200	10	1	1	2	8	....	1974-75	1979-80
• Owen, George	Bos.	5	183	44	33	77	151	21	2	5	7	25	1	1928-29	1932-33
Ozolinsh, Sandis	S.J., Col., Car., Fla., Ana., NYR	15	875	167	397	564	638	137	23	67	90	131	1	1992-93	2007-08
P															
Pachal, Clayton	Bos., Col.	3	35	2	3	5	95	....	....	....	....	....	....	1976-77	1978-79
‡ Paddock, Cam	St.L.	1	16	2	1	3	0	....	....	....	....	....	....	2008-09	2008-09
Paddock, John	Wsh., Phi., Que.	5	87	8	14	22	86	5	2	0	2	0	....	1975-76	1982-83
Paek, Jim	Pit., L.A., Ott.	5	217	5	29	34	155	27	1	4	5	8	2	1990-91	1994-95
Paiement, Rosaire	Phi., Van.	5	190	48	52	100	343	3	3	0	3	0	....	1967-68	1971-72
Paiement, Wilf	K.C., Col., Tor., Que., NYR, Buf., Pit.	14	946	356	458	814	1757	69	18	17	35	185	....	1974-75	1987-88
• Palangio, Pete	Mtl., Det., Chi.	5	71	13	10	23	28	7	0	0	0	0	1	1926-27	1937-38
• Palazzari, Aldo	Bos., NYR	1	35	8	3	11	4	....	....	....	....	....	....	1943-44	1943-44
Palazzari, Doug	St.L.	4	108	18	20	38	23	2	0	0	0	0	....	1974-75	1978-79
‡ Palffy, Ziggy	NYI, L.A., Pit.	12	684	329	384	713	322	24	9	10	19	8	....	1993-94	2005-06
Palmer, Brad	Min., Bos.	3	168	32	38	70	58	29	9	5	14	16	....	1980-81	1982-83
Palmer, Rob	Chi.	3	16	0	3	3	2	....	....	....	....	....	....	1973-74	1975-76
Palmer, Robert	L.A., N.J.	7	320	9	101	110	115	8	1	2	3	6	....	1977-78	1983-84
• Panagabko, Ed	Bos.	2	29	0	3	3	38	....	....	....	....	....	....	1955-56	1956-57
Pandolfo, Mike	CBJ	1	3	0	0	0	0	....	....	....	....	....	....	2003-04	2003-04
Pankewicz, Greg	Ott., Cgy.	2	21	0	3	3	22	....	....	....	....	....	....	1993-94	1998-99
Panteleev, Grigori	Bos., NYI	4	54	8	6	14	12	....	....	....	....	....	....	1992-93	1995-96
• Papike, Joe	Chi.	3	20	3	3	6	4	5	0	2	2	0	....	1940-41	1944-45
Papineau, Justin	St.L., NYI	3	81	11	8	19	12	1	0	0	0	0	....	2001-02	2003-04
Pappin, Jim	Tor., Chi., Cal., Cle.	14	767	278	295	573	667	92	33	34	67	101	2	1963-64	1976-77
Paradise, Bob	Min., Atl., Pit., Wsh.	8	368	8	54	62	393	12	0	1	1	19	....	1971-72	1978-79
• Pargeter, George	Mtl.	1	4	0	0	0	0	....	....	....	....	....	....	1946-47	1946-47
Parise, J.P.	Bos., Tor., Min., NYI, Cle.	14	890	238	356	594	706	86	27	31	58	87	....	1965-66	1978-79
Parizeau, Michel	St.L., Phi.	1	58	3	14	17	18	....	....	....	....	....	....	1971-72	1971-72
Park, Brad	NYR, Bos., Det.	17	1113	213	683	896	1429	161	35	90	125	217	....	1968-69	1984-85
Parker, Jeff	Buf., Hfd.	5	141	16	19	35	163	5	0	0	0	26	....	1986-87	1990-91
Parker, Scott	Col., S.J.	8	308	7	14	21	699	5	0	0	0	4	1	1998-99	2007-08
• Parkes, Ernie	Mtl.M.	1	17	0	0	0	2	....	....	....	....	....	....	1924-25	1924-25
Parks, Greg	NYI	3	23	1	2	3	6	2	0	0	0	0	....	1990-91	1992-93
Parrish, Mark	Fla., NYI, L.A., Min., Dal., T.B., Buf.	12	722	216	171	387	246	27	5	4	9	10	....	1998-99	2010-11
• Parsons, George	Tor.	3	78	12	13	25	20	7	3	2	5	11	....	1936-37	1938-39
‡ Parssinen, Timo	Ana.	1	17	0	3	3	2	....	....	....	....	....	....	2001-02	2001-02
• Pasek, Dusan	Min.	1	48	4	10	14	30	2	1	0	1	0	....	1988-89	1988-89
Pasin, Dave	Bos., L.A.	2	76	18	19	37	50	3	0	1	1	0	....	1985-86	1988-89
Paslawski, Greg	Mtl., St.L., Wpg., Buf., Que., Phi., Cgy.	11	650	187	185	372	169	60	19	13	32	25	....	1983-84	1993-94
‡ Patera, Pavel	Dal., Min.	2	32	2	7	9	8	....	....	....	....	....	....	1999-00	2000-01
Paterson, Joe	Det., Phi., L.A., NYR	9	291	19	37	56	829	22	3	4	7	77	....	1980-81	1988-89
Paterson, Mark	Hfd.	4	29	3	3	6	33	....	....	....	....	....	....	1982-83	1985-86
Paterson, Rick	Chi.	9	430	50	43	93	136	61	7	10	17	51	....	1978-79	1986-87
Patey, Doug	Wsh.	3	45	4	2	6	8	....	....	....	....	....	....	1976-77	1978-79
Patey, Larry	Cal., St.L., NYR	12	717	153	163	316	631	40	8	10	18	57	....	1973-74	1984-85
Patrick, Craig	Cal., St.L., K.C., Wsh.	8	401	72	91	163	61	2	0	1	1	0	....	1971-72	1978-79
Patrick, Glenn	St.L., Cal., Cle.	4	38	2	3	5	72	....	....	....	....	....	....	1973-74	1976-77
Patrick, James	NYR, Hfd., Cgy., Buf.	21	1280	149	490	639	759	117	6	32	38	86	....	1983-84	2003-04
• Patrick, Lester	NYR	1	1	0	0	0	2	....	....	....	....	....	....	1926-27	1926-27
• Patrick, Lynn	NYR	10	455	145	190	335	240	44	10	6	16	22	1	1934-35	1945-46
• Patrick, Muzz	NYR	5	166	5	26	31	133	25	4	0	4	34	1	1937-38	1945-46
Patrick, Steve	Buf., NYR, Que.	6	250	40	68	108	242	12	0	1	1	12	....	1980-81	1985-86
Patterson, Colin	Cgy., Buf.	10	504	96	109	205	239	85	12	17	29	57	1	1983-84	1992-93
Patterson, Dennis	K.C., Phi.	3	138	6	22	28	67	....	....	....	....	....	....	1974-75	1979-80
Patterson, Ed	Pit.	3	68	3	3	6	56	....	....	....	....	....	....	1993-94	1996-97
• Patterson, George	Tor., Mtl., NYA, Bos., Det., St.L.	9	284	51	27	78	218	3	0	0	0	2	....	1926-27	1934-35
• Paul, Butch	Det.	1	3	0	0	0	0	....	....	....	....	....	....	1964-65	1964-65
Paul, Jeff	Col.	1	2	0	0	0	7	....	....	....	....	....	....	2002-03	2002-03
• Paulhus, Rollie	Mtl.	1	33	0	0	0	0	....	....	....	....	....	....	1925-26	1925-26
Pavelich, Mark	NYR, Min., S.J.	7	355	137	192	329	340	23	7	17	24	14	....	1981-82	1991-92
Pavelich, Marty	Det.	10	634	93	159	252	454	91	13	15	28	74	4	1947-48	1956-57
Pavese, Jim	St.L., NYR, Det., Hfd.	8	328	13	44	57	689	36	0	6	6	81	....	1981-82	1988-89

Fred O'Donnell

Sean O'Donnell

Bill Orban

Ed Panagabko

Grigori Panteleev

Mark Parrish

Andre Peloffy

Jim Peplinski

			Regular Schedule					Playoffs					NHL Cup	First NHL	Last NHL
Name	NHL Teams	NHL Seasons	GP	G	A	TP	PIM	GP	G	A	TP	PIM	Wins	Season	Season
• Payer, Evariste	Mtl.	1	1	0	0	0	0	....	....	....	....	....	....	1917-18	1917-18
Payer, Serge	Fla., Ott.	4	124	7	6	13	49	....	....	....	....	....	....	2000-01	2006-07
Payne, Davis	Bos.	2	22	0	1	1	14	....	....	....	....	....	....	1995-96	1996-97
Payne, Steve	Min.	10	613	228	238	466	435	71	35	35	70	60	....	1978-79	1987-88
Paynter, Kent	Chi., Wsh., Wpg., Ott.	7	37	1	3	4	69	4	0	0	0	10	....	1987-88	1993-94
Peake, Pat	Wsh.	5	134	28	41	69	105	13	2	2	4	20	....	1993-94	1997-98
• Pearson, Mel	NYR, Pit.	5	38	2	6	8	25	....	....	....	....	....	....	1959-60	1967-68
Pearson, Rob	Tor., Wsh., St.L.	6	269	56	54	110	645	33	4	2	6	94	....	1991-92	1996-97
Pearson, Scott	Tor., Que., Edm., Buf., NYI	10	292	56	42	98	615	10	2	0	2	14	....	1988-89	1999-00
Peat, Stephen	Wsh.	4	130	8	2	10	234	....	....	....	....	....	....	2001-02	2005-06
Peca, Michael	Van., Buf., NYI, Edm., Tor., CBJ	14	864	176	289	465	798	97	15	19	34	80	....	1993-94	2008-09
Pedersen, Allen	Bos., Min., Hfd.	8	428	5	36	41	487	64	0	0	0	91	....	1986-87	1993-94
Pederson, Barry	Bos., Van., Pit., Hfd.	12	701	238	416	654	472	34	22	30	52	25	1	1980-81	1991-92
‡ Pederson, Denis	N.J., Van., Phx., Nsh.	8	435	57	71	128	398	27	1	5	6	8	....	1995-96	2002-03
Pederson, Mark	Mtl., Phi., S.J., Det.	5	169	35	50	85	77	2	0	0	0	0	....	1989-90	1993-94
Pederson, Tom	S.J., Tor.	5	240	20	49	69	142	24	1	11	12	10	....	1992-93	1996-97
• Peer, Bert	Det.	1	1	0	0	0	0	....	....	....	....	....	....	1939-40	1939-40
Peirson, Johnny	Bos.	11	545	153	173	326	315	49	10	16	26	26	....	1946-47	1957-58
Pelensky, Perry	Chi.	1	4	0	0	0	5	....	....	....	....	....	....	1983-84	1983-84
Pellerin, Scott	N.J., St.L., Min., Car., Bos., Dal., Phx.	11	536	72	126	198	320	37	1	2	3	26	....	1992-93	2003-04
Pelletier, Roger	Phi.	1	1	0	0	0	0	....	....	....	....	....	....	1967-68	1967-68
Peloffy, Andre	Wsh.	1	9	0	0	0	0	....	....	....	....	....	....	1974-75	1974-75
‡ Peltier, Derek	Col.	2	14	0	0	0	2	....	....	....	....	....	....	2008-09	2009-10
‡ Peltonen, Ville	S.J., Nsh., Fla.	8	382	52	96	148	119	....	....	....	....	....	....	1995-96	2008-09
Peluso, Mike	Chi., Ott., N.J., St.L., Cgy.	9	458	38	52	90	1951	62	3	4	7	107	1	1989-90	1997-98
Peluso, Mike	Chi., Phi.	2	38	4	2	6	19	....	....	....	....	....	....	2001-02	2003-04
Pelyk, Mike	Tor.	9	441	26	88	114	566	40	0	3	3	41	....	1967-68	1977-78
Penner, Jeff	Bos.	1	2	0	0	0	0	....	....	....	....	....	....	2009-10	2009-10
Penney, Chad	Ott.	1	3	0	0	0	2	....	....	....	....	....	....	1993-94	1993-94
Pennington, Cliff	Mtl., Bos.	3	101	17	42	59	6	....	....	....	....	....	....	1960-61	1962-63
Peplinski, Jim	Cgy.	11	711	161	263	424	1467	99	15	31	46	382	1	1980-81	1994-95
‡ Perezhogin, Alexander	Mtl.	2	128	15	19	34	86	6	1	1	2	4	....	2005-06	2006-07
Perlini, Fred	Tor.	2	8	2	3	5	0	....	....	....	....	....	....	1981-82	1983-84
‡ Perrault, Joel	Phx., St.L., Van.	6	96	12	14	26	68	....	....	....	....	....	....	2005-06	2010-11
Perreault, Fern	NYR	2	3	0	0	0	0	....	....	....	....	....	....	1947-48	1949-50
Perreault, Gilbert	Buf.	17	1191	512	814	1326	500	90	33	70	103	44	....	1970-71	1986-87
Perreault, Yanic	Tor., L.A., Mtl., Nsh., Phx., Chi.	14	859	247	269	516	402	54	11	19	30	18	....	1993-94	2007-08
‡ Perrin, Eric	T.B., Atl.	4	245	32	72	104	92	18	1	2	3	8	1	2003-04	2008-09
Perrott, Nathan	Nsh., Tor., Dal.	4	89	4	5	9	251	....	....	....	....	....	....	2001-02	2005-06
Perry, Brian	Oak., Buf.	3	96	16	29	45	24	8	1	1	2	4	....	1968-69	1970-71
Persson, Ricard	N.J., St.L., Ott.	7	229	10	44	54	262	26	1	3	4	59	....	1995-96	2001-02
Persson, Stefan	NYI	9	622	52	317	369	574	102	7	50	57	69	4	1977-78	1985-86
‡ Pesonen, Janne	Pit.	1	7	0	0	0	0	....	....	....	....	....	....	2008-09	2008-09
Pesut, George	Cal.	2	92	3	22	25	130	....	....	....	....	....	....	1974-75	1975-76
Peters, Andrew	Buf., N.J.	6	229	4	3	7	650	....	....	....	....	....	....	2003-04	2009-10
• Peters, Frank	NYR	1	43	0	0	0	59	4	0	0	0	2	....	1930-31	1930-31
Peters, Garry	Mtl., NYR, Phi., Bos.	8	311	34	34	68	261	9	2	2	4	31	1	1964-65	1971-72
• Peters, Jimmy	Mtl., Bos., Det., Chi.	9	574	125	150	275	186	60	5	9	14	22	3	1945-46	1953-54
Peters, Jimmy	Det., L.A.	9	309	37	36	73	48	11	0	2	2	2	....	1964-65	1974-75
Peters, Steve	Col.	1	2	0	1	1	0	....	....	....	....	....	....	1979-80	1979-80
Peterson, Brent	Det., Buf., Van., Hfd.	11	620	72	141	213	484	31	4	4	8	65	....	1978-79	1988-89
Peterson, Brent	T.B.	3	56	9	1	10	6	....	....	....	....	....	....	1996-97	1998-99
Petit, Michel	Van., NYR, Que., Tor., Cgy., L.A., T.B., Edm., Phi., Phx.	16	827	90	238	328	1839	19	0	2	2	61	....	1982-83	1997-98
Petrenko, Sergei	Buf.	1	14	0	4	4	0	....	....	....	....	....	....	1993-94	1993-94
‡ Petrov, Oleg	Mtl., Nsh.	8	382	72	115	187	101	20	1	6	7	2	....	1992-93	2002-03
‡ Petrovicky, Robert	Hfd., Dal., St.L., T.B., NYI	8	208	27	38	65	118	2	0	0	0	0	....	1992-93	2000-01
Petrovicky, Ronald	Cgy., NYR, Atl., Pit.	6	342	41	51	92	429	3	0	0	0	2	....	2000-01	2006-07
‡ Petruzalek, Jakub	Car.	1	2	0	1	1	0	....	....	....	....	....	....	2008-09	2008-09
Pettersson, Jorgen	St.L., Hfd., Wsh.	6	435	174	192	366	117	44	15	12	27	4	....	1980-81	1985-86
‡ Pettinen, Tomi	NYI	3	24	0	0	0	18	....	....	....	....	....	....	2002-03	2005-06
• Pettinger, Eric	Bos., Tor., Ott.	3	98	7	12	19	83	4	1	0	1	8	....	1928-29	1930-31
• Pettinger, Gord	NYR, Det., Bos.	8	292	42	74	116	77	47	4	5	9	11	4	1932-33	1939-40
‡ Pettinger, Matt	Wsh., Van., T.B.	9	422	65	58	123	210	1	0	0	0	0	....	2000-01	2009-10
Phair, Lyle	L.A.	3	48	6	7	13	12	1	0	0	0	0	....	1985-86	1987-88
Phillipoff, Harold	Atl., Chi.	3	141	26	57	83	267	6	0	2	2	9	....	1977-78	1979-80
• Phillips, Bill	Mtl.M.	1	27	1	1	2	6	4	0	0	0	2	....	1929-30	1929-30
• Phillips, Charlie	Mtl.	1	17	0	0	0	6	....	....	....	....	....	....	1942-43	1942-43
• Phillips, Merlyn	Mtl.M., NYA	8	302	52	31	83	232	24	5	1	6	19	1	1925-26	1932-33
Picard, Michel	Hfd., S.J., Ott., St.L., Edm., Phi.	9	166	28	42	70	103	5	0	0	0	2	....	1990-91	2000-01
Picard, Noel	Mtl., St.L., Atl.	7	335	12	63	75	616	50	2	11	13	167	1	1964-65	1972-73
Picard, Robert	Wsh., Tor., Mtl., Wpg., Que., Det.	13	899	104	319	423	1025	36	5	15	20	39	....	1977-78	1989-90
Picard, Roger	St.L.	1	15	2	2	4	21	....	....	....	....	....	....	1967-68	1967-68
Pichette, Dave	Que., St.L., N.J., NYR	7	322	41	140	181	348	28	3	7	10	54	....	1980-81	1987-88
Picketts, Hal	NYA	1	48	3	1	4	32	....	....	....	....	....	....	1933-34	1933-34
• Pidhirny, Harry	Bos.	1	2	0	0	0	0	....	....	....	....	....	....	1957-58	1957-58
Pierce, Randy	Col., N.J., Hfd.	8	277	62	76	138	223	2	0	0	0	0	....	1977-78	1984-85
‡ Pihlman, Tuomas	N.J.	3	15	1	1	2	12	....	....	....	....	....	....	2003-04	2006-07
‡ Pihlstrom, Antti	Nsh.	2	54	2	5	7	10	....	....	....	....	....	....	2007-08	2008-09
• Pike, Alf	NYR	6	234	42	77	119	145	21	4	2	6	12	1	1939-40	1946-47
‡ Pikkarainen, Ilkka	N.J.	1	31	1	3	4	10	....	....	....	....	....	....	2009-10	2009-10
‡ Pilar, Karel	Tor.	3	90	6	24	30	42	12	1	4	5	12	....	2001-02	2003-04
Pilon, Rich	NYI, NYR, St.L.	14	631	8	69	77	1745	15	0	0	0	50	....	1988-89	2001-02
Pilote, Pierre	Chi., Tor.	14	890	80	418	498	1251	86	8	53	61	102	1	1955-56	1968-69
Pinder, Gerry	Chi., Cal.	3	223	55	69	124	135	17	0	4	4	6	....	1969-70	1971-72
Pineault, Adam	CBJ	1	3	0	0	0	0	....	....	....	....	....	....	2007-08	2007-08
Pirjeta, Lasse	CBJ, Pit.	3	146	23	27	50	50	....	....	....	....	....	....	2002-03	2005-06
‡ Pirnes, Esa	L.A.	1	57	3	8	11	12	....	....	....	....	....	....	2003-04	2003-04
‡ Piros, Kamil	Atl., Fla.	3	28	4	4	8	10	....	....	....	....	....	....	2001-02	2003-04
Pirus, Alex	Min., Det.	4	159	30	28	58	94	2	0	1	1	2	....	1976-77	1979-80
‡ Pisa, Ales	Edm., NYR	2	53	1	3	4	26	....	....	....	....	....	....	2001-02	2002-03
‡ Pisani, Fernando	Edm., Chi.	8	462	87	82	169	200	33	15	4	19	12	....	2002-03	2010-11
Pitlick, Lance	Ott., Fla.	8	393	16	33	49	298	24	0	2	2	21	....	1994-95	2001-02
• Pitre, Didier	Mtl.	6	127	64	33	97	87	9	2	4	6	19	....	1917-18	1922-23
‡ Pittis, Domenic	Pit., Buf., Edm., Nsh.	7	86	5	11	16	71	3	0	0	0	2	....	1996-97	2003-04
‡ Pivko, Libor	Nsh.	1	1	0	0	0	0	....	....	....	....	....	....	2003-04	2003-04
Pivonka, Michal	Wsh.	13	825	181	418	599	478	95	19	36	55	86	....	1986-87	1998-99
• Plager, Barclay	St.L.	10	614	44	187	231	1115	68	3	20	23	182	....	1967-68	1976-77
Plager, Bill	Min., St.L., Atl.	9	263	4	34	38	294	31	0	2	2	26	....	1967-68	1975-76
Plager, Bob	NYR, St.L.	14	644	20	126	146	802	74	2	17	19	195	....	1964-65	1977-78
Plamondon, Gerry	Mtl.	5	74	7	13	20	10	11	5	2	7	2	1	1945-46	1950-51
Plante, Cam	Tor.	1	2	0	0	0	0	....	....	....	....	....	....	1984-85	1984-85
Plante, Dan	NYI	4	159	9	14	23	135	1	1	0	1	2	....	1993-94	1997-98
Plante, Derek	Buf., Dal., Chi., Phi.	8	450	96	152	248	138	41	6	10	16	18	1	1993-94	2000-01
Plante, Pierre	Phi., St.L., Chi., NYR, Que.	9	599	125	172	297	599	33	2	6	8	51	....	1971-72	1979-80
Plantery, Mark	Wpg.	1	25	1	5	6	14	....	....	....	....	....	....	1980-81	1980-81
‡ Platt, Geoff	CBJ, Ana.	3	46	4	10	14	28	....	....	....	....	....	....	2005-06	2007-08
Plavsic, Adrien	St.L., Van., T.B., Ana.	8	214	16	56	72	161	13	1	7	8	4	....	1989-90	1996-97
• Plaxton, Hugh	Mtl.M.	1	15	1	2	3	4	....	....	....	....	....	....	1932-33	1932-33
Playfair, Jim	Edm., Chi.	3	21	2	4	6	51	....	....	....	....	....	....	1983-84	1988-89
Playfair, Larry	Buf., L.A.	12	688	26	94	120	1812	43	0	6	6	111	....	1978-79	1989-90
Pleau, Larry	Mtl.	3	94	9	15	24	27	4	0	0	0	0	....	1969-70	1971-72
‡ Pletka, Vaclav	Phi.	1	1	0	0	0	0	....	....	....	....	....	....	2001-02	2001-02
• Pletsch, Charles	Ham.	1	1	0	0	0	0	....	....	....	....	....	....	1920-21	1920-21
Plett, Willi	Atl., Cgy., Min., Bos.	13	834	222	215	437	2572	83	24	22	46	466	....	1975-76	1987-88
‡ Plihal, Tomas	S.J.	3	89	7	9	16	26	4	0	0	0	0	....	2006-07	2008-09
Plumb, Rob	Det.	2	14	3	2	5	2	....	....	....	....	....	....	1977-78	1978-79
Plumb, Ron	Hfd.	1	26	3	4	7	14	....	....	....	....	....	....	1979-80	1979-80
Poapst, Steve	Wsh., Chi., Pit., St.L.	7	307	8	28	36	173	11	0	0	0	0	....	1995-96	2005-06
Pocza, Harvie	Wsh.	2	3	0	0	0	2	....	....	....	....	....	....	1979-80	1981-82
• Poddubny, Walt	Edm., Tor., NYR, Que., N.J.	11	468	184	238	422	454	19	7	2	9	12	....	1981-82	1991-92
Podein, Shjon	Edm., Phi., Col., St.L.	11	699	100	106	206	439	127	14	13	27	132	1	1992-93	2002-03
‡ Podkonicky, Andrej	Fla., Wsh.	2	8	1	0	1	2	....	....	....	....	....	....	2000-01	2003-04
Podloski, Ray	Bos.	1	8	0	1	1	17	....	....	....	....	....	....	1988-89	1988-89
Podollan, Jason	Fla., Tor., L.A., NYI	4	41	1	5	6	19	....	....	....	....	....	....	1996-97	2001-02
Podolsky, Nels	Det.	1	1	0	0	0	0	7	0	0	0	4	....	1948-49	1948-49

	Name	NHL Teams	NHL Seasons	Regular Schedule GP	G	A	TP	PIM	Playoffs GP	G	A	TP	PIM	NHL Cup Wins	First NHL Season	Last NHL Season
	Poeschek, Rudy	NYR, Wpg., T.B., St.L.	12	364	6	25	31	817	5	0	0	0	18	....	1987-88	1999-00
•	Poeta, Tony	Chi.	1	1	0	0	0	0	....	....	....	....	....	....	1951-52	1951-52
	Pohl, John	St.L., Tor.	4	115	17	21	38	24	....	....	....	....	....	....	2003-04	2007-08
•	Poile, Bud	Tor., Chi., Det., NYR, Bos.	7	311	107	122	229	91	23	4	5	9	8	1	1942-43	1949-50
	Poile, Don	Det.	2	66	7	9	16	12	4	0	0	0	0	....	1954-55	1957-58
•	Poirier, Gordie	Mtl.	1	10	0	0	0	0	....	....	....	....	....	....	1939-40	1939-40
‡	Polak, Vojtech	Dal.	2	5	0	0	0	0	....	....	....	....	....	....	2005-06	2006-07
	Polanic, Tom	Min.	2	19	0	2	2	53	5	1	1	2	4	....	1969-70	1970-71
•	Polich, John	NYR	2	3	0	1	1	0	....	....	....	....	....	....	1939-40	1940-41
	Polich, Mike	Mtl., Min.	5	226	24	29	53	57	23	2	1	3	2	1	1976-77	1980-81
	Polis, Greg	Pit., St.L., NYR, Wsh.	10	615	174	169	343	391	7	0	2	2	6	....	1970-71	1979-80
	Poliziani, Dan	Bos.	1	1	0	0	0	0	3	0	0	0	0	....	1958-59	1958-59
	Pollock, Jame	St.L.	1	9	0	0	0	6	....	....	....	....	....	....	2003-04	2003-04
	Polonich, Dennis	Det.	8	390	59	82	141	1242	7	1	0	1	19	....	1974-75	1982-83
	Pooley, Paul	Wpg.	2	15	0	3	3	0	....	....	....	....	....	....	1984-85	1985-86
	Popein, Larry	NYR, Oak.	8	449	80	141	221	162	16	1	4	5	6	....	1954-55	1967-68
	Popiel, Poul	Bos., L.A., Det., Van., Edm.	7	224	13	41	54	210	4	1	0	1	4	....	1965-66	1979-80
‡	Popovic, Mark	Ana., Atl.	5	81	2	5	7	20	....	....	....	....	....	....	2003-04	2009-10
	Popovic, Peter	Mtl., NYR, Pit., Bos.	8	485	10	63	73	291	35	1	4	5	18	....	1993-94	2000-01
•	Portland, Jack	Mtl., Bos., Chi.	10	381	15	56	71	323	33	1	3	4	25	1	1933-34	1942-43
	Porvari, Jukka	Col., N.J.	2	39	3	9	12	4	....	....	....	....	....	....	1981-82	1982-83
	Posa, Victor	Chi.	1	2	0	0	0	2	....	....	....	....	....	....	1985-86	1985-86
	Posavad, Mike	St.L.	2	8	0	0	0	0	....	....	....	....	....	....	1985-86	1986-87
	Posmyk, Marek	T.B.	2	19	1	2	3	20	....	....	....	....	....	....	1999-00	2000-01
‡	Pothier, Brian	Atl., Ott., Wsh., Car.	9	362	26	92	118	202	29	2	3	5	18	....	2000-01	2009-10
•	Potomski, Barry	L.A., S.J.	3	68	6	5	11	227	....	....	....	....	....	....	1995-96	1997-98
	Potvin, Denis	NYI	15	1060	310	742	1052	1356	185	56	108	164	253	4	1973-74	1987-88
	Potvin, Jean	L.A., Phi., NYI, Cle., Min.	11	613	63	224	287	478	39	2	9	11	17	2	1970-71	1980-81
•	Potvin, Marc	Det., L.A., Hfd., Bos.	6	121	3	5	8	456	13	0	1	1	50	....	1990-91	1995-96
	Poudrier, Daniel	Que.	3	25	1	5	6	10	....	....	....	....	....	....	1985-86	1987-88
	Poulin, Daniel	Min.	1	3	1	1	2	2	....	....	....	....	....	....	1981-82	1981-82
	Poulin, Dave	Phi., Bos., Wsh.	13	724	205	325	530	482	129	31	42	73	132	....	1982-83	1994-95
	Poulin, Patrick	Hfd., Chi., T.B., Mtl.	11	634	101	134	235	299	32	6	2	8	8	....	1991-92	2001-02
	Pouzar, Jaroslav	Edm.	4	186	34	48	82	135	29	6	4	10	16	3	1982-83	1986-87
•	Powell, Ray	Chi.	1	31	7	15	22	2	....	....	....	....	....	....	1950-51	1950-51
•	Powis, Geoff	Chi.	1	2	0	0	0	0	....	....	....	....	....	....	1967-68	1967-68
	Powis, Lynn	Chi., K.C.	2	130	19	33	52	25	1	0	0	0	0	....	1973-74	1974-75
	Prajsler, Petr	L.A., Bos.	4	46	3	10	13	51	4	0	0	0	0	....	1987-88	1991-92
•	Pratt, Babe	NYR, Tor., Bos.	12	517	83	209	292	463	63	12	17	29	90	2	1935-36	1946-47
•	Pratt, Jack	Bos.	2	37	2	0	2	42	4	0	0	0	0	....	1930-31	1931-32
	Pratt, Kelly	Pit.	1	22	0	6	6	15	....	....	....	....	....	....	1974-75	1974-75
	Pratt, Nolan	Hfd., Car., Col., T.B., Buf.	11	592	9	56	65	537	38	0	1	1	22	2	1996-97	2007-08
	Pratt, Tracy	Oak., Pit., Buf., Van., Col., Tor.	10	580	17	97	114	1026	25	0	1	1	62	....	1967-68	1976-77
‡	Preissing, Tom	S.J., Ott., L.A., Col.	6	326	31	101	132	78	42	3	12	15	14	....	2003-04	2009-10
	Prentice, Dean	NYR, Bos., Det., Pit., Min.	22	1378	391	469	860	484	54	13	17	30	38	....	1952-53	1973-74
•	Prentice, Eric	Tor.	1	5	0	0	0	4	....	....	....	....	....	....	1943-44	1943-44
	Presley, Wayne	Chi., S.J., Buf., NYR, Tor.	12	684	155	147	302	953	83	26	17	43	142	....	1984-85	1995-96
	Preston, Rich	Chi., N.J.	8	580	127	164	291	348	47	4	18	22	56	....	1979-80	1986-87
	Preston, Yves	Phi.	2	28	7	3	10	4	....	....	....	....	....	....	1978-79	1980-81
	Priakin, Sergei	Cgy.	3	46	3	8	11	2	3	0	0	0	0	....	1988-89	1990-91
•	Price, Jack	Chi.	3	57	4	6	10	24	4	0	0	0	0	....	1951-52	1953-54
	Price, Noel	Tor., NYR, Det., Mtl., Pit., L.A., Atl.	14	499	14	114	128	333	12	0	1	1	8	1	1957-58	1975-76
	Price, Pat	NYI, Edm., Pit., Que., NYR, Min.	13	726	43	218	261	1456	74	2	10	12	195	....	1975-76	1987-88
	Price, Tom	Cal., Cle., Pit.	5	29	0	2	2	12	....	....	....	....	....	....	1974-75	1978-79
	Priestlay, Ken	Buf., Pit.	6	168	27	34	61	63	14	0	0	0	21	1	1986-87	1991-92
•	Primeau, Joe	Tor.	9	310	66	177	243	105	38	5	18	23	12	1	1927-28	1935-36
	Primeau, Keith	Det., Hfd., Car., Phi.	15	909	266	353	619	1541	128	18	39	57	213	....	1990-91	2005-06
	Primeau, Kevin	Van.	1	2	0	0	0	4	....	....	....	....	....	....	1980-81	1980-81
	Primeau, Wayne	Buf., T.B., Pit., S.J., Bos., Cgy., Tor.	15	774	69	125	194	789	90	7	14	21	42	....	1994-95	2009-10
•	Pringle, Ellie	NYA	1	6	0	0	0	0	....	....	....	....	....	....	1930-31	1930-31
‡	Printz, David	Phi.	2	13	0	0	0	4	....	....	....	....	....	....	2005-06	2006-07
•	Probert, Bob	Det., Chi.	16	935	163	221	384	3300	81	16	32	48	274	....	1985-86	2001-02
	Prochazka, Martin	Tor., Atl.	2	32	2	5	7	8	....	....	....	....	....	....	1997-98	1999-00
•	Prodger, Goldie	Tor., Ham.	6	111	63	29	92	39	....	....	....	....	....	....	1919-20	1924-25
	Prokhorov, Vitali	St.L.	3	83	19	11	30	35	4	0	0	0	0	....	1992-93	1994-95
	Prokopec, Mike	Chi.	2	15	0	0	0	11	....	....	....	....	....	....	1995-96	1996-97
	Pronger, Sean	Ana., Pit., NYR, L.A., Bos., CBJ, Van.	8	260	23	36	59	159	14	0	2	2	8	....	1995-96	2003-04
	Pronovost, Andre	Mtl., Bos., Det., Min.	10	556	94	104	198	408	70	11	11	22	58	4	1956-57	1967-68
	Pronovost, Jean	Pit., Atl., Wsh.	14	998	391	383	774	413	35	11	9	20	14	....	1968-69	1981-82
	Pronovost, Marcel	Det., Tor.	21	1206	88	257	345	851	134	8	23	31	104	5	1949-50	1969-70
	Propp, Brian	Phi., Bos., Min., Hfd.	15	1016	425	579	1004	830	160	64	84	148	151	....	1979-80	1993-94
	Proulx, Christian	Mtl.	1	7	1	2	3	20	....	....	....	....	....	....	1993-94	1993-94
•	Provost, Claude	Mtl.	15	1005	254	335	589	469	126	25	38	63	86	9	1955-56	1969-70
‡	Prpic, Joel	Bos., Col.	3	18	0	3	3	4	....	....	....	....	....	....	1997-98	2000-01
‡	Prucha, Petr	NYR, Phx.	6	346	78	68	146	133	24	2	3	5	8	....	2005-06	2010-11
	Pryor, Chris	Min., NYI	6	82	1	4	5	122	....	....	....	....	....	....	1984-85	1989-90
	Prystai, Metro	Chi., Det.	11	674	151	179	330	231	43	12	14	26	8	2	1947-48	1957-58
•	Pudas, Al	Tor.	1	4	0	0	0	0	....	....	....	....	....	....	1926-27	1926-27
	Pulford, Bob	Tor., L.A.	16	1079	281	362	643	792	89	25	26	51	126	4	1956-57	1971-72
	Pulkkinen, Dave	NYI	1	2	0	0	0	0	....	....	....	....	....	....	1972-73	1972-73
	Purinton, Dale	NYR	5	181	4	16	20	578	....	....	....	....	....	....	1999-00	2003-04
•	Purpur, Fido	St.L., Chi., Det.	5	144	25	35	60	46	16	1	2	3	4	....	1934-35	1944-45
	Purves, John	Wsh.	1	7	1	0	1	0	....	....	....	....	....	....	1990-91	1990-91
‡	Pushkarev, Konstantin	L.A.	2	17	2	3	5	8	....	....	....	....	....	....	2005-06	2006-07
	Pushor, Jamie	Det., Ana., Dal., CBJ, Pit., NYR	10	521	14	46	60	648	14	0	1	1	16	1	1995-96	2005-06
•	Pusie, Jean	Mtl., NYR, Bos.	5	61	1	4	5	28	7	0	0	0	0	1	1930-31	1935-36
	Pyatt, Nelson	Det., Wsh., Col.	7	296	71	63	134	69	....	....	....	....	....	....	1973-74	1979-80
‡	Pyorala, Mika	Phi.	1	36	2	2	4	10	....	....	....	....	....	....	2009-10	2009-10

Q

	Name	NHL Teams	NHL Seasons	Regular Schedule GP	G	A	TP	PIM	Playoffs GP	G	A	TP	PIM	NHL Cup Wins	First NHL Season	Last NHL Season
•	Quackenbush, Bill	Det., Bos.	14	774	62	222	284	95	80	2	19	21	8	....	1942-43	1955-56
	Quackenbush, Max	Bos., Chi.	2	61	4	7	11	30	6	0	0	0	4	....	1950-51	1951-52
	Quenneville, Joel	Tor., Col., N.J., Hfd., Wsh.	13	803	54	136	190	705	32	0	8	8	22	....	1978-79	1990-91
•	Quenneville, Leo	NYR	1	25	0	3	3	10	3	0	0	0	0	....	1929-30	1929-30
‡	Quick, Kevin	T.B.	1	6	0	1	1	0	....	....	....	....	....	....	2008-09	2008-09
•	Quilty, John	Mtl., Bos.	4	125	36	34	70	81	13	3	5	8	9	....	1940-41	1947-48
	Quinn, Dan	Cgy., Pit., Van., St.L., Phi., Min., Ott., L.A.	14	805	266	419	685	533	65	22	26	48	62	....	1983-84	1996-97
	Quinn, Pat	Tor., Van., Atl.	9	606	18	113	131	950	11	0	1	1	21	....	1968-69	1976-77
	Quinney, Ken	Que.	3	59	7	13	20	23	....	....	....	....	....	....	1986-87	1990-91
‡	Quint, Deron	Wpg., Phx., N.J., CBJ, Chi., NYI	10	463	46	97	143	166	7	0	2	2	0	....	1995-96	2006-07
	Quintal, Stephane	Bos., St.L., Wpg., Mtl., NYR, Chi.	16	1037	63	180	243	1320	52	2	10	12	51	....	1988-89	2003-04
	Quintin, Jean-Francois	S.J.	2	22	5	5	10	4	....	....	....	....	....	....	1991-92	1992-93

R

	Name	NHL Teams	NHL Seasons	Regular Schedule GP	G	A	TP	PIM	Playoffs GP	G	A	TP	PIM	NHL Cup Wins	First NHL Season	Last NHL Season
•	Rachunek, Karel	Ott., NYR, N.J.	7	371	22	118	140	227	26	1	7	8	16	....	1999-00	2007-08
	Racine, Yves	Det., Phi., Mtl., S.J., Cgy., T.B.	9	508	37	194	231	439	25	5	4	9	37	....	1989-90	1997-98
‡	Radivojevic, Branko	Phx., Phi., Min.	6	393	52	68	120	252	31	2	1	3	36	....	2001-02	2007-08
•	Radley, Yip	NYA, Mtl.M.	2	18	0	1	1	13	....	....	....	....	....	....	1930-31	1936-37
‡	Radulov, Igor	Chi.	2	43	9	7	16	22	....	....	....	....	....	....	2002-03	2003-04
	Raduns, Nate	Phi.	1	1	0	0	0	0	....	....	....	....	....	....	2008-09	2008-09
	Rafalski, Brian	N.J., Det.	11	833	79	436	515	282	165	29	71	100	66	3	1999-00	2010-11
	Raglan, Herb	St.L., Que., T.B., Ott.	9	343	33	56	89	775	32	3	6	9	50	....	1985-86	1993-94
•	Raglan, Rags	Det., Chi.	3	100	4	9	13	52	3	0	0	0	0	....	1950-51	1952-53
	Ragnarsson, Marcus	S.J., Phi.	9	632	37	140	177	482	68	2	13	15	60	....	1995-96	2003-04
	Raleigh, Don	NYR	10	535	101	219	320	96	18	6	5	11	6	....	1943-44	1955-56
	Ralph, Brad	Phx.	1	1	0	0	0	0	....	....	....	....	....	....	2000-01	2000-01
	Ramage, Rob	Col., St.L., Cgy., Tor., Min., T.B., Mtl., Phi.	15	1044	139	425	564	2226	84	8	42	50	218	2	1979-80	1993-94
‡	Ramholt, Tim	Cgy.	1	1	0	0	0	0	....	....	....	....	....	....	2007-08	2007-08
•	Ramsay, Beattie	Tor.	1	43	0	2	2	10	....	....	....	....	....	....	1927-28	1927-28
	Ramsay, Craig	Buf.	14	1070	252	420	672	201	89	17	31	48	27	....	1971-72	1984-85
	Ramsay, Les	Chi.	1	11	2	2	4	2	....	....	....	....	....	....	1944-45	1944-45
	Ramsey, Mike	Buf., Pit., Det.	18	1070	79	266	345	1012	115	8	29	37	176	....	1979-80	1996-97

Jimmy Peters Sr.

Don Poile

Lynn Powis

Jack Price

Stephane Quintal

Ken Richardson

Gerry Rioux

Pierre Rioux

			Regular Schedule					Playoffs							
Name	NHL Teams	NHL Seasons	GP	G	A	TP	PIM	GP	G	A	TP	PIM	NHL Cup Wins	First NHL Season	Last NHL Season
Ramsey, Wayne	Buf.	1	2	0	0	0	0	....	....	....	....	....	....	1977-78	1977-78
• Randall, Ken	Tor., Ham., NYA	10	218	68	50	118	533	6	2	1	3	27	2	1917-18	1926-27
Ranheim, Paul	Cgy., Hfd., Car., Phi., Phx.	15	1013	161	199	360	288	36	3	8	11	6	....	1988-89	2002-03
Ranieri, George	Bos.	1	2	0	0	0	0	....	....	....	....	....	....	1956-57	1956-57
Rasmussen, Erik	Buf., L.A., N.J.	9	545	52	76	128	305	52	2	7	9	46	....	1997-98	2006-07
Ratchuk, Peter	Fla.	2	32	1	1	2	10	....	....	....	....	....	....	1998-99	2000-01
Ratelle, Jean	NYR, Bos.	21	1281	491	776	1267	276	123	32	66	98	24	....	1960-61	1980-81
Rathje, Mike	S.J., Phi.	13	768	30	150	180	491	77	9	14	23	51	....	1993-94	2006-07
Rathwell, Jake	Bos.	1	1	0	0	0	0	....	....	....	....	....	....	1974-75	1974-75
Ratushny, Dan	Van.	1	1	0	1	1	2	....	....	....	....	....	....	1992-93	1992-93
Rausse, Errol	Wsh.	3	31	7	3	10	0	....	....	....	....	....	....	1979-80	1981-82
Rautakallio, Pekka	Atl., Cgy.	3	235	33	121	154	122	23	2	5	7	8	....	1979-80	1981-82
Ravlich, Matt	Bos., Chi., Det., L.A.	10	410	12	78	90	364	24	1	5	6	16	....	1962-63	1972-73
Ray, Rob	Buf., Ott.	15	900	41	50	91	3207	55	3	2	5	169	....	1989-90	2003-04
• Raymond, Armand	Mtl.	2	22	0	2	2	10	....	....	....	....	....	....	1937-38	1939-40
• Raymond, Paul	Mtl.	4	76	2	3	5	6	5	0	0	0	2	....	1932-33	1938-39
• Read, Mel	NYR	1	1	0	0	0	0	....	....	....	....	....	....	1946-47	1946-47
Ready, Ryan	Phi.	1	7	0	1	1	0	....	....	....	....	....	....	2005-06	2005-06
• Reardon, Ken	Mtl.	7	341	26	96	122	604	31	2	5	7	62	1	1940-41	1949-50
• Reardon, Terry	Bos., Mtl.	7	193	47	53	100	73	30	8	10	18	12	1	1938-39	1946-47
Reaume, Marc	Tor., Det., Mtl., Van.	9	344	8	43	51	273	21	0	2	2	8	....	1954-55	1970-71
• Reay, Billy	Det., Mtl.	10	479	105	162	267	202	63	13	16	29	43	2	1943-44	1952-53
Recchi, Mark	Pit., Phi., Mtl., Car., Atl., T.B., Bos.	22	1652	577	956	1533	1033	189	61	86	147	93	3	1988-89	2010-11
Redahl, Gord	Bos.	1	18	0	1	1	2	....	....	....	....	....	....	1958-59	1958-59
• Redding, George	Bos.	2	55	3	2	5	23	....	....	....	....	....	....	1924-25	1925-26
‡ Reddox, Liam	Edm.	4	100	6	18	24	34	....	....	....	....	....	....	2007-08	2010-11
Redmond, Craig	L.A., Edm.	5	191	16	68	84	134	3	1	0	1	2	....	1984-85	1988-89
Redmond, Dick	Min., Cal., Chi., St.L., Atl., Bos.	13	771	133	312	445	504	66	9	22	31	27	....	1969-70	1981-82
Redmond, Keith	L.A.	1	12	1	0	1	20	....	....	....	....	....	....	1993-94	1993-94
Redmond, Mickey	Mtl., Det.	9	538	233	195	428	219	16	2	3	5	2	2	1967-68	1975-76
Reeds, Mark	St.L., Hfd.	8	365	45	114	159	135	53	8	9	17	23	....	1981-82	1988-89
Reekie, Joe	Buf., NYI, T.B., Wsh., Chi.	17	902	25	139	164	1326	51	3	4	7	63	....	1985-86	2001-02
• Regan, Bill	NYR, NYA	3	67	3	2	5	67	8	0	0	0	2	....	1929-30	1932-33
• Regan, Larry	Bos., Tor.	5	280	41	95	136	71	42	7	14	21	18	....	1956-57	1960-61
Regehr, Richie	Cgy.	2	20	1	3	4	6	....	....	....	....	....	....	2005-06	2006-07
Regier, Darcy	Cle., NYI	3	26	0	2	2	35	....	....	....	....	....	....	1977-78	1983-84
‡ Regier, Steve	NYI, St.L.	4	26	3	1	4	8	....	....	....	....	....	....	2005-06	2008-09
• Reibel, Dutch	Det., Chi., Bos.	6	409	84	161	245	75	39	6	14	20	4	2	1953-54	1958-59
‡ Reich, Jeremy	CBJ, Bos.	3	99	2	4	6	161	4	0	0	0	8	....	2003-04	2007-08
Reichel, Robert	Cgy., NYI, Phx., Tor.	11	830	252	378	630	388	70	8	23	31	20	....	1990-91	2003-04
Reichert, Craig	Ana.	1	3	0	0	0	0	....	....	....	....	....	....	1996-97	1996-97
‡ Reid, Brandon	Van.	3	13	2	4	6	0	10	0	2	2	0	....	2002-03	2006-07
Reid, Darren	T.B., Phi.	2	21	0	1	1	18	....	....	....	....	....	....	2005-06	2006-07
• Reid, Dave	Tor.	3	7	0	0	0	0	....	....	....	....	....	....	1952-53	1955-56
Reid, Dave	Bos., Tor., Dal., Col.	18	961	165	204	369	253	118	9	26	35	34	2	1983-84	2000-01
Reid, Gerry	Det.	1	....	....	....	....	....	2	0	0	0	2	....	1948-49	1948-49
Reid, Gord	NYA	1	1	0	0	0	2	....	....	....	....	....	....	1936-37	1936-37
• Reid, Reg	Tor.	2	39	1	0	1	4	2	0	0	0	0	....	1924-25	1925-26
Reid, Tom	Chi., Min.	11	701	17	113	130	654	42	1	13	14	49	....	1967-68	1977-78
Reierson, Dave	Cgy.	1	2	0	0	0	2	....	....	....	....	....	....	1988-89	1988-89
• Reigle, Ed	Bos.	1	17	0	2	2	25	....	....	....	....	....	....	1950-51	1950-51
Reinhart, Paul	Atl., Cgy., Van.	11	648	133	426	559	277	83	23	54	77	42	....	1979-80	1989-90
• Reinikka, Ollie	NYR	1	16	0	0	0	0	....	....	....	....	....	....	1926-27	1926-27
Reirden, Todd	Edm., St.L., Atl., Phx.	5	183	11	35	46	181	5	0	1	1	0	....	1998-99	2003-04
• Reise, Leo	Ham., NYA, NYR	8	223	36	29	65	181	6	0	0	0	16	....	1920-21	1929-30
Reise, Leo	Chi., Det., NYR	9	494	28	81	109	399	52	8	5	13	68	2	1945-46	1953-54
Reitz, Erik	Min., NYR	4	48	1	1	2	69	2	0	0	0	0	....	2005-06	2008-09
Renaud, Mark	Hfd., Buf.	5	152	6	50	56	86	....	....	....	....	....	....	1979-80	1983-84
Renberg, Mikael	Phi., T.B., Phx., Tor.	10	661	190	274	464	372	67	16	22	38	42	....	1993-94	2003-04
Reynolds, Bobby	Tor.	1	7	1	1	2	0	....	....	....	....	....	....	1989-90	1989-90
Rheaume, Pascal	N.J., St.L., Chi., Atl., NYR, Phx.	9	318	39	52	91	144	45	3	6	9	27	1	1996-97	2005-06
Ribble, Pat	Atl., Chi., Tor., Wsh., Cgy.	8	349	19	60	79	365	8	0	1	1	12	....	1975-76	1982-83
Ricci, Mike	Phi., Que., Col., S.J., Phx.	16	1099	243	362	605	974	110	23	43	66	77	1	1990-91	2006-07
Rice, Steven	NYR, Edm., Hfd., Car.	8	329	64	61	125	275	2	2	1	3	6	....	1990-91	1997-98
Richard, Henri	Mtl.	20	1256	358	688	1046	928	180	49	80	129	181	11	1955-56	1974-75
• Richard, Jacques	Atl., Buf., Que.	10	556	160	187	347	307	35	5	5	10	34	....	1972-73	1982-83
Richard, Jean-Marc	Que.	2	5	2	1	3	2	....	....	....	....	....	....	1987-88	1989-90
• Richard, Maurice	Mtl.	18	978	544	421	965	1285	133	82	44	126	188	8	1942-43	1959-60
Richard, Mike	Wsh.	2	7	0	2	2	0	....	....	....	....	....	....	1987-88	1989-90
Richards, Todd	Hfd.	2	8	0	4	4	4	11	0	3	3	6	....	1990-91	1991-92
Richards, Travis	Dal.	2	3	0	0	0	2	....	....	....	....	....	....	1994-95	1995-96
Richardson, Dave	NYR, Chi., Det.	4	45	3	2	5	27	....	....	....	....	....	....	1963-64	1967-68
Richardson, Glen	Van.	1	24	3	6	9	19	....	....	....	....	....	....	1975-76	1975-76
Richardson, Ken	St.L.	3	49	8	13	21	16	....	....	....	....	....	....	1974-75	1978-79
Richardson, Luke	Tor., Edm., Phi., CBJ, T.B., Ott.	21	1417	35	166	201	2055	69	0	8	8	130	....	1987-88	2008-09
Richer, Bob	Buf.	1	3	0	0	0	0	....	....	....	....	....	....	1972-73	1972-73
Richer, Stephane	Mtl., N.J., T.B., St.L., Pit.	17	1054	421	398	819	614	134	53	45	98	61	2	1984-85	2001-02
Richer, Stephane	T.B., Bos., Fla.	3	27	1	5	6	20	3	0	0	0	0	....	1992-93	1994-95
‡ Richmond, Danny	Car., Chi.	3	49	0	3	3	75	....	....	....	....	....	....	2005-06	2007-08
Richmond, Steve	NYR, Det., N.J., L.A.	5	159	4	23	27	514	4	0	0	0	12	....	1983-84	1988-89
Richter, Barry	NYR, Bos., NYI, Mtl.	5	151	11	34	45	76	....	....	....	....	....	....	1995-96	2000-01
Richter, Dave	Min., Phi., Van., St.L.	9	365	9	40	49	1030	22	1	0	1	80	....	1981-82	1989-90
Ridley, Mike	NYR, Wsh., Tor., Van.	12	866	292	466	758	424	104	28	50	78	70	....	1985-86	1996-97
‡ Riesen, Michel	Edm.	1	12	0	1	1	4	....	....	....	....	....	....	2000-01	2000-01
Riley, Bill	Wsh., Wpg.	5	139	31	30	61	320	....	....	....	....	....	....	1974-75	1979-80
• Riley, Jack	Det., Mtl., Bos.	4	104	10	22	32	8	4	0	3	3	0	....	1932-33	1935-36
• Riley, Jim	Chi., Det.	1	9	0	2	2	14	....	....	....	....	....	....	1926-27	1926-27
Riopelle, Rip	Mtl.	3	169	27	16	43	73	8	1	1	2	2	....	1947-48	1949-50
Rioux, Gerry	Wpg.	1	8	0	0	0	6	....	....	....	....	....	....	1979-80	1979-80
Rioux, Pierre	Cgy.	1	14	1	2	3	4	....	....	....	....	....	....	1982-83	1982-83
• Ripley, Vic	Chi., Bos., NYR, St.L.	7	278	51	49	100	173	20	4	1	5	10	....	1928-29	1934-35
Risebrough, Doug	Mtl., Cgy.	13	740	185	286	471	1542	124	21	37	58	238	4	1974-75	1986-87
Rissling, Gary	Wsh., Pit.	7	221	23	30	53	1008	5	0	1	1	4	....	1978-79	1984-85
‡ Rita, Jani	Edm., Pit.	4	66	9	5	14	10	....	....	....	....	....	....	2001-02	2005-06
Ritchie, Bob	Phi., Det.	2	29	8	4	12	10	....	....	....	....	....	....	1976-77	1977-78
‡ Ritchie, Byron	Car., Fla., Cgy., Van.	8	324	25	33	58	373	8	0	0	0	10	....	1998-99	2007-08
• Ritchie, Dave	Mtl.W., Ott., Tor., Que., Mtl.	6	58	15	6	21	50	1	0	0	0	0	....	1917-18	1925-26
Ritson, Alex	NYR	1	1	0	0	0	0	....	....	....	....	....	....	1944-45	1944-45
Rittinger, Alan	Bos.	1	19	3	7	10	0	....	....	....	....	....	....	1943-44	1943-44
Rivard, Bob	Pit.	1	27	5	12	17	4	....	....	....	....	....	....	1967-68	1967-68
• Rivers, Gus	Mtl.	3	88	4	5	9	12	16	2	0	2	2	2	1929-30	1931-32
Rivers, Jamie	St.L., NYI, Ott., Bos., Fla., Det., Phx.	11	454	17	49	66	385	15	1	1	2	8	....	1995-96	2006-07
Rivers, Shawn	T.B.	1	4	0	2	2	2	....	....	....	....	....	....	1992-93	1992-93
Rivers, Wayne	Det., Bos., St.L., NYR	7	108	15	30	45	94	....	....	....	....	....	....	1961-62	1968-69
Rivet, Craig	Mtl., S.J., Buf., CBJ	16	923	50	187	237	1171	69	4	19	23	69	....	1994-95	2010-11
Rizzuto, Garth	Van.	1	37	3	4	7	16	....	....	....	....	....	....	1970-71	1970-71
Roach, Andy	St.L.	1	5	1	2	3	10	....	....	....	....	....	....	2005-06	2005-06
• Roach, Mickey	Tor., Ham., NYA	8	211	77	34	111	54	....	....	....	....	....	....	1919-20	1926-27
Roberge, Mario	Mtl.	5	112	7	7	14	314	15	0	0	0	24	1	1990-91	1994-95
Roberge, Serge	Que.	1	9	0	0	0	24	....	....	....	....	....	....	1990-91	1990-91
• Robert, Claude	Mtl.	1	23	1	0	1	9	....	....	....	....	....	....	1950-51	1950-51
Robert, Rene	Tor., Pit., Buf., Col.	12	744	284	418	702	597	50	22	19	41	73	....	1970-71	1981-82
Roberto, Phil	Mtl., St.L., Det., K.C., Col., Cle.	8	385	75	106	181	464	31	9	8	17	69	1	1969-70	1976-77
Roberts, David	St.L., Edm., Van.	5	125	20	33	53	85	9	0	0	0	16	....	1993-94	1997-98
Roberts, Doug	Det., Oak., Cal., Bos.	10	419	43	104	147	342	16	2	3	5	46	....	1965-66	1974-75
Roberts, Gary	Cgy., Car., Tor., Fla., Pit., T.B.	22	1224	438	472	910	2560	130	32	61	93	332	1	1986-87	2008-09
Roberts, Gordie	Hfd., Min., Phi., St.L., Pit., Bos.	15	1097	61	359	420	1582	153	10	47	57	273	2	1979-80	1993-94
Roberts, Jim	Min.	3	106	17	23	40	33	2	0	0	0	0	....	1976-77	1978-79
Roberts, Jimmy	Mtl., St.L.	15	1006	126	194	320	621	153	20	16	36	160	5	1963-64	1977-78
• Robertson, Fred	Tor., Det.	2	34	1	0	1	35	7	0	0	0	0	1	1931-32	1933-34
Robertson, Geordie	Buf.	1	5	1	2	3	7	....	....	....	....	....	....	1982-83	1982-83
• Robertson, George	Mtl.	2	31	2	5	7	6	....	....	....	....	....	....	1947-48	1948-49
Robertson, Torrie	Wsh., Hfd., Det.	10	442	49	99	148	1751	22	2	1	3	90	....	1980-81	1989-90
Robertsson, Bert	Van., Edm., NYR	4	123	4	10	14	75	5	0	0	0	0	....	1997-98	2000-01
Robidoux, Florent	Chi.	3	52	7	4	11	75	....	....	....	....	....	....	1980-81	1983-84
Robinson, Doug	Chi., NYR, L.A.	7	239	44	67	111	34	11	4	3	7	0	....	1963-64	1970-71

Name	NHL Teams	NHL Seasons	Regular Schedule					Playoffs					NHL Cup Wins	First NHL Season	Last NHL Season
			GP	G	A	TP	PIM	GP	G	A	TP	PIM			
• Robinson, Earl	Mtl.M., Chi., Mtl.	11	417	83	98	181	133	25	5	4	9	0	1	1928-29	1939-40
Robinson, Larry	Mtl., L.A.	20	1384	208	750	958	793	227	28	116	144	211	6	1972-73	1991-92
Robinson, Moe	Mtl.	1	1	0	0	0	0	....	....	....	....	....	....	1979-80	1979-80
Robinson, Nathan	Det., Bos.	2	7	0	0	0	2	....	....	....	....	....	....	2003-04	2005-06
Robinson, Rob	St.L.	1	22	0	1	1	8	....	....	....	....	....	....	1991-92	1991-92
Robinson, Scott	Min.	1	1	0	0	0	2	....	....	....	....	....	....	1989-90	1989-90
Robitaille, Louis	Wsh.	1	2	0	0	0	5	....	....	....	....	....	....	2005-06	2005-06
Robitaille, Luc	L.A., Pit., NYR, Det.	19	1431	668	726	1394	1177	159	58	69	127	174	1	1986-87	2005-06
Robitaille, Mike	NYR, Det., Buf., Van.	8	382	23	105	128	280	13	0	1	1	4	....	1969-70	1976-77
‡ Robitaille, Randy	Bos., Nsh., L.A., Pit., NYI, Atl., Min., Phi., Ott.	11	531	84	172	256	201	13	1	4	5	8	....	1996-97	2007-08
Roche, Dave	Pit., Cgy., NYI	5	171	15	15	30	334	16	2	7	9	26	....	1995-96	2001-02
• Roche, Des	Mtl.M., Ott., St.L., Mtl., Det.	4	113	20	18	38	44	....	....	....	....	....	....	1930-31	1934-35
• Roche, Earl	Mtl.M., Bos., Ott., St.L., Det.	4	147	25	27	52	48	2	0	0	0	0	....	1930-31	1934-35
Roche, Ernie	Mtl.	1	4	0	0	0	2	....	....	....	....	....	....	1950-51	1950-51
Roche, Travis	Min., Phx.	4	60	6	14	20	24	....	....	....	....	....	....	2000-01	2006-07
Rochefort, Dave	Det.	1	1	0	0	0	0	....	....	....	....	....	....	1966-67	1966-67
Rochefort, Leon	NYR, Mtl., Phi., L.A., Det., Atl., Van.	15	617	121	147	268	93	39	4	4	8	16	2	1960-61	1975-76
Rochefort, Normand	Que., NYR, T.B.	13	598	39	119	158	570	69	7	5	12	82	....	1980-81	1993-94
• Rockburn, Harvey	Det., Ott.	3	94	4	2	6	254	....	....	....	....	....	....	1929-30	1932-33
• Rodden, Eddie	Chi., Tor., Bos., NYR	4	97	6	14	20	60	2	0	1	1	0	....	1926-27	1930-31
Rodgers, Marc	Det.	1	21	1	1	2	10	....	....	....	....	....	....	1999-00	1999-00
Roenick, Jeremy	Chi., Phx., Phi., L.A., S.J.	20	1363	513	703	1216	1463	154	53	69	122	115	....	1988-89	2008-09
‡ Roest, Stacy	Det., Min.	5	244	28	48	76	54	3	0	0	0	0	....	1998-99	2002-03
Rogers, John	Min.	2	14	2	4	6	0	....	....	....	....	....	....	1973-74	1974-75
Rogers, Mike	Hfd., NYR, Edm.	7	484	202	317	519	184	17	1	13	14	6	....	1979-80	1985-86
Rohlicek, Jeff	Van.	2	9	0	0	0	8	....	....	....	....	....	....	1987-88	1988-89
Rohlin, Leif	Van.	2	96	8	24	32	40	5	0	0	0	0	....	1995-96	1996-97
Rohloff, Jon	Bos.	3	150	7	25	32	129	10	1	2	3	8	....	1994-95	1996-97
Rohloff, Todd	Wsh., CBJ	2	75	0	6	6	40	....	....	....	....	....	....	2001-02	2003-04
Rolfe, Dale	Bos., L.A., Det., NYR	9	509	25	125	150	556	71	5	24	29	89	....	1959-60	1974-75
Rolston, Brian	N.J., Col., Bos., Min., NYI	17	1256	342	419	761	472	77	20	14	34	38	1	1994-95	2011-12
Romanchych, Larry	Chi., Atl.	6	298	68	97	165	102	7	2	2	4	4	....	1970-71	1976-77
Romaniuk, Russell	Wpg., Phi.	5	102	13	14	27	63	2	0	0	0	0	....	1991-92	1995-96
Rombough, Doug	Buf., NYI, Min.	4	150	24	27	51	80	....	....	....	....	....	....	1972-73	1975-76
Rominski, Dale	T.B.	1	3	0	1	1	2	....	....	....	....	....	....	1999-00	1999-00
• Romnes, Doc	Chi., Tor., NYA	10	360	68	136	204	42	43	7	18	25	4	2	1930-31	1939-40
Ronan, Ed	Mtl., Wpg., Buf.	6	182	13	23	36	101	27	4	3	7	16	1	1991-92	1996-97
• Ronan, Skene	Ott.	1	11	0	0	0	6	....	....	....	....	....	....	1918-19	1918-19
Ronning, Cliff	St.L., Van., Phx., Nsh., L.A., Min., NYI	18	1137	306	563	869	453	126	29	57	86	72	....	1985-86	2003-04
Ronnqvist, Jonas	Ana.	1	38	0	4	4	14	....	....	....	....	....	....	2000-01	2000-01
Ronson, Len	NYR, Oak.	2	18	2	1	3	10	....	....	....	....	....	....	1960-61	1968-69
Ronty, Paul	Bos., NYR, Mtl.	8	488	101	211	312	103	21	1	7	8	6	....	1947-48	1954-55
Rooney, Steve	Mtl., Wpg., N.J.	5	154	15	13	28	496	25	3	2	5	86	1	1984-85	1988-89
Root, Bill	Mtl., Tor., St.L., Phi.	6	247	11	23	34	180	22	1	2	3	25	....	1982-83	1987-88
‡ Rosa, Pavel	L.A.	4	36	5	13	18	6	....	....	....	....	....	....	1998-99	2003-04
• Ross, Art	Mtl.W.	1	3	1	0	1	12	....	....	....	....	....	....	1917-18	1917-18
‡ Ross, Jared	Phi.	2	13	0	0	0	2	9	1	0	1	0	....	2008-09	2009-10
Ross, Jim	NYR	2	62	2	11	13	29	....	....	....	....	....	....	1951-52	1952-53
Rossignol, Roly	Det., Mtl.	3	14	3	5	8	6	1	0	0	0	2	....	1943-44	1945-46
Rossiter, Kyle	Fla., Atl.	3	11	0	1	1	9	....	....	....	....	....	....	2001-02	2003-04
Rota, Darcy	Chi., Atl., Van.	11	794	256	239	495	973	60	14	7	21	147	....	1973-74	1983-84
Rota, Randy	Mtl., L.A., K.C., Col.	5	212	38	39	77	60	5	0	1	1	0	....	1972-73	1976-77
• Rothschild, Sam	Mtl.M., Pit., NYA	4	100	8	6	14	25	6	0	0	0	0	1	1924-25	1927-28
• Roulston, Rolly	Det.	3	24	0	6	6	10	....	....	....	....	....	1	1935-36	1937-38
Roulston, Tom	Edm., Pit.	5	195	47	49	96	74	21	2	2	4	2	....	1980-81	1985-86
Roupe, Magnus	Phi.	2	40	3	5	8	42	....	....	....	....	....	....	1987-88	1988-89
Rourke, Allan	Car., NYI, Edm.	4	55	1	4	5	31	....	....	....	....	....	....	2003-04	2007-08
Rouse, Bob	Min., Wsh., Tor., Det., S.J.	17	1061	37	181	218	1559	136	7	21	28	198	2	1983-84	1999-00
Rousseau, Bobby	Mtl., Min., NYR	15	942	245	458	703	359	128	27	57	84	69	4	1960-61	1974-75
Rousseau, Guy	Mtl.	2	4	0	1	1	0	....	....	....	....	....	....	1954-55	1956-57
• Rousseau, Roland	Mtl.	1	2	0	0	0	0	....	....	....	....	....	....	1952-53	1952-53
Routhier, Jean-Marc	Que.	1	8	0	0	0	9	....	....	....	....	....	....	1989-90	1989-90
• Rowe, Bobby	Bos.	1	4	1	0	1	0	....	....	....	....	....	....	1924-25	1924-25
Rowe, Mike	Pit.	3	11	0	0	0	11	....	....	....	....	....	....	1984-85	1986-87
• Rowe, Ron	NYR	1	5	1	0	1	0	....	....	....	....	....	....	1947-48	1947-48
Rowe, Tom	Wsh., Hfd., Det.	7	357	85	100	185	615	3	2	0	2	0	....	1976-77	1982-83
Roy, Andre	Bos., Ott., T.B., Pit., Cgy.	11	515	35	33	68	1169	41	1	3	4	98	1	1995-96	2008-09
Roy, Jean-Yves	NYR, Ott., Bos.	4	61	12	16	28	26	....	....	....	....	....	....	1994-95	1997-98
Roy, Stephane	Min.	1	12	1	0	1	0	....	....	....	....	....	....	1987-88	1987-88
Royer, Gaetan	T.B.	1	3	0	0	0	2	....	....	....	....	....	....	2001-02	2001-02
Royer, Remi	Chi.	1	18	0	0	0	67	....	....	....	....	....	....	1998-99	1998-99
• Rozzini, Gino	Bos.	1	31	5	10	15	20	6	1	2	3	6	....	1944-45	1944-45
Rucchin, Steve	Ana., NYR, Atl.	12	735	171	318	489	164	37	9	8	17	12	....	1994-95	2006-07
Rucinski, Mike	Chi.	2	1	0	0	0	0	2	0	0	0	0	....	1987-88	1988-89
Rucinski, Mike	Car.	3	26	0	2	2	10	....	....	....	....	....	....	1997-98	2000-01
‡ Rucinsky, Martin	Edm., Que., Col., Mtl., Dal., NYR, St.L., Van.	16	961	241	371	612	821	37	9	5	14	24	....	1991-92	2007-08
• Ruelle, Bernie	Det.	1	2	1	0	1	0	....	....	....	....	....	....	1943-44	1943-44
Ruff, Jason	St.L., T.B.	2	14	3	3	6	10	....	....	....	....	....	....	1992-93	1993-94
Ruff, Lindy	Buf., NYR	12	691	105	195	300	1264	52	11	13	24	193	....	1979-80	1990-91
Ruhnke, Kent	Bos.	1	2	0	1	1	0	....	....	....	....	....	....	1975-76	1975-76
Rumble, Darren	Phi., Ott., St.L., T.B.	8	193	10	26	36	216	....	....	....	....	....	1	1990-91	2003-04
Rundqvist, Thomas	Mtl.	1	2	0	1	1	0	....	....	....	....	....	....	1984-85	1984-85
• Runge, Paul	Bos., Mtl.M., Mtl.	7	140	18	22	40	57	7	0	0	0	6	....	1930-31	1937-38
Ruotsalainen, Reijo	NYR, Edm., N.J.	7	446	107	237	344	180	86	15	32	47	44	2	1981-82	1989-90
Rupp, Duane	NYR, Tor., Min., Pit.	10	374	24	93	117	220	10	2	2	4	8	....	1962-63	1972-73
Ruskowski, Terry	Chi., L.A., Pit., Min.	10	630	113	313	426	1354	21	1	6	7	86	....	1979-80	1988-89
Russell, Cam	Chi., Col.	10	396	9	21	30	872	44	0	5	5	16	....	1989-90	1998-99
• Russell, Church	NYR	3	90	20	16	36	12	....	....	....	....	....	....	1945-46	1947-48
Russell, Phil	Chi., Atl., Cgy., N.J., Buf.	15	1016	99	325	424	2038	73	4	22	26	202	....	1972-73	1986-87
Ruuttu, Christian	Buf., Chi., Van.	9	621	134	298	432	714	42	4	9	13	49	....	1986-87	1994-95
‡ Ruutu, Jarkko	Van., Pit., Ott., Ana.	11	652	58	84	142	1078	58	5	5	10	114	....	1999-00	2010-11
‡ Ruzicka, Stefan	Phi.	3	55	4	13	17	47	....	....	....	....	....	....	2005-06	2007-08
Ruzicka, Vladimir	Edm., Bos., Ott.	5	233	82	85	167	129	30	4	14	18	2	....	1989-90	1993-94
Ryan, Matt	L.A.	1	12	0	1	1	2	....	....	....	....	....	....	2005-06	2005-06
‡ Ryan, Michael	Buf., Car.	3	83	7	8	15	34	....	....	....	....	....	....	2006-07	2008-09
‡ Ryan, Prestin	Van.	1	1	0	0	0	2	....	....	....	....	....	....	2005-06	2005-06
Ryan, Terry	Mtl.	3	8	0	0	0	36	....	....	....	....	....	....	1996-97	1998-99
Rychel, Warren	Chi., L.A., Tor., Col., Ana.	9	406	38	39	77	1422	70	8	13	21	121	1	1988-89	1998-99
Rycroft, Mark	St.L., Col.	4	226	21	25	46	113	3	0	0	0	2	....	2001-02	2006-07
Rymsha, Andy	Que.	1	6	0	0	0	23	....	....	....	....	....	....	1991-92	1991-92
• Rypien, Rick	Van.	6	119	9	7	16	226	17	0	3	3	47	....	2005-06	2010-11
Ryznar, Jason	N.J.	1	8	0	0	0	2	....	....	....	....	....	....	2005-06	2005-06

S

Name	NHL Teams	NHL Seasons	GP	G	A	TP	PIM	GP	G	A	TP	PIM	NHL Cup Wins	First NHL Season	Last NHL Season
Saarinen, Simo	NYR	1	8	0	0	0	0	....	....	....	....	....	....	1984-85	1984-85
Sabol, Shaun	Phi.	1	2	0	0	0	0	....	....	....	....	....	....	1989-90	1989-90
Sabourin, Bob	Tor.	1	1	0	0	0	2	....	....	....	....	....	....	1951-52	1951-52
Sabourin, Gary	St.L., Tor., Cal., Cle.	10	627	169	188	357	397	62	19	11	30	58	....	1967-68	1976-77
Sabourin, Ken	Cgy., Wsh.	4	74	2	8	10	201	12	0	0	0	34	....	1988-89	1991-92
Sacco, David	Tor., Ana.	3	35	5	13	18	22	....	....	....	....	....	....	1993-94	1995-96
Sacco, Joe	Tor., Ana., NYI, Wsh., Phi.	13	738	94	119	213	421	26	2	0	2	8	....	1990-91	2002-03
Sacharuk, Larry	NYR, St.L.	5	151	29	33	62	42	2	1	1	2	2	....	1972-73	1976-77
‡ Safronov, Kirill	Phx., Atl.	2	35	2	2	4	16	....	....	....	....	....	....	2001-02	2002-03
Saganiuk, Rocky	Tor., Pit.	6	259	57	65	122	201	6	1	0	1	15	....	1978-79	1983-84
Sakic, Joe	Que., Col.	20	1378	625	1016	1641	614	172	84	104	188	78	2	1988-89	2008-09
‡ Salcido, Brian	Ana.	1	2	0	1	1	0	....	....	....	....	....	....	2008-09	2008-09
• Salei, Ruslan	Ana., Fla., Col., Det.	14	917	45	159	204	1065	62	7	9	16	52	....	1996-97	2010-11
Saleski, Don	Phi., Col.	9	543	128	125	253	629	82	13	17	30	131	2	1971-72	1979-80
‡ Salmela, Anssi	N.J., Atl.	3	112	4	17	21	44	....	....	....	....	....	....	2008-09	2010-11
‡ Salmelainen, Tony	Edm., Chi.	2	70	6	12	18	30	....	....	....	....	....	....	2003-04	2006-07
Salming, Borje	Tor., Det.	17	1148	150	637	787	1344	81	12	37	49	91	....	1973-74	1989-90
Salomonsson, Andreas	N.J., Wsh.	2	71	5	9	14	36	4	0	1	1	0	....	2001-02	2002-03
Salovaara, Barry	Det.	2	90	2	13	15	70	....	....	....	....	....	....	1974-75	1975-76

Doug Roberts

George Robertson

Earl Robinson

Brian Rolston

Terry Ruskowski

Bernie Saunders

Maynard Schurman

Brit Selby

			Regular Schedule					Playoffs							
Name	NHL Teams	NHL Seasons	GP	G	A	TP	PIM	GP	G	A	TP	PIM	NHL Cup Wins	First NHL Season	Last NHL Season
Salvian, Dave	NYI	1	....	....	....	....	....	1	0	1	1	2	....	1976-77	1976-77
Samis, Phil	Tor.	2	2	0	0	0	0	5	0	1	1	2	1	1947-48	1949-50
Sampson, Gary	Wsh.	4	105	13	22	35	25	12	1	0	1	0	....	1983-84	1986-87
Samsonov, Sergei	Bos., Edm., Mtl., Chi., Car., Fla.	13	888	235	336	571	209	76	18	29	47	20	....	1997-98	2010-11
Samuelsson, Kjell	NYR, Phi., Pit., T.B.	14	813	48	138	186	1225	123	4	20	24	178	1	1985-86	1998-99
Samuelsson, Martin	Bos.	2	14	0	1	1	2	....	....	....	....	....	....	2002-03	2003-04
Samuelsson, Ulf	Hfd., Pit., NYR, Det., Phi.	16	1080	57	275	332	2453	132	7	27	34	272	2	1984-85	1999-00
Sandelin, Scott	Mtl., Phi., Min.	4	25	0	4	4	2	....	....	....	....	....	....	1986-87	1991-92
Sanderson, Derek	Bos., NYR, St.L., Van., Pit.	13	598	202	250	452	911	56	18	12	30	187	2	1965-66	1977-78
Sanderson, Geoff	Hfd., Car., Van., Buf., CBJ, Phx., Phi., Edm.	17	1104	355	345	700	511	55	9	10	19	32	....	1990-91	2007-08
Sandford, Ed	Bos., Det., Chi.	9	502	106	145	251	355	42	13	11	24	27	....	1947-48	1955-56
Sandlak, Jim	Van., Hfd.	11	549	110	119	229	821	33	7	10	17	30	....	1985-86	1995-96
● Sands, Charlie	Tor., Bos., Mtl., NYR	12	427	99	109	208	58	34	6	6	12	4	1	1932-33	1943-44
Sandstrom, Tomas	NYR, L.A., Pit., Det., Ana.	15	983	394	462	856	1193	139	32	49	81	183	1	1984-85	1998-99
Sandwith, Terran	Edm.	1	8	0	0	0	6	....	....	....	....	....	....	1997-98	1997-98
Sanipass, Everett	Chi., Que.	5	164	25	34	59	358	5	2	0	2	4	....	1986-87	1990-91
‡ Santala, Tommi	Atl., Van.	2	63	2	7	9	46	1	0	0	0	0	....	2003-04	2006-07
‡ Saprykin, Oleg	Cgy., Phx., Ott.	7	325	55	82	137	240	41	4	4	8	18	....	1999-00	2006-07
Sarault, Yves	Mtl., Cgy., Col., Ott., Atl., Nsh.	8	106	10	10	20	51	5	0	0	0	2	....	1994-95	2001-02
Sargent, Gary	L.A., Min.	8	402	61	161	222	273	20	5	7	12	8	....	1975-76	1982-83
Sarner, Craig	Bos.	1	7	0	0	0	0	....	....	....	....	....	....	1974-75	1974-75
Sarno, Peter	Edm., CBJ	2	7	1	0	1	2	....	....	....	....	....	....	2003-04	2005-06
Sarrazin, Dick	Phi.	3	100	20	35	55	22	4	0	0	0	0	....	1968-69	1971-72
Sasakamoose, Fred	Chi.	1	11	0	0	0	6	....	....	....	....	....	....	1953-54	1953-54
Sasser, Grant	Pit.	1	3	0	0	0	0	....	....	....	....	....	....	1983-84	1983-84
‡ Satan, Miroslav	Edm., Buf., NYI, Pit., Bos.	14	1050	363	372	735	464	86	21	33	54	41	1	1995-96	2009-10
Sather, Glen	Bos., Pit., NYR, St.L., Mtl., Min.	10	658	80	113	193	724	72	1	5	6	86	....	1966-67	1975-76
Sauer, Kurt	Ana., Col., Phx.	7	357	5	28	33	250	43	2	1	3	18	....	2002-03	2009-10
Saunders, Bernie	Que.	2	10	0	1	1	8	....	....	....	....	....	....	1979-80	1980-81
Saunders, David	Van.	1	56	7	13	20	10	....	....	....	....	....	....	1987-88	1987-88
● Saunders, Ted	Ott.	1	18	1	3	4	4	....	....	....	....	....	....	1933-34	1933-34
Sauve, Jean-Francois	Buf., Que.	7	290	65	138	203	114	36	9	12	21	10	....	1980-81	1986-87
Savage, Andre	Bos., Phi.	4	66	10	14	24	14	....	....	....	....	....	....	1998-99	2002-03
Savage, Brian	Mtl., Phx., St.L., Phi.	12	674	192	167	359	321	39	3	8	11	12	....	1993-94	2005-06
Savage, Joel	Buf.	1	3	0	1	1	0	....	....	....	....	....	....	1990-91	1990-91
Savage, Reggie	Wsh., Que.	3	34	5	7	12	28	....	....	....	....	....	....	1990-91	1993-94
● Savage, Tony	Bos., Mtl.	1	49	1	5	6	6	2	0	0	0	0	....	1934-35	1934-35
Savard, Andre	Bos., Buf., Que.	12	790	211	271	482	411	85	13	18	31	77	....	1973-74	1984-85
Savard, Denis	Chi., Mtl., T.B.	17	1196	473	865	1338	1336	169	66	109	175	256	1	1980-81	1996-97
Savard, Jean	Chi., Hfd.	3	43	7	12	19	29	....	....	....	....	....	....	1977-78	1979-80
Savard, Serge	Mtl., Wpg.	17	1040	106	333	439	592	130	19	49	68	88	8	1966-67	1982-83
Savoia, Ryan	Pit.	1	3	0	0	0	0	....	....	....	....	....	....	1998-99	1998-99
Sawyer, Kevin	St.L., Bos., Phx., Ana.	6	110	3	3	6	403	....	....	....	....	....	....	1995-96	2002-03
Scamurra, Peter	Wsh.	4	132	8	25	33	59	....	....	....	....	....	....	1975-76	1979-80
Scatchard, Dave	Van., NYI, Bos., Phx., Nsh., St.L.	11	659	128	141	269	1040	17	2	2	4	34	....	1997-98	2010-11
Sceviour, Darin	Chi.	1	1	0	0	0	0	....	....	....	....	....	....	1986-87	1986-87
Schaefer, Peter	Van., Ott., Bos.	9	572	99	162	261	200	63	6	18	24	34	....	1998-99	2010-11
● Schaeffer, Butch	Chi.	1	5	0	0	0	6	....	....	....	....	....	....	1936-37	1936-37
Schamehorn, Kevin	Det., L.A.	3	10	0	0	0	17	....	....	....	....	....	....	1976-77	1980-81
‡ Schastlivy, Petr	Ott., Ana.	5	129	18	22	40	30	1	0	0	0	0	....	1999-00	2003-04
Schella, John	Van.	2	115	2	18	20	224	....	....	....	....	....	....	1970-71	1971-72
Scherza, Chuck	Bos., NYR	2	36	6	6	12	35	....	....	....	....	....	....	1943-44	1944-45
Schinkel, Ken	NYR, Pit.	12	636	127	198	325	163	19	7	2	9	4	....	1959-60	1972-73
Schlegel, Brad	Wsh., Cgy.	3	48	1	8	9	10	7	0	1	1	2	....	1991-92	1993-94
Schliebener, Andy	Van.	3	84	2	11	13	74	6	0	0	0	0	....	1981-82	1984-85
Schmautz, Bobby	Chi., Van., Bos., Edm., Col.	13	764	271	286	557	988	84	28	33	61	92	....	1967-68	1980-81
● Schmautz, Cliff	Buf., Phi.	1	56	13	19	32	33	....	....	....	....	....	....	1970-71	1970-71
Schmidt, Chris	L.A.	1	10	0	2	2	5	....	....	....	....	....	....	2002-03	2002-03
● Schmidt, Clarence	Bos.	1	7	1	0	1	2	....	....	....	....	....	....	1943-44	1943-44
Schmidt, Jackie	Bos.	1	45	6	7	13	6	5	0	0	0	0	....	1942-43	1942-43
Schmidt, Milt	Bos.	16	776	229	346	575	466	86	24	25	49	60	2	1936-37	1954-55
Schmidt, Norm	Pit.	4	125	23	33	56	73	....	....	....	....	....	....	1983-84	1987-88
Schmidt, Otto	Bos.	1	2	0	0	0	0	....	....	....	....	....	....	1943-44	1943-44
‡ Schnabel, Robert	Nsh.	3	22	0	3	3	34	....	....	....	....	....	....	2001-02	2003-04
● Schnarr, Werner	Bos.	2	26	0	0	0	0	....	....	....	....	....	....	1924-25	1925-26
Schneider, Andy	Ott.	1	10	0	0	0	15	....	....	....	....	....	....	1993-94	1993-94
Schneider, Mathieu	Mtl., NYI, Tor., NYR, L.A., Det., Ana., Atl., Van., Phx.	21	1289	223	520	743	1245	114	11	43	54	155	1	1987-88	2009-10
Schock, Danny	Bos., Phi.	2	20	1	2	3	0	1	0	0	0	0	1	1969-70	1970-71
Schock, Ron	Bos., St.L., Pit., Buf.	15	909	166	351	517	260	55	4	16	20	29	....	1963-64	1977-78
Schoenfeld, Jim	Buf., Det., Bos.	13	719	51	204	255	1132	75	3	13	16	151	....	1972-73	1984-85
Schofield, Dwight	Det., Mtl., St.L., Wsh., Pit., Wpg.	7	211	8	22	30	631	9	0	0	0	55	....	1976-77	1987-88
Schreiber, Wally	Min.	2	41	8	10	18	12	....	....	....	....	....	....	1987-88	1988-89
‡ Schremp, Rob	Edm., NYI, Atl.	5	114	20	34	54	26	....	....	....	....	....	....	2006-07	2010-11
● Schriner, Sweeney	NYA, Tor.	11	484	201	204	405	148	59	18	11	29	54	2	1934-35	1945-46
‡ Schubert, Christoph	Ott., Atl.	5	315	25	47	72	263	31	0	2	2	34	....	2005-06	2009-10
Schulte, Paxton	Que., Cgy.	2	2	0	0	0	4	....	....	....	....	....	....	1993-94	1996-97
Schultz, Dave	Phi., L.A., Pit., Buf.	9	535	79	121	200	2294	73	8	12	20	412	2	1971-72	1979-80
‡ Schultz, Jesse	Van.	1	2	0	0	0	0	....	....	....	....	....	....	2006-07	2006-07
Schultz, Ray	NYI	6	45	0	4	4	155	2	0	0	0	2	....	1997-98	2002-03
Schurman, Maynard	Hfd.	1	7	0	0	0	0	....	....	....	....	....	....	1979-80	1979-80
Schutt, Rod	Mtl., Pit., Tor.	8	286	77	92	169	177	22	8	6	14	26	....	1977-78	1985-86
Scissons, Scott	NYI	3	2	0	0	0	0	1	0	0	0	0	....	1990-91	1993-94
● Sclisizzi, Enio	Det., Chi.	6	81	12	11	23	26	13	0	0	0	6	1	1946-47	1952-53
● Scott, Ganton	Tor., Ham., Mtl.M.	3	57	1	1	2	0	....	....	....	....	....	....	1922-23	1924-25
● Scott, Laurie	NYA, NYR	2	62	6	3	9	28	....	....	....	....	....	....	1926-27	1927-28
Scott, Richard	NYR	2	10	0	0	0	28	....	....	....	....	....	....	2001-02	2003-04
Scoville, Darrel	Cgy., CBJ	3	16	0	1	1	12	....	....	....	....	....	....	1999-00	2003-04
Scremin, Claudio	S.J.	2	17	0	1	1	29	....	....	....	....	....	....	1991-92	1992-93
Scruton, Howard	L.A.	1	4	0	4	4	9	....	....	....	....	....	....	1982-83	1982-83
Seabrooke, Glen	Phi.	3	19	1	6	7	4	....	....	....	....	....	....	1986-87	1988-89
Secord, Al	Bos., Chi., Tor., Phi.	12	766	273	222	495	2093	102	21	34	55	382	....	1978-79	1989-90
Sedlbauer, Ron	Van., Chi., Tor.	7	430	143	86	229	210	19	1	3	4	27	....	1974-75	1980-81
Seftel, Steve	Wsh.	1	4	0	0	0	2	....	....	....	....	....	....	1990-91	1990-91
Seguin, Dan	Min., Van.	2	37	2	6	8	50	....	....	....	....	....	....	1970-71	1973-74
Seguin, Steve	L.A.	1	5	0	0	0	9	....	....	....	....	....	....	1984-85	1984-85
● Seibert, Earl	NYR, Chi., Det.	15	645	89	187	276	746	66	11	8	19	76	2	1931-32	1945-46
Seiling, Ric	Buf., Det.	10	738	179	208	387	573	62	14	14	28	36	....	1977-78	1986-87
Seiling, Rod	Tor., NYR, Wsh., St.L., Atl.	17	979	62	269	331	601	77	4	8	12	55	....	1962-63	1978-79
Sejba, Jiri	Buf.	1	11	0	2	2	8	....	....	....	....	....	....	1990-91	1990-91
‡ Sejna, Peter	St.L.	4	49	7	4	11	12	....	....	....	....	....	....	2002-03	2006-07
Sekeras, Lubomir	Min., Dal.	4	213	18	53	71	122	15	1	1	2	6	....	2000-01	2003-04
Selby, Brit	Tor., Phi., St.L.	8	350	55	62	117	163	16	1	1	2	8	....	1964-65	1971-72
Self, Steve	Wsh.	1	3	0	0	0	0	....	....	....	....	....	....	1976-77	1976-77
Selivanov, Alex	T.B., Edm., CBJ	7	459	121	114	235	379	13	2	3	5	16	....	1994-95	2000-01
Sellars, Luke	Atl.	1	1	0	0	0	2	....	....	....	....	....	....	2001-02	2001-02
Selmser, Sean	CBJ	1	1	0	0	0	5	....	....	....	....	....	....	2000-01	2000-01
Selwood, Brad	Tor., L.A.	3	163	7	40	47	153	6	0	0	0	4	....	1970-71	1979-80
Semak, Alexander	N.J., T.B., NYI, Van.	6	289	83	91	174	187	8	1	1	2	0	....	1991-92	1996-97
Semchuk, Brandy	L.A.	1	1	0	0	0	2	....	....	....	....	....	....	1992-93	1992-93
Semenko, Dave	Edm., Hfd., Tor.	9	575	65	88	153	1175	73	6	6	12	208	2	1979-80	1987-88
‡ Semenov, Alexei	Edm., Fla., S.J.	6	211	7	26	33	249	8	0	0	0	2	....	2002-03	2008-09
Semenov, Anatoli	Edm., T.B., Van., Ana., Phi., Buf.	8	362	68	126	194	122	49	9	13	22	12	....	1989-90	1996-97
● Senick, George	NYR	1	13	2	3	5	8	....	....	....	....	....	....	1952-53	1952-53
Seppa, Jyrki	Wpg.	1	13	0	2	2	6	....	....	....	....	....	....	1983-84	1983-84
Serafini, Ron	Cal.	1	2	0	0	0	2	....	....	....	....	....	....	1973-74	1973-74
Serowik, Jeff	Tor., Bos., Pit.	3	28	0	6	6	16	....	....	....	....	....	....	1990-91	1998-99
Servinis, George	Min.	1	5	0	0	0	0	....	....	....	....	....	....	1987-88	1987-88
Sevcik, Jaroslav	Que.	1	13	0	2	2	2	....	....	....	....	....	....	1989-90	1989-90
Severson, Cam	Ana., CBJ	3	37	3	0	3	63	1	0	0	0	0	....	2002-03	2005-06
Severyn, Brent	Que., Fla., NYI, Col., Ana., Dal.	7	328	10	30	40	825	8	0	0	0	12	1	1989-90	1998-99
Sevigny, Pierre	Mtl., NYR	4	78	4	5	9	64	3	0	1	1	0	....	1993-94	1997-98
Shack, Eddie	NYR, Tor., Bos., L.A., Buf., Pit.	17	1047	239	226	465	1437	74	6	7	13	151	4	1958-59	1974-75
● Shack, Joe	NYR	2	70	9	27	36	20	....	....	....	....	....	....	1942-43	1944-45
Shafranov, Konstantin	St.L.	1	5	2	1	3	0	....	....	....	....	....	....	1996-97	1996-97

Name	NHL Teams	NHL Seasons	Regular Schedule GP	G	A	TP	PIM	Playoffs GP	G	A	TP	PIM	NHL Cup Wins	First NHL Season	Last NHL Season
Shakes, Paul	Cal.	1	21	0	4	4	12	....	....	....	....	....	....	1973-74	1973-74
Shaldybin, Yevgeny	Bos.	1	3	1	0	1	0	....	....	....	....	....	....	1996-97	1996-97
Shanahan, Brendan	N.J., St.L., Hfd., Det., NYR	21	1524	656	698	1354	2489	184	60	74	134	279	3	1987-88	2008-09
Shanahan, Sean	Mtl., Col., Bos.	3	40	1	3	4	47	....	....	....	....	....	....	1975-76	1977-78
Shand, Dave	Atl., Tor., Wsh.	8	421	19	84	103	544	26	1	2	3	83	....	1976-77	1984-85
Shank, Daniel	Det., Hfd.	3	77	13	14	27	175	5	0	0	0	22	....	1989-90	1991-92
● Shannon, Chuck	NYA	1	4	0	0	0	2	....	....	....	....	....	....	1939-40	1939-40
Shannon, Darrin	Buf., Wpg., Phx.	10	506	87	163	250	344	45	7	10	17	38	....	1988-89	1997-98
Shannon, Darryl	Tor., Wpg., Buf., Atl., Cgy., Mtl.	13	544	28	111	139	523	29	4	7	11	16	....	1988-89	2000-01
● Shannon, Gerry	Ott., St.L., Bos., Mtl.M.	5	180	23	29	52	80	9	0	1	1	2	....	1933-34	1937-38
Shantz, Jeff	Chi., Cgy., Col.	10	642	72	139	211	341	44	5	8	13	24	....	1993-94	2002-03
Sharifijanov, Vadim	N.J., Van.	3	92	16	21	37	50	4	0	0	0	0	....	1996-97	1999-00
‡ Sharp, MacGregor	Ana.	1	8	0	0	0	0	....	....	....	....	....	....	2009-10	2009-10
Sharples, Jeff	Det.	3	105	14	35	49	70	7	0	3	3	6	....	1986-87	1988-89
Sharpley, Glen	Min., Chi.	6	389	117	161	278	199	27	7	11	18	24	....	1976-77	1981-82
Shaunessy, Scott	Que.	2	7	0	0	0	23	....	....	....	....	....	....	1986-87	1988-89
Shaw, Brad	Hfd., Ott., Wsh., St.L.	11	377	22	137	159	208	23	4	8	12	6	....	1985-86	1998-99
Shaw, David	Que., NYR, Edm., Min., Bos., T.B.	16	769	41	153	194	906	45	3	9	12	81	....	1982-83	1997-98
● Shay, Norm	Bos., Tor.	2	53	5	3	8	34	....	....	....	....	....	....	1924-25	1925-26
● Shea, Pat	Chi.	1	10	1	0	1	0	....	....	....	....	....	....	1931-32	1931-32
Shearer, Rob	Col.	1	2	0	0	0	0	....	....	....	....	....	....	2000-01	2000-01
Shedden, Doug	Pit., Det., Que., Tor.	8	416	139	186	325	176	....	....	....	....	....	....	1981-82	1990-91
Sheehan, Bobby	Mtl., Cal., Chi., Det., NYR, Col., L.A.	9	310	48	63	111	40	25	4	3	7	8	1	1969-70	1981-82
Sheehy, Neil	Cgy., Hfd., Wsh.	9	379	18	47	65	1311	54	0	3	3	241	....	1983-84	1991-92
Sheehy, Tim	Det., Hfd.	2	27	2	1	3	0	....	....	....	....	....	....	1977-78	1979-80
Shelton, Doug	Chi.	1	5	0	1	1	2	....	....	....	....	....	....	1967-68	1967-68
● Sheppard, Frank	Det.	1	8	1	1	2	0	....	....	....	....	....	....	1927-28	1927-28
Sheppard, Gregg	Bos., Pit.	10	657	205	293	498	243	82	32	40	72	31	....	1972-73	1981-82
● Sheppard, Johnny	Det., NYA, Bos., Chi.	8	308	68	58	126	224	10	0	0	0	0	1	1926-27	1933-34
Sheppard, Ray	Buf., NYR, Det., S.J., Fla., Car.	13	817	357	300	657	212	81	30	20	50	21	....	1987-88	1999-00
● Sherf, John	Det.	5	19	0	0	0	8	8	0	1	1	2	1	1935-36	1943-44
● Shero, Fred	NYR	3	145	6	14	20	137	13	0	2	2	8	....	1947-48	1949-50
● Sherritt, Gordon	Det.	1	8	0	0	0	12	....	....	....	....	....	....	1943-44	1943-44
Sherven, Gord	Edm., Min., Hfd.	5	97	13	22	35	33	3	0	0	0	0	....	1983-84	1987-88
Shevalier, Jeff	L.A., T.B.	3	32	5	9	14	8	....	....	....	....	....	....	1994-95	1999-00
● Shewchuk, Jack	Bos.	6	187	9	19	28	160	20	0	1	1	19	1	1938-39	1944-45
● Shibicky, Alex	NYR	8	324	110	91	201	161	39	12	12	24	12	1	1935-36	1945-46
● Shields, Al	Ott., Phi., NYA, Mtl.M., Bos.	11	459	42	46	88	637	17	0	1	1	14	1	1927-28	1937-38
● Shill, Bill	Bos.	3	79	21	13	34	18	7	1	2	3	2	....	1942-43	1946-47
● Shill, Jack	Tor., Bos., NYA, Chi.	6	160	15	20	35	70	25	1	6	7	23	1	1933-34	1938-39
Shinske, Rick	Cle., St.L.	3	63	5	16	21	10	....	....	....	....	....	....	1976-77	1978-79
Shires, Jim	Det., St.L., Pit.	3	56	3	6	9	32	....	....	....	....	....	....	1970-71	1972-73
‡ Shishkanov, Timofei	Nsh., St.L.	2	24	3	2	5	6	....	....	....	....	....	....	2003-04	2005-06
● Shmyr, Paul	Chi., Cal., Min., Hfd.	7	343	13	72	85	528	34	3	3	6	44	....	1968-69	1981-82
Shoebottom, Bruce	Bos.	4	35	1	4	5	53	14	1	2	3	77	....	1987-88	1990-91
● Shore, Eddie	Bos., NYA	14	550	105	179	284	1047	55	7	12	19	181	2	1926-27	1939-40
● Shore, Hamby	Ott.	1	18	3	8	11	51	....	....	....	....	....	....	1917-18	1917-18
Short, Steve	L.A., Det.	2	6	0	0	0	2	....	....	....	....	....	....	1977-78	1978-79
Shuchuk, Gary	Det., L.A.	5	142	13	26	39	70	20	2	2	4	12	....	1990-91	1995-96
Shudra, Ron	Edm.	1	10	0	5	5	6	....	....	....	....	....	....	1987-88	1987-88
Shutt, Steve	Mtl., L.A.	13	930	424	393	817	410	99	50	48	98	65	5	1972-73	1984-85
Shvidki, Denis	Fla.	4	76	11	14	25	30	....	....	....	....	....	....	2000-01	2003-04
● Siebert, Babe	Mtl.M., NYR, Bos., Mtl.	14	592	140	156	296	982	49	7	5	12	62	2	1925-26	1938-39
‡ Sifers, Jaime	Tor., Min.	2	37	0	2	2	24	....	....	....	....	....	....	2008-09	2009-10
‡ Sigalet, Jonathan	Bos.	1	1	0	0	0	4	....	....	....	....	....	....	2006-07	2006-07
‡ Siklenka, Mike	Phi., NYR	2	2	0	0	0	0	....	....	....	....	....	....	2002-03	2003-04
Silk, Dave	NYR, Bos., Det., Wpg.	7	249	54	59	113	271	13	2	4	6	13	....	1979-80	1985-86
Sillinger, Mike	Det., Ana., Van., Phi., T.B., Fla., Ott., CBJ, Phx., St.L., Nsh., NYI	18	1049	240	308	548	644	43	11	7	18	28	....	1990-91	2008-09
Siltala, Mike	Wsh., NYR	3	7	1	0	1	2	....	....	....	....	....	....	1981-82	1987-88
Siltanen, Risto	Edm., Hfd., Que.	8	562	90	265	355	266	32	6	12	18	30	....	1979-80	1986-87
Sim, Trevor	Edm.	1	3	0	1	1	2	....	....	....	....	....	....	1989-90	1989-90
Simard, Martin	Cgy., T.B.	3	44	1	5	6	183	....	....	....	....	....	....	1990-91	1992-93
Simicek, Roman	Pit., Min.	2	63	7	10	17	59	....	....	....	....	....	....	2000-01	2001-02
Simmer, Charlie	Cal., Cle., L.A., Bos., Pit.	14	712	342	369	711	544	24	9	9	18	32	....	1974-75	1987-88
Simmons, Al	Cal., Bos.	3	11	0	1	1	21	1	0	0	0	0	....	1971-72	1975-76
Simon, Ben	Atl., CBJ	4	81	3	1	4	47	....	....	....	....	....	....	2001-02	2005-06
‡ Simon, Chris	Que., Col., Wsh., Chi., NYR, Cgy., NYI, Min.	15	782	144	161	305	1824	75	10	7	17	191	1	1992-93	2007-08
● Simon, Cully	Det., Chi.	3	130	4	11	15	121	14	1	0	1	6	1	1942-43	1944-45
Simon, Jason	NYI, Phx.	2	5	0	0	0	34	....	....	....	....	....	....	1993-94	1996-97
● Simon, Thain	Det.	1	3	0	0	0	0	....	....	....	....	....	....	1946-47	1946-47
Simon, Todd	Buf.	1	15	0	1	1	0	5	1	0	1	0	....	1993-94	1993-94
Simonetti, Frank	Bos.	4	115	5	8	13	76	12	0	1	1	8	....	1984-85	1987-88
Simpson, Bobby	Atl., St.L., Pit.	5	175	35	29	64	98	6	0	1	1	2	....	1976-77	1982-83
● Simpson, Cliff	Det.	2	6	0	1	1	0	2	0	0	0	2	....	1946-47	1947-48
Simpson, Craig	Pit., Edm., Buf.	10	634	247	250	497	659	67	36	32	68	56	2	1985-86	1994-95
● Simpson, Joe	NYA	6	228	21	19	40	156	2	0	0	0	0	....	1925-26	1930-31
Simpson, Reid	Phi., Min., N.J., Chi., T.B., St.L., Mtl., Nsh., Pit.	12	301	18	18	36	838	10	0	0	0	31	....	1991-92	2003-04
Simpson, Todd	Cgy., Fla., Phx., Ana., Ott., Chi., Mtl.	10	580	14	63	77	1357	9	0	2	2	10	....	1995-96	2005-06
Sims, Al	Bos., Hfd., L.A.	10	475	49	116	165	286	41	0	2	2	14	....	1973-74	1982-83
‡ Sims, Shane	NYI	1	1	0	0	0	0	....	....	....	....	....	....	2010-11	2010-11
Sinclair, Reg	NYR, Det.	3	208	49	43	92	139	3	1	0	1	0	....	1950-51	1952-53
● Singbush, Alex	Mtl.	1	32	0	5	5	15	3	0	0	0	4	....	1940-41	1940-41
Sinisalo, Ilkka	Phi., Min., L.A.	11	582	204	222	426	208	68	21	11	32	6	....	1981-82	1991-92
Siren, Ville	Pit., Min.	5	290	14	68	82	276	7	0	0	0	6	....	1985-86	1989-90
Sirois, Bob	Phi., Wsh.	6	286	92	120	212	42	....	....	....	....	....	....	1974-75	1979-80
Sittler, Darryl	Tor., Phi., Det.	15	1096	484	637	1121	948	76	29	45	74	137	....	1970-71	1984-85
Sivek, Michal	Pit.	1	38	3	3	6	14	....	....	....	....	....	....	2002-03	2002-03
● Sjoberg, Lars-Erik	Wpg.	1	79	7	27	34	48	....	....	....	....	....	....	1979-80	1979-80
Sjodin, Tommy	Min., Dal., Que.	2	106	8	40	48	52	....	....	....	....	....	....	1992-93	1993-94
‡ Sjostrom, Fredrik	Phx., NYR, Cgy., Tor.	7	489	46	58	104	190	17	0	2	2	2	....	2003-04	2010-11
● Skaare, Bjorn	Det.	1	1	0	0	0	0	....	....	....	....	....	....	1978-79	1978-79
Skalde, Jarrod	N.J., Ana., Cgy., S.J., Chi., Dal., Atl., Phi.	9	115	13	21	34	62	....	....	....	....	....	....	1990-91	2001-02
Skarda, Randy	St.L.	2	26	0	5	5	11	....	....	....	....	....	....	1989-90	1991-92
● Skilton, Raymie	Mtl.W.	1	1	0	0	0	0	....	....	....	....	....	....	1917-18	1917-18
● Skinner, Alf	Tor., Bos., Mtl.M., Pit.	4	71	26	10	36	87	2	0	1	1	9	1	1917-18	1925-26
‡ Skinner, Brett	NYI	1	11	0	0	0	4	....	....	....	....	....	....	2008-09	2008-09
Skinner, Larry	Col.	4	47	10	12	22	8	2	0	0	0	0	....	1976-77	1979-80
Skolney, Wade	Phi.	1	1	0	0	0	2	....	....	....	....	....	....	2005-06	2005-06
‡ Skopintsev, Andrei	T.B., Atl.	3	40	2	4	6	32	....	....	....	....	....	....	1998-99	2000-01
‡ Skoula, Martin	Col., Ana., Dal., Min., Pit., N.J.	10	776	44	152	196	328	83	1	13	14	22	1	1999-00	2009-10
Skov, Glen	Det., Chi., Mtl.	12	650	106	136	242	413	53	7	7	14	48	3	1949-50	1960-61
● Skrastins, Karlis	Nsh., Col., Fla., Dal.	12	832	32	104	136	375	20	0	3	3	12	....	1998-99	2010-11
‡ Skrbek, Pavel	Pit., Nsh.	3	12	0	0	0	8	....	....	....	....	....	....	1998-99	2001-02
Skriko, Petri	Van., Bos., Wpg., S.J.	9	541	183	222	405	246	28	5	9	14	4	....	1984-85	1992-93
Skrlac, Rob	N.J.	1	8	1	0	1	22	....	....	....	....	....	....	2003-04	2003-04
Skrudland, Brian	Mtl., Cgy., Fla., NYR, Dal.	15	881	124	219	343	1107	164	15	46	61	323	2	1985-86	1999-00
Slaney, John	Wsh., Col., L.A., Phx., Nsh., Pit., Phi.	9	268	22	69	91	99	14	2	1	3	4	....	1993-94	2003-04
● Sleaver, John	Chi.	2	13	1	0	1	6	....	....	....	....	....	....	1953-54	1956-57
Slegr, Jiri	Van., Edm., Pit., Atl., Det., Bos.	11	622	56	193	249	838	42	4	14	18	39	1	1992-93	2005-06
Sleigher, Louis	Que., Bos.	6	194	46	53	99	146	17	1	1	2	64	....	1979-80	1985-86
‡ Sloan, Blake	Dal., CBJ, Cgy.	6	290	11	32	43	162	35	0	2	2	20	1	1998-99	2003-04
Sloan, Tod	Tor., Chi.	13	745	220	262	482	831	47	9	12	21	47	2	1947-48	1960-61
Sloane, David	Phi.	1	1	0	0	0	0	....	....	....	....	....	....	2008-09	2008-09
● Slobodian, Peter	NYA	1	41	3	2	5	54	....	....	....	....	....	....	1940-41	1940-41
● Slowinski, Ed	NYR	6	291	58	74	132	63	16	2	6	8	6	....	1947-48	1952-53
● Sly, Darryl	Tor., Min., Van.	4	79	1	2	3	20	....	....	....	....	....	....	1965-66	1970-71
‡ Smaby, Matt	T.B.	4	122	0	6	6	106	....	....	....	....	....	....	2007-08	2010-11
Smail, Doug	Wpg., Min., Que., Ott.	13	845	210	249	459	602	42	9	2	11	49	....	1980-81	1992-93
● Smart, Alex	Mtl.	1	8	5	2	7	0	....	....	....	....	....	....	1942-43	1942-43
Smedsmo, Dale	Tor.	1	4	0	0	0	0	....	....	....	....	....	....	1972-73	1972-73
Smehlik, Richard	Buf., Atl., N.J.	10	644	49	146	195	415	88	1	14	15	40	1	1992-93	2002-03

Jeff Sharples

Alex Smith

Wayne Smith

Art Somers

Tom Songin

Steve Staios

Jack Stanfield

Anton Stastny

			Regular Schedule					Playoffs							
Name	NHL Teams	NHL Seasons	GP	G	A	TP	PIM	GP	G	A	TP	PIM	NHL Cup Wins	First NHL Season	Last NHL Season
• Smillie, Don	Bos.	1	12	2	2	4	4	....	....	....	....	....	....	1933-34	1933-34
Smirnov, Alexei	Ana.	2	52	3	3	6	20	4	0	0	0	2	....	2002-03	2003-04
• Smith, Alex	Ott., Det., Bos., NYA	11	443	41	50	91	645	19	0	2	2	26	1	1924-25	1934-35
• Smith, Art	Tor., Ott.	4	144	15	10	25	249	4	1	1	2	8	....	1927-28	1930-31
Smith, Barry	Bos., Col.	3	114	7	7	14	10	....	....	....	....	....	....	1975-76	1980-81
Smith, Bobby	Min., Mtl.	15	1077	357	679	1036	917	184	64	96	160	245	1	1978-79	1992-93
Smith, Brad	Van., Atl., Cgy., Det., Tor.	9	222	28	34	62	591	20	3	3	6	49	....	1978-79	1986-87
Smith, Brandon	Bos., NYI	4	33	3	4	7	10	....	....	....	....	....	....	1998-99	2002-03
Smith, Brian	Det.	3	61	2	8	10	12	5	0	0	0	0	....	1957-58	1960-61
• Smith, Brian	L.A., Min.	2	67	10	10	20	33	7	0	0	0	0	....	1967-68	1968-69
• Smith, Carl	Det.	1	7	1	1	2	2	....	....	....	....	....	....	1943-44	1943-44
• Smith, Clint	NYR, Chi.	11	483	161	236	397	24	42	10	14	24	2	1	1936-37	1946-47
Smith, D.J.	Tor., Col.	3	45	1	1	2	67	....	....	....	....	....	....	1996-97	2002-03
Smith, Dallas	Bos., NYR	16	890	55	252	307	959	86	3	29	32	128	2	1959-60	1977-78
Smith, Dan	Col., Edm.	3	22	0	0	0	16	....	....	....	....	....	....	1998-99	2005-06
Smith, Dennis	Wsh., L.A.	2	8	0	0	0	4	....	....	....	....	....	....	1989-90	1990-91
Smith, Derek	Buf., Det.	8	335	78	116	194	60	30	9	14	23	13	....	1975-76	1982-83
Smith, Derrick	Phi., Min., Dal.	10	537	82	92	174	373	82	14	11	25	79	....	1984-85	1993-94
• Smith, Des	Mtl.M., Mtl., Chi., Bos.	5	196	22	25	47	236	25	1	4	5	18	1	1937-38	1941-42
• Smith, Don	Mtl.	1	12	1	0	1	6	....	....	....	....	....	....	1919-20	1919-20
• Smith, Don	NYR	1	11	1	1	2	0	1	0	0	0	0	....	1949-50	1949-50
Smith, Doug	L.A., Buf., Edm., Van., Pit.	9	535	115	138	253	624	18	4	2	6	21	....	1981-82	1989-90
Smith, Floyd	Bos., NYR, Det., Tor., Buf.	13	616	129	178	307	207	48	12	11	23	16	....	1954-55	1971-72
Smith, Geoff	Edm., Fla., NYR	10	462	18	73	91	282	13	0	1	1	8	1	1989-90	1998-99
Smith, Glen	Chi.	1	2	0	0	0	0	....	....	....	....	....	....	1950-51	1950-51
• Smith, Glenn	Tor.	1	9	0	0	0	0	....	....	....	....	....	....	1921-22	1921-22
Smith, Gord	Wsh., Wpg.	6	299	9	30	39	284	....	....	....	....	....	....	1974-75	1979-80
Smith, Greg	Cal., Cle., Min., Det., Wsh.	13	829	56	232	288	1110	63	4	7	11	106	....	1975-76	1987-88
• Smith, Hooley	Ott., Mtl.M., Bos., NYA	17	715	200	225	425	1013	54	11	8	19	109	2	1924-25	1940-41
Smith, Jason	N.J., Tor., Edm., Phi., Ott.	15	1008	41	128	169	1099	68	1	10	11	60	....	1993-94	2008-09
• Smith, Ken	Bos.	7	331	78	93	171	49	30	8	13	21	6	....	1944-45	1950-51
Smith, Mark	S.J., Cgy.	7	377	23	47	70	457	24	4	0	4	21	....	2000-01	2007-08
• Smith, Nakina	Det.	1	10	1	2	3	0	....	....	....	....	....	....	1943-44	1943-44
Smith, Nathan	Van., Pit., Min.	5	26	0	0	0	14	4	0	0	0	0	....	2003-04	2009-10
Smith, Nick	Fla.	1	15	0	0	0	0	....	....	....	....	....	....	2001-02	2001-02
Smith, Randy	Min.	2	3	0	0	0	0	....	....	....	....	....	....	1985-86	1986-87
Smith, Rick	Bos., Cal., St.L., Det., Wsh.	11	687	52	167	219	560	78	3	23	26	73	1	1968-69	1980-81
• Smith, Rodger	Pit., Phi.	6	210	20	4	24	172	4	3	0	3	0	....	1925-26	1930-31
Smith, Ron	NYI	1	11	1	1	2	14	....	....	....	....	....	....	1972-73	1972-73
• Smith, Sid	Tor.	12	601	186	183	369	94	44	17	10	27	2	3	1946-47	1957-58
Smith, Stan	NYR	2	9	2	1	3	0	1	0	0	0	0	1	1939-40	1940-41
Smith, Steve	Phi., Buf.	6	18	0	1	1	15	....	....	....	....	....	....	1981-82	1988-89
Smith, Steve	Edm., Chi., Cgy.	16	804	72	303	375	2139	134	11	41	52	288	3	1984-85	2000-01
Smith, Stu	Mtl.	2	4	2	2	4	2	1	0	0	0	0	....	1940-41	1941-42
Smith, Stu	Hfd.	4	77	2	10	12	95	....	....	....	....	....	....	1979-80	1982-83
• Smith, Tommy	Que.	1	10	0	1	1	11	....	....	....	....	....	....	1919-20	1919-20
Smith, Vern	NYI	1	1	0	0	0	0	....	....	....	....	....	....	1984-85	1984-85
Smith, Wayne	Chi.	1	2	1	1	2	2	1	0	0	0	0	....	1966-67	1966-67
Smith, Wyatt	Phx., Nsh., NYI, Min., Col.	8	211	10	22	32	65	5	0	0	0	0	....	1999-00	2007-08
‡ Smolenak, Radek	T.B., Chi.	2	7	0	1	1	15	....	....	....	....	....	....	2008-09	2009-10
Smolinski, Bryan	Bos., Pit., NYI, L.A., Ott., Chi., Van., Mtl.	15	1056	274	377	651	606	123	23	29	52	60	....	1992-93	2007-08
‡ Smotherman, Jordan	Atl.	2	4	1	1	2	0	....	....	....	....	....	....	2007-08	2008-09
Smrek, Peter	St.L., NYR	2	28	2	4	6	18	....	....	....	....	....	....	2000-01	2001-02
Smrke, John	St.L., Que.	3	103	11	17	28	33	....	....	....	....	....	....	1977-78	1979-80
• Smrke, Stan	Mtl.	2	9	0	3	3	0	....	....	....	....	....	....	1956-57	1957-58
Smyl, Stan	Van.	13	896	262	411	673	1556	41	16	17	33	64	....	1978-79	1990-91
• Smylie, Rod	Tor., Ott.	6	74	4	2	6	12	4	0	0	0	2	1	1920-21	1925-26
‡ Smyth, Brad	Fla., L.A., NYR, Nsh., Ott.	6	88	15	13	28	109	....	....	....	....	....	....	1995-96	2002-03
Smyth, Greg	Phi., Que., Cgy., Fla., Tor., Chi.	10	229	4	16	20	783	12	0	0	0	40	....	1986-87	1996-97
Smyth, Kevin	Hfd.	3	58	6	8	14	31	....	....	....	....	....	....	1993-94	1995-96
Snell, Chris	Tor., L.A.	2	34	2	7	9	24	....	....	....	....	....	....	1993-94	1994-95
Snell, Ron	Pit.	2	7	3	2	5	6	....	....	....	....	....	....	1968-69	1969-70
Snell, Ted	Pit., K.C., Det.	2	104	7	18	25	22	....	....	....	....	....	....	1973-74	1974-75
Snepsts, Harold	Van., Min., Det., St.L.	17	1033	38	195	233	2009	93	1	14	15	231	....	1974-75	1990-91
Snow, Sandy	Det.	1	3	0	0	0	2	....	....	....	....	....	....	1968-69	1968-69
Snuggerud, Dave	Buf., S.J., Phi.	4	265	30	54	84	127	12	1	3	4	6	....	1989-90	1992-93
• Snyder, Dan	Atl.	3	49	11	5	16	64	....	....	....	....	....	....	2000-01	2002-03
Sobchuk, Dennis	Det., Que.	2	35	5	6	11	2	....	....	....	....	....	....	1979-80	1982-83
Sobchuk, Gene	Van.	1	1	0	0	0	0	....	....	....	....	....	....	1973-74	1973-74
Solheim, Ken	Chi., Min., Det., Edm.	5	135	19	20	39	34	3	1	1	2	2	....	1980-81	1985-86
Solinger, Bob	Tor., Det.	5	99	10	11	21	19	....	....	....	....	....	....	1951-52	1959-60
• Somers, Art	Chi., NYR	6	222	33	56	89	189	30	1	5	6	20	1	1929-30	1934-35
‡ Somik, Radovan	Phi.	2	113	12	20	32	27	15	2	2	4	10	....	2002-03	2003-04
Sommer, Roy	Edm.	1	3	1	0	1	7	....	....	....	....	....	....	1980-81	1980-81
Songin, Tom	Bos.	3	43	5	5	10	22	....	....	....	....	....	....	1978-79	1980-81
Sonmor, Glen	NYR	2	28	2	0	2	21	....	....	....	....	....	....	1953-54	1954-55
Sonnenberg, Martin	Pit., Cgy.	3	63	2	3	5	21	7	0	0	0	0	....	1998-99	2003-04
Sorochan, Lee	Cgy.	2	3	0	0	0	0	....	....	....	....	....	....	1998-99	1999-00
• Sorrell, John	Det., NYA	11	490	127	119	246	100	42	12	15	27	10	2	1930-31	1940-41
Spacek, Jaroslav	Fla., Chi., CBJ, Edm., Buf., Mtl., Car.	13	880	82	273	355	618	61	4	14	18	44	....	1998-99	2011-12
Spanhel, Martin	CBJ	2	10	2	0	2	4	....	....	....	....	....	....	2000-01	2001-02
• Sparrow, Emory	Bos.	1	8	0	0	0	4	....	....	....	....	....	....	1924-25	1924-25
• Speck, Fred	Det., Van.	3	28	1	2	3	2	....	....	....	....	....	....	1968-69	1971-72
• Speer, Bill	Pit., Bos.	4	130	5	20	25	79	8	1	0	1	4	1	1967-68	1970-71
Speers, Ted	Det.	1	4	1	1	2	0	....	....	....	....	....	....	1985-86	1985-86
• Spence, Gordon	Tor.	1	3	0	0	0	0	....	....	....	....	....	....	1925-26	1925-26
• Spencer, Brian	Tor., NYI, Buf., Pit.	10	553	80	143	223	634	37	1	5	6	29	....	1969-70	1978-79
• Spencer, Irv	NYR, Bos., Det.	8	230	12	38	50	127	16	0	0	0	8	....	1959-60	1967-68
• Speyer, Chris	Tor., NYA	3	14	0	0	0	0	....	....	....	....	....	....	1923-24	1933-34
Spiller, Matthew	Phx., NYI	3	68	0	2	2	74	....	....	....	....	....	....	2003-04	2007-08
Spring, Corey	T.B.	2	16	1	1	2	12	....	....	....	....	....	....	1997-98	1998-99
Spring, Don	Wpg.	4	259	1	54	55	80	6	0	0	0	10	....	1980-81	1983-84
Spring, Frank	Bos., St.L., Cal., Cle.	5	61	14	20	34	12	....	....	....	....	....	....	1969-70	1976-77
• Spring, Jesse	Ham., Pit., Tor., NYA	6	133	11	4	15	74	2	0	2	2	2	....	1923-24	1929-30
Spruce, Andy	Van., Col.	3	172	31	42	73	111	2	0	2	2	0	....	1976-77	1978-79
‡ Sprukts, Janis	Fla.	2	14	1	2	3	2	....	....	....	....	....	....	2006-07	2008-09
Srsen, Tomas	Edm.	1	2	0	0	0	0	....	....	....	....	....	....	1990-91	1990-91
St. Amour, Martin	Ott.	1	1	0	0	0	2	....	....	....	....	....	....	1992-93	1992-93
‡ St. Jacques, Bruno	Phi., Car., Ana.	4	67	3	7	10	47	....	....	....	....	....	....	2001-02	2005-06
St. Laurent, Andre	NYI, Det., L.A., Pit.	11	644	129	187	316	749	59	8	12	20	48	....	1973-74	1983-84
St. Laurent, Dollard	Mtl., Chi.	12	652	29	133	162	496	92	2	22	24	87	5	1950-51	1961-62
St. Marseille, Frank	St.L., L.A.	10	707	140	285	425	242	88	20	25	45	18	....	1967-68	1976-77
St. Sauveur, Claude	Atl.	1	79	24	24	48	23	2	0	0	0	0	....	1975-76	1975-76
Stackhouse, Ron	Cal., Det., Pit.	12	889	87	372	459	824	32	5	8	13	38	....	1970-71	1981-82
• Stackhouse, Ted	Tor.	1	13	0	0	0	2	1	0	0	0	0	1	1921-22	1921-22
• Stahan, Butch	Mtl.	1	....	....	....	....	....	3	0	1	1	2	....	1944-45	1944-45
‡ Staios, Steve	Bos., Van., Atl., Edm., Cgy., NYI	16	1001	56	164	220	1322	33	1	5	6	32	....	1995-96	2011-12
Stajduhar, Nick	Edm.	1	2	0	0	0	4	....	....	....	....	....	....	1995-96	1995-96
Staley, Al	NYR	1	1	0	1	1	0	....	....	....	....	....	....	1948-49	1948-49
Stamler, Lorne	L.A., Tor., Wpg.	4	116	14	11	25	16	....	....	....	....	....	....	1976-77	1979-80
Standing, George	Min.	1	2	0	0	0	0	....	....	....	....	....	....	1967-68	1967-68
Stanfield, Fred	Chi., Bos., Min., Buf.	14	914	211	405	616	134	106	21	35	56	10	2	1964-65	1977-78
Stanfield, Jack	Chi.	1	....	....	....	....	....	1	0	0	0	0	....	1965-66	1965-66
• Stanfield, Jim	L.A.	3	7	0	1	1	0	....	....	....	....	....	....	1969-70	1971-72
Stankiewicz, Ed	Det.	2	6	0	0	0	2	....	....	....	....	....	....	1953-54	1955-56
Stankiewicz, Myron	St.L., Phi.	1	35	0	7	7	36	1	0	0	0	0	....	1968-69	1968-69
Stanley, Allan	NYR, Chi., Bos., Tor., Phi.	21	1244	100	333	433	792	109	7	36	43	80	4	1948-49	1968-69
• Stanley, Barney	Chi.	1	1	0	0	0	0	....	....	....	....	....	....	1927-28	1927-28
Stanley, Daryl	Phi., Van.	6	189	8	17	25	408	17	0	0	0	30	....	1983-84	1989-90
Stanowski, Wally	Tor., NYR	10	428	23	88	111	160	60	3	14	17	13	4	1939-40	1950-51
Stanton, Paul	Pit., Bos., NYI	5	295	14	49	63	262	44	2	10	12	66	2	1990-91	1994-95
Stapleton, Brian	Wsh.	1	1	0	0	0	0	....	....	....	....	....	....	1975-76	1975-76
Stapleton, Mike	Chi., Pit., Edm., Wpg., Phx., Atl., NYI, Van.	14	697	71	111	182	342	34	1	0	1	39	....	1986-87	2000-01
Stapleton, Pat	Bos., Chi.	10	635	43	294	337	353	65	10	39	49	38	....	1961-62	1972-73

			Regular Schedule					Playoffs							
Name	NHL Teams	NHL Seasons	GP	G	A	TP	PIM	GP	G	A	TP	PIM	NHL Cup Wins	First NHL Season	Last NHL Season
Starikov, Sergei	N.J.	1	16	0	1	1	8	....	....	....	....	....	....	1989-90	1989-90
• Starr, Harold	Ott., Mtl.M., Mtl., NYR	7	205	6	5	11	186	15	1	0	1	4	....	1929-30	1935-36
• Starr, Wilf	NYA, Det.	4	87	8	6	14	25	7	0	2	2	2	....	1932-33	1935-36
Stasiuk, Vic	Chi., Det., Bos.	14	745	183	254	437	669	69	16	18	34	40	2	1949-50	1962-63
Stastny, Anton	Que.	9	650	252	384	636	150	66	20	32	52	31	....	1980-81	1988-89
Stastny, Marian	Que., Tor.	5	322	121	173	294	110	32	5	17	22	7	....	1981-82	1985-86
Stastny, Peter	Que., N.J., St.L.	15	977	450	789	1239	824	93	33	72	105	123	....	1980-81	1994-95
‡ Stastny, Yan	Edm., Bos., St.L.	5	91	6	10	16	58	....	....	....	....	....	....	2005-06	2009-10
Staszak, Ray	Det.	1	4	0	1	1	7	....	....	....	....	....	....	1985-86	1985-86
• Steele, Frank	Det.	1	1	0	0	0	0	....	....	....	....	....	....	1930-31	1930-31
Steen, Anders	Wpg.	1	42	5	11	16	22	....	....	....	....	....	....	1980-81	1980-81
Steen, Thomas	Wpg.	14	950	264	553	817	753	56	12	32	44	62	....	1981-82	1994-95
Stefan, Patrik	Atl., Dal.	7	455	64	124	188	158	....	....	....	....	....	....	1999-00	2006-07
Stefaniw, Morris	Atl.	1	13	1	1	2	2	....	....	....	....	....	....	1972-73	1972-73
Stefanski, Bud	NYR	1	1	0	0	0	0	....	....	....	....	....	....	1977-78	1977-78
Stemkowski, Pete	Tor., Det., NYR, L.A.	15	967	206	349	555	866	83	25	29	54	136	1	1963-64	1977-78
Stenlund, Vern	Cle.	1	4	0	0	0	0	....	....	....	....	....	....	1976-77	1976-77
Stephens, Charlie	Col.	2	8	0	2	2	4	....	....	....	....	....	....	2002-03	2003-04
Stephenson, Bob	Hfd., Tor.	1	18	2	3	5	4	....	....	....	....	....	....	1979-80	1979-80
‡ Stephenson, Shay	L.A.	1	2	0	0	0	0	....	....	....	....	....	....	2006-07	2006-07
Stern, Ron	Van., Cgy., S.J.	12	638	75	86	161	2077	43	7	7	14	119	....	1987-88	1999-00
Sterner, Ulf	NYR	1	4	0	0	0	0	....	....	....	....	....	....	1964-65	1964-65
Stevens, John	Phi., Hfd.	5	53	0	10	10	48	....	....	....	....	....	....	1986-87	1993-94
Stevens, Kevin	Pit., Bos., L.A., NYR, Phi.	15	874	329	397	726	1470	103	46	60	106	170	2	1987-88	2001-02
Stevens, Mike	Van., Bos., NYI, Tor.	4	23	1	4	5	29	....	....	....	....	....	....	1984-85	1989-90
• Stevens, Phil	Mtl.W., Mtl., Bos.	3	25	1	0	1	3	....	....	....	....	....	....	1917-18	1925-26
Stevens, Scott	Wsh., St.L., N.J.	22	1635	196	712	908	2785	233	26	92	118	402	3	1982-83	2003-04
Stevenson, Grant	S.J.	1	47	10	12	22	14	5	0	0	0	4	....	2005-06	2005-06
Stevenson, Jeremy	Ana., Nsh., Min., Dal.	9	207	19	19	38	451	21	0	5	5	20	....	1995-96	2005-06
Stevenson, Shayne	Bos., T.B.	3	27	0	2	2	35	....	....	....	....	....	....	1990-91	1992-93
Stevenson, Turner	Mtl., N.J., Phi.	13	644	75	115	190	969	67	6	12	18	66	1	1992-93	2005-06
Stewart, Allan	N.J., Bos.	6	64	6	4	10	243	....	....	....	....	....	....	1985-86	1991-92
Stewart, Bill	Buf., St.L., Tor., Min.	8	261	7	64	71	424	13	1	3	4	11	....	1977-78	1985-86
Stewart, Blair	Det., Wsh., Que.	7	229	34	44	78	326	....	....	....	....	....	....	1973-74	1979-80
Stewart, Bob	Bos., Cal., Cle., St.L., Pit.	9	575	27	101	128	809	5	1	1	2	2	....	1971-72	1979-80
Stewart, Cam	Bos., Fla., Min.	7	202	16	23	39	120	13	1	3	4	9	....	1993-94	2001-02
• Stewart, Gaye	Tor., Chi., Det., NYR, Mtl.	11	502	185	159	344	274	25	2	9	11	16	2	1941-42	1953-54
‡ Stewart, Greg	Mtl.	3	26	0	1	1	48	2	0	0	0	2	....	2007-08	2009-10
• Stewart, Jack	Det., Chi.	12	565	31	84	115	765	80	5	14	19	143	2	1938-39	1951-52
Stewart, John	Pit., Atl., Cal.	5	258	58	60	118	158	4	0	0	0	10	....	1970-71	1974-75
Stewart, John	Que.	1	2	0	0	0	0	....	....	....	....	....	....	1979-80	1979-80
‡ Stewart, Karl	Atl., Pit., Chi., T.B.	4	69	2	4	6	68	....	....	....	....	....	....	2003-04	2007-08
Stewart, Ken	Chi.	1	6	1	1	2	2	....	....	....	....	....	....	1941-42	1941-42
• Stewart, Nels	Mtl.M., Bos., NYA	15	650	324	191	515	953	50	9	12	21	47	1	1925-26	1939-40
Stewart, Paul	Que.	1	21	2	0	2	74	....	....	....	....	....	....	1979-80	1979-80
Stewart, Ralph	Van., NYI	7	252	57	73	130	28	19	4	4	8	2	....	1970-71	1977-78
• Stewart, Ron	Tor., Bos., St.L., NYR, Van., NYI	21	1353	276	253	529	560	119	14	21	35	60	3	1952-53	1972-73
Stewart, Ryan	Wpg.	1	3	1	0	1	0	....	....	....	....	....	....	1985-86	1985-86
Stienburg, Trevor	Que.	4	71	8	4	12	161	1	0	0	0	0	....	1985-86	1988-89
Stiles, Tony	Cgy.	1	30	2	7	9	20	....	....	....	....	....	....	1983-84	1983-84
Stillman, Cory	Cgy., St.L., T.B., Car., Ott., Fla.	16	1025	278	449	727	489	82	19	32	51	43	2	1994-95	2010-11
Stock, P.J.	NYR, Mtl., Phi., Bos.	7	235	5	21	26	523	8	1	0	1	19	....	1997-98	2003-04
Stoddard, Jack	NYR	2	80	16	15	31	31	....	....	....	....	....	....	1951-52	1952-53
Stojanov, Alek	Van., Pit.	3	107	2	5	7	222	14	0	0	0	21	....	1994-95	1996-97
Stoltz, Roland	Wsh.	1	14	2	2	4	14	....	....	....	....	....	....	1981-82	1981-82
Stone, Ryan	Pit., Edm.	3	35	0	7	7	55	....	....	....	....	....	....	2007-08	2009-10
Stone, Steve	Van.	1	2	0	0	0	0	....	....	....	....	....	....	1973-74	1973-74
Storm, Jim	Hfd., Dal.	3	84	7	15	22	44	....	....	....	....	....	....	1993-94	1995-96
Stothers, Mike	Phi., Tor.	4	30	0	2	2	65	5	0	0	0	11	....	1984-85	1987-88
Stoughton, Blaine	Pit., Tor., Hfd., NYR	8	526	258	191	449	204	8	4	2	6	2	....	1973-74	1983-84
Stoyanovich, Steve	Hfd.	1	23	3	5	8	11	....	....	....	....	....	....	1983-84	1983-84
• Strain, Neil	NYR	1	52	11	13	24	12	....	....	....	....	....	....	1952-53	1952-53
‡ Straka, Martin	Pit., Ott., NYI, Fla., L.A., NYR	15	954	257	460	717	360	106	26	44	70	52	....	1992-93	2007-08
Strate, Gord	Det.	3	61	0	0	0	34	....	....	....	....	....	....	1956-57	1958-59
Stratton, Art	NYR, Det., Chi., Pit., Phi.	4	95	18	33	51	24	5	0	0	0	0	....	1959-60	1967-68
‡ Strbak, Martin	L.A., Pit.	1	49	5	11	16	46	....	....	....	....	....	....	2003-04	2003-04
• Strobel, Art	NYR	1	7	0	0	0	0	....	....	....	....	....	....	1943-44	1943-44
Strong, Ken	Tor.	3	15	2	2	4	6	....	....	....	....	....	....	1982-83	1984-85
Stroshein, Garret	Wsh.	1	3	0	0	0	14	....	....	....	....	....	....	2003-04	2003-04
Struch, David	Cgy.	1	4	0	0	0	4	....	....	....	....	....	....	1993-94	1993-94
Strudwick, Jason	NYI, Van., Chi., NYR, Edm.	14	674	13	42	55	811	7	0	0	0	0	....	1995-96	2010-11
Strueby, Todd	Edm.	3	5	0	1	1	2	....	....	....	....	....	....	1981-82	1983-84
• Stuart, Billy	Tor., Bos.	7	195	30	20	50	151	12	1	1	2	6	1	1920-21	1926-27
Stuart, Mike	St.L.	2	3	0	0	0	0	....	....	....	....	....	....	2003-04	2005-06
‡ Stumpel, Jozef	Bos., L.A., Fla.	16	957	196	481	677	245	55	6	24	30	24	....	1991-92	2007-08
Stumpf, Bob	St.L., Pit.	1	10	1	1	2	20	....	....	....	....	....	....	1974-75	1974-75
Sturgeon, Peter	Col.	2	6	0	1	1	2	....	....	....	....	....	....	1979-80	1980-81
Stutzel, Mike	Phx.	1	9	0	0	0	0	....	....	....	....	....	....	2003-04	2003-04
‡ Suchy, Radoslav	Phx., CBJ	6	451	13	58	71	104	10	1	1	2	0	....	1999-00	2005-06
‡ Suglobov, Alexander	N.J., Tor.	3	18	1	0	1	4	....	....	....	....	....	....	2003-04	2006-07
Suikkanen, Kai	Buf.	2	2	0	0	0	0	....	....	....	....	....	....	1981-82	1982-83
Sulliman, Doug	NYR, Hfd., N.J., Phi.	11	631	160	168	328	175	16	1	3	4	2	....	1979-80	1989-90
• Sullivan, Barry	Det.	1	1	0	0	0	0	....	....	....	....	....	....	1947-48	1947-48
Sullivan, Bob	Hfd.	1	62	18	19	37	18	....	....	....	....	....	....	1982-83	1982-83
Sullivan, Brian	N.J.	1	2	0	1	1	0	....	....	....	....	....	....	1992-93	1992-93
• Sullivan, Frank	Tor., Chi.	4	8	0	0	0	2	....	....	....	....	....	....	1949-50	1955-56
Sullivan, Mike	S.J., Cgy., Bos., Phx.	11	709	54	82	136	203	34	4	8	12	14	....	1991-92	2001-02
Sullivan, Peter	Wpg.	2	126	28	54	82	40	....	....	....	....	....	....	1979-80	1980-81
Sullivan, Red	Bos., Chi., NYR	11	557	107	239	346	441	18	1	2	3	6	....	1949-50	1960-61
Summanen, Raimo	Edm., Van.	5	151	36	40	76	35	10	2	5	7	0	....	1983-84	1987-88
• Summerhill, Bill	Mtl., Bro.	4	72	14	17	31	70	3	0	0	0	2	....	1937-38	1941-42
Sundblad, Niklas	Cgy.	1	2	0	0	0	0	....	....	....	....	....	....	1995-96	1995-96
Sundin, Mats	Que., Tor., Van.	18	1346	564	785	1349	1093	91	38	44	82	74	....	1990-91	2008-09
Sundin, Ronnie	NYR	1	1	0	0	0	0	....	....	....	....	....	....	1997-98	1997-98
‡ Sundstrom, Niklas	NYR, S.J., Mtl.	10	750	117	232	349	256	59	6	22	28	22	....	1995-96	2005-06
Sundstrom, Patrik	Van., N.J.	10	679	219	369	588	349	37	9	17	26	25	....	1982-83	1991-92
Sundstrom, Peter	NYR, Wsh., N.J.	6	338	61	83	144	120	23	3	3	6	8	....	1983-84	1989-90
Suomi, Al	Chi.	1	5	0	0	0	0	....	....	....	....	....	....	1936-37	1936-37
‡ Surma, Damian	Car.	2	2	1	1	2	0	....	....	....	....	....	....	2002-03	2003-04
‡ Surovy, Tomas	Pit.	3	126	27	32	59	71	....	....	....	....	....	....	2002-03	2005-06
‡ Sushinsky, Maxim	Min.	1	30	7	4	11	29	....	....	....	....	....	....	2000-01	2000-01
Suter, Gary	Cgy., Chi., S.J.	17	1145	203	641	844	1349	108	17	56	73	120	1	1985-86	2001-02
Sutherland, Bill	Mtl., Phi., Tor., St.L., Det.	6	250	70	58	128	99	14	2	4	6	0	....	1962-63	1971-72
• Sutherland, Max	Bos.	1	2	0	0	0	0	....	....	....	....	....	....	1931-32	1931-32
Sutter, Brent	NYI, Chi.	18	1111	363	466	829	1054	144	30	44	74	164	2	1980-81	1997-98
Sutter, Brian	St.L.	12	779	303	333	636	1786	65	21	21	42	249	....	1976-77	1987-88
Sutter, Darryl	Chi.	8	406	161	118	279	288	51	24	19	43	26	....	1979-80	1986-87
Sutter, Duane	NYI, Chi.	11	731	139	203	342	1333	161	26	32	58	405	4	1979-80	1989-90
Sutter, Rich	Pit., Phi., Van., St.L., Chi., T.B., Tor.	13	874	149	166	315	1411	78	13	5	18	133	....	1982-83	1994-95
Sutter, Ron	Phi., St.L., Que., NYI, Bos., S.J., Cgy.	19	1093	205	329	534	1352	104	8	32	40	193	....	1982-83	2000-01
Sutton, Andy	S.J., Min., Atl., NYI, Ott., Ana., Edm.	14	676	38	112	150	1185	11	0	0	0	20	....	1998-99	2012-13
Sutton, Ken	Buf., Edm., St.L., N.J., S.J., NYI	11	388	23	80	103	338	32	3	4	7	29	1	1990-91	2001-02
Suzor, Mark	Phi., Col.	2	64	4	16	20	60	....	....	....	....	....	....	1976-77	1977-78
Svartvadet, Per	Atl.	4	247	17	34	51	58	....	....	....	....	....	....	1999-00	2002-03
‡ Svatos, Marek	Col., Nsh., Ott.	7	344	100	72	172	217	14	2	5	7	4	....	2003-04	2010-11
Svehla, Robert	Fla., Tor.	9	655	68	267	335	649	38	1	14	15	42	....	1994-95	2002-03
Svejkovsky, Jaroslav	Wsh., T.B.	4	113	23	19	42	56	1	0	0	0	2	....	1996-97	1999-00
Svensson, Leif	Wsh.	2	121	6	40	46	49	....	....	....	....	....	....	1978-79	1979-80
Svensson, Magnus	Fla.	2	46	4	14	18	31	....	....	....	....	....	....	1994-95	1995-96
‡ Svitov, Alexander	T.B., CBJ	3	179	13	24	37	223	7	0	0	0	6	....	2002-03	2006-07
‡ Svoboda, Jaroslav	Car., Dal.	4	134	12	17	29	62	25	1	4	5	30	....	2001-02	2005-06
Svoboda, Petr	Mtl., Buf., Phi., T.B.	17	1028	58	341	399	1605	127	4	45	49	140	1	1984-85	2000-01
Svoboda, Petr	Tor.	1	18	1	2	3	10	....	....	....	....	....	....	2000-01	2000-01
Swain, Garry	Pit.	1	9	1	1	2	0	....	....	....	....	....	....	1968-69	1968-69
‡ Swanson, Brian	Edm., Atl.	4	70	4	13	17	16	....	....	....	....	....	....	2000-01	2003-04
Swarbrick, George	Oak., Pit., Phi.	4	132	17	25	42	173	....	....	....	....	....	....	1967-68	1970-71

Marion Stastny

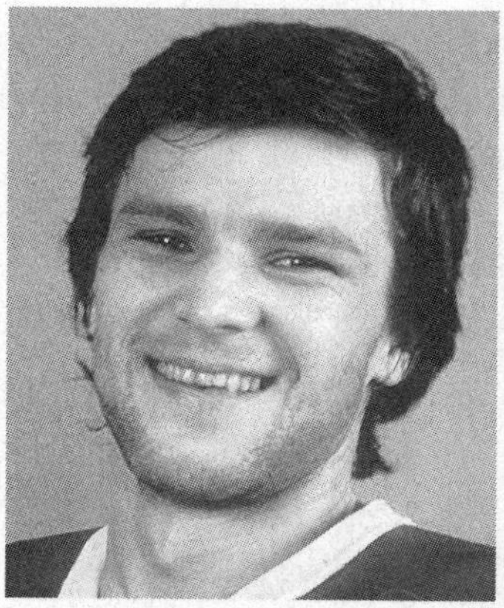
Peter Stastny

Ron Stewart

Art Stratton

Mike Sullivan

Bill Sutherland

Andy Sutton

Greg Tebbutt

			Regular Schedule					Playoffs							
Name	NHL Teams	NHL Seasons	GP	G	A	TP	PIM	GP	G	A	TP	PIM	NHL Cup Wins	First NHL Season	Last NHL Season
Sweatt, Lee	Van.	1	3	1	1	2	2	....	....	....	....	....	....	2010-11	2010-11
• Sweeney, Bill	NYR	1	4	1	0	1	0	....	....	....	....	....	....	1959-60	1959-60
Sweeney, Bob	Bos., Buf., NYI, Cgy.	10	639	125	163	288	799	103	15	18	33	197	....	1986-87	1995-96
Sweeney, Don	Bos., Dal.	16	1115	52	221	273	681	108	9	10	19	81	....	1988-89	2003-04
Sweeney, Tim	Cgy., Bos., Ana., NYR	8	291	55	83	138	123	4	0	0	0	2	....	1990-91	1997-98
Sydor, Darryl	L.A., Dal., CBJ, T.B., Pit., St.L.	18	1291	98	409	507	755	155	9	47	56	73	2	1991-92	2009-10
Sykes, Bob	Tor.	1	2	0	0	0	0	....	....	....	....	....	....	1974-75	1974-75
Sykes, Phil	L.A., Wpg.	10	456	79	85	164	519	26	0	3	3	29	....	1982-83	1991-92
Sykora, Michal	S.J., Chi., T.B., Phi.	7	267	15	54	69	185	7	0	1	1	0	....	1993-94	2000-01
‡ Sykora, Petr	N.J., Ana., NYR, Edm., Pit., Min.	15	1017	323	398	721	455	133	34	40	74	62	2	1995-96	2011-12
‡ Sykora, Petr	Nsh., Wsh.	2	12	2	2	4	6	....	....	....	....	....	....	1998-99	2005-06
Sylvester, Dean	Buf., Atl.	3	96	21	16	37	32	4	0	0	0	0	....	1998-99	2000-01
• Szura, Joe	Oak.	2	90	10	15	25	30	7	2	3	5	2	....	1967-68	1968-69

T

Taft, John	Det.	1	15	0	2	2	4	....	....	....	....	....	....	1978-79	1978-79
Taglianetti, Peter	Wpg., Min., Pit., T.B.	11	451	18	74	92	1106	53	2	8	10	103	2	1984-85	1994-95
Talafous, Dean	Atl., Min., NYR	8	497	104	154	258	163	21	4	7	11	11	....	1974-75	1981-82
• Talakoski, Ron	NYR	2	9	0	1	1	33	....	....	....	....	....	....	1986-87	1987-88
Talbot, Jean-Guy	Mtl., Min., Det., St.L., Buf.	17	1056	43	242	285	1006	150	4	26	30	142	7	1954-55	1970-71
‡ Tallackson, Barry	N.J.	4	20	1	1	2	2	....	....	....	....	....	....	2005-06	2008-09
Tallon, Dale	Van., Chi., Pit.	10	642	98	238	336	568	33	2	10	12	45	....	1970-71	1979-80
‡ Tambellini, Jeff	L.A., NYI, Van.	6	242	27	36	63	88	6	0	0	0	2	....	2005-06	2010-11
Tambellini, Steve	NYI, Col., N.J., Cgy., Van.	10	553	160	150	310	105	2	0	1	1	0	1	1978-79	1987-88
Tamer, Chris	Pit., NYR, Atl.	11	644	21	64	85	1183	37	0	8	8	52	....	1993-94	2003-04
Tanabe, David	Car., Phx., Bos.	8	449	30	84	114	245	7	2	1	3	12	....	1999-00	2007-08
Tancill, Chris	Hfd., Det., Dal., S.J.	8	134	17	32	49	54	11	1	1	2	8	....	1990-91	1997-98
Tanguay, Christian	Que.	1	2	0	0	0	0	....	....	....	....	....	....	1981-82	1981-82
Tannahill, Don	Van.	2	111	30	33	63	25	....	....	....	....	....	....	1972-73	1973-74
Tanti, Tony	Chi., Van., Pit., Buf.	11	697	287	273	560	661	30	3	12	15	27	....	1981-82	1991-92
Tapper, Brad	Atl.	3	71	14	11	25	72	....	....	....	....	....	....	2000-01	2002-03
Tardif, Marc	Mtl., Que.	8	517	194	207	401	443	62	13	15	28	75	2	1969-70	1982-83
Tardif, Patrice	St.L., L.A.	2	65	7	11	18	78	....	....	....	....	....	....	1994-95	1995-96
Tarnstrom, Dick	NYI, Pit., Edm., CBJ	5	306	35	105	140	254	17	0	2	2	12	....	2001-02	2007-08
Tatarinov, Mikhail	Wsh., Que., Bos.	4	161	21	48	69	184	....	....	....	....	....	....	1990-91	1993-94
• Tatchell, Spence	NYR	1	1	0	0	0	0	....	....	....	....	....	....	1942-43	1942-43
‡ Taticek, Petr	Fla.	1	3	0	0	0	0	....	....	....	....	....	....	2005-06	2005-06
• Taylor, Billy	Tor., Det., Bos., NYR	7	323	87	180	267	120	33	6	18	24	13	1	1939-40	1947-48
• Taylor, Billy	NYR	1	2	0	0	0	0	....	....	....	....	....	....	1964-65	1964-65
• Taylor, Bob	Bos.	1	8	0	0	0	6	....	....	....	....	....	....	1929-30	1929-30
Taylor, Chris	NYI, Bos., Buf.	8	149	11	21	32	48	2	0	0	0	2	....	1994-95	2003-04
Taylor, Dave	L.A.	17	1111	431	638	1069	1589	92	26	33	59	145	....	1977-78	1993-94
• Taylor, Harry	Tor., Chi.	3	66	5	10	15	30	1	0	0	0	0	1	1946-47	1951-52
Taylor, Mark	Phi., Pit., Wsh.	5	209	42	68	110	73	6	0	0	0	0	....	1981-82	1985-86
• Taylor, Ralph	Chi., NYR	3	99	4	1	5	169	4	0	0	0	10	....	1927-28	1929-30
Taylor, Ted	NYR, Det., Min., Van.	6	166	23	35	58	181	....	....	....	....	....	....	1964-65	1971-72
Taylor, Tim	Det., Bos., NYR, T.B.	13	746	73	94	167	433	89	2	12	14	73	2	1993-94	2006-07
Teal, Jeff	Mtl.	1	6	0	1	1	0	....	....	....	....	....	....	1984-85	1984-85
• Teal, Skip	Bos.	1	1	0	0	0	0	....	....	....	....	....	....	1954-55	1954-55
Teal, Vic	NYI	1	1	0	0	0	0	....	....	....	....	....	....	1973-74	1973-74
Tebbutt, Greg	Que., Pit.	2	26	0	3	3	35	....	....	....	....	....	....	1979-80	1983-84
‡ Tenkrat, Petr	Ana., Nsh., Bos.	3	177	22	30	52	84	....	....	....	....	....	....	2000-01	2006-07
‡ Tenute, Joey	Wsh.	1	1	0	0	0	0	....	....	....	....	....	....	2005-06	2005-06
Tepper, Stephen	Chi.	1	1	0	0	0	0	....	....	....	....	....	....	1992-93	1992-93
• Terbenche, Paul	Chi., Buf.	5	189	5	26	31	28	12	0	0	0	0	....	1967-68	1973-74
Terrion, Greg	L.A., Tor.	8	561	93	150	243	339	35	2	9	11	41	....	1980-81	1987-88
Terry, Bill	Min.	1	5	0	0	0	0	....	....	....	....	....	....	1987-88	1987-88
• Tertyshny, Dmitri	Phi.	1	62	2	8	10	30	1	0	0	0	0	....	1998-99	1998-99
Tessier, Orval	Mtl., Bos.	3	59	5	7	12	6	....	....	....	....	....	....	1954-55	1960-61
Tetarenko, Joey	Fla., Ott., Car.	4	73	4	1	5	176	....	....	....	....	....	....	2000-01	2003-04
Tezikov, Alexei	Wsh., Van.	3	30	1	1	2	2	....	....	....	....	....	....	1998-99	2001-02
Theberge, Greg	Wsh.	5	153	15	63	78	73	4	0	1	1	0	....	1979-80	1983-84
Thelin, Mats	Bos.	3	163	8	19	27	107	5	0	0	0	6	....	1984-85	1986-87
Thelven, Michael	Bos.	5	207	20	80	100	217	34	4	10	14	34	....	1985-86	1989-90
Therien, Chris	Phi., Dal.	11	764	29	130	159	585	104	4	10	14	68	....	1994-95	2005-06
Therrien, Gaston	Que.	3	22	0	8	8	12	9	0	1	1	4	....	1980-81	1982-83
Thibaudeau, Gilles	Mtl., NYI, Tor.	5	119	25	37	62	40	8	3	3	6	2	....	1986-87	1990-91
Thibeault, Lorrain	Det., Mtl.	2	5	0	2	2	2	....	....	....	....	....	....	1944-45	1945-46
Thiffault, Leo	Min.	1	....	....	....	....	....	5	0	0	0	0	....	1967-68	1967-68
• Thomas, Cy	Chi., Tor.	1	14	2	2	4	12	....	....	....	....	....	....	1947-48	1947-48
Thomas, Reg	Que.	1	39	9	7	16	6	....	....	....	....	....	....	1979-80	1979-80
Thomas, Scott	Buf., L.A.	3	63	6	4	10	32	12	1	0	1	4	....	1992-93	2000-01
Thomas, Steve	Tor., Chi., NYI, N.J., Ana., Det.	20	1235	421	512	933	1306	174	54	53	107	187	....	1984-85	2003-04
Thomlinson, Dave	St.L., Bos., L.A.	5	42	1	3	4	50	9	3	1	4	4	....	1989-90	1994-95
Thompson, Brent	L.A., Wpg., Phx.	6	121	1	10	11	352	4	0	0	0	4	....	1991-92	1996-97
• Thompson, Cliff	Bos.	2	13	0	1	1	2	....	....	....	....	....	....	1941-42	1948-49
Thompson, Errol	Tor., Det., Pit.	10	599	208	185	393	184	34	7	5	12	11	....	1970-71	1980-81
• Thompson, Ken	Mtl.W.	1	1	0	0	0	0	....	....	....	....	....	....	1917-18	1917-18
• Thompson, Paul	NYR, Chi.	13	582	153	179	332	336	48	11	11	22	54	3	1926-27	1938-39
Thompson, Rocky	Cgy., Fla.	4	25	0	0	0	117	....	....	....	....	....	....	1997-98	2001-02
• Thoms, Bill	Tor., Chi., Bos.	13	548	135	206	341	154	44	6	10	16	6	....	1932-33	1944-45
• Thomson, Bill	Det.	2	9	2	2	4	0	2	0	0	0	0	....	1938-39	1943-44
Thomson, Floyd	St.L.	8	411	56	97	153	341	10	0	2	2	6	....	1971-72	1979-80
Thomson, Jim	Wsh., Hfd., N.J., L.A., Ott., Ana.	7	115	4	3	7	416	1	0	0	0	0	....	1986-87	1993-94
• Thomson, Jimmy	Tor., Chi.	13	787	19	215	234	920	63	2	13	15	135	4	1945-46	1957-58
• Thomson, Rhys	Mtl., Tor.	2	25	0	2	2	38	....	....	....	....	....	....	1939-40	1942-43
‡ Thoresen, Patrick	Edm., Phi.	2	106	6	18	24	66	14	0	2	2	4	....	2006-07	2007-08
Thornbury, Tom	Pit.	1	14	1	8	9	16	....	....	....	....	....	....	1983-84	1983-84
Thornton, Scott	Tor., Edm., Mtl., Dal., S.J., L.A.	17	941	144	141	285	1459	79	13	14	27	82	....	1990-91	2007-08
• Thorsteinson, Joe	NYA	1	4	0	0	0	0	....	....	....	....	....	....	1932-33	1932-33
• Thurier, Fred	NYA, Bro., NYR	3	80	25	27	52	18	....	....	....	....	....	....	1940-41	1944-45
Thurlby, Tom	Oak.	1	20	1	1	2	4	....	....	....	....	....	....	1967-68	1967-68
Thyer, Mario	Min.	1	5	0	0	0	0	1	0	0	0	2	....	1989-90	1989-90
Tibbetts, Billy	Pit., Phi., NYR	3	82	2	8	10	269	....	....	....	....	....	....	2000-01	2002-03
Tichy, Milan	Chi., NYI	3	23	0	5	5	40	....	....	....	....	....	....	1992-93	1995-96
Tidey, Alex	Buf., Edm.	3	9	0	0	0	8	2	0	0	0	0	....	1976-77	1979-80
Tikkanen, Esa	Edm., NYR, St.L., N.J., Van., Fla., Wsh.	15	877	244	386	630	1077	186	72	60	132	275	5	1984-85	1998-99
Tiley, Brad	Phx., Phi.	3	11	0	0	0	0	1	0	0	0	0	....	1997-98	2000-01
Tilley, Tom	St.L.	4	174	4	38	42	89	14	1	3	4	19	....	1988-89	1993-94
Timander, Mattias	Bos., CBJ, NYI, Phi.	8	419	13	57	70	165	23	3	5	8	8	....	1996-97	2003-04
• Timgren, Ray	Tor., Chi.	6	251	14	44	58	70	30	3	9	12	6	2	1948-49	1954-55
‡ Timonen, Jussi	Phi.	1	14	0	4	4	6	....	....	....	....	....	....	2006-07	2006-07
Tinordi, Mark	NYR, Min., Dal., Wsh.	12	663	52	148	200	1514	70	7	11	18	165	....	1987-88	1998-99
Tippett, Dave	Hfd., Wsh., Pit., Phi.	12	721	93	169	262	317	62	6	16	22	34	....	1983-84	1993-94
Titanic, Morris	Buf.	2	19	0	0	0	0	....	....	....	....	....	....	1974-75	1975-76
Titov, German	Cgy., Pit., Edm., Ana.	9	624	157	220	377	311	34	11	12	23	18	....	1993-94	2001-02
‡ Tjarnqvist, Daniel	Atl., Min., Edm., Col.	6	352	18	72	90	130	....	....	....	....	....	....	2001-02	2008-09
‡ Tjarnqvist, Mathias	Dal., Phx.	4	173	13	19	32	60	....	....	....	....	....	....	2003-04	2007-08
Tkachuk, Keith	Wpg., Phx., St.L., Atl.	18	1201	538	527	1065	2219	89	28	28	56	176	....	1991-92	2009-10
Tkaczuk, Daniel	Cgy.	1	19	4	7	11	14	....	....	....	....	....	....	2000-01	2000-01
Tkaczuk, Walt	NYR	14	945	227	451	678	556	93	19	32	51	119	....	1967-68	1980-81
Toal, Mike	Edm.	1	3	0	0	0	0	....	....	....	....	....	....	1979-80	1979-80
Tobler, Ryan	T.B.	1	4	0	0	0	5	....	....	....	....	....	....	2001-02	2001-02
Tocchet, Rick	Phi., Pit., L.A., Bos., Wsh., Phx.	18	1144	440	512	952	2972	145	52	60	112	471	1	1984-85	2001-02
Todd, Kevin	N.J., Edm., Chi., L.A., Ana.	9	383	70	133	203	225	12	3	2	5	16	....	1988-89	1997-98
‡ Tollefsen, Ole-Kristian	CBJ, Phi.	5	163	4	8	12	296	....	....	....	....	....	....	2005-06	2009-10
‡ Tolpeko, Denis	Phi.	1	26	1	5	6	24	....	....	....	....	....	....	2007-08	2007-08
Tomalty, Glenn	Wpg.	1	1	0	0	0	0	....	....	....	....	....	....	1979-80	1979-80
Tomlak, Mike	Hfd.	4	141	15	22	37	103	10	0	1	1	4	....	1989-90	1993-94
Tomlinson, Dave	Tor., Wpg., Fla.	4	42	1	3	4	28	....	....	....	....	....	....	1991-92	1994-95
Tomlinson, Kirk	Min.	1	1	0	0	0	0	....	....	....	....	....	....	1987-88	1987-88
Toms, Jeff	T.B., Wsh., NYI, NYR, Pit., Fla.	8	236	22	33	55	59	1	0	0	0	0	....	1995-96	2002-03
• Tomson, Jack	NYA	3	15	1	1	2	0	2	0	0	0	0	....	1938-39	1940-41
Tonelli, John	NYI, Cgy., L.A., Chi., Que.	14	1028	325	511	836	911	172	40	75	115	200	4	1978-79	1991-92
Tookey, Tim	Wsh., Que., Pit., Phi., L.A.	7	106	22	36	58	71	10	1	3	4	2	....	1980-81	1988-89

Name	NHL Teams	NHL Seasons	Regular Schedule					Playoffs					NHL Cup Wins	First NHL Season	Last NHL Season
			GP	G	A	TP	PIM	GP	G	A	TP	PIM			
Toomey, Sean	Min.	1	1	0	0	0	0	....	....	....	....	....	....	1986-87	1986-87
Toporowski, Shayne	Tor.	1	3	0	0	0	7	....	....	....	....	....	....	1996-97	1996-97
● Toppazzini, Jerry	Bos., Chi., Det.	12	783	163	244	407	436	40	13	9	22	13	....	1952-53	1963-64
● Toppazzini, Zellio	Bos., NYR, Chi.	5	123	21	22	43	49	2	0	0	0	0	....	1948-49	1956-57
Torgaev, Pavel	Cgy., T.B.	2	55	6	14	20	20	1	0	0	0	0	....	1995-96	1999-00
Torkki, Jari	Chi.	1	4	1	0	1	0	....	....	....	....	....	....	1988-89	1988-89
Tormanen, Antti	Ott.	1	50	7	8	15	28	....	....	....	....	....	....	1995-96	1995-96
● Touhey, Bill	Mtl.M., Ott., Bos.	7	280	65	40	105	107	2	1	0	1	0	....	1927-28	1933-34
● Toupin, Jacques	Chi.	1	8	1	2	3	0	4	0	0	0	0	....	1943-44	1943-44
● Townsend, Art	Chi.	1	5	0	0	0	0	....	....	....	....	....	....	1926-27	1926-27
Townshend, Graeme	Bos., NYI, Ott.	5	45	3	7	10	28	....	....	....	....	....	....	1989-90	1993-94
Trader, Larry	Det., St.L., Mtl.	4	91	5	13	18	74	3	0	0	0	0	....	1982-83	1987-88
● Trainor, Wes	NYR	1	17	1	2	3	6	....	....	....	....	....	....	1948-49	1948-49
● Trapp, Bob	Chi., Mtl.	3	83	4	4	8	129	2	0	0	0	4	....	1926-27	1932-33
Trapp, Doug	Buf.	1	2	0	0	0	0	....	....	....	....	....	....	1986-87	1986-87
● Traub, Percy	Chi., Det.	3	130	3	3	6	217	4	0	0	0	6	....	1926-27	1928-29
‡ Traverse, Patrick	Ott., Ana., Bos., Mtl., Dal.	7	279	14	51	65	113	6	0	0	0	2	....	1995-96	2005-06
Trebil, Dan	Ana., Pit., St.L.	5	85	4	4	8	32	10	0	1	1	8	....	1996-97	2000-01
Tredway, Brock	L.A.	1	....	....	....	....	....	1	0	0	0	0	....	1981-82	1981-82
Tremblay, Brent	Wsh.	2	10	1	0	1	6	....	....	....	....	....	....	1978-79	1979-80
Tremblay, Gilles	Mtl.	9	509	168	162	330	161	48	9	14	23	4	4	1960-61	1968-69
● Tremblay, J.C.	Mtl.	13	794	57	306	363	204	108	14	51	65	58	5	1959-60	1971-72
● Tremblay, Marcel	Mtl.	1	10	0	2	2	0	....	....	....	....	....	....	1938-39	1938-39
Tremblay, Mario	Mtl.	12	852	258	326	584	1043	101	20	29	49	187	5	1974-75	1985-86
● Tremblay, Nils	Mtl.	2	3	0	1	1	0	2	0	0	0	0	....	1944-45	1945-46
Tremblay, Yannick	Tor., Atl., Van.	9	390	38	87	125	178	....	....	....	....	....	....	1996-97	2006-07
‡ Trepanier, Pascal	Col., Ana., Nsh.	6	229	12	22	34	252	2	0	0	0	0	....	1997-98	2002-03
Trimper, Tim	Chi., Wpg., Min.	6	190	30	36	66	153	2	0	0	0	2	....	1979-80	1984-85
‡ Tripp, John	NYR, L.A.	2	43	2	7	9	35	....	....	....	....	....	....	2002-03	2003-04
‡ Trnka, Pavel	Ana., Fla.	7	411	14	63	77	323	4	0	1	1	2	....	1997-98	2003-04
Trotter, Brock	Mtl.	1	2	0	0	0	0	....	....	....	....	....	....	2009-10	2009-10
Trottier, Bryan	NYI, Pit.	18	1279	524	901	1425	912	221	71	113	184	277	6	1975-76	1993-94
● Trottier, Dave	Mtl.M., Det.	11	446	121	113	234	517	31	4	3	7	39	1	1928-29	1938-39
Trottier, Guy	NYR, Tor.	3	115	28	17	45	37	9	1	0	1	16	....	1968-69	1971-72
Trottier, Rocky	N.J.	2	38	6	4	10	2	....	....	....	....	....	....	1983-84	1984-85
Trudel, Jean-Guy	Phx., Min.	3	5	0	0	0	4	....	....	....	....	....	....	1999-00	2002-03
● Trudel, Lou	Chi., Mtl.	8	306	49	69	118	122	24	1	3	4	4	2	1933-34	1940-41
● Trudell, Rene	NYR	3	129	24	28	52	72	5	0	0	0	2	....	1945-46	1947-48
Tselios, Nikos	Car.	1	2	0	0	0	6	....	....	....	....	....	....	2001-02	2001-02
Tsulygin, Nikolai	Ana.	1	22	0	1	1	8	....	....	....	....	....	....	1996-97	1996-97
Tsygurov, Denis	Buf., L.A.	3	51	1	5	6	45	....	....	....	....	....	....	1993-94	1995-96
Tsyplakov, Vladimir	L.A., Buf.	6	331	69	101	170	90	18	1	2	3	16	....	1995-96	2000-01
Tucker, Darcy	Mtl., T.B., Tor., Col.	14	947	215	261	476	1410	68	10	11	21	81	....	1995-96	2009-10
Tucker, John	Buf., Wsh., NYI, T.B.	12	656	177	259	436	285	31	10	18	28	24	....	1983-84	1995-96
● Tudin, Connie	Mtl.	1	4	0	1	1	4	....	....	....	....	....	....	1941-42	1941-42
Tudor, Rob	Van., St.L.	3	28	4	4	8	19	3	0	0	0	0	....	1978-79	1982-83
Tuer, Allan	L.A., Min., Hfd.	4	57	1	1	2	208	....	....	....	....	....	....	1985-86	1989-90
‡ Tukonen, Lauri	L.A.	2	5	0	0	0	0	....	....	....	....	....	....	2006-07	2007-08
Tuomainen, Marko	Edm., L.A., NYI	4	79	9	9	18	84	1	0	0	0	0	....	1994-95	2001-02
Turcotte, Alfie	Mtl., Wpg., Wsh.	7	112	17	29	46	49	5	0	0	0	0	....	1983-84	1990-91
Turcotte, Darren	NYR, Hfd., Wpg., S.J., St.L., Nsh.	12	635	195	216	411	301	35	6	8	14	12	....	1988-89	1999-00
Turgeon, Pierre	Buf., NYI, Mtl., St.L., Dal., Col.	19	1294	515	812	1327	452	109	35	62	97	36	....	1987-88	2006-07
Turgeon, Sylvain	Hfd., N.J., Mtl., Ott.	12	669	269	226	495	691	36	4	7	11	22	....	1983-84	1994-95
Turlick, Gord	Bos.	1	2	0	0	0	2	....	....	....	....	....	....	1959-60	1959-60
Turnbull, Ian	Tor., L.A., Pit.	10	628	123	317	440	736	55	13	32	45	94	....	1973-74	1982-83
Turnbull, Perry	St.L., Mtl., Wpg.	9	608	188	163	351	1245	34	6	7	13	86	....	1979-80	1987-88
Turnbull, Randy	Cgy.	1	1	0	0	0	2	....	....	....	....	....	....	1981-82	1981-82
● Turner, Bob	Mtl., Chi.	8	478	19	51	70	307	68	1	4	5	44	5	1955-56	1962-63
Turner, Brad	NYI	1	3	0	0	0	0	....	....	....	....	....	....	1991-92	1991-92
Turner, Dean	NYR, Col., L.A.	4	35	1	0	1	59	....	....	....	....	....	....	1978-79	1982-83
● Tustin, Norm	NYR	1	18	2	4	6	0	....	....	....	....	....	....	1941-42	1941-42
● Tuten, Aud	Chi.	2	39	4	8	12	48	....	....	....	....	....	....	1941-42	1942-43
Tutt, Brian	Wsh.	1	7	1	0	1	2	....	....	....	....	....	....	1989-90	1989-90
Tuttle, Steve	St.L.	3	144	28	28	56	12	17	1	6	7	2	....	1988-89	1990-91
Tuzzolino, Tony	Ana., NYR, Bos.	3	9	0	0	0	7	....	....	....	....	....	....	1997-98	2001-02
‡ Tverdovsky, Oleg	Ana., Wpg., Phx., N.J., Car., L.A.	11	713	77	240	317	291	45	0	14	14	6	2	1994-95	2006-07
‡ Tvrdon, Roman	Wsh.	1	9	0	1	1	2	....	....	....	....	....	....	2003-04	2003-04
Twist, Tony	St.L., Que.	10	445	10	18	28	1121	18	1	1	2	22	....	1989-90	1998-99

U V

Name	NHL Teams	NHL Seasons	GP	G	A	TP	PIM	GP	G	A	TP	PIM	NHL Cup Wins	First NHL Season	Last NHL Season
Ubriaco, Gene	Pit., Oak., Chi.	3	177	39	35	74	50	11	2	0	2	4	....	1967-68	1969-70
Ulanov, Igor	Wpg., Wsh., Chi., T.B., Mtl., Edm., NYR, Fla.	14	739	27	135	162	1151	39	1	4	5	84	....	1991-92	2005-06
Ullman, Norm	Det., Tor.	20	1410	490	739	1229	712	106	30	53	83	67	....	1955-56	1974-75
Ulmer, Jeff	NYR	1	21	3	0	3	8	....	....	....	....	....	....	2000-01	2000-01
‡ Ulmer, Layne	NYR	1	1	0	0	0	0	....	....	....	....	....	....	2003-04	2003-04
Unger, Garry	Tor., Det., St.L., Atl., L.A., Edm.	16	1105	413	391	804	1075	52	12	18	30	105	....	1967-68	1982-83
‡ Ustorf, Stefan	Wsh.	2	54	7	10	17	16	5	0	0	0	0	....	1995-96	1996-97
‡ Vaananen, Ossi	Phx., Col., Phi., Van.	7	479	13	55	68	482	20	0	1	1	26	....	2000-01	2008-09
Vachon, Nick	NYI	1	1	0	0	0	0	....	....	....	....	....	....	1996-97	1996-97
Vadnais, Carol	Mtl., Oak., Cal., Bos., NYR, N.J.	17	1087	169	418	587	1813	106	10	40	50	185	2	1966-67	1982-83
‡ Vaic, Lubomir	Van.	2	9	1	1	2	2	....	....	....	....	....	....	1997-98	1999-00
Vail, Eric	Atl., Cgy., Det.	9	591	216	260	476	281	20	5	6	11	6	....	1973-74	1981-82
● Vail, Sparky	NYR	2	50	4	1	5	18	10	0	0	0	2	....	1928-29	1929-30
Vaive, Rick	Van., Tor., Chi., Buf.	13	876	441	347	788	1445	54	27	16	43	111	....	1979-80	1991-92
Valentine, Chris	Wsh.	3	105	43	52	95	127	2	0	0	0	4	....	1981-82	1983-84
Valicevic, Rob	Nsh., L.A., Ana., Dal.	6	193	28	20	48	61	....	....	....	....	....	....	1998-99	2003-04
Valiquette, Jack	Tor., Col.	7	350	84	134	218	79	23	3	6	9	4	....	1974-75	1980-81
Valk, Garry	Van., Ana., Pit., Tor., Chi.	13	777	100	156	256	747	61	6	7	13	79	....	1990-91	2002-03
Vallis, Lindsay	Mtl.	1	1	0	0	0	0	....	....	....	....	....	....	1993-94	1993-94
Van Allen, Shaun	Edm., Ana., Ott., Dal., Mtl.	13	794	84	185	269	481	61	1	7	8	45	....	1990-91	2003-04
Van Boxmeer, John	Mtl., Col., Buf., Que.	11	588	84	274	358	465	38	5	15	20	37	....	1973-74	1983-84
Van Dorp, Wayne	Edm., Pit., Chi., Que.	6	125	12	12	24	565	27	0	1	1	42	....	1986-87	1991-92
Van Drunen, David	Ott.	1	1	0	0	0	0	....	....	....	....	....	....	1999-00	1999-00
Van Impe, Darren	Ana., Bos., NYR, Fla., NYI, CBJ	9	411	25	90	115	397	33	3	9	12	28	....	1994-95	2002-03
Van Impe, Ed	Chi., Phi., Pit.	11	700	27	126	153	1025	66	1	12	13	131	2	1966-67	1976-77
Van Ryn, Mike	St.L., Fla., Tor.	9	353	30	99	129	260	9	0	0	0	0	....	2000-01	2009-10
VandenBussche, Ryan	NYR, Chi., Pit.	9	310	10	10	20	702	1	0	0	0	0	....	1996-97	2005-06
Vandermeer, Peter	Phx.	1	2	0	0	0	0	....	....	....	....	....	....	2007-08	2007-08
‡ Varada, Vaclav	Buf., Ott.	10	493	58	125	183	410	87	11	19	30	82	....	1995-96	2005-06
Varis, Petri	Chi.	1	1	0	0	0	0	....	....	....	....	....	....	1997-98	1997-98
Varlamov, Sergei	Cgy., St.L.	4	63	8	7	15	26	1	0	0	0	2	....	1997-98	2002-03
Varvio, Jarkko	Dal.	2	13	3	4	7	4	....	....	....	....	....	....	1993-94	1994-95
● Vasicek, Josef	Car., Nsh., NYI	7	460	77	106	183	311	37	5	2	7	14	1	2000-01	2007-08
Vasilevski, Alexander	St.L.	2	4	0	0	0	2	....	....	....	....	....	....	1995-96	1996-97
Vasiliev, Alexei	NYR	1	1	0	0	0	2	....	....	....	....	....	....	1999-00	1999-00
Vasiljevs, Herbert	Fla., Atl., Van.	4	51	8	7	15	22	....	....	....	....	....	....	1998-99	2001-02
Vasilyev, Andrei	NYI, Phx.	4	16	2	5	7	6	....	....	....	....	....	....	1994-95	1998-99
Vaske, Dennis	NYI, Bos.	9	235	5	41	46	253	22	0	7	7	16	....	1990-91	1998-99
● Vasko, Moose	Chi., Min.	13	786	34	166	200	719	78	2	7	9	73	1	1956-57	1969-70
Vasko, Rick	Det.	3	31	3	7	10	29	....	....	....	....	....	....	1977-78	1980-81
● Vasyunov, Alexander	N.J.	1	18	1	4	5	0	....	....	....	....	....	....	2010-11	2010-11
Vauclair, Julien	Ott.	1	1	0	0	0	2	....	....	....	....	....	....	2003-04	2003-04
Vautour, Yvon	NYI, Col., N.J., Que.	6	204	26	33	59	401	....	....	....	....	....	....	1979-80	1984-85
Vaydik, Greg	Chi.	1	5	0	0	0	0	....	....	....	....	....	....	1976-77	1976-77
Veitch, Darren	Wsh., Det., Tor.	10	511	48	209	257	296	33	4	11	15	33	....	1980-81	1990-91
Velischek, Randy	Min., N.J., Que.	10	509	21	76	97	401	44	2	5	7	32	....	1982-83	1991-92
Vellucci, Mike	Hfd.	1	2	0	0	0	11	....	....	....	....	....	....	1987-88	1987-88
Venasky, Vic	L.A.	7	430	61	101	162	66	21	1	5	6	12	....	1972-73	1978-79
Veneruzzo, Gary	St.L.	2	7	1	1	2	0	9	0	2	2	2	....	1967-68	1971-72
Verbeek, Pat	N.J., Hfd., NYR, Dal., Det.	20	1424	522	541	1063	2905	117	26	36	62	225	1	1982-83	2001-02
Vermette, Mark	Que.	4	67	5	13	18	33	....	....	....	....	....	....	1988-89	1991-92
Vernarsky, Kris	Bos.	2	17	1	0	1	2	....	....	....	....	....	....	2002-03	2003-04
‡ Verot, Darcy	Wsh.	1	37	0	2	2	135	....	....	....	....	....	....	2003-04	2003-04
Verret, Claude	Buf.	2	14	2	5	7	2	....	....	....	....	....	....	1983-84	1984-85

Orval Tessier

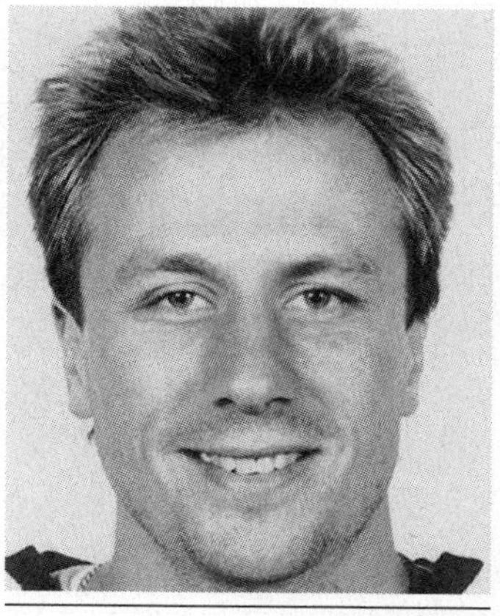

Michael Thelven

Esa Tikkanen

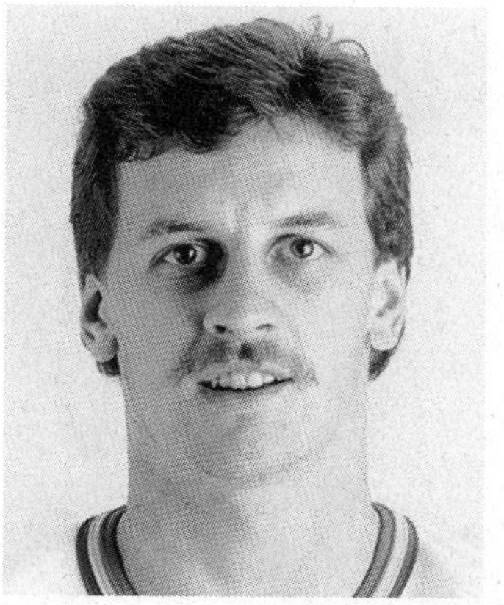

Larry Trader

Connie Tudin

Garry Unger

Yvon Vautour

Leigh Verstraete

			Regular Schedule					Playoffs					NHL	First	Last
Name	NHL Teams	NHL Seasons	GP	G	A	TP	PIM	GP	G	A	TP	PIM	Cup Wins	NHL Season	NHL Season
Verstraete, Leigh	Tor.	3	8	0	1	1	14	....	....	....	....	....	....	1982-83	1987-88
Ververgaert, Dennis	Van., Phi., Wsh.	8	583	176	216	392	247	8	1	2	3	6	....	1973-74	1980-81
‡ Vesce, Ryan	S.J.	2	19	3	2	5	4	....	....	....	....	....	....	2008-09	2009-10
Vesey, Jim	St.L., Bos.	3	15	1	2	3	7	....	....	....	....	....	....	1988-89	1991-92
Veysey, Sid	Van.	1	1	0	0	0	0	....	....	....	....	....	....	1977-78	1977-78
Vial, Dennis	NYR, Det., Ott.	8	242	4	15	19	794	....	....	....	....	....	....	1990-91	1997-98
Vickers, Steve	NYR	10	698	246	340	586	330	68	24	25	49	58	....	1972-73	1981-82
‡ Vigier, J.P.	Atl.	6	213	23	23	46	97	....	....	....	....	....	....	2000-01	2006-07
Vigneault, Alain	St.L.	2	42	2	5	7	82	4	0	1	1	26	....	1981-82	1982-83
Viitakoski, Vesa	Cgy.	3	23	2	4	6	8	....	....	....	....	....	....	1993-94	1995-96
Vilgrain, Claude	Van., N.J., Phi.	5	89	21	32	53	78	11	1	1	2	17	....	1987-88	1993-94
Vincelette, Dan	Chi., Que.	6	193	20	22	42	351	12	0	0	0	4	....	1986-87	1991-92
Vipond, Pete	Cal.	1	3	0	0	0	0	....	....	....	....	....	....	1972-73	1972-73
Virta, Hannu	Buf.	5	245	25	101	126	66	17	1	3	4	6	....	1981-82	1985-86
Virta, Tony	Min.	1	8	2	3	5	0	....	....	....	....	....	....	2001-02	2001-02
Virtue, Terry	Bos., NYR	2	5	0	0	0	0	....	....	....	....	....	....	1998-99	1999-00
Visheau, Mark	Wpg., L.A.	2	29	1	3	4	107	....	....	....	....	....	....	1993-94	1998-99
Vishnevski, Vitaly	Ana., Atl., Nsh., N.J.	8	552	16	52	68	494	40	0	5	5	18	....	1999-00	2007-08
‡ Vishnevskiy, Ivan	Dal.	2	5	0	2	2	2	....	....	....	....	....	....	2008-09	2009-10
Vitolinsh, Harijs	Wpg.	1	8	0	0	0	4	....	....	....	....	....	....	1993-94	1993-94
Viveiros, Emanuel	Min.	3	29	1	11	12	6	....	....	....	....	....	....	1985-86	1987-88
‡ Vlasak, Tomas	L.A.	1	10	1	3	4	2	....	....	....	....	....	....	2000-01	2000-01
● Vokes, Ed	Chi.	1	5	0	0	0	0	....	....	....	....	....	....	1930-31	1930-31
Volcan, Mickey	Hfd., Cgy.	4	162	8	33	41	146	....	....	....	....	....	....	1980-81	1983-84
Volchkov, Alexandre	Wsh.	1	3	0	0	0	0	....	....	....	....	....	....	1999-00	1999-00
Volek, David	NYI	6	396	95	154	249	201	15	5	5	10	2	....	1988-89	1993-94
Volmar, Doug	Det., L.A.	4	62	13	8	21	26	2	1	0	1	0	....	1969-70	1972-73
‡ Von Arx, Reto	Chi.	1	19	3	1	4	4	....	....	....	....	....	....	2000-01	2000-01
Von Stefenelli, Phil	Bos., Ott.	2	33	0	5	5	23	....	....	....	....	....	....	1995-96	1996-97
Vopat, Jan	L.A., Nsh.	5	126	11	20	31	70	2	0	1	1	2	....	1995-96	1999-00
Vopat, Roman	St.L., L.A., Chi., Phi.	4	133	6	14	20	253	....	....	....	....	....	....	1995-96	1998-99
Vorobiev, Pavel	Chi.	2	57	10	15	25	38	....	....	....	....	....	....	2003-04	2005-06
Vorobiev, Vladimir	NYR, Edm.	3	33	9	7	16	14	1	0	0	0	0	....	1996-97	1998-99
Voros, Aaron	Min., NYR, Ana.	4	162	18	19	37	395	9	1	0	1	30	....	2007-08	2010-11
● Voss, Carl	Tor., NYR, Det., Ott., St.L., NYA, Mtl.M., Chi.	8	261	34	70	104	50	24	5	3	8	0	1	1926-27	1937-38
‡ Vrana, Petr	N.J.	1	16	1	0	1	2	....	....	....	....	....	....	2008-09	2008-09
Vujtek, Vladimir	Mtl., Edm., T.B., Atl., Pit.	6	110	7	30	37	38	....	....	....	....	....	....	1991-92	2002-03
Vukota, Mick	NYI, T.B., Mtl.	11	574	17	29	46	2071	23	0	0	0	73	....	1987-88	1997-98
● Vyazmikin, Igor	Edm.	1	4	1	0	1	0	....	....	....	....	....	....	1990-91	1990-91
‡ Vyborny, David	CBJ	7	543	113	204	317	228	....	....	....	....	....	....	2000-01	2007-08
Vyshedkevich, Sergei	Atl.	2	30	2	5	7	16	....	....	....	....	....	....	1999-00	2000-01

W

Waddell, Don	L.A.	1	1	0	0	0	0	....	....	....	....	....	....	1980-81	1980-81
‡ Wagner, Steve	St.L.	2	46	4	8	12	26	....	....	....	....	....	....	2007-08	2008-09
● Waite, Frank	NYR	1	17	1	3	4	4	....	....	....	....	....	....	1930-31	1930-31
Walker, Gord	NYR, L.A.	4	31	3	4	7	23	....	....	....	....	....	....	1986-87	1989-90
Walker, Howard	Wsh., Cgy.	3	83	2	13	15	133	....	....	....	....	....	....	1980-81	1982-83
● Walker, Jack	Det.	2	80	5	8	13	18	....	....	....	....	....	....	1926-27	1927-28
Walker, Kurt	Tor.	3	71	4	5	9	142	16	0	0	0	34	....	1975-76	1977-78
Walker, Russ	L.A.	2	17	1	0	1	41	....	....	....	....	....	....	1976-77	1977-78
Walker, Scott	Van., Nsh., Car., Wsh.	15	829	151	246	397	1162	30	1	7	8	31	....	1994-95	2009-10
Wall, Bob	Det., L.A., St.L.	8	322	30	55	85	155	22	0	3	3	2	....	1964-65	1971-72
Wallin, Jesse	Det.	4	49	0	2	2	34	....	....	....	....	....	....	1999-00	2002-03
Wallin, Niclas	Car., S.J.	10	614	21	58	79	460	93	4	8	12	44	1	2000-01	2010-11
Wallin, Peter	NYR	2	52	3	14	17	14	14	2	6	8	6	....	1980-81	1981-82
‡ Wallin, Rickard	Min., Tor.	3	79	8	11	19	34	....	....	....	....	....	....	2002-03	2009-10
‡ Walser, Derrick	CBJ	4	91	8	21	29	56	....	....	....	....	....	....	2001-02	2006-07
Walsh, Jim	Buf.	1	4	0	1	1	4	....	....	....	....	....	....	1981-82	1981-82
Walsh, Mike	NYI	2	14	2	0	2	4	....	....	....	....	....	....	1987-88	1988-89
Walter, Ryan	Wsh., Mtl., Van.	15	1003	264	382	646	946	113	16	35	51	62	1	1978-79	1992-93
● Walton, Bobby	Mtl.	1	4	0	0	0	0	....	....	....	....	....	....	1943-44	1943-44
Walton, Mike	Tor., Bos., Van., St.L., Chi.	12	588	201	247	448	357	47	14	10	24	45	2	1965-66	1978-79
Walz, Wes	Bos., Phi., Cgy., Det., Min.	13	607	109	151	260	343	32	10	7	17	20	....	1989-90	2007-08
Wanvig, Kyle	Min., T.B.	5	75	6	9	15	94	....	....	....	....	....	....	2002-03	2007-08
Wappel, Gord	Atl., Cgy.	3	20	1	1	2	10	2	0	0	0	4	....	1979-80	1981-82
Ward, Aaron	Det., Car., NYR, Bos., Ana.	15	839	44	107	151	736	95	4	6	10	73	3	1993-94	2009-10
Ward, Dixon	Van., L.A., Tor., Buf., Bos., NYR	10	537	95	129	224	431	62	14	20	34	46	....	1992-93	2002-03
● Ward, Don	Chi., Bos.	2	34	0	1	1	16	....	....	....	....	....	....	1957-58	1959-60
Ward, Ed	Que., Cgy., Atl., Ana., N.J.	8	278	23	26	49	354	....	....	....	....	....	....	1993-94	2000-01
Ward, Jason	Mtl., NYR, L.A., T.B.	8	336	36	45	81	171	12	0	3	3	10	....	1999-00	2008-09
● Ward, Jimmy	Mtl.M., Mtl.	12	527	147	127	274	455	36	4	4	8	26	1	1927-28	1938-39
Ward, Joe	Col.	1	4	0	0	0	2	....	....	....	....	....	....	1980-81	1980-81
Ward, Lance	Fla., Ana.	4	209	4	12	16	391	....	....	....	....	....	....	2000-01	2003-04
Ward, Ron	Tor., Van.	2	89	2	5	7	6	....	....	....	....	....	....	1969-70	1971-72
Ware, Jeff	Tor., Fla.	3	21	0	1	1	12	....	....	....	....	....	....	1996-97	1998-99
Ware, Michael	Edm.	2	5	0	1	1	15	....	....	....	....	....	....	1988-89	1989-90
● Wares, Eddie	NYR, Det., Chi.	9	321	60	102	162	161	45	5	7	12	34	1	1936-37	1946-47
Warner, Bob	Tor.	2	10	1	1	2	4	4	0	0	0	0	....	1975-76	1976-77
Warner, Jim	Hfd.	1	32	0	3	3	10	....	....	....	....	....	....	1979-80	1979-80
Warrener, Rhett	Fla., Buf., Cgy.	12	714	24	82	106	899	101	1	7	8	68	....	1995-96	2007-08
Warriner, Todd	Tor., T.B., Phx., Van., Phi., Nsh.	9	453	65	89	154	249	21	2	1	3	6	....	1994-95	2002-03
● Warwick, Billy	NYR	2	14	3	3	6	16	....	....	....	....	....	....	1942-43	1943-44
● Warwick, Grant	NYR, Bos., Mtl.	9	395	147	142	289	220	16	2	4	6	6	....	1941-42	1949-50
Washburn, Steve	Fla., Van., Phi.	6	93	14	15	29	42	1	0	1	1	0	....	1995-96	2000-01
● Wasnie, Nick	Chi., Mtl., NYA, Ott., St.L.	7	248	57	34	91	176	20	6	3	9	20	2	1927-28	1934-35
Watson, Bill	Chi.	4	115	23	36	59	12	6	0	2	2	0	....	1985-86	1988-89
Watson, Bryan	Mtl., Det., Oak., Pit., St.L., Wsh.	16	878	17	135	152	2212	32	2	0	2	70	1	1963-64	1978-79
Watson, Dave	Col.	2	18	0	1	1	10	....	....	....	....	....	....	1979-80	1980-81
● Watson, Harry	Bro., Det., Tor., Chi.	14	809	236	207	443	150	62	16	9	25	27	5	1941-42	1956-57
Watson, Jim	Det., Buf.	8	221	4	19	23	345	....	....	....	....	....	....	1963-64	1971-72
Watson, Jimmy	Phi.	10	613	38	148	186	492	101	5	34	39	89	2	1972-73	1981-82
Watson, Joe	Bos., Phi., Col.	14	835	38	178	216	447	84	3	12	15	82	2	1964-65	1978-79
● Watson, Phil	NYR, Mtl.	13	590	144	265	409	532	54	10	25	35	67	2	1935-36	1947-48
Watt, Mike	Edm., NYI, Nsh., Car.	5	157	15	26	41	41	....	....	....	....	....	....	1997-98	2002-03
Watters, Tim	Wpg., L.A.	14	741	26	151	177	1289	82	1	5	6	115	....	1981-82	1994-95
Watts, Brian	Det.	1	4	0	0	0	0	....	....	....	....	....	....	1975-76	1975-76
Webb, Steve	NYI, Pit.	8	321	5	13	18	532	14	0	0	0	28	....	1996-97	2003-04
● Webster, Aubrey	Phi., Mtl.M.	2	5	0	0	0	0	....	....	....	....	....	....	1930-31	1934-35
● Webster, Don	Tor.	1	27	7	6	13	28	5	0	0	0	12	....	1943-44	1943-44
Webster, John	NYR	1	14	0	0	0	4	....	....	....	....	....	....	1949-50	1949-50
Webster, Tom	Bos., Det., Cal.	5	102	33	42	75	61	1	0	0	0	0	....	1968-69	1979-80
Weight, Doug	NYR, Edm., St.L., Car., Ana., NYI	20	1238	278	755	1033	970	97	23	49	72	94	1	1990-91	2010-11
● Weiland, Cooney	Bos., Ott., Det.	11	509	173	160	333	147	45	12	10	22	12	2	1928-29	1938-39
‡ Weinhandl, Mattias	NYI, Min.	4	182	19	37	56	70	5	0	0	0	2	....	2002-03	2006-07
Weinrich, Eric	N.J., Hfd., Chi., Mtl., Bos., Phi., St.L., Van.	17	1157	70	318	388	825	81	6	23	29	67	....	1988-89	2005-06
Weir, Stan	Cal., Tor., Edm., Col., Det.	10	642	139	207	346	183	37	6	5	11	4	....	1972-73	1982-83
Weir, Wally	Que., Hfd., Pit.	6	320	21	45	66	625	23	0	1	1	96	....	1979-80	1984-85
‡ Welch, Noah	Pit., Fla., T.B., Atl.	5	75	4	5	9	58	....	....	....	....	....	....	2005-06	2010-11
‡ Weller, Craig	Phx., Min.	2	95	4	10	14	127	....	....	....	....	....	....	2007-08	2008-09
● Wellington, Alex	Que.	1	1	0	0	0	0	....	....	....	....	....	....	1919-20	1919-20
Wells, Chris	Pit., Fla.	5	195	9	20	29	193	3	0	0	0	0	....	1995-96	1999-00
Wells, Jay	L.A., Phi., Buf., NYR, St.L., T.B.	18	1098	47	216	263	2359	114	3	14	17	213	1	1979-80	1996-97
Wensink, John	St.L., Bos., Que., Col., N.J.	8	403	70	68	138	840	43	2	6	8	86	....	1973-74	1982-83
● Wentworth, Cy	Chi., Mtl.M., Mtl.	13	575	39	68	107	355	35	5	6	11	20	1	1927-28	1939-40
Werenka, Brad	Edm., Que., Chi., Pit., Cgy.	7	320	19	61	80	299	19	2	1	3	14	....	1992-93	2000-01
Wesenberg, Brian	Phi.	1	1	0	0	0	5	....	....	....	....	....	....	1998-99	1998-99
Wesley, Blake	Phi., Hfd., Que., Tor.	7	298	18	46	64	486	19	2	2	4	30	....	1979-80	1985-86
Wesley, Glen	Bos., Hfd., Car., Tor.	20	1457	128	409	537	1045	169	15	37	52	141	1	1987-88	2007-08
‡ Westcott, Duvie	CBJ	6	201	11	45	56	299	....	....	....	....	....	....	2001-02	2007-08
Westfall, Ed	Bos., NYI	18	1226	231	394	625	544	95	22	37	59	41	2	1961-62	1978-79
Westlund, Tommy	Car.	4	203	9	13	22	48	25	1	0	1	17	....	1999-00	2002-03
Westrum, Erik	Phx., Min., Tor.	3	27	1	2	3	22	....	....	....	....	....	....	2003-04	2006-07

Name	NHL Teams	NHL Seasons	Regular Schedule GP	G	A	TP	PIM	Playoffs GP	G	A	TP	PIM	NHL Cup Wins	First NHL Season	Last NHL Season
Wharram, Kenny	Chi.	14	766	252	281	533	222	80	16	27	43	38	1	1951-52	1968-69
• Wharton, Len	NYR	1	1	0	0	0	0	....	....	....	....	....	....	1944-45	1944-45
Wheeldon, Simon	NYR, Wpg.	3	15	0	2	2	10	....	....	....	....	....	....	1987-88	1990-91
• Wheldon, Don	St.L.	1	2	0	0	0	0	....	....	....	....	....	....	1974-75	1974-75
Whelton, Bill	Wpg.	1	2	0	0	0	0	....	....	....	....	....	....	1980-81	1980-81
Whistle, Rob	NYR, St.L.	2	51	7	5	12	16	4	0	0	0	2	....	1985-86	1987-88
White, Bill	L.A., Chi.	9	604	50	215	265	495	91	7	32	39	76	....	1967-68	1975-76
White, Brian	Col.	1	2	0	0	0	0	....	....	....	....	....	....	1998-99	1998-99
White, Colin	N.J., S.J.	12	797	21	108	129	869	114	3	14	17	125	2	1999-00	2011-12
White, Moe	Mtl.	1	4	0	1	1	2	....	....	....	....	....	....	1945-46	1945-46
White, Peter	Edm., Tor., Phi., Chi.	9	220	23	37	60	36	19	0	2	2	0	....	1993-94	2003-04
• White, Sherman	NYR	2	4	0	2	2	0	....	....	....	....	....	....	1946-47	1949-50
• White, Tex	Pit., NYA, Phi.	6	203	33	12	45	141	4	0	0	0	4	....	1925-26	1930-31
White, Todd	Chi., Phi., Ott., Min., Atl., NYR	13	653	141	240	381	228	43	8	3	11	16	....	1997-98	2010-11
White, Tony	Wsh., Min.	5	164	37	28	65	104	....	....	....	....	....	....	1974-75	1979-80
Whitelaw, Bob	Det.	2	32	0	2	2	2	8	0	0	0	0	....	1940-41	1941-42
Whitlock, Bob	Min.	1	1	0	0	0	0	....	....	....	....	....	....	1969-70	1969-70
Whyte, Sean	L.A.	2	21	0	2	2	12	....	....	....	....	....	....	1991-92	1992-93
‡ Wick, Roman	Ott.	1	7	0	0	0	0	....	....	....	....	....	....	2010-11	2010-11
• Wickenheiser, Doug	Mtl., St.L., Van., NYR, Wsh.	10	556	111	165	276	286	41	4	7	11	18	....	1980-81	1989-90
• Widing, Juha	NYR, L.A., Cle.	8	575	144	226	370	208	8	1	2	3	2	....	1969-70	1976-77
Widmer, Jason	NYI, S.J.	3	7	0	1	1	7	....	....	....	....	....	....	1994-95	1996-97
• Wiebe, Art	Chi.	11	414	14	27	41	201	31	1	3	4	10	1	1932-33	1943-44
Wiemer, Jason	T.B., Cgy., Fla., NYI, Min., N.J.	11	726	90	112	202	1420	19	1	0	1	67	....	1994-95	2005-06
Wiemer, Jim	Buf., NYR, Edm., L.A., Bos.	11	325	29	72	101	378	62	5	8	13	63	....	1982-83	1993-94
• Wilcox, Archie	Mtl.M., Bos., St.L.	6	208	8	14	22	158	12	1	0	1	8	....	1929-30	1934-35
Wilcox, Barry	Van.	2	33	3	2	5	15	....	....	....	....	....	....	1972-73	1974-75
• Wilder, Arch	Det.	1	18	0	2	2	2	....	....	....	....	....	....	1940-41	1940-41
Wiley, Jim	Pit., Van.	5	63	4	10	14	8	....	....	....	....	....	....	1972-73	1976-77
Wilkie, Bob	Det., Phi.	2	18	2	5	7	10	....	....	....	....	....	....	1990-91	1993-94
Wilkie, David	Mtl., T.B., NYR	6	167	10	26	36	165	8	1	2	3	14	....	1994-95	2000-01
• Wilkins, Barry	Bos., Van., Pit.	9	418	27	125	152	663	6	0	1	1	4	....	1966-67	1975-76
• Wilkinson, John	Bos.	1	9	0	0	0	6	....	....	....	....	....	....	1943-44	1943-44
Wilkinson, Neil	Min., S.J., Chi., Wpg., Pit.	10	460	16	67	83	813	53	3	6	9	41	....	1989-90	1998-99
Wilks, Brian	L.A.	4	48	4	8	12	27	....	....	....	....	....	....	1984-85	1988-89
Willard, Rod	Tor.	1	1	0	0	0	0	....	....	....	....	....	....	1982-83	1982-83
• Williams, Burr	Det., St.L., Bos.	3	19	0	1	1	28	7	0	0	0	8	....	1933-34	1936-37
Williams, Butch	St.L., Cal.	3	108	14	35	49	131	....	....	....	....	....	....	1973-74	1975-76
Williams, Darryl	L.A.	1	2	0	0	0	10	....	....	....	....	....	....	1992-93	1992-93
Williams, David	S.J., Ana.	4	173	11	53	64	157	....	....	....	....	....	....	1991-92	1994-95
Williams, Fred	Det.	1	44	2	5	7	10	....	....	....	....	....	....	1976-77	1976-77
Williams, Gord	Phi.	2	2	0	0	0	2	....	....	....	....	....	....	1981-82	1982-83
‡ Williams, Jeremy	Tor., NYR	5	32	9	2	11	6	....	....	....	....	....	....	2005-06	2010-11
Williams, Sean	Chi.	1	2	0	0	0	4	....	....	....	....	....	....	1991-92	1991-92
Williams, Tiger	Tor., Van., Det., L.A., Hfd.	14	962	241	272	513	3966	83	12	23	35	455	....	1974-75	1987-88
Williams, Tom	NYR, L.A.	8	397	115	138	253	73	29	8	7	15	4	....	1971-72	1978-79
• Williams, Tommy	Bos., Min., Cal., Wsh.	13	663	161	269	430	177	10	2	5	7	2	....	1961-62	1975-76
Willis, Shane	Car., T.B.	5	174	31	43	74	77	2	0	0	0	0	....	1998-99	2003-04
‡ Willsie, Brian	Col., Wsh., L.A.	10	381	52	57	109	217	10	1	1	2	4	....	1999-00	2010-11
Willson, Don	Mtl.	2	22	2	7	9	0	3	0	0	0	0	....	1937-38	1938-39
Wilm, Clarke	Cgy., Nsh., Tor.	7	455	37	60	97	336	5	0	1	1	2	....	1998-99	2005-06
Wilson, Behn	Phi., Chi.	9	601	98	260	358	1480	67	12	29	41	190	....	1978-79	1987-88
• Wilson, Bert	NYR, St.L., L.A., Cgy.	8	478	37	44	81	646	21	0	2	2	42	....	1973-74	1980-81
Wilson, Bob	Chi.	1	1	0	0	0	0	....	....	....	....	....	....	1953-54	1953-54
Wilson, Carey	Cgy., Hfd., NYR	10	552	169	258	427	314	52	11	13	24	14	....	1983-84	1992-93
• Wilson, Cully	Tor., Mtl., Ham., Chi.	5	127	59	28	87	243	2	1	0	1	6	....	1919-20	1926-27
Wilson, Doug	Chi., S.J.	16	1024	237	590	827	830	95	19	61	80	88	....	1977-78	1992-93
Wilson, Gord	Bos.	1	....	....	....	....	....	2	0	0	0	0	....	1954-55	1954-55
• Wilson, Hub	NYA	1	2	0	0	0	0	....	....	....	....	....	....	1931-32	1931-32
Wilson, Jerry	Mtl.	1	3	0	0	0	2	....	....	....	....	....	....	1956-57	1956-57
• Wilson, Johnny	Det., Chi., Tor., NYR	13	688	161	171	332	190	66	14	13	27	11	4	1949-50	1961-62
Wilson, Landon	Col., Bos., Phx., Pit., Dal.	10	375	53	66	119	352	13	1	1	2	20	....	1995-96	2008-09
• Wilson, Larry	Det., Chi.	6	152	21	48	69	75	4	0	0	0	0	1	1949-50	1955-56
Wilson, Mike	Buf., Fla., Pit., NYR	8	336	16	41	57	264	29	0	2	2	15	....	1995-96	2002-03
Wilson, Mitch	N.J., Pit.	2	26	2	3	5	104	....	....	....	....	....	....	1984-85	1986-87
Wilson, Murray	Mtl., L.A.	7	386	94	95	189	162	53	5	14	19	32	4	1972-73	1978-79
Wilson, Rick	Mtl., St.L., Det.	4	239	6	26	32	165	3	0	0	0	0	....	1973-74	1976-77
Wilson, Rik	St.L., Cgy., Chi.	6	251	25	65	90	220	22	0	4	4	23	....	1981-82	1987-88
Wilson, Roger	Chi.	1	7	0	2	2	6	....	....	....	....	....	....	1974-75	1974-75
Wilson, Ron	Tor., Min.	7	177	26	67	93	68	20	4	13	17	8	....	1977-78	1987-88
Wilson, Ron	Wpg., St.L., Mtl.	14	832	110	216	326	415	63	10	12	22	64	....	1979-80	1993-94
• Wilson, Wally	Bos.	1	53	11	8	19	18	1	0	0	0	0	....	1947-48	1947-48
Wing, Murray	Det.	1	1	0	1	1	0	....	....	....	....	....	....	1973-74	1973-74
Winnes, Chris	Bos., Phi.	4	33	1	6	7	6	1	0	0	0	0	....	1990-91	1993-94
‡ Wirtanen, Petteri	Ana.	1	3	1	0	1	2	....	....	....	....	....	....	2007-08	2007-08
Wiseman, Brian	Tor.	1	3	0	0	0	0	....	....	....	....	....	....	1996-97	1996-97
‡ Wiseman, Chad	S.J., NYR	3	9	1	1	2	8	1	0	0	0	2	....	2002-03	2005-06
• Wiseman, Eddie	Det., NYA, Bos.	10	456	115	165	280	136	43	10	10	20	16	1	1932-33	1941-42
Wiste, Jim	Chi., Van.	3	52	1	10	11	8	....	....	....	....	....	....	1968-69	1970-71
Witehall, Johan	NYR, Mtl.	3	54	2	5	7	16	....	....	....	....	....	....	1998-99	2000-01
Witherspoon, Jim	L.A.	1	2	0	0	0	2	....	....	....	....	....	....	1975-76	1975-76
Witiuk, Steve	Chi.	1	33	3	8	11	14	....	....	....	....	....	....	1951-52	1951-52
Witt, Brendan	Wsh., Nsh., NYI	14	890	25	96	121	1424	41	4	1	5	44	....	1995-96	2009-10
Woit, Benny	Det., Chi.	7	334	7	26	33	170	41	2	6	8	18	3	1950-51	1956-57
Wojciechowski, Steve	Det.	2	54	19	20	39	17	6	0	1	1	0	....	1944-45	1946-47
Wolanin, Craig	N.J., Que., Col., T.B., Tor.	13	695	40	133	173	894	35	4	6	10	67	1	1985-86	1997-98
Wolf, Bennett	Pit.	3	30	0	1	1	133	....	....	....	....	....	....	1980-81	1982-83
Wong, Mike	Det.	1	22	1	1	2	12	....	....	....	....	....	....	1975-76	1975-76
Wood, Dody	S.J.	5	106	8	10	18	471	....	....	....	....	....	....	1992-93	1997-98
Wood, Randy	NYI, Buf., Tor., Dal.	11	741	175	159	334	603	51	8	9	17	40	....	1986-87	1996-97
• Wood, Robert	NYR	1	1	0	0	0	0	....	....	....	....	....	....	1950-51	1950-51
Woodley, Dan	Van.	1	5	2	0	2	17	....	....	....	....	....	....	1987-88	1987-88
Woods, Paul	Det.	7	501	72	124	196	276	7	0	5	5	4	....	1977-78	1983-84
Woolley, Jason	Wsh., Fla., Pit., Buf., Det.	14	718	68	246	314	430	79	11	36	47	44	....	1991-92	2005-06
Worrell, Peter	Fla., Col.	7	391	19	27	46	1554	4	1	0	1	8	....	1997-98	2003-04
Wortman, Kevin	Cgy.	1	5	0	0	0	2	....	....	....	....	....	....	1993-94	1993-94
Wotton, Mark	Van., Dal.	4	43	3	6	9	25	5	0	0	0	4	....	1994-95	2000-01
• Woytowich, Bob	Bos., Min., Pit., L.A.	8	503	32	126	158	352	24	1	3	4	20	....	1964-65	1971-72
‡ Wozniewski, Andy	Tor., St.L., Bos.	5	79	2	10	12	81	....	....	....	....	....	....	2005-06	2009-10
‡ Wren, Bob	Ana., Tor.	3	5	0	0	0	0	1	0	0	0	0	....	1997-98	2001-02
Wright, Jamie	Dal., Cgy., Phi.	6	124	12	20	32	54	5	0	0	0	0	....	1997-98	2002-03
Wright, John	Van., St.L., K.C.	3	127	16	36	52	67	....	....	....	....	....	....	1972-73	1974-75
Wright, Keith	Phi.	1	1	0	0	0	0	....	....	....	....	....	....	1967-68	1967-68
Wright, Larry	Phi., Cal., Det.	5	106	4	8	12	19	....	....	....	....	....	....	1971-72	1977-78
Wright, Tyler	Edm., Pit., CBJ, Ana.	13	613	79	70	149	854	30	3	2	5	40	....	1992-93	2005-06
• Wycherley, Ralph	NYA, Bro.	2	28	4	7	11	6	....	....	....	....	....	....	1940-41	1941-42
• Wylie, Bill	NYR	1	1	0	0	0	0	....	....	....	....	....	....	1950-51	1950-51
Wylie, Duane	Chi.	2	14	3	3	6	2	....	....	....	....	....	....	1974-75	1976-77
Wyrozub, Randy	Buf.	4	100	8	10	18	10	....	....	....	....	....	....	1970-71	1973-74

Y Z

‡ Yablonski, Jeremy	St.L.	1	1	0	0	0	5	....	....	....	....	....	....	2003-04	2003-04
Yachmenev, Vitali	L.A., Nsh.	8	487	83	133	216	88	....	....	....	....	....	....	1995-96	2002-03
• Yackel, Ken	Bos.	1	6	0	0	0	2	2	0	0	0	2	....	1958-59	1958-59
Yake, Terry	Hfd., Ana., Tor., St.L., Wsh.	11	403	77	120	197	220	32	4	4	8	36	....	1988-89	2000-01
‡ Yakubov, Mikhail	Chi., Fla.	2	53	2	10	12	20	....	....	....	....	....	....	2003-04	2005-06
Yakushin, Dmitri	Tor.	1	2	0	0	0	2	....	....	....	....	....	....	1999-00	1999-00
Yaremchuk, Gary	Tor.	4	34	1	4	5	28	....	....	....	....	....	....	1981-82	1984-85
Yaremchuk, Ken	Chi., Tor.	6	235	36	56	92	106	31	6	8	14	49	....	1983-84	1988-89
‡ Yashin, Alexei	Ott., NYI	12	850	337	444	781	401	48	11	16	27	24	....	1993-94	2006-07
Yates, Ross	Hfd.	1	7	1	1	2	4	....	....	....	....	....	....	1983-84	1983-84
Yawney, Trent	Chi., Cgy., St.L.	12	593	27	102	129	783	60	9	17	26	81	....	1987-88	1998-99
• Yegorov, Alexei	S.J.	2	11	3	3	6	2	....	....	....	....	....	....	1995-96	1996-97
Yelle, Stephane	Col., Cgy., Bos., Car.	14	991	96	169	265	490	171	11	21	32	90	2	1995-96	2009-10
Ylonen, Juha	Phx., T.B., Ott.	6	341	26	76	102	90	15	0	7	7	4	....	1996-97	2001-02

Jim Watson

Phil Watson

Len Wharton

Colin White

Rik Wilson

Wally Wilson

Gary Yaremchuk

Rob Zamuner

			Regular Schedule					Playoffs							
Name	NHL Teams	NHL Seasons	GP	G	A	TP	PIM	GP	G	A	TP	PIM	NHL Cup Wins	First NHL Season	Last NHL Season
York, Harry	St.L., NYR, Pit., Van.	4	244	29	46	75	99	5	0	0	0	2	....	1996-97	1999-00
York, Jason	Det., Ana., Ott., Nsh., Bos.	13	757	42	187	229	621	34	2	7	9	25	....	1992-93	2006-07
‡ York, Mike	NYR, Edm., NYI, Phi., Phx., CBJ	9	579	127	195	322	135	6	0	2	2	2	....	1999-00	2008-09
• Young, B.J.	Det.	1	1	0	0	0	0	....	....	....	....	....	....	1999-00	1999-00
Young, Brian	Chi.	1	8	0	2	2	6	....	....	....	....	....	....	1980-81	1980-81
‡ Young, Bryan	Edm.	2	17	0	0	0	10	....	....	....	....	....	....	2006-07	2007-08
Young, C.J.	Cgy., Bos.	1	43	7	7	14	32	....	....	....	....	....	....	1992-93	1992-93
• Young, Doug	Det., Mtl.	10	388	35	45	80	303	28	1	5	6	16	2	1931-32	1940-41
• Young, Howie	Det., Chi., Van.	8	336	12	62	74	851	19	2	4	6	46	....	1960-61	1970-71
Young, Scott	Hfd., Pit., Que., Col., Ana., St.L., Dal.	17	1181	342	415	757	448	141	44	43	87	64	2	1987-88	2005-06
Young, Tim	Min., Wpg., Phi.	10	628	195	341	536	438	36	7	24	31	27	....	1975-76	1984-85
Young, Warren	Min., Pit., Det.	7	236	72	77	149	472	....	....	....	....	....	....	1981-82	1987-88
Younghans, Tom	Min., NYR	6	429	44	41	85	373	24	2	1	3	21	....	1976-77	1981-82
Ysebaert, Paul	N.J., Det., Wpg., Chi., T.B.	11	532	149	187	336	217	30	4	3	7	20	....	1988-89	1998-99
Yushkevich, Dmitry	Phi., Tor., Fla., L.A.	11	786	43	182	225	659	72	4	19	23	52	....	1992-93	2002-03
Yzerman, Steve	Det.	22	1514	692	1063	1755	924	196	70	115	185	84	3	1983-84	2005-06
Zabransky, Libor	St.L.	2	40	1	6	7	50	....	....	....	....	....	....	1996-97	1997-98
Zaharko, Miles	Atl., Chi.	4	129	5	32	37	84	3	0	0	0	0	....	1977-78	1981-82
Zaine, Rod	Pit., Buf.	2	61	10	6	16	25	....	....	....	....	....	....	1970-71	1971-72
Zalapski, Zarley	Pit., Hfd., Cgy., Mtl., Phi.	12	637	99	285	384	684	48	4	23	27	47	....	1987-88	1999-00
‡ Zalesak, Miroslav	S.J.	2	12	1	2	3	0	....	....	....	....	....	....	2002-03	2003-04
Zamuner, Rob	NYR, T.B., Ott., Bos.	13	798	139	172	311	467	34	4	5	9	26	....	1991-92	2003-04
Zanussi, Joe	NYR, Bos., St.L.	3	87	1	13	14	46	4	0	1	1	2	....	1974-75	1976-77
Zanussi, Ron	Min., Tor.	5	299	52	83	135	373	17	0	4	4	17	....	1977-78	1981-82
Zavisha, Brad	Edm.	1	2	0	0	0	0	....	....	....	....	....	....	1993-94	1993-94
Zednik, Richard	Wsh., Mtl., NYI, Fla.	13	745	200	179	379	563	48	16	10	26	41	....	1995-96	2008-09
Zehr, Jeff	Bos.	1	4	0	0	0	2	....	....	....	....	....	....	1999-00	1999-00
Zeidel, Larry	Det., Chi., Phi.	5	158	3	16	19	198	12	0	1	1	12	1	1951-52	1968-69
Zelepukin, Valeri	N.J., Edm., Phi., Chi.	10	595	117	177	294	527	85	13	13	26	48	1	1991-92	2000-01
Zemlak, Richard	Que., Min., Pit., Cgy.	5	132	2	12	14	587	1	0	0	0	10	....	1986-87	1991-92
• Zeniuk, Ed	Det.	1	2	0	0	0	0	....	....	....	....	....	....	1954-55	1954-55
Zent, Jason	Ott., Phi.	3	27	3	3	6	13	....	....	....	....	....	....	1996-97	1998-99
Zetterstrom, Lars	Van.	1	14	0	1	1	2	....	....	....	....	....	....	1978-79	1978-79
Zettler, Rob	Min., S.J., Phi., Tor., Nsh., Wsh.	14	569	5	65	70	920	14	0	0	0	4	....	1988-89	2001-02
• Zezel, Peter	Phi., St.L., Wsh., Tor., Dal., N.J., Van.	15	873	219	389	608	435	131	25	39	64	83	....	1984-85	1998-99
Zhamnov, Alex	Wpg., Chi., Phi., Bos.	13	807	249	470	719	668	35	6	13	19	18	....	1992-93	2005-06
‡ Zherdev, Nikolai	CBJ, NYR, Phi.	6	421	115	146	261	225	15	1	2	3	4	....	2003-04	2010-11
Zhitnik, Alexei	L.A., Buf., NYI, Phi., Atl.	15	1085	96	375	471	1268	98	9	30	39	168	....	1992-93	2007-08
• Zholtok, Sergei	Bos., Ott., Mtl., Edm., Min., Nsh.	10	588	111	147	258	166	45	4	14	18	0	....	1992-93	2003-04
‡ Ziegler, Thomas	T.B.	1	5	0	0	0	0	....	....	....	....	....	....	2000-01	2000-01
Zinger, Dwayne	Wsh.	1	7	0	1	1	9	....	....	....	....	....	....	2003-04	2003-04
‡ Zinovjev, Sergei	Bos.	1	10	0	1	1	2	....	....	....	....	....	....	2003-04	2003-04
‡ Zizka, Tomas	L.A.	2	25	2	6	8	16	....	....	....	....	....	....	2002-03	2003-04
Zmolek, Doug	S.J., Dal., L.A., Chi.	8	467	11	53	64	905	14	0	1	1	16	....	1992-93	1999-00
Zoborosky, Marty	Chi.	1	1	0	0	0	2	....	....	....	....	....	....	1944-45	1944-45
Zombo, Rick	Det., St.L., Bos.	12	652	24	130	154	728	60	1	11	12	127	....	1984-85	1995-96
‡ Zubarev, Andrei	Atl.	1	4	0	1	1	4	....	....	....	....	....	....	2010-11	2010-11
‡ Zubov, Ilya	Ott.	2	11	0	2	2	0	....	....	....	....	....	....	2007-08	2008-09
Zubov, Sergei	NYR, Pit., Dal.	16	1068	152	619	771	337	164	24	93	117	62	2	1992-93	2008-09
Zuke, Mike	St.L., Hfd.	8	455	86	196	282	220	26	6	6	12	12	....	1978-79	1985-86
• Zunich, Rudy	Det.	1	2	0	0	0	2	....	....	....	....	....	....	1943-44	1943-44
‡ Zyuzin, Andrei	S.J., T.B., N.J., Min., Cgy., Chi.	10	496	38	82	120	446	29	2	1	3	30	....	1997-98	2007-08

Retired Players, Goaltenders and Coaches Research Project

Throughout the Retired Players and Retired Goaltenders sections of this book, you will notice many players with a bullet (•) by their names. These players, according to our records, are deceased. The editors recognize that our information on the death dates of NHLers is incomplete. If you have documented information on the passing of any player not marked with a bullet (•) in this edition, we would like to hear from you. We also welcome information on deceased NHL head coaches. Please send this information to:

Retired Player Research Project
c/o NHL Publishing
194 Dovercourt Road
Toronto, Ontario
M6J 3C8 Canada

Many thanks to the following contributors . . .

Tim Bateman, Corey Bryant, Paul R. Carroll, Jr., Bob Duff, Peter Fillman, Ernie Fitzsimmons, Chris Gory, Gary J. Pearce, Martin Schmid, Al Tario, Drew "Whitey" White.

Retired NHL Goaltender Index

Abbreviations: Teams/Cities: – **Ana.** – Anaheim; **Atl.** – Atlanta; **Bos.** – Boston; **Bro.** – Brooklyn; **Buf.** – Buffalo; **Cgy.** – Calgary; **Cal.** – California; **Car.** – Carolina; **Chi.** – Chicago; **Cle.** – Cleveland; **Col.** – Colorado; **CBJ** – Columbus; **Dal.** – Dallas; **Det.** – Detroit; **Edm.** – Edmonton; **Fla.** – Florida; **Ham.** – Hamilton; **Hfd.** – Hartford; **K.C.** – Kansas City; **L.A.** – Los Angeles; **Min.** – Minnesota; **Mtl.** – Montreal; **Mtl.M.** – Montreal Maroons; **Mtl.W.** – Montreal Wanderers; **Nsh.** – Nashville; **N.J.** – New Jersey; **NYA** – NY Americans; **NYI** – NY Islanders; **NYR** – New York Rangers; **Oak.** – Oakland; **Ott.** – Ottawa; **Phi.** – Philadelphia; **Phx.** – Phoenix; **Pit.** – Pittsburgh; **Que.** – Quebec; **St.L.** – St. Louis; **S.J.** – San Jose; **T.B.** – Tampa Bay; **Tor.** – Toronto; **Van.** – Vancouver; **Wsh.** – Washington; **Wpg.** – Winnipeg

Avg. – goals against per 60 minutes played; **GA** – goals agains; **GP** – games played; **Mins** – minutes played; **SO** – shutouts.
• – deceased. § – Forward, defenseman or coach who appeared in goal. For complete career, see Retired Player Index. ‡ – Remains active in other leagues.

NHL Seasons – A player or goaltender who does not play in a regular season but who does appear in that year's playoffs is credited with an NHL Season in this Index. Total seasons are rounded off to the nearest full season.

Name	NHL Teams	NHL Seasons	Regular Schedule								Playoffs								NHL Cup Wins	First NHL Season	Last NHL Season
			GP	W	L	T	Mins	GA	SO	Avg	GP	W	L	T	Mins	GA	SO	Avg			
Abbott, George	Bos.	1	1	0	1	0	60	7	0	7.00										1943-44	1943-44
Adams, John	Bos., Wsh.	3	22	9	10	1	1180	85	1	4.32	....	....	....	....	....	....	....	....	1	1969-70	1974-75
‡ Aebischer, David	Col., Mtl., Phx.	7	214	106	74	17	12230	513	13	2.52	13	6	5	....	697	24	1	2.07	1	2000-01	2007-08
Aiken, Don	Mtl.	1	1	0	1	0	34	6	0	10.59	....	....	....	....	....	....	....	....		1957-58	1957-58
• Aitkenhead, Andy	NYR	3	106	47	43	16	6570	257	11	2.35	10	6	2	2	608	15	3	1.48	1	1932-33	1934-35
• Almas, Red	Det., Chi.	3	3	0	2	1	180	13	0	4.33	5	1	3	....	263	13	0	2.97		1946-47	1952-53
• Anderson, Lorne	NYR	1	3	1	2	0	180	18	0	6.00	....	....	....	....	....	....	....	....		1951-52	1951-52
Askey, Tom	Ana.	2	7	0	1	2	273	12	0	2.64	1	0	1	....	30	2	0	4.00		1997-98	1998-99
Astrom, Hardy	NYR, Col.	3	83	17	44	12	4456	278	0	3.74	....	....	....	....	....	....	....	....		1977-78	1980-81
‡ Aubin, Jean-Sebastien	Pit., Tor., L.A.	9	218	80	83	16	11197	547	7	2.93	1	0	0	0	1	0	0	0.00		1998-99	2007-08
‡ Auld, Alex	Van., Fla., Phx., Bos., Ott., Dal., NYR, Mtl.	10	237	91	88	32	12986	606	6	2.80	4	1	2	0	242	10	0	2.48		2001-02	2011-12
‡ Bacashihua, Jason	St.L.	2	38	7	17	4	1860	99	0	3.19	....	....	....	....	....	....	....	....		2005-06	2006-07
Bach, Ryan	L.A.	1	3	0	3	0	108	8	0	4.44	....	....	....	....	....	....	....	....		1998-99	1998-99
‡ Backlund, Johan	Phi.	1	1	0	1	0	40	2	0	3.00	1	0	0	....	1	0	0	0.00		2009-10	2009-10
Bailey, Scott	Bos.	2	19	6	6	2	965	55	0	3.42	....	....	....	....	....	....	....	....		1995-96	1996-97
Baker, Steve	NYR	4	57	20	20	11	3081	190	3	3.70	14	7	7	....	826	55	0	4.00		1979-80	1982-83
Bales, Mike	Bos., Ott.	4	23	2	15	1	1120	77	0	4.13	....	....	....	....	....	....	....	....		1992-93	1996-97
Bannerman, Murray	Van., Chi.	8	289	116	125	33	16470	1051	8	3.83	40	20	18	....	2322	165	0	4.26		1977-78	1986-87
Baron, Marco	Bos., L.A., Edm.	6	86	34	38	9	4822	292	1	3.63	1	0	1	....	20	3	0	9.00		1979-80	1984-85
Barrasso, Tom	Buf., Pit., Ott., Car., Tor., St.L.	19	777	369	277	86	44180	2385	38	3.24	119	61	54	....	6953	349	6	3.01	2	1983-84	2002-03
• Bassen, Hank	Chi., Det., Pit.	9	156	46	66	31	8759	434	5	2.97	5	1	3	....	274	11	0	2.41		1954-55	1967-68
• Bastien, Baz	Tor.	1	5	0	4	1	300	20	0	4.00	....	....	....	....	....	....	....	....		1945-46	1945-46
• Bauman, Garry	Mtl., Min.	3	35	5	16	6	1719	102	0	3.56	....	....	....	....	....	....	....	....		1966-67	1968-69
Beaupre, Don	Min., Wsh., Ott., Tor.	17	667	268	277	75	37396	2151	17	3.45	72	33	31	....	3943	220	3	3.35		1980-81	1996-97
Beauregard, Stephane	Wpg., Phi.	5	90	19	39	11	4402	268	2	3.65	4	1	3	....	238	12	0	3.03		1989-90	1993-94
Beckford-Tseu, Chris	St.L.	1	1	0	0	0	27	1	0	2.22	....	....	....	....	....	....	....	....		2007-08	2007-08
Bedard, Jim	Wsh.	2	73	17	40	13	4232	278	1	3.94	....	....	....	....	....	....	....	....		1977-78	1978-79
Behrend, Marc	Wpg.	3	39	12	19	3	1991	160	1	4.82	7	1	3	....	312	19	0	3.65		1983-84	1985-86
Belanger, Yves	St.L., Atl., Bos.	6	78	29	33	6	4134	259	2	3.76	....	....	....	....	....	....	....	....		1974-75	1979-80
Belfour, Ed	Chi., S.J., Dal., Tor., Fla.	18	963	484	320	125	55695	2317	76	2.50	161	88	68	....	9945	359	14	2.17	1	1988-89	2006-07
Belhumeur, Michel	Phi., Wsh.	3	65	9	36	7	3306	254	0	4.61	1	0	0	....	10	1	0	6.00		1972-73	1975-76
• Bell, Gordie	Tor., NYR	2	8	3	5	0	480	31	0	3.88	2	1	1	....	120	9	0	4.50		1945-46	1955-56
• Benedict, Clint	Ott., Mtl.M.	13	362	190	143	28	22367	863	57	2.32	28	11	12	5	1707	53	9	1.86	4	1917-18	1929-30
• Bennett, Harvey	Bos.	1	25	10	12	2	1470	103	0	4.20	....	....	....	....	....	....	....	....		1944-45	1944-45
Bergeron, Jean-Claude	Mtl., T.B., L.A.	6	72	21	33	7	3772	232	1	3.69	....	....	....	....	....	....	....	....		1990-91	1996-97
Berkhoel, Adam	Atl.	1	9	2	4	1	473	30	0	3.81	....	....	....	....	....	....	....	....		2005-06	2005-06
Bernhardt, Tim	Cgy., Tor.	4	67	17	36	7	3748	267	0	4.27	....	....	....	....	....	....	....	....		1982-83	1986-87
Berthiaume, Daniel	Wpg., Min., L.A., Bos., Ott.	9	215	81	90	21	11662	714	5	3.67	14	5	9	....	807	50	0	3.72		1985-86	1993-94
Bester, Allan	Tor., Det., Dal.	10	219	73	99	17	11773	786	7	4.01	11	2	6	....	508	37	0	4.37		1983-84	1995-96
• Beveridge, Bill	Det., Ott., St.L., Mtl.M., NYR	9	297	87	166	42	18375	879	18	2.87	5	2	3	....	300	11	0	2.20		1929-30	1942-43
• Bibeault, Paul	Mtl., Tor., Bos., Chi.	7	214	81	107	25	12890	785	10	3.65	20	6	14	....	1237	71	2	3.44		1940-41	1946-47
Bierk, Zac	T.B., Min., Phx.	6	47	9	20	5	2135	113	1	3.18	....	....	....	....	....	....	....	....		1997-98	2003-04
Billington, Craig	N.J., Ott., Bos., Col., Wsh.	15	332	110	149	31	17097	1034	9	3.63	8	0	2	....	213	15	0	4.23		1985-86	2002-03
Binette, Andre	Mtl.	1	1	1	0	0	60	4	0	4.00	....	....	....	....	....	....	....	....		1954-55	1954-55
Binkley, Les	Pit.	5	196	58	94	34	11046	575	11	3.12	7	5	2	....	428	15	0	2.10		1967-68	1971-72
• Bittner, Richard	Bos.	1	1	0	0	1	60	3	0	3.00	....	....	....	....	....	....	....	....		1949-50	1949-50
Blackburn, Dan	NYR	2	63	20	32	4	3499	188	1	3.22	....	....	....	....	....	....	....	....		2001-02	2002-03
Blake, Mike	L.A.	3	40	13	15	5	2117	150	0	4.25	....	....	....	....	....	....	....	....		1981-82	1983-84
Blue, John	Bos., Buf.	3	46	16	18	7	2521	126	1	3.00	2	0	1	....	96	5	0	3.13		1992-93	1995-96
Boisvert, Gilles	Det.	1	3	0	3	0	180	9	0	3.00	....	....	....	....	....	....	....	....		1959-60	1959-60
Bouchard, Dan	Atl., Cgy., Que., Wpg.	14	655	286	232	113	37919	2061	27	3.26	43	13	30	....	2549	147	1	3.46		1972-73	1985-86
• Bourque, Claude	Mtl., Det.	2	62	16	38	8	3830	193	4	3.02	3	1	2	....	188	8	1	2.55		1938-39	1939-40
Boutin, Rollie	Wsh.	3	22	7	10	1	1137	75	0	3.96	....	....	....	....	....	....	....	....		1978-79	1980-81
• Bouvrette, Lionel	NYR	1	1	0	1	0	60	6	0	6.00	....	....	....	....	....	....	....	....		1942-43	1942-43
Bower, Johnny	NYR, Tor.	15	552	250	195	90	32016	1340	37	2.51	74	35	34	....	4378	180	5	2.47	4	1953-54	1969-70
§ • Branigan, Andy	NYA	1	1	0	0	0	7	0	0	0.00	....	....	....	....	....	....	....	....		1940-41	1940-41
Brathwaite, Fred	Edm., Cgy., St.L., CBJ	9	254	81	99	37	13840	629	15	2.73	1	0	0	0	1	0	0	0.00		1993-94	2003-04
• Brimsek, Frank	Bos., Chi.	10	514	252	182	80	31210	1404	40	2.70	68	32	36	....	4395	186	2	2.54	2	1938-39	1949-50
Brochu, Martin	Wsh., Van., Pit.	3	9	0	5	0	369	22	0	3.58	....	....	....	....	....	....	....	....		1998-99	2003-04
• Broda, Turk	Tor.	14	629	302	224	101	38167	1609	62	2.53	101	60	39	....	6389	211	13	1.98	5	1936-37	1951-52
Broderick, Ken	Min., Bos.	3	27	11	12	1	1464	74	1	3.03	....	....	....	....	....	....	....	....		1969-70	1974-75
Broderick, Len	Mtl.	1	1	1	0	0	60	2	0	2.00	....	....	....	....	....	....	....	....		1957-58	1957-58
‡ Brodeur, Mike	Ott.	2	7	3	1	0	277	10	1	2.17	....	....	....	....	....	....	....	....		2009-10	2010-11
Brodeur, Richard	NYI, Van., Hfd.	9	385	131	175	62	21968	1410	6	3.85	33	13	20	....	2009	111	1	3.32		1979-80	1987-88
Bromley, Gary	Buf., Van.	6	136	54	44	28	7427	425	7	3.43	7	2	5	....	360	25	0	4.17		1973-74	1980-81
• Brooks, Art	Tor.	1	4	2	2	0	220	23	0	6.27	....	....	....	....	....	....	....	....		1917-18	1917-18
Brooks, Ross	Bos.	3	54	37	7	6	3047	134	4	2.64	1	0	0	....	20	3	0	9.00		1972-73	1974-75
• Brophy, Frank	Que.	1	21	3	18	0	1249	148	0	7.11	....	....	....	....	....	....	....	....		1919-20	1919-20
Brown, Andy	Det., Pit.	3	62	22	26	9	3373	213	1	3.79	....	....	....	....	....	....	....	....		1971-72	1973-74
Brown, Ken	Chi.	1	1	0	0	0	18	1	0	3.33	....	....	....	....	....	....	....	....		1970-71	1970-71
Brunetta, Mario	Que.	3	40	12	17	1	1967	128	0	3.90	....	....	....	....	....	....	....	....		1987-88	1989-90
‡ Brust, Barry	L.A.	1	11	2	4	1	486	30	0	3.70	....	....	....	....	....	....	....	....		2006-07	2006-07
Bullock, Bruce	Van.	3	16	3	9	3	927	74	0	4.79	....	....	....	....	....	....	....	....		1972-73	1976-77
Burke, Sean	N.J., Hfd., Car., Van., Phi., Fla., Phx., T.B., L.A.	18	820	324	341	110	46442	2290	38	2.96	38	12	23	....	2151	119	1	3.32		1987-88	2006-07
• Buzinski, Steve	NYR	1	9	2	6	1	560	55	0	5.89	....	....	....	....	....	....	....	....		1942-43	1942-43
Caley, Don	St.L.	1	1	0	0	0	30	3	0	6.00	....	....	....	....	....	....	....	....		1967-68	1967-68
Caprice, Frank	Van.	6	102	31	46	11	5589	391	1	4.20	....	....	....	....	....	....	....	....		1982-83	1987-88
Carey, Jim	Wsh., Bos., St.L.	5	172	79	65	16	9668	416	16	2.58	10	2	5	....	455	35	0	4.62		1994-95	1998-99
Caron, Jacques	L.A., St.L., Van.	5	72	24	29	11	3846	211	2	3.29	12	4	7	....	639	34	0	3.19		1967-68	1973-74
‡ Caron, Sebastien	Pit., Chi., Ana., T.B.	5	95	26	48	12	5156	296	4	3.44	....	....	....	....	....	....	....	....		2002-03	2011-12
Carter, Lyle	Cal.	1	15	4	7	0	721	50	0	4.16	....	....	....	....	....	....	....	....		1971-72	1971-72
Casey, Jon	Min., Bos., St.L.	12	425	170	157	55	23255	1246	16	3.21	66	32	31	....	3743	192	3	3.08		1983-84	1996-97
Cassivi, Frederic	Atl., Wsh.	4	13	3	6	1	628	38	0	3.63	....	....	....	....	....	....	....	....		2001-02	2006-07
Cechmanek, Roman	Phi., L.A.	4	212	110	64	28	12085	419	25	2.08	23	9	14	....	1441	56	3	2.33		2000-01	2003-04
Centomo, Sebastien	Tor.	1	1	0	0	0	40	3	0	4.50	....	....	....	....	....	....	....	....		2001-02	2001-02
Chabot, Frederic	Mtl., Phi., L.A.	5	32	4	8	4	1262	62	0	2.95	....	....	....	....	....	....	....	....		1990-91	1998-99
• Chabot, Lorne	NYR, Tor., Mtl., Chi., Mtl.M., NYA	11	412	201	147	62	25411	859	71	2.03	37	13	17	6	2498	64	5	1.54	2	1926-27	1936-37
Chadwick, Ed	Tor., Bos.	6	184	57	92	35	11040	541	14	2.94	....	....	....	....	....	....	....	....		1955-56	1961-62
Champoux, Bob	Det., Cal.	2	17	2	11	3	923	80	0	5.20	1	1	0	....	55	4	0	4.36		1963-64	1973-74
Charpentier, Sebastien	Wsh.	3	26	6	14	1	1350	66	0	2.93	....	....	....	....	....	....	....	....		2001-02	2003-04
Cheevers, Gerry	Tor., Bos.	13	418	230	102	74	24394	1174	26	2.89	88	53	34	....	5396	242	8	2.69	2	1961-62	1979-80

Name	NHL Teams	NHL Seasons	Regular Schedule								Playoffs								NHL Cup Wins	First NHL Season	Last NHL Season
			GP	W	L	T	Mins	GA	SO	Avg	GP	W	L	T	Mins	GA	SO	Avg			
Cheveldae, Tim	Det., Wpg., Bos.	9	340	149	136	37	19172	1116	10	3.49	25	9	15	....	1418	71	2	3.00		1988-89	1996-97
Chevrier, Alain	N.J., Wpg., Chi., Pit., Det.	6	234	91	100	14	12202	845	2	4.16	16	9	7	....	1013	44	0	2.61		1985-86	1990-91
‡ Chiodo, Andy	Pit.	1	8	3	4	1	486	28	0	3.46	....	....	....	....	....	....	....	....		2003-04	2003-04
Chouinard, Mathieu	L.A.	1	1	0	0	0	3	0	0	0.00	....	....	....	....	....	....	....	....		2003-04	2003-04
§ • Clancy, King	Ott., Tor.	2	2	0	0	0	3	1	0	20.00	....	....	....	....	....	....	....	....		1924-25	1931-32
§ • Cleghorn, Odie	Pit.	1	1	1	0	0	60	2	0	2.00	....	....	....	....	....	....	....	....		1925-26	1925-26
§ • Cleghorn, Sprague	Ott., Mtl.	2	2	0	0	0	5	0	0	0.00	....	....	....	....	....	....	....	....		1918-19	1921-22
Clifford, Chris	Chi.	2	2	0	0	0	24	0	0	0.00	....	....	....	....	....	....	....	....		1984-85	1988-89
Cloutier, Dan	NYR, T.B., Van., L.A.	10	351	139	142	37	18927	874	15	2.77	25	10	13	0	1361	75	0	3.31		1997-98	2007-08
Cloutier, Jacques	Buf., Chi., Que.	12	255	82	102	24	12826	778	3	3.64	8	1	5	....	413	18	1	2.62		1981-82	1993-94
‡ Coleman, Gerald	T.B.	1	2	0	0	1	43	2	0	2.79	....	....	....	....	....	....	....	....		2005-06	2005-06
• Colvin, Les	Bos.	1	1	0	1	0	60	4	0	4.00	....	....	....	....	....	....	....	....		1948-49	1948-49
§ • Conacher, Charlie	Tor., Det.	3	4	0	0	0	10	0	0	0.00	....	....	....	....	....	....	....	....		1932-33	1938-39
Conklin, Ty	Edm., CBJ, Buf., Pit., Det., St.L.	9	215	96	67	21	11527	516	17	2.69	2	0	1	0	26	1	0	2.31		2001-02	2011-12
• Connell, Alec	Ott., Det., NYA, Mtl.M.	12	417	193	156	67	26050	830	81	1.91	21	8	5	8	1309	26	4	1.19	2	1924-25	1936-37
Corsi, Jim	Edm.	1	26	8	14	3	1366	83	0	3.65	....	....	....	....	....	....	....	....		1979-80	1979-80
• Courteau, Maurice	Bos.	1	6	2	4	0	360	33	0	5.50	....	....	....	....	....	....	....	....		1943-44	1943-44
Cousineau, Marcel	Tor., NYI, L.A.	4	26	4	10	1	1047	51	1	2.92	....	....	....	....	....	....	....	....		1996-97	1999-00
Cowley, Wayne	Edm.	1	1	0	1	0	57	3	0	3.16	....	....	....	....	....	....	....	....		1993-94	1993-94
• Cox, Abbie	Mtl.M., NYA, Det., Mtl.	3	5	1	1	2	263	11	0	2.51	....	....	....	....	....	....	....	....		1929-30	1935-36
Craig, Jim	Atl., Bos., Min.	3	30	11	10	7	1588	100	0	3.78	....	....	....	....	....	....	....	....		1979-80	1983-84
Crha, Jiri	Tor.	2	69	28	27	11	3942	261	0	3.97	5	0	4	....	186	21	0	6.77		1979-80	1980-81
• Crozier, Roger	Det., Buf., Wsh.	14	518	206	197	70	28567	1446	30	3.04	32	14	16	....	1789	82	1	2.75		1963-64	1976-77
• Cude, Wilf	Phi., Bos., Chi., Mtl., Det.	10	282	100	132	49	17586	798	24	2.72	19	7	11	1	1257	51	1	2.43		1930-31	1940-41
‡ Curry, John	Pit.	2	4	2	2	0	174	11	0	3.79	....	....	....	....	....	....	....	....		2008-09	2009-10
Cutts, Don	Edm.	1	6	1	2	1	269	16	0	3.57	....	....	....	....	....	....	....	....		1979-80	1979-80
• Cyr, Claude	Mtl.	1	1	0	0	0	20	1	0	3.00	....	....	....	....	....	....	....	....		1958-59	1958-59
Dadswell, Doug	Cgy.	2	27	8	8	3	1346	99	0	4.41	....	....	....	....	....	....	....	....		1986-87	1987-88
Dafoe, Byron	Wsh., L.A., Bos., Atl.	12	415	171	170	56	23478	1051	26	2.69	27	10	16	....	1686	65	3	2.31		1992-93	2003-04
D'Alessio, Corrie	Hfd.	1	1	0	0	0	11	0	0	0.00	....	....	....	....	....	....	....	....		1992-93	1992-93
Daley, Joe	Pit., Buf., Det.	4	105	34	44	19	5836	326	3	3.35	....	....	....	....	....	....	....	....		1968-69	1971-72
• Damore, Nick	Bos.	1	1	1	0	0	60	3	0	3.00	....	....	....	....	....	....	....	....		1941-42	1941-42
D'Amour, Marc	Cgy., Phi.	2	16	2	4	2	579	32	0	3.32	....	....	....	....	....	....	....	....		1985-86	1988-89
Damphousse, Jean-Fr.	N.J.	1	6	1	3	0	294	12	0	2.45	....	....	....	....	....	....	....	....		2001-02	2001-02
§ • Darragh, Jack	Ott.	1	1	0	0	0	2	0	0	0.00	....	....	....	....	....	....	....	....		1919-20	1919-20
Daskalakis, Cleon	Bos.	3	12	3	4	1	506	41	0	4.86	....	....	....	....	....	....	....	....		1984-85	1986-87
Davidson, John	St.L., NYR	10	301	123	124	39	17109	1004	7	3.52	31	16	14	....	1862	77	1	2.48		1973-74	1982-83
• DeCourcy, Bob	NYR	1	1	0	1	0	29	6	0	12.41	....	....	....	....	....	....	....	....		1947-48	1947-48
Defelice, Norm	Bos.	1	10	3	5	2	600	30	0	3.00	....	....	....	....	....	....	....	....		1956-57	1956-57
DeJordy, Denis	Chi., L.A., Mtl., Det.	12	316	124	128	51	17798	929	15	3.13	18	6	9	....	946	55	0	3.49	1	1960-61	1973-74
DelGuidice, Matt	Bos.	2	11	2	5	1	434	28	0	3.87	....	....	....	....	....	....	....	....		1990-91	1991-92
Denis, Marc	Col., CBJ, T.B., Mtl.	11	349	112	179	31	19526	982	16	3.02	....	....	....	....	....	....	....	....		1996-97	2008-09
DeRouville, Philippe	Pit.	2	3	1	2	0	171	9	0	3.16	....	....	....	....	....	....	....	....		1994-95	1996-97
Desjardins, Gerry	L.A., Chi., NYI, Buf.	10	331	122	153	44	19014	1042	12	3.29	35	15	15	....	1874	108	0	3.46		1968-69	1977-78
‡ DesRochers, Patrick	Phx., Car.	2	11	2	6	1	540	33	0	3.67	....	....	....	....	....	....	....	....		2001-02	2002-03
• Dickie, Bill	Chi.	1	1	1	0	0	60	3	0	3.00	....	....	....	....	....	....	....	....		1941-42	1941-42
Dion, Connie	Det.	2	38	23	11	4	2280	119	1	3.13	5	1	4	....	300	17	0	3.40		1943-44	1944-45
Dion, Michel	Que., Wpg., Pit.	6	227	60	118	32	12695	898	2	4.24	5	2	3	....	304	22	0	4.34		1979-80	1984-85
‡ Divis, Reinhard	St.L.	4	28	6	9	3	1212	67	0	3.32	1	0	0	....	18	0	0	0.00		2001-02	2005-06
• Dolson, Dolly	Det.	3	93	35	41	17	5820	192	16	1.98	2	0	2	0	120	7	0	3.50		1928-29	1930-31
Dopson, Rob	Pit.	1	2	0	0	0	45	3	0	4.00	....	....	....	....	....	....	....	....		1993-94	1993-94
Dowie, Bruce	Tor.	1	2	0	1	0	72	4	0	3.33	....	....	....	....	....	....	....	....		1983-84	1983-84
Draper, Tom	Wpg., Buf., NYI	6	53	19	23	5	2807	173	1	3.70	7	3	4	....	433	19	1	2.63		1988-89	1995-96
Dryden, Dave	NYR, Chi., Buf., Edm.	9	203	66	76	31	10424	555	9	3.19	3	0	2	....	133	9	0	4.06		1961-62	1979-80
Dryden, Ken	Mtl.	8	397	258	57	74	23352	870	46	2.24	112	80	32	....	6846	274	10	2.40	6	1970-71	1978-79
Dubielewicz, Wade	NYI, CBJ, Min.	6	43	18	16	2	2196	97	0	2.65	1	0	1	....	59	4	0	4.07		2003-04	2009-10
Duchesne, Jeremy	Phi.	1	1	0	0	0	17	1	0	3.53	....	....	....	....	....	....	....	....		2009-10	2009-10
Duffus, Parris	Phx.	1	1	0	0	0	29	1	0	2.07	....	....	....	....	....	....	....	....		1996-97	1996-97
Dumas, Michel	Chi.	3	8	2	1	2	362	24	0	3.98	1	0	0	....	19	1	0	3.16		1974-75	1976-77
Dunham, Mike	N.J., Nsh., NYR, Atl., NYI	10	394	141	178	44	21653	989	19	2.74	....	....	....	....	....	....	....	....		1996-97	2006-07
Dupuis, Bob	Edm.	1	1	0	1	0	60	4	0	4.00	....	....	....	....	....	....	....	....		1979-80	1979-80
• Durnan, Bill	Mtl.	7	383	208	112	62	22945	901	34	2.36	45	27	18	....	2871	99	2	2.07	2	1943-44	1949-50
Dyck, Ed	Van.	3	49	8	28	5	2453	178	1	4.35	....	....	....	....	....	....	....	....		1971-72	1973-74
Edwards, Don	Buf., Cgy., Tor.	10	459	208	155	74	26181	1449	16	3.32	42	16	21	....	2302	132	1	3.44		1976-77	1985-86
Edwards, Gary	St.L., L.A., Cle., Min., Edm., Pit.	13	286	88	125	51	16002	973	10	3.65	11	5	4	....	537	34	0	3.80		1968-69	1981-82
Edwards, Marv	Pit., Tor., Cal.	4	61	15	34	7	3467	218	2	3.77	....	....	....	....	....	....	....	....		1968-69	1973-74
• Edwards, Roy	Chi., Det., Pit.	8	236	97	88	38	13109	637	12	2.92	4	0	3	....	206	11	0	3.20	1	1960-61	1973-74
Eklund, Brian	T.B.	1	1	0	1	0	58	3	0	3.10	....	....	....	....	....	....	....	....		2005-06	2005-06
Eliot, Darren	L.A., Det., Buf.	5	89	25	41	12	4931	377	1	4.59	1	0	0	....	40	7	0	10.50		1984-85	1988-89
Ellacott, Ken	Van.	1	12	2	3	4	555	41	0	4.43	....	....	....	....	....	....	....	....		1982-83	1982-83
Erickson, Chad	N.J.	1	2	1	1	0	120	9	0	4.50	....	....	....	....	....	....	....	....		1991-92	1991-92
‡ Ersberg, Erik	L.A.	3	53	18	19	10	2827	120	2	2.55	1	0	0	....	13	2	0	9.23		2007-08	2009-10
‡ Esche, Robert	Phx., Phi.	8	186	78	64	22	10139	464	10	2.75	25	13	11	....	1405	64	1	2.73		1998-99	2006-07
Esposito, Tony	Mtl., Chi.	16	886	423	306	151	52585	2563	76	2.92	99	45	53	....	6017	308	6	3.07	1	1968-69	1983-84
Essensa, Bob	Wpg., Det., Edm., Phx., Van., Buf.	12	446	173	176	47	24215	1270	18	3.15	16	4	9	....	864	51	0	3.54		1988-89	2001-02
• Evans, Claude	Mtl., Bos.	2	5	1	2	1	260	16	0	3.69	....	....	....	....	....	....	....	....		1954-55	1957-58
Exelby, Randy	Mtl., Edm.	2	2	0	1	0	63	5	0	4.76	....	....	....	....	....	....	....	....		1988-89	1989-90
Fankhouser, Scott	Atl.	2	23	4	12	2	1180	65	0	3.31	....	....	....	....	....	....	....	....		1999-00	2000-01
Farr, Rocky	Buf.	3	19	2	6	3	722	42	0	3.49	....	....	....	....	....	....	....	....		1972-73	1974-75
Favell, Doug	Phi., Tor., Col.	12	373	123	153	69	20771	1096	18	3.17	21	6	15	....	1270	66	1	3.12		1967-68	1978-79
Fernandez, Manny	Dal., Min., Bos.	13	325	143	123	35	18580	775	15	2.50	11	3	4	....	571	19	0	2.00		1994-95	2008-09
Fichaud, Eric	NYI, Nsh., Car., Mtl.	6	95	22	47	10	4799	251	2	3.14	....	....	....	....	....	....	....	....		1995-96	2000-01
Finley, Brian	Nsh., Bos.	3	4	0	2	0	166	13	0	4.70	....	....	....	....	....	....	....	....		2002-03	2006-07
Fiset, Stephane	Que., Col., L.A., Mtl.	13	390	164	153	44	21785	1114	16	3.07	14	1	7	....	563	37	0	3.94	1	1989-90	2001-02
Fitzpatrick, Mark	L.A., NYI, Fla., T.B., Chi., Car.	12	329	113	136	49	18329	953	8	3.12	9	0	3	....	289	23	0	4.78		1988-89	1999-00
Flaherty, Wade	S.J., NYI, T.B., Fla., Nsh.	11	120	27	56	9	5941	348	5	3.51	7	2	3	....	377	31	0	4.93		1991-92	2002-03
• Forbes, Jake	Tor., Ham., NYA, Phi.	13	210	85	114	11	12922	594	19	2.76	2	0	2	0	120	7	0	3.50		1919-20	1932-33
Ford, Brian	Que., Pit.	2	11	3	7	0	580	61	0	6.31	....	....	....	....	....	....	....	....		1983-84	1984-85
Foster, Norm	Bos., Edm.	2	13	7	4	0	623	34	0	3.27	....	....	....	....	....	....	....	....		1990-91	1991-92
Fountain, Mike	Van., Car., Ott.	4	11	2	6	0	483	28	1	3.48	....	....	....	....	....	....	....	....		1996-97	2000-01
• Fowler, Hec	Bos.	1	7	1	6	0	409	42	0	6.16	....	....	....	....	....	....	....	....		1924-25	1924-25
Francis, Emile	Chi., NYR	6	95	31	52	11	5660	355	1	3.76	....	....	....	....	....	....	....	....		1946-47	1951-52
• Franks, Jimmy	Det., NYR, Bos.	4	42	12	23	7	2520	181	1	4.31	1	0	1	....	30	2	0	4.00	1	1936-37	1943-44
• Frederick, Ray	Chi.	1	5	0	4	1	300	22	0	4.40	....	....	....	....	....	....	....	....		1954-55	1954-55
Friesen, Karl	N.J.	1	4	0	2	1	130	16	0	7.38	....	....	....	....	....	....	....	....		1986-87	1986-87
Froese, Bob	Phi., NYR	8	242	128	72	20	13451	694	13	3.10	18	3	9	....	830	55	0	3.98		1982-83	1989-90
Fuhr, Grant	Edm., Tor., Buf., L.A., St.L., Cgy.	19	868	403	295	114	48945	2756	25	3.38	150	92	50	....	8834	430	6	2.92	5	1981-82	1999-00
Fukufuji, Yutaka	L.A.	1	4	0	3	0	96	7	0	4.38	....	....	....	....	....	....	....	....		2006-07	2006-07
Gage, Joaquin	Edm.	3	23	4	12	1	1076	67	0	3.74	....	....	....	....	....	....	....	....		1994-95	2000-01
Gagnon, Dave	Det.	1	2	0	1	0	35	6	0	10.29	....	....	....	....	....	....	....	....		1990-91	1990-91
• Gamble, Bruce	NYR, Bos., Tor., Phi.	10	327	110	150	46	18442	988	22	3.21	5	0	4	....	206	25	0	7.28		1958-59	1971-72
Gamble, Troy	Van.	4	72	22	29	9	3804	229	1	3.61	4	1	3	....	249	16	0	3.86		1986-87	1991-92
• Gardiner, Bert	NYR, Mtl., Chi., Bos.	6	144	49	68	27	8760	554	3	3.79	9	4	5	....	647	20	0	1.85		1935-36	1943-44
• Gardiner, Charlie	Chi.	7	316	112	152	52	19687	664	42	2.02	21	12	6	3	1472	35	5	1.43	1	1927-28	1933-34
• Gardner, George	Det., Van.	5	66	16	30	6	3313	207	0	3.75	....	....	....	....	....	....	....	....		1965-66	1971-72
Garner, Tyrone	Cgy.	1	3	0	2	0	139	12	0	5.18	....	....	....	....	....	....	....	....		1998-99	1998-99
‡ Garnett, Michael	Atl.	1	24	10	7	4	1271	73	2	3.45	....	....	....	....	....	....	....	....		2005-06	2005-06
Garrett, John	Hfd., Que., Van.	6	207	68	91	37	11763	837	1	4.27	9	4	3	....	461	33	0	4.30		1979-80	1984-85

Name	NHL Teams	NHL Seasons	Regular Schedule GP	W	L	T	Mins	GA	SO	Avg	Playoffs GP	W	L	T	Mins	GA	SO	Avg	NHL Cup Wins	First NHL Season	Last NHL Season
Gatherum, Dave	Det.	1	3	2	0	1	180	3	1	1.00	....	....	....	....	....	....	....	....	1	1953-54	1953-54
Gauthier, Paul	Mtl.	1	1	0	0	1	70	2	0	1.71	....	....	....	....	....	....	....	....		1937-38	1937-38
Gauthier, Sean	S.J.	1	1	0	0	0	3	0	0	0.00	....	....	....	....	....	....	....	....		1998-99	1998-99
• Gelineau, Jack	Bos., Chi.	4	143	46	64	33	8580	447	7	3.13	4	1	2	....	260	7	1	1.62		1948-49	1953-54
‡ Gerber, Martin	Ana., Car., Ott., Tor., Edm.	7	229	113	78	21	12920	566	10	2.63	12	1	5	....	479	28	1	3.51	1	2002-03	2010-11
Giacomin, Ed	NYR, Det.	13	609	289	209	96	35633	1672	54	2.82	65	29	35	....	3838	180	1	2.81		1965-66	1977-78
Gilbert, Gilles	Min., Bos., Det.	14	416	192	143	60	23677	1290	18	3.27	32	17	15	....	1919	97	3	3.03		1969-70	1982-83
Gill, Andre	Bos.	1	5	3	2	0	270	13	1	2.89	....	....	....	....	....	....	....	....		1967-68	1967-68
• Goodman, Paul	Chi.	3	52	23	20	9	3240	117	6	2.17	3	0	3	....	187	10	0	3.21	1	1937-38	1940-41
Gordon, Scott	Que.	2	23	2	16	0	1082	101	0	5.60	....	....	....	....	....	....	....	....		1989-90	1990-91
Gosselin, Mario	Que., L.A., Hfd.	9	241	91	107	14	12857	801	6	3.74	32	16	15	....	1816	99	0	3.27		1983-84	1993-94
Goverde, David	L.A.	3	5	1	4	0	278	29	0	6.26	....	....	....	....	....	....	....	....		1991-92	1993-94
‡ Grahame, John	Bos., T.B., Car.	8	224	97	86	18	12363	574	12	2.79	6	1	4	0	333	19	0	3.42	1	1999-00	2007-08
Grahame, Ron	Bos., L.A., Que.	4	114	50	43	15	6472	409	5	3.79	4	2	1	....	202	7	0	2.08		1977-78	1980-81
• Grant, Benny	Tor., NYA, Bos.	6	52	17	27	4	3036	188	4	3.72	....	....	....	....	....	....	....	....		1928-29	1943-44
Grant, Doug	Det., St.L.	7	77	27	34	8	4199	280	2	4.00	....	....	....	....	....	....	....	....		1973-74	1979-80
Gratton, Gilles	St.L., NYR	2	47	13	18	9	2299	154	0	4.02	....	....	....	....	....	....	....	....		1975-76	1976-77
Gray, Gerry	Det., NYI	2	8	1	5	1	440	35	0	4.77	....	....	....	....	....	....	....	....		1970-71	1972-73
Gray, Harrison	Det.	1	1	0	1	0	40	5	0	7.50	....	....	....	....	....	....	....	....		1963-64	1963-64
Greenlay, Mike	Edm.	1	2	0	0	0	20	4	0	12.00	....	....	....	....	....	....	....	....		1989-90	1989-90
Guenette, Steve	Pit., Cgy.	5	35	19	16	0	1958	122	1	3.74	....	....	....	....	....	....	....	....		1986-87	1990-91
Gustafson, Derek	Min.	2	5	1	3	0	265	10	0	2.26	....	....	....	....	....	....	....	....		2000-01	2001-02
Hackett, Jeff	NYI, S.J., Chi., Mtl., Bos., Phi.	15	500	166	244	56	28125	1361	26	2.90	12	3	7	....	610	36	0	3.54		1988-89	2003-04
• Hainsworth, George	Mtl., Tor.	11	465	246	145	74	29087	937	94	1.93	52	22	25	5	3486	112	8	1.93	2	1926-27	1936-37
Hall, Glenn	Det., Chi., St.L.	18	906	407	326	163	53484	2222	84	2.49	115	49	65	....	6899	320	6	2.78	2	1951-52	1970-71
Hamel, Pierre	Tor., Wpg.	4	69	13	41	7	3766	276	0	4.40	....	....	....	....	....	....	....	....		1974-75	1980-81
Hanlon, Glen	Van., St.L., NYR, Det.	14	477	167	202	61	26037	1561	13	3.60	35	11	15	....	1756	92	4	3.14		1977-78	1990-91
Harrison, Paul	Min., Tor., Pit., Buf.	7	109	28	59	9	5806	408	2	4.22	4	0	1	....	157	9	0	3.44		1975-76	1981-82
Hasek, Dominik	Chi., Buf., Det., Ott.	16	735	389	223	95	42837	1572	81	2.20	119	65	49	0	7318	246	14	2.02	2	1990-91	2007-08
Hauser, Adam	L.A.	1	1	0	0	0	51	6	0	7.06	....	....	....	....	....	....	....	....		2005-06	2005-06
Hayward, Brian	Wpg., Mtl., Min., S.J.	11	357	143	156	37	20025	1242	8	3.72	37	11	18	....	1803	104	0	3.46		1982-83	1992-93
Head, Don	Bos.	1	38	9	26	3	2280	158	2	4.16	....	....	....	....	....	....	....	....		1961-62	1961-62
Healy, Glenn	L.A., NYI, NYR, Tor.	15	437	166	190	47	24256	1361	13	3.37	37	13	15	....	1930	108	0	3.36	1	1985-86	2000-01
Hebert, Guy	St.L., Ana., NYR	10	491	191	222	56	27889	1307	28	2.81	14	4	7	....	744	33	1	2.66		1991-92	2000-01
• Hebert, Sammy	Tor., Ott.	2	4	2	1	0	200	19	0	5.70	....	....	....	....	....	....	....	....	1	1917-18	1923-24
Heinz, Rick	St.L., Van.	5	49	14	19	5	2356	159	2	4.05	1	0	0	....	8	1	0	7.50		1980-81	1984-85
Henderson, John	Bos.	2	46	15	15	15	2688	113	5	2.52	2	0	2	....	120	8	0	4.00		1954-55	1955-56
• Henry, Gord	Bos.	4	3	1	2	0	180	5	1	1.67	5	0	4	....	283	21	0	4.45		1948-49	1952-53
• Henry, Jim	NYR, Chi., Bos.	9	406	161	173	70	24355	1166	28	2.87	29	11	18	....	1741	81	2	2.79		1941-42	1954-55
Herron, Denis	Pit., K.C., Mtl.	14	462	146	203	76	25608	1579	10	3.70	15	5	10	....	901	50	0	3.33		1972-73	1985-86
Hextall, Ron	Phi., Que., NYI	13	608	296	214	69	34750	1723	23	2.97	93	47	43	....	5456	276	2	3.04		1986-87	1998-99
• Highton, Hec	Chi.	1	24	10	14	0	1440	108	0	4.50	....	....	....	....	....	....	....	....		1943-44	1943-44
§ • Himes, Normie	NYA	2	2	0	1	0	79	3	0	2.28	....	....	....	....	....	....	....	....		1927-28	1928-29
Hirsch, Corey	NYR, Van., Wsh., Dal.	7	108	34	45	14	5775	301	4	3.13	6	2	3	....	338	21	0	3.73		1992-93	2002-03
Hnilicka, Milan	NYR, Atl., L.A.	5	121	29	67	13	6509	359	5	3.31	....	....	....	....	....	....	....	....		1999-00	2003-04
Hodge, Charlie	Mtl., Oak., Van.	13	358	150	125	61	20573	925	24	2.70	16	7	8	....	804	32	2	2.39	6	1954-55	1970-71
Hodson, Kevin	Det., T.B.	6	71	17	18	10	2910	134	4	2.76	1	0	0	....	1	0	0	0.00	2	1995-96	2002-03
Hoffort, Bruce	Phi.	2	9	4	0	3	368	22	0	3.59	....	....	....	....	....	....	....	....		1989-90	1990-91
Hoganson, Paul	Pit.	1	2	0	1	0	57	7	0	7.37	....	....	....	....	....	....	....	....		1970-71	1970-71
Hogosta, Goran	NYI, Que.	2	22	5	12	3	1208	83	1	4.12	....	....	....	....	....	....	....	....		1977-78	1979-80
Holden, Mark	Mtl., Wpg.	4	8	2	2	1	372	25	0	4.03	....	....	....	....	....	....	....	....		1981-82	1984-85
Holland, Ken	Hfd., Det.	2	4	0	2	1	206	17	0	4.95	....	....	....	....	....	....	....	....		1980-81	1983-84
Holland, Rob	Pit.	2	44	11	22	9	2513	171	1	4.08	....	....	....	....	....	....	....	....		1979-80	1980-81
• Holmes, Hap	Tor., Det.	4	103	39	54	10	6510	264	17	2.43	2	1	1	0	120	7	0	3.50	1	1917-18	1927-28
‡ Holmqvist, Johan	NYR, T.B., Dal.	5	99	48	34	9	5264	262	3	2.99	6	2	4	....	370	18	0	2.92		2000-01	2007-08
Holt, Chris	NYR, St.L.	2	2	0	0	0	29	0	0	0.00	....	....	....	....	....	....	....	....		2005-06	2008-09
§ • Horner, Red	Tor.	2	2	0	0	0	3	1	0	20.00	....	....	....	....	....	....	....	....		1928-29	1931-32
Houle, Martin	Phi.	1	1	0	0	0	2	1	0	30.00	....	....	....	....	....	....	....	....		2006-07	2006-07
Hrivnak, Jim	Wsh., Wpg., St.L.	5	85	34	30	3	4217	262	0	3.73	....	....	....	....	....	....	....	....		1989-90	1993-94
Hrudey, Kelly	NYI, L.A., S.J.	15	677	271	265	88	38084	2174	17	3.43	85	36	46	....	5163	283	0	3.29		1983-84	1997-98
‡ Huet, Cristobal	L.A., Mtl., Wsh., Chi.	7	272	129	90	32	15260	625	24	2.46	17	6	10	....	987	44	0	2.67	1	2002-03	2009-10
‡ Hunwick, Shawn	CBJ	1	1	0	0	0	3	0	0	0.00	....	....	....	....	....	....	....	....		2011-12	2011-12
Hurme, Jani	Ott., Fla.	4	76	29	25	11	4041	176	6	2.61	....	....	....	....	....	....	....	....		1999-00	2002-03
Ing, Peter	Tor., Edm., Det.	4	74	20	37	9	3941	266	1	4.05	....	....	....	....	....	....	....	....		1989-90	1993-94
Inness, Gary	Pit., Phi., Wsh.	7	162	58	61	27	8710	494	2	3.40	9	5	4	....	540	24	0	2.67		1973-74	1980-81
Irbe, Arturs	S.J., Dal., Van., Car.	13	568	218	236	79	32066	1513	33	2.83	51	23	27	....	2981	142	1	2.86		1991-92	2003-04
Ireland, Randy	Buf.	1	2	0	0	0	30	3	0	6.00	....	....	....	....	....	....	....	....		1978-79	1978-79
Irons, Robbie	St.L.	1	1	0	0	0	3	0	0	0.00	....	....	....	....	....	....	....	....		1968-69	1968-69
• Ironstone, Joe	Ott., NYA, Tor.	3	2	0	0	1	110	3	1	1.64	....	....	....	....	....	....	....	....		1924-25	1927-28
Jablonski, Pat	St.L., T.B., Mtl., Phx., Car.	8	128	28	62	18	6634	413	1	3.74	4	0	0	....	139	6	0	2.59		1989-90	1997-98
Jackson, Doug	Chi.	1	6	2	3	1	360	42	0	7.00	....	....	....	....	....	....	....	....		1947-48	1947-48
• Jackson, Percy	Bos., NYA, NYR	4	7	1	3	1	392	26	0	3.98	....	....	....	....	....	....	....	....		1931-32	1935-36
Jaks, Pauli	L.A.	1	1	0	0	0	40	2	0	3.00	....	....	....	....	....	....	....	....		1994-95	1994-95
Janaszak, Steve	Min., Col.	2	3	0	1	1	160	15	0	5.63	....	....	....	....	....	....	....	....		1979-80	1981-82
Janecyk, Bob	Chi., L.A.	6	110	43	47	13	6250	432	2	4.15	3	0	3	....	184	10	0	3.26		1983-84	1988-89
§ • Jenkins, Roger	NYA	1	1	0	1	0	30	7	0	14.00	....	....	....	....	....	....	....	....		1938-39	1938-39
Jensen, Al	Det., Wsh., L.A.	7	179	95	53	18	9974	557	8	3.35	12	5	5	....	598	32	0	3.21		1980-81	1986-87
Jensen, Darren	Phi.	2	30	15	10	1	1496	95	2	3.81	....	....	....	....	....	....	....	....		1984-85	1985-86
Johnson, Bob	St.L., Pit.	2	24	9	9	1	1059	66	0	3.74	....	....	....	....	....	....	....	....		1972-73	1974-75
Johnson, Brent	St.L., Phx., Wsh., Pit.	12	309	140	112	31	16978	744	14	2.63	15	5	6	0	737	27	3	2.20		1998-99	2011-12
Johnston, Eddie	Bos., Tor., St.L., Chi.	16	592	234	257	80	34216	1852	32	3.25	18	7	10	....	1023	57	1	3.34	2	1962-63	1977-78
Joseph, Curtis	St.L., Edm., Tor., Det., Phx., Cgy.	19	943	454	352	96	54054	2516	51	2.79	133	63	66	....	8106	327	16	2.42		1989-90	2008-09
Junkin, Joe	Bos.	1	1	0	0	0	8	0	0	0.00	....	....	....	....	....	....	....	....		1968-69	1968-69
Kaarela, Jari	Col.	1	5	2	2	0	220	22	0	6.00	....	....	....	....	....	....	....	....		1980-81	1980-81
Kamppuri, Hannu	N.J.	1	13	1	10	1	645	54	0	5.02	....	....	....	....	....	....	....	....		1984-85	1984-85
• Karakas, Mike	Chi., Mtl.	8	336	114	169	53	20614	1002	28	2.92	23	11	12	0	1434	72	3	3.01	1	1935-36	1945-46
Keans, Doug	L.A., Bos.	9	210	96	64	26	11388	666	4	3.51	9	2	6	....	432	34	0	4.72		1979-80	1987-88
• Keenan, Don	Bos.	1	1	0	1	0	60	4	0	4.00	....	....	....	....	....	....	....	....		1958-59	1958-59
‡ Keetley, Matt	Cgy.	1	1	0	0	0	9	0	0	0.00	....	....	....	....	....	....	....	....		2007-08	2007-08
• Kerr, Dave	Mtl.M., NYA, NYR	11	427	203	148	75	26639	954	51	2.15	40	18	19	3	2616	76	8	1.74	1	1930-31	1940-41
Kidd, Trevor	Cgy., Car., Fla., Tor.	12	387	140	162	52	21426	1014	19	2.84	10	3	5	....	550	36	1	3.93		1991-92	2003-04
King, Scott	Det.	2	2	0	0	0	61	3	0	2.95	....	....	....	....	....	....	....	....		1990-91	1991-92
Kleisinger, Terry	NYR	1	4	0	2	0	191	14	0	4.40	....	....	....	....	....	....	....	....		1985-86	1985-86
Klymkiw, Julian	NYR	1	1	0	0	0	19	2	0	6.32	....	....	....	....	....	....	....	....		1958-59	1958-59
Knickle, Rick	L.A.	2	14	7	6	0	706	44	0	3.74	....	....	....	....	....	....	....	....		1992-93	1993-94
Kochan, Dieter	T.B., Min.	4	21	1	11	1	849	56	0	3.96	....	....	....	....	....	....	....	....		1999-00	2002-03
‡ Kolesnik, Vitali	Col.	1	8	3	3	0	370	20	0	3.24	....	....	....	....	....	....	....	....		2005-06	2005-06
Kolzig, Olaf	Wsh., T.B.	17	719	303	297	87	41671	1885	35	2.71	45	20	24	....	2799	100	6	2.14		1989-90	2008-09
Konstantinov, Evgeny	T.B.	2	2	0	0	0	21	1	0	2.86	....	....	....	....	....	....	....	....		2000-01	2002-03
Krahn, Brent	Dal.	1	1	0	0	0	20	3	0	9.00	....	....	....	....	....	....	....	....		2008-09	2008-09
Kuntar, Les	Mtl.	1	6	2	2	0	302	16	0	3.18	....	....	....	....	....	....	....	....		1993-94	1993-94
Kurt, Gary	Cal.	1	16	1	7	5	838	60	0	4.30	....	....	....	....	....	....	....	....		1971-72	1971-72
Labbe, Jean-Francois	NYR, CBJ	3	15	3	6	0	628	36	0	3.44	....	....	....	....	....	....	....	....		1999-00	2002-03
Labrecque, Patrick	Mtl.	1	2	0	1	0	98	7	0	4.29	....	....	....	....	....	....	....	....		1995-96	1995-96
Lacher, Blaine	Bos.	2	47	22	16	4	2636	123	4	2.80	5	1	4	....	283	12	0	2.54		1994-95	1995-96
LaCosta, Dan	CBJ	2	4	2	0	0	169	4	1	1.42	....	....	....	....	....	....	....	....		2007-08	2008-09
• Lacroix, Frenchy	Mtl.	2	5	1	4	0	280	16	0	3.43	....	....	....	....	....	....	....	....		1925-26	1926-27
LaFerriere, Rick	Col.	1	1	0	0	0	20	1	0	3.00	....	....	....	....	....	....	....	....		1981-82	1981-82

Name	NHL Teams	NHL Seasons	Regular Schedule GP	W	L	T	Mins	GA	SO	Avg	Playoffs GP	W	L	T	Mins	GA	SO	Avg	NHL Cup Wins	First NHL Season	Last NHL Season
LaForest, Mark	Det., Phi., Tor., Ott.	6	103	25	54	4	5032	354	2	4.22	2	1	0	....	48	1	0	1.25		1985-86	1993-94
Lajeunesse, Simon	Ott.	1	1	0	0	0	24	0	0	0.00	....	....	....	....	....	....	....	....		2001-02	2001-02
Lalime, Patrick	Pit., Ott., St.L., Chi., Buf.	12	444	200	174	48	25241	1085	35	2.58	41	21	20	....	2549	75	5	1.77		1996-97	2010-11
Lamothe, Marc	Chi., Det.	2	4	2	1	1	241	13	0	3.24	....	....	....	....	....	....	....	....		1999-00	2003-04
Langkow, Scott	Wpg., Phx., Atl.	4	20	3	12	1	943	68	0	4.33	....	....	....	....	....	....	....	....		1995-96	1999-00
• Larocque, Michel	Mtl., Tor., Phi., St.L.	11	312	160	89	45	17615	978	17	3.33	14	6	6	....	759	37	1	2.92	4	1973-74	1983-84
Larocque, Michel	Chi.	1	3	0	2	0	152	9	0	3.55	....	....	....	....	....	....	....	....		2000-01	2000-01
‡ Lasak, Jan	Nsh.	2	6	0	4	0	267	18	0	4.04	....	....	....	....	....	....	....	....		2001-02	2002-03
Laskoski, Gary	L.A.	2	59	19	27	5	2942	228	0	4.65	....	....	....	....	....	....	....	....		1982-83	1983-84
Laxton, Gord	Pit.	4	17	4	9	0	800	74	0	5.55	....	....	....	....	....	....	....	....		1975-76	1978-79
LeBlanc, Ray	Chi.	1	1	1	0	0	60	1	0	1.00	....	....	....	....	....	....	....	....		1991-92	1991-92
Leclaire, Pascal	CBJ, Ott.	7	173	61	76	15	9406	453	10	2.89	3	1	2	....	211	10	0	2.84		2003-04	2010-11
§ • Leduc, Albert	Mtl.	1	1	0	0	0	2	1	0	30.00	....	....	....	....	....	....	....	....		1931-32	1931-32
‡ Legace, Manny	L.A., Det., St.L., Car.	11	365	187	99	41	20140	809	24	2.41	11	4	6	....	639	27	0	2.54	1	1998-99	2009-10
Legris, Claude	Det.	2	4	0	1	1	91	4	0	2.64	....	....	....	....	....	....	....	....		1980-81	1981-82
• Lehman, Hugh	Chi.	2	48	20	24	4	3047	136	6	2.68	2	0	1	1	120	10	0	5.00		1926-27	1927-28
Lemelin, Reggie	Atl., Cgy., Bos.	15	507	236	162	63	28006	1613	12	3.46	59	23	25	....	3119	186	2	3.58		1978-79	1992-93
Lenarduzzi, Mike	Hfd.	2	4	1	1	1	189	10	0	3.17	....	....	....	....	....	....	....	....		1992-93	1993-94
‡ LeNeveu, David	Phx., CBJ	3	22	5	9	2	1067	61	0	3.43	....	....	....	....	....	....	....	....		2005-06	2010-11
Lessard, Mario	L.A.	6	240	92	97	39	13529	843	9	3.74	20	6	12	....	1136	83	0	4.38		1978-79	1983-84
Levasseur, Jean-Louis	Min.	1	1	0	1	0	60	7	0	7.00	....	....	....	....	....	....	....	....		1979-80	1979-80
§ • Levinsky, Alex	Tor.	1	1	0	0	0	1	1	0	60.00	....	....	....	....	....	....	....	....		1931-32	1931-32
• Lindbergh, Pelle	Phi.	5	157	87	49	15	9150	503	7	3.30	23	12	10	....	1214	63	3	3.11		1981-82	1985-86
• Lindsay, Bert	Mtl.W., Tor.	2	20	6	14	0	1238	118	0	5.72	....	....	....	....	....	....	....	....		1917-18	1918-19
Little, Neil	Phi.	2	2	0	2	0	93	6	0	3.87	....	....	....	....	....	....	....	....		2001-02	2003-04
Littman, David	Buf., T.B.	3	3	0	2	0	141	14	0	5.96	....	....	....	....	....	....	....	....		1990-91	1992-93
Liut, Mike	St.L., Hfd., Wsh.	13	664	294	271	74	38215	2221	25	3.49	67	29	32	....	3814	215	2	3.38		1979-80	1991-92
Lockett, Ken	Van.	2	55	13	15	8	2348	131	2	3.35	1	0	1	....	60	6	0	6.00		1974-75	1975-76
• Lockhart, Howard	Tor., Que., Ham., Bos.	5	59	16	41	0	3413	287	1	5.05	....	....	....	....	....	....	....	....		1919-20	1924-25
LoPresti, Pete	Min., Edm.	6	175	43	102	20	9858	668	5	4.07	2	0	2	....	77	6	0	4.68		1974-75	1980-81
• LoPresti, Sam	Chi.	2	74	30	38	6	4530	236	4	3.13	8	3	5	....	530	17	1	1.92		1940-41	1941-42
Lorenz, Danny	NYI	3	8	1	5	0	357	25	0	4.20	....	....	....	....	....	....	....	....		1990-91	1992-93
Loustel, Ron	Wpg.	1	1	0	1	0	60	10	0	10.00	....	....	....	....	....	....	....	....		1980-81	1980-81
Low, Ron	Tor., Wsh., Det., Que., Edm., N.J.	11	382	102	203	38	20502	1463	4	4.28	7	1	6	....	452	29	0	3.85		1972-73	1984-85
Lozinski, Larry	Det.	1	30	6	11	7	1459	105	0	4.32	....	....	....	....	....	....	....	....		1980-81	1980-81
• Lumley, Harry	Det., NYR, Chi., Tor., Bos.	16	803	330	329	142	48044	2206	71	2.75	76	29	47	....	4778	198	7	2.49	1	1943-44	1959-60
MacKenzie, Shawn	N.J.	1	4	0	1	0	130	15	0	6.92	....	....	....	....	....	....	....	....		1982-83	1982-83
Madeley, Darrin	Ott.	3	39	4	23	5	1928	140	0	4.36	....	....	....	....	....	....	....	....		1992-93	1994-95
Malarchuk, Clint	Que., Wsh., Buf.	10	338	141	130	45	19030	1100	12	3.47	15	2	9	....	781	56	0	4.30		1981-82	1991-92
Maneluk, George	NYI	1	4	1	1	0	140	15	0	6.43	....	....	....	....	....	....	....	....		1990-91	1990-91
Maniago, Cesare	Tor., Mtl., NYR, Min., Van.	15	568	190	257	97	32569	1773	30	3.27	36	15	21	....	2247	100	3	2.67		1960-61	1977-78
Maracle, Norm	Det., Atl.	5	66	14	33	8	3430	177	1	3.10	2	0	0	....	58	3	0	3.10		1997-98	2001-02
‡ Markkanen, Jussi	Edm., NYR	5	128	43	47	15	6610	297	7	2.70	7	3	3	....	374	14	1	2.25		2001-02	2006-07
Marois, Jean	Tor., Chi.	2	3	1	2	0	180	15	0	5.00	....	....	....	....	....	....	....	....		1943-44	1953-54
Martin, Seth	St.L.	1	30	8	10	7	1552	67	1	2.59	2	0	0	....	73	5	0	4.11		1967-68	1967-68
Mason, Bob	Wsh., Chi., Que., Van.	8	145	55	65	16	7988	500	1	3.76	5	2	3	....	369	12	1	1.95		1983-84	1990-91
Mattsson, Markus	Wpg., Min., L.A.	4	92	21	46	14	5007	343	6	4.11	....	....	....	....	....	....	....	....		1979-80	1983-84
May, Darrell	St.L.	2	6	1	5	0	364	31	0	5.11	....	....	....	....	....	....	....	....		1985-86	1987-88
Mayer, Gilles	Tor.	4	9	2	6	1	540	24	0	2.67	....	....	....	....	....	....	....	....		1949-50	1955-56
• McAuley, Ken	NYR	2	96	17	64	15	5740	537	1	5.61	....	....	....	....	....	....	....	....		1943-44	1944-45
McCartan, Jack	NYR	2	12	2	7	3	680	42	1	3.71	....	....	....	....	....	....	....	....		1959-60	1960-61
• McCool, Frank	Tor.	2	72	34	31	7	4320	242	4	3.36	13	8	5	....	807	30	4	2.23	1	1944-45	1945-46
McDuffe, Peter	St.L., NYR, K.C., Det.	5	57	11	36	6	3207	218	0	4.08	1	0	1	....	60	7	0	7.00		1971-72	1975-76
McGrattan, Tom	Det.	1	1	0	0	0	8	1	0	7.50	....	....	....	....	....	....	....	....		1947-48	1947-48
McKay, Ross	Hfd.	1	1	0	0	0	35	3	0	5.14	....	....	....	....	....	....	....	....		1990-91	1990-91
McKenzie, Bill	Det., K.C., Col.	6	91	18	49	13	4776	326	2	4.10	....	....	....	....	....	....	....	....		1973-74	1979-80
McKichan, Steve	Van.	1	1	0	0	0	20	2	0	6.00	....	....	....	....	....	....	....	....		1990-91	1990-91
McLachlan, Murray	Tor.	1	2	0	1	0	25	4	0	9.60	....	....	....	....	....	....	....	....		1970-71	1970-71
McLean, Kirk	N.J., Van., Car., Fla., NYR	16	612	245	262	72	35090	1904	22	3.26	68	34	34	....	4189	198	6	2.84		1985-86	2000-01
McLelland, Dave	Van.	1	2	1	1	0	120	10	0	5.00	....	....	....	....	....	....	....	....		1972-73	1972-73
McLennan, Jamie	NYI, St.L., Min., Cgy., NYR, Fla.	11	254	80	109	36	13834	617	13	2.68	5	0	2	....	134	7	0	3.13		1993-94	2006-07
McLeod, Don	Det., Phi.	2	18	3	10	1	879	74	0	5.05	....	....	....	....	....	....	....	....		1970-71	1971-72
McLeod, Jim	St.L.	1	16	6	6	4	880	44	0	3.00	....	....	....	....	....	....	....	....		1971-72	1971-72
McNamara, Gerry	Tor.	2	7	2	2	1	323	14	0	2.60	....	....	....	....	....	....	....	....		1960-61	1969-70
• McNeil, Gerry	Mtl.	8	276	119	105	52	16535	649	28	2.36	35	17	18	....	2284	72	5	1.89	3	1947-48	1957-58
McRae, Gord	Tor.	5	71	30	22	10	3799	221	1	3.49	8	2	5	....	454	22	0	2.91		1972-73	1977-78
McVicar, Rob	Van.	1	1	0	0	0	3	0	0	0.00	....	....	....	....	....	....	....	....		2005-06	2005-06
Melanson, Roland	NYI, Min., L.A., N.J., Mtl.	11	291	129	106	33	16452	995	6	3.63	23	4	9	....	801	59	0	4.42	3	1980-81	1991-92
Meloche, Gilles	Chi., Cal., Cle., Min., Pit.	18	788	270	351	131	45401	2756	20	3.64	45	21	19	....	2464	143	2	3.48		1970-71	1987-88
Micalef, Corrado	Det.	5	113	26	59	15	5794	409	2	4.24	3	0	0	....	49	8	0	9.80		1981-82	1985-86
Michaud, Alfie	Van.	1	2	0	1	0	69	5	0	4.35	....	....	....	....	....	....	....	....		1999-00	1999-00
Michaud, Olivier	Mtl.	1	1	0	0	0	18	0	0	0.00	....	....	....	....	....	....	....	....		2001-02	2001-02
Middlebrook, Lindsay	Wpg., Min., N.J., Edm.	4	37	3	23	6	1845	152	0	4.94	....	....	....	....	....	....	....	....		1979-80	1982-83
• Millar, Al	Bos.	1	6	1	4	1	360	25	0	4.17	....	....	....	....	....	....	....	....		1957-58	1957-58
Millen, Greg	Pit., Hfd., St.L., Que., Chi., Det.	14	604	215	284	89	35377	2281	17	3.87	59	27	29	....	3383	193	0	3.42		1978-79	1991-92
• Miller, Joe	NYA, NYR, Pit., Phi.	4	127	24	87	16	7871	383	16	2.92	3	2	1	0	180	3	1	1.00	1	1927-28	1930-31
Minard, Mike	Edm.	1	1	1	0	0	60	3	0	3.00	....	....	....	....	....	....	....	....		1999-00	1999-00
Mio, Eddie	Edm., NYR, Det.	7	192	64	73	30	10428	705	4	4.06	17	9	7	....	986	63	0	3.83		1979-80	1985-86
• Mitchell, Mike	Tor.	3	22	10	9	0	1190	88	0	4.44	....	....	....	....	....	....	....	....	1	1919-20	1921-22
Moffat, Mike	Bos.	3	19	7	7	2	979	70	0	4.29	11	6	5	....	663	38	0	3.44		1981-82	1983-84
Moog, Andy	Edm., Bos., Dal., Mtl.	18	713	372	209	88	40151	2097	28	3.13	132	68	57	....	7452	377	4	3.04	3	1980-81	1997-98
• Moore, Alfie	NYA, Chi., Det.	4	21	7	14	0	1290	81	1	3.77	3	1	2	....	180	7	0	2.33	1	1936-37	1939-40
Moore, Robbie	Phi., Wsh.	2	6	3	1	1	257	8	2	1.87	5	3	2	....	268	18	0	4.03		1978-79	1982-83
Morissette, Jean-Guy	Mtl.	1	1	0	1	0	36	4	0	6.67	....	....	....	....	....	....	....	....		1963-64	1963-64
Morrison, Mike	Edm., Ott., Phx.	2	29	11	7	3	1226	67	0	3.28	....	....	....	....	....	....	....	....		2005-06	2006-07
Moss, Tyler	Cgy., Car., Van.	4	30	6	16	1	1496	81	0	3.25	....	....	....	....	....	....	....	....		1997-98	2002-03
• Mowers, Johnny	Det.	4	152	65	61	26	9350	399	15	2.56	32	19	13	....	2000	85	2	2.55	1	1940-41	1946-47
Mrazek, Jerome	Phi.	1	1	0	0	0	6	1	0	10.00	....	....	....	....	....	....	....	....		1975-76	1975-76
§ • Mummery, Harry	Que., Ham.	2	4	2	1	0	192	20	0	6.25	....	....	....	....	....	....	....	....		1919-20	1921-22
‡ Munro, Adam	Chi.	2	17	4	10	3	927	51	1	3.30	....	....	....	....	....	....	....	....		2003-04	2005-06
§ • Munro, Dunc	Mtl.M.	1	1	0	0	0	2	0	0	0.00	....	....	....	....	....	....	....	....		1924-25	1924-25
• Murphy, Hal	Mtl.	1	1	1	0	0	60	4	0	4.00	....	....	....	....	....	....	....	....		1952-53	1952-53
• Murray, Mickey	Mtl.	1	1	0	1	0	60	4	0	4.00	....	....	....	....	....	....	....	....		1929-30	1929-30
Muzzatti, Jason	Cgy., Hfd., NYR, S.J.	5	62	13	25	10	3014	167	1	3.32	....	....	....	....	....	....	....	....		1993-94	1997-98
Myllys, Jarmo	Min., S.J.	4	39	4	27	1	1846	161	0	5.23	....	....	....	....	....	....	....	....		1988-89	1991-92
Mylnikov, Sergei	Que.	1	10	1	7	2	568	47	0	4.96	....	....	....	....	....	....	....	....		1989-90	1989-90
Myre, Phil	Mtl., Atl., St.L., Phi., Col., Buf.	14	439	149	198	76	25220	1482	14	3.53	12	6	5	....	747	41	1	3.29		1969-70	1982-83
Naumenko, Gregg	Ana.	1	2	0	1	0	70	7	0	6.00	....	....	....	....	....	....	....	....		2000-01	2000-01
Newton, Cam	Pit.	2	16	4	7	1	814	51	0	3.76	....	....	....	....	....	....	....	....		1970-71	1972-73
Niittymaki, Antero	Phi., T.B., S.J.	7	234	95	86	31	13113	645	5	2.95	4	1	0	....	164	6	0	2.20		2003-04	2010-11
‡ Noronen, Mika	Buf., Van.	5	71	23	32	6	3652	163	3	2.68	....	....	....	....	....	....	....	....		2000-01	2005-06
‡ Norrena, Fredrik	CBJ	3	100	35	45	11	5235	243	5	2.79	....	....	....	....	....	....	....	....		2006-07	2008-09
Norris, Jack	Bos., Chi., L.A.	4	58	20	25	4	3119	202	2	3.89	....	....	....	....	....	....	....	....		1964-65	1970-71
Nurminen, Pasi	Atl.	3	125	48	54	12	7059	338	5	2.87	....	....	....	....	....	....	....	....		2001-02	2003-04
Oleschuk, Bill	K.C., Col.	4	55	7	28	10	2835	188	1	3.98	....	....	....	....	....	....	....	....		1975-76	1979-80
• Olesevich, Dan	NYR	1	1	0	0	1	29	2	0	4.14	....	....	....	....	....	....	....	....		1961-62	1961-62
O'Neill, Mike	Wpg., Ana.	4	21	0	9	2	855	61	0	4.28	....	....	....	....	....	....	....	....		1991-92	1996-97
Osgood, Chris	Det., NYI, St.L.	17	744	401	216	95	42564	1768	50	2.49	129	74	49	....	7651	267	15	2.09	3	1993-94	2010-11
Ouellet, Maxime	Phi., Wsh., Van.	3	12	2	6	2	663	34	1	3.08	....	....	....	....	....	....	....	....		2000-01	2005-06

Name	NHL Teams	NHL Seasons	Regular Schedule								Playoffs								NHL Cup Wins	First NHL Season	Last NHL Season
			GP	W	L	T	Mins	GA	SO	Avg	GP	W	L	T	Mins	GA	SO	Avg			
Ouimet, Ted	St.L.	1	1	0	1	0	60	2	0	2.00	....	....	....	....	....	....	....	....		1968-69	1968-69
Pageau, Paul	L.A.	1	1	0	1	0	60	8	0	8.00	....	....	....	....	....	....	....	....		1980-81	1980-81
• Paille, Marcel	NYR	7	107	32	52	22	6342	362	2	3.42	....	....	....	....	....	....	....	....		1957-58	1964-65
Palmateer, Mike	Tor., Wsh.	8	356	149	138	52	20131	1183	17	3.53	29	12	17	....	1765	89	2	3.03		1976-77	1983-84
Pang, Darren	Chi.	3	81	27	35	7	4252	287	0	4.05	6	1	3	....	250	18	0	4.32		1984-85	1988-89
Parent, Bernie	Bos., Phi., Tor.	13	608	271	198	121	35136	1493	54	2.55	71	38	33	....	4302	174	6	2.43	2	1965-66	1978-79
Parent, Bob	Tor.	2	3	0	2	0	160	15	0	5.63	....	....	....	....	....	....	....	....		1981-82	1982-83
Parent, Rich	St.L., T.B., Pit.	4	32	7	11	5	1561	82	1	3.15	....	....	....	....	....	....	....	....		1997-98	2000-01
Parro, Dave	Wsh.	4	77	21	36	10	4015	274	2	4.09	....	....	....	....	....	....	....	....		1980-81	1983-84
Passmore, Steve	Edm., Chi., L.A.	6	93	23	44	12	5045	235	2	2.79	3	0	2	....	138	6	0	2.61		1998-99	2003-04
§ • Patrick, Lester	NYR	1	....	....	....	....	....	....	....	....	1	1	0	0	46	1	0	1.30	1	1927-28	1927-28
‡ Patzold, Dimitri	S.J.	1	3	0	0	0	44	4	0	5.45	....	....	....	....	....	....	....	....		2007-08	2007-08
Peeters, Pete	Phi., Bos., Wsh.	13	489	246	155	51	27699	1424	21	3.08	71	35	35	....	4200	232	2	3.31		1978-79	1990-91
Pelletier, Jean-Marc	Phi., Phx.	3	7	1	4	0	354	23	0	3.90	....	....	....	....	....	....	....	....		1998-99	2003-04
Pelletier, Marcel	Chi., NYR	2	8	1	6	0	395	32	0	4.86	....	....	....	....	....	....	....	....		1950-51	1962-63
Penney, Steve	Mtl., Wpg.	5	91	35	38	12	5194	313	1	3.62	27	15	12	....	1604	72	4	2.69		1983-84	1987-88
• Perreault, Bob	Mtl., Det., Bos.	3	31	8	16	7	1827	103	3	3.38	....	....	....	....	....	....	....	....		1955-56	1962-63
Pettie, Jim	Bos.	3	21	9	7	2	1157	71	1	3.68	....	....	....	....	....	....	....	....		1976-77	1978-79
‡ Pielmeier, Timo	Ana.	1	1	0	0	0	40	5	0	7.50	....	....	....	....	....	....	....	....		2010-11	2010-11
Pietrangelo, Frank	Pit., Hfd.	7	141	46	59	6	7141	490	1	4.12	12	7	5	....	713	34	1	2.86	1	1987-88	1993-94
• Plante, Jacques	Mtl., NYR, St.L., Tor., Bos.	18	837	437	246	145	49533	1964	82	2.38	112	71	36	....	6651	237	14	2.14	6	1952-53	1972-73
• Plasse, Michel	St.L., Mtl., K.C., Pit., Col., Que.	11	299	92	136	54	16760	1058	2	3.79	4	1	2	....	195	9	1	2.77	1	1970-71	1981-82
§ • Plaxton, Hugh	Mtl.M.	1	1	0	1	0	57	5	0	5.26	....	....	....	....	....	....	....	....		1932-33	1932-33
‡ Pogge, Justin	Tor.	1	7	1	4	1	372	27	0	4.35	....	....	....	....	....	....	....	....		2008-09	2008-09
‡ Popperle, Tomas	CBJ	1	2	0	0	0	45	1	0	1.33	....	....	....	....	....	....	....	....		2006-07	2006-07
Potvin, Felix	Tor., NYI, Van., L.A., Bos.	13	635	266	260	85	36765	1694	32	2.76	72	35	37	....	4435	195	8	2.64		1991-92	2003-04
Pronovost, Claude	Bos., Mtl.	2	3	1	1	0	120	7	1	3.50	....	....	....	....	....	....	....	....		1955-56	1958-59
Prusek, Martin	Ott., CBJ	4	57	31	12	4	2898	114	3	2.36	1	0	0	....	40	1	0	1.50		2001-02	2005-06
Puppa, Daren	Buf., Tor., T.B.	15	429	179	161	54	23819	1204	19	3.03	16	4	9	....	786	51	0	3.89		1985-86	1999-00
Pusey, Chris	Det.	1	1	0	0	0	40	3	0	4.50	....	....	....	....	....	....	....	....		1985-86	1985-86
Racicot, Andre	Mtl.	5	68	26	23	8	3357	196	2	3.50	4	0	1	....	31	4	0	7.74	1	1989-90	1993-94
Racine, Bruce	St.L.	1	11	0	3	0	230	12	0	3.13	1	0	0	....	1	0	0	0.00		1995-96	1995-96
Ram, Jamie	NYR	1	1	0	0	0	27	0	0	0.00	....	....	....	....	....	....	....	....		1995-96	1995-96
Ranford, Bill	Bos., Edm., Wsh., T.B., Det.	15	647	240	279	76	35936	2042	15	3.41	53	28	25	....	3110	159	4	3.07	2	1985-86	1999-00
‡ Raycroft, Andrew	Bos., Tor., Col., Van., Dal.	11	280	113	114	27	15191	732	9	2.89	8	3	4	....	472	17	1	2.16		2000-01	2011-12
Raymond, Alain	Wsh.	1	1	0	1	0	40	2	0	3.00	....	....	....	....	....	....	....	....		1987-88	1987-88
• Rayner, Chuck	NYA, Bro., NYR	10	424	138	208	77	25491	1294	25	3.05	18	9	9	....	1135	46	1	2.43		1940-41	1952-53
Reaugh, Daryl	Edm., Hfd.	3	27	8	9	1	1246	72	1	3.47	....	....	....	....	....	....	....	....		1984-85	1990-91
Reddick, Pokey	Wpg., Edm., Fla.	6	132	46	58	16	7162	443	0	3.71	4	0	2	....	168	10	0	3.57	1	1986-87	1993-94
§ • Redding, George	Bos.	1	1	0	0	0	11	1	0	5.45	....	....	....	....	....	....	....	....		1924-25	1924-25
Redquest, Greg	Pit.	1	1	0	0	0	13	3	0	13.85	....	....	....	....	....	....	....	....		1977-78	1977-78
Reece, Dave	Bos.	1	14	7	5	2	777	43	2	3.32	....	....	....	....	....	....	....	....		1975-76	1975-76
Reese, Jeff	Tor., Cgy., Hfd., T.B., N.J.	11	174	53	65	17	8667	529	5	3.66	11	3	5	....	515	35	0	4.08		1987-88	1998-99
Resch, Glenn	NYI, Col., N.J., Phi.	14	571	231	224	82	32279	1761	26	3.27	41	17	17	....	2044	85	2	2.50	1	1973-74	1986-87
• Rheaume, Herb	Mtl.	1	31	10	20	1	1889	92	0	2.92	....	....	....	....	....	....	....	....		1925-26	1925-26
Rhodes, Damian	Tor., Ott., Atl.	10	309	99	140	48	17339	820	12	2.84	13	5	7	....	741	27	0	2.19		1990-91	2001-02
Ricci, Nick	Pit.	4	19	7	12	0	1087	79	0	4.36	....	....	....	....	....	....	....	....		1979-80	1982-83
Richardson, Terry	Det., St.L.	5	20	3	11	0	906	85	0	5.63	....	....	....	....	....	....	....	....		1973-74	1978-79
Richter, Mike	NYR	15	666	301	258	73	38183	1840	24	2.89	76	41	33	....	4514	202	9	2.68	1	1988-89	2002-03
Ridley, Curt	NYR, Van., Tor.	6	104	27	47	16	5498	355	1	3.87	2	0	2	....	120	8	0	4.00		1974-75	1980-81
Riendeau, Vincent	Mtl., St.L., Det., Bos.	8	184	85	65	20	10423	573	5	3.30	25	11	12	....	1277	71	1	3.34		1987-88	1994-95
Riggin, Dennis	Det.	2	18	6	10	2	999	52	1	3.12	....	....	....	....	....	....	....	....		1959-60	1962-63
Riggin, Pat	Atl., Cgy., Wsh., Bos., Pit.	9	350	153	120	52	19872	1135	11	3.43	25	8	13	....	1336	72	0	3.23		1979-80	1987-88
Ring, Bob	Bos.	1	1	0	0	0	33	4	0	7.27	....	....	....	....	....	....	....	....		1965-66	1965-66
Rivard, Fern	Min.	4	55	9	27	11	2865	190	2	3.98	....	....	....	....	....	....	....	....		1968-69	1974-75
• Roach, John Ross	Tor., NYR, Det.	14	492	219	204	68	30444	1246	58	2.46	29	12	14	3	1901	60	7	1.89	1	1921-22	1934-35
• Roberts, Moe	Bos., NYA, Chi.	4	10	3	5	0	501	31	0	3.71	....	....	....	....	....	....	....	....		1925-26	1951-52
• Robertson, Earl	Det., NYA, Bro.	6	190	60	95	34	11820	575	16	2.92	15	7	7	....	995	29	2	1.75	1	1936-37	1941-42
• Rollins, Al	Tor., Chi., NYR	9	430	141	205	83	25723	1192	28	2.78	13	6	7	....	755	30	0	2.38	1	1949-50	1959-60
‡ Roloson, Dwayne	Cgy., Buf., Min., Edm., NYI, T.B.	14	606	227	257	82	34297	1552	29	2.72	50	28	18	....	2860	121	2	2.54		1996-97	2011-12
Romano, Roberto	Pit., Bos.	6	126	46	63	8	7111	471	4	3.97	....	....	....	....	....	....	....	....		1982-83	1993-94
Rosati, Mike	Wsh.	1	1	1	0	0	28	0	0	0.00	....	....	....	....	....	....	....	....		1998-99	1998-99
Roussel, Dominic	Phi., Wpg., Ana., Edm.	8	205	77	70	23	10665	555	7	3.12	1	0	0	....	23	0	0	0.00		1991-92	2000-01
Roy, Patrick	Mtl., Col.	19	1029	551	315	131	60235	2546	66	2.54	247	151	94	....	15209	584	23	2.30	4	1984-85	2002-03
Rudkowsky, Cody	St.L.	1	1	1	0	0	30	0	0	0.00	....	....	....	....	....	....	....	....		2002-03	2002-03
• Rupp, Pat	Det.	1	1	0	1	0	60	4	0	4.00	....	....	....	....	....	....	....	....		1963-64	1963-64
Rutherford, Jim	Det., Pit., Tor., L.A.	13	457	151	227	59	25895	1576	14	3.65	8	2	5	....	440	28	0	3.82		1970-71	1982-83
• Rutledge, Wayne	L.A.	3	82	28	37	9	4325	241	2	3.34	8	2	4	....	378	20	0	3.17		1967-68	1969-70
St. Croix, Rick	Phi., Tor.	8	130	49	54	18	7295	451	2	3.71	11	4	6	....	562	29	1	3.10		1977-78	1984-85
St. Laurent, Sam	N.J., Det.	5	34	7	12	4	1572	92	1	3.51	1	0	0	....	10	1	0	6.00		1985-86	1989-90
Salo, Tommy	NYI, Edm., Col.	10	526	210	225	73	30436	1296	37	2.55	22	5	16	....	1369	58	0	2.54		1994-95	2003-04
§ • Sands, Charlie	Mtl.	1	1	0	0	0	25	5	0	12.00	....	....	....	....	....	....	....	....		1939-40	1939-40
Sands, Mike	Min.	2	6	0	5	0	302	26	0	5.17	....	....	....	....	....	....	....	....		1984-85	1986-87
Sarjeant, Geoff	St.L., S.J.	2	8	1	2	1	291	20	0	4.12	....	....	....	....	....	....	....	....		1994-95	1995-96
Sauve, Bob	Buf., Det., Chi., N.J.	13	420	182	154	54	23711	1377	8	3.48	34	15	16	....	1850	95	4	3.08		1976-77	1988-89
Sauve, Philippe	Col., Cgy., Phx., Bos.	3	32	10	14	3	1616	93	0	3.45	....	....	....	....	....	....	....	....		2003-04	2006-07
• Sawchuk, Terry	Det., Bos., Tor., L.A., NYR	21	971	447	330	172	57194	2389	103	2.51	106	54	48	....	6290	266	12	2.54	4	1949-50	1969-70
• Schaefer, Joe	NYR	2	2	0	2	0	86	8	0	5.58	....	....	....	....	....	....	....	....		1959-60	1960-61
‡ Schaefer, Nolan	S.J.	1	7	5	1	0	352	11	1	1.88	....	....	....	....	....	....	....	....		2005-06	2005-06
Schafer, Paxton	Bos.	1	3	0	0	0	77	6	0	4.68	....	....	....	....	....	....	....	....		1996-97	1996-97
Schwab, Corey	N.J., T.B., Van., Tor.	8	147	42	63	13	7476	360	6	2.89	3	0	0	....	40	0	0	0.00	1	1995-96	2003-04
‡ Schwarz, Marek	St.L.	3	6	0	2	0	125	9	0	4.32	....	....	....	....	....	....	....	....		2006-07	2008-09
Scott, Ron	NYR, L.A.	5	28	8	13	4	1450	91	0	3.77	1	0	0	....	32	4	0	7.50		1983-84	1989-90
Scott, Travis	L.A.	1	1	0	0	0	25	3	0	7.20	....	....	....	....	....	....	....	....		2000-01	2000-01
Sevigny, Richard	Mtl., Que.	9	176	80	54	20	9485	507	5	3.21	4	0	3	....	208	13	0	3.75	1	1978-79	1986-87
Sharples, Scott	Cgy.	1	1	0	0	1	65	4	0	3.69	....	....	....	....	....	....	....	....		1991-92	1991-92
§ • Shields, Al	NYA	1	2	0	0	0	41	9	0	13.17	....	....	....	....	....	....	....	....		1931-32	1931-32
Shields, Steve	Buf., S.J., Ana., Bos., Fla., Atl.	10	246	80	104	40	13630	606	10	2.67	25	9	16	....	1445	74	1	3.07		1995-96	2005-06
Shtalenkov, Mikhail	Ana., Edm., Phx., Fla.	7	190	62	82	19	9966	480	8	2.89	4	0	3	....	211	10	0	2.84		1993-94	1999-00
Shulmistra, Richard	N.J., Fla.	2	2	1	1	0	122	3	0	1.48	....	....	....	....	....	....	....	....		1997-98	1999-00
Sidorkiewicz, Peter	Hfd., Ott., N.J.	8	246	79	128	27	13884	832	8	3.60	15	5	10	....	912	55	0	3.62		1987-88	1997-98
Sigalet, Jordan	Bos.	1	1	0	0	0	1	0	0	0.00	....	....	....	....	....	....	....	....		2005-06	2005-06
• Simmons, Don	Bos., Tor., NYR	11	249	101	101	41	14555	701	20	2.89	24	13	11	....	1436	62	3	2.59	3	1956-57	1968-69
Simmons, Gary	Cal., Cle., L.A.	4	107	30	57	15	6162	366	5	3.56	1	0	0	....	20	1	0	3.00		1974-75	1977-78
Skidmore, Paul	St.L.	1	2	1	1	0	120	6	0	3.00	....	....	....	....	....	....	....	....		1981-82	1981-82
Skorodenski, Warren	Chi., Edm.	5	35	12	11	4	1732	100	2	3.46	2	0	0	....	33	6	0	10.91		1981-82	1987-88
Skudra, Peter	Pit., Buf., Bos., Van.	6	146	51	47	20	7162	326	6	2.73	3	0	1	....	116	6	0	3.10		1997-98	2002-03
• Smith, Al	Tor., Pit., Det., Buf., Hfd., Col.	10	233	74	99	36	12752	735	10	3.46	6	1	4	....	317	21	0	3.97		1965-66	1980-81
Smith, Billy	L.A., NYI	18	680	305	233	105	38431	2031	22	3.17	132	88	36	....	7645	348	5	2.73	4	1971-72	1988-89
Smith, Gary	Tor., Oak., Cal., Chi., Van., Min., Wsh., Wpg.	14	532	173	261	74	29619	1675	26	3.39	20	5	13	....	1153	62	1	3.23		1965-66	1979-80
• Smith, Normie	Mtl.M., Det.	8	199	81	83	35	12357	479	17	2.33	12	9	2	0	820	18	3	1.32	2	1931-32	1944-45
Sneddon, Bob	Cal.	1	5	0	2	0	225	21	0	5.60	....	....	....	....	....	....	....	....		1970-71	1970-71
Snow, Garth	Que., Phi., Van., Pit., NYI	12	368	135	147	44	19837	925	16	2.80	20	9	8	....	1040	48	1	2.77		1993-94	2005-06
Soderstrom, Tommy	Phi., NYI	5	156	45	69	19	8189	496	10	3.63	....	....	....	....	....	....	....	....		1992-93	1996-97
Soetaert, Doug	NYR, Wpg., Mtl.	12	284	110	104	42	15583	1030	6	3.97	5	1	2	....	180	14	0	4.67	1	1975-76	1986-87
Soucy, Christian	Chi.	1	1	0	0	0	3	0	0	0.00	....	....	....	....	....	....	....	....		1993-94	1993-94
• Spooner, Red	Pit.	1	1	0	1	0	60	6	0	6.00	....	....	....	....	....	....	....	....		1929-30	1929-30
§ • Spring, Jesse	Ham.	1	1	0	0	0	2	0	0	0.00	....	....	....	....	....	....	....	....		1924-25	1924-25

Name	NHL Teams	NHL Seasons	Regular Schedule GP	W	L	T	Mins	GA	SO	Avg	Playoffs GP	W	L	T	Mins	GA	SO	Avg	NHL Cup Wins	First NHL Season	Last NHL Season
‡ Stana, Rastislav	Wsh.	1	6	1	2	0	211	11	0	3.13	....	....	....	....	....	....	....	....		2003-04	2003-04
Staniowski, Ed	St.L., Wpg., Hfd.	10	219	67	104	21	12075	818	2	4.06	8	1	6	....	428	28	0	3.93		1975-76	1984-85
§ • Starr, Harold	Mtl.M.	1	1	0	0	0	3	0	0	0.00	....	....	....	....	....	....	....	....		1931-32	1931-32
Stauber, Robb	L.A., Buf.	4	62	21	23	9	3295	209	1	3.81	4	3	1	....	240	16	0	4.00		1989-90	1994-95
Stefan, Greg	Det.	9	299	115	127	30	16333	1068	5	3.92	30	12	17	....	1681	99	1	3.53		1981-82	1989-90
• Stein, Phil	Tor.	1	1	0	0	1	70	2	0	1.71	....	....	....	....	....	....	....	....		1939-40	1939-40
‡ Stephan, Tobias	Dal.	2	11	1	3	2	499	29	0	3.49	....	....	....	....	....	....	....	....		2007-08	2008-09
• Stephenson, Wayne	St.L., Phi., Wsh.	10	328	146	103	49	18343	937	14	3.06	26	11	12	....	1522	79	2	3.11	1	1971-72	1980-81
• Stevenson, Doug	NYR, Chi.	3	8	2	6	0	480	39	0	4.88	....	....	....	....	....	....	....	....		1944-45	1945-46
• Stewart, Charles	Bos.	3	77	30	41	5	4742	194	10	2.45	....	....	....	....	....	....	....	....		1924-25	1926-27
Stewart, Jim	Bos.	1	1	0	1	0	20	5	0	15.00	....	....	....	....	....	....	....	....		1979-80	1979-80
Storr, Jamie	L.A., Car.	10	219	85	86	23	11512	488	16	2.54	5	0	3	....	182	11	0	3.63		1994-95	2003-04
• Stuart, Herb	Det.	1	3	1	2	0	180	5	0	1.67	....	....	....	....	....	....	....	....		1926-27	1926-27
Sylvestri, Don	Bos.	1	3	0	0	2	102	6	0	3.53	....	....	....	....	....	....	....	....		1984-85	1984-85
Tabaracci, Rick	Pit., Wpg., Wsh., Cgy., T.B., Atl., Col.	11	286	93	125	30	15255	760	15	2.99	17	4	12	....	1025	53	0	3.10		1988-89	1999-00
Takko, Kari	Min., Edm.	6	142	37	71	14	7317	475	1	3.90	4	0	1	....	109	7	0	3.85		1985-86	1990-91
Tallas, Robbie	Bos., Chi.	6	99	28	42	10	5069	246	3	2.91	....	....	....	....	....	....	....	....		1995-96	2000-01
Tanner, John	Que.	3	21	2	11	5	1084	65	1	3.60	....	....	....	....	....	....	....	....		1989-90	1991-92
Tataryn, Dave	NYR	1	2	1	1	0	80	10	0	7.50	....	....	....	....	....	....	....	....		1976-77	1976-77
Taylor, Bobby	Phi., Pit.	5	46	15	17	6	2268	155	0	4.10	....	....	....	....	....	....	....	....	2	1971-72	1975-76
‡ Tellqvist, Mikael	Tor., Phx., Buf.	6	113	45	41	10	6034	303	6	3.01	....	....	....	....	....	....	....	....		2002-03	2008-09
• Teno, Harvey	Det.	1	5	2	3	0	300	15	0	3.00	....	....	....	....	....	....	....	....		1938-39	1938-39
Terreri, Chris	N.J., S.J., Chi., NYI	14	406	151	172	43	22369	1143	9	3.07	29	12	12	....	1523	86	0	3.39	2	1986-87	2000-01
Thibault, Jocelyn	Que., Col., Mtl., Chi., Pit., Buf.	14	586	238	238	75	32892	1508	39	2.75	18	4	11	....	848	50	0	3.54		1993-94	2007-08
Thomas, Wayne	Mtl., Tor., NYR	9	243	103	93	34	13768	766	10	3.34	15	6	8	....	849	50	1	3.53		1972-73	1980-81
• Thompson, Tiny	Bos., Det.	12	553	284	194	75	34175	1183	81	2.08	44	20	24	0	2974	93	7	1.88	1	1928-29	1939-40
‡ Toivonen, Hannu	Bos., St.L.	3	61	18	24	10	3259	183	1	3.37	....	....	....	....	....	....	....	....		2005-06	2007-08
§ • Toppazzini, Jerry	Bos.	1	1	0	0	0	1	0	0	0.00	....	....	....	....	....	....	....	....		1960-61	1960-61
Torchia, Mike	Dal.	1	6	3	2	1	327	18	0	3.30	....	....	....	....	....	....	....	....		1994-95	1994-95
Tordjman, Josh	Phx.	1	2	0	2	0	118	8	0	4.07	....	....	....	....	....	....	....	....		2008-09	2008-09
‡ Toskala, Vesa	S.J., Tor., Cgy.	8	266	129	82	30	14767	679	13	2.76	11	6	5	....	686	28	1	2.45		2001-02	2009-10
Trefilov, Andrei	Cgy., Buf., Chi.	7	54	12	25	4	2663	153	2	3.45	1	0	0	....	5	0	0	0.00		1992-93	1998-99
Tremblay, Vincent	Tor., Pit.	5	58	12	26	8	2785	223	1	4.80	....	....	....	....	....	....	....	....		1979-80	1983-84
Tucker, Ted	Cal.	1	5	1	1	1	177	10	0	3.39	....	....	....	....	....	....	....	....		1973-74	1973-74
Tugnutt, Ron	Que., Edm., Ana., Mtl., Ott., Pit., CBJ, Dal.	16	537	186	239	62	29486	1497	26	3.05	25	9	13	....	1482	56	3	2.27		1987-88	2003-04
Turco, Marty	Dal., Chi., Bos.	11	543	275	167	66	30957	1216	41	2.36	47	21	26	....	3103	112	4	2.17		2000-01	2011-12
Turek, Roman	Dal., St.L., Cgy.	8	328	159	115	43	19095	734	27	2.31	22	12	9	....	1342	50	0	2.24	1	1996-97	2003-04
• Turner, Joe	Det.	1	1	0	0	1	70	3	0	2.57	....	....	....	....	....	....	....	....		1941-42	1941-42
Underhill, Matt	Chi.	1	1	0	1	0	61	4	0	3.93	....	....	....	....	....	....	....	....		2003-04	2003-04
Vachon, Rogie	Mtl., L.A., Det., Bos.	16	795	355	291	127	46298	2310	51	2.99	48	23	23	....	2876	133	2	2.77	3	1966-67	1981-82
‡ Valiquette, Steve	NYI, Edm., NYR	6	46	16	14	5	2256	103	4	2.74	2	0	0	....	40	0	0	0.00		1999-00	2009-10
Vanbiesbrouck, John	NYR, Fla., Phi., NYI, N.J.	20	882	374	346	119	50475	2503	40	2.98	71	28	38	....	3969	177	5	2.68		1981-82	2001-02
Veisor, Mike	Chi., Hfd., Wpg.	10	139	41	62	26	7806	532	5	4.09	4	0	2	....	180	15	0	5.00		1973-74	1983-84
Vernon, Mike	Cgy., Det., S.J., Fla.	19	781	385	273	92	44449	2206	27	2.98	138	77	56	....	8214	367	6	2.68	2	1982-83	2001-02
• Vezina, Georges	Mtl.	9	190	103	81	5	11592	633	13	3.28	13	10	3	0	780	35	2	2.69	1	1917-18	1925-26
Villemure, Gilles	NYR, Chi.	10	205	100	64	29	11581	542	13	2.81	14	5	5	....	656	32	0	2.93		1963-64	1976-77
Waite, Jimmy	Chi., S.J., Phx.	11	106	28	41	12	5253	293	4	3.35	6	0	3	....	211	14	0	3.98		1988-89	1998-99
Wakaluk, Darcy	Buf., Min., Dal., Phx.	8	191	67	75	21	9756	524	9	3.22	8	4	2	....	364	18	0	2.97		1988-89	1996-97
Wakely, Ernie	Mtl., St.L.	7	113	41	42	17	6244	290	8	2.79	10	2	6	....	509	37	1	4.36	2	1962-63	1971-72
Wall, Michael	Ana.	1	4	2	2	0	202	10	0	2.97	....	....	....	....	....	....	....	....		2006-07	2006-07
• Walsh, Flat	Mtl.M., NYA	7	108	48	43	16	6641	256	12	2.31	8	2	4	2	570	16	2	1.68		1926-27	1932-33
Wamsley, Rick	Mtl., St.L., Cgy., Tor.	13	407	204	131	46	23123	1287	12	3.34	27	7	18	....	1397	81	0	3.48	1	1980-81	1992-93
Watt, Jim	St.L.	1	1	0	0	0	20	2	0	6.00	....	....	....	....	....	....	....	....		1973-74	1973-74
Weekes, Kevin	Fla., Van., NYI, T.B., Car., NYR, N.J.	11	348	105	163	39	18837	903	19	2.88	9	3	3	....	468	15	2	1.92		1997-98	2008-09
Weeks, Steve	NYR, Hfd., Van., NYI, L.A., Ott.	14	290	111	119	33	15879	989	5	3.74	12	3	5	....	486	27	0	3.33		1980-81	1992-93
‡ Weiman, Tyler	Col.	1	1	0	0	0	16	0	0	0.00	....	....	....	....	....	....	....	....		2007-08	2007-08
Wetzel, Carl	Det., Min.	2	7	1	4	1	301	22	0	4.39	....	....	....	....	....	....	....	....		1964-65	1967-68
Whitmore, Kay	Hfd., Van., Bos., Cgy.	9	155	60	64	16	8596	508	4	3.55	4	0	2	....	174	13	0	4.48		1988-89	2001-02
Wilkinson, Derek	T.B.	4	22	3	12	3	933	57	0	3.67	....	....	....	....	....	....	....	....		1995-96	1998-99
Willis, Jordan	Dal.	1	1	0	1	0	19	1	0	3.16	....	....	....	....	....	....	....	....		1995-96	1995-96
Wilson, Dunc	Phi., Van., Tor., NYR, Pit.	10	287	80	150	33	15851	988	8	3.74	....	....	....	....	....	....	....	....		1969-70	1978-79
• Wilson, Lefty	Det., Tor., Bos.	3	3	0	0	1	81	1	0	0.74	....	....	....	....	....	....	....	....		1953-54	1957-58
• Winkler, Hal	NYR, Bos.	2	75	35	26	14	4739	126	21	1.60	10	2	3	5	640	18	2	1.69		1926-27	1927-28
Wolfe, Bernie	Wsh.	4	120	20	61	21	6104	424	1	4.17	....	....	....	....	....	....	....	....		1975-76	1978-79
• Wood, Alex	NYA	1	1	0	1	0	70	3	0	2.57	....	....	....	....	....	....	....	....		1936-37	1936-37
• Worsley, Gump	NYR, Mtl., Min.	21	861	335	352	150	50183	2407	43	2.88	70	40	26	....	4084	189	5	2.78	4	1952-53	1973-74
• Worters, Roy	Pit., NYA, Mtl.	12	484	171	229	83	30175	1143	67	2.27	11	3	6	2	690	24	3	2.09		1925-26	1936-37
• Worthy, Chris	Oak., Cal.	3	26	5	10	4	1326	98	0	4.43	....	....	....	....	....	....	....	....		1968-69	1970-71
Wregget, Ken	Tor., Phi., Pit., Cgy., Det.	17	575	225	248	53	31663	1917	9	3.63	56	28	25	....	3341	160	3	2.87	1	1983-84	1999-00
Yeats, Matthew	Wsh.	1	5	1	3	0	258	13	0	3.02	....	....	....	....	....	....	....	....		2003-04	2003-04
‡ Yeremeyev, Vitali	NYR	1	4	0	4	0	212	16	0	4.53	....	....	....	....	....	....	....	....		2000-01	2000-01
§ • Young, Doug	Det.	1	1	0	0	0	21	1	0	2.86	....	....	....	....	....	....	....	....		1933-34	1933-34
Young, Wendell	Van., Phi., Pit., T.B.	10	187	59	86	12	9410	618	2	3.94	2	0	1	....	99	6	0	3.64	2	1985-86	1994-95
‡ Zaba, Matt	NYR	1	1	0	0	0	34	2	0	3.53	....	....	....	....	....	....	....	....		2009-10	2009-10
Zanier, Mike	Edm.	1	3	1	1	1	185	12	0	3.89	....	....	....	....	....	....	....	....		1984-85	1984-85

Hank Bassen

Cristobal Huet

Manny Legace

Dwayne Roloson

Gary Simmons

Marty Turco

Hockey Hall of Fame, U.S. Hockey Hall of Fame and IIHF Hall of Fame 2013 Inductees and Award Winners

1954 Soviet National Team
IIHF Hall of Fame
Milestone Trophy Winner

Chris Chelios
Hockey Hall of Fame
2013 Inductee

Murray Costello
U.S. Hockey Hall of Fame
2012 Gretzky Award Winner

Cindy Curley
U.S. Hockey Hall of Fame
2013 Inductee

Jan-Ake Edvinsson
IIHF Hall of Fame
2013 Inductee

Peter Forsberg
IIHF Hall of Fame
2013 Inductee

Danielle Goyette
IIHF Hall of Fame
2013 Inductee

Jay Greenberg
2013 Elmer Ferguson
Memorial Award Winner

Bill Guerin
U.S. Hockey Hall of Fame
2013 Inductee

Geraldine Heaney
Hockey Hall of Fame
2013 Inductee

Paul Henderson
IIHF Hall of Fame
2013 Inductee

Peter Karmanos Jr
U.S. Hockey Hall of Fame
2013 Inductee

Ron Mason
U.S. Hockey Hall of Fame
2013 Inductee

Gord Miller
IIHF Hall of Fame
2013 Paul Loiqc Award Winner

Harry Neale
2013 Foster Hewitt
Memorial Award Winner

Scott Niedermayer
Hockey Hall of Fame
2013 Inductee

Teppo Numminen
IIHF Hall of Fame
2013 Inductee

Brendan Shanahan
Hockey Hall of Fame
2013 Inductee

Fred Shero
Hockey Hall of Fame
2013 Inductee

Mats Sundin
IIHF Hall of Fame
2013 Inductee

Doug Weight
U.S. Hockey Hall of Fame
2013 Inductee

Special thanks to Peter Jagla, Hockey Hall of Fame for inductee and honoree photos

Free Agent Signing Register, 2013

PLAYER	POS.	SIGNED BY	PREVIOUS ORGANIZATION	SIGNING DATE
Will Acton	C	Edmonton	Toronto (AHL)	July 5
Luke Adam	C	Buffalo	Buffalo	July 23
Craig Adams	RW	Pittsburgh	Pittsburgh	July 5
Daniel Alfredsson	RW	Detroit	Ottawa	July 5
Jake Allen	G	St. Louis	St. Louis	July 25
Karl Alzner	D	Washington	Washington	July 10
Joakim Andersson	C	Detroit	Detroit	Aug. 6
Nik Antropov	C	Astana (KHL)	Winnipeg	Aug. 7
Colby Armstrong	RW	Vaxjo (SWE)	Montreal	July 27
Keith Aucoin	C	St. Louis	NY Islanders	July 5
Richard Bachman	G	Edmonton	Dallas	July 6
Mikael Backlund	C	Calgary	Calgary	July 10
Josh Bailey	C	NY Islanders	NY Islanders	July 15
Keith Ballard	D	Minnesota	Vancouver	July 5
Mark Barberio	D	Tampa Bay	Tampa Bay	July 16
Kyle Beach	C	Chicago	Chicago	July 17
Eric Belanger	C	Yekaterinburg (KHL)	Edmonton	July 15
Matt Beleskey	LW	Anaheim	Anaheim	July 7
Andre Benoit	D	Colorado	Ottawa	July 5
Marc-Andre Bergeron	D	Zurich (SUI)	Carolina	July 18
Alex Biega	D	Vancouver	Buffalo	July 5
Jeremie Blain	D	Vancouver	Edmonton	July 5
Jonathon Blum	D	Minnesota	Nashville	July 12
Troy Bodie	RW	Toronto	Anaheim	July 10
Andrew Bodnarchuk	D	Los Angeles	Los Angeles	July 29
Zach Bogosian	D	Winnipeg	Winnipeg	July 29
Alexandre Bolduc	C	St. Louis	Phoenix	July 5
Mark Borowiecki	D	Ottawa	Ottawa	July 10
Pierre-Marc Bouchard	C	NY Islanders	Minnesota	July 5
Brian Boucher	G	Zug (SUI)	Philadelphia	July 17
Tyler Bozak	C	Toronto	Toronto	July 5
Chris Breen	D	Calgary	Calgary	July 17
T.J. Brennan	D	Toronto	Nashville	July 5
Tim Brent	C	Nizhny Novgorod (KHL)	Carolina	July 30
Danny Briere	C	Montreal	Philadelphia	July 4
T.J. Brodie	D	Calgary	Calgary	July 31
Evan Brophey	C	Salzburg (AUT)	Portland (AHL)	July 29
Chris Butler	D	Calgary	Calgary	July 5
Paul Byron	C	Calgary	Calgary	July 20
Carter Camper	RW	Boston	Boston	July 8
Chris Campoli	D	Lugano (SUI)	Biel-Bienne (SUI)	July 29
Jonathan Cheechoo	RW	Zagreb (KHL)	Oklahoma City (AHL)	July 9
Kyle Chipchura	C	Phoenix	Phoenix	July 5
Mat Clark	D	Anaheim	Anaheim	July 15
David Clarkson	RW	Toronto	New Jersey	July 5
Kyle Clifford	LW	Los Angeles	Los Angeles	Aug. 2
Ryane Clowe	RW	New Jersey	NY Rangers	July 5
Joe Colborne	C	Toronto	Toronto	July 10
Adam Comrie	D	San Jose	Worcester (AHL)	July 10
Erik Condra	RW	Ottawa	Ottawa	July 12
Chris Conner	RW	Pittsburgh	Phoenix	July 6
Matt Cooke	C	Minnesota	Pittsburgh	July 5
Patrice Cormier	C	Winnipeg	Winnipeg	July 16
Matthew Corrente	D	Carolina	New Jersey	July 10
Joe Corvo	D	Ottawa	Carolina	July 8
Corey Cowick	LW	Ottawa	Ottawa	July 23
Joey Crabb	RW	Florida	Washington	July 5
Nick Crawford	D	Buffalo	Buffalo	July 19
Matt Cullen	C	Nashville	Minnesota	July 5
Tyler Cuma	D	Minnesota	Minnesota	July 30
Mark Cundari	D	Calgary	Calgary	July 18
Stephane Da Costa	C	Ottawa	Ottawa	Aug. 7
Matt D'Agostini	RW	Pittsburgh	New Jersey	July 10
Zac Dalpe	RW	Carolina	Carolina	July 19

PLAYER	POS.	SIGNED BY	PREVIOUS ORGANIZATION	SIGNING DATE
Yann Danis	G	Philadelphia	Edmonton	July 5
Brandon Defazio	LW	Vancouver	NY Islanders	July 12
Guillaume Desbiens	RW	Colorado	Vancouver	July 6
Nicolas Deschamps	C	Washington	Washington	July 22
Cedrick Desjardins	G	Montreal	Colorado	July 5
Nick Drazenovic	C	Pittsburgh	St. Louis	July 5
Gabriel Dumont	C	Montreal	Montreal	July 10
David Dziurzynski	C	Ottawa	Ottawa	July 10
Andrew Ebbet	C	Pittsburgh	Vancouver	July 5
Dan Ellis	G	Dallas	Carolina	July 5
Ray Emery	G	Philadelphia	Chicago	July 5
Justin Falk	D	NY Rangers	NY Rangers	July 10
Andrew Ference	D	Edmonton	Boston	July 5
Benn Ferriero	C	Vancouver	Minnesota	July 12
Valtteri Filppula	C	Tampa Bay	Detroit	July 5
Mark Flood	D	Carolina	Yaroslavl (KHL)	July 10
Brian Flynn	RW	Buffalo	Buffalo	July 19
Kurtis Foster	D	Zagreb (KHL)	Philadelphia	July 30
Stefan Fournier	RW	Montreal	Halifax (QMJHL)	July 6
Mark Fraser	D	Toronto	Toronto	July 30
Sam Gagner	C	Edmonton	Edmonton	July 22
Aaron Gagnon	C	Jonkoping (SWE)	Winnipeg	Aug. 7
Nathan Gerbe	C	Carolina	Buffalo	July 26
Matt Gilroy	D	Florida	NY Rangers	July 8
Luke Glendening	RW	Detroit	Grand Rapids (AHL)	July 5
Cody Goloubef	D	Columbus	Columbus	July 25
Scott Gomez	C	Florida	San Jose	July 31
Andrew Gordon	RW	Winnipeg	Vancouver	July 6
Boyd Gordon	C	Edmonton	Phoenix	July 5
Alex Grant	D	Anaheim	Pittsburgh	July 10
Denis Grebeshkov	D	Edmonton	Khanti-Mansissik (KHL)	July 18
Thomas Greiss	G	Phoenix	San Jose	July 5
Nate Guenin	D	Colorado	Anaheim	July 5
Carl Gunnarson	D	Toronto	Toronto	July 22
Erik Gustafsson	D	Philadelphia	Philadelphia	July 9
Matt Hackett	G	Buffalo	Buffalo	July 23
Carl Hagelin	LW	NY Rangers	NY Rangers	July 10
Matt Halischuk	RW	Winnipeg	Nashville	July 11
Zach Hamill	C	Vancouver	Chicago	July 25
Ryan Hamilton	LW	Edmonton	Toronto	July 5
Travis Hamonic	D	NY Islanders	NY Islanders	July 5
Michal Handzus	C	Chicago	Chicago	July 5
Scott Hannan	D	San Jose	San Jose	July 5
Darren Haydar	RW	Munchen (GER)	Chicago (AHL)	July 25
Matt Hendricks	C	Nashville	Washington	July 5
Thomas Hickey	D	NY Islanders	NY Islanders	July 18
Mike Hoffman	C/LW	Ottawa	Ottawa	July 18
Nick Holden	D	Colorado	Columbus	July 6
Nathan Horton	RW	Columbus	Boston	July 5
Michel Hutchinson	G	Winnipeg	Boston	July 19
Carter Hutton	G	Nashville	Chicago	July 5
Jarome Iginla	RW	Boston	Pittsburgh	July 5
Jaromir Jagr	RW	New Jersey	Boston	July 23
Dustin Jeffrey	C	Pittsburgh	Pittsburgh	July 18
Jesse Joensuu	LW	Edmonton	NY Islanders	July 5
Aaron Johnson	D	NY Rangers	Boston	July 5
Nick Johnson	RW	Boston	Phoenix	July 5
Ryan Jones	RW	Edmonton	Edmonton	July 6
Derek Joslin	D	Solna(SWE)	Vancouver	July 28
Bracken Kearns	C	San Jose	San Jose	Aug. 2
Tim Kennedy	LW	Phoenix	San Jose	July 11
Tyler Kennedy	C	San Jose	Pittsburgh	July 5
Nikolai Khabibulin	G	Chicago	Edmonton	July 5
Anton Khudobin	G	Carolina	Boston	July 5

PLAYER	POS.	SIGNED BY	PREVIOUS ORGANIZATION	SIGNING DATE
Saku Koivu	C	Anaheim	Anaheim	July 5
David Kolomatis	D	Washington	Los Angeles	July 6
Mike Komisarek	D	Carolina	Toronto	July 5
Lauri Korpikoski	LW	Phoenix	Phoenix	July 11
Mike Kostka	D	Chicago	Toronto	July 19
Ilya Kovalchuk	LW	St. Petersburg (KHL)	New Jersey	July 15
Marcus Kruger	C	Chicago	Chicago	July 12
Jason LaBarbera	G	Edmonton	Phoenix	July 5
Jon Landry	D	Minnesota	NY Islanders	July 9
Maxim Lapierre	C	St. Louis	Vancouver	July 5
Peter LeBlanc	C	Washington	Washington	July 10
Vincent Lecavalier	C	Philadelphia	Tampa Bay	July 6
David Leggio	G	Washington	Buffalo	July 8
Trevor Lewis	C	Los Angeles	Los Angeles	July 23
Bryan Little	RW	Winnipeg	Winnipeg	July 22
Clarke MacArthur	LW	Ottawa	Toronto	July 5
Spencer Machacek	RW	Columbus	Columbus	July 20
Mark Mancari	RW	St. Louis	Buffalo	July 5
Jacob Markstrom	G	Florida	Florida	July 15
Kevin Marshall	D	Toronto	Toronto	July 5
Alec Martinez	D	Los Angeles	Los Angeles	July 15
Jon Matsumoto	C	Florida	San Jose	July 8
Ben Maxwell	C	Karpat (FIN)	St. John's (AHL)	Aug. 12
Ryan McDonagh	D	NY Rangers	NY Rangers	July 8
Frazer McLaren	LW	Toronto	Toronto	July 5
Patrick McNeill	D	Columbus	Washington	July 6
Derek Meech	D	Minsk (KHL)	Winnipeg	July 14
Andy Miele	LW	Phoenix	Phoenix	July 9
Antii Miettinen	RW	Fribourg (SUI)	Winnipeg	July 22
Brendan Mikkelson	D	Pittsburgh	Tampa Bay	July 20
Graham Mink	C	Dornbirner (AUT)	Providence (AHL)	Aug. 10
Steve Montador	D	Zagreb (KHL)	Rockford (AHL)	Aug.
11Dominic Moore	C	NY Rangers	San Jose	July 5
Mike Mottau	D	Florida	Toronto	July 5
Chris Mueller	C	Dallas	Washington	July 8
Andrew Murray	C	Zagreb (KHL)	St. Louis	July 29
Jake Muzzin	D	Los Angeles	Los Angeles	July 12
Evgeni Nabokov	G	NY Islanders	NY Islanders	July 5
Riley Nash	C	Carolina	Carolina	July 9
Greg Nemisz	C	Calgary	Calgary	July 5
Jordan Nolan	C	Los Angeles	Los Angeles	July 21
Eric Nystrom	LW	Nashville	Dallas	July 5
Brian O'Neill	RW	Los Angeles	Los Angeles	July 10
Rostislav Olesz	C	New Jersey	Chicago	July 5
Magnus Paajarvi	LW	St. Louis	St. Louis	Aug. 2
Kyle Palmieri	RW	Anaheim	Anaheim	July 26
Aaron Palushaj	RW	Carolina	Colorado	July 11
Adam Pardy	D	Winnipeg	Buffalo	July 6
Blake Parlett	D	Columbus	Columbus	July 20
Edward Pasquale	G	Winnipeg	Winnipeg	July 19
Theo Peckham	D	Chicago	Edmonton	July 19
Matt Pelech	D	San Jose	San Jose	July 10
Pascal Pelletier	LW	Vancouver	Langnau (SUI)	July 9
Rod Pelley	C	New Jersey	Anaheim	July 8
Anthony Peluso	RW	Winnipeg	Winnipeg	July 22
Dustin Penner	LW	Anaheim	Los Angeles	July 16
Steve Pinizzotto	C	Florida	Vancouver	Aug. 5
Alex Plante	D	Dornbirner (AUT)	Edmonton	July 18
Alexei Ponikarovsky	LW	St. Petersburg (KHL)	New Jersey	Aug. 5
Paul Postma	D	Winnipeg	Winnipeg	July 19
Benoit Pouliot	LW	NY Rangers	Tampa Bay	July 5
Karri Ramo	G	Calgary	Omsk (KHL)	July 5
Paul Ranger	D	Toronto	Toronto	July 24
Tuukka Rask	G	Boston	Boston	July 10
Zach Redmond	D	Winnipeg	Winnipeg	July 20
Peter Regin	C	NY Islanders	Ottawa	July 5
Mike Ribeiro	C	Phoenix	Washington	July 5
Brad Richardson	C	Vancouver	Los Angeles	July 5
Colby Robak	D	Florida	Florida	July 22
Bryan Rodney	D	Nashville	Manchester (AHL)	July 29
Derek Roy	C	St. Louis	Vancouver	July 6
Michal Rozsival	D	Chicago	Chicago	July 5
David Rundblad	D	Phoenix	Phoenix	July 22
Ryan Russell	LW	Leksand (SWE)	Columbus	July 29
Michael Ryder	RW	New Jersey	Montreal	July 5
Jerome Samson	RW	Winnipeg	Carolina	July 6
Mike Santorelli	C	Vancouver	Winnipeg	July 6
Jordan Schroeder	C	Vancouver	Vancouver	July 24
Jeff Schultz	D	Los Angeles	Washington	July 5
Rob Scuderi	D	Pittsburgh	Los Angeles	July 5
Jack Skille	RW	Columbus	Florida	July 7
Brendan Smith	D	Detroit	Detroit	July 16
Jeremy Smith	G	Columbus	Nashville	July 5
Trevor Smith	C	Toronto	Pittsburgh	July 5
Nick Spaling	C	Nashville	Nashville	July 25
Jared Spurgeon	D	Minnesota	Minnesota	July 5
Frederic St. Denis	D	Columbus	Montreal	July 7
Martin St. Pierre	C	Montreal	Rockford (AHL)	July 6
Jared Staal	RW	Carolina	Carolina	July 16
Viktor Stalberg	LW	Nashville	Chicago	July 5
Alex Stalock	G	San Jose	San Jose	July 10
Ryan Stanton	D	Chicago	Chicago	July 16
Chris Stewart	RW	St. Louis	St. Louis	July 19
Michael Stone	D	Phoenix	Phoenix	July 5
Zack Stortini	RW	Anaheim	Hamilton (AHL)	July 8
Tyson Strachan	D	Washington	Florida	July 8
Colin Stuart	LW	Vancouver	Iserlohn (GER)	July 25
Alexander Sulzer	D	Buffalo	Buffalo	July 6
Chris Summers	D	Phoenix	Phoenix	July 5
Eric Tangradi	C	Winnipeg	Winnipeg	July 16
Nick Tarnasky	C	Montreal	Buffalo	July 6
Scott Timins	C	Florida	Florida	July 24
Corey Tripp	RW	Buffalo	Buffalo	Aug. 6
Marek Viedensky	C	San Jose	San Jose	Aug. 2
Geoff Walker	RW	Tampa Bay	Colorado	July 5
Matt Watkins	RW	Washington	NY Islanders	July 8
Yannick Weber	D	Vancouver	Montreal	July 5
Dale Weise	RW	Vancouver	Vancouver	July 25
Stephen Weiss	C	Detroit	Florida	July 5
Blake Wheeler	RW	Winnipeg	Winnipeg	July 26
Ryan White	C	Montreal	Montreal	July 13
Patrick Wiercioch	D	Ottawa	Ottawa	July 22
Jesse Winchester	C	Florida	Turku (Finland)	July 5
J.T. Wyman	RW	Colorado	Tampa Bay	July 6
Brandon Yip	RW	Phoenix	Nashville	July 19
Nolan Yonkman	D	Anaheim	Florida	July 9
Steven Zalewski	C	Rauma (Finland)	New Jersey	July 18
Marek Zidlicky	D	New Jersey	New Jersey	July 10
Harry Zolnierczyk	LW	Pittsburgh	Pittsburgh	July 12
Mats Zuccarello	LW	NY Rangers	NY Rangers	July 30

Trades and free agent signings after Aug. 12, 2013 are listed on page 615.

Trade Register, 2012-13

January, 2013

13 – Carolina traded G **Brian Boucher** and D **Mark Alt** to Philadelphia for C **Luke Pothier**.
– Carolina traded RW **Anthony Stewart**, Carolina's 4th round choice (later traded to Edmonton – Edmonton selected C **Kyle Platzer**) in 2013 Entry Draft and Carolina's 6th round choice in 2014 Entry Draft to Los Angeles for RW **Kevin Westgarth**.
14 – Dallas traded D **Mark Fistric** to Edmonton for Edmonton's 3rd round choice (D **Niklas Hansson**) in 2013 Entry Draft.
– Florida traded D **Jason DeSantis** to Montreal for D **Brendon Nash**.
16 – Toronto traded C **Matthew Lombardi** to Phoenix for Phoenix's 4th round choice in 2014 Entry Draft.
– NY Rangers traded RW **Tommy Grant** and future considerations to San Jose for LW **Brian Mashinter**.
21 – Florida traded LW **Jean-Francois Jacques** to Tampa Bay for future considerations.
– Calgary traded G **Henrik Karlsson** to Chicago for Ottawa's 7th round choice (previously acquired, Calgary selected D **John Gilmour**) in 2013 Entry Draft.
24 – NY Rangers traded C **Chad Kolarik** to Pittsburgh for C **Benn Ferriero**.
– Pittsburgh traded D **Carl Sneep** to Dallas for future considerations.
31 – Florida traded C **Casey Wellman** to Washington for C **Zach Hamill**.
– Chicago traded C **Peter Leblanc** to Washington for future considerations.

February, 2013

4 – Minnesota traded C **Darroll Powe** and RW **Nick Palmieri** to NY Rangers for C **Mike Rupp**.
6 – Los Angeles traded C **Andrei Loktionov** to New Jersy for New Jersey's 5th round choice (later traded to Florida, later traded to Buffalo – Buffalo selected RW **Gustav Possler**) in 2013 Entry Draft.
– Pittsburgh traded D **Ben Lovejoy** to Anaheim for Anaheim's 5th round choice in 2014 Entry Draft
8 – Florida traded D **Keaton Ellerby** to Los Angeles for New Jersey's 5th round choice (previously acquired, later traded to Buffalo – Buffalo selected RW **Gustav Possler**) in 2013 Entry Draft.
13 – Pittsburgh traded C **Eric Tangradi** to Winnipeg for Winnipeg's 6th round choice (D **Dane Birks**) in 2013 Entry Draft.
– Winnipeg traded LW **Alexei Poikarovsky** to New Jersey for New Jersey's 7th round choice (D **Brenden Kichton**) in 2013 Entry Draft and New Jersey's 4th round choice in 2014 Entry Draft.
14 – Montreal traded G **Cedrik Desjardins** to Tampa Bay for G **Dustin Tokarski**.
19 – St. Louis traded D **Scott Ford** to Nashville for C **Jani Lajunen**.
25 – Calgary traded C **Mitch Wahl** to Philadelphia for RW **Mike Testwuide**.
26 – Los Angeles traded LW **Simon Gagne** to Philadelphia for future considerations.
– Montreal traded LW **Erik Cole** to Dallas for RW **Michael Ryder** and Dallas' 3rd round choice (LW **Connor Crisp**) in 2013 Entry Draft.
28 – Calgary traded D **Joe Piskula** to Nashville for RW **Brian McGrattan**.

March, 2013

4 – Toronto traded RW **Mike Brown** to Edmonton for future considerations.
10 – Columbus traded RW **Tomas Kubalik** to Winnipeg for RW **Spencer Machacek**.
11 – Anaheim traded RW **Dan Sexton** to Tampa Bay for C **Kyle Wilson**.
12 – Philadelphia traded RW **Matthew Ford** to Columbus for future considerations.
– Minnesota traded LW **Matt Kassian** to Ottawa for Ottawa's 6th round choice in 2014 Entry Draft.
14 – Minnesota traded D **Chad Genoway** to Washington for future considerations.
– Toronto traded C **Nicolas Deschamps** to Washington for D **Kevin Marshall**.
15 – Anaheim traded RW **Ryan Lasch** and a 7th round choice in 2014 Entry Draft to Toronto for C **David Steckel**.
– Buffalo traded D **T.J. Brennan** to Florida for New Jersey's 5th round choice (previously acquired, Buffalo selected RW **Gustav Possler**) in 2013 Entry Draft.
22 – St. Louis traded RW **Matt D'Agostini** and future considerations to New Jersey for future considerations.
24 – Dallas traded LW **Brenden Morrow** and Minnesota's 3rd round choice (previously acquired, Pittsburgh selected C **Jake Guentzel**) in 2013 Entry Draft to Pittsburgh for D **Joe Morrow** and Pittsburgh's 5th round choice (LW **Matej Paulovic**) in 2013 Entry Draft.
25 – San Jose traded D **Douglas Murray** to Pittsburgh for a 2nd round choice (later traded to Detroit – Detroit selected LW **Tyler Bertuzzi**) in 2013 Entry Draft.
28 – Calgary traded RW **Jarome Iginla** to Pittsburgh for LW **Kenny Agostino**, W **Ben Hankowski** and Pittsburgh's 1st round choice (LW **Morgan Klimchuk**) in 2013 Entry Draft.
29 – Edmonton traded C **Tobias Rieder** to Phoenix for LW **Kale Kessey**.
30 – Detroit traded D **Kent Huskins** to Philadelphia for future considerations.
– Buffalo traded D **Jordan Leopold** to St. Louis for St. Louis' 2nd (RW **Justin Bailey**) and 5th (D **Anthony Florentino**) round choices in 2013 Entry Draft.

April, 2013

1 – Anaheim traded LW **Jay Rosehill** to Philadelphia for LW **Harry Zolnierczyk**.
– San Jose traded C **Michael Handzus** to Chicago for Anaheim's 4th round choice (previously acquired, San Jose selected G **Fredrik Bergvik**) in 2013 Entry Draft.
– Calgary traded D **Jay Bouwmeester** to St. Louis for D **Mark Cundari**, G **Reto Berra** and St. Louis' 1st round choice (LW **Emile Poirier**) in 2013 Entry Draft.
– Buffalo traded D **Robyn Regher** to Los Angeles for 2nd round choices in 2014 and 2015 Entry Drafts.
2 – Carolina traded RW **Adam Hall** and Carolina's 7th round choice (RW **Joel Vermin**) in 2013 Entry Draft to Tampa Bay for D **Marc-Andre Bergeron**.
– Phoenix traded RW **Joel Rechlicz** to Washington for RW **Matthew Clackson**.
– Colorado traded D **Cameron Gaunce** to Dallas for C **Tomas Vincour**.
– Chicago traded LW **Phillippe Paradis** to Tampa Bay for the rights to D **Kirill Gotovets**.
– Dallas traded C **Derek Roy** to Vancouver for D **Kevin Connauton** and Vancouver's 2nd round choice (G **Philippe Desrosiers**) in 2013 Entry Draft.
– Dallas traded RW **Jaromir Jagr** to Boston for LW **Lane McDermid**, RW **Cody Payne** and future considerations.
– Edmonton traded LW **Dane Byers** to Washington for D **Garrett Stafford**.
– Los Angeles traded D **Davis Drewiske** to Montreal for Montreal's 5th round choice (G **Patrik Bartosak**) in 2013 Entry Draft.
– San Jose traded LW **Ryane Clowe** to NY Rangers for NY Rangers' 2nd round choice (LW **Gabryel Boudreau**) in 2013 Entry Draft and Florida's 3rd round choice (previously acquired, later traded to Phoenix – Phoenix selected C **Pavel Laplante**) in 2013 Entry Draft.
3 – Anaheim traded C **Brandon McMillan** to Phoenix for C **Matthew Lombardi**.
– Anaheim traded G **Jeff Deslauriers** to Minnesota for future considerations.
– Boston traded C **Maxime Sauve** to Chicago for C **Rob Flick**.
– Buffalo traded RW **Jason Pominville** and Buffalo's 4th round choice in 2014 Entry Draft to Minnesota for LW **Johan Larsson**, G **Matt Hackett**, Minnesota's 1st round choice (D **Nikita Zadorov**) in 2013 Entry Draft and Minnesota's 2nd round choice in 2014 Entry Draft.
– Calgary traded LW **Blake Comeau** to Columbus for Columbus' 5th round choice (D **Eric Roy**) choice in 2013 Entry Draft.
– Carolina traded LW **Jussi Jokinen** to Pittsburgh for future considerations.
– Colorado traded D **Ryan O'Byrne** to Toronto for a 4th round choice in 2014 Entry Draft.
– Columbus traded G **Steve Mason** to Philadelphia for G **Michael Leighton** and Philadelphia's 3rd round choice in 2015 Entry Draft.

– Columbus traded RW **Derek Dorsett**, C **Derick Brassard**, D **John Moore** and Columbus' 6th round choice in 2014 Entry Draft to NY Rangers for RW **Marian Gaborik**, D **Blake Parlett** and D **Steven Delisle**.

– Florida traded C **Jerred Smithson** to Edmonton for Edmonton's 4th round choice (C **Matt Buckles**) in 2013 Entry Draft.

– Nashville traded RW **Martin Erat** and C **Michael Latta** to Washington for C **Filip Forsberg**.

– Nashville traded D **Scott Hannan** to San Jose for future considerations.

– Ottawa traded G **Ben Bishop** to Tampa Bay for C **Cory Conacher** and Philadelphia's 4th round choice (previously acquired, Ottawa selected RW **Tobias Lindberg**) in 2013 Entry Draft.

– Phoenix traded LW **Raffi Torres** to San Jose for Florida's 3rd round choice (previously acquired, later traded to Phoenix – Phoenix selected C **Pavel Laplante**) in 2013 Entry Draft.

– Phoenix traded LW **Steve Sullivan** to New Jersey for New Jersey's 7th round choice in 2014 Entry Draft.

– Pittsburgh traded G **Patrick Killeen** to Columbus for future considerations.

– St. Louis traded D **Wade Redden** to Boston for future considerations.

May, 2013

7 – Ottawa traded D **Sergei Gonchar** to Dallas for Dallas' 6th round choice (RW **Chris Leblanc**) in 2013 Entry Draft.

12 – NY Islanders traded D **Mark Streit** to Philadelphia for RW **Shane Harper** and a 4th round choice in 2014 Entry Draft.

14 – Nashville traded RW **Bobby Butler** to Florida for D **T.J. Brennan**.

18 – Florida traded C **Corban Knight** to Calgary for Calgary's 4th round choice (D **Michael Downing**) in 2013 Entry Draft.

23 – Los Angeles traded G **Jonathan Bernier** to Toronto for G **Ben Scrivens**, RW **Matt Frattin** and Toronto's 2nd round choice in 2014 or 2015 Entry Draft.

24 – Anaheim traded LW **Harry Zolnierczyk** to Pittsburgh for D **Alex Grant**.

27 – Calgary traded LW **Alex Tanguay** and D **Cory Sarich** to Colorado for RW **David Jones** and D **Shane O'Brien**.

30 – Minnesota traded D **Justin Falk** to NY Rangers for C **Benn Ferriero** and a 6th round choice in 2014 Entry Draft.

– Pittsburgh traded C **Tyler Kennedy** to San Jose for San Jose's 2nd round choice (later traded to Columbus – Columbus selected D **Dillon Heatherington**) in 2013 Entry Draft.

– Vancouver traded G **Cory Schneider** to New Jersey for New Jersey's 1st round choice (C **Bo Horvat**) in 2013 Entry Draft.

– Minnesota traded RW **Cal Clutterbuck** to NY Islanders with New Jersey's 3rd round choice (previously acquired, NY Islanders selected G **Eamon McAdam**) in 2013 Entry Draft for RW **Nino Niederreiter**.

– Buffalo traded D **Andrej Sekera** to Carolina for D **Jamie McBain** and Carolina's 2nd round choice (LW **J.T. Compher**) in 2013 Entry Draft.

– Chicago traded C **Dave Bolland** to Toronto for Toronto's 2nd round choice (D **Carl Dahlstrom**) in 2013 Entry Draft, Anaheim's 4th round choice (previously acquired, later traded to San Jose – San Jose selected G **Fredrik Bergvik**) in 2013 Entry Draft and a 4th round choice in 2014 Entry Draft.

– Chicago traded LW **Michael Frolik** to Winnipeg for Winnipeg's 3rd (C **John Hayden**) and 5th (C **Luke Johnson**) round choices in 2013 Entry Draft.

July, 2013

1 – NY Rangers traded C **Kris Newbury** to Philadelphia for D **Danny Syvret**.

2 – San Jose traded LW **T.J. Galiardi** to Calgary for a 4th round choice in 2015 Entry Draft.

– Columbus traded D **Drew Olson** to Tampa Bay for future considerations.

– Montreal traded RW **Danny Kristo** to NY Rangers for RW **Christian Thomas**.

4 – Boston traded C **Tyler Seguin**, C **Rich Peverley** and D **Ryan Button** to Boston for LW **Loui Eriksson**, D **Joe Morrow**, RW **Reilly Smith** and LW **Matt Fraser**.

5 – Dallas traded D **Philip Larsen** and a 7th round choice in 2016 Entry Draft to Edmonton for C **Shawn Horcoff**.

– St. Louis traded D **Kris Russell** to Calgary for a 5th round choice in 2014 Entry Draft.

– Anaheim traded LW **Bobby Ryan** to Ottawa for LW **Jakob Silfverberg**, RW **Stefan Noesen** and a 1st round choice in 2014 Entry Draft.

– Florida traded RW **George Parros** to Montreal for LW **Phillipe Lefebvre** and a 7th round choice in 2014 Entry Draft.

– Minnesota traded LW **Devin Setoguchi** to Winnipeg for a 2nd round choice in 2014 Entry Draft.

6 – Edmonton traded D **Kyle Bigos** to San Jose for D **Lee Moffie**.

7 – Buffalo traded LW **Riley Boychuk** to New Jersey for D **Henrik Tallinder**.

8 – Ottawa traded RW **Patrick Cannone** to St. Louis for future considerations.

10 – Edmonton traded LW **Magnus Paajarvi** and a 2nd round choice in 2014 Entry Draft to St. Louis for LW **David Perron**.

16 – Chicago traded LW **Daniel Carcillo** to Los Angeles for future considerations.

Trades and free agent signings after Aug. 12, 2012 are listed on page 615.

League Abbreviations

AHA ....Alberta Amateur Hockey Association
AAHL ....Alaska Amateur Hockey League
AASHA..............Alaska All-Stars Hockey Association
ACHA ....American Collegiate Hockey Association
ACHL ....Atlantic Coast Hockey League
AFHL..............American Frontier Hockey League
AH ....Atlantic Hockey
AHL ....American Hockey League
AJHL ....Alberta Junior Hockey League
ALIH ....Asia League Ice Hockey
Alpenliga ....Alpenliga (Austria, Italy, Slovenia 1994-1999)
AMHA..............Alberta Minor Hockey Association
AMHL ....Alberta Midget AAA Hockey League
AMBHL ....Alberta Major Bantam Hockey League
AUAA..............Atlantic University Athletic Association
AtJHL ....Atlantic Junior Hockey League
AWHL ....American West Hockey League
AYHL..............Atlantic Youth Hockey League
BCAHA ....British Columbia Amateur Hockey Association
BCHL ....British Columbia (Junior) Hockey League (also BCJHL)
BCMML ....British Columbia Major Midget League
CABHL ....Central Alberta Bantam Hockey League
CBHL ....Calgary Bantam Hockey League
CCHA ....Central Collegiate Hockey Association
CEGEP ....Quebec College Prep
CHA..............College Hockey America
CHL ....Central Hockey League
CIS..............Commonwealth of Independent States
CIS..............Canadian Interuniversity Sport
CJHL ....Central Junior A Hockey League
CMHA..............Calgary Minor Hockey Association
ColHL..............Colonial Hockey League
CSHL..............Central States Hockey League
CSJHL ....Central States Junior Hockey League
CSSHL..............Canadian Sport School Hockey League
CWUAA ....Canadian Western University Athletic Association
ECAC ....Eastern College Athletic Conference
ECACHL ....ECAC Hockey League
ECHL..............East Coast Hockey League
EEHL ....Eastern European Hockey League
EJHL..............Eastern Junior Hockey League
EMHA ....Edmonton Minor Hockey Association
EmJHL..............Empire Junior B Hockey League
EuroHL..............European Hockey League
Exhib. ....Exhibition Games, Series or Season
GLHL..............Great Lakes Hockey League
GNML..............Greater North Midget League
GPAC ....Great Plains Athletic Conference
GTHL ....Greater Toronto Hockey League
H-East..............Hockey East
High-XX..............High School (state/province)
HJHL ....Heritage Junior Hockey League
HPHL ....High Performance Hockey League
IEHL ....Internationale Eishockey Liga
IHL..............International Hockey League
KIJHL ....Kootenay International Junior B Hockey League
LCJHL..............Little Caesar's Junior Hockey League
MAAC..............Metro Atlantic Athletic Conference
MAHA..............Manitoba Amateur Hockey Association
MAHL ....Mid America Hockey League
MBAHL ....Metropolitan Boston Amateur Hockey League
MBHL ....Metropolitan Boston Hockey League
MEHL..............Midwest Elite Hockey League
Metro-HL ....Metro Hockey League
MIAC ....Minnesota Intercollegiate Athletic Conference
Minor-XX ....Minor/Youth hockey (state/province)
MJHL ....Manitoba Junior Hockey League
MJrHL ....Maritime Junior A Hockey League
MMBHL ....Manitoba Major Bantam Hockey League
MMHL ....Manitoba Midget AAA Hockey League
MMHL ....Michigan Minor Hockey League
MMMHL ....Manitoba Minor Midget Hockey League
MNHL ....Michigan National Hockey League
MPHL..............Midwest Prep Hockey League
MtJHL ....Metropolitan Junior Hockey League (New York)
MTJHL..............Metropolitan Toronto Junior Hockey League
MTHL..............Metro Toronto Hockey League
MWEHL ....Midwest Elite Hockey League
NAHL..............North American Hockey League (Tier I Junior)
NAJHL..............North American Junior Hockey League
NAPHL..............North American Prospects Hockey League
Nat-Team ....National Team (also Nt.-Team)
NBAHA ....New Brunswick Amateur Hockey Association
NBMHL ....New Brunswick Midget Hockey League
NBPEI ....New Brunswick Prince Edward Island Midget Hockey League
NCAA ....National Collegiate Athletic Association
NCHA ....Northern Collegiate Hockey Association
NEJHL ....New England Junior Hockey League
NFAHA..............Newfoundland Amateur Hockey Association
NHL ....National Hockey League
NJCAA ....National Junior Collegiate Athletic Association
NOBHL..............Northern Ontario Bantam Hockey League
NOHA ....Northern Ontario Hockey Association
NOJHA..............Northern Ontario Junior Hockey Association
NOJHL ....Northern Ontario Junior Hockey League
NSBHL ....Nova Scotia Bantam Hockey League
NSMHL ....Nova Scotia Midget AAA Hockey League
NTHL ....North Texas Hockey League
NWJHL..............Northwest Junior B Hockey League
NYJHL..............New York Junior Hockey League
OCJHL..............Ontario Central Junior A Hockey League
OHA ....Ontario Hockey Association
OHL ....Ontario Hockey League
OMJHL..............Ontario Major Junior Hockey League
ON-Jr.A ....Ontario Junior A Hockey Leagues
ON-Jr.B ....Ontario Junior B Hockey Leagues
OPJHL ....Ontario Provincial Junior A Hockey League
OUAA ....Ontario Universities Athletic Association
PAHA ....Pennsylvania Amateur Hockey Association
PCJHL ....Pacific Coast Junior Hockey League
PEIHA ....Prince Edward Island Hockey Association
PIJHL..............Pacific International Junior Hockey League
QAA ....Quebec Junior AA
QAAA ....Quebec Midget AAA Hockey League
QAHA ....Quebec Amateur Hockey Association
QJHL ....Quebec Junior Hockey League
QMJHL..............Quebec Major Junior Hockey League
QNAHL ....(Quebec) North American Hockey League
Q-RHL..............(Quebec) Richelieu Elite Hockey League
QSPHL ....Quebec Semi-Pro Hockey League
RAMHL ....Rural Alberta Midget Hockey League
RMJHL ....Rocky Mountain Junior Hockey League
SAHA..............Saskatchewan Amateur Hockey Association
SAMHL ....Southern Alberta Midget Hockey League
SBHL..............Saskatchewan Bantam Hockey League
SCAHA..............Southern California Amateur Hockey Association
SIJHL ....Superior International Junior Hockey League
SJHL ....Saskatchewan Junior Hockey League
SMBHL..............Saskatchewan Major Bantam Hockey League
SMHL..............Saskatchewan Midget AAA Hockey League
SMMHL..............Saskatchewan Minor Midget Hockey League
SPHL..............Southern Professional Hockey League
SSJHL..............South Saskatchewan Junior B Hockey League
SSMHL..............South Saskatchewan Minor Hockey League
SunHL..............Sunshine Hockey League
T1EHL..............Tier 1 Elite Hockey League
TBAHA..............Thunder Bay Amateur Hockey Association
TBJHL..............Thunder Bay Junior Hockey League
TBMHL..............Thunder Bay Midget Hockey League
U-17..............Under 17
U-18..............Under 18
UHL ....United Hockey League
UMEHL ....Upper Midwest Elite Hockey League
UMHSEL ....Upper Midwest High School Elite League
USAHA ....United States Amateur Hockey Association
USHL ....United States (Junior A) Hockey League
VIJHL ....Vancouver Island Junior Hockey League
WCHA ....Western Collegiate Hockey Association
WCHL ....West Coast Hockey League
WHL ....Western Hockey League
WNYHA ....Western New York Hockey Association
WPHL ....Western Professional Hockey League
WSJHL ....Western States Junior Hockey League

NHL Goal of the Year, 2012-13

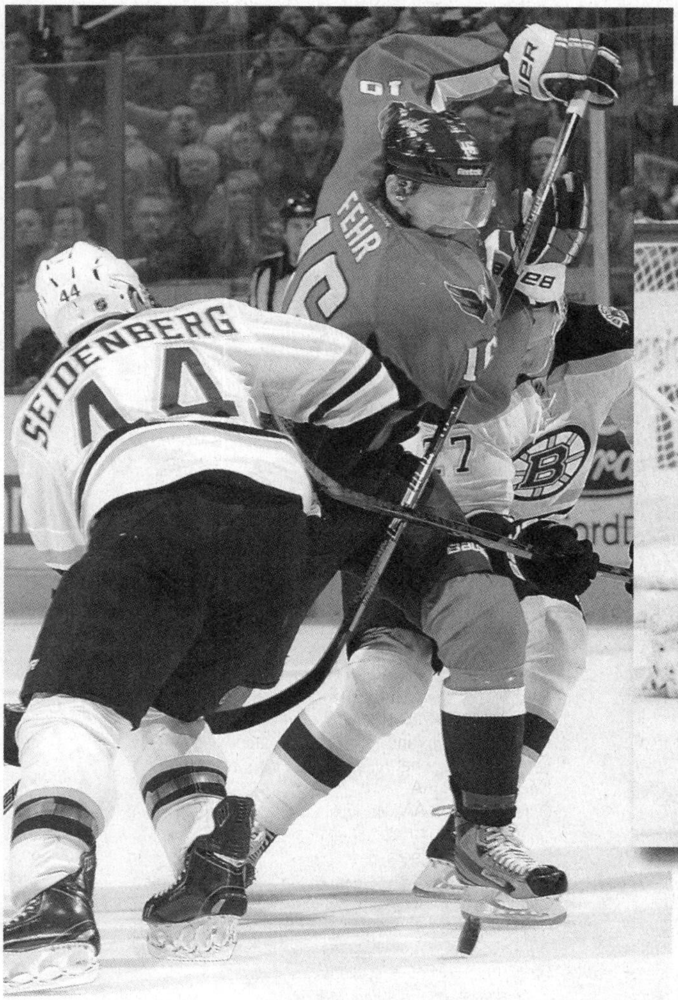

Early in overtime in a game between Boston and Washington on March 5, 2013, Capitals forward Eric Fehr split the Bruins defense of Denis Seidenberg and Dougie Hamilton. As Fehr was falling to the ice, he managed to put a shot past Tuukka Rask high to the glove side to win the game for Washington 4-3 at 4:23 of OT. Fehr's play headed the list of Top 10 goals of the year on the NHL Network's countdown.

Contributors

The NHL Official Guide & Record Book is produced with the help of many. Special thanks to: Kevin Abrams (Central Junior Hockey League), Manny Almela, Dave Andjelic, Scott Arnold, Brian Ash, Mike Asselin, Joe Babik (ECHL), Laurie Barron, Fenton Barrow, Brendan Batchelor, Bill Bestwick, John Blake, Rocky Bonanno, Nellie, Greg, Anne and Private Matt Bontje, Bob Borgen, Minako Borgen, Paul Bork, Mike Bose, Scott Bowley, Rob Brendt, Craig Campbell, Paul Cannata, Jason Chaimovitch (AHL), Tony Clarke, Ken Coleman, www.collegehockeystats.net, Rick Comfort, Brad Cook, Neil Corbett, Tyler Cragg, Brian Day, Danny Donato, Patrick Driscoll, David Erickson, Jason Farris, Peter Fillman, David Fischer (USA Hockey), Ernie Fitzsimmons, Cory Flett (WHL), Sean Forman, Michelle Fortin, Jon Frape, Brad Gaucher, John Gardner, Krista Gill, Todd Gill, Pete Gobiel, Bob Grove, Stu Hackel, Jacques Henri, Hockey Hall of Fame, www.hockey-reference.com, www.hockeydb.com, Eric Hornick, Calvin House, Tanner House, Greg Innis, Sean Jacques, Peter Jagla, Karl Jahnke (QMJHL), Todd Johnson, Casey Kesselring, Stefanie Kingersk, David W. Kosick, Paul Kroyz (CHL), Justin Kubatko, Cindy Kunitz, Igor Kuperman, Laurie Lakeman, Grace LeBlanc, Joe Lee, Liam Maguire, Jim Mancuso, Lance Marciano, Brett Martel, Kelly Masse, Robert McAfee, Brian McClogan, Ray McIsaac, Kibby McKibbon, Len McNeely, Larry Mitchell, Herb Morell (OHL), John Moritsugu, www.nahl.com, Glen Naka, Jeff Nash (Hockey Canada), NHL Broadcasters' Association, NHL Central Registry, www.nhlgms.com, NHL Officiating, NHL Players' Association, Buddy Oakes, www.ohahockey.org, Tim O'Donovan, R.G. (Bob) Olynyk (Alberta AAA Midget Hockey League), Doug Orr, Peter Peckett, Martine Pettem (Hockey Canada), Matt Plante, www.pointstreak.com, Kevin J. Potter, Phil Pritchard, Serge Proulx, Pearl Rajwanth, Devin Rask, George Richards (Pacific Junior Hockey League), Rita Rocys, Rob Rogers, John Ross, Dean and Jenny Rubisch, Martin Schmid, Naida Shannon, Tim Sinclair, Susan Snow, Society for International Hockey Research (SIHR), Trevor Sprague, Russ Stevenson, Greg Thompson (Manitoba AAA Midget Hockey League), Mike Traggio, www.ushl.com, Mike Vandekamp, Staale Volleng, Mike Walsh, John Walters, Bob Waterman (Elias Sports Bureau), Jesse Watts (WHL), Brian Werger (USHL), Jake Wesolek (U.S. National Team Development Program), Izak Westgate, Rick Westra, Carole Woodrow, Paul and Sonya Wright.

Photo Credits

Hockey Hall of Fame: Various Collections.
Getty Images: Graig Abel, Claus Andersen, Joel Auerbach, Scott Audette, Steve Babineau, Marissa Baecker, Brian Bahr, T. Biegun, Bruce Bennett, Paul Bereswill, Frederick Breedon, Denis Brodeur, Mark Buckner, Rob Carr, Glenn Cratty, Jonathan Daniel, Andy Devlin, Melchior DiGiacomo, Phil Ellsworth, Elsa, Greg Flume, Norm Hall, Drew Hallowell, Grant Halverson, Marianne Helm, Harry How, Kirk Irwin, Glenn James, Bruce Kluckhohn, Jonathan Kozub, Francois Lacasse, Rich Lam, Francois Laplante, Derek Leung, Scott Levy, Andy Marlin, Michael Martin, Patrick McDermott, Jim McIsaac, Ronald C. Modra, Perry Nelson, NHL Images, Christopher Pasatieri , Doug Pensinger, Mike Powell, Dave Reginek, Andre Ringuette, Debora Robinson, John Russell, Jamie Sabau, Dave Sanford, Eliot J. Schechter, Scott A. Schneider, Gregory Shamus, Bill Smith, Mike Stobe, Jamie Squire, Gerry Thomas, Ian Tomlinson, Jeff Vinnick, Brad Watson, RockyWidner, Bill Wippert, Richard Wolowicz.
Additional NHL team photographers: Chase Agnello-Dean, Rudi Ayasse, Brian Babineau, Greg Bartram, Andrew D. Bernstein Associates, Jack Cassidy, Tim DeFrisco, Gregg Forwerck, Freestyle Photography, Noah Graham, Travis Golby, George Kalinsky (MSG Photo Services), Andy King, Mitchell Layton, Dan Mannes, Juan Ocampo, Len Redkoles, Don Smith, Rafael Suanes, Lance Thomson.

Special thanks to Bruce Bennett, Paul Michinard, Michael Klein and Ashlyn Barefoot, Getty Images.

Researchers and historians: contact the Society for International Hockey Research (www.sihrhockey.org) and/or Hockey Reference (www.hockey-reference.com).

Patrick Kane cradles the Conn Smythe Trophy awarded to the most valuable player in the Stanley Cup Playoffs as team captain Jonathan Toews shares the moment. The Blackhawks clinched the Cup with two goals in the last two minutes of the third period of game six in Boston.

To order additional copies of the NHL Official Guide & Record Book

www.nhlofficialguide.com

ADDITIONAL INFORMATION AVAILABLE FROM

dda.nhl@sympatico.ca

or 416 531-6535